CARSWELL

Practitioner's

Income Tax Act

2021 · 60th Edition

The **Income Tax Act** and **Income Tax Application Rules**
fully annotated, as amended to **July 5, 2021**
Consolidated with
all draft legislation to the same date;
other proposed amendments
plus
The **Income Tax Regulations** and all draft regulations to July 5, 2021;
Remission Orders; **Multilateral Instrument**; Canada-US and Canada-UK tax treaties;
Canada-US Tax Information Exchange Agreement (FATCA); Tax Tables;
Interpretation Act; Topical Index

Editor and Author of Notes
David M. Sherman, B.A., LL.B., LL.M.
of the Ontario Bar

Contributing Editors
Seán DaCosta, B.J.   Scott McVicar, B.A.
Kayla Rice, B.A.

 **THOMSON REUTERS®**

42874896

ISSN 1193-1701

ISBN 978-1-7319-8290-2 (60th edition).—

A cataloguing record for this publication is available from Library and Archives Canada.

Printed in Canada by Thomson Reuters.

THOMSON REUTERS CANADA, A DIVISION OF THOMSON REUTERS CANADA LIMITED

One Corporate Plaza
2075 Kennedy Road
Toronto, Ontario
M1T 3V4

Customer Support
1-416-609-3800 (Toronto & International)
1-800-387-5164 (Toll Free Canada & U.S. Only)
Fax 1-416-298-5082 (Toronto)
Fax 1-877-750-9041 (Toll Free Canada Only)
E-mail CustomerSupport.LegalTaxCanada@TR.com

TABLE OF CONTENTS

INTRODUCTION

This is the 60th edition of the *Practitioner's Income Tax Act* (PITA), the most comprehensive and informative edition of the *Income Tax Act* available.

In this edition we have retained the innovations that have made PITA Canada's leading Income Tax Act:

- shaded boxes showing all draft legislation and draft regulations in context
- Department of Finance technical notes, in context, accompanying draft legislation and draft regulations
- shaded boxes with press releases and budget materials that announce pending changes, reproduced in context
- shaded boxes for "Enacted Amendments" that have been passed but are not yet in force
- shaded boxes for notable "Announced Administrative Changes", mostly from the Canada Revenue Agency, that are pending or current
- numerous "comfort letters" issued by the Department of Finance, placed in context with the provisions that will be amended
- "Notes" that explain many of the provisions, guide the reader's understanding, refer to Court cases, published articles and CRA interpretations, and list all changes since 1989 as well as all previous versions of the provision that are still relevant
- reference tables of individual, corporate and payroll tax rates, R&D incentive rates, treaty withholding rates, foreign exchange rates, interest rates, limitation periods and penalties (note: the Table of Dollar Amounts appears in the Topical Index under "Dollar amounts")
- comprehensive, expert annotations showing Related Provisions, Definitions (including terms defined in the *Interpretation Act*), Regulations, Remission Orders, Interpretation Bulletins, Income Tax Folios, Information Circulars, Income Tax Technical News, Advance Tax Rulings, Forms, Application Policies, Registered Plans Directorate newsletters and Actuarial Bulletins, Registered Charities newsletters, Transfer Pricing Memoranda, Info Sheets, Charities Policies, Registered Pension Plans Technical Manual, Provincial Income Allocation Newsletters, RDSP Bulletins and CRA Income Tax Audit Manual
- editorial headings for paragraphs in many long subsections, to make the subsection easier to scan (e.g., 53(1), 80(2), 85(1), 88(1), 94(2), 94(3), 95(2), 118.2(2)); and for dozens of provisions of the Regulations that do not have titles
- annotations, footnotes and titles to clarify errors and omissions in the legislation and to note when dollar amounts are not what they appear to be
- suppressing provisions that are no longer relevant, where they apply only to periods many years past
- editorial annotations to all Regulations to show the current reference to provisions in the Act that have been renumbered since the Regulation was enacted (e.g., Reg. 6900)
- the full text of numerous Remission Orders relating to the Act
- the full text of the *Interpretation Act* with annotations
- a comprehensive, expert Topical Index that includes many terms not explicitly found in the legislation as well as acronyms and Court cases overruled by legislation (e.g., *Alcatel*), and that reflects *all* the latest draft legislation.

What's New in This Edition?

This edition, current to July 5, 2021, reflects the following new developments since the 59th edition, which was current to February 2, 2021 [location of amendments or proposed amendments is shown in square brackets]:

- **Bill C-30**, the 2021 Budget bill #1, which also served in effect as the 2019 Budget bill #2, as it included measures from the 2019 Budget that were not enacted in the first 2019 Budget bill enacted in June 2019 (and then were interrupted by COVID-19). The Bill received First Reading in the House of Commons on April 30, 2021 and Royal Assent on June 29, 2021 (S.C. 2021, c. 23). It included the following changes:

April 19, 2021 Budget proposals:

- — Canada Emergency Wage Subsidy (CEWS) and Canada Emergency Rent Subsidy (CERS) extended and modified, and new Canada Hiring Recovery Program (CRHP) introduced [125.7; also 87(2)(g.6), 152(3.4), 163(2)(i)(i), 164(1.6), Reg. 8901.2]
- — Canada Workers Benefit enhanced, and inflation indexing rules restructured [122.7, 117.1]
- — charities: new rules re listed terrorist entities and false statements [149.1(1)"listed terrorist entity"; also 149.1(1)"ineligible individual", 149.1(1.02), (4.1), 168(3.1), 188(1), 188.2(2)(f)]
- — COVID-19 benefits taxation [56(1)(r)(iv), (iv.1), 60(n), 60(v.3), 115(1)(a)(iii.22)]

Previous outstanding proposals [including from 2019 Budget]:

- — annuities to be allowed for registered plans:
  - advanced life deferred annuity for DPSP, PRPP and RPP [146.5, 205–206; also 56(1)(z.5), 60(l)(v)(A.2), 118(7)"pension income"(a)(iii.3), 146(16)(a.1), 146.3(2)(f)(ix), 146.3(14.1)(c), 147(2)(k)(vi), 147(19)(d)(v), 147.3(1)(c)(iv), 147.4(1)(a), 147.5(1)"qualifying annuity", 147.5(21)(c)(vi), 153(1)(u), 212(1)(l.1), 248(1)"advanced life deferred annuity", 252(3), Reg. 100(1)"remuneration"(p), Reg. 216]
  - variable payment life annuity for PRPP and defined-contribution RPP [Reg. 8506(1)(e.2); also 147.5(5)(a), Reg. 8502(e)(i)(C), (e.1), 8506(2)(g), 8506(13)]
- — agricultural cooperative patronage dividends: rule for tax-deferred shares extended to shares issued before 2026 [135.1(1)"tax deferred cooperative share"(a)]
- — automobile standby charge for employees: relief for 2020 and 2021 due to COVID-19 [6(2.2), (2.3); also 87(2)(g.7)]

— basic personal amount increased to a sliding scale [118(1.1); also 63(3), 108(1), 117.1(1), 118(1), 146(1.1), 250(1)(f), Reg. 103.1(2)]

— child care expenses and disability supports deduction: relief for 2020-2021 due to COVID-19 [63(3.1), 64.01]

— employee life and health trusts [144.1, 207.9; also 111(7.4), 248(1)"employee benefit plan"]

— employee stock option deduction limits [110(0.1), 110(1)(d), (e), 110(1.1), 110(1.3)–(1.44), 110(1.9); also 7(7), 87(2)(j.97), 111(8)"non-capital loss"A:E(b), 126(1)(b)(ii)(A)(III), 126(2.1)(b)(ii)(A)(III), 115(1)(d), 143.3(5)(e)]

— flow-through shares: extending times for spending capital raised, due to COVID-19 [66(12.6001), (12.731), 211.91(2.1)]

— foreign affiliate dumping rules expanded [212.3; also 17.1(2), 128.1(1)(c.3), 219.1(2)(b)]

— journalism support: technical changes [168.1; also 118.02(1), 125.6, 149.1(1)"qualifying journalism organization"(h); 152(1)(b), 157(3)(e), (3.1)(c), 163(2)(h)(i), 164(1)(a)(ii), 241(3.4), 248(1)"qualified Canadian journalism organization"(a)(v), (vii)(C)]

— multi-unit residential properties: change in use of part of property, to or from personal use [45(2), (3)]

— mutual fund trusts: "allocation to redeemers" methodology of reporting capital gains — anti-avoidance rule to prevent deferral [132(5.3)]

— registered disability savings plan: effect where person ceases to be eligible for the disability credit [146.4; also 60.02(1)"specified RDSP payment"(e)]

— registered pension plan changes: pensionable service anti-avoidance rule, and contributions to a specified multi-employer plan for older members [147.3(3)(c), Reg. 8503(3)(a)(v)–(vi), 8510(7)(c)]

— Requirement for Information: electronic delivery of notice to bank or credit union that agrees to be served electronically [231.2(1.1); also 231.2(1), 231.6, 231.8(a), 244(6.1)]

— securities lending arrangements: rules expanded [212(2.1), 212(3)"fully exempt interest", 248(1)"fully collateralized arrangement", "specified securities lending arrangement", 260]

— shared-custody parenting rules for Canada Child Benefit, overruling *Morrissey* and *Lavrinenko* cases [122.6"shared-custody parent"(b)]

— transfer-pricing rules:

  • extended reassessment period expanded in application [152(4)(b)(iii)(A)]

  • order of application of transfer-pricing rules [247(2), (2.1), (8)]

— zero-emission vehicles capital cost allowance: adjustments to the rules added by the 2019 Budget first bill [13(7)(i)(ii)]

— postdoctoral fellowships as RRSP earned income [146(1)"earned income"(b.01)]

• **April 19, 2021 Budget** proposals in legislative form, but not included in Bill C-30:

— auditor to be able to require specific person to answer questions [231.1(1)(c), 231.1(2)]

• **April 19, 2021 Budget** proposals not yet in legislative form:

— avoidance of tax debts: rules to prevent avoidance of s. 160 [160(1)]

— beneficial ownership registry for corporations [150(1)(a) Notes]

— CRA funding: more money for automated T1 adjustments, Collections, evasion/avoidance, and protecting taxpayer information [220(1), 222(2), 239(1), 241(1)]

— capital cost allowance:

  • clean energy equipment [Reg. Sch. II:Cl. 43.1]

  • immediate expensing of $1.5 million of new investment for CCPCs [Reg. 1100(1)(a) opening words]

— carbon capture and storage technology: new investment tax credit [127(9)"investment tax credit"; also consultations launched June 7, 2021]

— charities disbursement quota increase (consultation) [149.1(1)"disbursement quota"]

— climate action incentive to be paid quarterly [122.8(4)]

— Digital Services Tax on large non-resident businesses [115(1)]

— disability tax credit expanded [118.3(1)]

— electronic filing, payment and communications: numerous changes to move towards all-digital [244(14.1)]

— employee ownership trusts [7(1)]

— film/video tax credit and production services credit: extensions of time limits for COVID-19 [Reg. 1106(1)"application for a certificate of completion"]

— general anti-avoidance rule to be "modernized" [245(2)]

— hybrid mismatch arrangements: preventing tax avoidance [248(1)"corporation"]

— Indigenous governments: Canada to continue to seek tax agreements [81(1)(a)]

— interest deductibility limited to 30% of tax EBITDA [20(1)(c)]

— manufacturers of zero-emission technology: corporate tax rate reduction [123.4(2)]

— Northern residents' deduction [110.7(1), Reg 7304(2)(c)]

— registered investments: fairer calculation of Part X.2 tax [204.6(1)]

— registered pension plans: fixing contribution errors in defined-contribution plans [147.2(1)]

— reportable transactions: strengthening the rules [237.3]

— student loans: waiving interest [118.62]

— Tax Court of Canada: more judges [169(1)]

— transfer pricing rules (consultation) [247(2)]

— vacant and unproductive housing owned by non-resident non-citizens [115(1)(b)]

• **Bill C-14, 2021 COVID bill #1** (Royal Assent May 6, 2021: S.C. 2021, c. 7):

— Canada Child Benefit: additional payments in 2021 [122.61(1.2); also 122.62(5)(b), 122.62(6)(b), 122.62(7)(b)]

— Canada Emergency Rent Subsidy — payable even if rent not yet paid [125.7(12), (13)]

— federal student loan interest waived for one year [118.62]

• **Bill C-31**, First Reading June 10, 2021, proposing amendments to the *Criminal Records Act* to change the term "record suspension" to "pardon", with consequential ITA amendments [149.1(1)"ineligible individual", 149.1(1.01)]

• **Bill C-35**, First Reading June 22, 2021, introducing the Canada Disability Benefit [118.3(1), 241(4)(d)(vii.51)]

• **Bill C-208**, the 2021 family business transfers bill, a private member's bill that (surprisingly) passed the House of Commons and received Royal Assent (S.C. 2021, c. 21). Its object was to "level the playing field by giving families the same tax treatment when they transfer their businesses or operations to their children as when they transfer it to a stranger" [55(5)(e), 84.1(2)(e), 84.1(2.3)]

• **Bill S-222**, a private member's bill that cleared the Senate and received First Reading in the House before summer 2021 recess, to permit charities to fund charitable activities abroad, without having to carry out the activities themselves through an agent [149.1(1)"charitable activities"; also 149.1 [throughout], 188(1.1), 188.1(5), (12), 189(6.2)]

• **National Day for Truth and Reconciliation** enacted as a public holiday (Sept. 30) by S.C. 2021, c. 11 [*Interpretation Act* 35(1)"holiday"]

• *Canada Revenue Agency Act* s. 63.1, enacted June 2021, permitting CRA to collect and disclose to a province (or territory) information for an organ/tissue donor registry run by the province [241(4) Notes]

• Consultation announced for the taxation of **insurance corporations** (tax implications of IFRS-17 international accounting rules for insurance contracts), May 28, 2021 [138(2)]

• Further changes announced to CEWS, CERS and CRHP, June 2, 2021 [125.7(2), (2.1), (2.2)]

• **Regulatory amendments** passed by the federal Cabinet:

— P.C. 2021-213, enacting Regulations for the *Disability Tax Credit Promoters Restrictions Act*, to limit fees that can be charged for claiming the disability credit [118.3(1) Notes]

— P.C. 2021-214, removing from the Regulations the CEWS and CERS rules that were put back into ITA 125.7 [Reg. 8901.2]

— P.C. 2021-304, amending the Canada Child Benefit rule that prefers the mother, to accommodate the "other parent" not being male [Reg. 6301(1)]

— P.C. 2021-522, amending the Registered Pension Plan regulations to provide relief related to COVID-19, as announced by Finance May 20, 2021 [Reg. 6801.1, 8308(4.1), (5.1)–(5.3), 8500(1.3), 8502(i.1)]

• **Agriculture Canada** announcement May 10, 2021 of livestock deferral regions for 2020 [Reg. 7305.01]

• **Announced Administrative Changes** from the CRA regarding numerous matters that do not require legislative amendment, mostly related to COVID-19, including updates to previous announcements:

— CRA administration and resuming activities [220(1)]

— clearance certificate requests by email [159(2)]

— filing and payment dates *not* extended in 2021 [150(1) opening words]

— interest waiver on income tax debt arising from COVID-19 support [220(3.1)]

— international tax issues [250(1)(a), consolidating and updating previous announcements reproduced under various provisions]

— T1 adjustments to be more automated [220(1)]

— Tax Court reopening, re-closing and deadlines [169(1)]

• global developments in **BEPS** (Base Erosion and Profit Shifting) and other international tax developments, including OECD Pillar One and Pillar Two [95, at end]

• references to various conference papers and CRA roundtable pronouncements

• Dept. of Finance, CRA and other government news releases and reports re various matters

• detailed revisions and extensions to the Notes commentary in many areas, including a complete **rewrite of the Notes** to 56(1)(a), 56(1)(b), 121, 122.6"shared-custody parent", 125.7(2), 144.1 [end], 146(1)"qualified investment", 149.1(4.1), 212.3 [end], 256(2.1), Reg. 8503(3), 8901.2

• dozens of new CRA interpretation letters and rulings ("VIEWS" docs) released by CRA, discussed in the Notes

• release by CRA of new or revised Income Tax Folios, newsletters, Forms, Guides, web pages and other administrative announcements

• responses to **Access to Information requests** I filed on numerous matters, including the makeup of numerous CRA committees

• **new case law** including decisions from the Supreme Court of Canada, Federal Court of Appeal, Federal Court, Tax Court of Canada and provincial courts — including new information on the current status of dozens of appeals

• publication of journal and newsletter articles and conference reports throughout the year, by the Canadian Tax Foundation, Carswell, CCH, Federated Press, STEP Canada and others.

In addition, I have added, reorganized and improved hundreds of "Notes" annotations, to provide additional explanations of how provisions operate; to summarize recent or older case law; to reflect new CRA interpretation and policy; and to refer to published articles.

I prepare all the Notes myself. I am constantly striving to reduce the size of the Notes by making them more concise and eliminating text that is no longer relevant or does not provide added value, to make room for more such explanations, references and summaries while allowing the book to remain in one (reasonably portable) softcover volume.

I have also updated the Topical Index to reflect the latest developments and to add new useful references.

As the **CRA website has moved** from cra.gc.ca to canada.ca/en/revenue-agency.html, I have, since the 55th edition, changed website references throughout the book, using tinyURL.com references since the new URLs are far too long for readers of the paper edition to type (e.g., canada.ca/en/revenue-agency/services/tax/businesses/topics/payroll/payroll-overview/penalties-interest-other-consequences/payroll-penalties/penalty-failure-file-information-return-date.html, which is now tinyurl.com/cra-late). The old cra.gc.ca references were guaranteed to work only until July 2018, and on April 1, 2019 almost all of them stopped working entirely.

Many legislative provisions that are no longer relevant, because they effectively expired long ago, are **suppressed from printing** in the paper edition, in order to leave more room for the current provisions and annotations while keeping the book portable. See sections 15.1 and 15.2, for example. (These provisions appear in the DVD-ROM version and on *Taxnet Pro*, but not the ProView version (e.g., iPad or Web browser) which mirrors the paper version.) I have continued to expand the suppression of more such provisions as their relevance recedes into the past (e.g. 12.5, 20.4, 142.51, Reg. 1201).

Since 2016, I have gradually converted existing case citations to "neutral" court citations where possible. See below under "Notes — References to Case Law".

Change in typesetting of federal legislation and regulations

In 2016, the federal Department of Justice, without any specific approval by Parliament, **changed the way defined terms are shown in all federal legislation and regulations**, including the *Income Tax Act* and the *Income Tax Regulations*. The changes appear on laws.justice.gc.ca, which is the "official" version of the law, and has been made in draft and enacted legislation since 2016. The change to existing legislation appears to have been done under the authority of the *Legislation Revision and Consolidation Act* (LRCA), although nothing in the LRCA quite authorizes this kind of change (para. 27(c) allows the Minister of Justice to "correct grammatical and typographical errors"). Instead of, for example:

"taxpayer" includes any person whether or not liable to pay tax;

the new form is

taxpayer includes any person whether or not liable to pay tax;

using italics and boldface to convey the information formerly conveyed by quotation marks.

We are not copying this change in Carswell publications at present, and will continue to show defined terms in quotation marks for clarity. My view is that the legislation is easier to read when quotation marks are used for definitions. There may be ambiguities or interpretation problems, of which the legislative revisors were unaware, that result from the new format. The LRCA, in ss. 30 and 31, provides that consolidated statutes "do not operate as new law", and that in the event of inconsistency, the original statute as enacted prevails. (Note however that new amendments since January 2016 have been enacted in the new format.)

Changes made by the Dept. of Justice under the LRCA since 2015 to correct typographical errors were finally published in 2020 at laws.justice.gc.ca/eng/corrections, almost two years after I first wrote to the Minister of Justice about there being no tracking of such changes. (These are mentioned in the Notes, in case the reader is surprised that the wording published in PITA does not match what was enacted by Parliament.)

Changes to cross-referenced sections in the text of the Act

Sometime around 2019, the Department of Justice, using the LRCA (above), silently changed dozens or perhaps hundreds of references throughout the Act (but not all), which are references to provisions within the same section, to be **fully-qualified** by repeating the section number. Thus, for example, the opening words of subparagraph 40(1)(a)(iii), as enacted, begin "Subject to **subsection (1.1)**", and this was silently changed to "Subject to **subsection 40(1.1)**".

In my view, the change is unnecessary, as there was no ambiguity in the legislation as enacted. A cross-reference beginning with a parenthesis is a reference to a provision within the same section, and this has been well understood for decades, Admittedly, there are places where the enacted version can cause confusion to the less-experienced reader, e.g. 110.6(2.1)(d), which contains references to both "paragraph 3(b)" and "paragraph (2)(d)", which are completely different (the second one is a reference to 110.6(2)(d)).

Furthermore, I do not believe that the Department of Justice had legal authority to do what it has done. LRCA paragraph 27(c) authorizes the Minister to "correct grammatical and typographical errors", but the changing of a correct reference "subsection (1.1)" to "subsection 40(1.1)" does not correct an error. It introduces a new style, arguably not necessary, of fully qualifying cross-references to provisions within the same section. This does not "correct grammatical and typographical errors", and arguably requires action by Parliament. Nor do I see any other provision of the LRCA that authorizes this change. I wrote to the Minister of Justice about this issue in January 2020.

The amendments do make the legislation slightly clearer, at the cost of adding more text. What is particularly egregious, however, is that **this was done without the involvement of the Department of Finance or Parliament**, and was done **without advising stakeholders** such as tax publishers, tax practitioners, Finance and CRA.

The *Income Tax Act* is an extraordinarily complex document, and the Department of Justice should not be messing with it, especially without telling anybody. Correcting an occasional typo is one thing; wholesale silent expansion of statutory references is another.

I became aware of this issue in 2020, when a reader (Cory G. Litzenberger, CPA) brought an example to my attention. Discussions are continuing with Finance and Justice to determine whether these changes will be retained. (See "Sherman Letter to Justice Minister", xlii(7) *The Canadian Taxpayer* (Carswell) 54-55 (April 3, 2020).) In the meantime, be aware that **the allegedly official version of the Act, as silently amended by the Department of Justice without telling stakeholders, has additional text** to fully qualify many cross-references, and that this additional text does not appear in this edition of PITA. This is not how legislation should be maintained in Canada, but is unfortunately the situation today.

If the changes are all identified and shown to be legally valid, we will in future editions update the cross-references to be fully qualified as per the "official" version of the Act.

Proposed amendments

Note that proposed amendments, as shown in shaded boxes through the Act, generally are expected to be enacted as proposed. It is only in rare cases that proposed legislation is not enacted, although it may take years and sometimes minor changes are made. Where there is some doubt that a proposal will be passed, the Notes generally provide useful information in this respect.

CRA's practice is to ask taxpayers to file based on proposed legislation. CRA does not accept "comfort letters" from the Department of Finance as having the force of proposed legislation, but generally will not reassess taxpayers who file on the basis of a comfort letter. (CRA Roundtable, 2009 Canadian Tax Foundation annual conference report, pp. 3:15-16 [*Income Tax Technical News* 44]; VIEWS docs 2009-0345781E5, 2011-0398491C6)

Revised Statutes of Canada, 1985, Fifth Supplement

When Canada's federal statutes were renumbered and consolidated into the *Revised Statutes of Canada, 1985* (RSC 1985), which were proclaimed into force on December 12, 1988, the *Income Tax Act* was not included. The consolidation was done under authority of the *Statute Revision Act*, now called the *Legislative Revision and Consolidation Act*.

The Statute Revision Commission had originally planned to renumber the Act, but after representations from those who work with it (both in and outside government), the Commission eventually agreed to include the Act in the RSC 1985 without renumbering it. Renumbering would have changed all the section numbers, so as to do away with references ending in ".1", ".2" and so on and to eliminate gaps left by repealed provisions.

As of March 1, 1994, the Governor in Council (cabinet) proclaimed into force the RSC 1985, Fifth Supplement, which contains the "revised" *Income Tax Act* and *Income Tax Application Rules*.

The RSC 1985 (5th Supp.) is generally effective for taxation years ending after November 1991. For certain purposes, it is effective for payments made, or other events occurring, after November 1991. ITAR section 73 sets out these application dates.

Although there was no general renumbering of the provisions, there were many other changes. Paragraph letters for definitions (e.g., in section 54) were entirely eliminated, so that definitions can be published in both French and English in their alphabetical order. Some formulas in the legislation were changed from "descriptive" to "algebraic" form. The language throughout the Act was made gender-neutral (as has been the Department of Finance's drafting style since 1989). Certain application provisions of previous enacting legislation were incorporated into the Act (e.g., section 237.2). In theory, all of the changes are non-substantive. However, for an example of a problem in this area involving the meaning of "corporation", see Robert Couzin & Allan Lanthier, "A Comment on the Impact of the *Legislative Revision and Consolidation Act*", Correspondence, 58(1) *Canadian Tax Journal* 223-27 (2010); Lanthier, "Statute Revision", 23(5) *Canadian Tax Highlights* (ctf.ca) 1-2 (May 2015).

Pursuant to section 4 of the *Revised Statutes of Canada, 1985 Act*, SC 1987, c. 48, the consolidation of the RSC 1985 is not intended to change the law. Therefore, the changes made to the Act in the 5th Supplement and by the *Income Tax Amendments Revision Act* should be considered non-substantive. See ITAR 75 and Notes thereto.

The RSC 1985 (5th Supp.) was first included in the 6th edition of PITA, published in August 1994.

Beyond the Act

The following appear after the text of the *Income Tax Act*:

* *Income Tax Application Rules:* referred to as the "ITARs". Part I provides transitional rules for the 1971 tax reform changes to the Act. Some of these rules, such as those dealing with dispositions of capital property owned since before 1972 (e.g., ITAR 26(3)), are still relevant. Part II of the ITARs provides transitional rules for the RSC 1985 (5th Supp.), as described above. "Notes" annotations are provided where appropriate. A comprehensive "Definitions" annotation appears at the end of every section, listing every term used in the section which has a legislative definition.

* *Income Tax Regulations:* Where the Regulations refer to provisions of the Act that were renumbered by the RSC 1985 (5th Supp.), the new numbering is shown in square brackets to assist the reader. "Notes" annotations have been provided where appropriate, recording all changes since 1990. As with the Act, draft regulations and other proposed amendments are reproduced in shaded boxes in context. Detailed "Related Provisions" annotations are provided for many of the Regulations. A "Definitions" annotation appears at the end of every section.

* *Remission Orders:* these provide relief from income tax as approved by the federal Cabinet. We reproduce both "General" remission orders, which apply to many taxpayers, and "Private" remission orders, which apply to only one or a few taxpayers, but are of general interest in that they show the kinds of relief that are available in particular situations.

* *Income Tax Conventions Interpretation Act:* this Act provides rules for the interpretation of Canada's tax treaties. It is annotated with Notes, Related Provisions and Definitions annotations.

* *Multilateral Convention to Implement Tax Treaty Measures* (MLI): not reproduced in full, but portions of it are, along with detailed explanation of how it applies to Canada's tax treaties starting 2020.

* *Canada-U.S. Tax Treaty:* consolidated with the amendments made by several Protocols. Detailed annotations, such as Definitions, Related Provisions, and Notes, are provided. The appropriate portions of the official Technical Explanations to the treaty are reproduced immediately after each Article of the treaty.

* *Canada-U.S. Enhanced Tax Information Exchange Agreement:* passed in 2014 to implement FATCA in Canada. See Notes to ITA s. 269 for explanation.

* *Canada-U.K. Tax Treaty:* Definitions, Notes and other annotations are provided to each section.

* *List of Canada's other tax treaties and current treaty negotiations:* the list has been updated.

* *Topical Index:* I strive to make the Index as helpful as possible, by including many terms that do not appear in the text of the Act but which will be sought by practitioners. I also include references to the Canada-U.S. tax treaty and the *Interpretation Act*. As well, the Index includes an innovative "Dollar amounts" entry which many practitioners find indispensable. All proposed amendments in draft legislation and regulations are reflected in the Index.

Notes — References to "VIEWS" Docs

In the Notes, I include extensive references to documents in the form "VIEWS doc" with a number. These are documents released by CRA to the tax publishers under the *Access to Information Act*. The VIEWS documents are interpretation letters, memoranda and rulings issued in response to a particular inquiry or request. They are not "published" as such by CRA, are not translated from the language in which they are written, and, like CRA publications, are not legally binding. However, they provide useful guidance in illuminating CRA policy and interpretation.

The document ("VIEWS doc") number is provided by CRA and is consistent for all tax publishers. Carswell publishes them on *TaxPartner* (DVD-ROM) and *Taxnet Pro* (Internet) under the heading "CRA VIEWS". They are not available on the CRA web site.

VIEWS document numbers before 2000 were in the form YYnumber, e.g. 9821446 issued in 1998. Beginning in 2000 they were in the form YYYY-number, e.g. 2001-0035621. For documents released from July 20, 2001 to early 2004, the last number is: 0 for Special Project; 1 for a supplemental ruling; 3 for an advance ruling; 4 for Ministerial correspondence; 5 for an external inquiry and 7 for an internal inquiry. Since early 2004, there is a two-character code at the end, e.g. 2004-0056051I7. The codes are:

R3	Ruling (binding; see Notes to ITA 220(1) under "Rulings")
M4	Ministerial correspondence (responding to a letter to the Minister of National Revenue)
E5	External interpretation letter (non-binding, sent to outside CRA)
C6	Conference public statement. I often indicate which conference and question number, e.g.:

APFF — Association de Planification Fiscale et Financière ["APFF Financial" refers to the APFF Financial Strategies and Instruments Roundtable, separate from the main Roundtable at the annual APFF *Congrès*]

CALU — Conference for Advanced Life Underwriting

CLHIA — Canadian Life and Health Insurance Association

CPTS — Canadian Petroleum Tax Society

CTF — Canadian Tax Foundation

IFA — International Fiscal Association

STEP — Society of Trust and Estate Practitioners

TEI — Tax Executives Institute

I7	Internal interpretation letter (non-binding, sent within CRA), but usually applied by Audit as though it were a ruling
A11	Appeals consultation (there is also one instance of "R11", which appears to be a Rulings consultation)
X0, Z0	Other [see Notes to ITA 89(14) and 220(1) for examples; X0 replaced Z0 in 2009]

The year is the year of the inquiry or request. The next six digits are a sequential file number, and the next number is almost always 1, unless the document has been revised (e.g., 2014-0527842I7) or translated (e.g., 2016-0675902I7). Thus, for example, 2008-0304621E5 is file 30462, with the inquiry received in 2008, and is an external interpretation letter.

Notes — References to Case Law

I include in the Notes many citations to case law. These are decisions of the Courts, usually on disputes between taxpayers and CRA but sometimes other cases such as criminal prosecutions, civil lawsuits, and disputes as to priorities over a debtor's funds.

Which courts do what:

- Appeals of income tax and GST/HST assessments go to the Tax Court of Canada (TCC) [see section 169], from there to the Federal Court of Appeal (FCA), and then to the Supreme Court of Canada (SCC), but only with leave of that Court (granted only if the matter is considered to be of national importance). Hence many citations include the reference "leave to appeal denied" with an SCC citation, meaning that the side losing at the FCA sought leave to appeal, and that the Supreme Court did not approve the FCA decision but merely refused to hear the case.

- Some tax matters, such as judicial review of CRA collection action and Taxpayer Relief (formerly called Fairness) decisions (220(3.1)), are heard by the Federal Court (FC) (called the Federal Court — Trial Division (FCTD) until July 2, 2003), whose decisions can be appealed to the FCA. See the Notes to 169(1) and 171(1).

- Some matters, such as prosecutions for tax evasion (s. 239), bankruptcy discharges (Notes to s. 128(2)) and disputes over priorities to assets on a bankruptcy (e.g. s. 224(1.2)), are heard by provincial courts. Each province has a "superior court", called the Supreme Court, Superior Court or Court of Queen's Bench. Appeals from the provincial superior court go to the provincial Court of Appeal, and then, only if leave is granted, to the Supreme Court of Canada.

- Provinces also have lower-level courts, called the Provincial Court, Court of Justice or Court of Quebec, which hear small civil claims and summary criminal matters. In most cases an appeal from this court is to the superior court of the province.

Precedent:

The higher the Court, the more binding and precedential the decision. A case normally stands for the legal principles stated, but will not necessarily apply to a new set of facts if the new facts can be "distinguished". A court's comments that are *obiter* (not required to decide the case) are persuasive, not binding, but may be binding if they are from the Supreme Court of Canada: see *Scott*, 2017 TCC 224, paras. 94-96. CRA is arguably limited in its legal ability to disregard a General Procedure decision unless it can distinguish the facts or can show that the earlier decision was flawed or prejudices its mandate: *Bio-Chem Supply*, 2016 FCA 257, paras. 47-53. The Tax Court is not *bound* to follow previous Tax Court decisions, but judges normally will (even Informal Procedure decisions), under the principle of "judicial comity", unless there is a cogent reason not to: *Friedman*, 2021 FCA 101, paras. 29-31; *Tudora*, 2020 TCC 11, paras. 38-43. For more on understanding how to read case law, see Ted Cook, *Canadian Tax Research* (Carswell, 5th ed., 2010).

Tax Court "Informal Procedure" decisions (see Notes to 169(1)) are technically non-precedential (*Tax Court of Canada Act* s. 18.28), but they are cited and used in argument, and a Tax Court judge will often follow a decision of a fellow judge for reasons of "judicial comity".

Case citations:

Case citations are usually in one of the following forms:

- "C.T.C." — Canada Tax Cases (published by Carswell). The citation "[2003] 2 C.T.C. 145 (FCA)" means volume 2 of the [2003] Canada Tax Cases, beginning at page 145, and that the decision was from the Federal Court of Appeal. This format is historically how all cases were cited before the advent of computer databases and neutral citations (below).

- "CarswellNat" (Carswell electronic citation, on *TaxPartner* or *Taxnet Pro*). The citation "2011 CarswellNat 145 (TCC)" means case number 145 decided in 2011 and stored on the CarswellNat (national jurisdiction, i.e. Tax Court or Federal Courts) database, and that the decision is of the Tax Court of Canada. If the case began in a provincial court, this would be CarswellOnt, Carswell-Que, CarswellBC, CarswellAlta, etc.

- The citation "G.S.T.C." refers to the Canada GST Cases, published by Carswell, which include my detailed Editorial Comment to each case. "[2014] G.S.T.C. 57" means the 57th case reported in the [2014] volumes.

- Neutral citations were introduced in 2001 to allow everyone to cite a case without being dependent on any particular publisher's pagination or case numbering, and the Tax Court of Canada began to use them in 2003. All Canadian courts now issue cases with neutral cites, and generally use neutral cites to cite past cases where possible.

A neutral cite format provides the name of the Court within the cite, so the Court need not be shown separately. It also provides the year in which the decision was issued; a traditional publisher citation like "[2015] 1 C.T.C. 101" may have a 2015 publishing date but may actually be a decision issued in 2014, and thus may be harder to find for a reader without access to the Canada Tax Cases.

Typical neutral cites are:

2015 TCC 123 — written decision #123 issued by the Tax Court of Canada in 2015

2015 FCA 123 — same, by the Federal Court of Appeal

2015 SCC 123 — same, by the Supreme Court of Canada

The neutral citation can *always* be used to identify the court, although some uncommon ones are a little obscure. Examples (e.g., see Notes to 224(1.2)):

YKSC — Yukon Supreme Court

BCCA — British Columbia Court of Appeal

ABPC — Alberta Provincial Court

SKQB — Saskatchewan Court of Queen's Bench

MBCA — Manitoba Court of Appeal

ONSC — Ontario Superior Court of Justice

ONCJ — Ontario Court of Justice

QCCQ — Court of Quebec

QCCA — Quebec Court of Appeal

NBCA — New Brunswick Court of Appeal

NSSC — Nova Scotia Supreme Court

PESCAD — Prince Edward Island Supreme Court, Appeal Division (more recent cases are simply PECA, for PEI Court of Appeal)

Cases from the UK, Australia and New Zealand are also cited (and noted as such). They also use neutral citations, but with brackets for the year, e.g.:

[2019] EWCA Civ 51 — England & Wales Court of Appeal, Civil Division

[2012] UKUT 363 — UK Upper Tribunal

[2021] UKSC 17 — UK Supreme Court

[2014] HCA 21 — High Court of Australia

[2017] FCA 645 — Federal Court of Australia

[2018] FCAFC 38 — Federal Court of Australia, Full Court

[2016] NZSC 91 — New Zealand Supreme Court.

Because neutral citations are more compact, more informative, and accessible to all readers without being dependent on any one legal publisher, they are the preferred form of citation. **Since December 2015, all *new* citations I have added to PITA are in neutral cite format if such a cite is available.** I have also converted existing cites to neutral cites as I update existing Notes, and as of 2021 virtually all of these have been done.

Almost all reported Canadian cases can be found on CanLii.org. Cases from the UK can be found on BaiLii.org, and Australian cases on AustLii.org.

Notes — Annotations with "History" Information

It is important that you not be misled in your expectations of what is in the Notes, to the extent they describe the past history of the provisions of the Act and Regulations. I therefore set out below a detailed explanation of the methodology used in constructing the Notes annotations, beyond the clarifications and explanations of the provision.

The primary goal is *relevance to today*. I have generally eliminated information that is of no relevance for current practitioners.

In building the Notes, I have followed these principles:

1. Notes are descriptive and clear, rather than formal.

2. Non-substantive changes are ignored.

3. Changes after 1988 Tax Reform are listed, but detail is generally omitted for changes before 2016.

4. Rules that still depend on the date of previous events are preserved.

5. Repealed provisions are summarized.

1. Notes are descriptive and clear, rather than formal

The Notes are descriptions of what has really changed, rather than formal "xxxx was substituted for yyyy" statements. With History annotations, you must study every past amendment, determine whether it is relevant, and determine how the legislation read with application to a given set of transactions. I have tried to save you time by summarizing the changes, where possible, clearly and concisely, without sacrificing completeness and accuracy.

Where a provision was repealed and replaced, but the substance was to add or delete a specific subparagraph or phrase, the change is described in terms of that addition or deletion rather than by reprinting the old version and leaving it to the reader to slog through the text word by word looking for differences. Changes are described in terms of their substantive effect, not their legal form. For example, 2019 budget bill #1 amended subparagraph 1100(1)(c)(i) of the Regulations, technically by repealing and replacing it. On examining the amendment, we can see that the existing subparagraph became new clause (i)(A), while new text was added as clause (i)(B), as an amount to be added to (A). My description of the amendment is, therefore, that Reg. 1100(1)(c)(i)(B) was added, which describes the substance of the change.

Furthermore, when a change was made retroactive to the date of introduction of an earlier amendment, the text of the earlier version is usually not reproduced in the Notes, since it is now deemed never to have had any application and thus never to have been in force. Where appropriate, I have added explanation of the nature of such amendments.

The Notes are intended to provide what you need when dealing with the Act as it stands today and for the past 4-5 years, typically the maximum period for dealing with an audit. If you are dealing with years long past and need to see the *exact* wording, consult the "History" annotation on the *TaxPartner* DVD-ROM or *Taxnet Pro* on the Internet.

2. Non-substantive changes are ignored

A formal description of changes in the legislation reflects drafting changes and other non-substantive changes. The Notes do not waste your time with such changes. These include, for example, changing "where" to "if", "he" to "the taxpayer", or "shall be deemed" to "is deemed". However, for very recent changes I usually reproduce the former version so that you can see how it read.

3. Changes after 1988 Tax Reform are described

The 1988 Tax Reform exercise produced an Act that looked quite different from the previous edition. Wholesale changes were made throughout the Act. 1988 is now over 30 years ago, and changes before 1989, or even 2016, are irrelevant to most practitioners in most cases.

You may want to know about changes over the past few years, however. If you are generally familiar with the operation of a provision but have not looked at it for some years, a quick outline of what has changed will help you orient yourself and more quickly familiarize yourself with the statute as it reads now.

As well, you may in 2021 be dealing with 2017–2020 tax issues, particularly when it comes to audits of corporate and personal tax returns. It may therefore be important to know whether the legislation you are reading has the same application for 2018 or 2019 as it does today. (Whether it had the same application in, say, 2010, however, is generally irrelevant.)

I have therefore included an outline of changes introduced since 1988 Tax Reform. A list of the important amending bills can be found following this Introduction.

Where the changes made were effective from 2016 or earlier, I have generally not provided the text of the former version, and have provided instead an outline of the change (but see 4 below). Where the changes are recent, enough information is provided about the earlier version to allow you to know exactly how it applied for 2016–2020. Also, if there are Proposed Amendments to earlier versions of the legislation, I continue to show those earlier versions.

Note that since the 27th edition, I am no longer maintaining the text of old versions of the legislation, going back to 1972, that affect the cost base of property (e.g. deemed disposition rules from the 1980s and 1990s). This change was made to save space and keep the book in one volume. Please consult any edition up to the 26th edition if you need this information.

4. Rules that still depend on the date of previous events are preserved

Simply deleting all History annotations from old years would have been easy. It would also have been irresponsible. The legislation that has amended the Act over the years is rife with "applicable after ...", "applicable with respect to shares issued after ...", "applicable with respect to acquisitions of property after ...", and the like.

The only way to delete the History, keep this book to manageable size and yet not mislead practitioners has been to analyze every amending provision to determine whether it is still relevant. Here are some examples of rules I have preserved:

- Income inclusion from life insurance policies applies differently for policies acquired before 1990 (12.2).
- Loans to a person "connected" with a shareholder may be taxed differently for loans made before November 2011: subsec. 15(2.1).
- The rules on expiry of an option issued by a trust to acquire units of the trust are different for options issued before Oct. 25, 2012: subsec. 49(2.1).
- The restrictive covenant rules apply differently depending on when the covenant was granted: 56.4(3), (7).
- The stop-loss rules in 112(2.2) apply differently to dividends on shares issuesd before June 17, 1987.
- The definition 146(1)"non-qualified investment" applies differently for investments acquired before March 23, 2011.
- Earlier versions of section 204.81 contain rules that still apply to labour-sponsored venture capital corporations that were incorporated before March 6, 1996.
- Subsection 250(5) in its pre-1998 form still applies to certain individuals depending on their residence status on February 24, 1998.
- Reg. 6202.1(5)"excluded obligation" reads differently for shares and rights issued under an agreement entered into before December 21, 2002.

In most cases, where changes were made applicable after a given date or as of a given taxation year that is before 2015, the older wording is not preserved. Where changes were made applicable with respect to transactions or events after a specific date (e.g., acquisition of control, issuance of shares, etc.), the provision has been analyzed to determine whether the earlier rules are still relevant today. If they are, they are reproduced, or enough information is given about the changes (e.g., "paragraph (c) added") so that you can apply the earlier rules.

5. Repealed provisions are summarized

I have violated, in one respect, the rule that older changes are generally irrelevant unless they have application today. Where a section or subsection was repealed and not replaced, you may wonder what you're missing. Even if the provision was repealed many years ago, I generally provide a brief outline of the subject matter of the provision, when it was repealed, and, if appropriate, where the provision was moved to.

I welcome comments from readers with suggestions for improvement or corrections to the Notes, or to any of the other annotations.

Finally, I wish to thank the superb team of editors at Carswell (Thomson Reuters), who maintain the legislation and process all my annotation updates throughout the year. Seán DaCosta and Scott McVicar have been editing and maintaining the Act for decades, and their work is integral to the success of the *Practitioner's Income Tax Act*. Carol Klein Beernink, who retired at the end of 2016, was a stalwart editor who worked on PITA from the very first edition in 1991 until her retirement, and helped immensely in keeping the text and many annotations accurate. I also thank Richard Yasny for exceptionally helpful feedback on all of the updates I have written since 2013.

David M. Sherman
July 2021
e-mail: ds@davidsherman.ca
web site: www.davidsherman.ca

consult issues of statute story, the pro ... ion has been analysed to determine whether the earlier rules are still relevant today. If they are repealed, or enough information is given about the changes ... in the graphic) added, so that you can apply the earlier rules.

5. Repealed provisions are annotated

have violated, in one respect the rule, but other changes and generally more important, unless they have implication today. Where a section or subsection was repealed and not replaced, you may wonder what you're missing. Even if the provision was repealed many years ago. I generally provide a hint of what the subject matter of the provision was when it was enacted and if inappropriate. Where the provision was moved to.

I welcome comments from readers with suggestions for improvement or corrections to the Notes, or to any of the other annotations.

Finally, I wish to thank the superb team of editors at Carswell/Thomson (Reuters) who maintain the publication and process all my annotation updates throughout the year. Seanna Parsons and Scott McVicar have been editing and maintaining the Act for decades and their work is integral to the success of the publication. Income Tax Act. Carol Klein-Beernink, who retired in the end of 2016 was a stalwart editor who worked on ITA from the very first edition in 1991 until 2016 team and helped immeasurably in keeping the text and many annotations accurate. I also thank Krishan Yadav for exceptionally helpful assistance on all of the updates I have written since 2017.

David M. Sherman
July 2021
e-mail: ds@davidsherman.ca
web site: www.davidsherman.ca

xiii

IMPORTANT AMENDING BILLS SINCE 1988 TAX REFORM

(as referred to in "Notes" annotations)

Bill or Budget	Bill No.	Citation	Royal Assent
1988 tax reform	C-139	S.C. 1988, c. 55	September 13, 1988
1988 Tax Court bill	C-146	S.C. 1988, c. 61	September 22, 1988 (in force January 1, 1991)
1989 budget	C-28	S.C. 1990, c. 39	October 23, 1990
1990 pension bill	C-52	S.C. 1990, c. 35	June 27, 1990
1990 garnishment/collection bill	C-51	S.C. 1990, c. 34	June 27, 1990
1990 GST	C-62	S.C. 1990, c. 45	December 17, 1990
1990 budget/1991 budget/1991 technical bill	C-18	S.C. 1991, c. 49	December 17, 1991
— (RSC-redrafted)	C-15	S.C. 1994, c. 7, Sch. II	May 12, 1994
1992 transportation support bill	C-75	S.C. 1992, c. 29	June 23, 1992
— (RSC-redrafted)	C-15	S.C. 1994, c. 7, Sch. VI	May 12, 1994
1992 Child Benefit bill	C-80	S.C. 1992, c. 48	October 15, 1992
— (RSC-redrafted)	C-15	S.C. 1994, c. 7, Sch. VII	May 12, 1994
1992 budget/1992 technical bill	C-92	S.C. 1993, c. 24	June 10, 1993
— (RSC-redrafted)	C-15	S.C. 1994, c. 7, Sch VIII	May 12, 1994

Note: The "RSC-redrafted" bills above were re-drafts of the original bills, revised to be consistent with the revisions to the Act made in the R.S.C. 1985 (5th Supp.) version which was proclaimed in force March 1, 1994, but which generally was effective retroactive to December 1, 1991. The redrafted versions of the bills are intended to be identical in meaning to the originals, differing only in that they make the bills conform to the new form of the Act. The consolidated Act as printed here reflects the redrafted amendments.

Bill or Budget	Bill No.	Citation	Royal Assent
1992 Economic Statement/1993 budget	C-9	S.C. 1994, c. 8	May 12, 1994
Department of National Revenue Act bill	C-2	S.C. 1994, c. 13	May 12, 1994
1993 technical bill	C-27	S.C. 1994, c. 21	June 15, 1994
1994 tobacco tax reduction bill	C-32	S.C. 1994, c. 29	June 23, 1994
1994 budget	C-59	S.C. 1995, c. 3	March 26, 1995
1994 technical bill	C-70	S.C. 1995, c. 21	June 22, 1995
1995 cultural property bill	C-93	S.C. 1995, c. 38	December 5, 1995
Department of Human Resources Development Act	C-11	S.C. 1996, c. 11	May 29, 1996
1995 budget	C-36	S.C. 1996, c. 21	June 20, 1996
Employment Insurance Act	C-12	S.C. 1996, c. 23	June 20, 1996
GST technical amendments	C-70	S.C. 1997, c. 10	March 20, 1997
Bankruptcy and insolvency bill	C-5	S.C. 1997, c. 12	April 25, 1997
1996 budget	C-92	S.C. 1997, c. 25	April 25, 1997
1997 budget bill #1	C-93	S.C. 1997, c. 26	April 25, 1997
1997 budget (main bill)	C-28 (Div. A)	S.C. 1998, c. 19	June 18, 1998
1995-97 technical bill	C-28 (Div. B)	S.C. 1998, c. 19	June 18, 1998
1998 budget bill #1	C-36	S.C. 1998, c. 21	June 18, 1998
Canada Customs & Revenue Agency Act	C-43	S.C. 1999, c. 17	April 29, 1999
1999 budget bill #1	C-71	S.C. 1999, c. 26	June 17, 1999
1998 budget (main bill)	C-72	S.C. 1999, c. 22	June 17, 1999
Same-sex partners bill	C-23	S.C. 2000, c. 12	June 29, 2000
1999 budget (main bill)	C-25	S.C. 2000, c. 19	June 29, 2000
2000 budget bill #1	C-32	S.C. 2000, c. 14	June 29, 2000
2000 GST bill	C-24	S.C. 2000, c. 30	October 20, 2000
2000 budget (main bill)/2001 technical bill	C-22 (Part 1)	S.C. 2001, c. 17	June 14, 2001
2001 *Civil Code* harmonization bill	C-22 (Part 2)	S.C. 2001, c. 17	June 14, 2001
2001 anti-terrorism bill	C-36	S.C. 2001, c. 41	December 18, 2001
2002 courts administration bill	C-30	S.C. 2002, c. 8	March 27, 2002
2001 budget	C-49	S.C. 2002, c. 9	March 27, 2002
2003 election financing bill	C-24	S.C. 2003, c. 19	June 19, 2003
2003 budget	C-28	S.C. 2003, c. 15	June 19, 2003

Bill or Budget	Bill No.	Citation	Royal Assent
2003 resource bill	C-48	S.C. 2003, c. 28	November 7, 2003
2004 budget bill #1	C-30	S.C. 2004, c. 22	May 14, 2004
2004 *Civil Code* harmonization bill	S-10	S.C. 2004, c. 25	December 15, 2004
2004 RESPs bill	C-5	S.C. 2004, c. 26	December 15, 2004
2004 budget	C-33	S.C. 2005, c. 19	May 13, 2005
2005 budget bill #1	C-43	S.C. 2005, c. 30	June 29, 2005
2005 same-sex marriage bill	C-38	S.C. 2005, c. 33	July 20, 2005
2004 CRA/CBSA bill	C-26	S.C. 2005, c. 38	November 3, 2005
2006 budget bill #1	C-13	S.C. 2006, c. 4	June 22, 2006
2006 budget bill #2	C-28	S.C. 2007, c. 2	February 21, 2007
2007 budget bill #1	C-52	S.C. 2007, c. 29	June 22, 2007
2007 budget bill #2	C-28 (Part 3)	S.C. 2007, c. 35	December 14, 2007
2007 RDSPs bill	C-28 (Part 4)	S.C. 2007, c. 35	December 14, 2007
2007 Economic Statement	C-28 (Part 14)	S.C. 2007, c. 35	December 14, 2007
2008 budget bill #1	C-50	S.C. 2008, c. 28	June 18, 2008
2009 budget bill #1/2008 budget bill #2	C-10	S.C. 2009, c. 2	March 12, 2009
2009 budget bill #2	C-51	S.C. 2009, c. 31	December 15, 2009
2010 budget bill #1	C-9	S.C. 2010, c. 12	July 12, 2010
2010 budget bill #2	C-47	S.C. 2010, c. 25	December 15, 2010
2011 budget bill #1	C-3	S.C. 2011, c. 15	June 26, 2011
2011 budget bill #2	C-13	S.C. 2011, c. 24	December 15, 2011
2012 budget bill #1	C-38	S.C. 2012, c. 19	June 29, 2012
2012 budget bill #2	C-45	S.C. 2012, c. 31	December 14, 2012
2013 budget bill #1	C-60	S.C. 2013, c. 33	June 26, 2013
2002-2013 technical bill	C-48	S.C. 2013, c. 34	June 26, 2013
2013 budget bill #2 (and technical amendments)	C-4	S.C. 2013, c. 40	December 12, 2013
2014 budget bill #1	C-31	S.C. 2014, c. 20	June 19, 2014
2014 budget bill #2	C-43	S.C. 2014, c. 39	December 16, 2014
2015 budget bill #1	C-59	S.C. 2015, c. 36	June 23, 2015
2016 budget bill #1/2015 budget bill #2	C-15	S.C. 2016, c. 7	June 22, 2016
2016 tax-rate bill	C-2	S.C. 2016, c. 11	December 15, 2016
2016 budget bill #2	C-29	S.C. 2016, c. 12	December 15, 2016
2016 CPP premium increases bill (for 2019)	C-26	S.C. 2016, c. 14	December 15, 2016
2017 budget bill #1	C-44	S.C. 2017, c. 20	June 22, 2017
2017 budget bill #2	C-63	S.C. 2017, c. 33	December 14, 2017
2018 budget bill #1	C-74	S.C. 2018, c. 12	June 21, 2018
2018 budget bill #2	C-86	S.C. 2018, c. 27	December 13, 2018
2019 budget bill #1	C-97	S.C. 2019, c. 29	June 21, 2019
2020 COVID bill #1	C-13	S.C. 2020, c. 5	March 25, 2020
2020 COVID bill #2	C-14	S.C. 2020, c. 6	April 11, 2020
2020 COVID bill #3	C-20 (replacing C-17)	S.C. 2020, c. 11	July 27, 2020
2020 COVID bill #4	C-4 (replacing C-2)	S.C. 2020, c. 12	October 2, 2020
2020 COVID bill #5	C-9	S.C. 2020, c. 13	November 19, 2020
2021 COVID bill #1	C-14	S.C. 2021, c. 7	May 6, 2021
2021 family business transfers bill	C-208	S.C. 2021, c. 21	June 29, 2021
2021 budget bill #1 [also 2019 budget bill #2]	C-30	S.C. 2021, c. 23	June 29, 2021

TABLE OF PROPOSED AMENDMENTS AND ANNOUNCED ADMINISTRATIVE CHANGES

The following table will assist readers in finding, in the shaded boxes throughout the Act and Regulations, the proposed amendments and notable current administrative changes announced at various times. If you know the subject-matter of announced changes but cannot find them in the legislation, scan the "Subject" column (or consult the Topical Index). If you know the approximate date on which the changes were announced, use the first column, which lists the proposals in chronological order. A separate Table of Comfort Letters appears following this table.

Where proposals do not include (and have not been superseded by) draft legislation, the relevant portions of the announcement or press release are reproduced in shaded boxes under the provisions of the Act or Regulations that are expected to be amended.

The Department of Finance announced on November 17, 2014 that all currently pending legislative proposals from before April 2013, other than certain ones listed in the announcement, are withdrawn. This applies to various proposals such as December 1991 interest deductibility (20(1)(c) and others); October 2003 REOP (3.1 and others); and September 2004 mutual fund status (132(7) and others). It does not apply to proposals that were not yet in legislative form (i.e., Budget and news release announcements) and are still listed below.

Except where indicated, all press/news releases and draft legislation emanate from the federal Department of Finance, fin.gc.ca.

Bill no. or date of Public Statement	Subject	Reproduced at section no.
News releases, March 2, 1993; Oct. 1, 1993	Limit on deductibility of provincial payroll and capital taxes	18 [end]
Federal budget, Feb. 28, 2000 (most measures enacted in 2001)	Extension of interest offset rule to individuals (still pending, in theory)	161.1
Federal Economic Statement, Oct. 18, 2000 (most measures enacted in 2001)	Cross-border share-for-share exchanges	86.1
Federal budget, Feb. 18, 2003	Cross-border share-for-share exchanges	86.1
CCRA Registered Plans Directorate newsletter, June 27, 2003	New participating pension supervisory authority	Reg. 8409(2)
Federal budget, March 23, 2004	Cross-border share-for-share exchanges	86.1
News release, Dec. 16, 2004	Limit on deductibility of provincial payroll and capital taxes	18 [end]
Federal budget, Feb. 23, 2005	Cross-border share-for-share exchanges	86.1
Federal budget, March 19, 2007	Limit on deductibility of provincial payroll and capital taxes	18 [end]
Draft regulations, July 16, 2010	Film or videotape — deemed cost reduction	Reg. 1100(21.1)
Bill C-74, First Reading June 18, 2015 (requires reintroduction to be enacted)	Canada-Quebec Gulf of St. Lawrence Petroleum Resources Accord	124(4), 241(4)(d)(vi), (11), 248(1)"joint management area"
Federal budget, March 22, 2016 (most items enacted by 2016 Budget bills #1 and 2)	Information return on disposition of certain interests in a life insurance policy	Reg. 217(2)
Draft legislation, Sept. 16, 2016 (other measures enacted by 2017 Budget bill #2)	Stock option deduction — prescribed shares: amendment to accommodate TELUS	Reg. 6204(1)(b)
Federal budget, March 22, 2017 (other measures enacted by 2017 Budget bills #1 and 2, and 2018 Budget bill #1)	OECD BEPS Action Plan	95 [end]
	Trust reporting of beneficial ownership	150(1.2) (see also draft legislation, July 27, 2018)
Agriculture and Agri-Food Canada news release, Nov. 6, 2017	2016-17 tax relief re bovine tuberculosis for livestock producers (Alberta, Saskatchewan)	80.3(3)
News release, Dec. 11, 2017	Trust reporting of beneficial ownership	150(1.2) (see also draft legislation, July 27, 2018)
News release, Dec. 22, 2017	Automobile dollar limits and amounts for 2018	Reg. 7306
Federal budget, Feb. 27, 2018 (other measures enacted by 2018 Budget bill #1)	Trust reporting of beneficial ownership	150(1.2) (see also draft legislation, July 27, 2018)
	More funding for the Tax Court	169(1)

Table of Proposed Amendments

Bill no. or date of Public Statement	Subject	Reproduced at section no.
Draft legislation, July 27, 2018 (other measures enacted by 2018 Budget bill #2)	Trust reporting of beneficial ownership	150(1.1), (1.2), 163(5), (6), Reg. 204.2, 4802(1.1)
Agriculture and Agri-Food Canada news releases, Sept. 14, 2018; Oct. 31, 2018	2018 tax relief re drought for livestock producers (see now Jan. 30, 2019 news release)	Reg. 7305.01(1)
News release, Dec. 27, 2018	Automobile dollar limits and amounts for 2019	Reg. 7305.1, 7306, 7307
Agriculture and Agri-Food Canada news release, Jan. 30, 2019	2018 tax relief re drought for livestock producers (BC, Alberta, Sask., Manitoba, Ontario, Quebec, New Brunswick)	Reg. 7305.01(1)
CRA news release and consultation, March 18, 2019	Northern residents' deduction — "Lowest airfare" requirement	Reg. 7304(2)(c)
Federal budget, March 19, 2019 (other measures enacted by 2019 Budget bill #1 and 2021 Budget bill #1)	Intergenerational business transfers	70(9)–(9.31)
	Aboriginal income taxation	81(1)(a)
	Fertility-related expenses	118.2(2.2)
	Audits in real estate sector	231.1(1)
	More resources to combat tax evasion	239(1)
Agriculture and Agri-Food Canada news release, July 22, 2019	2019 tax relief re drought for livestock producers (see now Feb. 18, 2020 news release)	Reg. 7305.01(1)
Liberal party election platform, Oct. 2019	Interest deductibility	20(1)(c)
	Maternity and parental EI benefits to be exempt	56(1)(a)(iv)
	Intergenerational business transfers	70(9)–(9.31)
	Increase northern residents' deduction for travel	110.7(1)
	Increase Canada Child Benefit by 15% for children under 1; Double the Child Disability benefit	122.61(1)
	Corporate tax rate cut in half for clean tech businesses	123.4(2)
Prime Minister's mandate letters to five Ministers, Dec. 2019	Interest deductibility	20(1)(c)
	Documenting fossil fuel subsidies	66.1(6)"Canadian exploration expense"
	Intergenerational business transfers	70(9)–(9.31)
	Increase northern residents' deduction for travel	110.7(1)
	Digital Services Tax on large non-resident businesses	115(1)
	Increase Canada Child Benefit by 15% for children under 1; Double the Child Disability benefit	122.61(1)
	Corporate tax rate cut in half for clean tech businesses	123.4(2)
	Anti-avoidance: large multinational companies	Multilateral Instrument (before Canada-US Treaty)
News release, Dec. 19, 2019	Automobile dollar limits and amounts for 2020	Reg. 7305.1, 7306, 7307
Draft legislation, Dec. 20, 2019	Amateur athlete trusts	143.1(3), (3.1)
Agriculture and Agri-Food Canada news release, Feb. 18, 2020	2019 tax relief re drought for livestock producers (BC, Alberta, Sask., Manitoba, Ontario, Quebec)	Reg. 7305.01(1)
Finance Backgrounder, March 18, 2020; CRA releases, March 18, 2020; Aug. 25, 2020; Jan. 19, 2021	Electronic signature to authorize corporate e-filing	241(5)
CRA notice, April 23, 2020	Deferral of source deduction-related payments under bankruptcy proposal	224(1.2)
Tax Court of Canada notice, Aug. 5, 2020	COVID-19 — TCC hearings and shutdown	169(1)
Fall Economic Statement, Nov. 30, 2020 (other measures enacted by 2021 Budget bill #1)	COVID-19 — Employee home office expenses in 2020	8(13)
	Additional tax on vacant housing owned by non-residents	115(1)(b)

Bill no. or date of Public Statement	Subject	Reproduced at section no.
	Digital Services Tax on large non-resident businesses	115(1)
	More resources to combat tax evasion	239(1)
	GAAR expanded	245(2)
CRA news release and backgrounder, Dec. 15, 2020	COVID-19 — Administrative policies re employee benefits and allowances in 2020	6(1)(a), (1.1), 8(1)(i), (10), (13)
News release, Dec. 21, 2020	Automobile dollar limits and amounts for 2021	Reg. 7305.1, 7306, 7307
Private Member's Bill S-222, First Senate Reading Feb. 8, 2021; First House Reading June 23, 2021	*Effective and Accountable Charities Act*	149.1(1)"charitable activities"; also throughout 149.1; 188(1.1), 188.1(5), (12), 189(6.2)
CRA news release, Feb. 9, 2021	Interest waiver on income tax debt arising from COVID-19 support	220(3.1)
CRA notice, April 2021	COVID-19 — 2021 filing and payment deadlines not extended	150(1) opening words
CRA notice, April 9, 2021	Requesting clearance certificate by email	159(2)
Federal budget, April 19, 2021 (other measures enacted by 2021 Budget bill #1)	Employee ownership trusts	7(1)
	Interest deduction limited to 30% of tax EBITDA	20(1)(c)
	Aboriginal income taxation	81(1)(a)
	OECD BEPS Action Plan	95 [end]
	Increase northern residents' deduction for travel	110.7(1)
	Additional tax on vacant housing owned by non-residents	115(1)(b)
	Digital Services Tax on large non-resident businesses	115(1)
	Disability Tax Credit — eligibility enacted	118.3(1)
	COVID-19 — Student loans — interest waiver	118.62
	Climate action incentive to be paid quarterly	122.8(4)
	Corporate tax rate cut in half for clean tech businesses	123.4(2)
	ITC for carbon-capture technology	127(9)"investment tax credit"
	Postdoctoral fellowship income	146(1)"earned income"(b.01)
	Fixing contribution errors in defined-contribution plans	147.2(1)
	Disbursement quota rules (consultation)	149.1(1)"disbursement quota"
	Corporation beneficial ownership registry	150(1)(a) Notes
	Avoidance of tax debts	160(1)
	More Tax Court judges	169(1)
	Taxes applicable to registered investments	204.6(1)
	More money for CRA, including for automated T1 Adjustments	220(1)
	More money for CRA Collections	222(2)
	Audit authorities	231.1(1), (2)
	Audits in real estate sector	231.1(1)
	Mandatory disclosure rules	237.3
	More money to CRA to combat tax evasion	239(1)
	More money to CRA for protecting information	241(1)
	Electronic filing and communications	244(14.1)
	GAAR expanded	245(2)
	Transfer Pricing Rules (consultation)	247(2)
	Hybrid mismatch arrangements	248(1)"corporation"
	$1.5m immediate expensing for CCPCs	Reg. 1100(1)(a)
	Film and video credits	Reg. 1106(1)"application for a certificate of completion"
	Northern Residents Deduction	Reg. 7304(2)

Table of Proposed Amendments

Bill no. or date of Public Statement	Subject	Reproduced at section no.
	Capital cost allowance for clean energy equipment	Reg. Sch. II:Cl. 43.1, 43.2
CRA notice, as of April 19, 2021	CRA response to COVID-19 crisis	220(1)
CRA notice, updated to April 26, 2021	COVID-19 — Payments to persons eligible for disability credit	118.3(1)
CRA notice, April 27, 2021	International issues raised by COVID-19 crisis (mostly due to travel restrictions)	250(1)(a)
Agriculture and Agri-Food Canada news release, May 10, 2021	2020 tax relief re drought for livestock producers (Quebec, New Brunswick, PEI, Nova Scotia)	Reg. 7305.01(1)
News release, backgrounder, consultation, May 28, 2021	Insurance corporations — consultation on implementation of IFRS 17 accounting rules	138(2)
Tax Court of Canada releases to June 1, 2021	Tax Court reopening, re-closing and deadlines	169(1)
News release and consultation, June 7, 2021	ITC for carbon-capture technology	127(9)"investment tax credit"
Bill C-31, First Reading June 10, 2021	*Reducing Barriers to Reintegration Act*: terminology change from "pardon" to "record suspension"	149.1(1)"ineligible individual", (1.01)
Employment and Social Development Canada news release, June 22, 2021	Canada Disability Benefit	118.3(1)
Bill C-35, First Reading June 22, 2021	*Canada Disability Benefit Act* — allowing CRA to disclose information for administration of new benefit by ESDC	241(4)(d)(vii.51)
CRA news release, June 25, 2021	Registered pension plan annual information return — T244 filing deadline in 2021	Reg. 8409(1)
News release, June 30, 2021	Private Member's Bill changes re transfer of business to family members	84.1(2)(e)

TABLE OF DEPARTMENT OF FINANCE COMFORT LETTERS

The following table will assist readers in finding, in the shaded boxes throughout the Act and Regulations, Department of Finance "comfort letters" issued for amendments that have not yet appeared as draft legislation. The comfort letters are placed and annotated by David M. Sherman, from information released under the *Access to Information Act*.

CANADA REVENUE AGENCY DIRECTORY

Website: canada.ca/tax

Government Electronic Directory Service (all federal government employees, though most CRA employees in local Tax Services Offices are not listed): geds.gc.ca

CRA commonly-used phone numbers: tinyurl.com/cra-contact

Individuals:

Order tax packages: 1-855-330-3305

Check tax account balance: 1-866-474-8272

Check status of filed return: 1-800-959-1956

Get various amounts and balances: 1-800-267-6999

Make payment arrangement (automated service): 1-866-256-1147

Discuss payment arrangements (human contact): 1-888-863-8657

Canada Child Benefit, GST/HST Credit: 1-800-387-1193 (YK, NT and NU: 1-866-426-1527)

Canada Emergency Response Benefit, Canada Emergency Student Benefit: 1-833-966-2099

International and non-resident withholding tax: 1-855-284-5946 (613-940-8499)

Requirement to Pay (garnishment) response: 1-800-675-6184

Ontario tax credits and benefits: 1-877-627-6645

Alberta tax credits and benefits: 1-800-959-2809

Phoenix (federal government payroll) tax issues: 1-888-556-5083

Other inquiries including online services help: 1-800-959-8281 (YK, NT and NU: 1-866-426-1527)

Businesses:

Canada Emergency Wage Subsidy: 1-833-966-2099

T2 e-filing help: 1-800-959-2803

Discuss payment arrangements (corporate tax debt): 1-866-291-6346

Discuss payment arrangements (GST/HST debt): 1-877-477-5068

Discuss payment arrangements (payroll debt): 1-877-548-6016

Other inquiries including online services help: 1-800-959-5525 (YK, NT and NU: 1-866-841-1876)

Charities: 1-800-267-2384

Tax Centres

Jonquière Tax Centre
2251 René-Lévesque Blvd.
Jonquière, QC G7S 5J2
Fax: (418) 548-0846

Prince Edward Island Tax Centre
275 Pope Road
Summerside, PE C1N 6A2
Fax: (902) 432-6287

Winnipeg Tax Centre
66 Stapon Road
Winnipeg, MB R3C 3M2
Fax: (204) 984-5164
Mailing: P.O. Box 14001, Stn Main
Winnipeg, MB R3C 3M3

Sudbury Tax Centre
1050 Notre Dame Avenue
Mailing: P.O. Box 20000, Station A
Sudbury, ON P3A 5C1*
*For T1 returns use P3A 5C2; for remittances, P3A 5C3; for GST filings, P3A 6B4
Fax: (705) 671-3994 or (855) 276-1529

Tax Services Offices

Newfoundland and Labrador

Newfoundland and Labrador Tax Services Office (served by Sudbury Tax Centre [individual]/PEI Tax Centre [business])
165 Duckworth Street
St. John's, NL A1C 1G4
Fax: (709) 754-5928
Mailing: P.O. Box 12075, Station A
St. John's, NL A1B 4R5

Prince Edward Island

Prince Edward Island Tax Services Office (served by Sudbury Tax Centre [individual]/PEI Tax Centre [business])
1-30 Brackley Point Road

Charlottetown, PE C1A 6X9
Fax: (902) 566-7197
Mailing: P.O. Box 8500, Station Central
Charlottetown, PE C1A 8L3

Nova Scotia

(served by Sudbury Tax Centre [individual]/PEI Tax Centre [business])

Halifax Tax Services Office
100-145 Hobsons Lake Drive
Halifax, NS B3S 0J1
Fax: (902) 450-8561
Mailing: P.O. Box 638, Station Central
Halifax, NS B3J 2T5

Sydney Tax Services Office
47 Dorchester Street
Sydney, NS B1P 7H5
Fax: (902) 564-3095
Mailing: P.O. Box 1300, Station A
Sydney, NS B1P 6K3

New Brunswick

(all served by Sudbury Tax Centre [individual]/PEI Tax Centre [business])

Bathurst Tax Services Office
955 Murray Avenue
Bathurst, NB E2A 0C8
Fax: (506) 548-7176

Moncton Tax Services Office
217-770 Main Street
Moncton, NB E1C 1E7
Fax: (506) 851-7018

Saint John Tax Services Office
65 Canterbury Street
Saint John, NB E2L 2C7
Fax: (506) 636-5200
Mailing: P.O. Box 6300, Retail Postal Outlet Brunswick Square
Saint John, NB E2L 4H9

Québec

Central and Southern Québec (Brossard) Tax Services Office*
3250 Lapinière Blvd.
Brossard, QC J4Z 3T8
Fax: (450) 926-7100

Central and Southern Québec (Sherbrooke) Tax Services Office**
50 Place de la Cité, P.O. Box 1300
Sherbrooke, QC J1H 5L8
Fax: (819) 564-4226

Central and Southern Québec (Trois-Rivières) Tax Services Office*
2250 St-Olivier Street
Trois-Rivières, QC G9A 4E9
Fax: (819) 371-2744

Eastern Québec (Chicoutimi) Tax Services Office*
100 La Fontaine Street
Chicoutimi, QC G7H 6X2
Fax: (418) 698-6387
Mailing: P.O. Box 1660, Stn Bureau-chef
Jonquière, QC G7S 4L3

Eastern Québec (Québec) Tax Services Office*
2575 Ste-Anne Blvd.
Québec, QC G1J 1Y5
Fax: (418) 649-6478

Eastern Québec (Rimouski) Tax Services Office*
Suite 101, 180 de la Cathédrale Avenue
Rimouski, QC G5L 5H9
Fax: (418) 722-3027

Montréal Tax Services Office**
305 René-Lévesque Blvd. W.
Montréal, QC H2Z 1A6
Fax: (514) 496-1309

Western Québec (Gatineau) Tax Services Office**
300-85 Chemin de La Savane
Gatineau, QC J8T 8L5
Fax: (819) 994-1103

Western Québec (Laval) Tax Services Office*
3400 Jean-Béraud Avenue
Laval, QC H7T 2Z2
Fax: (514) 496-1309

Western Québec (Rouyn-Noranda) Tax Services Office*
44 du Lac Avenue
Rouyn-Noranda, QC J9X 6Z9
Fax: (819) 797-8366

* served by Jonquière Tax Centre (individual)/PEI Tax Centre (business)
** served by Sudbury Tax Centre (individual)/PEI Tax Centre (business)

Ontario

East Central Ontario (Belleville) Tax Services Office*
11 Station Street
Belleville, ON K8N 2S3
Fax: (613) 969-7845

East Central Ontario (Peterborough) Tax Services Office*
1161 Crawford Drive
Peterborough, ON K9J 6X6
Fax: (705) 876-6422

Hamilton Niagara (St. Catharines) Tax Services Office*
32 Church Street
St. Catharines, ON L2R 3B9
Fax: (905) 688-5996

London-Windsor (London) Tax Services Office**
451 Talbot Street
London, ON N6A 5E5
Fax: (519) 645-4029

North Central Ontario (Barrie) Tax Services Office (served by
Sudbury Tax Centre)
81 Mulcaster Street
Barrie, ON L4M 6T7
Fax: (705) 721-0056

Ottawa Tax Services Office*
333 Laurier Avenue W.
Ottawa, ON K1A 0L9
Fax: (613) 952-1982

Toronto East Tax Services Office (served by Sudbury Tax Centre)
200 Town Centre Court
Toronto, ON M1P 4Y3
Fax: (416) 973-5126

Toronto West-Thunder Bay (Mississauga) Tax Services Office
(served by Sudbury Tax Centre)
5800 Hurontario Street
Mississauga, ON L5R 4B4
Fax: (905) 566-6182

East Central Ontario (Kingston) Tax Services Office*
102-1475 John Counter Blvd.
Kingston, ON K7M 0E6
Fax: (613) 541-7158

Hamilton Niagara (Hamilton) Tax Services Office**
55 Bay Street N.
Hamilton, ON L8R 3P7
Fax: (905) 546-1615

Kitchener/Waterloo Tax Services Office**
166 Frederick Street
Kitchener, ON N2H 0A9
Fax: (519) 579-4532

London-Windsor (Windsor) Tax Services Office**
441 University Avenue W., Suite 101
Windsor, ON N9A 5S8
Fax: (519) 257-6558

North Central Ontario (Sudbury) Tax Services Office
(Sudbury/Nickel Belt served by Sudbury Tax Centre; N.E. Ontario*)
1050 Notre Dame Avenue
Sudbury, ON P3A 5C1
Fax: (705) 671-3994/(855) 276-1529

Toronto Centre Tax Services Office (served by Sudbury Tax Centre)
1 Front Street W.
Toronto, ON M5J 2X6
Fax: (416) 360-8908

Toronto North Tax Services Office (served by Sudbury Tax Centre)
5001 Yonge Street
Toronto, ON M2N 6R9
Fax: (416) 512-2558

Toronto West-Thunder Bay (Thunder Bay) Tax Services Office**
130 Syndicate Avenue South
Thunder Bay, ON P7E 1C7
Fax: (807) 622-8512

* served by Sudbury Tax Centre (individual)/PEI Tax Centre (business)
** served by Winnipeg Tax Centre (individual)/PEI Tax Centre (business)

Manitoba

(served by Winnipeg Tax Centre [individual]/PEI Tax Centre [business])
Brandon Tax Services Office
210-153 11th Street
Brandon, MB R7A 7K6
Fax: (204) 726-7836

Winnipeg Tax Services Office
500-360 Main Street
Winnipeg, MB R3C 3Z3
Mailing: P.O. Box 1022, Stn Main
Winnipeg, MB R3C 2W2
Fax: (204) 984-5164

Saskatchewan

(served by Winnipeg Tax Centre [individual]/PEI Tax Centre [business])
Regina Tax Services Office
1955 Smith Street

Saskatoon Tax Services Office
340 3rd Avenue N.

Regina, SK S4P 2N9
Fax: (306) 757-1412

Saskatoon, SK S7K 0A8
Fax: (306) 652-3211

Alberta

(all served by Winnipeg Tax Centre [individual]/PEI Tax Centre [business])

Edmonton Tax Services Office
9700 Jasper Avenue, Suite 10
Edmonton, AB T5J 4C8
Fax: (780) 495-3533

Southern Alberta (Calgary) Tax Services Office
220 4th Avenue S.E.
Calgary, AB T2G 0L1
Fax: (403) 264-5843

Southern Alberta (Lethbridge) Tax Services Office
300-400 4th Avenue S.
Lethbridge, AB T1J 4E1
Fax: (403) 382-4765

Southern Alberta (Red Deer) Tax Services Office
201-4911 51 Street
Red Deer, AB T4N 6V4
Fax: (403) 309-7878

British Columbia

Fraser Valley Tax Services Office
9737 King George Boulevard
Surrey, BC V3T 5W6
Fax: (604) 587-2010

Vancouver Tax Services Office
468 Terminal Avenue
Vancouver, BC V6A 0C1
Fax: (604) 689-7536

Southern Interior B.C. Tax Services Offices
• 277 Winnipeg Street
  Penticton, BC V2A 1N6
  Fax: (250) 492-8346
• 200-471 Queensway Avenue
  Kelowna, BC V1Y 6S5
  Fax: (250) 862-4744

Vancouver Island and North Tax Services Offices
• 280 Victoria Street
  Prince George, BC V2L 4X3
  Fax: (250) 561-7869
• 1415 Vancouver Street
  Victoria, BC V8V 3W4
  Fax: (250) 363-3042

Mailing Address for all offices
(all served by Winnipeg Tax Centre [individual]/PEI Tax Centre [business])
9755 King George Boulevard
Surrey, BC V3T 5E1

Northwest Territories

(See Edmonton Tax Services Office above.)

Yukon

(See Vancouver Island and North (Prince George) Tax Services Office above.)

Nunavut

(See Ottawa Tax Services Office above.)

International Tax Services Office

Office address:
2204 Walkley Road
Ottawa, ON K1A 1A8

Mailing address:
International Tax Services Office
P.O. Box 20000, Station A
Sudbury, ON P3A 5C1

Individuals:
Telephone: (800) 959-8281 or (613) 940-8495
Fax: (705) 671-0794

Non-resident corporations and corporation accounts:
Telephone: (800) 959-5525 or (613) 940-8497
Fax: (705) 671-0490

Non-resident trusts:
Telephone: (800) 959-8281 or (613) 940-8495
Fax: (705) 671-0490

Part XIII tax and non-resident withholding accounts:
Telephone: (855) 284-5946 or (613) 940-8499
Fax: (705) 677-7712 or (866) 765-8460

CRA Legislative Policy and Regulatory Affairs Branch

Charities Directorate

Mailing address:

Charities Directorate
Canada Revenue Agency
320 Queen Street
Ottawa, ON K1A 0L5

Telephone: 1-800-267-2384

Fax: (613) 954-2586 (Director General's office)
(613) 948-1320 (Policy, Planning & Legislation)
(613) 952-6020 (Assessment & Determinations)
(613) 954-8037 (Client Service)
(613) 957-8925 (Monitoring)
(613) 946-2423 (Corporate and Information Programs)
(613) 941-0186 (Filing Enforcement)

Email: charities-bienfaisance@cra.gc.ca

Income Tax Rulings Directorate

Mailing address:

Income Tax Rulings Directorate
Canada Revenue Agency
112 Kent Street
Ottawa, ON K1A 0L5

Telephone — general enquiries: (613) 957-8953

(See also *Income Tax Technical News* No. 29 for workgroup cross-reference chart, to know which group to call for your issue.)

Email: itrulingsdirectorate@cra.gc.ca

Fax: (613) 957-2088
(613) 957-8946 (secure)

Legislative Policy Directorate — Legislative Amendments Division

Mailing address:

Legislative Policy Directorate
Income Tax Legislative Amendments
Canada Revenue Agency
320 Queen Street
Ottawa, ON K1A 0L5

Fax: (613) 954-0896

Registered Plans Directorate

Mailing address:
Registered Plans Directorate
112 Kent Street
Canada Revenue Agency
Ottawa, ON K1A 0L5

Courier:
Information Holdings Operation Section — Registered Plans
Registered Plans Directorate
Canada Revenue Agency
875 Heron Road, B70
Ottawa, ON K1A 1A2

Telephone: (613) 221-3105

Toll-free elsewhere in Canada: 1-800-267-3100

Fax: (613) 952-0199

Fax: (613) 952-1343 (secure)

Email: RPD.LPRA2@cra-arc.gc.ca

TAX REFERENCE TABLES

TAX REFERENCE TABLES

These tables provided by KPMG LLP[1]

INDIVIDUALS

I-1 — FEDERAL & PROVINCIAL/TERRITORIAL INCOME TAX RATES AND BRACKETS — 2021

Current to: April 30, 2021

	Tax Rates	Tax Brackets	Surtax Rate	Surtax Threshold
Federal[a]	15.00%	Up to $49,020		
	20.50	49,021–98,040		
	26.00	98,041–151,978		
	29.00	151,979–216,511		
	33.00	216,512 and over		
British Columbia[b]	5.06%	Up to $42,184		
	7.70	42,185–84,369		
	10.50	84,370–96,866		
	12.29	96,867–117,623		
	14.70	117,624–159,483		
	16.80	159,484–222,420		
	20.50	222,421 and over		
Alberta[c]	10.00%	Up to $131,220		
	12.00	131,221–157,464		
	13.00	157,465–209,952		
	14.00	209,953–314,928		
	15.00	314,929 and over		
Saskatchewan[d]	10.50%	Up to $45,677		
	12.50	45,678–130,506		
	14.50	130,507 and over		
Manitoba[f]	10.80%	Up to $33,723		
	12.75	33,724–72,885		
	17.40	72,886 and over		
Ontario[g, h]	5.05%	Up to $45,142		
	9.15	45,143–90,287	20%	$4,874
	11.16	90,288–150,000	36	6,237
	12.16	150,001–220,000		
	13.16	220,001 and over		
Québec[i]	15.00%	Up to $45,105		
	20.00	45,106–90,200		
	24.00	90,201–109,755		
	25.75	109,756 and over		
New Brunswick[d]	9.68%	Up to $43,835		
	14.82	43,836–87,671		
	16.52	87,672–142,534		
	17.84	142,535–162,383		
	20.30	162,384 and over		

[1] © 2021 KPMG LLP, a Canadian limited liability partnership and a member firm of the KPMG network of independent member firms affiliated with KPMG International Cooperative ("KPMG International"), a Swiss entity. All rights reserved. Reproduced by permission. Some Yukon, NWT and Nunavut information was obtained by Thomson Reuters, through the CRA and territorial government websites.

	Tax Rates	Tax Brackets	Surtax Rate	Surtax Threshold
Nova Scotia[e]	8.79%	Up to $29,590		
	14.95	29,591–59,180		
	16.67	59,181–93,000		
	17.50	93,001–150,000		
	21.00	150,001 and over		
Prince Edward Island[e, h]	9.80%	Up to $31,984		
	13.80	31,985–63,969		
	16.70	63,970 and over	10%	$12,500
Newfoundland & Labrador[j]	8.70%	Up to $38,081		
	14.50	38,082–76,161		
	15.80	76,162–135,973		
	17.30	135,974–190,363		
	18.30	190,364 and over		
Yukon[d]	6.40%	Up to $49,020		
	9.00	49,021–98,040		
	10.90	98,041–151,978		
	12.80	151,979–500,000		
	15.00	500,001 and over		
Northwest Territories[d]	5.90%	Up to $44,396		
	8.60	44,397–88,796		
	12.20	88,797–144,362		
	14.05	144,363 and over		
Nunavut[d]	4.00%	Up to $46,740		
	7.00	46,741–93,480		
	9.00	93,481–151,978		
	11.50	151,979 and over		

Notes:

a   The federal tax brackets are indexed each year by a calculated inflation factor, which is based on the change in the average federal inflation rate over the 12-month period ending September 30 of the previous year compared to the change in the rate for the same period of the year prior to that. The federal inflation factor is 1.0% for 2021.

b   British Columbia indexes its tax brackets using the same formula as that used federally, but uses the provincial inflation rate rather than the federal rate in the calculation.

 The province's inflation factor is 1.1% for 2021.

c   Alberta paused the annual indexation of non-refundable tax credits and tax bracket thresholds, and will carry forward 2019 amounts for the 2020 and future taxation years. The province also indicated that it will resume indexing the tax system once it achieves the required economic and fiscal conditions.

d   New Brunswick, Saskatchewan and the territories (Northwest Territories, Nunavut and Yukon) index their tax brackets using the same formula as that used federally. The inflation factor is 1.0% for 2021.

 Saskatchewan re-introduced indexation of the province's personal income tax system to the national rate of inflation, effective January 1, 2021.

e   Nova Scotia and Prince Edward Island do not index their tax brackets or, where applicable, surtax thresholds.

f   Manitoba indexes its tax brackets using the same formula as that used federally, but uses the provincial inflation rate rather than the federal rate in the calculation. The province's inflation factor is 1.0% for 2021.

g   Ontario indexes its tax brackets and surtax thresholds using the same formula as that used federally, but uses the provincial inflation rate rather than the federal rate in the calculation. The province's inflation factor is 0.9% for 2021. Ontario resident individuals with taxable income over $20,000 are also required to pay a Health Premium each year.

h   Ontario and Prince Edward Island have a surtax system where surtax applies to the provincial income tax (before surtax) in excess of the threshold noted in the table. For example, Ontario surtax of 20% applies to the provincial income tax (before surtax) in excess of $4,874. Ontario surtax of 36% applies in addition to the 20% surtax (i.e., a total surtax of 56%) to the provincial income tax (before surtax) in excess of $6,237.

 The surtax effectively increases the top marginal tax rate for residents of Ontario and Prince Edward Island to 20.53% (13.16% × 156%) and 18.37% (16.70% × 110%), respectively.

i   Québec indexes its tax brackets using the same formula as that used federally, but uses the provincial inflation rate, excluding changes in liquor and tobacco taxes, rather than the federal rate in the calculation. The province's inflation factor is 1.26% for 2021. Residents of Québec are required to make payments to the province's Health Services Fund.

j   Newfoundland and Labrador indexes its tax brackets using the same formula as that used federally, but uses the applicable provincial inflation rate rather than the federal rate in the calculation. Newfoundland and Labrador's inflation factor is 0.4% for 2021.

I-2A — FEDERAL & PROVINCIAL/TERRITORIAL NON-REFUNDABLE TAX CREDIT RATES AND AMOUNTS FOR 2021[a]

Current to: April 30, 2021

	Federal	B.C.	Alta.	Sask.	Man.	Ont.
Tax rate applied to credits[a]	15.00%	5.06%	10.00%	10.50%	10.80%	5.05%
Indexation factor[b]	1.00%	1.10%	n/a	1.00%	1.00%	0.90%
Basic personal[c]	$13,808	$11,070	$19,369	$16,225	$9,936	$10,880
Spousal/partner and wholly dependent person[d, e]	13,808	9,479	19,369	16,225	9,134	9,238
Net income threshold	—	*948*	—	*1,623*	—	*924*
Dependants[e]						
18 and over and infirm	(See	(See	11,212	9,559	3,605	(See
Net income threshold	Caregiver)	Caregiver)	*7,407*	*6,782*	*5,115*	Caregiver)
Caregiver[e]	7,348	4,844	11,212	9,559	3,605	5,128
Net income threshold	*17,256*	*16,394*	*17,826*	*16,325*	*12,312*	*17,544*
Child (max)[f]	—	—	—	6,155		—
Adoption (max)[g]	16,729	16,729	13,247	—	10,000	13,273
Disability[h]	8,662	8,303	14,940	9,559	6,180	8,790
Disability supplement[i]	5,053	4,845	11,212	9,559	3,605	5,126
Pension (max)[h]	2,000	1,000	1,491	1,000	1,000	1,504
Age 65 and over[h, j]	7,713	4,964	5,397	4,942	3,728	5,312
Net income threshold	*38,893*	*36,954*	*40,179*	*36,794*	*27,749*	*39,546*
Medical expense threshold[k]	2,421	2,302	2,504	2,291	1,728	2,463
Employment[l]	1,257	—	—	—	—	—
Canada Pension Plan contributions (max)[m]	3,166	3,166	3,166	3,166	3,166	3,166
Employment Insurance premiums (max)[m]	890	890	890	890	890	890
Children's fitness (max)[n]	—	—	—	Ref.*	500	—
Children's arts[o]	—	—	—	Ref.*	500	—
Children's wellness (max)[p]	—	—	—	—	—	—
Home buyers (max)[q]	5,000	—	—	10,000	—	—
Home accessibility (max)[r]	10,000	Ref.*	—	2,100	—	Ref.*
Tuition fees[s]	Yes	Yes	No	No	Yes	No
Education[s]						
Full-time — per month	—	—	—	—	400	—
Part-time — per month	—	—	—	—	120	—
Charitable donations[t]						
Credit rate on first $200	15.00%	5.06%	10.00%	10.50%	10.80%	5.05%
Credit rate on balance	29.00/33.00%	16.80/20.50%	21.00%	14.50%	17.40%	11.16%

Notes:

* "Ref." indicates a refundable credit — see the applicable note.

a See table preceding s. 118 for ITA section references to the above credits.

The table shows the dollar amounts of federal and provincial and territorial non-refundable tax credits for 2021 (except for Québec — see table I-3). In order to determine the credit value, each dollar amount must be multiplied by the tax rate indicated, which is the lowest tax rate applicable in the particular jurisdiction. For example, British Columbia's basic personal credit amount of $11,070 is multiplied by 5.06% to determine the credit value of $560.

Income earned by the taxpayer or dependant, as applicable, in excess of the net income thresholds shown in the table serves to reduce the availability of the credit on a dollar-for-dollar basis. The only exception to this is the age credit, which is reduced by 15% of the taxpayer's net income in excess of the threshold.

Ontario's tax rate that applies to credits is 7.88% (5.05% × 156%) for an individual who is subject to the 56% surtax.

Prince Edward Island's tax rate that applies to credits is 10.78% (9.80% × 110%) for an individual who is subject to the 10% surtax.

b-t See the Notes to table I-2B.

I-2B — FEDERAL & PROVINCIAL/TERRITORIAL NON-REFUNDABLE TAX CREDIT RATES AND AMOUNTS FOR 2021[a] (cont'd)

	N.B.	N.S.	P.E.I.	Nfld.	Yukon	NWT	Nunavut
Tax rate applied to credits	9.68%	8.79%	9.80%	8.70%	6.40%	5.90%	4.00%
Indexation factor[b]	1.00%	n/a	n/a	0.40%	1.00%	1.00%	1.00%
Basic personal[c]	$10,564	$8,481	$10,500	$9,536	$13,808	$15,243	$16,467
Spousal/partner and wholly dependent person[d, e]	8,970	8,481	8,918	7,792	13,808	15,243	16,467
Net income threshold	*898*	*848*	*891*	*780*	—	—	—
Dependants[e]							
18 and over and infirm	4,990	2,798	2,446	3,028	(See	5,053	5,053
Net income threshold	*7,078*	*5,683*	*4,966*	*6,508*	Caregiver)	*7,169*	*7,169*
Caregiver[e]	4,989	4,898	2,446	3,028	7,348	5,052	5,052
Net income threshold	*17,038*	*13,677*	*11,953*	*14,800*	*17,256*	*17,256*	*17,256*
Child (max)[f]	—	1,200	1,200	—	—	—	1,200
Adoption (max)[g]	—	—	—	12,869	16,729	—	—
Disability[h]	8,552	7,341	6,890	6,435	8,662	12,362	14,016
Disability supplement[i]	4,989	3,449	4,019	3,028	5,053	5,053	5,053
Pension (max)[h]	1,000	1,173	1,000	1,000	2,000	1,000	2,000
Age 65 and over[h, j]	5,158	4,141	3,764	6,087	7,713	7,456	10,512
Net income threshold	*38,400*	*30,828*	*28,019*	*33,359*	*38,893*	*38,893*	*38,893*
Medical expense threshold[k]	2,391	1,637	1,678	2,076	2,421	2,421	2,421
Employment[l]	—	—	—	—	1,257	—	—
Canada Pension Plan contributions (max)[m]	3,166	3,166	3,166	3,166	3,166	3,166	3,166
Employment Insurance premiums (max)[m]	890	890	890	890	890	890	890
Children's fitness (max)[n]	—	—	—	—	Ref.*	—	—
Children's arts (max)[o]	—	—	—	—	500	—	—
Children's wellness (max)[p]	—	—	500	—	—	—	—
Home buyers (max)[q]	—	—	—	—	—	—	—
Home accessibility[r]	Ref.*	—	—	—	—	—	—
Tuition fees[s]	Yes	Yes	Yes	Yes	Yes	Yes	Yes
Education[s]							
Full-time — per month	—	200	400	200	—	400	400
Part-time — per month	—	60	120	60	—	120	120
Charitable donations[t]							
Credit rate on first $200	9.68%	8.79%	9.80%	8.70%	6.40%	5.90%	4.00%
Credit rate on balance	17.95%	21.00%	16.70%	18.30%	12.80%	14.05%	11.50%

Notes:

* "Ref." indicates a refundable credit — see the applicable note.

a See table preceding s. 118 for ITA section references to the above credits.

The table shows the dollar amounts of federal and provincial and territorial non-refundable tax credits for 2021 (except for Québec — see table I-3). In order to determine the credit value, each dollar amount must be multiplied by the tax rate indicated, which is the lowest tax rate applicable in the particular jurisdiction. For example, British Columbia's basic personal credit amount of $11,070 is multiplied by 5.06% to determine the credit value of $560.

Income earned by the taxpayer or dependant, as applicable, in excess of the net income thresholds shown in the table serves to reduce the availability of the credit on a dollar-for-dollar basis. The only exception to this is the age credit, which is reduced by 15% of the taxpayer's net income in excess of the threshold.

Ontario's tax rate that applies to credits is 7.88% (5.05% × 156%) for an individual who is subject to the 56% surtax.

Prince Edward Island's tax rate that applies to credits is 10.78% (9.80% × 110%) for an individual who is subject to the 10% surtax.

b The indexation factors indicated in the table are used to index the credits in each jurisdiction. The calculation of these factors is based on the change in the average federal or provincial inflation rate over the 12-month period ending September 30 of the previous year compared to the change in the rate for the same period of the year prior to that.

British Columbia, Manitoba, Ontario and Newfoundland and Labrador use the applicable provincial inflation rate in their calculations, while Saskatchewan and New Brunswick use the federal inflation rate. Nova Scotia and Prince Edward Island do not index their credits.

Saskatchewan re-introduced indexation of the province's personal income tax system to the national rate of inflation, effective January 1, 2021.

Alberta paused the annual indexation of non-refundable tax credits and tax bracket thresholds, and carried forward 2019 amounts for the 2020 and future taxation years. Alberta indicated that it will resume indexing the tax system once it achieves the required economic and fiscal conditions.

Manitoba only indexes the basic personal amount and the personal income tax brackets. Other non-refundable tax credits are not indexed.

c   Nova Scotia provides an additional basic personal amount of $3,000 where a taxpayer's income is $25,000 or less. This amount will decrease proportionately if the taxpayer's income is between $25,000 and $75,000.

Prince Edward Island increased the province's basic personal amount to $10,500 (from $10,000) and proportionately changed the spouse and equivalent-to-spouse amounts to $8,918 (from $8,493), effective January 1, 2021. The province's basic personal amount will further increase to $11,250 (from $10,500), effective January 1, 2022.

The federal government proposed to gradually increase the federal basic personal amount to $15,000 by 2023. The basic personal amount is increased to $13,808 (from $13,299) for individuals with net income of $151,978 or less in 2021. The increase to the basic personal amount is gradually reduced for individuals with net income between $151,978 and $216,511 in 2021. Individuals with net income over $216,511 in 2021 will not be affected by these changes and their basic personal amount will remain at $12,421. These proposed measures have not been enacted into legislation but the CRA is administering the measures as though they are in force. Yukon proposed that it will harmonize with the federal changes to the basic personal amount, effective January 1, 2021.

d   The spousal/partner and wholly dependent person amounts are calculated by subtracting the spouse/partner and wholly dependant's net income from the maximum amount.

The spousal/partner credit may be claimed for a common-law partner as well as for a spouse. Taxpayers who are single, divorced or separated, and who support a dependant in their home may claim the wholly dependent person credit. The credit can be claimed for dependants under the age of 18 who are related to the taxpayer, for the taxpayer's parents or grandparents, or for any other infirm person who is related to the taxpayer (see note (e)).

The federal government proposed to gradually increase the maximum federal spouse or common-law partner amount and the eligible dependant credit to $15,000 by 2023. The maximum amount is increased to $13,808 (from $13,229) for individuals with net income of $151,978 or less in 2021. The increase to the maximum amount is gradually reduced for individuals with net income between $151,978 and $216,511 in 2021. Individuals with net income over $216,511 in 2021 will not be affected by these changes and the maximum amount will remain at $12,421. These proposed measures have not been enacted into legislation but the CRA is administering the measures as though they are in force. Yukon proposed that it will harmonize with the federal changes to the federal spouse or common-law partner amount and the eligible dependant credit, effective January 1, 2021.

Nova Scotia provides an additional non-refundable tax credit for spousal/partner and wholly dependant person in the year if their income is $25,000 or less. The amount for 2021 is $3,000. This amount will decrease proportionately if their income is between $25,000 and $75,000.

e   The caregiver credit is available to taxpayers who care for a related dependant. Generally, the dependant must be over the age of 18 and infirm, or, in the case of a parent or grandparent, over the age of 65 (except for federal, British Columbia, Ontario and Yukon purposes, where the credit is not available in respect of non-infirm dependants).

For the federal caregiver credit, the credit amount is $7,348 in respect of infirm dependants who are parents, grandparents, brothers/sisters, aunts/uncles, nieces/nephews, adult children and grandchildren of the claimant or of the claimant's spouse or common-law partner, and $2,295 in respect of an infirm dependent spouse or common-law partner in respect of whom the individual claims the spouse or common-law partner amount, an infirm dependant for whom the individual claims an eligible dependant credit, or an infirm child who is under the age of 18 years at the end of the year.

For Ontario and British Columbia, the credit amount is $5,128 and $4,844, respectively, in respect of relatives who are infirm dependants, including adult children of the claimant or of the claimant's spouse or common-law partner.

f   Nova Scotia, Prince Edward Island and Nunavut each provide a credit for children under the age of 6. If certain conditions are met, an individual in Nova Scotia and Prince Edward Island may claim $100 per eligible month for a maximum of $1,200 per year, and individuals in Nunavut may claim $1,200 per year. Unused credit amounts may be transferred between spouses.

Saskatchewan provides a credit for children under the age of 18 if certain conditions are met. Unused credit amounts may be transferred between spouses.

g   The adoption credit is available on eligible adoption expenses incurred in the year and not reimbursed to the taxpayer, up to the maximum amount indicated in the table.

h   The disability, pension and age credits are transferable to a spouse or partner. The amounts available for transfer are reduced by the excess of the spouse's or partner's net income over the basic personal credit amount. The disability credit is also transferable to a supporting person other than a spouse or partner; however, the amount of the credit is reduced by the excess of the disabled person's net income over the basic personal credit amount.

i   The disability supplement may be claimed by an individual who is under the age of 18 at the end of the year. The amount in the table represents the maximum amount that may be claimed, and is reduced by certain child and attendant care expenses claimed in respect of this individual.

j   Saskatchewan provides an additional non-refundable tax credit for individuals aged 65 or older in the year, regardless of their net income amount. The amount for 2021 is $1,305.

Nova Scotia provides an additional non-refundable tax credit for individuals aged 65 or older in the year if their taxable income is $25,000 or less. The amount for 2021 is $1,465. This amount will decrease proportionately if their income is between $25,000 and $75,000.

k   The medical expense credit is calculated based on qualified medical expenses exceeding 3% of net income or the threshold shown in the table, whichever is less. Medical expenses incurred by both spouses/partners and by their children under age 18 may be totalled and claimed by either spouse/partner.

Taxpayers can also claim medical expenses for other eligible dependants to the extent the amount exceeds the lesser of 3% of net income of the dependant or the threshold shown in the table. Ontario is currently the only province with a maximum allowable medical expense for other eligible dependants. The limit is $13,273 for 2021.

l The federal employment credit may be claimed by individuals based on the lesser of the amount indicated in the table and the amount of employment income earned in the year.

Yukon also provides the non-refundable federal employment credit.

Alberta had a refundable family employment credit for Alberta residents with children under the age of 18 who met the income eligibility criteria. The credit was generally paid out in January and July of each year. In July 2020, the Alberta child and family benefit replaced the Alberta child benefit and Alberta family employment credit. This benefit is non-taxable and paid quarterly.

m Self-employed taxpayers can deduct 50% of their Canada or Québec Pension Plan premiums in calculating net income. The balance is claimed as a non-refundable tax credit. Self-employed taxpayers can also claim Employment Insurance premiums paid.

n Taxpayers in Manitoba can claim a maximum of $500 for fees paid on registration or membership for an eligible program of physical activity for children under the age of 18 at the end of the year, spouse or common-law partner aged 18 to 24 at the end of the year, and self if under 25 years of age at the end of the year. For children or young adults eligible for the disability tax credit, taxpayers can claim an additional $500 if a minimum of $100 is paid for registration or membership fees for a prescribed program of physical activity.

Taxpayers in Yukon can claim a maximum of $1,000 for eligible fees paid on registration or membership for a prescribed program of physical activity for children under the age of 16 (or under the age of 18 if eligible for the disability tax credit) at the beginning of the year. For children eligible for the disability tax credit and under the age of 18, taxpayers can claim an additional $500 if a minimum of $100 is paid for registration or membership fees for a prescribed program of physical activity. The children's fitness tax credit is a refundable credit in Yukon.

Taxpayers in Saskatchewan can claim up to $150 annually per minor child for eligible families who pay fees to register children in eligible sports, recreational and cultural activities. Families with children with disabilities will receive an extra $50 annually.

o Taxpayers in Manitoba and Yukon can claim a maximum of $500 for fees paid relating to the cost of registration or membership in an eligible program of artistic, cultural, recreational, or developmental activity for children under the age of 16 (or 18 if eligible for the disability tax credit) at the beginning of the year. For children under 18 years of age at the beginning of the year eligible for the disability tax credit, taxpayers can claim an additional $500 if a minimum of $100 is paid for registration or membership fees for an eligible artistic program.

Taxpayers in Saskatchewan can claim up to $150 annually per minor child for eligible families who pay fees to register children in eligible sports, recreational and cultural activities. Families with children with disabilities will receive an extra $50 annually.

p Prince Edward Island introduced a new $500 non-refundable children's wellness tax credit, effective January 1, 2021. This credit will be available to families with children under the age of 18, for eligible activities (artistic, cultural, recreational or developmental activity or a physical activity) related to their children's well-being.

q First-time home buyers who acquire a qualifying home during the year may be entitled to claim a federal non-refundable tax credit up to $5,000 and worth up to $750 ($5,000 × 15%).

To qualify, neither the individual nor his or her spouse or common-law partner can have owned and lived in another home in the calendar year of the new home purchase or in any of the four preceding calendar years. The credit can be claimed by either the purchaser or by his or her spouse or common-law partner.

The credit will also be available for certain home purchases by or for the benefit of an individual eligible for the disability tax credit.

Saskatchewan's First-Time Home Buyers Tax Credit provides a non-refundable income tax credit of up to $1,050 (10.5% × $10,000) to eligible taxpayers. There are also provisions to allow persons with a disability to qualify for the purchase of more accessible homes, with eligibility rules similar to those for the existing federal incentive for first-time home buyers. The credit generally applies to qualifying homes acquired after December 31, 2011.

r The home accessibility tax credit provides a credit for qualifying expenses incurred for work performed or goods acquired in respect of a qualifying renovation of an eligible dwelling of someone who is 65 years or older before the end of the taxation year or eligible for the disability tax credit. British Columbia and New Brunswick provide a refundable credit of up to $1,000 for similar expenses. Ontario introduced a temporary new refundable credit of 25% on up to $10,000 on certain eligible expenses for a senior's principal residence beginning in 2021. Saskatchewan provides a 10.5% non-refundable home renovation tax credit on up to $20,000 of eligible home renovation expenses on a primary residence incurred between October 1, 2020 and December 31, 2022.

s The eligible portion of the tuition and education tax credits are transferable to a spouse or common-law partner, parent or grandparent. Any amounts not transferred may be carried forward indefinitely by the student.

t Charitable donations made by both spouses/partners may be totalled and claimed by either person. The maximum amount of donations that may be claimed in a year is 75% of net income. However, all donations may be carried forward for five years if they are not claimed in the year made.

The federal donation tax credit rate of 33% applies to charitable donations made after 2015 over $200 to the extent of the claimant's income that is subject to the top tax bracket (over $216,511 for 2021). Otherwise, the rate of 29% applies to the donations over $200.

British Columbia's tax credit for donations is 5.06% on the first $200 of donations in the year and a 20.5% donation credit can be claimed to the extent the donor's income exceeds $222,420. All remaining donations are subject to a 16.8% tax credit rate.

Ontario's tax credit rate for donations over $200 is 17.41% for an individual who is subject to the 56% surtax.

Prince Edward Island's tax credit rate for donations over $200 is 18.37% for an individual who is subject to the 10% surtax.

I-3 — QUÉBEC NON-REFUNDABLE TAX CREDIT RATES AND AMOUNTS FOR 2021

Current to: April 30, 2021

Tax rate applied to credits[a]	15.0%
Indexation factor[b]	1.26%
Basic personal amount	$15,728
Amounts for dependants:	
Child under 18 engaged in full-time training or post-secondary studies[c]	3,021
Child over 17 who is a full-time student[d]	See note [d]
Other dependants over 17[e]	4,403
Person living alone or with a dependant:[f]	
Basic amount[g]	1,802
Single-parent amount (supplement)[h]	2,225
Age 65 and over[f]	3,308
Career extension[i]	
Age 60 to 64	10,000
Age 65 and over	11,000
Pension (max)[f]	2,939
Disability	3,492
First-time home buyers[j]	5,000
Union and professional dues[k]	10%
Tuition fees[l]	8%
Interest paid on student loans[m]	20%
Medical expenses[n]	20%
Charitable donations:[o]	
Credit rate on first $200	20%
Credit rate on balance	24/25.75%

Notes:

a   In order to determine the credit value, each dollar value must be multiplied by Québec's tax credit rate. For example, the basic personal credit amount of $15,728 is multiplied by 15% to determine the credit value of $2,359.

    The unused portion of all non-refundable credits may be transferred from one spouse/partner to another, but only after all credits have been taken into account in the calculation of the individual's income tax otherwise payable.

b   Québec indexes its tax credits each year by using an inflation factor that is calculated based on the provincial rate of inflation, excluding changes in liquor and tobacco taxes. The Québec inflation factor is 1.26% for 2021. For the purpose of calculating the basic personal amount and personal tax credits, Québec's tax legislation stipulates automatic indexation.

c   This credit is available for a dependent child who is under the age of 18 and is engaged in full-time professional training or post-secondary studies for each completed term, to a maximum of two semesters per year per dependant. It is also available for infirm dependants who are engaged in such activities part-time.

d   An eligible student is able to transfer to either parent an amount relating to an unused portion of their basic personal credit amount for the year (transfer mechanism for the recognized parental contribution). Each taxation year, the amount that can be transferred must not exceed the limit applicable for that particular year ($10,796 for 2021).

e   This credit is available if the dependant, other than the spouse, is related to the taxpayer by blood, marriage or adoption and ordinarily lives with the taxpayer. In order to be eligible for the tax credit, the taxpayer must also not have benefited from a transfer of the recognized parental contribution from this dependant.

f   The total of the credit amounts for being 65 years of age or over, for living alone or with a dependent, and for receiving retirement income is reduced by 18.75% of the amount by which net family income exceeds $35,650.

g   The basic amount is available if the individual lives in a self-contained domestic establishment that he/she maintains and in which no other person, other than himself/herself, a minor person, or an eligible student lives of whom the individual is either the father, mother, grandfather or grandmother, or the great-grandfather or great-grandmother.

h   If an individual (i.e., father or mother) is living with an eligible student (i.e., a person who is 18 or over and is a post-secondary or vocational training student who transferred or could have transferred an amount to the single parent (see note (d)), the individual may be able to add an amount for a single-parent family of $2,225 to the basic amount for a person living alone (see note (g)).

i   For 2021, this credit is available for workers who are 60 years of age or older. For workers age 60 to 64, the credit applies at a 15% rate to $10,000 of "eligible work income" in excess of $5,000. For workers aged 65 and over, the credit applies at a 15% rate to $11,000 of "eligible work income" in excess of $5,000. The credit for workers aged 60 or older is reduced by 5% of "eligible work income" over $35,650. "Eligible work income" includes salary and business income, but excludes taxable benefits received for a previous employment as well as amounts deducted in computing taxable income, such as the stock option deduction.

    Any unused portion of the tax credit may not be carried forward or transferred to the individual's spouse.

j   Québec offers a first-time home buyers non-refundable tax credit of up to $5,000 and worth up to $750 ($5,000 × 15%) for a housing unit located in Québec and that is acquired after December 31, 2017. To qualify, the individual or his or her spouse has to intend to inhabit the home as a principal place of residence not later than one year after the time of acquisition and neither the individual nor his or her spouse can have owned and lived in another home in the calendar year of the new home purchase or in any of the four preceding calendar years.

k   The credit for union and professional dues is calculated based on the annual fees paid in the year. The portion of professional dues relating to liability insurance is allowed as a deduction from income and therefore not included in calculating the credit amount.

l   The tuition credit is calculated based on tuition, professional examination and mandatory ancillary fees paid for the calendar year. Tuition fees qualify for an 8% non-refundable credit for Québec tax purposes. The student may transfer the unused portion of the tuition credit to either one of his/her parents or grandparents. The portion of this credit that is not transferred will be available for future use by the student.

m   Interest paid on student loans is converted into a tax credit at a rate of 20%. Interest not claimed in a particular year may be carried forward indefinitely.

n   The medical expense credit is calculated based on qualified medical expenses in excess of 3% of family income. Family income is the total income of both spouses/partners. Eligible medical expenses and eligible expenses to obtain medical care not provided in the region where an individual lives will continue to be converted into a tax credit at the rate of 20%.

o   Charitable donations made by both spouses/partners may be totalled and claimed by either person. The maximum amount of donations that may be claimed in a year is 100% of net income. However, all donations may be carried forward for five years (or 10 years for certain particular donations) if they are not claimed in the year made.

Québec's tax credit for donations is 20% on the first $200 of eligible gifts in the year and a 25.75% donation credit can be claimed to the extent the donor's income exceeds $109,755 in 2021. All remaining donations are subject to a 24% tax credit on donations.

I-4 — QUÉBEC REFUNDABLE TAX CREDIT RATE AND AMOUNTS FOR 2021[a]

Current to: April 30, 2021

	Tax Rate	Maximum Expense	Maximum Credit
Medical expenses[b]	25%	certain eligible medical expenses	$1,241
Reduced by 5% of family income in excess of $24,000[c]			
Child care expense credit[c, d]	from 26 to 75%		
The lesser of the expenses incurred or:			
For a child who has a severe or prolonged mental or physical impairment		$13,615	
For a child under the age of seven		9,950	
For a child under the age of sixteen		5,235	
Adoption expense credit[e]	50%	20,000	10,000
Infertility treatment credit[f]	from 20% to 80%	20,000	16,000
Tax credit for caregivers[c, g, h]			
Basic amount			1,266
Reducible amount			1,266
Reduced by 16% of the eligible relative's income over $22,460[c]			
Home support of elderly persons living alone[h]			
Not recognized as dependant seniors	35%	19,500	6,825
Recognized as dependant seniors	35%	25,500	8,925
Reduced by 3% of the individual's family income in excess of $60,135[c]			
Short-term transition of seniors in rehabilitation centre[i]	20%	costs incurred in maximum 60-day period	
Safety equipment for seniors[j]	20%	costs incurred in excess of $250	
Residential waste water treatment system[k]	20%	costs incurred in excess of $2,500	5,500

Notes:

a   Québec's credit rate, maximum expense eligible and method of calculation of the credit vary from one type of refundable credit to another. Québec's credit rate is applied to the dollar amounts in the table to determine the maximum credit value. For example, the adoption expense credit amount of $20,000 is multiplied by 50% to determine the maximum credit value of $10,000. Some refundable credits are reduced when thresholds are exceeded.

b   Québec provides a refundable tax credit equal to the total of 25% of medical expenses eligible for the non-refundable credit (see table I-3) and 25% of the amount deducted for disability support products and services. A minimum amount of work income has to be earned in order to claim the refundable tax credit: $3,175 for 2021.

c   Québec indexes various tax credits each year by using an inflation factor that is calculated based on the provincial rate of inflation, excluding changes in liquor and tobacco taxes. The Québec inflation factor is 1.26% for 2021.

d   Unlike the federal treatment of qualifying child care expenses, which are eligible for a deduction in computing net income, Québec provides a refundable tax credit for such expenses. The rate of credit falls as net family income rises.

In general, the maximum amount of expenses eligible for the credit in 2021 is the lesser of:

- the total of:
  - $13,615 for an eligible child of any age who has a severe or prolonged mental or physical impairment, and
  - $9,950 for an eligible child under the age of seven, and
  - $5,235 for an eligible child aged seven or more but under the age of 16 or an eligible child who has a mental or physical infirmity, or
- the actual child care expenses incurred in the year.

The definition of eligible expenses includes costs incurred during the period an individual receives benefits under the Québec Parental Insurance Plan or the Employment Insurance Plan (see table I-9). The child care expenses are not limited by the earned income of the parent. For the purpose of calculating the refundable tax credit for childcare expenses, the definition of "eligible child" of an individual means a child of the individual or the individual's spouse, or a child who is a dependant of the individual or the individual's spouse and whose income for the year does not exceed $10,796, if, in any case, at any time during the year, the child is under 16 years of age or is dependent on the individual or the individual's spouse and has a mental or physical infirmity.

e   Qualifying expenses include court and legal fees paid to obtain the final adoption order, travel and accommodation expenses for foreign adoptions, translation expenses, and fees charged by foreign and domestic social agencies.

f   The applicable credit rate varies from 20% to 80% of eligible infertility expense, depending on family situation and income. The credit can be claimed on infertility expenses of up to $20,000.

g   Québec replaced the four components of the existing tax credit for informal caregivers of persons of full age with the new refundable tax credit called "tax credit for caregivers" effective in 2020. The new tax credit for caregivers will comprise of the following two components:

Component 1: A basic amount of $1,266 for a caregiver providing care to a person aged 18 or older who has a severe and prolonged impairment and needs assistance in carrying out a basic activity of daily living and a reducible amount of up to $1,266 is available where the caregiver co-resides with the eligible care receiver. Where the caregiver does not co-reside with the eligible care receiver aged 18 or older with a severe and prolonged impairment, then the caregiver is only eligible for the reducible amount of up to $1,266. The reducible amount is reduced by 16% for each dollar of income of the eligible care receiver in excess of $22,460 for 2021.

Component 2: A basic amount of $1,266 for a caregiver who supports and co-resides with an eligible care receiver aged 70 or older.

For the purpose of the new tax credit for caregivers, an eligible care receiver is a spouse, father, mother, grandparent, child, grandchild, nephew, niece, brother, sister, uncle, aunt, great-uncle, great-aunt or any other direct ascendant of the individual or the individual's spouse.

Québec's 2020 budget proposed to introduce a new form for certification of ongoing assistance in carrying out basic activity of daily living, where the eligible caregiver and care receiver have no family relationship but could qualify as an eligible care receiver for the purpose of Component 1.

The following table summarizes the maximum tax credit amount for caregivers for 2021:

| | Component 1: for caregiver to a care receiver with a severe and prolonged impairment | | Component 2: for caregiver to a care receiver aged 70+ |
	Caregiver co-residing with an eligible care receiver of 18+	Caregiver does not reside with an eligible care receiver of 18+	Caregiver co-residing with an eligible care receiver aged 70+
Basic amount	$1,266	Not entitled	$1,266
Reducible amount	$1,266	$1,266	Not entitled
Total – maximum	$2,532	$1,266	$1,266

h   The home support tax credit can be claimed by persons age 70 and over living in their home. For seniors recognized as dependant, and when this credit is determined in respect of a couple as soon as one of the members of the couple is recognized as dependant, no reduction is allowed. If the expense also qualifies for the non-refundable medical expense credit (see table I-3), it cannot be claimed for this credit as well. Québec's 2021-2022 budget proposed that starting in 2022 the credit rate be increased by 1% annually to reach 40% in 2026.

i   The rehabilitation centre tax credit can be claimed by seniors age 70 or older in respect of costs incurred for the first 60 days of any given stay in a public or private "functional rehabilitation transition unit". There is no limit to the number of stays that can be claimed.

j   The safety equipment tax credit can be claimed by seniors age 70 or older for the purchase or rental of equipment (including installation costs) used to improve their safety and security in their principal residence. Examples of qualifying equipment include remote monitoring systems, GPS tracking devices for persons, and walk-in bathtubs or showers.

k   The temporary refundable tax credit for the upgrading of residential waste water treatment systems of a principal residence or a cottage which includes the construction, renovation, modification or rebuilding of a system for the discharge, collection and disposal of waste water, toilet effluents or grey water, can be claimed if the work is carried out by a qualified contractor and paid under a service agreement entered into after March 31, 2017 and before April 1, 2022.

I-5 — COMBINED TOP MARGINAL TAX RATES FOR INDIVIDUALS — 2021

Current to: April 30, 2021

	Interest and Regular Income	Capital Gains[a]	Eligible Dividends	Non-Eligible Dividends
British Columbia	53.50%	26.75%	36.54%	48.89%
Alberta[b]	48.00	24.00	34.31	42.30
Saskatchewan[c]	47.50	23.75	29.64	42.29
Manitoba	50.40	25.20	37.79	46.67
Ontario	53.53	26.76	39.34	47.74
Québec[d]	53.31	26.65	40.11	48.02
New Brunswick	53.30	26.65	33.51	47.75
Nova Scotia	54.00	27.00	41.58	48.27
P.E.I.[e]	51.37	25.69	34.23	46.22
Newfoundland & Lab.	51.30	25.65	42.62	44.59
Yukon[f]	48.00	24.00	28.93	44.04
Northwest Territories	47.05	23.53	28.33	36.82
Nunavut	44.50	22.25	33.08	37.79

Notes:

a The lifetime capital gains exemption limit for qualified farm property, qualified fishing property and qualified small business corporation shares increased to $892,218 (from $883,384) for 2021. An additional lifetime capital gains exemption of $107,782 is available for qualified farm or fishing property disposed of in 2021.

b Alberta decreased the province's DTC rate that applies to eligible dividends to 8.12% (from 10%) of taxable dividends, effective January 1, 2021.

c Saskatchewan decreased the province's DTC rate that applies to non-eligible dividends to 1.70% (from 3.36%) of taxable dividends, effective January 1, 2021. The rate will increase to 2.11% effective January 1, 2022, 2.94% effective January 1, 2023 and 3.36% effective January 1, 2024. Accordingly, the combined top marginal tax rate on non-eligible dividends will decrease to 41.82% effective January 1, 2022, 40.86% effective January 1, 2023 and 40.37% effective January 1, 2024.

d Québec decreased the province's DTC rate that applies to non-eligible dividends to 4.01% (from 4.77%) of taxable dividends, effective January 1, 2021. Québec further decreased the province's DTC rate that applies to non-eligible dividends to 3.42% (from 4.01%) of taxable dividends, effective January 1, 2022. Accordingly, the combined top marginal tax rate on non-eligible dividends will increase to 48.70% effective January 1, 2022.

e Prince Edward Island decreased the province's DTC rate that applies to non-eligible dividends to 1.96% (from 2.74%) of taxable dividends, effective January 1, 2021.

f Yukon decreased the territory's DTC rate that applies to non-eligible dividends to 0.67% (from 2.30%) of taxable dividends, effective January 1, 2021.

I-6 — ELIGIBLE DIVIDEND TAX CREDIT RATES AND AMOUNT OF DIVIDENDS THAT MAY BE RECEIVED WITHOUT INCURRING TAX IN 2021[a]

Current to: April 30, 2021

	Dividend Tax Credit Rate[b]		Amount of Dividend Received Tax-Free	
	Actual Dividend	**Taxable Dividend**	**Actual Dividend**	**Taxable Dividend**
Federal	20.73%	15.02%	$53,808	$74,255
British Columbia	16.56	12.00	53,808	74,255
Alberta[c]	11.20	8.12	53,808	74,255
Saskatchewan	15.18	11.00	53,808	74,255
Manitoba	11.04	8.00	26,403	36,436
Ontario	13.80	10.00	53,808	74,255
Québec	16.15	11.70	40,287	55,596
New Brunswick	19.32	14.00	53,808	74,255
Nova Scotia	12.21	8.85	32,406	44,720
Prince Edward Island	14.49	10.50	48,658	67,148
Nfld. & Labrador	7.45	5.40	18,218	25,140
Yukon	16.59	12.02	53,808	74,255
Northwest Territories	15.87	11.50	53,808	74,255
Nunavut	7.60	5.51	53,808	74,255

Notes:

a   This table assumes only "eligible dividend" income is earned and takes into account all federal and provincial/territorial taxes, surtaxes, and alternative minimum taxes, but does not include provincial premiums. The respective basic personal and dividend tax credits and provincial tax reductions, where applicable, are also included.

In general, "eligible dividends" are dividends paid to Canadian residents by public companies, and by Canadian-controlled private corporations (CCPCs) out of income taxed at the federal general corporate tax rate. CCPCs cannot pay eligible dividends from income that is eligible for the federal small business deduction or subject to refundable tax treatment.

The gross-up rate for eligible dividends is 38%. The actual amount received is therefore multiplied by 1.38 to determine the taxable amount of the dividend.

b   The federal and provincial/territorial dividend tax credit (DTC) rates in the table's first column apply to the actual amount of the dividend received by an individual. The DTC rate can also be expressed as a percentage of the taxable dividend, as indicated in the table's second column.

c   Alberta decreased the province's DTC rate that applies to eligible dividends to 8.12% (from 10%) of taxable dividends, effective January 1, 2021. The increase was originally scheduled to be effective January 1, 2022, but Alberta's Bill 35 accelerated the increase to the DTC rate applicable to eligible dividends, effective July 1, 2020.

I-7 — NON-ELIGIBLE DIVIDEND TAX CREDIT RATES AND AMOUNT OF DIVIDENDS THAT MAY BE RECEIVED WITHOUT INCURRING TAX IN 2021[a]

Current to: April 30, 2021

	Dividend Tax Credit Rate[b]		Amount of Dividend Received Tax-Free	
	Actual Dividend	**Taxable Dividend**	**Actual Dividend**	**Taxable Dividend**
Federal	10.39%	9.03%	$30,170	$34,696
British Columbia	2.25	1.96	23,549	27,081
Alberta	2.51	2.18	21,548	24,780
Saskatchewan[c]	1.95	1.70	16,825	19,349
Manitoba	0.90	0.78	10,257	11,796
Ontario	3.43	2.99	30,170	34,696
Québec[d]	4.61	4.01	18,670	21,471
New Brunswick	3.16	2.75	19,585	22,523
Nova Scotia	3.44	2.99	16,580	19,067
Prince Edward Island[e]	2.25	1.96	15,296	17,590
Newfoundland & Labrador	4.03	3.50	20,470	23,540
Yukon[f]	0.77	0.67	13,411	15,423
Northwest Territories	6.90	6.00	30,170	34,696
Nunavut	3.00	2.61	30,170	34,696

Notes:

a   This table assumes only "non-eligible dividend" income is earned and takes into account all federal and provincial/territorial taxes, surtaxes, and alternative minimum taxes, but does not include provincial premiums. The respective basic personal and dividend tax credits and provincial tax reductions, where applicable, are also included.

"Non-eligible" dividends are those that are not subject to the dividend rules applying to "eligible" dividends (see table I-6).

The gross-up rate for non-eligible dividends is 15%. The actual amount received is therefore multiplied by 1.15 to determine the taxable amount of the dividend.

b   The federal and provincial dividend tax credit (DTC) rates in the table's first column apply to the actual amount of the dividend received by an individual. The DTC rate can also be expressed as a percentage of the taxable dividend, as indicated in the table's second column.

c   Saskatchewan reduced the province's DTC rate that applies to non-eligible dividends received to 1.70% (from 3.36%). This measure was introduced in Saskatchewan's Bill 2 which received assent on December 10, 2020.

d   Québec decreased the province's DTC rate that applies to non-eligible dividends received to 4.01% (from 4.77%) of taxable dividends, effective January 1, 2021. The rate will further decrease to 3.42%, effective January 1, 2022.

e   Prince Edward Island decreased the province's DTC rate that applies to non-eligible dividends received to 1.96% (from 2.74%) of taxable dividends, effective January 1, 2021. In its 2021-2022 Budget, the province proposed to further decrease this amount, effective January 1, 2022.

f   The Yukon 2020 Budget decreased the territory's DTC rate that applies to non-eligible dividends received to 0.67% (from 2.30%) of taxable dividends effective January 1, 2021. This measure was introduced in Yukon's Bill 8 which received assent on March 16, 2020.

I-8 — EMPLOYMENT WITHHOLDINGS — FEDERAL

Current to: April 30, 2021

Canada Pension Plan

Year	Maximum Annual Pensionable Earnings $	Basic Exemption $	Maximum Contributory Earnings $	Employer and Employee Contribution Rate %	Maximum Annual Employer / Employee Contributions $	Maximum Self-Employed Contribution Rate %	Maximum Annual Self-Employed Contributions $
2014	52,500	3,500	49,000	4.95	2,426	9.90	4,851
2015	53,600	3,500	50,100	4.95	2,480	9.90	4,960
2016	54,900	3,500	51,400	4.95	2,544	9.90	5,089
2017	55,300	3,500	51,800	4.95	2,564	9.90	5,128
2018	55,900	3,500	52,400	4.95	2,594	9.90	5,188
2019	57,400	3,500	53,900	5.10	2,749	10.20	5,498
2020	58,700	3,500	55,200	5.25	2,898	10.50	5,796
2021	61,600	3,500	58,100	5.45	3,166	10.90	6,333

Employment Insurance

Year	Maximum Annual Insurable Earnings $	Employee's Premium Rate %	Employer's Premium Rate %	Maximum Annual Employee Premiums $	Maximum Annual Employer Premiums $
2014	48,600	1.88	2.63	914	1,279
2015	49,500	1.88	2.63	931	1,303
2016	50,800	1.88	2.63	955	1,337
2017	51,300	1.63	2.28	836	1,171
2018	51,700	1.66	2.32	858	1,202
2019	53,100	1.62	2.27	860	1,204
2020	54,200	1.58	2.21	856	1,199
2021	56,300	1.58	2.21	890	1,245

I-9 — EMPLOYMENT WITHHOLDINGS — QUÉBEC

Current to: April 30, 2021

Québec Pension Plan

	2017	2018	2019	2020	2021
Maximum annual pensionable earnings	$55,300	$55,900	$57,400	$58,700	$61,600
Basic exemption	3,500	3,500	3,500	3,500	3,500
Maximum contributory earnings	51,800	52,400	53,900	55,200	58,100
Employer and employee contribution rate	5.40%	5.40%	5.55%	5.70%	5.90%
Maximum annual employer and employee contributions	$2,797	$2,830	$2,991	$3,146	$3,428
Maximum annual self-employed contributions	5,594	5,659	5,983	6,293	6,856

Employment Insurance

	2017	2018	2019	2020	2021
Maximum annual insurable earnings	$51,300	$51,700	$53,100	$54,200	$56,300
Employee's premium rate	1.27%	1.30%	1.25%	1.20%	1.18%
Maximum annual employee premiums	$652	$672	$664	$650	$664
Employer's premium rate	1.78%	1.82%	1.75%	1.68%	1.65%
Maximum annual employer premiums	$912	$941	$929	$911	$930

Québec Parental Insurance Plan

	2017	2018	2019	2020	2021
Maximum annual insurable earnings	$72,500	$74,000	$76,500	$78,500	$83,500
Employee's contribution rate	0.548%	0.548%	0.526%	0.494%	0.494%
Maximum annual employee contributions	$397	$406	$402	$388	$412
Employer's contribution rate	0.767%	0.767%	0.736%	0.692%	0.692%
Maximum annual employer contributions	$556	$568	$563	$543	$578
Self-employed contribution rate	0.973%	0.973%	0.934%	0.878%	0.878%
Maximum annual self-employed contributions	$705	$720	$715	$689	$733

Notes:

Québec's Parental Insurance Plan (QPIP) provides benefits to eligible Québec workers who take maternity, paternity, parental or adoption leave from their employment. The plan replaces maternity, parental and adoption benefits provided under the federal Employment Insurance (EI) program, and premiums are mandatory for all employers, employees and self-employed individuals in the province. Required withholdings under the QPIP are accompanied by reduced EI premiums for residents of Québec.

I-10 — OLD AGE SECURITY BENEFITS
Current to: April 30, 2021

Monthly Payments by Quarter	Old Age Security (OAS)[a]		Guaranteed Income Supplement (GIS)[b] Single		Married	
	2020	2021	2020	2021	2020	2021
1st	$613.53	$615.37	$916.38	$919.12	$551.63	$553.28
2nd	613.53	618.45	916.38	923.71	551.63	556.04
3rd	613.53		916.38		551.63	
4th	614.14		917.29		552.18	

Notes:

a   The Old Age Security (OAS) basic pension is a monthly taxable benefit available to individuals age 65 and over who have met certain Canadian residency requirements.

Generally, a minimum residence period of 40 years after age 18 is required in order to be eligible to receive the full pension entitlement. A minimum residence period of 10 years after age 18 is required in order to receive a partial pension entitlement.

Benefits may also be affected by a social security agreement with a previous country of residence. Individuals must apply in order to receive OAS benefits.

Individuals have the option to defer take-up of their OAS pension by up to five years past the age of eligibility, and subsequently receive a higher, actuarially adjusted pension.

The monthly OAS pension is increased by 0.6% for every month it is delayed up to a maximum of 36% at age 70.

For 2021, if an individual's net income is greater than $79,845, 15% of the excess over this amount must be repaid. The full OAS pension is eliminated when net income reaches $129,260.

Generally, full or partial OAS pension benefits may be paid indefinitely to non-residents, if the individual had lived in Canada for at least 20 years after age 18. Otherwise, payment may be made only for the month of the individual's departure from Canada and for six additional months. The benefit may be reinstated once the individual returns to live in Canada.

The 2021 federal budget enhanced OAS benefits by introducing a one-time $500 payment and then a 10% increase to regular, ongoing OAS payments. The enhancements apply to OAS pensioners who will be age 75 or over as of June 2022. The lump sum payment will go out in August 2021 while the 10% increase is effective July 1, 2022.

b   The Guaranteed Income Supplement (GIS) is a monthly non-taxable benefit paid to low-income OAS recipients. Eligibility to receive the benefit in 2021 is based on the annual income and marital status of the individual:

- single, divorced, separated or widowed individuals — net income (excluding OAS and GIS) must be less than $18,744;
- married individuals where both spouses/partners receive OAS benefits — combined net income (excluding OAS and GIS) must be less than $24,768.

The amounts indicated in the table reflect the maximum monthly benefits. As of July 2021-2022 benefit year, GIS recipients can earn up to $5,000 per year (previously $3,500 per year) in employment income or self-employment income before triggering a reduction in GIS benefits ("earnings exemption"). The federal government also introduced a partial earnings exemption of 50%, which applies to the first $10,000 of annual employment and self-employment income earned beyond the $5,000 threshold.

An Allowance is also available to low-income individuals between the ages of 60 and 64 whose spouses/partners are eligible to receive the OAS and the GIS. To be eligible for this non-taxable monthly benefit, you must have lived in Canada for at least 10 years after the age of 18, and family net income in 2021 must be less than $34,704.

Couples who receive GIS and Allowance benefits and are forced to live apart for reasons beyond their control (such as requirement for long-term care) may be eligible to receive higher benefits based on their individual income.

Individuals must apply in order to receive GIS and/or Allowance benefits. Generally, individuals may automatically renew the GIS and Allowance by filing their income tax return.

The GIS and Allowance are not payable to non-residents beyond a period of six months after the month of departure. However, individuals may reapply upon return to Canada.

I-11 — RETIREMENT AND SAVINGS PLANS — CONTRIBUTION LIMITS

Current to: April 30, 2021

	2017	2018	2019	2020	2021
Money Purchase Registered Pension Plans					
Contribution limit[a]	$26,230	$26,500	$27,230	$27,830	$29,210
Pensionable earnings[b]	145,722	147,222	151,278	154,611	162,278
Registered Retirement Savings Plans					
Contribution limit[c]	26,010	26,230	26,500	27,230	27,830
Previous year's earned income[d]	144,500	145,722	147,222	151,278	154,611
Deferred Profit Sharing Plans					
Contribution limit[e]	13,115	13,250	13,615	13,915	14,605
Pensionable earnings[f]	72,861	73,611	75,639	77,306	81,139
Tax-Free Savings Account					
Annual contribution limits[g]	5,500	5,500	6,000	6,000	6,000
Registered Education Savings Plans					
Annual limit[h]	N/A	N/A	N/A	N/A	N/A
Lifetime limit[i]	50,000	50,000	50,000	50,000	50,000
Registered Disability Savings Plans					
Annual limit[j]	N/A	N/A	N/A	N/A	N/A
Lifetime limit[k]	200,000	200,000	200,000	200,000	200,000

Notes:

a   The money purchase registered pension plan (RPP) contribution limit indicated in the table is the maximum limit applicable each year. The contribution limit is the greater of the limit for the preceding year, and the 2009 contribution limit of $22,000 adjusted for inflation. In general, the 2009 contribution limit will be indexed by an inflation factor equal to the average wage for the applicable year divided by the average wage for 2009.

b   The total of all employer and employee contributions to an RPP is limited to the lesser of the current year's contribution limit and 18% of the employee's pensionable earnings for the year. The amount of pensionable earnings that generates the contribution limit is indicated in the table.

c   The registered retirement savings plan (RRSP) contribution limit is equal to the RPP contribution limit for the preceding year.

d   The total of all contributions to an RRSP is limited to the lesser of the current year's contribution limit and 18% of an individual's earned income for the preceding year, plus any carry-forward contribution room. The amount of earned income that generates the contribution limit is indicated in the table.

e   The deferred profit sharing plan (DPSP) contribution limit is equal to one-half of the RPP contribution limit for the year.

f   The total of all employer contributions to a DPSP is limited to the lesser of the current year's contribution limit and 18% of an employee's pensionable earnings for the year. The amount of pensionable earnings that generates the contribution limit each year is indicated in the table.

g   Canadians age 18 and over can earn tax-free income in a Tax-Free Savings Account (TFSA) throughout their lifetime. Income, losses and gains on investment in the account, as well as amounts withdrawn, are not taxable and are not taken into account for determining eligibility for certain income-tested benefits or credits. Each calendar year, a taxpayer can contribute up to the TFSA limit, plus any unused TFSA contribution room from the previous years. The annual contribution limit increased to $10,000 (from $5,500) for 2015, however, it was reduced back to $5,500 effective January 1, 2016. The annual contribution room limit is indexed for inflation and rounded to the nearest $500. Generally, amounts withdrawn from a TFSA will be added to the individual's contribution room for future years. TFSA contributions are not tax-deductible.

h   Retirement education savings plans (RESPs) are commonly used by parents and other guardians to save for a child's post-secondary education. Like TFSAs, contributions to RESPs are not tax-deductible, but investment income can be earned in the plan tax-free. While there is no annual limit, contributions into the plan should be carefully considered in order to maximize government assistance payments under the Canada Education Savings Grant and Canada Learning Bond programs.

i   For each beneficiary there is a lifetime limit of $50,000, regardless of the number of plans in place for that beneficiary.

j   A registered disability savings plan (RDSP) is a savings plan to help parents and others save for the long-term financial security of a person who is eligible for the disability tax credit. Like RESPs, contributions to RDSPs are not tax-deductible, but investment income can be earned in the plan tax-free. While there is no annual limit, contributions into the plan should be carefully considered in order to maximize government assistance payments under the Canada Disability Savings Grant and Canada Savings Bonds programs.

k   Contributions on behalf of any one beneficiary are capped at a lifetime maximum of $200,000. Contributions can continue to be made until the end of the year the beneficiary turns 59, or until the beneficiary ceases to be a resident of Canada, dies or ceases to qualify for the disability tax credit.

   For 2021 and subsequent taxation years, the 2019 federal budget proposed to remove the time limitation on the period that an RDSP may remain open after its beneficiary ceases to qualify for the disability tax credit and to eliminate the requirement for a licensed medical doctor or nurse practitioner to certify in writing that the beneficiary is likely to become eligible for the disability credit in the future in order for the plan to remain open. A transition rule will ensure that an RDSP issuer will not be required to terminate an RDSP after March 18, 2019 and before 2021 solely because the RDSP beneficiary became ineligible for the disability tax credit.

I-12 — AUTOMOBILES — DEDUCTIONS AND BENEFITS

Current to: June 30, 2021

	2021	2020	2019	2018	2017	2016
Deduction limits:[a]						
Maximum cost for capital cost allowance purposes[b]	$30,000	$30,000	$30,000	$30,000	$30,000	$30,000
Maximum deductible monthly lease payment[c]	$800	$800	$800	$800	$800	$800
Maximum deductible monthly interest cost on automobile loans[d]	$300	$300	$300	$300	$300	$300
Maximum deductible allowances paid to employees[e]						
First 5,000 employment-related kilometres	59¢	59¢	58¢	55¢	54¢	54¢
Each additional employment-related kilometre	53¢	53¢	52¢	49¢	48¢	48¢
Taxable benefits:						
Standby charge benefit[f]						
Employer-owned automobile			2% per month of original cost			
Employer-leased automobile			⅔ of monthly lease cost			
Operating cost benefit per kilometre of personal use[f]	27¢	28¢	28¢	26¢	25¢	26¢
Allowances[g]			Taxable with certain exceptions			

Notes:

a   When a motor vehicle is purchased or leased for the purpose of earning income, certain expenses may be deducted. The more common types of motor vehicle expenses include fuel, insurance, maintenance and repairs, licence and registration fees, capital cost allowance, lease payments, and interest. The expenses also include all applicable federal and provincial sales taxes (GST, HST, PST and QST) to the extent the taxpayer is not a sales tax registrant and does not claim an input tax credit (input tax refund in Québec) for the taxes paid.

b   The maximum amounts shown in the table are determined before all applicable sales taxes, and are based on the automobile's year of purchase.

Each automobile with a cost in excess of the limit is allocated to a separate capital cost allowance (CCA) Class 10.1. The maximum capital cost of each automobile that may be included in Class 10.1 is $30,000 plus all applicable federal and provincial sales taxes. A Class 10.1 automobile is not subject to the normal recapture or terminal loss rules, and is eligible for a 15% CCA claim in the year of disposition.

Motor vehicles having a cost equal to or less than the limit are included in Class 10. The normal rules for recapture, terminal loss and CCA apply to these vehicles.

The CCA rate for both classes is 30% declining balance (15% in the year of acquisition).

For motor vehicles acquired after November 20, 2018, the CCA rate in the year of acquisition is increased to 45% (from 15%). The accelerated deduction will be gradually phased out starting in 2024 and will not apply to motor vehicles available for use after 2027.

The federal government introduced a temporary enhanced first-year CCA rate of 100% for eligible zero-emission vehicles purchased on or after March 19, 2019. A new Class 54 will be created for zero-emission passenger vehicles that would otherwise be included in Class 10 or 10.1 and the maximum CCA deductible in respect of each vehicle is $55,000 plus applicable sales tax. A new Class 55 will be also created for zero-emission vehicles that would otherwise be included in Class 16. The enhanced CCA rate will be gradually phased out for zero-emission vehicles that become available for use after 2023 and will not apply to zero-emission vehicles that become available for use after 2027.

The federal government has introduced a new Class 56 to provide a temporary enhanced first-year CCA rate of 100% for qualifying zero-emission off-road automotive vehicles purchased on or after March 2, 2020. The enhanced CCA rate will be gradually phased out for qualifying zero-emission off-road automotive vehicles that become available for use after 2023 but before 2028.

The 2021 federal budget provides immediate expensing of certain properties acquired by a Canadian-controlled private corporation (CCPC) that would otherwise qualify for CCA, up to a maximum of $1.5 million per taxation year. Eligible property includes any capital property subject to the CCA rules, except for property that would be included in Classes 1 to 6, 14.1, 17, 47, 49 and 51. Immediate expensing applies to eligible property acquired on or after April 19, 2021 and available for use before 2024.

c   The maximum amounts shown in the table are determined before all applicable sales taxes, and are based on the year the lease was entered into.

In general, the maximum deductible monthly lease charge is computed as the lesser of:

- the actual lease payments paid or incurred in the year (including insurance, maintenance and taxes if they are part of the actual lease payment);
- the prescribed monthly rate; or
- the annual lease limit, which is equal to the monthly pre-tax lease cost multiplied by the ratio of [CCA cost limit ÷ (85% × greater of the prescribed limit and the manufacturer's suggested list price)]

d   The maximum deductible monthly interest cost is based on the automobile's year of purchase.

e   For the Northwest Territories, Nunavut and Yukon, the tax-exempt allowance is set 4 cents higher (in 2021, 63 cents for the first 5,000 kilometres and 57 cents for each additional kilometre).

f   When an employee uses an employer-provided automobile for personal use, the employee must generally include a standby charge and operating expense benefit in income.

Generally, the standby charge can be reduced when the automobile is used for business purposes more than 50% of the time and the employee does not exceed 1,667 km per month for personal use. If an employee's use of the automobile is primarily for business purposes, the employee may also elect to calculate their operating expense benefit as an amount equal to 50% of the standby charge, rather than use the per-kilometre prescribed rate (27 cents per kilometre in 2021 and 28 cents in 2020). Operating expenses include items such as gasoline and oil, maintenance charges and licences and insurance. Operating expenses do not include items such as interest, lease costs for a leased automobile or parking costs. For taxpayers who are employed principally in selling or leasing automobiles, a reduced rate of 24 cents per kilometre in 2021 and 25 cents in 2020 applies.

The federal government has announced that employees will be able to use their 2019 automobile usage to determine whether their employer-provided automobile is eligible for the reduced standby charge in 2020 and 2021. The federal government also announced that employees will be able to use 2019 automobile usage to determine if they are eligible to calculate their operating cost benefit as 50% of the standby charge in 2020 and 2021.

g   An "allowance" is generally defined as an amount paid for which the employee does not have to account (by providing receipts, vouchers, etc.) to the employer for its actual use. This can be contrasted to a "reimbursement" for which the employee must usually provide the employer with receipts and that the employer repays to the employee on a dollar-for-dollar basis.

CORPORATIONS

C-1 — FEDERAL AND PROVINCIAL/TERRITORIAL TAX RATES FOR INCOME EARNED BY A GENERAL CORPORATION — 2021 AND 2022[a]

Current to: April 30, 2021

	M&P Income	Active Business Income	Investment Income[b]
Federal rates			
General corporate rate [ITA 123(1)]	38.0%	38.0%	38.0%
Federal abatement [ITA 124(1)]	(10.0)	(10.0)	(10.0)
	28.0	28.0	28.0
M&P deduction[c] [ITA 125.1]	(13.0)	0.0	0.0
Rate reduction[d] [ITA 123.4]	0.0	(13.0)	(13.0)
	15.0	15.0	15.0
Provincial/territorial rates			
British Columbia	12.0%	12.0%	12.0%
Alberta	8.0	8.0	8.0
Saskatchewan[e]	10.0	12.0	12.0
Manitoba	12.0	12.0	12.0
Ontario[f]	10.0	11.5	11.5
Québec	11.5	11.5	11.5
New Brunswick	14.0	14.0	14.0
Nova Scotia	14.0	14.0	14.0
Prince Edward Island	16.0	16.0	16.0
Newfoundland & Labrador	15.0	15.0	15.0
Yukon[g]	2.5	12.0	12.0
Northwest Territories	11.5	11.5	11.5
Nunavut	12.0	12.0	12.0

See the Notes after table C-2.

All rates must be prorated for taxation years that straddle the effective date of the rate changes.

The 2021 federal budget proposed to temporarily reduce the small business tax rate to 4.5% (from 9%) and the general corporate tax rate to 7.5% (from 15%) on eligible zero-emission technology manufacturing and processing income. The reduced tax rates apply to taxation years beginning after 2021. The reduced rates are gradually phased out starting in taxation years that begin in 2029, and are fully phased out for taxation years that begin after 2031. Legislation to enact this proposal has not been released as of April 30, 2021. Finance will accept stakeholder comments on this proposal until June 18, 2021.

C-2 — COMBINED FEDERAL AND PROVINCIAL/TERRITORIAL TAX RATES FOR INCOME EARNED BY A GENERAL CORPORATION — 2021 AND 2022[a]

Current to: April 30, 2021

	M&P Income	Active Business Income	Investment Income[b]
British Columbia	27.0%	27.0%	27.0%
Alberta	23.0	23.0	23.0
Saskatchewan[e]	25.0	27.0	27.0
Manitoba	27.0	27.0	27.0
Ontario[f]	25.0	26.5	26.5
Québec	26.5	26.5	26.5
New Brunswick	29.0	29.0	29.0
Nova Scotia	29.0	29.0	29.0
Prince Edward Island	31.0	31.0	31.0
Newfoundland & Labrador	30.0	30.0	30.0
Yukon[g]	17.5	27.0	27.0
Northwest Territories	26.5	26.5	26.5
Nunavut	27.0	27.0	27.0

Notes:

a   The federal and provincial/territorial tax rates shown in the tables apply to income earned by corporations other than Canadian-controlled private corporations (CCPCs). A general corporation typically includes public companies and their subsidiaries that are resident in Canada, and Canadian-resident private companies that are controlled by non-residents.

   For tax rates applicable to CCPCs, see tables C-4 and C-5.

b   The federal and provincial/territorial tax rates shown in the tables apply to investment income earned by general corporations other than capital gains and dividends received from Canadian corporations. The rates that apply to capital gains are one-half of the rates shown in the tables. Dividends received from Canadian corporations are deductible in computing regular Part I tax, but may be subject to Part IV tax, calculated at a rate of 38⅓%.

c   Corporations that derive at least 10% of their gross revenue for the year from manufacturing or processing goods in Canada for sale or lease can claim the manufacturing and processing (M&P) deduction against their M&P income.

d   A general tax rate reduction is available on qualifying income. Income that is eligible for other reductions or credits, such as small business income and M&P income, is not eligible for this rate reduction.

   Income of a corporation earned from a personal services business is not eligible for the general rate reduction and is subject to an additional 5% tax, which increases the federal tax rate on personal services business income to 33%.

e   Saskatchewan provides a manufacturing and processing profits tax reduction that effectively reduces the corporate tax rate on eligible corporations' Canadian manufacturing and processing profits earned in the province to 10%.

f   Ontario provides a manufacturing and processing tax credit that effectively reduces the corporate tax rate on the corporation's Canadian manufacturing and processing profits earned in the province to 10%.

g   Yukon provides a manufacturing and processing tax credit that effectively reduces the corporate tax rate on the corporation's Canadian manufacturing and processing profits earned in the Yukon to 2.5%.

C-3 — SUBSTANTIVELY ENACTED[a] INCOME TAX RATES FOR INCOME EARNED BY A GENERAL CORPORATION[b] FOR 2021 AND BEYOND — AS AT APRIL 30, 2021

Current to: April 30, 2021

	Active Business Income		M&P Income		Investment Income[c]	
	2021	2022 and Beyond	2021	2022 and Beyond	2021	2022 and Beyond
Federal rates						
General corporate rate	38.0%	38.0%	38.0%	38.0%	38.0%	38.0%
Federal abatement	(10.0)	(10.0)	(10.0)	(10.0)	(10.0)	(10.0)
	28.0	28.0	28.0	28.0	28.0	28.0
Rate reduction[d]	(13.0)	(13.0)	0.0	0.0	(13.0)	(13.0)
M&P deduction[e]	0.0	0.0	(13.0)	(13.0)	0.0	0.0
Gross federal rate	15.0	15.0	15.0	15.0	15.0	15.0
Provincial/territorial rates						
British Columbia	12.0%	12.0%	12.0%	12.0%	12.0%	12.0%
Alberta	8.0	8.0	8.0	8.0	8.0	8.0
Saskatchewan	12.0	12.0	10.0	10.0	12.0	12.0
Manitoba	12.0	12.0	12.0	12.0	12.0	12.0
Ontario	11.5	11.5	10.0	10.0	11.5	11.5
Québec	11.5	11.5	11.5	11.5	11.5	11.5
New Brunswick	14.0	14.0	14.0	14.0	14.0	14.0
Nova Scotia	14.0	14.0	14.0	14.0	14.0	14.0
Prince Edward Island	16.0	16.0	16.0	16.0	16.0	16.0
Newfoundland & Lab.	15.0	15.0	15.0	15.0	15.0	15.0
Yukon[f]	12.0	12.0	2.5	2.5	12.0	12.0
Northwest Territories	11.5	11.5	11.5	11.5	11.5	11.5
Nunavut	12.0	12.0	12.0	12.0	12.0	12.0

All rates must be prorated for taxation years that straddle the effective date of the rate changes. The tax rates in this table reflect federal and provincial/territorial income tax rate changes that were substantively enacted as at April 30, 2021.

The 2021 federal budget proposed to temporarily reduce the small business tax rate to 4.5% (from 9%) and the general corporate tax rate to 7.5% (from 15%) on eligible zero-emission technology manufacturing and processing income. The reduced tax rates apply to taxation years beginning after 2021. The reduced rates are gradually phased out starting in taxation years that begin in 2029, and are fully phased out for taxation years that begin after 2031. Legislation to enact this proposal has not been released as of April 30, 2021. Finance will accept stakeholder comments on this proposal until June 18, 2021.

Notes:

a   For Accounting Standards for Private Enterprise (ASPE) and International Financial Reporting Standards (IFRS) purposes, a corporation's recorded income tax liabilities and assets in their financial statements should be measured using tax rates that are considered to be "substantively enacted" at the balance sheet date. In general, where there is a majority government, federal and provincial/territorial tax changes are considered to be "substantively enacted" for ASPE and IFRS purposes when a tax bill containing the detailed legislation is tabled for first reading in the House of Commons or the provincial/territorial legislature. In the case of a minority government, however, the "substantively enacted" test is more stringent and requires the enabling legislation to have passed third reading in the House of Commons or the provincial/territorial legislature.

For U.S. Generally Accepted Accounting Principles (U.S. GAAP) purposes, a corporation's recorded income tax liabilities and assets in their financial statements should be measured using tax rates that are considered to be enacted at the balance sheet date. In general, tax rate changes are considered enacted once the relevant bill has received Royal Assent.

When tax rate changes are considered enacted or "substantively enacted", the effect of the change in tax rate is reflected in the period in which the changes are enacted or "substantively enacted". The effect of the change is recorded in income as a component of deferred tax expense in the period that includes the date of enactment or substantive enactment. For example, if a bill becomes "substantively enacted" for ASPE or IFRS purposes (enacted for U.S. GAAP purposes) on December 31, the tax rate changes should be reflected in the corporation's financial statements for the quarter that includes December 31.

b   The federal and provincial/territorial tax rates shown in the tables apply to income earned by corporations other than Canadian-controlled private corporations (CCPCs). A general corporation typically includes public companies, and their subsidiaries, that are resident in Canada, and Canadian resident private companies that are controlled by non-residents.

c   The federal and provincial/territorial rates shown in the tables apply to investment income earned by general corporations other than capital gains and dividends received from Canadian corporations. The rates that apply to capital gains are one-half of the rates shown in the table. Dividends received from Canadian corporations are generally deductible in computing regular Part I tax, but may be subject to Part IV tax, calculated at a rate of 38⅓%.

d   A general tax rate reduction is available on qualifying income. Income that is eligible for other reductions or credits, such as small business income, manufacturing and processing (M&P) income and investment income subject to the refundable provisions, is not eligible for this rate reduction.

Income of a corporation earned from a personal services business is not eligible for the general rate reduction and is subject to an additional 5% tax, which increases the federal tax rate on personal services business income to 33%.

e   Corporations that derive at least 10% of their gross revenue for the year from manufacturing or processing goods in Canada for sale or lease can claim the M&P deduction against their M&P income.

f   Yukon provides a manufacturing and processing tax credit that effectively reduces the corporate tax rate on the corporation's Canadian manufacturing and processing profits earned in the Yukon to 2.5%.

C-4 — FEDERAL AND PROVINCIAL/TERRITORIAL TAX RATES FOR INCOME EARNED BY A CCPC — 2021 AND 2022[a]

Current to: April 30, 2021

	Small Business Income up to $500,000[b]	Active Business Income[c]	Investment Income[d]
Federal rates			
General corporate rate [ITA 123(1)]	38.0%	38.0%	38.0%
Federal abatement [ITA 124(1)]	(10.0)	(10.0)	(10.0)
	28.0	28.0	28.0
Small business deduction[e] [ITA 125(1)]	(19.0)	0.0	0.0
Rate reduction[f] [ITA 123.4]	0.0	(13.0)	0.0
Refundable tax[g] [ITA 123.3]	0.0	0.0	10.7
	9.0	15.0	38.7
Provincial/territorial rates			
British Columbia	2.0%	12.0%	12.0%
Alberta	2.0	8.0	8.0
Saskatchewan[h]	0.0/1.0	12.0	12.0
Manitoba	0.0	12.0	12.0
Ontario	3.2	11.5	11.5
Québec[i]	4.0/3.2	11.5	11.5
New Brunswick	2.5	14.0	14.0
Nova Scotia	2.5	14.0	14.0
Prince Edward Island[j]	2.0/1.0	16.0	16.0
Newfoundland & Labrador	3.0	15.0	15.0
Yukon[k]	0.0	12.0	12.0
Northwest Territories[l]	2.0	11.5	11.5
Nunavut	3.0	12.0	12.0

See the Notes after table C-5.

All rates must be prorated for taxation years that straddle the effective date of the rate changes.

The 2021 federal budget proposed to temporarily reduce the small business tax rate to 4.5% (from 9%) and the general corporate tax rate to 7.5% (from 15%) on eligible zero-emission technology manufacturing and processing income. The reduced tax rates apply to taxation years beginning after 2021. The reduced rates are gradually phased out starting in taxation years that begin in 2029, and are fully phased out for taxation years that begin after 2031. Legislation to enact this proposal has not been released as of April 30, 2021. Finance will accept stakeholder comments on this proposal until June 18, 2021.

C-5 — COMBINED FEDERAL AND PROVINCIAL/TERRITORIAL TAX RATES FOR INCOME EARNED BY A CCPC — 2021 AND 2022[a]

Current to: April 30, 2021

	Small Business Income up to $500,000[b]	Active Business Income[c]	Investment Income[d]
Provincial/territorial rates			
British Columbia	11.0%	27.0%	50.7%
Alberta	11.0	23.0	46.7
Saskatchewan[h]	9.0/10.0	27.0	50.7
Manitoba	9.0	27.0	50.7
Ontario	12.2	26.5	50.2
Québec[i]	13.0/12.2	26.5	50.2
New Brunswick	11.5	29.0	52.7
Nova Scotia	11.5	29.0	52.7
Prince Edward Island[j]	11.0/10.0	31.0	54.7
Newfoundland & Labrador	12.0	30.0	53.7
Yukon[k]	9.0	27.0	50.7
Northwest Territories[l]	11.0	26.5	50.2
Nunavut	12.0	27.0	50.7

Notes:

a The federal and provincial/territorial tax rates shown in the tables apply to income earned by a Canadian-controlled private corporation (CCPC). In general, a corporation is a CCPC if the corporation is a private corporation and a Canadian corporation, provided it is not controlled by one or more non-resident persons, by a public corporation, by a corporation with a class of shares listed on a designated stock exchange, or by any combination of these, and provided it does not have a class of shares listed on a designated stock exchange. For tax rates applicable to general corporations, see tables C-1 and C-2.

b The small business threshold is $600,000 in Saskatchewan. Therefore, Saskatchewan's combined income tax rate on active business income between $500,000 and $600,000 is 15% (i.e., 15% federally and 0% provincially) effective October 1, 2020 to June 30, 2022. See table C-7 for the federal and provincial/territorial small business income thresholds.

c The general corporate tax rate applies to active business income earned in excess of the small business threshold. See table C-7 for the federal and provincial/territorial small business income thresholds.

CCPCs that earn income from manufacturing and processing activities (M&P income) are subject to the same rates as those that apply to general corporations (see tables C-1 and C-2).

d The federal and provincial/territorial tax rates shown in the tables apply to investment income earned by a CCPC, other than capital gains and dividends received from Canadian corporations. The rates that apply to capital gains are one-half of the rates shown in the tables. Dividends received from Canadian corporations are deductible in computing regular Part I tax, but may be subject to Part IV tax, calculated at a rate of $38\frac{1}{3}\%$.

e Corporations that are CCPCs throughout the year may claim the small business deduction (SBD). In general, the SBD is calculated based on the least of three amounts — active business income earned in Canada, taxable income and the small business income threshold.

f A general tax rate reduction is available on qualifying income. Income that is eligible for other reductions or credits, such as small business income, M&P income and investment income subject to the refundable provisions, is not eligible for this rate reduction.

Income of a corporation earned from a personal services business is not eligible for the general rate reduction and is subject to an additional 5% tax, which increases the federal tax rate on personal services business income to 33%.

g The refundable tax of $10\frac{2}{3}\%$ of a CCPC's investment income and taxable capital gains, as well as 20% of such income that is subject to regular Part I tax, is included in the corporation's non-eligible refundable dividend tax on hand (NERDTOH) account. When non-eligible dividends are paid out to shareholders, a dividend refund equal to the lesser of $38\frac{1}{3}\%$ of the dividends paid or the combined balance in NERDTOH and eligible refundable dividend tax on hand (ERDTOH) accounts is refunded to the corporation. The dividend refund on non-eligible dividends must come out of the corporation's NERDTOH account before it comes out of the corporation's ERDTOH balance.

h Saskatchewan has temporarily reduced the province's small business income tax rate to 0% (from 2%) effective October 1, 2020 to June 30, 2022. The small business income tax rate will increase to 1% (from 0%) beginning July 1, 2022 and will be further increased to 2% (from 1%) beginning July 1, 2023.

i Québec decreased the small business income tax rate to 4% (from 5%) effective January 1, 2021. Québec's 2021-2022 budget proposed to reduce the small business income tax rate to 3.2% (from 4%) effective after March 25, 2021.

Québec's small business deduction is generally available to corporations only if their employees were paid for at least 5,500 hours in the taxation year (proportionally reduced for short taxation years) or if their employees and those of their associated corporations were paid for at least 5,500 hours in the previous taxation year, to a maximum of 40 hours a week per employee (excluding the hours paid to a subcontractor). The small business deduction is reduced linearly between 5,500 and 5,000 hours, and falls to zero at 5,000 hours. Québec's 2021-2022 budget proposed that for a given taxation year that ended after June 30, 2020, but before July 1, 2021, a corporation may apply for the number of remunerated hours that were used to determine whether it was eligible for the small business deduction or to establish its small business deduction rate, for its taxation year, to be used to determine whether it qualifies for the small business deduction or to establish its small business deduction rate for the given year.

j Prince Edward Island decreased the province's small business income tax rate to 2% (from 3%) effective January 1, 2021. The province's small business income tax rate will further decrease to 1% (from 2%), effective January 1, 2022.

k Yukon decreased the territory's small business income tax rate to 0% (from 2%) effective January 1, 2021.

l Northwest Territories decreased the territory's small business income tax rate to 2% (from 4%) effective January 1, 2021.

C-6 — SUBSTANTIVELY ENACTED[a] INCOME TAX RATES FOR INCOME EARNED BY A CCPC FOR 2021 AND BEYOND — AS AT APRIL 30, 2021

Current to: April 30, 2021

	Small Business Income[b]		Active Business Income[c]	
	2021	2022 and Beyond	2021	2022 and Beyond
Federal rates				
General corporate rate	38.0%	38.0%	38.0%	38.0%
Federal abatement	(10.0)	(10.0)	(10.0)	(10.0)
	28.0	28.0	28.0	28.0
Small business reduction	(19.0)	(19.0)	0.0	0.0
Rate reduction[f]	0.0	0.0	(13.0)	(13.0)
	9.0	9.0	15.0	15.0
Provincial/territorial rates				
British Columbia	2.0%	2.0%	12.0%	12.0%
Alberta	2.0	2.0	8.0	8.0
Saskatchewan[g]	0.0	0.0/1.0/2.0	12.0	12.0
Manitoba	0.0	0.0	12.0	12.0
Ontario	3.2	3.2	11.5	11.5
Québec[h]	4.0	4.0	11.5	11.5
New Brunswick	2.5	2.5	14.0	14.0
Nova Scotia	2.5	2.5	14.0	14.0
Prince Edward Island[i]	2.0	2.0	16.0	16.0
Newfoundland & Labrador	3.0	3.0	15.0	15.0
Yukon[j]	0.0	0.0	12.0	12.0
Northwest Territories[k]	2.0	2.0	11.5	11.5
Nunavut	3.0	3.0	12.0	12.0

	M&P Income[d]		Investment Income[e]	
	2021	2022 and Beyond	2021	2022 and Beyond
Federal rates				
General corporate rate	38.0%	38.0%	38.0%	38.0%
Federal abatement	(10.0)	(10.0)	(10.0)	(10.0)
	28.0	28.0	28.0	28.0
M&P deduction[d]	(13.0)	(13.0)	0.0	0.0
Refundable tax	0.0	0.0	10.7	10.7
	15.0	15.0	38.7	38.7
Provincial/territorial rates				
British Columbia	12.0%	12.0%	12.0%	12.0%
Alberta	8.0	8.0	8.0	8.0
Saskatchewan[g]	10.0	10.0	12.0	12.0
Manitoba	12.0	12.0	12.0	12.0
Ontario	10.0	10.0	11.5	11.5
Québec[h]	11.5	11.5	11.5	11.5
New Brunswick	14.0	14.0	14.0	14.0
Nova Scotia	14.0	14.0	14.0	14.0
Prince Edward Island[i]	16.0	16.0	16.0	16.0
Newfoundland & Labrador	15.0	15.0	15.0	15.0
Yukon[j]	2.5	2.5	12.0	12.0
Northwest Territories[k]	11.5	11.5	11.5	11.5
Nunavut	12.0	12.0	12.0	12.0

All rates must be prorated for taxation years that straddle the effective date of the rate changes. The tax rates in this table reflect federal and provincial/territorial income tax rate changes that were substantively enacted as at April 30, 2021.

The 2021 federal budget proposed to temporarily reduce the small business tax rate to 4.5% (from 9%) and the general corporate tax rate to 7.5% (from 15%) on eligible zero-emission technology manufacturing and processing income. The reduced tax rates apply to taxation years beginning after 2021. The reduced rates are gradually phased out starting in taxation years that begin in 2029, and are fully phased out for taxation years that begin after 2031. Legislation to enact this proposal has not been released as of April 30, 2021. Finance will accept stakeholder comments on this proposal until June 18, 2021.

Notes:

a For Accounting Standards for Private Enterprise (ASPE) and International Financial Reporting Standards (IFRS) purposes, a corporation's recorded income tax liabilities and assets in their financial statements should be measured using tax rates that are considered to be "substantively enacted" at the balance sheet date. In general, where there is a majority government, federal and provincial/territorial tax changes are considered to be "substantively enacted" for ASPE and IFRS purposes when a tax bill containing the detailed legislation is tabled for first reading in the House of Commons or the provincial/territorial legislature. In the case of a minority government, however, the "substantively enacted" test is more stringent and requires the enabling legislation to have passed third reading in the House of Commons or the provincial/territorial legislature.

For U.S. Generally Accepted Accounting Principles (U.S. GAAP) purposes, a corporation's recorded income tax liabilities and assets in their financial statements should be measured using tax rates that are considered to be enacted at the balance sheet date. In general, tax rate changes are considered enacted once the relevant bill has received Royal Assent.

When tax rate changes are considered enacted or "substantively enacted", the effect of the change in tax rate is reflected in the period in which the changes are enacted or "substantively enacted". The effect of the change is recorded in income as a component of deferred tax expense in the period that includes the date of enactment or substantive enactment. For example, if a bill becomes "substantively enacted" for ASPE or IFRS purposes (enacted for U.S. GAAP purposes) on December 31, the tax rate changes should be reflected in the corporation's financial statements for the quarter that includes December 31.

b The federal and provincial/territorial tax rates shown in the tables apply to income earned by a Canadian-controlled private corporation (CCPC). In general, a corporation is a CCPC if the corporation is a private corporation and a Canadian corporation, provided it is not controlled by one or more non-resident persons, by a public corporation, by a corporation with a class of shares listed on a designated stock exchange, or by any combination of these, and provided it does not have a class of shares listed on a designated stock exchange.

c The general corporate tax rate applies to active business income earned in excess of the small business income threshold. See table C-7 for the federal and provincial/territorial small business income thresholds.

d Corporations that derive at least 10% of their gross revenue for the year from manufacturing or processing goods in Canada for sale or lease can claim the manufacturing and processing (M&P) deduction against their M&P income. Please refer to the notes to table C-2 for the provincial and territorial M&P tax credits and rate reduction details for Saskatchewan, Ontario and Yukon.

e The federal and provincial/territorial tax rates shown in this table apply to investment income earned by a CCPC other than capital gains and dividends received from Canadian corporations. The rates that apply to capital gains are one-half of the rates shown in the table. Dividends received from Canadian corporations are generally deductible in computing regular Part I tax, but may be subject to Part IV tax, calculated at a rate of 38⅓%.

f A general tax rate reduction is available on qualifying income. Income that is eligible for other reductions or credits, such as small business income, M&P income and investment income subject to the refundable provisions, is not eligible for this rate reduction.

Income of a corporation earned from a personal services business is not eligible for the general rate reduction and is subject to an additional 5% tax, which increases the federal tax rate on personal services business income to 33%.

g Saskatchewan has temporarily reduced the province's small business income tax rate to 0% (from 2%) effective October 1, 2020 to June 30, 2022. The small business income tax rate will increase to 1% (from 0%) beginning July 1, 2022 and will be further increased to 2% (from 1%) beginning July 1, 2023.

The small business threshold is $600,000 in Saskatchewan. Therefore, Saskatchewan's combined income tax rate on active business income between $500,000 and $600,000 is 15% (i.e., 15% federally and 0% provincially) effective October 1, 2020 to June 30, 2022.

h Québec decreased the small business income tax rate to 4% (from 5%) effective January 1, 2021. Québec's 2021-2022 budget proposed to reduce the small business income tax rate to 3.2% (from 4%) effective after March 25, 2021.

Québec's small business deduction is generally available to corporations only if their employees were paid for at least 5,500 hours in the taxation year (proportionally reduced for short taxation years) or if their employees and those of their associated corporations were paid for at least 5,500 hours in the previous taxation year, to a maximum of 40 hours a week per employee (excluding the hours paid to a subcontractor). The small business deduction is reduced linearly between 5,500 and 5,000 hours, and falls to zero at 5,000 hours. Québec's 2021-2022 budget proposed that for a given taxation year that ended after June 30, 2020, but before July 1, 2021, a corporation may apply for the number of remunerated hours that were used to determine whether it was eligible for the small business deduction or to establish its small business deduction rate, for its taxation year, to be used to determine whether it qualifies for the small business deduction or to establish its small business deduction rate for the given year.

i Prince Edward Island decreased the province's small business income tax rate to 2% (from 3%) effective January 1, 2021. Prince Edward Island's 2021 budget proposed to further decrease the province's small business income tax rate to 1% (from 2%) effective January 1, 2022.

j Yukon decreased the territory's small business income tax rate to 0% (from 2%) effective January 1, 2021.

Yukon provides a manufacturing and processing tax credit that effectively reduces the corporate tax rate on the corporation's Canadian manufacturing and processing profits earned in the Yukon to 2.5%.

k Northwest Territories decreased the territory's small business income tax rate to 2% (from 4%) effective January 1, 2021.

C-7 — SMALL BUSINESS INCOME THRESHOLDS FOR 2021 AND BEYOND[a]

Current to: April 30, 2021

	2021 and beyond
Federal[b] [ITA 125(2)]	$500,000
British Columbia	500,000
Alberta	500,000
Saskatchewan	600,000
Manitoba	500,000
Ontario	500,000
Québec[c]	500,000
New Brunswick	500,000
Nova Scotia	500,000
Prince Edward Island	500,000
Newfoundland & Labrador	500,000
Yukon	500,000
Northwest Territories	500,000
Nunavut	500,000

All thresholds must be prorated for taxation years that straddle the effective date of the threshold changes.

Notes:

a   The small business income thresholds shown in the table apply to active business income earned by a Canadian-controlled private corporation (CCPC) that is eligible for the small business rate of tax (see tables C-4 and C-5). All thresholds must be shared by associated corporations.

b   The federal small business threshold is reduced on a straight-line basis when the associated group's taxable capital employed in Canada in the preceding year is between $10 million and $15 million, and nil if the taxable capital is $15 million or more. This clawback applies to all provinces.

The small business limit is also reduced for CCPCs (and associated corporations) that earn passive investment income exceeding a certain threshold. Generally effective for taxation years that begin after 2018, the federal small business income threshold is also reduced on a straight-line basis when the associated corporate group's adjusted aggregate investment income in the preceding taxation year is between $50,000 and $150,000, and nil if the adjusted aggregate investment income is $150,000 or more.

The reduction in a corporation's federal small business income threshold will be the greater of the reductions under the taxable capital threshold and the investment income threshold.

c   Québec's small business deduction is available to CCPCs with paid-up capital (on an associated basis) of less than $10 million, and is gradually phased out for CCPCs with paid-up capital between $10 and $15 million.

Québec's small business deduction is generally available to corporations only if their employees were paid for at least 5,500 hours in the taxation year (proportionally reduced for short taxation years) or if their employees and those of their associated corporations were paid for at least 5,500 hours in the previous taxation year, to a maximum of 40 hours a week per employee (excluding the hours paid to a subcontractor). The small business deduction is reduced linearly between 5,500 and 5,000 hours, and falls to zero at 5,000 hours. Québec's 2021-2022 budget proposed that for a given taxation year that ended after June 30, 2020, but before July 1, 2021, a corporation may apply for the number of remunerated hours that were used to determine whether it was eligible for the small business deduction or to establish its small business deduction rate, for its taxation year, to be used to determine whether it qualifies for the small business deduction or to establish its small business deduction rate for the given year.

C-8 — FEDERAL RESEARCH AND DEVELOPMENT (R&D) TAX INCENTIVES

Current to: April 30, 2021

Federal Investment Tax Credits (ITCs)[a]

Type of Entity	Nature of Expenditure[b]	ITC Rate on Total Expenditures up to Expenditure Limit[c]	Refund Rate	ITC Rate on Total Expenditures in Excess of Expenditure Limit[c]	Refund Rate
Qualifying CCPCs	Current	35%	100%	15%	40%
Other corporations	Current	15%	—	15%	—
Individuals & unincorporated businesses	Current	15%	40%	15%	40%

Notes:

a Federal research and development (R&D) ITCs can either be applied against federal taxes payable in that taxation year, refunded to the claimant (if applicable), carried forward and claimed in the 20 subsequent years or carried back and applied against federal taxes payable in the three prior taxation years.

ITC claims must be identified on a prescribed form (T2 Schedule 31) and filed with the Canada Revenue Agency (CRA) within 12 months of the entity's filing due date for its regular income tax return. The related prescribed forms (Forms T661, T661 Part 2 and Schedule 31) must also be filed within this timeframe, to ensure a complete R&D filing.

ITCs claimed in a taxation year are deducted from the entity's R&D expenditure pool in the subsequent taxation year. The current portion of provincial ITCs, which are considered to be government assistance, are deducted from the R&D pool in the taxation year claimed. The portion of federal ITCs that related to qualifying Ontario R&D expenditures was not deducted from the entity's R&D pool for Ontario purposes, for taxation years ending before 2009. Under the single corporate tax administration system in Ontario (applicable for taxation years ending after 2008), Ontario replaced this treatment with a 4.5% non-refundable Ontario tax credit on R&D expenses incurred in Ontario that qualify for the federal ITC (reduced to 3.5% effective June 1, 2016).

b Expenditures for R&D capital property (including the right to use such property) made after 2013 are excluded for federal ITC purposes.

c The expenditure limit is generally $3 million and applies to current expenditures (capital expenditures are no longer eligible for taxation years after 2013). The expenditure limit must be shared and allocated among associated corporations. However, CCPCs that are associated due to a group of unconnected investors, such as venture capital investors, do not have to share the limit provided that the CRA is satisfied that the group of investors was not formed to gain access to multiple expenditure limits.

The expenditure limit is phased out for CCPCs with taxable capital employed in Canada of between $10 and $50 million in the prior year (on an associated group basis). The expenditure limit is reduced by $0.75 for every $10 by which taxable capital exceeds $10 million. The ability to claim the 35% ITC rate and related 100% ITC refund on current expenditures is eliminated once prior year taxable capital exceeds $50 million.

Federal R&D expenditure pool

Eligible Canadian R&D expenditures, which include current expenditures only, are aggregated in a pool each year and may be deducted in whole or in part. Expenditures for R&D capital property (including the right to use such property) made after 2013 are excluded from the federal R&D expenditures pool. These expenditures can still be claimed as regular business expenditures (presuming they qualify as such).

Any allowable amounts not deducted from the R&D pool in the current year may be carried forward indefinitely.

Foreign current expenditures may also be deducted as current R&D expenditures in the year they are incurred. Such expenditures generally do not give rise to federal ITCs. However, R&D labour expenditures incurred outside Canada may result in federal ITCs, as discussed below.

Government assistance (which includes provincial ITCs), non-government assistance and contract payments reduce the amount of eligible expenditures in the year. Eligible expenditures are also reduced when R&D assets, for which the taxpayer received an ITC in any of the 20 previous years (for taxation years after 1997), are converted to commercial use or sold during the year. In such instances the related recaptured ITCs will increase eligible expenditures.

Eligible expenditures incurred in the year, as well as project technical narratives and related project information, must be identified on prescribed forms (Forms T661, T661 Part 2 and Schedule 31) and filed with the CRA within 12 months of the entity's filing due date for its regular income tax return.

Qualifying current R&D expenditures

Qualifying Canadian current expenditures include the following:

- salaries and wages of employees directly engaged in R&D — salaries and wages of specified employees (those individuals who directly or indirectly own greater than 10% of the shares of any class of the capital stock of the company, or who do not deal at arm's length with the taxpayer) are limited to five times the year's maximum CPP pensionable earnings and exclude remuneration based on profits or bonuses;
- salaries and wages of Canadian-resident employees carrying on R&D activities outside Canada — these salaries and wages (limited to 10% of the total R&D salary and wages carried on in Canada in the year) are eligible provided the R&D activities are directly undertaken by the taxpayer and done solely in support of R&D carried on by the taxpayer in Canada;
- cost of materials consumed or transformed in R&D;

- capital expenditures used in R&D incurred before 2014;
- lease costs of machinery and equipment used in R&D incurred before 2014;
- eligible expenditures incurred by contractors performing R&D directly on behalf of the taxpayer (restricted for ITC purposes to only 80% of contractor R&D expenditures and excluding any R&D contractor expenditures that are considered R&D capital expenditures (also see note (b)), for expenditures incurred on or after January 1, 2013);
- contracts for services that are directly related to SR&ED activities;
- payroll burden (not included if proxy election made);
- eligible expenditures incurred by certain third parties where the taxpayer may exploit the results of the R&D (to be restricted for ITC purposes to only 80% of the third party payments for expenditures incurred after January 1, 2013).

Proxy election for overhead expenses

The proxy election adds 55% of qualifying R&D salaries and wages (excluding bonuses, taxable benefits and stock option benefits) to the expenditures eligible for federal ITCs (but not to the R&D pool itself). This "notional overhead" amount replaces non-SR&ED service contracts, payroll burden, administration and other overhead costs that are often difficult to support. Other less significant costs that are so replaced include utilities, office and other types of supplies. Once the election is made, it is irrevocable for that taxation year.

The salary of specified employees (as discussed above) is limited in a number of ways when calculating the amount of salaries and wages eligible for the proxy election. Only 75% of such employees' salaries can be included as eligible salaries, and the maximum per employee is 2.5 times the year's maximum CPP pensionable earnings. Remuneration based on profits and bonuses is excluded from the proxy computation for both specified and non-specified employees.

C-9 — PROVINCIAL/TERRITORIAL RESEARCH AND DEVELOPMENT (R&D) TAX INCENTIVES[k]

Current to: April 30, 2021

Province	Rate	Description
British Columbia[a]	10%	Refundable and non-refundable tax credit for eligible expenditures incurred in B.C. by a corporation with a permanent establishment (PE) in the province.
Alberta[b]	8%/20%	Refundable tax credit for eligible expenditures incurred in Alberta by a corporation with a PE in the province.
Saskatchewan[c]	10%	Refundable and non-refundable tax credit for eligible expenditures incurred in Saskatchewan by a corporation with a PE in the province.
Manitoba[d]	15%	Non-refundable and refundable tax credit for eligible expenditures incurred in Manitoba by a corporation with a PE in the province.
Ontario *Innovation Tax Credit (OITC)*[e]	8%	Refundable tax credit for eligible expenditures incurred in Ontario by a corporation with a PE in the province.
Ontario *Business-Research Institute Tax Credit (OBRITC)*[f]	20%	Refundable tax credit for eligible expenditures incurred in Ontario by a corporation with a PE in the province as part of an eligible contract with an eligible research institute.
Ontario *Research and Development Tax Credit (ORDTC)*[g]	3.5%	Non-refundable tax credit for eligible expenditures incurred in Ontario by a corporation with a PE in the province.
Québec *Credit for contract payments to/for R&D entities and projects*[h]	14%/30%	Refundable tax credit for contract and other payments to certain eligible entities (only 80% of payments to unrelated persons are eligible), subject to expenditure exclusion threshold.
Québec *R&D Wage Tax Credit*[i, j]	Canadian-controlled corporations — 30% Others — 14%	Refundable tax credit for R&D wages of Québec-based employees of a coporation that carries on business in Canada and performs R&D in Québec, or has such work carried out on their behalf in Québec. The corporation does not need to have a PE in Québec. This credit is also available for 50% of amounts paid to an unrelated subcontractor for R&D performed by employees in Québec and for 100% of amounts attributed to wages paid to employees of a related subcontractor in Québec.
New Brunswick[k]	15%	Refundable tax credit for eligible expenditures incurred in New Brunswick by a corporation with a PE in the province.
Nova Scotia[k]	15%	Refundable tax credit for eligible expenditures incurred in Nova Scotia by a corporation with a PE in the province.
Newfoundland & Labrador[k]	15%	Refundable tax credit for eligible expenditures incurred in Newfoundland & Labrador by a corporation with a PE in the province.
Yukon[k]	15%/20%	Refundable tax credit for eligible expenditures incurred in Yukon by a corporation with a PE in the territory.

Notes:

a Eligible expenditures in British Columbia are those that qualify for federal investment tax credit (ITC) purposes. Canadian-controlled private corporations (CCPCs) are eligible for the refundable credit on expenditures up to their expenditure limit (as it is defined for federal purposes). The credit is not refundable for other corporations or for a CCPC's expenditures in excess of the expenditure limit. Corporations that are active members of a partnership that incurs qualifying expenditures are also entitled to claim their porportionate share of the credit. Expenditures incurred by an individual or trust do not qualify.

The credit is considered to be government assistance and reduces federal expenditures for both the R&D deduction and ITCs. The credit can be claimed only once all other tax credits have been claimed. Unused non-refundable credits may be carried back three taxation years or carried forward ten taxation years. All or part of the non-refundable credit can be renounced each year.

British Columbia's provincial R&D tax credit is available for eligible expenditures incurred before September 1, 2022.

b Open as of January 1, 2021, the new Innovation Employment Grant is a refundable tax credit that replaces the Alberta SR&ED tax credit program terminated at the end of 2019. Those small and medium-sized Alberta-based companies who qualify for the grant could receive an amount equal to 8% of their base R&D expenditures (calculated as the company's average qualifying R&D spending over the previous two years), and 20% of spending that is above that base amount. Expenditures must qualify for the federal SR&ED program and relate to R&D carried out in Alberta after December 31, 2020 in order to be eligible for the grant.

Corporations may qualify for the grant on up to $4 million in annual R&D spending. Where the corporation is associated with one or more corporations, this annual limit must be shared among the associated group. The amount of the grant is gradually reduced for corporations or associated corporations with taxable capital between $10 million and $50 million, and is completely eliminated when taxable capital reaches $50 million.

c Eligible expenditures in Saskatchewan are determined by reference to the definition of "qualified expenditures" for federal ITC pur-poses. For eligible expenditures made between April 1, 2015 and March 31, 2017, the Saskatchewan ITC is a 10% non-refundable tax credit for all corporations. Effective April 1, 2017, qualifying R&D expenditures by Saskatchewan CCPCs are eligible for a 10% refundable R&D tax credit for the first $1 million annual qualifying expenditures. Qualifying expenditures in excess of the annual limit and qualifying expenditures by other corporations continue to be eligible for the 10% non-refundable R&D tax credit. The total refund-able and non-refundable R&D tax credits that may be claimed by a corporation will be limited to $1 million per year.

The credit is considered to be government assistance and reduces federal expenditures for both the R&D deduction and ITCs. Unused non-refundable credits may be carried back three taxation years or carried forward ten taxation years.

d Eligible expenditures in Manitoba are those that qualify for federal ITC purposes, with the following differences:

  • capital expenditures continue to be eligible expenditures in Manitoba;

  • contract payments to eligible educational institutions in Manitoba are fully claimable (for all other contract payments, only 80% of the payments is claimable).

The 15% tax credit is fully refundable if the eligible expenditures are incurred after 2009 and by a corporation with a PE in Manitoba and where the research and experimental development is carried on in Manitoba under contract with a qualifying research institute in Manitoba. The rate decreased to 15% (from 20%) for eligible expenditures made after April 11, 2017.

The credit is 100% refundable for R&D performed under contract with a prescribed Manitoba institution, including post-secondary institutions, and 50% refundable otherwise.

Unused non-refundable credits earned in taxation years ending after 2005 may be carried back three taxation years or carried forward ten taxation years.

The tax credit (refundable and non-refundable) is considered to be government assistance and reduces federal expenditures for both the R&D deduction and ITCs. All or part of the credit can be renounced each year, however, the renunciation must be made in the year the credit was earned and no later than 12 months after the filing due date of the corporate income tax return. The tax implications for federal purposes are different depending on whether the credit is renounced by the filing due date or after the filing due date. Requests to renounce the Manitoba ITCs after the deadline will be denied.

e The OITC is an 8% refundable tax credit for small- to medium-sized companies on eligible R&D expenditures. The OITC rate de-creased to 8% (from 10%) effective June 1, 2016. The tax credit rate is prorated for taxation years straddling June 1, 2016. Eligible expenditures in Ontario are those that qualify for federal ITC purposes and are not in excess of the $3 million expenditure limit. The credit is available to corporations with taxable income of less than $500,000 and taxable paid-up capital (for Ontario capital tax pur-poses) of less than $25 million, in the preceding year. The corporation's expenditure limit will be reduced where this restriction is exceeded by the associated group and, for taxation years ending after 2009, will be eliminated once taxable income exceeds $800,000 or paid-up capital exceeds $50 million, in the preceding year.

f In Ontario, an eligible research institute contract is an R&D contract with an eligible research institute (i.e., certain post-secondary and hospital research institutions, and prescribed non-profit research organizations). Eligible expenditures, as defined for federal ITC pur-poses, are limited to $20 million per year.

g The ORDTC rate decreased to 3.5% (from 4.5%) effective June 1, 2016. The tax credit rate is prorated for taxation years straddling June 1, 2016. Eligible expenditures in Ontario are those that qualify for federal ITC purposes. The credit is non-refundable and is applicable for taxation years ending after 2008. Unused credits may be carried forward 20 years and carried back three years (but only back to taxation years ending after 2008).

h The tax credit rate has harmonized for contracts concluded after December 4, 2014. After this date, payments will be subject to the same tax credit rate earned under the R&D Wage Tax Credit (see note (h) below).

In Québec, eligible entities include universities, public research centres and private research consortiums. These entities must carry on business in Canada and perform R&D in Québec, or have such work carried out on their behalf in Québec. An advance ruling from the Québec Ministry of Revenue is required in order to qualify. Claimants do not need to have a permanent establishment in Québec.

See note (j) below for expenditure exclusion thresholds in effect for taxation years beginning after December 2, 2014.

Other types of eligible payments include expenditures in respect of pre-competitive research projects. An advance ruling from the Québec Ministry of Revenue is required in order to qualify. Claimants do not need to have a permanent establishment in Québec.

The March 10, 2020 Québec budget confirmed the removal of the application of the expenditure exclusion threshold to pre-competitive projects.

i   In Québec, to be eligible for the 30% rate in respect of a maximum of $3 million in qualifying expenditures, the CCPC must have less than $50 million in assets on an associated worldwide basis in the preceding year. For corporations with assets between $50 million and $75 million, this rate is proportionally reduced to 14%. The limit must be shared by associated corporations.

   The credit reduces eligible expenditures for federal purposes. The credit is taxable in Québec.

   Claimants do not need to have a permanent establishment in Québec to claim for eligible expenditures incurred in Québec.

   See note (j) below for expenditure exclusion thresholds in effect for taxation years beginning after December 2, 2014.

j   Québec Information Bulletin 2014-11 introduced an exclusion threshold amount that reduces the expenditures that qualify for the tax credit. The threshold is prorated among the different Québec R&D tax credits claimed.

   The exclusion threshold amount varies depending on the taxpayer's assets, and is calculated on a non-consolidated basis:

   • $50,000 for corporations with assets of $50 million or less;

   • an amount that increases linearly between $50,000 and $225,000 for corporations with assets between $50 million and $75 million;

   • $225,000 for corporations with assets of $75 million or more.

k   In New Brunswick, Nova Scotia, Newfoundland & Labrador and the Yukon, eligible expenditures are those that are considered qualified expenditures for federal purposes. The credit is considered to be government assistance and reduces federal expenditures for both the R&D deduction and ITCs.

   The Yukon R&D tax credit is refundable at a rate of 15% of eligible expenditures. An additional tax credit of 5% is available on amounts paid or payable to the Yukon College. The Yukon credit cannot be carried back or forward.

l   There are no provincial/territorial R&D tax incentives in Prince Edward Island, Northwest Territories and Nunavut.

P-1 — PROVINCIAL/TERRITORIAL PAYROLL AND HEALTH FUND TAXES — 2021[a]

Current to: April 30, 2021

	British Columbia Employer Health Tax[e]	Manitoba Health & Post-Sec. Education Tax	Ontario Employer Health Tax	Québec Health Services Fund[l]	Nfld. & Lab. Health & Post-Sec. Education Tax	NWT Payroll Tax[a]	Nunavut Payroll Tax[a]
Tax rate	1.95%[f]	2.15%[h]	1.95%	4.26%[m]	2.00%	2.00%	2.00%
Exempt remuneration[b]	$500,000[f]	$1,500,000	$1,000,000[j]	—	$1,300,000	—	—
Instalment period	Quarterly[g]	Monthly[i]	Monthly[k]	Monthly[n]	Monthly[o]	Monthly[q]	Monthly[q]
Annual filing deadline	March 31	March 31	March 15	February 28	N/A[p]	February 28	February 28
Assessment period[c]	6 years	6 years	4 years	4 years	4 years	6 years	6 years
Refund period	—	2 years	4 years	4 years	3 years	3 years	3 years
Objection deadline[d]		90 days	180 days	90 days	90 days	90 days	90 days

Notes:

a Payroll, in general, includes all payments, benefits and allowances included in computing employment income under the *Income Tax Act*. Payroll may also be deemed to include such payments made by associated employers. Tax is paid by the employer except for NWT/Nunavut where the employee pays the tax.

b Each province/territory has specific eligibility criteria to obtain the exemption. In most cases, the exemption must be prorated among associated corporations and certain corporate partnerships.

c The assessment period may be extended if the employer is not registered for this tax or where there is suspicion of withholding or misrepresenting information on the returns.

d The objection deadline generally starts on the date of mailing of the Notice of Assessment.

e British Columbia introduced a new Employer Health Tax effective January 1, 2019. This tax is intended to help fund the elimination of the Medical Services Plan premiums, which were eliminated effective January 1, 2020.

   For purposes of the Employer Health Tax, a joint venture is not considered to be an employer. Each individual venturer is considered to be an employer.

f The Employer Health Tax is calculated as a percentage of payroll and varies based on the employer's annual payroll. Employers with annual payroll over $1.5 million are subject to the 1.95% rate with no exemption amount. Annual payroll of $500,000 or less is exempt from tax. Annual payroll between $500,000 and $1.5 million is subject to a rate of 2.925% of the amount in excess of $500,000. The annual thresholds for charitable or non-profit employers are $1.5 million and $4.5 million. If you are associated with other employers and the combined British Columbia remuneration of the associated employers is between $500,000 and $1.5 million, you must share the $500,000 exemption. If the combined British Columbia remuneration of the associated employers is greater than $1.5 million, there is no exemption available to any of the employers.

g Instalments are due during the calendar year on June 15, September 15, December 15 and March 31. If the amount of employer health tax in the previous calendar year exceeded $2,925, quarterly instalment payments are required based on the lesser of 25% of the previous year's tax or 25% of the current year's estimated tax.

h Employers with annual payroll over $3.0 million are subject to the 2.15% rate with no exemption amount. Annual payroll of $1.5 million or less is exempt from tax. Annual payroll between $1.5 million and $3.0 million is subject to a rate of 4.3% of the amount in excess of $1.5 million.

i Monthly instalments and returns are due on the 15th of the month following the month in which the remuneration is paid.

j Employers with annual Ontario payrolls over $5 million, including groups of associated employers, are not eligible for the exemption. The $5 million threshold does not apply to eligible registered charities. For the 2020 tax year, eligible employers were exempt from EHT on the first $1 million of total Ontario remuneration. In the 2020 Ontario Budget, the government announced it was making the EHT payroll exemption increase permanent.

k Monthly instalments and returns are due on the 15th of the month following the month in which the remuneration is paid. Employers with annual payroll of $600,000 or less are not required to make instalments. Instead, they must remit the tax once a year along with their annual return.

l In addition to the Health Services Fund, Québec also levies a Manpower Training Tax.

   Employers whose payroll exceeds $2 million must allot at least 1% of their payroll to eligible training expenditures. Employers whose eligible training expenditures are lower than the minimum required participation must make a contribution equal to the difference between the two amounts. The employer must remit this contribution by the last day of February of the following year.

   Most Québec employers also have a requirement to contribute to the financing of the Commission des normes du travail. For 2021, remuneration of up to $83,500 paid to an employee is subject to a contribution rate of 0.07%. The employer must remit this contribution by the last day of February in the following year.

m Public-sector employers must pay a contribution of 4.26%, regardless of their total payroll.

   Service and construction sectors are subject to the 4.26% rate if their annual payroll is over $6.5 million, and entitled to a gradual reduction in the contribution rate if their total annual payroll is less than $6.5 million.

   The contribution rate for all employers other than public sector employers and employers whose total payroll is more than 50% attributable to activities in the primary and manufacturing sectors with payroll between $1 million and $6.5 million is calculated using the formula [1.1755% + (0.4745% × total payroll/$1 million)]. If annual payroll is less than $1 million, the rate is 1.65%.

Tax Reference Tables

A reduction of the Health Services Fund contribution is granted until December 31, 2021 to eligible employers with payrolls under $6.5 million, for full-time jobs created in the natural and applied sciences sector. Employers with payrolls under $6.5 million and where more than 50% of the total payroll is attributable to activities in the manufacturing or primary sector (which includes activities in the agriculture, forestry, fishing and hunting sector and in the mining, quarrying and oil and gas extraction sector) are also eligible for the reduced contribution rate as follows:

Primary and manufacturing sectors are also subject to the 4.26% rate if their annual total payroll is over $6 million. The contribution rate for payroll between $1 million and $6.5 million is calculated using the formula $[0.7027\% + (0.5473\% \times$ total payroll$/\$1$ million$)]$. If annual payroll is less than $1 million, the rate is 1.25%.

n Monthly instalments and returns are due on the 15th of the month following the month in which the remuneration is paid. However, the frequency of instalments will depend upon an employer's average monthly remittances of income tax, Québec Pension Plan contributions and Health Services Fund.

o Monthly instalments and returns are due on the 20th of the month following the month in which the remuneration is paid.

p There is no requirement to file annual returns for the Newfoundland Health and Post-Secondary Education Tax. Returns and instalments are remitted on a monthly basis.

q Remittance periods vary according to the class of employer by amount of total remuneration paid to the employer's employees in the year. The monthly remittance period appearing in the table is for employers whose estimated total remuneration paid by the employer to its employees in the year exceeds $1,000,000. For remittance periods for other classes of employers, make reference to the Northwest Territories *Payroll Tax Regulations* and the Nunavut *Payroll Tax Regulations*.

OTHER

O-1 — PRESCRIBED INTEREST RATES[a]

Current to: April 30, 2021

	Federal[b]			Alberta[c]		Québec[d]	
	Base Rate	Tax Refunds[e]	Tax Debts	Tax Refunds	Tax Debts	Tax Refunds	Tax Debts
2015							
January to June	1	1/3	5	0.5	4.5	1.4	6
July to December	1	1/3	5	0.5	4.5	1.1	6
2016							
January to March	1	1/3	5	0.5	4.5	1.1	6
April to June	1	1/3	5	0.5	4.5	1.1	6
July to September	1	1/3	5	0.5	4.5	1.1	6
October to December	1	1/3	5	0.5	4.5	1.1	6
2017							
January to March	1	1/3	5	0.5	4.5	1.1	6
April to June	1	1/3	5	0.5	4.5	1.1	6
July to September	1	1/3	5	0.5	4.5	1.1	6
October to December	1	1/3	5	0.5	4.5	1.1	6
2018							
January to March	1	1/3	5	0.5	4.5	1.4	6
April to June	2	2/4	6	1.0	5.5	1.55	6
July to September	2	2/4	6	1.0	5.5	1.75	6
October to December	2	2/4	6	1.0	5.5	1.75	7
2019							
January to March	2	2/4	6	1.0	5.5	2	7
April to June	2	2/4	6	1.0	5.5	2	7
July to September	2	2/4	6	1.0	5.5	1.8	7
October to December	2	2/4	6	1.0	5.5	1.8	7
2020							
January to March	2	2/4	6	1.0	5.5	1.7	7
April to June	2	2/4	6	1.0	5.5	1.7	7
July to September	1	1/3	5	0.5	4.5	1.4	6
October to December	1	1/3	5	0.5	4.5	1.4	5
2021							
January to March	1	1/3	5	0.5	4.5	1.0	5
April to June	1	1/3	5	0.5	4.5	1.0	5
July to September	1	1/3	5	0.5	4.5	0.8	5

Notes:

a   See under Reg. 4301 for historical federal prescribed interest rates. For current federal rates, see tinyurl.com/cra-intrates.

   The rates in these tables do not apply to underpaid and overpaid capital taxes. For the applicable prescribed interest rates for capital tax debts and refunds see table O-2.

b   The federal base rate applies to taxable benefits for employees and shareholders, low-interest loans and other related-party transactions. The rate for tax debts applies to all tax debts, penalties, insufficient instalments, and unpaid employee income tax, Canada Pension Plan contributions and Employment Insurance premiums.

   All provinces other than Alberta and Québec use the federal interest rates for corporate income tax refunds and debts. All provinces other than Québec use the federal interest rate for individual income tax refunds and debts.

   Interest charged on tax debts is not deductible in calculating taxable income. Interest received on tax refunds must be included in taxable income in the year received. For any period of time where interest is calculated both on tax refunds and debts, the two amounts may be offset. Interest will be payable only on the net balance owing, with the rate of interest depending on whether there is a net overpayment or underpayment.

c   The Alberta rates indicated in the table apply to corporate income taxes.

d   The Québec rates indicated in the table apply to personal income taxes, as well as corporate income and capital taxes. Québec also charges an additional 10% per year on underpaid instalments if less than 75% of the required amount (90% for corporations) is paid.

e   The rate for tax refunds for non-corporate taxpayers is set at two percentage points higher than the rate for corporate taxpayers, for quarters beginning after June 30, 2010.

O-2 — PRESCRIBED INTEREST RATES FOR CAPITAL TAXES[a]
Current to: April 30, 2021

	Saskatchewan		Manitoba[b]		Ontario[c]		Québec[d]	
	Tax Debts	Tax Refunds	Tax Debts	Tax Refunds	Tax Debts	Tax Refunds	Tax Debts	Tax Refunds
2015								
January to March	6.0	3.0	9.0	N/A	6.0	0.0	6.0	1.4
April to June	6.0	3.0	9.0	N/A	6.0	0.0	6.0	1.4
July to September	5.85	2.85	8.85	N/A	6.0	0.0	6.0	1.1
October to December	5.85	2.85	8.85	N/A	6.0	0.0	6.0	1.1
2016								
January to March	5.7	2.7	8.7	N/A	6.0	0.0	6.0	1.1
April to June	5.7	2.7	8.7	N/A	6.0	0.0	6.0	1.1
July to September	5.7	2.7	8.7	N/A	6.0	0.0	6.0	1.1
October to December	5.7	2.7	8.7	N/A	6.0	0.0	6.0	1.1
2017								
January to March	5.7	2.7	8.7	N/A	6.0	0.0	6.0	1.1
April to June	5.7	2.7	8.7	N/A	6.0	0.0	6.0	1.1
July to September	5.7	2.7	8.7	N/A	6.0	0.0	6.0	1.1
October to December	5.7	2.7	8.7	N/A	6.0	0.0	6.0	1.1
2018								
January to March	6.2	3.2	9.2	N/A	6.0	0.0	6.0	1.4
April to June	6.2	3.2	9.2	N/A	6.0	0.0	6.0	1.55
July to September	6.45	3.45	9.45	N/A	6.0	0.0	6.0	1.75
October to December	6.45	3.45	9.45	N/A	7.0	1.0	7.0	1.75
2019								
January to March	6.95	3.95	9.95	N/A	6.0	2.0	7.0	2.0
April to June	6.95	3.95	9.95	N/A	6.0	2.0	7.0	2.0
July to September	6.95	3.95	9.95	N/A	6.0	2.0	7.0	1.8
October to December	6.95	3.95	9.95	N/A	6.0	2.0	7.0	1.8
2020								
January to March	6.95	3.95	8.95	N/A	6.0	2.0	7.0	1.7
April to June	6.95	3.95	8.95	N/A	6.0	2.0	7.0	1.7
July to September	5.45	2.45	7.45	N/A	5.0	1.0	6.0	1.4
October to December	5.45	2.45	7.45	N/A	5.0	1.0	5.0	1.4
2021								
January to March	5.45	2.45	6.45	N/A	5.0	5.0	5.0	5.0
April to June	5.45	2.45	6.45	N/A	1.0	1.0	1.0	1.0

	New Brunswick[b]		Nova Scotia[b]		P.E.I.[e]		Nfld. & Lab.	
	Tax Debts	Tax Refunds	Tax Debts	Tax Refunds	Tax Debts	Tax Refunds	Tax Debts	Tax Refunds
2015								
January to March	0.7591 per month	N/A	5.0	N/A	1.5 per month	1.5 per month	5.0	1.0
April to June	0.7591 per month	N/A	5.0	N/A	1.5 per month	1.5 per month	5.0	1.0
July to September	0.7591 per month	N/A	5.0	N/A	1.5 per month	1.5 per month	5.0	1.0
October to December	0.7591 per month	N/A	5.0	N/A	1.5 per month	1.5 per month	5.0	1.0
2016								
January to March	0.7591 per month	N/A	5.0	N/A	2.0 per month	2.0 per month	5.0	1.0
April to June	0.7591 per month	N/A	5.0	N/A	2.0 per month	2.0 per month	5.0	1.0
July to September	0.7591 per month	N/A	5.0	N/A	2.0 per month	2.0 per month	5.0	1.0

	New Brunswick[b]		Nova Scotia[b]		P.E.I.[e]		Nfld. & Lab.	
	Tax Debts	Tax Refunds	Tax Debts	Tax Refunds	Tax Debts	Tax Refunds	Tax Debts	Tax Refunds
October to December	0.7591 per month	N/A	5.0	N/A	2.0 per month	2.0 per month	5.0	1.0
2017								
January to March	0.7591 per month	N/A	5.0	N/A	2.0 per month	2.0 per month	5.0	1.0
April to June	0.7591 per month	N/A	5.0	N/A	2.0 per month	2.0 per month	5.0	1.0
July to September	0.7591 per month	N/A	5.0	N/A	2.0 per month	2.0 per month	5.0	1.0
October to December	0.7591 per month	N/A	5.0	N/A	2.0 per month	2.0 per month	5.0	1.0
2018								
January to March	0.7591 per month	N/A	5.0	N/A	2.0 per month	2.0 per month	5.0	1.0
April to June	0.7591 per month	N/A	6.0	N/A	2.0 per month	2.0 per month	6.0	2.0
July to September	0.7591 per month	N/A	6.0	N/A	2.0 per month	2.0 per month	6.0	2.0
October to December	0.7591 per month	N/A	6.0	N/A	2.0 per month	2.0 per month	6.0	2.0
2019								
January to March	0.7591 per month	N/A	6.0	N/A	2.0 per month	2.0 per month	6.0	2.0
April to June	0.7591 per month	N/A	6.0	N/A	2.0 per month	2.0 per month	6.0	2.0
July to September	0.7591 per month	N/A	6.0	N/A	2.0 per month	2.0 per month	6.0	2.0
October to December	0.7591 per month	N/A	6.0	N/A	2.0 per month	2.0 per month	6.0	2.0
2020								
January to March	0.7591 per month	N/A	6.0	2.0	1.5 per month	1.5 per month	6.0	2.0
April to June	0.7591 per month	N/A	6.0	2.0	1.5 per month	1.5 per month	6.0	2.0
July to September	0.7591 per month	N/A	5.0	1.0	1.5 per month	1.5 per month	5.0	1.0
October to December	0.7591 per month	N/A	5.0	1.0	1.5 per month	1.5 per month	5.0	1.0
2021								
January to March	0.7591 per month	N/A	5.0	1.0	1.5 per month	1.5 per month	5.0	1.0
April to June	0.7591 per month	N/A	5.0	1.0	1.5 per month	1.5 per month	5.0	1.0

Notes:

a The rates in these tables apply only to underpaid and overpaid capital taxes. Only financial institutions are subject to capital tax. These rates would also apply to underpaid or overpaid capital taxes of general corporations in earlier years. For the applicable prescribed interest rates for personal and corporate income tax debts and refunds, as well as for employee and shareholder taxable benefits, low-interest loans and other related-party transactions, see table O-1.

b Manitoba and New Brunswick do not pay refund interest on overpaid capital tax.

c The federal government administers Ontario's capital tax, therefore interest on underpaid and overpaid Ontario capital tax is calculated based on the federal prescribed rates.

d Québec also charges an additional 10% per year on underpaid corporate instalments if less than 90% of the amount is paid.

e Prince Edward Island only pays refund interest if it arises as a result of an objection or appeal.

O-3 — FOREIGN EXCHANGE RATES — MONTHLY AVERAGES
Current to: April 30, 2021

Month	Australian Dollar	European Euro	Japanese Yen	Norwegian Krone	Swedish Krona	Swiss Franc	U.K. Pound Sterling	U.S. Dollar
Jan. 2018	0.9888	1.5165	.0112	.1573	.1545	1.2940	1.7180	1.2427
Feb. 2018	0.9901	1.5533	.0117	.1605	.1563	1.3456	1.7571	1.2586
March 2018	1.0038	1.5950	.0122	.1665	.1570	1.3645	1.8070	1.2932
April 2018	0.9782	1.5628	.0118	.1623	.1506	1.3150	1.7922	1.2733
May 2018	0.9686	1.5212	.0117	.1589	.1469	1.2912	1.7335	1.2873
June 2018	0.9838	1.5329	.0119	.1618	.1491	1.3261	1.7443	1.3129
July 2018	0.9724	1.5347	.0118	.1616	.1490	1.3202	1.7292	1.3130
Aug. 2018	0.9550	1.5059	.0118	.1564	.1437	1.3206	1.6790	1.3041
Sept. 2018	0.9391	1.5207	.0116	.1582	.1458	1.3466	1.7035	1.3037
Oct. 2018	0.9248	1.4941	.0115	.1576	.1439	1.3087	1.6926	1.3010
Nov. 2018	0.9572	1.5010	.0117	.1557	.1458	1.3195	1.7029	1.3200
Dec. 2018	0.9637	1.5288	.0120	.1558	.1488	1.3541	1.7020	1.3432
Jan. 2019	0.9512	1.5186	.0122	.1556	.1479	1.3440	1.7154	1.3301
Feb. 2019	0.9428	1.4990	.0120	.1538	.1427	1.3187	1.7188	1.3206
March 2019	0.9467	1.5105	.0120	.1554	.1439	1.3361	1.7602	1.3368
April 2019	0.9512	1.5029	.0120	.1562	.1434	1.3271	1.7433	1.3378
May 2019	0.9348	1.5057	.0122	.1540	.1403	1.3316	1.7292	1.3459
June 2019	0.9230	1.5009	.0123	.1540	.1413	1.3448	1.6844	1.3287
July 2019	0.9146	1.4687	.0121	.1520	.1391	1.3260	1.6323	1.3101
Aug. 2019	0.8991	1.4767	.0125	.1480	.1376	1.3557	1.6141	1.3277
Sept. 2019	0.9022	1.4578	.0123	.1470	.1364	1.3366	1.6375	1.3241
Oct. 2019	0.8964	1.4583	.0122	.1441	.1350	1.3280	1.6684	1.3190
Nov. 2019	0.9035	1.4627	.0122	.1447	.1374	1.3328	1.7058	1.3239
Dec. 2019	0.9066	1.4640	.0121	.1458	.1397	1.3405	1.7270	1.3172
Jan. 2020	0.8968	1.4523	.0120	.1461	.1376	1.3495	1.7106	1.3087
Feb. 2020	0.8854	1.4494	.0121	.1429	.1371	1.3610	1.7210	1.3286
March 2020	0.8671	1.5417	.0130	.1367	.1419	1.4555	1.7239	1.3953
April 2020	0.8865	1.5276	.0131	.1348	.1403	1.4484	1.7453	1.4058
May 2020	0.9105	1.5236	.0130	.1385	.1437	1.4411	1.7188	1.3970
June 2020	0.9348	1.5257	.0126	.1422	.1456	1.4240	1.6969	1.3550
July 2020	0.9502	1.5499	.0127	.1455	.1498	1.4466	1.7135	1.3499
Aug. 2020	0.9527	1.5646	.0125	.1480	.1518	1.4534	1.7374	1.3222
Sept. 2020	0.9558	1.5591	.0125	.1445	.1495	1.4457	1.7126	1.3228
Oct. 2020	0.9413	1.5553	.0126	.1422	.1496	1.4484	1.7150	1.3215
Nov. 2020	0.9512	1.5471	.0125	.1440	.1512	1.4351	1.7262	1.3068
Dec. 2020	0.9645	1.5586	.0123	.1471	.1532	1.4417	1.7209	1.2808
Jan. 2021	0.9826	1.5484	.0123	.1495	.1534	1.4347	1.7352	1.2724
Feb. 2021	0.9844	1.5356	.0121	.1492	.1522	1.4140	1.7605	1.2699
March 2021	0.9691	1.4962	.0116	.1476	.1472	1.3522	1.7427	1.2574
April 2021	0.9627	1.4963	.0115	.1490	.1472	1.3566	1.7298	1.2496

Notes:

- The European Euro is the currency used in the following countries: Andorra, Austria, Belgium, Cyprus, Estonia, Finland, France, Germany, Greece, Ireland, Italy, Kosovo, Latvia, Lithuania, Luxembourg, Malta, Monaco, Montenegro, the Netherlands, Portugal, San Marino, Slovakia, Slovenia, Spain and Vatican City.

- This information is available on the Bank of Canada's website at bankofcanada.ca.

O-4 — FOREIGN EXCHANGE RATES — ANNUAL AVERAGES

Current to: April 30, 2021

Annual Average	Australian Dollar	European Euro	Japanese Yen	Norwegian Krone	Swedish Krona	Swiss Franc	U.K. Pound Sterling	U.S. Dollar
1989	.9385	—	.0086	.1716	.1838	.7246	1.9415	1.1842
1990	.9110	—	.0081	.1867	.1973	.8430	2.0808	1.1668
1991	.8925	—	.0085	.1774	.1900	.8027	2.0275	1.1458
1992	.8878	—	.0096	.1949	.2084	.8627	2.1302	1.2083
1993	.8766	—	.0117	.1819	.1659	.8734	1.9372	1.2898
1994	.9998	—	.0134	.1933	.1774	1.0024	2.0929	1.3659
1995	1.0173	—	.0147	.2168	.1926	1.1633	2.1671	1.3726
1996	1.0675	—	.0126	.2112	.2033	1.1051	2.1283	1.3636
1997	1.0295	—	.0115	.1959	.1814	.9548	2.2682	1.3844
1998	.9330	—	.0114	.1965	.1865	1.0258	2.4587	1.4831
1999	.9589	1.5847	.0131	.1905	.1799	.9901	2.4038	1.4858
2000	.8633	1.3704	.0138	.1689	.1624	.8793	2.2499	1.4852
2001	.8008	1.3868	.0128	.1723	.1500	.9184	2.2297	1.5484
2002	.8535	1.4832	.0126	.1977	.1619	1.0112	2.3582	1.5704
2003	.9105	1.5826	.0121	.1982	.1735	1.0418	2.2883	1.4015
2004	.9582	1.6169	.0120	.1931	.1772	1.0473	2.3842	1.3015
2005	.9243	1.5090	.0110	.1882	.1628	.9746	2.2067	1.2116
2006	.8543	1.4237	.0098	.1769	.1539	.9050	2.0886	1.1341
2007	.8982	1.4691	.0091	.1832	.1589	.8946	2.1487	1.0748
2008	.9002	1.5603	.0104	.1900	.1623	.9840	1.9617	1.0660
2009	.8969	1.5855	.0122	.1815	.1493	1.0505	1.7804	1.1420
2010	.9470	1.3661	.0118	.1706	.1432	.9896	1.5918	1.0299
2011	1.0206	1.3767	.0124	.1765	.1525	1.1187	1.5861	.9891
2012	1.0353	1.2850	.0125	.1718	.1476	1.0662	1.5840	.9996
2013	0.9966	1.3681	.0106	.1753	.1581	1.1117	1.6113	1.0299
2014	0.9963	1.4671	.0105	.1757	.1614	1.2078	1.8190	1.1045
2015	0.9604	1.4182	.0106	.1585	.1516	1.3286	1.9540	1.2787
2016	0.9852	1.4660	.0122	.1578	.1550	1.3450	1.7962	1.3248
2017	0.9951	1.4650	.0116	.1570	.1520	1.3189	1.6720	1.2986
2018	0.9687	1.5302	.0117	.1594	.1492	1.3246	1.7299	1.2957
2019	0.9228	1.4856	.0122	.1509	.1404	1.3352	1.6945	1.3269
2020	0.9247	1.5298	.0126	.1427	.1459	1.4294	1.7199	1.3415

Notes:

- The European Euro is the currency used in the following countries: Andorra, Austria, Belgium, Cyprus, Estonia, Finland, France, Germany, Greece, Ireland, Italy, Kosovo, Latvia, Lithuania, Luxembourg, Malta, Monaco, Montenegro, the Netherlands, Portugal, San Marino, Slovakia, Slovenia, Spain and Vatican City.
- This information is available on the Bank of Canada's website at bankofcanada.ca.

O-5 — TAX TREATY WITHHOLDING RATES
Current to: April 30, 2021

Non-Resident Withholding Tax Rates for Treaty Countries[a]

Country[b]	Interest[c]	Dividends[d]	Royalties[e]	Pensions/ Annuities[f]
Algeria	15%	15%	0/15%	15/25%
Argentina[g]	12.5	10/15	3/5/10/15	15/25
Armenia	10	5/15	10	15/25
Australia	10	5/15	10	15/25
Austria	10	5/15	0/10	25
Azerbaijan	10	10/15	5/10	25
Bangladesh	15	15	10	15/25
Barbados	15	15	0/10	15/25
Belgium[h]	10	5/15	0/10	25
Brazil	15	15/25	15/25	25
Bulgaria[g]	10	10/15	0/10	10/15/25
Cameroon	15	15	15	25
Chile[g]	10	10/15	15	15/25
China, People's Republic	10	10/15	10	25
Colombia[g]	10	5/15	10	15/25
Croatia	10	5/15	10	10/15/25
Cyprus	15	15	0/10	15/25
Czech Republic	10	5/15	10	15/25
Denmark	10	5/15	0/10	25
Dominican Republic	18	18	0/18	18/25
Ecuador[g]	15	5/15	10/15	15/25
Egypt	15	15	15	25
Estonia[g]	10	5/15	0/10	10/15/25
Finland	10	5/15	0/10	15/20/25
France	10	5/15	0/10	25
Gabon	10	15	10	25
Germany	10	5/15	0/10	15/25
Greece	10	5/15	0/10	15/25
Guyana	15	15	10	25
Hong Kong	10	5/15	10	25
Hungary	10	5/15	0/10	10/15/25
Iceland	10	5/15	0/10	15/25
India	15	15/25	10/15/20	25
Indonesia	10	10/15	10	15/25
Ireland	10	5/15	0/10	15/25
Israel	10	5/15	0/10	15/25
Italy	10	5/15	0/5/10	15/25
Ivory Coast	15	15	10	15/25
Jamaica	15	15	10	15/25
Japan	10	5/15	10	25
Jordan	10	10/15	10	25
Kazakhstan[g]	10	5/15	10	15/25
Kenya	15	15/25	15	15/25
Korea, Republic of	10	5/15	10	10/15/25
Kuwait	10	5/15	10	15/25
Kyrgyzstan[g]	15	15	0/10	15/25
Latvia[g]	10	5/15	10	10/15/25
Lebanon[i]	(10)	(5/15)	(5/10)	(15/25)
Lithuania[g]	10	5/15	10	10/15/25
Luxembourg	10	5/15	0/10	25
Madagascar	10	5/15	5/10	15/25
Malaysia	15	15	15	15/25
Malta	15	15	0/10	15/25
Mexico	10	5/15	0/10	15/25

Country[b]	Interest[c]	Dividends[d]	Royalties[e]	Pensions/Annuities[f]
Moldova	10	5/15	10	15/25
Mongolia	10	5/15	5/10	15/25
Morocco	15	15	5/10	25
Namibia[i]	(10)	(5/15)	(0/10)	(0/25)
Netherlands	10	5/15	0/10	15/25
New Zealand	10	5/15	5/10	15/25
Nigeria	12.5	12.5/15	12.5	25
Norway	10	5/15	0/10	15/25
Oman	10	5/15	0/10	15/25
Pakistan	15	15	0/15	25
Papua New Guinea	10	15	10	15/25
Peru[g]	15	10/15	15	15/25
Philippines	15	15	10	25
Poland	10	5/15	5/10	15/25
Portugal	10	10/15	10	15/25
Romania	10	5/15	5/10	15/25
Russian Federation	10	10/15	0/10	25
Senegal	15	15	15	15/25
Serbia	10	5/15	10	15/25
Singapore	15	15	15	25
Slovak Republic	10	5/15	0/10	15/25
Slovenia	10	5/15	10	10/15/25
South Africa	10	5/15	6/10	25
Spain	10	5/15	0/10	15/25
Sri Lanka	15	15	0/10	15/25
Sweden	10	5/15	0/10	25
Switzerland	10	5/15	0/10	15/25
Taiwan	10	10/15	10	15/25
Tanzania	15	20/25	20	15/25
Thailand	15	15	5/15	25
Trinidad & Tobago	10	5/15	0/10	15/25
Tunisia	15	15	0/15/20	25
Turkey	15	15/20	10	15/25
Ukraine	10	5/15	0/10	25
United Arab Emirates	10	5/15	0/10	25
United Kingdom[j]	10	5/15	0/10	0/10/25
United States[k]	0	5/15	0/10	15/25
Uzbekistan	10	5/15	5/10	25
Venezuela[g]	10	10/15	5/10	25
Vietnam[g]	10	5/10/15	7.5/10	15/25
Zambia	15	15	15	15/25
Zimbabwe	15	10/15	10	15/25

Notes:

a The relevant treaty should be consulted to determine if specific conditions, exemptions or tax-sparing provisions apply for each type of payment. In addition, the multilateral instrument (MLI) should be considered when determining treaty benefits under Canada's tax treaties as it entered into force for Canada on December 1, 2019 and began to affect a significant portion of Canada's treaties beginning in 2020.

Among other provisions adopted by Canada, the MLI includes preamble text that clarifies the purpose of the treaty and adds a principal purposes test (PPT) that could deny treaty benefits where one of the principal purposes of any arrangement or transaction is to obtain a treaty benefit. The MLI may impact the availability of reduced treaty withholding tax rates starting as early as January 1, 2020 if the treaty partner has also deposited its instrument of ratification with the OECD by September 30, 2019 and has listed its treaty with Canada as covered for purposes of the MLI.

The rates indicated in the table apply to payments from Canada to the treaty country. In some cases, a treaty may provide for a different rate of withholding tax on payments from the other country to Canada.

b As of April 30, 2021, Canada is negotiating or renegotiating tax treaties or protocols with the following countries: Australia, Brazil, China (PRC), Germany, Malaysia, Netherlands, San Marino, Switzerland.

c Canada imposes no domestic withholding tax on certain arm's length interest payments, however non-arm's length payments are subject to a 25% withholding tax.

d Dividends subject to Canadian withholding tax include taxable dividends (other than capital gains dividends paid by certain entities) and capital dividends.

The withholding tax rate on dividends under the terms of Canada's tax treaties generally varies depending on the percentage ownership of the total issued capital or voting rights in respect of shares owned by the recipient. For tax treaties covered by the MLI, the withholding tax rate on dividends may also be impacted by the 365-day holding period test in addition to other provisions in the MLI as early as January 1, 2020.

e Royalties generally include:

- Payments received as consideration for the use of or the right to use any property, invention, patent, trademark, design or model, plan, secret formula or process.
- Payments received as consideration for the use of or the right to use industrial, commercial or scientific equipment or for information concerning industrial, commercial or scientific experience.
- Payments in respect of motion picture films, and works on film or videotape for use in connection with television.
- In some cases, technical assistance in respect of these items is also included.

Canada generally exempts from withholding tax cultural royalties or similar payments for copyrights in respect of the production or reproduction of any literary, dramatic, musical or artistic work, other than motion-picture films and videotapes or other means of reproduction for use in connection with television. However, several treaties exempt all cultural royalties from tax.

Canada announced in its treaty negotiations that it is prepared to eliminate the withholding tax on arm's-length payments in respect of rights to use patented information or information concerning scientific experience. It also stated that it is prepared to negotiate, on a bilateral basis, exemptions from withholding taxes for payments for the use of computer software. As such, many treaties contain an exemption for such payments.

f In general, the terms "pension", "periodic pension payment" and "annuity" are defined in the applicable treaty. However, if they are defined in the treaty by reference to the laws of Canada, or are not specifically defined therein, the definition in the *Income Tax Conventions Interpretation Act* must be used.

Section 217 of the *Income Tax Act* allows non-residents who earn certain types of pension and other retirement benefits to elect to file a Canadian tax return and pay Part I tax thereon, rather than being subject to Canada's 25% withholding tax on the income.

The withholding tax rate varies depending on, among other attributes, whether the payment is a lump-sum or periodic payment, or if the payment is a pension or annuity.

Some treaties provide for an exemption for certain types of pensions or for an exemption up to a threshold amount. Some pensions are taxable only in the source country.

g The treaty currently in effect with these countries includes a Most Favoured Nation clause, which may provide for reduced withholding rates if the other country signs a treaty with another country and that treaty includes a lower withholding rate. This clause allows the lower rate to apply to the Canadian treaty. The items of income to which the clause applies vary by treaty. The lower withholding rate in the other country's treaty will apply to Canada if that treaty is signed after the date that Canada's treaty with the particular country is signed.

h A protocol or replacement treaty is signed but not yet ratified. If there are changes to withholding tax rates in the protocol or replacement treaty, the new rates are indicated in parentheses. Otherwise, the rates in the table continue to apply.

i A new treaty is signed but not yet in effect. The rates in the new treaty are indicated in parentheses. Until ratification, the withholding tax rate is generally 25%.

j The following terms apply under the provisions of the Canada-U.K. treaty, including the protocol to amend the tax treaty which entered into force on December 18, 2014:

Interest — Interest is defined as income from debt claims of every kind, whether or not secured by mortgage, and income from government securities, bonds or debentures, including premiums and prizes attaching to such securities, bonds or debentures, as well as income that is subjected to the same tax treatment as income from money lent by the tax laws of Canada or the U.K., as the case may be. There are certain exemptions under the treaty. See also note (c).

Dividends — The 5% withholding tax rate applies if the recipient of the dividend is a company that controls, directly or indirectly, at least 10% of the voting power of the payer. The protocol introduces an exemption from withholding tax for certain dividends received by organizations that operate exclusively to administer benefits under recognized pension plans. See also note (d).

Royalties — Cultural royalties, excluding royalties in respect of motion pictures and works on film, videotape or other media for use in television broadcasting, are taxable only in the resident country. This treatment also applies to payments for the use of any patent or for information concerning industrial, commercial or scientific experience, as well as payments for the use of computer software. See also note (e).

Pensions — Pensions are defined to include any payment under a superannuation, pension or retirement plan, and certain other amounts including payments made under social security legislation. Periodic pension payments are taxable only in the resident country.

Annuities — Annuities are defined as periodic payments payable during a person's lifetime or for a specified period of time, under an obligation to make the payments in return for money or money's worth. The definition excludes payments under pension or income-averaging annuity contracts. Annuities are subject to withholding tax in the payer country at a rate of 10%. See also note (f).

k The Protocol to the Canada-U.S. treaty entered into force on December 15, 2008.

It introduced a number of provisions that do not exist in Canada's other treaties, including the following:

- Art. IV:6: Treaty benefits apply to certain "fiscally transparent entities" (FTEs) such as limited liability companies, where the owner is resident in one country, the income of the FTE is subject to tax in the owners' hands, and the FTE is not resident in the other country.
- Art. IV:7: Treaty benefits are denied to certain FTEs, for example, if they are treated as flow-through entities under the laws of one country and as regular taxable entities under the laws of the other country.

- The permanent establishment provisions in Art. V:9 cover certain Canadian or U.S. service providers who are present in the other country for more than 183 days in any 12-month period.
- The 5% treaty withholding tax rate on dividends in Art. X:2(a) applies to corporate members of FTEs that hold at least 10% of the voting shares in the company paying the dividends.
- The treaty includes a limitation-on-benefits (LOB) clause (Art. XXIX-A) that generally allows treaty benefits to be claimed only by certain "qualifying" persons, or entities carrying on connected active business activities in both countries.

The following terms apply under the provisions of the Canada-U.S. treaty:

Interest — Interest is defined as income from debt claims of every kind, whether or not secured by mortgage, and whether or not carrying a right to participate in the debtor's profits, and income from government securities, bonds and debentures, including premiums and prizes attaching to such securities, bonds or debentures, as well as income assimilated to income from money lent by the tax laws of Canada or the U.S., as the case may be. Contingent interest arising in the U.S. that does not qualify as portfolio interest will be subject to a withholding rate of 15%. As well, interest arising in Canada that is determined by reference to receipts, sales, income, profits or other cash flow of the debtor will also be subject to a 15% withholding rate. See also note (c).

Dividends — The 5% withholding tax rate applies if the recipient of the dividends is a company that is the beneficial owner of at least 10% of the voting stock of the payer. The rate of Canadian branch tax is also limited to 5% on cumulative branch profits exceeding Cdn$500,000. The first Cdn$500,000 of cumulative branch profits are exempt from branch tax. See also note (d).

Royalties — Royalties are generally defined as payments for the use of, or right to use, any cultural property and any copyright of scientific work; any patent, trademark, design or model, plan, secret formula or process; and information concerning industrial, commercial or scientific experience. The definition also includes gains from the alienation of any intangible property or rights described in this paragraph to the extent that such gains are contingent on the productivity, use or subsequent disposition of such property or rights. See also note (e).

The following royalties are exempt from withholding tax:

- Cultural royalties, excluding royalties in respect of motion pictures and works on film, videotape or other media for use in television broadcasting.
- Payments for the use of, or right to use, computer software.
- Payments for the use of, or right to use, any patent or information concerning industrial, commercial or scientific experience (excluding any such information in relation to a rental or franchise agreement).
- Payments with respect to broadcasting as may be agreed to between the countries.

Pensions — Pensions are defined to include any payment under a superannuation, pension, or other retirement arrangement and certain other amounts, but exclude payments under income-averaging annuity contract payments. The definition of pensions also includes Roth IRAs and similar arrangements. Payments of Old Age Security and Canada/Québec Pension Plan benefits to U.S. residents are taxable only in the U.S. and are not subject to Canadian withholding tax. The U.S. does not withhold tax on social security benefits paid to Canadian residents, and only 85% of such benefits are taxable by Canada.

Annuities — Annuities are defined as periodic payments payable during a person's lifetime or for a specified period of time, under an obligation to make the payments in return for adequate and full consideration (other than services rendered). The definition excludes non-periodic payments or any annuity the cost of which was tax deductible in the country in which it was acquired. See also note (f).

O-6 — LIMITATIONS AND CONTINGENT DATES

Note: During 2020-21, certain deadlines were extended temporarily due to COVID-19. See Notes to ITA 150(1) opening words and paragraphs; "Announced Administrative Change" shaded boxes throughout, including under 159(1), 220(1), 250(1)(a), Reg. 1106(1); *Time Limits and Other Periods Act (TLOPA)*, shown as Enacted Amendment under ITA 169(1).

Subject	Required or Permitted Action	Within (Limitation)	Of (Precipitating Event)	Income Tax Act (Sections)
Appeal to Tax Court of Canada	Filing of notice of appeal to Tax Court of Canada	90 days	Sending of notice of confirmation or reassessment, or service of notice of objection	169(1)
		1 year	Individual's filing-due date	165(1)(a)(i)
Assessment for Previous Years (General)	Assessment, reassessment, or additional assessment of tax, interest, penalties under Part I by Minister	3 years	Sending of notice of original assessment	152(3.1), (4)(c)
(Mutual fund trusts and non-CCPCs)		4 years		152(3.1)
(Amounts carried back from subsequent years)		3 years	Expiration of normal assessment period (see above)	152(4)(b)
Collection	Refraining from commencement of collection proceedings regarding unpaid tax	90 days	Sending of notice of assessment or reassessment	225.1
	Collection of tax debt by Minister	10 years	Assessment, acknowledgement of debt or certain other events	222(3)–(8)
Death of Taxpayer	Filing of return by legal representatives	6 months	Death of taxpayer from November through June 15; April 30 or June 15 otherwise	150(1)(b), (d)
	Wind up estate (or lose GRE status)	36 months	Death of taxpayer	248(1)"graduated rate estate"(a)
Deferred Profit Sharing Plans	Remittance of tax equal to fair market value of security	10 days	Acquisition of non-qualified investment or use of trust property as security for loan	198(2)
Director's Liability	Assessment of director for corporation's failure to deduct, withhold or remit tax	2 years	Ceasing to be a director	227.1(4)
Interest Offset	Apply to offset refund interest against arrears interest	90 days	Sending of notice of assessment or final court decision	161.1(3)(c)
Keeping Books and Records	Retention of records for tax purposes	6 years	End of taxation year	230(4)(a), (b)
	Retention of duplicate charitable donation receipts	2 years	End of calendar year	230(4)(a), Reg. 5800(1)(f)
	Retention of general corporate records	2 years	Dissolution of corporation or charity	230(4)(a), Reg. 5800(1)(a), (b), (d), (e), (f)
Objection to Assessment	Filing Notice of Objection	90 days	Sending of notice of assessment	165(1)
		1 year (alternative for individuals and GREs)	Filing-due date for original return (see 248(1))	165(1)
Payment of Tax	Corporation pay balance for year	2 or 3 months	End of taxation year	248(1)"balance-due day"(d)
	Individual pay balance for year	April 30 (6 months if died Nov-April)	End of taxation year	248(1)"balance-due day"(b), (c)
	Trust pay balance for year	90 days	End of taxation year	248(1)"balance-due day"(a)
Prosecution of Offences	Laying of information or making complaint	8 years	Arising of the matter	244(4)

Subject	Required or Permitted Action	Within (Limitation)	Of (Precipitating Event)	Income Tax Act (Sections)
Recovery of Overpayment	Refund by Minister of overpayment upon taxpayer's filing return	*3 years*	End of taxation year	164(1)(a)
Refunds — Losses or Carry-backs (Mutual fund trusts and non-CCPCs)	Application for refund		Sending of notice of original assessment	164(1)(b)
		7 years		152(3.1)(a), (4)(b)
(Other)		*6 years*		152(3.1)(b), (4)(b)
Refunds — Other (Mutual fund trusts and non-CCPCs)	Application for refund			
		4 years		152(3.1)(a)
(Other)		*3 years*		152(3.1)(a)
(Individual or GRE)		*10 years*	End of taxation year, with CRA consent	152(4.2), 164(1.5)
Refunds — Non-resident Withholding Tax Improperly Withheld	Application for refund	*2 years*	End of calendar year in which amount paid to Receiver General	227(6)
Registered Retirement Savings Plan	Make RRSP contribution for the year	*60 days*	End of calendar year	146(5)(a), (5.1)(a)
Reportable Transaction	Filing of information return by taxpayer, advisor and promoter	*6 months [June 30]*	End of calendar year	237.3(5)
Sale by Non-residents	Notice to Minister of name and address of purchaser, description of property and sale price	*10 days*	Disposition of taxable Canadian property by non-resident	116(3)
Tax Shelter Reporting	Filing of information return by promoter	*2 months [Feb. 28 or 29]*	End of calendar year	237.1(7)
Taxpayer Relief (Fairness) Applications	Applying for any of: late reassessment; late refund; waiver of interest or penalty; late filing of election or revocation of election	*10 years*	End of taxation year	152(4.2), 164(1.5)(a), 220(3.1), 220(3.2)(b)
	Applying late for Canada Child Benefit	*10 years*	Beginning of month payment would have been made	122.62(2)
Withholdings	Remittance of tax withheld from employees' salaries	*7 days*	Employer ceasing to carry on business	Reg. 108(2)
	Remittance of tax withheld from payments to non-residents	*15 days*	End of month during which tax withheld	215(1): Information Circular 77-16R4, para. 54

O-7 — PENALTIES AND OFFENCES

Penalties

ITA Provisions	Violation	Penalty
66(12.75)	Flow-through share renunciation: late filing of documents	0.25% of renunciation or assistance (min. $100, max. $15,000)
66(14.5)	Late designation of Canadian exploration expense or Canadian development expense	.0025 times amount designated per month or partial month of lateness (maximum $100 per month, maximum $8,000)
85(8), 96(6)	Late filed election on rollover into corporation or on rollover into or out of partnership	.0025 times amount of deferral per month or partial month of lateness (maximum $100 per month, maximum $8,000)
93(6)	Late filed election to treat proceeds of disposition of share of foreign affiliate as a dividend	.0025 times amount elected per month of lateness (maximum $100 per month, maximum $8,000)
96(6)	(See under 85(8) above)	
146(13.1)	RRSP issuer extending a prohibited advantage to annuitant	Amount of the advantage (minimum $100)
149(7.1)	Non-profit SR&ED corporation: failure to file prescribed form on time	2% of taxable income (min. $500), times number of months or part months late (max. 12)
162(1)	Failure to file annual return	5% of year's unpaid tax plus 1% per complete month (up to 12 months) from due date

ITA Provisions	Violation	Penalty
162(2)	Failure to file annual return after demand (subsequent occurrence within 3 years)	10% of year's unpaid tax plus 2% per complete month (up to 20 months) from due date
162(2.1)	Failure to file annual return: non-resident corporation	Penalty under 162(1) or (2), but minimum $25 times number of days late (min. 4, max. 100 days)
162(3)	Failure of trustee in bankruptcy, etc., to file annual return	$10 for each day of default (maximum $50)
162(4)	Failure to complete or deliver non-resident ownership certificate (Forms NR601, NR602) or ownership certificate (T600) prior to negotiation of foreign bearer coupon or warrant (subsec. 234(1))	$50
162(5)	Failure to provide information on prescribed form	$100 for each failure (unless mitigating circumstances)
162(5.1)	Failure to provide SR&ED claim preparer information	$1,000
162(6)	Failure to provide Social Insurance Number, business number, trust account number or US tax number on request	$100 for each failure (unless applied for number within 15 days)
162(7)	Failure to file information return or comply with duty or obligation imposed by Act or Regulation (not specifically provided for)	$25 per day of default (minimum $100, maximum $2,500)
162(7.01), (7.02)	Failure to file information return required to be filed electronically	Varying depending on number of returns due
162(7.1)	Failure to file partnership return	$25 per day of default (minimum $100, maximum $2,500)
162(7.2)	Failure to file corporate income tax return electronically when gross revenue exceeds $1m	$1,000 ($250 for 2011, $500 for 2012)
162(7.3)	Tax return preparer's failure to file electronically	$25 per personal return over 10/year; $100 per corporate return over 10/year
162(8)	Failure to file partnership information return after demand (subsequent occurrence within 3 years)	Additional penalty of $100 per partner for each month or partial month of default, up to a maximum of 24 months
162(10)(a)	Failure to furnish foreign-based information under 233.1 to 233.4, knowingly or with gross negligence	$500 per month during which return not filed (maximum 24 months)
162(10)(b)	Failure to comply with demand to file return under 233 re dealings with non-residents	$1,000 per month during which return not filed (maximum 24 months)
162(10.1)	Additional penalty where number of months under subsec. 162(10) exceeds 24	5% of the value of property transferred or loaned to foreign trust, or of the cost of foreign property or foreign affiliate
163(1)	Failure to report amount in annual return, where taxpayer had failed to report an amount in returns filed in 3 previous years	10% of unreported amount (unless penalized under subsec. 163(2))
163(2)	False statement or omission in document knowingly or with gross negligence	50% of tax on understatement of income ($100 minimum)
163(2.2)	False statement or omission in respect of renunciation in respect of resource expenses, knowingly or with gross negligence	25% of excess renunciation
163(2.21), (2.22)	False statement or omission re flow-through share look-back rule, knowingly or with gross negligence	25% of excess renunciation
163(2.3)	False statement or omission relating to the allocation of assistance with respect to exercises expenditures under ss. 66(12.691) or (12.701)	25% of excess renunciation
163(2.4)	False statement or omission re foreign-based information (ss. 233–233.7)	5% of the value of the property, minimum $24,000 ($2,500 re distribution from non-resident trust)
163(5), (6) [proposed]	False statement or omission with gross negligence in trust return (starting 2021)	5% of highest value of trust in year, minimum $2,500
163.1	Late or insufficient instalments 190.21 — Part VI, 189(8) — Part V	50% of interest payable on instalments for year exceeding $1,000 or 25% of interest payable if no instalments had been made during year, whichever is greater
163.2(2), (3)	Third party civil penalty: "planner's penalty"	Minimum $1,000, maximum the person's "gross entitlements"

ITA Provisions	Violation	Penalty
163.2(4), (5)	Third party civil penalty: "filer's penalty"	Minimum $1,000, maximum the other person's penalty (capped at $100,000 plus "gross compensation")
163.3(2), (3)	Use or possession of zapper software or device	$5,000 ($50,000 second time)
163.3(4)	Manufacture or sale of zapper software or device	$10,000 ($50,000 or $100,000 second time)
180.2(6)	Penalties in respect of Part I.2 tax	Same as under sections 162 to 163.1
181.7	Penalties in respect of Part I.3 tax	Same as under sections 162 to 163.1
183.2(2)	Penalties in respect of Part II.1 tax	Same as under sections 162 to 163.1
185.2(2)	Penalties in respect of Part III.1 tax	Same as under sections 162 to 163.1
187(3)	Penalties in respect of Part IV tax	Same as under sections 162 to 163.1
187.6	Penalties in respect of Part IV.1 tax	Same as under sections 162 to 163.1
188.1	Charities penalties	Various
189(8)	Penalties in respect of Part V tax	Same as under sections 162 to 163.1
190.21	Penalties in respect of Part VI tax	Same as under sections 162 to 163.1
191.4(2)	Penalties in respect of Part VI.1 tax	Same as under sections 162 to 163.1
204.7(3)	Penalties in respect of Part X.2 tax	Same as under sections 162 to 163.1
204.82(4)	Registered labour-sponsored venture capital corporation: penalty equal to tax on recovery of credit	Amount of tax payable under 204.82(3)
204.84	LSVCC: penalty for corporation issuing information return in respect of a share, if revoked corporation or share not issued on time	Amount of consideration for which share was or was to be issued
204.87	Penalties in respect of Part X.3 tax	Same as under sections 162 to 163.1
204.93	Penalties in respect of Part X.4 tax	Same as under sections 162 to 163.1
207.07(3)	Penalties in respect of Part XI.01 tax	Same as under sections 162 to 163.1
207.2(3)	Penalties in respect of Part XI.1 tax	Same as under sections 162 to 163.1
207.4(2)	Penalties in respect of Part XI.2 tax	Same as under sections 162 to 163.1
207.7(4)	Penalties in respect of Part XI.3 tax	Same as under sections 162 to 163.1
209(5)	Penalties in respect of Part XII.1 tax	Same as under sections 162 to 163.1
210.2(7)	Penalties in respect of Part XII.2 tax	Same as under sections 162 to 163.1
211.6	Penalties in respect of Part XII.3 tax	Same as under sections 162 to 163.1
211.6(5)	Penalties in respect of Part XII.4 tax	Same as under sections 162 to 163.1
211.91(3)	Penalties in respect of Part XII.6 tax	Same as under sections 162 to 163.1
219(3)	Penalties in respect of Part XIV tax	Same as under sections 162 to 163.1
220(3.5)	Late-filed election under many specific provisions (listed in Reg. 600)	$100 per complete month of lateness (maximum $8,000)
227(8), (9)	Failure to withhold or deduct tax, or to remit tax, withheld or deducted (first occurrence)	10% of amount not withheld, deducted or remitted
	Subsequent occurrence after assessment of penalty in the same year	20% of amount not withheld, deducted or remitted and, after 1992, only if the failure was made knowingly or under circumstances amounting to gross negligence
235	Failure to file corporate return under Parts I, I.3 or VI	.0025 times total of Part I.3 and Part VI tax per complete month of lateness (maximum 40 months)
237.1(7.4)	False information on tax shelter application, or selling tax shelter before ID number issued	25% of consideration received from shelter ($500 minimum)
237.1(7.5)	Tax shelter promoter: failure to file information return with required information	25% of amounts received from shelter, or total value of stated donation amounts (whichever is higher)
247(3)	Transfer pricing adjustment	10% of adjustment minus 10% of revenues up to $5 million
247(11)	Penalties re transfer pricing (Part XVI.1)	Same as under sections 162 to 163.1
281(3)	Failure to provide Taxpayer Identification Number to financial institution for provision to foreign authorities	$500

Notes:

The burden of proof of a penalty under s. 163 is on the Minister: subsec. 163(3). Any penalty may be waived by the Minister: subsec. 220(3.1). A penalty can be imposed under s. 163 before a fine or imprisonment (see "Offences" table below), but once a conviction for an offence has been entered no penalty can apply: subsecs. 238(3), 239(3). See also Notes to 238(1).

Some penalties are implemented in the form of separate taxes. For example, the penalty for an excessive capital dividend election is enacted as the Part III tax, and the penalty for RRSP overcontributions is enacted as Part X.1 tax. See Parts II.1 to XII.6 generally (not all of these taxes are penalty taxes).

Offences

ITA Provisions	Violations	Penalty
238(1)	Failure to file return in required time and manner	On summary conviction, fine $1,000-$25,000, and imprisonment up to 12 months
	Failure of non-resident to notify Minister of particulars of sale of taxable Canadian property	
	Failure to issue receipts or make deposits with respect to political contributions in accordance with s. 127	
	Failure to deduct or withhold tax	
	Failure to keep proper books and records of account	
	Failure to comply with compliance order of court under subsec. 238(2)	
239(1), (1.1), (2)	False or deceptive statements in document. Alteration, falsification or destruction of books or records of account to evade payment of taxes. Claiming false refunds or credits. Wilful evasion or attempt to evade payment of taxes	On summary conviction, fine 50%-200% of tax sought to be evaded, and imprisonment up to 2 years. On indictment, fine 100%-200% of tax sought to be evaded, and imprisonment up to 5 years
239(2.1)	Providing incorrect tax shelter identification number	On summary conviction, fine 100%-200% of cost to other person of interest in shelter, and imprisonment up to 2 years
239(2.2), (2.21)	Unauthorized communication or use of information	On summary conviction, fine to $5,000 and imprisonment up to 1 year
239(2.3)	Unauthorized disclosure of Social Insurance Number	On summary conviction, fine to $5,000 and imprisonment up to 1 year
239.1(2), (3)	Use, possession, manufacture or sale of zapper software or device	On summary conviction, fine $10,000-$500,000, imprisonment up to 2 years. On indictment, fine $50,000-$1,000,000, imprisonment up to 5 years

Notes:

Saving provisions in subsecs. 238(3) and 239(3) prevent double penalties from being assessed, but only if the prosecution is instituted before the penalty is assessed.

Notes:

The burden of proof of a penalty under s. 163 is on the Minister: subsec. 163(3). Any penalty may be waived by the Minister: subsec. 220(3.1). A penalty can be imposed under s. 163 before a fine or imprisonment (see "Offences" table below), but once a conviction for an offence has been entered no penalty can apply: subsecs. 238(3), 239(3). See also Notes to 238(1).

Some penalties are implemented in the form of separate taxes. For example, the penalty for an excessive capital dividend election is enacted as the Part III tax, and the penalty for RRSP overcontributions is enacted as Part X.1 tax. See Parts II.1 to XII.6 generally (not all of these taxes are penalty taxes).

Offences

ITA Provisions	Violation	Penalty
238(1)	Failure to file return in required time and manner	On summary conviction, fine $1,000-$25,000, and imprisonment up to 12 months
	Failure of non-resident to notify Minister of particulars of sale of taxable Canadian property	
	Failure to issue receipts or make deposits with respect to political contributions in accordance with s. 127	
	Failure to deduct or withhold tax	
	Failure to keep proper books and records or account	
	Failure to comply with compliance order of court under subsec. 238(2)	
239(1), (1.1), (2)	False or deceptive statements in document. Alteration, falsification or destruction of books or records or account to evade payment of taxes. Claiming false refund or credits. Wilful evasion or attempt to evade payment of taxes.	On summary conviction, fine 50%-200% of tax sought to be evaded, and imprisonment up to 2 years. On indictment, fine 100%-200% of tax sought to be evaded, and imprisonment up to 5 years
239(2.1)	Providing incorrect tax shelter identification number	On summary conviction, fine 100%-200% of cost to other person of interest in shelter, and imprisonment up to 2 years
239(2.2), (2.21)	Unauthorized communication or use of information	On summary conviction, fine to $5,000 and imprisonment up to 1 year
239(2.3)	Unauthorized disclosure of Social Insurance Number	On summary conviction, fine to $5,000 and imprisonment up to 1 year
239(1.2), (5)	Use, possession, manufacture or sale of zapper software or device	On summary conviction, fine $10,000-$500,000, imprisonment up to 2 years. On indictment, fine $50,000-$1,000,000, imprisonment up to 5 years

Notes:

Saving provisions in subsecs. 238(3) and 239(3) prevent double penalties from being assessed, but only if the prosecution is instituted before the penalty is assessed.

OVERVIEW TABLE OF SECTIONS

Income Tax Act

1 — Short title

PART I — INCOME TAX

DIVISION A — LIABILITY FOR TAX
2

DIVISION B — COMPUTATION OF INCOME
Basic Rules
3 and 4

Subdivision A — Income or Loss from an Office or Employment
Basic Rules
5
Inclusions
6 and 7
Deductions
8

Subdivision B — Income or Loss from a Business or Property
Basic Rules
9 to 11
Inclusions
12 to 17.1
Deductions
18 to 21
Ceasing to Carry on Business
22 to 25
Special Cases
26 to 37

Subdivision C — Taxable Capital Gains and Allowable Capital Losses
38 to 55

Subdivision D — Other Sources of Income
56 to 59.1

Subdivision E — Deductions in Computing Income
60 to 66.8

Subdivision F — Rules Relating to Computation of Income
67 to 80.6

Subdivision G — Amounts Not Included in Computing Income
81

Subdivision H — Corporations Resident in Canada and Their Shareholders
82 to 89

Subdivision I — Shareholders of Corporations Not Resident in Canada
90 to 95

Subdivision J — Partnerships and Their Members
96 to 103

Subdivision K — Trusts and Their Beneficiaries
104 to 108

Division C — COMPUTATION OF TAXABLE INCOME
110 to 114.2

PART XVIII — ENHANCED INTERNATIONAL INFORMATION REPORTING [for U.S. FATCA]

PART XIX — COMMON REPORTING STANDARD

SCHEDULE — LISTED CORPORATIONS

DETAILED TABLE OF SECTIONS

INCOME TAX ACT

Deductions

Subdivision B — Income or Loss from a Business or Property
Basic Rules

Inclusions

Deductions

Ceasing to Carry on Business

Special Cases

Subdivision C — Taxable Capital Gains and Allowable Capital Losses

Subdivision D — Other Sources of Income

Subdivision F — Rules Relating to Computation of Income

Subdivision G — Amounts Not Included in Computing Income

ITA Sections

Subdivision J — Partnerships and Their Members

Subdivision K — Trusts and Their Beneficiaries

Detailed Table of Sections

DIVISION D — TAXABLE INCOME EARNED IN CANADA BY NON-RESIDENTS

ITA Sections

DIVISION E — COMPUTATION OF TAX
Subdivision A — Rules Applicable to Individuals

DIVISION E.1 — MINIMUM TAX

DIVISION F — SPECIAL RULES APPLICABLE IN CERTAIN CIRCUMSTANCES
Bankruptcies

Changes in Residence

Private Corporations

Non-Resident-Owned Investment Corporations

Patronage Dividends

Agricultural Cooperatives — Tax-deferred Patronage Dividends

Continuance of the Canadian Wheat Board

ITA Sections

Demutualization of Insurance Corporations

Financial Institutions
Interpretation

Registered Supplementary Unemployment Benefit Plans

Registered Retirement Savings Plans

Home Buyers' Plan

Registered Disability Savings Plan

Advanced Life Deferred Annuity

Deferred Profit Sharing Plans

Registered Pension Plans

Pooled Registered Pension Plans

Life Insurance Policies

Eligible Funeral Arrangements

DIVISION H — EXEMPTIONS
Miscellaneous Exemptions

Qualified Donees [Charities, etc.]

DIVISION I — RETURNS, ASSESSMENTS, PAYMENT AND APPEALS
Returns

Interest

Offset of Refund Interest and Arrears Interest

Small Amounts Owing

Penalties

Misrepresentation of a Tax Matter by a Third Party

Refunds

Objections to Assessments

General

Revocation of Registration of Certain Organizations and Associations

Designation of Qualified Canadian Journalism Organizations

DIVISION J — APPEALS TO THE TAX COURT OF CANADA AND THE FEDERAL COURT OF APPEAL

PART I.01 — TAX IN RESPECT OF STOCK OPTION BENEFIT DEFERRAL

PART I.1 — INDIVIDUAL SURTAX

PART I.2 — TAX [CLAWBACK] ON OLD AGE SECURITY BENEFITS

PART I.3 — TAX ON LARGE CORPORATIONS [PRE-2006]

PART II — TOBACCO MANUFACTURERS' SURTAX

PART II.1 — TAX ON CORPORATE DISTRIBUTIONS

PART III — ADDITIONAL TAX ON EXCESSIVE ELECTIONS

PART III.1 — ADDITIONAL TAX ON EXCESSIVE ELIGIBLE DIVIDEND DESIGNATIONS

Detailed Table of Sections

ITA Sections

PART X.3 — LABOUR-SPONSORED VENTURE CAPITAL CORPORATIONS

PART X.4 — TAX IN RESPECT OF OVERPAYMENTS TO REGISTERED EDUCATION SAVINGS PLANS

Collection

General

Offences and Punishment

Procedure and Evidence

PART XV.1 — REPORTING OF ELECTRONIC FUNDS TRANSFER

PART XVI — TAX AVOIDANCE

PART XVIII — ENHANCED INTERNATIONAL INFORMATION REPORTING [FOR U.S. FATCA]

ITA Sections

INCOME TAX ACT

An Act Respecting Income Taxes

REVISED STATUTES OF CANADA 1985, c. 1 (5TH SUPPLEMENT), AS AMENDED BY 1994, cc. 7, 8, 13, 21, 28, 29, 38, 41; 1995, cc. 1, 3, 11, 17, 18, 21, 38, 46; 1996, cc. 6, 11, 21, 23; 1997, cc. 10, 12, 25, 26; 1998, cc. 19, 21, 34; 1999, cc. 10, 17, 22, 26, 31; 2000, cc. 9, 12, 14, 19, 30; 2001, cc. 16, 17, 27, 41; 2002, cc. 8, 9; 2003, cc. 15, 19, 28; 2004, cc. 11, 22, 24, 25, 26; 2005, cc. 19, 21, 30, 33, 34, 35, 38, 47, 49; 2006, cc. 1, 4, 9, 12; 2007, cc. 2, 16, 29, 35, 36; 2008, c. 28; 2009, cc. 2, 31; 2010, cc. 12, 25; 2011, cc. 15, 24; 2012, cc. 19, 27, 31; 2013, cc. 33, 34, 40; 2014, cc. 12, 13, 20, 39; 2015, cc. 20, 36, 41; 2016, cc. 7, 11, 12, 14; 2017, cc. 12, 20, 33; 2018, cc. 12, 27; 2019, cc. 13, 29; 2020, cc. 5, 6, 11, 12, 13; 2021, cc. 7, 21, 23.

1. Short title — This Act may be cited as the *Income Tax Act*.

PART I — INCOME TAX

DIVISION A — LIABILITY FOR TAX

2. (1) Tax payable by persons resident in Canada — An income tax shall be paid, as required by this Act, on the taxable income for each taxation year of every person resident in Canada at any time in the year.

Related Provisions: 2(2) — Calculation of taxable income; 94(3)(a)(i) — Application to trust deemed resident in Canada; 96 — Partnerships and their members; 104 — Trusts and estates; 114 — Residence for part of year; 126 — Foreign tax credit; 127.5 — Alternative minimum tax; 149 — Exempt persons; 250 — Extended meaning of resident.

Notes: Tax on Canadian residents applies to income from all sources worldwide (actually universe-wide, including income from outer space: VIEWS doc 2011-0407961E5), subject to the foreign tax credit (see 126) and Canada's tax treaties with other countries. Losses outside Canada (e.g. on a rental property) can reduce Canadian-source income: 2012-0453461I7. See 2(2) and 2005-0116031E5, 2009-0332851M4, 2017-0736681M4. Tax on non-residents is limited to Canadian-source income; see 2(3), 115, 212 and 216–219. For the meaning of "resident in Canada", see Notes to 250(1). US citizens pay US tax on worldwide income regardless of where they are resident; see Notes to 128.1(1). Canada does not tax non-resident Canadian citizens differently than other non-residents: 2012-0438311E5. On "stateless" income arising outside any country see Burch, "Extranational Taxation", 67(3) *Canadian Tax Journal* 729-53 (2019).

Constitutional validity: The federal income tax is clearly within Parliament's jurisdiction under *Constitution Act, 1867* s. 91(3), and Canadian residents must pay tax: *Caron*, [1924] 4 D.L.R. 105 (JCPC); *Winterhaven Stables*, 1988 ABCA 334; *Kennedy*, [2000] 4 C.T.C. 186 (Ont. SCJ); *Bruno*, 2002 BCCA 47; *Hoffman*, 2004 MBQB 164; *Heckendorn*, 2006 FCA 407; *Gibbs*, 2006 BCPC 215 and 2006 BCSC 481; *Smith*, 2006 BCSC 1493; *Randall*, 2008 TCC 621; *Sandri*, 2009 CarswellOnt 5005 (Ont. SCJ) (lawsuit claiming ITA illegal struck out); *MacDonald*, 2009 TCC 458 and 2010 TCC 107 (appeal dismissed for delay: costs award at 2011 CarswellNat 660 (FCA)); *Martin*, 2012 NSPC 73; *Kennedy*, 2012 FC 1050; *Gerlitz*, 2014 ABQB 247; *Anderson*, 2014 BCSC 2002, paras. 28-33 (ITA not unconstitutionally vague or complex); *Bekkerus*, 2014 TCC 311; *Davis*, 2015 TCC 79; *Fong*, 2015 FCA 102 (leave to appeal denied 2015 CarswellNat 5253 (SCC)); *Lazar*, 2015 MBCA 45; *Langford*, 2015 MBPC 58 (federal government may impose direct tax, even though some revenues are transferred to the provinces); *Cridge*, 2016 FCA 87; *Walsh*, 2018 ONSC 2251; VIEWS docs 2014-0547641E5, 2015-0580471E5, 2017-0712781M4, 2020-0842721M4. See also Peter Hogg, *Constitutional Law of Canada* (Carswell, 2 vols. looseleaf), chap. 31.

An honest belief that the tax is constitutionally invalid is no defence to criminal charges of evasion or failing to file a return: *Klundert*, [2004] 5 C.T.C. 20 (Ont CA, leave to appeal denied 2005 CarswellOnt 1118 (SCC)); 2nd jury acquittal overturned 2008 ONCA 767 (leave to appeal denied 2009 CarswellOnt 1883); conviction in 3rd jury trial upheld but sentence reduced 2011 ONCA 646 (leave to appeal denied 2012 CarswellOnt 4074); attempt to relitigate denied 2014 FCA 155 (leave to appeal denied 2014 CarswellNat 4955); *Watson*, 2006 BCCA 233; *Kennedy*, 2004 BCCA 638 (leave to appeal denied 2006 CarswellBC 915); *Meikle*, 2006 BCCA 558 (leave to appeal denied 2007 CarswellBC 1579); 2008 BCPC 265 (leave to appeal denied 2010 BCCA 337); *Sydel*, 2006 BCPC 346 and 2013 FC 1116; *Lemieux*, 2007 SKPC 135; *Little*, 2009 NBCA 53 (leave to appeal denied 2010 CarswellNB 12) (taxes used to fund abortions); *Balla*, 2010 BCSC 486; *Amell*, 2013 SKCA 48; *Crischuk*, 2010 BCSC 1165 (tax preparer); *Drosdovech*, 2010 FC 858; *Lindsay*, 2010 BCSC 831 (leave to appeal denied 2011 BCCA 99 and 2011 CarswellBC 2525 (SCC)); *Fischer*, 2013 BCPC 154; *Tyskerud*, 2013 BCPC 277; *Mori*, 2017 ONSC 1551; *Steinkey*, 2018 ABCA 361; *Ciciarelli*, 2019 ONSC 6719; *Wallen*, 2020 ONCJ 652; *Merrill*, 2021 BCSC 1017. However, in *Patry*, 2018 BCSC 1524, an advisor who devised an absurd scheme to have his clients claim business losses on personal home purchases was acquitted because he genuinely believed his scheme worked (and was not challenging the tax's

constitutionality); and in *Maracle*, 2019 CarswellOnt 24314 (Ont. CJ), a status Indian was acquitted, as he believed his Band's advice to him that he was not required to collect GST/HST on sales.

The above cases have raised various bizarre and frivolous defences, which the Courts have rejected. CRA has no obligation to produce a certified or official copy of the Act: *Bruno* and *Gibbs* (above); *Dove*, 2004 CanLII 31861 (Ont. SCJ); *Iwanow*, 2008 TCC 22. The laws.justice.gc.ca version is "official" under the *Legislation Revision and Consolidation Act* (formerly *Statute Revision Act*): *Watts*, 2015 ONSC 5597; *Chaudhry*, 2016 TCC 28.

For a comprehensive review of the legal nonsense presented by such persons (dubbed "Organized Pseudolegal Commercial Argument" — OPCA), see *Meads v. Meads*, 2012 ABQB 571, recommending sanctions the Courts can apply including contempt of Court. For more detail on OPCA see: *Boisjoli*, 2015 ABQB 629, by the same judge (Rooke ACJ), finding B a vexatious litigant (see Notes to 169(1) re VLs) and calling paper attacks on court officials the offence of "criminal intimidation"; *Pomerleau*, 2017 ABQB 123. *Meads* was applied to strike out detaxers' appeals in *Cassa*, 2013 TCC 43; *Haynes*, 2013 TCC 229; *Dillon*, 2013 TCC 242 (costs awarded to Crown in Informal Procedure); *Dalle Rive*, 2013 TCC 243 (appeal dismissed for non-compliance 2014 CarswellNat 3284 (FCA); leave to appeal denied 2014 CarswellNat 2989); *Bertucci*, 2014 TCC 230; *Russell*, 2016 TCC 122; *Bradshaw*, 2017 TCC 123 (Fiscal Arbitrators); *Tyskerud*, 2019 TCC 84, para. 28. Nonsensical OPCA actions were struck in: *Heckendorn*, 2006 FCA 407; *Bloom [Natural and Sovran]*, 2010 FC 621; *Herbison*, 2014 BCCA 461; *Claeys*, 2013 MBQB 313; *Sinclair-McDonald*, 2013 ONSC 4900; *Dove*, 2016 FCA 231 (leave to appeal denied 2017 CarswellNat 2531 (SCC)); *Steinkey*, 2017 FCA 124; *MacMillan v. Johannson*, 2017 BCSC 1069; *Fazakas*, 2018 FC 364; *Howard*, 2019 ONCA 351; *AVI v. MHVB*, 2020 ABQB 489, 2020 ABQB 790 (calling it "pseudolaw", warning OPCA guru "Jacquie Phoenix" she'll be held in contempt of Court); *Steeves*, 2020 FC 1177; *Gauvreau*, 2021 ABQB 172, extension of time to appeal denied 2021 ABCA 130. Lawsuits claiming CRA discriminated against or prosecuted the plaintiff because of involvement in the "detax" movement were struck out: *Sydel*, 2011 BCCA 233 (leave to appeal denied 2011 CarswellBC 2576); *Ballantyne*, 2014 FC 242. Wrongly identifying an accused as an OPCA litigant did not breach her *Charter* rights: *Eddy*, 2016 ABQB 42, para. 128. In *Herbison*, 2014 BCCA 461, a challenge to the validity of CRA collection action under 223(3) was dismissed as vexatious with high costs awarded. A judge who refused to let an accused repeatedly make OPCA arguments, calling them "rubbish", acted properly: *Jefferd*, 2016 BCSC 1463. In *Shannon*, 2016 TCC 255, Chris Shannon was prohibited from representing anyone in the Tax Court due to repeated reliance on OPCA arguments. A lawyer who prepares OPCA paperwork may be sanctioned: *Steinkey*, 2017 FCA 124, para. 9. See also Notes to 248(1)"person"; to 163(2) re gross negligence penalty and Fiscal Arbitrators; and end of Notes to 169(1) re vexatious litigants.

Claims that income tax infringes freedoms by funding objectionable causes will also fail: Tonkovich, "Render Unto Caesar — Using the Freedom of Conscience and Religion to Challenge Canadian Taxes", 34(2) *National Journal of Constitutional Law* 121-43 (2015).

A taxpayer's constitutional challenge to legislation must respect objection and appeal limitation periods: *Horseman*, 2018 FCA 119.

The Minister of Justice must examine proposed legislation to determine if it complies with the *Charter* and *Bill of Rights*, but a report to Parliament is required only if "no credible argument" can be made that it complies: *Schmidt*, 2018 FCA 55, para. 66.

There is a "presumption against extraterritoriality" that may require interpreting a tax statute as not intending to tax a foreign tax refund. See *Oroville Reman & Reload*, 2016 TCC 75, where this applied to a softwood lumber charge; it likely is not relevant to the ITA, which explicitly taxes foreign income. In *Jiminez*, [2019] EWCA Civ 51 (England), *Oroville* was held not to prevent the UK tax authority from demanding information from a non-resident, "provided no steps are taken to seek to enforce the penalty in a foreign state" (para. 54: see Notes to 223(3)).

A court-approved plan cannot provide that trust distributions will not be subject to tax: *Canadian Red Cross Society*, [2007] 1 C.T.C. 27 (Ont. SCJ).

For discussion of how corporations are taxed, see Notes to 123(1).

Income Tax Folios: S5-F1-C1: Determining an individual's residence status [replaces IT-221R3]; S6-F1-C1: Residence of a trust or estate [replaces IT-447].

1

Interpretation Bulletins: IT-106R3: Crown corporation employees abroad.

(2) Taxable income — The taxable income of a taxpayer for a taxation year is the taxpayer's income for the year plus the additions and minus the deductions permitted by Division C.

Related Provisions: 3 — Income for taxation year; 110.5 — Addition to taxable income to create more foreign tax credit; 248(1) — "Taxable income" may not be less than nil; 261(2) — Canadian currency used to determine taxable income; 261(7) — Functional currency reporting.

Notes: Division C is sections 109 to 114.2.

(3) Tax payable by non-resident persons — Where a person who is not taxable under subsection (1) for a taxation year

(a) was employed in Canada,

(b) carried on a business in Canada, or

(c) disposed of a taxable Canadian property,

at any time in the year or a previous year, an income tax shall be paid, as required by this Act, on the person's taxable income earned in Canada for the year determined in accordance with Division D.

Announced Administrative Change — 2(3)(b) — COVID-19

CRA notice (tinyurl.com/cra-internat, April 27, 2021): See under 250(1)(a), sections II "Carrying on business in Canada/Permanent establishment" and VII.B "Permanent establishment".

Related Provisions [subsec. 2(3)]: 18(4) — Thin capitalization rule applies to non-resident corporation; 40(3)(e), 40(3.1)(b) — Deemed disposition of property or partnership interest when its ACB goes negative; 94(3)(a)(i) — Application to trust deemed resident in Canada; 96(1.6) — Members of partnership deemed carrying on business in Canada; 114 — Residence for part of year; 115(2)(d) — Non-resident deemed employed in Canada; 115(2.1), (2.2) — Non-resident actors; 120(1) — Federal surtax on non-resident's income not earned in a province; 150(1)(a), 150(1.1)(b) — Requirements for non-residents to file returns; 212–219 — Tax on non-residents; 217(3)(a) — Non-resident making election is deemed employed in Canada; 250.1 — Taxation year and income of non-resident person; 253 — Extended meaning of carrying on business in Canada; 261(2) — Canadian currency used to determine taxable income earned in Canada; Canada-U.S. Tax Treaty:Art. VII — Business profits of U.S. resident.

Notes: Division D is sections 115 to 116.

A person who was resident in Canada in any previous year can in some cases be deemed employed in Canada in respect of remuneration paid by a Canadian resident. See 115(2)(c) and (d).

For "carried on a business in Canada" in 2(3)(b), determine first whether there is a "business" under 248(1), and see Notes to 9(2) and to 9(1) under "Business income". Then see s. 253. Subject to 253, a business is carried on where the profit-producing activity takes place: VIEWS docs 2004-0082661R3, 2009-0307001R3, 2010-0383661R3, 2010-0386191M4, 2011-0426551R3, 2012-0441941E5, 2012-0459481E5.

Passive income, such as interest, dividends, rent and royalties, is not subject to tax under 2(3). It is taxed under Part XIII (withholding tax) instead, and the non-resident is generally not required or permitted to file a return. See ss. 212, 216 and 217.

See Vidal et al., *Introduction to International Tax in Canada* (Carswell, 8th ed., 2020), chap. 9, "Part I Tax for a Non-Resident of Canada"; Li & Cockfield, *International Taxation in Canada*, 4th ed. (LexisNexis, 2018), chaps. 5-8; Wanda Rumball, "Dealing with Non-Residents: The Basics", 2004 Cdn Tax Foundation conference report, 39:1-40 (detailed checklist).

See also s. 4 of the *Income Tax Conventions Interpretation Act*.

Income Tax Folios [subsec. 2(3)]: S5-F1-C1: Determining an individual's residence status [replaces IT-221R3].

Interpretation Bulletins [subsec. 2(3)]: IT-113R4: Benefits to employees — stock options; IT-168R3: Athletes and players employed by football, hockey and similar clubs; IT-171R2: Non-resident individuals — computation of taxable income earned in Canada and non-refundable tax credits (cancelled); IT-176R2: Taxable Canadian property — Interests in and options on real property and shares; IT-262R2: Losses of non-residents and part-year residents; IT-298: Canada-U.S. Tax Convention — number of days "present" in Canada (cancelled); IT-379R: Employees profit sharing plans — allocations to beneficiaries; IT-393R2: Election re tax on rents and timber royalties — non-residents; IT-420R3: Non-residents — income earned in Canada; IT-421R2: Benefits to individuals, corporations and shareholders from loans or debt; IT-434R: Rental of real property by individual.

Forms [subsec. 2(3)]: NR73: Determination of residency status (leaving Canada); NR74: Determination of residency status (entering Canada); T1-NT12: Residency information for tax administration agreements; T1248 Sched. D: Information about your residency status; T4058: Non-residents and temporary residents of Canada [guide].

Definitions [s. 2]: "business" — 248(1); "carried on a business in Canada" — 253; "employed" — 248(1); "employed in Canada" — 115(2)(d); "non-resident", "person", "property" — 248(1); "resident in Canada" — 94(3)(a), 250; "taxable Canadian pro-

perty" — 248(1); "taxable income" — 2(2), 248(1); "taxable income earned in Canada" — 115(1), 248(1); "taxation year" — 249, 250.1(a); "taxpayer" — 248(1).

DIVISION B — COMPUTATION OF INCOME

Basic Rules

3. Income for taxation year — The income of a taxpayer for a taxation year for the purposes of this Part is the taxpayer's income for the year determined by the following rules:

(a) determine the total of all amounts each of which is the taxpayer's income for the year (other than a taxable capital gain from the disposition of a property) from a source inside or outside Canada, including, without restricting the generality of the foregoing, the taxpayer's income for the year from each office, employment, business and property,

(b) determine the amount, if any, by which

(i) the total of

(A) all of the taxpayer's taxable capital gains for the year from dispositions of property other than listed personal property, and

(B) the taxpayer's taxable net gain for the year from dispositions of listed personal property,

exceeds

(ii) the amount, if any, by which the taxpayer's allowable capital losses for the year from dispositions of property other than listed personal property exceed the taxpayer's allowable business investment losses for the year,

(c) determine the amount, if any, by which the total determined under paragraph (a) plus the amount determined under paragraph (b) exceeds the total of the deductions permitted by Subdivision E in computing the taxpayer's income for the year (except to the extent that those deductions, if any, have been taken into account in determining the total referred to in paragraph (a)), and

(d) determine the amount, if any, by which the amount determined under paragraph (c) exceeds the total of all amounts each of which is the taxpayer's loss for the year from an office, employment, business or property or the taxpayer's allowable business investment loss for the year,

and for the purposes of this Part,

(e) where an amount is determined under paragraph (d) for the year in respect of the taxpayer, the taxpayer's income for the year is the amount so determined, and

(f) in any other case, the taxpayer shall be deemed to have income for the year in an amount equal to zero.

Related Provisions: 94(3)(a)(ii) — Application to trust deemed resident in Canada; 115(1)(b), (b.1), (c) — Application of s. 3 to a non-resident; 146.2(7) — No tax on income received in TFSA; 261(2) — Canadian currency used to determine income.

Notes: The term "income" as defined by s. 3 is called "net income" on CRA's income tax returns and forms.

Income is calculated annually, so a disability pension received as income did not change retroactively because it was later ordered repaid: *Lessard*, 2007 FCA 9, 2012 FCA 311.

Although 3(a) is worded very broadly, the courts apply it restrictively, so income from sources not specified in the Act is generally not taxable. "It is an open question whether any source of income exists that is not listed in para. 3(a) or section 56 ... it may never be necessary to determine that question because the words 'business' and 'property' are so broadly defined": *Johnson*, 2012 FCA 253, para. 25 (leave to appeal denied 2013 CarswellNat 633 (SCC)). The following have been held non-taxable:

- amateur hockey team's allowance and stipend paid to player: *Grenier*, 2007 TCC 72

- amount received following expropriation: *Bellingham*, [1996] 1 C.T.C. 187 (FCA)

- amounts paid for injurious affection to lands when expropriating other lands: *Hurley*, [2003] 2 C.T.C. 2620 (TCC)

- assistance (one-time) to hurricane and typhoon victims who are family members of employees: doc 2009-0349581E5

- attendant-care payments to taxpayer to care for disabled child or spouse: *Maurice*, [2002] 1 C.T.C. 2172 (TCC); *Pellerin*, 2006 TCC 383; docs 2007-0229251I7, 2009-0312891E5, 2011-0398241E5 (see also "home care" below), 2013-0485421E5, 2013-0491981E5, 2014-0520401E5
- autism intervention programs in BC: doc 2003-0054611E5
- bequest by will, or other inheritance: see Notes to 70(5)
- British Columbia tax refunds under the B.C. *International Financial Activity Act*: doc 2004-0086581E5
- British Columbia Temporary Parental Educational Support payments to parents during 2014 teacher strike (though payments could reduce child-care deduction under 63(1)(d)): doc 2014-054212I7
- British Columbia Training Tax Credit: doc 2007-0248001E5
- bus passes given by a church to street people who volunteer at a soup kitchen and shelter: doc 2004-005606I7
- COVID-19 payments to seniors and to persons qualifying for the disability credit (authorized by the *Public Health Events of National Concern Payments Act*): see Announced Administrative Changes under 56(1)(a)(i)(A) and 118.3(1) [note: the Canada Emergency Response Benefit and Canada Recovery Benefit are taxable under 56(1)(r)(iv) or (iv.1), and the Canada Emergency Wage Subsidy and Canada Emergency Rent Subsidy to businesses are taxable under 12(1)(x)]
- Canadian Forces disability-benefits class action settlement payments to surviving spouse or estate: 2015-057485117
- Chinese head tax immigration compensation $20,000 payments (Revenu Québec interpretation letter 06-010463; CRA would likely apply the same interpretation)
- class action pollution settlement received years after selling the land: doc 2007-0255051E5
- class action settlement for overpaid interest on student loans: doc 2008-0285311C6
- compensation by former employer to retirees for cancellation of private health coverage: doc 2006-0216481E5
- compensation by Ontario government to developer in Caledonia whose business was ruined by native occupation, to have developer "go away", drop claims and lift injunction against natives (*Henco Industries*, 2014 TCC 192, paras. 149-163, 170, 203)
- damages due to company's inability to relocate its business, paid by city for civic purpose not business purpose: *Toronto Refiners & Smelters*, 2002 FCA 476
- damages for breach of employment contract before it began: *Schwartz*, [1996] 1 C.T.C. 303 (SCC); *Schewe*, 2010 TCC 47; *Robinson*, 2010 QCCQ 6481; docs 2005-0135831E5, 2011-042940117
- damages for mental distress, harassment or to reimburse for losses (but for an employee, see also Notes to 248(1)"retiring allowance"): *Bédard*, [1991] 1 C.T.C. 2323 (TCC); *Mendes-Roux*, [1998] 2 C.T.C. 2274 (TCC); *Fournier*, [1999] 4 C.T.C. 2247 (TCC); *Saardi*, [1999] 4 C.T.C. 2488 (TCC); docs 2010-0389701E5, 2011-0415941E5
- damages for miscalculating pension entitlements: doc 2010-0361101R3
- damages for personal injury: IT-365R2, docs 2010-0384501E5, 2011-0423761E5, 2013-0514361E5, 2015-0564671E5; *Fawkes*, 2004 TCC 653; *Guay*, 2006 TCC 84; Larre, "Taxing Personal Injury Damages", 58(3) *Canadian Tax Journal* 577-608 (2010)
- damages for violating employee's rights under *Labour Relations Act* by unfair labour practices: doc 2018-0748731E5
- damages paid to X by customer of X's employer who induced employer to terminate X's employment: *Ahmad*, [2002] 4 C.T.C. 2497 (TCC) (see also Notes to 9(1) under "Damages")
- death benefit for employee, up to $10,000: 56(1)(a)(iii), 248(1)"death benefit"
- deceased person's retroactive pay increase or pay equity settlement: docs 2003-0018835, 2009-0324381E5
- disaster relief payments, from an employer or a charity, if purpose is philanthropic, not based on employment, and employer does not deduct payment: docs 2003-0005753, 2011-0409751M4, 2013-0496281E5, 2018-075422117 (payment to a business is taxable (offsetting expenses) or reduces cost of property replaced, so no net income: 2013-0494661E5, 2018-075422117) [see also "flood relief" below]
- dividends or interest from past years that cannot be paid because the beneficial owner is unknown (and any claim is statute-barred): doc 2011-0429031I7 (note the obligation to remit tax under 153(4))
- Duplessis Orphans national reconciliation program payments: doc 2007-0226801E5
- ecoAUTO (Transport Canada) rebate for fuel-efficient vehicles bought solely for personal use: doc 2007-026144117
- financial assistance to retired and incapacitated ministers: doc 2002-0151305
- flood relief payments: CRA news release, March 3, 2005; doc 2013-0494421E5 [see also "disaster relief" above]
- foreign government (apparently Macao) one-time payment to all its residents to share gains from buoyant economy: doc 2008-0293241E5

- gambling, if it is not a business (see Notes to 9(1) under "Gambling")
- gift from a family member: doc 2010-0379191E5
- golf marshal's free rounds of golf: doc 2009-0323331E5
- grant to company's employee from US charity to assist with unnamed event unrelated to employment history: doc 2013-0514581R3
- grant under Shipbuilders' Workers Adjustment Program: *Layton*, [1995] 2 C.T.C. 2408 (TCC)
- Health Canada payments to thalidomide survivors: doc 2015-056775117
- Hiring Credit for Small Business, where the taxpayer is not carrying on a business: doc 2012-047265117
- hockey training allowances: doc 2008-0264941E5
- home care assistance for injured spouse provided by auto insurer: doc 2011-043029117 (see also "attendant-care" above)
- Hong Kong government $10,000 COVID-19 cash payout in 2020: doc 2020-085107117 (and earlier "Scheme $6,000" payment: 2012-0433161E5, 2014-052776117)
- host home providers, boarding children from remote location (if not a business): doc 2007-0222411E5 (see also 81(1)(h))
- human rights violation damages: see Notes to 248(1)"retiring allowance"
- income tax refund (other than interest portion): doc 2016-0641771E5
- Indian residential school and day school settlements (for abuse): docs 2006-019925117, 2019-0827981E5
- insolvent employer's retirees: payments in lieu of continued PSHP coverage: doc 2010-0385181R3
- insurance agent's commission for selling policy to self: doc 2008-0279231E5
- lottery ticket retailer's prize for selling a winning ticket, through 2013 only: IT-404R paras. 3-4; docs 2013-049199117, 2014-0522731M4
- lottery winnings (see Notes to 40(2)(f))
- Macau government Wealth Sharing Scheme payments: doc 2014-052776117
- Nfld & Labrador Community Relocation Program payment (treated as disposition of principal residence): 2013-049579117, 2017-0682691E5
- non-compete agreement, now taxed by 56.4: *Fortino*, [2000] 1 C.T.C. 349 (FCA); *Manrell*, 2003 FCA 128 (giving up right to do business, shared with everyone, is not giving up "property")
- nun's gift from Order upon leaving the Order (because of her age and illness, without expectation and not as compensation for anything): 2011-039946117
- one-time unexpected and unsolicited payment to cover the cost of purchasing a vehicle or house: doc 2010-0389101E5
- organ donor's living allowance (max $6,600): doc 2006-0192721E5; Drache, "Common Sense Break for Organ Donors", 15(9) *Canadian Not-for-Profit News* (Carswell) 71 (Sept. 2007)
- payment for cancelled stock option rights (now overridden by 7(1.7)): *Buccini*, [2001] 1 C.T.C. 103 (FCA)
- pension plan deficit compensation paid by Quebec: doc 2008-0271781E5
- private health services plan retirement benefits discontinuance — lump sum paid: docs 2007-0220141R3, 2013-0514561R3
- Quebec "grant for multiple births" (baby bonus): doc 2009-034287117
- real estate brokerage "cash back" incentive to home buyer: doc 2019-0796631E5
- referral fees received from construction company for occasional referrals: doc 2007-0224771E5
- reimbursement of expenses to volunteers: doc 2005-0143851E5
- reimbursement (one-time) to employee of expense that is the employer's responsibility: doc 2006-0204381E5
- reimbursement to investor for trading losses incurred by broker: *Hazan*, 2008 CarswellNat 3057 (TCC)
- rental of a home to taxpayer's child for personal reasons: doc 2006-0171132E5
- scholarship or bursary from Conservatory's endowment fund for recreational music lessons: doc 2019-0802051E5
- school board payments compensating parents for the cost of transporting students where school bus service was discontinued: doc 2003-005416117
- settlement for defective steel pipe treatment system causing taxpayer to incur additional costs: *Ipsco Inc.*, [2002] 2 C.T.C. 2907 (TCC)
- settlement for employer's reneging on promise to leave employee a bequest on death: *Au*, [2005] 3 C.T.C. 2155 (TCC); aff'd [2006] 2 C.T.C. 235 (FCA)
- settlement of grievance concerning life insurance benefits, to cover financial loss: doc 2009-0322501E5
- status Indians' income situated on a reserve: see Notes to 81(1)(a)
- strike pay: *Fries*, [1990] 2 C.T.C. 439 (SCC); Income Tax Folio S3-F9-C1 ¶1.10 (see Notes to 8(1)(i) and "union's cash gift" below); and union paying employee's pension contributions during strike: doc 2013-0476281E5

- student loan program: interest-free loans and loan forgiveness under provincial program: docs 2018-0775971E5, 2018-077732I17
- TV game show prize (even where taxpayer trained to develop expertise in subject-matter): *Turcotte*, [1998] 3 C.T.C. 2359 (TCC)
- tax-free savings account income: 146.2(7)
- teachers buying school gala fundraiser tickets partly with parent donations (2013-0490621E5)
- tenant relocation and rental assistance paid by developer during renovations (doc 2019-0825431E5)
- transplant patient accommodation expenses reimbursement: doc 2009-0314691E5
- travel allowance paid by school board: doc 2010-0389601E5 (see also "school board" above)
- trust payment to mother of disabled adult to help cover personal expenses: doc 2005-011035I17
- union receipts from employers, held in trust to benefit union members: doc 2007-0249051E5
- union's cash gift to member (docs 2005-0114061I7, 2005-015557717, 2007-0249291E5, 2007-0261121E5 — but if the gift is large, members' dues might not be deductible under 8(5); and union's voluntary gift to terminated employee (2005-0155577I7 — but 2009-0348951E5 says certain union payments to terminated employees are a taxable "retiring allowance") or payment to employee for losing right to have grievance adjudicated (2007-0249291E5 — but distribution of assets to a member on windup of the union is a capital gain: 2005-0162511E5, 2010-0367981E5; and 6(1)(j) taxes receipts from a union if they are a reimbursement of dues (2009-0306601E5, 2009-0350371E5, 2010-0367981E5)); also, a payment by the union for services is taxable (2010-0384511E5). A union's payment of an employee's group plan contributions while the employee is sick is also non-taxable: 2012-0447371E5. An employer's payment to employees to settle union grievances, even if channeled through the union, is taxable under 5(1) in CRA's view: 2011-0401781E5
- US *CARES Act* (COVID-19) Economic Impact Payment, as it is a refundable tax credit: doc 2020-0851811I7
- US 2008 Economic Stimulus Package tax credits and advance payments (but amounts may reduce foreign tax credit): doc 2009-030642117
- Veterans Independence Program payments (due to 81(1)(d)): doc 2013-0489561M4
- veterans' Critical Injury Benefit and Family Caregiver Relief Benefit: 81(1)(d.1)
- voluntary compensation by government for stopping logging operations: *Frank Beban Logging*, [1998] C.T.C. 2493 (TCC)
- volunteer's compensation that is nominal ("significantly less" than what an employee would earn, and "not likely enough to induce the provision of services"): docs 2011-0400471E5, 2014-0550771E5
- witness protection program payments, possibly: doc 2014-053122117

In all these cases the amount in question was found not to be income from a taxable "source" and was thus a non-taxable windfall. See also Notes to 6(1)(a) re non-taxable employee benefits, 6(1)(b) for non-taxable allowances, 9(1) at "Damages" re the *surrogatum* principle, 12(1)(c) re pre-judgment interest, and 12(1)(x) re amounts paid by government. See also 81(1) re exempt income; 56(3)–(3.1) for exempt scholarship income; and 149(1) for exempt taxpayers. CRA states that fees for jury duty are taxable: archived IT-377R [cancelled Sept. 30/12]; VIEWS doc 2004-0067741E5. Compensation for property destroyed or taken may be proceeds triggering capital gain and/or recapture: see 54"proceeds of disposition", 13(21)"proceeds of disposition". A non-taxable windfall received by a corporation cannot be distributed tax-free to shareholders: 2011-0394951E5.

See also "Source Concept of Income", chap. 2 of Edgar et al., *Materials on Canadian Income Tax* (Carswell, 15th ed., 2015); Jin Wen, "Credit Card Rewards Not Related to Spending", 9(2) *Canadian Tax Focus* (ctf.ca) 18 (May 2019).

Ponzi schemes as a source of income (or losses): see Notes to 9(2).

If tax legislation is clear, the fact it gives the taxpayer a windfall does not matter: *Dowbrands Canada*, [1997] G.S.T.C. 85 (TCC); *Barrington Lane*, 2010 TCC 388; *Quinco*, 2014 FCA 108; *Metrogate*, 2018 TCC 91.

The factors to consider for a non-taxable windfall to X are: 1. Was there an enforceable claim to the payment? 2. Was there an organized effort to receive it? 3. Was the receipt sought after or solicited in any way? 4. Was the payment expected? 5. Was there a foreseeable element of recurrence? 6. Was this a customary source of income to X? 7. Was it in recognition of anything provided or to be provided by X? *Cranswick*, [1982] C.T.C. 69 (FCA); *Lavoie*, 2010 FCA 266; *Johnson*, 2012 FCA 253 (leave to appeal denied 2013 CarswellNat 633 (SCC)); *Morguard Corp.*, 2012 TCC 55 (aff'd on other grounds 2012 FCA 306, leave to appeal denied 2013 CarswellNat 1135; Income Tax Folio S3-F9-C1 ¶1.2; VIEWS docs 9926715, 2002-0151305, 2010-0389101E5, 2011-040427117, 2012-0433161E5, 2013-0490621E5, 2014-0522921E5.

In *656203 Ontario*, 2003 TCC 264, damages paid by an insurer in a settlement were held to be proceeds of disposition for destroyed property (and thus a capital gain), not punitive damages or another non-taxable windfall. In *Haché*, 2011 FCA 104, a fishing licence was held to be property, so an amount received from the government for surrendering it was a capital gain.

CRA considers payments for participating in clinical trials of experimental drugs to be taxable: VIEWS docs 2004-0107991E5, 2011-043087I17 (requires T4A for payment over $500). Accepting reduced interest in exchange for something else is taxable: see Notes to 12(1)(c). Prize winnings can be taxable if received in the course of a business: 2010-0355711E5, and see 9(1) Notes under "Gambling" and 56(1)(n). Rooftop solar panels: see 9(1) Notes under "Solar".

3(b) requires taxable capital gains (½ of current-year capital gains) and allowable capital losses (½ of current-year capital losses) to be netted against each other, with listed personal property losses factored into 3(b)(i)(B) (personal-use property losses are not otherwise deductible). Allowable business investment losses are claimed under 3(d) rather than 3(b). Losses (including capital losses) of prior and later years are allowed under s. 111 and claimed under 2(2) as optional deductions in computing *taxable* income rather than under s. 3.

3(f) added by 1991 technical bill, effective 1990, so that a taxpayer with no income is treated as having income of $0 (in response to the Court declining to consider a spouse with no income as having the "lower" income of two spouses for purposes of 63(2): *McLaren*, [1990] 2 C.T.C. 429 (FCTD)).

Definitions [s. 3]: "allowable business investment loss" — 38(c), 248(1); "allowable capital loss" — 38(b), 248(1); "amount", "business" — 248(1); "Canada" — 255; "employment" — 248(1); "foreign resource property" — 66(15), 248(1); "listed personal property" — 54, 248(1); "office", "property" — 248(1); "taxable capital gain" — 38(a), 248(1); "taxable net gain" — 41(1), 248(1); "taxation year" — 11(2), 249; "taxpayer" — 248(1).

I.T. Application Rules: 20(3)(c), 20(5)(c).

Income Tax Folios: S1-F3-C1: Child care expense deduction [replaces IT-495R3]; S3-F9-C1: Lottery winnings, miscellaneous receipts, and income (and losses) from crime [replaces IT-185R, IT-213R, IT-256R, IT-334R2]; S4-F3-C1: Price adjustment clauses [replaces IT-169]; S5-F2-C1: Foreign tax credit [replaces IT-270R3, IT-395R2, IT-520]; S4-F8-C1: Business investment losses [replaces IT-484R2].

Interpretation Bulletins: IT-98R2: Investment corporations (cancelled); IT-206R: Separate businesses; IT-232R3: Losses — their deductibility in the loss year or other years; IT-262R2: Losses of non-residents and part-year residents; IT-365R2: Damages, settlements and similar receipts; IT-377R: Director's, executor's or juror's fees (cancelled); IT-381R3: Trusts — capital gains and losses and the flow-through of taxable capital gains to beneficiaries; IT-393R2: Election re tax on rents and timber royalties — non-residents; IT-420R3: Non-residents — income earned in Canada; IT-434R: Rental of real property by individual; IT-490: Barter transactions.

Advance Tax Rulings: ATR-40: Taxability of receipts under a structured settlement; ATR-50: Structured settlement; ATR-68: Structured settlement.

Forms: T776: Statement of real estate rentals.

> ### Withdrawn Proposed Addition — 3.1 — REOP requirement
>
> **Notes:** Draft legislation of Oct. 31, 2003 would have introduced s. 3.1, requiring a reasonable expectation of profit (REOP) to claim a loss from business or property (and related amendments at 3(d), 9(3), 111(8)"non-capital loss"A:E). This responded to *Ludco Enterprises*, 2001 SCC 62 and *Stewart*, 2002 SCC 46. It raised a storm of protest from the tax, business and investment communities, and would have severely impacted borrowing for investment. Finance said in the 2005 Budget that it would make major changes and introduce "a more modest legislative initiative"; this could have been simply changing "for the purpose of earning income" in 20(1)(c)(i) to "for the purpose of earning profit other than capital gains". In Nov. 2014, Finance announced that these proposals were withdrawn. The April 2021 Budget proposes a limit on interest deduction to 30% of "tax EBITDA". See Proposed Amendment under 20(1)(c).
>
> For proposed 3.1 and related 2003-05 announcements, see up to PITA 46th ed.; Tamaki & Edgar, "Policy Forum", 52(4) *Canadian Tax Journal* 1121-72 (2004); Johnson & Tamaki, "Deductibility of Interest", 2004 Ontario Tax Conf. (ctf.ca), 1-6:1-21; Lefebvre, "REOP and Interest", 2004 Cdn Tax Foundation conference report, 3:1-10.

4. (1) Income or loss from a source or from sources in a place — For the purposes of this Act,

(a) a taxpayer's income or loss for a taxation year from an office, employment, business, property or other source, or from sources in a particular place, is the taxpayer's income or loss, as the case may be, computed in accordance with this Act on the assumption that the taxpayer had during the taxation year no income or loss except from that source or no income or loss except from those sources, as the case may be, and was allowed no deductions in computing the taxpayer's income for the taxation year except such deductions as may reasonably be regarded as wholly applicable to that source or to those sources, as the case may be, and except such part of any other deductions as may reasonably be regarded as applicable thereto; and

(b) where the business carried on by a taxpayer or the duties of the office or employment performed by the taxpayer was carried on or were performed, as the case may be, partly in one place and partly in another place, the taxpayer's income or loss for the taxation year from the business carried on, or the duties performed, by the taxpayer in a particular place is the taxpayer's income or loss, as the case may be, computed in accordance with this Act on the assumption that the taxpayer had during the taxation year no income or loss except from the part of the business that was carried on in that particular place or no income or loss except from the part of those duties that were performed in that particular place, as the case may be, and was allowed no deductions in computing the taxpayer's income for the taxation year except such deductions as may reasonably be regarded as wholly applicable to that part of the business or to those duties, as the case may be, and except such part of any other deductions as may reasonably be regarded as applicable thereto.

Related Provisions: 96(1)(f) — Source of income preserved when flows through partnership; 108(5) — Source of income lost when flows through trust.

Notes: On whether an activity is a business and therefore a "source" under 4(1), see 9(2) Notes. As to whether two activities are separate businesses, see Reg. 1101(1) Notes.

4(1)(b) requires profits to be allocated among countries "in a manner that reflect the contribution of the activities in each jurisdiction that gave rise to those profits": VIEWS doc 2007-0224221I7.

4(1) applied in *Nonis*, 2021 TCC 31: N, who received salary continuation over 2 years after being fired, was taxed only on the fraction of his income representing his days in Canada during those years.

Despite 4(1)(b), a non-resident that manufactures outside Canada and solicits sales in Canada through an agent must calculate Canadian tax based on the goods' fair market value: VIEWS docs 9235160, 2006-0196221C6.

In *Société Générale Valeurs*, 2017 FCA 3, 4(1) applied in determining which expenses were relevant to a source, in applying the Canada-Brazil treaty tax-sparing provision.

Interpretation Bulletins: IT-362R: Patronage dividends.

(2) Idem — Subject to subsection (3), in applying subsection (1) for the purposes of this Part, no deductions permitted by sections 60 to 64 apply either wholly or in part to a particular source or to sources in a particular place.

Notes: Deductions under 60–64 (e.g., spousal support, moving expenses, child care expenses) appear separately on the tax return and are not attributable to a particular "source", so they do not reduce employment, business or property income as such.

4(2) amended by 1993 technical bill, for 1989 and later tax years.

(3) Deductions applicable — In applying subsection (1) for the purposes of subsections 104(22) and (22.1) and sections 115 and 126,

(a) subject to paragraph (b), all deductions permitted in computing a taxpayer's income for a taxation year for the purposes of this Part, except any deduction permitted by any of paragraphs 60(b) to (o), (p), (r) and (v) to (z), apply either wholly or in part to a particular source or to sources in a particular place; and

(b) any deduction permitted by subsection 104(6) or (12) shall not apply either wholly or in part to a source in a country other than Canada.

Notes: 4(3) amended by 2002-2013 technical bill and 2007 RDSPs bill (both for 2007 and later tax years), 1993 technical bill.

Income Tax Folios: S5-F2-C1: Foreign tax credit [replaces IT-270R3, IT-395R2, IT-520].

(4) [Repealed]

Notes: 4(4) repealed by 1995 Budget, for tax years that end after July 19, 1995. See new 248(28), which is broader and has replaced it. It prevented double-counting of an income or loss amount. 4(4) earlier amended by 1991 technical bill.

Definitions [s. 4]: "amount", "business" — 248(1); "Canada" — 255; "employment", "office", "property" — 248(1); "taxation year" — 11(2), 249; "taxpayer" — 248(1).

Income Tax Folios [s. 4]: S3-F9-C1: Lottery winnings, miscellaneous receipts, and income (and losses) from crime [replaces IT-185R, IT-213R, IT-256R, IT-334R2].

Interpretation Bulletins [s. 4]: IT-377R: Director's, executor's or juror's fees (cancelled); IT-420R3: Non-residents — income earned in Canada.

Subdivision A — Income or Loss from an Office or Employment

Basic Rules

5. (1) Income from office or employment — Subject to this Part, a taxpayer's income for a taxation year from an office or employment is the salary, wages and other remuneration, including gratuities, received by the taxpayer in the year.

Related Provisions: 4(1) — Income or loss from a source; 6 — Amounts included as income from office or employment; 8(1)(n) — Reimbursement of salary for periods when not employed; 56.4(4)(a) — Amount paid by purchaser for non-compete agreement deemed to be wages paid to employee; 87(2)(k) — Amalgamation — Amount received by employee from new corporation; 110(1)(f)(v) — Deduction for Canadian Forces personnel and police on high-risk missions; 110.2(1)"qualifying amount" — Retroactive spreading of certain lump-sum payments over prior years; 115(1)(a)(i) — Non-resident's taxable income earned in Canada; 125.7(2) — COVID-19 Canada Emergency Wage Subsidy to employers for 2020; 149(1)(a), (b) — Exempt individuals; 153(1)(a) — Withholding; 153(1.02)–(1.04) — COVID-19 source deductions subsidy to employers for 2020; 248(7) — Payment to employee deemed received when mailed; Canada-U.S. Tax Treaty:Art. XV, XVI — Taxation of employment income.

Notes: Salary and wages from office or employment are subject to withholding of tax at source (153(1)(a)), as well as payroll withholding of provincial income tax, Canada Pension Plan contributions and Employment Insurance premiums, and must be reported on a T4 (Reg. 200).

Received: Salary/wages are taxed when "received" regardless of when the work is done: *Kuwalek*, 2006 TCC 624. An advance against wages is taxable in the year received: *Merchant*, 2009 TCC 31; *Ziobrowska*, 2010 TCC 64; VIEWS docs 9729246, 2015-062357I7. A cheque received but uncashed at year-end is still "received": *Deschesnes*, 2015 TCC 177, paras. 37-40. An amount overpaid in error is taxed but can be retroactively deleted if repaid (and a corrective T4 issued) by the end of the 3rd following year: 153(3.1) Notes; tinyurl.com/overpay-error, canada.ca/taxes-phoenix. No adjustment is made to past years on receiving a retroactive pay increase: 2003-0018235 (see 110.2 for averaging). Retroactive pay to a deceased person is non-taxable: 2003-0018835.

A bonus on top of wages is taxable as "remuneration" and included in employment income: *Baldassarra*, 2012 TCC 175; VIEWS doc 2009-0352571M4. A bonus may be "constructively received" in the year if the employee is entitled to it but asks for payment to be postponed to the next year: 2008-029784117.

In *Natarajan*, 2010 TCC 582, CRA agreed that employment income paid by the employer to a US Deferred Income Plan was not taxable because it had not been "received" — effectively turning the US plan into an RRSP! *Contra*, in doc 2010-0367831I7, CRA says contributions to French pension funds made by an employer are made as the employee's agent and are taxable under 5(1), not RCA contributions.

Information slips — effect: The fact an amount is shown on a T4 or T4A normally leads CRA to include it in the taxpayer's income, but is not binding if the evidence shows it is incorrect: VIEWS doc 2013-0494441E5; *Newcombe*, 2013 FC 955, para. 29; see also *Mitzelos*, [2002] 3 C.T.C. 2519 (TCC); *Feld*, [2003] 1 C.T.C. 2253 (TCC); *Boersen*, 2007 TCC 671; *Simone Sherman*, 2008 TCC 487; *Mikhailova*, 2009 TCC 120; *Sévère*, 2009 TCC 209; *Visser*, 2009 TCC 306 (T4RIF); *Suffolk*, 2010 TCC 295; *Morissette*, 2012 TCC 37, para. 7; *Gorfain*, 2013 TCC 136 ("It is simply insufficient to tax a person solely because another person under audit points to them and provides their name and address": para. 8); *Lunot*, 2018 TCC 241, para. 4; *Trower*, 2019 TCC 77, para. 34; *Morrisseau*, 2020 TCC 5. (*Contra*, in *Vincent*, 2020 QCCQ 3605, para. 21, the Court of Quebec wrongly stated that slips are binding if not corrected.) In *Hayfron-Benjamin*, aff'd 2015 FCA 196, the TCC did not believe HB's claim that he did not work for entities that issued T4s; but his appeal was accepted for later years: 2016 TCC 151. In *Newcombe*, 2013 FC 955, the FC ruled a T4 was issued in error (para. 26), but provided no remedy as N should have appealed to the TCC. See also 8(10) Notes re the T2200 not being conclusive.

In *Duguay*, [2001] 4 C.T.C. 2726 (TCC), hospital employees who were union officers were paid by the union as reimbursement for days they took off work to participate in union activities. These payments were taxable under 5(1). In *Vachon Estate [Conseil central des syndicats nationaux du Saguenay/Lac St-Jean]*, 2009 FCA 375 (leave to appeal denied 2010 CarswellNat 936 (SCC)), reimbursement by the union for expenses was taxable where the employees continued to be paid by their employer. In *Sévère*, 2009 TCC 209, reimbursement of losses incurred due to the employee's relocation and later dismissal was non-taxable because the employee was not enriched. Reimbursement by an employer of an employee's payments to buy back pensionable service is taxable: VIEWS doc 2005-0138861E5. An employer's payment to employees to settle union grievances, channeled through the union, is taxable: 2011-0401781E5. See also Notes to 6(1)(a) under "Reimbursement", and Notes to 248(1)"office".

Honoraria are normally taxable as payment for services: VIEWS docs 2009-0308691E5, 2010-0381611E5 (or under 6(1)(c)). If a university staff member forgoes entitlement to an honorarium for assuming extra duties, directing the money to a research account, it is not considered earned (but see also 2011-0409551E5 — depends on terms of contract), and is taxed under 5(1) only when received out of the account: 2001-0115875.

Interns: in *Mondo-Tech*, 2003 FCA 62, payments under an international youth internship program were taxable under 5(1), due to the relationship between the parties. In *Conseil Atlantique*, 2012 TCC 13, payments under the DND's Security and Defence Forum Internship Program were scholarship income, not employment income.

Maternity leave pay is taxable under 5(1): VIEWS doc 2016-0675801I7.

Offsetting pay: Where pay is legally reduced to set off a debt owing to the employer, the income may still be constructively "received" by the employee: *Tessier*, 2007 FCA 154; VIEWS doc 2011-0393781E5 (waiver of monthly condo fees). However, in *Dhillon*, [2002] 4 C.T.C. 2648 (TCC), training expenses deducted at source and never paid to the taxpayer were excluded from income despite being on the T4, because the taxpayer did not really benefit: "While it is true that one receives something when one derives the benefit from it, it is surely open in this case to suggest that the 'something' is the benefit itself, not the monies attributed as having been applied to provide the benefit" (para. 50). In *Simone Sherman*, 2008 TCC 487, CRA as employer withheld from an employee's pay an amount overpaid as workers' compensation benefits under the *Government Employees Compensation Act*. The amount would have been income under 5(1), but because it was statute-barred CRA had no right to withhold it, so it was not taxable. In *Morrison*, 2010 TCC 429, payments of back salary done by crediting shareholder loan accounts, without actually paying out money, were not "received"; but in *Sochatsky*, 2011 TCC 41 (FCA appeal discontinued A-33-11), once the company had withheld and remitted tax, the amount was considered received by the employee. In *Ackles*, 2011 TCC 57, amounts owing to an employee were offset by forgiveness of debt, but since the employee transferred shares back to the company and received nothing for them there was no benefit.

Overtime banked in lieu of time off with pay is taxed under 5(1) only when received, not when earned, but may be taxed under the salary deferral rules: doc 2002-0171745.

Pay equity compensation: In *Morency*, 2005 FCA 16, *van Elslande*, 2007 TCC 370, and *Eaton*, 2008 FCA 162, such payments to women were held to be taxable compensation for salary, not for moral prejudice or personal injury. The *surrogatum* principle applied (*Eaton*; see 9(1) Notes at "Damages"). However, in VIEWS doc 2008-0292081R3, the CRA ruled such payments to settle a human rights complaint were non-taxable.

Recharacterizing salary paid to a shareholder-employee as dividend or shareholder-loan repayment after year-end: see Notes to 169(1) under "If there is no rectification".

Rental payments to an employee for the use of his vehicle or tools are considered employment income, not rental income: VIEWS doc 2012-0442231E5. So are employee referral fees paid to an employee: 2012-0448621E5.

Stock options surrendered: the proceeds are not "remuneration": *Rogers Estate*, 2014 TCC 348, paras. 45-48 (FCA appeal discontinued A-533-14).

Students doing research: payments to graduate students were employment income in *Rizak*, 2013 TCC 273 (reviews previous case law). In *Russell*, 2016 TCC 143, an undergraduate student research award was not under 5(1) (it likely fell under 56(1)(n)). The test is the "dominant characteristic of the payments, whether it is compensation for work or student assistance": para. 15. Post-doctoral fellowships: see Notes to 56(3).

Wrongful dismissal (termination pay): see Notes to 248(1)"retiring allowance".

A lump sum for lost wages paid to an employee ordered reinstated is taxable as employment income (with the interest component taxed under 12(1)(c)): VIEWS doc 2011-0407421E5.

Where pay is clawed back because performance goals were not achieved or due to legal restrictions on executives' pay levels, there may be no way to "undo" taxability of amounts previously received, if 8(1)(n) does not apply: Paul Carenza, "Say-on-Pay, Clawbacks and Canadian Income Tax", 21(1) *Taxation of Executive Compensation & Retirement* (Federated Press) 1179-83 (July/Aug. 2009).

In *Dingman*, 2017 TCC 206 (FCA appeal dismissed for delay A-336-17), a "leased employee" wages-to-loan scheme promoted by Peter Eickmeier (Graycliff Financial) was held to be a sham. The promoter had purported to lease an employee's services and pay him by way of a supposedly non-taxable "loan". CRA warned the public about such scams in an Aug. 15, 2017 news release. In *J.R. Saint & Associates*, 2010 TCC 168, salary paid through an employees profit sharing plan was held partly genuine.

As to whether a person is an employee (or officer) as opposed to earning business income, see Notes to 248(1)"employee". For executors, directors and board members see Notes to 6(1)(c). A judge paid a *per diem* rate is taxable under 6(1)(c) rather than 5(1) in CRA's view: doc 2013-0482171I7.

An individual trustee of a mutual fund trust is considered an "officer" and taxed under 5(1), whether paid a lump sum or a *per diem* rate: VIEWS doc 2003-0032765.

See also Notes to 153(1) re payroll withholdings and tips.

S. 26 of the *Employment Insurance Act* (S.C. 1996, c. 23), as amended by 1997 Budget (first bill), states that for the purposes of the ITA, "benefits paid to a claimant while employed under employment benefits, or under similar benefits that are the subject of an agreement under section 63, are not earnings from employment". EI benefits are taxed under 56(1)(a)(iv).

Income Tax Folios: S1-F1-C3: Disability supports deduction [replaces IT-519R2]; S1-F2-C1: Education and textbook tax credits [replaces IT-515R2]; S1-F2-C3: Scholarships, research grants and other education assistance [replaces IT-340R]; S2-F3-C1: Payments from employer to employee [replaces IT-196R2 and its SR]; S3-F9-C1: Lottery winnings, miscellaneous receipts, and income (and losses) from crime [replaces IT-185R, IT-213R, IT-256R, IT-334R2].

Interpretation Bulletins: IT-113R4: Benefits to employees — stock options; IT-167R6: Registered pension plans — employee's contributions; IT-202R2: Employees' or workers' compensation; IT-257R: Canada Council grants; IT-266: Taxation of members of provincial legislative assemblies (cancelled); IT-292: Taxation of elected municipal officers; IT-316: Awards for employees' suggestions and inventions (cancelled); IT-365R2: Damages, settlements and similar receipts; IT-389R: Vacation-with-pay plans established under collective agreements; IT-470R: Employees' fringe benefits.

Registered Charities Newsletters: *Charities Connection* 2 (payroll and income taxes).

Advance Tax Rulings: ATR-21: Pension benefit from an unregistered pension plan; ATR-45: Share appreciation rights plan; ATR-64: Phantom stock award plan.

Forms: T1 General return, Line 10100 [former 101].

(2) Loss from office or employment — A taxpayer's loss for a taxation year from an office or employment is the amount of the taxpayer's loss, if any, for the taxation year from that source computed by applying, with such modifications as the circumstances require, the provisions of this Act respecting the computation of income from that source.

Related Provisions: 4(1) — Income or loss from a source or from sources in a place; 8(13) — Loss from home office disallowed; 111(1)(a), 111(8)"non-capital loss" — Carryover of loss from employment to prior or later years.

Notes: While losses from employment are unusual, they do arise, e.g. due to 8(1)(b) legal fees, or 8(1)(m) pension contributions (*Hatt*, 2015 TCC 207).

Definitions [s. 5]: "amount", "employment", "office" — 248(1); "taxation year" — 249; "taxpayer" — 248(1).

Inclusions

6. (1) Amounts to be included as income from office or employment — There shall be included in computing the income of a taxpayer for a taxation year as income from an office or employment such of the following amounts as are applicable:

(a) **value of benefits** — the value of board, lodging and other benefits of any kind whatever received or enjoyed by the taxpayer, or by a person who does not deal at arm's length with the taxpayer, in the year in respect of, in the course of, or by virtue of the taxpayer's office or employment, except any benefit

(i) derived from the contributions of the taxpayer's employer to or under a deferred profit sharing plan, an employee life and health trust, a group sickness or accident insurance plan, a group term life insurance policy, a pooled registered pension plan, a private health services plan, a registered pension plan or a supplementary unemployment benefit plan,

(ii) under a retirement compensation arrangement, an employee benefit plan or an employee trust,

(iii) that was a benefit in respect of the use of an automobile,

(iv) derived from counselling services in respect of

(A) the mental or physical health of the taxpayer or an individual related to the taxpayer, other than a benefit attributable to an outlay or expense to which paragraph 18(1)(l) applies, or

(B) the re-employment or retirement of the taxpayer,

(v) under a salary deferral arrangement, except to the extent that the benefit is included under this paragraph because of subsection (11), or

(vi) that is received or enjoyed by an individual other than the taxpayer under a program provided by the taxpayer's employer that is designed to assist individuals to further their education, if the taxpayer deals with the employer at arm's length and it is reasonable to conclude that the benefit is not a substitute for salary, wages or other remuneration of the taxpayer;

Announced Administrative Change — COVID-19 — Employee benefits and allowances in 2020

CRA Backgrounder, Dec. 15, 2020: *Employee-Provided Benefits and Allowances: CRA and COVID-19*

In light of the COVID-19 pandemic, the Canada Revenue Agency (CRA) recognizes that for many employers and employees, there have been changes in the way that work is being conducted. Consequently, employers may provide certain benefits, allowances, or reimbursements to ensure that their employees are not unduly subject to harm when performing their employment duties.

- A **benefit** is a good or service an employer gives, or arranges for a third party to give, to their employee such as free use of property that you own. A benefit also includes an allowance or a reimbursement of an employee's personal expense.

- An **allowance** or an **advance** is any periodic or lump-sum amount that an employer pays to their employee on top of salary or wages, to help the employee pay for certain anticipated expenses without having to account for the use of the funds. An allowance or advance is:

  — usually an arbitrary amount that is predetermined without using the actual cost

  — usually for a specific purpose

  — used as the employee chooses, since the employee does not provide receipts

- An **accountable advance** is an amount an employer gives to an employee who has to account for their expenses by producing receipts and return any amount they did not spend.

- A **reimbursement** is an amount an employer gives to their employee to repay expenses he or she paid while carrying out their duties of employment. The employee has to keep detailed records (including receipts) to support the expenses and give them to their employer.

If an employer provides benefits to their employees, they always have to go through the same steps:

- determine if the benefit is taxable [see 6(1)(a), 6(1)(b) — ed.]
- calculate the value of the benefit
- calculate payroll deductions
- file an information return

For more information on employer-provided benefits and allowances, see Guide T4130, *Employers' Guide–Taxable Benefits and Allowances.*

Under these extraordinary circumstances, the CRA has adopted the following positions for employer-provided benefits pertaining to commuting and home office costs. These positions are effective **from March 15, 2020 to December 31, 2020**.

Commuting costs (including parking)

It is the long-standing position of the CRA that travel between an employee's home and a regular place of employment is generally personal travel, and any expenses related to that travel are personal expenses [see 8(1)(h.1) Notes — ed.]. An employee's parking costs at a regular place of employment are also considered personal expenses [see 6(1.1) Notes — ed.].

When an employer pays for, reimburses, or provides an allowance to an employee for such transportation and parking expenses (collectively, commuting costs) or provides an employee with a motor vehicle that is used for such travel, the employee generally receives a taxable benefit.

However, the CRA acknowledges that employees who are required to commute to their regular places of employment to perform employment duties may incur additional commuting costs to minimize their risk of exposure during the COVID-19 pandemic. Employees may also incur costs to commute to their regular place of employment to pick up equipment that enables them to perform employment duties from home. The following tax treatment applies in these situations:

1. Employee continues performing their employment duties at their regular place of employment

   The CRA will not consider an employee to receive a taxable benefit where their employer pays for, reimburses, or provides a reasonable allowance for **additional commuting costs** incurred by that employee during the COVID-19 pandemic, that are over and above their normal commuting costs. This position is extended to the use of employer-provided motor vehicles for such travel, provided the employee did not normally commute to work using an employer-provided motor vehicle before the COVID-19 pandemic.

2. Employee is performing their employment duties at home because their regular place of employment is closed

   The CRA will not consider an employee to receive a taxable benefit where their employer pays for, reimburses, or provides a reasonable allowance for normal or additional commuting costs incurred by the employee to **travel to their regular place of employment for any purpose that enables them to perform their employment duties from home** (for example, to pick up equipment). This position is extended to the use of employer-provided motor vehicles for such travel.

   Similarly, when a regular place of employment is closed due to the COVID-19 pandemic, the CRA will not consider an **employer-provided parking spot** at that place of employment to be available for an employee's use. As such, the employer-provided parking will not result in a taxable benefit.

In both situations, employers are expected to maintain appropriate records to demonstrate that any allowances provided are reasonable in relation to the commuting costs incurred by the employee. Employees are expected to maintain appropriate records to account for their use of the employer-provided motor vehicles, including the total kilometers driven when commuting between home and their regular place of employment.

Home office equipment

The CRA recognizes that the COVID-19 pandemic has resulted in many employees having to work from home, where they may not have the necessary computer or home office equipment (desk, office chair, etc.) to perform their employment duties. In this particular context, the CRA will not consider an employee to receive a taxable benefit where their **employer pays for or reimburses up to $500 of computer or home office equipment** to enable the employee to carry out their employment duties, provided the employee submits receipts to the employer. This position is extended to accountable advances provided to an employee, but does not apply to allowances provided for this purpose.

It should be noted, however, that the $500 reimbursement amount is in respect of each employee rather than each piece of computer or office equipment that an employee may purchase. For example, if an employee purchases a computer for $400 and an office chair for $250, an employer can reimburse the employee up to $500 without the employee receiving a taxable benefit under the administrative position. By contrast, if the employer reimburses the employee the full amount for these purchases, the amount over $500 (that is, $150) must be included in the employee's income.

The CRA's existing policies recognize that an employer may pay for or reimburse the cost of an employee's cell phone service plan, or Internet service at home to help carry out their employment duties. The portion used for employment purposes is not a taxable benefit. For more information, go to *Cellular phone and Internet services* [tinyurl.com/cra-cellphone — ed.].

Meal costs

Where an employer pays for, reimburses, or provides a reasonable allowance for meals to employees working at their regular place of employment during regular hours of work, the amount must be included in their employment income as a taxable benefit. However, the CRA's existing policies maintain that there are certain circumstances where an employer can provide an overtime meal or allowance [tinyurl.com/overtime-meals-cra — ed.], or a subsidized meal [tinyurl.com/cra-meals — ed.], without the employee receiving a taxable benefit.

Related Provisions: 6(1)(e) — Standby charge for automobile; 6(1)(e.1) — Group sickness or accident insurance plan — whether premiums taxable; 6(1)(f) — Insurance benefits received by employer; 6(1)(g) — Employment benefit plan; 6(1)(i) — Salary deferral arrangement payments; 6(1)(k), (l) — Automobile operating expense benefits; 6(1.1) — Parking costs are taxable benefits; 6(4) — Group term life insurance — taxable benefit; 6(6) — Employment at special work site or remote location; 6(7) — Cost of property or service includes taxes; 6(11)–(14) — Salary deferral arrangement; 6(15), (15.1) — Forgiveness of employee debt; 6(16) — Disability-related employment benefits; 6(18)(a) — No benefit from top-up disability payments where insurer insolvent; 6(19)–(22) — Benefit from reimbursement for loss in value of housing; 6(23) — Benefit from housing subsidy; 7(3) — No benefit from stock option agreement except as provided under s. 7; 15(5) — Automobile benefit to shareholder; 20.01 — Deduction to self-employed person for private health services plan premiums; 56(1)(a) — Amounts included in income; 56(1)(w) — Salary deferral arrangement; 56(1)(x)–(z) — Retirement compensation arrangement; 81(3.1) — No tax on allowance or reimbursement for part-time employee's travel expenses; 153(1)(a) — Withholding of tax by employer; 248(1) — "retiring allowance" excludes counselling services.

Notes: Taxable benefits are subject to source withholding. See Notes to 153(1).

See generally CRA Income Tax Folio S2-F3-C2 [temporarily withdrawn in 2017 and still under review: see under "Discounts" below] (which confusingly provides only "interpretation" and not administrative policy: VIEWS docs 2016-0662341E5, 2016-0669931E5); T4130 *Employer's Guide — Taxable Benefits*, which lists benefits considered non-taxable under administrative policy. For software that assists in the determination see *Taxable Benefits Navigator* at bluejlegal.com; on whether a benefit "primarily" benefits the employer, see *Taxable Benefits: Primary Beneficiary Classifier*.

Where the employee is also a shareholder, 15(1) may apply instead of 6(1)(a). See Notes to 15(1).

Statutory exemptions in 6(1)(a)(i)-(vi)

6(1)(a)(i): See "Critical illness", "Group sickness", "Health care plan" and "Pension contributions" below, and Notes to 248(1)"private health services plan". Despite the exclusions for group sickness/accident insurance premiums and group term life insurance premiums, these may be taxed by 6(1)(e.1) and 6(4).

Non-taxable benefits such as 6(1)(a)(i) remain non-taxable if provided after retirement: VIEWS doc 2008-0299611E5. Reimbursement of medical expenses in a wrongful dismissal settlement is a "retiring allowance" and not considered exempt under 6(1)(a)(i) or (iv): 2010-0373341C6. An employer's unfunded short-term disability policy was not a wage loss replacement plan, so payments from it would be taxable: 2010-0388721E5.

The Parliamentary Budget Officer estimates that taxing employer contributions to a private health services plan would increase federal revenues by $3.8 billion: *Taxation of employer-provided health benefits* (May 24, 2018, 22pp) [but this assumes employers would not stop providing this benefit].

For the meaning of "derived" in 6(1)(a)(i) and (iv), see Notes to 18.1(12).

6(1)(a)(ii): an RCA contribution is excluded from income: VIEWS doc 2017-0702061E5. Payments from the RCA are taxable: see Notes to 248(1)"retirement compensation arrangement".

6(1)(a)(iv) exempts counselling for health, retirement or re-employment. In CRA's view this does not extend to preventative or curative treatment: doc 2016-0624811C6 [CPA QC 2016 q.12]. (Such benefits can be offered by an ELHT since Feb. 27, 2018: 144.1(1)"designated employee benefit"(d).)

6(1)(a)(vi), along with the reference to a person not at arm's length in the opening words of 6(1)(a) (all enacted in 2013), preserves the exemption for scholarships for employees' dependants in *Bartley and DiMaria*, 2008 FCA 390, but only if the benefit is not a substitute for salary, and the employee and employer deal at arm's length. See Notes to 56(1)(n) and Income Tax Folio S2-F3-C2 ¶2.49 [temporarily withdrawn in 2017 and still under review: see under "Discounts" below].

6(1)(a)(vi) might exempt only tuition for *adult* children, since employer-paid tuition for a young child might be "received or enjoyed by" the taxpayer, who has a legal obligation to educate his/her children. However, VIEWS doc 2012-0435091M4 states that discounts by elementary or secondary schools to an employee's family members will be non-taxable if not a substitute for salary.

One could argue that any benefit required by a collective agreement is a "substitute for salary", since it results from union negotiations that included tradeoffs on salary.

For more on 6(1)(a)(vi) see docs 2011-0431581I7, 2016-0623221E5, 2016-0634001E5.

Interpretation of 6(1)(a) aside from the exemptions

"As a general rule, any material acquisition in respect of employment which confers an economic benefit on a taxpayer and does not constitute an exemption falls within paragraph 6(1)(a)... Where something is provided to an employee primarily for the benefit of the employer, it will not be a taxable benefit if any personal enjoyment is merely incidental to the business purpose": *McGoldrick*, 2004 FCA 189, para. 9. A payment is taxable if it confers an economic advantage on the employee: *Ransom*, [1967] C.T.C. 346 (Exch. Ct.); *Phillips*, [1994] 1 C.T.C. 383 (FCA); or increases the recipient's net worth: *Savage*, [1983] C.T.C. 393 (SCC); *Hoefele*, [1996] 1 C.T.C. 131 (FCA); *Touchette*, [1994] 1 C.T.C. 2674 (TCC); *Suffolk*, 2010 TCC 295. There need be only a small connection between a benefit and the employment for 6(1)(a) to apply: *Blanchard*, [1995] 2 C.T.C. 262 (FCA), para. 6; VIEWS doc 2011-0398651E5.

Where a specific rule (e.g. 6(1)(f) or 6(4)) applies to a particular kind of payment but does not tax it, the general rule in 6(1)(a) does not apply: *Tsiaprailis*, 2003 FCA 136, para. 5 (aff'd on other grounds 2005 SCC 8); *Scott*, 2017 TCC 224, paras. 87-90, 124. See also Notes to 9(1), under "General vs specific".

An employer-paid trip provided to an employee's friend is a benefit to the employee: 2013-0515621E5 (note the words in 6(1)(a) "or by a person who does not deal at arm's length with the taxpayer"); see also 56(2), 246.

Note that taxable benefits remain taxable even if the employer does not deduct the cost as an expense.

A benefit from employment is taxable regardless of who provides it (e.g. a shareholder of the employer: VIEWS doc 2013-0497101E5); and see "Credit card use" below. In *Shaw*, 2013 TCC 256, a business owner who had sold the company wanted to give ex-employees a bonus from his shareholder loan account, believing it to be tax-free because the company had paid tax on the income. The bonus was taxable. However, an employee who donates vacation time to a co-worker is taxed on the benefit under 56(2), and the co-worker is not taxed; even if the benefit arises from employment, CRA will not "assess the same income twice": 2013-0514321E5.

Accessibility measures in the workplace are non-taxable, but hearing aids provided to an employee are considered to benefit primarily the employee: VIEWS doc 2010-0356121I7.

Advertising with employer signs on the employee's vehicle: payments for such ads are taxable (VIEWS doc 2012-0465031E5, and this could make a car allowance "unreasonable" under 6(1)(b)(x)).

Agent fees paid by a hockey player's team to his agent were a taxable benefit to him: *Pavel Bure*, [2000] 1 C.T.C. 2407 (TCC).

Aircraft personal use (by employees or shareholders): as of 2018, see CRA policy AD-18-01 (tinyurl.com/cra-aircraft). Depending on the facts, the benefit (in CRA's view) is based on a charter flight price, a first-class ticket, or an "available for use" charge plus an "operating cost" charge [Tollstam, "Aircraft Benefits", 26(4) *Canadian Tax Highlights* (ctf.ca) 9 (April 2018)]. Pre-2018 policy: IT-160R3, VIEWS docs 2011-0405391E5, 2014-0527842I7.

Alarm system provided at employee's home: see "Security system" below.

Alcohol meter (alcohol ignition interlock device, required for an employee convicted of impaired driving) is considered to benefit the employee, so it is a taxable benefit: doc 2014-0521631I7.

Allowances: see 6(1)(b).

Apprenticeship credits (B.C. Training Tax Credit) are not taxable because the apprentice need not be an employee: VIEWS doc 2007-0248001E5.

Attendant expenses for a disabled employee: see 6(16).

Automobile use by an employee is excluded by 6(1)(a)(iii); see instead 6(1)(e) and 6(2) for the "standby charge", and 6(1)(k)-(l) for operating costs. For a vehicle that is not an "automobile" (see 248(1)), the 6(1)(a) benefit should be calculated using the rate in Reg. 7305.1: VIEWS docs 2005-0151141E5, 2008-0272741E5; in 2019-0798361E5, there was no benefit to maintenance employees taking trucks home when on standby shifts. Purchase of a car coming off lease, for less than its value, is a taxable benefit: 2010-0370211E5.

Awards: see "Gifts" below.

Babysitting: see "Child care" below.

Beer given by a brewery to its employees were taxable (the employer argued it was part of its quality control): *Steam Whistle Brewing*, 2012 CarswellNat 2772 (TCC).

Board and lodging, employer-paid rent, or housing benefits are usually taxable, even if the rent allows the employee to live at a second home near the employment: *Cameron*, 2007 TCC 691 (suggesting that *Paul's Hauling*, [1979] C.T.C. 2164 (TRB) is no longer good law); except at a "special work site" or remote location: 6(6), T4130. This can include worksite lodging provided by the employer's client: VIEWS doc 2012-0460031E5. If provided to group home employees required to live in the home temporarily, only the meals are taxable: 2005-0144811E5, 2007-0231811I7. Charging below-FMV rent is also a benefit: 2014-0518621I7. The benefit may be reduced for "loss of privacy and quiet enjoyment" (e.g., dons in a student residence who are constantly on call): T4130, docs 2004-0108921E5, 2005-0147831E5; *Schutz*, 2008 TCC 523 (detailed calculations of reductions); or where the employee's presence provides security to the worksite: 2010-0382541E5. For hotel and restaurant employees given a rent-free room, Revenu Québec uses a formula to calculate the benefit for provincial income tax: RQ Bulletin IMP. 37-1/R26. A rent allowance to cover the higher cost of housing for a transferred employee may be non-taxable: 2011-039317I17. Reasonable living costs during a transition period of a move for employment, while the employee seeks a permanent home, are non-taxable: 2016-0639401E5. In *Christensen*, 2012 TCC 42 (FCA appeal dismissed for delay A-78-12), condo purchase costs paid by C's employer (a company owned by his father) were taxable. See 8(1)(c) for clergy residence deduction.

Cell phones are non-taxable if primarily for business purposes: T4130, VIEWS doc 2011-0399171E5; and personal use is non-taxable if it does not increase charges beyond a reasonable fixed plan cost: 2005-0155975E5, tinyurl.com/cra-cellphone (Nov. 2018) (also says reimbursing the employee's cell phone cost is taxable, but paying for their plan is not taxable if needed at home for employment). Earlier docs: reimbursement of employee phone expenses incurred for employment is non-taxable, even if the employee gets a free phone from the phone plan: 2013-0489981E5; but the employee may need to provide receipts to prove business use: 2014-0553481I7. If a monthly amount is paid with no receipts, it is a taxable 6(1)(b) allowance: 2014-0552731E5, even if the employee gives the employer a copy of the contract: 2015-0588201E5.

Charging station for electric vehicles, provided to employees, is a benefit, but in VIEWS doc 2014-0553241E5, nothing needed to be included in employees' income because the benefit "seems to be nominal"; or if the car is used in employment duties, there may be no benefit: 2017-0703881C6 [2017 CPA Alberta q.17] [Tollstam, "Taxable Benefit: Electric Vehicle Charging Station?", 26(2) *Canadian Tax Highlights* (ctf.ca) 6-7 (Feb. 2018)].

Child care is non-taxable if provided at the workplace, managed directly by the employer, provided to all employees at minimal or no cost, *and* available only to employees: T4130. Third-party child care paid by an employer is taxable: VIEWS docs RCT 5-8359, 2002-0161525, 2005-0124661E5; but possibly not where due to unusual overtime demands: 2008-0297761E5 (the same applies to elder care), 2013-0499631E5 (additional costs where employee required to travel to different city). Free child care to employees of a child-care centre is taxable: 2010-0390931E5. Any child care included in income is considered paid by the employee for purposes of s. 63: 2010-0390931E5, 2014-0528601C6.

Christmas parties: see "Social events" below.

Clothing paid for or supplied by an employer is non-taxable if it is a uniform required for employees, or special or protective clothing (T4130, Income Tax Folio S2-F3-C2 ¶2.19 [temporarily withdrawn in 2017 and still under review: see under "Discounts" below], VIEWS docs 2004-0060001E5, 2004-0098471E5); or special street clothes for a plainclothes policeman: *Huffman*, [1990] 2 C.T.C. 132 (FCA). Otherwise it is taxable: docs 2006-0168521E5, 2018-0775391E5. A shirt with company logo, if required to be worn, is considered a "uniform": 2007-0237891E5. Where an employer provides a uniform and also pays for shoes that have no company logo, the shoes are considered taxable: 2014-0552421E5.

Club dues: see "Fitness" and "Recreational" below.

Coffee and tea provided to employees is not a taxable benefit: *Income Tax Technical News* 40 (overriding VIEWS doc 9921735). ITTN-40 was cancelled when Folio S2-F3-C2 was issued, but the Folio does not discuss this issue.

Commissions on insurance sales: see "Insurance agents' commissions" below.

Commuting assistance: see "Transportation" below.

Computers provided by an employer may be non-taxable, if provided to enhance employees' quality of life and computer literacy, under guidelines for employment-related training (*Technical News* 13, VIEWS docs 2000-0037233, 2000-0073973, 2006-0169531E5). See Brender & Rudick, "Getting Employees Connected to the Internet Without a Taxable Benefit", 12(8) *Taxation of Executive Compensation & Retirement* (Federated Press) 416-20 (April 2001). For restrictions on this tax-free benefit, see doc 2001-0090497. Computers provided at work are of course non-taxable, but CRA considers payments to employees for bringing their own computer or other device to work ("BYOD") to be taxable: 2011-0425801C6 [2011 CTF conf report, p.4:8-9, q.5] (this view might not be correct). During the COVID-19 crisis, CRA allows reimbursement of up to $500 for equipment to enable an employee to work at home as non-taxable: 2020-0845431C6 [2020 APFF q.5]; 2020-0848111E5, 2020-0861021C6 [2020 CTF q.13] (applies to office furniture also), and Announced Administrative Change above.

Convention attendance for a business convention may be non-taxable even if there is an element of personal benefit: *Romeril*, [1999] 1 C.T.C. 2535 (TCC).

Counselling services re re-employment or retirement, or mental or physical health, are non-taxable: 6(1)(a)(iv), T4130, Income Tax Folio S2-F3-C2 ¶2.46-2.48 [temporarily withdrawn in 2017 and still under review: see under "Discounts" below], VIEWS docs 2000-0042265, 2012-0454661I7.

Credit card use by an employee without employer permission is a taxable benefit received by the employee, even though not conferred by the employer: *Walford*, 2010 TCC 635; *Tremblay*, 2013 TCC 133. Credit cards provided by an employer with a discounted interest rate may create a taxable benefit under 80.4(1), 6(9) or 6(1)(a): VIEWS doc 2012-0463501E5.

Criminal background checks required to employ a person are considered to be for the employer's benefit and not taxable: VIEWS doc 2002-0133095.

Critical illness insurance may qualify as "group sickness or accident insurance", so the premiums may be exempt under 6(1)(a)(i): VIEWS docs 2002-0160155, 2003-0026385, 2003-0034505, 2003-0054571E5, 2004-0105491E5, 2005-0112781E5. Non-group critical illness insurance does not fall within this exception; and return of premiums to the employee on cancellation of the policy may be taxable: 2009-0342541M4. Where the employee is also a shareholder, see 2008-0278801C6 q.1.

Crowdfunding contributions from an arm's-length employer may be tax-free if provided "for humanitarian or philanthropic reasons" and are not disguised pay: VIEWS doc 2018-0779191E5 (see also Notes to 9(1), "Crowdfunding").

Damages for personal loss are non-taxable: VIEWS doc 2009-0322501E5 (and see Notes to 248(1)"retiring allowance"); but compensation for the employer's unilateral reduction of non-taxable benefits is taxable: 2009-0329441E5. Payment in settlement of a grievance is normally taxable (2010-0373831I7, 2013-0492281M4, 2017-0685961E5), but see "settlement of grievance" bullet in s. 3 Notes. See also 9(1) Notes at "Damages" re the *surrogatum* principle; and *Saunders*, 2020 TCC 114 (damages for failing to pay overtime were taxable).

Debt forgiveness is taxable: 6(15).

Disability insurance benefits (including lump-sum settlements) may be taxable: see 6(1)(f).

Disability-related employment benefits: see 6(16).

Disaster relief payments can be non-taxable if the payment's purpose is philanthropic and not based on employment factors, and the employer does not deduct it: docs 2011-0409751M4, 2013-0496281E5.

Discounts offered to all employees (not below employer's cost) have long been non-taxable: T4130. (Folio S2-F3-C2 ¶2.28 (2016) said they are taxable, but in Oct. 2017 there was a media firestorm about this and the Folio was taken down for "review". See now VIEWS docs 2017-0726641M4 and 2017-0729161M4, confirming the policy is unchanged; but the Folio was still undergoing "additional review" as of June 2021: 2018-0782361C6, tinyurl.com/s2f3c2.) This policy does not apply to discounts on homes or major home upgrades: 2009-0316531I7; or to services: 2017-0729441E5; but does apply to groceries: 2011-0430971E5. An appliance manufacturer's cash rebate to employees purchasing its appliances at retail is effectively a (non-taxable) discount: 2007-0260051E5 (but see also 2011-0399661E6). Third-party discounts negotiated (not paid for) by the employer are non-taxable: 2005-0154061E5; but software offered at deep discount to employees because the employer has bought the same software is taxable: 2011-0409721E5. See also "Insurance agents' commissions" and "Meals" below. Tuition discounts to employees' children: see discussion of 6(1)(a)(vi) above and 56(1)(n) Notes.

Driver's licence costs: see "Licensing" below.

Early Childhood Worker Grant Program payments, which require the worker to be a permanent employee of a day care, are taxable: VIEWS doc 2014-0555921I7.

Educational costs: see "Computers" above; "School fees" and "Tuition" below.

Elder care: see "Child care" above.

Financial assistance to employees from a US charity for a social-assistance purpose was ruled exempt in VIEWS doc 2010-0384571R3; in 2013-0495661I7, similar assistance to retired employees who needed support was taxable under 56(1)(u) with offsetting 110(1)(f) deduction.

Fitness, gym or health club memberships are generally considered to benefit the employee and so are taxable, even if part of an employee wellness program to increase job performance: VIEWS docs 2003-0035455, 2004-0063471E5, 2006-0187401E5, 2009-0312311E5, 2009-0343851E5, 2014-0561571I7, and even if the employer does not deduct the expense: 6(2) *Toronto Centre CRA & Tax Professionals Group* newsletter (June 2007); and even if a physical fitness test is required before hiring where it is not required to stay employed: 2013-0497401I7. However, if the job has stringent fitness requirements, a membership to maintain fitness levels might be non-taxable: 2006-0216251E5, 2012-0460021E5. If the facilities are made available to *all* employees, the benefit is not taxable: IT-148R3 para. 12, docs 2009-0330341C6, 2011-0427381E5, 2013-0477351E5. An in-house facility provided to employees of only one department is taxable: 2011-0431681E5 (for criticism see Basssindale & Kreklewetz, "Employer's In-House Fitness Centre", 13(1) *Tax for the Owner-Manager* (ctf.ca) 4-5 (Jan. 2013)). Where employees can choose to participate and pay a reduced fee, the benefit is the amount paid by the employer divided by the number of employees who participate: 2006-0189291E5. Third-party fitness discounts negotiated (not paid for) by the employer are non-taxable: 2005-0154061E5. The cost of a personal trainer or nutritionist should be non-taxable under 6(1)(a)(iv) (counselling re physical health) in the author's view, but CRA disagrees: 2013-0514521E5. See also "Recreational" below.

Flex credits under a flexible benefit plan: see IT-529 and VIEWS docs 2006-0187401E5, 2007-0238961E5, 2014-0558931E5 (benefits must be chosen before start of year). Tax may apply if an existing contract is renegotiated to convert salary to flex benefits: 2001-0116363, 2011-0404361E5; or if flex credits can be converted to additional salary: 2009-0342701E5. A feature allowing employees to opt in to the plan at various times does not put it offside: 2012-0467271E5. A change in benefits within a flex plan to increase tax-free benefits, to correct an genuine error, will have no adverse tax consequence: 2002-0123617. Allocation of a bonus to health spending account credits is considered taxable as of 2013: see under "Health care plan premiums" below. An allocation of incentive pay to flex credits can be tax-free: 2006-0197511R3. Flex credits may be allocated to (taxable) TFSA contributions: 2008-0272891E5. A payment to replace the employer's unilateral reduction of non-taxable benefits is taxable: 2009-0329441E5. See also "Health care" below.

Fraud or theft from the employer is either a taxable benefit or income from business: see 9(1) Notes at "Criminal activity" (e.g., *Poynton* case). In *Filion*, 2020 QCCQ 3024, there was no benefit when a Member of the (Quebec) National Assembly illegally spent his MNA allowance on his personal residence, because the Assembly stopped a later payment to recover the overspending, so he had no economic gain.

Frequent-flyer points (FFPs) earned on employer-paid travel are technically a taxable benefit when used (*Giffen and Mommersteeg*, [1995] 2 C.T.C. 2767 (TCC)), but no benefit will be assessed on points earned on an employee's personal credit card, used for business travel and reimbursed by the employer, as long as the plan is not converted to cash or used as alternate remuneration or for tax avoidance: tinyurl.com/s6loyalty (also VIEWS docs 2002-0168007, 2010-0353041E5, 2010-0378631E5, 2010-0383501E5). Benefits earned on a company credit card are still considered taxable. See also *Atsaidis*, [2000] 4 C.T.C. 2490 (TCC) (value of moving expenses paid with FFPs was not proven); *Johnson*, 2010 TCC 321 (payment with FFPs was payment of medical expenses); *Hope Air*, 2011 TCC 248 (payment with Aeroplan points was "consideration", for Air Travellers Security Charge).

Gift bags at awards shows are taxable in CRA's view: 9(1) *Toronto West Tax Practitioners' Consultation Group* newsletter 5 (Jan. 2008).

Gifts and awards to employees including for a birthday or Christmas, if non-cash, are non-taxable up to total $500 annually per employee, but any excess is taxable: canada.ca/taxes-gifts > Gifts, awards > Rules for gifts (includes "Answer a few questions" Q&A advisor). As well, a separate non-cash long service/anniversary award can be non-taxable up to $500: it must be for at least 5 years of service and 5 years since the last such award. (These administrative exemptions do not apply to non-arm's length employees, such as shareholders and family members of closely-held corporations. They do apply to elected officials: VIEWS doc 2012-0443331E5.) In calculating the $500, mandatory environmental fees included in an item's purchase price are included: 2012-0466681E5. A family ski pass can qualify: 2015-0571471E5. Allowing the employee to choose from 15 non-cash gifts all valued under $500 is allowed: 2010-0359501E5 (this may override 2003-0004005, 2003-0029165, 2007-0247981E5); but not where the employee can accumulate points and choose from a catalogue of 40 services: 2012-0440731E5. These rules do not apply to cash or near-cash (e.g., "Companybucks" redeemable at employer's store (2011-0394901E5); gift certificates (2005-0153611E5), gold nuggets, securities, anything easily convertible to cash, or meals (2007-0247981E5)). (TEI has asked CRA to change this policy and allow retailer gift cards: Feb. 9, 2016 letter.) Points that can be redeemed for gifts might not be taxable until redeemed: 2007-0232051E5, 2013-0479271E5. An award for positive impact on the community, open only to employees, is taxable: 2013-0501351R5. A compassionate gift to an employee's child's RESP following a workplace accident is taxable: 2014-0526781E5. If the employee forgoes an award and the employer donates to charity instead, 2013-0510791E5 says 56(2) applies and the excess over $500 is a taxable benefit; but 2012-0440821E5 had said that as long as the employer gets the donation receipt, there is no taxable benefit. Performance-related rewards (for achieving an employment-related economic goal, e.g. sales targets) are always taxable: 2005-0161811E5, 2006-0181011E5, 2006-020601E5, 2011-0405361E5, 2011-0423981E5, 2012-0434471I7; *Shanahan*, 2011 TCC 530 (trip to Las Vegas for long service). For awards from prize draws and social committees see CRA page tinyurl.com/prizedraws; 2008-0293781E5, 2014-0534001E5; a door prize at an employer-held social event is likely taxable (to the employee if the spouse wins it): 2012-0442171E5. A gift from a customer is taxable even if the employee gives it to the employer's social committee: 2010-0388581E5 (if this arrangement is mandatory, the Courts might disagree on the basis that the gift was received as agent for the committee). (See Notes to 9(1) re deductibility to the employer.)

Group sickness or accident insurance premiums are exempt from 6(1)(a) under 6(1)(a)(i), but may be taxed under 6(1)(e.1). A plan with more than 2 employees can be a group plan even if the members have different employers: 2012-0465891E5. If travel accident insurance is not under 6(1)(a)(i), it may still be considered paid for the employer's benefit (thus non-taxable) if it is needed to get employees to work in high-risk places: 2016-0668351E5.

Guarantee of an employee's debt may be a taxable benefit, but in *Biniaz*, [2007] 1 C.T.C. 2469 (TCC), an employer's co-signing a car loan, paid out when the employee went bankrupt, was not taxable even though the employee later worked for free for the employer in gratitude.

Health and welfare trusts (HWTs) created before Feb. 28, 2018 can (through 2022) be a conduit for tax-free benefits (group sickness/accident insurance, private health services plan, group term life): see Income Tax Folio S2-F1-C1; VIEWS docs 2003-0051921R3, 2005-0121151E5, 2005-0117081E5, 2005-0129961E5, 2006-0206951E5, 2009-0343541E5, 2010-0355041M4, 2010-0355521E5, 2010-0376321E5, 2013-0502031E5; 2013-0506691I7 (HWT can deduct net capital losses); 2016-0645581E5. A long-term disability plan can be held under a HWT: 2010-0374891E5. A HWT can distribute funds to a government on windup: 2017-0702861E5. A 15(1) shareholder benefit can arise if insurance is provided only to a shareholder: *Spicy Sports*, 2004 TCC

463; but see *O'Flynn*, 2005 TCC 230, where amounts are received *qua* employee, and Baldry, "Too Good to be True?", 1(1) *It's Personal* (Carswell) 5 (Nov. 2007). A non-resident HWT may be subject to 75(2): 2004-0057511I7. See also Notes to 18(9), 248(1)"private health services plan"; and 144.1 for employee life and health trusts (ELHTs). See also *Canadian Health Insurance Tax Guide: Health and Welfare Trusts,* tinyurl.com/sunlife-taxguides; Geddes, "Health and Welfare Trusts", 15(7) *Taxation of Executive Compensation & Retirement* (Federated Press) 386-92 (March 2004). By the end of 2022, a HWT wanting to continue tax-free benefits must change its terms to qualify as an ELHT under 144.1(2) (until then it can elect under 144.1(14)-(15) to continue as is); or it can transfer its property to an ELHT under 144.1(16). See also Dollar, "Benefits Planning for Key Employees After Health and Welfare Trusts", XXIII(2) *Insurance Planning* (Federated Press) 2-13 (2018); BDO, "The End of Health and Welfare Trusts", tinyurl.com/bdo-hwt.

Health care plan premiums and benefits (private plans such as Blue Cross) are non-taxable: 6(1)(a)(i); 248(1)"private health services plan"; IT-339R2; VIEWS doc 2006-0175931E5 (including where reimbursed: doc 2009-0322451E5, but not if employer simply gives employee a cheque at year-end: 2010-0368871E5). The plan must be a group plan, not just for a "group" of one person: *Meyer*, [1977] C.T.C. 2581 (TRB); *Syrydiuk*, 2010 TCC 520; 2006-0174121C6; but an individual policy consistent with those for other employees may qualify: 2006-0214141E5. Reimbursement of premiums paid by an employee is non-taxable: 2007-0241701I7. Management and funding of the plan by the employer is not a taxable benefit: 2009-0311181R3. Payments to an insolvent employer's retirees in lieu of continued health plan coverage were non-taxable: 2010-0385181R3, 2012-0464921R3. Public health care premiums, and medical expenses paid by an employer, are taxable: T4130 (including the Ontario Health Premium: 2006-0181751E5, 2011-0404371E5). If part of salary is explicitly changed to health plan premiums, they may still be taxable in CRA's view: 9721115F, 2001-0080065, 2014-0528211E5. Before 2013, a bonus could be redirected to a tax-free health spending account: 2005-0160701R3, 2005-0161311E5, 2005-0163541R3, 2006-0169911R3, 2006-0207381R3, 2006-0208881R3, 2007-0255251E5, 2007-0257631R3; Boyd, "Converting Taxable Bonuses to Tax-free Credits Under Health Care Spending Accounts", 19(9) *Taxation of Executive Compensation & Retirement* (Federated Press) 999-1000 (May 2008). However, as of 2013 this is considered taxable as "foregone cash remuneration": 2011-0397751R3, 2012-0426571C6 [2011 CTF conf report p.4:7-8, q.10], 2012-0440721E5, 2012-0455951E5. The employee can claim the medical expense credit for taxable benefits from medical expenses provided by the employer: 118.2(3)(a). See also 144.1. (Self-employed persons can deduct the premiums in certain cases: see 20.01.)

Health club memberships: see "Fitness" above.

Home office equipment: CRA allows reimbursement of up to $500 to enable an employee to work at home during COVID-19. See Announced Administrative Change above, and VIEWS docs 2020-0848111E5 (telework equipment), 2020-0861021C6 [2020 CTF q.13].

Housing benefits: see "Board and lodging" above and "Moving expenses" below.

Income tax paid by the employer to cover an employee's tax payable on taxable benefits is itself a taxable benefit: VIEWS doc 2006-0188141E5.

Insurance premiums: see "Critical illness"; "Disability insurance"; "Group sickness"; "Life insurance"; "Pet care"; "Professional membership".

Insurance agents' commissions for policies purchased on themselves may be non-taxable if they are minor: Guide T4130; tinyurl.com/s6discounts; docs 9410837, 9913907F, 2001-0070655F, 2006-0197161C6, 2009-032451117; but were taxable as business income in *Bilodeau*, 2009 TCC 315, *Bégin*, 2012 TCC 18 and *Ghumman*, 2019 TCC 125, with no deduction for premiums paid to earn the income: Wark, "Recent Court Decisions on Insurance Commissions", XVIII(1) *Insurance Planning* (Federated Press) 1129-32 (2011). The administrative exemption applies only to *life* insurance, not home or auto: 2010-0374911E5, 2017-0729441E5. Post-*Bilodeau*, CRA noted that its position was "not intended to apply where the insurance was obtained for investment or business purposes" or if the commission income is "significant": 2010-0359451C6, 2010-0388111M4, 2011-0407121E5, 2011-0431701E5, 2012-0436141C6. See also Singh & Welch, "Interpretation Bulletin IT-470R", 20(7) *Taxation of Executive Compensation & Retirement* (Federated Press) at 1123-24 (March 2009).

Internet service at home is non-taxable if primarily to benefit the employer: T4130 (and provided it is essential for the job: VIEWS doc 2006-0174521E5). If it is partly for personal use, the personal-use portion is taxable: 2010-0377261E5. See also tinyurl.com/cra-cellphone.

Interest-free loans: see "Loans" below.

Law Society dues: see "Professional membership dues" below.

Legal fees paid by an employer are usually non-taxable if related to an employee act during the course of employment duties: VIEWS docs 2003-0035475, 2005-0131331E5, 2011-0406611I7, IT-99R5 para. 32; but possibly not if they are to defend criminal charges: 2010-0391441E5. (Disclosing details of legal fees to a CRA auditor should not waive solicitor-client privilege: see Notes to 232(2).) In *Bilodeau*, [2007] 2 C.T.C. 2111 (TCC), a company paid legal fees to successfully defend its CEO accused of sexual assault while on a business trip. The Court ruled this was not a taxable benefit: the acquittal was evidence that he had not committed an offence, and the CEO's critical role in the business gave the company a *bona fide* business interest in establishing his innocence. Reimbursement of legal fees in a settlement re a wage loss replacement plan is considered taxable even though part of the settlement is exempt under 6(1)(f): 2011-0408071E5.

Licensing and testing fees (e.g. for private investigators) are non-taxable if they primarily benefit the employer: VIEWS doc 2010-0377631E5. Drivers' licence cost reimbursement is considered taxable: 2011-0424791E5.

Life insurance that is not group term insurance is a taxable benefit: VIEWS docs 2008-0278501E5, 2008-0265651E5; but not if it is for employees working in a high-risk zone which nullifies their own life insurance, so that it is for the employer's benefit: 2009-0322781E5.

Loans at less than the prescribed rate of interest normally create a deemed interest benefit but may be offset by an interest deduction: 80.4, 80.5 (see T4130). If the employee is also a shareholder, the *entire* loan may be taxable: 15(2). Loan forgiveness is taxable: see 6(15).

Lodging: see "Board and lodging" above.

Lottery winnings are usually non-taxable (see Notes to 40(2)(f)), but gift certificates won in an employer-funded lottery open only to employees are taxable: VIEWS doc 2007-0227261E5.

Loyalty programs: see "Frequent-flyer points" above.

Meals are non-taxable if the employee pays a reasonable amount to cover the food cost: tinyurl.com/cra-meals, T4130; VIEWS docs 2017-0726641M4, 2017-0729161M4. Meals that primarily benefit the employee are taxable: 2011-0410781I7, 2013-0487931E5. Meal reimbursement may be non-taxable if it is for the employer's benefit: 2006-0187761E5 (inspectors at job sites); 2015-0587131E5 (meals while travelling). Meals in a casino staff cafeteria were a taxable benefit where the employee disliked them but had to eat them because outside food was prohibited: *McGoldrick*, 2004 FCA 189; but were only half taxed based on the employee's evidence that he ate in the cafeteria only half the time: *McGoldrick*, 2005 TCC 735. For hotel and restaurant employees, Revenu Québec uses a formula to calculate the benefit for provincial income tax: RQ Interpretation Bulletin IMP. 37-1/R26. For meal allowances (including overtime meal allowances) see Notes to 6(1)(b). Gala fundraiser tickets for a school's teachers, paid for by unsolicited parent donations, are non-taxable: 2013-0490621E5.

Medical examinations by an employer's physician are considered a taxable benefit when provided only to select executives at their request (but may create a medical expense credit under 118.2(2)(a)), but not when provided to new employees as a condition of employment: VIEWS docs 2001-0092805, 2013-0508501E5.

Medical expenses: see "Health care" above.

Membership fees are not taxable if primarily for the employer's benefit: VIEWS doc 2012-0453001E5. See also under "Professional" and "Reimbursement" below.

Moving expenses paid by an employer are partly non-taxable if the move is for the employer's benefit: see T4130 (the move can be from outside Canada: VIEWS docs 2006-0202091E5); or where the expenses would be deductible under 62(1): 2007-0236051E5, 2009-0315101E5, 2009-0342651E5, 2010-0369741I7, 2010-0379001E5, 2011-0427911E5, 2012-044536117; 2016-0629351E5 (public utility transferring technician to remote area is primary beneficiary of the move); 2017-0701181E5. Timing of the reimbursement (e.g., before the move) does not affect this: 2019-0821351E5. Purchase of new furniture by the employer is a taxable benefit: 2014-0523711E5. Reimbursement of a move from a remote location on retirement is non-taxable: 2011-0413871E5. *Moving allowances* of up to $650 may be non-taxable: see Notes to 6(1)(b). Other relocation expenses are taxable, e.g. paying the employee's spouse for a period until the spouse finds employment in the new city (2008-0276771E5); reimbursement of unused school fees (2009-0331701E5). Reimbursement of the cost of home appliances compatible with Canada's electrical system was taxable: *Suffolk*, 2010 TCC 295. See also 6(19)–(23) re home relocation loans and reimbursements.

Municipal officers and elected officials are subject to the same rules as employees: VIEWS doc 2012-0443331E5.

Parking paid by the employer may be a taxable benefit; see 6(1.1); 6(16) for employees with disabilities; and Announced Administrative Change above re 2020 (COVID-19). Bicycle stand parking is non-taxable: doc 2015-0595681C6 [2015 APFF q.20].

Parties: see "Social events" below.

Passport application fees for the employer's benefit, such as for a pilot or flight attendant, are a non-taxable benefit: VIEWS doc 2009-0337371E5. See also "Work permit" below.

Pension contributions are non-taxable if the plan is a registered pension plan, including a multi-employer plan: 6(1)(a)(i), VIEWS doc 2006-0212781E5. Pension or social security contributions to a foreign plan may be exempted by tax treaty: 2005-0151041E5 (France), 2012-0432281E5 (401(k) plan — Canada-US treaty Art. XVIII:10). Reimbursement of employee contributions is taxable: 2011-0407931I7.

Pet care or veterinary costs insurance is a taxable benefit: VIEWS doc 2009-0350391E5.

Phones: see "Cell phones" above.

Private health services plans: see "6(1)(a)(i)" above, and Notes to 248(1)"private health services plan".

Prizes: see "Gifts" above.

Professional membership dues and liability insurance premiums are not taxable if the employer is the primary beneficiary: IT-158R2; tinyurl.com/s6prof; VIEWS doc 2015-0608931I7. Professional initiation or admission fees are considered taxable: 2004-0058301E5. Law society dues paid by the employer were taxable for a Crown lawyer in *Tremblay*, 2002 CanLII 63208 (Que. CA), but not for a tribunal member in *Pelletier*, 2018 QCCQ 1655, as he did not practise law (both cases re Quebec income tax).

Protection of employees: see "Security" below.

RRSP contributions by the employer are a taxable benefit, but not where withheld from the employee's (taxable) salary as source deductions: T4130. RRSP, TFSA and LIRA management fees are a taxable benefit, but not DPSP or SERP fees: VIEWS doc 2014-0528521E5.

Rebates: see "Discounts" above.

Recreational facilities are taxable unless provided by the employer to all employees (whether or not in-house) and done principally for the employer's advantage: T4130, tinyurl.com/s6rec; VIEWS doc 2015-0595681C6 [2015 APFF q.20]. This can include a ski resort pass: 2015-0571471E5. For criteria to decide whether a golf club membership is for the employer's benefit, see 2007-0226111I7; in *Rachfalowski*, [2009] 1 C.T.C. 2073 (TCC), a golf club membership the employee did not want was non-taxable. Reimbursements of employee recreational facility dues are normally taxable: T4130, doc 2009-0329531E5. See also "Fitness" above.

Registered plan contributions (e.g., group RRSP) that are restorative due to employer error, and not deducted by the employer, are considered non-taxable damages for a tort: VIEWS doc 2012-0457981E5.

Reimbursement (R) of employment-related expenses (including for a charity's volunteers, who are considered "employees") is generally non-taxable: IT-522R para. 51; *Ransom*, [1967] C.T.C. 346 (Exch. Ct.); *Blanchard*, [1995] 2 C.T.C. 262 (FCA), para. 8; VIEWS docs 2002-0165645, 2005-0118981E5, 2005-0136951E5. R without receipts is an allowance and may be taxable under 6(1)(b): 2017-0682891E5. R of association membership is non-taxable if the employee needs it as part of the job description: 2008-0267901E5. R of home office expenses for corporation: May 2005 Alberta CPA Roundtable (tinyurl.com/cra-abtax), q. 15. R of political donations a company asked its employees to make was non-taxable: *Bernier*, 2007 QCCA 1003 (leave to appeal denied 2008 CarswellQue 338 (SCC)). R of relocated employee's foreign tax: see "Tax equalization payment" below. R of tax advisory services to help federal government employees with the Phoenix payroll disaster is non-taxable: 2017-0699741I7 (see also 153(3.1)). R of union members' expenses doing work for the union was taxable: *Vachon Estate [Conseil central]*, 2009 FCA 375 (leave to appeal denied 2010 CarswellNat 936 (SCC)). R of 1998 ice storm losses: *Ice Storm Employee Benefits Remission Order*. R to public-office holder for costs of blind trust to prevent conflict of interest is non-taxable if it matches actual costs: 2008-0274211E5. R by an insurer to cover costs resulting from the insurer thinking payments were not taxable under 6(1)(f) is itself considered taxable: 2013-0479111C6. R of mileage: see "Travel expense reimbursement" below. R of relocation-related expenses: see "Moving expenses" above. See also "Computers" and "Home office equipment" above; "Tuition reimbursement" below, and Notes to 5(1). CRA claims in Folio S2-F3-C2 ¶2.16 [temporarily withdrawn in 2017 and still under review: see under "Discounts" above] that "detailed receipts" are required for a R to be valid, and see 2016-0670911C6 [2016 TEI q.2b].

Relocation costs: see "Moving expenses" above.

Rent: see "Board and lodging" above.

Rewards to employees: see "Gifts and awards" above.

Scholarships: see Notes to 56(1)(n) and 56(3), and "Tuition reimbursement" below.

School fees reimbursement for an employee's children are normally taxable (VIEWS docs 2009-0320591E5, 2010-0372541E5; *Detchon*, [1996] 1 C.T.C. 2475 (TCC)) but may be non-taxable for employees posted outside Canada, for the closest suitable English or French school: T4130, Income Tax Folio S2-F3-C2 ¶2.49 [temporarily withdrawn in 2017 and still under review: see under "Discounts" above] (and see discussion of 6(1)(a)(vi) at beginning of these Notes). School fees were non-taxable when the employee was posted abroad rotationally and enrolled his children in a private school to ensure continuity in their education: *Guay*, [1997] 3 C.T.C. 276 (FCA); but once his work was no longer rotational, reimbursement was taxable: *Guay*, 2005 FCA 97. See also 6(1)(b)(ix). Tuition reimbursement for a foreign private school in a country where expatriates' children are not allowed into the public school system is non-taxable: doc 2004-0088561E5. Post-secondary tuition for employees' children: see discussion of 6(1)(a)(vi) above and Notes to 56(1)(n). School services provided by the employer in a remote location are non-taxable: T4130. See also "Tuition" below.

Security system provided at employee's home (including monitoring costs) and other reasonable protective measures are non-taxable (including where reimbursed by the employer) if safety risks arise from the employment: VIEWS docs 2010-0382741E5, 2011-0427391I7.

Snow clearing reimbursement for a school bus driver who takes the bus home is non-taxable, but is taxable as additional remuneration if the driver clears the snow: VIEWS doc 2011-0409231M4.

Social events are accepted as non-taxable if cost does not exceed $150/guest as of 2018: tinyurl.com/cra-social. The $150 includes sales taxes; the event must be open to all employees at the branch or division. From 1998-2017, the limit was $100. See T4130; *Income Tax Technical News* 15; VIEWS docs 2005-0161811E5, 2008-0294521E5, 2010-0373451C6; 2015-0595681C6 [2015 APFF q.20] (this policy covers a team lunch and a "5 to 7" after-work event); 2017-0731251I7 ($150 calculation is based on number of people attending, not number invited [note this means that if not enough people show up, the event becomes taxable!]; if cost is higher, invited person who does not attend has no benefit). Legally, social events are taxable: *Dunlap*, [1998] 4 C.T.C. 2644 (TCC).

Stock options and issuance of shares: see Notes to 7(1). Surrender of stock options (where not taxable under 7(1)) is not a 6(1)(a) benefit due to 7(3)(a): *Rogers Estate*, 2014 TCC 348, para. 38 (FCA appeal discontinued A-533-14).

Tax equalization payment covering higher tax payable in another country by a relocated employee is taxable: *Gernhart*, [1998] 2 C.T.C. 102 (FCA); VIEWS doc 2013-0495091E5.

Tax rate equalization payments for a multinational's employees assigned to different countries, from a fund paid for by employees, are not a taxable benefit: VIEWS doc 2003-0020053.

Theft from the employer: see "Fraud" above.

Tickets to concerts, games, etc. are non-taxable if the employee needs to attend for business purposes: see discussion in T4130.

Tool replacement, allowance or cost reimbursement is taxable: T4130, VIEWS doc 2005-0117441E5. This includes a Palm Pilot: doc 2004-0096221E5. Rental payments to an employee for the use of his tools are considered employment income, not rental income: 2012-0442231E5.

Training expenses: see "Tuition reimbursement" below.

Transportation passes for bus, rail and airline employees (including directors: VIEWS doc 2012-0471161I7) are taxable only if space is confirmed, and not taxable at all for retired airline employees: tinyurl.com/s6passes, 2016-0662341E5, 2016-0669931E5. (For ferry employees, this applies only to passenger transport, not vehicles: 2008-0298021E5.) This exemption applied to spouses only before 2010. It does not apply to employees of (or who move to) another city department: 2001-0099547, 2008-0267971E5, 2012-0471161I7. (As reported in the *Toronto Star* May 1, 2010, CRA determined that Toronto city councillors' free "Metropasses" were taxable, but agreed not to assess 2006-07 if their 2010 passes were immediately cancelled.) Transportation of at least 80km for an employee to get to work may be non-taxable: T4130. Transit passes can be non-taxable if the employer is the primary beneficiary: 2009-0315071E5. A group discount on transit passes, negotiated but not paid for by the employer, is non-taxable: 2011-0394411E5. Occasional commuting assistance (e.g., taxi) is non-taxable if the employee is required to work at least 3 hours overtime after regular work hours, and public transport is not available or the employee's physical safety is at risk: 2004-0076281E5. Taxi rides home from the nearest bus stop are otherwise taxable: 2006-0203901I7, as are taxi rides for bus drivers who start work early or finish late: 2012-0471161I7. See also 6(6) re transportation to a special or remote work site, 6(16) for disabled employees, and "Travel" below. See also Announced Administrative Change above re 2020 (COVID-19).

Travel allowances: see 6(1)(b). For deductibility of automobile allowances to employers see 18(1)(r).

Travel paid by the employer (including a rental car) while working away from home is not taxable: VIEWS docs 2004-0084201E5, 2011-0411961C6, 2013-0507421E5; and see Notes to 6(6). Reimbursement of regular travel to work is taxable: 2006-0216791E5, 2012-0432671E5, 2012-0438001E5, 2014-0518901E5, 2014-0521201E5 (see also Notes to 8(1)(h.1)). A helicopter pilot was taxed on flights every 6 weeks from Quebec to his Alberta work base: *Léonard*, 2008 TCC 321. Reimbursement of gas costs to encourage car-pooling and reduce emissions is taxable: 2011-0411941C6. Travel expenses paid for a spouse and children are taxable: T4130; but CRA declined to speculate on this situation for a university professor posted abroad for months, without specific facts: 2018-0768781C6 [2018 APFF q.7]. A business-class ticket is not taxable if the travel is for the employer's business; but paying for 2 economy tickets (i.e. also for the spouse), with total cost less than 1 business-class ticket, creates a taxable benefit: 2006-0210291E5. Travel for the employer's benefit is non-taxable: *Lowe*, [1996] 2 C.T.C. 33 (FCA) (guiding employee incentive trips); *Agostini*, 2009 TCC 87 (trade show); *Protection incendie Ideal*, 2016 QCCQ 6034, paras. 135-150 (hunting trips); *Aubin (Gagnon)*, 2019 QCCQ 6243 (client conference attended with spouse, despite ancillary sightseeing). On how to determine whether the travel primarily benefits the employer: 2016-0640201E5. Where an incentive trip is partly for business purposes, the personal portion is taxable: 2012-0472211I7, 2016-0670911C6 [2016 TEI q.2a] (fully taxable if paid to a corporation, so a T4A is required for the full trip value: 2014-0547931I7). See also Announced Administrative Change above re 2020 (COVID-19).

Travel reward points: see "Frequent-flyer points" above.

Tuition reimbursement or training expenses for an employee taking courses primarily to benefit the employer are non-taxable if the employee agrees to continue employment for a reasonable time afterwards: T4130, *Technical News* 13, VIEWS docs 2004-0066031E5, 2007-0228581E5, 2007-0230121I7, 2009-0344981E5, 2012-0435511E5, 2013-0484631E5, 2013-0500991E5; 2014-0529881I7 (employee cannot opt to treat the tuition as taxable and claim the tuition tax credit); 2014-0563251E5, 2018-0739061E5; or if it is a "legitimate commercial transaction": 2005-0152801E5. See also CRA employers' notice "Tuition fees, scholarships, bursaries", doc 2009-07-24 on *TaxPartner* and *Taxnet Pro*. The same applies to employer contributions to a professional development (PD) fund for employees, or a training fund for laid-off workers: 2006-0172701E5, 2009-0308741E5, 2012-0466421E5. Payments to employees for PD are taxable if not a reimbursement of actual costs: 2008-0295321E5; unless the training primarily benefits the employer: 2010-0371431E5. CRA opines that if a bonus is given up in exchange for a non-taxable scholarship (see Notes to 56(1)(n)), this will be taxable: 2008-0300041E5. Tuition reimbursement or bursary to a student who will later work for the employer is likely taxable under 6(3) or 6(1)(a): 2011-0424601E5. A scholarship available only to employees is taxable, unless the employer is the primary beneficiary of the education: 2013-0494891E5. See also "Computers" and "School fees" above.

Uniforms: see "Clothing" above.

Vehicles provided by the employer: see Notes to 6(2).

Volunteers (e.g., missionaries) paid living expenses are taxable: VIEWS doc 2005-0135801E5.

Wage loss replacement plans: see 6(1)(e.1) and 6(1)(f).

Weight loss programs arguably should be tax-free under 6(1)(a)(iv). CRA considers them taxable if counselling services are only "part of a weight management program": VIEWS docs 2005-0109731E5, 2013-0511191E5.

Work permit and visa fees are not a taxable benefit, but permanent resident authorization fees are considered taxable when paid by the employer: VIEWS docs 2003-0004715, 2003-0054021E5. See also "Passport application fees" above.

Payments to an employee's family members are taxable under 6(1)(a) or 56(2), but one-time humanitarian assistance to family members affected by hurricanes and typhoons is non-taxable: VIEWS doc 2009-0349581E5.

See also Siegmund, "Planes, Trains & Automobiles: A Journey Through Employee Benefits", 12 *Canadian Petroleum Tax Journal* (1999); Ebel & Stewart, "Update on Employee Stock Options and Employee Benefits", 2002 Cdn Tax Foundation conference report at 27:24-47; Brooks, "The Taxation of In-Kind Benefits", 49(2) *McGill Law Journal* 255-307 (2004) (ssrn.com/abstract=714662); Taylor, "Checklist of Tax-preferred Employee Compensation", 16(3) *Taxation of Executive Compensation & Retirement* (Federated Press) 468-75 (Oct. 2004); Samtani, "Not All Fringe Benefits Are Created Equal", 18(1) *TECR* 699-709 (July/Aug. 2006); Singh & Welch, "Interpretation Bulletin IT-470R", 20(7) *TECR* 1120-24 (March 2009); Allard, "Tax-effective Fringe Benefits for Executives", 20(10) and 21(1) *TECR* 1163-66, 1171-78 (June & July/Aug. 2009).

CRA conducts "Employer Compliance Audits" that focus on two main questions: the value of benefits, and "who is the primary beneficiary?". The most common adjustments relate to salary expenses, employment status (see Notes to 248(1)"employee"), automobile benefits (6(2)), parking benefits (6(1.1)) and vehicle allowance benefits (6(1)(b)). [Presentation at CRA Toronto Centre tax professionals group, Nov. 2/11] *Income Tax Audit Manual* §12.2.2 lists the most common taxable benefits that auditors look for: personal use of employer assets such as automobiles, aircraft, vacation properties, condominiums; allowances paid to employees; employer-provided parking; interest-free or low-interest loans; stock purchase options; incentives or prizes; gifts; relocation expenses; employer-paid insurance premiums; wage loss replacement plans; rent-free or low-rent housing; retirement allowances; termination payments; employer contributions to retirement plans; tuition fees, scholarships and bursaries where the primary beneficiary is the employee.

Employer Requested Resolution (ERR): Before 2007, CRA policy allowed large employers to pay employees' tax and interest resulting from taxable benefit errors; these were called "Negotiated Settlements", renamed ERR in 2001. This was intended to be a one-time adjustment "to assist in enhancing future compliance", to reduce the cost of amending hundreds or thousands of T4s and reassessing T1s. The ERR policy was cancelled, per Communication TSDMB-2007-113, Nov. 26, 2007, and an employer can no longer make a payment in lieu of amending employees' T4s. (*VDP Operations Manual* (2015), §1.9.9)

When an employee disagrees with an amount on a T4 and cannot resolve the matter with the employer, CRA states: "the employee can request an Employee Complaint Registration Form from Individual Income Tax Enquiries ... This Form is provided to the employee and he or she then returns the completed form to his or her tax centre": VIEWS doc 2011-0422901E5. (If the matter is not resolved quickly, the employee should file an objection by the deadline in 165(1) to preserve appeal rights.) The T4 is not binding: see Notes to 5(1).

Valuing a benefit for 6(1)(a): use fair market value, not the employer's cost: *Spence*, 2011 FCA 200 (reduced tuition for a teacher's children) (overruling *Detchon*, [1996] 1 C.T.C. 2475); *Schroter*, 2010 FCA 98 (parking); *Anthony*, 2011 FCA 336 (parking for teachers); *Steam Whistle Brewing*, 2012 CarswellNat 2772 (TCC) (beer); Folio S2-F3-C2 ¶2.26 [temporarily withdrawn in 2017 and still under review: see under "Discounts" above]; VIEWS docs 2010-0374311E5 (personal use of corporate asset); 2016-0624811C6 [CPA QC 2016 q.12] (Employee Assistance Program services). See also *Wisla*, [2000] 1 C.T.C. 2823 (TCC) (gold ring given by employer for long service was valued at scrap because it was stamped with employer's logo); 2010-0360261E5 (lottery win on employer-bought ticket is valued as of when it was given to employee, e.g. $5); 2010-0385881E5 (value of shuttle from home to work); Chen and Timm, "Valuation of Non-Cash Wages", 10(5) *Taxation of Executive Compensation & Retirement* (Federated Press) 73-88 (1999); Truster, "Taxable Benefits: How Much is Taxable?", 14(2) *Tax for the Owner-Manager* (ctf.ca) 2 (April 2014). For employer merchandise see "Discounts" above.

A person managing a company for no remuneration may be an "employee" for purposes of 6(1)(a): VIEWS doc 2007-0243871I7.

GST or HST must be remitted on some employee benefits. See *Excise Tax Act* s. 173 in *The Practitioner's Goods and Services Tax Annotated*, or guide T4130, Chapter 5.

Employers can generally deduct employee benefit expenses whether or not the benefit is taxable. See Notes to 9(1) under "Employee benefits".

6(1)(a) amended by 2012 budget bill #2 (effective Dec. 14, 2012, to refer to a PRPP), 2002-2013 technical bill (for benefits after Oct. 30, 2011), 2010 budget bill #2, 1993 and 1991 technical bills, 1989 Budget.

Regulations: 200(2)(g), 200(3) (information returns).

Remission Orders: *Ice Storm Employee Benefits Remission Order*, P.C. 1998-2047.

Income Tax Folios: S1-F2-C3: Scholarships, research grants and other education assistance [replaces IT-340R]; S2-F1-C1: Health and welfare trusts [replaces IT-85R2]; S3-F9-C1: Lottery winnings, miscellaneous receipts, and income (and losses) from crime [replaces IT-185R, IT-213R, IT-256R, IT-334R2].

Interpretation Bulletins: IT-54: Wage loss replacement plans — changes in plans established before June 19, 1971 (cancelled); IT-63R5: Benefits, including standby charge for an automobile, from the personal use of a motor vehicle supplied by an employer; IT-113R4: Benefits to employees — stock options; IT-160R3: Personal use of aircraft (cancelled); IT-167R6: Registered pension plans — employee's contributions; IT-339R2: Meaning of "private health services plan"; IT-357R2: Expenses of training; IT-365R2: Damages, settlements and similar receipts; IT-389R: Vacation-with-pay plans established under collective agreements; IT-421R2: Benefits to individuals, corporations and shareholders from loans or debt; IT-428: Wage loss replacement plans; IT-432R2: Benefits conferred on shareholders; IT-470R: Employees' fringe benefits; IT-502: Employee benefit plans and employee trusts; IT-529: Flexible employee benefit programs.

I.T. Technical News: 6 (payment of mortgage interest subsidy by employer); 12 (1998 deduction limits and benefit rates for automobiles); 13 (employer-paid educational costs); 15 (Christmas parties and employer-paid special events; employer payment of professional membership fees); 22 (employee benefits); 25 (health and welfare trusts); 40 (administrative policy changes: loyalty programs; vehicles required to be taken home at night; non-cash gifts and awards; surface transit passes).

Registered Charities Newsletters: 25 (volunteers).

Provincial Income Allocation Newsletters: 4 (salaries and wages — inclusion of taxable benefits).

CRA Audit Manual: 12.2.0: Auditing employee benefits; 27.10.0: Employee and shareholder benefits.

Advance Tax Rulings: ATR-8: Self-insured health and welfare trust fund; ATR-21: Pension benefit from an unregistered pension plan; ATR-23: Private health services plan; ATR-45: Share appreciation rights plan.

Forms: T4130: Employer's guide — taxable benefits.

(b) **personal or living expenses [allowances]** — all amounts received by the taxpayer in the year as an allowance for personal or living expenses or as an allowance for any other purpose, except

    (i) travel, personal or living expense allowances

        (A) expressly fixed in an Act of Parliament, or

        (B) paid under the authority of the Treasury Board to a person who was appointed or whose services were engaged pursuant to the *Inquiries Act*, in respect of the discharge of the person's duties relating to the appointment or engagement,

    (ii) travel and separation allowances received under service regulations as a member of the Canadian Forces,

    (iii) representation or other special allowances received in respect of a period of absence from Canada as a person described in paragraph 250(1)(b), (c), (d) or (d.1),

    (iv) representation or other special allowances received by a person who is an agent-general of a province in respect of a period while the person was in Ottawa as the agent-general of the province,

    (v) reasonable allowances for travel expenses received by an employee from the employee's employer in respect of a period when the employee was employed in connection with the selling of property or negotiating of contracts for the employee's employer,

    (v.1) allowances for board and lodging of the taxpayer, to a maximum total of $300[1] for each month of the year, if

        (A) the taxpayer is, in that month, a registered participant with, or member of, a sports team or recreation program

---

[1] Indexed by 117.1(1) after 2007 — ed.

of the employer in respect of which membership or participation is restricted to persons under 21 years of age,

(B) the allowance is in respect of the taxpayer's participation or membership and is not attributable to services of the taxpayer as a coach, instructor trainer, referee, administrator or other similar occupation,

(C) the employer is a registered charity or a non-profit organization described in paragraph 149(1)(l), and

(D) the allowance is reasonably attributable to the cost to the taxpayer of living away from the place where the employee would, but for the employment, ordinarily reside,

(vi) reasonable allowances received by a minister or clergyman in charge of or ministering to a diocese, parish or congregation for expenses for transportation incident to the discharge of the duties of that office or employment,

(vii) reasonable allowances for travel expenses (other than allowances for the use of a motor vehicle) received by an employee (other than an employee employed in connection with the selling of property or the negotiating of contracts for the employer) from the employer for travelling away from

(A) the municipality where the employer's establishment at which the employee ordinarily worked or to which the employee ordinarily reported was located, and

(B) the metropolitan area, if there is one, where that establishment was located,

in the performance of the duties of the employee's office or employment,

(vii.1) reasonable allowances for the use of a motor vehicle received by an employee (other than an employee employed in connection with the selling of property or the negotiating of contracts for the employer) from the employer for travelling in the performance of the duties of the office or employment,

(viii) [Repealed]

(ix) allowances (not in excess of reasonable amounts) received by an employee from the employee's employer in respect of any child of the employee living away from the employee's domestic establishment in the place where the employee is required by reason of the employee's employment to live and in full-time attendance at a school in which the language primarily used for instruction is the official language of Canada primarily used by the employee if

(A) a school suitable for that child primarily using that language of instruction is not available in the place where the employee is so required to live, and

(B) the school the child attends primarily uses that language for instruction and is not farther from that place than the community nearest to that place in which there is such a school having suitable boarding facilities;

and, for the purposes of subparagraphs (v), (vi) and (vii.1), an allowance received in a taxation year by a taxpayer for the use of a motor vehicle in connection with or in the course of the taxpayer's office or employment shall be deemed not to be a reasonable allowance

(x) where the measurement of the use of the vehicle for the purpose of the allowance is not based solely on the number of kilometres for which the vehicle is used in connection with or in the course of the office or employment, or

(xi) where the taxpayer both receives an allowance in respect of that use and is reimbursed in whole or in part for expenses in respect of that use (except where the reimbursement is in respect of supplementary business insurance or toll or ferry charges and the amount of the allowance was determined without reference to those reimbursed expenses);

Announced Administrative Change — COVID-19 — Employee allowances in 2020

CRA Backgrounder, Dec. 15, 2020: See under 6(1)(a).

Related Provisions: 6(6) — Employment at special work site or remote location; 6(16) — Disability-related employment benefits; 8(1) — Deductions allowed; 8(1)(c) — Clergyman's residence; 8(1)(f) — Salesman's expenses; 8(1)(g) — Transport employee's expenses; 8(1)(h), (h.1) — Travelling expenses; 8(11) — GST rebate deemed not a reimbursement; 18(1)(r) — Limitation on employer deductibility — automobile expenses; 81(3.1) — No tax on allowance or reimbursement for part-time employee's travel expenses; 81(4) — Exemption for payment to volunteer firefighter or emergency worker; 117.1(2)(a) — Inflation indexing of amount in 6(1)(b)(v.1); 153(1)(a) — Withholding of tax by employer.

Notes: See generally Income Tax Folio S2-F3-C2 [temporarily withdrawn in 2017 and still under review: see Notes to 6(1)(a) "Discounts"] and Guide T4130. 6(1)(b) seeks "to prevent excessive allowances that might amount to a tax-free and expense-free allowance": *Strong*, 2004 TCC 297, para. 13. For GST/HST treatment of allowances, see GST/HST Memorandum 9.3.

"Personal or living expenses" is given an extended definition in 248(1).

6(1)(b)(i)(A) exempts MPs' allowances, which are fixed in *Parliament of Canada Act* s. 63, but S.C. 2001, c. 20 eliminated most of them and provided salary increases. Before 2019, 81(2)-(3) exempted allowances for members of provincial legislatures and municipal officers. CRA "has no authority to require an itemized accounting of an allowance which is exempted from income by statute": VIEWS doc 9520875.

6(1)(b)(iii): for "representation or other special allowance", see VIEWS docs 2005-0158871E5, 2011-0393171I7, 2012-0435301I7, 2017-0695931E5. If X works overseas on a CIDA [now Global Affairs Canada] program, 250(1)(d) deems X resident and eligible for tax-free allowance, even if X is resident in Canada anyway: 2010-0361561E5, 2012-0435301I7.

A $100 allowance to cover the Ontario *Drug Benefit Plan* deductible is taxable: VIEWS doc 2009-0306351E5.

Book allowances are taxable: VIEWS doc 2011-0395471E5.

Bus washing allowance for school bus drivers, and for *electricity* to ensure bus will start in the morning, are considered taxable: VIEWS doc 2017-0682891E5.

Cell phone allowances are taxable: VIEWS docs 2014-054248I7, 2014-0552731E5, 2015-0588201E5, 2017-0682891E5.

Education allowances for a child's schooling are taxable unless they fall within 6(1)(b)(ix): doc 2010-0371001E5.

Equipment allowances are generally taxable: VIEWS doc 2010-0384711E5.

A modest *gas and laundry* allowance to house-cleaning employees is non-taxable: VIEWS doc 2005-0150091E5.

Home office allowances are taxable: VIEWS docs 2010-0361001E5, 2011-040258I7.

Housing allowance for a judge is taxable: doc 2013-049686I7.

Lodging allowances paid to an employee for arranging their own private non-commercial accommodation may be non-taxable: doc 2010-0368031E5; but likely not for a truck driver who sleeps in his truck, as the allowance should represent an estimate of actual cost: 2015-057720I7. See also Notes to 67.1 re *Transport Baie-Comeau* case on deductibility of lodging allowances to the employer. A reasonable temporary residence allowance for a member of a provincial legislative assembly, for an apartment in the capital far from the home constituency, is exempt: doc 2019-0820401E5.

Meal allowances while out of town, per 6(1)(b)(vii) (up to $23/meal since 2020 [see Announced Administrative Change under 62(3)], $17 for 2006-2019) are non-taxable for occasional (less than 3x/week) overtime of at least 2 hours before or after work: tinyurl.com/overtime-meals-cra; 2009-0333541E5, 2009-0348151E5, 2009-0348931E5, 2010-0366661E5, 2011-0398021E5, 2011-0423631E5; 2015-0608281E5 (higher allowance non-taxable if designed to cover actual expenses); 2019-0809831E5 (lists factors to consider for higher allowance; ambulance drivers on out-of-town emergency calls qualify). No proof is needed of meal consumption: 2009-0336061E5. Meal allowances or vouchers not within the above policy are taxable, even though subsidized meals provided by the employer are not (see Notes to 6(1)(a) under "Meals"): 2012-044071I7. However, in *Morissette*, 2012 TCC 37, a $20 allowance was found reasonable and was non-taxable; and in *Hamilton*, 2020 TCC 23, para. 14, a $40 overtime meal allowance qualified under 6(1)(b)(vii). A $25 bi-weekly meal allowance for expenses due to extended shifts is non-taxable: 2006-0165971E5. So is a nominal meal allowance or stipend to volunteers: 2006-0178011E5. Compensation for delayed meal breaks is taxable: 2010-0379521E5.

Moving allowance: up to $650 for incidental employee moving expenses is non-taxable if the employee certifies having spent at least that much: T4130; VIEWS doc 2010-036974117; GST/HST Memorandum 9.3 para. 4. See also 6(1)(a) Notes at "Moving expenses"; Watson, "Employer Support for Employee Movement", 17(6) *Tax Hyperion* (Carswell) 1-5 (Nov-Dec 2020) (effect of allowance vs reimbursement).

Municipal officers and elected officials are subject to the same rules as employees: VIEWS doc 2012-0443331E5.

Remote mine site allowances are taxable if not exempt under 6(6): doc 2011-0416061E5.

Travel allowances: see Income Tax Folio S2-F3-C2 ¶2.62-2.67 [temporarily withdrawn in 2017 and still under review: see Notes to 6(1)(a) "Discounts"]; tinyurl.com/auto-allow; VIEWS docs 2005-0124101E5, 2006-0185481E5, 2008-0276131E5, 2008-0278661E5, 2009-0345501I7, 2010-0359491E5, 2010-0362781E5, 2011-0400141E5, 2011-0427831E5, 2011-0428741E5, 2013-0476081E5, 2013-0491411E5, 2016-0673831E5, 2016-0674811C6 [CPA QC 2017 q.1.7]. Travel from home to place of employment is personal (see Notes to 8(1)(h.1)), so reimbursement is normally taxable (*Hogg*, 2002 FCA 177; *Daniels*, 2004 FCA 125; *Gutcher*, 2006 TCC 163; docs 2002-0177055, 2005-0164431E5 (even if the employee's home office is a regular place of employment), 2006-0203911E5, 2008-0266301E5, 2008-0270721E5, 2010-0368611E5, 2012-0432671E5, 2012-0463581E5, 2016-0643631E5, 2016-0670851E5); but where the home is also the employer's place of business, an allowance for employment-related travel to another location is exempt under 6(1)(b)(vii.1): 2007-0257661E5. Regular travel to meet a client at the client's residence was employment-related in 2009-0335451E5. A CPA firm client's premises, during a long audit, could be the employer's "establishment" at which the employee "ordinarily worked" so that travel allowances are taxable: 2014-0551941E5. Travel to part-time employment, such as substitute teachers, may be exempt under 81(3.1): 2006-0200171E5. A combined allowance is taxable if the travel portion cannot be determined: *Tozer*, 2004 TCC 411, para. 8. Allowances for school board members' travel between their "home offices" and the board were exempt under 6(1)(b)(vii.1) in *Campbell*, 2003 TCC 160 (no longer generally applicable in light of *Daniels*, above); and see Notes to 8(1)(h.1) for other exceptions. An allowance for travel to a special or remote work site may be exempt under 6(6). For deductibility of automobile allowances to employers see 18(1)(r).

The per-km amounts in Reg. 7306 are "reasonable" for 6(1)(b)(vii), (vii.1), but they are only a guide, and higher amounts are not necessarily unreasonable: VIEWS docs 2012-0454131C6, 2015-0565961E5. 6(1)(b)(x) clearly overrides (v)-(vii.1), so even if an allowance is otherwise "reasonable" it is deemed unreasonable if it is not based solely on the number of km driven: *Beauport (Ville)*, 2001 FCA 198; *Paré*, 2011 TCC 510; *Positano*, 2018 TCC 160. An unreasonable allowance must be entirely included in income, not split with the reasonable portion being exempt: *Al Saunders Contracting*, 2020 FCA 89. A flat-rate allowance not based on mileage (or a combined flat-rate and per-km allowance, or an allowance when operating expenses are being reimbursed) is taxable: 6(1)(b)(x), T4130, docs 2004-0057181E5 (the employee can claim allowable expenses under 8(1)(f)-(h.1)), 2005-0159931E5, 2006-0185301E5, 2007-0228521I7, 2007-0234891E5, 2008-0300671E5, 2009-0312541E5, 2009-0320531E5, 2009-0345481E5, 2009-0352721I7, 2010-0384711E5; [2010-0387391E5 for construction industry now overridden by 2012-0454141C6]; 2012-0460481E5; 2014-0555611I7 (minimum daily allowance intended to cover actual expenses). The calculation is done for each month: 2005-0115061E5. For "reasonable allowance" see also *Landry*, 2007 TCC 383 (aff'd 2009 FCA 174); *Henry*, 2007 TCC 451; *Agostini*, 2009 TCC 87; *Solomon*, 2009 TCC 320; Bruce Russell, "Of Cars and Tax", 4(9) *Tax Hyperion* (Carswell, Sept. 2007). Treasury Board reimbursement levels may be considered reasonable: 2007-0235131E5, 2008-0303901I7, 2013-0505481E5, 2015-0613001E5. For electric cars, CRA has not yet specified a "reasonable" per-km rate: 2016-0674801C6 [CPA QC 2017 q.1.5]. Paying the employee to advertise the employer with signs on the vehicle could make an allowance unreasonable in CRA's view: 2012-0465031E5. The CCA and lease payment limits in 13(7)(g) and 67.3 do not determine "reasonable": 2008-0300001I7. The per-km requirement applies to GST/HST input tax credits for the employer: *Tri-bec Inc.*, [2003] G.S.T.C. 75 (TCC); *I-D Foods*, 2013 TCC 15.

Union members working on union business and paid by their employers were taxable on allowances from the union in *Vachon Estate*, 2009 FCA 375 (leave to appeal denied 2010 CarswellNat 936 (SCC)), and *Sénéchal*, 2011 TCC 365 (see Notes to 248(1)"office").

An allowance exempted under 6(1)(b)(v)-(vii) is not taxable merely because the employee is also a shareholder: VIEWS doc 2005-0141491E5.

6(1)(b)(v.1) added, for tax years ending after June 22, 2007, by S.C. 2007, c. 16 (private member's bill). It is designed to exempt (and eliminate CPP on) room and board provided to amateur ("tier two") junior hockey players by teams, of up to $300/month, indexed by 117.1(1) after 2007 ($373 for 2020, $377 for 2021). See Hansard (parl.ca), June 1, 2006; Drache, "Tax Act Amended to Help Young Hockey Players", xxix(17) *The Canadian Taxpayer* (Carswell) 132-33 (Aug. 28, 2007). 6(1)(b)(v.1) might not be needed in light of *Grenier*, 2007 TCC 72, ruling an amateur hockey team's allowance non-taxable, but that was a non-binding Informal Procedure decision.

For 6(1)(b)(ix) see Notes to 6(1)(a) under "School fees reimbursement".

6(1)(b)(vii) and (vii.1) amended by 1991 technical bill. 6(1)(b)(viii) repealed by 1998 Budget, effective 1998 (the $500 exemption for volunteer firemen's allowances was expanded and moved to 81(4)). 6(1)(b)(xi) amended by 1991 technical bill and 1993 technical bill (parking was moved to 6(1.1)).

Remission Orders: *Ice Storm Employee Benefits Remission Order*, P.C. 1998-2047.

Income Tax Folios: S1-F2-C2: Tuition tax credit [replaces IT-516R2].

Interpretation Bulletins: IT-168R3: Athletes and players employed by football, hockey and similar clubs; IT-470R: Employees' fringe benefits; IT-518R: Food, beverages and entertainment expenses; IT-522R: Vehicle, travel and sales expenses of employees.

I.T. Technical News: 40 (administrative policy changes: meal and travel allowances).

Registered Charities Newsletters: 25 (volunteers).

Forms: T4130: Employer's guide — taxable benefits.

(c) **director's or other fees** — director's or other fees received by the taxpayer in the year in respect of, in the course of, or by virtue of an office or employment;

Related Provisions: 153(1)(a) — Withholding of tax by employer; 248(7)(a) — Payment deemed received when mailed.

Notes: A corporate director is an "officer" (see 248(1)"office"), and thus an "employee" (see 248(1)"employee"), and so generally cannot deduct expenses (see 8(2)). Since only a human being can be a director, CRA states that a director's income cannot be moved to a corporation or offshore, unless the director is representing a partnership or corporation and turns the fees over to it: VIEWS docs 2006-0193141E5, 2007-0246031E5, 2009-0308041E5; Drache, "Diverting Directors' Fees", xxxi(24) *The Canadian Taxpayer* (Carswell) 191-92 (Dec. 8, 2009); but see Notes to 9(1) under "Diverting income". Fees that the director asks be paid to a charity are taxable to the director under 56(2), but the director is making a donation under 118.1 (whereas if the fees are waived they will not be taxed): 2010-0367781E5.

Association council or committee members' fees are considered taxable under 6(1)(c) (requiring 153(1)(a) withholding), even if the members' practices are incorporated, as CRA considers that they receive such income on their own behalf: VIEWS doc 2013-0505471E5.

Directors' fees paid to a non-resident for services performed in Canada are reported on a T4 (guide T4061). If the director receives salary also, the fee is subject to graduated withholding tax under 153(1) rather than 15% under Reg. 105: T4001 ch. 5, IT-377R and IT-468. If the non-resident director stays outside Canada when joining meetings, no tax may apply but this is "under study": docs 2009-0308041E5, 2009-0345151E5.

Executor (estate trustee) fees are taxed by 9(1) if earned in the course of a business (e.g. a law practice), in which case GST/HST may need to be charged on the fees. Otherwise, they fall under 6(1)(c) or 5(1): IT-377R para. 5; docs 2004-0069781E5, 2005-0122221E5, 2005-0150881R3, 2006-0184481E5 (gift in lieu of fees is also taxable: 2007-0225651E5); 2012-0462961C6 [2012 Ontario Tax Conf. q.5]; 2012-0457901E5; *Messier*, 2008 TCC 349; *Boisvert*, 2011 TCC 290. Where a lawyer does not practise estates law but is appointed executor by a client, the fees may or may not be business income: 2014-0521791E5. If under 6(1)(c) or 5(1), the fees are taxable only when *received* regardless of when the work was done: 2013-0475341E5, and are subject to 153(1)(a) withholding (but not EI premiums): 2005-0164831E5, 2006-0209081E5, 2007-0250501E5, 2014-0521791E5. Expenses such as travel and meals are normally not deductible, due to 8(2): 2012-0438941E5, but see Notes to 8(1)(b) re deducting the cost of passing of accounts. An estate must issue a T4 or T4A for executor fees: 2012 Ontario Tax Conf. Q10 (no T4A needed for payment under $500 if no tax withheld). The executor can be liable under 159(3) for the estate's tax debts.

Honoraria to members of a board (including a university student government, municipal school board, health board or other public service board) are taxable under 6(1)(c) (or under 5(1) as salary), unless they are declined: docs 2002-0161565, 2010-0376881E5, 2011-0406741I7.

A part-time *judge's* per diem fees are taxable under 6(1)(c): doc 2012-0458071E5.

A *municipal councillor's* honorarium for representing the municipality on an external board is still taxable under 6(1)(c) and 56(2) if turned over to (or directed to be paid to) the municipality, but the councillor can claim a donation credit under 118.1: doc 2002-0174585.

Power of attorney fees, if not business income, fall under 6(1)(c): doc 2018-0749251E5 (and the payer must issue a T4).

Benefits to directors may be taxable under 6(1)(a): doc 2010-0355971E5.

Expenses can be deducted against 6(1)(c) income, e.g. under 8(1)(h) or (i).

Interpretation Bulletins: IT-377R: Director's, executor's or juror's fees (cancelled); IT-468R: Management or administration fees paid to non-residents; IT-470R: Employees' fringe benefits; IT-518R: Food, beverages and entertainment expenses.

Forms: T4001: Employers' guide — payroll deductions and remittances [guide]; T4061: Non-resident withholding tax guide.

(d) **allocations, etc., under [employees] profit sharing plan** — amounts allocated to the taxpayer in the year by a trustee under an employees profit sharing plan as provided by section 144 except subsection 144(4), and amounts required by subsection 144(7) to be included in computing the taxpayer's income for the year;

Related Provisions: 8(1)(o.1) — Deduction for forfeited amounts; 12(1)(n) — Income inclusion — amount received from EPSP; 128.1(10)"excluded right or interest"(a)(v) — No deemed disposition of rights on emigration; 144(9) — Deductions for forfeited amounts; 153(1)(a) — Withholding of tax at source.

Interpretation Bulletins: IT-379R: Employees profit sharing plans — allocations to beneficiaries.

Registered Plans Compliance Bulletins: 7 (pensionable earnings from an EPSP).

(e) **standby charge for automobile** — where the taxpayer's employer or a person related to the employer made an automobile available to the taxpayer, or to a person related to the taxpayer, in the year, the amount, if any, by which

(i) an amount that is a reasonable standby charge for the automobile for the total number of days in the year during which it was made so available

exceeds

(ii) the total of all amounts, each of which is an amount (other than an expense related to the operation of the automobile) paid in the year to the employer or the person related to the employer by the taxpayer or the person related to the taxpayer for the use of the automobile;

Related Provisions: 6(1)(a)(iii) — Automobile benefits excluded from general inclusion of benefits; 6(1)(k), (l) — Operating expense benefit; 6(2) — Calculation of reasonable standby charge; 6(2.1) — Reduced standby charge for automobile salesman; 6(7) — Cost of automobile includes GST effective 1996; 8(1)(f)(vii) — Salesman's expenses; 12(1)(y) — Partnerships — auto provided to partner or employee of partner; 15(5) — Automobile benefit to shareholder; 153(1)(a) — Withholding by employer.

Notes: See Notes to 6(2).

Regulations: 200(2)(g), 200(3) (information returns).

Interpretation Bulletins: See under 6(2).

I.T. Technical News: 12 (1998 deduction limits and benefit rates for automobiles).

Forms: RC18: Calculating automobile benefits.

(e.1) **group sickness or accident insurance plans** — the total of all amounts contributed in the year in respect of the taxpayer by the taxpayer's employer to a group sickness or accident insurance plan, except to the extent that the contributions are attributable to benefits under the plan that, if received by the taxpayer, would be included in the taxpayer's income under paragraph (f) in the year the benefits are received if that paragraph were read without regard to its subparagraph (v);

Notes: Under 6(1)(e.1), if benefits under the plan will be a lump sum so that they are not taxed by 6(1)(f), the employer's contributions are a taxable benefit.

For the meaning of "group sickness or accident insurance plan" and discussion of 6(1)(e.1) see *Canadian Health Insurance Tax Guide: Group Sickness or Accident Insurance Plans* (Jan. 2017), tinyurl.com/sunlife-taxguides; Balsara, "Changes to the Tax Rules for GSAIPs — Practical Results and Opportunities", XVIII(4) *Insurance Planning* (Federated Press) 1166-69 (2012).

For CRA interpretation see VIEWS doc 2012-0464171E5 (employer contributions to group business travel accident insurance plan and group occupational accident insurance plan likely fall under 6(1)(e.1)); 2013-0476131E5 (general discussion); 2013-0482151E5 (premiums paid through a trust for accidental death & dismemberment insurance and for group critical illness insurance likely fall under 6(1)(e.1)); 2016-0679291I7 (benefit is taxable even if plan primarily benefits employer by enabling it to attract employees to high-risk location).

6(1)(e.1) added by 2012 budget bill #2 for 2013 tax year; amended for 2014 and later years.

Former 6(1)(e.1) repealed by 1997 GST/HST bill, for 1996 and later tax years. It was added by 1990 GST and amended by 1992 technical bill. Before 1996, 6(1)(e.1) required inclusion of a 7% benefit to account for GST. The actual GST paid by the employer on the goods or services was not included in the benefit, per former 6(7). This rule has been reversed, and the GST/HST is now included in the benefit: 6(7).

Income Tax Folios: S2-F1-C1: Health and welfare trusts [replaces IT-85R2].

(f) **[private] employment insurance [plan] benefits** — the total of all amounts received by the taxpayer in the year that were payable to the taxpayer on a periodic basis in respect of the loss of all or any part of the taxpayer's income from an office or employment, pursuant to

(i) a sickness or accident insurance plan,

(ii) a disability insurance plan,

(iii) an income maintenance insurance plan or

(iii.1) a plan described in any of subparagraphs (i) to (iii) that is administered or provided by an employee life and health trust,

to or under which the taxpayer's employer has made a contribution, not exceeding the amount, if any, by which

(iv) the total of all such amounts received by the taxpayer pursuant to the plan before the end of the year and

(A) where there was a preceding taxation year ending after 1971 in which any such amount was, by virtue of this

paragraph, included in computing the taxpayer's income, after the last such year, and

(B) in any other case, after 1971,

exceeds

(v) the total of the contributions made by the taxpayer under the plan before the end of the year and

(A) where there was a preceding taxation year described in clause (iv)(A), after the last such year, and

(B) in any other case, after 1967;

Related Provisions: 6(1)(e.1) — Group sickness or accident insurance plan — whether premiums taxable; 6(18) — No taxable benefit on top-up disability payments where insurer insolvent; 8(1)(b) — Deduction for legal expenses to obtain benefits; 8(1)(n.1)(iii) — Deduction for certain amounts reimbursed to employer; 56(1)(a)(iv) — Income inclusion for benefit under *Employment Insurance Act*; 110.2(1)"qualifying amount"(c) — Retroactive spreading of lump-sum payment over prior years; 139.1(13) — Effect of demutualization of insurance corporation on group insurance policy; 144.1(1)"designated employee benefit" — Employee life and health trust (ELHT) may pay benefit from group sickness or accident insurance plan; 144.1(10) — Employee contributions to ELHT deemed to be payment of group sickness and accident premiums if so identified; 153(1)(a) — Withholding of tax at source.

Notes: Under 6(1)(f), employment insurance plan benefits such as disability insurance (not to be confused with federal EI benefits — see 56(1)(a)(iv)) are exempt if the employee paid *all* the premiums, and taxable if the employer paid *any* premiums (reduced by premiums the employee paid). See *Robson*, 2005 TCC 287; VIEWS docs 2005-0160551E5, 2006-0182841M4, 2006-0215691E5, 2009-0343571E5, 2010-0371201E5, 2010-0386411E5. The taxable portion is taxable even if the employment has been terminated: 2013-0485831I7. CRA says the gross benefit should be reported on Line 10400 [former 104] (if paid by a trustee) or Line 10100 [former 101] (if paid by the employer), and the premiums deducted on Line 23200 [former 232] of the T1 return: 2010-038046I7. Note that premiums deducted at payroll (from amounts included in the employee's income) are paid by the employee: 2005-0140591E5. If premiums paid by the employee are reimbursed by the employer and the reimbursements are taxed, the benefits are tax-free: *Brine*, 2006 TCC 458; but in CRA's view, if the employer pays the premiums and adds such amounts to the employee's income, the benefits are taxable: 2010-0362001E5. If employer contributions stop, a plan can be "purified" so that future benefits will be non-taxable: 2004-0098681R3, 2005-0125791C6; but simply returning the premiums does not change the tax status of the benefits unless the legal obligation to pay future premiums moves to the employees: 2010-0361971E5. If an employee-pay-all plan is converted to an employer-pay plan, CRA considers it to be a new plan: 2006-0189441E5. In *Eyckelhoff*, 2020 TCC 130, a claim that an annuity (from Aegon in the Netherlands) was from a disability insurance plan was rejected for lack of evidence.

An employer can enter into individual insurance policies that together are treated as a group plan: VIEWS doc 2006-017114I7; and such policies can include employees' spouses: 2011-0406551C6.

CRA's view is that if the employer makes contributions to the plan for *any* employees, other employees who paid all their own premiums are still subject to tax on benefits under 6(1)(f): VIEWS docs 2006-0172261E5, 2009-0347621E5. Benefits are taxable if employees can choose different levels of premiums and coverage, unless the regime is totally financed by employees: 2004-0097451E5. A "top-up" LTD plan paid for by employees can fall outside 6(1)(f) if there is no cross-subsidization with the main plan: 2005-0156311E5; or may be an employee benefit plan: 2008-0265651E5. If the insurer incorrectly assumes no tax is payable and later reimburses the employee for the extra costs of being assessed (including professional fees), CRA considers this taxable under 6(1)(a): 2013-0479111C6 (it is unclear whether this is correct).

If the insurer denies coverage and the employer pays benefits to the employee, CRA considers this taxable under 5(1) or 6(1): 2015-0580521E5. 6(1)(f) applied where a priest was suspended for alleged criminal acts, and his employer made "disability/sickness" payments while he was in treatment: *Touchette*, [1994] 1 C.T.C. 2674 (TCC).

Source withholding calculated under Reg. 102 applies to payments taxable under 6(1)(f): see Notes to 153(1) re 153(1)(a). Reporting is on a T4A per Reg. 200(2)(f): VIEWS doc 2011-0404951E5.

A lump-sum payment by an insurer in settlement of litigation is taxable if it is for arrears of benefits that would have been taxable had they been paid on a periodic basis, under the *surrogatum* principle ("the tax treatment of the item will depend on what the amount is intended to replace"): *Tsiaprailis*, 2005 SCC 8; *Williams*, 2008 TCC 418; *Frizzle*, 2008 TCC 651 [a nominal $10 was excluded as applying to the extinguishment of rights]; VIEWS docs 2009-0345541I7, 2013-047563I7. (These likely overrule *Peel*, [1987] 1 C.T.C. 2373 (TCC).) See Friedlan, "The Tsiaprailis Case", XII(1) *Insurance Planning* (Federated Press) 748-51 (2005). However, a lump-sum payment in respect of *future* benefits gives rise to a capital gain, which may be non-taxable under 39(1)(a)(iii) as proceeds of disposition of an "insurance policy": 2005-0121521E5, 2005-0141511E5, 2005-0154041E5, 2005-0160551E5, 2005-0159331E5, 2006-017555I7, 2006-0217191E5, 2012-047002I7, 2012-0471911E5. In *Scott*, 2017 TCC 224, a lump sum from the Nortel health & welfare trust, to compensate employees for losing their life insurance when it shut down unfunded, was non-taxable; and 2018-

0757561R3 approves the same for another employer. A post-death settlement is taxable to the estate: 2008-0293131E5; but an employer's payment to a deceased employee's estate to compensate for wrongly advising that no accident claim could be made is non-taxable: 2008-0289701E5.

To be an "insurance plan", a plan not provided by an insurance company must have funds accumulated in trust: IT-428 para. 7; VIEWS docs 2006-0174121C6, 2010-0388721E5, 2011-0397561E5. If an employer's self-funded LTD plan is not an insurance plan, benefits are taxable under 5(1) or 6(1)(a), and 6(1)(f) does not apply: 2006-0199501E5. Where a plan was instituted for the purpose of providing wage loss replacement benefits, CRA will assume 6(1)(f) applies unless the contrary is established: IT-428 para. 6, doc 2011-041475117.

An "income maintenance" plan (6(1)(f)(iii)) includes a plan insuring against involuntary job loss: VIEWS doc 2014-0551831E5.

Long-term disability payments are not taxed if provincial legislation provides that they must be assigned to an insurance company: VIEWS doc 2004-0085121R3.

Disability benefits under 6(1)(f), received by a plaintiff and held in trust for a defendant under a "*Cox v. Carter*" order (to prevent double recovery when a plaintiff receives disability benefits as well as damages from suing), can be excluded from income: VIEWS doc 2003-0010273. However, benefits received subject to a condition that they might have to be repaid if also recovered from a third party were taxable: *Théberge*, 2003 TCC 97; *Harnish*, 2007 TCC 546. In *Deschesnes*, 2015 TCC 177, benefits paid by an insurer, but subject to clawback if paid by the Québec Pension Plan, were not taxable; but QPP's reimbursements to the insurer on D's behalf were: paras. 23-25, 34.

See also "Watch out for offshore disability insurance plan schemes" (CRA, Aug. 26, 2020, tinyurl.com/cra-watchdip), re extracting funds from a corporation tax-free under the guise of disability insurance.

A "health and welfare trust" can be used until 2022 as a conduit for tax-free health benefits, but then must become an ELHT: see Notes to 6(1)(a) and 144.1.

Where the employee is also a shareholder, if coverage is higher than employees would get, the premium may be taxable under 15(1): doc 2005-0148221E5.

For a non-resident, 6(1)(f) benefits are taxed under 115(1), not 212(1)(h): *Price*, 2012 FCA 332 (overruling *Blauer*, 2007 TCC 706) [Thériault, "Disability Insurance Benefits and Non-Residents", 3(3) *Canadian Tax Focus* (ctf.ca) 10-11 (Aug. 2013)].

Where disability and loss of employment occurred before 1974, see ITAR 19.

6(1)(f)(iii.1) added by 2010 budget bill #2, effective 2010.

Regulations: 200(2)(f) (information return).

Remission Orders: *Janet Hall Remission Order*, P.C. 2004-1336 (remission where CPP lump sum disability repaid to wage loss replacement provider); *Ginette Archambault Remission Order*, P.C. 2010-273 (remission due to circumstances beyond taxpayer's control, provided she does not claim loss relating to repayment of wage loss replacement benefits).

I.T. Application Rules: 19 (where plan established before June 19, 1971).

Income Tax Folios: S2-F1-C1: Health and welfare trusts [replaces IT-85R2].

Interpretation Bulletins: IT-54: Wage loss replacement plans (cancelled); IT-99R5: Legal and accounting fees; IT-428: Wage loss replacement plans; IT-529: Flexible employee benefit programs.

Advance Tax Rulings: ATR-8: Self-insured health and welfare trust fund.

I.T. Technical News: 25 (health and welfare trusts).

Forms: T4E: Statement of employment insurance and other benefits; T4130: Employer's guide — taxable benefits.

> **(f.1)** **Canadian Forces members and veterans amounts** — the total of all amounts received by the taxpayer in the year on account of
>
> > (i) an earnings loss benefit, an income replacement benefit (other than an amount determined under subsection 19.1(1), paragraph 23(1)(b) or subsection 26.1(1) of the *Veterans Well-being Act*, as modified, where applicable, under Part 5 of that Act), a supplementary retirement benefit or a career impact allowance payable to the taxpayer under Part 2 of the *Veterans Well-being Act*, or
> >
> > (ii) an amount payable under any of subsections 99(6), 109(1) and 115(5) and sections 124 to 126 of the *Veterans Well-being Act*;

Related Provisions: 81(1)(d.1) — Exemption for other payments under CFMVRCA; 110.2(1)"qualifying amount"(c) — Retroactive spreading of lump-sum payment over prior years.

Notes: 6(1)(f.1) amended by 2018 budget bill #1, effective April 2019. Before then, read:

> (f.1) Canadian Forces members and veterans income replacement benefits — the total of all amounts received by the taxpayer in the year on account of an earnings loss benefit, a supplementary retirement benefit or a career impact allowance payable to the taxpayer under Part 2 of the *Veterans Well-being Act*;

6(1)(f.1) amended by 2017 budget bill #1, effective April 2018, to change "*Canadian Forces Members and Veterans Re-establishment and Compensation Act*" to "*Veterans Well-being Act*".

6(1)(f.1) amended by 2016 budget bill #1 (Part 4), effective April 2017, to change "permanent impairment allowance" to "career impact allowance".

6(1)(f.1) added by S.C. 2005, c. 21, effective (per P.C. 2006-136) April 2006.

> **(g)** **employee benefit plan benefits** — the total of all amounts each of which is an amount received by the taxpayer in the year out of or under an employee benefit plan or from the disposition of any interest in any such plan, other than the portion thereof that is
>
> > (i) a death benefit or an amount that would, but for the deduction provided in the definition of that term in subsection 248(1), be a death benefit,
> >
> > (ii) a return of amounts contributed to the plan by the taxpayer or a deceased employee of whom the taxpayer is an heir or legal representative, to the extent that the amounts were not deducted in computing the taxable income of the taxpayer or the deceased employee for any taxation year,
> >
> > (iii) a superannuation or pension benefit attributable to services rendered by a person in a period throughout which the person was not resident in Canada, or
> >
> > (iv) a designated employee benefit (as defined in subsection 144.1(1));

Related Provisions: 6(1.2) — Who is deemed to receive amount from EBP; 6(10) — Contributions; 6(14) — Salary deferral arrangement — part of benefit plan; 12(1)(n) — Employees profit sharing plan; 12(1)(n.1) — Employee's income from EBP; 18(1)(o) — EBP contributions; 32.1 — EBP deductions; 56(1)(a)(i)(D) — Exclusion for 6(1)(g) amounts; 104(13)(b) — Trusts — income payable to beneficiary; 107.1(b) — Distribution of property by EBP deemed at cost amount; 128.1(10)"excluded right or interest"(a)(vi), (b) — No deemed disposition of rights on emigration; 153(1)(a) — Withholding of tax by employer; 212(17) — No non-resident withholding tax.

Notes: See Notes to 248(1)"employee benefit plan". An amount is taxed under 6(1)(g) when received from an EBP or when "constructively" received, e.g. if the employee has the right to the funds but chooses not to receive them until a later year: IT-502 para. 10; Revenue Canada Round Table, 1984 Cdn Tax Foundation conference report, Q. 13, p. 795; VIEWS doc 2003-0039011E5. Note that 6(1.2) can deem another person to receive the benefit.

An amount from a US 401(k) plan may fall under 6(1)(g): doc 2011-0407461E5. The same can apply to a UK retirement plan, such as a FURBS (funded unapproved retirement benefit plan): 2018-0782381E5, 2019-0824281E5.

6(1)(g)(ii) excludes from income a return of amounts an employee contributed to an EBP. The exclusion is limited to returns of contributions that were not deducted. Contributions by a Canadian resident to a US pension plan, deductible per Canada-US Tax Treaty Art. XVIII:8, are included in income when returned to the contributor (or heir).

6(1)(g) amended by 2010 budget bill #2 (effective 2010), 2008 budget bill #2, 1990 pension bill.

Interpretation Bulletins: IT-499R: Superannuation or pension benefits; IT-502: Employee benefit plans and employee trusts; IT-529: Flexible employee benefit programs.

I.T. Technical News: 11 (reporting of amounts paid out of an employee benefit plan).

Advance Tax Rulings: ATR-17: Employee benefit plan — purchase of company shares; ATR-39: Self-funded leave of absence.

> **(h)** **employee trust** — amounts allocated to the taxpayer for the year by a trustee under an employee trust;

Related Provisions: 12(1)(n) — Employer income from employee trust; 107.1(a) — Distribution of property by employee trust deemed at FMV; 128.1(10)"excluded right or interest"(e)(i) — No deemed disposition of rights on emigration; 153(1)(a) — Withholding of tax by employer; 212(17) — No non-resident withholding tax.

Regulations: 200(2)(g) (information return).

Interpretation Bulletins: IT-502: Employee benefit plans and employee trusts; IT-529: Flexible employee benefit programs.

> **(i)** **salary deferral arrangement payments** — the amount, if any, by which the total of all amounts received by any person as benefits (other than amounts received by or from a trust governed by a salary deferral arrangement) in the year out of or

under a salary deferral arrangement in respect of the taxpayer exceeds the amount, if any, by which

(i) the total of all deferred amounts under the arrangement that were included under paragraph (a) as benefits in computing the taxpayer's income for preceding taxation years

exceeds

(ii) the total of

(A) all deferred amounts received by any person in preceding taxation years out of or under the arrangement, and

(B) all deferred amounts under the arrangement that were deducted under paragraph 8(1)(o) in computing the taxpayer's income for the year or preceding taxation years;

Related Provisions: 6(11)–(14) — Income inclusion for rights under SDA; 20(1)(oo), (pp) — SDA — deductions; 56(1)(w) — Benefits from SDA; 128.1(10)"excluded right or interest"(a)(vii), (b) — No deemed disposition of rights on emigration; 153(1)(a) — Withholding of tax by employer.

Notes: See 248(1)"salary deferral arrangement" Notes.

Interpretation Bulletins: IT-529: Flexible employee benefit programs.

(j) **reimbursements and awards** — amounts received by the taxpayer in the year as an award or reimbursement in respect of an amount that would, if the taxpayer were entitled to no reimbursements or awards, be deductible under subsection 8(1) in computing the income of the taxpayer, except to the extent that the amounts so received

(i) are otherwise included in computing the income of the taxpayer for the year, or

(ii) are taken into account in computing the amount that is claimed under subsection 8(1) by the taxpayer for the year or a preceding taxation year;

Related Provisions: 153(1)(a) — Withholding of tax by employer.

Notes: Reimbursement of union dues may or may not be taxable: VIEWS doc 2009-0306601E5; and see Notes to s. 3 under bullet "union's cash gift".

6(1)(j) added by 1989 Budget, effective for amounts received after 1989.

Interpretation Bulletins: IT-99R5: Legal and accounting fees.

(k) **automobile operating expense benefit** — where

(i) an amount is determined under subparagraph (e)(i) in respect of an automobile in computing the taxpayer's income for the year,

(ii) amounts related to the operation (otherwise than in connection with or in the course of the taxpayer's office or employment) of the automobile for the period or periods in the year during which the automobile was made available to the taxpayer or a person related to the taxpayer are paid or payable by the taxpayer's employer or a person related to the taxpayer's employer (each of whom is in this paragraph referred to as the "payor"), and

(iii) the total of the amounts so paid or payable is not paid in the year or within 45 days after the end of the year to the payor by the taxpayer or by the person related to the taxpayer,

the amount in respect of the operation of the automobile determined by the formula

$$A - B$$

where

A is

(iv) where the automobile is used primarily in the performance of the duties of the taxpayer's office or employment during the period or periods referred to in subparagraph (ii) and the taxpayer notifies the employer in writing before the end of the year of the taxpayer's intention to have this subparagraph apply, $\frac{1}{2}$ of the amount determined under subparagraph (e)(i) in respect of the automobile in computing the taxpayer's income for the year, and

(v) in any other case, the amount equal to the product obtained when the amount prescribed for the year is multiplied by the total number of kilometres that the automobile is driven (otherwise than in connection with or in the course of the taxpayer's office or employment) during the period or periods referred to in subparagraph (ii), and

B is the total of all amounts in respect of the operation of the automobile in the year paid in the year or within 45 days after the end of the year to the payor by the taxpayer or by the person related to the taxpayer; and

Related Provisions: 6(1)(a)(iii) — Automobile benefits excluded from general inclusion of benefits; 6(1)(l) — Benefit where 6(1)(k) does not apply; 6(1.1) — Parking is not an operating cost; 6(2.2) — COVID-19 — Calculation for 2020 or 2021 if A(iv) condition met in 2019; 12(1)(y) — Automobile benefit to partner or employee of partner; 15(5) — Automobile benefit to shareholder; 153(1)(a) — Withholding of tax by employer; 257 — Formula cannot calculate to less than zero; *Interpretation Act* 27(5) — Meaning of "within 45 days".

Notes: Where *any* operating costs in respect of an employer-owned automobile (see 248(1)"automobile") are paid by the employer, 6(1)(k) deems the taxable benefit to be a flat number of cents per personal-use kilometre as follows:

Taxation year	Regular employee	Auto salesperson
2017	25¢	22¢
2018	26¢	23¢
2019-2020	28¢	25¢
2021	27¢	24¢

(See Reg. 7305.1.) The rate is the same for an electric car: VIEWS doc 2016-0674801C6 [CPA QC 2017 q.1.5]; but if the employee pays for electricity to charge the car, that reduces the operating expense benefit: 2017-0703381C6 [2017 CPA Alberta q.17]. Driving between home and the employer's place of business is considered personal use for this purpose (see Notes to 8(1)(h.1)). The benefit inclusion can be avoided if the employee repays all the benefits by Feb. 14 of the new year (6(1)(k)(iii)). (This repayment may be made directly to third-party providers: 2008-0274071I7.) If, for example, the employer paid only the insurance, or the annual vehicle licence fee, or one repair bill, repayment by the employee can avoid an income inclusion potentially far greater than the value of the benefits.

GST: The amount per personal-use kilometre (28¢ for 2020, 27¢ for 2021) includes 3% (0.84¢ for 2020, 0.81¢ for 2021) of GST (in non-HST provinces) deemed collected by the employer, which must be remitted to CRA (or Revenu Québec) as GST collected under *Excise Tax Act* subpara. 173(1)(d)(vi)(A). The percentage is 9% in Ontario (for 13% HST) and 11% in the Atlantic provinces (15% HST). See the *Automobile Operating Expense Benefit (GST/HST) Regulations*, in David M. Sherman, *Practitioner's Goods and Services Tax Annotated*.

6(1)(k) applied in *Szymczyk*, 2014 TCC 380, para. 81 (FCA appeal discontinued A-35-15).

Certain employees can opt by Dec. 31 of the year to have their benefit calculated as half the standby charge: 6(1)(k)(iv) (for 2020-21, see also 6(2.2), which allows 2019 driving to be used as the test). For the meaning of "used primarily" see Notes to 73(3).

To calculate the taxable benefit, use CRA's tinyurl.com/autobenefits-calc or Form RC18E. See also T4130, *Employer's Guide — Taxable Benefits*.

For an example of 6(1)(k) applying see *Gariépy*, 2007 TCC 513.

See Notes to 6(2) re whether a mileage logbook is required.

6(1)(k) does not apply to employer-paid expenses for an employee-owned vehicle, which are taxed under 6(1)(a) instead.

6(1)(k) added by 1993 technical bill, effective 1993.

Regulations: 7305.1 (amount prescribed for 6(1)(k)(v)).

Interpretation Bulletins: IT-63R5: Benefits, including standby charge for an automobile, from the personal use of a motor vehicle supplied by an employer.

I.T. Technical News: 10 (1997 deduction limits and benefit rates for automobiles); 12 (1998 deduction limits and benefit rates for automobiles); 40 (employer vehicles required to be taken home at night).

Forms: RC18: Calculating automobile benefits.

(l) **where standby charge does not apply** — the value of a benefit in respect of the operation of an automobile (other than a benefit to which paragraph (k) applies or would apply but for subparagraph (k)(iii)) received or enjoyed by the taxpayer, or by a person related to the taxpayer, in the year in respect of, in the course of or because of, the taxpayer's office or employment.

Related Provisions: 6(1)(a)(iii) — Automobile benefits excluded from general inclusion of benefits; 15(5) — Automobile benefit to shareholder; 153(1)(a) — Withholding of tax by employer.

Notes: 6(1)(l) amended by 2002-2013 technical bill (Part 5 — technical), for benefits received or enjoyed after Oct. 30, 2011, to add "or by a person related to the taxpayer". (A parallel amendment was made to the opening words of 6(1)(a).)

6(1)(l) added by 1993 technical bill, effective 1993.

Interpretation Bulletins: IT-63R5: Benefits, including standby charge for an automobile, from the personal use of a motor vehicle supplied by an employer.

I.T. Technical News: 12 (1998 deduction limits and benefit rates for automobiles).

(1.1) Parking cost — For the purposes of this section, an amount or a benefit in respect of the use of a motor vehicle by a taxpayer does not include any amount or benefit related to the parking of the vehicle.

Announced Administrative Change — COVID-19 — Employee parking when workplace closed

CRA Backgrounder, Dec. 15, 2020: *Employee-Provided Benefits and Allowances: CRA and COVID-19*

Similarly, when a regular place of employment is closed due to the COVID-19 pandemic, the CRA will not consider an **employer-provided parking spot** at that place of employment to be available for an employee's use. As such, the employer-provided parking will not result in a taxable benefit.

[For the full text of this Backgrounder see under 6(1)(a) — ed.]

Related Provisions: 6(1)(a)(iii), 6(1)(e), (k) — Benefit in respect of the use of an automobile; 6(16)(a) — Parking benefits non-taxable for disabled employee; 15(5) — Automobile benefit to shareholder.

Notes: Since parking is deemed not to be a benefit from use of a motor vehicle, it is not included in the standby charge (6(1)(e), 6(2)), nor in the "operating costs" benefit (6(1)(k)). Instead, it falls under 6(1)(a).

Whether there is a benefit: In *Chow (Topechka)*, [2001] 1 C.T.C. 2741 (TCC), parking passes at work were non-taxable because the primary benefit of the employees being there outside normal work hours was to the employer. In *Saskatchewan Telecommunications*, [1999] G.S.T.C. 69 (TCC), SaskTel was held to have provided parking to employees for its own benefit. In *Adler*, 2007 TCC 272, 14 Telus employees had taxable benefit from their parking passes; 1 did not because he did not use it, and 1 did not because he was required to travel for employment and the pass benefited Telus. In *Schroter*, 2010 FCA 98, 1 Telus employee had a taxable benefit (the GST component was excluded), and 1 did not because he needed a vehicle for his duties.

In *Long*, 2010 TCC 153, a Toronto car mechanic who did not own a car (but occasionally drove his partner's) had no taxable benefit where no space was assigned to him and the employer did not officially make space available; his starting work early did not convert "scramble" parking to a guaranteed space. In *Toronto Parking Authority*, 2010 TCC 193, free parking for parking lot attendants and maintenance people (while working at the lot) was held taxable, despite higher risk of robbery if they had to walk to the bank to deposit money collected. In *Smith*, 2019 FCA 173, a flight attendant's airport parking pass was a taxable benefit.

CRA policy is that there is no benefit if free parking is available to the public (e.g., a shopping centre), or only "scramble" parking is provided; or if parking is provided for business purposes and employees "regularly" have to use their cars for employment: guide T4130, and working irregular hours is not enough: VIEWS doc 2016-0645911E5 (but see *Chow* case above). (Unassigned parking is not the same as scramble parking, which means significantly fewer spaces than employees seeking spaces. "The more important question is whether an employee is actually likely to get a parking spot on a given day": 2011-0422901E5.) Otherwise CRA maintains that parking is a taxable benefit, unless the employee is required to use the vehicle for employment more than half of the week's workdays: 2004-0101151E5, 2005-0110211E5, 2006-0187401E5, 2011-0424671E5. See also 2004-0101151E5, 2005-0110211E5, 2005-0134251E5, 2008-0286381E5, 2008-0288491E5.

Valuation: The benefit is determined based on fair market value, not the employer's cost or the actual value to the employee: *Anthony*, 2011 FCA 336; *Richmond*, [1998] 3 C.T.C. 2552 (TCC); *Bernier*, 2009 TCC 312. See Notes to 6(1)(a) and 69(1). In *Stauffer*, [2002] 4 C.T.C. 2608 (TCC), university employees were held to have paid the real cost of parking on gravelled lots (lower value than paved parking), so there was no taxable benefit.

A CRA interactive questionnaire, to help employers determine whether parking they provide is a taxable benefit, is at tinyurl.com/parking-qa. See also Jamie Golombek, "Employer-provided Parking", 22(1) *Taxation of Executive Compensation & Retirement* (Federated Press) 1312-16 (July/Aug. 2010).

6(1.1) added by 1993 technical bill, effective 1993.

Interpretation Bulletins: IT-63R5: Benefits, including standby charge for an automobile, from the personal use of a motor vehicle supplied by an employer.

I.T. Technical News: 12 (1998 deduction limits and benefit rates for automobiles).

(1.2) Deeming rule — amount received — For the purposes of paragraph (1)(g), an amount received by an individual out of or under an employee benefit plan is deemed to have been received by a taxpayer and not by the individual if

(a) the individual does not deal at arm's length with the taxpayer;

(b) the amount is received in respect of an office or employment of the taxpayer; and

(c) the taxpayer is living at the time the amount is received by the individual.

Notes: 6(1.2) added by 2002-2013 technical bill (Part 5 — technical), effective for benefits received or enjoyed after Oct. 30, 2011.

(2) Reasonable [automobile] standby charge — For the purposes of paragraph (1)(e), a reasonable standby charge for an automobile for the total number of days (in this subsection referred to as the "total available days") in a taxation year during which the automobile is made available to a taxpayer or to a person related to the taxpayer by the employer of the taxpayer or by a person related to the employer (both of whom are in this subsection referred to as the "employer") shall be deemed to be the amount determined by the formula

$$\frac{A}{B} \times \left[2\% \times (C \times D) + \frac{2}{3} \times (E - F)\right]$$

where

A is

(a) the lesser of the total kilometres that the automobile is driven (otherwise than in connection with or in the course of the taxpayer's office or employment) during the total available days and the value determined for the description of B for the year in respect of the standby charge for the automobile during the total available days, if

(i) the taxpayer is required by the employer to use the automobile in connection with or in the course of the office or employment, and

(ii) the distance travelled by the automobile in the total available days is primarily in connection with or in the course of the office or employment, and

(b) the value determined for the description of B for the year in respect of the standby charge for the automobile during the total available days, in any other case;

B is the product obtained when 1,667 is multiplied by the quotient obtained by dividing the total available days by 30 and, if the quotient so obtained is not a whole number and exceeds one, by rounding it to the nearest whole number or, where that quotient is equidistant from two consecutive whole numbers, by rounding it to the lower of those two numbers;

C is the cost of the automobile to the employer where the employer owns the vehicle at any time in the year;

D is the number obtained by dividing such of the total available days as are days when the employer owns the automobile by 30 and, if the quotient so obtained is not a whole number and exceeds one, by rounding it to the nearest whole number or, where that quotient is equidistant from two consecutive whole numbers, by rounding it to the lower of those two numbers;

E is the total of all amounts that may reasonably be regarded as having been payable by the employer to a lessor for the purpose of leasing the automobile during such of the total available days as are days when the automobile is leased to the employer; and

F is the part of the amount determined for E that may reasonably be regarded as having been payable to the lessor in respect of all or part of the cost to the lessor of insuring against

(a) loss of, or damage to, the automobile, or

(b) liability resulting from the use or operation of the automobile.

Related Provisions: 6(2.1) — Reduced benefit for automobile salesperson; 6(2.3) — COVID-19 — Calculation for 2020 or 2021 if A(a)(i)-(ii) conditions met in 2019; 12(1)(y) — Automobile benefit to partner or employee of partner; 15(5) — Rule applies to calculate automobile benefit to shareholder; 85(1)(e.4), (e.5) — Deemed cost following rollover of vehicle to corporation.

Notes: In simple terms, the standby charge (taxable income inclusion) for making a car available to an employee is 24% per year of the *original* cost of the vehicle to the employer, or ⅔ of the leasing cost if it is leased. See generally Form RC18; IT-63R5; T4130, *Employers' Guide — Taxable Benefits*; and VIEWS doc 2009-032308117. The employer's cost is net of any rebate received for fuel-efficient cars under Transport Canada's *ecoAuto* program: doc 2008-0265761E5. If the vehicle is not a 248(1)"automobile", 6(2) does not apply; see Notes to 6(1)(a).

The standby charge applies to partners: 12(1)(y); and to shareholders: 15(5); *Martin*, 2009 TCC 3; *J. Raymond Couvreur Inc.*, 2008 TCC 587.

To calculate the taxable benefit, use CRA's tinyurl.com/autobenefits-calc or Form RC18E. Where 1 car is provided to 2 employees, or 2 cars to 1 employee, see IT-63R5 para. 19 and VIEWS docs 2006-0214581C6, 2012-0454121C6 (doc 2011-0423461E5 fails to address this point and implies the full standby charge could apply to each car). Where a car is provided to an employee working for 2 related corps, one benefit should be counted and T4ed by one of them (and presumably business driving deducted for both): 2018-0777951E5. Weekends are included in the calculation of days the car is "made available": doc 2010-0361431E5.

The cost of the vehicle for C in the formula includes additions, options, accessories, fees and taxes (GST, HST, PST) on the vehicle (net of manufacturer rebates), but not financial fees or extended warranty costs: VIEWS doc 2011-039202117. If another vehicle was traded in to buy it so that BC, Sask or Manitoba sales tax was reduced, the cost includes the reduced PST (and likely the same for GST/HST): 2016-063691117. For an electric vehicle (EV), if one cannot determine recharging cost, the manufacturer's stated cost-per-km may be reasonable; also, purchase cost is not reduced by the Quebec govt subsidy for EVs, as that is paid to the dealer or lessor: 2016-0652861C6 [2016 APFF q.5]. Where the taxpayer is employed by two related companies and one transfers the vehicle to the other at reduced value after 3 years, the lower value applies, subject to 85(1)(e.4), GAAR and sham: 2012-0446921E5; but see also 2014-0529991E5, considering the related person to be the one that actually makes the vehicle available and thus whose cost should be used. Where related company Rco owns the car and leases it to the employer, there is technically a double charge under C and E (since "employer" in 6(2) opening words is defined to include Rco), but CRA accepts that only the leasing cost is included: 2017-0709061C6 [2017 APFF q.13].

Where a vehicle is purchased for a nominal amount at lease-end, that amount might or might not be accepted as the employer's cost for calculating the 2%: VIEWS docs 2009-0350541E5, 2010-0379641E5.

For E, leasing payments do not include insurance costs but may include certain other amounts: VIEWS doc 2008-0270151E5. Government rebates for leasing hybrid automobiles do not reduce E: 2008-0276661E5. Where the monthly lease charges paid off the vehicle and the lease continues for a nominal administrative fee, this amount can possibly be used for E: 2009-0338531E5, 2010-0379641E5.

A lump-sum terminal charge or credit at lease-end is part of the employer's lease cost for the year, or can be adjusted by amending past years' T4s: VIEWS docs 2004-0071441E5, 2005-0143231E5, 2007-0258991C6 (the past years must still be open for reassessment), 2010-0376211E5, 2010-0379641E5, 2011-039969117 [includes self-insured collision damage paid to lessor — for criticism see TEI submission to Finance, Dec. 5, 2012, p. 5, and Finance's continued non-response to TEI, Dec. 5, 2018, q. B.3]; T4130 under heading "Lump-sum lease payments". See also 2006-0167031E5, 2014-0516921R5.

Where the employer leases vehicles and rents them to employees to use solely in their employment duties, then provides an allowance to the employees to cover the cost, see VIEWS doc 2013-0492901E5.

The standby charge can be reduced if the vehicle is "primarily" used for business, and total personal driving (normally including from home to work: see 8(1)(h.1) Notes) does not exceed 20,004 km/year. (For 2020-2021, 2019 driving can be used to meet this condition: see 6(2.3).) "Primarily" may mean "more than 50%" or "first in importance"; see 73(3) Notes. Driving to a special or remote work site (see 6(6)) is not personal driving for this purpose: VIEWS doc 2005-0164991E5. Driving from home to a place requested by the employer, for the employer's benefit, is also not personal: 2010-037174117, 2013-0492901E5. Emblazoning a car with employer logo and advertising does not reduce the employee benefit in CRA's view: 2012-0471731E5, 2015-0582411E5.

Where the above does not apply, but the vehicle is not "available" to the employee throughout the year, formula element E provides a reduction: *Gill*, 2005 TCC 244. An unlicensed and uninsured vehicle is not "available": *Hewitt*, [1996] 1 C.T.C. 2675 (TCC). However, a vehicle is "available" even if it is not used: *Cheung*, [1998] 3 C.T.C. 2729 (TCC). "Made available" does not require unrestricted use, so a car dealer's vehicles that had to be kept free of personal items and on the dealer's premises daily were still "available" to the employees: *Adams*, [1998] 2 C.T.C. 353 (FCA). However, a BC Hydro van that M was required to take home so he could be available in emergencies, and that he was not allowed to use for personal purposes, was not "made available" to M: *MacMillan*, 2005 TCC 583 (CRA does not accept this principle and says that "getting to work is a personal responsibility": VIEWS docs 2005-0158771C6, 2005-0162611E5). In *Mazzafero*, 2019 TCC 147, M never used the company car for personal purposes and did not take possession of it from the dealer or sign the lease, so she was not liable for the standby charge. Where an executive's chauffeur takes the car home nightly, CRA says there is a benefit if the executive's home is the

pickup point each day: 2012-043434117. Where the employee drives their own car to a pickup point each day and switches to an employer car to drive to a work location, see 2013-0484761E5. A vehicle not suited to winter driving, put in storage from November to March, is not "available" during those times: 2011-0401191I7. CRA does not accept that an employee can voluntarily surrender a car and keys while on vacation, so as to reduce the standby charge: 2011-0409221E5. (Perhaps it would if the employer agrees to require that the car be surrendered during vacation! See Drache, "Hard to Escape the Standby Charge", xxxiii(23) *The Canadian Taxpayer* (Carswell) 183 (Dec, 9, 2011).)

Employees who worked out of their employer's pickup trucks, which they took home at night, did not receive a taxable benefit: *Anderson*, [2002] 4 C.T.C. 2008 (TCC). The same applied in *Fox*, 2003 TCC 351 (trucks driven home by forest technicians who had to be available to run errands and respond to emergencies); and *Gauthier*, 2007 TCC 573 (van used by repair technician). CRA still says there is a benefit in such cases at the lower "operating cost" 24¢/km rate in Reg. 7305.1: *Income Tax Technical News* 40 (June 2009); VIEWS docs 2010-0353961E5 and 2011-0419221E5 ("on-call" employees); 2010-0361991E5 (city public works pick-up trucks).

In *Szymczyk*, 2014 TCC 380 (FCA appeal discontinued A-35-15), General Motors and Revenue Canada signed an agreement in 1982 for simplified calculation of the benefit for executives who had multiple cars each year for "product evaluation"; in 2011, CRA ignored the agreement and assessed GM employees for 2008-09. The TCC held that the law and facts had both changed since 1982, so the agreement was no longer binding. (The appeal of the standby charge was allowed due to defective Crown pleadings.)

Keeping a travel log to record mileage is advisable but not mandatory if the taxpayer's evidence of employment-related use of the car is credible: *Keating*, [2001] 4 C.T.C. 2043 (TCC); *Keith*, 2004 TCC 793; *Solomon*, 2004 TCC 774; *Seto*, 2007 TCC 489, para. 25; *Diaz*, 2009 TCC 114; *Groscki*, 2009 TCC 165 [aff'd on other grounds 2011 FCA 174]; *Dale*, 2010 TCC 561; *Glawdecki*, 2010 TCC 650; *Emond*, 2011 TCC 142 (FCA appeal dismissed for delay A-163-11); *Hemmati*, 2013 TCC 66, para. 25; *Galvis*, 2020 TCC 20, para. 9; VIEWS docs 2012-0438001E5, 2012-0454151C6. However, not having *any* records may be fatal: *Singh*, 2008 TCC 149. Quebec requires for provincial tax that employees keep a logbook recording personal miles and provide it to the employer within 10 days after year-end to calculate the benefit: *Taxation Act* ss. 41.1.4, 1049.34 ($200 penalty for failing to do this). Odotrack.ca sells a device that can track business use, and some cars now keep GPS records of all travel. CRA states (tinyurl.com/cra-travel-log) that once a business has a full logbook to show business use of a vehicle for a year, a 3-month sample can be used in later years if usage is within 10% of the base year; this option is not for employee use of a vehicle [Lim & Mapa, "Sample Mileage Logbooks", 19(4) *Canadian Tax Highlights* (ctf.ca) 2-3 (April 2011)].

Where the standby charge does not apply because the vehicle is not an "automobile" (e.g., a clearly-marked emergency vehicle), there may still be a taxable benefit under 6(1)(a) if the vehicle is taken home, and driving the vehicle to work is considered personal use: VIEWS docs 2004-0107081E5, 2005-0117581R5, 2010-0361991E5, 2010-0364091E5, 2017-0689241E5; for calculation of the benefit see IT-63R5 para. 23, *Income Tax Technical News* 40, and doc 2007-0251471E5. Similarly, if the corporation does not own the vehicle but pays the lease and operating expenses, the benefit will be under 6(1)(a): docs 2005-015650117, 2007-026336117. Where s. 6 does not apply because the person receiving the benefit is an independent contractor or incorporated, the benefit is taxed under 9(1): 2016-063846117.

GST or HST must be remitted on automobile benefits. See *Excise Tax Act* s. 173 in David M. Sherman, *Practitioner's Goods and Services Tax Annotated*; guide T4130, Chapter 5; GST/HST Memorandum 9.2, "Automobile Benefits". See also 6(7).

Descriptions of A, B amended by 2003 Budget, for 2003 and later taxation years.

Regulations: 200(3) (information return).

Interpretation Bulletins: IT-63R5: Benefits, including standby charge for an automobile, from the personal use of a motor vehicle supplied by an employer; IT-291R3: Transfer of property to a corporation under subsection 85(1).

I.T. Technical News: 12 (1998 deduction limits and benefit rates for automobiles); 40 (employer vehicles required to be taken home at night).

CRA Audit Manual: 27.10.0: Employee and shareholder benefits.

Forms: RC18: Calculating automobile benefits; T4130: Employer's guide — taxable benefits.

(2.1) Automobile salesman — Where in a taxation year

  (a) a taxpayer was employed principally in selling or leasing automobiles,

  (b) an automobile owned by the taxpayer's employer was made available by the employer to the taxpayer or to a person related to the taxpayer, and

  (c) the employer has acquired one or more automobiles,

the amount that would otherwise be determined under subsection (2) as a reasonable standby charge shall, at the option of the employer, be computed as if

  (d) the reference in the formula in subsection (2) to "2%" were read as a reference to "1½%", and

(e) the cost to the employer of the automobile were the greater of

> (i) the quotient obtained by dividing

>> (A) the cost to the employer of all new automobiles acquired by the employer in the year for sale or lease in the course of the employer's business

> by

>> (B) the number of automobiles described in clause (A), and

> (ii) the quotient obtained by dividing

>> (A) the cost to the employer of all automobiles acquired by the employer in the year for sale or lease in the course of the employer's business

> by

>> (B) the number of automobiles described in clause (A).

Notes: As well as a reduced standby charge, automobile salespersons are also eligible for a reduced calculation of the benefit for operating costs. See Notes to 6(1)(k).

In the calculation, the employer must use the average cost of all automobiles (see 248(1)"automobile") it owned throughout the year, not the average cost of all automobiles it owned on a given day in the year: VIEWS doc 2004-0066911E5. Luxury vehicles must be counted in the calculation: 2006-0177111E5.

Interpretation Bulletins: IT-63R5: Benefits, including standby charge for an automobile, from the personal use of a motor vehicle supplied by an employer.

I.T. Technical News: 12 (1998 deduction limits and benefit rates for automobiles).

(2.2) COVID-19 — automobile operating expense benefit — If a taxpayer met the condition in subparagraph (iv) of the description of A in paragraph (1)(k) for the 2019 taxation year in respect of the use of an automobile made available to the taxpayer, or to a person related to the taxpayer, by an employer (within the meaning assigned by subsection (2)), then for the purpose of applying paragraph (1)(k) in respect of an automobile provided by that employer in 2020 or 2021 (referred to in this subsection as the "relevant year"), the amount determined for A in paragraph (1)(k) in respect of the automobile for the relevant year is deemed to be the lesser of

(a) $\frac{1}{2}$ of the amount determined under subparagraph (1)(e)(i) in respect of the automobile for the relevant year, and

(b) the amount determined under subparagraph (v) of the description of A in paragraph (1)(k) in respect of the automobile for the relevant year.

Related Provisions: 87(2)(g.7) — Amalgamation or windup — continuing corporation.

Notes: 6(2.2) provides COVID-19 relief for 2020-21. It reduces the 6(1)(k) taxable-benefit inclusion for automobile operating expenses, if 6(1)(k)A(iv) applied in 2019 (employer's car used primarily in employment duties). The optional calculation of the benefit as half the standby fee is reduced by half for 2020 and 2021. 6(2.2)-(2.3) were announced by Finance news release, Dec. 21, 2020, and enacted by 2021 budget bill #1, effective June 29, 2021.

Former 6(2.2) repealed by 1993 technical bill, effective 1993. It provided an alternate calculation of the operating expense benefit (now in 6(1)(k)(iv)).

(2.3) COVID-19 — reasonable standby charge — A taxpayer is deemed to meet the condition in subparagraph (a)(ii) of the description of A in subsection (2) in respect of an employer (within the meaning assigned by subsection (2)) for the 2020 or 2021 taxation year if the taxpayer met the conditions in subparagraphs (a)(i) and (ii) of the description of A in subsection (2) for the 2019 taxation year in respect of an automobile made available to the taxpayer, or to a person related to the taxpayer, by that employer.

Related Provisions: 87(2)(g.7) — Amalgamation or windup — continuing corporation.

Notes: 6(2.3) provides COVID-19 relief for 2020-21. It reduces the 6(2) "standby fee" for having an employer-provided automobile, if 6(2)A(a)(i)-(ii) applied in 2019 (employee required to use the car for work, and car primarily driven for employment duties). The test of the car being primarily driven for employment duties is then deemed to apply in 2020 and 2021. See also Notes to 6(2.2).

(3) Payments by employer to employee — An amount received by one person from another

> (a) during a period while the payee was an officer of, or in the employment of, the payer, or

> (b) on account, in lieu of payment or in satisfaction of an obligation arising out of an agreement made by the payer with the payee immediately prior to, during or immediately after a period that the payee was an officer of, or in the employment of, the payer,

shall be deemed, for the purposes of section 5, to be remuneration for the payee's services rendered as an officer or during the period of employment, unless it is established that, irrespective of when the agreement, if any, under which the amount was received was made or the form or legal effect thereof, it cannot reasonably be regarded as having been received

> (c) as consideration or partial consideration for accepting the office or entering into the contract of employment,

> (d) as remuneration or partial remuneration for services as an officer or under the contract of employment, or

> (e) in consideration or partial consideration for a covenant with reference to what the officer or employee is, or is not, to do before or after the termination of the employment.

Related Provisions: 6(3.1) — Timing of income inclusion from non-compete agreement; 56.4(4)(a) — Amount paid by purchaser for non-compete agreement deemed to be wages paid to employee; 87(2)(k) — Amalgamation — Amount received by employee from new corporation; 153(1)(a) — Withholding of tax by employer.

Notes: 6(3), 6(1)(a) and 5(1) together provide that virtually any payment from an employer to an employee may be taxable (see Income Tax Folio S2-F3-C1), but see Notes to 248(1)"retiring allowance" and to s. 3.

"Immediately after" did not apply to a payment under an agreement made a month after employment terminated: *No. 261*, 1955 CarswellNat 99 (Tax Appeal Board).

6(3) or its predecessors applied in: *Butters*, 1952 CarswellNat 12 (TAB) (trust company branch manager given paid leave plus retainer to ensure his availability); *Moss*, [1963] C.T.C. 535 (Exch. Ct) (on termination, payment to waive M's right to buy business was to release company from agreement under employment contract); *Bridgewater*, 1969 CarswellNat 214 (TAB) (lump sum on B leaving his father's business); *Richstone*, [1974] C.T.C. 155 (FCA) (10-year payouts to 2 brothers who agreed to sell shares in family business to third brother); *Demers*, [1981] C.T.C. 282 (FCTD) (cost-of-living adjustment paid after end of temporary employment contract); *Greiner*, [1984] C.T.C. 92 (FCA) (payment on employer's amalgamation as part of G moving to new employer); *Galanov*, [1987] 2 C.T.C. 2353 (TCC) (on firing G, employer forgave mortgage it had provided to assist G's relocation); *Morissette*, 2006 TCC 284 ($20,000 severance payment to investment advisor; further $5,000 for keeping his clients was for goodwill and non-taxable); *Desmarais*, 2006 TCC 417 ($350,000 lump sum); *Lockhart*, 2008 TCC 156 (shares issued to pay an owner for working without pay, in advance of merger with public company, were taxable even though he exchanged them for shares held in escrow that ultimately had no value).

6(3) applies to the following in CRA's view: payment to retired police officer to attend court as a witness (VIEWS doc 2005-0154091E5); payment to retired employee to compensate for cancelling life insurance benefit (2009-0339901E5); recruitment payment to recent graduate (2009-0352621E5); payments to employee or former employee for invention or design (2006-0201521E5, 2010-0391651E5, 2011-0397121E5); compensation for cancellation of group term life insurance plan on employer's bankruptcy (2012-0442671I7); payment to purchase employee's client list (2014-0526931E5); lump-sum amount from former employer in connection with non-competition agreement (2015-0599581E5, and see 6(3.1)).

Income Tax Folios: S1-F2-C1: Education and textbook tax credits [replaces IT-515R2]; S1-F2-C3: Scholarships, research grants and other education assistance [replaces IT-340R]; S2-F3-C1: Payments from employer to employee [replaces IT-196R2 and its SR]; S3-F9-C1: Lottery winnings, miscellaneous receipts, and income (and losses) from crime [replaces IT-185R, IT-213R, IT-256R, IT-334R2].

Interpretation Bulletins: IT-168R3: Athletes and players employed by football, hockey and similar clubs; IT-247: Employer's contributions to pensioners' premiums under provincial medical and hospital services plans (cancelled); IT-365R2: Damages, settlements and similar receipts; IT-470R: Employees' fringe benefits; IT-529: Flexible employee benefit programs.

(3.1) Amount receivable for covenant — If an amount (other than an amount to which paragraph (1)(a) applies because of subsection (11)) is receivable at the end of a taxation year by a taxpayer in respect of a covenant, agreed to by the taxpayer more than 36 months before the end of that taxation year, with reference to what the taxpayer is, or is not, to do, and the amount would be included in the taxpayer's income for the year under this Subdivision if it were received by the taxpayer in the year, the amount

(a) is deemed to be received by the taxpayer at the end of the taxation year for services rendered as an officer or during the period of employment; and

(b) is deemed not to be received at any other time.

Related Provisions: 6(3), 56.4(2) — Income inclusion from non-compete agreement; 60(f) — Deduction for bad debt.

Notes: Inclusion as employment income (whether under 6(3) or 6(3.1)) takes precedence over inclusion under 56.4: see 56.4(3)(a).

See Thompson, "The Impact of the Department of Finance Draft Legislation", 15(5) *Taxation of Executive Compensation & Retirement* (Federated Press) 364-68 (Jan. 2004). See also VIEWS doc 2015-0599581E5 (general comments).

6(3.1) added by 2002-2013 technical bill, for amounts received in respect of a covenant agreed to after Oct. 7, 2003.

Income Tax Folios: S2-F3-C1: Payments from employer to employee [replaces IT-196R2 and its SR].

(4) Group term life insurance — Where at any time in a taxation year a taxpayer's life is insured under a group term life insurance policy, there shall be included in computing the taxpayer's income for the year from an office or employment the amount, if any, prescribed for the year in respect of the insurance.

Related Provisions: 18(9)(a)(iii), 18(9.01) — Limitation on deduction for premiums paid; 139.1(15) — Effect of demutualization of insurance corporation; 139.1(16), (17) — Flow-through of demutualization benefits by employer to employee; 144.1(10) — Employee contributions to employee life and health trust deemed to be payment of group life insurance premiums if so identified; 153(1)(a) — Withholding of tax by employer.

Notes: CRA said a lump-sum payout of group term life insurance before death is taxable, while after death it may be a "death benefit" under 56(1)(a)(iii): VIEWS doc 2010-0359171E5. See also *Scott*, 2017 TCC 224 (lump sum from the Nortel health & welfare trust, upon employees losing coverage due to Nortel's bankruptcy).

"Reducing the Reporting Burden for Employers" (Jan. 23, 2018: tinyurl.com/cra-reducing) states: "Employers who pay group term life insurance premiums for retirees will [starting 2018] only have to report a paid premium if it is greater than $50 and it is the only income reported on a T4A slip."

Group term life insurance is now fully taxable, where before July 1994 the first $25,000 of coverage was exempt. See Guide T4130; VIEWS docs 2008-0274441E5, 2009-0312171E5, 2015-0618191E5.

6(4) amended by 1994 Budget, for insurance in respect of periods after June 1994.

Regulations: 2700–2704 (prescribed amount).

Income Tax Folios: S2-F1-C1: Health and welfare trusts [replaces IT-85R2].

Interpretation Bulletins: IT-529: Flexible employee benefit programs.

I.T. Technical News: 25 (health and welfare trusts).

(5) [Repealed]

Notes: 6(5) repealed by 1994 Budget, effective 1995. It provided an interpretation of "policy year" for the 1972–94 versions of 6(4).

(6) Employment at special work site or remote location — Notwithstanding subsection (1), in computing the income of a taxpayer for a taxation year from an office or employment, there shall not be included any amount received or enjoyed by the taxpayer in respect of, in the course or by virtue of the office or employment that is the value of, or an allowance (not in excess of a reasonable amount) in respect of expenses the taxpayer has incurred for,

(a) the taxpayer's board and lodging for a period at

(i) a special work site, being a location at which the duties performed by the taxpayer were of a temporary nature, if the taxpayer maintained at another location a self-contained domestic establishment as the taxpayer's principal place of residence

(A) that was, throughout the period, available for the taxpayer's occupancy and not rented by the taxpayer to any other person, and

(B) to which, by reason of distance, the taxpayer could not reasonably be expected to have returned daily from the special work site, or

(ii) a location at which, by virtue of its remoteness from any established community, the taxpayer could not reasonably be

expected to establish and maintain a self-contained domestic establishment,

if the period during which the taxpayer was required by the taxpayer's duties to be away from the taxpayer's principal place of residence, or to be at the special work site or location, was not less than 36 hours; or

(b) transportation between

(i) the principal place of residence and the special work site referred to in subparagraph (a)(i), or

(ii) the location referred to in subparagraph (a)(ii) and a location in Canada or a location in the country in which the taxpayer is employed,

in respect of a period described in paragraph (a) during which the taxpayer received board and lodging, or a reasonable allowance in respect of board and lodging, from the taxpayer's employer.

Related Provisions: 67.1(2)(e.1) — Construction work camp — meals fully deductible; 110.7(4) — Northern allowance reduced by amounts excluded under 6(6).

Notes: 6(6) can exempt only an allowance that is "reasonable": *Bergeron*, 2010 TCC 56; VIEWS docs 2008-0284191E5, 2014-055888117. An allowance "that approximates the transportation expenses to be incurred by the employee" is reasonable: 2013-0506241E5. 6(6) does not apply to an incorporated employee: *609309 Alberta*, 2010 TCC 166, para. 36.

6(6)(a)(i): a special work site need not be remote in the sense of isolated. For someone based in Calgary, for example, Toronto can be a "special work site". See *Jaffar*, [2002] 1 C.T.C. 2204 (TCC) (Rochester, NY qualified); *Rozumiak*, 2005 TCC 811 (Chicago qualified); and *Agostini*, 2009 TCC 87 (Collingwood, Ont. qualified). In *McEachern*, 2018 TCC 232, para. 16, Edmonton did not qualify as it was a "pick-up point" for a remote NWT mine site, not a work site. CRA policy (see IT-91R4) will not follow *Jaffar*, which was an informal procedure decision: VIEWS doc 2002-0125275. The exemption was unavailable in *Bourget*, 2009 TCC 533 (work site was too close to a home the taxpayer rented); and *Rio*, 2015 TCC 286 (FCA appeal discontinued A-526-15) (duties at site were not temporary). The employer need not be resident in Canada: 2006-0217331E5. A ship can qualify: 2010-0354771E5, IT-254R2 [cancelled Sept. 30/12]. For more interpretations on special work sites see 2004-0099101R3, 2005-0163341E5, 2006-01658211E5, 2006-0168981E5, 2007-0224441E5, 2007-0262851E5, 2008-0280221E5, 2008-0288681E5, 2008-0289311E5, 2008-0291081E5, 2008-0296431E5, 2009-0332901E5, 2009-0352811E5, 2010-0364801E5, 2010-0382181E5, 2011-0395571I7, 2012-0421921I7, 2013-0500761E5, 2014-0549061E5; Lee, "The Special Work Site Exemption...", 17(5) *Taxation of Executive Compensation & Retirement* (Federated Press) 619-27 (Dec-Jan. 2006); Winters & Novotny, "The 'Special Work Site' and 'Remote Location' Exemptions", 2014 Prairie Provinces Tax Conf. (ctf.ca), 10:1-34.

McEachern, 2018 TCC 232, paras. 6, 18-23, says 6(6) exemption requires Form TD4 from the employer, but in the author's view this is wrong: the cases cited re 8(10) are irrelevant because 8(10) requires a form and 6(6) does not.

CRA interprets "duties ... of a temporary nature" in 6(6)(a)(i) as not expected to be for more than 2 years: IT-91R4 paras. 5-6; VIEWS doc 2012-0449511E5. However, a transfer for several years can still be "temporary": 2006-0175331E5, 2008-0274361E5, 2009-0335751E5 (prepaying the allowance could lead to 80.4(1) deemed interest), 2011-0399091E5, 2011-0404151E5, 2012-0408181E5, 2012-0421921I7, 2013-0481321E5, 2012-0472981E5, 2014-054412117, 2014-054719117. In *Dubé*, [1999] 2 C.T.C. 2871 (TCC), and *Dupuis*, [2010] 1 C.T.C. 2021 (TCC), long-term work that was never guaranteed to continue was "temporary" [CRA confines *Dupuis* to its own facts: 2009-034892117]. Work was not "temporary" in *Burton*, [2006] 2 C.T.C. 286 (FCA) (despite owner's business plan to sell company), and *Léonard*, 2008 CarswellNat 2179 (TCC) (Quebec helicopter pilot's worksite in Alberta).

"Principal place of residence" in 6(6)(a)(i) PPR is based on the important connections the employee has, rather than the amount of time spent. In *Larson*, 2003 TCC 560, L's home remained his PPR even though he purchased a home at the work site. Where the employee's family resides is a persuasive factor but is not conclusive: VIEWS doc 2004-0067081E5. In *Spannier*, 2013 TCC 40, S qualified under 6(6)(a)(i) because she "maintained" a residence in Kelowna while working near Fort McMurray, even though she paid no rent, as "maintain" means "preserve for use" or "keep available" (para. 43), and in any event she provided services to the owner.

On "maintain a self-contained domestic establishment", see VIEWS doc 2018-0780481E5. In *Dupuis* (above) paras. 47-50, the fact the employee *did* set up a self-contained domestic establishment did not negate that Mistissini, QC was so remote that he could not reasonably be expected to for 6(6)(a)(ii)!

6(6)(a)(ii): CRA interprets "remote" as more than 80km, and "established community" as at least 1,000 people with a food store, clothing store, accommodations, and some medical and educational facilities: IT-91R4 paras. 14-17; VIEWS doc 2015-0570251E5.

See RC4054, *Ceiling Amounts for Housing Benefits Paid in Prescribed Zones*, and VIEWS doc 2011-0409561E5, for limits on rent and utilities paid to employees living in a prescribed zone without developed rental markets (for 2021: $558/month for an apartment rent-only, $829 with utilities, $933 for a house and $1,346 with utilities). The ceiling cannot be prorated where the employee lives in the accommodation only part of the month, but the employer may prorate the fair market value if that better reflects the value of the accommodation: 2012-0459981E5.

Allowances for living or travel do not fall under 6(6) if not used to pay for housing: *Théberge*, 2006 TCC 561. A board and lodging allowance (BLA) is exempt only if the employee actually incurs expenses and the amount is reasonable: VIEWS doc 2015-0614121E5. A remote mine site allowance that is not for BLA or transportation does not qualify: 2011-0414061E5. A travel allowance is not exempt under 6(6)(b) unless a BLA is also provided per 6(6)(a): 2011-0427831E5, 2019-0806021I7. BLAs calculated from the National Joint Council Travel Directive, paid by a charity to volunteers in remote sites, are reasonable and thus exempt, but Charities Policy CPC-012 does not apply to permit a volunteer to waive the allowance and take a donation receipt instead: 2014-0550771E5.

Transportation or a rental car provided from an employee's temporary boarding location to a special work site is not exempt under 6(6)(b): IT-91R4 para. 10, VIEWS doc 2016-0670851E5; but might not be taxable under 6(1)(a) in the first place: 2004-0084201E5 (effectively overruling 2004-0059521E5). An allowance for such travel is taxable if the work site is the employee's regular place of employment (see Notes to 8(1)(h.1)): 2011-0421441I7, 2011-0425961E5, but not if it falls under 6(6)(b): 2014-0563801E5. In *Hamilton*, 2020 TCC 23, para. 25, a travel allowance did not qualify because it was *calculated* (for all employees) based on distance from city hall rather than from home; this seems wrong given the purpose of the allowance. Where pick-up trucks are provided to groups of employees to travel between a mine and a nearby community, see 2009-0310401E5. Transportation of a family member could be exempt: 2009-0346161E5.

6(6) applies for purposes of the standby charge in 6(2), so driving to the special or remote work site is not considered personal driving: VIEWS doc 2005-0164991E5.

6(6) applies to exclude the allowance from a non-resident's taxable income earned in Canada: 115(1)(a)(i), VIEWS doc 2008-0297661E5.

See also T4130, *Employer's Guide — Taxable Benefits*. Qualifying communities are listed in T4039, *Northern Residents Deductions — Places in Prescribed Zones*.

Interpretation Bulletins: IT-91R4: Employment at special work sites or remote work locations; IT-168R3: Athletes and players employed by football, hockey and similar clubs; IT-254R2: Fishermen — employees and seafarers — value of rations and quarters (cancelled); IT-470R: Employees' fringe benefits; IT-518R: Food, beverages and entertainment expenses; IT-522R: Vehicle, travel and sales expenses of employees.

Forms: RC4054: Ceiling amounts for housing benefits paid in prescribed zones; TD4: Declaration of exemption — Employment at special work site; T4039: Northern residents deductions — places in prescribed zones [guide]; T4130: Employer's guide — taxable benefits.

(7) Cost of property or service [includes GST, etc.] — To
the extent that the cost to a person of purchasing a property or service or an amount payable by a person for the purpose of leasing property is taken into account in determining an amount required under this section to be included in computing a taxpayer's income for a taxation year, that cost or amount payable, as the case may be, shall include any tax that was payable by the person in respect of the property or service or that would have been so payable if the person were not exempt from the payment of that tax because of the nature of the person or the use to which the property or service is to be put.

Notes: 6(7) amended by 1997 GST/HST bill, for 1996 and later tax years. The change requires that GST payable by the employer be included in the calculation of a taxable benefit, rather than calculated and included as a separate benefit, as it was under 6(1)(e.1) before 1996. The reference to the "nature of the person" means that GST not paid by certain provincial governments and status Indians is still included in the value of the taxable benefit. Thus, the employee who is the consumer cannot benefit from the employer's special status.

6(7) added by 1990 GST, effective 1991.

Interpretation Bulletins: IT-63R5: Benefits, including standby charge for an automobile, from the personal use of a motor vehicle supplied by an employer.

I.T. Technical News: 12 (1998 deduction limits and benefit rates for automobiles).

(8) GST rebates re costs of property or service — If
(a) an amount in respect of an outlay or expense is deducted under section 8 in computing the income of a taxpayer for a taxation year from an office or employment, or

(b) an amount is included in the capital cost to a taxpayer of a property described in subparagraph 8(1)(j)(ii) or 8(1)(p)(ii),

and a particular amount is paid to the taxpayer in a particular taxation year as a rebate under the *Excise Tax Act* in respect of any goods and services tax included in the amount of the outlay or ex-

pense, or the capital cost of the property, as the case may be, the particular amount

(c) to the extent that it relates to an outlay or expense referred to in paragraph (a), shall be included in computing the taxpayer's income from an office or employment for the particular taxation year, and

(d) to the extent that it relates to the capital cost of property referred to in paragraph (b), is deemed, for the purposes of subsection 13(7.1), to have been received by the taxpayer in the particular taxation year as assistance from a government for the acquisition of the property.

Related Provisions: 8(11) — GST rebate deemed not to be reimbursement.

Notes: 6(8) amended by 2001 Budget, effective for 2002 and later taxation years.

6(8) added by 1990 GST, effective 1991.

(9) Amount in respect of interest on employee debt —
Where an amount in respect of a loan or debt is deemed by subsection 80.4(1) to be a benefit received in a taxation year by an individual, the amount of the benefit shall be included in computing the income of the individual for the year as income from an office or employment.

Related Provisions: 6(23) — Taxable benefit from employer-provided housing subsidy; 15(9) — Deemed benefit to shareholder.

Regulations: 200(2)(g) (information return).

Remission Orders: *Ice Storm Employee Benefits Remission Order*, P.C. 1998-2047.

Interpretation Bulletins: IT-171R2: Non-resident individuals — computation of taxable income earned in Canada and non-refundable tax credits (cancelled); IT-421R2: Benefits to individuals, corporations and shareholders from loans or debt.

I.T. Technical News: 6 (payment of mortgage interest subsidy by employer).

(10) Contributions to an employee benefit plan — For the
purposes of subparagraph (1)(g)(ii),

(a) an amount included in the income of an individual in respect of an employee benefit plan for a taxation year preceding the year in which it was paid out of the plan shall be deemed to be an amount contributed to the plan by the individual; and

(b) where an amount is received in a taxation year by an individual from an employee benefit plan that was in a preceding year an employee trust, such portion of the amount so received by the individual as does not exceed the amount, if any, by which the lesser of

(i) the amount, if any, by which

(A) the total of all amounts allocated to the individual or a deceased person of whom the individual is an heir or legal representative by the trustee of the plan at a time when it was an employee trust

exceeds

(B) the total of all amounts previously paid out of the plan to or for the benefit of the individual or the deceased person at a time when the plan was an employee trust, and

(ii) the portion of the amount, if any, by which the cost amount to the plan of its property immediately before it ceased to be an employee trust exceeds its liabilities at that time that

(A) the amount determined under subparagraph (i) in respect of the individual

is of

(B) the total of amounts determined under subparagraph (i) in respect of all individuals who were beneficiaries under the plan immediately before it ceased to be an employee trust

exceeds

(iii) the total of all amounts previously received out of the plan by the individual or a deceased person of whom the individual is an heir or legal representative at a time when the plan was an employee benefit plan to the extent that the amounts were deemed by this paragraph to be a return of amounts contributed to the plan shall be deemed to be the return of an amount contributed to the plan by the individual.

Interpretation Bulletins: IT-498: The deductibility of interest on money borrowed to reloan to employees or shareholders (cancelled); IT-502: Employee benefit plans and employee trusts.

(11) Salary deferral arrangement — Where at the end of a taxation year any person has a right under a salary deferral arrangement in respect of a taxpayer to receive a deferred amount, an amount equal to the deferred amount shall be deemed, for the purposes only of paragraph (1)(a), to have been received by the taxpayer as a benefit in the year, to the extent that the amount was not otherwise included in computing the taxpayer's income for the year or any preceding taxation year.

Related Provisions: 6(1)(a)(v) — Taxable benefit income inclusion; 6(1)(i) — SDA payment taxed; 6(12)–(14) — SDA rules; 8(1)(o) — Forfeited amounts; 20(1)(oo), (pp) — SDA — deduction to employer; 56(1)(w) — Benefit from SDA included in income.

Notes: See Notes to 248(1)"salary deferral arrangement" and "deferred amount". For the meaning of "not otherwise included" see Notes to 20(1)(j).

Advance Tax Rulings: ATR-39: Self-funded leave of absence; ATR-45: Share appreciation rights plan; ATR-64: Phantom stock award plan.

(12) Idem — Where at the end of a taxation year any person has a right under a salary deferral arrangement (other than a trust governed by a salary deferral arrangement) in respect of a taxpayer to receive a deferred amount, an amount equal to any interest or other additional amount that accrued to, or for the benefit of, that person to the end of the year in respect of the deferred amount shall be deemed at the end of the year, for the purposes only of subsection (11), to be a deferred amount that the person has a right to receive under the arrangement.

Notes: See Notes to 248(1)"salary deferral arrangement".

(13) Application — Subsection (11) does not apply in respect of a deferred amount under a salary deferral arrangement in respect of a taxpayer that was established primarily for the benefit of one or more non-resident employees in respect of services to be rendered in a country other than Canada, to the extent that the deferred amount

(a) was in respect of services rendered by an employee who

(i) was not resident in Canada at the time the services were rendered, or

(ii) was resident in Canada for a period (in this subsection referred to as an "excluded period") of not more than 36 of the 72 months preceding the time the services were rendered and was an employee to whom the arrangement applied before the employee became resident in Canada; and

(b) cannot reasonably be regarded as being in respect of services rendered or to be rendered during a period (other than an excluded period) when the employee was resident in Canada.

Related Provisions: 18(1)(o.1) — SDA — no deduction of outlays for non-residents.

(14) Part of plan or arrangement — Where deferred amounts under a salary deferral arrangement in respect of a taxpayer (in this subsection referred to as "that arrangement") are required to be included as benefits under paragraph (1)(a) in computing the taxpayer's income and that arrangement is part of a plan or arrangement (in this subsection referred to as the "plan") under which amounts or benefits not related to the deferred amounts are payable or provided, for the purposes of this Act, other than this subsection,

(a) that arrangement shall be deemed to be a separate arrangement independent of other parts of the plan of which it is a part; and

(b) where any person has a right to a deferred amount under that arrangement, an amount received by the person as a benefit at any time out of or under the plan shall be deemed to have been

received out of or under that arrangement except to the extent that it exceeds the amount, if any, by which

(i) the total of all deferred amounts under that arrangement that were included under paragraph (1)(a) as benefits in computing the taxpayer's income for taxation years ending before that time

exceeds

(ii) the total of

(A) all deferred amounts received by any person before that time out of or under the plan that were deemed by this paragraph to have been received out of or under that arrangement, and

(B) all deferred amounts under that arrangement that were deducted under paragraph 8(1)(o) in computing the taxpayer's income for the year or preceding taxation years.

Related Provisions: 6(1)(g) — Employee benefit plan benefits; 56(10) — Severability of retirement compensation arrangement.

Notes: See VIEWS doc 2017-0737571E5 (share appreciation rights plan providing for dividend equivalents).

(15) Forgiveness of employee debt — For the purpose of paragraph (1)(a),

(a) a benefit shall be deemed to have been enjoyed by a taxpayer at any time an obligation issued by any debtor (including the taxpayer) is settled or extinguished; and

(b) the value of that benefit shall be deemed to be the forgiven amount at that time in respect of the obligation.

Related Provisions: 6(15.1) — Meaning of "forgiven amount"; 15(1.2) — Forgiveness of shareholder loans; 79(3)F(b)(i) — Where property surrendered to creditor; 80(1)"forgiven amount"B(b) — Debt forgiveness rules do not apply to amount of benefit; 80.01 — Deemed settlement of debts.

Notes: For the meaning of "extinguished", see Notes to 80(2)(a).

In *Rémillard*, 2011 TCC 327, a corporation forgave a $5m debt to its President; the Court found the English and French text inconsistent and ruled that 6(15.1) does not apply if the debt was not a "commercial obligation", but 6(15) applied anyway. However, the French text was corrected by the 2002-2013 technical bill, retroactive to 1994, to ensure that 6(15.1) merely requires calculating the "forgiven amount" *as if* there were a commercial obligation.

See VIEWS docs 2008-0290481R3, 2009-0331661E5 for examples of 6(15). A low balance forgiven by a federal agency under *Financial Administration Act* s. 155.2 is not a 6(15) benefit as it is not forgiven due to employment: 2015-059673117; but 2016-063778117 says 6(15) covers a balance forgiven due to the employee's financial hardship, bankruptcy or the debt going statute-barred (*quaere* whether the last is correct).

CRA generally allows the employer a deduction for the amount taxed under 6(15), provided it is reasonable (s. 67): VIEWS doc 2002-0156785.

6(15) amended by 1994 technical bill, essentially to refer to the "forgiven amount" in 6(15.1), effective for taxation years that end after Feb. 21, 1994.

Interpretation Bulletins: IT-421R2: Benefits to individuals, corporations and shareholders from loans or debt.

(15.1) Forgiven amount — For the purpose of subsection (15), the "forgiven amount" at any time in respect of an obligation issued by a debtor has the meaning that would be assigned by subsection 80(1) if

(a) the obligation were a commercial obligation (within the meaning assigned by subsection 80(1)) issued by the debtor;

(b) no amount included in computing income because of the obligation being settled or extinguished at that time were taken into account;

(c) the definition "forgiven amount" in subsection 80(1) were read without reference to paragraphs (f) and (h) of the description of B in that definition; and

(d) section 80 were read without reference to paragraphs (2)(b) and (q) of that section.

Related Provisions: 80.01(1)"forgiven amount" — Application of definition for purposes of s. 80.01; 248(26) — Liability deemed to be obligation issued by debtor; 248(27) — Partial settlement of debt obligation.

Notes: See Notes to 6(15) re *Rémillard* case.

6(15.1) added by 1994 technical bill, for tax years that end after Feb. 21, 1994.

(16) Disability-related employment benefits [transportation, parking, attendant] — Notwithstanding subsection (1), in computing an individual's income for a taxation year from an office or employment, there shall not be included any amount received or enjoyed by the individual in respect of, in the course of or because of the individual's office or employment that is the value of a benefit relating to, or an allowance (not in excess of a reasonable amount) in respect of expenses incurred by the individual for,

(a) the transportation of the individual between the individual's ordinary place of residence and the individual's work location (including parking near that location) if the individual is blind or is a person in respect of whom an amount is deductible, or would but for paragraph 118.3(1)(c) be deductible, because of the individual's mobility impairment, under section 118.3 in computing a taxpayer's tax payable under this Part for the year; or

(b) an attendant to assist the individual in the performance of the individual's duties if the individual is a person in respect of whom an amount is deductible, or would but for paragraph 118.3(1)(c) be deductible, under section 118.3 in computing a taxpayer's tax payable under this Part for the year.

Related Provisions: 6(1.1) — Parking normally a taxable benefit; 64 — Disability supports deduction for attendant care and other expenses; 118.4(1) — Nature of impairment.

Notes: See VIEWS doc 2019-0807801E5 (CRA interpretation of "blind").

6(16) added by 1991 Budget, effective 1991.

(17) Definitions — The definitions in this subsection apply in this subsection and subsection (18).

"disability policy" means a group disability insurance policy that provides for periodic payments to individuals in respect of the loss of remuneration from an office or employment.

"employer" of an individual includes a former employer of the individual.

Notes: See Notes to 188.1(5) re meaning of "includes".

"top-up disability payment" in respect of an individual means a payment made by an employer of the individual as a consequence of the insolvency of an insurer that was obligated to make payments to the individual under a disability policy where

(a) the payment is made to an insurer so that periodic payments made to the individual under the policy will not be reduced because of the insolvency, or will be reduced by a lesser amount, or

(b) the following conditions are satisfied:

(i) the payment is made to the individual to replace, in whole or in part, periodic payments that would have been made under the policy to the individual but for the insolvency, and

(ii) the payment is made under an arrangement by which the individual is required to reimburse the payment to the extent that the individual subsequently receives an amount from an insurer in respect of the portion of the periodic payments that the payment was intended to replace.

For the purposes of paragraphs (a) and (b), an insurance policy that replaces a disability policy is deemed to be the same policy as, and a continuation of, the disability policy that was replaced.

Related Provisions: 8(1)(n) — Reimbursement under (b)(ii) not deductible as salary reimbursement; 8(1)(n.1) — Limited deduction for reimbursements under (b)(ii).

Notes [6(17)]: 6(17) added by 1995-97 technical bill, for payments made after Aug. 10, 1994. See Notes to 6(18).

(18) Group disability benefits — insolvent insurer — Where an employer of an individual makes a top-up disability payment in respect of the individual,

(a) the payment is, for the purpose of paragraph (1)(a), deemed not to be a benefit received or enjoyed by the individual;

(b) the payment is, for the purpose of paragraph (1)(f), deemed not to be a contribution made by the employer to or under the disability insurance plan of which the disability policy in respect of which the payment is made is or was a part; and

(c) if the payment is made to the individual, it is, for the purpose of paragraph (1)(f), deemed to be an amount payable to the individual pursuant to the plan.

Related Provisions: 6(17) — Definitions; 8(1)(n.1) — Reimbursement to employer.

Notes: 6(18) added by 1995-97 technical bill, for payments made after Aug. 10, 1994 (the day before the Superintendent of Financial Institutions took control of Confederation Life). It is worded in terms of a generic insolvent insurer, but was designed to deal with employer-sponsored disability plans insured by Confederation Life. (Finance news release, Oct. 4, 1994.)

(19) Benefit re housing loss — For the purpose of paragraph (1)(a), an amount paid at any time in respect of a housing loss (other than an eligible housing loss) to or on behalf of a taxpayer or a person who does not deal at arm's length with the taxpayer in respect of, in the course of or because of, an office or employment is deemed to be a benefit received by the taxpayer at that time because of the office or employment.

Related Provisions: 6(20) — Eligible housing loss only partly taxed; 6(21) — Meaning of "housing loss"; 6(23) — Employer-provided housing subsidy is taxable.

Notes: 6(19)-(22) provide that a benefit to cover a "housing loss" (6(21)) is fully taxable, unless it is an "eligible housing loss" (6(22)) 248(1)"eligible relocation" — generally a loss on a work-triggered move of 40 km or more), in which case the first $15,000 is exempt and the balance is only half-taxed. See Income Tax Folio S2-F3-C2 ¶2.39 [temporarily withdrawn in 2017 and still under review: see Notes to 6(1)(a) "Discounts"]; VIEWS docs 2006-0181611M4, 2016-0669531E5, 2017-0716001E5.

See also under "Moving expenses" in Notes to 6(1)(a).

6(19)-(22) added by 1998 Budget, last change effective 2001.

Interpretation Bulletins: IT-470R: Employees' fringe benefits.

(20) Benefit re eligible housing loss — For the purpose of paragraph (1)(a), an amount paid at any time in a taxation year in respect of an eligible housing loss to or on behalf of a taxpayer or a person who does not deal at arm's length with the taxpayer in respect of, in the course of or because of, an office or employment is deemed to be a benefit received by the taxpayer at that time because of the office or employment to the extent of the amount, if any, by which

(a) one half of the amount, if any, by which the total of all amounts each of which is so paid in the year or in a preceding taxation year exceeds $15,000

exceeds

(b) the total of all amounts each of which is an amount included in computing the taxpayer's income because of this subsection for a preceding taxation year in respect of the loss.

Notes: See Notes to 6(19).

Interpretation Bulletins: IT-470R: Employees' fringe benefits.

(21) Housing loss — In this section, "housing loss" at any time in respect of a residence of a taxpayer means the amount, if any, by which the greater of

(a) the adjusted cost base of the residence at that time to the taxpayer or to another person who does not deal at arm's length with the taxpayer, and

(b) the highest fair market value of the residence within the six-month period that ends at that time

exceeds

(c) if the residence is disposed of by the taxpayer or the other person before the end of the first taxation year that begins after that time, the lesser of

(i) the proceeds of disposition of the residence, and

(ii) the fair market value of the residence at that time, and

(d) in any other case, the fair market value of the residence at that time.

Related Provisions: 6(22) — Meaning of "eligible housing loss".

Notes: See Notes to 6(19). In *Thomas*, 2007 FCA 57, T's employer paid him $850,000 to buy his house as part of negotiating termination of his employment. Although this was the same as his cost, the excess over fair market value was a "housing loss" and was taxable.

On the issue of when to calculate the housing loss, see VIEWS doc 2005-0131231E5.

Interpretation Bulletins: IT-470R: Employees' fringe benefits.

(22) Eligible housing loss — In this section, "eligible housing loss" in respect of a residence designated by a taxpayer means a housing loss in respect of an eligible relocation of the taxpayer or a person who does not deal at arm's length with the taxpayer and, for these purposes, no more than one residence may be so designated in respect of an eligible relocation.

Related Provisions: 248(1) — Definition of "eligible relocation".

Notes: See Notes to 6(19).

Interpretation Bulletins: IT-470R: Employees' fringe benefits.

(23) Employer-provided housing subsidies — For greater certainty, an amount paid or the value of assistance provided by any person in respect of, in the course of or because of, an individual's office or employment in respect of the cost of, the financing of, the use of or the right to use, a residence is, for the purposes of this section, a benefit received by the individual because of the office or employment.

Related Provisions: 80.4(1), (1.1) — Taxable benefit on loan to employee.

Notes: 6(23) overrides case law finding non-taxable certain amounts paid to compensate for higher mortgage costs on relocation (*Krull*, [1996] 1 C.T.C. 131 (FCA)).

For CRA interpretation see docs 2008-0290481R3, 2009-034550117, 2010-0359491E5.

6(23) added by 1998 Budget, effective on the same basis as 6(19).

Definitions [s. 6]: "adjusted cost base" — 54, 248(1); "amount" — 248(1); "arm's length" — 251(1); "automobile" — 248(1); "benefit" — 6(18)(a); "business" — 248(1); "Canada" — 255; "contribution" — 6(18)(b); "cost" — 6(7); "cost amount", "death benefit", "deferred amount" — 248(1); "deferred payment" — 8(1)(n.1)(i); "deferred profit sharing plan" — 147(1), 248(1); "designated employee benefit" — 144.1(1); "disability policy" — 6(17); "dividend" — 248(1); "eligible housing loss" — 6(22); "eligible relocation", "employed", "employee", "employee benefit plan" — 248(1); "employee life and health trust" — 144.1(2), 248(1); "employee trust" — 248(1); "employees profit sharing plan" — 144(1), 248(1); "employer" — 6(2), (17), 248(1); "employment" — 248(1); "fair market value" — see 69(1) Notes; "forgiven amount" — 6(15.1); "goods and services tax", "group term life insurance policy" — 248(1); "housing loss" — 6(21); "individual", "insurance policy", "life insurance policy", "Minister" — 248(1); "month" — *Interpretation Act* 35(1); "motor vehicle", "non-resident" — 248(1); "obligation" — 248(26); "office", "officer" — 248(1); "Parliament" — *Interpretation Act* 35(1); "payor" — 6(1)(k)(ii); "person", "personal or living expenses" — 248(1); "policy year" — 6(5); "pooled registered pension plan" — 147.5(1), 248(1); "prescribed", "private health services plan" — 248(1); "proceeds of disposition" — 54 [technically does not apply to 6(21)(c)(i)]; "profit sharing plan" — 147(1), 248(1); "property" — 248(1); "province" — *Interpretation Act* 35(1); "received" — 248(7)(a); "registered charity", "registered pension plan", "regulation" — 248(1); "related" — 251(2); "resident in Canada" — 250; "retirement compensation arrangement", "salary deferral arrangement", "self-contained domestic establishment" — 248(1); "standby charge" — 6(2), (2.1); "superannuation or pension benefit" — 248(1); "supplementary unemployment benefit plan" — 145(1), 248(1); "taxation year" — 249; "taxpayer" — 248(1); "top-up disability payment" — 6(17); "Treasury Board" — 248(1); "writing" — *Interpretation Act* 35(1).

Income Tax Folios: S1-F1-C3: Disability supports deduction [replaces IT-519R2]; S1-F3-C1: Child care expense deduction [replaces IT-495R3].

7. (1) Agreement to issue securities to employees [stock options] — Subject to subsection (1.1), where a particular qualifying person has agreed to sell or issue securities of the particular qualifying person (or of a qualifying person with which the particular qualifying person does not deal at arm's length) to an employee of the particular qualifying person (or of a qualifying person with which the particular qualifying person does not deal at arm's length),

(a) if the employee has acquired securities under the agreement, a benefit equal to the amount, if any, by which

(i) the value of the securities at the time the employee acquired them

exceeds the total of

(ii) the amount paid or to be paid to the particular qualifying person by the employee for the securities, and

(iii) the amount, if any, paid by the employee to acquire the right to acquire the securities

is deemed to have been received, in the taxation year in which the employee acquired the securities, by the employee because of the employee's employment;

(b) if the employee has transferred or otherwise disposed of rights under the agreement in respect of some or all of the securities to a person with whom the employee was dealing at arm's length, a benefit equal to the amount, if any, by which

(i) the value of the consideration for the disposition

exceeds

(ii) the amount, if any, paid by the employee to acquire those rights

shall be deemed to have been received, in the taxation year in which the employee made the disposition, by the employee because of the employee's employment;

(b.1) if the employee has transferred or otherwise disposed of rights under the agreement in respect of some or all of the securities to the particular qualifying person (or a qualifying person with which the particular qualifying person does not deal at arm's length) with whom the employee was not dealing at arm's length, a benefit equal to the amount, if any, by which

(i) the value of the consideration for the disposition

exceeds

(ii) the amount, if any, paid by the employee to acquire those rights

is deemed to have been received, in the taxation year in which the employee made the disposition, by the employee because of the employee's employment;

(c) if rights of the employee under the agreement have, by one or more transactions between persons not dealing at arm's length, become vested in a person who has acquired securities under the agreement, a benefit equal to the amount, if any, by which

(i) the value of the securities at the time the person acquired them

exceeds the total of

(ii) the amount paid or to be paid to the particular qualifying person by the person for the securities, and

(iii) the amount, if any, paid by the employee to acquire the right to acquire the securities,

is deemed to have been received, in the taxation year in which the person acquired the securities, by the employee because of the employee's employment, unless at the time the person acquired the securities the employee was deceased, in which case such a benefit is deemed to have been received by the person in that year as income from the duties of an employment performed by the person in that year in the country in which the employee primarily performed the duties of the employee's employment;

(d) if rights of the employee under the agreement have, by one or more transactions between persons not dealing at arm's length, become vested in a particular person who has transferred or otherwise disposed of rights under the agreement to another person with whom the particular person was dealing at arm's length, a benefit equal to the amount, if any, by which

(i) the value of the consideration for the disposition

exceeds

(ii) the amount, if any, paid by the employee to acquire those rights

shall be deemed to have been received, in the taxation year in which the particular person made the disposition, by the employee because of the employee's employment, unless at the time the other person acquired the rights the employee was deceased, in which case such a benefit shall be deemed to have been received by the particular person in that year as income from the duties of an employment performed by the particular person in that year in the country in which the employee primarily performed the duties of the employee's employment;

(d.1) if rights of the employee under the agreement have, by one or more transactions between persons not dealing at arm's length, become vested in a particular person who has transferred or otherwise disposed of rights under the agreement to a particular qualifying person (or a qualifying person with which the particular qualifying person does not deal at arm's length) with whom the particular person was not dealing at arm's length, a benefit equal to the amount, if any, by which

    (i) the value of the consideration for the disposition

exceeds

    (ii) the amount, if any, paid by the employee to acquire those rights

is deemed to have been received, in the taxation year in which the particular person made the disposition, by the employee because of the employee's employment, unless at the time of the disposition the employee was deceased, in which case such a benefit is deemed to have been received by the particular person in that year as income from the duties of an employment performed by the particular person in that year in the country in which the employee primarily performed the duties of the employee's employment; and

(e) if the employee has died and immediately before death owned a right to acquire securities under the agreement, a benefit equal to the amount, if any, by which

    (i) the value of the right immediately after the death

exceeds

    (ii) the amount, if any, paid by the employee to acquire the right

shall be deemed to have been received, in the taxation year in which the employee died, by the employee because of the employee's employment, and paragraphs (b), (c) and (d) do not apply.

Proposed Amendment — Capping Stock Option Deduction

Federal Economic Statement, Supplementary Information, Nov. 30, 2020: See under 110(1.3)–(1.44).

Possible Future Amendment — Employee ownership trusts

Federal Budget, Chapter 3, April 19, 2021: *Employee Ownership Trusts*

Employee ownership trusts encourage employee ownership of a business, and facilitate the transition of privately owned businesses to employees. Both the United States and the United Kingdom support and encourage employee ownership though these types of arrangements.

Budget 2021 announces that the government will engage with stakeholders to examine what barriers exist to the creation of employee ownership trusts in Canada, and how workers and owners of private businesses in Canada could benefit from the use of employee ownership trusts.

Related Provisions: 7(1.1) — Stock option granted by CCPC; 7(1.4) — Exchange of options; 7(1.5) — Where shares exchanged; 7(1.7) — Deemed disposition where rights cease to be exercisable; 7(2) — Shares held by trustee; 8(1)(b) — Deduction for legal expenses to enforce stock option benefits; 8(12) — Return of employee shares by trustee; 53(1)(j) — Addition to ACB of share; 104(1), (2) — Employee of trustee deemed to be employee of mutual fund trust; 110(1)(d) — Deduction of ½ of taxable benefit; 110(1)(e) — Deduction to employer for options on non-qualified securities (above $200,000/year); 110(1.1), (1.2) — Election by employer to forgo deduction for cash-out payment; 110(1.7), (1.8) — Reduction in exercise price of stock option; 128.1(10)"excluded right or interest"(c) — Stock options excluded from deemed disposition on immigration or emigration; 143.3 — Whether stock option is an expenditure; 153(1)(a), 153(1.01), (1.31) — Withholding of tax on stock option benefits; 164(6.1) — Exercise or disposition of employee stock option by legal representative of deceased employee; 180.01 — Election to reduce tax on shares that have dropped in value; Canada-U.S. Tax Treaty:Art. XV:1, Fifth Protocol Annex B para. 6 — cross-border treatment of stock options.

Notes: Simplified, a stock option is taxed as follows: No benefit is recognized when the option is granted: 7(3)(a); *Ferlaino*, 2017 FCA 105, para. 4. A benefit is recognized when the option is exercised (7(1)(a)), unless the employer is a Canadian-controlled private corporation dealing at arm's length from the employee, in which case the bene-

fit is recognized only when the shares are disposed of (7(1.1)). Selling the option rather than exercising it puts the employee no further ahead, due to 7(1)(b)-(d.1). For non-CCPCs, deferral was available under 7(8)-(16) until March 4, 2010. In either case an offsetting deduction of ½ the benefit may be available under 110(1)(d) or (d.1). The benefit is normally added to the cost base of the shares under 53(1)(j). The same rules apply to units of mutual fund trusts, which are effectively treated like shares of public corporations. See IT-113R4 and guide T4130. An employee stock purchase plan is treated the same as a stock option, due to the opening words of 7(1).

Once the option is exercised and the shares acquired, a later drop in value is a capital loss (see Notes to 38), and cannot offset the s. 7 benefit. This is unfortunate but results from the market risk the employee takes in keeping the shares: VIEWS docs 2003-0007795, 2009-0319621M4, 2009-0325281M4, 2009-0331391M4; Tunney, "Underwater Stock Options Sink", 11(6) *Canadian Tax Highlights* (ctf.ca) 1-2 (June 2003). However, the *Certain Former Employees of SDL Optics, Inc. Remission Order* (Oct. 25, 2007) and "... *Remission Order No. 2*" (May 29, 2008) provided relief to named employees of JDS Uniphase in Saanich, BC [Bullard, "All taxpayers are created equal but some are more equal than others", 2008(6) *Tax Times* (Carswell) 4 (March 28/08)]. National Revenue Minister O'Connor stated in March 2008 that relief might be granted in other cases. However, in *Fink*, 2019 FCA 276, CRA's refusal to recommend remission for a stock *option* plan was found reasonable, as SDL Optics remission was only for a riskier stock *purchase* plan [CRA earlier agreed to discount Fink's shares' value by 30% to reflect blackout periods when he could not sell them: 2018 FC 936, para. 5]. (180.01 provided relief before 2015, but only for taxpayers who used the deferral mechanism in former 7(8).) In all of *Ellis*, 2008 FCA 92, *Baird*, 2010 FCA 35 and *Zhu*, 2015 TCC 16 (aff'd on other grounds 2016 FCA 113), the Court rejected the taxpayer's argument that he had purchased the shares for resale so that the loss was deductible; but in *Howard*, 2008 TCC 51, this argument succeeded. See also Nijhawan, "Baird v. R.", 20(8) *Taxation of Executive Compensation & Retirement* (Federated Press) 1136-38 (April 2009). On the employer re-pricing the options, see Huculak & Begun, "Rescuing Drowning Stock Options", XII(4) *Business Vehicles* (Federated Press) 654-58 (2009).

Options priced in foreign currency are taxed using the exchange rate on the day they are exercised, as that is the date of the "taxable transaction": *Ferlaino*, 2017 FCA 105.

Binding contract required: Without 7(1), no 110(1)(d) deduction is available. 7(1) applies only where the employer has "agreed" to issue shares, which had been thought to cover any stock option plan or arrangement. However, *TransAlta Corp.*, 2012 TCC 86 held that it means a *legally-binding* "agreement" (contract) (so 7(3) did not apply to a particular plan). CRA did not appeal *TransAlta* [2013 FCA 285 was an appeal on costs]: Padina, "Canada Revenue Agency Clarifies Position in Deciding Not to Appeal", 67(5) *Tax Notes International* (taxnotes.com) 453-56 (July 30, 2012). Thus, a fully-discretionary plan does not qualify: VIEWS docs 2016-060094117, 2016-064184117, 2016-0655901C6 [2016 APFF q.21]; Infanti, "Employee Stock Option Rules and Legally Binding Agreements", 17(2) *Tax for the Owner-Manager* (ctf.ca) 1-2 (April 2017). Where an employer pays a bonus by issuing shares, CRA's view was that 7(1) applies (2009-0330351C6), but this may be wrong: Craven, "Stock Bonuses Are Not Subject to Section 7", 18(3) *Taxation of Executive Compensation & Retirement* 735-39 (Oct. 2006).

The words "sell or issue" in 7(1) opening words include an employer providing shares of a related company that it has purchased, but the employer cannot deduct the cost due to 7(3)(b): VIEWS doc 2012-0432951E5. If Holdco sells shares of Opco to an Opco employee for less than fair market value, 7(1) applies: 2015-0581311E5.

In *Van de Velde*, 2007 TCC 533, the benefit from restricted stock units was valued when they vested in the taxpayer so that he had legal ownership of them.

If the employee sells the shares back to the employer corporation, there may be both a s. 7 benefit and an 84(3) deemed dividend: VIEWS docs 2002-0179145, 2003-0008795, 2003-0008805; Don Summerfeldt, "Sale of Shares Acquired on Exercise of Stock Option", 15(4) *Taxation of Executive Compensation & Retirement* (Federated Press) 353-56 (Nov. 2003).

A share's value for the 7(1) benefit can be discounted to reflect selling restrictions: VIEWS docs 2005-0112901E5, 2005-0132991C6; and is increased by the current value of an earnout clause: 2013-0502761E5.

Options granted to a non-employee who later becomes an employee may escape 7(1): Tax Ruling TR-75 (1978); but if the option is included in an offer of employment, 7(1) will apply: VIEWS doc 2000-0035405.

Where cross-border restricted share units are granted to employees who work in both Canada and another country, see VIEWS doc 2019-0832211I7 for CRA's "hybrid" sourcing to determine the extent to which 7(1) applies.

On the 2010 amendments restricting deduction for cash-outs [110(1)(d)(i), 110(1.1), 18(1)(m)], adding 7(1)(b.1), (d.1) and repealing 7(8)-(16) deferral, see Roth, "Proposed Changes to the Stock Option Rules" 7(4) *Tax Hyperion [TH]* (Carswell, April 2010); Keey, "Planning for Proposed Changes to the Stock Option Rules", 2010(15) *Tax Times [TT]* 1-2 (Aug. 13/10) and "Election to Forgo Deduction on Option Cash-Out", 2011(7) 3 (April 8/11); Mitchell Sherman, "Proposals to Amend the Stock Option Rules", XVI(3) *Corporate Finance* (Federated Press) 1851-54 (2010); Keey, "New Stock Option Rules", 8(3) *TH* (March 2011); Hickey, "Stock Option Roundup", 19(2) *Canadian Tax Highlights* (ctf.ca) 2 (Feb. 2011); Nijhawan, "Employee Stock Options", 22(6) *Taxation of Executive Compensation & Retirement* (Federated Press) 1370-72 (Feb. 2011); Forgie et al., "Structuring Stock Options in Light of the 2010 Budget", 2011 Cdn Tax Foundation conference report, 13:1-35.

Texts/papers on s. 7: Carenza, *Taxation of Private Corporations and their Shareholders* (ctf.ca, 5th ed., 2020), chap. 13; Singer, *Taxation of Executive Compensation* (researchcompensation.com), online; Ebel & Stewart, "Update on Employee Stock Options", 2002 Cdn Tax Foundation conference report, 27:1-24; Montgomery & Levin, "Cross-Border Compensation", 59(3) *Canadian Tax Journal* 645-71 (2011); Begun, "Equity-Based Compensation", 2017 conference report, 8:1-26; Coburn, "Stock Options, With a Focus on Startups", 2017 BC Tax Conference (ctf.ca); Milne, "Employee Stock Options", 2019 Prairie Provinces Tax Conf; Keey, Checklist 7 — Stock Options, *Taxnet Pro* Corporate Tax Centre (2020, 25pp); Desroches & Vaillancourt, "Stock Options ... for Employees of Private Corporations", 2019 conference report, 15:1-37.

Shorter articles: Sweatman & Hodge, "Employee Stock Options for Income Trusts", 17(7) *Taxation of Executive Compensation & Retirement [TECR]* (Federated Press) 651-55 (March 2006); D'Iorio & Kwiatkowski, "Equity Compensation for CCPCs", 18(5) *TECR* 763-70 (Dec. 2006); Krasa, "Implications ... to Stock Options Granted to Partnership Employees by a Corporate Partner", 19(2) *TECR* 879-83 (Sept. 2007); Begun, "Tax-effective Stock-based Compensation", 20(9) *TECR* 1143-49 (May 2009); Malazhavaya, "Stock Options and Foreign 'Treasury Stock': Is There an Agreement to 'Sell or Issue' Shares?", 23(1) *TECR* 1431-34 (July/Aug. 2011); Berry, "Bankruptcy and Its Implications for Stock Options", XXVI(3) *TECR* 11-14 (2018).

The identical-property averaging rule in 47(1) may apply where there are multiple blocks of shares due to exercising stock options at different times. See Marsha Reid, "Stock Options and the Application of the Identical Properties Rule", 12(1) *Taxation of Executive Compensation and Retirement* (Federated Press) 307-10 (July/Aug. 2000). But see also 7(1.3).

For non-residents (including taxpayers who emigrate before exercising the option), the 7(1) benefit triggers tax under 115(1)(a)(i) and 2(3), if the employment was in Canada: *Hurd*, [1981] C.T.C. 209 (FCA); *Hale*, [1992] 2 C.T.C. 379 (FCA); *Mullen*, 2013 FCA 101. The Canada-US tax treaty allocates tax based on where the work was done: see Notes to Art. XV:1, VIEWS doc 2012-0440741I7. Other treaty relief is limited: see *Hale* (Notes to Canada-UK treaty Art. 15:1), 2008-0276181E5. CRA sources benefits based on days of employment during the period between the option grant and its vesting: 2012-0459411C6; Yager, "OECD Sourcing of Employee Stock Options Benefits", 20(11) *Canadian Tax Highlights* (ctf.ca) 15-16 (Nov. 2012); Nijhawan, "Allocation of Benefits from Cross-border Stock Options", 23(9) *Taxation of Executive Compensation & Retirement [TECR]* (Federated Press) 1542-44 (May 2012). Immigrating non-residents: see 2009-0323151E5; they may benefit by exercising the option before immigrating, since the option is excluded from ACB step-up (128.1(10)"excluded right or interest"(c)) but the stock is not. See also Singh, "Stock Options and the Non-Resident Employee", 13(10) *TECR* 147-52 (June 2002); Blucher, "Stock Option Benefits Recognized by Non-resident Persons", XVII(3) *International Tax Planning* (Federated Press) 1193-96 (2012); Gosselin, "Review of the Stock Option Sourcing Rules for Immigrating and Emigrating Employees", 64(1) *Canadian Tax Journal* 245-66 (2016).

The amount "paid" in 7(1)(a)(iii) cannot include payment to a third party who helped the employee get the employment (and thus the stock options): *Morin*, 2006 FCA 25.

Where an option is exercised with no payment and a broker sells the shares for the employee, see VIEWS doc 2015-0572381E5; *Benham*, [2002] 3 C.T.C. 2461 (TCC) and Don Sommerfeldt, "Cashless Exercise of Employee Stock Options", 16(4) *Taxation of Executive Compensation & Retirement* 479-82 (Nov. 2004). Where payment is deferred, 7(1) still applies when the shares are "acquired" (2008-0279251E5, 2012-0458961E5), but if they are transferred to a trust for the employee, see 7(2).

7(1)(b) applies if the employee disposes of the right to the shares. An employee who elects to take cash in lieu of shares triggers this rule, and there is no offsetting deduction if the employer becomes insolvent and does not pay: VIEWS doc 2006-0196271C6. In *MacMillan*, 2008 TCC 56, tax would have applied to the sale of stock option rights but the reassessment was statute-barred (except with respect to cash actually received). In *Des Groseillers*, 2021 QCCA 906 (under the parallel Quebec rules, reversing the QCCQ), donating the options to charity still led to a 69(1)(b)(ii) deemed disposition at fair market value, as 69(1) applies even though s. 7 provides specific rules. See also 2009-0311941R3, 2011-0412031C6; 2015-0570801E5 (exchange of options where 7(1.4) does not apply: value of exchanged option is not considered part of what employee "pays" for new option [this might not be correct in the author's view]); 2015-0623031E5 (7(1)(b)(i) interpreted broadly and includes an unpaid holdback).

7(1)(b.1) was not yet in force in *Mathieu*, 2014 TCC 207, or in *Rogers Estate*, 2014 TCC 348 (FCA appeal discontinued A-533-14); so proceeds from surrendering stock options were not taxable under s. 7.

7(1)(c) applies if an employee stock option is exercised in a TFSA: VIEWS doc 2009-0307821E5.

A fundamental change to a stock option agreement creates a new agreement and causes a disposition of the employee's rights under the original agreement: *Wiebe*, [1987] 1 C.T.C. 145 (FCA). A change in the strike price of the option is not such a fundamental change (*Amirault*, [1990] 1 C.T.C. 2432 (TCC)); nor is an extension of the option expiry date (VIEWS doc 2002-0132805); nor is adding a share appreciation right (doc 2004-0073821R3). See also Notes to pre-2008 212(1)(b) re "novation".

7(1)(e): On death, see VIEWS docs 2009-0321721I7, 2014-0523011C6 [2014 STEP q.16]; Notes to 110(1)(d) and 110(1.1); Maclagan & Zimka, "Taxation of Stock Option Benefits on Death", 14(2) *Taxation of Executive Compensation & Retirement* (Federated Press) 171-75 (Sept. 2002); Georgina Tollstam, "Unexercised Employee Stock Options on Death", 21(5) *Canadian Tax Highlights* (ctf.ca) 13 (May 2013).

Where a subsidiary reimburses a parent (foreign or Canadian) for the value of options granted to employees to acquire shares in the parent, CRA will not treat this as a 15(1) benefit or subject to non-resident withholding tax, though it will examine the valuation method: VIEWS docs 2006-0217541R3, 2006-0217731E5, 2009-0321721I7, 2010-0356401E5, 2010-0391281R3. See also Dominic Belley, "Stock Option Plans: Reporting Requirements of Foreign Corporations", 2(3) *Tax for the Owner-Manager* (ctf.ca) 22-23 (July 2002).

The employer may need to withhold and remit tax as source deductions: see 153(1.01). This can include a Canadian subsidiary that reimburses a foreign parent, as discussed above. (Before 2011, see *Income Tax Technical News* 41; VIEWS doc 2009-0316621C6; William Holmes, "Must Tax Be Withheld in Respect of Stock Option Benefits?", 17(9) *Taxation of Executive Compensation & Retirement* 675-81 (May 2006); Chris D'Iorio, "Canadian Stock Benefit Withholding and Reporting Requirements", 19(3) *TECR* 891-95 (Oct. 2007).)

The employer must report the taxable benefit on the T4 (box 14, code 38): guide T4130 under "Security options".

Quebec payroll tax on stock options can be avoided by having the options issued by an employer with no establishment in Quebec and meeting certain conditions: *Pratt & Whitney*, 2013 QCCA 706; Landry, "QCCA Opens Door to Planning to Avoid Quebec Payroll Taxes", 3(3) *Canadian Tax Focus* (ctf.ca) 12 (Aug. 2013).

Where 7(1) does not apply, e.g., because the employer is an individual, or the "employee" is a corporation or an independent contractor, or the employer is a limited partnership granting rights to buy LP units, see VIEWS docs 2003-0054581E5, 2013-0513221I7, 2016-0673331E5, and Florence, "Taxation of Stock Options Where Section 7 Is Inapplicable — Robertson Revisited", 13(6) *Taxation of Executive Compensation & Retirement [TECR]* (Federated Press) 79-82 (Feb. 2002). The case referred to is *Robertson*, [1990] 1 C.T.C. 114 (FCA). See also Nijhawan & Larre, "Taxation of Stock Options Granted Qua Consultant", 16(5) *TECR* 496-8 (Dec. 2004); Bianchini & Abitbol, "Taxation of Stock Appreciation Rights", 24(8) *TECR* 1655-59 (2015); Berry & Walker, "Pitfalls for Canadians Offering Options in US LLCs", XXVII(1) *TECR* 2-3 (2019). In *Henley*, 2007 FCA 370, share warrants issued by a client to the taxpayer's employer, and allocated to H by the employer, were taxable under 6(1)(a) when issued, and a later gain on exercising the warrants and selling the shares was a capital gain. Shares issued to pay an employee for past service were a taxable benefit in *Lockhart*, 2008 TCC 156.

Contributions of stock options to a TFSA or RRSP: underwater options in publicly-traded companies arguably have nil to low value [see *Henley*, 2007 FCA 370; IT-96R6 para. 3; VIEWS docs 9503445, 9621975]. CRA has taken this position for RRSP contributions, but is revisiting it because taxpayers can contribute such options to a TFSA, potentially earning huge tax-free income from a $5,000 contribution. See Macnaughton & Mawani, "Contributions of Employee Stock Options to RRSPs and TFSAs", 56(4) *Canadian Tax Journal* 893-922 (2008) and "CRA: Employee Stock Options and TFSAs", 17(5) *Canadian Tax Highlights* (ctf.ca) 10 (May 2009) and "New tax savings opportunity", June/July 2009 *CAmagazine* (cica.ca) 44-47; Nijhawan & Somayaji, "Transfer of Employee Stock Options to Tax-Free Savings Accounts", 20(4) *Taxation of Executive Compensation & Retirement* (Federated Press) 1067-69 (Nov. 2008). 207.05 effectively prohibits a "swap transaction", but does not prohibit a contribution of options (though an under-valuation can cause an overcontribution triggering penalty tax, and might also fall under 207.01(1)"advantage"(b)(i)).

Payments by an employer to get rid of its stock option plan were on capital account and thus non-deductible in *Kaiser Petroleum*, [1990] 2 C.T.C. 439 (FCA), and *Imperial Tobacco (Imasco)*, 2011 FCA 308 (leave to appeal denied 2012 CarswellNat 1579 (SCC)); but were deductible in *Imperial Tobacco (Shoppers Drug Mart)*, 2007 TCC 636, as there was no enduring benefit. In *Devon Canada*, 2018 TCC 170, such payments to employees, by a company being acquired, were eligible capital expenditures (see Notes to 20(1)(b); today this would be Class 14.1 property).

7(1) opening words amended by 2010 budget bill #2, effective in respect of rights exercised after 4pm EST, March 4, 2010, to remove references to 7(8).

7(1)(b.1) and (d.1) added by 2010 budget bill #2, effective for dispositions of rights occurring after 4pm EST, March 4, 2010.

7(1) amended by 2000 Budget (effective for 2000 and later taxation years), 1998 Budget and 1991 technical bill. Opening words "Subject to subsection (1.1)", added by 1977 Budget, effective for agreements entered into after March 1977.

Income Tax Folios: S4-F7-C1: Amalgamations of Canadian corporations [replaces IT-474R2].

Interpretation Bulletins: IT-96R6: Options granted by corporations to acquire shares, bonds, or debentures and by trusts to acquire trust units; IT-113R4: Benefits to employees — stock options; IT-171R2: Non-resident individuals — computation of taxable income earned in Canada and non-refundable tax credits (cancelled).

Information Circulars: 89-3: Policy statement on business equity valuations.

I.T. Technical News: 1 (convertible preferred shares); 7 (stock options plans — receipt of cash in lieu of shares); 19 (Securities option plan — disposal of securities option rights for shares; Disposition of identical properties acquired under a section 7 securities option; Change in position in respect of GAAR — section 7).

Remission Orders: *Certain Former Employees of SDL Optics, Inc. Remission Order*, P.C. 2007-1635 and *Certain Former Employees of SDL Optics, Inc. Remission Order No. 2*, P.C. 2008-975 (relief for underwater stock options for certain JDS Uniphase employees).

Provincial Income Allocation Newsletters: 4 (salaries and wages — inclusion of taxable benefits).

Advance Tax Rulings: ATR-15: Employee stock option plan; ATR-64: Phantom stock award plan.

Forms: T4130: Employer's guide — taxable benefits.

(1.1) Employee stock options [in CCPC] — Where after March 31, 1977 a Canadian-controlled private corporation (in this subsection referred to as "the corporation") has agreed to sell or issue a share of the capital stock of the corporation or of a Canadian-controlled private corporation with which it does not deal at arm's length to an employee of the corporation or of a Canadian-controlled private corporation with which it does not deal at arm's length and at the time immediately after the agreement was made the employee was dealing at arm's length with

> (a) the corporation,

> (b) the Canadian-controlled private corporation, the share of the capital stock of which has been agreed to be sold by the corporation, and

> (c) the Canadian-controlled private corporation that is the employer of the employee,

in applying paragraph (1)(a) in respect of the employee's acquisition of the share, the reference in that paragraph to "the taxation year in which the employee acquired the securities" shall be read as a reference to "the taxation year in which the employee disposed of or exchanged the securities".

Related Provisions: 7(1.3) — Order of disposition of securities; 7(1.5) — Exchange of shares; 7(1.6) — Emigration does not trigger benefit from deemed disposition; 7(8) — Parallel rule for non-CCPCs where qualifying acquisition; 47(3)(a) — No averaging of cost on disposition of securities; 110(1)(d), (d.1) — Deduction of ½ of the taxable benefit; 128.1(1)(4)(d.1) — Emigration of taxpayer — calculation of gain; 153(1.01) — Withholding of tax on stock option benefits.

Notes: See Notes to 7(1). The deferral under 7(1.1) applies only to an employee, not to a consultant who only later became an employee: *Ward*, [1998] 4 C.T.C. 2129 (TCC). See Notes to 248(1)"employee" for the distinction.

Note that 7(1.5) can often prevent a 7(1.1) disposition on a rollover of the shares to a holding company, or on a disposition due to a reorganization.

See also VIEWS docs 2011-0428941E5 (7(1.1) can apply where employee transfers unexercised options to a protective trust); 2017-0692931E5 (employer's bankruptcy does not trigger disposition because 50(1) applies only to ss. 38-55; capital loss created on 50(1)(b) election or windup of employer).

7(1.1) closing words amended by 1998 Budget, for 1998 and later taxation years, to change "shares" to "securities" (twice).

7(1.1) added by 1977 Budget, effective for agreements entered into after March 1977.

Closing words (after para. (c)) amended by 1985 Budget, for shares acquired after May 22, 1985. For shares acquired earlier, read:

> paragraph (1)(a) does not apply in respect of the employee's acquisition of the share unless the employee disposes of the share, otherwise than as a consequence of his death, within two years from the date he acquired it.

That rule is now reflected in 110(1)(d.1).

Interpretation Bulletins: IT-96R6: Options granted by corporations to acquire shares, bonds, or debentures and by trusts to acquire trust units; IT-113R4: Benefits to employees — stock options; IT-171R2: Non-resident individuals — computation of taxable income earned in Canada and non-refundable tax credits (cancelled).

I.T. Technical News: 19 (Change in position in respect of GAAR — section 7).

Advance Tax Rulings: ATR-15: Employee stock option plan.

(1.11) Non-arm's length relationship with trusts — For the purposes of this section, a mutual fund trust is deemed not to deal at arm's length with a corporation only if the trust controls the corporation.

Proposed Amendment — 7(1.11)

Letter from Dept. of Finance, Dec. 4, 2006:

Dear [xxx]:

I am writing in response to your letters and e-mails concerning subsection 7(1.11) of the *Income Tax Act* (the "Act"). I also acknowledge phone conversations that you and your colleague, [xxx] have had with officials of this Branch.

Section 7 of the Act contains provisions dealing with agreements under which an employee of a corporation or mutual fund trust may acquire securities of the employer or of an entity that deals at non-arm's length with the employer. Subsection 7(1.11) deems a mutual fund trust to deal at non-arm's length with a corporation, for the purpose of section 7, only if the trust controls the corporation. Thus, in any other situation in

---

which a corporation and a mutual fund trust deal at non-arm's length, the provisions of section 7 will not apply.

You have suggested that subsection 7(1.11) excludes certain other non-arm's length relationships between a mutual fund trust and a corporation that may not be offensive from a policy perspective, and have asked that the scope of subsection 7(1.11) be expanded accordingly.

We have considered this issue carefully and are prepared to recommend that the scope of subsection 7(1.11) be expanded to include a corporation and a mutual fund trust where the corporation owns securities that would give it more than 50% of the votes that could be cast under all circumstances at a meeting of unitholders of the trust. As discussed, the securities to which such voting rights are attached would not be limited to units of the trust and could thus include, for example, securities that are exchangeable into units of the trust.

We will recommend to the Minister of Finance that the proposed amendment apply to rights exercised or disposed of after 2004 under agreements to sell or issue securities made after 2002.

While I cannot offer any assurance that the Minister or Parliament will agree with our recommendation in this regard, I hope that this statement of our position is helpful to you.

Yours sincerely,

> Brian Ernewein, General Director — Legislation, Tax Policy Branch

Notes: Finance confirmed on Nov. 1, 2019 that this amendment is still pending.

Notes: 7(1.11) added by 1998 Budget, for 1998 and later tax years.

(1.2) [Repealed under former Act]

Notes: 7(1.2) added by 1977 Budget, for agreements entered into after March 1977. Repealed by 1985 Budget, for shares acquired after May 22, 1985, as this rule is now reflected in 7(1.1) and 110(1)(d.1). Where it is in force, read:

> (1.2) **Idem** — Where a taxpayer has acquired a share in circumstances such that, if he had not disposed of it within two years from the date he acquired it, paragraph (1)(a) would not have applied to the acquisition by reason of subsection (1.1), the reference in paragraph (1)(a) to "the taxation year in which he acquired the shares" shall be read as "the taxation year in which he disposed of the shares".

(1.3) Order of disposition of securities — For the purposes of this subsection, subsection (1.1), Subdivision C, paragraph 110(1)(d.01), subparagraph 110(1)(d.1)(ii) and subsections 110(2.1) and 147(10.4), and subject to subsection (1.31), a taxpayer is deemed to dispose of securities that are identical properties in the order in which the taxpayer acquired them and, for this purpose,

> (a) if a taxpayer acquires a particular security (other than under circumstances to which subsection (1.1) or 147(10.1) applies) at a time when the taxpayer also acquires or holds one or more other securities that are identical to the particular security and are, or were, acquired under circumstances to which subsection (1.1) or 147(10.1) applied, the taxpayer is deemed to have acquired the particular security at the time immediately preceding the earliest of the times at which the taxpayer acquired those other securities; and

> (b) if a taxpayer acquires, at the same time, two or more identical securities under circumstances to which subsection (1.1) applied, the taxpayer is deemed to have acquired the securities in the order in which the agreements under which the taxpayer acquired the rights to acquire the securities were made.

Related Provisions: 7(1.31) — Disposition of newly-acquired security; 47(3) — No cost averaging for securities for which deferral provided; 248(12) — Identical properties.

Notes: 7(1.3) provides FIFO (first-in first-out) treatment for shares acquired under stock options, but 7(1.31) permits LIFO for shares donated to charity under 110(1)(d.01): VIEWS docs 2010-0370501C6; 2011-0399421C6 (discusses interaction with s. 47).

7(1.3) amended by 2010 budget bill #2, effective in respect of rights exercised after 4pm EST, March 4, 2010, to delete references to 7(8) and 7(14)(c).

7(1.3) amended by 2000 Budget, for securities acquired, but not disposed of, before Feb. 28, 2000 and for securities acquired after Feb. 27, 2000.

7(1.3) added by 1977 Budget, effective for agreements entered into after March 1977.

I.T. Technical News: 19 (Disposition of identical properties acquired under a s. 7 securities option).

(1.31) Disposition of newly-acquired security — Where a taxpayer acquires, at a particular time, a particular security under an agreement referred to in subsection (1) and, on a day that is no later than 30 days after the day that includes the particular time, the taxpayer disposes of a security that is identical to the particular security, the particular security is deemed to be the security that is so disposed of if

(a) no other securities that are identical to the particular security are acquired, or disposed of, by the taxpayer after the particular time and before the disposition;

(b) the taxpayer identifies the particular security as the security so disposed of in the taxpayer's return of income under this Part for the year in which the disposition occurs; and

(c) the taxpayer has not so identified the particular security, in accordance with this subsection, in connection with the disposition of any other security.

Related Provisions: 47(3)(b) — No averaging of cost on disposition of securities; 248(12) — Identical properties.

Notes: For detail on 7(1.31) see Geddes, "Changes to the Identical Property Rules for Stock Options", 13(1) *Taxation of Executive Compensation and Retirement* (Federated Press) 3-6 (July-Aug. 2001). 7(1.31) is elective, and may be needed to obtain 110(1)(d.01) relief for a donation: VIEWS docs 2010-0370501C6, 2011-0399421C6. An estate of a deceased employee can make a designation under 7(1.31): 2005-0115091E5. 7(1.31) will not apply to both a transfer and a donation of parts of the shares: 2015-0595841C6 [2015 APFF q.2].

For a taxpayer filing Quebec returns, an "identification" under 7(1.31)(b) must be copied to Revenu Québec: *Taxation Act* ss. 49.2.3, 21.4.6.

In 7(1.31)(b), identification "in the taxpayer's return" is valid in a return filed late: *Hayes*, 2005 FCA 227, para. 114; VIEWS doc 2013-0487871I7. However, where a provision requires an election to be "attached to a return filed with the Minister *in accordance with section 150*" (e.g. Reg. 1101(5b.1)), then a letter attached to a late-filed return arguably does not meet the test unless CRA extends the return deadline under 220(3). (CRA has not expressed a view on this point.) For identification "in" an electronic return, see Notes to 150.1.

7(1.31) added by 2000 Budget.

(1.4) Exchange of options — Where

(a) a taxpayer disposes of rights under an agreement referred to in subsection (1) to acquire securities of a particular qualifying person that made the agreement or of a qualifying person with which it does not deal at arm's length (which rights and securities are referred to in this subsection as the "exchanged option" and the "old securities", respectively),

(b) the taxpayer receives no consideration for the disposition of the exchanged option other than rights under an agreement with a person (in this subsection referred to as the "designated person") that is

(i) the particular person,

(ii) a qualifying person with which the particular person does not deal at arm's length immediately after the disposition,

(iii) a corporation formed on the amalgamation or merger of the particular person and one or more other corporations,

(iv) a mutual fund trust to which the particular person has transferred property in circumstances to which subsection 132.2(1) applied,

(v) a qualifying person with which the corporation referred to in subparagraph (iii) does not deal at arm's length immediately after the disposition, or

(vi) if the disposition is before 2013 and the old securities were equity in a SIFT wind-up entity that was at the time of the disposition a mutual fund trust, a SIFT wind-up corporation in respect of the SIFT wind-up entity

to acquire securities of the designated person or a qualifying person with which the designated person does not deal at arm's length (which rights and securities are referred to in this subsection as the "new option" and the "new securities", respectively), and

(c) the amount, if any, by which

(i) the total value of the new securities immediately after the disposition

exceeds

(ii) the total amount payable by the taxpayer to acquire the new securities under the new option

does not exceed the amount, if any, by which

(iii) the total value of the old securities immediately before the disposition

exceeds

(iv) the amount payable by the taxpayer to acquire the old securities under the exchanged option,

for the purposes of this section,

(d) the taxpayer is deemed (other than for the purposes of subparagraph (9)(d)(ii)) not to have disposed of the exchanged option and not to have acquired the new option,

(e) the new option is deemed to be the same option as, and a continuation of, the exchanged option, and

(f) if the designated person is not the particular person, the designated person is deemed to be the same person as, and a continuation of, the particular person.

Related Provisions: 110(1.7), (1.8) — Reduction in exercise price of option.

Notes: See Eva Krasa, "Exchange of Stock Options under Subsection 7(1.4)", 20(6) *Taxation of Executive Compensation & Retirement* (Federated Press) 1099-1107 (Feb. 2009); Gloria Geddes, "Dealing with Stock Options in Corporate Acquisitions", 21(9) *TECR* 1283-87 (May 2010) and 21(10) 1295-98 (June 2010).

For examples of 7(1.4) applying see VIEWS docs 2004-0058171R3, 2010-0366651R3.

7(1.4)(b)(vi) added by 2008 budget bill #2, effective Dec. 20, 2007, as part of the rules for SIFT windups (see Notes to 85.1(8)).

7(1.4) earlier amended by 2000 Budget (last change effective for 2000 and later tax years), 1998 Budget and 1991 technical bill.

Income Tax Folios: S4-F7-C1: Amalgamations of Canadian corporations [replaces IT-474R2].

Interpretation Bulletins: IT-96R6: Options granted by corporations to acquire shares, bonds, or debentures and by trusts to acquire trust units; IT-113R4: Benefits to employees — stock options.

(1.5) Rules where securities exchanged — For the purposes of this section and paragraphs 110(1)(d) to (d.1), where

(a) a taxpayer disposes of or exchanges securities of a particular qualifying person that were acquired by the taxpayer under circumstances to which subsection (1.1) applied (in this subsection referred to as the "exchanged securities"),

(b) the taxpayer receives no consideration for the disposition or exchange of the exchanged securities other than securities (in this subsection referred to as the "new securities") of

(i) the particular qualifying person,

(ii) a qualifying person with which the particular qualifying person does not deal at arm's length immediately after the disposition or exchange,

(iii) a corporation formed on the amalgamation or merger of the particular qualifying person and one or more other corporations,

(iv) a mutual fund trust to which the particular qualifying person has transferred property in circumstances to which subsection 132.2(1) applied, or

(v) a qualifying person with which the corporation referred to in subparagraph (iii) does not deal at arm's length immediately after the disposition or exchange, and

(c) the total value of the new securities immediately after the disposition or exchange does not exceed the total value of the old securities immediately before the disposition or exchange,

the following rules apply:

(d) the taxpayer is deemed not to have disposed of or exchanged the exchanged securities and not to have acquired the new securities,

(e) the new securities are deemed to be the same securities as, and a continuation of, the exchanged securities, except for the purpose of determining if the new securities are identical to any other securities,

(f) the qualifying person that issued the new securities is deemed to be the same person as, and a continuation of, the qualifying person that issued the exchanged securities, and

(g) where the exchanged securities were issued under an agreement, the new securities are deemed to have been issued under that agreement.

Related Provisions: 47(3)(a) — No averaging of cost on disposition of securities; 110(1)(d) — Employee stock options.

Notes: For CRA interpretation see VIEWS docs 2003-0003645 (whether receipt of non-share, non-cash consideration stops 7(1.5) from applying); 2006-0198411R3 (7(1.5) applies on exchange of butterfly options warrants); 2009-033357117 (application to fact situation); 2010-0366651R3 (7(1.5) applies); 2014-0533601R3 (7(1.5) applies in a spin-off).

7(1.5)(a) amended by 2010 budget bill #2, effective for rights exercised after 4pm EST, March 4, 2010, to change "either subsection (1.1) or (8)" to "subsection (1.1)".

7(1.5) earlier amended by 2000 Budget (for dispositions and exchanges after Feb. 27, 2000), 1993 technical bill, 1985 Budget (for shares acquired after May 22, 1985).

Interpretation Bulletins: IT-96R6: Options granted by corporations to acquire shares, bonds, or debentures and by trusts to acquire trust units; IT-113R4: Benefits to employees — stock options.

(1.6) Emigrant — For the purposes of this section and paragraph 110(1)(d.1), a taxpayer is deemed not to have disposed of a share acquired under circumstances to which subsection (1.1) applied solely because of subsection 128.1(4).

Related Provisions: 128.1(4)(d.1) — Calculation of gain from deemed disposition on emigration.

Notes: Under 128.1(4), emigration from Canada triggers a disposition of most capital property, triggering tax on accrued capital gains. This rule does not apply for purposes of triggering income under 7(1.1).

7(1.6) added by 2000 Budget, effective 1993.

(1.7) Rights ceasing to be exercisable — For the purposes of subsections (1) and 110(1), if a taxpayer receives at a particular time one or more particular amounts in respect of rights of the taxpayer to acquire securities under an agreement referred to in subsection (1) ceasing to be exercisable in accordance with the terms of the agreement, and the cessation would not, if this Act were read without reference to this subsection, constitute a transfer or disposition of those rights by the taxpayer,

(a) the taxpayer is deemed to have disposed of those rights at the particular time to a person with whom the taxpayer was dealing at arm's length and to have received the particular amounts as consideration for the disposition; and

(b) for the purpose of determining the amount, if any, of the benefit that is deemed to have been received as a consequence of the disposition referred to in paragraph (a), the taxpayer is deemed to have paid an amount to acquire those rights equal to the amount, if any, by which

(i) the amount paid by the taxpayer to acquire those rights (determined without reference to this subsection)

exceeds

(ii) the total of all amounts each of which is an amount received by the taxpayer before the particular time in respect of the cessation.

Notes: 7(1.7) overrules *Buccini*, [2001] 1 C.T.C. 103 (FCA), where a payment received on cancellation of stock option rights (on amalgamation of the employer) was found not to be taxable since there was no "disposition" by the taxpayer of his rights. See VIEWS doc 2012-046570117; Jim Yager, "Relief for Stock Option Buyout", 21(2) *Canadian Tax Highlights* (ctf.ca) 3-4 (Feb. 2013).

7(1.7) amended by 2010 budget bill #2, effective in respect of rights exercised after 4pm EST, March 4, 2010: in opening words, "paragraphs (1)(b) and 110(1)(d)" changed to "subsections (1) and 110(1)", and in para. (b), "is deemed by paragraph (1)(b)" changed to "is deemed".

7(1.7) added by 2000 Budget bill, effective for amounts received on or after March 16, 2001, other than amounts received on or after that day pursuant to an agreement in writing made before that day in settlement of claims arising as a result of a cessation occurring before that day, or pursuant to an order or judgment issued before that day for claims arising as a result of a cessation occurring before that day.

(2) Securities held by trustee [deemed held by employee] — If a security is held by a trustee in trust or otherwise, whether absolutely, conditionally or contingently, for an employee, the employee is deemed, for the purposes of this section and paragraphs 110(1)(d) to (d.1),

(a) to have acquired the security at the time the trust began to so hold it; and

(b) to have exchanged or disposed of the security at the time the trust exchanged it or disposed of it to any person other than the employee.

Related Provisions: 8(12) — Forfeiture of securities by employee; 104(21.2) — Capital gains exemption flowed through trust; 110.6(16) — Personal trust includes 7(2) trust for certain purposes.

Notes: See Ian Macdonald, "Trusts Holding Employee Shares — After the Initial Transfer", 22(10) *Taxation of Executive Compensation & Retirement* (Federated Press) 1415-19 (June 2011).

For examples of 7(2) applying see VIEWS docs 2008-0279251E5, 2009-0311921E5.

Opening words of 7(2) amended by 2000 Budget to change "and (d.1)" to "to (d.1)" (effectively adding 110(1)(d.01)), effective for 2000 and later taxation years.

7(2) amended by 1998 Budget, effective for 1998 and later taxation years, to change "share" to "security" throughout.

7(2)(b) added by 1985 Budget, effective for shares acquired after May 22, 1985.

Interpretation Bulletins: IT-113R4: Benefits to employees — stock options.

(3) Special provision [taxable benefit is under s. 7 only, and no deduction to employer] — If a particular qualifying person has agreed to sell or issue securities of the particular person, or of a qualifying person with which it does not deal at arm's length, to an employee of the particular person or of a qualifying person with which it does not deal at arm's length,

(a) except as provided by this section, the employee is deemed to have neither received nor enjoyed any benefit under or because of the agreement; and

(b) the income for a taxation year of any person is deemed to be not less than its income for the year would have been if a benefit had not been conferred on the employee by the sale or issue of the securities.

Related Provisions: 143.3(2) — Cost of stock option deemed not an expenditure.

Notes: 7(3)(a) is a relieving rule that ensures no benefit is taxable under other rules, such as s. 6. In *Mathieu*, 2014 TCC 207, and *Rogers Estate*, 2014 TCC 348, para. 38 (FCA appeal discontinued A-533-14), proceeds from surrendering stock options, before 7(1)(b.1) applied, were not taxable as employment income because 7(3) is more specific than 6(1)(a) (paras. 70, 77) (but 7(3)(a) did not prevent them from being a capital gain: *Rogers Estate*, paras. 76-77) [Fournier & Wilson, "Mathieu v. The Queen: When a Reassessment Results in a Windfall for the Taxpayer", 24(4) *Taxation of Executive Compensation & Retirement* (Federated Press) 1599-1603 (Nov. 2012); Carenza & Al-Shikarchy case comment, 62(4) *Canadian Tax Journal* 1079-84 (2014)].

7(3)(b) ensures that an employer (or non-arm's length person) cannot claim a deduction on the sale or issuance of its shares to an employee (or a person who has acquired the employee's rights), even though employee costs are normally deductible to an employer. See *Placer Dome*, [1992] 2 C.T.C. 99 (FCA); VIEWS docs 2008-030117117, 2010-0356401E5, 2012-0432951E5. *TransAlta*, 2012 TCC 86, held that 7(3) requires a legally-binding contract, so 7(3)(b) did not apply to a Performance Share Ownership Plan for senior executives [Keey, "Share Based Compensation: Fairness Restored?", 2012(15) *Tax Times* (Carswell) 1-3 (Aug. 10, 2012)]. CRA accepts this: 2015-060094117 [Lacoursière, "The CRA Issues Guidance on the Deductibility of Certain Share-Based Compensation", XXV(2) *Taxation of Executive Compensation & Retirement* (Federated Press) 9-10 (2017)]; 2018-078195117. CRA says in 2020-0840681E5 that 7(3)(b) prevents deduction of withholding tax paid on shares issued under a restricted share unit (RSU) plan (in lieu of issuing more shares: see 153(1.31) Notes); but in 2020-086483117, 7(3)(b) does not deny deduction if the Cdn employer has discretion as to whether an RSU is settled with US shares or cash (see also 2019-083221117).

7(3) amended by 1998 Budget, for 1995 and later tax years, except that, in respect of benefits conferred before March 1998, read "person" in 7(3)(b) as "corporation"; and the amendment has no effect on agreements entered into before March 1998 unless the employee makes the election referred to in Notes to 7(7)"qualifying person". Before the amendment, read:

(3) Where a corporation has agreed to sell or issue shares of the capital stock of the corporation or of a corporation with which it does not deal at arm's length to an employee of the corporation or of a corporation with which it does not deal at arm's length

(a) no benefit shall be deemed to have been received or enjoyed by the employee under or by virtue of the agreement for the purpose of this Part except as provided by this section; and

(b) the income for a taxation year of the corporation or of a corporation with which it does not deal at arm's length shall be deemed to be not less than its income for the year would have been if a benefit had not been conferred on the employee by the sale or issue of the shares to the employee or to a person in whom the employee's rights under the agreement have become vested.

Interpretation Bulletins: IT-96R6: Options granted by corporations to acquire shares, bonds, or debentures and by trusts to acquire trust units; IT-113R4: Benefits to employees — stock options.

I.T. Technical News: 7 (stock options plans — receipt of cash in lieu of shares).

Advance Tax Rulings: ATR-64: Phantom stock award plan.

(4) Application of subsec. (1) — For greater certainty it is hereby declared that, where a person to whom any provision of subsection (1) would otherwise apply has ceased to be an employee before all things have happened that would make that provision applicable, subsection (1) shall continue to apply as though the person were still an employee and as though the employment were still in existence.

Interpretation Bulletins: IT-113R4: Benefits to employees — stock options.

(5) Non-application of this section — This section does not apply if the benefit conferred by the agreement was not received in respect of, in the course of, or by virtue of, the employment.

(6) Sale to trustee for employees — If a particular qualifying person has entered into an arrangement under which securities of the particular person, or of a qualifying person with which it does not deal at arm's length, are sold or issued by either person to a trustee to be held by the trustee in trust for sale to an employee of the particular person or of a qualifying person with which it does not deal at arm's length,

(a) for the purposes of this section (other than subsection (2)) and paragraphs 110(1)(d) to (d.1),

(i) any particular rights of the employee under the arrangement in respect of those securities are deemed to be rights under a particular agreement with the particular person under which the particular person has agreed to sell or issue securities to the employee,

(ii) any securities acquired under the arrangement by the employee or by a person in whom the particular rights have become vested are deemed to be securities acquired under the particular agreement, and

(iii) any amounts paid or agreed to be paid to the trustee for any securities acquired under the arrangement by the employee or by a person in whom the particular rights have become vested are deemed to be amounts paid or agreed to be paid to the particular person for securities acquired under the particular agreement; and

(b) subsection (2) does not apply in respect of securities held by the trustee under the arrangement.

Notes: For an example of a plan to which 7(6) might apply, see VIEWS doc 2005-0124261E5. Where 7(6) applies, the corporate employer, not the trustee, must withhold tax under 153(1): 2013-0400641E5.

7(6)(a) amended by 2000 Budget to change "and (d.1)" to "to (d.1)" (effectively adding reference to 110(1)(d.01)), effective for 2000 and later taxation years.

7(6) earlier amended by 1998 Budget (effective 1998) and 1991 technical bill.

Advance Tax Rulings: ATR-15: Employee stock option plan.

(7) Definitions — The following definitions apply in this section and in subsection 47(3), paragraph 53(1)(j), subsection 110(0.1), paragraphs 110(1)(d), (d.01) and (e) and subsections 110(1.1) to (1.9) and (2.1).

Notes: 7(7) opening words amended by 2021 budget bill #1, effective July 2021, to apply to 110(0.1), 110(1)(e) and 110(1.9). Before then, after "53(1)(j)", read "and 110(1)(d) and (d.01) and subsections 110(1.1), (1.2), (1.5) to (1.8) and (2.1)".

Earlier amended by 2002-2013 technical bill (effective 1999), 2010 budget bill #2, 2000 Budget.

"qualifying person" means a corporation or a mutual fund trust.

Notes: Definition "qualifying person" added by 1998 Budget, effective 1995 but, except for the purpose of applying 7(3)(b), does not apply to a right under an agreement

made before March 1998 to sell or issue trust units to an individual unless an election was made by the end of 1999.

"security" of a qualifying person means

(a) if the person is a corporation, a share of the capital stock of the corporation; and

(b) if the person is a mutual fund trust, a unit of the trust.

Notes: Definition "security" added by 1998 Budget, effective on the same basis as the addition of 7(7)"qualifying person".

(8)–(15) [Repealed]

Notes: 7(8)-(15) (reproduced below) implemented a 2000 Budget proposal to defer tax on stock option benefits, when the option was exercised before 4pm EST March 4, 2010. The deferral still applies until the shares are disposed of [including to a spouse under a divorce settlement: VIEWS doc 2015-057290117], or until the employee dies or becomes non-resident; and see 110(1)(d) and 180.01. (Unlimited deferral applies for Canadian-controlled private corporations in 7(1.1).)

The deferral was available only if the employee was entitled to a deduction under 110(1)(d) [7(9)(b)] — generally, the shares are ordinary common shares, the employee dealt at arm's length with the employer when the option was granted, and the exercise price was not less than the value of the shares when the option was granted. In general terms, the deferral was not available to a "specified shareholder" [7(9)(c)] (person owning, with family members, 10% or more of any class of the employer at the time the stock option agreement was made). There was an annual limit of $100,000 [7(10)(c)(i)], based on the year the options become exercisable and on the value of the shares when the options were granted.

The deferral continues to be reported annually under 7(16)). The employee includes the amount in employment income for the year the deferral ceases: 7(8).

See detailed CRA Q&A "Deferral of taxation on employee stock options", doc 2001-02-26 on *TaxPartner* or *Taxnet Pro*; VIEWS doc 2005-0157521E5.

See Notes to 110(1.7) for an election available due to enactment of 110(1.7).

7(8)-(15) repealed by 2010 budget bill #2, effective in respect of rights exercised after 4pm EST, March 4, 2010. For rights exercised earlier, read:

(8) **Deferral in respect of non-CCPC employee options** — Where a particular qualifying person (other than a Canadian-controlled private corporation) has agreed to sell or issue securities of the particular qualifying person (or of a qualifying person with which it does not deal at arm's length) to a taxpayer who is an employee of the particular qualifying person (or of a qualifying person with which the particular qualifying person does not deal at arm's length), in applying paragraph (1)(a) in respect of the taxpayer's acquisition of a security under the agreement, the reference in that paragraph to "the taxation year in which the employee acquired the securities" shall be read as a reference to "the taxation year in which the employee disposed of or exchanged the securities" if

(a) the acquisition is a qualifying acquisition; and

(b) the taxpayer elects, in accordance with subsection (10), to have this subsection apply in respect of the acquisition.

Related Provisions [Former 7(8)]: 7(1.3) — Order of disposition of securities; 7(9) — Meaning of "qualifying acquisition"; 7(10) — Election for the purpose of subsec. (8); 7(13) — Revocation of election; 7(14) — Deferral deemed valid at CRA's discretion; 7(15) — No source withholding required when deferred benefit included; 7(16) — Prescribed form required while security held; 47(3)(a) — No averaging of cost on disposition of securities; 180.01(1) — Election to adjust tax where election made under 7(8) before March 4/10.

Regulations [Former 7(8)]: 200(5) (information return).

(9) **Meaning of "qualifying acquisition"** — For the purpose of subsection (8), a taxpayer's acquisition of a security under an agreement made by a particular qualifying person is a qualifying acquisition if

(a) the acquisition occurs after February 27, 2000;

(b) the taxpayer would, if this Act were read without reference to subsection (8), be entitled to deduct an amount under paragraph 110(1)(d) in respect of the acquisition in computing income for the taxation year in which the security is acquired;

(c) where the particular qualifying person is a corporation, the taxpayer was not, at the time immediately after the agreement was made, a person who would, if the references in the portion of the definition "specified shareholder" in subsection 248(1) before paragraph (a) to "in a taxation year" and "at any time in the year" were read as references to "at any time" and "at that time", respectively, be a specified shareholder of any of

(i) the particular qualifying person,

(ii) any qualifying person that, at that time, was an employer of the taxpayer and was not dealing at arm's length with the particular qualifying person, and

(iii) the qualifying person of which the taxpayer had, under the agreement, a right to acquire a security; and

(d) where the security is a share,

(i) it is of a class of shares that, at the time the acquisition occurs, is listed on a designated stock exchange, and

(ii) where rights under the agreement were acquired by the taxpayer as a result of one or more dispositions to which subsection (1.4) applied, none of the rights that were the subject of any of the dispositions included a right to acquire a share of a class of shares that, at the time the rights were disposed of, was not listed on any designated stock exchange.

(9.1) Reorganization — If, in the course of a reorganization that gives rise to a dividend that would, in the absence of paragraph 55(3)(b), be subject to subsection 55(2), rights to acquire securities listed on a designated stock exchange (referred to in this subsection as "public options") under an agreement to sell or issue securities referred to in subsection (1) are exchanged for rights to acquire securities that are not listed on a designated stock exchange (referred to in this subsection as "private options"), and the private options are subsequently exchanged for public options, the private options are deemed to be rights to acquire shares that are listed on a designated stock exchange for the purposes of subparagraph 7(9)(d)(ii).

(10) Election for the purpose of subsec. (8) — For the purpose of subsection (8), a taxpayer's election to have that subsection apply in respect of the taxpayer's acquisition of a particular security under an agreement referred to in subsection (1) is in accordance with this subsection if

(a) the election is filed, in prescribed form and manner at a particular time that is before January 16 of the year following the year in which the acquisition occurs, with a person who would be required to file an information return in respect of the acquisition if subsection (8) were read without reference to paragraph (8)(b);

(b) the taxpayer is resident in Canada at the time the acquisition occurs; and

(c) the specified value of the particular security does not exceed the amount by which

(i) $100,000

exceeds

(ii) the total of all amounts each of which is the specified value of another security acquired by the taxpayer at or before the particular time under an agreement referred to in subsection (1), where

(A) the taxpayer's right to acquire that other security first became exercisable in the year that the taxpayer's right to acquire the particular security first became exercisable, and

(B) at or before the particular time, the taxpayer has elected in accordance with this subsection to have subsection (8) apply in respect of the acquisition of that other security.

Related Provisions [Former 7(10)]: 7(11) — Meaning of "specified value"; 7(12) — Order of exercise of identical options; 7(13) — Revocation of election; 220(3.2), Reg. 600 — Late filing of election.

Forms [Former 7(10)]: RC310: Election for special relief for tax deferral election on employee security options; T1212: Statement of deferred security options benefits.

(11) Meaning of "specified value" — For the purpose of paragraph (10)(c), the specified value of a particular security acquired by a taxpayer under an agreement referred to in subsection (1) is the amount determined by the formula

$$A/B$$

where

A　is the fair market value, determined at the time the agreement was made, of a security that was the subject of the agreement at the time the agreement was made; and

B　is

(a) except where paragraph (b) applies, 1, and

(b) where the number or type of securities that are the subject of the agreement has been modified in any way after the time the agreement was made, the number of securities (including any fraction of a security) that it is reasonable to consider the taxpayer would, at the time the particular security was acquired, have a right to acquire under the agreement in lieu of one of the securities that was the subject of the agreement at the time the agreement was made.

(12) Identical options — order of exercise — Unless the context otherwise requires, a taxpayer is deemed to exercise identical rights to acquire securities under agreements referred to in subsection (1)

(a) where the taxpayer has designated an order, in the order so designated; and

(b) in any other case, in the order in which those rights first became exercisable and, in the case of identical rights that first became exercisable at the same time, in the order in which the agreements under which those rights were acquired were made.

Related Provisions [Former 7(12)]: 248(12) — Identical properties.

(13) Revoked election — For the purposes of this section (other than this subsection), an election filed by a taxpayer to have subsection (8) apply to the taxpayer's acquisition of a security is deemed never to have been filed if, before January 16 of the year following the year in which the acquisition occurs, the taxpayer files with the person with whom the election was filed a written revocation of the election.

Related Provisions [Former 7(13)]: 220(3.2), Reg. 600 — Late revocation of election.

(14) Deferral deemed valid — For the purposes of this section and paragraph 110(1)(d), where a taxpayer files an election to have subsection (8) apply in respect of the taxpayer's acquisition of a particular security and subsection (8) would not apply to the acquisition if this section were read without reference to this subsection, the following rules apply if the Minister so notifies the taxpayer in writing:

(a) the acquisition is deemed, for the purpose of subsection (8), to be a qualifying acquisition;

(b) the taxpayer is deemed to have elected, in accordance with subsection (10), at the time of the acquisition, to have subsection (8) apply in respect of the acquisition; and

(c) if, at the time the Minister sends the notice, the taxpayer has not disposed of the security, the taxpayer is deemed (other than for the purpose of subsection (1.5)) to have disposed of the security at that time and to have acquired the security immediately after that time other than under an agreement referred to in subsection (1).

(15) Withholding — Where, because of subsection (8), a taxpayer is deemed by paragraph (1)(a) to have received a benefit from employment in a taxation year, the benefit is deemed to be nil for the purpose of subsection 153(1).

7(9.1) (which implemented a Dec. 12, 2003 comfort letter published under 7(9)(d)(ii) in PITA 25th-38th ed.) added by 2010 budget bill #2, effective from 2000 to 3:59pm EST March 4, 2010, except that, before Dec. 14, 2007, read "designated stock exchange" as "prescribed stock exchange".

7(8)-(15) added by 2000 Budget, for 2000 and later taxation years. 7(9)(d)(i) and (ii) amended by 2007 budget bill #2, effective Dec. 14, 2007, to change "prescribed stock exchange" to "designated stock exchange".

(16) Prescribed form for deferral — Where, at any time in a taxation year, a taxpayer holds a security that was acquired under circumstances to which subsection (8) applied, the taxpayer shall file with the Minister, with the taxpayer's return of income for the year, a prescribed form containing prescribed information relating to the taxpayer's acquisition and disposition of securities under agreements referred to in subsection (1).

Notes: 7(16) added by 2000 Budget, effective for 2000 and later taxation years.

Forms: RC310: Election for special relief for tax deferral election on employee security options; T1212: Statement of deferred security options benefits.

Definitions [s. 7]: "amount" — 248(1); "arm's length" — 7(1.11), 251(1); "Canadian-controlled private corporation" — 125(7), 248(1); "Canadian corporation" — 89(1), 248(1); "class of shares" — 248(6); "corporation" — 248(1), *Interpretation Act* 35(1); "designated person" — 7(1.4)(b); "designated stock exchange" — 248(1), 262; "disposed", "disposition" — 7(1.6), 248(1); "dividend", "employee", "employer", "employment" — 248(1); "exchanged option" — 7(1.4)(a); "exchanged securities", "exchanged shares" — 7(1.5)(a); "fair market value" — see 69(1) Notes; "identical" — 248(12); "Minister" — 248(1); "mutual fund trust" — 132(6)–(7), 132.2(3)(n), 248(1); "new option" — 7(1,4)(b); "new securities", "new shares" — 7(1.4)(b); "old securities", "old shares" — 7(1.4)(a); "person", "prescribed" — 248(1); "property" — 248(1); "qualifying acquisition" — 7(9); "qualifying person" — 7(7); "resident in Canada" — 250; "SIFT wind-up corporation", "SIFT wind-up entity" — 248(1); "securities", "security" — 7(7); "share", "specified shareholder" — 248(1); "specified value" — 7(11); "taxation year" — 249; "taxpayer" — 248(1); "trust" — 104(1), 248(1), (3); "written" — *Interpretation Act* 35(1) "writing".

Income Tax Folios: S1-F1-C3: Disability supports deduction [replaces IT-519R2]; S1-F3-C1: Child care expense deduction [replaces IT-495R3].

Deductions

8. (1) Deductions allowed — In computing a taxpayer's income for a taxation year from an office or employment, there may be deducted such of the following amounts as are wholly applicable to that source or such part of the following amounts as may reasonably be regarded as applicable thereto:

Notes: Expenses not specifically listed under 8(1) are not deductible from employment income. See 8(2).

(a) [volunteer emergency workers — repealed]

Notes: 8(1)(a) added by 1998 Budget, but repealed by 2001 technical bill retroactive to its introduction. It provided a deduction for volunteer emergency workers for up to $1,000 of allowance per year, replacing an exemption within 6(1)(b)(viii). Since the inclusion/deduction required too much paperwork by municipalities and other public authorities, it was replaced by an exemption under 81(4).

Earlier 8(1)(a) repealed by 1988 tax reform, effective 1988. This was a general employment expense deduction of $500, available without any requirement that expenses have been incurred. See instead the Canada Employment Credit in 118(10). 8(2) prohibits deduction for employment expenses unless specifically allowed. 8(1)(b)-(s) allow specific expenses.

(b) **legal expenses of employee** — amounts paid by the taxpayer in the year as or on account of legal expenses incurred by the taxpayer to collect, or to establish a right to, an amount owed to the taxpayer that, if received by the taxpayer, would be required by this Subdivision to be included in computing the taxpayer's income;

Related Provisions: 6(1)(j) — Reimbursement or award may be taxable; 6(8) — GST rebate included in income; 60(o.1)(i)(B) — Legal expenses re retiring allowance.

Notes: The cases on 8(1)(b) before June 2013 were based on the wording "legal expenses incurred by the taxpayer to collect or establish a right to salary or wages owed to the taxpayer by the employer or former employer", which was changed in 2013 retroactive to 2001. However, since 248(1)"salary or wages" includes income taxed under s. 5, 6 or 7, those cases allowed legal expenses incurred to recover a s. 6 taxable benefit, or a s. 7 stock option benefit. The old wording "owed ... by the employer" included disability benefits payable by an insurer under contract with the employer, in *Farrell*, 2005 TCC 352; *Frizzle*, 2008 TCC 651. The new wording covers legal fees to obtain a disability insurance settlement taxable under the *surrogatum* principle because it replaces amounts that would have fallen under 6(1)(f): VIEWS doc 2013-0475631I7.

For an interesting suggestion on executors (estate trustees) using 8(1)(b) to deduct the cost of passing of accounts, see Jesse Brodlieb, "Amendment to the ITA Provides Opportunity for Trustees to Deduct Certain Expenses", IV(4) *Personal Tax and Estate Planning* (Federated Press) 204-06 (2013).

The words "to collect or establish a right to" relate to the purpose of incurring the legal fees, so the deduction is allowed even if the legal action has no chance of success: *Loo*, 2004 FCA 249; *Fortin*, [2002] 4 C.T.C. 2245 (TCC); *Rogers*, 2005 TCC 336; *Podlesny*, 2008 TCC 591. CRA now accepts this: VIEWS doc 2017-0699751E5 q.3 (overriding 2012-0433201I7 and IT-99R5 para. 23).

To "establish a right to" salary does not include: establishing right to a promotion (*Turner-Lienaux*, [1997] 2 C.T.C. 344 (FCA); hockey player negotiating contract (*Caruso*, 2012 TCC 233); *Jazairi*, 2001 FCA 31); oppression relief claims against other shareholders in family business, where no claim made against corp (*Hollinger Estate*, 2013 TCC 252); being restored to employment (VIEWS doc 2017-0699751E5 q.5).

Legal fees (**LF**) paid to protect one's job or right to earn income are not deductible: *Blagdon*, 2003 FCA 269 (shipmaster's LF to defend his competence and right to command a ship); *Esposito*, 2004 TCC 102 (police officer charged with assaulting prisoner); *Kaushik*, 2005 TCC 207 (professor's LF to defend student complaints that would have affected his career); *Cimolai*, 2006 FCA 348 (physician's LF to sue former colleagues for conspiracy in interfering with his job); *Blackburn*, 2006 TCC 332 and 2010 TCC 69 (police officer contesting criminal charges and disciplinary proceedings); *Lester*, 2011 TCC 543 (LF paid by Xco owner L to buy out another shareholder, to preserve L's ability to earn employment income from Xco); *Allan*, 2013 TCC 65 (FCA appeal discontinued A-115-13) (manager of escort business's LF to defend against criminal charges); *Ross*, 2016 TCC 170 (pharmacist contesting professional misconduct complaint); *Geick*, 2017 TCC 120 (police officer contesting criminal charges); *Dauphin*, 2019 TCC 93 (Montreal city councilor paid lawyers for services relating to searches of his home and office as part of police investigation into city administration); *Clément*, 2020 TCC 33 (judge trying to stay on past mandatory retirement age to earn pension). *Contra*, in *Blackburn*, 2004 TCC 180, a police officer was convicted of dangerous driving and automatically suspended without pay. His LF for the trial were non-deductible, but those for a successful appeal were allowed under 8(1)(b) because they resulted in his suspension changing retroactively to being with pay! See also VIEWS docs 2009-0310391I7, 2010-0361641E5, 2011-0423761E5, 2017-0699751E5; and Notes to 60(o).

LF to defend a claim to recover overpaid salary are non-deductible, as 8(1) applies only to costs incurred to "collect or establish a right to" employment income: *Barkley (Catlos)*, 2021 FCA 5 (ruling that *Fenwick*, 2008 FCA 370, is now "moot" as it dealt with the pre-2013 8(1)(b), and effectively overruling *Chagnon*, 2011 TCC 268).

In *Kurnik*, 2019 TCC 206, deduction was allowed for LF paid to settle suit against K's family trust because it was related to his suit for salary. In *Barrett*, 2019 TCC 228, fees paid for an oppression remedy action were not sufficiently connected with B's employment to be deductible.

LF paid to defend a director's liability assessment for a company's unremitted GST are non-deductible: *Shapiro*, 2011 TCC 79.

LF that cannot be deducted because there is no income can create a loss from employment, which can be carried over to another year under 111(1)(a) as a non-capital loss: VIEWS doc 2006-0179401E5.

LF paid in a suit for wrongful dismissal are deductible not under 8(1)(b), but under 60(o.1) and only to the extent of any award or settlement received: *Guenette*, 2004 TCC 111; *Bonsma*, 2010 TCC 342; VIEWS doc 2011-0423761E5.

8(1)(b) does not cover accounting fees: *Dnebosky*, 2019 TCC 78, para. 2; *Wallens*, 2019 TCC 193, para. 6.

See also VIEWS docs 2009-0345541I7 (fees deductible where incurred to obtain insurance settlement taxable under 6(1)(f)); 2011-0405861M4 (fees to obtain damages for complications following surgery do not qualify).

See also Notes to 60(o).

8(1)(b) amended by 2002-2013 technical bill (for amounts paid after 2000; see first para. above), 1989 Budget.

Interpretation Bulletins: IT-99R5: Legal and accounting fees.

Forms: T1 General return, Line 22900 [former 229]: Other employment expenses; T777: Statement of employment expenses; T4044: Employment expenses [guide].

(c) **clergy residence** — where, in the year, the taxpayer

(i) is a member of the clergy or of a religious order or a regular minister of a religious denomination, and

(ii) is

(A) in charge of a diocese, parish or congregation,

(B) ministering to a diocese, parish or congregation, or

(C) engaged exclusively in full-time administrative service by appointment of a religious order or religious denomination,

the amount, not exceeding the taxpayer's remuneration for the year from the office or employment, equal to

(iii) the total of all amounts including amounts in respect of utilities, included in computing the taxpayer's income for the year under section 6 in respect of the residence or other living accommodation occupied by the taxpayer in the course of, or because of, the taxpayer's office or employment as such a member or minister so in charge of or ministering to a diocese, parish or congregation, or so engaged in such administrative service, or

(iv) rent and utilities paid by the taxpayer for the taxpayer's principal place of residence (or other principal living accommodation), ordinarily occupied during the year by the taxpayer, or the fair rental value of such a residence (or other living accommodation), including utilities, owned by the taxpayer or the taxpayer's spouse or common-law partner, not exceeding the lesser of

(A) the greater of

(I) $1,000 multiplied by the number of months (to a maximum of ten) in the year, during which the taxpayer is a person described in subparagraphs (i) and (ii), and

(II) one-third of the taxpayer's remuneration for the year from the office or employment, and

(B) the amount, if any, by which

(I) the rent paid or the fair rental value of the residence or living accommodation, including utilities

exceeds

(II) the total of all amounts each of which is an amount deducted, in connection with the same accommodation or residence, in computing an individual's income for the year from an office or employment or from a business (other than an amount deducted under this paragraph by the taxpayer), to the extent that the amount can reasonably be considered to relate to the period, or a portion of the period, in respect of which an amount is claimed by the taxpayer under this paragraph;

Related Provisions: 8(10) — Employer's certificate required; 146(1)"earned income"(a)(i) — Earned income for RRSP purposes includes value of residence.

Notes: Deduction under 8(1)(c) requires an employer's Form T1223 certificate under 8(10). (For comment on improvements to the form, see tinyurl.com/cccc-t1223.) The T1223 is also used to calculate the deductible amount. If the employee wants source withholdings reduced to reflect this deduction, see Notes to 153(1.1).

To determine whether an organization is a religious order, the TCC (Bowman ACJ) set out six criteria in *McGorman*, [1999] 3 C.T.C. 2630, ruling that Canadian Baptist Overseas Mission Board and SIM Canada were religious orders. Paraphrased: (1) purpose of the organization must be primarily religious; (2) strict moral and spiritual regime of self-sacrifice and dedication to the organization's goals; (3) full-time, long-term commitment; (4) stricter spiritual and moral discipline than required of lay church members; (5) admission to the order in accordance with strict standards of spiritual and personal suitability; (6) general sense of communality. CRA accepts the criteria and repeats them in IT-141R para. 9. See also *Zylstra*, [1997] 2 C.T.C. 203 (FCA) (Ontario Bible College was not a religious order); VIEWS docs 2008-0301781E5, 2009-030576117; 2010-0363501E5 (non-denominational "Mission" is not a religious order); 2010-3552311I7 (need evidence of "communality" and of religion being primary purpose); 2009-033973117, 2009-036928117, 2010-0383881E5 and 2013-0494611I7 (organizations do not qualify); 2011-039555117 (Navigators of Canada now qualifies, after organizational changes since *Koop*, [1999] 3 C.T.C. 2084 (TCC)); 2012-0436451E5 (entity's Statement of Faith does not make it a religious denomination); 2012-0451081E5 (once accepted by Appeals Branch, status continues); 2012-0467711E5 (detailed description of criteria).

A "member of the clergy" is a person set apart from other members as a spiritual leader, and should be authorized to perform spiritual duties, conduct religious services, administer sacraments and carry out similar functions: VIEWS docs 2003-0026465, 2006-0178781I7, 2007-0223581E5, 2007-0227951E5, 2007-0228421E5 (various other functions do not qualify), 2008-0264171E5, 2008-0299791E5, 2010-035818117. The member must be considered a regular minister by the church but need not have been formally ordained: *Tidd*, 2012 TCC 16; 2004-0091791E5. The following did or may qualify: aboriginal spiritual caregiver (2015-0620371E5); Community Development Pastor (2011-042277117); Executive Pastor (2012-0436101E5, but does not satisfy "ministering" test below); hospital chaplain (*Moerman*, 2015 TCC 295); missionary with Christian and Missionary Alliance (*Reimer*, 2005 FCA 398); part-time or semi-retired minister (2003-0046121E5, 2004-0055401M4, 2004-0067671M4, 2005-0160401M4); Student Ministries Associate (2011-0394061E5). The following did not qualify: hospital chaplain appointed under agreement between archdiocese and Quebec government (*Pereira*, 2006 TCC 300); lay person acting as Coordinator of Youth Ministry and Pastoral Minister (2007-0241541E5); priest providing occasional liturgical services (2012-0447881E5); Roman Catholic pastoral associates (*Lefebvre*, 2009 FCA 307; *Proulx*, 2010 FCA 261); school chaplain who is not ordained priest (2010-0370201E5, 2015-0576461E5, 2015-0598631E5).

For "ministering to a congregation" in (ii)(B), see *McGorman* (above); *Alemu*, [1999] 2 C.T.C. 2245 (TCC) at para. 40; *Tidd* (above); *Lichtman*, 2017 TCC 252 (FCA appeal discontinued A-35-18) (rabbi employed by Jewish school is not "ministering", and school is not a "congregation" [also VIEWS doc 2009-031062117]); docs 2004-0055131E5, 2006-018604117; 2010-0387251E5 (Spiritual Care Coordinator in medical service centre: yes); 2011-039555117 (campus minister with Navigators of Canada: yes); 2011-040477117 (pastor in charge of children's ministry: yes); 2012-0436101E5 (Executive Pastor: no, as "ministering" duties are incidental).

For administrative personnel qualifying under (ii)(C), see *Fitch*, [1999] 2 C.T.C. 2419 (TCC); docs 2008-0270131E5, 2009-0307291E5, 2010-0363501E5, 2012-0436451E5.

CRA formerly operated an internal Clergy Residence Committee to consider clergy deduction issues raised by the Compliance Programs Branch on an "as-needed" basis. It was disbanded in 2007.

The deduction is available against remuneration from clergy employment only, not business (self-employment): *Abrahams*, 2013 TCC 391; VIEWS doc 2009-0350821E5 (see Notes to 248(1)"employee" for the distinction). In *Moerman*, 2015 TCC 295, M provided his services through his corporation, which paid him employment income that qualified. "Remuneration" is broad and includes taxable benefits: 2011-0413541E5. A person receiving income maintenance payments while on parental leave does not qualify in CRA's view: 2007-0219881E5; but see *Shaw*, 2010 TCC 210, where sick-leave income from a wage loss replacement plan qualified. *Shaw* does not extend to CPP disability benefits, as they are not provided by the employer: *Parker*, 2015 TCC 86, para. 26. Clergy who receive only voluntary payments from congregants earn income from business and cannot claim the deduction: 2007-022147117. Retired clergy cannot claim it because they have no clergy income: 2009-0314611E5; but free housing to retired clergy might not be a taxable benefit in the first place if it is no longer connected with employment: 2010-0382791E5. For the calculation where 2 spouses are both clergy and share a home, see 2009-0315181E5, Form T1223 Notes 1 and 3, and *Williams*, 2011 TCC 66. Where the spouses own 2 homes, both qualify: 2012-045596117. There is no requirement to have an office in the home: 2019-0796121E5.

A dormitory room can be a "residence" for 8(1)(c): doc 2015-056901117.

8(1)(c)(iii) and (iv) are alternatives, so a rabbi who owned a fraction of his home and rented the remaining fraction could not claim both: *Hoch*, 2019 TCC 99.

The parallel Quebec deduction is restricted to clergy who must use their residence in the course of employment: Robert Hayhoe, "Quebec Changes Tax Treatment of Clergy", xxix(4) *The Canadian Taxpayer* (Carswell) 20-21 (Feb. 13/07).

8(1)(c) amended by 2001 technical bill, effective for 2001 and later taxation years.

Interpretation Bulletins: IT-99R5: Legal and accounting fees; IT-141R: Clergy residence deduction.

Registered Charities Newsletters: 23 (did you know? clergy residence deduction).

Forms: T1 General return, Line 23100 [former 231]; T1223: Clergy residence deduction; T2200: Declaration of conditions of employment.

(d) **teachers' exchange fund contribution** — a single amount, in respect of all employments of the taxpayer as a teacher, not exceeding $250 paid by the taxpayer in the year to a fund established by the Canadian Education Association for the benefit of teachers from Commonwealth countries present in Canada under a teachers' exchange arrangement;

Notes: See *Interpretation Act* s. 35(1) and Schedule for "Commonwealth" countries.

(e) **expenses of railway employees** — amounts disbursed by the taxpayer in the year for meals and lodging while employed by a railway company

(i) away from the taxpayer's ordinary place of residence as a relieving telegrapher or station agent or on maintenance and repair work, or

(ii) away from the municipality and the metropolitan area, if there is one, where the taxpayer's home terminal was located, and at a location from which, by reason of distance from the place where the taxpayer maintained a self-contained domestic establishment in which the taxpayer resided and actually supported a spouse or common-law partner or a person dependent upon the taxpayer for support and connected with the taxpayer by blood relationship, marriage or common-law partnership or adoption, the taxpayer could not reasonably be expected to return daily to that place,

to the extent that the taxpayer has not been reimbursed and is not entitled to be reimbursed in respect thereof;

Related Provisions: 6(6) — Employment — remote and special work sites; 6(8) — GST rebate included in income; 8(1)(h) — Travelling expenses; 8(11) — GST; 67.1 — Expenses for food, etc.; 251(6) — Connected by blood relationship, etc.

Notes: For flat-rate meal deductions, see Notes to 8(1)(g).

8(1)(e) amended by 2000 same-sex partners bill to refer to "common-law partner" and "common-law partnership", effective as per Notes to 248(1)"common-law partner".

Interpretation Bulletins: IT-518R: Food, beverages and entertainment expenses.

Information Circulars: 73-21R9: Claims for meals and lodging expenses of transport employees.

Forms: TL2: Claim for meals and lodging expenses.

(f) **sales expenses [of commission employee]** — where the taxpayer was employed in the year in connection with the selling of property or negotiating of contracts for the taxpayer's employer, and

(i) under the contract of employment was required to pay the taxpayer's own expenses,

(ii) was ordinarily required to carry on the duties of the employment away from the employer's place of business,

(iii) was remunerated in whole or part by commissions or other similar amounts fixed by reference to the volume of the sales made or the contracts negotiated, and

(iv) was not in receipt of an allowance for travel expenses in respect of the taxation year that was, by virtue of subparagraph 6(1)(b)(v), not included in computing the taxpayer's income,

amounts expended by the taxpayer in the year for the purpose of earning the income from the employment (not exceeding the commissions or other similar amounts referred to in subparagraph (iii) and received by the taxpayer in the year) to the extent that such amounts were not

(v) outlays, losses or replacements of capital or payments on account of capital, except as described in paragraph (j),

(vi) outlays or expenses that would, by virtue of paragraph 18(1)(l), not be deductible in computing the taxpayer's income for the year if the employment were a business carried on by the taxpayer, or

(vii) amounts the payment of which reduced the amount that would otherwise be included in computing the taxpayer's income for the year because of paragraph 6(1)(e);

Related Provisions: 6(1)(b)(v) — Allowance for travelling expenses; 6(1)(j) — Reimbursement or award may be taxable; 6(8) — GST rebate included in income; 8(1)(h) — Travelling expenses; 8(1)(h.1) — Motor vehicle travelling expenses; 8(1)(j) — Auto and aircraft costs; 8(4) — Limitation — meals; 8(9) — Limitation — aircraft expenses; 8(10) — Employer's certificate; 8(13) — Work space in home; 18(1)(h) — Personal or living expenses; 18(1)(l) — Use of recreational facilities and club dues; 18(1)(r) — Limitation on employer deductibility; 67.1 — 50% limitation on expenses for meals and entertainment; 67.3 — Limitation re cost of leasing passenger vehicle; Reg. 102(2)(d)(i) — Effect of deduction on source withholdings.

Notes: See Guide T4044, Chapter 2 for detailed discussion of commission employees' eligible expenses and conditions. A deduction under 8(1)(f) requires an employer's T2200 certificate, but also needs proof the conditions are met: see Notes to 8(10). "The deduction of employment expenses by taxpayers should generally be supported by contemporaneous documentation so that the Court can be satisfied that the deductions are proper": *DiCosmo*, 2015 TCC 325, para. 29 (aff'd 2017 FCA 60).

"Required" by employment contract: this is determined based on the contract objectively, not the "personal perspective of the employer", and may be an "implicit or implied term": *Urquhart*, 2016 FCA 76, para. 6. Also, some expenses may be required under the contract and others not: para. 7. In *Brandt*, 2013 TCC 70, an IBM sales rep was found to be required to maintain a home office, and allowed vehicle expenses. Other expenses that IBM would have reimbursed had he asked did not qualify: para. 46. In *Lavigne*, 2013 TCC 308, expenses were disallowed because the Rogers Communications employment contract did not require the employee to pay his own expenses, even though he was required to pay those that Rogers considered unnecessary or unreasonable. In *Blott*, 2018 TCC 1, it was not proven the employee was required to hire an assistant. See also Notes to 8(1)(h.1) on "required"; Alvarez, "The Contractual Requirement Rule for Commission Employees' Deductions", 10(1) *Canadian Tax Focus* (ctf.ca) 2-3 (Feb. 2020).

An amount paid to an employee is generally a "commission" if computed with reference to the volume or dollar amount of sales the employee makes for the employer, and a "bonus" if it is payment above normal remuneration in recognition of achieving performance objectives (including sales targets): VIEWS docs April 1991-147, 9915377, 2004-0076301E5, 2004-0101641E5, 2005-0152821E5, 2011-0396821E5. However, in *Tulman*, 2014 TCC 140, paras. 39-41, a CEO's bonus was held not to be a commission. See also Notes to 20(1)(bb).

Commissions repaid to the employer are deductible under 8(1)(f): VIEWS doc 2010-0373481C6.

A stockbroker who pays a client for making an error on a trade may be able to deduct the payment: VIEWS doc 2009-0331661E5.

8(1)(f) expenses can be deducted only against commission income; the taxpayer may also claim amounts under 8(1)(j), or may bypass 8(1)(f) and use 8(1)(h) or (h.1): VIEWS doc 2006-0203361E5.

8(1)(f)(iv) disallows deduction if a non-taxable allowance is received, but only if the allowance relates to those expenses: IT-522R para. 36; doc 2015-0564161E5.

If a travel allowance is unreasonable, it is included in income and 8(1)(f)(iv) does not prevent deducting offsetting expenses: *Emond*, 2011 CarswellNat 6507, para. 15.

Most expenses "on account of capital" are disallowed: 8(1)(f)(v). In *Gifford*, 2004 SCC 15, para. 39, the Supreme Court stated that this is not the same as "capital expenditure"; for interest, the question is what the loan proceeds are to the borrower when received (e.g., inventory of a moneylender), not what they are spent on. Capital expenses were disallowed in *Emmons*, 2006 TCC 269 (computer equipment that would rapidly depreciate); *Collette*, 2006 TCC 641 (36 monthly payments for a computer were purchase instalments, not lease payments); *Paes*, 2007 TCC 311 (seminar and training expenses); *Emond* (above), para. 12 (loan repayment); VIEWS docs 2008-0273701E5 (ground source heat system), 2009-0315641E5 (ski equipment).

Internet connection fees paid to earn commission income can generally be deducted: VIEWS doc 2003-0022747. So can fees to a self-employed assistant: 2008-0287661E5.

Meals are subject to a special limitation: see 8(4).

For travel from home to place of work, see Notes to 8(1)(h.1).

In *Ross*, 2005 TCC 286 (Crown's FCA appeal discontinued A-231-05), a stockbroker was allowed his costs of maintaining thoroughbred horses (otherwise restricted as farm losses — see 31(1)) as expenses to earn commission income, by showing that much of his income came from contacts made through horse racing.

In *Emmons*, 2006 TCC 269, parking at the employer's office was deductible because E needed the car to travel from the office to clients.

Investment advisors who had to pay their former employers when leaving could deduct such costs in *Douthwright*, 2007 TCC 560 (repaid training costs) and *Raphael*, 2008 TCC 202 (compensation for lost commissions). This overrides CRA's view (2004-0103391E5) that "the employment" refers only to the current employer. In *Gagea*, 2007 TCC 620, G purchased shares for a client whose cheque was returned NSF. G was required by his employer to cover the loss and the shares were transferred to him. His loss on selling the shares was non-deductible (but he could claim a capital loss).

In *Cirone*, 2010 TCC 137, a taxpayer who sold mausoleums on commission was denied most expenses due to lack of documentation (some gifts and referral fees were allowed). In *Czerczak*, 2010 TCC 612 (FCA appeal discontinued A-487-10), expenses were denied because company policy was to reimburse reasonable expenses. In *LeRiche*, 2010 TCC 416, a CIBC Wood Gundy insurance specialist was allowed deductions for promotional expenses, skills training, equipment leases, supplies and assist-

ants' allowances, but not capital expenses (including personal development training) or personal expenses.

Most expenses were denied as personal, capital or unproven in: *Perera*, 2014 TCC 280 (RBC life insurance salesman); *Kalryzian*, 2016 TCC 186 (Future Shop salesman).

8(1)(f)(vii) added by 1991 technical bill, effective 1990, so that where an amount paid by the employee reduces the standby charge under 6(1)(e), that amount cannot also be deducted under 8(1)(f).

Regulations: 102(2)(c)B, 107(2) — Deduction allowed in calculating source withholdings.

Interpretation Bulletins: IT-352R2: Employee's expenses, including work space in home expenses; IT-421R2: Benefits to individuals, corporations and shareholders from loans or debt; IT-518R: Food, beverages and entertainment expenses; IT-522R: Vehicle, travel and sales expenses of employees.

I.T. Technical News: 12 (1998 deduction limits and benefit rates for automobiles).

Forms: T777: Statement of employment expenses; T2200: Declaration of conditions of employment; T2200S: Declaration of conditions of employment for working at home due to COVID-19; TD1X: Statement of commission income and expenses for payroll tax deductions; T4044: Employment expenses [guide].

(g) transport employee's expenses — where the taxpayer was an employee of a person whose principal business was passenger, goods, or passenger and goods transport and the duties of the employment required the taxpayer, regularly,

(i) to travel, away from the municipality where the employer's establishment to which the taxpayer reported for work was located and away from the metropolitan area, if there is one, where it was located, on vehicles used by the employer to transport the goods or passengers, and

(ii) while so away from that municipality and metropolitan area, to make disbursements for meals and lodging,

amounts so disbursed by the taxpayer in the year to the extent that the taxpayer has not been reimbursed and is not entitled to be reimbursed in respect thereof;

Related Provisions: 6(1)(b)(vii) — Allowance for travelling expenses; 6(1)(j) — Reimbursement or award may be taxable; 6(8) — GST rebate included in income; 8(1)(h) — Travelling expenses; 8(11) — GST rebate deemed not to be reimbursement; 67.1 — Expenses for food, etc.

Notes: See Guide T4044, Chapter 4 for detailed discussion of eligible expenses and conditions. The transport employee must be required to pay for both meals and lodging to qualify for this deduction: *Renko (Crawford)*, 2003 FCA 251. However, the deduction is allowed if the employee is required to stay away overnight and stays in their own truck (and showers are a lodging expense): *Kasaboski*, 2005 TCC 356; Information Circular 73-21R9 para. 3; VIEWS doc 2005-0149621E5. The meals need not be connected with the lodging requirement, but the disbursement must be made "while away from the municipality", so in-flight meals that a pilot brought from home did not qualify: *Elwood*, 2012 TCC 313. Where the employee does not stay away overnight, there is no deduction under 8(1)(g) but there may be one under 8(1)(h): 2007-0219611E5, 2009-0320011E5. Meals are subject to the limitation in 67.1. A long-haul truck driver can normally claim lodging including showers, meals, and supplies such as maps, pens, paper and cleaning supplies: 2016-0627441E5.

In *Niemeijer*, 2009 TCC 624, a KLM pilot resident in Canada could not deduct the cost of maintaining an apartment near Amsterdam airport, since it was near his workplace.

For travel from home to place of work, see Notes to 8(1)(h.1).

Claims by transport employees for meals under 8(1)(e), (g) or (h) can either be calculated from actual receipts, or use a "simplified method" (with a record of trips taken) claiming a flat $23 per meal, $69 per day (since 2020; $17 and $51 for 2006-2019: tinyurl.com/travel-cra; IC 73-21R9; *Hunter*, 2006 TCC 584, para. 8 (FCA appeal dismissed for delay A-559-06)), subject to the 50% rule in 67.1: IC 73-21R9, para. 11; *King*, 2008 TCC 79; *Neault*, 2009 TCC 586; *McKay*, 2009 TCC 612; *Stogrin*, 2011 TCC 532. One meal is allowed per 4 hours, up to 3 meals/day: IC 73-21R9 para. 14. *Kasaboski*, 2005 TCC 356, allowed $40/day in place of CRA's then-$33/day rate; but in *Kozmeniuk*, 2006 TCC 65, *Neault* (above) and *McKay* (above), CRA's $45/day was held to be reasonable. In *Beach*, [2009] 5 C.T.C. 2001, the TCC allowed $50 per day. The simplified method cannot be used by self-employed truckers: VIEWS docs 2011-0392521E5, 2011-0392961E5; or by non-transport employees: 2013-0511171E5.

The limitations in 8(1)(g) and 67.1, where federal government employees have a much larger meal allowance, are not a *Charter* violation: *Smith*, 2006 BCCA 237 (leave to appeal denied 2006 CarswellBC 3007 (SCC)); *Neault* (above); *Stogrin* (above).

Waste water pumping and removal is not considered a business of primarily transport of goods for purposes of 8(1)(g): VIEWS doc 2006-0174671E5, citing *Pepper*, [1984] C.T.C. 2694 (TCC) (BC Hydro not primarily in transportation business) and *Creamer*, [1976] C.T.C. 676 (FCTD) (Imperial Oil not primarily in transportation business). See also Notes to 20(1)(bb) re meaning of "principal business".

Ambulance paramedics do not qualify for 8(1)(g) deduction because transportation of persons for medical attention is not the transport of "passengers" (also, the paramedics do not need to stay overnight): VIEWS doc 2006-0175771E5.

Interpretation Bulletins: IT-254R2: Fishermen — employees and seafarers — value of rations and quarters (cancelled); IT-518R: Food, beverages and entertainment expenses.

Information Circulars: 73-21R9: Claims for meals and lodging expenses of transport employees.

Forms: TL2: Claim for meals and lodging expenses.

(h) **travel expenses** — where the taxpayer, in the year,

    (i) was ordinarily required to carry on the duties of the office or employment away from the employer's place of business or in different places, and

    (ii) was required under the contract of employment to pay the travel expenses incurred by the taxpayer in the performance of the duties of the office or employment,

amounts expended by the taxpayer in the year (other than motor vehicle expenses) for travelling in the course of the office or employment, except where the taxpayer

    (iii) received an allowance for travel expenses that was, because of subparagraph 6(1)(b)(v), (vi) or (vii), not included in computing the taxpayer's income for the year, or

    (iv) claims a deduction for the year under paragraph (e), (f) or (g);

Related Provisions: 6(1)(j) — Reimbursement or award may be taxable; 6(8) — GST rebate included in income; 8(1)(h.1) — Motor vehicle travel expenses; 8(1)(j) — Auto and aircraft costs; 8(4) — Limitation — meals; 8(9) — Limitation — aircraft expenses; 8(10) — Employer's certificate; 67.1 — 50% limitation on expenses for meals; 81(3.1) — No tax on allowance or reimbursement for part-time employee's travel expenses; Reg. 102(2)(d)(i) — Effect of deduction on source withholdings.

Notes: See Notes to 8(1)(h.1) for interpretation of 8(1)(h).

8(1)(h) amended by 1991 technical bill, effective 1988.

Regulations: 102(2)(c)B, 107(2) — Deduction allowed in calculating source withholdings.

Interpretation Bulletins: IT-266: Taxation of members of provincial legislative assemblies (cancelled); IT-421R2: Benefits to individuals, corporations and shareholders from loans or debt; IT-518R: Food, beverages and entertainment expenses; IT-522R: Vehicle, travel and sales expenses of employees.

Information Circulars: 73-21R9: Claims for meals and lodging expenses of transport employees; 74-6R2: Power saw expenses.

I.T. Technical News: 12 (1998 deduction limits and benefit rates for automobiles).

Forms: T777: Statement of employment expenses; T2200: Declaration of conditions of employment; TD1X: Statement of commission income and expenses for payroll tax deductions; T4044: Employment expenses [guide].

(h.1) **motor vehicle travel expenses** — where the taxpayer, in the year,

    (i) was ordinarily required to carry on the duties of the office or employment away from the employer's place of business or in different places, and

    (ii) was required under the contract of employment to pay motor vehicle expenses incurred in the performance of the duties of the office or employment,

amounts expended by the taxpayer in the year in respect of motor vehicle expenses incurred for travelling in the course of the office or employment, except where the taxpayer

    (iii) received an allowance for motor vehicle expenses that was, because of paragraph 6(1)(b), not included in computing the taxpayer's income for the year, or

    (iv) claims a deduction for the year under paragraph (f);

Related Provisions: 6(1)(j) — Reimbursement or award may be taxable; 6(8) — GST rebate included in income; 8(1)(j) — Motor vehicle and aircraft costs; 8(10) — Certificate of employer; 18(1)(r) — Limitation on employer deductibility; 67.3 — Limitation re cost of leasing passenger vehicle; 81(3.1) — No tax on allowance or reimbursement for part-time employee's travel expenses; Reg. 102(2)(d)(i) — Effect of deduction on source withholdings.

Notes: 8(1)(h) and (h.1) are almost identical; (h.1) is for an employee's motor vehicle expenses and (h) for other travel expenses. The cross-references in subparas. (iii) and (iv) differ slightly. When reading a VIEWS doc or article in French about 8(1)(h.1), note that subparas. (iii)-(iv) in English are (i)-(ii) in French, and the English (i)-(ii) are part of the opening words of (h.1).

"Expended" means "paid", and ownership of a vehicle does not affect 8(1)(h.1) deduction: VIEWS doc 2018-0768871C6 [2018 APFF q.16].

Required under the contract to pay: (h) and (h.1) require an employer's T2200 certificate, but also proof the condition is met: see Notes to 8(10). In *Barry*, 2014 FCA 280, (h.1) deduction was denied because the employment contract did not require B to use his own vehicle. A contractual requirement to drive to various locations can be implied: *Kreuz*, 2009 TCC 441. Travel expenses do not qualify if they are a "personal choice": *Blackburn*, 2007 TCC 284; *Vickers*, 2011 TCC 2. In *Adler*, 2009 TCC 613, a sole shareholder was held not "required" by his company to incur expenses, since there were no consequences to breaching the agreement (but see *Cofamek* below). Starting 2017, CRA was using *Adler* to deny expenses to employee-owners in a Canada-wide project; however, on Feb. 20, 2018, in "Employment expenses review" (tinyurl.com/review-adler), CRA announced: "Effective immediately, the Agency will stop reviewing and disallowing 'other employment expenses' claimed on line 229 [now 22900 — ed.] of the T1 ... by shareholder-employees. We will also reverse those reassessments specific to line 229 already issued during the review period Sept. 1, 2017 to Feb. 10, 2018.... Consultation will be undertaken with stakeholders in the tax professional community to clarify the requirement of employer certification under subsection 8(10) ... as it relates to shareholder-employees. It is expected that clarification will be issued to take effect in the 2019 tax year." See Friedlan & Friedlan, "CRA Audit of Other Employment Expenses", 18(2) *Tax for the Owner-Manager* (ctf.ca) 708 (April 2018). See also Notes to 8(1)(f) on "required".

"Ordinarily required" in subpara. (i) means "customarily or habitually, not continually but with some degree of regularity" (IT-522R para. 32(a)); "normally", "as a matter of regular occurrence", "commonly" and "usually": *Imray*, [1998] 4 C.T.C. 221 (FCTD); VIEWS docs 2007-0224411E5, 2009-0334751E5. Ordinarily required is "in the year" (opening words of (h) and (h.1)).

Employer's place of business (EPoB) in subpara. (i) generally means a permanent establishment (IT-522R para. 32(c)), and did not include construction trailers: *Champaigne*, 2006 TCC 74, approved in *Dionne*, 2006 FCA 79; and so does not include a temporary construction site that is not a field office: VIEWS doc 2007-0245181E5. In *Potter*, 2008 TCC 228, para. 6, the Crown conceded that driving from Edmonton to Ft. McMurray to work at the Syncrude project qualified, though this "surprised" the Court. If tools cannot be left at a worksite (so the employee has to keep them in his car), this may indicate it is not an EPoB: 2011-0418671E5. A remote logging camp is an EPoB, so charges to employees for daily travel and food to the camp are non-deductible: 2016-0642571E5. For employees working on ships, see 2010-0354771E5.

In the course of office or employment: The expenses "must have been incurred in the course of performing the duties of his office", and concerns of personal safety are not enough: *Hogg*, 2002 FCA 177; *Potter* (above); *Brandt*, 2013 TCC 70.

Travelling from home to place of employment is normally considered personal, not travel for employment; *Glawdecki*, 2010 TCC 650; *Brown*, 2012 TCC 452 (pilot had to commute from Calgary to Los Angeles to get to work); *Barry*, 2014 FCA 280, paras. 14-15; *Chao*, 2018 TCC 72, paras. 43-54; *Dnebosky*, 2019 TCC 78, para. 22 (FCA appeal discontinued A-111-19) (and travelling to *obtain* work also does not qualify: para. 25); *MacDonald*, 2019 TCC 169, paras. 32-49 (commuting from Ottawa to employer's office in Regina); and see Notes to 6(1)(b). Driving to a non-usual work location to respond to an emergency is not personal: doc 2010-0361431E5. Nor is a building inspector's drive home from a construction site: 2010-0374941E5. CRA considers that a client's premises to which an employee reports daily for a 6-month project "may" be a place of employment for this purpose: Guide T4130 under "Regular place of employment". If it is quicker to go from home to a client location than to the office first, the cost of travel from home is deductible: *McDonald*, [1998] 4 C.T.C. 2569 (TCC); *Homsy*, [2004] 2 C.T.C. 2871 (TCC).

Home office: if the employee works mostly at home as *required* by the employer, then travel to the employer's office is deductible: *Campbell*, 2003 TCC 160; *Toutov*, 2006 TCC 187; *McCreath*, 2008 TCC 595; *Emond*, 2011 TCC 142; *Gardner*, 2020 TCC 108. (CRA refused to accept *Campbell* and *Toutov*: doc 2008-0270191E5; but that view seems wrong.)

Where a company's owner's home was one of its places of business, the owner's driving from home to a client location was travel for employment: *Cofamek Inc.*, [2003] G.S.T.C. 115 (TCC). A provincial government employee who needed his car for work daily could deduct the cost of driving to work, as he would otherwise have taken cheaper transportation: *Hudson*, 2007 TCC 661; but CRA believes this decision was wrong: doc 2008-0285351C6. In *Chrapko*, [1988] 2 C.T.C. 342 (FCA), an employee was allowed to deduct travel to the location he worked at only 25% of the time.

The following have qualified: bulldozer operator required to be at job sites, who carried in his truck tools needed for bulldozer maintenance (*Zembal*, 2011 TCC 145); construction worker driving to construction sites (*Martorelli*, 2010 TCC 216); electrical lineman working across the US (*Freake*, 2009 TCC 568); firefighter required to attend emergencies away from the fire station, who maintained an apartment in town to use only when working (*Gariépy*, 2005 TCC 318); forestry equipment operator driving to cutting sites (*Veinot*, 2010 TCC 112); surveyor (*McKay*, 2009 TCC 612); teacher attending annual mandatory teachers' convention (*Imray*, above).

The following have not qualified: employee not required to carry on employment duties away from the employer (*St-Germain*, 2009 TCC 518; VIEWS doc 2015-0599631E5); logging camp equipment operator driving to winter camp, depot and marshalling point (*Brochu*, 2010 TCC 274).

Multiple work locations: note the "or in different places" option in subpara. (i), but this does not change driving to the employer's location from being "personal". In *Colavecchia*, 2010 TCC 194, a pipe-layer who worked at many sites could not deduct his costs of driving to the employer's location first. A plumber who worked at multiple sites was allowed the deduction in *Rousseau*, 2006 TCC 552. Travel *between* work locations is normally employment-related: VIEWS doc 2005-0152401E5, but driving from home to different assigned employer store locations each day of the week is considered personal driving: 2009-0313371E5, 2009-0311091E5, 2009-0339891E5, 2011-0400901E5. Similarly, an employee may have multiple regular places of employment so driving from home to any is personal driving: 2013-0495591C6, 2013-051011117, 2014-0529741E5; 2016 Alberta CPA (tinyurl.com/cra-abtax), q. 3; 2016-0643631E5. A supply teacher who goes to many schools can likely not deduct the cost of driving from home to a school since it is the place of employment: *Champaigne*, 2006 TCC 74; *Dionne*, 2006 FCA 79; *Kreuz*, 2012 TCC 238, para. 72; 2007-0224001E5, 2011-0413521E5 (*contra*, see *Kreuz*, 2009 TCC 441); Earle, "CRA Interpretation of a Substitute Teacher's Place of Business", 8(9) *Tax Hyperion* (Carswell, Sept. 2011).

Reimbursements: Where the reimbursement is unreasonably low, a deduction may be available, but H, who failed to seek full reimbursement from her employer, could not claim it: *Henry*, 2007 TCC 451 (and doc 2006-0185451E5). Where W's travel expenses were paid by the employer but he had to reimburse the employer, the amounts were "expended by" W and deductible under 8(1)(h): *Williams*, 2004 TCC 706.

Allowances: 8(1)(h)(iii) and (h.1)(iii) prevent deduction for travel expenses that exceed a "reasonable" (non-taxable — 6(1)(b)) allowance paid by the employer: *Landry*, 2009 FCA 174; *St-Julien*, 2005 TCC 511; *Logan*, 2008 TCC 546; *Steubing*, 2014 TCC 235, para. 15. The deduction is allowed if the only allowance received is unreasonably high (and thus taxable): *Veinot*, 2010 TCC 112; or if it is too low and the employee includes it in income: VIEWS doc 2016-0674811C6 [CPA QC 2017 q.1.7]. In *Meberatu*, 2017 TCC 211, para. 9-14, an allowance fell under 6(1)(b) so the deduction was disallowed (the Court did not believe the amounts claimed anyway). In *Kassa*, 2017 TCC 226, the allowance was reasonable but K reported it in income (though not required to) and claimed deductions, which were allowed because she had included it. See also *Tilahun*, 2018 TCC 118. Deduction must be based on actual expenses, not mileage: 2012-0442381E5.

8(1)(h.1)(iii) does not apply to an allowance received for different travel. Where a school psychologist visited many schools each day and was paid an allowance only for inter-school travel, she was allowed to deduct the costs of each day's travel from home to the first school and from the last school home: *Evans*, [1999] 1 C.T.C. 2609 (TCC).

Types of expense: 8(1)(h) does not allow entertainment such as a sporting event, fishing trip or cruise, but does allow meals and beverages for business guests while away from home (subject to 8(4) and 67.1): *Strong*, 2004 TCC 297; *Tozer*, 2004 TCC 411. It does not allow dog boarding, lawn care, snow removal and home security while travelling: VIEWS doc 2006-0190481E5; or a flight attendant's passport renewal: 2007-0222521E5. Travel-related cell phone costs were allowed in *Dryden*, 2008 TCC 386 and *Tilahun*, 2018 TCC 118, para. 11. Expenses for (h.1) include parking: 2011-0392721E5; car sharing per-hour, per-day or per-km fees: 2019-0812581E5; and may include a car lease cancellation penalty, subject to 67.3: 2004-0060021E5, 2008-0285361C6. For flat-rate meal deductions, see Notes to 8(1)(g).

For driving, see Notes to 6(2) re whether a mileage logbook is required. A taxpayer who chose to drive 4 vehicles was entitled to his work-related percentage of each one's maintenance, even though this gave him close to 100% work use of each: *Ragsdale*, 2008 TCC 232. A rural-route mail carrier was allowed 1/3 higher per-km gas costs than the average for city driving: *Dryden*, above.

See CRA Guide T4044, Chapter 8 for detailed discussion.

No deduction is available for travel by an *unemployed* person to find employment: VIEWS doc 2007-0239191M4. For a *self-employed* person, travel expenses are deductible under 9(1) as business expenses, except to the extent they are "personal": see Notes to 18(1)(h).

8(1)(h.1) added by 1991 technical bill, effective 1988.

Private Member's Bill C-303 (Nov. 18, 2002) proposed to add **8(1)(h.2)** and 8(1)(j.1) to allow travel expenses for a forestry worker required by employment to travel to a special or remote work site. Not being a Dept. of Finance proposal, it was not enacted.

Regulations: 102(2)(c)B, 107(2) — Deduction allowed in calculating source withholdings.

Interpretation Bulletins: IT-421R2: Benefits to individuals, corporations and shareholders from loans or debt; IT-522R: Vehicle, travel and sales expenses of employees.

I.T. Technical News: 12 (1998 deduction limits and benefit rates for automobiles).

Forms: TD1X: Statement of commission income and expenses for payroll tax deductions; T777: Statement of employment expenses; T2200: Declaration of conditions of employment; T4044: Employment expenses [guide].

(i) dues and other expenses of performing duties — an
amount paid by the taxpayer in the year, or on behalf of the taxpayer in the year if the amount paid on behalf of the taxpayer is required to be included in the taxpayer's income for the year, as

(i) annual professional membership dues the payment of which was necessary to maintain a professional status recognized by statute,

(ii) office rent, or salary to an assistant or substitute, the payment of which by the officer or employee was required by the contract of employment,

(iii) the cost of supplies that were consumed directly in the performance of the duties of the office or employment and that the officer or employee was required by the contract of employment to supply and pay for,

(iv) annual dues to maintain membership in a trade union as defined

(A) by section 3 of the *Canada Labour Code*, or

(B) in any provincial statute providing for the investigation, conciliation or settlement of industrial disputes,

or to maintain membership in an association of public servants the primary object of which is to promote the improvement of the members' conditions of employment or work,

(v) annual dues that were, pursuant to the provisions of a collective agreement, retained by the taxpayer's employer from the taxpayer's remuneration and paid to a trade union or association designated in subparagraph (iv) of which the taxpayer was not a member,

(vi) dues to a parity or advisory committee or similar body, the payment of which was required under the laws of a province in respect of the employment for the year, and

(vii) dues to a professions board, the payment of which was required under the laws of a province,

to the extent that the taxpayer has not been reimbursed, and is not entitled to be reimbursed in respect thereof;

Announced Administrative Change — COVID-19 — Employee home office expenses in 2020
CRA news release and Backgrounder, Dec. 15, 2020: *Introducing a simplified process for claiming the home office expenses for Canadians working from home due to the COVID-19 pandemic*

[See under 8(13). See also Canada.ca/cra-home-workspace-expenses > "Expenses you can claim" — ed.]

Related Provisions: 6(1)(j) — Reimbursement or award may be taxable; 6(8) — GST rebate included in income; 8(1)(l.1), (l.2) — Employer's portion of UI/EI and QPIP premiums and CPP contributions deductible; 8(1)(r) — Deduction for tools of apprentice auto mechanic; 8(1)(s) — Deduction for tradesperson's tool expenses; 8(5) — Certain dues not deductible; 8(10) — Employer's certificate required; 8(11) — GST rebate deemed not to be reimbursement; 8(13) — Limitation on home office expenses; Reg. 102(2)(d)(i) — Effect of deduction on source withholdings.

Notes: This deduction is claimed on Lines 21200 [former 212] of the T1 General income tax return for 8(1)(i)(i), Line 22900 [former 229] for the rest of 8(1)(i); the T1 Guide notes that only amounts "relating to employment" should be claimed. A person carrying on business in a professional practice should instead deduct professional membership dues in computing income from that business or practice. See Guide T4044, Chapter 3 for detailed discussion of eligible expenses and conditions. Note also the restriction in 8(5).

Mandatory insurance (e.g., physician's medical malpractice insurance) is allowed administratively by CRA if a T2200 employer certification is provided under 8(10), even though it may not quite fit within 8(1)(i)(i) or (iii): VIEWS doc 2005-0163641E5 (the CRA has raised this with Finance as a gap in the legislation).

8(1)(i)(i): "recognized by statute" does not mean the statute must *regulate* the profession. A real estate appraiser was allowed the deduction in *Montgomery*, [1999] 2 C.T.C. 196 (FCA), because provincial statutes required a qualified appraiser to conduct appraisals. An organization qualified where membership was required by 3 provinces' regulations to provide certain professional services: GST/HST Headquarters ruling 188320 (Aug. 8, 2019). Members of the Corporation des officiers municipaux du Québec (COMAQ) do not qualify in CRA's view, even though COMAQ was created by provincial statute: docs 2005-0112871E5, 2005-0157861E5. College of Physical Therapists of BC dues qualify, but Canadian Physiotherapy Association dues do not: *Shearman*, 2006 TCC 143. Annual membership fees paid by pastors and ministers qualify if provincial marriage legislation recognizes their status: 2006-0168311E5. Mess dues paid by members of the Canadian Forces do not qualify: 2007-0227181M4. "Statute" includes regulations: 2019-080464117. No deduction is allowed if membership is not *required* to maintain professional status, even if the organization or status is recognized by statute: 2006-0185911E5, 2012-0438722E5, 2014-0530691E5. See also 2006-0213981E5, 2008-0267901E5, 2009-033393117, IT-158R2. Student status does not qualify in CRA's view: IT-158R2 para. 8, 2009-0338271E5 (but fees may be eligible for 118.5 tuition credit). Note that 8(1)(i)(i) does not say the *payment* must be required by statute, only that it be required to maintain a *status recognized* by statute.

For 8(1)(i)(i), mandatory continuing education, required to maintain a professional status, is considered by CRA not to be annual membership dues and thus not deductible: VIEWS doc 2001-0112695. However, such costs were held deductible in *Bornstein*, [2002] 3 C.T.C. 2163 (TCC). Exam fees to obtain professional status qualify for tuition credit under 118.5(1)(d). Off-duty firearm practice does not qualify even if the employee must maintain firearm certification as a condition of employment: 2015-059848117.

See Notes to 8(1)(f) and (h.1) re meaning of "required".

8(1)(i)(ii): "office rent" does not include mortgage interest, property taxes or insurance expenses: *Horbay*, [2003] 2 C.T.C. 2248 (TCC); *Lester*, 2011 TCC 543; VIEWS doc 2019-0799241E5. The office need not be at home: 2012-0435521E5. The employer must provide Form T2200 certifying that the employment contract requires the expense: see 8(10) and *Ross*, 2014 TCC 317, para. 16.

Municipal councillors who receive a tax-free allowance have "in effect been reimbursed for their home office expenses" and should not get a T2200: VIEWS doc 2005-0131691E5.

The requirement to have an assistant for 8(1)(i)(ii) can be implied in the employment contract: *Schnurr*, 2004 TCC 684 (investment advisor); *Williams*, 2004 TCC 706; but no such requirement was found in *Blott*, 2018 TCC 1 (market dealer). The contractual requirement might be merely that the employee *pay* any assistant, not that the employee *have* an assistant: *Longtin*, 2006 TCC 335; VIEWS doc 2006-0174681E5; but *contra* see: *Sauvé*, 2006 TCC 528; *Morgan*, 2007 TCC 475; *Li*, 2009 TCC 530; *Massicolli*, 2012 TCC 344, para. 71; *Lagace*, 2019 TCC 249, para. 10:1. A self-employed assistant does not qualify: 2008-0287661E5. See also Notes to 8(1)(f), (h.1) and 8(13) re meaning of "required".

The "assistant" can be one's children and paid with gifts of goods and cash rather than cheques, if the employee's evidence is credible: *Aprile*, 2005 TCC 216. Deductions for payments to family members were disallowed as not credible in: *Zepotoczny*, 2007 TCC 696; *Burlando*, 2014 TCC 92; *Lagace*, 2019 TCC 249, para. 10.

8(1)(i)(iii) (which requires T2200: see 8(10)) does not allow deduction for special clothing, haircuts, tools, safety gear or equipment required for work, or basic phone line or cell phone costs: IT-352R2, para. 10(c); VIEWS docs 2003-0052451M4, 2006-0186091E5; *Luks*, [1958] C.T.C. 345 (Exch. Ct.); *Pyefinch*, [1995] 1 C.T.C. 2361 (TCC); *Cuddie*, [1998] 3 C.T.C. 2232 (TCC); *Ellis*, [1998] 4 C.T.C. 2373 (TCC); *Crawford*, [2003] 2 C.T.C. 2169 (TCC); *Barry*, 2014 FCA 280, paras. 16-17 (employee was not required by contract to own cell phone or incur expenses). However, an RCMP officer was allowed certain clothing in *Fardeau*, [2002] 3 C.T.C. 2169 (TCC); and cell phone expenses were allowed to a personal support worker in *Meberatu*, 2017 TCC 211, para. 18. (Cell phone costs were allowed as 8(1)(h) travel expenses in *Dryden*, 2008 TCC 386, and *Tilahun*, 2018 TCC 118, para. 11.) Masks, gloves and sanitizer for COVID-19 are allowed if the employer requires the employee to pay for them: 2020-0867061I7. A teacher may be allowed a deduction for classroom supplies: docs 2003-0016004, 2009-0327441E5 (see also the 122.9 credit). In CRA's view, long-distance calls, unlimited long-distance plan and cell phone airtime qualify as "office supplies", but monthly phone rates (including for a second line) and monthly Internet access fees do not because they are not "consumed": IT-352R2 para. 10(a), 2008-0276151E5, 2009-0317611E5, 2011-0403621M4 (but Guide T4044 now says that, starting 2020, employees working at home can deduct home Internet access fees as part of home office expenses); and cell phone data does not qualify unless the line is 100% for employment, as usage is not tracked separately: 2015-0603631I7, 2016-0634351E5. A hairstylist's shampoos qualify: 2008-0291191E5. A car salesman's promotional T-shirts and keychains qualified: *Fitzgerald*, 2009 TCC 321. A fishing guide's bait and fishing line may qualify: 2012-0472361E5. Training is not a "supply"; nor can it be "consumed"; and a pilot's repayment to his employer for training, required since he quit within 2 years, was not paid "directly in the performance of [his] duties": *Auclair*, 2013 TCC 188. Accounting/bookkeeping fees do not qualify: *Lagace*, 2019 TCC 249, paras. 11-12. See also Canada.ca/cra-home-workspace-expenses > "Expenses you can claim"; for employees not using 8(1)(f), CRA allows envelopes, highlighters, ink cartridges, notebooks, paper, paperclips, pens/pencils, stamps, stationery, sticky notes, toner; Internet service; cell phone basic service (subject to conditions); business long distance calls.

See also 8(1)(s) (tradespersons' tools) and 118.5(3) (ancillary tuition costs).

8(1)(i)(iv) allows deduction for union dues, but subject to 8(5); see generally VIEWS doc 2019-0814471M4. (Strike pay received and union gifts to members are not taxable: *Fries*, [1990] 2 C.T.C. 439 (SCC); Alarie & Sudak, "The Taxation of Strike Pay", 54(2) *Canadian Tax Journal* 426-n9 (2006); and see Notes to s. 3; but reimbursement of dues may be taxable under 6(1)(j).) Additional dues paid to fund a strike are deductible as "annual" dues even if this is a one-time assessment: *Lucas*, [1987] 2 C.T.C. 23 (FCTD). Local levy fees to repay a school board for releasing a teacher for union duties are deductible: 2005-012691E5. Non-mandatory dues are excluded, so under *Alberta Labour Relations Code* s. 26.1 (per S.A. 2020, c. 28, not yet in force), which makes the portion of union dues used for political and social causes voluntary, that portion is non-deductible: 2020-0871951I7. See also 8(5) Notes. Dues paid by the employer (compensating for an administrative error) and reported as a taxable benefit are deductible to the employee: 2006-0174331E5. Dues paid by provincial court judges to a judges' association to negotiate salary increases were held non-deductible in *Crowe*, 2003 FCA 191, because judges are not "public servants" (but the government is the judge's "employer": *St-Julien*, 2005 TCC 511). An "independent workers' association" that does not negotiate collectively is not a trade union: 2008-0304301E5. However, a mandatory or automatic employee association that is not certified as a union but negotiates employment agreements can qualify: 2013-0513781E5, 2016-0681161E5.

In CRA's view, union dues become non-deductible due to 8(5) if the union provides (untaxed) cash benefits to the member. See s. 3 Notes under bullet "union's cash gift".

A trade union for 8(1)(i)(iv) may be located outside Canada: doc 2003-0015727. An association of non-unionized employees does not qualify: 2009-0346331E5.

In *Brandt*, 2013 TCC 70, para. 46, expenses the employer would have reimbursed had the employee asked were not deductible (see the closing words of 8(1)(i)).

8(1)(i)(vii) allows deduction of dues that an employee is required to pay to a professions board such as L'Office de professions du Québec.

8(1)(i) opening words changed from "amounts paid by the taxpayer in the year as" by 2002-2013 technical bill (Part 5 — technical), effective June 26, 2013.

8(1)(i)(vii) added by 1995-97 technical bill, effective 1996.

Regulations: 100(3)(b) (deduction of dues by employer reduces source withholding); 102(2)(c)B, 107(2) — Deduction allowed in calculating source withholdings.

Interpretation Bulletins: IT-103R: Dues paid to a union or to a parity or advisory committee; IT-158R2: Employees' professional membership dues; IT-352R2: Employees' expenses, including work space in home expenses.

Information Circulars: 74-6R2: Power saw expenses.

Charities Policies: CPC-008: Gift — Payment to a registered charity instead of paying union dues.

Forms: T1 General return, Lines 21200 [former 212], 22900 [former 229]; T777: Statement of employment expenses; T777S: Statement of employment expenses for working at home due to COVID-19; T2200: Declaration of conditions of employment; T2200S: Declaration of conditions of employment for working at home due to COVID-19; T4044: Employment expenses [guide]; TD1X: Statement of commission income and expenses for payroll tax deductions.

(j) motor vehicle and aircraft costs — where a deduction may be made under paragraph (f), (h) or (h.1) in computing the taxpayer's income from an office or employment for a taxation year,

(i) any interest paid by the taxpayer in the year on borrowed money used for the purpose of acquiring, or on an amount payable for the acquisition of, property that is

(A) a motor vehicle that is used, or

(B) an aircraft that is required for use

in the performance of the duties of the taxpayer's office or employment, and

(ii) such part, if any, of the capital cost to the taxpayer of

(A) a motor vehicle that is used, or

(B) an aircraft that is required for use

in the performance of the duties of the office or employment as is allowed by regulation;

Related Provisions: 6(8) — GST rebate included in income or reduces capital cost of vehicle or aircraft; 8(1)(f) — Salesman's expenses; 8(1)(q) — Artists' employment expenses; 8(9) — Limitation — aircraft expenses; 13(7) — Capital cost allowance — rules applicable; 13(7.1) — Deemed capital cost of certain property; 13(11) — Deductions under 8(1)(j)(ii) deemed claimed as CCA; 67.2 — Interest on money borrowed for passenger vehicle; 67.3 — Limitation re cost of leasing passenger vehicle; 80(9)(c) — Reduction of capital cost on debt forgiveness ignored for purposes of para. 8(1)(j); 80.4 — Loans; Reg. 102(2)(d)(i) — Effect of deduction on source withholdings.

Notes: See Notes to 20(1)(a) re CCA calculation; the same rules apply to 8(1)(j).

CRA interprets "aircraft" as "any machine used or designed for travelling in the air but does not include a machine designed to derive support in the atmosphere from reactions against the earth's surface of air expelled from the machine (for example, a hovercraft)": IT-522R para. 22; and considers it to include a hot air balloon (VIEWS doc 2001-0083827) and a drone (2016-0633111E5). A helicopter is clearly an aircraft.

CRA will not allow an employee a terminal loss: see Notes to 20(16).

8(1)(j) amended by 1991 technical bill, retroactive to 1988.

Regulations: 102(2)(c)B, 107(2) — Deduction allowed in calculating source withholdings; 1100(1)(a)(x), (x.1) (CCA rate is 30% on declining balance).

Income Tax Folios: S3-F4-C1: General discussion of CCA [replaces IT-478R2].

Interpretation Bulletins: IT-421R2: Benefits to individuals, corporations and shareholders from loans or debt; IT-504R2: Visual artists and writers; IT-522R: Vehicle, travel and sales expenses of employees; IT-525R: Performing artists.

I.T. Technical News: 12 (1998 deduction limits and benefit rates for automobiles).

Forms: T777: Statement of employment expenses; TD1X: Statement of commission income and expenses for payroll tax deductions; T4044: Employment expenses [guide].

(k), (l) [Repealed under former Act]

Notes: 8(1)(k) and (l) repealed by 1988 tax reform, effective 1988. These were deductions for unemployment insurance premiums and *Canada Pension Plan* contributions.

A credit is now provided in 118.7 instead, and ½ deduction under 60(e) for self-employed CPP contributions.

(l.1) [employer's] C.P.P. contributions and U.I.A. [E.I.] premiums — any amount payable by the taxpayer in the year

(i) as an employer's premium under the *Employment Insurance Act*, or

(ii) as an employer's contribution under the *Canada Pension Plan* or under a provincial pension plan as defined in section 3 of the *Canada Pension Plan*,

in respect of salary, wages or other remuneration, including gratuities, paid to an individual employed by the taxpayer as an assistant or substitute to perform the duties of the taxpayer's office or employment if an amount is deductible by the taxpayer for the year under subparagraph (i)(ii) in respect of that individual;

Related Provisions: 8(1)(i) — Deduction for expenses of an employee's assistant or substitute; 8(1)(l.2) — Parallel rule for QPIP premiums; 60(e) — Deduction for ½ of self-employed person's CPP contributions; 118.7 — Credit for taxpayer's own CPP contributions and EI premiums.

Notes: EI premiums and CPP contributions paid by an employer carrying on business are deductible under 9(1) as ordinary business expenses. 8(1)(l.1) applies only to an employer whose deduction for employee expenses is a deduction from employment income under 8(1)(i)(ii). Premiums and contributions paid by an employee (via payroll deductions) generate a credit under s. 118.7 (for self-employed persons there is also a deduction under 60(e) for half of CPP contributions).

Unemployment Insurance Act changed to *Employment Insurance Act* by EI bill (S.C. 1996, c. 23), effective June 30, 1996.

Interpretation Bulletins: IT-352R2: Employee's expenses, including work space in home expenses.

(l.2) Quebec parental insurance plan — an amount payable by the taxpayer in the year as an employer's premium under the *Act respecting parental insurance*, R.S.Q., c. A-29.011 in respect of salary, wages or other remuneration, including gratuities, paid to an individual employed by the taxpayer as an assistant or substitute to perform the duties of the taxpayer's office or employment if an amount is deductible by the taxpayer for the year under subparagraph (i)(ii) in respect of that individual;

Related Provisions: 8(1)(i) — Deduction for expenses of an employee's assistant or substitute; 56(1)(a)(vii) — QPIP benefits taxable; 60(g) — Deduction for portion of self-employed person's QPIP premiums.

Notes: 8(1)(l.2) added by 2002-2013 technical bill (Part 5 — technical), effective for 2006 and later taxation years.

(m) employee's registered pension plan contributions — the amount in respect of contributions to registered pension plans that, by reason of subsection 147.2(4), is deductible in computing the taxpayer's income for the year;

Related Provisions: See under 147.2(4).

Notes: For a status Indian with exempt employment income (see Notes to 81(1)(a)), the 8(1)(m) deduction applies against the employment income, so cannot be used against other sources: *Smith*, 2018 TCC 61.

8(1)(m) amended by 1990 pension bill, effective 1991. See Notes to 147.2(4).

Interpretation Bulletins: IT-167R6: Registered pension plans — employee's contributions.

Information Circulars: 72-13R8: Employee's pension plans.

Registered Plans Compliance Bulletins: 2 (compensation for RPP purposes).

Advance Tax Rulings: ATR-2: Contribution to pension plan for past service.

Forms: See under 147.2(4).

(m.1) [Repealed under former Act]

Notes: 8(1)(m.1) repealed by 1990 pension bill, effective 1991. It provided a deduction for mandatory employee RPP contributions in excess of $3,500 per year (former 8(1)(m) allowed the first $3,500). See 147.2(4).

(m.2) employee RCA contributions — an amount contributed by the taxpayer in the year to a pension plan in respect of services rendered by the taxpayer where the plan is a prescribed plan established by an enactment of Canada or a province or where

(i) the plan is a retirement compensation arrangement,

(ii) the amount was paid to a custodian (within the meaning assigned by the definition "retirement compensation arrangement" in subsection 248(1)) of the arrangement who is resident in Canada, and

(iii) either

(A) the taxpayer was required, by the terms of the taxpayer's office or employment, to contribute the amount, and the total of the amounts contributed to the plan in the year by the taxpayer does not exceed the total of the amounts contributed to the plan in the year by any other person in respect of the taxpayer, or

(B) the plan is a pension plan the registration of which under this Act was revoked (other than a plan the registration of which was revoked as of the effective date of its registration) and the amount was contributed in accordance with the terms of the plan as last registered;

(C) [Repealed]

Related Provisions: 18(11)(e) — No deduction for interest on money borrowed to make deductible contribution; 20(1)(r) — Employer's RCA contribution deductible; 60(t)(ii) — Amount included under para. 56(1)(x) or (z) or subsec. 70(2); 60(u)(ii) — Deduction where amount included under para. 56(1)(y); 146(1)"earned income"(a)(i), 146(1)"earned income"(c)(i) — Earned income for RRSP counted before deduction for 8(1)(m.2); 207.6(6) — Rules re prescribed plan or arrangement.

Notes: See Notes to 248(1)"retirement compensation arrangement".

A "pension plan" in (m.2) opening words cannot be a plan that pays a single lump sum on retirement or loss of employment: VIEWS doc 2017-0702051E5.

Employee contributions to a SERP RCA on conversion of past service benefits from defined-contribution to defined-benefit basis likely satisfy the condition that the contribution be required as a condition of employment: VIEWS doc 2012-0444981E5.

8(1)(m.2) added by 1990 pension bill and amended by 1992 and 1993 technical bills.

Regulations: 100(3)(b.1) (payroll deduction of employee contribution reduces source withholding); 6802, 6802.1(1) (prescribed plans).

Forms: T4041: Retirement compensation arrangements [guide].

(n) salary reimbursement [repayment] — an amount paid by or on behalf of the taxpayer in the year pursuant to an arrangement (other than an arrangement described in subparagraph (b)(ii) of the definition "top-up disability payment" in subsection 6(17)) under which the taxpayer is required to reimburse any amount paid to the taxpayer for a period throughout which the taxpayer did not perform the duties of the office or employment, to the extent that

(i) the amount so paid to the taxpayer for the period was included in computing the taxpayer's income from an office or employment, and

(ii) the total of amounts so reimbursed does not exceed the total of amounts received by the taxpayer for the period throughout which the taxpayer did not perform the duties of the office or employment;

Related Provisions: 8(1)(n.1) — Reimbursement of top-up disability payments; 153(3.1) — Salary repayment net of source deductions.

Notes: 8(1)(n) allows a deduction only for amounts actually paid, not amounts payable: *Lunn*, 2011 TCC 552. However, 8(1)(n) applies only to overpayments for a period "throughout which the taxpayer did not perform any duties"; other repayment is not deductible, and the original year cannot be reassessed to not tax the income received by mistake: VIEWS doc 2014-0524371E5.

Where 8(1)(n) applies, the T4 should not be adjusted and the employer should give the employee a letter confirming the repayment. However, if a clerical or administrative error in pay is corrected, the adjustment can sometimes be made directly onto T4 and payroll records. See tinyurl.com/cra-t4error. An administrative or clerical error can be corrected by 152(4.2) reassessment because the employee received an amount to which s/he was not entitled: VIEWS doc 2012-044896I7. Consider also simply having the employer underpay the employee by the amount of previous overpayment, which is equivalent allowing the employee a current deduction for a repayment.

For more CRA interpretation of 8(1)(n) see docs 9409870 (repayment of EI benefits: non-deductible (ND)); 9426755 (repayment of wage loss replacement plan benefits taxed under 6(1)(f): deductible (D)); 9613507 (employee performed duties throughout year: ND); 9700155 (reimbursement to former employer for cost of training, because taxpayer leaves employment shortly after receiving training: ND); 2001-0069607 (medical resident's fellowships signed over to employer: ND); 2001-0078285 (repayment of non-taxable disability benefits: ND); 2004-0080871E5 (repayment of previously reimbursed relocation expenses: ND); 2004-008748I7 (repayment of top-up of workers' compensation benefits: D); 2005-0116061E5 (employee did not perform duties appropriately: ND); 2006-021601I7 (repayment to employer of assistance provided while taxpayer became a doctor, due to taxpayer not returning as employee: D);

2007-0237811E5 (repayment by terminated employee of income received during leave of absence plan: D); 2007-0262591E5 (repayment of retiring allowance in order to obtain disability insurance benefits: D); 2009-0352731I7 (repayment of income from leave-of-absence plan: D); 2010-037597I17 (repayment of signing bonus: D); 2010-0376491E5 (repayment of medical school education assistance: D, but ND if paid by physician's corporation); 2010-038580I17 (repayment of annual bonus: D); 2011-0401981I7 (repayment of vacation pay: D).

The word "period" refers to "the critical day or days under a contract that the employer must have worked to retain a bonus": VIEWS doc 2010-038580I17.

Where pay is clawed back because performance goals were not achieved or due to restrictions on executives' pay, see Notes to 5(1).

Opening words of 8(1)(n) amended by 1995-97 technical bill, effective for arrangements entered into after August 10, 1994, to add the parenthetical exclusion of arrangements under 6(17). A deduction for such repayments is provided under 8(1)(n.1).

Forms: T1 General return, Line 22900 [former 229]: Other employment expenses.

(n.1) **reimbursement of disability payments** — where,

    (i) as a consequence of the receipt of a payment (in this paragraph referred to as the "deferred payment") from an insurer, a payment (in this paragraph referred to as the "reimbursement payment") is made by or on behalf of an individual to an employer or former employer of the individual pursuant to an arrangement described in subparagraph (b)(ii) of the definition "top-up disability payment" in subsection 6(17), and

    (ii) the reimbursement payment is made

        (A) in the year, other than within the first 60 days of the year if the deferred payment was received in the immediately preceding taxation year, or

        (B) within 60 days after the end of the year, if the deferred payment was received in the year,

an amount equal to the lesser of

    (iii) the amount included under paragraph 6(1)(f) in respect of the deferred payment in computing the individual's income for any taxation year, and

    (iv) the amount of the reimbursement payment;

Notes: 8(1)(n.1) added by 1995-97 technical bill, effective for reimbursement payments made after August 10, 1994. It provides a deduction to an individual who reimburses a top-up disability payment (see 6(17), (18)). The deduction is limited to the amount included under 6(1)(f) on the payment by the insurer. For a plan funded solely by employee contributions, there is no 6(1)(f) inclusion, so there is no deduction for the reimbursement. If employer contributions were made to the plan, the reimbursement will be deductible, but reduced for the individual's contributions which reduced the 6(1)(f) inclusion.

Remission Orders: *Ginette Archambault Remission Order*, P.C. 2010-273 (remission due to circumstances beyond taxpayer's control, provided she does not claim loss relating to repayment of wage loss replacement benefits); *Kathryn Strigner Remission Order*, P.C. 2011-488 (same); *Pierre Dupuis Remission Order*, P.C. 2011-489 (same); *Allan Pysher Remission Order*, P.C. 2015-54 (same); *Céline Hamel Remission Order*, P.C. 2015-839 (same).

(o) **forfeited amounts [salary deferral arrangement]** — where at the end of the year the rights of any person to receive benefits under a salary deferral arrangement in respect of the taxpayer have been extinguished or no person has any further right to receive any amount under the arrangement, the amount, if any, by which the total of all deferred amounts under the arrangement included in computing the taxpayer's income for the year and preceding taxation years as benefits under paragraph 6(1)(a) exceeds the total of

    (i) all such deferred amounts received by any person in that year or preceding taxation years out of or under the arrangement,

    (ii) all such deferred amounts receivable by any person in subsequent taxation years out of or under the arrangement, and

    (iii) all amounts deducted under this paragraph in computing the taxpayer's income for preceding taxation years in respect of deferred amounts under the arrangement;

Related Provisions: 12(1)(n.2) — Inclusions — forfeited salary deferral amounts.

(o.1) **idem [employees profit sharing plan]** — an amount that is deductible in computing the taxpayer's income for the year because of subsection 144(9);

Related Provisions: 6(1)(d) — Income inclusion from allocations under employees profit sharing plan.

Notes: 8(1)(o.1) added by 1993 technical bill, effective 1992.

Interpretation Bulletins: IT-379R: Employees profit sharing plans — allocations to beneficiaries.

(o.2) **excess EPSP amounts** — an amount that is an excess EPSP amount (as defined in subsection 207.8(1)) of the taxpayer for the year, other than any portion of the excess EPSP amount for which the taxpayer's tax for the year under subsection 207.8(2) is waived or cancelled;

Notes: This deduction prevents double tax, since Part XI.4 tax is imposed on the excess EPSP amount by 207.8(2) at the highest personal tax rate.

8(1)(o.2) added by 2012 budget bill #2, effective for 2012 and later taxation years.

(p) **musical instrument costs** — where the taxpayer was employed in the year as a musician and as a term of the employment was required to provide a musical instrument for a period in the year, an amount (not exceeding the taxpayer's income for the year from the employment, computed without reference to this paragraph) equal to the total of

    (i) amounts expended by the taxpayer before the end of the year for the maintenance, rental and insurance of the instrument for that period, except to the extent that the amounts are otherwise deducted in computing the taxpayer's income for any taxation year, and

    (ii) such part, if any, of the capital cost to the taxpayer of the instrument as is allowed by regulation;

Related Provisions: 6(1)(j) — Reimbursement or award may be taxable; 6(8) — GST rebate included in income or reduces capital cost of instrument; 8(1)(q) — Artists' employment expenses deduction; 13(7), (7.1) — Capital cost allowance — rules applicable; 13(11) — Deduction under 8(1)(p)(ii) deemed claimed as CCA; 80(9)(c) — Reduction of capital cost on debt forgiveness ignored for purposes of 8(1)(p).

Notes: See Income Tax Folio S4-F14-C1 ¶1.49-1.56. See 20(1)(a) Notes re CCA calculation; the same rules apply to 8(1)(p). See 8(1)(f) and (h.1) Notes re meaning of "required".

CRA does not allow an employee a terminal loss: see Notes to 20(16).

A computer can be a musical instrument: *Belkin*, 2005 TCC 785. Tax issues for musicians: Sanderson, *Musicians and the Law* (Carswell, 4th ed., 2014), pp. 517-557.

Regulations: 1100(1)(a)(viii), Sch. II:Cl. 8(i) (CCA rate is 20%).

Income Tax Folios: S3-F4-C1: General discussion of CCA [replaces IT-478R2].

Interpretation Bulletins: IT-257R: Canada Council grants; IT-525R: Performing artists.

(q) **artists' employment expenses** — where the taxpayer's income for the year from the office or employment includes income from an artistic activity

    (i) that was the creation by the taxpayer of, but did not include the reproduction of, paintings, prints, etchings, drawings, sculptures or similar works of art,

    (ii) that was the composition by the taxpayer of a dramatic, musical or literary work,

    (iii) that was the performance by the taxpayer of a dramatic or musical work as an actor, dancer, singer or musician, or

    (iv) in respect of which the taxpayer was a member of a professional artists' association that is certified by the Minister of Communications,

amounts paid by the taxpayer before the end of the year in respect of expenses incurred for the purpose of earning the income from those activities to the extent that they were not deductible in computing the taxpayer's income for a preceding taxation year, but not exceeding a single amount in respect of all such offices and employments of the taxpayer equal to the amount, if any, by which

    (v) the lesser of $1,000 and 20% of the total of all amounts each of which is the taxpayer's income from an office or employment for the year, before deducting any amount under this section, that was income from an artistic activity described in any of subparagraphs (i) to (iv),

exceeds

(vi) the total of all amounts deducted by the taxpayer for the year under paragraph (j) or (p) in respect of costs or expenses incurred for the purpose of earning the income from such an activity for the year;

Related Provisions: 6(1)(j) — Reimbursement or award may be taxable.

Notes: See Income Tax Folio S4-F14-C1 ¶1.57–1.62 and Guide T4044, Chapter 6 for discussion of eligible expenses. Note that the activity must both be "artistic" *and* fall into one of (i)–(iv).

The *Department of Canadian Heritage Act* (S.C. 1995, c. 11), s. 46, provides: "Every reference made to the Minister of Communications ... in relation to any matter to which the powers, duties and functions of the Minister of Canadian Heritage extend by virtue of this Act, in any other Act of Parliament ... shall, unless the context otherwise requires, be read as a reference to the Minister of Canadian Heritage."

8(1)(q) added by 1991 technical bill, effective for amounts paid after 1990.

Interpretation Bulletins: IT-257R: Canada Council grants; IT-504R2: Visual artists and writers; IT-525R: Performing artists.

Forms: T777: Statement of employment expenses; T4044: Employment expenses [guide].

(r) apprentice mechanics' tool costs — if the taxpayer was an eligible apprentice mechanic at any time after 2001 and before the end of the taxation year, the amount claimed by the taxpayer for the taxation year under this paragraph not exceeding the lesser of

(i) the taxpayer's income for the taxation year computed without reference to this paragraph, and

(ii) the amount determined by the formula

$$(A - B) + C$$

where

A is the total of all amounts each of which is the cost to the taxpayer of an eligible tool acquired in the taxation year by the taxpayer or, if the taxpayer first becomes employed as an eligible apprentice mechanic in the taxation year, the cost to the taxpayer of an eligible tool acquired by the taxpayer in the last three months of the preceding taxation year,

B is the lesser of

(A) the value of A for the taxation year in respect of the taxpayer, and

(B) the greater of

(I) the amount that is the total of $500[2] and the amount determined for the taxation year for B in subsection 118(10), and

(II) 5% of the total of

1. the total of all amounts each of which is the taxpayer's income from employment for the taxation year as an eligible apprentice mechanic, computed without reference to this paragraph, and

2. the amount, if any, by which the amount required by paragraph 56(1)(n.1) to be included in computing the taxpayer's income for the taxation year exceeds the amount required by paragraph 60(p) to be deducted in computing that income, and

C is the amount by which the amount determined under this subparagraph for the preceding taxation year in respect of the taxpayer exceeds the amount deducted under this paragraph for that preceding taxation year by the taxpayer; and

Related Provisions: 6(1)(j) — Reimbursement or award may be taxable; 6(8) — GST rebate included in income or reduces capital cost of tools; 8(1)(s) — Deduction for tradesperson's tool expenses; 8(6) — Eligible apprentice mechanic and eligible

tool; 8(7) — Deemed cost of tool after deduction claimed; 53(2)(m) — Deduction does not reduce adjusted cost base of tools; 56(1)(k) — Income inclusion on sale of tools; 85(5.1), 97(5) — Rollover of tools to corporation or partnership.

Notes: 8(1)(r) allows a deduction to *apprentice* vehicle mechanics, for the portion of the cost of eligible tools that exceeds both (B)(I) and (B)(II). See 8(6), (7); and Guide T4044, Chapter 7. The amount in B(B)(I) is $1,745 for 2020, $1,757 for 2021. See 8(1)(s) for a more general tools deduction.

8(1)(r) amended by 2006 Budget second bill (this version effective for 2007 and later tax years). Added by 2001 Budget.

Interpretation Bulletins: IT-291R3: Transfer of property to a corporation under subsection 85(1).

Forms: T777: Statement of employment expenses; T4044: Employment expenses [guide].

(s) deduction — tradesperson's tools — if the taxpayer is employed as a tradesperson at any time in the taxation year, the lesser of $500[2] and the amount determined by the formula

$$A - \$1,000^{3}$$

where

A is the lesser of

(i) the total of all amounts each of which is the cost of an eligible tool acquired by the taxpayer in the year, and

(ii) the total of

(A) the amount that would, if this subsection were read without reference to this paragraph, be the taxpayer's income for the taxation year from employment as a tradesperson in the taxation year, and

(B) the amount, if any, by which the amount required by paragraph 56(1)(n.1) to be included in computing the taxpayer's income for the taxation year exceeds the amount required by paragraph 60(p) to be deducted in computing that income.

Related Provisions: 6(1)(j) — Reimbursement or award may be taxable; 6(8) — GST rebate included in income or reduces capital cost of tools; 8(1)(r) — Deduction for apprentice mechanics' tools; 8(6.1) — Meaning of "eligible tool"; 8(7) — Deemed cost of tool after deduction claimed; 56(1)(k) — Income inclusion on sale of tools; 85(5.1), 97(5) — Rollover of tools to corporation or partnership; 117.1(2)(b) — Indexing of $1,000 to inflation after 2007; 257 — Formula cannot calculate to less than zero.

Notes: 8(1)(s) implements a "tradesperson's tools deduction", for the first $500 (not indexed) spent in excess of $1,000 (indexed: $1,245 for 2020, $1,257 for 2021) on eligible tools (see 8(6.1)). See Guide T4044, Chapter 7. Below that indexed threshold, no deduction is allowed: *Steubing*, 2014 TCC 235, para. 11.

"Tradesperson" includes anyone engaged in an occupation that demands a level of skill: VIEWS doc 2006-0216591I7. A fishing guide can qualify: 2012-0472361E5.

For the meaning of "tools" see Notes to 8(6.1). 8(1)(s) applies to a hairstylist's hairdryers, curling irons and scissors: VIEWS doc 2008-0291191E5.

8(1)(s) added by 2006 budget bill #2, for 2006 and later taxation years.

Interpretation Bulletins: IT-422: Definition of tools.

Forms: T777: Statement of employment expenses; T4044: Employment expenses [guide].

(1.1) [Not included in R.S.C. 1985]

Notes: 8(1.1), added by 1990 pension bill, applied to the 1986 taxation year only.

(2) General limitation — Except as permitted by this section, no deductions shall be made in computing a taxpayer's income for a taxation year from an office or employment.

Notes: This rule is the converse of that for self-employed individuals, who can deduct any expenses to earn business income that are not specifically prohibited, when calculating income or loss under generally accepted commercial principles for 9(1) and 9(2). See Notes to 248(1)"employee". The Canada Employment Credit in 118(10) is a substitute for general employment-related expenses. Note also the broad deductions for commission employees in 8(1)(f), and see Notes to 8(1)(i).

CRA examples of non-deductible expenses: dog boarding, lawn care, snow removal and home security while travelling for employment (VIEWS doc 2006-0190481E5); driver training course (2014-0544501E5, but 118.5 tuition credit may be available); outplacement services to seek employment (2017-0730581E5); teacher's training expenses or costs of attending a mandatory convention (2006-0212301E5, but see Notes to 8(1)(h.1) re *Imray* case and 2007-0224411E5).

---

[2] Not indexed for inflation — ed.

[3] Indexed by s. 117.1 after 2007 — ed.

Income Tax Folios: S3-F4-C1: General discussion of CCA [replaces IT-478R2].

Interpretation Bulletins: IT-352R2: Employee's expenses, including work space in home expenses; IT-377R: Director's, executor's or juror's fees (cancelled).

(3) [Repealed under former Act]

Notes: 8(3) repealed by 1988 tax reform, effective 1988. It restricted the availability of the employment expense deduction under 8(1)(a) (repealed at the same time).

(4) Meals — An amount expended in respect of a meal consumed by a taxpayer who is an officer or employee shall not be included in computing the amount of a deduction under paragraph (1)(f) or (h) unless the meal was consumed during a period while the taxpayer was required by the taxpayer's duties to be away, for a period of not less than twelve hours, from the municipality where the employer's establishment to which the taxpayer ordinarily reported for work was located and away from the metropolitan area, if there is one, where it was located.

Related Provisions: 67.1 — 50% limitation on expenses for meals.

Notes: 8(4) applied to deny expenses in *Brandt*, 2013 TCC 70, para. 45.

8(4) and 67.1 both apply, to limit an 8(1)(f) expense of taking out a client to 25% (only the client's meal counts, and at 50%), and CRA cannot relax this rule but has referred it to Finance as requested: 2018-0768791C6 [2018 APFF q.8].

Interpretation Bulletins: IT-522R: Vehicle, travel and sales expenses of employees.

Information Circulars: 73-21R9: Claims for meals and lodging expenses of transport employees.

Forms: T777: Statement of employment expenses; TD1X: Statement of commission income and expenses for payroll tax deductions; T4044: Employment expenses [guide].

(5) Dues not deductible — Notwithstanding subparagraphs (1)(i)(i), (iv), (vi) and (vii), dues are not deductible under those subparagraphs in computing a taxpayer's income from an office or employment to the extent that they are, in effect, levied

(a) for or under a superannuation fund or plan;

(b) for or under a fund or plan for annuities, insurance (other than professional or malpractice liability insurance that is necessary to maintain a professional status recognized by statute) or similar benefits; or

(c) for any other purpose not directly related to the ordinary operating expenses of the committee or similar body, association, board or trade union, as the case may be.

Related Provisions: 8(1)(i)(i), (iv) — Professional and union dues deductible.

Notes: CRA's view is that 8(5)(c) makes union dues non-deductible if a union gives (untaxed) cash gifts or reimbursements to members, because the cash has not been used for union purposes: VIEWS docs 2006-0182451E5, 2007-0261121E5; 2011-0400091E5 (dues used to establish benevolent fund for injured workers). A levy on union members to cover a shortfall in the union's *employees'* pension plan does not violate 8(5)(a): 2013-0492411E5.

8(5) amended by 1995-97 technical bill, effective 1996.

Interpretation Bulletins: IT-103R: Dues paid to a union or to a parity or advisory committee; IT-158R2: Employees' professional membership dues.

(6) Apprentice mechanics — For the purpose of paragraph (1)(r),

(a) a taxpayer is an eligible apprentice mechanic in a taxation year if, at any time in the taxation year, the taxpayer

(i) is registered in a program established in accordance with the laws of Canada or of a province that leads to designation under those laws as a mechanic licensed to repair self-propelled motorized vehicles, and

(ii) is employed as an apprentice mechanic;

(b) an eligible tool is a tool (including ancillary equipment) that

(i) is acquired by a taxpayer for use in connection with the taxpayer's employment as an eligible apprentice mechanic,

(ii) has not been used for any purpose before it is acquired by the taxpayer,

(iii) is certified in prescribed form by the taxpayer's employer to be required to be provided by the taxpayer as a condition of, and for use in, the taxpayer's employment as an eligible apprentice mechanic, and

(iv) is, unless the device or equipment can be used only for the purpose of measuring, locating or calculating, not an electronic communication device or electronic data processing equipment; and

(c) a taxpayer who, for a taxation year, is not an eligible apprentice mechanic and has an excess amount determined under the description of C in subparagraph (1)(r)(ii) is, for the taxation year, entitled to claim a deduction under that paragraph as if that excess amount were wholly applicable to an employment of the taxpayer.

Related Provisions: 8(6.1) — Meaning of eligible tool for tradesperson's deduction; 8(7) — Cost of eligible tool; 85(5.1), 97(5) — Rollover of tools to corporation or partnership.

Notes: For the meaning of "tools" see Notes to 8(6.1). For the meaning of "required" see Notes to 8(1)(f), (h.1), (i) and 8(13).

The Dept. of Finance Technical Notes state that "ancillary equipment" in 8(6)(b) includes a tool box.

8(6)(a)(i) amended to add "Canada or of", and (b)(iv) added, by 2006 budget bill #2, for property acquired after May 1, 2006. The reference to Canada means that federally-established apprenticeship programs qualify: VIEWS doc 2006-0175501E5.

8(6) added by 2001 Budget, for "eligible tools" (see 8(6)(b)) acquired after 2001. See Notes to 8(1)(r).

Former 8(6), repealed by 1990 pension bill effective 1991, defined "contribution limit" for the pre-1991 8(1)(m).

Interpretation Bulletins: IT-422: Definition of tools.

(6.1) Eligible tool of tradesperson — For the purposes of paragraph (1)(s), an eligible tool of a taxpayer is a tool (including ancillary equipment) that

(a) is acquired by the taxpayer on or after May 2, 2006 for use in connection with the taxpayer's employment as a tradesperson;

(b) has not been used for any purpose before it is acquired by the taxpayer;

(c) is certified in prescribed form by the taxpayer's employer to be required to be provided by the taxpayer as a condition of, and for use in, the taxpayer's employment as a tradesperson; and

(d) is, unless the device or equipment can be used only for the purpose of measuring, locating or calculating, not an electronic communication device or electronic data processing equipment.

Related Provisions: 8(6)(b) — Meaning of eligible tool for apprentice mechanic's deduction.

Notes: See 8(1)(s) Notes. CRA states (IT-422) that "tool" is "an instrument of manual operation ... to be used and managed by hand instead of being moved and controlled by machinery", and it "must be designed to create a physical change in something or to be used as an instrument of measurement or manipulation. Examples are hammers, saws, squares, screwdrivers and hand-held power tools." A fishing guide's bait and fishing line are not considered "tools": VIEWS doc 2012-0472361E5.

8(6.1) added by 2006 budget bill #2, for 2006 and later tax years.

Interpretation Bulletins: IT-422: Definition of tools.

(7) Cost of tool — Except for the purposes of the description of A in subparagraph (1)(r)(ii) and the description of A in paragraph (1)(s), the cost to a taxpayer of an eligible tool the cost of which was included in determining the value of one or both of those descriptions in respect of the taxpayer for a taxation year is the amount determined by the formula

$$K - (K \times L/M)$$

where

K is the cost to the taxpayer of the tool determined without reference to this subsection;

L is

(a) if the tool is a tool to which only paragraph (1)(r) applies in the taxation year, the amount that would be determined under subparagraph (1)(r)(ii) in respect of the taxpayer for the taxation year if the value of C in that subparagraph were nil,

(b) if the tool is a tool to which only paragraph (1)(s) applies in the taxation year, the amount determined under that paragraph to be deductible by the taxpayer in the taxation year, or

(c) if the tool is a tool to which both paragraphs (1)(r) and (s) apply in the taxation year, the amount that is the total of

(i) the amount that would be determined under subparagraph (1)(r)(ii) in respect of the taxpayer for the taxation year if the value of C in that subparagraph were nil, and

(ii) the amount determined under paragraph (1)(s) to be deductible by the taxpayer in the taxation year; and

M is the amount that is

(a) if the tool is a tool to which only paragraph (1)(r) applies in the taxation year, the value of A determined under subparagraph (1)(r)(ii) in respect of the taxpayer for the taxation year,

(b) if the tool is a tool to which only paragraph (1)(s) applies in the taxation year, the amount determined under subparagraph (i) of the description of A in paragraph (1)(s) in respect of the taxpayer for the taxation year, and

(c) if the tool is a tool to which both paragraphs (1)(r) and (s) apply in the taxation year, the amount that is the greater of the value of A determined under subparagraph (1)(r)(ii) in respect of the taxpayer for the taxation year and the amount determined under subparagraph (i) of the description of A in paragraph (1)(s) in respect of the taxpayer for the taxation year.

Related Provisions: 8(6)(b) — Meaning of eligible tool for apprentice mechanic's deduction; 8(6.1) — Meaning of eligible tool for tradesperson's deduction; 85(5.1), 97(5) — Rollover of tools to corporation or partnership; 257 — Formula cannot calculate to less than zero.

Notes: See Notes to 8(1)(r). 8(7) amended by 2006 budget bill #2 (for 2006 and later taxation years), 2001 Budget.

Former 8(7), repealed by 1990 pension bill, applied to teachers' pension contributions.

Interpretation Bulletins: IT-291R3: Transfer of property to a corporation under subsection 85(1).

(8) [Repealed under former Act]

Notes: 8(8), repealed by 1990 pension bill effective 1991, allowed a deduction for mandatory employee contributions to a registered pension plan for arrears.

(9) Presumption — Notwithstanding any other provision of this Act, the total of all amounts that would otherwise be deductible by a taxpayer pursuant to paragraph (1)(f), (h) or (j) for travelling in the course of the taxpayer's employment in an aircraft that is owned or rented by the taxpayer, may not exceed an amount that is reasonable in the circumstances having regard to the relative cost and availability of other modes of transportation.

Related Provisions: 67 — General requirement that expenses be reasonable.

Notes: For the meaning of "aircraft", see Notes to 8(1)(j).

Interpretation Bulletins: IT-522R: Vehicle, travel and sales expenses of employees.

(10) Certificate of employer [T2200 or T2200S] — An amount otherwise deductible for a taxation year under paragraph (1)(c), (f), (h) or (h.1) or subparagraph (1)(i)(ii) or (iii) by a taxpayer shall not be deducted unless a prescribed form, signed by the taxpayer's employer certifying that the conditions set out in the applicable provision were met in the year in respect of the taxpayer, is filed with the taxpayer's return of income for the year.

Announced Administrative Change — COVID-19 (2020)

CRA news release and Backgrounder, Dec. 15, 2020: *Introducing a simplified process for claiming the home office expenses for Canadians working from home due to the COVID-19 pandemic*

[See under 8(13): no T2200 needed if using simplified $2/day for home office expenses; if using detailed method, simplified T2200S can be used for 2020 — ed.]

CRA Backgrounder, Dec. 15, 2020: *Consultation on the Simplification of Form T2200, Declaration of Conditions of Employment, As a Response to the COVID-19 Pandemic*

The COVID-19 pandemic has resulted in many Canadian employees working from home to help minimize the spread of the virus, raising questions about how salaried and commissioned employees affected by the new realities can claim work-space-in-the-home and supplies expenses, on their 2020 T1 Individual Income Tax and Benefit Return.

One of the requirements is that Form T2200, *Declaration of Conditions of Employment*, must be completed and signed by an employer, to enable their employee to claim certain employment related expenses (including work-space-in-the-home expenses and supplies) on line 22900 of their Individual Income Tax and Benefit Return.

In an effort to make it easier for employers to complete Form T2200, the Canada Revenue Agency drafted an early version of the simplified Form T2200 (also referred to as Form T2200 Short) [now T2200S — ed.] and engaged with stakeholder organizations including employers, the payroll industry, and tax professionals for their feedback. The consultation period took place between August 24 and September 18, 2020. The version of T2200 Short that was available at that time has since been modified.

What we heard

Ideas and input were sought around three topics:

1. How to clearly communicate the rules for employees who wish to claim supplies and work-space-in-the-home expenses within the COVID-19 context

2. An exploration of general feedback on the draft Form T2200 Short

3. An exploration of opportunities to collaborate on communicating, and amplifying messaging about the application of rules related to the T2200 forms (standard and short).

Importantly, the consultation was focused solely on feedback related to administrative solutions, as the requirement for the T2200 form is a legislated requirement under the *Income Tax Act*.

Stakeholders shared several key points of concern related to the early draft of the T2200 Short.

- The requirement of a T2200 could be too much of an administrative burden on employers because verifying the conditions, storing and signing the form is highly labour intensive, especially for employers with a large number of employees.

- Completion of the T2200 Short may have a high margin of error and unintentionally lead to perceived or actual unfairness due to the many technical terms and definitions on the forms that may cause confusion, and the complexity of application of the rules and eligibility of expenses (for example, with multiple people working from the same home).

- Greater emphasis is needed on communicating guidance, including providing tangible examples, outreach, education, opportunities to have questions answered and communication targeted to specific employee and employer industries or audiences.

Proposed Amendment — 8(10) — No handwritten signature needed for T2200

Federal Budget, Supplementary Information, April 19, 2021: See under 244(14.1), under heading "Handwritten Signatures".

Related Provisions: 8(6)(b)(iii) — Employer's certificate required for apprentice mechanic's tools deduction; 67 — General requirement that expenses be reasonable; 81(4)(b) — Certification re exemption for volunteer emergency worker; 122.9(3) — Employer certificate may be requested for teacher school-supplies credit.

Notes: For 2020, for people working at home due to COVID-19, see Form T2200S and Announced Administrative Change under 8(13).

In *Ali*, 2015 TCC 196, para. 38, the TCC said 8(10) "is a mandatory provision failing which a taxpayer cannot claim any employment-related expenses pursuant to s. 8", but in fact it applies only to 8(1)(c), (f), (h), (h.1), (i)(ii) and (i)(iii). Without the T2200 the claim will be denied: *Meberatu*, 2017 TCC 211, para. 15; *Bobic*, 2017 TCC 107, para. 8 footnote 5 (there may be an exception if the employee was unable to obtain it: *Richardson*, 2018 TCC 135, para. 8; *Perron-Ali*, 2021 TCC 6, para. 18 footnote 10).

The T2200's instructions say it need not be filed with the return, and this waives the requirement under 220(2.1): *Leith*, 2015 TCC 314, para. 7.

The T2200 is required and is *prima facie* evidence but not conclusive; the employee may need to prove the conditions for deduction are met. See *Schnurr*, 2004 TCC 684; *Potter*, 2008 TCC 228; *Fitzgerald*, 2009 TCC 321 ("erroneous and unreliable" T2200 is invalid); *Czerczak*, 2010 TCC 612 (FCA appeal discontinued A-487-10); *Vickers*, 2011 TCC 2, para. 18 (statement in T2200 that employee was not required to incur the expense can be refuted with evidence); *Tulman*, 2014 TCC 140, para. 29 (expenses must be required by the employer, not merely permitted); *Leith* (above) (altered T2200s and backdated calendars); *Meberatu*, 2017 TCC 211, para. 15 (T2200s were inconsistent); *Brown*, 2017 TCC 237; *Ross*, 2018 TCC 165 (FCA appeal dismissed for delay A-303-18); *Le Bouthillier*, 2019 TCC 176, para. 35 (aff'd 2021 FCA 119) (person who signed T2200 did not check it); VIEWS doc 2011-0399271E5.

An employee is entitled to a T2200 if the employee's failure to meet the requirement in the employment contract could lead to termination, poor performance evaluation or other disciplinary action: 2005-0117501E5, 2005-0124821E5. See also 8(1)(h.1) Notes.

The employer is not legally obliged to issue a Form T2200 certificate, but CRA "expects" the employer to issue one if the conditions are met: VIEWS doc 2013-0507001E5. The obligation may exist as a matter of contract between employer and employee. For an example of this problem see 2003-0021005. "It may be possible that in exceptional circumstances a paragraph 8(1)(h.1) claim could succeed if an employer unreasonably refused, or was unable, to complete and sign a T2200 form": *Brochu*, 2010 TCC 274, para. 11; *Smith*, 2019 TCC 274, para. 10; but in *Kreuz*, 2012 TCC 238, paras. 76-77, the employer's refusal was reasonable; and in *Chao*, 2018 TCC 72, paras.

83-99, C had asked the (film production) payroll company that paid her for a T2200, but not her actual employers. (Similarly, see *Dnebosky*, 2019 TCC 78, paras. 16-19 (FCA appeal discontinued A-111-19).) In *Richardson*, 2018 TCC 135, para. 13, waiting 5 years to ask the employer for the form was too long. In CRA's view, the employer should be "reasonably certain the employee meets the conditions before signing": 2011-0392721E5, 2012-0437201E5.

In *Wallens*, 2019 TCC 193, para. 5, CRA accepted that a sole director could sign her company's T2200 for herself.

"Normally" on the form means "commonly, under normal or ordinary conditions and with some degree of regularity": VIEWS doc 2010-0383031E5.

8(10) amended by 2001 technical bill (effective for 2001 and later taxation years) and by 1991 technical bill.

Interpretation Bulletins: IT-141R: Clergy residence deduction; IT-352R2: Employees' expenses, including work space in home expenses; IT-522R: Vehicle, travel and sales expenses of employees.

Information Circulars: 73-21R9: Claims for meals and lodging expenses of transport employees; 74-6R2: Power saw expenses.

Forms: T1223: Clergy residence deduction; T2200: Declaration of conditions of employment; T2200S: Declaration of conditions of employment for working at home due to COVID-19; T4044: Employment expenses [guide].

(11) Goods and services tax — For the purposes of this section and section 6, the amount of any rebate paid or payable to a taxpayer under the *Excise Tax Act* in respect of the goods and services tax shall be deemed not to be an amount that is reimbursed to the taxpayer or to which the taxpayer is entitled.

Related Provisions: 6(8) — GST rebate included in income.

Notes: The term "goods and services tax" is defined in 248(1) to include HST.

8(11) added by 1990 GST, effective 1991.

(12) Forfeiture of securities by employee — If, in a taxation year,

(a) an employee is deemed by subsection 7(2) to have disposed of a security (as defined in subsection 7(7)) held by a trust,

(b) the trust disposed of the security to the person that issued the security,

(c) the disposition occurred as a result of the employee not meeting the conditions necessary for title to the security to vest in the employee, and

(d) the amount paid by the person to acquire the security from the trust or to redeem or cancel the security did not exceed the amount paid to the person for the security,

the following rules apply:

(e) there may be deducted in computing the employee's income for the year from employment the amount, if any, by which

(i) the amount of the benefit deemed by subsection 7(1) to have been received by the employee in the year or a preceding taxation year in respect of the security

exceeds

(ii) any amount deducted under paragraph 110(1)(d) or (d.1) in computing the employee's taxable income for the year or a preceding taxation year in respect of that benefit, and

(f) notwithstanding any other provision of this Act, the employee's gain or loss from the disposition of the security is deemed to be nil and section 84 does not apply to deem a dividend to have been received in respect of the disposition.

Notes: 8(12) amended by 1998 Budget, retroactive to 1988.

8(12) added by 1991 technical bill, effective for 1988 and later taxation years.

Interpretation Bulletins: IT-113R4: Benefits to employees — stock options.

(13) Work space in home — Notwithstanding paragraphs (1)(f) and (i),

(a) no amount is deductible in computing an individual's income for a taxation year from an office or employment in respect of any part (in this subsection referred to as the "work space") of a self-contained domestic establishment in which the individual resides, except to the extent that the work space is either

(i) the place where the individual principally performs the duties of the office or employment, or

(ii) used exclusively during the period in respect of which the amount relates for the purpose of earning income from the office or employment and used on a regular and continuous basis for meeting customers or other persons in the ordinary course of performing the duties of the office or employment;

(b) where the conditions set out in subparagraph (a)(i) or (ii) are met, the amount in respect of the work space that is deductible in computing the individual's income for the year from the office or employment shall not exceed the individual's income for the year from the office or employment, computed without reference to any deduction in respect of the work space; and

(c) any amount in respect of a work space that was, solely because of paragraph (b), not deductible in computing the individual's income for the immediately preceding taxation year from the office or employment shall be deemed to be an amount in respect of a work space that is otherwise deductible in computing the individual's income for the year from that office or employment and that, subject to paragraph (b), may be deducted in computing the individual's income for the year from the office or employment.

Announced Administrative Change — COVID-19 — Employee home office expenses in 2020

Federal Economic Statement, Chapter 4, Nov. 30, 2020: *4.8.3 Simplifying the Home Office Expense Deduction*

Millions of Canadians are unexpectedly working from home because of COVID-19. They are turning their bedrooms, basements and kitchens into offices, and taking on increased household expenses to do their jobs. Canadians working from home can already deduct certain home office expenses for tax purposes, but first-time claimants may not be familiar with the rules and the claim process imposes an administrative burden on employers who are already dealing with the broader impacts of the pandemic and have to fill out additional information for their employees who qualify.

To simplify the process for both taxpayers and businesses, the CRA will allow employees working from home in 2020 due to COVID-19 with modest expenses to **claim up to $400**, based on the amount of time working from home, without the need to track detailed expenses, and will generally not request that people provide a signed form from their employers. This measure will help taxpayers access deductions they are entitled to receive and simplify the tax filing process. Further detail will be communicated by the CRA in the coming weeks.

Notes: A table after §4.8.3 says this measure will cost the federal government $210 million in 2020-21.

CRA news release and Backgrounder, Dec. 15, 2020: *Introducing a simplified process for claiming the home office expenses for Canadians working from home due to the COVID-19 pandemic*

This year has been filled with unprecedented challenges due to the COVID-19 pandemic. Many Canadians unexpectedly had to work from home which resulted in millions of Canadians setting up their work space in their kitchens, bedrooms and living rooms.

In response, the Honourable Diane Lebouthillier, Minister of National Revenue, provided today additional details on how the Canada Revenue Agency (CRA) has made the home office expenses deduction available to more Canadians, and simplified the way employees can claim these expenses on their personal income tax return for the 2020 tax year. Employees with larger claims for home office expenses can still choose to use the existing detailed method to calculate their home office expenses deduction.

Employees who worked from home more than 50% of the time over a period of at least four consecutive weeks in 2020 due to COVID-19 will now be eligible to claim the home office expenses deduction for 2020. The use of a shorter qualifying period will ensure that more employees can claim the deduction than would otherwise have been possible under longstanding practice.

A new temporary flat rate method will allow eligible employees to claim a deduction of **$2 for each day they worked at home** in that period, plus any other days they worked from home in 2020 due to COVID-19 **up to a maximum of $400**. Under this new method, employees will not have to get Form T2200 or Form T2200S completed and signed by their employer.

To simplify the process for employees choosing the **detailed** method, the CRA launched today simplified forms (Form T2200S and Form T777S) and a calculator designed specifically to assist with the calculation of eligible home office expenses.

For more information on working from home expenses go to Canada.ca/cra-home-workspace-expenses.

Quick facts

- Home office expenses can be claimed as a deduction on an employee's personal income tax return. Deductions reduce the amount of income they pay tax on.

- For those using the detailed method to calculate their home office expenses, the CRA has expanded the list of eligible expenses that can be claimed to include home internet access fees. A comprehensive list of all eligible expenses is available online.

- According to Statistics Canada, "Working from home continues to be an important adaptation to COVID-19 health risks, with 2.4 million Canadians who do not normally work from home doing so in October."

- The CRA engaged many stakeholders in the fall of 2020 about the simplified Form T2200 and work-space-in-the-home expenses prior to introducing these temporary measures. For more information, go to the Backgrounder–Consultation on the simplification of Form T2200.

- The new temporary flat rate method to calculate the deduction for home office expenses was announced on November 30th in the Fall Economic Statement.

Contacts: Jeremy Bellefeuille, Press Secretary, Office of the Minister of National Revenue, 343-551-0898, Jeremy.Bellefeuille@cra-arc.gc.ca; Media Relations, Canada Revenue Agency, 613-948-8366, cra-arc.media@cra-arc.gc.ca.

Backgrounder — Simplifying the Process for Claiming a Deduction for Home Office Expenses for Employees Working from Home Due to COVID-19

As a result of the unprecedented challenges due to COVID-19, many people have been working at home and using their kitchens, bedrooms and living rooms as their work space. In response, the Canada Revenue Agency (CRA) has introduced a new temporary flat rate method to simplify claiming the deduction for home office expenses for the 2020 tax year.

As an employee, you may be able to claim a deduction for home office expenses (work-space-in-the-home expenses, office supplies, and certain phone expenses). This deduction is claimed on your personal income tax return. Deductions reduce the amount of income you pay tax on, so they reduce your overall income tax liability.

Eligibility

You are eligible to claim a deduction for home office expenses for the period you worked from home, if you meet all of the criteria:

- you worked from home in 2020 due to the COVID-19 pandemic or your employer required you to work from home

- you worked more than 50% of the time from home for a period of at least four consecutive weeks in 2020

- have a completed and signed Form T2200S or Form T2200 from your employer (only applicable if the detailed method is used to complete the claim)

- the expenses are used directly in your work during the period

The use of a shorter qualifying period will ensure that more employees can claim the deduction than would otherwise have been possible under longstanding practice.

New temporary flat rate method

The new temporary flat rate method simplifies your claim for home office expenses. You are eligible to use this new method if you worked more than 50% of the time from home for a period of at least four consecutive weeks in 2020 due to the COVID-19 pandemic. You can claim **$2 for each day you worked from home** during that period plus any additional days you worked at home in 2020 due to the COVID-19 pandemic. The maximum you can claim using the new temporary flat rate method is **$400 (200 working days)** per individual.

Each individual working from home who meets the eligibility criteria can use the temporary flat rate method to calculate their deduction for home office expenses. This means multiple people working from the same home can each make a claim.

This method can only be used for the 2020 tax year.

Simplified process for the temporary flat rate method

You do not have to: calculate the size of your work space, keep supporting documents or get Form T2200 completed and signed by your employer.

What counts as a work day

- days you worked full-time hours from home
- days you worked part-time hours from home

What days do not count

- days off
- vacation days
- sick leave days
- other leave or absence

Expenses that are covered by the $2 a day flat rate

The temporary flat rate method is used to claim home office expenses. You cannot claim any other employment expenses (line 22900) if you are using the flat rate method.

Using the detailed method to claim your deduction for home office expenses

You can use the detailed method to claim the home office expenses you paid for the period that you worked from home.

Simplified process for using the detailed method if you worked from home due to the COVID-19 pandemic

---

To support you, the CRA:

- created a simplified Form T2200S and Form T777S

- created a calculator to help you claim the home office expense deduction that you are entitled to

- will accept an electronic signature on the Form T2200S and Form T2200 to reduce the necessity for employees and employers to meet in person (applies to the 2020 tax year only)

What is Form T2200S?

Form T2200S, *Declaration of Conditions of Employment for Working at Home During COVID-19* is a shorter version of Form T2200 that you get your employer to complete and sign if you worked from home in 2020 due to the COVID-19 pandemic and are not using the temporary flat rate method. Your employer completes and signs this form to certify that you worked from home in 2020 due to COVID-19 and had to pay your own home office expenses.

What is Form T777S?

Form T777S, *Statement of Employment Expenses for Working at Home Due to COVID-19*, is used to calculate your claim for home office expenses.

How to determine the employment use of a work space

Whether you work at the dining table or in a spare bedroom, there are several factors to consider when calculating your employment use of the work space:

- Size of your home and work space
- Types of work spaces
- Hours per week you use the space for work

New eligible expenses

The CRA has expanded the list of eligible expenses that can be claimed to include home internet access fees.

A comprehensive list of eligible home office expenses has also been created.

For more information on working from home expenses go to Canada.ca/cra-home-workspace-expenses.

Notes: For detailed information see Canada.ca/cra-home-workspace-expenses.

See also Rusu, "The CRA's Draft Form T2200 Short", 10(4) *Canadian Tax Focus* (ctf.ca) 11-12 (Nov. 2020) (draft 1-page T2200 due to COVID-19); Mancell, "Deducting Home Office Expenses as an Employee in 2020", 2546-47 *Tax Topics* (CCH) 6-8 (Dec. 22, 2020).

Related Provisions: 18(12) — Parallel rule for self-employed individual.

Notes: 8(13) is restrictive, not permissive. It does not create any deduction that is not first allowed by another provision, usually 8(1)(i) [8(1)(f) for commission employees].

"Principally" in 8(13)(a)(i) means "more than 50% of the time" according to CRA: VIEWS docs 2004-0066731E5, 2004-0066821E5, 2007-0227511E5, 2007-0228231I7, 2007-023186117, 2009-0329111E5. However, "the" office or employment means that a second job with the same employer can be excluded from the calculation: 2007-0254531E5. In *Lester*, 2011 TCC 543, para. 29, the Court agreed that the "principally performed" test was met. In *Brown*, 2017 TCC 237, B performed only 20% of his duties at home according to the T2200 (see 8(10)), so no expenses were allowed.

With COVID-19, many people worked at home for months. 8(13) is ambiguous as to whether "principally" must apply to the entire year. However, CRA administrative policy now allows home office expenses for 2020 if the employee worked at home over 50% of the time for at least 4 consecutive weeks due to COVID-19. See Dec. 15, 2020 Announced Administrative Change above, which also allows a simplified $2/day (max $400) without calculations, and simplified Form T2200S for those claiming specific expenses. See also Canada.ca/cra-home-workspace-expenses.

See Notes to 18(12) for interpretation of 8(13)(a)(ii) and if the property is owned or co-owned by another person. (The employer need not impose the "used exclusively" requirement: VIEWS doc 2009-033775117.)

The deduction is limited to the income from the employment (8(13)(b)), but any amount so disallowed can be carried forward indefinitely and claimed against later income from the same employment: 8(13)(c).

VIEWS docs 2000-0022015 and 2011-0394321E5 note that whether the home meets local zoning regulations is irrelevant to deducting home office expenses [see also Notes to 9(1) under "Diverting income"]; and that working at home can be "required" (for 8(1)(i)) under an arrangement that was voluntarily entered into. An informal work-at-home arrangement that does not "require" the employee to work at home does not permit the deduction (see Notes to 8(1)(f) and (h.1) for more on "required"). Inventory storage space can be part of the home office: 2012-0471391E5.

A home office allowance is taxable whether or not the employee can deduct an amount under 8(13): VIEWS doc 2011-040258117.

See also Crowell, "Home Office Expenses of Employees", 8(6) *Tax Hyperion* (Carswell, June 2011); Johnson, "Home Office and Office Space Expenses of Employees During the COVID-19", 17(3) *Tax Hyperion* (Carswell) 1-5 (May-June 2020).

8(13) added by 1991 technical bill, effective 1991.

Interpretation Bulletins: IT-352R2: Employee's expenses, including work space in home expenses.

Forms: T777: Statement of employment expenses; T2200: Declaration of conditions of employment; T2200S: Declaration of conditions of employment for working at home due to COVID-19; T4044: Employment expenses [guide].

Definitions [s. 8]: "additional voluntary contribution", "amount", "annuity", "automobile" — 248(1); "blood relationship" — 251(6)(a); "borrowed money", "business" — 248(1); "Canada" — 255, *Interpretation Act* 35(1); "capital cost" — 13(7)–(7.4), 128.1(1)(c), 128.1(4)(c); "common-law partner", "common-law partnership" — 248(1); "Commonwealth" — *Interpretation Act* 35(1); "connected" — 251(6); "custodian" — 248(1)"retirement compensation arrangement"; "deferred amount" — 248(1); "eligible apprentice mechanic" — 8(6)(a); "eligible tool" — 8(6)(b), 8(6.1); "employed", "employee", "employer", "employment" — 248(1); "excess EPSP amount" — 207.8(1); "goods and services tax", "individual", "Minister" — 248(1); "month" — *Interpretation Act* 35(1); "motor vehicle", "office", "person", "prescribed", "property" — 248(1); "province" — *Interpretation Act* 35(1)"province"; "provincial" — *Interpretation Act* 33(3), 35(1)"province"; "provincial pension plan" — *Canada Pension Plan* s. 3; "registered pension plan", "regulation" — 248(1); "reimbursement payment" — 8(1)(n.1)(i); "resident" — 250; "retirement compensation arrangement" — 248(1); "salary, wages" — 248(1)"salary or wages"; "salary deferral arrangement", "salary or wages" — 248(1); "security" — 7(7); "self-contained domestic establishment", "share" — 248(1); "taxable income" — 2(2), 248(1); "taxation year" — 249; "taxpayer" — 248(1); "trust" — 104(1), 248(1), (3).

Interpretation Bulletins [s. 8]: IT-168R3: Athletes and players employed by football, hockey and similar clubs.

Subdivision B — Income or Loss from a Business or Property

Basic Rules

9. (1) Income — Subject to this Part, a taxpayer's income for a taxation year from a business or property is the taxpayer's profit from that business or property for the year.

Related Provisions: 9(3) — Capital gains and losses not included; 10.1 — Derivatives — mark-to-market only if election made; 18(17)–(23) — Straddle transactions — no income deferral; 18 — Limitations on various deductions; 18.1 — Limitation on deduction for matchable expenditure; 19, 19.01, 19.1 — Limitations on deductions for advertising expenses; 23 — Sale of inventory after ceasing to carry on business; 27.1 — Treatment of emissions allowance; 80(13) — Income inclusion on forgiveness of debt; 95(1) — Extended definition of "income from property" for FAPI purposes; 112(4)–(5.6) — Restrictions on losses on shares held as inventory; 115(1)(a)(ii) — Non-resident's taxable income earned in Canada; 142.5(1) — Mark-to-market rules for securities held by financial institutions; 143.2(6) — Reduction in expenditure allowed for tax shelter investment; 143.3 — Stock options and shares issued, whether deductible; 247 — Calculation of profit on transactions with non-residents; 248(24) — Equity and consolidation methods of accounting not to be used; 261(7) — Functional currency reporting; Canada-U.S. Tax Treaty:Art. VII — Business profits of U.S. resident; Canada-U.S. Tax Treaty:Art. XVI — Artistes and athletes.

Notes: "Profit" is normally calculated in accordance with "well accepted principles of business (or accounting) practice" or "well accepted principles of commercial trading": *Symes*, [1994] 1 C.T.C. 40 (SCC), para. 43; *Canderel Ltd.*, [1998] 2 C.T.C. 35 (SCC). These are usually but not always the same as generally accepted accounting principles (GAAP), set out in the *CPA Canada Handbook — Accounting*. See also *Kruger* (under "Cash-based accounting" below); *Romar*, 2009 FCA 48; *Ugro*, 2009 FC 826 (FCA appeal discontinued A-396-09) and 2011 TCC 317 (taxpayer's invented accounting method rejected). See also Tamaki & Richards, "The Significance of Commercial and Accounting Principles in Canadian Tax Cases", 58(Supp. [Bowman]) *Canadian Tax Journal* 101-09 (2010); Arnold et al., *Timing and Income Taxation* (ctf.ca, 2nd ed., 2015), chaps. 2-3; Edgar et al., *Materials on Canadian Income Tax* (Carswell, 15th ed., 2015), chap. 6. The Act has many rules that override the accounting treatment. See Form T2 Schedule 1; *Corporate Tax Returns and Provisions Guide* (Carswell, annual).

IFRS: GAAP has been partly superseded by International Financial Reporting Standards, mandatory for public companies since 2011: see www.frascanada.ca; IFRS Bulletins; Chant & Hughes, *iGAAP 2008* (CCH, 2008, 2850pp); Doucet et al., *International Financial Reporting Standards* (Cdn Tax Foundation, 2011), chap. 3; PwC, *Manual of Accounting IFRS* (3 vols., LexisNexis UK, 2019); Gergovich, "International Financial Reporting Standards", 2007 Cdn Tax Foundation conference report, 1:1-40; Hinz, "International Financial Reporting Standards and Accounting for Income Taxes", 2008 conference report, 16:1-23; Gall & Dawe, "Transition to IFRS", 2010 conference report, 9:1-20; Landry & MacPhee, "International Financial Reporting Standards", 2011 Atlantic Provinces Tax Conference (ctf.ca), 1B:1-7; Lacroix, "Converting to IFRS", 2011 conference report, 8:1-8; Okafor et al., "How Did the CRA Expect the Adoption of IFRS To Affect Corporate Tax?", 66(1) *Canadian Tax Journal* 1-22 (2018). In many areas the Act provides specific treatment (9(3), 10-37, 38-55 for capital gains, etc.), so IFRS has limited impact: inventories; foreign exchange gains and losses; capital tax effect on business limit (125(5.1)(a), VIEWS doc 2010-0390601E5) and SR&ED expenditure limit (127(10.2)); thin capitalization (18(4), 2010-0384001E5); and some other rules. CRA discussion: tinyurl.com/cra-ifrs (queries: IFRS@cra.gc.ca); *Technical News* 41, 42 and 44; docs 2006-0178661E5, 2009-0316371C6, 2009-0330391C6 [2009 APFF q.47]; 2010-0361401E5 (early adoption of

IFRS for N.S. large corps tax); 2010-0358861R3 (trust variation to comply with IFRS does not trigger tax); 2011-0399761C6 (adjustments in first year taxpayer uses IFRS); 2009 conference report pp. 3:18-19 (roundtable q.21). It is unclear whether IFRS provides a "truer picture of profit" for tax purposes than GAAP. For private companies there are new Accounting Standards for Private Enterprises (ASPE): see 2011-0425511E5 (conversion from GAAP to ASPE), 2012-0425081E5 (ASPE business combination costs deductibility does not make them current expenses for tax); Cummings & Bowen, "Financial Reporting Framework", 2010 Ontario Tax conf. 11:1-34; Shepherd, "International Financial Reporting Standards or ASPE?", 2010 Prairie Provinces Tax Conf. 11:1-39; Driedger & Wong (see 20(1)(l) Notes).

Under *Canderel*, the determination of profit is a question of law, not to be delegated to accountants. "The main object remains to have an accounting method that presents an accurate picture of a taxpayer's profit for a given year": *Mann*, 2007 TCC 732, para. 21. See George Walker, "Timing and Recognition of Income", 2001 Cdn Tax Foundation conference report, 29:1-54; David Nathanson, "Determining Business 'Profit' for Income Tax Purposes", X(4) *Tax Litigation* (Federated Press) 646-56 (2002); Joseph Frankovic, "Principles in the Computation of Profit: Unanswered Questions?", 2261 *Tax Topics* (CCH) 1-3 (July 9, 2015). See also under "Cash-based accounting" and "Matching principle" below.

Under *Canderel*, a taxpayer may adopt any method of calculating profit that is in accordance with the Act, established case law principles (rules of law) and well-accepted business principles (including GAAP). A method that is "so out of whack with economic reality" that it does not meet the fundamental criterion of accuracy in reporting income is unacceptable; thus a partnership could not prepare financial statements on the basis that the cost of zero-coupon bonds was their maturity value in 29 years: *Bernick*, [2004] 3 C.T.C. 191 (FCA). Accounting for leasing income on a straight-line basis as per *CICA Handbook* §3065.55 would not be in accordance with 9(1): VIEWS doc 2006-0169231E5. Based on *Canderel*, an insurance broker can deduct a rebate paid to a customer out of commissions: docs 2008-0271381E5, 2010-0359401C6.

A corporation that reports using U.S. GAAP for Canadian securities purposes can file those financial statements, but must still determine whether U.S. GAAP provides an accurate picture for s. 9: VIEWS doc 2011-0403641E5.

Accrual accounting: see "Cash-based accounting" below.

Advertising/promotion expenses: see 18(1)(a) Notes.

Agency: where a person carries on business as another's agent, it is the *principal* who carries on the business: *Avotus Corp.*, 2006 TCC 505; *Fourney*, 2011 TCC 520 (corp carried on business as shareholder's agent). See also under "Bare trustee" and "Diverting income" below.

Artists: see 10(6); Income Tax Folio S4-F14-C1; VIEWS docs 2010-0381591E5; 2017-0706471E5 (residency); 2018-0759891M4, 2018-0790641M4.

Authors who write actively as a business have business income: *Rocco Gagliese Productions*, 2018 TCC 136. CRA accepts this: Income Tax Folio S4-F14-C1; VIEWS docs 9722915, 2007-0238221E5, 2019-0798321C6 [2019 STEP q.7]; T5 Box 17 instructions say "Enter on line 135 [Business income] your royalties that have expenses associated." "If income from property has any meaning at all, it can only mean the production of revenue from the use of such property which produces income without the active and extensive business-like intervention of its owner or someone on his behalf": *Hollinger*, 1972 CarswellNat 173, para. 40 (FCTD; aff'd 1974 CarswellNat 216 (FCA)). See also "Business income vs property income" below; *Switzer*, 1994 CarswellNat 1297 (TCC) (geologist's royalty income was RRSP "earned income" because it was remuneration for his work); and GST/HST Policy P-176R under "Artists and Writers", though its focus is on whether the author has a reasonable expectation of profit (see 9(2) Notes). If the publisher issues a T5 (Reg. 201(1)(c)), CRA's "matching program" (see 231.1(1) Notes) may think the author has received royalties as income from property, and CRA may assess the author without notice to deny expenses, to delete RRSP contribution room (despite 146(1)"earned income"(a)(iii)), to deny childcare expenses (63(3)"earned income") and/or to double-tax income already reported as business income. See for example Drache, "T-5 Form over Substance", xxxviii *The Canadian Taxpayer* 133-34 (Sept 9, 2016). For sale of copyright, see 54"capital property" Notes.

Bare trustee, beneficial vs legal ownership of property, and who reports the income: see end of 54"capital property" Notes and 104(1) Notes.

Barter transactions are taxable if what is bartered generates income: *Levert*, 2017 TCC 208 (ITEX exchange network); IT-490; VIEWS docs 2008-0280701E5, 2014-0537231M4. See also "Damages" below re the *surrogatum* principle, and 12(1)(c) Notes under "Accepting reduced or no interest".

Benefits to employees: see "Employee benefits" below. Benefits received (e.g. an independent contractor or incorporated employee who gets employee-like benefits) are income under 9(1): VIEWS doc 2016-063846117.

Bitcoin and other digital currency: see "Cryptocurrency" below.

Break fees received in mergers and acquisitions may be proceeds of disposition of rights, or may be taxable under 9(1) (the *surrogatum* principle; see "Damages" below) or 12(1)(x): VIEWS docs 2010-036632117, 2012-0467961E5. In *Morguard Corp.*, 2012 TCC 55; aff'd 2012 FCA 306 (leave to appeal denied 2013 CarswellNat 1135 (SCC)), a break fee was taxable because it was integral to MC's business operations. (The TCC had doubts about the *surrogatum* argument (para. 46); the FCA did not discuss this point.) See also Hickey, "Break Fees and Failed Transaction Costs", 20(1) *Canadian Tax Highlights* (ctf.ca) 9-10 (Jan. 2012); Biringer & Lee, "Break-fee Receipts: Expanding the Concept of Income", XVIII(1) *Corporate Finance* (Federated Press) 2066-75 (2012).

Business income vs. no business: see 3 and 9(2) Notes. *Business income vs. employment income*: see 248(1)"employee" Notes.

Business income vs. property income: the same expenses can usually be deducted: *Venditti*, 2008 TCC 553, but the distinction has consequences, e.g., 74.1-74.5 attribution rules apply only to property income; 123.3 tax on a CCPC's property income; 125(1) small business deduction; Reg. 1100(11)-(20) CCA limitations. Renting apartments is normally property income (*Burri*, 1985 CarswellNat 303 (FCTD)); operating a hotel is business income (IT-73R6 para. 13); storage lockers were unlike a hotel even where the owner provided extra services to many customers: *0742443 B.C. [R-Xtra Co.]*, 2015 FCA 231. (For software that assists in the determination see *Business vs Property: Rental Classifier* at bluejlegal.com.) The Supreme Court of Canada stated in *Canadian Marconi*, [1986] 2 C.T.C. 465, para. 12, that this determination "must be made from an examination of the taxpayer's whole course of conduct viewed in the light of surrounding circumstances... the number of transactions, their volume, their frequency, the turnover of the investments and the nature of the investments themselves." Generally, Ponzi scheme income is property income while pyramid scheme income is business income: *Mazo*, 2016 TCC 232, para. 17. Rental income depends on this rule and how actively the property is managed; it was business income in *Cadboro Bay*, [1977] C.T.C. 186 (FCTD), *Étoile Immobilière*, [1992] 2 C.T.C. 2367 (TCC), *Valec SA*, [1998] 2 C.T.C. 2322 (TCC) and *Arbutus Gardens*, [1998] 3 C.T.C. 2972 (TCC); and was property income in *Wertman*, [1964] C.T.C. 252 (Exch), *Walsh*, [1965] C.T.C. 478 (Exch), *Venditi* (above), *Orcheson*, 2004 TCC 427 (cottages) and *McInnes*, 2014 TCC 247 (cottages); and see 129(6). See also VIEWS docs 2010-0382091E5 (providing furnished apartments was likely property income); 2010-0380391I7 (co-owners of triplex: effect of Quebec *Civil Code*); 2011-0403841E5 (triple net lease is normally property income). See also "Authors" above.

Interest income ancillary to a business is business income: *Irving Oil*, 2001 FCA 364; *Munich Reinsurance*, 2001 FCA 365; *3850625 Canada Inc.*, 2011 FCA 117 (tax refund interest under 164(3)). In *Inter-Leasing*, 2014 ONCA 683 (leave to appeal denied to Ontario 2015 CarswellOnt 2996 (SCC)) and *Safeway Ontario*, 2014 ONSC 5204, interest income moved to an offshore company in an "Ontario shuffle" was income from property, as little activity was required to earn it. See also docs 2010-0385151E5 (whether activity incidental to farming business); 2010-0381031E5 (foreign currency trading may be business income); 2013-0508841I7 (business loss of limited partner is still business loss); 2014-0536581I7 (threshold for any corporation "to be considered to be carrying on business is extremely low").

For more on business vs property income see "Authors" above; Notes to 18(12), 108(5), 125(7)"active business...", 125(7)"specified investment business", 129(4)"aggregate investment income", 129(4)"income", 149.1(1)"related business", 248(1)"active business", 248(1)"automobile" [re para. (d)], and Proposed Non-Amendment under 125(7)"specified investment business". See also Gamble, "Income from a Business or Property", 2014 Cdn Tax Foundation conference report, 5:1-32; Lanthier, "Business or Property Income", 23(4) *Canadian Tax Highlights* (ctf.ca) 5-6 (April 2015); Friedlan, "When Does the Operation of a Rental Property Become a Business?", 16(2) *Tax for the Owner-Manager* (ctf.ca) 1-2 (April 2016).

Business income vs other: In *Freitas*, 2018 FCA 110, para. 30, a retired accountant's income taxed under 96(1.1) was not business income (so no CPP contributions were required).

Capital expenses disallowed: see 18(1)(b) Notes.

Capital gain vs. income: see 54"capital property" Notes and (for home builders) 40(2)(b) Notes.

Capital pool company deductions: see VIEWS doc 2010-0379141E5; Raymond Adlington, "Capital Pool Companies — Expense Deductibility", 8(6) *Tax Hyperion* (Carswell, June 2011).

Car expenses: see 18(1)(h) Notes.

Cash expenses (or if records have been lost) can be allowed without receipts if the Court believes they were incurred: *House*, 2011 FCA 234; *Muller's Meats*, [1969] Tax A.B.C. 171; *Merchant*, [1998] 3 C.T.C. 2505 (TCC), para. 23; *Tozer*, 2004 TCC 411, para. 20; *Redrupp*, 2004 TCC 640, paras. 18-19, 22; *Chrabalowski*, 2004 TCC 644, para. 10; *Chandan*, 2005 TCC 685, para. 34; *Benjamin*, 2006 TCC 69, paras. 6-7; *Pytel*, 2009 TCC 615; *Rotondi*, 2010 TCC 378; *Brenneur*, 2011 TCC 330, para. 23; *Saleem*, 2019 TCC 25, para. 14; *Wilson*, 2019 TCC 42, para. 12; *Voyer*, 2019 TCC 221, para. 47. This is so even if the 230(1) record-keeping obligation is not followed: *Chandan*; *Pytel*; VIEWS doc 2010-0384481I7. Similarly, expenses required by oral amendment to a written lease were allowed in *8076958 Ontario*, 2018 TCC 253. CRA's *Income Tax Audit Manual* §10.5.2 accepts: "The taxpayer/registrant's own testimony constitutes audit evidence that, if credible, can support what was said, and even serve as proof." "In the absence of an invoice, the cancelled cheque or any other reasonably verifiable information would be given consideration": 2009-0335711E5. CRA allowed estimated development costs against a real estate sale in *Wall*, 2019 TCC 168, para. 12 (FCA appeal on other grounds heard June 10/21); and conceded a geologist's expenses that were not proven in Court (though perhaps they were proven at audit) in *Larkin*, 2020 TCC 98, para. 42. When doing an arbitrary assessment (see 152(7) Notes), CRA may allow 80-90% of a business's sales as expenses without evidence: *Estra Flooring*, 2021 TCC 20, paras. 4, 27.

However, the Courts usually disallow undocumented expenses, e.g. *Njenga*, [1997] 2 C.T.C. 8 (FCA) ("As a public policy matter the burden of proof of deductions and claims properly rests with the taxpayer..., [who] is responsible for documenting her own personal affairs in a reasonable manner. Self written receipts and assertion without proof are not sufficient"); *Hafizy*, 2014 FCA 109; *Loates*, 2016 FCA 47 (2015 TCC 30, para. 26 said undocumented claims "must fail", but FCA interpreted this as "declining to accept the taxpayer's uncorroborated evidence"); *1345805 Ontario*, [2005] 5 C.T.C. 2334; *Lauzon*, 2014 TCC 3 (FCA appeal discontinued A-87-14) (includes detailed reasons for rejecting claim, e.g. business not having enough liquidity to have paid cash); *Francis*, 2014 TCC 137; *Amiripour*, 2015 TCC 187, paras. 21-26; *Ngai*, 2018 TCC 26, paras. 106-115; *Lavigne*, 2020 TCC 57, para. 9. If receipts printed on heat-sensitized paper have faded to invisible by the time of audit, expenses may be disallowed: doc 2005-0156201E5. See also Rachert, "Proving Business Expenses", 2012 B.C. Tax Conf. (ctf.ca) 11:1-26, Part III.

Paying cash for home construction costs was not conspiracy to evade GST disentitling V (as not having "clean hands") from an equitable claim to land based on a promised gift: *Vestby v. Galloway*, 2020 ABQB 361, paras. 119-129.

Cash-based accounting is not normally allowed (except farmers/fishermen under 28(1); and financial institutions (FIs) have mark-to-market accounting under 142.5(2)): *Ken Steeves Sales*, [1955] C.T.C. 47 (Exch. Ct.); *Freeway Properties*, [1985] 1 C.T.C. 222 (FCTD); *Corriveau*, 2004 TCC 550; *Srougi*, 2007 TCC 186. In *Kruger Inc.*, 2016 FCA 186, a non-FI was allowed to "mark to market" foreign exchange option contracts, as this was an appropriate accounting method, but starting 2017 this requires an election under 10.1. (See also 10(15) and 18(1)(x), reversing *Kruger*'s ruling that a derivative held on income account could be written down as inventory.) *Gooch*, 2009 TCC 367, para. 16, said the taxpayer was "entitled" to report income on a cash basis "if that method yielded an accurate picture of his profit for the year", citing *Canderel*, but *Reilly*, 2010 TCC 326 (FCA appeal discontinued A-322-10) held that *Canderel* did not permit a realtor to use the cash basis. Hedge accounting: see under "Hedges" below.

Compensation for Employers of Reservists Program grants are considered taxable: VIEWS doc 2014-0656001I7.

Conditional income: see "Contingent income" below.

Conditional sales vs. leases: see 49(3) Notes.

Construction contractors: see "Disbursements" below, and 12(1)(b) Notes.

Contingent expenses: see 18(1)(e) Notes.

Contingent income: A conditional or contingent fee is recognized only when billed or when it becomes billable, unless it is received (see 12(1)(b)): VIEWS doc 2003-0015775. Such a fee is not income until it is "absolute and under no restriction": *Commonwealth Construction*, [1984] C.T.C. 338 (FCA); *Lockwood Financial*, 2020 TCC 128, paras. 46-53.

Correcting errors: In *2187878 Nova Scotia*, 2007 TCC 249, a deduction was allowed for prior years' nonexistent income that had been falsely reported by the company's Controller in a fraud on the company.

Cost of goods is normally deductible only on sale of the goods: see 10(1) Notes.

Criminal activity creates income from business (or possibly a 6(1)(a) benefit, if theft is from the employer): Income Tax Folio S3-F9-C1 ¶1.30; *Poynton*, [1972] C.T.C. 411 (Ont CA); *Molenaar*, 2004 FCA 349; *Zins*, 2007 FCA 314; *Brizzi*, 2008 FCA 200; *Brown*, 2013 FCA 111; *No. 275*, 1955 CarswellNat 151 (Tax App. Bd); *Humphrey*, 2006 TCC 168; *Peek*, 2007 TCC 152; *Biros*, 2007 TCC 248; *Anjaria*, 2007 TCC 746; *Ko*, 2007 TCC 753; *Ouellette*, 2009 TCC 443, para. 17; *Chronis*, 2010 TCC 218; *Bilodeau*, 2014 TCC 210; *Mosly*, 2015 TCC 136. (Conviction of fraud is *prima facie* evidence of having earned the income: see "Issue estoppel" in 239(1) Notes.) Where money came into G's bank account due to fraud (an altered cheque) but benefited someone else, it was not G's income: *Gainor*, 2011 TCC 442. Ponzi scheme profits and losses: see Notes to 9(2); in *Mazo*, 2016 TCC 232, income from a pyramid scheme was business income. Expenses of criminal activity are deductible: Income Tax Folio S4-F2-C1 ¶1.8-1.13; *Eldridge*, [1964] C.T.C. 545 (Exch. Ct.) (call girl business); *65302 British Columbia (formerly Veekens Poultry) ["BC Eggs"]*, [2000] 1 C.T.C. 57 (SCC), para. 56; *Canadian Imperial Bank of Commerce*, 2013 FCA 122, paras. 76-77 (even if conduct was "egregious and repulsive", as the morality of the taxpayer's conduct is irrelevant [CRA agrees: Folio S4-F2-C1 ¶1.13]); *Chronis* (above) (illegal satellite decoder business) (see also *Orman v. Marnat*, 2012 ONSC 549, in Notes to 9(2)). This does not include penalties and fines (see "Penalties and fines" below); or legal fees to avoid going to jail: *Neeb*, 1997 CarswellNat 67 (TCC); *Chan*, 2010 TCC 3 (aff'd on other grounds 2011 FCA 88). A net worth analysis of criminal activity (see Notes to 152(7)) "must still be completed in a principled and rational manner": *Sarwari*, 2009 TCC 357, para. 3. CRA can assess based on evidence of illegal activity provided by the police: *Brown* (above); see Notes to 231.2(1) re the *Jarvis* principle. The fact something is illegal does not mean it does not happen for tax purposes; see under "Diverting income" below. CRA may disclose information about many criminal offences to the police: 241(9.5). VIEWS doc 2015-0566531E5 queried whether CRA collecting tax from someone selling sex would be receiving a financial benefit in violation of *Criminal Code* s. 286.2! (CRA did not answer.)

Crowdfunding revenues under which the donor gets an incentive gift and no equity are taxable as business income: VIEWS doc 2013-0484941E5. Docs 2013-0508971E5 and 2013-0509101E5 note that crowdfunding payments "could represent a loan, capital contribution, gift, income, or a combination thereof" and that each case will depend on its facts; and see 2013-0495701C6, 2013-0507541E5 to similar effect. However, 2015-0579031I7 and Income Tax Folio S3-F9-C1 ¶1.5 state that unless it is clearly a loan or equity contribution, crowdfunding to develop a new product for a business is income. In the author's view, the amount should not be income if the taxpayer is really raising capital that may be returned to the investors if there is a profit (or is for a non-profit purpose such as humanitarian aid), but is business income if the funding is really advance sales of a product to be supplied later. If it is business fundraising with no obligation to return anything, CRA may be correct that it is taxable, but this is uncertain. Such funding might be "assistance" that reduces expenses or capital costs under 12(1)(x). See also Gill, "CRA: Crowdfunding Receipts", 3(4) *Canadian Tax Focus* (ctf.ca) 6-7 (Nov. 2013); Arnould & Oliver, "Crowdfunding Receipts", XIX(2) *Corporate Finance* (Federated Press) 2219-21 (2013); 1 *Privately Held Companies & Taxes* (Carswell, March 2014) (treatment of crowdfunding in Canada, US, Netherlands & Sweden); Drache, "Crowdfunding", 23(4) *Canadian Not-for-Profit News* (Carswell) 25-27 (April 2015); Bernstein, "Crowdfunding", 23(6) *Canadian Tax Highlights* (ctf.ca) 4-5 (June 2015). Non-tax issues: Gillen & Pogorski, "Crowd-Funding Offers Under Canadian and US Securities Regulation", 93 *Canadian Bar Review* 107-81 (2015). If the employer contributes, see 6(1)(a) Notes under "Crowdfunding".

Cryptocurrency such as Bitcoin: see CRA *Guide for cryptocurrency users*, tinyurl.com/cra-crypto. CRA considers it to be property, not money, and subject to barter transaction rules (see "Barter" above), and discusses capital vs inventory (see Notes to 54"capital property"). Bitcoin *mining* may be business income, and the inventory valuation rules in s. 10 may apply. See also VIEWS docs 2013-051470117, 2014-0525191E5; 2018-0776661I7 (Bitcoin mining revenue valued using the value of the Bitcoin received); Fournier & Lennard, "Rebooting Money", 2014 Cdn Tax Foundation conference report, 11:1-27; Alatopulos & Scholl, "Bitcoins and Blockchains", *Taxnet Pro* Tax Disputes Centre (Nov. 2017, 13pp); Donnelly, "A Guide to Cryptocurrencies and Tax", 2395 *Tax Topics* (CCH) 1-3 (Feb. 1, 2018); Arnould & Kirby, "Taxation of Cryptocurrencies & Tokens", 11(2) *Taxes & Wealth Management* (Carswell) 6-8 (March 2018), 11(3) 4-6 (Oct.) and 11(4) 9-13 (Nov. 2018); Gibney & Walker, "Canadian Taxation of Cryptocurrency", VII(1) *Personal Tax & Estate Planning* (Federated Press) 2-7 (2018); Chan, "Tax Implications of Cryptocurrencies", The Tax Advocate, *Taxnet Pro* Tax Disputes Centre (Nov. 2018, 10pp); Dueck & Allan, "Taxation of the Token Economy", 2018 BC Tax Conf. 4:1-74; Oakey et al., "Decrypting the Taxation of Cryptocurrency Mining", 2018 Atlantic Provinces Tax Conf. 2:1-52; Coles, "Succession Issues Relating to Cryptocurrency", 6(16) *Tax Hyperion* (Carswell) 1-4 (Nov-Dec 2019); Raveendran & Navkar, "The Rise of Crypto Funds and the Offshore Investment Rules", 27(12) *Canadian Tax Highlights* (ctf.ca) 13-15 (Dec. 2019); Spenceley, "Cryptocurrencies", 300 *The Estate Planner* (CCH) 1-3 (Jan. 2020). The March 2019 federal Budget says CRA will be "hiring additional auditors, conducting outreach and building technical expertise to target non-compliance associated with cryptocurrency transactions and the digital economy." See also 231.2(2) Notes re CRA seeking customer data from Coinsquare. For US treatment see IRS Notice 2014-21 and "IRS Letters Warning of Cryptocurrency", tinyurl.com/gavioli-crypto (July 30, 2019). For GST/HST purposes, Finance announced on May 17, 2019 exemption of cryptocurrency transactions as financial services, by including a "virtual payment instrument" in *Excise Tax Act* 123(1)"financial instrument".

Damages are taxable if they replace an amount that would have been taxable as business income. (See also "Break fees" above.) Under the *surrogatum* principle, "the tax treatment of the item will depend on what the amount is intended to replace": *Tsiprailis*, 2005 SCC 8 [O'Brien, "Surrogatum", 54(4) *Canadian Tax Journal* 862-906 (2006)]. See also IT-365R2 paras. 8-10, IT-273R2 para. 2; *Income Tax Audit Manual* §27.3; *Pe Ben Industries*, [1988] 2 C.T.C. 120 (FCTD) (compensation for termination of distinct business was capital gain); *Canadian National Railway*, [1988] 2 C.T.C. 111 (FCTD) (compensation for future business profit was income); *Mohawk Oil*, [1992] 1 C.T.C. 195 (FCA) (compensation for loss of processing plant was part capital gain, part income); *Schwartz*, [1996] 1 C.T.C. 303 (SCC) and *Schewe*, 2010 TCC 47 (no tax on damages for breach of employment contract before it began, but see VIEWS doc 2005-0135831E5); *BP Canada*, 2002 CarswellNat 2784 (TCC) ("decontracting" settlement paid to gas producer was capital gain); *Bourgault Industries*, 2007 FCA 373 (settlement for patent infringement was taxable as compensation for lost profits); *Valley Equipment*, 2008 FCA 65 (damages for cancellation of dealer agreement were capital gain); *Gestion E.S.C.*, 2008 TCC 315 (compensation to contractor for loss of business caused by supplying wrong cement); *Santagapita*, 2008 TCC 662 (insurance proceeds covering loss of rental income); *Lavoie*, 2010 FCA 266 (payment to RRSP investor for damage caused to RRSP); *Alberta Power*, 2009 TCC 412 (government termination payment was for assets of generating plant, not for loss of future profits); *River Hills Ranch*, 2013 TCC 248 (settlement was for contract cancellation that destroyed taxpayer's business, so was on capital account); *Henco Industries*, 2014 TCC 192, paras. 149-163, 170, 203 (Ontario govt payment to developer in Caledonia whose business was destroyed by native occupation, to have developer "go away", give up its land and drop its injunction against the natives, was non-taxable); *Béliveau*, 2018 TCC 87 (disability insurance payments to dental surgeon to cover her business expenses were taxable); *Grenier*, 2016 FCA 297 (payment to farmer for use of his land for wind turbine was ⅔ taxable, ⅓ disposition of property, nil for personal injury). See also docs 2005-0139411E5, 2006-0194051E5, 2009-0322751E5, 2009-0350531I7, 2014-0520921I7 (compensation to farmer for crop loss), 2011-0399991E5, 2011-0406231E5; 2011-0429691I7 (discusses factors for determining whether settlement of lawsuit over cancellation of licence agreement is on account of capital); 2014-0523861E5, 2014-0546091I7 (determination of *surrogatum* is question of fact); 2016-0652851C6 [2016 APFF q.3] and 2017-0709051C6 [2017 APFF q.7] (payment for breach of contract to buy principal residence); and Notes to 5(1) and 6(1) re applying *surrogatum* to employment income and to employer-paid insurance benefits. *Surrogatum* should lead to tax neutrality, so damages reimbursing capital costs that were deductible under 20(1)(cc) were taxable: *Goff Construction*, 2009 FCA 60 (leave to appeal denied 2009 CarswellNat 3108 (SCC)). However, in *Tesainer*, 2009 FCA 33 (leave to appeal denied 2009 CarswellNat 3106 (SCC)), *surrogatum* did not change a settlement compensating investors in a partnership for its failure (paid by lawyers for giving wrong securities law advice) into a distribution of partnership capital. Damages for personal injury are non-taxable (see Notes to s. 3 and 248(1)"retiring allowance"), but *Mathew*, 2012 TCC 289, rejected a sham attempt to convert business income into payment for injury. See also Doody, "A New Direction for the Surrogatum Principle", 19(3) *Taxation Law* (oba.org) (July 2009); McMechan, "The Tax Treatment of Damages", in Aron, *Tax Aspects of Litigation* (Carswell looseleaf or *Taxnet Pro* Reference Centre), chap. 2. Damages paid out: see Notes to 18(1)(a).

In *Kennett v. Diarco Farms*, 2018 SKQB 179, the parties agreed to settle for $500,000 but disagreed on what the payment was for tax purposes. The Court held the character was an essential term so no settlement had been reached. In the author's view, this is incorrect because settlement terms do not bind CRA or the TCC, which will determine the tax treatment based on the Statement of Claim and other relevant facts (and may apply *surrogatum*).

Deferring income: while in principle income received can be amortized over the period it applies to, VIEWS doc 2015-0618601E5 noted that a particular payment was taxable under 56.4(2) (restrictive covenant) or 12(1)(x) (assistance). See also 12(1)(a), which requires income inclusion, though a reserve may be available under 20(1)(m); and "Matching" below.

Digital currency: see "Cryptocurrency" above.

Disbursements are either "incurred as agent for the client" or "the business's own expense, to be reimbursed". An amount incurred as agent (e.g. lawyer pays land transfer tax for client buying property) is *not* an expense of the business and should not be deducted, but passed on to the client: *2321184 Ontario*, 2020 TCC 52, para. 37(e). An amount *not* incurred as agent (e.g., travel cost, or expert report to be used by a lawyer) is a deductible expense of the business, and reimbursement is income to the business: VIEWS doc 2014-0535591E5. This applies not only to professionals such as lawyers, but also to construction: it must be clear whether a contractor is acquiring (and deducting) subtrades' services and resupplying them as part of its construction services, or is merely an agent / project manager, passing on subtrades' invoices to be reimbursed by the owner and not itself deducting the costs (e.g., *Anand*, 2019 TCC 119). For GST/HST, an expense incurred as agent maintains its status (e.g., an exempt government fee) when reimbursed, while a business expense takes on the same status as the business's fees charged to the client (including zero-rated in most cases if the client is non-resident): CRA Policy P-209R; *Libra Transport*, 2002 FCA 347; *Merchant Law*, 2010 FCA 206 (leave to appeal denied [2011] G.S.T.C. 57 (SCC)).

Discontinuing business: see 18(1)(a) Notes under "Wind-down".

Diverting income, and illegal actions being valid for tax purposes: CRA's view is that an individual who is legally or contractually prohibited from incorporating cannot transfer business income to a corporation for tax purposes in violation of the prohibition. In the author's view this is wrong, since tax applies based on what the taxpayer *did*, not on what was legally allowed (see "Criminal activity" above). An *illegal* action is not *void* and has still happened. See *Campbell*, [1980] C.T.C. 319 (SCC) (fees diverted by surgeon to private hospital that was not legally entitled to practise medicine); *Cooper*, 1988 CarswellNat 478 (FCTD), para. 61 (tax on loan from trust determined without regard to whether it was taken legally); *Continental Bank*, [1998] 4 C.T.C. 119 (SCC), para. 118 ("public policy requires that breaches of the *Bank Act* should not lead to the invalidation of contracts and other transactions"); *Mennillo v. Intramodal*, 2016 SCC 51, para. 74 ("Even if the transfer was subject to nullity, it did not mean that it was inexistent"); *Wallsten*, [2001] 1 C.T.C. 2847 (TCC) (agreement between W and his corp violated W's contracts but did not affect tax liability); *Johnson v. Lazzarino* (1999), 43 O.R. (3d) 253 (Ont CA) (CA could validly sue under a contract for a contingency fee prohibited by his professional institute); *Unit Construction v. Bullock*, [1959] 3 All E.R. 831 (HL) at 834 ("It does not in any way alter their character that ... they are irregular or unauthorized or unlawful. The business is not the less managed in London because it ought to be managed in Kenya"); *Richter & Associates*, 2005 TCC 92, para. 34 (legal prohibition against bankruptcy trustee engaging in business did not affect GST status: "the Act is not to be applied to transactions that ought to have taken place, nor is it to be applied only to transactions that could be legally carried out... the Act ought to be applied to what has actually taken place"); *Angels of Flight*, 2009 TCC 279 (AF provided GST-exempt "ambulance services" even though it was not licensed by province to do so); *Durocher*, 2015 TCC 297 (aff'd on other grounds 2016 FCA 299) (illegal option to acquire control of corp triggered 251(5)(b)); *Groupe PPP*, 2017 TCC 2, paras. 35-54 (non-insurer sold insurance policies under Quebec law); *Parthiban*, 2017 TCC 30 (P's primary place of residence was in Canada even though he was on visitor visa); *Enriquez*, 2019 TCC 114 (illegally employed workers entitled to EI); *Lohas Farm*, 2019 TCC 197, paras. 113-129 (purchases of iPhones for resale, in violation of Apple policy, were not void). However, in Quebec, *Civil Code* art. 1413 nullifies a contract to perform illegal acts, e.g. *Raposo*, 2019 FCA 208. CRA did not appeal *Wallsten* but will not follow it: *Income Tax Technical News* 22; VIEWS docs 2003-0028805, 2004-0080701E5, 2006-0176531I7, 2009-0314661E5, 2011-0423361E5, 2017-0693761E5. Some cases contradict this principle, wrongly in the author's view (though some also lacked evidence the income was properly diverted): *Trudel-Leblanc*, 2004 FCA 115 (pharmacist's income was not company's income because *Pharmacy Act* prohibited it from selling drugs); *Hedges*, 2016 FCA 19 (leave to appeal denied [2016] G.S.T.C. 61) (alleged illegality of marijuana sales meant they were not zero-rated for GST); *Morriset*, 2006 TCC 483 (chiropractor could not divert income to company because *Chiropractic Act* did not let him share fees with non-member); *Dion*, 2012 TCC 6 (income from second truck was not company's because it had licence for only one truck); *McLeod*, 2017 TCC 192 (corp's alleged "management fee" was really individual's proceeds of share sale); *All Nations Supermarket*, 2019 TCC 10, para. 26 (worker with no work permit could not be employee). Where there is no legal prohibition, income can be diverted if the documentation is done right: *Grupp*, [1999] 4 C.T.C. 2022 (TCC) (teacher could have contracted for his corp to provide services to school, but he contracted personally); *Boutilier*, 2007 TCC 96, para. 17 (financial planner failed in transferring trailer fees to company because he transferred only the fees: "it would be possible to transfer an opportunity to service clients and earn trailer fees, but that is not what happened here"); *Langille*, 2009 TCC 398 (insurance agent's intention to have commissions earned by company failed, as they were received before incorporation); *Welch*, 2011 FCA 330 (lawyer's attempt to divert income to company failed through lack of documentation); *Mason*, 2016 FCA 15 (leave to appeal denied 2016 CarswellNat 2621 (SCC)) (accountant's income was earned by him, not by corporations and purported trusts). Income can be diverted via an undisclosed agency agreement: *Lussier*, [1999] 3 C.T.C. 2213 (TCC) (psychologist provided psychoanalysis to patients without telling them this was being done by his company); *Hooke*, [1995] 2 C.T.C. 2705 (TCC) (lecturer claimed his fees from a university were earned by his wife's corp under an agency arrangement; this failed only due to lack of documentation); *David*, 2016 TCC 79 (D's income from pyramid scheme was earned through his corp); *Andre Lamy Medicine*, 2020 TCC 61, paras. 14, 53. (For more on undisclosed agency, see *Ziner Lumber v. Kotov*, 2000 CanLII 16894 (Ont CA).) A lawyer does not transfer property by giving his corp the "right to invoice" for his services: *Aitchison Prof. Corp.*, 2018 TCC 131.

If existing rights are transferred to a corp (like *Boutilier* above), CRA may apply 56(2) or 56(4) to attribute income back to the taxpayer: 2007-0238221E5; such a transfer attempt failed in Australia in *Howard*, [2014] HCA 21 (High Ct); similarly, employees could not divert bonuses to a trust in *Murray Group*, [2015] CSIH 77 (Scotland Court of Session). Where business income is shared with a spouse, 74.1 attribution does not apply but the spouses may be partnership (see 96(1) Notes) or 56(2) may apply. See also 56(2) and (4) Notes, IT-189R2, and "Agency" above. Human parent P can divert income by paying P's company to care for P's child and claiming a 63(1) deduction: 2011-0417371E5.

Dividends are not deductible to the payor but are paid out of after-tax profits: *Struck*, 2017 TCC 94, para. 106.

Documentation lacking: see "Cash expenses" above.

Employee benefits are generally deductible to the employer whether or not the benefit is taxable under 6(1)(a): VIEWS docs 2011-0399661E5 (manufacturer rebates); 2011-0425571E5 (CCA on house occupied by employee, but not if *qua* shareholder); 2012-0466891E5 (non-cash gifts and awards that are not taxable to the employee); 2015-0595681C6 [2015 APFF q.20].

Exchanging cheques when there are not enough funds to cover a cheque used for payment might or might not constitute payment; see Notes to 104(24).

Executors (estate trustees) may have business income: see Notes to 6(1)(c).

Financing leases are treated as leases (not sales): see Notes to 49(3).

Foreign exchange gains and losses: see Notes to 39(2).

Form over substance: In general, the Courts look to the legal form of a transaction rather than economic substance: *Shell Canada*, [1999] 4 C.T.C. 313 (SCC); *1524994 Ontario*, 2007 FCA 74; *Wabush Iron*, 2009 TCC 239 (FCA appeal discontinued A-242-09). However, calling a transaction something it is not does not change it; "it is the true legal relationship, not its nomenclature, that governs": *Farm Business Consultants*, [1994] 2 C.T.C. 2450 (TCC), para. 13; *Catalyst Paper*, 2015 BCCA 372, para. 46 (leave to appeal denied 2016 CanLII 20437 (SCC)). Monthly payments on a rental property are normally property income, but could be deposits toward purchase of the property if so intended: VIEWS doc 2007-0244941E5. See also Notes to 245(2).

Fundraising for a charity generates business income that can be offset by donating the funds raised to the charity: VIEWS doc 2014-0518841E5. See also "Crowdfunding" above; and Notes to 149(1)(l) re non-profit organizations.

GST or HST included in an expense is deductible if the expense is, but if the taxpayer can claim an input tax credit, rebate or bad debt credit (*Excise Tax Act* s. 231) to recover the GST/HST, that amount is deemed government assistance by 248(16) and included back in income under 12(1)(x) (in practice it is simpler not to deduct it in the first place): VIEWS docs 2004-0076561E5, 2009-0309291I7. An assessment for failing to remit GST/HST is considered non-deductible: 2011-0400561I7. Interest and penalty on a GST/HST assessment are non-deductible except in respect of pre-April 2007 periods: 18(1)(t), 67.6.

Gambling was held to be a business in *Luprypa*, [1997] 3 C.T.C. 2363 (TCC) (pool playing done in professional manner, including playing only drunk opponents). Gambling was not a business in: *Leblanc*, 2006 TCC 680 ($50 million spent on sports lotteries over 4 years for $55 million in winnings was merely compulsive gambling with no "system"); *Cohen*, 2011 TCC 262 (poker playing not done in businesslike way); *Tarascio*, 2012 FCA 30 (no systematic method); *Radonjic*, 2013 FC 916 (online poker: CRA refusal to open past years to delete reported winnings was unreasonable); *Hakki*, [2014] EWCA Civ 530 (England) (poker player). For software that assists in the determination, see Windfall Classifier at bluejlegal.com. See also Income Tax Folio S3-F9-C1 ¶1.12-1.15; *Income Tax Technical News* 41; CRA Roundtable q.7, 2008 Cdn Tax Foundation conference report at 3:6-7; VIEWS docs 1999-0009745, 2007-0238601E5, 2009-0337281E5, 2010-0377321E5, 2010-0379181E5, 2012-0432251E5, 2013-0512371E5; Alarie, "The Taxation of Winnings from Poker and Other Gambling Activities", 59(4) *Canadian Tax Journal* 731-63 (2011); Woolley, "Income from a Business or Property", 2014 conference report at 6:32-49. A casino worker's tips from patrons' winnings are taxable: *Xia*, 2020 FCA 35. The US taxes gross gambling winnings of non-US persons whether or not there is a business; but for Canadian residents, US withholding tax applies to net winnings (net of gambling losses): Canada-US Tax Treaty Art. XXII:3; VIEWS doc 9730188.

General vs specific: if a provision specifically applies to a type of income but does not tax it, the general rule in 9(1) will not tax it: *Foulds*, 1997 CarswellNat 43 (TCC) (prize for achievement taxable only under 56(1)(n)). See also Notes to 6(1)(a), at "Where a specific rule...".

Guaranteed payments from Ontario Hydro under a power purchase agreement, required even when a flood prevented delivery of power, were loan repayment and not income in *1200757 Ontario Ltd.*, 2011 CarswellOnt 9218 (Ont. SCJ).

Health care plan premiums deduction for individuals: see 20.01.

Hedges can generally not be used to claim a loss in one year and defer the profit to the next: 18(17)-(23) (since 2017) (these rules do not apply to capital property: 18(18)(c)). Hedge accounting could not offset foreign currency gains and losses even though it complied with GAAP: *Saskferco Products*, 2008 FCA 297 (this seems hard to reconcile with *Kruger*, under "Cash-based accounting" above). In *MacDonald*, 2020 SCC 6, M had a loss on a forward contract on BNS shares, done to help secure a loan when he owned shares in BNS used as security for the loan. The forward contract was held to be a hedge, not speculation; since the BNS shares were capital property the loss was a capital loss (confirming *George Weston Ltd.*, 2015 TCC 42). Whether there is a hedge is determined objectively, based on the linkage between the derivative and the underlying asset: *MacDonald*, para. 22. See also Biringer & Sheridan, "MacDonald", XXIII(1) *Corporate Finance* (Federated Press) 14-21 (2020); Ross, "Macdonald — SCC establishes effects-based test for hedging", tinyurl.com/ross-mcd. See also 39(2) Notes re foreign-currency hedging; and (pre-*Macdonald*) Johnston & Taylor, "Taxation of Hedges and Derivatives", 2016 Cdn Tax Foundation conference report, 13:1-36.

Home boarding is a business if there is "an element of income or profit": VIEWS doc 2008-0277621E5.

Independent contractor (income under 9(1)) vs. employee (income under ss. 5-7): see Notes to 248(1)"employee".

Inducement payments: see 12(1)(x) and *Income Tax Audit Manual* §27.9. Lease inducements: see under "Leasing" below.

Insurance agents' commissions are taxable, even if not yet earned (12(1)(a)), and no reserve is available: 32(1). See also Notes to 6(1)(a) under this heading.

Insurance premiums for overhead expenses are deductible per IT-223 even though it has been archived [and cancelled Sept. 30/12]: VIEWS docs 2009-0337691E5, 2010-0378521C6.

Interest expenses: see Notes to 20(1)(c).

Interest rate swaps are considered to be on income account: VIEWS doc 2003-0030597; but only where the income or loss is realized: 2009-0336671I7.

Internet sales (web-based sales) by a corporation must be specifically reported on T2 Schedule 88: Paul Hickey, "CRA Expands Reporting of Internet Information", 22(1) *Canadian Tax Highlights* (ctf.ca) 10-11 (Jan. 2014).

Inventory and work in progress: see Notes to 10(1).

Investment income is normally based on what is reported on a T5 slip (Reg. 201), unless the taxpayer can show the income was not earned: *Schmidt*, 2012 CarswellNat 1305 (TCC, under appeal to FCA). See also "Business income vs. property income" above.

Leasing or rent prepayments and premiums received: see IT-261R, IT-359R2 and VIEWS docs 2011-0398711E5, 2012-0462781E5. Payments under a lease with option to purchase must be allocated between the two components: 2010-0370561E5. Lease inducement payments were deductible in *Canderel*, [1998] 2 C.T.C. 35 (SCC) and *Toronto College Park*, [1998] 2 C.T.C. 78 (SCC); non-deductible capital expenses (see 18(1)(b)) in *Motter*, 2021 QCCA 72 (even though reimbursement by tenant was apparently included in income); and see Woolley, "Income from a Business or Property", 2014 Cdn Tax Foundation conference report at 6:2-7. Leasing commission costs reimbursed to landlord: 2011-0430901E5. Lease monetization using a trust and a "concurrent lease": see 2009-0329491R3, 2009-0351741R3, 2010-0356241R3. Lease cancellation payments paid by a tenant to a landlord are normally fully deductible and taxable: IT-359R2; *Monart Corp.*, [1967] C.T.C. 263 (Ex. Ct.); *R. Reusse Construction*, [1999] 2 C.T.C. 2928 (TCC); *Spezzano (Bueti)*, 2007 FCA 294 (taxable under *Tsiaprailis*). Such payments by a landlord to a tenant must be amortized over the remaining term of the cancelled lease (max 40 years): 18(1)(q), 20(1)(z), (z.1); and may be proceeds of disposition to the tenant (leading to recapture, capital gain and/or terminal loss) or may be taxed under 12(1)(x); see IT-359R2 and *Westfair Foods*, [1991] 2 C.T.C. 343 (FCA), and docs 2006-0196281C6, 2012-0436781E5, 2014-0519401E5 (says apply the *surrogatum* principle). A sublease for the entire lease term is a disposition: *Sussex Square*, [1999] 2 C.T.C. 2143 (TCC), paras. 31-32 (aff'd without discussing this point [2000] 4 C.T.C. 203 (FCA)). Rental payments by an employer to an employee for the use of the employee's vehicle or tools are considered employment income, not rental income: 2012-0442231E5. An owner can normally deduct expenses even while the property is vacant: 2013-0475101E5 (but see 18(2)–(3.3) while property is under construction).

Legal fees: see Notes to 18(1)(a), 18(1)(b), 18(1)(h), 56(1)(b) and 60(o).

Life insurance premiums on a key employee may be deductible: see 20(1)(e.2).

Loan securitization proceeds: see VIEWS doc 2007-0259241E5.

Matching principle: See the "matchable expenditure" rules in 18.1. In *Ferro*, [2003] 2 C.T.C. 2461 (TCC), a litigation lawyer working on contingency could deduct expenses of conducting personal-injury litigation even though the "matching" revenues came years later. In *Glueckler Metal*, 2003 TCC 256, a voluntary payment to Glueckler's parent, to adjust for past years' management services and interest, was deductible in the year paid despite the matching principle. In *GMAC Leaseco*, 2015 TCC 146, residual value support payments from GM, to compensate for lower income due to higher residual values on leases, were taxable only at end of lease when GMAC had the right to keep the money; and provincial capital tax was deductible in the year it was payable, even when it arose from an adjustment made years later. Costs of finding a tenant are deductible even though the matching revenues come later: 2011-0424461E5. Expenses cannot normally be postponed to a later year: 2005-0139681E5. See also 2014-0538111C6 [2014 APFF q.13] (general comments); Arnold et al., *Timing and Income Taxation* (ctf.ca, 2nd ed., 2015, 696pp); Frankovic, "Capitalization", 2473 *Tax Topics* (CCH) 1-3 (Aug. 1, 2019); and "Contingent income" above.

Meals and entertainment: see 67.1, and note that the simplified meals calculation discussed under 8(1)(g) cannot be used by self-employed persons (VIEWS docs 2011-0392521E5, 2011-0392961E5).

Morality is not relevant to expense deductibility: see "Criminal activity" above.

Oil and gas expenses: see 66-66.8 including 66.1(6)"Canadian exploration expense". For surface lease bonus payments, see VIEWS doc 2009-0345121E5.

Payment by cheque where there is not enough in the account to cover the cheque: see "Exchanging cheques" above.

Penalties and fines are non-deductible: see 67.6, overruling *65302 British Columbia Ltd. (Veekans Poultry) ["BC Eggs"]*, [2000] 1 C.T.C. 57 (SCC). Penalties and fines imposed under the ITA have always been non-deductible: 18(1)(t). A GST/HST assessment, including pre-April 1997 penalty and interest, is normally deductible: VIEWS doc 2003-0036237, Reg. 7309, 18(1)(t). Proceeds of crime forfeited to the Crown: see Notes to 67.6.

Political contributions cannot be deducted: 18(1)(n); but may create a credit: 127(3).

Ponzi scheme income tax treatment: see under "Criminal activity" above.

Pre-incorporation expenses: see Notes to 248(1)"corporation".

Prizes to franchisees paid by the franchisor are likely taxable: doc 2011-0425361E5. Prizes won in lotteries (including by lottery ticket sellers): see Notes to 40(2)(f).

Property income: see "Business income vs. property income" above.

Provincial taxes and WCB premiums, whether deductible: see Notes to 18(1)(t).

"Reasonable expectation of profit" is no longer the test to determine whether there is a business: see Notes to 9(2).

Rebates: Pharmacists' rebates from drug companies are taxable: *Chalati*, 2011 FCA 180; *Mikhail*, 2019 TCC 49; *Quraishi*, 2019 TCC 272. Commission kickbacks from a realtor to a purchaser of rental condos were taxable in *Zhang*, 2020 TCC 49, para. 32. See also 12(1)(x).

Referral fees, under an agreement whereby a house purchaser receives part of a real estate agent's commission, are taxable to the purchaser but will normally be taxed under 56(2) to the agent instead: VIEWS doc 2013-0488011E5. Doc 2007-0224771E5 suggests fees for occasional referrals to a construction company are non-taxable.

Reimbursements of expenses: see "Disbursements" above, and 12(1)(x).

Rentals: see "Leasing" above.

Safety deposit box costs are disallowed since 2014. See 18(1)(l.1).

Services donated by a business for promotion are not a deduction: see 18(1)(a) Notes.

Settlement payments: see "Damages" above.

Shutdown costs: see 18(1)(a) Notes under "Wind-down costs".

Solar panels on a homeowner's roof, feeding electricity into the grid under Ontario's microFIT program, are considered to generate taxable rental income: VIEWS docs 2008-0275351E5, 2008-0287671E5, 2010-0353421E5, 2009-0343881E5, 2013-0501131R5; Drache, "Tax Ruling Hits Solar Initiative", xxxi(10) *The Canadian Taxpayer* (Carswell) 76-78 (May 12, 2009). A Net Metering Program credit is taxable only to a business: 2017-0685341E5, 2019-0828841E5. Where advance payments are made for panels that are never delivered, CRA says the resulting loss is a capital loss (possibly an ABIL): 2015-0572221E5.

Startup costs: Preparatory work aimed at starting a business, even if it fails, may constitute carrying on business: *Harquail (Hudon)*, 2001 FCA 320, para. 62; *Caballero*, 2009 TCC 390, para. 6. When does a business begin? See IT-364, VIEWS doc 2010-0379141E5; *Gartry*, [1994] 2 C.T.C. 2021 (TCC); *Kaye*, [1998] 3 C.T.C. 2248 (TCC); *Spasic*, 2009 TCC 193; *Wescast Industries*, 2010 TCC 538 (FCA appeal discontinued A-452-10); *Standard Life*, 2015 TCC 97, paras. 81-88, 97-156 (aff'd on other grounds as *SCDA*, 2017 FCA 177). See also 18(1)(b) Notes at "Business or project startup".

Straddle transactions crossing a year-end to defer tax: see "Hedges" above.

Surrogatum principle: see under "Damages" above.

Swap agreement payments are deductible or included in income: 2020 IFA Roundtable q.2.

Termination payments to employees are normally deductible (for taxability to the employee see Notes to 248(1)"retiring allowance"), but if the employee is surrendering shares in the company, amounts paid to redeem those shares are not deductible: *RNC Média*, 2011 TCC 92.

Theft losses are usually allowed as an inherent risk of business, unless stolen by an owner or senior employee: Income Tax Folio S3-F9-C1 ¶1.33-1.41.

Timing of income: see "Cash-based accounting" and "Matching principle" above and the beginning of these Notes.

Trust income calculation including deduction of trustee or executor fees: see VIEWS doc 2008-0278801C6 q.3.

Undocumented expenses: see "Cash expenses" above.

Vehicle expenses: see Notes to 18(1)(h).

Wind-down costs: see Notes to 18(1)(a) under "Wind-down".

Workers' Compensation premiums paid by a self-employed individual are deductible as laid out for the purpose of earning income: VIEWS doc 2001-0083897.

Where a corporation's charter is cancelled but the business continues, the owners may be carrying on the business as partners. See Notes to 88(2).

On the effect on regulated utility charges of changing past years' income tax profit calculations, see *ATCO Gas*, 2009 CarswellAlta 1870 (Alta. Utilities Commission).

CRA's view is that travel expenses for *investment* purposes cannot be deducted because 18(1)(h) permits them only for *business*: VIEWS doc 2009-0324901E5 (but see Notes to 18(1)(h)).

See also Notes to 18(1)(a) (deductible expenses) and (b) (capital expenses); Woolley, "Income from a Business or Property", 2014 CTF conference report, 6:1-73.

Income Tax Folios: S1-F2-C3: Scholarships, research grants and other education assistance [replaces IT-340R]; S3-F6-C1: Interest deductibility [replaces IT-533]; S3-F9-C1: Lottery winnings, miscellaneous receipts, and income (and losses) from crime [replaces IT-185R, IT-213R, IT-256R, IT-334R2]; S4-F2-C1: Deductibility of fines and penalties [replaces IT-104R3]; S4-F11-C1: Meaning of farming and farming business [replaces IT-373R2]; S4-F14-C1: Artists and writers [replaces IT-504R2].

Interpretation Bulletins: IT-92R2: Income of contractors; IT-95R: Foreign exchange gains and losses; IT-99R5: Legal and accounting fees; IT-102R2: Conversion of property, other than real property, from or to inventory; IT-129R: Lawyers' trust accounts and disbursements; IT-200: Surface rentals and farming operations; IT-216: Corporation holding property as agent for shareholder (cancelled); IT-218R: Profit, capital gains and losses from the sale of real estate, including farmland and inherited land and conversion of real estate from capital property to inventory and vice versa; IT-223: Overhead expense insurance vs. income insurance (cancelled); IT-233R: Lease-option agreements; sale-leaseback agreements (cancelled); IT-257R: Canada Council grants; IT-261R: Prepayment of rents; IT-273R2: Government assistance — general comments; IT-293R: Debtor's gain on settlement of debt; IT-297R2: Gifts in kind to charity and others; IT-314: Income of dealers in oil and gas leases (cancelled); IT-346R: Commodity futures and certain commodities; IT-359R2: Premiums and other amounts re leases; IT-365R2: Damages, settlements and similar receipts; IT-403R: Options on real estate; IT-404R: Payments to lottery ticket vendors; IT-417R2: Prepaid expenses and deferred charges; IT-423: Sale of sand, gravel or topsoil (cancelled); IT-425: Miscellaneous farm income; IT-434R: Rental of real property by individual; IT-446R: Legacies; IT-454: Business transactions prior to incorporation; IT-459: Adventure or concern in the nature of trade; IT-461: Forfeited deposits (cancelled); IT-479R: Transactions in securities; IT-490: Barter transactions; IT-493: Agency cooperative corporations (cancelled); IT-504R2: Visual artists and writers.

Information Circulars: 77-11: Sales tax reassessments — deductibility in computing income.

I.T. Technical News: 1 (sales commission expenses of mutual-fund limited partnerships); 5 (lease agreements); 8 (proceeds of sale of a condominium — first closing date or second closing date; treatment of United States unitary state taxes); 12 ("millennium bug" expenditures); 16 (*Canderel*, *Toronto College Park* and *Ikea* cases; *Continental Bank* case); 21 (cancellation of Interpretation Bulletin IT-233R); 22 (commission income transferred to corporation); 25 (reasonable expectation of profit); 30 (prepaid income — whether 9(1) or 12(1)(a) applies); 34 (emission reduction and offset credits); 38 (criteria for determining hedge effectiveness for tax purposes); 39 (settlement of a shareholder class action suit); 41 (meaning of "business" — gambling; conversion from Canadian GAAP to IFRS); 42 (International Financial Reporting Standards); 44 (IFRS and foreign GAAP).

Registered Charities Newsletters: 18 (can businesses receive receipts for donations made out of their inventory?).

Info Sheets: TI-001: Sale of a residence by an owner builder.

Application Policies: SR&ED 2004-02R5: Filing requirements for claiming SR&ED; SR&ED 2004-03: Prototypes, pilot plants/commercial plants, custom products and commercial assets.

CRA Audit Manual: Chapter 27.0: Income/supplies.

Advance Tax Rulings: ATR-4: Exchange of interest rates; ATR-15: Employee stock option plan; ATR-20: Redemption premium on debentures; ATR-23: Private health services plan; ATR-45: Share appreciation rights plan; ATR-50: Structured settlement; ATR-62: Mutual fund distribution limited partnership — amortization of selling commissions.

Forms: T2 Sched. 14: Miscellaneous payments to residents; T776: Statement of real estate rentals; T2042: Statement of farming activities; T2121: Statement of fishing activities; T2125: Statement of business or professional activities; T4002: Business and professional income [guide]; T4036: Rental income [guide].

(2) Loss — Subject to section 31, a taxpayer's loss for a taxation year from a business or property is the amount of the taxpayer's loss, if any, for the taxation year from that source computed by applying the provisions of this Act respecting computation of income from that source with such modifications as the circumstances require.

Related Provisions: 18 — Limitations on various deductions; 18.1 — Limitation on deduction for matchable expenditure; 96(8)(b), (c) — Business loss of partnership that previously had only non-resident partners; 103(2) — Meaning of "losses" in subsec. 103(1); 111(1)(a) — Carryover of loss to prior or later year; 111(8) — "non-capital loss"; 112(4)–(4.3) — Loss on share held as inventory.

Notes: Losses under 9(2) can be offset against other sources of income, such as employment or investment income.

Test for claiming losses: Until 2002, CRA denied business or property losses where it found no "reasonable expectation of profit" (REOP). There was extensive case law interpreting REOP. The Supreme Court of Canada ruled in *Stewart*, 2002 SCC 46 that REOP is not the test to determine whether activities are a source of income for s. 9. CRA accepts that REOP "will no longer be used to determine if there is a source of income under the Act. CRA will, however, question whether a taxpayer is operating in a sufficiently commercial manner when the activity has some personal or hobby element." Also, "If a taxpayer is motivated by tax considerations when he or she enters into a business or property venture, this will not detract from the venture's commercial nature or characterization as a source of income." See *Income Tax Technical News* 25, VIEWS docs 2010-0372461E5, 2012-0442371M4, 2017-0731171E5; 2019-0812761C6 [2019 APFF q.17] (CRA will not issue guidelines on meaning of "business"). For artists and writers see Income Tax Folio S4-F14-C1 ¶1.18-1-26.

The SCC set out a 2-stage approach to determine whether activities are a source of business or property income: (i) Is the taxpayer's activity undertaken in pursuit of profit, or a personal endeavour? (ii) If it is not a personal endeavour, is the source of the income a business or property? The first stage is relevant only if the activity has a personal or hobby element. If an activity's nature is clearly commercial, the pursuit of profit is established, and there is no need to analyze the taxpayer's business decisions. However, if the nature of the venture contains elements that suggest it may be a hobby or other personal pursuit, it will be considered a source of income only if it is undertaken in a sufficiently commercial manner. The taxpayer must have the subjective intention to profit and there must be evidence of businesslike behaviour supporting that intention. REOP is only one factor, among others, to be considered at this stage. Deductibility of expenses is a separate question from whether a business exists (s. 67 denies unreasonable expenses).

In addition, since a tax motivation does not affect the validity of transactions for tax purposes, the appellant's hope in *Stewart* of realizing an eventual capital gain and expectation of deducting interest expenses did not detract from the commercial nature of his rental operation or its characterization as a source of income.

The SCC simultaneously decided *Walls (Buvyer)*, 2002 SCC 47, along the same lines, ruling that if activities have no personal aspect, REOP is not considered: it was self-evident that a storage park operation was commercial.

For more on *Stewart* see Laiken & Laiken, "Working with the source test", 50(3) *Canadian Tax Journal* 1147-81 (2002); Nitikman, "REOP After Standard Life", 2302 *Tax Topics* (CCH) 1-6 (April 21, 2016). Note that an artistic venture is often commercial: *LeBlanc*, [2003] 4 C.T.C. 2593 (TCC). See also 18(1)(a); and "Profits from non-business" below where the activity generates a profit.

For CRA guidelines on whether a farming business is carried on in a business-like manner, see Income Tax Folio S4-F11-C1 ¶1.21.

Proposed s. 3.1 (2003) would have reintroduced a REOP requirement for claiming business or property losses, overruling *Stewart*, but was withdrawn.

REOP still applies for: 18(1)(h) (see 248(1)"personal or living expenses"(a)); the change in control rules in 111(5)(a)(i), (b)(i), 37(6.1)(b)(i), 88(1.1)(e)(i), 190.1(6)(a)(i)(A)(I), (b)(i)(A)(I); GST/HST for individuals, under *Excise Tax Act* 123(1)"commercial activity" (see *Practitioner's Goods and Services Tax Annotated*).

Business purpose test: Even if the only purpose of an activity is avoiding tax, it can still be a "business" as long as there is no personal element (due to *Stewart* and *Walls*): *Paletta*, 2021 TCC 11 (under appeal by Crown to FCA), paras. 142, 199-204 [Bélanger, "Paletta", 2560 *Tax Topics* (CCH) 2-4 (March 30, 2021)].

Capital expenses: see Notes to 18(1)(b) and 54"capital property".

Defrauded investors: losses were disallowed because there was no "business" in: *Hammill*, 2005 FCA 252 (leave to appeal denied 2006 CarswellNat 58 (SCC)) (fraudulent scheme to profit from precious gems; finding of fraud "precludes the existence of a business, regardless of any other consideration"); *Rouleau*, 2008 FCA 288 ("Cablotel" — R&D supposedly to develop system to provide cable TV in outlying areas); *Vankerk*, 2005 TCC 292 (investors in nonexistent partnerships were deceived); *Heppner*, 2007 TCC 667 and *Mattu*, 2009 TCC 605 (FCA appeal discontinued A-516-09) (Nigerian advance-fee scam); *Zakrzewski*, 2008 TCC 385 (alleged pharmaceutical export business); *Hayter*, 2010 TCC 255 (deal to buy TVs); *Swain*, 2012 TCC 46 (lawyer who advanced funds to client Discovery Biotech was apparently duped); *Ruff*, 2012 TCC 105 (Nigerian [Ivory Coast] advance-fee scam: lawyer had source of income but expenses were unreasonable); *Garber*, 2014 TCC 1 (FCA appeal discontinued A-83-14) (Overseas Credit & Guaranty Corp [Einar Bellfield] fraud re luxury yachts that were never built [see also *Belchetz (Brandimarte)*, 2020 FCA 225 re this scam]). See also Magee, "Tax Writeoffs for Investment Losses", 62(1) *Canadian Tax Journal* 221-44 (2014); Woolley, "Income from a Business or Property", 2014 Cdn Tax Foundation conference report at 6:15-25; Tonkovich, "Theft by Owners or Senior Employees", 6(1) *Canadian Tax Focus* (ctf.ca) 1-2 (Feb. 2016).

A defrauded investor was allowed losses in *Hayter*, 2010 TCC 255 (laptop deal); and a capital loss was allowed in *Simmonds*, [1997] 2 C.T.C. 2293 (TCC) (Ponzi scheme where accountant absconded with taxpayer's money).

On fraudulent investments see also VIEWS docs 2009-0317891I7, 2014-0531171M6, 2018-0752991E5, 2018-0753001E5, 2018-0753011E5, 2018-0753021E5, 2018-0753051E5, 2018-0753081E5, 2018-0776571M4, 2019-0805221E5. See also 2013-0490361E5 and Notes to 39(1) re allowing a capital loss or business investment loss; 2012-0453191C6 [2012 APFF q.21] (20(1)(p) can be used to claim bad debt deduction for past years' wrongly-reported income (Mount Real fraud), in the year the fraud is discovered, and resulting non-capital loss can be carried over to other years). Lawsuits against tax advisers and loss promoters: see Notes to 237.1(1)"tax shelter".

Farming losses: see Notes to 31(1).

Gambling: see Notes to 9(1).

Hallmarks of business: Losses were disallowed as not having these in: *Alsaadi*, 2007 TCC 384 (buying goods at Wal-Mart and allegedly selling them at home parties); *Coome*, 2007 TCC 493 (FCA appeal discontinued A-414-07) (real estate agent); *Madell*, 2009 FCA 193 (also *Caputo*, 2008 TCC 263, *Falkenberg*, 2008 TCC 265, and *Storwick*, 2008 TCC 268 — FCA appeals discontinued) (tax shelter claiming to market customer loyalty discount cards); *Lubega-Matovu*, 2011 FCA 265 (business ventures with "lack of commerciality") and 2015 TCC 147 (same ventures, later years); *Palangio*, 2013 FCA 268 (writing columns for local newspaper was part of town councillor's political activities); *Malin*, 2007 TCC 516 (plans for various activities); *Foster (Atherton)*, 2007 TCC 659 (purported SR&ED partnership); *Olver*, 2008 TCC 352 (Internet multi-level marketing); *Thompson*, 2008 TCC 392 (network marketing sales, gardening); *Spasic*, 2009 TCC 193 (part-time inventor trying to develop transducer for sonic imaging device); *Payette*, 2009 TCC 348 (attempt to patent spacecraft propulsion system); *Rocheleau*, 2009 TCC 484 (licence for lottery terminals in Russia); *Binning*, 2009 TCC 487 (producing music albums); *Morgan*, 2009 TCC 552 (daycare at home); *Opacic*, 2010 TCC 74 (rental properties in Bosnia and Serbia); *Sinclair*, 2010 TCC 418 (playwright); *Hourie*, 2010 TCC 525 (FCA appeal dismissed for delay A-223-11) (snowmobile tourism); *Bertucci*, 2010 TCC 597 (opera-singer management services); *Bangura*, 2010 TCC 551 (moving and delivery); *Dickson*, 2011 TCC 153 (flight instruction, church organist and book writing); *Robert*, 2011 TCC 166 (bizarre creation of fictitious corporation); *Cohen*, 2011 TCC 262 (poker playing); *Roy*, 2011 TCC 299 (yacht chartering); *Walsh*, 2011 TCC 341 (researching technology to start a business); *Kuhlmann*, 2011 TCC 410 (looking for work); *Sumner*, 2011 TCC 484 (excavation and clearing); *Tcheng*, 2013 TCC 196 (sales of beauty products); *Longo*, 2013 TCC 213 (consulting); *Turner*, 2016 TCC 77 (FCA appeal discontinued A-124-16) ("trading" in securities consisted of buying more and more of one stock); *Pakzad*, 2016 TCC 144 (real estate consulting and personal fitness training; see also 2017 TCC 83: P sought publication ban because the reasons "portrayed him as an incompetent businessman"); *Fil*, 2016 TCC 200 (buying and selling jewellery and watches); *Peckitt*, 2017 TCC 60 (financial consulting); *Renaud*, 2019 FCA 154 (professor's part-time law practice with no attempt to make a profit was personal, not commercial); *Barbour*, 2018 TCC 77 (producing artistic video); *Free*, 2018 TCC 238 (alleged engineering services); *Tremblay*, 2020 TCC 100 (marketing sewage treatment technology: business had not yet begun). See also Notes to Reg. Sch. II:Cl. 12 re disallowed software investments.

Losses were allowed as having hallmarks of business in: *Kaegi*, 2008 TCC 566 (music recording, 9 years of losses); *Malltezi*, 2009 TCC 149 (glass cleaning machine); *Ngai*, 2009 TCC 370 (importing Chinese furniture for resale); *Caballero*, 2009 TCC 390 (mobile massage therapy buses); *Ollivierre*, 2009 TCC 490 (festival programming); *Tri-O-cycles Concept.*, 2009 TCC 632 (adult tricycle development); *Newell*, 2010 TCC 196 (gold mining); *Perreault*, 2011 TCC 270 ("Advantage Conference" multi-level marketing, recruiting evangelical Christians for "financial success through biblical business principles"); *Beauregard*, 2013 TCC 287 (intention to build and rent medical office building, frustrated by lack of financing); *Drouin*, 2013 TCC 139 (Prospector Networks software franchise); *Michaud*, 2014 TCC 83 (gold prospecting); *Berger*, 2015 TCC 153 (experienced sportswriter travelled with the Leafs and wrote blog at a loss, hoping for sponsors); *Okafor*, 2018 TCC 31, para. 35 (but most expenses disallowed as unproven); *Callaghan*, 2020 TCC 28 (food recipe business); *Larkin*, 2020 TCC 98 (geologist's speculative work on graphene, mining, oil sands, water separation; having no revenue is not determinative (para. 35)). In *Malo*, 2012 TCC 75 (FCA appeal discontinued A-98-12), a tree-planting investment (Maya) was a business but losses were disallowed because the taxpayer did not file a tax-shelter form (see 237.1(6)) and the expenses were for inventory (see Notes to 10(1)).

Hobby or personal activity: losses were disallowed in: *Lang*, 2008 FCA 29 (war veteran collected and sold military artifacts); *Palangio*, 2013 FCA 268 (tool rentals to friends); *Salloum*, 2016 FCA 85 (amateur mechanic); *Weaver*, 2019 QCCA 1687 (daughters' equestrian riding); *Harrison*, 2007 TCC 19 (book writing); *Dean*, 2007 TCC 257 (condo in Whistler); *Brooks*, 2007 TCC 557 (buying memorabilia on eBay); *Dreaver*, 2008 TCC 39 (environmental scientist writing books on the environment); *Clancy*, 2008 TCC 518 (6 "businesses", based on World Network Business Club suggestions); *Neilson*, 2008 TCC 512 (race car); *Graham*, 2009 TCC 580 (musical performer); *Grau*, 2009 TCC 60 (sailboat chartering); *Cudjoe*, 2009 TCC 550 (recording studio); *Sokil*, 2009 TCC 601 (web-based "Fun For Life" vacation marketing); *Tiede*, 2011 TCC 84 (photography); *Skaling*, 2011 TCC 180 (drag racing); *Bouchard*, 2013 TCC 247 (investment in Eugénie Bouchard's tennis career by her father in hope she would pay profits once she turned pro); *Bui*, 2013 TCC 326 (administration of father's estate); *Syed*, 2013 TCC 403 (buying and repairing damaged vehicles); *Leith*, 2015 TCC 314 (farming); *Soheili*, 2017 TCC 172 (home sold at a loss was intended to be personal home); *Beil*, 2017 TCC 136 (caring for son after he was injured by police); *Savage*, 2017 TCC 247 (dog kennel); *Hurwitz*, 2020 TCC 31 (photography, and playing in string quartet); *Brown*, 2020 TCC 123 (under appeal to FCA) (lawyer managing wife's money-losing art gallery for free). See also Wen, "Business or Hobby?", 18(2) *Tax for the Owner-Manager* (ctf.ca) 10-11 (April 2018); Drache, "Fighting the Same Battle Again", xl(11) *The Canadian Taxpayer* 84-85 (June 1, 2018) (re CBC report: sculptor Steve Higgins denied losses, CRA saying his work was hobby).

Inventory losses may be denied because the costs are deductible only against sales (see Notes to 10(1)): *Malo*, 2012 TCC 75, para. 26 (FCA appeal discontinued A-98-12).

Investment opportunities: losses from efforts to "commercialize innovation" might have been allowed, but were denied because the expenses were capital (18(1)(b)): *Robinson*, 2019 TCC 181.

Lawyers: being an *employed* lawyer is not a business, so continuing legal education costs and professional membership fees were disallowed in *Jamieson*, 2013 TCC 52 (but see 8(1)(i)(i)).

Personal expenses: see "Hobby" above, and Notes to 18(1)(h).

Purpose of expenses: see Notes to 18(1)(a).

Reasonability of expenses: See Notes to s. 67.

Residential rents: losses were disallowed in: *Daoust*, 2011 FCA 67 (cottage was really for personal use); *Peach*, 2016 FCA 173 and 2020 TCC 12 (renting to sons below market, no pursuit of profit); *Ziu*, 2009 TCC 147; *Rapuano*, 2009 TCC 150 (family arrangement not intended for profit); *Grégoire*, 2009 TCC 251 (FCA appeal dismissed for delay A-161-09) (evidence inadequate); *Landriault*, 2009 TCC 378 (rentals to family members for less than FMV); *LeCaine*, 2009 TCC 382 (rental to family members for less than FMV); *Burnett*, 2009 TCC 430 (short-term rental of parts of home while travelling was not business-like); *Bourdages*, 2009 TCC 543 (condo in ski area partly used personally; *Emond*, 2011 TCC 142 (FCA appeal dismissed for delay A-163-11) (rental of inn to E's company was not in commercial manner); *Hanna*, 2011 TCC 382 (property used to house refugees); *Leisser*, 2011 TCC 472 (rental to daughter); *Clarke*, 2011 TCC 548 (documentation re basement rentals lacking); *Manning*, 2013 TCC 51 (rental to son "not in accordance with objective standards of businesslike behaviour"); *Tcheng*, 2013 TCC 196 (no effort made to rent out condo); *Bradshaw*, 2013 TCC 244 (purported rental of home was personal use); *Virani*, 2014 TCC 195 (appellant not credible); *Bobic*, 2017 TCC 107, para. 46 (evidence of rental disbelieved); *Hustak*, 2018 TCC 199 (7 years of losses, charging well below market rent).

Rental losses were allowed in *Morris*, 2014 TCC 142 (accountants undertook repairs and renovations so they could rent out former home); *Crockett*, 2019 TCC 203 (vacation home: intention was to earn a profit). Some rental losses were allowed in: *LeCaine* (above); *Preiss*, 2009 TCC 488; *MacIntyre*, 2010 TCC 277; *Kelly*, 2012 TCC 66 (condo at ski resort); *Okafor*, 2018 TCC 31. See also VIEWS docs 2006-0171131E5 (no income where no intention to profit); 2009-0327161E5 (allocation of losses among co-owners in Quebec).

Second-guessing business decisions should not be done by CRA or the Courts: *Stewart*, 2002 SCC 46, para. 55; *Corbett*, [1997] 1 C.T.C. 2 (FCA) at 12; *Mastri*, [1997] 3 C.T.C 234 (FCA), para. 12; *Tonn*, [1996] 1 C.T.C. 205 (FCA), para. 61; *Keeping*, 2001 FCA 182; *Nichol*, [1993] 2 C.T.C. 2906 (TCC) at 2910; *Green*, [1997] 1 C.T.C. 2668 (TCC) at 2672; *Jolly Farmer Products*, 2008 TCC 409, para. 24; *Bilous (Yorkton Distributors)*, 2011 TCC 154, para. 60; *Kelly*, 2012 TCC 66, paras. 7-8; *Drouin*, 2013 TCC 139, para. 260; *Kyard*, 2019 QCCQ 1617, para. 35; *Wise*, 2019 TCC 196, para. 61.

Spouses' expenses were disallowed in: *Cook*, 2008 TCC 458 (C's husband's election campaign expenses); *Claeys*, 2010 TCC 586 (loan to wife for her business did not entitle C to deduct her expenses).

Startup work for a business: see Notes to 9(1) under "Startup costs".

Termination and post-termination expenses: see "Wind-down" in Notes to 18(1)(a).

Note also specific rules that prevent or limit a loss, e.g. from home office expenses (18(12)); tax shelters (143.2(6), 237.1(6)); CCA on rental property, leasing property, computer tax shelter property or specified energy property (Reg. 1100(1.1), (11), (15), (20.1), (24)); restricted farm losses (31(1)); vacant land (18(2)) or land under construction (18(3.1)).

Profits from non-business, including Ponzi schemes (see also "Defrauded investors" above): No business means no source of income, so arguably any "profit" from the activity is not taxed (see also Notes to 3 and 9(1)). VIEWS doc 2013-0503031I7 says T4A revenue need not be reported if the "business" is just a hobby whose purpose is to make money for a personal matter. In *Radonjic*, 2013 FC 916, CRA's refusal to reassess to delete previously-reported poker winnings was found unreasonable. In *Johnson*, 2012 FCA 253 (leave to appeal denied 2013 CarswellNat 633 (SCC)), a Ponzi scheme early investor who benefited innocently from fraud on others was taxable on the income, because she received the return on investment she bargained for even though the promoter acted fraudulently. The same applied in *Auto Maculate*, 2020 TCC 105, paras. 188-205; but in *Roszko*, 2014 TCC 59, interest received from a Ponzi scheme was treated as non-taxable return of capital. In *Orman v. Marnat*, 2012 ONSC 549, the

Court issued a "declaratory order" [see Notes to 169(1) on rectification] that early investors in a Ponzi scheme received returns of capital and not investment income. CRA now says early Ponzi investors can claim a 20(1)(p) bad debt deduction for reinvested income once the promoters are charged: VIEWS docs 2017-0691941I7, 2018-0760751E5. See also Aptowitzer, "Ponzi Schemes and Taxation", xxxii(13) *The Canadian Taxpayer* (Carswell) 97-98 (June 29, 2010), re CRA allowing investors defrauded by Earl Jones to retract reported fictitious income. In *763993 Alberta*, 2012 TCC 308, a corp deducted amounts paid to a shareholder, above her employment income, under an agreement where she claimed no intention to profit. This was denied as "a cute and somewhat clever attempt to avoid paying tax on a distribution to shareholders" (paras. 14-15). Similarly, detaxers' claims that their business was a "non-commercial personal endeavour" were rejected in: *Meerman*, 2019 FCA 119; leave to appeal denied 2020 CarswellNat 370 (SCC) (mechanic); *De Geest*, 2019 TCC 33 (under appeal to FCA) (window installer).

Income Tax Folios: S4-F14-C1: Artists and writers [replaces IT-504R2].

Interpretation Bulletins: IT-328R3: Losses on shares on which dividends have been received. See also under 9(1).

I.T. Technical News: 16 (*Tonn, Mastri, Mohammad* and *Kaye* cases); 25 (reasonable expectation of profit); 41 (meaning of "business" — gambling).

CRA Audit Manual: 11.6.4 and Appendix A-11.2.22: Reasonable expectation of profit report.

Advance Tax Rulings: See under 9(1).

(3) Gains and losses not included — In this Act, "income from a property" does not include any capital gain from the disposition of that property and "loss from a property" does not include any capital loss from the disposition of that property.

Related Provisions: 40(1)(a) — Expenses deducted in determining capital gain.

Notes: Capital gains and losses are excluded from the s. 9 income calculation because they are dealt with separately under 3(b) and 38–55. Capital gains are not income from a "source": *Cassan*, 2017 TCC 174 (FCA appeal settled A-304-17), para. 414. Costs are deducted in determining gain or loss under 40(1). Because of 9(3), interest on money borrowed to realize a capital gain is non-deductible: *Firth*, 2009 TCC 137. See also Notes to 38 and 39(1).

Definitions [s. 9]: "amount", "business" — 248(1); "capital gain" — 39(1)(a), 248(1); "capital loss" — 39(1)(b), 248(1); "property" — 248(1); "taxation year" — 11(2), 249; "taxpayer" — 248(1).

10. (1) Valuation of inventory — For the purpose of computing a taxpayer's income for a taxation year from a business that is not an adventure or concern in the nature of trade, property described in an inventory shall be valued at the end of the year at the cost at which the taxpayer acquired the property or its fair market value at the end of the year, whichever is lower, or in a prescribed manner.

Related Provisions: 10(1.01) — Adventure in the nature of trade — no writedown until sale; 10(1.1) — Certain expenses included in cost; 10(2) — Valuation of inventory property; 10(6) — Inventory of artists; 10(15), 18(1)(x) — Derivatives excluded; 12(1)(r) — Income inclusion — inventory adjustment; 27.1 — Emissions allowances; 28(1.1), (1.2) — Inventory of farming or fishing business; 86.1(4) — Value of shares in inventory after foreign spin-off; 87(2)(b) — Amalgamations — inventory; 96(8)(b) — Cost of inventory of partnership that previously had only non-resident partners; 107(1.2) — fair market value of interest in trust held as inventory; 112(4.1) — Fair market value of share held as inventory; 112(11)–(13) — Cost reductions for partnership interest that is inventory; 142.5(1) — Mark-to-market rules for securities held by financial institutions.

Notes: See Notes to 54"capital property" on the distinction between inventory and capital property.

The cost of purchasing inventory is normally required to be included in the cost of inventory under 10(1) and deducted only when the inventory is sold, rather than when incurred (but see 10(6) for artists).

In *Yorkwest Plumbing*, 2020 TCC 122, YP, having overlooked an inventory deduction for 2010, could not remedy it by overstating cost of goods sold for 2012.

The Supreme Court of Canada ruled in *Friesen*, [1995] 2 C.T.C. 369, that 10(1) could be used to claim a deduction by writing down inventory, including land inventory, even if the taxpayer owned only one asset. However, this was reversed by 10(1.01), for cases where the property is held as an adventure in the nature of trade.

For an example of inventory writedown allowed see *This Is It Design*, 2010 TCC 652. In *Kruger Inc.*, 2016 FCA 186, foreign exchange option contracts were not inventory, but the mark-to-market method was allowed to write them down (as of 2017, this can be done only by election under 10.1). See also VIEWS doc 2010-0386121E5.

Work in progress (WIP) is included in inventory (10(5)) and thus in income, but can be written down to fair market value, overriding s. 9: *CDSL Canada*, 2008 FCA 400; Perry Truster, "Valuation of a Service Business's WIP Revisited", 9(2) *Tax for the Owner-Manager* (ctf.ca) 1-2 (April 2009). In *Gestion Raynald Lavoie*, 2008 TCC 204, the production cost of a TV series was deductible over 5 years as it gradually became clear it would not be paid for and thus lost value.

Professionals: with the phaseout of s. 34 (see 10(14.1)), a professional's WIP is now taxed. See VIEWS docs 2008-0294011E5, 2017-0709101C6, 2018-0743031E5 (cost of WIP includes employees but not overhead and not the professional's own time; FMV of contingency fee is normally nil until it's known). The Finance Minister stated on Dec. 18, 1981 (news release 81-126): "The cost of the work in progress will not include fixed or indirect overheads, such as rental, secretarial and general office expenses. It will generally be restricted to those costs, such as the salaries paid to professional employees, that are expected to be recovered in future billings. No cost is required to be imputed to partners' or proprietors' time." Thus, WIP for a sole practitioner is usually nil (lower of cost or market: 10(1)). See also Infanti, "CRA Confirms Partner Time Not Part of Professional's WIP Cost", 18(3) *Tax for the Owner-Manager* (ctf.ca) 1-3 (July 2018); Campbell, "WIP Update", 15(5) *Tax Hyperion* (Carswell) 4-6 (Sept-Oct 2018).

CRA accepts that nursery stock can be valued at $1, whether growing in the field or in pots, because its saleability is uncertain: *Income Tax Audit Manual* §20.1.5.

Discounts or rebates on inventory purchases, such as volume rebates not calculated at time of purchase, are considered income rather than part of cost of goods: VIEWS doc 2010-0382161I7.

Land inventory transferred by a developer at no cost to a golf club should be expensed by reallocating the cost to remaining land in inventory, in CRA's view: doc 2011-0398111I7.

See also Arnold et al., *Timing and Income Taxation* (ctf.ca, 2nd ed., 2015), chap. 12.

10(1) amended by 1995-97 technical bill, effective on the same basis as 10(1.01).

Regulations: 1102(1)(b) (no capital cost allowance for property described in inventory); 1801 (inventory generally may be valued at fair market value); 1802 (valuation of animals).

Income Tax Folios: S4-F7-C1: Amalgamations of Canadian corporations [replaces IT-474R2].

Interpretation Bulletins: IT-51R2: Supplies on hand at end of a fiscal period; IT-102R2: Conversion of property, other than real property, from or to inventory; IT-142R3: Settlement of debts on the winding-up of a corporation; IT-153R3: Land developers — subdivision and development costs and carrying charges on land; IT-165R: Returnable containers (cancelled); IT-328R3: Losses on shares on which dividends have been received; IT-459: Adventure or concern in the nature of trade; IT-482R: Pipelines; IT-504R2: Visual artists and writers. See also at end of s. 10.

Registered Charities Newsletters: 18 (can businesses receive receipts for donations made out of their inventory?).

CRA Audit Manual: Chapter 20.0: Valuation of inventory.

(1.01) Adventures in the nature of trade
— For the purpose of computing a taxpayer's income from a business that is an adventure or concern in the nature of trade, property described in an inventory shall be valued at the cost at which the taxpayer acquired the property.

Related Provisions: 10(9) — Grandfathering of writedown taken before 10(1.01) applies; 10(10) — Writedown required before change in control; 18(14)–(16) — Superficial loss rule for property held as adventure in the nature of trade.

Notes: 10(1.01) implements a Dec. 20, 1995 press release effectively overturning the Supreme Court of Canada decision in *Friesen*, [1995] 2 C.T.C. 369. Under 10(1.01), inventory that has dropped in value cannot be written down (to generate a loss for tax purposes) if the property is held as an adventure in the nature of trade. Thus, for example, if a taxpayer owns a single piece of land that was purchased for resale purposes, and it drops in value, it cannot be written down until it is sold.

The distinction between "business" and "adventure in the nature of trade" was not previously important in income tax law, despite the extensive case law on "income" vs. "capital property". It is relevant for GST purposes, however. For CRA discussion see GST/HST Policy Statement P-059, "Business vs. Adventure or Concern in the Nature of Trade Relating to Sales of Real Property", and GST/HST New Memorandum chapter 19.5 Appendix C, in David M. Sherman, *GST Memoranda, Bulletins, Policies & Info Sheets* (Carswell, annual). See also IT-459.

10(1.01) does not restrict the annual deduction of carrying costs; it applies only to writedown of the inventory: *Stremler*, [2000] 2 C.T.C. 2172 (TCC). Carrying costs are deductible under accounting principles per *Canderel*, [1998] 2 C.T.C. 35 (SCC).

10(1.01) added by 1995-97 technical bill, effective for taxation years that end after Dec. 20, 1995, and in some cases effective for earlier taxation years.

Interpretation Bulletins: IT-459: Adventure or concern in the nature of trade.

CRA Audit Manual: 20.1.1: Valuation of inventory.

(1.1) Certain expenses included in cost
— For the purposes of subsections (1), (1.01) and (10), where land is described in an inventory of a business of a taxpayer, the cost at which the taxpayer acquired the land shall include each amount that is

(a) described in paragraph 18(2)(a) or (b) in respect of the land and for which no deduction is permitted to the taxpayer, or to another person or partnership that is

(i) a person or partnership with whom the taxpayer does not deal at arm's length,

(ii) if the taxpayer is a corporation, a person or partnership that is a specified shareholder of the taxpayer, or

(iii) if the taxpayer is a partnership, a person or partnership whose share of any income or loss of the taxpayer is 10% or more; and

(b) not included in or added to the cost to that other person or partnership of any property otherwise than because of paragraph 53(1)(d.3) or subparagraph 53(1)(e)(xi).

Notes: "Land" in 10(1.1)(a) is subject to 18(3), which applies to 18(2).

10(1.1) amended by 1995-97 technical bill (for tax years ending after Dec. 20, 1994, earlier in some cases), 1991 technical bill.

Interpretation Bulletins: IT-153R3: Land developers — subdivision and development costs and carrying charges on land. See also at end of s. 10.

(2) Continuation of valuation
— Notwithstanding subsection (1), for the purpose of computing income for a taxation year from a business, the inventory at the commencement of the year shall be valued at the same amount as the amount at which it was valued at the end of the preceding taxation year for the purpose of computing income for that preceding year.

Related Provisions: 10(2.1) — Valuation methods to be the same from year to year.

Interpretation Bulletins: See list at end of s. 10.

(2.1) Methods of valuation to be same
— Where property described in an inventory of a taxpayer's business that is not an adventure or concern in the nature of trade is valued at the end of a taxation year in accordance with a method permitted under this section, that method shall, subject to subsection (6), be used in the valuation of property described in the inventory at the end of the following taxation year for the purpose of computing the taxpayer's income from the business unless the taxpayer, with the concurrence of the Minister and on any terms and conditions that are specified by the Minister, adopts another method permitted under this section.

Notes: See IT-473R para. 8 for when the CRA will permit a change in method. On the impact of CICA *Handbook* §3031 see VIEWS doc 2009-0330401C6.

10(2.1) amended by 1995-97 technical bill, effective on the same basis as the addition of 10(1.01), to exclude the rule from applying to property held as an adventure in the nature of trade.

Interpretation Bulletins: IT-459: Adventure or concern in the nature of trade. See also list at end of s. 10.

(3) Incorrect valuation
— Where the inventory of a business at the commencement of a taxation year has, according to the method adopted by the taxpayer for computing income from the business for that year, not been valued as required by subsection (1), the inventory at the commencement of that year shall, if the Minister so directs, be deemed to have been valued as required by that subsection.

Interpretation Bulletins: See list at end of s. 10.

CRA Audit Manual: 20.1.1: Valuation of inventory; 20.1.6: Appendix 1 — sample letter.

(4) Fair market value
— For the purpose of subsection (1), the fair market value of property (other than property that is obsolete, damaged or defective or that is held for sale or lease or for the purpose of being processed, fabricated, manufactured, incorporated into, attached to, or otherwise converted into property for sale or lease) that is

(a) work in progress at the end of a taxation year of a business that is a profession means the amount that can reasonably be expected to become receivable in respect thereof after the end of the year; and

(b) advertising or packaging material, parts, supplies or other property (other than work in progress of a business that is a profession) that is included in inventory means the replacement cost of the property.

Related Provisions: 10(5) — Property deemed to be inventory; 34 — Election to exclude work in progress from professional income until 2017; 107(1.2) — fair market value of interest in trust held as inventory.

Notes: See Notes to 10(1).

Interpretation Bulletins: IT-51R2: Supplies on hand at end of fiscal period. See also list at end of s. 10.

(5) [Meaning of] Inventory — Without restricting the generality of this section,

(a) property (other than capital property) of a taxpayer that is advertising or packaging material, parts or supplies or work in progress of a business that is a profession is, for greater certainty, inventory of the taxpayer;

(b) anything used primarily for the purpose of advertising or packaging property that is included in the inventory of a taxpayer shall be deemed not to be property held for sale or lease or for any of the purposes referred to in subsection (4); and

(c) property of a taxpayer, the cost of which to the taxpayer was deductible by virtue of paragraph 20(1)(mm), is, for greater certainty, inventory of the taxpayer having a cost to the taxpayer, except for the purposes of that paragraph, of nil.

Related Provisions: 10(4) — Fair market value of work in progress, advertising or packaging materials, parts and supplies; 34 — Election to exclude work in progress from professional income until 2017.

Notes: See Notes to 10(1) re the *CDSL Canada* case. For the meaning of "used primarily" in 10(5)(b) see Notes to 73(3).

I.T. Application Rules: 23(3), (4).

Interpretation Bulletins: IT-51R2: Supplies on hand at end of fiscal period; IT-457R: Election by professionals to exclude work in progress from income. See also at end of s. 10.

CRA Audit Manual: 27.12.4: Farming and fishing income — income tax implications — ceasing to carry on a farming or fishing business.

(6) Artistic endeavour — Notwithstanding subsection (1), for the purpose of computing the income of an individual other than a trust for a taxation year from a business that is the individual's artistic endeavour, the value of the inventory of the business for that year shall, if the individual so elects in the individual's return of income under this Part for the year, be deemed to be nil.

Related Provisions: 10(7) — Effect of election; 10(8) — Artistic endeavour; 118.1(7), (7.1) — Donation of inventory by artist.

Notes: The effect of an artist electing under 10(6) to value inventory at nil is to allow the costs associated with creating the inventory to be deducted in the year they are incurred, rather than waiting for the inventory to be sold. This recognizes the difficulty in valuing works of art and the long period of time it can take for art to be sold.

10(6) was enacted after artist Toni Onley threatened to burn his works to reduce his inventory and thus his tax bill: Arthur Drache, "Onley's Death Ends Tax Saga", xxvi(7) *The Canadian Taxpayer* (Carswell) 51-52 (March 30, 2004).

In *Tramble*, [2001] 4 C.T.C. 2160 (TCC), Bowman J. noted that 10(6) means that artists need not reduce cost of goods sold by paintings in inventory at year-end, so effectively artists can report on the cash basis. 10(6) thus can create losses. 10(6) was also applied in *Faber*, 2008 TCC 403.

For the application of 10(6) on the artist's death, see VIEWS doc 2004-0099191E5.

If the artist is resident in Quebec, an election under 10(6) must be copied to Revenu Québec: *Taxation Act* ss. 85.5, 21.4.6.

Interpretation Bulletins: IT-212R3: Income of deceased persons — rights or things; IT-504R2: Visual artists and writers. See also at end of s. 10.

(7) Value in later years — Where an individual has made an election pursuant to subsection (6) for a taxation year, the value of the inventory of a business that is the individual's artistic endeavour shall, for each subsequent taxation year, be deemed to be nil unless the individual, with the concurrence of the Minister and on such terms and conditions as are specified by the Minister, revokes the election.

Notes: If the artist is resident in Quebec, a revocation under 10(7) must be copied to Revenu Québec: *Taxation Act* ss. 85.6, 21.4.6.

Interpretation Bulletins: IT-504R2: Visual artists and writers. See also at end of s. 10.

(8) Definition of "business that is an individual's artistic endeavour" — For the purpose of this section, "business that is an individual's artistic endeavour" means the business of creating paintings, prints, etchings, drawings, sculptures or similar works of art, where such works of art are created by the individual, but does not include a business of reproducing works of art.

Interpretation Bulletins [subsec. 10(8)]: IT-504R2: Visual artists and writers. See also at end of s. 10.

(9) Transition — Where, at the end of a taxpayer's last taxation year at the end of which property described in an inventory of a business that is an adventure or concern in the nature of trade was valued under subsection (1), the property was valued at an amount that is less than the cost at which the taxpayer acquired the property, after that time the cost to the taxpayer at which the property was acquired is, subject to subsection (10), deemed to be that amount.

Notes: 10(9) added by 1995-97 technical bill, effective on the same basis as 10(1.01). It grandfathers an inventory writedown taken before 10(1.01) applied. The amount to which the writedown was taken is deemed to be the new cost for 10(1.01).

Interpretation Bulletins: IT-459: Adventure or concern in the nature of trade.

(10) Loss restriction event — Notwithstanding subsection (1.01), property described in an inventory of a taxpayer's business that is an adventure or concern in the nature of trade at the end of the taxpayer's taxation year that ends immediately before the time at which the taxpayer is subject to a loss restriction event is to be valued at the cost at which the taxpayer acquired the property, or its fair market value at the end of the year, whichever is lower, and after that time the cost at which the taxpayer acquired the property is, subject to a subsequent application of this subsection, deemed to be that lower amount.

Related Provisions: 251.2 — Loss restriction event.

Notes: 10(10) requires inventory writedown before a change in control of a corporation or trust. This prevents loss trading in entities that have an unrealized loss in property held as an adventure in the nature of trade. The reference to the year that ends immediately before the loss restriction event is to the year-end triggered under 249(4).

10(10) amended by 2013 budget bill #2, effective March 21, 2013, essentially to change "corporation" to "taxpayer" and reference to control being acquired to a "loss restriction event" (see 251.2), to extend the rule to trusts.

10(10) added by 1995-97 technical bill, effective on the same basis as 10(1.01).

Interpretation Bulletins: IT-459: Adventure or concern in the nature of trade.

(11) Loss restriction event — For the purposes of subsections 88(1.1) and 111(5), a taxpayer's business that is at any time an adventure or concern in the nature of trade is deemed to be a business carried on at that time by the taxpayer.

Notes: 10(11) deems an adventure in the nature of trade to be a business for purposes of the rules that allow a loss carryforward to be used (after change in control) only against the same or a similar business.

10(11) amended by 2013 budget bill #2, effective March 21, 2013, to change "corporation" to "taxpayer" twice. (See Notes to 10(10).)

10(11) added by 1995-97 technical bill, effective on the same basis as 10(1.01).

Interpretation Bulletins: IT-459: Adventure or concern in the nature of trade.

(12) Removing property from [Canadian] inventory [of non-resident] — If at any time a non-resident taxpayer ceases to use, in connection with a business or part of a business carried on by the taxpayer in Canada immediately before that time, a property that was immediately before that time described in the inventory of the business or the part of the business, as the case may be, (other than a property that was disposed of by the taxpayer at that time), the taxpayer is deemed

(a) to have disposed of the property immediately before that time for proceeds of disposition equal to its fair market value at that time; and

(b) to have received those proceeds immediately before that time in the course of carrying on the business or the part of the business, as the case may be.

Related Provisions: 10(14) — Inventory includes work in progress of a professional; 142.6(1.1) — Parallel rule for non-resident financial institution.

Notes: 10(12) replaces a more specific rule for farming inventory that appeared in 28(4.1). It was added by 2001 technical bill, effective December 24, 1998.

(13) Adding property to [Canadian] inventory [of non-resident] — If at any time a property becomes included in the inventory of a business or part of a business that a non-resident taxpayer carries on in Canada after that time (other than a property that was, otherwise than because of this subsection, acquired by the taxpayer at that time), the taxpayer is deemed to have acquired the property at that time at a cost equal to its fair market value at that time.

Related Provisions: 10(14) — Inventory includes work in progress of a professional.

Notes: 10(13) added by 2001 technical bill, effective December 24, 1998.

(14) Work in progress — For the purposes of subsections (12) and (13), property that is included in the inventory of a business includes property that would be so included if paragraph 34(a) did not apply.

Enacted Repeal — 10(14) (effective 2024)

Application: S.C. 2017, c. 33 (Bill C-63, Royal Assent Dec. 14, 2017), subsec. 2(1), has repealed subsec. 10(14), in force Jan. 1, 2024.

Technical Notes: Section 34 provides an exception to full accrual accounting in computing the income of a business that is a professional practice of an accountant, dentist, lawyer, medical doctor, veterinarian or chiropractor by allowing the income to be determined without taking into account any work in progress at year end.

Subsection 10(14) provides, for the purposes of 10(12) and 10(13), that a property included in the inventory of a business includes professional work in progress that would be included if paragraph 34(a) (the basic rule described above) did not apply.

Consequential on the repeal of section 34 [with a 5-year phase-out — ed.], subsection 10(14) is repealed.

Federal Budget, Supplementary Information, March 22, 2017: See under s. 34.

Related Provisions: 142.6(1.2) — Parallel rule for non-resident financial institution.

Notes: 34(a) refers to the work in progress that a professional (lawyer, physician, etc.) has elected to exclude from inventory.

10(14) added by 2001 technical bill, effective December 24, 1998.

(14.1) Work in progress — transitional — If paragraph 34(a) applies in computing a taxpayer's income from a business for the last taxation year of the taxpayer that begins before March 22, 2017, then

(a) for the purpose of computing the income of the taxpayer from the business, at the end of the first taxation year that begins after March 21, 2017,

(i) the amount of the cost of the taxpayer's work in progress is deemed to be one-fifth of the amount of its cost determined without reference to this paragraph, and

(ii) the amount of the fair market value of the taxpayer's work in progress is deemed to be one-fifth of the amount of its fair market value determined without reference to this paragraph;

(b) for the purpose of computing the income of the taxpayer from the business, at the end of the second taxation year that begins after March 21, 2017,

(i) the amount of the cost of the taxpayer's work in progress is deemed to be two-fifths of the amount of its cost determined without reference to this paragraph, and

(ii) the amount of the fair market value of the taxpayer's work in progress is deemed to be two-fifths of the amount of its fair market value determined without reference to this paragraph;

(c) for the purpose of computing the income of the taxpayer from the business, at the end of the third taxation year that begins after March 21, 2017,

(i) the amount of the cost of the taxpayer's work in progress is deemed to be three-fifths of the amount of its cost determined without reference to this paragraph, and

(ii) the amount of the fair market value of the taxpayer's work in progress is deemed to be three-fifths of the amount of its fair market value determined without reference to this paragraph; and

(d) for the purpose of computing the income of the taxpayer from the business, at the end of the fourth taxation year that begins after March 21, 2017,

(i) the amount of the cost of the taxpayer's work in progress is deemed to be four-fifths of the amount of its cost determined without reference to this paragraph, and

(ii) the amount of the fair market value of the taxpayer's work in progress is deemed to be four-fifths of the amount of its fair market value determined without reference to this paragraph.

Enacted Repeal — 10(14.1) (effective 2024)

Application: S.C. 2017, c. 33 (Bill C-63, Royal Assent Dec. 14, 2017), subsec. 2(3), has repealed subsec. 10(14.1), in force Jan. 1, 2024.

Technical Notes: Section 34 provides an exception to full accrual accounting in computing the income of a business that is a professional practice of an accountant, dentist, lawyer, medical doctor, veterinarian or chiropractor by allowing the income from that business to be determined without taking into account any work in progress at year end.

Consequential on the repeal of section 34, new subsection 10(14.1) provides a five-year transitional rule for the purpose of valuing work in progress from a business that is a professional practice of one of the designated professions listed above. Subsection 10(14.1) provides that for the purposes of computing the income of a taxpayer from a business the cost and the fair market value of the taxpayer's work in progress from the business is deemed to be:

- 20% of the cost and fair market value of the taxpayer's work in progress at the end of the first taxation year that begins after March 21, 2017;
- 40% of the cost and fair market value of the taxpayer's work in progress at the end of the second taxation year that begins after March 21, 2017;
- 60% of the cost and fair market value of the taxpayer's work in progress at the end of the third taxation year that begins after March 21, 2017; and
- 80% of the cost and fair market value of the taxpayer's work in progress at the end of the fourth taxation year that begins after March 21, 2017.

For the fifth taxation year that begins after March 21, 2017, the full amount in respect of work in progress must be included in computing income from a professional business.

This transitional relief is available to a taxpayer who elected to exclude work in progress in computing income in respect of the last taxation year that begins before March 22, 2017.

Federal Budget, Supplementary Information, March 22, 2017: See under s. 34.

Notes: 10(14.1) provides a 5-year transition for the repeal of s. 34, which allowed certain professionals to avoid recognizing work in progress until it was billed. It can only be used by a taxpayer who had elected under 34(a) for their last taxation year that began before March 22, 2017. See also Notes to 10(1) and to Enacted Repeal of s. 34.

10(14.1) added by 2017 budget bill #2, for tax years ending after March 2017.

(15) Derivatives — For the purposes of this section, property of a taxpayer that is a swap agreement, a forward purchase or sale agreement, a forward rate agreement, a futures agreement, an option agreement, or any similar agreement is deemed not to be inventory of the taxpayer.

Related Provisions: 18(1)(x) — No writedown to market value allowed under general principles.

Notes: 10(15) and 18(1)(x) implement a 2016 Budget proposal to overturn *Kruger Inc.*, 2015 TCC 119, para 124 (rev'd in part 2016 FCA 186), which ruled that a derivative held on income account could be treated as inventory. Absent 10(15), where a derivative is held on income account, its loss in value could be deducted but increases would be taxed only when realized.

10(15) added by 2016 budget bill #2, for agreements entered into after March 21, 2016.

Definitions [s. 10]: "adventure or concern in the nature of trade" — see 10(1.01) Notes; "amount" — 248(1); "artistic endeavour" — 10(8); "business" — 248(1); "Canada" — 255, *Interpretation Act* 35(1); "capital property" — 54, 248(1); "control" — 256(6)–(9), 256.1(3); "corporation" — 248(1), *Interpretation Act* 35(1); "cost" — 10(9); "fair market value" — 10(4), 107(1.2) and see 69(1) Notes; "filing-due date" — 248(1); "fiscal period" — 249.1; "individual" — 248(1); "inventory" — 10(5), 248(1); "land" — 18(3); "loss restriction event" — 251.2; "Minister", "non-resident" — 248(1); "partnership" — see 96(1) Notes; "person", "prescribed", "property", "regulation", "specified shareholder" — 248(1); "taxation year" — 11(2), 249; "taxpayer" — 248(1); "trust" — 104(1), 248(1), (3).

Interpretation Bulletins [s. 10]: IT-98R2: Investment corporations (cancelled); IT-189R2: Corporations used by practising members of professions; IT-283R2: CCA — video tapes, videotape cassettes, films, computer software and master recording tapes (cancelled); IT-452: Utility service connections (cancelled); IT-473R: Inventory valuation.

10.1 (1) Mark-to-market election [for derivatives] — Subsection (4) applies to a taxpayer in respect of a taxation year and subsequent taxation years if the taxpayer elects to have subsection (4) apply to the taxpayer and has filed that election in prescribed form on or before its filing-due date for the taxation year.

Related Provisions: 10.1(2) — Revocation of election; 10.1(4), (6) — Consequences of election; 10.1(7) — Rules for first year election is made; 10.1(8) — No mark-to-market treatment without election; 96(3) — Election by members of partnership.

Notes: See Notes at end of 10.1.

Forms: T217: Election, or Revocation of an Election, to use the Mark-to-Market method.

(2) Revocation — The Minister may, on application by the taxpayer in prescribed form, grant permission to the taxpayer to revoke its election under subsection (1). The revocation applies to each taxation year of the taxpayer that begins after the day on which the taxpayer is notified in writing that the Minister concurs with the revocation, on such terms and conditions as are specified by the Minister.

Related Provisions: 10.1(3) — Subsequent election.

Forms: T217: Election, or Revocation of an Election, to use the Mark-to-Market method.

(3) Subsequent election — Notwithstanding subsection (1), if a taxpayer has, under subsection (2), revoked an election, any subsequent election under subsection (1) shall result in subsection (4) applying to the taxpayer in respect of each taxation year that begins after the day on which the prescribed form in respect of the subsequent election is filed by the taxpayer.

(4) Application — If this subsection applies to a taxpayer in respect of a taxation year,

(a) if the taxpayer is a "financial institution" (as defined in subsection 142.2(1)) in the taxation year, each eligible derivative held by the taxpayer at any time in the taxation year is, for the purpose of applying the provisions of this Act and with such modifications as the context requires, deemed to be "mark-to-market property" (as defined in subsection 142.2(1)) of the taxpayer for the taxation year; and

(b) in any other case, subsection (6) applies to the taxpayer in respect of each eligible derivative held by the taxpayer at the end of the taxation year.

Related Provisions: 10.1(1) — Conditions for 10.1(3) to apply; 10.1(6) — Consequences of election; 10.1(9) — Rule where eligible derivative is not property.

(5) Definition of eligible derivative — For the purposes of this section, an "eligible derivative", of a taxpayer for a taxation year, means a swap agreement, a forward purchase or sale agreement, a forward rate agreement, a futures agreement, an option agreement or a similar agreement, held at any time in the taxation year by the taxpayer, if

(a) the agreement is not a capital property, a Canadian resource property, a foreign resource property or an obligation on account of capital of the taxpayer;

(b) either

(i) the taxpayer has produced audited financial statements prepared in accordance with generally accepted accounting principles in respect of the taxation year, or

(ii) if the taxpayer has not produced audited financial statements described in subparagraph (i), the agreement has a readily ascertainable fair market value; and

(c) where the agreement is held by a "financial institution" (as defined in subsection 142.2(1)), the agreement is not a "tracking property" (as defined in subsection 142.2(1)), other than an "ex-

cluded property" (as defined in subsection 142.2(1)), of the financial institution.

Related Provisions: 10(15), 18(1)(x) — Property excluded from inventory writedown; 10.1(9) — Rule where ED is not property; 85(1.12), 85(2)(a), 97(2) — ED does not qualify for s. 85 or 97(2) rollover if election made.

(6) Deemed disposition — If this subsection applies to a taxpayer in respect of each eligible derivative held by the taxpayer at the end of a taxation year, for each eligible derivative held by the taxpayer at the end of the taxation year, the taxpayer is deemed

(a) to have disposed of the eligible derivative immediately before the end of the year and received proceeds or paid an amount, as the case may be, equal to its fair market value at the time of disposition; and

(b) to have reacquired, or reissued or renewed, the eligible derivative at the end of the year at an amount equal to the proceeds or the amount, as the case may be, determined under paragraph (a).

Related Provisions: 10.1(4)(b) — Conditions for 10.1(6) to apply; 10.1(7) — Rules for first year election is made; 10.1(9) — Rule where eligible derivative is not property; 85(1.12), 85(2)(a), 97(2) — Derivative does not qualify for s. 85 or 97(2) rollover if election made; 87(2)(e.41) — Effect of amalgamation; 88(1)(j) — Effect of windup.

(7) Election year — gains and losses — If a taxpayer holds, at the beginning of its first taxation year in respect of which an election referred to in subsection (1) applies (in this subsection referred to as the "election year"), an eligible derivative and, in the taxation year immediately preceding the election year, the taxpayer did not compute its profit or loss in respect of that eligible derivative in accordance with a method of profit computation that produces a substantially similar effect to subsection (6), then

(a) the taxpayer is deemed

(i) to have disposed of the eligible derivative immediately before the beginning of the election year and received proceeds or paid an amount, as the case may be, equal to its fair market value at that time, and

(ii) to have reacquired, or reissued or renewed, the eligible derivative at the beginning of the election year at an amount equal to the proceeds or the amount, as the case may be, determined under subparagraph (i);

(b) the profit or loss that would arise (determined without reference to this paragraph) on the deemed disposition in subparagraph (a)(i)

(i) is deemed not to arise in the taxation year immediately preceding the election year, and

(ii) is deemed to arise in the taxation year in which the taxpayer disposes of the eligible derivative (otherwise than because of paragraphs (6)(a) or 142.5(2)(a)); and

(c) for the purpose of applying subsection 18(15) in respect of the disposition of the eligible derivative referred to in subparagraph (b)(ii), the profit or loss deemed to arise because of that subparagraph is included in determining the amount of the transferor's loss, if any, from the disposition.

Related Provisions: 10.1(9) — Rule where eligible derivative is not property; 87(2)(e.42) — Amalgamation — continuing corporation.

(8) Default realization method — If subsection (4) does not apply to a taxpayer referred to in paragraph (4)(b) in respect of a taxation year, a method of profit computation that produces a substantially similar effect to subsection (6) shall not be used for the purpose of computing the taxpayer's income from a business or property in respect of a swap agreement, a forward purchase or sale agreement, a forward rate agreement, a futures agreement, an option agreement or a similar agreement for the taxation year.

Notes: See Notes at end of 10.1.

(9) Interpretation — For the purposes of subsections (4) to (7), if an agreement that is an eligible derivative of a taxpayer is not a property of the taxpayer, the taxpayer is deemed

(a) to hold the eligible derivative at any time while the taxpayer is a party to the agreement; and

(b) to have disposed of the eligible derivative when it is settled or extinguished in respect of the taxpayer.

Notes [s. 10.1]: 10.1 overrides *Kruger Inc.*, 2016 FCA 186, which allowed a non-"financial institution" to use the mark-to-market (M2M) method for derivatives (see now 10.1(8)). It provides instead an election under 10.1(1) (Form T217) to use M2M only for "eligible derivatives" (defined in 10.1(5); see 10.1(4)). The election remains binding forever unless CRA permits revocation (10.1(2)). This ensures consistency and prevents tax advantages from switching back and forth. It does not apply to a financial institution (10.1(4)(a)); see the M2M rule in 142.5(2).

See Marcovitz & Wong, "Computation of Income from Derivatives", 25(6) *Canadian Tax Highlights* (ctf.ca) 7 (June 2017); Frankovic, "Amendments to the Taxation of Derivatives", 2366 *Tax Topics* (CCH) 1-4 (July 13, 2017); Marcovitz, "Taxation of Liabilities and Derivatives on Income Account", 2017 Cdn Tax Foundation conference report, at 12:15-17.

10.1 added by 2017 budget bill #2, for tax years that begin after March 21, 2017.

Definitions [s. 10.1]: "amount", "business" — 248(1); "Canadian resource property" — 66(15), 248(1); "capital property" — 54, 248(1); "disposition" — 248(1); "eligible derivative" — 10.1(5); "excluded property" — 142.2(1); "fair market value" — see 69(1) Notes; "filing-due date" — 150(1), 248(1); "financial institution" — 142.2(1); "foreign resource property" — 66(15), 248(1); "Minister", "prescribed", "property" — 248(1); "taxation year" — 249; "taxpayer" — 248(1); "tracking property" — 142.2(1); "writing" — *Interpretation Act* 35(1).

11. (1) Proprietor of business — Subject to section 34.1, if an individual is a proprietor of a business, the individual's income from the business for a taxation year is deemed to be the individual's income from the business for the fiscal periods of the business that end in the year.

(2) Reference to "taxation year" — Where an individual's income for a taxation year includes income from a business the fiscal period of which does not coincide with the calendar year, unless the context otherwise requires, a reference in this Subdivision or section 80.3 to a "taxation year" or "year" shall, in respect of the business, be read as a reference to a fiscal period of the business ending in the year.

Related Provisions [s. 11]: 20(16.2) — Terminal loss rules — reference to "taxation year" and "year"; 34.1 — Additional income adjustment where fiscal year is not calendar year; 96(1)(f) — Income inclusion from partnership in taxation year in which partnership's year ends; 25(1) — Fiscal period for individual proprietor of business disposed of; 249(2)(b) — Where end of fiscal period coincides with end of taxation year.

Notes [s. 11]: 11(1) amended to delete reference to 34.2 by 2013 budget bill #2, for tax years ending after March 22, 2011. Earlier amended by 1995 Budget, 1993 technical bill, 1989 Budget.

Definitions [s. 11]: "business" — 248(1), 249.1; "calendar year" — *Interpretation Act* 37(1)(a); "fiscal period" — 248(1), 249.1; "individual" — 248(1); "taxation year" — 249.

Regulations [s. 11]: 1104(1) (taxation year of individual for capital cost allowance purposes).

Interpretation Bulletins [s. 11]: IT-184R: Deferred cash purchase tickets issued by Canadian Wheat Board.

Inclusions

12. (1) Income inclusions — There shall be included in computing the income of a taxpayer for a taxation year as income from a business or property such of the following amounts as are applicable:

(a) **services, etc., to be rendered [or goods to be delivered]** — any amount received by the taxpayer in the year in the course of a business

(i) that is on account of services not rendered or goods not delivered before the end of the year or that, for any other reason, may be regarded as not having been earned in the year or a previous year, or

(ii) under an arrangement or understanding that it is repayable in whole or in part on the return or resale to the taxpayer of articles in or by means of which goods were delivered to a customer;

Related Provisions: 12(1)(x) — Inducements, reimbursements, etc. included in income; 12(2) — Rule is for greater certainty only; 20(1)(m) — Deductions — reserve for goods and services; 20(1)(m.1) — Deductions — manufacturer's warranty reserve; 20(1)(m.2) — Deductions — repayment of amount previously included in income;

20(24) — Amounts paid for undertaking future obligations; 68 — Allocation of amounts paid for combination of services and property; 248(7)(a) — Amount deemed received when mailed.

Notes: Although 12(1)(a)(i) requires an income inclusion, an offsetting reserve may be allowed by 20(1)(m), and a deduction by 20(1)(m.2) when amounts are repaid. Where no 20(1)(m) reserve is sought, it does not matter whether an amount is included under 12(1)(a) or under 9(1): VIEWS doc 2014-0524751I7 (minimally revised 2015-0566681I7).

12(1)(a)(ii) refers to container and bottle deposits.

In *Destacamento*, 2009 TCC 242, and *Demeterio*, 2011 TCC 192, advance commissions on insurance sales fell under 12(1)(a) even though they might have to be paid back; no reserve was allowed due to 32(1). CRA applies this rule: doc 2013-0475571E5.

For discussion of 12(1)(a) see Joseph Frankovic, "The Taxation of Prepaid Income", 50(4) *Canadian Tax Journal* 1239-1306 (2002).

Money from the sale of gift certificates falls under 12(1)(a), but a 20(1)(m) reserve can be claimed: VIEWS docs 2007-0254551I7, 2008-0300811I7, 2009-0349561E5.

On the interaction with 20(24) where a purchaser assumes a vendor's obligations, see doc 2010-0375921E5; and 9909965, 9924585 (prepaid rent may be considered proceeds of disposition).

Interpretation Bulletins: IT-154R: Special reserves; IT-165R: Returnable containers (cancelled); IT-321R: Insurance agents and brokers — unearned commissions (cancelled); IT-457R: Election by professionals to exclude work in progress from income; IT-531: Eligible funeral arrangements.

I.T. Technical News: 18 (*Oerlikon Aérospatiale* case); 30 (prepaid income — whether 9(1) or 12(1)(a) applies).

CRA Audit Manual: 27.25.0: Income of professionals and fiscal period issues.

Forms: T2125: Statement of business or professional activities.

(b) **amounts receivable** — any amount receivable by the taxpayer in respect of property sold or services rendered in the course of a business in the year, notwithstanding that the amount or any part thereof is not due until a subsequent year, unless the method adopted by the taxpayer for computing income from the business and accepted for the purpose of this Part does not require the taxpayer to include any amount receivable in computing the taxpayer's income for a taxation year unless it has been received in the year, and for the purposes of this paragraph, an amount shall be deemed to have become receivable in respect of services rendered in the course of a business on the day that is the earlier of

(i) the day on which the account in respect of the services was rendered, and

(ii) the day on which the account in respect of those services would have been rendered had there been no undue delay in rendering the account in respect of the services;

Related Provisions: 12(2) — Rule is for greater certainty only; 34 — Professional business — election to exclude work in progress until 2017; 68 — Allocation of amounts in consideration for disposition of property; 78 — Unpaid amounts; 138(11.5)(k) — Transfer of business by non-resident insurer.

Notes: Although 12(1)(b) requires income inclusion of any amount receivable for services rendered even if not due, IT-92R2 para. 12 allows the "completion method" to be used for construction contracts when the contract is expected to be completed within two years from start. All revenue is recognized in the year the work is physically completed. (The method cannot be used for a business of processing data to create survey maps: VIEWS doc 2006-0191371E5. Nor can it be used for water or sewer works, building renovations or any other non-construction contract of the same contractor: 2011-0404021E5; or for communication and electricity structures: 2012-0463181I7. "Construction" is a very general term that can include demolition; and this method can be used by a non-resident: 2009-0316421E5.) "Receivable" means there is a legal right to enforce payment; "where a contract provides for a holdback pending architect or engineer approval or expiry of a lien period, the amount held back is not considered receivable until such condition is met": 2007-0228811E5. See also 9(1) Notes at "Disbursements".

The "unless..." exception allows amounts receivable to be excluded if the taxpayer is using the cash method, under s. 28 or otherwise, "accepted for the purpose of this Part". It is unclear whether "accepted" means the CRA has to accept it.

No reserve is allowed for goods sold and expected to be returned, or based on actual returns shortly after year-end. See 18(1)(e); VIEWS doc 2002-0129813; *Sinnott News*, [1956] C.T.C. 81 (SCC); *Harlequin Enterprises*, [1977] C.T.C. 208 (FCA).

"Receivable" requires an unconditional right to receive income, and a binding agreement fixing the amount: *Maple Leaf Mills*, [1976] C.T.C. 324 (SCC), para. 13. See *Huang & Danczkay*, [2000] 4 C.T.C. 219 (FCA) (amounts owing on debt instruments were "receivable", despite no immediate right to payment); *Heritage Education Funds*, 2010 TCC 161 (unpaid RESP enrolment fees were "receivable", but previous years' amounts needed to be excluded from the year's income for the same reason); *Lockwood Financial*, 2020 TCC 128, para. 53 (fee subject to condition precedent was not yet "receivable") [Yang & Wang, "Share Compensation Taxable as Business Income When Receivable", 11(1) *Canadian Tax Focus* (ctf.ca) 15-16 (Feb. 2021)].

Receivables for services rendered are included under 12(1)(b) even if they are not recorded for accounting purposes due to being likely uncollectable: *Chartwell Management*, 2004 TCC 728; and even if provincial legislation (the *Ontario Legal Aid Act*) prohibits the account from being paid when rendered: *Hamilton*, 2005 TCC 625. See also VIEWS doc 2007-0262931E5.

Legal fees under a contingency fee arrangement need only be recognized when billed or billable, unless they have been received: VIEWS doc 2003-0015775. In *Baribeau*, 2011 TCC 125, 12(1)(b) did not apply to shares transferred by a company to its shareholder, as he had not rendered an account for services.

Accounting for leasing income on a straight-line basis as per *CICA Handbook* §3065.55 would not be in accordance with 12(1)(b): VIEWS doc 2006-0169231E5.

For GST interpretation of "undue delay", used in 12(1)(b)(ii), see *Lacroix (Canadevim)*, 2011 FCA 128 (leave to appeal denied [2012] G.S.T.C. 12 (SCC)) (failure to bill for partly-completed golf course construction that stopped was undue delay); *DHM Energy*, [1995] G.S.T.C. 3 (TCC) (delay at recipient's request was not undue delay); *International Hi-Tech*, 2018 TCC 240 (FCA appeal discontinued A-426-18), paras. 57-63 (accounting firm not rendering invoice). In *Spur Oil*, [1981] C.T.C. 336 (FCA), para. 12, "undue" (in the phrase "unduly reduces income") was held to mean "excessive".

See also VIEWS doc 2008-0287901R3 (12(1)(b) applies to consideration for immovable under emphyteutic lease with purchase option).

Interpretation Bulletins: IT-92R2: Income of contractors; IT-129R: Lawyers' trust accounts and disbursements; IT-170R: Sale of property — when included in income computation.

CRA Audit Manual: 27.25.0: Income of professionals and fiscal period issues.

(c) **interest** — subject to subsections (3) and (4.1), any amount received or receivable by the taxpayer in the year (depending on the method regularly followed by the taxpayer in computing the taxpayer's income) as, on account of, in lieu of payment of or in satisfaction of, interest to the extent that the interest was not included in computing the taxpayer's income for a preceding taxation year;

Related Provisions: 12(3) — Accrued interest taxable to corporation, partnership and certain trusts; 12(4) — Annual accrual of interest even if unpaid; 12(4.1) — Impaired debt obligations; 12(9.1) — Exception for certain interests in prescribed debt obligations; 12.1 — Cash bonus on Canada Savings Bonds; 16 — Income and capital combined; 16(3) — Bonds purchased at a discount; 16(6) — Indexed debt obligations — amount deemed received as interest; 17 — Interest deemed received on loan to non-resident; 17.1(1) — Deemed interest inclusion from "pertinent loan or indebtedness"; 18(9.1)(e) — Pre-payment penalty on debt repayment deemed to be interest; 20(1)(c) — Deduction for interest paid; 20(1)(l) — Reserve for doubtful debts; 20(1)(p) — Deduction for bad debts; 20(14) — Accrued bond interest; 20(14.1) — Interest on debt obligation; 137(4.1) — Interest deemed received on certain reductions of capital by credit union; 142.5(3)(a), (b) — Mark-to-market debt obligation; 146.2(7) — No tax on interest income received in TFSA; 218 — Loan to wholly-owned subsidiary; 248(7)(a) — Interest payment deemed received when mailed; 258(3) — Certain dividends on preferred shares deemed to be interest; 258(5) — Deemed interest on certain shares; Canada-U.S. Tax Treaty:Art. XI — Taxation of interest.

Notes: *Meaning of "interest"*: compensation for the use of money belonging to or owed to another: *Sherway Centre*, [1998] 2 C.T.C. 343 (FCA); *Cassan*, 2017 TCC 174 (FCA appeal settled A-304-17), para. 381. Or "the return or consideration or compensation for the use or retention by one person of a sum of money, belonging to, in a colloquial sense, or owed to, another": *Shell Canada*, [1999] 4 C.T.C. 313 (SCC), para. 30. "Symmetry is the essence of interest ... an amount is not interest if it does not have the character of interest to both the recipient and the payer": *Plains Midstream*, 2019 FCA 57, para. 90. In *Pike*, [2014] EWCA Civ 824, para. 18, the England & Wales Court of Appeal stated: "First, it is calculated by reference to an underlying debt. Second, it is a payment made according to time, by way of compensation for the use of money. Third, the sum payable accrues from day to day or at other periodic intervals. Fourth, whilst the payment so accrues, it does not ... have to be paid at any intervals: it is possible for interest not to become payable until the principal becomes payable. Fifth, what the payment is called is not determinative.... Sixth, the fact that an interest payment may be aggregated with a payment of a different nature does not [matter]." In *Solar Power v. ClearFlow*, 2018 ONCA 727, paras. 35, 42 (non-tax case; leave to appeal denied 2019 CarswellOnt 4702 (SCC)), a daily "discount fee" was held to be interest; an administration fee was not. See also VIEWS docs 2002-0162255 (meaning of "loan"); 2015-0589841E5 (general comments); 2015-0609071E5 (credit union savings account mortgage incentive is not interest but may be taxable under 12(1)(x)); 2018-0776381R3 (negative repo spread in "reverse repo" securities repurchase is not interest); 2020 IFA Roundtable q.2 (interest component of swap payment is not interest unless that is its legal character); 2020-0867071C6 [2020 APFF q.16] (payments under swap agreement are not interest, so 212(1)(b) does not apply [reversing 1984 CTF Roundtable q.60]); and 79(1)"debt" Notes on the meaning of "debt". Where a payment combines interest and principal, see 16(1). See also Friedlander, *Taxation of Corporate Finance* (Carswell, looseleaf or *Taxnet Pro* Reference Centre), §2.1.1; Caines, "Very Short-Term Crypto Loans", 11(2) *Canadian Tax Focus* (ctf.ca) 3-4 (May 2021) (payment for a cryptocurrency "flash" loan, repaid at the same instant made).

Interest accruing on a bond (including a strip bond or banker's acceptance) is normally taxed annually: see 12(3) for corporations, 12(4) for individuals.

The payer of interest must normally issue a T5: see Reg. 201(1)(b).

Pre-judgment interest ***(PJI)***: Before 2004, PJI on a wrongful dismissal **(WD)** award was considered non-taxable. The CRA now says PJI is taxable if the underlying award is taxable: *Income Tax Technical News* 30. Thus, PJI for WD is considered taxable, while such interest on an award for personal injury or death, or retroactive workers' compensation claims, is not (VIEWS docs 2003-0035267, 2003-0038025, 2004-0060321E5, 2006-0182471E5, 2013-0475631I7).

CRA's position might not be correct. Earlier cases *Coughlan*, [2001] 4 C.T.C. 2004 (TCC), and *Ahmad*, [2002] 4 C.T.C. 2497 (TCC), ruled that PJI is not taxable if no debt is owed the taxpayer until judgment is issued, but if the interest is based on an amount that was already owing, it is taxable. However, CRA's policy change was upheld in *Davies*, 2007 TCC 409. In *Naraine*, 2015 TCC 104, para. 12 (aff'd on other grounds 2016 FCA 6), the TCC ruled PJI on a WD award taxable under 12(1)(c) without explaining why. In *Valley Equipment*, 2008 FCA 65, the basis for a PJI award (on top of damages for cancellation of a dealer agreement) was unclear; the Court gave VE the benefit of the doubt and treated it as additional damages (capital gain).

PJI on a *pay equity award* is taxable: *Montgomery*, 2007 TCC 317; *Cloutier-Hunt*, 2007 TCC 345; *Darcy*, 2007 CarswellNat 2258 (TCC); *Loubier*, 2007 TCC 350; *van Elslande*, 2007 TCC 370; and this did not violate the *Charter of Rights* when CRA policy exempted other PJI: *Burrows*, 2005 TCC 761 (FCA appeal discontinued A-19-06). Retroactive salary increase for Quebec judges [under *Courts of Justice Act*] was not tax-exempt damages, so PJI was taxable: *Gaboury*, 2015 TCC 235. Interest included in a QPP disability award for past years was taxable: *St-Pierre*, 2008 TCC 209.

In *Bernardin*, 2021 QCCA 625, PJI on a Quebec class action (damage from snowmobile nuisance) was non-taxable for Quebec purposes even after judgment was pronounced, until the award was final and all appeal periods had expired.

Interest is considered taxable if included in a lump-sum payment of support arrears (VIEWS doc 2011-0407661E5) or lost wages (2011-0407421E5).

Post-judgment interest is taxable in CRA's view: docs 9727105, 2003-0031035, 2011-0429401I7, 2013-0475631I7 (but see *Bernardin* case above).

In *MacKinnon*, 2007 TCC 658, M sued to recover her deceased son's RRSP, which had been mistakenly paid to his estate although M was named beneficiary. The sum awarded to M by the Court as "interest" on the RRSP from date of death was taxable under 12(1)(c).

In *Roszko*, 2014 TCC 59, interest received by an innocent investor in a Ponzi scheme was treated as non-taxable return of capital. However, in *Johnson*, 2012 FCA 253 (leave to appeal denied 2013 CarswellNat 633 (SCC)), a Ponzi scheme early investor who benefited innocently from fraud on others was taxable on the income, because she received the return she bargained for even though the promoter acted fraudulently.

An interest indemnity under Quebec *Civil Code* §1619 is taxable: VIEWS doc 2005-0162821I7. A recovery (settling a class action) of interest paid on student loans is not (though interest on the settlement is): 2008-0285311C6. Interest on an unpaid equalization payment under a spousal separation agreement is taxable: 2009-0324621E5.

A participation payment may be interest in some cases: VIEWS doc 2008-0293561E5. Notes payable via delivery of gold are the forward sale of gold, not payments of interest (for non-resident withholding tax purposes): 2009-0326881R3, 2009-0348861R3.

Accepting reduced or no interest in exchange for something else (e.g., lower club dues or lower apartment rent) is considered taxable as interest: VIEWS docs 2005-0165371E5, 2006-0189101E5, 2006-0171231E5 (life lease arrangement), 2012-0455921E5 (free rent in lieu of interest on a mortgage). However, in 2008-0266481R3 and 2009-0342461R3, if a major bank charges a lower mortgage rate to customers with matching savings accounts (a "Performance Offset Mortgage"), only the interest actually paid to customers is taxable to them.

Damages for breaching an obligation to pay interest would be "in lieu of" interest, but when a debt is repaid before its term, an amount paid to compensate for the loss of potential future interest is not "in lieu of" interest: *Puder*, [1963] C.T.C. 445 (Ex. Ct.); *Transocean Offshore Ltd.*, 2005 FCA 104, leave to appeal denied 2005 CarswellNat 3125 (SCC). An early redemption penalty paid by the lender does not reduce interest earned in CRA's view: VIEWS doc 2007-0228831E5. In *Holzhey*, 2007 TCC 247, a right to receive accrued interest on a loan, when deemed disposed of on emigration, was taxable "in lieu of interest".

Where a government bond is purchased at a discount, the difference to maturity may be deemed to be interest; see 16(3). Where a bond is sold with accrued interest, payment received in respect of the interest is taxable; see 20(14). The discount on a banker's acceptance is taxable under 12(1)(c): VIEWS doc 2010-0379151E5 (disposition before maturity could give rise to a capital gain).

A "bonus" received on a loan is normally taxable: *West Coast Parts*, [1964] C.T.C. 519 (Exch. Ct.); *Western Union Insurance*, [1983] C.T.C. 363 (FCTD); VIEWS doc 2010-0368641E5.

Interest income that is accruing must be reported annually: 12(3) (for corporations), 12(4) (for individuals). This rule could also apply to a no-interest non-arm's length loan: see Notes to 12(4). If it is not received when due, it can be deducted under

20(1)(p)(i) as a bad debt (with a 20(1)(l) doubtful-debt reserve until it is known to be bad): docs 2010-0379941E5, 2012-0449671E5.

If a debt goes bad after interest is received, the interest remains taxable: docs 2013-0489731M4, 2018-0760751E5, 2018-0761111E5 (the debt may be a capital loss, or deducted under 20(1)(p) or 39(1)(c)).

Interest income that is ancillary to a business may be part of business income. See Notes to 9(1) under "Interest income".

Refund interest from CRA on a reassessment is taxable in the year received: *Greenwood*, 2011 TCC 214; VIEWS doc 2012-0469301M4.

Interest earned by a fund set up by a group of truck owners to cover an emergency, if the arrangement is not a partnership or trust, should be allocated and reported by each co-owner of the fund: VIEWS doc 2009-0346641E5. Interest on a mortgage pool was taxable, net of servicing fees, in 2011-0431891R3. Interest earned in a UK Individual Savings Account (similar to a TFSA) is taxable (even if it was opened for retirement purposes), as there is no treaty relief: 2013-0478241E5, 2013-0485661E5. A bonus or incentive payment, calculated as a percentage of a balance in an account over time, is interest: 2014-0517121E5. *Negative interest* on overnight deposits may be deductible under 9(1) depending on the facts: 2016-0666411E5 [Arnould, "Can Interest be Negative?", XX(4) *Corporate Finance* (Federated Press) 8-12 (2017)].

Where parties created false contracts to evade reporting interest income, access to the courts to enforce any part of the contracts was denied: *Wojnarowski v. Bomar Alarms*, 2010 ONSC 273, para. 71.

A deduction was once available in 110.1 for individuals to offset the first $1,000 of interest income from Canadian sources, but this was eliminated in 1988.

12(1)(c) amended by 2001 technical bill (effective for taxation years that end after Sept. 1997) and 1995-97 technical bill.

Regulations: 201(1)(b) (information return).

Interpretation Bulletins: IT-265R3: Payments of income and capital combined (cancelled); IT-396R: Interest income.

I.T. Technical News: 30 (pre-judgment interest).

Advance Tax Rulings: ATR-61: Interest accrual rules.

Forms: RC257: Request for an information return program account (RZ); T5: Statement of investment income; T5 Summ: Return of investment income.

(d) **reserve for doubtful debts** — any amount deducted under paragraph 20(1)(l) as a reserve in computing the taxpayer's income for the immediately preceding taxation year;

Related Provisions: 87(2.2) — Amalgamation of insurers; 88(1)(g) — Windup of subsidiary insurer; 138(11.5)(k) — Transfer of business by non-resident insurer; 138(11.91)(d) — Income of non-resident insurer; 142.3(1)(c) — Amount deductible in respect of specified debt obligation.

Notes: See Notes to 20(1)(l) and 20(1)(p).

Interpretation Bulletins: IT-442R: Bad debts and reserve for doubtful debts.

Forms: T2 Sched. 13: Continuity of reserves.

(d.1) **reserve for guarantees, etc.** — any amount deducted under paragraph 20(1)(l.1) as a reserve in computing the taxpayer's income for the immediately preceding taxation year;

Related Provisions: 138(11.91)(d) — Income of non-resident insurer.

(d.2) **[unamortized bond premium reserve]** — any amount deducted under paragraph 20(1)(m.3) as a reserve in computing the taxpayer's income for the immediately preceding taxation year;

Related Provisions: 138(11.91)(d) — Income of non-resident insurer.

Notes: 12(1)(d.2) added by 2017 budget bill #2, for bonds issued after 2000.

(e) **reserves for certain goods and services, etc.** — any amount

(i) deducted under paragraph 20(1)(m) (including any amount substituted by virtue of subsection 20(6) for any amount deducted under that paragraph), paragraph 20(1)(m.1) or subsection 20(7), or

(ii) deducted under paragraph 20(1)(n),

in computing the taxpayer's income from a business for the immediately preceding year;

Related Provisions: 66.2(2)(b)(ii)(B), 66.4(2)(a)(ii)(B) — Deductions for resource expenses; 87(2.2) — Amalgamation of insurers; 88(1)(g) — Windup of subsidiary insurer; 138(11.91)(d) — Computation of income of non-resident insurer.

Notes: If a 20(1)(m) reserve is allowed in a year for which a waiver was filed, the parallel 12(1)(e) inclusion in the next year (otherwise statute-barred) is allowed by 152(4.3): VIEWS doc 2012-0463681I7.

Interpretation Bulletins: IT-73R6: The small business deduction; IT-154R: Special reserves.

I.T. Technical News: 30 (prepaid income — whether 9(1) or 12(1)(a) applies).

CRA Audit Manual: 27.25.0: Income of professionals and fiscal period issues.

Forms: T2 Sched. 13: Continuity of reserves.

(e.1) **[insurer's] negative reserves** — where the taxpayer is an insurer, the amount prescribed in respect of the insurer for the year;

Related Provisions: 20(22) — Deduction in following year; 87(2.2) — Amalgamation of insurers; 88(1)(g)(i) — Windup of subsidiary insurer; 138(11.5)(j.1) — Transfer of business by non-resident insurer; 138(11.91)(d.1)(ii) — Computation of income for non-resident insurer.

Notes: 12(1)(e.1) added by 1996 Budget, for 1996 and later tax years. It requires income inclusion of an insurer's "negative reserves"; an offsetting deduction is allowed the next year under 20(22). Negative policy reserves arise where the present value of future premiums exceeds the present value of future estimated benefits and expenses in respect of the insurer's policies. See Reg. 1400(2).

An earlier 12(1)(e.1), proposed in the July 12, 1994 draft legislation on debt forgiveness, was not enacted. See now 56.3.

Regulations: 1400(2) (amount prescribed).

(f) **insurance proceeds expended** — such part of any amount payable to the taxpayer as compensation for damage to, or under a policy of insurance in respect of damage to, property that is depreciable property of the taxpayer as has been expended by the taxpayer

(i) within the year, and

(ii) within a reasonable time after the damage,

on repairing the damage;

Related Provisions: 13(21)"proceeds of disposition"(c), (f) — Depreciable property — proceeds of disposition.

Notes: The income inclusion is normally offset by the repair expense: VIEWS doc 2015-0605581E5.

(g) **payments based on production or use** — any amount received by the taxpayer in the year that was dependent on the use of or production from property whether or not that amount was an instalment of the sale price of the property, except that an instalment of the sale price of agricultural land is not included by virtue of this paragraph;

Related Provisions: 12(2.01) — No deferral of amounts taxable anyway under s. 9; 212(1)(b)(ii), 212(3)"participating debt interest" — Parallel rule for non-resident withholding tax; 212(1)(d)(v) — Earn-out payments to non-resident; Canada-U.S. Tax Treaty:Art. XI:6(b) — U.S. resident's interest income based on sales or cash flow.

Notes: See IT-462. Although 12(1)(g) technically taxes any amount based on production or use of property, CRA accepts a "cost recovery method", when (capital property) shares of a corp are sold at arm's length with an earnout agreement (based on the underlying goodwill), as not triggering 12(1)(g) but instead reducing the cost as proceeds are received over up to 5 years, with the excess being capital gain. See IT-426R. This method cannot be used on sale of goodwill: VIEWS docs 2004-0098121E5, 2014-0555071E5. It can be used on sale of Aco, which owns Bco, based on Bco's earnings: 2015-0589471R3, 2019-0824531C6 [2019 CTF q.12] (reversing 2013-0480561E5). If the vendor is non-resident, it can be used only if the shares are taxable Canadian property, and otherwise 212(1)(d)(v) imposes withholding tax: 2005-0145311C6 [2005 APFF q.30], 2006-0196211C6 [2006 APFF q.17], 2019-0824461C6 [2019 CTF q.10]. If the vendor does not choose this method, amounts received under the earnout are income under 12(1)(g) and ineligible for the 40(1)(a)(iii) capital gains reserve: 2000-0051115, 2013-0505391E5. CRA will not reassess to apply the method if it was not used on initial filing: 2014-0529221E5.

12(1)(g) is not a relieving provision. If an amount would be included in income anyway under ordinary commercial principles, 12(1)(g) does not affect it: 12(2.01). Income under 12(1)(g) is accounted on the accrual basis as per 9(1): VIEWS docs 2001-0072367, 2008-027826117, but this is wrong in the author's view due to the words "received ... in the year".

CRA will apply 12(1)(g) to: sale of a partnership interest (VIEWS docs 9718365, 2011-0423771E5); royalties paid to investors based on sales volumes (2011-0422891E5); royalties based on production from a well (2014-0532221E5).

12(1)(g) applied in *Smith*, 2011 TCC 461, where the sale price of an insurance brokerage's client list was based on amounts received from the list.

A sale of all timber on a property fell outside 12(1)(g), as it was a one-time sale rather than an ongoing continuous right to use the land: *Wright*, [2003] 1 C.T.C. 2726 (TCC). CRA's view is that a sale of trees may be on capital account, not subject to 12(1)(g), if: the land was not acquired with the specific intention of selling the timber, the sale is an isolated transaction, the price is a fixed amount that does not depend on the use or production of the land, and the timber is removed over a short period: VIEWS docs 2003-0011795, 2003-0036395. (See also doc 2002-0173367 for review of the case law.) Similarly, a one-time contract to remove the gravel or sand in a gravel or sand pit is not subject to 12(1)(g): 2003-007093, 2014-0552551E5.

The fact a payout is income to the vendor under 12(1)(g) does not make it deductible to the purchaser. Often the outlay is capital; see Notes to 18(1)(b).

Reverse earnouts (vendor gets full price but must repay some later if target not met) can allow the proceeds to remain capital if the "full price" is fair market value at time of sale; and repayment required from the vendor is a later capital loss. See IT-462 para 9; VIEWS docs 2009-0337651R3, 2013-0505391E5; *Fiducie Claude Deragon*, 2015 TCC 294; O'Connor & Gwyer, "Earnout Trends", 2014(20) *Tax Times* (Carswell) 1-3 (Oct. 24, 2014); Korhonen, "Reverse Earnouts and the CDA", 5(4) *Canadian Tax Focus* (ctf.ca) 4-5 (Nov. 2015) (interaction with capital dividend account).

For more on 12(1)(g) and earnouts see Joseph Frankovic, "Payments Based on Use or Production", 1713 *Tax Topics* (CCH) 1-4 (Jan. 6, 2005); Pashkowich & Bellefontaine, "Participation-Based Payments", 2017 Cdn Tax Foundation conference report, 9:1-25.

If capital property is sold but not delivered until later, and the price paid includes a financing component, 12(1)(z.7) may tax it as income: see 248(1)"derivative forward agreement".

Interpretation Bulletins: IT-423: Sale of sand, gravel or topsoil (cancelled); IT-426R: Shares sold subject to an earnout agreement; IT-462: Payment based on production or use.

(g.1) proceeds of disposition of right to receive production — any proceeds of disposition to which subsection 18.1(6) applies;

Notes: 12(1)(g.1) added by 1995-97 technical bill, for dispositions after Nov. 17, 1996.

(h) previous reserve for quadrennial survey — any amount deducted as a reserve under paragraph 20(1)(o) in computing the taxpayer's income for the immediately preceding year;

(i) bad debts recovered — any amount, other than an amount referred to in paragraph (i.1), received in the year on account of a debt or a loan or lending asset in respect of which a deduction for bad debts or uncollectable loans or lending assets had been made in computing the taxpayer's income for a preceding taxation year;

Related Provisions: 12.4 — Bad debt inclusion; 20(1)(p) — Bad debts; 22(1) — Sale of accounts receivable; 26(3) — Banks — write-offs and recoveries; 87(2.2) — Amalgamation of insurers; 88(1)(g) — Windup of subsidiary insurer; 111(5.3) — Doubtful debts and bad debts; 138(11.5)(k) — Transfer of business by non-resident insurer; 142.3(1)(c), (g) — Amount deductible in respect of specified debt obligation; 142.5(8)(d)(iv) — First deemed disposition of mark-to-market debt obligation.

Notes: Where a 20(1)(p) bad debt deduction was made by mistake (by a taxpayer not in the business of lending money) and the debt was later recovered, 12(1)(i) did not apply because 20(1)(p) had not permitted the deduction (even though the earlier year was now statute-barred): *Barrington Lane Developments*, 2010 TCC 388.

Income Tax Folios: S3-F4-C1: General discussion of CCA [replaces IT-220R2]; S3-F9-C1: Lottery winnings, miscellaneous receipts, and income (and losses) from crime [replaces IT-185R, IT-213R, IT-256R, IT-334R2].

Interpretation Bulletins: IT-109R2: Unpaid amounts; IT-302R3: Losses of a corporation — the effect that acquisitions of control, amalgamations, and windings-up have on their deductibility; IT-442R: Bad debts and reserve for doubtful debts.

(i.1) bad debts recovered — where an amount is received in the year on account of a debt in respect of which a deduction for bad debts was made under subsection 20(4.2) in computing the taxpayer's income for a preceding taxation year, the amount determined by the formula

$$A \times B/C$$

where

A is ½ of the amount so received,

B is the amount that was deducted under subsection 20(4.2) in respect of the debt, and

C is the total of the amount that was so deducted under subsection 20(4.2) and the amount that was deemed by that subsection or subsection 20(4.3) to be an allowable capital loss in respect of the debt;

Related Provisions: 39(11) — Bad debt recovery; 89(1)"capital dividend account"(c) — Capital dividend account.

Notes: 12(1)(i.1) amended by 2000 Budget, effective for taxation years that end after October 17, 2000.

Interpretation Bulletins: IT-442R: Bad debts and reserve for doubtful debts.

(j) dividends from resident corporations — any amount of a dividend in respect of a share of the capital stock of a corporation resident in Canada that is required by Subdivision H to be included in computing the taxpayer's income for the year;

Related Provisions: 82(1) — Taxable dividends received; 84, 84.1(1)(b) — Deemed dividends; 139.1(4)(f), (g) — Deemed dividend on demutualization of insurance corporation; 139.2 — Deemed dividend on distribution by mutual holding corporation.

Notes: Subdivision h is sections 82 to 89. See Notes to 82(1).

12(1)(j) amended by 2002-2013 technical bill (Part 5 — technical), effective Nov. 6, 2010. (The new wording is consistent with 12(1)(k).)

Interpretation Bulletins: IT-67R3: Taxable dividends from corporations resident in Canada.

Advance Tax Rulings: ATR-15: Employee stock option plan.

(k) foreign corporations, trusts and investment entities — any amount required by Subdivision I to be included in computing the taxpayer's income for the year;

Related Provisions: 90 — Dividends received from non-resident corporation; 91(1), (3) — FAPI inclusions; 91(1), (3), 94(15), (16), 94.2 — Income inclusions in subdivision i; 115(1)(a)(vii)(B) — Authorized foreign bank's taxable income earned in Canada; 258(3) — Certain dividends on preferred shares deemed to be interest; 258(5) — Deemed interest on certain shares.

Notes: Subdivision i is sections 90 to 95. This income inclusion can be from a dividend (90(1)); loan from a foreign affiliate (90(6)-(15)); FAPI (s. 91, including from a non-resident commercial trust under 94.2); or from a non-resident trust (94(15), (16)).

12(1)(k) amended by 2002-2013 technical bill, for tax years that end after 2006.

(l) partnership income — any amount that is, by virtue of Subdivision J, income of the taxpayer for the year from a business or property;

Related Provisions: 96(1)(c)(ii) — Partner taxed on share of partnership's income from business or property; 96(1.1)(b), 96(1.2) — Income inclusion for retired partner.

Notes: Subdivision j is sections 96 to 103.

Interpretation Bulletins: IT-278R2: Death of a partner or of a retired partner.

Forms: T2125: Statement of business or professional activities.

(l.1) partnership — [thin capitalization] interest deduction add back — the total of all amounts, each of which is the amount, if any, determined in respect of a partnership by the formula

$$A \times B/C - D$$

where

A is the total of all amounts each of which is an amount of interest that is

(i) deductible by the partnership, and

(ii) paid by the partnership in, or payable by the partnership in respect of, the taxation year of the taxpayer (depending on the method regularly followed by the taxpayer in computing the taxpayer's income) on a debt amount included in the taxpayer's outstanding debts to specified non-residents (as defined in subsection 18(5)),

B is the amount determined under paragraph 18(4)(a) in respect of the taxpayer for the year,

C is the amount determined under paragraph 18(4)(b) in respect of the taxpayer for the year, and

D is the total of all amounts each of which is an amount included under subsection 91(1) in computing the income of the taxpayer for the year or a subsequent taxation year, or of the partnership for a fiscal period, that may reasonably be considered to be in respect of interest described in A;

Related Provisions: 12(2.02) — Sourcing of income flowing through 12(1)(l.1); 18(5.4) — Trust can designate thin-cap interest paid to non-resident as being payment to beneficiary instead; 18(7) — Partners deemed to owe proportion of partnership debt; 214(16)(a)(ii) — Interest included under 12(1)(l.1) deemed to be dividend subject to withholding tax; 257 — Formula cannot calculate to less than zero.

Notes: 12(1)(l.1) applies the thin capitalization rules in 18(4)-(8) to debts of a partnership that has a Canadian resident corporate partner, by adding back an amount to the corporate partner's income rather than limiting the interest deduction as does 18(4).

Selling the partnership interest to a non-resident before year-end does not avoid 12(1)(l.1): VIEWS doc 2015-0567811E5 [Jamal, "Partnership Withdrawal Creates a Paragraph 12(1)(l.1) Anomaly", 5(4) *Canadian Tax Focus* (ctf.ca) 3-4 (Nov. 2015)].

12(1)(l.1) added by 2012 budget bill #2, for tax years that begin after March 28, 2012.

(m) **benefits from trusts** — any amount required by Subdivision K or subsection 132.1(1) to be included in computing the taxpayer's income for the year, except

(i) any amount deemed by that Subdivision to be a taxable capital gain of the taxpayer, and

(ii) any amount paid or payable to the taxpayer out of or under an RCA trust (within the meaning assigned by subsection 207.5(1));

Related Provisions: 12(1)(n.3) — Retirement compensation arrangement — refund of contributions; 56(1)(x), (z) — Retirement compensation arrangement; 104(7.2) — Income inclusion re capital interest in trust; 104(13), (14) — Income from trusts; 105(1) — Value of benefits from trust; 106(2) — Disposition of income interest in trust — income inclusion.

Notes: Subdivision k is sections 104 to 108.

Reference to 132.1(1) added to 12(1)(m) by 1993 technical bill, effective 1988. 132.1(1) provides that a mutual fund trust may designate an amount for its taxation year in respect of a trust unit, which generally results in a deduction of that amount in computing the trust's income and a corresponding income inclusion for the taxpayer.

(n) **employees profit sharing plan [or employee trust]** — any amount received by the taxpayer in the year out of or under

(i) an employees profit sharing plan, or

(ii) an employee trust

established for the benefit of employees of the taxpayer or of a person with whom the taxpayer does not deal at arm's length;

Related Provisions: 6(1)(d) — Inclusions — allocations etc. under profit sharing plan; 6(1)(g) — Inclusions — employee benefit plan benefits; 20(1)(w) — Deduction to employer; 32.1 — Employee benefit plan deductions; 107.1(a) — Distribution of property by employee trust deemed at FMV; 144(1) — "Employees profit sharing plan" defined; 144(6), (7) — Beneficiary's receipts.

Interpretation Bulletins: IT-502: Employee benefit plans and employee trusts.

(n.1) **employee benefit plan [amount received by employer]** — the amount, if any, by which the total of amounts received by the taxpayer in the year out of or under an employee benefit plan to which the taxpayer has contributed as an employer (other than amounts included in the income of the taxpayer by virtue of paragraph (m)) exceeds the amount, if any, by which the total of all amounts

(i) so contributed by the taxpayer to the plan, or

(ii) included in computing the taxpayer's income for any preceding taxation year by virtue of this paragraph

exceeds the total of all amounts

(iii) deducted by the taxpayer in respect of the taxpayer's contributions to the plan in computing the taxpayer's income for the year or any preceding taxation year, or

(iv) received by the taxpayer out of or under the plan in any preceding taxation year (other than an amount included in the taxpayer's income by virtue of paragraph (m));

Related Provisions: 6(1)(g) — Employee's income inclusion; 18(1)(o) — No deduction for EBP contributions; 32.1 — EBP deductions; 87(2)(j.3) — Amalgamation — continuation of corporation; 107.1(b) — Distribution of property by EBP deemed at cost amount.

Interpretation Bulletins: IT-502: Employee benefit plans and employee trusts.

(n.2) **forfeited salary deferral amounts** — where deferred amounts under a salary deferral arrangement in respect of another person have been deducted under paragraph 20(1)(oo) in computing the taxpayer's income for preceding taxation years, any amount in respect of the deferred amounts that was deductible under paragraph 8(1)(o) in computing the income of the person for a taxation year ending in the year;

Related Provisions: 6(1)(a) — Inclusions — value of benefits; 6(1)(i) — Salary deferral arrangement payments; 6(11) — Salary deferral arrangement; 87(2)(j.3) — Amalgamation — continuing corporation.

(n.3) **retirement compensation arrangement** — the total of all amounts received by the taxpayer in the year in the course of a business out of or under a retirement compensation arrangement to which the taxpayer, another person who carried on a business that was acquired by the taxpayer, or any person with whom the taxpayer or that other person does not deal at arm's length, has contributed an amount that was deductible under paragraph 20(1)(r) in computing the contributor's income for a taxation year;

Related Provisions: 56(1)(x)–(z) — Employee's income inclusion — amounts received from RCA; 87(2)(j.3) — Amalgamation — continuing corporation; 207.5–207.7 — Tax in respect of retirement compensation arrangements.

Notes: See Notes to 248(1)"retirement compensation arrangement". An amount included under 12(1)(n.3) is considered business income: VIEWS doc 2009-0338841E5.

Forms: T4A-RCA: Statement of distributions from an RCA.

(o) [Repealed]

Notes: 12(1)(o), which required inclusion in income of Crown royalties and taxes on production or resource property ownership, amended by 2003 resource bill for amounts that become receivable after Dec. 20, 2002, and repealed for taxation years that begin after 2006 (phased out from 2003-06). See Notes to 18(1)(m) and 20(1)(v.1). Earlier amended by 1996 Budget, 1991 technical bill. Alberta Crown Royalty is not "royalty" for 12(1)(o) because it is a "mere fiction": *Enermark Inc.*, 2009 ABQB 210.

(o.1) **foreign oil and gas production taxes** — the total of all amounts, each of which is the taxpayer's production tax amount for a foreign oil and gas business of the taxpayer for the year, within the meaning assigned by subsection 126(7);

Notes: 12(1)(o.1) added by 2000 Budget, for taxation years that begin after 1999, or earlier by designation (see Notes to 126(5)).

(p) **certain payments to farmers** — any amount received by the taxpayer in the year as a stabilization payment, or as a refund of a levy, under the *Western Grain Stabilization Act* or as a payment, or a refund of a premium, in respect of the gross revenue insurance program established under the *Farm Income Protection Act*;

Related Provisions: 20(1)(ff) — Deductions — payments by farmers; 135.2(7), (9) — Income from selling unit of Canadian Wheat Board Farmers' Trust.

Notes: 12(1)(p) amended by 1992 technical bill, effective 1991.

Regulations: 234–236 (information slips for farm support payments).

Remission Orders: *Farmers' Income Taxes Remission Order*, P.C. 1993-1647 (remission of tax on certain income under 12(1)(p) for 1992).

(q) **employment tax deduction** — [No longer relevant]

Notes: The employment tax credit under former 127(13)–(16) was repealed effective 1989, so this paragraph is inoperative.

I.T. Application Rules: 69 (meaning of "chapter 148 of ...").

(r) **inventory adjustment [depreciation, etc.]** — the total of all amounts each of which, in respect of a property described in the taxpayer's inventory at the end of the year and valued at its cost amount to the taxpayer for the purposes of computing the taxpayer's income for the year, is an allowance in respect of depreciation, obsolescence or depletion included in that cost amount;

Related Provisions: 10(1) — Inventory valuation; 20(1)(ii) — Deduction allowed in next year; 87(2)(j.1) — Amalgamations — inventory adjustment.

Notes: 12(1)(r) and 20(1)(ii) overturn *Quebec North Shore Paper*, [1978] C.T.C. 628 (FCTD), where depreciation on inventory was allowed.

(s) [Repealed]

Notes: 12(1)(s), "reinsurance commission", repealed by 2002-2013 technical bill (Part 5 — technical), for reinsurance commissions paid after 1999. It and 20(1)(jj) were no longer appropriate due to 18(9.02).

(t) **investment tax credit** — the amount deducted under subsection 127(5) or (6) in respect of a property acquired or an expenditure made in a preceding taxation year in computing the taxpayer's tax payable for a preceding taxation year to the extent that it was not included in computing the taxpayer's income for a preceding taxation year under this paragraph or is not included in an amount determined under paragraph 13(7.1)(e) or 37(1)(e), subparagraph 53(2)(c)(vi) or (h)(ii) or for I in the definition "undepreciated capital cost" in subsection 13(21) or L in the definition "cumulative Canadian exploration expense" in subsection 66.1(6);

Related Provisions: 12(1)(x) — Other government assistance; 70(1) — Death of a taxpayer; 87(2)(j.6) — Amalgamation — continuing corporation; 88(2)(c) — Winding-up of a Canadian corporation.

Notes: Investment tax credits claimed may be allocated (under "well-accepted business principles") to reduce the cost of depreciable property (s. 13) or capital property (s. 53) or allocated against R&D expenses (s. 37) or Canadian exploration expenses (66.1). If not used in any of these ways, the ITC is taxable under 12(1)(t) as a benefit received from government. See IT-273R2 paras. 2, 21; VIEWS doc 2007-0244621I7. For other kinds of assistance, see 12(1)(x).

Interpretation Bulletins: IT-210R2: Income of deceased persons — periodic payments and investment tax credit; IT-273R2: Government assistance — general comments.

Information Circulars: 78-4R3: Investment tax credit rates.

(u) **home insulation or energy conversion grants** — the amount of any grant received by the taxpayer in the year under a prescribed program of the Government of Canada relating to home insulation or energy conversion in respect of a property used by the taxpayer principally for the purpose of gaining or producing income from a business or property;

Related Provisions: 13(7.1) — Deemed capital cost of certain property; 53(2)(k) — Adjustments to cost base; 56(1)(s) — Amounts to be included in income for year — grants under prescribed programs.

Regulations: 224 (information return); 5500, 5501 (prescribed program).

(v) **research and development deductions** — the amount, if any, by which the total of amounts determined at the end of the year in respect of the taxpayer under paragraphs 37(1)(d) to (h) exceeds the total of amounts determined at the end of the year in respect of the taxpayer under paragraphs 37(1)(a) to (c.1);

Related Provisions: 37(1)(c.1) — Deduction allowed in later year.

Forms: T2 Sched. 14: Miscellaneous payments to residents.

(w) **subsec. 80.4(1) benefit** — where the taxpayer is a corporation that carried on a personal services business at any time in the year or a preceding taxation year, the amount deemed by subsection 80.4(1) to be a benefit received by it in the year from carrying on a personal services business;

Interpretation Bulletins: IT-421R2: Benefits to individuals, corporations and shareholders from loans or debt.

(x) **inducement, reimbursement, [refund] etc.** — any particular amount (other than a prescribed amount) received by the taxpayer in the year, in the course of earning income from a business or property, from

(i) a person or partnership (in this paragraph referred to as the "payer") who pays the particular amount

(A) in the course of earning income from a business or property,

(B) in order to achieve a benefit or advantage for the payer or for persons with whom the payer does not deal at arm's length, or

(C) in circumstances where it is reasonable to conclude that the payer would not have paid the amount but for the receipt by the payer of amounts from a payer, government, municipality or public authority described in this subparagraph or in subparagraph (ii), or

(ii) a government, municipality or other public authority,

where the particular amount can reasonably be considered to have been received

(iii) as an inducement, whether as a grant, subsidy, forgivable loan, deduction from tax, allowance or any other form of inducement, or

(iv) as a refund, reimbursement, contribution or allowance or as assistance, whether as a grant, subsidy, forgivable loan, deduction from tax, allowance or any other form of assistance, in respect of

(A) an amount included in, or deducted as, the cost of property, or

(B) an outlay or expense,

to the extent that the particular amount

(v) was not otherwise included in computing the taxpayer's income, or deducted in computing, for the purposes of this Act, any balance of undeducted outlays, expenses or other amounts, for the year or a preceding taxation year,

(v.1) is not an amount received by the taxpayer in respect of a restrictive covenant, as defined by subsection 56.4(1), that was included, under subsection 56.4(2), in computing the income of a person related to the taxpayer,

(vi) except as provided by subsection 127(11.1), (11.5) or (11.6), does not reduce, for the purpose of an assessment made or that may be made under this Act, the cost or capital cost of the property or the amount of the outlay or expense, as the case may be,

(vii) does not reduce, under subsection (2.2) or 13(7.4) or paragraph 53(2)(s), the cost or capital cost of the property or the amount of the outlay or expense, as the case may be, and

(viii) may not reasonably be considered to be a payment made in respect of the acquisition by the payer or the public authority of an interest in the taxpayer, an interest in, or for civil law a right in, the taxpayer's business or an interest in, or for civil law a real right in, the taxpayer's property;

Related Provisions: 12(1)(t) — Investment tax credits; 12(1)(x.2) — Crown royalty refund — income inclusion; 12(2.1) — Where partner or trust beneficiary receives inducement; 12(2.2) — Election to exclude amount from income; 13(7.1), (7.4) — Capital cost of depreciable property reduced by assistance; 20(1)(hh) — Repayments of inducements, etc.; 37(1)(d.1) — Reduction of R&D pool for provincial super R&D allowance; 53(2)(k) — Reduction in ACB — assistance; 53(2.1) — Election to reduce capital cost; 80(1)"excluded obligation"(a)(i) — Debt forgiveness rules do not apply where amount included under 12(1)(x); 80.2 — Royalty reimbursements; 80.3(2) — Deferral of income from assistance to farmers for destroying livestock; 87(2)(j.6) — Amalgamation — continuing corporation; 125.4(5) — Canadian film/video credit deemed to be assistance; 125.5(5) — Film/video production services credit deemed to be assistance; 125.6(3) — Journalism labour credit deemed received as assistance before year-end; 125.7(3) — COVID-19 wage subsidy deemed to be assistance; 127(9) — Meaning of "non-government assistance" for ITC purposes; 127(18) — Reduction of qualified expenditures for ITC to reflect assistance; 143.4(4) — Contingency added later to previously-claimed expenditure triggers 12(1)(x) inclusion; 248(16), (16.1), (18), (18.1) — GST and QST input tax credit, refund and rebate deemed to be assistance.

Notes: 12(1)(x) applies to a wide range of government and other assistance including leasehold inducements, GST/HST input tax credits and rebates (see 248(16) and VIEWS doc 2009-0309291I7), Canadian film/video production credit (125.4(5)), film/video production services credit (125.5(5)), journalism labour credit (125.6(3)), Canada Emergency Wage Subsidy (CEWS) (125.7(3)). Such amounts can first be applied against the cost of depreciable property (13(7.1) or (7.4)) or the adjusted cost base of capital property (53(2)(s)); for investment tax credits, see 12(1)(t). Any amount not so allocated (12(1)(x)(v)) is taxable. For provincial R&D incentives, see 127(9)"super-allowance benefit amount". See also Reg. 7300, prescribing excluded amounts. See s. 3 Notes for amounts not taxed at all. 12(1)(x) overrules *Consumer's Gas*, [1987] 1 C.T.C. 79 (FCA).

CEWS is taxed in the year 125.7(3) deems it received (in the relevant "qualifying period"), even if it is not claimed until later: VIEWS doc 2020-0865661I7.

A 12(2.2) election prevents 12(1)(x) from applying by deeming the refund or assistance to reduce the original expense. This is useful if 12(1)(x) makes taxable a refund of an amount that was not earlier deductible. See VIEWS docs 2003-0048545, 2004-0086361E5; Stack, "An Update on Paragraph 12(1)(x) and Subsection 12(2.2)", III(4) *Resource Sector Taxation* (Federated Press) 244-48 (2005).

Repayment of an amount taxed under 12(1)(x) is deductible under 20(1)(hh).

Opening words: "received" must mean more than accepting possession of an amount and using it for a period of time, so payments GMAC received but might have to repay were not "received": *GMAC Leaseco*, 2015 TCC 146, para. 40. On *when* a tax credit or reduction is "received", see *Income Tax Technical News* 29. In *Herdt & Charton inc.*, 2007 QCCQ 14504, GST and Quebec Sales Tax refunds were taxable even though the business they related to had been sold.

12(1)(x)(i) does not catch payment by a subsidiary to a parent to compensate for benefit to the sub's employees from exercising options to buy shares in the parent, and share appreciation rights: doc 2006-0217541R3.

12(1)(x)(iii), (iv): in *PCI Géomatics*, 2020 QCCA 1342 (reversing the QCCQ), an Industry Canada loan that was forgiven if revenues steadily decreased was a "forgivable loan" (FL). Canada Emergency Business Account (CEBA) forgivable portion of loan is taxable: VIEWS docs 2020-0861481E5, 2020-0862931C6 [2020 APFF q.18], 2020-0864141E5, 2020-0869931E5; Roseman & Loney, "Taxing the CEBA and the CEWS", tinyurl.com/mclennan-ceba; Qian & Luan, "Achieving Temporary Relief from Tax on CEBA Loans" 11(1) *Canadian Tax Focus* (ctf.ca) 14-15 (Feb. 2021). See also 2006-018443I17 (loan is not FL); 2010-0364761E5 (Part XII.4 tax credit under 127.41 is not an "inducement"); 2021-087923117 (Regional Relief and Recovery Fund, forgivable portion of contribution).

12(1)(x)(iv): "refund", added in 1997, overrules *Canada Safeway*, [1998] 1 C.T.C. 120 (FCA), where a federal sales tax refund was ruled non-taxable. In *Iron Ore Co.*, 2001 FCA 224, "refund" included a refund of provincial sales tax paid in error (s. 9 might also have applied). In *Bois Aisé De Roberval*, [1999] 4 C.T.C. 2161 (TCC), refunds under the *Softwood Lumber Products Export Charge Act* for export charges paid in error were "refunds". (See also *Leggett v. Brink Forest*, 2008 BCSC 1783, where such refunds were evidently taxable; and 12(1)(z.6) Notes.)

In *Glubis*, 2015 SKPC 143, BASF farm chemicals rebates, and refunds of levies from the Saskatchewan Flax, Canola and Mustard Development Commissions were all taxable (12(1)(x) was not cited, but G was guilty of evasion for not reporting them).

"Assistance": in *CCLC Technologies*, [1996] 3 C.T.C. 246 (FCA), provincial government payments were "assistance", where the contract with CCLC did not give the province any lasting property rights in the technology if it was commercially valuable. In *PSC Elstow Research*, 2008 TCC 694, provincial government R&D assistance was not taxable under 12(1)(x) because it reduced SR&ED qualified expenditures under 127(19). In *Immunovaccine Technologies*, 2014 FCA 196 (leave to appeal denied 2015 CarswellNat 643 (SCC)), funds from Atlantic Canada Opportunities Agency under the Atlantic Innovation Fund were government assistance, even though repayable, because the terms were not a "regular loan" but were based on supporting the project.

"Reimbursement": In *Westcoast Energy*, [1992] 1 C.T.C. 261 (FCA), a settlement for negligence in faulty pipeline construction was held to be damages for negligence rather than "reimbursement" of an expenditure, so was not taxable (*quaere* whether today it might be taxable under *surrogatum*: see 9(1) Notes at "Damages"). In *Alberta Power*, 2009 TCC 412, a government termination payment for the assets of a coal-fired generating plant was held not to be an inducement or reimbursement. See also 9(1) Notes at "Disbursements".

In *Hudson Bay Mining*, 2003 TCC 21, Manitoba investment credits were not taxable under 12(1)(x)(iv) because the taxpayer was acting as agent in a flow-through share arrangement.

12(1)(x)(v): an amount taxed under 9(1) is excluded and thus ineligible for 12(1)(x) treatment: eg. real estate agent's commission "rebate" to business lessee: VIEWS doc 2008-0288691E5. Carbon credits earned by a farmer and sold are taxable as business income: 2007-0232091E5 (see now 27.1).

In *Henco Industries*, 2014 TCC 192, paras. 119-129, an unconditional $650,000 payment from the Ontario government, to assist a Caledonia developer whose business was ruined by native occupation, was not "in the course of earning income from a business or property" because Henco could no longer operate the business, so 12(1)(x) did not apply and the payment was a "freebie".

12(1)(x)(viii): In *Ritchie*, 2018 TCC 113, a "signing bonus" towards granting an easement for a pipeline was excluded by (viii) and was a capital gain. Purchase proceeds paid to a film producer by a broadcaster, to acquire ownership of the production, are excluded by 12(1)(x)(viii): VIEWS doc 2003-0023253.

Generally: If doctor, medical resident or student D receives money from a government or municipality on condition that D practise medicine in a particular place once D qualifies, this may fall under 12(1)(x) or 56(1)(n): docs 2005-0153931E5, 2007-0225741E5 [Manitoba Medical Student/Resident Financial Assistance], 2008-0270781E5, 2008-0295581E5, 2012-0432981E5. See also Reg. 7300(c), which excludes from 12(1)(x) certain forgiveness of loans to D.

Rebates from a remission order, such as the *Coin-Operated Devices GST Remission Order*, may be a gift from the Crown that falls under 12(1)(x): *Income Tax Audit Manual* §27.2.1. Provincial credits earned under the Ontario Community Small Business Investments Programs are excluded from 12(1)(x) to the extent they reduce deductible provincial capital tax: doc 2003-0034663.

CRA considers that the following can fall under 12(1)(x): Aboriginal Business Canada grant (VIEWS doc 2007-0256101E5); BC Forestry Revitalization Trust payment (2006-0172351E5, 2006-0194051E5, 2007-023699117 and see *British Columbia Forestry Revitalization Remission Order*); break fees from mergers and acquisitions (2010-0366321I7, 2012-0467961E5, but see also 9(1) Notes under "Break fees"); Canada Council payments to authors for books in libraries, under the Public Lending Rights Commission (2002-0139485); Canadian Agricultural Income Stabilization payments by Alberta Agriculture Financial Services Corp (2005-0155851E5, and see *Funk*, 2009 MBQB 136); Canadian Farm Families Options Program payments (2007-0228241E5); COVID-19 Canada Emergency Wage Subsidy (125.7(3)); COVID-19 source-deduction wage subsidy in 153(1.02) (tinyurl.com/cra-wagesub (May 26, 2020), q.16); credit union savings account mortgage incentive (2015-0609071E5); disaster or flood compensation to businesses (2013-0481831M4, 2013-0494661E5, 2018-0754221I7); ecoAUTO rebate (2007-026144117); ecoEnergy Retrofit grants (2009-0343911M4); ecological program (2009-0333701M4); exploration inducement payments (2004-0108281R3); fuel-efficient vehicle rebate (2008-0276661E5); GST/HST interest and penalty forgiven under a *Bankruptcy and Insolvency Act* compromise: 2013-0516121E5; interest refunded on overpayment of Crown royalty charges (2002-0164407), even if the payment was non-deductible (2003-0048545), unless a 12(2.2) election is made; life insurance policy broker's commission rebate (2002-015164, 2008-0271381E5, 2010-0359401C6; and see *Scotti*, 2019 QCCQ 7579, where rebates to a client were taxable); mortgage renewal cash-back incentives on rental properties (2016-0681271E5); Newfoundland Community Relocation Program assistance to commercial property owners (2017-0682691E5); Ontario Apprenticeship Training Tax Credit (2010-0378831E5, 2014-0522541E5); Ont. Commercialization Investment Funds program grant (2007-0223081E5); Ont. Home Energy Retrofit grants (2009-0343911M4); Ont. Special Additional Tax on Life Insurance Corporations — credit

against Ont. corporate income tax (2011-0395011E5); PEI Agri-Food Promotion Program (2008-029515117); PEI Alternative Land Use Services Program (2008-029915117); PEI Farm Support Payments (2010-0355841E5 and Reg. 234(2)); provincial *Climate Act* fund to reduce carbon emissions (2010-0376811R3); Quebec capital tax credits (2006-0212641E5); QC government subsidy to build a manure pit (2014-0521041E5); QC immigrant investor payments (2006-0165521E5); QC investment tax credits (2009-0350241E5); QC performances production credit (2012-0440031E5); Quebec Sales Tax input tax refunds (2001-0083295, and see now 248(16.1)); QC on-the-job training periods tax credit (2007-023839117); research grant from provincial government (2008-0288041E5, and see 56(1)(o)); self-employment program for support amounts (2014-0517101E5); signing bonus as inducement for farmer to allow use of his land (2009-035053117); solar panel power credited to homeowner's electricity bill (see 9(1) Notes under "Solar"); stock purchase warrant issued as an incentive (2007-025460117); Strategic Aerospace and Defence Initiative payments (2012-045973117); supplier loyalty inducement (2015-0618601E5); tax liability settlement paid to purchaser of corp for breach of vendor's warranty (2005-0141091C6, 2010-0371461R3); tax losses compensation — contribution of capital to subsidiary (2008-028928117, but position reversed in 2010-035551117).

See also 127(9)"government assistance" Notes.

12(1)(x) amended by 2002-2013 technical bill (last change effective June 26, 2013), 1998 Budget, 1995-97 technical bill, 1995 Budget, 1990 GST. Added by 1985 Budget, for amounts received after May 22, 1985 but with grandfathering for amounts received under terms of an earlier written agreement or prospectus.

Regulations: 234–236 (information slips for farm support payments); 7300 (prescribed amount).

Remission Orders: *British Columbia Forestry Revitalization Remission Order*, P.C. 2013-2 (remission of tax on payments from 2011 Contractor Mitigation Account Subtrust); *Payments Received under the Atlantic Groundfish Licence Retirement Program Remission Order*, P.C. 2013-936 (tax on payments received for 1998-2002 partly reduced for 156 taxpayers).

Interpretation Bulletins: IT-232R3: Losses — their deductibility in the loss year or in other years; IT-273R2: Government assistance — general comments.

I.T. Technical News: 5 (western grain transition payments); 7 (lease inducement payments — renewal term); 16 (*Canderel*, *Toronto College Park* and *Ikea* cases); 29 (application of paragraph 12(1)(x)).

Transfer Pricing Memoranda: TPM-17: The impact of government assistance on transfer pricing.

Application Policies: SR&ED 2005-02: General rules concerning the treatment of government and non-government assistance.

CRA Audit Manual: 27.2.1: Rebates from coin-operated devices remission order; 27.12.4: Farming and fishing income — income tax implications — government assistance; 27.20.0: Inducement payments.

(x.1) **fuel tax rebates** — [No longer relevant]

Notes: 12(1)(x.1) provides income inclusion for now-expired fuel tax rebates. Added by 1992 transportation support bill, which enacted *Excise Tax Act* s. 68.4, a fuel tax rebate for small truckers of up to $500, and the Loss Offset program, under which businesses could claim a fuel tax rebate of 3¢ per litre of fuel purchased, in exchange for which the business had to bring into income 10x the rebate received. The second program was only of interest to businesses with large losses that would not otherwise be used. Both programs applied to 1991-92.

12(1)(x.1) amended by 1997 budget bill #1. The 1997 rebate was part of a package to rescue Canadian Airlines International Ltd. from bankruptcy, but could be used by any airline company. For excise taxes paid 1996-99, airlines could obtain a rebate of up to $20m/year of federal excise tax paid on aviation fuel, by surrendering $10 of accumulated income tax losses for each $1 of rebate. (They could choose to repay the rebate and reinstate the losses within 90 days of their income tax assessment for the year.)

(x.2) **Crown charge [royalty] rebates** — the total of all amounts each of which is an amount that

(i) was received by the taxpayer, including by way of a deduction from tax, in the year as a refund, reimbursement, contribution or allowance, in respect of an amount that was at any time receivable, directly or indirectly in any manner whatever, by Her Majesty in right of Canada or of a province in respect of

(A) the acquisition, development or ownership of a Canadian resource property, or

(B) the production in Canada from a mineral resource, a natural accumulation of petroleum or natural gas, or an oil or a gas well, and

(ii) was not otherwise included in computing the taxpayer's income for the year or a preceding taxation year;

Related Provisions: 12(1)(x)(iii), (iv) — Alternative income inclusion.

Notes: 12(1)(x.2) applies to include a refund of a Crown royalty in income where the Crown royalty was not included into income. Under the 2003 resource bill amendments, once the prohibition in 18(1)(m) is phased out, a taxpayer may either deduct the gross royalty or tax and include any refund or reimbursement into income under 12(1)(x), or elect to reduce the original deduction to the extent of the refund or reimbursement under 12(2.2). In either case, the result is that the net deduction is limited to the mining taxes paid minus any refund or reimbursement. 12(1)(x)(iv) does not apply to a refund or reimbursement of a Crown royalty described in 12(1)(o), since the original Crown royalty does not constitute an outlay or expense. Since the income inclusion in 12(1)(o) is not reduced by any refund or reimbursement, the exclusion of refunds from 12(1)(x)(iv) serves the same purpose as 12(2.2) in the context of mining taxes, namely to avoid double taxation of the refund. However, once the requirement to include the Crown royalty in 12(1)(o) is phased-out (2007), any refund or reimbursement of that Crown royalty is included in income by 12(1)(x.2), consistent with the treatment of refunds or reimbursements of mining taxes. See also Notes to 20(1)(v.1).

For the meaning of "indirectly" in subpara. (i) see Notes to 17.1(1).

12(1)(x.2) does not apply to the Credit on Duties Refundable for Losses under the Quebec *Mining Duties Act*: VIEWS doc 2005-0158451E5.

12(1)(x.2) added by 2003 resource bill, for taxation years that begin after 2002, with phase-in rules (reproduced here up to the 50th ed.) until 2012.

(y) **automobile provided to partner** — where the taxpayer is an individual who is a member of a partnership or an employee of a member of a partnership and the partnership makes an automobile available in the year to the taxpayer or to a person related to the taxpayer, the amounts that would be included by reason of paragraph 6(1)(e) in the income of the taxpayer for the year if the taxpayer were employed by the partnership;

Notes: The benefit in respect of automobile operating costs, under 6(1)(k) or (l), does not apply to partners. Only benefits under 6(1)(e) are included here.

12(1)(y) amended by 1990 GST to add a reference to 6(1)(e.1), and amended by 1997 GST/HST bill, effective for 1996 and later taxation years, to delete the reference. GST is now included in the taxable benefit calculation under 6(7) rather than included in income under 6(1)(e.1).

Interpretation Bulletins: IT-63R5: Benefits, including standby charge for an automobile, from the personal use of a motor vehicle supplied by an employer.

(z) **amateur athlete trust payments** — any amount in respect of an amateur athlete trust required by section 143.1 to be included in computing the taxpayer's income for the year;

Related Provisions: 143.1(2) — Amounts included in beneficiary's income; 146(1)"earned income"(a), (b.2), (c) — Earned income for RRSP purposes.

Notes: 12(1)(z) added by 1992 technical bill, effective 1988.

Forms: T1061: Canadian amateur athletic trust group information return.

(z.1) **qualifying environmental trusts** — the total of all amounts received by the taxpayer in the year as a beneficiary under a qualifying environmental trust, whether or not the amounts are included because of subsection 107.3(1) in computing the taxpayer's income for any taxation year;

Related Provisions: 20(1)(ss) — Deduction for contribution to qualifying environmental trust; 87(2)(j.93) — Amalgamation — continuing corporation; 107.3(2) — Where property of qualifying environmental trust transferred to beneficiary; 107.3(3) — Income where trust ceases to be qualifying environmental trust; 107.3(4) — No income inclusion under 104(13) for amounts payable by trust.

Notes: 12(1)(z.1) added by 1994 Budget, for tax years that end after Feb. 22, 1994; and amended by 1997 Budget, for tax years that end after Feb. 18, 1997.

Reg. 1204(3)(b) provides that amounts included under 12(1)(z.1) are not included for purposes of the pre-2008 resource allowance.

(z.2) **dispositions of interests in qualifying environmental trusts** — the total of all amounts each of which is the consideration received by the taxpayer in the year for the disposition to another person or partnership of all or part of the taxpayer's interest as a beneficiary under a qualifying environmental trust, other than consideration that is the assumption of a reclamation obligation in respect of the trust;

Related Provisions: 20(1)(tt) — Deduction for acquisition of interest in qualifying environmental trust; 39(1)(a)(v) — No capital gain on disposition of interest; 50(1) — Conditions for business investment loss where shares or debt still owned; 87(2)(j.93) — Amalgamation — continuing corporation; 107.3(1)(b) — Where beneficiary not resident in Canada.

Notes: Reg. 1204(3)(b) provides that amounts included under 12(1)(z.2) are not included for purposes of the pre-2008 resource allowance.

12(1)(z.2) added by 1994 Budget, for tax years that end after Feb. 22, 1994; and amended by 1997 Budget, for tax years that end after Feb. 18, 1997.

(z.3) **debt forgiveness** — any amount required because of subsection 80(13) or (17) to be included in computing the taxpayer's income for the year;

Notes: 12(1)(z.3) added by 1994 technical bill, for tax years that end after Feb. 21, 1994.

(z.4) **eligible funeral arrangements** — any amount required because of subsection 148.1(3) to be included in computing the taxpayer's income for the year;

Notes: 12(1)(z.4) added by 1994 technical bill, effective 1993.

Interpretation Bulletins: IT-531: Eligible funeral arrangements.

(z.5) **TFSA amounts** — any amount required by subsection 146.2(9) or section 207.061 to be included in computing the taxpayer's income for the year;

Related Provisions: 212(1)(p) — Non-resident withholding tax.

Notes: 12(1)(z.5) amended to add reference to 207.061 by 2010 budget bill #2, effective Oct. 17, 2009.

12(1)(z.5) added by 2008 budget bill #2, for 2009 and later taxation years.

Former 12(1)(z.5) repealed by 2003 resource bill (see Notes to 20(1)(v.1)), for taxation years that begin after 2006 (phased out from 2003-06). It required inclusion of 25% of a taxpayer's prescribed resource loss. Added by 1996 Budget.

(z.6) **refunds [of countervailing or anti-dumping duties]** — any amount received by the taxpayer in the year in respect of a refund of an amount that was deducted under paragraph 20(1)(vv) in computing income for any taxation year; and

Related Provisions: 13(21)"undepreciated capital cost"K — Deduction of refund from UCC of depreciable property.

Notes: A deposit to a bank to secure a potential countervailing duty obligation was not deductible under 20(1)(vv), so its release did not fall under 12(1)(z.6): *Industries Perron*, 2013 FCA 176, paras. 35-39.

A softwood lumber duty refund, including the interest component, is business income, not property income: VIEWS doc 2007-0252431E5.

12(1)(z.6) added by 1998 Budget, for amounts received after Feb. 23, 1998.

(z.7) **derivative forward agreement [character conversion transaction]** — the total of all amounts each of which is

(i) if the taxpayer acquires a property under a derivative forward agreement in the year, the portion of the amount by which the fair market value of the property at the time it is acquired by the taxpayer exceeds the cost to the taxpayer of the property that is attributable to an underlying interest other than an underlying interest referred to in subparagraphs (b)(i) to (iii) of the definition "derivative forward agreement" in subsection 248(1), or

(ii) if the taxpayer disposes of a property under a derivative forward agreement in the year, the portion of the amount by which the "proceeds of disposition" (within the meaning assigned by Subdivision C) of the property exceeds the fair market value of the property at the time the agreement is entered into by the taxpayer that is attributable to an underlying interest other than an underlying interest referred to in clauses (c)(i)(A) to (C) of the definition derivative forward agreement in subsection 248(1).

Related Provisions: 20(1)(xx) — Deduction for loss; 53(1)(s), (t) — Addition to ACB.

Notes: See Notes to 248(1)"derivative forward agreement".

12(1)(z.7)(i), (ii) both amended by 2017 budget bill #2, for acquisitions and dispositions after Sept. 15, 2016, to add "the portion of" and "that is attributable ... subsection 248(1)".

12(1)(z.7) added by 2013 budget bill #2, for acquisitions and dispositions under a derivative forward agreement entered into after March 20, 2013, with certain grandfathering and certain application to earlier agreements (see these Notes up to the 58th ed.).

(2) Interpretation — Paragraphs (1)(a) and (b) are enacted for greater certainty and shall not be construed as implying that any amount not referred to in those paragraphs is not to be included in computing income from a business for a taxation year whether it is received or receivable in the year or not.

(2.01) No deferral of s. 9 income under para. (1)(g) — Paragraph (1)(g) does not defer the inclusion in income of any amount that would, if this section were read without reference to that paragraph, be included in computing the taxpayer's income in accordance with section 9.

Notes: See Notes to 12(1)(g).

12(2.01) added by 2002-2013 technical bill, effective June 26, 2013.

(2.02) Source of income [flowing through 12(1)(l.1)] — For the purposes of this Act, if an amount is included in computing the income of a taxpayer for a taxation year because of paragraph (1)(l.1) and the amount is in respect of interest that is deductible by a partnership in computing its income from a particular source or from sources in a particular place, the amount is deemed to be from the particular source or from sources in the particular place, as the case may be.

Notes: 12(2.02) ensures that any income inclusion under 12(1)(l.1) (partner's thin capitalization add-back) for a non-resident partner will be taxable in Canada to the same extent as income earned through the partnership. Its "source" rule may be useful in sheltering the income with losses after acquisition of control of a corporate partner.

12(2.02) added by 2013 budget bill #2, for taxation years that begin after 2013.

(2.1) Receipt of inducement, reimbursement, etc. — For the purposes of paragraph (1)(x), where at a particular time a taxpayer who is a beneficiary of a trust or a member of a partnership has received an amount as an inducement, whether as a grant, subsidy, forgivable loan, deduction from tax, allowance or any other form of inducement, in respect of the activities of the trust or partnership, or as a reimbursement, contribution, allowance or as assistance, whether as a grant, subsidy, forgivable loan, deduction from tax, allowance or any other form of assistance, in respect of the cost of property or in respect of an expense of the trust or partnership, the amount shall be deemed to have been received at that time by the trust or partnership, as the case may be, as such an inducement, reimbursement, contribution, allowance or assistance.

Notes: For CRA interpretation see VIEWS doc 2012-0448351E5 (mutual fund rebate paid to investor). This was essentially the same as *Invesco Canada*, 2014 TCC 375; the mutual fund manager was providing rebates to large investors to effectively reduce the fees it was charging the trusts. This could trigger 12(2.1), so the manager reduced its fees to the trusts and arranged for the trusts to provide rebates to the large investors; CRA ruled that this solved the problem. (The case held that GST applied only to the reduced fees.)

12(2.1) added by 1985 Budget, for amounts received after May 22, 1985 other than pursuant to the terms of an agreement in writing entered into by that date or to the terms of a prospectus, preliminary prospectus or registration statement filed before May 24, 1985.

Interpretation Bulletins: IT-273R2: Government assistance — general comments.

(2.2) Deemed outlay or expense — Where

(a) in a taxation year a taxpayer receives an amount that would, but for this subsection, be included under paragraph (1)(x) in computing the taxpayer's income for the year in respect of an outlay or expense (other than an outlay or expense in respect of the cost of property of the taxpayer) made or incurred by the taxpayer before the end of the following taxation year, and

(b) the taxpayer elects under this subsection on or before the day on or before which the taxpayer's return of income under this Part for the year is required to be filed, or would be required to be filed if tax under this Part were payable by the taxpayer for the year or, where the outlay or expense is made or incurred in the following taxation year, for that following year,

the amount of the outlay or expense shall be deemed for the purpose of computing the taxpayer's income, other than for the purposes of this subsection and paragraphs (1)(x) and 20(1)(hh), to have always been the amount, if any, by which

(c) the amount of the outlay or expense

exceeds

(d) the lesser of the amount elected by the taxpayer under this subsection and the amount so received by the taxpayer,

and, notwithstanding subsections 152(4) to (5), such assessment or reassessment of the taxpayer's tax, interest and penalties under this Act for any taxation year shall be made as is necessary to give effect to the election.

Related Provisions: 20(1)(hh) — Repayments of inducements, etc.; 87(2)(j.6) — Amalgamation — Continuing corporation; 220(3.2), Reg. 600 — Late filing or revocation of election.

Notes: See 12(1)(x) Notes. 12(2.2) added by 1990 GST; amended by 1992 technical bill.

Interpretation Bulletins: IT-273R2: Government assistance — general comments.

CRA Audit Manual: 27.20.5: Inducement payments — elective provisions.

(3) Interest income [corporation etc. — accrual to year-end] — Subject to subsection (4.1), in computing the income for a taxation year of a corporation, partnership, unit trust or any trust of which a corporation or a partnership is a beneficiary, there shall be included any interest on a debt obligation (other than interest in respect of an income bond, an income debenture, a small business bond, a small business development bond, a net income stabilization account or an indexed debt obligation) that accrues to it to the end of the year, or becomes receivable or is received by it before the end of the year, to the extent that the interest was not included in computing its income for a preceding taxation year.

Related Provisions: 12(4) — Annual accrual for individuals and other trusts; 12(4.1) — Impaired debt obligations; 12(9) — Deemed accrual; 12.2(8) — Deemed acquisition of interest in annuity; 16(1) — Blended payments; 20(1)(l) — Reserve for doubtful debts; 20(14.1) — Interest on debt obligation; 20(19) — Annuity contract; 87(2)(j.4) — Amalgamation — continuing corporation; 138(11.5)(k) — Transfer of business by non-resident insurer; 138(12)"gross investment revenue"E(b) — Inclusion in gross investment revenue of insurer; 142.3(1)(c) — No income accrual from specified debt obligation; 142.4(1)"tax basis"(b) — Disposition of specified debt obligation by financial institution; 142.5(3)(a) — Mark-to-market debt obligation; 148(9)"adjusted cost basis"D — Inclusion in "adjusted cost basis".

Notes: See Notes to 12(4).

12(3) amended by 1995-97 technical bill (last change effective for tax years that end after Sept. 1997), 1993 and 1992 technical bills.

Regulations: 303 (amount deductible under subsec. 20(19)).

Interpretation Bulletins: IT-87R2: Policyholders' income from life insurance policies; IT-142R3: Settlement of debts on the winding-up of a corporation; IT-265R3: Payments of income and capital combined (cancelled); IT-396R: Interest income.

(4) Interest from investment contract [annual accrual] — Subject to subsection (4.1), if in a taxation year a taxpayer (other than a taxpayer to whom subsection (3) applies) holds an interest in, or for civil law a right in, an investment contract on any anniversary day of the contract, there shall be included in computing the taxpayer's income for the year the interest that accrued to the taxpayer to the end of that day with respect to the investment contract, to the extent that the interest was not otherwise included in computing the taxpayer's income for the year or any preceding taxation year.

Related Provisions: 12(4.1) — Impaired debt obligations; 12(9) — Deemed accrual; 12(11) — Investment contract; 20(14.1) — Interest on debt obligation.

Notes: For investments (e.g., term deposits, GICs) acquired since 1990, accrued interest must be reported by individuals every year on the anniversary date. (For those acquired earlier, it is reported every 3 years: see former version and VIEWS doc 2011-0424081E5.) For corporations, partnerships and certain trusts, accrued income must be reported under 12(3) at year-end, meaning that the year *in which the investment was acquired* must include the income accrued from acquisition date to year-end.

12(4) applied in *Goulet*, 2011 FCA 164 (leave to appeal denied 2011 CarswellNat 5307 (SCC)), so the difference between discounted acquisition price and proceeds of non-interest-bearing debt obligations was taxed as accrued interest, not capital gain.

See Notes to 79(1)"debt" on the meaning of "debt" (to which 12(3) might apply).

On a structured note with interest linked to an index and no determinable rate, interest need not be reported until received: VIEWS doc 2001-0076265. (Selling such a note just before maturity may produce capital gain instead of interest.) Where it is uncertain whether the interest will be paid, a reserve may be available under 20(1)(l): 2012-0449671E5.

Accruing interest must be reported annually on a T5: Reg. 201(4), VIEWS docs 2012-0449671E5, 2014-0519881E5.

CRA considers that 12(3)-(4) apply to strip bonds and banker's acceptances (and disposition triggers an anniversary day under 12(11) as well as a possible capital gain, and see 12(9.1)): VIEWS docs 2002-0123165, 2005-0137041C6, 2010-0379151E5.

12(4) may apply to a Roth IRA, but the income can be deferred by election under Canada US tax treaty Art. XVIII.7.

CRA may apply 12(4) to commodity- or stock-linked debt obligations: Paul Hickey, "Index-Linked Debt", 16(12) *Canadian Tax Highlights* (ctf.ca) 1 (Dec. 2008).

CRA considers that all interest accrued under 12(4) to a non-resident before immigrating to Canada should be included in income on the first anniversary date after immigration: doc 2011-040287117 (the Courts might disagree).

Where a non-arm's length loan is made at no interest, the CRA says (doc 2014-0532651E5) that 69(1)(a) may apply, so that 12(9) applies and the lender is deemed to earn interest! (This seems wrong.)

Where interest is not reported annually due to the financial institution's error (thinking that an account was RRSP-registered), the CRA suggests that interest on past years' tax might be waived under 220(3.1): VIEWS doc 2004-0082611E5.

Accrued bond interest is also taxed if the bond is bought back by the issuer: VIEWS doc 2007-0241891C6.

For a ruling that 12(4) does not apply to a supplemental pension plan see VIEWS doc 2006-0203271R3.

12(4) amended by 2002-2013 technical bill (Part 4 — bijuralism), effective June 26, 2013, to add "or for civil law a right in".

12(4) amended by 1995-97 technical bill, effective on the same basis as the addition to 12(4.1), to add "Subject to subsection (4.1)".

12(4) amended and 12(5)-(8) repealed by 1989 Budget, effective (per 1991 technical bill) for investment contracts last acquired after 1989. For those last acquired before 1990, accruing interest must still be reported every 3 years, rather than every year. For the text, see these Notes up to the 52nd ed.

The change to subsecs. (4)-(8) was from mandatory reporting of accruing interest every three years to reporting of accruing interest every year.

Regulations: 201(4) (information return).

Interpretation Bulletins: IT-265R3: Payments of income and capital combined (cancelled); IT-415R2: Deregistration of RRSPs (cancelled).

Advance Tax Rulings: ATR-61: Interest accrual rules.

(4.1) Impaired debt obligations — Paragraph (1)(c) and subsections (3) and (4) do not apply to a taxpayer in respect of a debt obligation for the part of a taxation year throughout which the obligation is impaired where an amount in respect of the obligation is deductible because of subparagraph 20(1)(l)(ii) in computing the taxpayer's income for the year.

Notes: 12(4.1) added by 1995-97 technical bill, effective for taxation years that end after September 1997, or earlier by election (see Notes to 20(1)(l)).

(5)–(8) [Repealed under former Act]

Notes: See under 12(4).

(9) Deemed accrual — For the purposes of subsections (3), (4) and (11) and 20(14) and (21), if a taxpayer acquires an interest in, or for civil law a right in, a prescribed debt obligation, an amount determined in prescribed manner is deemed to accrue to the taxpayer as interest on the obligation in each taxation year during which the taxpayer holds the interest or the right in the obligation.

Related Provisions: 16(3) — Obligation issued at discount; 18.1(14) — Right to receive production deemed to be debt obligation; 20(14.2) — Deemed interest on sale of linked note; 87(2)(j.4) — Amalgamations — accrual rules; 142.3(1)(c) — No income accrual from specified debt obligation.

Notes: 12(9) will apply to strip bond coupons and residuals. See Duncan Osborne, "CARS and PARS: Focus on Stripping Corporate Bonds", XI(1) *Corporate Finance* (Federated Press) 1023-25 (2003); VIEWS docs 2002-0123165, 2008-0293561E5.

12(9) applied in *Goulet*, 2011 FCA 164 (leave to appeal denied 2011 CarswellNat 5307 (SCC)), so the difference between discounted acquisition price and proceeds of non-interest-bearing debt obligations was interest, not capital gain. See also Reg. 7000(1) Notes.

12(9) amended by 2002-2013 technical bill, effective June 26, 2013, to add "or for civil law a right in" and "or the right".

12(9) amended by 1989 Budget, effective (per 1991 technical bill) for investment contracts last acquired after 1989, to delete reference to repealed subsec. (8).

Regulations: 7000 (prescribed debt obligation, prescribed manner).

Interpretation Bulletins: IT-396R: Interest income; IT-410R: Debt obligations — accrued interest on transfer (cancelled).

Advance Tax Rulings: ATR-61: Interest accrual rules.

(9.1) Exclusion of proceeds of disposition — If a taxpayer disposes of an interest in, or for civil law a right in, a debt obligation that is a debt obligation in respect of which the proportion of the payments of principal to which the taxpayer is entitled is not equal to the proportion of the payments of interest to which the taxpayer is entitled, the portion of the proceeds of disposition received by the taxpayer that can reasonably be considered to represent a recovery of the cost to the taxpayer of the interest or the right in the

debt obligation shall, notwithstanding any other provision of this Act, not be included in computing the taxpayer's income, and for the purpose of this subsection, a debt obligation includes, for greater certainty, all of the issuer's obligations to pay principal and interest under that obligation.

Notes: In CRA's view, 12(9.1) does not apply to an investment acquired at a premium on the secondary market, as only a debt obligation falling within Reg. 7000(1)(b) qualifies: VIEWS doc 2006-0197031C6.

12(9.1) applies to dispositions of stripped bonds.

12(9.1) amended by 2002-2013 technical bill (Part 4 — bijuralism), effective June 26, 2013.

12(9.1) amended by 1992 technical bill so that it continues to apply to all stripped bonds, including those that are indexed debt obligations. The amendment applies to "dispositions of debt obligations occurring after October 16, 1991", and so technically might be said not to apply to a disposition of an *interest* in a debt obligation.

Interpretation Bulletins: IT-396R: Interest income.

(10) [Repealed under former Act]

Notes: 12(10) repealed by 1989 Budget, effective (per 1991 technical bill) for investment contracts last acquired after 1989. It grandfathers certain interests in an investment contract acquired before Nov. 12, 1981. See Notes to 12(4) re the former 3-year accruing-interest rule.

(10.1) Income from RHOSP — [No longer relevant]

Notes: 12(10.1) provides that income accrued in a registered home ownership savings plan (see Notes to 146.2) before 1986 is not taxable.

(10.2) NISA receipts — There shall be included in computing a taxpayer's income for a taxation year from a property the total of all amounts each of which is the amount determined by the formula

$$A - B$$

where

A   is an amount paid at a particular time in the year out of the taxpayer's NISA Fund No. 2; and

B   is the amount, if any, by which

    (a) the total of all amounts each of which is

        (i) deemed by subsection (10.4) or 104(5.1) or (14.1) (as it read for the taxpayer's 2015 taxation year) to have been paid out of the taxpayer's NISA Fund No. 2 before the particular time, or

        (ii) deemed by subsection 70(5.4) or 73(5) to have been paid out of another person's NISA Fund No. 2 on being transferred to the taxpayer's NISA Fund No. 2 before the particular time,

  exceeds

    (b) the total of all amounts each of which is the amount by which an amount otherwise determined under this subsection in respect of a payment out of the taxpayer's NISA Fund No. 2 before the particular time was reduced because of this description.

Related Provisions: 104(6)(b)A — Limitation on deduction by trust for amount payable to beneficiaries; 104(14.1) — NISA election; 108(1) — "accumulating income"; 125(7)"income of the corporation for the year from an active business"(b) — "Income of the corporation for the year from an active business"; 129(4)"aggregate investment income"(b)(ii) — Exclusion from calculation of refundable dividend tax on hand; 212(1)(t) — NISA Fund No. 2 payments to non-residents; 214(3)(l) — Non-resident withholding tax; 248(9.1) — Whether trust created by taxpayer's will.

Notes: See Notes to 12(10.3) and 248(1)"NISA Fund No. 2".

12(10.2)B(a)(i) amended by 2014 budget bill #2, for 2016 and later taxation years, to add "(as it read for the taxpayer's 2015 taxation year)".

12(10.2)B(a) amended by 2007 budget bill #2 to refer to 12(10.4) (and para. (a) was split into two subparas.), effective on the same basis as 12(10.4) added.

12(10.2) added by 1992 technical bill, effective 1991.

Regulations: 201(1)(e) (information return).

Interpretation Bulletins: IT-212R3: Income of deceased persons — rights or things; IT-243R4: Dividend refund to private corporations; IT-305R4: Testamentary spouse trusts.

(10.3) Amount credited or added not included in income — Notwithstanding any other provision of this Act, an amount credited or added to a taxpayer's NISA Fund No. 2 shall not be included in

computing the taxpayer's income solely because of that crediting or adding.

Notes: See Notes to 248(1)"NISA Fund No. 2". Due to 12(10.3), the farmer is not taxed on Fund No. 2 moneys until they are paid out (see 12(10.2)). One might think that the moneys are held in trust for the farmer and that such trust should pay tax, but the trustee is the federal government, which is not subject to tax.

12(10.3) added by 1992 technical bill, effective 1991.

Forms: RC322: AgriInvest adjustment request; T1163: Statement A — AgriStability and AgriInvest programs information and statement of farming activities for individuals; T1164: Statement B — AgriStability and AgriInvest programs information and statement of farming activities for additional farming operations; T1175: Farming — Calculation of CCA and business-use-of-home expenses; T1273: Statement A — Harmonized AgriStability and AgriInvest programs information and statement of farming activities for individuals; T1274: Statement B — Harmonized AgriStability and AgriInvest programs information and statement of farming activities for additional farming operations; T1275: AgriStability and AgriInvest programs additional information and adjustment request form.

(10.4) Acquisition of control — corporate NISA Fund No. 2 — For the purpose of subsection (10.2), if at any time there is an acquisition of control of a corporation, the balance of the corporation's NISA Fund No. 2, if any, at that time is deemed to be paid out to the corporation immediately before that time.

Related Provisions: 12(10.2)B(a) — Effect on NISA income inclusion.

Notes: See Notes to 248(1)"NISA Fund No. 2". This rule prevents acquisition of a corporation for its NISA funds (see Notes to 111(5) for other similar rules).

12(10.4) added by 2007 budget bill #2, applicable to the balance in a NISA Fund No. 2 to the extent that that balance consists of contributions made to the fund, and amounts earned on those contributions, in the 2008 and later taxation years.

(11) Definitions — In this section,

"anniversary day" of an investment contract means

(a) the day that is one year after the day immediately preceding the date of issue of the contract,

(b) the day that occurs at every successive one year interval from the day determined under paragraph (a), and

(c) the day on which the contract was disposed of;

Notes: 12(11)"anniversary day" was 12(11)(b) before re-enactment in RSC 1985 (5th Supp), effective for taxation years beginning after November 1991.

12(11)(b), originally "third anniversary day", amended by 1989 Budget, effective (per 1991 technical bill) for investment contracts last acquired after 1989. See Notes to 12(4) re the former 3-year accruing-interest rule.

"investment contract", in relation to a taxpayer, means any debt obligation other than

(a) a salary deferral arrangement or a plan or arrangement that, but for any of paragraphs (a), (b) and (d) to (l) of the definition "salary deferral arrangement" in subsection 248(1), would be a salary deferral arrangement,

(b) a retirement compensation arrangement or a plan or arrangement that, but for any of paragraphs (a), (b), (d) and (f) to (n) of the definition "retirement compensation arrangement" in subsection 248(1), would be a retirement compensation arrangement,

(c) an employee benefit plan or a plan or arrangement that, but for any of paragraphs (a) to (e) of the definition "employee benefit plan" in subsection 248(1), would be an employee benefit plan,

(d) a foreign retirement arrangement,

(d.1) a TFSA,

(e) an income bond,

(f) an income debenture,

(g) a small business development bond,

(h) a small business bond,

(i) an obligation in respect of which the taxpayer has (otherwise than because of subsection (4)) at periodic intervals of not more than one year, included, in computing the taxpayer's income throughout the period in which the taxpayer held an interest in, or for civil law a right in, the obligation, the income accrued on it for those intervals,

(j) an obligation in respect of a net income stabilization account,

(k) an indexed debt obligation, and

(l) a prescribed contract.

Notes [12(11)"investment contract"]: The CRA considers a banker's acceptance to be a "debt obligation" for this definition: VIEWS doc 2005-0137041C6. See also 2011-0431891R3 (mortgage pool is not "investment contract").

Para. (i) amended by 2002-2013 technical bill (Part 4 — bijuralism), effective June 26, 2013, to add "or for civil law a right in".

Para. (d.1) added by 2008 budget bill #2, for 2009 and later taxation years.

Definition "investment contract" amended by 1993, 1992 and 1991 technical bills. Paras. (a) and (b) are effective 1986; para. (d) effective 1990; para. (j) effective 1991; para (k) for debt obligations issued after Oct. 16, 1991 (see 16(6)); para. (l) was formerly (k); and for debt obligations acquired before 1990, read "3 years" in place of "one year" in para. (i). 12(11)"investment contract" was 12(11)(a) before re-enactment in RSC 1985 (5th Supp) for tax years beginning after Nov. 1991.

Related Provisions: 12(9) — Deemed accrual.

Regulations: 7000(6) (prescribed contract).

Interpretation Bulletins [subsec. 12(11)]: IT-396R: Interest income; IT-415R2: Deregistration of RRSPs (cancelled).

Definitions [s. 12]: "adjusted cost base" — 54, 248(1); "allowable capital loss" — 38(b), 248(1); "amateur athlete trust" — 143.1(1.2)(a), 248(1); "amount" — 248(1); "anniversary day" — 12(11); "arm's length" — 251(1); "assessment" — 248(1); "assistance" — 79(4), 125.4(5), 248(16), (16.1), (18), (18.1); "automobile", "bankrupt", "business" — 248(1); "Canada" — 255; "Canadian resource property" — 66(15), 248(1); "controlled" — 256(6), (6.1); "corporation" — 248(1), *Interpretation Act* 35(1); "credit union" — 137(6), 248(1); "debt amount" — 18(7)(a); "deferred amount" — 248(1); "depreciable property" — 13(21), 248(1); "derivative forward agreement", "dividend", "employee", "employee benefit plan", "employee trust" — 248(1); "employees profit sharing plan" — 144(1), 248(1); "employer" — 248(1); "fair market value" — see 69(1) Notes; "fiscal period" — 249.1; "foreign affiliate" — 95(1), 248(1); "foreign oil and gas business" — 126(7); "foreign retirement arrangement" — 248(1); "Her Majesty" — *Interpretation Act* 35(1); "income from property" — 9(1), 9(3); "income bond", "income debenture", "indexed debt obligation", "individual", "insurance corporation", "insurer" — 248(1); "investment contract" — 12(11); "investment corporation" — 130(3), 248(1); "lending asset", "life insurance corporation" — 248(1); "life insurance policy" — 138(12), 248(1); "mineral resource", "mineral" — 248(1); "mortgage investment corporation" — 130.1(6), 248(1); "mutual fund corporation" — 131(8), 248(1); "net income stabilization account", "NISA Fund No. 2", "non-resident" — 248(1); "outstanding debts to specified non-residents" — 18(5); "partnership" — see 96(1) Notes; "payer" — 12(1)(x)(i); "person" — 248(1); "personal services business" — 125(7), 248(1); "prescribed" — 248(1); "prescribed debt obligation" — Reg. 7000; "production tax amount" — 126(7); "property" — 248(1); "province" — *Interpretation Act* 35(1); "qualifying environmental trust — 211.6(1), 248(1); "real right" — 248(4.1); "received" — 248(7)(a); "related" — 251(2); "resident in Canada" — 94(3)(a), 250; "restrictive covenant" — 56.4(1); "retirement compensation arrangement", "salary deferral arrangement", "share" — 248(1); "small business bond" — 15.2, 248(1); "small business development bond" — 15.1, 248(1); "TFSA" — 146.2(5), 248(1); "tar sands" — 248(1); "tax payable" — 248(2); "taxable capital gain" — 38(a), 248(1); "taxation year" — 249; "taxpayer" — 248(1); "trust" — 104(1), 248(1), (3); "unit trust" — 108(2), 248(1).

12.1 Cash bonus on Canada Savings Bonds — Notwithstanding any other provision of this Act, where in a taxation year a taxpayer receives an amount from the Government of Canada in respect of a Canada Savings Bond as a cash bonus that the Government of Canada has undertaken to pay (other than any amount of interest, bonus or principal agreed to be paid at the time of the issue of the bond under the terms of the bond), the taxpayer shall, in computing the taxpayer's income for the year, include as interest in respect of the Canada Savings Bond ½ of the cash bonus so received.

Related Provisions: 12(1)(c) — Interest.

Notes: The half-taxation of cash bonuses on CSBs is intended to give such bonuses treatment similar to capital gains.

No new CSBs will be sold after November 2017.

Definitions [s. 12.1]: "amount" — 248(1); "taxation year" — 249; "taxpayer" — 248(1).

Regulations: 220 (information return).

12.2 (1) Amount to be included [annually from life insurance policy] — Where in a taxation year a taxpayer holds an interest, last acquired after 1989, in a life insurance policy that is not

(a) an exempt policy,

(b) a prescribed annuity contract, and

(c) a contract under which the policyholder has, under the terms and conditions of a life insurance policy that was not an annuity contract and that was last acquired before December 2, 1982, received the proceeds therefrom in the form of an annuity contract,

on any anniversary day of the policy, there shall be included in computing the taxpayer's income for the taxation year the amount, if any, by which the accumulating fund on that day in respect of the interest in the policy, as determined in prescribed manner, exceeds the adjusted cost basis to the taxpayer of the interest in the policy on that day.

Related Provisions: 12.2(5) — Amounts to be included; 12.2(8)–(11) — Rules and definitions; 20(1)(c)(iv) — Interest deductibility; 20(20) — Disposal of life insurance policy or annuity contract; 56(1)(d.1) — Annuity payments included in income; 87(2)(j.4) — Amalgamation — accrual rules; 148(9)"adjusted cost basis"G, 148(9)"adjusted cost basis"L(b) — Adjusted cost basis; 148(10) — Life annuity contracts.

Notes: A lottery prize paid in annual instalments is an annuity taxed under 12.2(1): *Rumack*, [1992] 1 C.T.C. 57 (FCA) (leave to appeal to SCC denied); VIEWS doc 2004-0085091E5.

See Gail Grobe, "The Exempt Test for Life Insurance Policies", XVI(1) and (2) *Insurance Planning [IP]* (Federated Press) 996-1000 and 1011-14 (2009); Martin Reeves, "A Payout Annuity is Like a Personal Pension Plan", XVII(3) *IP* 1090-95 (2011).

See also VIEWS docs 2006-0170861E5, 2007-0220301R3, 2008-0286071E5; 2009-0347061M4 (exempt policies); 2009-0340381R3 (purchase of life insurance policy and using it as security to borrow from bank to acquire an annuity); 2010-0371161E5 (US annuity); 2010-0375511E5 (Swiss annuity); 2011-0398471C6 (timing of annuity payment); 2014-0549941E5 (foreign-issued deferred annuities).

Amended by 1991 technical bill, for life insurance policies last acquired after 1989. The present 12.2(1) was formerly 12.2(3); the rules for corporate and individual policyholders have now been combined into one rule. For earlier policies, read:

> 12.2 (1) **Amount to be included** — In computing the income for a taxation year of a corporation, partnership, unit trust or any trust of which a corporation or partnership is a beneficiary that holds
>
> > (a) an interest, last acquired after December 1, 1982, in a life insurance policy or
> >
> > (b) an interest, last acquired after December 19, 1980 and before December 2, 1982, in an annuity contract under which annuity payments did not commence before December 2, 1982,
>
> that is not
>
> > (c) an interest in an exempt policy, or
> >
> > (d) an interest, last acquired before December 2, 1982, in a contract under which the policyholder has, under the terms and conditions of a life insurance policy that was not an annuity contract, received the proceeds therefrom in the form of an annuity contract,
>
> there shall be included the amount by which the accumulating fund at the end of the calendar year ending in the taxation year, as determined in prescribed manner, in respect of the interest exceeds the adjusted cost basis of the interest to the corporation, partnership, unit trust or trust at the end of that calendar year.

See under 12.2(2)–(4.1).

Regulations [subsec. 12.2(1)]: 201(5) (information return); 304 (prescribed annuity contract); 307 (accumulating fund).

Interpretation Bulletins [subsec. 12.2(1)]: IT-87R2: Policyholders' income from life insurance policies; IT-355R2: Interest on loans to buy life insurance policies and annuity contracts, and interest on policy loans (cancelled); IT-365R2: Damages, settlements and similar receipts; IT-415R2: Deregistration of RRSPs (cancelled).

Advance Tax Rulings: ATR-50: Structured settlement; ATR-68: Structured settlement.

(2)–(4.1) [Repealed under former Act]

Related Provisions: 87(2)(j.4) — Amalgamation — accrual rules; 220(3.2), Reg. 600(b) — Late filing or revocation of election under 12.2(4); Reg. 1408(5) — Similar rule for policy reserves.

Notes: 12.2(2), (3), (4) and (4.1) repealed and replaced by 12.2(3) by 1989 Budget. 12.2(3) then merged into 12.2(1) by 1991 technical bill, for life insurance policies last acquired after 1989. For policies acquired earlier, read:

> (2) **Interest not disposed of before 1985** — Where, before 1985, a corporation, partnership, unit trust or any trust of which a corporation or partnership is a beneficiary has not disposed of an interest in an annuity contract that was last acquired by it before December 20, 1980,
>
> > (a) subsection (1) shall be read without reference to the words "after December 19, 1980 and", and

> (b) all that portion of subsection (1) following paragraph (d) thereof shall be read as follows:
>
> > "there shall be included the amount by which the accumulating fund at the end of the calendar year ending in the taxation year, as determined in prescribed manner, in respect of the interest exceeds the aggregate of the adjusted cost basis of the interest to the corporation, partnership, unit trust or trust at the end of the calendar year ending in the taxation year and the amount, if any, at the end of that calendar year of unallocated income accrued in respect of the interest before 1982, as determined in prescribed manner.",
>
> for taxation years ending after December 30, 1984, with respect to that interest.

(3) **Third anniversary amounts to be included** — Where in a taxation year a taxpayer (other than a corporation, partnership, unit trust or any trust of which a corporation or partnership is a beneficiary) holds an interest in

> (a) a life insurance policy last acquired after December 1, 1982, or
>
> (b) an annuity contract last acquired before December 2, 1982 under which annuity payments did not commence before December 2, 1982,

other than

> (c) an exempt policy,
>
> (d) a prescribed annuity contract, or
>
> (e) a contract under which the policyholder has, under the terms and conditions of a life insurance policy that was not an annuity contract and that was last acquired before December 2, 1982, received the proceeds therefrom in the form of an annuity contract

on a third anniversary of the policy or contract and in the taxation year or any preceding taxation year he has not made an election under subsection (4) in respect of his interest, there shall be included in computing his income for the taxation year the amount by which the accumulating fund on that third anniversary, as determined in prescribed manner, in respect of his interest exceeds the aggregate of the adjusted cost basis of the interest to the taxpayer on that third anniversary and the amount, if any, on that third anniversary of unallocated income accrued in respect of the interest before 1982, as determined in prescribed manner.

(4) **Election** — Where in a taxation year a taxpayer (other than a corporation, partnership, unit trust or any trust of which a corporation or partnership is a beneficiary) who holds an interest in

> (a) a life insurance policy (other than an annuity contract) last acquired after December 1, 1982, or
>
> (b) an annuity contract (other than a prescribed annuity contract)

has, in the year or a preceding taxation year, elected in respect of that interest by notifying the issuer thereof in writing, he shall, in computing his income for the year, include the amount by which the accumulating fund at the end of the year, as determined in prescribed manner, in respect of that interest exceeds the aggregate of

> (c) the adjusted cost basis to him of the interest at the end of the year, and
>
> (d) the amount, if any, at that time of unallocated income accrued in respect of the interest before 1982, as determined in prescribed manner.

(4.1) **Revocation of election** — Where not later than 120 days after the end of a taxation year a taxpayer revokes an election made under subsection (4) in respect of his interest in a life insurance policy or an annuity contract by notifying the issuer thereof in writing, the following rules apply for that year and each subsequent taxation year:

> (a) he shall be deemed for the purposes of subsection (3) not to have made an election under subsection (4) in respect of his interest; and
>
> (b) he is not entitled to make an election under subsection (4) in respect of his interest.

Regulations: 304 (prescribed annuity contract).

(5) Idem — Where in a taxation year subsection (1) applies with respect to a taxpayer's interest in an annuity contract (or would apply if the contract had an anniversary day in the year at a time when the taxpayer held the interest), there shall be included in computing the taxpayer's income for the year the amount, if any, by which

(a) the total of all amounts each of which is an amount determined at the end of the year, in respect of the interest, for any of H to L in the definition "adjusted cost basis" in subsection 148(9)

exceeds

(b) the total of all amounts each of which is an amount determined at the end of the year, in respect of the interest, for any of A to G in the definition referred to in paragraph (a).

Notes: 12.2(5) amended by 1989 Budget and by 1991 technical bill, effective for life insurance policies last acquired after 1989. For policies acquired earlier, read:

(5) **Amounts to be included** — Where in a taxation year subsection (1), (3) or (4) applies with respect to a taxpayer's interest in an annuity contract, or would apply if the contract had a third anniversary in the year, and at the end of the year

(a) the aggregate of all amounts each of which is an amount determined under any of subparagraphs 148(9)(a)(vi) to (xi) in respect of his interest

exceeds

(b) the aggregate of all amounts each of which is an amount determined under any of subparagraphs 148(9)(a)(i) to (v.1) in respect of his interest,

there shall be included in computing the income of the taxpayer for the year the amount by which the aggregate determined under paragraph (a) exceeds the aggregate determined under paragraph (b).

(6) **Application** — Subsection (1) does not apply in computing the income of a taxpayer for a taxation year if his interest in the annuity contract was last acquired before December 20, 1980, and

(a) he could not, in the period after December 19, 1980 and before the end of the taxation year, require the repayment, acquisition, cancellation or conversion of his interest (other than by reason of a failure or default under the terms or conditions thereof) and the maturity date of the contract has not been extended and the terms or conditions relating to payments in respect of his interest have not been changed in that period; or

(b) the cash surrender value of his interest has not, in the period referred to in paragraph (a), exceeded the aggregate of premiums paid in respect of the interest.

(7) **Idem** — Subsection (3) does not apply in computing the income of a taxpayer for a taxation year if his interest in the annuity contract was last acquired before December 2, 1982 and

(a) he could not, in the period after December 1, 1982 and before the end of the taxation year, require the repayment, acquisition, cancellation or conversion of his interest (other than by reason of a failure or default under the terms or conditions thereof) and the maturity date of the contract has not been extended and the terms or conditions relating to payments in respect of his interest have not been changed in that period; or

(b) the cash surrender value of his interest has not, in the period referred to in paragraph (a), exceeded the aggregate of premiums paid in respect of the interest.

Regulations: 201(5) (information return).

Interpretation Bulletins: IT-355R2: Interest on loans to buy life insurance policies and annuity contracts, and interest on policy loans (cancelled).

(6), (7) [Repealed under former Act]

Notes: See under 12.2(5).

(8) **Deemed acquisition of interest in annuity** — For the purposes of this section, the first premium that was not fixed before 1990 and that was paid after 1989 by or on behalf of a taxpayer under an annuity contract, other than a contract described in paragraph (1)(d) of this section, or paragraph 12.2(3)(e) of the *Income Tax Act*, chapter 148 of the Revised Statutes of Canada, 1952, or to which subsection (1) of this section or subsection 12.2(4) of the *Income Tax Act*, chapter 148 of the Revised Statutes of Canada, 1952, applies (as those paragraphs and subsections, the numbers of which are those in force immediately before December 17, 1991, read in their application to life insurance policies last acquired before 1990) or to which subsection 12(3) applies, last acquired by the taxpayer before 1990 (in this subsection referred to as the "original contract") shall be deemed to have been paid to acquire, at the time the premium was paid, an interest in a separate annuity contract issued at that time, to the extent that the amount of the premium was not fixed before 1990, and each subsequent premium paid under the original contract shall be deemed to have been paid under that separate contract to the extent that the amount of that subsequent premium was not fixed before 1990.

Notes: 12.2(8) amended by 1989 Budget and 1991 technical bill, effective for premiums paid after 1989, and re-enacted in the RSC 1985 (5th Supp) consolidation. The references to R.S.C. 1952, c. 148 are to the Act before the RSC 1985 (5th Supp) came into force; Dec. 17, 1991 was the date of Royal Assent to the 1991 technical bill.

I.T. Application Rules: 69 (meaning of "chapter 148 of ...").

Interpretation Bulletins: IT-355R2: Interest on loans to buy life insurance policies and annuity contracts, and interest on policy loans (cancelled).

(9) [Repealed under former Act]

Notes: 12.2(9) repealed by 1989 Budget, effective (per 1991 technical bill) for life insurance policies last acquired after 1989. For policies acquired earlier, read:

(9) **Rules where premium paid** — Where, at any time after December 1, 1982, a prescribed premium (other than a premium referred to in subsection (8)) has been paid by or on behalf of a taxpayer in respect of an interest in a life insurance policy last acquired on or before that date, and

(a) the policy is not an exempt policy, or

(b) there has been a prescribed increase in any benefit on death under the policy,

this Act applies after that time with respect to his interest in the policy as if

(c) subsections (1), (3) and (4) and 148(4), paragraph 148(2)(b) and clause 148(9)(e.2)(iv)(A) were read without reference to the words "last acquired after December 1, 1982";

(d) subsection (1) were read without reference to paragraph (d) thereof;

(e) subsection (3) were read without reference to paragraph (e) thereof;

(f) subsection 148(6) were not applicable;

(g) subparagraph 148(9)(a)(ix) were read as follows:

"(ix) in the case of an interest in a life insurance policy (other than an annuity contract), the aggregate of all amounts each of which is the net cost of pure insurance in respect of the interest, as determined in prescribed manner, immediately before the end of the calendar year ending in a taxation year commencing after the later of

(A) May 31, 1985, and

(B) the end of the year before the year in which subsection 12.2(9) first applied in respect of the interest, and

before that time,";

(h) subparagraph 148(9)(c)(ix) were read without reference to clause (A) thereof; and

(i) all that portion of subparagraph 148(9) (e.1)(iii) preceding clause (A) thereof were read as follows:

(iii) that portion of any amount paid, after the later of May 31, 1985 and the time at which subsection 12.2(9) first applied in respect of the interest, under the policy with respect to

and, for the purposes of this subsection, paragraph 148(10)(d) shall be read without reference to the expression "(other than a conversion into an annuity contract)".

Regulations: 309 (prescribed premium, prescribed increase).

(10) **Riders** — For the purposes of this Act, a rider added at any time after 1989 to a life insurance policy last acquired before 1990 that provides additional life insurance is deemed to be a separate life insurance policy issued at that time unless

(a) the policy is an exempt policy last acquired after December 1, 1982 or an annuity contract; or

(b) the only additional life insurance provided by the rider is an accidental death benefit.

Related Provisions: 87(2)(j.4) — Amalgamation — accrual rules; Reg. 1408(5) — Similar rule for policy reserves.

Notes: 12.2(10) amended by 1989 Budget, and paras. (a), (b) added by 1995-97 technical bill, both effective for riders added after 1989. For riders added after Dec. 1, 1982 and before 1990, read "acquired before December 2, 1982" in place of "before 1990".

(11) **Definitions** — In this section and paragraph 56(1)(d.1) of the *Income Tax Act*, chapter 148 of the Revised Statutes of Canada, 1952,

Related Provisions: 20(1.2) — Definitions in 12.2(11) apply to 20(1)(c).

I.T. Application Rules: 69 (meaning of "chapter 148 of ...").

"anniversary day" of a life insurance policy means

(a) the day that is one year after the day immediately preceding the day on which the policy was issued, and

(b) each day that occurs at each successive one-year interval after the day determined under paragraph (a);

Notes: 12.2(11)"anniversary day" was 12.2(11)(b) before RSC 1985 (5th Supp) consolidation for tax years ending after Nov. 1991.

12.2(11)(b) (now 12.2(11)"anniversary day") amended by 1989 Budget and 1991 technical bill, effective for life insurance policies last acquired after 1989. For earlier policies, read:

(b) "third anniversary" — "third anniversary" of a life insurance policy means

(i) the end of the day that is three years after the end of the calendar year of issue of the policy, and

(ii) the end of the day that occurs at every successive three year interval from the time determined under subparagraph (i)

and for the purposes of this paragraph, where before 1985 a taxpayer has not disposed of an interest in an annuity contract last acquired by him before December 2, 1982, the contract shall be deemed to have been issued on December 31, 1984.

"exempt policy" has the meaning prescribed by regulation.

Related Provisions: 148(9)"adjusted cost basis".

Notes: See Notes to Reg. 306(1).

12.2(11)"exempt policy" was 12.2(11)(a) before RSC 1985 (5th Supp) consolidation for tax years ending after Nov. 1991.

Regulations: 306 (meaning of "exempt policy").

(12) Application of subsecs. 138(12) and 148(9) — The definitions in subsections 138(12) and 148(9) apply to this section.

Notes: 12.2(12) added in the RSC 1985 (5th Supp) consolidation, for tax years beginning after Nov. 1991. This rule was formerly in the opening words to 138(12) and 148(9).

(13) Application of subsec. 148(10) — Subsection 148(10) applies to this section.

Notes: 12.2(13) added in the RSC 1985 (5th Supp) consolidation, for tax years beginning after Nov. 1991. This rule was formerly in the opening words to 148(10).

Definitions [s. 12.2]: "accumulating fund" — Reg. 307; "acquired" — 12.2(13), 148(10)(c), (e); "adjusted cost basis" — 148(9), 248(1); "amount" — 12.2(12), 148(9), 248(1); "anniversary day" — 12.2(11); "annuity" — 248(1); "cash surrender value" — 12.2(12), 148(9); "corporation" — 248(1), *Interpretation Act* 35(1); "exempt policy" — 12.2(11), Reg. 306; "insurer" — 12.2(13), 148(10)(a); "life insurance policy" — 138(12), 248(1); "life insurer" — 12.2(13), 148(10)(a), 248(1); "person" — 248(1); "person whose life was insured" — 12.2(13), 148(10)(b); "premium" — 12.2(12), 148(9); "prescribed" — 248(1); "prescribed annuity contract" — Reg. 304; "regulation" — 248(1); "taxation year" — 249; "taxpayer" — 248(1); "trust" — 104(1), 248(1), (3); "unit trust" — 108(2), 248(1).

Income Tax Folios [s. 12.2]: S3-F6-C1: Interest deductibility [replaces IT-533]; S3-F9-C1: Lottery winnings, miscellaneous receipts, and income (and losses) from crime [replaces IT-185R, IT-213R, IT-256R, IT-334R2].

Interpretation Bulletins [s. 12.2]: IT-355R2: Interest on loans to buy life insurance policies and annuity contracts, and interest on policy loans (cancelled); IT-363R2: Deferred profit sharing plans — deductibility of employer contributions and taxation of amounts received by a beneficiary (cancelled); IT-415R2: Deregistration of RRSPs (cancelled).

12.3 [Repealed]

Notes: 12.3 repealed by 2002-2013 technical bill for tax years that begin after Oct. 2011. It provided a transitional income inclusion from 1995-2004 for an insurer's 1994 unpaid claims reserve. Earlier amended by 1994 Budget.

12.4 Bad debt inclusion — Where, in a taxation year, a taxpayer disposes of a property that was a property described in an inventory of the taxpayer and in the year or a preceding taxation year an amount has been deducted under paragraph 20(1)(p) in computing the taxpayer's income in respect of the property, there shall be included in computing the taxpayer's income for the year from the business in which the property was used or held, the amount, if any, by which

(a) the total of all amounts deducted under paragraph 20(1)(p) by the taxpayer in respect of the property in computing the taxpayer's income for the year or a preceding taxation year

exceeds

(b) the total of all amounts included under paragraph 12(1)(i) by the taxpayer in respect of the property in computing the taxpayer's income for the year or a preceding taxation year.

Related Provisions: 26(3) — Banks — write-offs and recoveries; 87(2)(g.1) — Amalgamations; 138(11.5)(k) — Transfer of business by non-resident insurer; 142.5(8)(d)(ii) — First deemed disposition of mark-to-market debt obligation.

Definitions [s. 12.4]: "amount", "business", "inventory", "property" — 248(1); "taxation year" — 11(2), 249; "taxpayer" — 248(1).

Interpretation Bulletins: IT-442R: Bad debts and reserves for doubtful debts.

12.5 [Insurer's reserves — transition 2006-2011] — [No longer relevant]

Notes: 12.5, 20.4, 138(16)-(25) and 142.51 allow a 5-year phase-in for tax purposes of changes in accounting for financial instruments, required by CPA Canada *Handbook*

§3855, which applies to tax years beginning after Sept. 2006. Under the new accounting model, the balance sheet should reflect financial instrument values rather than cost.

See Backgrounder to Finance news release 2006-091 (Dec. 28/06) on fin.gc.ca; Deloitte & Touche, "Taxation of Financial Institutions", 2008(1) *Tax Times* (Carswell) 1-3 (Jan. 11/08); Janet Newcombe, "The New FI Rules", 5(2) *Tax Hyperion* (Carswell, Feb. 2008); Notes to 142.2(1)"mark-to-market property"; and *Dept. of Finance Technical Notes* (Carswell, annual).

12.5 added by 2008 budget bill #2, for tax years that begin after Sept. 2006.

12.6 [SIFTs — stapled securities anti-avoidance rule] — **(1) Definitions** — The definitions in section 18.3 apply in this section.

(2) Where subsec. (3) applies [— temporary unstapling] — Subsection (3) applies for a taxation year of an entity in respect of a security of the entity if

(a) the security becomes, at a particular time in the year, a stapled security of the entity and, as a consequence, amounts described in paragraphs 18.3(3)(a) and (b) are not deductible because of subsection 18.3(3);

(b) the security (or any security for which the security was substituted) ceased, at an earlier time, to be a stapled security of any entity and, as a consequence, subsection 18.3(3) ceased to apply to deny the deductibility of amounts that would be described in paragraphs 18.3(3)(a) and (b) if the security were a stapled security; and

(c) throughout the period that began immediately after the most recent time referred to in paragraph (b) and that ends at the particular time, the security (or any security for which the security was substituted) was not a stapled security of any entity.

Related Provisions: 248(5) — Substituted property.

(3) Income inclusion [— unstapled security] — If this subsection applies for a taxation year of an entity in respect of a security of the entity, the entity shall include in computing its income for the year each amount that

(a) was deducted by the entity (or by another entity that issued a security for which the security was substituted) in computing its income for a taxation year that includes any part of the period described in paragraph (2)(c); and

(b) would not have been deductible if subsection 18.3(3) had applied in respect of the amount.

Related Provisions: 12.6(2) — Conditions for 12.6(3) to apply; 18.3(1)"security"(b)(ii) — Anti-avoidance.

Notes: 12.6 is an anti-avoidance rule linked to 18.3, which denies deductions for certain amounts paid or payable in respect of stapled securities (see Notes at end of 18.3).

For an entity to avoid 18.3, it must "unstaple" the securities. However, stapled securities could be temporarily unstapled and later restapled. The effect of 12.6 is to disregard unstapling that is not permanent and irrevocable. 12.6(3) requires income inclusion of amounts deducted during a period of "temporary unstapling". Due to 12.6(4), interest under 161(1) applies on the additional tax as though the deduction had been disallowed originally.

See Notes at end of 12.6.

The reference in 12.6(3)(a) to "paragraph 2(c)" should read "paragraph (2)(c)", i.e. 12.6(2)(c).

(4) Deemed excess [— interest payable] — For the purposes of subsection 161(1), if an amount described in paragraph (3)(a) is included in the income of an entity for a taxation year under subsection (3), the entity is deemed to have an excess immediately after the entity's balance-due day for the year computed as if

(a) the entity were resident in Canada throughout the year;

(b) the entity's tax payable for the year were equal to the tax payable by the entity on its taxable income for the year;

(c) the amount were the entity's only taxable income for the year;

(d) the entity claimed no deductions under Division E for the year;

(e) the entity had not paid any amounts on account of its tax payable for the year; and

(f) the tax payable determined under paragraph (b) had been outstanding throughout the period that begins immediately after the end of the taxation year for which the amount was deducted and that ends on the entity's balance-due day for the year.

Notes: See Notes to 12.6(3). 12.6 added by 2013 budget bill #2, effective July 20, 2011.

Definitions [s. 12.6]: "amount", "balance-due day" — 248(1); "entity", "equity value", "real estate investment trust" — 12.6(1), 18.3(1), 122.1(1); "resident in Canada" — 94(3)(a), 250; "security" — 12.6(1), 18.3(1); "stapled security" — 12.6(1), 18.3(1), (2); "subsidiary" — 12.6(1), 18.3(1); "substituted" — 248(5); "taxable income" — 2(2), 248(1); "taxation year" — 249; "transition period" — 12.6(1), 18.3(1).

13. (1) Recaptured depreciation — If, at the end of a taxation year, the total of the amounts determined for E to K in the definition "undepreciated capital cost" in subsection (21) in respect of a taxpayer's depreciable property of a particular prescribed class exceeds the total of the amounts determined for A to D.1 in that definition in respect of that property, the excess shall be included in computing the taxpayer's income of the year.

Related Provisions: 13(3) — Interpretation where taxpayer is an individual; 13(5.2) — Where taxpayer paid rent for property before acquiring it; 13(5.3) — Rules applicable; 13(8) — Property disposed of after ceasing business; 13(13) — Vessel construction; 20(16) — Terminal loss where A to D exceed E to J and no property left in class; 28(1)(d) — Inclusion in farming or fishing income when using cash method; 37(6) — Recapture on sale of property expensed via SR&ED deductions; 104(5)(b), (c) — Trusts — 21-year deemed disposition rule; 110.1(3), 118.1(6) — Election for reduced recapture on donated property; 110.6(1) — "investment income"; 115(1)(a)(iii.2) — Non-resident's taxable income earned in Canada; 216(6) — Non-residents. See also at end of s. 13.

Notes: When depreciable property is sold, the proceeds of disposition, up to the original cost, are deducted from the UCC of the class (see 13(21)"undepreciated capital cost"F). (Any excess over the original cost is a capital gain under 39(1).) If as a result the UCC goes negative, 13(1) requires the balance to be included in income. This is "recapture" (clawback) of CCA that was claimed; conceptually, too much CCA was claimed, since the property was sold for more than the UCC. The pooling of properties into one class can distort the timing of the recapture, however. If the last asset in the class has been disposed of and the UCC is still positive, a terminal loss can be claimed under 20(16). See also Income Tax Folio S3-F4-C1.

Recapture is triggered on death: 70(5)(c). Methods of avoiding this include leaving the property to a spouse or spouse trust (70(6)), rolling it into a corporation before death (85(1)), buying life insurance, and donating the property to a charity (118.1(6)(b)(i)): Arthur Drache, "Recapture Options", xxiv(19) *The Canadian Taxpayer* (Carswell) 145-47 (Sept. 24/02). It cannot be reported on a separate "rights or things" return: *Mercure*, 2003 TCC 655. Sale of assets of a "separate business" effectively triggers recapture: Reg. 1101(1).

Recapture should be added to either *business* income or *property* income, based on the proportion in which CCA was claimed: VIEWS docs 9221275, 2011-0413891I7, 2012-0440781E5, 2015-0605581E5.

If property was wrongly classified as depreciable and the CCA claims are statute-barred, CRA will apply recapture of the wrongly-claimed CCA on sale if the property was acquired after 2015: VIEWS doc 2015-0575921I7.

13(1) amended by 2002-2013 technical bill (Part 5 — technical), for taxation years that end after Feb. 23, 1998, effectively to cover formula elements K and D.1.

I.T. Application Rules: 20(2) (income from farming or fishing — property acquired before 1972).

Income Tax Folios: S3-F4-C1: General discussion of CCA [replaces IT-418 and IT-478R2].

Interpretation Bulletins: IT-121R3: Election to capitalize cost of borrowed money (cancelled); IT-267R2: CCA — vessels; IT-288R2: Gifts of capital properties to a charity and others; IT-481: Timber resource property and timber limits.

I.T. Technical News: 12 (1998 deduction limits and benefit rates for automobiles); 16 (*Continental Bank* case).

(2) Idem [luxury automobile] — Notwithstanding subsection (1), where an excess amount is determined under that subsection at the end of a taxation year in respect of a passenger vehicle having a cost to a taxpayer in excess of $20,000 or such other amount as may be prescribed, that excess amount shall not be included in computing the taxpayer's income for the year but shall be deemed, for the purposes of B in the definition "undepreciated capital cost" in subsection (21), to be an amount included in the taxpayer's income for the year by reason of this section.

Related Provisions: 13(3) — Interpretation where taxpayer is an individual; 13(7)(g) — Limitation on capital cost of automobile; 13(8) — Disposition after ceasing business; 20(16.1)(a) — Terminal loss — vehicles; 67.2 — Interest on money borrowed for passenger vehicle; Reg. 1100(2.5) — 50% CCA in year of disposition. See also at end of s. 13.

Notes: See Notes to 13(7)(g) re prescribed amount for each year. See also VIEWS doc 2012-0470591E5, where 13(5.2) applied.

Regulations: 7307(1) (prescribed amount).

Income Tax Folios: S3-F4-C1: General discussion of CCA [replaces IT-478R2].

Interpretation Bulletins: IT-521R: Motor vehicle expenses claimed by self-employed individuals; IT-522R: Vehicle, travel and sales expenses of employees.

I.T. Technical News: 10 (1997 deduction limits and benefit rates for automobiles).

(3) "Taxation year", "year" and "income" of individual — Where a taxpayer is an individual whose income for a taxation year includes income from a business the fiscal period of which does not coincide with the calendar year and depreciable property acquired for the purpose of gaining or producing income from the business has been disposed of,

(a) for greater certainty, each reference in subsections (1) and (2) to a "taxation year" and "year" shall be read as a reference to a "fiscal period"; and

(b) a reference in subsection (1) to "the income" shall be read as a reference to "the income from the business".

Related Provisions: 13(8) — Property disposed of after ceasing business; 20(16.2) — Same rule applies for purposes of subsecs. 20(16) and (16.1). See also at end of s. 13.

Notes: Since 1995, almost all individuals use a calendar year as their fiscal period. See Notes at end of 249.1.

Before re-enactment in RSC 1985 (5th Supp), 13(3)(a) applied explicitly for purposes of 20(16) and (16.1); this rule is now in 20(16.2).

Income Tax Folios: S3-F4-C1: General discussion of CCA [replaces IT-418 and IT-478R2].

(4) Exchanges of [depreciable] property — Where an amount in respect of the disposition in a taxation year (in this subsection referred to as the "initial year") of depreciable property (in this section referred to as the "former property") of a prescribed class of a taxpayer would, but for this subsection, be the amount determined for F or G in the definition "undepreciated capital cost" in subsection (21) in respect of the disposition of the former property that is either

(a) property the proceeds of disposition of which were proceeds referred to in paragraph (b), (c) or (d) of the definition "proceeds of disposition" in subsection (21), or

(b) a property that was, immediately before the disposition, a former business property of the taxpayer,

and the taxpayer so elects under this subsection in the taxpayer's return of income for the taxation year in which the taxpayer acquires a depreciable property of a prescribed class of the taxpayer that is a replacement property for the taxpayer's former property,

(c) the amount otherwise determined for F or G in the definition "undepreciated capital cost" in subsection (21) in respect of the disposition of the former property shall be reduced by the lesser of

(i) the amount, if any, by which the amount otherwise determined for F or G in that definition exceeds the undepreciated capital cost to the taxpayer of property of the prescribed class to which the former property belonged at the time immediately before the time that the former property was disposed of, and

(ii) the amount that has been used by the taxpayer to acquire

(A) if the former property is described in paragraph (a), before the later of the end of the second taxation year following the initial year and 24 months after the end of the initial year, or

(B) in any other case, before the later of the end of the first taxation year following the initial year and 12 months after the end of the initial year,

a replacement property of a prescribed class that has not been disposed of by the taxpayer before the time at which the taxpayer disposed of the former property, and

(d) the amount of the reduction determined under paragraph (c) shall be deemed to be proceeds of disposition of a depreciable property of the taxpayer that had a capital cost equal to that amount and that was property of the same class as the replacement property, from a disposition made on the later of

    (i) the time the replacement property was acquired by the taxpayer, and

    (ii) the time the former property was disposed of by the taxpayer.

Related Provisions: 13(4.1) — Replacement property; 13(4.2), (4.3) — Exchange of franchise, concession or licence; 13(18) — Reassessments; 20(4.2) — Bad debt on sale of pre-2016 eligible capital property; 44(1) — Parallel rule for capital gains purposes; 44(4) — Deemed election; 44(6) — Deemed proceeds of disposition; 87(2)(g.5) — Amalgamation — continuing corporation; 87(2)(l.3) — Amalgamations — replacement property; 96(3) — Election by members of partnership; 220(3.2), Reg. 600(b) — Late filing or revocation of election. See also at end of s. 13.

Notes: 13(4) allows a "rollover" of undepreciated capital cost for CCA purposes where replacement property is acquired, to prevent recapture under 13(1). See Notes to 44(1), the parallel rule for the property's adjusted cost base, preventing a gain from being recognized. For pre-2017 eligible capital property, see (repealed) 14(6).

An election "in the taxpayer's return" is valid even if the return is filed late. See Notes to 7(1.31).

For a taxpayer filing Quebec returns, an election under 13(4) must be copied to Revenu Québec: *Taxation Act* ss. 96(4), 21.4.6.

The 24-month and 12-month rules in (c)(ii)(A) and (B) accommodate short taxation years (see Notes to 249(4)).

13(4) amended by 2002-2013 technical bill (for dispositions in tax years ending after Dec. 19, 2001), 1995-97 technical bill.

Remission Orders: *Telesat Canada Remission Order*, P.C. 1999-1335.

Interpretation Bulletins: IT-259R4: Exchanges of property; IT-267R2: CCA — vessels; IT-271R: Expropriations — time and proceeds of disposition (cancelled).

Information Circulars: 07-1R1: Taxpayer relief provisions.

(4.1) Replacement for a former property — For the purposes of subsection (4), a particular depreciable property of a prescribed class of a taxpayer is a replacement for a former property of the taxpayer if

(a) it is reasonable to conclude that the property was acquired by the taxpayer to replace the former property;

(a.1) it was acquired by the taxpayer and used by the taxpayer or a person related to the taxpayer for a use that is the same as or similar to the use to which the taxpayer or a person related to the taxpayer put the former property;

(b) where the former property was used by the taxpayer or a person related to the taxpayer for the purpose of gaining or producing income from a business, the particular depreciable property was acquired for the purpose of gaining or producing income from that or a similar business or for use by a person related to the taxpayer for such a purpose;

(c) where the former property was a taxable Canadian property of the taxpayer, the particular depreciable property is a taxable Canadian property of the taxpayer; and

(d) where the former property was a taxable Canadian property (other than treaty-protected property) of the taxpayer, the particular depreciable property is a taxable Canadian property (other than treaty-protected property) of the taxpayer.

Related Provisions: See at end of s. 13.

Notes: See Notes to 44(5), which provides the same rule for non-depreciable property.

13(4.1) amended by 1998 Budget (effective for dispositions in a taxation year that ends after 1997), 1995-97 technical bill (last change effective for a former property disposed of after June 17, 1998) and 1991 technical bill.

Interpretation Bulletins: IT-259R4: Exchanges of property.

(4.2) Election — limited period franchise, concession or license — Subsection (4.3) applies if

(a) a taxpayer (in this subsection and subsection (4.3) referred to as the "transferor") has, pursuant to a written agreement with a person or partnership (in this subsection and subsection (4.3) referred to as the "transferee"), at any time disposed of or terminated a former property that is a franchise, concession or licence

for a limited period that is wholly attributable to the carrying on of a business at a fixed place;

(b) the transferee acquired the former property from the transferor or, on the termination, acquired a similar property in respect of the same fixed place from another person or partnership; and

(c) the transferor and the transferee jointly elect in their returns of income for their taxation years that include that time to have subsection (4.3) apply in respect of the acquisition and the disposition or termination.

Related Provisions: 96(3) — Election by members of partnership; 248(1)"former business property" — Property that is the subject of election under 13(4.2).

Notes: See Notes to 13(4.3). For a taxpayer filing Quebec returns, an election under 13(4.2)(c) must be copied to Revenu Québec: *Taxation Act* ss. 96.0.2, 21.4.6.

13(4.2) added by 2002-2013 technical bill (Part 5 — technical), for dispositions and terminations after Dec. 20, 2002.

(4.3) Effect of election — If this subsection applies in respect of an acquisition and a disposition or termination,

(a) if the transferee acquired a similar property referred to in paragraph (4.2)(b), the transferee is deemed to have also acquired the former property at the time that the former property was terminated and to own the former property until the transferee no longer owns the similar property;

(b) if the transferee acquired the former property referred to in paragraph (4.2)(b), the transferee is deemed to own the former property until such time as the transferee owns neither the former property nor a similar property in respect of the same fixed place to which the former property related;

(c) for the purpose of calculating the amount deductible under paragraph 20(1)(a) in respect of the former property in computing the transferee's income, the life of the former property remaining on its acquisition by the transferee is deemed to be equal to the period that was the life of the former property remaining on its acquisition by the transferor; and

(d) any amount that would, if this Act were read without reference to this subsection, be included in the cost of a property of the transferor included in Class 14.1 of Schedule II to the *Income Tax Regulations* (including a deemed acquisition under subsection (35)) or included in the proceeds of disposition of a property of the transferee included in that Class (including a deemed disposition under subsection (37)) in respect of the disposition or termination of the former property by the transferor is deemed to be

    (i) neither included in the cost nor the proceeds of disposition of property included in that Class,

    (ii) an amount required to be included in computing the capital cost to the transferee of the former property, and

    (iii) an amount required to be included in computing the proceeds of disposition to the transferor in respect of a disposition of the former property.

Related Provisions: 13(4.2) — Conditions for 13(4.3) to apply; 20(16.1)(b) — Restriction on terminal loss; Reg. 1101(1ag) — Separate class for property subject to 13(4.2) election.

Notes: 13(4.2)-(4.3) effectively allow the 13(4) "replacement property" rule to apply to a defined-period franchise, concession or license (normally Class 14 property) in limited circumstances. Such property is included in 248(1)"former business property" and deemed a separate class by Reg. 1101(1ag). For detailed explanation see Finance Technical Notes.

13(4.3)(d) amended by 2016 budget bill #2, for dispositions and terminations after 2016 (as part of changing ECP rules to CCA Class 14.1: see Notes to 20(1)(b)). Before the amendment, read:

    (d) any amount that would, if this Act were read without reference to this subsection, be an eligible capital amount to the transferor or an eligible capital expenditure to the transferee in respect of the disposition or termination of the former property by the transferor is deemed to be

        (i) neither an eligible capital amount nor an eligible capital expenditure,

        (ii) an amount required to be included in computing the capital cost to the transferee of the former property, and

(iii) an amount required to be included in computing the proceeds of disposition to the transferor in respect of a disposition of the former property.

13(4.3) added by 2002-2013 technical bill (Part 5 — technical), for dispositions and terminations after Dec. 20, 2002.

(5) Reclassification of property

(5) **Reclassification of property** — Where one or more depreciable properties of a taxpayer that were included in a prescribed class (in this subsection referred to as the "old class") become included at any time (in this subsection referred to as the "transfer time") in another prescribed class (in this subsection referred to as the "new class"), for the purpose of determining at any subsequent time the undepreciated capital cost to the taxpayer of depreciable property of the old class and the new class

(a) the value of A in the definition "undepreciated capital cost" in subsection (21) shall be determined as if each of those depreciable properties were

(i) properties of the new class acquired before the subsequent time, and

(ii) never included in the old class; and

(b) there shall be deducted in computing the total depreciation allowed to the taxpayer for property of the old class before the subsequent time, and added in computing the total depreciation allowed to the taxpayer for property of the new class before the subsequent time, the greater of

(i) the amount determined by the formula

$$A - B$$

where

A is the total of all amounts each of which is the capital cost to the taxpayer of each of those depreciable properties, and

B is the undepreciated capital cost to the taxpayer of depreciable property of the old class at the transfer time, and

(ii) the total of all amounts each of which is an amount that would have been deducted under paragraph 20(1)(a) in respect of a depreciable property that is one of those properties in computing the taxpayer's income for a taxation year that ended before the transfer time and at the end of which the property was included in the old class if

(A) the property had been the only property included in a separate prescribed class, and

(B) the rate allowed by the regulations made for the purpose of paragraph 20(1)(a) in respect of that separate class had been the effective rate that was used by the taxpayer to calculate a deduction under that paragraph in respect of the old class for the year.

Related Provisions: 87(2)(d)(ii)(C) — Amalgamations — depreciable property; 257 — Formula cannot calculate to less than zero. See also at end of s. 13.

Notes: See Income Tax Folio S3-F4-C1 ¶1.123-1.128. See VIEWS doc 2008-0301331E5 for an example of 13(5) applying.

13(5) amended by 1996 Budget, effective for properties of a prescribed class that, after 1996, become included in property of another prescribed class. The amendment clarifies that 13(5) applies as a result of a change to the Act or Regulations; accommodates the simultaneous change in status of more than one property of a prescribed class; and causes 13(5) to apply immediately after a change in status, to deal with a change in status at the very beginning of a taxpayer's taxation year.

Regulations: 1103 (property reclassifications by Regulation).

Income Tax Folios: S3-F4-C1: General discussion of CCA [replaces IT-190R2].

Information Circulars: 84-1: Revision of capital cost allowance claims and other permissive deductions.

(5.1) Rules applicable [leasehold interest]

(5.1) **Rules applicable [leasehold interest]** — Where at any time in a taxation year a taxpayer acquires a particular property in respect of which, immediately before that time, the taxpayer had a leasehold interest that was included in a prescribed class, for the purposes of this section, section 20 and any regulations made under paragraph 20(1)(a), the following rules apply:

(a) the leasehold interest shall be deemed to have been disposed of by the taxpayer at that time for proceeds of disposition equal to the amount, if any, by which

(i) the capital cost immediately before that time of the leasehold interest

exceeds

(ii) the total of all amounts claimed by the taxpayer in respect of the leasehold interest and deductible under paragraph 20(1)(a) in computing the taxpayer's income in previous taxation years;

(b) the particular property shall be deemed to be depreciable property of a prescribed class of the taxpayer acquired by the taxpayer at that time and there shall be added to the capital cost to the taxpayer of the property an amount equal to the capital cost referred to in subparagraph (a)(i); and

(c) the total referred to in subparagraph (a)(ii) shall be added to the total depreciation allowed to the taxpayer before that time in respect of the class to which the particular property belongs.

Related Provisions: See at end of s.13.

Notes: For a ruling applying 13(5.1) see VIEWS doc 2008-0303431R3.

Income Tax Folios: S3-F4-C1: General discussion of CCA.

Interpretation Bulletins: IT-464R: CCA — leasehold interests.

(5.2) Deemed cost and depreciation [past rent deemed to be CCA]

(5.2) **Deemed cost and depreciation [past rent deemed to be CCA]** — If, at any time, a taxpayer has acquired a capital property that is depreciable property or real or immovable property in respect of which, before that time, the taxpayer or any person with whom the taxpayer was not dealing at arm's length was entitled to a deduction in computing income in respect of any amount paid or payable for the use of, or the right to use, the property and the cost or the capital cost (determined without reference to this subsection) at that time of the property to the taxpayer is less than the fair market value thereof at that time determined without reference to any option with respect to that property, for the purposes of this section, section 20 and any regulations made under paragraph 20(1)(a), the following rules apply:

(a) the property shall be deemed to have been acquired by the taxpayer at that time at a cost equal to the lesser of

(i) the fair market value of the property at that time determined without reference to any option with respect to that property, and

(ii) the total of the cost or the capital cost (determined without reference to this subsection) of the property to the taxpayer and all amounts (other than amounts paid or payable to a person with whom the taxpayer was not dealing at arm's length) each of which is an outlay or expense made or incurred by the taxpayer or by a person with whom the taxpayer was not dealing at arm's length at any time for the use of, or the right to use, the property,

and for the purposes of this paragraph and subsection (5.3), where a particular corporation has been incorporated or otherwise formed after the time any other corporation with which the particular corporation would not have been dealing at arm's length had the particular corporation been in existence before that time, the particular corporation shall be deemed to have been in existence from the time of the formation of the other corporation and to have been not dealing at arm's length with the other corporation;

(b) the amount by which the cost to the taxpayer of the property determined under paragraph (a) exceeds the cost or the capital cost thereof (determined without reference to this subsection) shall be added to the total depreciation allowed to the taxpayer before that time in respect of the prescribed class to which the property belongs; and

(c) where the property would, but for this paragraph, not be depreciable property of the taxpayer, it shall be deemed to be depreciable property of a separate prescribed class of the taxpayer.

Related Provisions: See at end of s. 13.

Notes: 13(5.2) applies where a taxpayer pays rent for property and then acquires it. In essence, if the property is later sold for a profit, the rent paid is taxed by treating it as CCA claimed, which is recaptured under 13(1).

For application of 13(5.2) to an automobile see VIEWS doc 2012-0470591E5.

13(5.2) opening words amended by 2002-2013 technical bill (Part 4 — bijuralism), effective June 26, 2013, to add "or immovable" (and to change "the depreciable property or real property" to "the property" — non-substantive change).

Regulations: 1101(5g) and Sch. II:Cl. 36 (property under 13(5.2)(c) deemed to be a separate class).

Interpretation Bulletins: IT-233R: Lease-option agreements; sale-leaseback agreements (cancelled).

I.T. Technical News: 21 (cancellation of Interpretation Bulletin IT-233R).

Forms: T776: Statement of real estate rentals.

(5.3) Deemed recapture [disposition of option] — If, at any time in a taxation year, a taxpayer has disposed of a capital property that is an option with respect to depreciable property or real or immovable property in respect of which the taxpayer or any person with whom the taxpayer was not dealing at arm's length was entitled to a deduction in computing income in respect of any amount paid for the use of, or the right to use, the property, for the purposes of this section, the amount, if any, by which the proceeds of disposition to the taxpayer of the option exceed the taxpayer's cost in respect thereof is deemed to be an excess referred to in subsection (1) in respect of the taxpayer for the year.

Related Provisions: 49 — Options. See also at end of s. 13.

Notes: 13(5.3) amended by 2002-2013 technical bill (Part 4 — bijuralism), effective June 26, 2013, to add "or immovable" (and to change "the depreciable property or real property" to "the property" — non-substantive change).

Interpretation Bulletins: IT-233R: Lease-option agreements; sale-leaseback agreements (cancelled).

I.T. Technical News: 21 (cancellation of Interpretation Bulletin IT-233R).

Forms: T776: Statement of real estate rentals.

(5.4) Idem — Where, before the time of disposition of a capital property that was depreciable property of a taxpayer, the taxpayer, or any person with whom the taxpayer was not dealing at arm's length, was entitled to a deduction in computing income in respect of any outlay or expense made or incurred for the use of, or the right to use, during a period of time, that capital property (other than an outlay or expense made or incurred by the taxpayer or a person with whom the taxpayer was not dealing at arm's length before the acquisition of the property), except where the taxpayer disposed of the property to a person with whom the taxpayer was not dealing at arm's length and that person was subject to the provisions of subsection (5.2) with respect to the acquisition by that person of the property, the following rules apply:

(a) an amount equal to the lesser of

(i) the total of all amounts (other than amounts paid or payable to the taxpayer or a person with whom the taxpayer was not dealing at arm's length) each of which was a deductible outlay or expense made or incurred before the time of disposition by the taxpayer, or by a person with whom the taxpayer was not dealing at arm's length, for the use of, or the right to use, during the period of time, the property, and

(ii) the amount, if any, by which the fair market value of the property at the earlier of

(A) the expiration of the last period of time in respect of which the deductible outlay or expense referred to in subparagraph (i) was made or incurred, and

(B) the time of the disposition

exceeds the capital cost to the taxpayer of the property immediately before that time

shall, immediately before the time of the disposition, be added to the capital cost of the property to the person who owned the property at that time; and

(b) the amount added to the capital cost to the taxpayer of the property pursuant to paragraph (a) shall be added immediately before the time of the disposition to the total depreciation allowed to the taxpayer before that time in respect of the prescribed class to which the property belongs.

Related Provisions: 13(5.5) — Lease cancellation payment deemed not to be made for the use of property. See also at end of s. 13.

(5.5) Lease cancellation payment — For the purposes of subsection (5.4), an amount deductible by a taxpayer under paragraph 20(1)(z) or (z.1) in respect of a cancellation of a lease of property shall, for greater certainty, be deemed not to be an outlay or expense that was made or incurred by the taxpayer for the use of, or the right to use, the property.

Related Provisions: See at end of s. 13.

(6) Misclassified property — Where, in calculating the amount of a deduction allowed to a taxpayer under subsection 20(16) or regulations made for the purposes of paragraph 20(1)(a) in respect of depreciable property of the taxpayer of a prescribed class (in this subsection referred to as the "particular class"), there has been added to the capital cost to the taxpayer of depreciable property of the particular class the capital cost of depreciable property (in this subsection referred to as "added property") of another prescribed class, for the purposes of this section, section 20 and any regulations made for the purposes of paragraph 20(1)(a), the added property shall, if the Minister so directs with respect to any taxation year for which, under subsection 152(4), the Minister may make any reassessment or additional assessment or assess tax, interest or penalties under this Part, be deemed to have been property of the particular class and not of the other class at all times before the beginning of the year and, except to the extent that the added property or any part thereof has been disposed of by the taxpayer before the beginning of the year, to have been transferred from the particular class to the other class at the beginning of the year.

Related Provisions: See at end of s. 13.

Notes: Where property was wrongly classified and the CCA claims are now statute-barred, see VIEWS doc 2015-057592117 to determine UCC and recapture.

13(6) amended by 1991 technical bill to correct the reference to 152(4), retroactive to April 20, 1983.

Income Tax Folios: S3-F4-C1: General discussion of CCA [replaces IT-190R2].

Information Circulars: 84-1: Revision of capital cost allowance claims and other permissive deductions.

(7) Rules applicable — Subject to subsection 70(13), for the purposes of paragraphs 8(1)(j) and (p), this section, section 20 and any regulations made for the purpose of paragraph 20(1)(a),

Notes: Opening words of 13(7) amended to add "Subject to subsection 70(13)" by 1993 technical bill, effective 1993.

(a) [change in use from income-producing] — where a taxpayer, having acquired property for the purpose of gaining or producing income, has begun at a later time to use it for some other purpose, the taxpayer shall be deemed to have disposed of it at that later time for proceeds of disposition equal to its fair market value at that time and to have reacquired it immediately thereafter at a cost equal to that fair market value;

Related Provisions: 13(9) — Application to non-resident taxpayer; 45 — Change in use rules. See also at end of s. 13.

Notes: A change of use under 13(7)(a) requires that the asset be used "for some other purpose". Where a company acquired new vehicles each year just before year-end, and traded in its old vehicles just after year-end, there was no such "other purpose" merely because at year-end it was now holding the vehicles for disposal, and 13(7)(a) did not apply: *Hewlett Packard*, 2004 FCA 240.

Where property that is leased out switches between capital property and inventory, 13(7) and 45(1) apply: *CAE Inc.*, 2013 FCA 92, paras. 85-102. However, the CRA disagrees: see Notes to 45(1).

13(7)(a) applied in: *Evans*, 2008 TCC 310 (taxpayers used garage on their property for electrical business, and sons took over business so they were no longer carrying it on; CCA recaptured); *Murphy*, 2010 TCC 564, para. 19 (lawyer who closed her practice in Oct. and became an employee had a change in use and was denied CCA for that year); *Donaldson*, 2016 TCC 5, para. 33 (rental property changed to principal residence).

Note that on conversion of inventory to capital property, GST/HST may be triggered as well: see *Excise Tax Act* s. 196.1, in David M. Sherman, *Practitioner's Goods and Services Tax Annotated*. On conversion of inventory to personal use see ETA 172(1).

13(7)(a) applies on a Canadian branch moving depreciable property to its US head office, due to 13(9): VIEWS doc 2010-0383571I7.

13(7)(a) amended by 1991 technical bill, last change effective May 1988.

Interpretation Bulletins: IT-525R: Performing artists.

(b) **[change in use to income-producing]** — where a taxpayer, having acquired property for some other purpose, has begun at a later time to use it for the purpose of gaining or producing income, the taxpayer shall be deemed to have acquired it at that later time at a capital cost to the taxpayer equal to the lesser of

   (i) the fair market value of the property at that later time, and

   (ii) the total of

      (A) the cost to the taxpayer of the property at that later time determined without reference to this paragraph, paragraph (a) and subparagraph (d)(ii), and

      (B) $\frac{1}{2}$ of the amount, if any, by which

         (I) the fair market value of the property at that later time

   exceeds the total of

         (II) the cost to the taxpayer of the property as determined under clause (A), and

         (III) twice the amount deducted by the taxpayer under section 110.6 in respect of the amount, if any, by which the fair market value of the property at that later time exceeds the cost to the taxpayer of the property as determined under clause (A);

Related Provisions: 13(7)(e) — Rules applicable; 13(9) — Application to non-resident taxpayer; 45 — Change in use rules; 70(13) — Capital cost of depreciable property on death; 248(1) — "cost amount"(a). See also at end of s. 13.

Notes: See Notes to 13(7)(a), and Notes to 45(1) re conditions for a change in use. See VIEWS doc 2009-0344171I7 where a computer acquired personally is changed to business use. In *Donaldson*, 2016 TCC 5, para. 32, 13(7)(b) applied on a change from principal residence to rental property.

13(7)(b)(ii)(B) amended by 2000 Budget (for tax years ending after Oct. 17, 2000), 1991 technical bill.

Interpretation Bulletins: IT-148R3: Recreational properties and club dues; IT-160R3: Personal use of aircraft (cancelled); IT-209R: Inter-vivos gifts of capital property to individuals directly or through trusts; IT-525R: Performing artists.

I.T. Technical News: 18 (*Cudd Pressure* case).

(c) **[partial use to produce income]** — where property has, since it was acquired by a taxpayer, been regularly used in part for the purpose of gaining or producing income and in part for some other purpose, the taxpayer shall be deemed to have acquired, for the purpose of gaining or producing income, the proportion of the property that the use regularly made of the property for gaining or producing income is of the whole use regularly made of the property at a capital cost to the taxpayer equal to the same proportion of the capital cost to the taxpayer of the whole property and, if the property has, in such a case, been disposed of, the proceeds of disposition of the proportion of the property deemed to have been acquired for gaining or producing income shall be deemed to be the same proportion of the proceeds of disposition of the whole property;

Related Provisions: 13(9) — Application to non-resident taxpayer; 45 — Change in use rules. See also at end of s. 13.

Notes: 13(7)(c) amended by 1991 technical bill, retroactive to May 1988.

Interpretation Bulletins: IT-148R3: Recreational properties and club dues; IT-160R3: Personal use of aircraft (cancelled); IT-217R: Depreciable property owned on Dec. 31, 1971 (cancelled); IT-525R: Performing artists.

(d) **[partial change in use]** — where, at any time after a taxpayer has acquired property, there has been a change in the relation between the use regularly made by the taxpayer of the property for gaining or producing income and the use regularly made of the property for other purposes,

   (i) if the use regularly made by the taxpayer of the property for the purpose of gaining or producing income has increased, the taxpayer shall be deemed to have acquired at that time depreciable property of that class at a capital cost equal to the total of

      (A) the proportion of the lesser of

         (I) its fair market value at that time, and

         (II) its cost to the taxpayer at that time determined without reference to this subparagraph, subparagraph (ii) and paragraph (a)

      that the amount of the increase in the use regularly made by the taxpayer of the property for that purpose is of the whole of the use regularly made of the property, and

      (B) $\frac{1}{2}$ of the amount, if any, by which

         (I) the amount deemed under subparagraph 45(1)(c)(ii) to be the taxpayer's proceeds of disposition of the property in respect of the change

   exceeds the total of

         (II) that proportion of the cost to the taxpayer of the property as determined under subclause (A)(II) that the amount of the increase in the use regularly made by the taxpayer of the property for that purpose is of the whole of the use regularly made of the property, and

         (III) twice the amount deducted by the taxpayer under section 110.6 in respect of the amount, if any, by which the amount determined under subclause (I) exceeds the amount determined under subclause (II), and

   (ii) if the use regularly made of the property for the purpose of gaining or producing income has decreased, the taxpayer shall be deemed to have disposed at that time of depreciable property of that class and the proceeds of disposition shall be deemed to be an amount equal to the proportion of the fair market value of the property as of that time that the amount of the decrease in the use regularly made by the taxpayer of the property for that purpose is of the whole use regularly made of the property;

Related Provisions: 13(4) — Exchange of property; 13(7)(e) — Rules applicable; 13(9) — Application to non-resident taxpayer; 44(1) — Exchanges of property; 45 — Change in use rules; 70(12) — Capital cost of depreciable property on death; 248(1)"cost amount"(a) — Application of 13(7) to determination of cost amount; 256(6) — Controlled corporation. See also at end of s. 13.

Notes: 13(7)(d)(i)(B) amended by 2000 Budget to change "¾" to "½" and "⅓ of" to "twice", effective 2000-01 with transitional rules for 2000.

13(7)(d)(i)(B)(II) and (III) amended by 1991 technical bill, last change effective for changes in use after 1989.

Interpretation Bulletins: IT-160R3: Personal use of aircraft (cancelled); IT-209R: Inter-vivos gifts of capital property to individuals directly or through trusts.

(e) **[non-arm's length acquisition]** — notwithstanding any other provision of this Act except subsection 70(13), where at a particular time a person or partnership (in this paragraph referred to as the "taxpayer") has, directly or indirectly, in any manner whatever, acquired (otherwise than as a consequence of the death of the transferor) a depreciable property (other than a timber resource property) of a prescribed class from a person or partnership with whom the taxpayer did not deal at arm's length (in this paragraph referred to as the "transferor") and, immediately before the transfer, the property was a capital property of the transferor,

   (i) where the transferor was an individual resident in Canada or a partnership any member of which was either an individual resident in Canada or another partnership and the cost of the property to the taxpayer at the particular time determined without reference to this paragraph exceeds the cost, or where the property was depreciable property, the capital cost of the property to the transferor immediately before the transferor disposed of it, the capital cost of the property to the taxpayer at the particular time shall be deemed to be the amount that is equal to the total of

(A) the cost or capital cost, as the case may be, of the property to the transferor immediately before the particular time, and

(B) ½ of the amount, if any, by which

(I) the transferor's proceeds of disposition of the property

exceed the total of

(II) the cost or capital cost, as the case may be, to the transferor immediately before the particular time,

(III) twice the amount deducted by any person under section 110.6 in respect of the amount, if any, by which the amount determined under subclause (I) exceeds the amount determined under subclause (II), and

(IV) the amount, if any, required by subsection 110.6(21) to be deducted in computing the capital cost to the taxpayer of the property at that time

and, for the purposes of paragraph (b) and subparagraph (d)(i), the cost of the property to the taxpayer shall be deemed to be the same amount,

(ii) where the transferor was neither an individual resident in Canada nor a partnership any member of which was either an individual resident in Canada or another partnership and the cost of the property to the taxpayer at the particular time determined without reference to this paragraph exceeds the cost, or where the property was depreciable property, the capital cost of the property to the transferor immediately before the transferor disposed of it, the capital cost of the property to the taxpayer at that time shall be deemed to be the amount that is equal to the total of

(A) the cost or capital cost, as the case may be, of the property to the transferor immediately before the particular time, and

(B) ½ of the amount, if any, by which the transferor's proceeds of disposition of the property exceed the cost or capital cost, as the case may be, to the transferor immediately before the particular time

and, for the purposes of paragraph (b) and subparagraph (d)(i), the cost of the property to the taxpayer shall be deemed to be the same amount, and

(iii) where the cost or capital cost, as the case may be, of the property to the transferor immediately before the transferor disposed of it exceeds the capital cost of the property to the taxpayer at that time determined without reference to this paragraph, the capital cost of the property to the taxpayer at that time shall be deemed to be the amount that was the cost or capital cost, as the case may be, of the property to the transferor immediately before the transferor disposed of it and the excess shall be deemed to have been allowed to the taxpayer in respect of the property under regulations made under paragraph 20(1)(a) in computing the taxpayer's income for taxation years ending before the acquisition of the property by the taxpayer;

Related Provisions: 13(7)(e.1) — Where election made to trigger capital gains exemption; 13(7.3) — Control of corporations by one trustee; 13(21.2) — Transfer of property where UCC exceeds fair market value; 70(13) — Capital cost of depreciable property on death; 85(5) — Similar rule on section 85 rollover; 97(4) — Transfer of depreciable property to partnership; 248(8) — Meaning of "consequence" of death; 256(6) — Controlled corporation. See also at end of s. 13.

Notes: 13(7)(e) applies on a non-arm's-length transfer of depreciable property. It prevents an increase in the depreciable base of property where the transferor benefits from the half-taxation of capital gains (38(a)) and possibly the capital gains exemption (110.6). If the cost of depreciable property to the transferee would otherwise exceed the capital cost to the transferor, 13(7)(e)(i)-(ii) provide that the capital cost to the transferee is limited to the sum of the capital cost to the transferor and the transferor's *taxable* capital gain on the property minus any related claim by the transferor under 110.6. (See VIEWS docs 2006-0176171E5, 2012-0463191E5. There may also be a 15(1) ben-

efit: 2011-040808117.) If the cost to the transferor would otherwise exceed the capital cost to the transferee, 13(7)(e)(iii) provides that the property is treated as having been acquired by the transferee at the transferor's capital cost; the excess is deemed to be CCA claimed by the transferee (and thus subject to recapture under 13(1)). Shifting depreciable property to use up capital losses within a corporate group does not trigger GAAR: 2000-0014543, 2017-0693691R3, 2018-0772921R3 [Smit & Kimiagar, "Using Capital Losses to Step up Depreciable Cost", XVI(2) *Corporate Structures & Groups* (Federated Press) 3-5 (2020)].

For the meaning of "indirectly" in opening words, see Notes to 17.1(1).

13(7)(e) and (e.1) applied in *Sicurella*, 2013 TCC 79, so a 110.6(19) election to use the $100,000 capital gains exemption to 1994 did not change UCC or the annual CCA entitlement. The parallel Quebec rule did not apply to pre-2017 eligible capital property (see 20(1)(b) Notes) in *7958501 Canada*, 2020 QCCQ 2424.

13(7)(e) does not apply to a 104(5) deemed disposition by a trust but can apply to a 107(2.1) distribution in CRA's view: doc 2015-0576751E5.

13(7)(e)(ii) will apply to an acquisition of software from a related non-resident even though the non-resident may have been allowed to expense the cost of developing the software: VIEWS doc 2003-0014995.

13(7)(e) amended by 2000 Budget (for acquisitions in tax years ending after Oct. 17, 2000), 1994 Budget, 1993 and 1991 technical bills.

Regulations: 1102(14) — Class of property preserved on non-arm's length acquisition.

Interpretation Bulletins: IT-209R: Inter-vivos gifts of capital property to individuals directly or through trusts; IT-217R: Depreciable property owned on Dec. 31, 1971 (cancelled); IT-291R3: Transfer of property to a corporation under subsection 85(1).

(e.1) **[capital gains exemption election]** — where a taxpayer is deemed by paragraph 110.6(19)(a) to have disposed of and reacquired a property that immediately before the disposition was a depreciable property, the taxpayer shall be deemed to have acquired the property from himself, herself or itself and, in so having acquired the property, not to have been dealing with himself, herself or itself at arm's length;

Related Provisions: 69(1) — Effect of acquiring property not at arm's length.

Notes: This rule applied in *Sicurella* (see Notes to 13(7)(e)).

13(7)(e.1) added by 1994 Budget, effective 1994.

Regulations: 1102(14) — Class of property preserved on deemed reacquisition.

(f) **[change in control]** — if a taxpayer is deemed under paragraph 111(4)(e) to have disposed of and reacquired depreciable property (other than a timber resource property), the capital cost to the taxpayer of the property at the time of the reacquisition is deemed to be equal to the total of

(i) the capital cost to the taxpayer of the property at the time of the disposition, and

(ii) ½ of the amount, if any, by which the taxpayer's proceeds of disposition of the property exceed the capital cost to the taxpayer of the property at the time of the disposition;

Related Provisions: See at end of s. 13.

Notes: 13(7)(f) amended by 2013 budget bill #2 (effective March 21, 2013, to change all "corporation" to "taxpayer" since 111(4) now applies to trusts as well); 2000 Budget; 1995-97 and 1991 technical bills.

Interpretation Bulletins: IT-302R3: Losses of a corporation — the effect that acquisitions of control, amalgamations, and windings-up have on their deductibility.

(g) **[$30,000 cost cap on automobile]** — where the cost to a taxpayer of a passenger vehicle exceeds $20,000 or such other amount as may be prescribed, the capital cost to the taxpayer of the vehicle shall be deemed to be $20,000 or that other prescribed amount, as the case may be;

Related Provisions: 13(2) — No recapture on luxury automobile; 13(7)(h) — Where vehicle acquired not at arm's length; 13(7)(i) — $55,000 cost cap for zero-emission passenger vehicle; 20(4) — No bad debt deduction on disposition of luxury automobile; 20(16.1)(a) — No terminal loss on luxury automobile; 67.2 — Limitation on interest expense; 67.3 — Limitation on leasing cost; 67.4 — Where vehicle is jointly owned; 85(1)(e.4) — Rollover of vehicle by shareholder to corp; Reg. 1100(2.5) — 50% CCA in year of disposition.

Notes: 13(7)(g) limits the capital cost of an automobile (see 248(1)"passenger vehicle" and "automobile") to a fixed dollar amount for CCA purposes, on the theory that any additional amount is paid for "luxury" features not necessary for business purposes. The limit is $30,000 plus GST/HST & PST, for autos bought in 2001-2021.

(See Notes to Reg. 7307(1) for earlier acquisitions.) For parallel limitations on leasing costs and interest paid, see 67.2 and 67.3. Under s. 201 of the *Excise Tax Act* the same limitation applies for GST/HST input tax credits.

Each vehicle over the threshold is deemed to be in a separate Class 10.1 by Reg. 1101(1af), so CCA is calculated separately for it rather than pooled with other vehicles.

The definition of "passenger vehicle" depends on 248(1)"automobile", which excludes (para. (d)) a vehicle in a business of selling, renting or leasing motor vehicles. See Notes to that definition.

A GPS that is an "integral part of the vehicle" is included in the cost for purposes of the cap: VIEWS doc 2007-0243391C6.

Regulations: 1101(1af) (separate class); 7307(1) (prescribed amount); Sch. II:Cl. 10.1 (class for CCA).

Interpretation Bulletins: IT-521R: Motor vehicle expenses claimed by self-employed individuals.

I.T. Technical News: 10 (1997 deduction limits and benefit rates for automobiles); 12 (1998 deduction limits and benefit rates for automobiles).

(h) [luxury automobile — non-arm's length acquisition] — notwithstanding paragraph (g), where a passenger vehicle is acquired by a taxpayer at any time from a person with whom the taxpayer does not deal at arm's length, the capital cost at that time to the taxpayer of the vehicle shall be deemed to be the least of

(i) the fair market value of the vehicle at that time,

(ii) the amount that immediately before that time was the cost amount to that person of the vehicle, and

(iii) $20,000 or such other amount as is prescribed; and

Related Provisions: 20(16.1)(a) — Terminal loss; 67.4 — More than one owner. See also at end of s. 13.

Notes: See Notes to 13(7)(g) re prescribed amount.

Regulations: 7307(1) (prescribed amount).

Interpretation Bulletins [para. 13(7)(h)]: IT-521R: Motor vehicle expenses claimed by self-employed individuals.

I.T. Technical News: 10 (1997 deduction limits and benefit rates for automobiles).

(i) [$55,000 cost cap on zero-emission automobile] — if the cost to a taxpayer of a zero-emission passenger vehicle exceeds the prescribed amount,

(i) the capital cost to the taxpayer of the vehicle is deemed to be equal to the prescribed amount, and

(ii) for the purposes of paragraph (a) of the description of F in the definition "undepreciated capital cost" in subsection (21), the proceeds of disposition of the vehicle are deemed to be the amount determined by the formula

$$A \times B/C$$

where

A   is the amount that would, in the absence of this subparagraph, be the proceeds of disposition of the vehicle,

B   is

      (A) if the vehicle is disposed of to a person or partnership with which the taxpayer deals at arm's length, the capital cost to the taxpayer of the vehicle, and

      (B) in any other case, the amount determined for C, and

C   is the amount determined by the formula

$$D + (E + F) - (G + H)$$

where

D   is the cost to the taxpayer of the vehicle,

E   is the amount determined under paragraph (7.1)(d) in respect of the vehicle at the time of disposition,

F   is the maximum amount determined for C in the definition "undepreciated capital cost" in subsection (21) in respect of the vehicle,

G   is the amount determined under paragraph (7.1)(f) in respect of the vehicle at the time of disposition, and

H   is the maximum amount determined for J in the definition "undepreciated capital cost" in subsection (21) in respect of the vehicle.

Related Provisions: 20(4.11) — Bad debt deduction on disposition of vehicle to which 13(7)(i) applies; 67.2 — Limitation on interest expense; 67.41 — Where vehicle is jointly owned; 85(1)(e.5) — Rollover of vehicle by shareholder to corp; 257 — Formula cannot calculate to less than zero.

Notes: 13(7)(i) provides the same rule as 13(7)(g), but for an electric, hydrogen or hybrid car. See 248(1)"zero-emission passenger vehicle" (ZEPV). The CCA cost cap, announced each December for the next year, is $55,000 for 2019-2021: Reg. 7307(1.1).

13(7)(i)(ii) provides that, on disposition of the vehicle to an arm's length person or partnership, the proceeds of disposition for determining UCC are multiplied by the deemed cost divided by the actual cost (adjusted for government assistance [GA]). E.g., if X acquires a ZEPV for $60,000 [with no GA] and, in a later year sells it for $30,000, the proceeds of disposition for determining Class 54 UCC are $30,000 × $55,000 / $60,000 = $27,500.

Note that, unlike Class 10.1, disposition of a ZEPV can lead to 13(1) recapture or 20(16) terminal loss; but one can elect under Reg. 1103(2j) to put a ZEPV in Class 10.1 instead of Class 54.

13(7)(i) amended by 2021 budget bill #1, for dispositions after July 29, 2019, to address GA. For dispositions March 19-July 29, 2019, read (ii)B(B) and (ii)C as:

      (B) in any other case, the cost to the taxpayer of the vehicle, and

    C is the cost to the taxpayer of the vehicle.

13(7)(i) added by 2019 budget bill #1, effective March 19, 2019.

Regulations: 7307(1.1) (prescribed amount is $55,000 plus sales taxes).

Income Tax Folios [subsec. 13(7)]: S1-F3-C2: Principal residence [replaces IT-120R6, IT-437R]; S3-F4-C1: General discussion of CCA [replaces IT-478R2].

Interpretation Bulletins [subsec. 13(7)]: IT-102R2: Conversion of property, other than real property, from or to inventory; IT-218R: Profit, capital gains and losses from the sale of real estate, including farmland and inherited land and conversion of real estate from capital property to inventory and vice versa; IT-522R: Vehicle, travel and sales expenses of employees.

(7.1) Deemed capital cost of certain property [if government assistance] — For the purposes of this Act, where section 80 applied to reduce the capital cost to a taxpayer of a depreciable property or a taxpayer deducted an amount under subsection 127(5) or (6) in respect of a depreciable property or received or is entitled to receive assistance from a government, municipality or other public authority in respect of, or for the acquisition of, depreciable property, whether as a grant, subsidy, forgivable loan, deduction from tax, investment allowance or as any other form of assistance other than

(a) an amount described in paragraph 37(1)(d),

(b) an amount deducted as an allowance under section 65, or

(b.1) an amount included in income by virtue of paragraph 12(1)(u) or 56(1)(s),

the capital cost of the property to the taxpayer at any particular time shall be deemed to be the amount, if any, by which the total of

(c) the capital cost of the property to the taxpayer, determined without reference to this subsection, subsection (7.4) and section 80, and

(d) such part, if any, of the assistance as has been repaid by the taxpayer, pursuant to an obligation to repay all or any part of that assistance, in respect of that property before the disposition thereof by the taxpayer and before the particular time

exceeds the total of

(e) where the property was acquired in a taxation year ending before the particular time, all amounts deducted under subsection 127(5) or (6) by the taxpayer for a taxation year ending before the particular time,

(f) the amount of assistance the taxpayer has received or is entitled, before the particular time, to receive, and

(g) all amounts by which the capital cost of the property to the taxpayer is required because of section 80 to be reduced at or before that time,

in respect of that property before the disposition thereof by the taxpayer.

Related Provisions: 6(8)(d) — GST rebate deemed to be assistance; 12(1)(t) — Investment tax credit; 13(7.2) — Receipt of public assistance; 13(7.4) — Deemed capital cost of certain property; 65 — Allowances; 80(1)"excluded obligation"(a)(iii) — Debt forgiveness rules do not apply where amount has reduced capital cost of property; 80(5) — Reduction in capital cost on settlement of debt; 80(9) — Additional reduction in capital cost for limited purposes; 87(2)(j.6) — Amalgamation — continuing corporation; 127(11.5) — Ignore 13(7.1) for purposes of ITC qualified expenditures;

127(12) — Investment tax credit; 143.2(6) — Reduction in cost of tax shelter investment; 248(16), (16.1), (18), (18.1) — GST and QST input tax credit, refund and rebate deemed to be government assistance. See also at end of s. 13.

Notes: See 12(1)(x) Notes for meaning of "assistance" and related words.

Where a GST/HST input tax credit or other government assistance cannot be applied to reduce the capital cost of depreciable property (under this subsection) or the adjusted cost base of capital property (under 53(2)(k)), it is generally included in income under 12(1)(t) or (x).

For an example of 13(7.1) see VIEWS doc 2008-0301331E5 (rebate for solar water heater under ecoEnergy incentive). For the timing of "entitled to receive" for Quebec tax credits, see 2007-0227241E5, 2007-0234681E5, 2009-0331731E5, 2010-0389011E5, 2012-0466641I7.

References to s. 80 in 13(7.1) added, and 13(7.1)(g) added, by 1994 technical bill, effective for taxation years that end after February 21, 1994.

Income Tax Folios: S3-F4-C1: General discussion of CCA [replaces IT-478R2].

Interpretation Bulletins: IT-273R2: Government assistance — General comments.

CRA Audit Manual: 27.20.3: Inducement payments — depreciable property.

(7.2) Receipt of public assistance — For the purposes of subsection (7.1), where at any time a taxpayer who is a beneficiary of a trust or a member of a partnership has received or is entitled to receive assistance from a government, municipality or other public authority whether as a grant, subsidy, forgivable loan, deduction from tax, investment allowance or as any other form of assistance, the amount of the assistance that may reasonably be considered to be in respect of, or for the acquisition of, depreciable property of the trust or partnership shall be deemed to have been received at that time by the trust or partnership, as the case may be, as assistance from the government, municipality or other public authority for the acquisition of depreciable property.

Related Provisions: 53(2)(c)(ix) — Reduction of ACB of partnership interest; 53(2)(h)(v) — Reduction of ACB of capital interest in trust. See also Related Provisions at end of s. 13.

Notes: For CRA interpretation see doc 2009-0331731E5 (Quebec capital tax credits).

(7.3) Control of corporations by one trustee — For the purposes of paragraph (7)(e), where at a particular time one corporation would, but for this subsection, be related to another corporation by reason of both corporations being controlled by the same executor, liquidator of a succession or trustee and it is established that

    (a) the executor, liquidator or trustee did not acquire control of the corporations as a result of one or more estates or trusts created by the same individual or by two or more individuals not dealing with each other at arm's length, and

    (b) the estate or trust under which the executor, liquidator or trustee acquired control of each of the corporations arose only on the death of the individual creating the estate or trust,

the two corporations are deemed not to be related to each other at the particular time.

Related Provisions: 256(6)–(9) — Whether control acquired. Also see Related Provisions at end of s. 13.

Notes: Reference to "liquidator of a succession" added to 13(7.3) by 2001 *Civil Code* harmonization bill, effective June 14, 2001. The change is non-substantive; see *Interpretation Act* s. 8.2.

13(7.3) added by 1985 Budget, effective for property acquired after May 22, 1985, with grandfathering for property acquired before 1986.

(7.4) Deemed capital cost — Notwithstanding subsection (7.1), where a taxpayer has in a taxation year received an amount that would, but for this subsection, be included in the taxpayer's income under paragraph 12(1)(x) in respect of the cost of a depreciable property acquired by the taxpayer in the year, in the three taxation years immediately preceding the year or in the taxation year immediately following the year and the taxpayer elects under this subsection on or before the day on or before which the taxpayer is required to file the taxpayer's return of income under this Part for the year, or, where the property is acquired in the taxation year immediately following the year, for that following year, the capital cost of

the property to the taxpayer shall be deemed to be the amount by which the total of

    (a) the capital cost of the property to the taxpayer otherwise determined, applying the provisions of subsection (7.1), where necessary, and

    (b) such part, if any, of the amount received by the taxpayer as has been repaid by the taxpayer pursuant to a legal obligation to repay all or any part of that amount, in respect of that property and before the disposition thereof by the taxpayer, and as may reasonably be considered to be in respect of the amount elected under this subsection in respect of the property

exceeds the amount elected by the taxpayer under this subsection, but in no case shall the amount elected under this subsection exceed the least of

    (c) the amount so received by the taxpayer,

    (d) the capital cost of the property to the taxpayer otherwise determined, and

    (e) where the taxpayer has disposed of the property before the year, nil.

Related Provisions: 87(2)(j.6) — Amalgamation — continuing corporation; 125.4(5) — Canadian film/video credit is deemed to be assistance; 125.5(5) — Film/video production services credit is deemed to be assistance; 127(11.5) — Ignore 13(7.4) for purposes of ITC qualified expenditures; 220(3.2), Reg. 600(b) — Late filing or revocation of election. See also at end of s. 13.

Notes: 13(7.4) allows an amount that would be included in income under 12(1)(x) (see Notes to 12(1)(x)) to be optionally allocated to reduce the cost of depreciable property instead, reducing future CCA claims (see Notes to 20(1)(a)). Later repayment of the 12(1)(x) inducement re-increases the cost; 13(7.4)(b).

When filing electronically, this election must be submitted on paper to the CRA: VIEWS doc 2012-0454041C6.

Income Tax Folios: S3-F4-C1: General discussion of CCA [replaces IT-478R2].

Interpretation Bulletins: IT-273R2: Government assistance — general comments.

Information Circulars: 07-1R1: Taxpayer relief provisions.

CRA Audit Manual: 27.20.3: Inducement payments — depreciable property; 27.20.5: Inducement payments — elective provisions.

(7.41) Deemed capital cost — Subsection (38) applies in respect of an amount repaid after 2016 as if that amount was repaid immediately before 2017, if

    (a) the amount is repaid by the taxpayer under a legal obligation to repay all or part of an amount the taxpayer received or was entitled to receive that was assistance from a government, municipality or other public authority (whether as a grant, subsidy, forgivable loan, deduction from tax, investment allowance or as any other form of assistance) in respect of, or for the acquisition of, property the cost of which was an eligible capital expenditure of the taxpayer in respect of the business;

    (b) the amount of an eligible capital expenditure of the taxpayer in respect of the business was reduced by paragraph 14(10)(c) because of the assistance referred to in paragraph (a); and

    (c) paragraph 20(1)(hh.1) does not apply in respect of the amount repaid.

Related Provisions: 13(7.42) — No 20(1)(a) deduction until assistance repaid.

Notes: 13(7.41) and (7.42) are part of changing eligible capital property rules to CCA Class 14.1 as of 2017; see Notes to 20(1)(b) and 12(1)(x). Added by 2016 budget bill #2, effective 2017.

(7.42) Timing of deduction — No amount may be deducted under paragraph 20(1)(a) in respect of an amount of repaid assistance referred to in subsection (7.41) for any taxation year prior to the taxation year in which the assistance is repaid.

Notes: See Notes to 13(7.41).

(7.5) Deemed capital cost — For the purposes of this Act,

    (a) where a taxpayer, to acquire a property prescribed in respect of the taxpayer, is required under the terms of a contract made after March 6, 1996 to make a payment to Her Majesty in right of Canada or a province or to a Canadian municipality in respect of costs incurred or to be incurred by the recipient of the payment

(i) the taxpayer is deemed to have acquired the property at a capital cost equal to the portion of that payment made by the taxpayer that can reasonably be regarded as being in respect of those costs, and

(ii) the time of acquisition of the property by the taxpayer is deemed to be the later of the time the payment is made and the time at which those costs are incurred;

(b) where

(i) at any time after March 6, 1996 a taxpayer incurs a cost on account of capital for the building of, for the right to use or in respect of, a prescribed property, and

(ii) the amount of the cost would, if this paragraph did not apply, not be included in the capital cost to the taxpayer of depreciable property of a prescribed class,

the taxpayer is deemed to have acquired the property at that time at a capital cost equal to the amount of the cost;

(c) if a taxpayer acquires an intangible property, or for civil law an incorporeal property, as a consequence of making a payment to which paragraph (a) applies or incurring a cost to which paragraph (b) applies,

(i) the property referred to in paragraph (a) or (b) is deemed to include the intangible or incorporeal property, and

(ii) the portion of the capital cost referred to in paragraph (a) or (b) that applies to the intangible or incorporeal property is deemed to be the amount determined by the formula

$$A \times B/C$$

where

A is the lesser of the amount of the payment made or cost incurred and the amount determined for C,

B is the fair market value of the intangible or incorporeal property at the time the payment was made or the cost was incurred, and

C is the fair market value at the time the payment was made or the cost was incurred of all intangible or incorporeal properties acquired as a consequence of making the payment or incurring the cost; and

(d) any property deemed by paragraph (a) or (b) to have been acquired at any time by a taxpayer as a consequence of making a payment or incurring a cost

(i) is deemed to have been acquired for the purpose for which the payment was made or the cost was incurred, and

(ii) is deemed to be owned by the taxpayer at any subsequent time that the taxpayer benefits from the property.

Related Provisions: 66.1(6)"Canadian exploration expense"(l), 66.2(5)"Canadian development expense"(j) — Where property is depreciable property, its cost will not be CEE or CDE. See also at end of s. 13.

Notes: 13(7.5) overrides *Teck-Bullmoose Coal*, [1997] 1 C.T.C. 2603 (TCC) (aff'd on other grounds [1998] 3 C.T.C. 195 (FCA)), where the TCC denied CCA on a road built on leased land. See VIEWS doc 2011-0426921E5 (general comments).

13(7.5)(c) amended by 2002-2013 technical bill, effective June 26, 2013. 13(7.5) added by 1996 Budget, for tax years that end after March 6, 1996.

Regulations: 1102(14.2) (prescribed property for 13(7.5)(a)); 1102(14.3) (prescribed property for 13(7.5)(b)).

Income Tax Folios: S3-F4-C1: General discussion of CCA.

Interpretation Bulletins: IT-143R3: Meaning of eligible capital expenditure; IT-476R: CCA — Equipment used in petroleum and natural gas activities.

(8) Disposition after ceasing business — Notwithstanding subsections (3) and 11(2), where a taxpayer, after ceasing to carry on a business, has disposed of depreciable property of the taxpayer of a prescribed class that was acquired by the taxpayer for the purpose of gaining or producing income from the business and that was not subsequently used by the taxpayer for some other purpose, in applying subsection (1) or (2), each reference therein to a "taxation year" and "year" shall not be read as a reference to a "fiscal period".

Related Provisions: 13(1) — Recaptured depreciation; 20(16.3) — Same rule for purposes of subsecs. 20(16) and (16.1); 25(3) — Disposition in extended fiscal period. See also at end of s. 13.

Notes: Before re-enactment in RSC 1985 (5th Supp), 13(8) applied for purposes of 20(16) and (16.1) as well. See now 20(16.3).

Income Tax Folios: S3-F4-C1: General discussion of CCA [replaces IT-478R2].

(9) Meaning of "gaining or producing income" — In applying paragraphs (7)(a) to (d) in respect of a non-resident taxpayer, a reference to "gaining or producing income" in relation to a business shall be read as a reference to gaining or producing income from a business wholly carried on in Canada or such part of a business as is wholly carried on in Canada.

Related Provisions: See at end of s. 13.

Income Tax Folios: S3-F4-C1: General discussion of CCA [replaces IT-478R2].

I.T. Technical News: 18 (*Cudd Pressure* case).

(10) Deemed capital cost — For the purposes of this Act, where a taxpayer has, after December 3, 1970 and before April 1, 1972, acquired prescribed property

(a) for use in a prescribed manufacturing or processing business carried on by the taxpayer, and

(b) that was not used for any purpose whatever before it was acquired by the taxpayer,

the taxpayer shall be deemed to have acquired that property at a capital cost to the taxpayer equal to 115% of the amount that, but for this subsection and section 21, would have been the capital cost to the taxpayer of that property.

Related Provisions: See at end of s. 13.

Regulations: 1102(15) (prescribed property, prescribed manufacturing or processing business).

(11) Deduction in respect of property used in performance of duties — Any amount deducted under subparagraph 8(1)(j)(ii) or (p)(ii) of this Act or subsection 11(11) of *The Income Tax Act*, chapter 52 of the Statutes of Canada, 1948, shall be deemed, for the purposes of this section to have been deducted under regulations made under paragraph 20(1)(a).

Related Provisions: See at end of s.13.

Interpretation Bulletins: IT-522R: Vehicle, travel and sales expenses of employees.

(12) Application of para. 20(1)(cc) [lobbying expenses] — Where, in computing the income of a taxpayer for a taxation year, an amount has been deducted under paragraph 20(1)(cc) or the taxpayer has elected under subsection 20(9) to make a deduction in respect of an amount that would otherwise have been deductible under that paragraph, the amount shall, if it was a payment on account of the capital cost of depreciable property, be deemed to have been allowed to the taxpayer in respect of the property under regulations made under paragraph 20(1)(a) in computing the income of the taxpayer

(a) for the year, or

(b) for the year in which the property was acquired,

whichever is the later.

Related Provisions: See at end of s. 13.

Interpretation Bulletins: IT-99R5: Legal and accounting fees.

(13) Deduction under *Canadian Vessel Construction Assistance Act* — Where a deduction has been made under the *Canadian Vessel Construction Assistance Act* for any taxation year, subsection (1) is applicable in respect of the prescribed class created by that Act or any other prescribed class to which the vessel may have been transferred.

(14) Conversion cost — For the purposes of this section, section 20 and any regulations made under paragraph 20(1)(a), a vessel in respect of which any conversion cost is incurred after March 23, 1967 shall, to the extent of the conversion cost, be deemed to be included in a separate prescribed class.

Related Provisions: 13(17) — Transfer of separate class to same class as vessel.

Regulations: 1100(1)(v), 1101(2a).

Interpretation Bulletins: IT-267R2: CCA — vessels.

(15) [No longer relevant.]

Notes: 13(15) provides an election on disposition of a vessel before 1974.

(16) Election concerning vessel — Where a vessel owned by a taxpayer is disposed of by the taxpayer, the taxpayer may, if subsection (15) does not apply to the proceeds of disposition or if the taxpayer did not make an election under paragraph (15)(b) in respect of the vessel, within the time specified for the filing of a return of the taxpayer's income for the taxation year in which the vessel is disposed of, elect to have the proceeds that would be included in computing the taxpayer's income for the year under this Part treated as proceeds of disposition of property of another prescribed class that includes a vessel owned by the taxpayer.

Related Provisions: 13(17) — Transfer of separate prescribed class on disposition of vessel; 96(3) — Election by members of partnership. See also at end of s. 13.

Notes: 13(16) allows a taxpayer to elect to transfer the proceeds of disposition of a vessel to another class that has another vessel. The "other class" may be a separate prescribed class under Reg. 1101(2a): VIEWS doc 2004-0059661E5.

Interpretation Bulletins: IT-267R2: CCA — vessels.

(17) Separate prescribed class concerning vessel — Where a separate prescribed class has been constituted either under this Act or the *Canadian Vessel Construction Assistance Act* by reason of the conversion of a vessel owned by a taxpayer and the vessel is disposed of by the taxpayer, if no election in respect of the vessel was made under paragraph (15)(b), the separate prescribed class constituted by reason of the conversion shall be deemed to have been transferred to the class in which the vessel was included immediately before the disposition thereof.

Related Provisions: See at end of s. 13.

Interpretation Bulletins: IT-267R2: CCA — vessels.

(18) Reassessments — Notwithstanding any other provision of this Act, where a taxpayer has

(a) used an amount as described in paragraph (4)(c), or

(b) made an election under paragraph (15)(b) in respect of a vessel and the proceeds of disposition of the vessel were used before 1975 for replacement under conditions satisfactory to the appropriate minister,

such reassessments of tax, interest or penalties shall be made as are necessary to give effect to subsections (4) and (15).

Notes: 13(18) redrafted in the RSC 1985 (5th Supp) consolidation, effective for tax years ending after Nov. 1991, to change the reference to which Minister.

(18.1) Ascertainment of certain [energy conservation] property — For the purpose of determining whether property meets the criteria set out in the *Income Tax Regulations* in respect of prescribed energy conservation property, the *Technical Guide to Class 43.1 and 43.2*, as amended from time to time and published by the Department of Natural Resources, shall apply conclusively with respect to engineering and scientific matters.

Related Provisions: 241(4)(d)(vi.1) — Disclosure of information to Department of Natural Resources. See also at end of s. 13.

Notes: The Technical Guide is available at tinyurl.com/43-1guide.

13(18.1) amended by 2013 budget bill #2, effective Dec. 12, 2014 (to change Guide title). Added by 1994 Budget.

Regulations: Reg. 8200.1 (prescribed energy conservation property).

(19) Disposition of deposit [vessel construction] — All or any part of a deposit made under subparagraph (15)(a)(ii) or under the *Canadian Vessel Construction Assistance Act* may be paid out to or on behalf of any person who, under conditions satisfactory to the appropriate minister and as a replacement for the vessel disposed of, acquires a vessel before 1975

(a) that was constructed in Canada and is registered in Canada or is registered under conditions satisfactory to the appropriate minister in any country or territory to which the British Com-

monwealth Merchant Shipping Agreement, signed at London on December 10, 1931, applies, and

(b) in respect of the capital cost of which no allowance has been made to any other taxpayer under this Act or the *Canadian Vessel Construction Assistance Act*,

or incurs any conversion cost with respect to a vessel owned by that person that is registered in Canada or is registered under conditions satisfactory to the appropriate minister in any country or territory to which the agreement referred to in paragraph (a) applies, but the ratio of the amount paid out to the amount of the deposit shall not exceed the ratio of the capital cost to that person of the vessel or the conversion cost to that person of the vessel, as the case may be, to the proceeds of disposition of the vessel disposed of, and any deposit or part of a deposit not so paid out before July 1, 1975 or not paid out pursuant to subsection (20) shall be paid to the Receiver General and form part of the Consolidated Revenue Fund.

Related Provisions: 13(21)"appropriate minister". See also at end of s. 13.

Notes: 13(19) redrafted in the RSC 1985 (5th Supp) consolidation, effective for tax years ending after Nov. 1991, to change the reference to which Minister.

(20) Idem — Notwithstanding any other provision of this section, where a taxpayer made a deposit under subparagraph (15)(a)(ii) and the proceeds of disposition in respect of which the deposit was made were not used by any person before 1975 under conditions satisfactory to the appropriate minister as a replacement for the vessel disposed of,

(a) to acquire a vessel described in paragraphs (19)(a) and (b), or

(b) to incur any conversion cost with respect to a vessel owned by that person that is registered in Canada or is registered under conditions satisfactory to the appropriate minister in any country or territory to which the agreement referred to in paragraph (19)(a) applies,

the appropriate minister may refund to the taxpayer the deposit, or the part thereof not paid out to the taxpayer under subsection (19), as the case may be, in which case there shall be added, in computing the income of the taxpayer for the taxation year of the taxpayer in which the vessel was disposed of, that proportion of the amount that would have been included in computing the income for the year under this Part had the deposit not been made under subparagraph (15)(a)(ii) that the portion of the proceeds of disposition not so used before 1975 as such a replacement is of the proceeds of disposition, and, notwithstanding any other provision of this Act, such reassessments of tax, interest or penalties shall be made as are necessary to give effect to this subsection.

Related Provisions: See at end of s. 13.

Notes: 13(20) redrafted in the RSC 1985 (5th Supp) consolidation, effective for tax years ending after Nov. 1991, to change the reference to which Minister.

(21) Definitions — In this section,

Related Provisions: 20(1.1) — Definitions in 13(21) apply to regulations made under 20(1)(a); 20(27.1) — Definitions in 13(21) apply to s. 20.

"appropriate minister" means the Canadian Maritime Commission, the Minister of Industry, Trade and Commerce, the Minister of Regional Industrial Expansion, the Minister of Industry, Science and Technology or the Minister of Industry or any other minister or body that was or is legally authorized to perform the act referred to in the provision in which this expression occurs at the time the act was or is performed;

Notes: 13(21)"appropriate minister" added in RSC 1985 (5th Supp) consolidation, effective for tax years ending after Nov. 1991. Reference to "Minister of Industry" added by *Department of Industry Act* (1995, c. 1), effective March 29, 1995.

"conversion", in respect of a vessel, means a conversion or major alteration in Canada by a taxpayer;

Notes: "Conversion" amended by 1991 technical bill, effective for property acquired after July 13, 1990, to remove requirement for approval by the Minister of Industry, Science and Technology (the "appropriate Minister"). Accelerated CCA for vessels and conversion costs is now verified by the CRA as part of the normal audit process.

13(21)"conversion" was 13(21)(a) before RSC 1985 (5th Supp) consolidation, effective for tax years ending after Nov. 1991.

Interpretation Bulletins: IT-267R2: CCA — vessels; IT-273R2: Government assistance — general comments.

"conversion cost", in respect of a vessel, means the cost of a conversion;

Notes: "Conversion cost" was included in the definition of "conversion" in 13(21)(a) before RSC 1985 (5th Supp) consolidation for tax years ending after Nov. 1991.

Interpretation Bulletins: IT-267R2: CCA — vessels.

"depreciable property" of a taxpayer as of any time in a taxation year means property acquired by the taxpayer in respect of which the taxpayer has been allowed, or would, if the taxpayer owned the property at the end of the year and this Act were read without reference to subsection (26), be entitled to, a deduction under paragraph 20(1)(a) in computing income for that year or a preceding taxation year;

Related Provisions: 13(1) — Recapture; 13(5.2)(c) — Certain real property deemed to be depreciable property; 20(1)(a) — Capital cost allowance; 54 — "Capital property"; 88(1)(c.7) — Extended meaning for certain windup rules; 107.4(3)(d) — Rollover of depreciable property to trust; 248(1)"depreciable property" — Definition applies to entire Act. See also at end of s. 13.

Notes: The reference to "the end of the year" should not mean that one must determine whether CCA was *actually* available at year-end. If depreciable property is converted to inventory during the year, it should remain depreciable property until the day it is converted. See, however, *Sako Auto Leasing*, [1993] G.S.T.C. 17 (CITT).

Property held for sale is inventory and cannot be depreciable property, due to Reg. 1102(1)(b): *CAE Inc.*, 2013 FCA 92, para. 104.

"Depreciable property" amended by 1991 technical bill, effective for property acquired after 1989, to clarify that property not yet "available for use" under 13(26) is still considered depreciable property.

13(21)"depreciable property" was 13(21)(b) before RSC 1985 (5th Supp) consolidation for tax years ending after Nov. 1991.

Regulations: Part XI (capital cost allowance allowed on depreciable property).

I.T. Application Rules: 18, 20 (property acquired before 1972).

Income Tax Folios: S3-F4-C1: General discussion of CCA [replaces IT-128R and IT-220R2].

Interpretation Bulletins: IT-102R2: Conversion of property, other than real property, from or to inventory.

"disposition of property" — [Repealed]

Notes: 13(21)"disposition of property" repealed by 2001 technical bill, effective for transactions and events that occur after December 23, 1998. It has been superseded by 248(1)"disposition". The definition was para. 13(21)(c) before RSC 1985 (5th Supp) consolidation for tax years ending after Nov. 1991.

"proceeds of disposition" of property includes

    (a) the sale price of property that has been sold,

    (b) compensation for property unlawfully taken,

    (c) compensation for property destroyed and any amount payable under a policy of insurance in respect of loss or destruction of property,

    (d) compensation for property taken under statutory authority or the sale price of property sold to a person by whom notice of an intention to take it under statutory authority was given,

    (e) compensation for property injuriously affected, whether lawfully or unlawfully or under statutory authority or otherwise,

    (f) compensation for property damaged and any amount payable under a policy of insurance in respect of damage to property, except to the extent that the compensation or amount, as the case may be, has within a reasonable time after the damage been expended on repairing the damage,

    (g) an amount by which the liability of a taxpayer to a mortgagee or hypothecary creditor is reduced as a result of the sale of mortgaged or hypothecated property under a provision of the mortgage or hypothec, plus any amount received by the taxpayer out of the proceeds of the sale, and

    (h) any amount included because of section 79 in computing a taxpayer's proceeds of disposition of the property;

Related Provisions: 12(1)(f) — Insurance proceeds received for amount expended; 13(4) — Exchanges of property; 13(21) — Undepreciated capital cost; 13(21.1) — Disposition of a building; 44 — Exchanges of property; 54"proceeds of disposition" — Parallel definition for capital property; 79(3) — Deemed proceeds of disposition when

property surrendered to creditor; 248(1) — "Cost amount"(a); 248(39)(b) — Anti-avoidance — selling property and donating proceeds. See also at end of s. 13.

Notes: See Notes to 54"proceeds of disposition". For case law on the timing of a disposition for CCA purposes, see Notes to 248(1)"disposition".

"Hypothec", "hypothecated property" and "hypothecary creditor" added to para. (g) by 2001 *Civil Code* harmonization bill, effective June 14, 2001. The change is non-substantive; see *Interpretation Act* s. 8.2.

Reference in para. (h) to 79(c) changed to 79 by 1994 technical bill, effective for taxation years that end after Feb. 21, 1994.

13(21)"proceeds of disposition" was 13(21)(d) before RSC 1985 (5th Supp) consolidation for tax years ending after Nov. 1991.

Income Tax Folios: S3-F4-C1: General discussion of CCA; S7-F1-C1: Split-receipting and deemed fair market value.

Interpretation Bulletins: IT-170R: Sale of property — when included in income computation; IT-259R4: Exchanges of property; IT-271R: Expropriations (cancelled); IT-460: Dispositions — absence of consideration; IT-505: Mortgage foreclosures and conditional sales repossessions (cancelled).

"timber resource property" of a taxpayer means

    (a) a right or licence to cut or remove timber from a limit or area in Canada (in this definition referred to as an "original right") if

        (i) that original right was acquired by the taxpayer (other than in the manner referred to in paragraph (b)) after May 6, 1974, and

        (ii) at the time of the acquisition of the original right

            (A) the taxpayer may reasonably be regarded as having acquired, directly or indirectly, the right to extend or renew that original right or to acquire another such right or licence in substitution therefor, or

            (B) in the ordinary course of events, the taxpayer may reasonably expect to be able to extend or renew that original right or to acquire another such right or licence in substitution therefor, or

    (b) any right or licence owned by the taxpayer to cut or remove timber from a limit or area in Canada if that right or licence may reasonably be regarded

        (i) as an extension or renewal of or as one of a series of extensions or renewals of an original right of the taxpayer, or

        (ii) as having been acquired in substitution for or as one of a series of substitutions for an original right of the taxpayer or any renewal or extension thereof;

Related Provisions: 128.1(4)(b)(i) — timber resource property excluded from deemed disposition on emigration; 248(1)"timber resource property" — Definition applies to entire Act; 248(10) — Series of transactions.

Notes: In *ITT Industries*, [2000] 3 C.T.C. 400 (FCA; leave to appeal denied 2001 CarswellNat 494 (SCC)), a replacement 25-year BC tree farm licence, issued when the previous *Forest Act* was repealed, was held to be a timber resource property (TRP), not a timber limit. For more on "timber limit" vs. TRP see *Fletcher Challenge*, [2000] 3 C.T.C. 281 (FCA; leave to appeal denied 2001 CarswellNat 492 (SCC)); *Twin Islands*, 2004 TCC 141; footnotes in *Myles*, [2002] 1 C.T.C. 2570 (TCC); VIEWS docs 2007-0252051E5, 2014-0528021E5 (including tax treatment of gain on sale of land with standing timber). Land owned outright cannot be TRP: *MacAlpine*, 2004 FCA 221.

The following are considered TRP: Replaceable Interior BC Timber Harvesting Contract (VIEWS doc 2009-0343311E5); woodlot licence under BC *Forest Act* (2012-0461021E5); Alberta coniferous timber quota (2017-0732151E5).

Certain payments from B.C. Forest Revitalization Trust are proceeds of disposition (PoD) of a TRP: 2007-0236991I7; but see *British Columbia Forestry Revitalization Remission Order*. When selling a TRP, reforestation obligations assumed by the purchaser do not increase the vendor's PoD; a TRP is a "hybrid" that is capital property for CCA purposes but is excluded from capital gains treatment: *Daishowa-Marubeni*, 2013 SCC 29.

For the meaning of "indirectly" in (a)(ii)(A) see Notes to 17.1(1).

13(21)"timber resource property" was para. 13(21)(d.1) before RSC 1985 (5th Supp) consolidation for tax years ending after Nov. 1991.

Interpretation Bulletins: IT-393R2: Election re tax on rents and timber royalties — non-residents; IT-481: Timber resource property and timber limits.

"total depreciation" allowed to a taxpayer before any time for property of a prescribed class means the total of all amounts each of which is an amount deducted by the taxpayer under paragraph 20(1)(a) in respect of property of that class or an amount deducted under subsection 20(16), or that would have been so deducted but for subsection 20(16.1), in computing the taxpayer's income for taxation years ending before that time;

Related Provisions: See also at end of s. 13.

Notes: 13(21)"total depreciation" was para. 13(21)(e) before RSC 1985 (5th Supp) consolidation for tax years ending after Nov. 1991.

Regulations: Part XI.

Income Tax Folios: S3-F4-C1: General discussion of CCA [replaces IT-478R2].

"undepreciated capital cost" to a taxpayer of depreciable property of a prescribed class as of any time means the amount determined by the formula

$$(A + B + C + D + D.1) - $$
$$(E + E.1 + F + G + H + I + J + K)$$

where

A   is the total of all amounts each of which is the capital cost to the taxpayer of a depreciable property of the class acquired before that time,

B   is the total of all amounts included in the taxpayer's income under this section for a taxation year ending before that time, to the extent that those amounts relate to depreciable property of the class,

C   is the total of all amounts each of which is such part of any assistance as has been repaid by the taxpayer, pursuant to an obligation to repay all or any part of that assistance, in respect of a depreciable property of the class subsequent to the disposition thereof by the taxpayer that would have been included in an amount determined under paragraph (7.1)(d) had the repayment been made before the disposition,

D   is the total of all amounts each of which is an amount repaid in respect of a property of the class subsequent to the disposition thereof by the taxpayer that would have been an amount described in paragraph (7.4)(b) had the repayment been made before the disposition,

D.1   is the total of all amounts each of which is an amount paid by the taxpayer before that time as or on account of an existing or proposed countervailing or anti-dumping duty in respect of depreciable property of the class,

E   is the total depreciation allowed to the taxpayer for property of the class before that time, including, if the taxpayer is an insurer, depreciation deemed to have been allowed before that time under subsection (22) or (23) as they read in their application to the taxpayer's last taxation year that began before November 2011,

E.1   is the total of all amounts each of which is an amount by which the undepreciated capital cost to the taxpayer of depreciable property of that class is required (otherwise than because of a reduction in the capital cost to the taxpayer of depreciable property) to be reduced at or before that time because of subsection 80(5),

F   is the total of all amounts each of which is an amount in respect of a disposition before that time of property (other than a timber resource property) of the taxpayer of the class, and is the lesser of

     (a) the proceeds of disposition of the property minus any outlays and expenses to the extent that they were made or incurred by the taxpayer for the purpose of making the disposition, and

     (b) the capital cost to the taxpayer of the property,

G   is the total of all amounts each of which is the proceeds of disposition before that time of a timber resource property of the taxpayer of the class minus any outlays and expenses to the extent that they were made or incurred by the taxpayer for the purpose of making the disposition,

H   is, where the property of the class was acquired by the taxpayer for the purpose of gaining or producing income from a mine and the taxpayer so elects in prescribed manner and within a pre-

scribed time in respect of that property, the amount equal to that portion of the income derived from the operation of the mine that is, by virtue of the provisions of the *Income Tax Application Rules* relating to income from the operation of new mines, not included in computing income of the taxpayer or any other person,

I   is the total of all amounts deducted under subsection 127(5) or (6), in respect of a depreciable property of the class of the taxpayer, in computing the taxpayers' tax payable for a taxation year ending before that time and subsequent to the disposition of that property by the taxpayer,

J   is the total of all amounts of assistance that the taxpayer received or was entitled to receive before that time, in respect of or for the acquisition of a depreciable property of the class of the taxpayer subsequent to the disposition of that property by the taxpayer, that would have been included in an amount determined under paragraph (7.1)(f) had the assistance been received before the disposition, and

K   is the total of all amounts each of which is an amount received by the taxpayer before that time in respect of a refund of an amount added to the undepreciated capital cost of depreciable property of the class because of the description of D.1;

Related Provisions: 12(1)(f) — Damage to depreciable property — insurance proceeds; 12(1)(t) — Investment tax credit; 13(1) — Recapture where E to J exceed A to D; 13(2) — Recaptured depreciation for vehicle; 13(4) — Exchanges of property; 13(5) — Transferred property; 13(5.2) — Where rent paid on property before its acquisition; 13(7) — Rules affecting capital cost; 13(7)(i)(ii) — Proceeds of disposition of zero-emission automobile for F(a); 13(21) — "timber resource property"; 13(22), (23) — Deductions deemed allowed to insurer for 1977 and 1978; 13(24) — Acquisition of control — calculation of UCC; 13(26) — Restriction on deduction before available for use; 13(33) — Consideration given for depreciable property; 20(16) — Terminal loss; 70(13) — Capital cost of depreciable property on death; 87(2)(j.6) — Amalgamation — continuing corp; 138(11.31)(b) — Change-in-use rule for insurance properties does not apply for purposes of UCC definition; 248(1)"undepreciated capital cost" — Definition applies to entire Act; 257 — Formula cannot calculate to less than zero; 261(7)(d) — Functional currency reporting. See also at end of s. 13.

Notes: Capital cost allowance (CCA) is normally claimed as a percentage of UCC: see Notes to 20(1)(a). Put simply and ignoring the special-case exceptions, UCC of a class (see Reg. Sch. II) is: (A) the original cost of each property in the class, plus (B) prior years' recapture under 13(1), minus (E) CCA claimed till now, minus (F) the proceeds of disposition of property sold, up to a limit of the original cost. (Excess proceeds over original cost are a capital gain under 39(1), not covered by s. 13.) See Notes to 13(1) and 13(21)"depreciable property"; and Income Tax Folio S3-F4-C1 ¶1.62-1.65.

" 'Cost' in the context of CCA is a well-understood legal concept. It has been carefully defined by the Act and the jurisprudence... we see nothing in the GAAR or the object of the CCA provisions that permits us to rewrite them to interpret 'cost' to mean 'amount economically at risk' ": *Canada Trustco*, 2005 SCC 54, para. 75. Similarly, anticipated costs of cleaning up contamination (under a legal obligation) were not part of a building's "cost": *A & D Holdings*, 2005 TCC 768. Where loyalty points are used to buy a vehicle, the points are considered to be cash so the vehicle cost includes the points: VIEWS doc 2006-0175841E5.

UCC carries through an amalgamation to the new companies, whether or not the amalgamation falls under 87(1): *Envision Credit Union*, 2011 FCA 321, para. 67 (aff'd on other grounds 2013 SCC 48).

E.1 reduces UCC as required by 80(5), but does not apply to the extent the reduction results from reduction under 80(5) or (9) of the capital cost of depreciable property. Those reductions are under 13(7.1)(g).

For the meaning of "derived" in H, see Notes to 18.1(12).

Definition amended by 2002-2013 technical bill (for tax years starting after Oct. 2011), 1998 Budget, 1994 technical bill. 13(21)"undepreciated capital cost" was 13(21)(f) before RSC 1985 (5th Supp) consolidation for tax years ending after Nov. 1991.

Regulations: Part XI (amounts of depreciation allowed, for E).

I.T. Application Rules: 18 (property acquired before 1972).

Income Tax Folios: S3-F4-C1: General discussion of CCA [replaces IT-418 and IT-478R2].

Interpretation Bulletins: IT-327: CCA — Elections under Regulation 1103 (cancelled); IT-481: Timber resource property and timber limits.

Information Circulars: 87-5: Capital cost of property where trade-in is involved.

"vessel" means a vessel as defined in the *Canada Shipping Act*.

Notes: The *Canada Shipping Act, 2001*, s. 2, provides:

     "vessel" means a boat, ship or craft designed, used or capable of being used solely or partly for navigation in, on, through or immediately above water, without regard to method or lack of propulsion, and includes such a vessel that is under construction. It does not include a floating object of a prescribed class.

13(21)"vessel" was 13(21)(g) before RSC 1985 (5th Supp) consolidation for tax years ending after Nov. 1991.

Interpretation Bulletins: IT-267R2: CCA — vessels.

Advance Tax Rulings: ATR-52: Accelerated rate of CCA for vessels.

Related Provisions [subsec. 13(21)]: 20(1.1) — Definitions in 13(21) apply to regulations made under 20(1)(a); 20(27.1) — Definitions in 13(21) apply to s. 20.

(21.1) Disposition of building — Notwithstanding subsection (7) and the definition "proceeds of disposition" in section 54, where at any particular time in a taxation year a taxpayer disposes of a building of a prescribed class and the proceeds of disposition of the building determined without reference to this subsection and subsection (21.2) are less than the lesser of the cost amount and the capital cost to the taxpayer of the building immediately before the disposition, for the purposes of paragraph (a) of the description of F in the definition "undepreciated capital cost" in subsection (21) and Subdivision C,

(a) where in the year the taxpayer or a person with whom the taxpayer does not deal at arm's length disposes of land subjacent to, or immediately contiguous to and necessary for the use of, the building, the proceeds of disposition of the building are deemed to be the lesser of

(i) the amount, if any, by which

(A) the total of the fair market value of the building at the particular time and the fair market value of the land immediately before its disposition

exceeds

(B) the lesser of the fair market value of the land immediately before its disposition and the amount, if any, by which the cost amount to the vendor of the land (determined without reference to this subsection) exceeds the total of the capital gains (determined without reference to subparagraphs 40(1)(a)(ii) and (iii)) in respect of dispositions of the land within 3 years before the particular time by the taxpayer or by a person with whom the taxpayer was not dealing at arm's length to the taxpayer or to another person with whom the taxpayer was not dealing at arm's length, and

(ii) the greater of

(A) the fair market value of the building at the particular time, and

(B) the lesser of the cost amount and the capital cost to the taxpayer of the building immediately before its disposition,

and, notwithstanding any other provision of this Act, the proceeds of disposition of the land are deemed to be the amount, if any, by which

(iii) the total of the proceeds of disposition of the building and of the land determined without reference to this subsection and subsection (21.2)

exceeds

(iv) the proceeds of disposition of the building as determined under this paragraph,

and the cost to the purchaser of the land shall be determined without reference to this subsection; and

(b) where paragraph (a) does not apply with respect to the disposition and, at any time before the disposition, the taxpayer or a person with whom the taxpayer did not deal at arm's length owned the land subjacent to, or immediately contiguous to and necessary for the use of, the building, the proceeds of disposition of the building are deemed to be an amount equal to the total of

(i) the proceeds of disposition of the building determined without reference to this subsection and subsection (21.2), and

(ii) ½ of the amount by which the greater of

(A) the cost amount to the taxpayer of the building, and

(B) the fair market value of the building

immediately before its disposition exceeds the proceeds of disposition referred to in subparagraph (i).

Related Provisions: 70(5)(c), (d) — Capital property of a deceased taxpayer.

Notes: 13(21.1) provides special rules where a building is disposed of for less than its 248(1)"cost amount". If land and building are sold together, any (terminal) loss on the building (20(16)) is reduced by any (capital) gain on the land. This is done by increasing the building's proceeds of disposition by the lesser of the loss on the building and the gain on the land (and reducing the gain on the land by the same amount). In CRA's view, this rule applies to a vendor who allocates the entire sale price to the land because the building is demolished after purchase: doc 2006-0203301I7. 13(21.1)(b) also applies if the building is demolished and the land is not sold: *9136-6872 Québec*, 2010 TCC 91; *Grondin*, 2019 QCCQ 1059 (involuntary disposition due to fire); 2007-0222251E5. (If a purchaser always intended to demolish a building and never uses it, no CCA can be claimed: Reg. 1102(1)(c).) See also Income Tax Folio S3-F4-C1 ¶1.85-1.94; Jeyarajah & Pham, "The tax consequences of demolition costs" (Nov. 2019), tinyurl.com/rsm-demo.

13(21.1) applies before (21.2) but does not stop 13(21.2) from applying. If, after 13(21.1) applies to a disposition, there is still a terminal loss, and the disposition is one to which 13(21.2) applies, 13(21.2) may defer the recognition of the remaining loss.

13(21.1) can apply on a s. 85 rollover: VIEWS doc 2012-0469231E5; or on a 55(3)(b) spinoff: 2016-0635101R3. Where a taxpayer disposes of land, building, machinery and equipment, an election under Reg. 1103(1) to combine all the assets in Class 1 can reduce the impact of 13(21.1): 2004-0072411E5.

13(21.1) amended by 2000 Budget (last change effective for tax years that end after Oct. 17, 2000) and 1995-97 technical bill.

Income Tax Folios [subsec. 13(21.1)]: S3-F4-C1: General discussion of CCA [replaces IT-220R2].

Interpretation Bulletins: IT-349R3: Intergenerational transfers of farm property on death.

(21.2) Loss on certain transfers [within affiliated group] — Where

(a) a person or partnership (in this subsection referred to as the "transferor") disposes at a particular time (otherwise than in a disposition described in any of paragraphs (c) to (g) of the definition "superficial loss" in section 54) of a depreciable property — other than, for the purposes of computing the exempt surplus or exempt deficit and taxable surplus or taxable deficit of a foreign affiliate of a taxpayer, in respect of the taxpayer, where the transferor is the affiliate or is a partnership of which the affiliate is a member, depreciable property that is, or would be, if the transferor were a foreign affiliate of the taxpayer, excluded property (within the meaning assigned by subsection 95(1)) of the transferor — of a particular prescribed class of the transferor,

(b) the lesser of

(i) the capital cost to the transferor of the transferred property, and

(ii) the proportion of the undepreciated capital cost to the transferor of all property of the particular class immediately before that time that

(A) the fair market value of the transferred property at that time

is of

(B) the fair market value of all property of the particular class immediately before that time

exceeds the amount that would otherwise be the transferor's proceeds of disposition of the transferred property at the particular time, and

(c) on the 30th day after the particular time, a person or partnership (in this subsection referred to as the "subsequent owner") who is the transferor or a person affiliated with the transferor owns or has a right to acquire the transferred property (other than a right, as security only, derived from a mortgage, hypothec, agreement for sale or similar obligation),

the following rules apply:

(d) sections 85 and 97 do not apply to the disposition,

(e) for the purposes of applying this section and section 20 and any regulations made for the purpose of paragraph 20(1)(a) to the transferor for taxation years that end after the particular time,

(i) the transferor is deemed to have disposed of the transferred property for proceeds equal to the lesser of the amounts determined under subparagraphs (b)(i) and (ii) with respect to the transferred property,

(ii) where two or more properties of a prescribed class of the transferor are disposed of at the same time, subparagraph (i) applies as if each property so disposed of had been separately disposed of in the order designated by the transferor or, if the transferor does not designate an order, in the order designated by the Minister,

(iii) the transferor is deemed to own a property that was acquired before the beginning of the taxation year that includes the particular time at a capital cost equal to the amount of the excess described in paragraph (b), and that is property of the particular class, until the time that is immediately before the first time, after the particular time,

(A) at which a 30-day period begins throughout which neither the transferor nor a person affiliated with the transferor owns or has a right to acquire the transferred property (other than a right, as security only, derived from a mortgage, hypothec, agreement for sale or similar obligation),

(B) at which the transferred property is not used by the transferor or a person affiliated with the transferor for the purpose of earning income and is used for another purpose,

(C) at which the transferred property would, if it were owned by the transferor, be deemed by section 128.1 or subsection 149(10) to have been disposed of by the transferor,

(D) that is immediately before the transferor is subject to a loss restriction event, or

(E) if the transferor is a corporation,

(I) for the purposes of computing the transferor's foreign accrual property income, exempt surplus or exempt deficit, and taxable surplus or taxable deficit, in respect of a taxpayer for a taxation year of the transferor where the transferor is a foreign affiliate of the taxpayer, at which the liquidation and dissolution of the transferor begins, unless the liquidation and dissolution is

1. a qualifying liquidation and dissolution (within the meaning assigned by subsection 88(3.1)) of the transferor, or

2. a designated liquidation and dissolution (within the meaning assigned by subsection 95(1)) of the transferor, and

(II) for any other purposes, at which the winding-up (other than a winding-up to which subsection 88(1) applies) of the transferor begins, and

(iv) the property described in subparagraph (iii) is considered to have become available for use by the transferor at the time at which the transferred property is considered to have become available for use by the subsequent owner,

(f) for the purposes of subparagraphs (e)(iii) and (iv), where a partnership otherwise ceases to exist at any time after the particular time, the partnership is deemed not to have ceased to exist, and each person who was a member of the partnership immediately before the partnership would, but for this paragraph, have ceased to exist is deemed to remain a member of the partnership, until the time that is immediately after the first time described in clauses (e)(iii)(A) to (E), and

(g) for the purposes of applying this section and section 20 and any regulations made for the purpose of paragraph 20(1)(a) to the subsequent owner,

(i) the subsequent owner's capital cost of the transferred property is deemed to be the amount that was the transferor's capital cost of the transferred property, and

(ii) the amount by which the transferor's capital cost of the transferred property exceeds its fair market value at the particular time is deemed to have been deducted under paragraph 20(1)(a) by the subsequent owner in respect of property of that class in computing income for taxation years that ended before the particular time.

Related Provisions: 18(13)–(16) — Parallel rule for share or debt owned by financial institution; 40(3.3), (3.4) — Parallel rule re capital losses; 69(5)(d) — No application where corporate property appropriated by shareholder on windup; 87(2)(g.3) — Amalgamation — continuing corporation; 88(1)(d.1) — No application to property acquired on windup of subsidiary; 93.1(3)(b) — Tiered partnership — look-through rule; 95(2)(e)(v)(A)(II) — Designated liquidation and dissolution of foreign affiliate; 251.1 — Affiliated persons; 251.2 — Loss restriction event.

Notes: 13(21.2) prevents a transfer of property with a latent or accrued loss (also called a pregnant loss) from being used as a way to transfer a high capital cost where property has declined in value. (Before this rule, pre-1997 85(5.1) could prevent 20(16) from giving the transferor a terminal loss, transferring high cost base to the transferee and effectively allowing the sale of tax losses: see *Husky Oil*, [1999] 4 C.T.C. 2691 (TCC), and *OSFC Holdings*, 2001 FCA 260 (leave to appeal denied 2002 CarswellNat 1388 (SCC)).) For the parallel rule for capital losses, see 40(3.3)–(3.4); for certain inventory, 18(13)–(16); for pre-2017 eligible capital property, repealed 14(12).

For interpretation of 13(21.2) see VIEWS docs 9831627F (interaction with Reg. 1100(11)), 2005-0125501E5 (time at which suspended loss may be realized), 2008-0266441R3 (recapitalization of public company under plan of arrangement); 2009-0347301R3 (whether 13(21.2) applies on a 98(5) rollover); 2012-0452611E5 (denied terminal loss cannot be claimed on death); 2012-0460011E5 (where property transferred to affiliated entity that is exempt); 2012-0469231E5 (application to multiple properties); 2015-0571501E5 (13(21.2)(f): whether partnership that has ceased to exist can claim deduction).

13(21.2) did not apply to a trust before 2013: doc 2004-0091061E5. See now 251.2.

For the meaning of "derived" in (c) and (e)(iii)(A), see Notes to 18.1(12).

For a transferor filing Quebec returns, a designation under 13(21.2)(e)(ii) must be copied to Revenu Québec: *Taxation Act* ss. 93.3.1, 21.4.6.

13(21.2) amended by 2013 budget bill #2 (effective March 21, 2013), 2002-2013 technical bill, 2001 *Civil Code* harmonization bill, 2001 and 1995-97 technical bills.

Interpretation Bulletins: IT-291R3: Transfer of property to a corporation under subsection 85(1).

(22), (23), (23.1) [Repealed]

Notes: 13(22), (23) and (23.1) repealed by 2002-2013 technical bill (Part 5 — technical), for taxation years that begin after Oct. 2011.

13(22) and (23) deemed certain CCA to have been allowed to an insurer for its last taxation year before 1977. 13(22) deemed an insurer who had made a branch accounting election for 1975, and had a 1975 branch accounting election deficiency, to have claimed CCA for pre-1977 taxation years beyond what it claimed in its return. 13(23) was part of the transitional rules changing to the method of taxing life insurers that began in 1978, and deemed an insurer to have been allowed a certain amount of CCA under 20(1)(a) for pre-1978 years. 13(23.1) provided "The definitions in subsection 138(12) apply to this section", to cover "1975-76 excess capital cost allowance" and "1975 branch accounting election deficiency", used in 13(22).

A consequential amendment to 13(21)"undepreciated capital cost"E ensures that amounts determined under 13(22) and (23) continue to be included in an insurer's UCC.

(24) Loss restriction event [change in control] — If at any time a taxpayer is subject to a loss restriction event and, within the 12-month period that ended immediately before that time, the taxpayer, a partnership of which the taxpayer was a majority-interest partner or a trust of which the taxpayer was a majority-interest beneficiary (as defined in subsection 251.1(3)) acquired depreciable property (other than property that was held, by the taxpayer, partnership or trust or by a person that would be affiliated with the taxpayer if section 251.1 were read without reference to the definition "controlled" in subsection 251.1(3), throughout the period that began immediately before the 12-month period began and ended at the time the property was acquired by the taxpayer, partnership or trust) that was not used, or acquired for use, by the taxpayer, partnership or trust in a business that was carried on by it immediately before the 12-month period began

(a) subject to paragraph (b), for the purposes of the description of A in the definition "undepreciated capital cost" in subsection (21) and of sections 127 and 127.1, the property is deemed

(i) not to have been acquired by the taxpayer, partnership or trust, as the case may be, before that time, and

(ii) to have been acquired by it immediately after that time; and

(b) if the property was disposed of by the taxpayer, partnership or trust, as the case may be, before that time and was not reacquired by it before that time, for the purposes of the description of A in that definition, the property is deemed to have been acquired by it immediately before the property was disposed of.

Related Provisions: 13(25) — Change of control within 12 months of incorporation; 87(2)(j.6) — Amalgamation — continuing corporation; 111(5.1) — Restriction after change in control of corporation or trust; 251.2 — Loss restriction event. See also at end of s. 13.

Notes: 13(24) amended by 2013 budget bill #2 to be based on "loss restriction event" (see Notes to 251.2(2)) instead of control of a corporation being acquired, this version effective Sept. 13, 2013.

13(24) amended by 1995-97 technical bill, for acquisitions of control after April 26, 1995.

Interpretation Bulletins: IT-302R3: Losses of a corporation — the effect that acquisitions of control, amalgamations, and windings-up have on their deductibility.

I.T. Technical News: 7 (control by a group — 50/50 arrangement).

(25) Affiliation — subsec. (24) — For the purposes of subsection (24), if the taxpayer referred to in that subsection was formed or created in the 12-month period referred to in that subsection, the taxpayer is deemed to have been, throughout the period that began immediately before the 12-month period and ended immediately after it was formed or created,

(a) in existence; and

(b) affiliated with every person with whom it was affiliated (otherwise than because of a right referred to in paragraph 251(5)(b)) throughout the period that began when it was formed or created and that ended immediately before the time at which the taxpayer was subject to the loss restriction event referred to in that subsection.

Notes: 13(25) amended by 2013 budget bill #2, effective March 21, 2013 (changing its application from control being acquired to "loss restriction event").

13(25)(b) amended by 1995-97 technical bill, for acquisitions of control after April 26, 1995, as a result of the amendment to 13(24).

(26) Restriction on deduction before available for use — In applying the definition "undepreciated capital cost" in subsection (21) for the purpose of paragraph 20(1)(a) and any regulations made for the purpose of that paragraph, in computing a taxpayer's income for a taxation year from a business or property, no amount shall be included in calculating the undepreciated capital cost to the taxpayer of depreciable property of a prescribed class in respect of the capital cost to the taxpayer of a property of that class (other than property that is a certified production, as defined by regulations made for the purpose of paragraph 20(1)(a)) before the time the property is considered to have become available for use by the taxpayer.

Related Provisions: 13(27), (28) — Interpretation — available for use; 13(30) — Transfers of property; 13(32) — Leased property; 20(28) — Deduction against rental income from building; 37(1.2) — No R&D deduction for capital expenditure until property available for use; 127(11.2) — No investment tax credit until property available for use; 248(19) — When property available for use. See also at end of s. 13; Reg. 1100(2) — CCA in year property becomes available for use.

Notes: 13(26) provides, in effect, that no CCA can be claimed for the year an asset is acquired, or the next year, if the property is not "available for use" as defined in 13(27)-(28). When the property first becomes available for use, the half-year rule in Reg. 1100(2) formula "-(0.5)C" limits the CCA to half, but 2019 amendments to Reg. 1100(2) allow CCA on 1x or 1.5x cost for the acquisition year as an investment incentive, and in some cases on 100%. By year 3, the "two-year rolling start" rule in 13(27)(b) and 13(28)(c) allows the CCA regardless, and Reg. 1100(2)C:F(b)(v) provides that it is the full CCA. See also Income Tax Folio S3-F4-C1 ¶1.32-1.37.

13(26)-(29) added by 1991 technical bill, for property acquired after 1989, except for non-arm's length or rollover acquisition from a person who owned the property before 1990.

Income Tax Folios: S3-F4-C1: General discussion of CCA.

Advance Tax Rulings: ATR-44: Utilization of deductions and credits within a related corporate group.

Application Policies: SR&ED 2005-01: Shared-use equipment.

(27) Interpretation — available for use — For the purposes of subsection (26) and subject to subsection (29), property (other than a building or part thereof) acquired by a taxpayer shall be considered to have become available for use by the taxpayer at the earliest of

(a) the time the property is first used by the taxpayer for the purpose of earning income,

(b) the time that is immediately after the beginning of the first taxation year of the taxpayer that begins more than 357 days after the end of the taxation year of the taxpayer in which the property was acquired by the taxpayer,

(c) the time that is immediately before the disposition of the property by the taxpayer,

(d) the time the property

(i) is delivered to the taxpayer, or to a person or partnership (in this paragraph referred to as the "other person") that will use the property for the benefit of the taxpayer, or, where the property is not of a type that is deliverable, is made available to the taxpayer or the other person, and

(ii) is capable, either alone or in combination with other property in the possession at that time of the taxpayer or the other person, of being used by or for the benefit of the taxpayer or the other person to produce a commercially saleable product or to perform a commercially saleable service, including an intermediate product or service that is used or consumed, or to be used or consumed, by or for the benefit of the taxpayer or the other person in producing or performing any such product or service,

(e) in the case of property acquired by the taxpayer for the prevention, reduction or elimination of air or water pollution created by operations carried on by the taxpayer or that would be created by such operations if the property had not been acquired, the time at which the property is installed and capable of performing the function for which it was acquired,

(f) in the case of property acquired by

(i) a corporation a class of shares of the capital stock of which is listed on a designated stock exchange,

(ii) a corporation that is a public corporation because of an election made under subparagraph (b)(i) of the definition "public corporation" in subsection 89(1) or a designation made by the Minister in a notice to the corporation under subparagraph (b)(ii) of that definition, or

(iii) a subsidiary wholly-owned corporation of a corporation described in subparagraph (i) or (ii),

the end of the taxation year for which depreciation in respect of the property is first deducted in computing the earnings of the corporation in accordance with generally accepted accounting principles and for the purpose of the financial statements of the corporation for the year presented to its shareholders,

(g) in the case of property acquired by the taxpayer in the course of carrying on a business of farming or fishing, the time at which the property has been delivered to the taxpayer and is capable of performing the function for which it was acquired,

(h) in the case of property of a taxpayer that is a motor vehicle, trailer, trolley bus, aircraft or vessel for which one or more permits, certificates or licences evidencing that the property may be operated by the taxpayer in accordance with any laws regulating the use of such property are required to be obtained, the time all those permits, certificates or licences have been obtained,

(i) in the case of property that is a spare part intended to replace a part of another property of the taxpayer if required due to a breakdown of that other property, the time the other property became available for use by the taxpayer,

(j) in the case of a concrete gravity base structure and topside modules intended to be used at an oil production facility in a commercial discovery area (within the meaning assigned by section 2 of the *Canada Petroleum Resources Act*) on which the drilling of the first well that indicated the discovery began before March 5, 1982, in an offshore region prescribed for the purposes of subsection 127(9), the time the gravity base structure deballasts and lifts the assembled topside modules, and

(k) where the property is (within the meaning assigned by subsection (4.1)) a replacement for a former property described in paragraph (4)(a) that was acquired before 1990 or that became available for use at or before the time the replacement property is acquired, the time the replacement property is acquired,

and, for the purposes of paragraph (f), where depreciation is calculated by reference to a portion of the cost of the property, only that portion of the property shall be considered to have become available for use at the end of the taxation year referred to in that paragraph.

Related Provisions: 13(21.2)(e)(iv) — When property considered available for use following transfer to affiliated person; 13(30), (31) — Transfers of property; 20(28) — Deduction before available for use; 87(2)(j.6) — Continuing corporation; 248(19) — When property available for use. See also at end of s. 13; Reg. 1100(2)C:F(b)(v) — CCA in year property becomes available for use under 13(27)(b).

Notes: See 13(26) Notes. For a ruling applying 13(27) to a licence see VIEWS doc 2006-0185201R3. 13(27)(f) cannot apply to a partnership (of corporations): 2011-0401381E5.

13(27)(f)(i) amended by 2007 budget bill #2 (effective Dec. 14, 2007), 1995-97 technical bill.

Income Tax Folios: S3-F4-C1: General discussion of CCA.

Application Policies: SR&ED 2000-04R2: Recapture of investment tax credit.

(28) Idem — For the purposes of subsection (26) and subject to subsection (29), property that is a building or part thereof of a taxpayer shall be considered to have become available for use by the taxpayer at the earliest of

(a) the time all or substantially all of the building is first used by the taxpayer for the purpose for which it was acquired,

(b) the time the construction of the building is complete,

(c) the time that is immediately after the beginning of the taxpayer's first taxation year that begins more than 357 days after the end of the taxpayer's taxation year in which the property was acquired by the taxpayer,

(d) the time that is immediately before the disposition of the property by the taxpayer, and

(e) where the property is (within the meaning assigned by subsection (4.1)) a replacement for a former property described in paragraph (4)(a) that was acquired before 1990 or that became available for use at or before the time the replacement property is acquired, the time the replacement property is acquired,

and, for the purpose of this subsection, a renovation, alteration or addition to a particular building shall be considered to be a building separate from the particular building.

Related Provisions: 13(21.2)(e)(iv) — When property considered available for use following transfer to affiliated person; 13(30), (31) — Transfers of property; 87(2)(j.6) — Continuing corporation; Reg. 1100(2)C:F(b)(v) — CCA in year property becomes available for use under 13(28)(c).

Notes: See 13(26) Notes. CRA considers that "substantially all", used in 13(28)(a), means 90% or more.

Income Tax Folios: S3-F4-C1: General discussion of CCA.

(29) Idem — For the purposes of subsection (26), where a taxpayer acquires property (other than a building that is used or is to be used by the taxpayer principally for the purpose of gaining or producing gross revenue that is rent) in the taxpayer's first taxation year (in this subsection referred to as the "particular year") that begins more than 357 days after the end of the taxpayer's taxation year in which

the taxpayer first acquired property after 1989, that is part of a project of the taxpayer, or in a taxation year subsequent to the particular year, and at the end of any taxation year (in this subsection referred to as the "inclusion year") of the taxpayer

(a) the property can reasonably be considered to be part of the project, and

(b) the property has not otherwise become available for use,

if the taxpayer so elects in prescribed form filed with the taxpayer's return of income under this Part for the particular year, that particular portion of the property the capital cost of which does not exceed the amount, if any, by which

(c) the total of all amounts each of which is the capital cost to the taxpayer of a depreciable property (other than a building that is used or is to be used by the taxpayer principally for the purpose of gaining or producing gross revenue that is rent) that is part of the project, that was acquired by the taxpayer after 1989 and before the end of the taxpayer's last taxation year that ends more than 357 days before the beginning of the inclusion year and that has not become available for use at or before the end of the inclusion year (except where the property has first become available for use before the end of the inclusion year because of this subsection or paragraph (27)(b) or (28)(c))

exceeds

(d) the total of all amounts each of which is the capital cost to the taxpayer of a depreciable property, other than the particular portion of the property, that is part of the project to the extent that the property is considered, because of this subsection, to have become available for use before the end of the inclusion year

shall be considered to have become available for use immediately before the end of the inclusion year.

Related Provisions: 220(3.2), Reg. 600(b) — Late filing or revocation of election.

Notes: See 13(26) Notes. The 13(29) election is available to a partnership: VIEWS doc 2011-0416051E5. The election need be filed only once, not annually: 2019-0821651I7 (despite the current Form T1031 wording).

Regulations: 4609 (prescribed offshore region).

Income Tax Folios: S3-F4-C1: General discussion of CCA.

Forms: T1031: Subsection 13(29) election re certain depreciable properties, acquired for use in a long term project.

(30) Transfers of property — Notwithstanding subsections (27) to (29), for the purpose of subsection (26), property of a taxpayer shall be deemed to have become available for use by the taxpayer at the earlier of the time the property was acquired by the taxpayer and, if applicable, a prescribed time, where

(a) the property was acquired

(i) from a person with whom the taxpayer was not dealing at arm's length (otherwise than because of a right referred to in paragraph 251(5)(b)) at the time the property was acquired by the taxpayer, or

(ii) in the course of a reorganization in respect of which, if a dividend were received by a corporation in the course of the reorganization, subsection 55(2) would not apply to the dividend because of paragraph 55(3)(b); and

(b) before the property was acquired by the taxpayer, it became available for use (determined without reference to paragraphs (27)(c) and (28)(d)) by the person from whom it was acquired.

Notes: 13(30) added by 1991 technical bill and amended retroactively by 1992 technical bill, for property acquired after 1989.

Regulations: 1100(2.2)(j).

(31) Idem — For the purposes of paragraphs (27)(b) and (28)(c) and subsection (29), where a property of a taxpayer was acquired from a person (in this subsection referred to as "the transferor")

(a) with whom the taxpayer was, at the time the taxpayer acquired the property, not dealing at arm's length (otherwise than because of a right referred to in paragraph 251(5)(b)), or

(b) in the course of a reorganization in respect of which, if a dividend were received by a corporation in the course of the re-organization, subsection 55(2) would not apply to the dividend because of the application of paragraph 55(3)(b),

the taxpayer shall be deemed to have acquired the property at the time it was acquired by the transferor.

Notes: 13(31) added by 1991 technical bill, for property acquired after 1989.

(32) Leased property — Where a taxpayer has leased property that is depreciable property of a person with whom the taxpayer does not deal at arm's length, the amount, if any, by which

(a) the total of all amounts paid or payable by the taxpayer for the use of, or the right to use, the property in a particular taxation year and before the time the property would have been considered to have become available for use by the taxpayer if the taxpayer had acquired the property, and that, but for this subsection, would be deductible in computing the taxpayer's income for any taxation year

exceeds

(b) the total of all amounts received or receivable by the taxpayer for the use of, or the right to use, the property in the particular taxation year and before that time and that are included in the income of the taxpayer for any taxation year

shall be deemed to be a cost to the taxpayer of a property included in Class 13 in Schedule II to the *Income Tax Regulations* and not to be an amount paid or payable for the use of, or the right to use, the property.

Notes: 13(32) added by 1991 technical bill, for property acquired after 1989.

(33) Consideration given for depreciable property — For greater certainty, where a person acquires a depreciable property for consideration that can reasonably be considered to include a transfer of property, the portion of the cost to the person of the depreciable property attributable to the transfer shall not exceed the fair market value of the transferred property.

Related Provisions: 68 — Allocation of amounts in consideration for disposition of property; 69(1) — Inadequate considerations.

Notes: 13(33) added by 1993 technical bill, for property acquired after Nov. 1992. It ensures that on a trade-in (e.g., of a vehicle), no more than the value of the trade-in can be allocated to the transfer of the trade-in for the person who acquires it.

Income Tax Folios: S3-F4-C1: General discussion of CCA.

(34) Goodwill — Where a taxpayer carries on a particular business,

(a) there is deemed to be a single goodwill property in respect of the particular business;

(b) if at any time the taxpayer acquires goodwill as part of an acquisition of all or a part of another business that is carried on, after the acquisition, as part of the particular business — or is deemed by subsection (35) to acquire goodwill in respect of the particular business — the cost of the goodwill is added at that time to the cost of the goodwill property in respect of the particular business;

(c) if at any time the taxpayer disposes of goodwill as part of the disposition of part of the particular business, receives proceeds of disposition a portion of which is attributable to goodwill and continues to carry on the particular business or is deemed by subsection (37) to dispose of goodwill in respect of the particular business,

(i) the taxpayer is deemed to dispose at that time of a portion of the goodwill property in respect of the particular business having a cost equal to the lesser of the cost of the goodwill property in respect of the particular business otherwise determined and the portion of the proceeds attributable to goodwill, and

(ii) the cost of the goodwill property in respect of the particular business is reduced at that time by the amount determined under subparagraph (i); and

(d) if paragraph (c) applies to more than one disposition of goodwill at the same time, that paragraph and subsection (39) apply as if each disposition had occurred separately in the order designated by the taxpayer or, if the taxpayer does not designate an order, in the order designated by the Minister.

Related Provisions: 13(35) — Deemed acquisition of goodwill; 13(37) — Deemed disposition of goodwill; 13(38)–(41) — Transition from eligible capital property rules; 248(1)"property"(e) — Goodwill is deemed to be property.

Notes: 13(34)-(42) are part of changing eligible capital property (ECP) rules in s. 14 to CCA Class 14.1 as of 2017. See Notes to 20(1)(b).

13(34)-(37) provide rules for expenditures and receipts of a business that do *not* relate to "property" as defined in 248(1) and that, before 2017, would adjust cumulative eligible capital (CEC) under the ECP rules. Such amount is accounted for by adjusting the capital cost of the goodwill.

13(34) treats every business as having a single goodwill property, on which Class 14.1 CCA can be claimed. Expenditures of the business not related to property increase this goodwill: 13(35). Purchased goodwill does also: 13(34)(a). Dispositions of a business can reduce it: 13(34)(c), (d). This goodwill is deemed to be property: 248(1)"property"(e).

13(36) and 18(1)(y) ensure that consideration for shares (even if the purchased shares no longer exist) cannot be allocated to goodwill, and that no deduction is allowed.

13(37) provides that a receipt not related to property (i.e., not otherwise allocated) reduces the cost of goodwill (and thus Class 14.1 UCC). If the receipt exceeds the goodwill's cost, the excess is a capital gain. Previously deducted CCA may be recaptured under 13(1).

13(38)-(41) provide transitional rules from the ECP system to Class 14.1:

13(38) effectively transfers a pre-2017 CEC balance to Class 14.1. First, 13(38)(a) deems the total capital cost of all Class 14.1 property to be 4/3 of the total of the CEC balance and past amounts claimed under 20(1)(b) that have not been recaptured. 13(38)(b) then allocates this cost as between goodwill and any identifiable property that was ECP. Then 13(38)(c) deems CCA to have been claimed under 20(1)(a) before 2017, so that the UCC balance at the start of 2017 is equal to the previous CEC balance. This allows CCA (20(1)(a)), recapture (13(1)) and capital gains to work properly going forward.

13(38)(d) provides an income inclusion for a taxation year X that straddles Jan. 1, 2017, e.g. if a taxpayer receives proceeds in that taxation year before 2017, which would trigger a 14(1)(b) income inclusion if the taxation year ended before 2017. A taxpayer may choose to have the income inclusion reported as business income or as taxable capital gain. An election to defer this inclusion is available in a way conceptually similar to the ECP rules. Where, after 2016 and in taxation year X, a taxpayer acquires property of the new class or is deemed by 13(35) to have acquired goodwill, the taxpayer may elect to reduce the 13(38)(d) inclusion by up to half the capital cost of the new property. The capital cost of the new property is then reduced by twice the amount by which the income inclusion is reduced.

See Notes to 13(38) for more detail.

13(39) is intended to ensure that receipts related to expenditures incurred before 2017 do not trigger excess recapture when applied to reduce the Class 14.1 balance. 13(39) provides, in effect, that certain qualifying receipts reduce Class 14.1 UCC at a 75% rate (the rate at which eligible capital expenditures were added to CEC). Receipts that qualify are generally those from disposition of property that was ECP, and receipts that do not represent proceeds of disposition (PoD) of property. This is achieved by increasing Class 14.1 UCC by, generally, 25% of the lesser of the PoD and the cost of the property disposed of.

13(40) prevents the use of 13(39) and non-arm's length transfers to increase UCC. This is done by deeming the taxpayer to have claimed Class 14.1 CCA equal to the lesser of 1/4 of the cost of the property acquired and the amount deemed by 13(39) to have been added to Class 14.1 UCC of the taxpayer or another person or partnership.

13(42) provides various adjusting rules where a taxpayer owns Class 14.1 property at the start of 2017 that was ECP before 2017.

See Dept. of Finance Technical Notes for much more detail and examples.

13(34) replaced by 2016 budget bill #2, effective 2017. Former 13(34) applied to resource expenditures in years ending before Dec. 6, 1996 (see now Reg. 1102(1)(a)).

(35) Outlays not relating to property — If at any time a taxpayer makes or incurs an outlay or expense on account of capital for the purpose of gaining or producing income from a business carried on by the taxpayer, the taxpayer is deemed to acquire at that time goodwill in respect of the business with a cost equal to the amount of the outlay or expense if no portion of the amount is

(a) the cost, or any part of the cost, of a property;

(b) deductible in computing the taxpayer's income from the business (determined without reference to this subsection);

(c) not deductible in computing the taxpayer's income from the business because of any provision of this Act (other than paragraph 18(1)(b)) or the *Income Tax Regulations*;

(d) paid or payable to a creditor of the taxpayer as, on account of or in lieu of payment of, any debt, or on account of the redemption, cancellation or purchase of any bond or debenture; or

(e) where the taxpayer is a corporation, partnership or trust, paid or payable to a person as a shareholder, partner or beneficiary, as the case may be, of the taxpayer.

Notes: See Notes to 13(34). 13(35) added by 2016 budget bill #2, effective 2017.

(36) No addition to goodwill [for share purchase] — For greater certainty, no amount paid or payable may be included in Class 14.1 of Schedule II to the *Income Tax Regulations*, if the amount is

(a) in consideration for the purchase of shares; or

(b) in consideration for the cancellation or assignment of an obligation to pay consideration referred to in paragraph (a).

Related Provisions: 18(1)(y) — No deduction for 13(36) amount.

Notes: See Notes to 13(34). 13(36) added by 2016 budget bill #2, effective 2017. This was 13(35.1) in the July 29/16 draft legislation. It was not in the March 22/16 draft.

(37) Receipts not relating to property — If at any time in a taxation year a taxpayer has or may become entitled to receive an amount (in this subsection referred to as the "receipt") on account of capital in respect of a business that is or was carried on by the taxpayer, the taxpayer is deemed to dispose, at that time, of goodwill in respect of the business for proceeds of disposition equal to the amount by which the receipt exceeds the total of all outlays or expenses that were made or incurred by the taxpayer for the purpose of obtaining the receipt and that were not otherwise deductible in computing the taxpayer's income, if the following conditions are satisfied (determined without reference to this subsection):

(a) the receipt is not included in computing the taxpayer's income, or deducted in computing, for the purposes of this Act, any balance of undeducted outlays, expenses or other amounts for the taxation year or a preceding taxation year;

(b) the receipt does not reduce the cost or capital cost of a property or the amount of an outlay or expense; and

(c) the receipt is not included in computing any gain or loss of the taxpayer from a disposition of a capital property.

Notes: See Notes to 13(34). 13(37) added by 2016 budget bill #2, effective 2017. This was 13(36) in the March 22/16 and July 29/16 draft legislation.

(38) Class 14.1 — transitional rules [pre-2017 expenditures] — If a taxpayer has incurred an eligible capital expenditure in respect of a business before January 1, 2017,

(a) at the beginning of that day, the total capital cost of all property of the taxpayer included in Class 14.1 of Schedule II to the *Income Tax Regulations* in respect of the business, each of which was an eligible capital property of the taxpayer immediately before that day or is the goodwill property in respect of the business, is deemed to be the amount determined by the formula

$$4/3 \times (A + B - C)$$

where

A   is the amount that is the cumulative eligible capital in respect of the business at the beginning of that day,

B   is the amount determined for F in the definition "cumulative eligible capital" in subsection 14(5) (as that subsection applied immediately before that day) in respect of the business at the beginning of that day, and

C   is the amount by which the total of all amounts determined, in respect of the business, for E or F in the definition "cumulative eligible capital" in subsection 14(5) (as that subsection applied immediately before that day), exceeds the total of all amounts determined for A to D.1 in that definition in respect of the business at the beginning of that day, including any adjustment required by subparagraph (d)(i);

(b) at the beginning of that day, the capital cost of each property of the taxpayer included in the class in respect of the business, each of which was an eligible capital property of the taxpayer

immediately before that day or is the goodwill property in respect of the business, is to be determined as follows:

(i) the taxpayer shall designate the order in which the capital cost of each property that is not the goodwill property is determined and, if the taxpayer does not designate an order, the Minister may designate the order,

(ii) the capital cost of a particular property that is not the goodwill property in respect of the business is deemed to be the lesser of the eligible capital expenditure of the taxpayer in respect of the particular property and the amount by which the total capital cost of the class determined under paragraph (a) exceeds the total of all amounts each of which is an amount deemed by this subparagraph to be the capital cost of a property that is determined in advance of the determination of the capital cost of the particular property, and

(iii) the capital cost of the goodwill property is deemed to be the amount by which the total capital cost of the class exceeds the total of all amounts each of which is an amount deemed by subparagraph (ii) to be the capital cost of a property;

(c) an amount is deemed to have been allowed to the taxpayer in respect of property of the class under regulations made under paragraph 20(1)(a) in computing the taxpayer's income for taxation years ending before that day equal to the amount by which

(i) the total of the total capital cost of the class and the amount determined for C in paragraph (a)

exceeds

(ii) the amount determined for A in paragraph (a); and

(d) if no taxation year of the taxpayer ends immediately before that day and the taxpayer would have had a particular amount included, because of paragraph 14(1)(b) (as that paragraph applied immediately before that day), in computing the taxpayer's income from the business for the particular taxation year that includes that day if the particular year had ended immediately before that day,

(i) for the purposes of the formula in paragraph (a), ³/₂ of the particular amount is to be included in computing the amount for B of the definition "cumulative eligible capital" in subsection 14(5) (as that subsection applied immediately before that day),

(ii) the taxpayer is deemed to dispose of a capital property in respect of the business immediately before that day for proceeds of disposition equal to twice the particular amount,

(iii) if the taxpayer elects in writing to have this subparagraph apply and files that election with the Minister on or before the filing-due date for the particular year, subparagraph (ii) does not apply and an amount equal to the particular amount is to be included in computing the taxpayer's income from the business for the particular year,

(iv) if, on or after that day and in the particular year, the taxpayer acquires a property included in the class in respect of the business, or is deemed by subsection (35) to acquire goodwill in respect of the business, and the taxpayer elects in writing to have this subparagraph apply and files that election with the Minister on or before the filing-due date for the particular year,

(A) for the purposes of subparagraphs (ii) and (iii), the particular amount is to be reduced by the lesser of the particular amount otherwise determined and ¹/₂ of the capital cost of the property or goodwill acquired (determined without reference to clause (B)), and

(B) the capital cost of the property or goodwill acquired, as the case may be, is to be reduced by twice the amount by which the particular amount is reduced under clause (A), and

(v) if, in the particular year and before that day, the taxpayer disposed of a "qualified farm or fishing property" (as defined in subsection 110.6(1)) that was an eligible capital property of the taxpayer, the capital property disposed of under subparagraph (ii), if any, is deemed to be a qualified farm or fishing property to the extent of the lesser of

(A) the proceeds of disposition of the capital property, and

(B) the amount by which the proceeds of disposition of the qualified farm or fishing property exceed its cost.

Proposed Addition — Election on disposition of eligible capital property before March 22, 2016

Letter from Dept. of Finance, July 29, 2019: See under s. 14.

Related Provisions: 13(7.41) — Application of 13(38) to repayment of assistance after 2016; 257 — Formula cannot calculate to less than zero; Reg. 1100(1)(c.1) — Additional 2% CCA for pre-2017 amounts.

Notes: See Notes to 13(34). For CRA interpretation see VIEWS docs 2016-0660861E5 (partial disposition of farm quota: units are generally indistinguishable); 2016-0664451E5 (application of 13(38) and (42) where former 14(3) applied); 2016-0666901E5 (replacement-property rules cannot apply to disposition of farm quota after 2016); 2016-0669721C6 [2016 CTF q.13] (no (d)(iii) election where only intangible asset is internally-generated goodwill with no cost [Benqassmi, "The ECP Transitional Rules and Internally Generated Goodwill", 7(2) *Canadian Tax Focus* (ctf.ca) 13 (May 2017)]); 2016-0680071E5 (requirement to make election); 2016-0680141E5 (OK if any ECE incurred before 2017) [Infanti, "ECP Transitional Election May Apply to Internally Generated Goodwill", 17(3) *Tax for the Owner-Manager* (ctf.ca) 9-10 (July 2017)]; 2017-0688971E5 (effect of rollover of goodwill acquired before 2017); 2017-0709091C6 [2017 APFF q.11] (disposition of ECP by calendar-year partnership with off-calendar-year corporate partners).

13(38) added by 2016 budget bill #2, effective 2017. This was 13(37) in the March 22/16 and July 29/16 draft legislation. The March version had two technical flaws: Lorne Richter, "ECP Transitional Rules and 2016 Asset Sales", 24(7) *Canadian Tax Highlights* (ctf.ca) 12-13 (July 2016); VIEWS doc 2016-0641851E5. These have both been corrected.

Income Tax Folios: S3-F2-C1: Capital Dividends [replaces IT-66R6].

(39) Class 14.1 — transitional rule [disposition of pre-2017 property — ¼ add-back] — If at any time a taxpayer disposes of a particular property included in Class 14.1 of Schedule II to the *Income Tax Regulations* in respect of a business and none of subsections 24(2), 70(5.1), 73(3.1), 85(1), 88(1), 98(3) and (5), 107(2) and 107.4(3) apply to the disposition, then for the purpose of determining the undepreciated capital cost of the class, the taxpayer is deemed to have acquired a property of the class immediately before that time with a capital cost equal to the least of ¼ of the proceeds of disposition of the particular property, ¼ of the capital cost of the particular property and

(a) if the particular property is not goodwill and is acquired before January 1, 2017 by the taxpayer, ¼ of the capital cost of the particular property;

(b) if the particular property is not goodwill, is acquired on or after that day by the taxpayer and subsection (40) deems an amount to have been allowed under paragraph 20(1)(a) in respect of the taxpayer's acquisition of the particular property, that amount;

(c) if the particular property (other than a property to which paragraph (b) applies) is not goodwill and is acquired on or after that day by the taxpayer — in circumstances under which any of subsections 24(2), 70(5.1), 73(3.1), 85(1), 88(1), 98(3) and (5), 107(2) and 107.4(3) apply — from a person or partnership that would have been deemed under this subsection to have acquired a property if none of those subsections had applied, the capital cost of the property that would have been deemed under this subsection to have been acquired by the person or partnership;

(d) if the particular property is goodwill, the amount by which

(i) the total of all amounts each of which is

(A) ¼ of the amount determined under subparagraph (38)(b)(iii) in respect of the business,

(B) if goodwill is acquired on or after that day by the taxpayer and subsection (40) deems an amount to have been allowed under paragraph 20(1)(a) in respect of the taxpayer's acquisition of the goodwill, that amount, or

(C) if goodwill is acquired (other than an acquisition in respect of which clause (B) applies) on or after that day by the taxpayer — in circumstances under which any of subsections 24(2), 70(5.1), 73(3.1), 85(1), 88(1), 98(3) and (5), 107(2) and 107.4(3) apply — from a person or partnership that would have been deemed under this subsection to have acquired a property if none of those subsections had applied, the capital cost of the property that would have been deemed under this subsection to have been acquired by the person or partnership

exceeds

(ii) the total of all amounts each of which is the capital cost of a property deemed by this subsection to have been acquired by the taxpayer at or before that time in respect of another disposition of goodwill in respect of the business; and

(e) in any other case, nil.

Related Provisions: 14(13), (14) [before 2017] — Disposition of pre-1988 ECP; 14(15), (16) [before 2017] — Disposition where there is an "exempt gains balance" from 1994 capital gains exemption; 20(4.2) — Bad debt on sale of pre-2016 eligible capital property.

Notes: See Notes to 13(34). 13(39) added by 2016 budget bill #2, effective 2017. This was 13(38) in the March 22/16 and July 29/16 draft legislation.

(40) Class 14.1 — transitional rule [non-arm's length transfer] — If at any time a taxpayer acquires a particular property included in Class 14.1 of Schedule II to the *Income Tax Regulations* in respect of a business, the acquisition of the particular property is part of a transaction or series of transactions or events that includes a disposition (in this subsection referred to as the "prior disposition") at or before that time of the particular property, or a similar property, by the taxpayer or a person or partnership that does not deal at arm's length with the taxpayer and subsection (39) applies in respect of the prior disposition, then for the purpose of determining the undepreciated capital cost of the class, an amount is deemed to have been allowed under paragraph 20(1)(a) to the taxpayer in respect of the particular property in computing the taxpayer's income for taxation years ending before the acquisition equal to the lesser of the capital cost of the property deemed by subsection (39) to be acquired in respect of the prior disposition and ¼ of the capital cost of the particular property.

Notes: See Notes to 13(34). 13(40) added by 2016 budget bill #2, effective 2017. This was 13(39) in the March 22/16 and July 29/16 draft legislation.

(41) Class 14.1 — transitional rule [meaning of CEC, ECE, etc.] — For the purposes of subsections (38) to (40) and (42), paragraph 20(1)(hh.1), subsections 40(13) to (16) and paragraph 79(4)(b), "cumulative eligible capital", "eligible capital expenditure", "eligible capital property" and "exempt gains balance" have the meanings that would be assigned to those expressions if the Act read as it did immediately before 2017.

Notes: See Notes to 13(34). For the pre-2017 definitions, see Notes to repealed s. 14 [for 14(5)"cumulative eligible capital", 14(5)"eligible capital expenditure", 14(5)"exempt gains balance"] and to 54"eligible capital property".

13(41) added by 2016 budget bill #2, effective 2017. It was 13(40) in the March 22/16 and July 29/16 draft legislation.

(42) Class 14.1 — transitional rules — If a taxpayer owns property included in Class 14.1 of Schedule II to the *Income Tax Regulations* in respect of a business at the beginning of 2017, that was an eligible capital property in respect of the business immediately before 2017,

(a) for the purposes of the Act and its regulations (other than this section, section 20 and any regulations made for the purposes of paragraph 20(1)(a)), if the amount determined for A in the definition "cumulative eligible capital" in subsection 14(5) would have been increased immediately before 2017 if the property had been disposed of immediately before that time, the capital cost of the property is deemed to be increased by ⁴⁄₃ of the amount of that increase;

(b) for purposes of this section, section 20 and any regulations made for the purposes of paragraph 20(1)(a), if the taxpayer was deemed by subsection 14(12) to continue to own eligible capital property in respect of the business and not to have ceased to carry on the business until a time that is after 2016, the taxpayer is deemed to continue to own the property and to continue to carry on the business until the time that is immediately before the first time one of the events that would be described in any of paragraphs 14(12)(c) to (g) (as they read immediately before 2017, if the reference to "eligible capital property" in paragraph 14(12)(d) were read as "eligible capital property or capital property") occurs;

(c) for the purposes of the descriptions of D.1 and K in the definition "undepreciated capital cost" in subsection (21), the taxpayer is deemed not to have paid or received any amounts before 2017 as or on account of an existing or proposed countervailing or antidumping duty in respect of depreciable property of the class; and

(d) subsection (7.1) does not apply to assistance that a taxpayer received or is entitled to receive before 2017 in respect of a property that was an eligible capital property immediately before 2017.

Notes: See Notes to 13(34) and (38). 13(42) added by 2016 budget bill #2, effective 2017. This was 13(41) in the March 22/16 and July 29/16 draft legislation.

Related Provisions [s. 13]: 37(6) — Scientific research capital expenditures; 70(5) — Depreciable and other capital property of deceased taxpayer; 70(9.1), (9.11) — Transfer of farm property from spouse trust to children of settlor; 73(2) — Capital cost and amount deemed allowed to spouse or trust; 73(3.1)(h) — *Inter vivos* transfer of farm property by farmer to child; 80(9)(c) — Reduction of capital cost on debt forgiveness ignored for purposes of s. 13; 85(5) — Rules on transfers of depreciable property; 87(2)(d) — Amalgamation — depreciable property; 87(2)(l.3) — Amalgamation — replacement property; 88(1)(f) — Winding-up; 97(4) — Where capital cost to partner exceeds proceeds of disposition; 98(3)(e), (5)(e) — Rules where partnership ceases to exist; 107(2) — Distribution by trust in satisfaction of capital interest; 107.2 — Distribution by RCA; 138(11.8) — Transfer of insurance business.

Definitions [s. 13]: "affiliated" — 13(25), 251.1; "amount" — 248(1); "appropriate minister" — 13(21); "arm's length" — 13(7)(e.1), 251; "assessment" — 248(1); "assistance" — 79(4), 125.4(5), 248(16), (16.1), (18), (18.1); "available for use" — 13(21.2)(e)(iv), 13(27)–(31), 248(19); "beneficiary" — 248(25) [Notes]; "business" — 248(1); "calendar year" — *Interpretation Act* 37(1)(a); "Canada" — 255; "capital cost" — 13(7)–(7.4), (10), 13(21.2)(g)(i), 70(12), 128.1(1)(c), 128.1(4)(c), 132.1(1)(d); "capital gain" — 39(1), 248(1); "capital property" — 54, 248(1); "certified production" — Reg. 1104(2); "class of shares" — 248(6); "control" — 256(6)–(9), 256.1(3); "conversion", "conversion cost" — 13(21); "consequence of the death" — 248(8); "corporation" — 248(1), *Interpretation Act* 35(1); "cost amount" — 248(1); "cumulative eligible capital" — 13(41), 14(5), 248(1); "deficit" — Reg. 5907(1)"exempt deficit", "taxable deficit"; "depreciable property" — 13(21), 248(1); "designated liquidation and dissolution" — 95(1); "designated stock exchange" — 248(1), 262; "disposition", "dividend" — 248(1); "eligible capital expenditure" — 13(41), 14(5), 248(1); "eligible capital property" — 13(41); "estate" — 104(1), 248(1); "excluded property" — 95(1); "exempt deficit" — Reg. 5907(1); "exempt surplus" — 113(1)(a), Reg. 5907(1), (1.01); "fair market value" — see 69(1) Notes; "farming" — 248(1); "filing-due date" — 150(1), 248(1); "fiscal period" — 249.1; "fishing" — 248(1); "foreign accrual property income", "foreign affiliate" — 95(1), 248(1); "former business property" — 248(1); "former property" — 13(4); "gaining or producing income" — 13(9); "goodwill" — 13(34); "goodwill property" — 13(34)(a); "gross revenue" — 248(1); "Her Majesty" — *Interpretation Act* 35(1); "immovable" — Quebec *Civil Code* art. 900–907; "income" — 13(3)(b); "incorporeal property" — Quebec *Civil Code* art. 899, 906; "individual", "insurer", "life insurer" — 248(1); "loss restriction event" — 251.2; "majority-interest beneficiary" — 251.1(3); "majority-interest partner", "Minister", "motor vehicle" — 248(1); "non-resident" — 248(1); "partnership" — see 96(1) Notes; "passenger vehicle", "person", "prescribed" — 248(1); "prescribed energy conservation property" — Reg. 8200.1; "property" — 248(1); "province" — *Interpretation Act* 35(1); "public corporation" — 89(1), 248(1); "qualified farm or fishing property" — 110.6(1); "qualifying liquidation and dissolution" — 88(3.1); "regulation" — 248(1); "related" — 13(25), 251(2); "replacement" — 13(4.1); "resident in Canada" — 94(3)(a), 250; "series" — 248(10); "share", "shareholder", "subsidiary wholly-owned corporation" — 248(1); "tax payable" — 248(2); "taxable Canadian property" — 248(1); "taxable deficit" — Reg. 5907(1); "taxable surplus" — 113(1)(b)(i), Reg. 5907(1), (1.01); "taxation year" — 249; "taxpayer" — 248(1); "timber resource property" — 13(21), 248(1); "transferee" — 13(4.2)(a); "transferor" — 13(4.2)(a), 13(7)(e), 13(21.2)(a), 13(31); "treaty-protected property" — 248(1); "trust" — 104(1), 248(1), (3); "undepreciated capital cost" — 13(21), 248(1); "writing", "written" — *Interpretation Act* 35(1)"writing"; "year" — 11(2), 13(3)(a), 13(8); "zero-emission passenger vehicle" — 248(1).

Regulations [s. 13]: 1105 (prescribed classes of depreciable property).

I.T. Application Rules [s. 13]: 20(1), (1.1), (3).

Income Tax Folios [s. 13]: S4-F7-C1: Amalgamations of Canadian corporations [replaces IT-474R2].

Interpretation Bulletins [s. 13]: IT-297R2: Gifts in kind to charity and others; IT-325R2: Property transfers after separation, divorce and annulment.

Forms [s. 13]: T2 Sched. 8: Capital cost allowance.

14. [Repealed]

Notes: S. 14 repealed by 2016 budget bill #2, effective 2017, as part of changing eligible capital property to CCA Class 14.1. See 20(1)(b) Notes. It read:

14. (1) Eligible capital property — inclusion in income from business — Where, at the end of a taxation year, the total of all amounts each of which is an amount determined, in respect of a business of a taxpayer, for E in the definition "cumulative eligible capital" in subsection (5) (in this section referred to as an "eligible capital amount") or for F in that definition exceeds the total of all

amounts determined for A to D in that definition in respect of the business (which excess is in this subsection referred to as "the excess"), there shall be included in computing the taxpayer's income from the business for the year the total of

(a) the amount, if any, that is the lesser of

(i) the excess, and

(ii) the amount determined for F in the definition "cumulative eligible capital" in subsection (5) at the end of the year in respect of the business, and

(b) the amount, if any, determined by the formula

$$2/3 \times (A - B - C - D)$$

where

A   is the excess,

B   is the amount determined for F in the definition "cumulative eligible capital" in subsection (5) at the end of the year in respect of the business,

C   is $\frac{1}{2}$ of the amount determined for Q in the definition "cumulative eligible capital" in subsection (5) at the end of the year in respect of the business, and

D   is the amount claimed by the taxpayer, not exceeding the taxpayer's exempt gains balance for the year in respect of the business.

Related Provisions [Former 14(1)]: 14(1.01) — Election to recognize capital gain in place of reducing CEC pool; 14(1.1) — Expenditure relating to qualified farm or fishing property; 14(3) — Non-arm's length acquisition of ECP; 14(8) — Deemed residence in Canada; 14(9) — Effect of excessive election for capital gains exemption.

Notes [Former 14(1)]: See Notes to 20(1)(b) for an explanation of 14(1), which applied until the end of 2016. The 75% inclusion up to the 20(1)(b) deduction claimed comes through 14(1)(a) and 14(5)"cumulative eligible capital"E (which refers to "3/4 of the amount"). The 50% inclusion of the balance comes through "2/3 × A" in 14(1)(b), since 2/3 × 3/4 = 2/4 = 50%. These amounts are included in business income, so are eligible for the small business deduction (125(1)) for a CCPC. For interpretation of 14(1)(b) see VIEWS doc 2005-0140891C6.

On a sale of ECP, there is no 5-year reserve for unpaid amounts as under 40(1)(a)(iii) on a sale of capital property. Nor is the capital gains exemption available: *Leclerc*, [1988] 2 C.T.C. 2318 (TCC).

In *Toronto Refiners*, 2002 FCA 476, 14(1) did not apply to an amount paid by a city following an expropriation, as it was paid for a civic and not a business purpose. A "mirror image" test applied, so 14(1) applied only if the amount paid was deductible as an eligible capital expenditure. This rule was followed in *Winsor*, 2007 TCC 692, and *Haché*, 2011 FCA 104, where 14(1) did not apply to surrender of a fishing licence to the government, which had no profit motive (the disposition was a capital gain). See also *White*, 2011 FC 556, where CRA's denial of *Winsor* treatment to others was sent back for a new decision; and Notes to 85(1.1) re fishing licences. However, the "mirror image" rule was deleted from 14(5)"cumulative eligible capital"E in 2006. In *Henco Industries*, 2014 TCC 192, paras. 181-201, a developer had its business ruined by native occupation in Caledonia, and its land became worthless. The Ontario government's $15.8 million payment to make HI "go away" was not taxable under the "mirror image" rule (which HI elected to use under the transitional rule amending 14(5)).

On whether there is more than one "business", see Notes to Reg. 1101(1).

In *RCI Environnement*, 2008 FCA 419 (leave to appeal denied 2009 CarswellNat 1832 (SCC)), disposition of a non-compete right (pre-56.4) led to 14(1) inclusion.

On ceasing to carry on business before 2017, there may be a deemed disposition of goodwill at market value and 14(1) inclusion (if a related person continues the business): *Charron*, [1990] 2 C.T.C. 2609 (TCC); or a 24(1) deduction.

14(1) amended by 2000 Budget (for tax years that end after Oct. 17, 2000), 1995-97 technical bill, 1994 Budget and 1991 technical bill.

I.T. Application Rules [Former 14(1)]: 21(1).

Interpretation Bulletins [Former 14(1)]: IT-73R6: The small business deduction; IT-291R3: Transfer of property to a corporation under subsection 85(1); IT-365R2: Damages, settlements and similar receipts; IT-386R: Eligible capital amounts. See also at end of s. 14.

(1.01) Election re capital gain — A taxpayer may, in the taxpayer's return of income for a taxation year, or with an election under subsection 83(2) filed on or before the taxpayer's filing-due date for the taxation year, elect that the following rules apply to a disposition made at any time in the year of an eligible capital property in respect of a business, if the taxpayer's actual proceeds of the disposition exceed the taxpayer's eligible capital expenditure in respect of the acquisition of the property, that eligible capital expenditure can be determined and, for taxpayers who are individuals, the taxpayer's exempt gains balance in respect of the business for the taxation year is nil:

(a) for the purpose of subsection (5) other than the description of A in the definition "cumulative eligible capital", the proceeds of disposition of the

property are deemed to be equal to the amount of that eligible capital expenditure;

(b) the taxpayer is deemed to have disposed at that time of a capital property that had, immediately before that time, an adjusted cost base to the taxpayer equal to the amount of that eligible capital expenditure, for proceeds of disposition equal to the actual proceeds; and

(c) if the eligible capital property is a qualified farm or fishing property (within the meaning assigned by subsection 110.6(1)) of the taxpayer at that time, the capital property deemed by paragraph (b) to have been disposed of by the taxpayer is deemed to be a qualified farm or fishing property of the taxpayer at that time.

Related Provisions [Former 14(1.01)]: 14(1.02) — Parallel election for property acquired before 1972; 14(1.03) — Non-application of 14(1.01); 14(3) — Effect of 14(1.01) on non-arm's length acquisition of ECP; 96(3) — Election by members of partnership.

Notes [Former 14(1.01)]: 14(1.01) and (1.02) effectively allow a taxpayer to treat the excess of proceeds of ECE on a disposition (see Notes to 20(1)(b)) as a capital gain, so as to use up capital losses, claim a reserve under 40(1)(a)(iii), or accelerate the capital dividend account and not need to wait until after year-end to pay a capital dividend (83(2)). The T2054 capital dividend election form now allows inclusion of the 14(1.01) or (1.02) election.

14(1) applies only if a taxpayer has a negative CEC pool balance. Thus, additions to the CEC pool are still made at the $\frac{3}{4}$ rate and dispositions of ECP still reduce pool balances on a $\frac{3}{4}$ basis. A taxpayer may prefer to recognize the entire economic capital gain on ECP on a $\frac{1}{2}$ or $\frac{2}{3}$ basis, e.g. if the taxpayer has outstanding capital losses to be used but wants to conserve the CEC pool balance. 14(1.01) permits a taxpayer to elect to, in effect, remove an asset from the CEC pool and recognize a capital gain on the asset in the year as if it were ordinary non-depreciable capital property. This election is only available to recognize gains, not losses, and is not available for goodwill or other types of property for which the original cost cannot be determined. It also cannot be used to recognize a gain that can be sheltered by the taxpayer's exempt gains balance.

An election "in the taxpayer's return" is valid even if the return is filed late. See Notes to 7(1.31).

If the election is filed with the tax return for the year, the property is still ECP, so no amount can be added to the capital dividend account (CDA) under 89(1): VIEWS doc 2003-0030245. Under the amendment made by 2006 budget bill #2, both elections can be made on the same day, so the CDA addition can be made at the same time: 2005-0147671I7. If the election is filed with the return rather than with the 83(2) election, the deeming rule in 14(1.01) does not change the application of 83(2) or cancel the 184(2) tax, in CRA's view: 2010-0364411I7 (Yull, "Deeming Something to Happen Doesn't Necessarily Make it So", 8(2) *Tax Hyperion* (Carswell, Feb. 2011); MacPherson, "ECP Capital Gains Election Timing", 11(2) *Tax for the Owner-Manager* (ctf.ca) 3-4 (April 2011); Louis, "The Endnote that Became an Article", 200 *The Estate Planner* (CCH) 5 (Sept. 2011)). See *5551928 Manitoba*, 2019 BCCA 376, where rectification was used to change a capital dividend declaration from a (wrong) dollar amount to the actual CDA amount.

The words "at that time" in 14(1.01)(b) refer to the time of disposition, not the time of filing the return: VIEWS doc 2002-0163825.

See also docs 2005-011785I17 (interaction with 110.6(19) election), 2005-0154301I7 (meaning of "can be determined"), 2006-0197401E5 (partial disposition of farm quota), 2011-0394231E5 (partial disposition of milk quota and rollover of the rest).

14(1.01) amended by 2014 budget bill #2 (for dispositions and transfers in 2014 and later tax years), 2006 budget bill #2.

(1.02) Election re property acquired with pre-1972 outlays or expenditures — If at any time in a taxation year a taxpayer has disposed of an eligible capital property in respect of which an outlay or expenditure to acquire the property was made before 1972 (which outlay or expenditure would have been an eligible capital expenditure if it had been made or incurred as a result of a transaction that occurred after 1971), the taxpayer's actual proceeds of the disposition exceed the total of those outlays or expenditures, that total can be determined, subsection 21(1) of the *Income Tax Application Rules* applies in respect of the disposition and, for taxpayers who are individuals, the taxpayer's exempt gains balance in respect of the business for the taxation year is nil, the taxpayer may, in the taxpayer's return of income for the taxation year, or with an election under subsection 83(2) filed on or before the taxpayer's filing-due date for the taxation year, elect that the following rules apply:

(a) for the purpose of subsection (5) other than the description of A in the definition "cumulative eligible capital", the proceeds of disposition of the property are deemed to be nil;

(b) the taxpayer is deemed to have disposed at that time of a capital property that had, immediately before that time, an adjusted cost base to the taxpayer equal to nil, for proceeds of disposition equal to the amount determined, in respect of the disposition, under subsection 21(1) of the *Income Tax Application Rules*; and

(c) if the eligible capital property is a qualified farm or fishing property (within the meaning assigned by subsection 110.6(1)) of the taxpayer at that time, the capital property deemed by paragraph (b) to have been disposed of by the taxpayer is deemed to be a qualified farm or fishing property of the taxpayer at that time.

Related Provisions [Former 14(1.02)]: 14(1.03) — Non-application of 14(1.02); 14(3) — Effect of 14(1.02) on non-arm's length acquisition of ECP; 96(3) — Election by members of partnership.

Notes [Former 14(1.02)]: 14(1.02) effectively allows a 14(1.01) election for property acquired before 1972. See Notes to 14(1.01).

14(1.02)(c) amended by 2014 budget bill #2, for dispositions and transfers in 2014 and later tax years. Added by 2006 budget bill #2.

(1.03) Non-application of subsecs. (1.01) and (1.02) — Subsections (1.01) and (1.02) do not apply to a disposition by a taxpayer of a property

  (a) that is goodwill; or

  (b) that was acquired by the taxpayer

    (i) in circumstances where an election was made under subsection 85(1) or (2) and the amount agreed on in that election in respect of the property was less than the fair market value of the property at the time it was so acquired, and

    (ii) from a person or partnership with whom the taxpayer did not deal at arm's length and for whom the eligible capital expenditure in respect of the acquisition of the property cannot be determined.

Notes [Former 14(1.03)]: 14(1.03) added by 2006 budget bill #2.

(1.1) Deemed taxable capital gain [qualified farm or fishing property] — For the purposes of section 110.6 and paragraph 3(b) as it applies for the purposes of that section, an amount included under paragraph (1)(b) in computing a taxpayer's income for a particular taxation year from a business is deemed to be a taxable capital gain of the taxpayer for the year from the disposition in the year of qualified farm or fishing property to the extent of the lesser of

  (a) the amount included under paragraph (1)(b) in computing the taxpayer's income for the particular year from the business, and

  (b) the amount determined by the formula

$$A - B$$

where

A is the amount by which the total of

    (i) $\frac{3}{4}$ of the total of all amounts each of which is the taxpayer's proceeds from a disposition in a preceding taxation year that began after 1987 and ended before February 28, 2000 of eligible capital property in respect of the business that, at the time of the disposition, was a qualified farm property (within the meaning assigned by subsection 110.6(1)) of the taxpayer,

    (ii) $\frac{2}{3}$ of the total of all amounts each of which is the taxpayer's proceeds from a disposition in the particular year or a preceding taxation year that ended after February 27, 2000 and before October 18, 2000 of eligible capital property in respect of the business that, at the time of the disposition, was a qualified farm property (within the meaning assigned by subsection 110.6(1)) of the taxpayer, and

    (iii) $\frac{1}{2}$ of the total of all amounts each of which is the taxpayer's proceeds from a disposition in the particular year or a preceding taxation year that ended after October 17, 2000 of eligible capital property in respect of the business that, at the time of the disposition, was a qualified farm property, a qualified fishing property or a qualified farm or fishing property (within the meaning assigned by subsection 110.6(1)) of the taxpayer

  exceeds the total of

    (iv) $\frac{3}{4}$ of the total of all amounts each of which is

      (A) an eligible capital expenditure of the taxpayer in respect of the business that was made or incurred in respect of a property that was, at the time of disposition, a qualified farm property disposed of by the taxpayer in a preceding taxation year that began after 1987 and ended before February 28, 2000, or

      (B) an outlay or expense of the taxpayer that was not deductible in computing the taxpayer's income and that was made or incurred for the purpose of making a disposition referred to in clause (A),

    (v) $\frac{2}{3}$ of the total of all amounts each of which is

      (A) an eligible capital expenditure of the taxpayer in respect of the business that was made or incurred in respect of a property that was, at the time of disposition, a qualified farm property disposed of by the taxpayer in the particular year or a preceding taxation year that ended after February 27, 2000 and before October 18, 2000, or

      (B) an outlay or expense of the taxpayer that was not deductible in computing the taxpayer's income and that was made or incurred for the purpose of making a disposition referred to in clause (A), and

    (vi) $\frac{1}{2}$ of the total of all amounts each of which is

      (A) an eligible capital expenditure of the taxpayer in respect of the business that was made or incurred in respect of a property that was, at the time of disposition, a qualified farm property, a qualified fishing property or a qualified farm or fishing property disposed of by the taxpayer in the particular year or a preceding taxation year that ended after October 17, 2000, or

      (B) an outlay or expense of the taxpayer that was not deductible in computing the taxpayer's income and that was made or incurred for the purpose of making a disposition referred to in clause (A), and

B is the total of all amounts each of which is

    (i) that portion of an amount deemed by subparagraph (1)(a)(v) (as it applied in respect of the business to fiscal periods that began after 1987 and ended before February 23, 1994) to be a taxable capital gain of the taxpayer that can reasonably be attributed to a disposition of a property that was, at the time of disposition, a qualified farm property of the taxpayer, or

    (ii) an amount deemed by this section to be a taxable capital gain of the taxpayer for a taxation year preceding the particular year from the disposition of a property that was, at the time of disposition, a qualified farm property, a qualified fishing property or a qualified farm or fishing property of the taxpayer.

Related Provisions [Former 14(1.1)]: 110.6(2) — Capital gains exemption for qualified farm or fishing property; 257 — Formula cannot calculate to less than zero.

Notes [Former 14(1.1)]: For interpretation of "reasonably be attributed" in (b)B(i), see *729658 Alberta Ltd.*, [2004] 4 C.T.C. 2261 (TCC).

14(1.1) opening words and para. (b) amended by 2014 budget bill #2 (for dispositions and transfers in the 2014 and later taxation years), 2000 Budget. Added by 1995-97 technical bill.

(1.2) [Repealed]

Notes [Former 14(1.2)]: 14(1.2) repealed by 2014 budget bill #2, for dispositions and transfers in the 2014 and later tax years.

(2) Amount deemed payable — Where any amount is, by any provision of this Act, deemed to be a taxpayer's proceeds of disposition of any property disposed of by the taxpayer at any time, for the purposes of this section, that amount shall be deemed to have become payable to the taxpayer at that time.

Interpretation Bulletins [Former 14(2)]: See list at end of s. 14.

(3) Acquisition of eligible capital property [not at arm's length] — Notwithstanding any other provision of this Act, where at any particular time a person or partnership (in this subsection referred to as the "taxpayer") has, directly or indirectly, in any manner whatever, acquired an eligible capital property in respect of a business from a person or partnership with which the taxpayer did not deal at arm's length (in this subsection referred to as the "transferor") and the property was an eligible capital property of the transferor (other than property acquired by the taxpayer as a consequence of the death of the transferor), the eligible capital expenditure of the taxpayer in respect of the business is, in respect of that acquisition, deemed to be equal to $\frac{4}{3}$ of the amount, if any, by which

  (a) the amount determined for E in the definition "cumulative eligible capital" in subsection (5) in respect of the disposition of the property by the transferor or, if the property is the subject of an election under subsection (1.01) or (1.02) by the transferor, $\frac{3}{4}$ of the actual proceeds referred to in that subsection,

exceeds the total of

  (b) the total of all amounts that can reasonably be considered to have been claimed as deductions under section 110.6 for taxation years that ended before February 28, 2000 by any person with whom the taxpayer was not dealing at arm's length in respect of the disposition of the property by the transferor, or any other disposition of the property before the particular time,

  (b.1) $\frac{9}{8}$ of the total of all amounts that can reasonably be considered to have been claimed as deductions under section 110.6 for taxation years that ended after February 27, 2000 and before October 18, 2000 by any person with whom the taxpayer was not dealing at arm's length in respect of the disposition of the property by the transferor, or any other disposition of the property before the particular time, and

  (b.2) $\frac{1}{2}$ of the total of all amounts that can reasonably be considered to have been claimed as deductions under section 110.6 for taxation years that end after October 17, 2000 by any person with whom the taxpayer was not dealing at arm's length in respect of the disposition of the property by the transferor, or any other disposition of the property before that particular time, except that, where the taxpayer disposes of the property after the particular time, the amount of the eligible capital expenditure deemed by this subsection to be made by the taxpayer in respect of the property shall be determined at any time after the disposition as if the total of the amounts determined under paragraphs (b), (b.1) and (b.2) in respect of the disposition were the lesser of

(c) the amount otherwise so determined, and

(d) the amount, if any, by which

(i) the amount determined under paragraph (a) in respect of the disposition of the property by the transferor

exceeds

(ii) the amount determined for E in the definition "cumulative eligible capital" in subsection (5) in respect of the disposition of the property by the taxpayer.

Related Provisions [Former 14(3)]: 248(8) — Meaning of "consequence" of death.

Notes [Former 14(3)]: For interpretation of 14(3) see VIEWS docs 2000-0024257, 2006-0212001E5, 2008-0285331C6.

14(3)(a) amended by 2002-2013 technical bill (Part 5 — technical) to add everything from "or, if the property...", for tax years that end after Feb. 27, 2000; but ignore the reference to 14(1.02) for tax years that end before Dec. 20, 2002.

14(3) amended by 2000 Budget, for tax years that end after Feb. 27, 2000.

Interpretation Bulletins [Former 14(3)]: See list at end of s. 14.

(4) References to "taxation year" or "year" — Where a taxpayer is an individual and the taxpayer's income for a taxation year includes income from a business the fiscal period of which does not coincide with the calendar year, for greater certainty a reference in this section to a "taxation year" or "year" shall be read as a reference to a "fiscal period" or "period".

Related Provisions [Former 14(4)]: 11(2) — References to "taxation year" or "year" of an individual.

Notes [Former 14(4)]: Since 1995, most individuals use a calendar year as their fiscal period. See Notes at end of 249.1.

(5) Definitions — In this section,

"adjustment time", of a taxpayer in respect of a business, means

(a) for a corporation, the time immediately after the commencement of its first taxation year commencing after June 1988, and

(b) for any other taxpayer, the time immediately after the commencement of the taxpayer's first fiscal period commencing after 1987 in respect of the business;

Related Provisions [Former 14(5)"adjustment time"]: 248(1)"adjustment time" — Definition applies to entire Act.

Notes [Former 14(5)"adjustment time"]: Definition amended by 2002-2013 technical bill (Part 5 — technical), effective Nov. 2011, effectively to repeal former para. (a) (consequential on the 1994 amendment to 87(2)(f) and repeal of 87(2)(f.1)).

14(5)"adjustment time" was 14(5)(c) before RSC 1985 (5th Suppl) consolidation for tax years ending after Nov. 1991.

"cumulative eligible capital" of a taxpayer at any time in respect of a business of the taxpayer means the amount determined by the formula

$$(A + B + C + D + D.1) - (E + F)$$

where

A   is the amount, if any, by which $\frac{3}{4}$ of the total of all eligible capital expenditures in respect of the business made or incurred by the taxpayer after the taxpayer's adjustment time and before that time exceeds the total of all amounts each of which is determined by the formula

$$1/2 \times (A.1 - A.2) \times (A.3/A.4)$$

where

A.1 is the amount required, because of paragraph (1)(b) or 38(a), to be included in the income of a person or partnership (in this definition referred to as the "transferor") not dealing at arm's length with the taxpayer in respect of the disposition after December 20, 2002 of a property that was an eligible capital property acquired by the taxpayer directly or indirectly, in any manner whatever, from the transferor and not disposed of by the taxpayer before that time,

A.2 is the total of all amounts that can reasonably be considered to have been claimed as deductions under section 110.6 by the transferor in respect of that disposition,

A.3 is the transferor's proceeds from that disposition, and

A.4 is the transferor's total proceeds of disposition of eligible capital property in the taxation year of the transferor in which the property described in A.1 was disposed of,

B   is the total of

(a) $\frac{3}{2}$ of all amounts included under paragraph (1)(b) in computing the taxpayer's income from the business for taxation years that ended before that time and after October 17, 2000,

(b) $\frac{9}{8}$ of all amounts included under paragraph (1)(b) in computing the taxpayer's income from the business for taxation years that ended

(i) before that time, and

(ii) after February 27, 2000 and before October 18, 2000,

(c) all amounts included under paragraph (1)(b) in computing the taxpayer's income from the business for taxation years that ended

(i) before the earlier of that time and February 28, 2000, and

(ii) after the taxpayer's adjustment time,

(d) all amounts each of which is the amount that would have been included under subparagraph (1)(a)(v) (as that subparagraph applied for taxation years that ended before February 28, 2000) in computing the taxpayer's income from the business, if the amount determined for D in that subparagraph for the year were nil, for taxation years that ended

(i) before the earlier of that time and February 28, 2000, and

(ii) after February 22, 1994, and

(e) all taxable capital gains included, because of the application of subparagraph (1)(a)(v) (as that subparagraph applied for taxation years that ended before February 28, 2000) to the taxpayer in respect of the business, in computing the taxpayer's income for taxation years that began before February 23, 1994,

C   is $\frac{3}{2}$ of the amount, if any, of the taxpayer's cumulative eligible capital in respect of the business at the taxpayer's adjustment time,

D   is the amount, if any, by which

(a) the total of all amounts deducted under paragraph 20(1)(b) in computing the taxpayer's income from the business for taxation years ending before the taxpayer's adjustment time

exceeds

(b) the total of all amounts included under subsection (1) in computing the taxpayer's income from the business for taxation years ending before the taxpayer's adjustment time,

D.1 is, where the amount determined by B exceeds zero, $\frac{1}{2}$ of the amount determined for Q in respect of the business,

E   is the total of all amounts each of which is $\frac{3}{4}$ of the amount, if any, by which

(a) an amount that the taxpayer has or may become entitled to receive, after the taxpayer's adjustment time and before that time, on account of capital in respect of the business carried on or formerly carried on by the taxpayer, other than an amount that

(i) is included in computing the taxpayer's income, or deducted in computing, for the purposes of this Act, any balance of undeducted outlays, expenses or other amounts for the year or a preceding taxation year,

(ii) reduces the cost or capital cost of a property or the amount of an outlay or expense, or

(iii) is included in computing any gain or loss of the taxpayer from a disposition of a capital property

exceeds

(b) all outlays and expenses that were not otherwise deductible in computing the taxpayer's income and were made or incurred by the taxpayer for the purpose of obtaining the amount described by paragraph (a), and

F   is the amount determined by the formula

$$(P + P.1 + Q) - R$$

where

P   is the total of all amounts deducted under paragraph 20(1)(b) in computing the taxpayer's income from the business for taxation years ending before that time and after the taxpayer's adjustment time,

P.1 is the total of all amounts each of which is an amount by which the cumulative eligible capital of the taxpayer in respect of the business is required to be reduced at or before that time because of subsection 80(7),

Q   is the amount, if any, by which

(a) the total of all amounts deducted under paragraph 20(1)(b) in computing the taxpayer's income from the business for taxation years ending before the taxpayer's adjustment time

exceeds

(b) the total of all amounts included under subsection (1) in computing the taxpayer's income for taxation years ending before the taxpayer's adjustment time, and

R   is the total of all amounts each of which is an amount included, in computing the taxpayer's income from the business for a taxation year that ended before that time and after the taxpayer's adjustment time

> (a) in the case of a taxation year that ends after February 27, 2000, under paragraph (1)(a), or
>
> (b) in the case of a taxation year that ended before February 28, 2000,
>
>> (i) under subparagraph (1)(a)(iv), as that subparagraph applied in respect of that taxation year, or
>>
>> (ii) under paragraph (1)(b), as that paragraph applied in respect of that taxation year, to the extent that the amount so included is in respect of an amount included in the amount determined for P;

Related Provisions [Former 14(5)"cumulative eligible capital"]: 13(38)–(41) — Transition to new Class 14.1 as of 2017.

Notes [Former 14(5)"cumulative eligible capital"]: See Notes to 20(1)(b). A loss in the ECP's value does not affect the CEC balance: VIEWS doc 2013-0510371E5. For the effect of a transfer-pricing adjustment, see 2013-0490751I7. On the interpretation of element A.1 see 2014-0518921E5.

Definition amended by 2002-2013 technical bill (for tax years ending after Feb. 27, 2000), 2006 budget bill #2 (for amounts that became receivable after May 1, 2006, or Aug. 30, 2006 by election), 2000 and 1994 Budgets, 1994 technical bill. The 2006 amendments replaced the "mirror image" rule (see 14(1) Notes): Strawson, "Mirror Image Rule", 7(4) *Tax for the Owner-Manager* (ctf.ca) 1-2 (Oct. 2007); Bauer & Smith, "Eligible Capital Expenditures", 2013 Cdn Tax Foundation conference report, 11:1-30.

14(5)"cumulative eligible capital" was 14(5)(a) before RSC 1985 (5th Supp) consolidation for tax years ending after Nov. 1991.

D.1 (originally 14(5)(a)(iii.2)) added by 1991 technical bill, effective 1988.

Income Tax Folios [Former 14(5)"cumulative eligible capital"]: S4-F7-C1: Amalgamations of Canadian corporations [replaces IT-474R2]; S7-F1-C1: Split-receipting and deemed fair market value.

Interpretation Bulletins [Former 14(5)"cumulative eligible capital"]: IT-99R5: Legal and accounting fees; IT-143R3: Meaning of eligible capital expenditure; IT-291R3: Transfer of property to a corporation under subsec. 85(1); IT-365R2: Damages, settlements and similar receipts; IT-386R: Eligible capital amounts' IT-471R: Merger of partnerships. See also at end of s. 14.

Forms [Former 14(5)"cumulative eligible capital"]: T2 Sched. 10: Cumulative eligible capital deduction.

"eligible capital expenditure" of a taxpayer in respect of a business means the portion of any outlay or expense made or incurred by the taxpayer, as a result of a transaction occurring after 1971, on account of capital for the purpose of gaining or producing income from the business, other than any such outlay or expense

> (a) in respect of which any amount is or would be, but for any provision of this Act limiting the quantum of any deduction, deductible (otherwise than under paragraph 20(1)(b)) in computing the taxpayer's income from the business, or in respect of which any amount is, by virtue of any provision of this Act other than paragraph 18(1)(b), not deductible in computing that income,
>
> (b) made or incurred for the purpose of gaining or producing income that is exempt income, or
>
> (c) that is the cost of, or any part of the cost of,
>
>> (i) tangible property, or for civil law corporeal property, of the taxpayer,
>>
>> (ii) intangible property, or for civil law incorporeal property, that is depreciable property of the taxpayer,
>>
>> (iii) property in respect of which any deduction (otherwise than under paragraph 20(1)(b)) is permitted in computing the taxpayer's income from the business or would be so permitted if the taxpayer's income from the business were sufficient for the purpose, or
>>
>> (iv) an interest in, or for civil law a right in, or a right to acquire any property described in any of subparagraphs (i) to (iii)

but, for greater certainty and without restricting the generality of the foregoing, does not include any portion of

> (d) any amount paid or payable to any creditor of the taxpayer as, on account or in lieu of payment of any debt or as or on account of the redemption, cancellation or purchase of any bond or debenture,
>
> (e) where the taxpayer is a corporation, any amount paid or payable to a person as a shareholder of the corporation, or
>
> (f) any amount that is the cost of, or any part of the cost of,
>
>> (i) an interest in a trust,
>>
>> (ii) an interest in a partnership,
>>
>> (iii) a share, bond, debenture, mortgage, hypothecary claim, note, bill or other similar property, or

> (iv) an interest in, or for civil law a right in, or a right to acquire, any property described in any of subparagraphs (i) to (iii);

Related Provisions [Former 14(5)"eligible capital expenditure"]: 14(3) — Non-arm's length acquisition of eligible capital property; 56.4(4)(b) — Restrictive covenant or non-competition agreement — treatment of purchaser; 87(2)(f) — Amalgamations — cumulative eligible capital; 98(3)(b) — Rules applicable where partnership ceases to exist; 107(2)(f) — Capital interest distribution by personal or prescribed trust; 139.1(4)(b) — Amount payable by insurer on demutualization deemed not to be eligible capital expenditure; 248(1)"eligible capital expenditure" — Definition applies to entire Act.

Notes [Former 14(5)"eligible capital expenditure"]: See Notes to 20(1)(b).

Definition amended by 2002-2013 technical bill (effective June 26, 2013), 2001 *Civil Code* harmonization bill. 14(5)"eligible capital expenditure" was 14(5)(b) before RSC 1985 (5th Supp) consolidation for tax years ending after Nov. 1991.

Interpretation Bulletins [Former 14(5)"eligible capital expenditure"]: IT-99R5: Legal and accounting fees; IT-143R3: Meaning of eligible capital expenditure; IT-187: Customer lists and ledger accounts; IT-291R3: Transfer of property to a corporation under subsec. 85(1); IT-341R4: Expenses of issuing shares, units in a trust, interests in a partnership or syndicate and expenses of borrowing money; IT-364: Commencement of business operations; IT-386R: Eligible capital amounts; IT-467R2: Damages, settlements and similar payments; IT-482R: Pipelines. See also list at end of s. 14.

"exempt gains balance" of an individual in respect of a business of the individual for a taxation year means the amount determined by the formula

$$A - B$$

where

A   is the lesser of

> (a) the amount by which
>
>> (i) the amount that would have been the individual's taxable capital gain determined under paragraph 110.6(19)(b) in respect of the business if
>>
>>> (A) the amount designated in an election under subsection 110.6(19) in respect of the business were equal to the fair market value at the end of February 22, 1994 of all the eligible capital property owned by the elector at that time in respect of the business, and
>>>
>>> (B) this Act were read without reference to subsection 110.6(20)
>>
>> exceeds
>>
>> (ii) the amount determined by the formula
>>
>> $$0.75(C - 1.1D)$$
>>
>> where
>>
>> C   is the amount designated in the election that was made under subsection 110.6(19) in respect of the business, and
>>
>> D   is the fair market value at the end of February 22, 1994 of the property referred to in clause (i)(A), and
>
> (b) the individual's taxable capital gain determined under paragraph 110.6(19)(b) in respect of the business, and

B   is the total of all amounts each of which is the amount determined for D in subparagraph (1)(a)(v) in respect of the business for a preceding taxation year that ended before February 28, 2000 or the amount determined for D in paragraph (1)(b) for a preceding taxation year that ended after February 27, 2000.

Related Provisions [Former 14(5)"exempt gains balance"]: 14(9) — Effect of excessive election; 257 — Formulas cannot calculate to less than zero.

Notes [Former 14(5)"exempt gains balance"]: The "exempt gains balance" deals with the election to use the capital gains exemption for 1994-95 under 110.6(19). It determines the amount by which the income inclusion under 14(1)D can be reduced. In general, it is the unclaimed portion of the taxable capital gain that was included in income because of the 110.6(19) election. Thus, the gain is not taxed again on a later disposition of the eligible capital property.

Definition amended by 2000 Budget (for tax years ending after Feb. 27, 2000). Added by 1994 Budget.

(5.1) Restrictive covenant amount — The description of E in the definition "cumulative eligible capital" in subsection (5) does not apply to an amount that is received or receivable by a taxpayer in a taxation year if that amount is required to be included in the taxpayer's income because of subsection 56.4(2).

Related Provisions [Former 14(5.1)]: 56.4(7)(d) — Allocation of goodwill amount in restrictive covenant.

Notes [Former 14(5.1)]: 14(5.1) added by 2002-2013 technical bill (Part 5 — technical), effective Oct. 8, 2003.

(6) Exchange of property — If in a taxation year (in this subsection referred to as the "initial year") a taxpayer disposes of an eligible capital property (in this

section referred to as the taxpayer's "former property") and the taxpayer so elects under this subsection in the taxpayer's return of income for the year in which the taxpayer acquires an eligible capital property that is a replacement property for the taxpayer's former property, the amount, not exceeding the amount that would otherwise be included in the amount determined for E in the definition "cumulative eligible capital" in subsection (5) (if the description of E in that definition were read without reference to "¾ of") in respect of a business, that has been used by the taxpayer to acquire the replacement property before the later of the end of the first taxation year after the initial year and 12 months after the end of the initial year

(a) shall, subject to paragraph (b), not be included in the amount determined for E in that definition for the purpose of determining the cumulative eligible capital of the taxpayer in respect of the business; and

(b) shall, to the extent of ¾ thereof, be included in the amount determined for E in that definition for the purpose of determining the cumulative eligible capital of the taxpayer in respect of the business at a time that is the later of

(i) the time the replacement property was acquired by the taxpayer, and

(ii) the time the former property was disposed of by the taxpayer.

Related Provisions [Former 14(6)]: 13(4.2), (4.3) — Exchange of franchise, concession or licence with fixed term; 14(7) — Meaning of a "replacement property"; 96(3) — Election by members of partnership; 220(3.2), Reg. 600(b) — Late filing or revocation of election.

Notes [Former 14(6)]: See Notes to 13(4) and 44(1). Shares cannot be replacement property for ECP under 14(7): VIEWS doc 2011-0427411E5. Starting 2017, no replacement property rules are available: 2016-0666901E5.

An election "in the taxpayer's return" is valid even if the return is filed late. See Notes to 7(1.31).

For a taxpayer filing Quebec returns, an election under 14(6) must be copied to Revenu Québec: *Taxation Act* ss. 110.1(3), 21.4.6.

14(6) opening words amended by 2002-2013 technical bill (for dispositions in tax years that end after Dec. 20, 2001), 1995-97 technical bill.

Interpretation Bulletins [Former 14(6)]: IT-259R4: Exchanges of property. See also at end of s. 14.

(7) **Replacement property for a former property** — For the purposes of subsection (6), a particular eligible capital property of a taxpayer is a replacement property for a former property of the taxpayer if

(a) it is reasonable to conclude that the property was acquired by the taxpayer to replace the former property;

(a.1) it was acquired by the taxpayer for a use that is the same as or similar to the use to which the taxpayer put the former property;

(b) it was acquired for the purpose of gaining or producing income from the same or a similar business as that in which the former property was used; and

(c) where the former property was used by the taxpayer in a business carried on in Canada, the particular property was acquired for use by the taxpayer in a business carried on by the taxpayer in Canada.

Notes [Former 14(7)]: See Notes to 14(6). 14(7) amended by 1995-97 technical bill (effective 1994) and 1991 technical bill.

Interpretation Bulletins [Former 14(7)]: IT-259R4: Exchanges of property. See also at end of s. 14.

(8) **Deemed residence in Canada** — Where an individual was resident in Canada at any time in a particular taxation year and throughout

(a) the preceding taxation year, or

(b) the following taxation year,

for the purpose of paragraph (1)(a), the individual shall be deemed to have been resident in Canada throughout the particular year.

Related Provisions [Former 14(8)]: 110.6(5) — Parallel rule for capital gains exemption.

Notes [Former 14(8)]: 14(8) added by 1993 technical bill, effective for 1988 and later taxation years. It is a relieving provision for individuals who either cease to be (14(8)(a)), or begin to be (14(8)(b)), resident in Canada during the taxation year, allowing them the benefit of 14(1)(a) rather than 14(1)(b) for the year.

(9) **Effect of election under subsec. 110.6(19)** — Where an individual elects under subsection 110.6(19) in respect of a business, the individual shall be deemed to have received proceeds of a disposition on February 23, 1994 of eligible capital property in respect of the business equal to the amount determined by the formula

$$(A - B)\frac{4}{3}$$

where

A   is the amount determined in respect of the business under subparagraph (a)(ii) of the description of A in the definition "exempt gains balance" in subsection (5), and

B   is the amount determined in respect of the business under subparagraph (a)(i) of the description of A in the definition "exempt gains balance" in subsection (5).

Notes [Former 14(9)]: 14(9) deems an individual who made a 110.6(19) election (to use the $100,000 general capital gains exemption before it was repealed) to have received certain proceeds of disposition on Feb. 23, 1994. Added by 1994 Budget, for fiscal periods ending after Feb. 22, 1994. An earlier proposed 14(9) was enacted as 14(10).

(10) **Deemed eligible capital expenditure** — For the purposes of this Act, where a taxpayer received or is entitled to receive assistance from a government, municipality or other public authority in respect of, or for the acquisition of, property the cost of which is an eligible capital expenditure of the taxpayer in respect of a business, whether as a grant, subsidy, forgivable loan, deduction from tax, investment allowance or as any other form of assistance, that eligible capital expenditure shall at any time be deemed to be the amount, if any, by which the total of

(a) that eligible capital expenditure, determined without reference to this subsection, and

(b) such part, if any, of the assistance as the taxpayer repaid before

(i) the taxpayer ceased to carry on the business, and

(ii) that time

under a legal obligation to pay all or any part of the assistance

exceeds

(c) the amount of the assistance the taxpayer received or is entitled to receive before the earlier of that time and the time the taxpayer ceases to carry on the business.

Related Provisions [Former 14(10)]: 14(5) — Definition of "exempt gains balance"; 14(11) — Assistance deemed received by trust or partnership; 20(1)(hh.1) — Deduction for repayment after ceasing to carry on business.

Notes [Former 14(10)]: 14(10) added by 1994 technical bill, effective for assistance that a taxpayer receives or becomes entitled to receive after February 21, 1994 and repayments of such assistance. See Notes to 12(1)(x). (This was 14(9) in the draft legislation of July 12, 1994.)

Interpretation Bulletins [Former 14(10)]: IT-273R2: Government assistance — general comments. See also at end of s. 14.

(11) **Receipt of public assistance** — For the purpose of subsection (10), where at any time a taxpayer who is a beneficiary under a trust or a member of a partnership received or is entitled to receive assistance from a government, municipality or other public authority, whether as a grant, subsidy, forgivable loan, deduction from tax, investment allowance or as any other form of assistance, the amount of the assistance that can reasonably be considered to be in respect of, or for the acquisition of, property the cost of which was an eligible capital expenditure of the trust or partnership shall be deemed to have been received at that time by the trust or partnership, as the case may be, as assistance from the government, municipality or other public authority for the acquisition of such property.

Notes [Former 14(11)]: 14(11) added by 1994 technical bill, effective on the same basis as 14(10). (This was originally 14(10) in the draft legislation of July 12, 1994.)

Interpretation Bulletins [Former 14(11)]: IT-273R2: Government assistance — general comments. See also at end of s. 14.

(12) **Loss on certain transfers [within affiliated group]** — Where

(a) a corporation, trust or partnership (in this subsection referred to as the "transferor") disposes at any time in a taxation year of a particular eligible capital property — other than, for the purposes of computing the exempt surplus or exempt deficit and taxable surplus or taxable deficit of a foreign affiliate of a taxpayer, in respect of the taxpayer, where the transferor is the affiliate or is a partnership of which the affiliate is a member, eligible capital property that is, or would be, if the transferor were a foreign affiliate of the taxpayer, excluded property (within the meaning assigned by subsection 95(1)) of the transferor — in respect of a business of the transferor in respect of which it would, but for this subsection, be permitted a deduction under paragraph 24(1)(a) as a consequence of the disposition, and

(b) during the period that begins 30 days before and ends 30 days after the disposition, the transferor or a person affiliated with the transferor acquires a property (in this subsection referred to as the "substituted property") that is, or is identical to, the particular property and, at the end of that period, a person or partnership that is either the transferor or a person or partnership affiliated with the transferor owns the substituted property,

the transferor is deemed, for the purposes of this section and sections 20 and 24, to continue to own eligible capital property in respect of the business, and not to have ceased to carry on the business, until the time that is immediately before the first time, after the disposition,

(c) at which a 30-day period begins throughout which neither the transferor nor a person affiliated with the transferor owns

(i) the substituted property, or

(ii) a property that is identical to the substituted property and that was acquired after the day that is 31 days before the period begins,

(d) at which the substituted property is not eligible capital property in respect of a business carried on by the transferor or a person affiliated with the transferor,

(e) at which the substituted property would, if it were owned by the transferor, be deemed by section 128.1 or subsection 149(10) to have been disposed of by the transferor,

(f) that is immediately before the transferor is subject to a loss restriction event, or

(g) if the transferor is a corporation,

(i) for the purposes of computing the transferor's foreign accrual property income, exempt surplus or exempt deficit, and taxable surplus or taxable deficit, in respect of a taxpayer for a taxation year of the transferor where the transferor is a foreign affiliate of the taxpayer, at which the liquidation and dissolution of the transferor begins, unless the liquidation and dissolution is

(A) a qualifying liquidation and dissolution (within the meaning assigned by subsection 88(3.1)) of the transferor, or

(B) a designated liquidation and dissolution (within the meaning assigned by subsection 95(1)) of the transferor, and

(ii) for any other purposes, at which the winding-up (other than a winding-up to which subsection 88(1) applies) of the transferor begins.

Related Provisions [Former 14(12)]: 13(21.2) — Parallel rule for depreciable capital property; 14(13) — Deemed identical property; 18(13)–(16) — Parallel rule for share or debt owned by financial institution; 40(3.3), (3.4) — Parallel rule re capital losses; 69(5)(d) — No application where corporate property appropriated by shareholder on windup; 87(2)(g.3) — Amalgamations — continuing corporation; 88(1)(d.1) — No application to property acquired on windup of subsidiary; 93.1(3)(b) — Tiered partnership — look-through rule; 95(2)(e)(v)(A)(II) — Designated liquidation and dissolution of foreign affiliate; 248(12) — Whether properties are identical; 251.1 — Affiliated persons; 251.2 — Loss restriction event.

Notes [Former 14(12)]: See Notes to 13(21.2).

14(12) amended by 2013 budget bill #2 (effective March 21, 2013), 2002-2013 technical bill. Added by 1995-97 technical bill.

Interpretation Bulletins [Former 14(12)]: IT-291R3: Transfer of property to a corporation under subsec. 85(1).

(13) **Deemed identical property** — For the purpose of subsection (12),

(a) a right to acquire a property (other than a right, as security only, derived from a mortgage, hypothec, agreement for sale or similar obligation) is deemed to be a property that is identical to the property; and

(b) where a partnership otherwise ceases to exist at any time after the disposition, the partnership is deemed not to have ceased to exist and each person who, immediately before the partnership would, but for this paragraph, have ceased to exist, was a member of the partnership is deemed to remain a member of the partnership, until the time that is immediately after the first time described in paragraphs (12)(c) to (g).

Notes [Former 14(13)]: 14(13) added by 1995-97 technical bill, effective (subject to grandfathering) for dispositions after April 26, 1995.

Reference to "hypothec" added to 14(13)(a) by 2001 *Civil Code* harmonization bill, effective June 14, 2001. The change is non-substantive; see *Interpretation Act* s. 8.2.

(14) **[Non-resident] Ceasing to use [eligible capital] property in Canadian business** — If at a particular time a non-resident taxpayer ceases to use, in connection with a business or part of a business carried on by the taxpayer in Canada immediately before the particular time, a property that was immediately before the particular time eligible capital property of the taxpayer (other than a property that was disposed of by the taxpayer at the particular time), the taxpayer is deemed to have disposed of the property immediately before the particular time for proceeds of disposition equal to the amount determined by the formula

$$A - B$$

where

A is the fair market value of the property immediately before the particular time, and

B is

(a) where at a previous time before the particular time the taxpayer ceased to use the property in connection with a business or part of a business carried on by the taxpayer outside Canada and began to use it in connection with a business or part of a business carried on by the taxpayer in Canada, the amount, if any, by which the fair market value of the property at the previous time exceeded its cost to the taxpayer at the previous time, and

(b) in any other case, nil.

Related Provisions [Former 14(14)]: 10(12) — Parallel rule for inventory; 142.6(1.1) — Parallel rule for non-resident financial institution; 257 — Formula cannot calculate to less than zero.

Notes [Former 14(14)]: 14(14) added by 2001 technical bill, effective June 28, 1999 for an authorized foreign bank, and August 9, 2000 in any other case.

(15) **[Non-resident] Beginning to use [eligible capital] property in Canadian business** — If at a particular time a non-resident taxpayer ceases to use, in connection with a business or part of a business carried on by the taxpayer outside Canada immediately before the particular time, and begins to use, in connection with a business or part of a business carried on by the taxpayer in Canada, a property that is an eligible capital property of the taxpayer, the taxpayer is deemed to have disposed of the property immediately before the particular time and to have reacquired the property at the particular time for consideration equal to the lesser of the cost to the taxpayer of the property immediately before the particular time and its fair market value immediately before the particular time.

Related Provisions [Former 14(15)]: 10(14) — Parallel rule for inventory; 142.6(1.2) — Parallel rule for non-resident financial institution.

Notes [Former 14(15)]: 14(15) added by 2001 technical bill, effective June 28, 1999 for an authorized foreign bank, and August 9, 2000 in any other case.

Definitions [Former 14]: "adjusted cost base" — 54, 248(1); "adjustment time" — 14(5), 248(1); "affiliated" — 251.1; "amount" — 248(1); "arm's length" — 251(1); "assistance" — 79(4), 125.4(5), 248(16), (16.1), (18), (18.1); "business" — 248(1); "calendar year" — *Interpretation Act* 37(1)(a); "Canada" — 255; "Canadian partnership" — 102(1), 248(1); "capital gain" — 39(1)(a), 248(1); "capital property" — 54, 248(1); "consequence of the death" — 248(8); "control" — 256(6)–(9). 256.1(3); "corporation" — 248(1), *Interpretation Act* 35(1); "corporeal property" — Quebec *Civil Code* art. 899, 906; "cumulative eligible capital" — 14(5), 248(1); "deficit" — Reg. 5907(1)"exempt deficit", "taxable deficit" — depreciable property" — 13(21), 248(1); "disposition" — 248(1); "eligible capital amount" — 14(1), 248(1); "eligible capital expenditure" — 14(5), 248(1); "eligible capital property" — 54, 248(1); "excluded property" — 95(1); "exempt deficit" — Reg. 5907(1); "exempt gains balance" — 14(5); "exempt income" — 248(1); "exempt surplus" — 113(1)(a), Reg. 5907(1), (1.01); "fair market value" — see Notes to 69(1); "filing-due date" — 248(1); "fiscal period" — 249.1; "fishing" — 248(1); "foreign accrual property income", "foreign affiliate" — 95(1), 248(1); "former property" — 14(6); "identical" — 14(13), 248(12); "incorporeal property" — Quebec *Civil Code* art. 899, 906; "individual" — 248(1); "loss restriction event" — 251.2; "month" — *Interpretation Act* 35(1); "non-resident" — 248(1); "partnership" — see Notes to 96(1); "person", "property" — 248(1); "qualified farm or fishing property" — 110.6(1); "replacement property" — 14(6), (7); "resident in Canada" — 14(8), 94(3)(a), 250; "shareholder" — 248(1); "substituted property" — 14(12)(b); "taxable capital gain" — 38(a), 248(1); "taxable deficit" — Reg. 5907(1); "taxable surplus" — 113(1)(b)(i), Reg. 5907(1), (1.01); "taxation year" — 11(2), 14(4), 249; "taxpayer" — 248(1); "transferor" — 14(3), 14(12)(a); "trust" — 104(1), 248(1), (3); "year" — 11(2), 14(4).

I.T. Application Rules [Former 14]: 21(1) (business carried on since before 1972).

Interpretation Bulletins [Former 14]: IT-66R6: Capital dividends; IT-123R4: Disposition of eligible capital property; IT-123R6: Transactions involving eligible capital property; IT-187: Customer lists and ledger accounts; IT-206R: Separate businesses; IT-313R2: Eligible capital property — rules where a taxpayer has ceased carrying on a business or has died; IT-330R: Dispositions of capital property subject to warranty, covenant, etc. (cancelled); IT-364: Commencement of business operations; IT-488R2: Winding-up of 90%-owned taxable Canadian corporations (cancelled).

15. (1) Benefit conferred on shareholder — If, at any time, a benefit is conferred by a corporation on a shareholder of the corporation, on a member of a partnership that is a shareholder of the corporation or on a contemplated shareholder of the corporation, then the amount or value of the benefit is to be included in computing the income of the shareholder, member or contemplated shareholder, as the case may be, for its taxation year that includes the time, except to the extent that the amount or value of the benefit is deemed by section 84 to be a dividend or that the benefit is conferred on the shareholder

(a) where the corporation is resident in Canada at the time,

(i) by the reduction of the paid-up capital of the corporation,

(ii) by the redemption, acquisition or cancellation by the corporation of shares of its capital stock,

(iii) on the winding-up, discontinuance or reorganization of the corporation's business, or

(iv) by way of a transaction to which subsection 88(1) or (2) applies;

(a.1) where the corporation is not resident in Canada at the time,

(i) by way of a distribution to which subsection 86.1(1) applies,

(ii) by a reduction of the paid-up capital of the corporation to which subclause 53(2)(b)(i)(B)(II) or subparagraph 53(2)(b)(ii) applies,

(iii) by the redemption, acquisition or cancellation by the corporation of shares of its capital stock, or

(iv) on the winding-up, or liquidation and dissolution, of the corporation;

(b) by the payment of a dividend or a stock dividend;

(c) by conferring, on all owners of common shares of the capital stock of the corporation at that time, a right in respect of each common share, that is identical to every other right conferred at that time in respect of each other such share, to acquire additional shares of the capital stock of the corporation, and, for the purposes of this paragraph,

(i) the shares of a particular class of common shares of the capital stock of the corporation are deemed to be property that is identical to the shares of another class of common shares of the capital stock of the corporation if

(A) the voting rights attached to the particular class differ from the voting rights attached to the other class, and

(B) there are no other differences between the terms and conditions of the classes of shares that could cause the fair market value of a share of the particular class to differ materially from the fair market value of a share of the other class, and

(ii) rights are not considered identical if the cost of acquiring the rights differs; or

(d) by an action to which paragraph 84(1)(c.1), (c.2) or (c.3) applies.

Related Provisions: 15(1.1) — Where stock dividend paid; 15(1.2), (1.21) — Forgiveness of shareholder debt; 15(1.3) — GST on shareholder benefit; 15(1.4) — Interpretation rules including "contemplated shareholder"; 15(5) — Calculation of benefit where automobile available to shareholder; 15(7) — Application; 15(9) — Deemed benefit; 69(4), (5) — Property deemed disposed of by corporation at fair market value; 80.04(5.1) — No benefit conferred where debtor transfers property to eligible transferee under 80.04; 80.1(4) — Assets acquired from foreign affiliate as dividend in kind or as benefit to shareholder; 80.4(2) — Loans; 84(2) — Distribution on winding-up, etc.; 120.4(1)"split income"(a)(ii), (c)(ii)(B) — Application of income-splitting tax; 135.2(2) — No income inclusion on Canadian Wheat Board transfer of debt to farmers' trust; 139(a), 139.1(11) — No application on mutualization or demutualization of insurance corp; 142.7(4) — Deemed value of property on rollover from foreign bank subsidiary to branch; 214(3)(a) — Deemed dividend for purposes of non-resident withholding tax; 247(15) — No application to transfer pricing amount deemed to be dividend for non-resident withholding tax.

Notes: Shareholder S can legitimately extract money or property from corporation C by: dividend (taxable under 82(1) or 90(1)); repayment of loan owing by C; capital repayment (s. 84); reimbursement of C's expenses incurred by S (*Arpeg Holdings*, 2008 FCA 31); salary/benefits (5(1), 6(1)); and if S is an independent contractor (see Notes to 248(1)"employee"), business income (9(1)). 15(1) is aimed at other "payments, distributions, benefits and advantages flowing from a corporation to a shareholder": *Pillsbury Holdings*, [1964] C.T.C. 294 (Exch. Ct.), para. 18. To be caught by 15(1), the benefit must be real, not a "legal fiction": *Colubriale*, 2005 FCA 329, para. 28; *Laliberté*, 2020 FCA 97, para. 35. Note that 15(1) also applies to a "contemplated" shareholder, and see 15(1.4)(a) for interpretation.

15(1) applies to appropriations of corporate property (including money) by S. See IT-432R2. If a corp mistakenly pays too much to S when repaying a loan from S, 15(1) should not apply because there is no "benefit" conferred. The corp has a right to recover the overpayment from S, and 15(2) and 20(1)(j) would apply instead. Similarly, if an amount is posted in error to the shareholder account without S's knowledge, there is no benefit: *Cook*, 2006 TCC 344; *Poulin*, 2010 TCC 313; *Charania*, 2015 TCC 80. See also VIEWS doc 2007-0224101E5 and Notes to 15(2). However, where a corp's investment funds were transferred to the owners' joint account, then 3 years later transferred to a new account for the corp, the first transfer created a benefit even though the funds were never used: *Dyck*, 2007 TCC 458 (FCA appeal dismissed for delay A-432-07).

If S already had a contractual right to what the corp provided, there is no benefit: *Del Grande*, [1993] 1 C.T.C. 2096 (TCC). "The word 'confer' implies the bestowal of bounty or largesse, to the economic benefit of the conferee and a corresponding economic detriment of the corporation": para. 29.

15(1)(a)(iii): for the meaning of "winding-up, discontinuance or reorganization", see Notes to 84(2).

It may or may not be acceptable to recharacterize draws as salary, dividend, or loan repayment after year-end: see Notes to 169(1) under "If there is no rectification".

Double tax: If a corp pays personal expenses of (or transfers funds to) a shareholder, the expense may be denied to the corp and also be a 15(1) benefit, thus double tax: *Chopp*, [1995] 2 C.T.C. 2946 (TCC), para. 12 (aff'd by FCA without discussing this point); *Potvin*, 2008 TCC 319, paras. 38-40; *JDI 2000 Transport*, 2010 TCC 310, paras. 13-16; *Delso Restoration*, 2011 TCC 435; *Telepath Corp.*, 2012 TCC 423; *McLeod*, 2013 TCC 269; *Vicars*, 2013 TCC 329 (FCA appeal discontinued A-386-13); *Centrepoint Foods*, 2015 TCC 296, para. 10. However, a corp can deduct personal expenses of an *employee* as an employee benefit (see Notes to 9(1) under "Employee benefits"); one can argue that a benefit was conferred on a given shareholder *qua* employee. CRA has said "it is the department's policy not to tax the same amount twice" (1986 Cdn Tax Foundation conference report pp. 51:21-22 conf [q.39]; doc 2012-0440071E5), referring to two taxpayers. However, *Ascot Enterprises*, [1996] 1 C.T.C. 384 (FCA), para. 16, says tax in different persons' hands is not double tax to be avoided. In *Mikhail*, 2019 TCC 49, the Court avoided double tax by finding that rebate incentives paid to a pharmacy were earned only by the corp, not its shareholders (in *Quraishi*, 2019 TCC 272, such rebates were taxable to the shareholders). See also Notes to 248(28); Paul Grower, "Subsections 15(1) and 56(2) — The Risks of Double Taxation", 2012 Prairie Provinces Tax Conf. (ctf.ca), 10:1-34.

15(1) applies only if a benefit is conferred on the shareholder in that capacity: *Pillsbury Holdings*, [1964] C.T.C. 294 (Exch.), para. 22; *Struck*, 2017 TCC 94, para. 49. To determine whether a benefit is received *qua* shareholder or *qua* employee, see *Pellizzari*, [1987] 1 C.T.C. 2106 (TCC); *Del Grande*, [1993] 1 C.T.C. 2096 (TCC); *Hilderman*, 2020 TCC 58, paras. 84-87; VIEWS docs 2005-0115691E5, 2006-0204951I7: "a benefit will be considered to be received *qua* employee if it is reasonable to conclude that it has been provided as part of a reasonable remuneration package for the individual as an employee"; 2012-0465891E5 (a benefit not offered to other employees is presumed received as shareholder). If 6(1)(a) applies rather than 15(1), the employer can deduct the benefit, but may be liable for failing to withhold source deductions under 153(1). 15(1.4)(c) gives priority to 6(1)(a) over 15(1) and prevents double income inclusion: 2014-0538101C6 [2014 APFF q.1]. In *Kootenay Management*, 2019 TCC 97, assessments under 6(1)(a) were vacated: 6(1)(a) did not apply because the corp's payments to its sole shareholder were taxable only under 15(1)!

Penalties and criminal charges: A shareholder not reporting the benefit can incur 163(2) penalty (*JDI 2000 Transport*, above) and prosecution: *Alberta Hot Oil*, 2007 ABQB 155; *Goett*, 2010 ABQB 100; *Tyskerud*, 2013 BCPC 27, para. 231; *Gunner Industries*, 2015 SKQB 349 (SKCA denied leave to appeal; SCC denied leave 2019 CarswellSask 116); *Bekkerus*, 2018 ABPC 201; *Isaak*, 2020 BCSC 686; CRA news releases June 29/12 (Frederick Lewis conviction), Feb. 21/20 (Vincenzo Mariani and Mariani Metal Fabricators conviction — corp paid for M's son's wedding).

Shareholder loan account: An amount appropriated by shareholder S was not taxed under 15(1) where the company owed money to S: *Chopp*, [1998] 1 C.T.C. 407 (FCA) (tax should not be payable on the basis of incorrect financial statements); *Franklin*, 2002 FCA 38; *Mastracci*, 2006 TCC 594; *Hillier*, 2008 TCC 648; *Kotilainen*, 2017 TCC 7. See also *Long*, [1998] 1 C.T.C. 2995 (TCC); *Lee*, [1999] 3 C.T.C. 2204 (TCC). *Contra*, money taken could not be offset by unrelated shareholder loan balances in: *Donovan*, [1996] 1 C.T.C. 264 (FCA); *Burrows*, 2006 TCC 463; *Dumais*, 2008 FCA 174; *Nielsen Development*, 2009 TCC 160; *Hansen*, 2011 TCC 194; *Babich*, 2012 FCA 276, para. 14; *Post*, 2016 TCC 92, para. 28; *Bonhomme*, 2016 TCC 152, para. 16 (FCA appeal dismissed for delay A-321-16). A false increase in the shareholder loan account (with no withdrawal) does not confer a benefit until money is paid out to the shareholder: *Chaplin*, 2017 TCC 194, paras. 114-118 (see also 184(3) Notes re "carry on the books option"). In *Walker*, 2014 TCC 182, payments by Opco (O) to its Holdco (H)'s shareholder (S)'s RPP and RRSP fell under 15(1) despite S having outstanding loans to H and H to O, as there was no "current intention to reduce" the loans (para. 12). In *Vialink*, 2009 TCC 117, where the controlling shareholder did not keep proper records, withdrawals from the corp's bank account were taxed to him under 15(1) while deposits were ignored. In all of *Pereira*, 2009 TCC 388, *Rudolph*, 2009 TCC 452 and *De Couto*, 2013 TCC 198, amounts claimed to be shareholder loan repayments were taxable when the evidence did not prove the loans had existed; while in *Barkaoui*, 2011 TCC 207 (FCA appeal discontinued A-204-11), decrease of a loan to the shareholder in the corporate records was taxable to him. In both *Fahey*, 2010 TCC 407 and *Merchant*, 2010 TCC 467, where an individual owned two companies and one repaid his shareholder loan owing by the other, the Court found 15(1) did not apply.

Timing: in *Engelberg*, 2017 QCCQ 14819, the benefit was incurred in the year of sale of a condo for less than FMV to the shareholder, not the year the corp signed the agreement to sell it, as at that time it did not yet exist. Renovations (leasehold improvements) by a tenant corp to a building owned by a shareholder can be a benefit despite the lease still running, if the value of the reversionary interest can be quantified: *Kennedy*, [1973] C.T.C. 437 (FCA); *Melançon*, 2018 TCC 73; *Wise*, 2019 TCC 196.

Valuing a shareholder benefit: the Tax Court can determine the value from the available evidence, even if the Crown does not lead any: *Laliberté*, 2020 FCA 97, para. 56. The value may be calculated as a return on the amount the corporation paid (e.g., to construct a home the shareholder uses), rather than by fair market value (market rent on the home). See *Donovan*, [1996] 1 C.T.C. 264 (FCA); *Youngman*, [1990] 2 C.T.C. 10 (FCA); *Fingold*, [1997] 3 C.T.C. 441 (FCA); *Arpeg Holdings*, 2008 FCA 31; *Bonhomme*, 2016 TCC 152, paras. 60-82 (FCA appeal dismissed for delay A-321-16);

Melançon, 2018 TCC 73, para. 38; VIEWS docs 2008-0267401E5, 2010-0373251C6; 2014-0527842I7, 2018-0768851C6 [2018 APFF q.14] (use of company aircraft); 2015-0595541C6 [2015 APFF q.4] (return cannot necessarily use the Reg. 4301 prescribed rate). The taxable benefit is reduced by payments by the shareholder to the corporation specifically for using the home (*Donovan*); or by the annual value of a loan from the shareholder to build the home (*Youngman*); or by corporate expenses incurred by the shareholder (*Arpeg*). The value of a golf club membership was reduced where the shareholder spent 60% of his golfing time with the corporation's customers: *Gillis*, 2005 TCC 782. In *Jarjoura*, 2008 TCC 415, it was reasonable for a corp to maintain an executive home it owned at a high standard, and this was not a benefit to the shareholder living there. In *Pelletier*, 2011 FCA 21, the value of a shareholder's use of a cottage was reduced to reflect constant disturbance by tourists. In (a different) *Pelletier*, 2021 QCCQ 670, use of a corporate helicopter was valued based on its actual depreciated value, not its lower (tax) undepreciated capital cost. (See also Notes to 6(1)(a) under "Aircraft" and "Board and lodging".)

An expense paid by a subsidiary on behalf of a parent corporation creates a 15(1) benefit: VIEWS doc 2011-0401131I7 (even where a dividend to the parent would have been tax-free due to 112(1)).

A shareholder may also have a deemed interest inclusion under 80.4(2), which is deemed to be a 15(1) benefit by 15(9). An interest-free loan is not considered a benefit (VIEWS doc 2012-0464411I7), but may be included in income under 15(2).

Where X owned Xco which owned Yco, transfer by Xco of Yco shares to X for less than market value conferred a 15(1) benefit even though X was not accessing Yco's assets: *No. 513*, 1958 CarswellNat 98 (TAB); *Cléroux*, 2013 TCC 365 (and not realizing this was carelessness or neglect for 152(4)(a)(i)). See also *Bourgault* below.

Other cases where 15(1) applied: *Perrault*, [1978] C.T.C. 395 (FCA) (shareholder P caused corp to pay tax-free dividend to Cco to cover an amount P owed Cco); *Gravil*, 2010 FCA 239 (individual bought corp and used its shares to fund the purchase); *Tyskerud*, 2012 TCC 196 (corp paid off shareholder's personal line of credit); *Carrier*, 2013 TCC 203 (repayment of investment by corp was deposited by shareholder into his own account); *Struck*, 2017 TCC 94 (corp paid shareholder's mortgage); *Laliberté*, 2020 FCA 97 ($42 million cost of sending main Cirque du Soleil shareholder to International Space Station was 10% business promotion, 90% 15(1) benefit).

Other cases where 15(1) did not apply: *Colubriale*, 2005 FCA 329 (building rebuilt by shareholder after fire and sold to corp for more than CRA thought was FMV); *9100-2402 Québec Inc.*, 2006 TCC 302 (bookkeeping errors); *Gravil*, 2010 FCA 239; *House*, 2011 FCA 234 (company shut down with assets on its books, and Court believed shareholders that no assets ended up in their hands despite lack of documentation); *Murugesu*, 2013 TCC 21 (cash taken from company went to wages for owner, spouse and other workers); *Osinski*, 2013 TCC 71 (company had unreported revenues, but any funds taken from it had gone to the taxpayer's (now-divorced) spouse, not him); *Tremblay*, 2013 TCC 133 (corp must "do something" to confer benefit, so 6(1)(a) applied instead: para. 7); *Rogers Estate*, 2014 TCC 348, para. 52 (FCA appeal discontinued A-533-14) (payment on surrendering stock options to company); *Bourgault*, 2019 TCC 6 (B bought Qco from his corp Pco without payment; Qco payments to Pco were commissions, not payment of disguised purchase price on B's behalf).

Who is taxed: 15(1) did not apply to a non-shareholder, such as a related person: *Mullen*, [1990] 2 C.T.C. 2141 (TCC); *Ntakos Estate*, 2012 TCC 409; but now the shareholder may be taxed: 15(1.4)(c). When a company made a car available to its sole shareholder's spouse or parent, 15(1) applied to him rather than the spouse or parent: *Potvin*, 2008 TCC 319; *Babich*, 2012 FCA 276. Similarly, if a company makes a home available to its shareholder's parents, gives cash to a shareholder's relative, or pays the relative's university tuition, the shareholder is taxed under 15(1) and 56(2): VIEWS docs 2008-0264161E5, 2009-0315531E5, 2013-0502151E5. Where a benefit is conferred on the child of a shareholder of a corporate shareholder of the corp, see 2016-0666841E5. See also 246(1).

15(1) does not apply when a redemption of shares results in an 84(3) deemed dividend: *Gestion Léon Gagnon*, 2006 TCC 682; or on reduction of paid-up capital, due to 15(1)(a): VIEWS doc 2008-0297811R3.

For discussion of 15(1)(a.1) see Michael Colborne & Mark Barbour, "More Collateral Damage", XVII(4) *International Tax Planning* (Federated Press) 1209-10 (2012).

There is no tax on a "legitimate commercial transaction" with a shareholder: VIEWS doc 2005-0152801E5, and 15(1) applies only to payments "outside the ordinary course of business": *Bibby*, 2009 TCC 588, para. 20 (but 6(1) can apply to shareholders who are directors or employees). Where a corp sells property to a shareholder for less than fair market value (FMV — see Notes to 69(1)), there is a 15(1) benefit, and 69(1) and/or 69(4) applies to the corp. However, in *Boulet*, 2009 TCC 261, the FMV of property transferred by a corp to shareholders was reduced to the value set in a prior agreement they had reached to acquire the land.

Meals paid by a corporation, outside normal work hours where the shareholders had to return to work after the meal, were not a shareholder benefit in *McIntosh*, 2011 CarswellNat 5427 (TCC) (they were not provided to them *qua* shareholders, and the Crown did not allege they were employee benefits).

A cost-plus private health services plan, although allowed by Income Tax Folio S1-F1-C1 ¶1.133 (formerly IT-85R2) (see Notes to 6(1)(a) on Health and welfare trusts), may be a 15(1) benefit where it is purchased only for the shareholder: *Spicy Sports*, 2004 TCC 463; VIEWS doc 2005-0151161E5; but see *O'Flynn*, 2005 TCC 230, where amounts are received *qua* employee. See also 144.1 for employee life and health trusts, which are not allowed to prefer shareholders (144.1(2)(d), (e)).

Is an intercompany loan a benefit to the ultimate shareholder? *Béliveau*, [1991] 1 C.T.C. 2683 (TCC), says not; *Vine*, [1990] 1 C.T.C. 18 (FCTD) found a benefit, but the facts are unclear and it may not have been a loan. CRA says 15(1) can apply to an interest-free loan from a Canadian subsidiary to a foreign parent (see 80.4(2) and 15(9)): docs 2007-0243331C6, 2008-0280041R3; *contra*, see 2012-0464411I7. See also Truster, "The Trouble with Some Intercompany Loans", 13(1) *Tax for the Owner-Manager* (ctf.ca) 5-6 (Jan. 2013).

Amending a unanimous shareholder agreement is a legitimate corporate expense, not a benefit to the shareholders: *Truckbase Corp.*, [2006] 3 C.T.C. 2409 (TCC).

Where a single-purpose corporation is used to hold property (e.g. a Florida condominium) for the shareholder's personal use, 15(1) formerly did not apply if the corp did not report any profit or loss from the property (Revenue Canada Round Table, 1980 Cdn Tax Foundation conference report, p. 606, Q.20). The original reason for this relief, relating to US estate tax, was fixed by Canada-US tax treaty Art. XXIX-B. The policy no longer applies to acquisitions after 2004: *Income Tax Technical News* 31R2, 32. It applies to pre-existing arrangements until the disposition of the US real estate or of the corp's shares (other than transfer to spouse, spouse trust [VIEWS doc 2005-0136421E5] or common-law partner on the shareholder's death). No grandfathering is available on a transfer to a divorcing spouse (2010-0386871E5) or an *alter ego* trust (2011-0393401E5), or after a deemed disposition on emigration (2011-0426971E5). Transitional relief is provided if construction began before 2005. See also 2004-0106241E5, 2004-0086791C6, 2006-0185661C6 (conditions that must be satisfied), 2008-0285281C6 (corp whose only asset is helicopter, to limit shareholder's civil liability); 2010-0360001E5 (same, re an airplane); Goldberg, "Single-Purpose and Professional Corporations", 2004 Cdn Tax Foundation conference, 11:1-12; Stavropoulos & Jarman, "The Purchase of U.S. Vacation Property by Canadians", 1898 *Tax Topics* (CCH) 1-7 (July 24, 2008); Roberts, "Structuring Ownership of US Vacation Property", 2008 Prairie Provinces Tax Conference (ctf.ca), 7:1-30; Ideias, "U.S. Vacation Properties: What a Tax Planner Needs to Know" (*Taxnet Pro* Tax & Estate Planning Centre, 2020, 12pp). See also Notes to Canada-US treaty Art. XIII:1.

CRA will not apply 15(1) to a wrong price on a non-arm's length transaction if there is a price adjustment clause (PAC) with a *bona fide* intention to reach accurate fair market value: Income Tax Folio S4-F3-C1 ¶1.5. Notifying the CRA of the PAC (previously required by IT-169) is no longer required: VIEWS docs 9527537, 2013-0480291C6 [2013 STEP q.7]. For more on PACs see Notes to 69(1).

Where a yacht is jointly owned (and paid for) by shareholder and corporation, as long as personal use does not exceed the shareholder's percentage interest in the property there is no 15(1) benefit: VIEWS doc 2002-0143137.

Improving a shareholder's building that the corporation rents is a 15(1) benefit: IT-432R2 para. 10; VIEWS docs 2014-0528841E5; 2014-0522261E5 (where shareholder reimburses the cost).

A "dividend reinvestment plan" (DRIP) of a public corporation is technically taxable under 15(1), if the exception in 15(1)(c) does not apply because non-resident shareholders are excluded due to foreign securities laws. However, CRA's practice is not to assess a benefit, provided the amount paid for the additional shares is not less than 95% of their value: *Income Tax Technical News* 25.

In *Golini*, 2016 TCC 174 (FCA appeal discontinued A-349-16), an "RCA Optimizer Plan" was held to trigger 15(1): "immediate access to $6,000,000 tax-free, with only the obligation of a guarantee fee of $40,000 for 15 years, is a benefit ... Holdco is using its assets to pay his debt" (paras. 91, 97).

Payment of life insurance premiums on a shareholder's life by a corporation is not a 15(1) benefit if the corp is the policyholder and beneficiary: VIEWS docs 2004-0065461C5, 2004-0072971I7, 2006-0178561E5, 2007-0257251E5, 2011-0407291C6, 2011-0413281C6; but may be if two different corps are used: 2010-0359421C6, 2012-0435661C6. The same applies to an annuity contract: 2006-0180031I7. The existence of a cash surrender value in the policy is not a determining factor: 2007-0241951C6. Pledging the policy towards the shareholder's credit line is likely a benefit (or else GAAR might apply): 2006-0175401I7. Transferring a critical insurance policy to the shareholder for no consideration is a benefit: 2016-0651771C6 [2016 APFF q.1]. A shareholder benefit was included in *Reakes Enterprises*, 2006 TCC 295. See Kevin Wark, "Avoiding Benefit from Corporate-Owned Insurance", XII(3) *Insurance Planning [IP]* (Federated Press) 786-87 (2006). Where the shareholder owns the policy, premiums paid by the corp are a benefit but a policy loan to the shareholder is not: 2011-0416791E5. Where the premium is paid by a corp and the beneficiary is its parent corp, the CRA now says there is a 15(1) benefit, as of Jan. 2010 for new policies and Jan. 2011 for existing policies: 2009-0329911C6, 2009-0347291C6 (2009 CTF annual conference; *Income Tax Technical News* 44); Janet Newcombe, "Parentco Beneficiary of Subco Life Insurance Policy — CRA Reverses Position", 7(1) *Tax Hyperion* (Carswell, Jan. 2010); Kevin Wark, "The Canada Revenue Agency Announces New Assessing Position", XVI(2) *IP* 1002-04 and XIII(2) *Business Vehicles* (Federated Press) 686-88 (2010); Cheryl Scholten, "Corporately Held Life Insurance", 8(8) *Tax Hyperion* (Aug. 2011). For critical illness insurance provided to a shareholder see 2008-0278801C6 q.1 (2008 STEP). In *Lapalme*, 2011 TCC 396, a company bought life insurance on its shareholders and the insurance broker made "gifts" of $58,000 to the shareholders; these were taxable under 15(1). Payment of liability insurance for a director and shareholder may be a taxable benefit depending on the facts: 2010-0390171E5. See also Nathan Wright, "Using Life Insurance to Extract Corporate Funds Tax-Free", 2(3) *Canadian Tax Focus* (ctf.ca) 7-8 (Aug. 2012) (selling policy to corporation); Lindsay & Welch, "Taxable Benefits and Corporate-Owned Life Insurance", XXI(2) *IP* 1334-39 (2015).

As to whether rights are "identical" for 15(1), see IT-116R3, IT-432R2, IT-96R6 and VIEWS doc 2004-0093731E5.

A guarantee fee paid by a corporation to a shareholder is probably income under s. 9, not under 15(1): VIEWS doc 2005-0116281E5. A corporation's guarantee of a shareholder's loan may be a benefit: 2006-0174011C6. See also Notes to 247(2) re *General Electric* case.

15(1) can apply to: an employee who uses the loan to acquire shares and so becomes a shareholder (doc 2006-0172841E5); issuance of discretionary shares for less than their value (2002-0179095, 2010-0364131E5, 2012-0454181C6); use by shareholders of cottages on property owned by a non-profit corp (2011-0397881E5); members of a non-share-capital corp (2011-0415831E5; see Notes to 248(1)"shareholder"); payment by an LLC or Alberta ULC of Canadian shareholder's US tax imposed because these corps are transparent for US tax purposes (2011-0411491E5; May 2013 ICAA Roundtable q.22 (tinyurl.com/cra-abtax); condo corporation members to whom it distributed a capital gain (2014-0532691E5).

Non-resident (NR) shareholder: CRA will apply 15(1) to a NR corp that allows a NR shareholder to use property located in Canada, and due to 214(3)(a) this is a deemed dividend subject to 212(2) withholding tax: VIEWS doc 2006-0196241C6, 2012-0451241C6. CRA will not apply 15(1) and 214(3)(a) to reimbursement to a NR parent for the current value of stock options granted to Canco's employees (2009-0321721I7, 2010-0356401E5); or where Canco is sold by a NR corp to an affiliate for more than its value, and the excess did not come from Canco's funds (2011-040930II7). On applying 246(1) to an indirect benefit, see 2019-0798821C6 [2019 IFA q.7]. A group contribution payment from one foreign affiliate to another can be included in the recipient's income under 15(1), but is active business income for FAPI due to 95(2)(a)(ii)(B): 2010-0363361R3. Where 15(1) does not apply, 56(2) may still apply to trigger 214(3)(a).

15(1) can apply to a shareholder that is a corporation (e.g., it was considered in VIEWS docs 2016-0630761R3, 2017-0693751R3, 2017-0703821R3), but in practice is rare (the 15(1)(a)-(d) exceptions apply to most intercorporate transfers).

See also docs 2010-0369661R3 (no 15(1) on reorganization of incestuous shareholdings of Western Coal: Smit, "Recent Transactions of Interest", 2011 Cdn Tax Foundation conference report at 10:5-10); 2018-0775221R3 (no 15(1) on specific foreign investment with foreign government involvement).

See also s. 67 Notes on owner-manager remuneration; Haynes et al., *Taxation of Private Corporations* (ctf.ca, 5th ed., 2020), pp. 7:36-51; Heddema, "Section 15 Shareholder Benefits", 2004 British Columbia Tax Conference (ctf.ca), 12:1-32; Junkin, "Section 15", 2009 BC Tax Conf 12:1-18; Mitchell, "The Dark Path", 2012(5) *Tax Times* (Carswell) 1-3 (March 16, 2012); Brudner, "Shareholder Benefits... A Primer", *Taxnet Pro* Tax Disputes Centre (Sept. 2017, 7pp.). For software that assists in applying 15(1) see *Shareholder Benefits Classifier* at bluejlegal.com.

Note that if the corp has unpaid income tax (or GST) debts, the shareholder can be assessed under s. 160 (or *Excise Tax Act* s. 325) for 100% of the same transfer in addition to being taxed under 15(1): VIEWS docs 2010-0354691I7, 2010-035875II7. One can argue that there is no 15(1) inclusion because the value of the benefit, net of the s. 160 assessment, is nil: the TCC seemed receptive to this idea in *Budwal*, 2014 TCC 370, footnote 2 to para. 9. See also Erica Hennessey, "Another Reason to Avoid Shareholder Benefits", 6(1) *Canadian Tax Focus* (ctf.ca) 3-4 (Feb. 2016).

15(1) amended by 2002-2013 technical bill, for benefits conferred after Oct. 30, 2011. The changes include new 15(1)(a.1); references to "contemplated shareholder"; rules addressing partnerships; and narrowing the 15(1)(a) exception to respond to *Morasse* (see Notes to 86.1). Earlier amended by 1993, 1992 and 1991 technical bills.

Income Tax Folios: S2-F1-C1: Health and welfare trusts [replaces IT-85R2]; S3-F9-C1: Lottery winnings, miscellaneous receipts, and income (and losses) from crime [replaces IT-185R, IT-213R, IT-256R, IT-334R2]; S4-F3-C1: Price adjustment clauses [replaces IT-169].

Interpretation Bulletins: IT-63R5: Benefits, including standby charge for an automobile, from the personal use of a motor vehicle supplied by an employer; IT-96R6: Options to acquire shares, bonds or debentures and by trusts to acquire trust units; IT-116R3: Rights to buy additional shares; IT-119R4: Debts of shareholders and certain persons connected with shareholders; IT-160R3: Personal use of aircraft (cancelled); IT-291R3: Transfer of property to a corporation under subsection 85(1); IT-335R2: Indirect payments; IT-357R2: Expenses of training; IT-421R2: Benefits to individuals, corporations and shareholders from loans or debt; IT-432R2: Benefits conferred on shareholders; IT-498: The deductibility of interest on money borrowed to reloan to employees or shareholders (cancelled); IT-529: Flexible employee benefit programs.

Information Circulars: 76-19R3: Transfer of property to a corporation under s. 85; 87-2R: International transfer pricing (archived).

I.T. Technical News: 25 (dividend reinvestment plans); 31R2 (single-purpose corporations); 32 (new administrative policy on single-purpose corporations); 44 (corporate-held life insurance).

Transfer Pricing Memoranda: TPM-03: Downward transfer pricing adjustments under subsec. 247(2).

CRA Audit Manual: 24.11.0: Indirect payments and benefits; 27.10.0: Employee and shareholder benefits.

Advance Tax Rulings: ATR-9: Transfer of personal residence from corporation to its controlling shareholder; ATR-14: Non-arm's length interest charges; ATR-15: Employee stock option plan; ATR-22R: Estate freeze using share exchange; ATR-27: Ex-change and acquisition of interests in capital; ATR-29: Amalgamation of social clubs; ATR-35: Partitioning of assets to get specific ownership — "butterfly"; ATR-36: Estate freeze.

Forms: T2 Sched. 11: Transactions with shareholders, officers, or employees.

(1.1) Conferring of benefit — Notwithstanding subsection (1), if in a taxation year a corporation has paid a stock dividend to a person and it may reasonably be considered that one of the purposes of that payment was to significantly alter the value of the interest of any specified shareholder of the corporation, the fair market value of the stock dividend shall, except to the extent that it is otherwise included in computing that person's income under any of paragraphs 82(1)(a), (a.1) and (c) to (e), be included in computing the income of that person for the year.

Related Provisions: 52(3) — Cost of stock dividend.

Notes: In interpreting "it may reasonably be considered" in 15(1.1), the taxpayer has the onus of proving, with "objectively reasonable" evidence, that none of the purposes of the stock dividend was to alter the value of a shareholder's interest: *Wu*, [1998] 1 C.T.C. 99 (FCA).

15(1.1) can apply where a foreign corp pays a stock dividend to another foreign corp: VIEWS doc 2013-0507981C6 [2013 CTF]. For an estate freeze where it would likely not apply see 2014-0538041C6 [2014 APFF q.19].

15(1.1) amended to add reference to 82(1)(a.1) and (c)-(e) by 2006 budget bill #2 (Part 2 — eligible dividends), effective for dividends paid after 2005.

Interpretation Bulletins: IT-88R2: Stock dividends; IT-432R2: Benefits conferred on shareholders.

(1.2) Forgiveness of shareholder debt — For the purpose of subsection (1), the value of the benefit where an obligation issued by a debtor is settled or extinguished at any time shall be deemed to be the forgiven amount at that time in respect of the obligation.

Related Provisions: 6(15) — Forgiveness of employee loans; 15(1.21) — Meaning of "forgiven amount"; 79(3)F(b)(i) — Where property surrendered to creditor; 80(1)"forgiven amount"B(b) — Debt forgiveness rules do not apply to amount of benefit; 80.01 — Deemed settlement of debts.

Notes: For the meaning of "extinguished", see Notes to 80(2)(a).

15(1.2) was applied in *Gilbert*, 2009 TCC 328.

15(1.2) amended by 1994 technical bill.

Interpretation Bulletins: IT-119R4: Debts of shareholders and certain persons connected with shareholders; IT-421R2: Benefits to individuals, corporations and shareholders from loans or debt; IT-432R2: Benefits conferred on shareholders.

(1.21) Forgiven amount — For the purpose of subsection (1.2), the "forgiven amount" at any time in respect of an obligation issued by a debtor has the meaning that would be assigned by subsection 80(1) if

(a) the obligation were a commercial obligation (within the meaning assigned by subsection 80(1)) issued by the debtor;

(b) no amount included in computing income (otherwise than because of paragraph 6(1)(a)) because of the obligation being settled or extinguished were taken into account;

(c) the definition "forgiven amount" in subsection 80(1) were read without reference to paragraphs (f) and (h) of the description B in that definition; and

(d) section 80 were read without reference to paragraphs (2)(b) and (q) of that section.

Related Provisions: 80.01(1)"forgiven amount" — Application of definition for purposes of s. 80.01; 248(26) — Liability deemed to be obligation issued by debtor; 248(27) — Partial settlement of debt obligation.

Notes: 15(1.21) added by 1994 technical bill.

Forms: T2 Sched. 11: Transactions with shareholders, officers, or employees.

(1.3) Cost of property or service — To the extent that the cost to a person of purchasing a property or service or an amount payable by a person for the purpose of leasing property is taken into account in determining an amount required under this section to be included in computing a taxpayer's income for a taxation year, that cost or amount payable, as the case may be, shall include any tax that was payable by the person in respect of the property or service or that would have been so payable if the person were not exempt from the payment of that tax because of the nature of the person or the use to which the property or service is to be put.

Notes: Before 1996, 15(1.4) required inclusion of a benefit of 7% to account for GST. The actual GST paid on the goods or services was not included in the calculation of the benefit due to former 15(1.3). This rule has been reversed, and the GST is specifically included in the benefit.

15(1.3) amended by 1997 GST/HST bill, effective for 1996 and later taxation years. Added by 1990 GST, effective for benefits conferred after 1990.

Interpretation Bulletins: IT-63R5: Benefits, including standby charge for an automobile, from the personal use of a motor vehicle supplied by an employer; IT-432R2: Benefits conferred on shareholders.

Forms: T2 Sched. 11: Transactions with shareholders, officers, or employees.

(1.4) Interpretation — subsec. (1) — For the purposes of this subsection and subsection (1),

(a) a contemplated shareholder of a corporation is

(i) a person or partnership on whom a benefit is conferred by the corporation in contemplation of the person or partnership becoming a shareholder of the corporation, or

(ii) a member of a partnership on whom a benefit is conferred by the corporation in contemplation of the partnership becoming a shareholder of the corporation;

(b) a person or partnership that is (or is deemed by this paragraph to be) a member of a particular partnership that is a member of another partnership is deemed to be a member of the other partnership;

(c) a benefit conferred by a corporation on an individual is a benefit conferred on a shareholder of the corporation, a member of a partnership that is a shareholder of the corporation or a contemplated shareholder of the corporation — except to the extent that the amount or value of the benefit is included in computing the income of the individual or any other person — if the individual is an individual, other than an excluded trust in respect of the corporation, who does not deal at arm's length with, or is affiliated with, the shareholder, member of the partnership or contemplated shareholder, as the case may be; and

(d) for the purposes of paragraph (c), an excluded trust in respect of a corporation is a trust in which no individual (other than an excluded trust in respect of the corporation) who does not deal at arm's length with, or is affiliated with, a shareholder of the corporation, a member of a partnership that is a shareholder of the corporation or a contemplated shareholder of the corporation, is beneficially interested.

(e) [Repealed]

Notes: See Notes to 15(1). For criticism of 15(1.4) as inadvertently taxing a benefit received *qua* employee and requiring inclusion in multiple taxpayers' income, see CBA/CICA Joint Committee letter to Finance, Dec. 1, 2011. 15(1.4)(c) and (d) were changed from the Oct. 31/11 draft to introduce the term "excluded trust", and 15(1.4)(e) was new as of Oct. 24/12, but the above concerns were not addressed.

Before Oct. 31, 2011, 15(1) did not apply where a corp paid its sole shareholder's father's mortgage: *Struck*, 2017 TCC 94, paras. 47-53. See also 15(1) Notes at "Who is taxed".

15(1.4)(c) prevents double tax (6(1)(a) and 15(1)) of a benefit: VIEWS doc 2014-0538101C6 [2014 APFF q.1]. If a corp owned by 4 brothers confers a benefit on brother X's wife, the CRA will tax only X, not all 4: 2015-0575911E5.

For interpretation of para. (e) see VIEWS doc 2013-0483741C6 [2013 IFA q.2].

15(1.4)(e) repealed by 2018 budget bill #2, effective Oct. 24, 2012. The rule it provided was expanded and moved to 15(1.5).

15(1.4) added by 2002-2013 technical bill, for benefits conferred after Oct. 30, 2011, but para. (e) for divisions of non-resident corps after Oct. 23, 2012.

Former 15(1.4) repealed by 1997 GST/HST bill for 1996 and later tax years. See Notes to 15(1.3). Former 15(1.4) earlier amended by 1993 and 1992 technical bills; added by 1990 GST.

(1.5) Division of corporation under foreign laws — If a non-resident corporation (in this subsection referred to as the "original corporation") governed by the laws of a foreign jurisdiction undergoes a division under those laws that results in all or part of its property and liabilities becoming the property and liabilities of one or more other non-resident corporations (each of which is referred to in this subsection as a "new corporation") and, as a consequence of the division, a shareholder of the original corporation acquires one or more shares (referred to in this subsection as "new shares")

of the capital stock of a new corporation at a particular time, the following rules apply:

(a) except to the extent that any of subparagraphs (1)(a.1)(i) to (iii) and paragraph (1)(b) applies (determined without reference to this subsection) to the acquisition of the new shares

(i) in the case where, for each class of shares of the capital stock of the original corporation of which shares are held by the shareholder immediately before the division, new shares are received at the particular time by shareholders of that class on a pro rata basis in respect of all the shares (referred to in this subsection as the "original shares") of that class

(A) at the particular time, the original corporation is deemed to have distributed, and the shareholder is deemed to have received, as a dividend in kind in respect of the original shares, the new shares acquired by the shareholder at the particular time, and

(B) the amount of the dividend in kind received by the shareholder in respect of an original share is deemed to be equal to the fair market value, immediately after the particular time, of the new shares acquired by the shareholder at the particular time in respect of the original share, and

(ii) in any case where subparagraph (i) does not apply, the original corporation is deemed, at the particular time, to have conferred a benefit on the shareholder equal to the total fair market value, at that time, of the new shares acquired by the shareholder as a consequence of the division;

(b) any gain or loss of the original corporation from a distribution of the new shares as a consequence of the division is deemed to be nil; and

(c) each property of the original corporation that becomes at any time (referred to in this paragraph as the "disposition time") property of the new corporation as a consequence of the division is deemed to be

(i) disposed of by the original corporation immediately before the disposition time for proceeds of disposition equal to the property's fair market value, and

(ii) acquired by the new corporation at the disposition time at a cost equal to the amount determined under subparagraph (i) to be the original corporation's proceeds of disposition.

Related Provisions: Reg. 5907(1)"designated person or partnership"(c), 5907(2.011) — Application of FAPI to 15(1.5) division.

Notes: 15(1.5) addresses a Mexico *escisión*: see Notes at end of 86.1.

15(1.5) added by 2018 budget bill #2, for divisions after Oct. 23, 2012. This was proposed as an amendment to 15(1.4)(e) before the July 27, 2018 draft.

(2) Shareholder debt — Where a person (other than a corporation resident in Canada) or a partnership (other than a partnership each member of which is a corporation resident in Canada) is

(a) a shareholder of a particular corporation,

(b) connected with a shareholder of a particular corporation, or

(c) a member of a partnership, or a beneficiary of a trust, that is a shareholder of a particular corporation

and the person or partnership has in a taxation year received a loan from or become indebted to (otherwise than by way of a pertinent loan or indebtedness) the particular corporation, any other corporation related to the particular corporation or a partnership of which the particular corporation or a corporation related to the particular corporation is a member, the amount of the loan or indebtedness is included in computing the income for the year of the person or partnership.

Proposed Amendment — 15(2)

Letter from Dept. of Finance, May 2, 2013: Mr. Drew Morier, Osler, Hoskin & Harcourt LLP, Toronto, ON

Dear Mr. Morier:

Thank you for your letter dated April 24, 2013 regarding [xxx] the application of subsection 15(2) of the *Income Tax Act*. In particular, you are concerned that subsection

15(2) may apply inappropriately to certain loans to a partnership that is held, directly or indirectly, solely by corporations resident in Canada.

We are prepared to recommend legislative amendments to clarify that subsection 15(2) does not apply to loans received by the partnership in the specific circumstances described in your letter. We would also recommend that this amendment apply concurrently with the application of the amendment to subsection 15(2.1), as proposed in Bill C-48, which is currently before Parliament.

While I cannot offer any assurance that the legislative amendments that we intend to recommend will be adopted, I trust that this statement of our intention is helpful to you.

Yours sincerely,

Brian Ernewein, General Director–Legislation, Tax Policy Branch

Notes: Finance has confirmed (Nov. 13/18) that this amendment is still pending.

Related Provisions: 15(2.1) — Meaning of "connected"; 15(2.11), 17.1 — Exclusion for "pertinent loan or indebtedness"; 15(2.16)–(2.192) — Back-to-back loans; 15(2.2)–(2.6) — Exceptions to 15(2); 15(7) — Application of subsec. 15(2); 20(1)(j) — Repayment of loan by shareholder; 80(1)"excluded obligation"(a)(i) — Debt forgiveness rules do not apply where amount included in debtor's income; 80.4(2), (3) — Deemed interest; 90(6)–(15) — Loan from foreign affiliate included in income; 120.4(1)"split income"(a)(ii), (c)(ii)(B) — Application of income-splitting tax; 139(a) — Mutualization of insurance corporations; 214(3)(a) — Deemed dividend for withholding tax where shareholder is non-resident; 227(6.1) — Repayment of non-resident shareholder loan.

Notes: A loan to a (non-corporate) shareholder is fully included in income (unless one of the exceptions in 15(2.2)-(2.6) applies), though an offsetting deduction is allowed by 20(1)(j) on repayment. If 15(2) applies, there is no annual deemed interest inclusion: 80.4(3). A 15(2) assessment is better for the taxpayer than 15(1) because of the 20(1)(j) deduction if the amount is repaid: *Lust*, 2007 FCA 62. See also VIEWS doc 2010-0375621E5.

For a corporate shareholder (or related person), if the loan is from a foreign affiliate, it may be included in income by 90(6).

For a non-resident shareholder, 214(3)(a) deems the amount included by 15(2) to be a dividend, so the corporation must remit non-resident withholding tax under 212(2): VIEWS doc 9203335. If the loan is repaid, see 227(6.1). For more on 15(2) in an international context, see VIEWS docs 2010-0353141R3, 2010-0377581R3, 2010-0391551R3 and 2011-0418711R3 (all related foreign entity financing); 2010-0376391R3 (15(2) does not apply to loans between non-residents); 2015-0595621C6 [2015 APFF q.19] (cash pooling in multinational group); Tremblay & Wilkie, "The Canadian Triangle", 2002 Cdn Tax Foundation conference report at 18:1-17; Heakes, "CRA Issues Favourable Outbound Financing Ruling", XV(4) *International Tax Planning* (Federated Press) 1801-83 (2010); Van Loan, "CRA Rules Positively on a Second Tier Financing", XVI(4) *Corporate Finance* (Federated Press) 1896-98 (2010).

In *Attis*, [1992] 1 C.T.C. 2244, and *Nigel Hill [Uphill Holdings]*, [1993] 1 C.T.C. 2021, the Tax Court ruled that where a shareholder took advances during the year but cleared out the shareholder loan account with dividends and bonuses after year-end, 15(2) did not apply (this was not a "series of loans and repayments" (see 15(2.6)) because the income was taxed to the shareholder): IT-119R4 para. 29, VIEWS docs 2003-001670, 2007-0241041R3; but see also docs 2008-0267271E5, 2012-0443581E5 (temporary repayment may be evidence of a series of loans and repayments). 15(2) applied to corporate loans to shareholders in *Sandia Mountain*, 2006 TCC 348; *Gilbert*, 2009 TCC 328; *Bibby*, 2009 TCC 588; *Struck*, 2017 TCC 94; *Mazzafero*, 2019 TCC 147 (loan to shareholder's sister).

Transferring personal-use assets to a corporation to reduce the indebtedness under 15(2) is fraught with various dangers, as discussed in *VanNieuwkerk*, 2003 TCC 670.

15(2) cannot apply to assess an opening balance in the year's shareholder loan account even if the earlier year when the balance arose is statute-barred: VIEWS doc 2006-0215161I7.

On whether 15(2) applies when a corporation makes a loan to a partnership of which the controlling shareholder is a partner, see Truster, "Secrets of Subsection 15(2)", 1(3) *Tax for the Owner-Manager* (ctf.ca) 15-16 (July 2001). 15(2) can apply to an employee who uses the loan to acquire shares and so becomes a shareholder: doc 2006-0172841E5.

In *Erb*, [2000] 1 C.T.C. 2597 (TCC), a deficit in a partner's capital account was held not to be "indebtedness" to other partners (which included a corporation controlled by the partner); thus there was no indebtedness to the corporation and 15(2) did not apply.

In *St-Pierre*, 2018 FCA 144, a capital dividend was overpaid due to miscalculation of the capital dividend account; after the Quebec Superior Court nullified the dividend, the TCC held the cash paid to S was taxed under 15(2), but the FCA overruled this as there was no "unjust enrichment", since S was required to repay the corp.

15(2) can possibly be used for one-time advance income averaging by shareholders or family members with low income in early years and high income later (e.g., students), by taking a loan from a corp when the individual wants to recognize income, and paying it back in a later year for a 20(1)(j) deduction; however, see 80.4 and TOSI in 120.4. See *Hevey*, 2005 TCC 76 (FCA appeal discontinued A-76-05). See Notes to 110.2 and 146(16) for other averaging methods.

See also Haynes et al., *Taxation of Private Corporations* (ctf.ca, 5th ed., 2020), pp. 7:51-67; Morphy, "The Modern Approach to Statutory Interpretation, Applied to the Section 15 Anomaly in Foreign Affiliate Financing", 61(2) *Canadian Tax Journal* 367-

85 (2013); Bunn & Dumalski, "Subsection 15(2) and Partnerships in the Foreign Affiliate Context", 69(1) *Canadian Tax Journal* 253-77 (2021) (suggests 15(2) does not apply as broadly as its wording appears to).

15(2) closing words amended by 2012 budget bill #2, for loans received and indebtedness incurred after March 28, 2012, to add "(otherwise than by way of a pertinent loan or indebtedness)" (see 15(2.11)).

15(2) amended by 1995-97 technical bill, for loans made and indebtedness arising in 1990 and later taxation years. The exceptions in former 15(2)(a) and (b) were expanded and moved to new 15(2.2)-(2.7). A loan to an employee who is also a shareholder was caught by former 15(2), even if it was made to the employee *qua* employee. This is no longer the case due to 15(2.4)(e).

15(2) earlier amended by 1991 technical bill, effective 1985.

Interpretation Bulletins: IT-119R4: Debts of shareholders and certain persons connected with shareholders; IT-421R2: Benefits to individuals, corporations and shareholders from loans or debt; IT-503: Exploration and development shares (cancelled).

Transfer Pricing Memoranda: TPM-02: Repatriation of funds by non-residents — Part XIII assessments.

CRA Audit Manual: 24.12.0: Shareholder debt.

Forms: T2 Sched. 11: Transactions with shareholders, officers, or employees.

(2.1) Meaning of connected

(2.1) Meaning of connected — For the purposes of subsection (2), a person or partnership is connected with a shareholder of a particular corporation if that person or partnership does not deal at arm's length with, or is affiliated with, the shareholder, unless, in the case of a person, that person is

(a) a foreign affiliate of the particular corporation; or

(b) a foreign affiliate of a person resident in Canada with which the particular corporation does not deal at arm's length.

Notes: CRA might apply GAAR or 95(6)(b) to an international transaction that bypasses 15(2.1): VIEWS doc 2004-0064811E5.

Even before the 2013 amendment, CRA's view (docs 9610685, 2004-0088411C6, 2011-039792117) was that a partnership can be a person "connected" for purposes of 15(2), despite *Gillette Canada*, [2001] 4 C.T.C. 2884 (TCC) (aff'd on other grounds 2003 FCA 22, refusing to decide this issue). For criticism of the 2013 amendment as overly broad, see TEI submission to Finance, Dec. 5, 2012, p. 9.

15(2.1) opening words amended by 2002-2013 technical bill, for loans made and indebtedness arising after Oct. 2011. Before the amendment, read:

(2.1) Persons connected with a shareholder — For the purposes of subsection (2), a person is connected with a shareholder of a particular corporation if that person does not deal at arm's length with the shareholder and if that person is a person other than

Interpretation Bulletins: IT-119R4: Debts of shareholders and certain persons connected with shareholders.

(2.11) Pertinent loan or indebtedness

(2.11) Pertinent loan or indebtedness — For the purposes of subsection (2) and subject to subsection 17.1(3), "pertinent loan or indebtedness" means a loan received, or an indebtedness incurred, at any time, by a non-resident corporation (in this subsection referred to as the "subject corporation"), or by a partnership of which the subject corporation is, at that time, a member, that is an amount owing to a corporation resident in Canada (in this subsection and subsections (2.12) and (2.14) referred to as the "CRIC") or to a qualifying Canadian partnership in respect of the CRIC and in respect of which amount owing all of the following apply:

(a) subsection (2) would, in the absence of this subsection, apply to the amount owing;

(b) the amount becomes owing after March 28, 2012;

(c) at that time, the CRIC is controlled by a non-resident corporation that

(i) is the subject corporation, or

(ii) does not deal at arm's length with the subject corporation; and

(d) either

(i) in the case of an amount owing to the CRIC, the CRIC and a non-resident corporation that controls the CRIC jointly elect in writing under this subparagraph in respect of the amount owing and file the election with the Minister on or before the filing-due date of the CRIC for the taxation year that includes that time, or

(ii) in the case of an amount owing to the qualifying Canadian partnership, all the members of the qualifying Canadian partnership and a non-resident corporation that controls the CRIC jointly elect in writing under this subparagraph in respect of the amount owing and file the election with the Minister on or before the filing-due date of the CRIC for its taxation year in which ends the fiscal period of the qualifying Canadian partnership that includes that time.

Related Provisions: 15(2.12)–(2.13) — Late-filed election under (2.11)(d); 15(2.14)(a) — Meaning of "qualifying Canadian partnership"; 15(2.14)(b) — Look-through rule for partnerships; 15(2.15) — Effect of amalgamation or windup; 17.1(1) — Deemed interest income on PLOI; 17.1(3) — PLOI not PLOI where treaty applies; 212.3(11) — Definition of PLOI for foreign-affiliate-dumping rules.

Notes: By making a 15(2.11)(d) election, instead of a one-time deemed dividend and withholding tax via 15(2) > 214(3) > 212(2), interest imputation applies *annually* under 17.1. See Liang, "Outbound Loans", 20(9) *Canadian Tax Highlights [CTH]* (ctf.ca) 6-7 (Sept. 2012); Perron, "Subsection 15(2) Election", 2(4) *Canadian Tax Focus* (ctf.ca) 2-3 (Nov. 2012); Ko, "Pertinent Loan and Indebtedness", XXI(1) *Corporate Finance* (Federated Press) 17-22 (2018); Katlai, "Simple Planning Around Outbound Loans Using Tax Incentives", 27(12) *CTH* 8-9 (Dec. 2019).

For a corporation or partnership filing a Quebec return, a 15(2.11)(d)(i) or (ii) election must be copied to Revenu Québec: *Taxation Act* ss. 113.1, 21.4.6.

For CRA interpretation see VIEWS docs 2013-0482991E5 (effect of replacement or novation of the debt); 2013-0506551E5 (transitioning from 15(2) to a PLOI); 2014-053454117 (one document can make multiple elections; partners, not partnership, file the election).

15(2.11) added by 2012 budget bill #2, for loans received and indebtedness incurred after March 28, 2012.

(2.12) Late-filed elections

(2.12) Late-filed elections — Where an election referred to in paragraph (2.11)(d) was not made on or before the day on or before which the election was required by that paragraph to be made, the election is deemed to have been made on that day if the election is made on or before the day that is three years after that day and the penalty in respect of the election is paid by the CRIC when the election is made.

Related Provisions: 15(2.13) — Penalty for late-filed election.

Notes: For CRA interpretation see VIEWS docs 2014-0519431E5 (no amended return required; calculation of arrears interest; application of withholding tax when election not yet filed); 2014-0542061E5 (late election).

15(2.12) added by 2012 budget bill #2, for loans received and indebtedness incurred after March 28, 2012.

(2.13) Penalty for late-filed election

(2.13) Penalty for late-filed election — For the purposes of subsection (2.12), the penalty in respect of an election referred to in that subsection is the amount equal to the product obtained by multiplying $100 by the number of months each of which is a month all or part of which is during the period commencing with the day on or before which the election is required by paragraph (2.11)(d) to be made and ending on the day the election is made.

Notes: On calculating the penalty when there are multiple "amounts" owing from different transactions, see VIEWS doc 2016-0642031C6 [2016 IFA q.11].

15(2.13) added by 2012 budget bill #2, for loans received and indebtedness incurred after March 28, 2012.

(2.14) Partnerships

(2.14) Partnerships — For the purposes of this subsection, subsection (2.11) and section 17.1 and subsection 18(5),

(a) a **"qualifying Canadian partnership"**, at any time in respect of a CRIC, means a partnership each member of which is, at that time, the CRIC or another corporation resident in Canada to which the CRIC is, at that time, related; and

(b) a person or partnership that is (or is deemed by this paragraph to be) a member of a particular partnership that is a member of another partnership is deemed to be a member of the other partnership.

Related Provisions: 15(2.15) — Effect of amalgamation or windup.

Notes: Opening words amended to refer to 18(5) by 2014 budget bill #2, effective for taxation years that end after March 28, 2012, except that, if taxpayer elects under subsec. 49(3) of 2012 budget bill #2 [see Notes at end of 212.3], it does not apply to the taxpayer's taxation years that ended before Aug. 14, 2012.

15(2.14) added by 2012 budget bill #2, for loans received and indebtedness incurred after March 28, 2012.

(2.15) Mergers

(2.15) Mergers — For the purposes of subsections (2.11) and (2.14),

(a) if there has been an amalgamation to which subsection 87(1) applies, the new corporation referred to in that subsection is deemed to be the same corporation as, and a continuation of, each predecessor corporation referred to in that subsection; and

(b) if there has been a winding-up to which subsection 88(1) applies, the parent referred to in that subsection is deemed to be the same corporation as, and a continuation of, the subsidiary referred to in that subsection.

Notes: 15(2.15) added by 2012 budget bill #2, effective for amalgamations that occur, and windups that begin, after March 28, 2012.

(2.16) Back-to-back arrangement — application [of 15(2.17)]

(2.16) Back-to-back arrangement — application [of 15(2.17)] — Subsection (2.17) applies at any time if

(a) at that time, a person or partnership (referred to in this subsection and subsections (2.17) to (2.192) as the "intended borrower") has an amount outstanding as or on account of a debt or other obligation to pay an amount (in this subsection and subsections (2.17) to (2.192) referred to as the "shareholder debt") to a person or partnership (in this subsection and subsections (2.17) to (2.192) referred to as the "immediate funder");

(b) subsection (2) would not, in the absence of this subsection and subsection (2.17), apply to the shareholder debt;

(c) at that time, a funder, in respect of a particular funding arrangement,

(i) has an amount outstanding as or on account of a debt or other obligation to pay an amount (other than a debt or other obligation to pay an amount to which subsection (2) applies or would apply if it were not a "pertinent loan or indebtedness", as defined in subsection (2.11)) to a person or partnership that meets either of the following conditions:

(A) recourse in respect of the debt or other obligation is limited in whole or in part, either immediately or in the future and either absolutely or contingently, to a funding arrangement, or

(B) it can reasonably be concluded that all or a portion of the particular funding arrangement was entered into or was permitted to remain outstanding because

(I) all or a portion of the debt or other obligation was entered into or was permitted to remain outstanding, or

(II) the funder anticipated that all or a portion of the debt or other obligation would become owing or remain outstanding, or

(ii) has a specified right in respect of a particular property that was granted directly or indirectly by a person or partnership and

(A) the existence of the specified right is required under the terms and conditions of the particular funding arrangement, or

(B) it can reasonably be concluded that all or a portion of the particular funding arrangement was entered into, or was permitted to remain in effect, because

(I) the specified right was granted, or

(II) the funder anticipated that the specified right would be granted; and

(d) at that time, one or more funders is an ultimate funder.

Related Provisions: 15(2.192) — Definitions.

Notes: 15(2.16)-(2.192) provide "back-to-back" loan rules, modelled on those in 212(3.1)-(3.81). These rules are intended to ensure that 15(2) and 80.4(2) are not avoided where a corporation, rather than providing a loan directly to its shareholder, or to a connected person or partnership, provides debt funding indirectly through one or more intermediaries. The rules apply, for example, where Xco lends funds to arm's length person Y on condition that Y make a loan to shareholder X of Xco (i.e., a "back-to-back loan" arrangement).

Where they apply, the rules generally deem Xco to make a loan to X (or to a connected person or partnership) for purposes of 15 and 80.4, in an amount equal to the funding indirectly provided by Xco to X. The rules also include "deemed repayment" rules, which generally deem repayment on a loan previously deemed made under these rules to occur when the funding indirectly provided by Xco to X is reduced.

15(2.16) sets out the conditions for the application of the operative "deemed loan" rule in 15(2.17). 15(2.18) sets out the conditions for the application of the rule for deemed repayments in 15(2.19). 15(2.191) provides a separate rule for deemed repayments in certain special circumstances. 15(2.192) contains definitions.

See Dept. of Finance Technical Notes for much more detail and examples.

These rules may catch some "cash pooling" arrangements: 2016(44) *EY Tax Alert — Canada* (Oct. 4, 2016). See also Amanda Doucette & Britney Wangler, "Normal Borrowing by CCPC Owners Can Create an Income Inclusion", 7(1) *Canadian Tax Focus* (ctf.ca) 1-2 (Feb. 2017).

For the meaning of "indirectly" in (c)(ii), see Notes to 17.1(1).

For CRA interpretation see VIEWS docs 2017-0690691E5 (15(2.17) applies where term deposit pledged by family corp to secure shareholder's business loan); 2017-0703901C6 [2017 CPA Alberta q.11] (OK for corp to provide "typical commercial security" for bank loan to shareholder); 2018-0745491C6 [2018 CALU q.1] (interpretation of (c)(i)).

See also Boland and Montes, "A Detailed Review of the Back-to-Back Loan Rules", 2016 Cdn Tax Foundation conference report, at 26:23-27.

15(2.16)-(2.192) added by 2016 budget bill #2, effective in respect of

(a) if the immediate funder in respect of a shareholder debt is a debtor, or holder of a specified right, under a funding arrangement under which an ultimate funder is the creditor or the grantor of the specified right,

(i) loans received and indebtedness incurred in respect of the shareholder debt after March 21, 2016, and

(ii) any portion of a particular loan received or indebtedness incurred in respect of the shareholder debt before March 22, 2016 that remains outstanding on that day, as if that portion were a separate loan or indebtedness that was received or incurred, as the case may be, on March 22, 2016 in the same manner and on the same terms as the particular loan or indebtedness; and

(b) in any other case [i.e., where there are multiple intermediaries],

(i) loans received and indebtedness incurred after 2016, and

(ii) any portion of a particular loan received or indebtedness incurred before Jan. 1, 2017 that remains outstanding on that day, as if that portion were a separate loan or indebtedness that was received or incurred, as the case may be, on Jan. 1, 2017 in the same manner and on the same terms as the particular loan or indebtedness.

(2.17)   Back-to-back   arrangement — consequences [deemed loan] — If this subsection applies at a particular time, then for the purposes of this section and section 80.4, the intended borrower is deemed to receive a loan from each particular ultimate funder at the particular time, the amount of which is equal to the amount determined by the formula

$$A \times B/C - (D - E)$$

where

A is the lesser of

(a) the amount outstanding as or on account of the shareholder debt at the particular time, and

(b) the total of all amounts, each of which is, at the particular time,

(i) an amount outstanding as or on account of a debt or other obligation that is owed by a funder (other than an ultimate funder) to an ultimate funder under a funding arrangement in respect of the shareholder debt, or

(ii) the fair market value of a particular property in respect of which an ultimate funder has granted a specified right to a funder (other than an ultimate funder) under a funding arrangement in respect of the shareholder debt;

B is the total of all amounts, each of which is, at the particular time,

(a) an amount outstanding as or on account of a debt or other obligation that is owed by a funder (other than an ultimate funder) to the particular ultimate funder under a funding arrangement in respect of the shareholder debt, or

(b) the fair market value of a particular property in respect of which the particular ultimate funder has granted a specified right to a funder (other than an ultimate funder) under a funding arrangement in respect of the shareholder debt;

C is the total amount determined under paragraph (b) of the description of A;

D is the total of all amounts, each of which is, in respect of the shareholder debt, an amount that the intended borrower has been deemed by this subsection to have received from the particular ultimate funder as a loan at any time before the particular time; and

E is the total amount of any repayments deemed by subsections (2.19) and (2.191) to have occurred before the particular time, in respect of any deemed loans from the particular ultimate funder that are referred to in the description of D.

Related Provisions: 15(2.16) — Conditions for 15(2.17) to apply; 15(2.18), (2.19) — Deemed repayment of deemed loan; 15(2.191) — Effect if formula is negative; 15(2.192) — Definitions; 80.4(2)(e) — Deemed interest on loan to shareholder; 212(3.1)–(3.94) — Non-resident withholding tax — back to back arrangements; 257 — Formula cannot calculate to less than zero.

Notes: See Notes to 15(2.16).

(2.18)   Back-to-back   arrangement — conditions   for [15(2.19)] deemed repayment — Subsection (2.19) applies in respect of an intended borrower and a particular ultimate funder at a particular time if

(a) prior to the particular time, subsection (2.17) has applied in respect of a shareholder debt to deem one or more loans to have been received by the intended borrower from the particular ultimate funder; and

(b) at the particular time,

(i) an amount owing in respect of the shareholder debt is repaid in whole or in part,

(ii) an amount owing in respect of a debt or other obligation owing to the particular ultimate funder by a funder (other than an ultimate funder) under a funding arrangement in respect of the shareholder debt is repaid in whole or in part, or

(iii) either

(A) there is a decrease in the fair market value of a property in respect of which a specified right was granted by the particular ultimate funder to a funder (other than an ultimate funder) under a funding arrangement in respect of the shareholder debt, or

(B) a right described in clause (A) is extinguished.

Related Provisions: 15(2.192) — Definitions.

Notes: See Notes to 15(2.16).

(2.19) Back-to-back arrangement — deemed repayment — If this subsection applies in respect of an intended borrower and a particular ultimate funder at a particular time,

(a) the intended borrower is deemed, for the purposes of this section, paragraph 20(1)(j), section 80.4 and subsection 227(6.1), to repay, in whole or in part, one or more of the deemed loans referred to in paragraph (2.18)(a) at the particular time; and

(b) the total amount of the deemed repayments referred to in paragraph (a) is to be determined by the following formula:

$$A - B - C$$

where

A is the total of all amounts, each of which is the amount of a loan deemed by subsection (2.17) to have been received, at any time before the particular time, by the intended borrower from the particular ultimate funder in respect of the shareholder debt,

B is the total of all amounts deemed by this subsection to have been repaid, at any time before the particular time, by the intended borrower in respect of any loans referred to in the description of A, and

C is the amount determined by the formula

$$D \times E/F$$

where

D   is the lesser of

(i) the amount outstanding as or on account of the shareholder debt, immediately after the particular time, and

(ii) the total of all amounts, each of which is, immediately after the particular time,

(A) an amount outstanding as or on account of a debt or other obligation that is owed by a funder (other than an ultimate funder) to an ultimate funder under a funding arrangement in respect of the shareholder debt, or

(B) the fair market value of a particular property in respect of which an ultimate funder has granted a specified right to a funder (other than an ultimate funder) under a funding arrangement in respect of the shareholder debt,

E   is the total of all amounts, each of which is, immediately after the particular time

(i) an amount outstanding as or on account of a debt or other obligation that is owed by a funder (other than an ultimate funder) to the particular ultimate funder under a funding arrangement in respect of the shareholder debt, or

(ii) the fair market value of a particular property in respect of which the particular ultimate funder has granted a specified right to a funder (other than an ultimate funder) under a funding arrangement in respect of the shareholder debt, and

F   is the amount determined under subparagraph (ii) in the description of D.

> **Proposed Amendment — Rules similar to 15(2.18)-(2.19) to apply to upstream loan rules**
>
> **Letter from Dept. of Finance, May 1, 2018**: See under 90(8)(a).

Related Provisions: 15(2.18) — Conditions for 15(2.19) to apply; 15(2.192) — Definitions; 257 — Formula cannot calculate to less than zero.

Notes: See Notes to 15(2.16).

(2.191) Negative amounts — If, in the absence of section 257, the formula in subsection (2.17) would result in a negative amount at a particular time,

(a) the intended borrower is deemed, for the purposes of this section, paragraph 20(1)(j), section 80.4 and subsection 227(6.1), to repay, in whole or in part, one or more of the loans deemed by subsection (2.17) to have been received by the intended borrower from the particular ultimate funder before the particular time; and

(b) the total amount of the deemed repayments referred to in paragraph (a) is equal to the absolute value of that negative amount.

Related Provisions: 15(2.192) — Definitions.

Notes: See Notes to 15(2.16).

(2.192) Back-to-back arrangement — definitions — The following definitions apply in this subsection and subsections (2.16) to (2.191).

"funder", in respect of a funding arrangement, means

(a) if the funding arrangement is described in paragraph (a) of the definition "funding arrangement", the immediate funder;

(b) if the funding arrangement is described in paragraph (b) of the definition "funding arrangement", the creditor in respect of the debt or other obligation or the grantor of the specified right, as the case may be; and

(c) a person or partnership that does not deal at arm's length with a person or partnership referred to in paragraph (a) or (b).

"funding arrangement" means

(a) the shareholder debt; and

(b) each debt or other obligation or specified right, owing by or granted to a funder, in respect of a particular funding arrangement, if the debt or other obligation or specified right meets the conditions in subparagraph (2.16)(c)(i) or (ii) in respect of a funding arrangement.

"specified right" has the same meaning as in subsection 18(5).

"ultimate funder" means a funder, if subsection (2) would apply to the shareholder debt if the creditor under the shareholder debt were the funder instead of the immediate funder.

Notes: See Notes to 15(2.16).

(2.2) When s. 15(2) not to apply — non-resident persons — Subsection (2) does not apply to indebtedness between non-resident persons.

Related Provisions: 90(6)–(15) — Loan from foreign affiliate included in income; 95(2)(a)(ii) — Whether FAPI on income from loans between non-resident corps.

Notes: For examples of 15(2.2) applying see VIEWS docs 2010-0353141R3, 2010-0377581R3, 2010-0381821R3, 2010-0387971R3.

15(2.2) added by 1995-97 technical bill, effective for loans made and indebtedness arising in 1990 or later taxation years. This rule was formerly in 15(8).

CRA Audit Manual: 24.12.2: Subsection 15(2) — shareholder debt.

(2.3) When s. 15(2) not to apply — ordinary lending business — Subsection (2) does not apply to a debt that arose in the ordinary course of the creditor's business or a loan made in the ordinary course of the lender's ordinary business of lending money where, at the time the indebtedness arose or the loan was made, *bona fide* arrangements were made for repayment of the debt or loan within a reasonable time.

Related Provisions: 80.4(2), (3) — Deemed interest; 90(8)(b) — Parallel exception for loan from foreign affiliate.

Notes: Where 15(2.3) applies, a deemed benefit from interest on the loan will still be included in income unless a market rate of interest is paid. See 80.4(2) and (3).

"Ordinary implies that the business of lending money be one of the ways in which the company as an ordinary part of its business operations earns its income. It also implies that the lending of money be identifiable as a business": *Loman Warehousing*, [1999] 4 C.T.C. 2049 (TCC); aff'd [2001] 1 C.T.C. 50 (FCA). For CRA's interpretation of the ordinary business of lending money, see docs 2003-0047891E5, 2004-0064811E5, 2010-0385211E5, 2011-0393881E5; and see 20(1)(p) Notes. For rulings applying 15(2.3) to related financing companies see 2006-0191881R3, 2007-0238971R3, 2007-0244561R3.

For more on 15(2.3) see Morphy, "The Modern Approach to Statutory Interpretation, Applied to the Section 15 Anomaly", 61(2) *Canadian Tax Journal* 367-85 (2013).

15(2.3) added by 1995-97 technical bill, effective for loans made and indebtedness arising in 1990 or later taxation years. This rule was formerly in 15(2)(a)(i).

Interpretation Bulletins: IT-119R4: Debts of shareholders and certain persons connected with shareholders.

CRA Audit Manual: 24.12.2: Subsection 15(2) — shareholder debt.

(2.4) When s. 15(2) not to apply — certain employees — Subsection (2) does not apply to a loan made or a debt that arose

(a) in respect of an individual who is an employee of the lender or creditor but not a specified employee of the lender or creditor,

(b) in respect of an individual who is an employee of the lender or creditor or who is the spouse or common-law partner of an employee of the lender or creditor to enable or assist the individual to acquire a dwelling or a share of the capital stock of a cooperative housing corporation acquired for the sole purpose of acquiring the right to inhabit a dwelling owned by the corporation, where the dwelling is for the individual's habitation,

(c) where the lender or creditor is a particular corporation, in respect of an employee of the particular corporation or of another corporation that is related to the particular corporation, to enable or assist the employee to acquire from the particular corporation, or from another corporation related to the particular corporation, previously unissued fully paid shares of the capital stock of the particular corporation or the related corporation, as the case may be, to be held by the employee for the employee's own benefit, or

(d) in respect of an employee of the lender or creditor to enable or assist the employee to acquire a motor vehicle to be used by the employee in the performance of the duties of the employee's office or employment,

where

(e) it is reasonable to conclude that the employee or the employee's spouse or common-law partner received the loan, or became indebted, because of the employee's employment and not because of any person's share-holdings, and

(f) at the time the loan was made or the debt was incurred, *bona fide* arrangements were made for repayment of the loan or debt within a reasonable time.

Related Provisions: 15(2.7) — Deemed specified employee of a partnership; 80.4(2), (3) — Deemed interest.

Notes: Where 15(2.4) applies, a deemed benefit from interest on the loan will still be included in income unless a market rate of interest is paid. See 80.4(2) and (3).

Bona fide repayment arrangements for 15(2.4) do not necessarily have to be in writing, contractually binding or with firm repayment dates: *Davidson*, [1999] 3 C.T.C. 2159 (TCC); *Dionne*, [1998] 3 C.T.C. 2610 (TCC); but their existence at the time of the loan needs to be proven: *Barbeau*, 2006 TCC 126.

If 15(2.4) applies, assignment of the debt from one corporation to another does not create a new loan, so the exemption still applies: VIEWS doc 2005-0129551E5.

15(2.4)(a) and (e) effectively reverse *Silden*, [1993] 2 C.T.C. 123 (FCA), which had held that a loan to an employee who is also a shareholder was caught by 15(2) even if the loan was made to the employee *qua* employee. A $300,000 house loan would be considered to result from shareholdings rather than employment: VIEWS doc 2005-0159061E5. A benefit is considered conferred *qua* employee if it can be considered part of a reasonable employee remuneration package (a one-employee corporation can qualify): doc 2008-0270201E5. In *Mast*, 2013 TCC 309, a $1 million interest-free loan to a company's sole shareholder to build a home was held to have been due to his shareholdings and not as employee, so 15(2) applied.

The reference to "any person's share-holdings" in 15(2.4)(e) can include an arm's length employee receiving a loan, at the direction of the controlling shareholder, in order to buy shares from that shareholder: VIEWS doc 2002-0118495. A 3% shareholder without "significant influence" over the corp can receive the loan *qua* employee: 2019-0808411E5.

For 15(2.4)(b), a home purchase loan does not normally include a loan to refinance an earlier acquisition: IT-119R4 para. 18; VIEWS doc 2011-0406271E5.

15(2.4) amended by 2000 same-sex partners bill to refer to "common-law partner", effective as per Notes to 248(1)"common-law partner".

15(2.4) added by 1995-97 technical bill, effective for loans made and indebtedness arising in 1990 or later taxation years, except that 15(2.4)(e) does not apply to loans made and indebtedness arising before April 26, 1995. 15(2.4)(b), (c) and (d) were formerly in 15(2)(a)(ii), (iii) and (iv).

Interpretation Bulletins: IT-119R4: Debts of shareholders and certain persons connected with shareholders.

CRA Audit Manual: 24.12.2: Subsection 15(2) — shareholder debt.

(2.5) When s. 15(2) not to apply — certain trusts — Subsection (2) does not apply to a loan made or a debt that arose in respect of a trust where

(a) the lender or creditor is a private corporation;

(b) the corporation is the settlor and sole beneficiary of the trust;

(c) the sole purpose of the trust is to facilitate the purchase and sale of the shares of the corporation, or of another corporation related to the corporation, for an amount equal to their fair market value at the time of the purchase or sale, as the case may be, from or to the employees of the corporation or of the related corporation (other than employees who are specified employees of the corporation or of another corporation related to the corporation), as the case may be; and

(d) at the time the loan was made or the debt incurred, *bona fide* arrangements were made for repayment of the loan or debt within a reasonable time.

Related Provisions: 15(2.7) — Deemed specified employee of a partnership; 80.4(2), (3) — Deemed interest.

Notes: 15(2.5) added by 1995-97 technical bill, for loans made and indebtedness arising in 1990 or later tax years, except that for loans made and indebtedness arising before June 20, 1996, ignore the parenthesized words in 15(2.5)(c).

Interpretation Bulletins: IT-119R4: Debts of shareholders and certain persons connected with shareholders.

CRA Audit Manual: 24.12.2: Subsection 15(2) — shareholder debt.

(2.6) When s. 15(2) not to apply — repayment within one year [of year-end] — Subsection (2) does not apply to a loan or an indebtedness repaid within one year after the end of the taxation year of the lender or creditor in which the loan was made or the indebtedness arose, where it is established, by subsequent events or otherwise, that the repayment was not part of a series of loans or other transactions and repayments.

Related Provisions: 80.4(2), (3) — Deemed interest; 90(8)(a) — Similar exception for loan from foreign affiliate; 248(10) — Series of transactions; *Interpretation Act* 27(5) — Meaning of "within one year".

Notes: Repayments are considered to apply "first-in first-out": VIEWS doc 2015-0595621C6 [2015 APFF q.19].

Where 15(2.6) applies, a deemed benefit from interest on the loan may still be included in income unless a market rate of interest is paid. See 80.4(2) and (3); VIEWS doc 2018-0738871E5; *Income Tax Audit Manual* §24.12.6.

If the shareholder dies, repayment by the estate qualifies for purposes of 15(2.6): VIEWS doc 2012-0442911C6 [2012 STEP q.6].

For "series of loans and repayments", see Notes to 15(2) re *Attis* and related cases. However, annually declaring dividends or bonus to clear out the loans is considered acceptable and not "part of a series of loans or other transactions and repayments": IT-119R4 para. 29, VIEWS docs 2010-0382431E5, 2013-0506571E5. For more on 15(2.6) see 2011-0414431R3, 2012-0442521E5, 2013-0482991E5; 2013-0505181R3 [Bernstein, "Cash Pooling", 23(5) *Canadian Tax Highlights [CTH]* (ctf.ca) 9-10 (May 2015)]; 2017-0682631I7 [Cepparo, "CRA: Cross-Border Cash Pooling", 26(9) *CTH* 8-9 (Sept. 2018); Richardson, "Canada Revenue Agency Says 'Likely' to Series in Physical Cash Pooling", XXI(4) *Corporate Finance* (Federated Press) 15-18 (2018)].

See 248(10) Notes re the meaning of "series of transactions".

In *Holmes v. Schonfeld*, 2016 ONCA 148, persons whose assets were being managed could not sue the receiver for not repaying a loan in time for 15(2.6) to apply.

15(2.6) added by 1995-97 technical bill, for loans made and indebtedness arising in 1990 or later taxation years. This rule was formerly in 15(2)(b).

Interpretation Bulletins: IT-119R4: Debts of shareholders and certain persons connected with shareholders.

I.T. Technical News: 3 (paragraphs 15(2)(b) and 20(1)(j)).

CRA Audit Manual: 24.12.2: Subsection 15(2) — shareholder debt.

(2.7) Employee of partnership — For the purpose of this section, an individual who is an employee of a partnership is deemed to be a specified employee of the partnership where the individual is a specified shareholder of one or more corporations that, in total, are entitled, directly or indirectly, to a share of any income or loss of the partnership, which share is not less than 10% of the income or loss.

Related Provisions: 248(1) — Definition of "specified employee".

Notes: For the meaning of "indirectly" see Notes to 17.1(1).

15(2.7) added by 1995-97 technical bill, effective for loans made and indebtedness arising in 1990 or later taxation years.

Interpretation Bulletins: IT-119R4: Debts of shareholders and certain persons connected with shareholders.

(3) Interest or dividend on income bond or debenture — An amount paid as interest or a dividend by a corporation resident in Canada to a taxpayer in respect of an income bond or income debenture shall be deemed to have been paid by the corporation and received by the taxpayer as a dividend on a share of the capital stock of the corporation, unless the corporation is entitled to deduct the amount so paid in computing its income.

Related Provisions: 15(4) — Where paid by corporation not resident in Canada; 18(1)(g) — Payment on income bonds; 112(2.1) — Where no deductions permitted; 214(3) — Non-residents' Canadian income; 258(2) — Deemed dividend on preferred share.

Interpretation Bulletins: IT-52R4: Income bonds and income debentures (cancelled); IT-243R4: Dividend refund to private corporations; IT-527: Distress preferred shares.

(4) Idem, where corporation not resident — An amount paid as interest or a dividend by a corporation not resident in Canada to a taxpayer in respect of an income bond or income debenture shall be deemed to have been received by the taxpayer as a dividend on a share of the capital stock of the corporation unless the amount so paid was, under the laws of the country in which the corporation was resident, deductible in computing the amount for the year on which the corporation was liable to pay income or profits tax imposed by the government of that country.

Related Provisions: 15(3) — Where paid by corporation resident in Canada; 18(1)(g) — Payment on income bonds; 214(3) — Non-residents' Canadian income; 258 — Deemed dividend on preferred share.

Notes: For the meaning of "income or profits tax", see Notes to 126(4).

Interpretation Bulletins: IT-52R4: Income bonds and income debentures (cancelled).

(5) Automobile benefit — For the purposes of subsection (1), the value of the benefit to be included in computing a shareholder's income for a taxation year with respect to an automobile made available to the shareholder, or a person related to the shareholder, by a corporation shall (except where an amount is determined under subparagraph 6(1)(e)(i) in respect of the automobile in computing the shareholder's income for the year) be computed on the assumption that subsections 6(1), (1.1), (2) and (7) apply, with such modifications as the circumstances require, and as though the references therein to "the employer of the taxpayer", "the taxpayer's employer" and "the employer" were read as "the corporation".

Related Provisions: 15(7) — Application; 214(3)(a) — Non-residents' Canadian income.

Notes: See Notes to 6(2) and 6(1)(k). For examples of 15(5) applying see *Babich*, 2012 CarswellNat 4578 (FCA) and VIEWS doc 2006-0187051E5. 15(1.4)(c) prevents double tax (6(1)(a) and 15(5)) of an automobile benefit provided to a shareholder's child: VIEWS doc 2014-0538101C6 [2014 APFF q.1].

Where 15(5) does not apply because a pickup truck is not an "automobile", 15(1) still applies to the benefit even though the standby rule does not: *Servais*, 2003 FCA 329.

15(5) amended by 1993 technical bill, effective 1993, to add reference to 6(1.1); and by 1997 GST bill, effective for 1996 and later taxation years, to add reference to 6(7).

Regulations: 200(2)(h), 200(4) (information returns).

Interpretation Bulletins: IT-63R5: Benefits, including standby charge for an automobile, from the personal use of a motor vehicle supplied by an employer.

Forms: T2 Sched. 11: Transactions with shareholders, officers, or employees.

(6) [Repealed under former Act]

Notes: 15(6) repealed in 1982. This rule is now included in 15(5).

(7) Application of subsecs. (1), (2) and (5) — For greater certainty, subsections (1), (2) and (5) are applicable in computing, for the purposes of this Part, the income of a shareholder or of a person or partnership whether or not the corporation, or the lender or creditor, as the case may be, was resident or carried on business in Canada.

Interpretation Bulletins: IT-63R5: Benefits, including standby charge for an automobile, from the personal use of a motor vehicle supplied by an employer; IT-119R4: Debts of shareholders and certain persons connected with shareholders; IT-432R2: Benefits conferred on shareholders.

Forms: T2 Sched. 11: Transactions with shareholders, officers, or employees.

(8) [Repealed]

Notes: 15(8) repealed by 1995-97 technical bill, effective for loans made and indebtedness arising in 1990 or later taxation years. This rule was moved to 15(2.2).

(9) Deemed benefit to shareholder by corporation — Where an amount in respect of a loan or debt is deemed by section 80.4 to be a benefit received by a person or partnership in a taxation year, the amount is deemed for the purpose of subsection (1) to be a benefit conferred in the year on a shareholder, unless subsection 6(9) or paragraph 12(1)(w) applies to the amount.

Related Provisions: 247(15) — No application to transfer pricing amount deemed to be dividend for non-resident withholding tax.

Notes: An interest-free loan by a Canadian subsidiary to a foreign parent can trigger 80.4(2), deemed via 15(9) to be a 15(1) benefit, which via 214(3)(a) triggers withholding tax under 212(2) (and a 17(1) benefit also applies): VIEWS docs 2007-0243331C6, 2008-0280041R3.

15(9) amended by 1995-97 technical bill, for taxation years that end after Nov. 1991.

Regulations: 200(2)(i) (information return).

Interpretation Bulletins: IT-119R4: Debts of shareholders and certain persons connected with shareholders; IT-421R2: Benefits to individuals, corporations and shareholders from loans or debt.

Transfer Pricing Memoranda: TPM-02: Repatriation of funds by non-residents — Part XIII assessments.

CRA Audit Manual: 24.12.5: Section 80.4 — benefit on interest-free or low-interest loans — non-residents.

Definitions [s. 15]: "Act" — *Interpretation Act* 35(1); "affiliated" — 251.1; "amount" — 248(1); "arm's length" — 251(1); "beneficially interested" — 248(25); "business" — 248(1); "CRIC" — 15(2.11); "Canada" — 255; "Canadian partnership" — 102(1), 248(1); "carried on business in Canada" — 253; "class" — 248(6); "common share", "common-law partner" — 248(1); "connected" — 15(2.1); "contemplated shareholder" — 15(1.4)(a); "corporation" — 248(1), *Interpretation Act* 35(1); "dividend", "employee" — 248(1); "excluded trust" — 15(1.4)(d); "fair market value" — see 69(1) Notes; "filing-due date" — 150(1), 248(1); "fiscal period" — 249.1; "forgiven amount" — 15(1.21); "funder", "funding arrangement" — 15(2.192); "goods and services tax" — 248(1); "identical" — 248(12); "immediate funder" — 15(2.16); "income bond", "income debenture" — 248(1); "income or profits tax" — 126(4); "individual" — 248(1); "intended borrower" — 15(2.16); "legislature" — *Interpretation Act* 35(1); "Minister" — 248(1); "month" — *Interpretation Act* 35(1); "motor vehicle", "non-resident" — 248(1); "obligation" — 248(26); "paid-up capital" — 89(1), 248(1); "parent" — 88(1); "partnership" — see 96(1); "person" — 248(1); "pertinent loan or indebtedness" — 15(2.11); "proceeds of disposition" — 54; "property" — 248(1); "province" — *Interpretation Act* 35(1); "qualifying Canadian partnership" — 15(2.14)(a); "related" — 251(2)–(6); "resident in Canada" — 94(3)(a), 250; "series" — 248(10); "share", "shareholder" — 248(1); "shareholder debt" — 15(2.16); "specified employee" — 15(2.7), 248(1); "specified right" — 15(2.192); "specified shareholder", "stock dividend" — 248(1); "taxation year" — 249; "taxpayer" — 248(1); "trust" — 104(1), 248(1), (3); "ultimate funder" — 15(2.192); "writing" — *Interpretation Act* 35(1).

15.1, 15.2 [No longer relevant.]

Notes: 15.1 and 15.2, both enacted by 1992 Budget/technical bill, provide for "small business development bonds" and "small business bonds" respectively, up to $500,000 of which could be issued from Feb. 26/92 through 1994 by a corporation (SBDB), or by an individual or partnership (SBB), in financial difficulty, with a term of up to 5 years. Interest paid on SBDBs or SBBs was non-deductible (15.1(2)(a), 15.2(2)(a)) and was deemed to be a taxable dividend except for dividend refund purposes: 15.1(1), 15.1(2)(b), 15.2(1). 15.1(4) and 15.2(4) still provide that interest paid on borrowed money to acquire an SBDB or SBB is deemed paid on borrowed money used to earn income from business or property (thus deductible under 20(1)(c)). Earlier SBDBs and SBBs could be issued from Dec. 12, 1979 to 1987. See IT-507R.

16. (1) Income and capital combined — Where, under a contract or other arrangement, an amount can reasonably be regarded as being in part interest or other amount of an income nature and in part an amount of a capital nature, the following rules apply:

(a) the part of the amount that can reasonably be regarded as interest shall, irrespective of when the contract or arrangement was made or the form or legal effect thereof, be deemed to be interest on a debt obligation held by the person to whom the amount is paid or payable; and

(b) the part of the amount that can reasonably be regarded as an amount of an income nature, other than interest, shall, irrespective of when the contract or arrangement was made or the form or legal effect thereof, be included in the income of the taxpayer to whom the amount is paid or payable for the taxation year in which the amount was received or became due to the extent it has not otherwise been included in the taxpayer's income.

Related Provisions: 12(1)(c) — Interest income; 12(1)(g) — Amount fully taxable where based on production or use; 12(3) — Accrual of interest income; 16(4), (5) — Application of subsec. (1); 20(1)(c) — Deduction for interest; 138(12) — "Gross investment revenue" of an insurer; 214(2) — Tax on non-residents.

Notes: 16(1) applies to a blended payment such as a mortgage payment. The interest portion is deemed to be interest, for both payer (20(1)(c)) and payee (12(1)(c)). See IT-265R3 (officially cancelled but still generally accurate).

For detailed discussion of the history and purpose of 16(1), see *Plains Midstream*, 2019 FCA 57 (16(1) did not create a deduction for interest based on economic substance on assuming a loan due in 42 years, as PM got much more than the actual cash it received for assuming the loan: para. 106) [Nesbitt, "Asymmetry", XXI(2) *Corporate Finance* (Federated Press) 9-14 (2018); Davis, case comment, 67(4) *Canadian Tax Journal* 1215-25].

Despite 16(1), the interest component of structured settlement payments to injury victims is non-taxable if certain conditions are met. See IT-365R2 para. 5.

See also Vantil & Boehmer, "Caveat Venditor", VII(3) *Corporate Structures & Groups* (Federated Press) 372-74 (2002); VIEWS doc 2013-0485481I7.

Where a stream of interest payments on a loan was bought by a third party, which treated the cost as part capital and part interest, 16(1) did not reduce interest deductibility to the payer: *Lehigh Cement*, 2009 TCC 237, paras. 21-23 (reversed on other grounds 2010 FCA 124).

Regulations: 201(1)(d) (information return).

Income Tax Folios: S3-F6-C1: Interest deductibility [replaces IT-533].

Interpretation Bulletins: IT-233R: Lease-option agreements; sale-leaseback agreements (cancelled); IT-265R3: Payments of income and capital combined (cancelled); IT-365R2: Damages, settlements and similar receipts; IT-396R: Interest income.

Forms: RC257: Request for an information return program account (RZ); T5: Statement of investment income; T5 Summ: Return of investment income.

(2) Obligation issued at discount [before June 19, 1971] — [No longer relevant]

Notes: This rule applies to bonds or debt issued by an exempt entity, such as a municipality, before June 19, 1971. Reproduced here up to the 52nd ed.

(3) Obligation issued at discount — Where, in the case of a bond, debenture, bill, note, mortgage, hypothecary claim or similar obligation (other than an obligation that is a prescribed debt obligation for the purpose of subsection 12(9)) issued after June 18, 1971 by a person exempt, because of section 149, from Part I tax on part or on all of the person's income, a non-resident person not carrying on business in Canada or a government, municipality or municipal or other public body performing a function of government,

(a) the obligation was issued for an amount that is less than the principal amount of the obligation, and

(b) the yield from the obligation, expressed in terms of an annual rate on the amount for which the obligation was issued (which annual rate shall, if the terms of the obligation or any agreement relating thereto conferred on the holder thereof a right to demand payment of the principal amount of the obligation or the amount outstanding as or on account of the principal amount, as the case may be, before the maturity of the obligation, be calculated on the basis of the yield that produces the highest annual rate obtainable either on the maturity of the obligation or conditional on the exercise of any such right) exceeds $4/3$ of the interest stipulated to be payable on the obligation, expressed in terms of an annual rate on

(i) the principal amount of the obligation, if no amount is payable on account of the principal amount before the maturity of the obligation, or

(ii) the amount outstanding from time to time as or on account of the principal amount thereof, in any other case,

the amount by which the principal amount of the obligation exceeds the amount for which the obligation was issued shall be included in computing the income of the first owner of the obligation

(c) who is resident in Canada,

(d) who is not a government nor a person exempt, because of section 149, from tax under this Part on all or part of the person's taxable income, and

(e) of whom the obligation is a capital property,

for the taxation year in which the owner acquired the obligation.

Related Provisions: 16(5) — Application of subsec. 16(1); 20(14) — Treatment of accrued bond interest; 53(1)(g) — Addition to adjusted cost base; 142.4(1)"tax basis"(b) — Disposition of specified debt obligation by financial institution.

Notes: For the meaning of "municipal or public body...", see Notes to 149(1)(c).

16(3) amended by 2001 *Civil Code* harmonization bill (effective June 14, 2001), 1993 and 1992 technical bills.

Regulations: 7000(1) (prescribed debt obligation).

Interpretation Bulletins: IT-265R3: Payments of income and capital combined (cancelled).

(4) Where subsec. (1) does not apply — Subsection (1) does not apply to any amount received by a taxpayer in a taxation year

(a) as an annuity payment; or

(b) in satisfaction of the taxpayer's rights under an annuity contract.

(5) Idem — Subsection (1) does not apply in any case where subsection (2) or (3) applies.

(6) Indexed debt obligations — Subject to subsection (7) and for the purposes of this Act, where at any time in a taxpayer's taxation year

(a) an interest in an indexed debt obligation is held by the taxpayer,

(i) an amount determined in prescribed manner shall be deemed to be received and receivable by the taxpayer in the year as interest in respect of the obligation, and

(ii) an amount determined in prescribed manner shall be deemed to be paid and payable in respect of the year by the taxpayer as interest under a legal obligation of the taxpayer to pay interest on borrowed money used for the purpose of earning income from a business or property;

(b) an indexed debt obligation is an obligation of the taxpayer,

(i) an amount determined in prescribed manner shall be deemed to be payable in respect of the year by the taxpayer as interest in respect of the obligation, and

(ii) an amount determined in prescribed manner shall be deemed to be received and receivable by the taxpayer in the year as interest in respect of the obligation; and

(c) the taxpayer pays or credits an amount in respect of an amount determined under subparagraph (b)(i) in respect of an indexed debt obligation, the payment or crediting shall be deemed to be a payment or crediting of interest on the obligation.

Related Provisions: 20(1)(c) — Interest deduction; 53(1)(g.1) — Addition to adjusted cost base; 53(2)(l.1) — Deduction from adjusted cost base; 138(12)"gross investment revenue"G(a) — Gross investment revenue of insurer; 142.3(2) — Indexed debt obligation not subject to rules re income from specified debt obligations; 142.4(1)"tax basis"(e), (n) — Disposition of specified debt obligation by financial institution; 214(7) — Sale of obligation by non-resident.

Notes: Where interest on a security is tied to inflation, the interest paid and the interest received (by the issuer and the purchaser respectively) are determined for tax purposes by Reg. 7001.

Opening words of 16(6) amended by 1995-97 technical bill, effective on the same basis as 16(7). 16(6) added by 1992 technical bill, effective for debt obligations issued after Oct. 16, 1991. (It was originally proposed as 248(25).)

Regulations: 7001 (amounts determined in prescribed manner).

(7) Impaired indexed debt obligations — Paragraph (6)(a) does not apply to a taxpayer in respect of an indexed debt obligation for the part of a taxation year throughout which the obligation is impaired where an amount in respect of the obligation is deductible because of subparagraph 20(1)(l)(ii) in computing the taxpayer's income for the year.

Notes: Under 16(7), interest is not included under 16(6) for the portion of the year in which the indexed debt obligation is impaired. This is consistent with the new accounting rules which provide that recognition of interest income in accordance with the terms of the original debt obligation ceases on the impairment of the obligation.

16(7) added by 1995-97 technical bill, effective for tax years that end after Sept. 1997, or earlier by election (see Notes to 20(1)(l)).

Definitions [s. 16]: "amount", "annuity", "borrowed money", "business" — 248(1); "Canada" — 255; "capital property" — 54, 248(1); "carrying on business in Canada" — 253; "indexed debt obligation", "non-resident", "prescribed" — 248(1); "prescribed debt obligation" — Reg. 7000(1); "principal amount" — 248(1), (26); "property" — 248(1); "received" — 248(7); "regulation" — 248(1); "resident of Canada" — 94(3)(a), 250; "taxation year" — 249; "taxpayer" — 248(1).

Income Tax Folios [s. 16]: S3-F6-C1: Interest deductibility [replaces IT-533].

Interpretation Bulletins [s. 16]: IT-265R3: Payments of income and capital combined (cancelled).

16.1 (1) Leasing properties — Where a taxpayer (in this section referred to as the "lessee") leases tangible property, or for civil law corporeal property, that is not prescribed property and that would, if the lessee acquired the property, be depreciable property of the lessee, from a person resident in Canada other than a person whose taxable income is exempt from tax under this Part, or from a non-resident person who holds the lease in the course of carrying on a business through a permanent establishment in Canada, as defined by regulation, any income from which is subject to tax under this Part, who owns the property and with whom the lessee was dealing

at arm's length (in this section referred to as the "lessor") for a term of more than one year, if the lessee and the lessor jointly elect in prescribed form filed with their returns of income for their respective taxation years that include the particular time when the lease began, the following rules apply for the purpose of computing the income of the lessee for the taxation year that includes the particular time and for all subsequent taxation years:

(a) in respect of amounts paid or payable for the use of, or for the right to use, the property, the lease shall be deemed not to be a lease;

(b) the lessee shall be deemed to have acquired the property from the lessor at the particular time at a cost equal to its fair market value at that time;

(c) the lessee shall be deemed to have borrowed money from the lessor at the particular time, for the purpose of acquiring the property, in a principal amount equal to the fair market value of the property at that time;

(d) interest shall be deemed to accrue on the principal amount of the borrowed money outstanding from time to time, compounded semi-annually, not in advance, at the prescribed rate in effect

    (i) at the earlier of

        (A) the time, if any, before the particular time, at which the lessee last entered into an agreement to lease the property, and

        (B) the particular time, or

    (ii) where the lease provides that the amount payable by the lessee for the use of, or the right to use, the property varies according to prevailing interest rates in effect from time to time, and the lessee so elects, in respect of all of the property that is subject to the lease, in the lessee's return of income under this Part for the taxation year of the lessee in which the lease began, at the beginning of the period for which the interest is being calculated;

(e) all amounts paid or payable by or on behalf of the lessee for the use of, or the right to use, the property in the year shall be deemed to be blended payments, paid or payable by the lessee, of principal and interest on the borrowed money outstanding from time to time, calculated in accordance with paragraph (d), applied firstly on account of interest on principal, secondly on account of interest on unpaid interest and thirdly on account of unpaid principal, if any, and the amount, if any, by which any such payment exceeds the total of those amounts shall be deemed to be paid or payable on account of interest, and any amount deemed by reason of this paragraph to be a payment of interest shall be deemed to have been an amount paid or payable, as the case may be, pursuant to a legal obligation to pay interest in respect of the year on the borrowed money;

(f) at the time of the expiration or cancellation of the lease, the assignment of the lease or the sublease of the property by the lessee, the lessee shall (except where subsection (4) applies) be deemed to have disposed of the property at that time for proceeds of disposition equal to the amount, if any, by which

    (i) the total of

        (A) the amount referred to in paragraph (c), and

        (B) all amounts received or receivable by the lessee in respect of the cancellation or assignment of the lease or the sublease of the property

exceeds

    (ii) the total of

        (A) all amounts deemed under paragraph (e) to have been paid or payable, as the case may be, by the lessee on account of the principal amount of the borrowed money, and

        (B) all amounts paid or payable by or on behalf of the lessee in respect of the cancellation or assignment of the lease or the sublease of the property;

(g) for the purposes of subsections 13(5.2) and (5.3), each amount paid or payable by or on behalf of the lessee that would, but for this subsection, have been an amount paid or payable for the use of, or the right to use, the property shall be deemed to have been deducted in computing the lessee's income as an amount paid or payable by the lessee for the use of, or the right to use, the property after the particular time;

(h) any amount paid or payable by or on behalf of the lessee in respect of the granting or assignment of the lease or the sublease of the property that would, but for this paragraph, be the capital cost to the lessee of a leasehold interest in the property shall be deemed to be an amount paid or payable, as the case may be, by the lessee for the use of, or the right to use, the property for the remaining term of the lease; and

(i) where the lessee elects under this subsection in respect of a property and, at any time after the lease was entered into, the owner of the property is a non-resident person who does not hold the lease in the course of carrying on a business through a permanent establishment in Canada, as defined by regulation, any income from which is subject to tax under this Part, for the purposes of this subsection the lease shall be deemed to have been cancelled at that time.

Related Provisions: 16.1(5) — Replacement property; 16.1(6) — Additional property; 16.1(7) — Renegotiation of lease; Reg. 1100(1.1)–(1.13) — CCA restrictions on leasing property; Reg. 1100(2)C:F(b)(iv) — Year of acquisition — no half-year rule for 16.1(1)(b) property.

Notes: The election under 16.1(1) allows taxpayers to reduce the negative effects of the "specified leasing property" CCA restrictions in Reg. 1100(1.1)-(1.3). The lessee can elect to be treated as having acquired the leased property at fair market value and as having financed the purchase through a loan at a prescribed interest rate. Prescribed property (Reg. 8200) is excluded. See also Income Tax Folio S3-F4-C1 ¶1.26.

For the interaction between 16.1(1) and 18(9) on a prepaid lease, see VIEWS doc 2004-0109381E5. For a ruling approving a 16.1(1) election see doc 2006-0201361R3. On the tax shelter rules applying to a 16.1(1) election, see 2008-0265681E5. The investment tax credit cannot be claimed by the lessee: 2012-0440531E5 (revoking the position in 2011-0417811E5). The election must be filed by both lessor and lessee with their return for the year that includes the day the lease began: 2013-0516251E5. It cannot be late-filed: 2014-0548041E5. Although the lessee effectively treats the property as depreciable property, CRA does not consider it to be "capital property" for GST/HST purposes: GST/HST HQ letter 187306.

16.1(1) amended by 2002-2013 technical bill (Part 4 — bijuralism, effective June 26, 2013), 1998 Budget, 1991 technical bill.

Regulations: 4302 (prescribed rate of interest for 16.1(1)(d)); 8200 (prescribed property); 8201 (permanent establishment).

Income Tax Folios: S3-F4-C1: General discussion of CCA.

Interpretation Bulletins: IT-233R: Lease-option agreements; sale-leaseback agreements (cancelled); IT-265R3: Payments of income and capital combined (cancelled).

I.T. Technical News: 21 (cancellation of Interpretation Bulletin IT-233R).

Forms: T2145: Election in respect of the leasing of property.

(2) Assignments and subleases — Subject to subsections (3) and (4), where at any particular time a lessee who has made an election under subsection (1) in respect of a leased property assigns the lease or subleases the property to another person (in this section referred to as the **"assignee"**),

(a) subsection (1) shall not apply in computing the income of the lessee in respect of the lease for any period after the particular time; and

(b) if the lessee and the assignee jointly elect in prescribed form filed with their returns of income under this Part for their respective taxation years that include the particular time, subsection (1) shall apply to the assignee as if

    (i) the assignee leased the property at the particular time from the owner of the property for a term of more than one year, and

    (ii) the assignee and the owner of the property jointly elected under subsection (1) in respect of the property with their returns of income under this Part for their respective taxation years that include the particular time.

Notes: 16.1(2) amended by 1991 technical bill, retroactive to introduction of the section (see Notes at end of 16.1).

Forms: T2146: Election in respect of assigned leases or subleased property.

(3) Idem — Subject to subsection (4), where at any particular time a lessee who has made an election under subsection (1) in respect of a leased property assigns the lease or subleases the property to another person with whom the lessee is not dealing at arm's length, the other person shall, for the purposes of subsection (1) and for the purposes of computing that person's income in respect of the lease for any period after the particular time, be deemed to be the same person as, and a continuation of, the lessee, except that, notwithstanding paragraph (1)(b), that other person shall be deemed to have acquired the property from the lessee at the time that it was acquired by the lessee at a cost equal to the amount that would be the lessee's proceeds of disposition of the property determined under paragraph (1)(f) if that amount were determined without reference to clauses (1)(f)(i)(B) and (ii)(B).

(4) Amalgamations and windings-up — Notwithstanding subsection (2), where at any time a particular corporation that has made an election under subsection (1) in respect of a lease assigns the lease

(a) by reason of an amalgamation (within the meaning assigned by subsection 87(1)), or

(b) in the course of the winding-up of a Canadian corporation in respect of which subsection 88(1) applies,

to another corporation with which it does not deal at arm's length, the other corporation shall, for the purposes of subsection (1) and for the purposes of computing its income in respect of the lease after that time, be deemed to be the same person as, and a continuation of, the particular corporation.

(5) Replacement property — For the purposes of subsection (1), where at any time a property (in this subsection referred to as a "replacement property") is provided by a lessor to a lessee as a replacement for a similar property of the lessor (in this subsection referred to as the "original property") that was leased by the lessor to the lessee, and the amount payable by the lessee for the use of, or the right to use, the replacement property is the same as the amount that was so payable in respect of the original property, the replacement property shall be deemed to be the same property as the original property.

Notes: See Notes at end of 16.1.

(6) Additional property — For the purposes of subsection (1), where at any particular time

(a) an addition or alteration (in this subsection referred to as "additional property") is made by a lessor to a property (in this subsection referred to as the "original property") of the lessor that is the subject of a lease,

(b) the lessor and the lessee of the original property have jointly elected under subsection (1) in respect of the original property, and

(c) as a consequence of the addition or alteration, the total amount payable by the lessee for the use of, or the right to use, the original property and the additional property exceeds the amount so payable in respect of the original property,

the following rules apply:

(d) the lessee shall be deemed to have leased the additional property from the lessor at the particular time,

(e) the term of the lease of the additional property shall be deemed to be greater than one year,

(f) the lessor and the lessee shall be deemed to have jointly elected under subsection (1) in respect of the additional property,

(g) the prescribed rate in effect at the particular time in respect of the additional property shall be deemed to be equal to the

prescribed rate in effect in respect of the original property at the particular time,

(h) the additional property shall be deemed not to be prescribed property, and

(i) the excess referred to in paragraph (c) shall be deemed to be an amount payable by the lessee for the use of, or the right to use, the additional property.

Regulations: 4301(c) (prescribed rate for 16.1(6)(g)); 4302 (prescribed rate for 16.1(6)(d).

(7) Renegotiation of lease — For the purposes of subsection (1), where at any time

(a) a lease (in this subsection referred to as the "original lease") of property is renegotiated in the course of a *bona fide* renegotiation, and

(b) as a result of the renegotiation, the amount payable by the lessee of the property for the use of, or the right to use, the property is altered in respect of a period after that time (otherwise than because of an addition or alteration to which subsection (6) applies),

the original lease shall be deemed to have expired and the renegotiated lease shall be deemed to be a new lease of the property entered into at that time.

Related Provisions: 16(1) — Income and capital combined; 20(1)(c) — Deductions permitted — interest.

Notes: 16.1 added by 1989 Budget, effective for leases and subleases entered into after 10pm EDST, April 26, 1989, with grandfathering for certain leases under an agreement in writing entered into before then (see up to PITA 39th ed. for specifics). 16.1(5)-(7) added by 1991 technical bill, retroactive to introduction of the section.

Definitions [s. 16.1]: "amount" — 248(1); "arm's length" — 251(1); "assignee" — 16.1(2); "borrowed money", "business" — 248(1); "Canada" — 255; "corporeal property" — Quebec *Civil Code* art. 899, 906; "depreciable property" — 13(21), 248(1); "fair market value" — see 69(1) Notes; "lessee", "lessor" — 16.1(1); "non-resident" — 248(1); "permanent establishment" — Reg. 8201; "person", "prescribed" — 248(1); "prescribed rate" — Reg. 4301, 4302; "principal amount" — 248(1), (26); "property", "regulation" — 248(1); "resident in Canada" — 94(3)(a), 250; "taxable income — 248(1); "taxation year" — 11(2), 249; "taxpayer" — 248(1).

Regulations [s. 16.1]: 4302 (prescribed interest rate); 8200 (prescribed property).

17. (1) Amount owing by non-resident [deemed interest income] — If this subsection applies to a corporation resident in Canada in respect of an amount owing to the corporation (in this subsection referred to as the "debt"), the corporation shall include in computing its income for a taxation year the amount determined by the formula

$$A - B$$

where

A is the amount of interest that would be included in computing the corporation's income for the year in respect of the debt if interest on the debt were computed at the prescribed rate for the period in the year during which the debt was outstanding; and

B is the total of all amounts each of which is

(a) an amount included in computing the corporation's income for the year as, on account of, in lieu of or in satisfaction of, interest in respect of the debt,

(b) an amount received or receivable by the corporation from a trust that is included in computing the corporation's income for the year or a subsequent taxation year and that can reasonably be attributed to interest on the debt for the period in the year during which the debt was outstanding, or

(c) an amount included in computing the corporation's income for the year or a subsequent taxation year under subsection 91(1) that can reasonably be attributed to interest on an amount owing (in this paragraph referred to as the "original debt") — or if the amount of the original debt exceeds the amount of the debt, a portion of the original debt that is equal to the amount of the debt — for the period in the year during which the debt was outstanding if

(i) without the existence of the original debt, subsection (2) would not have deemed the debt to be owed by the non-resident person referred to in paragraph (1.1)(a),

(ii) the original debt was owed by a non-resident person or a partnership each member of which is a non-resident person, and

(iii) where subsection (11.2) applies to the original debt,

(A) an amount determined under paragraph (11.2)(a) or (b) in respect of the original debt is an amount referred to in paragraph (2)(a), and because of the amount referred to in paragraph (2)(a), the debt is deemed to be owed by the non-resident person referred to in paragraph (1.1)(a), and

(B) the original debt was owing by an intermediate lender to an initial lender or by an intended borrower to an intermediate lender (within the meanings of those terms assigned by subsection (11.2)).

Related Provisions: 17(1.1) — Conditions for 17(1) to apply; 17(2)–(6) — Anti-avoidance rules; 17(7)–(9) — Exceptions; 17(10)–(15) — Interpretation; 17.1(1)(a) — No application to "pertinent loan or indebtedness" under 15(2.11) or 212.3(11); 257 — Formula cannot calculate to less than zero.

Notes: In simple terms, 17(1) applies when a Canadian resident corporation lends money to a non-resident at no interest or less than "reasonable" interest and the loan is outstanding for more than a year. The corporation is deemed to have received interest on the loan at the prescribed rate (Reg. 4301(c)). 17(1) will apply to an interest-free loan by a Canadian subsidiary to a foreign parent (see also Notes to 15(9)): VIEWS docs 2007-0243331C6, 2008-0280041R3. "Owes an amount" does not require a loan to have been made: 2003-0017231E5.

See Vidal et al., *Introduction to International Tax in Canada* (Carswell, 8th ed., 2020), chap. 12; Woolford-Marshall, "Amendments to Section 17", 47(3) *Canadian Tax Journal* 640-62 (1999); Tremblay, "Amendments to Section 17", VIII(3) *International Tax Planning* (Federated Press) 573-78 (1999); Toselli, "Section 17: The New Rules", 1999 Prairie Provinces Tax Conference (ctf.ca), 1:1-35; Moskowitz, "Financing of Non-Residents and the Recent Amendments to Section 17", 1999 Cdn Tax Foundation conference report, 43:1-61; Tremblay & Wilkie, "The Canadian Triangle: the Uneasy Interaction of Subsection 15(2), Section 17 and Subsection 95(2)", 2002 conference report, 18:1-17; McDowell, "Section 17: Practical Issues", 2004 conference report, 19:1-27; Watson & Baum, "Section 17: Interpretive Considerations", 58(3) *CTJ* 653-73 (2010); Tyler, "CRA Seeks to Clarify Application of Section 17", 2062 *Tax Topics* (CCH) 1-3 (Sept. 15, 2011); VIEWS docs 2007-0253161I7, 2007-0257241R3, 2009-0332861R3, 2009-0349701R3, 2010-0381821R3, 2010-0386201R3, 2011-0418711R3, 2012-0452291R3, 2018-0772971I7. A doubtful debt reserve under 20(1)(l) will not trigger 17(1): 2004-0093541E5.

New 247(2.1), introduced in 2019, may effectively make 17(1) redundant, since the transfer pricing rules apply first.

Where 17(1) does not apply (e.g., loan by an individual), CRA may still apply 247(2): docs 2003-0033891E5, 2020-0852221C6 [2020 APFF q.10]. For a ruling that neither applies see 2007-0241991R3.

For interpretation of "reasonably be attributed" in 17(1)(b)(ii) and (iii), see *729658 Alberta*, 2004 TCC 474.

17(1) amended by 2014 budget bill #2 (for tax years that begin after Feb. 23, 1998, as per a Sept. 3, 2002 Finance comfort letter; late-reassessment rule for all related amendments reproduced here up to PITA 56th ed.), 1998 Budget.

Regulations: 4301(c) (prescribed rate of interest for 17(1)(a)).

(1.1) Amount owing by non-resident [conditions for 17(1) to apply] — Subsection (1) applies to a corporation resident in Canada in respect of an amount owing to the corporation if, at any time in a taxation year of the corporation,

(a) a non-resident person owes the amount to the corporation;

(b) the amount has been or remains outstanding for more than a year; and

(c) the amount that would be determined for B in subsection (1), if that subsection applied, for the year in respect of the amount owing is less than the amount of interest that would be included in computing the corporation's income for the year in respect of the amount owing if that interest were computed at a reasonable rate for the period in the year during which the amount was outstanding.

Notes: 17(1.1) added by 2014 budget bill #2, for tax years beginning after Feb. 23, 1998.

(2) Anti-avoidance rule — indirect loan — For the purpose of this section and subject to subsection (3), where

(a) a non-resident person owes an amount at any time to a particular person or partnership (other than a corporation resident in Canada), and

(b) it is reasonable to conclude that the amount or a portion of the amount became owing, or was permitted to remain owing, to the particular person or partnership because

(i) a corporation resident in Canada made a loan or transfer of property, or

(ii) the particular person or partnership anticipated that a corporation resident in Canada would make a loan or transfer of property,

either directly or indirectly, in any manner whatever, to or for the benefit of any person or partnership (other than an exempt loan or transfer),

the non-resident person is deemed at that time to owe to the corporation an amount equal to the amount, or the portion of the amount, as the case may be, owing to the particular person or partnership.

Related Provisions: 17(3) — Exception; 17(11.3) — Determination of whether persons are related; 17(15)"exempt loan or transfer" — Definition.

Notes: For rulings applying 17(2) see VIEWS docs 2005-0149491R3, 2010-0353141R3, 2010-0376391R3, 2010-0377581R3, 2011-0414431R3, 2011-0418711R3, 2012-0452291R3.

For the meaning of "indirectly" in (b) closing words, see Notes to 17.1(1)

17(2) amended by 2014 budget bill #2 (for tax years that begin after July 12, 2013), 1998 Budget.

(3) Exception to anti-avoidance rule — indirect loan — Subsection (2) does not apply to an amount owing at any time by a non-resident person to a particular person or partnership where

(a) at that time, the non-resident person and the particular person or each member of the particular partnership, as the case may be, are controlled foreign affiliates of the corporation resident in Canada; or

(b) at that time,

(i) the non-resident person and the particular person are not related or the non-resident person and each member of the particular partnership are not related, as the case may be,

(ii) the terms or conditions made or imposed in respect of the amount owing, determined without reference to any loan or transfer of property by a corporation resident in Canada described in paragraph (2)(b) in respect of the amount owing, are such that persons dealing at arm's length would have been willing to enter into them at the time that they were entered into, and

(iii) if there were an amount of interest payable on the amount owing at that time that would be required to be included in computing the income of a foreign affiliate of the corporation resident in Canada for a taxation year, that amount of interest would not be required to be included in computing the foreign accrual property income of the affiliate for that year.

Related Provisions: 17(10), (12), (13), (15) — Definition of "controlled foreign affiliate"; 17(11), (11.1), (11.3) — Meaning of "related"; 17(11.2) — Back-to-back loans — look-through rule.

Notes: For a ruling that 17(3)(a) applies see VIEWS doc 2009-0347271R3.

17(3) amended by 1998 Budget, effective for taxation years that begin after 1999.

(4) Anti-avoidance rule — loan through partnership — For the purpose of this section, where a non-resident person owes an amount at any time to a partnership and subsection (2) does not deem the non-resident person to owe an amount equal to that amount to a corporation resident in Canada, the non-resident person is deemed at that time to owe to each member of the partnership, on the same terms as those that apply in respect of the amount owing

to the partnership, that proportion of the amount owing to the partnership at that time that

(a) the fair market value of the member's interest in the partnership at that time

is of

(b) the fair market value of all interests in the partnership at that time.

Notes: 17(4) added by 1998 Budget, for taxation years that begin after Feb. 23, 1998.

(5) Anti-avoidance rule — loan through trust — For the purpose of this section, where a non-resident person owes an amount at any time to a trust and subsection (2) does not deem the non-resident person to owe an amount equal to that amount to a corporation resident in Canada,

(a) where the trust is a non-discretionary trust at that time, the non-resident person is deemed at that time to owe to each beneficiary of the trust, on the same terms as those that apply in respect of the amount owing to the trust, that proportion of the amount owing to the trust that

(i) the fair market value of the beneficiary's interest in the trust at that time

is of

(ii) the fair market value of all the beneficial interests in the trust at that time; and

(b) in any other case, the non-resident person is deemed at that time to owe to each settlor in respect of the trust, on the same terms as those that apply in respect of the amount owing to the trust, an amount equal to the amount owing to the trust.

Notes: 17(5) added by 1998 Budget, for taxation years that begin after Feb. 23, 1998.

(6) Anti-avoidance rule — loan to partnership — For the purpose of this section, where a particular partnership owes an amount at any time to any person or any other partnership (in this subsection referred to as the "lender"), each member of the particular partnership is deemed to owe at that time to the lender, on the same terms as those that apply in respect of the amount owing by the particular partnership to the lender, that proportion of the amount owing to the lender that

(a) the fair market value of the member's interest in the particular partnership at that time

is of

(b) the fair market value of all interests in the particular partnership at that time.

Notes: 17(6) added by 1998 Budget, for taxation years that begin after Feb. 23, 1998.

(7) Exception — Subsection (1) does not apply in respect of an amount owing to a corporation resident in Canada by a non-resident person if a tax has been paid under Part XIII on the amount owing, except that, for the purpose of this subsection, tax under Part XIII is deemed not to have been paid on that portion of the amount owing in respect of which an amount was repaid or applied under subsection 227(6.1).

Notes: 17(7) does not apply to an interest-free loan that creates Part XIII tax on a deemed dividend, in the CRA's view: VIEWS doc 2007-0243331C6.

17(7) added by 1998 Budget, for taxation years that end after March 9, 1999.

(8) Exception — Subsection (1) does not apply to a corporation resident in Canada for a taxation year of the corporation in respect of an amount owing to the corporation by a non-resident person if the non-resident person is a controlled foreign affiliate of the corporation throughout the period in the year during which the amount is owing to the extent that it is established that the amount owing

(a) arose as a loan or advance of money to the affiliate that the affiliate has used, throughout the period that began when the loan or advance was made and that ended at the earlier of the end of the year and the time at which the amount was repaid,

(i) for the purpose of earning

(A) income from an active business, as defined in subsection 95(1), of the affiliate, or

(B) income that was included in computing the income from an active business of the affiliate under subsection 95(2), or

(ii) for the purpose of making a loan or advance to another controlled foreign affiliate of the corporation where, if interest became payable on the loan or advance at any time in the period and the affiliate was required to include the interest in computing its income for a taxation year, that interest would not be required to be included in computing the affiliate's foreign accrual property income for that year; or

(b) arose in the course of an active business, as defined in subsection 95(1), carried on by the affiliate throughout the period that began when the amount owing arose and that ended at the earlier of the end of the year and the time at which the amount was repaid.

Related Provisions: 17(8.1), (8.2) — Replacement borrowings still eligible for 17(8); 17(10), (12), (13), (15) — Definition of "controlled foreign affiliate"; 17(11.3) — Effect of 17(8) on whether persons related for 17(3)(b); 212(1)(b) — Part XIII (withholding) tax on interest payments to non-resident; 247(7) — Loan described in 17(8) not subject to transfer pricing rules.

Notes: Where 17(8) applies, 247(2) generally does not: see 247(7) and VIEWS doc 2017-0691071C6 [2017 IFA q.1].

To determine the purpose for which funds are used for 17(8), the CRA will apply the same IT-533 tests as for 20(1)(c): VIEWS doc 2009-0348851C6. The *Trans-Prairie* "fill the hole" test [see Notes to 20(1)(c)] can apply to (a)(i)(A): 2016-0676701E5 (reversing 2000-0060475). "Making a loan or advance" in 17(8)(a)(ii) does not include acquiring an existing debt: 2011-0414111I7.

17(8) opening words amended by 2007 budget bill #2 for taxation years beginning after Feb. 23, 1998.

17(8) added by 1998 Budget, for taxation years that begin after Feb. 23, 1998.

(8.1) Borrowed money — Subsection (8.2) applies in respect of money (referred to in this subsection and in subsection (8.2) as "new borrowings") that a controlled foreign affiliate of a particular corporation resident in Canada has borrowed from the particular corporation to the extent that the affiliate has used the new borrowings

(a) to repay money (referred to in this subsection and in subsection (8.2) as "previous borrowings") previously borrowed from any person or partnership, if

(i) the previous borrowings became owing after the last time at which the affiliate became a controlled foreign affiliate of the particular corporation, and

(ii) the previous borrowings were, at all times after they became owing, used for a purpose described in subparagraph (8)(a)(i) or (ii); or

(b) to pay an amount owing (referred to in this subsection and in subsection (8.2) as the "unpaid purchase price") by the affiliate for property previously acquired from any person or partnership, if

(i) the property was acquired, and the unpaid purchase price became owing, by the affiliate after the last time at which it became a controlled foreign affiliate of the particular corporation,

(ii) the unpaid purchase price is in respect of the property, and

(iii) throughout the period that began when the unpaid purchase price became owing by the affiliate and ended when the unpaid purchase price was so paid, the property had been used principally to earn income described in clause (8)(a)(i)(A) or (B).

Notes: For CRA interpretation see doc 2015-056906I7 (no-interest loan to CFA).

For the meaning of "used principally" in (b)(iii), see Notes to 73(3).

17(8.1), (8.2) added by 2007 budget bill #2, for tax years beginning after Feb. 23, 1998.

(8.2) Deemed use — To the extent that this subsection applies in respect of new borrowings, the new borrowings are, for the purpose of subsection (8), deemed to have been used for the purpose for which the proceeds from the previous borrowings were used or were deemed by this subsection to have been used, or to acquire the property in respect of which the unpaid purchase price was payable, as the case may be.

Related Provisions: 17(8.1) — Conditions for 17(8.2) to apply.

Notes: See Notes to 17(8.1).

(9) Exception — Subsection (1) does not apply to a corporation resident in Canada for a taxation year of the corporation in respect of an amount owing to the corporation by a non-resident person if

(a) the corporation is not related to the non-resident person throughout the period in the year during which the amount owing is outstanding;

(b) the amount owing arose in respect of goods sold or services provided to the non-resident person by the corporation in the ordinary course of the business carried on by the corporation; and

(c) the terms and conditions in respect of the amount owing are such that persons dealing at arm's length would have been willing to enter into them at the time that they were entered into.

Related Provisions: 17(10), (12), (13), (15) — Definition of "controlled foreign affiliate"; 17(11), (11.1) — Meaning of "related".

Notes: 17(9) added by 1998 Budget, for taxation years that begin after Feb. 23, 1998.

(10) Determination of whether related and controlled foreign affiliate status — For the purpose of this section, in determining whether persons are related to each other and whether a non-resident corporation is a controlled foreign affiliate of a corporation resident in Canada at any time,

(a) each member of a partnership is deemed to own that proportion of the number of shares of a class of the capital stock of a corporation owned by the partnership at that time that

(i) the fair market value of the member's interest in the partnership at that time

is of

(ii) the fair market value of all interests in the partnership at that time; and

(b) each beneficiary of a non-discretionary trust is deemed to own that proportion of the number of shares of a class of the capital stock of a corporation owned by the trust at that time that

(i) the fair market value of the beneficiary's interest in the trust at that time

is of

(ii) the fair market value of all the beneficial interests in the trust at that time.

Related Provisions: 17(12), (13) — Determination of controlled foreign affiliate status.

Notes: 17(10) added by 1998 Budget, for taxation years that begin after Feb. 23, 1998.

(11) Determination of whether related — For the purpose of this section, in determining whether persons are related to each other at any time, each settlor in respect of a trust, other than a non-discretionary trust, is deemed to own the shares of a class of the capital stock of a corporation owned by the trust at that time.

Related Provisions: 17(11.1) — Limitation on meaning of "related".

Notes: 17(11) added by 1998 Budget, for taxation years that begin after Feb. 23, 1998.

(11.1) Determination of whether persons related — For the purposes of this section, in determining whether persons are related to each other at any time, any rights referred to in subparagraph 251(5)(b)(i) that exist at that time are deemed not to exist at that time to the extent that the exercise of those rights is prohibited at that time under a law of the country under the law of which the corporation was formed or last continued and is governed, that restricts the foreign ownership or control of the corporation.

Related Provisions: 17(11.3) — Additional rule re whether persons related for 17(3)(b).

Notes: 17(11.1) added by 2001 technical bill, for taxation years that begin after Feb. 23, 1998.

(11.2) Back-to-back loans — For the purposes of subsection (2) and paragraph (3)(b), where a non-resident person, or a partnership each member of which is non-resident, (in this subsection referred to as the "intermediate lender") makes a loan to a non-resident person, or a partnership each member of which is non-resident, (in this subsection referred to as the "intended borrower") because the intermediate lender received a loan from another non-resident person, or a partnership each member of which is non-resident, (in this subsection referred to as the "initial lender")

(a) the loan made by the intermediate lender to the intended borrower is deemed to have been made by the initial lender to the intended borrower (to the extent of the lesser of the amount of the loan made by the initial lender to the intermediate lender and the amount of the loan made by the intermediate lender to the intended borrower) under the same terms and conditions and at the same time as it was made by the intermediate lender; and

(b) the loan made by the initial lender to the intermediate lender and the loan made by the intermediate lender to the intended borrower are deemed not to have been made to the extent of the amount of the loan deemed to have been made under paragraph (a).

Notes: A bank deposit is considered a "loan" for 17(11.2): VIEWS doc 2003-0017231E5.

17(11.2) added by 2001 technical bill, for taxation years that begin after Feb. 23, 1998.

(11.3) Determination of whether persons related — For the purpose of applying paragraph (3)(b) in respect of a corporation resident in Canada described in paragraph (2)(b), in determining whether persons described in subparagraph (3)(b)(i) are related to each other at any time, any rights referred to in paragraph 251(5)(b) that otherwise exist at that time are deemed not to exist at that time where, if the rights were exercised immediately before that time,

(a) all of those persons would at that time be controlled foreign affiliates of the corporation resident in Canada; and

(b) because of subsection (8), subsection (1) would not apply to the corporation resident in Canada in respect of the amount that would, but for this subsection, have been deemed to have been owing at that time to the corporation resident in Canada by the non-resident person described in subparagraph (3)(b)(i).

Notes: 17(11.3) added by 2001 technical bill, for tax years that begin after Feb. 23, 1998.

(12) Determination of controlled foreign affiliate status — For the purpose of this section, in determining whether a non-resident person is a controlled foreign affiliate of a corporation resident in Canada at any time, each settlor in respect of a trust, other than a non-discretionary trust, is deemed to own that proportion of the number of shares of a class of the capital stock of a corporation owned by the trust at that time that one is of the number of settlors in respect of the trust at that time.

Notes: 17(12) added by 1998 Budget, for taxation years that begin after Feb. 23, 1998.

(13) Extended definition of controlled foreign affiliate — For the purpose of this section, where, at any time, two corporations resident in Canada are related (otherwise than because of a right referred to in paragraph 251(5)(b)), any corporation that is a controlled foreign affiliate of one of the corporations at that time is deemed to be a controlled foreign affiliate of the other corporation at that time.

Notes: 17(13) added by 1998 Budget, for taxation years that begin after Feb. 23, 1998.

(14) Anti-avoidance rule — where rights or shares issued, acquired or disposed of to avoid tax — For the purpose of this section,

(a) where any person or partnership has a right under a contract, in equity or otherwise, either immediately or in the future and either absolutely or contingently, to, or to acquire, shares of the capital stock of a corporation and it can reasonably be considered that the principal purpose for the existence of the right is to avoid or reduce the amount of income that subsection (1) would otherwise require any corporation to include in computing its income for any taxation year, those shares are deemed to be owned by that person or partnership; and

(b) where any person or partnership acquires or disposes of shares of the capital stock of a corporation, either directly or indirectly, and it can reasonably be considered that the principal purpose for the acquisition or disposition of the shares is to avoid or reduce the amount of income that subsection (1) would otherwise require any corporation to include in computing its income for any taxation year, those shares are deemed not to have been acquired or disposed of, as the case may be, and where the shares were unissued by the corporation immediately before the acquisition, those shares are deemed not to have been issued.

Related Provisions: 95(6) — Similar rule re foreign accrual property income.

Notes: For rulings that 17(14)(b) does not apply see VIEWS docs 2009-0347271R3, 2012-0452291R3. For the meaning of "indirectly" in (b) see Notes to 17.1(1).

17(14) added by 1998 Budget, for taxation years that begin after Feb. 23, 1998.

(15) Definitions — The definitions in this subsection apply in this section.

"controlled foreign affiliate", at any time, of a taxpayer resident in Canada, means a corporation that would, at that time, be a controlled foreign affiliate of the taxpayer within the meaning assigned by the definition "controlled foreign affiliate" in subsection 95(1) if the word "or" were added at the end of paragraph (a) of that definition and

(a) subparagraph (b)(ii) of that definition were read as "all of the shares of the capital stock of the foreign affiliate that are owned at that time by persons resident in Canada who do not deal at arm's length with the taxpayer,"; and

(b) subparagraph (b)(iv) of that definition were read as "all of the shares of the capital stock of the foreign affiliate that are owned at that time by persons resident in Canada who do not deal at arm's length with any relevant Canadian shareholder;".

Related Provisions: 17(9) — Rules for determining CFA status; 17(10), (12), (13) — Extended meaning of controlled foreign affiliate.

Notes: 17(15)"controlled foreign affiliate" amended by 2007 budget bill #2, last change effective for FAs' tax years that begin after Feb. 27, 2004. Added by 1998 Budget.

"exempt loan or transfer" means

(a) a loan made by a corporation resident in Canada where the interest rate charged on the loan is not less than the interest rate that a lender and a borrower would have been willing to agree to if they were dealing at arm's length with each other at the time the loan was made;

(b) a transfer of property (other than a transfer of property made for the purpose of acquiring shares of the capital stock of a foreign affiliate of a corporation or a foreign affiliate of a person resident in Canada with whom the corporation was not dealing at arm's length) or payment of an amount owing by a corporation resident in Canada pursuant to an agreement made on terms and conditions that persons who were dealing at arm's length at the time the agreement was entered into would have been willing to agree to;

(c) a dividend paid by a corporation resident in Canada on shares of a class of its capital stock; and

(d) a payment made by a corporation resident in Canada on a reduction of the paid-up capital in respect of shares of a class of its capital stock (not exceeding the total amount of the reduction).

Notes: For CRA interpretations on "exempt loan or transfer" (Y or N) see VIEWS docs 2001-0078027 (Y), 2004-0072331E5 (N), 2010-0381821R3 (Y).

17(15)"exempt loan or transfer" added by 1998 Budget and amended by 2001 technical bill, effective for taxation years that begin after February 23, 1998.

"non-discretionary trust", at any time, means a trust in which all interests were vested indefeasibly at the beginning of the trust's taxation year that includes that time.

Related Provisions: 248(1)"non-discretionary trust" — Definition applies to entire Act; 248(9.2) — Meaning of "vested indefeasibly".

Notes: Definition "non-discretionary trust" added by 1998 Budget, for tax years that begin after Feb. 23, 1998.

"settlor" in respect of a trust at any time means any person or partnership that has made a loan or transfer of property, either directly or indirectly, in any manner whatever, to or for the benefit of the trust at or before that time, other than, where the person or partnership deals at arm's length with the trust at that time,

(a) a loan made by the person or partnership to the trust at a reasonable rate of interest; or

(b) a transfer made by the person or partnership to the trust for fair market value consideration.

Notes: This definition is much broader than 108(1)"settlor", which applies to the taxation of trusts. For the meaning of "indirectly", see Notes to 17.1(1).

Definition added by 1998 Budget, for tax years that begin after Feb. 23, 1998.

Definitions [s. 17]: "active business", "amount" — 248(1); "arm's length" — 251(1); "business" — 248(1); "Canada" — 255; "class" — 248(6); "controlled foreign affiliate" — 17(15); "corporation" — 248(1), *Interpretation Act* 35(1); "debt" — 17(1); "disposition", "dividend" — 248(1); "exempt loan or transfer" — 17(15); "foreign accrual property income" — 95(1), (2), 248(1); "foreign affiliate" — 95(1), 248(1); "new borrowings" — 17(8.1); "non-discretionary trust" — 17(15); "non-resident" — 248(1); "original debt" — 17(1)(c); "paid-up capital" — 89(1), 248(1); "partnership" — see 96(1) Notes; "person", "prescribed" — 248(1); "prescribed rate" — Reg. 4301; "previous borrowings" — 17(8.1)(a); "property" — 248(1); "related" — 17(10), (11), (11.1), (11.3) 251(2)–(6); "resident", "resident in Canada" — 250; "settlor" — 17(15); "share" — 248(1); "taxation year" — 249; "taxpayer" — 248(1); "trust" — 104(1), 248(1), (3); "unpaid purchase price" — 17(8.1)(b); "vested indefeasibly" — 248(9.2).

17.1 (1) Deemed interest income — ss. 15 and 212.3 — Subject to subsection (2), if — at any time in a taxation year of a corporation resident in Canada (in this section referred to as the **"CRIC"**) or in a fiscal period of a qualifying Canadian partnership in respect of the CRIC — a non-resident corporation, or a partnership of which the non-resident corporation is a member, owes an amount to the CRIC or the qualifying Canadian partnership and the amount owing is a pertinent loan or indebtedness (as defined in subsection 15(2.11) or 212.3(11)),

(a) section 17 does not apply in respect of the amount owing; and

(b) the amount, if any, determined by the following formula is to be included in computing the income of the CRIC for the year or of the qualifying Canadian partnership for the fiscal period, as the case may be:

$$A - B$$

where

A is the amount that is the greater of

   (i) the amount of interest that would be included in computing the income of the CRIC for the year or of the qualifying Canadian partnership for the fiscal period, as the case may be, in respect of the amount owing for the particular period in the year, or the fiscal period, during which the amount owing was a pertinent loan or indebtedness if that interest were computed at the prescribed rate for the particular period, and

   (ii) the total of all amounts of interest payable in respect of the period in the year, or the fiscal period, during which the amount owing was a pertinent loan or indebtedness, by the CRIC, the qualifying Canadian partnership, a person resident in Canada with which the CRIC did not, at the time the amount owing arose, deal at arm's length or a partnership of which the CRIC or the person is a member, in respect of a debt obligation — entered into as part of a series of transactions or events that includes the transaction by which the amount owing arose — to the extent that the proceeds of the debt obligation can reasonably be considered to have directly or indirectly funded, in whole or in part, the amount owing, and

B is an amount included in computing the income of the CRIC for the year or of the qualifying Canadian partnership for the fiscal period, as the case may be, as, on account of, in lieu of or in satisfaction of, interest in respect of the amount owing for the period in the year, or the fiscal period, during which the amount owing was a pertinent loan or indebtedness.

Related Provisions: 15(2.14)(a) — Meaning of "qualifying Canadian partnership"; 15(2.14)(b) — Look-through rule for partnerships; 17.1(2) — Rule on change in control; 17.1(3) — Rule where tax treaty reduces income; 18(5)"outstanding debts to specified non-residents"(b)(ii) — Exclusion from thin capitalization rules; 212.3(25) — Application to partnerships for purposes of 212.3(11); 212.3(26) — Determining "related" and "control" for a trust for certain purposes; 257 — Formula cannot calculate to less than zero.

Notes: 17.1(1) provides interest deeming rules for the elective "pertinent loan or indebtedness" (PLOI) regimes of 15(2) and 212.3. 17.1(1) applies to PLOI as defined in 15(2.11) or 212.3(11). It generally requires the interest inclusion for a corporation resident in Canada (CRIC) from such loan or debt to be at least the interest calculated under Reg. 4301(b.1) (if the CRIC (or certain non-arm's length persons or partnerships) has incurred debt to fund the PLOI, the interest payable on that debt if it is higher). The prescribed rate is 4 percentage points higher than for s. 17 and there is no rounding-up rule: see Reg. 4301(b.1).

The references to "indirectly funded" and to interest payable by persons or partnerships other than the CRIC are intended to deal with situations where, for example, a Canadian corporation not at arm's length with the CRIC borrows money, makes an equity contribution to the CRIC, and the CRIC then makes the loan to the non-resident debtor. The imputed interest under 17.1(1) is intended to be based on the interest payable by the other corporation if that actual borrowing cost exceeds the interest determined using the prescribed rate.

For more on "indirectly": *Louie*, 2019 FCA 255, paras. 44-86 (re 207.01(1)"advantage": broad interpretation) (leave to appeal denied 2020 CarswellNat 1258 (SCC)); *Garron*, 2009 TCC 450 [aff'd on other grounds by FCA and SCC], paras. 289-301 (re 75(2): narrow interpretation); 256(5.1)–(6) (meaning of "controlled directly or indirectly"); VIEWS docs 2003-0032047, 2003-0032565 (for 67.3); 2018-0771861E5 (for 120.4); and Notes to 81(1)(h) (re foster care) and 95(2) (re 95(2)(a)(ii) opening words — FAPI).

Provision is also made for amounts owing to a qualifying Canadian partnership in respect of the CRIC and for amounts owed by a partnership of which a non-resident corporation is a member, in the context of PLOIs referred to in 15(2.11). For PLOIs in 212.3(11), the partnership look-through rule in 212.3(25) applies.

For CRA interpretation see VIEWS docs 2013-0483751C6 [2013 IFA q.6] (question 6(e)); 2014-0517151E5 (where PLOI is denominated in foreign currency); 2014-0519431E5 (calculation of interest on late-filed PLOI election).

See also Notes at end of 17.1.

Regulations: 4301(b.1) — Prescribed interest rate.

(2) Acquisition of control — If at any time a parent or group of parents referred to in section 212.3 acquires control of a CRIC and the CRIC was not controlled by a non-resident person, or a group of non-resident persons not dealing with each other at arm's length, immediately before that time, no amount is to be included under subsection (1) in computing the income of the CRIC in respect of a "pertinent loan or indebtedness" (as defined in subsection 212.3(11)) for the period that begins at that time and ends on the day that is 180 days after that time.

Related Provisions: 256(6)–(9) — Whether control acquired.

Notes: 17.1(2) amended by 2021 budget bill #1, for transactions or events after March 18, 2019, due to 212.3 being expanded to include control by non-resident individuals. Before the amendment, read:

> (2) If at any time a parent referred to in section 212.3 acquires control of a CRIC and the CRIC was not controlled by a non-resident corporation immediately before that time, no amount is to be included under subsection (1) in computing the income of the CRIC in respect of a pertinent loan or indebtedness (as defined in subsection 212.3(11)) for the period that begins at that time and ends on the day that is 180 days after that time.

(3) Tax treaties — A particular loan or indebtedness that would, in the absence of this subsection, be a pertinent loan or indebtedness is deemed not to be a pertinent loan or indebtedness if, because of a provision of a tax treaty, the amount included in computing the income of the CRIC for any taxation year or of the qualifying Canadian partnership for any fiscal period, as the case may be, in respect of the particular loan or indebtedness is less than it would be if no tax treaty applied.

Notes: 17.1 added by 2012 budget bill #2, for tax years and fiscal periods that end after March 28, 2012, but for acquisitions of control of a CRIC that occur before Oct. 15, 2012, read 17.1(2) differently.

Definitions [s. 17.1]: "amount" — 248(1); "arm's length" — 251(1); "Canadian partnership" — 102(1), 248(1); "control" — 212.3(26), 256(6)–(9); "corporation" — 248(1), *Interpretation Act* 35(1); "CRIC" — 17.1(1); "fiscal period" — 249.1; "non-resident" — 248(1); "parent" — 212.3(1)(b); "partnership" — see 96(1) Notes; "person" — 248(1); "pertinent loan or indebtedness" — 15(2.11), 17.1(3), 212.3(11); "prescribed" — 248(1); "qualifying Canadian partnership" — 15(2.14)(a); "resident in Canada" — 94(3)(a), 250; "series of transactions" — 248(10); "tax treaty" — 248(1); "taxation year" — 249.

Deductions

18. (1) General limitations — In computing the income of a taxpayer from a business or property no deduction shall be made in respect of

    (a) **general limitation** — an outlay or expense except to the extent that it was made or incurred by the taxpayer for the purpose of gaining or producing income from the business or property;

Related Provisions: 7(3)(b) — No deduction to employer for cost of issuing stock options to employees; 18(1)(c) — Limitation re exempt income; 18(9) — Limitation re prepaid expenses; 18.3(3) — No deduction for rent or other amount payable to REIT on stapled security; 19, 19.01, 19.1 — Limitation on advertising expense deduction; 20(1) — Deductions permitted; 20.01 — Deduction for private health services plan premiums; 67 — Unreasonable expenses not allowed; 67.1 — 50% limit on expenses for food and entertainment; 143.3 — Limitation on deductibility for issuing shares and stock options; Reg. 1102(1)(c) — No CCA unless property acquired for purpose of gaining or producing income.

Notes: 18(1)(a) does not *allow* a deduction; that is done by 9(1) in calculating "profit": *Lacroix*, 2013 TCC 312, para. 9. 18(1)(a) *prohibits* deductions that are not incurred to earn income. 18(1)(a) is based on expenses *incurred* (obligation to pay), not paid, so a spouse paying one's expense does not make the expense non-deductible, but CRA thinks there could be an offsetting 9(1) or s. 80 income inclusion: VIEWS doc 2018-0768871C6 [2018 APFF q.16].

The "income" required by 18(1)(a) is gross income, not net income or profit after expenses: *Novopharm Ltd.*, 2003 FCA 112 (leave to appeal denied 2003 CarswellNat 4612 (SCC)), based on *Ludco Enterprises*, 2001 SCC 62, where this interpretation applied to interest deductibility (see Notes to 20(1)(c)). Proposed s. 3.1 [2003], which would have changed this rule, has been withdrawn.

See 9(2) Notes under "Second-guessing business decisions". The criteria for deductibility were broadened by deleting "wholly, exclusively and necessarily" from the predecessor to 18(1)(a): *BJ Services*, 2003 TCC 900. Expenses of doing work *pro bono* can be deductible: VIEWS doc 2008-0278561E5. Costs of providing management assistance to related companies were disallowed in *Lyncorp International*, 2011 FCA 352, even though those companies' profits could be paid as dividends to the taxpayer, because the evidence of the work done was unclear and permitting the expenses was "not consistent with commercial reality". The same applied in *Motech Molding*, 2012 TCC 351 (potential receipt of dividends as a result of sponsorship fees was too remote). *Contra*, in *Potash Corp.*, 2011 TCC 213, consulting fees to reorganize related companies to repatriate offshore profits tax-efficiently were allowed (although only as eligible capital expenditures under then-20(1)(b)).

For discussion of losses denied because there is no real business, see Notes to 9(2).

In *Industries Perron*, 2013 FCA 176, para. 29, 18(1)(a) prevented a deduction for preliminary countervailing duty (later cancelled) that was "paid" by purchasing term deposits to lodge with a bank to guarantee payment, because the amounts "were not made 'once and for all, without recourse' as Perron retained an interest in the funds".

Advertising/promotion expenses were allowed, though remote from the business, in: *Matt Harris & Son*, [2001] 1 C.T.C. 2513 (TCC) (stock car and snowmobile racing, for wood and gravel business); *Otterbrook Percherons*, 2004 TCC 517 (exhibiting horses, for wood supply business); *Ross*, 2005 TCC 286 (Crown's FCA appeal discontinued) (maintaining thoroughbred horses, for stockbroker earning commission income); *Bilous [Yorkton Distributors]*, 2011 TCC 154 (snowmobile museum, for farm chemicals business). They were disallowed in: *Ace Salvage*, 1985 CarswellNat 398 (TCC) (horse racing, for scrap metal business); *Ngai*, 2018 TCC 26 (various, for real estate broker, though sponsoring a horse show was allowed: para. 49). Incentives paid to clients by a real estate agent are normally deductible: VIEWS doc 2012-0432621E5; *Ngai* (above), paras. 75, 81-83. See also Notes to 18(1)(b) under "Advertising".

Capital expenditures: see Notes to 18(1)(b).

Ceasing business — later expenses: See under "Wind-down" below.

Commissions and finder's fees must be calculated objectively and not be discretionary to be deductible: *Edison Transportation*, 2016 TCC 80, para. 49. A musician's fees to "associate musicians" who were close friends were disallowed as too vague in *Costanzo*, 2017 TCC 58.

Consulting fees that were disguised payment towards a share purchase were denied as not connected with an income source: *Groupe Immobilier Grilli*, 2019 TCC 223.

Damages paid out: In *Canadian Imperial Bank of Commerce*, 2013 FCA 122, a $3 billion settlement paid by CIBC in the Enron debacle could not be non-deductible by being "egregious and repulsive": the "morality" of the taxpayer's conduct is not relevant (paras. 1, 21) (further preliminary decision at 2015 TCC 280). Damages were deductible in: *McNeill*, [2000] 2 C.T.C. 304 (FCA) (paid for violating restrictive covenant); *ZR*, 2007 TCC 598 (paid to settle US lawsuit against ZR to collect a judgment against her spouse, relating to hotels they operated). Damages were not deductible in:

St-Georges, 2006 FCA 207 (leave to appeal denied 2007 CarswellNat 345 (SCC)) (paid by director to company's creditors for wrongfully causing company to pay a dividend); *Nisker*, 2008 FCA 37 (leave to appeal denied 2008 CarswellNat 2559) (paid by corporation's officer to settle tort claim for acting in bad faith on real estate deal); *Fonds de solidarité*, 2019 FCA 36 ($9m payment to town by lender F, from failed assets of paper mill, was made to walk away from project, not as marketing to maintain F's reputation); *Hanmar Motor*, 2007 TCC 618 (payments to insolvent subsidiary's employees for unpaid wages, legally required). See also IT-467R2 para. 5, VIEWS docs 2008-0280801E5, 2012-0443721E5. The liability to pay must be unconditional and not contingent: IT-467R2 para. 10, doc 2007-0253271E5. Damages paid by an intended buyer for breach of the purchase agreement are not a capital loss because no property was disposed of: 2016-0652851C6 [2016 APFF q.3].

Defending against a threat to a business's working capital is deductible, since the expenses preserve profit-earning potential: *Premium Iron Ores*, [1966] C.T.C. 391 (SCC); but see Notes to 18(1)(b). This principle may apply to tax-risk insurance.

Directors' fees to children of shareholders are allowed under 18(1)(a) regardless of how little work the directors do, but may be limited by s. 67: *Manchester Chivers Insurance Brokers*, [2005] 5 C.T.C. 2180 (TCC). Scholarships to children of shareholders may be deductible if they are sufficiently open and merit-based to be taxed under 56(1)(n) rather than 15(1): VIEWS doc 2007-0223341E5.

Employee expenses and benefits are normally deductible if included in the employee's income (e.g. VIEWS doc 2013-0510921E5), but see Notes to 18(1)(h) and 67. Where company Cco takes over X's employees and provides their services to X (to shift income to a family management company), the cost of paying Cco remains deductible to X: 2013-0513411R3 [but note the 2016 Budget changes to s. 125].

Estate administration costs such as fees to gather, distribute and settle assets are generally non-deductible: *Waxman Estate*, [1994] 1 C.T.C. 2817 (TCC); aff'd 1994 CarswellNat 2992 (FCA); *Bui*, [2014] 2 C.T.C. 2097 (TCC); VIEWS doc 2013-0477561I7.

Group sickness and accident insurance trusts set up offshore for select employees did not entitle the employer to deduct contributions, in *Labow*, 2010 TCC 408; aff'd 2011 FCA 305: "there was no commercial reason for Dr. Labow to spend $400,000 to provide [his wife] with disability and medical insurance ... [this was] simply a way of accumulating capital in a tax-free jurisdiction" (TCC, paras. 34, 36).

Insurance premiums for employees and shareholders: see Notes to 20(1)(e.2).

Legal fees (LF) up to $3,000 to incorporate a business are allowed under 20(1)(b); any excess goes into Class 14.1. LF to set up a trust were considered non-deductible, as not in respect of a business, in VIEWS doc 2009-0306591E5. LF include court costs awarded to the other side: 2015-0578131I7. LF were allowed in: *Bilodeau*, 2004 TCC 685 (company successfully defended its CEO accused of sexual assault while on a business trip, as the company had a *bona fide* interest in establishing his innocence); *MacKinnon*, 2007 TCC 658 (LF to recover an RRSP (and interest), mistakenly not paid to the beneficiary on the RRSP owner's death).

LF were disallowed in: *Begley*, 2008 TCC 605 (self-employed dentist sued for long-term disability benefits that would be non-taxable); *Doiron*, 2012 FCA 71 (lawyer defending criminal charges arising from client association: LF not laid out to earn income); *Ironside*, 2013 TCC 339 [includes detailed discussion of case law]; attempt to reargue 2015 TCC 116 (CA defending Alberta Securities Commission charges: insufficient connection to ability to earn income as a CA); *Gouveia*, 2013 TCC 414 [aff'd on other grounds 2014 FCA 289] (former President of public corp defending Ont. Securities Commission charges and shareholder class action: these related to his work as corporate employee, not later work as consultant); *Lacroix*, 2013 TCC 312 (shareholder paid LF re bankruptcy of failed company); *Danilov*, 2017 TCC 114 (litigation against in-laws re private family loan was not for D's business); *Nandlal*, 2017 TCC 162 (shareholder required to pay fees incurred by failed corp, unrelated to his current business); *Horn*, 2017 TCC 167 (shareholder paid LF to protect his interest in corp).

For LF, see also Notes to 8(1)(b), 18(1)(b), 18(1)(h) and 60(o) and "Defending against a threat" above. LF relating to a past business: see "Wind-down" below.

Meals for employees and contractors are generally deductible (subject to the 50% rule in 67.1(1)): VIEWS doc 2013-0508451E5, but may be a taxable benefit (see Notes to 6(1)(a)).

Merger expenses were held deductible in *International Colin Energy*, [2003] 1 C.T.C. 2406 (TCC), since they were incurred to improve the value of the company's shares and the company's income potential. CRA generally disagrees and believes that costs relating to a corp's own shares are on account of capital: IT-99R5 para. 16; docs 2002-0151425, 2006-0195981C6. However, in *BJ Services*, 2003 TCC 900, expenses of defending against a hostile takeover (including "break" fees) were deductible, as the deduction created an accurate portrayal of the company's income. Expenses of maintaining shareholder relations were part of the company's business operations. See also *Boulangerie St-Augustin*, 1996 CarswellNat 2523 (FCA), to the same effect; Citrone & D'Elia, "Now That I Have Paid You ... Are Your Fees Deductible?" IX(4) *Business Vehicles* (Federated Press) 466-73 (2004); Steeves & Van Esch, "Deductibility of Expenses in Merger and Acquisition Transactions", 65(1) *Canadian Tax Journal* 241-69 (2017).

Motor vehicle accident repair expenses are deductible if the vehicle was being used for business purposes at the time of the accident: IT-521R para. 7. In *Harvey*, 2013 TCC 298, paras. 69-74, H's daughter and friends took his leased Jeep without permission and crashed it. He was allowed to deduct the repair costs in the same proportion (80%) as his annual use of the Jeep for business purposes. (Had he allowed the daughter to use the Jeep, the expense would have been personal.)

Networking and socializing costs paid to a retired owner were allowed to an investment counselling company in *Bush Associates*, 2010 TCC 159.

Penalties and fines are generally non-deductible: see Notes to 67.6.

Personal expenses such as clothes and meals: see Notes to 18(1)(h).

Prepaid expenses: see 18(9).

Real estate broker commission rebates to clients are deductible: *Ngai*, 2018 TCC 26, para. 53.

Reclamation and ongoing clean-up costs are normally considered laid out to earn income and thus deductible: VIEWS doc 9413377 (but not if the business has not been operated for years: 2007-0232611E5). They are part of the cost of the land, and should not be counted in the cost of a building built on the land: 2007-0228881E5. Other decontamination, environmental testing and greenhouse gas costs may be capital expenses: docs 9328197, 2006-0196081C6, 2006-0196082C6, 2008-0276631C6. Screening for bacteria in cooling towers and condensers is likely deductible: 2010-0358981E5. CRA accepts that *Daishowa-Marubeni*, 2013 SCC 29 (see Notes to 54"proceeds of disposition") applies to embedded reclamation obligations: 2017-0695131C6 [2017 CPTS q.1]. See also Diep & Keyes, "Reclamation", XIV(1) *Resource Sector Taxation* (Federated Press) 2-13 (2020).

Regional development charges on land were deductible in *Urbandale Realty Corp.*, [2000] 2 C.T.C. 250 (FCA).

Royalties paid under the Canada Petroleum Resources Act are deductible: VIEWS doc 2018-0742881E5.

Services provided by a business are not a deduction even if done for promotion purposes. Only the *costs* of providing the services are deductible. If the services are considered bartered for advertising, then the value of the services is included in income and an offsetting deduction allowed: VIEWS doc 2019-0800941E5 (see also 9(1) Notes under "Barter").

Shareholder benefits may be non-deductible and also taxable to the shareholder: see Notes to 15(1).

Shutdown costs: see under "Wind-down" below.

Startup costs: see Notes to 9(1).

Taxes on income are generally not deductible: see Notes to 18(1)(t) and 20(1)(v).

Termination payments made on selling or shutting down a business may be non-deductible: VIEWS doc 2003-0011007. However, 18(1)(a) "should not be so readily applied simply because the income producing asset [a hurricane-damaged rental property] is up for sale during an extended period of income deprivation caused by extraordinary conditions beyond the control and expectation of the taxpayer ... even if the income stream of an enterprise was at an absolute end, a reasonable sell-off period should be recognized during which holding expenses should be allowed": *Mikhail*, [2002] 2 C.T.C. 2612 (TCC), para. 29. Lease cancellation payments: see Notes to 9(1).

Wind-down or post-termination costs may be deductible: *Selig*, 1955 CarswellNat 14 (TAB); *Poulin*, 1996 CarswellNat 1017 (FCA) (real estate broker who had ceased the business was allowed to deduct damages paid out for a lawsuit in the course of his business); *Heard*, [2001] 4 C.T.C. 2426 (TCC), para. 15; *Mikhail*, [2002] 2 C.T.C. 2612 (TCC), para. 34; *Langille*, 2009 TCC 398, paras. 9-12; *Génier*, 2010 TCC 641, para. 29 ("It is simply incontrovertible that business closing costs are deductible business expenses"); *Raegele*, [2002] 2 C.T.C. 2955 (TCC), para. 19 (purpose of 18(1)(a) "is met where the cause of the expenses incurred is directly linked to the income producing activity of the business"); *Hébert*, 2018 TCC 48 (radio repair corp's only activity for years was trying to sell its remaining inventory of parts; this was active business for ABIL purposes); *Tournier*, 2018 TCC 229 (retired lawyer: file storage fees). See also VIEWS docs 9707457; 2015-0618981E5 (post-retirement E&O insurance premiums to protect against lawsuits); Goodman, "Losses Arising from Claims", XII(1) *Goodman on Estate Planning* (Federated Press) 937 (2003). Contra, see *Darling*, [2003] 1 C.T.C. 2367 (TCC) (no source of income exists).

For payments to family members, see Notes to s. 67.

See also Harris, "Deduction of Business Expenses", 43(5) *Canadian Tax Journal* 1190-1215 (1995); Briggs, "Expense Deductibility", 2012 Atlantic Provinces Tax Conference (ctf.ca), 5:1-27; J. Rachert, "Proving Business Expenses", 2012 BC Tax Conf. 11:1-26; Neilson, "Deductibility of Expenses", 2013 Prairie Provinces Tax Conf. 14:1-21; Gervais & Power, "Can I Deduct That?", 2013 Ontario Tax Conf. 10:1-15.

See also Notes to 18(1)(h) re personal expenses, and to 9(1) generally.

Income Tax Folios: S2-F1-C1: Health and welfare trusts [replaces IT-85R2]; S3-F9-C1: Lottery winnings, miscellaneous receipts, and income (and losses) from crime [replaces IT-185R, IT-213R, IT-256R, IT-334R2]; S4-F2-C1: Deductibility of fines and penalties [replaces IT-104R3].

Interpretation Bulletins: IT-80: Interest on money borrowed to redeem shares, or to pay dividends (cancelled); IT-99R5: Legal and accounting fees; IT-153R3: Land developers — subdivision and development costs and carrying charges on land; IT-211R: Membership dues — associations and societies; IT-223: Overhead expense insurance vs. income insurance (cancelled); IT-233R: Lease-option agreements; sale-leaseback agreements (cancelled); IT-261R: Prepayment of rents; IT-265R3: Payments of income and capital combined (cancelled); IT-316: Awards for employees' suggestions and inventions (cancelled); IT-339R2: Meaning of "private health services plan"; IT-341R4: Expenses of issuing shares, units in a trust, interests in a partnership or syndicate and expenses of borrowing money; IT-364: Commencement of business operations; IT-389R: Vacation-with-pay plans established under collective agreements; IT-461: Forfeited deposits (cancelled); IT-467R2: Damages, settlements and similar payments; IT-475: Expenditures on research and for business expansion; IT-487: General limitation on deduction of outlays or expenses; IT-521R: Motor vehicle expenses claimed by self-employed individuals; IT-525R: Performing artists.

Information Circulars: 77-11: Sales tax reassessments.

I.T. Technical News: 12 (meals and beverages at golf clubs); 16 (*Tonn*, *Mastri*, *Mohammad* and *Kaye* cases; *Scott* case); 34 (emission reduction and offset credits: q3).

Advance Tax Rulings: ATR-4: Exchange of interest rates; ATR-20: Redemption premium on debentures; ATR-21: Pension benefit from an unregistered pension plan; ATR-23: Private health services plan; ATR-45: Share appreciation rights plan; ATR-50: Structured settlement.

Forms: T2125: Statement of business or professional activities.

(b) **capital outlay or loss** — an outlay, loss or replacement of capital, a payment on account of capital or an allowance in respect of depreciation, obsolescence or depletion except as expressly permitted by this Part;

Related Provisions: 16(1) — Income and capital combined; 20(1) — Deductions permitted; 20(10) — Convention expenses; 20(16) — Terminal loss; 26(2) — Banks; 30 — Clearing land, levelling land and laying tile drainage; 37(1)(b) — Deductible R&D expenditures on capital; 66.1(6.2) — Certain pre-production mining expenses deemed not to be capital expenditures.

Notes: 18(1)(b) prohibits deduction of capital expenses (except where specifically allowed, such as by s. 30); instead, they are included in the cost of property for capital gains calculation (40(1)(a), 39(1)(a)), and, for depreciable property, for capital cost allowance (CCA: 20(1)(a)). A current expense is not prohibited by 18(1)(b) but must still pass 18(1)(a) to be deductible.

The classic definition of capital expenditure is one incurred for procuring "the advantage of an enduring benefit", and includes "preserving an asset": *Dominion Natural Gas*, [1940-41] C.T.C. 155 (SCC), paras. 10, 16; but not an expense that creates no identifiable asset: *Algoma Central*, [1968] S.C.R. 447. However, the line between a non-deductible capital expense ("**CAP**") and a deductible current expense ("**CUR**") can be hard to draw.

See generally Income Tax Folio S3-F4-C1 ¶1.2-1.12; *Canderel Ltd.*, [1998] 2 C.T.C. 35 (SCC); *Toronto College Park*, [1998] 2 C.T.C. 78 (SCC); *Central Amusement*, [1992] 1 C.T.C. 218 (FCTD); *Rio Tinto*, 2016 TCC 172, paras. 73-89 (aff'd 2018 FCA 124, para. 61; leave to appeal denied 2019 CarswellNat 809 (SCC)); and "Recurring expenses" in alphabetical list below.

In *Gifford*, 2004 SCC 15, the Supreme Court of Canada stated that to read "on account of capital" literally "could render every expenditure that could not be directly traced to revenue non-deductible as an outlay of capital. This has not been the approach under [18(1)(b)] in the past, and the analysis should continue to look at what is acquired rather than examining where the money to make the payment originates."

Advertising costs and market surveys are generally CUR: *No. 511* (1958), 19 Tax A.B.C. 248, para. 28; *Algoma Central*, [1967] C.T.C. 130 (Exch. Ct.), para. 26 (aff'd on other grounds [1968] S.C.R. 447); *Bowater Power*, [1971] C.T.C. 818 (FCTD), paras. 53-54; *Wacky Wheatley's*, [1987] 2 C.T.C. 2311 (TCC), para. 29.

Buildings: see Durnford, "The Deductibility of Building Repair and Renovation Costs", 45(3) *Canadian Tax Journal* 395-416 (1997); Wen, "Maintenance vs Capital Improvement of a Building", 7(4) *Canadian Tax Focus* (ctf.ca) 10 (Nov. 2017). "If as a result of the repairs, something is created that did not exist previously, the expenditure will tend to be" CAP, but "if the repairs resulted in virtually the same old building as before" they are CUR: *Cousineau*, 2013 TCC 375, para. 13. Where repair is necessary, replacement with a different material may be CUR: *Gold Bar Developments*, [1987] 1 C.T.C. 262 (FCTD). Demolition costs: see Notes to 13(21.1).

The following building expenses were held to be CAP: renovations to rent out properties (*Fiore*, [1993] 2 C.T.C. 68 (FCA); *Hare*, 2013 FCA 80); repairs and renovations that materially improved building beyond original condition, or to rebuild property damaged by fire or hurricane (*Fotherby*, 2008 TCC 343; *Scharfe*, 2010 TCC 39; *Bishop*, 2010 FCA 137; *Pilon*, 2011 TCC 67 (FCA appeal dismissed for delay A-109-11); *Mbénar*, 2012 FCA 180; *Drago*, 2013 TCC 257); replacing wood-framed windows with vinyl-framed (*Peach*, 2020 TCC 12, para. 67 (under appeal to FCA)).

The following were CUR: replacing deck (*Lewin*, 2008 TCC 618); repairs to put duplex back to original state (*Janota*, 2010 TCC 395); repairs of hurricane damage that did not improve house beyond original condition (*Martinello*, 2010 TCC 432); returning roof to original condition (*Palangio*, 2012 TCC 405, para. 47 [aff'd on other grounds 2013 FCA 268]); replacing part of parking garage roof with a longer-lasting one (*Aon Inc.*, 2017 TCC 166); misc repairs to interior of vacant townhouse that was undergoing CAP exterior renovation (*DiCaita*, 2021 TCC 5).

For CRA views see Income Tax Folio S3-F4-C1 ¶1.4-1.8, 2009-0348491E5, 2010-0377171E5 and 2010-0382411I7 (renovations); 2010-0382041E5 (new roof); 2011-0414561E5 (rental property repairs); 2012-0432831E5 (repairs).

Business or project startup: in *Wescast Industries*, 2010 TCC 538 (FCA appeal discontinued A-452-10), $13 million in factory startup costs in Hungary, for "human resources development", "promotion and advertising" and "technology development", were CAP. (Such costs may be Class 14.1 property for CCA.) Preliminary costs such as feasibility studies were CAP where related to a specific project in *Trustpower*, [2016] NZSC 91, para. 71 (New Zealand). CRA is vague in VIEWS doc 2019-0816111C6

[2019 CPTS], q.5. See also "Transaction costs" below; and 9(1) Notes at "Startup costs". Incorporation costs: see 20(1)(b).

Client lists are purchased as CAP: *Gifford*, [2004] 2 C.T.C. 1 (SCC).

Compensation paid to clients by a securities broker for losses on bad investments were CAP, as they were to preserve his reputation and customer base: *Voyer*, 2019 TCC 221, para. 31; similarly, VIEWS doc 2011-040928117.

Conferences and conventions: see Notes to 20(10).

Contracts: In *Basell Canada*, 2007 TCC 685, payment for a supply contract to acquire raw materials at favourable prices, made when acquiring a business, was CUR. In *Gestions Pierre St-Cyr*, 2010 TCC 146, alarm system monitoring contracts were CAP. Costs of a 10-year contract to cut Christmas trees are CAP: VIEWS doc 2011-042464117. Cost of terminating a business arrangement: payments may be CUR even though they are capital to the recipient: IT-467R2 para. 16, docs 2003-004476117, 2006-0163291E5. See also "Termination payments" in 18(1)(a) Notes.

Education and training expenses create a lasting asset and so are CAP: IT-357R2, VIEWS doc 2005-0159941E5. (Tuition credits may be available under 118.5.) In *Tiede*, 2011 TCC 84, a photography training course was CAP and treated as an eligible capital expenditure (ECE: see Notes to 20(1)(b)). However, in *Setchell*, 2006 TCC 37, a 4-week computer training course was CUR.

Equipment: In *Kelowna Flightcraft*, 2003 TCC 347, a "Quiet Wing System" added to an aircraft to make it quieter to meet US regulations was allowed as an operating expense, because it did not add to the value of the aircraft. Computer equipment for which CCA is available is CAP even though it will rapidly depreciate: *Emmons*, 2006 TCC 269 (but note the fast depreciation in Reg. Sch. II:Cl. 50). Small portable items for a rental property needing constant replacing, such as kitchenware, sheets and lamps, were CUR in *Gruber*, 2007 TCC 340, while items of enduring benefit were CAP. Repairing rather than refurbishing equipment was CUR in *Alberta Printed Circuits*, 2009 TCC 195. See also VIEWS docs 2004-0070211E5 (computer hardware, software, office furniture, equipment); 2007-0243391C6 (car GPS and its map updates).

Financial reporting costs including appraisal fees are CUR: doc 2011-0411971C6.

Guarantee payments: In *Groupe TVA*, 2008 TCC 509, payments to a bank on a guarantee were CUR because the guarantee was needed to enable production of a film.

Incorporation costs: see 20(1)(b).

Investment opportunity expenses were CAP in *Robinson*, 2019 TCC 181, paras. 46-60; see also *Neonex*, [1978] C.T.C. 485 (FCA); *Firestone*, [1987] 2 C.T.C. 1 (FCA); and "Business startup" above.

Land: for decontamination, reclamation and clean-up costs see 18(1)(a) Notes under "Reclamation". For site investigation costs see 20(1)(dd). For farmers, see ss. 28-30. See also "Buildings" above.

Lease payments: see Notes to 9(1) and 18(9). In *Armour Group*, 2018 FCA 134, a purported lease cancellation fee was held to be a capital payment to acquire a leasehold interest.

Leasehold improvements and other lease costs: see 9(1) Notes at "Leasing".

Leasing commissions: see "Real estate commissions" below.

Legal fees (LF): the following have been ruled CUR: LF to recover mining claims the taxpayer had sold, as the taxpayer was in the business of staking claims and transferring them to mining companies (*Bolen*, 2007 FCA 293); LF to defend a trademark or sue another company for using a trade name (*Kellogg Co.*, [1943] C.T.C. 1 (SCC); *Hudson's Bay*, [1947] C.T.C. 86 (Exch. Ct.): fees not "laid out with the object of acquiring or bringing into existence an asset"); "board oversight" costs: *Rio Tinto* (see "Transaction costs" below); LF to recover theft of most of a company's assets (funds recovered were used to earn income): *102751 Canada*, 2021 QCCA 605.

The following have been held to be CAP: LF paid by physician in libel action to defend his professional reputation (*Upenieks*, 1994 CarswellNat 1110 (FCA)); LF for lawyer to defend against criminal charges to protect his ability to practise law (*Doiron*, 2012 FCA 71); LF to preserve company's reputation and income-earning potential (*Gouveia*, 2014 FCA 289); LF to cancel contract for purchase of rental property (*Dubois*, 2007 TCC 461); LF to protect rental property from foreclosure (*Keay*, 2009 FCA 170); LF to recover proceeds of disposition of capital property (*Audet*, 2012 TCC 162); LF re bankruptcy of failed company by its shareholder (*Lacroix*, 2013 TCC 312); LF in spousal dispute, to protect value of corporate shares so as to earn income from them (*Kondor*, 2014 TCC 303); LF to remove lien from property in order to sell it (VIEWS doc 2008-0290441E5); LF for company to acquire and redeem its own shares as part of shareholder dispute (*A.P. Toldo Holding*, 2013 TCC 416); LF whose goal was to increase value of estate being inherited (*Deschênes*, 2015 FCA 147 (leave to appeal denied 2016 CarswellNat 315 (SCC)). See also Notes to 18(1)(a).

Liability assumption: In *Daishowa-Marubeni*, 2011 FCA 267, para. 89 (rev'd on other grounds 2013 SCC 29), the cost of having a purchaser assume DM's reforestation liabilities was an "enduring benefit" and thus CAP.

License fees to market customer loyalty cards in a particular territory were CAP (Class 14) in *Madell*, 2009 FCA 193 (also *Caputo*, 2008 TCC 263, *Falkenberg*, 2008 TCC 265, and *Storwick*, 2008 TCC 268 — FCA appeals discontinued). Gaming machine licences were CAP in *Sharpcan*, [2019] HCA 36 (Australia, High Court).

Licensing fees for a professional: see "Business startup" above.

Life insurance premiums are deductible in limited cases: see Notes to 20(1)(e.2).

Loans: In *Newmont Canada [Hemlo Gold]*, 2012 FCA 214, Hemlo's loss on a loan to another mining company was CAP because the agreement for the loan resulted in Hemlo "acquiring assets of enduring benefit" (para. 29). In *Valiant Cleaning*, 2008 TCC 637, cash advances to keep a UK subsidiary running were CUR because they were needed to keep VC as a "Tier 1" supplier to the auto industry. Loans to a subsidiary (in the form of unpaid receivables) were CAP in *Cathelle Inc.*, 2005 TCC 360, and *966838 Ontario*, 2009 TCC 256. So were payments to honour guarantees of a sister corp's debts in *Shaw-Almex*, 2009 TCC 538 (FCA appeal discontinued A-479-09).

Lobbying costs for a business: see 20(1)(cc).

Market surveys and marketing costs: see "Advertising" above.

Merger expenses: see Notes to 18(1)(a), and "Transaction costs" below.

Oversight costs: see "Transaction costs" below.

Pension actuarial surplus paid for on buying a business is CAP: doc 2019-0817641I7.

Pipeline: In *Rainbow Pipe Line*, 2002 FCA 259, replacing 44km of 781km oil pipeline was CAP; other repairs were CUR. See also VIEWS doc 2008-02802721E5 (distribution line in existing sewage system).

Preliminary costs, e.g. feasibility studies: see "Business or project startup" above.

Prepaid expenses: see 18(9).

Productivity improvement costs and ISO 9000 registration costs are CUR: docs 9702057F, 2006-0190161M4, 2009-031226I17.

Real estate commissions paid to purchase a rental property are CAP, but to find a tenant are CUR: *Cummings*, [1981] C.T.C. 285 (FCA); VIEWS docs 2011-0424461E5, 2014-053592117.

Recurring expenses are generally CUR even if they look like CAP. See *Johns-Manville*, [1985] 2 C.T.C. 111 (SCC) (land needed to steadily expand open-pit mining operation); *Pantorama Industries*, 2005 FCA 135 (regular expenses paid to contractor that found locations, negotiated leases and renewals for PI's stores, where the business was not expanding); *Norton*, 2010 TCC 62 (lobster traps and fishing nets, to the extent they were replaced each year); *ATCO Electric*, 2007 TCC 243 (aff'd on unrelated issue 2008 FCA 188) ($1.2m cost of replacing transformers, as some needed replacing each year; though they were expensive, replacing a few "in a multi-million dollar electrical system is akin to changing a few bulbs in an otherwise functioning string of Christmas tree lights" (para. 66)); IT-475; VIEWS doc 2013-049421E5 (cranberry plants). *Contra*, see *Rona Inc.*, 2003 TCC 121 (costs re construction of new stores were CAP, though Rona was steadily expanding and building stores every year, and even where plans for a project never came to fruition); *Healius Ltd.*, [2020] FCAFC 173 (Australia) (chain of medical centres: payments to doctors to keep them for 5 years).

Rezoning costs for a rental property were CUR in *Jennings*, 2015 TCC 96 (had it been a business, 20(1)(cc) could have applied).

Scientific research expenses that are CAP were allowed under 37(1)(b) before 2014.

Share purchases: see 54"capital property" Notes.

Shares of the taxpayer: see Notes to 18(1)(a), and "Transaction costs" below. In *BJ Services*, [2004] 2 C.T.C. 2169 (TCC), expenses of defending against a hostile takeover were CUR. The Court suggested that even share issue costs are CUR: "Once the initial sale occurs by the company in the public market, the shares inherit a quasi-independent existence within the 'corporate marketplace' and cannot be perceived as providing the issuing company with any enduring or lasting benefit" (para. 44). The CRA considers fees to convert to an income trust to be CAP: VIEWS doc 2007-0233551I7; but see Hanna & Morin, "Reorganization Costs", VI(1) *Resource Sector Taxation* (Federated Press) 410-16 (2008). In *Potash Corp.*, 2011 CarswellNat 1215 (TCC), consulting fees to reorganize related companies to repatriate offshore profits tax-efficiently were held to be CAP, and allowed only as ECE under 20(1)(b). In the CRA's view, attempted takeover costs for shares that would have been capital property are CAP, while other takeover and transaction costs that cannot be linked to a capital transaction are CUR: 2011-039170117, 2017-0727041E5. Business combination costs are CAP even if under the Accounting Standards for Private Enterprises they are current expenses: 2012-0435081E5. See also "Legal fees" above, and "Merger expenses" in Notes to 18(1)(a).

Startup costs: see "Business startup" above.

Stock option payments: In *Imperial Tobacco (Shoppers Drug Mart)*, 2007 TCC 636, payments to reimburse the taxpayer's parent company for surrender of employees' stock options were CUR, and did not become CAP merely because they were part of a corporate reorganization. *Contra*, in *Kaiser Petroleum*, [1990] 2 C.T.C. 439 (FCA), and *Imperial Tobacco (Imasco)*, 2011 FCA 308 (leave to appeal denied 2012 CarswellNat 1579 (SCC)), payments by the employer to get rid of its stock option plan were CAP because they were part of a capital restructuring. (See now 143.3.)

Tools were held to be CAP (claimable as CCA) in *Couture*, 2009 TCC 598.

Training and coaching costs (on investing in real estate) were CAP in *Perron-Ali*, 2021 TCC 6, para. 66.

Transaction costs: Oversight costs to assist a company's board in its decision-making process to buy a company or spin off a business, as distinct from "execution costs", are CUR: *Rio Tinto*, 2018 FCA 124, paras. 77-79 (leave to appeal denied 2019 CarswellNat 809 (SCC)) [Lille, "The Slow Demise of the Enduring Benefit Test", XXI(3) *Corporate Finance* (Federated Press) 2-6 (2018); Pandher, "Rio Tinto", XXI(4) *Tax Litigation* (Federated Press) 2-7 (2018)].

Website development costs may be CAP depending on the web page's expected useful life: VIEWS docs 2010-0380521E5, 2013-0507121E5.

More information: see Notes to 54"capital property"; Spiro & Vanderkooy, "Updating the Trilogy", XIII(1) *Corporate Finance* (Federated Press) 1274-76 (2005); Michael Flatters, "The Distinction Between Income and Capital", 2005 Prairie Provinces Tax Conference (ctf.ca), 16:1-15; Carr & McIssac, "What is Depreciable Property?", XI(1) *Resource Sector Taxation* (Federated Press) 7-13 (2017); St-Cyr and Jadd, "Treatment of Costs incurred in the Course of a Corporate Transaction", 2016 Cdn Tax Foundation conference report, 11:1-24. For software that assists in the determination see *Tangible Expenditure Classifier* and *Intangible Expenditure Classifier* at bluejlegal.com.

Income Tax Folios: S2-F1-C1: Health and welfare trusts [replaces IT-85R2]; S3-F4-C1: General discussion of CCA [replaces IT-285R2]; S4-F2-C1: Deductibility of fines and penalties [replaces IT-104R3].

Interpretation Bulletins: IT-187: Purchase of customer lists and ledger accounts; IT-233R: Lease-option agreements; sale-leaseback agreements (cancelled); IT-261R: Prepayment of rents; IT-341R4: Expenses of issuing or selling shares, units in a trust, interests in a partnership or syndicate and expenses of borrowing money; IT-357R2: Expenses of training; IT-364: Commencement of business operations; IT-467R2: Damages, settlements and similar payments; IT-475: Expenditures on research and for business expansion.

I.T. Technical News: 5 (lease agreements).

Advance Tax Rulings: ATR-20: Redemption premium on debentures; ATR-50: Structured settlement; ATR-59: Financing exploration and development through limited partnerships.

(c) limitation re exempt income — an outlay or expense to the extent that it may reasonably be regarded as having been made or incurred for the purpose of gaining or producing exempt income or in connection with property the income from which would be exempt;

Related Provisions: 81(1) — Exempt income; 248(1)"exempt income" — Definition excludes dividends and support amounts.

Notes: 248(1)"exempt income" excludes support amounts so that legal expenses of obtaining non-taxable child support can be deducted: *Nadeau*, 2003 FCA 400. See Notes to 56(1)(b).

Income Tax Folios: S4-F2-C1: Deductibility of fines and penalties [replaces IT-104R3].

Interpretation Bulletins: IT-341R4: Expenses of issuing shares, units in a trust, interests in a partnership or syndicate and expenses of borrowing money; IT-467R2: Damages, settlements and similar payments.

(d) annual value of property — the annual value of property except rent for property leased by the taxpayer for use in the taxpayer's business;

Related Provisions: 20(1)(a) — Deduction for capital cost allowance.

(e) reserves, etc. — an amount as, or on account of, a reserve, a contingent liability or amount or a sinking fund except as expressly permitted by this Part;

Related Provisions: 18(9) — Prepaid expenses — deduction denied; 20(1)(l), (l.1), (m), (m.1), (n), (o) — Reserves specifically allowed; 20(7)(c) — Policy reserves for insurance corporations; 20(26) — Deduction for unpaid claims reserve adjustment; 40(1)(a)(iii) — Capital gains reserve; 61.2–61.4 — Reserves re forgiven debt included in income; 138(3)(a)(ii) — Reserves in respect of life insurance claims; 143.4(2) — Contingent amounts (including right to reduce expenditure) excluded from expenditures generally; 248(1) — "Insurance policy" includes life insurance policy.

Notes: A contingent liability is "a liability which depends for its existence upon an event which may or may not happen": *McLarty*, 2008 SCC 26. The test is "whether a legal obligation comes into existence at a point in time or whether it will not come into existence until the occurrence of an event which may never occur": para. 18.

Liabilities held to be contingent, non-deductible: amounts accrued under GM's collective agreement to a "special contingency fund", based on employees' overtime worked (*General Motors*, 2004 FCA 370 (leave to appeal denied 2005 CarswellNat 1376 (SCC)): there was no identifiable creditor who could enforce payment. GM then obtained a retroactive order from a labour arbitrator that GM had an absolute liability to the union to expend the funds, but its appeal of a later year was denied because the amounts were still contingent, as GM had no obligation in the year to actually expend funds: 2008 FCA 142.

Also contingent, non-deductible: security deposit under Ontario *Pits and Quarries Control Act* (*Nomad Sand*, [1991] 1 C.T.C. 60 (FCA): it was refundable); amount payable only if certain contractual conditions applied, with no unconditional promise to pay (*Ticketnet Corp.*, [1999] 3 C.T.C. 564 (FCTD)); liability on promissory note relating to software acquisition, due to vendor's representations that the software would result in a certain level of annual sales (*Peter Brown*, [2002] 1 C.T.C. 2451 (TCC), paras. 153-189 (limited partnership investment contingent so subject to at-risk rules; aff'd on other grounds 2003 FCA 192; leave to appeal denied 2004 CarswellNat 84 (SCC)); *Morley*, 2006 FCA 171 (leave to appeal denied 2006 CarswellNat 3839)); purchase price of software that was subject to warranty, when the Court held the software had no value (*Sherman*, 2008 TCC 186 (aff'd on other grounds 2009 FCA 9)); amount set aside to account for future expenses (*Aktary*, 2006 TCC 359); allowance for preliminary countervailing duty that was later cancelled (*Industries Perron*, 2013 FCA 176, para. 30).

Liabilities held deductible, not contingent: seismic shelter promissory note whose security might not be sufficient at maturity for the creditor to make full recovery (*McLarty*, 2008 SCC 26; the Crown later changed its position to allege sham, but lost: 2014 TCC 30); holdbacks required by workers' compensation legislation but not payable until after year-end (*Wawang Forest Products*, 2001 FCA 80: the expense is incurred once there is a legal obligation to pay a sum of money; uncertainty as to whether payment will be made, amount payable or when it will be paid do not create contingent liability [this was approved in *McLarty*]; deferred liability account set up to provide for workers' compensation liabilities (*Canadian Pacific v. Ontario*, [2000] 2 C.T.C. 331 (Ont CA, under Ontario *Corporations Tax Act*); employer premiums (unemployment insurance, pension plan, etc.) payable on accrued vacation pay which employees had not yet used (*Fédération des Caisses Populaires*, 2001 FCA 27: the obligation was real and not potential, even though not payable until a later year when the employees took vacations); liability under a guarantee (*Shaw-Almex Industries*, 2009 TCC 538 (FCA appeal discontinued A-479-09): it had become a "real legal obligation"); software shelter promissory note subject to agreement under which it might not be payable — this was a condition subsequent which did not make the note contingent (*Baxter*, 2006 TCC 230 (rev'd on other grounds 2007 FCA 172; leave to appeal denied 2007 CarswellNat 3625 (SCC)).

18(1)(e) applies only to amounts set aside internally, not those paid out to third parties: *Crane Ltd.*, [1960] C.T.C. 371 (Exch. Ct.), para. 16.

See also 18(9), which may restrict deductions, and the overlapping broader limitation in 143.4, which reduces any expenditure by an amount the taxpayer has a "right to reduce" in addition to contingent amounts.

Financial institutions normally mark their properties to market under 142.5, so 18(1)(e) generally does not apply. However, in VIEWS doc 2000-0001327, CRA stated that 18(1)(e) would deny a deduction for "accrued interest" on an index-linked GIC, since the index could fall and eliminate the interest liability. Unrealized losses on interest rate swaps are contingent: 2009-0336671I7.

CRA considers the following to be contingent: refundability of membership fees in the event of death (doc 2003-0043431E5: death is certain but its timing is not); employer's contribution to claim stabilization fund for private health services plan (2005-0155961E5); employer's payable set up for future "retiring allowance" where employee has not yet retired (2009-0328501E5).

CRA will not apply 18(1)(e) to a health and welfare trust (HWT) if the amounts paid are actuarially determined: 2002 Cdn Tax Foundation conference report pp. 15:8-12; *Income Tax Technical News* 25. Note that HWTs must convert to ELHTs by 2022: see 144.1.

Where contingent liabilities are acquired, see VIEWS doc 2002-0164607 and Jocelyn Blanchet, "Purchase and Sale of Assets: The Treatment to the Vendor of Contingent Liabilities Assumed", 2009 Cdn Tax Foundation conference report, 11:1-24.

For more on "contingent" see Harris, "Words in Context: 'Contingent' and 'Dividend'", 2002 Cdn Tax Foundation conference report at 38:1-19; Frankovic, "The Case for 'Reverse Depreciation' of Reclamation Costs", 52(1) *Canadian Tax Journal* 1-58 (2004) at 41-50; Jacina & Misutka, "Contingent Liabilities: The Gathering Storm", 1793 *Tax Topics* (CCH) 1-3 (July 20, 2006); Morin & Sandler, "The Vendor's Treatment of Assumed Silviculture Obligations — A Comment on *Daishowa-Marubeni*", VIII(2) *Resource Sector Taxation [RST]* (Federated Press) 562-65 (2010) [see Notes to 54"proceeds of disposition" re *Daishowa*]; Johnson & Ritchie, "The Cost of Acquiring An Asset With Environmental Liabilities Post-*Daishowa*, XI(2) *RST* 7-10 (2017).

Income Tax Folios: S3-F6-C1: Interest deductibility [replaces IT-533].

Interpretation Bulletins: IT-109R2: Unpaid amounts; IT-215R: Reserves, contingent accounts and sinking funds (cancelled); IT-321R: Insurance agents and brokers — unearned commissions (cancelled); IT-442R: Bad debts and reserves for doubtful debts; IT-467R2: Damages, settlements and similar payments; IT-518R: Food, beverages and entertainment expenses.

I.T. Technical News: 25 (health and welfare trusts).

Advance Tax Rulings: ATR-50: Structured settlement.

(e.1) **unpaid claims under insurance policies** — an amount in respect of claims that were received by an insurer before the end of the year under insurance policies and that are unpaid at the end of the year, except as expressly permitted by this Part;

Related Provisions: 20(7)(c) — Policy reserves for insurance corporations; 20(26) — Deduction for unpaid claims reserve adjustment; 138(3)(a)(ii) — Reserves in respect of life insurance claims.

(f) **payments on discounted bonds** — an amount paid or payable as or on account of the principal amount of any obligation described in paragraph 20(1)(f) except as expressly permitted by that paragraph;

Interpretation Bulletins: IT-341R4: Expenses of issuing shares, units in a trust, interests in a partnership or syndicate and expenses of borrowing money; IT-518R: Food, beverages and entertainment expenses.

I.T. Technical News: 25 (foreign exchange losses).

(g) **payments on income bonds** — an amount paid by a corporation as interest or otherwise to holders of its income bonds or income debentures unless the bonds or debentures have been issued or the income provisions thereof have been adopted since 1930

    (i) to afford relief to the debtor from financial difficulties, and

    (ii) in place of or as an amendment to bonds or debentures that at the end of 1930 provided unconditionally for a fixed rate of interest;

Related Provisions: 15(3), (4) — Interest or dividend on income bond or debenture.

Interpretation Bulletins: IT-52R4: Income bonds and debentures (cancelled); IT-518R: Food, beverages and entertainment expenses.

(h) **personal and living expenses** — personal or living expenses of the taxpayer, other than travel expenses incurred by the taxpayer while away from home in the course of carrying on the taxpayer's business;

Related Provisions: 20(1) — Deductions permitted; 20(16) — Terminal loss; 20.01 — Deduction allowed for private health services plan premiums; 56(1)(o)(i) — No deduction for personal or living expenses against research grant income; 67 — Unreasonable expenses not allowed; 67.1 — 50% limit on expenses for food and entertainment; 248(1)"personal or living expenses" — Reasonable expectation of profit required.

Notes: Before 2002, 18(1)(h) and 248(1)"personal or living expenses" were used by CRA to deny deductions for expenses of a business where there was no "reasonable expectation of profit" (REOP). See Notes to 9(2).

An *employee's* personal expense can be a legitimate business expense of the *employer*, even if the employee is a shareholder: *Jolly Farmer*, 2008 TCC 409, since the benefit is "received as remuneration" under 6(1)(a): *Lavoie*, 2014 TCC 68, para. 31. However, often the expense is denied to the corp and also treated as a 15(1) benefit to the shareholder, leading to double tax: e.g., *JDI 2000 Transport*, 2010 TCC 310.

"Claims for a large number of personal expenses can cast doubt on claims for expenses": *Perera*, 2014 TCC 280, para. 26.

Personal expenses needed for business: The Supreme Court of Canada ruled in *Symes*, [1994] 1 C.T.C. 40 that child-care expenses were not deductible even though they were required to enable S to earn business income, since there was already a scheme in s. 63 for deducting such expenses. Foot/bicycle couriers and rickshaw drivers can claim $23 per day for extra food provided they keep a log of hours worked, per CRA Guide T4002 Chap. 3 Line 8523 and tinyurl.com/cra-bus-exp under "Extra food...", based on *Alan Scott*, [1998] 4 C.T.C. 103 (FCA) where a foot courier was allowed extra food needed as "fuel" for his body. (This rule does not apply to ordinary workers' expenses where the "need to consume food ... exists independently from the business": *Rogers*, 2014 TCC 101, para. 30.) A taxi driver's lunch is not deductible: 2007-0237631I7. A fisherman's meals on a factory freezer trawler are: 2008-0269021E5. Meals when travelling normally are, but CRA suggests the taxpayer may have to prove they were incurred for the purpose of producing income: 2008-0298891E5 [Drache, "CRA Ruling Tough on Meal Expenses", xxxii(22) *The Canadian Taxpayer* (Carswell) 174-75 (Nov. 2, 2010)]. See also "Clothing" below.

Advertising: For personal hobbies considered legitimate advertising expenses for a business, see Notes to 18(1)(a) under "Advertising".

Aircraft: In *Blanchette*, 2008 FCA 45, the costs of owning an airplane were held to be personal rather than business expenses. In *SLX Management*, 2010 TCC 148 (varied by FCA on consent A-158-10), various expenses were denied or partly denied as being for the shareholder's personal use, including aircraft costs, cruises, condominium costs and medical expenses. For the benefit from a company-owned plane see Notes to 6(1)(a).

Artist's residency: see VIEWS doc 2017-0706471E5.

Child care: see "Personal expenses needed for business" above.

Clothing bought by a self-employed person for business use is not deductible if it is generally usable for personal purposes: VIEWS docs 2004-0063131E5, 2006-0217641E5, 2008-0298891E5; 2010-0377011I7 (welder's work boots); *Rupprecht*, 2009 FCA 314 (leave to appeal denied 2010 CarswellNat 1092 (SCC)) (financial planner wore expensive suits and ties). Lawyers were allowed CCA for barrister's robes in *Charron*, [1998] 2 C.T.C. 2240 (TCC), and *Desgagné*, 2012 TCC 63 (Class 12), but nothing for other black clothes needed for Court in *Desgagné*. Uniforms can be claimed under Class 12: 2005-0155251E5. In *Vézina*, 2007 TCC 655, a child actor was not allowed deductions for clothing worn on film sets or for eyeglasses or dental care, but was allowed costs of parental accompaniment (analogized by the Court to bodyguard services), psychologist services, makeup and skates. In *Shenanigans Media*, 2017 TCC 180, para. 25, a teenage actor was not allowed deductions for clothing (CRA had allowed some), grooming or makeup. In *Rail*, 2011 TCC 130, a dentist was not allowed deductions for clothing he claimed as a professional hygiene requirement because it could handle high-temperature washing. The CRA considers an erotic model's expenses for a fitness centre, breast implants, cosmetic treatments and lingerie to be non-deductible: 2010-0387551I7. For employees, see "Clothing" in Notes to 6(1)(a), and Notes to 8(1)(i) re 8(1)(i)(iii).

Food for couriers: see "Personal expenses needed for business" above.

Home office expenses: see Notes to 18(12).

Legal fees (LF): In *Leduc*, 2005 TCC 96, a lawyer was denied deductions for LF paid to defend against charges of sexual exploitation; the Court ruled the LF non-deductible due to 18(1)(a) and (h) even though he could have been disbarred and lost his business income had he been convicted. "If a need exists even in the absence of business activity, then an expense incurred to meet the need would traditionally be viewed as a personal expense" (para. 17). Similarly, in *Thimio*, 2017 TCC 164, a swim school owner's LF to be acquitted of sexual assault on an employee, needed to reopen the business, were held not connected to the business for GST/HST purposes; and in *Patry*, 2013 TCC 107, LF to defend a suit for malicious prosecution and infliction of mental suffering arose from a "personal vendetta" (para. 36) and were only "incidental" to the taxpayer's rental operations. See also Notes to 9(1) under "Criminal activity" and to 18(1)(a) under "Legal fees".

Life insurance premiums on self and family members, paid by an insurance agent, are personal expenses, but the commissions are also not income: VIEWS doc 2009-0324511I7. In *Bégin*, 2012 TCC 18, B bought (and then cancelled) life insurance on himself so as to profit from the commission, but was not allowed to deduct the premiums he paid due to 18(1)(h). (See also 6(1)(a) Notes at 'Insurance agents' commissions".)

Meal expenses of taxpayer and spouse together: see Notes to s. 67 and 67.1.

Psychotherapy costs for a psychologist, to improve the quality of his services, were considered deductible in VIEWS doc 2014-0562151R5.

Rental property: In *Preiss*, 2009 TCC 488, expenses of a rental property were disallowed because it was rented to P's mother. In *Lessard*, 2010 TCC 544, expenses to renovate a rental property before it was converted to personal use were personal expenses.

Travel: The CRA interprets "travel expenses" in 18(1)(h) to include food and accommodation, and "while away from home" to exclude travelling *from* home (unless home is a place of business) to a business location: VIEWS docs 2002-0143427, 2008-0271941E5, 2011-0393331E5 [see also Notes to 8(1)(h.1)]; and to exclude returning home from vacation for an urgent business matter: 2011-0426471E5. In *Morrissey*, 2011 TCC 373, para. 12, a newspaper distributor was allowed expenses because her residence was her place of business. In *Phillips*, 2012 TCC 337, a Winnipeg conference organizer who accepted employment in Regina could deduct expenses of attending the conferences in Wpg but not of travel to his Wpg office; although "personal choice" travel does not qualify (*Blackburn*, 2007 TCC 284), moving to Regina for his job was not a "personal choice". An accountant renting an apartment near his firm so as not to have to travel a long way home in bad weather is considered a personal expense: 2008-0280251E5; but see *Gariépy* in Notes to 8(1)(h.1). Accident repair expenses are deductible if the vehicle was being used for business purposes at the time of the accident: IT-521R para. 7. Costs of a boat to get to the taxpayer's cottage and back to clients are non-deductible: 2013-0503581E5.

In *Faber*, 2008 TCC 403, a successful Inuit artist was allowed travel and other expenses relating to hunting and being in nature to get inspiration for his art. In *Henrie*, 2009 TCC 356, 25% of travel expenses were allowed to a novelist who travelled to enrich his experiences. In *McLean*, 2009 TCC 509, travel to attend a wedding was 10% deductible (trying to sell multi-level marketing products), and trips with friends that were also business-related were 25% deductible, while other expenses were denied as personal. In *Stevens*, 2012 TCC 312, no deduction for travel was allowed to a writer who went to Paris with his wife and son, supposedly to do research for a book. In *Johnson*, 2012 TCC 399, no deduction was allowed for annual trips to Mexico: "Simply working while on vacation does not make a vacation trip a business trip" (para. 36). In *DiCaita*, 2021 TCC 5, para. 66, part of the cost of travel to Las Vegas was allowed as relating to D's rental property in Phoenix.

Although 18(1)(h) allows travel expenses only for a business, CRA administratively allows vehicle expenses for rental properties a taxpayer personally maintains: Guide T4036, line 9281; docs 2006-0191571I7, 2009-0324901E5, 2012-0454932117. (See Notes to 9(1) on the distinction between business and property income.)

Vehicle expenses are deductible to the extent required for business (normally not including driving from home unless that is one's place of business). Odotrack.ca sells a device that can track business use, and some cars now keep GPS records of all travel. CRA states that once a business has maintained a full logbook to show business vs. personal use of a vehicle for a year, a 3-month sample can be used in future years providing the usage is within 10% of the base year: tinyurl.com/cra-doc-use.

Wedding and barmitzvah expenses were disallowed in *Roebuck* (1961), 26 Tax A.B.C. 11 and *Fingold*, [1992] 2 C.T.C. 2393 (TCC), despite evidence that many invitees were clients or business contacts. Wedding expenses were partly allowed in *Grunbaum*, [1994] 1 C.T.C. 2687 (TCC), where half the invitations were sent in the business name to business contacts; but were disallowed in *Spiegel Sohmer (Raich)*, 2021 QCCQ 69: insufficient evidence that inviting clients and business contacts to R's daughter's wedding was to promote R's law firm's business.

See also VIEWS docs 2009-0319301E5 (self-employed taxi driver's expenses); 2013-0500701E5 (deduction allowed where personal component is incidental or secondary).

Income Tax Folios: S3-F9-C1: Lottery winnings, miscellaneous receipts, and income (and losses) from crime [replaces IT-185R, IT-213R, IT-256R, IT-334R2]; S4-F2-C1: Deductibility of fines and penalties [replaces IT-104R3].

Interpretation Bulletins: IT-223: Overhead expense insurance vs. income insurance (cancelled); IT-341R4: Expenses of issuing shares, units in a trust, interests in a partnership or syndicate and expenses of borrowing money; IT-357R2: Expenses of training; IT-467R2: Damages, settlements and similar payments; IT-518R: Food, beverages

and entertainment expenses; IT-521R: Motor vehicle expenses claimed by self-employed individuals.

I.T. Technical News: 16 (*Tonn, Mastri, Mohammad* and *Kaye* cases; *Scott* case); 25 (reasonable expectation of profit).

CRA Audit Manual: 29.4.0: Farm losses and restricted farm losses.

Forms: T2125: Statement of business or professional activities.

(i) limitation re employer's contribution under supplementary unemployment benefit plan — an amount paid by an employer to a trustee under a supplementary unemployment benefit plan except as permitted by section 145;

Related Provisions: 20(1)(x), 145(5) — Employer's contribution to supplementary unemployment benefit plan deductible.

(j) limitation re employer's contribution under deferred profit sharing plan — an amount paid by an employer to a trustee under a deferred profit sharing plan except as expressly permitted by section 147;

Related Provisions: 147(8) — Employer's DPSP contribution deductible.

(k) limitation re employer's contribution under profit sharing plan — an amount paid by an employer to a trustee under a profit sharing plan that is not

(i) an employees profit sharing plan,

(ii) a deferred profit sharing plan, or

(iii) a pooled registered pension plan or registered pension plan;

Notes: 18(1)(k)(iii) amended by 2012 budget bill #2, effective Dec. 14, 2012, to add reference to a PRPP.

Interpretation Bulletins: IT-502: Employee benefit plans and employee trusts.

(l) use of recreational facilities and club dues — an outlay or expense made or incurred by the taxpayer after 1971,

(i) for the use or maintenance of property that is a yacht, a camp, a lodge or a golf course or facility, unless the taxpayer made or incurred the outlay or expense in the ordinary course of the taxpayer's business of providing the property for hire or reward, or

(ii) as membership fees or dues (whether initiation fees or otherwise) in any club the main purpose of which is to provide dining, recreational or sporting facilities for its members;

Related Provisions: 8(1)(f)(vi) — Salesman's expenses; Reg. 1102(1)(f) — No capital cost allowance for property subject to 18(1)(l).

Notes: The restriction on a "yacht" is "bateau de plaisance" in French. For discussion of these terms see *C.I.P. Inc.*, [1988] 1 C.T.C. 32 (FCTD), which held that it is the *use* of the vessel that is most important, and since the converted tugboat in that case was used as a residence, 18(1)(l) did not apply. See also VIEWS doc 2013-0503581E5.

The cost of entertaining clients at a fishing lodge is non-deductible, as the expenses are for the "use" of the lodge: *Sie-Mac Pipeline*, [1993] 1 C.T.C. 226 (SCC). However, "lodge" means a rustic facility, not a full-service luxury resort such as Deerhurst, Chateau Whistler, the Delta Hotel at Kananaskis or Le Château Montebello: *Hewlett-Packard*, 2005 TCC 398. CRA accepts this: VIEWS docs 2011-0420521E5, 2013-0477911E5 (so IT-148R3 para. 3 appears to be partly obsolete). Note that no CCA is allowed for property subject to 18(1)(l), as Reg. 1102(1)(f) deems it not to be depreciable property of any prescribed class.

In *Harland*, 2010 TCC 105, a corporation's deduction of the cost of its shareholder's boat was indirectly denied by recalculating the shareholder's dividends from the corp.

CRA will generally apply 18(1)(l)(ii) to club dues "unless it can be factually established to our satisfaction that it is not the main purpose of such a club to provide dining, recreational or sporting facilities to its members": VIEWS docs 2007-0236851E5, 2007-0238871E5. 18(1)(l)(i) is considered to apply to a golf transfer fee paid to a golf course on purchasing a golf share, with no addition to the share's ACB: 2012-0436791E5. A self-employed golfer cannot deduct green fees in CRA's view: 2012-0457751E5. A golf club's dining room, conference room, lounge, etc., are not subject to 18(1)(l) but only to the 50% rule in 67.1: *Income Tax Technical News* 12, docs 2009-0346971I7, 2012-0442681M4.

Some MPs have sought to repeal the golf rule: Paul Vieira, "Canadian Push to Make Golf Tax Deductible", Sports, *Wall Street Journal*, Jan. 3, 2012.

18(1)(l)(ii) applies to fitness club dues: VIEWS doc 2012-0460021E5. See also Notes to 6(1)(a) re taxable benefits, under "Fitness" and "Recreational".

See also 18(1)(h), which restricts personal expenses generally.

Interpretation Bulletins: IT-148R3: Recreational properties and club dues; IT-211R: Membership dues — Associations and societies; IT-470R: Employees' fringe benefits.

I.T. Technical News: 12 (meals and beverages at golf clubs).

(l.1) **safety deposit box [fees]** — an amount paid or payable in respect of the use of a safety deposit box of a financial institution;

Notes: Safety deposit box costs were deductible where needed for investment certificates. As electronic records become the norm and boxes are more used to safeguard personal valuables, 2013 budget bill #1 added 18(1)(l.1), for tax years that begin after March 20, 2013, to deny deduction, even for businesses that need one.

The term "financial institution" is not defined for this provision (the definition in 142.2(1) does not apply), so it has its ordinary meaning.

Former 18(1)(l.1), repealed by 2003 resource bill for amounts payable after Dec. 20, 2002, prohibited deduction for amounts paid or payable under the *Petroleum and Gas Revenue Tax Act*.

(m) **limitation re employee stock option expenses** — an amount in respect of which an election was made by or on behalf of the taxpayer under subsection 110(1.1);

Notes: 18(1)(m) denies a deduction to an employer for a stock option "cash-out" where the employer has elected under 110(1.1) for the employee to be able to claim the 110(1)(d) deduction.

18(1)(m) added by 2010 budget bill #2, effective in respect of transfers or dispositions of rights occurring after 4pm EST, March 4, 2010.

Former 18(1)(m), "royalties, etc.", restricted deductions for resource royalties. It was phased out 2003-07 and repealed by 2003 resource bill for tax years that begin after 2007. See 20(1)(v.1) Notes. Royalties paid under the *Canada Petroleum Resources Act* are now deductible: VIEWS doc 2018-0742881E5. See now Spinelli & Elanga, "An Update to the Deductibility of Crown Charges", XIII(1) *Resource Sector Taxation* (Federated Press) 11-15 (2019).

For discussion of the 2003 resource bill changes to 12(1)(o) and 18(1)(m), see Edward Rowe, "Deductibility of Crown Charges", II(1) *Resource Sector Taxation* 91-97 (2003); Dept. of Finance, *Improving the Income Taxation of the Resource Sector in Canada* (March 2003), on fin.gc.ca at Publications > Archived publications > 2003.

In *Mobil Oil*, 2001 FCA 333, amounts paid under the Saskatchewan *Road Allowances Crown Oil Act* were "royalties" and non-deductible due to then-18(1)(m)(v). The Court interpreted "royalty" under former 18(1)(m) as including "any share of resource production that is paid to the province in connection with its interest in the resource". In *Cogema Resources*, 2005 FCA 316, surcharges on uranium yellowcake under Sask. legislation were deductible despite 18(1)(m)(ii)(B)(II), because they were levied on the yellowcake's sale rather than on its production.

Former 18(1)(m) did not apply to Crown surface rentals under the Saskatchewan *Mineral Taxation Act* and *Crown Minerals Act*: VIEWS doc 2002-0122035; Stack, "Deductibility of Surface Rights Rentals", II(4) *Resource Sector Taxation* (Federated Press) 165-67 (2004). Income taxes on resource royalties are generally not deductible: 18(1)(t) Notes.

Former 18(1)(m) earlier amended by 1996 Budget and 1991 technical bill.

(n) **political contributions** — a political contribution;

Related Provisions: 127(3) — Tax credit for political contributions.

Notes: Donations to *federal* parties and candidates generate a credit under 127(3); for provincial candidates, see the provincial Income Tax Act. There is no credit or deduction for donations to municipal candidates: VIEWS doc 2018-0779741M4.

(o) **employee benefit plan contributions** — an amount paid or payable as a contribution to an employee benefit plan;

Related Provisions: 6(1)(a)(ii), 6(1)(g) — EBP benefits taxable to employee; 12(1)(n.1) — Income inclusion — amounts received by employer from EBP; 18(10) — Exceptions where 18(1)(o) does not apply; 32.1 — EBP deductions.

Interpretation Bulletins: IT-502: Employee benefit plans and employee trusts.

(o.1) **salary deferral arrangement** — except as expressly permitted by paragraphs 20(1)(oo) and (pp), an outlay or expense made or incurred under a salary deferral arrangement in respect of another person, other than such an arrangement established primarily for the benefit of one or more non-resident employees in respect of services to be rendered outside Canada;

Related Provisions: 6(1)(a)(v) — Value of benefits; 6(1)(i), 56(1)(w) — Salary deferral arrangements — amounts included in income.

Notes: 18(1)(o.1) amended by 1991 technical bill, retroactive to 1986, to add reference to 20(1)(pp) and to change "in a country other than Canada" to "outside Canada".

(o.2) **retirement compensation arrangement** — except as expressly permitted by paragraph 20(1)(r), contributions made under a retirement compensation arrangement;

Notes: 18(1)(o.2) applied in VIEWS doc 2007-0245551C6 (employer contributes to trust to acquire letter of credit to fund pension benefits).

(o.3) **employee life and health trust** — except as expressly permitted by paragraph 20(1)(s), contributions to an employee life and health trust;

Notes: 18(1)(o.3) added by 2010 budget bill #2, effective 2010. It denies deduction for contributions to an ELHT except as per 144.1(4)-(7), but does not deny contributions to a plan that does not qualify as an ELHT.

(p) **limitation re personal services business expenses** — an outlay or expense to the extent that it was made or incurred by a corporation in a taxation year for the purpose of gaining or producing income from a personal services business, other than

(i) the salary, wages or other remuneration paid in the year to an incorporated employee of the corporation,

(ii) the cost to the corporation of any benefit or allowance provided to an incorporated employee in the year,

(iii) any amount expended by the corporation in connection with the selling of property or the negotiating of contracts by the corporation if the amount would have been deductible in computing the income of an incorporated employee for a taxation year from an office or employment if the amount had been expended by the incorporated employee under a contract of employment that required the employee to pay the amount, and

(iv) any amount paid by the corporation in the year as or on account of legal expenses incurred by it in collecting amounts owing to it on account of services rendered

that would, if the income of the corporation were from a business other than a personal services business, be deductible in computing its income;

Related Provisions: 123.4(1)"full rate taxable income"(a)(iii) — PSB income ineligible for general corporate rate reduction; 123.5 — Additional 5% tax on PSB income; 207.6(3) — Retirement compensation arrangement for incorporated employee; 248(1) — extended definition of "salary or wages".

Notes: See Notes to 125(7)"personal services busines" (PSB). As well as having its deductions limited by 18(1)(p), a corporation carrying on a PSB (effectively an incorporated employee (**IE**)) is ineligible for the small business deduction (125(1)(a)(i), 125(7)"active business"), cannot claim the 13-point general corporate rate reduction (123.4(1)"full rate taxable income"(a)(iii)), and pays additional 5% corporate tax (123.5). It can however deduct the costs of a pension plan for the IE: VIEWS doc 2005-012273117; and the employer's portion of source deductions: 2001-0086745 (note that there will be no EI). If there are two IEs (e.g. spouses), the salaries of both can be deducted: 2011-0411871C6. The expenses allowed by 18(1)(p)(iii), for commission income, match those allowed for employees by 8(1)(f): 2011-0411891C6.

For interpretation of "cost of any benefit or allowance" in 18(1)(p)(ii) see VIEWS docs 2004-0098531E5 (includes payroll taxes); 2011-0423941E5 (various interpretations); 2013-0490301E5 (includes lease and loan interest costs of company car, but not CCA).

The French versions of 18(1)(p)(i) and (ii) are incorrect, using "actionnaire constitué en société" instead of "employé constitué en société" (IE), as defined in 125(7)"personal services business". This has been pointed out to Finance.

An IE could not claim the pre-2016 overseas employment tax credit. See 122.3(1.1).

The IE may be able to claim home office expenses under 8(13) and vehicle expenses under 8(1)(h.1): doc 2011-0411891C6.

See also Magee, "Personal Services Businesses", 55(1) *Canadian Tax Journal* 160-83 (2007); docs 2009-0320491E5, 2009-0326681M4, 2009-032924117, 2009-0340221E5.

Interpretation Bulletins: IT-73R6: The small business deduction; IT-168R3: Athletes and players employed by football, hockey and similar clubs; IT-189R2: Corporations used by practising members of professions.

(q) **limitation re cancellation of lease** — an amount paid or payable by the taxpayer for the cancellation of a lease of property of the taxpayer leased by the taxpayer to another person, except to the extent permitted by paragraph 20(1)(z) or (z.1);

Interpretation Bulletins: IT-359R2: Premiums on leases.

(r) **certain automobile expenses** — an amount paid or payable by the taxpayer as an allowance for the use by an individual of an automobile to the extent that the amount exceeds an amount determined in accordance with prescribed rules, except where the amount so paid or payable is required to be included in computing the individual's income;

Notes: See Notes to Reg. 7306 re limits on deductible tax-exempt car allowances.

Regulations: 7306 (prescribed rules).

I.T. Technical News: 10 (1997 deduction limits and benefit rates for automobiles).

(s) **loans or lending assets** — any loss, depreciation or reduction in a taxation year in the value or amortized cost of a loan or lending asset of a taxpayer made or acquired by the taxpayer in the ordinary course of the taxpayer's business of insurance or the lending of money and not disposed of by the taxpayer in the year, except as expressly permitted by this Part;

Notes: 18(1)(s) amended by 1991 technical bill, retroactive to 1988.

(t) **payments under different acts** — any amount paid or payable

(i) under this Act (other than tax paid or payable under Part XII.2 or Part XII.6),

(ii) as interest under Part IX of the *Excise Tax Act*, or

(iii) as interest under the *Air Travellers Security Charge Act*;

Related Provisions: 20(1)(v) — Deduction for mining taxes; 20(1)(ll) — Deduction for interest repaid; 20(1)(nn) — Deduction for Part XII.6 tax; 20(1)(vv) — Deduction for countervailing and anti-dumping duties; 60(o) — Expenses of objection or appeal; 67.6 — Fines and penalties non-deductible; 104(30) — Deduction for Part XII.2 tax paid by trust; 161.1 — Offsetting of non-deductible interest against taxable interest of other years.

Notes: 18(1)(t)(i) prohibits deduction for interest, penalties or fines paid under the ITA, as well as for tax itself (except Part XII.2 or XII.6 tax). Provincial income tax is non-deductible due to 18(1)(a), as it is not paid for the purpose of earning income: *Roenisch*, [1928-34] C.T.C. 69 (Exch. Ct.); *First Pioneer Petroleums*, [1974] C.T.C. 108 (FCTD). The same applies to provincial mining taxes calculated on income: *Teck Corp. v. BC*, 2004 BCCA 514 (leave to appeal denied 2005 CarswellBC 1022 (SCC)); and to provincial corporate minimum tax (VIEWS doc 2008-0300361I7). Alberta Freehold Mineral Rights Tax is deductible: 2010-0375471E5. See also 20(1)(v) Notes.

Repayments of taxable refund interest are deductible under 20(1)(ll), but interest on provincial income tax is not prohibited by 18(1)(t), but one would still need to show [20(1)(c)] that the interest was on money borrowed to earn income, which is not normally true. Provincial capital tax (and interest thereon) is deductible: *GMAC Leaseco*, 2015 TCC 146 (deductible in the year to which it applied even if not imposed till later); VIEWS doc 2009-032694I17, and see Proposed Amendment at end of s. 18. So is the Ontario Special Additional Tax on Life Insurance Corporations: 2005-0160621E5, 2011-0395011E5. Foreign income tax may create a foreign tax credit under s. 126 or deduction under 20(12). State sales and franchise taxes are deductible: 2006-0198331E5. The cost of contesting an income tax audit, objection or appeal is deductible under 60(o). Provincial taxes paid by the owner of a hydro-electric generating station under s. 92.1 of the *Ontario Electricity Act, 1998* (portions of the Gross Revenue Charge tax regime) are deductible: 2001-0115235.

18(1)(t) did not apply when a payroll processing company paid interest and penalties on remittances it made late on behalf of clients, because it was not liable under the ITA to pay these amounts: *ADP Canada*, 2008 TCC 236 (reversed on unrelated issue 2009 FCA 117). 18(1)(t) applied to interest paid under the ITA despite the taxpayer's claim he "borrowed" money from CRA by not paying his taxes and being assessed interest, and used those funds to earn interest he reported: *Doulis*, 2014 TCC 26.

Most other penalties and fines are non-deductible: see 67.6. For taxation years beginning April 2007 or later, interest on GST (or HST) assessments (which have replaced late-payment penalties: *Excise Tax Act* s. 280) is non-deductible (18(1)(t)(ii)).

18(1)(t)(ii) and (iii) apply only to tax years that begin after March 2007, as added by 2006 budget bill #1. CRA's view is that GST interest accruing in a year that began before April 2007 is deductible even if not paid until later: *Income Tax Technical News* 38; 2007 Cdn Tax Foundation conference report at 4:3-5.

For interest accruing since 2001, 161.1 allows interest of different years to offset each other, so that (non-deductible) interest payable can cancel out (otherwise-taxable) interest on refunds. (This applies to corporations, and is supposed to be extended to individuals.)

18(1)(t) amended by 1996 Budget (for 1997 and later tax years); added by 1989 Budget.

Income Tax Folios: S4-F2-C1: Deductibility of fines and penalties [replaces IT-104R3].

Information Circulars: 77-11: Sales tax reassessments — deductibility in computing income.

I.T. Technical News: 38 (income tax treatment of GST).

(u) **fees — individual savings plans** — any amount paid or payable by the taxpayer for services in respect of a retirement savings plan, retirement income fund or TFSA under or of which the taxpayer is the annuitant or holder;

Related Provisions: 18(11) — No deduction for interest paid on money borrowed to make deferred income plan contribution; 146(21.2) — Saskatchewan Pension Plan account deemed to be RRSP for purposes of 18(1)(u); 147.5(12) — PRPP deemed to be RRSP for purposes of 18(1)(u).

Notes: 18(1)(u) prevents deduction for administration fees and investment counselling fees for an RRSP, RRIF, TFSA, PRPP (see 147.5(12)) and a Sask. Pension Plan account (see 146(21.2)). See VIEWS doc 2009-0324901E5. It does not apply to an RDSP, but investment counselling fees are not deductible by the holder under 20(1)(bb) because the RDSP, not the holder, owns the shares: 2014-0526891E6.

Historically, management fees and investment counsel fees for an RRSP or RRIF (or now, a TFSA) could be paid either from the plan (without conferring a taxable benefit on the annuitant) or by the annuitant (without being considered a contribution to the plan): VIEWS doc 9727875. However, the CRA announced at the 2016 Cdn Tax Foundation conference Roundtable [q.5, doc 2016-0670801C6] that paying the fees outside the plan will be considered to confer a 207.01(1)"advantage" on the controlling individual as of 2018, so it is effectively prohibited (see 207.05(2)).

In *Wickham Estate*, 2014 TCC 352, fees paid to manage an infirm person's assets were deductible under 20(1)(bb), but the portion relating to the person's RRIF was disallowed under 18(1)(u).

18(1)(u) amended by 2008 budget bill #1, for 2009 and later years, to add references to a TFSA and "holder". Added by 1996 Budget.

(v) **interest — authorized foreign bank** — where the taxpayer is an authorized foreign bank, an amount in respect of interest that would otherwise be deductible in computing the taxpayer's income from a business carried on in Canada, except as provided in section 20.2;

Notes: 18(1)(v) added by 2001 technical bill, effective June 28, 1999. Interest is deductible to an authorized foreign bank (foreign bank branch) under the rules in 20.2.

(w) **underlying payments on qualified securities** — except as expressly permitted, an amount that is deemed by subsection 260(5.1) to have been received by another person as an amount described in any of paragraphs 260(5.1)(a) to (c); and

Related Provisions: 260(6), (6.1) — Deductible compensation payments.

Notes: A compensation payment under a securities lending arrangement can be deducted only as allowed under s. 260(6) and (6.1).

18(1)(w) added by 2002-2013 technical bill (Part 5 — technical), effective 2002.

(x) **derivatives — lower of cost and market** — any reduction in a taxation year in the value of a property if

(i) the method used by the taxpayer to value the property at the end of the year for purposes of computing the taxpayer's profit from a business or property is the cost at which the taxpayer acquired it or its fair market value at the end of the year, whichever is lower,

(ii) the property is described in subsection 10(15), and

(iii) the property is not disposed of by the taxpayer in the year; and

Notes: See 10(15) Notes. 18(1)(x) added by 2016 budget bill #2, for agreements entered into after March 21, 2016.

(y) **payment for shares** — an amount referred to in subsection 13(36).

Notes: See Notes to 13(34). Although it was not Finance's intention, 18(1)(y) could be taken to mean that a business of buying and selling shares (as inventory) cannot deduct the cost of the shares, nor any amount described in 13(36)(b)! This has been pointed out to Finance.

18(1)(y) added by 2016 budget bill #2, effective 2017.

(2) Limit on certain interest and property tax — Notwithstanding paragraph 20(1)(c), in computing the taxpayer's income for a particular taxation year from a business or property, no amount shall be deductible in respect of any expense incurred by the taxpayer in the year as, on account or in lieu of payment of, or in satisfaction of,

(a) interest on debt relating to the acquisition of land, or

(b) property taxes (not including income or profits taxes or taxes computed by reference to the transfer of property) paid or payable by the taxpayer in respect of land to a province or to a Canadian municipality,

unless, having regard to all the circumstances (including the cost to the taxpayer of the land in relation to the taxpayer's gross revenue, if any, from the land for the particular year or any preceding taxation year), the land can reasonably be considered to have been, in the year,

(c) used in the course of a business carried on in the particular year by the taxpayer, other than a business in the ordinary course of which land is held primarily for the purpose of resale or development, or

(d) held primarily for the purpose of gaining or producing income of the taxpayer from the land for the particular year,

except to the extent of the total of

(e) the amount, if any, by which the taxpayer's gross revenue, if any, from the land for the particular year exceeds the total of all amounts deducted in computing the taxpayer's income from the land for the year, and

(f) in the case of a corporation whose principal business is the leasing, rental or sale, or the development for lease, rental or sale, or any combination thereof, of real or immovable property owned by it, to or for a person with whom the corporation is dealing at arm's length, the corporation's base level deduction for the particular year.

Related Provisions: 10(1.1) — Cost of land inventory; 18(2.1) — Limitations; 18(2.2)–(2.5) — Base level deduction; 18(3) — Definitions; 53(1)(d.3) — Addition to adjusted cost base of share; 53(1)(e)(xi) — Addition to adjusted cost base of partnership interest; 53(1)(h) — Addition to adjusted cost base of land; 80(2)(b) — Application of debt forgiveness rules; 212(1)(b)(iii)(E) — Non-resident withholding tax — interest; 241(4)(b) — Communication of information; 248(1)"business".

Notes: 18(2) limits the deduction of interest and property taxes on vacant land to the income from the land (amounts disallowed are added to the adjusted cost base of the land: 53(1)(h)). For corporations whose "principal business" (see IT-153R3 and Notes to 20(1)(bb)) is the leasing, rental or sale (or the development for lease, rental or sale) of real property, such expenses may also be deducted up to the "base level deduction" for the year in 18(2.2) (generally, $1 million for the associated group, times the prescribed interest rate in Reg. 4301(c)). See also 18(3.1) re soft costs during construction.

See generally VIEWS doc 2009-0333031R5. The "total" for 18(2)(e) generally includes costs under 20(1)(cc) and (dd): 2007-0262121E5. The gross revenue for 18(2)(e) does not include that of the "assisted entity" in 18(3)"interest on..."(b): 2008-0280971E5. Proceeds of sale of the land do not qualify for 18(2)(e): 2012-0469811E5.

18(2) applied in *Kokai-Kuun*, 2015 TCC 217, para. 50.

18(2)(f) amended by 2002-2013 technical bill (to add "or immovable", effective June 26, 2013), and in 1988 with a transitional rule for 1988-92.

Interpretation Bulletins: IT-142R3: Settlement of debts on the winding-up of a corporation; IT-153R3: Land developers — subdivision and development costs and carrying charges on land; IT-355R2: Interest on loans to buy life insurance policies and annuity contracts, and interest on policy loans (cancelled); IT-360R2: Interest payable in a foreign currency.

(2.1) Where taxpayer member of partnership — Where a taxpayer who is a member of a partnership was obligated to pay any amount as, on account or in lieu of payment of, or in satisfaction of, interest (in this subsection referred to as an "interest amount") on money that was borrowed by the taxpayer before April 1, 1977 and that was used to acquire land owned by the partnership before that day or on an obligation entered into by the taxpayer before April 1, 1977 to pay for land owned by the partnership before that day, and, in a taxation year of the taxpayer, either,

(a) the partnership has disposed of all or any portion of the land, or

(b) the taxpayer has disposed of all or any portion of the taxpayer's interest in the partnership

to a person other than a person with whom the taxpayer does not deal at arm's length, in computing the taxpayer's income for the year or any subsequent year, there may be deducted such portion of the taxpayer's interest amount

(c) that was, by virtue of subsection (2), not deductible in computing the income of the taxpayer for any previous taxation year,

(d) that was not deductible in computing the income of any other taxpayer for any taxation year,

(e) that was not included in computing the adjusted cost base to the taxpayer of any property, and

(f) that was not deductible under this subsection in computing the income of the taxpayer for any previous taxation year

as is reasonable having regard to the portion of the land or interest in the partnership, as the case may be, so disposed of.

(2.2) Base level deduction — For the purposes of this section, a corporation's base level deduction for a taxation year is the amount that would be the amount of interest, computed at the prescribed rate, for the year in respect of a loan of $1,000,000 outstanding throughout the year, unless the corporation is associated in the year with one or more other corporations in which case, except as otherwise provided in this section, its base level deduction for the year is nil.

Related Provisions: 18(2.3), (2.4) — Associated corporations; 18(2.5) — Special rules for base level deduction.

Regulations: 4301(c) (prescribed rate of interest).

Interpretation Bulletins: IT-153R3: Land developers — subdivision and development costs and carrying charges on land.

(2.3) Associated corporations — Notwithstanding subsection (2.2), if all of the corporations that are associated with each other in a taxation year have filed with the Minister in prescribed form an agreement whereby, for the purposes of this section, they allocate an amount to one or more of them for the taxation year and the amount so allocated or the total of the amounts so allocated, as the case may be, does not exceed $1,000,000, the base level deduction for the year for each of the corporations is the base level deduction that would be computed under subsection (2.2) in respect of the corporation if the reference in that subsection to $1,000,000 were read as a reference to the amount so allocated to it.

Related Provisions: 18(2.4) — Failure to file agreement.

Interpretation Bulletins: IT-153R3: Land developers — subdivision and development costs and carrying charges on land.

Forms: T2005: Agreement among associated corporations to allocate an amount to calculate their base level deduction; T2013: Agreement among associated corporations.

(2.4) Failure to file agreement — If any of the corporations that are associated with each other in a taxation year has failed to file with the Minister an agreement as contemplated by subsection (2.3) within 30 days after notice in writing by the Minister has been forwarded to any of them that such an agreement is required for the purpose of any assessment of tax under this Part, the Minister shall, for the purpose of this section, allocate an amount to one or more of them for the taxation year, which amount or the total of which amounts, as the case may be, shall equal $1,000,000 and in any such case, the amount so allocated to any corporation shall be deemed to be an amount allocated to the corporation pursuant to subsection (2.3).

Related Provisions: *Interpretation Act* 27(5) — Meaning of "within 30 days".

Interpretation Bulletins: IT-153R3: Land developers — subdivision and development costs and carrying charges on land.

(2.5) Special rules for base level deduction — Notwithstanding any other provision of this section,

(a) where a corporation, in this paragraph referred to as the "first corporation", has more than one taxation year ending in the same calendar year and is associated in two or more of those taxation years with another corporation that has a taxation year ending in that calendar year, the base level deduction of the first corporation for each taxation year in which it is associated with the other corporation ending in that calendar year is, subject to the application of paragraph (b), an amount equal to its base level deduction for the first such taxation year determined without reference to paragraph (b); and

(b) where a corporation has a taxation year that is less than 51 weeks, its base level deduction for the year is that proportion of its base level deduction for the year determined without reference to this paragraph that the number of days in the year is of 365.

Related Provisions: 18(2.2) — Base level deduction.

Interpretation Bulletins: IT-153R3: Land developers — subdivision and development costs and carrying charges on land.

Forms: T2005: Agreement among associated corporations to allocate an amount to calculate their base level deduction.

(3) Definitions — In subsection (2),

"interest on debt relating to the acquisition of land" includes

(a) interest paid or payable in a year in respect of borrowed money that cannot be identified with particular land but that may nonetheless reasonably be considered (having regard to all the circumstances) as interest on borrowed money used in respect of or for the acquisition of land, and

(b) interest paid or payable in the year by a taxpayer in respect of borrowed money that may reasonably be considered (having regard to all the circumstances) to have been used to assist, directly or indirectly,

  (i) another person with whom the taxpayer does not deal at arm's length,

  (ii) a corporation of which the taxpayer is a specified shareholder, or

  (iii) a partnership of which the taxpayer's share of any income or loss is 10% or more,

to acquire land to be used or held by that person, corporation or partnership otherwise than as described in paragraph (2)(c) or (d), except where the assistance is in the form of a loan to that person, corporation or partnership and a reasonable rate of interest on the loan is charged by the taxpayer;

Related Provisions: 53(1)(h) — Addition to adjusted cost base of land.

Notes: See Notes to 188.1(5) re meaning of "includes"; and Notes to 17.1(1) re meaning of "indirectly" in (b) opening words.

18(3)"interest on debt ..." was 18(3)(b) before RSC 1985 (5th Supp) consolidation for tax years ending after Nov. 1991.

Interpretation Bulletins: IT-153R3: Land developers — subdivision and development costs, etc.

"land" does not, except to the extent that it is used for the provision of parking facilities for a fee or charge, include

(a) any property that is a building or other structure affixed to land,

(b) the land subjacent to any property described in paragraph (a), or

(c) such land immediately contiguous to the land described in paragraph (b) that is a parking area, driveway, yard, garden or similar land as is necessary for the use of any property described in paragraph (a).

Interpretation Bulletins: IT-153R3: Land developers — subdivision and development costs, etc.

Notes: 18(3)"land" was 18(3)(a) before RSC 1985 (5th Supp) consolidation for tax years ending after Nov. 1991.

(3.1) Costs relating to construction of building or ownership of land — Notwithstanding any other provision of this Act, in computing a taxpayer's income for a taxation year,

(a) no deduction shall be made in respect of any outlay or expense made or incurred by the taxpayer (other than an amount deductible under paragraph 20(1)(a), (aa) or (qq) or subsection 20(29)) that can reasonably be regarded as a cost attributable to the period of the construction, renovation or alteration of a building by or on behalf of the taxpayer, a person with whom the taxpayer does not deal at arm's length, a corporation of which the taxpayer is a specified shareholder or a partnership of which the taxpayer's share of any income or loss is 10% or more and relating to the construction, renovation or alteration, or a cost attributable to that period and relating to the ownership during that period of land

  (i) that is subjacent to the building, or

  (ii) that

    (A) is immediately contiguous to the land subjacent to the building,

    (B) is used, or is intended to be used, for a parking area, driveway, yard, garden or any other similar use, and

    (C) is necessary for the use or intended use of the building; and

(b) the amount of such an outlay or expense shall, to the extent that it would otherwise be deductible in computing the taxpayer's income for the year, be included in computing the cost or capital cost, as the case may be, of the building to the taxpayer, to the person with whom the taxpayer does not deal at arm's length, to the corporation of which the taxpayer is a specified shareholder or to the partnership of which the taxpayer's share of any income or loss is 10% or more, as the case may be.

Related Provisions: 18(3.2)–(3.7) — Interpretation and application; 20(29) — Deduction against rental income from building; 53(1)(d.3) — Addition to adjusted cost base of share; 53(1)(e)(xi) — Addition to adjusted cost base of partnership interest; 80(2)(b) — Application of debt forgiveness rules; 241(4) — Communication of information.

Notes: 18(3.1) denies a deduction for construction-period soft costs, which must be added to the building's capital cost and claimed as CCA under 20(1)(a). See 18(3.2)-(3.7) for interpretation rules. See also VIEWS docs 2005-0141071C6, 2013-0489821I7. Expenses that would not otherwise be deductible cannot be capitalized: 18(3.1)(b); *Mikhail*, [2002] 2 C.T.C. 2612 (TCC), para. 36; *Eskandari*, 2007 TCC 419; *Firth*, 2009 TCC 137. Deductions were allowed in *Janota*, 2010 TCC 395 and *Morris*, 2014 TCC 142 (repairs and minor renovations did not trigger 18(3.1), and in any event the Crown did not show that the mortgage paid for the construction); and CRA agrees that maintenance and repairs do not fall under 18(3.1): 2015-0595761C6 [2015 APFF q.3]. While the land is vacant, see 18(2).

In *Mikhail* (above), 18(3.1) applied to a Florida property that was temporarily unrentable due to hurricane damage. General repairs are not "construction, renovation or alteration": *Preiss*, 2009 TCC 488. In *Santagapita*, 2008 TCC 662, 18(3.1) applied, but partial deduction was allowed for rental income due to 20(29).

18(3.1)(b) does not permit the deduction of accrued but unpaid compound interest, which would be deductible under 20(1)(d) only when paid: VIEWS doc 2002-0147295.

Demolition costs may fall within 18(3.1), but are deductible if they relate to replacing a building that was used by the taxpayer to earn income: docs 2004-0082201E5, 2006-0167321I7.

See also Ian MacInnis, "Financing Costs Incurred During Construction Period", 1990 *Tax Topics* (CCH) 1-2 (April 29, 2010); VIEWS doc 2010-0386121E5.

18(3.1) amended by 2000 Budget (for outlays and expenses made or incurred after Dec. 21, 2000), 1993 and 1991 technical bills.

Income Tax Folios: S3-F4-C1: General discussion of CCA.

Interpretation Bulletins: IT-121R3: Election to capitalize cost of borrowed money (cancelled); IT-142R3: Settlement of debts on the winding-up of a corporation; IT-355R2: Interest on loans to buy life insurance policies and annuity contracts, and interest on policy loans (cancelled).

(3.2) Included costs — For the purposes of subsection (3.1), costs relating to the construction, renovation or alteration of a building or to the ownership of land include

(a) interest paid or payable by a taxpayer in respect of borrowed money that cannot be identified with a particular building or particular land, but that can reasonably be considered (having regard to all the circumstances) as interest on borrowed money used by the taxpayer in respect of the construction, renovation or alteration of a building or the ownership of land; and

(b) interest paid or payable by a taxpayer in respect of borrowed money that may reasonably be considered (having regard to all the circumstances) to have been used to assist, directly or indirectly,

  (i) another person with whom the taxpayer does not deal at arm's length,

  (ii) a corporation of which the taxpayer is a specified shareholder, or

  (iii) a partnership of which the taxpayer's share of any income or loss is 10% or more,

to construct, renovate or alter a building or to purchase land, except where the assistance is in the form of a loan to that other person, corporation or partnership and a reasonable rate of interest on the loan is charged by the taxpayer.

Notes: For the meaning of "indirectly" in (b), see Notes to 17.1(1).

Income Tax Folios: S3-F4-C1: General discussion of CCA.

(3.3) Completion — For the purposes of subsection (3.1), the construction, renovation or alteration of a building is completed at the earlier of the day on which the construction, renovation or alteration is actually completed and the day on which all or substantially all of the building is used for the purpose for which it was constructed, renovated or altered.

Notes: CRA considers that "substantially all" means 90% or more.

For a case applying 18(3.3) see *Lee*, 2008 CarswellNat 1902 (TCC).

Income Tax Folios: S3-F4-C1: General discussion of CCA.

(3.4) Where subsec. (3.1) does not apply — [Applies to expenses incurred before 1992]

Income Tax Folios: S3-F4-C1: General discussion of CCA.

(3.5)–(3.7) [Applies to construction begun before 1983]

(4) Limitation on deduction of interest [thin capitalization] — Notwithstanding any other provision of this Act (other than subsection (8)), in computing the income for a taxation year of a corporation or a trust from a business (other than the Canadian banking business of an authorized foreign bank) or property, no deduction shall be made in respect of that proportion of any amount otherwise deductible in computing its income for the year in respect of interest paid or payable by it on outstanding debts to specified non-residents that

(a) the amount, if any, by which

(i) the average of all amounts each of which is, in respect of a calendar month that ends in the year, the greatest total amount at any time in the month of the outstanding debts to specified non-residents of the corporation or trust,

exceeds

(ii) 1.5 times the equity amount of the corporation or trust for the year,

is of

(b) the amount determined under subparagraph (a)(i) in respect of the corporation or trust for the year.

Related Provisions: 12(1)(l.1) — Income inclusion for corporate partner; 12(2.02) — Characterization of income flowing through 12(1)(l.1); 18(5) — Meaning of certain expressions; 18(5.1) — Person deemed not to be specified shareholder; 18(5.2) — Non-resident corp or trust is deemed specified shareholder or beneficiary of itself; 18(5.4) — Trust can designate interest paid to non-resident as being payment to beneficiary instead; 18(6), (6.1) — Back-to-back loans; 18(7) — Partners deemed to owe proportion of partnership debt; 18(8) — FAPI exception; 214(16)(a)(i), 214(17) — Interest disallowed under 18(4) deemed to be dividend subject to withholding tax; 261(2) — Canadian currency used unless election made; Canada-U.S. Tax Treaty:Art. XXV:8 — Thin cap rules grandfathered from treaty non-discrimination provision.

Notes: 18(4)–(8) provide the "thin capitalization" rules. In general, they limit the debt:equity ratio for Canadian subsidiaries of non-residents to 1.5:1, by limiting the deductibility (under 20(1)(c)) of interest paid to non-resident shareholders. In effect, this forces a non-resident setting up a Canadian subsidiary to provide 40% of financing through equity rather than using only debt (so debt:equity does not exceed 60:40). This limits interest deductions that reduce Canadian tax on a Canadian subsidiary of a foreign entity, and increases withholding tax (212(2)) on dividends (there is generally no withholding tax on interest: 212(1)(b)). Disallowed interest is deemed by 214(16) to be a dividend and subject to withholding tax, even if not yet paid (214(17)). The 2013 amendments extended these rules from corporations to trusts, and to non-resident corps and trusts carrying on business in Canada; and the 2014 amendments extended them to back-to-back loans. See also Notes to 18(6).

Foreign currency debt is measured for 18(4) based on the exchange rate at the time the loan was made, due to 261(2) (provided no 261(3) election is made): VIEWS doc 2015-0610601C6 [2015 CTF q.10], reversing previous policy.

See Vidal et al., *Introduction to International Tax in Canada* (Carswell, 8th ed., 2020), chap. 12; Monaghan, "The Thin Capitalization Rules", VIII(1) *Corporate Structures & Groups* (Federated Press) 404-412 (2002); Edgar et al., "Foreign Direct Investment, Thin Capitalization and the Interest Expense Deduction", 56(4) *Canadian Tax Journal* 803-69 (2008); Biringer, "Thin Capitalization", XV(4) *Corporate Finance [CF]* (Federated Press) 1702-09 (2009); Johnson, "Selected Tax Issues Relating to Capitalizing Private Equity Investments", VI(4) *Resource Sector Taxation* (Federated Press) 466-71 (2009); Pantry & Jamal, "The Thin Cap Rules: Revisiting the Foreign Exchange Anomaly", XVII(1) *CF* 1934-37 (2011); Diksic, "Thin Cap Calculation Revisited", 19(8) *Canadian Tax Highlights* (ctf.ca) 1-2 (Aug. 2011) (re doc 2010-0365371R3); Alty & Studniberg, "The Corporate Capital Structure", 62(4) *CTJ* 1159-1202 (2014).

For the 2012 amendments see Dawe, "Changes to the Thin Capitalization Rules", 9(8) *Tax Hyperion* (Carswell) 5-6 (Aug. 2012) and "Additional Changes...", 10(5) 2-4 (May 2013); Sherman & Smit, "Thin Cap Gains Weight", 2012 Cdn Tax Foundation conference report, 25:1-19; Colden, "Changes to the Thin Capitalization Rules", XVIII(2) *Corporate Finance* (Federated Press) 2104-08 (2012).

In *Wildenburg Holdings*, [2000] 3 C.T.C. 148 (Ont CA), these rules applied (for Ont. corporate tax) to holdings through a partnership. However, CRA generally does not apply them if there is a *bona fide* partnership and the partners are liable for the partnership debts: 1992 Cdn Tax Foundation conference round table, p. 54:8, Q. 12; 1998 conference (p. 52:14); *Income Tax Technical News* 16.

In *Mac's Convenience*, 2015 QCCA 837 (leave to appeal denied 2017 CarswellQue 960 (SCC)), inadvertent triggering of 18(4) could not be fixed by rectification (see 169(1) Notes).

At the Cdn Tax Foundation conference, Nov. 28, 2006 (slides distributed), CRA stated that when "push down accounting" is implemented after a foreign takeover, and Canco's retained earnings are transferred to contributed surplus, "good retained earnings remain as good retained earnings. Reflecting them as contributed surplus does not expose the company to thin capitalization problems. However, when push down accounting requires that a purchase price adjustment be credited to Canco's contributed surplus, the accounting adjustments to contributed surplus are not associated with contributions of capital by a shareholder and accordingly would not qualify as 18(4)(a)(ii)(B) contributed surplus even if required under Canadian GAAP". See also VIEWS doc 2007-0232081I7.

If a partnership is inserted to acquire debts to specified non-residents, so as to avoid 18(4), CRA will apply GAAR: VIEWS doc 2005-0123631R3.

Retained earnings (RE) for 18(4)(a)(ii)(A) carry through an amalgamation: VIEWS doc 2005-0121941E5. Canadian GAAP applies in determining the amount of partnership income included in a corporate partner's RE: 2013-0512552I7; but a corp's unconsolidated and consolidated financial statements must use the same accounting standards: 2015-0618511I7. Undistributed partnership income did not reduce RE in ruling 2007-0248961R3. For rulings on 18(4)(a)(ii)(C) see 2007-0237921R3, 2010-0365371R3. An addition to contributed surplus that does not accord with GAAP or IFRS would not count for 18(4): 2012-0445891E5. Where US GAAP is used, accumulated "other comprehensive income" is not included in RE: 2017-0721641I7.

For deemed interest on interest-free loans to non-residents, see s. 17.

18(4) amended by 2013 budget bill #2 (for tax years that begin after 2013, to extend its application to trusts), 2012 budget bill #2, 2000 Budget.

Interpretation Bulletins: IT-59R3: Interest on debts owing to specified non-residents (thin capitalization); IT-121R3: Election to capitalize cost of borrowed money (cancelled).

Information Circulars: 87-2R: International transfer pricing (archived).

Advance Tax Rulings: ATR-43: Utilization of a non-resident-owned investment corporation as a holding corporation.

I.T. Technical News: 15 (back-to-back loans in relation to subsecs. 18(4) and 18(6)); 16 (*Wildenburg Holdings* case); 38 (thin capitalization); 42 (International Financial Reporting Standards — thin capitalization).

(5) Definitions — Notwithstanding any other provision of this Act (other than subsection (5.1)), in this subsection and subsections (4) and (5.1) to (6.1),

Notes: Opening words amended by 2014 budget bill #2, for tax years that begin after 2014, to apply to 18(5.1)-(5.4) and (6.1). Earlier amended by 2012 budget bill #2, but that change reversed by 2002-2013 technical bill.

"beneficiary" has the same meaning as in subsection 108(1);

Notes: Definition added by 2013 budget bill #2, effective for taxation years that begin after 2013.

"equity amount", of a corporation or trust for a taxation year, means

(a) in the case of a corporation resident in Canada, the total of

(i) the retained earnings of the corporation at the beginning of the year, except to the extent that those earnings include retained earnings of any other corporation,

(ii) the average of all amounts each of which is the corporation's contributed surplus (other than any portion of that contributed surplus that arose at a time when the corporation was non-resident, or that arose in connection with a disposition to which subsection 212.1(1.1) applies or an "investment", as defined in subsection 212.3(10), to which subsection 212.3(2) applies) at the beginning of a calendar month that ends in the year, to the extent that it was contributed by a specified non-resident shareholder of the corporation, and

(iii) the average of all amounts each of which is the corporation's paid-up capital at the beginning of a calendar month that ends in the year, excluding the paid-up capital in respect of shares of any class of the capital stock of the corporation owned by a person other than a specified non-resident shareholder of the corporation,

(b) in the case of a trust resident in Canada, the amount, if any, by which

   (i) the total of

      (A) the average of all amounts each of which is the total amount of all equity contributions to the trust made before a calendar month that ends in the year, to the extent that the contributions were made by a specified non-resident beneficiary of the trust, and

      (B) the tax-paid earnings of the trust for the year,

exceeds

   (ii) the average of all amounts each of which is the total of all amounts that were paid or became payable by the trust to a beneficiary of the trust in respect of the beneficiary's interest under the trust before a calendar month that ends in the year except to the extent that the amount is

      (A) included in the beneficiary's income for a taxation year because of subsection 104(13),

      (B) an amount from which tax was deducted under Part XIII because of paragraph 212(1)(c), or

      (C) paid or payable to a person other than a specified non-resident beneficiary of the trust, and

(c) in the case of a corporation or trust that is not resident in Canada, including a corporation or trust that files a return under this Part in accordance with subsection 216(1) in respect of the year, 40% of the amount, if any, by which

   (i) the average of all amounts each of which is the cost of a property, other than an interest as a member of a partnership, owned by the corporation or trust at the beginning of a calendar month that ends in the year

      (A) that is used by the corporation or trust in the year in, or held by it in the year in the course of, carrying on business in Canada, or

      (B) that is an interest in real property, or a real right in immovables, in Canada, or an interest in, or for civil law a right in, timber resource properties and timber limits, in Canada, and in respect of which the corporation or trust files a return under this Part in accordance with subsection 216(1) in respect of the year,

exceeds

   (ii) the average of all amounts each of which is the total of all amounts outstanding, at the beginning of a calendar month that ends in the year, as or on account of a debt or other obligation to pay an amount that was payable by the corporation or trust that may reasonably be regarded as relating to a business carried on by it in Canada or to an interest or right described in clause (i)(B), other than a debt or obligation that is included in the outstanding debts to specified non-residents of the corporation or trust;

Related Provisions: 15(2.14)(b) — Partnership look-through rule; 18(5.3) — Interpretation for subpara. (c)(i).

Notes: The 40% figure in para. (c) applies the 1.5 limit in 18(4)(a)(ii) to equity relative to debt+equity (on $100 equity + $150 debt, $100 is 40% of $250).

"Beginning of a calendar month" (BCM) mean the first moment of the month, so equity provided during the first day does not qualify: VIEWS doc 2002-0135330. Where a taxation year ends mid-month, BCM can be in the previous tax year: 2008-0286611E5. For a new corp, BCM means the date of incorporation: *Income Tax Technical News* 38 [2007 Cdn Tax Foundation conf. report, 4:11]. For criticism see Diksic, "Thin Cap Calculation", 17(3) *Canadian Tax Highlights* (ctf.ca) 9-10 (March 2009).

For (a)(i), partnership income under 96(1) cannot be added to retained earnings as otherwise determined: doc 2015-0618511I7.

For (a)(ii), CRA says the person must be a specified NR shareholder "at the beginning of the month for which the amount is determined": VIEWS doc 2019-0798721C6 [2019 IFA q.4].

For interpretation of (b)(i)(A), see doc 2015-0585471E5.

"Cost" in (c)(i) means original cost, not after claiming CCA: VIEWS docs 2013-0513761E5, 2014-0526631E5.

Subpara. (a)(ii) amended by 2018 budget bill #2, for transactions or events that occur after Feb. 26, 2018, to change "in connection with an investment" to "at a time when the corporation was non-resident, or that arose in connection with a disposition to which subsection 212.1(1.1) applies or an investment". In effect, this puts contributed surplus on the same footing as paid-up capital (reduced under 212.1(1.1)(b)) for the cross-border anti-surplus-stripping rule in 212.1. (Finance Technical Notes)

Definition added by 2013 budget bill #2, for taxation years that begin after 2013, with an elective transitional rule for before March 21, 2013.

"equity contribution", to a trust, means a transfer of property to the trust that is made

   (a) in exchange for an interest as a beneficiary under the trust,

   (b) in exchange for a right to acquire an interest as a beneficiary under the trust, or

   (c) for no consideration by a person beneficially interested in the trust;

Notes: Definition added by 2013 budget bill #2, effective for taxation years that begin after 2013 (but see Notes to 18(5) "equity amount").

"outstanding debts to specified non-residents", of a corporation or trust at any particular time in a taxation year, means

   (a) the total of all amounts each of which is an amount outstanding at that time as or on account of a debt or other obligation to pay an amount

      (i) that was payable by the corporation or trust to a person who was, at any time in the year,

         (A) a specified non-resident shareholder of the corporation or a specified non-resident beneficiary of the trust, or

         (B) a non-resident person who was not dealing at arm's length with a specified shareholder of the corporation or a specified beneficiary of the trust, as the case may be, and

      (ii) on which any amount in respect of interest paid or payable by the corporation or trust is or would be, but for subsection (4), deductible in computing the income of the corporation or trust for the year,

but does not include

   (b) an amount outstanding at the particular time as or on account of a debt or other obligation

      (i) to pay an amount to

         (A) a non-resident insurance corporation to the extent that the obligation was, for the non-resident insurance corporation's taxation year that included the particular time, designated insurance property in respect of an insurance business carried on in Canada through a permanent establishment as defined by regulation, or

         (B) an authorized foreign bank, if the bank uses or holds the obligation at the particular time in its Canadian banking business, or

      (ii) that is a debt obligation described in subparagraph (ii) of the description of A in paragraph 17.1(1)(b) to the extent that the proceeds of the debt obligation can reasonably be considered to directly or indirectly fund at the particular time, in whole or in part, a pertinent loan or indebtedness (as defined in subsection 212.3(11)) owing to the corporation or another corporation resident in Canada that does not, at the particular time, deal at arm's length with the corporation;

Related Provisions: 15(2.14) — Interpretation — partnerships; 18(7) — Partnership debts and property.

Notes: For CRA interpretation see VIEWS docs 2010-0355691I7 (loans from Canadian branch of foreign bank to related company); 2016-0626841E5 (accrued but unpaid compound interest is not included); 2019-0798721C6 [2019 IFA q.4] (application to 78(1)(b) deemed interest).

Accounting Standards Board 2014 proposals may treat preferred shares as debt for accounting purposes as of 2016, but CRA has said that "debt" for 18(4) is based on legal form, not accounting principles: 1996 Corporate Management Tax Conference q.6, pp. 24:7-9; VIEWS docs 9530990, 9619120, 2015-0572201C6 [2015 STEP q.3].

For the meaning of "indirectly" in (b)(ii) see Notes to 17.1(1).

Definition amended by 2014 budget bill #2 (last change effective for tax years ending after Aug. 13, 2012), 2013 budget bill #2 (for tax years that begin after 2013), 2001 technical bill, 1996 Budget. 18(5) "outstanding debts..." was 18(5)(a) before RSC 1985 (5th Supp) consolidation for tax years ending after Nov. 1991.

Regulations: 8201 (permanent extablishment).

Interpretation Bulletins: IT-59R3: Interest on debts owing to specified non-residents (thin capitalization).

Advance Tax Rulings: ATR-43: Utilization of a non-resident-owned investment corporation as a holding corporation.

"security interest", in respect of a property, means an interest in, or for civil law a right in, the property that secures payment of an obligation;

Notes: 18(5)"security interest" added by 2014 budget bill #2, effective for taxation years that begin after 2014.

"specified beneficiary", of a trust at any time, means a person who at that time, either alone or together with persons with whom that person does not deal at arm's length, has an interest as a beneficiary under the trust with a fair market value that is not less than 25% of the fair market value of all interests as a beneficiary under the trust and for the purpose of determining whether a particular person is a specified beneficiary of a trust,

(a) if the particular person, or a person with whom the particular person does not deal at arm's length, has at that time a right under a contract, in equity or otherwise, either immediately or in the future and either absolutely or contingently, to, or to acquire, an interest as a beneficiary under a trust, the particular person or the person with whom the particular person does not deal at arm's length, as the case may be, is deemed at that time to own the interest,

(b) if the particular person, or a person with whom the particular person does not deal at arm's length, has at that time a right under a contract, in equity or otherwise, either immediately or in the future and either absolutely or contingently to cause a trust to redeem, acquire or terminate any interest in it as a beneficiary (other than an interest held by the particular person or a person with whom the particular person does not deal at arm's length), the trust is deemed at that time to have redeemed, acquired or terminated the interest, unless the right is not exercisable at that time because the exercise of the right is contingent on the death, bankruptcy or permanent disability of an individual, and

(c) if the amount of income or capital of the trust that the particular person, or a person with whom the particular person does not deal at arm's length, may receive as a beneficiary of the trust depends on the exercise by any person of, or the failure by any person to exercise, a discretionary power, that person is deemed to have fully exercised, or to have failed to exercise, the power, as the case may be;

Related Provisions: 18(5.2) — Non-resident trust is deemed SB of itself.

Notes: Definition added by 2013 budget bill #2, effective for taxation years that begin after 2013.

"specified non-resident beneficiary", of a trust at any time, means a specified beneficiary of the trust who at that time is a non-resident person;

Notes: Definition added by 2013 budget bill #2, effective for taxation years that begin after 2013.

"specified non-resident shareholder" of a corporation at any time means a specified shareholder of the corporation who was at that time a non-resident person or a non-resident-owned investment corporation;

Notes: 18(5)"specified non-resident shareholder" was 18(5)(b) before RSC 1985 (5th Supp) consolidation for tax years ending after Nov. 1991.

"specified proportion" — [Repealed]

Notes: Definition added by 2012 budget bill #2, for taxation years that begin after March 28, 2012, and repealed by 2002-2013 technical bill (co-ordinating amendment in s. 427(2)(b)) effective June 26, 2013, as "specified proportion" is now defined in 248(1).

"specified right", at any time in respect of a property, means a right to, at that time, mortgage, hypothecate, assign, pledge or in any way encumber the property to secure payment of an obligation — other than the particular debt or other obligation described in paragraph (6)(a) or a debt or other obligation described in sub-paragraph (6)(d)(ii) — or to use, invest, sell or otherwise dispose of, or in any way alienate, the property unless it is established by the taxpayer that all of the proceeds (net of costs, if any) received, or that would be received, from exercising the right must first be applied to reduce an amount described in subparagraph (6)(d)(i) or (ii);

Notes: Definition added by 2014 budget bill #2, for tax years that begin after 2014.

"specified shareholder" of a corporation at any time means a person who at that time, either alone or together with persons with whom that person is not dealing at arm's length, owns

(a) shares of the capital stock of the corporation that give the holders thereof 25% or more of the votes that could be cast at an annual meeting of the shareholders of the corporation, or

(b) shares of the capital stock of the corporation having a fair market value of 25% or more of the fair market value of all of the issued and outstanding shares of the capital stock of the corporation,

and, for the purpose of determining whether a particular person is a specified shareholder of a corporation at any time, where the particular person or a person with whom the particular person is not dealing at arm's length has at that time a right under a contract, in equity or otherwise, either immediately or in the future and either absolutely or contingently

(c) to, or to acquire, shares in a corporation or to control the voting rights of shares in a corporation, or

(d) to cause a corporation to redeem, acquire or cancel any of its shares (other than shares held by the particular person or a person with whom the particular person is not dealing at arm's length),

the particular person or the person with whom the particular person is not dealing at arm's length, as the case may be, shall be deemed at that time to own the shares referred to in paragraph (c) and the corporation referred to in paragraph (d) shall be deemed at that time to have redeemed, acquired or cancelled the shares referred to in paragraph (d), unless the right is not exercisable at that time because the exercise thereof is contingent on the death, bankruptcy or permanent disability of an individual.

Related Provisions: 18(5.1) — Person deemed not to be specified shareholder; 18(5.2) — Non-resident corp is deemed specified shareholder of itself.

Notes: A person must own at least 1 share to be a specified shareholder: VIEWS docs 9521415, 2019-0798831C6 [2019 IFA q.1].

"tax-paid earnings", of a trust resident in Canada for a taxation year, means the total of all amounts each of which is the amount in respect of a particular taxation year of the trust that ended before the year determined by the formula

$$A - B$$

where

A   is the taxable income of the trust under this Part for the particular year, and

B   is the total of tax payable under this Part by the trust, and all income taxes payable by the trust under the laws of a province, for the particular year.

Notes: Definition added by 2013 budget bill #2, effective for taxation years that begin after 2013.

Notes: 18(5) amended by 1992 technical bill, last change effective for 1993 and later taxation years. 18(5)"specified shareholder" was 18(5)(c) before RSC 1985 (5th Supp) consolidation for tax years ending after Nov. 1991.

Interpretation Bulletins: IT-59R3: Interest on debts owing to specified non-residents (thin capitalization).

(5.1) [Person deemed not to be] Specified shareholder or specified beneficiary — For the purposes of subsections (4) to (6), if

(a) a particular person would, but for this subsection, be a specified shareholder of a corporation or a specified beneficiary of a trust at any time,

(b) there was in effect at that time an agreement or arrangement under which, on the satisfaction of a condition or the occurrence of an event that it is reasonable to expect will be satisfied or will occur, the particular person will cease to be a specified shareholder of the corporation or a specified beneficiary of the trust, and

(c) the purpose for which the particular person became a specified shareholder or specified beneficiary was the safeguarding of rights or interests of the particular person or a person with whom the particular person is not dealing at arm's length in respect of any indebtedness owing at any time to the particular person or a person with whom the particular person is not dealing at arm's length,

the particular person is deemed not to be a specified shareholder of the corporation or a specified beneficiary of the trust, as the case may be, at that time.

Related Provisions: 18(7) — Partners deemed to owe proportion of partnership debt.

Notes: 18(5.1) amended by 2013 budget bill #2 (for tax years that begin after 2013, to add references to "specified beneficiary" as part of extending the thin-cap rules to trusts). Added by 1992 technical bill.

(5.2) Specified shareholder or specified beneficiary — For the purposes of subsections (4) to (6), a non-resident corporation is deemed to be a specified shareholder of itself and a non-resident trust is deemed to be a specified beneficiary of itself.

Notes: 18(5.2) added by 2013 budget bill #2, for tax years that begin after 2013.

(5.3) Property used in business — cost attribution [for "equity amount"(c)(i)] — For the purposes of subparagraph (c)(i) of the definition "equity amount" in subsection (5),

(a) if a property is partly used or held by a taxpayer in a taxation year in the course of carrying on business in Canada, the cost of the property to the taxpayer is deemed for the year to be equal to the same proportion of the cost to the taxpayer of the property (determined without reference to this subsection) that the proportion of the use or holding made of the property in the course of carrying on business in Canada in the year is of the whole use or holding made of the property in the year; and

(b) if a corporation or trust is deemed to own a portion of a property of a partnership because of subsection (7) at any time,

(i) the property is deemed to have, at that time, a cost to the corporation or trust equal to the same proportion of the cost of the property to the partnership as the proportion of the debts and other obligations to pay an amount of the partnership allocated to it under subsection (7) is of the total amount of all debts and other obligations to pay an amount of the partnership, and

(ii) in the case of a partnership that carries on business in Canada, the corporation or trust is deemed to use or hold the property in the course of carrying on business in Canada to the extent the partnership uses or holds the property in the course of carrying on business in Canada for the fiscal period of the partnership that includes that time.

Notes: 18(5.3) added by 2013 budget bill #2, for tax years that begin after 2013.

(5.4) Rules — trust income [redesignation of thin-cap interest as payment to beneficiary] — For the purposes of this Act, a trust resident in Canada may designate in its return of income under this Part for a taxation year that all or any portion of an amount paid or credited as interest by the trust, or by a partnership, in the year to a non-resident person is deemed to be income of the trust that has been paid to the non-resident person as a beneficiary of the trust, and not to have been paid or credited by the trust or the partnership as interest, to the extent that an amount in respect of the interest

(a) is included in computing the income of the trust for the year under paragraph 12(1)(l.1); or

(b) is not deductible in computing the income of the trust for the year because of subsection (4).

Notes: For a trust filing a Quebec return, an 18(5.4) designation must be copied to Revenu Québec: *Taxation Act* ss. 173.3, 21.4.6.

18(5.4) added by 2013 budget bill #2, for tax years that begin after 2013.

(6) Back-to-back loan arrangement — Subsection (6.1) applies at any time in respect of a taxpayer if at that time

(a) the taxpayer has a particular amount outstanding as or on account of a particular debt or other obligation to pay an amount to a person (in this subsection and subsection (6.1) referred to as the **"intermediary"**);

(b) the intermediary is neither

(i) a person resident in Canada with whom the taxpayer does not deal at arm's length, nor

(ii) a person that is, in respect of the taxpayer, described in subparagraph (a)(i) of the definition "outstanding debts to specified non-residents" in subsection (5);

(c) the intermediary or a person that does not deal at arm's length with the intermediary

(i) has an amount outstanding as or on account of a debt or other obligation to pay an amount to a particular non-resident person that is, in respect of the taxpayer, described in subparagraph (a)(i) of the definition "outstanding debts to specified non-residents" in subsection (5) that meets any of the following conditions (in this subsection and subsection (6.1) referred to as the "intermediary debt"):

(A) recourse in respect of the debt or other obligation is limited in whole or in part, either immediately or in the future and either absolutely or contingently, to the particular debt or other obligation, or

(B) it can reasonably be concluded that all or a portion of the particular amount became owing, or was permitted to remain owing, because

(I) all or a portion of the debt or other obligation was entered into or was permitted to remain outstanding, or

(II) the intermediary anticipated that all or a portion of the debt or other obligation would become owing or remain outstanding, or

(ii) has a specified right in respect of a particular property that was granted directly or indirectly by a person that is, in respect of the taxpayer, a particular non-resident person described in subparagraph (a)(i) of the definition "outstanding debts to specified non-residents" in subsection (5) and

(A) the existence of the specified right is required under the terms and conditions of the particular debt or other obligation, or

(B) it can reasonably be concluded that all or a portion of the particular amount became owing, or was permitted to remain owing, because

(I) the specified right was granted, or

(II) the intermediary anticipated that the specified right would be granted; and

(d) the total of all amounts — each of which is, in respect of the particular debt or other obligation, an amount outstanding as or on account of an intermediary debt or the fair market value of a particular property described in subparagraph (c)(ii) — is equal to at least 25% of the total of

(i) the particular amount, and

(ii) the total of all amounts each of which is an amount (other than the particular amount) that the taxpayer, or a person that does not deal at arm's length with the taxpayer, has outstanding as or on account of a debt or other obligation to pay an amount to the intermediary under the agreement, or an agreement that is connected to the agreement, under which the particular debt or other obligation was entered into if

(A) the intermediary is granted a security interest in respect of a property that is the intermediary debt or the

127

particular property, as the case may be, and the security interest secures the payment of two or more debts or other obligations that include the debt or other obligation and the particular debt or other obligation, and

(B) each security interest that secures the payment of a debt or other obligation referred to in clause (A) secures the payment of every debt or other obligation referred to in that clause.

Related Provisions: 18(5) — Definitions; 18(5.1) — Person deemed not to be specified shareholder; 18(7) — Partners deemed to owe proportion of partnership debt.

Notes: See Notes to 18(6.1) for the rules effective 2015.

The pre-2015 version of this rule could be avoided with conditional loans: Kohn, "Application of Subsection 18(6)", VI(4) *Corporate Finance* (Federated Press), 558-60 (1998); Ng & Schweitzer, "Thin Capitalization Rules", 1715 *Tax Topics* (CCH) 1-4 (Jan. 20, 2005); VIEWS docs 2006-0182431R3, 2007-0237921R3, 2009-0349141R3 [Gamble, "Inbound Financing", XVI(2) *International Tax Planning* (Federated Press) 1100-04 (2010)], 2010-035569117, 2010-0366541C6 [2010 IFA], 2010-0384001E5. See also 18(4) Notes.

18(6) amended by 2014 budget bill #2 for tax years that begin after 2014, and 2013 budget bill #2 for tax years that begin after 2013.

Interpretation Bulletins: IT-59R3: Interest on debts owing to specified non-residents (thin capitalization).

I.T. Technical News: 15 (back-to-back loans in relation to subsecs. 18(4) and 18(6)).

(6.1) Back-to-back loan arrangement — If this subsection applies at any time in respect of a taxpayer,

(a) then for the purpose of applying subsections (4) and (5),

(i) the portion of the particular amount, at that time, referred to in paragraph (6)(a) that is equal to the lesser of the following amounts is deemed to be an amount outstanding as or on account of a debt or other obligation to pay an amount to the particular non-resident person referred to in subparagraph (6)(c)(i) or (ii), as the case may be, and not to the intermediary:

(A) the amount outstanding as or on account of the intermediary debt or the fair market value of the particular property referred to in subparagraph (6)(c)(ii), as the case may be, and

(B) the proportion of the particular amount that the amount outstanding or the fair market value, as the case may be, is of the total of all amounts each of which is

(I) an amount outstanding as or on account of an intermediary debt in respect of the particular debt or other obligation, owed to the particular non-resident or any other non-resident person that is, in respect of the taxpayer, described in the definition "outstanding debts to specified non-residents" in subsection (5), or

(II) the fair market value of a particular property referred to in subparagraph (6)(c)(ii) in respect of the particular debt or other obligation, and

(ii) the portion of the interest paid or payable by the taxpayer, in respect of a period throughout which subparagraph (a)(i) applies, on the particular debt or other obligation referred to in paragraph (6)(a) that is equal to the amount determined by the following formula is deemed to be paid or payable by the taxpayer to the particular non-resident, and not to the intermediary, as interest for the period on the amount deemed by subparagraph (a)(i) to be outstanding to the particular non-resident:

$$A \times B/C$$

where

A is the interest paid or payable,

B is the average of all amounts each of which is an amount that is deemed by subparagraph (a)(i) to be outstanding to the particular non-resident at a time during the period, and

C is the average of all amounts each of which is the particular amount outstanding at a time during the period; and

(b) for the purposes of Part XIII and subject to subsections 214(16) and (17), interest deemed under subparagraph (a)(ii) to be paid or payable to the particular non-resident in respect of a period is, to the extent that the interest is not deductible in computing the income of the taxpayer for the year because of subsection 18(4), deemed to be paid or payable by the taxpayer to the particular non-resident, and not to the intermediary, in respect of the period.

Related Provisions: 18(6) — Conditions for 18(6.1) to apply; 18(7) — Partners deemed to owe proportion of partnership debt.

Notes: 18(6) and (6.1) implement a 2014 Budget proposal to strengthen the previous back-to-back loan rule in 18(6). See Courage, "The Thin Capitalization", 7(4) *Taxes & Wealth Management* (Carswell) 12-17 (Sept. 2014); Suarez, "Canada's Latest International Tax Proposals", 75(13) *Tax Notes International* (taxnotes.com) 1131 (Sept. 29, 2014) at 1132-36 and "Canada Releases Revised Back-to-Back Loan Rules", 76(4) 357-63 (Oct. 27, 2014); Harris, "Thin Capitalization and Back-to-Back Loan Arrangements", 12(4) *Tax Hyperion* (Carswell) 1-2 (March 2015); Heakes, "The Proposed Revisions to Back-to-Back Loan Rules", XIX(4) *International Tax Planning* (Federated Press) 1357-60 (2014); Boland and Montes, "A Detailed Review of the Back-to-Back Loan Rules", 2016 Cdn Tax Foundation conference report, at 26:1-9 and 25-27.

For CRA interpretation see VIEWS docs 2015-0581531C6 [2015 IFA q.5] (linkage required to establish back-to-back loans); 2015-0614241C6 [2015 TEI q.6] (notional cash-pooling arrangement creates "intermediary debt" under 18(6) and 212(3.1)(c)(i)).

For the meaning of "indirectly" in 18(6)(c)(ii) see Notes to 17.1(1).

See also Notes to 212(3.2) re the back-to-back rules for non-resident withholding tax.

18(6.1) added by 2014 budget bill #2, for taxation years that begin after 2014.

(7) Partnership debts and property — For the purposes of this subsection, paragraph (4)(a), subsections (5) to (6.1) and paragraph 12(1)(l.1), each member of a partnership at any time is deemed at that time

(a) to owe the portion (in this subsection and paragraph 12(1)(l.1) referred to as the "debt amount") of each debt or other obligation to pay an amount of the partnership and to own the portion of each property of the partnership that is equal to

(i) the member's specified proportion for the last fiscal period, if any, of the partnership ending

(A) at or before the end of the taxation year referred to in subsection (4), and

(B) at a time when the member is a member of the partnership, and

(ii) if the member does not have a specified proportion described in subparagraph (i), the proportion that

(A) the fair market value of the member's interest in the partnership at that time

is of

(B) the fair market value of all interests in the partnership at that time;

(b) to owe the debt amount to the person to whom the partnership owes the debt or other obligation to pay an amount; and

(c) to have paid interest on the debt amount that is deductible in computing the member's income to the extent that an amount in respect of interest paid or payable on the debt amount by the partnership is deductible in computing the partnership's income.

Related Provisions: 12(1)(l.1) — Income inclusion for corporate partner.

Notes: 18(7) extends the 18(4) thin-cap rule to include a corporation's share of debts of partnerships of which it is a member, either directly or through tiers of partnerships, in determining whether it has exceeded the 1.5 debt:equity threshold.

18(7) amended by 2014 budget bill #2 (for tax years that begin after 2014), 2013 budget bill #2; added by 2012 budget bill #2.

(8) Exception — foreign accrual property income — An amount in respect of interest paid or payable to a controlled foreign affiliate of a corporation resident in Canada that would otherwise not be deductible by the corporation for a taxation year because of subsection (4) may be deducted to the extent that an amount included under subsection 91(1) in computing the corporation's income for the year or a subsequent year can reasonably be considered to be in respect of the interest.

Notes: 18(8) added by 2012 budget bill #2, for taxation years that end after 2004.

Former 18(8), repealed by 2000 Budget for taxation years beginning after 2000, provided that 18(4) did not apply to a corporation whose principal business was developing or manufacturing aircraft or aircraft components.

(9) Limitation respecting prepaid expenses — Notwithstanding any other provision of this Act,

(a) in computing a taxpayer's income for a taxation year from a business or property (other than income from a business computed in accordance with the method authorized by subsection 28(1)), no deduction shall be made in respect of an outlay or expense to the extent that it can reasonably be regarded as having been made or incurred

(i) as consideration for services to be rendered after the end of the year,

(ii) as, on account of, in lieu of payment of or in satisfaction of, interest, taxes (other than taxes imposed on an insurer in respect of insurance premiums of a non-cancellable or guaranteed renewable accident and sickness insurance policy, or a life insurance policy other than a group term life insurance policy that provides coverage for a period of 12 months or less), rent or royalties in respect of a period that is after the end of the year,

(iii) as consideration for insurance in respect of a period after the end of the year, other than

(A) where the taxpayer is an insurer, consideration for reinsurance, and

(B) consideration for insurance on the life of an individual under a group term life insurance policy where all or part of the consideration is for insurance that is (or would be if the individual survived) in respect of a period that ends more than 13 months after the consideration is paid; or

(iv) subject to clause (iii)(B) and subsections 144.1(4) to (7), as consideration for a "designated employee benefit" (as defined in subsection 144.1(1)) to be provided after the end of the year (other than consideration payable in the year, to a corporation that is licensed to provide insurance, for insurance coverage in respect of the year);

(b) such portion of each outlay or expense (other than an outlay or expense of a corporation, partnership or trust as, on account of, in lieu of payment of or in satisfaction of, interest) made or incurred as would, but for paragraph (a), be deductible in computing a taxpayer's income for a taxation year shall be deductible in computing a taxpayer's income for the subsequent year to which it can reasonably be considered to relate;

(c) for the purposes of section 37.1, such portion of each qualified expenditure (within the meaning assigned by subsection 37.1(5)) as was made by a taxpayer in a taxation year and as would, but for paragraph (a), have been deductible in computing the taxpayer's income for the year shall be deemed

(i) not to be a qualified expenditure made by the taxpayer in the year, and

(ii) to be a qualified expenditure made by the taxpayer in the subsequent year to which the expenditure can reasonably be considered to relate;

(d) for the purpose of paragraph (a), an outlay or expense of a taxpayer is deemed not to include any payment referred to in subparagraph 37(1)(a)(ii) or (iii) that

(i) is made by the taxpayer to a person or partnership with which the taxpayer deals at arm's length, and

(ii) is not an expenditure described in subparagraph 37(1)(a)(i); and

(e) for the purposes of section 37 and the definition "qualified expenditure" in subsection 127(9), the portion of an expenditure that is made or incurred by a taxpayer in a taxation year and that would, but for paragraph (a), have been deductible under section 37 in computing the taxpayer's income for the year, is deemed

(i) not to be made or incurred by the taxpayer in the year, and

(ii) to be made or incurred by the taxpayer in the subsequent taxation year to which the expenditure can reasonably be considered to relate;

(f) [Repealed]

Related Provisions: 6(1)(a)(i), 6(4) — Group term life insurance premiums — taxable benefit; 18(9.01) — Group term life insurance — deductibility of premiums; 18(9.02) — Application to insurers; 18(9.2)–(9.8) — Prepaid interest; 20(1)(m.1) — Manufacturer's warranty reserve; 20(1)(m.2) — Repayment of amount previously included in income; 87(2)(j.2) — Amalgamations — prepaid expenses; 144.1(4)(b) — Contribution to employee life and health trust prohibited by 18(9) can be deducted in later year; 261(7)(f) — Functional currency reporting.

Notes: 18(9) prohibits the deduction of certain prepaid expenses before the year to which they relate. It applies only if the expense is otherwise deductible: *Patry*, 2013 TCC 107, para. 24. (In *Mussali*, [2020] FCA 544 (Australia), prepaid rent was considered a capital expense, disallowed by the equivalent of 18(1)(b).) See also 18.1 for the "matchable expenditure" rules.

The parenthesized words in 18(9)(a)(ii) are consequential on 18(9.02), which requires the deferral of policy acquisition costs (which include premium taxes) generally in respect of non-life insurance policies.

18(9) applies to a lump-sum lease prepayment, which must be amortized over the term of the lease: VIEWS docs 2003-0015675, 2012-0435241I7, 2012-044283117. It also prevents averaging the deductions for escalating lease payments: 2008-0272771I7, 2009-031285117. A supposed lease might be considered a form of sale financing: 2012-0438741E5 (but see 49(3) Notes).

18(9)(a) did not apply to regional development charges on land, in *Urbandale Realty*, [2000] 2 C.T.C. 250 (FCA); or to a reforestation liability in *Daishowa-Marubeni*, 2010 TCC 317 (decided on other grounds by FCA and 2013 SCC 29).

CRA will use 18(9) to deny deduction for prepayments to a health and welfare trust (HWT) to fund later costs, but will not disqualify the HWT: *Income Tax Technical News* 25, VIEWS docs 2004-009477117, 2011-0402691M4 (CRA will consider advance rulings on this issue). Note that HWTs must convert to ELHTs by 2021: see Proposed Amendment at end of 144.1.

18(9)(f) repealed by 2017 budget bill #1 (as part of repeal of the investment tax credit for child-care spaces), for expenditures incurred after March 21, 2017, unless incurred before 2020 under a written agreement entered into by that date. It read:

(f) for the purpose of the definition "eligible child care space expenditure" in subsection 127(9), the portion of an expenditure (other than for the acquisition of depreciable property) that is made or incurred by a taxpayer in a taxation year and that would, but for paragraph (a), have been deductible under this Act in computing the taxpayer's income for the year, is deemed

(i) not to be made or incurred by the taxpayer in the year, and

(ii) to be made or incurred by the taxpayer in the subsequent taxation year to which the expenditure can reasonably be considered to relate.

18(9)(a)(iv) added by 2010 budget bill #2, effective 2010.

18(9)(f) added by 2007 budget bill #2, for expenses incurred after March 18, 2007.

18(9) earlier amended by 2001 technical bill (effective for taxation years that begin after 1999), 1995 and 1994 Budgets and 1992 technical bill.

Interpretation Bulletins: IT-109R2: Unpaid amounts; IT-211R: Membership dues — associations and societies; IT-233R: Lease-option agreements; sale-leaseback agreements (cancelled); IT-341R4: Expenses of issuing shares, units in a trust, interests in a partnership or syndicate and expenses of borrowing money; IT-417R2: Prepaid expenses and deferred charges.

I.T. Technical News: 25 (health and welfare trusts).

(9.01) [No longer relevant.]

Notes: 18(9.01) (added by 1994 Budget) limits an employer's deductions for group term life insurance premiums paid from March 1994 through 1996.

(9.02) Application of subsec. (9) to insurers — For the purpose of subsection (9), an outlay or expense made or incurred by an insurer on account of the acquisition of an insurance policy (other than a non-cancellable or guaranteed renewable accident and sickness insurance policy or a life insurance policy other than a group term life insurance policy that provides coverage for a period of 12 months or less) is deemed to be an expense incurred as consideration for services rendered consistently throughout the period of coverage of the policy.

Notes: Before 18(9.02), policy acquisition costs were deductible. 18(9.02) deems an expense made by an insurer on the acquisition of an insurance policy (other than the list excluded) to be an expense incurred for services rendered consistently throughout the period of coverage of the policy. Where the policy covers a period extending beyond the end of the insurer's taxation year, 18(9) will apply to prorate the deductibility of the costs over the period of coverage of the policy. Under GAAP, policy acquisition costs include premium taxes, commissions and other costs directly related to the acquisition of premiums written.

18(9.02) added by 2001 technical bill, for tax years that begin after 1999, or earlier by election.

(9.1) Penalties, bonuses and rate-reduction payments —
Subject to subsection 142.4(10), where at any time a payment, other than a payment that

(a) can reasonably be considered to have been made in respect of the extension of the term of a debt obligation or in respect of the substitution or conversion of a debt obligation to another debt obligation or share, or

(b) is contingent or dependent on the use of or production from property or is computed by reference to revenue, profit, cash flow, commodity price or any other similar criterion or by reference to dividends paid or payable to shareholders of any class of shares of the capital stock of a corporation,

is made to a person or partnership by a taxpayer in the course of carrying on a business or earning income from property in respect of borrowed money or on an amount payable for property acquired by the taxpayer (in this subsection referred to as a "debt obligation")

(c) as consideration for a reduction in the rate of interest payable by the taxpayer on the debt obligation, or

(d) as a penalty or bonus payable by the taxpayer because of the repayment by the taxpayer of all or part of the principal amount of the debt obligation before its maturity,

the payment shall, to the extent that it can reasonably be considered to relate to, and does not exceed the value at that time of, an amount that, but for the reduction described in paragraph (c) or the repayment described in paragraph (d), would have been paid or payable by the taxpayer as interest on the debt obligation for a taxation year of the taxpayer ending after that time, be deemed,

(e) for the purposes of this Act, to have been paid by the taxpayer and received by the person or partnership at that time as interest on the debt obligation, and

(f) for the purpose of computing the taxpayer's income in respect of the business or property for the year, to have been paid or payable by the taxpayer in that year as interest pursuant to a legal obligation to pay interest,

(i) in the case of a reduction described in paragraph (c), on the debt obligation, and

(ii) in the case of a repayment described in paragraph (d),

(A) where the repayment was in respect of all or part of the principal amount of the debt obligation that was borrowed money, except to the extent that the borrowed money was used by the taxpayer to acquire property, on borrowed money used in the year for the purpose for which the borrowed money that was repaid was used, and

(B) where the repayment was in respect of all or part of the principal amount of the debt obligation that was either borrowed money used to acquire property or an amount payable for property acquired by the taxpayer, on the debt obligation to the extent that the property or property substituted therefor is used by the taxpayer in the year for the purpose of gaining or producing income therefrom or for the purpose of gaining or producing income from a business.

Related Provisions: 18(9.2) — Prepaid interest on debt obligations; 20(1)(e) — Expenses re financing; 87(2)(j.6) — Amalgamation — continuing corporation; 248(5) — Substituted property; 261(7)–(10) — Functional currency reporting.

Notes: 18(9.1) applies where a penalty or bonus is paid in respect of the repayment of all or part of a debt obligation before maturity. It provides, in certain circumstances, that the penalty or bonus is deemed paid and received as interest, to the extent it does not exceed the future interest that would otherwise have been payable on the obligation. 18(9.1) also applies to certain interest rate reduction payments. For interpretation see Income Tax Folio S4-F2-C1 ¶1.30-1.38; VIEWS docs 2003-0023137, 2005-0129061E5, 2005-0156071E5, 2006-0196691R3, 2008-030105117, 2012-0436771E5;

2017-068916117 [Cepparo, "Prepayment Penalty Deductible on New Lender's Refinancing", 26(3) *Canadian Tax Highlights* (ctf.ca) 5-6 (March 2018)]; 2018-0755631E5 (substituted loan). See also Samuel & Beswick, "Selected Issues in Transactions Involving Debt", 2019 Cdn Tax Foundation conference report, 19:1-27.

18(9.1)(b) uses the same wording as 212(3)"participating debt interest"; see Notes to 212(1)(b) for interpretation.

18(9.1) amended by 1995-97 technical bill, effective for taxation years ending after Feb. 22, 1994. 18(9.1) added by 1991 technical bill.

Income Tax Folios: S4-F2-C1: Deductibility of fines and penalties [replaces IT-104R3].

Interpretation Bulletins: IT-341R4: Expenses of issuing shares, units in a trust, interests in a partnership or syndicate and expenses of borrowing money.

(9.2) Interest on debt obligations —
For the purposes of this Part, the amount of interest payable on borrowed money or on an amount payable for property (in this subsection and subsections (9.3) to (9.8) referred to as the "debt obligation") by a corporation, partnership or trust (in this subsection and subsections (9.3) to (9.7) referred to as the "borrower") in respect of a taxation year shall, notwithstanding subparagraph (9.1)(f)(i), be deemed to be an amount equal to the lesser of

(a) the amount of interest, not in excess of a reasonable amount, that would be payable on the debt obligation by the borrower in respect of the year if no amount had been paid before the end of the year in satisfaction of the obligation to pay interest on the debt obligation in respect of the year and if the amount outstanding at each particular time in the year that is after 1991 on account of the principal amount of the debt obligation were the amount, if any, by which

(i) the amount outstanding at the particular time on account of the principal amount of the debt obligation

exceeds the total of

(ii) all amounts each of which is an amount paid before the particular time in satisfaction, in whole or in part, of the obligation to pay interest on the debt obligation in respect of a period or part thereof that is after 1991, after the beginning of the year, and after the time the amount was so paid (other than a period or part thereof that is in the year where no such amount was paid before the particular time in respect of a period, or part of a period, that is after the end of the year), and

(iii) the amount, if any, by which

(A) the total of all amounts of interest payable on the debt obligation (determined without reference to this subsection) by the borrower in respect of taxation years ending after 1991 and before the year (to the extent that the interest does not exceed a reasonable amount)

exceeds

(B) the total of all amounts of interest deemed by this subsection to have been payable on the debt obligation by the borrower in respect of taxation years ending before the year, and

(b) the amount, if any, by which

(i) the total of all amounts of interest payable on the debt obligation (determined without reference to this subsection) by the borrower in respect of the year or taxation years ending after 1991 and before the year (to the extent that the interest does not exceed a reasonable amount)

exceeds

(ii) the total of all amounts of interest deemed by this subsection to have been payable on the debt obligation by the borrower in respect of taxation years ending before the year.

Related Provisions: 18(9.3)–(9.8) — Prepaid interest on debt obligations; 261(7)–(10) — Functional currency reporting.

Notes: 18(9.2)-(9.8), limiting deduction of prepaid interest, were introduced to counter Canadian option interest note (COIN) financings: Wach, "Legislating Change", 2001 Cdn Tax Foundation conference report, 35:8-11.

For CRA's interpretation of 18(9.2)(a)(ii), see VIEWS doc 2004-008291117.

18(9.2) added by 1992 technical bill, for 1992 and later taxation years.

Interpretation Bulletins: IT-417R2: Prepaid expenses and deferred charges.

(9.3) Interest on debt obligations — Where at any time in a taxation year of a borrower a debt obligation of the borrower is settled or extinguished or the holder of the obligation acquires or reacquires property of the borrower in circumstances in which section 79 applies in respect of the debt obligation and the total of

(a) all amounts each of which is an amount paid at or before that time in satisfaction, in whole or in part, of the obligation to pay interest on the debt obligation in respect of a period or part of a period that is after that time, and

(b) all amounts of interest payable on the debt obligation (determined without reference to subsection (9.2)) by the borrower in respect of taxation years ending after 1991 and before that time, or in respect of periods, or parts of periods, that are in such years and before that time (to the extent that the interest does not exceed a reasonable amount),

exceeds the total of

(c) all amounts of interest deemed by subsection (9.2) to have been payable on the debt obligation by the borrower in respect of taxation years ending before that time, and

(d) the amount of interest that would be deemed by subsection (9.2) to have been payable on the debt obligation by the borrower in respect of the year if the year had ended immediately before that time,

(which excess is in this subsection referred to as the "excess amount"), the following rules apply:

(e) for the purpose of applying section 79 in respect of the borrower, the principal amount at that time of the debt obligation shall be deemed to be equal to the amount, if any, by which

(i) the principal amount at that time of the debt obligation

exceeds

(ii) the excess amount, and

(f) the excess amount shall be deducted at that time in computing the forgiven amount in respect of the obligation (within the meaning assigned by subsection 80(1)).

Related Provisions: 80(1)"forgiven amount"B(c) — Deduction from forgiven amount as per 18(9.3)(f); 261(7)–(10) — Functional currency reporting.

Notes: For the meaning of "extinguished", see Notes to 80(2)(a).

18(9.3) amended by 1994 technical bill (effective on same basis as new 80-80.04); added by 1992 technical bill.

Interpretation Bulletins: IT-417R2: Prepaid expenses and deferred charges.

(9.4) Idem — Where an amount is paid at any time by a person or partnership in respect of a debt obligation of a borrower

(a) as, on account of, in lieu of payment of or in satisfaction of, interest on the debt obligation in respect of a period or part thereof that is after 1991 and after that time, or

(b) as consideration for a reduction in the rate of interest payable on the debt obligation (excluding, for greater certainty, a payment described in paragraph (9.1)(a) or (b)) in respect of a period or part thereof that is after 1991 and after that time,

that amount shall be deemed, for the purposes of subsection (9.5) and, subject to that subsection, for the purposes of clause (9.2)(a)(iii)(A), subparagraph (9.2)(b)(i), paragraph (9.3)(b) and subsection (9.6), to be an amount of interest payable on the debt obligation by the borrower in respect of that period or part thereof and shall be deemed, for the purposes of subparagraph (9.2)(a)(ii) and paragraph (9.3)(a), to be an amount paid at that time in satisfaction of the obligation to pay interest on the debt obligation in respect of that period or part thereof.

Related Provisions: 261(7)–(10) — Functional currency reporting.

Notes: 18(9.4) added by 1992 technical bill, for 1992 and later taxation years.

Interpretation Bulletins: IT-417R2: Prepaid expenses and deferred charges.

(9.5) Idem — Where the amount of interest payable on a debt obligation (determined without reference to subsection (9.2)) by a bor-

rower in respect of a particular period or part thereof that is after 1991 can reasonably be regarded as an amount payable as consideration for

(a) a reduction in the amount of interest that would otherwise be payable on the debt obligation in respect of a subsequent period, or

(b) a reduction in the amount that was or may be paid before the beginning of a subsequent period in satisfaction of the obligation to pay interest on the debt obligation in respect of that subsequent period

(determined without reference to the existence of, or the amount of any interest paid or payable on, any other debt obligation), that amount shall, for the purposes of clause (9.2)(a)(iii)(A), subparagraph (9.2)(b)(i), paragraph (9.3)(b) and subsection (9.6), be deemed to be an amount of interest payable on the debt obligation by the borrower in respect of the subsequent period and not to be an amount of interest payable on the debt obligation by the borrower in respect of the particular period and shall, when paid, be deemed for the purposes of subparagraph (9.2)(a)(ii) and paragraph (9.3)(a) to be an amount paid in satisfaction of the obligation to pay interest on the debt obligation in respect of the subsequent period.

Related Provisions: 18(9.4) — Prepaid interest on debt obligations; 261(7)–(10) — Functional currency reporting.

Notes: 18(9.5) added by 1992 technical bill, for 1992 and later taxation years.

Interpretation Bulletins: IT-417R2: Prepaid expenses and deferred charges.

(9.6) Idem — Where the liability in respect of a debt obligation of a person or partnership is assumed by a borrower at any time,

(a) the amount of interest payable on the debt obligation (determined without reference to subsection (9.2)) by any person or partnership in respect of a period shall, to the extent that that period is included in a taxation year of the borrower ending after 1991, be deemed, for the purposes of clause (9.2)(a)(iii)(A), subparagraph (9.2)(b)(i) and paragraph (9.3)(b), to be an amount of interest payable on the debt obligation by the borrower in respect of that year, and

(b) the application of subsections (9.2) and (9.3) to the borrower in respect of the debt obligation after that time shall be determined on the assumption that subsection (9.2) applied to the borrower in respect of the debt obligation before that time,

and, for the purposes of this subsection, where the borrower came into existence at a particular time that is after the beginning of the particular period beginning at the beginning of the first period in respect of which interest was payable on the debt obligation by any person or partnership and ending at the particular time, the borrower shall be deemed

(c) to have been in existence throughout the particular period, and

(d) to have had, throughout the particular period, taxation years ending on the day of the year on which its first taxation year ended.

Related Provisions: 261(7)–(10) — Functional currency reporting.

Notes: 18(9.6) added by 1992 technical bill, for 1992 and later taxation years.

Interpretation Bulletins: IT-417R2: Prepaid expenses and deferred charges.

(9.7) Idem — Where the amount paid by a borrower at any particular time, in satisfaction of the obligation to pay a particular amount of interest on a debt obligation in respect of a subsequent period or part thereof, exceeds the particular amount of that interest, discounted

(a) for the particular period beginning at the particular time and ending at the end of the subsequent period or part thereof, and

(b) at the rate or rates of interest applying under the debt obligation during the particular period (or, where the rate of interest of any part of the particular period is not fixed at the particular time, at the prescribed rate of interest in effect at the particular time), that excess shall

(c) for the purposes of applying subsections (9.2) to (9.6) and (9.8), be deemed to be neither an amount of interest payable on the debt obligation nor an amount paid in satisfaction of the obligation to pay interest on the debt obligation, and

(d) be deemed to be a payment described in paragraph (9.1)(d) in respect of the debt obligation.

Notes: 18(9.7) added by 1992 technical bill, for 1992 and later taxation years.

Regulations: 4301(c) (prescribed rate of interest).

Interpretation Bulletins: IT-417R2: Prepaid expenses and deferred charges.

(9.8) Idem — Nothing in any of subsections (9.2) to (9.7) shall be construed as providing that

(a) the total of all amounts each of which is the amount of interest payable on a debt obligation by an individual (other than a trust), or deemed by subsection (9.2) to be payable on the debt obligation by a corporation, partnership or trust, in respect of a taxation year ending after 1991 and before any particular time,

may exceed

(b) the total of all amounts each of which is the amount of interest payable on the debt obligation (determined without reference to subsection (9.2)) by a person or partnership in respect of a taxation year ending after 1991 and before that particular time.

Notes: 18(9.8) added by 1992 technical bill, for 1992 and later taxation years.

Interpretation Bulletins: IT-417R2: Prepaid expenses and deferred charges.

(10) Employee benefit plan — Paragraph (1)(o) does not apply in respect of a contribution to an employee benefit plan

(a) to the extent that the contribution

(i) is made in respect of services performed by an employee who is not resident in Canada and is regularly employed in a country other than Canada, and

(ii) cannot reasonably be regarded as having been made in respect of services performed or to be performed during a period when the employee is resident in Canada;

(b) the custodian of which is non-resident, to the extent that the contribution

(i) is in respect of an employee who is non-resident at the time the contribution is made, and

(ii) cannot reasonably be regarded as having been made in respect of services performed or to be performed during a period when the employee is resident in Canada; or

(c) the custodian of which is non-resident, to the extent that the contribution can reasonably be regarded as having been made in respect of services performed by an employee in a particular calendar month where

(i) the employee was resident in Canada throughout no more than 60 of the 72 calendar months ending with the particular month, and

(ii) the employee became a member of the plan before the end of the month following the month in which the employee became resident in Canada,

and, for the purpose of this paragraph, where benefits provided to an employee under a particular employee benefit plan are replaced by benefits provided under another employee benefit plan, the other plan shall be deemed, in respect of the employee, to be the same plan as the particular plan.

Notes: 18(10) amended by 1993 technical bill, for contributions made after 1992. The extension of the exemption from 36 to 60 months after becoming a Canadian resident is consistent with the RCA rules; see 207.6(5.1)(b)(ii).

Interpretation Bulletins: IT-502: Employee benefit plans and employee trusts.

(11) Limitation [on interest expense] — Notwithstanding any other provision of this Act, in computing the income of a taxpayer for a taxation year, no amount is deductible under paragraph 20(1)(c), (d), (e), (e.1) or (f) in respect of borrowed money (or other property acquired by the taxpayer) in respect of any period after

which the money (or other property) is used by the taxpayer for the purpose of

(a) making a payment after November 12, 1981 as consideration for an income-averaging annuity contract, unless the contract was acquired pursuant to an agreement in writing entered into before November 13, 1981;

(b) paying a premium (within the meaning assigned by subsection 146(1) read without reference to the portion of the definition "premium" in that subsection following paragraph (b) of that definition) under a registered retirement savings plan after November 12, 1981;

(c) making a contribution to a deferred profit sharing plan, a pooled registered pension plan or a registered pension plan, other than

(i) a contribution described in subparagraph 8(1)(m)(ii) or (iii) (as they read in their application to the 1990 taxation year) that was required to be made pursuant to an obligation entered into before November 13, 1981, or

(ii) a contribution deductible under paragraph 20(1)(q) or (y) in computing the taxpayer's income;

(d) making a payment as consideration for an annuity the payment for which was deductible in computing the taxpayer's income by virtue of paragraph 60(l);

(e) making a contribution to a retirement compensation arrangement where the contribution was deductible under paragraph 8(1)(m.2) in computing the taxpayer's income;

(f) making a contribution to a net income stabilization account;

(g) [Repealed]

(h) making a contribution into a registered education savings plan;

(i) making a contribution to a registered disability savings plan; or

(j) making a contribution under a TFSA,

and, for the purposes of this subsection, to the extent that an indebtedness is incurred by a taxpayer in respect of a property and at any time that property or a property substituted therefor is used for any of the purposes referred to in this subsection, the indebtedness shall be deemed to be incurred at that time for that purpose.

Related Provisions: 18(1)(u) — Investment counselling and administration fees for RRSP, RRIF or TFSA are non-deductible; 110.6(1)"investment expense"(a); 146(21.1) — Contribution to Saskatchewan Pension Plan deemed to be RRSP premium for purposes of 18(11)(b); 248(5) — Substituted property.

Notes: Although interest on money borrowed to *contribute* to an RRSP is non-deductible (18(11)(b)), interest on money borrowed under a mortgage *from* one's RRSP may be deductible: VIEWS doc 2011-0413761E5.

18(11)(c) disallows interest on money borrowed to make a past service RPP contribution, but payments (including interest) to acquire past service may be deductible under 147.2(4): VIEWS doc 2020-0868601E5 [note that 18(11) restricts only 20(1) deductions, not 147.2(4)].

Former 18(11)(g), which disallowed interest on money borrowed to contribute to the Sask. Pension Plan, is now covered by 18(11)(b), as 146(21.1) deems the contribution to be an RRSP contribution.

18(11) amended by 2012 budget bill #2 (effective Dec. 14, 2012), 2011 budget bill #2, 2008 budget bill #1, 2007 RDSPs bill, 1997 Budget, 1993, 1992 and 1991 technical bills, 1990 pension bill.

Interpretation Bulletins: IT-124R6: Contributions to registered retirement savings plans; IT-167R6: Registered pension plans — employee's contributions; IT-307R4: Spousal or common-law partner registered retirement savings plans; IT-355R2: Interest on loans to buy life insurance policies and annuity contracts, and interest on policy loans (cancelled).

(12) Work space in home — Notwithstanding any other provision of this Act, in computing an individual's income from a business for a taxation year,

(a) no amount shall be deducted in respect of an otherwise deductible amount for any part (in this subsection referred to as the "work space") of a self-contained domestic establishment in which the individual resides, except to the extent that the work space is either

(i) the individual's principal place of business, or

(ii) used exclusively for the purpose of earning income from business and used on a regular and continuous basis for meeting clients, customers or patients of the individual in respect of the business;

(b) if the conditions set out in subparagraph (a)(i) or (ii) are met, the amount for the work space that is deductible in computing the individual's income for the year from the business shall not exceed the individual's income for the year from the business, computed without reference to the amount and section 34.1; and

(c) any amount not deductible by reason only of paragraph (b) in computing the individual's income from the business for the immediately preceding taxation year shall be deemed to be an amount otherwise deductible that, subject to paragraphs (a) and (b), may be deducted for the year for the work space in respect of the business.

Related Provisions: 8(13) — Parallel rule for employee.

Notes: See generally Income Tax Folio S4-F2-C2. 18(12) restricts home office expenses (HOE) to certain cases, and prevents them from creating a business loss.

18(12) applies only to business, not rental income (for an employee see 8(13)): Folio S4-F2-C2 ¶2.2. HOE for a rental operation that produces property income (see Notes to 9(1) under "Business income vs property income") are deductible under general principles: VIEWS docs 2002-0118727, 2002-0120025. Thus, *Jha*, [2003] 1 C.T.C. 2574 (TCC), which denied HOE because the rental income was not income from business, was wrongly decided: 2007-0235681I7. A home rooftop solar panel "business" will not likely justify HOE: 2009-0344011E5. If corporation C has an office in shareholder S's home, 18(12) does not apply to C, and if S generates income from renting the office to C, S can deduct related expenses: 2013-0500831E5.

18(12)(a)(i) [principal place of business (PPOB)]: if this test is met, the "regular and continuous" test below need not be. In *Jenkins*, 2005 TCC 167, a couple working on fishing boats were held to have PPOB in their home office, where the paperwork was done (not on the boats). Where an office is X's PPOB and is not used for personal purposes, the fact X works mostly at client locations does not preclude claiming HOE: VIEWS doc 2000-0008905.

A *bed-and-breakfast* is not subject to 18(12) if the owners live in a "self-contained domestic establishment" within the house, inaccessible to guests or considered "separate": *Sudbrack*, [2000] 4 C.T.C. 2668 (TCC); *Rudiak*, [2002] 3 C.T.C. 2454 (TCC); *Vallee-Moczulski*, 2003 TCC 175; *Denis*, 2007 TCC 656; *Vandonkersgoed*, 2010 TCC 208; or if the owner lives elsewhere: *Trudeau*, [2003] 4 C.T.C. 2138 (TCC). See Income Tax Folio S4-F2-C2 ¶¶2.7-2.9; VIEWS docs 2006-0211371E5, 2010-0364721E5. Bed-and-breakfasts fell under 18(12) in: *Maitland*, [2000] 3 C.T.C. 2840 (TCC); *Broderick*, [2001] 3 C.T.C. 2033 (TCC); *Doleman*, 2011 TCC 349.

18(12)(a)(ii) [regular and continuous]: In *Vanka*, [2001] 4 C.T.C. 2832 (TCC), use of a doctor's home office for average 1 patient per week and 7 phone calls per evening was held to be regular and continuous: "meeting patients" could be done by phone. The same applied in *Hémond*, 2003 TCC 705, and *Ryan*, 2006 TCC 132. In *Landry*, 2007 TCC 383 (aff'd on other grounds 2009 FCA 174), a school superintendent who had to check the weather before 5am daily and make calls about school closings, and also made calls from his home office on evenings and weekends, was allowed the parallel employment deduction in 8(13). In *Middleton*, 2010 TCC 363, a spa operator was allowed a deduction for a bedroom she used at home for testing hair and saliva. In *Lavigne*, 2004 TCC 306, a home office next door to the owner's store met the "regular and continuous" test, as it was open to the public and used regularly by customers for various purposes.

Contra, in *Molckovsky*, 2004 TCC 13, seeing 1 patient a week and receiving on average 1 phone call per day was not "regular and continuous". In *Rail*, 2011 TCC 130, a dentist was denied deductions for a home office that was not his primary place of business. In *Layton*, 2015 TCC 184, the Court disbelieved a lawyer's evidence that she regularly met clients at her home office. The CRA does not accept *Vanka* and *Hémond* (both non-binding Informal Procedure decisions) and says "meeting" means "in person": Folio S4-F2-C2 ¶2.14; May 2006 ICAA roundtable (tinyurl.com/cra-abtax), q. 27; docs 2007-0228231I7, 2009-0337751I7, 2013-0481171E5.

With COVID-19, given that most people working were at home, and the wide use of video conferencing, one hopes CRA will accept that "meeting" includes phone and video meetings, and stop trying to overrule the Tax Court.

Calculation of business portion of home for prorating expenses: Square footage is usually used (the usable part of a house's basement should be counted in the calculation: *Murphy*, 2010 TCC 564, para. 9; *Lippert*, 2010 TCC 484, para. 29); but other methods are possible, e.g. number of rooms, electrical energy use (VIEWS doc 2010-0379101E5), or even use by different people: *Henkels*, 2009 TCC 558 (a rental property case). Inventory storage space can count: 2012-0471391E5. Square footage percentages were allowed in: *Walker*, 2011 TCC 10; *Morrissey*, 2011 TCC 373, para. 34; *Last*, 2012 TCC 352 (aff'd on other grounds 2014 FCA 129); *Metza*, 2011 TCC 331

(60%, as the business had "effectively taken over" the taxpayer's small home); *Ali*, 2015 TCC 196, para. 41 (less than 1%, as the taxpayer used 10% of her home as a day-care 15 days a year); *Basic*, 2015 TCC 202, para. 10 (aluminum siding contractor allowed 15% for home office plus garage); *Chaloux*, 2015 TCC 284, para. 62 (FCA appeal discontinued A-540-15) (electrical contractor allowed 30% for office and "shop" in the home); *Cocos*, 2016 TCC 107, para. 14 (35% for office space plus garage used for storing supplies); *Harris*, 2018 TCC 148, para. 22 (22% of 700 sq ft); *Wallens*, 2019 TCC 193, para. 10 (W was "fortunate" that CRA allowed 20%); *Hébert*, 2019 TCC 266, para. 10 (35.83%: basement of engineer's home). In *Jacobsen*, 2012 TCC 25, it was unreasonable to claim "all of the kitchen area because he sometimes served clients a cup of coffee [and] all of the basement because his consultancy files were stored there along with household items". Since Dec. 2020, CRA provides detailed instructions for employees: Canada.ca/cra-home-workspace-expenses > "Determine your work space use"; CRA will likely apply these to self-employed persons also.

What is deductible: Expenses not part of maintaining the whole home are fully deductible if used for business, e.g. telephone, Internet (but in *Harris*, 2018 TCC 148, para. 24, 20% was disallowed as personal). Repair or maintenance of the *office* is fully deductible: Income Tax Folio S4-F2-C2 ¶2.28. Apportioned expenses typically include mortgage interest (Folio S4-F2-C2 ¶2.22-2.27, VIEWS doc 2009-0310321E5) or rent, property taxes (including local improvement fees: 2012-0436401E5), utilities, insurance, maintenance and capital cost allowance. (CCA claims may lead to losing the principal-residence capital gains exemption for that portion of the home: Folio S1-F3-C2 ¶2.59.) In *Andreone*, 2005 TCC 240, outside maintenance costs were non-deductible as they would be needed anyway and did not enhance the business's income-generating potential; in the author's view, if the home office is used by a professional to meet clients, the outside should look decent and lawn and garden care qualify; the TCC agreed in *Hébert*, 2019 TCC 266, para. 29. However, see *Lavoie*, 2014 TCC 68, para. 19: "to claim significant landscaping costs for the home, on the basis potential buyers look for a professional setting when visiting is just too tenuous a business connection". (20(1)(aa) allows landscaping costs only for a building "primarily" used for earning income.) Guard dog expenses can qualify: VIEWS doc 2012-0457171E5. Legal fees re structural defects in the home do not, in the CRA's view, because they "would have been incurred irrespective of the existence of your business": 2011-0416701E5 (this may be wrong, though they should possibly be disallowed under 18(1)(b)). In *Hyska*, 2009 TCC 71, utilities for an attached garage were considered part of HOE subject to 18(12)(b).

Where another person (such as a spouse) owns or co-owns the property, the 18(12) deduction is allowed, but if the other person pays the expenses, CRA thinks there could be an income inclusion: doc 2018-0768871C6 [2018 APFF q.16].

Quebec allows only 50% of home office expenses for provincial tax purposes: *Taxation Act* s. 175.5(a)(i).

18(12)(b): HOE cannot create or increase a loss from the business: *Haight-Smith*, 2006 TCC 451. 18(12)(c) allows indefinite carryforward of allowable HOE against eventual income from the business, provided it is the "same" business (with the same meaning as under Reg. 1101(1): *Arbeau*, 2010 TCC 307). Each year, the amount not deductible last year due to 18(12)(b) is deductible, but if the business does not generate enough income, 18(12)(b) restricts it again. (If the business stops and later restarts, the carryforward may be lost: VIEWS doc 2002-0140967.) An appeal of expenses disallowed by this rule can be made only in the later year in which they actually reduce income: *Fotherby*, 2008 TCC 343, para. 37 and Notes to 152(1.1). For employees, 8(13)(c) provides the same carryforward.

See also Caron-Morin, "Work Space in Home and Elsewhere", 3(3) *Canadian Tax Focus* (ctf.ca) 7-8 (Aug. 2013); Tomlinson, "Home Office Expenses", 2495 *Tax Topics* (CCH) 1-3 (Jan. 2, 2020); Johnson, "Business-use-of-home expenses of the owner-manager during COVID-19", 17(4) *Tax Hyperion* (Carswell) 8-12 (July-Aug 2020). For software that assists in applying 18(12) see *Home Office Classifier* at bluejlegal.com.

A parallel limitation applies to GST input tax credits for HOE. See *Excise Tax Act* 170(1)(a.1), in David M. Sherman, *Practitioner's Goods and Services Tax Annotated*.

18(12)(b) amended by 2017 budget bill #2 to change "34.1 and 34.2" to "34.1", for 2011 and later taxation years. Earlier amended by 1995 Budget.

Income Tax Folios: S1-F3-C2: Principal residence [replaces IT-120R6, IT-437R]; S3-F6-C1: Interest deductibility [replaces IT-533]; S4-F2-C2: Business use of home expenses [replaces IT-514].

Interpretation Bulletins: IT-504R2: Visual artists and writers.

(13) When subsec. (15) applies to money lenders — Subsection (15) applies, subject to subsection 142.6(7), when

(a) a taxpayer (in this subsection and subsection (15) referred to as the "transferor") disposes of a particular property (other than, for the purposes of computing the exempt surplus or exempt deficit and taxable surplus or taxable deficit of a foreign affiliate of a taxpayer, in respect of the taxpayer, where the transferor is the affiliate or is a partnership of which the affiliate is a member, property that is, or would be, if the transferor were a foreign affiliate of the taxpayer, excluded property (within the meaning assigned by subsection 95(1)) of the transferor);

(b) the disposition is not described in any of paragraphs (c) to (g) of the definition "superficial loss" in section 54;

(c) the transferor is not an insurer;

(d) the ordinary business of the transferor includes the lending of money and the particular property was used or held in the ordinary course of that business;

(e) the particular property is a share, or a loan, bond, debenture, mortgage, hypothecary claim, note, agreement for sale or any other indebtedness;

(f) the particular property was, immediately before the disposition, not a capital property of the transferor;

(g) during the period that begins 30 days before and ends 30 days after the disposition, the transferor or a person affiliated with the transferor acquires a property (in this subsection and subsection (15) referred to as the "substituted property") that is, or is identical to, the particular property; and

(h) at the end of the period, the transferor or a person affiliated with the transferor owns the substituted property.

Related Provisions: 18(14) — Alternate application of subsec. 18(15); 40(2)(g)(i), 54"superficial loss" — Parallel rule for capital property; 93.1(3)(b) — Tiered partnership — look-through rule; 248(12) — Identical properties.

Notes: See Notes to 13(21.2). In simple terms, 18(13)-(16) deny a loss to persons in the business of lending money (18(13)) or holding property as an adventure in the nature of trade (18(14)), where the property sold or identical property is reacquired within the period from 30 days before to 30 days after the sale, either by the same person or an "affiliated" person (see 251.1). For the superficial loss rule for capital property, see 40(2)(g)(i) and 54"superficial loss". The accrued loss is suspended in the seller's hands (18(15)), as is done by 40(3.4) for accrued capital losses and 13(21.2) for terminal losses (see Notes to those provisions).

For interpretation of "ordinary business includes the lending of money" in para. (d), see 15(2.3) Notes.

18(13)(a) amended by 2002-2013 technical bill (for dispositions after Aug. 19, 2011), 2001 *Civil Code* harmonization bill, 1995-97 and 1994 technical bills.

(14) When subsec. (15) applies to adventurers in trade — Subsection (15) applies where

(a) a person (in this subsection and subsection (15) referred to as the "transferor") disposes of a particular property;

(b) the particular property is described in an inventory of a business that is an adventure or concern in the nature of trade;

(c) the disposition is not a disposition that is deemed to have occurred by subsection 10.1(6) or (7), section 70, subsection 104(4), section 128.1, paragraph 132.2(3)(a) or (c) or subsection 138(11.3) or 138.2(4) or 149(10);

(d) during the period that begins 30 days before and ends 30 days after the disposition, the transferor or a person affiliated with the transferor acquires property (in this subsection and subsection (15) referred to as the "substituted property") that is, or is identical to, the particular property; and

(e) at the end of the period, the transferor or a person affiliated with the transferor owns the substituted property.

Related Provisions: 10(1.01) — No writedown of inventory held as adventure in the nature of trade; 18(13) — Alternate application of subsec. 18(15); 40(2)(g)(i), 54"superficial loss" — Parallel rule for capital property; 248(12) — Identical properties.

Notes: See 18(13) Notes.

18(14)(c) amended by 2017 budget bill #2 to refer to 10.1(6) and (7) for taxation years that begin after March 21, 2017; and to 138.2(4) for taxation years that begin after 2017.

18(14)(c) amended by 2002-2013 technical bill, for dispositions after 1998, to change "132.2(1)(f)" to "132.2(3)(a) or (c)".

18(14) added by 1995-97 technical bill, effective for dispositions of property after June 20, 1996 (with limited grandfathering for a disposition before 1997).

(15) Loss on certain properties [transferred within affiliated group] — If this subsection applies because of subsection (13) or (14) to a disposition of a particular property,

(a) the transferor's loss, if any, from the disposition is deemed to be nil, and

(b) the amount of the transferor's loss, if any, from the disposition (determined without reference to this subsection) is deemed

to be a loss of the transferor from a disposition of the particular property at the first time, after the disposition,

(i) at which a 30-day period begins throughout which neither the transferor nor a person affiliated with the transferor owns

(A) the substituted property, or

(B) a property that is identical to the substituted property and that was acquired after the day that is 31 days before the period begins,

(ii) at which the substituted property would, if it were owned by the transferor, be deemed by section 128.1 or subsection 149(10) to have been disposed of by the transferor,

(iii) that is immediately before the transferor is subject to a loss restriction event, or

(iv) if the transferor is a corporation,

(A) for the purposes of computing the transferor's foreign accrual property income, exempt surplus or exempt deficit, and taxable surplus or taxable deficit, in respect of a taxpayer for a taxation year of the transferor where the transferor is a foreign affiliate of the taxpayer, at which the liquidation and dissolution of the transferor begins, unless the liquidation and dissolution is

(I) a qualifying liquidation and dissolution (within the meaning assigned by subsection 88(3.1)) of the transferor, or

(II) a designated liquidation and dissolution (within the meaning assigned by subsection 95(1)) of the transferor, and

(B) for any other purposes, at which the winding-up (other than a winding-up to which subsection 88(1) applies) of the transferor begins, and

and for the purpose of paragraph (b), where a partnership otherwise ceases to exist at any time after the disposition, the partnership is deemed not to have ceased to exist, and each person who was a member of the partnership immediately before the partnership would, but for this subsection, have ceased to exist is deemed to remain a member of the partnership, until the time that is immediately after the first time described in subparagraphs (b)(i) to (iv).

Related Provisions: 13(21.2) — Parallel rule for depreciable capital property; 14(12) [before 2017] — Parallel rule for eligible capital property; 18(16) — Deemed identical property; 18(19)A(a) — Combined effect of 18(15) and straddle-transaction rules; 40(3.3), (3.4) — Parallel rule for capital losses; 69(5)(d) — No application where corporate property appropriated by shareholder on windup; 87(2)(g.3) — Amalgamation — continuing corporation; 95(2)(e)(v)(A)(II) — Designated liquidation and dissolution of foreign affiliate; 248(12) — Whether properties are identical; 251.1 — Affiliated persons; 251.2 — Loss restriction event.

Notes: See 18(13) Notes. For 18(15)(b)(iii), see 251.2(2) Notes.

18(15) amended by 2013 budget bill #2 (effective March 21, 2013), 2002-2013 technical bill. Added by 1995-97 technical bill.

(16) Deemed identical property — For the purposes of subsections (13), (14) and (15), a right to acquire a property (other than a right, as security only, derived from a mortgage, hypothec, agreement for sale or similar obligation) is deemed to be a property that is identical to the property.

Notes: See Notes to 18(13). For the meaning of "derived", see Notes to 18.1(12).

18(16) amended non-substantively by 2001 *Civil Code* harmonization bill, effective June 14, 2001. Added by 1995-97 technical bill.

(17) [Year-end straddle transaction rules —] Definitions — The following definitions apply in this subsection and subsections (18) to (23).

"offsetting position", in respect of a particular position of a person or partnership (in this definition referred to as the "holder"), means one or more positions that

(a) are held by

(i) the holder,

(ii) a person or partnership that does not deal at arm's length with, or is affiliated with, the holder (in this subsection and subsections (20), (22) and (23) referred to as the **"connected person"**), or

(iii) for greater certainty, by any combination of the holder and one or more connected persons;

(b) have the effect, or would have the effect if each of the positions held by a connected person were held by the holder, of eliminating all or substantially all of the holder's risk of loss and opportunity for gain or profit in respect of the particular position; and

(c) if held by a connected person, can reasonably be considered to have been held with the purpose of obtaining the effect described in paragraph (b).

Related Provisions: 18(21)(c) — Anti-avoidance — extended meaning of "offsetting position".

Notes: See Notes to 18(19).

CRA considers that "substantially all", used in para. (b), means 90% or more.

"position", of a person or partnership, means one or more properties, obligations or liabilities of the person or partnership, if

(a) each property, obligation or liability is

(i) a share in the capital stock of a corporation,

(ii) an interest in a partnership,

(iii) an interest in a trust,

(iv) a commodity,

(v) foreign currency,

(vi) a swap agreement, a forward purchase or sale agreement, a forward rate agreement, a futures agreement, an option agreement or a similar agreement,

(vii) a debt owed to or owing by the person or partnership that, at any time,

(A) is denominated in a foreign currency,

(B) would be described in paragraph 7000(1)(d) of the *Income Tax Regulations* if that paragraph were read without reference to the words "other than one described in paragraph (a), (b) or (c)", or

(C) is convertible into or exchangeable for an interest, or for civil law a right, in any property that is described in any of subparagraphs (i) to (iv),

(viii) an obligation to transfer or return to another person or partnership a property identical to a particular property described in any of subparagraphs (i) to (vii) that was previously transferred or lent to the person or partnership by that other person or partnership, or

(ix) an interest, or for civil law a right, in any property that is described in any of subparagraphs (i) to (vii); and

(b) it is reasonable to conclude that, if there is more than one property, obligation or liability, each of them is held in connection with each other.

"successor position", in respect of a position (in this definition referred to as the "initial position"), means a particular position if

(a) the particular position is an offsetting position in respect of a second position;

(b) the second position was an offsetting position in respect of the initial position that was disposed of at a particular time; and

(c) the particular position was entered into during the period that begins 30 days before, and ends 30 days after, the particular time.

Related Provisions: 18(21)(d) — Anti-avoidance — extended meaning of "successor position".

"unrecognized loss", in respect of a position of a person or partnership at a particular time in a taxation year, means the loss, if any, that would be deductible in computing the income of the person or partnership for the year with respect to the position if it were disposed of immediately before the particular time at its fair market value at the time of disposition.

"unrecognized profit", in respect of a position of a person or partnership at a particular time in a taxation year, means the profit, if any, that would be included in computing the income of the person or partnership for the year with respect to the position if it were disposed of immediately before the particular time at its fair market value at the time of disposition.

Related Provisions: 18(23) — Rule where taxpayer and connected person have different year-ends.

Notes: See Notes to 18(19).

(18) Application of subsec. (19) — Subject to subsection (20), subsection (19) applies in respect of a disposition of a particular position by a person or partnership (in this subsection and subsections (19), (20) and (22) referred to as the **"transferor"**), if

(a) the disposition is not a disposition that is deemed to have occurred by section 70, subsection 104(4), section 128.1 or subsection 138(11.3) or 149(10);

(b) the transferor is not a "financial institution" (as defined in subsection 142.2(1)), a mutual fund corporation or a mutual fund trust; and

(c) the particular position was, immediately before the disposition, not a capital property, or an obligation or liability on account of capital, of the transferor.

Related Provisions: 18(17) — Definitions; 18(20) — Exceptions where 18(19) does not apply.

Notes: See Notes to 18(19).

(19) Straddle losses — If this subsection applies in respect of a disposition of a particular position by a transferor, the portion of the transferor's loss, if any, from the disposition of the particular position that is deductible in computing the transferor's income for a particular taxation year is the amount determined by the formula

$$A + B - C$$

where

A is

(a) if the particular taxation year is the taxation year in which the disposition occurs, the amount of the loss determined without reference to this subsection (which is, for greater certainty, subject to subsection (15)), and

(b) in any other taxation year, nil;

B is

(a) if the disposition occurred in a preceding taxation year, the amount determined for C in respect of the disposition for the immediately preceding taxation year, and

(b) in any other case, nil; and

C is the lesser of

(a) the amount determined for A for the taxation year in which the disposition occurs, and

(b) the amount determined by the formula

$$D - (E + F)$$

where

D is the total of all amounts each of which is the amount of unrecognized profit at the end of the particular taxation year in respect of

(i) the particular position,

(ii) positions that are offsetting positions in respect of the particular position (or would be, to the extent that there is no successor position in respect of the particular position, if the particular position continued to be held by the transferor),

(iii) successor positions in respect of the particular position (for this purpose, a successor position in respect of a position includes a successor position that is in respect of a successor position in respect of the position), and

(iv) positions that are offsetting positions in respect of any successor position referred to in subparagraph (iii) (or would be, if any such successor position continued to be held by the holder),

E　is the total of all amounts each of which is the amount of unrecognized loss at the end of the particular taxation year in respect of positions referred to in subparagraphs (i) to (iv) of the description of D, and

F　is the total of all amounts each of which is an amount determined by the formula

$$G - H$$

where

G　is the amount determined for A for the taxation year in which the disposition occurs in respect of any position that was disposed of prior to the disposition of the particular position, if

(i) the particular position was a successor position in respect of that position (for this purpose, a successor position in respect of a position includes a successor position that is in respect of a successor position in respect of the position), and

(ii) that position was

(A) an offsetting position in respect of the particular position,

(B) an offsetting position in respect of a position in respect of which the particular position was a successor position (for this purpose, a successor position in respect of a position includes a successor position that is in respect of a successor position in respect of the position), or

(C) the particular position, and

H　is the total of all amounts each of which is, in respect of a position described in G, an amount determined under the first formula in this subsection for the particular taxation year or a preceding taxation year.

Related Provisions: 18(17) — Definitions; 18(18) — Conditions for 18(19) to apply; 18(20) — Exceptions where 18(19) does not apply; 18(21) — Application rules; 18(23) — Rule where taxpayer and connected person have different year-ends; 257 — Formula amounts cannot calculate to less than zero.

Notes: 18(17)-(23) target "straddle transaction" deferrals using derivatives traded on income account, where offsetting positions are held, the losing position is closed out before year-end and the winning one after year-end. Before these rules, deferral was permitted in *Friedberg*, [1993] 2 C.T.C. 306 (SCC), para. 5, and *Paletta*, 2021 TCC 11 (under appeal by Crown to FCA), but is now restricted by 18(19). These rules do not apply to capital property: 18(18)(c).

See also Marcovitz, "Taxation of Liabilities and Derivatives on Income Account", 2017 Cdn Tax Foundation conference report, at 12:17-22; CRA, "Warning: Watch Out for Straddle-Loss Schemes" (June 1, 2021), tinyurl.com/cra-straddle.

18(17)-(23) added by 2017 budget bill #2, effective in respect of a "position" (as defined in 18(17)) of a person or partnership if

(a) the position is acquired, entered into, renewed or extended, or becomes owing, by the person or partnership after March 21, 2017; or

(b) an "offsetting position" (as defined in 18(17)) in respect of the position is acquired, entered into, renewed or extended, or becomes owing, by the person or partnership or a "connected person" (as defined in 18(17)) after March 21, 2017.

(20) Exceptions — Subsection (19) does not apply in respect of a particular position of a transferor if

(a) it is the case that

(i) either the particular position, or the offsetting position in respect of the particular position, consists of

(A) commodities that the holder of the position manufactures, produces, grows, extracts or processes, or

(B) debt that the holder of the position incurs in the course of a business that consists of one or any combination of the activities described in clause (A), and

(ii) it can reasonably be considered that the position not described in subparagraph (i) — the particular position if the offsetting position is described in subparagraph (i) or the offsetting position if the particular position is described in that subparagraph — is held to reduce the risk, with respect to the position described in subparagraph (i), from

(A) in the case of a position described in clause (i)(A), price changes or fluctuations in the value of currency with respect to the goods described in clause (i)(A), or

(B) in the case of a position described in clause (i)(B), fluctuations in interest rates or in the value of currency with respect to the debt described in clause (i)(B);

(b) the transferor or a connected person (in this paragraph referred to as the "holder") continues to hold a position — that would be an offsetting position in respect of the particular position if the particular position continued to be held by the transferor — throughout a 30-day period beginning on the date of disposition of the particular position, and at no time during the period

(i) is the holder's risk of loss or opportunity for gain or profit with respect to the position reduced in any material respect by another position entered into or disposed of by the holder, or

(ii) would the holder's risk of loss or opportunity for gain or profit with respect to the position be reduced in any material respect by another position entered into or disposed of by a connected person, if the other position were entered into or disposed of by the holder; or

(c) it can reasonably be considered that none of the main purposes of the series of transactions or events, or any of the transactions or events in the series, of which the holding of both the particular position and offsetting position are part, is to avoid, reduce or defer tax that would otherwise be payable under this Act.

Related Provisions: 18(17) — Definitions.

Notes: See Notes to 18(19).

(21) Application — For the purposes of subsections (17) to (23),

(a) if a position of a person or partnership is not a property of the person or partnership, the person or partnership is deemed

(i) to hold the position at any time while it is a position of the person or partnership, and

(ii) to have disposed of the position when the position is settled or extinguished in respect of the person or partnership;

(b) a disposition of a position is deemed to include a disposition of a portion of the position;

(c) a position held by one or more persons or partnerships referred to in paragraph (a) of the definition "offsetting position" in subsection (17) is deemed to be an offsetting position in respect of a particular position of a person or partnership if

(i) there is a high degree of negative correlation between changes in value of the position and the particular position, and

(ii) it can reasonably be considered that the principal purpose of the series of transactions or events, or any of the transactions in the series, of which the holding of both the position and the particular position are part, is to avoid, reduce or defer tax that would otherwise be payable under this Act; and

(d) one or more positions held by one or more persons or partnerships referred to in paragraph (a) of the definition "offsetting position" in subsection (17) are deemed to be a successor position in respect of a particular position of a person or partnership if

(i) a portion of the particular position was disposed of at a particular time,

(ii) the position is, or the positions include, as the case may be, a position that consists of the portion of the particular position that was not disposed of (in this paragraph referred to as the "remaining portion of the particular position"),

(iii) where there is more than one position, the position or positions that do not consist of the remaining portion of the particular position were entered into during the period that begins 30 days before, and ends 30 days after, the particular time,

(iv) the position is, or the positions taken together would be, as the case may be, an offsetting position in respect of a second position (within the meaning of the definition "successor position" in subsection (17)),

(v) the second position was an offsetting position in respect of the particular position, and

(vi) it can reasonably be considered that the principal purpose of the series of transactions or events, or any of the transactions in the series, of which the disposition of a portion of the particular position and the holding of one or more positions are part, is to avoid, reduce or defer tax that would otherwise be payable under this Act.

Related Provisions: 18(17) — Definitions.

Notes: See Notes to 18(19).

(22) [Straddles —] Different taxation years — Subsection (23) applies if

(a) at any time in a particular taxation year of a transferor, a position referred to in any of subparagraphs (ii) to (iv) of the description of D in subsection (19) (in this subsection and subsection (23) referred to as the **"gain position"**) is held by a connected person;

(b) the connected person disposes of the gain position in the particular taxation year; and

(c) the taxation year of the connected person in which the disposition referred to in paragraph (b) occurs ends after the end of the particular taxation year.

Related Provisions: 18(17) — Definitions.

Notes: See Notes to 18(19).

(23) [Straddles —] Different taxation years — If this subsection applies, for the purposes of the definition "unrecognized profit" in subsection (17) and subsection (19), the portion of the profit, if any, realized from the disposition of the gain position referred to in paragraph (22)(b) that is determined by the following formula is deemed to be unrecognized profit in respect of the gain position until the end of the taxation year of the connected person in which the disposition occurs:

$$A \times B/C$$

where

A is the amount of the profit otherwise determined;

B is the number of days in the taxation year of the connected person in which the disposition referred to in paragraph (22)(b) occurs that are after the end of the particular taxation year; and

C is the total number of days in the taxation year of the connected person in which the disposition referred to in paragraph (22)(b) occurs.

Related Provisions: 18(17) — Definitions; 18(22) — Conditions for 18(23) to apply.

Notes: See Notes to 18(19).

Proposed Amendment — Section 18 — Limitation on deductibility of provincial payroll and capital taxes

Dept. of Finance press release, March 2, 1993: Finance Minister Don Mazankowski today announced that the government would take action, on an interim basis, to effectively deny the deductibility of any increases in provincial payroll and capital taxes. This measure would take effect if provincial payroll and capital tax revenues were increased by way of a rate increase, base change, or the introduction of a new tax.

The 1991 federal Budget proposed a mechanism to limit the impact on federal revenue of the provinces' increasing reliance on such taxes. Discussions with the provinces and affected taxpayers have been held since that time to consider possible modifications of the federal proposal to limit deductibility. Those discussions are continuing, and it is anticipated that a comprehensive solution will be ready for implementation in 1994. Today's measure is intended to apply until that final proposal is brought forward.

Mr. Mazankowski said, "I remain concerned that any provincial actions to increase existing payroll and capital taxes or the introduction of new taxes would further erode federal revenues and put additional pressure on the fiscal framework."

If a province institutes or increases payroll or capital taxes in 1993, an income tax amendment would be sought to ensure that corporations and certain trusts operating in that province are allowed to deduct only a certain percentage of such taxes in computing their income for federal tax purposes. To compute its deductible amount, a taxpayer would simply multiply its total amount of those taxes paid to the province by a percentage prescribed under the *Income Tax Act*. That percentage, which would be determined after consultation with the province on expected revenues, would ensure that the total amount of payroll and capital taxes deducted by all businesses in the province remained the same. It would not, in contrast, ensure that the level of each taxpayer's deductible taxes remained the same. The restriction on deductibility would apply on a prorated basis from the date the provincial tax increase took effect.

The Minister noted that this measure would not restrict the tax policy options of any province. A province may continue to levy these taxes as it sees fit. "However, provinces that increase these taxes will no longer be able to pass part of the cost on to the federal government and taxpayers in other provinces," added Mr. Mazankowski.

The Minister stressed that this is an interim measure and that federal and provincial officials are continuing to work on a longer-term solution.

For further information: Jack Jung, (613) 992-7162; Lawrence Purdy, (613) 996-0602.

Dept. of Finance press release, Oct. 1, 1993: *Extension of Interim Measure to Limit the Deductibility of Provincial Payroll and Capital Taxes*

Finance Minister Gilles Loiselle today announced that proposed limits to the deductibility for federal tax purposes of provincial payroll and capital taxes will be delayed for another year, to allow time for additional consultations with provincial and business representatives. An interim measure announced earlier this year to limit the impact of any increases in these taxes will continue to apply until the revised proposal is in effect. The Minister indicated that federal and provincial officials will continue their discussions on a longer term solution.

The 1991 federal budget proposed to limit the impact of deductible provincial payroll and capital taxes on federal revenue without adding to the overall tax burden. Implementation of the proposal was to begin on January 1, 1992, but was postponed for two years, pending revisions. Today's announcement delays the implementation of the revised proposal until January 1, 1995.

Under the interim measure announced in March 1993, the government would deny the deductibility of any increases in provincial payroll and capital taxes, whether by way of rate increases, base changes, or the introduction of new taxes. "The problems associated with deductible provincial payroll and capital taxes still need to be addressed," Mr. Loiselle said. "Until the revised proposal is in effect, the interim measure protects the federal tax base from any further erosion resulting from provincial actions to increase these taxes."

For further information: Denis Boucher, (613) 996-7861; Jack Jung, (613) 992-7162.

[Parallel news releases issued on October 14, 1994, December 27, 1995, November 29, 1996, November 25, 1997, December 18, 1998, December 17, 1999, December 12, 2000, December 18, 2001, December 23, 2002 and December 18, 2003 — ed.]

Dept. of Finance press release 2004-080, Dec. 16, 2004: *Extension of Interim Measure on Deductibility of Provincial Payroll and Capital Taxes*

Minister of Finance Ralph Goodale announced today that the interim measure that limits the deductibility of increases in provincial payroll and capital taxes will continue to apply.

Under the interim measure, any existing provincial payroll and capital taxes will remain deductible for federal income tax purposes, but increases in these taxes by way of provincial actions to increase the rate, change the definition of the base or introduce new taxes generally would not be deductible.

The announcement of the extension of the interim measure ensures that all businesses and provinces are informed of the rules that apply to the deductibility of provincial payroll and capital taxes.

For further information: David Gamble, Public Affairs and Operations Division, (613) 996-8080; Pat Breton, Press Secretary, Office of the Minister of Finance, (613) 996-7861.

Federal Budget, Supplementary Information, March 19, 2007: *Provincial Capital Taxes*

Many provinces are in the process of reducing or phasing out their capital taxes. To help provinces eliminate their capital taxes as soon as possible, Budget 2007 proposes a temporary financial incentive for provincial governments to eliminate their capital taxes. To be eligible for the federal payment, a province must eliminate its currently existing general capital tax or capital tax on financial institutions, or restructure a currently existing capital tax on financial institutions into a minimum tax on financial institutions. The elimination or restructuring must take effect on or before January 1, 2011, and the enabling legislation must be enacted on or after March 19, 2007 and before 2011.

In order for a province to receive the new financial incentive for restructuring an existing capital tax on financial institutions into a minimum tax, the restructured tax must have both of the following characteristics:

- the level of revenues it raises is broadly commensurate with the corporate income tax; and

- the financial institution is able to reduce the tax by the amount of income tax it pays, if any.

The amount of the new financial incentive will correspond to the federal corporate income tax revenue gain from qualifying provincial capital tax reductions. The new financial incentive will be calculated as a specified rate times the estimated provincial revenue loss from capital tax reductions that meet the criteria for this financial incentive and that relate to the period from March 19, 2007 to January 1, 2011, inclusive. The specified rate will be equivalent to the estimated average effective federal corporate income tax rate applicable to these qualifying capital tax reductions.

The estimated provincial revenue loss from a qualifying capital tax reduction will be the difference between an estimate of the provincial capital tax revenue that would have been raised in a given fiscal year based on legislation in effect before March 19, 2007, and the actual provincial capital tax revenue raised in that fiscal year. In the case of a capital tax on financial institutions that is restructured into a minimum tax eligible for the financial incentive, the estimated revenue loss will be equal to the provincial capital tax revenue that would have been raised in a given fiscal year based on legislation in effect before March 19, 2007.

The incentive will be paid out annually, in respect of each full or partial fiscal year between March 19, 2007 and January 1, 2011, inclusive. An advance payment will be made on each March 31 beginning in 2008 and ending in 2011, if the province has enacted legislation before the payment date and provided sufficient information to estimate the provincial revenue loss of the qualifying capital tax reduction or restructuring prior to the preceding January 31. The final adjustment for a qualifying capital tax reduction in a given fiscal year will be made on the first March 31 following the release of the province's public accounts in respect of that fiscal year (except where those accounts are released less than 60 days before that date, in which case the final adjustment will be made on the next following March 31).

Notes: To implement this incentive, 2007 budget bill #2 enacted Part IV (ss. 9-12.01) of the *Federal-Provincial Fiscal Arrangements Act*.

The provinces have complied with this incentive: Provenzano & Lim, "Capital Taxes Eliminated by 2012", 15(8) *Canadian Tax Highlights* (ctf.ca) 5-6 (Aug. 2007); Carson & Lim, "The Demise of General Capital Taxes", 18(9) *CTH* 9 (Sept. 2010). Ontario eliminated capital tax as of 2007 for companies primarily engaged in manufacturing and resource activities, and as of July 2010 for all others (March 26/08 Ont. Budget). See also VIEWS doc 2009-0326941I7.

Definitions [s. 18]: "affiliated" — 251.1; "amortized cost", "amount", "annuity" — 248(1); "arm's length" — 251(1); "assessment" — 248(1); "associated" — 256; "automobile", "authorized foreign bank" — 248(1); "base level deduction" — 18(2.2); "beneficially interested" — 248(25); "beneficiary" — 18(5), 108(1); "borrowed money", "business" — 248(1); "calendar year" — *Interpretation Act* 37(1)(a); "Canada" — 255, *Interpretation Act* 35(1); "Canadian banking business" — 248(1); "Canadian resource property" — 66(15), 248(1); "capital property" — 54, 248(1); "carries on business in Canada" — 253; "class of shares" — 248(6); "connected person" — 18(17)"offsetting position"; "control" — 256(6)–(9); "controlled" — 256(6), (6.1); "controlled foreign affiliate" — 95(1), 248(1); "corporation" — 248(1), *Interpretation Act* 35(1); "custodian" — 248(1)"employee benefit plan"; "debt amount" — 18(7)(a); "debt obligation" — 18(9.1), (9.2); "deferred profit sharing plan" — 147(1), 248(1); "depreciable property" — 13(21), 248(1); "designated employee benefit" — 144.1(1); "designated insurance property" — 138(12), 248(1); "disposition" — 18(21)(b), 248(1); "dividend", "employee", "employee benefit plan" — 248(1); "employee life and health trust" — 144.1(2), 248(1); "employees profit sharing plan" — 144(1), 248(1); "employer" — 248(1); "equity amount", "equity contribution" — 18(5); "excluded property" — 95(1); "exempt deficit" — Reg. 5907(1); "exempt income" — 248(1); "exempt surplus" — 113(1)(a), Reg. 5907(1), (1.01); "fair market value" — see 69(1) Notes; "financial institution" — 142.2(1); "fiscal period" — 249.1; "foreign accrual property income" — 95(1), 248(1); "foreign currency" — 248(1); "gain position" — 18(22)(a); "gross revenue", "group term life insurance policy" — 248(1); "Her Majesty" — *Interpretation Act* 35(1); "identical" — 18(16), 248(12); "immovable" — Quebec *Civil Code* art. 900–907; "income-averaging annuity contract", "income bond", "income debenture" — 248(1); "incorporated employee" — 125(7)"personal services business"(a); "individual", "insurance corporation", "insurance policy", "insurer" — 248(1); "interest in real property" — 248(4); "interest on debt relating to the acquisition of land" — 18(3); "intermediary" — 18(6)(a); "intermediary debt" — 18(6)(c)(i); "inventory" — 248(1); "investment" — 212.3(10); "land" — 18(3); "lending asset", "life insurance corporation" — 248(1); "life insurance policy" — 138(12), 248(1); "loss restriction event" — 251.2; "mineral resource", "mineral", "Minister" — 248(1); "month" — *Interpretation Act* 35(1); "mutual fund corporation" — 131(8), 248(1); "mutual fund trust" — 132(6)–(7), 132.2(3)(n), 248(1); "net income stabilization account", "non-resident" — 248(1); "non-resident-owned investment corporation" — 133(8), 248(1); "offsetting position" — 18(17), (21)(c); "outstanding debts to specified non-residents" — 18(5); "paid-up capital" — 89(1), 248(1); "partnership" — see 96(1) Notes; "permanent establishment" — Reg. 8201; "person", "personal or living expenses", "personal services business" — 248(1); "pertinent loan or indebtedness" — 212.3(11); "pooled registered pension plan" — 147.5(1), 248(1); "position" — 18(17);

"prescribed" — 248(1); "prescribed rate" — Reg. 4301; "principal amount" — 248(1), (26); "profit sharing plan" — 147(1); "property" — 248(1); "province" — *Interpretation Act* 35(1); "real right" — 248(4.1); "received" — 248(7); "registered disability savings plan" — 146.4(1), 248(1); "registered education savings plan" — 146.1(1), 248(1); "registered pension plan" — 248(1); "registered retirement savings plan" — 146(1), 248(1); "regulation" — 248(1); "relating to the construction, renovation or alteration" — 18(3.2); "resident in Canada" — 94(3)(a), 250; "retirement compensation arrangement", "retirement income fund", "retirement savings plan", "salary, wages" — 248(1)"salary or wages"; "salary deferral arrangement" — 248(1); "security interest" — 18(5); "self-contained domestic establishment" — 248(1); "series of transactions" — 248(10); "share", "shareholder" — 248(1); "specified beneficiary", "specified non-resident beneficiary", "specified non-resident shareholder" — 18(5); "specified pension plan" — 248(1), Reg. 7800; "specified proportion" — 18(5), 248(1); "specified right" — 18(5); "specified shareholder" — 18(5), 18(5.1), 248(1); "substituted" — 18(13)(g), 248(5); "successor position" — 18(17); "supplementary unemployment benefit fund" — 145(1), 248(1); "TFSA" — 146.2(5), 248(1); "tar sands" — 248(1); "tax-paid earnings" — 18(5); "tax shelter investment" — 143.2(1); "taxable deficit" — Reg. 5907(1); "taxable income" — 2(2), 248(1); "taxable surplus" — 113(1)(b)(i), Reg. 5907(1), (1.01); "taxation year" — 11(2), 249; "taxpayer" — 248(1); "timber resource property" — 13(21), 248(1); "transferor" — 18(13)(a), 18(14)(a), 18(18); "trust" — 104(1), 248(1), (3); "unrecognized loss", "unrecognized profit" — 18(17); "writing" — *Interpretation Act* 35(1).

Interpretation Bulletins [s. 18]: IT-105: Administrative costs of pension plans.

18.1 [Matchable expenditures] — (1) Definitions — The definitions in this subsection apply in this section.

"matchable expenditure" of a taxpayer means the amount of an expenditure that is made by the taxpayer to

(a) acquire a right to receive production,

(b) fulfil a covenant or obligation arising in circumstances in which it is reasonable to conclude that a relationship exists between the covenant or obligation and a right to receive production, or

(c) preserve or protect a right to receive production,

but does not include an amount for which a deduction is provided under section 20 in computing the taxpayer's income.

Notes: See Notes at end of 18.1.

"right to receive production" means a right under which a taxpayer is entitled, either immediately or in the future and either absolutely or contingently, to receive an amount all or a portion of which is computed by reference to use of property, production, revenue, profit, cash flow, commodity price, cost or value of property or any other similar criterion or by reference to dividends paid or payable to shareholders of any class of shares where the amount is in respect of another taxpayer's activity, property or business but such a right does not include an income interest in a trust, a Canadian resource property or a foreign resource property.

Related Provisions: 88(1)(a)(i) — Treatment of right to receive production on windup of corporation; 248(1)"cost amount"(e)(iv) — Definition of cost amount does not apply to right to receive production.

I.T. Technical News: 10 (net profits interests and proposed section 18.1).

"tax benefit" means a reduction, avoidance or deferral of tax or other amount payable under this Act or an increase in a refund of tax or other amount under this Act.

"tax shelter" means a property that would be a tax shelter (as defined in subsection 237.1(1)) if

(a) the cost of a right to receive production were the total of all amounts each of which is a matchable expenditure to which the right relates; and

(b) subsections (2) to (13) did not apply for the purpose of computing an amount, or in the case of a partnership a loss, represented to be deductible.

"taxpayer" includes a partnership.

(2) Limitation on the deductibility of matchable expenditure — In computing a taxpayer's income from a business or property for a taxation year, no amount of a matchable expenditure may be deducted except as provided by subsection (3).

Related Provisions: 18.1(15) — No application to risks ceded between insurers; 18.1(16) — No application where not a tax shelter; 87(2)(j.2) — Amalgamation —

continuing corporation; 88(1)(a)(i) — Treatment of right to receive production on windup of corporation.

Notes: See Notes at end of 18.1.

I.T. Technical News: 10 (net profits interests and proposed section 18.1).

(3) Deduction of matchable expenditure — If a taxpayer's matchable expenditure would, but for subsection (2) and this subsection, be deductible in computing the taxpayer's income, there may be deducted in respect of the matchable expenditure in computing the taxpayer's income for a taxation year the amount that is determined under subsection (4) for the year in respect of the expenditure.

Related Provisions: 18.1(6) — Income inclusion; 18.1(10) — Amount of deduction if non-arm's length disposition; 18.1(14) — Where right to receive production is reasonably certain.

(4) Amount of deduction — For the purpose of subsection (3), the amount determined under this subsection for a taxation year in respect of a taxpayer's matchable expenditure is the amount, if any, that is the least of

(a) the total of

(i) the lesser of

(A) $\frac{1}{5}$ of the matchable expenditure, and

(B) the amount determined by the formula

$$(A/B) \times C$$

where

A   is the number of months that are in the year and after the day on which the right to receive production to which the matchable expenditure relates is acquired,

B   is the lesser of 240 and the number of months that are in the period that begins on the day on which the right to receive production to which the matchable expenditure relates is acquired and that ends on the day the right is to terminate, and

C   is the amount of the matchable expenditure, and

(ii) the amount, if any, by which the amount determined under this paragraph for the preceding taxation year in respect of the matchable expenditure exceeds the amount of the matchable expenditure deductible in computing the taxpayer's income for that preceding year,

(b) the total of

(i) all amounts each of which is included in computing the taxpayer's income for the year (other than any portion of such amount that is the subject of a reserve claimed by the taxpayer for the year under this Act) in respect of the right to receive production to which the matchable expenditure relates, and

(ii) the amount by which the amount determined under this paragraph for the preceding taxation year in respect of the matchable expenditure exceeds the amount of the matchable expenditure deductible in computing the taxpayer's income for that preceding year, and

(c) the amount, if any, by which

(i) the total of all amounts each of which is an amount of the matchable expenditure that would, but for this section, have been deductible in computing the taxpayer's income for the year or a preceding taxation year

exceeds

(ii) the total of all amounts each of which is an amount of the matchable expenditure deductible under subsection (3) in computing the taxpayer's income for a preceding taxation year.

Related Provisions: 18.1(5) — Rules for determining amount; 18.1(17) — Non-application of 18.1(4)(a) (film shelters, etc.).

Notes: See Notes at end of 18.1. 18.1(4) limits deduction for a matchable expenditure to the least of 3 amounts. Generally, the first amount is the expenditure prorated over the term of the right to receive production to which the expenditure relates, but the term

cannot be less than 5 years (but see also 18.1(17) re the 80% rule). Added to this are amounts that would have been deductible in preceding years but for the second constraint. The second constraint is the income included in respect of the right for the year. Added to this is income for previous years against which amounts could not be deducted because of the first constraint. The third constraint is the amount that would otherwise have been deductible in computing income up to and including the current tax year in respect of the taxpayer's right to receive production minus the amounts deductible under 18.1(3) in computing income for preceding years.

(5) Special rules — For the purpose of this section,

(a) where a taxpayer's matchable expenditure is made before the day on which the related right to receive production is acquired by the taxpayer, the expenditure is deemed to have been made on that day;

(b) where a taxpayer has one or more rights to renew a particular right to receive production to which a matchable expenditure relates for one or more additional terms, after the term that includes the time at which the particular right was acquired, the particular right is deemed to terminate on the latest day on which the latest possible such term could terminate if all rights to renew the particular right were exercised;

(c) where a taxpayer has 2 or more rights to receive production that can reasonably be considered to be related to each other, the rights are deemed to be one right; and

(d) where the term of a taxpayer's right to receive production is for an indeterminate period, the right is deemed to terminate 240 months after it is acquired.

(6) Proceeds of disposition considered income — Where in a taxation year a taxpayer disposes of all or part of a right to receive production to which a matchable expenditure relates, the proceeds of the disposition shall be included in computing the taxpayer's income for the year.

Related Provisions: 12(1)(g.1) — Inclusion in income of proceeds of disposition; 87(2)(j.2) — Amalgamation — continuing corporation.

Notes: See Notes at end of 18.1.

(7) Arm's length disposition — Subject to subsections (8) to (10), where in a taxation year a taxpayer disposes (otherwise than in a disposition to which subsection 87(1) or 88(1) applies) of all of the taxpayer's right to receive production to which a matchable expenditure (other than an expenditure no portion of which would, if this section were read without reference to this subsection, be deductible under subsection (3) in computing the taxpayer's income) relates, or the taxpayer's right expires, the amount deductible in respect of the expenditure under subsection (3) in computing the taxpayer's income for the year is deemed to be the amount, if any, determined under paragraph (4)(c) for the year in respect of the expenditure.

Related Provisions: 87(2)(j.2) — Amalgamation — continuing corporation; 88(1)(a)(i) — Treatment of right to receive production on windup of corporation; 251.1 — Affiliated persons.

Notes: See Notes at end of 18.1. 18.1(7) provides that, on disposition or expiry, a taxpayer may claim a terminal deduction in respect of a right to receive production to which a matchable expenditure relates. However, this terminal deduction is not available where 18.1(8) or (9) applies.

(8) Non-arm's length disposition — Subsection (10) applies where

(a) a taxpayer's particular right to receive production to which a matchable expenditure (other than an expenditure no portion of which would, if this section were read without reference to subsections (7) and (10), be deductible under subsection (3) in computing the taxpayer's income) relates has expired or the taxpayer has disposed of all of the right (otherwise than in a disposition to which subsection 87(1) or 88(1) applies);

(b) during the period that begins 30 days before and ends 30 days after the disposition or expiry, the taxpayer or a person affiliated, or who does not deal at arm's length, with the taxpayer acquires a right to receive production (in this subsection and subsection (10) referred to as the "substituted property") that is, or is identical to, the particular right; and

(c) at the end of the period, the taxpayer or a person affiliated, or who does not deal at arm's length, with the taxpayer owns the substituted property.

(9) Special case — Subsection (10) applies where

(a) a taxpayer's particular right to receive production to which a matchable expenditure (other than an expenditure no portion of which would, if this section were read without reference to subsections (7) and (10), be deductible under subsection (3) in computing the taxpayer's income) relates has expired or the taxpayer has disposed of all of the right (otherwise than in a disposition to which subsection 87(1) or 88(1) applies); and

(b) during the period that begins at the time of the disposition or expiry and ends 30 days after that time, a taxpayer that had an interest, directly or indirectly, in the right has another interest, directly or indirectly, in another right to receive production, which other interest is a tax shelter or a tax shelter investment (as defined by section 143.2).

Related Provisions: 18.1(12) — Identical properties.

Notes: For the meaning of "indirectly" in (b), see Notes to 17.1(1).

(10) Amount of deduction if non-arm's length disposition — Where this subsection applies because of subsection (8) or (9) to a disposition or expiry in a taxation year or a preceding taxation year of a taxpayer's right to receive production to which a matchable expenditure relates,

(a) the amount deductible under subsection (3) in respect of the expenditure in computing the taxpayer's income for a taxation year that ends at or after the disposition or expiry of the right is the least of the amounts determined under subsection (4) for the year in respect of the expenditure; and

(b) the least of the amounts determined under subsection (4) in respect of the expenditure for a taxation year is deemed to be the amount, if any, determined under paragraph (4)(c) in respect of the expenditure for the year where the year includes the time that is immediately before the first time, after the disposition or expiry,

(i) at which the right would, if it were owned by the taxpayer, be deemed by section 128.1 or subsection 149(10) to have been disposed of by the taxpayer,

(ii) that is immediately before the taxpayer is subject to a loss restriction event,

(iii) at which winding-up of the taxpayer begins (other than a winding-up to which subsection 88(1) applies), if the taxpayer is a corporation,

(iv) if subsection (8) applies, at which a 30-day period begins throughout which neither the taxpayer nor a person affiliated, or who does not deal at arm's length, with the taxpayer owns

(A) the substituted property, or

(B) a property that is identical to the substituted property and that was acquired after the day that is 31 days before the period began, or

(v) if subsection (9) applies, at which a 30-day period begins throughout which no taxpayer who had an interest, directly or indirectly, in the right has an interest, directly or indirectly, in another right to receive production if one or more of those direct or indirect interests in the other right is a tax shelter or tax shelter investment (as defined by section 143.2).

Related Provisions: 18.1(11) — Partnerships; 18.1(12) — Identical properties; 251.2 — Loss restriction event.

Notes: For the meaning of "indirectly" in (b)(v), see 17.1(1) Notes. For "loss restriction event" see 251.2(2) Notes.

18.1(10)(b)(ii) amended by 2013 budget bill #2, effective March 21, 2013.

(11) Partnerships — For the purpose of paragraph (10)(b), where a partnership otherwise ceases to exist at any time after a disposition or expiry referred to in subsection (10), the partnership is deemed not to have ceased to exist, and each taxpayer who was a member of the partnership immediately before the partnership would, but for this subsection, have ceased to exist is deemed to remain a member of the partnership until the time that is immediately after the first of the times described in subparagraphs (10)(b)(i) to (v).

(12) Identical property — For the purposes of subsections (8) and (10), a right to acquire a particular right to receive production (other than a right, as security only, derived from a mortgage, hypothec, agreement of sale or similar obligation) is deemed to be a right to receive production that is identical to the particular right.

Related Provisions: 248(12) — Extended definition of identical properties.

Notes: "Derived" in para. (c) may be interpreted broadly: see *Gilhooly*, [1945] C.T.C. 203 (Exch. Ct.); *Kemp*, [1947] C.T.C. 343 (Exch. Ct.); *Hollinger North Shore*, [1963] C.T.C. 51 (SCC); *Bessemer Trust*, [1972] C.T.C. 473 (FCTD); *Westar Mining*, [1992] 2 C.T.C. 11 (FCA) (insurance proceeds for mine shut down by fire were "income derived from the operation of a mine"); *Garcia*, 2007 TCC 548, paras. 28-37 ("having its source"); *News Australia*, [2017] FCA 645 (Australia FC); *Apex City Homes*, 2018 TCC 247, paras. 18-23; *Ardmore Construction*, [2018] EWCA Civ 1438 (UK). *Exxonmobil*, 2019 TCC 108, para. 49, held that income "derived from transporting petroleum" meant that the transporting "in and of itself generated income", not merely that transporting petroleum was necessary to sell it.

Reference to "hypothec" added to 18.1(12) by 2001 *Civil Code* harmonization bill, effective June 14, 2001 (non-substantive change; see *Interpretation Act* s. 8.2).

(13) Application of s. 143.2 — For the purpose of applying section 143.2 to an amount that would, if this section were read without reference to this subsection, be a matchable expenditure any portion of the cost of which is deductible under subsection (3), the expenditure is deemed to be a tax shelter investment and that section shall be read without reference to subparagraph 143.2(6)(b)(ii).

(14) Debt obligations — Where the rate of return on a taxpayer's right to receive production to which a matchable expenditure (other than an expenditure no portion of which would, if this section were read without reference to this subsection, be deductible under subsection (3) in computing the taxpayer's income) relates is reasonably certain at the time the taxpayer acquires the right,

(a) the right is, for the purposes of subsection 12(9) and Part LXX of the *Income Tax Regulations*, deemed to be a debt obligation in respect of which no interest is stipulated to be payable in respect of its principal amount and the obligation is deemed to be satisfied at the time the right terminates for an amount equal to the total of the return on the obligation and the amount that would otherwise be the matchable expenditure that is related to the right; and

(b) notwithstanding subsection (3), no amount may be deducted in computing the taxpayer's income in respect of any matchable expenditure that relates to the right.

(15) Non-application — risks ceded between insurers — Subsections (2) to (13) do not apply to a taxpayer's matchable expenditure in respect of a right to receive production if

(a) the expenditure is in respect of commissions, or other expenses, related to the issuance of an insurance policy for which all or a portion of a risk has been ceded to the taxpayer; and

(b) the taxpayer and the person to whom the expenditure is made, or is to be made, are both insurers who are subject to the supervision of

(i) the Superintendent of Financial Institutions, if the taxpayer or that person, as the case may be, is an insurer who is required by law to report to the Superintendent of Financial Institutions, or

(ii) the Superintendent of Insurance, or other similar officer or authority, of the province under whose laws the insurer is incorporated, in any other case.

Related Provisions [subsec. 18.1(15)]: 12(1)(s), 20(1)(jj) — Reinsurance commissions.

Notes: 18.1(15) amended and 18.1(16)-(17) added by 2002-2013 technical bill (Part 5 — technical), generally effective for expenditures made after Sept. 17, 2001, but with extensive grandfathering rules (reproduced here up to the 45th ed.).

What is now 18.1(15) is the former 18.1(15)(b), and 18.1(16) is the former 18.1(15)(a).

(16) Non-application — no rights, tax benefits or shelters — Subsections (2) to (13) do not apply to a taxpayer's matchable expenditure in respect of a right to receive production if

(a) no portion of the matchable expenditure can reasonably be considered to have been paid to another taxpayer, or to a person or partnership with whom the other taxpayer does not deal at arm's length, to acquire the right from the other taxpayer;

(b) no portion of the matchable expenditure can reasonably be considered to relate to a tax shelter or a tax shelter investment (within the meaning assigned by subsection 143.2(1)); and

(c) none of the main purposes for making the matchable expenditure can reasonably be considered to have been to obtain a tax benefit for the taxpayer, a person or partnership with whom the taxpayer does not deal at arm's length, or a person or partnership that holds, directly or indirectly, an interest in the taxpayer.

Notes: See Notes to 18.1(15).

(17) Revenue exception — Paragraph (4)(a) does not apply in determining the amount for a taxation year that may be deducted in respect of a taxpayer's matchable expenditure in respect of a right to receive production if

(a) before the end of the taxation year in which the matchable expenditure is made, the total of all amounts each of which is included in computing the taxpayer's income for the year (other than any portion of any of those amounts that is the subject of a reserve claimed by the taxpayer for the year under this Act) in respect of the right to receive production that relates to the matchable expenditure exceeds 80% of the matchable expenditure; and

(b) no portion of the matchable expenditure can reasonably be considered to have been paid to another taxpayer, or to a person or partnership with whom the other taxpayer does not deal at arm's length, to acquire the right from the other taxpayer.

Notes: See Notes to 18.1(15). 18.1(17) shut down numerous film shelters that were developed to circumvent the matchable expenditure rules by using the 20% deductibility under 18.1(4)(a). For some fallout and history of these deals see *Strother*, 2007 SCC 24 and 2009 BCSC 1286 (advisor required to disgorge profits); *Sentinel Hill*, 2007 TCC 742 (Crown's FCA appeal discontinued); *Strother (Sentinel Hill)*, 2011 TCC 251; *University Hill*, 2017 FCA 232 (leave to appeal denied 2018 CarswellNat 4689 (SCC)).

Notes [s. 18.1]: 18.1 restricts the deductibility of an otherwise deductible matchable expenditure incurred in respect of a right to receive production by prorating the deductibility of the amount of the expenditure over the economic life of the right. (See Notes to 18.1(4).) It does not create an entitlement to deduct an amount in respect of an expenditure, unless the expenditure is otherwise deductible under existing jurisprudence. The "Backgrounder" accompanying Finance news release 96-082 (Nov. 18, 1996) provides general details about the tax policy concerns that led to 18.1, and news releases of Dec. 19, 1996 and July 30, 1997 announced the transitional relief below. Generally, these concern the use of royalty-type arrangements to effect tax-assisted financing by structuring the arrangements as tax shelters or as debt substitutes.

The original transactions that started this kind of planning were for mutual fund limited partnership commissions, financed through these shelters. Originally they were allowed a 100% writeoff, later restricted by Revenue Canada administrative policy to ⅓ deduction each year. In the months leading up to the Nov. 1996 announcement, the concept had been extended to other areas. See also Notes to 18.1(17).

18.1 added by 1995-97 technical bill, effective for every expenditure made by a taxpayer or a partnership after November 17, 1996, with grandfathering for certain expenditures made before 1998.

Definitions [s. 18.1]: "affiliated" — 251.1; "amount" — 248(1); "arm's length" — 251(1); "business" — 248(1); "Canadian resource property" — 66(15), 248(1); "class of shares" — 248(6); "control" — 256(6)–(9); "dividend" — 248(1); "foreign resource property" — 66(15), 248(1); "identical" — 18.1(12); "insurer" — 248(1); "loss restriction event" — 251.2; "matchable expenditure" — 18.1(1); "partnership" — see 96(1) Notes; "officer", "person" — 248(1); "principal amount" — 248(1), (26); "property" — 248(1); "province" — *Interpretation Act* 35(1); "related" — 251(2)–(6); "right to receive production" — 18.1(1); "share", "shareholder" — 248(1); "substituted property" — 18.1(8)(b); "tax benefit", "tax shelter" — 18.1(1); "taxation year" — 249; "taxpayer" — 18.1(1), 248(1); "trust" — 104(1), 248(1), (3).

18.2 [Repealed]

Notes: 18.2 added by 2007 budget bill #2 but repealed by 2009 budget bill #1, both for interest paid or payable in respect of a period or periods that begin after 2011. It would have disallowed "double-dip" interest, had it not been repealed.

A simple "double dip" occurs where Canco (Canadian co) has two foreign subsidiaries: Opco (operating co in high-tax jurisdiction) and Finco (financing co in low-tax jurisdiction that has a tax treaty with Canada, such as Barbados). Canco borrows from the bank, invests in shares of Finco, and deducts interest paid to the bank. Finco lends the same funds to Opco at a commercial interest rate, and records the income but pays little tax. Opco deducts the interest paid to Finco. Under 95(2)(a)(ii), Finco's interest income is deemed to be active business income and thus not FAPI.

The US attacks double-dips through "dual consolidated loss" rules: Mitchell, "Department of Treasury Attacks 'Double Dips' Too?", XIV(2) *International Tax Planning* (Federated Press) 976-80 (2007).

18.2(2) would have disallowed interest expense except to the extent "specified financing expense" (18.2(3)) exceeded "aggregate double-dip income" (18.2(1)). The denial would have been permanent; there was no carryforward of the loss deduction. One way to avoid 18.2 would be not to have 95(2)(a)(ii) "re-characterized" income.

18.2 was criticized by many, and the 2008 Advisory Panel on Canada's System of International Taxation recommended it be repealed. This was done in 2009.

For discussion before the announced repeal see these Notes up to the 46th ed. For the text of 18.2 (deemed never to have come into force), see PITA 33rd-39th ed.

18.3 [SIFTs — Stapled securities] — (1) Definitions — The following definitions apply in this section.

"entity" has the same meaning as in subsection 122.1(1).

"equity value" has the same meaning as in subsection 122.1(1).

"real estate investment trust" has the same meaning as in subsection 122.1(1).

"security", of an entity, means

(a) a liability of the entity;

(b) if the entity is a corporation,

(i) a share of the capital stock of the corporation, and

(ii) a right to control in any manner whatever the voting rights of a share of the capital stock of the corporation if it can reasonably be concluded that one of the reasons that a person or partnership holds the right to control is to avoid the application of subsection (3) or 12.6(3);

(c) if the entity is a trust, an income or a capital interest in the trust; and

(d) if the entity is a partnership, an interest as a member of the partnership.

"stapled security", of a particular entity at any time, means a particular security of the particular entity if at that time

(a) another security (referred to in this section as the **"reference security"**)

(i) is or may be required to be transferred together or concurrently with the particular security as a term or condition of the particular security, the reference security, or an agreement or arrangement to which the particular entity (or if the reference security is a security of another entity, the other entity) is a party, or

(ii) is listed or traded with the particular security on a stock exchange or other public market under a single trading symbol;

(b) the particular security or the reference security is listed or traded on a stock exchange or other public market; and

(c) any of the following applies:

(i) the reference security and the particular security are securities of the particular entity and the particular entity is a corporation, SIFT partnership or SIFT trust,

(ii) the reference security is a security of another entity, one of the particular entity or the other entity is a subsidiary of the other, and the particular entity or the other entity is a corporation, SIFT partnership or SIFT trust, or

(iii) the reference security is a security of another entity and the particular entity or the other entity is a real estate investment trust or a subsidiary of a real estate investment trust.

Related Provisions: 18.3(2) — Deemed stapled security where receipt or similar property represents security.

"subsidiary", of a particular entity at any time, means

(a) an entity in which the particular entity holds at that time securities that have a total fair market value greater than 10% of the equity value of the entity; and

(b) an entity that at that time is a subsidiary of an entity that is a subsidiary of the particular entity.

"transition period", of an entity, means

(a) if one or more securities of the entity would have been stapled securities of the entity on October 31, 2006 and July 19, 2011 had the definition "stapled security" in this subsection come into force on October 31, 2006, the period that begins on July 20, 2011 and ends on the earliest of

(i) January 1, 2016,

(ii) the first day after July 20, 2011 on which any of those securities is materially altered, and

(iii) the first day after July 20, 2011 on which any security of the entity becomes a stapled security other than by way of

(A) a transaction

(I) that is completed under the terms of an agreement in writing entered into before July 20, 2011 if no party to the agreement may be excused from completing the transaction as a result of amendments to this Act, and

(II) that is not the issuance of a security in satisfaction of a right to enforce payment of an amount by the entity, or

(B) the issuance of the security in satisfaction of a right to enforce payment of an amount that became payable by the entity on another security of the entity before July 20, 2011, if the other security was a stapled security on July 20, 2011 and the issuance was made under a term or condition of the other security in effect on July 20, 2011;

(b) if paragraph (a) does not apply to the entity and one or more securities of the entity would have been stapled securities of the entity on July 19, 2011 had the definition "stapled security" in this subsection come into force on July 19, 2011, the period that begins on July 20, 2011 and ends on the earliest of

(i) July 20, 2012,

(ii) the first day after July 20, 2011 on which any of those securities is materially altered, and

(iii) the first day after July 20, 2011 on which any security of the entity becomes a stapled security other than by way of

(A) a transaction

(I) that is completed under the terms of an agreement in writing entered into before July 20, 2011 if no party to the agreement may be excused from completing the transaction as a result of amendments to this Act, and

(II) that is not the issuance of a security in satisfaction of a right to enforce payment of an amount by the entity, or

(B) the issuance of the security in satisfaction of a right to enforce payment of an amount that became payable by the entity on another security of the entity before July 20, 2011, if the other security was a stapled security on July 20, 2011 and the issuance was made under a term or condition of the other security in effect on July 20, 2011; and

(c) in any other case, if the entity is a subsidiary of another entity on July 20, 2011 and the other entity has a transition period, the period that begins on July 20, 2011 and ends on the earliest of

(i) the day on which the other entity's transition period ends,

(ii) the first day after July 20, 2011 on which the entity ceases to be a subsidiary of the other entity, and

(iii) the first day after July 20, 2011 on which any security of the entity becomes a stapled security other than by way of

(A) a transaction

(I) that is completed under the terms of an agreement in writing entered into before July 20, 2011 if no party to the agreement may be excused from completing the transaction as a result of amendments to this Act, and

(II) that is not the issuance of a security in satisfaction of a right to enforce payment of an amount by the entity, or

(B) the issuance of the security in satisfaction of a right to enforce payment of an amount that became payable by the entity on another security of the entity before July 20, 2011, if the other security was a stapled security on July 20, 2011 and the issuance was made under a term or condition of the other security in effect on July 20, 2011.

Related Provisions: 12.6(1) — Definitions in 18.3(1) apply to 12.6.

(2) Property representing security — For the purpose of determining whether a particular security of an entity is a stapled security, if a receipt or similar property (referred to in this subsection as the "receipt") represents all or a portion of the particular security and the receipt would be described in paragraphs (a) and (b) of the definition "stapled security" in subsection (1) if it were a security of the entity, then

(a) the particular security is deemed to be described in those paragraphs; and

(b) a security that would be a reference security in respect of the receipt is deemed to be a reference security in respect of the particular security.

(3) Amounts not deductible — Notwithstanding any other provision of this Act, in computing the income of a particular entity for a taxation year from a business or property, no deduction may be made in respect of an amount

(a) that is paid or payable after July 19, 2011, unless the amount is paid or payable in respect of the entity's transition period; and

(b) that is

(i) interest paid or payable on a liability of the particular entity that is a stapled security, unless each reference security in respect of the stapled security is a liability, or

(ii) if a security of the particular entity, a subsidiary of the particular entity or an entity of which the particular entity is a subsidiary is a reference security in respect of a stapled security of a real estate investment trust or a subsidiary of a real estate investment trust, an amount paid or payable to

(A) the real estate investment trust,

(B) a subsidiary of the real estate investment trust, or

(C) any person or partnership on condition that any person or partnership pays or makes payable an amount to the real estate investment trust or a subsidiary of the real estate investment trust.

Related Provisions: 12.6(3) — Anti-avoidance rule; 18.3(1)"security"(b)(ii) — Anti-avoidance.

Notes: 18.3 (added by 2013 budget bill #2 effective July 20, 2011) provides rules for stapled securities (separate securities that are "stapled" together and not independently transferable). Stapled securities allow deductions that frustrate the policy objectives of the tax on SIFTs (see Notes to 104(16)) and the tax regime for REITs (see 122.1(1)"real estate investment trust").

18.3(3) denies the deduction of certain amounts (generally interest paid or payable on a debt obligation that is a stapled security, or rent paid or payable to an entity that is part of a stapled security structure that includes a REIT), and provides a transition period to defer the application of the deduction denial rule in certain circumstances. Where a stapled security is unstapled and later restapled, see 12.6.

In a typical stapled-security arrangement involving a public corp, a share and debt of the corporation (or a subsidiary) are stapled together. 18.3(3)(b)(i) denies a deduction for interest paid on the debt.

In a typical stapled-security arrangement involving a REIT, an equity interest in the REIT (or a subsidiary) is stapled to an equity interest in a taxable entity (or a sub). The taxable entity (or its sub) carries on a business that the REIT could not carry on directly without losing its REIT status, leasing property from the REIT. 18.3(3)(b)(ii) denies deduction for payments, such as rent or interest, made by the taxable entity (or its sub) to the REIT (or its sub).

For discussion see CBA/CICA Joint Committee submission to Finance, Sept. 25, 2012; Mitchell Sherman & Jarrett Freeman, "Stapled Securities Under Fire", XVIII(2) *Corporate Finance* (Federated Press) 2109-13 (2012).

Definitions [s. 18.3]: "amount", "business" — 248(1); "capital interest" — 108(1), 248(1); "corporation" — 248(1), *Interpretation Act* 35(1); "entity", "equity value" — 18.3(1), 122.1(1); "estate" — 104(1), 248(1); "fair market value" — see 69(1) Notes; "partnership" — see 96(1) Notes; "person", "property" — 248(1); "public market" — 122.1(1), 248(1); "real estate investment trust" — 18.3(1), 122.1(1); "receipt" — 18.3(2); "reference security" — 18.3(1)"stapled security"(a); "security" — 18.3(1); "share" — 248(1); "SIFT partnership" — 197(1), (8), 248(1); "SIFT trust" — 122.1(1), (2), 248(1); "stapled security" — 18.3(1), (2); "subsidiary" — 18.3(1); "taxation year" — 249; "transition period" — 18.3(1); "trust" — 104(1), 248(1), (3); "writing" — *Interpretation Act* 35(1).

19. (1) Limitation re advertising expense — newspapers —
In computing income, no deduction shall be made in respect of an otherwise deductible outlay or expense of a taxpayer for advertising space in an issue of a newspaper for an advertisement directed primarily to a market in Canada unless

(a) the issue is a Canadian issue of a Canadian newspaper; or

(b) the issue is an issue of a newspaper that would be a Canadian issue of a Canadian newspaper except that

(i) its type has been wholly set in the United States or has been partly set in the United States with the remainder having been set in Canada, or

(ii) it has been wholly printed in the United States or has been partly printed in the United States with the remainder having been printed in Canada.

Related Provisions: 19.01 — Limitation for magazines and other periodicals.

Notes: 19(1) disallows a deduction for advertising in a foreign newspaper aimed at the Canadian market (but not the U.S., since the 1989 Canada-US Free Trade Agreement). This is a political/cultural rule designed to force Canadian advertisers to patronize Canadian publications. However, for magazines, 19.01 is less restrictive; s. 19 now applies only to newspapers.

Foreign newspaper ads listing Canadian real estate for sale are deductible, since they are aimed at a market outside Canada: VIEWS doc 2004-0071381E5.

Online and social media advertising are not caught by 19, 19.01 or 19.1: VIEWS docs 9618735, 2017-0691521M4, 2017-0691771M4, 2017-0695331M4, 2017-0697311M4, 2017-0697751M4, 2017-0697761M4, 2017-0700121M4, 2017-0708891M4, 2017-0719471E5 (the issue has been referred to Finance).

19(1) amended by 2001 technical bill, effective for advertisements placed in an issue dated after May 2000, to delete reference to periodicals.

(2) [Repealed under former Act]

(3) Where subsec. (1) does not apply — Subsection (1) does
not apply with respect to an advertisement in a special issue or edition of a newspaper that is edited in whole or in part and printed and published outside Canada if that special issue or edition is devoted to features or news related primarily to Canada and the publishers thereof publish such an issue or edition not more frequently than twice a year.

(4) [Repealed under former Act]

(5) Definitions — In this section,

"Canadian issue" of a newspaper means an issue, including a special issue,

(a) the type of which, other than the type for advertisements or features, is set in Canada,

(b) all of which, exclusive of any comics supplement, is printed in Canada,

(c) that is edited in Canada by individuals resident in Canada, and

(d) that is published in Canada;

Notes: 19(5)"Canadian issue" amended by 2001 technical bill, for advertisements placed in an issue dated after May 2000. This was 19(5)(a) before RSC 1985 (5th Supp) consolidation for tax years ending after Nov. 1991.

"Canadian newspaper" means a newspaper the exclusive right to produce and publish issues of which is held by one or more of the following:

(a) a Canadian citizen,

(b) a partnership

(i) in which interests representing in value at least ¾ of the total value of the partnership property are beneficially owned by, and

(ii) at least ¾ of each income or loss of which from any source is included in the determination of the income of,

corporations described in paragraph (e) or Canadian citizens or any combination thereof,

(c) an association or society of which at least ¾ of the members are Canadian citizens,

(d) Her Majesty in right of Canada or a province, or a municipality in Canada, or

(e) a corporation

(i) that is incorporated under the laws of Canada or a province,

(ii) of which the chairperson or other presiding officer and at least ¾ of the directors or other similar officers are Canadian citizens, and

(iii) that, if it is a corporation having share capital, is

(A) a public corporation a class or classes of shares of the capital stock of which are listed on a designated stock exchange in Canada, other than a corporation controlled by citizens or subjects of a country other than Canada, or

(B) a corporation of which at least ¾ of the shares having full voting rights under all circumstances, and shares having a fair market value in total of at least ¾ of the fair market value of all of the issued shares of the corporation, are beneficially owned by Canadian citizens or by public corporations a class or classes of shares of the capital stock of which are listed on a designated stock exchange in Canada, other than a public corporation controlled by citizens or subjects of a country other than Canada,

and, for the purposes of clause (B), where shares of a class of the capital stock of a corporation are owned, or deemed by this definition to be owned, at any time by another corporation (in this definition referred to as the "holding corporation"), other than a public corporation a class or classes of shares of the capital stock of which are listed on a designated stock exchange in Canada, each shareholder of the holding corporation shall be deemed to own at that time that proportion of the number of such shares of that class that

(C) the fair market value of the shares of the capital stock of the holding corporation owned at that time by the shareholder

is of

(D) the fair market value of all the issued shares of the capital stock of the holding corporation outstanding at that time,

and, where at any time shares of a class of the capital stock of a corporation are owned, or are deemed by this definition to be owned, by a partnership, each member of the partnership shall be deemed to own at that time the least proportion of the number of such shares of that class that

(E) the member's share of the income or loss of the partnership from any source for its fiscal period that includes that time

is of

(F) the income or loss of the partnership from that source for its fiscal period that includes that time,

and for this purpose, where the income and loss of a partnership from any source for a fiscal period are nil, the partnership shall be deemed to have had income from that source for that period in the amount of $1,000,000;

Related Provisions: 19(5.1) — Extended meaning of "Canadian citizen"; 19(6) — Trust property; 19(7) — Grace period on ceasing to be Canadian newspaper; 19(8) — Anti-avoidance — certain newspapers and periodicals deemed not to be Canadian.

Notes: When a newspaper ceases to be a "Canadian newspaper", there is a 12-month grace period under 19(7), after which 19(1) applies: VIEWS doc 2003-004425.

Periodicals are now under 19.01.

19(5)"Canadian newspaper"(e) amended by 2007 budget bill #2 to change "prescribed stock exchange" to "designated stock exchange", effective Dec. 14, 2007.

Definition earlier amended by 2001 technical bill, 1991 technical bill. 19(5)"Canadian newspaper or periodical" was 19(5)(b) before RSC 1985 (5th Supp) consolidation for tax years ending after Nov. 1991.

"issue of a non-Canadian newspaper or periodical [para. 19(5)(c)]" — [Repealed under former Act]

Notes: 19(5)(c) repealed effective 1989, due to Canada-U.S. Free Trade Agreement. It defined "issue of a non-Canadian newspaper or periodical", no longer used in 19(1).

"substantially the same" — [Repealed]

Notes: 19(5)"substantially the same" (more than 20% the same) repealed by 2001 technical bill, for advertisements placed in an issue dated after May 2000. It was 19(5)(d) before RSC 1985 (5th Supp) consolidation for tax years ending after Nov. 1991.

"United States" means

(a) the United States of America, but does not include Puerto Rico, the Virgin Islands, Guam or any other United States possession or territory, and

(b) any areas beyond the territorial sea of the United States within which, in accordance with international law and its domestic laws, the United States may exercise rights with respect to the seabed and subsoil and the natural resources of those areas.

Notes: 19(5)"United States" was 19(5)(e) before RSC 1985 (5th Supp) consolidation for tax years ending after Nov. 1991.

(5.1) Interpretation ["Canadian citizen"] — In this section, each of the following is deemed to be a Canadian citizen:

(a) a trust or corporation described in paragraph 149(1)(o) or (o.1) formed in connection with a pension plan that exists for the benefit of individuals a majority of whom are Canadian citizens;

(b) a trust described in paragraph 149(1)(r) or (x), the annuitant in respect of which is a Canadian citizen;

(c) a mutual fund trust, within the meaning assigned by subsection 132(6), other than a mutual fund trust the majority of the units of which are held by citizens or subjects of a country other than Canada;

(d) a trust, each beneficiary of which is a person, partnership, association or society described in any of paragraphs (a) to (e) of the definition "Canadian newspaper" in subsection (5); and

(e) a person, association or society described in paragraph (c) or (d) of the definition "Canadian newspaper" in subsection (5).

Notes: Paras. (a) and (b) refer to pension plans, RRSPs and RRIFs.

19(5.1) ensures that Canadian pension funds and certain other entities that own Canadian newspapers are "Canadian citizens" for the ownership requirements of s. 19.

19(5.1) added by 2001 technical bill, this version effective in respect of advertisements placed in an issue dated after June 2000.

(6) Trust property — Where the right that is held by any person, partnership, association or society described in the definition "Canadian newspaper" in subsection (5) to produce and publish issues of a newspaper is held as property of a trust or estate, the newspaper is not a Canadian newspaper unless each beneficiary under the trust or estate is a person, partnership, association or society described in that definition.

Notes: 19(6) amended by 2001 technical bill, effective for advertisements placed in an issue dated after May 2000.

(7) Grace period — A Canadian newspaper that would, but for this subsection, cease to be a Canadian newspaper, is deemed to

continue to be a Canadian newspaper until the end of the 12th month that follows the month in which it would, but for this subsection, have ceased to be a Canadian newspaper.

Notes: 19(7) amended by 2001 technical bill, effective for advertisements placed in an issue dated after May 2000.

(8) Non-Canadian newspaper — Where at any time one or more persons or partnerships that are not described in any of paragraphs (a) to (e) of the definition "Canadian newspaper" in subsection (5) have any direct or indirect influence that, if exercised, would result in control in fact of a person or partnership that holds a right to produce or publish issues of a newspaper, the newspaper is deemed not to be a Canadian newspaper at that time.

Related Provisions: 256(5.1) — General test for "control in fact"; 256(5.11) — Factors to consider in determining direct or indirect influence (for a corporation only).

Notes: 19(8) amended by 2001 technical bill, for ads placed in an issue dated after May 2000 (see these Notes up to the 58th ed. re *Reader's Digest*, *Sports Illustrated*, *Time*). Added by 1995 split-run periodicals bill (S.C. 1995, c. 46).

Definitions [s. 19]: "beneficially owned" — 248(3); "Canada" — 255, *Interpretation Act* 35(1); "Canadian citizen" — 19(5.1); "Canadian issue" — 19(5); "Canadian newspaper" — 19(5), (8); "class", "class of shares" — 248(6); "corporation" — 248(1), *Interpretation Act* 35(1); "designated stock exchange" — 248(1), 262; "direct or indirect influence" — 256(5.11); "estate" — 104(1), 248(1); "fair market value" — see 69(1) Notes; "Her Majesty" — *Interpretation Act* 35(1); "individual" — 248(1); "month" — *Interpretation Act* 35(1); "mutual fund trust" — 132(6)–(7), 248(1); "paid-up capital" — 89(1), 248(1); "partnership" — see 96(1) Notes; "person" — 248(1); "property" — 248(1); "province" — *Interpretation Act* 35(1); "public corporation" — 89(1), 248(1); "resident in Canada" — 94(3)(a), 250; "share", "shareholder" — 248(1); "substantially" — 19(5); "taxpayer" — 248(1); "territorial sea" — *Interpretation Act* 35(1); "trust" — 104(1), 248(1), (3); "United States" — 19(5).

19.01 (1) Definitions — The definitions in this subsection apply in this section.

"advertisement directed at the Canadian market" has the same meaning as the expression "directed at the Canadian market" in section 2 of the *Foreign Publishers Advertising Services Act* and includes a reference to that expression made by or under that Act.

Notes: Section 2 of the *FPASA*, S.C. 1999, c. 23, provides:

"directed at the Canadian market", in relation to advertising services, means that the target market related to those advertising services consists primarily of consumers in Canada.

For the meaning of "primarily" see 73(3) Notes.

See also Notes at end of 19.01.

"original editorial content" in respect of an issue of a periodical means non-advertising content

(a) the author of which is a Canadian citizen or a permanent resident of Canada within the meaning assigned by the *Immigration Act* and, for this purpose, "author" includes a writer, a journalist, an illustrator and a photographer; or

(b) that is created for the Canadian market and has not been published in any other edition of that issue of the periodical published outside Canada.

"periodical" has the meaning assigned by section 2 of the *Foreign Publishers Advertising Services Act*.

Related Provisions: 19.01(6) — Meaning of "edition".

Notes: Section 2 of the *FPASA*, S.C. 1999, c. 23, provides:

"periodical" means a printed publication that appears in consecutively numbered or dated issues, published under a common title, usually at regular intervals, not more than once every week, excluding special issues, and at least twice every year. It does not include a catalogue, a directory, a newsletter or a newspaper.

(2) Limitation re advertising expenses — periodicals — Subject to subsections (3) and (4), in computing income, no deduction shall be made by a taxpayer in respect of an otherwise deductible outlay or expense for advertising space in an issue of a periodical for an advertisement directed at the Canadian market.

Notes: See Notes at end of 19.01.

(3) 100% deduction — A taxpayer may deduct in computing income an outlay or expense of the taxpayer for advertising space in

an issue of a periodical for an advertisement directed at the Canadian market if

(a) the original editorial content in the issue is 80% or more of the total non-advertising content in the issue; and

(b) the outlay or expense would, but for subsection (2), be deductible in computing the taxpayer's income.

Related Provisions: 19.01(5) — Calculation of percentage.

Notes: See Notes at end of 19.01 and to 19(1).

(4) 50% deduction — A taxpayer may deduct in computing income 50% of an outlay or expense of the taxpayer for advertising space in an issue of a periodical for an advertisement directed at the Canadian market if

(a) the original editorial content in the issue is less than 80% of the total non-advertising content in the issue; and

(b) the outlay or expense would, but for subsection (2), be deductible in computing the taxpayer's income.

Related Provisions: 19.01(5) — Calculation of percentage.

(5) Application — For the purposes of subsections (3) and (4),

(a) the percentage that original editorial content is of total non-advertising content is the percentage that the total space occupied by original editorial content in the issue is of the total space occupied by non-advertising content in the issue; and

(b) the Minister may obtain the advice of the Department of Canadian Heritage for the purpose of

(i) determining the result obtained under paragraph (a), and

(ii) interpreting any expression defined in this section that is defined in the *Foreign Publishers Advertising Services Act*.

(6) Editions of issues — For the purposes of this section,

(a) where an issue of a periodical is published in several versions, each version is an edition of that issue; and

(b) where an issue of a periodical is published in only one version, that version is an edition of that issue.

Notes [s. 19.01]: 19.01 implements the Canada-U.S. Agreement of June 3, 1999 regarding periodicals (Department of Foreign Affairs and International Trade news releases, May 26, 1999 and June 4, 1999). It allows full deductibility of expenses for advertisements published in issues of U.S. periodicals that contain at least 80% original or Canadian editorial content, and 50% deductibility for advertising expenses in other periodicals, regardless of the ownership of the periodical. See also Notes to 19(1).

Under the agreement, the *Foreign Publishers Advertising Services Act* (S.C. 1999, c. 23), which would have prohibited foreign publishers from selling advertising aimed primarily at the Canadian market, now allows two limited forms of access: a *de minimis* exemption allowing foreign publishers to publish up to 18% of ads aimed at the Canadian market and an exemption giving foreign publishers access to a greater percentage of the Canadian advertising services market, provided that they create majority Canadian content and establish a new periodicals business in Canada. Acquisitions of Canadian publishers will not be permitted.

A Canadian magazine (Vue) tried to force CRA to disallow advertisers' expenses paid to a competitor (SEE) under 19.01 on the basis that SEE was not Canadian once Conrad Black renounced his Canadian citizenship: *783783 Alberta* [also reported as *7837783 Alberta*], 2010 ABCA 226. The Court ruled that CRA does not owe a duty of care to other taxpayers to assess taxpayers any particular way.

19.01 added by 2001 technical bill, for advertisements placed in an issue dated after May 2000. For earlier issues, s. 19 applied to both newspapers and periodicals.

Definitions [s. 19.01]: "advertisement directed at the Canadian market" — 19.01(5); "Canada" — 255, *Interpretation Act* 35(1); "edition" — 19.01(6); "Minister" — 248(1); "original editorial content", "periodical" — 19.01(1); "taxpayer" — 248(1).

19.1 (1) Limitation re advertising expense on broadcasting undertaking — Subject to subsection (2), in computing income, no deduction shall be made in respect of an otherwise deductible outlay or expense of a taxpayer made or incurred after September 21, 1976 for an advertisement directed primarily to a market in Canada and broadcast by a foreign broadcasting undertaking.

Notes: 19.1 does not apply to online advertising: see Notes to 19(1). Advertising on a radio station near the border may fall under 19.1(1) based on the number of listeners on each side of the border; but 19.1(1) does not apply to an ad agency if it is simply an agent of its customer: VIEWS doc 2006-0185441E5.

(2) Exception — In computing income, a deduction may be made in respect of an outlay or expense made or incurred before September 22, 1977 for an advertisement directed primarily to a market in Canada and broadcast by a foreign broadcasting undertaking pursuant to

(a) a written agreement entered into on or before January 23, 1975; or

(b) a written agreement entered into after January 23, 1975 and before September 22, 1976 if the agreement is for a term of one year or less and by its express terms is not capable of being extended or renewed.

(3) [Repealed under former Act]

(4) Definitions — In this section,

"foreign broadcasting undertaking" means a network operation or a broadcasting transmitting undertaking located outside Canada or on a ship or aircraft not registered in Canada;

"network" includes any operation involving two or more broadcasting undertakings whereby control over all or any part of the programs or program schedules of any of the broadcasting undertakings involved in the operation is delegated to a network operator.

Notes: See Notes to 188.1(5) re meaning of "includes".

Definitions [s. 19.1]: "broadcasting" — *Interpretation Act* 35(1); "Canada" — 255; "foreign broadcasting undertaking", "network" — 19.1(4); "taxpayer" — 248(1).

20. (1) Deductions permitted in computing income from business or property — Notwithstanding paragraphs 18(1)(a), (b) and (h), in computing a taxpayer's income for a taxation year from a business or property, there may be deducted such of the following amounts as are wholly applicable to that source or such part of the following amounts as may reasonably be regarded as applicable thereto:

Notes: In 20(1) opening words, "that source" refers to the "income ... from a business or property" (and this overrides previous contrary interpretations), and expenses not wholly applicable to a source of income must be prorated: VIEWS doc 2010-0384681I7. Thus, 20(1)(z) cannot apply to a lease cancellation payment made for a personal-use condo: 2019-0812611C6 [2019 APFF q.2].

(a) **capital cost of property [CCA]** — such part of the capital cost to the taxpayer of property, or such amount in respect of the capital cost to the taxpayer of property, if any, as is allowed by regulation;

Proposed Amendment — $1.5m immediate expensing for CCPCs

Federal Budget, Supplementary Information, April 19, 2021: See under Reg. 1100(1)(a) opening words.

Related Provisions: 13(4.3)(c) — Where franchise, concession or license is exchanged; 13(5) — Transferred property; 13(5.2) — Rules applicable; 13(6) — Misclassified property; 13(7) — Change in use of depreciable property (DP); 13(11) — Automobile deduction; 13(12) — Lobbying expenses; 13(14) — Conversion cost of vessel; 13(21.2) — Transfer of property where UCC exceeds fair market value; 13(26)–(32) — Restriction on deduction before available for use; 18(3.1)(a) — Costs relating to construction of building or ownership of land; 18(12) — Home office expense; 20(1.1) — Definitions in 13(21) apply to regulations; 20(16), (16.1) — Terminal loss; 21 — Cost of borrowed money; 28(1)(g) — Deduction from farming or fishing income when using cash method; 37(6) — Scientific research capital expenditures; 68 — Allocation of cost between property and services; 70(13) — Capital cost of DP on death; 80(9)(c) — Reduction of capital cost on debt forgiveness ignored for CCA purposes; 85(5) — Rules on transfers of DP; 87(2)(d.1) — Amalgamations — DP acquired from predecessor corporation; 104(5)(a) — DP — deemed disposition by trust; 107.2(e) — Distribution of DP by retirement compensation arrangement; 107.4(3)(d) — Rollover of DP to trust; 125.4(4) — No Canadian film/video production credit to corporation if investor can claim CCA; 127.52(1)(b), (c) — Minimum tax — add-back of some CCA; 132.2(3)(d), (5)(d) — Deemed capital cost of DP following mutual fund reorganization; 138(11.8) — Transfer of DP by non-resident insurer; 164(6) — Refund — disposition of property by legal representative of deceased taxpayer. See also at end of s. 20.

Notes: Capital cost allowance (CCA) is claimed in place of accounting depreciation or amortization. Capital expenses are otherwise non-deductible: 18(1)(b). See Notes to 54"capital property" on the distinction between capital property (eligible for CCA) and inventory; and Notes to 13(21)"depreciable property".

CCA is allowed by class (pool) rather than by individual asset; the rates are set out in Reg. 1100 and the classes of property are in Schedule II at the end of the Regulations.

Some assets, however, are each deemed to be a separate class; see Reg. 1101. CCA for most classes is claimed as a percentage of a declining balance. See also Notes to 13(21)"undepreciated capital cost" (UCC). Note that in determining CCA for a building, the land value is excluded: Reg. 1102(2). For software that assists in determining which class, see *CCA Navigator* at bluejlegal.com.

CCA can be claimed only by the owner: *Saskatoon Community Broadcasting* (1958), 20 Tax A.B.C. 97; *Shenanigans Media*, 2017 TCC 180, para. 12; VIEWS doc 2018-0768871C6 [2018 APFF q.16]. The fact a vehicle is registered in another person's name does not preclude a claim by the beneficial owner: 2005-0122211E5; Income Tax Folio S3-F4-C1 ¶1.22; *Andrews*, 2007 TCC 312 (and see Notes to 54"capital property" at "Bare trustee"). See also Notes to 13(7)(a) and *Interpretation Act* s. 8.1 re "acquisition" of property.

One can choose to claim less than the maximum allowable (see opening words of Reg. 1100(1)(a)), and thus keep a higher UCC for future years; for CRA policy on changing the claim see Information Circular 84-1 (still current: VIEWS doc 2014-0550381C6 [2014 TEI q.E2]). No direct deduction is available for the cost of capital property other than via CCA: 18(1)(b). CCA claims, once made, cannot be unilaterally reduced later so as to extend loss carryforwards: see 111(5) Notes at "Refreshing losses".

When determining CCA on a new asset, note in particular the "available for use" rule in 13(26)-(32), the rule in Reg. 1100(2) for the year the property is acquired and the change-in-control rules in 13(24)-(25). Property is "acquired" when title passes or when the purchaser has all incidents of title such as possession, use and risk: *Terexcavation Antoine Grant*, 2002 CarswellNat 5183 (TCC), and possession under a Quebec instalment sale (*Civil Code* s. 1745) is sufficient: VIEWS doc 2007-0237551E5. CCA can be claimed only if the property was acquired in order to earn income from it: Reg. 1102(1)(c).

There is no clear policy underlying 20(1)(a) that makes it abusive to claim CCA based on "legal" cost (purchase price paid) rather than the "economic" cost of an asset: *Canada Trustco*, 2005 SCC 54 (see Notes to 245(4)).

On a dispute where CCA was claimed for years with no indication of irregularity, and purchase receipts from many years back are unavailable, CRA must show some "basis" for challenging UCC: *Benedict*, 2012 TCC 174, para. 15. In *Sicurella*, 2013 TCC 79, the ACB recorded in a taxpayer's 1994 election under 110.6(19) was taken as her cost, absent other evidence.

CCA can be claimed on a car used for earning rental income (not only business income): VIEWS doc 2012-0443281E5.

See also Income Tax Folio S3-F4-C1; Mancell, *Capital Cost Allowance* (WoltersKluwer, 4th ed., 2019); Bonvie et al., "The Capital Cost Allowance System", 43(5) *Canadian Tax Journal* 1245-64 (1995); Keey, "Depreciable Property: Tips and Traps", 2010(13) *Tax Times* (Carswell) 1-2 (July 16, 2010); Gamble, *Taxation of Canadian Mining* (Carswell, looseleaf or Taxnet Pro Reference Centre [TPRC]), chap. 4; Carr & Calverley, *Canadian Resource Taxation* (Carswell, looseleaf or TPRC), §4.13; Arnold et al., *Timing and Income Taxation* (ctf.ca, 2nd ed., 2015), chap. 10.

Regulations: Part XI (CCA rules); Part XVII (farming and fishing property owned since before 1972); Reg. Sch. II–Sch. VI (classes of property).

I.T. Application Rules: 18(2), 20, 26.1(2).

Income Tax Folios: S3-F4-C1: General discussion of CCA [replaces IT-128R and IT-285R2]; S4-F7-C1: Amalgamations of Canadian corporations [replaces IT-474R2].

Interpretation Bulletins: IT-79R3: CCA — Buildings or other structures; IT-121R3: Election to capitalize cost of borrowed money (cancelled); IT-187: Customer lists and ledger accounts; IT-195R4: Rental property — CCA restrictions; IT-267R2: CCA — Vessels; IT-283R2: CCA — video tapes, video tape cassettes, films, computer software and master recording media (cancelled); IT-291R3: Transfer of property to a corporation under subsection 85(1); IT-304R2: Condominiums; IT-306R2: CCA — Contractor's movable equipment; IT-317R: CCA — Radio and television equipment (cancelled); IT-324: Emphyteutic lease (cancelled); IT-325R2: Property transfers after separation, divorce and annulment; IT-327: CCA — Elections under regulation 1103 (cancelled); IT-336R: CCA — Pollution control property (cancelled); IT-371: Rental property — meaning of "principal business"; IT-422: Definition of tools; IT-464R: CCA — Leasehold interests; IT-465R: Non-resident beneficiaries of trusts; IT-469R: CCA — Earth-moving equipment; IT-472: CCA — Class 8 property; IT-477: CCA — Patents, franchises, concessions and licences; IT-481: Timber resource property and timber limits; IT-485: Cost of clearing or levelling land [to be amended re golf courses, per I.T. Technical News 20]; IT-492: CCA — Industrial mineral mines; IT-501: CCA — Logging assets.

Information Circulars: 84-1: Revision of capital cost allowance claims and other permissive deductions; 87-5: Capital cost of property where trade-in is involved.

I.T. Technical News: 1 (sales commission expenses of mutual-fund limited partnerships); 3 (loss utilization within a corporate group); 12 ("millennium bug" expenditures); 20 (tax treatment of golf courses).

CRA Audit Manual: 11.3.5: Revision of CCA and other permissive deductions; 12.1.0: Taxpayer requests (TPR) and general adjustment forms (GAF); 12.15.9: Revising capital cost allowance and other permissive deductions.

Advance Tax Rulings: ATR-1: Transfer of legal title in land to bare trustee corporation — mortgagee's requirements sole reason for transfer.

Forms: T1-CP Summ: Summary of certified productions; T1-CP Supp: Statement of certified productions; T2 Sched. 8: Capital cost allowance; T776: Statement of real

estate rentals; T777: Statement of employment expenses; T2125: Statement of business or professional activities, area A; T4044: Employment expenses [guide].

(b) **incorporation expenses** — the lesser of

(i) the portion of the amount (that is not otherwise deductible in computing the income of the taxpayer) that is an expense incurred in the year for the incorporation of a corporation, and

(ii) $3,000 less the total of all amounts each of which is an amount deducted by another taxpayer in respect of the incorporation of the corporation;

Notes: Since 2017, 20(1)(b) provides a deduction for up to $3,000 of incorporation expenses to whoever incurs the expense, whether the corporation or a shareholder. (Presumably "incurred" means "incurred by the taxpayer".)

If incorporation expenses exceed $3,000, the 2016 Budget Supplementary Information and Finance Technical Notes both say the first $3,000 is deductible under 20(1)(b) and the balance is included in Class 14.1 for future CCA. However, Class 14.1(c)(iii) excludes "property in respect of which *any* amount is deductible" in computing business income, which arguably excludes the balance from being added (though perhaps a corporation's existence is not "property").

Change from "eligible capital property" to Class 14.1 (2017)

Before 2017, 20(1)(b) provided an annual deduction for "eligible capital property" (ECP), generally at 7% of a declining balance which was 3/4 of amounts paid for intangibles such as goodwill, customer lists and indefinite-life franchises or licences. (See "Pre-2017 ECP rules" below.) S. 14 implemented this system, which was in place since 1972 and had become more and more complex. It was simplified by creating a new capital cost allowance (CCA) class 14.1 and applying the regular CCA rules.

Class 14.1 generally includes goodwill, property that was ECP before 2017 and property acquired after 2016 whose cost would have fallen under the ECP rules. The full cost (instead of 3/4) is added to the undepreciated capital cost (UCC) of the class, and Reg. 1100(1)(a)(xii.1) allows CCA (via 20(1)(a)) at 5% on the declining balance (instead of 7% under former 20(1)(b)), while Reg. 1100(1)(c.1)(i) allows an extra 2% through 2026 on expenditures incurred before 2017. Each business's property is a separate class: Reg. 1101(1). On sale of Class 14.1 property, recapture can apply under 13(1). Gains beyond original cost are capital gains under 39(1), half-taxed under 38(a).

A consequence of this change for private corps is that a gain on sale of ECP, half-taxed before 2017 as business income under 14(1)(b), is now half-taxed as capital gain, with the half subject to a high passive-income tax rate of about 50% (see Notes to 123.3), until dividends are paid out. Businesses with unrealized gains were advised to consider crystallizing or selling ECP by the end of 2016 to avoid this: Wen, "Pre-2017 ECP Crystallizations for CCPCs", 6(3) *Canadian Tax Focus* (ctf.ca) 1 (Aug. 2016).

Another consequence arises on sale of a business with an amount allocated to goodwill. Available losses restricted to income from the business, such as home office expense carryforwards (18(12)(c)) or restricted farm losses (111(1)(c)), could previously be deducted against the 14(1) income inclusion, but cannot be claimed against the taxable capital gain.

On the effect of these amendments on FAPI, see Baker & Bunn, "FAs and the Repeal of the ECP Regime", 24(9) *Canadian Tax Highlights* (ctf.ca) 4 (Sept. 2016).

See also Spiers, "ECP Planning", 6(4) *Canadian Tax Focus* (ctf.ca) 1-2 (Nov. 2016); Mancell, "CRA Interpretations of the New Class 14.1 Rules", 2345 *Tax Topics* (CCH) 1-3 (Feb. 16, 2017); Chow, "Selected Issues for Private Corporations: Eligible Capital Property", 2016 Cdn Tax Foundation conference report, at 28:1-10; Paproski, "Effectively Dealing with Eligible Capital Property Under the New Regime", 2017 Prairie Provinces Tax Conference (ctf.ca).

Transitional rules for the change from ECP to Class 14.1: see Notes to 13(34).

20(1)(b) amended by 2016 budget bill #2, for expenses incurred after 2016. It read:

(b) **cumulative eligible capital amount** — such amount as the taxpayer claims in respect of a business, not exceeding 7% of the taxpayer's cumulative eligible capital in respect of the business at the end of the year except that, where the year is less than 12 months, the amount allowed as a deduction under this paragraph shall not exceed that proportion of the maximum amount otherwise allowable that the number of days in the taxation year is of 365;

Related Provisions: 14(1) — Inclusion in income from business; 14(5) — Definitions — "cumulative eligible capital", "eligible capital expenditure"; 24 — Ceasing to carry on business; 28(1)(g) — Deduction from farming or fishing income when using cash method; 70(5.1) — Eligible capital property of deceased; 70(9.8) — Farm or fishing property used by corporation or partnership; 87(2)(f) — Amalgamations — cumulative eligible capital; 107(2)(f) — Capital interest distribution by personal or prescribed trust; 111(5.2) — CEC after change in control. See also at end of s. 20.

Interpretation Bulletins: IT-99R5: Legal and accounting fees; IT-123R4: Disposition of and transactions involving eligible capital property; IT-123R6: Transactions involving eligible capital property; IT-291R3: Transfer of property to a corporation under subsection 85(1); IT-302R3: Losses of a corporation — the effect that acquisitions of control, amalgamations, and windings-up have on their deductibility; IT-313R2: Eligible capital property — rules where a taxpayer has ceased carrying on a business or has died; IT-341R4: Expenses of issuing shares, units in a trust, interests in a partnership or syndicate and expenses of borrowing money.

I.T. Technical News: 38 (purchase price allocation for rental properties).

Pre-2017 ECP rules (applicable until Dec. 31, 2016)

Eligible capital property (ECP) is goodwill and other purchased intangibles without a fixed lifespan. See IT-143R3 for details, and 14(5)"eligible capital expenditure" for the substantive definition. (Patents and other intangibles with a *fixed* life generally fall under the CCA system and are grouped in Class 14 or 44.) An amount expended on ECP is an eligible capital expenditure. 3/4 of all eligible capital expenditures constitute the taxpayer's cumulative eligible capital (CEC). Under pre-2017 20(1)(b), 7% of the declining balance of cumulative eligible capital can be claimed as a deduction each year. On a sale of ECP, there may be an income inclusion (recapture) under 14(1): 75% inclusion up to the 20(1)(b) deduction claimed, and 50% inclusion thereafter (same rate as capital gains). A capital gain excludes a gain on ECP, so "capital property" excludes ECP: 39(1)(a)(i), VIEWS doc 2016-0637031E5. On ceasing to carry on business, the taxpayer may deduct the entire remaining balance of CEC under 24(1).

The following were ECP: customer list, easement, incorporation expense, milk quota, non-competition payment, professional organization admission fee, stock exchange entrance fee, and trademark purchased (IT-143R3); client list (*Martin*, 2009 TCC 152; VIEWS doc 2010-0380081E5); consulting fees to reorganize related companies to improve after-tax return from U.S. subsidiary (*Potash Corp.*, 2011 TCC 213); employee option surrender payments by company (*Devon Canada*, 2018 TCC 170); farm quota (2010-0369801E5); franchise fee with automatic indefinite renewal (2010-0365771E5); master recordings of music (*Unidisc*, 2021 QCCA 393 (leave to appeal to SCC requested)); photography training course (*Tiede*, 2011 TCC 84); professional licence exam fee (2004-0072821E5, 2005-0121351E5, 2008-0295831E5); prospectus cost if not deductible under 20(1)(e) (2009-0340251I7); takeover attempt costs where the shares would have been capital property (2011-039170117, 2017-0727041E5); taxi licence (*Mourtzis*, [1994] 1 C.T.C. 2801 (TCC)). See Class 14 if the item purchased has a fixed life.

The following were not ECP: acquisition of rights to pension surplus (2019-081764117); contract to acquire raw materials at favourable prices — a current expense (*Basell Canada*, 2007 TCC 685); earnout payments in a merger transaction (2015-060967117 [Killy He, "Earnouts Not ECE", 7(7) *Canadian Tax Focus* (ctf.ca) 5 (May 2017)]); expenditures on electricity generation projects that were deducted as CRCE (2013-0489911E5); fishing licence — property whose surrender led to a capital gain (*Winsor*, 2007 TCC 692; *Haché*, 2011 FCA 104; 2008-0274651M4 [overruling 2000-0038827]); goodwill included in the value of shares acquired (unless the business assets are acquired: 2006-0213071E5); investment in lottery terminal in Russia, as it was not for purposes of earning business income (*Rocheleau*, 2009 TCC 484); share acquisition costs (*Rio Tinto*, 2016 TCC 172, para. 206 (aff'd on other grounds 2018 FCA 124; leave to appeal denied 2019 CarswellNat 809 (SCC)); spinoff costs (*Rio Tinto* TCC, para. 207).

Goodwill is an unidentified intangible that arises from the expectation of future earnings and cannot be sold separately from the business: *Transalta Corp.*, 2012 FCA 20, para. 54. "Any attempt to define goodwill is doomed to failure. Rather, various characteristics inherent to the notion of goodwill should be identified and then used to ascertain goodwill on a case-by-case basis": para. 53.

A 20(1)(b) deduction was disallowed in *Atlantic Thermal*, 2016 TCC 135, para. 47, as the value of the goodwill had not been established.

On a real estate transaction, CRA will generally not consider that ECP is purchased and sold as a result of an accounting requirement (EIC 140, CICA Handbook §1581): *Income Tax Technical News* 38; 2007 Cdn Tax Foundation conference report at 4:20. On a share purchase, no amount can be allocated to goodwill: doc 2010-0383891E5 (and see now 13(36)). ECP acquired on an 85(1) rollover and then quickly sold may retain its status as ECP: 2008-0285151C6.

See also Severin, "Eligible Capital Property", 2003 Prairie Provinces Tax Conference (ctf.ca), 4:1-35; Kerr, "Eligible Capital Property", 2006 BC Tax Conf. 17:1-29; Bauer & Smith, "Eligible Capital Expenditures: Some Practical Issues", 2013 Cdn Tax Foundation conference report, 11:1-30.

20(1)(b) amended by 2000 Budget bill, for tax years beginning after Dec. 21, 2000.

(c) **interest** — an amount paid in the year or payable in respect of the year (depending upon the method regularly followed by the taxpayer in computing the taxpayer's income), pursuant to a legal obligation to pay interest on

(i) borrowed money used for the purpose of earning income from a business or property (other than borrowed money used to acquire property the income from which would be exempt or to acquire a life insurance policy),

(ii) an amount payable for property acquired for the purpose of gaining or producing income from the property or for the purpose of gaining or producing income from a business (other than property the income from which would be exempt or property that is an interest in a life insurance policy),

(iii) an amount paid to the taxpayer under

(A) an appropriation Act and on terms and conditions approved by the Treasury Board for the purpose of advancing or sustaining the technological capability of Canadian manufacturing or other industry, or

(B) the *Northern Mineral Exploration Assistance Regulations* made under an appropriation Act that provides for payments in respect of the Northern Mineral Grants Program, or

(iv) borrowed money used to acquire an interest in an annuity contract in respect of which section 12.2 applies (or would apply if the contract had an anniversary day in the year at a time when the taxpayer held the interest) except that, where annuity payments have begun under the contract in a preceding taxation year, the amount of interest paid or payable in the year shall not be deducted to the extent that it exceeds the amount included under section 12.2 in computing the taxpayer's income for the year in respect of the taxpayer's interest in the contract,

or a reasonable amount in respect thereof, whichever is the lesser;

Proposed Amendment — 20(1)(c) — Interest deduction limited to 30% of tax EBITDA (earnings-stripping rule)

Federal Budget, Supplementary Information, April 19, 2021: *Interest Deductibility Limits*

In general, businesses obtain external funding for their operations through either debt or equity. In Canada, as in most jurisdictions, interest expenses in respect of such debt are generally deductible against the income of the borrower. However, the deductibility of interest raises the potential that excessive debt or interest expense can be placed in Canadian businesses in a way that erodes the tax base, for example, through:

- interest payments to related non-residents in low-tax jurisdictions;
- the use of debt to finance investments that earn non-taxable income; or
- having Canadian businesses bear a disproportionate burden of a multinational group's third-party borrowings.

A number of rules provide some measure of protection of the Canadian tax base from erosion due to excessive debt and interest expense. These include the thin capitalization rules, which limit the deductibility of interest expense where the amount of debt owing to specified non-residents exceeds a 1.5-to-1 debt-to-equity ratio [18(4)-(8) — ed.]. However, the scope of these rules is limited.

A number of countries — notably other members of the G7 and the European Union member states — have introduced, or are in the process of introducing, limitations on interest deductibility that are consistent with the recommendations in the Action 4 Report of the BEPS Action Plan [see Proposed Amendments at end of s. 95, under Action 4 — ed.]. The recommended approach described in that report limits the amount of net interest expense (i.e., interest expense, including payments economically equivalent to interest, as well as other financing-related expenses, less interest and financing-related income) that may be deducted to a fixed share of earnings. This "earnings-stripping" approach to limiting interest deductibility provides broad protection against base erosion, while still allowing businesses to deduct reasonable amounts of interest.

Budget 2021 proposes to introduce an earnings-stripping rule consistent with the recommendations in the Action 4 Report. The new rule would limit the amount of net interest expense that a corporation may deduct in computing its taxable income to no more than a fixed ratio of "tax EBITDA", which is that corporation's taxable income before taking into account interest expense, interest income and income tax, and deductions for depreciation and amortization, where each of these items is as determined for tax purposes. For these purposes:

- As it is based on a corporation's taxable income, tax EBITDA would exclude, among other things, dividends to the extent they qualify for the inter-corporate dividend deduction or the deduction for certain dividends received from foreign affiliates.
- Interest expense and interest income would include not only amounts that are legally interest, but also certain payments that are economically equivalent to interest, and other financing-related expenses and income.
- The measure of interest expense would exclude interest that is not deductible under existing income tax rules, including the thin capitalization rules, which would continue to apply.
- Interest expense and interest income related to debts owing between Canadian members of a corporate group would generally be excluded. This is intended to ensure, among other things, that the new rule does not impact on corporate transactions that are undertaken within Canadian corporate groups to allow the losses of one group member to be offset against the income of another group member. In addition, a mechanism would be included to ensure that the new rule does not

impact on certain variants of these transactions that involve the generation of a loss in a group entity through the payment of interest on intra-group debt and the subsequent absorption of this entity by another group entity in order to claim a carryforward of the loss.

The new earnings-stripping rule would also apply to trusts, partnerships and Canadian branches of non-resident taxpayers.

Exemptions from the new rule would be available for:

- Canadian-controlled private corporations that, together with any associated corporations, have taxable capital employed in Canada of less than $15 million (i.e., the top end of the phase-out range for the small business deduction [125(5.1) — ed.]); and

- groups of corporations and trusts whose aggregate net interest expense among their Canadian members is $250,000 or less.

Interest denied under the earnings-stripping rule would be able to be carried forward for up to 20 years or back for up to 3 years. Denied interest would be allowed to be carried back to taxation years that begin prior to the effective date of the rule, to the extent that the taxpayer would have had the capacity to absorb these denied expenses, had the proposed rule been in effect for those years. In determining whether the taxpayer would have had the capacity to absorb the denied expenses in those years, any such capacity would be reduced by overall net interest expense, in aggregate for all those years, of Canadian members of the taxpayer's group that exceeded the fixed ratio (or the group ratio, discussed below, if higher).

Canadian members of a group that have a ratio of net interest to tax EBITDA below the fixed ratio would generally be able to transfer the resultant unused capacity to deduct interest to other Canadian members of the group whose net interest expense deductions, including denied deductions carried over from another year, would otherwise be limited by the rule. The definition of a group for this purpose will be included in the draft legislative proposals.

The proposed measure also includes a "group ratio" rule that would allow a taxpayer to deduct interest in excess of the fixed ratio of tax EBITDA where the taxpayer is able to demonstrate that the ratio of net third party interest to book EBITDA of its consolidated group implies that a higher deduction limit would be appropriate. The determination of the amount of unused capacity to deduct interest, which can be transferred between the Canadian members of a group, would take into consideration the higher group ratio.

The consolidated group, for purposes of the group ratio rule, would comprise the parent company and all of its subsidiaries that are fully consolidated in the parent's audited consolidated financial statements. Measures of net third party interest expense and book EBITDA under this rule would be based on the group's audited consolidated financial statements with appropriate adjustments, including an exclusion for certain interest payments to creditors that are outside the consolidated group but are related to, or are significant shareholders of, Canadian group entities. As set out in the Action 4 report, adjustments would also be necessary to address the impact of entities with negative book EBITDA. These adjustments would ensure that, where a group has negative book EBITDA, such that it is not possible to calculate a meaningful group ratio, the group can nonetheless benefit from the group ratio rule. Adjustments would also be made to ensure that, where the group as a whole has positive book EBITDA but includes one or more entities with negative book EBITDA, the group does not benefit from an inappropriately high group ratio.

Consistent with the rationale of the group ratio rule, it is expected that **standalone Canadian corporations and Canadian corporations that are members of a group none of whose members is a non-resident** would, in most cases, not have their interest expense deductions limited under the proposed rule. Measures to reduce the compliance burden on these entities and groups will be explored.

While there are base erosion risks associated with interest deductions by financial institutions, there are challenges in applying an earnings-stripping rule to certain types of financial institutions, and there is no clear way to address these challenges. One reason is that many financial institutions earn substantial amounts of interest income as part of their regular business activity and these amounts may frequently exceed their interest expense. As the proposal is based on a concept of net interest expense, this could result in the proposed earnings-stripping rule having no impact on these financial institutions, and could provide significant capacity to shelter the interest expense of other members of the financial institution's group. It is therefore proposed to not allow banks and life insurance companies to transfer unused capacity to deduct interest to other members of their corporate groups that are not also regulated banking or insurance entities. Further consideration will be given to whether there are targeted measures that could address base erosion concerns associated with excessive interest deductions by regulated banks and life insurance companies, and comments are invited from stakeholders in this regard.

In order to facilitate transition to the new rule and in particular having regard to the impact of the pandemic on corporate earnings, it would be phased in, with a fixed ratio of 40% for taxation years beginning on or after January 1, 2023 but before January 1, 2024 (the transition year), and 30% for taxation years beginning on or after January 1, 2024. In addition, taxpayers that have interest deductions denied for the transition year would be able to carry back the denied interest and deduct it in any of the three preceding years, as discussed above, using the 40% fixed ratio (or the group ratio for that earlier year, if higher) to determine their capacity to absorb carried-back interest in those preceding years. Where interest deductions are denied for a year following the transition year, carrybacks of denied interest to the transition year or an earlier year

would be allowed using the 30% fixed ratio (or the group ratio for the transition year or that earlier year, as the case may be, if higher) to determine their capacity to absorb carried-back interest in those preceding years. Carrybacks to the transition year would also be subject to the constraint, similar to the provision described above in relation to pre-transition years, that the taxpayer's capacity in the transition year to absorb carried-back denied interest would be reduced by the overall deductible net interest expense of Canadian members of the taxpayer's group that exceeded the 30% ratio (or the group ratio, if higher) in the transition year. For example, the unused capacity in the transition year of an entity with a tax-EBITDA ratio of 25% (and ignoring the group ratio for purposes of this example) would be reduced to the extent another Canadian group entity incurred net interest expense in the transition year in excess of 30% of its tax EBITDA and the deduction of this excess interest expense was not denied in the transition year by virtue of the 40% fixed ratio in that year.

This measure would apply to taxation years that begin on or after January 1, 2023 (with an anti-avoidance rule to prevent taxpayers from deferring the application of the measure, or of the 30% fixed ratio) and would apply with respect to existing as well as new borrowings. Draft legislative proposals are expected to be released for comment in the summer.

Federal Budget, Chapter 10, April 19, 2021: *Limitations on Excessive Interest Deductions*

Many firms borrow in order to fund their operations. Generally, the interest charges on those borrowings are considered a cost of doing business and, therefore, are deductible from income for tax purposes. However, some large companies, typically multinationals, use excessive deductions of interest to reduce the taxes they pay in Canada.

All G7 countries — except Canada — have taken action, as a result of the Base Erosion and Profit Shifting (BEPS) Project, to limit excessive interest deductions by large companies.

Budget 2021 proposes that, starting in 2023, the amount of interest that certain businesses can deduct be limited to 40% of their earnings in the first year of the measure and 30% thereafter. Relief will be provided for small businesses and for other situations that do not represent significant tax base erosion risks. The government expects to release draft legislation this summer and will seek stakeholder input on the new rules. This strengthening of the rules on interest deductibility will ensure that large companies pay their fair share and bring Canada in line with other jurisdictions, including all our G7 peers. It is estimated that this measure will increase federal revenues by $5.3 billion over five years, starting in 2021-22.

Prime Minister's mandate letter to Minister of Finance, Dec. 2019: I will expect you to work with your colleagues and through established legislative, regulatory and Cabinet processes to deliver on your top priorities. In particular, you will: .....

- Close corporate tax loopholes that allow companies to excessively deduct debt [should be "interest" — ed.] to artificially reduce the tax that they pay.

Liberal.ca election platform, Oct. 2019: *New Revenue: Making Taxes More Fair*

To ensure that we continue to have the resources needed to invest in people and keep our economy strong and growing, we will move forward with a transparent and publicly reported review of several existing tax measures and will take action to make taxes more fair. This includes taking steps to crack down on corporate tax evasion and avoidance, and asking the wealthiest Canadians to pay a little bit more. We will: ...

- crack down on corporate tax loopholes that allow companies to excessively deduct debt to artificially reduce the tax they pay;

Notes: Bringing Canada into line with other countries' limitations on interest expense has been considered for some time. For discussion just before this proposal, see the articles in 2(1) *Perspectives on Tax Law & Policy* (ctf.ca) 1-19 (March 2021). For much earlier proposals, see withdrawn proposed s. 3.1.

For discussion of these proposals see Nikolakakis, "Interest Deductibility Proposals", 117 *International Tax* (CCH, April 2021) (gives examples).

Budget Table 1 projects that this measure will generate revenue for the federal government of $26 million in 2021-22, $398m in 2022-23, $1.3 billion in 2023-24, $1.75b in 2024-25 and $1.8b in 2025-26; with a note that "an important proportion of the overall projected revenue impact (75%) relates to the expectation that the measure will help in preventing the shifting of debt into Canada".

Related Provisions: 9(3) — Capital gains not included in income from property; 16(1) — Income and capital combined; 16(6) — Indexed debt obligations — amount deemed paid as interest; 17 — Loan to non-resident; 18(1)(e) — No deduction for contingent reserve; 18(1)(g) — Interest on income bonds; 18(1)(t) — No deduction for interest paid on income tax arrears; 18(1)(v) — No deduction to authorized foreign bank except under 20.2; 18(2) — Limitation — interest and property taxes on land; 18(4)–(8) — Thin capitalization — limitation on interest deductibility; 18(5.4) — Trust can designate thin-cap interest paid to non-resident as being payment to beneficiary instead; 18(9)–(9.2) — Prepaid interest; 18(9.1)(e), (f) — Pre-payment penalty on debt repayment deemed to be interest paid on borrowed money; 18(11) — No deduction for interest on money borrowed to make RRSP or certain other contributions; 18.3(3) — No deduction for certain interest paid or payable on stapled security; 20(1)(e) — Expense of borrowing money; 20(1)(f) — Amounts paid in satisfaction of the "principal amount"; 20(1.2) — Definitions in 12.2(11) apply; 20(2) — Borrowed money; 20(2.01) — No deduction for interest on 10/8 policy; 20(2.1) — Limitation [re policy loan]; 20(2.2) — Life insurance policy; 20(3), (3.1) — Borrowed money; 20(14) — Accrued bond interest; 20.1(1) — Borrowed money where property is disposed of; 20.3 — Weak currency debt — limitation on interest deduction; 21(1)–(4) — Capitalizing interest; 60(d) — Annual interest accruing in respect of estate tax or succession duties; 67.2 — Interest on money borrowed for passenger vehicle; 80.5 — Deemed interest — employee deduction re funds borrowed to purchase auto or aircraft; 110.6(1) — "investment expense"; 118.62 — Credit for interest paid on student loans; 127.52(1)(b), (c), (c.2), (e.1) — Limitation on deduction for minimum tax purposes; 137(4.1) — Interest deemed paid on certain reductions of capital by credit union; 138(5)(b) — Insurers — limitation; 143.4(2) — Limitation on contingent amount or where taxpayer has right to reduce expenditure; 212(1)(b) — Non-resident withholding tax on interest; 212.3 — Anti-avoidance — foreign affiliate dumping; 218 — Loan to wholly-owned subsidiary; 261(7)–(10) — Functional currency reporting. See also at end of s. 20.

Notes: The basic entitlement to deduct interest is in 20(1)(c)(i): a reasonable amount of interest paid (or payable), under a legal obligation, on borrowed money used for the "purpose" of earning income from business or property. (See "Business income vs property income" in Notes to 9(1): either one works.) 20(1)(c)(ii) applies to interest on "an amount payable for property", e.g. a mortgage on a building bought to produce income (or debt assumed on rollout of property by a trust: VIEWS doc 2016-0635051R3). See Income Tax Folio S3-F6-C1 (replaces IT-533) for detailed CRA interpretation. For software that assists in determining deductibility, see *Interest Deductibility Navigator* at bluejlegal.com.

Meaning of "interest" and whether an obligation is "debt": See Notes to 12(1)(c).

"Borrowed money": see 20(2). In *Doulis*, 2014 TCC 26, D claimed he "borrowed" money from CRA by not paying his taxes, and used those funds to earn interest he reported. The Court disallowed the deduction for the interest he paid to CRA, as there was no borrower-lender relationship (and see 18(1)(t)). See also VIEWS doc 2011-0416781E5 (no deduction for payments in lieu of interest where no borrower-lender relationship). If debt can automatically convert to shares, 20(1)(c) may not apply because the lender cannot enforce repayment; but if this can happen only on insolvency or bankruptcy, that is remote enough that interest is deductible: 2014-0523691R3 (nonviable contingent capital [Sherman & Jamal, "Cuckoo for CoCos", XX(2) *International Tax Planning* (Federated Press) [FP] 1388-91 (2015)]), 2014-0563351E5 [Shaunessy, "Hybrid Securities Afford Interest Deductions", XX(2) *Corporate Finance [CF]* (FP) 11-14 (2016); D'Avignon, "Recent Hybrid Note Offerings", XV(1) *Resource Sector Taxation* (FP) 2-5 (2021)], 2015-0602711R3. See also Wortsman, "Working Remotely — CRA's Evolving View of Borrowed Money", XXII(2) *CF* 14-18 (2019); Kelly, "Limited Recourse Capital Notes", XXIII(3) *CF* 32-37 (2020) (re Royal Bank offering).

Legal obligation: 20(1)(c) allows deduction only if there is a legal obligation to pay interest. See *Barbican Properties*, [1997] 1 C.T.C. 2383 (FCA), and Notes to 18(1)(e). The obligation need not be in writing: *Black*, 2019 TCC 135 [see Notes to 169(1) (last para. before heading "Jurisdiction") re oral agreements]. The obligation must have been in existence during the year: VIEWS doc 2006-0190791I7. Contingent interest is disallowed: 143.4, overruling *Collins*, 2010 FCA 12 (leave to appeal denied 2010 CarswellNat 5845 (SCC)); as is interest that the payor can opt to cancel: 2016-0649061R3, 2017-0732001R3. CRA's view is that a company under *Companies' Creditors Arrangement Act* (CCAA) protection cannot deduct accrued interest: 2006-0214681I7, 2008-0304841I7 [Lang, "Interest Deductibility and CCAA Proceedings", XVI(1) *Corporate Finance* (Federated Press) 1753-54 (2009)]; and see *Nortel Networks*, 2015 ONCA 681 (leave to appeal denied 2016 CarswellOnt 7202), ruling that interest stops accruing during CCAA protection. Note also that there is no legal obligation to pay interest that (combined with other fees) violates *Criminal Code* s. 347 (rate over 60%: see *Garland v. Consumers Gas*, 2004 SCC 25, paras. 55-57) or, for a mortgage loan, *Interest Act* s. 8 (see *P.A.R.C.E.L. v. Acquaviva*, 2015 ONCA 331, para. 48).

Where a bond with accrued interest is purchased, payment made in respect of the interest may be deductible; see 20(14).

Reasonableness: 20(1)(c) closing words allow only a "reasonable amount"; see Notes to s. 67, which provides the same rule generally. Reasonableness is determined based on the terms on which the money is lent and the purpose for which the borrower uses it: *Shell Canada*, [1999] 4 C.T.C. 313 (SCC), para. 28. In *TDL Group*, 2016 FCA 67, para. 26, a 7-month period where the borrowed funds were lent out interest-free did not make the borrowing rate unreasonable. In *Teranet Inc.*, 2016 TCC 42 (procedural decision), the issue was the reasonableness of the rate on promissory notes issued in a reorganization. In *ENMAX Energy*, 2018 ABCA 147 (leave to appeal denied 2019 CarswellAlta 355 (SCC)), the deductible amount was reduced to a market interest rate [Virji & Elsaghir, "Crossing Provincial Lines", 2414 *Tax Topics* (CCH) 1-2 (June 14, 2018); Nikolakakis, "ENMAX", 26(9) *Canadian Tax Highlights* (ctf.ca) 4-5 (Sept. 2018)]. In *Gervais Auto*, 2021 QCCA 459 (reversing the QCCQ), GA paying 10% interest to its shareholders was reasonable, as its CPAs had found that a commercial rate was 7.89%-12.39%. Where debt is deliberately priced to give rise to a premium, CRA considers part of the interest to be unreasonable: Folio S3-F6-C1 ¶1.96; VIEWS doc 2015-0586301I7 (premium received on re-opening debt to extend term [Sherman & Saddington, "The Grand Reopening", XX(3) *Corporate Finance* (Federated Press) 12-15 (2017)]). See also Katlai, "Interest Deductibility Test", *Taxnet Pro* Tax Disputes Centre (Nov 2018, 3pp).

Exceptions: 18(11) prohibits deduction of interest on loans taken for certain purposes (e.g., to make RRSP or TFSA contributions, or past-service pension contributions: VIEWS doc 2020-0868601E5). 18(4)-(8) ((thin capitalization rules) limit deduction for interest paid by a company to a non-resident shareholder where the debt:equity ratio exceeds 1.5:1. Interest in respect of certain investments is non-deductible for purposes of the Alternative Minimum Tax: 127.52(1)(b), (c), (c.2), (e.1). See also the April 2021

Budget Proposed Amendment above, restricting interest expense to 30% of "tax EBITDA".

Timing of deduction: 20(1)(c) allows a taxpayer to choose to deduct interest on the cash basis rather than the accrual basis: *Crown Forest*, 2006 TCC 47. Interest can be deducted only in the year 20(1)(c) permits it, but if it was missed, one can request a 152(4.2) reassessment of a past year: VIEWS doc 2014-0521341E5.

Purpose requirement (that money be used for earning income): There must be a "direct link" between the borrowed money and an eligible use: *Shell Canada*, [1999] 4 C.T.C. 313 (SCC), para. 31. Purpose is determined at the time the investment is made: *Ludco Enterprises*, 2001 SCC 62, para. 54; *Keybrand Foods*, 2020 FCA 201, para. 71. In *Sinha*, 1981 CarswellNat 374 (TRB), money borrowed to repay a student loan was instead invested at a higher rate; the interest paid was deductible, due to the purpose for which the money was *used* (rather than the original intention). In *Black*, 2019 TCC 135, Conrad Black's payment of a damage award was held to be an interest-bearing loan to his corp that was jointly liable with him, so interest was deductible (income need not actually be earned as long as the purpose test is met: para. 143). In *Novopharm Ltd.*, 2003 FCA 112 (leave to appeal denied 2003 CarswellNat 4612 (SCC)), even though the purpose of incurring loans was tax avoidance, each transaction had to be considered independently, and on that basis the loans were incurred to earn income and the interest was deductible. (The taxpayer lost under the pre-GAAR 245(1), however.) In *Struck*, 2017 TCC 94, paras. 81, 85, borrowed money was not used for business purposes. In *Cassan*, 2017 TCC 174 (FCA appeal settled A-304-17), para. 426, interest was deductible on loans taken in a donation shelter, as the taxpayers' (underlying) *motive* for entering the program (obtaining donation credits) was not the same as the *purpose* of borrowing (buying LP units that would eventually pay interest).

Using borrowed money to buy shares: interest is deductible if the shares can be expected to pay dividends, even if the dividends expected are low: *Ludco Enterprises*, 2001 SCC 62. The Supreme Court ruled that earning dividends need not be the primary purpose of the investment; an ancillary purpose is sufficient: para. 52. It is not the purpose of the borrowing that is relevant, but the taxpayer's purpose in using the borrowed money in a particular manner: para. 44. The purpose need only be to earn (gross) income, not net income or profit: para. 59. CRA accepts this: Folio S3-F6-C1 ¶1.27, VIEWS docs 2008-0275171E5, 2014-0534811C6 [2014 APFF q.1]; this would have been overruled by proposed s. 3.1 (2003), but that proposal was withdrawn. (Expectation of capital gains does not qualify: *Cassan*, 2017 TCC 174, para. 414.) In *Swirsky*, 2014 FCA 36, deduction was denied because the shares had no history of paying dividends (it paid bonus to the owner-manager instead), so there was no subjective "reasonable expectation" of income (REOI). Similarly, in *Keybrand Foods*, 2020 FCA 201, paras. 71-82, KF bought shares in a failing company but deduction was denied due to no REOI. CRA's position in S3-F6-C1 ¶1.70 (former IT-533 para. 31) is supposedly unchanged despite *Swirsky*; no history of dividend payment is needed, and common shares are normally presumed to meet the test; but there are exceptions, such as a stated policy of not paying dividends. It has been suggested that CRA could reassess investors in startups, junior resource companies, and other growth companies with no REOI: Macknight, "Swirsky", 13(2) *Tax for the Owner-Manager* 2 (April 2013); Morand & Falk, "Interest Deductibility", 2199 *Tax Topics* 1-6 (May 1, 2014) and 2200:1-4 (May 8, 2014). *Swirsky* does not appear to apply broadly, but in light of *Keybrand Foods* (though it did not cite *Swirsky*), one needs to be concerned. In *Brown*, 2020 TCC 84, interest on loans B took to lend to his corps was deductible due to 20(3), even though they were insolvent and so could not pay dividends: para. 21. In *TDL Group*, 2016 FCA 67, interest on a loan to buy more shares of a wholly-owned US sub was deductible; it was irrelevant that the ultimate purpose was to allow the sub to lend money interest-free to TDL's parent corp. See also docs 2010-0376711I7, 2011-0415801R3. Investing in a mutual fund trust that distributes capital might not qualify: 2008-0268511E5, 2009-0329781C6.

Using borrowed money to make interest-bearing loan: interest is deductible even if the loan pays a lower rate of interest: doc 2012-0443771E5 [Hudson, "Deductibility of Interest Paid to Earn Interest Income", 13(2) *Tax for the Owner-Manager* (ctf.ca) 8-9 (April 2013)]; but see 20(2.01) re a "10/8 policy". In *McLarty*, 2014 TCC 30, interest was deductible on a limited-recourse note in years when revenue from the seismic data purchased with the loan was only a small fraction of that interest. (For Quebec provincial tax purposes, interest expense relating to investments is usually deductible only to offset investment income, with a carryover to other years: *Taxation Act* ss. 313.10, 336.6.) See also 2015-0601211E5 [Tollstam, "Deduction for Interest Paid to RRSP on Mortgage Loan", 24(11) *Canadian Tax Highlights* (ctf.ca) 3-4 (Nov. 2016)]. In *Black*, 2019 TCC 135, Conrad Black's payment of a damage award was held to be a loan to his company that was jointly liable with him, and was made to earn interest as later documented.

Using borrowed money to make interest-free loan: interest is deductible if it can be linked to future income earning: Folio S3-F6-C1 ¶1.54; *Canadian Helicopters*, 2002 FCA 30 (money borrowed by CH to lend to its parent's parent corp for acquisition that would benefit CH's business). In *Scragg*, 2009 FCA 180, the taxpayer lending money to his own companies was insufficient without proving an income-earning purpose. In *Bernacchi*, 2010 TCC 306, a wife's payments on a line of credit (as required by a separation agreement), for borrowings used to fund her ex-husband's business, were non-deductible. See also Paul Barnicke & Melanie Huynh, "Non-Interest-Bearing Loans", 18(12) *Canadian Tax Highlights* (ctf.ca) 10-11 (Dec. 2010); Notes to 18(1)(a) re *Lyncorp* case; VIEWS docs 2008-0297631E5 (interest-free loan to related company to acquire operating company — no deduction); 2010-0367351E5 (interest-free loan to trust which will use funds to earn income); 2017-0712141E5 (general discussion).

Cycling funds: In *Singleton*, 2001 SCC 61, money was "cycled" to make it deductible: a lawyer withdrew cash from his firm partnership to pay for his home purchase, then borrowed funds to reinvest in the partnership the same day. The interest on the new loan was deductible, since the "shuffle of cheques" defined the legal relationship that must be given effect [para. 32]. The SCC confirmed this is acceptable in *Lipson*, 2009 SCC 1 (but GAAR applied due to misuse of the 74.1 attribution rule; see now VIEWS doc 2009-0327071C6). In *Husky Energy*, 2012 ABCA 231 (leave to appeal denied to Crown 2013 CarswellAlta 265 (SCC)), a *Singleton*-like circular refinancing to move interest expense from Alberta to Ontario was valid and did not violate GAAR. CRA accepts such a "restructuring" of borrowings: Folio S3-F6-C1 ¶1.33; docs 2009-0307951E5, 2009-0352171E5, 2013-0477601E5. However, in *Sherle*, 2009 TCC 377, S switched her home and a rental property, switching the mortgages so that she continued to live in a mortgage-free home, but could not deduct the interest because the *direct* use of the funds was not to acquire an income-generating property. See also 2010-0373551C6 (if spouses swap shares to refinance their mortgage, result will depend on the details).

Using borrowed money or incurring debt to acquire property (20(1)(c)(ii)): See Folio S3-F6-C1 ¶1.62-1.65. If the property goes down in value, the interest deduction can continue: *Tennant*, [1996] 1 C.T.C. 290 (SCC). Where the value of acquired property increases and part is sold, see VIEWS doc 2007-0230341E5 [R. Ian Crosbie, "Is the Canada Revenue Agency Narrowing Its View on Interest Deductibility?", XV(2) *Corporate Finance* (Federated Press) 1642-44 (2008)]. If the source of income disappears, see 20.1, as the deduction under 20(1)(c) would otherwise be lost: *Moufarrège*, [2005] 5 C.T.C. 212 (SCC). (20.1 was apparently overlooked in *St-Hilaire*, 2014 CarswellNat 5303 (TCC), para. 42.) If the property is replaced by other income-earning property, interest remains deductible: S3-F6-C1 ¶1.36-1.39, docs 2005-0152251R3, 2006-0216551R3; 2007-0219791E5 (deductibility after rollover of shares — "flexible approach to linking"). If non-income property is substituted the deduction is lost: 2008-0267961E5 (mortgage interest on rental property non-deductible after moving in and renting out previous home) (and see *Sherle*, above). If a loan is taken to buy preferred shares but the corporation then distributes capital to the investor, the deduction may be lost: 2012-0446741E5. See also Galambos, case comment on *Moufarrège*, 54(1) *Canadian Tax Journal* 228-34 (2006); *Tesainer*, [2008] 3 C.T.C. 2433 (TCC) (reversed on unrelated issue [2009] 3 C.T.C. 109 (FCA); leave to appeal denied 2009 CarswellNat 3106 (SCC)) (no deduction after a litigation settlement reduced capital cost of partnership units); *1200757 Ontario Ltd.*, 2011 CarswellOnt 9218 (Ont. SCJ) (deduction of interest under power-purchase agreement continued when plant inoperative); and doc 2007-0256671R3.

Loss shifting: The Courts may disallow interest deduction if the loan's purpose is to shift losses between companies: *C.R.B. Logging*, [2000] 4 C.T.C. 157 (FCA); *Mark Resources*, [1993] 2 C.T.C. 2259 (TCC); *Canwest Broadcasting*, [1995] 2 C.T.C. 2780 (TCC). But see Notes to 111(5) for dozens of rulings permitting such shifting; doc 2015-0589611E5 discusses policy points.

Return of capital: Interest on money borrowed to acquire shares or income trust units can become partly non-deductible if the taxpayer receives a PUC reduction or capital distribution that is not used to reduce the loan: *Van Steenis*, 2019 FCA 107 (leave to appeal denied 2019 CarswellNat 7412 (SCC)); VIEWS docs 9817625F, 2002-0142475, 2005-0156891E5, 2006-0191681E5, 2007-0230431E5, 2007-0236351E5; 2007-0243181C6 (capital repayments apply *pro rata* to ineligible portion of borrowing); 2007-0252211E5. See also Frankovic, "Interest Deductibility and Changing Uses of Borrowed Money", 2411 *Tax Topics* (CCH) 1-2 (May 24, 2018); and 20.1.

Tracking borrowed funds: "cash damming" by keeping funds separate can allow tracing of the use of particular borrowed funds. See Folio S3-F6-C1 ¶1.34; VIEWS docs 2006-0186681R3, 2006-0208461R3; 2006-0218241E5 (sole proprietor mixes sales revenues with personal funds [see Jim Yager, "Sole Proprietor's Cash Damming", 15(11) *Canadian Tax Highlights* (ctf.ca) 9-10 (Nov. 2007)]); 2010-0373541C6 (cash damming position is still correct since *Lipson*). See also 2006-0198861E5 (mixed-use personal line of credit — percentage of interest relating to investments is deductible); 2006-0218381E5 and 2007-0221071E5 (personal mortgage is increased and additional funds are invested [see Jim Yager, "Interest on Line of Credit", 15(12) *CTH* 1 (Dec. 2007)]); 2010-0354361E5 (interest deductible where money borrowed to acquire upper half of duplex the taxpayer lives in, to rent out); 2010-0362101E5 (mortgage loan used partly to finance rental property).

Borrowing to pay dividends or redeem shares or debt: see Folio S3-F6-C1 ¶1.48-1.53 (interest allowed if the funds replace money used for an eligible purpose: "filling the hole" of capital withdrawn from the business). In *Penn Ventilator*, [2002] 2 C.T.C. 2636 (TCC), interest paid on a note issued by PV to repurchase its stock was deductible under 20(1)(c)(ii). See also VIEWS docs 2007-0227501R3 (corporate reorganization replaces paid-up capital with debt); 2007-0228931E5 and 2009-0348551I7 (corporation borrowing to pay dividend: effect of CICA *Handbook* §3840.08, .09); 2008-0293901E5, 2008-0296731E5, 2009-0344721E5. In *Trans-Prairie Pipelines*, [1970] C.T.C. 537 (Exch. Ct.), interest borrowed to redeem preferred shares was deductible. In *A.P. Toldo Holding Corp.*, 2013 TCC 416, interest on borrowed money used to redeem common shares to resolve a shareholder dispute was not deductible, as the company was a holding company and did not have a "financing and banking" business; only in "exceptional circumstances" would *Penn Ventilator* apply, and there was no direct effect on the company's income-earning potential (however, this has not changed CRA's position in Folio S3-F6-C1 ¶1.65: 2016-0638241I7). Interest on a loan taken out to pay dividends may be deductible where the effect is to replace retained earnings with debt financing: 2005-0157301R3, 2008-0296731E5, 2010-0378661R3; Daniel Lang, "Interest Deductibility", XVI(4) *Corporate Finance* (Federated Press) 1899-1901 (2010). See also 2006-0182321I7 (corp borrowing from shareholders to pay them dividends — no deduction); 2009-0344721E5 (corp borrowing to pay dividends used to buy annuity on life of related individual — GAAR may apply); 2011-0412041C6, 2012-0436411E5 (accounting adjustments affecting retained earnings); 2011-0426151C6 (distribution under 84(4.1) does not affect this principle); 2012-0453481I7 (borrowed money commingled with cash on hand can be applied first to "filling the hole" so deduction allowed); 2014-0527251E5 (dividend declared with pref shares that are immediately redeemed for promissory note — deductible); 2015-0595771C6 [2015 APFF q.11] (borrowing from target to buy its shares); 2015-0621401I7 (84(6)(b) repurchasing shares for cancellation is the same as redeeming shares, for purposes of this rule); 2018-0779991C6 [2018 CTF q. 13] (loan taken to redeem pref shares issued by Targetco on triangular amalgamation — deductible); 2018-0740931R3 (borrowing to repay debenture and conversion premium). See also Thomas McDonnell, "Borrowing to Return Paid-Up Capital", 8(1) *Tax for the Owner-Manager* (ctf.ca) 7 (Jan. 2008). (Might 20.1(1)(b)(iv) apply?)

Trust borrowing to repay capital: CRA stated at the 2005 Cdn Tax Foundation conference (*Income Tax Technical News* No. 34) that, based on *Penn Ventilator* (above), interest is deductible in an income trust structure where a leveraged buy-out and amalgamation are used and redemptions or repurchases are used to "fill the hole". However, interest paid on a note issued by a trust in settlement of a capital interest is not normally deductible because there is no borrowed money to earn income from a property: VIEWS doc 2014-0538261C6 [2014 APFF q. 9].

Monetizations: see docs 2007-0246461R3, 2008-0276821R3, 2010-0356191R3, 2010-0379341C6, 2011-0408871R5, 2013-0507191C6 [2010 CTF conf p.4:31-32, q.36]; Wortsman et al., "Complex Financial Instruments", 2009 conf report, 8:3-21.

Premium arising on issuing debt, if deliberately planned, may make part of the interest non-deductible. See under "Reasonableness" above.

Ceasing to carry on business: see 20.1(2) for ongoing deductibility.

Amalgamation: see VIEWS docs 2006-0196291C6, 2009-0317541E5 (deductibility after amalgamation); 2009-0344721E5 (deduction after amalgamation limited by 20(1)(c)(iv)); 2014-0551121I7 (amalgamation of debtor and creditor after amounts due but before they are paid: deduction allowed).

Guarantees: CRA's view is that no 20(1)(c) deduction is allowed for amounts paid under a guarantee: docs 2011-0398721I7, 2011-0411151R11, 2014-0519231I7; Jessica Upshaw, "Advance Ruling on the Deductibility of Post-Judgment Interest", 9(8) *Tax Hyperion* (Carswell) 7-8 (2012). Such amounts could be a capital loss (39(1)), ABIL (39(12)) or non-capital loss (*Lachapelle*, [1990] 2 C.T.C. 2396 (TCC), para. 30).

Life insurance: In doc 2009-0340381R3, CRA approved deduction of interest when purchasing life insurance and using it as security to borrow from bank to acquire an annuity. See now Notes to 248(1)"leveraged insurance annuity" and "10/8 policy".

Tax shelters: See *Cassan* case under "Purpose requirement" above. In *Lee*, 2020 QCCQ 780, paras. 441-445 (Prospector Networks software), interest expense was disallowed where the tax-shelter filing rule (Quebec equivalent to 237.1(6)) was not followed; at para. 505, the expense was otherwise allowed.

More cases: In *Sherway Centre*, [1998] 2 C.T.C. 343 (FCA), participating interest payments on a bond were deductible. CRA applied *Sherway* in VIEWS doc 2012-0468131I7. In *Shell Canada*, [1999] 4 C.T.C. 313 (SCC), high-rate interest on a "Kiwi loan" (NZ$ weak currency loan) was deductible under 20(1)(c) even though it was hedged back to US dollars. GAAR did not apply to this scheme: *Canadian Pacific*, [2002] 2 C.T.C. 197 (FCA). It is now prevented by 20.3.

In *Heaps*, 2008 TCC 130, the taxpayers sold their home and bought and subdivided a property, living on 1 lot and developing and selling 4. The mortgage was registered against the entire property. Based on the joint venture agreement, all the mortgage interest was "reasonably attributable to a business use" and was deductible. In *Grant*, 2007 FCA 174, interest deduction on a "departure trade" was denied: see Notes to 128.1(4).

For more rulings and interpretations on 20(1)(c) see VIEWS docs 2006-0171431R3 ("innovative instrument"); 2006-0180221 (maturity of bond purchased on the market at a premium — no deduction); 2006-0187411R3 ("xx-year notes"); 2006-0188621E5 and 2007-0254941E5 (borrowing to make payments on earlier loan); 2006-0195471R3 (corporation/trust transaction); 2006-0199621E5 (circular non-arm's length transactions); 2006-0204621E5 (mortgage interest on home not allowed against other rental income); 2006-0209001E5 (no deductibility after principal repaid); 2006-0216781E5 (money loaned to sister corporation to fund expansion); 2007-0223521R3 (interest on multi-year notes is deductible); 2007-0234061R3 (cost reimbursement — innovative instrument); 2007-0239291R3 (assumption of debt for assets); 2007-0239321R3 (replacement capital); 2007-0243361C6 (corporate structure held by family trust); 2007-0244231I7 (loan transactions within corporate group); 2007-0245691R3 (corporate reorganization); 2007-0251761I7 (interest added to debt not deductible); 2007-0255401R3 (swap termination); 2008-0273431R3 and 2009-0321111R3 (cash sweeping); 2008-0300101R3 and 2008-0300102R3 (notes issued in public offering); 2009-0309811E5 [Islamic finance — unclear whether interest deductible [see Drache, "Interest and Islam as Seen by the CRA", xxxiv(6) *The Canadian Taxpayer* (Carswell) 47-48 (March 23, 2012)]); 2009-0322591I7 (issuing new note to pay debt — whether novation in Quebec); 2009-0331651E5 (interest on increased borrowing on line of credit used to pay interest on the line of credit); 2010-0353101R3 (ULC can deduct interest in Art. IV:7(b) restructuring); 2010-0357241I7 (exchangeable debentures); 2010-0360361R3 (Indian band subsidiary can deduct interest on note owing to band); 2010-0377281R3 (structure used to acquire limited partnership); 2011-0423511R3 (notes with conversion clause are debt); 2011-0413761E5 (individual can deduct interest on mortgage funded by RRSP); 2012-044339117 (cross-border loans where interest paid by issuing shares); 2012-0443481E5 (no deduction on loan to reduce equity in property); 2012-0443931E5 (no deduction on funds borrowed to buy home using financing provided on basis of income from investment fund); 2012-0449811C6 (interest deductible where income attributed to borrower by 75(2)); 2012-0452821R3 and 2012-0462141R3 (recapitalization with debt forgiveness); 2012-0458361R3 (cross-border financing); 2014-0538141C6 [2014 APFF q.8] (beneficiary assuming mortgage on receiving rental property from trust or estate can deduct mortgage interest); 2014-055529117 (interest on debt to acquire shares remains deductible after amalgamation and partial return of capital); 2016-0635081R3 (issuances of notes — deductible).

Where a payment combines interest and principal, see 16(1).

If 20(1)(c) does not apply, interest was traditionally considered paid on account of capital and thus not deductible under s. 9: *Bowater Cdn.*, [1987] 2 C.T.C. 47 (FCA); *Shell Canada*, [1999] 4 C.T.C. 313 (SCC); *A.P. Toldo Holding Corp.*, 2013 TCC 416, paras. 56-58 (interest was not paid in the course of a money-lending business). In *Gifford*, 2004 SCC 15, the Supreme Court ruled that if the loan "adds to the financial capital" of the borrower, then the payment is on account of capital. If the loan proceeds constitute inventory of the borrower, as for moneylenders, then the interest is deductible. The Court stated: "it is not necessary to determine whether the payment is a capital expenditure but to determine whether the payment is being made 'on account of capital'"; and that when the FCA had said "in the absence of statutory provisions permitting the deduction of interest, interest is considered a non-deductible capital expense", it "may be doubtful that the authorities support a statement as broad as that". See Friedlander, "What Does *Gifford* Mean?", 53(4) *Canadian Tax Journal* 897-940 (2005). Negative interest on overnight deposits: see Notes to 12(1)(c).

Further discussion: Tamaki, "Interest Deductibility", 2003 Cdn Tax Foundation conference report, 1:1-21; Bodie & Haymour, "Recent Trends in Interest Expense Deductibility", 15 *Canadian Petroleum Tax Journal [CPTJ]* 51-66 (2002); Jack, "Selected Current Issues Regarding Interest Deductibility", 15 *CPTJ* 89-109 (2002); Thomson & Quinn, "Financing Alternatives for Small and Medium-Sized Businesses", 2007 conference report, 33:1-25; Maclagan, "Interest Deductibility", 2009 BC Tax Conference (ctf.ca), 10:1-20; Kellough, "Justice Bowman's Decisions on the Deductibility of Interest", 58(Supp.) *Canadian Tax Journal* 211-23 (2010); Huynh et al., "Foreign Affiliates: Tracing the Purpose and Use of Funds", 59(3) *CTJ* 571-89 (2011); Fréchette & Rabinovitch, "Recent Issues Relating to Interest Deductibility and Non-Traditional Forms of Indebtedness", 2011 conference report, 27:1-45; Boidman et al., "Interest Deductibility in Canada", 79(2) *Tax Notes International* (taxnotes.com) 161-67 (July 13, 2015); Gosselin & Lynch, "A Review of Interest Deductibility Since *Ludco*", 2015 conference report, 7:1-23; Arnold, "The Relationship Between Restrictions on the Deduction of Interest Under Canadian Law and Canadian Tax Treaties", 67(4) *Canadian Tax Journal* 1051-76 (2019); Luu, "Interest Deductibility", *Practical Insights*, Taxnet Pro Tax Disputes Centre (Nov. 2020, 31pp).

The Dept. of Finance was considering a response to *Singleton* and *Ludco*, as well as to *Bronfman Trust*, [1987] 1 C.T.C. 117 (SCC). Draft 20(1)(c)(v), (vi), 20(1)(qq), 20(3.1), 20.1 and 20.2 [1991] would have created a legal framework to support Revenue Canada's then administrative practice following *Bronfman Trust*. These proposals were largely superseded by later case law, and Finance abandoned its review of this area. Proposed s. 3.1 (2003), requiring a reasonable expectation of profit to claim losses, was also withdrawn. See also articles in *Canadian Tax Journal* 39(6) 1473-96 (1991); 40(2) 267-303 (1992); 40(3) 533-53 (1992); 43(5) 1216-44 (1995); 44(2) 227-347 (1996); 48(2) 231-73 (2000). See now the 2021 Budget Proposed Amendment above.

20(1)(c) amended by 1989 Budget and 1991 technical bill, for contracts last acquired after 1989. For those acquired earlier, in 20(1)(c)(iv), in place of the parenthesized words, add "or would apply if the contract had a third anniversary in the year".

Regulations: 201(1)(b) (information return).

Income Tax Folios: S3-F6-C1: Interest deductibility [replaces IT-533]; S4-F2-C1: Deductibility of fines and penalties [replaces IT-104R3]; S4-F7-C1: Amalgamations of Canadian corporations [replaces IT-474R2].

Interpretation Bulletins: IT-80: Interest on money borrowed to redeem shares or pay dividends (cancelled); IT-121R3: Election to capitalize cost of borrowed money (cancelled); IT-153R3: Land developers — subdivision and development costs and carrying charges on land; IT-265R3: Payments of income and capital combined (cancelled); IT-315: Interest expense incurred for the purpose of winding-up or amalgamation (cancelled); IT-341R4: Expenses of issuing shares, units in a trust, interests in a partnership or syndicate and expenses of borrowing money; IT-355R2: Interest on loans to buy life insurance policies and annuity contracts, and interest on policy loans (cancelled); IT-362R: Patronage dividends; IT-421R2: Benefits to individuals, corporations and shareholders from loans or debt; IT-445: Deduction of interest on borrowed funds which are loaned at less than a reasonable rate (cancelled); IT-488R2: Winding-up of 90%-owned taxable Canadian corporations (cancelled); IT-498: Deductibility of interest on money borrowed to reloan to employees or shareholders (cancelled).

Information Circulars: 88-2, paras. 19, 20: General anti-avoidance rule — section 245 of the *Income Tax Act*; 88-2, Supplement, para. 5: General anti-avoidance rule.

I.T. Technical News: 3 (loss utilization within a corporate group; use of a partner's assets by a partnership; interest-bearing note issued in consideration for the redemption or repurchase of shares); 16 (*Sherway Centre* case; *Shell Canada* and *Canadian Pacific* cases; *Parthenon Investments* case); 18 (*C.R.B. Logging*, *Ludco Enterprises*, *Byram* and *Singleton* cases); 34 (income trusts and interest deductibility); 41 (deductibility of interest on money borrowed to acquire common shares).

Advance Tax Rulings: ATR-4: Exchange of interest rates; ATR-14: Non-arm's length interest charges; ATR-16: Inter-company dividends and interest expense; ATR-41: Convertible preferred shares; ATR-43: Utilization of a non-resident-owned investment corporation as a holding corporation; ATR-44: Utilization of deductions and credits within a related corporate group; ATR-59: Financing exploration and development through limited partnerships.

Forms: T2210: Verification of policy loan interest by the insurer.

(d) compound interest — an amount paid in the year pursuant to a legal obligation to pay interest on an amount that would be deductible under paragraph (c) if it were paid in the year or payable in respect of the year;

Related Provisions: 18(11) — Limitation; 20(2.01) — No deduction for interest on 10/8 policy; 20(2.1) — Limitation [re policy loan]; 20(2.2) — Life insurance policy; 21(1)–(4) — Cost of borrowed money; 67.2 — Interest on money borrowed for automobile; 127.52(1)(b), (c), (c.2), (e.1) — Limitation on deduction for minimum tax purposes; 138(5)(b) — Insurers — limitation; 248(1) — "Borrowed money". See also at end of s. 20.

Notes: The deduction under 20(1)(d) is only for amounts *paid*, while 20(1)(c) allows amount *paid or payable*. This can lead to a technical mismatch of deductions.

In *Hill*, [2003] 4 C.T.C. 2548 (TCC), payment of compound interest arrears was deductible even though an identical loan advance was taken back from the mortgagee.

For CRA interpretation see VIEWS docs 2005-0154191E5, 2006-0188621E5, 2007-025176117, 2008-0304841I7, 2009-0331651E5.

Income Tax Folios: S3-F6-C1: Interest deductibility [replaces IT-533].

Interpretation Bulletins: IT-121R3: Election to capitalize cost of borrowed money (cancelled); IT-355R2: Interest on loans to buy life insurance policies and annuity contracts, and interest on policy loans (cancelled); IT-362R: Patronage dividends.

Advance Tax Rulings: ATR-4: Exchange of interest rates.

Forms: T2210: Verification of policy loan interest by the insurer.

(e) expenses re financing — such part of an amount (other than an excluded amount) that is not otherwise deductible in computing the income of the taxpayer and that is an expense incurred in the year or a preceding taxation year

(i) in the course of an issuance or sale of units of the taxpayer where the taxpayer is a unit trust, of interests in a partnership or syndicate by the partnership or syndicate, as the case may be, or of shares of the capital stock of the taxpayer,

(ii) in the course of a borrowing of money used by the taxpayer for the purpose of earning income from a business or property (other than money used by the taxpayer for the purpose of acquiring property the income from which would be exempt),

(ii.1) in the course of incurring indebtedness that is an amount payable for property acquired for the purpose of gaining or producing income therefrom or for the purpose of gaining or producing income from a business (other than property the income from which would be exempt or property that is an interest in a life insurance policy), or

(ii.2) in the course of a rescheduling or restructuring of a debt obligation of the taxpayer or an assumption of a debt obligation by the taxpayer, where the debt obligation is

(A) in respect of a borrowing described in subparagraph (ii), or

(B) in respect of an amount payable described in subparagraph (ii.1),

and, in the case of a rescheduling or restructuring, the rescheduling or restructuring, as the case may be, provides for the modification of the terms or conditions of the debt obligation or the conversion or substitution of the debt obligation to or with a share or another debt obligation,

(including a commission, fee, or other amount paid or payable for or on account of services rendered by a person as a salesperson, agent or dealer in securities in the course of the issuance, sale or borrowing) that is the lesser of

(iii) that proportion of 20% of the expense that the number of days in the year is of 365 and

(iv) the amount, if any, by which the expense exceeds the total of all amounts deductible by the taxpayer in respect of the expense in computing the taxpayer's income for a preceding taxation year,

and, for the purposes of this paragraph,

(iv.1) "excluded amount" means

(A) an amount paid or payable as or on account of the principal amount of a debt obligation or interest in respect of a debt obligation,

(B) an amount that is contingent or dependent on the use of, or production from, property, or

(C) an amount that is computed by reference to revenue, profit, cash flow, commodity price or any other similar criterion or by reference to dividends paid or payable to shareholders of any class of shares of the capital stock of a corporation,

(v) where in a taxation year all debt obligations in respect of a borrowing described in subparagraph (ii) or in respect of indebtedness described in subparagraph (ii.1) are settled or extinguished (otherwise than in a transaction made as part of a series of borrowings or other transactions and repayments), by the taxpayer for consideration that does not include any unit, interest, share or debt obligation of the taxpayer or any person with whom the taxpayer does not deal at arm's length or any partnership or trust of which the taxpayer or any person with whom the taxpayer does not deal at arm's length is a member or beneficiary, this paragraph shall be read without reference to the words "the lesser of" and to subparagraph (iii), and

(vi) where a partnership has ceased to exist at any particular time in a fiscal period of the partnership,

(A) no amount may be deducted by the partnership under this paragraph in computing its income for the period, and

(B) there may be deducted for a taxation year ending at or after that time by any person or partnership that was a member of the partnership immediately before that time, that proportion of the amount that would, but for this subparagraph, have been deductible under this paragraph by the partnership in the fiscal period ending in the year had it continued to exist and had the partnership interest not been redeemed, acquired or cancelled, that the fair market value of the member's interest in the partnership immediately before that time is of the fair market value of all the interests in the partnership immediately before that time;

Related Provisions: 18(11) — Limitation; 20(1)(e.1) — Deduction for annual fees, etc.; 20(1)(e.2) — Premiums on life insurance used as collateral; 20(1)(g) — Deduction for share transfer, listing and annual report fees; 20(3) — Use of borrowed money; 21(1)–(4) — Cost of borrowed money; 53(2)(c)(x) — Deduction from adjusted cost base of partnership interest; 87(2)(j.6) — Amalgamation — continuing corporation; 110.6(1) — "investment expense"; 127.52(1)(b), (c), (c.2), (e.1) — Limitation on deduction for minimum tax purposes; 142.7(8)(c) — Application to debt transferred to foreign bank branch by Canadian affiliate; 143.3(3) — Whether stock value deductible; 248(1) — "Borrowed money"; 248(10) — Series of transactions; 261(7)–(10) — Functional currency reporting; Canada-U.S. Tax Treaty:Art. XXII:4 — No withholding tax on guarantee fee. See also at end of s. 20.

Notes: *20(1)(e)(i)*: CRA applies a restrictive interpretation in VIEWS docs 2002-0151415 (takeover fees paid by purchaser to prepare and distribute information circular); 2002-0151485, 2004-0087011C6 (investment banker fees paid by target during share issuance). These may be wrong in light of *Boulangerie St-Augustin*, 1996 CarswellNat 2523 (FCA) and *BJ Services*, 2003 TCC 900. In *BJ*, the words "issuance or sale" in 20(1)(e)(i) were not limited to a sale from treasury, but included a sale by shareholders. In *Banque Laurentienne*, 2020 TCC 73, deduction was allowed for transaction fees paid to major investors for investing in BL shares.

CRA examples of costs that may be allowed (for (e)(i) or (ii)) include: legal fees for preparing a prospectus (**PR**), accounting and auditing fees required for a PR, printing PR and share certificates, transfer agent fees, and government filing fees (IT-341R4); Gilt lock derivative termination fee (2008-027244I7); lender's legal costs (2009-0341951E5); loan guarantee fee at arm's length (2002-0175705, 2003-0037283); PR that was not used, or other "abandoned plan to borrow money" (2009-034025117).

See also docs 2009-032867117 (20(1)(e) is available to company under bankruptcy or CCAA protection; discussion of its scope); 2005-015121117, 2005-0161661E5, 2006-0201321R3, 2011-0412061C6.

20(1)(e)(ii) deduction was allowed in *MacMillan Bloedel*, [1990] 1 C.T.C. 468 (FCTD) (foreign exchange losses from forward hedging contracts); *Cousineau*, 2013 TCC 375 (mortgage insurance premium). In *Rio Tinto*, 2016 TCC 172, para. 201 (aff'd on other grounds 2018 FCA 124; leave to appeal denied 2019 CarswellNat 809 (SCC)), the costs of buying another company were disallowed, due to lack of evidence supporting claimed allocation of costs.

20(1)(e)(ii.2): see VIEWS docs 2008-027977117, 2011-0412021C6.

20(1)(e)(iv.1) and "excluded amount" overrule *Sherway Centre*, [1998] 2 C.T.C. 343 (FCA), which allowed participatory interest payments to finance a shopping centre. (iv.1)(C) uses the same language as 212(3)"participating debt interest"; see 212(1)(b) Notes and VIEWS doc 2014-054743117.

20(1)(e)(v): see doc 2015-0595751C6 [2015 APFF q.1]. For the meaning of "extinguished", see 80(2)(a) Notes.

See also St-Cyr and Jadd, "Treatment of Costs incurred in the Course of a Corporate Transaction", 2016 Cdn Tax Foundation conference report, at 11:20-21; Colborne, "Paragraph 20(1)(e)", XI(2) *Corporate Finance [CF]* (Federated Press) 1066-70 (2003); Hickey, "Indirect Use of Funds", 14(2) *Canadian Tax Highlights* (ctf.ca) 1-2 (Feb. 2006); Hsu, "Update on Deductibility of Financing Expenses", XIV(2) *CF* 1486-88 (2007) (re new IT-341R4 and 2005-0161661E5).

Alternative claim: Costs relating to a corp's shares may be deductible as business expenses under 9(1): see Notes to 18(1)(a) and (b). The TCC declined to rule on 20(1)(e) in *International Colin Energy*, [2003] 1 C.T.C. 2406 (merger expenses allowed as current expenses), and *Devon Canada*, 2018 TCC 170 (payments to employees to surrender their stock options were eligible capital expenditures (see 20(1)(b) Notes), 75% deductible under pre-2017 111(5.2)).

20(1)(e) amended by 1995-97, 1993 technical bills, for expenses incurred after 1987.

Income Tax Folios: S3-F6-C1: Interest deductibility [replaces IT-533].

Interpretation Bulletins: IT-99R5: Legal and accounting fees; IT-121R3: Election to capitalize cost of borrowed money (cancelled); IT-341R4: Expenses of issuing shares, units in a trust, interests in a partnership or syndicate and expenses of borrowing money.

I.T. Technical News: 16 (*Sherway Centre* case).

Advance Tax Rulings: ATR-49: Long-term foreign debt; ATR-59: Financing exploration and development through limited partnerships.

(e.1) **annual fees, etc. [re borrowings]** — an amount payable by the taxpayer (other than a payment that is contingent or dependent on the use of, or production from, property or is computed by reference to revenue, profit, cash flow, commodity price or any other similar criterion or by reference to dividends paid or payable to shareholders of any class of shares of the capital stock of a corporation) as a standby charge, guarantee fee, registrar fee, transfer agent fee, filing fee, service fee or any similar fee, that can reasonably be considered to relate solely to the year and that is incurred by the taxpayer

(i) for the purpose of borrowing money to be used by the taxpayer for the purpose of earning income from a business or property (other than borrowed money used by the taxpayer for the purpose of acquiring property the income from which would be exempt income),

(ii) in the course of incurring indebtedness that is an amount payable for property acquired for the purpose of gaining or producing income therefrom or for the purpose of gaining or producing income from a business (other than property the income from which would be exempt or property that is an interest in a life insurance policy), or

(iii) for the purpose of rescheduling or restructuring a debt obligation of the taxpayer or an assumption of a debt obligation by the taxpayer, where the debt obligation is

(A) in respect of a borrowing described in subparagraph (i), or

(B) in respect of an amount payable described in subparagraph (ii),

and, in the case of a rescheduling or restructuring, the rescheduling or restructuring, as the case may be, provides for the modification of the terms or conditions of the debt obligation or the conversion or substitution of the debt obligation to or with a share or another debt obligation.

Related Provisions: 18(11) — Limitation; 20(3) — Use of borrowed money; 21 — Cost of borrowed money; 87(2)(j.6) — Amalgamation — continuing corporation; 110.6(1) — "investment expense"; 127.52(1)(b), (c), (c.2), (e.1) — Limitation on deduction for minimum tax purposes; 248(1) — "Borrowed money"; Canada-U.S. Tax Treaty:Art. XXII:4 — No withholding tax on guarantee fee. See also at end of s. 20.

Notes: See VIEWS doc 2013-0507931E5 (intercompany fees for keeping cash in account to reduce bank's interest charges to related corp are arguably deductible).

An 20(1)(e.1) dispute that was conditionally settled (FCA, A-72-20) after procedural decisions was *Burlington Resources*, 2020 TCC 32: CRA argued that amounts an unlimited liability corp paid its parent P to guarantee its bonds were not "guarantee fees" because P was liable for its debts anyway.

20(1)(e.1) amended by 1993 technical bill, effective for expenses incurred after 1987, essentially to add subparas. (ii) and (iii) and the closing words.

Interpretation Bulletins: IT-121R3: Election to capitalize cost of borrowed money (cancelled); IT-341R4: Expenses of issuing shares, units in a trust, interests in a partnership or syndicate and expenses of borrowing money.

Advance Tax Rulings: ATR-49: Long-term foreign debt.

(e.2) **premiums on life insurance — collateral** — the least of the following amounts in respect of a life insurance policy (other than an annuity contract or LIA policy):

(i) the premiums payable by the taxpayer under the policy in respect of the year, if

(A) an interest in the policy is assigned to a restricted financial institution in the course of a borrowing from the institution,

(B) the interest payable in respect of the borrowing is or would, but for subsections 18(2) and (3.1) and sections 21 and 28, be deductible in computing the taxpayer's income for the year, and

(C) the assignment referred to in clause (A) is required by the institution as collateral for the borrowing,

(ii) the net cost of pure insurance in respect of the year (other than in respect of a period after 2013 during which the policy is a 10/8 policy), as determined in accordance with the regulations, in respect of the interest in the policy referred to in clause (i)(A), and

(iii) the portion, of the lesser of the amounts determined under subparagraphs (i) and (ii) in respect of the policy, that can reasonably be considered to relate to the amount owing from time to time during the year by the taxpayer to the institution under the borrowing;

Related Provisions: 127.52(1)(b), (c), (c.2), (e.1) — Limitation on deduction for minimum tax purposes.

Notes: The deduction was denied in: *Quantz*, [2003] 1 C.T.C. 2714 (TCC) (no assignment of policy to financial institution); *Norton*, 2010 TCC 62, para. 49 (unclear whether credit union *required* the insurance or merely *recommended* it); *Emjo Holdings*, 2018 TCC 97 (policy was assigned, but amount of loan owing had been reduced to 10% or nil, and no evidence as to "net cost of pure insurance").

Premiums incurred to secure a loan from a financial institution may not be deductible under 20(1)(e.2) if the institution assigns its rights under the loan agreement to a securitization vehicle, and the taxpayer does not continue to owe the amount to the institution: VIEWS doc 2002-0167085.

The condition in 20(1)(e.2)(i)(B) is satisfied where only a portion of the interest is deductible due to 20(1)(c)(iv): VIEWS docs 2004-0077031E5, 2005-0116651C6.

See also VIEWS docs 2004-0068141E5, 2005-0143281R3, 2005-0162001E5, 2006-0174781C6, 2006-0175101C6, 2006-0191541E5, 2007-0219601C6, 2007-0241911C6, 2008-0270441C6, 2008-0303961E5, 2009-0340381R3, 2011-0428931E5, 2012-0325671C6, 2012-0449631E5; Scholten, "Corporately Held Life Insurance", 8(8) *Tax Hyperion* (Carswell, Aug. 2011); Marino & Natale, *Canadian Taxation of Life Insurance* (Carswell, 10th ed., 2020), §6.4.

See also Notes to 89(1)"capital dividend account", 248(1)"LIA policy" and 248(1)"10/8 policy".

20(1)(e.2) amended by 2013 budget bill #2, for tax years ending after March 20, 2013, essentially to exclude a LIA policy or 10/8 policy.

20(1)(e.2) added by 1991 technical bill, effective for premiums payable after 1989.

Regulations: 308 (net cost of pure insurance).

Interpretation Bulletins: IT-309R2: Premiums on life insurance used as collateral; IT-341R4: Expenses of issuing shares, units in a trust, interests in a partnership or syndicate and expenses of borrowing money.

(f) **discount on certain obligations** — an amount paid in the year in satisfaction of the principal amount of any bond, debenture, bill, note, mortgage, hypothecary claim or similar obligation issued by the taxpayer after June 18, 1971 on which inter-

est was stipulated to be payable, to the extent that the amount so paid does not exceed,

(i) in any case where the obligation was issued for an amount not less than 97% of its principal amount, and the yield from the obligation, expressed in terms of an annual rate on the amount for which the obligation was issued (which annual rate shall, if the terms of the obligation or any agreement relating thereto conferred on its holder a right to demand payment of the principal amount of the obligation or the amount outstanding as or on account of its principal amount, as the case may be, before the maturity of the obligation, be calculated on the basis of the yield that produces the highest annual rate obtainable either on the maturity of the obligation or conditional on the exercise of any such right) does not exceed $4/3$ of the interest stipulated to be payable on the obligation, expressed in terms of an annual rate on

(A) the principal amount of the obligation, if no amount is payable on account of the principal amount before the maturity of the obligation, or

(B) the amount outstanding from time to time as or on account of the principal amount of the obligation, in any other case,

the amount by which the lesser of the principal amount of the obligation and all amounts paid in the year or in any preceding year in satisfaction of its principal amount exceeds the amount for which the obligation was issued, and

(ii) in any other case, $1/2$ of the lesser of the amount so paid and the amount by which the lesser of the principal amount of the obligation and all amounts paid in the year or in any preceding taxation year in satisfaction of its principal amount exceeds the amount for which the obligation was issued;

Related Provisions: 18(1)(f) — Payments on discounted bonds; 18(11) — Limitation; 110.6(1) — "Investment expense"; 127.52(1)(b), (c), (c.2), (e.1) — Limitation on deduction for minimum tax purposes; 142.7(8)(c) — Application to debt transferred to foreign bank branch by Canadian affiliate; 261(7)–(10) — Functional currency reporting. See also at end of s. 20.

Notes: Foreign exchange losses incurred on purchasing and redeeming debt issued by the taxpayer cannot be deducted under 20(1)(f); they are a capital loss under 39(2): *Imperial Oil (Inco)*, 2006 SCC 46. The majority (4:3) wrote: "Although the word 'discount' does not appear in s. 20(1)(f), the opening words of s. 20(1)(f)(i) set out what is commonly accepted as the definition of a discount... Where an obligation is denominated (and repayable) in Canadian dollars ... the formulas in s. 20(1)(f) have the effect of isolating the difference between the face value (principal amount) of the obligation and the amount for which it was issued (i.e., the 'discount'). Where the discount is 3% or less (a 'shallow discount'), it is fully deductible from income under s. 20(1)(f)(i), and where it is more than 3% (a 'deep discount'), it is deductible at the capital rate... [for] debts issued and repayable in Canadian dollars, each branch of s. 20(1)(f) has a clear application and together they encompass what are generally referred to as original issue discounts. In this context, the deduction in s. 20(1)(f) is in respect of a point-in-time expense that is actually incurred only when the debt is repaid — it does not encompass the appreciation or depreciation of the principal amount over time... Parliament intended s. 20(1)(f)(i) to apply to shallow discounts" (paras. 62, 64). The words 'in any other case' in 20(1)(f)(ii) mean 'any case in which the obligation was issued for an amount less than 97%', not "any case in which the cost of repaying the principal amount exceeds the amount for which the debt was issued" (paras. 63-64).

Under *Imperial Oil* (para. 59), 20(1)(f) does not apply to commodity-based loans or exchangeable debentures, but CRA stated at the Cdn Tax Foundation conference, Nov. 28, 2006 (slides distributed) that such financings currently in place will still be eligible for 20(1(f)(ii) treatment. CRA is talking to Justice and Finance and any change in policy to reflect *Imperial Oil* will be announced. See also doc 2010-0357241I7.

In *Tembec Inc. [Provigo Inc., Cascades Inc.]*, 2008 FCA 205, leave to appeal denied by SCC 2009 CarswellNat 72, a loss on the fluctuation of the taxpayer's convertible debentures, when converted, was denied on the basis that the "principal amount" cannot fluctuate. "It is at the time the obligations are issued that it must be determined whether or not they are issued at a discount" (TCC, para. 37). See McGuffin & Samtani, "Federal Court of Appeal Ruling May Lead to Review of Exchangeable Debt", XI(1) *Corporate Structures & Groups* (Federated Press) 599-601 (2008). For exchangeable debentures, CRA has reversed its view that 20(1)(f) applies, for debentures issued after 2009. On exchange, the issuer of the debentures is not entitled to any deduction or capital loss for the appreciation in principal amount over face value. The issuer has a disposition of the underlying shares at FMV: VIEWS doc 2009-0347251C6 (2009 CTF; *Income Tax Technical News* 44); Gabrielle Richards, "Canada Revenue Agency Revises Its Position on Convertible and Exchangeable Debt", XI(3) *CS&G* (Federated Press) 627-30 (2009).

See Marc Ton-That, "Recent Developments Affecting the Taxation of Convertible Debentures", X(3) *Corporate Structures & Groups* (Federated Press) 556-65 (2007).

For rulings on 20(1)(f) see VIEWS docs 2005-0152441R3, 2007-0223521R3, 2009-0323901I7.

The term "bond, debenture, bill, note, mortgage or similar obligation" may not include bankers' acceptances: *Federated Co-operatives*, 2001 FCA 217; leave to appeal denied 2001 CarswellNat 1788 (SCC).

Reference to "hypothecary claim" added to 20(1)(f) opening words by 2001 *Civil Code* harmonization bill, effective June 14, 2001. The change is non-substantive; see *Interpretation Act* s. 8.2.

20(1)(f)(ii) amended by 2000 Budget, for amounts that become payable after Oct. 17, 2000.

Income Tax Folios: S3-F6-C1: Interest deductibility [replaces IT-533].

Interpretation Bulletins: IT-341R4: Expenses of issuing shares, units in a trust, interests in a partnership or syndicate and expenses of borrowing money.

I.T. Technical News: 25 (foreign exchange losses); 41 (exchangeable debentures [but policy reversed at 2009 CTF conference]); 44 (exchangeable debentures).

(g) **share transfer and other fees** — where the taxpayer is a corporation,

(i) an amount payable in the year as a fee for services rendered by a person as a registrar of or agent for the transfer of shares of the capital stock of the taxpayer or as an agent for the remittance to shareholders of the taxpayer of dividends declared by it,

(ii) an amount payable in the year as a fee to a stock exchange for the listing of shares of the capital stock of the taxpayer, and

(iii) an expense incurred in the year in the course of printing and issuing a financial report to shareholders of the taxpayer or to any other person entitled by law to receive the report;

Related Provisions: See at end of s. 20.

Notes: In 20(1)(g)(iii), "financial report" means annual and similar reports, and does not cover a takeover bid or spinoff offer or circular: *Boulangerie St-Augustin*, [1995] 2 C.T.C. 2149 (TCC), paras. 15-23 (aff'd on other grounds 1996 CarswellNat 2523 (FCA)); *Rio Tinto*, 2018 FCA 124 (leave to appeal denied 2019 CarswellNat 809 (SCC)), paras. 112-118.

(h), (i) [Repealed under former Act]

Notes: 20(1)(h) and (i), repealed in 1984, allowed deductions for certification fees and discounts on bankers' acceptance fees. These are now included in the definition of "borrowed money" in 248(1), and thus deductible over five years under 20(1)(e).

(j) **repayment of loan by shareholder** — such part of any loan or indebtedness repaid by the taxpayer in the year as was by virtue of subsection 15(2) included in computing the taxpayer's income for a preceding taxation year (except to the extent that the amount of the loan or indebtedness was deductible from the taxpayer's income for the purpose of computing the taxpayer's taxable income for that preceding taxation year), if it is established by subsequent events or otherwise that the repayment was not made as part of a series of loans or other transactions and repayments;

Related Provisions: 20(3) — Use of borrowed money; 110.6(1) — "investment expense"; 227(6.1) — Repayment of loan by shareholder when shareholder is non-resident; 248(10) — Series of transactions. See also at end of s. 20.

Notes: If the shareholder dies, repayment by the estate (but not by a beneficiary) qualifies for 20(1)(j) deduction by the estate (not by the deceased): IT-119R4 para. 32, VIEWS docs 9918015, 2012-0442911C6 [2012 STEP q.6].

20(1)(j) can be used for income averaging. See Notes to 15(2).

20(1)(j) might not work if the 15(2) loan is split income: Lee, "Shareholder Loans", 9(2) *Canadian Tax Focus* (ctf.ca) 1-2 (May 2019).

Does "included" in 20(1)(j) mean "as reported", "as finally assessed by CRA" or "as determined by the Court"? In *Quigley*, [1996] 1 C.T.C. 2378, and *Skinner*, 2009 TCC 269, the TCC interpreted it as "finally assessed". See Nathanson, "Included Versus Reported", 24(9) *Canadian Tax Highlights* (ctf.ca) 5 (Sept. 2016). The same issue arises in interpreting "claimed" or "deducted"; does this mean claimed on a return, or (validly) claimed and allowed? There are cases and arguments to support both readings. See David Sherman's *Canada GST Service* Analysis to ETA V-I-2 (on *Taxnet Pro*).

After a shareholder becomes non-resident, 20(1)(j) cannot be used to reduce income taxed under s. 115 since the non-resident is not taxed under Part I (only Part XIII) on income from property: VIEWS doc 2002-0156915.

Interpretation Bulletins: IT-119R4: Debts of shareholders and certain persons connected with shareholders.

I.T. Technical News: 3 (paragraphs 15(2)(b) and 20(1)(j)).

CRA Audit Manual: 24.12.3: Repayment of loan by shareholder.

(k) [Repealed under former Act]

Notes: 20(1)(k), repealed by 1988 tax reform, allowed a deduction for the interest portion of a blended payment combining interest and principal. Such amounts are now deductible under the general rule in 20(1)(c) for interest deductibility, since 16(1) deems the interest portion of such a payment to be interest on a debt obligation.

(l) **doubtful or impaired debts** — a reserve determined as the total of

(i) a reasonable amount in respect of doubtful debts (other than a debt to which subparagraph (ii) applies) that have been included in computing the taxpayer's income for the year or a preceding taxation year, and

(ii) where the taxpayer is a financial institution (as defined in subsection 142.2(1)) in the year or a taxpayer whose ordinary business includes the lending of money, an amount in respect of properties (other than mark-to-market properties, as defined in that subsection) that are

(A) impaired loans or lending assets that are specified debt obligations (as defined in that subsection) of the taxpayer, or

(B) impaired loans or lending assets that were made or acquired by the taxpayer in the ordinary course of the taxpayer's business of insurance or the lending of money

equal to the total of

(C) the percentage (not exceeding 100%) that the taxpayer claims of the prescribed reserve amount for the taxpayer for the year, and

(D) in respect of loans, lending assets or specified debt obligations that are impaired and for which an amount is not deductible for the year because of clause (C) (each of which in this clause is referred to as a "loan"), the taxpayer's specified percentage for the year of the lesser of

(I) the total of all amounts each of which is a reasonable amount as a reserve (other than any portion of which is in respect of a sectoral reserve) for a loan in respect of the amortized cost of the loan to the taxpayer at the end of the year, and

(II) the amount determined by the formula

$$0.9M - N$$

where

M is the amount that is the taxpayer's reserve or allowance for impairment (other than any portion of the amount that is in respect of a sectoral reserve) for all loans that is determined for the year in accordance with generally accepted accounting principles, and

N is the total of all amounts each of which is the specified reserve adjustment for a loan (other than an income bond, an income debenture, a small business bond or small business development bond) for the year or a preceding taxation year;

Related Provisions: 12(1)(d) — Income inclusion in following year; 12(4.1) — Regular interest income rules do not apply where 20(1)(l)(ii) applies; 16(7) — Indexed debt obligation rules do not apply where 20(1)(l)(ii) applies; 18(1)(s) — Limitation on deduction by insurer or money lender; 20(1)(p) — Bad debt deduction; 20(2.3) — Sectoral reserve; 20(2.4) — Specified percentage; 20(27) — Non-arm's length acquisition of loan or lending asset; 20(30) — Specified reserve adjustment; 22(1) — Sale of accounts receivable; 79.1(8) — Creditor cannot deduct amount for bad or impaired debt where property seized; 87(2)(g) — Amalgamations — reserves; 87(2)(h) — Amalgamations — debts; 87(2.2) — Amalgamation of insurers; 88(1)(e.1), (g) — Application of reserve on windup; 111(5.3) — Restriction after change in control of corporation or trust; 138(5)(a) — Deductions not allowed; 138(11.31)(b) — Change in use rule for insurance properties does not apply for purposes of 20(1)(l); 142.3(1)(c) — Amount deductible in respect of specified debt obligation; 142.3(4) — Specified debt obligation rules do not apply where 20(1)(l)(ii) applies; 142.5(8.2)(a) — Rules on certain deemed dispositions of debt obligation; 142.7(7) — Application to foreign bank branch on transfer of business from affiliate; 257 — Formula cannot calculate to less than zero; 261(7)(e) — Functional currency reporting. See also at end of s. 20.

Notes: See Notes to 20(1)(p), and IT-442R paras. 22-27.

In *Cloverdale Paint*, 2006 TCC 628 (Crown's appeal to FCA discontinued), a $4 million reserve for a doubtful debt on receivables from a US subsidiary was allowed (the debt was eventually paid). The factors to be considered, based on *Coppley Noyes*, [1991] 1 C.T.C. 541 (FCTD), are "the time element, a history of the account, financial position of the customer and the general business condition in the locality where the debtor lives or operates, as well as general economic conditions".

In *Martin*, 2007 TCC 339, no deduction was allowed to a lawyer who lent money to start-up companies she was involved with, because she was not in the ordinary business of lending money.

In *Heron Bay Investments*, 2009 TCC 337; rev'd 2010 FCA 203, the TCC held that the taxpayer met the "ordinary business includes the lending of money" condition in 20(1)(l)(ii); the FCA ruled that the judge intervened too much in the trial by asking questions of witnesses, and ordered a new trial.

In *Meilleur*, 2016 TCC 287, para. 5, no 20(1)(l)(i) deduction was allowed because the amounts had not earlier been included in income.

A debt can be found doubtful at year-end based on information available as of the return filing date: *Delle Donne*, 2015 TCC 150, para. 70. The suicide of the debtor's further debtor company's owner and evidence he had been running a Ponzi scheme made it reasonable to call the debt doubtful (paras. 86-88). Attaching a letter to the return explaining that interest income was not being reported because it was not collectible was as good as reporting it and claiming a 20(1)(l) deduction: para. 92.

On 20(1)(l)(ii)(D), see Driedger & Wong, "IFRS 9: Financial Instruments", 26(6) *Canadian Tax Highlights* (ctf.ca) 6-7 (June 2018); Chen & Ross, "Mortgage Investment Corporations Affected by IFRS 9 Uncertainty", 9(4) *Canadian Tax Focus* (ctf.ca) 3-4 (Nov. 2019).

20(1)(l) amended by 1995-97 technical bill, for tax years that end after Sept. 1997, or earlier by election.

Regulations: 8000(a) (prescribed reserve amount).

I.T. Application Rules: 23(5)"investment interest".

Interpretation Bulletins: IT-109R2: Unpaid amounts; IT-188R: Sale of accounts receivable; IT-291R3: Transfer of property to a corporation under subsection 85(1); IT-302R3: Losses of a corporation — the effect that acquisitions of control, amalgamations, and windings-up have on their deductibility; IT-442R: Bad debts and reserve for doubtful debts; IT-505: Mortgage foreclosures and conditional sales repossessions (cancelled).

CRA Audit Manual: 12.15.9: Revising capital cost allowance and other permissive deductions.

Advance Tax Rulings: ATR-6: Vendor reacquires business assets following default by purchaser.

(l.1) reserve for guarantees, etc. — a reserve in respect of credit risks under guarantees, indemnities, letters of credit or other credit facilities, bankers' acceptances, interest rate or currency swaps, foreign exchange or other future or option contracts, interest rate protection agreements, risk participations and other similar instruments or commitments issued, made or assumed by a taxpayer who was an insurer or whose ordinary business included the lending of money in favour of persons with whom the taxpayer deals at arm's length in the ordinary course of the taxpayer's business of insurance or the lending of money, equal to the lesser of

(i) a reasonable amount as a reserve for credit risk losses of the taxpayer expected to arise after the end of the year under or in respect of such instruments or commitments, and

(ii) 90% of the reserve for credit risk losses of the taxpayer expected to arise after the end of the year under or in respect of those instruments or commitments determined for the year in accordance with generally accepted accounting principles,

or such lesser amount as the taxpayer may claim;

Related Provisions: 12(1)(d.1) — Income inclusion in following year; 20(27) — Non-arm's length acquisition of loan or lending assets; 87(2)(g) — Amalgamations — reserves; 87(2)(h) — Amalgamation — debts; 87(2.2) — Amalgamation of insurers; 88(1)(e.1), (g) — Application of reserve on windup; 142.7(7) — Application to foreign bank branch on transfer of business from affiliate; 261(7)(e) — Functional currency reporting. See also at end of s. 20.

Notes: For interpretation of "ordinary business included the lending of money", see Notes to 15(2.3) and 20(1)(p).

20(1)(l.1)(ii) amended by 1995-97 technical bill, effective on the same basis as the amendments to 20(1)(l) (see Notes to 20(1)(l)). The "prescribed recovery rate" under former 20(1)(l.1)(ii) was found in Reg. 8001.

Proposed Addition — Reserve on premium received on reopening bond issue

Letter from Dept. of Finance, Oct. 24, 2001:

Dear [xxx]:

I am writing in response to your letter dated October 17, 2001 concerning the income tax treatment of a premium received by a taxpayer upon the re-opening of a bond issue where the bond's interest rate is higher than the market rate of interest for similar debt instruments at the time of such re-opening.

You have requested that we consider recommending a provision that would permit a taxpayer to claim a reserve in respect of such a premium with the intended effect that the income tax treatment would follow the accounting treatment. This would avoid having the premium included in income at the outset, only to be offset by increased interest expense over the remaining term of the debt.

We are sympathetic to your request. Consequently it will be recommended to the Minister of Finance that an amendment be introduced to the Act that will have the effect of matching the premium income and the enhanced interest expense that gives rise to the premium. Our recommendation regarding the timing of the effective date will likely depend on the exact nature of our recommendation, however, we would, at a minimum, recommend that a taxpayer be able to elect to have the amendment apply to debts issued after 2000.

While I can, as you know, offer no assurance that either the Minister or Parliament will accept our recommendation, I have no reason to believe that this would be controversial.

We trust that this letter addresses your concerns.

Yours sincerely,

Brian Ernewein, Director, Tax Legislation Division, Tax Policy Branch

Notes: Finance has confirmed (Nov. 26, 2014) that this amendment is still pending.

(m) reserve in respect of certain [future] goods and services — subject to subsection (6), where amounts described in paragraph 12(1)(a) have been included in computing the taxpayer's income from a business for the year or a previous year, a reasonable amount as a reserve in respect of

(i) goods that it is reasonably anticipated will have to be delivered after the end of the year,

(ii) services that it is reasonably anticipated will have to be rendered after the end of the year,

(iii) periods for which rent or other amounts for the possession or use of land or of chattels or movables have been paid in advance, or

(iv) repayments under arrangements or understandings of the class described in subparagraph 12(1)(a)(ii) that it is reasonably anticipated will have to be made after the end of the year on the return or resale to the taxpayer of articles other than bottles;

Related Provisions: 12(1)(e)(i) — Income inclusion in following year; 20(1)(m.2) — Deduction for amounts repaid; 20(6) — Reserve for food, drink or transportation; 20(7) — Where 20(1)(m) does not apply; 20(24) — Amounts paid for undertaking future obligations; 32(1) — Insurance agents and brokers; 34 — Professional business — election to exclude work in progress until 2017; 87(2)(g) — Amalgamations — reserves; 88(1)(e.1) — Subsidiary can claim reserve on windup; 142.7(7) — Application to foreign bank branch on transfer of business from affiliate; 261(7)(e) — Functional currency reporting. See also at end of s. 20.

Notes: "Land" in 20(1)(m)(iii) may include buildings: see 70(5.2) Notes.

This reserve is for prepaid income from business only (see "Business income vs property income" in 9(1) Notes): *Auto Maculate*, 2020 TCC 105, para. 148.

In *Blue Mountain Resorts*, [2002] 4 C.T.C. 2016 (TCC), a ski resort was allowed a reserve under 20(1)(m) for season passes sold before its October year-end for the winter ski season. The passes were contracts with the holders for the provision of future services.

Ellis Vision, 2003 TCC 912, allowed a reserve for licence fees received for use of a TV production in a future period, saying that amounts included in income under 9(1) may simultaneously fall under 12(1)(a) and thus be eligible for reserve. CRA has taken the opposite view: VIEWS docs 2001-0091415, 2003-0037947, *Income Tax Technical News* 30, 32. CRA did not appeal *Ellis Vision* but does not accept that it applies in all cases, yet appeared to accept it in 2015-0595661C6 [2015 APFF q.9]. Note that 20(1)(m) refers to amounts "*described* in paragraph 12(1)(a)", not necessarily *taxed* by 12(1)(a). The earlier case of *Burrard Yarrows Corp.*, [1988] 2 C.T.C. 90 (FCA) may thus no longer be good law. Thus, in *Doteasy Technology*, 2009 TCC 324, a reserve was allowed to a website hosting company for prepaid service contracts extending past year-end, even though the income was taxable under 9(1). The same should apply to an amount taxable under 56.4(2) (but see 2015-0618601E5, where CRA rejects this but without addressing this point).

Where a club charged initiation fees and prorated the income over 10 years, this was effectively a claim of a 20(1)(m) reserve: *Argus Holdings*, [2001] 1 C.T.C. 115 (FCA).

Where a business is sold on a tax-deferred basis, the 20(1)(m) reserve does not follow the business. Neither seller nor buyer can claim a reserve under 20(1)(m) at year-end. If the seller has paid a reasonable amount to the buyer as consideration for undertaking to provide the goods or services, they may file a joint election under 20(24) to alleviate this consequence: VIEWS doc 2004-0057741E5.

See also Frankovic, "The Taxation of Prepaid Income", 50(4) *Canadian Tax Journal* 1239-1306 (2002).

20(1)(m) reserve was allowed in VIEWS docs 2002-0140805 (prepaid funeral arrangements — IT-531 para. 20); 2004-0105461R3 (rent prepayment); 2003-0048241E5 (reclamation costs); 2008-0277531E5 (upfront loan fee); 2008-0300811I7 (gift certificates); 2009-033954117 (services to be rendered).

No reserve was allowed in docs 2005-0141171C6 (obligation to perform services was to a government entity and prepayment would not have to be repaid); 2009-0329391E5 (possible customer returns — IT-215R para. 13 ["archived", cancelled Sept. 30/12] is still valid); 2014-0538131C6 (App Store sale of gaming points to be used up over time). See also 20(6) (food, drink, transportation), 20(7) (various exclusions) and 32(1) (no reserve to insurance agent or broker for unearned commissions).

20(1)(m)(iii) amended by 2002-2013 technical bill (Part 4 — bijuralism), effective June 26, 2013, to add "or movables".

Interpretation Bulletins: IT-92R2: Income of contractors; IT-154R: Special reserves; IT-165R: Returnable containers (cancelled); IT-215R: Reserves, contingent accounts (cancelled); IT-261R: Prepayment of rents; IT-321R: Insurance agents and brokers — unearned commissions (cancelled); IT-531: Eligible funeral arrangements.

I.T. Technical News: 18 (*Oerlikon Aérospatiale* case); 30 (prepaid income — whether 9(1) or 12(1)(a) applies); 32 (reserve for prepaid amount: impact of the *Ellis Vision* case).

CRA Audit Manual: 27.25.0: Income of professionals and fiscal period issues.

Forms: T2 Sched. 13: Continuity of reserves.

(m.1) **manufacturer's warranty reserve** — where an amount described in paragraph 12(1)(a) has been included in computing the taxpayer's income from a business for the year or a preceding taxation year, a reasonable amount as a reserve in respect of goods or services that it is reasonably anticipated will have to be delivered or rendered after the end of the year pursuant to an agreement for an extended warranty

(i) entered into by the taxpayer with a person with whom the taxpayer was dealing at arm's length, and

(ii) under which the only obligation of the taxpayer is to provide such goods or services with respect to property manufactured by the taxpayer or by a corporation related to the taxpayer,

not exceeding that portion of the amount paid or payable by the taxpayer to an insurer that carries on an insurance business in Canada to insure the taxpayer's liability under the agreement in respect of an outlay or expense made or incurred after December 11, 1979 and in respect of the period after the end of the year;

Related Provisions: 12(1)(e)(i) — Income inclusion in following year; 20(24) — Amounts paid for undertaking future obligations; 87(2)(g), (j) — Amalgamations — reserves; 88(1)(e.1) — Subsidiary can claim reserve on windup; 261(7)(e) — Functional currency reporting. See also at end of s. 20.

Interpretation Bulletins: IT-154R: Special reserves.

(m.2) **repayment of amount previously included in income** — a repayment in the year by the taxpayer of an amount required by paragraph 12(1)(a) to be included in computing the taxpayer's income from a business for the year or a preceding taxation year;

Related Provisions: 20(1)(m) — Reserve; 87(2)(j) — Amalgamations; 88(1)(e.1) — Subsidiary can claim reserve on windup. See also at end of s. 20.

Notes: For a ruling allowing a 20(1)(m.2) deduction see VIEWS doc 2008-0303431R3.

In *Silverman*, 2013 TCC 366, S was denied deduction for repayment of a publisher's advance received before S was resident in Canada. (The Court did not consider 20(1)(m.2) or whether 12(1)(a) would be considered to have applied.)

Interpretation Bulletins: IT-154R: Special reserves.

(m.3) **[unamortized bond premium]** — the unamortized amount at the end of the year in respect of the amount that was received in excess of the principal amount of a bond (in this paragraph referred to as the "premium") received by the issuer in the year, or a previous year, for issuing the bond (in this paragraph referred to as the "new bond") if

(i) the terms of the new bond are identical to the terms of bonds previously issued by the taxpayer (in this paragraph referred to as the "old bonds"), except for the date of issuance and total principal amount of the bonds,

(ii) the old bonds were part of an issuance (in this paragraph referred to as the "original issuance") of bonds by the taxpayer,

(iii) the interest rate on the old bonds was reasonable at the time of the original issuance,

(iv) the new bond is issued on the re-opening of the original issuance,

(v) the amount of the premium at the time of issuance of the new bond is reasonable, and

(vi) the amount of the premium has been included in the taxpayer's income for the year or a previous taxation year;

Related Provisions: 12(1)(d.2) — Income inclusion in next year.

Notes: See 12(1)(d.2) for the next year's matching income inclusion from this reserve. 20(1)(m.3) added by 2017 budget bill #2, for bonds issued after 2000.

(n) **reserve for unpaid amounts** — if an amount included in computing the taxpayer's income from the business for the year or for a preceding taxation year in respect of property sold in the course of the business is payable to the taxpayer after the end of the year and, except where the property is real or immovable property, all or part of the amount was, at the time of the sale, not due until at least two years after that time, a reasonable amount as a reserve in respect of any part of the amount that can reasonably be regarded as a portion of the profit from the sale;

Related Provisions: 12(1)(e)(ii) — Income inclusion in following year; 20(8) — No deduction in certain circumstances; 66.2(2) — Deduction for cumulative Canadian development expenses; 66.4(2) — Deduction for cumulative Canadian oil and gas property expenses; 72(1)(a) — No reserve for year of death; 79.1(4), (6)(c) — Deemed amount where property repossessed by creditor; 87(2)(g), (i), (ll) — Amalgamations — reserves; 88(1)(e.1) — Subsidiary can claim reserve on windup; 142.7(7) — Application to foreign bank branch on transfer of business from affiliate; 261(7)(e) — Functional currency reporting. See also at end of s. 20.

Notes: The reserve under 20(1)(n) is limited to 3 years: see 20(8). However, the "reasonable" reserve need not be an inflexible formula such as CRA applies to 40(1)(a)(iii): *Ennisclare Corp.*, [1984] C.T.C. 286 (FCA).

No reserve can be claimed under 20(1)(n) for recaptured depreciation under 13(1), since such amount is not "profit from the sale": *Odyssey Industries*, [1996] 2 C.T.C. 2401 (TCC).

CRA says no reserve can be claimed on a sale of goodwill (or pre-2017 eligible capital property), because such sale is not "in the course of the business": IT-123R6 para. 37; VIEWS doc 2007-0250301E5. See however "Wind-down or post-termination costs" in Notes to 18(1)(a).

If the purchaser owing the unpaid amount is related to the taxpayer, 78(1) could apply to the purchaser.

20(1)(n) amended by 2002-2013 technical bill (Part 4 — bijuralism), effective June 26, 2013, to add "or immovable". Earlier amended by 1994 technical bill.

Proposed **20(1)(n.1)** in the July 12, 1994 draft legislation on debt forgiveness was not enacted. See instead 61.4.

Income Tax Folios: S4-F7-C1: Amalgamations of Canadian corporations [replaces IT-474R2].

Interpretation Bulletins: IT-109R2: Unpaid amounts; IT-123R6: Transactions involving eligible capital property; IT-152R3: Special reserves — sale of land; IT-154R: Special reserves; IT-442R: Bad debts and reserves for doubtful debts; IT-505: Mortgage foreclosures and conditional sales repossessions (cancelled).

Information Circulars: 88-2, para. 24: General anti-avoidance rule — section 245 of the *Income Tax Act*.

Forms: T2 Sched. 13: Continuity of reserves; T2069: Election in respect of amounts not deductible as reserves for the year of death.

(o) **reserve for quadrennial survey** — such amount as may be prescribed as a reserve for expenses to be incurred by the taxpayer by reason of quadrennial or other special surveys required under the *Canada Shipping Act*, or the regulations under that Act, or under the rules of any society or association for the classification and registry of shipping approved by the Minister of Transport for the purposes of the *Canada Shipping Act*;

Related Provisions: 12(1)(h) — Inclusion into income — previous reserve; 87(2)(g) — Amalgamations — reserves; 88(1)(e.1) — Subsidiary can claim reserve on windup; 261(7)(e) — Functional currency reporting. See also at end of s. 20.

Notes: This is a discretionary deduction, so if a tugboat operator did not claim the reserve in the three years before a quadrennial survey, it can claim the full deduction in the fourth year: VIEWS doc 2011-0395271E5.

Regulations: 3600 (prescribed amount).

(p) **bad debts** — the total of

(i) all debts owing to the taxpayer that are established by the taxpayer to have become bad debts in the year and that have been included in computing the taxpayer's income for the year or a preceding taxation year, and

(ii) all amounts each of which is that part of the amortized cost to the taxpayer at the end of the year of a loan or lending asset (other than a mark-to-market property, as defined in subsection 142.2(1)) that is established in the year by the taxpayer to have become uncollectible and that,

(A) where the taxpayer is an insurer or a taxpayer whose ordinary business includes the lending of money, was made or acquired in the ordinary course of the taxpayer's business of insurance or the lending of money, or

(B) where the taxpayer is a financial institution (as defined in subsection 142.2(1)) in the year, is a specified debt obligation (as defined in that subsection) of the taxpayer;

Related Provisions: 12(1)(i) — Income inclusion — bad debts recovered; 12.4 — Bad debt inclusion; 20(1)(l) — Reserve for doubtful debts; 20(4)–(4.2) — Bad debt on disposition of depreciable property or eligible capital property; 20(27) — Non-arm's length acquisition of loan or lending assets; 22(1) — Sale of accounts receivable; 50(1) — Bad debt creating ABIL; 50(1)(a) — Deemed disposition where debt becomes bad debt; 60(f) — Deduction for bad debt on restrictive covenant; 79.1(7)(d) — Deduction by creditor for bad debt where property seized; 79.1(8) — No deduction for principal amount of bad debt where property seized by creditor; 87(2)(g), (h) — Amalgamations; 87(2.2) — Amalgamation of insurers; 88(1)(g) — Windup of subsidiary insurer; 111(5.3) — Restriction after change in control of corporation or trust; 142.3(1)(c) — Amount deductible in respect of specified debt obligation; 142.4(1)"tax basis"(p) — Disposition of specified debt obligation by financial institution; 142.5(8)(d)(i) — First deemed disposition of mark-to-market debt obligation; 142.5(8.2)(a) — Rules on certain deemed dispositions of debt obligation; 142.7(7) — Application to foreign bank branch on transfer of business from affiliate. See also at end of s. 20.

Notes: A doubtful debt can be deducted under 20(1)(l), included in income the next year under 12(1)(d), then deducted again under 20(1)(l) if still doubtful. If it becomes a bad debt (see IT-442R and IT-159R3), it is deducted permanently under 20(1)(p), and any later recovery is included in income by 12(1)(i). A bad debt cannot be claimed for the increase in doubtful accounts from a prior year as a substitute for the rules in 20(1)(l) and 12(1)(d): *Groscki*, 2011 FCA 174. Nor can a bad debt be offset against revenues so that the revenues are not reported: *Groscki*, 2017 TCC 249, para. 8. Where debt is forgiven, see s. 80 and VIEWS doc 2011-0393561E5.

The bad debt can be deducted under either subpara. (i) or (ii).

20(1)(p)(i) allows a deduction if the debt was previously included in income (e.g., as interest or as a receivable from sale of inventory): *Newmont Canada (Hemlo Gold)*, 2012 FCA 214. Attaching a letter to the return explaining that interest income was not being reported because it was not collectible was as good as reporting it and claiming the deduction: *Delle Donne*, 2015 TCC 150, paras. 89-92. "A debt owed to a taxpayer can be said to have been included in the taxpayer's income only where the debt represents unpaid revenue that has been earned by the taxpayer in connection with a business or property": *Brake*, 2013 FCA 172, para. 6. In *Supercom Canada*, 2005 TCC 589, bad debts from an insolvent UK subsidiary were deductible because they arose from sales to the sub, despite the CRA's claim that they were advances of capital. In *Morrissey*, 2011 TCC 373, para. 37, no deduction was allowed because the loan (to a subcontractor) was a personal loan. In *Groscki*, 2017 TCC 249, para. 13, there was no evidence of the claimed bad debts.

20(1)(p)(ii) allows a deduction only if the taxpayer is a financial institution, insurer or one "whose ordinary business includes the lending of money". Taxpayers failed the "ordinary business" test in: *Loman Warehousing*, [2001] 1 C.T.C. 50 (FCA); *Zaenker*, 2007 TCC 440; *725685 Alberta*, 2009 FCA 194; *966838 Ontario*, 2009 TCC 256 (deduction denied to 1 taxpayer and allowed to 1); *Smith*, 2010 TCC 9; *Newmont Canada*, 2011 TCC 148 (rev'd on other grounds by FCA, above) (gold producer); *Yazdani*, 2012 TCC 371, para. 21; *Heron Bay*, rev'd 2010 FCA 203 (loans were structured for tax advantage; FCA ordered new trial because judge intervened too much); *Meilleur*, 2016 TCC 287 (loans to fund real estate projects). See also Notes to 15(2.3) for the meaning of the phrase.

No debt? In *Terrador Investments (Serin Holdings)*, [1999] 3 C.T.C. 520 (FCA; leave to appeal denied 2000 CarswellNat 869 (SCC)), no 20(1)(l) or (p) deduction was allowed for bad debt on a 12(1)(k) deemed dividend triggered by a 93(1) election, where an offsetting deduction was allowed under 113(1). Similarly, in *Mills*, 2011 FCA 219

(leave to appeal denied 2012 CarswellNat 385), a promissory note that was deemed by 84.1(1)(b) to be "paid" as a dividend could not be an "unpaid" bad debt for 20(1)(p).

Bad debt determination: The taxpayer must take steps to establish the debt is bad in the taxation year: *Clackett*, 2007 TCC 499. See Notes to 50(1) re whether this means the establishing must be done in the year or that the debt became bad in the year (though one can argue it does not become bad until the taxpayer so establishes). Deduction was disallowed in: *Jones*, 2008 TCC 293 (J had not made sufficient efforts to collect the debt); *Atlantic Thermal*, 2016 TCC 135 (bad debt not proven); *Hokhold*, 2018 FCA 163 (H could not identify which debts were bad).

One can determine a bad debt using information available on the return filing date re events "that reveal the true state of affairs as of the end of the relevant taxation year": *Delle Donne*, 2015 TCC 150, para. 81. Since the taxpayer "acted reasonably and in a pragmatic, business-like manner" in determining the debt was uncollectible, the deduction was allowed.

Alternative deductions: Where 20(1)(p) relief is denied, a capital loss may be available, e.g. *Smith*, 2010 TCC 9. In *Excell Duct Cleaning*, 2005 TCC 776, bad loans to franchisees were deductible as business expenses, not under 20(1)(p). In *SRI Homes*, 2014 TCC 180, after the FCA ordered a new trial, the TCC found shareholder loans were not made in the ordinary course of SRI's moneylending business, but were for income producing purpose so losses were deductible under ordinary principles under 9(1).

For CRA interpretation of 20(1)(l) and (p) see VIEWS docs 2007-0223281I7, 2009-0328191E5, 2009-0349861E5, 2012-0449671E5, 2012-043499117, 2014-0525361E5. See also Notes to 9(2) at "Losses were allowed to a defrauded investor" and "Profits from non-business", for CRA allowing 20(1)(p) to undo past reporting of income that never existed due to fraud. See also "Warning: Watch out for bad-debt tax schemes" (Sept. 29, 2020), tinyurl.com/cra-bad-debt.

The GST/HST component of a bad debt should not be claimed under 20(1)(p) but as a net tax deduction under *Excise Tax Act* s. 231 (see David M. Sherman, *Practitioner's Goods and Services Tax Annotated*): VIEWS docs 2002-0180587, 2009-033607117; but see also doc 2009-030929117.

20(1)(p) amended by 1995-97 technical bill, for tax years ending after Feb. 22, 1994.

Income Tax Folios: S3-F9-C1: Lottery winnings, miscellaneous receipts, and income (and losses) from crime [replaces IT-185R, IT-213R, IT-256R, IT-334R2].

Interpretation Bulletins: IT-109R2: Unpaid amounts; IT-123R4: Disposition of and transactions involving eligible capital property; IT-123R6: Transactions involving eligible capital property; IT-159R3: Capital debts established to be bad debts; IT-188R: Sale of accounts receivable; IT-291R3: Transfer of property to a corporation under subsection 85(1); IT-302R3: Losses of a corporation — the effect that acquisitions of control, amalgamations, and windings-up have on their deductibility; IT-442R: Bad debts and reserve for doubtful debts; IT-488R2: Winding-up of 90%-owned taxable Canadian corporations (cancelled); IT-505: Mortgage foreclosures and conditional sales repossessions (cancelled).

Advance Tax Rulings: ATR-6: Vendor reacquires business assets following default by purchaser.

(q) **employer's contributions to RPP or PRPP** — such amount in respect of employer contributions to registered pension plans or pooled registered pension plans as is permitted under subsection 147.2(1) or 147.5(10);

Related Provisions: See under 147.2(1).

Notes: 20(1)(q) limits deductibility of employer RPP contributions, but not administrative costs, subject to 18(1)(a): IT-105 [cancelled Sept. 30/12], VIEWS doc 2009-0314851E5.

For deductibility of employer contributions to an Individual Pension Plan see Notes to Reg. 8515(1).

20(1)(q) amended by 2012 budget bill #2 (effective Dec. 14, 2012), 1990 pension bill. Pre-1991, it provided a deduction for employer contributions to an employee's RPP, capped at $3,500, linked with 20(1)(s) and 20(22). See now 147.1.

Interpretation Bulletins: IT-105: Administrative costs of pension plans.

Information Circulars: 72-13R8: Employee's pension plans.

Registered Plans Compliance Bulletins: 2 (compensation for RPP purposes); 3 (employer over-contributions to a registered pension plan: double taxation).

(r) **employer's contributions under retirement compensation arrangement** — amounts paid by the taxpayer in the year as contributions under a retirement compensation arrangement in respect of services rendered by an employee or former employee of the taxpayer, other than where it is established, by subsequent events or otherwise, that the amounts were paid as part of a series of payments and refunds of contributions under the arrangement;

Related Provisions: 8(1)(m.2) — Employee's RCA contribution deductible; 12(1)(n.3) — Retirement compensation arrangement; 18(1)(o.2) — Retirement compensation arrangement; 87(2)(j.3) — Amalgamation — continuing corporation; 153(1)(p) — Withholding; 227(8.2) — RCA — failure to withhold; 248(10) — Series of transactions. See also at end of s. 20.

Notes: See Notes to 248(1)"retirement compensation arrangement". CRA will not allow the deduction to an employer who contributes to a trust to fund a letter of credit to fund pension benefits (VIEWS doc 2007-0245551C6), or where most of the employee's service was rendered to subsidiaries rather than to the employer itself (2007-0259851I7, 2010-0388761R3).

Forms: T737-RCA: Statement of contributions paid to a custodian of a retirement compensation arrangement.

(s) **employer's contributions under employee life and health trust** — such amount in respect of employer contributions paid to a trustee under an employee life and health trust as is permitted by subsections 144.1(4) to (7);

Related Provisions: 18(1)(o.3) — No deduction to ELHT except as permitted by 20(1)(s).

Notes: 20(1)(s) added by 2010 budget bill #2, effective 2010.

Former 20(1)(s) repealed by 1990 pension bill, effective 1991. Employer contributions to registered pension plans are now deducted per 147.2. See Notes to 20(1)(q).

(t) [Repealed under former Act]

Notes: 20(1)(t), repealed by 1988 tax reform, allowed a deduction for SR&ED expenses as permitted by 37 and 37.1. The deduction under 37 is still explicitly available under that section, which is part of the same subdivision as s. 20.

(u) **patronage dividends** — such amounts in respect of payments made by the taxpayer pursuant to allocations in proportion to patronage as are permitted by section 135;

Related Provisions: See at end of s.20.

(v) **mining taxes** — such amount as is allowed by regulation in respect of taxes on income for the year from mining operations;

Proposed Addition — Deduction of mining taxes paid for statute-barred years

Letter from Dept. of Finance, Sept. 3, 2019: Mr. Pierre Gratton, President and CEO, The Mining Association of Canada, Ottawa ON

Dear Mr. Gratton:

Deductibility of Mining Taxes

I am writing in response to requests by your organization in respect of the deductibility of mining taxes in computing the income of a taxpayer. More particularly, I understand that the issue is in respect of reassessments, under the relevant statutes, of mining taxes that are made, in some instances, many years after the taxation year in which the relevant operations occur, so late that income tax reassessments cannot be made to take into account the changes to the taxpayer's mining tax liability for that year.

Mining taxes are generally levied by a province or territory in respect of production from mining operations. Under the combined operation of paragraph 20(1)(v) of the *Income Tax Act* (the Act) and subsection 3900(2) of the *Income Tax Regulations* (the Regulations), taxpayers are allowed a deduction "in respect of taxes on income for the year from mining operations". Thus, where a taxpayer is assessed an additional amount of mining taxes, say, two years after the year in which the relevant mining activities are carried on, the taxpayer must amend its tax return for the earlier year in order to claim a deduction in respect of the payment of the additional mining tax.

I understand that there are taxpayers who have been reassessed additional mining taxes a number of years after the year in which the relevant mining operations took place. In some of these situations, the taxation year in which the relevant mining operations were carried on is barred from reassessment under the Act at the time the taxpayer attempted to deduct the amounts in computing its income tax liability. In such cases, the Canada Revenue Agency has found itself unable to accept deductions for these increased mining taxes. You object to this treatment.

Our Comments

We are sympathetic and are prepared to recommend to the Minister of Finance that amendments be made to the Act and the Regulations to address this issue. Specifically, we will recommend that a deduction for mining taxes be allowed for the taxation year in which the mining taxes are paid if the mining taxes paid are in respect of income from mining operations that were carried on in a prior taxation year of the taxpayer that is barred from reassessment under the Act. The deduction will be equal to the amount that would have been allowed for the taxation year in which the relevant mining operations were carried on if that year had not be [should say "been" — ed.] barred from reassessment. We will also recommend that this amendment be made retroactive to taxation years that end after 2007.

While we cannot offer any assurance that either the Minister of Finance or Parliament will agree with our recommendation in respect of this matter, we hope that this statement of our intentions is helpful.

Yours sincerely,

Brian Ernewein, Assistant Deputy Minister — Legislation, Tax Policy Branch

Related Provisions: See at end of s. 20.

Notes: Taxes on income are not incurred to earn income, and so are normally non-deductible due to 18(1)(a) (see Notes to 18(1)(t)). 20(1)(v) overrides this for provincial mining taxes: see opening words of 20(1). See also Reg. 3900, Notes to 20(1)(v.1).

See VIEWS docs 2004-008632I7 (deductibility of Ont. mining taxes and QC royalties on surface mineral substances extraction); 2014-0559451E5 (timing of deduction for QC mining tax).

With the repeal of former 18(1)(m) since 2008, Crown royalties and resource taxes are deductible under s. 9.

Regulations: 3900 (amount allowed).

(v.1) [Repealed]

Notes: 20(1)(v.1) which allowed the resource allowance, repealed by 2003 resource bill (see Notes to 20(1)(v)), effective for taxation years that begin after 2006 (phased out from 2003-06). The resource allowance is explained in *Cameco*, 2018 TCC 195, paras. 858-860 (aff'd 2020 FCA 112 without discussing it; leave to appeal denied 2021 CarswellNat 377 (SCC)).

The resource allowance was replaced with an investment tax credit for pre-production mining expenditures: 127(9)"investment tax credit"(a.3). See Gamble, *Taxation of Canadian Mining* (Carswell, looseleaf or *Taxnet Pro* Reference Centre), chap. 5; Carr & Calverley, *Canadian Resource Taxation* (Carswell, looseleaf or *Taxnet Pro* Reference Centre), chap. 6; Carr, "Recent Amendments to the Resource Tax Regime", 2003 Cdn Tax Foundation conference report, 34:1-34; Dept. of Finance, *Improving the Income Taxation of the Resource Sector in Canada* (March 2003). For commodity hedging under the pre-2007 rules see Rowe & Richardson, "Resource Allowance and Swap Transactions", IV(4) *Resource Sector Taxation* (Federated Press) 310-15 (2006).

Parallel deletions over 2003-07 were the income inclusion of a resource loss (12(1)(z.5)); and income inclusion of, or prohibition on the deduction of, Crown royalties and taxes on production or resource property ownership (12(1)(o), 18(1)(m)). Actual Crown royalties and mining taxes paid will be deductible (20(1)(v) — refunds included in income under 12(1)(x) or (x.2)); and the federal corporate tax rate on resource income will be reduced from 28% to 21% (125.11, 123.4). A new tax credit of 10% applies to qualifying mineral exploration expenditures (127(9)"pre-production mining expenditure"). A transitional rule reduces the income inclusion for the Alberta Royalty Tax Credit for 2003-2012 (12(1)(x.2)).

20(1)(v.1) deductions were allowed in: *Barrick Gold*, 2017 TCC 18 (forward hedging gains were mine production profits); *Cameco*, 2018 TCC 195, paras. 857-887; aff'd 2020 FCA 112; leave to appeal denied 2021 CarswellNat 377 (SCC) (losses on uranium sales); *Exxonmobil*, 2019 TCC 108 (transporting Hibernia crude to an "offshore loading system" was not transporting petroleum for Reg. 1204(3)(a)). In *Baytex Energy*, 2015 ABQB 278, rectification (or rescission in the alternative) was granted to cancel transfers that should not have continued when the resource allowance was eliminated. (See Notes to 169(1) re rectification; due to *Fairmont Hotels* this would no longer be granted.)

Ontario did not copy these changes, so the pre-2003 federal rules continued to apply through 2008 for Ont. corporate tax purposes (2004 Ont. budget). As of Jan. 2009, the 25% Ontario resource allowance was eliminated as part of harmonization whereby the CRA administers Ont. corporate tax: Canada-Ontario Memorandum of Agreement, Oct. 6, 2006. See John Gravelle, "Ontario-Federal Memorandum of Agreement", IV(4) *Resource Sector Taxation* 316-18 (2006).

(w) **employer's contributions under profit sharing plan** — an amount paid by the taxpayer to a trustee in trust for employees of the taxpayer or of a corporation with whom the taxpayer does not deal at arm's length, under an employees profit sharing plan as permitted by section 144;

Related Provisions: 12(1)(n) — Receipts from employees profit sharing plan — inclusion in income of employer; 144(5) — Employer's contribution to trust deductible. See also at end of s. 20.

(x) **employer's contributions under registered supplementary unemployment benefit plan** — an amount paid by the taxpayer to a trustee under a registered supplementary unemployment benefit plan as permitted by section 145;

Related Provisions: 6(1)(a)(i) — Employer's contribution not a taxable benefit to employee; 18(1)(i) — No deduction except as permitted by s. 145; 145(5) — Payments by employer deductible. See also at end of s. 20.

(y) **employer's contributions under deferred profit sharing plan** — an amount paid by the taxpayer to a trustee under a deferred profit sharing plan as permitted by subsection 147(8);

Related Provisions: See at end of s. 20.

(z) **cancellation of lease** — the proportion of an amount not otherwise deductible that was paid or that became payable by the taxpayer before the end of the year to a person for the cancellation of a lease of property of the taxpayer leased by the taxpayer to that person that

(i) the number of days that remained in the term of the lease (including all renewal periods of the lease), not exceeding 40 years, immediately before its cancellation and that were in the year

is of

(ii) the number of days that remained in the term of the lease (including all renewal periods of the lease), not exceeding 40 years, immediately before its cancellation,

in any case where the property was owned at the end of the year by the taxpayer or by a person with whom the taxpayer was not dealing at arm's length and no part of the amount was deductible by the taxpayer under paragraph (z.1) in computing the taxpayer's income for a preceding taxation year;

Related Provisions: 13(5.5) — Lease cancellation payment not included as rental payment under 13(5.4) for CCA purposes; 18(1)(q) — No deduction other than under 20(1)(z) or (z.1); 20(1)(z.1) — Cancellation payment where property not owned at end of year; 87(2)(j.5) — Amalgamations — cancellation of lease. See also at end of s. 20.

Notes: 20(1)(z) does not apply to a lease cancellation payment made for a personal-use condo, since 20(1) applies only to income "from a business or property": VIEWS doc 2019-0812611C6 [2019 APFF q.2].

Interpretation Bulletins: IT-359R2: Premiums and other amounts re leases; IT-467R2: Damages, settlements, and similar payments.

(z.1) idem [lease cancellation payment where property not owned at year-end] — an amount not otherwise deductible that was paid or that became payable by the taxpayer before the end of the year to a person for the cancellation of a lease of property of the taxpayer leased by the taxpayer to that person, in any case where

(i) the property was not owned at the end of the year by the taxpayer or by a person with whom the taxpayer was not dealing at arm's length, and

(ii) no part of the amount was deductible by the taxpayer under this paragraph in computing the taxpayer's income for any preceding taxation year,

to the extent of the amount thereof (or in the case of capital property, $\frac{1}{2}$ of the amount thereof) that was not deductible by the taxpayer under paragraph (z) in computing the taxpayer's income for any preceding taxation year;

Related Provisions: See under 20(1)(z) and at end of s. 20.

Notes: 20(1)(z.1) amended by 2000 Budget to change "¾" to "¹¹½", effective for amounts that become payable after Oct. 17, 2000. For amounts that became payable from Feb. 27, 2000 through Oct. 17, 2000, read "²/₃".

Interpretation Bulletins: IT-359R2: Premiums and other amounts re leases; IT-467R2: Damages, settlements, and similar payments.

(aa) landscaping of grounds — an amount paid by the taxpayer in the year for the landscaping of grounds around a building or other structure of the taxpayer that is used by the taxpayer primarily for the purpose of gaining or producing income therefrom or from a business;

Related Provisions: 18(3.1)(a) — Costs relating to construction of building or ownership of land. See at end of s. 20.

Notes: This deduction is on a cash basis, not based on amounts billed. It overrides capital treatment under 18(1)(b). The taxpayer must own the building to claim the deduction, but need not own the land: *Toronto College Park*, [1994] 1 C.T.C. 194 (TCC) (appealed on other grounds to FCA and SCC).

"Used primarily" is usually taken by CRA to mean "more than 50%", but can also mean "first in importance". See Notes to 73(3) on "used principally".

Since 20(1)(aa) is a *permissive* provision, it does not restrict deductions that pass 18(1)(a) and (b) and would otherwise be allowed. For landscaping costs for a home office, see Notes to 18(12).

See also VIEWS doc 2012-0442571E5.

Interpretation Bulletins: IT-296: Landscaping of grounds (cancelled); IT-304R2: Condominiums; IT-485: Cost of clearing or levelling land [to be amended re golf courses, per I.T. Technical News 20].

I.T. Technical News: 20 (tax treatment of golf courses).

(bb) fees paid to investment counsel — an amount, other than a commission, that

(i) is paid by the taxpayer in the year to a person or partnership the principal business of which

(A) is advising others as to the advisability of purchasing or selling specific shares or securities, or

(B) includes the provision of services in respect of the administration or management of shares or securities, and

(ii) is paid for

(A) advice as to the advisability of purchasing or selling a specific share or security of the taxpayer, or

(B) services in respect of the administration or management of shares or securities of the taxpayer;

Proposed Amendment — Investment management fees of registered plan paid by taxpayer

Letter from Dept. of Finance, Aug. 26, 2019: See under 207.01(1)"advantage"(b).

Related Provisions: 18(1)(u) — Investment counsel fees for RRSP, RRIF or TFSA are non-deductible; 87(2.2) — Amalgamation of insurers; 88(1)(g) — Windup of subsidiary insurer; 110.6(1) — "investment expense". See also at end of s. 20.

Notes: Commissions are excluded by the opening words of 20(1)(bb), but fees may be based on the portfolio value and not be commissions: IT-238R2 para. 4. For the meaning of "commission" (generally a percentage, not just on contingency) see *Rio Tinto*, 2018 FCA 124, paras. 81-94 (leave to appeal denied 2019 CarswellNat 809 (SCC)).

Beyond general investment counselling fees, 20(1)(bb) may apply to fees paid to investment banks for advice on buying a company: Jakolev & Prgomet, "Takeover Costs", 9(1) *Canadian Tax Highlights* (ctf.ca) 4-5 (Jan. 2001). Many such fees were allowed in *Rio Tinto*, 2016 TCC 172, paras. 154-175 (aff'd 2018 FCA 124; leave to appeal denied 2019 CarswellNat 809), on both acquisition and butterfly spinoff (overriding VIEWS docs 2002-0151435, 2006-0170871I7). See also *Boulangerie St-Augustin*, 1996 CarswellNat 2523 (FCA); Notes to 20(1)(e), (g) and (cc).

CRA thinks 20(1)(bb) applies only to investment portfolio advice, so a public company cannot deduct costs of advice re acquiring its own shares on the market: 2006-0196261C6 (this may be wrong in light of *Rio Tinto*). For more VIEWS on 20(1)(bb) see 2006-0207071E5; 2010-0381561E5 (some trustee fees may be deductible); 2013-047756117 (whether estate can deduct trustee fees, and general comments).

Deduction was denied in: *Walmsley Estate*, [1999] 2 C.T.C. 2956 (TCC) (insufficient evidence as to what portion of fees related to earning income); *Ellis*, 2007 TCC 289, aff'd on other grounds 2008 FCA 92 (accounting advice on structuring sale of shares was not advice on the advisability of selling them); *Davies*, 2007 TCC 503 (payee's principal business was not advising on purchasing and selling shares); *DiCosmo*, 2015 TCC 325, para. 49 (aff'd 2017 FCA 60) (insufficient evidence).

Deduction was allowed in *Wickham Estate*, 2014 TCC 352, where S was paid $40,000 as "committee", to manage the assets and income of mentally infirm W, and S had no other business; however, 20% was disallowed under 18(1)(u) as relating to W's RRSP.

"Principal business", in CRA's view, refers to more than 50% of time spent or gross revenue earned: VIEWS doc 2005-0124131E5. In determining "principal business", a business carried on by a partnership is considered carried on by the corporate partners: 2011-0409011E5.

Due to "of the taxpayer", the securities must belong to the person claiming the deduction, so RDSP investment counselling fees are not deductible by the RDSP holder: VIEWS doc 2014-0526891E6. A segregated fund is not considered a "security" for 20(1)(bb): 2014-0523321C6 [2014 CALU q.5], 2014-0542581E5.

20(1)(bb) amended by 2002-2013 technical bill (Part 5 — technical), effective for amounts paid after June 2005, to extend the rule to an amount paid to a partnership.

Interpretation Bulletins: IT-124R6: Contributions to registered retirement savings plans; IT-238R2: Fees paid to investment counsel.

(cc) expenses of representation [or lobbying] — an amount paid by the taxpayer in the year as or on account of expenses incurred by the taxpayer in making any representation relating to a business carried on by the taxpayer,

(i) to the government of a country, province or state or to a municipal or public body performing a function of government in Canada, or

(ii) to an agency of a government or of a municipal or public body referred to in subparagraph (i) that had authority to make rules, regulations or by-laws relating to the business carried on by the taxpayer, including any representation for the purpose of obtaining a licence, permit, franchise or trade mark relating to the business carried on by the taxpayer;

Related Provisions: 13(12) — Application to depreciable property; 20(9) — Amortizing claim over 10 years. See also at end of s. 20.

Notes: For the meaning of "municipal or public body...", see Notes to 149(1)(c).

Many costs of a takeover and a spinoff were allowed under 20(1)(cc) in *Rio Tinto*, 2016 TCC 172, paras. 176-189 (aff'd on other grounds 2018 FCA 124; leave to appeal denied 2019 CarswellNat 809 (SCC)). Acquisition of a large French company met the test of "relating to" RT's business, as it enhanced that business: TCC para. 178.

20(1)(cc) should apply to GST/HST objection and appeal expenses. (Income tax objection and appeal expenses fall under 60(o).) 20(1)(cc) does not say the business of the taxpayer must be *currently* carried on; *quaere* whether it applies to start-up lobbying or to a GST appeal after the business shuts down. Note that 20(1)(cc) requires a *business*, so it does not apply to property costs that are otherwise capital expenses under 18(1)(b); see Notes to 9(1) under "Business income vs property income".

Deductible lobbying costs may include wages, travel costs and other related expenses paid to make the representation: VIEWS doc 2004-0074581E5.

Patent application costs are deductible under 20(1)(cc): IT-99R5, IT-477 and VIEWS doc 2001-0109617. Stone quarry approval costs can qualify: 2014-0520941E5. Voluntary disclosure costs relating to a business can qualify: 2014-0528451C6.

A person making representations to a federal department or agency may have to register under the *Lobbying Act (LA)* (lobbying by a former "designated public office holder" is prohibited for 5 years: *LA* s. 10.11; *Carson*, 2019 ONCA 396). Contact the Office of the Commissioner of Lobbying at 613-957-2760, or ocl-cal.gc.ca (where all existing and past registered lobbyists can be viewed). See also Meunier et al., *Lobbying in Canada* (Carswell, looseleaf); Coleman, "Are You a Lobbyist?", 5(4) *Tax for the Owner-Manager* (ctf.ca) 4-5 (Oct. 2005); Chenier, "Political Activities May Lead to Lobbying Registration Requirements", 27(2) *Canadian Not-for-Profit News* (Carswell) 9-11 (Feb. 2019) and "Lobbying by Charities and NPOs", 27(3) 17-19 (March 2019).

Reimbursed legal costs deducted under 20(1)(cc) are taxable: *Goff Construction*, 2009 FCA 60 (leave to appeal denied 2009 CarswellNat 3108 (SCC)).

Interpretation Bulletins: IT-99R5: Legal and accounting fees; IT-477: Capital cost allowance — patents, franchises, concessions and licences.

(dd) **investigation of site** — an amount paid by the taxpayer in the year for investigating the suitability of a site for a building or other structure planned by the taxpayer for use in connection with a business carried on by the taxpayer;

Related Provisions: 53(1)(n) — Valuation or surveying costs — addition to adjusted cost base. See also at end of s. 20.

Notes: This is a "cash basis" deduction, since it is based on when the amount is paid. The taxpayer need not own the property or be the builder for site investigation costs to be deductible, as long as the taxpayer will use the building; and the deduction is available even if no building is ever built: *Parker Brothers*, 2007 TCC 74.

Interpretation Bulletins: IT-350R: Investigation of site.

(ee) **utilities service connection** — an amount paid by the taxpayer in the year to a person (other than a person with whom the taxpayer was not dealing at arm's length) for the purpose of making a service connection to the taxpayer's place of business for the supply, by means of wires, pipes or conduits, of electricity, gas, telephone service, water or sewers supplied by that person, to the extent that the amount so paid was not paid

(i) to acquire property of the taxpayer, or

(ii) as consideration for the goods or services for the supply of which the service connection was undertaken or made;

Related Provisions: See at end of s. 20.

Notes: See VIEWS docs 2004-0084151E5 (20(1)(ee) applies to cost of constructing irrigation pipe on farmer's land, where farmer does not acquire the pipe); 2012-0442571E5 (whether cost of land includes certain costs).

Tax Executives Institute recommended to Finance (Dec. 5, 2018, q. C.4) an amendment to eliminate the requirement that the person receiving payment must be the same one that supplies the utility service. Finance is open to this.

Interpretation Bulletins: IT-452: Utility service connections (cancelled); IT-482R: Pipelines.

(ff) **payments by farmers** — an amount paid by the taxpayer in the year as a levy under the *Western Grain Stabilization Act*, as a premium in respect of the gross revenue insurance program established under the *Farm Income Protection Act* or as an administration fee in respect of a net income stabilization account;

Related Provisions: 12(1)(p) — Certain payments made to farmers — income inclusion. See also at end of s. 20.

Notes: See Notes to 248(1)"net income stabilization account". 20(1)(ff) amended by 1992 technical bill, effective 1991.

Forms: RC322: AgriInvest adjustment request; T1163: Statement A — AgriStability and AgriInvest programs information and statement of farming activities for individuals; T1164: Statement B — AgriStability and AgriInvest programs information and statement of farming activities for additional farming operations; T1175: Calculation of CCA and business-use-of-home expenses; T1273: Statement A — Harmonized AgriStability and AgriInvest programs information and statement of farming activities for individuals; T1274: Statement B — Harmonized AgriStability and AgriInvest programs information and statement of farming activities for additional farming operations; T1275: AgriStability and AgriInvest programs additional information and adjustment request form.

(gg) [Repealed]

Notes: 20(1)(gg) added by 1991 Budget, but moved to 20(1)(qq) by 1992 technical bill, retroactive to its introduction. See Notes to 20(1)(qq). An earlier 20(1)(gg), repealed by 1986 Budget, provided a 3% inventory allowance.

(hh) **repayments of inducements, etc.** — an amount repaid by the taxpayer in the year pursuant to a legal obligation to repay all or part of a particular amount

(i) included under paragraph 12(1)(x) in computing the taxpayer's income for the year or a preceding taxation year, or

(ii) that is, by reason of subparagraph 12(1)(x)(vi) or subsection 12(2.2), not included under paragraph 12(1)(x) in computing the taxpayer's income for the year or a preceding taxation year, where the particular amount relates to an outlay or expense (other than an outlay or expense that is in respect of the cost of property of the taxpayer or that is or would be, if amounts deductible by the taxpayer were not limited by reason of paragraph 66(4)(b), subsection 66.1(2), subparagraph 66.2(2)(a)(ii), the words "30% of" in clause 66.21(4)(a)(ii)(B), clause 66.21(4)(a)(ii)(C) or (D) or subparagraph 66.4(2)(a)(ii), deductible under section 66, 66.1, 66.2, 66.21 or 66.4) that would, if the particular amount had not been received, have been deductible in computing the taxpayer's income for the year or a preceding taxation year;

Related Provisions: 60(s) — Repayment of policy loan; 79(4)(d) — Subsequent payment by debtor following surrender of property deemed to be repayment of assistance; 87(2)(j.6) — Amalgamation — continuing corporation; 148(9)"adjusted cost basis"E — "adjusted cost basis"; 248(18) — Repaid GST/HST input tax credit deemed to be repaid assistance. See also at end of s. 20.

Notes: 20(1)(hh) allows a deduction for amounts taxable under 12(1)(x) and repaid, but only if the repayment is "pursuant to a legal obligation": VIEWS doc 2012-0432981E5.

20(1)(hh) applies to repayment of GST/HST input tax credits on meals and entertainment. See Karen Yull, "M&E Expense Reporting for Income and Sales Tax Purposes", 7(9) *Tax Hyperion* (Carswell, Sept. 2010).

20(1)(hh) amended by 2000 Budget (effective for taxation years that begin after 2000), 1992 Economic Statement and 1990 GST.

Interpretation Bulletins: IT-273R2: Government assistance — general comments.

CRA Audit Manual: 27.20.0: Inducement payments.

(hh.1) **repayment of obligation** — ³⁄₄ of any amount repaid by the taxpayer in the year (on or after the time the taxpayer ceases to carry on a business) under a legal obligation to repay all or part of an amount the taxpayer received or was entitled to receive that was assistance from a government, municipality or other public authority (whether as a grant, subsidy, forgivable loan, deduction from tax, investment allowance or as any other form of assistance) in respect of, or for the acquisition of, property the cost of which was an eligible capital expenditure of the taxpayer in respect of the business if the amount of the eligible capital expenditure of the taxpayer in respect of the business was reduced by paragraph 14(10)(c) because of the amount of the assistance the taxpayer received or was entitled to receive;

Related Provisions: 79(4)(b) — Subsequent payment by debtor following surrender of property deemed to be repayment of assistance.

Notes: See 12(1)(x) Notes for meaning of "assistance" and related words.

20(1)(hh.1) amended by 2016 budget bill #2, effective 2017, as part of changing eligible capital property (ECP) to CCA Class 14.1 (see Notes to 20(1)(b)). Before 2017, read:

(hh.1) ³⁄₄ of any amount (other than an amount to which paragraph 14(10)(b) applies in respect of the taxpayer) repaid by the taxpayer in the year under a legal obligation to repay all or part of an amount to which paragraph 14(10)(c) applies in respect of the taxpayer;

Until the end of 2016, 20(1)(hh.1) allowed a deduction for repayment of assistance received in respect of ECP related to a business carried on by the taxpayer. The deduction (¾ of the amount repaid) applied only where the taxpayer ceased to carry on the business before the repayment. Repayments of assistance before that time were added to eligible capital expenditure under 14(10)(b).

20(1)(hh.1) added by 1994 technical bill, for amounts repaid after Feb. 21, 1994.

Interpretation Bulletins: IT-273R2: Government assistance — general comments.

(ii) **inventory adjustment** — the amount required by paragraph 12(1)(r) to be included in computing the taxpayer's income for the immediately preceding year;

Related Provisions: 87(2)(j.1) — Amalgamations — inventory adjustment. See also at end of s. 20.

(jj) [Repealed]

Notes: 20(1)(jj), "reinsurance commission", repealed by 2002-2013 technical bill (Part 5 — technical), for reinsurance commissions paid after 1999. It and 12(1)(s) were no longer appropriate due to 18(9.02).

(kk) **exploration and development grants** — the amount of any assistance or benefit received by the taxpayer in the year as a deduction from or reimbursement of an expense that is a tax (other than the goods and services tax) or royalty to the extent that

(i) the tax or royalty is, by reason of the receipt of the amount by the taxpayer, not deductible in computing the taxpayer's income for a taxation year, and

(ii) the deduction or reimbursement was included by the taxpayer in the amount determined for J in the definition "cumulative Canadian exploration expense" in subsection 66.1(6), for M in the definition "cumulative Canadian development expense" in subsection 66.2(5) or for I in the definition "cumulative Canadian oil and gas property expense" in subsection 66.4(5);

Related Provisions: See at end of s. 20.

Notes: 20(1)(kk) amended by 1990 GST, effective 1991.

(ll) **repayment of interest** — such part of any amount payable by the taxpayer because of a provision of this Act, or of an Act of a province that imposes a tax similar to the tax imposed under this Act, as was paid in the year and as can reasonably be considered to be a repayment of interest that was included in computing the taxpayer's income for the year or a preceding taxation year;

Related Provisions: 129(2.2), 131(3.2), 132(2.2), 133(7.02), 164(3.1) — Provisions requiring repayment of interest. See also at end of s. 20.

Notes: 20(1)(ll) amended by 1993 technical bill, for tax years that begin after 1991, to apply to any provision requiring repayment of interest rather than just 164(3.1), as a result of the addition of 129(2.2), 131(3.2), 132(2.2) and 133(7.02).

(mm) **cost of substances injected in reservoir** — the portion claimed by the taxpayer of an amount that is an outlay or expense made or incurred by the taxpayer before the end of the year that is a cost to the taxpayer of any substance injected before that time into a natural reservoir to assist in the recovery of petroleum, natural gas or related hydrocarbons to the extent that that portion was not

(i) otherwise deducted in computing the taxpayer's income for the year, or

(ii) deducted in computing the taxpayer's income for any preceding taxation year,

except that where the year is less than 51 weeks, the amount that may be claimed under this paragraph by the taxpayer for the year shall not exceed the greater of

(iii) that proportion of the maximum amount that may otherwise be claimed under this paragraph by the taxpayer for the year that the number of days in the year is of 365, and

(iv) the amount of such outlay or expense that was made or incurred by the taxpayer in the year and not otherwise deducted in computing the taxpayer's income for the year;

Related Provisions: 10(5)(c) — Property deemed to be inventory with cost of nil; 66(13.1) — Short taxation years; 87(2)(j.2) — Amalgamation — continuing corporation. See also at end of s. 20.

Notes: 20(1)(mm) amended by 1996 Budget, effective for 1996 and later taxation years, and by 1991 technical bill.

(nn) **Part XII.6 tax** — the tax, if any, under Part XII.6 paid in the year or payable in respect of the year by the taxpayer (depending on the method regularly followed by the taxpayer in computing the taxpayer's income);

Related Provisions: 18(1)(t) — Part XII.6 tax not non-deductible. See also at end of s. 20.

Notes: 20(1)(nn) added by 1996 Budget, for 1997 and later taxation years. See 211.91.

Former 20(1)(nn), repealed by 1988 tax reform, provided a deduction for Part VI tax paid. Part VI tax is now reduced by Part I tax instead; see 190.1(3).

(nn.1) [Repealed]

Notes: 20(1)(nn.1) repealed by 2017 budget bill #1, for expenditures incurred after March 21, 2017 (as part of repeal of the investment tax credit for child-care spaces), unless incurred before 2020 under a written agreement entered into by that date. For earlier expenditures, read:

(nn.1) recapture of investment tax credits — child care space amount — total of all amounts (other than an amount in respect of a disposition of a depreciable property) added because of subsection 127(27.1) or (28.1) to the taxpayer's tax otherwise payable under this Part for any preceding taxation year;

See Notes to 127(27.1). 20(1)(nn.1) added by 2007 budget bill #2, effective March 19, 2007.

(oo) **salary deferral arrangement** — any deferred amount under a salary deferral arrangement in respect of another person to the extent that it was

(i) included under paragraph 6(1)(a) as a benefit in computing the income of the other person for the taxation year of the other person that ends in the taxpayer's taxation year, and

(ii) in respect of services rendered to the taxpayer;

Related Provisions: 6(1)(i) — Salary deferral arrangement payments; 6(11) — Salary deferral arrangement; 12(1)(n.2) — Forfeited salary deferral amounts; 18(1)(o.1) — Deductions — General limitations — Salary deferral arrangement; 87(2)(j.3) — Amalgamation — continuation of corporation. See also at end of s. 20.

(pp) **idem** — any amount under a salary deferral arrangement in respect of another person (other than an arrangement established primarily for the benefit of one or more non-resident employees in respect of services to be rendered outside Canada) to the extent that it was

(i) included under paragraph 6(1)(i) in computing the income of the other person for the taxation year of the other person that ends in the taxpayer's taxation year, and

(ii) in respect of services rendered to the taxpayer;

Related Provisions: 18(1)(o.1) — Salary deferral arrangement; 87(2)(j.3) — Amalgamation — continuation of corporation.

Notes: 20(1)(pp) added by 1991 technical bill, effective 1986.

(qq) **disability-related modifications to buildings** — an amount paid by the taxpayer in the year for prescribed renovations or alterations to a building used by the taxpayer primarily for the purpose of gaining or producing income from the building or from a business that are made to enable individuals who have a mobility impairment to gain access to the building or to be mobile within it;

Related Provisions: 18(3.1)(a) — Costs relating to construction of building or ownership of land; 20(1)(rr) — Disability-related equipment.

Notes: 20(1)(qq) enacted by 1992 Budget/technical bill, this version effective for renovations and alterations made after February 25, 1992. 20(1)(qq) was originally 20(1)(gg) as added by 1991 Budget but was moved to (qq) retroactively. For the 1991 proposed 20(1)(qq), see Notes to 20(1)(c).

Regulations: 8800 (prescribed renovations and alterations).

(rr) **disability-related equipment** — an amount paid by the taxpayer in the year for any prescribed disability-specific device or equipment;

Related Provisions: 20(1)(qq) — Disability-related modifications to buildings. See also at end of s. 20.

Notes: 20(1)(rr) added by 1992 Budget/technical bill and amended by 1993 technical bill, both effective for amounts paid after February 25, 1992. The later amendment uses "disability-specific" in place of "acquired primarily to assist individuals who have a sight or hearing impairment". Thus, devices can be prescribed for persons who have other kinds of impairments such as mobility impairments; see Reg. 8801(c).

Some of the devices that qualify under 20(1)(rr) are eligible for the medical expense credit under 118.2 for individuals. See Reg. 5700.

Regulations: 8801 (prescribed devices and equipment).

(ss) **qualifying environmental trusts** — a contribution made in the year by the taxpayer to a qualifying environmental trust under which the taxpayer is a beneficiary;

Related Provisions: 12(1)(z.1) — Inclusion in income of amount received from qualifying environmental trust; 87(2)(j.93) — Amalgamation — continuing corporation; Reg. 1204(1)(f), 1204(1.1)(a)(ii) — Amount deducted under 20(1)(ss) excluded from resource allowance computation.

Notes: For examples of 20(1)(ss) deductions see rulings in Notes to 248(1)"qualifying environmental trust".

20(1)(ss) added by 1994 Budget, and amended by 1997 Budget to change "mining reclamation trust" to "qualifying environmental trust"; the same change was made throughout the Act.

Proposed 20(1)(ss) in the July 12, 1994 debt forgiveness draft legislation was enacted as 20(1)(uu).

(tt) **acquisition of interests in qualifying environmental trusts** — the consideration paid by the taxpayer in the year for the acquisition from another person or partnership of all or part of the taxpayer's interest as a beneficiary under a qualifying environmental trust, other than consideration that is the assumption of a reclamation obligation in respect of the trust;

Related Provisions: 12(1)(z.2) — Inclusion in income on disposition of interest in qualifying environmental trust; 87(2)(j.93) — Amalgamation — continuing corporation; Reg. 1204(1)(f), 1204(1.1)(a)(ii) — Amount deducted under 20(1)(tt) excluded from resource allowance computation.

Notes: 20(1)(tt) added by 1994 Budget, effective for taxation years that end after February 22, 1994, and amended by 1997 Budget, effective for taxation years that end after February 18, 1997, to change "mining reclamation trust" to "qualifying environmental trust" (the same change was made throughout the Act).

(uu) **debt forgiveness** — any amount deducted in computing the taxpayer's income for the year because of paragraph 80(15)(a) or subsection 80.01(10);

Related Provisions: 28(1)(g) — Deduction from farming or fishing income when using cash method.

Notes: 20(1)(uu) added by 1994 technical bill, for tax years that end after Feb. 21, 1994. It was first proposed as 20(1)(ss), before enactment of 20(1)(ss) and (tt) by 1994 Budget.

(vv) **countervailing or anti-dumping duty** — an amount paid in the year by the taxpayer as or on account of an existing or proposed countervailing or anti-dumping duty in respect of property (other than depreciable property);

Related Provisions: 12(1)(z.6) — Refund of duties included in income; 13(21)"undepreciated capital cost"D.1, K — Inclusion of duties in UCC of depreciable property.

Notes: For detailed discussion of these duties see Saroli & Tereposky, "Changes to Canada's Anti-Dumping and Countervailing Duty Laws for the New Millennium", 79(3) *Canadian Bar Review* 352-68 (2000).

In *Industries Perron*, 2013 FCA 176, para. 39, no deduction was allowed for preliminary countervailing duty (later cancelled), where the taxpayer did not pay the duty directly but purchased term deposits to lodge with a bank to guarantee payment.

20(1)(vv) added by 1998 Budget, for amounts that become payable after Feb. 23, 1998. For the parallel reduction in u.c.c. for depreciable property, see 13(21)"undepreciated capital cost"K.

(ww) **split income** — where the taxpayer is a specified individual in relation to the year, the individual's split income for the year; and

Related Provisions: 118(2)B, 118(4)(a.2), 122.5(1)"adjusted income"(b), 122.6"adjusted income"(b), 122.7(1)"adjusted net income"(c), 180.2(1)"adjusted income"(b) — Deduction under 20(1)(ww) disallowed for purposes of various credits, benefits and OAS clawback; 120(3)(c) — No deduction in determining income not earned in a province and income subject to Quebec abatement; 120.4 — Income-splitting tax payable by child.

Notes: 20(1)(ww) added by 1999 Budget, for 2000 and later tax years. It allows a deduction for amounts of "split income" that are taxed at a high rate under 120.4. This ensures that such amounts are not also taxed at regular rates. The deduction does not apply for purposes of obtaining the old age credit, other personal credits, the GST/HST Credit, Canada Child Benefit, Canada Workers Benefit, and for the Old Age Security clawback: see Related Provisions above. It does however reduce net income for the medical expense credit threshold (118.2(1):C) and charitable donations (75% of net income allowed: 118.1(1)"total gifts"(a)(iii)).

Where a taxable capital gain is subject to TOSI (120.4(1)"split income"(e)(i)(A)), but the taxpayer also has capital losses, the effect of 20(1)(ww) allowing a deduction is that the losses can no longer be used against the gain.

(xx) **derivative forward agreement** — in respect of a derivative forward agreement of a taxpayer, the amount determined by the formula

$$A - B$$

where

A is the lesser of

(i) the total of all amounts each of which is

(A) if the taxpayer acquires a property under the agreement in the year or a preceding taxation year, the portion of the amount by which the cost to the taxpayer of the property exceeds the fair market value of the property at the time it is acquired by the taxpayer that is attributable to an underlying interest other than an underlying interest referred to in subparagraphs (b)(i) to (iii) of the definition "derivative forward agreement" in subsection 248(1), or

(B) if the taxpayer disposes of a property under the agreement in the year or a preceding taxation year, the portion of the amount by which the fair market value of the property at the time the agreement is entered into by the taxpayer exceeds the "proceeds of disposition" (within the meaning assigned by Subdivision C) of the property that is attributable to an underlying interest other than an underlying interest referred to in clauses (c)(i)(A) to (C) of the definition "derivative forward agreement" in subsection 248(1), and

(ii) the amount that is,

(A) if final settlement of the agreement occurs in the year and it cannot reasonably be considered that one of the main reasons for entering into the agreement is to obtain a deduction under this paragraph, the amount determined under subparagraph (i), or

(B) in any other case, the total of all amounts included under paragraph 12(1)(z.7) in computing the taxpayer's income in respect of the agreement for the year or a preceding taxation year, and

B is the total of all amounts deducted under this paragraph in respect of the agreement for a preceding taxation year.

Related Provisions: 12(1)(z.7) — Income inclusion; 53(2)(w), (x) — Reduction in ACB; 257 — Formula cannot calculate to less than zero.

Notes: See Notes to 248(1)"derivative forward agreement". For the meaning of "one of the main reasons" in A(ii)(A), see Notes to 83(2.1).

20(1)(xx) added by 2013 budget bill #2, effective on the same basis as 12(1)(z.7). 20(1)(xx)(i)(A), (B) both amended by 2017 budget bill #2, for acquisitions and dispositions after Sept. 15, 2016, to add "the portion of" and "that is attributable ... subsection 248(1)".

(1.1) Application of subsec. 13(21) — The definitions in subsection 13(21) apply to any regulations made under paragraph (1)(a).

Notes: 20(1.1) added in the RSC 1985 (5th Supp) consolidation, effective for tax years ending after Nov. 1991. This rule had been in the opening words of 13(21).

(1.2) Application of subsec. 12.2(11) — The definitions in subsection 12.2(11) apply to paragraph (1)(c).

Notes: 20(1.2) added in the RSC 1985 (5th Supp) consolidation, effective for tax years ending after Nov. 1991. This rule had been in the opening words of 12.2(11).

(2) Borrowed money — For the purposes of paragraph (1)(c), where a person has borrowed money in consideration of a promise by the person to pay a larger amount and to pay interest on the larger amount,

(a) the larger amount shall be deemed to be the amount borrowed; and

(b) where the amount actually borrowed has been used in whole or in part for the purpose of earning income from a business or property, the proportion of the larger amount that the amount actually so used is of the amount actually borrowed shall be deemed to be the amount so used.

Related Provisions: See at end of s. 20.

Income Tax Folios: S3-F6-C1: Interest deductibility [replaces IT-533].

(2.01) Limitation of expression "interest" — 10/8 policy —
For the purposes of paragraphs (1)(c) and (d), interest does not include an amount if

(a) the amount

(i) is paid, after March 20, 2013 in respect of a period after 2013, in respect of a life insurance policy that is, at the time of the payment, a 10/8 policy, and

(ii) is described in paragraph (a) of the definition "10/8 policy" in subsection 248(1); or

(b) the amount

(i) is payable, in respect of a life insurance policy, after March 20, 2013 in respect of a period after 2013 during which the policy is a 10/8 policy, and

(ii) is described in paragraph (a) of the definition "10/8 policy" in subsection 248(1).

Notes: See Notes to 248(1)"10/8 policy". 20(2.01) added by 2013 budget bill #2, effective for taxation years ending after March 20, 2013.

Income Tax Folios: S3-F6-C1: Interest deductibility [replaces IT-533].

(2.1) Limitation of expression "interest" [re policy loan] —
For the purposes of paragraphs (1)(c) and (d), "interest" does not include an amount that is paid after the taxpayer's 1977 taxation year or payable in respect of a period after the taxpayer's 1977 taxation year, depending on the method regularly followed by the taxpayer in computing the taxpayer's income, in respect of interest on a policy loan made by an insurer except to the extent that the amount of that interest is verified by the insurer in prescribed form and within the prescribed time to be

(a) interest paid in the year on that loan; and

(b) interest (other than interest that would, but for paragraph (2.2)(b), be interest on money borrowed before 1978 to acquire a life insurance policy or on an amount payable for property acquired before 1978 that is an interest in a life insurance policy) that is not added to the adjusted cost basis (within the meaning given that expression in subsection 148(9)) to the taxpayer of the taxpayer's interest in the policy.

Related Provisions: See at end of s. 20.

Notes: For interest on a policy loan to be deductible, Form T2210 must be completed by the tax return deadline, but need not be filed with the CRA unless requested: VIEWS docs 2004-0058631M4, 2009-0322421E5.

Regulations: 4001 (prescribed time).

Income Tax Folios: S3-F6-C1: Interest deductibility [replaces IT-533].

Interpretation Bulletins: IT-355R2: Interest on loans to buy life insurance policies and annuity contracts, and interest on policy loans (cancelled).

Forms: T2210: Verification of policy loan interest by the insurer.

(2.2) Limitation of expression "life insurance policy" —
For the purposes of paragraphs (1)(c) and (d), a "life insurance policy" does not include a policy

(a) that is or is issued pursuant to a pooled registered pension plan, a registered pension plan, a registered retirement savings plan, an income-averaging annuity contract or a deferred profit sharing plan;

(b) that was an annuity contract issued before 1978 that provided for annuity payments to commence not later than the day on which the policyholder attains 75 years of age; or

(c) that is an annuity contract all of the insurer's reserves for which vary in amount depending on the fair market value of a specified group of properties.

Related Provisions: 138(12)"life insurance policy". See also at end of s. 20.

Notes: 20(2.2)(a) amended by 2012 budget bill #2, effective Dec. 14, 2012, to add reference to a PRPP.

20(2.2)(c) added by 1991 technical bill, effective 1987.

Income Tax Folios: S3-F6-C1: Interest deductibility [replaces IT-533].

Interpretation Bulletins: IT-355R2: Interest on loans to buy life insurance policies and annuity contracts, and interest on policy loans (cancelled).

(2.3) Sectoral reserve —
For the purpose of clause (1)(l)(ii)(D), a sectoral reserve is a reserve or an allowance for impairment for a loan that is determined on a sector-by-sector basis (including a geographic sector, an industrial sector or a sector of any other nature) and not on a property-by-property basis.

Notes: 20(2.3) added by 1995-97 technical bill, effective on the same basis as the amendment to 20(1)(l).

(2.4) Specified percentage —
For the purpose of clause (1)(l)(ii)(D), a taxpayer's specified percentage for a taxation year is

(a) where the taxpayer has a prescribed reserve amount for the year, the percentage that is the percentage of the prescribed reserve amount of the taxpayer for the year claimed by the taxpayer under clause (1)(l)(ii)(C) for the year, and

(b) in any other case, 100%.

Notes: 20(2.4) added by 1995-97 technical bill, effective on the same basis as the amendment to 20(1)(l).

Regulations: 8000(a) (prescribed reserve amount).

(3) Borrowed money —
For greater certainty, if a taxpayer uses borrowed money to repay money previously borrowed, or to pay an amount payable for property described in subparagraph (1)(c)(ii) previously acquired (which previously borrowed money or amount payable in respect of previously acquired property is, in this subsection, referred to as the "previous indebtedness"), subject to subsection 20.1(6), for the purposes of paragraphs (1)(c), (e) and (e.1), subsections 20.1(1) and (2), section 21 and subparagraph 95(2)(a)(ii), and for the purpose of paragraph 20(1)(k) of the *Income Tax Act*, Chapter 148 of the Revised Statutes of Canada, 1952, the borrowed money is deemed to be used for the purpose for which the previous indebtedness was used or incurred, or was deemed by this subsection to have been used or incurred.

Related Provisions: See at end of s. 20.

Notes: Although 20(3) technically applies to refinancing *principal*, CRA allows deduction for interest on a loan taken out to pay *interest* on a loan for which interest is deductible under 20(1)(c): VIEWS docs 2005-0116661C6, 2018-0740931E4; as well as a loan taken to replace an interest-free loan (2006-0173731E5) and interim financing using US certificates of deposit (2006-0201321R3).

20(3) was enacted for greater certainty, to "make it clear that interest that is deductible under s. 20(1)(c) does not cease to be deductible because the original loan was refinanced. It serves a practical function in the commercial world of facilitating refinancing": *Lipson*, 2009 SCC 1, para. 30. Shuffling debt as in *Singleton*, 2001 SCC 61 to make it deductible was therefore allowable and did not violate GAAR (although the misuse of 74.1 in *Lipson* did: see 245(2) Notes). 20(3) applied in *Brown*, 2020 TCC 84.

20(3) amended by 2009 budget bill #1 (for periods that begin after Jan. 27, 2009), 2007 budget bill #2 (amendment never in effect), 1994 and 1993 technical bills.

Proposed **20(3.1), (3.2)** [1991] would have allowed interest deductibility where a shareholder is effectively required to borrow money to fund a company's operations. They were withdrawn; in light of later case law (see Notes to 20(1)(c)) they are likely not necessary. See Finance's (Brian Ernewein) comments in Couzin et al., "Interest Expense", 1992 Corporate Management Tax Conference (ctf.ca), 2:1-42.

Income Tax Folios: S3-F6-C1: Interest deductibility [replaces IT-533].

I.T. Application Rules: 69 (meaning of "chapter 148 of ...").

I.T. Technical News: 3 (use of a partner's assets by a partnership).

(4) Bad debts — dispositions of depreciable property —
If an amount that is owing to a taxpayer as or on account of the proceeds of disposition of depreciable property (other than a timber resource property, a passenger vehicle to which paragraph 13(7)(g) applies or a zero-emission passenger vehicle to which paragraph 13(7)(i) applies) of the taxpayer of a prescribed class is established by the taxpayer to have become a bad debt in a taxation year, there may be deducted in computing the taxpayer's income for the year the lesser of

(a) the amount so owing to the taxpayer, and

(b) the amount, if any, by which the capital cost to the taxpayer of that property exceeds the total of the amounts, if any, realized by the taxpayer on account of the proceeds of disposition.

Related Provisions: 20(1)(a) — Capital cost of property; 20(4.11) — Bad debt deduction on disposition of zero-emission automobile to which 13(7)(i) applies; 50(1)(a) — Deemed disposition where debt becomes bad debt; 79.1(7)(d) — Deduction by creditor for bad debt where property seized; 79.1(8) — No deduction for principal amount of bad debt where property seized by creditor. See also at end of s. 20.

Notes: For interpretation see VIEWS doc 2008-030263I17 (bad debt not established) and Notes to 20(1)(p).

Exclusion for expensive passenger vehicle added by 1991 technical bill, for amounts established as bad debts after July 13, 1990. (There is no depreciation recapture or terminal loss on such property; see 13(2) and 20(16.1).)

See Notes to 13(7)(g) re prescribed amount for each year.

20(4) opening words amended by 2019 budget bill #1, effective March 19, 2019, to change "or a passenger vehicle having a cost to the taxpayer in excess of $20,000 or such other amount as may be prescribed" to "a passenger vehicle to which paragraph 13(7)(g) applies or a zero-emission passenger vehicle to which paragraph 13(7)(i) applies". This excludes a ZEPV, but see 20(4.11), which allows the bad debt.

Regulations: 7307(1) (prescribed amount).

Income Tax Folios: S3-F4-C1: General discussion of CCA [replaces IT-220R2].

Interpretation Bulletins: IT-159R3: Capital debts established to be bad debts; IT-442R: Bad debts and reserve for doubtful debts.

I.T. Technical News: 10 (1997 deduction limits and benefit rates for automobiles).

(4.1) Idem — Where an amount that is owing to a taxpayer as or on account of the proceeds of disposition of a timber resource property of the taxpayer is established by the taxpayer to have become a bad debt in a taxation year, the amount so owing to the taxpayer may be deducted in computing the taxpayer's income for the year.

Related Provisions: 50(1)(a) — Deemed disposition where debt becomes bad debt; 79.1(7)(d) — Deduction by creditor for bad debt where property seized; 79.1(8) — No deduction for principal amount of bad debt where property seized by creditor. See at end of s. 20.

Income Tax Folios: S3-F4-C1: General discussion of CCA.

Interpretation Bulletins: IT-442R: Bad debts and reserve for doubtful debts.

(4.11) Bad debts — zero-emission passenger vehicles — If an amount that is owing to a taxpayer as or on account of the proceeds of disposition of a zero-emission passenger vehicle of the taxpayer to which paragraph 13(7)(i) applies is established by the taxpayer to have become a bad debt in a taxation year, there may be deducted in computing the taxpayer's income for the year the lesser of

(a) the amount that would be determined by the formula in subparagraph 13(7)(i)(ii) in respect of the disposition if the amount determined for A in the formula were the amount owing to the taxpayer, and

(b) the amount determined by the formula

$$A - B$$

where

A   is the capital cost to the taxpayer of the vehicle, and

B   is the amount that would be determined by the formula in subparagraph 13(7)(i)(ii) in respect of the disposition if the amount determined for A in the formula were the total amount, if any, realized by the taxpayer on account of the proceeds of disposition.

Related Provisions: 257 — Formula cannot calculate to less than zero.

Notes: 20(4.11) allows a bad debt on sale of a zero-emission passenger vehicle (defined in 248(1)) that cost more than $55,000 before sales taxes. It is similar to 20(4), but prorates the amount deductible based on the fraction used to adjust the proceeds of disposition for Class 54 UCC purposes (see 13(7)(i)(ii)). Added by 2019 budget bill #1, effective March 19, 2019.

(4.2) [Bad debt on sale of] Former eligible capital property — If an amount is deductible under subsection (4) in respect of the disposition of a depreciable property and subsection 13(39) applied to the disposition of the depreciable property, the amount deductible under subsection (4) is equal to ¾ of the amount that would be deductible without reference to this subsection.

Related Provisions: 12(1)(i.1) — Bad debts recovered; 39(11) — Bad debt recovery; 50(1)(a) — Deemed disposition where debt becomes bad debt; 79.1(7)(d) — Deduction by creditor for bad debt where property seized; 79.1(8) — No deduction for principal amount of bad debt where property seized by creditor; 89(1)"capital dividend

account"(c) — Capital dividend account; 257 — Formula cannot calculate to less than zero. See also at end of s. 20.

Notes: 20(4.2) amended by 2016 budget bill #2, for dispositions after 2016, as part of changing eligible capital property rules to CCA Class 14.1 (see Notes to 20(1)(b)). For earlier dispositions, read:

(4.2) **Bad debts re eligible capital property** — Where, in respect of one or more dispositions of eligible capital property by a taxpayer, an amount that is described in paragraph (a) of the description of E in the definition "cumulative eligible capital" in subsection 14(5) in respect of the taxpayer is established by the taxpayer to have become a bad debt in a taxation year, there shall be deducted in computing the taxpayer's income for the year the amount determined by the formula

$$(A + B) - (C + D + E + F + G + H)$$

where

A   is the lesser of

(a) ½ of the total of all amounts each of which is such an amount that was so established to have become a bad debt in the year or a preceding taxation year, and

(b) the amount that is

(i) where the year ended after February 27, 2000, the amount, if any, that would be the total of all amounts determined by the formula in paragraph 14(1)(b) (if that formula were read without reference to the description of D) for the year, or for a preceding taxation year that ended after February 27, 2000, and

(ii) where the year ended before February 28, 2000, nil;

B   is the amount, if any, by which

(a) ¾ of the total of all amounts each of which is such an amount that was so established to be a bad debt in the year or a preceding taxation year

exceeds the total of

(b) ½ of the amount by which

(i) the value of A

exceeds

(ii) the amount included in the value of A because of subparagraph (b)(i) of the description of A in respect of taxation years that ended after February 27, 2000 and before October 18, 2000, and

(c) ⁹⁄₈ of the amount included in the value of A because of subparagraph (b)(i) of the description of A in respect of taxation years that ended after February 27, 2000 and before October 18, 2000;

C   is the total of all amounts each of which is an amount determined under subsection 14(1) or (1.1) for the year, or a preceding taxation year, that ends after October 17, 2000 and in respect of which a deduction can reasonably be considered to have been claimed under section 110.6 by the taxpayer;

D   is the total of all amounts each of which is an amount determined under subsection 14(1) or (1.1) for the year, or a preceding taxation year, that ended after February 27, 2000 and before October 18, 2000 and in respect of which a deduction can reasonably be considered to have been claimed under section 110.6 by the taxpayer;

E   is the total of all amounts each of which is an amount determined under subsection 14(1) or (1.1) for a preceding taxation year that ended before February 28, 2000 and in respect of which a deduction can reasonably be considered to have been claimed under section 110.6 by the taxpayer;

F   is the total of

(a) ⅔ of the total of all amounts each of which is the value determined in respect of the taxpayer for D in the formula in paragraph 14(1)(b) for the year, or a preceding taxation year, that ends after October 17, 2000, and

(b) ⁸⁄₉ of the total of all amounts each of which is the value determined in respect of the taxpayer for D in the formula in paragraph 14(1)(b) for the year, or a preceding taxation year, that ended after February 27, 2000 and before October 18, 2000;

G   is the total of all amounts each of which is the value determined in respect of the taxpayer for D in the formula in subparagraph 14(1)(a)(v) (as that subparagraph applied for taxation years that ended before February 28, 2000) for a preceding taxation year; and

H   is the total of all amounts deducted by the taxpayer under this subsection for preceding taxation years.

20(4.2) earlier amended by 2000 Budget (for tax years ending after Oct. 17, 2000), 1994 Budget.

Interpretation Bulletins: IT-123R6: Transactions involving eligible capital property.

(4.3) [Repealed]

Notes: 20(4.3) repealed by 2016 budget bill #2, for dispositions after 2016, as part of changing eligible capital property rules to CCA Class 14.1 (see Notes to 20(1)(b)). It read:

> **(4.3) Deemed allowable capital loss [on disposition of ECP]** — Where, in respect of one or more dispositions of eligible capital property by a taxpayer, an amount that is described in paragraph (a) of the description of E in the definition "cumulative eligible capital" in subsection 14(5) in respect of the taxpayer is established by the taxpayer to have become a bad debt in a taxation year, the taxpayer is deemed to have an allowable capital loss from a disposition of capital property in the year equal to the lesser of
>
>> (a) the total of the value determined for A and ⅔ of the value determined for B in the formula in subsection (4.2) in respect of the taxpayer for the year; and
>>
>> (b) the total of all amounts each of which is
>>
>>> (i) the value determined for C or paragraph (a) of the description of F in the formula in subsection (4.2) in respect of the taxpayer for the year,
>>>
>>> (ii) ¾ of the value determined for D or paragraph (b) of the description of F in the formula in subsection (4.2) in respect of the taxpayer for the year, or
>>>
>>> (iii) ⅔ of the value determined for E or G in the formula in subsection (4.2) in respect of the taxpayer for the year.

20(4.3) added by 2000 Budget, last change effective for tax years ending after Oct. 17, 2000.

(5) Sale of agreement for sale, mortgage or hypothecary claim included in proceeds of disposition — Where depreciable property, other than a timber resource property, of a taxpayer has, in a taxation year, been disposed of to a person with whom the taxpayer was dealing at arm's length, and the proceeds of disposition include an agreement for the sale of, or a mortgage or hypothecary claim on, land that the taxpayer has, in a subsequent taxation year, sold to a person with whom the taxpayer was dealing at arm's length, there may be deducted in computing the income of the taxpayer for the subsequent year an amount equal to the lesser of

(a) the amount, if any, by which the principal amount of the agreement for sale, mortgage or hypothecary claim outstanding at the time of the sale exceeds the consideration paid by the purchaser to the taxpayer for the agreement for sale, mortgage or hypothecary claim, and

(b) the amount determined under paragraph (a) less the amount, if any, by which the proceeds of disposition of the depreciable property exceed the capital cost to the taxpayer of that property.

Related Provisions: See at end of s. 20.

Notes: 20(5) allows a deduction for a loss on sale of a mortgage taken back on the sale of depreciable property.

References to "hypothecary claim" added by 2001 *Civil Code* harmonization bill, effective June 14, 2001. The change is non-substantive; see *Interpretation Act* s. 8.2.

Interpretation Bulletins: IT-323: Sale of mortgage included in proceeds of disposition of depreciable property (cancelled).

(5.1) Sale of agreement for sale, mortgage or hypothecary claim included in proceeds of disposition — Where a timber resource property of a taxpayer has, in a taxation year, been disposed of to a person with whom the taxpayer was dealing at arm's length, and the proceeds of disposition include an agreement for sale of, or a mortgage or hypothecary claim on, land that the taxpayer has, in a subsequent taxation year, sold to a person with whom the taxpayer was dealing at arm's length, there may be deducted in computing the income of the taxpayer for the subsequent year the amount, if any, by which the principal amount of the agreement for sale, mortgage or hypothecary claim outstanding at the time of the sale exceeds the consideration paid by the purchaser to the taxpayer for the agreement for sale, mortgage or hypothecary claim.

Related Provisions: See at end of s. 20.

Notes: References to "hypothecary claim" added to 20(5.1) by 2001 *Civil Code* harmonization bill, effective June 14, 2001. The change is non-substantive; see *Interpretation Act* s. 8.2.

(6) Special reserves — Where an amount is deductible in computing income for a taxation year under paragraph (1)(m) as a reserve in respect of

(a) articles of food or drink that it is reasonably anticipated will have to be delivered after the end of the year, or

(b) transportation that it is reasonably anticipated will have to be provided after the end of the year,

there shall be substituted for the amount determined under that paragraph an amount not exceeding the total of amounts included in computing the taxpayer's income from the business for the year that were received or receivable (depending on the method regularly followed by the taxpayer in computing the taxpayer's profit) in the year in respect of

(c) articles of food or drink not delivered before the end of the year, or

(d) transportation not provided before the end of the year,

as the case may be.

Related Provisions: 12(1)(e) — Reserves in respect of certain goods and services, etc., rendered. See also at end of s. 20.

Interpretation Bulletins: IT-154R: Special reserves.

(7) Where para. (1)(m) does not apply — Paragraph (1)(m) does not apply to allow a deduction

(a) as a reserve in respect of guarantees, indemnities or warranties;

(b) in computing the income of a taxpayer for a taxation year from a business in any case where the taxpayer's income for the year from that business is computed in accordance with the method authorized by subsection 28(1);

(c) as a reserve in respect of insurance, except that in computing an insurer's income for a taxation year from an insurance business, other than a life insurance business, carried on by it, there may be deducted as a policy reserve any amount that the insurer claims not exceeding the amount prescribed in respect of the insurer for the year; or

(d) as a reserve in respect of a reclamation obligation.

Related Provisions: 12(1)(e) — Income inclusion in following year; 12(1)(s) — Reinsurance commission; 18(1)(e.1) — Unpaid policy claims; 20(26) — Deduction for unpaid claims reserve adjustment; 87(2.2) — Amalgamation of insurers; 88(1)(g) — Windup of subsidiary insurer; 138(3)(a)(i) — Policy reserves for life insurance business; 139.1(8)(b) — No deduction for policy dividend paid on demutualization. See also at end of s. 20.

Notes: 20(7)(d) was added because reclamation obligations can be deducted using the Qualifying Environmental Trust rules (20(1)(xx), (tt)). Aadded by 2013 budget bill #1, for amounts received after March 20, 2013, except an amount directly attributable to a reclamation obligation, that was authorized by a government or regulatory authority before March 21, 2013 and that is received

(a) under a written agreement between the taxpayer and another party (other than a government or regulatory authority) that was entered into before March 21, 2013 and not extended or renewed on or after that day; or

(b) before 2018.

20(7)(c) amended by 1996 Budget, effective for 1996 and later taxation years, to correspond to changes to Reg. 1400.

Regulations: 1400(1) (amount prescribed for 20(7)(c)); for structured settlement reserves, see Reg. 1400(3)E; for earthquake reserves, see Reg. 1400(3)L.

Interpretation Bulletins: IT-154R: Special reserves.

(8) No deduction in respect of [sale of] property in certain circumstances — Paragraph (1)(n) does not apply to allow a deduction in computing the income of a taxpayer for a taxation year from a business in respect of a property sold in the course of the business if

(a) the taxpayer, at the end of the year or at any time in the immediately following taxation year,

(i) was exempt from tax under any provision of this Part, or

(ii) was not resident in Canada and did not carry on the business in Canada;

(b) the sale occurred more than 36 months before the end of the year;

(c) the purchaser of the property sold was a corporation that, immediately after the sale,

(i) was controlled, directly or indirectly, in any manner whatever, by the taxpayer,

(ii) was controlled, directly or indirectly, in any manner whatever, by a person or group of persons that controlled the taxpayer, directly or indirectly, in any manner whatever, or

(iii) controlled the taxpayer, directly or indirectly, in any manner whatever; or

(d) the purchaser of the property sold was a partnership in which the taxpayer was, immediately after the sale, a majority-interest partner.

Related Provisions: 149 — Exemptions; 256(5.1) — Meaning of "controlled, directly or indirectly". See also at end of s. 20.

Notes: 20(8) amended by 2013 budget bill #2 (effective Dec. 12, 2013), 2002-2013 technical bill.

Interpretation Bulletins: IT-152R3: Special reserves — sale of land; IT-154R: Special reserves.

(9) Application of para. (1)(cc) — In lieu of making any deduction of an amount permitted by paragraph (1)(cc) in computing a taxpayer's income for a taxation year from a business, the taxpayer may, if the taxpayer so elects in prescribed manner, make a deduction of $^{1}/_{10}$ of that amount in computing the taxpayer's income for that taxation year and a like deduction in computing the taxpayer's income for each of the 9 immediately following taxation years.

Related Provisions: 13(12) — Application of 20(1)(cc); 96(3) — Election by members of partnership. See also at end of s. 20.

Regulations: 4100 (prescribed manner).

Interpretation Bulletins: IT-99R5: Legal and accounting fees.

(10) Convention expenses — Notwithstanding paragraph 18(1)(b), there may be deducted in computing a taxpayer's income for a taxation year from a business an amount paid by the taxpayer in the year as or on account of expenses incurred by the taxpayer in attending, in connection with the business, not more than two conventions held during the year by a business or professional organization at a location that may reasonably be regarded as consistent with the territorial scope of that organization.

Related Provisions: 67.1(3) — Meals and entertainment included in fee for convention; Canada-U.S. Tax Treaty:Art. XXV:9 — Fees for convention held in U.S. deductible if would be deductible in Canada. See also at end of s. 20.

Notes: 20(10) is a *permissive* provision, not restrictive. If convention expenses can be justified as incurred to earn income and not being on account of capital (18(1)(a), (b)), they should be deductible even if they do not meet the restrictions in 20(10). See however *Griffith*, [1956] C.T.C. 47 (Exch. Ct.); *Shaver*, 2004 FCA 371 (Amway monthly business seminars); IT-357R2: training expenses may be eligible capital expenditures (now Class 14.1) if they do not fall under 20(10). See also VIEWS docs 2009-0347581E5, 2017-0709111C6 [2017 APFF q.12].

In *Leduc*, 2008 TCC 142, investment seminar costs in Cancun were deductible to a financial advisor whose spouse attended to take notes for him.

"Convention" in 20(10) is a "formal meeting of members for professional or business purposes" (IT-131R2 para. 1) and can include a seminar, conference, information session or annual meeting: VIEWS doc 2005-0132981E5. The annual meeting of the CMMTQ (Quebec plumbing and heating contractors' association) with related trade show qualifies: 2011-0393731E5.

A national organization's convention may be in the US: Canada-US tax treaty, Art. XXV:8, VIEWS doc 2007-0239511M4. A cruise ship is outside Canada so expenses do not qualify: IT-131R2 para. 2; doc July 1990-119.

In "business or professional organization", "business" is an adjective modifying "organization", as is clear from the French ("organisation commerciale ou professionnelle"). A website that claims convention expenses are deductible under 20(10) for conventions held "by *a* business or by *a* professional organization" is wrong; still, expenses genuinely deductible as non-capital business expenses do not need 20(10).

Interpretation Bulletins: IT-131R2: Convention expenses; IT-357R2: Expenses of training.

(11) Foreign taxes on income from property exceeding 15% — In computing the income of an individual from a property other than real or immovable property for a taxation year after 1975

that is income from a source outside Canada, there may be deducted the amount, if any, by which,

(a) such part of any income or profits tax paid by the taxpayer to the government of a country other than Canada for the year as may reasonably be regarded as having been paid in respect of an amount that has been included in computing the taxpayer's income for the year from the property,

exceeds

(b) 15% of the amount referred to in paragraph (a).

Related Provisions: 20(12) — Deduction for foreign tax as alternative to credit; 94(3)(b) — Application to trust deemed resident in Canada; 104(22)–(22.4) — Foreign tax credit (FTC) for beneficiaries of trust; 126(1) — FTC; 126(7)"non-business-income tax"(b) — Limitation on FTC; 144(8.1) — Employees profit sharing plan — FTC; Canada-U.S. Tax Treaty:Art. XXIX:5(c) — Optional rule for US "S" corporation. See also at end of s. 20.

Notes: The effect of 126(7)"non-business-income tax"(b) is that for individuals, a foreign tax credit on interest, dividend and royalty income can only be claimed up to 15% of such income. Any excess is deductible under 20(11). (This is calculated on a property-by-property basis due to the words "a property"). If this leads to double tax on a US citizen in Canada, see Canada-US tax treaty Art. XXIV. See also 20(12).

For the meaning of "income or profits tax" in para. (a), see Notes to 126(4).

For examples of 20(11) applying see VIEWS docs 2003-0051851E5 (Canadian resident pays US tax on income from S-corp that Canada does not tax); 2013-0480371C6 (income from US LLC); 2009-0320581E5 (German tax on dividends and interest); 2006-0174701E5 and 2007-0233701C6 (trust's foreign income attributed to taxpayer under 75(2), 56(4.1), 74.1(1) or (2)); 2009-0316841E5 (RCA's calculation of Part XI.3 tax); 2015-0572461I7 (LP holds US LP which holds US LLCs). It does not apply to beneficiaries of an employees profit sharing plan: 2016-0676431E5.

20(11) opening words amended by 2002-2013 technical bill (Part 4 — bijuralism), effective June 26, 2013, to add "or immovable".

Income Tax Folios: S5-F2-C1: Foreign tax credit [replaces IT-270R3, IT-395R2, IT-520].

Interpretation Bulletins: IT-201R2: Foreign tax credit — trusts and beneficiaries; IT-506: Foreign income taxes as a deduction from income.

(12) Foreign non-business income tax — In computing the income of a taxpayer who is resident in Canada at any time in a taxation year from a business or property for the year, there may be deducted any amount that the taxpayer claims that does not exceed the non-business income tax paid by the taxpayer for the year to the government of a country other than Canada (within the meaning assigned by subsection 126(7) read without reference to paragraphs (c) and (e) of the definition "non-business income tax" in that subsection) in respect of that income, other than any of those taxes paid that can, in whole or in part, reasonably be regarded as having been paid by a corporation in respect of income from a share of the capital stock of a foreign affiliate of the corporation.

Related Provisions: 20(11) — Deduction to limit foreign tax credit of individual; 93.1(1) — Where shares are owned by partnership; 94(3)(b) — Application to trust deemed resident in Canada; 94(16)(e) — Application to electing contributor of non-resident trust; 104(22)–(22.4) — Foreign tax credit for beneficiaries of trust; 126(1) — Foreign tax credit; 126(1.1) — Application to authorized foreign bank; 126(7)"non-business-income tax"(c) — Limitation on foreign tax credit. See also at end of s. 20.

Notes: It is usually more advantageous to claim a foreign tax credit under 126 than this deduction. However, sometimes no FTC can be claimed, e.g. because foreign withholding tax applies to income that is Canadian-source income under the ITA.

In *FLSmidth Ltd.*, 2013 FCA 160, no 20(12) deduction was allowed on a tower structure that included a US limited partnership, Nova Scotia ULC and an LLC. The TCC ruled that: (1) 20(12) contemplates a calculation of income from a specific business or property source, and the foreign tax must be paid in respect of income from that source; (2) the foreign tax need not be paid on the taxpayer's income from a business or property, but the payment of the tax must be "connected with or related to" that income; (3) the "can reasonably be regarded" wording allows looking through the NSULC, so the US tax paid by the limited partnership was "paid in respect of" income from the shares of the LLC, so no 20(12) deduction was allowed [the FCA specifically upheld this point]; (4) this result did not violate Canada-US tax treaty Art. XXIV:2 or 3. See (all published before the FCA decision): Tyler, "FLSmidth", 2089 *Tax Topics* (CCH) 1-6 (March 22, 2012); Scheuerman, "Flsmidth", 2(2) *Canadian Tax Focus* (ctf.ca) 4-5 (May 2012); Stirling case comment, 60(2) *Canadian Tax Journal* 404-14 (2012). CRA now allows a 20(12) deduction for US tax paid on income earned through an LLC: VIEWS doc 2014-056037117 [Pereira, "Foreign Taxes Paid in US LLC Structure", 24(7) *Canadian Tax Highlights* (ctf.ca) 4-5 (July 2016)].

In *Emergis Inc.*, 2021 TCC 23 (under appeal to FCA), no 20(12) deduction was allowed on a different tower structure, for US withholding tax paid on interest income from a US partnership that EI controlled; the test of "in respect of" income from a share of a foreign affiliate was satisfied [Lim, "No Deduction for US Withholding Tax", 11(2) *Canadian Tax Focus* (ctf.ca) 13-14 (May 2021)].

For CRA interpretation see VIEWS docs 2002-0144257 (20(12) applies to interest income accrued annually in Canada); 2003-0003095 (foreign tax paid on capital gain is not deductible); 2008-0284351I7 (20(12) applies to US income tax paid on taxpayer's share of income of S corp that did not distribute income in the year); 2009-0316841E5 (RCA's calculation of Part XI.3 tax); 2009-0320581E5 (German tax); 2011-039463I7 (20(12) cannot be used for US LP treated as earning business income in US and property income in Canada); 2014-0548111E5 (20(12) can apply to US tax paid by Cdn resident individual on US LLC income); 2015-0572461I7 (similar, but 20(12) now allowed where Canadian LP holds US LP which holds US LLCs); 2016-0676431E5 (no 20(12) for EPSP beneficiaries).

Where a partner claims a deduction under 20(12) for foreign non-business income tax allocated by a partnership, there is no reduction in the ACB of the partner's partnership interest: VIEWS doc 2004-0075931E5.

With the amendment enacted in 2013, 20(12) does not apply to trust income attributed from a non-resident trust under 75(2), 56(4.1), or 74.1(1) or (2): VIEWS docs 2006-0174701E5, 2007-0233701C6 (see also Notes to 20(11)).

20(12) amended by 2002-2013 technical bill, effective Dec. 21, 2002.

20(12) amended by 1992 technical bill, effective 1992, to add "from a business or property" and "in respect of that income", thus limiting the deduction to foreign taxes paid in respect of income from a business or property and clarifying that the amount claimed is to be deducted in computing income from the source to which the foreign tax relates.

Income Tax Folios: S5-F2-C1: Foreign tax credit [replaces IT-270R3, IT-395R2, IT-520].

Interpretation Bulletins: IT-201R2: Foreign tax credit — trusts and beneficiaries; IT-506: Foreign income taxes as a deduction from income.

(12.1) Foreign tax where no economic profit

(12.1) Foreign tax where no economic profit — In computing a taxpayer's income for a taxation year from a business, there may be deducted the amount that the taxpayer claims not exceeding the lesser of

(a) the amount of foreign tax (within the meaning assigned by subsection 126(4.1)) that

(i) is in respect of a property used in the business for a period of ownership by the taxpayer or in respect of a related transaction (as defined in subsection 126(7)),

(ii) is paid by the taxpayer for the year,

(iii) is, because of subsection 126(4.1), not included in computing the taxpayer's business-income tax or non-business-income tax, and

(iv) where the taxpayer is a corporation, is not an amount that can reasonably be regarded as having been paid in respect of income from a share of the capital stock of a foreign affiliate of the taxpayer, and

(b) the portion of the taxpayer's income for the year from the business that is attributable to the property for the period or to a related transaction (as defined in subsection 126(7)).

Related Provisions: 20(13) — Deduction for foreign tax on dividend from foreign affiliate; 126(1.1) — Application to authorized foreign bank.

Notes: 20(12.1) added by 1998 Budget, for 1998 and later tax years. It provides a business deduction for certain foreign taxes that are not eligible for foreign tax credit due to 126(4.1). Note that if a related transaction involves acquisition of another property in respect of which 126(4.1) could apply independently, foreign tax in respect of that property may not be deducted a second time if it has already been deducted as tax in respect of a related transaction relative to the first property: see 248(28). There is no carryforward of foreign tax amounts not deductible in the year.

(13) Deductions under Subdivision I

(13) Deductions under Subdivision I — In computing the income for a taxation year of a taxpayer resident in Canada, there may be deducted such amounts as are provided by Subdivision I.

Related Provisions: 20(12.1) — Deduction for foreign tax where no economic profit; 91(5) — Amount deductible in respect of dividends received from foreign affiliate; 93.1(2) — Dividends received from foreign affiliate by partnership; 113(1) — Deduction re dividend received from foreign affiliate. See also at end of s. 20.

Notes: Subdivision i is s. 90-95. For deductions see 90(9), (14), 91(2), (4), (5), 94(16)(f).

20(13) amended by 2002-2013 technical bill, for tax years that end after 1994 (simplified to recognize that deductions are now not always tied to dividends).

(14) Accrued bond interest

(14) Accrued bond interest — Where, by virtue of an assignment or other transfer of a debt obligation, other than an income bond, an income debenture, a small business development bond or a small business bond, the transferee has become entitled to an amount of interest that accrued on the debt obligation for a period commencing before the time of transfer and ending at that time that is not payable until after that time, that amount

(a) shall be included as interest in computing the transferor's income for the transferor's taxation year in which the transfer occurred, except to the extent that it was otherwise included in computing the transferor's income for the year or a preceding taxation year; and

(b) may be deducted in computing the transferee's income for a taxation year to the extent that the amount was included as interest in computing the transferee's income for the year.

Related Provisions: 12(9) — Deemed accrual; 16(3) — Purchase of bond at a discount; 20(14.2) — Sale of linked note; 20(21) — Deduction on disposition of debt obligation; 53(2)(l) — Adjusted cost base — amounts to be deducted; 138(12)"gross investment revenue"E(b) — Inclusion in gross investment revenue of insurer; 142.4(1)"tax basis"(m) — Disposition of specified debt obligation by financial institution; 142.4(3)(b) — Disposition of specified debt obligation by financial institution; 142.5(3)(a) — Mark-to-market debt obligation; 214(6) — Deemed interest; 214(9) — Deemed resident. See also at end of s. 20.

Notes: 20(14)(a) includes in income the amount received, on sale of a bond with accrued interest, in respect of that accrued interest. Where what is sold is a linked note, see 20(14.2).

Paras. (a) and (b) are to be read independently of each other: *Antosko (Trzop)*, [1994] 2 C.T.C. 25 (SCC). However, an amount deducted under 20(14)(b) reduces ACB of the property under 53(2)(l), and if ACB goes below zero, 40(3) creates a capital gain: *Trzop*, 2001 FCA 380, leave to appeal denied 2002 CarswellNat 1986 (SCC).

Accrued interest in foreign currency should be converted to C$ on the date of the debt transfer: VIEWS doc 2018-0779911C6 [2018 CTF q.14].

The CRA considers a banker's acceptance to be a "debt obligation" for 20(14): VIEWS doc 2005-0137041C6.

Regulations: 211 (information return by financial institution).

Interpretation Bulletins: IT-396R: Interest income; IT-410R: Debt obligations — accrued interest on transfer (cancelled).

(14.1) Interest on debt obligation

(14.1) Interest on debt obligation — Where a person who has issued a debt obligation, other than an income bond, an income debenture, a small business development bond or a small business bond, is obligated to pay an amount that is stipulated to be interest on that debt obligation in respect of a period before its issue (in this subsection referred to as the "unearned interest amount") and it is reasonable to consider that the person to whom the debt obligation was issued paid to the issuer consideration for the debt obligation that included an amount in respect of the unearned interest amount,

(a) for the purposes of subsection (14) and section 12, the issue of the debt obligation shall be deemed to be an assignment of the debt obligation from the issuer, as transferor, to the person to whom the obligation was issued, as transferee, and an amount equal to the unearned interest amount shall be deemed to be interest that accrued on the obligation for a period commencing before the issue and ending at the time of issue; and

(b) notwithstanding paragraph (a) or any other provision of this Act, no amount that can reasonably be considered to be an amount in respect of the unearned interest amount shall be deducted or included in computing the income of the issuer.

Related Provisions: 261(7)–(10) — Functional currency reporting. See also at end of s. 20.

(14.2) Sales of linked notes [— deemed interest]

(14.2) Sales of linked notes [— deemed interest] — For the purposes of subsection (14), the amount determined by the following formula is deemed to be interest that accrued on an assigned or otherwise transferred debt obligation — that is, at any time, described in paragraph 7000(1)(d) of the *Income Tax Regulations* — to which the transferee has become entitled to for a period commencing before the time of the transfer and ending at that particular time that is not payable until after that particular time:

$$A - B$$

where

A is the price for which the debt obligation was assigned or otherwise transferred at the particular time; and

B is the amount by which the price (converted to Canadian currency using the exchange rate prevailing at the particular time, if the debt obligation is denominated in a foreign currency) for which the debt obligation was issued exceeds the portion, if any, of the principal amount of the debt obligation (converted to Canadian currency using the exchange rate prevailing at the particular time, if the debt obligation is denominated in a foreign currency) that was repaid by the issuer on or before the particular time.

Related Provisions: 257 — Formula cannot calculate to less than zero.

Notes: A linked note (LN) is a debt obligation, typically issued by a financial institution, the return on which is linked to performance of a reference asset or index (RAI) over the term of the obligation. The RAI — e.g., basket of stocks, stock index, commodity, currency or investment fund units — is generally unrelated to the issuer's operations or securities. 12(3)-(4) deem interest to accrue on a "prescribed debt obligation" (12(9), Reg. 7000(1)), which includes a typical LN, and an investor in a LN must accrue the maximum interest that could be payable on the note for a year (Reg. 7000(2)). Investors generally take the position that there is no deemed interest accrual on a LN before the maximum interest is determinable. Instead, the full return on the note is included in income for the year it becomes determinable, which is generally shortly before maturity.

However, some investors would sell LNs before the determination date to, in effect, convert the return from ordinary income to capital gains, taking the position that no amount was accrued interest on the date of sale of the LN for purposes of 20(14) (accrued interest on sales of debt obligations). Issuers would establish a secondary market where investors could sell LNs before maturity to an affiliate of the issuer.

20(14.2) implements a 2016 Budget proposal (modified by Finance news release, Sept. 16, 2016) to have a LN's return retain the same character whether earned at maturity or via a secondary market sale. A deeming rule applies for purposes of 20(14). A gain on sale of a LN is treated as interest that accrued (ignoring foreign currency fluctuations).

20(14.2) added by 2016 budget bill #2, for transfers after 2016.

Regulations: 201(1)(g) (information return).

(15) [Repealed]

Notes: 20(15) repealed by 2003 resource bill, effective for taxation years that end after 2002. It provided for regulations re the amount deductible under 20(1)(v.1).

(16) Terminal loss — Notwithstanding paragraphs 18(1)(a), (b) and (h), where at the end of a taxation year,

(a) the total of all amounts used to determine A to D.1 in the definition "undepreciated capital cost" in subsection 13(21) in respect of a taxpayer's depreciable property of a particular class exceeds the total of all amounts used to determine E to K in that definition in respect of that property, and

(b) the taxpayer no longer owns any property of that class,

in computing the taxpayer's income for the year

(c) there shall be deducted the amount of the excess determined under paragraph (a), and

(d) no amount shall be deducted for the year under paragraph (1)(a) in respect of property of that class.

Related Provisions: 13(1) — Recapture where E to J exceed A to D; 13(6) — Misclassified property; 13(21.1) — Limitation on disposition of a building; 13(21.2) — Limitation where affiliated person acquires the property; 20(16.1) — Limitations on terminal loss; 20(16.2) — Meaning of "taxation year" and "year"; 20(16.3) — Property disposed of after ceasing business; 28(1)(g) — Deduction from farming or fishing income when using cash method; 70(13) — Capital cost of depreciable property on death; 80(9)(c) — Reduction of capital cost on debt forgiveness ignored for CCA purposes; 132.2(5)(d) — Deemed capital cost of depreciable property following mutual fund reorganization; 138(11.8) — Rules on transfer of depreciable property; 164(6)(b) — Disposition of property by legal representative of deceased taxpayer. See also at end of s. 20.

Notes: A terminal loss is available as a deduction if all depreciable property in a class is disposed of and there is still some unused cost (undepreciated capital cost, UCC) "left over". See also Notes to 13(1), 13(21)"undepreciated capital cost" and 20(1)(a). The UCC must be established to prove the terminal loss: *DeForest*, 2009 FCA 64. The terminal loss can be claimed only for the year the last assets in the class are disposed of, not carried forward: *Claeys*, 2010 TCC 586.

See also Income Tax Folio S3-F4-C1 ¶1.98-1.103, 1.111. CRA allows no terminal loss to an employee who claims CCA under 8(1)(j) or (p), because those provisions permit capital cost deductions "as allowed by regulation", and 20(16) is not in the Regulations. (8(2) prohibits deductions to employees except as specifically allowed.)

For the parallel rule for pre-2017 eligible capital property, see repealed 24(1).

A terminal loss is automatic, not elective, so failing to claim it does not prevent it being carried forward as a non-capital loss to a later year: *Benedict*, 2012 TCC 174, para. 9 (and see 152(1.1) Notes).

The provision of "separate classes" for many kinds of assets under Reg. 1101 permits a terminal loss to be claimed on the sale of any such property for less than its undepreciated capital cost even if the taxpayer owns other similar property.

Terminal losses were allowed in: *Landrus*, 2009 FCA 113 (disposition by partnership to related partnership; GAAR did not apply); *568864 B.C. Ltd.*, 2014 TCC 373 ($3.8 million allowed on patents held as loan security and seized when loan went bad); *Donaldson*, 2016 TCC 5, para. 34 (rental property changed to principal residence).

A terminal loss is allowed on "rental property" even though Reg. 1100(11) denies deduction of CCA on such property: VIEWS docs 2002-0177677, 2002-0177695. Similarly, accumulated rental losses of past years do not affect the availability of the terminal loss: 2004-0073141E5. For various issues in establishing the loss, see 2009-0305951E5.

No terminal loss is available on ceasing to carry on business, until the property is disposed of: doc 2008-0277681E5. One may be allowed on windup: 2014-0553731I7.

Once a film stops generating revenue, there may be a change of use under 45(1) and a terminal loss can be claimed: VIEWS doc 2010-0354881E5.

20(16) amended by 2002-2013 technical bill for tax years that end after Feb. 23, 1998, 1991 technical bill.

Income Tax Folios: S3-F4-C1: General discussion of CCA [replaces IT-478R2].

Interpretation Bulletins: IT-195R4: Rental property — CCA restrictions; IT-288R2: Gifts of capital properties to a charity and others; IT-464R: CCA — leasehold interests; IT-465R: Non-resident beneficiaries of trusts; IT-522R: Vehicle, travel and sales expenses of employees.

(16.1) Non-application of subsec. (16) [No terminal loss] — Subsection (16) does not apply

(a) in respect of a passenger vehicle of a taxpayer that has a cost to the taxpayer in excess of $20,000 or any other amount that is prescribed;

(b) in respect of a taxation year in respect of a property that was a former property deemed by paragraph 13(4.3)(a) or (b) to be owned by the taxpayer, if

(i) within 24 months after the taxpayer last owned the former property, the taxpayer or a person not dealing at arm's length with the taxpayer acquires a similar property in respect of the same fixed place to which the former property applied, and

(ii) at the end of the taxation year, the taxpayer or the person owns the similar property or another similar property in respect of the same fixed place to which the former property applied; and

(c) in respect of a taxation year in respect of property included in Class 14.1 of Schedule II to the *Income Tax Regulations* unless the taxpayer has ceased to carry on the business to which the class relates.

Related Provisions: 13(2) — No recapture on luxury automobile; 13(7)(g) — Maximum capital cost of passenger vehicle; 13(8) — Disposition after ceasing business; 20(16.2) — Meaning of "taxation year" and "year"; 87(2)(g.5) — Amalgamation — continuing corp for 20(16.1)(b); Reg. 1100(2.5) — 50% CCA in year of disposition; *Interpretation Act* 27(5) — Meaning of "within 24 months". See also at end of s. 20.

Notes: See Notes to 13(7)(g) re changes in prescribed amount. Although 20(16.1)(a) disallows a terminal loss on a luxury automobile, 1/2 of the otherwise allowable CCA is allowed in the year of disposition, by Reg. 1100(2.5); see Notes thereto.

20(16.1)(c) (added by 2016 budget bill #2 effective 2017) is part of the replacement of the eligible capital property (ECP) rules by CCA Class 14.1 (see Notes to 20(1)(b)). Only if the business ceases is a terminal loss available for goodwill and similar property; this is similar to former 24(1).

20(16.1)(b) added by 2002-2013 technical bill (and "such other amount" changed to "any other amount" in 20(16.1)(a)), for tax years that end after Dec. 20, 2002.

20(16.1) earlier amended by 1992 technical bill.

Regulations: 7307(1) (prescribed amount).

Income Tax Folios: S3-F4-C1: General discussion of CCA [replaces IT-478R2].

Interpretation Bulletins: IT-521R: Motor vehicle expenses claimed by self-employed individuals; IT-522R: Vehicle, travel and sales expenses of employees.

I.T. Technical News: 10 (1997 deduction limits and benefit rates for automobiles).

(16.2) Reference to "taxation year" and "year" of individual — Where a taxpayer is an individual and the taxpayer's income for a taxation year includes income from a business the fiscal period of which does not coincide with the calendar year, if depreciable property acquired for the purpose of gaining or producing income from the business has been disposed of, each reference in

subsections (16) and (16.1) to a "taxation year" and "year" shall, for greater certainty, be read as a reference to a "fiscal period".

Related Provisions: 11(2) — References to "taxation year" and "year"; 20(16.3) — Exception — disposition after ceasing business; 249 — Taxation year; 249.1 — Fiscal period.

Notes: 20(16.2) added in the RSC 1985 (5th Supp) consolidation, effective for tax years ending after Nov. 1991. This rule was formerly in 13(3)(a).

Income Tax Folios: S3-F4-C1: General discussion of CCA [replaces IT-478R2].

(16.3) Disposition after ceasing business — Where a taxpayer, after ceasing to carry on a business, has disposed of depreciable property of the taxpayer of a prescribed class that was acquired by the taxpayer for the purpose of gaining or producing income from the business and that was not subsequently used by the taxpayer for some other purpose, in applying subsection (16) or (16.1), each reference in that subsection to a "taxation year" and "year" shall, notwithstanding anything in subsection (16.2), not be read as a reference to a "fiscal period".

Notes: 20(16.3) added in the RSC 1985 (5th Supp) consolidation, effective for tax years ending after Nov. 1991. This rule was formerly in 13(8).

Income Tax Folios: S3-F4-C1: General discussion of CCA [replaces IT-478R2].

(17), (18) [Repealed]

Notes: 20(17), (18) repealed by 2002-2013 technical bill (Part 5 — technical), effective June 26, 2013. They related to a version of 20(1)(gg), the inventory allowance deduction, that was repealed in 1986.

(19) Annuity contract — Where a taxpayer has in a particular taxation year received a payment under an annuity contract in respect of which an amount was by virtue of subsection 12(3) included in computing the taxpayer's income for a taxation year commencing before 1983, there may be deducted in computing the taxpayer's income for the particular year such amount, if any, as is allowed by regulation.

Related Provisions: 20(20) — Disposal of annuity where payments have not commenced; 148(9)"adjusted cost basis"I — Amount deducted reduces adjusted cost basis. See also at end of s. 20.

Regulations: 303 (amounts that may be deducted).

(20) Life insurance policy [disposed of] — Where in a taxation year a taxpayer disposes of an interest in a life insurance policy that is not an annuity contract (otherwise than as a consequence of a death) or of an interest in an annuity contract (other than a prescribed annuity contract), there may be deducted in computing the taxpayer's income for the year an amount equal to the lesser of

(a) the total of all amounts in respect of the interest in the policy that were included under section 12.2 of this Act or paragraph 56(1)(d.1) of the *Income Tax Act*, chapter 148 of the Revised Statutes of Canada, 1952, in computing the taxpayer's income for the year or a preceding taxation year, and

(b) the amount, if any, by which the adjusted cost basis (within the meaning assigned by section 148) to the taxpayer of that interest immediately before the disposition exceeds the proceeds of the disposition (within the meaning assigned by section 148) of the interest that the policyholder, a beneficiary or an assignee became entitled to receive.

Related Provisions: 148(2) — Deemed proceeds of disposition; 248(8) — Meaning of "consequence" of death. See also at end of s. 20.

Notes: 20(20) amended by 1991 technical bill, effective for dispositions after 1989, to extend to accrued but unreceived income in respect of an annuity (other than a prescribed annuity) under which annuity payments have begun at the time of disposition.

Regulations: 304 (prescribed annuity contract).

I.T. Application Rules: 69 (meaning of "chapter 148 of ...").

Interpretation Bulletins: IT-87R2: Policyholders' income from life insurance policies.

(21) [Deduction on disposition of] Debt obligation — If a taxpayer has in a particular taxation year disposed of a property that is an interest in, or for civil law a right in, a debt obligation for consideration equal to its fair market value at the time of disposi-

tion, there may be deducted in computing the taxpayer's income for the particular year the amount, if any, by which

(a) the total of all amounts each of which is an amount that was included in computing the taxpayer's income for the particular year or a preceding taxation year as interest in respect of that property

exceeds the total of all amounts each of which is

(b) the portion of an amount that was received or became receivable by the taxpayer in the particular year or a preceding taxation year that can reasonably be considered to be in respect of an amount described in paragraph (a) and that was not repaid by the taxpayer to the issuer of the debt obligation because of an adjustment in respect of interest received before the time of disposition by the taxpayer, or

(c) an amount in respect of that property that was deductible by the taxpayer by virtue of paragraph (14)(b) in computing the taxpayer's income for the particular year or a preceding taxation year.

Related Provisions: 51(1)(c) — Exchange of convertible property is disposition for purposes of 20(21); 142.5(3)(a) — Mark-to-market debt obligation (MMDO); 142.5(8)(c) — First deemed disposition of MMDO; 142.5(8.2)(a) — First deemed disposition of specified debt obligation. See also at end of s. 20.

Notes: CRA considers a banker's acceptance to be a "debt obligation" for 20(21): VIEWS doc 2005-0137041C6.

This deduction can apply on early redemption of a compound interest investment: VIEWS doc 2008-0284421C6.

20(21) amended by 2002-2013 technical bill (effective June 26, 2013, to add "or for civil law a right in"), 1992 and 1991 technical bills.

Interpretation Bulletins: IT-396R: Interest income.

(22) Deduction for [insurer's] negative reserves — In computing an insurer's income for a taxation year, there may be deducted the amount included under paragraph 12(1)(e.1) in computing the insurer's income for the preceding taxation year.

Related Provisions: 87(2.2) — Amalgamation of insurers; 88(1)(g)(i) — Windup of subsidiary insurer; 138(11.91)(d.1) — Computation of income for non-resident insurer. See also at end of s. 20.

Notes: 20(22) added by 1996 Budget, effective for 1996 and later taxation years. See Notes to 12(1)(e.1). For former 20(22), see Notes to 20(23).

Regulations: 1400(2) (negative reserves).

(23) [Repealed under former Act]

Notes: 20(22) and (23) repealed by 1990 pension bill, effective 1991. For registered pension plan contributions before 1991, they provided a limitation on deductibility to a member of a related group of employers. See also Notes to 20(1)(q) and (s).

(24) Amounts paid for undertaking future obligations — Where an amount is included under paragraph 12(1)(a) in computing a taxpayer's income for a taxation year in respect of an undertaking to which that paragraph applies and the taxpayer paid a reasonable amount in a particular taxation year to another person as consideration for the assumption by that other person of the taxpayer's obligations in respect of the undertaking, if the taxpayer and the other person jointly so elect,

(a) the payment may be deducted in computing the taxpayer's income for the particular year and no amount is deductible under paragraph (1)(m) or (m.1) in computing the taxpayer's income for that or any subsequent taxation year in respect of the undertaking; and

(b) where the amount was received by the other person in the course of business, it shall be deemed to be an amount described in paragraph 12(1)(a).

Related Provisions: 20(25) — Manner of election; 87(2)(j) — Amalgamations — special reserve; 220(3.2), Reg. 600 — Late filing or revocation of election. See also at end of s. 20.

Notes: 20(24) allows a deduction for payments made to obtain another person's agreement to assume obligations for which an amount has been included under 12(1)(a). The other person must include the amount received in income and may be entitled to a 20(1)(m) reserve. The purpose of 20(24) is to allow the taxpayer a deduction "for the particular year" for an obligation previously taxed under 12(1)(a) in "a taxation year", where the taxpayer cannot claim the 20(1)(m) reserve in the "particular" year because the obligation has been transferred. 20(24) is not restricted to a transferred obligation taxed under 12(1)(a) in the current year; the "particular year" and "a taxation year" can be different. Thus, 20(24) may also apply to a transferred obligation for which an amount has been included under 12(1)(e). Also, the 20(24) deduction can be claimed in a later year for an amount previously taxed under 12(1)(a) even where the taxpayer did not claim a 20(1)(m) reserve. (VIEWS doc 2005-0114981E5.)

For a taxpayer filing Quebec returns, an election under 20(24) must be copied to Revenu Québec: *Taxation Act* ss. 157.10, 21.4.6.

See "Practical Issues: Subsection 20(24) Election", in Ron Choudhury, "Non-Resident Issues in Acquisition Transactions", 2005 Cdn Tax Foundation conference report, at 42:9-16; VIEWS docs 9909965 and 9924585 (deduction for prepaid rent on sale of property); 2008-0279671R3 (98(3) partnership windup); 2008-0304371R3 (20(24) applies on a butterfly); 2010-0375921E5 (effect of making or not making the election).

20(24) reworded and amended by 1992 technical bill, effective for 1991 and later taxation years, so that it applies to all cases where 12(1)(a) applies (not just undelivered goods and services) and to refer to 20(1)(m.1).

Interpretation Bulletins: IT-154R: Special reserves; IT-321R: Insurance agents and brokers — unearned commissions (cancelled).

Forms: T2 Sched. 13: Continuity of reserves.

(25) Manner of election — An election under subsection (24) shall be made by notifying the Minister in writing on or before the earlier of the days on or before which either the payer or the recipient is required to file a return of income pursuant to section 150 for the taxation year in which the payment to which the election relates was made.

Related Provisions: See at end of s. 20.

Interpretation Bulletins: IT-154R: Special reserves.

(26) [Repealed]

Notes: 20(26) repealed by 2002-2013 technical bill, for tax years that begin after Oct. 2011. It provided a transitional rule for 1994-95 only, re insurers' unpaid claims reserves. Earlier amended by 1994 Budget.

(27) Loans, etc., acquired in ordinary course of business — For the purposes of computing a deduction under paragraph (1)(l), (l.1) or (p) from the income for a taxation year of a taxpayer who was an insurer or whose ordinary business included the lending of money, a loan or lending asset or an instrument or commitment described in paragraph (1)(l.1) acquired from a person with whom the taxpayer did not deal at arm's length for an amount equal to its fair market value shall be deemed to have been acquired by the taxpayer in the ordinary course of the taxpayer's business of insurance or the lending of money where

(a) the person from whom the loan or lending asset or instrument or commitment was acquired carried on the business of insurance or the lending of money; and

(b) the loan or lending asset was made or acquired or the instrument or commitment was issued, made or assumed by the person in the ordinary course of the person's business of insurance or the lending of money.

Related Provisions: See at end of s. 20.

Interpretation Bulletins: IT-442R: Bad debts and reserves for doubtful debts.

(27.1) Application of subsecs. 13(21) and 138(12) — The definitions in subsections 13(21) and 138(12) apply to this section.

Notes: 20(27.1) added in RSC 1985 (5th Supp) consolidation, for tax years ending after Nov. 1991. This rule was formerly in the opening words of 13(21) and 138(12).

(28) Deduction [for building] before available for use — In computing a taxpayer's income from a business or property for a taxation year ending before the time a building or a part thereof acquired after 1989 by the taxpayer becomes available for use by the taxpayer, there may be deducted an amount not exceeding the amount by which the lesser of

(a) the amount that would be deductible under paragraph (1)(a) for the year in respect of the building if subsection 13(26) did not apply, and

(b) the taxpayer's income for the year from renting the building, computed without reference to this subsection and before deducting any amount in respect of the building under paragraph (1)(a)

exceeds

(c) the amount deductible under paragraph (1)(a) for the year in respect of the building, computed without reference to this subsection,

and any amount so deducted shall be deemed to be an amount deducted by the taxpayer under paragraph (1)(a) in computing the taxpayer's income for the year.

Related Provisions: 20(29) — Deduction before available for use. See also at end of s. 20.

Notes: 20(28) added by 1991 technical bill, effective for taxation years ending after 1989.

(29) Idem — Where, because of subsection 18(3.1), a deduction would, but for this subsection, not be allowed to a taxpayer in respect of an outlay or expense in respect of a building, or part thereof, and the outlay or expense would, but for that subsection and without reference to this subsection, be deductible in computing the taxpayer's income for a taxation year, there may be deducted in respect of such outlays and expenses in computing the taxpayer's income for the year an amount equal to the lesser of

(a) the total of all such outlays or expenses, and

(b) the taxpayer's income for the year from renting the building or the part thereof computed without reference to subsection (28) and this subsection.

Related Provisions: 18(3.1)(a) — Costs relating to construction of building or ownership of land. See also at end of s. 20.

Notes: In *Santagapita*, 2008 TCC 662, 20(29) allowed costs restricted by 18(3.1) to be deducted against rental income.

20(29) added by 1991 technical bill, effective for outlays and expenses after 1989.

(30) Specified reserve adjustment — For the purpose of the description of N in subclause (1)(l)(ii)(D)(II), the specified reserve adjustment for a loan of a taxpayer for a taxation year is the amount determined by the formula

$$0.1(A \times B \times C/365)$$

where

A is the carrying amount of the impaired loan that is used or would be used in determining the interest income on the loan for the year in accordance with generally accepted accounting principles;

B is the effective interest rate on the loan for the year determined in accordance with generally accepted accounting principles; and

C is the number of days in the year on which the loan is impaired.

Related Provisions: See at end of s. 20.

Notes: 20(30) added by 1995-97 technical bill, effective on the same basis as the amendment to 20(1)(l).

Related Provisions [s. 20]: 18 — Limitations on deductions; 67 — Expenses must be reasonable; 67.1 — Limitation on expenses for meals and entertainment; 67.3 — Limitation re motor vehicle expenses; 78 — Unpaid amounts; 107.2 — Distribution by a retirement compensation arrangement; 138(11.5)(k) — Transfer of business by non-resident insurer; 138(11.91)(f) — Computation of income of non-resident insurer.

Definitions [s. 20]: "adjusted cost base" — 54, 248(1); "allowable capital loss" — 38(b), 248(1); "amortized cost", "amount" — 248(1); "amount payable" — (in respect of a policy loan) 20(27.1), 138(12); "anniversary day" — 12.2(11), 20(1.2); "annuity" — 248(1); "arm's length" — 251(1); "assistance" — 79(4), 125.4(5), 248(16), (16.1), (18), (18.1); "authorized foreign bank" — 248(1); "available for use" — 13(27)–(31), 248(19); "borrowed money" — 20(2), 20.1(1), 248(1); "business" — 248(1); "business-income tax" — 126(7); "calendar year" — *Interpretation Act* 37(1)(a); "Canada" — 255; "Canadian oil and gas property expense" — 66.4(5), 248(1); "Canadian partnership" — 102(1), 248(1); "capital cost" — 13(7)–(7.4), 70(5), 128.1(1)(c), 128.1(4)(c), 132.2(1)(d); "capital property" — 54, 248(1); "class of shares" — 248(6); "consequence of the death" — 248(8); "controlled" — 256(5.1), (6), (6.1); "corporation" — 248(1), *Interpretation Act* 35(1); "cumulative eligible capital" — 14(5), 248(1); "deferred amount" — 248(1); "deferred profit sharing plan" — 147(1), 248(1); "depreciable property" — 13(21), 248(1); "derivative forward agreement", "disposition", "dividend" — 248(1); "eligible capital expenditure" — 14(5), 248(1) [repealed]; "eligible capital property" — 54, 248(1); "employee" — 248(1); "employee life and health trust" — 144.1(2), 248(1); "employees profit sharing plan" — 144(1), 248(1); "employer" — 248(1); "excluded amount" — 20(1)(e)(iv.1); "exempt income" — 248(1); "fair market value" — see 69(1) Notes; "financial institution" — 142.2(1); "fiscal period" — 249(2), 249.1; "foreign affiliate" — 93.1(1),

95(1), 248(1); "foreign currency" — 248(1); "foreign tax" — 126(4.1); "goods and services tax" — 248(1); "immovable" — Quebec *Civil Code* art. 900–907; "income" — from business or property 9(1), (3); "income-averaging annuity contract", "income bond", "income debenture" — 248(1); "income or profits tax" — 126(4); "individual", "insurance corporation", "insurer" — 248(1); "interest in real property" — 248(4); "interest" — in respect of a policy loan 20(27.1), 138(12); "interest paid" — 20(2.1); "inventory" — 248(1); "land" — see 70(5.2) Notes; "lending asset", "LIA policy", "life insurance business" — 248(1); "life insurance policy" — 20(2.2), 138(12), 248(1); "majority-interest partner" — 248(1); "mark-to-market property" — 142.2(1); "mineral resource", "Minister" — 248(1); "month" — *Interpretation Act* 35(1); "motor vehicle" — 248(1); "movable" — Quebec *Civil Code* art. 900–907; "net cost of pure insurance" — Reg. 308; "net income stabilization account" — 248(1); "non-business-income tax" — 126(7); "non-resident", "oil or gas well" — 248(1); "partnership" — see 96(1) Notes; "passenger vehicle", "person" — 248(1); "policy loan" — 138(12); "pooled registered pension plan" — 147.5(1), 248(1); "prescribed" — 248(1); "prescribed annuity contract" — Reg. 304; "principal amount" — 248(1), (26); "proceeds of disposition" — 13(21), 20(27.1), 54; "property" — 248(1); "province" — *Interpretation Act* 35(1); "qualifying environmental trust" — 211.6(1), 248(1); "registered pension plan" — 248(1); "registered retirement savings plan" — 146(1), 248(1); "registered supplementary unemployment benefit plan" — 145(1), 248(1); "regulation" — 248(1); "resident", "resident in Canada" — 250; "restricted financial institution", "retirement compensation arrangement", "salary deferral arrangement" — 248(1); "sectoral reserve" — 20(2.3); "series" — 248(10); "share", "shareholder" — 248(1); "small business bond" — 15.2(3), 248(1); "small business development bond" — 15.1(3), 248(1); "specified individual" — 120.4(1), 248(1); "specified percentage" — 20(2.4); "specified reserve adjustment" — 20(30); "split income" — 120.4(1), 248(1); "subsidiary controlled corporation", "superannuation or pension benefit" — 248(1); "taxable Canadian corporation" — 89(1), 248(1); "taxable income" — 2(2), 248(1); "taxation year" — 11(2), 20(16.2), (16.3), 249; "taxpayer" — 248(1); "timber resource property" — 13(21), 248(1); "Treasury Board" — 248(1); "trust" — 104(1), 248(1, (3); "undepreciated capital cost" — 13(21); "unit trust" — 108(2), 248(1); "writing" — *Interpretation Act* 35(1); "year" — 11(2), 20(16.2), (16.3); "zero-emission passenger vehicle", "10/8 policy" — 248(1).

I.T. Application Rules [s. 20]: 20(3)(b), 20(5)(b).

20.01 (1) PHSP [private health services plan] premiums —

Notwithstanding paragraphs 18(1)(a) and (h) and subject to subsection (2), there may be deducted in computing an individual's income for a taxation year from a business carried on by the individual and in which the individual is actively engaged on a regular and continuous basis, directly or as a member of a partnership, an amount payable by the individual or partnership in respect of the year as a premium, contribution or other consideration under a private health services plan in respect of the individual, the individual's spouse or common-law partner or any person who is a member of the individual's household if

(a) in the year or in the preceding taxation year

(i) the total of all amounts each of which is the individual's income from such a business for a fiscal period that ends in the year exceeds 50% of the individual's income for the year, or

(ii) the individual's income for the year does not exceed the total of $10,000 and the total referred to in subparagraph (i) in respect of the individual for the year,

on the assumption that the individual's income from each business is computed without reference to this subsection and the individual's income is computed without reference to this subsection and Subdivision E; and

(b) the amount is payable under a contract between the individual or partnership and

(i) a person licensed or otherwise authorized under the laws of Canada or a province to carry on in Canada an insurance business or the business of offering to the public its services as trustee,

(ii) a person or partnership engaged in the business of offering to the public its services as an administrator of private health services plans, or

(iii) a person the taxable income of which is exempt under section 149 and that is a business or professional organization of which the individual is a member or a trade union of which the individual or a majority of the individual's employees are members.

Related Provisions: 53(2)(c)(xii) — Reduction in ACB of partnership interest; 118.2(2)(q) — Medical expense credit for premiums.

Notes: See Notes at end of 20.01.

Interpretation Bulletins: IT-339R2: Meaning of "private health services plan"; IT-502: Employee benefit plans and employee trusts.

(2) Limit — For the purpose of calculating the amount deductible under subsection (1) in computing an individual's income for a taxation year from a particular business,

(a) no amount may be deducted to the extent that

(i) it is deducted under this section in computing another individual's income for any taxation year, or

(ii) it is included in calculating a deduction under section 118.2 in computing an individual's tax payable under this Part for any taxation year;

(b) where an amount payable under a private health services plan relates to a period in the year throughout which

(i) each of one or more persons

(A) is employed on a full-time basis (other than on a temporary or seasonal basis) in the particular business or in another business carried on by

(I) the individual (otherwise than as a member of a partnership),

(II) a partnership of which the individual is a majority-interest partner, or

(III) a corporation affiliated with the individual, and

(B) has accumulated not less than three months of service in that employment since the person last became so employed, and

(ii) the total number of persons employed in a business described in clause (i)(A), with whom the individual deals at arm's length and to whom coverage is extended under the plan, is not less than 50% of the total number of persons each of whom is a person

(A) who carries on the particular business or is employed in a business described in clause (i)(A), and

(B) to whom coverage is extended under the plan,

the amount so deductible in relation to the period shall not exceed the individual's cost of equivalent coverage under the plan in respect of each employed person who deals at arm's length with the individual and who is described in subparagraph (i) in relation to the period;

(c) subject to paragraph (d), where an amount payable under a private health services plan relates to a particular period in the year, other than a period described in paragraph (b), the amount so deductible in relation to the particular period shall not exceed the amount determined by the formula

$$(A/365) \times (B + C)$$

where

A   is the number of days in the year that are included in the particular period,

B   is the product obtained when $1,500 is multiplied by the number of persons each of whom is covered under the plan, and

(i) is the individual or the individual's spouse or common-law partner, or

(ii) is a member of the individual's household and has attained the age of 18 years before the beginning of the particular period, and

C   is the product obtained when $750 is multiplied by the number of members of the individual's household who, but for the fact that they have not attained the age of 18 years before the particular period began, would be included in computing the product under the description of B; and

(d) where an amount payable under a private health services plan relates to a particular period in the year (other than a period described in paragraph (b)) and one or more persons with whom the individual deals at arm's length are described in subparagraph (b)(i) in relation to the particular period, the amount so deductible in relation to the particular period shall not exceed the lesser of the amount determined under the formula set out in paragraph (c) and the individual's cost of equivalent coverage in respect of any such person in relation to the particular period.

Related Provisions: 20.01(3) — Cost of equivalent coverage; 118.2(2)(q) — Medical expense credit for premiums.

Notes: See Notes at end of 20.01. 20.01(2)(b)(i)(A)(II) amended by 2013 budget bill #2, effective Dec. 12, 2013 (non-substantive change).

(3) Equivalent coverage — For the purpose of subsection (2), an amount payable in respect of an individual under a private health services plan in relation to a period does not exceed the individual's cost of equivalent coverage under the plan in respect of another person in relation to the period to the extent that, in relation to the period, the amount does not exceed the product obtained when

(a) the amount that would be the individual's cost of coverage under the plan if the benefits and coverage in respect of the individual, the individual's spouse or common-law partner and the members of the individual's household were identical to the benefits and coverage made available in respect of the other person, the other person's spouse or common-law partner and the members of the other person's household

is multiplied by

(b) the percentage of the cost of coverage under the plan in respect of the other person that is payable by the individual or a partnership of which the individual is a member.

Notes [20.01]: 20.01 allows a deduction for PHSP premiums (e.g. for an extended health plan, drug plan or dental plan — see 248(1)"private health services plan") for self-employed individuals, to parallel the non-inclusion of such premiums as a taxable benefit to employees under 6(1)(a)(i). 20.01(2)(b) and (d) effectively ensure that the deduction is only available if equivalent coverage is offered to arm's length employees. Where 20.01(2)(b) does not apply, 20.01(2)(c) limits the deduction to $1,500 per year per adult family member and $750 per child. Where amounts are not deductible under 20.01, they should be claimed for medical expense credit under 118.2(2)(q) instead.

Although 20.01(2)(a) prevents two people from deducting premiums to the *same* PSHP, spouses who are both self-employed can deduct premiums to parallel plans covering both of them: VIEWS doc 2015-0581431E5.

For detailed discussion see Marcel Théroux & Karen Millard, "Trends and Developments in Group Benefit Plans", 2002 Cdn Tax Foundation conference report, 29:41-48.

No 20.01 deduction was allowed in *Murray*, 2014 TCC 197, as the evidence did not support that the taxpayer had paid premiums to a PSHP, and his business income did not exceed 50% of his income.

The deduction includes sales taxes on the PSHP premiums, subject to the dollar limits: VIEWS doc 2006-0217631E5.

Where a "cost-plus" plan is used, whereby the employer pays the actual costs of medical care plus an administration fee to the insurer, 20.01 will still allow a deduction: VIEWS doc 2001-0101935. However, a sole proprietor's cost-plus plan will not qualify, in CRA's view, if there are no employees: docs 2002-0158495, 2011-0400311E5, 2011-0406101M4. For general discussion of the administration of a PSHP see doc 2004-0071731E5. See also 2012-0454051C6.

20.01 amended by 2000 same-sex partners bill, effective 2001 or earlier. Added by 1998 Budget, for amounts payable after 1997.

Definitions [s. 20.01]: "affiliated" — 251.1; "amount" — 248(1); "arm's length" — 251(1); "business" — 248(1); "Canada" — 255, *Interpretation Act* 35(1); "common-law partner" — 248(1); "corporation" — 248(1), *Interpretation Act* 35(1); "cost of equivalent coverage" — 20.01(3); "employed", "employee", "employment" — 248(1); "fiscal period" — 249.1; "immovable" — Quebec *Civil Code* art. 900–907; "individual", "majority-interest partner" — 248(1); "month" — *Interpretation Act* 35(1); "partnership" — see 96(1) Notes; "person", "private health services plan" — 248(1); "province" — *Interpretation Act* 35(1); "taxable income" — 248(1); "taxation year" — 249.

Interpretation Bulletins [s. 20.01]: See under 20.01(1).

20.1 (1) Borrowed money used to earn income from property — Where

(a) at any time after 1993 borrowed money ceases to be used by a taxpayer for the purpose of earning income from a capital pro-

perty (other than real or immovable property or depreciable property), and

(b) the amount of the borrowed money that was so used by the taxpayer immediately before that time exceeds the total of

(i) where the taxpayer disposed of the property at that time for an amount of consideration that is not less than the fair market value of the property at that time, the amount of the borrowed money used to acquire the consideration,

(ii) where the taxpayer disposed of the property at that time and subparagraph (i) does not apply, the amount of the borrowed money that, if the taxpayer had received as consideration an amount of money equal to the amount by which the fair market value of the property at that time exceeds the amount included in the total by reason of subparagraph (iii), would be considered to be used to acquire the consideration,

(iii) where the taxpayer disposed of the property at that time for consideration that includes a reduction in the amount of the borrowed money, the amount of the reduction, and

(iv) where the taxpayer did not dispose of the property at that time, the amount of the borrowed money that, if the taxpayer had disposed of the property at that time and received as consideration an amount of money equal to the fair market value of the property at that time, would be considered to be used to acquire the consideration,

an amount of the borrowed money equal to the excess shall, to the extent that the amount is outstanding after that time, be deemed to be used by the taxpayer for the purpose of earning income from the property.

Notes: See Notes at end of 20.1.

20.1(1)(a) amended by 2002-2013 technical bill, effective June 26, 2013.

(2) Borrowed money used to earn income from business — Where at any particular time after 1993 a taxpayer ceases to carry on a business and, as a consequence, borrowed money ceases to be used by the taxpayer for the purpose of earning income from the business, the following rules apply:

(a) where, at any time (in this paragraph referred to as the "time of disposition") at or after the particular time, the taxpayer disposes of property that was last used by the taxpayer in the business, an amount of the borrowed money equal to the lesser of

(i) the fair market value of the property at the time of disposition, and

(ii) the amount of the borrowed money outstanding at the time of disposition that is not deemed by this paragraph to have been used before the time of disposition to acquire any other property

shall be deemed to have been used by the taxpayer immediately before the time of disposition to acquire the property;

(b) subject to paragraph (a), the borrowed money shall, after the particular time, be deemed not to have been used to acquire property that was used by the taxpayer in the business;

(c) the portion of the borrowed money outstanding at any time after the particular time that is not deemed by paragraph (a) to have been used before that subsequent time to acquire property shall be deemed to be used by the taxpayer at that subsequent time for the purpose of earning income from the business; and

(d) the business shall be deemed to have fiscal periods after the particular time that coincide with the taxation years of the taxpayer, except that the first such fiscal period shall be deemed to begin at the end of the business's last fiscal period that began before the particular time.

Related Provisions: 20.1(3) — Deemed dispositions — rules.

Notes: See Notes at end of 20.1.

(3) Deemed dispositions — For the purpose of paragraph (2)(a),

(a) where a property was used by a taxpayer in a business that the taxpayer has ceased to carry on, the taxpayer shall be deemed to dispose of the property at the time at which the taxpayer begins to use the property in another business or for any other purpose;

(b) where a taxpayer, who has at any time ceased to carry on a business, regularly used a property in part in the business and in part for some other purpose,

(i) the taxpayer shall be deemed to have disposed of the property at that time, and

(ii) the fair market value of the property at that time shall be deemed to equal the proportion of the fair market value of the property at that time that the use regularly made of the property in the business was of the whole use regularly made of the property; and

(c) where the taxpayer is a trust, subsections 104(4) to (5.2) do not apply.

(4) Amount payable for property — Where an amount is payable by a taxpayer for property, the amount shall be deemed, for the purposes of this section and, where subsection (2) applies with respect to the amount, for the purposes of this Act, to be payable in respect of borrowed money used by the taxpayer to acquire the property.

Income Tax Folios: S3-F6-C1: Interest deductibility [replaces IT-533].

(5) Interest in partnership — For the purposes of this section, where borrowed money that has been used to acquire an interest in a partnership is, as a consequence, considered to be used at any time for the purpose of earning income from a business or property of the partnership, the borrowed money shall be deemed to be used at that time for the purpose of earning income from property that is the interest in the partnership and not to be used for the purpose of earning income from the business or property of the partnership.

(6) Refinancings — Where at any time a taxpayer uses borrowed money to repay money previously borrowed that was deemed by paragraph (2)(c) immediately before that time to be used for the purpose of earning income from a business,

(a) paragraphs (2)(a) to (c) apply with respect to the borrowed money; and

(b) subsection 20(3) does not apply with respect to the borrowed money.

Related Provisions [s. 20.1]: 20(3) — Use of borrowed money; 87(2)(j.6) — Amalgamation — continuing corporation.

Notes: 20.1 (the "disappearing source" rule) ensures that if borrowed money ceases to be used for income-earning purposes because the income source is gone, interest paid on the money may remain deductible. No 20(1)(c) deduction would otherwise be allowed: *Moufarrège*, 2005 SCC 53. See also Chang & Briant, "Interest Deductibility", 43(1) *Canadian Tax Journal* 154-76 (1995).

In *Moras*, 2019 TCC 111, interest deduction was allowed where M ceased carrying on business but continued to pay interest on his line of credit.

In *St-Hilaire*, 2014 TCC 336, para. 42, interest expense was denied because S had waived the loan made with the borrowed funds, but the Court did not discuss 20.1. See also Notes to 20(1)(c) at "Return of capital".

20.1 does not allow a deduction where a guarantor is ordered to pay interest under a guarantee: VIEWS doc 2011-0398721I7. It allows a deduction to a sole shareholder who borrows money to fund an interest-free loan to the company and later forgives the loan: 2015-0588951C6 [2015 APFF q.3] (but see *St-Hilare* above). See also 2009-0335101E5 [Wong, "Interest Deductibility: Decreased Fair Market Value", 8(3) *Tax Hyperion* (Carswell, March 2011)].

20.1 added by 1993 technical bill, effective 1994 (but not if the property was disposed of before 1994: VIEWS doc 2009-0329171E5).

A different 20.1-20.2 were proposed in 1991 to allow deduction for interest on money borrowed by a corporation or partnership to distribute retained earnings or capital. They were overtaken by case law and withdrawn. See end of Notes to 20(1)(c).

Definitions [s. 20.1]: "amount", "borrowed money", "business" — 248(1); "capital property" — 54, 248(1); "depreciable property" — 13(21), 248(1); "fair market value" — see 69(1) Notes; "fiscal period" — 249.1; "immovable" — Quebec *Civil Code* art. 900–907; "property", "taxpayer" — 248(1); "time of disposition" — 20.1(2)(a).

Income Tax Folios: S3-F6-C1: Interest deductibility [replaces IT-533].

20.2 (1) Interest — authorized foreign bank — interpretation — The following definitions apply in this section.

"branch advance" of an authorized foreign bank means an amount allocated or provided by, or on behalf of, the bank to, or for the benefit of, its Canadian banking business under terms that were documented, before the amount was so allocated or provided, to the same extent as, and in a form similar to the form in which, the bank would ordinarily document a loan by it to a person with whom it deals at arm's length.

Notes: For an example of an "allocation" under this definition (as opposed to a "loan"), see VIEWS doc 2010-035569117.

20.2(1)"branch advance" added by 2001 technical bill, this version effective for amounts allocated or provided after Aug. 21, 2000.

"branch financial statements" of an authorized foreign bank for a taxation year means the unconsolidated statements of assets and liabilities and of income and expenses for the year, in respect of its Canadian banking business,

(a) that form part of the bank's annual report for the year filed with the Superintendent of Financial Institutions as required under section 601 of the *Bank Act*, and accepted by the Superintendent, and

(b) if no filing is so required for the taxation year, that are prepared in a manner consistent with the statements in the annual report or reports so filed and accepted for the period or periods in which the taxation year falls,

except if the Minister demonstrates that the statements are not prepared in accordance with generally-accepted accounting principles in Canada as modified by any specifications applicable to the bank made by the Superintendent of Financial Institutions under subsection 308(4) of the *Bank Act* (in this definition referred to as "modified GAAP"), in which case it means the statements subject to such modifications as are required to make them comply with modified GAAP.

Related Provisions: 115(1)(a)(ii) — Foreign bank's Canadian income calculated using branch financial statements.

"calculation period" of an authorized foreign bank for a taxation year means any one of a series of regular periods into which the year is divided in a designation by the bank in its return of income for the year or, in the absence of such a designation, by the Minister,

(a) none of which is longer than 31 days;

(b) the first of which commences at the beginning of the year and the last of which ends at the end of the year; and

(c) that are, unless the Minister otherwise agrees in writing, consistent with the calculation periods designated for the bank's preceding taxation year.

(2) Formula elements — The following descriptions apply for the purposes of the formulae in subsection (3) for any calculation period in a taxation year of an authorized foreign bank:

A is the amount of the bank's assets at the end of the period;

BA is the amount of the bank's branch advances at the end of the period;

IBA is the total of all amounts each of which is a reasonable amount on account of notional interest for the period, in respect of a branch advance, that would be deductible in computing the bank's income for the year if it were interest payable by, and the advance were indebtedness of, the bank to another person and if this Act were read without reference to paragraph 18(1)(v) and this section;

IL is the total of all amounts each of which is an amount on account of interest for the period in respect of a liability of the bank to another person or partnership that would be deductible in computing the bank's income for the year if this Act were read without reference to paragraph 18(1)(v) and this section; and

L is the amount of the bank's liabilities to other persons and partnerships at the end of the period.

Related Provisions: 20.2(4) — Branch amounts; 20.2(5) — Notional interest for IBA.

(3) Interest deduction — In computing the income of an authorized foreign bank from its Canadian banking business for a taxation year, there may be deducted on account of interest for each calculation period of the bank for the year,

(a) where the total amount at the end of the period of its liabilities to other persons and partnerships and branch advances is 95% or more of the amount of its assets at that time, an amount not exceeding

(i) if the amount of liabilities to other persons and partnerships at that time is less than 95% of the amount of its assets at that time, the amount determined by the formula

$$IL + IBA \times (0.95 \times A - L) / BA$$

and

(ii) if the amount of those liabilities at that time is greater than or equal to 95% of the amount of its assets at that time, the amount determined by the formula

$$IL \times (0.95 \times A) / L$$

and

(b) in any other case, the total of

(i) the amount determined by the formula

$$IL + IBA$$

and

(ii) the product of

(A) the amount claimed by the bank, in its return of income for the year, not exceeding the amount determined by the formula

$$(0.95 \times A) - (L + BA)$$

and

(B) the average, based on daily observations, of the Bank of Canada bank rate for the period.

Related Provisions: 18(1)(v) — No other interest deduction allowed; 20.2(2) — Formula element descriptions; 20.2(4) — Branch amounts; 218.2(2) — Part XIII.1 tax on taxable interest expense; 219 — Branch tax on Canadian branch; 257 — Formulas cannot calculate to less than zero.

Notes: See Notes at end of 20.2.

(4) Branch amounts — Only amounts that are in respect of an authorized foreign bank's Canadian banking business, and that are recorded in the books of account of the business in a manner consistent with the manner in which they are required to be treated for the purposes of the branch financial statements, shall be used to determine

(a) the amounts in subsection (2); and

(b) the amounts in subsection (3) of an authorized foreign bank's assets, liabilities to other persons and partnerships, and branch advances.

(5) Notional interest — For the purposes of the description of IBA in subsection (2), a reasonable amount on account of notional interest for a calculation period in respect of a branch advance is the amount that would be payable on account of interest for the period by a notional borrower, having regard to the duration of the advance, the currency in which repayment is required and all other terms, as adjusted by paragraph (c), of the advance, if

(a) the borrower were a person that dealt at arm's length with the bank, that carried on the bank's Canadian banking business and that had the same credit-worthiness and borrowing capacity as the bank;

(b) the advance were a loan by the bank to the borrower; and

(c) any of the terms of the advance (excluding the rate of interest, but including the structure of the interest calculation, such as whether the rate is fixed or floating and the choice of any reference rate referred to) that are not terms that would be made between the bank as lender and the borrower, having regard to all the circumstances, including the nature of the Canadian banking

business, the use of the advanced funds in the business and normal risk management practices for banks, were instead terms that would be agreed to by the bank and the borrower.

Notes: 20.2 added by 2001 technical bill, effective June 28, 1999 (see also Notes to 20.2(1)"branch advance"). It allows specific deductions for interest expense for an authorized foreign bank operating a branch ("Canadian banking business") in Canada. 18(1)(v) prohibits any other interest deduction. See the Finance Technical Notes.

On the principle that an authorized foreign bank's capital structure will include at least 5% equity, interest is not deductible to the extent it reflects debt in excess of 95% of the value of the assets of the Canadian banking business at the end of the period.

In CRA's view, transactions between the Canadian branch and another branch are part of the Canadian branch's profits for treaty purposes: doc 2004-0078321E5.

(See also 218.2 and 219. See Notes to 20.1 re 1991 proposed 20.2.)

Definitions [s. 20.2]: "amount" — 248(1); "arm's length" — 251(1); "authorized foreign bank", "bank" — 248(1); "branch advance", "branch financial statements" — 20.2(1); "business" — 248(1); "calculation period" — 20.2(1); "Canadian banking business", "Minister" — 248(1); "partnership" — see 96(1) Notes; "person" — 248(1); "taxation year" — 249; "writing" — *Interpretation Act* 35(1).

20.3 (1) Weak currency debt [Kiwi loans] — interpretation — The definitions in this subsection apply in this section.

"exchange date" in respect of a debt of a taxpayer that is at any time a weak currency debt means, if the debt is incurred or assumed by the taxpayer

(a) in respect of borrowed money that is denominated in the final currency, the day that the debt that is incurred or assumed by the taxpayer; and

(b) in respect of borrowed money that is not denominated in the final currency, or in respect of the acquisition of property, the day on which the taxpayer uses the borrowed money or the acquired property, directly or indirectly, to acquire funds that are, or to settle an obligation that is, denominated in the final currency.

Notes: For the meaning of "indirectly", see Notes to 17.1(1).

"hedge" in respect of a debt of a taxpayer that is at any time a weak currency debt means any agreement made by the taxpayer

(a) that can reasonably be regarded as having been made by the taxpayer primarily to reduce the taxpayer's risk, with respect to payments of principal or interest in respect of the debt, of fluctuations in the value of the weak currency; and

(b) that is identified by the taxpayer as a hedge in respect of the debt in a designation in prescribed form filed with the Minister on or before the 30th day after the day the taxpayer enters into the agreement.

Notes: This definition was used as "indirect guidance" to the meaning of "hedge" when considering a currency swap: *George Weston Ltd.*, 2015 TCC 42, para. 64.

"weak currency debt" of a taxpayer at a particular time means a particular debt in a foreign currency (in this section referred to as the **"weak currency"**), incurred or assumed by the taxpayer at a time (in this section referred to as the **"commitment time"**) after February 27, 2000, in respect of a borrowing of money or an acquisition of property, where

(a) any of the following applies, namely,

(i) the borrowed money is denominated in a currency (in this section referred to as the **"final currency"**) other than the weak currency, is used for the purpose of earning income from a business or property and is not used to acquire funds in a currency other than the final currency,

(ii) the borrowed money or the acquired property is used, directly or indirectly, to acquire funds that are denominated in a currency (in this section referred to as the **"final currency"**) other than the weak currency, that are used for the purpose of earning income from a business or property and that are not used to acquire funds in a currency other than the final currency,

(iii) the borrowed money or the acquired property is used, directly or indirectly, to settle an obligation that is denominated in a currency (in this section referred to as the **"final** currency") other than the weak currency, that is incurred or assumed for the purpose of earning income from a business or property and that is not incurred or assumed to acquire funds in a currency other than the final currency, or

(iv) the borrowed money or the acquired property is used, directly or indirectly, to settle another debt of the taxpayer that is at any time a weak currency debt in respect of which the final currency (which is deemed to be the final currency in respect of the particular debt) is a currency other than the currency of the particular debt;

(b) the amount of the particular debt (together with any other debt that would, but for this paragraph, be at any time a weak currency debt, and that can reasonably be regarded as having been incurred or assumed by the taxpayer as part of a series of transactions that includes the incurring or assumption of the particular debt) exceeds $500,000; and

(c) either of the following applies, namely,

(i) if the rate at which interest is payable at the particular time in the weak currency in respect of the particular debt is determined under a formula based on the value from time to time of a reference rate (other than a reference rate the value of which is established or materially influenced by the taxpayer), the interest rate at the commitment time, as determined under the formula as though interest were then payable, exceeds by more than two percentage points the rate at which interest would have been payable at the commitment time in the final currency if

(A) the taxpayer had, at the commitment time, instead incurred or assumed an equivalent amount of debt in the final currency on the same terms as the particular debt (excluding the rate of interest but including the structure of the interest calculation, such as whether the rate is fixed or floating) with those modifications that the difference in currency requires, and

(B) interest on the equivalent amount of debt referred to in clause (A) was payable at the commitment time, or

(ii) in any other case, the rate at which interest is payable at the particular time in the weak currency in respect of the particular debt exceeds by more than two percentage points the rate at which interest would have been payable at the particular time in the final currency if at the commitment time the taxpayer had instead incurred or assumed an equivalent amount of debt in the final currency on the same terms as the particular debt (excluding the rate of interest but including the structure of the interest calculation, such as whether the rate is fixed or floating), with those modifications that the difference in currency requires.

Related Provisions: Reg. 3100(1)(a)(iv) — Prescribed benefit for tax shelter rules.

Notes: For the meaning of "indirectly" in para. (a), see Notes to 17.1(1).

(2) Interest and gain — Notwithstanding any other provision of this Act, the following rules apply in respect of a particular debt of a taxpayer (other than a corporation described in one or more of paragraphs (a), (b), (c) and (e) of the definition "specified financial institution" in subsection 248(1)) that is at any time a weak currency debt:

(a) no deduction on account of interest that accrues on the debt for any period that begins after the day that is the later of June 30, 2000 and the exchange date during which it is a weak currency debt shall exceed the amount of interest that would, if at the commitment time the taxpayer had instead incurred or assumed an equivalent amount of debt, the principal and interest in respect of which were denominated in the final currency, on the same terms as the particular debt (excluding the rate of interest but including the structure of the interest calculation, such as whether the rate is fixed or floating) have accrued on the equivalent debt during that period, with those modifications that the difference in currency requires;

(b) the amount, if any, of the taxpayer's gain or loss (in this section referred to as a "foreign exchange gain or loss") for a taxation year on the settlement or extinguishment of the debt that arises because of the fluctuation in the value of any currency shall be included or deducted, as the case may be, in computing the taxpayer's income for the year from the business or the property to which the debt relates; and

(c) the amount of any interest on the debt that was, because of this subsection, not deductible is deemed, for the purpose of computing the taxpayer's foreign exchange gain or loss on the settlement or extinguishment of the debt, to be an amount paid by the taxpayer to settle or extinguish the debt.

Notes: See Notes at end of 20.3.

(3) Hedges — In applying subsection (2) in circumstances where a taxpayer has entered into a hedge in respect of a debt of the taxpayer that is at any time a weak currency debt, the amount paid or payable in the weak currency for a taxation year on account of interest on the debt, or paid in the weak currency in the year on account of the debt's principal, shall be decreased by the amount of any foreign exchange gain, or increased by the amount of any foreign exchange loss, on the hedge in respect of the amount so paid or payable.

(4) Repayment of principal — If the amount (expressed in the weak currency) outstanding on account of principal in respect of a debt of the taxpayer that is at any time a weak currency debt is reduced before maturity (whether by repayment or otherwise), the amount (expressed in the weak currency) of the reduction is deemed, except for the purposes of determining the rate of interest that would have been charged on an equivalent loan in the final currency and applying paragraph (b) of the definition "weak currency debt" in subsection (1), to have been a separate debt from the commitment time.

Notes [20.3]: 20.3 added by 2000 Budget, for tax years that end after Feb. 27, 2000. It limits deduction for interest paid on "weak currency loans", or "Kiwi loans", overruling *Shell Canada*, [1999] 4 C.T.C. 313 (SCC), which dealt with New Zealand dollars (see also *Canadian Pacific*, using Australian dollars, in Notes to 245(2)). Where a currency is weak (expected to decline in value relative to C$), the interest rate on a loan in the currency will be higher than on a loan on similar terms in C$. The higher rate reflects the market's expectation that the amount of the loan expressed in the weak currency will be worth less in C$ when the loan is repaid. If, as expected, the weak currency depreciates, the borrower will realize a foreign exchange gain when the loan principal is repaid in the depreciated foreign currency. In economic terms, this gain compensates for the higher interest payments made during the term of the loan. Hedging transactions can fix the C$ cost of the interest and principal payments that will be made in the weak currency. See Purda, "Quantifying the Tax Benefits of Borrowing in Foreign Currencies", 49(4) *Canadian Tax Journal* 925-44 (2001); Chapman & Marcovitz, "Weak-currency Borrowing Transaction", *ibid.* pp. 961-89.

Definitions [s. 20.3]: "amount", "borrowed money", "business" — 248(1); "commitment time" — 20.3(1)"weak currency debt"; "corporation" — 248(1), *Interpretation Act* 35(1); "exchange date" — 20.3(1); "final currency" — 20.3(1)"weak currency"(a)(i), (ii), (iii); "foreign currency" — 248(1); "foreign exchange gain or loss" — 20.3(2)(b); "hedge" — 20.3(1); "Minister", "prescribed", "property" — 248(1); "series of transactions" — 248(10); "specific financial institution" — 248(1); "taxation year" — 249; "taxpayer" — 248(1); "weak currency", "weak currency debt" — 20.3(1).

20.4 [Insurer — accounting transition 2006-2011] — [No longer relevant]

Notes: See Notes to 12.5. 20.4 added by 2008 budget bill #2, for tax years that begin after Sept. 2006.

21. (1) Cost of borrowed money — Where in a taxation year a taxpayer has acquired depreciable property, if the taxpayer elects under this subsection in the taxpayer's return of income under this Part for the year,

(a) in computing the taxpayer's income for the year and for such of the 3 immediately preceding taxation years as the taxpayer had, paragraphs 20(1)(c), (d), (e) and (e.1) do not apply to the amount or to the part of the amount specified in the taxpayer's election that, but for an election under this subsection in respect thereof, would be deductible in computing the taxpayer's income (other than exempt income) for any such year in respect of borrowed money used to acquire the depreciable property or the amount payable for the depreciable property; and

(b) the amount or the part of the amount, as the case may be, described in paragraph (a) shall be added to the capital cost to the taxpayer of the depreciable property so acquired by the taxpayer.

Related Provisions: 13(10) — Deemed capital cost of certain property; 13(21) — Definitions; 20(3) — Life insurance policy; 21(5) — Reassessments; 80(2)(b) — Application of debt forgiveness rules; 96(3) — Election by members of partnership; 127(11.5)(b)(i) — Ignore s. 21 for purposes of ITC qualified expenditures; 220(3.2), Reg. 600(a) — Late filing or revocation of election.

Notes: 21(1) provides an election to capitalize interest and similar expenses and fold them into the cost of depreciable property. It cannot be used to capitalize costs that are not claimable for CCA purposes: see Notes to 54"adjusted cost base".

An election "in the taxpayer's return" is valid even if the return is filed late. See Notes to 7(1.31).

21(1) amended by 1991 technical bill, effective 1988.

Interpretation Bulletins: See list at end of s. 21.

Information Circulars: 07-1R1: Taxpayer relief provisions.

Advance Tax Rulings: ATR-1: Transfer of legal title in land to bare trustee corporation — mortgagee's requirements sole reason for transfer.

(2) Borrowed money used for exploration or development

— Where in a taxation year a taxpayer has used borrowed money for the purpose of exploration, development or the acquisition of property and the expenses incurred by the taxpayer in respect of those activities are Canadian exploration and development expenses, Canadian exploration expenses, Canadian development expenses, Canadian oil and gas property expenses, foreign resource expenses in respect of a country, or foreign exploration and development expenses, as the case may be, if the taxpayer so elects under this subsection in the taxpayer's return of income for the year,

(a) in computing the taxpayer's income for the year and for such of the three immediately preceding taxation years as the taxpayer had, paragraphs 20(1)(c), (d), (e) and (e.1) do not apply to the amount or to the part of the amount specified in the taxpayer's election that, but for that election, would be deductible in computing the taxpayer's income (other than exempt income or income that is exempt from tax under this Part) for any such year in respect of the borrowed money used for the exploration, development or acquisition of property, as the case may be; and

(b) the amount or the part of the amount, as the case may be, described in paragraph (a) is deemed to be Canadian exploration and development expenses, Canadian exploration expenses, Canadian development expenses, Canadian oil and gas property expenses, foreign resource expenses in respect of a country, or foreign exploration and development expenses, as the case may be, incurred by the taxpayer in the year.

Related Provisions: 13(10) — Deemed capital cost of property; 13(21) — Definitions; 21(5) — Reassessments; 66(18) — Expenses incurred by partnerships; 80(2)(b) — Application of debt forgiveness rules; 96(3) — Election by members of partnership; 220(3.2), Reg. 600(a) — Late filing or revocation of election.

Notes: In the author's view, interest deemed to be CEE under 21(2) qualifies as a pre-production mining expenditure under 127(9), since the scope of the "deeming" is not limited. See however Notes to 244(15) and the Carr/Hass article cited there.

21(2) amended by 2000 Budget/2001 technical bill, for tax years that begin after 2000. Earlier amended by 1991 technical bill.

Interpretation Bulletins: See list at end of s. 21.

Information Circulars: 07-1R1: Taxpayer relief provisions.

(3) Borrowing for depreciable property

— In computing the income of a taxpayer for a particular taxation year, where the taxpayer

(a) in any preceding taxation year

(i) made an election under subsection (1) in respect of borrowed money used to acquire depreciable property or an amount payable for depreciable property acquired by the taxpayer, or

(ii) was, by virtue of subsection 18(3.1), required to include an amount in respect of the construction of a depreciable pro-

perty in computing the capital cost to the taxpayer of the depreciable property, and

(b) in each taxation year, if any, after that preceding taxation year and before the particular year, made an election under this subsection covering the total amount that, but for an election under this subsection in respect thereof, would have been deductible in computing the taxpayer's income (other than exempt income) for each such year in respect of the borrowed money used to acquire the depreciable property or the amount payable for the depreciable property acquired by the taxpayer,

if an election under this subsection is made in the taxpayer's return of income under this Part for the particular year, paragraphs 20(1)(c), (d), (e) and (e.1) do not apply to the amount or to the part of the amount specified in the election that, but for an election under this subsection in respect thereof, would be deductible in computing the taxpayer's income (other than exempt income) for the particular year in respect of the borrowed money used to acquire the depreciable property or the amount payable for the depreciable property acquired by the taxpayer, and the amount or part of the amount, as the case may be, shall be added to the capital cost to the taxpayer of the depreciable property.

Related Provisions: 96(3) — Election by members of partnership; 127(11.5)(b)(i) — Ignore s. 21 for purposes of ITC qualified expenditures; 220(3.2), Reg. 600(a) — Late filing or revocation of election.

Notes: An election "in the taxpayer's return" is valid even if the return is filed late. See Notes to 7(1.31).

21(3) amended by 1991 technical bill, effective 1988.

Interpretation Bulletins: See list at end of s. 21.

(4) Borrowing for exploration, etc.

— In computing the income of a taxpayer for a particular taxation year, where the taxpayer

(a) in any preceding taxation year made an election under subsection (2) in respect of borrowed money used for the purpose of exploration, development or acquisition of property,

(b) in each taxation year, if any, after that preceding taxation year and before the particular year, made an election under this subsection covering the total amount that, but for that election, would have been deductible in computing the taxpayer's income (other than exempt income or income that is exempt from tax under this Part) for each such year in respect of the borrowed money used for the exploration, development or acquisition of property, as the case may be, and

(c) so elects in the taxpayer's return of income for the particular year,

the following rules apply:

(d) paragraphs 20(1)(c), (d), (e) and (e.1) do not apply to the amount or to the part of the amount specified in the election that, but for the election, would be deductible in computing the taxpayer's income (other than exempt income or income that is exempt from tax under this Part) for the particular year in respect of the borrowed money used for the exploration, development or acquisition of property, and

(e) the amount or part of the amount, as the case may be, is deemed to be Canadian exploration and development expenses, Canadian exploration expenses, Canadian development expenses, Canadian oil and gas property expenses, foreign resource expenses in respect of a country, or foreign exploration and development expenses, as the case may be, incurred by the taxpayer in the particular year.

Related Provisions: 96(3) — Election by members of partnership; 220(3.2), Reg. 600(a) — Late filing or revocation of election.

Notes: For 21(4)(c), an election "in the taxpayer's return" is valid even if the return is filed late. See Notes to 7(1.31).

21(4) amended by 2000 Budget (for tax years beginning after 2000), 1991 technical bill.

Interpretation Bulletins: See list at end of s. 21.

(5) Reassessments

— Notwithstanding any other provision of this Act, where a taxpayer has made an election in accordance with the provisions of subsection (1) or (2), such reassessments of tax, interest or penalties shall be made as are necessary to give effect thereto.

Definitions [s. 21]: "amount", "borrowed money" — 248(1); "Canadian exploration expense" — 66.1(6), 248(1); "Canadian exploration and development expenses" — 66(15), 248(1); "Canadian development expense" — 66.2(5), 248(1); "Canadian oil and gas property expense" — 66.4(5), 248(1); "depreciable property" — 13(21), 248(1); "exempt income" — 248(1); "foreign exploration and development expenses" — 66(15), 248(1); "prescribed", "property", "regulation" — 248(1); "taxation year" — 11(2), 249; "taxpayer" — 248(1).

Interpretation Bulletins [s. 21]: IT-109R2: Unpaid amounts; IT-121R3: Election to capitalize cost of borrowed money (cancelled); IT-142R3: Settlement of debts on the winding-up of a corporation; IT-341R4: Expenses of issuing shares, units in a trust, interests in a partnership or syndicate and expenses of borrowing money; IT-360R2: Interest payable in a foreign currency.

Ceasing to Carry on Business

22. (1) Sale of accounts receivable [on sale of business] — Where a person who has been carrying on a business has, in a taxation year, sold all or substantially all the property used in carrying on the business, including the debts that have been or will be included in computing the person's income for that year or a previous year and that are still outstanding, and including the debts arising from loans made in the ordinary course of the person's business if part of the person's ordinary business was the lending of money and that are still outstanding, to a purchaser who proposes to continue the business which the vendor has been carrying on, if the vendor and the purchaser have executed jointly an election in prescribed form to have this section apply, the following rules are applicable:

(a) there may be deducted in computing the vendor's income for the taxation year an amount equal to the difference between the face value of the debts so sold (other than debts in respect of which the vendor has made deductions under paragraph 20(1)(p)), and the consideration paid by the purchaser to the vendor for the debts so sold;

(b) an amount equal to the difference described in paragraph (a) shall be included in computing the purchaser's income for the taxation year;

(c) the debts so sold shall be deemed, for the purposes of paragraphs 20(1)(l) and (p), to have been included in computing the purchaser's income for the taxation year or a previous year but no deduction may be made by the purchaser under paragraph 20(1)(p) in respect of a debt in respect of which the vendor has previously made a deduction; and

(d) each amount deducted by the vendor in computing income for a previous year under paragraph 20(1)(p) in respect of any of the debts so sold shall be deemed, for the purpose of paragraph 12(1)(i), to have been so deducted by the purchaser.

Related Provisions: 13(8) — Disposition of depreciable property after ceasing to carry on business; 22(2) — Required statement by vendor and purchaser; 96(3) — Election by members of partnership.

Notes: 22(1) provides an election, on sale of a business including its receivables, so that after the sale the buyer and not the seller can claim the doubtful debts reserve and bad debt deduction (20(1)(l), (p)). If the buyer pays $x less than face value for the receivables, the seller gets a deduction for $x on the sale and the buyer includes $x in income (typically offset by later 20(1)(l) and (p) claims).

For "part of the person's ordinary business was the lending of money", see Notes to 15(2.3) and 20(1)(p).

For interpretation of 22(1) see VIEWS docs 2006-0168491E5; 2014-0560491E5 (business outside Canada qualifies for 22(1), despite IT-188R para. 1); Income Tax Folio S4-F7-C1 ¶1.62.1 (election valid after amalgamation); 2011 Cdn Tax Foundation conference report, CRA/RQ Round Table qq.20-21 (p. 4:15-16); 2017-0719531I7 (s. 22 cannot technically be used after an amalgamation, but CRA permitted it anyway). In *SRI Homes*, 2012 FCA 208, the TCC had denied a s. 22 deduction because the sale was only of receivables and shares, but the FCA sent the matter back for a new hearing because the reasons were insufficient.

CRA considers that "substantially all", used in 22(1) opening words, means 90% or more.

For a taxpayer filing Quebec returns, an election under 22(1) must be copied to Revenu Québec: *Taxation Act* ss. 184, 21.4.6.

Interpretation Bulletins: IT-188R: Sale of accounts receivable; IT-291R3: Transfer of property to a corporation under subsection 85(1); IT-442R: Bad debts and reserve for doubtful debts; IT-471R: Merger of partnership; IT-488R2: Winding-up of 90%-owned taxable Canadian corporations (cancelled).

Forms: T2022: Election in respect of the sale of debts receivable.

(2) Statement by vendor and purchaser — An election executed for the purposes of subsection (1) shall contain a statement by the vendor and the purchaser jointly as to the consideration paid for the debts sold by the vendor to the purchaser and that statement shall, subject to subsection 69(1), as against the Minister, be binding upon the vendor and the purchaser in so far as it may be relevant in respect of any matter arising under this Act.

Definitions [s. 22]: "amount", "business", "Minister", "person", "prescribed", "property" — 248(1); "taxation year" — 11(2), 249.

23. (1) Sale of inventory — Where, on or after disposing of or ceasing to carry on a business or a part of a business, a taxpayer has sold all or any part of the property that was included in the inventory of the business, the property so sold shall, for the purposes of this Part, be deemed to have been sold by the taxpayer in the course of carrying on the business.

Related Provisions: 12.4 — Bad debt inclusion on sale of inventory.

Notes: In *Henco Industries*, 2014 TCC 192, paras. 164-169, a developer in Caledonia had its business ruined by native occupation, and its land became worthless. The Ontario government's $15.8 million payment to make the developer "go away" was not taxable under 23(1), even though it transferred the land to Ontario, as "The land lost its character as inventory by being made legally useless for development."

See also Notes to 24(1) re Reg. 205(2) filing requirement.

Interpretation Bulletins: IT-287R2: Sale of inventory; IT-457R: Election by professionals to exclude work in progress from income.

(2) [Repealed under former Act]

Notes: 23(2) repealed effective May 7, 1974.

(3) Reference to property in inventory — A reference in this section to property that was included in the inventory of a business shall be deemed to include a reference to property that would have been so included if the income from the business had not been computed in accordance with the method authorized by subsection 28(1) or paragraph 34(a).

Definitions [s. 23]: "business" — 248(1); "inventory" — 23(3), 248(1); "Minister", "person", "property", "taxpayer" — 248(1).

24. (1) [Repealed]

Notes: 24(1) repealed by 2016 budget bill #2, effective 2017, as part of changing eligible capital property rules to CCA Class 14.1 as of 2017 (see Notes to 20(1)(b)). See now 20(16.1)(c). Before 2017, read:

(1) Ceasing to carry on business [deduction for cumulative eligible capital] — Notwithstanding paragraph 18(1)(b), where at any time after a taxpayer ceases to carry on a business the taxpayer no longer owns any property that was eligible capital property in respect of the business and that has value, in computing the taxpayer's income for taxation years ending after that time,

(a) there shall be deducted, for the first such taxation year, the amount of the taxpayer's cumulative eligible capital in respect of the business at that time;

(b) no amount may be deducted under paragraph 20(1)(b) in respect of the business;

(c) for the purposes of determining the value of P in the definition "cumulative eligible capital" in subsection 14(5), the amount deducted by the taxpayer under paragraph (a) shall be deemed to be an amount deducted under paragraph 20(1)(b) in computing the taxpayer's income from the business for the taxation year that included that time; and

(d) for the purposes of subsection 14(1), section 14 shall be read without reference to subsection 14(4).

(2) Business carried on by spouse or common-law partner or controlled corporation [after taxpayer ceases] — If, at any time, an individual ceases to carry on a business and the individual's spouse or common-law partner, or a corporation controlled directly or indirectly in any manner whatever by the individual, carries on the business and acquires all of the property included in Class 14.1 of Schedule II to the *Income Tax Regulations* in respect of the business owned by the individual immediately before that time and that had value at that time, the following rules apply:

(a) the individual is deemed to have, immediately before that time, disposed of the property and received proceeds of disposition equal to the lesser of the capital cost and the cost amount to the individual of the property immediately before the disposition;

(b) the spouse, common-law partner or corporation, as the case may be, is deemed to have acquired the property at a cost equal to those proceeds; and

(c) if the amount that was the capital cost to the individual of the property exceeds the amount determined under paragraph 70(5)(b) to be the cost to the person that acquired the property, for the purposes of sections 13 and 20 and any regulations made for the purpose of paragraph 20(1)(a),

(i) the capital cost to the person of the property is deemed to be the amount that was the capital cost to the individual of the property, and

(ii) the excess is deemed to have been allowed to the person in respect of the property under regulations made for the purposes of paragraph 20(1)(a) in computing income for taxation years that ended before the person acquired the property.

Related Provisions: 25 — Fiscal period for individual proprietor of business disposed of; 256(5.1), (6.2) — Controlled directly or indirectly.

Notes: On the interaction of 24(2) and pre-2017 14(3) see VIEWS docs 2005-0152261E5, 2008-0285331C6.

24(2) amended by 2016 budget bill #2, effective 2017 (see Notes to 24(1)). Before 2017, read:

(2) Notwithstanding subsection (1), where at any time an individual ceases to carry on a business and thereafter the individual's spouse or common-law partner, or a corporation controlled directly or indirectly in any manner whatever by the individual, carries on the business and acquires all of the property that was eligible capital property in respect of the business owned by the individual before that time and that had value at that time,

(a) in computing the individual's income for the individual's first taxation year ending after that time, subsection (1) shall be read without reference to paragraph (1)(a) and the reference in paragraph (1)(c) to "the amount deducted by the taxpayer under paragraph (a)" shall be read as a reference to "an amount equal to the taxpayer's cumulative eligible capital in respect of the business immediately before that time";

(b) in computing the cumulative eligible capital of the spouse or common-law partner or the corporation, as the case may be, in respect of the business, the spouse or common-law partner or corporation shall be deemed to have acquired an eligible capital property and to have made an eligible capital expenditure at that time at a cost equal to ⁴/₃ of the total of

(i) the cumulative eligible capital of the taxpayer in respect of the business immediately before that time, and

(ii) the amount, if any, determined for F in the definition "cumulative eligible capital" in subsection 14(5) in respect of the business of the individual at that time;

(c) for the purposes of determining the cumulative eligible capital in respect of the business of the spouse or common-law partner or corporation after that time, an amount equal to the amount determined under subparagraph (b)(ii) shall be added to the amount otherwise determined in respect thereof for P in the definition "cumulative eligible capital" in subsection 14(5); and

(d) for the purpose of determining after that time the amount required to be included under paragraph 14(1)(b) in computing the income of the spouse, the common-law partner or the corporation in respect of any subsequent disposition of property of the business, there shall be added to the amount otherwise determined for Q in the definition "cumulative eligible capital" in subsection 14(5) the amount, if any, determined for Q in that definition in respect of the business of the individual immediately before the individual ceased to carry on business.

24(2) amended by 2000 Budget (for tax years that end after Feb. 27, 2000), 2000 same-sex partners bill, 1994 Budget and 1992 and 1991 technical bills.

(3) [Repealed]

Notes: 24(3) repealed by 2016 budget bill #2, effective 2017 (see Notes to 24(1)). Before 2017, read:

(3) **Where partnership has ceased to exist** — Notwithstanding subsection (1), where at any time a partnership ceases to exist in circumstances to which neither subsection 98(3) nor subsection 98(5) applies, there may be deducted, in computing the income for the first taxation year beginning after that time of a

taxpayer who was a member of the partnership immediately before that time, an amount determined by the formula

$$A \times B/C$$

where

A   is the amount that would, had the partnership continued to exist, have been deductible under subsection (1) in computing its income;

B   is the fair market value of the taxpayer's interest in the partnership immediately before that time; and

C   is the fair market value of all interests in the partnership immediately before that time.

24(3) added by 1992 technical bill, effective July 14, 1990.

Definitions [s. 24]: "amount", "business", "common-law partner" — 248(1); "controlled directly or indirectly" — 256(5.1)–(6); "corporation" — 248(1), *Interpretation Act* 35(1); "cost amount" — 248(1); "cumulative eligible capital" — 14(5), 248(1); "disposition" — 248(1); "fair market value" — see 69(1) Notes; "individual", "person", "property", "regulation" — 248(1); "taxation year" — 11(2), 249; "taxpayer" — 248(1).

24.1 [Repealed]

Notes: 24.1 repealed by 1995 Budget, for judicial appointments after 1995. It allowed deferral of income for lawyers appointed as judges (salary taxed under 5(1) on a current-year basis). It is no longer needed because lawyers no longer can defer income through choice of a year-end (see 249.1, 34.1).

25. (1) Fiscal period of business disposed of by individual — Where an individual was the proprietor of a business and disposed of it during a fiscal period of the business, the fiscal period may, if the individual so elects and subsection 249.1(4) does not apply in respect of the business, be deemed to have ended at the time it would have ended if the individual had not disposed of the business during the fiscal period.

Related Provisions: 13(8) — Disposition of depreciable property after ceasing to carry on business; 99(2) — Parallel rule where partnership ceases to exist.

Notes: For an individual filing a Quebec return, an election under 25(1) must be copied to Revenu Québec: *Taxation Act* ss. 190, 21.4.6.

25(1) amended by 1995 Budget, for fiscal periods that begin after 1994.

Interpretation Bulletins: IT-179R: Change of fiscal period; IT-313R2: Eligible capital property — rules where a taxpayer has ceased carrying on a business or has died.

Information Circulars: 76-19R3: Transfer of property to a corporation under s. 85.

(2) Election — An election under subsection (1) is not valid unless the individual, at the time when the fiscal period of the business would, if the election were valid, be deemed to have ended, is resident in Canada.

(3) Dispositions in the extended fiscal period — If subsection (1) applies in respect of a fiscal period of a business of an individual, for the purpose of computing the individual's income for the fiscal period, section 13 is to be read without reference to its subsection (8).

Notes: 25(3) amended by 2016 budget bill #2, effective 2017 (as part of changing eligible capital property rules to CCA Class 14.1 — see Notes to 20(1)(b)), to repeal "(b) section 24 shall be read without reference to paragraph 24(1)(d)" and fold para. (a) ("section 13...") into the subsec.

Income Tax Folios: S3-F4-C1: General discussion of CCA [replaces IT-478R2].

Interpretation Bulletins: IT-313R2: Eligible capital property — rules where a taxpayer has ceased carrying on a business or has died.

Definitions [s. 25]: "business" — 248(1); "Canada" — 255; "fiscal period" — 249.1; "individual" — 248(1); "resident in Canada" — 94(3)(a), 250; "taxpayer" — 248(1).

Special Cases

26. (1) Banks — inclusions in income — There shall be included in computing the income of a bank for its first taxation year that commences after June 17, 1987 and ends after 1987 the total of

(a) the total of the specific provisions of the bank, as determined, or as would be determined if such a determination were required, under the Minister's rules, as at the end of its immediately preceding taxation year,

(b) the total of the general provisions of the bank, as determined, or as would be determined if such a determination were required, under the Minister's rules, as at the end of its immediately preceding taxation year,

(c) the amount, if any, by which

(i) the amount of the special provision for losses on transborder claims of the bank, as determined, or as would be determined if such a determination were required, under the Minister's rules, that was deductible by the bank under subsection (2) in computing its income for its immediately preceding taxation year

exceeds

(ii) that part of the amount determined under subparagraph (i) that was a realized loss of the bank for that immediately preceding taxation year, and

(d) the amount, if any, of the tax allowable appropriations account of the bank, as determined, or as would be determined if such a determination were required, under the Minister's rules, at the end of its immediately preceding taxation year.

Related Provisions: 20(1)(l) — Reserve for doubtful accounts; 20(1)(l.1) — Reserve for guarantees; 26(4) — Minister's rules; 87(2)(g.1) — Amalgamation — continuing corporation; 95(2.31), (2.43)–(2.45), (3.01) — FAPI flexibility for banks; 142.2–142.6 — Additional rules for financial institutions; 142.7 — Foreign banks — conversion from subsidiary to branch; 248(1)"authorized foreign bank" — Foreign bank branches.

(2) Banks — deductions from income — In computing the income for a taxation year of a bank, there may be deducted an amount not exceeding the total of

(a) that part of the total of the amounts of the five-year average loan loss experiences of the bank, as determined, or as would be determined if such a determination were required, under the Minister's rules, for all taxation years before its first taxation year that commences after June 17, 1987 and ends after 1987 that is specified by the bank for the year and was not deducted by the bank in computing its income for any preceding taxation year,

(b) that part of the total of the amounts transferred by the bank to its tax allowable appropriations account, as permitted under the Minister's rules, for all taxation years before its first taxation year that commences after June 17, 1987 and ends after 1987 that is specified by the bank for the year and was not deducted by the bank in computing its income for any preceding taxation year,

(c) that part of the amount, if any, by which

(i) the amount of the special provision for losses on transborder claims, as determined, or as would be determined if such a determination were required, under the Minister's rules, that was deductible by the bank under this subsection in computing its income for its last taxation year before its first taxation year that commences after June 17, 1987 and ends after 1987

exceeds

(ii) that part of the amount determined under subparagraph (i) that was a realized loss of the bank for that last taxation year

that is specified by the bank for the year and was not deducted by the bank in computing its income for any preceding taxation year,

(d) where the tax allowable appropriations account of the bank at the end of its last taxation year before its first taxation year that commences after June 17, 1987 and ends after 1987, as determined, or as would be determined if such a determination were required, under the Minister's rules, is a negative amount, that part of such amount expressed as a positive number that is specified by the bank for the year and was not deducted by the bank in computing its income for any preceding taxation year, and

(e) that part of the total of the amounts calculated in respect of the bank for the purposes of the Minister's rules, or that would be calculated for the purposes of those rules if such a calculation were required, under Procedure 8 of the Procedures for the Determination of the Provision for Loan Losses as set out in Appendix 1 of those rules, for all taxation years before its first taxation year that commences after June 17, 1987 and ends after 1987 that is specified by the bank for the year and was not deducted by the bank in computing its income for any preceding taxation year.

Related Provisions: 20.2 — Foreign bank branch — interest deduction; 87(2)(g.1) — Amalgamation — continuing corporation.

(3) Write-offs and recoveries — In computing the income of a bank, the following rules apply:

(a) any amount that was recorded by the bank as a realized loss or a write-off of an asset that was included by the bank in the calculation of an amount deductible under the Minister's rules, or would have been included in the calculation of such an amount if such a calculation had been required, for any taxation year before its first taxation year that commences after June 17, 1987 and ends after 1987, shall, for the purposes of paragraph 12(1)(i) and section 12.4, be deemed to have been deducted by the bank under paragraph 20(1)(p) in computing its income for the year for which it was so recorded; and

(b) any amount that was recorded by the bank as a recovery of a realized loss or a write-off of an asset that was included by the bank in the calculation of an amount deductible under the Minister's rules, or would have been included in the calculation of such an amount if such a calculation had been required, for any taxation year before its first taxation year that commences after June 17, 1987 and ends after 1987 shall, for the purposes of section 12.4, be deemed to have been included by the bank under paragraph 12(1)(i) in computing its income for the year for which it was so recorded.

(4) Definition of "Minister's rules" — For the purposes of this section, "Minister's rules" means the *Rules for the Determination of the Appropriations for Contingencies of a Bank* issued under the authority of the Minister of Finance pursuant to section 308 of the *Bank Act* for the purposes of subsections (1) and (2) of this section.

Definitions [s. 26]: "amount", "bank" — 248(1); "Minister of Finance" — *Financial Administration Act* 14; "Minister's rules" — 26(4); "taxation year" — 249.

27. (1) Application of Part I to Crown corporation — This Part applies to a federal Crown corporation as if

(a) any income or loss from a business carried on by the corporation as agent of Her Majesty, or from a property of Her Majesty administered by the corporation, were an income or loss of the corporation from the business or the property, as the case may be; and

(b) any property, obligation or debt of any kind whatever held, administered, entered into or incurred by the corporation as agent of Her Majesty were a property, obligation or debt, as the case may be, of the corporation.

Related Provisions: 124(3) — No tax abatement for income earned in a province; 149(1)(c)–(d.4) — Crown corporations and subsidiaries generally exempt; 181(1) — Meaning of "long-term debt"; 181.71, 190.211 — Capital taxes apply to federal Crown corporations; 187.61, 191.4(3) — Part IV.1 and VI.1 taxes on preferred share dividends apply to federal Crown corporations.

Notes: On whether a corp carries on business as agent of Her Majesty, see *Nova Scotia Power*, 2004 SCC 51, paras. 12-13: "There are two ways in which an entity can become an agent of the Crown. The first is when the Crown exercises sufficient control over it so that it can be said to be in *de jure* control, which requires a careful examination of the relationship between the parties ... The second way is for the legislature to expressly legislate it to be an agent." Note that CRA is deemed by *Canada Revenue Agency Act* s. 4(2) to be "for all purposes an agent of Her Majesty in right of Canada".

See VIEWS doc 2014-0549701I7 re obligations (under the ITA) of Crown corporations that are Crown agents.

CP Rail is contesting its Large Corporations Tax based on exemptions enacted to enable the railway to be built across Canada in the 1880s: *Canadian Pacific Railway*, 2013 FC 161, 2019 FC 1531, 2020 FC 690, 2020 FC 1058. The appeal was heard starting Oct. 5, 2020, and final argument was heard in Feb. 2021. (CP has a similar dispute against Saskatchewan: 2019 SKQB 233.)

Export Development Act s. 22 provides that s. 27 does not apply to Export Development Canada.

See also Notes to 27(2).

27(1) amended by 1995-97 technical bill, effective April 27, 1995, or earlier.

Interpretation Bulletins: IT-347R2: Crown corporations (cancelled).

(2) Presumption — Notwithstanding any other provision of this Act, a prescribed federal Crown corporation and any corporation controlled by such a corporation are each deemed not to be a private corporation and paragraphs 149(1)(d) to (d.4) do not apply to those corporations.

Related Provisions: 181.71, 190.211 — Capital taxes apply to prescribed federal Crown corporations (PFCCs); 187.61, 191.4(3) — Part IV.1 and VI.1 taxes on preferred share dividends apply to PFCCs; 256(6), (6.1) — Meaning of "control".

Notes: 27(2) forces Crown corporations that operate in the commercial sector to pay income tax, to eliminate a competitive advantage over private-sector corps. The list of such corporations is in Reg. 7100. Some provincial Crown corps are similarly taxed under provincial rules: e.g., *ENMAX Energy*, 2018 ABCA 147, para. 3 (leave to appeal denied 2019 CarswellAlta 355 (SCC)).

Where assets of a Crown corp are privatized, bonds of the corp may qualify as qualified investments for RRSPs and other deferred income plans. See Reg. 4900(1)(q).

27(2) amended by 2001 technical bill, for tax years and fiscal periods that begin after 1998, to add reference to 149(1)(d.1)–(d.4).

Regulations: 7100 (prescribed federal Crown corporation).

Interpretation Bulletins: IT-347R2: Crown corporations (cancelled).

(3) Transfers of land for disposition — Where land of Her Majesty has been transferred to a prescribed federal Crown corporation for purposes of disposition, the acquisition of the property by the corporation and any disposition thereof shall be deemed not to have been in the course of the business carried on by the corporation.

Notes: "Land" may include buildings: see 70(5.2) Notes.

Regulations: 7100 (prescribed federal Crown corporation).

Interpretation Bulletins: IT-347R2: Crown corporations (cancelled).

Definitions [s. 27]: "business" — 248(1); "controlled" — 256(6), (6.1); "corporation" — 248(1), *Interpretation Act* 35(1); "disposition" — 248(1); "Her Majesty" — *Interpretation Act* 35(1); "land" — see 70(5.2) Notes; "prescribed" — 248(1); "private corporation" — 89(1), 248(1); "property" — 248(1).

27.1 (1) Emissions allowances — Notwithstanding section 10, for the purpose of computing a taxpayer's income from a business, an emissions allowance shall be valued at the cost at which the taxpayer acquired it.

Related Provisions: 27.1(2) — Determination of cost of emissions allowance.

Notes: See Notes at end of 27.1.

(2) Determination of cost of emissions allowances — If at any particular time a taxpayer that owns one emissions allowance, or two or more identical emissions allowances (for the purposes of this subsection two or more emissions allowances will be considered identical if they could be used to settle the same emissions obligations), acquires one or more other emissions allowances (in this subsection referred to as "newly acquired emissions allowances"), each of which is identical to each of the previously-acquired emissions allowances, for the purposes of computing, at any subsequent time, the cost of the taxpayer of each of the identical emissions allowances,

(a) the taxpayer is deemed to have disposed of each of the previously-acquired emissions allowances immediately before the particular time for proceeds equal to its cost to the taxpayer immediately before the particular time; and

(b) the taxpayer is deemed to have acquired each of the identical emissions allowances at the particular time at a cost equal to the amount determined by the formula

$$(A + B)/C$$

where

A is the total cost to the taxpayer immediately before the particular time of the previously-acquired emissions allowances,

B is the total cost to the taxpayer (determined without reference to this section) of the newly-acquired emissions allowances, and

C is the number of the identical emissions allowances owned by the taxpayer immediately after the particular time.

Related Provisions: 248(1)"inventory"(b) — Emissions allowance excluded from definition of inventory.

(3) Expense restriction — Notwithstanding any other provision of this Act, in computing a taxpayer's income from a business for a taxation year, the total amount deductible in respect of a particular emissions obligation for a taxation year shall not exceed the amount determined by the formula

$$A + B \times C$$

where

A is the total cost of emissions allowances either

(a) used by the taxpayer to settle the particular emissions obligation in the year, or

(b) held by the taxpayer at the end of the taxation year that can be used to satisfy the particular emissions obligation in respect of the year;

B is the amount determined by the formula

$$D - (E + F)$$

where

D is the number of emissions allowances required to satisfy the particular emissions obligation in respect of the taxation year,

E is the number of emissions allowances used by the taxpayer to settle the particular emissions obligation in the year, and

F is the number of emissions allowances held by the taxpayer at the end of the taxation year that can be used to satisfy the particular emissions obligation in respect of the year; and

C is the fair market value of an emissions allowance at the end of the taxation year that could be used to satisfy the particular emissions obligation in respect of the year.

Related Provisions: 27.1(4) — Income inclusion in next year; 257 — Formula cannot calculate to less than zero.

Notes: See Notes at end of 27.1.

(4) Income inclusion in following year — There shall be included in computing the income of a taxpayer for a taxation year as income from a business the amount deducted in respect of an emissions obligation referred to in subsection (3) for the immediately preceding taxation year to the extent that the emissions obligation was not settled in the immediately preceding taxation year.

(5) Proceeds of disposition — If a taxpayer surrenders an emissions allowance to settle an emissions obligation, the taxpayer's proceeds from the disposition of the emissions allowance are deemed to be equal to the taxpayer's cost of the emissions allowance.

Notes: See Notes at end of 27.1.

(6) Loss restriction event [change in control rule] — Notwithstanding subsection (1), each emissions allowance held at the end of the taxpayer's taxation year that ends immediately before the time at which the taxpayer is subject to a loss restriction event is to be valued at the cost at which the taxpayer acquired the property, or its fair market value at the end of the year, whichever is lower, and after that time the cost at which the taxpayer acquired the property is, subject to a subsequent application of this subsection and subsection (2), deemed to be that lower amount.

Notes [s. 27.1]: Under emissions trading regimes, governments impose an obligation on regulated emitters to deliver emissions allowances (EAs) to the government. The amount of EAs required is determined by reference to emissions of a regulated substance (e.g., greenhouse gases) produced. EAs may be purchased by emitters in the market or at auction, earned by emissions reduction activities, or provided by the government at a reduced price or no cost.

Before 2017, EAs were taxed under general principles: 9(1). EAs (see 248(1)"emissions allowance") are now treated as inventory for all taxpayers: 248(1)"inventory"(b); but the "lower of cost and market" method for inventory valuation in 10(1) cannot be used: 27.1(1).

If a regulated emitter receives a free EA, there is no income inclusion. The deduction for an accrued EO (248(1)"emissions obligation") is limited to the extent the EO exceeds the cost of any EAs the taxpayer can use to settle it: 27.1(3). A taxpayer claiming an EO deduction will quantify it at year-end based on the cost of EAs it has acquired and that can be used to settle its EOs, plus the current market price of any EAs it still must acquire to fully satisfy its obligations. A deduction for an EO that accrues in year X and will be satisfied in a later year is brought back into income the next year: 27.1(4); and the obligation must be evaluated again each year until it is satisfied.

If a taxpayer disposes of an EA to satisfy an EO, the proceeds are deemed to be the same as cost so there is no income inclusion: 27.1(5). Otherwise, since an EA is inventory, proceeds minus cost are included in income.

27.1 added by 2016 budget bill #2, for EAs acquired in tax years that begin after 2016. However, if X elects in its return of income for its 2016 or 2017 tax year, then 27.1, 248(1)"emissions allowance", "emission obligation", "inventory"(b) and Reg. 7300(d) apply to EAs acquired by X in tax years that end after 2012.

Definitions [s. 27.1]: "amount", "business", "disposition", "emissions allowance", "emissions obligation" — 248(1); "fair market value" — see 69(1) Notes; "identical" — 248(12); "loss restriction event" — 251.2; "property" — 248(1); "taxation year" — 249; "taxpayer" — 248(1).

28. (1) Farming or fishing business [cash method] — For the purpose of computing the income of a taxpayer for a taxation year from a farming or fishing business, the income from the business for that year may, if the taxpayer so elects, be computed in accordance with a method (in this section referred to as the **"cash method"**) whereby the income therefrom for that year shall be deemed to be an amount equal to the total of

(a) all amounts that

(i) were received in the year, or are deemed by this Act to have been received in the year, in the course of carrying on the business, and

(ii) were in payment of or on account of an amount that would, if the income from the business were not computed in accordance with the cash method, be included in computing income from the business for that or any other year,

(b) with respect to a farming business, such amount, if any, as is specified by the taxpayer in respect of the business in the taxpayer's return of income under this Part for the year, not exceeding the amount, if any, by which

(i) the fair market value at the end of the year of inventory owned by the taxpayer in connection with the business at that time

exceeds

(ii) the amount determined under paragraph (c) for the year,

(c) with respect to a farming business, the amount, if any, that is the lesser of

(i) the taxpayer's loss from the business for the year computed without reference to this paragraph and to paragraph (b), and

(ii) the value of inventory purchased by the taxpayer that was owned by the taxpayer in connection with the business at the end of the year, and

(d) the total of all amounts each of which is an amount included in computing the taxpayer's income for the year from the business because of subsection 13(1), 80(13) or 80.3(3) or (5),

minus the total of

(e) all amounts, other than amounts described in section 30, that

(i) were paid in the year, or are deemed by this Act to have been paid in the year, in the course of carrying on the business,

(ii) in the case of amounts paid, or deemed by this Act to have been paid, for inventory, were in payment of or on account of an amount that would be deductible in computing

the income from the business for the year or any other taxation year if that income were not computed in accordance with the cash method, and

(iii) in any other case, were in payment of or on account of an amount that would be deductible in computing the income from the business for a preceding taxation year, the year or the following taxation year if that income were not computed in accordance with the cash method,

(e.1) all amounts, other than amounts described in section 30, that

(i) would be deductible in computing the income from the business for the year if that income were not computed in accordance with the cash method,

(ii) are not deductible in computing the income from the business for any other taxation year, and

(iii) were paid in a preceding taxation year in the course of carrying on the business,

(f) the total of all amounts each of which is the amount, if any, included under paragraph (b) or (c) in computing the taxpayer's income from the business for the immediately preceding taxation year, and

(g) the total of all amounts each of which is an amount deducted for the year under paragraph 20(1)(a) or (uu), subsection 20(16), section 30 or subsection 80.3(2) or (4) in respect of the business,

Possible Future Amendment — 28(1)(g)

Notes: The Dept. of Finance has acknowledged that a reference to 80.3(4.1) was inadvertently deleted from para. 28(1)(g) by 2016 budget bill #2, and will be restored in a future technical bill.

except that paragraphs (b) and (c) do not apply in computing the income of the taxpayer for the taxation year in which the taxpayer dies.

Related Provisions: 20(7)(b) — No reserve available under 20(1)(m) when using cash method; 23(3) — Reference to property included in inventory; 28(2) — Limitation where business carried on jointly with other persons; 28(4) — Non-resident; 29–31 — Additional special rules for farmers; 76(1) — Security in satisfaction of income debt; 79(3)F(b)(v)(B)(II) — Proceeds of disposition to debtor on surrender of property — unpaid interest included under 28(1)(e); 80(1)"excluded obligation"(b) — Obligation not subject to debt forgiveness rules; 80.3 — Income deferral from destruction of livestock or drought-induced sales of breeding animals; 85(1)(c.2) — Transfer of property to corporation by shareholders; 87(2)(b) — Amalgamations — inventory; 88(1.6) — Winding-up; 125.7(4)(e) — Election to use cash method to qualify for COVID-19 Canada Emergency Wage Subsidy; 248(1)"cash method" — Definition applies to entire Act.

Notes: 28(1) allows a farmer or fisherman (or corporation) to use the cash method instead of accrual accounting (whereby income is recognized once it is earned and/or billed). See also ss. 29–31 and Notes to 248(1)"farming" and "fishing"; Munro & Oelschlagel, *Taxation of Farmers and Fishermen* (Carswell, looseleaf or *Taxnet Pro* Reference Centre). (See Notes to 9(1) re whether cash-based accounting is allowed without 28(1).)

For 28(1)(b), specifying an amount "in the taxpayer's return" is valid even if the return is filed late. See Notes to 7(1.31).

For a taxpayer filing Quebec returns, an election under 28(1) must be copied to Revenu Québec: *Taxation Act* ss. 194, 21.4.6.

Under the cash method, a post-dated cheque is considered received when it comes due: IT-433R, para. 6.

Compensation for damaged crops is considered income if the farmer expensed the crops: VIEWS doc 2014-0520921I7.

Cash purchase tickets under 76(4) are not inventory for purposes of the optional 28(1)(b) inventory adjustment or the mandatory 28(1)(c) inventory adjustment: VIEWS doc 2010-0381741E5.

For the 28(1)(c) inventory adjustment see VIEWS docs 9328315, 2013-0509021E5.

A farmer using the cash method cannot deduct prepaid expenses (other than for inventory) relating to a taxation year more than 1 year after the year paid: 28(1)(e), VIEWS doc 2003-0046941E5. The cash method does not apply to CCA recapture under 13(1) on sale of depreciable property, due to 28(1)(d): 2008-030263I7. On amalgamation of farming corporations that both use the cash method, see 2011-0429071E5.

A CBC News report "Tax charges dropped against Lark Harbour man" (March 7, 2012) states that it is "accepted practice [in Newfoundland] that fishermen can claim a $20 deduction for new lobster pots, even though there are no receipts". This does not appear in any CRA publication and, if it was accepted by CRA auditors, no longer seems to be. However, see 9(1) Notes at "Cash expenses".

28(1) amended by 2016 budget bill #2 effective 2017, as part of changing eligible capital property rules to CCA Class 14.1 (see Notes to 20(1)(b)), to delete from para. (d) a reference to 14(1), and from para. (g) references to 20(1)(b), 24(1), and (inadvertently — this has been pointed out to Finance) 80.3(4.1).

28(1) earlier amended by 2014 budget bill #2 (for 2014 and later tax years), 2013 budget bill #2, 1995-97, 1994 and 1991 technical bills, 1989 Budget.

Regulations: 1700–1704 (capital cost allowance rates for pre-1972 property of farming or fishing business).

Remission Orders: *Payments Received under the Atlantic Groundfish Licence Retirement Program Remission Order*, P.C. 2013-936 (tax on payments received for 1998-2002 partly reduced for 156 taxpayers).

Income Tax Folios: S4-F7-C1: Amalgamations of Canadian corporations [replaces IT-474R2]; S4-F11-C1: Meaning of farming and farming business [replaces IT-373R2].

Interpretation Bulletins: IT-154R: Special reserves; IT-184R: Deferred cash purchase tickets issued by Canadian Wheat Board; IT-291R3: Transfer of property to a corporation under subsection 85(1); IT-427R: Livestock of farmers; IT-526: Farming — cash method inventory adjustments.

CRA Audit Manual: 27.12.0: Farming and fishing income; 29.4.0: Farm losses and restricted farm losses.

Forms: RC322: AgriInvest adjustment request; RC602: Checklist for Tax Preparers — Cattle Ranching and Dairy Farming; RC4004: Seasonal agricultural workers program [guide]; RC4060 (for PE, ON, AB): Farming income and the AgriStability and AgriInvest programs guide; RC4408 (for BC, SK, MB, NS, NL, YK): Farming income and the AgriStability and AgriInvest programs harmonized guide — joint forms and guide; T1163: Statement A — AgriStability and AgriInvest programs information and statement of farming activities for individuals; T1164: Statement B — AgriStability and AgriInvest programs information and statement of farming activities for additional farming operations; T1175: Calculation of CCA and business-use-of-home expenses; T1273: Statement A — Harmonized AgriStability and AgriInvest programs information and statement of farming activities for individuals; T1274: Statement B — Harmonized AgriStability and AgriInvest programs information and statement of farming activities for additional farming operations; T1275: AgriStability and AgriInvest programs additional information and adjustment request form; T2034: Election to establish inventory unit prices for animals; T2042: Statement of farming activities; T2121: Statement of fishing activities; T4003: Farming and fishing income [guide]; TD3F: Fisher's election to have tax deducted at source.

(1.1) Acquisition of inventory — Where at any time, and in circumstances where paragraph 69(1)(a) or (c) applies, a taxpayer acquires inventory that is owned by the taxpayer in connection with a farming business the income from which is computed in accordance with the cash method, for the purposes of this section an amount equal to the cost to the taxpayer of the inventory shall be deemed

(a) to have been paid by the taxpayer at that time and in the course of carrying on that business, and

(b) to be the only amount so paid for the inventory by the taxpayer,

and the taxpayer shall be deemed to have purchased the inventory at the time it was so acquired.

Notes: 28(1.1) added by 1991 technical bill, for tax years and fiscal periods ending after 1990. Former 28(1.1), repealed by 1991 technical bill effective for taxation years beginning after 1988, defined "inventory" for 28(1). 248(1)"inventory" was amended to cover that rule.

Interpretation Bulletins: IT-427R: Livestock of farmers.

Forms: T2034: Election to establish inventory unit prices for animals.

(1.2) Valuation of inventory — For the purpose of paragraph (1)(c) and notwithstanding section 10, inventory of a taxpayer shall be valued at any time at the lesser of the total amount paid by the taxpayer at or before that time to acquire it (in this section referred to as its **"cash cost"**) and its fair market value, except that an animal (in this section referred to as a **"specified animal"**) that is a horse or, where the taxpayer has so elected in respect thereof for the taxation year that includes that time or for any preceding taxation year, is a bovine animal registered under the *Animal Pedigree Act*, shall be valued

(a) at any time in the taxation year in which it is acquired, at such amount as is designated by the taxpayer not exceeding its cash cost to the taxpayer and not less than 70% of its cash cost to the taxpayer; and

(b) at any time in a subsequent taxation year, at such amount as is designated by the taxpayer not exceeding its cash cost to the taxpayer and not less than 70% of the total of

(i) its value determined under this subsection at the end of the preceding taxation year, and

(ii) the total amount paid on account of the purchase price of the animal during the year.

Related Provisions: 85(1)(c.2) — Transfer of property to corporation by shareholders; 88(1.6) — Winding-up.

Notes: 28(1.2) amended by 1991 technical bill, effective for fiscal periods commencing after 1988.

Regulations: 1801, 1802 (valuation of inventory).

Interpretation Bulletins: IT-291R3: Transfer of property to a corporation under subsection 85(1).

Forms: T2034: Election to establish inventory unit prices for animals.

(1.3) Short fiscal period — For each taxation year that is less than 51 weeks, the reference in subsection (1.2) to "70" shall be read as a reference to the number determined by the formula

$$100 - \left(30 \times \frac{A}{365} \right)$$

where

A is the number of days in the taxation year.

Notes: 28(1.3) is presumably intended to apply to *both* references to "70%" in 28(1.2).

(2) Where joint farming or fishing business — Subsection (1) does not apply for the purpose of computing the income of a taxpayer for a taxation year from a farming or fishing business carried on by the taxpayer jointly with one or more other persons, unless each of the other persons by whom the business is jointly carried on has elected to have his or her income from the business for that year computed in accordance with the cash method.

(3) Concurrence of Minister [to stop using cash method] — Where a taxpayer has filed a return of income under this Part for a taxation year wherein the taxpayer's income for that year from a farming or fishing business has been computed in accordance with the cash method, income from the business for each subsequent taxation year shall, subject to the other provisions of this Part, be computed in accordance with that method unless the taxpayer, with the concurrence of the Minister and on such terms and conditions as are specified by the Minister, adopts some other method.

Notes: For a taxpayer filing a Quebec return, adoption of a different method must be copied to Revenu Québec: *Taxation Act* ss. 195, 21.4.6.

(4) Non-resident — Notwithstanding subsections (1) and (5), where at the end of a taxation year a taxpayer who carried on a business the income from which was computed in accordance with the cash method is non-resident and does not carry on that business in Canada, an amount equal to the total of all amounts each of which is the fair market value of an amount outstanding during the year as or on account of a debt owing to the taxpayer that arose in the course of carrying on the business and that would have been included in computing the taxpayer's income for the year if the amount had been received by the taxpayer in the year, shall (to the extent that the amount was not otherwise included in computing the taxpayer's income for the year or a preceding taxation year) be included in computing the taxpayer's income from the business

(a) for the year, if the taxpayer was non-resident throughout the year; and

(b) for the part of the year throughout which the taxpayer was resident in Canada, if the taxpayer was resident in Canada at any time in the year.

Related Provisions: 28(5) — Accounts receivable; 128.1(4)(b) — Deemed disposition of property where taxpayer ceases to be resident in Canada; 253 — Extended meaning of "carrying on business in Canada".

Notes: 28(4) amended by 2001 technical bill (for 1998 and later tax years), 1991 technical bill.

Interpretation Bulletins: IT-427R: Livestock of farmers.

(4.1) [Repealed]

Notes: 28(4.1) repealed by 2001 technical bill, effective Dec. 24, 1998. (It has been superseded by 10(12) and amended 128.1.) It dealt with a cash-method non-resident ceasing to use inventory. Originally added by 1991 technical bill, effective for taxpayers who cease to reside in Canada after July 13, 1990 and for property that ceases after July 13, 1990 to be used in connection with a business carried on in Canada.

(5) Accounts receivable — There shall be included in computing the income of a taxpayer for a taxation year such part of an amount received by the taxpayer in the year, on or after disposing of or ceasing to carry on a business or a part of a business, for, on account or in lieu of payment of, or in satisfaction of debts owing to the taxpayer that arose in the course of carrying on the business as would have been included in computing the income of the taxpayer for the year had the amount so received been received by the taxpayer in the course of carrying on the business.

Notes: 28(5) requires full income inclusion when accounts receivable are sold by a cash-basis farmer, even if the transfer is to a wholly-owned corporation in exchange for a note: VIEWS doc 2008-0302641E5.

CRA Audit Manual: 27.12.4: Farming and fishing income — income tax implications — ceasing to carry on a farming or fishing business.

Definitions [s. 28]: "amount", "business" — 248(1), 253; "Canada" — 255; "cash cost" — 28(1.2); "cash method" — 28(1), 248(1); "fair market value" — see 69(1) Notes; "farming", "fishing", "inventory", "Minister", "non-resident", "person", "property" — 248(1); "specified animal" — 28(1.2); "taxation year" — 11(2), 249; "taxpayer" — 248(1).

Income Tax Folios [s. 28]: S4-F11-C1: Meaning of farming and farming business [replaces IT-433R]; S4-F15-C1: Manufacturing and processing [replaces IT-147R3].

Interpretation Bulletins [s. 28]: IT-156R: Feedlot operators (cancelled); IT-188R: Sale of accounts receivable; IT-433R: Farming or fishing — use of cash method; IT-505: Mortgage foreclosures and conditional sales repossessions (cancelled); IT-526: Farming — cash method inventory adjustments.

29. (1) Disposition of animal of basic herd class — Where a taxpayer has a basic herd of a class of animals and disposes of an animal of that class in the course of carrying on a farming business in a taxation year, if the taxpayer so elects in the taxpayer's return of income under this Part for the year the following rules apply:

(a) there shall be deducted in computing the taxpayer's basic herd of that class at the end of the year such number as is designated by the taxpayer in the taxpayer's election, not exceeding the least of

(i) the number of animals of that class so disposed of by the taxpayer in that year,

(ii) ¹/₁₀ of the taxpayer's basic herd of that class on December 31, 1971, and

(iii) the taxpayer's basic herd of that class of animal at the end of the immediately preceding taxation year; and

(b) there shall be deducted in computing the taxpayer's income from the farming business for the taxation year the product obtained when

(i) the number determined under paragraph (a) in respect of the taxpayer's basic herd of that class for the year

is multiplied by

(ii) the quotient obtained when the fair market value on December 31, 1971 of the taxpayer's animals of that class on that day is divided by the number of the taxpayer's animals of that class on that day.

Related Provisions: 28(1)(b) — Optional inclusion of inventory in income; 80.3 — Income deferral from destruction of livestock or drought-induced sales of breeding animals; 96(3) — Election by members of partnership.

Notes: An election "in the taxpayer's return" is valid even if the return is filed late. See Notes to 7(1.31).

For a taxpayer filing Quebec returns, an election under 29(1) must be copied to Revenu Québec: *Taxation Act* ss. 199, 21.4.6.

Forms: T2034: Election to establish inventory unit prices for animals.

(2) Reduction in basic herd — Where a taxpayer carries on a farming business in a taxation year and the taxpayer's basic herd of any class at the end of the immediately preceding year, minus the deduction, if any, required by paragraph (1)(a) to be made in computing the taxpayer's basic herd of that class at the end of the year, exceeds the number of animals of that class owned by the taxpayer at the end of the year,

(a) there shall be deducted in computing the taxpayer's basic herd of that class at the end of the year the number of animals comprising the excess, and

(b) there shall be deducted in computing the taxpayer's income from the farming business for the taxation year the product obtained when

(i) the number of animals comprising the excess

is multiplied by

(ii) the quotient obtained when the fair market value on December 31, 1971 of the taxpayer's animals of that class on that day is divided by the number of the taxpayer's animals of that class on that day.

(3) Interpretation — For the purposes of this section,

(a) a taxpayer's **"basic herd"** of any class of animals at a particular time means such number of the animals of that class that the taxpayer had on hand at the end of [the taxpayer's] 1971 taxation year as were, for the purpose of assessing the taxpayer's tax under this Part for that year, accepted by the Minister, as a consequence of an application made by the taxpayer, to be capital properties and not to be stock-in-trade, minus the numbers, if any, required by virtue of this section to be deducted in computing the taxpayer's basic herd of that class at the end of taxation years of the taxpayer ending before the particular time;

(b) **"class of animals"** means animals of a particular species, namely, cattle, horses, sheep or swine, that are

(i) purebred animals of that species for which a certificate of registration has been issued by a person recognized by breeders in Canada of purebred animals of that species to be the registrar of the breed to which such animals belong, or issued by the Canadian National Livestock Records Corporation, or

(ii) animals of that species other than purebred animals described in subparagraph (i),

each of which descriptions in subparagraphs (i) and (ii) shall be deemed to be of separate classes, except that where the number of the taxpayer's animals described in subparagraph (i) or (ii), as the case may be, of a particular species is not greater than 10% of the total number of the taxpayer's animals of that species that would otherwise be of two separate classes by virtue of this paragraph, the taxpayer's animals described in subparagraphs (i) and (ii) of that species shall be deemed to be of a single class; and

(c) in determining the **number of animals** of any class on hand at any time, an animal shall not be included if it was acquired for a feeder operation, and an animal shall be included only if its actual age is not less than,

(i) in the case of cattle, 2 years,

(ii) in the case of horses, 3 years, and,

(iii) in the case of sheep or swine, one year,

except that 2 animals of a class under the age specified in subparagraph (i), (ii) or (iii), as the case may be, shall be counted as one animal of the age so specified.

Definitions [s. 29]: "basic herd" — 29(3)(a); "business" — 248(1); "capital property" — 54, 248(1); "class of animals" — 29(3)(b); "fair market value" — see 69(1) Notes; "farming", "Minister", — 248(1); "number" — 29(3)(c); "person" — 248(1); "taxation year" — 11(2), 249; "taxpayer" — 248(1).

Interpretation Bulletins [s. 29]: IT-427R: Livestock of farmers.

30. Improving land for farming — Notwithstanding paragraphs 18(1)(a) and (b), there may be deducted in computing a taxpayer's income for a taxation year from a farming business any amount paid by the taxpayer before the end of the year for clearing land, levelling land or installing a land drainage system for the purposes of the business, to the extent that such amount has not been deducted in a preceding taxation year.

Related Provisions: 28(1)(g) — Deduction from farming or fishing income when using cash method.

Notes: This is a "cash basis" deduction, since it is based on when the amount is *paid*. (The taxpayer need not own the land: VIEWS doc 2011-0427821E5.) It is overridden by 18(3.1) for construction period soft costs that must be capitalized: 2007-0231881I7. Payments received under Agriculture Canada's Orchards and Vineyards Transition Program reduce the amount deductible: 2008-0300731E5. A land drainage system would include plastic pipes: 2013-0476561E5. For discussion of the extent to which expenses for a cranberry farm fall within s. 30, see 2013-0479421E5.

Since this is a *permissive* provision, it does not restrict deductions that pass 18(1)(a) and (b) and would otherwise be allowed.

Definitions [s. 30]: "amount", "business", "farming" — 248(1); "taxation year" — 11(2), 249; "taxpayer" — 248(1).

Interpretation Bulletins [s. 30]: IT-485: Cost of clearing or levelling land.

31. (1) Restricted farm loss

— If a taxpayer's chief source of income for a taxation year is neither farming nor a combination of farming and some other source of income that is a subordinate source of income for the taxpayer, then for the purposes of sections 3 and 111 the taxpayer's loss, if any, for the year from all farming businesses carried on by the taxpayer is deemed to be the total of

(a) the lesser of

(i) the amount by which the total of the taxpayer's losses for the year, determined without reference to this section and before making any deduction under section 37, from all farming businesses carried on by the taxpayer exceeds the total of the taxpayer's incomes for the year, so determined from all such businesses, and

(ii) $2,500 plus the lesser of

(A) ½ of the amount by which the amount determined under subparagraph (i) exceeds $2,500, and

(B) $15,000, and

(b) the amount, if any, by which

(i) the amount that would be determined under subparagraph (a)(i) if it were read without reference to "and before making any deduction under section 37",

exceeds

(ii) the amount determined under subparagraph (a)(i).

Related Provisions: 31(1.1) — Restricted farm loss (RFL); 31(2) — Farming qualifies if it is subordinate to manufacturing or processing farm output; 53(1)(i) — Addition to ACB for non-deductible losses; 53(2)(c)(i)(B) — S. 31 generally ignored in determining reduction in ACB of partnership interest; 87(2.1)(a) — Amalgamation — RFL carried forward; 96(1) — RFL of partner; 101 — Disposition of land used in farming business of partnership; 111(1)(c) — Carryover of RFL; 111(9) — RFL where taxpayer not resident in Canada; 127.52(1)(i)(ii)(B) — Calculation of previous year's RFL for minimum tax purposes.

Notes: See Notes to 248(1)"farming" for what constitutes farming; and Munro & Oelschlagel, *Taxation of Farmers and Fishermen* (Carswell, looseleaf or *Taxnet Pro* Reference Centre), chap. 5.

There are 3 categories of farm losses. No deduction is allowed if the farming is not a business (see Notes to 9(2)). If farming is a business but not (alone or in combination with a *subordinate* activity) the chief source of income, 31(1) restricts the loss to $2,500 plus 1/2 of the next $30,000 (maximum $17,500) [for years ending before March 21/13: $2,500 + 1/2 of the next $12,500, max $8,750]. This is a "restricted farm loss" (RFL): 31(1.1). Unused RFLs can be carried forward 20 years and back 3 years, but only against farming income: 111(1)(c). Non-RFLs are fully deductible against other income, and can also be carried forward 20 years and back 3: 111(1)(d), 111(8)"farm loss".

The 2013 Budget amendment restored the rule from *Moldowan*, [1977] C.T.C. 310 (SCC): the other source of income must be subordinate to farming for it, combined with farming, to be the "chief" source of income so that a farm loss is not an RFL. (There is an exception in 31(2), if the other business is manufacturing or processing the farming output.) See VIEWS docs 2014-0534261E5; 2016-0625131C6 [CPA QC 2016 q.7] (person with substantial pension income devoting most time to farming after retirement would not automatically make losses deductible).

Before this amendment, the Supreme Court of Canada overruled *Moldowan* in 2012 and held that farming need not be predominant for full losses to be allowed: *Craig*, 2012 SCC 43, agreeing with *Gunn*, 2006 FCA 281. Thus, unrelated activities (e.g. farming and law) could in combination be a chief source of income. Determining the chief source(s) of income required "inquiry into the amount of capital, time, effort,

commitment and general emphasis on the part of the taxpayer" (*Craig*, para. 37); the taxpayer must "devote significant time and resources to the farming business" (para. 41); factors to consider in determining the emphasis are "the capital invested in farming and the second source of income, the income from each, the time spent on the two sources, and the taxpayer's ordinary mode of living, farming history, and future intention and expectations" (para. 42).

Pre-*Craig*, full farming losses were allowed in many cases that now apply only to years before 2013 (see these Notes up to the 58th ed.).

In *Richard*, 2008 TCC 257, full losses were allowed because the taxpayer's business was essentially logging (selling wood), not farming (producing maple syrup).

See also CRA *Income Tax Audit Manual* §29.4; Graham, "Restricted Farm Losses", 10(1) *Taxes & Wealth Management* (Carswell) 1-4 (April 2017). For criticism of the 2013 amendment see Stavropoulos, "Tax Policy Bewilderment", 2156 *Tax Topics* (CCH) 1-7 (July 4, 2013).

31(1) amended by 2013 budget bill #2 (for tax years ending after March 20, 2013), 1994 technical bill.

Interpretation Bulletins: IT-302R3: Losses of a corporation — the effect that acquisitions of control, amalgamations, and windings-up have on their deductibility.

I.T. Technical News: 30 (restricted farm losses).

CRA Audit Manual: 11.6.5 and Appendix A-11.2.23: Farm losses and restricted farm loss report; 29.4.0: Farm losses and restricted farm losses.

(1.1) Restricted farm loss

— For the purposes of this Act, a taxpayer's "restricted farm loss" for a taxation year is the amount, if any, by which

(a) the amount determined under subparagraph (1)(a)(i) in respect of the taxpayer for the year

exceeds

(b) the total of the amount determined under subparagraph (1)(a)(ii) in respect of the taxpayer for the year and all amounts each of which is an amount by which the taxpayer's restricted farm loss for the year is required to be reduced because of section 80.

Related Provisions: 80(3)(c) — Reduction in restricted farm loss on debt forgiveness; 248(1)"restricted farm loss" — Definition applies to entire Act. See also at 31(1).

Notes: 31(1.1) added by 1994 technical bill, for tax years that end after Feb. 21, 1994. See Notes to 31(1).

CRA Audit Manual: 11.6.5 and Appendix A-11.2.23: Farm losses and restricted farm loss report; 29.4.0: Farm losses and restricted farm losses.

(2) Farming and manufacturing or processing

— Subsection (1) does not apply to a taxpayer for a taxation year if the taxpayer's chief source of income for the year is a combination of farming and manufacturing or processing in Canada of goods for sale and all or substantially all output from all farming businesses carried on by the taxpayer is used in the manufacturing or processing.

Notes: See Notes to 31(1); and see Notes to 125.1(3)"manufacturing or processing" re the meaning of that phrase. 31(2) replaced by 2013 budget bill #2, effective for taxation years ending after March 20, 2013.

Definitions [s. 31]: "amount", "business", "farming", "Minister" — 248(1); "restricted farm loss" — 31(1.1), 248(1); "taxation year" — 11(2), 249; "taxpayer" — 248(1).

Interpretation Bulletins [s. 31]: IT-156R: Feedlot operators (cancelled); IT-232R3: Losses — their deductibility in the loss year or in other years; IT-262R2 — Losses of non-residents and part-year residents.

32. (1) Insurance agents and brokers [unearned commissions]

— In computing a taxpayer's income for a taxation year from the taxpayer's business as an insurance agent or broker, no amount may be deducted under paragraph 20(1)(m) for the year in respect of unearned commissions from the business, but in computing the taxpayer's income for the year from the business there may be deducted, as a reserve in respect of such commissions, an amount equal to the lesser of

(a) the total of all amounts each of which is that proportion of an amount that has been included in computing the taxpayer's income for the year or a preceding taxation year as a commission in respect of an insurance contract (other than a life insurance contract) that

(i) the number of days in the period provided for in the insurance contract that are after the end of the taxation year

is of

(ii) the number of days in that period, and

(b) the total of all amounts each of which is the amount that would, but for this subsection, be deductible under paragraph 20(1)(m) for the year in respect of a commission referred to in paragraph (a).

Related Provisions: 72(1)(b) — No reserve for year of death; 87(2)(j.6) — Amalgamation — continuing corp; 88(1)(e.1) — Subsidiary can claim reserve on windup.

Notes: In *Destacamento*, 2009 TCC 242, and *Demeterio*, 2011 TCC 192, insurance agents could not claim a reserve on cash advances received towards commissions on sale of life insurance, due to 32(1)(a). CRA applies this rule: VIEWS docs 2013-0475571E5, 2015-0588871E5. See also Notes to 6(1)(a) under "Insurance agents' commissions", for employed agents.

32(1) amended by 1991 technical bill, for tax years ending after 1990.

Forms: T2069: Election in respect of amounts not deductible as reserves for the year of death.

(2) Reserve to be included — There shall be included as income of a taxpayer for a taxation year from a business as an insurance agent or broker, the amount deducted under subsection (1) in computing the taxpayer's income therefrom for the immediately preceding year.

(3) Additional reserve — [No longer relevant]

Notes: 32(3) allows an insurance agent or broker an extra reserve for taxation years ending in 1991-99.

Definitions [s. 32]: "amount", "business" — 248(1); "taxation year" — 11(2), 249; "taxpayer" — 248(1).

Interpretation Bulletins [s. 32]: IT-321R: Insurance agents and brokers — unearned commissions (cancelled).

32.1 (1) Employee benefit plan deductions — Where a taxpayer has made contributions to an employee benefit plan in respect of the taxpayer's employees or former employees, the taxpayer may deduct in computing the taxpayer's income for a taxation year

(a) such portion of an amount allocated to the taxpayer for the year under subsection (2) by the custodian of the plan as does not exceed the amount, if any, by which

(i) the total of all amounts each of which is a contribution by the taxpayer to the plan for the year or a preceding year

exceeds the total of all amounts each of which is

(ii) an amount in respect of the plan deducted by the taxpayer in computing the taxpayer's income for a preceding year, or

(iii) an amount received by the taxpayer in the year or a preceding year that was a return of amounts contributed by the taxpayer to the plan; and

(b) where at the end of the year all of the obligations of the plan to the taxpayer's employees and former employees have been satisfied and no property of the plan will thereafter be paid to or otherwise be available for the benefit of the taxpayer, the amount, if any, by which

(i) the total of all amounts each of which is a contribution by the taxpayer to the plan for the year or a preceding year

exceeds the total of all amounts each of which is

(ii) an amount in respect of the plan deducted by the taxpayer in computing the taxpayer's income for a preceding year, or, by virtue of paragraph (a), for the year, or

(iii) an amount received by the taxpayer in the year or a preceding year that was a return of amounts contributed by the taxpayer to the plan.

Related Provisions: 6(1)(a)(ii), 6(1)(g) — EBP benefits taxable; 12(1)(n) — Employer's income inclusion — amounts received from employees profit sharing plan; 12(1)(n.1) — Income inclusion to employer; 18(1)(o) — EBP contributions non-deductible; 87(2)(j.3) — Amalgamation — continuation of corporation; 94(1)"exempt foreign trust"(f) — EBP excluded from non-resident trust rules; 107.1(b) — Distribution of property by EBP deemed at cost amount; 207.6(4) — Deemed contribution.

Notes: VIEWS doc 2018-0781951I7 allowed deduction for "performance share plan" reimbursements to a parent corp, not under 32.1 but as ordinary business expense.

Advance Tax Rulings: ATR-17: Employee benefit plan — purchase of company shares.

(2) Allocation — Every custodian of an employee benefit plan shall each year allocate to persons who have made contributions to the plan in respect of their employees or former employees the amount, if any, by which the total of

(a) all payments made in the year out of or under the plan to or for the benefit of their employees or former employees (other than the portion thereof that, by virtue of subparagraph 6(1)(g)(ii), is not required to be included in computing the income of a taxpayer), and

(b) all payments made in the year out of or under the plan to the heirs or the legal representatives of their employees or former employees

exceeds the income of the plan for the year.

Related Provisions: 32.1(3) — Income of employee benefit plan; 94(1)"exempt foreign trust"(f) — Employee benefit plan excluded from non-resident trust rules.

(3) Income of employee benefit plan — For the purposes of subsection (2), the income of an employee benefit plan for a year

(a) in the case of a plan that is a trust, is the amount that would be its income for the year if section 104 were read without reference to subsections 104(4) to (24); and

(b) in any other case, is the total of all amounts each of which is the amount, if any, by which a payment under the plan by the custodian thereof in the year exceeds

(i) in the case of an annuity, that part of the payment determined in prescribed manner to have been a return of capital, and

(ii) in any other case, that part of the payment that could, but for paragraph 6(1)(g), reasonably be regarded as being a payment of a capital nature.

Regulations: 300 (prescribed manner).

Definitions [s. 32.1]: "amount", "annuity" — 248(1); "custodian" — 248(1)"employee benefit plan"; "employee benefit plan", "person", "prescribed", "property" — 248(1); "taxation year" — 11(2), 249.

Interpretation Bulletins [s. 32.1]: IT-502: Employee benefit plans and employee trusts.

33. [Repealed under former Act]

Notes: 33 repealed by 1988 tax reform. This was a special reserve that could be deducted by taxpayers whose business includes the lending of money on security. The normal reserve for doubtful debts can still be claimed under 20(1)(l) by such taxpayers.

33.1 [Repealed]

Notes: 33.1 provided the International Banking Centre (IBC) rules, exempting prescribed financial institutions from tax on certain income earned through a branch or office in Montreal or Vancouver. It was repealed by 2013 budget bill #1, for tax years that begin after March 20, 2013. The Budget stated: "Eliminating the IBC rules is consistent with the goals of simplifying Canada's tax system and making it more neutral across business sectors and regions. In addition, the international community has identified the provision as resembling preferential regimes in some tax havens. (Also repealed were 87(2)(j.8), 126(7)"non-business-income tax"(h), Reg. 400(1.1), 413.1 and 8600"Canadian assets"(c); and Reg. 413(1) and 7900 were amended.)

34. Professional business — In computing the income of a taxpayer for a taxation year from a business that is the professional practice of an accountant, dentist, lawyer, medical doctor, veterinarian or chiropractor, the following rules apply:

(a) if the taxpayer so elects in the taxpayer's return of income under this Part for the year and the year begins before March 22, 2017, there shall not be included any amount in respect of work in progress at the end of the year; and

(b) where the taxpayer has made an election under this section, paragraph (a) shall apply in computing the taxpayer's income from the business for all subsequent taxation years unless the taxpayer, with the concurrence of the Minister and on such terms and conditions as are specified by the Minister, revokes the election to have that paragraph apply.

Application: S.C. 2017, c. 33 (Bill C-63, Royal Assent Dec. 14, 2017), subsec. 7(2), has repealed s. 34, in force Jan. 1, 2024.

Technical Notes: Section 34 is repealed, effective January 1, 2024. For more information, see the commentary on the transitional rules in subsection 10(14.1).

Federal Budget, Supplementary Information, March 22, 2017: *Billed-basis Accounting*

Taxpayers are generally required to include the value of work in progress in computing their income for tax purposes. However, taxpayers in certain designated professions (i.e., accountants, dentists, lawyers [including Quebec notaries — ed.], medical doctors, veterinarians and chiropractors) may elect to exclude the value of work in progress in computing their income. This election effectively allows income to be recognized when the work is billed (billed-basis accounting). Billed-basis accounting enables taxpayers to defer tax by permitting the costs associated with work in progress to be expensed without the matching inclusion of the associated revenues.

Budget 2017 proposes to eliminate the ability for designated professionals to elect to use billed-basis accounting.

This measure will apply to taxation years that begin on or after March 22, 2017.

To mitigate the effect on taxpayers, a transitional period will be provided to phase in the inclusion of work in progress into income. For the first taxation year that begins on or after March 22, 2017, 50% of the lesser of the cost and the fair market value of work in progress will be taken into account [10(14.1) — ed.] for the purposes of determining the value of inventory held by the business under the *Income Tax Act*. For the second, and each successive, taxation year that begins on or after March 22, 2017, the full amount of the lesser of the cost and the fair market value of work in progress will be taken into account for the purposes of valuing inventory. [In the Sept. 8, 2017 draft legislation, later 2017 budget bill #2, the 2-year phase-in was changed to a 5-year phase-in — ed.]

Federal Budget, Chapter 4, "Tax Fairness for the Middle Class", March 22, 2017: *Updating Tax Measures to Reflect Changes in the Economy*

Over time, changes in the economy have made a number of provisions in Canada's tax statutes less relevant than when they were first introduced. To address these changes, Budget 2017 proposes to:

- Eliminate the use of billed-basis accounting for income tax purposes by a limited group of professionals in order to avoid giving these professionals a deferral of tax that is not available to other taxpayers. . . .

Notes: Measuring the "cost" of a lawyer or accountant's work in progress may be challenging: see Notes to 10(1). For discussion of the history of s 34 and difficulties caused by its repeal, see Keung & Moody, "Whip that WIP", tinyurl.com/moodys-wip. See also Drache, "Budget Proposal on Professional WIP Sparks Backlash", xxxix(10) *The Canadian Taxpayer* (Carswell) 73-75 (May 19, 2017); CBA/CPA Joint Committee submission to Finance, May 31, 2017; CBA lobbying efforts at tinyurl.com/cba-ita34; Moody, "Federal Budget Proposes to Tax Professionals' WIP", 17(3) *Tax for the Owner-Manager* (ctf.ca) 1-2 (July 2017); Korhonen, "Professionals' Rough Work-in-Progress Transition", 7(3) *Canadian Tax Focus* (ctf.ca) 8-9 (Aug. 2017); Brown & Blanchette, "Budget 2017: The Elimination of the Section 34 Election ... and Its Impact on Death", 6(1) *Personal Tax & Estate Planning* (Federated Press) 2-6 (2018); Kietaibl, Arnold & Martenstyn, "Professional Corporations and Personal Services Businesses", 2019 Prairie Provinces Tax Conference (ctf.ca) at "The WIP Deduction".

Contingency fees: normally no amount can be determined until the case is won, so there is no WIP inclusion: tinyurl.com/cra-wip17, #5. However, VIEWS doc 2019-0798481C6 [2019 STEP q.8] suggests there are cases where the WIP value can be determined at year-end.

Budget Table 1 predicts that this change will save the federal government $35 million in 2017-18, $220m in 2018-19 and $170m in 2019-20.

Related Provisions: 10(4)(a) — Valuation of work in progress; 10(5)(a) — Work in progress deemed to be inventory; 10(14.1) — Transitional rule for 2017; 23(3) — Reference to property included in inventory; 70(2) — Rights or things included in income on death; 96(3) — Election by members of partnership.

Notes: See shaded box above. S. 34 provided an election for the listed professionals to *not* include work in progress (WIP) in income until it is billed. The deferral is phased out over 5 years for taxation years ending after March 21, 2017 (10(14.1)), and is now available only if the election was made in an earlier year. The election is made by attaching a letter to the return, or filling in the appropriate lines on Form T2125: Guide T4002. When made in the past, the election normally stayed in effect for later years. A partner joining the partnership (even after 2017), after the election is made for a tax year beginning before March 22, 2017, is covered by the election: VIEWS doc 2017-0734381E5.

S. 34 applies to a Quebec notary: see 248(1)"lawyer", but not an Ontario paralegal regulated by the Law Society: VIEWS doc 2014-0531461E5. CRA says that "accountant" includes a CA, CMA or CGA (who are now all CPAs), but not a bookkeeper who is a member of a voluntary association, and that a lawyer's business as a real estate agent or trustee in bankruptcy does not qualify: 2009-0311151E35.

On the professional's death, WIP excluded under s. 34 is considered taxable under 70(2) as a "right or thing": IT-212R3.

In *Ferro*, [2003] 2 C.T.C. 2461 (TCC), a litigation lawyer who worked on contingency and did not include WIP in income was entitled to deduct expenses even though the "matching" revenues came years later.

Where a partner withdraws from a professional partnership, see VIEWS docs 2006-0187181E5, 2013-049195117.

An election "in the taxpayer's return" is valid even if the return is filed late. See Notes to 7(1.31).

There is no limit on the income excluded by this election, which can result in the business having a loss: VIEWS doc 2008-0294011E5.

For a taxpayer filing Quebec returns, the election or revocation must be copied to Revenu Québec: *Taxation Act* ss. 215, 216, 21.4.6.

Many provinces permit professionals to incorporate. See Notes to 125(1).

See Notes to 10(1) re calculating WIP.

2017 budget bill #2 amended 34(a) to add "and the year begins before March 22, 2017", and repealed s. 34 effective 2024; see 10(14.1) for the 5-year phase-out.

Definitions [s. 34]: "amount", "business" — 248(1); "lawyer" — 232(1), 248(1); "Minister", "property" — 248(1); "taxation year" — 11(2), 249; "taxpayer" — 248(1).

I.T. Application Rules [s. 34]: 23(3)–(5) (where business carried on since before 1972).

Interpretation Bulletins [s. 34]: IT-188R: Sale of accounts receivable; IT-189R2: Corporations used by practising members of professions; IT-212R3: Income of deceased persons — rights or things; IT-278R2: Death of a partner or of a retired partner; IT-457R: Election by professionals to exclude work in progress from income; IT-471R: Merger of partnerships.

CRA Audit Manual [s. 34]: 27.25.0: Income of professionals and fiscal period issues; 40.1.0: Sector profiles — accounting and bookkeeping services; 40.4.0: Sector profiles — dentists; 40.11.0: Sector profiles — healthcare professionals — physicians and surgeons; 40.12.0: Sector profiles — veterinary services.

Forms [s. 34]: T2125: Statement of business or professional activities.

34.1 (1) Additional business income [off-calendar fiscal period] — Where

(a) an individual (other than a graduated rate estate) carries on a business in a taxation year,

(b) a fiscal period of the business begins in the year and ends after the end of the year (in this subsection referred to as the "particular period"), and

(c) the individual has elected under subsection 249.1(4) in respect of the business and the election has not been revoked,

there shall be included in computing the individual's income for the year from the business, the amount determined by the formula

$$(A - B) \times C / D$$

where

A   is the total of the individual's income from the business for the fiscal periods of the business that end in the year,

B   is the lesser of

(i) the total of all amounts each of which is an amount included in the value of A in respect of the business and that is deemed to be a taxable capital gain for the purpose of section 110.6, and

(ii) the total of all amounts deducted under section 110.6 in computing the individual's taxable income for the year,

C   is the number of days on which the individual carries on the business that are both in the year and in the particular period, and

D   is the number of days on which the individual carries on the business that are in fiscal periods of the business that end in the year.

Related Provisions: 11(1) — Determination of income from fiscal period of proprietor; 34.1(3) — Offsetting deduction in following year; 34.1(8) — No additional inclusion on death, bankruptcy or cease of business; 96(1.01)(a) — Income allocation to former partner; 96(1.1), (1.6) — Allocation of share of income to retiring partner; 257 — Formula cannot calculate to less than zero; Reg. 1104(1) — CCA calculation where fiscal year is not calendar year.

Notes: 34.1(1) provides the calculation of additional business income to be included each year for individuals using an off-calendar year-end. See Notes at end of 34.1. The amount included is deducted in the next year under 34.1(3).

34.1(1)(a) amended by 2014 budget bill #2, for 2016 and later taxation years, to change "testamentary trust" to "graduated rate estate".

Forms: RC4015: Reconciliation of business income for tax purposes [guide]; T1139: Reconciliation of business income for tax purposes.

(2) Additional income election — Where

(a) an individual (other than a graduated rate estate) begins carrying on a business in a taxation year and not earlier than the beginning of the first fiscal period of the business that begins in the year and ends after the end of the year (in this subsection referred to as the "particular period"), and

(b) the individual has elected under subsection 249.1(4) in respect of the business and the election has not been revoked,

there shall be included in computing the individual's income for the year from the business the lesser of

(c) the amount designated in the individual's return of income for the year, and

(d) the amount determined by the formula

$$(A - B) \times C / D$$

where

A   is the individual's income from the business for the particular period,

B   is the lesser of

(i) the total of all amounts each of which is an amount included in the value of A in respect of the business and that is deemed to be a taxable capital gain for the purpose of section 110.6, and

(ii) the total of all amounts deducted under section 110.6 in computing the individual's taxable income for the taxation year that includes the end of the particular period,

C   is the number of days on which the individual carries on the business that are both in the year and in the particular period, and

D   is the number of days on which the individual carries on the business that are in the particular period.

Related Provisions: 34.1(3) — Offsetting deduction in following year; 34.1(8) — No additional inclusion on death, bankruptcy or cease of business; 96(1.01)(a) — Income allocation to former partner; 96(1.1), (1.6) — Allocation of share of income to retiring partner; 257 — Formula cannot calculate to less than zero.

Notes: See Notes at end of 34.1.

34.1(2)(a) amended by 2014 budget bill #2, for 2016 and later taxation years, to change "testamentary trust" to "graduated rate estate".

Forms: RC4015: Reconciliation of business income for tax purposes [guide]; T1139: Reconciliation of business income for tax purposes.

(3) Deduction — There shall be deducted in computing an individual's income for a taxation year from a business the amount, if any, included under subsection (1) or (2) in computing the individual's income for the preceding taxation year from the business.

(4)–(7) [Repealed]

Notes: 34.1(4), (5), (6) and (7) repealed by 2013 budget bill #2, effective Dec. 12, 2013. They applied to determine "December 31, 1995 income" for purposes of transitional rules added in 1995.

(8) No additional income inclusion — Subsections (1) and (2) do not apply in computing an individual's income for a taxation year from a business where

(a) the individual dies or otherwise ceases to carry on the business in the year; or

(b) the individual becomes a bankrupt in the calendar year in which the taxation year ends.

Related Provisions: 34.1(9) — Income inclusion on death where election made or separate return filed.

(9) Death of partner or proprietor — Where

(a) an individual carries on a business in a taxation year,

(b) the individual dies in the year and after the end of a fiscal period of the business that ends in the year,

(c) another fiscal period of the business ends because of the individual's death (in this subsection referred to as the "short period"), and

(d) the individual's legal representative

(i) elects that this subsection apply in computing the individual's income for the year, or

(ii) files a separate return of income under subsection 150(4) in respect of the individual's business,

notwithstanding subsection (8), there shall be included in computing the individual's income for the year from the business, the amount determined by the formula

$$(A - B) \times C / D$$

where

A   is the total of the individual's income from the business for fiscal periods (other than the short period) of the business that end in the year,

B   is the lesser of

(i) the total of all amounts, each of which is an amount included in the value of A in respect of the business that is deemed to be a taxable capital gain for the purpose of section 110.6, and

(ii) the total of all amounts deducted under section 110.6 in computing the individual's taxable income for the year,

C   is the number of days in the short period, and

D   is the total number of days in fiscal periods of the business (other than the short period) that end in the year.

Related Provisions: 96(1.01)(a) — Income allocation to former partner; 257 — Formula cannot calculate to less than zero; 150(4)(c)C — Additional amount deductible on deceased's separate return.

Notes: When reading a VIEWS doc or article in French about 34.1(9), note that paras. (b)-(d) in English are (a)-(c) in French.

34.1(9) added by 1995-97 technical bill, effective for 1996 and later taxation years, but 34.1(9)(d)(ii) does not apply to the 1996 and 1997 taxation years.

Notes [s. 34.1]: 34.1 added by 1995 Budget, effective 1995. It provides rules for computing the "additional business income" of individuals who carry on an unincorporated business for which an election to have an off-calendar fiscal period is filed under 249.1(4). An off-calendar year can be retained for business purposes (e.g., for a seasonal business that runs through the winter), but tax must be prepaid through a recognition of income under 34.1 to approximate the income earned to December 31. The CRA indicated in Nov. 2007, in response to an *Access to Information* request, that it has no statistics on how many taxpayers use s. 34.1. Parallel rules for corporations were introduced in the 2011 Budget; see 34.2.

34.1 applied in *MacKay*, 2015 FCA 94, even though M thought its application was unfair.

34.1 applies to a retiring partner even if the agreement to allocate income to the partner is made after year-end: VIEWS doc 2014-0522551E5.

For taxpayers claiming a 34.2 reserve in 1995-2003 who were subject to 34.1, a dip in business income in any year after 1995 effectively capped the reserve and forced 1995 income to be recognized earlier: *McLauchlin*, [2002] 2 C.T.C. 2935 (TCC).

Definitions [s. 34.1]: "amount", "bankrupt", "business" — 248(1); "calendar year" — *Interpretation Act* 37(1)(a); "fiscal period" — 249.1; "graduated rate estate", "individual", "legal representative" — 248(1); "particular period" — 34.1(1)(b), 34.1(2)(a); "partnership" — see 96(1) Notes; "professional corporation" — 248(1); "short period" — 34.1(9)(c); "specified shareholder" — 248(1); "taxable capital gain" — 38, 248(1); "taxation year" — 249.

34.2 [Corporation — inclusion of partnership stub-period income] — **(1) Definitions** — The definitions in this subsection apply in this section.

"adjusted stub period accrual" of a corporation in respect of a partnership — in which the corporation has a significant interest at the end of the last fiscal period of the partnership that ends in the corporation's taxation year in circumstances where another fiscal period (in this definition referred to as the "particular period") of the partnership begins in the year and ends after the year — means

(a) if paragraph (b) does not apply, the amount determined by the formula

$$[(A - B) \times C/D] - (E + F)$$

where

A is the total of all amounts each of which is the corporation's share of an income or taxable capital gain of the partnership for a fiscal period of the partnership that ends in the year (other than any amount for which a deduction is available under section 112 or 113),

B is the total of all amounts each of which is the corporation's share of a loss or allowable capital loss — to the extent that the total of all allowable capital losses does not exceed the total of all taxable capital gains included in the description of A — of the partnership for a fiscal period of the partnership that ends in the year,

C is the number of days that are in both the year and the particular period,

D is the number of days in fiscal periods of the partnership that end in the year,

E is the amount of the qualified resource expense in respect of the particular period of the partnership that is designated by the corporation for the year under subsection (6) in its return of income for the year filed with the Minister on or before its filing-due date for the year, and

F is an amount designated by the corporation in its return of income for the year (other than an amount included in the description of E) and filed with the Minister on or before its filing-due date for the year; and

(b) if a fiscal period of the partnership ends in the corporation's taxation year and the year is the first taxation year in which the fiscal period of the partnership is aligned with the fiscal period of one or more other partnerships under a multi-tier alignment (in this paragraph referred to as the "eligible fiscal period"),

(i) where a fiscal period of the partnership ends in the year and before the eligible fiscal period, the amount determined by the formula

$$[(A - B) \times C/D] - (E + F)$$

where

A is the total of all amounts each of which is the corporation's share of an income or taxable capital gain of the partnership for the first fiscal period of the partnership that ends in the year (other than any amount for which a deduction is available under section 112 or 113),

B is the total of all amounts each of which is the corporation's share of a loss or allowable capital loss — to the extent that the total of all allowable capital losses does not exceed the total of all taxable capital gains included in the description of A — of the partnership for the first fiscal period of the partnership that ends in the year,

C is the number of days that are in both the year and the particular period,

D is the number of days in the first fiscal period of the partnership that ends in the year,

E is the amount of the qualified resource expense in respect of the particular period of the partnership that is designated by the corporation for the year under subsection (6) in its return of income for the year filed with the Minister on or before its filing-due date for the year, and

F is an amount designated by the corporation in its return of income for the year (other than an amount included in the description of E) and filed with the Minister on or before its filing-due date for the year, and

(ii) where the eligible fiscal period of the partnership is the first fiscal period of the partnership that ends in the corporation's taxation year, the amount determined by the formula

$$(A - B - C) \times D/E - (F + G)$$

where

A is the total of all amounts each of which is the corporation's share of an income or taxable capital gain of the partnership for the eligible fiscal period (other than any amount for which a deduction is available under section 112 or 113),

B is the total of all amounts each of which is the corporation's share of a loss or allowable capital loss — to the extent that the total of all allowable capital losses does not exceed the total of all taxable capital gains included in the description of A — of the partnership for the eligible fiscal period,

C is the corporation's eligible alignment income for the eligible fiscal period,

D is the number of days that are in both the year and the particular period,

E is the number of days that are in the eligible fiscal period that ends in the year,

F is the amount of the qualified resource expense in respect of the particular period of the partnership that is designated by the corporation for the year under subsection (6) in its return of income for the year filed with the Minister on or before its filing-due date for the year, and

G is an amount designated by the corporation in its return of income for the year (other than an amount included in the description of F) and filed with the Minister on or before its filing-due date for the year.

Related Provisions: 34.2(1)"qualifying transitional income"(b), 34.2(16), (17) — Adjusted stub period accrual (ASPA) included in QTI; 34.2(2) — ASPA included in income; 34.2(6), 34.2(17)E — Corporation can designate amount of qualified resource expense to reduce ASPA; 34.2(10) — Designations under (a)E-F, (b)(i)E-F and (b)(ii)F-G may not be amended or revoked; 34.3(1)"actual stub period adjustment" — Determination of actual adjustment where designation made under F to include less; 87(2)(j), 88(1)(e.2) — Amalgamation or windup — continuing corporation; 257 — Formulas cannot calculate to less than zero.

Notes: See VIEWS docs 2011-0425411E5 (interpretation of (a)A, C, D); 2012-0436121E5 (where corporation's interest in partnership increases, then decreases); 2018-0788161E5 (LP losses and other deductions in computing taxable income do not reduce ASPA). See also Notes at end of 34.2.

Forms: T2 Sched. 71, Part 3: Income inclusion for corporations that are members of single-tier partnerships; T2 Sched. 72, Part 3: Income inclusion for corporations that are members of multi-tier partnerships.

"eligible alignment income", of a corporation, means

(a) if a partnership is subject to a single-tier alignment, the first aligned fiscal period of the partnership ends in the first taxation year of the corporation ending after March 22, 2011 (in this paragraph referred to as the **"eligible fiscal period"**) and the corporation is a member of the partnership at the end of the eligible fiscal period,

(i) where the eligible fiscal period is preceded by another fiscal period of the partnership that ends in the corporation's first taxation year that ends after March 22, 2011 and the corporation is a member of the partnership at the end of that preceding fiscal period, the amount determined by the formula

$$A - B - C$$

where

A is the total of all amounts each of which is the corporation's share of an income or taxable capital gain of the partnership for the eligible fiscal period (other than any amount for which a deduction is available under section 112 or 113),

B is the total of all amounts each of which is the corporation's share of a loss or allowable capital loss — to the extent that the total of all allowable capital losses does not exceed the total of all taxable capital gains included in the description of A — of the partnership for the eligible fiscal period, and

C is, where an outlay or expense of the partnership is deemed by subsection 66(18) to be made or incurred by the corporation at the end of the eligible fiscal period, the total of all amounts each of which is an amount that would be deductible by the corporation for the taxation year under any of sections 66.1, 66.2, 66.21 and 66.4 determined as if each such outlay or expense were the only amount relevant in determining the amount deductible, or

(ii) where the eligible fiscal period is the first fiscal period of the partnership that ends in the corporation's first taxation year ending after March 22, 2011, nil; and

(b) if a partnership is subject to a multi-tier alignment, the first aligned fiscal period of the partnership ends in the taxation year of the corporation (in this paragraph referred to as the **"eligible fiscal period"**) and the corporation is a member of the partnership at the end of the eligible fiscal period, the amount determined by the formula

$$A - B - C$$

where

A is the total of all amounts each of which is the corporation's share of an income or taxable capital gain of the partnership for the eligible fiscal period, other than any amount

(i) for which a deduction is available under section 112 or 113, or

(ii) that would be included in computing the income of the corporation for the year if there were no multi-tier alignment,

B is the total of all amounts each of which is the corporation's share of a loss or allowable capital loss — to the extent that the total of all allowable capital losses does not exceed the total of all taxable capital gains included in the description of A — of a partnership for the eligible fiscal period, and

C is, where an outlay or expense of the partnership is deemed by subsection 66(18) to be made or incurred by the corporation at the end of the eligible fiscal period, the total of all amounts each of which is an amount that would be deductible by the corporation for the taxation year under any of sections 66.1, 66.2, 66.21 and 66.4 determined as if each such outlay or expense were the only amount relevant in determining the amount deductible.

Related Provisions: 34.2(1)"qualifying transitional income"(a) — Eligible alignment income included in QTI; 257 — Formula cannot calculate to less than zero.

Forms: T2 Sched. 71, Part 2: Income inclusion for corporations that are members of single-tier partnerships.

"multi-tier alignment", in respect of a partnership, means the alignment under subsection 249.1(9) or (11) of the fiscal period of the partnership and the fiscal period of one or more other partnerships.

Related Provisions: 34.2(9) — Special rule for multi-tier alignment; 34.2(13) — Limitation on transitional reserve under 34.2(11).

"qualified resource expense", of a corporation for a taxation year in respect of a fiscal period of a partnership that begins in the year and ends after the year, means an expense incurred by the partnership in the portion of the fiscal period that is in the year and that is described in any of the following definitions:

(a) "Canadian exploration expense" in subsection 66.1(6);

(b) "Canadian development expense" in subsection 66.2(5);

(c) "foreign resource expense" in subsection 66.21(1); and

(d) "Canadian oil and gas property expense" in subsection 66.4(5).

Related Provisions: 34.2(6), 34.2(17)E — Corporation can designate amount of QRE to reduce stub period income.

"qualifying transitional income", of a corporation that is a member of a partnership on March 22, 2011, means the amount that is

the total of the following amounts, computed in accordance with subsection (15),

(a) the corporation's eligible alignment income in respect of the partnership, and

(b) the corporation's adjusted stub period accrual in respect of the partnership for

(i) if there is a multi-tier alignment in respect of the partnership, the corporation's taxation year during which ends the fiscal period of the partnership that is aligned with the fiscal period of one or more other partnerships under the multi-tier alignment, or

(ii) in any other case, the corporation's first taxation year that ends after March 22, 2011.

Related Provisions: 34.2(11) — Deduction of QTI as reserve; 34.2(15) — Rules for computing QTI; 34.2(16), (17) — Adjustment of stub period accrual included in QTI.

Forms: T2 Sched. 71, Part 5: Income inclusion for corporations that are members of single-tier partnerships.

"significant interest", of a corporation in a partnership at any time, means a membership interest of the corporation in the partnership if the corporation, or the corporation together with one or more persons or partnerships related to or affiliated with the corporation, is entitled at that time to more than 10% of

(a) the income or loss of the partnership; or

(b) the assets (net of liabilities) of the partnership if it were to cease to exist.

Related Provisions: 34.2(2)(a) — Corporation with significant interest in partnership must include stub period accrual in income; 34.2(3) — Where new partner has significant interest at year-end.

"single-tier alignment", in respect of a partnership, means the ending of a fiscal period of the partnership under subsection 249.1(8).

"specified percentage", of a corporation for a particular taxation year in respect of a partnership, means

(a) if the first taxation year for which the corporation has qualifying transitional income ends in 2011 and the particular year ends in

(i) 2011, 100%,

(ii) 2012, 85%,

(iii) 2013, 65%,

(iv) 2014, 45%,

(v) 2015, 25%, and

(vi) 2016, 0%;

(b) if the first taxation year for which the corporation has qualifying transitional income ends in 2012 and the particular year ends in

(i) 2012, 100%,

(ii) 2013, 85%,

(iii) 2014, 65%,

(iv) 2015, 45%,

(v) 2016, 25%, and

(vi) 2017, 0%; and

(c) if the first taxation year for which the corporation has qualifying transitional income ends in 2013 and the particular year ends in

(i) 2013, 85%,

(ii) 2014, 65%,

(iii) 2015, 45%,

(iv) 2016, 25%, and

(v) 2017, 0%.

Related Provisions: 34.2(11)(a) — Transitional reserve — deduction of specified percentage of qualifying transitional income.

(2) Income inclusion — adjusted stub period accrual — Subject to subsections (5) and (9), a corporation (other than a professional corporation) shall include in computing its income for a taxation year its adjusted stub period accrual in respect of a partnership if

(a) the corporation has a significant interest in the partnership at the end of the last fiscal period of the partnership that ends in the year;

(b) another fiscal period of the partnership begins in the year and ends after the year; and

(c) at the end of the year, the corporation is entitled to a share of an income, loss, taxable capital gain or allowable capital loss of the partnership for the fiscal period referred to in paragraph (b).

Related Provisions: 34.2(3) — Optional income inclusion for new partner; 34.2(4) — Deduction in following year; 34.2(5)(a)(i) — Income and capital gains of partnership carried through to stub period; 34.2(5)B(b)(ii) — Taxable capital gain inclusion reduces allowable capital loss; 34.2(7) — No income inclusion when corporation becomes bankrupt; 34.2(8) — No stub period accrual in determining FAPI; 34.2(9) — Special rule for multi-tier alignment; 34.3 — Adjustment for income shortfall where designation made under 34.2(1)"adjusted stub period accrual"F to reduce inclusion; 87(2)(j), 88(1)(e.2) — Amalgamation or windup — continuing corporation; 96(1)(f) — Inclusion of income from partnership ending in corporation's year.

Notes: See Notes at end of 34.2.

Forms: T2 Sched. 71, Part 3: Income inclusion for corporations that are members of single-tier partnerships; T2 Sched. 72, Part 3: Income inclusion for corporations that are members of multi-tier partnerships; T2 Sched. 73: Income inclusion summary for corporations that are members of partnerships.

(3) Income inclusion — new partner designation — Subject to subsection (5), if a corporation (other than a professional corporation) becomes a member of a partnership during a fiscal period of the partnership (in this subsection referred to as the "particular period") that begins in the corporation's taxation year and ends after the taxation year but on or before the filing-due date for the taxation year and the corporation has a significant interest in the partnership at the end of the particular period, the corporation may include in computing its income for the taxation year the lesser of

(a) the amount, if any, designated by the corporation in its return of income for the taxation year, and

(b) the amount determined by the formula

$$A \times B/C$$

where

A　is the corporation's income from the partnership for the particular period (other than any amount for which a deduction is available under section 112 or 113),

B　is the number of days that are both in the corporation's taxation year and the particular period, and

C　is the number of days in the particular period.

Related Provisions: 34.2(4) — Deduction in following year; 34.2(5)(a)(ii) — Income and capital gains of partnership carried through to stub period; 34.2(7) — No income inclusion when corporation becomes bankrupt; 87(2)(j), 88(1)(e.2) — Amalgamation or windup — continuing corporation.

(4) Treatment in following year — If an amount was included in computing the income of a corporation in respect of a partnership for the immediately preceding taxation year under subsection (2) or (3),

(a) the portion of the amount that, because of subparagraph (5)(a)(i) or (ii), was income for that preceding year is deductible in computing the income of the corporation for the current taxation year; and

(b) the portion of the amount that, because of subparagraph (5)(a)(i) or (ii), was taxable capital gains for that preceding year is deemed to be an allowable capital loss of the corporation for the current taxation year from the disposition of property.

Related Provisions: 34.2(5)(a)(iii) — Deduction to match income and capital gains included; 34.2(5)(b) — Deemed allowable capital loss.

Notes: 34.2(4) amended by 2013 budget bill #2, effective for taxation years ending after March 22, 2011 (i.e., retroactive to its introduction).

(5) Character of amounts — For the purposes of this Act, the following rules apply:

(a) in computing the income of a corporation for a taxation year,

(i) an adjusted stub period accrual included under subsection (2) in respect of a partnership for the year is deemed to be income, and taxable capital gains from the disposition of property, having the same character and to be in the same proportions as any income and taxable capital gains that were allocated by the partnership to the corporation for all fiscal periods of the partnership ending in the year,

(ii) an amount included under subsection (3) in respect of a partnership for the year is deemed to be income, and taxable capital gains from the disposition of property, having the same character and to be in the same proportions as any income and taxable capital gains that were allocated by the partnership to the corporation for the particular period referred to in that subsection,

(iii) an amount, a portion of which is deductible or is an allowable capital loss under subsection (4) in respect of a partnership for the year, is deemed to have the same character and to be in the same proportions as the income and taxable capital gains included in the corporation's income for the immediately preceding taxation year under subsection (2) or (3) in respect of the partnership,

(iv) an amount claimed as a reserve under subsection (11) in respect of a partnership for the year is deemed to have the same character and to be in the same proportions as the qualifying transitional income in respect of the partnership for the year, and

(v) an amount, a portion of which is included in income under paragraph (12)(a), or is deemed to be a taxable capital gain under paragraph (12)(b), in respect of a partnership for the year, is deemed to have the same character and to be in the same proportions as the amount claimed as a reserve under subsection (11) in respect of the partnership for the immediately preceding taxation year;

(b) a corporation's capital dividend account, as defined in subsection 89(1), is to be determined without reference to this section; and

(c) the reference in subparagraph 53(2)(c)(i.4) to an amount deducted under subsection (11) by a taxpayer includes an amount deemed to be an allowable capital loss under subparagraph (11)(b)(ii).

Related Provisions: 34.2(4) — Treatment in following year; 87(2)(j), 88(1)(e.2) — Amalgamation or windup — continuing corporation.

Notes: 34.2(5) amended by 2013 budget bill #2, effective for taxation years ending after March 22, 2011 (i.e., retroactive to its introduction).

Income Tax Folios: S3-F2-C1: Capital Dividends [replaces IT-66R6].

(6) Designation — qualified resource expense — A corporation may designate an amount for a taxation year in respect of a qualified resource expense under the definition "adjusted stub period accrual" in subsection (1) subject to the following rules:

(a) the corporation cannot designate an amount for the year in respect of a qualified resource expense in respect of a partnership except to the extent the corporation obtains from the partnership, before the corporation's filing-due date for the year, information in writing identifying the corporation's qualified resource expenses described

(i) in paragraph (h) of the definition "Canadian exploration expense" in subsection 66.1(6), determined as if those expenses had been incurred by the partnership in its last fiscal period that ended in the year,

(ii) in paragraph (f) of the definition "Canadian development expense" in subsection 66.2(5), determined as if those expenses had been incurred by the partnership in its last fiscal period that ended in the year,

(iii) in paragraph (e) of the definition "foreign resource expense" in subsection 66.21(1), determined as if those expenses had been incurred by the partnership in its last fiscal period that ended in the year, and

(iv) in paragraph (b) of the definition "Canadian oil and gas property expense" in subsection 66.4(5), determined as if those expenses had been incurred by the partnership in its last fiscal period that ended in the year; and

(b) the amount designated for the year by the corporation is not to exceed the maximum amount that would be deductible by the corporation under any of sections 66.1, 66.2, 66.21 and 66.4 in computing its income for the year if

(i) the amounts referred to in paragraph (a) in respect of the partnership were the only amounts relevant in determining the maximum amount, and

(ii) the fiscal period of the partnership that begins in the year and ends after the year had ended at the end of the year and each qualified resource expense were deemed under subsection 66(18) to be incurred by the corporation at the end of the year.

Related Provisions: 34.2(17)E — Amount designated reduces stub period income included in qualifying transitional income.

(7) No additional income — bankrupt — Subsections (2) and (3) do not apply in computing a corporation's income for a taxation year in respect of a partnership if the corporation becomes a bankrupt in the year.

(8) Foreign affiliates — This section does not apply for the purposes of computing, for a taxation year of a foreign affiliate of a corporation resident in Canada,

(a) the foreign accrual property income of the affiliate in respect of the corporation; and

(b) except to the extent that the context otherwise requires, the exempt surplus or exempt deficit, the hybrid surplus or hybrid deficit, and the taxable surplus or taxable deficit (as those terms are defined in subsection 5907(1) of the *Income Tax Regulations*) of the affiliate in respect of the corporation.

Notes: 34.2(8)(b) amended by 2002-2013 technical bill (Part 3 — FA reorganizations), to add "the hybrid surplus or hybrid deficit", effective for taxation years that end after Aug. 19, 2011.

(9) Special case — multi-tier alignment — If a corporation is a member of a partnership subject to a multi-tier alignment, subsection (2) does not apply to the corporation in respect of the partnership for taxation years preceding the taxation year that includes the end of the first aligned fiscal period of the partnership under the multi-tier alignment.

(10) Designations — Once a corporation makes a designation in calculating its adjusted stub period accrual in respect of a partnership for a taxation year under any of the description of E or F of paragraph (a), the description of E or F of subparagraph (b)(i) and the description of F or G of subparagraph (b)(ii) of the definition "adjusted stub period accrual" in subsection (1), the designation cannot be amended or revoked.

(11) Transitional reserve — If a corporation has qualifying transitional income in respect of a partnership for a particular taxation year,

(a) the corporation may, in computing its income for the particular year, claim an amount, as a reserve, not exceeding the least of

(i) the specified percentage for the particular year of the corporation's qualifying transitional income in respect of the partnership,

(ii) if, for the immediately preceding taxation year, an amount was claimed under this subsection in computing the

corporation's income in respect of the partnership, the amount that is the total of

(A) the amount included under subsection (12) in computing the corporation's income for the particular year in respect of the partnership, and

(B) the amount by which the corporation's qualifying transitional income in respect of the partnership is increased in the particular year because of the application of subsections (16) and (17), and

(iii) the amount determined by the formula

$$A - B$$

where

A is the corporation's income for the particular year computed before deducting or claiming any amount under this subsection in respect of the partnership or under section 61.3 and 61.4, and

B is the total of all amounts each of which is an amount deductible by the corporation for the year under section 112 or 113 in respect of a dividend received by the corporation after December 20, 2012; and

(b) the portion of the amount claimed under paragraph (a) for the particular year that, because of subparagraph (5)(a)(iv), has

(i) a character other than capital is deductible in computing the income of the corporation for the particular year, and

(ii) the character of capital is deemed to be an allowable capital loss of the corporation for the particular year from the disposition of property.

Related Provisions: 34.2(5)(a)(iv) — Reserve deemed to have same character as qualifying transitional income; 34.2(5)(b)B(iii) — Net taxable capital gain inclusion; 34.2(12) — Reserve included in next year's income; 34.2(13) — Where no reserve allowed; 34.2(16), (17) — QTI adjustment; 53(2)(c)(i.4) — Addition to adjusted cost base; 87(2)(j), 88(1)(e.2) — Amalgamation or windup — continuing corporation; 88(1)(e.1) — Subsidiary can claim reserve on windup; 257 — Formula cannot calculate to less than zero.

Notes: See VIEWS docs 2011-0425411E5, 2012-0454481E5 (deduction is discretionary), 2012-0454811E5, 2012-0471021E5, 2013-0479711E5, 2013-0499681E5, 2013-0503421E5 and Notes at end of 34.2.

34.2(11) amended by 2013 budget bill #2, for tax years ending after March 22, 2011.

Forms: RC354: Election for transitional relief by a participant taxpayer of a joint venture; T2 Sched. 71, Part 7: Income inclusion for corporations that are members of single-tier partnerships.

(12) Inclusion of prior year reserve — Subject to subsection (5), if a reserve was claimed by a corporation under subsection (11) in respect of a partnership for the immediately preceding taxation year,

(a) the portion of the reserve that was deducted under subparagraph (11)(b)(i) for that preceding year is to be included in computing the income of the corporation for the current taxation year; and

(b) the portion of the reserve that was deemed by subparagraph (11)(b)(ii) to be an allowable capital loss of the corporation for that preceding year is deemed to be a taxable capital gain of the corporation for the current taxation year from the disposition of property.

Related Provisions: 34.2(5)(a)(v) — Income inclusion deemed to have same character as previous year's reserve; 34.2(5)(b)B(iii) — Taxable capital gain inclusion reduces allowable capital loss; 34.2(11)(b)(i) — Inclusion under (12) forms limitation on next year's reserve.

Notes: See VIEWS docs 2011-0425411E5, 2012-0454811E5; Notes at end of 34.2.

34.2(12) amended by 2013 budget bill #2, for tax years ending after March 22, 2011.

(13) No reserve — No claim shall be made under subsection (11) in computing a corporation's income for a taxation year in respect of a partnership

(a) unless,

(i) in the case of a corporation that is a member of a partnership in respect of which there is a multi-tier alignment, the corporation has been a member of the partnership continuously since before March 22, 2011 to the end of the year,

(ii) in the case of a corporation that is a member of a partnership in respect of which there is no multi-tier alignment, the corporation is a member of the partnership

(A) at the end of the partnership's fiscal period that begins before March 22, 2011 and ends in the year of the corporation that includes March 22, 2011,

(B) at the end of the partnership's fiscal period commencing immediately after the fiscal period referred to in clause (A) and continues to be a member until after the end of the year of the corporation that includes March 22, 2011, and

(C) continuously since before March 22, 2011 until the end of the year;

(b) if at the end of the year or at any time in the following taxation year,

(i) the corporation's income is exempt from tax under this Part, or

(ii) the corporation is non-resident and the partnership does not carry on business through a permanent establishment (as defined for the purpose of subsection 16.1(1)) in Canada; or

(c) if the year ends immediately before another taxation year

(i) at the beginning of which the partnership no longer principally carries on the activities to which the reserve relates,

(ii) in which the corporation becomes a bankrupt, or

(iii) in which the corporation is dissolved or wound up (other than in circumstances to which subsection 88(1) applies).

Related Provisions: 34.2(14) — Ex-partner deemed to be a partner; 34.2(18) — Anti-avoidance rule for 34.2(13).

Notes: For CRA interpretation see VIEWS doc 2011-0423021E5 (subpara. (c)(i)).

34.2(13) amended by 2013 budget bill #2, effective for taxation years ending after March 22, 2011, to change "deduction" to "claim".

(14) Deemed partner — A corporation that cannot claim an amount under subsection (11) for a taxation year in respect of a partnership solely because it has disposed of its interest in the partnership is deemed for the purposes of paragraph (13)(a) to be a member of the partnership continuously until the end of the taxation year if

(a) the corporation disposed of its interest to another corporation related to, or affiliated with, the corporation at the time of the disposition; and

(b) a corporation related to, or affiliated with, the corporation has the partnership interest referred to in paragraph (a) at the end of the taxation year.

Notes: 34.2(14) will not be extended to joint ventures: VIEWS doc 2011-0431141E5 (see Notes to 249.1(1)). For a ruling applying 34.2(14) see 2013-0516071R3.

34.2(14) opening words amended by 2013 budget bill #2, for tax years ending after March 22, 2011, to change "deduct" to "claim".

(15) Computing qualifying transitional income — special rules — For the purposes of determining a corporation's qualifying transitional income, the income or loss, as the case may be, of a partnership for a fiscal period shall be computed as if

(a) the partnership had deducted for the period the maximum amount deductible in respect of any expense, reserve, allowance or other amount;

(b) this Act were read without reference to paragraph 28(1)(b); and

(c) the partnership had made an election under paragraph 34(a).

(16) Qualifying transition income adjustment — conditions for application — Subsection (17) applies for a particular taxation year of a corporation and for each subsequent taxation year for which the corporation may claim an amount under subsection (11) in respect of a partnership if the particular year is the first taxation year

(a) that is after the taxation year in which the corporation has, or would have if the partnership had income, an adjusted stub period accrual that is included in the corporation's qualifying transitional income in respect of the partnership by reason of paragraph (b) of the definition "qualifying transitional income" in subsection (1); and

(b) in which ends the fiscal period of the partnership that began in the taxation year referred to in paragraph (a).

Related Provisions: 34.2(11)(b)(ii) — Increase under (16) increases next year's reserve.

Notes: 34.2(16) opening words amended by 2013 budget bill #2, for tax years ending after March 22, 2011, to change "deduct" to "claim".

(17) Adjustment of qualifying transitional income — If this subsection applies in respect of a partnership for a taxation year of a corporation, the adjusted stub period accrual included in the corporation's qualifying transitional income in respect of the partnership for the year is computed as if

(a) the descriptions in paragraph (a) and subparagraph (b)(i) of the definition "adjusted stub period accrual" in subsection (1) read as follows:

A　is the total of all amounts each of which is the corporation's share of an income or taxable capital gain of the partnership for the particular period (other than any amount for which a deduction is available under section 112 or 113),

B　is the total of all amounts each of which is the corporation's share of a loss or allowable capital loss — to the extent that the total of all allowable losses does not exceed the total of all taxable capital gains included in the description of A — of the partnership for the particular period,

C　is the number of days that are in both the year and the particular period,

D　is the number of days in the particular period,

E　is the amount of the qualified resource expense in respect of the particular period of the partnership that is designated by the corporation for the year under subsection (6) in its return of income for the year filed with the Minister on or before its filing-due date for the year, and

F　is nil; and

(b) the descriptions in subparagraph (b)(ii) of the definition "adjusted stub period accrual" in subsection (1) read as follows:

A　is the total of all amounts each of which is the corporation's share of an income or taxable capital gain of the partnership for the particular period (other than any amount for which a deduction is available under section 112 or 113),

B　the total of all amounts each of which is the corporation's share of a loss or allowable capital loss — to the extent that the total of all allowable losses does not exceed the total of all taxable capital gains included in the description of A — of the partnership for the particular period,

C　is nil,

D　is the number of days that are in both the year and the particular period,

E　is the number of days in the particular period,

F　is the amount of the qualified resource expense in respect of the particular period of the partnership that is designated by the corporation for the year under subsection (6) in its return of income for the year filed with the Minister on or before its filing-due date for the year, and

G　is nil.

Related Provisions: 34.2(11)(b)(ii) — Increase under (17) increases next year's reserve; 34.2(16) — Conditions for 34.2(17) to apply; 34.3(2)(b) — Application of income shortfall adjustment; 87(2)(j), 88(1)(e.2) — Amalgamation or windup — continuing corporation.

Notes: For discussion of 34.2(17) see TEI submission to Finance, Dec. 5, 2012, pp. 7-10.

34.2(17)(b)C changed from "is the corporation's eligible alignment income for the eligible fiscal period" by 2013 budget bill #2, effective for taxation years ending after March 22, 2011.

(18) Anti-avoidance — If it is reasonable to conclude that one of the main reasons a corporation is a member of a partnership in a taxation year is to avoid the application of subsection (13), the corporation is deemed not to be a member of the partnership for the purposes of that subsection.

Notes: For the meaning of "one of the main reasons" see Notes to 83(2.1).

Notes [s. 34.2]: 34.2 and 34.3 implement a 2011 Budget proposal to catch corporate income being deferred through partnership by having different fiscal year-ends. Under 96(1)(f), only the partnership's income for the year ending in the corporation's fiscal year is included in income. *Fredette*, [2001] 3 C.T.C. 2468 (TCC) and *Rousseau-Houle*, 2001 CarswellNat 1126 (TCC, Crown's appeal to FCA discontinued), had held that using partnerships to defer income by only one year was not abuse under GAAR.

34.2(2) requires inclusion of the "adjusted stub period accrual" (34.2(1)), which is essentially the partnership's income already included in the corporation's income for the year, prorated for the rest of the year (the "stub period"). (This does not increase the ACB of the partnership interest: VIEWS doc 2017-0687051E5.) 34.2(4) allows a deduction of this amount the next year, so the inclusion affects only the timing of the income recognition. However, where a partnership uses a "floating" year-end, see Jonathan Bright, "Floating Year-Ends: A Floating Quirk in the ASPA Rules", tinyurl.com/bright-aspa, April 2017.

The corporation can reduce the income inclusion by designating under 34.2(1)"adjusted stub period accrual"F, where the partnership income is expected to be lower for the stub period, but if there is a shortfall, interest effectively applies under 34.3.

There is no income inclusion if no partnership fiscal period ends in the taxation year: VIEWS doc 2014-0539191E5.

For discussion of 34.2 and 249.1(8)-(10) see CBA/CICA Joint Committee submission to Finance, Nov. 14, 2011 (25pp.); Anderson & Strawson, "Partnership Income Deferral Limited", 19(11) *Canadian Tax Highlights [CTH]* (ctf.ca) 6-7 (Nov. 2011); Calvert & Young, "New Anti-Deferral Rules for Partnership Income", 2011 Cdn Tax Foundation conference report, 40:1-28; Jamal & Maclagan, "Eliminating the Partnership Deferral Rules", XIV(2) *Business Vehicles* (Federated Press) 734-38 (2011); Mitchell Sherman & Mark Biderman, "Corporate Partnership Deferral Eliminated", XVII(3) *Corporate Finance* (Federated Press) 2022-25 (2011); Shreeram, "The Partnership Accrual Rules", VIII(4) *Resource Sector Taxation* (Federated Press) 602-09 (2011); Gan, Hsieh & Tse, "Ending the Year Ending after the End of the Year", 2011 British Columbia Tax Conference (ctf.ca), 12:1-31 and "Adjusting to the Adjusted Stub Period", 2012 BC Tax Conf. 8:1-18; Scholten, "The End of Income Deferral for Corporate Partners", 9(1) *Tax Hyperion* (Carswell, Jan. 2012); Oldewening & Carr, "Limitation on Deferral of Partnership Income by a Corporation", 60(1) *Canadian Tax Journal* (2012) 219-56; Lindsey & Pashkowich, "Anti-Deferral Rules for Partnership Income", 2012 conference report, 15:1-23; Derek Smith, "Corporate Partnerships: Deferral Still?", 4(1) *Canadian Tax Focus* (ctf.ca) 2-3 (Feb. 2014); Pantry & Campbell, "Partnerships and ASPA on Acquisition of Control", 24(10) *CTH* 3-4 (Oct. 2016).

As a result of 34.2, CRA has withdrawn its administrative position on joint-venture fiscal periods. See Notes to 249.1(1).

34.2 replaced by 2011 budget bill #2, effective for taxation years ending after March 22, 2011, replacing former 34.2, which provided a similar transitional reserve for individuals from 1995-2004 (the stub-period inclusion for individuals is in 34.1).

Former 34.2 was added by 1995 Budget, effective 1995. It provided a 10-year reserve for individuals (and certain partnerships and professional corporations) that switched from an off-calendar year-end to a December 31 year-end as of 1995, as required by 249.1. (An election out of this rule is available under 249.1(4), but then an additional annual income inclusion is required under 34.1.) Because most affected taxpayers would otherwise be required to report for more than 12 months of business income for 1995, former 34.2 provided a 10-year transitional reserve (i.e., allowed the extra income to be recognized gradually over a 10-year period).

Definitions [s. 34.2]: "adjusted stub period accrual" — 34.2(1); "affiliated" — 251.1; "allowable capital loss" — 38(b), 248(1); "amount", "bankrupt", "business" — 248(1); "Canada" — 255, *Interpretation Act* 35(1); "capital dividend account" — 89(1); "corporation" — 248(1), *Interpretation Act* 35(1); "disposition", "dividend" — 248(1); "eligible alignment income" — 34.2(1); "eligible fiscal period" — 248(1); "eligible alignment income"(a), (b), "exempt deficit", "exempt surplus" — Reg. 5907(1); "filing-due date" — 248(1); "fiscal period" — 249(2)(b), 249.1; "foreign accrual property income", "foreign affiliate" — 95(1), 248(1); "hybrid surplus" — 113(1)(a.1)(i), Reg. 5907(1), (1.01); "Minister" — 248(1); "multi-tier alignment" — 34.2(1); "non-resident" — 248(1); "partnership" — see 96(1) Notes; "permanent establishment" — Reg. 8201; "person", "professional corporation", "property" — 248(1); "qualified resource expense", "qualifying transitional income" — 34.2(1); "related" — 251(2); "resident in Canada" — 250; "share" — 248(1); "significant interest", "single-tier alignment", "specified percentage" — 34.2(1); "taxable capital gain" — 38(a), 248(1); "taxable deficit", "taxable surplus" — Reg. 5907(1); "taxation year" — 249; "taxpayer" — 248(1); "writing" — *Interpretation Act* 35(1).

34.3 (1) Definitions — The definitions in this subsection and in subsection 34.2(1) apply in this section.

"actual stub period accrual", of a corporation in respect of a qualifying partnership for a taxation year, means the positive or negative amount determined by the formula

$$(A - B) \times C/D - E$$

where

A is the total of all amounts each of which is the corporation's share of an income or taxable capital gain of the qualifying partnership for the last fiscal period of the partnership that began in the base year (other than any amount for which a deduction was available under section 112 or 113);

B is the total of all amounts each of which is the corporation's share of a loss or allowable capital loss of the qualifying partnership for the last fiscal period of the partnership that began in the base year (to the extent that the total of all allowable capital losses included under this description in respect of all qualifying partnerships for the taxation year does not exceed the corporation's share of all taxable capital gains of all qualifying partnerships for the taxation year);

C is the number of days that are in both the base year and the fiscal period;

D is the number of days in the fiscal period; and

E is the amount of the qualified resource expense in respect of the qualifying partnership that was designated by the corporation for the base year under subsection 34.2(6) in its return of income for the base year filed with the Minister on or before its filing-due date for the base year.

Notes: Because of the words "positive or negative amount", s. 257 does not apply and the formula can be negative.

"base year", of a corporation in respect of a qualifying partnership for a taxation year, means the preceding taxation year of the corporation in which began a fiscal period of the partnership that ends in the corporation's taxation year.

"income shortfall adjustment", of a corporation in respect of a qualifying partnership for a taxation year, means the positive or negative amount determined by the formula

$$(A - B) \times C \times D$$

where

A is the amount that is the lesser of

    (a) the actual stub period accrual in respect of the qualifying partnership, and

    (b) the amount that would be the corporation's adjusted stub period accrual for the base year in respect of the qualifying partnership if the value of F in paragraph (a) of the definition "adjusted stub period accrual" in subsection 34.2(1) were nil;

B is the amount included under subsection 34.2(2) in computing the corporation's income for the base year in respect of the qualifying partnership;

C is the number of days in the period that

    (a) begins on the day after the day on which the base year ends, and

    (b) ends on the day on which the taxation year ends; and

D is the average daily rate of interest determined by reference to the rate of interest prescribed under paragraph 4301(a) of the *Income Tax Regulations* for the period referred to in the description of C.

Related Provisions: 34.3(3) — Income shortfall adjustment added to income, plus additional amount if shortfall is excessive.

Notes: Because of the words "positive or negative amount", s. 257 does not apply and the formula amount for any partnership can be negative. The actual income inclusion under 34.3(3) cannot be negative.

Applying the prescribed interest rate to calculate *income* (added under 34.3(3)) results in the correct calculation of interest when the corporate tax rate is applied to the resulting additional income!

"qualifying partnership", in respect of a corporation for a particular taxation year, means a partnership

(a) a fiscal period of which began in a preceding taxation year and ends in the particular taxation year; and

(b) in respect of which the corporation was required to calculate an adjusted stub period accrual for the preceding taxation year.

(2) Application of subsec. (3) — Subsection (3) applies to a corporation for a taxation year if

(a) the corporation has designated an amount for the purpose of the description of F in paragraph (a) of the definition "adjusted stub period accrual" in subsection 34.2(1) in calculating its adjusted stub period accrual for the base year in respect of a qualifying partnership for the taxation year; and

(b) where the corporation has qualifying transitional income, the taxation year is after the first taxation year of the corporation to which subsection 34.2(17) applies.

(3) Income shortfall adjustment — inclusion — If this subsection applies to a corporation for a taxation year, the corporation shall include in computing its income for the taxation year the amount determined by the formula

$$A + 0.50 \times (A - B)$$

where

A is the amount that is the total of all amounts each of which is the corporation's income shortfall adjustment in respect of a qualifying partnership for the year; and

B is the amount that is the lesser of A and the total of all amounts each of which is 25% of the positive amount, if any, that would be the income shortfall adjustment in respect of a qualifying partnership for the year if the value of the description of B in the definition "income shortfall adjustment" in subsection (1) were nil.

Related Provisions: 34.3(2) — Conditions for 34.3(3) to apply.

Notes: The 50% amount is effectively a penalty for significantly under-calculating the partnership income for the stub period.

Forms: T2 Sched. 71, Part 8: Income inclusion for corporations that are members of single-tier partnerships.

Notes [s. 34.3]: See Notes at end of 34.2. 34.3 added by 2011 budget bill #2, effective for taxation years ending after March 22, 2011.

Definitions [s. 34.3]: "actual stub period accrual" — 34.3(1); "allowable capital loss" — 38(b), 248(1); "amount" — 248(1); "base year" — 34.3(1); "corporation" — 248(1), *Interpretation Act* 35(1); "filing-due date" — 248(1); "fiscal period" — 249(2)(b), 249.1; "income shortfall adjustment" — 34.3(1); "Minister" — 248(1); "partnership" — see 96(1) Notes; "prescribed" — 248(1); "qualified resource expense" — 34.2(1), 34.3(1); "qualifying partnership" — 34.3(1); "share" — 248(1); "taxable capital gain" — 38(a), 248(1); "taxation year" — 249.

35. (1) Prospectors and grubstakers — Where a share of the capital stock of a corporation

(a) is received in a taxation year by an individual as consideration for the disposition by the individual to the corporation of a mining property or an interest, or for civil law a right, therein acquired by the individual as a result of the individual's efforts as a prospector, either alone or with others, or

(b) is received in a taxation year

(i) by a person who has, either under an arrangement with a prospector made before the prospecting, exploration or development work or as an employer of a prospector, advanced money for, or paid part or all of, the expenses of prospecting or exploring for minerals or of developing a property for minerals, and

(ii) as consideration for the disposition by the person referred to in subparagraph (i) to the corporation of a mining property or an interest, or for civil law a right, therein acquired under the arrangement under which that person made the advance

or paid the expenses, or if the prospector's employee, acquired by the person through the employee's efforts,

the following rules apply:

(c) notwithstanding any other provision of this Act, no amount in respect of the receipt of the share shall be included

(i) in computing the income for the year of the individual or person, as the case may be, except as provided in paragraph (d), or

(ii) in computing at any time the amount to be determined for F in the definition "cumulative Canadian development expense" in subsection 66.2(5) in respect of the individual or person, as the case may be,

(d) in the case of an individual or partnership (other than a partnership each member of which is a taxable Canadian corporation), an amount in respect of the receipt of the share equal to the lesser of its fair market value at the time of acquisition and its fair market value at the time of disposition or exchange of the share shall be included in computing the income of the individual or partnership, as the case may be, for the year in which the share is disposed of or exchanged,

(e) notwithstanding Subdivision C, in computing the cost to the individual, person or partnership, as the case may be, of the share, no amount shall be included in respect of the disposition of the mining property or the interest, or for civil law the right, therein, as the case may be,

(f) notwithstanding sections 66 and 66.2, in computing the cost to the corporation of the mining property or the interest, or for civil law the right, therein, as the case may be, no amount shall be included in respect of the share, and

(g) for the purpose of paragraph (d), an individual or partnership shall be deemed to have disposed of or exchanged shares that are identical properties in the order in which they were acquired.

Related Provisions: 35(2) — "prospector"; 81(1)(l) — Income exemption; 110(1)(d.2) — Deduction in computing taxable income; 248(12) — Identical properties.

Notes: 35(1) "in effect defers any form of taxation resulting from the exchange until the shares are disposed of or further exchanged. Upon disposition, the prospector must include in income the lesser of the fair market value of the shares at the time of the exchange or at the time of the disposition (or further exchange)": *Bolen*, 2007 FCA 293, para. 20. As a result, "mining property is no longer treated as capital property": para. 25. 35(1) does not apply to the sale of a mining claim by a corporation: VIEWS doc 2012-0452841E5. Granting an option is a "disposition" of mining property: 2012-0480021I7. Note also the one-half deduction under 110(1)(d.2). A 35(1) transaction is not reported to CRA: 2017-0733221E5.

On death, see VIEWS doc 2008-0269451E5.

For discussion of the rules and case law see Carr & Calverley, *Canadian Resource Taxation* (Carswell, looseleaf or *Taxnet Pro* Reference Centre), chap. 17; Olga Koubrak, "Tax Deferral for Mining Prospectors and Grubstakers", 3(3) *Canadian Tax Focus* (ctf.ca) 12-13 (Aug. 2013).

35(1) amended by 2002-2013 technical bill (Part 4 — bijuralism), effective June 26, 2013, to add references to a "right" under civil law (paras. (a), (e) and (f) and subpara. (b)(ii)) and to change "if the prospector was the person's employee" to "if the prospector's employee" (subpara. (b)(ii)).

Interpretation Bulletins: IT-171R2: Non-resident individuals — computation of taxable income earned in Canada and non-refundable tax credits (cancelled).

(2) Definitions — In this section,

"mining property" means

(a) a right, licence or privilege to prospect, explore, drill or mine for minerals in a mineral resource in Canada, or

(b) real property or an immovable in Canada (other than depreciable property) the principal value of which depends on its mineral resource content;

Related Provisions: 66.21 — Foreign mining properties.

Notes: See Notes to 35(1).

For the meaning of "right, licence or privilege" in para. (a), see Notes to 66(15)"Canadian resource property". For the meaning of "real property" see Notes to 248(4).

Para. (b) amended by 2002-2013 technical bill (Part 4 — bijuralism), effective June 26, 2013, to add "or an immovable".

Definition amended by 2000 Budget, effective for shares received after Dec. 21, 2000. 35(2)"mining property" was 35(2)(a) before RSC 1985 (5th Supp) consolidation for tax years ending after Nov. 1991.

"prospector" means an individual who prospects or explores for minerals or develops a property for minerals on behalf of the individual, on behalf of the individual and others or as an employee.

Notes: 35(2)"prospector" was 35(2)(b) before RSC 1985 (5th Supp) consolidation for tax years ending after Nov. 1991.

Definitions [s. 35]: "amount" — 248(1); "Canada" — 255, *Interpretation Act* 35(1); "corporation" — 248(1), *Interpretation Act* 35(1); "depreciable property" — 13(21), 248(1); "employee", "employer" — 248(1); "fair market value" — see 69(1) Notes; "identical" — 248(12); "immovable" — Quebec *Civil Code* art. 900–907; "individual", "mineral", "mineral resource" — 248(1); "mining property" — 35(2); "person", "property" — 248(1); "prospector" — 35(2); "share" — 248(1); "taxable Canadian corporation" — 89(1), 248(1); "taxation year" — 11(2), 249.

36. [Repealed]

Notes: 36 repealed by 2013 budget bill #2, for expenditures incurred in tax years that begin after Dec. 21, 2012. It provided rules for depreciable property of railway companies. They are now subject to the same rules as other taxpayers, but see Canada-US tax treaty Art, VIII:4-6. (See 27(1) Notes re *CP Rail* case.)

Definitions [s. 36]: "amount" — 248(1); "depreciable property" — 13(21), 248(1); "prescribed", "regulation" — 248(1); "taxation year" — 249; "taxpayer" — 248(1).

Regulations: Sch. II:Cl. 1, Sch. II:Cl. 4, Sch. II:Cl. 6, Sch. II:Cl. 35.

37. (1) Scientific research and experimental development — Where a taxpayer carried on a business in Canada in a taxation year, there may be deducted in computing the taxpayer's income from the business for the year such amount as the taxpayer claims not exceeding the amount, if any, by which the total of

(a) the total of all amounts each of which is an expenditure of a current nature made by the taxpayer in the year or in a preceding taxation year ending after 1973

(i) on scientific research and experimental development related to a business of the taxpayer, carried on in Canada and directly undertaken by the taxpayer,

(i.01) on scientific research and experimental development related to a business of the taxpayer, carried on in Canada and directly undertaken on behalf of the taxpayer,

(i.1) by payments to a corporation resident in Canada to be used for scientific research and experimental development carried on in Canada that is related to a business of the taxpayer, but only where the taxpayer is entitled to exploit the results of that scientific research and experimental development,

(ii) by payments to

(A) an approved association that undertakes scientific research and experimental development,

(B) an approved university, college, research institute or other similar institution,

(C) a corporation resident in Canada and exempt from tax under paragraph 149(1)(j), or

(D) [Repealed]

(E) an approved organization that makes payments to an association, institution or corporation described in any of clauses (A) to (C)

to be used for scientific research and experimental development carried on in Canada that is related to a business of the taxpayer, but only where the taxpayer is entitled to exploit the results of that scientific research and experimental development, or

(iii) where the taxpayer is a corporation, by payments to a corporation resident in Canada and exempt from tax because of paragraph 149(1)(j), for scientific research and experimental development that is basic research or applied research carried on in Canada

(A) the primary purpose of which is the use of results therefrom by the taxpayer in conjunction with other scien-

tific research and experimental development activities undertaken or to be undertaken by or on behalf of the taxpayer that relate to a business of the taxpayer, and

(B) that has the technological potential for application to other businesses of a type unrelated to that carried on by the taxpayer,

(b) [Repealed]

(c) the total of all amounts each of which is an expenditure made by the taxpayer in the year or in a preceding taxation year ending after 1973 by way of repayment of amounts described in paragraph (d),

(c.1) all amounts included by virtue of paragraph 12(1)(v), in computing the taxpayer's income for any previous taxation year,

(c.2) all amounts added because of subsection 127(27), (29) or (34) to the taxpayer's tax otherwise payable under this Part for any preceding taxation year, and

(c.3) in the case of a partnership, all amounts each of which is an excess referred to in subsection 127(30) in respect of the partnership for any preceding fiscal period,

exceeds the total of

(d) the total of all amounts each of which is the amount of any government assistance or non-government assistance (as defined in subsection 127(9)) in respect of an expenditure described in paragraph (a) or (b), as paragraph (a) or (b), as the case may be, read in its application in respect of the expenditure, that at the taxpayer's filing-due date for the year the taxpayer has received, is entitled to receive or can reasonably be expected to receive,

(d.1) the total of all amounts each of which is the super-allowance benefit amount (within the meaning assigned by subsection 127(9)) for the year or for a preceding taxation year in respect of the taxpayer in respect of a province,

(e) that part of the total of all amounts each of which is an amount deducted under subsection 127(5) in computing the tax payable under this Part by the taxpayer for a preceding taxation year where the amount can reasonably be attributed to

(i) a prescribed proxy amount for a preceding taxation year,

(ii) an expenditure of a current nature incurred in a preceding taxation year that was a qualified expenditure incurred in that preceding year in respect of scientific research and experimental development for the purposes of section 127, or

(iii) an amount included because of paragraph 127(13)(e) in the taxpayer's SR&ED qualified expenditure pool at the end of a preceding taxation year within the meaning assigned by subsection 127(9),

(f) the total of all amounts each of which is an amount deducted under this subsection in computing the taxpayer's income for a preceding taxation year, except amounts described in subsection (6),

(f.1) the total of all amounts each of which is the lesser of

(i) the amount deducted under section 61.3 in computing the taxpayer's income for a preceding taxation year, and

(ii) the amount, if any, by which the amount that was deductible under this subsection in computing the taxpayer's income for that preceding year exceeds the amount claimed under this subsection in computing the taxpayer's income for that preceding year,

(g) the total of all amounts each of which is an amount equal to twice the amount claimed under subparagraph 194(2)(a)(ii) by the taxpayer for the year or any preceding taxation year, and

(h) if the taxpayer was subject to a loss restriction event before the end of the year, the amount determined for the year under subsection (6.1) with respect to the taxpayer.

Related Provisions: 12(1)(t) — Investment tax credit included in income; 12(1)(v) — Income inclusion where calculation under 37(1) would be negative; 18(9)(d), (e) — Certain prepaid expenses deemed incurred in later taxation year; 37(1.1) — Business of related corporations; 37(1.2) — Deemed time of capital expenditure; 37(1.3) — SR&ED within 200 nautical miles offshore is deemed done in Canada; 37(1.4), (1.5) — Limited deduction for research performed by employees outside Canada; 37(2) — Research outside Canada; 37(4) — No deduction for acquisition of rights: 37(6) — Expenditures of a capital nature; 37(6.1) — Change of control of corporation; 37(7), (8) — Interpretation; 37(9.1) — Limitation on remuneration to specified employee; 37(11) — Prescribed form required; 37(14) — Current expenses — look-through to expenses of recipient; 87(2)(l) — Amalgamation — continuing corporation; 96(1)(e.1) — Partnerships — carryforward of expenses not allowed; 125.4(2)(c) — No film production credit where R&D deduction allowed; 127(9) — "contract payment", "qualified expenditure"; 127(10.1), (10.8) — Additions to investment tax credits; 127(11.2) — Investment tax credit; 127(12.1) — Allocation of portion from trust or partnership; 143.3 — Stock option benefits, whether SR&ED expenditures; 149(1)(j) — Non-profit corporation for SR&ED — exemption; 248(1)"scientific research and experimental development" — Definition; 248(16), (16.1) — GST or QST input tax credit/refund and rebate; 248(18), (18.1) — GST or QST — repayment of input tax credit or refund; 251.2 — Loss restriction event; 261(7)(a) — Functional currency reporting; Reg. 1102(1)(d) — No CCA for capital property deducted under former 37(1)(b).

Notes: 37(1) entitles a taxpayer to a deduction for current (not capital, since 2014) R&D expenditures in Canada (and, via 37(1.4)–(1.5), limited R&D by employees outside Canada; see 37(2) generally for research outside Canada), even if otherwise barred by 18(1)(a) as not incurred to produce income. Note the extended definition of "in Canada" (up to 200 nautical miles offshore) in 37(1.3). Form T661 for these claims must be filed by 1 year after the return filing-due date, and no extension is allowed: 37(11), 220(2.2).

37(1)(a)(i) amounts are 100% "qualified expenditures" (as defined in 127(9)), qualifying for SR&ED investment tax credits. 37(1)(a)(i.01)-(iii) amounts are 80% QEs: 127(9)"qualified expenditure"(a)(ii). QEs generate ITCs of 15-35%: 127(9)"investment tax credit"(a.1), 127(10.1)

For the meaning of SR&ED, see 248(1)"scientific research and experimental development". For discussion of the SR&ED program, see Notes to 127(9)"SR&ED qualified expenditure pool".

37(1) uses the "pool" method: all expenses over time go into the pool, from which any amount can be claimed in any year, after which it cannot be claimed again due to 37(1)(f). (A partnership must claim the maximum each year: 96(1)(e.1).)

37(1)(a): for the meaning of "expenditure" see 37(8).

37(1)(a)(ii)(A), (B), (E): for approved entities see Notes to 37(7)"approved".

37(1)(a)(ii)(C) (payment to non-profit R&D corp): for a ruling see VIEWS doc 2010-0376811R3 (and see Notes to 149(1)(j)).

37(1)(b), before 2014, allowed capital expenditures, otherwise barred by 18(1)(b).

37(1)(d): in *Borealis Geopower*, 2018 TCC 189, government assistance was held to be "received" (and thus reduced the SR&ED claim) once BG had access to it, even though funding conditions had not yet been met.

37(1)(e): for interpretation of "reasonably be attributed" see *729658 Alberta*, 2004 TCC 474.

37(1) can apply where costs are reimbursed by a foreign parent that retains ownership of the rights: VIEWS doc 2008-0276121E5. Transportation costs for testing a prototype outside Canada are deductible under 37(2) but not 37(1): 2007-0239641E5. For rulings approving SR&ED deductions see 2009-0313261R3, 2010-0366511R3.

37(1)(b) (allowing capital expenditures) repealed by 2012 budget bill #2, for expenditures made after 2013 and expenditures that 37(1.2) deems not made before 2014.

37(1) earlier amended by 2012 budget bill #2 (last change effective 2014), 2013 budget bill #2 (effective March 21, 2013), 2000, 1998 and 1995 Budgets, 1994 technical bill, 1994 Budget, 1992 Economic Statement and 1991 technical bill.

Regulations: 2900(4) (prescribed proxy amount for 37(1)(e)).

Interpretation Bulletins: IT-121R3: Election to capitalize cost of borrowed money (cancelled).

Information Circulars: 86-4R2 Supplement 1: Automotive industry application paper; 86-4R2 Supplement 2: Aerospace industry application paper; 86-4R3: Scientific research and experimental development; 94-1: Plastics industry application paper; 94-2: Machinery and equipment industry application paper; 97-1: Administrative guidelines for software development.

I.T. Technical News: 23 (list of "approved" entities for SR&ED).

Application Policies: SR&ED 95-05: SR&ED capital expenditures — retroactive deductions under subsec. 37(1); SR&ED 96-04: Payments to third parties for SR&ED; SR&ED 96-05: Penalties under subsection 163(2); SR&ED 96-10: Third party payments — approval process; SR&ED 2000-02R3: Guidelines for resolving claimants' SR&ED concerns; SR&ED 2000-04R2: Recapture of investment tax credit; SR&ED 2002-01: Expenditures incurred for administrative salaries or wages — "directly related" test; SR&ED 2002-02R2: Experimental production and commercial production with experimental development work — allowable SR&ED expenditures; SR&ED 2004-01: Retiring allowance; SR&ED 2004-02R5: Filing requirements for claiming SR&ED; SR&ED 2004-03: Prototypes, pilot plants/commercial plants, custom products and commercial assets; SR&ED 2005-02: General rules concerning the treatment of government and non government assistance.

CRA Audit Manual: 11.3.5: Revision of CCA and other permissive deductions; 12.15.9: Revising capital cost allowance and other permissive deductions.

Forms: RC532: Request for administrative review; T2 Sched. 301: Newfoundland and Labrador research and development tax credit; T2 Sched. 340: Nova Scotia research and development tax credit; T2 Sched. 360: New Brunswick research and development tax credit; T2 Sched. 380: Manitoba research and development tax credit; T2 Sched. 403: Saskatchewan research and development tax credit; T661: SR&ED expenditures claim; T666: British Columbia scientific research and experimental development tax credit; T1129: Newfoundland and Labrador research and development tax credit (individuals); T1263: Third-party payments for SR&ED; T4088: Claiming scientific research and experimental development expenditures — guide to form T661.

(1.1) Business of related corporations
— Notwithstanding paragraph (8)(c), for the purposes of subsection (1), where a taxpayer is a corporation, scientific research and experimental development, related to a business carried on by another corporation to which the taxpayer is related (otherwise than by reason of a right referred to in paragraph 251(5)(b)) and in which that other corporation is actively engaged, at the time at which an expenditure or payment in respect of the scientific research and experimental development is made by the taxpayer, shall be considered to be related to a business of the taxpayer at that time.

(1.2) Deemed time of capital expenditure
— For the purposes of paragraph (1)(b), an expenditure made by a taxpayer in respect of property shall be deemed not to have been made before the property is considered to have become available for use by the taxpayer.

Related Provisions: 13(26) — No CCA until property available for use; 87(2)(l) — Amalgamations; 127(11.2) — No investment tax credit until property available for use; 248(19) — When property available for use.

Notes: The reference to "(1)(b)" is to 37(1)(b), which allowed deduction for capital expenses but was repealed by 2012 budget bill #2 for expenditures incurred after 2013, and also for expenditures deemed by 37(1.2) not to have been incurred before 2014. Thus, 37(1.2) still applied in 2013 to postpone capital expenditures past 2013 and thus disallow them entirely.

37(1.2) added by 1991 technical bill, effective for expenditures made by a taxpayer after 1989 other than expenditures in respect of property acquired

(a) from a person with whom the taxpayer was not dealing at arm's length (otherwise than by reason of a right referred to in 251(5)(b)) at the time the property was acquired, or

(b) in the course of a reorganization in respect of which, if a dividend were received by a corporation in the course of the reorganization, 55(2) would not be applicable to the dividend by reason of the application of 55(3)(b),

where the property was depreciable property of the person from whom it was acquired (or would, but for s. 37, be depreciable property of the person from whom it was acquired) and was owned by that person before 1990.

Application Policies: SR&ED 2003-01: Capital property intended to be used all or substantially all for SR&ED.

(1.3) SR&ED in the exclusive economic zone
— For the purposes of this section and section 127 of this Act and Part XXIX of the *Income Tax Regulations*, an expenditure is deemed to have been made by a taxpayer in Canada if the expenditure is

(a) made by the taxpayer in the course of a business carried on by the taxpayer in Canada; and

(b) made for the prosecution of scientific research and experimental development in the exclusive economic zone of Canada, within the meaning of the *Oceans Act*, or in the airspace above that zone or the seabed or subsoil below that zone.

Notes: This rule applies to SR&ED deductions and investment tax credits: 37(1)(a)(i), 37(1)(b)(i), 127(9)"first term shared-use-equipment" and "second term shared-use-equipment", all referred to in 127(9)"qualified expenditure"(a) [deduction for capital expenditures repealed effective 2014]; and Reg. 2900(4) and 2902(b)(i)(B). A "qualified expenditure" goes into 127(9)"SR&ED qualified expenditure pool", and ITC is allowed under 127(9)"investment tax credit"(a.1), 127(5) and 127(10.1).

This definition is broader than *Interpretation Act* 35(1)"exclusive economic zone" by including airspace. *Oceans Act* s. 13 provides:

13. (1) Exclusive economic zone of Canada — The exclusive economic zone of Canada consists of an area of the sea beyond and adjacent to the territorial sea of Canada that has as its inner limit the outer limit of the territorial sea of Canada and as its outer limit

(a) subject to paragraph (b), the line every point of which is at a distance of 200 nautical miles from the nearest point of the baselines of the territorial sea of Canada; or

(b) in respect of a portion of the exclusive economic zone of Canada for which geographical coordinates of points have been prescribed pursuant to subparagraph 25(a)(iii), lines determined from the geographical coordinates of points so prescribed.

(2) Determination of the outer limit of the exclusive economic zone of Canada — For greater certainty, paragraph (1)(a) applies regardless of whether regulations are made pursuant to subparagraph 25(a)(iv) prescribing geographical coordinates of points from which the outer limit of the exclusive economic zone of Canada may be determined.

37(1.3) added by 2005 budget bill #1, for expenditures made after Feb. 22, 2005.

(1.4) Salary or wages for SR&ED outside Canada — For the purposes of this section, section 127 and Part XXIX of the *Income Tax Regulations*, the amount of a taxpayer's expenditure for a taxation year determined under subsection (1.5) is deemed to be made in the taxation year in respect of scientific research and experimental development carried on in Canada by the taxpayer.

Related Provisions: 37(2) — Other SR&ED performed outside Canada.

Notes: Even before 37(1.4), CRA administratively allowed certain expenses outside Canada: former IT-151R5 para. 46; Mel Machado, "SR&ED Work Outside Canada", 16(12) *Canadian Tax Highlights* (ctf.ca) 6-7 (Dec. 2008).

37(1.4) added by 2008 budget bill #1, for taxation years that end after Feb. 25, 2008.

(1.5) Salary or wages outside Canada — limit determined — The amount of a taxpayer's expenditure for a taxation year determined under this subsection is the lesser of

(a) the amount that is the total of all expenditures each of which is an expenditure made by the taxpayer, in the taxation year and after February 25, 2008, in respect of an expense incurred in the taxation year for salary or wages paid to the taxpayer's employee who was resident in Canada at the time the expense was incurred in respect of scientific research and experimental development,

(i) that was carried on outside Canada,

(ii) that was directly undertaken by the taxpayer,

(iii) that related to a business of the taxpayer, and

(iv) that was solely in support of scientific research and experimental development carried on in Canada by the taxpayer, and

(b) the amount that is 10 per cent of the total of all expenditures, made by the taxpayer in the year, each of which would, if this Act were read without reference to subsection (1.4), be an expenditure made in respect of an expense incurred in the year for salary or wages paid to an employee in respect of scientific research and experimental development that was carried on in Canada, that was directly undertaken by the taxpayer and that related to a business of the taxpayer.

Related Provisions: 37(1.4) — Deduction for salary or wages outside Canada; 37(9)(b) — "Salary or wages" does not include amount subject to foreign income tax.

Notes: See Notes to 37(1.4). 37(1.5) added by 2008 budget bill #1, for taxation years that end on or after Feb. 25, 2008, with a transitional reading for tax years that include that date.

(2) Research outside Canada — In computing the income of a taxpayer for a taxation year from a business of the taxpayer, there may be deducted expenditures of a current nature made by the taxpayer in the year

(a) on scientific research and experimental development carried on outside Canada, directly undertaken by or on behalf of the taxpayer, and related to the business (except to the extent that subsection (1.4) deems the expenditures to have been made in Canada); or

(b) by payments to an approved association, university, college, research institute or other similar institution to be used for scientific research and experimental development carried on outside Canada related to the business provided that the taxpayer is entitled to exploit the results of that scientific research and experimental development.

Related Provisions: 37(1.3) — SR&ED within 200 nautical miles offshore is deemed done in Canada; 87(2)(l) — Amalgamations; 127(12.1) — Allocation of portion from trust or partnership.

Notes: See Notes to 37(1). Amounts under 37(1) are eligible for investment tax credits under 127(9)"qualified expenditure"(a), while those under 37(2) are not. (Note that

37(1.4)-(1.5) allow some research performed outside Canada by Canadian employees to qualify under 37(1).)

The costs of a project can be split between portions carried on in and outside Canada, rather than characterized as wholly one or the other: *LGL Ltd.*, [2000] 2 C.T.C. 27 (FCA). See also VIEWS doc 2005-0152601E5.

Where an amount is deductible under 37(2), CRA's view is that the amount cannot be deducted under 9(1) instead (to avoid 96(1)(g)(ii)): doc 2010-0389611E5.

37(2)(a) amended by 2008 budget bill #1, for tax years that end after Feb. 25, 2008, to add the parenthesized exception.

(3) Minister may obtain advice — The Minister may obtain the advice of the Department of Industry, the National Research Council of Canada, the Defence Research Board or any other agency or department of the Government of Canada carrying on activities in the field of scientific research as to whether any particular activity constitutes scientific research and experimental development.

Related Provisions: 241(4)(a) — Disclosure of taxpayer information to obtain advice.

Notes: 37(3) amended effective March 29, 1995 (S.C. 1995, c. 1).

(4) Where no deduction allowed under section — No deduction may be made under this section in respect of an expenditure made to acquire rights in, or arising out of, scientific research and experimental development.

Notes: In VIEWS doc 2002-0169537, CRA says 37(4) applies because an expenditure is for rights to SR&ED embedded into the taxpayer's product.

Application Policies: SR&ED 2000-04R2: Recapture of investment tax credit.

(5) Where no deduction allowed under sections 110.1 and 118.1 — Where, in respect of an expenditure on scientific research and experimental development made by a taxpayer in a taxation year, an amount is otherwise deductible under this section and under section 110.1 or 118.1, no deduction may be made in respect of the expenditure under section 110.1 or 118.1 in computing the taxable income of, or the tax payable by, the taxpayer for any taxation year.

(6) Expenditures of a capital nature — For the purposes of section 13, an amount claimed under subsection (1) that may reasonably be considered to be in respect of a property described in paragraph (1)(b), as that paragraph read in its application in respect of the property, is deemed to be an amount allowed to the taxpayer in respect of the property under regulations made under paragraph 20(1)(a), and for that purpose the property is deemed to be of a separate prescribed class.

Related Provisions: 87(2)(d)(ii)(D) — Amalgamations — depreciable property.

Notes: As a result of 37(6), the recapture provisions of the CCA system (see 13(1)) apply if depreciable property acquired before 2014 is later sold. See Notes preceding Reg. 1101 re the effect of separate classes.

37(6) amended by 2012 budget bill #2, effective 2014, consequential on repeal of 37(1)(b).

Application Policies: SR&ED 2000-04R2: Recapture of investment tax credit.

(6.1) Loss restriction event [change in control] — If a taxpayer was, at any time (in this subsection referred to as "that time") before the end of a taxation year of the taxpayer, last subject to a loss restriction event, the amount determined for the purposes of paragraph (1)(h) for the year with respect to the taxpayer in respect of a business is the amount, if any, by which

(a) the amount, if any, by which

(i) the total of all amounts each of which is

(A) an expenditure described in paragraph (1)(a) or (c) that was made by the taxpayer before that time,

(B) the lesser of the amounts determined immediately before that time in respect of the taxpayer under subparagraphs (1)(b)(i) and (ii), as those paragraphs read on March 29, 2012, in respect of expenditures made, and property acquired, by the taxpayer before 2014, or

(C) an amount determined in respect of the taxpayer under paragraph (1)(c.1) for its taxation year that ended immediately before that time exceeds the total of all amounts each of which is

    (ii) the total of all amounts determined in respect of the taxpayer under paragraphs (1)(d) to (g) for its taxation year that ended immediately before that time, or

    (iii) the amount deducted under subsection (1) in computing the taxpayer's income for its taxation year that ended immediately before that time

exceeds

  (b) the total of

    (i) if the business to which the amounts described in any of clauses (a)(i)(A) to (C) can reasonably be considered to have been related was carried on by the taxpayer for profit or with a reasonable expectation of profit throughout the year, the total of

      (A) the taxpayer's income for the year from the business before making any deduction under subsection (1), and

      (B) if properties were sold, leased, rented or developed, or services were rendered, in the course of carrying on the business before that time, the taxpayer's income for the year, before making any deduction under subsection (1), from any other business substantially all the income of which was derived from the sale, leasing, rental or development, as the case may be, of similar properties or the rendering of similar services, and

    (ii) the total of all amounts each of which is an amount determined in respect of a preceding taxation year of the taxpayer that ended after that time equal to the lesser of

      (A) the amount determined under subparagraph (i) with respect to the taxpayer in respect of the business for that preceding year, and

      (B) the amount in respect of the business deducted under subsection (1) in computing the taxpayer's income for that preceding year.

Related Provisions: 251.2 — Loss restriction event.

Notes: *Cl. (b)(i)(B)*: CRA considers that "substantially all" means 90% or more. For the meaning of "derived", see Notes to 18.1(12).

37(6.1) amended by 2013 budget bill #2, last change effective 2014, to change references from control of a corporation being acquired to a "loss restriction event" for any taxpayer, so as to extend the rule to trusts (see Notes to 251.2(2)).

2013 Budget bill, s. 120, deems an amendment to 37(6.1)(a)(i)(B) by 2012 budget bill #2, enacted to come into force in 2014, to never have come into force (it is covered off by the above amendment).

I.T. Technical News: 7 (control by a group — 50/50 arrangement).

(7) Definitions — In this section,

"approved" means approved by the Minister after the Minister has, if the Minister considers it necessary, obtained the advice of the Department of Industry or the National Research Council of Canada;

Notes: For 37(1)(a)(ii)(B), all Canadian universities and affiliated colleges are approved (SR&ED *Third-Party Payments Policy*, §11.3.1), as well as 18 institutions listed in *Technical News* 23 for 37(1)(a)(ii)(A) and (B); and the Institute in VIEWS doc 2018-0740791E5. Other "university-colleges" are not included: 2003-0004967. The entity must carry on activities that are unquestionably only SR&ED: 2013-0515771E5.

For the criteria and approval process for a non-profit corporation, see docs 2002-0152995, 2004-0096811E5, 2005-0159581E5, 2006-0168111E5, 2008-0270711E5, 2010-0371671E5, 2010-0373811E5, 2011-0392191E5, 2011-0424481E5, 2012-0433841E5, 2012-0454441E5, 2013-0487671E5, 2013-0505451E5, 2014-0537371E5.

For 37(1)(a)(ii)(E), the Natural Sciences and Engineering Research Council and Social Sciences and Humanities Research Council are approved: SR&ED *Third-Party Payments Policy*, §11.5. No other organization can be approved for (E) unless it is directly funded by the federal government: VIEWS doc 2006-0168111E5.

Amended effective March 29, 1995 (S.C. 1995, c. 1) to "Department of Industry". 37(7)"approved" was 37(7)(a) before RSC 1985 (5th Supp) consolidation for tax years ending after Nov. 1991.

I.T. Technical News: 23 (list of "approved" entities for SR&ED).

Application Policies: SR&ED 96-10: Third party payments — approval process.

"scientific research and experimental development" — [Repealed]

Notes: Definition repealed by 1995 Budget, for work performed after Feb. 27, 1995 except that, for the purposes of 149(1)(j) and (8)(b), the definition (which simply said it was defined by regulation, which was Reg. 2900) still applies to work performed pursuant to an agreement in writing entered into before Feb. 28, 1995. It has been replaced by a definition in 248(1) that applies for all purposes of the Act. See also 37(8).

37(7)"scientific research and experimental development" was 37(7)(b) before RSC 1985 (5th Supp) consolidation for tax years ending after Nov. 1991. For former 37(7)(c)–(f), see 37(8)(a)–(d).

(8) Interpretation — In this section,

  (a) references to expenditures on or in respect of scientific research and experimental development

    (i) where the references occur in subsection (2), include only

      (A) expenditures each of which was an expenditure incurred for and all or substantially all of which was attributable to the prosecution of scientific research and experimental development, and

      (B) expenditures of a current nature that were directly attributable, as determined by regulation, to the prosecution of scientific research and experimental development, and

    (ii) where the references occur other than in subsection (2), include only

      (A) expenditures incurred by a taxpayer in a taxation year (other than a taxation year for which the taxpayer has elected under clause (B)), each of which is

        (I) an expenditure of a current nature all or substantially all of which was attributable to the prosecution, or to the provision of premises, facilities or equipment for the prosecution, of scientific research and experimental development in Canada, or

        (II) an expenditure of a current nature directly attributable, as determined by regulation, to the prosecution, or to the provision of premises, facilities or equipment for the prosecution, of scientific research and experimental development in Canada, and

        (III) [Repealed]

      (B) where a taxpayer has elected in prescribed form and in accordance with subsection (10) for a taxation year, expenditures incurred by the taxpayer in the year each of which is

        (I) [Repealed]

        (II) an expenditure of a current nature for the prosecution of scientific research and experimental development in Canada directly undertaken on behalf of the taxpayer,

        (III) [Repealed]

        (IV) that portion of an expenditure made in respect of an expense incurred in the year for salary or wages of an employee who is directly engaged in scientific research and experimental development in Canada that can reasonably be considered to relate to such work having regard to the time spent by the employee thereon, and, for this purpose, where that portion is all or substantially all of the expenditure, that portion shall be deemed to be the amount of the expenditure, or

        (V) the cost of materials consumed or transformed in the prosecution of scientific research and experimental development in Canada,

        (VI) [Repealed]

  (b) for greater certainty, references to scientific research and experimental development related to a business include any scientific research and experimental development that may lead to or facilitate an extension of that business;

  (c) except in the case of a taxpayer who derives all or substantially all of the taxpayer's revenue from the prosecution of scientific research and experimental development (including the sale of rights arising out of scientific research and experimental development carried on by the taxpayer), the prosecution of scientific research and experimental development shall not be considered to be a business of the taxpayer to which scientific research and experimental development is related; and

(d) references to expenditures of a current nature include any expenditure made by a taxpayer other than an expenditure made by the taxpayer for

(i) the acquisition from a person or partnership of a property that is a capital property of the taxpayer, or

(ii) the use of, or the right to use, property that would be capital property of the taxpayer if it were owned by the taxpayer.

Related Provisions: 37(1.1) — Business of related corporations; 37(1.3) — SR&ED within 200 nautical miles offshore is deemed done in Canada; 37(9)(a) — Meaning of "expenditure" for 37(8)(a)(ii)(A), (B); 37(9.1)–(9.5) — Limitation on payments to specified employees; 37(10) — Time for election; 37(14) — Current expenses — lookthrough to expenses of recipient; 96(3) — Election by members of partnership; 143.3 — Stock option benefits, whether SR&ED expenditures; 149(1)(j)(ii)(A) — Non-profit SR&ED corporation's expenditures; 248(1)"scientific research and experimental development" — Definition.

Notes: Wages to owners or key employees were allowed as "directly undertaken" in *Tri-O-cycles Concept*, 2009 TCC 632; *Sunatori*, 2010 TCC 346, footnote 21 to para. 57 (aff'd 2011 FCA 254) (corp accruing liability to pay shareholder for services, even without payment); *AG Shield*, 2017 TCC 68 (owners chose not to take salary for time spent running the company). They were denied in *Laboratoire Du-Var*, 2012 TCC 366 and *Indusol*, 2020 TCC 103, paras. 129-137 (not proven to be legitimate R&D expenses).

In *Alcatel*, 2005 TCC 149, stock option benefits to employees were included in "expenditures" under 37(8)(a), even though there was no cash outlay. CRA accepts *Alcatel* (VIEWS doc 2005-0141141C6); but for options granted and shares issued after Nov. 17, 2005, *Alcatel* is overruled by 143.3.

In *PSC Elstow*, 2008 TCC 694, 37(8)(a) applied and 37(8)(c) did not apply to a sole-purpose R&D company set up for pig research by a Univ. of Saskatchewan non-profit.

In *Inflection Analytics*, 2015 TCC 129, fees for real-time data on stocks were not for lease of "equipment", so deduction was denied.

CRA considers that "substantially all" means 90% or more.

37(8)(a)(ii)(A): see VIEWS doc 2009-0313261R3.

37(8)(a)(ii)(A)(III) [repealed]: In *VLN Advanced Technologies*, 2018 TCC 33, property was held not to meet the condition of intended to be used for substantially all its operating life for carrying on SR&ED in Canada.

The *37(8)(a)(ii)(B)* election is for the "proxy" method. See Notes to Reg. 2900(4).

37(8)(a)(ii)(B)(II): Before Sept. 17, 2016, "*in respect of* [SR&ED] directly undertaken on behalf of the taxpayer" was interpreted broadly and did not require the third party's work to be SR&ED: *Feedlot Health*, 2015 TCC 32, paras. 61-63. This has been overruled by the 2017 amendment below.

CRA accepts a contract with a specialized placement agency as a contract for SR&ED, rather than for services, if certain conditions are met: Mel Machado, "The CRA's Revised Position on SR&ED Contracts", 1830 *Tax Topics* (CCH) 1-4 (April 5/07). See also VIEWS doc 2008-026972117.

37(8)(a)(ii)(B)(IV): In *CalAmp Wireless Networks*, 2013 TCC 201, bonuses were disallowed as not being for SR&ED purposes, as their purpose was to reward workers after the sale of the company and encourage them to stay.

37(8)(a)(ii)(B)(VI): For "used primarily", see Notes to 73(3).

37(8)(a)(ii)(B)(II) amended by 2017 budget bill #2, for expenditures incurred after Sept. 16, 2016, to change "in respect of" to "for" (see above re *Feedlot Health*).

37(8) amended by 2012 budget bill #2, effective on the same basis as the repeal of 37(1)(b) (which allowed deduction for capital expenditures made before 2014), to repeal (a)(ii)(A)(III), (a)(ii)(B)(I), (a)(ii)(B)(III) and (a)(ii)(B)(VI), to add "of a current nature" in (a)(ii)(B)(II) and to amend para. (d).

37(8)(a)(ii)(B)(V) amended to add "or transformed" by 2002-2013 technical bill (Part 5 — technical), for costs incurred after Feb. 23, 1998. 37(8) earlier amended by 1992 Economic Statement (with limited grandfathering to 1996 by 1996 Budget bill). 37(8)(a)-(d) were 37(7)(c)-(f) before RSC 1985 (5th Supp) consolidation for tax years ending after Nov. 1991.

Regulations: 2900(2)–(10) (meaning of "expenditures directly attributable"); 2903 (prescribed special-purpose building, before 2014).

Information Circulars: 86-4R2 Supplement 1: Automotive industry application paper; 86-4R2 Supplement 2: Aerospace industry application paper; 86-4R3: Scientific research and experimental development; 94-1: Plastics industry application paper; 94-2: Machinery and equipment industry application paper; 97-1: Administrative guidelines for software development.

Application Policies: SR&ED 95-04R: Conflict of interest with regard to outside consultants; SR&ED 96-06: Directly undertaking, supervising or supporting v. "directly engaged" SR&ED salary and wages; SR&ED 2000-01: Cost of materials;

SR&ED 2002-01: Expenditures incurred for administrative salaries or wages — "directly related" test; SR&ED 2002-02R2: Experimental production and commercial production with experimental development work — allowable SR&ED expenditures; SR&ED 2003-01: Capital property intended to be used all or substantially all for SR&ED; SR&ED 2004-01: Retiring allowance; SR&ED 2004-03: Prototypes, pilot plants/commercial plants, custom products and commercial assets.

Forms: RC4613: Election to use the SR&ED proxy to report the recapture of input tax credits; T661: SR&ED expenditures claim, Line 160 (election to use prescribed proxy amount).

(9) Salary or wages — An expenditure of a taxpayer

(a) does not include, for the purposes of clauses (8)(a)(ii)(A) and (B), remuneration based on profits or a bonus, where the remuneration or bonus, as the case may be, is in respect of a specified employee of the taxpayer, and

(b) includes, for the purpose of paragraph (1.5)(a), an amount paid in respect of an expense incurred for salary or wages paid to an employee only if the taxpayer reasonably believes that the salary or wages is not subject to an income or profits tax imposed, because of the employee's presence or activity in a country other than Canada, by a government of that other country.

Notes: 37(9)(b) added by 2008 budget bill #1, for tax years that end after Feb. 25, 2008.

37(9) (originally proposed as 37(8) before reconsolidation in RSC 1985 (5th Supp)) added by 1992 Economic Statement, for taxation years ending after Dec. 2, 1992.

(9.1) Limitation re specified employees — For the purposes of clauses (8)(a)(ii)(A) and (B), expenditures incurred by a taxpayer in a taxation year do not include expenses incurred in the year in respect of salary or wages of a specified employee of the taxpayer to the extent that those expenses exceed the amount determined by the formula

$$A \times \frac{B}{365}$$

where

A is 5 times the Year's Maximum Pensionable Earnings (as determined under section 18 of the *Canada Pension Plan*) for the calendar year in which the taxation year ends; and

B is the number of days in the taxation year on which the employee is a specified employee of the taxpayer.

Related Provisions: 38(9.2)–(9.5) — Allocation of salary of specified employee of associated corporations.

Notes: 37(9.1) limits the amount of claim for SR&ED expense for salary of a "specified employee" (see 248(1)) to 5 times the Year's Maximum Pensionable Earnings (YMPE). This maximum amount is prorated for short taxation years.

The YMPE for 2020 is $58,700, and for 2021 is $61,600. For other years, see Table I-8 at beginning of book.

See VIEWS doc 2012-0439781E5 (whether shareholder of majority partner is "specified employee").

37(9.1) added by 1996 Budget, for taxation years that begin after March 5, 1996.

(9.2) Associated corporations — Where

(a) in a taxation year of a corporation that ends in a calendar year, the corporation employs an individual who is a specified employee of the corporation,

(b) the corporation is associated with another corporation (in this subsection and subsection (9.3) referred to as the "associated corporation") in a taxation year of the associated corporation that ends in the calendar year, and

(c) the individual is a specified employee of the associated corporation in the taxation year of the associated corporation that ends in the calendar year,

for the purposes of clauses (8)(a)(ii)(A) and (B), the expenditures incurred by the corporation in its taxation year or years that end in the calendar year and by each associated corporation in its taxation year or years that end in the calendar year do not include expenses incurred in those taxation years in respect of salary or wages of the specified employee unless the corporation and all of the associated corporations have filed with the Minister an agreement referred to in subsection (9.3) in respect of those years.

Related Provisions: 37(9.5) — Certain individuals and partnerships deemed to be associated corporations; 87(2)(l) — Amalgamations.

Notes: 37(9.2) added by 1996 Budget, effective for taxation years that begin after March 5, 1996.

(9.3) Agreement among associated corporations — Where all of the members of a group of associated corporations of which an individual is a specified employee file, in respect of their taxation years that end in a particular calendar year, an agreement with the Minister in which they allocate an amount in respect of the individual to one or more of them for those years and the amount so allocated or the total of the amounts so allocated, as the case may be, does not exceed the amount determined by the formula

$$A \times B / 365$$

where

A   is 5 times the Year's Maximum Pensionable Earnings (as determined under section 18 of the *Canada Pension Plan*) for the particular calendar year, and

B   is the lesser of 365 and the number of days in those taxation years on which the individual was a specified employee of one or more of the corporations,

the maximum amount that may be claimed in respect of salary or wages of the individual for the purposes of clauses (8)(a)(ii)(A) and (B) by each of the corporations for each of those years is the amount so allocated to it for each of those years.

Related Provisions: 37(9.5) — Certain individuals and partnerships deemed to be associated corporations; 87(2)(l) — Amalgamations.

Notes: For discussion of this allocation on Form T1174, see May 2011 ICAA roundtable (tinyurl.com/cra-abtax), q. 25.

For the Year's Maximum Pensionable Earnings in A, see 37(9.1) Notes.

37(9.3) added by 1996 Budget, for taxation years that begin after March 5, 1996.

Forms: T1174: Agreement between associated corporations to allocate salary or wages of specified employees for SR&ED.

(9.4) Filing — An agreement referred to in subsection (9.3) is deemed not to have been filed by a taxpayer unless

(a) it is in prescribed form; and

(b) where the taxpayer is a corporation, it is accompanied by

(i) where its directors are legally entitled to administer its affairs, a certified copy of their resolution authorizing the agreement to be made, and

(ii) where its directors are not legally entitled to administer its affairs, a certified copy of the document by which the person legally entitled to administer its affairs authorized the agreement to be made.

Notes: 37(9.4) added by 1996 Budget, for tax years that begin after March 5, 1996.

(9.5) Deemed corporation — For the purposes of subsections (9.2) and (9.3) and this subsection, each

(a) individual related to a particular corporation,

(b) partnership of which a majority-interest partner is

(i) an individual related to a particular corporation, or

(ii) a corporation associated with a particular corporation, and

(c) limited partnership of which a member whose liability as a member is not limited is

(i) an individual related to a particular corporation, or

(ii) a corporation associated with a particular corporation,

is deemed to be a corporation associated with the particular corporation.

Notes: 37(9.5)(b) amended by 2013 budget bill #2, effective Dec. 12, 2013, to change "majority interest partner" to "majority-interest partner" (with a hyphen).

37(9.5) added by 1996 Budget, for taxation years that begin after March 5, 1996.

(10) Time for [proxy] election — Any election made under clause (8)(a)(ii)(B) for a taxation year by a taxpayer shall be filed by the taxpayer on the day on which the taxpayer first files a prescribed form referred to in subsection (11) for the year.

Notes: A 37(10) election cannot be revoked under 220(3.2) because it is not listed in Reg. 600: *Advanced Agricultural Testing*, [2009] 6 C.T.C. 2318 (TCC).

37(10) amended by 1995 Budget and 1995-97 technical bill, cumulatively effective for taxation years that begin after 1995.

37(10) (originally proposed as 37(9)) added by 1992 Economic Statement, effective for taxation years ending after December 2, 1992.

(11) Filing requirement — A prescribed form must be filed by a taxpayer with the Minister in respect of any expenditure, that would be incurred by the taxpayer in a taxation year that begins after 1995 if this Act were read without reference to subsection 78(4), that is claimed by the taxpayer for the year as a deduction under this section, on or before the day that is 12 months after the taxpayer's filing-due date for the taxation year, containing

(a) prescribed information in respect of the expenditure; and

(b) "claim preparer information", as defined in subsection 162(5.3).

Enacted Amendment — *Time Limits and Other Periods Act (COVID-19)* [TLOPA]

[See under 169(1). TLOPA 7(1) specifically permits the Minister of National Revenue to extend the deadline in 37(11) by up to 6 months during the COVID-19 pandemic, though no extension can run past Dec. 31, 2020 — ed.]

CRA notices, Aug. 13 and Sept. 11, 2020: See under 127(9)"investment tax credit"(m).

Related Provisions: 37(11.1) — No deduction if 37(11)(a) information not filed; 127(9)"investment tax credit"(m) — Filing deadline applies to all investment tax credits; 162(5.1)–(5.3) — Penalty for not providing details regarding SR&ED claim preparer fees; 220(2.2) — No extension of deadline allowed.

Notes: See Notes to 127(9)"SR&ED qualified expenditure pool". For CRA policy see: tinyurl.com/sred-file; T4088 guide to the T661 claim form. If the T661 is not filed by the deadline *with all prescribed information* (determined by CRA: see 248(1)"prescribed", tinyurl.com/qa-t661 and *Westsource Group*, 2018 FCA 57), the work does not qualify as SR&ED (see 37(11.1), (12)), even if CRA has the data on forms elsewhere: *Easy Way Cattle*, 2016 FCA 301 (*Interpretation Act* s. 32 did not help); *1373744 Ontario [One Source Metal]*, 2009 TCC 511; *AFD Petroleum*, 2016 FC 547 (FCA appeal discontinued A-215-16); *Westsource* (above; only 1 of 2 projects fully described in time). 162(5.1) imposes a $1,000 penalty on the preparer for a false statement or omission in the T661. See also 127(9)"investment tax credit"(m).

For a corporation, the filing deadline is 18 months from year-end due to 150(1)(a) (see also Notes to *Interpretation Act* s. 27(4)). The same deadline applies under 127(9)"investment tax credit"(m) for the ITC. CRA cannot extend the deadline, due to 220(2.2): doc 2009-0343331I7. Claims must be made early enough to allow time for a CRA letter seeking more detail to be answered by the deadline. In *AFD Petroleum* (above), filing on the last day meant that missing information CRA sought could not be provided. See also Feely & Pringle, "The CRA's SR&ED Claim-Processing Procedures", 7(1) *Tax for the Owner-Manager* (ctf.ca) 7-8 (Jan. 2007).

COVID-19 extensions: (1) The *Time Limits and Other Periods Act (COVID-19)* (see Enacted Amendment under 169(1)) allows CRA to exclude March 13-Sept. 13, 2020 from the calculation, but no extended deadline could run past Dec. 31, 2020. (2) For corporate income tax returns due after March 18, 2020, the corporate filing deadline was extended by CRA to June 1, 2020 (returns due March 19-May 29) or Sept. 1, 2020 (returns due May 31-Aug. 31). Thus, the SR&ED filing deadline is June 1, 2021 or Sept. 1, 2021 for such corps: tinyurl.com/sred-file.

For a partnership, CRA states in T4068 (guide to the T5013 partnership information return): "Form T661 should be filed no later than 12 months after the earliest of all filing due dates for the return of income of the members for the tax year in which the partnership's fiscal period ends so that each member would then be able to meet their deadline to claim the SR&ED investment tax credit allocated to them."

If the deadline is missed, an expenditure deductible under 37(1) is normally still a business expense under 9(1), but does not qualify for investment tax credit under s. 127: see Application Policy SR&ED 2004-02R5.

The current version of CRA Form T661 must be used. However, failing to file documents proving "systematic investigation" did not invalidate a claim: *6379249 Canada*, 2015 TCC 77, para. 93.

A parent company's claim under 37(13) for work done for a subsidiary is not affected by the sub's failure to file a T661: VIEWS doc 2007-0226201E5.

In opening words, "filing due-date" corrected to "filing-due date", Nov. 2020: laws.justice.gc.ca/eng/corrections.

37(11) amended by 2017 budget bill #2, effective Dec. 14, 2017. Before then, read:

(11) Subject to subsection (12), no amount in respect of an expenditure that would be incurred by a taxpayer in a taxation year that begins after 1995 if this Act were read without reference to subsection 78(4) may be deducted under subsection (1) unless the taxpayer files with the Minister a prescribed form contain-

ing prescribed information in respect of the expenditure on or before the day that is 12 months after the taxpayer's filing-due date for the year.

37(11) added by 1995 Budget, for taxation years beginning after 1995. The filing requirement was formerly in the opening words of 37(1). For an earlier 37(11) dealing with reclassified expenditures, see 37(12).

Application Policies: SR&ED 2000-02R3: Guidelines for resolving claimants' SR&ED concerns; SR&ED 2004-02R5: Filing requirements for claiming SR&ED.

Forms: RC532: Request for administrative review; T2 Sched. 380: Manitoba research and development tax credit; T661: SR&ED expenditures claim; T1263: Third-party payments for SR&ED; T4088: Claiming scientific research and experimental development expenditures — guide to form T661.

(11.1) Failure to file — Subject to subsection (12), if the prescribed information in respect of an expenditure referred to in paragraph (11)(a) is not contained in the form referred to in subsection (11), no amount in respect of the expenditure may be deducted under subsection (1).

Notes: 37(11.1) is worded incorrectly. Finance's intention is that the "no deduction without the form filed on time" rule not apply to "claim preparer information" required by 37(11)(b). However, since that information is requested by the CRA on the T661, it is still "prescribed information" on a "prescribed form" (see 248(1)"prescribed"(a)), and so it falls under 37(11)(a) (as well as (b)) and 37(11.1) applies to it! This has been pointed out to Finance.

Note also that 37(11) and (11.1) apply only to deductions under s. 37; the parallel rule in 127(9)"investment tax credit"(m) for investment tax credits (ITCs) was not amended when 37(11.1) was added in 2017. ITCs are allowed per 127(9)"qualified expenditure"(a)(i) based on expenditures "described" in 37(1)(a)(i), not those "deductible" under 37(1)(a)(i).

37(11.1) added by 2017 budget bill #2, effective Dec. 14, 2017.

(12) Misclassified expenditures [Work deemed not SR&ED if T661 not completed] — If a taxpayer has not filed a prescribed form in respect of an expenditure in accordance with subsection (11), for the purposes of this Act, the expenditure is deemed not to be an expenditure on or in respect of scientific research and experimental development.

Notes: 37(12) deems an expenditure for which the taxpayer has not met the 37(11) requirements not to be SR&ED. It is classified as a business expense under 9(1), still deductible but ineligible for investment tax credit (127(9)"SR&ED qualified expenditure pool").

37(12) amended by 1997 Budget, for 1997 and later taxation years. Added by 1995 Budget, replacing 37(11) which was added by 1994 Budget effective Feb. 22, 1994.

Application Policies: SR&ED 2004-02R5: Filing requirements for claiming SR&ED.

(13) Non-arm's length contract — linked work — For the purposes of this section and sections 127 and 127.1, where

(a) work is performed by a taxpayer for a person or partnership at a time when the person or partnership does not deal at arm's length with the taxpayer, and

(b) the work would be scientific research and experimental development if it were performed by the person or partnership,

the work is deemed to be scientific research and experimental development.

Notes: A parent company's claim under 37(13) for work done for a subsidiary is not affected by the subsidiary's failure to file the T661: VIEWS doc 2007-0226201E5.

37(13) added by 1995 Budget and amended by 1995-97 technical bill, effective for taxation years that begin after 1995.

(14) Look-through rule [capital expenditures disallowed] — For the purposes of subparagraphs (1)(a)(i.01) to (iii), the amount of a particular expenditure made by a taxpayer shall be reduced by the amount of any related expenditure of the person or partnership to whom the particular expenditure is made that is not an expenditure of a current nature of the person or partnership.

Related Provisions: 37(15) — Recipient required to notify taxpayer of amount of reduction.

Notes: 37(14) added by 2012 budget bill #2, effective on the same basis as repeal of 37(1)(b) (which allowed deduction for capital expenditures made before 2014).

(15) Reporting of certain payments — If an expenditure is required to be reduced because of subsection (14), the person or the partnership referred to in that subsection is required to inform the taxpayer in writing of the amount of the reduction without delay if

requested by the taxpayer and in any other case no later than 90 days after the end of the calendar year in which the expenditure was made.

Notes: 37(15) added by 2012 budget bill #2, effective on the same basis as the repeal of 37(1)(b) (which allowed deduction for capital expenditures before 2014).

Definitions [s. 37]: "amount" — 248(1); "approved" — 37(7); "arm's length" — 251(1); "associated" — 13(9.5), 256; "available for use" — 13(27)–(32), 248(19); "business" — 248(1); "calendar year" — *Interpretation Act* 37(1)(a); "Canada" — 37(1.3), (1.4), 255, *Interpretation Act* 35(1); "capital property" — 54, 248(1); "carried on a business in Canada" — 253; "claim preparer information" — 162(5.3); "control" — 256(6)–(9), 256.1(3); "corporation" — 248(1), *Interpretation Act* 35(1); "current" — 37(8)(d), 37(14); "depreciable property" — 13(21), 248(1); "employee" — 248(1); "expenditure" — 37(8)(a), (d), (9)(a); "filing-due date" — 150(1), 248(1); "government assistance" — 127(9); "individual" — 248(1); "loss restriction event" — 251.2; "majority-interest partner", "Minister" — 248(1); "month" — *Interpretation Act* 35(1); "non-government assistance" — 127(9); "partnership" — see 96(1) Notes; "person", "prescribed" — 248(1); "prescribed proxy amount" — Reg. 2900(4)–(10); "property" — 248(1); "qualified expenditure" — 127(9); "received" — 248(7); "regulation" — 248(1); "related to a business" — 37(1.1), 37(8)(b); "resident in Canada" — 94(3)(a), 250; "salary or wages" — 37(9)(b), 248(1); "scientific research and experimental development" — 37(8), (13), 248(1), Reg. 2900; "specified employee" — 248(1); "super-allowance benefit amount" — 127(9); "tax payable" — 248(2); "taxable income" — 2(2), 248(1); "taxation year" — 11(2), 249; "taxpayer" — 248(1); "writing" — *Interpretation Act* 35(1).

37.1, 37.2, 37.3 [Repealed]

Notes: 37.1–37.3 repealed by 1995-97 technical bill, for 1995 and later tax years. 37.1 provided additional R&D allowance, eliminated in 1983 (grandfathering to 1988 under 37.2, 37.3) and replaced with enhanced s. 127 investment tax credit.

Subdivision C — Taxable Capital Gains and Allowable Capital Losses

38. Taxable capital gain and allowable capital loss — For the purposes of this Act,

(a) **[taxable capital gain — general]** — subject to paragraphs (a.1) to (a.3), a taxpayer's taxable capital gain for a taxation year from the disposition of any property is $\frac{1}{2}$ of the taxpayer's capital gain for the year from the disposition of the property;

(a.1) **[taxable capital gain — donation of listed securities]** — a taxpayer's taxable capital gain for a taxation year from the disposition of a property is equal to zero if

(i) the disposition is the making of a gift to a qualified donee of a share, debt obligation or right listed on a designated stock exchange, a share of the capital stock of a mutual fund corporation, a unit of a mutual fund trust, an interest in a related segregated fund trust (within the meaning assigned by paragraph 138.1(1)(a)) or a prescribed debt obligation,

(ii) the disposition is deemed by section 70 to have occurred and the property is

(A) a security described in subparagraph (i), and

(B) the subject of a gift to which subsection 118.1(5.1) applies and that is made by the taxpayer's estate to a qualified donee, or

(iii) the disposition is the exchange, for a security described in subparagraph (i), of a share of the capital stock of a corporation, which share included, at the time it was issued and at the time of the disposition, a condition allowing the holder to exchange it for the security, and the taxpayer

(A) receives no consideration on the exchange other than the security, and

(B) makes a gift of the security to a qualified donee not more than 30 days after the exchange;

(a.2) **[taxable capital gain — ecological gift]** — a taxpayer's taxable capital gain for a taxation year from the disposition of a property is equal to zero if

(i) the disposition is the making of a gift to a qualified donee (other than a private foundation) of a property described, in respect of the taxpayer, in paragraph 110.1(1)(d) or in the definition "total ecological gifts" in subsection 118.1(1), or

(ii) the disposition is deemed by section 70 to have occurred and the property is

(A) described in subparagraph (i), and

(B) the subject of a gift to which subsection 118.1(5.1) applies and that is made by the taxpayer's estate to a qualified donee (other than a private foundation);

(a.3) [taxable capital gain — exchange of partnership units for securities later donated] — a taxpayer's taxable capital gain for a taxation year, from the disposition of an interest in a partnership (other than a prescribed interest in a partnership) that would be an exchange described in subparagraph (a.1)(iii) if the interest were a share in the capital stock of a corporation, is equal to the lesser of

(i) that taxable capital gain determined without reference to this paragraph, and

(ii) ½ of the amount, if any, by which

(A) the total of

(I) the cost to the taxpayer of the partnership interest, and

(II) each amount required by subparagraph 53(1)(e)(iv) or (x) to be added in determining the taxpayer's adjusted cost base of the partnership interest,

exceeds

(B) the adjusted cost base to the taxpayer of the partnership interest (determined without reference to subparagraphs 53(2)(c)(iv) and (v));

(b) [allowable capital loss] — a taxpayer's allowable capital loss for a taxation year from the disposition of any property is ½ of the taxpayer's capital loss for the year from the disposition of that property; and

(c) [allowable business investment loss] — a taxpayer's allowable business investment loss for a taxation year from the disposition of any property is ½ of the taxpayer's business investment loss for the year from the disposition of that property.

Income Tax Folios [para. 38(c)]: S4-F8-C1: Business investment losses [replaces IT-484R2].

Related Provisions [s. 38]: 11(2) — Fiscal (business) year of individual does not apply to subdivision c; 38.1, 40(12) — Capital gain on donating flow-through shares; 38.2 — Allocation of gain to 38(a.1) or (a.2) where advantage received; 39 — Capital gains and losses; 53(2)(c)(i)(A) — 38(b) generally ignored in determining reduction in ACB of partnership interest; 83(2), 89(1)"capital dividend account"(a)(i) — Untaxed fraction of gain can be distributed free of tax by corporation as capital dividend; 93(2)–(2.31) — Loss limitations on disposition of foreign affiliate shares; 96(1.7) — Partnership gains and losses; 100(1) — Disposition of interest in a partnership; 104(21) — Flow-through of gain from trust to beneficiary; 110(1)(d.01) — Deduction on donating employee stock-option shares to charity; 110.6 — Capital gains exemption; 111(8)"net capital loss" — Carryover of unused allowable capital loss; 127.52(1)(d)(i) — 30% of gain added to income for minimum tax purposes; 142.5(9)(e) — Deemed taxable capital gain where mark-to-market property acquired by financial institution on rollover; 149.1(6.4) — Rule re gifts of public securities applies to gifts to registered national arts service organizations; 248(1)"allowable business investment loss", 248(1)"allowable capital loss", 248(1)"taxable capital gain" — Definitions in s. 38 apply to entire Act; 248(37)(d) — Rule limiting value of donated property does not apply where 38(a.1) or (a.2) applies; Canada-U.S. Tax Treaty:Art. XIII — Gains.

Notes: Taxable capital gains (½ of capital gains) and allowable capital losses (½ of capital losses) of the current year must be netted against each other. Excess allowable capital losses can be carried back 3 years or forward indefinitely as "net capital losses", and optionally used against taxable capital gains in those other years (or against *any* income in the year of death and the previous year: 111(2)(b)). See 111 and Notes to s. 3. Allowable business investment losses (38(c)) can be used against any income (see 3(d)) or carried back 3 years or forward 10 years as non-capital losses (see 111(1)(a) and 111(8)"non-capital loss"E). Certain taxable capital gains of individuals are eligible for an offsetting deduction under 110.6 (the capital gains exemption).

The capital gains inclusion rate was ¾ from 1990 to Feb. 27, 2000; ⅔ from Feb. 28 to Oct. 17, 2000; and has been ½ since then. Complex transitional rules, reproduced here in the 20th-29th eds., provide the inclusion rate for 2000 when more than one fraction applies. For a history of Canadian capital gains taxation to 2000, see *Foisy*, [2001] 1 C.T.C. 2606 (TCC), paras. 16-23.

A corporation with taxable capital gains can generally pay out tax-free capital dividends. See Notes to 83(2).

For the exemption on sale of a principal residence, see 40(2)(b). For the exemption on sale of small business shares and qualified farm/fishing property, see 110.6(2)–(2.3).

38(a.1) provides that there is no tax on capital gains on publicly-traded securities donated to a charity (including foreign securities listed on a "designated stock exchange" — see 262 Notes). See Policy Forum, 51(2) *Canadian Tax Journal* 902-36 (2003). *38(a.2)* does the same for gifts of ecological property, and 39(1)(a)(i.1) effectively does the same for donations of cultural property to certain institutions. This calculation applies before going to s. 3, so the gain need not be netted against losses before being deemed nil, and losses can still be used. See also VIEWS docs 2008-0270551C6 (donation of interest in segregated fund trust); 2009-0312081R3 (donation of exchangeable shares), 2009-0330511R3 and 2011-0394671R3 (restructuring and donation of shares); 2016-0632621C6 [2016 CALU q.3] (designation of charity as beneficiary of segregated fund policy: 38(a.1) does not apply); 2019-0798491C6 [2019 STEP q.2] (whether 38(a.1) applies on donation by *alter ego* trust after death). No relief is available for donation of ecological land that is inventory: 2009-0330321C6. In *Staltari*, 2015 TCC 123, para. 40, S argued that 38(a.2) is not limited to capital property; the Court did not answer this point, but in the author's view it is wrong because s. 38 is part of the rules in 38-55 that apply only to capital property.

38(a.1) was especially useful before the 2011 Budget when donating flow-through shares (see Notes to 66(12.6)), which have deemed cost of nil (66.3(3)) and thus a large capital gain to be eliminated. 40(12) now triggers a capital gain on donating flow-through shares acquired under an agreement entered into after March 21, 2011, reducing the benefit of this arrangement. Flow-through shares "paired" with a donation are a "tax shelter" under 237.1(1), so one must file a T5004: *Income Tax Technical News* 41, VIEWS doc 2008-0289451C6 [2008 CTF q.10, conf. report p. 3:9-10]. Pre-2011 rulings approving such shelters: 2007-0232271R3, 2007-0242361R3, 2008-0269281R3, 2008-0281941R3, 2009-0316961R3, 2012-0466731R3. (38(a.3) prevents the deemed gain from being eliminated on partnership interests exchangeable for flow-through shares, but not on the shares themselves.) A donation of a *private* company's flow-through shares creates no tax credit, due to 66.3(3), 248(35) [248(37)(d) does not apply] and 248(31): 2012-0454451E5.

See also docs 2014-0532201R3, 2015-0619931R3 (ruling approving donation of publicly traded shares to foundation which sells them to another company in same group); 2016-0642621E5 (subsidiary of charity donates listed shares to charity: 38(a.1) takes priority over 69(4)); 2017-0683501E5 (donation of a "flow-through share class of property"); 2017-0698191E5 (38(a.1) applies to estate's donation carried back to deceased's return under 118.1(5)); Tehranchian, "Flow Through Share Donation", 12(4) *Taxes & Wealth Management* (Carswell) 6-8 (Dec. 2019) (notes that such packages are offered by Bertov, PearTree, Oberon and WCPD); Carr, "Flow-Through Shares in Structured Donation Transactions", XIV(1) *Resource Sector Taxation* (Federated Press) 20-34 (2020) (if liquidity provider agreeing to buy shares is a Reg. 6202.1(5)"specified person", flow-through share status is lost).

38(a.1)(iii) applies 38(a.1) to unlisted exchangeable shares, if the new publicly-traded shares received in exchange are donated within 30 days.

A side effect of 38(a.1), (a.2) and (a.4) is to increase, from 1/2 to 1, the portion of the gain added to a donating corporation's CDA that can be distributed to shareholders tax-free. See Notes to 89(1)"capital dividend account".

Timing: When determining the value of a 38(a.1) transfer, the transfer appears to take place when the donor has done everything required to effect it, even if the broker is slow to respond and the price changes before the charity receives the stocks. See Drache, "The Timing of a Gift", 8(11) *Canadian Not-for-Profit News* (Carswell) 84 (Nov. 2000) (referring to *D'Esterre* (1956), 15 Tax A.B.C. 356); "The Timing of a Gift of Shares", 16(11) *CNfPN* 87-88 (Nov. 2008) (citing *Walsh*, 2008 TCC 282). See also *Paxton*, 1996 CarswellNat 2400 (FCA), where a binding contract was held to have completed a sale once it was signed. *Contra*, see Malcolm Burrows' letter to the editor, 9(2) *CNfPN* 14-15 (Feb. 2001), noting that in practice the gift is considered made when received in the charity's brokerage account. CRA's view is generally that the gift is made when the charity receives it: *Registered Charities Newsletter* 12, but this may be wrong. A mailed gift is deemed received upon being mailed: 248(7). See also *Labis v. Labis*, 2018 QCCA 992, where instruction to a broker to transfer securities was valid in Quebec despite the transferor's death before the transfer was done.

38(a.3) applies the rule in 38(a.1) to unlisted partnership interests that are exchangeable for publicly traded securities, if the new securities are donated within 30 days. It ensures that only capital gains reflecting economic appreciation of the partnership interests are exempt, and not gains arising because of reductions to the ACB of partnership interests. In general, the taxable capital gain on the exchange is increased to half of any amount by which the cost of the exchanged units exceeds the ACB of those interests (determined without reference to distributions of partnership capital). The reduction is not added to ACB: see Notes to 53(1)(e).

Proposed 38(a.4), 38.3 and 38.4, a Conservative proposal that would have (starting 2017) eliminated the capital gain on private company shares and real estate to the extent the proceeds were donated to charity, was dropped per the Liberals' 2016 Budget.

38(a.1)(ii)(B) and (a.2)(ii)(B) amended by 2016 budget bill #2, for 2016 and later tax years, to change "graduated rate estate" to "estate". This allows donations by an estate after 36 months (when it is no longer a GRE) up to 60 months after death (see 118.1(5.1)).

38(a.1)(ii) and (a.2)(ii) amended by 2014 budget bill #2, for 2016 and later taxation years. Both previously read: "the disposition is deemed by section 70 to have occurred and the taxpayer is deemed by subsection 118.1(5) to have made a gift described in subparagraph (i) of the property".

38(a.1) earlier amended by 2008 budget bill #1 (for gifts made after Feb. 25, 2008), 2007 budget bill #2, 2006 budget bill #1, and 2001, 2000 and 1997 Budgets.

Definitions [s. 38]: "adjusted cost base" — 54, 248(1); "amount" — 248(1); "business investment loss" — 39(1)(c), 39(9), (10); "capital gain" — 39(1)(a), 248(1); "capital loss" — 39(1)(b), 248(1); "corporation" — 248(1), *Interpretation Act* 35(1); "designated stock exchange" — 248(1), 262; "disposition" — 248(1); "estate" — 104(1), 248(1); "mineral resource" — 248(1); "mutual fund corporation" — 131(8), 248(1); "mutual fund trust" — 132(6)–(7), 132.2(3)(n), 248(1); "partnership" — see 96(1) Notes; "prescribed" — 248(1); "prescribed debt obligation" — Reg. 6210; "private foundation" — 149.1(1), 248(1); "property" — 248(1); "qualified donee" — 149.1(1), 188.2(3)(a), 248(1); "related segregated fund trust" — 138.1(1)(a); "resident in Canada" — 94(3)(a), 250; "share" — 248(1); "taxation year" — 249; "taxpayer" — 248(1); "total ecological gifts" — 118.1(1).

Regulations: 6210 (prescribed debt obligations for 38(a.1); no prescribed interests in partnerships yet for 38(a.3).

I.T. Technical News: 41 (donation of flow-through shares).

Registered Charities Newsletters: 12 (valuing gifts of public securities); 28 (capital gains exemption on gifts of securities).

Income Tax Folios: S3-F2-C1: Capital Dividends [replaces IT-66R6]; S7-F1-C1: Split-receipting and deemed fair market value.

Forms [s. 38]: T1 Sched. 3: Capital gains (or losses); T3 Sched. 1A: Capital gains on gifts of certain capital property; T1170: Capital gains on gifts of certain capital property; T4037: Capital gains [guide].

38.1 Tax-deferred transaction — flow-through shares — If a taxpayer acquires a property (in this section referred to as the **"acquired property"**) that is included in a flow-through share class of property in the course of a transaction or series of transactions to which any of section 51, subsections 73(1), 85(1) and (2) and 85.1(1), sections 86 and 87 and subsections 88(1) and 98(3) apply

(a) if the transfer of the acquired property is part of a gifting arrangement (within the meaning assigned by section 237.1) or of a transaction or series of transactions to which subsection 98(3) applies, or the transferor is a person with whom the taxpayer was, at the time of the acquisition, not dealing at arm's length, there shall be added, at the time of the transfer, to the taxpayer's exemption threshold in respect of the flow-through share class of property, and deducted from the transferor's exemption threshold in respect of the flow-through share class of property, the amount determined by the formula

$$A \times B$$

where

A is the amount by which the transferor's exemption threshold in respect of the flow-through share class of property immediately before that time exceeds the capital gain, if any, of the transferor as a result of the transfer, and

B is the proportion that the fair market value of the acquired property immediately before the transfer is of the fair market value of all property of the transferor immediately before the transfer that is included in the flow-through share class of property; and

(b) if the transferor receives particular shares of the capital stock of the taxpayer as consideration for the acquired property and those particular shares are listed on a designated stock exchange or are shares of a mutual fund corporation, then for the purposes of this section and subsection 40(12)

(i) the particular shares are deemed to be flow-through shares of the transferor, and

(ii) there shall be added to the transferor's exemption threshold in respect of the flow-through share class of property that includes the particular shares the amount that is determined under paragraph (a) or that would be so determined if paragraph (a) applied to the taxpayer.

Related Provisions [s. 38.1]: 248(30)–(33) — Eligible amount of gift and advantage in respect of gift.

Notes: 38.1 added by 2011 budget bill #2, effective March 22, 2011. It ties in with 40(12), which prevents the tax-free capital gain on donation of publicly-traded shares from applying to the capital gain created by flow-through shares having a low or nil cost base (see Notes to 66(12.66) and s. 38). 38.1 supports the policy of 40(12) by preserving the status of the shares through a s. 85 or other rollover under which the low cost base is maintained.

For discussion see VIEWS doc 2017-0683501E5.

Former proposed 38.1 from what became the 2002-2013 technical bill is now 38.2.

Definitions [s. 38.1]: "acquired property" — 38.1; "amount" — 248(1); "arm's length" — 251(1); "capital gain" — 39(1)(a), 248(1); "designated stock exchange" — 248(1), 262; "exemption threshold" — 54; "fair market value" — see 69(1) Notes; "flow-through share" — 66(15), 248(1); "flow-through share class of property" — 54; "mutual fund corporation" — 131(8), 248(1); "person", "property" — 248(1); "series of transactions" — 248(10); "share", "taxpayer" — 248(1).

38.2 Allocation of gain re certain gifts — If a taxpayer is entitled to an amount of an advantage in respect of a gift of property described in paragraph 38(a.1) or (a.2),

(a) those paragraphs apply only to that proportion of the taxpayer's capital gain in respect of the gift that the eligible amount of the gift is of the taxpayer's proceeds of disposition in respect of the gift; and

(b) paragraph 38(a) applies to the extent that the taxpayer's capital gain in respect of the gift exceeds the amount of the capital gain to which paragraph 38(a.1) or (a.2) applies.

Notes: 38.2 added by 2002-2013 technical bill (Part 5 — technical), for gifts made after Dec. 20, 2002. This was 38.1 in the July16/10 (and earlier) draft, but became 38.2 due to enactment of another 38.1.

Proposed **38.3, 38.4**, with 38(a.4), were a 2015 Conservative Budget proposal to exempt gains on private company shares and real estate donated to charity. This was dropped by the Liberals after they were elected in 2015.

Definitions [s. 38.2]: "advantage" — 248(32); "amount" — 248(1); "capital gain" — 39(1)(a), 248(1); "eligible amount" — 248(31), (41); "proceeds of disposition" — 54; "property", "taxpayer" — 248(1).

39. (1) Meaning of capital gain and capital loss [and business investment loss] — For the purposes of this Act,

(a) a taxpayer's **capital gain** for a taxation year from the disposition of any property is the taxpayer's gain for the year determined under this Subdivision (to the extent of the amount thereof that would not, if section 3 were read without reference to the expression "other than a taxable capital gain from the disposition of a property" in paragraph 3(a) and without reference to paragraph 3(b), be included in computing the taxpayer's income for the year or any other taxation year) from the disposition of any property of the taxpayer other than

(i) [Repealed]

(i.1) an object that the Canadian Cultural Property Export Review Board has determined meets the criterion set out in paragraph 29(3)(b) of the *Cultural Property Export and Import Act* if

(A) the disposition is to an institution or a public authority in Canada that was, at the time of the disposition, designated under subsection 32(2) of that Act either generally or for a specified purpose related to that object, or

(B) the disposition is deemed by section 70 to have occurred and the object is the subject of a gift to which subsection 118.1(5.1) applies and that is made by the taxpayer's estate to an institution that would be described in clause (A) if the disposition were made at the time the estate makes the gift,

(ii) a Canadian resource property,

(ii.1) a foreign resource property,

(ii.2) a property if the disposition is a disposition to which subsection 142.4(4) or (5) or 142.5(1) applies,

(iii) an insurance policy, including a life insurance policy, except for that part of a life insurance policy in respect of which a policyholder is deemed by paragraph 138.1(1)(e) to have an interest in a related segregated fund trust,

(iv) a timber resource property, or

(v) an interest of a beneficiary under a qualifying environmental trust;

(b) a taxpayer's **capital loss** for a taxation year from the disposition of any property is the taxpayer's loss for the year determined under this Subdivision (to the extent of the amount thereof that would not, if section 3 were read in the manner described in paragraph (a) of this subsection and without reference to the expression "or the taxpayer's allowable business investment loss for the year" in paragraph 3(d), be deductible in computing the taxpayer's income for the year or any other taxation year) from the disposition of any property of the taxpayer other than

(i) depreciable property, or

(ii) property described in any of subparagraphs 39(1)(a)(ii) to (iii) and (v); and

(c) a taxpayer's **business investment loss** for a taxation year from the disposition of any property is the amount, if any, by which the taxpayer's capital loss for the year from a disposition after 1977

(i) to which subsection 50(1) applies, or

(ii) to a person with whom the taxpayer was dealing at arm's length

of any property that is

(iii) a share of the capital stock of a small business corporation, or

(iv) a debt owing to the taxpayer by a Canadian-controlled private corporation (other than, where the taxpayer is a corporation, a debt owing to it by a corporation with which it does not deal at arm's length) that is

(A) a small business corporation,

(B) a bankrupt that was a small business corporation at the time it last became a bankrupt, or

(C) a corporation referred to in section 6 of the *Winding-up and Restructuring Act* that was insolvent (within the meaning of that Act) and was a small business corporation at the time a winding-up order under that Act was made in respect of the corporation,

exceeds the total of

(v) in the case of a share referred to in subparagraph (iii), the amount, if any, of the increase after 1977 by virtue of the application of subsection 85(4) in the adjusted cost base to the taxpayer of the share or of any share (in this subparagraph referred to as a "replaced share") for which the share or a replaced share was substituted or exchanged,

(vi) in the case of a share referred to in subparagraph (iii) that was issued before 1972 or a share (in this subparagraph and subparagraph (vii) referred to as a "substituted share") that was substituted or exchanged for such a share or for a substituted share, the total of all amounts each of which is an amount received after 1971 and before or on the disposition of the share or an amount receivable at the time of such a disposition by

(A) the taxpayer,

(B) where the taxpayer is an individual, the taxpayer's spouse or common-law partner, or

(C) a trust of which the taxpayer or the taxpayer's spouse or common-law partner was a beneficiary

as a taxable dividend on the share or on any other share in respect of which it is a substituted share, except that this subparagraph shall not apply in respect of a share or substituted share that was acquired after 1971 from a person with whom the taxpayer was dealing at arm's length,

(vii) in the case of a share to which subparagraph (vi) applies and where the taxpayer is a trust for which a day is to be, or

has been, determined under paragraph 104(4)(a), or (a.4) by reference to a death or later death, as the case may be, the total of all amounts each of which is an amount received after 1971 or receivable at the time of the disposition, as a taxable dividend on the share or on any other share in respect of which it is a substituted share, by an individual whose death is that death or later death, as the case may be, or a spouse or common-law partner of the individual, and

(viii) the amount determined in respect of the taxpayer under subsection (9) or (10), as the case may be.

Related Provisions: 12(1)(z.1) — Disposition of interest in qualifying environmental trust; 12(1)(z.7) — Derivative forward agreement — full income inclusion; 39(1.1), (2) — Capital gains and losses in respect of foreign currencies; 39(3) — Gain — purchase of bonds by issuer; 39(9), (10) — Deduction from BIL where capital gains exemption claimed; 39(12) — Amount paid under guarantee deemed to be business investment loss; 40(10), (11) — Calculation of gain or loss on foreign currency debt after change of control; 40 — Calculation of gain or loss; 44.1(2) — Capital gain on disposition of small business investment that is replaced by another; 50(1) — Conditions for business investment loss where shares or debt still owned; 53(1)(e)(i)(A.1) — Adjustment to ACB for cultural property under 39(1)(a)(i.1); 55(2) — Deemed capital gain on certain dividends; 80.03(2), (4) — Deemed capital gain on disposition of property following debt forgiveness; 93(2)–(2.31) — Loss limitations on disposition of foreign affiliate shares; 100(4), (5) — Capital loss on disposition of partnership interest; 110.6 — Capital gains exemption; 112(3)–(4.22) — Capital loss on shares reduced by certain dividends previously paid; 118.1(7.1)(a) — Donation of cultural property; 136 — Co-operative can be private corporation for 39(1)(c); 139.1(4)(a) — Capital gain and loss on ownership rights resulting from demutualization of insurer deemed nil; 142.2 — Financial institutions — mark-to-market property; 144(4) — Deemed capital gain from employees profit sharing plan; 152(4)(b.3) — Extended reassessment period if disposition of real property not reported; 248(1)"capital gain", "capital loss" — Definitions in 39(1) definitions apply to entire Act; 248(37)(c) — Rule limiting value of donated property does not apply where 39(1)(a)(i.1) applies; Canada-U.S. Tax Treaty:Art. XIII — Gains.

Notes: In general, a capital gain is a gain on the sale of "capital property" as defined in 54. See Notes to that definition for the distinction between a capital gain and an income gain. See also Notes to s. 38 re application of taxable capital gains, allowable capital losses and allowable business investment losses. A capital gain on foreign property must be included, but a foreign tax credit may be available under 126(1): VIEWS doc 2008-0301441I7. (See 39(2) Notes for foreign exchange gains and losses.)

For depreciable property, the capital gain is only the amount above original cost; see Notes to 13(1).

In *Antle*, 2010 FCA 280 (leave to appeal denied 2011 CarswellNat 1491 (SCC); motion for reconsideration dismissed 2012 CarswellNat 183), an attempted "capital property step-up" using a Barbados spousal trust failed because the trust was not validly formed and was a sham (the TCC had also applied GAAR).

If a taxpayer sells capital property, then in a later year receives additional proceeds of disposition, this may be a capital gain: VIEWS doc 2008-0288501M4 (but see doc 2002-0135637I7). See also 12(1)(g), which may deem a later receipt to be income.

39(1)(a)(i.1) eliminates the capital gain on cultural property donated to a qualifying institution (see list at tinyurl.com/cult-desig). Although certification can be done *after* the donation (118.1(11), VIEWS doc 2004-0101211E5), 39(1)(a)(i.1) applies only if the *institution* has been designated under the *Cultural Property Export and Import Act* (CPEIA) *before* the donation: 2003-0004375; *Williamson*, 2005 FC 954. See also Notes to 118.1(10).

CPEIA ss. 29(3), 11(1) and 32(2) provide:

29(3) Determination of the Review Board — In reviewing an application for an export permit, the Review Board shall determine whether the object in respect of which the application was made

(a) is included in the Control List;

(b) is of outstanding significance for one or more of the reasons set out in paragraph 11(1)(a); and

(c) meets the degree of national importance referred to in paragraph 11(1)(b).

11(1) Where object included in Control List — Where an expert examiner determines that an object that is the subject of an application for an export permit that has been referred to him is included in the Control List, the expert examiner shall forthwith further determine

(a) whether that object is of outstanding significance by reason of its close association with Canadian history or national life, its aesthetic qualities, or its value in the study of the arts or sciences; and

(b) whether the object is of such a degree of national importance that its loss to Canada would significantly diminish the national heritage.

32(2) Designated authorities and institutions — For the purposes of subparagraph 39(1)(a)(i.1), paragraph 110.1(1)(c), the definition "total cultural gifts" in subsection 118.1(1), subsection 118.1(10) and section 207.3 of the *Income Tax*

Act, the Minister may designate any institution or public authority indefinitely or for a period of time, and generally or for a specified purpose.

The 2019 amendment to 39(1)(a)(i.1) removed the requirement to comply with CPEIA 29(3)(c), that an object be of "national importance" to be cultural property. This preserved the tax-free gain after *Heffel Gallery*, 2018 FC 605 (later overturned anyway at 2019 FCA 82), which had held that foreign works did not have "national importance".

A corporation's donation of cultural property does not increase its capital dividend account, as does a 38(a.1) donation of listed securities, because 39(1)(a)(i.1) eliminates the gain and 89(1)"capital dividend account"(a)(i)(A) is based on the capital gain.

39(1)(a)(ii) excludes a mining claim that is "Canadian resource property"; its sale reduces cumulative CDE (66.2(5)"cumulative Canadian development expense"F) and if that goes negative, is taxable under 59(3.2)(c) and 66.2(1): VIEWS doc 2012-0452841E5.

39(1)(a)(iii) generally excludes a gain on an insurance policy. If it is a *life* insurance policy, 148(1) applies, but otherwise (e.g. critical illness insurance) there is no capital gain: VIEWS doc 2015-0588941C6 [2015 APFF q.1].

39(1)(b) requires the taxpayer to have owned the property, so where a financial advisor left his last employment and his clients could not follow him to a new firm, he did not have a capital loss on the value of the client list: *Martin*, 2015 FCA 204 (leave to appeal denied 2016 CarswellNat 1182 (SCC)). If purchaser P defaults on buying a rental property and pays damages, P has no capital loss because there is no property that P owned and disposed of: VIEWS doc 2016-0652851C6 [2016 APFF q.3].

39(1)(b)(i) denies a capital loss on depreciable property because a terminal loss is available under 20(16) instead, once all the property in the class has been disposed of.

39(1)(c) creates a business investment loss (**BIL**), half of which is fully deductible against any income source as an allowable business investment loss (**ABIL**): see Notes to 38. A corporation must have been a small business corporation at any time in the past 12 months for the loss on its shares or debt to qualify as a BIL: see the closing words of 248(1)"small business corporation". This may require recognizing a loss quickly after the business fails, or the ABIL may be lost. See also Income Tax Folio S4-F8-C1, IT-159R3 and VIEWS docs 2010-0379201E5, 2010-0382361E5, 2011-0426871I7, 2012-0441591E5.

Note that no loss on debt is allowed if 40(2)(g)(ii) applies (no income purpose for the loan, or non-arm's-length disposition). See Notes to 40(2)(g).

A BIL can be triggered under 50(1), by election, even where the shares or debt are still owned, if the debt has been written off or the shares are of a corporation that is bankrupt, under a winding-up process or that is inactive, expected to be dissolved, insolvent and worthless. A non-arm's length relationship with the company does not disentitle the taxpayer to the BIL: *Sunatori*, 2010 TCC 346, para. 30 (aff'd 2011 FCA 254).

A payment to an arm's-length creditor under a guarantee can create a BIL: see 39(12). Even if 39(12) is not satisfied, the TCC suggested in *Dietrich*, 2005 TCC 326, that payment under a guarantee that otherwise meets the conditions of 39(1) will qualify. This may be difficult to apply in practice: Craven, "Subsection 39(12) not a prerequisite for guarantors claiming ABILs", 1753 *Tax Topics* (CCH) 4-6 (Oct. 27, 2005); but see *Abrametz* in 39(12) Notes.

Many ABIL claims are reviewed by CRA (though not all: CRA Roundtable, 2012 Ontario Tax Conference (ctf.ca), Q11) and many are disallowed. See *Income Tax Audit Manual* §29.3. In *Ollenberger*, 2013 FCA 74 (rev ersing the TCC), an ABIL was allowed to a company that bought distressed oil & gas properties, as "active business" need not actually be active.

Cases allowing ABILs: *Brand*, 2005 TCC 494 (loan through son was made "in trust" to be loaned on to corp); *Litowitz*, 2005 TCC 557 (debt had become bad despite recovery 5 years later); *Chandan*, 2005 TCC 685 (evidence accepted despite "abysmal" record-keeping); *Netolitzky*, 2006 TCC 172 (taxpayer reasonably concluded loans had gone bad); *Tardif*, 2005 TCC 10 (50(1) applied, debt was deemed disposed of at end of 2000, so 50% rate applied to ABIL rather than higher rate); *Fidyk*, 2006 TCC 418 (Court agreed taxpayer advanced some funds to corps); *Jodoin*, 2006 TCC 555 (ABIL allowed for 2004 where 50(1) election could have been made in 2003 but was made in 2004); *Spillman*, 2006 TCC 519 (taxpayer "acquired" debt by assuming guarantee); *Kyriazakos*, 2007 TCC 66 (50(1) satisfied); *Daniels*, 2007 TCC 179 (corporate debenture acquired from brother to repay loan); *Boily*, 2008 TCC 92 (debt really existed); *Lesnick*, 2008 TCC 522 (Court agreed taxpayer advanced funds); *Lirette*, 2008 TCC 593 (complex ABIL calculations based on amounts invested); *Langille*, 2009 TCC 139 (corp's trading in liquidated goods was not specified investment business); *Giasson*, 2009 TCC 504 (losses on guarantees); *Scott*, 2010 TCC 401 (loss on loan to son's corp); *MacCallum*, 2011 TCC 316 (guarantee was made to earn income, so 40(2)(g)(ii) did not apply); *Dhaliwal*, 2012 TCC 84 (ABIL even though corp did not file its tax return); *Gingras*, 2016 TCC 250 (loan to corp was a "novation" of loan to daughter to open restaurant); *Hébert*, 2018 TCC 48 (radio repair corp's only activity for years was trying to sell parts after business dried up); *Dépatie*, 2019 TCC 123 (D's loan to her mother's corp was to allow D to share in corp's profits).

Cases denying ABILs: *Venneri*, 2006 FCA 165 (holding land for speculation was not "active business", so corp was not small business corporation (SBC)); *Singh*, 2006 FCA 230 (inadequate documentation); *Hopmeyer*, 2007 FCA 34 (corp was still carrying on business during taxation year); *Sunatori*, 2011 FCA 254 (loan cannot go bad on same day it is made); *Covely*, 2014 FCA 281 (debts not shown to have become bad in year claimed; also loans to corp were at zero interest and one taxpayer was not a shareholder]); *Barnwell*, 2016 FCA 150 (loans were made to B, not his corp); *DiCosmo*, 2017 FCA 60 (insufficient evidence); *Blais*, 2020 FCA 38 (sole proprietorship was not SBC); *Keybrand Foods*, 2020 FCA 201 (KF and Vco did not deal at arm's length, so cost of worthless Vco shares deemed nil when acquired); *Hoffman*, 2009 FC 832 (documentation lacking); *Lemieux*, 2006 TCC 298 (insufficient evidence); *MacKay*, 2006 TCC 530 (M lending money to common-law spouse to invest in corp where M had no investment in it); *Soja*, 2007 TCC 61 (50(1) election not made in return); *Glynn*, 2007 TCC 83 (corp inactive except for rentals, so carried on specified investment business); *Wilkins*, 2007 TCC 187 (50(1) did not apply); *Gilbert*, 2009 TCC 102 (debt not proven and bad debt recognition was arbitrary); *Cilevitz*, 2009 TCC 214 (advances to corp not proven to have created debt, and no proof that corp was SBC); *Mattu*, 2009 TCC 605 (FCA appeal discontinued A-516-09) (evidence inadequate); *Charran*, 2010 TCC 201 (loans had likely been made to C's spouse rather than to corp); *Polowick*, 2010 TCC 304 (owner's advance was loan, not equity, and conditions for debt ABIL not met); *Demers*, 2010 TCC 402 (D's RRSP was defrauded, not D); *Bourget*, 2010 TCC 642 (director's payment to CRA of corp's source-deduction liability was not loan to corp); *Lobo*, 2011 TCC 132 (FCA appeal discontinued A-153-11) (evidence inadequate); *Grist*, 2011 TCC 304 (insufficient evidence that corp was SBC); *Allisen*, 2011 TCC 508 (investment was in limited partnership); *Audet*, 2012 TCC 162 (A was not shareholder of corp to which he provided guarantee, though Court did not consider 39(12)); *McDowell*, 2012 TCC 244 (corp ceased business more than 12 months before loan written off); *Stinson*, 2013 TCC 22 (insufficient documentation); *Nicholls*, 2013 TCC 166 (loss on trust's promissory note); *Affordable Sign*, 2014 TCC 18 (insufficient evidence); *St-Hilaire*, 2014 TCC 336 (taxpayer had waived right to corp's debt as part of its bankruptcy proposal, so he did not own the debt at year-end); *Gougeon PGL Consultant*, 2015 TCC 266 (insufficient evidence); *Delisle*, 2015 TCC 281 (corp's bankruptcy proposal was accepted in 2006 so debt went bad then; ABIL disallowed for 2007); *D'Amour*, 2016 TCC 18 (debt not disposed of until corp dissolved; business had ceased years earlier so corp was not SBC, and 40(2)(g) denied loss because loan was no-interest); *Huxham Inc.*, 2016 TCC 36 (debt not established to exist); *Di Cienzo*, 2016 TCC 187 (FCA appeal dismissed for delay A-368-16) (unclear whether shareholder loan cancelled when corp was sold); *Meilleur*, 2016 TCC 287, para. 6 (no evidence loan was to SBC); *Grubner*, 2018 TCC 39, para. 18 (payments of corp's unremitted source deductions and GST/HST, to avoid director liability, did not create loan to corp [*quaere* whether this is right: if the director has a right to be reimbursed by the corp, that is a debt]); *Nabil Warda Inc.*, 2019 TCC 95 (no expectation of income when corp made advances to Holdco, so 40(2)(g)(ii) applied); *Moose Factory*, 2019 TCC 156 (FCA appeal discontinued A-297-19) (security agreement did not create debt owing to MF by corp that went bankrupt).

A loan to a holding company that lent money to a company to profit from buying and selling a golf course was an ABIL, not fully deductible to the lenders: *Laramee (Casey)*, 2008 FCA 299.

A corporation's ABIL appears to reduce its CDA, due to 89(1)"capital dividend account"(a)(ii) as it interacts with 39(1)(b) and 3(b)-(d).

For a very detailed discussion of the relevant factors, and flowchart, see Donnelly & Young, "Substantiating an ABIL Deduction", 58(2) *Canadian Tax Journal* 229-76 (2010). See also Posthumus, "An Update on Claiming ABILs", 2008 Prairie Provinces Tax Conference (ctf.ca), 12:1-24; Weder & MacDonald, "Allowable Business Investment Losses", 2009 B.C. Tax Conf. 7:1-21; Schusheim & Hurst, "Allowable Business Investment Losses", 2009 Ontario Tax Conf. 6:1-25; Kakkar & Yan, "Practical Considerations in Claiming an ABIL", 2012 Ontario Tax Conf. 5:1-28.

When reading 39(1)(c)(iv)(C), see Notes to 50(1) for s. 6 of the *Winding-up and Restructuring Act*.

39(1)(a)(i.1) opening words amended by 2019 budget bill #1, effective March 19, 2019, to change "criteria set out in paragraphs 29(3)(b) and (c)" to "criterion set out in paragraph 29(3)(b)".

39(1)(c)(iv)(B) amended by 2017 budget bill #2, for bankruptcies after April 26, 1995, to delete "(within the meaning assigned by subsection 128(3))" after the first "a bankrupt". ("Bankrupt" is now defined in 248(1).)

39(1)(a)(i) ["(i) eligible capital property"] repealed, and (b)(ii) amended to delete reference to it, by 2016 budget bill #2, effective 2017, as part of changing ECP rules to CCA Class 14.1 (see Notes to 20(1)(b)).

39(1)(a)(i.1)(B) amended by 2016 budget bill #2, for 2016 and later taxation years, to change "graduated rate estate" to "estate". This allows donations by an estate after 36 months (when it is no longer a GRE) up to 60 months after death (see 118.1(5.1)).

39(1)(a)(i.l) and (c)(vii) amended by 2014 budget bill #2 (for 2016 and later tax years). 39(1) earlier amended by 2014 budget bill #2 (for 2014 and 2015 tax years), 2008 budget bill #2, 1994 Budget, 1994 and 1991 technical bills.

Income Tax Folios: S3-F4-C1: General discussion of CCA [replaces IT-220R2]; S4-F8-C1: Business investment losses [replaces IT-484R2].

Interpretation Bulletins: IT-123R5: Transactions involving eligible capital property; IT-125R4: Dispositions of resource properties; IT-159R3: Capital debts established to be bad debts; IT-297R2: Gifts in kind to charity and others; IT-346R: Commodity futures and certain commodities; IT-359R2: Premiums and other amounts re leases; IT-407R4: Dispositions of cultural property to designated Canadian institutions; IT-426R: Shares sold subject to an earnout agreement; IT-444R: Corporations — involuntary dissolutions; IT-481: Timber resource property and timber limits.

I.T. Technical News: 16 (*Continental Bank* case); 34 (creation of capital losses — applying GAAR).

CRA Audit Manual: 29.2.0: Capital losses; 29.3.0: Business investment losses.

Advance Tax Rulings: ATR-15: Employee stock option plan; ATR-28: Redemption of capital stock of family farm corporation.

Forms: T1 Sched. 3: Capital gains (or losses); T2 Sched. 6: Summary of dispositions of capital property; T3 Sched. 1: Dispositions of capital property; T1161: List of properties by an emigrant of Canada; T4037: Capital gains [guide].

(1.1) Foreign currency dispositions by an individual

— If, because of any fluctuation after 1971 in the value of one or more currencies other than Canadian currency relative to Canadian currency, an individual (other than a trust) has made one or more particular gains or sustained one or more particular losses in a taxation year from dispositions of currency other than Canadian currency and the particular gains or losses would, in the absence of this subsection, be capital gains or losses described under subsection (1)

(a) subsection (1) does not apply to any of the particular gains or losses;

(b) the amount determined by the following formula is deemed to be a capital gain of the individual for the year from the disposition of currency other than Canadian currency:

$$A - (B + C)$$

where

A is the total of all the particular gains made by the individual in the year,

B is the total of all the particular losses sustained by the individual in the year, and

C is $200; and

(c) the amount determined by the following formula is deemed to be a capital loss of the individual for the year from the disposition of currency other than Canadian currency:

$$D - (E + F)$$

where

D is the total of all the particular losses sustained by the individual in the year,

E is the total of all the particular gains made by the individual in the year, and

F is $200.

Related Provisions: 39(2) — Capital gains and losses from foreign currency debt; 257 — Formula amounts cannot calculate to less than zero.

Notes: CRA says 39(1.1) does not apply to foreign currency held in an account at a financial institution: doc 2017-0712621C6 [2017 APFF q.8] (this may not be correct in the author's view). See also Notes to 39(2).

39(1.1) added (some of it was formerly in 39(2)) by 2002-2013 technical bill, for gains and losses in tax years that begin after Aug. 19, 2011 (earlier for certain gains/losses of a foreign affiliate). (The $200 amount has not increased for inflation since its introduction in 1972.)

Income Tax Folios: S5-F2-C1: Foreign tax credit [replaces IT-270R3, IT-395R2, IT-520].

(2) Foreign exchange capital gains and losses

— If, because of any fluctuation after 1971 in the value of a currency other than Canadian currency relative to Canadian currency, a taxpayer has made a gain or sustained a loss in a taxation year (other than a gain or loss that would, in the absence of this subsection, be a capital gain or capital loss to which subsection (1) or (1.1) applies, or a gain or loss in respect of a transaction or event in respect of shares of the capital stock of the taxpayer)

(a) the amount of the gain (to the extent of the amount of that gain that would not, if section 3 were read in the manner described in paragraph (1)(a), be included in computing the taxpayer's income for the year or any other taxation year), if any, is deemed to be a capital gain of the taxpayer for the year from the disposition of currency other than Canadian currency; and

(b) the amount of the loss (to the extent of the amount of that loss that would not, if section 3 were read in the manner described in paragraph (1)(a), be deductible in computing the taxpayer's income for the year or any other taxation year), if any, is deemed to be a capital loss of the taxpayer for the year from the disposition of currency other than Canadian currency.

Related Provisions: 20.3(2)(b) — Foreign exchange (FX) gain on weak currency loan deemed to be income; 39(1.1) — Foreign currency dispositions by an individual; 39(2.01)–(2.03) — Deemed gain where debt obligation is parked; 39(2.1)–(2.3) — Upstream loans — transitional set-off of foreign currency gain/loss on repayment of loan; 80.01(11) — FX fluctuation ignored for purposes of debt parking and statute-barred debt rules; 93(2.01)(b)(ii)(A)(I)1, (2.11)(b)(ii)(A)(I), (2.21)(b)(ii)(A)(I)1, (2.31)(b)(ii)(A)(I) — Loss limitation on disposition of foreign affiliate shares; 95(2)(f.11)(i)(B) — Application of 39(2) to income of foreign affiliate; 95(2)(f.15) — Application to foreign affiliate for FAPI; 95(2)(g)–(g.02), 95(2)(i) — Gain or loss of foreign affiliate on FX fluctuation; 111(12) — FX gains and losses after change in control; 142.3(1)(a), (b) — FX gain or loss by financial institution on specified debt obligation; 142.4(1)"tax basis"(f), (o) — Disposition of specified debt obligation by financial institution; 144(4) — Deemed capital loss from employees profit sharing plan; 248(1)"amortized cost"(c.1), (f.1) — Effect on amortized cost of loan or lending asset; 261(2) — Canadian currency used to determine income; 261(5)(e) — Effect of using functional currency reporting.

Notes: Foreign exchange **(FX)** gains/losses are discussed here whether taxable under 39(1) or (2).

39(2) amended by 2002-2013 technical bill, for tax years that end after Aug. 20, 2011 (earlier in some cases). It previously applied to *any* capital gain/loss resulting from FX, and deemed the net of all such gains/losses to be from disposition of *currency* (so when it applied to a loss on shares in a tower structure, 112(3.1) did not apply to deny the loss since the disposition was deemed not to be of shares, and GAAR did not apply as there was no "tax benefit": *Bank of Montreal*, 2020 FCA 82) [Yau, "Bank of Montreal", XXIV(2) *International Tax Planning* (Federated Press) 10-16 (2020)]. It also had a $200 *de minimis* exclusion for individuals; this was moved to 39(1.1).

New 39(2) *excludes* gains/losses caught by 39(1) and (1.1) (including all capital property dispositions), so it applies only to debt obligations denominated in foreign currency. It excludes FX gains/losses by a corp on its own stock (this overrules *MacMillan Bloedel*, [1999] 3 C.T.C. 652 (FCA)). It no longer combines FX gains/losses into one net amount; instead there is a separate one from each foreign currency disposition. (This facilitates applying the 95(2)(f.1) "carve-out" rule: Finance Technical Notes.) On the 2013 amendments see Guimont, "Denial of Capital Losses", 3(2) *Canadian Tax Focus* (ctf.ca) 4-5 (May 2013); Snider, "Foreign Exchange Revisited", 2149 *Tax Topics* (CCH) 1-4 (May 16, 2013); Keey, "Foreign Exchange Gains and Losses", General Corporate Tax newsletter (*Taxnet Pro* Corporate Tax Centre), Oct. 2013, pp. 1-6.

To calculate FX gains/losses (261(1)"relevant spot rate"), see rates at (e.g.) bankofcanada.ca or xe.com. Certain corps can elect to report in their "functional currency": 261(5). Absent such election, 261(2) says C$ is used to determine "Canadian tax results" and each amount relevant in that determination.

20(1)(f) cannot be used to deduct FX losses on debt redemption: *Imperial Oil (Inco)*, 2006 SCC 46 (see 20(1)(f) Notes). CRA's view is that the underlying transaction (see 54"capital property" Notes) determines whether FX gains/losses are income or capital: IT-95R, docs 2008-029708117, 2008-030465117; 2016-064963117 (FX gain on income tax refund is capital gain); *Ethicon Sutures*, [1985] 2 C.T.C. 6 (FCTD). In *CCLI*, 2007 FCA 185, FX losses of a financial leasing corp were held to be on capital account.

Where capital property is bought and sold in foreign currency, the gain or loss is calculated by converting the cost to C$ on the purchase date and converting the proceeds on the sale date: *Gaynor*, [1991] 1 C.T.C. 470 (FCA); VIEWS docs 2014-0529961M4, 2014-0538631C6 [2014 APFF q.9]. If only one asset is sold in the year, the rate on the sale date rather than the annual average rate should be used: May 2011 ICAA roundtable (tinyurl.com/cra-abtax), q. 5. On a stock market sale, the proceeds are converted on the settlement date, not the sale date, in CRA's view, and the noon Bank of Canada exchange rate should be used per 261(2)(b) and 261(1)"relevant spot rate": 2015-0588981C6 [2015 APFF q.5]. For non-capital property (inventory) or a formula in the ITA, the entire calculation should be applied and the final profit or loss converted to C$: *Imperial Oil (Inco)*, 2006 SCC 46, paras. 37, 52, 60. See Chasmar, "Foreign Exchange Gains and Losses", 2006 Cdn Tax Foundation conference report, 12:1-23; Slade, "Hedging Foreign Exchange Exposure of Balance Sheet Items", XVII(1) *Corporate Finance* (Federated Press) 1941-43 (2011); White, "Recent Income Tax Developments Relevant to the Mutual Fund Industry", 2011 conference report at 39:2-17. (Note these articles predate the 2013 amendments discussed above.)

Since 2017, hedges generally cannot defer income past a year-end: see the straddle-transaction rules in 18(17)-(23) (these rules do not apply to capital property: 18(18)(c)). Hedge accounting cannot be used to offset FX income gains with capital losses: *Saskferco Products*, 2008 FCA 297. If a derivative (forward contract, or cross-currency swap) is used to hedge a capital investment, gain/loss on the derivative is on capital account: *MacDonald*, 2020 SCC 6; *George Weston Ltd.*, 2015 TCC 42, para. 98. This is consistent with pre-*MacDonald* CRA policy: docs 2010-036761117, 2015-0577691C6 [IFA 2015 q.1], 2017-0705181C6 [2017 APFF q.16]. [Earlier docs: 2006-0215491C6, 2009-034592117, 2009-034896117, 2010-035587117, 2012-046556117, 2013-0481691E5.] See also 9(1) Notes at "Hedges"; and note that 40(2)(g) (superficial loss) can apply to a capital loss.

CRA takes the position [this would seem to survive the 2013 amendments] that where money is borrowed in foreign currency and repaid in that currency, 39(2) applies to the FX fluctuation as against the C$. "The government would be concerned if the tax community held the view that this permits capital losses to be recognized, but does not require the reporting of capital gains" (Cdn Tax Foundation conference, Nov. 28, 2006, slides distributed). CRA stated at the 2007 conference (*Income Tax Technical News* 38; conference report at 4:11-12) that the SCC's comments in *Imperial Oil*, that a mere repayment of principal in the same currency creates no profit or loss, are *obiter*, not binding. See also doc 2009-0327061C6; and 39(2.01)-(2.03), addressing debt parking to avoid foreign exchange gains.

In *Agnico-Eagle Mines*, 2016 FCA 130, AE issued US$ convertible debentures when the C$ was low and accepted them for conversion to shares when the C$ was high. The FCA ruled that the FX conversion date could not be the debenture issue date because at the time it was not known whether the conversion right would be exercised. Applying s. 261, the value of the rights the debenture holders gave up on conversion was based on the value of the shares issued at that time. See doc 2016-0670201C6 [2016 CTF q.3] (this method would not allow issuer to claim a loss, and 143.3(3) must be considered); Rabinovitch & Haikal, "Converting Foreign-Denominated Debentures into Common Shares", *International Tax Newsletter* (Taxnet Pro), June 2016, pp. 7-10; Sandler & Korkh, "No Forex Gain on US-Dollar Debenture Conversion", 24(7) *Canadian Tax Highlights* (ctf.ca) 1-2 (July 2016); Carr & McIsaac, "Musings on Agnico-Eagle and Univar", 66(1) *Canadian Tax Journal* 215-49 (2018).

The interest component in a currency forward agreement may be taxed by 12(1)(z.7); see 248(1)"derivative forward agreement".

See also *Ludmer*, 2018 QCCS 3381, paras. 522-531; aff'd 2020 QCCA 697, para. 88 (conversion to C$ required before calculating Reg. 7000 deemed annual interest) (leave to appeal denied 2021 CarswellQue 2160 (SCC)).

For CRA interpretation on 39(2) *[some pre-2013 docs may no longer apply, or may apply now under 39(1)]*, see 2005-0156921R3 (assumption of one US$ debt to extinguish another issued by same subsidiary), 2005-0165041R3 (cross-currency swap and termination payment); 2006-0176081R3 (US cash contributed to corp and used to acquire target company); 2006-0190971E5 and 2006-0204361E5 (individual's transactions on income account — method in IT-95R para. 8); 2007-021993I7 (US$ debt owing by partnership to partners); 2007-0234001E5 and 2008-0284291C6 (conversion of proceeds of interest bearing account at maturity); 2007-023469117 (impact of FX losses on capital dividend account); 2007-023779117 (conversion of one foreign currency to another, and IT-95R para. 13); 2007-0239291R3 (assumption of debt for assets); 2007-0242441C6 (investor's realized exchange gains or losses); 2007-0243711C6 (using foreign currency to acquire US company); 2007-0255401R3 (swap termination); 2008-0267831E5 (settlement of debt on amalgamation of debtor and creditor); 2008-0269971R3 (same); 2008-028011117 and 2017-0705201C6 [2017 APFF q.10] (capital loss on foreign currency is not denied by 40(3.3)-(3.4) or 40(2)(g)(i) [Barnicke & Huynh, "Cash Not Property for Stop-Loss Rules", 17(2) *Canadian Tax Highlights* [CTH] (ctf.ca) 5-6 (Feb. 2009)]); 2008-0284271C6 (FX gain/loss solely attributable to currency fluctuations); 2008-0295641E5 (accrued FX gain in a mortgage held on death); 2008-030251117 (Liquid Yield Options Notes repurchased on the market); 2009-0317591E5 (partnership must recognize FX gains/losses when foreign debt is assumed by partners on 98(3) rollover); 2009-035255117 (transfers to related persons are "purchase or payment" per IT-95R para. 13(b), so 39(2) applies); 2010-036512117 (non-resident partner's FX gain on repayment of debt); 2010-0365791E5 (administrative fees and margin interest cannot be added to cost base for FX gain/loss); 2010-0374471E5 (CRA treats rollover of one term deposit to another in the same currency as not a disposition); 2009-0350501E5 (application in different scenarios); 2009-0350711R3 (39(2) will apply when debt is exchanged for a different debt); 2010-0353291E5 (FX losses and superficial losses); 2010-0386881E5 (no 39(2) on debt forgiveness); 2011-0395771R3 (no 39(2) when pref shares converted to common shares); 2012-043692117 (no loss on redemption of shares where 40(3.6) applies [Barnicke & Huynh, "Currency Losses on FA Share Redemption", 20(10) *CTH* 5-6 (Oct. 2012)]); 2013-0501241E5 (FX gain or loss on an unpaid dividend); 2013-050766117 (automatic renewal of loan does not trigger 39(2)); 2014-056057117 (no 39(2) gain where corp received amount on reduction of FA's PUC, as 53(2)(b)(ii) applied [Haughey, "No Foreign Exchange Gain on PUC Reduction", 23(6) *CTH* 3-4 (June 2015); Naqvi, "Foreign Affiliate Treatment of Foreign Currency Gains and Losses on a Reduction of PUC", XX(2) *International Tax Planning* (Federated Press) 1396-97 (2015)]); 2018-0750261C6 [2018 IFA q.7] (FX loss if related corp R assumes debt so it is extinguished, but not if R only undertakes to repay loan).

Texts and papers *[note: some pre-2013 points may be obsolete, or may apply now under 39(1)]*: Arnold et al., *Timing and Income Taxation* (ctf.ca, 2nd ed., 2015), chap. 11; Schreiner, "Foreign Currency Management", 2007 Cdn Tax Foundation conference report, 18:1-16; Schreiner & Conway, "Foreign Currency Management", 2008 BC Tax Conference (ctf.ca), 10:1-21; Bretsen & Kerr, "Tax Planning for Foreign Currency", 2009 conference report, 35:1-47; Murdoch & Babour, "Foreign Exchange", 2010 Ontario Tax Conf 12:1-19; Calverley et al., "Taxation of Derivative Transactions", 26(2) *Canadian Petroleum Tax Journal* (2013); Fréchette & Rabinovitch, "Current Issues Involving FX Gains", 2015 conference report, 26:1-58; Ancimer & Beswick, "Foreign Exchange Legislation", 2017 conference report, 17:1-25.

Shorter articles: Korkh & Nikolakakis, "Taxation of Derivatives", 23(5) *Canadian Tax Highlights* [CTH] (ctf.ca) 5-6 (May 2015); Bernstein & Gucciardo, "Foreign Exchange Transactions", 24(4) *CTH* 7-9 (April 2016) and "Canadian Taxation of Foreign Exchange Transactions", 83(1) *Tax Notes International* (taxnotes.com) 65-68 (July 4, 2016); Bloch & Gandhi, "A Cross Border Review of Foreign Exchange Gains and Losses", 9(2) *BorderCrossings* (Carswell) 1-7 (July 2016); Drache, "Foreign Exchange Reporting Options", xl(7) *The Canadian Taxpayer* (Carswell) 54-56 (April 6, 2018).

Income Tax Folios: S5-F2-C1: Foreign tax credit [replaces IT-270R3, IT-395R2, IT-520].

Interpretation Bulletins: IT-95R: Foreign exchange gains and losses.

I.T. Technical News: 15 (tax consequences of the adoption of the "euro" currency); 25 (foreign exchange losses); 38 (*Imperial Oil* and the treatment of foreign currency loans); 44 (foreign exchange gains and losses).

CRA Audit Manual: 27.15.0: Foreign currency exchange.

(2.01) Deemed gain — parked [foreign-currency] obligation — For the purposes of subsection (2), if a debt obligation owing by a taxpayer (referred to in this subsection and subsections (2.02) and (2.03) as the "debtor") is denominated in a foreign currency and the debt obligation has become a parked obligation at a particular time, the debtor is deemed at that time to have made the gain, if any, that the debtor otherwise would have made if it had paid an amount at the particular time in satisfaction of the debt obligation equal to

(a) if the debt obligation has become a parked obligation at the particular time as a result of its acquisition by the holder of the debt obligation, the amount paid by the holder to acquire the debt obligation; and

(b) in any other case, the fair market value of the debt obligation at the particular time.

Related Provisions: 39(2.02) — Meaning of "parked obligation"; 39(2.03) — Interpretation; 80.01 — General debt-parking rules; 261(10.1) — Application to pre-transition debt; 261(14.1) — Application to pre-reversion debt.

Notes: 39(2.01)-(2.03) address debt parking (see 80.01) to avoid foreign exchange (FX) gains. In a typical debt-parking transaction, instead of directly repaying a debt with an accrued FX gain, the debtor would arrange for a related person to acquire the debt from the creditor for a price equal to its principal amount. From the creditor's perspective, the debt was effectively repaid, but from the debtor's perspective, it remained owing, so the FX gain was not realized. The related person, as the new creditor, would leave the debt outstanding to avoid the debtor realizing the gain. 39(2.01) now deems the gain to be triggered. It applies only if there is a "parked obligation", which under 39(2.02)(b) requires that one of the main purposes is to avoid 39(2). For the meaning of "one of the main purposes", see Notes to 83(2.1).

39(2.01) added by 2016 budget bill #2, effective March 22, 2016. However, it does not apply to a debtor in respect of a debt obligation owing by that debtor at the time the obligation meets the conditions to become a "parked obligation" because of a written agreement entered into before March 22, 2016, if that time is before 2017.

(2.02) Parked obligation — For the purposes of subsection (2.01), a debt obligation owing by a debtor is a parked obligation at a particular time if

(a) both

(i) at that time, the holder of the debt obligation does not deal at arm's length with the debtor or, if the debtor is a corporation, has a significant interest in the debtor, and

(ii) at any previous time, a person who held the debt obligation dealt at arm's length with the debtor and, where the debtor is a corporation, did not have a significant interest in the debtor; and

(b) it can reasonably be considered that one of the main purposes of the transaction or event or series of transactions or events that resulted in the debt obligation meeting the condition in subparagraph (a)(i) is to avoid the application of subsection (2).

Related Provisions: 39(2.03) — Interpretation.

Notes: 39(2.02) added by 2016 budget bill #2, effective March 22, 2016. See Notes to 39(2.01). For the meaning of "one of the main purposes", see Notes to 83(2.1).

(2.03) Interpretation — For the purposes of subsections (2.01) and (2.02),

(a) paragraph 80(2)(j) applies for the purpose of determining whether two persons are related to each other or whether any person is controlled by any other person; and

(b) paragraph 80.01(2)(b) applies for the purpose of determining whether a person has a significant interest in a corporation.

Notes: 39(2.03) added by 2016 budget bill #2, effective March 22, 2016.

(2.1) Upstream loan [repayment by Aug. 19/16] — transitional set-off — If at any time a corporation resident in Canada or a partnership of which such a corporation is a member (such corporation or partnership referred to in this subsection and subsections (2.2) and (2.3) as the "borrowing party") has received a loan from, or become indebted to, a creditor that is a foreign affiliate (referred to in this subsection and subsections (2.2) and (2.3) as a "creditor affiliate") of a qualifying entity, or that is a partnership (referred to in this subsection and subsection (2.3) as a "creditor partnership") of which such an affiliate is a member, and the loan or indebtedness is at a later time repaid, in whole or in part, then the amount of the borrowing party's capital gain or capital loss determined, in the absence of this subsection, under subsection (2) in respect of the repayment, is to be reduced

    (a) in the case of a capital gain

        (i) if the creditor is a creditor affiliate, by an amount, not exceeding that capital gain, that is equal to twice the amount that would — in the absence of subparagraph 40(2)(g)(ii) and paragraph 95(2)(g.04) and on the assumption that the creditor affiliate's capital loss in respect of the repayment of the loan or indebtedness were a capital gain of the creditor affiliate, the creditor affiliate had no other income, loss, capital gain or capital loss for any taxation year, and no other foreign affiliate of a qualifying entity had any income, loss, capital gain or capital loss for any taxation year — be the total of all amounts each of which is an amount that would be included in computing a qualifying entity's income under subsection 91(1) for its taxation year that includes the last day of the taxation year of the creditor affiliate that includes the later time, or

        (ii) if the creditor is a creditor partnership, by an amount, not exceeding that capital gain, that is equal to twice the amount that is the total of each amount, determined in respect of a particular member of the creditor partnership that is a foreign affiliate of a qualifying entity, that would — in the absence of subparagraph 40(2)(g)(ii) and paragraph 95(2)(g.04) and on the assumption that the creditor partnership's capital loss in respect of the repayment of the loan or indebtedness were a capital gain of the creditor partnership, the particular member had no other income, loss, capital gain or capital loss for any taxation year, and no other foreign affiliate of a qualifying entity had any income, loss, capital gain or capital loss for any taxation year — be the total of all amounts each of which is an amount that would be included in computing a qualifying entity's income under subsection 91(1) for its taxation year that includes the last day of the taxation year of the particular member that includes the last day of the creditor partnership's fiscal period that includes that later time; and

    (b) in the case of a capital loss

        (i) if the creditor is a creditor affiliate, by an amount, not exceeding that capital loss, that is equal to twice the amount, in respect of the creditor affiliate's capital gain in respect of the repayment of the loan or indebtedness, that would — in the absence of paragraph 95(2)(g.04) and on the assumption that the creditor affiliate had no other income, loss, capital gain or capital loss for any taxation year, and no other foreign affiliate of a qualifying entity had any income, loss, capital gain or capital loss for any taxation year — be the total of all amounts each of which is an amount that would be included in computing a qualifying entity's income under subsection 91(1) for its taxation year that includes the last day of the taxation year of the creditor affiliate that includes the later time, or

        (ii) if the creditor is a creditor partnership, by an amount, not exceeding that capital loss, that is equal to twice the amount, in respect of the creditor partnership's capital gain in respect of the repayment of the loan or indebtedness, that is the total of each amount, determined in respect of a particular member of the creditor partnership that is a foreign affiliate of a qualifying entity, that would — in the absence of paragraph 95(2)(g.04) and on the assumption that the particular member had no other income, loss, capital gain or capital loss for any taxation year, and no other foreign affiliate of a qualifying entity had any income, loss, capital gain or capital loss for

any taxation year — be the total of all amounts each of which is an amount that would be included in computing a qualifying entity's income under subsection 91(1) for its taxation year that includes the last day of the taxation year of the particular member that includes the last day of the creditor partnership's fiscal period that includes the later time.

Related Provisions: 39(2.3) — Transitional setoff election; 90(7) — Back-to-back loans — deeming rule; 93.1(1) — Shares owned by partnership deemed owned by partners; 93.1(3)(c) — Tiered partnership — look-through rule.

Notes: 39(2.1) is a temporary measure that, in certain cases, can set off T's foreign exchange (FX) gains or losses on repayment of a debt obligation owing to a foreign affiliate (FA) against the FA's related losses or gains from the repayment. It is intended to provide relief if T finds it necessary to repay an "upstream loan" to avoid 90(6).

This rule applies only if T's gain is equal to the FA's loss, or T's loss is equal to the FA's gain. A companion rule in 95(2)(g.04) deems the FA's gain or loss to be nil. Given its connection to the upstream loan rules in 90(6)-(15), the application dates for 39(2.1) correspond with the transitional rule for those rules. Thus, it applies only to T's FX gain or loss on repayment of the portion of a debt obligation outstanding on Aug. 19, 2011 where that repayment occurs by Aug. 19, 2016. (Finance Technical Notes)

For CRA interpretation see VIEWS doc 2015-0581561C6 [2015 IFA q.8].

See also Jim Samuel, "When Do the Stop-Loss Rules Apply? Transactions Involving Foreign Affiliates", 64(3) *Canadian Tax Journal* 561-600 (2016).

39(2.1) amended by 2017 budget bill #2, retroactive to its introduction, to expand the scope of its application and add reference to 39(2.2)-(2.3).

39(2.1) added by 2002-2013 technical bill (Part 3 — FA reorganizations), for the portions of loans received and indebtedness incurred by Aug. 19, 2011 that remain outstanding on that date and that are repaid, in whole or in part, by Aug. 19, 2016.

Income Tax Folios: S5-F2-C1: Foreign tax credit [replaces IT-270R3, IT-395R2, IT-520].

(2.2) Definition of qualifying entity — For purposes of subsections (2.1) and (2.3), "qualifying entity" means

    (a) in the case of a borrowing party that is a corporation,

        (i) the borrowing party,

        (ii) a corporation resident in Canada of which

            (A) the borrowing party is a subsidiary wholly-owned corporation, or

            (B) a corporation described in this paragraph is a subsidiary wholly-owned corporation,

        (iii) a corporation resident in Canada

            (A) each share of the capital stock of which is owned by

                (I) the borrowing party, or

                (II) a corporation that is described in this subparagraph or subparagraph (ii), or

            (B) all or substantially all of the capital stock of which is owned by one or more corporations resident in Canada that are borrowing parties in respect of the creditor affiliate because of subsection 90(7), or

        (iv) a partnership each member of which is

            (A) a corporation described in any of subparagraphs (i) to (iii), or

            (B) another partnership described in this subparagraph; and

    (b) in the case of a borrowing party that is a partnership,

        (i) the borrowing party,

        (ii) if each member — determined as if each member of a partnership that is a member of another partnership is a member of that other partnership — of the borrowing party is either a particular corporation resident in Canada (in this paragraph referred to as the "parent") or a corporation resident in Canada that is a "subsidiary wholly-owned corporation", as defined in subsection 87(1.4), of the parent,

            (A) the parent, or

            (B) a corporation resident in Canada that is a "subsidiary wholly-owned corporation", as defined in subsection 87(1.4), of the parent, or

(iii) a partnership each member of which is any of

(A) the borrowing party,

(B) a corporation described in subparagraph (ii), and

(C) another partnership described in this subparagraph.

Related Provisions: 90(7) — Back-to-back loans — deeming rule.

Notes: 39(2.2) added by 2017 budget bill #2, effective on same basis as 39(2.1).

(2.3) Upstream loan — transitional set-off election — Subsection (2.1) and paragraph 95(2)(g.04) do not apply in respect of a repayment, in whole or in part, of a loan or indebtedness if an election has been filed with the Minister before 2019 jointly by

(a) the borrowing party;

(b) if the creditor is a creditor affiliate, each qualifying entity of which the creditor affiliate is a foreign affiliate; and

(c) if the creditor is a creditor partnership, each qualifying entity of which a member of the creditor partnership is a foreign affiliate.

Notes: 39(2.3) added by 2017 budget bill #2, effective on same basis as 39(2.1).

(3) Gain in respect of purchase of bonds, etc., by issuer — Where a taxpayer has issued any bond, debenture or similar obligation and has at any subsequent time in a taxation year and after 1971 purchased the obligation in the open market, in the manner in which any such obligation would normally be purchased in the open market by any member of the public,

(a) the amount, if any, by which the amount for which the obligation was issued by the taxpayer exceeds the purchase price paid or agreed to be paid by the taxpayer for the obligation shall be deemed to be a capital gain of the taxpayer for the taxation year from the disposition of a capital property, and

(b) the amount, if any, by which the purchase price paid or agreed to be paid by the taxpayer for the obligation exceeds the greater of the principal amount of the obligation and the amount for which it was issued by the taxpayer shall be deemed to be a capital loss of the taxpayer for the taxation year from the disposition of a capital property,

to the extent that the amount determined under paragraph (a) or (b) would not, if section 3 were read in the manner described in paragraph (1)(a) and this Act were read without reference to subsections 80(12) and (13), be included or be deductible, as the case may be, in computing the taxpayer's income for the year or any other taxation year.

Related Provisions: 80(1)"forgiven amount"B(d) — Debt forgiveness rules do not apply where subsec. 39(3) applies; 95(2)(f.11)(i)(B) — Application of 39(3) to income of foreign affiliate; 248(27) — Purchase of partial obligation treated as purchase of obligation.

Notes: For CRA interpretation see VIEWS docs 2008-0302511I7 (Liquid Yield Options Notes repurchased on the market); 2014-0550401C6 [2014 TEI q.E3] ("in the open market" requires competing with the public through the market).

In *Goulet*, 2011 FCA 164 (leave to appeal denied 2011 CarswellNat 5307 (SCC)), the deemed interest accrual in 12(4) and 12(9) effectively overrode 39(3), so the difference between acquisition price and proceeds of non-interest-bearing debt obligations was interest, not capital gain.

39(3) amended by 1994 technical bill, for tax years ending after Feb. 21, 1994.

I.T. Application Rules: 26(1.1) (when obligation was outstanding on January 1, 1972).

Interpretation Bulletins: IT-479R: Transactions in securities.

(4) Election concerning disposition of Canadian securities — Except as provided in subsection (5), where a Canadian security has been disposed of by a taxpayer in a taxation year and the taxpayer so elects in prescribed form in the taxpayer's return of income under this Part for that year,

(a) every Canadian security owned by the taxpayer in that year or any subsequent taxation year shall be deemed to have been a capital property owned by the taxpayer in those years; and

(b) every disposition by the taxpayer of any such Canadian security shall be deemed to be a disposition by the taxpayer of a capital property.

Related Provisions: 12(1)(z.7) — Income inclusion from derivative forward agreement, overriding 39(4); 39(4.1) — Look through partnerships for purposes of 39(4); 39(5) — Taxpayers to whom subsec. (4) inapplicable; 39(6) — Definition of "Canadian security"; 54.2 — Certain shares deemed to be capital property.

Notes: The election on Form T123 causes permanent treatment of gains (losses) on Canadian securities as capital gains (losses), rather than fully includable in (deductible from) business income. Once made, it is effective forever. Note the many exclusions from "Canadian security" in 39(6) due to Reg. 6200, and the exceptions in 39(5). Note also that on a character-conversion transaction (248(1)"derivative forward agreement"), 12(1)(z.7) requires income inclusion that effectively overrides 39(4).

The election can apply to short sales: IT-479R para. 6; VIEWS doc 2006-0198391E5.

For a similar administrative rule for commodity trading see IT-346R para. 7.

Interest accrued on interest-bearing bonds before disposition does not become capital gain as a result of the election, but remains fully taxable: *Satinder*, 2002 FCA 491.

A partner can make the election: 39(4.1). A mutual fund trust can make the election: VIEWS doc 2012-0470991E5.

An election "in the taxpayer's return" is valid even if the return is filed late. See Notes to 7(1.31).

Where the election was not filed on time, the Tax Court might rule that it should be accepted late. See *Sandnes*, 2004 TCC 244, para. 28.

Once the election is made, management of investments cannot be a business "since businesses buy and sell inventory, not capital assets": *McNeil*, 2005 TCC 124.

For a taxpayer filing Quebec returns, the election must be copied to Revenu Québec: *Taxation Act* ss. 250.1, 21.4.6.

Interpretation Bulletins: IT-346R: Commodity futures and certain commodities; IT-479R: Transactions in securities.

Forms: T123: Election on disposition of Canadian securities.

(4.1) Members of partnerships — For the purpose of determining the income of a taxpayer who is a member of a partnership, subsections (4) and (5) apply as if

(a) every Canadian security owned by the partnership were owned by the taxpayer; and

(b) every Canadian security disposed of by the partnership in a fiscal period of the partnership were disposed of by the taxpayer at the end of that fiscal period.

Notes: 39(4.1) applies to a limited partner: VIEWS doc 2014-0559961E5. (Note that if the partnership is a "trader or dealer", the limited partner is considered to be carrying on the partnership's business: *cf. Robinson*, [1998] 1 C.T.C. 272 (FCA), para. 18; and 253.1 does not apply to 39(4).)

39(4.1) added by 1991 technical bill, for dispositions after July 13, 1990.

(5) Exception — An election under subsection (4) does not apply to a disposition of a Canadian security by a taxpayer (other than a mutual fund corporation or a mutual fund trust) who at the time of the disposition is

(a) a trader or dealer in securities,

(b) a financial institution (as defined in subsection 142.2(1)),

(c)–(e) [Repealed]

(f) a corporation whose principal business is the lending of money or the purchasing of debt obligations or a combination thereof, or

(g) a non-resident,

or any combination thereof.

Related Provisions: 39(4.1) — Members of partnerships; 96(3) — Election by members of partnership.

Notes: The term "trader or dealer in securities" covers much more than a *licensed* trader or dealer, can include an insider who promotes the stock, and depends on how actively the person trades. See *Vancouver Art Metal*, [1993] 1 C.T.C. 346 (FCA); *Kane*, [1995] 1 C.T.C. 1 (FCTD); *Robertson*, [1996] 2 C.T.C. 2269 (TCC); *Arcorp Investments*, [2001] 2 C.T.C. 1 (FCTD); IT-479R para. 5; and Revenue Canada Round Table, 1993 Cdn Tax Foundation conference report, p. 58:31, Q. 52. But see *Sandnes*, 2004 TCC 244 (many sales of a holding to meet financial needs did not make taxpayer a "trader", as a trader must be both *buying* and selling). The term is defined in Reg. 230(1), but only for information returns. See also VIEWS docs 2008-0269301E5, 2009-0308851E5, 2009-0321871E5, 2010-0381231E5.

For "principal business" in 39(5)(f), see Notes to 20(1)(bb).

An active trader who cannot file a 39(4) election can incorporate the business to obtain the small business deduction, income splitting and other benefits. See VIEWS doc 2000-0030125, and Drache, "Incorporating Day Trading", XXIII(4) *The Canadian Taxpayer* (Carswell) 30-31 (Feb. 2001).

39(5) amended by 1997 Budget (for 1991 and later tax years), 1994 technical bill.

Interpretation Bulletins: IT-479R: Transactions in securities.

(6) Definition of "Canadian security" — For the purposes of this section, "Canadian security" means a security (other than a prescribed security) that is a share of the capital stock of a corporation resident in Canada, a unit of a mutual fund trust or a bond, debenture, bill, note, mortgage, hypothecary claim or similar obligation issued by a person resident in Canada.

Notes: Prescribed securities, under Reg. 6200, include private corporation shares whose value is primarily attributable to real property or resource property; non-arm's length debt; shares or debt acquired not at arm's length or in a section 85 rollover (but see 54.2); flow-through shares (VIEWS doc 2012-0465551E5; such shares purchased for resale at a tax gain but no cash gain are capital property anyway per *Loewen*, [1994] 2 C.T.C. 75 (FCA) and *Gervais*, 2016 FCA 1); and shares or debt substituted for any of the above. The 39(4) election does not apply to such securities.

The term "bond, debenture, bill, note, mortgage or similar obligation" may not include bankers' acceptances: *Federated Co-operatives*, 2001 FCA 217; leave to appeal denied 2001 CarswellNat 1788 (SCC).

"Hypothecary claim" added to 39(6) by 2001 *Civil Code* harmonization bill, effective June 14, 2001. The change is non-substantive; see *Interpretation Act* s. 8.2.

Regulations: 6200 (prescribed security).

Interpretation Bulletins: IT-346R: Commodity futures and certain commodities; IT-479R: Transactions in securities.

(7) Unused share-purchase tax credit — [No longer relevant]

Notes: Since the SPTC is no longer available, this provision deeming an unused SPTC to be a capital loss is obsolete. See Notes to 127.2.

(8) Unused scientific research and experimental development tax credit — [No longer relevant]

Notes: Since the SRTC is no longer available, this provision deeming an unused SRTC to be a capital loss is obsolete. See Notes to 127.3.

(9) Deduction from business investment loss — In computing the business investment loss of a taxpayer who is an individual (other than a trust) for a taxation year from the disposition of a particular property, there shall be deducted an amount equal to the lesser of

(a) the amount that would be the taxpayer's business investment loss for the year from the disposition of that particular property if paragraph (1)(c) were read without reference to subparagraph (1)(c)(viii), and

(b) the amount, if any, by which the total of

(i) the total of all amounts each of which is twice the amount deducted by the taxpayer under section 110.6 in computing the taxpayer's taxable income for a preceding taxation year that

(A) ended before 1988, or

(B) begins after October 17, 2000,

(i.1) the total of all amounts each of which is

(A) $^3/_2$ of the amount deducted under section 110.6 in computing the taxpayer's taxable income for a preceding taxation year that

(I) ended after 1987 and before 1990, or

(II) began after February 27, 2000 and ended before October 18, 2000, or

(B) the amount determined by multiplying the reciprocal of the fraction in paragraph 38(a) that applies to the taxpayer for each of the taxpayer's taxation years that includes February 28, 2000 or October 18, 2000 by the amount deducted under section 110.6 in computing the taxpayer's taxable income for that year, and

(i.2) the total of all amounts each of which is $^4/_3$ of the amount deducted under section 110.6 in computing the taxpayer's taxable income for a preceding taxation year that ended after 1989 and before February 28, 2000

exceeds

(ii) the total of all amounts each of which is an amount deducted by the taxpayer under paragraph (1)(c) by virtue of

subparagraph (1)(c)(viii) in computing the taxpayer's business investment loss

(A) from the disposition of property in taxation years preceding the year, or

(B) from the disposition of property other than the particular property in the year,

except that, where a particular amount was included under subparagraph 14(1)(a)(v) in the taxpayer's income for a taxation year that ended after 1987 and before 1990, the reference in subparagraph (i.1) to "$^3/_2$" shall, in respect of that portion of any amount deducted under section 110.6 in respect of the particular amount, be read as "$^4/_3$".

Related Provisions: 39(10) — Deduction from business investment loss of trust.

Notes: 39(9) prevents "double-dipping" by claiming the capital gains exemption (CGE) to absorb capital gains while also claiming an allowable business investment loss (see 38(c), 39(1)(c)) against other income. The idea is that capital gains and losses are supposed to be netted against each other first. See VIEWS doc 2013-0480431E5 for an example (involving a trust and 39(10)).

A parallel rule prevents the CGE from being claimed to the extent ABILs have been claimed in the past. See 110.6(1)"annual gains limit"B(b) and "cumulative gains limit"(b).

The wording of 39(9)(b) reflects the fact that capital gains were ½ taxed from 1972 to 1988, ⅔ taxed in 1988 and 1989, ¾ taxed from 1990 to Feb. 27, 2000, ⅔ taxed from Feb. 28 to Oct. 17, 2000, and ½ taxed since Oct. 18, 2000 (see s. 38). 39(9) amended by 2000 Budget (for tax years that end after Feb. 27, 2000), 1993 technical bill.

Income Tax Folios: S4-F8-C1: Business investment losses [replaces IT-484R2].

(10) Idem, of a trust — In computing the business investment loss of a trust for a taxation year from the disposition of a particular property, there shall be deducted an amount equal to the lesser of

(a) the amount that would be the trust's business investment loss for the year from the disposition of that particular property if paragraph (1)(c) were read without reference to subparagraph (1)(c)(viii), and

(b) the amount, if any, by which the total of

(i) the total of all amounts each of which is twice the amount designated by the trust under subsection 104(21.2) in respect of a beneficiary in its return of income for a preceding taxation year that

(A) ended before 1988, or

(B) begins after October 17, 2000,

(i.1) the total of all amounts each of which is

(A) $^3/_2$ of the amount designated by the trust under subsection 104(21.2) in respect of a beneficiary in its return of income for a preceding taxation year that

(I) ended after 1987 and before 1990, or

(II) began after February 27, 2000 and ended before October 18, 2000, or

(B) the amount determined by multiplying the reciprocal of the fraction in paragraph 38(a) that applies to the trust for each of the trust's taxation years that includes February 28, 2000 or October 18, 2000 by the amount designated by the trust under subsection 104(21.2) in respect of a beneficiary in its return of income for that year, and

(i.2) the total of all amounts each of which is $^4/_3$ of the amount designated by the trust under subsection 104(21.2) in respect of a beneficiary in its return of income for a preceding taxation year that ended after 1989 and before February 28, 2000

exceeds

(ii) the total of all amounts each of which is an amount deducted by the trust under paragraph (1)(c) by virtue of subparagraph (1)(c)(viii) in computing its business investment loss

(A) from the disposition of property in taxation years preceding the year, or

(B) from the disposition of property other than the particular property in the year,

except that, where a particular amount was included under subparagraph 14(1)(a)(v) in the trust's income for a taxation year that ended after 1987 and before 1990, the reference in subparagraph (i.1) to "³/₂" shall, in respect of that portion of any amount deducted under section 110.6 in respect of the particular amount, be read as "⁴/₃".

Notes: See Notes to 39(9).

39(10) amended by 2000 Budget (for taxation years that end after Feb. 27, 2000), 1993 technical bill.

Income Tax Folios: S4-F8-C1: Business investment losses [replaces IT-484R2].

(11) Recovery of bad debt — Where an amount is received in a taxation year on account of a debt (in this subsection referred to as the "recovered amount") in respect of which a deduction for bad debts had been made under subsection 20(4.2) in computing a taxpayer's income for a preceding taxation year, the amount, if any, by which ½ of the recovered amount exceeds the amount determined under paragraph 12(1)(i.1) in respect of the recovered amount is deemed to be a taxable capital gain of the taxpayer from a disposition of capital property in the year.

Notes: 39(11) amended by 2000 Budget to change "³/₄" to "¹/₂", effective for taxation years that end after October 17, 2000, with transitional rules for 2000.

39(11) amended by 1994 Budget, effective 1995, consequential on the elimination of the capital gains exemption in 110.6.

Interpretation Bulletins: IT-442R: Bad debts and reserves for doubtful debts; Foreign tax credit — foreign-source capital gains and losses.

(12) Guarantees — For the purpose of paragraph (1)(c), where

(a) an amount was paid by a taxpayer in respect of a debt of a corporation under an arrangement under which the taxpayer guaranteed the debt,

(b) the amount was paid to a person with whom the taxpayer was dealing at arm's length, and

(c) the corporation was a small business corporation

(i) at the time the debt was incurred, and

(ii) at any time in the 12 months before the time an amount first became payable by the taxpayer under the arrangement in respect of a debt of the corporation,

that part of the amount that is owing to the taxpayer by the corporation shall be deemed to be a debt owing to the taxpayer by a small business corporation.

Related Provisions: 80(2)(l) — Application of debt forgiveness rules on payment by guarantor.

Notes: Under 39(12), payment under a guarantee of corporate debt is deemed to be a debt owing to the taxpayer by a small business corp (SBC) if the payment is made to an arm's length person, and the corp was a SBC both when the corporate debt was incurred and at any time in the 12 months before the time any amount first became payable under the guarantee. See *Armstrong*, [2000] 1 C.T.C. 1 (FCA). In *Abrametz*, 2009 FCA 111, the TCC had held that the taxpayer failed to show he paid an amount under a guarantee, so 39(12) did not apply; but the FCA allowed the appeal and sent the matter back to CRA because a capital loss or BIL could have arisen under 39(1)(b) or (c) without needing 39(12). See also Notes to 39(1) re *Dietrich*, approved by the FCA in *Abrametz*. In *Woloshyn*, 2011 TCC 306, an ABIL under a guarantee was allowed only when it was "finally determined" (related legal fees were not deductible). *Audet*, 2012 TCC 162, denied an ABIL on a guarantee but failed to consider 39(12).

"Payable" in 39(12)(c)(ii) "refers to the moment when a creditor can, for the first time, require payment from the guarantor": VIEWS doc 2006-00196101C6.

See also VIEWS doc 2012-0436251E5 (guarantee likely qualifies).

See also Notes to 20(1)(c) under "Guarantees".

39(12) added by 1991 technical bill, effective for amounts paid after 1985.

Income Tax Folios: S4-F8-C1: Business investment losses [replaces IT-484R2].

CRA Audit Manual: 29.3.5: Business investment losses — debts from a guarantee.

(13) Repayment of assistance — The total of all amounts paid by a taxpayer in a taxation year each of which is

(a) such part of any assistance described in subparagraph 53(2)(k)(i) in respect of, or for the acquisition of, a capital property (other than depreciable property) by the taxpayer that was repaid by the taxpayer in the year where the repayment is made

after the disposition of the property by the taxpayer and under an obligation to repay all or any part of that assistance, or

(b) an amount repaid by the taxpayer in the year in respect of a capital property (other than depreciable property) acquired by the taxpayer that is repaid after the disposition thereof by the taxpayer and that would have been an amount described in subparagraph 53(2)(s)(ii) had the repayment been made before the disposition of the property,

shall be deemed to be a capital loss of the taxpayer for the year from the disposition of property by the taxpayer in the year and, for the purpose of section 110.6, that property shall be deemed to have been disposed of by the taxpayer in the year.

Related Provisions: 79(4)(a) — Subsequent payment by debtor following surrender of property deemed to be repayment of assistance.

Notes: 39(13) added by 1992 technical bill, effective 1991. Assistance repaid while capital property is owned reduces the adjusted cost base of the property (and see 40(3)). If the assistance is repaid after the property is disposed of, 39(13) allows a capital loss.

Definitions [s. 39]: "adjusted cost base" — 54, 248(1); "amount" — 248(1); "arm's length" — 251(1); "bank", "bankrupt" — 248(1); "borrowing party" — 39(2.1); "business investment loss" — 39(1)(c), 39(9), (10); "Canada" — 255; "Canadian-controlled private corporation" — 248(1); "Canadian resource property" — 66(15), 248(1); "Canadian security" — 39(6); "capital gain" — 39(1)(a), 248(1); "capital loss" — 39(1)(b), 248(1); "capital property" — 54, 248(1); "common-law partner" — 248(1); "corporation" — 248(1), Interpretation Act 35(1); "credit union" — 137(6), 248(1); "creditor affiliate", "creditor partnership" — 39(2.1); "debtor" — 39(2.01); "depreciable property" — 13(21), 248(1); "disposition" — 248(1); "eligible capital property" — 54, 248(1); "fair market value" — see 69(1) Notes; "financial institution" — 142.2(1); "fiscal period" — 249(2)(b), 249.1; "foreign affiliate" — 95(1), 248(1); "foreign currency" — 248(1); "foreign currency debt" — 111(8), 248(1); "foreign resource property" — 66(15), 248(1); "individual", "insurance corporation" — 248(1); "life insurance policy" — 138(12), 248(1); "Minister" — 248(1); "mutual fund corporation" — 131(8), 248(1); "mutual fund trust" — 132(6)–(7), 132.2(3)(n), 248(1); "parked obligation" — 39(2.02); "partnership" — see 96(1) Notes; "person", "prescribed" — 248(1); "principal amount" — 248(1), (26), ITAR 26(1.1); "property" — 211.6(1), 248(1); "qualifying entity" — 39(2.2); "qualifying environmental trust" — 211.6(1), 248(1); "received" — 248(7); "related" — 251(2)–(6); "related segregated fund trust" — 138.1(1)(a); "resident in Canada" — 94(3)(a), 250; "series of transactions" — 248(10); "settlor" — 108(1); "share", "small business corporation" — 248(1); "subsidiary wholly-owned corporation" — 87(1.4), 248(1); "substituted" — 39(1)(c)(vi), 248(5); "taxable capital gain" — 38(a), 248(1); "taxable dividend" — 89(1), 248(1); "taxable income" — 2(2), 248(1); "taxation year" — 249; "taxpayer" — 248(1); "timber resource property" — 13(21), 248(1); "trust" — 104(1), 248(1), (3); "unused scientific research and experimental development tax credit" — 127.3(2), 248(1); "unused share-purchase tax credit" — 127.2(6), 248(1).

39.1 (1) Definitions — In this section,

"exempt capital gains balance" of an individual for a taxation year that ends before 2005 in respect of a flow-through entity means the amount determined by the formula

$$A - B - C - F$$

where

A is

(a) if the entity is a trust referred to in any of paragraphs (f) to (j) of the definition "flow-through entity" in this subsection, the amount determined under paragraph 110.6(19)(c) in respect of the individual's interest or interests therein, and

(b) in any other case, the lesser of

(i) ⁴/₃ of the total of the taxable capital gains that resulted from elections made under subsection 110.6(19) in respect of the individual's interests in or shares of the capital stock of the entity, and

(ii) the amount that would be determined under subparagraph (i) if

(A) the amount designated in the election in respect of each interest or share were equal to the amount determined by the formula

$$D - E$$

where

D is the fair market value of the interest or share at the end of February 22, 1994, and

E is the amount, if any, by which the amount designated in the election that was made in respect of the interest or share exceeds $^{11}/_{10}$ of its fair market value at the end of February 22, 1994, and

 (B) this Act were read without reference to subsection 110.6(20),

B is the total of all amounts each of which is the amount by which the individual's capital gain for a preceding taxation year, determined without reference to subsection (2), from the disposition of an interest in or a share of the capital stock of the entity was reduced under that subsection, and

C is

(a) if the entity is a trust described in any of paragraphs (d) and (h) to (j) of the definition "flow-through entity" in this subsection, the total of

(i) $^{3}/_{2}$ of the total of all amounts each of which is the amount by which the individual's taxable capital gain (determined without reference to this section), for a preceding taxation year that began after February 27, 2000 and ended before October 18, 2000 that resulted from a designation made under subsection 104(21) by the trust, was reduced under subsection (3),

(ii) $^{4}/_{3}$ of the total of all amounts each of which is the amount by which the individual's taxable capital gain (determined without reference to this section), for a preceding taxation year that ended before February 28, 2000 that resulted from a designation made under subsection 104(21) by the trust, was reduced under subsection (3),

(iii) the amount claimed by the individual under subparagraph 104(21.4)(a)(ii) or (21.7)(b)(ii) for a preceding taxation year, and

(iv) twice the total of all amounts each of which is the amount by which the individual's taxable capital gain (determined without reference to this section) for a preceding taxation year that began after October 17, 2000 and that resulted from a designation made under subsection 104(21) by the trust, was reduced under subsection (3),

(b) if the entity is a partnership, the total of

(i) $^{3}/_{2}$ of the total of

(A) the total of all amounts each of which is the amount by which the individual's share of the partnership's taxable capital gains (determined without reference to this section), for its fiscal period that began after February 27, 2000 and ended before October 18, 2000, was reduced under subsection (4), and

(B) the total of all amounts each of which is the amount by which the individual's share of the partnership's income from a business (determined without reference to this section), for its fiscal period that began after February 27, 2000 and ended before October 18, 2000, was reduced under subsection (5),

(ii) $^{4}/_{3}$ of the total of

(A) the total of all amounts each of which is the amount by which the individual's share of the partnership's taxable capital gains (determined without reference to this section), for its fiscal period that ended before February 28, 2000 and in a preceding taxation year was reduced under subsection (4), and

(B) the total of all amounts each of which is the amount by which the individual's share of the partnership's income from a business (determined without reference to this section), for its fiscal period that ended before February 28, 2000 and in a preceding taxation year, was reduced under subsection (5),

(iii) the product obtained when the reciprocal of the fraction in paragraph 38(a) that applies to the partnership for

its fiscal period that includes February 28, 2000 or October 17, 2000 is multiplied by the total of

(A) the total of all amounts each of which is the amount by which the individual's share of the partnership's taxable capital gains (determined without reference to this section), for its fiscal period that includes February 28, 2000 or October 17, 2000 and ended in a preceding taxation year, was reduced under subsection (4), and

(B) the total of all amounts each of which is the amount by which the individual's share of the partnership's income from a business (determined without reference to this section), for its fiscal period that includes February 28, 2000 or October 17, 2000 and ended in a preceding taxation year was reduced under subsection (5), and

(iv) twice the total of

(A) the total of all amounts each of which is the amount by which the individual's share of the partnership's taxable capital gains (determined without reference to this section), for its fiscal period that began after October 17, 2000 and ended in a preceding taxation year, was reduced under subsection (4), and

(B) the total of all amounts each of which is the amount by which the individual's share of the partnership's income from a business (determined without reference to this section), for its fiscal period that began after October 17, 2000 and ended in a preceding taxation year, was reduced under subsection (5), and

(c) in any other case, the total of all amounts each of which is the amount by which the total of the individual's capital gains otherwise determined under subsection 130.1(4) or 131(1), subsections 138.1(3) and (4) or subsection 144(4), as the case may be, for a preceding taxation year in respect of the entity was reduced under subsection (6), and

F is

(a) if the entity is a trust described in any of paragraphs (g) to (j) of the definition "flow-through entity" in this subsection, the total of all amounts each of which is an amount included before the year in the cost to the individual of a property under subsection 107(2.2) or paragraph 144(7.1)(c) because of the individual's exempt capital gains balance in respect of the entity, and

(b) in any other case, nil;

Related Provisions: 39.1(7) — Balance deemed nil after ceasing to be shareholder or beneficiary; 53(1)(p) — Addition to ACB after balance expires at end of 2004; 53(1)(r) — Increase in ACB immediately before disposing of all interests or shares of a flow-through entity; 54"adjusted cost base"(c) — ACB adjustment to flow-through entity preserved through disposition and reacquisition; 87(2)(bb.1) — Amalgamation — flow-through entity considered to be same corporation; 107(2.2) — Cost bump on distribution of property from trust that is a flow-through entity; 132.2(3)(g)(iv) — Effect of mutual fund reorganization; 144(1) — Employees profit sharing plan — unused portion of a beneficiary's exempt capital gains balance; 144(7.1) — Employees profit sharing plan — where property received by beneficiary; 257 — Formulas cannot calculate to less than zero.

Notes: See Notes at end of 39.1. The exempt capital gains balance is the unclaimed balance of the capital gains on flow-through entities that were included in income by making a 110.6(19) election to recognize accrued gains to Feb. 22, 1994 when the $100,000 capital gain exemption was eliminated. Under 39.1(2)–(6), the balance could be used against later capital gains until 2004, after which it is added to ACB under 53(1)(p). See also Notes to 39.1(7) for cases where the taxpayer disposes of all of the units of the flow-through entity.

39.1(1)"exempt capital gains balance"C(a) and (b) amended by 2000 Budget, effective for taxation years that end after Feb. 27, 2000.

Formula element F added by 1995-97 technical bill, retroactive to 1994. Where the flow-through entity is a trust listed in 39.1(1)"flow-through entity"(g) to (j) and it distributed property in a previous year to the individual in satisfaction of all or a portion of the individual's interests in the trust, F will reduce the exempt capital gains balance by the total of all amounts included in the individual's cost of the property because of elections under 107(2.2) or 144(7.1)(c) (see those provisions).

"flow-through entity" means

(a) an investment corporation,

(b) a mortgage investment corporation,

(c) a mutual fund corporation,

(d) a mutual fund trust,

(e) a partnership,

(f) a related segregated fund trust for the purpose of section 138.1,

(g) a trust governed by an employees profit sharing plan,

(h) a trust maintained primarily for the benefit of employees of a corporation or two or more corporations that do not deal at arm's length with each other, where one of the main purposes of the trust is to hold interests in, or for civil law rights in, shares of the capital stock of the corporation or corporations, as the case may be, or any corporation not dealing at arm's length therewith,

(i) a trust established exclusively for the benefit of one or more persons each of whom was, at the time the trust received property or a creditor of that person, where one of the main purposes of the trust is to secure the payments required to be made by or on behalf of that person to such creditor, and

(j) a trust all or substantially all of the properties of which consist of shares of the capital stock of a corporation, where the trust was established pursuant to an agreement between 2 or more shareholders of the corporation and one of the main purposes of the trust is to provide for the exercise of voting rights in respect of those shares pursuant to that agreement.

Related Provisions: 54"adjusted cost base"(c) — ACB adjustment preserved through disposition and reacquisition; 87(2)(bb.1) — Amalgamation — flow-through entity considered to be same corporation; 107(2.2) — Cost bump on distribution of property from trust that is a flow-through entity. See also Definitions at end of 39.1.

Notes: See Notes at end of 39.1. Essentially, flow-through entities are entities on which a taxpayer can have both a capital gain on the sale of the interest in the entity, and capital gains flowed out by the entity as a conduit from its own dispositions. For the meaning of "one of the main purposes" see Notes to 83(2.1).

Para. (h) amended by 2002-2013 technical bill (Part 4 — bijuralism), effective June 26, 2013, to add "or for civil law rights in".

(2) Reduction of capital gain — Where at any time after February 22, 1994 an individual disposes of an interest in or a share of the capital stock of a flow-through entity, the individual's capital gain, if any, otherwise determined for a taxation year from the disposition shall be reduced by such amount as the individual claims, not exceeding the amount determined by the formula

$$A - B - C$$

where

A is the exempt capital gains balance of the individual for the year in respect of the entity,

B is

(a) if the entity made a designation under subsection 104(21) in respect of the individual for the year, twice the amount, if any, claimed under subsection (3) by the individual for the year in respect of the entity,

(b) if the entity is a partnership, twice the amount, if any, claimed under subsection (4) by the individual for the year in respect of the entity, and

(c) in any other case, the amount, if any, claimed under subsection (6) by the individual for the year in respect of the entity, and

C is the total of all reductions under this subsection in the individual's capital gains otherwise determined for the year from the disposition of other interests in or shares of the capital stock of the entity.

Related Provisions: 39.1(6) — Reduction of capital gains on ongoing basis; 110.6(19)–(30) — Election to trigger capital gains exemption; 132.2(3)(g)(iv) — Effect of mutual fund reorganization; 257 — Formula cannot calculate to less than zero.

Notes: 39.1(2) allowed the elected capital gains exemption under 110.6(19) to be used when the taxpayer's interest in a flow-through entity is sold. For gains flowed out to X while X still owns the interest, see 39.1(3)–(6). These provisions are now inoperative because 39.1(1)"exempt capital gains balance" is defined only in terms of years before 2005. The balance is instead added to the property's ACB by 53(1)(p).

39.1(2)B(b)(ii) repealed (and (i) folded into the para.) by 2016 budget bill #2, for taxation years that begin after 2016, to delete a reference to 39.1(5) as part of changing eligible capital property rules to CCA Class 14.1 (see Notes to 20(1)(b)).

39.1(2) earlier amended by 2000 Budget.

(3) Reduction of taxable capital gain — The taxable capital gain otherwise determined under subsection 104(21) of an individual for a taxation year as a result of a designation made under that subsection by a flow-through entity shall be reduced by such amount as the individual claims, not exceeding ½ of the individual's exempt capital gains balance for the year in respect of the entity.

Notes: See Notes at end of 39.1. 39.1(3) allowed the elected capital gains exemption under 110.6(19) to be used on capital gains allocated by a trust under 104(21).

39.1(3) amended by 2000 Budget to change "¾" to "½", last change effective for taxation years that end after Oct. 17, 2000.

(4) Reduction in share of partnership's taxable capital gains — An individual's share otherwise determined for a taxation year of a taxable capital gain of a partnership from the disposition of a property (other than property acquired by the partnership after February 22, 1994 in a transfer to which subsection 97(2) applied) for its fiscal period that ends after February 22, 1994 and in the year shall be reduced by such amount as the individual claims, not exceeding the amount determined by the formula

$$A - B$$

where

A is ½ of the individual's exempt capital gains balance for the year in respect of the partnership, and

B is the total of amounts claimed by the individual under this subsection in respect of other taxable capital gains of the partnership for that fiscal period.

Related Provisions: 39.1(1)"exempt capital gains balance"C(b)(i), 39.1(2)B(b)(i) — Reduction in balance to reflect application of subsec. (4); 257 — Formula cannot calculate to less than zero.

Notes: 39.1(4) allowed the elected capital gains exemption under 110.6(19) to be used on capital gains allocated to the taxpayer by a partnership under 96(1).

39.1(4)A amended by 2000 Budget to change "¾" to "½", last change effective for taxation years that end after Oct. 17, 2000.

(5) [Repealed]

Notes: 39.1(5) repealed by 2016 budget bill #2, for taxation years that begin after 2016, as part of changing eligible capital property rules to CCA Class 14.1 (see Notes to 20(1)(b)).

39.1(5) amended by 2000 Budget, last change effective for taxation years that end after Oct. 17, 2000.

(6) Reduction of capital gains — The total capital gains otherwise determined under subsection 130.1(4) or 131(1), subsections 138.1(3) and (4) or subsection 144(4), as the case may be, of an individual for a taxation year as a result of one or more elections, allocations or designations made after February 22, 1994 by a flow-through entity shall be reduced by such amount as the individual claims, not exceeding the individual's exempt capital gains balance for the year in respect of the entity.

Related Provisions: 39.1(1)"exempt capital gains balance"C(c), 39.1(2)B(c) — Reduction in balance to reflect application of subsec. (4).

Notes: 39.1(6) allowed the elected capital gains exemption under 110.6(19) to be used on various capital gains flowed out to the taxpayer by a mortgage investment corporation (130.1(4)), a mutual fund trust (131(1)), a related segregated fund trust (138.1(3), (4)) or an employees profit sharing plan (144(4)). For a mutual fund trust (or any other trust) where the allocation to the beneficiary is done under 104(21), see 39.1(3).

(7) Nil exempt capital gains balance — Notwithstanding subsection (1), where at any time an individual ceases to be a member of, or shareholder of, or a beneficiary under, a flow-through entity, the exempt capital gains balance of the individual in respect of the entity for each taxation year that begins after that time is deemed to be nil.

Related Provisions: 53(1)(r) — Increase in ACB on disposition before 2005.

Notes: See Notes at end of 39.1 and to 39.1(1)"exempt capital gains balance". Once the last unit of a particular flow-through entity is sold, the exempt capital gains balance goes to nil. A taxpayer with a leftover balance who is selling all the units of (say) a mutual fund may therefore wish to keep 1 unit, so that if the taxpayer later repurchases units of the same fund, the exempt capital gains balance will be available. Alternatively, 53(1)(r) can increase the ACB of the final shares or units disposed of.

Notes [s. 39.1]: 39.1 added by 1994 Budget, effective 1994. It provided for the 1994 elected capital gains exemption under 110.6(19) to be used with respect to "flow-through entities", as defined in 39.1(1), until 2004.

Definitions [s. 39.1]: "amount" — 248(1); "capital gain" — 39(1)(a), 248(1); "disposition" — 248(1); "employees profit sharing plan" — 144(1), 248(1); "exempt capital gains balance" — 39.1(1), (7); "fair market value" — see 69(1) Notes; "fiscal period" — 249(2)(b), 249.1; "flow-through entity" — 39.1(1); "individual" — 248(1); "investment corporation" — 130(3)(a), 248(1); "mortgage investment corporation" — 130.1(6), 248(1); "mutual fund corporation" — 131(8), (8.1), 248(1); "mutual fund trust" — 132(6)–(7), 132.2(3)(n), 248(1); "partnership" — see 96(1) Notes; "person" — 248(1); "related segregated fund trust" — 138.1(1)(a); "share" — (of corporation) 248(1); "share" — (of partnership's gains) 39.1(4); "shareholder" — 248(1); "taxable capital gain" — 38(a), 248(1); "taxation year" — 11(2), 249; "trust" — 104(1), 248(1).

40. (1) General rules [gain and loss calculation] — Except as otherwise expressly provided in this Part

(a) a taxpayer's gain for a taxation year from the disposition of any property is the amount, if any, by which

(i) if the property was disposed of in the year, the amount, if any, by which the taxpayer's proceeds of disposition exceed the total of the adjusted cost base to the taxpayer of the property immediately before the disposition and any outlays and expenses to the extent that they were made or incurred by the taxpayer for the purpose of making the disposition, or

(ii) if the property was disposed of before the year, the amount, if any, claimed by the taxpayer under subparagraph (iii) in computing the taxpayer's gain for the immediately preceding year from the disposition of the property,

exceeds

(iii) subject to subsection (1.1), such amount as the taxpayer may claim

(A) in the case of an individual (other than a trust) in prescribed form filed with the taxpayer's return of income under this Part for the year, and

(B) in any other case, in the taxpayer's return of income under this Part for the year,

as a deduction, not exceeding the lesser of

(C) a reasonable amount as a reserve in respect of such of the proceeds of disposition of the property that are payable to the taxpayer after the end of the year as can reasonably be regarded as a portion of the amount determined under subparagraph (i) in respect of the property, and

(D) an amount equal to the product obtained when $\frac{1}{5}$ of the amount determined under subparagraph (i) in respect of the property is multiplied by the amount, if any, by which 4 exceeds the number of preceding taxation years of the taxpayer ending after the disposition of the property; and

(b) a taxpayer's loss for a taxation year from the disposition of any property is,

(i) if the property was disposed of in the year, the amount, if any, by which the total of the adjusted cost base to the taxpayer of the property immediately before the disposition and any outlays and expenses to the extent that they were made or incurred by the taxpayer for the purpose of making the disposition, exceeds the taxpayer's proceeds of disposition of the property, and

(ii) in any other case, nil.

Related Provisions: 7(1.3) — Order of disposition of securities acquired under stock option agreement; 40(1.1) — Reserve where small business share or farm/fishing property transferred to child; 40(2) — Limitations; 40(3.3), (3.4) — Limitation on loss where property acquired by affiliated person; 40(10), (11) — Gain or loss on foreign currency debt after change of control; 44(1) — Exchanges of property; 53(1)(n) — Survey and valuation costs for disposition included in adjusted cost base; 69(11) — Deemed proceeds of disposition; 72(1)(c) — No reserve for year of death; 79.1(3), (6)(c) — Capital gains reserve where property repossessed by creditor; 84.1(2.1) — Non-arm's length sale of shares; 87(2)(e) — Amalgamation — capital property; 87(2)(m) — Amalgamation — proceeds not due until after end of year; 87(2)(ll) — Amalgamation — continuation of predecessor corporations; 88(1)(d)(i)(C) — Winding-up; 93(2)–(2.31) — Loss limitations on disposition of foreign affiliate shares; 100(2) — Gain from disposition of interest in partnership; 104(6) — Reduction in loss where property disposed of owned by a trust; 110.6(31) — Limit to capital gains deduction; 112(3)–(4.22) — Capital loss on shares reduced by certain dividends previously paid; 142.2 — Financial institutions — mark-to-market property; 152(4)(b.3) — Extended reassessment period if disposition of real property not reported.

Notes: The basic calculation of a capital gain is in 40(1)(a)(i). "Proceeds of disposition" (s. 54) and "adjusted cost base" (ss. 53, 54) both have detailed defined meanings. (See Notes to 54"capital property" on the distinction between a capital gain and an income gain.) Where proceeds payable over time are dependent on earnings from the property sold, they may be fully taxable under 12(1)(g).

Note when selling publicly-traded stocks that the trade does not "settle" for 2 business days (reduced from 3 days Sept. 5, 2017), so sales must be done by Dec. 27, 2019, or Dec. 29, 2020 or 2021, to trigger gain or loss for the calendar year.

Undeducted current expenses to maintain a property cannot be treated as part of its cost on selling it. See Notes to 54"adjusted cost base".

40(1)(a)(i): See Notes to 54"adjusted cost base" re what costs are included. "Outlays and expenses for the purpose of making the disposition" (OEPMD) refers to the *immediate* purpose, and not outlays "that simply facilitated the disposition or were incurred in the course of the disposition": *Avis Immobilien*, 1996 CarswellNat 2529 (FCA), para. 15 (so currency exchange loss on paying off the mortgage on a property being sold did not qualify); VIEWS doc 2014-0527041I7. In *Wagner*, 2013 FCA 11, an amount paid back to purchasers of a business, to split the tax savings from changing an asset sale to a share sale, was not OEPMD. In *Giguère*, 2018 QCCQ 874, repayments to company Nco's receiver by Nco's owner's wife, for fraudulent Nco payments that she used to buy buildings, were not OEPMD on selling the buildings. The CRA's view is that OEPMD do not include an estate's costs relating to a 70(5) deemed disposition on death creating the gain (2006-0185591C6) or legal fees for disputing an easement to property that is later sold (2012-0461291E5); but might include repayment of a forgivable loan that was conditional on not selling the property (2016-0661001E5). In the author's view, OEPMD should include staging or repairs to real property to make it more saleable, but in light of *Avis Immobilien* this is uncertain. However, surveying and valuation costs can be claimed via 53(1)(n): 2012-0457901E5.

40(1)(a)(iii): a reserve must both be "reasonable" ((iii)(C), and see IT-236R4 for CRA's formula) and be within the "1/5 cumulative per year" rule ((iii)(D)). A "reasonable" reserve need not use the CRA's inflexible formula: *Ennisclare Corp.*, [1984] C.T.C. 286 (FCA). See also docs 2010-0369551E5; 2010-0384701E5 (effect of 70(5.1) and of price adjustment in fifth year); 2012-0462781E5 (purchaser resells property and new purchaser assumes mortgage); 2013-0492721E5 (reserve is included in next year's gain from the disposition, and can qualify for 110.6 capital gains deduction); 2013-050408117 (interaction with 55(2) and 84(3)); 2015-0595471E5 (partnership's reserve is claimed at partnership level); 2015-0594461E5, 2018-0744141C6 [STEP 2018 q.17] (application of 84.1(2.1)); 2018-075535117 (trust flowing capital gains out to beneficiary). If transfer of title is deferred and the sale price includes an interest component, see 12(1)(z.7) and 248(1)"derivative forward agreement".

Ineligible for reserve are: where 40(2)(a) applies (e.g. non-resident vendor, or sale to controlled corp); amounts held in escrow (*Pineo*, [1986] 2 C.T.C. 71 (FCTD); doc 2002-0161395); addition to capital gain based on negative ACB (2005-0116081E5); mortgage transferred to *alter ego* trust or joint partner trust (2011-0394081E5); share sale reverse earnout payments (2000-0051115, 2013-0505391E5). The July 12, 1994 draft legislation proposed a formula for 40(1)(a)(iii)(C) that was the same as the calculation used administratively for calculating a "reasonable" reserve (IT-236R4, para. 4). That calculation was not included in the 1994 technical bill, however, so the determination of a "reasonable" reserve is still open to interpretation.

Where the vendor is financing only a small portion of the sale proceeds, so only a small reserve is available, the reserve can be increased by using a "wrap mortgage" in which the vendor participates in a larger mortgage.

For 40(1)(a)(iii)(B), a claim "in the taxpayer's return" is valid even if the return is filed late. See Notes to 7(1.31).

In *Struck*, 2017 FCA 69, a consent judgment fixing "taxable capital gains" (TCG) for a year precluded the taxpayer later claiming a 40(1)(a)(iii) reserve, since TCG is based on the gain in 40(1).

On sale of a partnership interest, the capital gain calculation is of the interest as a whole, not the individual units: *Iberville Developments*, 2020 FCA 115, para. 53 (leave to appeal denied 2021 CarswellNat 863 (SCC)) [Morris & Wahidie case comment, 68(4) *Canadian Tax Journal* 1123-30 (2020)].

Where property is bought and sold in foreign currency, see Notes to 39(2).

Where a person is on title to property but has no beneficial ownership, see Notes to 54"capital property".

40(1)(a)(iii)(C) amended by 1994 technical bill, for tax years ending after Feb. 21, 1994.

I.T. Application Rules: 26(3), 26(11).

Income Tax Folios: S3-F2-C1: Capital Dividends [replaces IT-66R6]; S3-F4-C1: General discussion of CCA [replaces IT-220R2]; S4-F2-C1: Deductibility of fines and penalties [replaces IT-104R3]; S4-F7-C1: Amalgamations of Canadian corporations [replaces IT-474R2].

Interpretation Bulletins: IT-95R: Foreign exchange gains and losses; IT-99R5: Legal and accounting fees; IT-236R4: Reserves — disposition of capital property (cancelled); IT-259R4: Exchanges of property; IT-268R4: *Inter vivos* transfer of farm property to child; IT-328R3: Losses on shares on which dividends have been received; IT-426R: Shares sold subject to an earnout agreement; IT-461: Forfeited deposits (cancelled); IT-467R2: Damages, settlements, and similar payments; IT-505: Mortgage foreclosures and conditional sales repossessions (cancelled).

Information Circulars: 88-2, paras. 24, 27: General anti-avoidance rule — section 245 of the *Income Tax Act*.

CRA Audit Manual: 11.3.5: Revision of CCA and other permissive deductions; 12.15.9: Revising capital cost allowance and other permissive deductions; 29.2.0: Capital losses.

Forms: RC257: Request for an information return program account (RZ); T2 Sched. 13: Continuity of reserves; T3 Sched. 2: Reserves on dispositions of capital property; T2017: Summary of reserves on dispositions of capital property; T2069: Election in respect of amounts not deductible as reserves for the year of death; T4037: Capital gains [guide]; T4091: Return of securities transactions [guide]; T5008: Statement of securities transactions.

(1.01) [Reserve on] Gift of non-qualifying security — A taxpayer's gain for a particular taxation year from a disposition of a non-qualifying security of the taxpayer (as defined in subsection 118.1(18)) that is the making of a gift (other than an excepted gift, within the meaning assigned by subsection 118.1(19)) to a qualified donee (as defined in subsection 149.1(1)) is the amount, if any, by which

(a) where the disposition occurred in the particular year, the amount, if any, by which the taxpayer's proceeds of disposition exceed the total of the adjusted cost base to the taxpayer of the security immediately before the disposition and any outlays and expenses to the extent they were made or incurred by the taxpayer for the purpose of making the disposition, and

(b) where the disposition occurred in the 60-month period that ends at the beginning of the particular year, the amount, if any, deducted under paragraph (c) in computing the taxpayer's gain for the preceding taxation year from the disposition of the security

exceeds

(c) the amount that the taxpayer claims in prescribed form filed with the taxpayer's return of income for the particular year, not exceeding the eligible amount of the gift, where the taxpayer is not deemed by subsection 118.1(13) to have made a gift of property before the end of the particular year as a consequence of a disposition of the security by the donee or as a consequence of the security ceasing to be a non-qualifying security of the taxpayer before the end of the particular year.

Related Provisions: 72(1)(c) — No reserve for year of death; 87(2)(m.1) — Amalgamation — continuing corporation; 110.1(6), 118.1(13)–(13.3) — Donation of non-qualifying security disallowed; 248(30)–(33) — Determination of eligible amount of gift.

Notes: If donor D makes a charitable gift of a non-qualifying security (defined in 118.1(18)), the gift is ignored for purposes of the donation deduction or credit: 110.1(6), 118.1(13). However, if the donee disposes of the security within 5 years, D will be treated as having made a gift at that later time. 40(1.01) allows D a reserve for the gain realized on making the gift so that the income inclusion can be shifted to a later year — normally the year in which D receives the deduction or credit. The reserve cannot be claimed once D receives tax recognition for the gift or if D becomes non-resident or tax-exempt. If the security is not disposed of within the 5-year period by the donee, D is not required to bring the reserve back into income in the year following expiration of the period.

(For the regular capital gains reserve where proceeds of disposition are not all received in the year, see 40(1)(a)(iii).)

40(1.01)(c) amended by 2002-2013 technical bill, for gifts made after Dec. 20, 2002.

40(1.01) added by 1997 Budget, for 1997 and later taxation years.

(1.1) Reserve — property disposed of to a child — In computing the amount that a taxpayer may claim under subparagraph (1)(a)(iii) in computing the taxpayer's gain from the disposition of a property, that subparagraph shall be read as if the references therein to "$^1/_5$" and "4" were references to "$^1/_{10}$" and "9" respectively, if,

(a) the property was disposed of by the taxpayer to the taxpayer's child,

(b) that child was resident in Canada immediately before the disposition, and

(c) the property was immediately before the disposition,

(i) any land in Canada or depreciable property in Canada of a prescribed class that was used by the taxpayer, the spouse or common-law partner of the taxpayer, a child or a parent of the taxpayer in a farming or fishing business carried on in Canada,

(ii) a share of the capital stock of a family farm or fishing corporation of the taxpayer or an interest in a family farm or fishing partnership of the taxpayer (such a share or an interest having the meaning assigned by subsection 70(10)), or

(iii) a qualified small business corporation share of the taxpayer (within the meaning assigned by subsection 110.6(1)).

(iv) [Repealed]

Related Provisions: 40(8), 70(10) — Extended meaning of "child".

Notes: See David Louis et al., "Succession Planning — Intergenerational Cash-Outs", 177 *The Estate Planner* (CCH) 5-6 (Oct. 2009).

40(1.1) amended by 2014 budget bill #2 (for dispositions and transfers in the 2014 and later tax years), 2006 budget bill #2, 2000 same-sex partners bill.

Interpretation Bulletins: IT-236R4: Reserves — disposition of capital property (cancelled); IT-268R4: *Inter vivos* transfer of farm property to child; IT-328R3: Losses on shares on which dividends have been received.

(2) Limitations — Notwithstanding subsection (1),

(a) **[reserve limitations]** — subparagraph (1)(a)(iii) does not apply to permit a taxpayer to claim any amount under that subparagraph in computing a gain for a taxation year if

(i) the taxpayer, at the end of the year or at any time in the immediately following year, was not resident in Canada or was exempt from tax under any provision of this Part,

(ii) the purchaser of the property sold is a corporation that, immediately after the sale,

(A) was controlled, directly or indirectly, in any manner whatever, by the taxpayer,

(B) was controlled, directly or indirectly, in any manner whatever, by a person or group of persons by whom the taxpayer was controlled, directly or indirectly, in any manner whatever, or

(C) controlled the taxpayer, directly or indirectly, in any manner whatever, where the taxpayer is a corporation, or

(iii) the purchaser of the property sold is a partnership in which the taxpayer was, immediately after the sale, a majority-interest partner;

Related Provisions: 256(5.1), (6.2) — Controlled directly or indirectly.

Notes: 40(2)(a)(iii) added by 2002-2013 technical bill, for sales after Dec. 20, 2002; amended non-substantively by 2013 budget bill #2, effective Dec. 12, 2013.

Interpretation Bulletins: IT-236R4: Reserves — disposition of capital property (cancelled).

(b) **[principal residence]** — where the taxpayer is an individual, the taxpayer's gain for a taxation year from the disposition of a property that was the taxpayer's principal residence at any time after the date (in this section referred to as the "acquisition date") that is the later of December 31, 1971 and the day on which the taxpayer last acquired or reacquired it, as the case may be, is the amount determined by the formula

$$A - \frac{A \times B}{C} - D$$

where

A is the amount that would, if this Act were read without reference to this paragraph and subsections 110.6(19) and (21), be the taxpayer's gain therefrom for the year,

B is

(i) if the taxpayer was resident in Canada during the year that includes the acquisition date, one plus the number of taxation years that end after the acquisition date for which the property is the taxpayer's principal residence and during which the taxpayer was resident in Canada, or

(ii) if it is not the case that the taxpayer was resident in Canada during the year that includes the acquisition date, the number of taxation years that end after the acquisition date for which the property was the taxpayer's principal residence and during which the taxpayer was resident in Canada,

C is the number of taxation years that end after the acquisition date during which the taxpayer owned the property whether jointly with another person or otherwise, and

D is

(i) if the acquisition date is before February 23, 1994 and the taxpayer or the taxpayer's spouse or common-law partner elected under subsection 110.6(19) in respect of the property or an interest, or for civil law a right, therein that was owned, immediately before the disposition, by the taxpayer, $\frac{4}{3}$ of the lesser of

(A) the total of all amounts each of which is the taxable capital gain of the taxpayer or of their spouse or common-law partner that would have resulted from an election by the taxpayer or spouse or common-law partner under subsection 110.6(19) in respect of the property or the interest or right if

(I) this Act were read without reference to subsection 110.6(20), and

(II) the amount designated in the election were equal to the amount, if any, by which the fair market value of the property or the interest or right at the end of February 22, 1994 exceeds the amount determined by the formula

$$E - 1.1F$$

where

E is the amount designated in the election that was made in respect of the property or the interest or right, and

F is the fair market value of the property or the interest or right at the end of February 22, 1994, and

(B) the total of all amounts each of which is the taxable capital gain of the taxpayer or of their spouse or common-law partner that would have resulted from an election that was made under subsection 110.6(19) in respect of the property or the interest or right if the property were the principal residence of neither the taxpayer nor the spouse or common-law partner for each particular taxation year unless the property was designated, in a return of income for the taxation year that includes February 22, 1994 or for a preceding taxation year, to be the principal residence of either of them for the particular taxation year, and

(ii) in any other case, zero;

Announced Administrative Change — Audits in Real Estate Sector

Federal Budget, March 19, 2019, Chapter 1, Part 1: See under 231.1(1).

Possible Future Amendment — Additional tax on housing owned by non-residents

Federal Economic Statement, Chapter 4, Nov. 30, 2020: See under 115(1)(b).

Related Provisions: 40(4) — Disposal of principal residence (PR) to spouse or trust for spouse; 40(5) — Where PR is property of trust for spouse; 40(6) — Special rule re PR; 40(6.1) — Determination of gain for principal residence owned by a trust since before 2017; 40(7) — Property acquired in satisfaction of trust interest; 40(7.1) — Capital gains exemption election ignored for purposes of determining when property last acquired; 45(3) — Election re PR; 152(4)(b.3) — Extended reassessment period if disposition not reported; 257 — Formula amounts cannot calculate to less than zero.

Notes: 40(2)(b) allows full exemption for the gain on a "principal residence" (PR) (see Notes to definition in s. 54; this need not be the main place the taxpayer lives). As long as the family unit has only one PR at a time (see 54"principal residence"(c)(ii) and VIEWS doc 2010-0380171E5), the "one-plus" rule in 40(2)(b)B ensures that the calendar year in which two residences are owned (one sold, another bought) does not disentitle the full exemption (unless the taxpayer was non-resident at time of acquisition: see B(ii)). For discussion of how element B applies, see *Cassidy*, 2011 FCA 271 (what land forms part of the PR is determined for *each* taxation year).

The exemption applies only if the taxpayer owns the property: VIEWS docs 2009-0335041E5, 2011-0408311I7, 2013-0501471E5. If someone else is on title as bare trustee, the exemption is available to the beneficial owner: 2010-0389041E5; but not for beneficial ownership of only part of a property: 2017-0687961E5. See Notes to 54"capital property" at "Bare trustee".

The exemption applies only for years the taxpayer is resident in Canada: see formula element B, VIEWS doc 2013-0493911E5. It applies separately to each property if two residences are sold in the same year: 2004-0088031E5. If one lives in the home, then tears it down, rebuilds and lives in the new home, residence in both homes can be counted: doc 2006-0215721E5. The exemption can apply to a grant of servitude in Quebec: 2006-0196071C6; on extinguishment of a usufruct: 2010-0367371E5; and to a tenant's receipt of an amount due to early termination of lease: 2006-0211451M4, 2007-0254721R3, 2019-0812611C6 [2019 APFF q.2]. On a rollover to a corporation of a property that includes a PR, one cannot sever the residence portion so as to elect a high amount under 85(1) for the residence: doc 2005-0132391E5.

Reporting: 54"principal residence"(c) and Reg. 2301 require filing a prescribed form to designate a PR. See T1 Schedule 3; Form T2091. Since the 2016 tax year, the disposition must always be reported: Income Tax Folio S1-F3-C2 ¶2.15; VIEWS docs 2017-0709011C6 [2017 APFF q.3]. The form can be filed late with a penalty: 220(3.21)(a.1), 220(3.5). The penalty was normally waived for dispositions in 2016-17: 2018-0761571C6 [2018 APFF Financial q.11].

Before the 2016 tax year, CRA administrative policy (based on 220(2.1)) was to not require the form if the exemption eliminated the gain, unless the 1994 election to use the $100,000 capital gains exemption had been filed for the property. (This did not apply to a trust claiming the exemption, which had to file Form T1079: 2010-0373591C6.) Despite this concession, the Courts could deny the exemption if the form had not been filed: *Smellie Estate*, [1977] C.T.C. 2435 (TRB); *Rhéaume*, 2003 FCA 219. The form could not be filed late, since 54"principal residence"(c) and Reg. 2301 were not listed in Reg. 600: 2012-0448391I7.

A PR capital gains exemption is allowed administratively to foreign officials living in Canada who are exempt under 149(1)(a) (where the sale takes place after the official leaves Canada, so that 149(1)(a) no longer applies), if the foreign country grants a reciprocal exemption to Canadian officials living there; VIEWS doc 2010-0391502I7.

An exemption is also allowed administratively where a partner lives in a home owned by a partnership: doc 2012-0473291E5.

For discussion see Katz, "The Principal Residence Exemption", 49(4) *Canadian Tax Journal* 990-1024 (2001); Woolley, "Principal Residences", 2010 BC Tax Conference (ctf.ca), 6:1-55; Wong. "Cross Border Issues Related to the Rental and Sale of a Principal Residence", 5(3) *BorderCrossings* (Carswell) 1-5 (Sept. 2012); Bergeron, "Principal Residence: When Civil Law Muddles Tax Law", 3(2) *Canadian Tax Focus* (ctf.ca) 8-9 (May 2013); Friedlan & Friedlan, Wang & Bernier, "Principal and Cottage Residence Planning" [2 papers], 2013 Ontario Tax Conf. 8A:1-23, 8B:1-24; Ideias, "Principal Residence Exemption: What a Tax Planner Needs to Know" (*Taxnet Pro Tax & Estate Planning Centre*, 2021, 14pp); Checklist 46 — *Principal Residence Planning* (*ibid.*, 2021, 5pp).

If a house is destroyed and the land is later sold, the exemption is available for the years during which it was a PR: VIEWS docs 2005-0148091E5, 2005-0157441I7, 2006-0200271E5, 2007-0224601E5, 2007-0237251E5, 2012-0473291E5, 2017-0702001E5.

For more CRA interpretation see Income Tax Folio S1-F3-C2; docs 2009-0342121E5 and 2013-0480951E5 (whether rooftop solar panels disentitle taxpayer to part of exemption); 2010-0357631E5 (part-year counts as a year in the calculation, even if 45(2) election filed or property sold on leaving Canada); 2010-0383481E5 (parent transfers part ownership in home to adult child); 2012-0473291E5 (home destroyed by fire and replaced with new home); 2013-0495791I7 (Nfld & Labrador community relocation payment treated as disposition of PR); 2016-0652851C6 [2016 APFF q.3] (payment received on breach of agreement to buy PR: no exemption). See also Notes to 54"principal residence".

Inventory, and CRA real estate audits: The exemption applies only to a PR that is *capital* property: see Notes to 54"capital property". A "flipper" or "house hopper", who builds or buys a home or condo intending to sell it, is fully taxed on the gain as business profit under 9(1), even if they live there, as the home is inventory, not capital property: *Lacina*, [1997] G.S.T.C. 69 (FCA); *Schlamp*, [1982] C.T.C. 304 (FCTD); TCC cases *Deleurme*, [1996] 3 C.T.C. 2856; *Fournier*, [1998] 2 C.T.C. 2001; *Watson*,

[1998] 3 C.T.C. 2370; *Mullin*, [1998] 3 C.T.C. 2812; *Vogan*, 2004 TCC 657; *Scopacasa*, 2004 TCC 655; *Cayer*, 2007 TCC 136 (FCA appeal discontinued A-201-07); *Giusti*, 2011 TCC 62; *Gilbert*, 2011 TCC 155; *Giguère*, 2012 TCC 309; *Sangha*, 2013 TCC 69; *DaCosta*, 2017 TCC 235; *Wall*, 2019 TCC 168, paras. 157-174 (FCA appeal heard June 10/21); *Hansen*, 2020 TCC 102 (6 houses sold in 6 years, but gross-negligence penalties and statute-barred assessments cancelled). See also Info Sheet TI-001; VIEWS doc 2004-0099751E5. As well, the self-supply rule imposes GST/HST on the home's value when the builder moves in (or rents it out): see *Excise Tax Act* s. 191(1) in David M. Sherman, *Practitioner's Goods and Services Tax Annotated*. A person who can show **no intention to resell** and compelling reason to have unexpectedly sold the home can claim the exemption: e.g. *Freer*, 2003 TCC 20; *Arnold*, 2005 TCC 725; *Nowoczin*, 2007 TCC 275; *Stan Wire*, 2009 TCC 425; *Ballone*, 2010 TCC 66; *Palardy*, 2011 TCC 108; *Cameron*, 2011 TCC 107; *Piché*, 2020 QCCQ 1283 (parallel Quebec rule); *Ouellette*, 2020 QCCQ 8765 (O built and sold 3 homes in 4 years; Court believed reasons given for selling); or if the exemption does not apply, can treat the gain as capital gain: *Bygrave*, 2019 TCC 138; *Bishara*, 2020 QCCA 854 (Quebec rule); *Swift*, 2020 TCC 115 (construction company owner built home for family, not resale); *Gosai*, 2020 CarswellNat 4376 (TCC) (G bought condo pre-construction for investment, then sold it to her son when he broke up and needed a home; "period of ownership" for new condo was based on date of original agreement of purchase). See also Perumal, "Is the Doctrine of Secondary Intention Still Appropriate?", 13(4) *Taxes & Wealth Management* (Carswell) 13-14 (Dec. 2020).

Further to the above, CRA has since 2013 run a large "property flipping" project in the Toronto and Vancouver areas, finding taxpayers who held a condo or other home for only a short time before selling it (even if the purchase agreement was signed years before the condo was built), and assessing to deny the PR exemption and treat the gain as business income. (CRA also audits for "shadow flipping", selling the purchase right before closing.) GST/HST is assessed as well in some cases, and the GST/HST new housing rebate is usually denied. See CRA news releases "The Canada Revenue Agency updates audit results relating to the real estate sector in British Columbia and Ontario" (May 17, 2018) [past 3 years: 30,000 files, $593m additional tax assessed, $44m penalties; CRA issues unnamed-person requirements to find pre-construction assignments]; "The Government of Canada identifies more than a billion dollars in additional taxes in British Columbia and Ontario real estate markets" (May 30, 2019); "How the Canada Revenue Agency addresses non-compliance in the real estate sector" (tinyurl.com/cra-REnon). Conviction for not reporting flipping income: Harjinder Dhudwal (CRA news release, Aug. 30, 2017: 15 months conditional + fine). See also Kiselbach & Ghag, "CRA's Continuing Audit Project — Real Estate Transactions", 12(4) *Taxes & Wealth Management* (Carswell) 2-3 (Dec. 2019). CRA is also seeking to examine US real estate records for Canadian ownership: "Bulk US Real Property Data re Canadian residents" (tender notice, June 2020, tinyurl.com/cra-bulk-us).

The Oct. 2019 Liberal election platform states: "And we will work with interested provinces, territories and communities to establish a national approach to beneficial ownership so that law enforcement and tax authorities have the tools necessary to crack down on financial crime in the real estate sector, while respecting Canadian privacy rights." The Liberals were elected with a minority government on Oct. 21, 2019, so this measure may well be implemented.

(The 2018 BC budget introduced a requirement for beneficial ownership information to be provided on real property transfers: see the *Land Owner Transparency Act*, in force Nov. 30, 2020; Dy, "Beneficial Ownership Transparency", 1(4) *Perspectives on Tax Law & Policy* (ctf.ca) 6-8 (Dec. 2020). This will give CRA additional audit tools. The Prime Minister's Dec. 2019 "mandate letter" to the Minister of Finance told him to: "Work with the Minister of Families ... to limit housing speculation by developing a framework and introducing a 1% annual vacancy and speculation tax on applicable residential properties owned by non-resident non-Canadians"; see now the April 2021 Budget proposal under 115(1)(b). See also Quebec *Déclarations du cédant et du cessionnaire* (tinyurl.com/qc-declar), required on every real estate purchase or sale since Oct. 1, 2020. Ontario has a non-resident speculation tax, a 15% tax on non-residents who buy homes in or near Toronto without moving in: tinyurl.com/ont-nrst.)

For US citizens, see Feigenbaum, "What Dual Citizens Should Know About the US Principal Residence Exemption", *Ameri-Can Tax Talk Newsletter* (*Taxnet Pro* Corporate Tax Centre), Feb. 2011; Jesson, "US Taxpayers and the Principal-Residence Exemption", 5(3) *Canadian Tax Focus* (ctf.ca) 2-3 (Aug. 2015); Notes to 128.1(1).

The exemption can be claimed by a trust, but only in limited circumstances for gains after 2016: see Notes to 54"principal residence". It cannot be claimed by a corporation: VIEWS doc 2011-0414691E5.

40(2)(b)B amended by 2017 budget bill #2, for dispositions after Oct. 2, 2016, effectively to add the rule in B(ii). Earlier amended by 2002-2013 technical bill (effective June 26, 2013), 2000 same-sex partners bill, 1994 Budget.

I.T. Application Rules: 26.1(1) (change of use of property before 1972).

Income Tax Folios: S1-F3-C2: Principal residence [replaces IT-120R6, IT-437R].

Interpretation Bulletins: IT-268R3: *Inter vivos* transfer of farm property to child; IT-332R: Personal-use property (cancelled).

Info Sheets: TI-001: Sale of a residence by an owner builder.

Forms: T1 Sched. 3: Capital gains (or losses); T1255: Designation of a property as a principal residence by the legal representative of a deceased individual; T2091(IND): Designation of a property as a principal residence by an individual (other than a personal trust); T2091 (IND)-WS: Principal residence worksheet.

(c) **[land used in farming business]** — where the taxpayer is an individual, the taxpayer's gain for a taxation year from the disposition of land used in a farming business carried on by the taxpayer that includes property that was at any time the taxpayer's principal residence is

(i) the taxpayer's gain for the year, otherwise determined, from the disposition of the portion of the land that does not include the property that was the taxpayer's principal residence, plus the taxpayer's gain for the year, if any, determined under paragraph (b) from the disposition of the property that was the taxpayer's principal residence, or

(ii) if the taxpayer so elects in prescribed manner in respect of the land, the taxpayer's gain for the year from the disposition of the land including the property that was the taxpayer's principal residence, determined without regard to paragraph (b) or subparagraph (i) of this paragraph, less the total of

(A) $1,000, and

(B) $1,000 for each taxation year ending after the acquisition date for which the property was the taxpayer's principal residence and during which the taxpayer was resident in Canada;

Related Provisions: 40(4) — Disposal of residence to spouse or spousal trust.

Notes: 40(2)(c) offers an alternative principal-residence exemption for farmers. Instead of having the gain on the residence exempt and the gain on the farmland taxable, the farmer may elect to have a gain of $1,000 per year exempted on the entire property. (This figure has not increased since 1972.) "Land" includes farm buildings as well as the home: see 70(5.2) Notes.

Regulations: 2300 (prescribed manner).

Income Tax Folios: S1-F3-C2: Principal residence [replaces IT-120R6, IT-437R].

Interpretation Bulletins: IT-268R3: *Inter vivos* transfer of farm property to child; IT-332R: Personal-use property (cancelled).

(d) **[disposition of bond]** — where the taxpayer is a corporation, its loss for a taxation year from the disposition of a bond or debenture is its loss therefrom for the year otherwise determined, less the total of such amounts received by it as, on account or in lieu of payment of, or in satisfaction of interest thereon as were, by virtue of paragraph 81(1)(m), not included in computing its income;

(e) **[disposition to controller or controlled corporation]** — [Repealed]

Notes: 40(2)(e) repealed by 1995-97 technical bill, effective (subject to grandfathering) for dispositions of property after April 26, 1995. It has been replaced by 40(3.4) and 54"superficial loss".

(e.1) **[disposition of debt of related person]** — a particular taxpayer's loss, if any, from the disposition at any time to a particular person or partnership of an obligation — other than, for the purposes of computing the exempt surplus or exempt deficit and taxable surplus or taxable deficit of the particular taxpayer in respect of another taxpayer, where the particular taxpayer or, if the particular taxpayer is a partnership, a member of the particular taxpayer is a foreign affiliate of the other taxpayer, an obligation that is, or would be, if the particular taxpayer were a foreign affiliate of the other taxpayer, excluded property (within the meaning assigned by subsection 95(1)) of the particular taxpayer — that was, immediately after that time, payable by another person or partnership to the particular person or partnership is nil if the particular taxpayer, the particular person or partnership and the other person or partnership are related to each other at that time or would be related to each other at that time if paragraph 80(2)(j) applied for the purpose of this paragraph;

Related Provisions: 40(2)(e.2), 40(2)(g)(ii) — Further limitations on loss on disposition of debt; 53(1)(f.1), (f.11) — Addition to adjusted cost base; 54"superficial loss"(e) — Superficial loss rule does not apply; 80.01(8) — Deemed settlement after debt parking; 93.1(3)(b) — Tiered partnership — look-through rule.

Notes: Where a loss is denied by 40(2)(e.1), the transferee is generally entitled to increase its ACB under 53(1)(f.1) or (f.11). The purpose of 40(2)(e.1) is to provide balanced treatment for debtors and creditors under the debt parking rule in 80.01(8) and the stop-loss rules in 40(2) (and former 85(4), 97(3)).

For planning around 40(2)(e.1) see Advance Tax Ruling ATR-66 (cancelled but CRA policy has not changed: VIEWS doc 2014-0522501E5) and docs 2004-0081691R3, 2008-0300161R3, 2009-0343201R3, 2009-0347271R3, 2013-0514191R3, 2014-0547871R3. For examples of 40(2)(e.1) applying see 2009-0350711R3, 2011-0395701E5, 2011-0426051R3, 2012-0452821R3, 2012-0462141R3; 2013-0479701R3 (where 40(2)(g)(ii) also applies); 2014-0524391E5 (debt parking).

See also Mike Hegedus, "Paragraph 40(2)(e.1) Versus Subparagraph 40(2)(g)(ii): Potential Conflict?", IX(4) *Resource Sector Taxation* (Federated Press) 684-90 (2014).

40(2)(e.1) amended by 2002-2013 technical bill, for dispositions after Aug. 19, 2011, effectively to add the " — other than" exclusion. Added by 1994 technical bill.

I.T. Application Rules: 26(5)(c)(ii)(A) (where property owned since June 18, 1971).

(e.2) **[settlement of commercial obligation]** — subject to paragraph (e.3), a taxpayer's loss on the settlement or extinguishment of a particular commercial obligation (in this paragraph having the meaning assigned by subsection 80(1)) issued by a person or partnership and payable to the taxpayer is deemed to be the amount determined by the following formula if any part of the consideration given by the person or partnership for the settlement or extinguishment of the particular obligation consists of one or more other commercial obligations issued by the person or partnership to the taxpayer:

$$A \times \frac{(B - C)}{B}$$

where

A   is the amount, if any, that would be the taxpayer's loss from the disposition of the particular obligation if this Act were read without reference to this paragraph,

B   is the total fair market value of all the consideration given by the person or partnership for the settlement or extinguishment of the particular obligation, and

C   is the total fair market value of the other obligations;

Related Provisions: 40(2)(e.2), 40(2)(g)(ii) — Further limitations on loss on disposition of debt; 53(1)(f.12) — Addition to adjusted cost base; 80(2)(h) — Application of debt forgiveness rules; 257 — Formula cannot calculate to less than zero.

Notes: For the meaning of "extinguishment", see Notes to 80(2)(a).

40(2)(e.2) amended by 2002-2013 technical bill (for settlements and extinguishments after Aug. 19, 2011). Added by 1994 technical bill.

I.T. Application Rules: 26(5)(c)(ii)(A) (where property owned since June 18, 1971).

(e.3) **[exception to 40(2)(e.2)]** — paragraph (e.2) does not apply, for the purposes of computing the exempt surplus or exempt deficit and taxable surplus or taxable deficit of the taxpayer in respect of another taxpayer, where the taxpayer or, if the taxpayer is a partnership, a member of the taxpayer is a foreign affiliate of the other taxpayer, to the particular commercial obligation if the particular commercial obligation is, or would be, if the taxpayer were a foreign affiliate of the other taxpayer, excluded property (within the meaning assigned by subsection 95(1)) of the taxpayer;

Related Provisions: 93.1(3)(b) — Tiered partnership — look-through rule.

Notes: 40(2)(e.3) added by 2002-2013 technical bill (Part 3 — FA reorganizations), effective for settlements and extinguishments that occur after Aug. 19, 2011.

(f) **[right to a prize]** — a taxpayer's gain or loss from the disposition of

(i) a chance to win a prize or bet, or

(ii) a right to receive an amount as a prize or as winnings on a bet,

in connection with a lottery scheme or a pool system of betting referred to in section 205 of the *Criminal Code* is nil;

Notes: See Income Tax Folio S3-F9-C1 ¶1.17-1.21.

The present wording of 40(2)(f) reverts to an earlier version. It appears that in the R.S.C. 1985 consolidation which came into force in 1994, amendments made in 1985 were overlooked. Those amendments deleted "or bet" from subpara. (i), "or as winnings on a bet" from subpara. (ii), and "or a pool system of betting referred to in section 188.1 [now 205] of the *Criminal Code*". The section of the *Criminal Code* referred to has been repealed.

The receipt of a lottery prize is not taxed because it is not income from a "source" for ss. 3 and 4(1), unless the prize is an employment benefit (6(1)(a)), a business incentive

(9(1)) or caught by 56(1)(n): Folio S3-F9-C1 ¶1.16, VIEWS docs 2005-0111311E5, 2010-0357141E5, 2011-0425361E5. (A lottery win on a ticket given by an employer is valued as of when the ticket was given, e.g. $5: doc 2010-0360261E5.) See also Notes to s. 3. A prize is deemed acquired at its fair market value, however; see 52(4). Note also that a lottery prize that is paid as annual payments may be taxable under 12.2(1) or 56(1)(d) as an annuity: *Rumack*, [1992] 1 C.T.C. 57 (FCA) (leave to appeal to SCC denied); doc 2004-0085091E5. In *Leblanc*, [2007] 2 C.T.C. 2248 (TCC), $5 million net winnings on sports lotteries were not taxable. A lottery ticket retailer's prize for selling a winning ticket was administratively untaxed (IT-404R paras. 3-4), but is taxed as business income starting 2014: VIEWS docs 2013-049199117, 2014-0522731M4.

Income Tax Folios: S3-F9-C1: Lottery winnings, miscellaneous receipts, and income (and losses) from crime [replaces IT-185R, IT-213R, IT-256R, IT-334R2].

Interpretation Bulletins: IT-404R: Payments to lottery ticket vendors.

(g) **[various losses deemed nil]** — a taxpayer's loss, if any, from the disposition of a property (other than, for the purposes of computing the exempt surplus or exempt deficit, hybrid surplus or hybrid deficit, and taxable surplus or taxable deficit of the taxpayer in respect of another taxpayer, where the taxpayer or, if the taxpayer is a partnership, a member of the taxpayer is a foreign affiliate of the other taxpayer, a property that is, or would be, if the taxpayer were a foreign affiliate of the other taxpayer, excluded property (within the meaning assigned by subsection 95(1)) of the taxpayer), to the extent that it is

(i) a superficial loss,

(ii) a loss from the disposition of a debt or other right to receive an amount, unless the debt or right, as the case may be, was acquired by the taxpayer for the purpose of gaining or producing income from a business or property (other than exempt income) or as consideration for the disposition of capital property to a person with whom the taxpayer was dealing at arm's length,

(iii) a loss from the disposition of any personal-use property of the taxpayer (other than listed personal property or a debt referred to in subsection 50(2)), or

(iv) a loss from the disposition of property to

(A) a trust governed by a deferred profit sharing plan, an employees profit sharing plan, a registered disability savings plan, a registered retirement income fund or a TFSA under which the taxpayer is a beneficiary or immediately after the disposition becomes a beneficiary, or

(B) a trust governed by a registered retirement savings plan under which the taxpayer or the taxpayer's spouse or common-law partner is an annuitant or becomes, within 60 days after the end of the taxation year, an annuitant,

is nil;

Related Provisions: 3(b)(ii) — Limitation on use of listed personal property losses; 13(21.2) — Superficial loss rule for depreciable property; 18(13)–(16) — Superficial loss in moneylending business or adventure in nature of trade; 40(2)(e.1) — Limitation on loss where commercial obligation disposed of in exchange for another commercial obligation; 40(3.3), (3.4) — Limitation on loss where property acquired by affiliated person; 41 — Listed personal property losses can offset listed personal property gains; 53(1)(f) — Addition to adjusted cost base — superficial loss; 80(1) — "Unrecognized loss"; 93.1(3)(b) — Tiered partnership — look-through rule; 112(3)–(4.22) — Reduction in capital loss on shares where dividends previously paid.

Notes: 40(2)(g) disallows a capital loss (CL) for various unrelated reasons.

40(2)(g)(i): See Notes to 54"superficial loss".

40(2)(g)(ii) requires only that earning income be *one* of the purposes of the loan, even if not the primary purpose: *Rich*, 2003 FCA 38, para. 8; *Scott*, 2010 TCC 401; *MacCallum*, 2011 TCC 316.

Interest-free loans: in *Byram*, [1999] 2 C.T.C. 149, the FCA allowed a CL on interest-free loans made by a shareholder to a corporation so it could earn income and pay dividends. The test in 40(2)(g)(ii) is not like that in 20(1)(c), which requires, for interest deductibility, that the borrowed money have been used directly for purposes of producing income. CRA requires a "clear nexus" between the loan and potential dividend income from the shares: VIEWS docs 2002-0151337, 2003-0038755, 2005-0117541I7, 2006-0172111E5; 2007-0239681I7 (shares acquired through RRSP have enough nexus); 2012-0436251E5; 2014-052465117; 2015-059797117 (insufficient where interest-free loans made to building tenant). A CL was allowed in *Martel*, 2006 TCC 556 (taxpayer's intention was to earn dividend income from the shares); *Alessandro*, 2007 TCC 411 (enough nexus between taxpayer and corp). CL was denied in *Grubner*, 2018 TCC 39 (paying corp's unremitted source deductions and GST/HST, to avoid director liability, with no real hope of recovery from corp).

The *Byram* principle did not extend to loans made to (or guarantees of the debts of) a corporation owned by the taxpayer's spouse in: *Service*, 2005 FCA 163; *Elliott*, 2005 TCC 35; *Proulx-Drouin*, 2005 TCC 116; *Coveley*, 2013 TCC 417, para. 103 (aff'd on other grounds 2014 FCA 281); or to a corp owned by a family trust of which the taxpayer was only a discretionary beneficiary: *Toews*, 2005 TCC 597 (see VIEWS doc 2007-0243361C6); or to a corp that the taxpayer supported but was not a shareholder of: *Gaudette*, 2018 TCC 208. Nor did it extend to a loan made to earn future employment income: *Coveley*, para. 105. In *MacCallum*, 2011 TCC 316, a CL was allowed on a guarantee of a loan to the taxpayer's son's company, made to protect a loan owing to the taxpayer's company. CRA accepts that the taxpayer need not be a direct shareholder but says the burden of demonstrating the connection to income-earning potential "will be much higher": Income Tax Folio S4-F8-C1 ¶1.47.

In *Daniels*, 2007 TCC 179, a CL was allowed on a worthless debenture D acquired from his brother in exchange for releasing his brother's debt to him, where he could have claimed the loss on the first debt. In *Dolbec*, 2008 TCC 464, a CL was allowed on the strength of D's evidence and the logic that she would not have transferred $245,000 to a corporation unless it was to earn income. In *Nabil Warda Inc.*, 2019 TCC 95, a CL (and ABIL) was denied on loans a corp made to its Holdco, as there was no expectation of profit. In *Dépatie*, 2019 TCC 123, D's loan to her mother's corp was intended to allow D to share in corp's profits even though D was not a shareholder.

For a plan avoiding 40(2)(g)(i) see Katlai, "Succession Planning in a Down Economy", 21(1) *Tax for the Owner-Manager* (ctf.ca) 3-4 (Jan. 2021).

See also VIEWS docs 2007-0237791I7 (no CL on foreign exchange on loans to parent corp); 2012-0442951C6 (no CL to estate on debt forgiveness in testator's will); 2012-0463431E5 (no CL on loan made to sister corp); 2012-043499II7 (CL on loans made to earn income); 2014-052465II7 (CL on loan to foreign affiliate).

40(2)(g)(iii): Personal-use property (s. 54) losses are disallowed except for listed personal property (LPP) losses, which can be offset against LPP gains. See Notes to 54"personal-use property" and 41(1). See also docs 2006-0198381E5 (after sale of home, payment under warranty triggers loss under s. 42 but deemed nil by 40(2)(g)(iii)); 2013-0504531E5 (no CL on cottage destroyed by flood).

40(2)(g)(iv): Note that this does not apply on a disposition to a RESP.

40(2)(g) opening words amended by 2002-2013 technical bill (Part 3 — FA reorganizations) to add "(other than ... of the taxpayer)", for dispositions after Aug. 19, 2011. 40(2)(g)(iv) earlier amended by 2007 RDSPs bill (for 2008 and later taxation years), 2001 technical bill, 2000 same-sex partners bill.

I.T. Application Rules: 26(6).

Income Tax Folios: S1-F3-C2: Principal residence [replaces IT-120R6, IT-437R]; S4-F8-C1: Business investment losses [replaces IT-484R2].

Interpretation Bulletins: IT-124R6: Contributions to registered retirement savings plans; IT-159R3: Capital debts established to be bad debts; IT-160R3: Personal use of aircraft (cancelled); IT-218R: Profit, capital gains and losses from the sale of real estate; IT-239R2: Deductibility of capital losses from guaranteeing loans and loaning funds in non-arm's length circumstances (cancelled); IT-291R3: Transfer of property to a corporation under subsection 85(1); IT-325R2: Property transfers after separation, divorce and annulment; IT-332R: Personal-use property (cancelled).

I.T. Technical News: 18 (*Byram* case).

CRA Audit Manual: 29.2.4: Specific exceptions to capital gain and loss rules.

(h) **[shares of controlled corporation]** — where the taxpayer is a corporation, its loss otherwise determined from the disposition at any time in a taxation year of shares of the capital stock of a corporation (in this paragraph referred to as the "controlled corporation") that was controlled, directly or indirectly in any manner whatever, by it at any time in the year, is its loss therefrom otherwise determined less the amount, if any, by which

(i) all amounts added under paragraph 53(1)(f.1) to the cost to a corporation, other than the controlled corporation, of property disposed of to that corporation by the controlled corporation that were added to the cost of the property during the period while the controlled corporation was controlled by the taxpayer and that can reasonably be attributed to losses on the property that accrued during the period while the controlled corporation was controlled by the taxpayer,

exceeds

(ii) all amounts by which losses have been reduced by virtue of this paragraph in respect of dispositions before that time of shares of the capital stock of the controlled corporation; and

Related Provisions: 40(3.3), (3.4) — Limitation on loss where property acquired by affiliated person; 87(2)(kk) — Amalgamations — Continuation of predecessor corporations; 112(3)–(4.22) — Reduction in capital loss on shares where dividends previously paid; 256(5.1), (6.2) — Controlled directly or indirectly.

Notes: For interpretation of "reasonably be attributed" in (h)(i), see *729658 Alberta Ltd.*, 2004 TCC 474.

40(2)(h)(i) amended by 1995-97 technical bill, effective (subject to grandfathering) for dispositions of property after April 26, 1995, to clarify that a corporation's loss from the disposition of a controlled corporation's shares is subject to adjustment to take account of previous dispositions of property by the controlled corporation to any other corporation, including the shareholder corporation.

(i) **[shares of certain corporations]** — where at a particular time a taxpayer has disposed of a share of the capital stock of a corporation that was at any time a prescribed venture capital corporation or a prescribed labour-sponsored venture capital corporation or a share of the capital stock of a taxable Canadian corporation that was held in a prescribed stock savings plan or of a property substituted for such a share, the taxpayer's loss from the disposition thereof shall be deemed to be the amount, if any, by which

(i) the loss otherwise determined

exceeds

(ii) the amount, if any, by which

(A) the amount of prescribed assistance that the taxpayer (or a person with whom the taxpayer was not dealing at arm's length) received or is entitled to receive in respect of the share

exceeds

(B) the total of all amounts determined under subparagraph (i) in respect of any disposition of the share or of the property substituted for the share before the particular time by the taxpayer or by a person with whom the taxpayer was not dealing at arm's length.

Related Provisions: 53(2)(k) — Reduction in adjusted cost base — government assistance; 112(3)–(4.22) — Reduction in capital loss on shares where dividends previously paid; 248(5) — Substituted property; Reg. 3101 — Property is prescribed property for tax shelter rules.

Notes: 40(2)(i)(ii) amended by 1993 technical bill, effective for 1991 and later taxation years, to add the words "or is entitled to receive". Thus, prescribed assistance receivable (as well as received) in respect of a share reduces the capital loss on disposition of the share. A parallel amendment to 53(2)(k)(i)(C) provides that such assistance does not reduce ACB.

Regulations: 6700, 6700.1 (prescribed venture capital corporation); 6701 (prescribed labour-sponsored venture capital corporation); 6702 (prescribed assistance); 6705 (prescribed stock savings plan).

Interpretation Bulletins: IT-273R2: Government assistance — general comments.

(j) [Repealed under former Act]

Notes: 40(2)(j), repealed by 1985 Budget, dealt with losses on transfers to an indexed security investment plan, a concept no longer used.

(3) Deemed gain where amounts to be deducted from ACB exceed cost plus amounts to be added to ACB — Where

(a) the total of all amounts required by subsection 53(2) (except paragraph 53(2)(c)) to be deducted in computing the adjusted cost base to a taxpayer of any property at any time in a taxation year

exceeds

(b) the total of

(i) the cost to the taxpayer of the property determined for the purpose of computing the adjusted cost base to the taxpayer of that property at that time, and

(ii) all amounts required by subsection 53(1) to be added to the cost to the taxpayer of the property in computing the adjusted cost base to the taxpayer of that property at that time,

the following rules apply:

(c) subject to paragraph 93(1)(b), the amount of the excess is deemed to be a gain of the taxpayer for the year from a disposition at that time of the property,

(d) for the purposes of section 93 and subsections 116(6) and (6.1), the property is deemed to have been disposed of by the taxpayer at that time, and

(e) for the purposes of subsection 2(3) and sections 110.6 and 150, the property is deemed to have been disposed of by the taxpayer in the year.

Related Provisions: 40(3.1)–(3.2) — Deemed capital gain or loss for passive partners; 53(1)(a) — Deemed gain added to adjusted cost base of property; 93(1) — Election re disposition of share in foreign affiliate; 98(1)(c) — Where partnership ceases to exist; 98.1(1)(c) — Residual interest in partnership; 100(2) — Deemed gain on disposition of partnership interest.

Notes: 40(3) provides that "negative" ACB under 53(2) triggers an immediate capital gain. The ACB is then reset to zero by 53(1)(a). 40(3) does not apply to a partnership interest (see Notes to 53(2)(c)) for an active partner, which can remain negative unless the partnership ceases to exist (98(1)(c)) or the partner withdraws from the partnership (98.1(1)(c)). However, for limited partners and other passive partners (and possibly LLP professionals), see 40(3.1)–(3.2). Where a partner redeems only a portion of her partnership units, see VIEWS doc 2010-0373461C6.

Where an investor's interest in a mutual fund trust is negative, 40(3) applies; any return of capital appears in box 42 of the T3 information slip: VIEWS docs 2005-0125951E5, 2008-0284261C6.

See also Paul Cormack & Janette Pantry, "Negative Partnership Interest ACB", 24(8) *Canadian Tax Highlights* (ctf.ca) 1-2 (Aug. 2016).

40(3)(d), (e) amended by 2017 budget bill #2, for gains from dispositions after Sept. 15, 2016, to add references to 2(3), 116 and 150. 40(3) earlier amended by 2002-2013 technical bill (effective Aug. 20, 2011), 1991 technical bill.

Interpretation Bulletins: IT-242R: Retired partners; IT-278R2: Death of a partner or of a retired partner.

(3.1) Deemed gain for certain partners

— Where, at the end of a fiscal period of a partnership, a member of the partnership is a limited partner of the partnership, or is a member of the partnership who was a specified member of the partnership at all times since becoming a member, except where the member's partnership interest was held by the member on February 22, 1994 and is an excluded interest at the end of the fiscal period,

(a) the amount determined under subsection (3.11) is deemed to be a gain from the disposition, at the end of the fiscal period, of the member's interest in the partnership; and

(b) for the purposes of subsection 2(3), section 110.6, subsections 116(6) and (6.1) and section 150, the interest is deemed to have been disposed of by the member at that time.

Related Provisions: 40(3.12) — Election for deemed capital loss where ACB is later positive; 40(3.131) — Specified member of partnership — anti-avoidance rule; 40(3.14) — Limited partner; 40(3.15) — Excluded interest; 40(3.18) — Grandfathered partners; 40(3.19) — Subsec. 40(3.1) takes precedence over 40(3); 40(3.2) — Paras. 98(1)(c) and 98.1(1)(c) take precedence; 53(1)(e)(vi) — Addition to adjusted cost base; 53(2)(c)(i.3), (i.4) — Reduction in adjusted cost base; 89(1)"capital dividend account"(a)(i)(A) — CDA not increased by 40(3.1)(a) disposition.

Notes: A negative ACB normally causes an immediate capital gain, but not for partnership interests; see Notes to 40(3). For limited partners and other passive partners (see 248(1)"specified member"), 40(3.1) deems there to be a capital gain, subject to the rules in 40(3.11)-(3.19) and (3.2). A way to defer the gain might be to have the partnership lend funds to partners rather than distributing profits, but the CRA disagrees: VIEWS doc 2016-0637341E5 [Cepparo, "Loans to Limited Partner May Create Negative ACB", 24(12) *Canadian Tax Highlights* (ctf.ca) 7-8 (Dec. 2016)].

See also Notes to 40(3.12) re *Gladwin Realty* case.

For the impact on ACB see VIEWS doc 2009-0349911E5. For a ruling that 40(3.1) does not apply on a corporate reorganization, see 2007-0245691R3. Since 40(3.1)(b) applies only to 110.6, it does not trigger a non-resident's gain on taxable Canadian property: 2011-0417491E5, 2011-0421481E5.

40(3.1)(b) amended by 2017 budget bill #2, for gains from dispositions after Sept. 15, 2016, to add references to 2(3), 116 and 150.

40(3.1) added by 1994 Budget and amended retroactively by 1995-97 technical bill, effective Feb. 22, 1994 with grandfathering through the partnership's 5th fiscal period ending after 1994 for film production partnerships that met certain conditions.

Former 40(3.1), repealed by 1985 Budget, dealt with losses on the transfer of securities to an indexed security investment plan (see 47.1).

I.T. Technical News: 5 (adjusted cost base of partnership interest).

(3.11) Amount of gain

— For the purpose of subsection (3.1), the amount determined at any time under this subsection in respect of a member's interest in a partnership is the amount determined by the formula

$$A - B$$

where

A is the total of

(a) all amounts required by subsection 53(2) to be deducted in computing the adjusted cost base to the member of the interest in the partnership at that time, and

(b) if the member is a member of a professional partnership, and that time is the end of the fiscal period of the partnership, the amount referred to in subparagraph 53(2)(c)(i) in respect of the taxpayer for that fiscal period; and

B is the total of

(a) the cost to the member of the interest determined for the purpose of computing the adjusted cost base to the member of the interest at that time,

(b) all amounts required by subsection 53(1) to be added to the cost to the member of the interest in computing the adjusted cost base to the member of the interest at that time, and

(c) if the member is a member of a professional partnership, and that time is the end of the fiscal period of the partnership, the amount referred to in subparagraph 53(1)(e)(i) in respect of the taxpayer for that fiscal period.

Related Provisions: 40(3.111) — Meaning of "professional partnership"; 257 — Formula cannot calculate to less than zero.

Notes: In simple terms, any negative adjusted cost base of a limited or passive partner is deemed to be a capital gain.

The rules for professional partnerships (40(3.11)A(b) and B(c); see definition in 40(3.111)) were added by 2002-2013 technical bill, for fiscal periods that end after Nov. 2001. See Yull, "Limited Liability Partnerships and Professional Services Firms", 5(3) *Tax Hyperion* (Carswell, March 2008); Nightingale, "Ontario Limited Liability Partnerships", 1921 *Tax Topics* (CCH) 1-3 (Jan. 2, 2009); Templeton et al., "Proposed Rules Will Improve Timing of Professional Partnership Income", 21(2) *Taxation Law* (Ontario Bar Assn. oba.org, April 2011).

40(3.11) added by 1994 Budget, effective Feb. 22, 1994.

(3.111) Meaning of "professional partnership"

— In this section, "professional partnership" means a partnership through which one or more persons carry on the practice of a profession that is governed or regulated under a law of Canada or a province.

Notes: 40(3.111) added by 2002-2013 technical bill (Part 5 — technical), for fiscal periods that end after Nov. 2001. See Notes to 40(3.11).

(3.12) Deemed loss for certain partners

— If a corporation, an individual (other than a trust) or a graduated rate estate (each of which is referred to in this subsection as the "taxpayer") is a member of a partnership at the end of a fiscal period of the partnership, the taxpayer is deemed to have a loss from the disposition at that time of the member's interest in the partnership equal to the amount that the taxpayer elects in the taxpayer's return of income under this Part for the taxation year that includes that time, not exceeding the lesser of

(a) the amount, if any, by which

(i) the total of all amounts each of which was an amount deemed by subsection (3.1) to be a gain of the taxpayer from a disposition of the interest before that time

exceeds

(ii) the total of all amounts each of which was an amount deemed by this subsection to be a loss of the taxpayer from a disposition of the interest before that time, and

(b) the adjusted cost base to the taxpayer of the interest at that time.

Related Provisions: 53(2)(c)(i.2) — Reduction in adjusted cost base; 89(1)"capital dividend account"(a)(ii)(A) — CDA not reduced by 40(3.12) disposition; 96(1.01)(b) — Deemed end of fiscal period when taxpayer ceases to be partner.

Notes: An election "in the taxpayer's return" is valid even if the return is filed late. See Notes to 7(1.31).

For a taxpayer filing Quebec returns, the election must be copied to Revenu Québec: *Taxation Act* ss. 261.2, 21.4.6.

A partnership that is a member of another partnership cannot elect under 40(3.12): VIEWS doc 2012-0449701E5 (the CBA/CICA Joint Committee asked Finance in 2006 to change this).

In *Gladwin Realty*, 2020 FCA 142, misusing 40(3.1), 40(3.12) and the pre-2011 Capital Dividend Account rules to inflate the CDA violated GAAR in 245(2).

40(3.12) opening words amended by 2014 budget bill #2, for 2016 and later taxation years, to change "testamentary trust" to "graduated rate estate".

40(3.12) added by 1994 Budget, effective February 22, 1994.

(3.13) Artificial transactions — For the purpose of applying section 53 at any time to a member of a partnership who would be a member described in subsection (3.1) of the partnership if the fiscal period of the partnership that includes that time ended at that time, where at any time after February 21, 1994 the member of the partnership makes a contribution of capital to the partnership and

(a) the partnership or a person or partnership with whom the partnership does not deal at arm's length

(i) makes a loan to the member or to a person with whom the member does not deal at arm's length, or

(ii) pays an amount as, on account of, in lieu of payment of or in satisfaction of, a distribution of the member's share of the partnership profits or partnership capital, or

(b) the member or a person with whom the member does not deal at arm's length becomes indebted to the partnership or a person or partnership with whom the partnership does not deal at arm's length,

and it is established, by subsequent events or otherwise, that the loan, payment or indebtedness, as the case may be, was made or arose as part of a series of contributions and such loans, payments or other transactions, the contribution of capital shall be deemed not to have been made.

Related Provisions: 251 — Arm's length.

Notes: 40(3.13) added by 1994 Budget, effective Feb. 22, 1994. It is an anti-avoidance rule designed to prevent artificial increases in the ACB of a partnership interest that would avoid 40(3.1). It is in part a legislative codification of the principle in *Stursberg*, [1993] 2 C.T.C. 76 (FCA), as it applied to a particular set of facts. It does not apply to a loan from partnership to partner absent capital contribution by the partner: VIEWS doc 2016-0637341E5.

(3.131) Specified member of a partnership — Where it can reasonably be considered that one of the main reasons that a member of a partnership was not a specified member of the partnership at all times since becoming a member of the partnership is to avoid the application of subsection (3.1) to the member's interest in the partnership, the member is deemed for the purpose of that subsection to have been a specified member of the partnership at all times since becoming a member of the partnership.

Related Provisions: 127.52(2.1) — Parallel rule for minimum tax purposes.

Notes: For the meaning of "one of the main reasons" see Notes to 83(2.1).

40(3.131) added by 1995-97 technical bill, effective April 27, 1995. This anti-avoidance rule was originally proposed as 248(28) in the draft legislation of April 26, 1995. A parallel rule appears in 127.52(2.1).

(3.14) Limited partner — For the purpose of subsection (3.1), a member of a partnership at a particular time is a limited partner of the partnership at that time if, at that time or within 3 years after that time,

(a) by operation of any law governing the partnership arrangement, the liability of the member as a member of the partnership is limited (except by operation of a provision of a statute of Canada or a province that limits the member's liability only for debts, obligations and liabilities of the partnership, or any member of the partnership, arising from negligent acts or omissions, from misconduct or from fault of another member of the partnership or an employee, an agent or a representative of the partnership in the course of the partnership business while the partnership is a limited liability partnership);

(b) the member or a person not dealing at arm's length with the member is entitled, either immediately or in the future and either absolutely or contingently, to receive an amount or to obtain a benefit that would be described in paragraph 96(2.2)(d) if that paragraph were read without reference to subparagraphs (ii) and (vi);

(c) one of the reasons for the existence of the member who owns the interest

(i) can reasonably be considered to be to limit the liability of any person with respect to that interest, and

(ii) cannot reasonably be considered to be to permit any person who has an interest in the member to carry on the person's business (other than an investment business) in the most effective manner; or

(d) there is an agreement or other arrangement for the disposition of an interest in the partnership and one of the main reasons for the agreement or arrangement can reasonably be considered to be to attempt to avoid the application of this subsection to the member.

Related Provisions: 96(2.4) — Definition of limited partner for purposes of at-risk amount.

Notes: The parenthesized exception for limited liability partnerships (LLPs) in para. (a) was added as a result of provincial legislation permitting accounting and law firms to form LLPs, whereby partners are not liable for negligence of other partners. Most law and accounting firms are now LLPs. See also 96(2.4)(a) and 40(3.11).

For the meaning of "one of the main reasons" in para. (d), see Notes to 83(2.1).

For CRA interpretation of 40(3.14) see VIEWS docs 2000-0026905, 2000-0026775, 2001-0070933, 2010-0391271R3, 2013-0495861C6 [2013 APFF q. 20].

Ontario LLP partners are limited partners: Bonanno & Buckley, "Limited Liability Partnerships", 25(2) *Canadian Tax Highlights* (ctf.ca) 7-8 (Feb. 2017).

40(3.14)(a) amended by 2002-2013 technical bill, effective June 21, 2001, to add "fault" (for Quebec civil law). 40(3.14) earlier amended by 2001 technical bill (to add the LLP exception), 1995-97 technical bill. Added by 1994 Budget.

(3.15) Excluded interest — For the purpose of subsection (3.1), an excluded interest in a partnership at any time means an interest in a partnership that actively carries on a business that was carried on by it throughout the period beginning February 22, 1994 and ending at that time, or that earns income from a property that was owned by it throughout that period, unless in that period there was a substantial contribution of capital to the partnership or a substantial increase in the indebtedness of the partnership.

Related Provisions: 40(3.16) — Amounts considered not substantial; 40(3.17) — Whether carrying on business before Feb. 22, 1994; 53(2)(c)(i.4)(E) — Effect of excluded interest on ACB of partnership with 1995 stub period income.

Notes: For interpretation of 40(3.15) see VIEWS docs 2004-0094791E5, 2014-0524331E5.

40(3.15) added by 1994 Budget, effective February 22, 1994.

(3.16) Amounts considered not to be substantial — For the purpose of subsection (3.15), an amount will be considered not to be substantial where

(a) the amount

(i) was raised pursuant to the terms of a written agreement entered into by a partnership before February 22, 1994 to issue an interest in the partnership and was expended on expenditures contemplated by the agreement before 1995 (or before March 2, 1995 in the case of amounts expended to acquire a film production prescribed for the purpose of subparagraph 96(2.2)(d)(ii) the principal photography of which or, in the case of such a production that is a television series, one episode of the series, commences before 1995 and the production is completed before March 2, 1995, or an interest in one or more partnerships all or substantially all of the property of which is such a film production),

(ii) was raised pursuant to the terms of a written agreement (other than an agreement referred to in subparagraph (i)) entered into by a partnership before February 22, 1994 and was expended on expenditures contemplated by the agreement before 1995 (or before March 2, 1995 in the case of amounts expended to acquire a film production prescribed for the purpose of subparagraph 96(2.2)(d)(ii) the principal photography of which or, in the case of such a production that is a television series, one episode of the series, commences before 1995 and the production is completed before March 2, 1995, or an interest in one or more partnerships all or substantially all of the property of which is such a film production),

(iii) was used by the partnership before 1995 (or before March 2, 1995 in the case of amounts expended to acquire a film production prescribed for the purpose of subparagraph 96(2.2)(d)(ii) the principal photography of which or, in the case of such a production that is a television series, one episode of the series, commences before 1995 and the production is completed before March 2, 1995, or an interest in one or more partnerships all or substantially all of the property of which is such a film production) to make an expenditure required to be made pursuant to the terms of a written agreement entered into by the partnership before February 22, 1994, or

(iv) was used to repay a loan, debt or contribution of capital that had been received or incurred in respect of any such expenditure;

(b) the amount was raised before 1995 pursuant to the terms of a prospectus, preliminary prospectus, offering memorandum or registration statement filed before February 22, 1994 with a public authority in Canada pursuant to and in accordance with the securities legislation of Canada or of a province and, where required by law, accepted for filing by the public authority, and expended before 1995 (or before March 2, 1995 in the case of amounts expended to acquire a film production prescribed for the purpose of subparagraph 96(2.2)(d)(ii), or an interest in one or more partnerships all or substantially all of the property of which is such a film production) on expenditures contemplated by the document that was filed before February 22, 1994;

(c) the amount was raised before 1995 pursuant to the terms of an offering memorandum distributed as part of an offering of securities where

(i) the memorandum contained a complete or substantially complete description of the securities contemplated in the offering as well as the terms and conditions of the offering,

(ii) the memorandum was distributed before February 22, 1994,

(iii) solicitations in respect of the sale of the securities contemplated by the memorandum were made before February 22, 1994,

(iv) the sale of the securities was substantially in accordance with the memorandum, and

(v) the funds are expended in accordance with the memorandum before 1995 (except that the funds may be expended before March 2, 1995 in the case of a partnership all or substantially all of the property of which is a film production prescribed for the purpose of subparagraph 96(2.2)(d)(ii) the principal photography of which or, in the case of such a production that is a television series, one episode of the series, commences before 1995 and the production is completed before March 2, 1995, or an interest in one or more partnerships all or substantially all of the property of which is such a film production); or

(d) the amount was used for an activity that was carried on by the partnership on February 22, 1994 but not for a significant expansion of the activity nor for the acquisition or production of a film production.

Related Provisions: 40(3.17) — Partnership deemed to have carried on business before Feb. 22, 1994; 40(3.18)(d) — Grandfathering of certain partnership interests.

Notes: 40(3.16) added by 1994 Budget, effective February 22, 1994.

CRA considers that "substantially all" means 90% or more.

(3.17) Whether carrying on business before February 22, 1994 — For the purpose of subsection (3.15), a partnership in respect of which paragraph (3.16)(a), (b) or (c) applies shall be considered to have actively carried on the business, or earned income from the property, contemplated in the document referred to in that paragraph throughout the period beginning February 22, 1994 and

ending on the earlier of the closing date, if any, stipulated in the document and January 1, 1995.

Notes: 40(3.17) added by 1994 Budget, effective February 22, 1994.

(3.18) Deemed partner — For the purpose of subsection (3.1), a member of a partnership who acquired an interest in the partnership after February 22, 1994 shall be deemed to have held the interest on February 22, 1994 where the member acquired the interest

(a) in circumstances in which

(i) paragraph 70(6)(d.1) applied,

(ii) where the member is an individual, the member's spouse or common-law partner held the partnership interest on February 22, 1994,

(iii) where the member is a trust, the taxpayer by whose will the trust was created held the partnership interest on February 22, 1994, and

(iv) the partnership interest was, immediately before the death of the spouse or common-law partner or the taxpayer, as the case may be, an excluded interest;

(b) in circumstances in which

(i) paragraph 70(9.2)(c) applied,

(ii) the member's parent held the partnership interest on February 22, 1994, and

(iii) the partnership interest was, immediately before the parent's death, an excluded interest;

(c) in circumstances in which

(i) paragraph 70(9.3)(e) applied,

(ii) the trust referred to in subsection 70(9.3) or the taxpayer by whose will the trust was created held the partnership interest on February 22, 1994, and

(iii) the partnership interest was, immediately before the death of the spouse or common-law partner referred to in subsection 70(9.3), an excluded interest; or

(d) before 1995 pursuant to a document referred to in subparagraph (3.16)(a)(i) or paragraph (3.16)(b) or (c).

Related Provisions: 252(2)(a) — Extended meaning of "parent".

Notes: 40(3.18) amended by 2000 same-sex partners bill to refer to "common-law partner", effective 2001 or earlier by election.

40(3.18) added by 1994 Budget, effective February 22, 1994.

(3.19) Non-application of subsec. (3) — Subsection (3) does not apply in any case where subsection (3.1) applies.

Notes: 40(3.19) added by 1994 Budget, effective February 22, 1994.

(3.2) Non-application of subsec. (3.1) — Subsection (3.1) does not apply in any case where paragraph 98(1)(c) or 98.1(1)(c) applies.

Notes: 40(3.2) added by 1994 Budget, effective February 22, 1994.

(3.21) [No longer relevant]

Notes: 40(3.21), added by 2010 budget bill #2 effective March 4, 2010 and for certain earlier tax years, provides that a gain triggered by the pre-2015 election in 180.01 (changing a deferred stock option benefit to a deemed gain) is a s. 40 gain, not a taxable capital gain.

(3.3) When subsec. (3.4) applies — Subsection (3.4) applies when

(a) a corporation, trust or partnership (in this subsection and subsection (3.4) referred to as the "transferor") disposes of a particular capital property — other than depreciable property of a prescribed class and other than, for the purposes of computing the exempt surplus or exempt deficit, hybrid surplus or hybrid deficit, and taxable surplus or taxable deficit of a foreign affiliate of a taxpayer, in respect of the taxpayer, where the transferor is the affiliate or is a partnership of which the affiliate is a member, property that is, or would be, if the transferor were a foreign affiliate of the taxpayer, excluded property (within the meaning assigned by subsection 95(1)) of the transferor — otherwise than in a disposition described in any of paragraphs (c) to (g) of the definition "superficial loss" in section 54;

(b) during the period that begins 30 days before and ends 30 days after the disposition, the transferor or a person affiliated with the transferor acquires a property (in this subsection and subsection (3.4) referred to as the "substituted property") that is, or is identical to, the particular property; and

(c) at the end of the period, the transferor or a person affiliated with the transferor owns the substituted property.

Related Provisions: 93(2)–(2.3) — Loss on disposition of share of foreign affiliate; 93.1(3)(b) — Tiered partnership — look-through rule; 251.1 — Affiliated persons.

Notes: See Notes to 40(3.4). 40(3.3)(a) amended to add "and other than ... of the transferor" by 2002-2013 technical bill (Part 3 — FA reorganizations), for dispositions that occur after Aug. 19, 2011.

40(3.3) added by 1995-97 technical bill, effective (subject to grandfathering) for dispositions of property after April 26, 1995.

I.T. Application Rules: 26(5)(c)(ii)(A) (where property owned since June 18, 1971).

CRA Audit Manual: 29.2.4: Specific exceptions to capital gain and loss rules.

(3.4) Loss on certain properties — If this subsection applies because of subsection (3.3) to a disposition of a particular property,

(a) the transferor's loss, if any, from the disposition is deemed to be nil, and

(b) the amount of the transferor's loss, if any, from the disposition (determined without reference to paragraph (2)(g) and this subsection) is deemed to be a loss of the transferor from a disposition of the particular property at the time that is immediately before the first time, after the disposition,

(i) at which a 30-day period begins throughout which neither the transferor nor a person affiliated with the transferor owns

(A) the substituted property, or

(B) a property that is identical to the substituted property and that was acquired after the day that is 31 days before the period begins,

(ii) at which the property would, if it were owned by the transferor, be deemed by section 128.1 or subsection 149(10) to have been disposed of by the transferor,

(iii) that is immediately before the transferor is subject to a loss restriction event,

(iv) at which the transferor or a person affiliated with the transferor is deemed by section 50 to have disposed of the property, where the substituted property is a debt or a share of the capital stock of a corporation, or

(v) if the transferor is a corporation,

(A) for the purposes of computing the transferor's foreign accrual property income, exempt surplus or exempt deficit, hybrid surplus or hybrid deficit, and taxable surplus or taxable deficit, in respect of a taxpayer for a taxation year of the transferor where the transferor is a foreign affiliate of the taxpayer, at which the liquidation and dissolution of the transferor begins, unless the liquidation and dissolution is

(I) a qualifying liquidation and dissolution (within the meaning assigned by subsection 88(3.1)) of the transferor, or

(II) a designated liquidation and dissolution (within the meaning assigned by subsection 95(1)) of the transferor, and

(B) for any other purposes, at which the winding-up (other than a winding-up to which subsection 88(1) applies) of the transferor begins,

and, for the purpose of paragraph (b), where a partnership otherwise ceases to exist at any time after the disposition, the partnership is deemed not to have ceased to exist, and each person who was a member of the partnership immediately before the partnership would, but for this subsection, have ceased to exist is deemed to remain a member of the partnership, until the time that is immediately after the first time described in subparagraphs (b)(i) to (v).

Related Provisions: 13(21.2) — Parallel rule for depreciable capital property; 18(13)–(15) — Parallel rule for share or debt owned by financial institution; 40(3.5) — Deemed identical property; 40(3.6) — Where share in corporation disposed of to the corporation; 40(3.61) — Exception where estate loss carried back; 54"superficial loss"(h) — Superficial loss rule inapplicable if 40(3.4) applies; 69(5)(d) — No application where corporate property appropriated by shareholder on windup; 87(2)(g.3) — Amalgamation — continuing corporation; 93(2)–(2.3), (4) — Loss on disposition of share of foreign affiliate; 95(2)(e)(v)(A)(II) — Designated liquidation and dissolution of foreign affiliate; 112(3)–(4.22) — Reduction in capital loss on shares where dividends previously paid; 248(12) — Whether properties are identical; 251.2 — Loss restriction event.

Notes: 40(3.4) prevents the transfer of property with an accrued loss from being used as a method of transferring a high cost base within a group where property has declined in value. The loss is kept suspended in the transferor's hands, and can be claimed once the property is no longer in the affiliated group. For the parallel rule for depreciable property, see 13(21.2); for certain inventory, 18(13)–(16); for pre-2017 eligible capital property, repealed 14(12). See Notes to 13(21.2). See also 40(3.5).

See Ton-That and McLean, "Navigating the Stop-Loss Rules", VI(3) *Corporate Structures & Groups* (Federated Press) 324-28 (2000); Forget, "Strategies and Issues Relating to the Transfer of Businesses or Assets Within a Corporate Group", 2007 Cdn Tax Foundation conference report at 7:4-6; Laren, "Gap in Subsections 40(3.3) and (3.4) for Wound-Up Trust?", 9(2) *Canadian Tax Focus* (ctf.ca) 9-10 (May 2019); Fenton, "Transfers of Capital Property", 2505 *Tax Topics* (CCH) 1-4 (March 12, 2020).

When reading a VIEWS doc or article in French about 40(3.4), note that the closing words in English are 40(3.4)(c) in French.

In *Cascades Inc.*, 2009 FCA 135, the TCC held that 40(3.4) did not apply to shares of subsidiary A, sold to subsidiary B, where A and B amalgamated before the 30 days so 40(3.3)(c) did not apply because the shares of A no longer existed! The FCA found this conclusion illogical and reversed it.

In *10737 Newfoundland*, 2011 TCC 346, 40(3.4) did not apply to exchangeable shares (Newbridge-Alcatel merger) that mirrored the rights of other shares, as they were not a "right to acquire property" under 40(3.5)(a) [Smit, "Exchangeable Shares: Not Just Rights to Foreign Shares", 2065 *Tax Topics* (CCH) 1-5 (Oct. 6, 2011)].

Due to the closing words of 40(3.4), the ex-partners of a wound-up partnership can claim their share of the deferred loss: doc 2010-0386311C6 [2010 CTF conf. report p.4:8-9, q.8].

The taxpayer can choose the order of disposition of shares for 40(3.4)(b)(i): VIEWS doc 2003-0002915.

Where shares are acquired and sold at a loss in the same period, but not all are sold, part of the loss may be denied and allocated to the shares still held, based on the assumption that each share still held is a substituted property for one share sold: doc 2001-0088155. See also 2009-033772I17 (shares after merger are not identical shares).

See also VIEWS docs 2001-0088155 (administrative formula for determining capital loss to be suspended); 2003-0051915 (no 40(3.4) on loan repayment); 2007-0221361R3 (no 40(3.4) when *alter ego* trust donates shares); 2007-0237011R3 (no 40(3.4) on foreign buy-out of mutual fund trust); 2007-0239291R3 (no 40(3.4) on assumption of debt for assets); 2007-0245281R3 (no 40(3.4) on income trust windup); 2007-0255401R3 (no 40(3.4) on swap termination); 2008-0274451E5 (no 40(3.4) when 50(1) applies); 2008-0275881R3 (no 40(3.4) on butterfly); 2008-028011117 and 2017-0705201C6 [2017 APFF q.10] (no 40(3.4) on capital loss on foreign currency — see Notes to 39(2)); 2009-031543117 (interaction with 100(4)); 2010-035931117 (no application to capital loss of estate under 107(2.1)(a)); 2011-0399611E5 (formula in 2001-0088155 does not apply to 40(3.4)(b)); 2012-0456221R3 (post-mortem planning); 2014-0529731E5 (taxpayer can designate order in which shares disposed of, and can recognize partial loss where some shares disposed of by group); 2014-053498117 (application of the closing words); 2015-058879117 (units of Delaware LP are not "identical" to shares of Delaware LLC for 40(3.3)(b)); and Notes to 40(3.5).

40(3.4)(b)(iii) changed from referring to change in control of a corporation by 2013 budget bill #2, effective March 21, 2013. (See Notes to 251.2(2) re "loss restriction event".)

40(3.4)(b)(v) amended by 2002-2013 technical bill, for windups, liquidations and dissolutions that begin after Aug. 19, 2011, effectively to add (v)(A).

40(3.4) added by 1995-97 technical bill, effective (subject to grandfathering) for dispositions of property after April 26, 1995.

Interpretation Bulletins: IT-291R3: Transfer of property to a corporation under subsection 85(1).

CRA Audit Manual: 29.2.4: Specific exceptions to capital gain and loss rules.

(3.5) Deemed identical property — For the purposes of subsections (3.3) and (3.4),

(a) a right to acquire a property (other than a right, as security only, derived from a mortgage, hypothec, agreement for sale or similar obligation) is deemed to be a property that is identical to the property;

(b) a share of the capital stock of a corporation that is acquired in exchange for another share in a transaction is deemed to be a property that is identical to the other share if

(i) section 51, 86, or 87 applies to the transaction, or

(ii) the following conditions are met, namely,

(A) section 85.1 applies to the transaction,

(B) subsection (3.4) applied to a prior disposition of the other share, and

(C) none of the times described in any of subparagraphs (3.4)(b)(i) to (v) has occurred in respect of the prior disposition;

(b.1) a share of the capital stock of a SIFT wind-up corporation in respect of a SIFT wind-up entity is, if the share was acquired before 2013, deemed to be a property that is identical to equity in the SIFT wind-up entity;

(c) if subsections (3.3) and (3.4) apply to the disposition by a transferor of a share of the capital stock of a particular corporation and after the disposition

(i) the particular corporation is merged or combined with one or more other corporations, otherwise than in a transaction in respect of which paragraph (b) applies to the share, then the corporation formed on the merger or combination is deemed to own the share while the corporation so formed is affiliated with the transferor,

(ii) the particular corporation is wound up in a winding-up to which subsection 88(1) applies, then the parent (within the meaning assigned by subsection 88(1)) is deemed to own the share while the parent is affiliated with the transferor, or

(iii) the particular corporation is liquidated and dissolved, the liquidation and dissolution is a qualifying liquidation and dissolution (within the meaning assigned by subsection 88(3.1)) of the corporation or a designated liquidation and dissolution (within the meaning assigned by subsection 95(1)) of the corporation, and the transferor is a foreign affiliate of a taxpayer, then for the purposes of computing the transferor's foreign accrual property income, exempt surplus or exempt deficit, hybrid surplus or hybrid deficit, and taxable surplus or taxable deficit, in respect of the taxpayer for a taxation year of the transferor, the taxpayer referred to in subsection 88(3.1) or the particular shareholder referred to in the definition "designated liquidation and dissolution" in subsection 95(1), as the case may be, is deemed to own the share while the taxpayer or particular shareholder is affiliated with the transferor; and

(d) where subsections (3.3) and (3.4) apply to the disposition by a transferor of a share of the capital stock of a corporation, and after the disposition the share is redeemed, acquired or cancelled by the corporation, otherwise than in a transaction in respect of which paragraph (b) or (c) applies to the share, the transferor is deemed to own the share while the corporation is affiliated with the transferor.

Related Provisions: 87(2)(g.4) — Amalgamation — continuing corporation; 95(2)(e)(v)(A)(III) — Designated liquidation and dissolution of foreign affiliate.

Notes: *40(3.5)(a)*: Exchangeable shares are not a "right to acquire property": *10737 Newfoundland*, 2011 TCC 346. For the meaning of "derived", see Notes to 18.1(12).

40(3.5)(c): The words "where subsections 40(3.3) and (3.4) apply" do not require all 3 conditions of 40(3.3) to apply, so (c) can apply even if the corp is amalgamated or wound up before the period expires: *Cascades Inc.*, 2009 FCA 135; Kandev & Wiener, "Purposive Interpretation", 17(8) *Canadian Tax Highlights [CTH]* (ctf.ca) 6-7 (Aug. 2009); VIEWS docs 2003-0182977, 2005-0141191C6. "Merged or combined" in (c)(i) can include a windup or liquidation: 2017-0735771I7, 2017-0737151I7, 2018-0745501C6 [2018 IFA q.5] [Barnicke & Huynh, "Merger Includes a Winding-Up", 26(12) *CTH* 1 (Dec. 2018)], 2019-0793481I7, 2020-0852071I7. See also Bradley & Bright, "The Stop-Loss Rules", 67(2) *Canadian Tax Journal* 383-410 (2019); Szpakowski & Korovilas, "Paragraph 40(3.5)(c)", 21(1) *Tax for the Owner-Manager* (ctf.ca) 11-12 (Jan. 2021).

40(3.5) amended by 2002-2013 technical bill (generally effective Aug. 20, 2011), 2008 budget bill #2, 2001 *Civil Code* harmonization bill. Added by 1995-97 technical bill.

CRA Audit Manual: 29.2.4: Specific exceptions to capital gain and loss rules.

(3.6) Loss on [redeemed] shares — If at any time a taxpayer disposes, to a corporation that is affiliated with the taxpayer immediately after the disposition, of a share of a class of the capital stock of the corporation (other than a share that is a distress preferred share (within the meaning assigned by subsection 80(1)) and other than, for the purposes of computing the exempt surplus or exempt deficit, hybrid surplus or hybrid deficit, and taxable surplus or taxable deficit of the taxpayer in respect of another taxpayer, where the taxpayer or, if the taxpayer is a partnership, a member of the taxpayer is a foreign affiliate of the other taxpayer, a property that is, or would be, if the taxpayer were a foreign affiliate of the other taxpayer, excluded property (within the meaning assigned by subsection 95(1)) of the taxpayer),

(a) the taxpayer's loss, if any, from the disposition is deemed to be nil; and

(b) in computing the adjusted cost base to the taxpayer after that time of a share of a class of the capital stock of the corporation owned by the taxpayer immediately after the disposition, there shall be added the proportion of the amount of the taxpayer's loss from the disposition (determined without reference to paragraph (2)(g) and this subsection) that

(i) the fair market value, immediately after the disposition, of the share

is of

(ii) the fair market value, immediately after the disposition, of all shares of the capital stock of the corporation owned by the taxpayer.

Related Provisions: 40(3.61) — Exception where estate loss carried back; 53(1)(f.2) — Addition to adjusted cost base; 69(5)(d) — No application where corporate property appropriated by shareholder on windup; 84(3) — Deemed dividend of excess of proceeds over paid-up capital; 93.1(3)(b) — Tiered partnership — look-through rule; 251.1 — Affiliated persons.

Notes: 40(3.6) effectively replaces former 85(4)(b). See also Notes to 40(3.4).

40(3.6) opening words refer to a corp buying back its own shares: *Hess*, 2008 TCC 4.

The use of an algebraic formula to allocate the capital loss, approved administratively for 40(3.4) in VIEWS doc 2001-0088155 (see Notes to 40(3.4)), is not permitted for 40(3.6): doc 2002-0161447.

Where the taxpayer has made a capital dividend election under 83(2) for the deemed dividend under 84(3), the stop-loss rule in 112(3) applies and so there is no addition to the ACB under 40(3.6)(b): VIEWS doc 2003-0035135.

Where a testamentary trust acquires shares of a corporation from a deceased's estate and the remaining shares are redeemed by the estate, 40(3.6) will not apply since the estate and the corporation are not "affiliated" after the redemption, even though the estate and the trust have the same trustees: VIEWS doc 2002-0151025 (see also 2013-0493651C6 [2013 APFF q.4]). 40(3.6) does not apply when 50(1) applies: doc 2008-0274451E5; or where 69(5) applies to a controlled foreign affiliate windup: 2014-0560421I7. For examples of 40(3.6) applying on share exchanges see 2009-0308611R3, 2009-0354091R3, 2011-0427461E5; on distribution of pre-1972 CSOH see 2012-0443081R3, 2013-0512531R3; on interaction with 75(2) see 2014-0538241C6; on a loss consolidation, 2014-0536651R5.

In *Fairmont Hotels*, 2016 SCC 56, steps that accidentally triggered 40(3.6), causing a hedged foreign exchange gain to be taxed, could not be unwound by rectification (see Notes to 169(1)).

In *Pomerleau*, 2018 FCA 129, using 40(3.6) to shift a loss to avoid 84.1 triggered GAAR (245(2)).

See also "Stop-Loss Rule in Subsection 40(3.6) and Trusts", in Gosselin, "APFF Quebec Tax Conference", 14(1) *Tax for the Owner-Manager* (ctf.ca) 2-3 (Jan. 2014).

40(3.6) opening words amended by 2002-2013 technical bill, for dispositions after Aug. 19, 2011.

40(3.6) added by 1995-97 technical bill, effective (subject to grandfathering) for dispositions after April 26, 1995.

CRA Audit Manual: 29.2.4: Specific exceptions to capital gain and loss rules.

(3.61) Exception — estate loss carried back — If, in the course of administering the estate of a deceased taxpayer, the taxpayer's legal representative elects in accordance with subsection 164(6) to treat all or any portion of the estate's capital loss (determined without reference to subsections (3.4) and (3.6)) from the disposition of a share of the capital stock of a corporation as a capital loss of the deceased taxpayer from the disposition of the share, subsections (3.4) and (3.6) apply to the estate in respect of the loss only to the extent that the amount of the loss exceeds the portion of the loss to which the election applies.

Notes: 40(3.61) ensures that 40(3.4) and (3.6) do not apply to any portion of an estate's capital loss carried back under 164(6). See Wark, "Concerns with Proposed Subsection 40(3.61)", XI(2) *Insurance Planning* (Federated Press) 703-5 (2005); Tunney, "Stop-Loss Rules", 13(2) *Canadian Tax Highlights* (ctf.ca) 6-7 (Feb. 2005); Ireland, "Selected Developments in Post-Mortem Planning", 2005 Cdn Tax Foundation conference report, 13:25-34. The Joint Committee on Taxation has asked Finance to extend this rule: see VIEWS doc 2012-0457541C6.

On potential circularity with 164(6) see Notes to 164(6). For examples of rulings applying 40(3.61) see docs 2007-0237511R3, 2010-0377601R3, 2010-0388591R3, 2013-0509251R3, 2014-0540861R3, 2015-0602831R3, 2015-0606721R3.

40(3.61) added by 2004 Budget, effective for dispositions after March 22, 2004.

(3.7) Losses of non-resident — If an individual disposes of a property at any time after having ceased to be resident in Canada, for the purposes of applying subsections 100(4), 107(1) and 112(3) to (3.32) and (7) in computing the individual's loss from the disposition,

(a) the individual is deemed to be a corporation in respect of dividends received by the individual, or deemed under Part XIII to have been paid to the individual, at a particular time that is after the time at which the individual last acquired the property and at which the individual was non-resident; and

(b) an amount on account of

(i) each taxable dividend received by the individual at a particular time described in paragraph (a), and

(ii) each amount deemed under Part XIII to have been paid to the individual at a particular time described in paragraph (a), as a dividend from a corporation resident in Canada, to the extent that the amount can reasonably be considered to relate to the property,

is deemed to be a taxable dividend that was received by the individual and that was deductible under section 112 in computing the individual's taxable income or taxable income earned in Canada for the taxation year that includes that particular time.

Related Provisions: 119 — Credit to former resident where stop-loss rule applies; 128.1(6)(b), 128.1(7)(e) — Returning former resident of Canada.

Notes: 40(3.7) is a "stop-loss" rule to reduce an individual's loss from the disposition of a property after becoming non-resident. Generally, it applies where an individual has received dividends in respect of a property (whether a share or an interest in a partnership or trust) while non-resident and owning the property. 112 contains a comprehensive stop-loss system for corporations; instead of duplicating it, 40(3.7) adapts it to apply to such losses.

For purposes of 100(4), 107(1), 112(3)–(3.32) and 112(7), 40(3.7) deems individual X to be a corporation in respect of dividends received in respect of a property since the time X acquired the property and while X was non-resident, and deems any taxable dividends received to have been deductible under s. 112 when received. The effect is that some or all dividends received while non-resident may reduce X's loss on a share, partnership interest or trust interest.

40(3.7) added by 2001 technical bill, for dispositions after Dec. 23, 1998 by individuals who cease to be resident in Canada after Oct. 1, 1996.

(4) Disposal of principal residence to spouse or trust for spouse [or common-law partner] — Where a taxpayer has, after 1971, disposed of property to an individual in circumstances to which subsection 70(6) or 73(1) applied, for the purposes of computing the individual's gain from the disposition of the property under paragraph (2)(b) or (c), as the case may be,

(a) the individual shall be deemed to have owned the property throughout the period during which the taxpayer owned it;

(b) the property shall be deemed to have been the individual's principal residence

(i) in any case where subsection 70(6) is applicable, for any taxation year for which it would, if the taxpayer had designated it in prescribed manner to have been the taxpayer's principal residence for that year, have been the taxpayer's principal residence, and

(ii) in any case where subsection 73(1) is applicable, for any taxation year for which it was the taxpayer's principal residence; and

(c) where the individual is a trust, the trust shall be deemed to have been resident in Canada during each taxation year during which the taxpayer was resident in Canada.

Related Provisions: 40(7.1) — Effect of election to trigger capital gains exemption.

Notes: After a spousal rollover, 40(4) allows the combined holding period of both spouses to be counted for purposes of the principal-residence exemption. See VIEWS doc 2004-0075051E5. 40(7) applies a similar rule when a trust rolls out a principal resident to a beneficiary who lived in the home.

40(4) applied to exempt part of the gain, without a designation of the property having been made, in *Levatte Estate*, 2019 TCC 177, paras. 39-42.

Regulations: 2301 (prescribed manner of designation).

Income Tax Folios: S1-F3-C2: Principal residence [replaces IT-120R6, IT-437R].

(5) [Repealed]

Notes: 40(5) repealed by 1992 technical bill, for dispositions after 1990. See now amended 54"principal residence" re the principal residence of a spousal trust.

(6) Principal residence — property owned at end of 1981 — Subject to subsection (6.1), if a property was owned by a taxpayer, whether jointly with another person or otherwise, at the end of 1981 and continuously from the beginning of 1982 until disposed of by the taxpayer, the amount of the gain determined under paragraph (2)(b) in respect of the disposition shall not exceed the amount, if any, by which the total of

(a) the taxpayer's gain calculated in accordance with paragraph (2)(b) on the assumption that the taxpayer had disposed of the property on December 31, 1981 for proceeds of disposition equal to its fair market value on that date, and

(b) the taxpayer's gain calculated in accordance with paragraph (2)(b) on the assumption that that paragraph applies and that

(i) the taxpayer acquired the property on January 1, 1982 at a cost equal to its proceeds of disposition as determined under paragraph (a), and

(ii) the description of B in paragraph (2)(b) is read without reference to "one plus"

exceeds

(c) the amount, if any, by which the fair market value of the property on December 31, 1981 exceeds the proceeds of disposition of the property determined without reference to this subsection.

Related Provisions: 40(7.1) — Effect of election to trigger capital gains exemption.

Notes: 40(6) opening words amended by 2017 budget bill #2, effective Dec. 14, 2017, to add "Subject to subsection (6.1)" and change "thereafter" to "from the beginning of 1982".

40(6)(b)(ii) amended by 1994 Budget, for dispositions after Feb. 22, 1994.

Income Tax Folios: S1-F3-C2: Principal residence [replaces IT-120R6, IT-437R].

(6.1) Principal residence — property owned [by trust] at end of 2016 — If a trust owns property at the end of 2016, the trust is not in its first taxation year that begins after 2016 a trust described in subparagraph (c.1)(iii.1) of the definition "principal residence" in section 54, the trust disposes of the property after 2016, the disposition is the trust's first disposition of the property after 2016 and the trust owns the property, whether jointly with another person or otherwise, continuously from the beginning of 2017 until the disposition,

(a) subsection (6) does not apply to the disposition; and

(b) the trust's gain determined under paragraph (2)(b) in respect of the disposition is the amount, if any, determined by the formula

$$A + B - C$$

where

A is the trust's gain calculated in accordance with paragraph (2)(b) on the assumption that

(i) the trust disposed of the property on December 31, 2016 for proceeds of disposition equal to its fair market value on that date, and

(ii) paragraph (a) did not apply in respect of the disposition described in subparagraph (i),

B is the trust's gain in respect of the disposition calculated in accordance with paragraph (2)(b) on the assumption that

(i) the description of B in that paragraph is read without reference to "one plus", and

(ii) the trust acquired the property on January 1, 2017 at a cost equal to its fair market value on December 31, 2016, and

C is the amount, if any, by which the fair market value of the property on December 31, 2016 exceeds the proceeds of disposition of the property determined without reference to this subsection.

Related Provisions: 257 — Formula cannot calculate to less than zero.

Notes: 40(6.1) is consequential on 54"principal residence"(c.1)(iii.1), which limits the types of trust that can claim the principal residence (PR) exemption after 2016. It applies if a trust owned a property at end of 2016, the trust is not listed in (c.1)(iii.1) for its first taxation year that begins after 2016, and on its first disposition of the property after 2016 the trust chooses to designate the property as its PR for any years in which it owned the property. 40(6.1) then determines the trust's gain.

The formula splits the gain into 2 periods. Under element A, the "first" gain under 40(2)(b) pretends that the trust disposed of the property on Dec. 31, 2016 at fair market value (FMV), so the PR exemption applies as it did before 2017. Under B, the "second" gain treats the trust as having acquired the property at the start of 2017 at that FMV, and is computed using the post-2016 40(2)(b), but without the "one-plus" in 40(2)(b)B(i). Element C reduces the gain to the extent the proceeds from the "first" disposition (end-2016 FMV) exceed those from the actual disposition: A+B is reduced by any actual loss that accrued after December 31, 2016.

If a trust to which 40(6.1) applies would otherwise have qualified for transitional relief under 40(6) for a property owned since before 1982, 40(6.1)A(ii) provides that the "first" disposition gain is computed as though 40(6) applied.

For CRA interpretation see VIEWS doc 2017-0698181E5.

40(6.1) added by 2017 budget bill #2, effective Dec. 14, 2017.

(7) Property in satisfaction of interest in trust — Where property has been acquired by a taxpayer in satisfaction of all or any part of the taxpayer's capital interest in a trust, in circumstances to which subsection 107(2) applies and subsection 107(4) does not apply, for the purposes of paragraph (2)(b) and the definition "principal residence" in section 54, the taxpayer shall be deemed to have owned the property continuously since the trust last acquired it.

Related Provisions: 40(7.1) — Effect of election to trigger capital gains exemption; 107(2.01) — Principal residence distribution by spouse trust.

Income Tax Folios: S1-F3-C2: Principal residence [replaces IT-120R6, IT-437R].

(7.1) Effect of election under subsec. 110.6(19) — Where an election was made under subsection 110.6(19) in respect of a property of a taxpayer that was the taxpayer's principal residence for the 1994 taxation year or that, in the taxpayer's return of income for the taxation year in which the taxpayer disposes of the property or grants an option to acquire the property, is designated as the taxpayer's principal residence, in determining, for the purposes of paragraph (2)(b) and subsections (4) to (7), the day on which the property was last acquired or reacquired by the taxpayer and the period throughout which the property was owned by the taxpayer this Act shall be read without reference to subsection 110.6(19).

Notes: 40(7.1) added by 1994 Budget, for dispositions after Feb. 22, 1994. It provides that the capital gains exemption election in 110.6(19) is to be ignored in determining when a principal residence was "last acquired". As a result, the increase in ACB of the property resulting from the election will be ignored in computing the capital gain from the disposition; and the tax years that ended before Feb. 23, 1994 and during which the taxpayer owned the property will still be relevant in computing the principal residence portion of the gain under 40(2)(b)B.

Income Tax Folios: S1-F3-C2: Principal residence [replaces IT-120R6, IT-437R].

(8) Application of subsec. 70(10) — The definitions in subsection 70(10) apply to this section.

Notes: 40(8) added in RSC 1985 (5th Supp) consolidation, for tax years ending after Nov. 1991. This rule was formerly in the opening words of 70(10).

(9) Additions to taxable Canadian property — If a non-resident person disposes of a taxable Canadian property

(a) that the person last acquired before April 27, 1995,

(b) that would not be a taxable Canadian property immediately before the disposition if section 115 were read as it applied to dispositions that occurred on April 26, 1995, and

(c) that would be a taxable Canadian property immediately before the disposition if section 115 were read as it applied to dispositions that occurred on January 1, 1996,

the person's gain or loss from the disposition is deemed to be the amount determined by the formula

$$A \times B/C$$

where

A is the amount of the gain or loss determined without reference to this subsection;

B is the number of calendar months in the period that begins with May 1995 and ends with the calendar month that includes the time of the disposition; and

C is the number of calendar months in the period that begins with the calendar month in which the person last acquired the property and ends with the calendar month that includes the time of the disposition.

Related Provisions: ITAR 26(30) — Relief for property held since pre-1972 does not apply to property that became taxable Canadian property due to amendments effective 1995.

Notes: Due to amendments to 115(1)(b) (now 248(1)"taxable Canadian property"), some property acquired before April 27, 1995 became TCP on that date. 40(9) prorates X's gain or loss based on the number of months X held the property before May 1995.

40(9) amended by 2000 Budget/2001 technical bill, effective for dispositions that occur after April 26, 1995 (i.e. retroactive to its introduction), effectively to add para. (c). The amendment clarifies that the formula applies only to gains or losses realized on the disposition of properties that became taxable Canadian properties on April 27, 1995.

40(9) added by 1995-97 technical bill, effective (subject to grandfathering) for dispositions of property after April 26, 1995.

(10) Application of subsec. (11) — Subsection (11) applies in computing at any particular time a taxpayer's gain or loss (in this subsection and subsection (11) referred to as the "new gain" or "new loss", as the case may be), in respect of any part (which in this subsection and subsection (11) is referred to as the "relevant part" and which may for greater certainty be the whole) of a foreign currency debt of the taxpayer, arising from a fluctuation in the value of the currency of the foreign currency debt (other than, for greater certainty, a gain or a capital loss that arises because of the application of subsection 111(12)), if at any time before the particular time the taxpayer realized a capital loss or gain in respect of the foreign currency debt because of subsection 111(12).

Notes: See Notes to 40(11). 40(10) amended by 2013 budget bill #2, effective March 21, 2013, to change "corporation" to "taxpayer" thrice (effectively extending the rule to trusts).

40(10) added by 2008 budget bill #2, effective 2006. See Notes to 40(11).

Income Tax Folios: S4-F7-C1: Amalgamations of Canadian corporations [replaces IT-474R2].

(11) Gain or loss on foreign currency debt — If this subsection applies, the new gain is the positive amount, or the new loss is the negative amount, as the case may be, determined by the formula

$$A + B - C$$

where

A is

(a) if the taxpayer would, but for any application of subsection 111(12), recognize a new gain, the amount of the new gain, determined without reference to this subsection, or

(b) if the taxpayer would, but for any application of subsection 111(12), recognize a new loss, the amount of the new loss, determined without reference to this subsection, multiplied by (−1);

B is the total of all amounts each of which is that portion of the amount of a capital loss realized by the taxpayer at any time before the particular time, in respect of the foreign currency debt and because of subsection 111(12), that is reasonably attributable to

(a) the relevant part of the foreign currency debt at the particular time, or

(b) the forgiven amount, if any, (as defined in subsection 80(1)) in respect of the foreign currency debt at the particular time; and

C   is the total of all amounts each of which is that portion of the amount of a gain realized by the taxpayer at any time before the particular time, in respect of the foreign currency debt and because of subsection 111(12), that is reasonably attributable to

(a) the relevant part of the foreign currency debt at the particular time, or

(b) the forgiven amount, if any, (as defined in subsection 80(1)) in respect of the foreign currency debt at the particular time.

Related Provisions: 40(10) — Conditions for 40(11) to apply; 257 — Formula cannot calculate to less than zero.

Notes: 40(10)-(11) are consequential on 111(12), which extends the treatment of accrued capital gains and losses on change in control of a corporation to apply to accrued capital gains and losses from foreign currency fluctuations on debt denominated in foreign currency. 40(11) provides a mechanism for computing gain or loss on a foreign currency debt that takes into account the impact of gains and losses already recognized by 111(12). This is needed because, unlike gains and losses on property, gains and losses from fluctuation in the value of the currency of a foreign currency debt are not referable to a cost base that may be adjusted under s. 53 to account for previously recognized gains and losses.

An amalgamated corp is considered to have realized a predecessor's 111(4) and 111(12) gain for purposes of 40(10) and (11), due to 87(7)(d): VIEWS doc 2010-0387601E5.

40(11) amended by 2013 budget bill #2, effective March 21, 2013, to extend the rule to trusts.

40(11) added by 2008 budget bill #2, effective 2006.

Income Tax Folios: S4-F7-C1: Amalgamations of Canadian corporations [replaces IT-474R2].

(12) Donated flow-through shares — If at any time a taxpayer disposes of one or more capital properties that are included in a flow-through share class of property and subparagraph 38(a.1)(i) or (iii) applies to the disposition (in this subsection referred to as the "actual disposition"), then the taxpayer is deemed to have a capital gain from a disposition at that time of another capital property equal to the lesser of

(a) the taxpayer's exemption threshold at that time in respect of the flow-through share class of property, and

(b) the total of all amounts each of which is a capital gain from the actual disposition (for greater certainty, calculated without reference to this subsection).

Related Provisions: 38.1 — Acquisition of flow-through share on rollover; 89(1)"capital dividend account"(a)(i)(A), (B.1) — Disposition under 40(12) excluded from CDA.

Notes: 40(12) prevents "double-dipping" by donating flow-through shares (FTS: see Notes to 66(12.66)) to charity, which would otherwise eliminate the capital gain (see 38(a.1)). It applies to shares issued under a FTS agreement entered into after March 21, 2011 (see 54"exemption threshold" and "flow-through share class of property").

40(12) creates a capital gain up to the "exemption threshold", which in general is the total original cost of such flow-through shares (not counting the deemed reduction in cost resulting from the flow-through deduction), minus any capital gains realized on such shares. The exemption threshold is reset to zero at any time (54"fresh-start date") that the taxpayer no longer holds any shares of the class. 38.1 applies to the donation of property acquired by a donor in a rollover of such shares.

For CRA interpretation see docs 2011-0426631E5 and 2012-0446211E5 (general explanation of 40(12) and 38.1); 2012-0441151E5 (interaction with capital dividend account); 2017-0683501E5 (donation of a "flow-through share class of property").

See also Edwin Harris, "New Rulings for Flow-Through Shares", 8(11) *Tax Hyperion* (Carswell, Nov. 2011).

40(12) added by 2011 budget bill #2, for dispositions after March 21, 2011.

Income Tax Folios: S3-F2-C1: Capital Dividends [replaces IT-66R6].

(13) Class 14.1 — transitional rules [conditions for 40(14) to apply] — Subsection (14) applies in respect of a disposition by a taxpayer of a property that is included in Class 14.1 of Schedule II

to the *Income Tax Regulations* in respect of a business of the taxpayer if

(a) the property was an eligible capital property of the taxpayer immediately before January 1, 2017;

(b) the amount determined for Q in the definition "cumulative eligible capital" in subsection 14(5) in respect of the business immediately before January 1, 2017 is greater than nil;

(c) the amount determined for B in that definition in respect of the business immediately before January 1, 2017 is nil; and

(d) no amount is included in the taxpayer's income for a taxation year because of paragraph 13(38)(d).

Related Provisions: 13(41) — Definitions of pre-2017 terms.

Notes: 40(13)-(16) added by 2016 budget bill #2, effective 2017, to provide transition from the eligible capital property rules to CCA Class 14.1 (see Notes to 20(1)(b)).

(14) Class 14.1 — transitional rules [disposition of pre-1988 ECP] — If this subsection applies in respect of a disposition at any time by a taxpayer of a property, the taxpayer's capital gain from the disposition is to be reduced by such amount as the taxpayer claims, not exceeding the amount by which

(a) $\frac{2}{3}$ of the amount determined for Q in the definition "cumulative eligible capital" in subsection 14(5) in respect of the business immediately before 2017

exceeds

(b) the total of all amounts each of which is an amount claimed under this subsection in respect of another disposition at or before that time.

Related Provisions: 13(41) — Definitions of pre-2017 terms; 40(13) — Conditions for 40(14) to apply; 40(16) — Rule where taxpayer had exempt gains balance.

Notes: See Notes to 40(13).

(15) Class 14.1 — transitional rules [conditions for 40(16) to apply] — Subsection (16) applies in respect of a disposition by an individual of a property that is included in Class 14.1 of Schedule II to the *Income Tax Regulations* in respect of a business of the individual if

(a) the property was an eligible capital property of the individual immediately before January 1, 2017; and

(b) the individual's exempt gains balance in respect of the business is greater than nil for the taxation year that includes January 1, 2017.

Related Provisions: 13(41) — Definitions of pre-2017 terms.

Notes: See Notes to 40(13).

(16) Class 14.1 — transitional rules [disposition of pre-2017 ECP where there was an exempt gains balance] — If this subsection applies in respect of a disposition at any time by an individual of a property, the individual's capital gain from the disposition is to be reduced by such amount as the individual claims, not exceeding the amount by which

(a) twice the amount of the individual's exempt gains balance in respect of the business for the taxation year that includes January 1, 2017

exceeds

(b) the total of

(i) if paragraph 13(38)(d) applies in respect of the business for the individual's taxation year that includes January 1, 2017, the amount determined for D in paragraph 14(1)(b) for the purposes of paragraph 13(38)(d), and

(ii) the total of all amounts each of which is an amount claimed under this subsection in respect of another disposition at or before that time.

Related Provisions: 13(41) — Definitions of pre-2017 terms; 40(15) — Conditions for 40(16) to apply.

Notes: See Notes to 40(13).

Definitions [s. 40]: "acquired" — 40(7.1), 256(7)–(9); "acquisition date" — 40(2)(b); "adjusted cost base" — 54, 248(1); "affiliated" — 251.1; "amount" — 248(1); "arm's length" — 251(1); "business" — 248(1); "Canada" — 255, *Interpreta-*

tion Act 35(1); "capital gain" — 39(1), 248(1); "capital loss" — 39(1)(b), 248(1); "capital property" — 54, 248(1); "child" — 40(8), 70(10), 252(1); "class of shares" — 248(6); "commercial obligation" — 80(1); "common-law partner" — 248(1); "control" — 256(6)–(9), 256.1(3); "controlled directly or indirectly" — 256(5.1)–(6); "corporation" — 248(1), *Interpretation Act* 35(1); "cumulative eligible capital" — 13(40), 14(5); "deferred profit sharing plan" — 147(1), 248(1); "deficit" — Reg. 5907(1)"exempt deficit", "taxable deficit"; "depreciable property" — 13(21), 248(1); "disposition" — 248(1); "distress preferred share" — 80(1); "dividend" — 248(1); "eligible amount" — 248(31), (41); "eligible capital expenditure" — 13(40), 14(5); "eligible capital property" — 54 [repealed]; "employee" — 248(1); "employees profit sharing plan" — 144(1), 248(1); "estate" — 104(1), 248(1); "excepted gift" — 118.1(19); "excluded interest" — 40(3.5), 248(12); "excluded property" — 95(1); "exempt deficit" — Reg. 5907(1); "exempt gains balance" — 13(40), 14(5); "exempt income" — 248(1); "exempt surplus" — 113(1)(a), Reg. 5907(1), (1.01); "exemption threshold" — 54; "fair market value" — see 69(1) Notes; "farming" — 248(1); "fiscal period" — 249(2)(b), 249.1; "fishing" — 248(1); "flow-through share class of property" — 54; "foreign accrual property income", "foreign affiliate" — 95(1), 248(1); "foreign currency debt" — 111(8), 248(1); "forgiven amount" — 80(1); "graduated rate estate" — 248(1); "hybrid deficit" — Reg. 5907(1); "hybrid surplus" — 113(1)(a.1)(i), Reg. 5907(1), (1.01); "identical" — 40(3.5), 248(12); "individual" — 248(1); "interest in a family farm or fishing partnership" — 70(10); "land" — see 70(5.2) Notes; "last acquired" — 40(7.1); "legal representative" — 248(1); "limited partner" — 40(3.14); "listed personal property" — 54, 248(1); "loss restriction event" — 251.2; "majority-interest partner" — 248(1); "new gain", "new loss" — 40(10), (11); "non-qualifying security" — 118.1(18); "non-resident" — 248(1); "parent" — 252(2)(a); "partnership" — see 96(1) Notes; "person" — 248(1); "personal-use property" — 54, 248(1); "prescribed" — 248(1); "prescribed labour-sponsored venture capital corporation" — Reg. 6701; "preferred share" — 248(1); "prescribed labour-sponsored venture capital corporation" — Reg. 6701; "prescribed venture capital corporation" — Reg. 6700, 6700.1, 6700.2; "principal residence", "proceeds of disposition" — 54; "professional partnership" — 40(3.111); "property" — 248(1); "province" — *Interpretation Act* 35(1); "qualified donee" — 149.1(1), 248(1); "qualified small business corporation share" — 110.6(1); "registered disability savings plan" — 146.4(1), 248(1); "registered retirement income fund" — 146.3(1), 248(1); "registered retirement savings plan" — 146(1), 248(1); "related" — 251(2)–(6); "relevant part" — 40(10); "resident in Canada" — 94(3)(a), 250; "SIFT wind-up corporation", "SIFT wind-up entity" — 248(1); "series of contributions" — 248(10); "share" — 248(1); "share of the capital stock of a family farm or fishing corporation" — 70(10); "shareholder", "small business corporation" — 248(1); "specified member" — 40(3.131), 248(1); "substantial" — 40(3.16); "substituted" — 248(5); "substituted property" — 40(3.3)(b); "superficial loss" — 54; "TFSA" — 146.2(5), 248(1); "taxable Canadian corporation" — 89(1), 248(1); "taxable Canadian property" — 248(1); "taxable deficit" — Reg. 5907(1); "taxable dividend" — 89(1), 248(1); "taxable income", "taxable income earned in Canada" — 248(1); "taxable surplus" — 113(1)(b)(i), Reg. 5907(1), (1.01); "taxation year" — 249; "taxpayer" — 248(1); "transferor" — 40(3.3)(a); "trust" — 104(1), 248(1), (3); "written" — *Interpretation Act* 35(1) [writing].

41. (1) Taxable net gain from disposition of listed personal property — For the purposes of this Part, a taxpayer's taxable net gain for a taxation year from dispositions of listed personal property is $\frac{1}{2}$ of the amount determined under subsection (2) to be the taxpayer's net gain for the year from dispositions of such property.

Related Provisions: 127.52(1)(d)(i) — Untaxed 30% of gain added to income for minimum tax purposes; 248(1)"taxable net gain" — Definition applies to entire Act.

Notes: Listed personal property losses (see 41(3), 54"listed personal property") can be used under 41(2) only to offset LPP gains. Like other losses from personal-use property, they cannot be used against ordinary capital gains: see 3(b)(ii) and 40(2)(g)(iii).

41(1) amended by 2000 Budget, this version effective for tax years that end after Oct. 17, 2000.

Interpretation Bulletins: See list at end of s. 41.

(2) Determination of net gain — A taxpayer's net gain for a taxation year from dispositions of listed personal property is an amount determined as follows:

(a) determine the amount, if any, by which the total of the taxpayer's gains for the year from the disposition of listed personal property, other than property described in subparagraph 39(1)(a)(i.1), exceeds the total of the taxpayer's losses for the year from dispositions of listed personal property, and

(b) deduct from the amount determined under paragraph (a) such portion as the taxpayer may claim of the taxpayer's listed-personal-property losses for the 7 taxation years immediately preceding and the 3 taxation years immediately following the taxation year, except that for the purposes of this paragraph

    (i) an amount in respect of a listed-personal-property loss is deductible for a taxation year only to the extent that it ex-

ceeds the total of amounts deducted under this paragraph in respect of that loss for preceding taxation years,

    (ii) no amount is deductible in respect of the listed-personal-property loss of any year until the deductible listed-personal-property losses for previous years have been deducted, and

    (iii) no amount is deductible in respect of listed-personal-property losses from the amount determined under paragraph (a) for a taxation year except to the extent of the amount so determined for the year,

and the remainder determined under paragraph (b) is the taxpayer's net gain for the year from dispositions of listed personal property.

Related Provisions: 46(1) — Personal-use property.

Interpretation Bulletins: IT-407R4: Dispositions of cultural property to designated Canadian institutions. See also at end of s. 41.

Forms: T1A: Request for loss carryback; T3A: Request for loss carryback by a trust.

(3) Definition of "listed-personal-property loss" — In this section, "listed-personal-property loss" of a taxpayer for a taxation year means the amount, if any, by which the total of the taxpayer's losses for the year from dispositions of listed personal property exceeds the total of the taxpayer's gains for the year from dispositions of listed personal property, other than property described in subparagraph 39(1)(a)(i.1).

Related Provisions: 152(6) — Reassessment; 164(5), (5.1) — Effect of carryback of loss.

Interpretation Bulletins [subsec. 41(3)]: IT-159R3: Capital debts established to be bad debts. See also list at end of s. 41.

Definitions [s. 41]: "amount", "disposition" — 248(1); "listed personal property" — 54, 248(1); "listed-personal-property loss" — 41(3); "property" — 248(1); "taxable net gain" — 41(1), 248(1); "taxation year" — 249; "taxpayer" — 248(1).

Interpretation Bulletins [s. 41]: IT-332R: Personal-use property (cancelled).

42. (1) Dispositions subject to warranty — For the purposes of this Subdivision,

(a) an amount received or receivable by a person or partnership (referred to in this subsection as the "vendor"), as the case may be, as consideration for a warranty, covenant or other conditional or contingent obligation given or incurred by the vendor in respect of a property (referred to in this section as the **"subject property"**) disposed of by the vendor,

    (i) if it is received or receivable on or before the specified date, is deemed to be received as consideration for the disposition by the vendor of the subject property (and not to be an amount received or receivable by the vendor as consideration for the obligation) and is to be included in computing the vendor's proceeds of disposition of the subject property for the taxation year or fiscal period in which the disposition occurred, and

    (ii) in any other case, is deemed to be a capital gain of the vendor from the disposition of a property by the vendor that occurs at the earlier of the time when the amount is received or becomes receivable; and

(b) an outlay or expense paid or payable by the vendor under a warranty, covenant or other conditional or contingent obligation given or incurred by the vendor in respect of the subject property disposed of by the vendor,

    (i) if it is paid or payable on or before the specified date, is deemed to reduce the consideration for the disposition by the vendor of the subject property (and not to be an outlay or expense paid or payable by the vendor under the obligation) and is to be deducted in computing the vendor's proceeds of disposition of the subject property for the taxation year or fiscal period in which the disposition occurred, and

    (ii) in any other case, is deemed to be a capital loss of the vendor from the disposition of a property by the vendor that occurs at the earlier of the time when the outlay or expense is paid or becomes payable.

Notes: See Notes at end of s. 42. "This subdivision" is sections 38-55.

(2) Meaning of "specified date" — In subsection (1),"specified date" means,

(a) if the vendor is a partnership, the last day of the vendor's fiscal period in which the vendor disposed of the subject property; and

(b) in any other case, the vendor's filing-due date for the vendor's taxation year in which the vendor disposed of the subject property.

Related Provisions: 56.4(10) — Restrictive covenant or non-competition agreement — s. 42 does not apply; 87(2)(n) — Amalgamations — outlays made pursuant to warranty.

Notes [s. 42]: 42(1)(a) provides that if V sells a property and charges separately for a warranty or other contingent obligation, that charge is deemed part of the sale price if it is received/receivable before the return due date for the year of sale ("specified date" in 42(2)), and is deemed to be a separate capital gain after that. 42(1)(b) provides that if V spends money to honour the warranty, the expense reduces the sale price if it is paid/payable before the return due date, and is a capital loss afterwards.

These rules are not explicitly limited to *capital* property, but apply only for purposes of ss. 38-55 so that is their effect.

For CRA interpretation see docs 2006-0198381E5 (payment under warranty after sale of home triggers loss under s. 42, but it is deemed nil by 40(2)(g)(iii) because the home was personal-use property); 2013-0511381E5 (estate cannot claim 42(1)(b) loss for settling warranty claim against deceased); 2013-0513281E5 (payment under breach of share sale covenant is now deemed to be loss on disposition of "a property", not of the shares, so no ABIL); 2014-0551641E5 (corp that has been wound up but not yet dissolved [IT-126R2 para. 5] can claim 42(1)(b) loss); 2015-0585431E5 (42 applies to rental property hidden-defect lawsuit defence costs).

42 amended by 2002-2013 technical bill (Part 5 — technical), this version effective for taxation years and fiscal periods that end after Nov. 4, 2010.

Definitions [s. 42]: "amount" — 248(1); "capital gain" — 39(1)(a), 248(1); "capital loss" — 39(1)(b), 248(1); "disposition", "filing-due date", "fiscal period", "person", "property" — 248(1); "specified date" — 42(2); "subject property" — 42(1)(a); "taxation year" — 249; "vendor" — 42(1)(a).

Interpretation Bulletins [s. 42]: IT-330R: Disposition of capital property subject to warranty, covenant, etc (cancelled).

CRA Audit Manual [s. 42]: 29.2.4: Specific exceptions to capital gain and loss rules — disposition of capital property subject to warranty.

43. (1) General rule for part dispositions — For the purpose of computing a taxpayer's gain or loss for a taxation year from the disposition of part of a property, the adjusted cost base to the taxpayer, immediately before the disposition, of that part is the portion of the adjusted cost base to the taxpayer at that time of the whole property that can reasonably be regarded as attributable to that part.

Related Provisions: 43(3) — Where trust makes payment out of income or gains; 53(2)(d) — Reduction in adjusted cost base; 98.2(c), 100(3)(c) — No application to transfer of partnership interest on death.

Notes: See IT-264R and VIEWS docs 2008-0296741E5 and 2009-0350531I7 (allocation of proceeds on expropriation or granting of easement); 2006-0196071C6 (application of 43(1) to grant of servitude in Quebec); 2008-0299771E5 (receipt of part payment is considered disposition of part of debt); 2008-0297011E5 (amending partnership agreement to split income and capital interests may trigger 43(1)); 2010-0373461C6 (where partner redeems only some of partnership units); 2009-0338871R3 (ruling on donation of conservation land); 2012-0446131E5 ("at that time" means the time just before disposition); 2013-0491571E5 (partial disposition of partnership interest — partnership income for fiscal period is added to ACB of remaining interest).

In *Grenier*, 2016 FCA 297, para. 4 (leave to appeal denied 2018 CarswellNat 64 (SCC)), 43(1) applied to ⅓ of compensation paid to a farmer for having a wind turbine on his land (⅔ was business income).

43(1) was cited as support for saying that on sale of a partnership interest, the capital gain calculation is of the entire interest rather than individual units: *Iberville Developments*, 2020 FCA 115, para. 53 (leave to appeal denied 2021 CarswellNat 863).

CRA considers that 43(1) applies to "A" and "B" units of a partnership, which are treated a having a single bundle of rights: *Income Tax Technical News* 25.

43 renumbered as 43(1) by 2001 technical bill, effective Feb. 28, 1995.

Income Tax Folios: S3-F4-C1: General discussion of CCA [replaces IT-418].

Interpretation Bulletins: IT-200: Surface rentals and farming operations; IT-226R: Gift to a charity of a residual interest in real property or an equitable interest in a trust; IT-242R: Retired partners; IT-264R: Part dispositions; IT-278R2: Death of a partner or of a retired partner; IT-338R2: Partnership interests — changes in cost base resulting from the admission or retirement of a partner (cancelled); IT-359R2: Premiums and other amounts re leases.

I.T. Technical News: 25 (partnership issues).

(2) Ecological gifts — For the purposes of subsection (1) and section 53, if at any time a taxpayer disposes of a covenant or an easement to which land is subject or, in the case of land in the Province of Quebec, a real or personal servitude, in circumstances where subsection 110.1(5) or 118.1(12) applies,

(a) the portion of the adjusted cost base to the taxpayer of the land immediately before the disposition that can reasonably be regarded as attributable to the covenant, easement or servitude, as the case may be, is deemed to be equal to the amount determined by the formula

$$A \times B/C$$

where

A   is the adjusted cost base to the taxpayer of the land immediately before the disposition,

B   is the amount determined under subsection 110.1(5) or 118.1(12) in respect of the disposition, and

C   is the fair market value of the land immediately before the disposition; and

(b) for greater certainty, the cost to the taxpayer of the land shall be reduced at the time of the disposition by the amount determined under paragraph (a).

Related Provisions: 107(2), (2.1), (2.11) — No capital gain on disposition of capital interest.

Notes: 43(2) applies where the part of a property disposed of is a servitude, covenant or easement (SCE) to which land is subject. The 1995 budget introduced enhanced incentives for the donation of ecologically sensitive land (see 118.1(1)"total ecological gifts" and 110.1(1)(d)). Besides transfers of title, landowners may donate SCEs. "Land" can include buildings: see 70(5.2) Notes.

Normally the value of a donated property is the price a purchaser would pay for it on the open market, but there is no market for SCEs. To provide certainty in these valuations, the 1997 budget introduced a measure to deem the value of these gifts to be not less than the resulting decrease in the value of the land (see 118.1(12) and 110.1(5)).

Like other capital property, the ACB of a SCE is relevant in calculating the gain or loss arising on its disposition. 43(2) ensures that a portion of the ACB of the land to which the SCE relates is to be allocated to the donated SCE. For this purpose, the allocation is calculated in proportion to the percentage decrease in the value of the land due to the donation.

43(2) amended by 2017 budget bill #2, for gifts made after March 21, 2017, to add "or personal" (servitude) in opening words, and delete "real" before "servitude" in (a) (to extend the rule to personal servitudes).

43(2) amended by 2002-2013 technical bill, for gifts made after Dec. 20, 2002, to more clearly apply to a "real servitude" in Quebec.

43(2) added by 2001 technical bill, for gifts made after Feb. 27, 1995.

(3) Payments out of trust income, etc. — Notwithstanding subsection (1), where part of a capital interest of a taxpayer in a trust would, but for paragraph (h) or (i) of the definition "disposition" in subsection 248(1), be disposed of solely because of the satisfaction of a right to enforce payment of an amount by the trust, no part of the adjusted cost base to the taxpayer of the taxpayer's capital interest in the trust shall be allocated to that part of the capital interest.

Notes: 43(3) applies where part of a capital interest in a trust would, but for 248(1)"disposition"(h) or (i), be disposed of solely because of a satisfaction by the trust of a right to enforce a payment from the trust. No portion of the ACB of the taxpayer's capital interest is allocated to such a right. Accordingly, the ACB of the remaining part of the taxpayer's capital interest in the trust is not reduced after satisfaction of the right.

43(3) added by 2001 technical bill, for satisfactions of rights after 1999.

Definitions [s. 43]: "adjusted cost base" — 54, 248(1); "capital interest" — 108(1), 248(1); "disposition" — 248(1); "fair market value" — see 69(1) Notes; "land" — see 70(5.2) Notes; "property" — 248(1); "real servitude" — Quebec *Civil Code* art. 1177; "taxation year" — 249; "taxpayer" — 248(1); "trust" — 104(1), 248(1), (3).

43.1 (1) Life estates in real property — Notwithstanding any other provision of this Act, if at any time a taxpayer disposes of a remainder interest in real property (except as a result of a transaction to which subsection 73(3) would otherwise apply or by way of a gift to a qualified donee) to a person or partnership and retains a

life estate or an estate *pur autre vie* (in this section referred to as the "life estate") in the property, the taxpayer is deemed

(a) to have disposed at that time of the life estate in the property for proceeds of disposition equal to its fair market value at that time; and

(b) to have reacquired the life estate immediately after that time at a cost equal to the proceeds of disposition referred to in paragraph (a).

Related Provisions: 248(4) — Interest in real property.

Notes: See Notes at end of 43.1.

43.1(1) amended by 2011 budget bill #2, last change effective 2012.

Reference to "total ecological gifts" added by 2011 budget bill #2, for dispositions after Feb. 27, 1995.

(2) Idem — Where, as a result of an individual's death, a life estate to which subsection (1) applied is terminated,

(a) the holder of the life estate immediately before the death shall be deemed to have disposed of the life estate immediately before the death for proceeds of disposition equal to the adjusted cost base to that person of the life estate immediately before the death; and

(b) where a person who is the holder of the remainder interest in the real property immediately before the death was not dealing at arm's length with the holder of the life estate, there shall, after the death, be added in computing the adjusted cost base to that person of the real property an amount equal to the lesser of

(i) the adjusted cost base of the life estate in the property immediately before the death, and

(ii) the amount, if any, by which the fair market value of the real property immediately after the death exceeds the adjusted cost base to that person of the remainder interest immediately before the death.

Related Provisions: 53(1)(o) — Addition to adjusted cost base.

Notes: 43.1(1) applies on selling or giving a "remainder interest" in real property, i.e., ownership after death (effectively like leaving it in one's will) or after someone else's death (*pur autre vie*)). It provides that the taxpayer is deemed to have sold the life interest at the same time, for fair market value, and reacquired it at the same cost. Thus, gain up to fair market value is triggered on the *entire* property. On death, 43.1(2) deems the life interest to be sold at cost (so there is no further gain or loss), and if the remainder interest is held by a non-arm's length person (e.g., close family member) who now has the entire property, there is an addition to the property's ACB to reduce any future capital gain. These rules do not apply to a 73(3) rollover or a donation to a "qualified donee" such as a charity.

43.1 reportedly was enacted to prevent the planning technique of giving a cottage to the children while retaining a life interest, to avoid tax on deemed disposition at death: Drache, xxvi(18) *The Canadian Taxpayer* (Carswell) 142-44 (Sept. 7, 2004), and xxxvi(1) 2 (Jan. 3, 2014). See also Ranjan Thiruchelvam, "Income Tax Considerations in Structuring Real Estate Transactions With Life Interest", 29(9) *Money & Family Law* (Carswell) 71 (Sept. 2014). For valuation of a life interest, based on capitalized rents and mortality tables, see *Nauss*, 2005 TCC 488.

43.1 applied in *DePedrina*, 2005 TCC 590, resulting in the effective loss of the principal-residence exemption that would have been available to the transferor.

For CRA interpretation of 43.1 see VIEWS docs 2006-0155601E5 and 2008-0291091E5 (consequences to taxpayer of transfer of remainder interest in mother's home back to her); 2006-0188391E5 (life lease agreement with refundable entrance fee); 2006-0152101E5 (interpretation of 43.1(2)(b)); 2007-0242921E5 and 2008-0278801C6 q.5 (gain on property held by child where parent transferred remainder interest to child before death); 2011-0401401C6 (various issues re life estates and death).

43.1 added by 1992 technical bill (and amended retroactively by 1993 technical bill), effective for dispositions and terminations after Dec. 20, 1991. The amendment extended the exemption to donations to governments and certain other organizations.

Definitions [s. 43.1]: "adjusted cost base" — 54, 248(1); "arm's length" — 251(1); "fair market value" — see 69(1) Notes; "individual" — 248(1); "life estate" — 43.1(1); "partnership" — see 96(1) Notes; "person", "property" — 248(1); "qualified donee" — 149.1(1), 188.2(3)(a), 248(1); "registered charity", "taxpayer" — 248(1); "total charitable gifts", "total Crown gifts", "total ecological gifts" — 118.1(1).

44. (1) Exchanges of property [rollover] — Where at any time in a taxation year (in this subsection referred to as the "initial year") an amount has become receivable by a taxpayer as proceeds of disposition of a capital property that is not a share of the capital stock

of a corporation (which capital property is in this section referred to as the taxpayer's "former property") that is either

(a) property the proceeds of disposition of which are described in paragraph (b), (c) or (d) of the definition "proceeds of disposition" in subsection 13(21) or paragraph (b), (c) or (d) of the definition "proceeds of disposition" in section 54, or

(b) a property that was, immediately before the disposition, a former business property of the taxpayer,

and the taxpayer has

(c) if the former property is described in paragraph (a), before the later of the end of the second taxation year following the initial year and 24 months after the end of the initial year, and

(d) in any other case, before the later of the end of the first taxation year following the initial year and 12 months after the end of the initial year,

acquired a capital property that is a replacement property for the taxpayer's former property and the replacement property has not been disposed of by the taxpayer before the time the taxpayer disposed of the taxpayer's former property, notwithstanding subsection 40(1), if the taxpayer so elects under this subsection in the taxpayer's return of income for the year in which the taxpayer acquired the replacement property,

(e) the gain for a particular taxation year from the disposition of the taxpayer's former property shall be deemed to be the amount, if any, by which

(i) where the particular year is the initial year, the lesser of

(A) the amount, if any, by which the proceeds of disposition of the former property exceed

(I) in the case of depreciable property, the lesser of the proceeds of disposition of the former property computed without reference to subsection (6) and the total of its adjusted cost base to the taxpayer immediately before the disposition and any outlays and expenses to the extent that they were made or incurred by the taxpayer for the purpose of making the disposition, and

(II) in any other case, the total of its adjusted cost base to the taxpayer immediately before the disposition and any outlays and expenses to the extent that they were made or incurred by the taxpayer for the purpose of making the disposition, and

(B) the amount, if any, by which the proceeds of disposition of the former property exceed the total of the cost to the taxpayer, or in the case of depreciable property, the capital cost to the taxpayer, determined without reference to paragraph (f), of the taxpayer's replacement property and any outlays and expenses to the extent that they were made or incurred by the taxpayer for the purpose of making the disposition, or

(ii) where the particular year is subsequent to the initial year, the amount, if any, claimed by the taxpayer under subparagraph (iii) in computing the taxpayer's gain for the immediately preceding year from the disposition of the former property,

exceeds

(iii) subject to subsection (1.1), such amount as the taxpayer claims,

(A) in the case of an individual (other than a trust), in prescribed form filed with the taxpayer's return of income under this Part for the particular year, and

(B) in any other case, in the taxpayer's return of income under this Part for the particular year,

as a deduction, not exceeding the lesser of

(C) a reasonable amount as a reserve in respect of such of the proceeds of disposition of the former property that are payable to the taxpayer after the end of the particular year as can reasonably be regarded as a portion of the amount determined under subparagraph (i) in respect of the property, and

(D) an amount equal to the product obtained when $\frac{1}{5}$ of the amount determined under subparagraph (i) in respect of the property is multiplied by the amount, if any, by which 4 exceeds the number of preceding taxation years of the taxpayer ending after the disposition of the property, and

(f) the cost to the taxpayer or, in the case of depreciable property, the capital cost to the taxpayer, of the taxpayer's replacement property at any time after the time the taxpayer disposed of the taxpayer's former property, shall be deemed to be

(i) the cost to the taxpayer or, in the case of depreciable property, the capital cost to the taxpayer of the taxpayer's replacement property otherwise determined,

minus

(ii) the amount, if any, by which the amount determined under clause (e)(i)(A) exceeds the amount determined under clause (e)(i)(B).

Related Provisions: 13(4) — Parallel rule for CCA recapture; 44(4) — Deemed election; 44(5) — Replacement property; 44(6) — Deemed proceeds of disposition; 72(1)(c) — No reserve for year of death; 72(2)(b) — Election by legal representative and transferee re reserves; 79.1(3), (6)(c) — Capital gains reserve where property repossessed by creditor; 87(2)(l.3) — Amalgamations — replacement property acquired by new corporation; 87(2)(m) — Amalgamations — proceeds not due until after end of year; 87(2)(ll) — Amalgamations — continuation of predecessor corporations; 88(1)(d)(i)(C) — Winding-up; 96(3) — Election by members of partnership; 220(3.2), Reg. 600(b) — Late filing or revocation of election.

Notes: 44(1) allows a rollover of the cost base of property, and deferral of accrued capital gain, where the property is replaced (see 44(5)) and was a "former business property" (FBP) (as defined in 248(1)), or was expropriated, or was stolen or destroyed and paid for by insurance. It does not apply to rental property that is simply replaced (rental property is excluded from the definition of FBP): VIEWS docs 2007-0250661M4, 2010-0388881E5, 2010-0391191E5. Nor does it apply to partition under Quebec *Civil Code* art. 1030-37 and 884-88, splitting up assets held by taxpayers in undivided co-ownership: 2007-0231831E5. Nor does it apply to property sold "involuntarily" due to franchisor pressure: 2011-039952117. Where a property is destroyed by fire, only the building and not the land falls under 44(1): 2012-0473291E5. For the parallel rule preventing recapture of capital cost allowance, see 13(4).

See Income Tax Folio S3-F3-C1 (replaces IT-259R4). Note the time limits in 44(1)(c), (d) and 44(2) (the replacement can be acquired *before* the sale, e.g. on business expansion: CRA, 2019-0824481C6 [2019 CTF q.14]). The taxpayer should report the gain until the replacement property is acquired, but can defer payment by posting security: Folio S3-F3-C1 ¶1.16 (see 220(4)); VIEWS docs 2008-028390117, 2010-0391061E5.

When the 44(1) election is made, CRA can be *asked* to reassess the "initial year", but since 44(1) is not listed in 152(6), cannot be *forced* to. This has been pointed out to Finance. If one knows a replacement property will be acquired, it may be wise to object to the "as filed" assessment (see Notes to 165(1) under "Objection to own filing"), to keep open the appeal right for the initial year.

The "later of" in each of 44(1)(c) and (d) normally comes out to the same date as the months calculation, but 12 or 24 "months after" will be later if the corporation has a short taxation year, e.g. due to 249(3.1) or (4).

For discussion see Shapiro, "The Replacement Property Rules", 50(6) *Canadian Tax Journal* 2141-66 (2002); Scherer & Rayman, "Tax Implications of Expropriation", 56(4) *CTJ* 870-92 (2008); Truster, "The Replacement Property Rules: Some Quirks", 9(1) *Tax for the Owner-Manager* (ctf.ca) 1-2 (Jan. 2009); Purse, "How the Replacement Property Rules Work", 9(2) *Taxes & Wealth Management* (Carswell) 17-19 (May 2016).

In *Randhawa*, 2014 ABPC 163, aff'd ABQB (unreported), leave to appeal denied 2016 ABCA 273, R did not report gains on sales of agricultural land because he bought replacement land and thought the deferral applied. He was convicted of tax evasion, as he had not sought professional advice and mistake of law is not a defence.

An election "in the taxpayer's return" is valid even if the return is filed late. See Notes to 7(1.31).

For a taxpayer filing Quebec returns, the election must be copied to Revenu Québec: *Taxation Act* ss. 279, 21.4.6.

The phrase "immediately before the disposition" in 44(1)(b) has been interpreted very liberally, so that it does not mean "immediately before". See *Macklin*, [1993] 1 C.T.C. 21 (FCTD).

The deemed capital cost under 44(1)(f) was held not to apply for purposes of determining investment tax credits, in *Gaston Cellard Inc.*, 2002 CarswellNat 4726 (TCC).

44(1) can apply to an exchange of interests between two related persons who are dividing jointly-owned property: VIEWS doc 2002-0127033. See doc 2004-0099311E5 on

the timing of replacement of a rental property destroyed by fire. On interaction with 69(11), see 2014-0551841E5.

For a CCPC with a high-income shareholder, it may be better *not* to use 44(1) and to recognize a capital gain and pay a tax-free capital dividend. See Walters & Thornton, "Replacement Property Eschewed", 10(12) *Canadian Tax Highlights* (ctf.ca) 91-92 (Dec. 2002).

The exclusion of shares in the opening words was announced by Finance news release, April 15, 1999. Specific rollover provisions in 85-87 can apply to an exchange of shares; and see the small-business share rollover in 44.1.

44(1)(e)(iii)(C) allows a "reasonable" reserve for amounts not yet paid, using the same rule as 40(1)(a)(iii) for capital gains reserves. See Notes to 40(1) for discussion.

44(1) amended by 2002-2013 technical bill (last change effective for dispositions in tax years that end after Dec. 19, 2001); 2001, 1995-97 and 1991 technical bills.

Remission Orders: *Telesat Canada Remission Order*, P.C. 1999-1335.

Income Tax Folios: S4-F7-C1: Amalgamations of Canadian corporations [replaces IT-474R2].

Interpretation Bulletins: IT-259R4: Exchanges of property; IT-271R: Expropriations — time and proceeds of disposition (cancelled); IT-491: Former business property. See also at end of s. 44.

Information Circulars: 07-1R1: Taxpayer relief provisions.

Forms: T1030: Election to claim a capital gains reserve for individuals (other than trusts) when calculating the amount of a capital gain using the replacement property rules; T2069: Election in respect of amounts not deductible as reserves for the year of death.

(1.1) Reserve — property disposed of to a child — In computing the amount that a taxpayer may claim under subparagraph (1)(e)(iii) in computing the taxpayer's gain from the disposition of a former property of the taxpayer, that subparagraph shall be read as if the references in that subparagraph to "$\frac{1}{5}$" and "4" were references to "$\frac{1}{10}$" and "9" respectively if that former property is real or immovable property in respect of the disposition of which, because of subsection 73(3), the rules in subsection 73(3.1) applied to the taxpayer and a child of the taxpayer.

Notes: 44(1.1) amended by 2006 budget bill #2, for dispositions after May 1, 2006.

(2) Time of disposition and of receipt of proceeds — For the purposes of this Act, the time at which a taxpayer has disposed of a property for which there are proceeds of disposition as described in paragraph (b), (c) or (d) of the definition "proceeds of disposition" in subsection 13(21) or paragraph (b), (c) or (d) of the definition "proceeds of disposition" in section 54, and the time at which an amount, in respect of those proceeds of disposition has become receivable by the taxpayer shall be deemed to be the earliest of

(a) the day the taxpayer has agreed to an amount as full compensation to the taxpayer for the property lost, destroyed, taken or sold,

(b) where a claim, suit, appeal or other proceeding has been taken before one or more tribunals or courts of competent jurisdiction, the day on which the taxpayer's compensation for the property is finally determined by those tribunals or courts,

(c) where a claim, suit, appeal or other proceeding referred to in paragraph (b) has not been taken before a tribunal or court of competent jurisdiction within two years of the loss, destruction or taking of the property, the day that is two years following the day of the loss, destruction or taking,

(d) the time at which the taxpayer is deemed by section 70 or paragraph 128.1(4)(b) to have disposed of the property, and

(e) where the taxpayer is a corporation other than a subsidiary corporation referred to in subsection 88(1), the time immediately before the winding-up of the corporation,

and the taxpayer shall be deemed to have owned the property continuously until the time so determined.

Related Provisions: 59.1 — Involuntary disposition of resource property; 70(10), (11) — Definitions.

Notes: If property is destroyed by fire in 2006 and the insurer's compensation offer is made in 2007, disposition takes place in 2007: VIEWS doc 2007-0221141E5; and see 2012-0473291E5. "Finally determined" in 44(2)(b) means when the appeal period expires: doc 2006-0196141C6. Since 44(2) applies to the entire Act, the taxpayer can claim CCA for all years during which the disposition is deferred: 2006-0196141C6. Where proceeds are received through both insurance and a civil suit, the two sources are combined into one for 44(2) purposes: 2007-0227601E5. Where insurance proceeds are received over a period of time, see 2010-0390181I7, 2012-0461511E5.

44(2)(d) amended by 1993 technical bill to change reference from s. 48 to 128.1(4)(b), effective 1993. Where a corporation continued before 1993 elects for new 250(5.1) to apply earlier (see Notes to 250(5.1)), the amendment is effective from the corporation's "time of continuation".

Income Tax Folios: S3-F9-C1: Lottery winnings, miscellaneous receipts, and income (and losses) from crime [replaces IT-185R, IT-213R, IT-256R, IT-334R2].

Interpretation Bulletins: IT-125R4: Dispositions of resource properties; IT-259R4: Exchanges of property; IT-271R: Expropriations — time and proceeds of disposition (cancelled).

(3) Where subsec. 70(3) does not apply — Subsection 70(3) does not apply to compensation referred to in paragraph (b), (c) or (d) of the definition "proceeds of disposition" in subsection 13(21) or paragraph (b), (c) or (d) of the definition "proceeds of disposition" in section 54 that has been transferred or distributed to beneficiaries or other persons beneficially interested in an estate or trust.

(4) Deemed election — Where a former property of a taxpayer was a depreciable property of the taxpayer

(a) if the taxpayer has elected in respect of that property under subsection (1), the taxpayer shall be deemed to have elected in respect thereof under subsection 13(4); and

(b) if the taxpayer has elected in respect of that property under subsection 13(4), the taxpayer shall be deemed to have elected in respect thereof under subsection (1).

(5) Replacement property — For the purposes of this section, a particular capital property of a taxpayer is a replacement property for a former property of the taxpayer, if

(a) it is reasonable to conclude that the property was acquired by the taxpayer to replace the former property;

(a.1) it was acquired by the taxpayer and used by the taxpayer or a person related to the taxpayer for a use that is the same as or similar to the use to which the taxpayer or a person related to the taxpayer put the former property;

(b) where the former property was used by the taxpayer or a person related to the taxpayer for the purpose of gaining or producing income from a business, the particular capital property was acquired for the purpose of gaining or producing income from that or a similar business or for use by a person related to the taxpayer for such a purpose;

(c) where the former property was a taxable Canadian property of the taxpayer, the particular capital property is a taxable Canadian property of the taxpayer; and

(d) where the former property was a taxable Canadian property (other than treaty-protected property) of the taxpayer, the particular capital property is a taxable Canadian property (other than treaty-protected property) of the taxpayer.

Related Provisions: 87(2)(l.3) — Amalgamation — replacement property deemed acquired by new corporation.

Notes: For a property to qualify as replacement property (RP) under 44(5)(a), CRA's view is that there must be a correlation or causal relationship between the disposition and the new acquisition. See Income Tax Folio S3-F3-C1 ¶1.36, VIEWS docs 2010-0374241E5, 2010-0378261E5, 2014-0495681C6 [2013 APFF q. 17], 2014-0517491E5. Business expansion may qualify in some cases; *Technical News* 25; docs 2002-0156414, 2003-0006993 (ruling accepting a particular business expansion), 2008-0277991E5, 2008-0288341I7. The RP can be bought before the former property is sold: 2019-0824481C6 [2019 CTF q.14]. A retirement home cannot "replace" a motel because the use and business are different: 2003-0053261E5. An RV park can "replace" a motel if it includes similar services: 2006-0173181E5. A share in a vacation home can replace an expropriated vacation home: 2009-0352221E5. A rental building cannot "replace" a parking lot or farmland because the physical characteristics are different: 2010-0354951E5, 2016-0648971E5; but a rental office building can replace a rental warehouse: 2014-0561101E5, and cottages can replace other rental properties: 2014-0535041E5. The RP can be outside Canada if the former property was: 2006-0213921E5. RP status survives amalgamation: 87(2)(l.3), 2010-0357921I7. For a favourable ruling on 44(5)(a) see 2006-0185251R3. "Replace" requires direct substitution: *Livingston*, 2015 TCC 24, para. 42.

For property to qualify under 44(5)(a.1), it must be used, not merely acquired, during the period listed in 44(1)(c) or (d); *Glaxo Wellcome*, [1999] 4 C.T.C. 371 (FCA); *Klanten Farms*, 2017 TCC 348 (there is no distinction between voluntary and involuntary disposition for (a.1)); *Jorgensen*, 2009 TCC 37; VIEWS doc 2003-0012135. Va-

cant land is not "used": 2004-0088421E5. For examples of farming property "used" the same way as former property, and thus RP, see *Depaoli*, [2000] 1 C.T.C. 6 (FCA); 2016-0632001R3 (2 farms for 1). The property must be used by the same taxpayer or a related person: 2013-0505151E5. Rental property of a different type is "similar" to other rental property (cottages vs. building): 2014-0535041E5. In *Livingston* (above), para. 50, farm business assets (milk quotas, tractors) were not for "similar" use as farmland, and so did not qualify.

For the parallel rule for depreciable property (e.g., the building portion of land + building), see 13(4.1).

Leasehold improvements can qualify as RP: VIEWS doc 2005-0156171E5. (A leasehold is depreciable property under Reg. 1102(5), and 13(4) refers to depreciable property. Note also that 248(4) deems a leasehold to be an "interest" in real property.)

Shares probably cannot qualify as RP: *Dallas*, 2003 TCC 726; aff'd on the ground that the taxpayer did not intend to treat the shares as RP, 2004 FCA 364. Shares are explicitly excluded in 44(1) opening words from being the "former property".

Note that there is no geographical limitation on the RP, and that one can buy the RP before disposing of the former property, as long as there is a causal connection. See Income Tax Folio S3-F3-C1 ¶1.5; Weissman, Lang & Wong, "Managing the Sales of Canadian Businesses", 2015 Cdn Tax Foundation conference report, 8:1-42 at 8:27.

44(5) amended by 1998 Budget (effective for dispositions in a taxation year that ends after 1997), and 1995-97 and 1991 technical bills.

Interpretation Bulletins: IT-259R4: Exchanges of property; IT-271R: Expropriations — time and proceeds of disposition (cancelled).

I.T. Technical News: 25 (replacement property rules and business expansions).

(6) Deemed proceeds of disposition — If a taxpayer has disposed of property that was a former business property and was in part a building and in part the land (or an interest, or for civil law a right, therein) subjacent to, or immediately contiguous to and necessary for the use of, the building, for the purposes of this Subdivision, the amount if any, by which

(a) the proceeds of disposition of one such part determined without regard to this subsection

exceed

(b) the adjusted cost base to the taxpayer of that part

shall, to the extent that the taxpayer so elects in the taxpayer's return of income under this Part for the year in which the taxpayer acquired a replacement property for the former business property, be deemed not to be proceeds of disposition of that part and to be proceeds of disposition of the other part.

Related Provisions: 96(3) — Election by members of partnership; 220(3.2), Reg. 600(b) — Late filing or revocation of election; 248(4) — Interest in real property.

Notes: See Notes to 248(1)"former business property". The reallocated proceeds of disposition in respect of the land and building apply for purposes of the capital gains determination under 40(1) as well as for 44(1).

An election "in the taxpayer's return" is valid even if the return is filed late. See Notes to 7(1.31).

For a taxpayer filing Quebec returns, the election must be copied to Revenu Québec: *Taxation Act* ss. 280.3, 21.4.6.

44(6) opening words amended by 2002-2013 technical bill (Part 4 — bijuralism), effective June 26, 2013, to add "or for civil law a right".

44(6) amended by 1993 technical bill, effective for dispositions after Dec. 21, 1992.

Interpretation Bulletins: IT-271R: Expropriations — time and proceeds of disposition (cancelled); IT-259R4: Exchanges of property.

Information Circulars: 07-1R1: Taxpayer relief provisions.

(7) Where subpara. (1)(e)(iii) does not apply — Subparagraph (1)(e)(iii) does not apply to permit a taxpayer to claim any amount under that subparagraph in computing a gain for a taxation year where

(a) the taxpayer, at the end of the year or at any time in the immediately following year, was not resident in Canada or was exempt from tax under any provision of this Part;

(b) the person to whom the former property of the taxpayer was disposed of was a corporation that, immediately after the disposition,

(i) was controlled, directly or indirectly in any manner whatever, by the taxpayer,

(ii) was controlled, directly or indirectly in any manner whatever, by a person or group of persons by whom the taxpayer was controlled, directly or indirectly in any manner whatever, or

(iii) controlled the taxpayer, directly or indirectly in any manner whatever, where the taxpayer is a corporation; or

(c) the former property of the taxpayer was disposed of to a partnership in which the taxpayer was, immediately after the disposition, a majority-interest partner.

Related Provisions: 256(5.1), (6.2) — Controlled directly or indirectly.

Notes: 44(7)(c) amended by 2013 budget bill #2, effective Dec. 12, 2013, to change "majority interest partner" to "majority-interest partner" (with a hyphen).

44(7)(c) added by 2002-2013 technical bill, for dispositions after Dec. 20, 2002, with grandfathering for property transferred before 2004.

(8) Application of subsec. 70(10) — The definitions in subsection 70(10) apply to this section.

Notes: 44(8) added in the RSC 1985 (5th Supp) consolidation, for tax years ending after Nov. 1991. This rule was formerly in 70(10) opening words.

Definitions [s. 44]: "amount" — 248(1); "adjusted cost base" — 54, 248(1); "beneficially interested" — 248(25); "business" — 248(1); "capital property" — 54, 248(1); "child" — 44(8), 70(10), 252(1); "controlled directly or indirectly" — 256(5.1)–(6); "corporation" — 248(1); *Interpretation Act* 35(1); "depreciable property" — 13(21), 248(1); "disposition", "farming", "former business property" — 248(1); "former property" — 44(1); "immovable" — Quebec *Civil Code* art. 900–907; "individual" — 248(1); "interest" — (in real property) 248(4); "majority-interest partner", "prescribed" — 248(1); "proceeds of disposition" — 54; "property" — 248(1); "resident in Canada" — 94(3)(a), 250; "replacement property" — 44(5); "share", "taxable Canadian property" — 248(1); "taxation year" — 249; "taxpayer", "treaty-protected property" — 248(1); "trust" — 104(1), 248(1), (3).

44.1 (1) [Small-business share rollover] Definitions — The definitions in this subsection apply in this section.

"ACB reduction" of an individual in respect of a replacement share of the individual in respect of a qualifying disposition of the individual means the amount determined by the formula

$$D \times (E/F)$$

where

D   is the permitted deferral of the individual in respect of the qualifying disposition;

E   is the cost to the individual of the replacement share; and

F   is the cost to the individual of all the replacement shares of the individual in respect of the qualifying disposition.

Notes: E and F amended by 2003 Budget to change "qualifying cost" to "cost", for dispositions after Feb. 18, 2003. See also Notes at end of 44.1.

"active business corporation" at any time means, subject to subsection (10), a corporation that is, at that time, a taxable Canadian corporation all or substantially all of the fair market value of the assets of which at that time is attributable to assets of the corporation that are

(a) assets used principally in an active business carried on by the corporation or by an active business corporation that is related to the corporation;

(b) shares issued by or debt owing by other active business corporations that are related to the corporation; or

(c) a combination of assets described in paragraphs (a) and (b).

Related Provisions: 44.1(8) — Special rule re carrying on an active business; 44.1(10) — Exclusions to definition.

Notes: For the meaning of "used principally" in para. (a), see Notes to 73(3).

"carrying value" of the assets of a corporation at any time means the amount at which the assets of the corporation would be valued for the purpose of the corporation's balance sheet as of that time if that balance sheet were prepared in accordance with generally accepted accounting principles used in Canada at that time, except that an asset of a corporation that is a share or debt issued by a related corporation is deemed to have a carrying value of nil.

Related Provisions: 248(24) — Equity and consolidation methods of accounting not to be used.

"common share" means a share prescribed for the purpose of paragraph 110(1)(d).

Regulations: 6204 (prescribed share).

"eligible pooling arrangement" in respect of an individual means an agreement in writing made between the individual and another person or partnership (which other person or partnership is referred to in this definition and subsection (3) as the "investment manager") where the agreement provides for

(a) the transfer of funds or other property by the individual to the investment manager for the purpose of making investments on behalf of the individual;

(b) the purchase of eligible small business corporation shares with those funds, or the proceeds of a disposition of the other property, within 60 days after receipt of those funds or the other property by the investment manager; and

(c) the provision of a statement of account to the individual by the investment manager at the end of each month that ends after the transfer disclosing the details of the investment portfolio held by the investment manager on behalf of the individual at the end of that month and the details of the transactions made by the investment manager on behalf of the individual during the month.

"eligible small business corporation" at any time means, subject to subsection (10), a corporation that, at that time, is a Canadian-controlled private corporation all or substantially all of the fair market value of the assets of which at that time is attributable to assets of the corporation that are

(a) assets used principally in an active business carried on primarily in Canada by the corporation or by an eligible small business corporation that is related to the corporation;

(b) shares issued by or debt owing by other eligible small business corporations that are related to the corporation; or

(c) a combination of assets described in paragraphs (a) and (b).

Related Provisions: 44.1(8) — Special rule re carrying on an active business; 44.1(10) — Exclusions to definition.

Notes: See Notes at end of 44.1. For dispositions before October 18, 2000, ignore the words "subject to subsection (10)".

For the meaning of "used principally" in para. (a), see Notes to 73(3).

"eligible small business corporation share" of an individual means a common share issued by a corporation to the individual if

(a) at the time the share was issued, the corporation was an eligible small business corporation; and

(b) immediately before and after the share was issued, the total carrying value of the assets of the corporation and corporations related to it did not exceed $50,000,000.

Notes: See Notes at end of 44.1. For dispositions before October 18, 2000, para. (b) read differently.

"permitted deferral" of an individual in respect of a qualifying disposition of the individual means the amount determined by the formula

$$(G/H) \times I$$

where

G   is the lesser of the individual's proceeds of disposition from the qualifying disposition and the total of all amounts each of which is the cost to the individual of a replacement share in respect of the qualifying disposition;

H   is the individual's proceeds of disposition from the qualifying disposition; and

I   is the individual's capital gain from the qualifying disposition.

Related Provisions: 44.1(12) — Anti-avoidance — permitted deferral deemed nil.

Notes: Descriptions of G, H and I amended by 2003 Budget, for dispositions after Feb. 18, 2003. The amendments eliminate the $2-million limit on the amount of the original investment on which the deferral is allowed ("qualifying cost"), as well as on the amount that can be reinvested in shares of eligible small business corporations.

"qualifying cost" [Repealed]

Notes: Definition "qualifying cost" repealed by 2003 Budget, for dispositions that occur after Feb. 18, 2003. See Notes to 44.1(1)"permitted deferral" and at end of 44.1.

"qualifying disposition" of an individual (other than a trust) means, subject to subsection (9), a disposition of shares of the capital stock of a corporation where each such share disposed of was

(a) an eligible small business corporation share of the individual;

(b) throughout the period during which the individual owned the share, a common share of an active business corporation; and

(c) throughout the 185-day period that ended immediately before the disposition of the share, owned by the individual.

Related Provisions: 44.1(9) — Special rule re qualifying disposition.

Notes: For dispositions before Oct. 18, 2000, ignore "subject to subsection (9)".

"qualifying portion of a capital gain" [Repealed]

"qualifying portion of the proceeds of disposition" [Repealed]

Notes: Definitions "qualifying portion of a capital gain" and "qualifying portion of the proceeds of disposition" repealed by 2003 Budget, effective for dispositions that occur after Feb. 18, 2003. See Notes to "permitted deferral" and at end of 44.1.

"replacement share" of an individual in respect of a qualifying disposition of the individual in a taxation year means an eligible small business corporation share of the individual that is

(a) acquired by the individual in the year or within 120 days after the end of the year; and

(b) designated by the individual in the individual's return of income for the year to be a replacement share in respect of the qualifying disposition.

Notes: A late designation will be allowed by the CRA in limited circumstances: VIEWS doc 2008-0267811I7.

Para. (a) amended by 2003 Budget, for dispositions after Feb. 18, 2003.

(2) Capital gain deferral — Where an individual has made a qualifying disposition in a taxation year,

(a) the individual's capital gain for the year from the qualifying disposition is deemed to be the amount by which the individual's capital gain for the year from the qualifying disposition, determined without reference to this section, exceeds the individual's permitted deferral in respect of the qualifying disposition;

(b) in computing the adjusted cost base to the individual of a replacement share of the individual in respect of the qualifying disposition at any time after its acquisition, there shall be deducted the amount of the ACB reduction of the individual in respect of the replacement share; and

(c) where the qualifying disposition was a disposition of a share that was a taxable Canadian property of the individual, the replacement share of the individual in respect of the qualifying disposition is deemed to be, at any time that is within 60 months after the disposition, taxable Canadian property of the individual.

Related Provisions: 44.1(13) — Order of disposition of shares; 53(2)(a)(v) — Reduction in ACB of replacement share as per 44.1(2)(b); 107.4(3)(f) — Deemed taxable Canadian property retains status when rolled into trust.

Notes: See Notes at end of 44.1.

44.1(2)(c) amended by 2010 budget bill #1, effective March 5, 2010 to add "at any time that is within 60 months after the disposition". This change was made throughout the Act (44.1(2)(c), 51(1)(f), 85(1)(i), 85.1(1)(a), 85.1(5), 85.1(8)(b), 87(4), 87(5), 97(2)(c), 107(3.1)(d), 107.4(3)(f), 248(25.1)), in conjunction with narrowing 248(1)"taxable Canadian property". However, every time a rollover takes place the 60-month sunset clock is reset, so it could be extended many times.

(3) Special rule — re eligible pooling arrangements — Except for the purpose of the definition "eligible pooling arrangement" in subsection (1), any transaction entered into by an investment manager under an eligible pooling arrangement on behalf of an individual is deemed to be a transaction of the individual and not a transaction of the investment manager.

Related Provisions: 44.1(1)"eligible pooling arrangement" — Meaning of "investment manager".

(4) Special rule — re acquisitions on death — For the purpose of this section, a share of the capital stock of a corporation, acquired by an individual as a consequence of the death of a person who is the individual's spouse, common-law partner or parent, is deemed to be a share that was acquired by the individual at the time it was acquired by that person and owned by the individual throughout the period that it was owned by that person, if

(a) where the person was the spouse or common-law partner of the individual, the share was an eligible small business share of the person and subsection 70(6) applied to the individual in respect of the share; or

(b) where the person was the individual's parent, the share was an eligible small business share of the parent and subsection 70(9.2) applied to the individual in respect of the share.

(5) Special rule — re breakdown of relationships — For the purpose of this section, a share of the capital stock of a corporation, acquired by an individual from a person who was the individual's former spouse or common-law partner as a consequence of the settlement of rights arising out of their marriage or common-law partnership, is deemed to be a share that was acquired by the individual at the time it was acquired by that person and owned by the individual throughout the period that it was owned by that person if the share was an eligible small business share of the person and subsection 73(1) applied to the individual in respect of the share.

(6) Special rule — re eligible small business corporation share exchanges — For the purpose of this section, where an individual receives shares of the capital stock of a particular corporation that are eligible small business corporation shares of the individual (in this subsection referred to as the "new shares") as the sole consideration for the disposition by the individual of shares issued by the particular corporation or by another corporation that were eligible small business corporation shares of the individual (in this subsection referred to as the "exchanged shares"), the new shares are deemed to have been owned by the individual throughout the period that the exchanged shares were owned by the individual if

(a) section 51, paragraph 85(1)(h), subsection 85.1(1), section 86 or subsection 87(4) applied to the individual in respect of the new shares; and

(b) the individual's total proceeds of disposition of the exchanged shares was equal to the total of all amounts each of which was the individual's adjusted cost base of an exchanged share immediately before the disposition.

Related Provisions: 51(1)(c) — Exchange of convertible property is disposition for purposes of 44.1(6).

Notes: For discussion of 44.1(6)-(12) see Baek, "The Small Business Investment Deferral Incentive", 11(3) *Tax Law Update* (Ontario Bar Association) 1-5 (May 2001).

44.1(6) amended by 2002-2013 technical bill, for dispositions after Feb. 27, 2000.

(7) Special rule — re active business corporation share exchanges — For the purpose of this section, where an individual receives common shares of the capital stock of a particular corporation (in this subsection referred to as the "new shares") as the sole consideration for the disposition by the individual of common shares of the particular corporation or of another corporation (in this subsection referred to as the "exchanged shares"), the new shares are deemed to be eligible small business corporation shares of the individual and shares of the capital stock of an active business corporation that were owned by the individual throughout the period that the exchanged shares were owned by the individual, if

(a) section 51, paragraph 85(1)(h), subsection 85.1(1), section 86 or subsection 87(4) applied to the individual in respect of the new shares;

(b) the total of the individual's proceeds of disposition in respect of the disposition of the exchanged shares was equal to the total of the individual's adjusted cost bases immediately before the disposition of such shares; and

(c) the disposition of the exchanged shares was a qualifying disposition of the individual.

Related Provisions: 51(1)(c) — Exchange of convertible property is disposition for purposes of 44.1(7).

Notes: See Notes to 44.1(6). 44.1(7) amended by 2002-2013 technical bill, for dispositions after Feb. 27, 2000.

(8) Special rule — re carrying on an active business — For the purpose of the definitions in subsection (1), a property held at any particular time by a corporation that would, if this Act were read without reference to this subsection, be considered to carry on an active business at that time, is deemed to be used or held by the corporation in the course of carrying on that active business if the property (or other property for which the property is substituted property) was acquired by the corporation, at any time in the 36-month period ending at the particular time, because the corporation

(a) issued a debt or a share of a class of its capital stock in order to acquire money for the purpose of acquiring property to be used in or held in the course of, or making expenditures for the purpose of, earning income from an active business carried on by it;

(b) disposed of property used or held by it in the course of carrying on an active business in order to acquire money for the purpose of acquiring property to be used in or held in the course of, or making expenditures for the purpose of, earning income from an active business carried on by it; or

(c) accumulated income derived from an active business carried on by it in order to acquire property to be used in or held in the course of, or to make expenditures for the purpose of, earning income from an active business carried on by it.

Related Provisions: 248(5) — Substituted property.

Notes: See Notes to 44.1(6) and at end of 44.1. For the meaning of "derived" in para. (c), see Notes to 18.1(12).

(9) Special rule — re qualifying disposition — A disposition of a common share of an active business corporation (in this subsection referred to as the "subject share") by an individual that, but for this subsection, would be a qualifying disposition of the individual is deemed not to be a qualifying disposition of the individual unless the active business of the corporation referred to in paragraph (a) of the definition "active business corporation" in subsection (1) was carried on primarily in Canada

(a) at all times in the period that began at the time the individual last acquired the subject share and ended at the time of disposition, if that period is less than 730 days; or

(b) in any other case, for at least 730 days in the period referred to in paragraph (a).

Notes: For dispositions before October 18, 2000, 44.1(9) does not apply.

(10) Special rule — re exceptions — For the purpose of this section, an eligible small business corporation and an active business corporation at any time do not include a corporation that is, at that time,

(a) a professional corporation;

(b) a specified financial institution;

(c) a corporation the principal business of which is the leasing, rental, development or sale, or any combination of those activities, of real or immovable property owned by it; or

(d) a corporation more than 50% of the fair market value of the property of which (net of debts incurred to acquire the property) is attributable to real or immovable property.

Notes: For the meaning of "principal business" see IT-153R3 and Notes to 20(1)(bb).

44.1(10)(c), (d) amended by 2002-2013 technical bill (Part 4 — bijuralism), effective June 26, 2013, to add "or immovable".

(11) Determination rule — In determining whether a share owned by an individual is an eligible small business corporation share of the individual, this Act shall be read without reference to section 48.1.

(12) Anti-avoidance rule — The permitted deferral of an individual in respect of a qualifying disposition of shares issued by a cor-poration (in this subsection referred to as "new shares") is deemed to be nil where

(a) the new shares (or shares for which the new shares are substituted property) were issued to the individual or a person related to the individual as part of a series of transactions or events in which

(i) shares of the capital stock of a corporation (in this subsection referred to as the "old shares") were disposed of by the individual or a person related to the individual, or

(ii) the paid-up capital of old shares or the adjusted cost base to the individual or to a person related to the individual of the old shares was reduced;

(b) the new shares (or shares for which the new shares are substituted property) were

(i) issued by the corporation that issued the old shares,

(ii) issued by a corporation that, at or immediately after the time of issue of the new shares, was a corporation that was not dealing at arm's length with

(A) the corporation that issued the old shares, or

(B) the individual, or

(iii) issued, by a corporation that acquired the old shares (or by another corporation related to that corporation), as part of the transaction or event or series of transactions or events that included that acquisition of the old shares; and

(c) it is reasonable to conclude that one of the main reasons for the series of transactions or events or a transaction in the series was to permit the individual, persons related to the individual, or the individual and persons related to the individual to become eligible to deduct under subsection (2) permitted deferrals in respect of qualifying dispositions of new shares (or shares substituted for the new shares) the total of which would exceed the total that those persons would have been eligible to deduct under subsection (2) in respect of permitted deferrals in respect of qualifying dispositions of old shares.

Related Provisions: 248(5) — Substituted property.

Notes: See Notes to 44.1(6). For the meaning of "one of the main reasons" in para. (c), see Notes to 83(2.1).

44.1(12)(b)(ii)(B) and (iii) added by 2002-2013 technical bill (Part 5 — technical), for dispositions after Feb. 27, 2004.

(13) Order of disposition of shares — For the purpose of this section, an individual is deemed to dispose of shares that are identical properties in the order in which the individual acquired them.

Notes: 44.1(13) added by 2002-2013 technical bill (Part 5 — technical), effective for dispositions after Dec. 20, 2002. However, if an individual so elects in writing and files the election with the Minister by the individual's filing-due date for the individual's taxation year that includes June 26, 2013, it applies, in respect of the individual, to dispositions after Feb. 27, 2000.

Notes [44.1]: 44.1(2) provides a rollover (deferral) of the capital gain when individual X's investment in a small business is cashed in, but another investment is made (no longer limited to $2 million: 44.1(1)"permitted deferral"). X must be selling shares of an ESBC: see 44.1(1)"eligible small business corporation", "eligible small business corporation share". The shares must be common shares owned for at least 185 days: see 44.1(1)"qualifying disposition". Certain corporations are excluded: see 44.1(10). 44.1(4)–(7) allow a flow-through of ownership (as though X had owned the shares throughout) if shares are acquired on the death of a spouse or parent, due to marital breakdown, or on certain corporate reorganizations.

Once X sells the shares, a new investment must be made in another eligible small business. (There is no requirement to track the proceeds and actually use the same cash.) The new shares must be acquired after the start of the year in which the old investment was sold, and up to 120 days after the end of the calendar year (see 44.1(1)"replacement share"). The capital gains deferral under 44.1(2) is then the "permitted deferral" as defined in 44.1(1).

See Harris, "Small-Business Share Rollovers", 10(4) *Tax Hyperion* (Carswell) 6-7 (April 2013); Courage, "Are You a Serial Entrepreneur?", 7(2) *Taxes & Wealth Management* (Carswell) 11-14 (May 2014).

For CRA discussion of the conditions for 44.1 see VIEWS docs 2004-0057171E5, 2009-0339151E5, 2010-0385861E5, 2012-0445941E5. For an example of 44.1 applying (and 44.1(12) not applying) see doc 2007-0194571I7.

44.1 added by 2000 Budget, effective for dispositions that occur after Feb. 27, 2000; for dispositions that occurred before Oct. 18, 2000, a different version applied.

Definitions [s. 44.1]: "ACB reduction" — 44.1(1); "active business" — 248(1); "active business corporation" — 44.1(1), (10); "adjusted cost base" — 54, 248(1); "amount" — 248(1); "arm's length" — 251(1); "business" — 248(1); "Canada" — 255, *Interpretation Act* 35(1); "Canadian-controlled private corporation" — 125(7), 248(1); "capital gain" — 39(1)(a), 248(1); "carrying value", "common share" — 44.1(1); "common-law partner", "common-law partnership" — 248(1); "corporation" — 248(1), *Interpretation Act* 35(1); "disposition" — 248(1); "eligible pooling arrangement" — 44.1(1); "eligible small business corporation" — 44.1(1), (10); "eligible small business corporation share" — 44.1(1), (11); "fair market value" — see 69(1) Notes; "immovable" — Quebec *Civil Code* art. 900–907; "individual" — 248(1); "investment manager" — 44.1(1)"eligible pooling arrangement"; "month" — *Interpretation Act* 35(1); "paid-up capital" — 89(1), 248(1); "parent" — 252(2)(a); "partnership" — see 96(1) Notes; "permitted deferral" — 44.1(1); "person", "prescribed", "professional corporation", "property" — 248(1); "qualifying cost" — 44.1(1); "qualifying disposition" — 44.1(1), (9); "qualifying portion of a capital gain", "qualifying portion of the proceeds" — 44.1(1); "related" — 251(2)–(6); "replacement share" — 44.1(1); "series of transactions" — 248(10); "share", "small business corporation", "specified financial institution" — 248(1); "substituted", "substituted property" — 248(5); "taxable Canadian corporation" — 89(1), 248(1); "taxable Canadian property" — 248(1); "taxation year" — 249; "trust" — 104(1), 248(1), (3); "writing" — *Interpretation Act* 35(1).

45. (1) Property with more than one use [change in use] —
For the purposes of this Subdivision the following rules apply:

(a) where a taxpayer,

(i) having acquired property for some other purpose, has commenced at a later time to use it for the purpose of gaining or producing income, or

(ii) having acquired property for the purpose of gaining or producing income, has commenced at a later time to use it for some other purpose,

the taxpayer shall be deemed to have

(iii) disposed of it at that later time for proceeds equal to its fair market value at that later time, and

(iv) immediately thereafter reacquired it at a cost equal to that fair market value;

(b) where property has, since it was acquired by a taxpayer, been regularly used in part for the purpose of gaining or producing income and in part for some other purpose, the taxpayer shall be deemed to have acquired, for that other purpose, the proportion of the property that the use regularly made of the property for that other purpose is of the whole use regularly made of the property at a cost to the taxpayer equal to the same proportion of the cost to the taxpayer of the whole property, and, if the property has, in such a case, been disposed of, the proceeds of disposition of the proportion of the property deemed to have been acquired for that other purpose shall be deemed to be the same proportion of the proceeds of disposition of the whole property;

(c) where, at any time after a taxpayer has acquired property, there has been a change in the relation between the use regularly made by the taxpayer of the property for gaining or producing income and the use regularly made of the property for other purposes,

(i) if the use regularly made of the property for those other purposes has increased, the taxpayer shall be deemed to have

(A) disposed of the property at that time for proceeds equal to the proportion of the fair market value of the property at that time that the amount of the increase in the use regularly made by the taxpayer of the property for those other purposes is of the whole use regularly made of the property, and

(B) immediately thereafter reacquired the property so disposed of at a cost equal to the proceeds referred to in clause (A), and

(ii) if the use regularly made of the property for those other purposes has decreased, the taxpayer shall be deemed to have

(A) disposed of the property at that time for proceeds equal to the proportion of the fair market value of the property at that time that the amount of the decrease in use regularly made by the taxpayer of the property for those

other purposes is of the whole use regularly made of the property, and

(B) immediately thereafter reacquired the property so disposed of at a cost equal to the proceeds referred to in clause (A); and

(d) in applying this subsection in respect of a non-resident taxpayer, a reference to "gaining or producing income" shall be read as a reference to "gaining or producing income from a source in Canada".

Related Provisions: 13(7)(a), (b), (d) — Change in use rules for depreciable property; 45(2), (3) — Elections to postpone deemed disposition; 54"superficial loss"(c) — Superficial loss rule does not apply.

Notes: 45(1) provides for a deemed disposition at fair market value (see Notes to 69(1)) on change in use of capital property to or from income-earning. See Income Tax Folio S1-F3-C2, ¶2.48-2.60. (For depreciable property, see 13(7)(a)-(d).) The FMV must be determined as of the change in use: VIEWS doc 2011-0429321E5. A gain on change in use *to* income-earning may be deferred by election under 45(2): 2009-0344001E5. A gain on change in use *from* income-earning to a principal residence may be deferred by election under 45(3), unless CCA has been claimed (45(4)). See VIEWS doc 2005-0125831E5.

Where property that is leased out changes between capital property and inventory, 13(7) and 45(1) apply: *CAE Inc.*, 2013 FCA 92, paras. 85-102. However, CRA disagrees, considers this to be *obiter*, and is not changing IT-102R2 and IT-218R due to the "difficult compliance and administrative obligations" in applying 13(7) to every change from personal to business use and back: VIEWS doc 2013-0493811C6 [2013 CTF q.2] [Asif Abdulla, "No CRA Change on Change in Use", 22(9) *Canadian Tax Highlights* (ctf.ca) 11 (Sept. 2014)].

In *Henco Industries*, 2014 TCC 192, paras. 165-168, a developer in Caledonia had its business ruined by native occupation and the province failed to honour Court injunctions, and its land became worthless. The Ontario government paid $15.8 million to make Henco "go away", and Henco gave up the land. Henco argued that it changed the land from inventory to capital before this payment; the Court ruled there was no change in use, "as the land went from use as a trading asset to no use at all". There was instead "a conversion in which the land completely lost its character as inventory." (This seems to conflict with *Friesen* and *CAE Inc.* saying all property is either inventory or capital property: see Notes to 54"capital property".)

The capital gains exemption can be claimed on the deemed disposition: VIEWS doc 2007-0248391E5.

CRA does not apply 45(1) on a change of use of real estate inventory to a principal residence (e.g., a builder decides to move in): docs 9335765, 2015-0596921E5.

45(2) and (3) provide elections for 45(1) not to apply in certain cases, to defer the gain until actual disposition. As amended in 2021 for changes in use after March 18, 2019, these elections now apply to a partial change in use as well. Before, CRA policy was not to apply 45(1) when a principal residence was partly changed to an ancillary income-earning use, provided no CCA was claimed on the building: Income Tax Folio S1-F3-C2 ¶2.59, VIEWS docs 2008-028578117, 2009-0321481E5, 2013-0475301E5, 2016-0673231E5 (CCA can be claimed on other assets: 2005-0134681E5; and US depreciation can be claimed on the home: 2010-0369351E5). Whether a change in use was sufficiently "substantial" for this policy to apply depends on the facts: 2010-0360441E5, 2010-0360451E5. (See also 2011-0409671E5.)

A structural change to a property, such as an addition or opening an exterior wall to give access to the business portion, may create a change in use: doc 2014-0528841E5. Changing a duplex from living in unit 1 and renting unit 2 to the reverse is not considered a change in use, as rental use remains 50%: 2015-0589821E5, 2016-0674831C6 [CPA QC 2017 q.1.4]; and the same for other changes where total rental use does not change: 2016-0652841C6 [2016 APFF q.2]. Rooftop solar panels do not trigger 45(1) unless the owner leases the roof to a third party: 2009-0342121E5.

A "clear and unequivocal positive act implementing a change of intention" is necessary for a change in use from inventory to capital property: *Edmund Peachey Ltd.*, [1979] C.T.C. 51 (FCA); *Peluso*, 2012 TCC 153. A mere decision to a sell a property is not a change in use: VIEWS doc 2005-0113981E5. Renting a property for four years indicates an intention to produce income, so a change to personal use triggers 45(1): 2006-0208681E5. Constructing a home on vacant land is not a change in use: 2006-0203191E5. Where part of the property was depreciable property subject to 13(7)(b), see 2005-0157751E5. "The time at which a change in use takes place for the purposes of section 45 is a question of fact depending on all of the circumstances": *Roos*, [1994] 1 C.T.C. 2105 (TCC), para. 36.

45(1) does not apply to a change in use from capital property to inventory, but the capital gain to the date of change in use is taxed when the property is sold: IT-218R para. 15, and is eligible for the capital gains exemption: VIEWS docs 2007-0248391E5, 2008-027545117. Conversion of a rental building to condominiums (for sale likely leads to a sale on income account: *Hughes*, [1984] C.T.C. 101 (FCTD) (despite *Cantor*, [1985] 1 C.T.C. 2059 (TCC)).

45(1) can be used to advantage by a taxpayer assessed for a capital gain on a property held for many years. If one can show a change in use from personal to income-earning in a year that is statute-barred but more recent than the year of purchase, the capital gain can be reduced! See *Willis*, 2003 TCC 575.

45(1)(c) amended by 1991 technical bill, retroactive to 1972, to correct technical errors. 45(1)(d) added by 2001 technical bill, effective October 2, 1996.

Income Tax Folios: S1-F3-C2: Principal residence [replaces IT-120R6, IT-437R].

Interpretation Bulletins: IT-83R3: Non-profit organizations — taxation of income from property; IT-160R3: Personal use of aircraft (cancelled); IT-218R: Profit, capital gains and losses from the sale of real estate, including farmland and inherited land and conversion of real estate from capital property to inventory and vice versa.

(2) Election where change of use — For the purposes of this Subdivision and section 13, if a taxpayer elects in respect of any property of the taxpayer in the taxpayer's return of income for a taxation year under this Part,

(a) if subparagraph (1)(a)(i) or paragraph 13(7)(b) would otherwise apply to the property for the taxation year, the taxpayer is deemed not to have begun to use the property for the purpose of gaining or producing income;

(b) if subparagraph (1)(c)(ii) or 13(7)(d)(i) would otherwise apply to the property for the taxation year, the taxpayer is deemed not to have increased the use regularly made of the property for the purpose of gaining or producing income relative to the use regularly made of the property for other purposes; and

(c) if the taxpayer rescinds the election in respect of the property in the taxpayer's return of income under this Part for a subsequent taxation year,

(i) if paragraph (a) applied to the taxpayer in the taxation year, the taxpayer is deemed to have begun to use the property for the purpose of gaining or producing income on the first day of the subsequent taxation year, and

(ii) if paragraph (b) applied to the taxpayer in the taxation year, the taxpayer is deemed to have increased the use regularly made of the property for the purpose of gaining or producing income on the first day of the subsequent taxation year by the amount that would have been the increase in the taxation year if the election had not been made.

Related Provisions: 13(1) — Recapture of depreciation; 54"principal residence"(b) — Effect of election on principal residence; 220(3.2), Reg. 600(b) — Late filing or revocation of election.

Notes: See Notes to 45(1). 45(2) does not apply to a change from one kind of income-producing use to another (e.g., from property income to business income).

Principal-residence status can extend up to 4 years that the property is rented out: 54"principal residence"(d).

An election or rescission "in the taxpayer's return" is valid even if the return is filed late. See Notes to 7(1.31).

CRA may accept a late 45(2) election if no CCA has been claimed: Income Tax Folio S1-F3-C2, ¶2.49, VIEWS docs 2008-0265741I7, 2011-0396221I7, 2012-0448391I7; 2014-0541171E5 (executor can make election on behalf of deceased).

For a taxpayer filing Quebec returns, the election and any rescission must be copied to Revenu Québec: *Taxation Act* ss. 284, 21.4.6.

For a non-resident, no 116(3) notice is required if an election is made under 45(2): VIEWS doc 2005-0113981E5; but if the non-resident revokes the election, a s. 116 certificate is required.

Returning in the 5th year to live in the property infrequently while it is still rented out would not entitle the owner to designate the property as principal residence (PR): 2008-0286721E5. For the calculation of the PR exemption see 2011-0415731E5. On the election's application to a duplex or triplex, see 2013-0495621C6 [2013 APFF q.2].

In *Gjernes*, 2007 FC 609, CRA was ordered to reconsider its disallowance of a late 45(2) election.

See also Yang, "Late Filing of Election for a Temporary Home Rental", 10(3) *Canadian Tax Focus* (ctf.ca) 1-2 (Aug. 2020).

45(2) amended by 2021 budget bill #1, for changes in use after March 18, 2019, to extend to a *partial* change in use by adding (b) and (c)(ii). For earlier changes in use, read:

(2) For the purposes of this Subdivision and section 13, where subparagraph (1)(a)(i) or paragraph 13(7)(b) would otherwise apply to any property of a taxpayer for a taxation year and the taxpayer so elects in respect of the property in the taxpayer's return of income for the year under this Part, the taxpayer shall be deemed not to have begun to use the property for the purpose of gaining or producing income except that, if in the taxpayer's return of income under this Part for a subsequent taxation year the taxpayer rescinds the election in respect of the property, the taxpayer shall be deemed to have begun so to use the property on the first day of that subsequent year.

45(2) earlier amended by 1993 technical bill.

Income Tax Folios: S1-F3-C2: Principal residence [replaces IT-120R6, IT-437R].

Information Circulars: 07-1R1: Taxpayer relief provisions.

(3) Election concerning principal residence — If at any time a property that was acquired by a taxpayer for the purpose of gaining or producing income, or that was acquired in part for that purpose, ceases in whole or in part to be used for that purpose and becomes, or becomes part of, the principal residence of the taxpayer, paragraphs (1)(a) and (c) shall not apply to deem the taxpayer to have disposed of the property at that time and to have reacquired it immediately thereafter if the taxpayer so elects by notifying the Minister in writing on or before the earlier of

(a) the day that is 90 days after a demand by the Minister for an election under this subsection is sent to the taxpayer, and

(b) the taxpayer's filing-due date for the taxation year in which the property is actually disposed of by the taxpayer.

Related Provisions: 45(4) — Where election cannot be made; 54"principal residence"(b), (d) — Effect of election and parallel rule when moving out of principal residence; 220(3.2), Reg. 600(b) — Late filing or revocation of election.

Notes: See Notes to 45(1). By making a 45(3) election, capital gain accrued while the property was rented out can be deferred: VIEWS docs 2005-0134361E5, 2007-0237341E5. The election cannot be made if CCA was claimed: 45(4), 2013-0484531M4. It can be made by a non-resident: 2005-0128711E5. It can be made for a property that was a principal residence (PR), then rented out, and is now a PR again: 2012-0433451E5. No election can be made on partial change of use since Feb. 21, 2012: Income Tax Folio S1-F3-C2, ¶2.57; docs 2007-0224761E5, 2011-0417471E5 (duplex is one property, so no election on moving into one unit), 2012-0440471I7 (incorporating second half of duplex into PR; but see now 2019-0812621C6 [2019 APFF q.3] saying the election can be made). This applies even if the taxpayer made a 45(2) election before CRA changed its policy: 2016-0651791C6 [2016 APFF q.4]. (However, the PR exemption does not apply to a duplex or triplex with separate units: see Notes to 54"principal residence" at "Two distinguishable parts".) See also 2006-0214351E5; 2013-0495621C6 [2013 APFF q.2] (application to duplex or triplex); 2014-0535611E5 (interaction with 73(1)). PR status can be carried back up to 4 years that the property was rented out: 54"principal residence"(d).

For a taxpayer filing Quebec returns, the election must be copied to Revenu Québec: *Taxation Act* ss. 286.1, 21.4.6.

See also Painter, "Principal-Residence Tax-Deferral Election May Be Inadvisable", 6(1) *Canadian Tax Focus* (ctf.ca) 7 (Feb. 2016) (election can increase tax later).

45(3) opening words amended by 2021 budget bill #1, for changes in use after March 18, 2019, to extend to a change in use of *part* of the property. For earlier changes in use, read:

(3) Where at any time a property that was acquired by a taxpayer for the purpose of gaining or producing income ceases to be used for that purpose and becomes the principal residence of the taxpayer, subsection (1) shall not apply to deem the taxpayer to have disposed of the property at that time and to have reacquired it immediately thereafter if the taxpayer so elects by notifying the Minister in writing on or before the earlier of

45(3)(b) amended by 1995 Budget, effective 1995.

Income Tax Folios: S1-F3-C2: Principal residence [replaces IT-120R6, IT-437R].

Information Circulars: 07-1R1: Taxpayer relief provisions.

(4) Where election cannot be made — Notwithstanding subsection (3), an election described in that subsection shall be deemed not to have been made in respect of a change in use of property if any deduction in respect of the property has been allowed for any taxation year ending after 1984 and on or before the change in use under regulations made under paragraph 20(1)(a) to the taxpayer, the taxpayer's spouse or common-law partner or a trust under which the taxpayer or the taxpayer's spouse or common-law partner is a beneficiary.

Notes: 45(4) denies the 45(3) election to defer a capital gain if CCA has been claimed on "the" property, i.e. the entire property, so VIEWS doc 2011-0417471E5 said one unit of a duplex does not qualify. (It has been suggested that a building and its land are separate "properties", so only the building would be subject to 45(4); but this is doubtful given the common-law doctrine of "merger" when adjoining properties are owned by the same person: *Fraser-Reid v. Droumtsekas*, [1980] 1 S.C.R. 720, and also given that a building and its land are usually part of the same legal property description.)

45(4) amended by 2000 same-sex partners bill to refer to "common-law partner", effective 2001 or earlier by election.

Income Tax Folios: S1-F3-C2: Principal residence [replaces IT-120R6, IT-437R].

Definitions [s. 45]: "amount", "business", "common-law partner" — 248(1); "fair market value" — see 69(1) Notes; "filing-due date" — 150(1), 248(1); "gaining or producing income" — 45(1)(d); "Minister" — 248(1); "principal residence", "proceeds of disposition" — 54; "property", "regulation" — 248(1); "taxation year" — 249; "taxpayer" — 248(1); "writing" — *Interpretation Act* 35(1).

Interpretation Bulletins [s. 45]: IT-102R2: Conversion of property, other than real property, from or to inventory.

46. (1) Personal-use property

46. (1) Personal-use property — Where a taxpayer has disposed of a personal-use property (other than an excluded property disposed of in circumstances to which subsection 110.1(1), or the definition "total charitable gifts", "total cultural gifts" or "total ecological gifts" in subsection 118.1(1), applies) of the taxpayer, for the purposes of this Subdivision

> (a) the adjusted cost base to the taxpayer of the property immediately before the disposition shall be deemed to be the greater of $1,000 and the amount otherwise determined to be its adjusted cost base to the taxpayer at that time; and

> (b) the taxpayer's proceeds of disposition of the property shall be deemed to be the greater of $1,000 and the taxpayer's proceeds of disposition of the property otherwise determined.

Related Provisions: 40(2)(g)(iii) — No loss allowed on most personal-use property; 46(3) — Properties ordinarily disposed of as a set; 46(5) — Excluded property; 50(2) — Personal-use property debts.

Notes: The effect of the minimum $1,000 to both cost and proceeds of personal-use property is that, if such property is sold for proceeds of $1,000 or less, no gain or loss results and there are no tax consequences. See 54"personal-use property" Notes. Note that losses on personal-use property cannot be used anyway (see 40(2)(g)(iii)), except for listed-personal-property losses, which can be used only against listed-personal-property gains (see 3(b)(ii) and 41(2)). For art flips, see 46(5).

46(1) amended by 2000 Budget, for property acquired after Feb. 27, 2000.

Income Tax Folios: S3-F9-C1: Lottery winnings, miscellaneous receipts, and income (and losses) from crime [replaces IT-185R, IT-213R, IT-256R, IT-334R2].

Interpretation Bulletins: IT-332R: Personal Use Property (cancelled).

(2) Where part only of property disposed of

(2) Where part only of property disposed of — Where a taxpayer has disposed of part of a personal-use property (other than a part of an excluded property disposed of in circumstances to which subsection 110.1(1), or the definition "total charitable gifts", "total cultural gifts" or "total ecological gifts" in subsection 118.1(1), applies) owned by the taxpayer and has retained another part of the property, for the purposes of this Subdivision

> (a) the adjusted cost base to the taxpayer, immediately before the disposition, of the part so disposed of shall be deemed to be the greater of

>> (i) the adjusted cost base to the taxpayer at that time of that part otherwise determined, and

>> (ii) that proportion of $1,000 that the amount determined under subparagraph (i) is of the adjusted cost base to the taxpayer at that time of the whole property; and

> (b) the proceeds of disposition of the part so disposed of shall be deemed to be the greater of

>> (i) the proceeds of disposition of that part otherwise determined, and

>> (ii) the amount determined under subparagraph (a)(ii).

Notes: Opening words of 46(2) amended by 2000 Budget, effective for property acquired after February 27, 2000.

(3) Properties ordinarily disposed of as a set

(3) Properties ordinarily disposed of as a set — For the purposes of this Subdivision, where a number of personal-use properties of a taxpayer that would, if the properties were disposed of, ordinarily be disposed of in one disposition as a set,

> (a) have been disposed of by more than one disposition so that all of the properties have been acquired by one person or by a group of persons not dealing with each other at arm's length, and

> (b) had, immediately before the first disposition referred to in paragraph (a), a total fair market value greater than $1,000,

the properties shall be deemed to be a single personal-use property and each such disposition shall be deemed to be a disposition of a part of that property.

Notes: A group of prints that were acquired and donated together (before 46(5) was introduced) was considered a single set with cost and proceeds over $1,000 even

though the cost of each print was less than $1,000: *Nash (Tolley, Quinn)*, 2005 FCA 386, para. 36; leave to appeal denied 2006 CarswellNat 932 (SCC).

An insect collection assembled over time from 46 countries was not a "set", so each insect was eligible for the $1,000 cost base: *Plamondon*, 2011 TCC 47.

VIEWS doc 2013-0481001C6 [2013 STEP q.8] states that a "set" is "a number of properties belonging together and relating to each other", and gives examples for paintings and stamps.

(4) Decrease in value of personal-use property of corporation, etc.

(4) Decrease in value of personal-use property of corporation, etc. — Where it may reasonably be regarded that, by reason of a decrease in the fair market value of any personal-use property of a corporation, partnership or trust,

> (a) a taxpayer's gain, if any, from the disposition of a share of the capital stock of a corporation, an interest in a trust or an interest in a partnership has become a loss, or is less than it would have been if the decrease had not occurred, or

> (b) a taxpayer's loss, if any, from the disposition of a share or interest described in paragraph (a) is greater than it would have been if the decrease had not occurred,

the amount of the gain or loss, as the case may be, shall be deemed to be the amount that it would have been but for the decrease.

(5) Excluded property [art flips]

(5) Excluded property [art flips] — For the purpose of this section, "excluded property" of a taxpayer means property acquired by the taxpayer, or by a person with whom the taxpayer does not deal at arm's length, in circumstances in which it is reasonable to conclude that the acquisition of the property relates to an arrangement, plan or scheme that is promoted by another person or partnership and under which it is reasonable to conclude that the property will be the subject of a gift to which subsection 110.1(1), or the definition "total charitable gifts", "total cultural gifts" or "total ecological gifts" in subsection 118.1(1), applies.

Related Provisions: 163.2 — Penalties for third-party promoters and valuators; 248(35)–(37) — Value of gift limited to cost if acquired within 3 years or as tax shelter.

Notes: 46(5) and the reference to "excluded property" in 46(1) limit "art flips", whereby a property was acquired for, say, $250 and donated to a charity for a tax receipt valuing it at $1,000. 46(5) creates a capital gain on the property. See now 248(35) and Notes to 118.1(1)"total charitable gifts".

46(5) added by 2000 Budget, effective for property acquired after Feb. 27, 2000.

Definitions [s. 46]: "adjusted cost base" — 54, 248(1); "amount" — 248(1); "arm's length" — 251(1); "corporation" — 248(1), *Interpretation Act* 35(1); "disposition" — 248(1); "excluded property" — 46(5); "fair market value" — see 69(1) Notes; "partnership" — see 96(1) Notes; "person" — 248(1); "personal-use property" — 54, 248(1); "proceeds of disposition" — 54; "property", "share", "taxpayer" — 248(1); "trust" — 104(1), 248(1), (3).

Interpretation Bulletins [s. 46]: IT-332R: Personal-use property (cancelled).

47. (1) Identical properties [averaging rule]

47. (1) Identical properties [averaging rule] — Where at any particular time after 1971 a taxpayer who owns one property that was or two or more identical properties each of which was, as the case may be, acquired by the taxpayer after 1971, acquires one or more other properties (in this subsection referred to as "newly-acquired properties") each of which is identical to each such previously-acquired property, for the purposes of computing, at any subsequent time, the adjusted cost base of the taxpayer of each such identical property,

> (a) the taxpayer shall be deemed to have disposed of each such previously-acquired property immediately before the particular time for proceeds equal to its adjusted cost base to the taxpayer immediately before the particular time;

> (b) the taxpayer shall be deemed to have acquired the identical property at the particular time at a cost equal to the quotient obtained when

>> (i) the total of the adjusted cost bases to the taxpayer immediately before the particular time of the previously-acquired properties, and the cost to the taxpayer (determined without reference to this section) of the newly-acquired properties

> is divided by

>> (ii) the number of the identical properties owned by the taxpayer immediately after the particular time;

(c) there shall be deducted, after the particular time, in computing the adjusted cost base to the taxpayer of each such identical property, the amount determined by the formula

$$A/B$$

where

A is the total of all amounts deducted under paragraph 53(2)(g.1) in computing immediately before the particular time the adjusted cost base to the taxpayer of the previously-acquired properties, and

B is the number of such identical properties owned by the taxpayer immediately after the particular time or, where subsection (2) applies, the quotient determined under that subsection in respect of the acquisition; and

(d) there shall be added, after the particular time, in computing the adjusted cost base to the taxpayer of each such identical property the amount determined under paragraph (c) in respect of the identical property.

Related Provisions: 7(1.3) — Order of disposition of securities acquired under stock-option agreement; 47(2) — Where identical properties are bonds, etc.; 47(3) — Certain securities acquired by employee deemed not identical; 53(1)(q) — Addition to ACB for amount under 47(1)(d); 53(2)(g.1) — Reduction in ACB under 47(1)(c); 80.03(2)(a) — Deemed gain on disposition following debt forgiveness; 138(11.1) — Properties of life insurance corporation; 248(12) — Meaning of "identical properties".

Notes: Shares held in escrow (such as where a company has recently gone public) have been held not to be identical to shares that can be freely disposed of, for purposes of this rule: *Michael Taylor*, [1988] 2 C.T.C. 2227 (TCC); but see also Notes to 40(1).

Note the extended definition of "identical" in 248(12) for debt obligations, and 47(2). Classes of shares with identical characteristics are not identical if they have different paid-up capital: VIEWS docs 2010-0373301C6, 2011-0412141C6. In *Gervais*, 2016 FCA 1, para. 38, 47(1) applied because all the shares in question were capital property (it does not apply to inventory as it is in subdivision c, ss. 38-55: para. 20).

On rehearing for GAAR, *Gervais [Gendron]*, 2018 FCA 3, 47(1) averaging was used to transfer half of a capital gain between spouses so the wife could claim the capital gains exemption: this violated GAAR (245(2)) by avoiding 74.2(1) attribution.

47(1) applies only to property acquired after 1971; where it does not apply, see doc 2011-0410531I7 on the difference between a stock dividend and a stock split.

47(1)(c) and (d) added by 1994 technical bill, for tax years that end after Feb. 21, 1994. They effectively preserve the history of deductions in computing ACB under 53(2)(g.1), which relates to reductions in ACB under the debt forgiveness rules in s. 80. The only relevance of 47(1)(c) and (d) is for the potential future application of 80.03. Similar amendments were made at 49(3.01), 51(1), 53(4)–(6), 86(4), 87(5.1) and 87(6.1). See also Notes to 53(2)(g.1).

I.T. Application Rules: 26(8)–(8.5) (property owned since before 1972).

I.T. Technical News: 19 (Disposition of identical properties acquired under a section 7 securities option; Change in position in respect of GAAR — section 7).

Forms: T4037: Capital gains [guide], chap. 3.

(2) Where identical properties are bonds, etc. — For the purposes of subsection (1), where a group of identical properties referred to in that subsection is a group of identical bonds, debentures, bills, notes or similar obligations issued by a debtor, subparagraph (1)(b)(ii) shall be read as follows:

"(ii) the quotient obtained when the total of the principal amounts of all such identical properties owned by the taxpayer immediately after the particular time is divided by the principal amount of the identical property."

Related Provisions: 248(12) — Whether bonds, etc., are identical properties.

(3) Securities acquired by employee — For the purpose of subsection (1), a security (within the meaning assigned by subsection 7(7)) acquired by a taxpayer after February 27, 2000 is deemed not to be identical to any other security acquired by the taxpayer if

(a) the security is acquired in circumstances to which any of subsections 7(1.1), (1.5) or (8) or 147(10.1) applies; or

(b) the security is a security to which subsection 7(1.31) applies.

Related Provisions: 7(1.3) — Order of disposition of securities; 53(1)(j) — Addition of deferred employment benefit to ACB of security.

Notes: 47(3) added by 2000 Budget, effective 2000. It exempts certain securities from the cost-averaging rule by deeming them not to be identical to any other securities (thus giving each security its own unique ACB):

- Securities acquired under an employee option agreement for which a deferral is provided under 7(1.1) or (8), and securities acquired in exchange for such securities under circumstances to which 7(1.5) applied.

- Securities acquired under an employee option agreement where the securities are designated by the taxpayer and deemed by 7(1.31) to be the securities that are the subject of a disposition of identical securities occurring within 30 days after the acquisition.

- Employer shares received by an employee as part of a lump-sum payment on withdrawing from a DPSP, where the employee filed an election under 147(10.1) to allow deferral of tax on the growth of the shares until disposition.

Under 7(1.3) and (1.31), one can determine when each security to which 47(3) applies is disposed of. 7(1.3) deals with securities for which a deferral is provided under 7(1.1) or (8) or 147(10.1). In general terms, 7(1.3) deems a taxpayer to dispose of such "deferral" securities only after having disposed of other securities, and then to dispose of deferral securities in the order in which they were acquired. Since one can determine exactly when a particular security to which 47(3) applies is disposed of, the fact that the security has its own unique ACB is not problematic.

Former 47(3), which defined "identical properties", was moved to 248(12) in 1987.

(4) [Repealed under former Act]

Notes: 47(4), repealed by 1985 Budget, excluded indexed securities from "property". Indexed security investment plans no longer exist.

Definitions [s. 47]: "adjusted cost base" — 54, 248(1); "identical" — 138(11.1), 248(12); "principal amount" — 248(1), (26); "property" — 248(1); "security" — 7(7); "taxpayer" — 248(1).

Interpretation Bulletins [s. 47]: IT-78: Capital property owned on December 31, 1971 — identical properties (cancelled); IT-88R2: Stock dividends; IT-115R2: Fractional interest in shares; IT-199: Identical properties acquired in non-arm's length transactions (cancelled); IT-387R2: Meaning of "identical properties".

47.1 Indexed Security Investment Plans — (1)–(28) [Repealed or obsolete]

Notes: 47.1 implemented indexed security investment plans (ISIPs), which existed from 1983-85 and were discarded with the introduction of the capital gains exemption in 110.6. 47.1(1)–(26) repealed by 1985 Budget. 47.1(26.1)-(28) are no longer relevant.

48. [Repealed]

Notes: 48 repealed by 1993 technical bill, effective 1993 or earlier. 128.1 now provides the rules that were in 48: a deemed disposition of property when a taxpayer ceases to be resident in Canada, and a deemed acquisition on becoming resident.

48.1 (1) Gain when small business corporation becomes public[ly listed] — Where

(a) at any time in a taxation year an individual owns capital property that is a share of a class of the capital stock of a corporation that,

(i) at that time, is a small business corporation, and

(ii) immediately after that time, ceases to be a small business corporation because a class of its or another corporation's shares is listed on a designated stock exchange, and

(b) the individual elects in prescribed form to have this section apply,

the individual is deemed, except for the purposes of sections 7 and 35, paragraph 110(1)(d.1) and subsections 120.4(4) and (5),

(c) to have disposed of the share at that time for proceeds of disposition equal to the greater of

(i) the adjusted cost base to the individual of the share at that time, and

(ii) the lesser of the fair market value of the share at that time and such amount as is designated in the prescribed form by the individual in respect of the share, and

(d) to have reacquired the share immediately after that time at a cost equal to those proceeds of disposition.

Related Provisions: 44.1(11) — 48.1 inapplicable in determining eligible small business corporation share for small business investment rollover; 53(4) — Effect on ACB where 48.1(1)(c) applies; 110.6(2.1) — Capital gains deduction — qualified small business corporation shares.

Notes: See Notes at end of 48.1. 48.1(1) amended by 2011 budget bill #2 (for dispositions after March 21, 2011), 2007 budget bill #2, 2001 and 1995-97 technical bills.

Forms: T2101: Election for gains on shares of a corporation becoming public.

(2) Time for election — An election made under subsection (1) by an individual for a taxation year shall be made on or before the individual's filing-due date for the year.

(3) Late filed election — Where the election referred to in subsection (2) was not made on or before the day referred to therein, the election shall be deemed for the purposes of subsections (1) and (2) to have been made on that day if, on or before the day that is 2 years after that day,

(a) the election is made in prescribed form; and

(b) an estimate of the penalty in respect of that election is paid by the individual when the election is made.

(4) Penalty for late filed election — For the purposes of this section, the penalty in respect of an election referred to in paragraph (3)(a) is an amount equal to the lesser of

(a) ¼ of 1% of the amount, if any, by which

(i) the proceeds of disposition determined under subsection (1)

exceed

(ii) the amount referred to in subparagraph (1)(c)(i)

for each month or part of a month during the period commencing on the day referred to in subsection (2) and ending on the day the election is made, and

(b) an amount equal to the product obtained by multiplying $100 by the number of months each of which is a month all or part of which is during the period referred to in paragraph (a).

(5) Unpaid balance of penalty — The Minister shall, with all due dispatch, examine each election referred to in paragraph (3)(a), assess the penalty payable and send a notice of assessment to the individual, who shall pay forthwith to the Receiver General the amount, if any, by which the penalty so assessed exceeds the total of all amounts previously paid on account of that penalty.

Notes [s. 48.1]: 48.1 allows the owner of qualified small business corporation shares (defined in 110.6(1)) to crystallize the accrued capital gain for purposes of the lifetime capital gains exemption in 110.6(2.1) without having to actually sell the shares before the corporation has its shares listed on a stock exchange. (Once the shares are listed the corporation no longer qualifies as a small business corporation.) See Notes to 110.6(2.1) re some of the dangers of crystallization.

See Funt, "Section 48.1", VI(3) *Business Vehicles* (Federated Press) 305-07 (2000); Kaplan, "Going Public", 56(4) *Canadian Tax Journal* 990-1008 (2008); Lee, Kakkar & Raveendran, "Section 48.1: TOSI Trap in Going Public", 20(1) *Tax for the Owner-Manager* (ctf.ca) 4-5 (Jan. 2020).

When an initial public offering closes before the shares are listed, the corporation may cease to be an SBC (due to change in control or ineligible investments) and not meet the "immediately after" test in 48.1(1)(a)(ii), unless "immediately" is interpreted broadly as in *Macklin*, [1993] 1 C.T.C. 21 (FCTD). See VIEWS docs 2000-0057105 and 2001-0087585. Where a corp amalgamates with a public corp whose shares are listed, 48.1(1)(a)(ii) does not apply in CRA's view: 2001-0083915.

CRA takes the view that a 48.1 election cannot be revoked (48.1 is not listed in Reg. 600): VIEWS doc 9916575. Thus, if an error is made in determining the availability of the exemption, there is no way to undo the election. The CBA/CICA Joint Committee on Taxation submitted to the Dept. of Finance (Dec. 2/99) that this should be changed.

Where a trust makes the election, see VIEWS docs 2015-0604971E5, 2016-0634921C6 [2016 STEP q.12].

48.1(2) amended by 1995 Budget, effective 1995; added by 1991 Budget.

Definitions [s. 48.1]: "adjusted cost base" — 54, 248(1); "amount", "assessment" — 248(1); "capital property" — 54, 248(1); "class of shares" — 248(6); "corporation" — 248(1), *Interpretation Act* 35(1); "designated stock exchange" — 248(1), 262; "fair market value" — see 69(1) Notes; "filing-due date" — 150(1), 248(1); "individual", "Minister", "prescribed" — 248(1); "share", "small business corporation" — 248(1); "taxation year" — 11(2), 249.

49. (1) Granting of options — Subject to subsections (3) and (3.1), for the purposes of this Subdivision, the granting of an option, other than

(a) an option to acquire or to dispose of a principal residence,

(b) an option granted by a corporation to acquire shares of its capital stock or bonds or debentures to be issued by it, or

(c) an option granted by a trust to acquire units of the trust to be issued by the trust,

is a disposition of a property the adjusted cost base of which to the grantor immediately before the grant is nil.

Related Provisions: 13(5.3) — Disposition of option on depreciable property or real property; 49(2), (2.1) — Where option expires; 49(5) — Extension or renewal of options; 118.1(22)–(24) — Granting option to charity or other qualified donee.

Notes: *For the vendor*: Granting a call option (other than on a principal residence, corporation's own shares or trust's own units) is a disposition with ACB of nil (49(1)), so it triggers a capital gain. If the option is later exercised, the capital gain is un-done (amended return reassessment allowed by 49(4)) and the underlying property's proceeds of disposition include both the actual proceeds and the option proceeds: 49(3). However, arrears interest still runs on the earlier year as if the tax were payable then: 161(7)(a)(iii); and refund interest is payable only from 30 days after the later filing: 164(5)(c). If the option expires, there are no consequences. (If the option is sold back to the vendor, the option rights are extinguished due to the doctrine of merger: *Devon Canada*, 2018 TCC 170, paras. 118-126.)

The 49(1) disposition is of a generic property, not the underlying property, so no capital gains exemption can be claimed if the option was on qualified farm/fishing property: VIEWS doc 2006-0191891E5. However, if the property was a farm that included a home, 49(1)(a) will exclude the principal residence portion: 2007-0230381E5.

Using options to rejuvenate an expiring non-capital loss could trigger GAAR: VIEWS doc 2007-0251081E5.

Where a corporation issues options on its own stock, see 49(1)(b), 49(2) and VIEWS docs 2003-0054581E5, 2004-0076271I7.

For the purchaser: Acquiring a call option is an acquisition of property with ACB of the amount paid for the option. If it is later exercised, the option cost is transferred to the ACB of the property (49(3)(b)(ii)), with special-case adjustments under 49(3)(b)(i) and 49(3.01). If the option expires, there is a disposition (248(1)"disposition"(b)(iv)) at nil, and thus a capital loss.

49(1) amended by 1991 technical bill, effective for options granted after 1989.

49(1) amended by 1985 Budget to add reference to 45(3.1), effective for dispositions of property under options granted, extended or renewed after November 21, 1985.

Interpretation Bulletins: IT-96R6: Options granted by corporations to acquire shares, bonds or debentures and by trusts to acquire trust units; IT-403R: Options on real estate; IT-479R: Transactions in securities.

(2) Expired option — shares — If at any time an option described in paragraph (1)(b) expires, the corporation that granted the option is deemed to have disposed of capital property at that time for proceeds equal to the proceeds received by it for the granting of the option, and the adjusted cost base to the corporation of that capital property immediately before that time is deemed to be nil, unless

(a) the option is held, at that time, by a person who deals at arm's length with the corporation and the option was granted by the corporation to a person who was dealing at arm's length with the corporation at the time that the option was granted, or

(b) the option is an option to acquire shares of the capital stock of the corporation in consideration for the incurring, pursuant to an agreement described in paragraph (e) of the definition "Canadian exploration and development expenses" in subsection 66(15), paragraph (i) of the definition "Canadian exploration expense" in subsection 66.1(6), paragraph (g) of the definition "Canadian development expense" in subsection 66.2(5) or paragraph (c) of the definition "Canadian oil and gas property expense" in subsection 66.4(5), of any expense described in whichever of those paragraphs is applicable.

Related Provisions: 49(5) — Extension or renewal of option; 54"superficial loss"(d) — Superficial loss rule does not apply; 87(2)(o) — Effect of amalgamation of corporation granting option; 143.3(2) — Issuing option is not expenditure of corporation.

Notes: 49(2) amended by 2002-2013 technical bill (Part 5 — technical), for options issued after Oct. 24, 2012. Before the amendment, read:

(2) Where at any time an option described in paragraph (1)(b) (other than an option to acquire shares of the capital stock of a corporation in consideration for the incurring, pursuant to an agreement described in paragraph (e) of the definition "Canadian exploration and development expenses" in subsection 66(15), paragraph (i) of the definition "Canadian exploration expense" in subsection 66.1(6), paragraph (g) of the definition "Canadian development expense" in subsection 66.2(5) or paragraph (c) of the definition "Canadian oil and gas property expense" in subsection 66.4(5), of any expense described in whichever of those

paragraphs is applicable) that has been granted by a corporation after 1971 expires,

(a) the corporation shall be deemed to have disposed of capital property at that time for proceeds equal to the proceeds received by it for the granting of the option; and

(b) the adjusted cost base to the corporation of that capital property immediately before that time shall be deemed to be nil.

Income Tax Folios: S3-F9-C1: Lottery winnings, miscellaneous receipts, and income (and losses) from crime [replaces IT-185R, IT-213R, IT-256R, IT-334R2].

Interpretation Bulletins: IT-96R6: Options granted by corporations to acquire shares, bonds or debentures and by trusts to acquire trust units; IT-98R2: Investment corporations (cancelled).

(2.1) Expired option — trust units — If, at a particular time, an option referred to in paragraph (1)(c) expires, and the option is held at that time by a person who does not deal at arm's length with the trust or was granted to a person who did not deal at arm's length with the trust at the time that the option was granted,

(a) the trust is deemed to have disposed of capital property at the particular time for proceeds equal to the proceeds received by it for the granting of the option; and

(b) the adjusted cost base to the trust of that capital property immediately before the particular time is deemed to be nil.

Related Provisions: 49(5) — Extension or renewal; 54"superficial loss"(d) — Superficial loss rule does not apply.

Notes: 49(2.1) amended by 2002-2013 technical bill (Part 5 — technical), for options issued after Oct. 24, 2012. For earlier options, read:

(2.1) **Idem** — Where at any time an option referred to in paragraph (1)(c) expires,

(a) the trust shall be deemed to have disposed of capital property at that time for proceeds equal to the proceeds received by it for the granting of the option; and

(b) the adjusted cost base to the trust of that capital property immediately before that time shall be deemed to be nil.

49(2.1) added by 1991 technical bill, effective for options granted after 1989.

Interpretation Bulletins: IT-96R6: Options granted by corporations to acquire shares, bonds or debentures and by trusts to acquire trust units.

(3) Where option to acquire exercised — Where an option to acquire property is exercised so that property is disposed of by a taxpayer (in this subsection referred to as the "vendor") or so that property is acquired by another taxpayer (in this subsection referred to as the "purchaser"), for the purpose of computing the income of each such taxpayer the granting and the exercise of the option shall be deemed not to be dispositions of property and there shall be included

(a) in computing the vendor's proceeds of disposition of the property, the consideration received by the vendor for the option; and

(b) in computing the cost to the purchaser of the property,

(i) where paragraph 53(1)(j) applied to the acquisition of the property by the purchaser because a person who did not deal at arm's length with the purchaser was deemed because of the acquisition to have received a benefit under section 7, the adjusted cost base to that person of the option immediately before that person last disposed of the option, and

(ii) in any other case, the adjusted cost base to the purchaser of the option.

Related Provisions: 49(3.2) — Election to have 49(3) not apply where option granted before Feb. 23/94; 49(4) — Reassessment of earlier year to remove gain when option granted; 49(5) — Extension or renewal of option; 110.1(10)–(13) — Effect of corporation granting option to charity; 118.1(21)–(24) — Effect of individual granting option to charity; 143.3(2) — Issuing share is not expenditure of corporation; 164(5)(c), 164(5.1)(c) — Effect of carryback of loss.

Notes: See Notes to 49(1).

A financing lease is a lease, not a sale, but a lease with purchase option may be a sale. See *Income Tax Technical News* 21 [cancelling IT-233R due to *Shell Canada*, [1999] 4 C.T.C. 313 (SCC) (*Technical News* 21 has been cancelled but CRA maintains the same view: doc 2014-0516921E5)]; *Construction Bérou*, [2000] 2 C.T.C. 174 (FCA) (lease with purchase option was acquisition); *Mimetix Pharmaceuticals*, 2003 FCA 106 (lease without purchase option was lease); *Divall*, 2005 TCC 551 (real property lease-option agreement was "in substance" a sale); *Collette*, 2006 TCC 641 (computer lease contract

with Future Shop was conditional sale, not lease); *On-Line Finance*, 2010 TCC 475 (leases were really loans); docs 2001-0115657, 2004-0076531E5, 2006-017496117, 2008-0303651E5, 2010-037604117; Gilbert, "Characterization for Tax Purposes", VI(2) *Business Vehicles* (Federated Press) 295-99 (2000); Templeton, "Financial Leases", 48(1) *Canadian Tax Journal* 148-54 (2000); David Sherman's *Canada GST Service* analysis of *Excise Tax Act* s. 123(1)"debt security" (also on *Taxnet Pro*).

See also VIEWS doc 2010-038925117 (farm-out agreements and warrants).

49(3)(b)(i) added by 1991 technical bill, effective July 14, 1990.

Income Tax Folios: S3-F9-C1: Lottery winnings, miscellaneous receipts, and income (and losses) from crime [replaces IT-185R, IT-213R, IT-256R, IT-334R2].

Interpretation Bulletins: IT-96R6: Options granted by corporations to acquire shares, bonds or debentures and by trusts to acquire trust units; IT-403R: Options on real estate; IT-479R: Transactions in securities.

(3.01) Option to acquire specified property exercised — Where at any time a taxpayer exercises an option to acquire a specified property,

(a) there shall be deducted after that time in computing the adjusted cost base to the taxpayer of the specified property the total of all amounts deducted under paragraph 53(2)(g.1) in computing, immediately before that time, the adjusted cost base to the taxpayer of the option; and

(b) the amount determined under paragraph (a) in respect of that acquisition shall be added after that time in computing the adjusted cost base to the taxpayer of the specified property.

Related Provisions: 53(1)(q) — Addition to adjusted cost base for amount under 49(3.01)(b); 53(2)(g.1) — Reduction in adjusted cost base under 49(3.01)(a); 80.03(2)(a) — Deemed gain on disposition following debt forgiveness.

Notes: 49(3.01) added by 1994 technical bill, effective for taxation years that end after February 21, 1994. See Notes to 47(1).

Interpretation Bulletins: IT-96R6: Options granted by corporations to acquire shares, bonds or debentures and by trusts to acquire trust units.

(3.1) Where option to dispose exercised — Where an option to dispose of property is exercised so that property is disposed of by a taxpayer (in this subsection referred to as the "vendor") or so that property is acquired by another taxpayer (in this subsection referred to as the "purchaser"), for the purpose of computing the income of each such taxpayer the granting and the exercise of the option shall be deemed not to be dispositions of property and there shall be deducted

(a) in computing the vendor's proceeds of disposition of the property, the adjusted cost base to the vendor of the option; and

(b) in computing the cost to the purchaser of the property, the consideration received by the purchaser for the option.

Related Provisions: 49(5) — Extension or renewal of option.

Notes: 49(3.1) added by 1985 Budget, effective for dispositions of property under options granted, extended or renewed after November 21, 1985.

Interpretation Bulletins: IT-96R6: Options granted by corporations to acquire shares, bonds or debentures and by trusts to acquire trust units; IT-403R: Options on real estate.

(3.2) Option granted before February 23, 1994 — Where an individual (other than a trust) who disposes of property pursuant to the exercise of an option that was granted by the individual before February 23, 1994 so elects in the individual's return of income for the taxation year in which the disposition occurs, subsection (3) does not apply in respect of the disposition in computing the income of the individual.

Notes: 49(3.2) added by 1994 Budget, effective for dispositions after Feb. 22, 1994. It is consequential on the elimination of the $100,000 capital gains exemption. It allows the grantor of an option granted before Feb. 23, 1994 to elect not to have 49(3) apply to the option. Thus, the gain arising on the granting of the option can be a gain from a disposition before Feb. 23, 1994, and eligible for the exemption under 110.6(3).

Interpretation Bulletins: IT-96R6: Options granted by corporations to acquire shares, bonds or debentures and by trusts to acquire trust units.

(4) Reassessment where option exercised in subsequent year — Where

(a) an option granted by a taxpayer in a taxation year (in this subsection referred to as the "initial year") is exercised in a subsequent taxation year (in this subsection referred to as the "subsequent year"),

(b) the taxpayer has filed a return of the taxpayer's income for the initial year as required by section 150, and

(c) on or before the day on or before which the taxpayer was required by section 150 to file a return of the taxpayer's income for the subsequent year, the taxpayer has filed an amended return for the initial year excluding from the taxpayer's income the proceeds received by the taxpayer for the granting of the option,

such reassessment of the taxpayer's tax, interest or penalties for the year shall be made as is necessary to give effect to the exclusion.

Related Provisions: 49(5) — Extension or renewal of option; 161(7)(b)(iii) — Effect of carryback of loss, etc.

Notes: 49(4) should say that it applies despite 152(4)–(5), as other such provisions do. (It has not been amended since 1988; if it had been, those words likely would have been added.) This has been pointed out to Finance.

Interpretation Bulletins: IT-96R6: Options granted by corporations to acquire shares, bonds or debentures and by trusts to acquire trust units. See also at end of s. 49; IT-384R: Reassessment where option exercised in subsequent year.

(5) [Extension or renewal of option] — Where a taxpayer has granted an option (in this subsection referred to as the "original option") to which subsection (1), (2) or (2.1) applies, and grants one or more extensions or renewals of that original option,

(a) for the purposes of subsections (1), (2) and (2.1), the granting of each extension or renewal shall be deemed to be the granting of an option at the time the extension or renewal is granted;

(b) for the purposes of subsections (2) to (4) and subparagraph (b)(iv) of the definition "disposition" in subsection 248(1), the original option and each extension or renewal of it is deemed to be the same option; and

(c) subsection (4) shall be read as if the year in which the original option was granted and each year in which any extension or renewal thereof was granted were all initial years.

Notes: If a lease is amended to add a purchase option and increase the lease payments to reflect the option, the increased payments are considered to be made in respect of the option: VIEWS doc 2003-0028033.

49(5)(b) amended by 2001 technical bill (effective for options granted after December 23, 1998) and 1991 technical bill.

Interpretation Bulletins: IT-96R6: Options to acquire shares, bonds or debentures and by trusts to acquire trust units.

Definitions [s. 49]: "adjusted cost base" — 54, 248(1); "arm's length" — 251(1); "assessment" — 248(1); "capital property" — 54, 248(1); "corporation" — 248(1), *Interpretation Act* 35(1); "disposition", "person" — 248(1); "principal residence" — 54; "property", "share" — 248(1); "specified property" — 54; "taxation year" — 249; "taxpayer" — 248(1); "trust" — 104(1), 248(1), (3).

Income Tax Folios [s. 49]: S4-F7-C1: Amalgamations of Canadian corporations [replaces IT-474R2].

49.1 No disposition where obligation satisfied — For greater certainty, where a taxpayer acquires a particular property in satisfaction of an absolute or contingent obligation of a person or partnership to provide the particular property pursuant to a contract or other arrangement one of the main objectives of which was to establish a right, whether absolute or contingent, to the particular property and that right was not under the terms of a trust, partnership agreement, share or debt obligation, the satisfaction of the obligation is not a disposition of that right.

Notes: 49.1 added by 1999 Budget bill, for obligations satisfied after Dec. 15, 1998. It is relevant to demutualization of insurance corporations (see 139.1) as it ensures there are no tax consequences from satisfying an undertaking to issue shares. It is also generally intended to apply in connection with property acquired as a result of the execution of a contract. For the meaning of "one of the main objectives" see Notes to 83(2.1).

Definitions: "disposition" — 248(1); "partnership" — see 96(1) Notes; "person", "property", "share", "taxpayer" — 248(1); "trust" — 104(1), 248(1), (3).

50. (1) Debts established to be bad debts and shares of bankrupt corporation — For the purposes of this Subdivision, where

(a) a debt owing to a taxpayer at the end of a taxation year (other than a debt owing to the taxpayer in respect of the disposition of personal-use property) is established by the taxpayer to have become a bad debt in the year, or

(b) a share (other than a share received by a taxpayer as consideration in respect of the disposition of personal-use property) of the capital stock of a corporation is owned by the taxpayer at the end of a taxation year and

(i) the corporation has during the year become a bankrupt,

(ii) the corporation is a corporation referred to in section 6 of the *Winding-up and Restructuring Act* that is insolvent (within the meaning of that Act) and in respect of which a winding-up order under that Act has been made in the year, or

(iii) at the end of the year,

(A) the corporation is insolvent,

(B) neither the corporation nor a corporation controlled by it carries on business,

(C) the fair market value of the share is nil, and

(D) it is reasonable to expect that the corporation will be dissolved or wound up and will not commence to carry on business

and the taxpayer elects in the taxpayer's return of income for the year to have this subsection apply in respect of the debt or the share, as the case may be, the taxpayer shall be deemed to have disposed of the debt or the share, as the case may be, at the end of the year for proceeds equal to nil and to have reacquired it immediately after the end of the year at a cost equal to nil.

Related Provisions: 20(1)(p) — Deduction for bad debt on trade account; 39(1)(c) — Business investment loss; 40(2)(e.2), (g)(ii) — Restrictions on capital losses on debt; 50(1.1) — Where insolvent corporation begins carrying on business again; 54"superficial loss"(c) — Superficial loss rule does not apply; 79.1(8) — No bad debt deduction where property seized by creditor; 80.01(6)(b) — Debt deemed a specified obligation after subsec. 50(1) applies; 80.01(8) — Deemed settlement after debt parking; 96(3) — Election by members of partnership; 111(5.3) — Limitation on bad debt deduction after change in control of corporation; 220(3.2), Reg. 600(b) — Late filing or revocation of election.

Notes: The deemed disposition on bad debt, bankruptcy or insolvency triggers a capital loss under 39(1)(b). If the corporation was a "small business corporation" (defined in 248(1)), the loss is a business investment loss under 39(1)(c), and half the loss is an allowable business investment loss (38(c)), which can be used under 3(d) against income from other sources rather than just against taxable capital gains. See Notes to 39(1) and Income Tax Folio S4-F8-C1.

50(1) applies "For purposes of this subdivision" (ss. 38-55), so it does not apply to 180.01: VIEWS doc 2011-0420241E5; or to 7(1.1): 2017-0692931E5.

It is not certain whether "established by the taxpayer to have become a bad debt in the year" in 50(1)(a) [the same words appear in 20(1)(p)] means that (A) the act of establishing must be done in the year, or (B) the debt became bad in the year. Cases such as *Rich* and *Litowitz* (below) are ambiguous on the question. In *Francis*, 2014 TCC 137, paras. 32-33, the TCC held (A), which is wrong in the author's view. The French text supports (B), as does the placement of "in the year" next to "bad debt" in English. *Delle Donne*, 2015 TCC 150, paras. 81-84, held (B) for purposes of 20(1)(p).

Determination of a bad debt is made by the creditor, acting "reasonably and in a pragmatic, business-like manner, applying the proper factors", determining the debt is uncollectible: *Flexi-Coil*, [1996] 3 C.T.C. 57 (FCA), para. 5. In *Rich*, 2003 FCA 38, the Court stated the factors to consider include: "1. the history and age of the debt; 2. the financial position of the debtor, its revenues and expenses, whether it is earning income or incurring losses, its cash flow and its assets, liabilities and liquidity; 3. changes in total sales as compared with prior years; 4. the debtor's cash, accounts receivable and other current assets at the relevant time and as compared with prior years; 5. the debtor's accounts payable and other current liabilities at the relevant time and as compared with prior years; 6. the general business conditions in the country, the community of the debtor, and in the debtor's line of business; and 7. the past experience of the taxpayer with writing off bad debts. This list is not exhaustive and, in different circumstances, one factor or another may be more important. While future prospects of the debtor company may be relevant in some cases, the predominant considerations would normally be past and present." A non-arm's length relationship may justify closer scrutiny, but that alone does not mean that the creditor did not honestly and reasonably determine the debt to be bad. For cases applying the *Rich* criteria see *Kyriazakos*, 2007 TCC 66; *Fisher*, 2015 FCA 276. When Xco was still operating with good prospects and the owners were still advancing funds, the fact the owners were sure they would never recover the millions they had lent to Xco did not mean the debt went bad as it was being advanced: *Coveley*, 2013 TCC 417, paras. 129-133; aff'd 2014 FCA 281.

"One should, in general, not apply the wisdom of hindsight in determining whether a debt is bad at a particular point in time ...a determination whether a debt is bad ...cannot be based upon events five years later that could not possibly have been foreseen": *Litowitz*, 2005 TCC 557, para. 17.

For CRA's views on when a debt becomes bad, see Income Tax Folio S4-F8-C1 ¶1.33-1.40; IT-442R; docs 2010-0380821E5; 2014-053512117 (second mortgagee must force sale rather than writing off debt — but see *Litowitz* above).

Taxpayers seeking to support a bad debt or ABIL claim should obtain documentation (ideally from when the financial problems began) to justify that the debt has gone bad.

Where only part of the debt is uncollectible, see MacEachern, "Partial Bad Debt Claim", 12(4) *Tax for the Owner-Manager* (ctf.ca) 2-3 (Oct. 2012); doc 2013-0495671C6.

Once a loan has clearly gone bad, the taxpayer need not force the debtor into bankruptcy to prove it: *Cosentino*, [2003] 2 C.T.C. 2447 (TCC).

As to when a corporation goes bankrupt for 50(1)(b)(i), see *Bankruptcy and Insolvency Act* s. 2 ("bankrupt" means a person who has made an assignment or against whom a bankruptcy order has been made or the legal status of that person); and provisions deeming a person to have made an assignment in bankruptcy: VIEWS doc 2006-016808117.

There is no provision like 50(1)(b) for partnership units, and due to 98(1)(a), a partnership that has ceased activity may still be deemed to exist: doc 2013-0482081E5.

In *Jacques St-Onge Inc.*, 2001 CarswellNat 3869 (TCC), a river salvage project that had been abandoned met the test of "reasonable to expect" in 50(1)(b)(iii)(D), even though negotiations for the project were later revived. The fact the company still had accounts payable did not affect the test. 50(1)(b)(iii) focuses on whether business operations have ceased and are unlikely to resume, not on whether formal winding-up procedures have taken place: *Simmonds*, 2006 FC 130. In both *St-Hilaire*, 2014 TCC 336 and *Gaumond*, 2014 TCC 339, the taxpayer had waived his right to a share of the corporation's assets as part of its bankruptcy proposal to creditors, so he did not own the debt at year-end [see Joan Jung, "Effect of BIA Proposal on ABIL Claim", 15(3) *Tax for the Owner-Manager* (ctf.ca) 5-6 (July 2015)].

A cease-trading order does not necessarily mean the company is insolvent or worthless for purposes of 50(1)(b): VIEWS doc 2006-0175701M4.

Failure to make the election in 50(1) closing words is fatal to a capital loss claim: *Harris*, 2005 TCC 501; *Kokai-Kuun*, 2015 TCC 217, para. 61. However, in the author's view, if the loss is on shares and the conditions of 50(1)(b)(iii) continue to be met, the election can be made in any later year when they are still met; only 50(1)(b)(i) and (ii) require that the bankruptcy or winding-up have happened in the year.

The election is made "in" the return. For a paper return, this means filing a letter with the return. CRA may accept that a valid election was made "when the taxpayer's actions clearly indicate the intention to have the elective provision apply": Cdn Tax Foundation 1983 conference report p. 766. CRA can also extend time under 220(3.2), since 50(1) is listed in Reg. 600. An election is valid if the return is filed late: see Notes to 7(1.31). To elect "in" a return filed electronically, see Notes to 150.1.

One might not elect if electing would result in 80.01(8) applying to a non-arm's length debtor or a debtor in which the taxpayer has a significant interest. See 80.01(6)–(8).

Since the deemed disposition under 50(1) occurs at year-end, any application during 2000 led to a 50% ABIL rather than ⅔ or ¾: *Tardif*, 2005 TCC 10.

When 50(1) applies, the capital loss will not be subject to 40(3.4) or (3.6): VIEWS doc 2008-0274451E5.

See also Drache, "Holding Shares or Debt when a Company Becomes Insolvent", xxxiv(17) *The Canadian Taxpayer* (Carswell) 133-34 (Sept. 14, 2012).

50(1) amended by 2013 budget bill #2 (effective Dec. 21, 2012, non-substantive change), 1994 and 1991 technical bills.

Winding-up and Restructuring Act (WRA) s. 6 (last amended in 2015) provides:

6. **Application** — (1) This Act applies to all corporations incorporated by or under the authority of an Act of Parliament, of the former Province of Canada or of the Province of Nova Scotia, New Brunswick, British Columbia, Prince Edward Island or Newfoundland, and whose incorporation and affairs are subject to the legislative authority of Parliament, and to incorporated banks and savings banks, to authorized foreign banks, and to trust companies, insurance companies, loan companies having borrowing powers, building societies having a capital stock and incorporated trading companies doing business in Canada wherever incorporated where any of those bodies

(a) is insolvent;

(b) is in liquidation or in the process of being wound up and, on petition by any of its shareholders or creditors, assignees or liquidators — or, if it is a federal credit union, by any of its members, shareholders, creditors, assignees or liquidators — asks to be brought under this Act; or

(c) if it is a financial institution, is under the control, or its assets are under the control, of the Superintendent and is the subject of an application for a winding-up order under section 10.1.

(2) **Application to authorized foreign banks** — In its application to an authorized foreign bank, this Act only applies to the winding-up of its business in Canada and to the liquidation of its assets, and any reference to the winding-up of a company or to the winding-up of the business of a company is deemed, in relation to an authorized foreign bank, to be a reference to the winding-up of the business in Canada of the authorized foreign bank and to include the liquidation of the assets of the authorized foreign bank.

WRA s. 3 (last amended in 2016) defines "insolvent":

3. **When company deemed insolvent** — A company is deemed insolvent

(a) if it is unable to pay its debts as they become due;

(b) if it calls a meeting of its creditors for the purpose of compounding with them;

(c) if it exhibits a statement showing its inability to meet its liabilities;

(d) if it has otherwise acknowledged its insolvency;

(e) if it assigns, removes or disposes of, or attempts or is about to assign, remove or dispose of, any of its property, with intent to defraud, defeat or delay its creditors, or any of them;

(f) if, with the intent referred to in paragraph (e), it has procured its money, goods, chattels, land or property to be seized, levied on or taken, under or by any process of execution;

(g) if it has made any general conveyance or assignment of its property for the benefit of its creditors, or if, being unable to meet its liabilities in full, it makes any sale or conveyance of the whole or the main part of its stock in trade or assets without the consent of its creditors or without satisfying their claims;

(h) if it permits any execution issued against it, under which any of its goods, chattels, land or property are seized, levied on or taken in execution, to remain unsatisfied until within four days of the time fixed by the sheriff or other officer for the sale thereof, or for fifteen days after the seizure;

(i) if, in the case of a company that is a "federal member institution", as defined in section 2 of the *Canada Deposit Insurance Corporation Act*, in respect of which an order has been made under paragraph 39.13(1)(a) of that Act but in respect of which no order has been made under subsection 39.13(1.3) of that Act, a notice has not been published under subsection 39.2(3) of that Act in respect of the institution on or before

(i) the 60th day after the day on which the order was made under paragraph 39.13(1)(a) of that Act, or

(ii) the day on which any extension of that period ends;

(j) if, in the case of a company that is a "federal member institution", as defined in section 2 of the *Canada Deposit Insurance Corporation Act*, in respect of which an order has been made under paragraph 39.13(1)(b) of that Act but in respect of which no order has been made under subsection 39.13(1.3) of that Act, a notice has not been published under subsection 39.2(3) of that Act in respect of the institution on or before

(i) the 60th day after the day on which the order was made under paragraph 39.13(1)(b) of that Act, or

(ii) the day on which any extension of that period ends;

(j.1) if, in the case of a company that is a "federal member institution", as defined in section 2 of the *Canada Deposit Insurance Corporation Act*, in respect of which an order has been made under paragraph 39.13(1)(d) or subsection 39.13(1.3) of that Act, a notice has not been published under subsection 39.2(3) of that Act in respect of the institution on or before

(i) the day that is one year after the day on which the order is made under subsection 39.13(1) of that Act or any shorter period that is specified in the order made under paragraph 39.13(1)(d) or subsection 39.13(1.3) of that Act, as the case may be, or

(ii) the day on which any extension of the applicable period ends; or

(k) if, in the case of a company that is a federal member institution, as defined in section 2 of the *Canada Deposit Insurance Corporation Act*, in respect of which the Canada Deposit Insurance Corporation has been appointed as receiver, a transfer of part of the business of the federal member institution to a bridge institution has been substantially completed.

Income Tax Folios: S3-F4-C1: General discussion of CCA [replaces IT-220R2]; S4-F8-C1: Business investment losses [replaces IT-484R2].

Interpretation Bulletins: IT-159R3: Capital debts established to be bad debts; IT-188R: Sale of accounts receivable; IT-239R2: Deductibility of capital losses from guaranteeing loans for inadequate consideration and from loaning funds at less than a reasonable rate of interest in non-arm's length circumstances (cancelled); IT-442R: Bad debts and reserves for doubtful debts.

CRA Audit Manual: 29.3.0: Business investment losses.

(1.1) Idem — Where

(a) a taxpayer is deemed because of subparagraph (1)(b)(iii) to have disposed of a share of the capital stock of a corporation at the end of a taxation year, and

(b) the taxpayer or a person with whom the taxpayer is not dealing at arm's length owns the share at the earliest time, during the 24-month period immediately following the disposition, that the corporation or a corporation controlled by it carries on business, the taxpayer or the person, as the case may be, shall be deemed to have disposed of the share at that earliest time for proceeds of disposition equal to its adjusted cost base to the taxpayer determined immediately before the time of the disposition referred to in paragraph (a) and to have reacquired it immediately after that earliest time at a cost equal to those proceeds.

Notes: 50(1.1) effectively eliminates the capital loss triggered by 50(1)(b)(iii) if the corporation begins to carry on business again within 2 years (see Income Tax Folio S4-F8-C1 ¶1.29-1.32). Added by 1991 technical bill, effective 1990.

Income Tax Folios: S4-F8-C1: Business investment losses [replaces IT-484R2].

(2) Where debt a personal-use property — Where at the end of a taxation year a debt that is a personal-use property of a taxpayer is owing to the taxpayer by a person with whom the taxpayer deals at arm's length and is established by the taxpayer to have become a bad debt in the year,

(a) the taxpayer shall be deemed to have disposed of it at the end of the year for proceeds equal to the amount, if any, by which

(i) its adjusted cost base to the taxpayer immediately before the end of the year

exceeds

(ii) the amount of the taxpayer's gain, if any, from the disposition of the personal-use property the proceeds of disposition of which included the debt; and

(b) the taxpayer shall be deemed to have reacquired the debt immediately after the end of the year at a cost equal to the amount of the proceeds determined under paragraph (a).

Related Provisions: 46 — Disposition of personal-use property; 54 "superficial loss"(c) — Superficial loss rule does not apply.

Interpretation Bulletins: IT-159R3: Capital debts established to be bad debts.

(3) [No longer relevant]

Notes: 50(3) deems a registered home ownership savings plan to have disposed of its property at fair market value at the end of 1985, when RHOSPs were eliminated.

Definitions [s. 50]: "adjusted cost base" — 54, 248(1); "amount", "bankrupt" — 248(1); "carrying on business" — 253; "controlled" — 256(6), (6.1); "corporation" — 248(1), *Interpretation Act* 35(1); "disposition" — 248(1); "fair market value" — see 69(1) Notes; "personal-use property" — 54, 248(1); "share" — 248(1); "taxation year" — 249; "taxpayer" — 248(1).

51. (1) Convertible property — Where a share of the capital stock of a corporation is acquired by a taxpayer from the corporation in exchange for

(a) a capital property of the taxpayer that is another share of the corporation (in this section referred to as a "convertible property"), or

(b) a capital property of the taxpayer that is a bond, debenture or note of the corporation the terms of which confer on the holder the right to make the exchange (in this section referred to as a "convertible property")

and no consideration other than the share is received by the taxpayer for the convertible property,

(c) except for the purposes of subsections 20(21) and 44.1(6) and (7) and paragraph 94(2)(m), the exchange is deemed not to be a disposition of the convertible property,

(d) the cost to the taxpayer of all the shares of a particular class acquired by the taxpayer on the exchange shall be deemed to be the amount determined by the formula

$$A \times B / C$$

where

A is the adjusted cost base to the taxpayer of the convertible property immediately before the exchange,

B is the fair market value, immediately after the exchange, of all the shares of the particular class acquired by the taxpayer on the exchange, and

C is the fair market value, immediately after the exchange, of all the shares acquired by the taxpayer on the exchange,

(d.1) there shall be deducted, after the exchange, in computing the adjusted cost base to the taxpayer of a share acquired by the taxpayer on the exchange, the amount determined by the formula

$$A \times B / C$$

where

A is the total of all amounts deducted under paragraph 53(2)(g.1) in computing, immediately before the exchange, the adjusted cost base to the taxpayer of the convertible property,

B is the fair market value, immediately after the exchange, of that share, and

C is the fair market value, immediately after the exchange, of all the shares acquired by the taxpayer on the exchange,

(d.2) the amount determined under paragraph (d.1) in respect of a share shall be added, after the exchange, in computing the adjusted cost base to the taxpayer of the share,

(e) for the purposes of sections 74.4 and 74.5, the exchange shall be deemed to be a transfer of the convertible property by the taxpayer to the corporation, and

(f) where the convertible property is taxable Canadian property of the taxpayer, the share acquired by the taxpayer on the exchange is deemed to be, at any time that is within 60 months after the exchange, taxable Canadian property of the taxpayer.

Related Provisions: 51(2) — Where benefit conferred on related person; 51(3) — Computation of PUC after exchange of shares; 51(4) — Exceptions; 51.1 — Conversion of debt obligation; 53(1)(q) — Addition to adjusted cost base for amount under 51(1)(d.2); 53(2)(g.1) — Reduction in ACB under 51(1)(d.1); 80(2)(g) — Shares issued in settlement of debt; 80.03(2)(a) — Deemed gain on disposition following debt forgiveness; 80.6(2)(d) — No deemed disposition on synthetic disposition arrangement if 51(1) applies; 86(2) — Exchange of shares — reorganization of capital; 93.2(3) — Application to non-resident corp without share capital; 107.4(3)(f) — Deemed taxable Canadian property (TCP) retains status when rolled out of or into trust; 112(7) — Application of stop-loss rule where shares exchanged; 128.3 — Deferral applies to post-emigration disposition for certain purposes; 131(4.1) — Mutual fund switch-fund shares — no rollover; 211.7(1) "qualifying exchange" — Exchangeable LSVCC shares; 248(25.1) — Deemed TCP retains status through trust-to-trust transfer.

Notes: When reading a VIEWS doc or article in French about 51(1), note that the para. numbering is totally different in French from English!

For CRA interpretation see VIEWS doc 2008-0300391C6 (if common shares with nil value exchanged for pref shares, the pref shares will have $0 ACB due to 51(1)(d)); 2003-0030145 and 2010-0373231C6 (new share must be legally authorized for 51(1) to apply); 2011-0412191C6 (Quebec *Business Corporations Act* s. 91 conversion falls under 51 rather than s. 86); 2012-0454181C6 (on issuing shares with discretionary dividends, 15(1), 110.6(7) or GAAR may apply); 2014-0524651I7 (convertible debenture converted to share but not pursuant to its terms: 51(1) does not apply); 2018-0772921R3 (capital loss consolidation ruling); 2020-0852271C6 [2020 APFF q.15] (estate freeze by spouses creating discretionary trusts that benefit both of them: 74.4(2) may apply).

Where the shareholder is non-resident, 116(5) or 212(1) may require the corp to withhold tax: MacArthur, "A Comment on Subsection 51(1)", 15(3) *Taxation Law* (oba.org) 19-22 (May 2005); Vohrah, "Convertible Debt and Withholding Tax", X(3) *Corporate Structures & Groups* (Federated Press) 571-73 (2007).

51(1) does not apply when 85(1) or (2) or 86 applies: see 51(4).

51(1)(f): see 44.1(2) Notes re the 60-month rule.

51(1) amended by 2002-2013 technical bill (last change for tax years ending after 2006); 2010 budget bill #1 (effective March 5, 2010); 1995-97, 1994 and 1993 technical bills.

Regulations: 230(3) (no information return required).

I.T. Application Rules: 26(28).

Interpretation Bulletins: IT-115R2: Fractional interest in shares. See also at end of s. 51.

(2) Idem — Notwithstanding subsection (1), where

(a) shares of the capital stock of a corporation have been acquired by a taxpayer in exchange for a convertible property in circumstances such that, but for this subsection, subsection (1) would have applied,

(b) the fair market value of the convertible property immediately before the exchange exceeds the fair market value of the shares immediately after the exchange, and

(c) it is reasonable to regard any portion of the excess (in this subsection referred to as the "gift portion") as a benefit that the taxpayer desired to have conferred on a person related to the taxpayer,

the following rules apply:

(d) the taxpayer shall be deemed to have disposed of the convertible property for proceeds of disposition equal to the lesser of

(i) the total of its adjusted cost base to the taxpayer immediately before the exchange and the gift portion, and

(ii) the fair market value of the convertible property immediately before the exchange,

(e) the taxpayer's capital loss from the disposition of the convertible property shall be deemed to be nil, and

(f) the cost to the taxpayer of all the shares of a particular class acquired in exchange for the convertible property shall be deemed to be that proportion of the lesser of

(i) the adjusted cost base to the taxpayer of the convertible property immediately before the exchange, and

(ii) the total of the fair market value immediately after the exchange of all the shares acquired by the taxpayer in exchange for the convertible property and the amount that, but for paragraph (e), would have been the taxpayer's capital loss on the disposition of the convertible property,

that

(iii) the fair market value, immediately after the exchange, of all the shares of the particular class acquired by the taxpayer on the exchange

is of

(iv) the fair market value, immediately after the exchange, of all the shares acquired by the taxpayer on the exchange.

Related Provisions: 112(7) — Application of stop-loss rule where shares exchanged.

Income Tax Folios: S4-F3-C1: Price adjustment clauses [replaces IT-169]; S4-F7-C1: Amalgamations of Canadian corporations [replaces IT-474R2].

(3) Computation of paid-up capital — Where subsection (1) applies to the exchange of convertible property described in paragraph (1)(a) (referred to in this subsection as the "old shares"), in computing the paid-up capital in respect of a particular class of shares of the capital stock of the corporation at any particular time that is the time of, or any time after, the exchange

(a) there shall be deducted the amount determined by the formula

$$(A - B) \times C/A$$

where

A is the total of all amounts each of which is the amount of the increase, if any, as a result of the exchange, in the paid-up capital in respect of a class of shares of the capital stock of the corporation, computed without reference to this subsection as it applies to the exchange,

B is the paid-up capital immediately before the exchange in respect of the old shares, and

C is the increase, if any, as a result of the exchange, in the paid-up capital in respect of the particular class of shares, computed without reference to this subsection as it applies to the exchange; and

(b) there shall be added an amount equal to the lesser of

(i) the amount, if any, by which

(A) the total of all amounts deemed by subsection 84(3), (4) or (4.1) to be a dividend on shares of that class paid by the corporation before the particular time

exceeds

(B) the total that would be determined under clause (A) if this Act were read without reference to paragraph (a), and

(ii) the total of all amounts required by paragraph (a) to be deducted in respect of that particular class of shares before the particular time.

Related Provisions: 257 — Formula cannot calculate to less than zero.

Notes: The effect of 51(3), which reduces the paid-up capital (PUC) of the new shares, is to permit a PUC deficiency on the old shares (such as may have arisen where 85(2.1) applied to reduce PUC following a rollover under 85(1)) to flow through to the new shares. Thus, the 51(1) exchange will not result in an increase in PUC to which 84(1) would apply; and the amount received for the old shares for purposes of 84(3) will be equal to the PUC of the old shares (see 84(5)). 86(2.1) applies the same rule to share exchanges under s. 86.

On the interaction of 51(3) with 84(1), see VIEWS doc 2008-0293401E5.

51(3) added by 1993 technical bill, last change effective for exchanges after Dec. 19, 1992.

(4) Application — Subsections (1) and (2) do not apply to any exchange to which subsection 85(1) or (2) or section 86 applies.

Related Provisions: 86(3) — Application of section 86.

Notes: 51(4) added by 1993 technical bill, for exchanges occurring, and reorganizations that begin, after December 21, 1992.

Interpretation Bulletins: IT-115R2: Fractional interest in shares.

Definitions [s. 51]: "adjusted cost base" — 54, 248(1); "capital loss" — 39(1)(b), 248(1); "capital property" — 54, 248(1); "class of shares" — 248(6); "convertible property" — 51(1)(b); "corporation" — 248(1), *Interpretation Act* 35(1); "disposition" — 248(1); "fair market value" — see 69(1) Notes; "paid-up capital" — 89(1), 248(1); "property", "share", "specified participating interest", "taxable Canadian property", "taxpayer" — 248(1).

Interpretation Bulletins [s. 51]: IT-96R6: Options to acquire shares, bonds or debentures and by trusts to acquire trust units; IT-146R4: Shares entitling shareholders to choose taxable or capital dividends; IT-243R4: Dividend refund to private corporations.

51.1 Conversion of debt obligation — Where

(a) a taxpayer acquires a bond, debenture or note of a debtor (in this section referred to as the "new obligation") in exchange for a capital property of the taxpayer that is another bond, debenture or note of the same debtor (in this section referred to as the "convertible obligation"),

(b) the terms of the convertible obligation conferred on the holder the right to make the exchange, and

(c) the principal amount of the new obligation is equal to the principal amount of the convertible obligation,

the cost to the taxpayer of the new obligation and the proceeds of disposition of the convertible obligation shall be deemed to be equal to the adjusted cost base to the taxpayer of the convertible obligation immediately before the exchange.

Notes: For rulings that 51.1 applies see VIEWS docs 2008-0300161R3, 2013-0514191R3, 2014-0547871R3.

51.1 added by 1994 technical bill, for exchanges occurring after Oct. 1994. For earlier exchanges, see former s. 77.

Definitions [s. 51.1]: "adjusted cost base" — 54, 248(1); "amount" — 248(1); "capital property" — 54, 248(1); "convertible obligation", "new obligation" — 51.1(a); "principal amount" — 248(1), (26); "proceeds of disposition" — 54; "taxpayer" — 248(1).

Regulations: 230(3) (no information return required).

I.T. Application Rules: 26(25) (where bond owned since before 1972).

52. (1) Cost of certain property the value of which included in income — In applying this Subdivision, an amount equal to the particular amount described by paragraph (d) shall be added in computing the cost at any time to a taxpayer of a property if

(a) the taxpayer acquired the property after 1971;

(b) the amount was not at or before that time otherwise added to the cost, or included in computing the adjusted cost base, to the taxpayer of the property;

(c) the property is not an annuity contract, a right as a beneficiary under a trust to enforce payment of an amount by the trust to the taxpayer, property acquired in circumstances to which subsection (2) or (3) applies, or property acquired from a trust in satisfaction of all or part of the taxpayer's capital interest in the trust; and

(d) a particular amount in respect of the property's value was

(i) included, otherwise than under section 7, in computing

(A) the taxpayer's taxable income or taxable income earned in Canada, as the case may be, for a taxation year during which the taxpayer was non-resident, or

(B) the taxpayer's income for a taxation year throughout which the taxpayer was resident in Canada, or

(ii) for the purpose of computing the tax payable under Part XIII by the taxpayer, included in an amount that was paid or credited to the taxpayer.

Related Provisions: 69(5)(c) — No application to property appropriated by shareholder on winding-up.

Notes: "This subdivision" (in the opening words) is sections 38-55.

52(1) amended by 2002-2013 technical bill (Part 5 — technical), for tax years that begin after 2006. The amendments were non-substantive. 52(1) earlier amended by 2001 technical bill (effective 2000) and 1992 technical bill.

Interpretation Bulletins: IT-96R6: Options to acquire shares, bonds or debentures and by trusts to acquire trust units; IT-432R2: Benefits conferred on shareholders.

(1.1) [Repealed]

Notes: 52(1.1) repealed by 2001 technical bill, effective 2000. It applied to certain acquisitions by a non-resident.

(2) Cost of property received as dividend in kind

— Where any property has, after 1971, been received by a shareholder of a corporation at any time as, on account or in lieu of payment of, or in satisfaction of, a dividend payable in kind (other than a stock dividend) in respect of a share owned by the shareholder of the capital stock of the corporation, the shareholder shall be deemed to have acquired the property at a cost to the shareholder equal to its fair market value at that time, and the corporation shall be deemed to have disposed of the property at that time for proceeds equal to that fair market value.

Related Provisions: 69(5)(c) — No application to property appropriated by shareholder on winding-up; 80.1(4) — Assets acquired from foreign affiliate of taxpayer as dividend in kind or as benefit to taxpayer; 86.1(1)(b) — No application to eligible distribution (foreign spin-off).

Notes: 52(2) applied to a dividend in kind in the 2007 Tyco-Covidien spinoff, e.g. *Rezayat*, 2011 TCC 286 (see Notes to 86.1).

For CRA policy on a return of capital "in kind", see VIEWS doc 2013-0506561I7.

I.T. Technical News: 11 (U.S. spin-offs (divestitures) — dividends in kind).

(3) Cost of stock dividend

— Where a shareholder of a corporation has, after 1971, received a stock dividend in respect of a share owned by the shareholder of the capital stock of the corporation, the shareholder shall be deemed to have acquired the share or shares received by the shareholder as a stock dividend at a cost to the shareholder equal to the total of

(a) where the stock dividend is a dividend,

(i) in the case of a shareholder that is an individual, the amount of the stock dividend, and

(ii) in any other case, the total of all amounts each of which is

(A) the amount, if any, by which

(I) the amount that is the lesser of the amount of the stock dividend and its fair market value

exceeds

(II) the amount of the dividend that the shareholder may deduct under subsection 112(1) in computing the shareholder's taxable income, except any portion of the dividend that, if paid as a separate dividend, would not be subject to subsection 55(2) because the amount of the separate dividend would not exceed the amount of the income earned or realized by any corporation — after 1971 and before the safe-income determination time for the transaction, event or series of transactions or events as part of which the dividend is received —

that could reasonably be considered to contribute to the capital gain that could be realized on a disposition at fair market value, immediately before the dividend, of the share on which the dividend is received, and

(B) the amount determined by the formula

$$A + B$$

where

A is the amount of the deemed gain under paragraph 55(2)(c) in respect of that stock dividend, and

B is the amount, if any, by which the amount of the reduction under paragraph 55(2.3)(b) in respect of that stock dividend to which paragraph 55(2)(a) would otherwise apply exceeds the amount determined for clause (A) in respect of that dividend.

(a.1) where the stock dividend is not a dividend, nil, and

(b) where an amount is included in the shareholder's income in respect of the stock dividend under subsection 15(1.1), the amount so included.

Related Provisions: 95(7) — Stock dividends from foreign affiliates.

Notes: 52(3) establishes the cost of a share received as a stock dividend by a shareholder of a corporation. If the stock dividend is a "dividend" under 248(1), 52(3)(a) provides that its cost is the amount of the dividend.

For 52(3)(a.1), when is a stock dividend not a dividend? See exclusion in 248(1)"dividend" (paid by non-resident corp to corp or MFT). One might think that if 55(2) applies, 55(2)(a) deems the dividend not to be a dividend so (a.1) would apply, but since 2015 52(3)(a) specifically contemplates 55(2) applying: VIEWS doc 2018-0780071C6 [2018 CTF q.2] (overruling 9830665).

52(3) was successfully used in an estate plan in *Evans*, 2005 TCC 684.

For a ruling that 52(3) applies see VIEWS doc 2010-0374141R3 (distribution of stock dividend from share premium account of a controlled foreign affiliate).

Under 52(3) as amended in 2016, for a corporate recipient of a stock dividend, the adjusted cost base generally becomes the safe-income portion of the stock dividend, plus the amount that 55(2) has converted into a capital gain.

52(3)(a) amended by 2016 budget bill #1, for stock dividends received after April 20, 2015, except that, for those *declared* from April 21, 2015 through July 30, 2015 and *received* before Sept. 30, 2015, read (a)(ii)(A) as "the lesser of the amount of the stock dividend and its fair market value" and ignore "to which paragraph 55(2)(a) would otherwise apply" in (a)(ii)(B)B. Before the amendment, read:

(a) where the stock dividend is a dividend, the amount, if any, by which

(i) the amount of the stock dividend

exceeds

(ii) the amount of the dividend that the shareholder may deduct under subsection 112(1) in computing the shareholder's taxable income, except any portion of the dividend that, if paid as a separate dividend, would not be subject to subsection 55(2) because the capital gain referred to in that subsection could reasonably be considered not to be attributable to anything other than income earned or realized by any corporation after 1971 and before the safe-income determination time for the transaction or event or series of transactions or events as part of which the dividend was received,

52(3)(a)(ii), added by 2002-2013 technical bill (Part 5 — technical) for amounts received after Nov. 8, 2006, provides that the cost of a stock dividend to a corporate shareholder excludes any dividend deductible under 112(1), other than safe-income dividends. Related amendments were made to 53(1)(b) and 89(1)"capital dividend account". Finance said these amendments were consequential on 143.3. The earlier version of this proposal (to 2007) did not have the safe-income exclusion. See also Rick McLean, "Accessing Safe Income through PUC Increases and Stock Dividends", 2012 *Tax Topics* 1-2 (Sept. 30, 2010); Kakkar & Kotecha, "Proposed Changes to the Treatment of PUC Increases and Stock Dividends", 11(4) *Tax for the Owner-Manager* (ctf.ca) 1-2 (Oct. 2011); docs 2011-0415891E5, 2011-0423861E5. (The 2016 amendments to s. 55 make some of this discussion obsolete.)

52(3) amended by 1991 technical bill.

Income Tax Folios: S3-F2-C1: Capital Dividends [replaces IT-66R6].

Interpretation Bulletins: IT-88R2: Stock dividends.

(4) Cost of property acquired as prize

— Where any property has been acquired by a taxpayer at any time after 1971 as a prize in connection with a lottery scheme, the taxpayer shall be deemed to have acquired the property at a cost to the taxpayer equal to its fair market value at that time.

Related Provisions: 40(2)(f) — No gain or loss on disposition of chance to win or right to receive a prize.

Notes: Lottery winnings are not taxed, unless they are annuity payments. See Notes to s. 3 and 12.2(1). 52(4) does not apply to a "prize" paid by a franchisor in a contest open only to franchisees: VIEWS doc 2011-0425361E5.

Income Tax Folios: S3-F9-C1: Lottery winnings, miscellaneous receipts, and income (and losses) from crime [replaces IT-185R, IT-213R, IT-256R, IT-334R2].

Registered Charities Newsletters: 22 (property won through a lottery).

(5) [Repealed under former Act]

Notes: 52(5) repealed in 1973, retroactive to 1972.

(6) [Repealed]

Notes: 52(6), "Cost of right to receive from trust", repealed by 2001 technical bill, last change effective March 2000.

(7) Cost of shares of subsidiary — Notwithstanding any other provision of this Act, where a corporation disposes of property to another corporation in a transaction to which paragraph 219(1)(l) applies, the cost to it of any share of a particular class of the capital stock of the other corporation received by it as consideration for the property is deemed to be the lesser of the cost of the share to the corporation otherwise determined immediately after the disposition and the amount by which the paid-up capital in respect of that class increases because of the issuance of the share.

Notes: 52(7) amended by 1995-97 technical bill, for taxation years that begin after 1995.

Interpretation Bulletins: IT-137R3: Additional tax on certain corporations carrying on business in Canada.

(8) Cost of shares of immigrant corporation — Notwithstanding any other provision of this Act, where at any time a corporation becomes resident in Canada, the cost to any shareholder who is not at that time resident in Canada of any share of the corporation's capital stock, other than a share that was taxable Canadian property immediately before that time, is deemed to be equal to the fair market value of the share at that time.

Related Provisions: 53(1)(b.1), (c) — Additions to ACB of share; 128.1(1)–(3) — Effect of corporation's immigration; 250(4), (5) — Residence of corporation.

Notes: When a corporation becomes resident in Canada, 52(8) resets the cost of its shares to any non-resident (NR) shareholder to their fair market value. There may thus be a lower capital gain on the NR's later disposition of the shares (115(1)(b), 248(1)"taxable Canadian property"(d)), though most shares are now excluded from TCP since amendments in 2010.

52(8) amended by 1998 Budget, effective for corporations that become resident in Canada after Feb. 23, 1998. Added by 1993 technical bill.

Definitions [s. 52]: "adjusted cost base" — 54, 248(1); "amount" — 95(7), 248(1); "annuity" — 248(1); "Canada" — 255; "capital gain" — 39(1)(a), 248(1); "capital interest" — 108(1), 248(1); "class of shares" — 248(6); "corporation" — 248(1), *Interpretation Act* 35(1); "disposition" — 248(1); "dividend" — 248(1); "employees profit sharing plan" — 144(1), 248(1); "fair market value" — see 69(1) Notes; "individual", "non-resident" — 248(1); "paid-up capital" — 89(1), 248(1); "person", "property" — 248(1); "resident in Canada" — 94(3)(a), 250; "series of transactions" — 248(10); "share", "shareholder", "stock dividend", "subsidiary wholly-owned corporation" — 248(1); "taxable Canadian property" — 248(1); "taxable income", "taxable income earned in Canada" — 248(1); "taxation year" — 249; "taxpayer" — 248(1); "trust" — 104(1), 248(1), (3); "unit trust" — 108(2), 248(1).

53. (1) Adjustments to cost base [additions to ACB] — In computing the adjusted cost base to a taxpayer of property at any time, there shall be added to the cost to the taxpayer of the property such of the following amounts in respect of the property as are applicable:

Notes: Additions to ACB are good for the taxpayer since they result in a lower capital gain. For deductions from ACB, see 53(2).

(a) **[negative ACB]** — any amount deemed by subsection 40(3) to be a gain of the taxpayer for a taxation year from a disposition before that time of the property;

Notes: Under 40(3), negative ACB normally triggers an immediate capital gain, except for active partners' partnership interests. 53(1)(a) then resets the ACB to zero.

(b) **[share, where 84(1) applied]** — where the property is a share of the capital stock of a corporation resident in Canada, the amount, if any, by which

(i) the total of all amounts each of which is the amount of a dividend on the share deemed by subsection 84(1) to have been received by the taxpayer before that time

exceeds

(ii) the portion of the total determined under subparagraph (i) that relates to dividends in respect of which the taxpayer was permitted a deduction under subsection 112(1) in computing the taxpayer's taxable income, except any portion of the dividend that, if paid as a separate dividend, would not be subject to subsection 55(2) because the amount of the separate dividend would not exceed the amount of the income earned or realized by any corporation — after 1971 and before the safe-income determination time for the transaction, event or series of transactions or events as part of which the dividend is received — that could reasonably be considered to contribute to the capital gain that could be realized on a disposition at fair market value, immediately before the dividend, of the share on which the dividend is received;

Related Provisions: 52(3)(a) — Cost of share received as stock dividend excludes amount deductible under 112(1).

Notes: 84(1) generally deems a dividend to have been paid if the paid-up capital of a share is increased (since increased PUC can be withdrawn tax-free: see Notes to 84(3)). 53(1)(b) allows this deemed dividend to increase ACB, to prevent double tax on sale of the shares, as 55(2) may have converted the deemed dividend into a capital gain. However, if the dividend is an intercorporate dividend deducted under 112(1), the ACB increase is ground down by 53(1)(b)(ii), except to the extent the company has safe income (see Notes to 55(2)). [The same rule applies to a stock dividend under 52(3)(a).] The ACB increase under 53(1)(b)(i) reduces the capital gain for CDA purposes and thus reduces available tax-free capital dividends; this happens *even if* there is no safe income and the ACB increase is ground down per above, since 89(1)"capital dividend account"(a)(i)(A) says 53(1)(b)(ii) is to be ignored.

"Contributed surplus" in 53(1)(b)(ii)(B) should have its meaning based on GAAP: VIEWS doc 2008-0285231C6.

For examples of rulings that 53(1)(b) will apply see VIEWS docs 2003-0051381R3, 2004-0088551R3, 2004-0093021R3, 2005-0113301R3, 2006-0181061R3, 2006-0188371R3, 2006-0189151R3, 2007-0237361R3, 2009-0350471R3, 2009-0350921R3.

53(1)(b)(ii) amended by 2016 budget bill #1 for dividends received after April 20, 2015, consequential on amendments to s. 55. Added by 2002-2013 technical bill (see Notes to 52(3) for discussion), this version for dividends received after July 15, 2010.

Income Tax Folios: S3-F2-C1: Capital Dividends [replaces IT-66R6].

(b.1) **[share of immigrant corporation]** — where the property is a share of the capital stock of a corporation, the amount of any dividend deemed by paragraph 128.1(1)(c.2) to have been received in respect of the share by the taxpayer before that time and while the taxpayer was resident in Canada;

Related Provisions: 52(8) — Cost of share to non-resident.

Notes: 53(1)(b.1) added by 1998 Budget, effective February 24, 1998.

(c) **[share, where contribution of capital made]** — where the property is a share of the capital stock of a corporation and the taxpayer has, after 1971, made a contribution of capital to the corporation otherwise than by way of a loan, by way of a disposition of shares of a foreign affiliate of the taxpayer to which subsection 85.1(3) or paragraph 95(2)(c) applies or, subject to subsection (1.1), a disposition of property in respect of which the taxpayer and the corporation have made an election under section 85, that proportion of such part of the amount of the contribution as cannot reasonably be regarded as a benefit conferred by the taxpayer on a person (other than the corporation) who was related to the taxpayer that

(i) the amount that may reasonably be regarded as the increase in the fair market value, as a result of the contribution, of the share

is of

(ii) the amount that may reasonably be regarded as the increase in the fair market value, as a result of the contribution, of all shares of the capital stock of the corporation owned by the taxpayer immediately after the contribution;

Related Provisions: 52(8) — Cost to non-resident of share of corporation that becomes resident in Canada; 53(1)(j) — Addition to ACB of share on which stock option benefit received; 53(1.1) — Deemed contribution of capital; 92(1)(a), (1.2) — Additions to ACB.

Notes: For CRA interpretation see VIEWS doc 2009-032495117.

Interpretation Bulletins: IT-291R3: Transfer of property to a corporation under subsection 85(1); IT-456R: Capital property — some adjustments to cost base; IT-527: Distress preferred shares.

(d) **[share of foreign affiliate]** — if the property is a share of the capital stock of a foreign affiliate of the taxpayer, any amount required by section 92 to be added in computing the adjusted cost base to the taxpayer of the share;

Related Provisions: 91(6) — Amounts deductible in respect of dividends received; Canada-U.S. Tax Treaty:Art. XXIX:5(d) — Reduction in ACB of share of U.S. "S" corporation.

Notes: For an example of 53(1)(d) applying see VIEWS doc 2007-0247551E5.

53(1)(d) amended by 2002-2013 technical bill, effective Dec. 21, 2002.

(d.01) **[share of demutualized insurer]** — where the property is a share of the capital stock of a corporation, any amount required by paragraph 139.1(16)(l) to be added in computing the adjusted cost base to the taxpayer of the share;

Notes: 53(1)(d.01) added by 1999 Budget, effective December 16, 1998.

(d.1) **[capital interest in a non-resident trust]** — if the property is a capital interest in a trust, any amount included under subsection 91(1) or (3) in computing the taxpayer's income for a taxation year that ends at or before that time (or that would have been required to have been included under those subsections but for subsection 56(4.1) and sections 74.1 to 75 of this Act and section 74 of the *Income Tax Act*, chapter 148 of the Revised Statutes of Canada, 1952) in respect of that interest;

Related Provisions: 53(2)(h), (i), (j) — Deductions from ACB — interest in a trust.

Notes: 53(1)(d.1) amended by 2002-2013 technical bill, for tax years that end after 2006 (earlier years in some cases), with different reading for a capital interest disposed of before Aug. 28, 2010.

(d.2) **[unit in mutual fund trust]** — where the property is a unit in a mutual fund trust, any amount required by subsection 132.1(2) to be added in computing the adjusted cost base to the taxpayer of the unit;

(d.3) **[share]** — where the property is a share of the capital stock of a corporation of which the taxpayer was, at any time, a specified shareholder, any expense incurred by the taxpayer in respect of land or a building of the corporation that was by reason of subsection 18(2) or (3.1) not deductible by the taxpayer in computing the taxpayer's income for any taxation year commencing before that time;

Related Provisions: 10(1.1) — Effect of 53(1)(d.3) on cost of land inventory; 53(1)(h) — Where land owned directly by taxpayer.

Interpretation Bulletins: IT-153R3: Land developers — subdivision and development costs and carrying charges on land.

(e) **[partnership interest]** — where the property is an interest in a partnership,

(i) an amount in respect of each fiscal period of the partnership ending after 1971 and before that time, equal to the total of all amounts each of which is the taxpayer's share (other than a share under an agreement referred to in subsection 96(1.1)) of the income of the partnership from any source for that fiscal period, computed as if this Act were read without reference to

(A) paragraphs 38(a.1) to (a.3) and the fractions set out in the formula in paragraph 14(1)(b) and in subsection 14(5), paragraph 38(a) and subsection 41(1),

(A.1) subparagraph 39(1)(a)(i.1) in respect of an object referred to in that subparagraph that is not the subject of a gifting arrangement, as defined in subsection 237.1(1), nor a property that is a tax shelter,

(A.2) the description of C in the formula in paragraph 14(1)(b), and

(B) paragraph (i), paragraphs 12(1)(o) and (z.5), 18(1)(m), 20(1)(v.1) and 29(1)(b) and (2)(b), section 55, subsections 69(6) and (7) and paragraph 82(1)(b) of this Act and paragraphs 20(1)(gg) and 81(1)(r) and (s) of the *Income Tax Act*, chapter 148 of the Revised Statutes of Canada, 1952, and the provisions of the *Income Tax Application Rules* relating to income from the operation of new mines,

(ii) the taxpayer's share of any capital dividends and any life insurance capital dividends received by the partnership before that time on shares of the capital stock of a corporation that were partnership property,

(iii) the taxpayer's share of the amount, if any, by which

(A) any proceeds of a life insurance policy received by the partnership after 1971 and before that time in consequence of the death of any person whose life was insured under the policy,

exceeds the total of all amounts each of which is

(B) the "adjusted cost basis" (in this subparagraph as defined in subsection 148(9)), immediately before the death, of

(I) if the death occurs before March 22, 2016, the policy to the partnership, and

(II) if the death occurs after March 21, 2016, a policyholder's interest in the policy,

(C) the amount by which the fair market value of consideration given in respect of a disposition of an interest in the policy exceeds the greater of the amount determined under subparagraph 148(7)(a)(i) in respect of the disposition and the adjusted cost basis to the policyholder of the interest immediately before the disposition, if

(I) the death occurs after March 21, 2016, and

(II) the disposition was by a policyholder (other than a taxable Canadian corporation) after 1999 and before March 22, 2016, or

(D) if the death occurs after March 21, 2016, an interest in the policy was disposed of by a policyholder (other than a taxable Canadian corporation) after 1999 and before March 22, 2016 and subsection 148(7) applied to the disposition, the amount, if any, determined by the formula

$$A - B$$

where

A is the amount, if any, by which the lesser of the adjusted cost basis to the policyholder of the interest immediately before the disposition and the fair market value of consideration given in respect of the disposition exceeds the amount determined under subparagraph 148(7)(a)(i) in respect of the disposition, and

B is the absolute value of the negative amount, if any, that would be, in the absence of section 257, the adjusted cost basis, immediately before the death, of the interest in the policy,

(iv) where the taxpayer has, after 1971, made a contribution of capital to the partnership otherwise than by way of loan, such part of the amount of the contribution as cannot reasonably be regarded as a benefit conferred on any other member of the partnership who was related to the taxpayer,

(iv.1) each amount that is in respect of a specified amount described in subsection 80.2(1) and that is paid by the taxpayer to the partnership, to the extent that the amount paid is not deductible in computing the income of the taxpayer,

(v) where the time is immediately before the taxpayer's death and the taxpayer was at that time a member of a partnership, the value, at the time of the taxpayer's death, of the rights or things referred to in subsection 70(2) in respect of a partnership interest held by the taxpayer immediately before the taxpayer's death, other than an interest referred to in subsection 96(1.5),

(vi) any amount deemed by subsection 40(3.1) to be a gain of the taxpayer for a taxation year from a disposition before that time of the property,

(vii) any amount deemed by paragraph 98(1)(c) or 98.1(1)(c) to be a gain of the taxpayer for a taxation year from a disposition before that time of the property,

(vii.1) a share of the taxpayer's Canadian development expense or Canadian oil and gas property expense that was deducted at or before that time in computing the adjusted cost base to the taxpayer of the interest because of subparagraph (2)(c)(ii) and in respect of which the taxpayer elected under paragraph (f) of the definition "Canadian development expense" in subsection 66.2(5) or paragraph (b) of the definition "Canadian oil and gas property expense" in subsection 66.4(5), as the case may be,

(viii) an amount deemed, before that time, by subsection 66.1(7), 66.2(6) or 66.4(6) to be an amount referred to in the description of G in the definition "cumulative Canadian exploration expense" in subsection 66.1(6), paragraph (a) of the description of F in the definition "cumulative Canadian development expense" in subsection 66.2(5) or the description of G in that definition, or paragraph (a) of the description of F in the definition "cumulative Canadian oil and gas property expense" in subsection 66.4(5) or the description of G in that definition in respect of the taxpayer,

(viii.1) an amount deemed, before that time, by subsection 59(1.1) to be proceeds of disposition receivable by the taxpayer in respect of the disposition of a foreign resource property,

(ix) the amount, if any, by which

(A) the taxpayer's share of the amount of any assistance or benefit that the partnership received or became entitled to receive after 1971 and before that time from a government, municipality or other public authority, whether as a grant, subsidy, forgivable loan, deduction from royalty or tax, investment allowance or any other form of assistance or benefit, in respect of or related to a Canadian resource property or an exploration or development expense incurred in Canada

exceeds

(B) the part, if any, of the amount included in clause (A) in respect of the interest that was repaid before that time by the taxpayer under a legal obligation to repay all or any part of the amount,

(x) any amount required by section 97 to be added before that time in computing the adjusted cost base to the taxpayer of the interest,

(xi) of which the taxpayer's share of any income or loss of the partnership was, at any time, 10% or more, any expense incurred by the taxpayer in respect of land or a building of the partnership that was by reason of subsection 18(2) or (3.1) not deductible by the taxpayer in computing the taxpayer's income for any taxation year commencing before that time,

(xii) any amount required by paragraph 110.6(23)(a) to be added at that time in computing the adjusted cost base to the taxpayer of the interest, and

(xiii) any amount required by subsection 127(30) to be added to the taxpayer's tax otherwise payable under this Part for a taxation year that ended before that time.

(xiv) [Repealed]

Related Provisions: 10(1.1) — Cost of land inventory; 40(3.13) — Artificial transactions affecting partnership capital; 53(2)(c) — Reduction in adjusted cost base — partnership interest; 70(6)(d.1)(iii) — Where transfer or distribution to spouse or trust; 70(9.21)(a)(iii)(C), (b)(iii)(C) — Transfer of family farm or fishing corporation or partnership; 70(9.31)(a)(iii)(C), (b)(iii)(C) — Transfer of family farm or fishing corporation or partnership from spouse's trust to children of settlor; 87(2)(e.1) — Amalgamations — cost of partnership interest; 96(1.01)(b) — Deemed end of fiscal period when taxpayer ceases to be partner; 112(11)–(13) — Cost reductions for partnership interest that is not capital property; 248(8) — Meaning of "consequence" of death; 248(16), (16.1) — GST or QST input tax credit/refund and rebate deemed to be assistance; 248(18), (18.1) — GST or QST — repayment of input tax credit or refund; 257 — Formula cannot calculate to less than zero.

Notes: See Notes to 53(2)(c).

In CRA's view, 53(1)(e)(iii) does not apply to the deceased partner's interest, since the partner is no longer a partner by the time the insurance proceeds are received: 1984 Cdn Tax Foundation conference, Round Table q. 25 (p. 801); Where there are tiered partnerships or corporate partners, see VIEWS doc 2005-0125401E5. On the interaction with 96(1.01) and s. 34, see 2006-0214411E5. Where a partnership ceases to exist, see 2008-0275471E5. A 34.2(2) stub period income inclusion does not increase ACB: 2017-0687051E5. On the interaction with 40(3.1) and (3.11) see 2009-0349911E5. Where a limited partner's partnership share increases, see 2010-0373371C6. On an arrangement using life insurance proceeds in a partnership to fund the disposition of a partnership interest held by a corporate partner, see 2011-0398421C6. On the interaction with the at-risk amount see 2011-042279117. Different classes of units (even tracking units) are all considered one property for ACB purposes: *Income Tax Technical News* 25 (partnership issues q.6), 2014-0538161C6 [2014 APFF q.22].

On partial disposition of a partnership interest, the partner's share of the income for the fiscal period is added to the ACB of the remaining interest: 2013-0491571E5.

53(1)(e)(ix)(A): see 12(1)(x) Notes for meaning of "assistance" and related words.

53(1)(e)(iii) amended by 2016 budget bill #2, effective Dec. 15, 2016. Before that date, read:

(iii) the taxpayer's share of the amount, if any, by which

(A) any proceeds of a life insurance policy received by the partnership after 1971 and before that time in consequence of the death of any person whose life was insured under the policy,

exceeds

(B) the adjusted cost basis (within the meaning assigned by subsection 148(9)) of the policy to the partnership immediately before that person's death,

53(1)(e) amended by 2013 budget bill #2 (for gifts after Feb 25, 2008), 2002-2013 technical bill (last change effective for dispositions after 2003), 2008 and 2007 budget bills #2, 2006 budget bill #1, 2000, 1998, 1996 and 1994 Budgets, 1992 and 1991 technical bills.

I.T. Application Rules: 26(9)–(9.4) (where taxpayer became partner before 1972); 69 (meaning of "chapter 148 of ..." in cl. 53(1)(e)(i)(B))).

Income Tax Folios: S3-F2-C1: Capital Dividends [replaces IT-66R6].

Interpretation Bulletins: IT-153R3: Land developers — subdivision and development costs and carrying charges on land; IT-242R: Retired partners; IT-278R2: Death of a partner or of a retired partner; IT-338R2: Partnership interests — effects on ACB of admission or retirement of a partner (cancelled); IT-353R2: Partnership interests — some adjustments to cost base (cancelled); IT-430R3: Life insurance proceeds received by a private corporation or a partnership as a consequence of death; IT-471R: Merger of partnerships.

I.T. Technical News: 5 (adjusted cost base of partnership interest); 9 (calculation of ACB of a partnership interest); 12 (adjusted cost base of partnership interest — subparagraph 53(1)(e)(viii)); 25 (partnership issues).

Forms: T2065: Determination of adjusted cost base of a partnership interest.

(f) **[substituted property]** — where the property is substituted property (within the meaning assigned by paragraph (a) of the definition "superficial loss" in section 54) of the taxpayer, the amount, if any, by which

(i) the amount of the loss that was, because of the acquisition by the taxpayer of the property, a superficial loss of any taxpayer from a disposition of a property

exceeds

(ii) where the property disposed of was a share of the capital stock of a corporation, the amount that would, but for paragraph 40(2)(g), be deducted under subsection 112(3), (3.1) or (3.2) in computing the loss of any taxpayer in respect of the disposition of the share;

Related Provisions: 40(2)(g)(i) — Superficial loss denied; 40(2)(h) — Loss on disposition of share of controlled corporation; 40(3.3), (3.4) — Rule on disposition by corporation; 142.4(1)"tax basis"(h) — Disposition of specified debt obligation by financial institution.

Notes: 53(1)(f) does not apply to a disposition by a corporation because 40(3.4) applies instead: see 40(3.3)(b) and 54"superficial loss"(h).

53(1)(f)(ii) added by 1991 technical bill, effective July 14, 1990.

Interpretation Bulletins: IT-291R3: Transfer of property to a corporation under subsection 85(1); IT-456R: Capital property — some adjustments to cost base.

(f.1) [property disposed of at loss by other corporation] — where the taxpayer is a taxable Canadian corporation and the property was disposed of by another taxable Canadian corporation to the taxpayer in circumstances such that

(i) paragraph (f.2) does not apply to increase the adjusted cost base to the other corporation of shares of the capital stock of the taxpayer, and

(ii) the capital loss from the disposition was deemed by paragraph 40(2)(e.1) (or, where the property was acquired by the taxpayer before 1996, by paragraph 40(2)(e) or 85(4)(a) as those paragraphs read in their application to property acquired before April 26, 1995) to be nil,

the amount that would otherwise have been the capital loss from the disposition;

Related Provisions: 53(1)(f.11) — Alternative addition to ACB on dispositions subject to para. 40(2)(e.1); 142.4(1)"tax basis"(h) — Disposition of specified debt obligation by financial institution.

Notes: For rulings applying 53(1)(f.1) see VIEWS docs 2011-0426051R3, 2012-0452821R3, 2012-0462141R3, 2013-0479701R3, 2013-0514191R3, 2014-0547871R3. See also 2014-0524391E5 (interaction with debt parking rules).

53(1)(f.1) amended by 1995-97 technical bill (for dispositions after April 26, 1995, subject to grandfathering), 1994 technical bill.

Advance Tax Rulings: ATR-57: Transfer of property for estate planning purposes; ATR-66: Non-arm's length transfer of debt followed by a winding-up and a sale of shares.

(f.11) [property disposed of at loss by other person] — where the property was disposed of by a person (other than a non-resident person or a person exempt from tax under this Part on the person's taxable income) or by an eligible Canadian partnership (as defined in subsection 80(1)) to the taxpayer in circumstances such that

(i) paragraph (f.1) does not apply to increase the adjusted cost base to the taxpayer of the property,

(ii) paragraph (f.2) does not apply to increase the adjusted cost base to that person of shares of the capital stock of the taxpayer, and

(iii) the capital loss from the disposition was deemed by paragraph 40(2)(e.1) (or, where the property was acquired by the taxpayer before 1996, by paragraph 85(4)(a) as it read in its application to property acquired before April 26, 1995) to be nil,

the amount that would otherwise be the capital loss from the disposition;

Notes: For rulings applying 53(1)(f.11) see VIEWS docs 2008-0300161R3, 2009-0343201R3, 2009-0350711R3, 2011-0426051R3.

53(1)(f.11) amended by 1995-97 technical bill, effective (subject to grandfathering) for dispositions after April 26, 1995. Added by 1994 technical bill, for tax years that end after Feb. 21, 1994.

(f.12) [commercial obligation owing to taxpayer] — where the property is a particular commercial obligation (in this paragraph having the meaning assigned by subsection 80(1)) payable to the taxpayer as consideration for the settlement or extinguishment of another commercial obligation payable to the taxpayer and the taxpayer's loss from the disposition of the other obligation was reduced because of paragraph 40(2)(e.2), the proportion of the reduction that the principal amount of the particular obligation is of the total of all amounts each of which is the principal amount of a commercial obligation payable to the taxpayer as consideration for the settlement or extinguishment of that other obligation;

Notes: For the meaning of "extinguishment", see Notes to 80(2)(a).

53(1)(f.12) added by 1994 technical bill, for tax years that end after Feb. 21, 1994.

(f.2) [share, after transfer of other shares to corporation] — where the property is a share, any amount required by paragraph 40(3.6)(b) (or, where the property was acquired by the taxpayer before 1996, by paragraph 85(4)(b) as it read in its application to property disposed of before April 26, 1995) to be

added in computing the adjusted cost base to the taxpayer of the share;

Related Provisions: 53(1)(f.1), (f.11) — (f.2) takes precedence over (f.1) and (f.11).

Notes: 53(1)(f.2) amended by 1995-97 technical bill, effective (subject to grandfathering) for dispositions after April 26, 1995.

Interpretation Bulletins: IT-456R: Capital property — some adjustments to cost base.

(g) [bond, mortgage, etc.] — where the property is a bond, debenture, bill, note, mortgage, hypothecary claim or similar obligation, the amount, if any, by which the principal amount of the obligation exceeds the amount for which the obligation was issued, if the excess was required by subsection 16(2) or (3) to be included in computing the income of the taxpayer for a taxation year commencing before that time;

Notes: The term "bond, debenture, bill, note, mortgage or similar obligation" may not include bankers' acceptances: *Federated Co-operatives*, 2001 FCA 217; leave to appeal denied 2001 CarswellNat 1788 (SCC).

"Hypothecary claim" added to 53(1)(g) by 2001 *Civil Code* harmonization bill, effective June 14, 2001. The change is non-substantive; see *Interpretation Act* s. 8.2.

(g.1) [indexed debt obligation] — where the property is an indexed debt obligation, any amount determined under subparagraph 16(6)(a)(i) in respect of the obligation and required to be included in computing the taxpayer's income for a taxation year beginning before that time;

Related Provisions: 53(2)(l.1) — Reduction in adjusted cost base — indexed debt obligation.

Notes: 53(1)(g.1) added by 1992 technical bill, for IDOs issued after Oct. 16, 1991.

(h) [land] — where the property is land of the taxpayer, any amount paid by the taxpayer or by another taxpayer in respect of whom the taxpayer was a person, corporation or partnership described in subparagraph (b)(i), (ii) or (iii) of the definition "interest on debt relating to the acquisition of land" in subsection 18(3), after 1971 and before that time pursuant to a legal obligation to pay

(i) interest on debt relating to the acquisition of land (within the meaning assigned by subsection 18(3)), or

(ii) property taxes (not including income or profits taxes or taxes imposed by reference to the transfer of property) paid by the taxpayer in respect of the property to a province or to a Canadian municipality

to the extent that the amount was, because of subsection 18(2),

(iii) not deductible in computing the taxpayer's income from the land or from a business for any taxation year beginning before that time, or

(iv) not deductible in computing the income of the other taxpayer and was not included in or added to the cost to the other taxpayer of any property otherwise than because of subparagraph (d.3) or subparagraph (e)(xi);

Related Provisions: 43.1(2) — Life estates in real property; 53(1)(d.3) — Where land owned through a corporation.

Notes: See Notes to 18(2). Where property was not used to generate income, the non-deductibility of property taxes was based on that fact, not on 18(2), so 53(1)(h) did not add these amounts to ACB: *Bauerle*, [1986] 1 C.T.C. 2175 (TCC); VIEWS doc 2010-0359631I7.

53(1)(h) amended by 1991 technical bill, for taxation years ending after 1987.

Interpretation Bulletins: IT-456R: Capital property — some adjustments to cost base.

(i) [land used in farming] — where the property is land used in a farming business carried on by the taxpayer, an amount in respect of each taxation year ending after 1971 and commencing before that time, equal to the taxpayer's loss, if any, for that year from the farming business, to the extent that the loss

(i) was not, by virtue of section 31, deductible in computing the taxpayer's income for that year,

(ii) was not deducted in computing the taxpayer's taxable income for the taxation year in which the taxpayer disposed of the property or any preceding taxation year,

(iii) did not exceed the total of

(A) taxes (other than income or profits taxes or taxes imposed by reference to the transfer of the property) paid by the taxpayer in that year or payable by the taxpayer in respect of that year to a province or a Canadian municipality in respect of the property, and

(B) interest, paid by the taxpayer in that year or payable by the taxpayer in respect of that year, pursuant to a legal obligation to pay interest on borrowed money used to acquire the property or on any amount as consideration payable for the property,

to the extent that those taxes and interest were included in computing the loss, and

(iv) did not exceed the remainder obtained when

(A) the total of each of the taxpayer's losses from the farming business for taxation years preceding that year (to the extent that they are required by this paragraph to be added in computing the taxpayer's adjusted cost base of the property),

is deducted from

(B) the amount, if any, by which the taxpayer's proceeds of disposition of the property exceed the adjusted cost base to the taxpayer of the property immediately before that time, determined without reference to this paragraph;

Related Provisions: 96(1)(e) — Partnerships — gains to be computed without reference to para. 53(1)(i); 101 — Corresponding rule for partnerships; 111(1)(c), (d) — Farming loss carryovers; 111(3) — Limitations on deductibility of loss carryover; 111(6) — Limitation.

Interpretation Bulletins: IT-232R2: Non-capital losses, net capital losses, restricted farm losses, farm losses and limited partnership losses — their composition and deductibility in computing taxable income.

(j) **share or fund unit taxed as stock option benefit** — if the property is a security (within the meaning assigned by subsection 7(7)) and, in respect of its acquisition by the taxpayer, a benefit was deemed by section 7 to have been received in any taxation year that ends after 1971 and begins before that time by the taxpayer or by a person that did not deal at arm's length with the taxpayer or, if the security was acquired after February 27, 2000, would have been so deemed if section 7 were read without reference to subsections 7(1.1) and (8), the amount of the benefit that was, or would have been, so deemed to have been received;

Related Provisions: 7(1.6), 128.1(4)(d.1) — Effect of emigration on disposition of share or fund unit; 49(3)(b) — Where option to acquire exercised.

Notes: There does not appear to be an offsetting reduction in ACB for the deduction allowed by 110(1)(d) or (d.1).

If a trustee hold shares for the employee, the 53(1)(j) addition occurs when the trust acquires the shares, due to 7(2): VIEWS doc 2005-0126131E5.

53(1)(j) amended by 2000 Budget, effective 2000. This amendment provides that, for all employee option securities acquired after Feb. 27, 2000, the employment benefit is included in the ACB of the security from the time of acquisition, even if recognition of the benefit is deferred until the disposition of the security. This is relevant primarily where securities for which deferral is provided under 7(1.1) or 7(8) are exchanged for new securities under 7(1.5), but there is no rollover available for the disposition of the old securities. The immediate inclusion in the ACB of the old securities ensures that the determination of the capital gain or loss on their disposition is not distorted by exclusion of the deferred benefit associated with their acquisition.

53(1)(j) amended to add "or unit" by 1998 Budget, effective in computing the ACB of a unit acquired after February 1998.

Interpretation Bulletins: IT-96R6: Options to acquire shares, bonds or debentures and by trusts to acquire trust units; IT-113R4: Benefits to employees — stock options.

I.T. Technical News: 19 (Disposition of identical properties acquired under a section 7 securities option).

(k) **[expropriation asset]** — where the property is an expropriation asset of the taxpayer (within the meaning assigned by section 80.1) or an asset of the taxpayer assumed for the purposes of that section to be an expropriation asset thereof, any amount required by paragraph 80.1(2)(b) to be added in computing the adjusted cost base to the taxpayer of the asset;

Related Provisions: 53(2)(n) — Reduction in ACB of expropriation asset.

(l) **[interest in related segregated fund trust]** — where the property is an interest in a related segregated fund trust referred to in section 138.1,

(i) each amount deemed by paragraph 138.1(1)(f) to be an amount payable to the taxpayer before that time in respect of that interest,

(ii) each amount required by subparagraph 138.1(1)(g)(ii) to be added before that time in respect of that interest,

(iii) each amount in respect of that interest that is a capital gain deemed to have been allocated under subsection 138.1(4) to the taxpayer before that time, and

(iv) each amount in respect of that interest that before that time was deemed by subsection 138.1(3) to be a capital gain of the taxpayer;

Related Provisions: 53(2)(q) — Deductions from ACB of related segregated fund trust; 138.1(5) — ACB of property in related segregated fund trust.

I.T. Application Rules: 26(4) (property owned since before 1972).

(m) **[offshore investment fund property]** — where the property is an offshore investment fund property (within the meaning assigned by subsection 94.1(1)),

(i) any amount included in respect of the property by virtue of subsection 94.1(1) in computing the taxpayer's income for a taxation year commencing before that time, or

(ii) where the taxpayer is a controlled foreign affiliate (within the meaning of subsection 95(1)), of a person resident in Canada, any amount included in respect of the property in computing the foreign accrual property income of the controlled foreign affiliate by reason of the description of C in the definition "foreign accrual property income" in subsection 95(1) for a taxation year commencing before that time;

(n) **[surveying and valuation costs]** — the reasonable costs incurred by the taxpayer, before that time, of surveying or valuing the property for the purpose of its acquisition or disposition (to the extent that those costs are not deducted by the taxpayer in computing the taxpayer's income for any taxation year or attributable to any other property);

Related Provisions: 20(1)(dd) — Deduction for site investigation expenses; 40(1)(a)(i), (b)(i) — Expenses of disposition deductible in computing gain or loss.

Notes: 53(1)(n) added by 1985 technical bill, effective for costs incurred after 1984.

Interpretation Bulletins: IT-407R4: Dispositions of cultural property to designated Canadian institutions.

(o) **[real property — remainder interest]** — where the property is real property of the taxpayer, any amount required by paragraph 43.1(2)(b) to be added in computing the adjusted cost base to the taxpayer of the property;

Notes: 53(1)(o) added by 1992 technical bill, effective Dec. 21, 1991.

(p) **[flow-through entity after 2004]** — where the time is after 2004 and the property is an interest in or a share of the capital stock of a flow-through entity (within the meaning assigned by subsection 39.1(1)), the amount determined by the formula

$$A \times B / C$$

where

A is the amount, if any, that would, if the definition "exempt capital gains balance" in subsection 39.1(1) were read without reference to "that ends before 2005", be the taxpayer's exempt capital gains balance in respect of the entity for the taxpayer's 2005 taxation year,

B is the fair market value at that time of the property, and

C is the fair market value at that time of all the taxpayer's interests in or shares of the capital stock of the entity;

Related Provisions: 53(1)(r) — Increase in ACB before 2005.

Notes: 53(1)(p) added by 1994 Budget, effective 1994. See Notes to 39.1(1) "exempt capital gains balance" and "flow-through entity".

(q) **[history preservation rules — debt forgiveness]** — any amount required under paragraph (4)(b), (5)(b), (6)(b),

47(1)(d), 49(3.01)(b), 51(1)(d.2), 86(4)(b) or 87(5.1)(b) or (6.1)(b) to be added in computing the adjusted cost base to the taxpayer of the property;

Notes: 53(1)(q) added by 1994 technical bill, effective for taxation years that end after February 21, 1994. See Notes to 47(1).

(r) **[flow-through entity before 2005]** — [no longer relevant]

Notes: 53(1)(r) applies only in respect of dispositions before 2005. See Notes to 39.1(2). After 2004, 53(1)(p) increases the ACB of any remaining interests in, or shares of the capital stock of, a flow-through entity by the unused portion of the individual's exempt capital gains balance in respect of the entity.

53(1)(r) amended by 2013 budget bill #2, for dispositions occurring after 2001, and by 2000 Budget. Added by 1995-97 technical bill.

(s) **[gain on derivative forward agreement]** — if the property was acquired under a derivative forward agreement, any amount required to be included in respect of the property under subparagraph 12(1)(z.7)(i) in computing the income of the taxpayer for a taxation year; and

Related Provisions: 53(1)(t) — Where property disposed of under DFA.

Notes: See Notes to 248(1)"derivative forward agreement". 53(1)(s) added by 2013 budget bill #2, effective March 21, 2013.

(t) **[gain on derivative forward agreement]** — if the property is disposed of under a derivative forward agreement, any amount required to be included in respect of the property under subparagraph 12(1)(z.7)(ii) in computing the income of the taxpayer for the taxation year that includes that time.

Related Provisions: 53(1)(s) — Where property acquired under DFA.

Notes: See Notes to 248(1)"derivative forward agreement". 53(1)(t) added by 2013 budget bill #2, effective March 21, 2013.

(1.1) **Deemed contribution of capital** — For the purposes of paragraph (1)(c), where there has been a disposition of property before May 7, 1974, and

(a) the taxpayer and the corporation referred to in that paragraph have made an election under section 85 in respect of that property, and

(b) the consideration received by the taxpayer for the property did not include shares of the capital stock of the corporation,

the disposition of property shall be deemed to be a contribution of capital equal to the amount, if any, by which

(c) the amount that the taxpayer and the corporation have agreed on in the election

exceeds

(d) the fair market value at the time of the disposition of any consideration received by the taxpayer for the property so disposed of.

Interpretation Bulletins: IT-456R: Capital property — some adjustments to cost base.

(1.2) **Flow-through entity before 2005** — [No longer relevant.]

Notes: 53(1.2) applies only for purposes of 53(1)(r). Added by 2013 budget bill #2, for dispositions occurring after 2001.

(2) **Amounts to be deducted [from ACB]** — In computing the adjusted cost base to a taxpayer of property at any time, there shall be deducted such of the following amounts in respect of the property as are applicable:

Notes: See Notes to opening words of 53(1).

(a) **[share]** — where the property is a share of the capital stock of a corporation resident in Canada,

(i) any amount received by the taxpayer after 1971 and before that time as, on account or in lieu of payment of, or in satisfaction of, a dividend on the share (other than a taxable dividend or a dividend in respect of which the corporation paying the dividend has elected in accordance with subsection 83(2) or (2.1) in respect of the full amount thereof),

(ii) any amount received by the taxpayer after 1971 and before that time on a reduction of the paid-up capital of the corporation in respect of the share, except to the extent that

the amount is deemed by subsection 84(4) or (4.1) to be a dividend received by the taxpayer,

(iii) any amount required to be deducted before that time under section 84.1 of the *Income Tax Act*, chapter 148 of the Revised Statutes of Canada, 1952, as it applied before May 23, 1985 in computing the adjusted cost base to the taxpayer of the share,

(iv) any amount, to the extent that such amount is not proceeds of disposition of a share, received by the taxpayer before that time that would, but for subsection 84(8), be deemed by subsection 84(2) to be a dividend received by the taxpayer, and

(v) any amount required by paragraph 44.1(2)(b) to be deducted in computing the adjusted cost base to the taxpayer of the share;

Related Provisions: 40(2)(h), (i) — Limitation on capital loss on certain shares; 52(8) — Cost to non-resident of share of corporation that becomes resident in Canada; 91(6) — Amounts deductible in respect of dividends received.

Notes: 53(2)(a)(ii) amended by 1991 technical bill, effective 1990.

53(2)(a)(v) added by 2000 Budget, for dispositions that occur after Feb. 27, 2000.

I.T. Application Rules: 69 (meaning of "chapter 148 of ...").

Interpretation Bulletins: IT-456R: Capital property — some adjustments to cost base.

Advance Tax Rulings: ATR-54: Reduction of paid-up capital.

(b) **[share of non-resident corporation]** — where the property is a share of the capital stock of a non-resident corporation,

(i) if the corporation is a foreign affiliate of the taxpayer,

(A) any amount required under paragraph 80.1(4)(d) or section 92 to be deducted in computing the adjusted cost base to the taxpayer of the share, and

(B) any amount received by the taxpayer before that time, on a reduction of the paid-up capital of the corporation in respect of the share, that is so received

(I) after 1971 and on or before August 19, 2011, or

(II) after August 19, 2011, where the reduction is a qualifying return of capital (within the meaning assigned by subsection 90(3)) in respect of the share, or

(ii) in any other case, any amount received by the taxpayer after 1971 and before that time on a reduction of the paid-up capital of the corporation in respect of the share;

Related Provisions: 15(1)(a.1)(ii) — No shareholder-benefit income inclusion where 53(2)(b)(ii) applies; 52(8) — Cost to non-resident of share of corporation that becomes resident in Canada; 56(6)–(9) — Whether control acquired; 92(1)(b), 92(2), (3) — Deductions from ACB; 258(4)(b), 258(6) — Exceptions to rules deeming interest on certain shares.

Notes: For examples of 53(2)(b)(ii) applying see VIEWS docs 2008-0297811R3, 2010-0374301R3, 2012-0463611R3, 2014-056057117.

53(2)(b)(i)(B) added by 2002-2013 technical bill, effective Aug. 20, 2011.

(b.1) **[capital interest in non-resident trust]** — if the property is a capital interest in a trust, any amount deducted by the taxpayer by reason of subsection 91(2) or (4) in computing the taxpayer's income for a taxation year that ends at or before that time (or that would have been so deductible by the taxpayer but for subsection 56(4.1) and sections 74.1 to 75 of this Act and section 74 of the *Income Tax Act*, chapter 148 of the Revised Statutes of Canada, 1952) in respect of that interest;

Notes: 53(2)(b.1) amended by 2002-2013 technical bill, for tax years that end after 2006, and also in computing the ACB of a capital interest in a trust for an earlier tax year if amended 94(1) applies to the trust for a tax year that ends in that earlier year.

(b.2) **[property of corporation or trust after change in control]** — if the property is property of a taxpayer that was subject to a loss restriction event at or before that time, any amount required by paragraph 111(4)(c) to be deducted in computing the adjusted cost base of the property;

Related Provisions: 142.4(1)"tax basis"(q) — Disposition of specified debt obligation by financial institution; 251.2 — Loss restriction event.

Notes: 53(2)(b.2) amended by 2013 budget bill #2, effective March 21, 2013, to extend the rule to trust interests. (See Notes to 251.2(2) re loss restriction event.)

(c) **[partnership interest]** — where the property is an interest in a partnership,

(i) an amount in respect of each fiscal period of the partnership ending after 1971 and before that time, equal to the total of amounts each of which is the taxpayer's share (other than a share under an agreement referred to in subsection 96(1.1)) of any loss of the partnership from any source for that fiscal period, computed as if this Act were read without reference to

(A) the fractions set out in subsection 14(5), paragraph 38(b) and in the formula in paragraph 14(1)(b),

(A.1) [Repealed]

(A.2) the description of C in the formula in paragraph 14(1)(b),

(B) paragraphs 12(1)(o) and (z.5), 18(1)(m) and 20(1)(v.1), section 31, subsection 40(2), section 55 and subsections 69(6) and (7) of this Act and paragraphs 20(1)(gg) and 81(1)(r) and (s) of the *Income Tax Act*, chapter 148 of the Revised Statutes of Canada, 1952, and

(C) subsections 100(4), 112(3.1), (4), (4.2) as it read in its application to dispositions of property that occurred before April 27, 1995 and (5.2),

except to the extent that all or a portion of such a loss may reasonably be considered to have been included in the taxpayer's limited partnership loss in respect of the partnership for the taxpayer's taxation year in which that fiscal period ended,

(i.1) an amount in respect of each fiscal period of the partnership ending before that time that is the taxpayer's limited partnership loss in respect of the partnership for the taxation year in which that fiscal period ends to the extent that such loss was deducted by the taxpayer in computing the taxpayer's taxable income for any taxation year that commenced before that time,

(i.2) any amount deemed by subsection 40(3.12) to be a loss of the taxpayer for a taxation year from a disposition before that time of the property,

(i.3) if at that time the property is not a tax shelter investment as defined by section 143.2 and the taxpayer would be a member, described in subsection 40(3.1), of the partnership if the fiscal period of the partnership that includes that time ended at that time, the unpaid principal amount of any indebtedness of the taxpayer for which recourse is limited, either immediately or in the future and either absolutely or contingently, and that can reasonably be considered to have been used to acquire the property,

(i.4) unless that time is immediately before a disposition of the interest, if the taxpayer is a member of the partnership and the taxpayer has been a specified member of the partnership at all times since becoming a member of the partnership, or the taxpayer is at that time a limited partner of the partnership for the purposes of subsection 40(3.1),

(A) where that time is in the taxpayer's first taxation year for which the taxpayer is eligible to deduct an amount in respect of the partnership under subsection 34.2(11), the portion of the amount deducted in computing the taxpayer's income for the taxation year under subsection 34.2(11) in respect of the partnership that would have been deductible if the definition "qualifying transitional income" in subsection 34.2(1) were read without reference to paragraph (b), and

(B) where that time is in any other taxation year, the portion of the amount deducted in computing the taxpayer's income for the taxation year immediately preceding that other year under subsection 34.2(11) in respect of the partnership that would have been deductible if the defini-

tion "qualifying transitional income" in subsection 34.2(1) were read without reference to paragraph (b),

(ii) an amount in respect of each fiscal period of the partnership ending after 1971 and before that time, other than a fiscal period after the fiscal period in which the taxpayer ceased to be a member of the partnership, equal to the taxpayer's share of the total of

(A) amounts that, but for paragraph 96(1)(d), would be deductible in computing the income of the partnership for the fiscal period by virtue of the provisions of the *Income Tax Application Rules* relating to exploration and development expenses,

(B) the Canadian exploration and development expenses and foreign resource pool expenses, if any, incurred by the partnership in the fiscal period,

(C) the Canadian exploration expense, if any, incurred by the partnership in the fiscal period,

(D) the Canadian development expense, if any, incurred by the partnership in the fiscal period, and

(E) the Canadian oil and gas property expense, if any, incurred by the partnership in the fiscal period,

(iii) any amount deemed by subsection 110.1(4) or 118.1(8) to have been the eligible amount of a gift made by the taxpayer by reason of the taxpayer's membership in the partnership at the end of a fiscal period of the partnership ending before that time,

(iv) any amount required by section 97 to be deducted before that time in computing the adjusted cost base to the taxpayer of the interest,

(v) any amount received by the taxpayer after 1971 and before that time as, on account or in lieu of payment of, or in satisfaction of, a distribution of the taxpayer's share (other than a share under an agreement referred to in subsection 96(1.1)) of the partnership profits or partnership capital,

(vi) an amount equal to that portion of all amounts deducted under subsection 127(5) in computing the tax otherwise payable by the taxpayer under this Part for the taxpayer's taxation years ending before that time that may reasonably be attributed to amounts added in computing the investment tax credit of the taxpayer by virtue of subsection 127(8),

(vii) any amount added pursuant to subsection 127.2(4) in computing the taxpayer's share-purchase tax credit for a taxation year ending before or after that time,

(viii) an amount equal to 50% of the amount deemed to be designated pursuant to subsection 127.3(4) before that time in respect of each share, debt obligation or right acquired by the partnership and deemed to have been acquired by the taxpayer under that subsection,

(ix) the amount of all assistance received by the taxpayer before that time that has resulted in a reduction of the capital cost of a depreciable property to the partnership by virtue of subsection 13(7.2),

(x) any amount deductible by the taxpayer under subparagraph 20(1)(e)(vi) in respect of the partnership for a taxation year of the taxpayer ending at or after that time,

(xi) any amount required by paragraph 110.6(23)(b) to be deducted at that time in computing the adjusted cost base to the taxpayer of the interest,

(xii) any amount payable by the partnership, to the extent that the amount is deductible under subsection 20.01(1) in computing the taxpayer's income for a taxation year that began before that time, and

(xiii) the amount of any reduction (within the meaning of paragraph 247(13)(a)) of the amount of a dividend deemed to have been received by the taxpayer in respect of a transaction (as defined in subsection 247(1)) or series of transactions in which the partnership was a participant;

Related Provisions: 40(3) — Deemed gain when ACB becomes negative; 40(3.13) — Artificial transactions affecting partnership capital; 53(1)(e) — Addition to ACB — partnership interest; 66.8(1) — Resource expenses of limited partner; 70(6)(d.1) — Where transfer or distribution to spouse or trust; 70(9.21)(a)(iii)(C), (b)(iii)(C) — Transfer of family farm or fishing corporation or partnership; 70(9.31)(a)(iii)(C), (b)(iii)(C) — Transfer of family farm or fishing corporation or partnership from spouse's trust to children of settlor; 80(1)"excluded obligation"(a)(iii) — Debt forgiveness rules do not apply where amount deducted in computing ACB (e.g., under 53(2)(c)(i.3)); 87(2)(e.1), 87(2)(j.6) — Amalgamations; 96(1.01)(b) — Deemed end of fiscal period when taxpayer ceases to be partner; 96(2.2)(c) — At-risk amount — amount deducted under 53(2)(c)(i.3); 98(1)(c) — Disposition of partnership property; 100(2) — Gain from disposition of interest in partnership; 112(11)–(13) — Cost reductions for partnership interest that is not capital property; 127(12.2) — Investment tax credit; 248(16), (16.1) — GST or QST input tax credit/refund and rebate deemed to be assistance; 248(18), (18.1) — GST or QST — repayment of input tax credit or refund; 248(30)–(33) — Determination of eligible amount of gift.

Notes: Simplified, the ACB of a partnership interest is the original investment plus the partner's share of the profits (53(1)(e)(i)) plus contributions of capital (53(1)(e)(iv)), minus the taxpayer's share of partnership losses (53(2)(c)(i)) and partnership drawings (53(2)(c)(v) (this could include loans: VIEWS doc 2016-0637341E5)).

Unlike every other reduction that takes ACB below zero, 53(2)(c) does not necessarily trigger an immediate capital gain. The ACB of an active partner's partnership interest can remain negative (see 40(3)-(3.2)) unless the partnership ceases to exist (see 98(1)(c)).

See also Norman Tobias, *Taxation of Corporations, Partnerships and Trusts* (Carswell, 5th ed., 2017), chap. 3.

In *Tesainer*, 2009 FCA 33 (leave to appeal denied 2009 CarswellNat 3106 (SCC)), a settlement compensating investors in a partnership for its failure, paid by lawyers for giving wrong securities law advice, did not fall under 53(2)(c)(v).

For the impact on ACB of a limited partner's restricted farm loss, see VIEWS doc 2008-0296981E5.

53(2)(c)(i.4) reduces the ACB of a partnership interest held by a passive corporate partner that has "qualifying transitional income" (QTI) under 34.2, where a corporate partner's QTI in respect of a particular partnership includes "eligible alignment income" (EAI) under 34.2. The corporation's EAI increases the corporation's ACB due to 53(1)(e), even though the corporation may deduct an amount, as a reserve, under 34.2(11) for the QTI that includes the EAI. 53(2)(c)(i.4) effectively reduces the corporation's ACB to what it would have been without 53(1)(e). This reduction of the ACB of a partner's interest is tied to the corporation's entitlement to a reserve for QTI for the partnership under 34.2. For the first taxation year for which the corporation is eligible to deduct an amount as a reserve for its QTI for the partnership under 34.2(11), the ACB reduction is the portion of the amount deducted by the corporation for the first taxation year in which it has the QTI that would have been deductible for that year if 34.2(1)"QTI" did not include adjusted stub period accrual. For any other taxation year, the ACB reduction is the portion of the amount that would have been deducted for the preceding year if 34.2(1)"QTI" did not include adjusted stub period accrual. The ACB of a passive corporate partner's partnership interest will not be reduced in two cases. First, there is no reduction immediately before the interest is disposed of. Second, there is no reduction in respect of adjusted stub period accrual amounts included in a corporation's QTI in respect of a partnership. This is not necessary since such amounts are not added to the ACB of the partner's partnership interest. (Finance Technical Notes)

For interpretation of "reasonably be attributed" in 53(2)(c)(vi), see *729658 Alberta*, 2004 TCC 474.

See also Notes to 53(1)(e).

53(2)(c)(i)(C) amended by 2017 budget bill #2, effective Sept. 16, 2016, to add references to 112(4) and (5.2). For discussion of this amendment see Gina Yew & Richard Marcovitz, "Cost of Partnership Interest and the Dividend Stop-Loss Rules", 24(11) *Canadian Tax Highlights* (ctf.ca) 10-11 (Nov. 2016).

53(2)(c) amended by 2002-2013 technical bill (last changes effective for amounts that became payable, or gifts made, after Dec. 20, 2002); 2012 budget bill #2 (effective March 29, 2012); 2011 budget bill #2; 2000 and 1998 Budgets; 1995-97 technical bill; 1996, 1995 and 1994 Budgets.

I.T. Application Rules: 26(9)–(9.4) (where taxpayer became partner before 1972); 69 (meaning of "chapter 148 of ...").

Interpretation Bulletins: IT-242R: Retired partners; IT-278R2: Death of a partner or of a retired partner; IT-338R2: Partnership interests — effects on ACB of admission or retirement of a partner (cancelled); IT-341R4: Expenses of issuing shares, units in a trust, interests in a partnership or syndicate and expenses of borrowing money; IT-353R2: Partnership interests — some adjustments to cost base (cancelled).

I.T. Technical News: 5 (adjusted cost base of partnership interest); 9 (calculation of ACB of a partnership interest).

Forms: T2065: Determination of adjusted cost base of a partnership interest.

(d) **[part of property retained]** — where the property is such that the taxpayer has, after 1971 and before that time, disposed of a part of it while retaining another part of it, the amount deter-

mined under section 43 to be the adjusted cost base to the taxpayer of the part so disposed of;

Interpretation Bulletins: IT-200: Surface rentals and farming operations.

(e) **[share acquired before August 1976]** — if the property is a share, or an interest in or a right to — or, for civil law, a right in or to — a share, of the capital stock of a corporation acquired before August 1976, an amount equal to any expense incurred by the taxpayer in consideration therefor, to the extent that the expense was, by virtue of

(i) paragraph (e) of the definition "Canadian exploration and development expenses" in subsection 66(15), a Canadian exploration and development expense,

(ii) paragraph (i) of the definition "Canadian exploration expense" in subsection 66.1(6), a Canadian exploration expense,

(iii) paragraph (g) of the definition "Canadian development expense" in subsection 66.2(5), a Canadian development expense, or

(iv) paragraph (c) of the definition "Canadian oil and gas property expense" in subsection 66.4(5), a Canadian oil and gas property expense

incurred by the taxpayer;

Notes: 53(2)(e) opening words amended by 2002-2013 technical bill (Part 4 — bijuralism), effective June 26, 2013, to add "or, for civil law, a right in or to".

(f) **[consideration from joint exploration corporation]** — where the property was received by the taxpayer as consideration for any payment or loan

(i) made before April 20, 1983 by the taxpayer as a shareholder corporation (within the meaning assigned by subsection 66(15)) to a joint exploration corporation of the shareholder, and

(ii) described in paragraph (a) of the definition "agreed portion" in subsection 66(15),

or the property was substituted for such a property, such portion of the payment or loan as may reasonably be considered to be related to an agreed portion (within the meaning assigned by subsection 66(15)) of the joint exploration corporation's

(iii) Canadian exploration and development expenses,

(iv) Canadian exploration expense,

(v) Canadian development expense, or

(vi) Canadian oil and gas property expense,

as the case may be;

Related Provisions: 248(5) — Substituted property.

(f.1) **[share of joint exploration corporation]** — where the property is a share of the capital stock of a joint exploration corporation resident in Canada and the taxpayer has, after 1971, made a contribution of capital to the corporation otherwise than by way of a loan, which contribution was included in computing the adjusted cost base of the property by virtue of paragraph (1)(c), such portion of the contribution as may reasonably be considered to be part of an agreed portion (within the meaning assigned by subsection 66(15)) of the corporation's

(i) Canadian exploration and development expenses,

(ii) Canadian exploration expense,

(iii) Canadian development expense, or

(iv) Canadian oil and gas property expense,

as the case may be;

(f.2) **[resource expenses renounced by joint exploration corporation]** — any amount required by paragraph 66(10.4)(a) to be deducted before that time in computing the adjusted cost base to the taxpayer of the property;

Advance Tax Rulings: ATR-60: Joint exploration corporations.

(g) **[debt forgiveness]** — where section 80 is applicable in respect of the taxpayer, the amount, if any, by which the adjusted cost base to the taxpayer of the property is required in prescribed manner to be reduced before that time;

Regulations: none (Reg. 5400(1) repealed).

(g.1) [history preservation rules — debt forgiveness] — any amount required under paragraph (4)(a), (5)(a), (6)(a), 47(1)(c), 49(3.01)(a), 51(1)(d.1), 86(4)(a) or 87(5.1)(a) or (6.1)(a) to be deducted in computing the adjusted cost base to the taxpayer of the property or any amount by which that adjusted cost base is required to be reduced because of subsection 80(9), (10) or (11);

Related Provisions: 80.03(2), (3) — Gain on subsequent "surrender" of property; 107(1)(a) — Reduction in gain on disposition of capital interest in trust.

Notes: The provisions listed in 53(2)(g.1) are referred to informally as the "history preservation rules", since under 80.03(2)(a) they may result in a subsequent deemed capital gain.

53(2)(g.1) added by 1994 technical bill, effective for taxation years that end after February 21, 1994. See Notes to 47(1).

Interpretation Bulletins: IT-96R6: Options to acquire shares, bonds or debentures and by trusts to acquire trust units.

(h) [capital interest in trust] — where the property is a capital interest of the taxpayer in a trust (other than an interest in a personal trust that has never been acquired for consideration or an interest of a taxpayer in a trust described in any of paragraphs (a) to (e.1) of the definition "trust" in subsection 108(1)),

(i) any amount paid to the taxpayer by the trust after 1971 and before that time as a distribution or payment of capital by the trust (otherwise than as proceeds of disposition of the interest or part thereof), to the extent that the amount became payable before 1988,

(i.1) any amount that has become payable to the taxpayer by the trust after 1987 and before that time in respect of the interest (otherwise than as proceeds of disposition of the interest or part thereof), except to the extent of the portion thereof

(A) that was included in the taxpayer's income by reason of subsection 104(13) or from which an amount of tax was deducted under Part XIII by reason of paragraph 212(1)(c),

(A.1) that was deemed by subsection 104(16) to be a dividend received by the taxpayer, or

(B) where the trust was resident in Canada throughout its taxation year in which the amount became payable

(I) that is equal to the amount designated by the trust under subsection 104(21) in respect of the taxpayer,

(II) that was designated by the trust under subsection 104(20) in respect of the taxpayer, or

(III) that is an assessable distribution (as defined in subsection 218.3(1)) to the taxpayer,

(ii) an amount equal to that portion of all amounts deducted under subsection 127(5) in computing the tax otherwise payable by the taxpayer under this Part for the taxpayer's taxation years ending before that time that may reasonably be attributed to amounts added in computing the investment tax credit of the taxpayer by virtue of subsection 127(7),

(iii) any amount added pursuant to subsection 127.2(3) in computing the taxpayer's share-purchase tax credit for a taxation year ending before or after that time,

(iv) an amount equal to 50% of the amount deemed to be designated pursuant to subsection 127.3(3) before that time in respect of each share, debt obligation or right acquired by the trust and deemed to have been acquired by the taxpayer under that subsection, and

(v) an amount equal to the amount of all assistance received by the taxpayer before that time that has resulted in a reduction of the capital cost of a depreciable property to the trust by virtue of subsection 13(7.2);

Related Provisions: 53(1)(d.1) — Additions to ACB — capital interest in non-resident trust; 53(2)(i), (j) — further deduction from ACB of interest in a trust;

87(2)(j.6) — Amalgamation — continuing corporation; 94(3)(a)(iv) — Application to trust deemed resident in Canada; 104(20) — Designation re non-taxable dividends; 104(24) — Whether amount payable to beneficiary; 107(1.2) — Fair market value of trust interest that is not capital property; 108(6) — Where terms of trust are varied; 108(7) — Meaning of "acquired for consideration"; 127(12.2) — Interpretation; 248(1)"personal trust" — Where interest deemed acquired for no consideration; 248(25.3) — Deemed cost of trust interest; 250(6.1) — Trust that ceases to exist deemed resident throughout year.

Notes: For examples of 53(2)(h)(i.1) applying, see VIEWS docs 2007-0253861I7, 2008-0264181E5, 2008-0281441E5, 2008-0284261C6, 2009-0330291C6. Where a corporate beneficiary has a different year-end than the trust, see CRA May 2007 ICAA roundtable (tinyurl.com/cra-abtax), Q8.

For interpretation of "reasonably be attributed" in 53(2)(h)(ii), see *729658 Alberta Ltd.*, 2004 TCC 474.

53(2)(h) amended by 2007 Budget (effective Oct. 31, 2006), 2004 Budget, 2001 technical bill, 2000 Budget.

Interpretation Bulletins: IT-342R: Trusts: Income payable to beneficiaries; IT-381R3: Trusts — capital gains and losses and the flow-through of taxable capital gains to beneficiaries; IT-390: Unit trusts — cost of rights and adjustments to cost base (cancelled); IT-456R: Capital property — some adjustments to cost base.

(i) [capital interest in non-resident trust] — where the property is a capital interest in a trust (other than a unit trust) not resident in Canada that was purchased after 1971 and before that time by the taxpayer from a non-resident person at a time (in this paragraph referred to as the "purchase time") when the property was not taxable Canadian property and the fair market value of such of the trust property as was

(i) a Canadian resource property,

(ii) [Repealed under former Act]

(iii) an income interest in a trust resident in Canada,

(iv) taxable Canadian property, or

(v) a timber resource property

was not less than 50% of the fair market value of all the trust property, that proportion of the amount, if any, by which

(vi) the fair market value at the purchase time of such of the trust properties as were properties described in any of subparagraphs (i) to (v)

exceeds

(vii) the total of the cost amounts to the trust at the purchase time of such of the trust properties as were properties described in any of subparagraphs (i) to (v),

that the fair market value at the purchase time of the interest is of the fair market value at the purchase time of all capital interests in the trust;

Notes: 53(2)(i) amended by 2001 technical bill, effective for the purpose of computing the ACB of property after April 26, 1995.

(j) [unit of non-resident unit trust] — where the property is a unit of a unit trust not resident in Canada that was purchased after 1971 and before that time by the taxpayer from a non-resident person at a time (in this paragraph referred to as the "purchase time") when the property was not taxable Canadian property and the fair market value of such of the trust property as was

(i) a Canadian resource property,

(ii) [Repealed under former Act]

(iii) an income interest in a trust resident in Canada,

(iv) taxable Canadian property, or

(v) a timber resource property

was not less than 50% of the fair market value of all the trust property, that proportion of the amount, if any, by which

(vi) the fair market value at the purchase time of such of the trust properties as were properties described in any of subparagraphs (i) to (v)

exceeds

(vii) the total of the cost amounts to the trust at the purchase time of such of the trust properties as were properties described in any of subparagraphs (i) to (v), that the fair market value at the purchase time of the unit is of the fair market value at the purchase time of all the issued units of the trust;

Notes: Opening words of 53(2)(j) amended by 2001 technical bill, effective for the purpose of computing the ACB of property after April 26, 1995.

53(2)(j) after para. (v) amended by 2001 technical bill, effective for the purpose of computing ACB of property after April 26, 1995.

(k) **[government assistance received or receivable]** — where the property was acquired by the taxpayer after 1971, the amount, if any, by which the total of

(i) the amount of any assistance which the taxpayer has received or is entitled to receive before that time from a government, municipality or other public authority, in respect of, or for the acquisition of, the property, whether as a grant, subsidy, forgivable loan, deduction from tax not otherwise provided for under this paragraph, investment allowance or as any other form of assistance other than

(A) an amount described in paragraph 37(1)(d),

(B) an amount deducted as an allowance under section 65,

(C) the amount of prescribed assistance that the taxpayer has received or is entitled to receive in respect of, or for the acquisition of, shares of the capital stock of a prescribed venture capital corporation or a prescribed labour-sponsored venture capital corporation or shares of the capital stock of a taxable Canadian corporation that are held in a prescribed stock savings plan, or

(D) an amount included in income by virtue of paragraph 12(1)(u) or 56(1)(s), and

(ii) all amounts deducted under subsection 127(5) or (6) in respect of the property before that time,

exceeds such part, if any, of the assistance referred to in subparagraph (i) as has been repaid before that time by the taxpayer pursuant to an obligation to repay all or any part of that assistance;

Related Provisions: 39(13) — Repaid assistance deemed a capital loss; 125.4(5) — Canadian film/video credit deemed to be assistance; 125.5(5) — Film/video production services credit deemed to be assistance; 127(12.2) — Interpretation; 127.4(1)"net cost"(b) — Labour-sponsored venture capital corporation; 248(16), (16.1) — GST or QST input tax credit/refund and rebate deemed to be assistance; 248(18), (18.1) — GST or QST — repayment of input tax credit or refund.

Notes: 53(2)(k)(i)(C) amended by 1993 technical bill, for 1991 and later tax years, to change "has been provided" to "that the taxpayer has received or is entitled to receive". Thus, prescribed assistance (Reg. 6702) receivable (as well as received) in respect of a share does not reduce the share's ACB. 40(2)(i)(ii) provides that such assistance reduces any capital loss on disposition of the share. See VIEWS doc 2005-0153771E5. See also 12(1)(x) Notes for meaning of "assistance" and related words.

Regulations: 6700, 6700.1 (prescribed venture capital corporation); 6701 (prescribed labour-sponsored venture capital corporation); 6702 (prescribed assistance); 6705 (prescribed stock savings plan).

Interpretation Bulletins: IT-273R2: Government assistance — general comments.

CRA Audit Manual: 27.20.4: Inducement payments — capital property other than depreciable property.

(l) **[debt obligation]** — where the property is a debt obligation, any amount that was deductible by virtue of subsection 20(14) in computing the taxpayer's income for any taxation year commencing before that time in respect of interest on that debt obligation;

(l.1) **[indexed debt obligation]** — where the property is an indexed debt obligation,

(i) any amount determined under subparagraph 16(6)(a)(ii) in respect of the obligation and deductible in computing the income of the taxpayer for a taxation year beginning before that time, and

(ii) the amount of any payment that was received or that became receivable by the taxpayer at or before that time in respect of an amount that was added under paragraph (1)(g.1) to the cost to the taxpayer of the obligation;

Related Provisions: 53(1)(g.1) — Addition to adjusted cost base — indexed debt obligation.

Notes: 53(2)(l.1) added by 1992 technical bill, for indexed debt obligations issued after Oct. 16, 1991.

(m) **[amounts deducted from income]** — any part of the cost to the taxpayer of the property that was deductible (otherwise than because of this Subdivision or paragraph 8(1)(r)) in computing the taxpayer's income for any taxation year commencing before that time and ending after 1971;

Notes: 53(2)(m) amended by 2001 Budget, effective 2002, to add reference to 8(1)(r).

Interpretation Bulletins: IT-350R: Investigation of site; IT-456R: Capital property — some adjustments to cost base.

(n) **[expropriation asset]** — where the property is an expropriation asset of the taxpayer (within the meaning assigned by section 80.1) or an asset of the taxpayer assumed for the purposes of that section to be an expropriation asset thereof, any amount required by paragraph 80.1(2)(b) to be deducted in computing the adjusted cost base to the taxpayer of the asset;

Related Provisions: 53(1)(k) — Addition to ACB of expropriation asset.

(o) **[right to receive partnership property]** — where the property is a right to receive partnership property within the meaning assigned by paragraph 98.2(a) or 100(3)(a), any amount received by the taxpayer in full or partial satisfaction of that right;

(p) **[debt owing by corporation]** — where the property is a debt owing to the taxpayer by a corporation, any amount required to be deducted before that time under section 84.1 of the *Income Tax Act*, chapter 148 of the Revised Statutes of Canada, 1952, as it applied before May 23, 1985 or subsection 84.2(2) in computing the adjusted cost base to the taxpayer of the debt;

I.T. Application Rules: 69 (meaning of "chapter 148 of ...").

(q) **[interest in related segregated fund trust]** — where the property is an interest in a related segregated fund trust referred to in section 138.1,

(i) each amount in respect of that interest that is a capital loss deemed to have been allocated under subsection 138.1(4) to the taxpayer before that time, and

(ii) each amount in respect of that interest that before that time was deemed by subsection 138.1(3) to be a capital loss of the taxpayer;

Related Provisions: 53(1)(l) — Addition to ACB of interest in related segregated fund trust; 138.1(5) — ACB of property in related segregated fund trust.

(r) [Repealed under former Act]

Notes: 53(2)(r) repealed by 1986 Budget, for dividends paid after May 23, 1985. It related to dividends on a share where the corporation had made an 83(2.1) election.

(s) **[government assistance — amount elected under 53(2.1)]** — the amount, if any, by which

(i) the amount elected by the taxpayer before that time under subsection (2.1)

exceeds

(ii) any repayment before that time by the taxpayer of an amount received by the taxpayer as described in subsection (2.1) that may reasonably be considered to relate to the amount elected where the repayment is made pursuant to a legal obligation to repay all or any part of the amount so received;

Related Provisions: 12(1)(t) — Income inclusion — investment tax credit; 12(1)(x) — Payments as inducement or as reimbursement etc.; 39(13) — Repayment of assistance; 40(3) — Deemed capital gain when ACB goes negative; 53(2.1) — Election; 87(2)(j.6) — Amalgamation — continuing corporation.

Interpretation Bulletins: IT-273R2: Government assistance — general comments.

CRA Audit Manual: 27.20.4: Inducement payments — capital property other than depreciable property.

(t) **[right to acquire shares or fund units]** — if the property is a right to acquire shares or units under an agreement, any amount required by paragraph 164(6.1)(b) to be deducted in computing the adjusted cost base to the taxpayer of the right;

Notes: 53(2)(t) amended to add "or units" by 1998 Budget, effective March 1998. This was consequential on extending s. 7 to mutual fund units (see Notes to 7(1)).

53(2)(t) added by 1992 technical bill, effective July 14, 1990.

I.T. Application Rules: 26(3).

Interpretation Bulletins: IT-456R: Capital property — some adjustments to cost base.

(u) **[non-qualifying real property]** — where the property was at the end of February 22, 1994 a non-qualifying real property (within the meaning assigned by subsection 110.6(1) as that subsection applies to the 1994 taxation year) of a taxpayer, any amount required by paragraph 110.6(21)(b) to be deducted in computing the adjusted cost base to the taxpayer of the property;

Notes: 53(2)(u) added by 1994 Budget, effective 1994.

(v) **[excessive capital gains election]** — where the taxpayer elected under subsection 110.6(19) in respect of the property, any amount required by subsection 110.6(22) to be deducted in computing the adjusted cost base to the taxpayer of the property at that time;

Notes: 53(2)(v) added by 1994 Budget, effective 1994.

(w) **[where loss on derivative forward agreement]** — if the property was acquired under a derivative forward agreement, any amount deductible in respect of the property under paragraph 20(1)(xx) in computing the income of the taxpayer for a taxation year; and

Related Provisions: 53(2)(x) — Where property disposed of under DFA.

Notes: See Notes to 248(1)"derivative forward agreement". 53(2)(w) added by 2013 budget bill #2, effective March 21, 2013.

(x) **[where loss on derivative forward agreement]** — if the property is disposed of under a derivative forward agreement, any amount deductible in respect of the property under paragraph 20(1)(xx) in computing the income of the taxpayer for the taxation year that includes that time.

Related Provisions: 53(2)(w) — Where property acquired under DFA.

Notes: See Notes to 248(1)"derivative forward agreement". 53(2)(x) added by 2013 budget bill #2, effective March 21, 2013.

Notes [subsec. 53(2)]: Subsec. 4(4) of the *Western Grain Transition Payments Act* (1995, c. 17, Sch. II), as amended by 1995-97 technical bill (s. 303), provides rules for the tax treatment of transition payments received in respect of farmland, effective for payments made after June 22, 1995.

I.T. Technical News: 5 (western grain transition payments).

(2.1) Election — For the purpose of paragraph (2)(s), where in a taxation year a taxpayer receives an amount that would, but for this subsection, be included in the taxpayer's income under paragraph 12(1)(x) in respect of the cost of a property (other than depreciable property) acquired by the taxpayer in the year, in the 3 taxation years preceding the year or in the taxation year following the year, the taxpayer may elect under this subsection on or before the date on or before which the taxpayer's return of income under this Part for the year is required to be filed or, where the property is acquired in the following year, for that following year, to reduce the cost of the property by such amount as the taxpayer specifies, not exceeding the least of

(a) the adjusted cost base, determined without reference to paragraph (2)(s), at the time the property was acquired,

(b) the amount so received by the taxpayer, and

(c) where the taxpayer has disposed of the property before the year, nil.

Related Provisions: 87(2)(j.6) — Amalgamation — continuing corporation; 220(3.2), Reg. 600(b) — Late filing or revocation of election.

Notes: Opening words of 53(2.1) amended by 1992 technical bill, effective 1991, to introduce the exclusion "(other than depreciable property)".

Interpretation Bulletins: IT-273R2: Government assistance — general comments; IT-456R: Capital property — some adjustments to cost base.

CRA Audit Manual: 27.20.4: Inducement payments — capital property other than depreciable property; 27.20.5: Inducement payments — elective provisions.

(3) [Repealed]

Notes: 53(3) repealed by 2001 technical bill, effective October 2, 1996 (consequential on new definition 248(1)"taxable Canadian property"). It deemed property to be TCP for purposes of 53(2)(i) and (j).

(4) Recomputation of adjusted cost base on transfers and deemed dispositions — If at any time in a taxation year a person or partnership (in this subsection referred to as the "vendor") disposes of a specified property and the proceeds of disposition of the property are determined under paragraph 48.1(1)(c), section 70 or 73, subsection 85(1), paragraph 87(4)(a) or (c) or 88(1)(a), subsection 97(2) or 98(2), paragraph 98(3)(f) or (5)(f), subsection 104(4), paragraph 107(2)(a) or (2.1)(a), 107.4(3)(a) or 111(4)(e) or section 128.1,

(a) there shall be deducted after that time in computing the adjusted cost base to the person or partnership (in this subsection referred to as the "transferee") who acquires or reacquires the property at or immediately after that time the amount, if any, by which

(i) the total of all amounts deducted under paragraph (2)(g.1) in computing, immediately before that time, the adjusted cost base to the vendor of the property,

exceeds

(ii) the amount that would be the vendor's capital gain for the year from that disposition if this Act were read without reference to subparagraph 40(1)(a)(iii) and subsection 100(2); and

(b) the amount determined under paragraph (a) in respect of that disposition shall be added after that time in computing the adjusted cost base to the transferee of the property.

Related Provisions: 53(1)(q) — Addition to adjusted cost base for amount under 53(4)(b); 53(2)(g.1) — Reduction in adjusted cost base under 53(4)(a); 53(5) — Recomputation of ACB on other transfers; 80.03(2)(a) — Deemed gain on disposition following debt forgiveness; 251(1) — Arm's length.

Notes: 53(4) applies only to "specified property" as defined in 54 (shares, partnership or trust interests, or options on any of these), and its only significance is for the future application of 80.03. See Notes to 47(1).

53(4) opening words amended by 2002-2013 technical bill (Part 5 — technical), effective Feb. 28, 2004.

53(4) amended by 2001 technical bill (effective 1998 and later taxation years) and 1995-97 technical bill. Added by 1994 technical bill.

(5) Recomputation of adjusted cost base on other transfers — Where

(a) at any time in a taxation year a person or partnership (in this subsection referred to as the "vendor") disposes of a specified property to another person or partnership (in this subsection referred to as the "transferee"),

(b) immediately before that time, the vendor and the transferee do not deal with each other at arm's length or would not deal with each other at arm's length if paragraph 80(2)(j) applied for the purpose of this subsection,

(c) paragraph (b) would apply in respect of the disposition if each right referred to in paragraph 251(5)(b) that is a right of the transferee to acquire the specified property from the vendor or a right of the transferee to acquire other property as part of a transaction or event or series of transactions or events that includes the disposition were not taken into account, and

(d) the proceeds of the disposition are not determined under any of the provisions referred to in subsection (4),

the following rules apply:

(e) there shall be deducted after that time in computing the adjusted cost base to the transferee of the property the amount, if any, by which

(i) the total of all amounts deducted under paragraph (2)(g.1) in computing the adjusted cost base to the vendor of the property immediately before that time

exceeds

(ii) the amount that would be the vendor's capital gain for the year from that disposition if this Act were read without reference to subparagraph 40(1)(a)(iii) and subsection 100(2), and

(f) the amount determined under paragraph (e) in respect of that disposition shall be added after that time in computing the adjusted cost base to the transferee of the property.

Related Provisions: 53(1)(q) — Addition to ACB for amount under 53(5)(b); 53(2)(g.1) — Reduction in ACB under 53(5)(a); 80.03(2)(a) — Deemed gain on disposition following debt forgiveness.

Notes: 53(5) added by 1994 technical bill, for taxation years that end after Feb. 21, 1994, and amended retroactive to its introduction by 1995-97 technical bill. See Notes to 47(1).

(6) Recomputation of adjusted cost base on amalgamation — Where a capital property that is a specified property is acquired by a new corporate entity at any time as a result of the amalgamation or merger of 2 or more predecessor corporations,

(a) there shall be deducted after that time in computing the adjusted cost base to the new entity of the property the total of all amounts deducted under paragraph (2)(g.1) in computing, immediately before that time, the adjusted cost base to a predecessor corporation of the property, unless those amounts are otherwise deducted under that paragraph in computing the adjusted cost base to the new entity of the property; and

(b) the amount deducted under paragraph (a) in respect of the acquisition shall be added after that time in computing the adjusted cost base to the new entity of the property.

Related Provisions: 53(1)(q) — Addition to ACB for amount under 53(6)(b); 53(2)(g.1) — Reduction in ACB under 53(6)(a); 80.03(2)(a) — Deemed gain on disposition following debt forgiveness.

Notes: 53(6) added by 1994 technical bill, effective for taxation years that end after February 21, 1994. See Notes to 47(1).

Definitions [s. 53]: "acquired for consideration" — 108(7); "adjusted cost base" — 54, 248(1); "adjusted cost basis" — 53(1)(e)(iii)(B), 148(9); "agreed portion" — 66(15); "amount" — 248(1); "arm's length" — 251(1); "assessable distribution" — 218.3(1); "assistance" — 79(4), 125.4(5), 248(16), (16.1), (18), (18.1); "business" — 248(1); "Canada" — 255; "Canadian development expense" — 66.2(5), 248(1); "Canadian exploration and development expense" — 66(15), 248(1); "Canadian exploration expense" — 66.1(6), 248(1); "Canadian oil and gas property expense" — 66.4(5), 248(1); "Canadian resource property" — 66(15), 248(1); "capital dividend" — 83(2), 248(1); "capital gain" — 39(1)(a), 248(1); "capital interest" — 108(1), 248(1); "commercial obligation" — 80(1); "consequence of the death" — 248(8); "consideration" — 108(7); "control" — 256(6)–(9); "controlled foreign affiliate" — 17(15); "corporation" — 248(1), *Interpretation Act* 35(1); "cost amount" — 248(1); "depreciable property" — 13(21), 248(1); "derivative forward agreement", "disposition", "dividend" — 248(1); "eligible amount" — 248(31), (41); "expropriation asset" — 80.1(1); "fair market value" — see 69(1) Notes; "farming" — 248(1); "fiscal period" — 249(2)(b), 249.1; "flow-through entity" — 39.1(1); "foreign accrual property income" — 95(1), (2), 248(1); "foreign affiliate" — 95(1), 248(1); "foreign exploration and development expense" — 66(15), 248(1); "foreign investment entity", "foreign resource pool expense" — 248(1); "foreign resource property" — 66(15), 248(1); "gifting arrangement" — 237.1(1); "income bond", "income debenture" — 248(1); "income interest in a trust" — 108(1), 248(1); "indexed debt obligation" — 248(1); "joint exploration corporation" — 66(15); "land" — 18(3), and see 70(5.2) Notes; "life insurance capital dividend" — 83(2.1), 248(1); "life insurance policy" — 138(12), 248(1); "limited partnership loss" — 248(1); "loss restriction event" — 251.2; "mutual fund trust" — 132(6)–(7), 132.2(3)(n), 248(1); "non-qualifying real property" — 110.6(1); "non-resident" — 248(1); "paid-up capital" — 89(1), 248(1); "participating interest" — 248(1); "partnership" — see 96(1) Notes; "person", "personal trust", "prescribed" — 248(1); "prescribed labour-sponsored venture capital corporation" — Reg. 6701; "prescribed venture capital corporation" — Reg. 6700, 6700.1, 6700.2; "principal amount" — 248(1), (26); "property" — 248(1); "province" — *Interpretation Act* 35(1); "qualifying fiscal period" — 34.2(1); "qualifying return of capital" — 90(3); "related" — 251(1); "related segregated fund trust" — 138.1(1)(a); "resident in Canada" — 94(3)(a), 250; "security" — 7(7); "series of transactions" — 248(10); "share", "shareholder", "specified member" — 248(1); "specified amount" — 80.2(1); "specified property" — 54; "specified shareholder" — 248(1); "substituted" — 248(5); "substituted property" — 54"superficial loss"(a); "superficial loss" — 54; "tax shelter" — 237.1(1), 248(1); "taxable Canadian corporation" — 89(1), 248(1); "taxable Canadian property" — 248(1); "taxable dividend" — 89(1), 248(1); "taxable income" — 2(2), 248(1); "taxation year" — 249; "taxpayer" — 248(1); "timber resource property" — 13(21), 248(1); "trust" — 104(1), 248(1), (3); "unit trust" — 108(2), 248(1); "vendor" — 53(4), (5).

54. Definitions — In this Subdivision,

"adjusted cost base" to a taxpayer of any property at any time means, except as otherwise provided,

(a) where the property is depreciable property of the taxpayer, the capital cost to the taxpayer of the property as of that time, and

(b) in any other case, the cost to the taxpayer of the property adjusted, as of that time, in accordance with section 53,

except that

(c) for greater certainty, where any property (other than an interest in or a share of the capital stock of a flow-through entity within the meaning assigned by subsection 39.1(1) that was last reacquired by the taxpayer as a result of an election under subsection 110.6(19)) of the taxpayer is property that was reacquired by the taxpayer after having been previously disposed of by the taxpayer, no adjustment to the cost to the taxpayer of the property that was required to be made under section 53 before its reacquisition by the taxpayer shall be made under that section to the cost to the taxpayer of the property as reacquired property of the taxpayer, and

(d) in no case shall the adjusted cost base to a taxpayer of any property at any time be less than nil;

Related Provisions: 40(1) — Calculation of gain or loss for capital gain/loss purposes; 40(3), (3.1) — Deemed capital gain where ACB is negative; 43 — ACB on partial disposition; 47(1) — ACB of identical properties; 49(1) — Granting of options; 49(2) — Where option expires; 53 — Adjustments to ACB; 69(1)(c) — Deemed acquisition at fair market value in certain circumstances; 84.1(2) — Non-arm's length sale of shares; 91(6) — Amounts deductible in respect of dividends received; 92 — ACB of share of foreign affiliate; 93(4)(b) — Loss on disposition of shares of foreign affiliate; 110.6(19)(a)(ii) — Increase in cost base on capital gains exemption election; 139.1(4)(d) — Cost of share acquired on insurance demutualization deemed nil; 142.4(1)"tax basis" — cost base for securities held by financial institutions; 143.2(6) — Deemed cost reduction of tax shelter investment; 248(1)"adjusted cost base" — Definition applies to entire Act; 261(7)(b), (c) — Cost of property when functional currency election made; Canada-U.S. Tax Treaty:Art. XXIX:5(d) — Reduction in ACB of share of U.S. "S" corporation.

Notes: In simple terms, ACB is the cost of (non-depreciable capital) property, adjusted up by 53(1) and down by 53(2).

"Cost" means "the price that the taxpayer gave up in order to get the asset; it does not include any expense that he may have incurred in order to put himself in a position to pay that price or to keep the property afterwards": *Stirling*, [1985] 1 C.T.C. 275 (FCA); *Coast Capital*, 2016 FCA 181, para. 31. Thus, "interest on money borrowed to acquire property for the purpose of making a capital gain" is not part of ACB: *Kokai-Kuun*, 2015 TCC 217, para. 45, though such interest was allowed in *Turner*, 2016 TCC 77, para. 24 (FCA appeal discontinued A-124-16) (the Crown seems to have agreed: para. 14). See also McNair, *The Meaning of Cost* (ctf.ca, Canadian Tax Paper No. 69, 1982, 277pp.); Lamarre, "Critical Issues in the Determination of Cost", 2012 Cdn Tax Foundation conference report, 17:1-33.

Capital expenses denied by 18(1)(b) are included in ACB even if they were wrongly deducted from income in an earlier year that is now statute-barred: *Peach*, 2020 TCC 12, para. 67 (under appeal to FCA).

Current expenses (see Notes to 18(1)(b)) to maintain a property, such as mortgage interest or condo fees, that are not deductible because the property is not used to earn income, *cannot* be treated as part of the cost on selling it: *Eskandari*, 2007 TCC 419; *Firth*, 2009 TCC 137; *Brousseau Estate*, 2012 TCC 390; *D'Anjou*, 2008 QCCQ 7197 and 2019 TCC 208, para. 29; but see 53(1)(h), which adds to ACB certain expenses denied by 18(2); Lewin, "Tax Attributes", 1998 Cdn Tax Foundation conference report, 8:1-17; VIEWS docs 2010-0352971I7, 2012-0471741E5, 2013-0485721E5, 2015-0606511I7. Similarly, interest that CRA allows to be capitalized under s. 21 solely for a non-resident's s. 216 return cannot be deducted against the capital gain when selling the building: CRA Round Table, 2010 conference report, q.24, p. 4:23-24.

For the ACB of property seized by the Nazis and returned years later, see Notes to 81(1)(g).

Where the taxpayer has no records of the original cost of gold, CRA will accept an estimated cost: VIEWS doc 2010-0380771M4.

Paras. (c), (d) amended by 1994 Budget, effective 1994 and later taxation years. 54"adjusted cost base" was 54(a) before RSC 1985 (5th Supp) consolidation for tax years ending after Nov. 1991.

Regulations: 4400, Sch. VII (ACB of publicly-traded shares at end of 1971).

I.T. Application Rules: 26(3)–(27) (where property owned since before 1972).

Income Tax Folios: S3-F4-C1: General discussion of CCA [replaces IT-418].

Interpretation Bulletins: IT-65: Stock splits and consolidations; IT-102R2: Conversion of property, other than real property, from or to inventory; IT-218R: Profit, capital gains and losses from the sale of real estate, including farmland and inherited land and conversion of real estate from capital property to inventory and vice versa.

I.T. Technical News: 9 (calculation of ACB of a partnership interest); 39 (settlement of a shareholder class action suit).

Advance Tax Rulings: ATR-67: Increase in the cost of property on the winding-up of a wholly-owned subsidiary.

Forms: T2065: Determination of adjusted cost base of a partnership interest.

"capital property" of a taxpayer means

(a) any depreciable property of the taxpayer, and

(b) any property (other than depreciable property), any gain or loss from the disposition of which would, if the property were disposed of, be a capital gain or a capital loss, as the case may be, of the taxpayer;

Related Provisions: 27.1 — Emissions allowances treated as inventory; 39(1) — Determination of capital gain and capital loss; 39(4) — Election to treat Canadian securities as capital property; 54.2 — Shares deemed to be capital property where all assets of business transferred; 66.3(1)(a)(i) — Certain exploration and development shares deemed not to be capital property; 96(1.4) — Certain rights to share in income or loss of partnership deemed not to be capital property; 142.5(1) — Mark-to-market rules for financial institutions; 152(4)(b.3) — Extended reassessment period if disposition not reported; 248(1)"capital property" — Definition applies to entire Act.

Notes: Gains on capital property (**CP**) are only half-taxed (38(a)), but proceeds are fully taxable if they are based on use or production from the CP: 12(1)(g). Capital expenses are non-deductible (18(1)(b)), but are added to ACB (54"adjusted cost base") to reduce future gain, and for depreciable CP are allowed over time as capital cost allowance (20(1)(a)). See also Notes to 248(1)"property", 54"proceeds of disposition".

This definition looks circular. The real definition is in 39(1)(a), which in effect defines CP by excluding everything else. For example, a mining claim that is Canadian resource property is excluded: see Notes to 39(1).

CP is distinguished from inventory (**INV**) that, when sold, leads to business income. All property is one or the other: *Friesen*, [1995] 2 C.T.C. 369 (SCC); *Hollinger Inc.*, [1999] 4 C.T.C. 61 (FCA), paras. 36-37; *CAE Inc.*, 2013 FCA 92, paras. 75-84 (on a change in use from one to the other, 13(7) or 45(1) applies); but *contra* see *Kruger Inc.*, 2016 FCA 186, paras. 95-100, ruling that foreign exchange contracts not held for sale were neither CP nor INV despite *Friesen*. "Business" is defined in 248(1) to include an "adventure in the nature of trade", so a one-time purchase for resale is INV. Property that a lessee has a binding right to purchase under an option is INV, even if a sale is unlikely: *CAE Inc.*, para. 108. See also Carl Irvine case comment on *CAE Inc.*, 61(3) *Canadian Tax Journal* 729-39 (2013). On the distinction between "business" and "adventure in the nature of trade", see Notes to 10(1.01).

Intention is the key test: property purchased with the intention (including secondary intention) of selling at a profit is INV, while property purchased to generate income (e.g. dividends, rent) is CP: *Irrigation Industries*, [1962] C.T.C. 215 (SCC); *Canada Safeway*, 2008 FCA 24 (for "secondary intention" to apply, it "must have been an operating motivation in the acquisition of the property": para. 61); *Fiducie Charbonneau*, 2010 QCCA 400; *Taylor*, [1956] C.T.C. 189 (Ex. Ct.); *Happy Valley Farms*, [1986] 2 C.T.C. 259 (FCTD); *Paletta*, 2019 TCC 205, paras. 280-316 (under appeal to FCA). For CRA interpretation see IT-218R, IT-459. See also 18(1)(b) Notes re capital vs. current expenses; and 40(2)(b) Notes at "Inventory".

Inventory must be "held for sale": *Kruger Inc.*, 2016 FCA 186, paras. 87-91. For a detailed challenge to this view based on *Friesen*, see Hegedus, "Only Property Held for Sale?", XV(1) *Resource Sector Taxation* (Federated Press) 9-20 (2021). Acquisition in order to donate to charity is not "adventure in the nature of trade" as there is no profit, so the property is CP: *Whent*, [2000] 1 C.T.C. 329 (FCA) (leave to appeal denied 2000 CarswellNat 2397 (SCC)); VIEWS doc 2012-0438651E5; GST/HST Headquarters letter 53926. The same applies to flow-through shares (see 66(12.6)) purchased for immediate sale at a cash loss but a tax gain: *Loewen*, [1994] 2 C.T.C. 75 (FCA) [dealt with the pre-1986 Scientific Research Tax Credit, but the same principle applies]; *Gervais* (see next para.).

Length of ownership: If property is acquired for resale, the passage of even 13 or 30 years without sale does not change its status as INV: *Esar*, [1974] C.T.C. 34 (FCTD); *Orzeck*, [1987] 2 C.T.C. 2318 (TCC); *Chen*, 2012 TCC 215, para. 21. Conversely, property can be CP despite an unexpected sale soon after acquisition: *Gold*, 1962 CarswellNat 182 (TAB); *Rochefort*, 2019 QCCQ 2660, para. 169; *Cristofaro*, 2019 QCCQ 6242. Acquisition by a creditor for immediate sale was income in *Saskatchewan Wheat Pool*, 2008 TCC 8. CP rolled into a corporation remains CP even if the corp sells it immediately: see Notes to 85(1). If substantially all assets of a business are rolled into a corp under 85(1), the shares taken back are CP: see 54.2. In *Gervais*, 2016 FCA 1, shares bought under a pre-arrangement to sell them soon for no cash profit (but a tax gain) were CP (para. 32); shares received as a gift under the same pre-arrangement to sell were also CP (para. 37). (The matter was sent back to consider GAAR, which applied: 2018 FCA 3.) In *Gosai*, 2020 CarswellNat 4376 (TCC), the Court agreed that for a new condo, the length of ownership is measured from signing the pre-construction agreement of purchase.

Change in intention: a clear change can turn CP into INV (or vice-versa) as of that date. See Notes to 45(1). In *Hughes*, [1984] C.T.C. 101 (FCTD), an apartment building was CP until the owner decided to convert it to condos and sell the units, so the gain up to that decision was capital gain; in *Bodine*, 2011 FCA 157, rolling long-held farmland into a partnership so as to sell it caused it to be INV when sold (but for an 85(1) rollover see previous para.; perhaps the difference is that partners still own the partnership property). *Contra*, in *Latulippe*, 2019 QCCA 2177, subdividing a co-ownership capital property into saleable units before selling (a step with low cost and risk) did not change its status. In the author's view, *Hughes* is correct: if a taxpayer starts actively trying to develop and market property held for years as capital property, that may be business activity; but there is a *current* change in use under 45(1)(a)(i) triggering capital gain to current date, rather than treating earlier accrued gain as income. See also IT-218R para. 15 and docs 9600785, 2011-0430411E5, 2012-0467841E5: CRA considers conversion from CP to INV to trigger capital gain to that date but not to be reportable until *actual* disposition; this view was upheld in *Polonovski*, 2020 QCCQ 8943, paras. 206-211 (so P could not claim gain was in statute-barred year).

Buildings (existing) were held to be CP in: *Perelmutter*, 2010 TCC 349 (nursing home); *9067-9051 Québec*, 2011 TCC 456 (building destroyed by fire; owner had intended to use it); *Belcourt Properties*, 2014 TCC 208 (company was in business of buying and selling real estate, but 2 properties were bought for rental; CRA had failed to assume "secondary intention" when assessing); *Cristofaro*, 2019 QCCQ 6242 (C intended to renovate and rent out property, but cost became too high; second property was intended for mother to live in).

Buildings (existing) were held to be INV in: *Dubé*, 2005 TCC 779 (buying and selling several buildings); *Zaenker*, 2007 TCC 440 (business of buying and selling properties); *Smitlener*, 2009 TCC 268 (apartments could not have been profitable as rentals); *Chartrand*, 2010 TCC 92 (many small apartment buildings rented out were still INV); *Ayala*, 2010 TCC 206 (taxpayer bought, renovated and resold buildings); *Wiens*, 2011 TCC 152 (purchased with resale intention); *Constantin*, 2014 TCC 327 (multiple buildings, short holding periods); *9228-2987 Québec*, 2019 TCC 281 (intention was to renovate apartment buildings and sell them); *Immeubles Zamora*, 2020 QCCA 894 (secondary intention).

Buildings (new): see *Bélanger*, 2012 TCC 93 (builder with pattern of building and selling had secondary intention to sell apartment complex that he claimed he had intended to hold as capital). See also 40(2)(b) Notes re homes/condos that taxpayers treated as principal residences but CRA assessed as INV; and "Land" below.

Client lists are normally CP. Before 2017 they could be eligible capital property (see Notes to 20(1)(b)): *Gifford*, 2004 SCC 15. In *Bergeron*, 2013 TCC 13 (FCA appeal discontinued A-68-13), deferred closing fees paid to a broker after transfer of client accounts were payment for services, not property. See also VIEWS doc 2007-0242451C6 (broker's "management right" to a client list is CP).

Commodities including gold are normally INV: *Southco Holdings*, [1975] C.T.C. 2205 (TRB); IT-346R para. 5; VIEWS docs 2008-0292461E5, 2010-0352971I7, 2010-0381521E5, 2011-0392061E5. However, gold was held to be CP in *Harms*, [1984] C.T.C. 2714 (TCC) (taxpayer was convinced the economy would collapse and acquired gold as security for use in a future barter system); and was accepted as CP (other issues were in dispute) in *Campbell*, 1984 CarswellNat 528 (TCC) and *Stirling*, [1985] 1 C.T.C. 275 (FCA).

Condominiums: see Notes to 40(2)(b).

Copyright: An author or software developer selling copyright is normally considered to have written the work for this purpose, so the gain is business income; payment based on future sales is taxable under 12(1)(g) anyway. See VIEWS docs "RCT 7-532", "August 1990-408", 2013-0485501E5.

Damages received: the *surrogatum* principle applies. See Notes to 9(1).

Debt securities held short-term were INV in *Loblaw Financial*, 2018 TCC 182, paras. 272-277 (rev'd on other grounds 2020 FCA 79; SCC appeal heard May 13/21). A mortgage owed by an insolvent developer was INV in *Leonard*, 2021 TCC 33 (under appeal to FCA), paras. 54, 78, as L intended to acquire and resell the underlying land. See also Notes to 20(1)(f) and 39(2); Nanji, "Capital vs Income Determinations Related to Debt", *YP Focus Virtual Conference* (ctf.ca, Sept. 2020), 3B:1-27.

Derivative transactions: see "Hedges" below.

Dogs held by a breeder as breeding stock are considered INV: VIEWS doc 2008-0288071I7 (this may not be correct in the author's view).

Easement granting is considered partial disposition of CP. See Notes to 43(1).

Equipment: in *CAE Inc.*, [2013] 4 C.T.C. 160 (FCA), sale-leaseback arrangements were not part of CAE's trading operations, so were on capital account (para. 69); some leased-out flight simulators were CP, but those subject to a true purchase option were INV (paras. 103-111)). In *Good Equipment*, [2008] 4 C.T.C. 2154 (TCC), leased INV was converted to CP on entering into a financing lease. In *Klemen*, 2014 CarswellNat 2948 (TCC), K owned equipment that he allowed his company to use for free; when he transferred it to the company it was CP. In docs 2003-0048331I7, 2004-0097181I7 and 2010-0379411E5, the CRA said that a heavy equipment dealer's leased equipment was probably INV.

Gold: see "Commodities" above.

Hedges and other derivative transactions take on the status of the underlying asset being hedged: *Shell Canada*, [1999] 4 C.T.C. 313 (SCC), para. 68; *MacDonald*, 2020 SCC 6 (forward contract was a hedge). See also Notes to 9(1) at "Hedges", and to 39(2) re foreign currency hedging. A "derivative forward agreement" (248(1)) is INV even if a 39(4) election was made: 12(1)(z.7).

Houses and condos: see Notes to 40(2)(b).

Insurance policy: a right under a policy can be CP: VIEWS doc 2012-0470021I7. See also Notes to 6(1)(f).

Land was held to be CP in: *Schwartz*, 2008 TCC 432 (land bought for resale once developer obtained approval, but S did nothing towards plan so sale was capital); *Beauregard*, 2013 TCC 287 (land purchased to build rental properties but B could not get financing); *Staltari*, 2015 TCC 123 (despite S being in real estate business, he bought wetlands from his father as a favour and not for resale, then later donated them, which cancelled his secondary intention to develop the property); *Paletta*, 2019 TCC 205 (under appeal to FCA), para. 316 (2 of 9 sales were woodlots acquired 28 years earlier for farming); *Chevalier*, 2020 QCCQ 2220 (C owned land 13 years; developer D offered to buy it subdivided and serviced; C divided it into 28 lots and put in infrastructure, but D made all arrangements). See also IT-218R, doc 2013-0501311E5 (general comments). (See also para. "Change in intention" above.)

Land was held to be INV in: *Dalron Construction*, 2008 TCC 476 (DC was in business of buying and developing land); *Bodine*, 2011 FCA 157 (rolling long-held farmland into a partnership to sell it caused it to be INV when sold); *Karam*, 2013 TCC 354 (intention in buying land was to develop and resell it); *Zielinski*, 2013 TCC 384 (same); *Henco Industries*, 2014 TCC 192, para. 138 (developer holding land to build golf course was just as likely to have sold it as to have operated it); VIEWS docs 2007-022675117; 2008-0275452117 (farmland changed to INV when subdivided into building lots); 2011-0411931E5 (land bought with intention of subdividing and selling); *Paletta*, 2019 TCC 205 (under appeal to FCA), paras. 280-316 (7 of 9 sales: sophisticated developer had secondary intention to resell if plans failed); *6610048 Canada*, 2019 TCC 225 (under appeal to FCA) (land acquired for development; also secondary intention of resale).

Land gain was part capital, part income in *Von Realty*, 2011 TCC 345. See also under "Change in intention" near beginning of these Notes.

For software that assists in the determination see the *Real Estate Classifier* and *Securities Trading Classifier* at bluejlegal.com.

Leases: In *GMAC Leaseco*, 2015 CarswellNat 2148 (TCC), excess-km charges paid on car leases were income, as they compensated GMAC for lost interest and other income. Residual value support payments from GM, to compensate for increased losses at lease-end due to higher residual values, were also income as they replaced lost interest and other income. An amount received to give up an office space co-tenancy is likely capital: VIEWS doc 2012-0436781E5.

Mines are capital assets: *Newmont Canada [Hemlo Gold]*, [2012] 6 C.T.C. 72 (FCA), para. 39 (but see also 39(1)(a)(ii), (ii.1)).

Mutual fund trust's trades: see VIEWS doc 2012-0470991E5.

Natural gas: a distributor's "cushion gas" (base pressure gas) is considered CP: doc 2007-025712117.

Non-competition agreement proceeds: see 56.4.

Patents: an amount received for non-exclusive patent rights or licensing was income: *Canadian Industries*, [1980] C.T.C. 222 (FCA); *Canadian General Electric*, [1987] 1 C.T.C. 180 (FCA). Foreign patent: see IT-477 para. 10; VIEWS doc 2010-0353301E5.

Real property: see "Buildings" and "Land" above.

Settlement payments: See Notes to 9(1) under "Damages".

Shares are often bought as CP. Where shares of a company are sold but the underlying asset is real property, the CRA will use the criteria for real property to classify the shares: VIEWS doc 2011-0397351E5.

Share trading actively on the market is on income account, if no 39(4) election has ever been filed: *Hawa*, 2006 TCC 612; *Empire Paving*, 2008 TCC 355; *Richer*, 2008 TCC 547 (a broker); *Zsebok*, 2012 TCC 99 (trading was "flurried" and "feverish"); *Mittal*, 2012 TCC 417; *Wong*, 2013 TCC 130 (over 600 transactions in 5 years, with short holding periods); *Foote*, 2017 TCC 61 (co-head of institutional trading at brokerage); *Duffy*, 2019 TCC 75, para. 12 (564 trades over 3 years). In *Greenberg*, 2006 TCC 608, funding businesses to enable them to go public so as to sell the shares was on income account, since the taxpayer had no intention of deriving dividend income. In *Atlantic Packaging*, 2020 FCA 75 (leave to appeal denied 2020 CarswellNat 4337 (SCC)), shares of a subsidiary issued on a rollover were INV when resold, as 54.2 did not apply. In *Leola Purdy Sons Ltd.*, 2009 TCC 21, when CRA reassessed 2002 to treat securities gains as income, the taxpayer was allowed to restate 1998 capital losses as business losses (though 1998 was statute-barred) and carry forward the resulting loss to offset 2002 income.

Shares traded were held to be CP in: *Robertson*, [1998] 3 C.T.C. 147 (FCA); *Corvalan*, 2006 TCC 200 (employee acquired shares under stock option); *Leng*, 2007 TCC 59 (infrequent trades, short holding periods); *Pollock*, 2008 TCC 115 (infrequent purchases, shares held for long periods); *Azrak*, 2008 TCC 217 (little activity); *Kriplani*, 2011 TCC 542 (17 purchases and 19 sales over a year, mostly short holding periods, where previous years reported as capital); *Prochuk*, 2014 TCC 17 (active trading in RRSP did not put *taxpayer* in business of trading); *Turner*, 2016 TCC 77 (FCA appeal discontinued A-124-16) ("trading" was simply buying more and more of one stock). Switching from capital to income reporting requires a "heavy onus" of showing purchase with intent to sell: *Rajchgot*, 2005 FCA 289; in *Thibault*, 2007 TCC 515, gross-negligence penalty applied to an active trader who switched to reporting gains as capital gains.

Share trading part income, part capital? *Strassburger*, 2004 TCC 614, was assessed on the basis that securities held less than 365 days were INV; the TCC rejected this approach as "arbitrary". In CRA's view, a taxpayer cannot segregate day trading and long-term investments and treat some as capital and others as income: doc 2006-0185041E5. However, in *1338664 Ontario*, 2008 TCC 350, stocks held for less than a week were held to be INV, while those held longer were capital!

For an interesting mathematical model for stock market losses, suggesting "points" to allocate to various factors, see Fitzsimmons, "Stock Market Losses", 1882 *Tax Topics* (CCH) 1-5 (April 3, 2008).

Shares held by financial institutions are marked up and down on income account regardless of dispositions: 142.2(1)"mark-to-market property", 142.5(1), (2).

A short sale of shares is normally on income account: IT-479R para. 18, VIEWS doc 2010-0364991E5 (see s. 260 re securities lending arrangements).

In many cases investors own "security entitlements" and do not own the shares they think they own. This could have implications for determining whether there is a capital gain. See Notes to 233.3(1)"specified foreign property".

For more on shares see IT-479R; docs 2008-0269481E5 (general comments); 2010-0371111E5 (whether former investment-dealer employee would be trading); 2011-0424591M4 (how "carried interest" is treated); 2019-0826051E5 (corp actively trading).

A member's interest in a non-share corporation is likely CP, so property received on its windup is proceeds of disposition: IT-409 paras. 9-11, VIEWS doc 2009-0332161E5.

Stock options: Gain on surrender of stock options, not taxed under s. 7, was capital gain in *Rogers Estate*, 2014 TCC 348, paras. 65-73 (FCA appeal discontinued A-533-14). See also VIEWS doc 2013-0502761E5. Where employees convert options and sell the shares, see 7(1) Notes re "underwater" options.

Term deposit or GIC: see VIEWS doc 2012-0469691E5.

Vehicles: see doc 2013-0487571E5 (vehicle acquired for purposes of resale is INV).

Bare trustee or nominee: A person whose name is on title to property solely for legal purposes with no beneficial ownership does not own the property for capital gain purposes: Income Tax Folio S1-F3-C2 ¶2.79-2.82; VIEWS docs 2008-0272121E5; 2008-0281841E5 and 2008-0282461E5 (transfer of home from father to daughter where he always held it for her and she paid the expenses); 2009-0327041C6 (Quebec); 2010-0358161E5, 2010-0368681E5, 2010-0377971E5, 2010-0379711E5, 2010-0385711E5, 2010-0389041E5; 2009-035087117 (legal owner is presumed to be beneficial owner unless facts show otherwise); 2011-0427801E5, 2013-0511771E5, 2014-0533561E5 and 2014-0553131E5 (transfer of only legal title is not a disposition [see also 248(1)"disposition"(e)]); 2014-0521891E5 (joint ownership); 2014-0550971E5; 2015-0576281I7 (whether relationship must be disclosed to CRA); 2015-0580531E5 and 2016-0647461E5 (joint ownership). This can be a bare trust (common law; see Notes to 104(1)) or prête-nom (Quebec civil law). The evidence must establish that it is "more likely than not" that beneficial ownership differs from legal ownership: *Gabrini*, 2011 TCC 188; *Eliyin*, 2014 TCC 125, paras. 9-11; *Langard*, 2015 TCC 161. Legal ownership prevails over accounting treatment: *Finch*, 2003 TCC 353, para. 14; *Otte & Associates*, 2016 TCC 162, para. 40. For more on beneficial ownership see 2009-032485117 and Notes to 104(1). The Ontario *Family Law Act* does not give a spouse half-ownership in property, but merely entitles a separating spouse to an equalization payment, so it does not split a gain between spouses where only one is on title: 2004-006756117. In Quebec, a nominee agreement and its details must be disclosed on Form TP-1079.PN-V to Revenu Québec within 90 days of signing (*Taxation Act (TA)* s. 1079.8.6.4; first deadline Dec. 23, 2020), with a non-compliance penalty of $1,000 plus $100 per day, max $5,000 (*TA* s. 1079.8.13.3): Finances Québec Information Bulletin 2019-5 and Aug. 22/19 Revenu Québec news release [Lafrance, "Mandatory Disclosure of Nominee Agreements", 9(4) *Canadian Tax Focus* (ctf.ca) 5-6 (Nov. 2019)]; RQ Round Table, 2019 Cdn Tax Foundation conference report at 4:1-7 (qq. 1-9). In British Columbia, beneficial ownership of real property must be disclosed to a government registry under the *Land Owner Transparency Act*, in force Nov. 30, 2020.

54"capital property" was 54(b) before RSC 1985 (5th Supp) consolidation for tax years ending after Nov. 1991.

I.T. Application Rules: 26(5), (6) and (7).

Interpretation Bulletins: IT-102R2: Conversion of property, other than real property, from or to inventory; IT-218R: Profit, capital gains and losses from the sale of real estate, including farmland and inherited land and conversion of real estate from capital property to inventory and vice versa; IT-325R2: Property transfers after separation, divorce and annulment; IT-442R: Bad debts and reserves for doubtful debts; IT-459: Adventure or concern in the nature of trade.

I.T. Technical News: 7 (rollovers of capital property — *Mara Properties*); 12 ("millennium bug" expenditures).

Info Sheets: TI-001: Sale of a residence by an owner builder.

CRA Audit Manual: 11.6.3: Capital gain vs. income report; 27.4.0: Capital gain or business income.

Advance Tax Rulings: ATR-59: Financing exploration and development through limited partnerships.

"disposition" — [Repealed]

Notes: See 248(1)"disposition". 54"disposition" repealed by 2001 technical bill for transactions and events that occur after Dec. 23, 1998. It was 54(c) before RSC 1985 (5th Supp) consolidation for tax years ending after Nov. 1991.

"eligible capital property" — [Repealed]

Related Provisions: [all before 2017] 14(3) — Non-arm's length acquisition of eligible capital property; 87(2)(f) — Amalgamation — continuing corporation; 98(3)(b) — Rules applicable where partnership ceases to exist; 248(1)"eligible capital property" — Definition applies to entire Act; Reg. Sch. II:Cl. 14.1(b) — ECP becomes Class 14.1 property in 2017.

Notes: Definition repealed by 2016 budget bill #2, effective 2017, as part of changing ECP rules to CCA Class 14.1 (see Notes to 20(1)(b)). It read:

"eligible capital property" of a taxpayer means any property, a part of the consideration for the disposition of which would, if the taxpayer disposed of the property, be an eligible capital amount in respect of a business;

The definition is tortuous and somewhat circular. In essence, it is goodwill and other purchased intangibles, including incorporation expenses.

54"eligible capital property" was 54(d) before RSC 1985 (5th Supp) consolidation for tax years ending after Nov. 1991.

"exemption threshold", of a taxpayer at a particular time in respect of a flow-through share class of property, means the amount determined by the formula

$$A - B$$

where

A is the total of

(a) the total of all amounts, each of which is an amount that would be the cost to the taxpayer, computed without reference to subsection 66.3(3), of a flow-through share that was included at any time before the particular time in the flow-through share class of property and that was issued by a corporation to the taxpayer on or after the taxpayer's fresh-start date in respect of the flow-through share class of property at that time, other than a flow-through share that the taxpayer was obligated, before March 22, 2011, to acquire pursuant to the terms of a flow-through share agreement entered into between the corporation and the taxpayer, and

(b) the total of all amounts, each of which is an amount that would be the adjusted cost base to the taxpayer of an interest in a partnership — computed as if subparagraph 53(1)(e)(vii.1) and clauses 53(2)(c)(ii)(C) and (D) did not apply to any amount incurred by the partnership in respect of a flow-through share held by the partnership, either directly or indirectly through another partnership — that was included at any time before the particular time in the flow-through share class of property, if

(i) the taxpayer

(A) acquired the interest on or after the taxpayer's fresh-start date in respect of the flow-through share class of property at the particular time (other than an interest that the taxpayer was obligated, before August 16, 2011, to acquire pursuant to the terms of an agreement in writing entered into by the taxpayer), or

(B) made a contribution of capital to the partnership on or after August 16, 2011,

(ii) at any time after the taxpayer acquired the interest or made the contribution of capital, the taxpayer is deemed by subsection 66(18) to have made or incurred an outlay or expense in respect of a flow-through share held by the partnership, either directly or indirectly through another partnership, and

(iii) at any time between the time that the taxpayer acquired the interest or made the contribution of capital and the particular time, more than 50% of the fair market value of the assets of the partnership is attributable to property included in a flow-through share class of property, and

B is the total, if any, of all amounts, each of which is the lesser of

(a) the total of all amounts, each of which is a capital gain from a disposition of a property included in the flow-through share class of property, other than a capital gain referred to in paragraph 38.1(a), at an earlier time that is

(i) before the particular time, and

(ii) after the first time that the taxpayer acquired a flow-through share referred to in paragraph (a) of the description of A or acquired a partnership interest referred to in paragraph (b) of the description of A, and

(b) the exemption threshold of the taxpayer in respect of the flow-th[r]ough share class of property immediately before that earlier time;

Related Provisions: 40(12) — Deemed capital gain on donation of flow-through share; 257 — Formula cannot calculate to less than zero.

Notes: See Notes to 40(12). 54"exemption threshold" added by 2011 budget bill #2, effective March 22, 2011.

"flow-through share class of property" means a group of properties,

(a) in respect of a class of shares of the capital stock of a corporation, each of which is

(i) a share of the class, if any share of the class or any right described in subparagraph (ii) is, at any time, a flow-through share to any person,

(ii) a right to acquire a share of the class, if any share of that class or any right described in this subparagraph is, at any time, a flow-through share to any person, or

(iii) a property that is an identical property of a property described in subparagraph (i) or (ii), or

(b) each of which is an interest in a partnership, if at any time more than 50% of the fair market value of the partnership's assets is attributable to property included in a flow-through share class of property;

Notes: See Notes to 40(12). 54"flow-through share class of property" added by 2011 budget bill #2, effective March 22, 2011.

"fresh-start date", of a taxpayer at a particular time in respect of a flow-through share class of property, means

(a) in the case of a partnership interest that is included in the flow-through share class of property, the day that is the later of

(i) August 16, 2011, and

(ii) the last day, if any, before the particular time, on which the taxpayer held an interest in the partnership, and

(b) in the case of any other property that is included in the flow-th[r]ough share class of property, the day that is the later of

(i) March 22, 2011, and

(ii) the last day, if any, before the particular time, on which the taxpayer disposed of all property included in the flow-through share class of property;

Notes: See Notes to 40(12). 54"fresh-start date" added by 2011 budget bill #2, effective March 22, 2011.

"listed personal property" of a taxpayer means the taxpayer's personal-use property that is all or any portion of, or any interest in or right to — or, for civil law, any right in or to — any

(a) print, etching, drawing, painting, sculpture, or other similar work of art,

(b) jewellery,

(c) rare folio, rare manuscript, or rare book,

(d) stamp, or

(e) coin;

Related Provisions: 40(2)(g)(iii) — Limitations; 41 — Gain from listed personal property; 248(1)"listed personal property" — Definition applies to entire Act.

Notes: Listed personal property (LPP) typically appreciates rather than depreciates in value. See Notes to 41(1) re use of LPP losses.

Reg. 1102(1)(e) generally prohibits CCA claims on art, except for Canadian art. Of course, listed personal property is, by definition, personal-use property and thus ineligible for CCA anyway because its use is personal and not for business or property income (see Reg. 1102(1)(c)).

Opening words amended by 2002-2013 technical bill (Part 4 — bijuralism), effective June 26, 2013, to add "or, for civil law, any right in or to".

54"listed personal property" was 54(e) before RSC 1985 (5th Supp) consolidation for tax years ending after Nov. 1991.

Interpretation Bulletins: IT-159R3: Capital debts established to be bad debts.

"personal-use property" of a taxpayer includes

(a) property owned by the taxpayer that is used primarily for the personal use or enjoyment of the taxpayer or for the personal use or enjoyment of one or more individuals each of whom is

(i) the taxpayer,

(ii) a person related to the taxpayer, or

(iii) where the taxpayer is a trust, a beneficiary under the trust or any person related to the beneficiary,

(b) any debt owing to the taxpayer in respect of the disposition of property that was the taxpayer's personal-use property, and

(c) any property of the taxpayer that is an option to acquire property that would, if the taxpayer acquired it, be personal-use property of the taxpayer,

and "personal-use property" of a partnership includes any partnership property that is used primarily for the personal use or enjoyment of any member of the partnership or for the personal use or enjoyment of one or more individuals each of whom is a member of the partnership or a person related to such a member;

Related Provisions: 3(b)(ii), 40(2)(g)(iii) — No capital loss on personal-use property; 46 — Disposition of personal-use property; 50(2) — Where debt personal-use property; 248(1)"personal-use property" — Definition applies to entire Act.

Notes: No capital loss is allowed on personal-use property (PUP) (except for listed personal property losses against LPP gains): 40(2)(g)(iii), VIEWS docs 2006-0216941E5, 2011-0400251E5. (This rule applies to *capital* property only, but PUP would not normally be inventory given the definition of PUP.) PUP need not be reported as foreign property on a T1135: 233.3(1)"specified foreign property"(p).

A home the taxpayer vacated remains PUP while the taxpayer is trying to sell it for several years: *Solomons*, [2003] 2 C.T.C. 2268 (TCC); doc 2012-0455621E5. A loan is not PUP unless it arises on disposition of PUP: 2013-0513361E5. Where X owns a foreign home that is rented to his brother at FMV, it is a question of fact whether it is "primarily" personal-use: VIEWS doc 2014-0536261E5.

For the meaning of "includes" see 188.1(5) Notes. For "used primarily" see 73(3) Notes.

Bowman ACJ stated in *Klotz*, 2004 TCC 147 (aff'd on other grounds 2005 FCA 158) that PUP need not be physically used or enjoyed by the taxpayer, and that "one way of using an object is to give it away, whether the motive be altruistic, charitable or fiscal", so art the taxpayer did not see or take possession of was PUP. However, in *Plamondon*, 2011 TCC 47, paras. 13-19, Hogan J held that there must be actual physical enjoyment of the property. The CRA agrees and requires actual use or enjoyment: VIEWS docs 2002-0148955, 2004-0077831E5, 2005-0141261C6, 2013-0513361E5.

Planning tip: After death, PUP that the beneficiaries do not use is not PUP to the estate: doc 2011-0401871C6. If a home or cottage is not used after death and is sold soon, its cost to the estate is the FMV (70(5)(b)) but the sale proceeds will be the same net of real estate commission and lawyer fees, creating a capital loss the estate can use against the deceased's capital gains (see 164(6)).

In *Donato*, 2009 TCC 590 (aff'd on other grounds 2010 FCA 312), a newspaper cartoonist's cartoons were not PUP because their primary use was for a commercial purpose. (Drache, "Personal Use Property or Capital Property", xxxii(5) *The Canadian Taxpayer* (Carswell) 38-39 (March 2, 2010), notes that Donato's gifts could have been certified as cultural property to eliminate tax on the gain.)

54"personal-use property" was 54(f) before RSC 1985 (5th Supp) consolidation for tax years ending after Nov. 1991.

Interpretation Bulletins: IT-159R3: Capital debts established to be bad debts; IT-218R: Profit, capital gains and losses from the sale of real estate, including farmland and inherited land and conversion of real estate from capital property to inventory and vice versa; IT-332R: Personal-use property (cancelled).

"principal residence" of a taxpayer for a taxation year means a particular property that is a housing unit, a leasehold interest in a housing unit or a share of the capital stock of a co-operative housing corporation acquired for the sole purpose of acquiring the right to inhabit a housing unit owned by the corporation and that is owned, whether jointly with another person or otherwise, in the year by the taxpayer, if

(a) where the taxpayer is an individual other than a personal trust, the housing unit was ordinarily inhabited in the year by the taxpayer, by the taxpayer's spouse or common-law partner or former spouse or common-law partner or by a child of the taxpayer,

(a.1) where the taxpayer is a personal trust, the housing unit was ordinarily inhabited in the calendar year ending in the year by a specified beneficiary of the trust for the year, by the spouse or common-law partner or former spouse or common-law partner of such a beneficiary or by a child of such a beneficiary, or

(b) where the taxpayer is a personal trust or an individual other than a trust, the taxpayer

(i) elected[4] under subsection 45(2) that relates to the change in use of the particular property in the year or a preceding taxation year, other than an election rescinded under subsection 45(2) in the taxpayer's return of income for the year or a preceding taxation year, or

(ii) elected[4] under subsection 45(3) that relates to a change in use of the particular property in a subsequent taxation year,

except that, subject to section 54.1, a particular property shall be considered not to be a taxpayer's principal residence for a taxation year

(c) where the taxpayer is an individual other than a personal trust, unless the particular property was designated by the taxpayer in prescribed form and manner to be the taxpayer's principal residence for the year and no other property has been designated for the purposes of this definition for the year

(i) where the year is before 1982, by the taxpayer, or

(ii) where the year is after 1981,

(A) by the taxpayer,

(B) by a person who was throughout the year the taxpayer's spouse or common-law partner (other than a spouse or common-law partner who was throughout the year living apart from, and was separated under a judicial separation or written separation agreement from, the taxpayer),

(C) by a person who was the taxpayer's child (other than a child who was at any time in the year a married person, a person who is in a common-law partnership or 18 years of age or older), or

(D) where the taxpayer was not at any time in the year a married person, a person who is in a common-law partnership or 18 years of age or older, by a person who was the taxpayer's

(I) mother or father, or

(II) brother or sister, where that brother or sister was not at any time in the year a married person, a person who is in a common-law partnership or 18 years of age or older,

(c.1) where the taxpayer is a personal trust, unless

(i) the particular property was designated by the trust in prescribed form and manner to be the taxpayer's principal residence for the year,

(ii) the trust specifies in the designation each individual (in this definition referred to as a "specified beneficiary" of the trust for the year) who, in the calendar year ending in the year,

(A) is beneficially interested in the trust, and

(B) except where the trust is entitled to designate it for the year solely because of paragraph (b), ordinarily inhabited the housing unit or has a spouse or common-law partner, former spouse or common-law partner or child who ordinarily inhabited the housing unit,

(iii) no corporation (other than a registered charity) or partnership is beneficially interested in the trust at any time in the year,

(iii.1) if the year begins after 2016, the trust is, in the year,

(A) a trust

(I) for which a day is to be determined under paragraph 104(4)(a), (a.1) or (a.4) by reference to the death or later death, as the case may be, that has not occurred before the beginning of the year, of an individual who is resident in Canada during the year, and

---

[4] *Sic*. Should read "made an election" — ed.

(II) a specified beneficiary of which for the year is the individual referred to in subclause (I),

(B) a trust

(I) that is a "qualified disability trust" (as defined in subsection 122(3)) for the year, and

(II) an "electing beneficiary" (in this clause, as defined in subsection 122(3)) of which for the year is

1 resident in Canada during the year,

2 a specified beneficiary of the trust for the year, and

3 a spouse, common-law partner, former spouse or common-law partner or child of the "settlor" (in this subparagraph, as defined in subsection 108(1)) of the trust, or

(C) a trust

(I) a specified beneficiary of which for the year is an individual

1 who is resident in Canada during the year,

2 who has not attained 18 years of age before the end of the year, and

3 a mother or father of whom is a settlor of the trust, and

(II) in respect of which either of the following conditions is met:

1 no mother or father of the individual referred to in subclause (I) is alive at the beginning of the year, or

2 the trust arose before the beginning of the year on and as a consequence of the death of a mother or father of the individual referred to in subclause (I), and

(iv) no other property has been designated for the purpose of this definition for the calendar year ending in the year by any specified beneficiary of the trust for the year, by a person who was throughout that calendar year such a beneficiary's spouse or common-law partner (other than a spouse or common-law partner who was throughout that calendar year living apart from, and was separated pursuant to a judicial separation or written separation agreement from, the beneficiary), by a person who was such a beneficiary's child (other than a child who was during that calendar year a married person or a person who is in a common-law partnership or a person 18 years or over) or, where such a beneficiary was not during that calendar year a married person or a person who is in a common-law partnership or a person 18 years or over, by a person who was such a beneficiary's

(A) mother or father, or

(B) brother or sister, where that brother or sister was not during that calendar year a married person or a person who is in a common-law partnership or a person 18 years or over, or

Proposed Amendment — 54 "principal residence" (c.1) — *inter vivos* trust for person with disability

Letter from Dept. of Finance, Sept. 4, 2019: Ms. Carmen S. Thériault, Norton Rose Fulbright Canada LLP, Vancouver, BC

Dear Ms. Thériault:

Principal Residence Exemption for Trusts

I am writing in response to the issue raised in your correspondence and discussions with officials of Tax Legislation Division concerning the ability of an *inter vivos* trust established for the benefit of an individual eligible for the Disability Tax Credit (DTC) to qualify for the principal residence exemption. Specifically, you are concerned that the [xxx] Trust, an *inter vivos* trust established by your client for the benefit of his DTC-eligible son, is ineligible for the principal residence exemption.

On October 3, 2016, income tax measures were announced, and subsequently introduced into law as part of *Budget Implementation Act, 2017, No. 2*, to ensure that the

principal residence exemption is available only in appropriate cases. As part of these rules, the definition "principal residence" in section 54 of the *Income Tax Act* was amended to add additional eligibility requirements for trusts claiming the principal residence exemption for a taxation year that begins after 2016, including limiting eligibility for the principal residence exemption to three categories of trusts.

In order to accommodate trusts that hold property for the benefit of a Canadian resident who is disabled, the measure preserved the ability of a qualified disability trust to be eligible to claim the principal residence exemption. A qualified disability trust must be a testamentary trust (generally a trust that arose on and as a consequence of the death of an individual, subject to certain exceptions) where, among other criteria, a beneficiary of the trust is DTC-eligible.

You note that following the introduction of the measures described above, the [xxx] Trust would no longer qualify for the principal residence exemption since the trust was established during the lifetime of the settlor, rather than as a testamentary trust.

Our Comments

We agree that it would be appropriate to make certain *inter vivos* trusts eligible to claim the principal residence exemption. We are therefore prepared to recommend to the Minister of Finance that the *Income Tax Act* be amended in a manner that allows an *inter vivos* trust for the benefit of an individual who is DTC-eligible to be eligible to claim the principal residence exemption as long as certain conditions are met. To this end, we will recommend that the definition "principal residence" be amended so that a trust will be allowed to designate a property as a principal residence for a taxation year provided that all other designation requirements are fulfilled (including the requirements relating to occupation of the property and one property per family unit) and the following conditions are met:

- a beneficiary of the trust is an individual resident in Canada during the year who is eligible for the DTC;

- the beneficiary is a child, spouse, common-law partner, or former spouse or common-law partner, of the settlor of the trust; and

- no person other than a beneficiary described above may, during the beneficiary's lifetime, receive or otherwise obtain the use of any of the income or capital of the trust.

We will also recommend that the amendment applies to taxation years that begin after 2016.

While we cannot offer any assurances that either the Minister of Finance or Parliament will agree with our recommendation in respect of this matter, we hope that this statement of our intention is helpful.

Yours sincerely,

Brian Ernewein, Assistant Deputy Minister — Legislation, Tax Policy Branch

Notes: See Sweeney, "Finance to Recommend Extension of Principal Residence Exemption", 13(1) *Taxes & Wealth Management* (Carswell) 5-6 (March 2020).

(d) because of paragraph (b), if solely because of that paragraph the property would, but for this paragraph, have been a principal residence of the taxpayer for 4 or more preceding taxation years,

and, for the purpose of this definition,

(e) the principal residence of a taxpayer for a taxation year shall be deemed to include, except where the particular property consists of a share of the capital stock of a co-operative housing corporation, the land subjacent to the housing unit and such portion of any immediately contiguous land as can reasonably be regarded as contributing to the use and enjoyment of the housing unit as a residence, except that where the total area of the subjacent land and of that portion exceeds ½ hectare, the excess shall be deemed not to have contributed to the use and enjoyment of the housing unit as a residence unless the taxpayer establishes that it was necessary to such use and enjoyment, and

(f) a particular property designated under paragraph (c.1) by a trust for a year shall be deemed to be property designated for the purposes of this definition by each specified beneficiary of the trust for the calendar year ending in the year;

Related Provisions: 40(2)(b), 40(4)–(6) — Principal residence rules; 40(6.1) — Determination of gain for principal residence owned by a trust since before 2017; 40(7) — Property acquired in satisfaction of trust interest; 45(3), (4) — Election where change in use; 54.1 — Exception to principal residence rules; 107(2.01) — Distribution of principal residence by trust; 107(4.1)(a.1) — Exception to trust rollout rules; 152(4)(b.3) — Extended reassessment period if disposition is not reported; 220(3.21)(a.1) — Late filing, amendment or revocation of designation under (c) or (c.1); 248(25) — Beneficially interested; 252(2) — Mother, father, etc.

Notes: See Notes to 40(2)(b), which provides the principal-residence (PR) exemption.

A condo parking space is part of the residence if certain conditions are met: VIEWS doc 2015-0590371E5; *Grands Palais du nouveau Saint-Laurent*, 2020 QCCQ 281.

Opening words: "Owned" applies only after closing, not from when a purchase agreement is signed: *Higgins*, [2019] EWCA Civ 1890 (England), para. 21.

Para. (a): "Ordinarily inhabited" does not mean the taxpayer must spend most of their time in the home (but there must be more than an intention to inhabit: *Kuntz*, 2013 TCC 218; VIEWS doc 2008-0289971E5). One may designate a cottage or other vacation property under 40(2)(b): Income Tax Folio S1-F3-C2 ¶2.7; 2014-0528241E5. If the owner moves permanently to a nursing home, the test is no longer met: 2010-0359101E5. In *Feizmohammadi*, 2017 TCC 28, F was found not to have inhabited the home.

A PR can be outside Canada: Income Tax Folio S1-F3-C2 ¶2.74, VIEWS doc 2010-0369351E5. A non-resident can have a PR in Canada, but the 40(2)(b) formula exempts the gain only for years of residence in Canada: 2012-0472221E5.

"Child" includes an adult child: 2014-0541901E5 (and see 252(1)). Charging market rent to the child does not stop the home being a PR: 2015-0567791I7, 2016-0625161C6 [CPA QC 2016 q.10]. Para. (a) includes a child (C) but not a parent (P), so if P transfers her home to joint ownership with C, and C does not live there, it will not be a PR to C and disposition will lead to a capital gain. In *Royer*, 2019 QCCQ 4163 (parallel Quebec rule), a grandmother who lived in the home to care for R's disabled child caused her portion of the home not to be a PR to R.

Subpara. (b)(i): an election "in the taxpayer's return" is valid even if the return is filed late: see Notes to 7(1.31).

Para. (c): See Notes to 40(2)(b) re requirement to file a prescribed form. Each family unit can have only one PR: 2010-0364781E5, 2011-0408461E5 (see below re (c.1) on a family trust also having a PR). Where two spouses owned different PRs before 1982, 40(6) still provides partial exemption for both.

Where a home is used partly to earn income (rented out, or bed-and-breakfast, or to operate another business), CRA's view is that the property "retains its nature" as a PR as long as the income-producing use is ancillary to its main use as a residence, there is no structural change, and no CCA (20(1)(a)) is claimed: Income Tax Folio S1-F3-C2 ¶2.11, 2.59; VIEWS docs 2008-0274141E5, 2008-0285781I7, 2009-0321481E5, 2009-0344001E5, 2011-0421051E5, 2013-0475301E5; 2014-0527591E5 (taxpayer rents home to his son and others). However, 2015-0567791I7 says CCA can be claimed on a home rented to one's child, and the exemption will still be available.

Two distinguishable parts of a house were separate "housing units", so only one was eligible for the exemption, in *Boulet*, 2009 TCC 261; and a triplex was not all one PR in *Denis*, 2019 QCCQ 6708. Two apartments in a duplex (even if owned by two individuals as tenants in common) are each a "housing unit": VIEWS docs 2010-0354361E5, 2010-0380991M4, 2011-0395001I7, 2016-0625141C6 [CPA QC 2016 q.9] (despite internal access between them and the owner and her aging parent sharing most meals); unless the units are integrated into one: 2012-0445241E5. So is a unit of a triplex (2010-0375591E5, 2012-0453961C6) and a basement apartment with separate entrance (2010-0364711E5). Where an individual lives downstairs and rents out the upstairs, only the downstairs is the PR: 2012-0420171E5. See also Kay Gray, "Laneway Houses", 2014 Cdn Tax Foundation conference report, 13:1-24. On X converting a duplex (X lived in part) to 1 home (X lives in all), the part is a separate PR for the period X lived there: 2019-0812621C6 [2019 APFF q.3].

Two condominium units connected and occupied as one are still considered two units for purposes of para. (c) unless they are "sufficiently integrated that one cannot enjoy the living accommodation of one unit without the use and access to the other": VIEWS docs 2005-0148091E5, 2009-0311301E5, 2012-0447471E5.

CRA's view (possibly incorrect) is that a waterfront property where the taxpayer lives in a houseboat does not qualify: VIEWS doc 2008-0271331E5.

A leasehold interest can qualify as a principal residence: VIEWS docs 2006-0211451M4, 2007-0254721R3, 2019-0812611C6 [2019 APFF q.2]; as can a usufruct: 2010-0367371E5.

A "cooperative housing corporation" means one incorporated under cooperative housing legislation, not under ordinary companies legislation, according to Income Tax Folio S1-F3-C2 ¶2.7 and VIEWS docs 970410A, 9726975 and 2002-0164895. However, docs 2001-0096333F, 2003-0000955 and 2007-0234031R3 (2007-0244641R3) state that, in Quebec, a share of a corporation incorporated under the CBCA, combined with a lease entitling the owner to inhabit a unit, is considered a "housing unit" that can be inhabited. This can apply generally if specific conditions are satisfied: 2010-0396361M4.

For (c)(ii)(B), there was insufficient evidence of a "written separation agreement", so a wife was not entitled to claim a PR during the period when her estranged husband also did: *Balanko Estate*, 2015 CarswellNat 560 (TCC).

Para. (c.1): Since 2017, only a few trusts can designate a PR under para. (c.1) and claim the exemption where a specified beneficiary (**SB**: (c.1)(ii)) lives in the home: (A) *alter ego* and joint partner trusts, (B) qualified disability trusts [this will be extended retroactively to *inter vivos* trusts for a person eligible for the disability credit: see Sept. 4/19 comfort letter above], and (C) certain "orphan" trusts. A trust that was previously eligible (see next para.) can claim the exemption for the increase in value through 2016: 40(6.1). See also VIEWS docs 2017-0724121C6 [2017 CTF q.2]; 2020-0852171C6 [2020 APFF q.5] (deceased's will creates usufruct for spouse). On disposing of the PR the trust files a T1079 with its T3 return: VIEWS doc 2010-0384891E5. (107(2.01) allows the trust to elect to "bump up" the cost on distributing the PR to the SB, so the trust gets the exemption and the SB acquires the home at FMV.) The SB cannot also designate another residence: (c.1)(iv). If the trust rolls the property out to SB under 107(2), SB is deemed by 40(7) to have owned it throughout, affecting the exemption claim: 2011-0403301E5. For detailed discussion see Thompson, "October 3, 2016 Changes to the Principal Residence Deduction", 36(3) *Estates, Trusts & Pensions Journal* 264-98 (May 2017); Woolley, "Principal Residences", 2017 BC Tax Conference (ctf.ca). See also Spinner, "Revisiting Residence Trusts", 5(5) *Personal Tax and Estate Planning* (Federated Press) 2-4 (2016); Dykema, "Changes to the Principal Residence Exemption and the Impact on Trusts", 14(3) *Tax Hyperion* (Carswell) 1-3 (April-June 2017).

Under (c.1) before 2017 (and for increase in value to end of 2016 under 40(6.1)), most trusts with SBs can claim the exemption: see VIEWS docs 2004-0063491E5 (trust created for two adult siblings); 2006-0194211M4 (house owned by trust and inhabited by person with life interest); 2008-0289721E5 (whether parents can be SBs); 2010-0356041E5 (trust cannot designate 2 properties for 2 beneficiaries for same year); 2010-0362011E5 (exemption claimed by trust created by taxpayer's will); 2010-0365181E5 (estate, after owner's death); 2010-0368141E5 (application of half-hectare rule); 2011-0415231E5 (only 1 beneficiary need occupy the home); 2012-0453941C6 (determination of SB, impact on SB's own PR claim, and effect of renunciation of rights by SB); 2012-0464321E5 (rollout of PR by trust to multiple SBs); 2015-0584611E5 (testamentary trust, spouse occupied house after death). See also Corbin, "The Parent Trap", 21(12) *Money & Family Law* (Carswell) 91-93 (Dec. 2006); Drache, "Principal Residence Exemption for Home Held in Personal Trust", xxix(23) *The Canadian Taxpayer* (Carswell) 182-83 (Nov. 20/07); Bernstein & Atsaidis, "Residence Trusts", 16(8) *Canadian Tax Highlights [CTH]* (ctf.ca) 9-10 (Aug. 2008); Bernstein & Pernica, "Personal Trust: Cottages", 19(5) *CTH* 6-7 (May 2011); Baxter, "Reversionary Trusts and the Principal Residence Exemption", 8(6) *Tax Hyperion* (Carswell, June 2011); Bernstein & Pernica, "Personal Trusts and Cottage Properties Residences", 2057 *Tax Topics* (CCH) 1-2 (Aug. 11, 2011).

Para. (e): land over 0.5 hectare is considered necessary if the home's size or character and its location on the lot make the excess land essential to its use and enjoyment as a residence; where the home's location requires the excess land for access to/from public roads; or where there is a legal minimum lot size or unavoidable severance restriction; keeping pets or country living is not sufficient: Income Tax Folio S1-F3-C2 ¶2.33-2.35, VIEWS docs 2005-0125521E5, 2006-0204111M4, 2008-0263781E5; 2008-0286351I7 (not where lot size bylaw increases after acquisition); 2010-0387891I7 (detailed discussion of "objective test"); 2011-0401071E5; 2011-0416011E5; 2011-0417481E5; 2011-0423381E5, 2013-0498701E5, 2016-0629951I7. See *Yates*, [1986] 2 C.T.C. 46 (FCA); *Augart*, [1993] 2 C.T.C. 34 (FCA); *Carlile*, [1995] 2 C.T.C. 273 (FCA); *Stuart*, 2004 FCA 80 (financial circumstances of sale not relevant to "necessary"); *Cassidy*, 2011 FCA 271 ("legal minimum lot size" test met because by-law applied on acquisition; later change irrelevant); *Rode*, [1985] 1 C.T.C. 2324 (TCC) (test of what is necessary is objective); *Todesco*, [2000] 1 C.T.C. 2144 (TCC) (extra land must be necessary, not just enjoyable); *Makosz*, 2018 TCC 250 (woodlot sold off separately was not necessary where not proven to have been needed to heat the house). The land to be part of the PR must be "immediately contiguous", meaning touching the land under the home, even though the French term "adjacent" is ambiguous: 2014-0528271E5. CRA will challenge an excessive allocation of value to the house: e.g., *Munro*, 2006 TCC 294. An adjoining lot under separate title, sold with the home, might be part of the PR: 2007-0227451E5, 2010-0373041E5; but not if one spouse owns the home and the other the lot: 2012-0433681E5. A trailer can qualify as a PR but likely only for 0.5 hectare: *Windrim*, [1991] 1 C.T.C. 271 (FCTD), doc 2009-0341621E5. See also Baxter, "Half a Hectare", 3(9) *Canadian Tax Highlights* (ctf.ca) 65-66 (Sept. 19, 1995); Bergen, "The Tax Treatment of Principal Residences", 1993 Cdn Tax Foundation conference report, at 12:22-27; Elawny & Virji, "Principal Residence Exemption and Zoning Requirements", 2148 *Tax Topics* (CCH) 1-3 (May 9, 2013).

See also Magee, "Investing in Residential Real Estate", 64(4) *Canadian Tax Journal* 859-85 (2016); Sinclair & Paisley, "Planning for Principal Residences", 2017 Ontario Tax Conf.

Subpara. (c.1)(iii.1) added by 2017 budget bill #2, effective Dec. 14, 2017 (but see opening words of (iii.1)).

Paras. (a) and (c) amended by 2000 same-sex partners bill to refer to "common-law partner(ship)", effective 2001 or earlier by election.

Definition amended by 2001 and 1992 technical bills, both for dispositions after 1990. 54"principal residence" was 54(g) before RSC 1985 (5th Supp) consolidation for tax years ending after Nov. 1991.

Regulations: 2301 (prescribed manner of designation).

I.T. Application Rules: 26.1(1) (change of use of property before 1972).

Income Tax Folios: S1-F3-C2: Principal residence [replaces IT-120R6, IT-437R].

Interpretation Bulletins: IT-218R: Profit, capital gains and losses from the sale of real estate, including farmland and inherited land and conversion of real estate from capital property to inventory and vice versa; IT-268R3: *Inter vivos* transfer of farm property to child.

I.T. Technical News: 7 (principal residence and the capital gains election).

Info Sheets: TI-001: Sale of a residence by an owner builder.

Forms: T1079: Designation of a property as a principal residence by a personal trust; T1079-WS: Principal residence worksheet; T1255: Designation of a property as a principal residence by the legal representative of a deceased individual; T2091(IND): Designation of a property as a principal residence by an individual (other than a personal trust); T2091 (IND)-WS: Principal residence worksheet.

"proceeds of disposition" of property includes,

(a) the sale price of property that has been sold,

(b) compensation for property unlawfully taken,

(c) compensation for property destroyed, and any amount payable under a policy of insurance in respect of loss or destruction of property,

(d) compensation for property taken under statutory authority or the sale price of property sold to a person by whom notice of an intention to take it under statutory authority was given,

(e) compensation for property injuriously affected, whether lawfully or unlawfully or under statutory authority or otherwise,

(f) compensation for property damaged and any amount payable under a policy of insurance in respect of damage to property, except to the extent that such compensation or amount, as the case may be, has within a reasonable time after the damage been expended on repairing the damage,

(g) an amount by which the liability of a taxpayer to a mortgagee or hypothecary creditor is reduced as a result of the sale of mortgaged or hypothecated property under a provision of the mortgage or hypothec, plus any amount received by the taxpayer out of the proceeds of the sale,

(h) any amount included in computing a taxpayer's proceeds of disposition of the property because of section 79, and

(i) in the case of a share, an amount deemed by subparagraph 88(2)(b)(ii) not to be a dividend on that share,

but notwithstanding any other provision of this Part, does not include

(j) any amount that would otherwise be proceeds of disposition of a share to the extent that the amount is deemed by subsection 84(2) or (3) to be a dividend received except to the extent the dividend is deemed

(i) by paragraph 55(2)(b) to be proceeds of disposition of the share, or

(ii) by subparagraph 88(2)(b)(ii) not to be a dividend, or

(k) any amount that would otherwise be proceeds of disposition of property of a taxpayer to the extent that the amount is deemed by subsection 84.1(1), 212.1(1.1) or 212.2(2) to be a dividend paid to the taxpayer or, if the taxpayer is a partnership, to a member of the taxpayer;

Related Provisions: 13(21)"proceeds of disposition" — Parallel definition for depreciable property; 13(21.1) — Disposition of a building; 43.1 — Life estates in real property; 44(6) — Deemed proceeds on replacement of land and building; 48.1(1) — Optional gain when small business corporation becomes public; 49.1 — Satisfaction of obligation is not a disposition of property; 50(1) — Debts established to be bad debts and shares of bankrupt corporation; 51.1 — Deemed proceeds on conversion of convertible bond; 55(2) — Deemed proceeds or capital gain; 56.4(3) — Where non-competition agreement deemed part of sale of shares; 59(5), 66.4(5) — Definition applies to 59 and 66.4; 69(1)(b) — Inadequate considerations — taxpayer deemed to have received proceeds; 69(4) — Shareholder appropriation — deemed proceeds to corporation; 69(11) — Deemed proceeds; 70(5) — Deemed disposition on death; 79(3) — Deemed proceeds to debtor on surrender of property to creditor; 79.1(5) — Deemed proceeds where property sold and repossessed in same taxation year; 85(1)(a) — Transfer of property to corporation by shareholders; 85.1(1)(a)(i) — Share for share exchange; 86(1)(c) — Exchange of shares by a shareholder in course of reorganization of capital; 87(4)(a), (c) — Shares of predecessor corporation; 88(1)(a), (b) — Winding-up; 128.1(4)(b) — Deemed disposition of property on ceasing to be resident in Canada; 128.1(8) — Retroactive adjustment to proceeds for deemed disposition on emigration where taxpayer returns to Canada; 132.2(3)(a), (c), (f), (g), (4)(b), (5)(c) — Deemed proceeds on mutual fund reorganization; 248(1) — Definition of "disposition"; 248(39)(b) — Anti-avoidance — selling property and donating proceeds.

Notes: See Notes to 188.1(5) re meaning of "includes" in the opening words.

In *Daishowa-Marubeni*, 2013 SCC 29, proceeds of disposition (**PoD**) did not include the purchaser's assumption of reforestation liabilities, since this obligation was "embedded" in the asset and so the sale price already reflected it (similar to a property in need of repair). However, the assumption of an external liability such as a mortgage *does* increase PoD: para. 26. CRA issued a directive to its offices on Nov. 21/13 to apply *Daishowa* to oil & gas reclamation obligations (Jeff Sadrian, CRA Roundtable, 2013 Cdn Tax Foundation annual conference).

Damages for breach of an agreement to buy a principal residence are PoD of the contract, not of the residence (so not exempt): VIEWS doc 2016-0652851C6 [2016 APFF q.3]; and cannot reduce the cost of the property per IT-365R2 para. 9: 2017-0709051C6 [2017 APFF q.7].

The "sale price" of shares under para. (a) was reduced by an amount paid to retire the corporation's debt in VIEWS doc 2010-037078117, based on *Fradet*, [1986] 2 C.T.C. 321 (FCA). See also Notes to 40(1).

PoD do not include an amount paid by a government, on purchasing land for a highway, for "injurious affection" to other lands the vendor retains: *Hurley*, 2003 TCC 22.

PoD can be triggered by a deemed disposition on death (70(5)), emigration (128.1(4)), gift (69(1)), synthetic disposition arrangement (80.6) or others: see "Disposition: deemed" in Topical Index. Where the property is replaced with similar property, a rollover may be available: see 44(1) and 13(4).

In *Valley Equipment*, 2008 FCA 65, court-awarded damages for cancellation of a dealer agreement by John Deere were "compensation for property unlawfully taken" and thus were PoD.

Funds received by a member on windup of an unincorporated association are PoD: VIEWS docs 2009-031086117, 2018-0779221R3. Property received on windup of a non-share corporation is likely PoD: IT-409 paras. 9-11, doc 2009-0332161E5.

In *Singh*, 2008 TCC 629, payment for access to the taxpayer's land by a pipeline owner was not PoD and was fully taxable; but in *Ritchie*, 2018 TCC 113, a "signing bonus" towards granting an easement for a pipeline was PoD (not taxable under 12(1)(x)).

Para. (e): compensation for property injuriously affected includes: payment by landfill site owner to vendor of land next door sold for less than market value due to the landfill (VIEWS doc 2004-0067411E5); payments to landowners by oil & gas companies for conducting exploration on their land (2008-0297051E5); settlement by financial advisor for failing to dispose of an estate's shares when the market was dropping (2010-0377131E5); payment by an expropriating municipality for the remaining land that has been injuriously affected (2016-0625261E5); Newfoundland Community Relocation Program payment to owner for diminishing value of property (2017-0682691E5).

Prepaid rent compensated by a buyer may be PoD: docs 9909965, 9924585.

Where additional amounts are received long after disposition (e.g., following a class action), this may be additional PoD for the year of sale, which may be statute-barred: VIEWS doc 2002-013563717; or may be capital gain in the year received: 2008-0288501M4. Where proceeds include a promissory note that is unpaid, the loss on the note is a new capital loss: *Basi*, 2012 TCC 345, para. 27. Where a deposit is forfeited see doc 9600785. Proceeds agreed to but not yet paid are included in PoD but a reserve may be allowed under 40(1)(a)(iii). Where proceeds must be repaid later, there is a capital loss in the later year (e.g., reverse earnout agreement: see Notes to 12(1)(g)).

Monthly payments made as deposits towards purchase of property would cumulatively be PoD: VIEWS doc 2007-0244941E5.

PoD include an amount received but released to a spouse as part of a divorce settlement: doc 2011-0405071E5.

See also Adam Scherer & Shane Rayman, "Tax Implications of Expropriation", 56(4) *Canadian Tax Journal* 870-92 (2008).

Para. (k) amended by 2018 budget bill #2, for dispositions after Feb. 26, 2018, to add "or, if the taxpayer is a partnership, to a member of the taxpayer".

Para. (k) amended by 2016 budget bill #2, for dispositions after March 21, 2016, to change "212.1(1)" to "212.1(1.1)".

Para. (j) amended by 2016 budget bill #1 for dividends received after April 20, 2015, consequential on amendments to s. 55.

Definition amended by 2001 *Civil Code* harmonization bill (effective June 14, 2001), 1999 Budget, 1994 technical bill. 54"proceeds of disposition" was 54(h) before RSC 1985 (5th Supp) consolidation for tax years ending after Nov. 1991.

Income Tax Folios: S3-F9-C1: Lottery winnings, miscellaneous receipts, and income (and losses) from crime [replaces IT-185R, IT-213R, IT-256R, IT-334R2]; S7-F1-C1: Split-receipting and deemed fair market value.

Interpretation Bulletins: IT-125R4: Dispositions of resource properties; IT-149R4: Winding-up dividend; IT-170R: Sale of property — when included in income computation; IT-200: Surface rentals and farming operations; IT-259R4: Exchanges of property; IT-271R: Expropriations (cancelled); IT-444R: Corporations — involuntary dissolutions; IT-460: Dispositions — absence of consideration; IT-505: Mortgage foreclosures and conditional sales repossessions (cancelled).

I.T. Technical News: 39 (settlement of a shareholder class action suit).

Advance Tax Rulings: ATR-28: Redemption of capital stock of family farm corporation; ATR-35: Partitioning of assets to get specific ownership — "butterfly".

"specified property" of a taxpayer is capital property of the taxpayer that is

(a) a share,

(b) a capital interest in a trust,

(c) an interest in a partnership, or

(d) an option to acquire specified property of the taxpayer;

Notes: 54"specified property" added by 1994 technical bill, for taxation years that end after Feb. 21, 1994. The term is used in 49(3.01) and 53(4)-(6).

"superficial loss" of a taxpayer means the taxpayer's loss from the disposition of a particular property where

(a) during the period that begins 30 days before and ends 30 days after the disposition, the taxpayer or a person affiliated with the taxpayer acquires a property (in this definition referred to as the "substituted property") that is, or is identical to, the particular property, and

(b) at the end of that period, the taxpayer or a person affiliated with the taxpayer owns or had a right to acquire the substituted property,

except where the disposition was

(c) a disposition deemed to have been made by subsection 45(1), section 48 as it read in its application before 1993, section 50 or 70, subsection 104(4), section 128.1, paragraph 132.2(3)(a) or (c), subsection 138(11.3) or 138.2(4) or 142.5(2), section 142.6 or any of subsections 144(4.1) and (4.2) and 149(10),

(d) the expiry of an option,

(e) a disposition to which paragraph 40(2)(e.1) applies,

(f) a disposition by a taxpayer that was subject to a loss restriction event within 30 days after the disposition,

(g) a disposition by a person that, within 30 days after the disposition, became or ceased to be exempt from tax under this Part on its taxable income, or

(h) a disposition to which subsection 40(3.4) or 69(5) applies,

and, for the purpose of this definition,

(i) a right to acquire a property (other than a right, as security only, derived from a mortgage, hypothec, agreement for sale or similar obligation) is deemed to be a property that is identical to the property, and

(j) a share of the capital stock of a SIFT wind-up corporation in respect of a SIFT wind-up entity is, if the share was acquired before 2013, deemed to be a property that is identical to equity in the SIFT wind-up entity.

Related Provisions: 13(21.2) — Superficial loss rule for depreciable property; 18(13)–(16) — Superficial loss in moneylending business or adventure in nature of trade; 40(2)(g)(i) — Superficial loss deemed to be nil; 40(3.3), (3.4) — Limitation on loss where property acquired by affiliated person; 53(1)(f) — Addition to ACB of substituted property; 248(12) — Identical properties; 251.1 — Affiliated persons; 251.2 — Loss restriction event.

Notes: 40(2)(g)(i) disallows a superficial loss as a capital loss (e.g. *Krauss*, 2009 TCC 597 (aff'd on other grounds 2010 FCA 284)). There is no parallel rule preventing recognition of a gain where property disposed of is immediately reacquired. There is also no superficial-loss rule for income losses (see Notes to 54"capital property").

For a disposition by a corporation, para. (h) excludes the superficial-loss rule from applying since 40(3.4) applies instead. See Notes to 13(21.2) for more on the rules for superficial losses and transfers of accrued losses.

A capital loss can be transferred to a spouse by transferring loss property to the spouse, electing under 73(1) at the current low value (causing the superficial loss rule to apply to this transfer), waiting 30 days and having the spouse sell the property, with the spouse's ACB increased by 53(1)(f). See VIEWS docs 2001-0106905, 2003-0017075, 2009-0327081C6 [accepts this despite *Lipson* (SCC), where "backwards" use of the spousal attribution rule triggered GAAR].

See 251.1 for "affiliated", and note that the superficial loss rules do not apply if a child or parent purchases the property disposed of by the taxpayer. This can be a useful planning tool. Before March 23/04, a trust and its beneficiary were not affiliated, but transfers were held to violate GAAR in *Triad Gestco*, 2012 CarswellNat 3853 (FCA), and *1207192 Ontario Ltd.*, [2013] 1 C.T.C. 1 (FCA) (leave to appeal denied 2013 CarswellOnt 3394 (SCC)), so losses were denied.

IT-387R2 para. 7 states that shares in different classes are identical if one class has rights allowing conversion into the other. Two options on the same share, with different exercise prices or dates, may not be identical if "a prospective buyer would have a preference for acquiring one rather than the other": VIEWS doc 2008-0284441C6. See also 2009-0337721I7 (shares after merger are not identical shares).

Where shares are acquired and sold at a loss in the same period, but not all are sold, part of the loss may be denied and allocated to the shares still held, based on the assumption that each share still held is a substituted property for one share sold: VIEWS docs 2001-0088155, 2004-0073011E5. For the administrative calculation see doc 2005-0150811E5. A loss on foreign currency is not a superficial loss: 2008-028011I7, 2017-0705201C6 [2017 APFF q.10] (see Notes to 39(2)).

See also VIEWS docs 2009-0343051M4 (SL on sale by taxpayer and repurchase by TFSA); 2009-0330501E5 (whether X's spouse affiliated with X's company); 2009-

0348901E5 (SL on swap to a RESP); 2010-0352921E5 (SL on transfer to RESP); 2010-0353291E5 (SL on foreign currency losses); 2012-0454061C6 (may be SL on attempted loss consolidation); 2014-0518561E5 (sale of Opco shares to Holdco, then Opco is wound up into Holdco: likely no SL but GAAR might apply).

For the meaning of "derived" in para. (i), see Notes to 18.1(12).

Para. (c) amended by 2017 budget bill #2 to refer to 138.2(4), for tax years that begin after 2017.

Definition earlier amended by 2013 budget bill #2 (last change effective for tax years that begin after March 20, 2013), 2002-2013 technical bill, 2009 budget bill #1, 2008 budget bill #2, 2001 *Civil Code* harmonization bill, 1995-97, 1994, 1993 and 1991 technical bills. 54"superficial loss" was 54(i) before RSC 1985 (5th Suppl) consolidation for tax years ending after Nov. 1991.

I.T. Application Rules: 26(6) (superficial loss where disposition from June 19 to December 31, 1971).

Interpretation Bulletins: IT-159R3: Capital debts established to be bad debts; IT-325R2: Property transfers after separation, divorce and annulment; IT-387R2: Meaning of "identical properties".

I.T. Technical News: 7 (control by a group — 50/50 arrangement (re para. (f))).

Definitions [s. 54]: "adjusted cost base" — 54, 248(1); "affiliated" — 251.1; "amount" — 248(1); "beneficially interested" — 248(25); "brother" — 252(2); "business" — 248(1); "calendar year" — *Interpretation Act* 37(1)(a); "Canada" — 255; "capital gain" — 39(1)(a), 248(1); "capital interest" — in a trust 108(1), 248(1); "capital loss" — 39(1)(b), 248(1); "capital property" — 54, 248(1); "child" — 252(1); "class of shares" — 248(6); "common-law partner", "common-law partnership" — 248(1); "control" — 256(6)–(9); "corporation" — 248(1), *Interpretation Act* 35(1); "deferred profit sharing plan" — 147(1), 248(1); "depreciable property" — 13(21), 248(1); "disposition", "dividend" — 248(1); "eligible beneficiary" — 122(3); "electing beneficiary" — 122(3); "eligible capital property" — 54, 248(1); "employees profit sharing plan" — 144(1), 248(1); "exemption threshold" — 54; "fair market value" — see 69(1) Notes; "father" — 252(2)(a); "flow-through share" — 66(15), 248(1); "flow-through share class of property", "fresh-start date" — 54; "identical" — 54"superficial loss"(i), (j), 248(12); "individual" — 248(1); "loss restriction event" — 251.2; "mother" — 252(2)(a); "partnership" — see 96(1) Notes; "person", "personal trust" — 248(1); "personal-use property" — 54, 248(1); "prescribed", "property" — 248(1); "qualified disability trust" — 122(3); "registered charity" — 248(1); "registered retirement income fund" — 146.3(1), 248(1); "registered retirement savings plan" — 146(1), 248(1); "resident in Canada" — 94(3)(a), 250; "separation agreement" — 248(1); "share" — 248(1); "sister" — 252(2); "specified beneficiary" — 54"principal residence"(c.1)(ii); "substituted property" — 54"superficial loss"(a); "taxation year" — 249; "taxpayer" — 248(1); "trust" — 104(1), 248(1), (3); "writing", "written" — *Interpretation Act* 35(1)"writing".

54.1 (1) Exception to principal residence rules — A taxation year in which a taxpayer does not ordinarily inhabit the taxpayer's property as a consequence of the relocation of the place of employment of the taxpayer or the taxpayer's spouse or common-law partner while the taxpayer or the taxpayer's spouse or common-law partner, as the case may be, is employed by an employer who is not a person to whom the taxpayer or the taxpayer's spouse or common-law partner is related is deemed not to be a previous taxation year referred to in paragraph (d) of the definition "principal residence" in section 54 if

(a) the property subsequently becomes ordinarily inhabited by the taxpayer during the term of the taxpayer's or the taxpayer's spouse's or common-law partner's employment by that employer or before the end of the taxation year immediately following the taxation year in which the taxpayer's or the spouse's or common-law partner's employment by that employer terminates; or

(b) the taxpayer dies during the term of the taxpayer's or the spouse's or common-law partner's employment by that employer.

Notes: 54.1(1) opening words amended by 2002-2013 technical bill (Part 5 — technical), restructuring the wording to accommodate a missing reference to "common-law partner", effective as per Notes to 248(1)"common-law partner" (2001 or earlier).

(2) Definition of "property" — In this section, "property", in relation to a taxpayer, means a housing unit

(a) owned by the taxpayer,

(b) in respect of which the taxpayer has a leasehold interest, or

(c) in respect of which the taxpayer owned a share of the capital stock of a co-operative housing corporation if the share was acquired for the sole purpose of acquiring the right to inhabit a housing unit owned by the corporation whether jointly with another person or otherwise in the year and that at all times was at least 40 kilometres farther from the taxpayer's or the taxpayer's spouse's or common-law partner's new place of employment than was the taxpayer's subsequent place or places of residence.

Related Provisions: 40(2)(b), 40(4)-(6) — Principal residence rules.

Notes: The 40km in 54.1(2) closing words should be measured based on normal road distance. See Notes to 248(1)"eligible relocation".

54.1 amended by 2000 same-sex partners bill (and by Part 3 of 2001 technical bill) to add references to "common-law partner", effective 2001 or earlier by election.

Definitions [s. 54.1]: "common-law partner" — 248(1); "corporation" — 248(1), *Interpretation Act* 35(1); "employed", "employer", "employment", "person" — 248(1); "property" — 54.1(2); "share" — 248(1); "taxation year" — 249; "taxpayer" — 248(1).

Income Tax Folios [s. 54.1]: S1-F3-C2: Principal residence [replaces IT-120R6, IT-437R].

54.2 Certain shares deemed to be capital property —
Where any person has disposed of property that consisted of all or substantially all of the assets used in an active business carried on by that person to a corporation for consideration that included shares of the corporation, the shares shall be deemed to be capital property of the person.

Related Provisions: 39(4) — Election re disposition of Canadian securities; 85(1) — Rollovers of property to corporation; 110.6(14)(f)(ii) — Shares qualify for capital gains exemption without waiting for 2-year holding period; 248(1) — "Business" does not include adventure or concern in the nature of trade.

Notes: 54.2 ensures that when a proprietor rolls business assets into a corp under 85(1) and then sells its shares, the gain will be capital gain even if the shares are held for only a short time, and can qualify for the 110.6(2.1) capital gains exemption (110.6(14)(f)(ii)(A) provides an exception from the 2-year holding requirement).

Even if 54.2 does not apply, the gain may be capital: see Notes to 54"capital property". This includes if the rollover + sale generates no economic profit: see those Notes under "Inventory must be "held for sale" ".

"Business": On whether what is transferred is one "business" when a taxpayer has multiple activities, see Notes to Reg. 1101(1).

"Person" includes a partnership for 54.2: VIEWS docs December 1990-265 [903344], 2003-0009513.

"Substantially all": CRA says this means 90% or more. The test can be met using the transferred assets' value, or by them being sufficient to carry on the business: *Atlantic Packaging*, 2018 TCC 183, paras. 26-27 (aff'd 2020 FCA 75 without discussing this point; leave to appeal denied 2020 CarswellNat 4337 (SCC); 54.2 did not apply because only 68% of the value of a division's assets were rolled over).

Definitions [s. 54.2]: "active business", "business" — 248(1); "capital property" — 54, 248(1); "corporation" — 248(1), *Interpretation Act* 35(1); "disposition", "person", "property", "share" — 248(1).

Information Circulars: 88-2 Supplement, para. 7: General anti-avoidance rule — section 245 of the *Income Tax Act*.

55. [Capital gain strips and butterflies] — (1) Definitions —
In this section,

"distribution" means a direct or indirect transfer of property of a corporation (referred to in this section as the **"distributing corporation"**) to one or more corporations (each of which is referred to in this section as a **"transferee corporation"**) where, in respect of each type of property owned by the distributing corporation immediately before the transfer, each transferee corporation receives property of that type the fair market value of which is equal to or approximates the amount determined by the formula

$$A \times \frac{B}{C}$$

where

A is the fair market value, immediately before the transfer, of all property of that type owned at that time by the distributing corporation,

B is the fair market value, immediately before the transfer, of all the shares of the capital stock of the distributing corporation owned at that time by the transferee corporation, and

C is the fair market value, immediately before the transfer, of all the issued shares of the capital stock of the distributing corporation;

Related Provisions: 55(3.02) — Where distributing corporation is a specified corporation; 88(1)(c)(iv) — Winding-up.

Notes: In simple terms, a distribution is a divisive reorganization whereby each corporate shareholder of the corporation that receives property on the distribution receives its *pro rata* share of each type of property owned by the distributing corporation immediately before the distribution. The CRA is flexible on the classification of assets for this purpose: VIEWS doc 2011-0399401C6.

Definition "distribution" added by 1994 Budget, effective for dividends received after February 21, 1994, other than dividends received before 1995 in the course of a reorganization that was required on February 22, 1994 to be carried out pursuant to a written agreement entered into before February 22, 1994.

"permitted acquisition", in relation to a distribution by a distributing corporation, means an acquisition of property by a person or partnership on, or as part of,

(a) a distribution, or

(b) a permitted exchange or permitted redemption in relation to a distribution by another distributing corporation;

Notes: Definition "permitted acquisition" added by 1994 Budget, effective on the same basis as 55(1)"distribution" (see Notes thereto).

"permitted exchange", in relation to a distribution by a distributing corporation, means

(a) an exchange of shares for shares of the capital stock of the distributing corporation to which subsection 51(1) or 86(1) applies or would, if the shares were capital property to the holder thereof, apply, other than an exchange that resulted in an acquisition of control of the distributing corporation by any person or group of persons, and

(b) an exchange of shares of the capital stock of the distributing corporation by one or more shareholders of the distributing corporation (each of whom is referred to in this paragraph as a "participant") for shares of the capital stock of another corporation (referred to in this paragraph as the "acquiror") in contemplation of the distribution where

(i) no share of the capital stock of the acquiror outstanding immediately after the exchange (other than directors' qualifying shares) is owned at that time by any person or partnership other than a participant,

and either

(ii) the acquiror owns, immediately before the distribution, all the shares each of which is a share of the capital stock of the distributing corporation that was owned immediately before the exchange by a participant, or

(iii) the fair market value, immediately before the distribution, of each participant's shares of the capital stock of the acquiror is equal to or approximates the amount determined by the formula

$$\left(A \times \frac{B}{C}\right) + D$$

where

A is the fair market value, immediately before the distribution, of all the shares of the capital stock of the acquiror then outstanding (other than shares issued to participants in consideration for shares of a specified class all the shares of which were acquired by the acquiror on the exchange),

B is the fair market value, immediately before the exchange, of all the shares of the capital stock of the distributing corporation (other than shares of a specified class none or all of the shares of which were acquired by the acquiror on the exchange) owned at that time by the participant,

C is the fair market value, immediately before the exchange, of all the shares (other than shares of a specified class none or all of the shares of which were acquired by the acquiror on the exchange and shares to be redeemed, acquired or cancelled by the distributing corporation pursuant to the exercise of a statutory right of dissent by the holder of the share) of the capital stock of the distributing corporation outstanding immediately before the exchange, and

D   is the fair market value, immediately before the distribution, of all the shares issued to the participant by the acquiror in consideration for shares of a specified class all of the shares of which were acquired by the acquiror on the exchange;

Related Provisions: 256(6)–(9) — Whether control acquired.

Notes: This definition covers two types of share-for-share exchanges. The first is an exchange to which 51(1) or 86(1) applies (or would apply if the shares were capital property), except where it results in an acquisition of control of the distributing corp. The second is an exchange of shares of the distributing corp for shares of another corp (the acquiror) made in contemplation of the tax-deferred distribution of property by the distributing corp to one or more of its corporate shareholders. For the second type to qualify, each participating shareholder must receive their *pro rata* share of shares of the acquiror on the exchange and, immediately after, all the issued shares of the acquiror must be owned by those who participated in the exchange. If not all the shares of the distributing corp owned by a participant immediately before the exchange are transferred to the acquiror on the exchange, all the shareholders of the distributing corp (other than those holding only shares of a "specified class") must participate in the exchange on a *pro rata* basis. Where a participant holds shares of a specified class before the exchange and none or all of the shares of that class are transferred on the exchange, the shares of that class are ignored in determining whether the participants have participated in the exchange on a *pro rata* basis.

The definition's requirements generally limit the use of the butterfly exemption to two basic types of butterfly:

- the spin-off, in which some of each type of property owned by the distributing corp is transferred to a new corp having the same shareholders; and

- the split-up, in which one or more of the shareholders of the distributing corp cease to be shareholders and, in so doing, receive their *pro rata* share of each type of property the corp owns.

The definition's requirements must be satisfied whenever a person acquires a share of the distributing corp in contemplation of the distribution from another person to whom the acquiror is not related. For this purpose, the acquiror is considered not related to the other person unless

- the acquiror acquires all of the shares of the distributing corp that are owned by the other person,

- the acquiror is related, after the reorganization that includes the distribution, to the distributing corp (see 55(3.2)(c)), or

- the acquiror acquired the share on a capital distribution by a personal trust (see 55(3.2)(d)).

For "directors' qualifying shares" in (b)(i), see Notes to 85(1.3).

For CRA interpretation see VIEWS docs 2010-0373211C6 (where family trust acquires shares of transferee after butterfly); 2017-0699201R3 (cross-border butterfly). See also rulings in Notes to 55(3).

Definition "permitted exchange" added by 1994 Budget, effective on the same basis as 55(1)"distribution" (see Notes thereto).

"permitted redemption", in relation to a distribution by a distributing corporation, means

(a) a redemption or purchase for cancellation by the distributing corporation, as part of the reorganization in which the distribution was made, of all the shares of its capital stock that were owned, immediately before the distribution, by a transferee corporation in relation to the distributing corporation,

(b) a redemption or purchase for cancellation by a transferee corporation in relation to the distributing corporation, or by a corporation that, immediately after the redemption or purchase, was a subsidiary wholly-owned corporation of the transferee corporation, as part of the reorganization in which the distribution was made, of all of the shares of the capital stock of the transferee corporation or the subsidiary wholly-owned corporation that were acquired by the distributing corporation in consideration for the transfer of property received by the transferee corporation on the distribution, and

(c) a redemption or purchase for cancellation by the distributing corporation, in contemplation of the distribution, of all the shares of its capital stock each of which is

(i) a share of a specified class the cost of which, at the time of its issuance, to its original owner was equal to the fair market value at that time of the consideration for which it was issued, or

(ii) a share that was issued, in contemplation of the distribution, by the distributing corporation in exchange for a share described in subparagraph (i);

Notes: Definition "permitted redemption" added by 1994 Budget, effective on the same basis as 55(1)"distribution" (see Notes thereto).

Paras. (a) and (b) amended by 1995-97 technical bill, effective for dividends received after February 21, 1994. (This appears to override the grandfathering originally provided when the definition was enacted.)

"qualified person", in relation to a distribution, means a person or partnership with whom the distributing corporation deals at arm's length at all times during the course of the series of transactions or events that includes the distribution if

(a) at any time before the distribution,

(i) all of the shares of each class of the capital stock of the distributing corporation that includes shares that cause that person or partnership to be a specified shareholder of the distributing corporation (in this definition all of those shares in all of those classes are referred to as the "exchanged shares") are, in the circumstances described in paragraph (a) of the definition "permitted exchange", exchanged for consideration that consists solely of shares of a specified class of the capital stock of the distributing corporation (in this definition referred to as the "new shares"), or

(ii) the terms or conditions of all of the exchanged shares are amended (which shares are in this definition referred to after the amendment as the "amended shares") and the amended shares are shares of a specified class of the capital stock of the distributing corporation,

(b) immediately before the exchange or amendment, the exchanged shares are listed on a designated stock exchange,

(c) immediately after the exchange or amendment, the new shares or the amended shares, as the case may be, are listed on a designated stock exchange,

(d) the exchanged shares would be shares of a specified class if they were not convertible into, or exchangeable for, other shares,

(e) the new shares or the amended shares, as the case may be, and the exchanged shares are non-voting in respect of the election of the board of directors of the distributing corporation except in the event of a failure or default under the terms or conditions of the shares, and

(f) no holder of the new shares or the amended shares, as the case may be, is entitled to receive on the redemption, cancellation or acquisition of the new shares or the amended shares, as the case may be, by the distributing corporation or by any person with whom the distributing corporation does not deal at arm's length an amount (other than a premium for early redemption) that is greater than the total of the fair market value of the consideration for which the exchanged shares were issued and the amount of any unpaid dividends on the new shares or on the amended shares, as the case may be;

Notes: See Notes to 55(6). Definition "qualified person" added by 2002-2013 technical bill (Part 5 — technical), effective for dividends received after 1999; but before Dec. 14, 2007, read "designated stock exchange" as "prescribed stock exchange".

"safe-income determination time" for a transaction or event or a series of transactions or events means the time that is the earlier of

(a) the time that is immediately after the earliest disposition or increase in interest described in any of subparagraphs (3)(a)(i) to (v) that resulted from the transaction, event or series, and

(b) the time that is immediately before the earliest time that a dividend is paid as part of the transaction, event or series;

Notes: See Notes to 55(2), and VIEWS doc 2016-0672321C6 [2016 TEI q.B3] (where company pays regular dividend). Definition "safe-income determination time" added by 1995-97 technical bill, effective for dividends received after June 20, 1996.

"specified class" means a class of shares of the capital stock of a distributing corporation where

(a) the paid-up capital in respect of the class immediately before the beginning of the series of transactions or events that includes a distribution by the distributing corporation was not less than the fair market value of the consideration for which the shares of that class then outstanding were issued,

(b) under neither the terms and conditions of the shares nor any agreement in respect of the shares are the shares convertible into or exchangeable for shares other than shares of a specified class or shares of the capital stock of a transferee corporation in relation to the distributing corporation,

(c) no holder of the shares is entitled to receive on the redemption, cancellation or acquisition of the shares by the corporation or by any person with whom the corporation does not deal at arm's length an amount (other than a premium for early redemption) that is greater than the total of the fair market value of the consideration for which the shares were issued and the amount of any unpaid dividends on the shares, and

(d) the shares are non-voting in respect of the election of the board of directors except in the event of a failure or default under the terms or conditions of the shares;

Notes: For a ruling that para. (b) is met when shares of a series are convertible into another series, see VIEWS doc 2006-0177341R3.

Para. (c) amended and (d) added by 2002-2013 technical bill (Part 5 — technical), for shares issued after Dec. 20, 2002.

Definition "specified class" added by 1994 Budget, effective on the same basis as 55(1)"distribution" (see Notes thereto).

"specified corporation" in relation to a distribution means a distributing corporation

(a) that is a public corporation or a specified wholly-owned corporation of a public corporation,

(b) shares of the capital stock of which are exchanged for shares of the capital stock of another corporation (referred to in this definition and subsection (3.02) as an "acquiror") in an exchange to which the definition "permitted exchange" in this subsection would apply if that definition were read without reference to paragraph (a) and subparagraph (b)(ii) of that definition,

(c) that does not make a distribution, to a corporation that is not an acquiror, after 1998 and before the day that is three years after the day on which the shares of the capital stock of the distributing corporation are exchanged in a transaction described in paragraph (b), and

(d) no acquiror in relation to which makes a distribution after 1998 and before the day that is three years after the day on which the shares of the capital stock of the distributing corporation are exchanged in a transaction described in paragraph (b),

and, for the purposes of paragraphs (c) and (d),

(e) a corporation that is formed by an amalgamation of two or more other corporations is deemed to be the same corporation as, and a continuation of, each of the other corporations, and

(f) where there has been a winding-up of a corporation to which subsection 88(1) applies, the parent is deemed to be the same corporation as, and a continuation of, the subsidiary;

Notes: 55(1)"specified corporation" added by 2001 technical bill, for transfers that occur after 1998. As a result of "specified corporation", "specified wholly-owned corporation" and 55(3.02), the requirement that each transferee corporation must receive its *pro rata* share of each type of property owned by the distributing corporation on a butterfly no longer applies for certain public corporation butterflies. In particular, the type of property requirement no longer applies for butterfly reorganizations of specified corporations.

See Wortsman, "The Public Company Spinoff", 2000 Cdn Tax Foundation conference report, 24:1-50; Harris, "Changes to the Butterfly Rules", VII(4) *Business Vehicles* (Federated Press) 358 (2001).

"specified wholly-owned corporation" of a public corporation means a corporation all of the outstanding shares of the capital stock of which (other than directors' qualifying shares and shares of a specified class) are held by

(a) the public corporation,

(b) a specified wholly-owned corporation of the public corporation, or

(c) any combination of corporations described in paragraph (a) or (b).

Notes: For "directors' qualifying shares", see Notes to 85(1.3).

55(1)"specified wholly-owned corporation" added by 2001 technical bill, for transfers after 1998. See Notes to 55(1)"specified corporation".

Notes [subsec. 55(1)]: Former 55(1), an anti-avoidance rule dealing with artificial reduction of a gain, was repealed by 1988 tax reform, for transactions entered into after Sept. 12, 1988, with limited grandfathering that was intended to, but does not quite, match the introduction of GAAR in 245(2). In *Toronto Dominion Bank*, 2011 FCA 221, 55(1) did not apply because the transactions in question were not "pre-ordained" and thus were not a "series of transactions" (since 248(10) did not apply to the grandfathering rule).

(2) Deemed proceeds or gain [capital gain strip] — If this subsection applies to a taxable dividend received by a dividend recipient, notwithstanding any other provision of this Act, the amount of the dividend (other than the portion of it, if any, subject to tax under Part IV that is not refunded as a consequence of the payment of a dividend by a corporation where the payment is part of the series referred to in subsection (2.1)) is deemed

(a) not to be a dividend received by the dividend recipient;

(b) if the dividend is received on a redemption, acquisition or cancellation of a share, by the corporation that issued the share, to which subsection 84(2) or (3) applies, to be proceeds of disposition of the share that is redeemed, acquired or cancelled except to the extent that the dividend is otherwise included in computing those proceeds; and

(c) if paragraph (b) does not apply to the dividend, to be a gain of the dividend recipient, for the year in which the dividend was received, from the disposition of a capital property.

Related Provisions: 52(3)(a) — Cost of stock dividend; 53(2)(c)(i)(B) — S. 55 generally ignored in determining reduction in ACB of partnership interest; 55(2.1) — Conditions for 55(2) to apply; 55(2.2) — Amount of stock dividend and recipient's entitlement; 55(2.5) — Whether dividend causes significant reduction in FMV.

Notes: 55(2), together with (2.1)-(2.5), is an anti-avoidance rule aimed at "capital gains stripping", whereby paying an intercorporate dividend, tax-free due to 112(1), would reduce or avoid a capital gain on selling the shares. As amended in 2016, it now extends to dividends that reduce the value of shares (something any dividend can do, by definition) or increase the cost base of property, and can apply in many situations where there is no avoidance intention. When 55(2) applies (see conditions in 55(2.1)), it turns the dividend into a capital gain (or, for an 84(2) or (3) deemed dividend, proceeds of disposition). See also the stop-loss rules in s. 112, which can prevent the intercorporate dividend from being deductible in the first place.

"Safe income" (income earned by any corporation since 1972: see Notes to 55(5)) can be paid out as a dividend without triggering 55(2), as long as it does not exceed the accrued capital gain on the shares (FMV minus cost base): see 55(2.1)(c).

If 55(2) will trigger a capital gain on a dividend, 55(5)(f) automatically splits the dividend into two parts, one for the amount deemed by 55(2)(c) to be a capital gain, and one for the safe income up to the capital gain (which is treated as a normal intercorporate dividend). On a stock dividend, 55(2.3) does the same.

To the extent 55(2) applies, Part IV.1 tax will not apply but Part VI.1 tax can: VIEWS doc 2007-0250831E5.

Part IV tax exception in 55(2) opening words: 55(2) will not apply to the extent Part IV tax applies and is not refunded due to payment of a dividend as part of the same series of transactions. *Canutilities (Canadian Utilities)*, 2004 FCA 234 (leave to appeal denied 2005 CarswellNat 554 (SCC)) addressed whether Part IV tax had been refunded due to dividends paid as "part of the series". Regular, normal course dividends paid in the year, which triggered recovery of Part IV tax, were "preordained" and were part of the same "series" in which the dividend deductible under 112(1) was received (even without considering 248(10)). See Mark Brender, "Federal Court of Appeal Expands Scope of Series of Transactions", IX(1) *Corporate Structures & Groups [CS&G]* (Federated Press) 456-63 (2004); Ton-That & Erinc, "Towards a More Reasoned Approach on 'Series' in the Context of Section 55", XI(4) *CS&G* 632-39 (2010); CBA/CPA Canada Joint Committee letter to Finance, Oct. 13, 2016; Tmej & Wen, "Subsection 55(2), Part IV Tax, and the CDA", 25(7) *Canadian Tax Highlights* (ctf.ca) 10 (July 2017); Halil & Kakkar, "Accessing CDA on a Subsection 55(2) Dividend: Avoiding the Part IV Tax Exception", 17(3) *Tax for the Owner-Manager* (ctf.ca) 8-9 (July 2017). See also Notes to 248(10). For CRA interpretation see doc 2016-0653451E5 (exception does not apply when Part IV tax is refunded on paying dividend to individual; election for capital dividend would not refund all Part IV tax); 2017-0714971E5 (several examples where amended return needed to accommodate 55(2) calculation); 2017-0724071C6 [2017 CTF q.6] (55(2) and Part IV tax are not circular).

The 2016 amendments (effective April 21, 2015) restructured 55(2) to be 55(2)-(2.1), and added (2.2)-(2.4). The stated purpose was to overrule *D & D Livestock* (see Notes to 55(2.3)). However, the new rule is broader. The substantive changes were:

- limiting the Part IV tax exclusion (opening words of 55(2)): "to a corporation" changed to "by a corporation", so that a later refund of Part IV tax to an individual or trust makes the dividend potentially subject to 55(2)

- if 55(2) applies, dividends (other than deemed by 84(2) or (3)) are recharacterized into capital gains rather than proceeds of disposition (there are subtle differences re timing, the application of the stop-loss rules and the capital dividend account)

- the rule is subject to a "purpose" test (55(2.1)(b)(i) or (ii)) or an "effects" test (55(2.1)(b)(i))

- the rule can apply when there is a significant reduction in a share's value (55(2.1)(b)(ii)(A), 55(2.5)), or increase in the cost of the dividend recipient's property (55(2.1)(b)(ii)(B))

- safe income cannot be paid out tax-free on a share if there is no accrued capital gain, as only the amount up to the gain avoids the rule (55(2.1)(c))

- special rules apply to stock dividends (55(2.2)-(2.4)), with a "high-low" (high FMV, low PUC) stock dividend separated into two, one up to safe income and the other triggering a capital gain

- effective April 18, 2016, a dividend in excess of safe income is automatically deemed to be a separate dividend so that the safe-income up-to-the-gain amount is not subject to 55(2), instead of this requiring a designation by the dividend recipient (55(5)(f)).

Texts and papers on s. 55 (since 2016): Lamarre et al., *Taxation of Corporate Reorganizations* (Carswell, 3rd ed., 2019), chap. 8; Loewen & Walker, *Taxation of Private Corporations and their Shareholders* (ctf.ca, 5th ed., 2020), chap. 10; McLean, "Subsection 55(2)", 2015 Cdn Tax Foundation conference report, 22:1-71; Keung, "Subsection 55(2)", 2016 Prairie Provinces Tax Conference (ctf.ca); McLean & Bell, "Amendments to Section 55 and Implications on Estate Planning", 2016 STEP Canada conference (contact memberservices@step.ca), 101 slides; Tipton, "How 'Safe' Is Your Inter-Corporate Dividend?", 2016 BC Tax Conf; Barkai & Demner, "Dealing with new Subsection 55(2)", 2016 conference report, 6:1-56; McLean & Oldewening, "Capital Gains Stripping and Surplus Stripping", 2017 conference report, 4:1-35; Talbot & Conrad, "Subsection 55(2)", 2017 Atlantic Provinces Tax Conf; Carenza & Jacinto, "New 55(2)", 2017 Ontario Tax Conf; Keung, "Selected Safe Income Issues", 2017 Prairie Provinces Tax Conf; Strawson, "The New Section 55: Select Planning Considerations", *ibid.*

Shorter articles/comments: CBA/CPA Canada Joint Committee on Taxation letters to Finance, May 27 and Nov. 12, 2015 and April 20, 2017; TEI letter to Finance, Oct. 12, 2015; Ross & Watson, "Draft Legislation Amending Subsection 55(2)", XXI(3) *Insurance Planning* (Federated Press) 1350-59 (2015); Maclagan & Jamal, "An Update on Proposed Amendments", XIII(4) *Corporate Structures and Groups* (Federated Press) 754-58 (2015); Truster, "Cash Dividends and Amended Subsection 55(2)", 16(2) *Tax for the Owner-Manager* (ctf.ca) 6-7 (April 2016); Mancell, "An Overview of Section 55 and Safe Income", 2465 *Tax Topics* (CCH) 1-5 (June 6, 2019). See also articles cited in 55(2.1) and (5) Notes.

Deliberate use of 55(2) (including *Evans*- or *Descarries*-like surplus stripping) to use up losses or to convert a dividend to a capital dividend does not trigger GAAR [245(2)]: VIEWS docs 2015-0595641C6 [2015 APFF q.15], 2015-0610701C6 [2015 CTF q.4] (overruling 2012-04331261E5), but the CRA has raised concerns with Finance about such transactions (which presumably was the reason for the 55(5)(f) amendment effective April 18, 2016, making the dividend-split automatic). In *Ottawa Air Cargo*, 2008 FCA 54, the taxpayer wanted to have 55(2) apply, but it did not because, for the Part IV exclusion to apply, Part I tax must be first paid and then refunded. See also Wen & Liu, "Deliberate Triggering of Subsection 55(2)", 6(1) *Canadian Tax Focus* (ctf.ca) 11-12 (Feb. 2016); Félix Turcot, "Key Reminders About the Deliberate Triggering of 55(2)", 7(2) *Canadian Tax Focus* (ctf.ca) 5-6 (May 2017); 2016-0671491C6 [2016 CTF q.4] (using 55(2) to trigger Part IV refund).

For more CRA interpretation since 2016 see docs 2015-0610681C6 [2015 CTF q.6(d)] (55(3)(a) exemption for 84(3) deemed dividend cannot be used to avoid 55(2.1)(b)(ii)); 2016-0630281E5 (84(3) deemed dividend exceeding SI is subject to 55(2) but can be separate taxable dividend under (5)(f)). See also Notes to 55(2.1)-(2.5); 2017-0693421C6 [2017 STEP q.7] and 2018-0743951C6 [STEP 2018 q.4] (pipeline for an estate does not trigger 55(2)); 2017-0723491C6 [2017 TEI q.B6] (policy on when CRA will issue rulings on 55(2)); 2017-0724051C6 [2017 CTF q.4] (capital dividend account increase due to 55(2)(c) happens at time of dividend, not year-end [reversing 2011-0412131C6], so it can be the same year); 2018-0780071C6 [2018 CTF q.2] (impact of 55(2) deeming rules on calculation of cost, capital dividend account and 112(3) [see also Income Tax Folio S3-F2-C1 ¶1.30, 1.30.1]); 2019-0824391C6 [2019 CTF q.3] (where dividend paid by foreign corp, use foreign exchange rate at safe-income determination time); 2020-0860991C6 [2020 CTF q.1] (ACB increase on spinoff; GAAR may apply to duplication of cost base).

Pre-2016 55(2) applied, despite causing double tax at shareholder and corporate level, in *101139810 Saskatchewan*, 2017 TCC 3 [Welters, "Results Test in Subsection

---

55(2)", 25(3) *Canadian Tax Highlights* (ctf.ca) 6-7 (March 2016); Wen, "Asset Removal Under Subsection 55(2) Gone Wrong", 7(7) *Canadian Tax Focus* (ctf.ca) 10 (May 2017)].

Articles on pre-2016 55(2) (still partly accurate): Brender, "Subsection 55(2)", 45(2) *Canadian Tax Journal* 343-373 and 45(4) 806-843 (1997); Truster, "Divisive Reorganizations", 2005 Cdn Tax Foundation conference report, 12:1-30; Engel, "A Review of Common Mistakes", 2015 Prairie Provinces Tax Conf. (ctf.ca) at 7:14-25.

CRA interpretation pre-2016 (still partly accccurate): docs 2006-0170921E5 (55(2) applies); 2007-0245691R3 (no 55(2)); 2008-0270081R3 (no 55(2)); 2008-0289771R3 (55(2) on loss consolidation); 2008-0293911E5 (various scenarios); 2008-0294631E5 and 2013-0498191E5 (55(2) and Part IV tax); 2011-0394191E5 (whether 55(2) applies if dividend is paid before disposition of shares); 2011-0403291R3, 2013-0477241R3 (using Canada-US treaty to avoid 55(2) on spinoff); 2011-0415891E5 (double tax on increase of stated capital); 2011-0422021E5 (55(2) purpose test might not be met if the series of transactions contains no sale of Opco shares or increase in direct interest in Opco); 2012-0434501E5 (application to 84(3) deemed dividend); 2013-0503511E5 (rollover, discretionary dividends and sale of shares).

55(2) amended by 2016 budget bill #1, for dividends received after April 20, 2015. Earlier amended by 1995-97 technical bill, for dividends received after June 20, 1996.

Income Tax Folios: S3-F2-C1: Capital Dividends [replaces IT-66R6].

Information Circulars: 88-2, paras. 7, 13: General anti-avoidance rule — section 245 of the *Income Tax Act*.

I.T. Technical News: 3 (loss utilization within a corporate group; butterfly reorganizations); 7 (subsection 55(2) — recent cases); 33 (income earned or realized — the *Kruco* case); 34 (safe income calculation — the *Kruco* case); 37 (safe income calculation — treatment of non-deductible expenses).

Advance Tax Rulings: ATR-22R: Estate freeze using share exchange; ATR-27: Exchange and acquisition of interests in capital properties through rollovers and winding-up ("butterfly"); ATR-35: Partitioning of assets to get specific ownership — "butterfly"; ATR-47: Transfer of assets to Realtyco; ATR-56: Purification of a family farm corporation; ATR-57: Transfer of property for estate planning purposes; ATR-58: Divisive reorganization.

(2.1) Application of subsec. (2) — Subsection (2) applies to a taxable dividend received by a corporation resident in Canada (in subsections (2) to (2.2) and (2.4) referred to as the "dividend recipient") as part of a transaction or event or a series of transactions or events if

(a) the dividend recipient is entitled to a deduction in respect of the dividend under subsection 112(1) or (2) or 138(6);

(b) it is the case that

(i) one of the purposes of the payment or receipt of the dividend (or, in the case of a dividend under subsection 84(3), one of the results of which) is to effect a significant reduction in the portion of the capital gain that, but for the dividend, would have been realized on a disposition at fair market value of any share of capital stock immediately before the dividend, or

(ii) the dividend (other than a dividend that is received on a redemption, acquisition or cancellation of a share, by the corporation that issued the share, to which subsection 84(2) or (3) applies) is received on a share that is held as capital property by the dividend recipient and one of the purposes of the payment or receipt of the dividend is to effect

(A) a significant reduction in the fair market value of any share, or

(B) a significant increase in the cost of property, such that the amount that is the total of the cost amounts of all properties of the dividend recipient immediately after the dividend is significantly greater than the amount that is the total of the cost amounts of all properties of the dividend recipient immediately before the dividend; and

(c) the amount of the dividend exceeds the amount of the income earned or realized by any corporation — after 1971 and before the safe-income determination time for the transaction, event or series — that could reasonably be considered to contribute to the capital gain that could be realized on a disposition at fair market value, immediately before the dividend, of the share on which the dividend is received.

Related Provisions: 55(2.2) — Amount of stock dividend and recipient's entitlement.

Notes: See Notes to 55(2). 55(2.1) contains 3 conditions for 55(2) to apply.

First [55(2.1)(a): *deductible*], the dividend must be deductible to the recipient as an intercorporate dividend under 112(1) or (2) (or 138(6) for a life insurer).

Second [55(2.1)(b): *purpose*], a "one of the purposes" test must be satisfied: either (b)(i) a reduction in the capital gain that would have been realized (because paying the dividend strips down the value of the shares on which the dividend was paid) [if it is an 84(3) deemed dividend on redemption of shares, this is a "results" test instead]; or (b)(ii) the dividend reduces the value of the shares (even without a pending capital gain), or increases the cost of the dividend recipient's property. The CRA considers cash to be property for purposes of 55(2.1)(b)(ii)(B): 2016-0671501C6 [2016 CTF q.8]. See also 2016-0658841E5 (purpose test and allocation of safe income); 2017-0683511E5 (purpose test of a dividend or repurchase of share); 2017-0724021C6 [2017 CTF q.3] (purpose of a dividend paid to purify a corp so it can qualify for 110.6(2.1); purpose for 55(2.1) is determined objectively); 2017-0726381C6 [2017 CTF q.5] (whether purpose test applies to the whole dividend); 2018-0765271C6 [CPA 2018 q.11] (how to determine purpose). See also *Placer Dome*, 1996 CanLII 4094 (FCA): "one of the purposes" in 55(2) means the taxpayer must show that *none* of the purposes was to effect a significant reduction in a capital gain, but purpose and effect are not the same thing.

Read literally, 55(2.1)(b) can be triggered by any dividend, since a dividend's purpose is always to transfer value from the corporation to shareholders. See Keung, "Section 55 May Now Apply to Every Intercorporate Dividend", 15(3) *Tax for the Owner-Manager [TfOM]* (ctf.ca) 3-4 (July 2015); VIEWS docs 2015-0595601C6 [2015 APFF q.12] (55(2) applies in 3 scenarios); 2015-0610651C6 [2015 CTF q.6(a)]; 2016-0627571E5 (various scenarios). (Before the 2016 amendments, 55(3)(a) provided a related-party exception). However, CRA accepts normal dividends "paid pursuant to a well-established policy of paying regular dividends", based on a "reasonable dividend income return on equity on a comparable listed share": 2015-0613821C6 [2015 TEI], 2016-0627571E5. Thus, every intercorporate dividend potentially needs to be examined to ensure it is not offside, unless there is clearly enough safe income (see below). (Where safe income is low because the corporation received tax benefits, 55(2) may apply: 2016-0627571E5.) Also acceptable are standard loss consolidation arrangements [see Notes to 111(5)]: 2015-0604071R3, 2015-0610671C6 [2015 CTF q.6(b)]. A creditor-proofing dividend can trigger 55(2): 2015-0617731E5, 2015-0623551C6 [2015 CTF q.6(e)]; Ewens & Keung, "Our Response to the CRA's Position on Creditor-Proofing Reorganizations — Part 1", tinyurl.com/moodys-cp. See also 2018-0761561C6 [2018 APFF Financial s.5] (extraordinary dividend paid out of disability insurance payment received: 55(2) may apply). See also Abdulla, "New Subsection 55(2) Issues", 24(1) *Canadian Tax Highlights [CTH]* (ctf.ca) 2-3 (Jan. 2016); Kakkar & Halil, "Subsection 55(2): The CRA's Recent Positions", 16(1) *TfOM* 1-2 (Jan. 2016); McLean, "CRA: The Importance of Safe Income" 24(8) *CTH* 3-4 (Aug. 2016); Kiefer & Taylor, "Lumpy Creditor-Protection Dividends and Subsection 55(2)", 16(3) *TfOM* (ctf.ca) 4-5 (July 2016); Didkovsky, "Subsection 55(2): The Reasonable Regular Dividends Exemption", 6(4) *Canadian Tax Focus* (ctf.ca) 13-14 (Nov. 2016) [includes an example of finding dividend data from comparable public companies]; Campbell & Dean, "Interpreting the Purpose Test", 2016 Atlantic Provinces Tax Conf.

Third [55(2.1)(c): *safe income*], the dividend exceeds the paying corporation's "safe income" (SI) and also exceeds the accrued (unrealized) gain on the shares. The words "income earned or realized by any corporation after 1971" (defined in 55(5)(b), (c)) describe SI: income that can be extracted by intercorporate dividend tax-free under 112(1) without being recharacterized as capital gain. ("Any corporation" includes a foreign non-affiliate: *Lamont Management*, [2000] 3 C.T.C. 18 (FCA).) See Notes to 55(5) for discussion of SI.

Allocation of gain: In *729658 Alberta*, 2004 TCC 474, where the shares had been acquired by the paying corp in an 85(1) rollover, the TCC allowed allocation of all of the gain to SI. The words "reasonable be considered to be attributable" did not require *pro rata* allocation as there was no tax avoidance. However, the Court suggested its answer might change if the series of transactions included crystallization of the capital gains exemption. See also VIEWS docs 2005-0112141E5, 2010-0388821E5; and since the 2016 amendments: 2015-0593941E5, 2016-0633101E5, 2016-0652981C6 [2016 APFF q.13] and 2016-0653001C6 [2016 APFF q. 16] (allocation of SI to different dividends where dividend is paid disproportionately on one class of shares); 2018-0768891C6 [2018 APFF q.4] (allocation between stock dividend shares and shares on which the high-low stock dividend is paid); 2021-0876441E5 (SI allocation on corporate reorg). CRA was studying this issue: 2017-0693391C6 [2017 STEP q.5], and advised at 2018 CTF [q.1: 2018-0780061C6] that its positions on discretionary shares are unchanged, but it will provide assurance only in rulings.

In *Granite Bay Charters*, [2001] 3 C.T.C. 2516 (TCC), a deemed dividend, followed by a sale of shares to an unanticipated purchaser, was held to be part of the same "series of transactions" and caught by 55(2).

55(2.1) added by 2016 budget bill #1, for dividends received after April 20, 2015. (For earlier dividends, these rules were part of 55(2).)

(2.2) Special rule [for 55(2)] — amount of the stock dividend — For the purpose of applying subsections (2), (2.1), (2.3) and (2.4), the amount of a stock dividend and the dividend recipient's entitlement to a deduction under subsection 112(1) or (2) or 138(6) in respect of the amount of that dividend are to be deter-

mined as if paragraph (b) of the definition "amount" in subsection 248(1) read as follows:

(b) in the case of a stock dividend paid by a corporation, the greater of

(i) the amount by which the paid-up capital of the corporation that paid the dividend is increased by reason of the payment of the dividend, and

(ii) the fair market value of the share or shares issued as a stock dividend at the time of payment,

Notes: See Notes to 55(2.3).

(2.3) Stock dividends and safe income — If this subsection applies in respect of a stock dividend

(a) the amount of the stock dividend is deemed for the purpose of subsection (2) to be a separate taxable dividend to the extent of the portion of the amount that does not exceed the amount of the income earned or realized by any corporation — after 1971 and before the safe-income determination time for the transaction, event or series — that could reasonably be considered to contribute to the capital gain that could be realized on a disposition at fair market value, immediately before the dividend, of the share on which the dividend is received; and

(b) the amount of the separate taxable dividend referred to in paragraph (a) is deemed to reduce the amount of the income earned or realized by any corporation — after 1971 and before the safe-income determination time for the transaction, event or series — that could reasonably be considered to contribute to the capital gain that could be realized on a disposition at fair market value, immediately before the dividend, of the share on which the dividend is received.

Related Provisions: 55(2.2) — Amount of stock dividend and recipient's entitlement; 55(2.4) — Conditions for 55(2.3) to apply; 55(5)(f) — No designation of separate taxable dividend if 55(2.3) applies.

Notes: 55(2.2)-(2.4) and 55(2.1)(b)(ii)(A) overrule *D & D Livestock*, 2013 TCC 318, where safe income of a subsidiary's shares was not reduced by a stock dividend paid on the shares of the parent, even though this meant the safe income could be used twice. (CRA will apply GAAR to such cases before the amendments: VIEWS doc 2014-0534671C6 [2014 APFF q.20].)

55(2.3) applies automatically when a stock dividend is paid, the value of the new shares exceeds the PUC increase (see Notes to 89(1)"paid-up capital"), and 55(2.1)(a) and (b) apply. 55(2.3) deems the stock dividend to be two separate taxable dividends for purposes of s. 55: one up to the safe income that contributes to the accrued capital gain (see Notes to 55(2.1) and 55(5)) and other, subject to 55(2), for the excess. This is the same mechanism as applies under 55(5)(f) for regular dividends.

For discussion see Kenneth Keung, "Subsection 55(2) — The Road Ahead", 2016 Prairie Provinces tax conference (ctf.ca).

For CRA interpretation see VIEWS docs 2016-0658351E5 (safe income effect on stock dividend); 2016-0668341E5 (effect of stock dividend of pref shares with high value and low PUC).

55(2.2)-(2.4) added by 2016 budget bill #1, effective for dividends received after April 20, 2015.

(2.4) Application of subsec. (2.3) — Subsection (2.3) applies in respect of a stock dividend if

(a) a dividend recipient holds a share upon which it receives the stock dividend;

(b) the fair market value of the share or shares issued as a stock dividend exceeds the amount by which the paid-up capital of the corporation that paid the stock dividend is increased because of the dividend; and

(c) subsection (2) would apply to the dividend if subsection (2.1) were read without reference to its paragraph (c).

Related Provisions: 55(2.2) — Amount of stock dividend and recipient's entitlement.

Notes: See Notes to 55(2.3).

(2.5) Determination of reduction in fair market value [whether significant reduction] — For the purpose of applying clause (2.1)(b)(ii)(A), whether a dividend causes a significant reduction in the fair market value of any share is to be determined as if the fair market value of the share, immediately before the dividend, was increased by an amount equal to the amount, if any, by which the fair market value of the dividend received on the share exceeds the fair market value of the share.

Notes: This provision makes it possible for the 55(2.1)(b)(ii)(A) purpose test to be met even if the share starts with a nil or insignificant value. See Notes to 55(2.1); Kakkar & Halil, "Proposed Subsection 55(2.5)", 15(4) *Tax for the Owner-Manager* (ctf.ca) 4-5 (Oct. 2015).

55(2.5) added by 2016 budget bill #1, for dividends received after April 20, 2015.

(3) Application [butterfly] — Subsection (2) does not apply to any dividend received by a corporation (in this subsection and subsection (3.01) referred to as the "dividend recipient")

(a) in the case of a dividend that is received on a redemption, acquisition or cancellation of a share, by the corporation that issued the share, to which subsection 84(2) or (3) applies, if, as part of a transaction or event or a series of transactions or events as a part of which the dividend is received, there was not at any particular time

(i) a disposition of property, other than

(A) money disposed of on the payment of a dividend or on a reduction of the paid-up capital of a share, and

(B) property disposed of for proceeds that are not less than its fair market value,

to a person or partnership that was an unrelated person immediately before the particular time,

(ii) a significant increase (other than as a consequence of a disposition of shares of the capital stock of a corporation for proceeds of disposition that are not less than their fair market value) in the total direct interest in any corporation of one or more persons or partnerships that were unrelated persons immediately before the particular time,

(iii) a disposition, to a person or partnership who was an unrelated person immediately before the particular time, of

(A) shares of the capital stock of the corporation that paid the dividend (referred to in this paragraph and subsection (3.01) as the "dividend payer"), or

(B) property (other than shares of the capital stock of the dividend recipient) more than 10% of the fair market value of which was, at any time during the series, derived from any combination of shares of the capital stock and debt of the dividend payer,

(iv) after the time the dividend was received, a disposition, to a person or partnership that was an unrelated person immediately before the particular time, of

(A) shares of the capital stock of the dividend recipient, or

(B) property more than 10% of the fair market value of which was, at any time during the series, derived from any combination of shares of the capital stock and debt of the dividend recipient, and

(v) a significant increase in the total of all direct interests in the dividend payer of one or more persons or partnerships who were unrelated persons immediately before the particular time; or

(b) if the dividend was received

(i) in the course of a reorganization in which

(A) a distributing corporation made a distribution to one or more transferee corporations, and

(B) the distributing corporation was wound up or all of the shares of its capital stock owned by each transferee corporation immediately before the distribution were redeemed or cancelled otherwise than on an exchange to which subsection 51(1), 85(1) or 86(1) applies, and

(ii) on a permitted redemption in relation to the distribution or on the winding-up of the distributing corporation.

Related Provisions: 13(30) — Transfers of property; 55(3.01) — Rules of interpretation for 55(3)(a); 55(3.1), (3.2) — Exception for purchase butterfly; 55(6) — Reor-

ganization share deemed listed on designated stock exchange for certain purposes; 88(1)(d) — Winding-up; 88(1)(c)(iii), 88(1)(c.2) — Cost base of property after windup; 110.6(7)(a) — Capital gains exemption disallowed on butterfly; 248(10) — Series of transactions; 256(7)(a)(i)(E) — No acquisition of control on spin-off distribution; Reg. 1100(2.2), 1102(14)(a) — Depreciable property acquired on reorganization.

Notes: In general terms, 55(3) allows a "divisive reorganization", to split up and distribute a company's assets to its shareholders without realizing accrued gains. 55(3)(a) is for related parties and 55(3)(b) for unrelated parties (but see 55(5)(e) — e.g., siblings are deemed unrelated). It is called a "butterfly" due to the way it looks when the corporate holdings and transactions are drawn on paper. A "partial" butterfly transfers only some of the assets to the shareholders. 55(3) provides exemptions from the deemed capital gain under 55(2). GAAR (245(2)) may apply if the result is an ACB increase: VIEWS docs 2015-0604521E5, 2017-0693411C6 [2017 STEP q.6], and see Jesse Brodlieb, "Proposed Amendments to Section 55 Contain Unwanted Surprise", 2257 *Tax Topics* (CCH) 1-3 (June 11, 2015); and articles cited in Notes to 55(2). See also Notes to 55(1)"permitted exchange".

Since the 2016 amendments (dividends received after April 20, 2015), 55(3)(a) applies only on redemption or cancellation of shares where 84(2) or (3) is used. This makes it much less useful, as it no longer applies to cash dividends, and most pre-2016 rulings no longer apply.

55(3)(a) since the 2016 amendments: docs 2014-0563061R3 (restructuring); 2015-0604051R3 and 2017-0715791R3 (internal reorg), 2015-0608841R3 (spinoff); 2015-0623731R3 and 2017-0715951R3 (followup to 2015-0601441R3 — see Notes to 98(5)); 2016-0675881R3 and 2017-0683941R3 and 2017-0704351R3 (split-up); 2016-0648991R3 and 2018-0772501E5 (internal spinoff); 2018-0749491R3 [revised 2018-0778931R3]; 2018-0789981R3, 2019-0791661R3, 2019-0800141R3, 2020-0844991R3, 2020-0852281R3 (reorgs). See also Bilodeau & Dupuis, "The 55(3)(a) Related-Party Exemption in the New 55 Context", XIV(3) *Corporate Structures & Groups* (Federated Press) 8-15 (2017); Morin & Rautenberg, "Paragraph 55(3)(a): Developments Over the Last Ten Years", 2018 Cdn Tax Foundation conference report, 9:1-36; Hamelin, "Paragraph 55(3)(a): A Safe Harbour for Related-Party Dividends or a GAAR Trap?", 20(2) *Tax for the Owner-Manager* (ctf.ca) 2-3 (April 2020); Hamelin & Thuot, "Réduire l'impact du paragraphe 55(2) vie le revenu protégé ou l'alinéa 55(3)(a)", 2019 Cdn Tax Foundation conference report, 17:1-44.

55(3)(a)(i)(B) refers to "proceeds", not "proceeds of disposition" (PoD), but the CRA says a 69(1)(b)(ii) determination of PoD applies to it: doc 2014-0557251E5.

55(3)(a) before the 2016 amendments: see these Notes up to PITA 59th ed.

In *Eyeball Networks*, 2021 FCA 17 (reversing the TCC), 160(1) did not apply to a 55(3)(a) butterfly with cross-cancellation of promissory notes, as the TCC was wrong to say one was valuable and one was worthless at the time of transfer. (Thus, CRA could not collect Oldco's unpaid tax debt from Newco.)

55(3)(b): The purchase butterfly was generally eliminated by 55(3.1); see Notes to 55(1)"permitted exchange". Cross-border butterflies were mostly eliminated by 55(3.2)(h), but can still work: VIEWS docs 2012-0439381R3, 2012-0461881R3, 2015-0585681R3 (cross-border spin-off), 2009-0335441R3 [Russell, "Cross-Border Butterfly Ruling", 19(1) *Canadian Tax Highlights [CTH]* (ctf.ca) 8-9 (Jan. 2011)], 2011-0431101R3, 2011-0425441R3, 2013-0491651R3, 2014-0530961R3; 2013 Cdn Tax Foundation conference Roundtable (Mark Symes; not in the published conference report); McLean, "Cross-Border Butterfly Redux", 22(5) *CTH* 6-8 (May 2014). (These all predate the 2016 amendments.)

For more advance rulings approving a butterfly (bf), see VIEWS docs 2004-0060571R3, 2004-0078331R3, 2005-0114861R3, 2005-0126061R3, 2005-0126111R3, 2005-0144831R3, 2005-0149551R3, 2005-0151921R3, 2005-0161581R3, 2006-0175261R3, 2006-0181061R3, 2006-0199781R3, 2006-0203981R3, 2007-0240881R3, 2005-0141531R3, 2007-0241221R3, 2007-0241351R3, 2007-0241741R3, 2007-0243901R3, 2008-0265041R3, 2008-0266471R3, 2008-0275881R3, 2008-0281481R3, 2008-0299721R3, 2009-0328831R3, 2009-0346671R3, 2010-0364681R3, 2010-0376231R3, 2011-0425221R3, 2012-0446701R3, 2013-0490391R3, 2013-0513211R3, 2014-0517691R3, 2014-0528291R3, 2014-0539031R3. 2014-0563171R3, 2015-0578031R3, 2015-0582431R3, 2016-0650571R3, 2018-0767501R3, 2018-0788191R3, 2020-0852601R3 [2021-0884881R3]. Split-up bf: see also 2005-0142491R3, 2005-0157121R3, 2006-0189011R3, 2006-0195571R3, 2007-0221331R3, 2007-0241291R3, 2007-0245711R3, 2008-0268321R3, 2008-0284591R3, 2008-0290491R3, 2008-0296141R3, 2009-0313981R3, 2009-0325191R3, 2010-0353931R3, 2010-0357061R3, 2010-0358061R3, 2010-0369071R3, 2010-0370961R3, 2011-0403371R3, 2011-0408991R3, 2011-0416001R3, 2012-0440021R3, 2013-0476331R3, 2013-0498951R3, 2013-0500251R3, 2014-0520971R3, 2014-0526491R3, 2014-0537201R3 [2015-0598641R3], 2014-0548491R3, 2014-0552871R3, 2014-0554231R3, 2015-0569561R3, 2015-0579791R3, 2017-0681451R3 [2018-0753831R3], 2017-0693271R3, 2017-0714411R3, 2017-0733011R3, 2018-0774201R3, 2018-0790021R3 and 2019-0795521R3; 2016-0674681R3 (sequential split-up bf); 2007-0249451R3 (split-up bf, 2-stage transfer); 2007-0251621R3 (split-up bf, 4 siblings); 2005-0127871R3, 2007-0219671R3, 2009-0339201R3, 2012-0449681R3, 2013-0502921R3, 2019-0818261R3 (split-up bf, farm property); 2013-0475681R3 (family holding bf, pref shares); 2006-0209121R3 (split-up, family-owned corp); 2018-0745061R3, 2018-0780761R3 and 2020-0843991R3 (single-wing split-up bf); 2014-0540881R3, 2018-0758411R3, 2019-0811641R3, 2019-0816991R3 (multi-wing split-up bf); 2018-0772291R3 (multi-wing split-up net asset bf); 2019-0781491R3. For spinoffs see 2005-0140641R3 (internal spin-off); 2005-0141921R3, 2006-0182211R3, 2006-0207721R3, 2007-0237501R3, 2009-0338731R3, 2010-0380621R3, 2012-0460811R3 (public company spin-offs); 2007-0223921R3 (sequential spin-off bf); 2018-0772151R3 (multi-wing spin-off); 2005-0143191R3, 2008-0276061R3, 2010-0366651R3, 2010-0374291R3, 2013-0490341R3, 2014-0553601R3, 2014-0558831R3 (other spin-offs). Other public bfs: 2007-0247611R3, 2007-0256411R3. Single-wing bf: 2005-0158461R3, 2005-0162951R3, 2006-0172201R3, 2008-0304371R3, 2012-0435341R3 [farm], 2012-0449611R3, 2013-0490651R3 [farm], 2013-0498651R3, 2015-0582421R3. Multiple-wing bf: 2005-0158841R3 (followed by winding-up), 2006-0188101R3, 2006-0197501R3, 2009-0329601R3. Cross-border bf: 2012-0459781R3, 2017-0699201R3, 2018-0761621R3, 2019-0794571R3 [2019-0833091R3], and see 55(3.1) Notes. See also 2007-0226581R3 (distribution of corporate assets before share-holders' divorce); 2007-0227371R3 (bf using treaty-protected gain); 2007-0237361R3 (sequential bf: Michael Kandev & Alan Shragie, "RDTOH on Butterfly", 16(11) *Canadian Tax Highlights* (ctf.ca) 2-3 (Nov. 2008)); 2007-0251681R3 (bf and estate freeze); 2009-0306341R3 (trusts as shareholders on a bf); 2009-0351351R3 (post-bf stock options); 2011-0413661R3 (bf of assets of a financial institution); 2006-0172881E5 (interaction with 85(1)(d), (e)); 2009-0327951R3 (application of 73(4.1)); 2015-0617601E5, 2016-0646891R3 (pipeline followed by butterfly); 2018-0756881R3 (net asset bf — farm).

A butterfly may be exempt from Ontario land transfer tax on the transfer of a beneficial interest in land: Ont. Reg. 70/91 under the *Land Transfer Tax Act*, s. 2.

Alternatives to a butterfly: Boehmer, "The Divisive Reorganization of a Closely-held Corporation", XII(1) *Corporate Structures & Groups* (Federated Press) 651-54 (2010). Or consider the strategy in *McMullen* (see Notes to 84(2)): Alary, "A Corporate Divorce Alternative When the Butterfly Won't Fly", tinyurl.com/alary-alternat.

See also Chong, "US Disregards Butterfly Wings", 20(11) *Canadian Tax Highlights* (ctf.ca) 14-15 (Nov. 2012); Vair, "The Essential Structure of a Public Butterfly Transaction", XIII(2) *Corporate Structures & Groups* (Federated Press) 722-25 (2014); Oldewening, "Integrating a Canadian Butterfly into a Foreign Reverse Spinoff", XXII(1) *International Tax Planning* (Federated Press) 2-12 (2018); and Notes to 55(2).

55(3) amended by 2016 budget bill #1 (for dividends received after April 20, 2015, to add "in the case ... 84(2) or (3) applies" in (a)); 2013 budget bill #2 (for dividends received after Dec. 20, 2012); 2002-2013 and 1995-97 technical bills; 1994 Budget.

Information Circulars: 88-2, para. 7: General anti-avoidance rule — section 245 of the *Income Tax Act*.

I.T. Technical News: 3 (butterfly reorganizations); 16 (*Parthenon Investments* case).

Advance Tax Rulings: ATR-22R: Estate freeze using share exchange; ATR-27: Exchange and acquisition of interests in capital properties through rollovers and winding-up ("butterfly"); ATR-35: Partitioning of assets to get specific ownership — "butterfly"; ATR-47: Transfer of assets to Realtyco; ATR-56: Purification of a family farm corporation; ATR-57: Transfer of property for estate planning purposes; ATR-58: Divisive reorganization.

(3.01) Interpretation for para. (3)(a) — For the purposes of paragraph (3)(a),

(a) an **unrelated person** means a person (other than the dividend recipient) to whom the dividend recipient is not related or a partnership any member of which (other than the dividend recipient) is not related to the dividend recipient;

(b) a corporation that is formed by an amalgamation of 2 or more other corporations is deemed to be the same corporation as, and a continuation of, each of the other corporations;

(c) where there has been a winding-up of a corporation to which subsection 88(1) applies, the parent is deemed to be the same corporation as, and a continuation of, the subsidiary;

(d) proceeds of disposition are to be determined without reference to

(i) subparagraph (j)(i) of the definition "proceeds of disposition" in section 54, and

(ii) section 93;

(e) notwithstanding any other provision of this Act, where a non-resident person disposes of a property in a taxation year and the gain or loss from the disposition is not included in computing the person's taxable income earned in Canada for the year, the person is deemed to have disposed of the property for proceeds of disposition that are less than its fair market value unless, under the income tax laws of the country in which the person is resident, the gain or loss is computed as if the property were disposed of for proceeds of disposition that are not less than its fair market value and the gain or loss so computed is recognized for the purposes of those laws;

(f) a significant increase in the total direct interest in a corporation that would, but for this paragraph, be described in subparagraph (3)(a)(ii) is deemed not to be described in that subpara-

graph if the increase was the result of the issuance of shares of the capital stock of the corporation solely for money and the shares were redeemed, acquired or cancelled by the corporation before the dividend was received;

(g) a disposition of property that would, but for this paragraph, be described in subparagraph (3)(a)(i), or a significant increase in the total direct interest in a corporation that would, but for this paragraph, be described in subparagraph (3)(a)(ii), is deemed not to be described in those subparagraphs if

(i) the dividend payer was related to the dividend recipient immediately before the dividend was received,

(ii) the dividend payer did not, as part of the series of transactions or events that includes the receipt of the dividend, cease to be related to the dividend recipient,

(iii) the disposition or increase occurred before the dividend was received,

(iv) the disposition or increase was the result of the disposition of shares to, or the acquisition of shares of, a particular corporation, and

(v) at the time the dividend was received, all the shares of the capital stock of the dividend recipient and the dividend payer were owned by the particular corporation, a corporation that controlled the particular corporation, a corporation controlled by the particular corporation or any combination of those corporations; and

(h) a winding-up of a subsidiary wholly-owned corporation to which subsection 88(1) applies, or an amalgamation to which subsection 87(11) applies of a corporation with one or more subsidiary wholly-owned corporations, is deemed not to result in a significant increase in the total direct interest, or in the total of all direct interests, in the subsidiary or subsidiaries, as the case may be.

Related Provisions: 55(3.2)(c), (d) — Persons deemed related or unrelated for 55(3.1); 55(4) — Anti-avoidance — persons deemed unrelated.

Notes: 55(3.01)(g) permits unrelated individuals to spin off real estate from an Opco to a new corp with new Holdcos: VIEWS docs 2015-0570021E5, 2015-0605901R3.

55(3.01)(d)(i) amended by 2016 budget bill #1, for dividends received after April 20, 2015, to change "the expression 'paragraph 55(2)(a) or' in paragraph (j)" to "subparagraph (j)(i)".

55(3.01)(f), (g) and (h) added by 2013 budget bill #2, for dividends received after 2003 (implementing Finance comfort letters of Oct. 16, 2007, Sept. 6, 2006 and April 21, 2005 respectively).

55(3.01)(d)(ii) added by 2002-2013 technical bill (Part 5 — technical), for dividends received after Feb. 21, 1994.

55(3.01) added by 1995-97 technical bill, on the same basis as the amendments to 55(3) and subject to the same application and transitional rules (see Notes to 55(3)).

(3.02) Distribution by a specified corporation — For the purposes of the definition "distribution" in subsection (1), where the transfer referred to in that definition is by a specified corporation to an acquiror described in the definition "specified corporation" in subsection (1), the references in the definition "distribution" to

(a) "each type of property" shall be read as "property"; and

(b) "property of that type" shall be read as "property".

Notes: 55(3.02) enabled BCE Inc. to spin off common shares of Nortel Networks Corp. in 1999-2000. See Christopher Steeves, "The BCE-Nortel Spin-Off and the New Public Company Butterfly", VI(2) *Corporate Structures & Groups* 312-15 (2000).

55(3.02) added by 2001 technical bill, effective for transfers that occur after 1998. See Notes to 55(1)"specified corporation".

(3.1) Where para. (3)(b) not applicable — Notwithstanding subsection (3), a dividend to which subsection (2) would, but for paragraph (3)(b), apply is not excluded from the application of subsection (2) where

(a) in contemplation of and before a distribution (other than a distribution by a specified corporation) made in the course of the reorganization in which the dividend was received, property became property of the distributing corporation, a corporation controlled by it or a predecessor corporation of any such corporation otherwise than as a result of

    (i) an amalgamation of corporations each of which was related to the distributing corporation,

    (ii) an amalgamation of a predecessor corporation of the distributing corporation and one or more corporations controlled by that predecessor corporation,

    (iii) a reorganization in which a dividend was received to which subsection (2) would, but for paragraph (3)(b), apply, or

    (iv) a disposition of property by

      (A) the distributing corporation, a corporation controlled by it or a predecessor corporation of any such corporation to a corporation controlled by the distributing corporation or a predecessor corporation of the distributing corporation,

      (B) a corporation controlled by the distributing corporation or by a predecessor corporation of the distributing corporation to the distributing corporation or predecessor corporation, as the case may be, or

      (C) the distributing corporation, a corporation controlled by it or a predecessor corporation of any such corporation for consideration that consists only of money or indebtedness that is not convertible into other property, or of any combination thereof,

(b) the dividend was received as part of a series of transactions or events in which

    (i) a person or partnership (referred to in this subparagraph as the "vendor") disposed of property and

      (A) the property is

        (I) a share of the capital stock of a distributing corporation that made a distribution as part of the series or of a transferee corporation in relation to the distributing corporation, or

        (II) property 10% or more of the fair market value of which was, at any time during the course of the series, derived from one or more shares described in subclause (I),

      (B) the vendor (other than a qualified person in relation to the distribution) was, at any time during the course of the series, a specified shareholder of the distributing corporation or of the transferee corporation, and

      (C) the property or any other property (other than property received by the transferee corporation on the distribution) acquired by any person or partnership in substitution therefor was acquired (otherwise than on a permitted acquisition, permitted exchange or permitted redemption in relation to the distribution) by a person (other than the vendor) who was not related to the vendor or, as part of the series, ceased to be related to the vendor or by a partnership,

    (ii) control of a distributing corporation that made a distribution as part of the series or of a transferee corporation in relation to the distributing corporation was acquired (otherwise than as a result of a permitted acquisition, permitted exchange or permitted redemption in relation to the distribution) by any person or group of persons, or

    (iii) in contemplation of a distribution by a distributing corporation, a share of the capital stock of the distributing corporation was acquired (otherwise than on a permitted acquisition or permitted exchange in relation to the distribution or on an amalgamation of 2 or more predecessor corporations of the distributing corporation) by

      (A) a transferee corporation in relation to the distributing corporation or by a person or partnership with whom the

transferee corporation did not deal at arm's length from a person to whom the acquiror was not related or from a partnership,

      (B) a person or any member of a group of persons who acquired control of the distributing corporation as part of the series,

      (C) a particular partnership any interest in which is held, directly or indirectly through one or more partnerships, by a person referred to in clause (B), or

      (D) a person or partnership with whom a person referred to in clause (B) or a particular partnership referred to in clause (C) did not deal at arm's length,

(c) the dividend was received by a transferee corporation from a distributing corporation that, immediately after the reorganization in the course of which a distribution was made and the dividend was received, was not related to the transferee corporation and the total of all amounts each of which is the fair market value, at the time of acquisition, of a property that

    (i) was acquired, as part of the series of transactions or events that includes the receipt of the dividend, by a person (other than the transferee corporation) who was not related to the transferee corporation or, as part of the series, ceased to be related to the transferee corporation or by a partnership, otherwise than

      (A) as a result of a disposition

        (I) in the ordinary course of business, or

        (II) before the distribution for consideration that consists solely of money or indebtedness that is not convertible into other property, or of any combination of the two,

      (B) on a permitted acquisition in relation to a distribution, or

      (C) as a result of an amalgamation of 2 or more corporations that were related to each other immediately before the amalgamation, and

    (ii) is a property (other than money, indebtedness that is not convertible into other property, a share of the capital stock of the transferee corporation and property more than 10% of the fair market value of which is attributable to one or more such shares)

      (A) that was received by the transferee corporation on the distribution,

      (B) more than 10% of the fair market value of which was, at any time after the distribution and before the end of the series, attributable to property (other than money and indebtedness that is not convertible into other property) described in clause (A) or (C), or

      (C) to which, at any time during the course of the series, the fair market value of property described in clause (A) was wholly or partly attributable

is greater than 10% of the fair market value, at the time of the distribution, of all the property (other than money and indebtedness that is not convertible into other property) received by the transferee corporation on the distribution, or

(d) the dividend was received by a distributing corporation that, immediately after the reorganization in the course of which a distribution was made and the dividend was received, was not related to the transferee corporation that paid the dividend and the total of all amounts each of which is the fair market value, at the time of acquisition, of a property that

    (i) was acquired, as part of the series of transactions or events that includes the receipt of the dividend, by a person (other than the distributing corporation) who was not related to the distributing corporation or, as part of the series, ceased to be related to the distributing corporation or by a partnership, otherwise than

    (A) as a result of a disposition

        (I) in the ordinary course of business, or

        (II) before the distribution for consideration that consists solely of money or indebtedness that is not convertible into other property, or of any combination of the two,

    (B) on a permitted acquisition in relation to a distribution, or

    (C) as a result of an amalgamation of 2 or more corporations that were related to each other immediately before the amalgamation, and

(ii) is a property (other than money, indebtedness that is not convertible into other property, a share of the capital stock of the distributing corporation and property more than 10% of the fair market value of which is attributable to one or more such shares)

    (A) that was owned by the distributing corporation immediately before the distribution and not disposed of by it on the distribution,

    (B) more than 10% of the fair market value of which was, at any time after the distribution and before the end of the series, attributable to property (other than money and indebtedness that is not convertible into other property) described in clause (A) or (C), or

    (C) to which, at any time during the course of the series, the fair market value of property described in clause (A) was wholly or partly attributable

is greater than 10% of the fair market value at the time of the distribution, of all the property (other than money and indebtedness that is not convertible into other property) owned immediately before that time by the distributing corporation and not disposed of by it on the distribution.

Related Provisions: 55(3.2) — Interpretation; 88(1)(c)(iv), 88(1)(c.2) — Limitation of cost base of property on winding-up; 256(6)–(9) — Whether control acquired.

Notes: 55(3.1) contains "butterfly denial" rules that prevent using the 55(3)(b) butterfly (bf) exception on a "purchase butterfly". See Notes to 55(1) "permitted exchange".

For discussion of 55(3.1) see Carr & Monaghan, "Today's Butterfly", 1994 Cdn Tax Foundation conference report, 4:1-68; Ton-That & Sider, "Butterfly Revisited", 1999 conference report, 24:1-33; Powrie, "Nether 'Split' Nor 'Spin': Butterflies Involving a Controlling Shareholder", X(4) *Corporate Structures & Groups* (Federated Press) 582-86 (2008); Chong, "Paragraphs 55(3.1)(d) and (e) Exception?", 19(4) *Canadian Tax Highlights* (ctf.ca) 7-8 (April 2011); Haughey, "Spinoff Butterflies in Trouble?", 3(4) *Canadian Tax Focus* (ctf.ca) 3-4 (Nov. 2013); Desjardins & Diksic, "Cross-Border Butterflies in the Context of Public Spin-off Transactions", 2015 conference report, 29:1-34. See also Notes to 55(2).

For some CRA VIEWS that 55(3.1) does not apply see docs 2006-0169241R3 (pre-bf sales of property to shareholder at FMV for cash); 2006-0215751R3 (cross-border bf); 2007-0247611R3 (public bf); 2007-0232261R3 (post-bf transaction); 2007-0237021R3 and 2008-0288701R3 (estate freeze after bf); 2007-0239871R3 (post-bf transaction); 2007-0255931R3 (bf); 2007-0256411R3 (public bf); 2007-0261171R3 (post-bf transaction); 2008-0268321R3 (split-up bf); 2008-0275881R3 (bf); 2008-0279961R3 (bf); 2008-0281481R3 (bf); 2008-0284591R3 (split-up bf); 2009-0306341R3 (trusts as shareholders on a bf); 2009-0351351R3 (post-bf stock options); 2010-0357061R3 (co-ownership agreement that is not partnership will not taint the bf); 2010-0370331R3 (post-bf transaction); 2010-0373211C6 (family trust acquires shares of transferee); 2011-0399401C6 (distributing corporation cannot incur debt to balance the assets transferred); 2011-0409641R3 (internal reorg); 2011-0421341E5 (disposition by distributing corp, to non-related person, of real estate for cash before a bf); 2012-0432441R3 (split-up of brothers' interests); 2012-0460811R3 (public company spinoff); 2014-0528291R3, 2014-0539031R3 (bf); 2014-0530961R3 (cross-border bf); 2015-0582431R3 (bf); 2015-0616291R3 and 2016-0626681R3 (cross-border bf).

See Notes to 111(5) and 125(7) "Canadian-controlled private corporation" re the meaning of "control". For "derived" in (b)(i)(A)(II), see Notes to 18.1(12).

55(3.1)(a) opening words amended to add "(other than a distribution by a specified corporation)", and (c)(i)(A)(II) and (d)(i)(A)(II) added, by 2013 budget bill #2, for dividends received after 2003. The first amendment implements a Nov. 26, 2004 comfort letter; for a case where it will apply see VIEWS doc 2010-0388951R3. The other amendments implement a June 8, 2005 comfort letter; for discussion see Mark Brender, "Pre-Butterfly Reorganization Transactions", IX(3) *Corporate Structures & Groups* (Federated Press) 488-91 (2005); Kabir Jamal, "Prohibited Post-Butterfly Dispositions

or Acquisitions of Property", *Mergers and Acquisitions Newsletter* (*Taxnet Pro*), April 2013; CICA/CBA Joint Committee letter to Finance, Feb. 15, 2013, pp. 2-3.

55(3.1)(b)(i)(B) amended by 2002-2013 technical bill (Part 5 — technical), for dividends received after 1999, to add "(other than a qualified person in relation to the distribution)".

55(3.1)(c)(ii)(B) and (C) and 55(3.1)(d)(ii)(B) and (C) amended by 1995-97 technical bill, effective for dividends received after April 26, 1995, with certain grandfathering for dividends received before June 20, 1996.

Previously amended by 1994 Budget, replacing a different 55(3.1) introduced by 1993 technical bill. The earlier 55(3.1) prohibited the use of the butterfly exception in 55(3)(b) on a so-called "cross-border butterfly".

I.T. Technical News: 3 (butterfly reorganizations); 9 (the backdoor butterfly rule); 16 (*Parthenon Investments* case).

(3.2) Interpretation of para. (3.1)(b) — For the purpose of paragraph (3.1)(b),

    (a) in determining whether the vendor referred to in subparagraph (3.1)(b)(i) is at any time a specified shareholder of a transferee corporation or of a distributing corporation, the references in the definition "specified shareholder" in subsection 248(1) to "taxpayer" shall be read as "person or partnership";

    (b) a corporation that is formed by the amalgamation of 2 or more corporations (each of which is referred to in this paragraph as a "predecessor corporation") shall be deemed to be the same corporation as, and a continuation of, each of the predecessor corporations;

    (c) subject to paragraph (d), each particular person who acquired a share of the capital stock of a distributing corporation in contemplation of a distribution by the distributing corporation shall be deemed, in respect of that acquisition, not to be related to the person from whom the particular person acquired the share unless

        (i) the particular person acquired all the shares of the capital stock of the distributing corporation that were owned, at any time during the course of the series of transactions or events that included the distribution and before the acquisition, by the other person, or

        (ii) immediately after the reorganization in the course of which the distribution was made, the particular person was related to the distributing corporation;

    (d) where a share is acquired by an individual from a personal trust in satisfaction of all or a part of the individual's capital interest in the trust, the individual shall be deemed, in respect of that acquisition, to be related to the trust;

    (e) subject to paragraph (f), where at any time a share of the capital stock of a corporation is redeemed or cancelled (otherwise than on an amalgamation where the only consideration received or receivable for the share by the shareholder on the amalgamation is a share of the capital stock of the corporation formed by the amalgamation), the corporation shall be deemed to have acquired the share at that time;

    (f) where a share of the capital stock of a corporation is redeemed, acquired or cancelled by the corporation pursuant to the exercise of a statutory right of dissent by the holder of the share, the corporation shall be deemed not to have acquired the share;

    (g) control of a corporation shall be deemed not to have been acquired by a person or group of persons where it is so acquired solely because of

        (i) the incorporation of the corporation, or

        (ii) the acquisition by an individual of one or more shares for the sole purpose of qualifying as a director of the corporation; and

    (h) in relation to a distribution each corporation (other than a qualified person in relation to the distribution) that is a shareholder and a specified shareholder of the distributing corporation at any time during the course of a series of transactions or events, a part of which includes the distribution made by the distributing corporation, is deemed to be a transferee corporation in relation to the distributing corporation.

Related Provisions: 88(1)(c)(iv), 88(1)(c.2) — Winding-up; 256(6)–(9) — Whether control acquired.

Notes: For a ruling on 55(3.2)(h) see VIEWS doc 2006-0215751R3.

55(3.2)(h) amended by 2002-2013 technical bill (Part 5 — technical), for dividends received after 1999, to add "(other than a qualified person in relation to the distribution)" (and add "a" before "specified shareholder").

55(3.2)(h) added by 1995-97 technical bill, effective for dividends received after June 20, 1996 other than dividends received in the course of a reorganization carried out under a series of transactions or events substantially advanced, as evidenced in writing, before June 21, 1996 or that was required on June 20, 1996 to be carried out under a written agreement made before June 21, 1996; and for the purpose of this rule, a reorganization is deemed not to be required to be carried out if the parties to the agreement can be relieved of that requirement if there is a change to the Act.

55(3.2) originally added by 1994 Budget.

(3.3) Interpretation of "specified shareholder" changed —
In determining whether a person is a specified shareholder of a corporation for the purposes of subparagraph (3.1)(b)(i) and paragraph (3.2)(h), the reference in the definition "specified shareholder" in subsection 248(1) to "or of any other corporation that is related to the corporation" shall be read as "or of any other corporation that is related to the corporation and that has a significant direct or indirect interest in any issued shares of the capital stock of the corporation".

Notes: 55(3.3) added by 1995-97 technical bill, for dividends received after 1996.

(3.4) Specified shareholder exclusion — In determining
whether a person is a specified shareholder of a corporation for the purposes of the definition "qualified person" in subsection (1), subparagraph (3.1)(b)(i) and paragraph (3.2)(h) as it applies for the purpose of subparagraph (3.1)(b)(iii), the reference to "not less than 10% of the issued shares of any class of the capital stock of the corporation" in the definition "specified shareholder" in subsection 248(1) is to be read as "not less than 10% of the issued shares of any class of the capital stock of the corporation, other than shares of a specified class (within the meaning of subsection 55(1))".

Notes: See Notes to 55(6). 55(3.4) added by 2002-2013 technical bill (Part 5 — technical), for dividends received after 1999.

(3.5) Amalgamation of related corporations — For the purposes of paragraphs (3.1)(c) and (d), a corporation formed by an amalgamation of two or more corporations (each of which is referred to in this subsection as a "predecessor corporation") that were related to each other immediately before the amalgamation, is deemed to be the same corporation as, and a continuation of, each of the predecessor corporations.

Notes: See Notes to 55(6). 55(3.5) added by 2002-2013 technical bill (Part 5 — technical), for dividends received after April 26, 1995.

(4) Avoidance of subsec. (2) — For the purposes of this section, where it can reasonably be considered that one of the main purposes of one or more transactions or events was to cause 2 or more persons to be related to each other or to cause a corporation to control another corporation, so that subsection (2) would, but for this subsection, not apply to a dividend, those persons shall be deemed not to be related to each other or the corporation shall be deemed not to control the other corporation, as the case may be.

Related Provisions: 55(5)(e) — Determination of "related" and "arm's length".

Notes: For the meaning of "one of the main purposes" see Notes to 83(2.1).

For CRA interpretation see VIEWS docs 2005-0149021R3 (no 55(4) on internal reorganization); 2009-0317541E5 and 2011-0399401C6 (general comments); 2010-0380661E5 (no 55(4) if main reason for holding shares is to protect economic interests); 2012-0450041E5 (no 55(4) on rollout of shares by personal trust under 107(2)).

55(4) amended by 1994 Budget, effective for dividends received after Feb. 21, 1994, other than dividends received as part of a transaction or event or a series of transactions or events that was required on Feb. 22, 1994 to be carried out pursuant to a written agreement entered into before Feb. 22, 1994.

(5) Applicable rules — For the purposes of this section,

(a) where a dividend referred to in subsection (2) was received by a corporation as part of a transaction or event or a series of transactions or events, the portion of a capital gain attributable to any income expected to be earned or realized by a corporation after the safe-income determination time for the transaction,

event or series is deemed to be a portion of a capital gain attributable to anything other than income;

(b) the income earned or realized by a corporation for a period throughout which it was resident in Canada and not a private corporation shall be deemed to be the total of

(i) its income for the period otherwise determined on the assumption that no amounts were deductible by the corporation by reason of section 37.1 of this Act or paragraph 20(1)(gg) of the *Income Tax Act*, chapter 148 of the Revised Statutes of Canada, 1952,

(ii) the amount, if any, by which

(A) the amount, if any, by which the total of the capital gains of the corporation for the period exceeds the total of the taxable capital gains of the corporation for the period

exceeds

(B) the amount, if any, by which the total of the capital losses of the corporation for the period exceeds the total of the allowable capital losses of the corporation for the period,

(iii) the total of all amounts each of which is an amount required to have been included under this subparagraph as it read in its application to a taxation year that ended before February 28, 2000,

(iv) the amount, if any, by which

(A) ½ of the total of all amounts each of which is an amount required by paragraph 14(1)(b) to be included in computing the corporation's income in respect of a business carried on by the corporation for a taxation year that is included in the period and that ended after February 27, 2000 and before October 18, 2000,

exceeds

(B) where the corporation has deducted an amount under subsection 20(4.2) in respect of a debt established by it to have become a bad debt in a taxation year that is included in the period and that ended after February 27, 2000 and before October 18, 2000, or has an allowable capital loss for such a year because of the application of subsection 20(4.3), the amount determined by the formula

$$V + W$$

where

V is ½ of the value determined for A under subsection 20(4.2) in respect of the corporation for the last such taxation year that ended in the period, and

W is ⅓ of the value determined for B under subsection 20(4.2) in respect of the corporation for the last such taxation year that ended in the period, and

(C) in any other case, nil, and

(v) the amount, if any, by which

(A) the total of all amounts each of which is an amount required by paragraph 14(1)(b) to be included in computing the corporation's income in respect of a business carried on by the corporation for a taxation year that is included in the period and that ends after October 17, 2000,

exceeds

(B) where the corporation has deducted an amount under subsection 20(4.2) in respect of a debt established by it to have become a bad debt in a taxation year that is included in the period and that ends after October 17, 2000, or has an allowable capital loss for such a year because of the application of subsection 20(4.3), the amount determined by the formula

$$X + Y$$

where

X   is the value determined for A under subsection 20(4.2) in respect of the corporation for the last such taxation year that ended in the period, and

Y   is $\frac{1}{3}$ of the value determined for B under subsection 20(4.2) in respect of the corporation for the last such taxation year that ended in the period, and

(C) in any other case, nil;

(c) the income earned or realized by a corporation for a period throughout which it was a private corporation is deemed to be its income for the period otherwise determined on the assumption that no amounts were deductible by the corporation under section 37.1 of this Act, as that section applies for taxation years that ended before 1995, or paragraph 20(1)(gg) of the *Income Tax Act*, chapter 148 of the Revised Statutes of Canada, 1952;

(d) the income earned or realized by a corporation (referred to in this paragraph as the "affiliate") for a period ending at a time when the affiliate was a foreign affiliate of another corporation is deemed to be the lesser of

(i) the amount that would, if the *Income Tax Regulations* were read without reference to their subsection 5905(5.6), be the tax-free surplus balance (within the meaning of their subsection 5905(5.5)) of the affiliate in respect of the other corporation at that time, and

(ii) the fair market value at that time of all the issued and outstanding shares of the capital stock of the affiliate;

(e) in determining whether 2 or more persons are related to each other, in determining whether a person is at any time a specified shareholder of a corporation and in determining whether control of a corporation has been acquired by a person or group of persons,

(i) a person shall be deemed to be dealing with another person at arm's length and not to be related to the other person if the person is the brother or sister of the other person, except in the case where the dividend was received or paid, as part of a transaction or event or a series of transactions or events, by a corporation of which a share of the capital stock is a qualified small business corporation share or a "share of the capital stock of a family farm or fishing corporation" within the meaning of subsection 110.6(1),

(ii) where at any time a person is related to each beneficiary (other than a registered charity) under a trust who is or may (otherwise than by reason of the death of another beneficiary under the trust) be entitled to share in the income or capital of the trust, the person and the trust shall be deemed to be related at that time to each other and, for this purpose, a person shall be deemed to be related to himself, herself or itself,

(iii) a trust and a person shall be deemed not to be related to each other unless they are deemed by paragraph (3.2)(d) or subparagraph (ii) to be related to each other or the person is a corporation that is controlled by the trust, and

(iv) this Act shall be read without reference to subsection 251(3) and paragraph 251(5)(b); and

Proposed Amendment — 55(5)(e) — Application date for 2021 amendment

Dept. of Finance news release, June 30, 2021: See under 84.1(2)(e).

(f) unless subsection (2.3) applies, if a corporation has received a dividend any portion of which is a taxable dividend (such a portion referred to as the "taxable part" in this paragraph), as part of a transaction or event or series of transactions or events

(i) a portion of the dividend is deemed to be a separate taxable dividend equal to the lesser of

(A) the taxable part, and

(B) the amount of the income earned or realized by any corporation — after 1971 and before the safe-income determination time for the transaction, event or series — that could reasonably be considered to contribute to the

capital gain that could be realized on a disposition at fair market value, immediately before the dividend, of the share on which the dividend is received, and

(ii) the amount, if any, by which the taxable part exceeds the portion referred to in subparagraph (i) is deemed to be a separate taxable dividend.

Related Provisions [subsec. 55(5)]: 141.1 — Insurance corporation deemed not to be private corporation; 256(6)–(9) — Whether control acquired.

Notes: *55(5)(b) and (c),* in defining "income earned or realized...", define "*safe income*" (SI), which can be paid out as an intercorporate dividend (to the extent it contributes to the accrued capital gain) without triggering 55(2) (see 55(2.1)(c) and Notes to 55(2.1)). The core rules are "Robertson's Rules", set by Revenue Canada's John Robertson, 1981 Cdn Tax Foundation conference report (pp. 83-91) and clarified by Robert Read, 1988 conference report, 18:3-7. For a spreadsheet to calculate SI see taxtemplates.ca "Safe Income".

SI is computed *after* deducting corporate income tax ultimately payable on the income (even if not yet payable): *Kruco Inc.*, 2003 FCA 284, para. 38; *626468 New Brunswick*, 2019 FCA 306 [Katlai, "Safe income calculation must include taxes payable", 2506 *Tax Topics* (CCH) 1-3 (March 19, 2020); Wahidie case comment, 68(3) *Canadian Tax Journal* 891-98 (2020)].

The starting point in the SI calculation is income for tax purposes (not financial statement or accounting purposes). Mark Brender, in "Subsection 55(2)", 2011 Cdn Tax Foundation conference report, 12:1-35, suggests that the concept of SI has become overcomplicated over 30+ years, and should simply be income taxed under s. 3, minus taxes paid and dividends paid out, so that income subject to the tax system can be extracted tax-free. Stock dividends can reduce SI: see 55(2.2)-(2.4), specifically (2.3)(b).

SI need not be "disposable", and is not reduced by investment tax credits included in income, or other "phantom income" for which there is no corresponding cash inflow: *Kruco Inc.*, 2003 FCA 284. "Parliament did not want to impede the tax-free flow of dividends that were attributable to income which had already been taxed."

CRA said at the 2005 Cdn Tax Foundation conference (*Income Tax Technical News* 34) that it would follow *Kruco* for all corporations; *ITTN* 33 provided transitional relief. However, at the 2006 conference (Nov. 28/06, slides available), Wayne Adams noted that this cannot be extended to allow techniques that manufacture unlimited SI, such as through timing changes (12(1)(a), 20(1)(m)). For dividends paid after Feb. 15/08, non-deductible cash outflows must be deducted in computing SI: *ITTN* 37 (gives a detailed rationale based on *Kruco*); Janet Newcombe, "CRA Flip-Flops on Non-deductible Expenses and Safe Income", 5(4) *Tax Hyperion* (Carswell, April 2008). In *VIH Logging*, 2005 FCA 36, SI was not reduced by a deduction for a later purchase of seismic data as a tax shelter.

SI computation ends at the "safe-income determination time" (55(1)), which applies to a "series of transactions" (defined broadly in 248(10)). See Kenneth Keung, "Subsection 55(2) — The Road Ahead", 2016 Prairie Provinces tax conference (ctf.ca).

See also Osborne, "Practical Issues in Computing Safe Income", 2002 Cdn Tax Foundation conference report, 42:1-23; Rogers, "Safe Income", 2004 B.C. Tax Conference (ctf.ca) 16:1-20; Boehmer & Campbell, "Safe Income", 2005 Ontario Tax Conf. 5:1-33; Allard, "L'utilisation du revenu protégé", 54(1) *Canadian Tax Journal [CTJ]* 87-114 (2006); Pantry & Maclagan, "Issues and Updates — Safe Income", 2008 BC Tax Conf. 4:1-35; Swanston, "Safe Income: Public Company Takeovers", 16(5) *Canadian Tax Highlights [CTH]* (ctf.ca) 7-8 (May 2008); Sohmer, "Safe Income", xxxix *The Canadian Taxpayer* (Carswell) 86-87 (June 2, 2017); McLean, "CRA Provides Comments on Safe-Income", 25(6) *CTH* 13-14 (June 2017); Cormack, "A Practical Approach to Calculating Safe Income", 2017 BC Tax Conf.; Samuel, "Interaction of the Foreign Affiliate Surplus and Safe-Income Regimes", 66(2) *CTJ* 269-307 (2018); Shew, "Safe Income May Vary Within Shares of the Same Class", 8(3) *Canadian Tax Focus* (ctf.ca) 3 (Aug. 2018) (and see correction posted with article on CTF website: CRA policy allows pooling of SI within a class); Oldewening & Ariyakumaran, "Safe Income of a Foreign Affiliate", XXIII(1) *International Tax Planning* (Federated Press) 6-10 (2019); Mancell, "An Overview of Section 55 and Safe Income Part II — Safe Income Calculation", 2467 *Tax Topics* (CCH) 1-4 (June 20, 2019); and "Part III — Safe Income on Hand Allocation", 2471 1-3 (July 18, 2019).

For CRA comments on SI *[the pre-2007 ones may be superseded by the new Kruco policy above]*, see docs 2005-0113931I7 (premiums paid under life insurance policy reduce SI); 2005-0122691R3 (SI of 2 classes of shares can be combined if the shares are rolled into a new class); 2006-0168551E5 (13(7)(g) excess of automobile cost over $30,000 need not be deducted from SI); 2007-0233881R3, 2007-0245191R3 (55(2) will not apply to portions of dividend protected by SI); 2007-0243151C6 (SI after *Kruco*); 2007-0243161C6 (SI and s. 85.1); 2008-0271401E5 (SI and GRIP); 2009-0330171C6 (financing expenses); 2009-0330201C6 (freeze shares); 2010-0373191C6 (SI computation); 2011-0395701E5 (SI where capital loss on loan would be realized after safe-income determination time); 2011-039953I7 (losses should be reflected in SI when incurred, not when deducted, even for construction business using IT-92R2 method); 2011-0415071E5 (taxable income addition under 110.5 is not SI); 2011-0416801E5 (SI on hand — stub period); 2010-0374231E5, 2011-0423181E5 (SI after s. 51 exchange); 2012-0448651E5 (allocation of SI among classes of shares); 2012-0454481E4, 2012-0471021E5 (impact of 34.2(11) transitional reserve); 2013-0495851C6 [2013 APFF q.18] (impact on SI of additional income tax paid by Opco for years before acquisition of its shares); 2013-049914I7 (impact of US *Internal Revenue*

Code §338(h)(10) election); 2014-0522991C6 [2014 STEP q.7] (whether recipient of dividend exceeding SI can self-assess it as proceeds of disposition); 2014-0538061C6 (SI dividend to trust that distributes it under 104(19) to corporate beneficiary: SI status preserved [Kakkar & Halil, "Corporate Beneficiary Can Add to Its Safe Income on Hand", 15(3) Tax for the Owner-Manager (ctf.ca) 7-8 (July 2015)]); 2015-0573821C6 (effect of transfer of life insurance policy from Opco to parent); 2015-0610661C6 [2015 CTF q.6(c)] (dividends paid on discretionary-dividend shares may reduce safe income of other shares); 2016-0633961E5 (recapture and terminal loss, technically at year-end, can count as before safe-income determination time); 2016-0652991C6 [2016 APFF q.15] (SI not transferred from common to pref shares on stock dividend); 2016-0655921C6 [2016 APFF q.14] (no SI that would contribute to capital gain on non-participating pref shares); 2016-0669651C6 [2016 CTF q.2] (discretionary dividend shares: various anti-avoidance provisions may apply); 2016-0672321C6 [2016 TEI q.B3] (CRA procedures for helping corps calculate safe income; audit practices; effects of annual dividends and of amounts under 13(1) and 14(1)); 2018-0743951C6 [STEP 2018 q.4] (safe income of corp owned by person who dies does not flow through to estate); 2019-0812691C6 [2019 APFF q.10] (losses in sub do not always reduce parent's SI [Thivierge & Roy, "Should the Safe Income of Unprofitable Subsidiaries Be Consolidated?", 10(2) Canadian Tax Focus (ctf.ca) 16-17 (May 2020)]); 2019-0833061E5 (trust designating dividend to 2 beneficiaries: see 104(19)); 2020-0861001C6 [2020 CTF q.2] (consolidation of SI in corporate group) and 2020-0861031C6 [2020 CTF q.3] (impact of reorganization on SI: detailed examples); 2020-0852151C6 [2020 APFF q.3] (loan to pay dividend reduces SI when repaid from SI earnings).

55(5)(e): See Notes to 55(3). In (e)(ii), "beneficiary" includes "beneficially interested" due to Propep (see Notes to 248(25)): VIEWS doc 2014-0538021C6 [2014 APFF q.3], reversing 2004-0086961C6. See also John Oakey, "Understanding Subsection 55", 13(12) Tax Hyperion (Carswell) 1-2 (Dec. 2016).

55(5)(f) applies automatically (since the 2016 amendment) to split a dividend that exceeds safe income into two parts, both taxable dividends. The portion up to safe income is a normal intercorporate dividend, deductible under 112(1); the remainder may be subject to 55(2) (see Notes to 55(2.1)).

For CRA views on 55(5)(f) since the 2016 amendments, see 2016-0630281E5; 2017-0726381C6 [2017 CTF q.5] (interaction with 55(2.1) and (2.3)).

For dividends paid before April 21, 2015, 55(5)(f) applied only if the dividend recipient designated a specific amount to be a separate taxable dividend. Late designations were permitted in Administration Gilles Leclair, [1997] 3 C.T.C. 3053 (TCC); Nassau Walnut Investments, [1998] 1 C.T.C. 33 (FCA); 101139810 Saskatchewan Ltd., 2017 TCC 3, para. 83. The CRA now accepts late designations generally (but not elections): doc 2015-0573861C6 [2015 CLHIA q.3]; but may apply GAAR if the purpose of a late 55(5)(f) designation is dividend stripping: 2011-0412091C6 [2011 APFF q.10].

For examples of pre-2016 55(5)(f) see VIEWS docs 2008-0271401E5, 2008-0284961C6, 2009-0310251E5, 2012-0433261E5, 2012-0434501E5, 2012-0435381E5, 2013-0480051E5 [Daniel Gosselin, "CRA Confirms GRIP Trap When Dividend Not Paid Out of Safe Income", 14(3) Tax for the Owner-Manager (ctf.ca) 1-2 (July 2014)]. See also Adam Drori, "CRA's Reinterpretation of Paragraph 55(5)(f)", 5(3) Canadian Tax Focus (ctf.ca) 7 (Aug. 2015).

For a corporation filing Quebec returns, a designation under (pre-2016) 55(5)(f)(i) must be copied to Revenu Québec: Taxation Act ss. 308.6, 21.4.6.

55(5)(e)(i) amended to add everything from "except in the case" by 2021 family business transfers bill, effective June 29, 2021. See 84.1(2) Notes re 84.1(2)(e).

55(5)(f) amended by 2016 budget bill #1, this version effective for dividends received after April 17, 2016. For those received from April 21, 2015 through April 17, 2016, read [this was the draft version before April 18, 2016]:

> (f) unless subsection (2.3) applies, if a corporation has received a dividend any portion of which is a taxable dividend
>
> > (i) the corporation may designate in its return of income under this Part for the taxation year during which the dividend was received any portion of the taxable dividend to be a separate taxable dividend, and
>
> > (ii) the amount, if any, by which the portion of the dividend that is a taxable dividend exceeds the portion designated under subparagraph (i) shall be deemed to be a separate dividend.

55(5)(d) amended by 2002-2013 technical bill (Part 3 — FA reorganizations), effective for a dividend received after Aug. 19, 2011 by a corporation resident in Canada, with a grandfathering exception.

55(5) earlier amended by 2001 technical bill, 2000 budget, 1995-97 technical bill, 1994 Budget.

I.T. Application Rules: 69 (meaning of "chapter 148 of ...").

I.T. Technical News: 7 (subsection 55(2) — recent cases); 16 (Brelco Drilling); 33 (income earned or realized — Kruco); 34 (safe income calculation — Kruco).

(6) Unlisted shares deemed listed — A share (in this subsection referred to as the "reorganization share") is deemed, for the purposes of subsection 116(6) and the definition "taxable Canadian property" in subsection 248(1), to be listed on a designated stock exchange if

(a) a dividend, to which subsection (2) does not apply because of paragraph (3)(b), is received in the course of a reorganization;

(b) in contemplation of the reorganization

(i) the reorganization share is issued to a taxpayer by a public corporation in exchange for another share of that corporation (in this subsection referred to as the "old share") owned by the taxpayer, and

(ii) the reorganization share is exchanged by the taxpayer for a share of another public corporation (in this subsection referred to as the "new share") in an exchange that would be a permitted exchange if the definition "permitted exchange" were read without reference to paragraph (a) and subparagraph (b)(ii) of that definition;

(c) immediately before the exchange, the old share

(i) is listed on a designated stock exchange, and

(ii) is not taxable Canadian property of the taxpayer; and

(d) the new share is listed on a designated stock exchange.

Notes: For commentary on the 2002-2013 technical bill amendments to s. 55 including 55(3)-(3.5) and 55(6), see Marc Ton-That & Rick McLean, "Technical Amendments Designed to Accommodate Public Company Spin-offs Leave Uncertainties", VIII(2) Corporate Structures & Groups (Federated Press) 421-26 (2002).

For CRA interpretation of 55(6) see VIEWS doc 2010-0366651R3.

55(6) added by 2002-2013 technical bill, for shares issued after April 26, 1995.

Definitions [s. 55]: "acquired" — 55(3.2)(e), (f), 256(7); "acquiror" — 55(1)"permitted exchange"(b); "acquisition of control" — 55(3.2)(g), 55(5)(e), 256(7), (8); "affiliate" — 55(5)(d); "allowable capital loss" — 38(b), 248(1); "amount" — 248(1); "arm's length" — 55(4), 55(5)(e), 251(1); "brother" — 252(2); "business" — 248(1); "Canada" — 255; "capital gain", "capital loss" — 39(1), 248(1); "capital property" — 54, 248(1); "class of shares" — 248(6); "control", "controlled" — 55(3.2)(g), 55(4), 55(5)(e), 139.1(18), 256(6)-(9); "corporation" — 55(3.2)(b), 248(1), Interpretation Act 35(1); "cost amount" — 248(1); "cumulative eligible capital" — 14(5), 248(1); "designated stock exchange" — 248(1), 262; "disposition" — 248(1); "distributing corporation" — 55(1)"distribution"; "distribution" — 55(1); "dividend" — 55(2.1), 248(1); "dividend payer" — 55(3)(a)(iii)(A); "dividend recipient" — 55(2.1), (3); "eligible capital property" — 54, 248(1); "fair market value" — see 69(1) Notes; "foreign affiliate" — 95(1), 248(1); "foreign vendor" — 55(3.1)(a); "income earned or realized..." — 55(5)(b), (c); "individual", "non-resident" — 248(1); "paid-up capital" — 89(1), 248(1); "participant" — 55(1)"permitted exchange"(b); "partnership" — see 96(1) Notes; "permitted acquisition", "permitted exchange", "permitted redemption" — 55(1); "person", "personal trust" — 248(1); "private corporation" — 89(1), 248(1); "proceeds of disposition" — 54, 55(3.01)(d); "property" — 248(1); "public corporation" — 89(1), 248(1); "qualified person" — 55(1); "qualifying share" — 192(6), 248(1) [not intended to apply to s. 55]; "related" — 55(3.01)(a), 55(3.2)(c), (d), 55(4), 55(5)(e), 251(2)-(6); "resident in Canada" — 250; "safe-income determination time" — 55(1); "series of transactions" — 248(10); "share", "shareholder" — 248(1); "significant reduction" — 55(2.5); "sister" — 252(2); "specified class", "specified corporation" — 55(1); "specified shareholder" — 55(3.2)(a), 55(3.3), 248(1); "specified wholly-owned corporation" — 55(1); "stock dividend", "subsidiary wholly-owned corporation" — 248(1); "taxable Canadian corporation" — 89(1), 248(1); "taxable Canadian property" — 248(1); "taxable capital gain" — 38(a), 248(1); "taxable dividend" — 89(1), 248(1); "tax-free surplus balance" — Reg. 5905(5.5); "taxpayer" — 248(1); "transferee" — 55(1)"distribution"; "transferee corporation" — 55(1)"distribution", 55(3.2)(h); "trust" — 104(1), 248(1), (3); "unrelated" — 55(3.01)(a); "vendor" — 55(3.1)(b)(i).

Subdivision D — Other Sources of Income

56. (1) Amounts to be included in income for year — Without restricting the generality of section 3, there shall be included in computing the income of a taxpayer for a taxation year,

(a) **pension benefits, unemployment insurance benefits, etc.** — any amount received by the taxpayer in the year as, on account or in lieu of payment of, or in satisfaction of,

(i) a superannuation or pension benefit including, without limiting the generality of the foregoing,

(A) the amount of any pension, supplement or spouse's or common-law partner's allowance under the Old Age Security Act and the amount of any similar payment under a law of a province,

(B) the amount of any benefit under the *Canada Pension Plan* or a provincial pension plan as defined in section 3 of that Act,

(C) the amount of any payment out of or under a specified pension plan, and

(C.1) the amount of any payment out of or under a foreign retirement arrangement established under the laws of a country, except to the extent that the amount would not, if the taxpayer were resident in the country, be subject to income taxation in the country,

but not including

(D) the portion of a benefit received out of or under an employee benefit plan that is required by paragraph 6(1)(g) to be included in computing the taxpayer's income for the year, or would be required to be so included if that paragraph were read without reference to subparagraph 6(1)(g)(ii),

(E) the portion of an amount received out of or under a retirement compensation arrangement that is required by paragraph (x) or (z) to be included in computing the taxpayer's income for the year,

(F) a benefit received under section 71 of the *Canada Pension Plan* or under a similar provision of a provincial pension plan as defined in section 3 of that Act, and

(G) an amount received out of or under a registered pension plan as a return of all or a portion of a contribution to the plan to the extent that the amount

(I) is a payment made to the taxpayer under subsection 147.1(19) or subparagraph 8502(d)(iii) of the *Income Tax Regulations*, and

(II) is not deducted in computing the taxpayer's income for the year or a preceding taxation year,

(ii) a retiring allowance, other than an amount received out of or under an employee benefit plan, a retirement compensation arrangement or a salary deferral arrangement,

(iii) a death benefit,

(iv) a benefit under the *Unemployment Insurance Act*, other than a payment relating to a course or program designed to facilitate the re-entry into the labour force of a claimant under that Act, or a benefit under Part I, VII.1, VIII or VIII.1 of the *Employment Insurance Act*,

---

Possible Future Amendment — 56(1)(a)(iv) — Maternity and parental EI benefits to be exempt

Liberal.ca election platform, Oct. 2019: We will ...

• make sure families get more money right away, by making maternity and parental benefits tax-free;

Notes: The Liberals were elected with a minority government on Oct. 21, 2019, so this measure may be implemented. However, it was not included in the Prime Minister's Dec 2019 "mandate letter" to the Minister of Finance.

(v) a benefit under regulations made under an appropriation Act providing for a scheme of transitional assistance benefits to persons employed in the production of products to which the Canada-United States Agreement on Automotive Products, signed on January 16, 1965 applies,

(vi) except to the extent otherwise required to be included in computing the taxpayer's income, a prescribed benefit under a government assistance program,

(vii) a benefit under the *Act respecting parental insurance*, R.S.Q., c. A-29.011, or

(viii) an income replacement benefit payable to the taxpayer under Part 2 of the *Veterans Well-being Act*, if the amount is determined under subsection 19.1(1), paragraph 23(1)(b) or subsection 26.1(1) of that Act (as modified, where applicable, under Part 5 of that Act);

Related Provisions: 56(1)(r), 110(1)(g) — *EI Act* Part II tuition assistance; 56(8) — Averaging of CPP/QPP benefits where paid for earlier years; 56(12) — Distribution

---

from foreign retirement arrangement; 57 — Certain superannuation or pension benefits; 60(g) — Deduction for Quebec Parental Insurance Plan premiums; 60(j) — Transfer of superannuation benefits; 60(j.04) — Deduction for repayments of pension benefits; 60(j.1) — Transfer of retiring allowances; 60(n), (n.1) — Deduction for repayment of pension or benefits; 60(v.1) — UI/EI benefit repayment; 60.01 — Rollover of 56(1)(a)(i)(C.1) amount to RPP or RRSP; 60.02(1)"eligible proceeds"(c) — Rollover of RPP payment to RDSP on death; 60.2(1) — Refund of undeducted past service AVCs; 78(4) — Unpaid amounts; 81(1)(d)–(g) — Certain pensions exempt from tax; 104(28) — Death benefit flowed through estate; 110(1)(f) — Deductions for certain payments; 110(1)(h) — Grandfathering of 50% inclusion in income of US social security for taxpayers receiving benefits since before 1996; 110.2(1)"qualifying amount" — Retroactive spreading of certain lump-sum payments over prior years; 118(3) — Pension income credit; 118.7 — Credit for EI premium and CPP contributions; 128.1(10)"excluded right or interest"(a)(viii), (d), (g), (h) — Emigration — no deemed disposition of right to pension or retiring allowance; 146(5.2) — Transfer of commuted RPP to RRSP when employer insolvent; 147.3(13.1) — Withdrawal of excessive transfer to RRSP or RRIF; 153(1) — Withholding of tax at source; 212(1)(h), (j) — Pension and benefit payments to non-residents — withholding tax; 254 — Contract under pension plan; Canada-U.S. Tax Treaty:Art. XVIII — Pensions and annuities; Canada-U.S. Tax Treaty:Art. XXIX:7 — exemption for half of old age security paid to citizen of U.S. resident in Canada.

Notes: *56(1)(a)(i)(A)* taxes both private pension benefits (see 147.1 for RPPs) and Old Age Security (OAS). For OAS benefits (including Guaranteed Income Supplement (GIS)) see tinyurl.com/oas-canada; Killeen & James, *Annotated Canada Pension Plan and Old Age Security Act* (17th ed., LexisNexis, 2018); Fitzgerald & Hawker, "Government Retirement Income", 23(5) *Canadian Tax Highlights* (ctf.ca) 7-8 (May 2015) and 23(6) 7-8 (June 2015). For the clawback of OAS benefits, which are not paid to high-income seniors or couples, see 180.2.

COVID-19 Seniors' Benefit: A one-time $300 was paid in July 2020 to those eligible for OAS in June, plus $200 for those eligible for GIS. This was paid under the *Public Health Events of National Concern Payments Act* (enacted by 2020 COVID bill #1), not the *OAS Act*. CRA says it is tax-free, no tax slip will be issued and it need not be reported on the 2020 return: tinyurl.com/senior-ben. However, since it is income-based (being only for those not subject to full 180.2 clawback), 56(1)(u) could require it to be added to net income (with offsetting 110(1)(f) deduction in computing taxable income), which could reduce 2021 OAS, GST/HST Credit and other credits. Since CRA says the payment is tax-free, Finance saw no need for corrective legislation.

Pension income qualifies for the 118(3) pension credit: see 118(7)"eligible pension income". It can be split between spouses or common-law partners: see 60.03. Pension income earned through a trust or estate loses its character and is taxed under 104(13) due to 108(5), unless designated under 104(27)(c)(i): VIEWS doc 2011-0420781C6. Pension income earned by a status Indian: see 81(1)(a) Notes.

Foreign pensions (FP): Pensions from the US are taxable under 56(1)(a)(i) only if they are also taxable under US law: Canada-US tax treaty Art. XVIII:1, VIEWS doc 2002-0142171I7. See also Reg. 6803. (Exempt pensions are included in income and deducted under 110(1)(f) in computing taxable income: 2007-0262251M4.) The same applies to other countries if the tax treaty so provides, e.g. Belgium (2012-0449621E5), Germany (2007-0236891E5, 2011-0400781E5 (part exempt, part eligible for foreign tax credit), 2012-0438671E5 (same, and see next para.)), Hong Kong (taxable: 2014-0522671E5, 2014-0529791E5), Hungary (2005-0160601E5), Singapore (2011-0416841E5), Switzerland (2008-0274271E5, 2011-0405551E5); UK (see Notes to Canada-UK tax treaty Art. 17:1). A commutation payment from a FP is taxable: 2009-0311631E5. A FP can be rolled into an RRSP: 60(j), 2011-0409121E5; there is no deferral if the FP is transferred to an annuity: 2019-0802301E5. FPs can be reported using Bank of Canada or other official exchange rate, but not (in CRA's view) the rate actually received from the bank: 2007-0242861M4. Certain pensions, e.g. for wartime service, are exempt: see 81(1)(d)-(g). See also below re FPs from specific countries.

Australia: In *Rasmussen*, 2019 TCC 124, payments from the government employees' "QSuper" fund were taxable and not treaty-exempt, including a "tax-free component" that is non-taxable in Australia; the same applies to a "Self-Managed Super Fund": doc 2018-0747781E5. **Colombia**: In *Reyes*, 2019 FCA 7, a pension was taxable, not exempted by treaty. **Germany** taxes social security pensions paid from Germany. See tinyurl.com/cra-agreements under "Germany"; 2012-0438671E5. (The heirs are liable if a deceased owed German tax; and under the Canada-Germany treaty, Germany can ask CRA to collect German tax: see Canada-US treaty Art. XXVI-A:1 Notes.) **India**: military service pension and military disability pension payments are exempt under the Canada-India treaty: 2020-0860081E5. **Ireland**: payments from a Personal Retirement Savings Account and Approved Retirement Fund are non-taxable if there were no employer contributions: 2018-0781941E5. **Isle of Man**: Withdrawals from a "retirement account" are taxable: 2014-0555271E5, as are payments from a "provident fund": 2020-0852671E5 (though it could be an EBP taxed by 6(1)(g)). **Malaysia**: payments from Employees Provident Fund: 2015-0571591E5 (unresolved). **Netherlands**: pensions including Stichting Bedrijfspensioenfonds voor medewerkers were taxable in *Eyckelhoff*, 2020 TCC 130. **New Zealand**: payments from a "personal retirement plan" are likely not taxable: 2010-0385371E5. **Switzerland**: a pension was taxable in *Schaub*, 2014 TCC 212, even though S had not been able to deduct his contributions. (Art. 27:4 of the Canada-Swiss tax treaty and tinyurl.com/switzer27-4 now provide relief for 5 years of contributions.) CRA says payments from a "Pillar 2" policy are taxable, but income accruing in it is not: 2016-0640651E5. **UK**: see Notes to Canada-UK Treaty Art. 17:1. **US**: 401(k) plan payments were not taxable in *Jacques*, 2016 TCC 245 (see also 56(12) Notes).

For pension/social security *contributions*, including to other countries, see 118.7 Notes.

Unclaimed pension or survivor benefits that are eventually paid out are taxable when paid: VIEWS doc 2016-0649821I7. If an employer winds up its pension plan and transfers the funds to an annuity in the employee's name without using 147.4(1), the full amount is taxable: 2012-0458781E5. A class action settlement with employees re pension plan funding was taxable under 56(1)(a)(i): 2015-0586831R3.

Division of a pension on marriage breakdown, where the pension authority continues to pay only one spouse who then transfers half to the other, may be recognized so that each is taxed on half the income, if the transfer is spousal support or was intended to have the tax shared: *Walker*, [2000] 1 C.T.C. 271 (FCA); *Lane*, 2007 TCC 674; VIEWS docs 2005-0144501E5, 2009-0331771E5; Théroux, "Deferred Income Benefits", 14(10) *Canadian Tax Highlights* (ctf.ca) 2-3 (Oct. 2006). *Contra*, payments were equalization of property in *St-Jacques*, [2001] 1 C.T.C. 2704 (TCC); *Andrews*, 2005 TCC 246; *O'Brien*, 2006 TCC 661; *Emond*, 2012 TCC 304.

See also 248(1)"superannuation or pension benefit" Notes.

A lump sum pension payment on death to an estate or beneficiary (including a retroactive GIS correction) is normally taxed in the recipient's hands in the year received. (It can instead go on the deceased's 70(2) "rights or things" return: IT-212R3 para. 15, docs 2006-0192051I7, 2007-0254491E5, 2013-0515681E5, 2015-0615201I7; but not if payment was to a non-spouse designated beneficiary: 2012-0441381E5, 2012-0447551C6.) In the recipient's hands it is neither (exempt) life insurance nor a ($10,000-exempt) death benefit, but taxable under 56(1)(a)(i): *Woods*, 2011 FCA 90.

A one-time payment from the employer to retired plan members, such as to compensate for non-indexation, falls under 56(1)(a)(i): 2007-0262301R3, 2009-0337641R3. However, amounts paid by Quebec to compensate for pension deficits are not taxable: 2008-0271781E5. If purchase of an annuity contract represents the payment of a pension benefit, the FMV of the contract falls under 56(1)(a)(i): 2008-0286071E5.

In *Dunne*, 2007 SCC 19, a retired Ontario accountant who had never worked or lived in Quebec was subject to QC tax on his pension because the partnership carried on business in QC.

A distribution of surplus to an employer, or sale of pension plan actuarial surplus, is taxable, subject to 147.2(1) deduction if recontributed to another RPP: docs 2007-025640I7, 2008-029492117, 2009-0342511R3, 2019-081764117 [Théroux, "CRA Pension Positions Change", 16(6) *Canadian Tax Highlights* (ctf.ca) 5 (June 2008)].

56(1)(a)(i)(B): For info on CPP benefits see: tinyurl.com/info-cpp-ben; first para. of these Notes; "CPP enhancements" in 147.5 Notes. CPP benefits are divided between spouses on divorce: *Canada Pension Plan* s. 55.1; *Upshall*, 2013 FCA 174. CPP disability benefits are taxable even if they replace non-taxable LTD benefits: *Parker*, 2015 TCC 86, paras. 30-33.

56(1)(a)(i)(B) applied to a Quebec Pension Plan disability benefit that L cashed, even though she disputed it and it was eventually ordered repaid: *Lessard*, 2007 FCA 9 (leave to appeal denied 2007 CarswellNat 1534 (SCC)); and this was not a *Charter* violation: *Lessard*, 2012 FCA 311.

US social security benefits are 85% taxable, 50% if received continuously since before 1996: Canada-US tax treaty Art. XVIII:5, 110(1)(h). The income is included under 56(1)(a)(i)(B) and 15% deduction allowed under 110(1)(f): VIEWS doc 2011-0392071E5. This applies also to disability benefits (overruling 2004-0058651E5), since cancellation of IT-122 in 2004 by *Income Tax Technical News* 31. A retroactive lump-sum is eligible for averaging: see 56(8) Notes.

56(1)(a)(i)(C) taxes payments from a "specified pension plan" (the Saskatchewan Pension Plan). See 248(1)"specified pension plan" Notes.

56(1)(a)(i)(C.1) taxes payment from a US IRA (248(1)"foreign retirement arrangement"), including received by an heir on the holder's death: *Gill*, 2013 FCA 135; *Kaiser*, 1994 CarswellNat 1093 (TCC); *McKenzie*, 2017 TCC 56 (no other way to tax it, and this is not double tax); *Owen*, 2018 TCC 90; docs 2015-0570291R3; 2017-0682301E5 (deemed distribution under US expatriation rules on giving up green card). Amounts accruing in an IRA are not taxed until withdrawn, even without a Canada-US tax treaty Art. XVIII:7 election: 2015-0576551E5.

56(1)(a)(i)(F) provides that a CPP/QPP death benefit is not taxed by 56(1)(a). It is included in the estate's income by 56(1)(a.1).

56(1)(a)(i)(G) allows a refund of a pension contribution made due to reasonable error to be tax-free, provided the contribution was not deducted.

56(1)(a)(ii) taxes retirement and termination payments (severance pay) and wrongful dismissal settlements/damage awards. See 248(1)"retiring allowance" Notes.

56(1)(a)(iii) taxes a death benefit; $10,000 is exempt. See 248(1)"death benefit" Notes.

56(1)(a)(iv) taxes most EI benefits. If they are later repaid they can be deducted under 60(n)(iv), if the taxpayer has income against which to deduct. Relief in one case was granted by the *Danielle Gareau Remission Order*, P.C. 2003-774. For EI benefits earned by a status Indian, see 81(1)(a) Notes.

56(1)(a)(vii) refers to benefits under the Quebec Parental Insurance Plan (QPIP).

56(1)(a)(viii) added by 2018 budget bill #1, effective April 2019. 56(1)(a) earlier amended by 2013 budget bill #2 (effective 2014), 2002-2013 technical bill, 2011 budget bill #2, 2000 same-sex partners bill, 1995-97 technical bill, 1997 Budget, 1996 EI bill, 1993 and 1991 technical bills.

Regulations: 100(1)"remuneration"(b), (c), (d), (g) (withholding at source); 103(4), (6)(e) (withholding required for retiring allowance); 200(2)(e) (information return);

5502 (prescribed benefits for 56(1)(a)(vi)); 7800 (Saskatchewan Pension Plan is specified pension plan for 56(1)(a)(i)(C)).

Remission Orders: *Willard Thorne Remission Order*, P.C. 2002-2177 (remission of tax on retroactive lump sum payment of CPP benefits); *Danielle Gareau Remission Order*, P.C. 2003-774 (remission of tax on EI benefits repaid in a later year); *Janet Hall Remission Order*, P.C. 2004-1336 (remission where CPP lump sum disability repaid to wage loss replacement provider).

Income Tax Folios: S1-F2-C3: Scholarships, research grants and other education assistance [replaces IT-340R]; S2-F1-C2: Retiring allowances [replaces IT-337R4].

Interpretation Bulletins: IT-91R4: Employment at special work sites or remote work locations; IT-167R6: Registered pension plans — employee's contributions; IT-247: Employer's contribution to pensioners' premiums under provincial medical and hospital services plans (cancelled); IT-365R2: Damages, settlements and similar receipts; IT-397R: Amounts excluded from income — statutory exemptions and certain service or RCMP pensions, allowances and compensation; IT-499R: Superannuation or pension benefits; IT-508R: Death benefits; IT-528: Transfers of funds between registered plans; IT-529: Flexible employee benefit programs.

Information Circulars: 13-2R1: Government programs collection policies.

Registered Plans Compliance Bulletins: 3 (purchase of annuity under subsec. 147.4(1)).

Advance Tax Rulings: ATR-12: Retiring allowance; ATR-21: Pension benefit from an unregistered pension plan.

Forms: RC4157: Deducting income tax on pension and other income, and filing the T4A slip and summary; T4A(OAS) Supp: Statement of old age security; T4A: Information.

(a.1) [death] benefits under CPP/QPP — where the taxpayer is an estate that arose on or as a consequence of the death of an individual, each benefit received under section 71 of the *Canada Pension Plan*, or under a similar provision of a provincial pension plan as defined in section 3 of that Act, after July 1997 and in the year in respect of the death of the individual;

Related Provisions: 56(8) — Averaging of benefits where paid for earlier years.

Notes: A CPP death benefit cannot be included in the deceased's income: 56(1)(a)(i)(F). It can be flowed out by the estate, deducted under 104(5) and taxed to the beneficiary under 104(13); or the estate may elect under 104(13.1) to pay tax on it: VIEWS doc 2005-0157581E5.

CRA's view is that a CPP death benefit paid to a person other than the estate can fall within 56(1)(a.1), due to the extended meaning of "estate" in 104(1): doc 2004-0097381I7. However, in *Goldberg Estate*, 2005 TCC 460, a Quebec Pension Plan death benefit paid to the heirs was not taxable to the estate.

56(1)(a.1) added by 1997 Budget, for 1997 and later tax years.

(a.2) [split] pension income reallocation — where the taxpayer is a pension transferee (as defined in subsection 60.03(1)), any amount that is a split-pension amount (as defined in that subsection) in respect of the pension transferee for the taxation year;

Related Provisions: 60.03(2) — Effect of pension income splitting; 153(2) — Source deductions deemed withheld on behalf of transferee.

Notes: 56(1)(a.2) added by 2007 budget bill #1, for 2007 and later tax years. Together with 60(c) and 60.03, it implements pension income splitting with the spouse.

(a.3) parents of victims of crime — amounts received by the taxpayer in the year under a program established under the authority of the *Department of Employment and Social Development Act* in respect of children who are deceased or missing as a result of an offence, or a probable offence, under the *Criminal Code*;

Related Provisions: 60(v) — Repayment of benefit is deductible; 153(1)(d.2), Reg. 100(1)"remuneration"(g.1) — Withholding of tax at source; 241(4)(d)(x.1) — Disclosure of information to ESDC official.

Notes: 56(1)(a.3) added effective 2013 by S.C. 2012, c. 27, the *Helping Families in Need Act*, which also amended the *Canada Labour Code* to provide for employee leave when a child is critically ill, dies or disappears due to a crime. Amended by 2012 budget bill #1 effective March 2013 and then by 2013 budget bill #2 effective Dec. 12, 2013, both to change legislative reference.

Forms: T1 General return, Line 13000 [former 130]: Other income.

(b) [spousal or child] support — the total of all amounts each of which is an amount determined by the formula

$$A - (B + C)$$

where

A is the total of all amounts each of which is a support amount received after 1996 and before the end of the year by the taxpayer from a particular person where the taxpayer and the particular person were living separate and apart at the time the amount was received,

B is the total of all amounts each of which is a child support amount that became receivable by the taxpayer from the particular person under an agreement or order on or after its commencement day and before the end of the year in respect of a period that began on or after its commencement day, and

C is the total of all amounts each of which is a support amount received after 1996 by the taxpayer from the particular person and included in the taxpayer's income for a preceding taxation year;

Related Provisions: 56.1(4) — Definitions of "commencement day", "support amount" and "child support amount"; 60(b) — Parallel deduction for payer; 60(c.2) — Repayment of support payments; 110.2(1)"qualifying amount"(c) — Retroactive spreading of lump-sum payments over prior years; 146(1)"earned income" — RRSP earned income includes amounts under 56(1)(b); 212(1)(f) — No withholding tax on support paid to non-resident; 241(4)(e)(vii) — Disclosure of name and address for enforcement of support payments; 248(1)"exempt income" — Support amount is not exempt income; 252(3) — Extended meaning of "spouse", "former spouse"; 257 — Formula cannot calculate to less than zero; Canada-U.S. Tax Treaty:Art. XVIII:6 — Child support exempt if paid by U.S. resident.

Notes: See 56.1(4)"support amount" Notes for what payments qualify.

Where 56(1)(b) includes an amount in income, 60(b) allows a parallel deduction. While inclusion and deduction depend on the same conditions, they do not depend on what happens on the other side. CRA may use 174(1) to bring both parties to Tax Court for consistency.

Amounts taxable under 56(1)(b) are deemed by 56.1(1) to be received as soon as they are paid, even if not actually received until the next year (e.g., by being delayed in the bureaucracy of the Ontario Family Responsibility Office).

If the recipient is non-resident, there is no Canadian tax: see repealed 212(1)(f).

If the payer is non-resident and cannot claim a deduction, the recipient is still taxed on the income: VIEWS doc 2011-0430161E5. However, if a tax treaty exempts the income, 110(1)(f)(i) allows the recipient an offsetting deduction: 2015-0617821E5 (Hong Kong). Alimony (spousal support) paid under a separation or divorce agreement executed after 2018 is no longer deductible/taxable in the US (*Internal Revenue Code* §§61(a)(8) amended and §215 repealed in 2017), so if paid by a US resident to a Canadian resident it is exempt under Canada-US tax treaty Art. XVIII:6(b). A dual resident taxed in Japan, with no deduction there for support paid to a Cdn resident, got no treaty relief: 2011-0420971E5. Non-taxability of child support under a tax treaty does not entitle the Cdn resident payer to deduct support payments: *Studer*, 2011 TCC 322.

B in the formula can never exceed A because 56.1(4)"child support amount" requires the amount to first be a "support amount". In *Glasel*, 2016 TCC 147, para. 11 (FCA appeal dismissed for delay A-312-16), the Court missed this point.

See also Notes to 56.1(3) re prior payments, and 110.2 re averaging of a payment received as a lump sum.

Legal costs incurred to obtain spousal or child support, or to update a child support award so it will be non-taxable, are deductible (as an expense incurred to earn income — the cost of establishing a right to support would be non-deductible, but the right already exists): *Income Tax Technical News* 24; VIEWS docs 2004-010935117, 2006-0208471E5, 2010-0390451E5; *Grenon*, 2016 FCA 4, para. 4 (leave to appeal denied 2016 CarswellNat 2619 (SCC)); *Donald*, [1999] 1 C.T.C. 2025 (TCC); *Nissim*, [1998] 4 C.T.C. 2496 (TCC); *Gallien*, [2001] 2 C.T.C. 2676 (TCC); *Nadeau*, 2003 FCA 400; *Rabb*, 2006 TCC 140; *Gal*, 2006 TCC 157; *Trignani*, 2010 TCC 209; *Persaud*, 2011 TCC 163; *Ruel*, 2017 TCC 93, para. 35; *Mader* (originally reported as *Richards*), 2019 TCC 289 (costs to force husband's corp to pay M dividends were partly deductible as being for M's claim for spousal support [Friedlan, "A Question of Deductibility", 2504 *Tax Topics* (CCH) 1-3 (March 5, 2020)]). (Child support being non-taxable does not prevent the deduction: see 18(1)(c) and 248(1)"exempt income".) Legal costs are deductible if the purpose was to obtain periodic support, even if the result is a lump sum payment: 2018-0787011E5. They may be deducted on an accrual basis: 2004-0104261E5; and may create a non-capital loss to carry forward under 111(1)(a): 2010-0386271E5, 2011-0399111E5. (Disclosing details of legal fees to a CRA auditor should not waive solicitor-client privilege: see 232(2) Notes.)

Legal costs of **defending** a claim for support are not deductible: IT-99R5 para. 21; *Nadeau*, 2003 FCA 400; *Grenon* (above); *Beauchamp*, 2007 TCC 747; *Loewig*, 2006 TCC 476; *Dalfort*, 2009 TCC 416 (FCA appeal dismissed for delay A-398-09); *McLaren*, 2009 TCC 514; *Sarophim*, 2012 TCC 92; *Ruel* (above); docs 2008-0294511E5, 2009-0342281M4, 2010-0390451E5; 2011-0417661E5. This does not violate the *Charter of Rights*: *Nadeau*, *Grenon*, *Sarophim*. Nor are the costs of recovering overpayments of support deductible: *Solmon*, 2000 CarswellNat 780 (TCC); *Lauber*, 2005 TCC 191; or of terminating child support once the child is independent; *McIntyre*, 2007 TCC 754 (FCA appeal dismissed for delay 2009 CarswellNat 4869; leave to appeal denied 2010 CarswellNat 536); *Landry*, 2014 TCC 275; or of reducing support payments: *Mills*, 2015 FCA 255; *Bayer*, [1991] 2 C.T.C. 2304 (TCC); *Berry*, 2005 TCC 787; or of custody disputes: *Yovo*, 2018 FCA 59; or of dividing spousal assets: *Barrett*, 2019 TCC 228, para. 17; or professional fees required to pay equalization: *Burley*, 2020 TCC 68.

However, see Ranot & DeBresser, "Deductibility of Legal Fees", 23(4) *Money & Family Law [MFL]* (Carswell) 31-32 (April 2008), describing deductibility allowed to a father for the costs of obtaining "notional" child support to reduce his obligation to the children's mother. The TCC has noted the unfairness of legal fees being deductible to *obtain* support but not to prevent *paying* it (e.g., *Mills*, *Grenon*), but that is the law. The costs to common-law spouses in Quebec of negotiating support are not deductible because there is no legal right to support: 2010-0373641C6. The costs of dividing marital property are not deductible: 2008-0270061E5.

See also St-Hilaire, "La Deductibilité des frais juridiques en matière de droit de la famille", 86(3) *Canadian Bar Review* 539-92 (2007); Corbin, "Legal Fees Incurred to Obtain Support", 25(6) *Money & Family Law [MFL]* (Carswell) 41-42 (June 2010) (based on *Trignani*, the deduction does not depend on success of the claim, but it must be a *bona fide* claim); Ranot, "Income Tax Issues in Matrimonial Settlements — Part IV", 33(11) *MFL* 83-84 (Nov. 2018).

The 2000 same-sex partners bill (Royal Assent June 29, 2000), which extended references to "spouse" to add "common-law partner" throughout the Act, provides:

145. Where, but for the application of sections 130 to 142, paragraphs 56(1)(b) and 60(b) of the *Income Tax Act* would not apply to amounts paid and received pursuant to an order or a written agreement, made before the coming into force of this section, those paragraphs do not apply unless the payor and the recipient of the amounts jointly elect to have those paragraphs apply to those amounts for the 2001 and following taxation years by notifying the Minister of National Revenue in prescribed manner on or before their filing due date for the year in which this Act receives royal assent.

56(1)(b) rewritten by 1996 Budget for amounts received after 1996. The essence of the change is that *child* support is no longer deductible to the payer (60(b)) and taxable to the recipient (56(1)(b)) (**"D/T"**) and if the order or agreement was made or varied after April 30, 1997 (56.1(4)"commencement day"). *Spousal* support that meets the conditions continues to be D/T. Any amount that was non-D/T before the amendments, due to not meeting the conditions (e.g., certain pre-1993 agreements) remains non-D/T due to the in-force application rule for 56.1(4)"support amount". In *Thibaudeau*, [1995] 1 C.T.C. 382, the Supreme Court of Canada had ruled 5:2 that former 56(1)(b) did not violate s. 15 of the *Charter of Rights* in its application to child support. See also Durnford and Toope, "Spousal Support", 42(1) *Canadian Tax Journal* 1-107 (1994). The 1996 Budget amendments responded to concerns about unfairness of the rules to women, although they addressed only child support, not spousal support.

Former 56(1)(b), (c) consolidated into 56(1)(b) by 1992 technical bill, for breakdown after 1992 of a "marriage" (under the 252(4)(b) extended definition; *Interpretation Act* 42(3)). For earlier breakdown, see these Notes to PITA 59th ed.

Income Tax Folios: S1-F3-C3: Support payments [replaces IT-530R].

Interpretation Bulletins: IT-99R5: Legal and accounting fees; IT-325R2: Property transfers after separation, divorce and annulment.

Forms: P102: Support payments (pamphlet); T1 General return, Lines 12799, 12800 [former 128]; T1157: Election for child support payments; T1158: Registration of family support payments.

(c), (c.1) [Repealed]

Notes: 56(1)(c), "maintenance", repealed by 1996 Budget, effective for amounts received after 1996. See now 56(1)(b).

Former 56(1)(c.1) amended and renumbered as 56(1)(c) by 1992 technical bill, for orders made after 1992.

Former 56(1)(c.1) added by 1981 Budget, effective (a) for all orders made after December 11, 1979, and (b) for earlier orders, where the taxpayer and the person agree in writing at any time in a taxation year, for that year and all subsequent years. In other words, for orders made before December 11, 1979, the amendment does not apply unless the parties elect (or have ever previously elected) for it to apply.

Former 56(1)(c.1) amended by 1988 tax reform, except that for orders made after December 11, 1979 under the laws of Ontario, read "December 11, 1979" and "December 12, 1979" in place of "February 10, 1988" and "February 11, 1988" respectively.

(c.2) **reimbursement of support payments** — an amount received by the taxpayer in the year under a decree, order or judgment of a competent tribunal as a reimbursement of an amount deducted under paragraph 60(b) or (c), or under paragraph 60(c.1) as it applies, in computing the taxpayer's income for the year or a preceding taxation year to decrees, orders and judgments made before 1993;

Related Provisions: 60(c.2) — Parallel deduction to spouse; 146(1)"earned income"(b) — Amount under 56(1)(c.2) included in RRSP earned income.

Notes: 56(1)(c.2) added by 1992 technical bill, for payments received after 1990.

Income Tax Folios: S1-F3-C3: Support payments [replaces IT-530R].

(d) **annuity payments** — any amount received by the taxpayer in the year as an annuity payment other than an amount

(i) otherwise required to be included in computing the taxpayer's income for the year,

(ii) with respect to an interest in an annuity contract to which subsection 12.2(1) applies (or would apply if the contract had an anniversary day in the year at a time when the taxpayer held the interest),

(iii) received out of or under an annuity contract issued or effected as a TFSA, or

(iv) described in subsection 146.5(3) that is not required by that subsection to be included in the taxpayer's income;

Related Provisions: 12.2(1) — Life insurance annuities; 56(1.1) — Definitions in 12.2(11) apply; 60(a) — Deduction of capital element; 128.1(10)"excluded right or interest"(f)(i) — Emigration — no deemed disposition of right to annuity contract; 146.2(7) — Amount accruing inside TFSA not taxable; 147.5(23) — Annuity from pooled registered pension plan taxable only under 147.5(23); 153(1)(f) — Withholding at source; 207.061 — Certain amounts included in TFSA holder's income; 212(1)(o) — Withholding tax on annuity payment to non-resident.

Notes: Although the annuity payment is included under 56(1)(d), an offsetting deduction for the capital portion is allowed under 60(a), so the return of capital is not taxed.

See Martin Reeves, "A Payout Annuity is Like a Personal Pension Plan", XVII(3) *Insurance Planning* (Federated Press) 1090-95 (2011).

Annuity payments are not "income" in determining entitlement to the Guaranteed Income Supplement under the *Old Age Security Act* (OAS Regs s. 14), but this does not include an RRSP withdrawal that was derived from a pension plan: *McArthur*, 2017 TCC 213.

A charitable annuity issued after Dec. 20, 2002 is taxed like other annuities: VIEWS doc 2003-0038517. If it is a "prescribed annuity contract", payments are included in income, with a deduction under 60(a) for the capital element.

Despite 56(1)(d), structured settlement payments to injury victims can be non-taxable: IT-365R2 para. 5; Weir, *Structured Settlements* (Carswell, 1984, 293pp); Marino & Natale, *Canadian Taxation of Life Insurance* (Carswell, 10th ed., 2020), chap. 18; VIEWS docs 2004-0072271R3, 2004-0074331R3, 2004-0084861E5, 2004-0094081R3, 2004-0096111R3, 2004-0101651E5, 2005-0121571R3, 2005-0155471R3, 2006-0217071R3, 2006-0218321R3, 2007-0226271R3, 2007-0250671R3, 2008-0284611R3, 2009-0342011R3, 2010-0358871R3, 2010-0359271R3, 2010-0362861R3, 2010-0382511R3, 2011-0404701R3, 2012-0437891R3, 2012-0437941R3, 2012-0450371R3, 2013-0479481R3, 2015-0581271R3, 2015-0621341R3, 2016-0676001R3, 2018-0749691R3, 2018-0761771R3. A transfer of the structured settlement obligation to another insurer is allowed: 2004-0086091R3, 2005-0142851E5, 2006-0185881R3, 2007-0254851E5, 2019-0801391E5. A variance of a settlement to add a beneficiary was allowed in 2007-0224941E5. See also 81(1)(g.1) and (g.2), which exempt income from a personal injury award while the taxpayer is under 21.

For rulings that particular life insurance products with monthly payments do not fall within 56(1)(d) see VIEWS docs 2007-0220301R3, 2007-0223091R3.

See Notes to 56(1)(v) re US workers' compensation and *War Hazards Compensation Act* payments, which are considered annuity payments, as are Dependency and Indemnity Compensation from the US Dept. of Veterans Affairs: 2014-0563131I7.

56(1)(d)(iv) (added by 2021 budget bill #1, effective 2020) excludes Advanced Life Deferred Annuity payments. This ensures the 146.5 regime is self-contained, and ALDA payments are included only under 56(1)(z.5). This amendment was not in the July 30/19 draft legislation.

56(1)(d) amended by 2008 budget bill #2, 1989 Budget. For contracts acquired before 1990, an earlier version still applies: see up to PITA 59th ed.

Income Tax Folios: S3-F9-C1: Lottery winnings, miscellaneous receipts, and income (and losses) from crime [replaces IT-185R, IT-213R, IT-256R, IT-334R2].

Interpretation Bulletins: IT-365R2: Damages, settlements and similar receipts.

I.T. Technical News: 25 (health and welfare trusts).

Advance Tax Rulings: ATR-40: Taxability of receipts under a structured settlement; ATR-50: Structured settlement; ATR-68: Structured settlement.

Forms: T1 General return, Line 13000 [former 130]: Other income.

(d.1) [Repealed under former Act]

Notes: 56(1)(d.1) repealed by 1989 Budget, effective (per 1991 technical bill) for contracts last acquired after 1989. For contracts last acquired before 1990, read:

(d.1) [annuity payments] — any amount paid in the year as an annuity payment with respect to

(i) an interest in an annuity contract (other than a contract to which subsection 12.2(3) does not apply in the year by virtue of subsection 12.2(7)) to which subsection 12.2(3) does not apply but would apply if the contract had a third anniversary in the year, or

(ii) an interest in an annuity contract (other than a contract to which subsection 12.2(1) does not apply in the year by virtue of subsection 12.2(6)) to which subsection 12.2(1) does not apply but would apply if the interest had been last acquired after December 19, 1980 and before December 2, 1982

where such interest was held by the taxpayer at the time of the payment, except to the extent that the aggregate of such amounts with respect to such an interest

in a particular annuity contract exceeds the amount by which the accumulating fund at the end of the calendar year ending in the year, as determined in prescribed manner, with respect to the interest exceeds the aggregate of its adjusted cost basis at the end of that calendar year and the amount at the end of that calendar year of unallocated income accrued in respect of the interest before 1982, as determined in prescribed manner;

Income Tax Folios: S3-F9-C1: Lottery winnings, miscellaneous receipts, and income (and losses) from crime [replaces IT-185R, IT-213R, IT-256R, IT-334R2].

(d.2) idem [annuity payments] — any amount received out of or under, or as proceeds of disposition of, an annuity the payment for which was

(i) deductible in computing the taxpayer's income because of paragraph 60(l) or because of subsection 146(5.5) of the *Income Tax Act*, Chapter 148 of the Revised Statutes of Canada, 1952,

(ii) made in circumstances to which subsection 146(21) applied, or

(iii) made pursuant to or under a deferred profit sharing plan by a trustee under the plan to purchase the annuity for a beneficiary under the plan;

Related Provisions: 60.2(1) — Refund of undeducted past service AVCs; 147(2)(k)(vi) — Purchase of annuity by DPSP; 147(10.6) — Purchase of annuity by DPSP before 1997.

Notes: 56(1)(d.2)(ii) added by 1993 technical bill, effective 1992. 146(21) applies to transfers from the Saskatchewan Pension Plan.

56(1)(d.2)(iii) added by 1996 Budget, effective for 1996 and later taxation years.

I.T. Application Rules: 69 (meaning of "chapter 148 of ...").

Interpretation Bulletins: IT-517R: Pension tax credit (cancelled).

(e) disposition of income-averaging annuity contract — any amount received by the taxpayer in the year as, on account or in lieu of payment of, or in satisfaction of, proceeds of the surrender, cancellation, redemption, sale or other disposition of an income-averaging annuity contract;

Related Provisions: 153(1)(k) — Withholding of tax at source; Canada-U.S. Tax Treaty:Art. XVIII:3 — Pension income excludes payment from IAAC.

Notes: See Notes to 61(1).

(f) idem — any amount deemed by subsection 61.1(1) to have been received by the taxpayer in the year as proceeds of the disposition of an income-averaging annuity contract;

Related Provisions: 212(1)(n), 214(3)(b) — Non-resident withholding tax.

(g) supplementary unemployment benefit plan — amounts received by the taxpayer in the year from a trustee under a supplementary unemployment benefit plan as provided by section 145;

Related Provisions: 6(1)(a)(i) — Employer-paid premiums not a taxable benefit; 145(3) — Amounts received taxable; 146(1)"earned income"(b) — Amount under 56(1)(g) included in RRSP earned income; 153(1)(e) — Withholding of tax at source.

Regulations: 100(1)"remuneration"(e) (withholding at source).

(h) registered retirement savings plan, etc. — amounts required by section 146 in respect of a registered retirement savings plan or a registered retirement income fund to be included in computing the taxpayer's income for the year;

Related Provisions: 56(1)(t) — RRIF inclusion under 146.3; 60.2(1) — Refund of undeducted past service AVCs; 139.1(12) — Conversion benefit on demutualization of insurance corporation; 146(8) — Benefits taxable; 148(8.1) — *Inter vivos* transfer to spouse; 153(1)(j) — Withholding of tax at source.

Notes: 56(1)(h) is a "provision of general application" that catches all amounts that s. 146 includes in income: *Gramiak*, 2015 FCA 40, paras. 35-36.

Regulations: 214 (information return).

Interpretation Bulletins: IT-307R4: Spousal or common-law partner registered retirement savings plans.

Advance Tax Rulings: ATR-37: Refund of premiums transferred to spouse.

(h.1) Home Buyers' Plan — amounts required by section 146.01 to be included in computing the taxpayer's income for the year;

Related Provisions: 146.01(4), (5), (6) — Income inclusions.

Notes: 56(1)(h.1) added by 1992 technical bill, effective 1992.

(h.2) Lifelong Learning Plan — amounts required by section 146.02 to be included in computing the taxpayer's income for the year;

Related Provisions: 146.02(4), (5), (6) — Income inclusions.

Notes: 56(1)(h.2) added by 1998 Budget, effective for 1999 and later taxation years.

(i) deferred profit sharing plan — amounts received by the taxpayer in the year under a deferred profit sharing plan as provided by section 147;

Related Provisions: 147(10) — Amounts received from DPSP taxable; 153(1)(h) — Withholding of tax at source; 212(1)(m) — DPSP payments to non-residents.

Regulations: 100(1)"remuneration"(f) (withholding at source).

Interpretation Bulletins: IT-281R2: Elections on single payments from a deferred profit-sharing plan (cancelled).

Advance Tax Rulings: ATR-31: Funding of divorce settlement amount from DPSP.

(j) life insurance policy proceeds — any amount required by subsection 148(1) or (1.1) to be included in computing the taxpayer's income for the year;

Related Provisions: 148(9)"adjusted cost basis"C — increase in AC basis.

Notes: See Notes to 148(1).

Regulations: 217 (information return).

Interpretation Bulletins: IT-87R2: Policyholders' income from life insurance policies.

Forms: RC257: Request for an information return program account (RZ); T5: Statement of investment income; T5 Summ: Return of investment income.

(k) certain tools of an employee, re proceeds — all amounts received in the year by a person or partnership (in this paragraph referred to as the "vendor") as consideration for the disposition by the vendor of a property the cost of which was included in computing an amount under paragraph 8(1)(r) or (s) in respect of the vendor or in respect of a person with whom the vendor does not deal at arm's length, to the extent that the total of those amounts received in respect of the disposition in the year and in preceding taxation years exceeds the total of the cost to the vendor of the property immediately before the disposition and all amounts included in respect of the disposition under this paragraph in computing the vendor's income for a preceding taxation year, unless the property was acquired by the vendor in circumstances to which subsection 85(5.1) or subsection 97(5) applied;

Notes: 56(1)(k) applies to amounts received by an apprentice mechanic who claimed the 8(1)(r) tools deduction, or a person not at arm's length with the mechanic, as consideration for disposition of the tools. In general, the vendor must include in income the amount received only to the extent the total received in the year and preceding years from the disposition exceeds the cost of the property (as reduced by 8(7)) and the total previously included in income. However, this rule does not apply to a vendor who acquired the property in a 85(5.1) or 97(5) rollover.

56(1)(k) amended by 2006 budget bill #2 (for 2006 and later tax years), 2001 Budget.

Former 56(1)(k), repealed in 1977, dealt with allocations under insurance policies as provided by 148(1)(b). These are now covered by 56(1)(j).

(l) legal expenses [awarded or reimbursed] — amounts received by the taxpayer in the year as

(i) legal costs awarded to the taxpayer by a court on an appeal in relation to an assessment of any tax, interest or penalties referred to in paragraph 60(o),

(ii) reimbursement of costs incurred in relation to a decision of the Canada Employment Insurance Commission under the *Employment Insurance Act* or to an appeal of such a decision to the Social Security Tribunal,

(iii) reimbursement of costs incurred in relation to an assessment or a decision under the *Canada Pension Plan* or a provincial pension plan as defined in section 3 of that Act,

if with respect to that assessment or decision, as the case may be, an amount has been deducted or may be deductible under paragraph 60(o) in computing the taxpayer's income;

Related Provisions: 60(o) — Expense of objection or appeal; 152(1.2) — Rule applies to determination of losses as well as assessment.

Notes: 56(1)(l) amended by 2012 budget bill #1 (for appeals filed after March 2013 or where leave granted by April 2014), 1995-97 technical bill, 1996 EI bill.

Interpretation Bulletins: IT-99R5: Legal and accounting fees.

(l.1) idem — amounts received by the taxpayer in the year as an award or a reimbursement in respect of legal expenses (other than those relating to a division or settlement of property arising out of, or on a breakdown of, a marriage or common-law partnership) paid to collect or establish a right to a retiring allowance or a benefit under a pension fund or plan (other than a benefit under the *Canada Pension Plan* or a provincial pension plan as defined in section 3 of that Act) in respect of employment;

Related Provisions: 60(o.1) — Deductions in computing income — legal expenses in respect of retiring allowances and pension benefits.

Notes: Legal fees paid directly to a lawyer by a former employer are generally taxable under 56(1)(l.1), subject to offsetting 60(o.1) deduction: VIEWS doc 2005-0139921E5.

56(1)(l.1) amended by 2000 same-sex partners bill (effective 2001), 1992 technical bill. Added by 1989 Budget.

Interpretation Bulletins: IT-99R5: Legal and accounting fees.

(m) bad debt recovered [non-competition agreement] — any amount received by the taxpayer, or by a person who does not deal at arm's length with the taxpayer, in the year on account of a debt in respect of which a deduction was made under paragraph 60(f) in computing the taxpayer's income for a preceding taxation year;

Related Provisions: 212(1)(i), (13)(g) — Non-resident withholding tax.

Notes: 56(1)(m) added by 2002-2013 technical bill, effective Oct. 8, 2003.

Former 56(1)(m), repealed by 1996 EI bill effective 1998, dealt with a training allowance under the *National Training Act*.

A proposed 56(1)(m), in the Aug. 31/06 draft legislation, was renumbered 56(1)(n.1) in 2006 budget bill #2.

(n) scholarships, bursaries, etc. — the amount, if any, by which

(i) the total of all amounts (other than amounts described in paragraph (q), amounts received in the course of business, and amounts received in respect of, in the course of or by virtue of an office or employment) received by the taxpayer in the year, each of which is an amount received by the taxpayer as or on account of a scholarship, fellowship or bursary, or a prize for achievement in a field of endeavour ordinarily carried on by the taxpayer (other than a prescribed prize),

exceeds

(ii) the taxpayer's scholarship exemption for the year computed under subsection (3);

Related Provisions: 56(3), (3.1) — Amount of scholarship exemption; 60(q) — Deduction for scholarship refunded; 62(1) — Moving expenses; 63(3)"earned income"(b), 64(b)(i)(A) — Amount under 56(1)(n) is earned income for child care expenses and for disability supports deduction; 115(2)(a)–(b.1), 115(2)(e)(ii) — Non-resident's taxable income earned in Canada; 248(1) — Extended meaning of "personal or living expenses"; Canada-U.S. Tax Treaty:Art. XX — Students.

Notes: The scholarship exemption (56(3)) is unlimited in most cases, but only $500 if the scholarship is not received in connection with enrolment at a qualifying educational institution or an elementary or secondary school (e.g. *El Qandil*, 2021 TCC 12). See also 56(3.1), requiring the scholarship to be intended to support enrolment in the program and limiting the exemption for part-time students to the cost of the program and materials; and 118.6(1)"qualifying educational program", excluding post-doctoral fellowships from exemption.

There is no withholding tax for 56(1)(n) amounts (153(1)), but a T4A information slip must be issued even if the scholarship is exempt: Reg. 200(2), VIEWS docs 2005-0115261E5, 2007-0248181E5, 2008-0266811E5. Where tuition reduction is provided, the unreduced tuition amount should be shown on the T2202A, and a T4A issued for the scholarship: 2009-0308201E5.

A scholarship falls under 56(1)(n) even if it is provided directly by the school as free tuition and the student gets no money: *Jones*, [2002] 3 C.T.C. 2483 (TCC); *Mbarga*, 2005 TCC 595 (but now, if 56(3) provides unlimited exemption, there is no income inclusion in such cases).

Meaning of "scholarship": "a sum of money or its equivalent offered (as by an educational institution, a public agency, or a private organization or foundation) to enable a student to pursue his studies at a school, college, or university": *Amyot*, [1976] C.T.C. 352 (FCTD), para. 12. "Scholarships and bursaries are amounts paid or benefits given to students to enable them to pursue their education": Income Tax Folio S1-F2-C3 ¶3.7.

See also VIEWS docs 2011-0427891E5 (payments to international students in a summer undergrad research program were scholarships); 2010-0371151E5 (summer program to allow undergrad students to study a particular field for 3 months was a scholarship); 2017-0706531E5 (undergrad student research awards); 2017-0738071E5 (Japanese government scholarships).

Employment-related: A scholarship or tuition reimbursement received by an employee is excluded by 56(1)(n)(i) but may be taxed under 6(1)(a): see Notes to 6(1)(a) under "Tuition". (Where paid to a student who will later work for the employer, 6(3) may apply (2011-0424601E5), but Income Tax Folio S1-F2-C3 ¶3.14-3.16 and 2009-0347781E5 are lenient if the employment relationship has not yet started.) Scholarships to arm's length employees' dependants (or tuition fee discount for university employees' spouses or children) may be exempt since Oct. 31, 2011: 6(1)(a)(vi), Folio S1-F2-C3 ¶3.17-3.20. (56(3.1) may apply to these arrangements.) Before then, these were held exempt in *Bartley (DiMaria)*, 2008 FCA 390 and *Okonski*, 2008 TCC 142, overturning CRA policy, and CRA conceded this point for arm's length employees: *Kaushik*, 2009 TCC 318; docs 2008-0296041E5, 2009-0312451E5, 2009-0339001E5, 2010-0364111E5, 2012-0434941E5. In *Rooke*, 2019 TCC 52 (FCA appeal filed too late 19-A-72; leave to appeal denied 2020 CanLII 84083 (SCC)), payments were held to be for work as a teaching assistant, not a scholarship. An amount may be a "forgivable loan" (not taxed) or "repayable award", taxed as per Income Tax Folio S1-F2-C3 ¶3.39-3.52 [former IT-340R paras. 8-13]; 2009-0348931E5, 2010-0361371E5.

Medical students and doctors: For payment to encourage them to practise in remote areas, see Notes to 12(1)(x) under "If doctor". Assistance by a municipality to a medical resident, on condition he practise medicine in the municipality after qualifying, falls under 56(1)(n), not 12(1)(x): 2008-0270781E5. However, in 2010-0366441E5, an Ontario tuition subsidy for medical students and residents, on condition they practise in an underserviced area, was taxable under 6(3) or 12(1)(x) and not 56(1)(n), as it was paid *after* medical school.

"Bursary", taxable under 56(1)(n) and eligible for 56(3) exemption, is "broad enough to encompass any form of financial assistance to enable a student to pursue his or her education", so it covers tuition reduction offered by a college to all students: VIEWS docs 2005-0122271E5, 2017-0735391E5. (There seems to be little difference between bursary and scholarship in practice.) It includes: Canada Job Grant (2014-0559561I7); financial assistance to international and aboriginal students as directed by donors under a particular program (2006-0187471E5); Ontario Student Assistance Program bursary to permit student to attend school for the deaf in the US (*Waters*, 2006 TCC 553); *Programme québécois de prêts et bourses* (2006-017637117); support to seminary students for theological or priesthood studies (2005-012136117, 2007-024218117 [see 110(2) for students who take a vow of perpetual poverty]); Special Opportunities Grant for Disabled Students with Permanent Disabilities (*Simser*, 2004 FCA 414 (leave to appeal denied 2005 CarswellNat 1727 (SCC)) [see now s. 64 for offsetting deduction]); student loan reductions under Canada Millennium Scholarship and Manitoba Bursary programs (2005-0114411E5); tuition assistance provided by elementary or secondary school for financial reasons (2013-0513061E5); tuition paid by a particular Crown corp (2008-0267551E5).

Contra, a bursary or scholarship from a Conservatory's endowment fund for recreational music lessons is non-taxable as not being to "pursue education" (doc 2019-0802051E5); a *Children of Deceased Veterans Education Assistance Act* bursary is exempt under 81(1)(d) (2003-0040151E5); assistance with child-care costs to students in financial difficulty falls under 56(1)(u) rather than 56(1)(n) (2010-0389161E5).

Fellowship: "In general terms, a fellowship is an amount paid or a benefit given to persons to enable them to advance their education. It is normally awarded for doctoral studies or postdoctoral work. Income from an office or employment, on the other hand, results from a contract of service between an employee and employer. In such cases, the services are rendered primarily for the benefit of the employer and the payments represent consideration for the services, usually based on the time spent providing the services or the value or volume of the services": VIEWS doc 2004-007054117. See also 2007-0252651E5; and 118.6(1)"qualifying educational program", excluding post-doctoral fellowships from 56(3) exemption.

Grants might be taxed as employment income or under 56(1)(o) rather than under 56(1)(n) (note that 56(1)(n)(i) excludes amounts received in respect of an office or employment). VIEWS doc 2004-007054117. See Notes to 56(1)(o); and to 5(1) re payments to interns or students doing research. See also Dumalski & Sarabalos, "Are Payments to Research Assistants Tax-Free?", 3(2) *Canadian Tax Focus* (ctf.ca) 11-12 (May 2013). National Sciences and Engineering Research Council (NSERC) grants: see 2006-0195781E5. Art production grants are exempt under 56(3)(b): Income Tax Folios S1-F2-C3 ¶3.98-3.100, S4-F14-C1 ¶1.66-1.77; 2007-0219861E5.

Prizes: Student prizes in a college contest fall under 56(1)(n): VIEWS doc 2014-0539611E5. See also Notes to Reg. 7700 re prizes generally.

Social assistance: Assistance under the B.C. Young Adult Program likely falls under 56(1)(u) rather than 56(1)(n): 2009-034556117.

A *hockey training allowance* paid by a third party is not taxable under 56(1)(n): doc 2008-0264941E5.

56(1)(n) amended by 2000 Budget (for 2000 and later tax years), 1991 technical bill.

Regulations: 200(2)(a) (information return); 7700 (prescribed prize).

Income Tax Folios: S1-F1-C3: Disability supports deduction [replaces IT-519R2]; S1-F2-C1: Education and textbook tax credits [replaces IT-515R2]; S1-F2-C2: Tuition tax credit [replaces IT-516R2]; S1-F2-C3: Scholarships, research grants and other education assistance [replaces IT-340R]; S1-F3-C1: Child care expense deduction [re-

places IT-495R3]; S1-F3-C4: Moving expenses [replaces IT-178R3]; S3-F9-C1: Lottery winnings, miscellaneous receipts, and income (and losses) from crime [replaces IT-185R, IT-213R, IT-256R, IT-334R2].

Interpretation Bulletins: IT-257R: Canada Council grants.

Forms: T1 General return, Line 13010 [former 130]: Other income.

(n.1) **apprenticeship grants** — the total of all amounts, each of which is an amount received by the taxpayer in the year under the Apprenticeship Incentive Grant program or the Apprenticeship Completion Grant program administered by the Department of Employment and Social Development;

Related Provisions: 8(1)(r)(ii)B(B)(II)2 — apprentice mechanics' tools deduction based on amount of Apprenticeship Incentive Grant; 60(p) — Deduction where grant repaid; 63(3)"earned income"(b) — Grant is earned income for child care expenses.

Notes: See tinyurl.com/appren-grants for these grants.

56(1)(n.1) amended by 2013 budget bill #2 (s. 237(1)(j)) to change "Department of Human Resources and Skills Development" to "Department of Employment and Social Development", effective Dec. 12, 2013.

56(1)(n.1) added by 2006 budget bill #2 (it was 56(1)(m) in the Aug. 31/06 draft legislation), and reworded by 2002-2013 technical bill (Part 5 — technical), both effective for 2007 and later taxation years; and amended by the latter bill to add "or the Apprenticeship Completion Grant program" for 2009 and later taxation years.

The amendment adding Apprenticeship Completion Grants was first released on Oct. 24, 2012, with a parallel amendment to 60(p). No amendment was needed to 63(3)"earned income"(b), as it refers to amounts included under 56(1)(n.1).

Regulations: 200(2)(b.1) (information return).

Income Tax Folios: S1-F3-C1: Child care expense deduction [replaces IT-495R3].

Forms: T1 General return, Line 13000 [former 130]: Other income.

(o) **research grants** — the amount, if any, by which any grant received by the taxpayer in the year to enable the taxpayer to carry on research or any similar work exceeds the total of expenses incurred by the taxpayer in the year for the purpose of carrying on the work, other than

(i) personal or living expenses of the taxpayer except travel expenses (including the entire amount expended for meals and lodging) incurred by the taxpayer while away from home in the course of carrying on the work,

(ii) expenses in respect of which the taxpayer has been reimbursed, or

(iii) expenses that are otherwise deductible in computing the taxpayer's income for the year;

Related Provisions: 60(q) — Refund of income payments; 62(1) — Moving expenses; 63(3)"earned income"(b), 64(b)(i)(A) — Amount under 56(1)(o) is earned income for child care expenses and disability supports deduction; 115(2)(b.1), 115(2)(e)(ii) — Non-resident's taxable income earned in Canada; 146(1)"earned income"(b) — Amount under 56(1)(o) is earned income for RRSP; 248(1) — Extended meaning of "personal or living expenses"; Canada-U.S. Tax Treaty:Art. XX — Students.

Notes: The purpose of a research grant must be to enable the taxpayer to carry on research. If the purpose is to assist in advancing the taxpayer's academic career and the research is merely an (essential) means to carry out that purpose, then it is a fellowship or scholarship under 56(1)(n). See *Amyot*, [1976] C.T.C. 352 (FCTD); *Albert Taylor*, [1979] C.T.C. 2356 (TRB); *Horlings*, 1991 CarswellNat 1309 (TCC). See also Income Tax Folio S1-F2-C3; VIEWS docs 2005-0127621E5, 2006-0204151I7, 2008-0276691E5, 2010-035909117, 2010-0382351E5, 2011-0395881E5; 2013-0509291E5 (whether faculty member can allocate part of salary to research grant).

Even if the researcher endorses the grant cheque over to the institution, 56(1)(o) still applies: VIEWS doc 2008-0268251E5. However, a research allowance or reimbursement that is solely to cover expenses is non-taxable: 2009-0333891E5.

Amounts paid to a university professor for research expenses during a sabbatical year were research grants under 56(1)(o): *Ghali*, 2004 FCA 60: that "research or any similar work" means "a set of scientific, literary and artistic works and activities having as its purpose the discovery and development of knowledge" (para. 44). See also VIEWS docs 2005-0118921E5, 2005-0136091E5 re payments while on sabbatical leave.

An amount paid to a professor in settlement of a copyright claim, although called a research grant, was not one, so no expenses were deductible: *Santerre*, 2005 TCC 606.

Where a grant is paid to a self-employed writer, it may be not taxable under 56(1)(o) but business income under 12(1)(x) (subject to making a 12(2.2) election): VIEWS doc 2004-0076661E5.

Deductible expenses against a grant, while on sabbatical doing research, include travel, but not if the person is residing or "sojourning" in the place rather than "travelling": VIEWS docs 2009-0339721E5, 2009-0346301E5, 2011-0404241E5. See also 62(1) for moving expenses.

A research grant must be reported on a T4A (Reg. 200(2)(b)) but is not subject to source withholdings under 153(1): VIEWS doc 2011-0409741E5.

See also Notes to 56(1)(n). Post-doctoral fellowships: see Notes to 56(3).

Regulations: 200(2)(b) (information return).

Income Tax Folios: S1-F1-C3: Disability supports deduction [replaces IT-519R2]; S1-F2-C3: Scholarships, research grants and other education assistance [replaces IT-340R]; S1-F3-C1: Child care expense deduction [replaces IT-495R3]; S1-F3-C4: Moving expenses [replaces IT-178R3].

Interpretation Bulletins: IT-257R: Canada Council grants.

(p) **refund of scholarships, bursaries and research grants** — amounts as described in paragraph 60(q) received by the taxpayer in the year from an individual;

Related Provisions: 56(1)(n) — Scholarships, bursaries, etc.; 60(q) — Refund of income payments.

Income Tax Folios: S1-F2-C3: Scholarships, research grants and other education assistance [replaces IT-340R].

(q) **education savings plan payments** — amounts in respect of a registered education savings plan required by section 146.1 to be included in computing the taxpayer's income for the year;

Related Provisions: 146.1(7) — Amounts to be included in beneficiary's income; 212(1)(r) — RESP payments to non-residents.

Notes: Educational assistance payments from a RESP are taxable to the student, with no scholarship exemption. See Notes at end of 146.1.

Income Tax Folios: S1-F2-C3: Scholarships, research grants and other education assistance [replaces IT-340R].

(q.1) **registered disability savings plan payments** — amounts in respect of a registered disability savings plan required by section 146.4 to be included in computing the taxpayer's income for the year;

Related Provisions: 60(z) — Repayment deductible; 122.5(1)"adjusted income"(a)(i) — Income not counted for purposes of GST/HST Credit; 122.6"adjusted income"(a)(i) — Income not counted for purposes of Canada Child Benefit; 122.7(1)"adjusted net income"(b) — Income not counted for purposes of Canada Workers Benefit; 146.4(6) — Amount of disability assistance payment exceeding non-taxable portion is taxable; 180.2(1)"adjusted income"(a)(i) — Income not counted for purposes of Old Age Security clawback; 212(1)(r.1) — Non-resident withholding tax; Reg. 100(1)"remuneration"(o), 103.1 — Source withholding.

Notes: See 146.4(6). 56(1)(q.1) added by 2007 RDSPs bill, effective for 2008 and later taxation years.

(r) **[government] financial assistance** — amounts received in the year by the taxpayer as

(i) earnings supplements provided under a project sponsored by a government or government agency in Canada to encourage individuals to obtain or keep employment,

(ii) financial assistance under a program established by the Canada Employment Insurance Commission under Part II of the *Employment Insurance Act*,

(iii) financial assistance under a program that is

(A) established by a government or government agency in Canada or by an organization,

(B) similar to a program established under Part II of that Act, and

(C) the subject of an agreement between the government, government agency or organization and the Canada Employment Insurance Commission because of section 63 of that Act,

(iv) financial assistance provided under a program established by a government, or government agency, in Canada that provides income replacement benefits similar to income replacement benefits provided under a program established under the *Employment Insurance Act*, other than amounts referred to in subparagraph (iv.1),

(iv.1) financial assistance provided under

(A) the *Canada Emergency Response Benefit Act*,

(B) Part VIII.4 of the *Employment Insurance Act*,

(C) the *Canada Emergency Student Benefit Act*, or

(D) the *Canada Recovery Benefits Act*, or

(E) a program established by a government, or government agency, of a province, that provides income replacement benefits similar to income replacement benefits provided under a program established under an Act referred to in any of clauses (A) to (D), or

(v) amounts received by the taxpayer in the year under the *Wage Earner Protection Program Act* in respect of wages (within the meaning of that Act);

Related Provisions: 56(1)(u) — Inclusion of social assistance payments generally (subject to offsetting deduction); 60(n)(vi) — Deduction for amounts repaid; 60(v.2), (v.3) — Deduction for COVID-19 benefits repaid; 62(1)(c)(i) — 56(1)(r)(v) amount treated as employment income for moving expenses; 63(3)"earned income"(b), 64(b)(i)(A) — 56(1)(r) amount is earned income for child care expenses and for disability supports deduction; 110(1)(g) — Deduction for tuition assistance for adult basic education; 115(1)(a)(ii.22) — COVID benefits (56(1)(r)(iv.1)) taxable to non-resident; 115(1)(a)(iii.21) — 56(1)(r)(v) amount is non-resident's taxable income earned in Canada; 118(10)B(b) — 56(1)(r)(v) amount treated as employment income for Canada Employment Credit; 122.51(1)"eligible individual"(c)(iii) — 56(1)(r)(v) amount treated as employment income for refundable medical expense supplement; 122.7(1)"working income"(b) — 56(1)(r)(v) amount treated as employment income for Canada Workers Benefit; 146(1)"earned income"(b) — 56(1)(r)(v) amount is earned income for RRSP; 153(1)(s) — Withholding of tax at source.

Notes: 56(1)(r) amounts are treated as employment income for many purposes. See Related Provisions annotation above.

Taxable under 56(1)(r)(i): HRDC's Supporting Communities Partnership Initiative (VIEWS doc 2003-0046691E5); Employability Skills Through Work Experience (2007-0227901E5); training allowance under Targeted Initiative for Older Workers (2010-0382681I7).

Taxable under (r)(ii): tuition assistance from a non-profit organization under HRDC funding (2006-0205981E5) or from Service Canada (2007-0230731M4), though the tuition may be eligible for credit (118.5) or deduction (110(1)(g)).

Taxable under (r)(iii): provincial tuition and transportation assistance for worker on EI to attend re-employment course offered by construction industry (*Michaud*, 2002 CarswellNat 2473 (TCC)); Canada-[province] Labour Market Development Agreement (2014-0516501E5, 2014-0517081E5, 2014-0517091E5, 2014-0517101E5, 2014-0517111E5) [56(1)(n) or (u) for payments not falling under (r)]; Emploi-Québec active employment measures (2014-0527751I7); unnamed provincial program (2015-0601671E5). (iii) applies only if all of (A), (B) and (C) are satisfied: 2013-0495661I7.

Taxable under (r)(iv): assistance for laid-off workers (2017-0735991E5). Until (r)(iv.1) was introduced retroactively, (r)(iv) was also considered to cover CERB, CRB, CESB and other COVID assistance.

Taxable under (r)(iv.1) (COVID-19 benefits), introduced April 2021 retroactive to Jan. 2020: Canada Emergency Response Benefit (CERB, tinyurl.com/cra-cerb-tax [and see Godbout, "CERB", 1(3) *Perspectives on Tax Law & Policy* (ctf.ca) 16-19 (Sept. 2020)]); Canada Recovery Benefit (CRB, tinyurl.com/cra-crb-tax; see Reg. 103(4.1), 103(6)(h) for source withholding); Canada Emergency Student Benefit (CESB, tinyurl.com/cra-cesb); Canada Recovery Caregiving Benefit (CRCB, tinyurl.com/crcb-tax); Employment Insurance Emergency Response Benefit. See tinyurl.com/covid-ben-tax.

A 56(1)(r) amount must be reported on a T4A: Reg. 200(2)(c), doc 2015-0601671E5.

56(1)(r)(iv.1) added, and (iv) amended to exclude (iv.1) amounts, by 2021 budget bill #1, effective 2020.

56(1)(r)(iv) added by 2008 budget bill #2, for 2003 and later tax years.

Regulations: 100(1)"remuneration"(h) (withholding at source).

Income Tax Folios: S1-F1-C3: Disability supports deduction [replaces IT-519R2]; S1-F2-C3: Scholarships, research grants and other education assistance [replaces IT-340R]; S1-F3-C1: Child care expense deduction [replaces IT-495R3]; S1-F3-C4: Moving expenses [replaces IT-178R3].

(s) **grants under prescribed programs** — the amount of any grant received in the year under a prescribed program of the Government of Canada relating to home insulation or energy conversion by

(i) the taxpayer, other than a married taxpayer or a taxpayer who is in a common-law partnership who resided with the taxpayer's spouse or common-law partner at the time the grant was received and whose income for the year is less than the taxpayer's spouse's or common-law partner's income for the year, or

(ii) the spouse or common-law partner of the taxpayer with whom the taxpayer resided at the time the grant was received, if the spouse's or common-law partner's income for the year is less than the taxpayer's income for the year

to the extent that the amount is not required by paragraph 12(1)(u) to be included in computing the taxpayer's or the taxpayer's spouse's or common-law partner's income for the year or a subsequent year;

Related Provisions: 13(7.1)(b.1) — Deemed capital cost of certain property; 56(9) — Definition of "income for the year"; 81(1)(g.4) — Exemption for 2000-01 heating expenses credit.

Notes: Examples of grants not prescribed in Reg. 5500-01 and thus exempt: grants covering personal losses or replacing destroyed rental or business properties from the 1998 ice storm (Revenue Canada news release, March 11, 1999); Home Energy Efficiency Retrofit Grants, unless the home is used principally to earn income (12(1)(u)); 2006 Ontario Home Electricity Relief grants (CRA Notice, "Ontario Home Electricity Relief program", Oct. 26, 2006). See also Notes to s. 3.

56(1)(s) amended by 2000 same-sex partners bill, effective 2001.

Regulations: 224 (information return); 5500, 5501 (prescribed program).

Interpretation Bulletins: IT-273R2: Government assistance — general comments.

(t) **registered retirement income fund** — amounts in respect of a registered retirement income fund required by section 146.3 to be included in computing the taxpayer's income for the year;

Related Provisions: 60.2(1) — Refund of undeducted past service AVCs; 139.1(11), (12) — Conversion benefit on demutualization of insurance corporation; 146.3(5), (5.1), (7) — Benefits taxable; 153(1)(l) — Withholding of tax at source; 212(1)(q) — RRIF payments to non-residents.

Regulations: 215 (information return).

Forms: T1234 Sched. B: Allowable amounts of non-refundable tax credits; T2205: Amounts from a spousal or common-law partner RRSP, RRIF or SPP to include in income.

(u) **social assistance [welfare] payments** — a social assistance payment made on the basis of a means, needs or income test and received in the year by

(i) the taxpayer, other than a married taxpayer or a taxpayer who is in a common-law partnership who resided with the taxpayer's spouse or common-law partner at the time the payment was received and whose income for the year is less than the spouse's or common-law partner's income for the year, or

(ii) the taxpayer's spouse or common-law partner, if the taxpayer resided with the spouse or common-law partner at the time the payment was received and if the spouse's or common-law partner's income for the year is less than the taxpayer's income for the year,

except to the extent that the payment is otherwise required to be included in computing the income for a taxation year of the taxpayer or the taxpayer's spouse or common-law partner;

Related Provisions: 56(1)(r) — Inclusion of social assistance payments intended to supplement employment income (with no offsetting deduction); 56(9) — Definition of "income for the year"; 81(1)(g.6) — Ontario Electricity Support Program payments exempt; 81(1)(h) — Exemption for payments for foster care or other in-home care; 110(1)(f) — Offsetting deduction.

Notes: Although 56(1)(u) includes an amount in income, 110(1)(f) allows an offsetting deduction in computing *taxable* income. Thus, the only effect is on net income (s. 3), which affects entitlement to various credits. See Notes to 56(1)(v).

Reporting is required on a T5007 slip: Reg. 233, though some amounts are excluded by Reg. 233(2). CRA policy is not to require some amounts to be reported and included in net income: VIEWS docs 2003-0053511E5, 2010-0384571R3 (assistance from US charity to Canadian employees), 2011-0419111I7; but in 2013-0495661I7, assistance from a US charity to former employees had to be included and deducted.

A 56(1)(u) amount is generally excluded from the income calculation for the Guaranteed Income Supplement if it arises in Canada, but not if it is foreign: *Fang*, 2016 TCC 166; *Fu*, 2020 FC 235. In *Kenny*, 2018 TCC 2, foreign (non-taxable) social assistance caused a non-resident to be denied personal credits by 118.94.

Due to the closing words, a payment that falls into both 56(1)(u) and 56(1)(r) is taxable under (r) with no 110(1) deduction.

A social assistance payment for a couple can be split between them for tax purposes (keeping net income low) even if it is all allocated to one person by the paying agency: *Gefter*, 2006 TCC 650.

56(1)(u) covers not only welfare (social assistance) payments from government and municipalities, but also payments by charities to poor people. See Drache, "Payments for Relief of Poverty", 7(4) *Canadian Not-for-Profit News* (Carswell), 29-30 (April 1999); and VIEWS doc 9825265. Social assistance for foster care and similar caregiving is exempt: 81(1)(h), but not if the cared-for person is related: 2010-0384491E5.

Private assistance to refugees, not through a government agency or charity, is not "social assistance" and not under 56(1)(u): VIEWS doc 2017-0690811I7.

The following fall under 56(1)(u) and 110(1)(f): Aboriginal off-reserve housing program (VIEWS doc 2010-0357911E5); BC Young Adult Program assistance (2009-034556117); Canada-[province] Labour Market Development Agreement payments that are not under 56(1)(r) (2014-0517081E5); caregiver payments to taxpayer for own child (2010-0359971M4, 2011-0414651E5) [but see now 81(1)(h.1)]; charity's financial assistance to needy persons, or Individual Development Account (2006-0180281E5, 2011-0418701E5); child-care assistance to student in financial difficulty (2010-0389161E5); church payments to Syrian refugee family (2016-0651661E5); Cree Hunters and Trappers Income Security Board benefits (9505637); employment assistance services program financial assistance (2009-0338621E5); Indian band rental assistance payments to member (2014-055411117); Ontario Basic Income Pilot program (2017-0704801E5); program providing medical devices to disabled persons (2009-0305961E5); provincial Disability Support Program payments (2018-0764761E5); Quebec "Devenir", "Alternative Jeunesse", "Programme d'aide financière d'urgence" and "Soutien financier aux mineurs enceintes" programs (2006-0169341I7, 2006-020816117, 2007-023045117, 2008-0265861E5, 2009-0345741I7); social assistance provided by way of gift cards (2014-0537191E5).

Social assistance received by an Indian on a reserve is exempt (see Notes to 81(1)(a)), not included under 56(1)(u): VIEWS doc 2015-061502117.

Funding under the B.C. Interim Early Intensive Intervention and Extended Autism Intervention programs for children with autism is non-taxable because it is not based on a means, needs or income test: VIEWS doc 2003-0054611E5.

CRA considers that welfare fraud creates business income, taxable under 9(1) rather than 56(1)(u), so no 110(1)(f) deduction is available: news release, June 12, 2003.

An amount for in-home care may be exempt under 81(1)(h) rather than falling under 56(1)(u); or it may be business income under 9(1).

A T5007 must be issued for 56(1)(u) income and a T4A for business income: VIEWS docs 2011-0407071E5, 2015-0575631E5 (see Reg. 233, 200(1)).

56(1)(u) amended by 2000 same-sex partners bill (effective 2001), 1995-97 and 1991 technical bills.

Regulations: 233 (information return).

CRA Audit Manual: 27.34.0: Social assistance payments.

Forms: RC257: Request for an information return program account (RZ); T1 General return, Line 14500 [former 145]; T4115: T5007 guide — return of benefits; T5007: Statement of benefits; T5007 Summ: Summary of benefits.

(v) **workers' compensation** — compensation received under an employees' or workers' compensation law of Canada or a province in respect of an injury, a disability or death;

Related Provisions: 110(1)(f)(ii) — Offsetting deduction.

Notes: In most provinces, benefits are paid by the Workers' Compensation Board (WCB); in Ontario, Workplace Safety and Insurance Board (WSIB); in Quebec, Commission des normes, de l'équité, de la santé et de la sécurité du travail (CNESST).

Although 56(1)(v) includes an amount in income, 110(1)(f)(ii) allows an offsetting deduction in computing *taxable* income. Thus no tax is payable on the amount, but "net income" (s. 3) is increased. This can: reduce the age credit (118(2)); GST/HST Credit (122.5) [*Farah*, 2013 TCC 16; *Dakiri*, 2013 TCC 18], Canada Child Benefit (122.61) [*Nicholson*, 2006 TCC 398], Canada Workers Benefit (122.7 and medical expense credit (118.2(1)C)); reduce the *Old Age Security Act* Guaranteed Income Supplement [*Dupuis*, 2011 TCC 485]; trigger Old Age Security clawback [see Notes to 180.2]; increase charitable donation room (118.1(1)"total gifts"(a)(iii)A). See also VIEWS docs 2009-032473117, 2011-0411231M4.

CRA's view (doc 2013-0486851E5) is that 56(1)(v) applies only to "workers' compensation benefits", which include wage loss benefits, permanent disability benefits, dependency benefits and rehabilitation benefits, but *not* a "non-economic loss" (NEL) award for pain and suffering, which is non-taxable damages (see Notes to s. 3).

A payment covering several years of benefits is all included in the same year, since 56(1)(v) is based on the year of receipt: *Franklin*, 2003 TCC 598 (the large inclusion clawed back the taxpayer's Old Age Security under 180.2).

In *Hepburn*, 77 D.T.C. 29 (TRB), payments from the Toronto Fire Dept. Superannuation and Benefit Fund to an injured fireman were considered to be a substitution for a provincial workers' compensation plan, and thus were exempt under the predecessor to 56(1)(v) (former 81(1)(h)).

However, in *Whitney*, 2002 FCA 266 (leave to appeal denied 2003 CarswellNat 734 (SCC)), amounts paid by an employer, under a collective agreement which used the provincial WCB approval process, were considered not to fall under 56(1)(v). IT-202R2 para. 4 was held incorrect in allowing such payments to qualify. Similarly, in *Suchon*, 2002 FCA 282, disability payments made by an employer who was outside the WCB system were taxable under 6(1)(a) and did not fall under 56(1)(v). See also VIEWS docs 2003-01828285, 2007-0239601E5, and *Gingras*, [1998] 2 C.T.C. 2557 (TCC) (RCMP officer). Payments by a bank to employees under the *Canada Labour Code* can fall within 56(1)(v): 2006-020861117.

In *Coulter*, 2004 TCC 510, C received payments from her employer for 9 years which were eventually repaid by WCB to her employer and thus were only advances. The Court agreed the payments were not taxable, dismissed her appeal because she had not objected to the earlier years, but recommended a remission order.

In *Butler*, 2016 FCA 65, para. 11, a retroactive award for pain, taken as lump sum, fell into 56(1)(v).

For CRA policy on employer "top-up" amounts, see Guide T4001, *Employer's Guide — Payroll Deductions* (policy changed in response to *Fraser*, [1996] 2 C.T.C. 2631 (TCC)). Where the employer advances pay, pending WCB benefits, see VIEWS doc 2006-0213961E5. However, in *Québec (Ville)*, 2007 TCC 329, CRA's policy was held to be wrong and the City was not liable for source deductions when it reduced injured employees' pay to their net pay while they were off work.

Where the provincial WCB sets up a "retirement annuity fund" for workers on long-term compensation, to be paid after regular benefits stop (Manitoba and Sask. do this), the transfer of accumulated annuity funds to an external investment organization does not trigger 56(1)(v) or Reg. 232 (but that organization will need to issue T5007s under Reg. 232 when it makes payments): VIEWS doc 2011-0431221R3.

Federal government employees: workers' comp benefits are paid by the government under the *Government Employees Compensation Act*, through the provincial WCB as agent: *Simone Sherman*, 2008 TCC 487. In *McCarthy*, 2019 TCC 69, government in-jury-on-duty leave pay was 85% workers' comp and deductible under 110(1)(f)(ii); the remaining 15% was salary.

A loan by the employer to the employee in advance of an expected Board award is neither taxable nor generates deemed interest: VIEWS doc 2013-0496251E5 (but it is taxable to the extent it exceeds the Board's award).

Retroactive WCB benefits are taxable under 56(1)(v) (VIEWS doc 2006-0189531I7), but a lump sum payment on death, for which Reg. 232(4)(e) provides that no T5007 is issued, is not (2006-0191501I7). See also 2006-0211061I7. A post-mortem WCB set-tlement for earlier injury is taxable to the estate under 56(1)(v): 2006-0215791E5, as is a "loss of retirement income" benefit paid to an estate: 2011-0421671E5.

CRA views US *War Hazards Compensation Act* workers' compensation benefits as taxable annuity payments, not eligible for 110(1)(f) or treaty relief: doc 2006-0217681E5; but US workers' compensation to an injured US federal government worker, which would be exempt in the US, is exempt under Canada-US tax treaty Art. XVIII:1: 2010-0389831E5.

Regulations: 232 (information return).

Interpretation Bulletins: IT-202R2: Employees' or workers' compensation.

Forms: RC257: Request for an information return program account (RZ); T1 General return, Line 14400 [former 144]; T4115: T5007 guide — return of benefits; T5007: Statement of benefits; T5007 Summ: Summary of benefits.

(w) **salary deferral arrangement** — the total of all amounts each of which is an amount received by the taxpayer as a benefit (other than an amount received by or from a trust governed by a salary deferral arrangement) in the year out of or under a salary deferral arrangement in respect of a person other than the tax-payer except to the extent that the amount, or another amount that may reasonably be considered to relate thereto, has been in-cluded in computing the income of that other person for the year or for any preceding taxation year;

Related Provisions: 6(1)(i) — Inclusions — salary deferral arrangement payments; 6(11) — Salary deferral arrangement.

(x) **retirement compensation arrangement** — any amount, including a return of contributions, received in the year by the taxpayer or another person, other than an amount required to be included in that other person's income for a taxation year under paragraph 12(1)(n.3), out of or under a retirement com-pensation arrangement that can reasonably be considered to have been received in respect of an office or employment of the taxpayer;

Related Provisions: 56(11) — Disposition of property by RCA trust; 60(j.1) — Transfer of retiring allowances; 60(t) — Deductions — amount included under 56(1)(x); 60.03(1)"eligible pension income"(b)(i)(A) — pension income splitting on RCA income; 149(1)(q.1) — RCA trust — exempt from Part I tax; 107.2 — Distribu-tion by RCA to beneficiary; 153(1)(q) — Withholding of tax at source; 160.3 — Lia-bility in respect of amounts received out of or under RCA trust; 207.6(7) — Transfer from RCA to another RCA; 212(1)(j) — Non-resident withholding tax.

Notes: See Notes to 248(1)"retirement compensation arrangement".

In *Haley*, 2006 TCC 464, payments from a government-funded RCA (Early Retirement Incentive Program for federal employees) fell under 56(1)(x).

Where the RCA custodian buys an annuity contract for the beneficiary, the CRA con-siders the amount paid to be taxable under 56(1)(x): VIEWS doc 2007-0244651C6.

Regulations: 100(1)"remuneration"(b.1) (withholding at source).

Interpretation Bulletins: IT-499R: Superannuation or pension benefits.

Forms: T1 General return, Line 13000 [former 130]: Other income; T4A-RCA: State-ment of distributions from an RCA; T4A-RCA Summ: Information return of distribu-tions from an RCA; T4041: Retirement compensation arrangements [guide].

(y) **idem** — any amount received or that became receivable in the year by the taxpayer as proceeds from the disposition of an interest in a retirement compensation arrangement;

Related Provisions: 60(u) — Deductions — amount included under 56(1)(y); 153(1)(r) — Withholding of tax at source; 214(3)(b.1) — Non-resident withholding tax — deemed payments.

Forms: T1 General return, Line 13000 [former 130]: Other income; T4A-RCA: State-ment of distributions from an RCA; T4A-RCA Summ: Information return of distribu-tions from an RCA; T4041: Retirement compensation arrangements [guide].

(z) **idem** — the total of all amounts, including a return of con-tributions, each of which is an amount received in the year by the taxpayer out of or under a retirement compensation arrange-ment that can reasonably be considered to have been received in respect of an office or employment of a person other than the taxpayer, except to the extent that the amount was required

(i) under paragraph 12(1)(n.3) to be included in computing the taxpayer's income for a taxation year, or

(ii) under paragraph (x) or subsection 70(2) to be included in computing the income for the year of a person resident in Canada other than the taxpayer;

Related Provisions: 56(11) — Disposition of property by RCA trust; 60(t) — De-ductions — amount included under 56(1)(z); 60.03(1)"eligible pension in-come"(b)(i)(A) — pension income splitting on RCA income; 153(1)(q) — Withholding of tax at source; 212(1)(j) — Non-resident withholding tax.

Regulations: 100(1)"remuneration"(b.1) (withholding at source).

Forms: T1 General return, Line 13000 [former 130]: Other income; T4A-RCA: State-ment of distributions from an RCA; T4A-RCA Summ: Information return of distribu-tions from an RCA; T4041: Retirement compensation arrangements [guide].

Interpretation Bulletins: IT-499R: Superannuation or pension benefits.

(z.1) **[benefit from registered national arts service or-ganization]** — the value of benefits received or enjoyed by any person in the year in respect of workshops, seminars, training programs and similar development programs because of the tax-payer's membership in a registered national arts service organization;

Related Provisions: 149.1(6.4) — National arts service organizations.

Notes: 56(1)(z.1) was 56(1)(aa) (added by 1991 technical bill effective July 14, 1990); renumbered by 2010 budget bill #2 effective 2010 when 56(1)(z.2) was added.

Income Tax Folios: S1-F2-C3: Scholarships, research grants and other education assistance [replaces IT-340R].

(z.2) **employee life and health trust** — the total of all amounts, each of which is an amount received in the year by the taxpayer that is required to be included in income under subsec-tion 144.1(11) except to the extent that the amount was required under subsection 70(2) to be included in computing the income for the year by the taxpayer or other person resident in Canada;

Related Provisions: 128.1(10)"excluded right or interest"(a)(vi.1) — No deemed disposition of rights on emigration or immigration of ELHT beneficiary; 153(1)(s) — Withholding of tax at source; 212(1)(w) — Withholding tax on payment to non-resident.

Notes: 56(1)(z.2) added by 2010 budget bill #2, effective 2010.

(z.3) **pooled registered pension plan** — any amount re-quired by section 147.5 to be included in computing the tax-payer's income for the year other than an amount distributed under a PRPP as a return of all or a portion of a contribution to the plan to the extent that the amount

(i) is a payment described under clause 147.5(3)(d)(ii)(A) or (B), and

(ii) is not deducted in computing the taxpayer's income for the year or a preceding taxation year;

Related Provisions: 147.3(13.1) — Withdrawal of excessive transfer to RRSP or RRIF; 147.5(13)(a) — Income inclusion of PRPP member's benefit; 147.5(13)(b) — Income inclusion where employer contribution withdrawn; Reg. 100(1)"remunera-tion"(b)(i) — No source withholdings on PRPP distribution not taxed under 56(1)(z.3).

Notes: 56(1)(z.3) added by 2012 budget bill #2, effective Dec. 14, 2012; and amended by 2017 budget bill #2, retroactive to its introduction, to add "other than..." and subparas. (i), (ii).

(z.4) **tax informant program** — any amount received in the year by the taxpayer under a contract, to provide information to the Canada Revenue Agency, entered into by the taxpayer under a program administered by the Canada Revenue Agency to obtain information relating to tax non-compliance; and

Related Provisions: 60(z.1) — Deduction for repayment of amount; 152(10)(b) — Province does not get paid until assessment collected; 153(1)(s) — Withholding of tax at source; 212(1)(x) — Withholding tax if paid to non-resident.

Notes: 56(1)(z.4) (added by 2014 budget bill #1 effective June 19, 2014) includes in income payments received under the Offshore Tax Informant Program. CRA will contract to pay 5-15% of $100,000 or more federal tax collected from a lead on unreported income on property outside Canada. See tinyurl.com/cra-otip; VIEWS doc 2015-0572181C6 [2015 STEP q.16]; Harris, "The Offshore Tax Informant Program", 12(10) *Tax Hyperion* (Carswell) 1-2 (Oct. 2015); Campbell, *Administration of Income Tax 2020* (Carswell), §7.14. The US has had such "bounty payments" since 1867: tinyurl.com/irs-whistle.

The amount paid out is far less than 15% of what CRA collects, since it applies only to federal tax, not to interest, penalties or provincial tax. At 33% top federal rate, there must be at least $303,030 of unreported income (over multiple years) for any payment to be made.

From the program's 2014 start to end of 2019, CRA received 1,600 calls from potential informants and 750 written submissions; signed 50 contracts with informants; completed 150 audits (300 more were in progress); and assessed $60 million of federal tax of which $20m was collected: VIEWS doc 2020-0839921C6 [2020 STEP q.16].

Quebec has a "Reward Program for Informants of Transactions Covered by the General Anti-Avoidance Rule and Sham Transactions": tinyurl.com/rq-reward. Since such rewards do not fall under 56(1)(z.4), they arguably are non-taxable under the ITA; but see Notes to s. 3.

Regulations: 103(9) (50% source withholding required; 30% in Quebec).

(z.5) **advanced life deferred annuity** — any amount required by section 146.5 to be included in computing the taxpayer's income for the year.

Related Provisions: 56(1)(d)(iv) — Non-taxable ALDA payments not taxed as annuity income; 146.5(5) — Where ALDA refund transferred to another registered plan; 153(1)(u) — Withholding on payment to Canadian resident; 212(1)(l.1) — Withholding tax on payment to non-resident.

Notes: See Notes to 146.5. 56(1)(z.5) added by 2021 budget bill #1, effective 2020.

Regulations: 100(1)"remuneration"(p) (includes 56(1)(z.5) amount for source withholding); 216(3) (information return on payment from ALDA).

(1.1) Application of subsec. 12.2(11) — The definitions in subsection 12.2(11) apply to paragraph (1)(d).

Notes: 56(1.1) added in the RSC 1985 (5th Supp) consolidation, effective for tax years ending after Nov. 1991. This was formerly in the opening words of 12.2(11).

(2) Indirect payments — A payment or transfer of property made pursuant to the direction of, or with the concurrence of, a taxpayer to another person for the benefit of the taxpayer or as a benefit that the taxpayer desired to have conferred on the other person (other than by an assignment of any portion of a retirement pension under section 65.1 of the *Canada Pension Plan* or a comparable provision of a provincial pension plan as defined in section 3 of that Act) shall be included in computing the taxpayer's income to the extent that it would be if the payment or transfer had been made to the taxpayer.

Related Provisions: 56(5) — 56(2) does not apply to income subject to income-splitting tax; 74.1–74.5 — Attribution rules; 80.04(5.1) — No benefit conferred where debtor transfers property to eligible transferee under 80.04; 120.4 — Tax on split income; 135(4)"payment"(c) — Patronage dividend payments; 212(2), 214(3)(a) — Non-resident withholding tax; 246 — Benefit conferred; 247(15) — No application to transfer pricing amount deemed to be dividend for non-resident withholding tax.

Notes: In *Neuman*, [1998] 3 C.T.C. 177, the Supreme Court of Canada ruled that 56(2) could not apply to dividends in a family income-splitting situation. Specifically, a shareholder need not contribute services to the corporation to be entitled to a dividend; and a dividend, had it not been declared, would not otherwise have been included in any other taxpayer's income (since the dividend belongs to the corporation until it is declared). This was consistent with the Supreme Court's earlier decision in *McClurg*, 1990 CarswellNat 520, that dividend declaration is done by a corp's directors, not in their capacity as shareholders, and is normally not subject to 56(2). However, see now 120.4; and in *Champ*, [1983] C.T.C. 1 (FCTD), where the articles did not permit dividends to be paid selectively, the husband was liable for tax on dividends paid to his wife. In *Demers*, 2006 TCC 504, 56(2) applied to dividends paid to D's young daughters, as their ownership of shares was a "sham", "abusive and artificial" (paras. 27-28)

and was used to transfer D's employment compensation to them. See also Notes to 74.1(1) re income splitting generally.

Pre-2018, CRA accepted *Neuman* and would not apply GAAR to such cases (*Income Tax Technical News* 16). The person directing a payment must have a pre-existing entitlement to the funds for 56(2) to apply. However, 74.4 can apply to some income-splitting done through a corp; and, since 2018, 120.4 tax on split income (TOSI) catches much income sprinkling. CRA may also apply 15(1), 69(1), 74.1(1): VIEWS docs 2006-0175601E5, 2010-0364131E5, 2016-0626781E5 [Cameron, "Discretionary Dividend Shares — Beware!", 13(7) *Tax Hyperion* (Carswell) 5-7 (July 2016)]. Different classes of shares used for *Neuman*-type dividends no longer need to have different rights in some provinces, e.g. Ontario *Business Corporations Act* s. 22(7), Quebec *Business Corporations Act* s. 49: 2007 STEP q.15 (www.step.ca).

"56(2) is rooted in the doctrine of 'constructive receipt' and was meant to cover principally cases where a taxpayer seeks to avoid receipt of ... income by arranging to have the amount paid to some other person either for his own benefit ... or for the benefit of that other person ... however, the wording of the provision does not allow to its being confined to such clear cases of tax-avoidance": *Outerbridge Estate*, [1991] 1 C.T.C. 113 (FCA), approved by the SCC in *Neuman*.

A loan to B is not a "payment or transfer" for 56(2): *Williams*, 2004 TCC 838; but CRA says it may be, if at the time of the loan it appears B will be unable to repay it: VIEWS doc 2013-0506401E5.

Non-residents: An amount deemed by 56(2) to be a NR's income is deemed by 214(3)(a) to be a corporate dividend, triggering 212(2) withholding tax. See 214(3) Notes.

In *Kuryliw*, 2007 TCC 352, 56(2) did not apply to amounts K had withdrawn from a corp's account as bank drafts to third parties, because the Crown's assumptions did not establish intent to confer a benefit on any third party.

56(2) applied to sole shareholder X when he allowed his company to have sale proceeds paid to his sons' company: *Hasiuk*, 2008 FCA 294. The 4 *Neuman* tests applied: (1) payment to someone other than X; (2) allocation was at X's direction or with his concurrence; (3) payment for the benefit of X or of a person he wished to benefit; (4) payment would have been included in X's income had he received it; also, from *Winter*, [1991] 1 C.T.C. 113 (FCA): (5) the transferee was not taxed on the payment (and see *Delso Restoration*, 2011 TCC 435 re (5)). See also *Laflamme*, 2008 TCC 255; *Sochatsky*, 2011 TCC 41 (FCA appeal discontinued A-33-11) (attempt to redirect employment income to company after year-end). 56(2) applied in *Bonavia*, 2010 FCA 129 and *Gougeon*, 2010 TCC 359 (both RRSP/RRIF strips); *D'Andrea*, 2011 TCC 298 (proceeds of sale of property directed to a company). It would have applied to an RRSP strip if other provisions had not already taxed it: *Astorino*, 2010 TCC 144. It would have applied to pension-plan strips in *Ross*, 2013 TCC 333, para. 80, but the assessments were statute-barred. In *Ludmer*, 2018 QCCS 3381, paras. 604-618 (aff'd on other grounds 2020 QCCA 697; leave to appeal denied 2021 CarswellQue 2160 (SCC)), it was reasonable for CRA to apply 56(2).

56(2) did not apply in: *Husky Oil*, 2009 TCC 118 (*Neuman* conditions not met) (rev'd on other grounds 2010 FCA 125); *Guilbault*, 2011 TCC 394 (no transfer of art from G's corp to his ex-wife as part of their settlement, even though the art remained at her home); *Mattacchione*, 2015 TCC 283, para. 80 (M could not invoke 56(2) to shift income away, and M directed payment in any event); *Grenon*, 2021 TCC 30, paras. 404-436 (under appeal to FCA on other grounds) (56(2) did not apply to income generated by non-qualified investments held in G's RRSP, as it was payable to the RRSP, not G).

56(2) did not apply to a transfer of stolen funds in *Gainor*, 2011 TCC 442, para. 49, as the funds did not belong to G in the first place.

A 56(2) income inclusion may have GST and other taxes added to it due to 15(1.3): VIEWS doc 2007-0236841I7.

56(2) might apply where a father's company lends money interest-free to (or invests in retractable preferred shares in) his son's company: VIEWS doc 2005-0140961C6. It applied where a public company issued stock options to a consulting company's shareholder instead of the company: 2013-0513221I7. It does not apply by a renunciation by a settlor of a trust so that 75(2) no longer applies: 2008-0279741E5. Providing collateral to secure a joint line of credit for the spouse does not trigger 56(2): 2009-0317041E5. The CRA refuses to say it will *not* apply to a sole trustee discretionary beneficiary of a trust who makes distributions to other beneficiaries: 2012-0457551C6, 2012-0462891C6 [2012 Ontario Tax Conf. q.19]. For criticism see Daren Baxter, "Application of 56(2) to Trustee of Discretionary Trust", 10(1) *Tax Hyperion* (Carswell) 1-4 (Jan. 2013); Sunita Doobay, "Subsection 56(2) and a Discretionary Trust", 21(10) *Canadian Tax Highlights* (ctf.ca) 8-9 (Oct. 2013). See also 2016-0654331E5 (sale of land to related corp with vendor retaining right to rents).

Where 56(2) results in double tax, CRA may agree to cancel the assessment, e.g. *Singleton*, 2010 TCC 638, paras. 24-25. See also Grower, "Subsections 15(1) and 56(2) — The Risks of Double Taxation", 2012 Prairie Provinces Tax Conference (ctf.ca), 10:1-34. VIEWS docs 2013-0488011E5 and 2013-0514321E5 note that when 56(2) applies and an amount could be included in the income of both the actual recipient and under 56(2), "it is the practice of the CRA not to assess the same income twice".

Directors' fees that a director asks be paid to a charity are taxable to the director under 56(2) (but the director is making a donation under 118.1), and if the fees are waived the CRA will not apply 56(2)): VIEWS doc 2010-0367781E5. Similarly, if an employee asks for part of their income to be paid to a charity, 56(2) will apply, but not for an award that would otherwise be non-taxable if the employer gets the donation receipt: 2012-0440821E5.

Rulings: In many pre-2016 rulings listed in Notes to 125(7)"personal services business" (e.g. 2009-0349951R3), CRA ruled that 56(2) does not apply when a partner's professional corp provides services to the partnership. 2011-0424341I7 said 56(2) did not apply to a particular Quebec trust. 2016-0630761R3 and 2017-0693751R3 ruled 56(2) did not apply to a rollover of foreign-affiliate shares to another FA followed by transfer to a related Cdn resident corp.

Amounts payable by a company to a union under a collective agreement, held in trust to benefit the union's members who are self-employed, do not fall under 56(2): VIEWS doc 2007-0249051E5. Similarly, amounts payable by a producer to the Caisse de sécurité des artistes for the benefit of an artist are not subject to 56(2): 2012-0461711E5.

Where a real estate agent directs their brokerage to pay part of their commission to the home purchaser as a referral fee, this is taxable to the agent under 56(2): VIEWS doc 2013-0488011E5.

See also Smith & Pidborochynski, "Indirect Shareholder Benefits", 2009 Ontario Tax Conference (ctf.ca), 10:1-21; Baass, "Are Management Fees a Useful Tool or Audit Time Bomb?", 22(8) *Taxation of Executive Compensation & Retirement* (Federated Press) 1391-95 (April 2011).

56(2) amended by 2011 budget bill #2, for payments and transfers made after 2010. The substantive change was to delete "a prescribed provincial pension plan" from the parenthesized words; Sask. Pension Plan income is now treated as RRSP income for the attribution rules (see 146(21.1)-(21.3)).

Income Tax Folios: S1-F2-C3: Scholarships, research grants and other education assistance [replaces IT-340R].

Interpretation Bulletins: IT-335R2: Indirect payments; IT-362R: Patronage dividends; IT-415R2: Deregistration of registered retirement savings plans (cancelled); IT-432R: Benefits conferred on shareholders.

I.T. Technical News: 16 (*Neuman* case).

Transfer Pricing Memoranda: TPM-02: Repatriation of funds by non-residents — Part XIII assessments; TPM-03: Downward transfer pricing adjustments under subsec. 247(2).

CRA Audit Manual: 24.11.0: Indirect payments and benefits.

Advance Tax Rulings: ATR-3: Winding-up of an estate; ATR-14: Non-arm's length interest charges; ATR-15: Employee stock option plan; ATR-17: Employee benefit plan — purchase of company shares; ATR-22R: Estate freeze using share exchange; ATR-27: Exchange and acquisition of interests in capital properties through rollovers and winding-up ("butterfly"); ATR-29: Amalgamation of social clubs; ATR-35: Partitioning of assets to get specific ownership ("butterfly"); ATR-36: Estate freeze.

(3) Exemption for scholarships, fellowships, bursaries and prizes — For the purpose of subparagraph (1)(n)(ii), a taxpayer's scholarship exemption for a taxation year is the total of

(a) the total of all amounts each of which is the amount included under subparagraph (1)(n)(i) in computing the taxpayer's income for the taxation year in respect of a scholarship, fellowship or bursary received in connection with the taxpayer's enrolment

   (i) in an educational program in respect of which the taxpayer is a "qualifying student" (as defined in subsection 118.6(1)) in the taxation year, in the immediately preceding taxation year or in the following taxation year, or

   (ii) in an elementary or secondary school educational program,

(b) the total of all amounts each of which is the lesser of

   (i) the amount included under subparagraph (1)(n)(i) in computing the taxpayer's income for the taxation year in respect of a scholarship, fellowship, bursary or prize that is to be used by the taxpayer in the production of a literary, dramatic, musical or artistic work, and

   (ii) the total of all amounts each of which is an expense incurred by the taxpayer in the taxation year for the purpose of fulfilling the conditions under which the amount described in subparagraph (i) was received, other than

      (A) personal or living expenses of the taxpayer (except expenses in respect of travel, meals and lodging incurred by the taxpayer in the course of fulfilling those conditions and while absent from the taxpayer's usual place of residence for the period to which the scholarship, fellowship, bursary or prize, as the case may be, relates),

      (B) expenses for which the taxpayer is entitled to be reimbursed, and

      (C) expenses that are otherwise deductible in computing the taxpayer's income, and

(c) the lesser of $500 and the amount by which the total described in subparagraph (1)(n)(i) for the taxation year exceeds the total of the amounts determined under paragraphs (a) and (b).

Related Provisions: 56(3.1) — Limitations on scholarship exemption.

Notes: 56(3)(c) exempts at least $500 of scholarship, fellowship or bursary income. If the income is intended to support enrolment (see Notes to 56(3.1)) qualifying for the tuition credit (56(3)(a)(i), VIEWS doc 2011-043079I7) or an elementary or secondary school program (56(3)(a)(ii), 2013-0513061E5), the scholarship is fully exempt. 56(3)(b) exempts it to the extent of expenses to produce a literary, dramatic, musical or artistic work contemplated by the payment.

Even if a scholarship is entirely exempt, a T4A must be issued; see Notes to Reg. 200(2). Similarly, a student whose tuition is all covered by scholarship is still entitled to a T2202A: 2010-0382261E5. Enrolment information is now reported under Reg. 203.

A scholarship received after the end of the educational program will not qualify for the full exemption: VIEWS doc 2003-0036737. See also Notes to 56(1)(n).

In *Larsen*, 2012 TCC 74, only the $500 exemption was allowed for a teacher taking a course at a university in Spain because the course was less than 13 weeks (before the threshold was changed to 3 weeks).

Post-doctoral fellowship (**PDF**) status is uncertain: employment income (5(1)), scholarship/bursary/fellowship (56(1)(n)), research grant (56(1)(o)) or independent contractor (9(1))? Each case depends on its facts. A PDF was employment income in *Chabaud*, 2011 TCC 438 (very comprehensive analysis; para. 109 encouraged an FCA appeal to clarify the law, but this was not done); and *Caropreso*, 2012 TCC 212. A PDF (working at AECL) was fellowship income, with only $500 exempt, in *Ismail*, 2019 TCC 159 (payer's intention is the most important factor: para. 41). See also VIEWS doc 2014-0537851E5. PDFs before 2010 were exempt scholarship income in *Zhang*, 2010 TCC 592, *Huang*, 2012 TCC 81, and *Lahlou*, 2013 TCC 161. They were *not* employment income for EI/CPP purposes in *Ontario Cancer*, 1993 CarswellNat 2659 (it was a "contract for education and training"), *Bekhor*, 2005 TCC 443 (fellowship income), and *Naghash*, 2005 TCC 694. The TCC declined to hold a PDF was employment income in *Lewis*, 2013 TCC 137, due to insufficient evidence. In CRA's view, PDF income may be employment income: 2008-0302591E5, 2010-0364651M4. A medical resident's income from a hospital is normally employment income: 2008-0299301E5 (see also 118.5(1)(a) Notes re medical residents). The Finance materials quoted in *Chabaud* indicate that PDFs are intended to be taxable. Graduate student support is different from a PDF: see discussion in *Rizak*, 2013 TCC 273. The 2021 Budget makes PDF income eligible for RRSP deduction regardless of its classification, retroactive to 2011 at the taxpayer's request: 146.01(1)"earned income"(b.01).

Since 2010, a PDF is disqualified from 56(3) by 118.6(1)"qualifying educational program", requiring that research be towards a degree (as announced in the 2010 Budget). This rule applied in *Lewis* (above). Even before 2010, CRA considered that a PDF may be employment income, research grant or a scholarship but did not fall under 56(3): VIEWS docs 2007-0228871E5, 2007-0242801E5, 2007-0252651E5, 2007-0261421E5, 2008-0276691E5, 2008-0300441E5, 2008-0301601M4, 2008-0305252E5, 2008-0302591E5, 2010-036999I7. See 2009-0308561E5 ("the full scholarship exemption was never intended to apply to postdoctoral fellows"). In *Zhang* (above), only the $500 exemption was allowed because Z had no T2202A certificate required by 118.6(2) [now 118.6(1)"qualifying student"(b)]. The amendment confirms CRA's position: 2008-0302461M4, 2008-0302951E5, 2008-0303451M4, 2009-0307471M4, 2009-0308991M4, 2009-0310891M4, 2009-0311901E5 (quotes the Finance Minister confirming this in Parliament), 2009-0314831M4, 2009-0350191M4, 2011-0394491E5, 2011-0404131M4, 2011-0404751M4. See also 2011-0404241E5 re deducting expenses against PDF funding.

For application of 56(3) to non-residents see VIEWS doc 2007-022951I7.

56(3)(a)(i) amended by 2016 budget bill #1, for 2017 and later taxation years, and

   (a) for the 2016 taxation year, a taxpayer is considered to be entitled to deduct an amount under 118.6(2) in respect of an educational program for the immediately following taxation year if the taxpayer is a "qualifying student" (as defined in 118.6(1)) in respect of the program in that year; and

   (b) for the 2017 taxation year, a taxpayer is considered to be a qualifying student in respect of an educational program in the immediately preceding taxation year if the taxpayer was entitled to deduct an amount under 118.6(2) in respect of the program for the year.

(This amendment was non-substantive, consequential on repeal of the education credit in 118.6.) For 2007-2016 taxation years, read:

   (i) in an educational program in respect of which an amount may be deducted under subsection 118.6(2) in computing the taxpayer's tax payable under this Part for the taxation year, for the immediately preceding taxation year or for the following taxation year, or

56(3) amended by 2007 budget bill #2 (for 2007 and later tax years), 2006 budget bill #2 (to increase the $3,000 exemption to unlimited if certain conditions are met). Added by 2000 Budget (some of its rules were formerly in 56(1)(n)(ii) and (iii); the principal change was the general increase in exemption from $500 to $3,000).

Regulations: 203 (institution required to issue information slip for scholarship).

Income Tax Folios: S1-F2-C1: Education and textbook tax credits [replaces IT-515R2]; S1-F2-C2: Tuition tax credit [replaces IT-516R2]; S1-F2-C3: Scholarships, research grants and other education assistance [replaces IT-340R].

(3.1) Limitations of scholarship exemption — For the purpose of determining the total in paragraph (3)(a) for a taxation year,

(a) a scholarship, fellowship or bursary (in this subsection referred to as an "award") is not considered to be received in connection with the taxpayer's enrolment in an educational program described in subparagraph (3)(a)(i) except to the extent that it is reasonable to conclude that the award is intended to support the taxpayer's enrolment in the program, having regard to all the circumstances, including the terms and conditions that apply in respect of the award, the duration of the program and the period for which support is intended to be provided; and

(b) if an award is received in connection with an educational program in respect of which the taxpayer is a qualifying student because of subparagraph (a)(ii) of the definition "qualifying student" in subsection 118.6(1) in the taxation year, in the immediately preceding taxation year or in the following taxation year (in this paragraph referred to as the "claim year"), the amount included under subparagraph (1)(n)(i) in computing the taxpayer's income for the taxation year in respect of the award may not exceed the amount that is the total of amounts, each of which is the cost of materials related to the program or a fee paid to a "designated educational institution" in respect of the program, as defined in subsection 118.6(1), in respect of the claim year.

Notes: 56(3.1), added by 2011 budget bill #2 for 2010 and later taxation years, implements a 2010 Budget proposal. To be exempt, 56(3.1) requires a scholarship to be intended to support enrolment in the program, and limits the exemption for part-time students to the cost of the program and materials (including amounts paid in other years and not yet claimed: VIEWS doc 2015-062427117). See also 118.6(1)"qualifying educational program", which as amended excludes research that does not lead to a degree, so postdoctoral fellowships do not qualify for the exemption (see Notes to 56(3)).

CRA considers a scholarship or bursary as intended to support enrolment "unless it significantly exceeds the individual's tuition fees, living expenses and other expenses associated with undertaking the program": Folio S1-F2-C3 ¶3.97, VIEWS doc 2014-0529481E5.

For interpretation of "materials related to the program" in (b), see Income Tax Folio S1-F2-C3 ¶3.94.

56(3.1)(b) amended by 2016 budget bill #1, to change "may deduct an amount by reason of" 118.6(2)B(b) for the taxation year to "is a qualifying student because of" 118.6(1)"qualifying student"(a)(ii) in the taxation year, for 2017 and later taxation years, and

(a) for the 2016 taxation year, a taxpayer is considered to be entitled to deduct an amount by reason of 118.6(2)B(b) in respect of an educational program for the immediately following taxation year if the taxpayer is a qualifying student in respect of the program because of 118.6(1)"qualifying student"(a)(ii) for that year; and

(b) for the 2017 taxation year, a taxpayer is considered to be a qualifying student in respect of an educational program because of 118.6(1)"qualifying student"(a)(ii) in the immediately preceding taxation year if the taxpayer was entitled to deduct an amount by reason of 118.6(2)B(b) of the Act in respect of the program for that year.

(This amendment was non-substantive, consequential on repeal of the education credit in 118.6.)

Income Tax Folios: S1-F2-C3: Scholarships, research grants and other education assistance [replaces IT-340R].

(4) Transfer of rights to income — Where a taxpayer has, at any time before the end of a taxation year, transferred or assigned to a person with whom the taxpayer was not dealing at arm's length the right to an amount (other than any portion of a retirement pension assigned by the taxpayer under section 65.1 of the *Canada Pension Plan* or a comparable provision of a provincial pension plan as defined in section 3 of that Act) that would, if the right had not been so transferred or assigned, be included in computing the taxpayer's income for the taxation year, the part of the amount that relates to the period in the year throughout which the taxpayer is resident in Canada shall be included in computing the taxpayer's income for the year unless the income is from property and the taxpayer has also transferred or assigned the property.

Notes: 56(4) was initially applied in *Spuehler*, 2003 TCC 611, where S's wife reported the income from rental of trucks that S owned. The income was attributed back to S. However, the FCA (2004 FCA 428) ruled the Tax Court judge had failed to take into account relevant evidence, and sent the matter back for a new hearing.

56(4) applied to a financial planner who directed that trailer fees from sales commissions be paid to his corporation: *Boutilier*, 2007 TCC 96. In *Demers*, 2006 TCC 504, 56(4) may have applied to D transferring employment compensation to his two young daughters by way of dividends; the Court ruled the arrangement a sham without saying whether 56(4) applied.

For CRA interpretation see docs 2002-0149781R3, 2007-0238221E5, 2013-051322117, 2016-0654331E5.

56(4) amended by 1993 technical bill, effective for 1992 and later taxation years.

Interpretation Bulletins: IT-440R2: Transfer of rights to income; IT-499R: Superannuation or pension benefits.

(4.1) Interest free or low interest loans — Where

(a) a particular individual (other than a trust) or a trust in which the particular individual is beneficially interested has, directly or indirectly by means of a trust or by any means whatever, received a loan from or become indebted to

(i) another individual (in this subsection referred to as the "creditor") who

(A) does not deal at arm's length with the particular individual, and

(B) is not a trust, or

(ii) a trust (in this subsection referred to as the "creditor trust") to which another individual (in this subsection referred to as the "original transferor") who

(A) does not deal at arm's length with the particular individual,

(B) was resident in Canada at any time in the period during which the loan or indebtedness is outstanding, and

(C) is not a trust,

has, directly or indirectly by means of a trust or by any means whatever, transferred property, and

(b) it can reasonably be considered that one of the main reasons for making the loan or incurring the indebtedness was to reduce or avoid tax by causing income from

(i) the loaned property,

(ii) property that the loan or indebtedness enabled or assisted the particular individual, or the trust in which the particular individual is beneficially interested, to acquire, or

(iii) property substituted for property referred to in subparagraph (i) or (ii)

to be included in the income of the particular individual,

the following rules apply:

(c) any income of the particular individual for a taxation year from the property referred to in paragraph (b) that relates to the period or periods in the year throughout which the creditor or the creditor trust, as the case may be, was resident in Canada and the particular individual was not dealing at arm's length with the creditor or the original transferor, as the case may be, shall be deemed,

(i) where subparagraph (a)(i) applies, to be income of the creditor for that year and not of the particular individual except to the extent that

(A) section 74.1 applies or would, but for subsection 74.5(3), apply, or

(B) subsection 75(2) applies

to that income, and

(ii) where subparagraph (a)(ii) applies, to be income of the creditor trust for that year and not of the particular individual except to the extent that

(A) subparagraph (i) applies,

(B) section 74.1 applies or would, but for subsection 74.5(3), apply, or

(C) subsection 75(2) applies (otherwise than because of paragraph (d))

to that income; and

(d) where subsection 75(2) applies to any of the property referred to in paragraph (b) and subparagraph (c)(ii) applies to income from the property, subsection 75(2) applies after subparagraph (c)(ii) is applied.

Related Provisions: 56(4.2) — Exception where interest charged; 56(4.3) — Repayment of existing indebtedness; 56(5) — Exception where income-splitting tax applies; 74.4(2) — Transfer or loan to corporation; 82(2) — Dividends deemed received by taxpayer; 96(1.8) — Transfer or loan of partnership interest; 120.4 — Tax on split income; 212(12) — No non-resident withholding tax where income attributed; 248(5) — Substituted property; 248(25) — Meaning of "beneficially interested"; 250(6.1) — Creditor trust that ceases to exist deemed resident throughout year.

Notes: 56(4.1) is an attribution rule of more limited application than 74.1-74.5. It applies only to loans (not transfers), and only where income-splitting is one of the main reasons for the loan (or indebtedness). However, it applies to income-splitting with adult taxpayers, whereas 74.1-74.5 apply only to spouses and minor children. Providing collateral to secure a joint line of credit for the spouse does not trigger 56(4.1): VIEWS doc 2009-0317041E5. See also doc 2008-0300401E5.

For the meaning of "indirectly" in para. (a), see Notes to 17.1(1). For "one of the main reasons" in para. (b), see Notes to 83(2.1).

The phrase "beneficially interested" used in 56(4.1)(a), is defined in 248(25). Before 1991, 56(4.1)(a) referred explicitly to 74.5(10), which provided the same definition.

56(4.1) amended by 1993 technical bill (for income relating to periods that begin after Dec. 21, 1992) and 1991 technical bill.

Interpretation Bulletins: IT-394R2: Preferred beneficiary election; IT-511R: Interspousal and certain other transfers and loans of property.

CRA Audit Manual: 15.7.13: Application of attribution rules to trusts.

(4.2) Exception — Notwithstanding any other provision of this Act, subsection (4.1) does not apply to any income derived in a particular taxation year where

(a) interest was charged on the loan or indebtedness at a rate equal to or greater than the lesser of

(i) the prescribed rate of interest in effect at the time the loan was made or the indebtedness arose, and

(ii) the rate that would, having regard to all the circumstances, have been agreed on, at the time the loan was made or the indebtedness arose, between parties dealing with each other at arm's length;

(b) the amount of interest that was payable in respect of the particular year in respect of the loan or indebtedness was paid not later than 30 days after the end of the particular year; and

(c) the amount of interest that was payable in respect of each taxation year preceding the particular year in respect of the loan or indebtedness was paid not later than 30 days after the end of each of those preceding taxation years.

Notes: 56(4.2) amended by 1991 technical bill, effective for income relating to periods beginning in 1991, in consequence of changes to 56(4.1).

Regulations: 4301(c) (prescribed rate of interest).

Interpretation Bulletins: IT-511R: Interspousal and certain other transfers and loans of property.

(4.3) Repayment of existing indebtedness — For the purposes of subsection (4.1), where at any time a particular property is used to repay, in whole or in part, a loan or indebtedness that enabled or assisted an individual to acquire another property, there shall be included in computing the income from the particular property that proportion of the income or loss, as the case may be, derived after that time from the other property or from property substituted therefor that the amount so repaid is of the cost to the individual of the other property, but for greater certainty nothing in this subsection shall affect the application of subsection (4.1) to any income or loss derived from the other property or from property substituted therefor.

Related Provisions: 248(5) — Substituted property.

Notes: For the meaning of "derived", see Notes to 18.1(12).

56(4.3) amended by 1991 technical bill, effective for income relating to periods beginning in 1991, in consequence of changes to 56(4.1).

Interpretation Bulletins: IT-511R: Interspousal and certain other transfers and loans of property.

(5) Exception for split income — Subsections (2), (4) and (4.1) do not apply to any amount that is included in computing a specified individual's split income for a taxation year.

Notes: See Notes to 120.4. 56(5) added by 1999 Budget, effective for 2000 and later taxation years. For former 56(5) see Notes to 56(6), (7) below.

(6) [Pre-July 2016 Universal] Child care benefit — There shall be included in computing the income of a taxpayer for a taxation year the total of all amounts each of which is a benefit paid under section 4 of the *Universal Child Care Benefit Act* that is received in the taxation year by

(a) the taxpayer, if

(i) the taxpayer does not have a "cohabiting spouse or common-law partner" (within the meaning assigned by section 122.6) at the end of the year and the taxpayer does not make a designation under subsection (6.1) for the taxation year, or

(ii) the income, for the taxation year, of the person who is the taxpayer's cohabiting spouse or common-law partner at the end of the taxation year is equal to or greater than the income of the taxpayer for the taxation year;

(b) the taxpayer's cohabiting spouse or common-law partner at the end of the taxation year, if the income of the cohabiting spouse or common-law partner for the taxation year is greater than the taxpayer's income for the taxation year; or

(c) an individual who makes a designation under subsection (6.1) in respect of the taxpayer for the taxation year.

Related Provisions: 3(f) — Nil income deemed to be $0 income for comparative purposes; 56(8) — Averaging of benefits where paid for earlier years; 56(9.1) — Meaning of "income" for 56(6); 60(y) — Deduction where income repaid; 74.1(2) — No income attribution on UCCB; 75(3)(d) — Trust from UCCB payments — exclusion from reversionary trust rules; 122.5(1)"adjusted income"(a)(i), 122.6"adjusted income"(a)(i), 122.7(1)"adjusted net income"(b) — UCCB does not affect entitlement to GST/HST Credit, Child Tax Benefit or Working Income Tax Benefit; 122.61(1) — Canada Child Benefit; 180.2(1)"adjusted income"(a)(i) — UCCB does not create OAS clawback; 241(4)(d)(vii.4) — Disclosure of taxpayer information by CRA.

Notes: 56(6) includes the pre-July 2016 Universal Child Care Benefit (UCCB) in the lower-income spouse's income, as the child-care deduction under 63(1) is for the lower-income spouse; but note the special meaning of "income" in 56(9.1). (For a single parent, it can be included in the child's income via a 56(6.1) designation: 56(6)(c).) It was added by 2006 budget bill #1, effective for amounts received after June 2006.

The *Universal Child Care Benefit Act* was added by 2006 (Conservative) budget bill #1; amended by 2010 budget bill #2 to address shared-custody parents; amended by 2015 Budget bill to increase the monthly benefit from $100 to $160 for children under 6 and introduce a $60 monthly benefit for children 6-17. (In theory the money was to be spent on child-care of the parents' choosing, but nothing required this.) The increased payments started July 2015, before the Oct. 2015 federal election. It was then amended by the 2016 (Liberal) budget bill #1 to cancel the UCCB for months after June 2016 — see *UCCB Act* 4(2) (replaced with a much larger Canada Child Benefit under 122.61(1)). From July 2015-June 2016, total UCCBs paid out were $10 billion: tinyurl.com/uccb-stats.

Although CRA administered the UCCB, its denial or recovery could not be appealed to the Tax Court: *Moise*, 2009 TCC 187, para. 4; *Fatima*, 2012 TCC 49, para. 6; *Goldstein*, 2013 TCC 165, para. 3; *Jersak (Best)*, 2020 TCC 136, para. 6.

The UCCB did not count as income to reduce the GST/HST Credit (see 122.5"adjusted income"(a)(i)), nor the Child Tax Benefit (122.6"adjusted income"(a)(i)), nor the Working Income Tax benefit (122.7"adjusted net income"(b)), nor the OAS clawback (180.2(1)"adjusted income"(a)(i)).

The UCCB could be put into a child's bank account to earn investment income that will not be attributed back to the parent: 74.1(2) opening words, VIEWS doc 2006-0200541E5. The UCCB itself was still taxable if the parent was not a single parent: 2010-0367561E5.

In determining the lower-income spouse for 56(6), "income" is the same as T1 return "net income", and is calculated after child-care expenses deducted by the higher-income spouse: VIEWS doc 2010-0372351E5. Income exempt under 81(1)(a) (e.g., a status Indian) is not income: 2009-0318751E5. Where one spouse dies during the year, see 2013-0484971E5.

The 2008 Conservative election platform (*The True North Strong and Free*, Oct. 7, 2008) proposed to index the UCCB to inflation and to make it tax-free for single parents. The "tax-free" part was implemented by 56(6.1), added in the Conservative minority government 2010 Budget, which allows a single parent to include the UCCB in the child's income, making it tax-free unless the child has substantial income from other sources. Indexing of the UCCB was not included in the 2011 Conservative election platform (*Here for Canada*, April 2011). However, the Oct. 30, 2014 announcement, enacted by the 2015 Budget bill, increased the UCCB substantially as well as extending it to children age 6-17. The Liberal government elected in Oct. 2015 campaigned on a proposal to replace the UCCB with a higher income-tested Canada Child Benefit, and did that in its March 2016 Budget (see 122.61(1)).

56(6) amended by 2010 budget bill #1 for 2010 and later years, essentially to add para. (c). See Notes to 56(6.1).

Regulations: 200(6) (information return).

Forms: T1 General return, Line 117 (pre-2016).

(6.1) Designation [to include UCCB in child's income] — If, at the end of the taxation year, a taxpayer does not have a "cohabiting spouse or common-law partner" (within the meaning assigned by section 122.6), the taxpayer may designate, in the taxpayer's return of income for the taxation year, the total of all amounts, each of which is a benefit received in the taxation year by the taxpayer under section 4 of the *Universal Child Care Benefit Act*, to be income of

>   (a) if the taxpayer deducts an amount for the taxation year under subsection 118(1) because of paragraph (b) of the description of B in that subsection in respect of an individual, the individual; or
>
>   (b) in any other case, a child who is a "qualified dependant" (as defined in section 2 of the *Universal Child Care Benefit Act*) of the taxpayer.

Related Provisions: 56(6)(c) — Effect of designation.

Notes: The *Universal Child Care Benefit Act* has been amended (s. 4(2)) to eliminate payments for months after June 2016. See Notes to 56(6).

56(6.1) (added by 2010 budget bill #1, for 2010 and later years) implements a 2010 Budget proposal to allow a single parent to include the UCCB in the child's income, usually making it tax-free (see VIEWS doc 2011-0395761I7). An election "in the taxpayer's return" is valid even if the return is filed late: see Notes to 7(1.31).

(7) [Repealed]

Notes: Former 56(5), (6) and (7) repealed by 1992 Child Benefit bill, effective 1993. They provided that family allowance payments (baby bonus) were included in the income of the higher-income spouse. Family allowances were discontinued in January 1993, and replaced with non-taxable Child Tax Benefit payments under 122.61.

56(7)(a) previously amended by 1991 technical bill, effective 1988.

(8) CPP/QPP and UCCB amounts for previous years [averaging] — Notwithstanding subsections (1) and (6), if

>   (a) one or more amounts
>
>>   (i) are received by an individual (other than a trust) in a taxation year as, on account of, in lieu of payment of or in satisfaction of, any benefit under the *Canada Pension Plan* or a provincial pension plan as defined in section 3 of that Act, or
>>
>>   (ii) would be, but for this subsection, included in computing the income of an individual for a taxation year under subsection (6), and
>
>   (b) a portion, not less than $300, of the total of those amounts relates to one or more preceding taxation years,

that portion shall, at the option of the individual, not be included in the individual's income.

Related Provisions: 120.2 — General deferral rule for lump-sum payments; 120.3 — CPP/QPP benefits for previous years; 146(1)"earned income"(b.1) — RRSP — earned income includes amount under 56(8)(a).

Notes: 56(8) and 120.3 allow a lump sum CPP/QPP benefit (and pre-July 2016 Universal Child Care Benefits taxed under 56(6)) to be taxed in the current year as if spread over the years to which they apply, so that "bunching" of the income need not push the taxpayer into a higher bracket. Although the closing words say "at the option of the individual", no election is needed; CRA will "calculate the tax payable on those parts as if you received them in those years only if the result is better for you": *T1 General Income Tax Guide*, Line 11400, tinyurl.com/cra-Line11400.

The election can be made in respect of a retroactive lump-sum U.S. Social Security benefit: VIEWS docs 2010-0385701E5, 2011-0392071E5.

A more general (but largely ineffective) retroactive averaging rule for lump-sum payments is found in 110.2.

56(8) amended by 2013 budget bill #2 (for 2006 and later tax years), 2006 Budget bill #2, 1997 Budget. Added by 1991 Budget.

Remission Orders: *Willard Thorne Remission Order*, P.C. 2002-2177 (remission of tax on retroactive lump sum payment of CPP benefits); *Janet Hall Remission Order*, P.C. 2004-1336 (remission where CPP lump sum disability repaid to wage loss replace-

ment provider); *Wendy Drever Remission Order*, P.C. 2009-299 (remission where CPP lump sum disability repaid to wage loss replacement provider and transaction bridged 2 taxation years).

Forms: T1 General return, Line 11400 [former 114].

(9) Meaning of "income for the year" — For the purposes of paragraphs (1)(s) and (u), "income for the year" of a person means the amount that would, but for those paragraphs, paragraphs 60(v.1) and (w) and section 63, be the income of that person for the year.

Notes: 56(9) amended by 1992 Child Benefit bill, effective 1993.

(9.1) Meaning of "income" — For the purposes of subsection (6), "income" of a person for a taxation year means the amount that would, in the absence of that subsection, paragraphs (1)(s) and (u), 60(v.1), (w) and (y) and section 63, be the income of the person for the taxation year.

Notes: See Notes to 56(6). 56(9.1) added by 2002-2013 technical bill (Part 5 — technical), for 2006 and later tax years.

(10) Severability of retirement compensation arrangement — Where a retirement compensation arrangement is part of a plan or arrangement (in this subsection referred to as the "plan") under which amounts not related to the retirement compensation arrangement are payable or provided, for the purposes of this Act, other than this subsection,

>   (a) the retirement compensation arrangement shall be deemed to be a separate arrangement independent of other parts of the plan of which it is a part; and
>
>   (b) subject to subsection 6(14), amounts paid out of or under the plan shall be deemed to have first been paid out of the retirement compensation arrangement unless a provision in the plan otherwise provides.

(11) Disposition of property by RCA trust — For the purposes of paragraphs (1)(x) and (z), where, at any time in a year, a trust governed by a retirement compensation arrangement

>   (a) disposes of property to a person for consideration less than the fair market value of the property at the time of the disposition, or for no consideration,
>
>   (b) acquires property from a person for consideration greater than the fair market value of the property at the time of the acquisition, or
>
>   (c) permits a person to use or enjoy property of the trust for no consideration or for consideration less than the fair market value of such use or enjoyment,

the amount, if any, by which such fair market value differs from the consideration or, if there is no consideration, the amount of the fair market value shall be deemed to be an amount received at that time by the person out of or under the arrangement that can reasonably be considered to have been received in respect of an office or employment of a taxpayer.

Related Provisions: 69(1) — General rule deeming disposition to be at fair market value.

Notes: This rule is similar to 69(1) but does not require that the disposition be to a non-arm's length person.

(12) Foreign retirement arrangement — If an amount in respect of a foreign retirement arrangement is, as a result of a transaction, an event or a circumstance, considered to be distributed to an individual under the income tax laws of the country in which the arrangement is established, the amount is, for the purpose of paragraph (1)(a), deemed to be received by the individual as a payment out of the arrangement in the taxation year that includes the time of the transaction, event or circumstance.

Related Provisions: 94(1)"exempt foreign trust"(h)(ii)(D) — Roth IRA excluded from non-resident trust rules; Canada-U.S. Tax Treaty:Art. XVIII:3(b) — Roth IRA deemed to be pension under treaty.

Notes: See VIEWS docs 2011-0407461E5 (tax on 401(k) transfer to IRA, and on IRA withdrawal); 2018-0750411E5 (deemed distribution on giving up green card, and withdrawal in same year: CRA says no 60(j) rollover available).

Roth IRA: Income earned is taxable on a current basis, but a (permanent) election to defer the tax can be filed under Canada-US Tax Treaty Art. XVIII:7 (see Art.

XVIII:3(b)): Income Tax Folio S5-F3-C1 (replaces *Income Tax Technical News* 43); VIEWS docs 2002-0152515, 2006-0186661M4, 2011-0398691E5, 2013-0476351E5, 2015-0580301E5. Roth 401(k): see 2020-0846401E5.

56(12) added by 2002-2013 technical bill, this version effective for 2002 and later tax years.

Former 56(12) repealed by 1996 Budget, for amounts received after 1996. This rule, which required an "allowance" to be at the recipient's discretion, is now in 56.1(4)"support amount" opening words. Former 56(12) added by 1988 tax reform, for decrees, orders, judgments and written agreements made or entered into before March 28, 1986 or after 1987. For those made or entered into from March 29, 1986 through the end of 1987, where amounts were paid before 1997, see *Gagnon*, [1986] 1 C.T.C. 410 (SCC).

I.T. Technical News: 43 (taxation of Roth IRAs).

Definitions [s. 56]: "allowance" — 56(12); "amount" — 248(1); "anniversary day" — 12.2(11), 56(1.1); "annuity" — 248(1); "arm's length" — 251(1); "assessment" — 248(1); "beneficially interested" — 248(25); "borrowed money", "business" — 248(1); "Canada" — 255, *Interpretation Act* 35(1); "child" — 252(1); "child support amount" — 56.1(4); "cohabiting spouse or common-law partner" — 122.6; "commencement day" — 56.1(4); "common-law partner", "common-law partnership" — 248(1); "consequence of the death" — 248(8); "death benefit" — 248(1); "deferred profit sharing plan" — 147(1), 248(1); "designated educational institution" — 118.6(1); "employee benefit plan", "employment" — 248(1); "estate" — 104(1), 248(1); "fair market value" — see 69(1) Notes; "foreign retirement arrangement" — 248(1), Reg. 6803; "income" — 3, 56(9.1); "income for the year" — 56(9); "income-averaging annuity contract" — 61(4), 248(1); "individual", "insurer" — 248(1); "office" — 248(1); "PRPP" — 248(1)"pooled registered pension plan"; "parent" — 252(2)(a); "pension transferee" — 60.03(1); "person", "personal or living expenses", "prescribed" — 248(1); "prescribed benefit" — Reg. 5502; "prescribed rate" — Reg. 4301; "property" — 248(1); "province" — *Interpretation Act* 35(1); "provincial pension plan" — *Canada Pension Plan* s. 3; "qualifying student" — 118.6(1); "received" — 248(7); "registered disability savings plan" — 146.4(1), 248(1); "registered education savings plan" — 146.1(1), 248(1); "registered pension plan" — 248(1); "registered retirement income fund" — 146.3(1), 248(1); "registered retirement savings plan" — 146(1), 248(1); "regulation" — 248(1); "related" — 251(2); "resident in Canada" — 94(3)(a), 250; "retirement compensation arrangement", "retiring allowance", "salary deferral arrangement" — 248(1); "scholarship exemption" — 56(3), (3.1); "specified individual" — 120.4(1), 248(1); "specified pension plan" — 248(1), Reg. 7800; "split income" — 120.4(1), 248(1); "split-pension amount" — 60.03(1); "substituted" — 248(5); "superannuation or pension benefit" — 248(1); "supplementary unemployment benefit plan" — 145(1), 248(1); "support amount" — 56.1(4); "TFSA" — 146.2(5), 248(1); "taxation year" — 249; "taxpayer" — 248(1); "trust" — 104(1), 248(1), (3); "writing" — *Interpretation Act* 35(1).

56.1 (1) Support [payment made to third party] — For the purposes of paragraph 56(1)(b) and subsection 118(5), where an order or agreement, or any variation thereof, provides for the payment of an amount to a taxpayer or for the benefit of the taxpayer, children in the taxpayer's custody or both the taxpayer and those children, the amount or any part thereof

(a) when payable, is deemed to be payable to and receivable by the taxpayer; and

(b) when paid, is deemed to have been paid to and received by the taxpayer.

Related Provisions: 60.1(1) — Parallel rule for payer.

Notes: Where an amount is included in income by 56.1(1), an offsetting deduction is allowed to the payor by 60.1(1). See Notes to 60.1(1) for interpretation of 56.1(1).

56.1(1) amended by 1996 Budget, for amounts received after 1996.

Income Tax Folios: S1-F3-C3: Support payments [replaces IT-530R].

(2) Agreement [to make third-party support payments] — For the purposes of section 56, this section and subsection 118(5), the amount determined by the formula

$$A - B$$

where

A is the total of all amounts each of which is an amount (other than an amount that is otherwise a support amount) that became payable by a person in a taxation year, under an order of a competent tribunal or under a written agreement, in respect of an expense (other than an expenditure in respect of a self-contained domestic establishment in which the person resides or an expenditure for the acquisition of tangible property, or for civil law corporeal property, that is not an expenditure on account of a medical or education expense or in respect of the acquisition, improvement or maintenance of a self-contained domestic estab-

lishment in which the taxpayer described in paragraph (a) or (b) resides) incurred in the year or the preceding taxation year for the maintenance of a taxpayer, children in the taxpayer's custody or both the taxpayer and those children, if the taxpayer is

(a) the person's spouse or common-law partner or former spouse or common-law partner, or

(b) where the amount became payable under an order made by a competent tribunal in accordance with the laws of a province, an individual who is the parent of a child of whom the person is a legal parent,

and

B is the amount, if any, by which

(a) the total of all amounts each of which is an amount included in the total determined for A in respect of the acquisition or improvement of a self-contained domestic establishment in which the taxpayer resides, including any payment of principal or interest in respect of a loan made or indebtedness incurred to finance, in any manner whatever, such acquisition or improvement

exceeds

(b) the total of all amounts each of which is an amount equal to $1/_5$ of the original principal amount of a loan or indebtedness described in paragraph (a),

is, where the order or written agreement, as the case may be, provides that this subsection and subsection 60.1(2) shall apply to any amount paid or payable thereunder, deemed to be an amount payable to and receivable by the taxpayer as an allowance on a periodic basis, and the taxpayer is deemed to have discretion as to the use of that amount.

Related Provisions: 60.1(2) — Parallel rule for payer; 252(3) — Extended meaning of "spouse" and "former spouse".

Notes: See Notes to 60.1(2) for interpretation of 56.1(2).

56.1(2) amended by 2002-2013 technical bill (Part 4 — bijuralism) (effective June 26, 2013), 2005 and 2000 same-sex partners bills, 1996 Budget.

See also Notes at end of 56.1.

Income Tax Folios: S1-F3-C3: Support payments [replaces IT-530R].

(3) Prior payments — For the purposes of this section and section 56, where a written agreement or order of a competent tribunal made at any time in a taxation year provides that an amount received before that time and in the year or the preceding taxation year is to be considered to have been paid and received thereunder,

(a) the amount is deemed to have been received thereunder; and

(b) the agreement or order is deemed, except for the purpose of this subsection, to have been made on the day on which the first such amount was received, except that, where the agreement or order is made after April 1997 and varies a child support amount payable to the recipient from the last such amount received by the recipient before May 1997, each varied amount of child support received under the agreement or order is deemed to have been receivable under an agreement or order the commencement day of which is the day on which the first payment of the varied amount is required to be made.

Related Provisions: 60.1(3) — Parallel rule for payer.

Notes: For the parallel rule for the payor, see 60.1(3).

Without explicit recognition in the agreement that payments made before signing will be deductible/taxable [**D/T**], they are not: *Nagy*, 2003 TCC 282. Where lawyers exchanged correspondence but did not reach final agreement in time, prior-year payments were not D/T even if the recipient paid tax on them: *Tuck*, 2007 TCC 259; *Burton*, 2019 TCC 67. Where clauses citing the prior payments were struck from an agreement before the wife would sign, the prior payments were not D/T even though a clause accidentally remained saying they were: *Witzke*, 2008 TCC 596. The prior-payments rule cannot go back more than 1 year, even if CRA failed to advise the taxpayer of the deadline during an audit: *Connor*, 2009 TCC 319. Where agreement was reached in a 2014 settlement conference, confirmed by Court Order in 2015, payments in 2013 were D/T: *Ryan*, 2018 TCC 257. See also VIEWS docs 2006-0217701I7, 2012-0465511E5, 2014-0543931E5.

56.1(3) amended by 1996 Budget, for amounts received after 1996. The amended version has an unusual effect. If an agreement was entered into in, say, October 1997, it normally would be subject to the new non-deductibility/non-taxability treatment for the child support portion (see 56.1(4)"commencement day"). However, if prior payments began in, for example, August 1996, and the agreement provides that the prior payments are under the agreement (which normally will be done to ensure the spousal portion is deductible to the payer), and the amount of support is not varied, then 56.1(3) deems the agreement to be made in August 1996, and the child support becomes D/T! If the amount of support is varied, then a new agreement is deemed to be made, and the child support is not D/T.

Income Tax Folios: S1-F3-C3: Support payments [replaces IT-530R].

(4) Definitions — The definitions in this subsection apply in this section and section 56.

"child support amount" means any support amount that is not identified in the agreement or order under which it is receivable as being solely for the support of a recipient who is a spouse or common-law partner or former spouse or common-law partner of the payer or who is a parent of a child of whom the payer is a legal parent.

Related Provisions: 60.1(4) — Definition applies to sections 60 and 60.1; 252(3) — Extended meaning of "spouse" and "former spouse".

Notes: A child support (CS) amount payable under an agreement made or varied after April 1997 is generally non-taxable and non-deductible, while other (i.e., spousal) support is generally taxable to the recipient and deductible to the payer. See Notes to 56.1(4)"commencement day".

CS under a pre-April/97 agreement continues to be deductible/taxable after the child turns 18: *Boisvert*, 2008 TCC 323. CS due but not received is not taxed; there is no deduction for not receiving it: VIEWS doc 2012-0440761E5.

In *Berty*, 2013 TCC 202, an amount described as lump sum CS and spousal support (SS) was entirely CS due to this rule; and in *Elcich*, 2009 TCC 531, an order that did not allocate amounts between CS and SS was held to be all CS. In *Larivière*, 2015 TCC 287, amounts specified by Court order as being for the children were CS even when one of the children was living with the payor. *Contra*, despite the words "not identified ... as being solely ...", amounts (including car payments) not specifically identified as SS were treated as SS when they were clearly intended to be SS and a separate amount was identified as CS: *Krpan*, 2006 TCC 595. See also VIEWS doc 2011-0405131E5 (a formula can allow the CS vs. SS to be calculated).

Non-taxability of CS under a tax treaty does not mean that the Canadian resident *payer* can deduct CS payments: *Studer*, 2011 TCC 322.

Definition amended to change "natural parent" to "legal parent" by 2005 same-sex marriage bill, effective July 20, 2005. Amended by 2000 same-sex partners bill to refer to "common-law partner", effective as per Notes to 248(1)"common-law partner". Definition added by 1996 Budget, effective for amounts received after 1996.

"commencement day" at any time of an agreement or order means

    (a) where the agreement or order is made after April 1997, the day it is made; and

    (b) where the agreement or order is made before May 1997, the day, if any, that is after April 1997 and is the earliest of

        (i) the day specified as the commencement day of the agreement or order by the payer and recipient under the agreement or order in a joint election filed with the Minister in prescribed form and manner,

        (ii) where the agreement or order is varied after April 1997 to change the child support amounts payable to the recipient, the day on which the first payment of the varied amount is required to be made,

        (iii) where a subsequent agreement or order is made after April 1997, the effect of which is to change the total child support amounts payable to the recipient by the payer, the commencement day of the first such subsequent agreement or order, and

        (iv) the day specified in the agreement or order, or any variation thereof, as the commencement day of the agreement or order for the purposes of this Act.

Related Provisions: 60.1(4) — Definition applies to sections 60 and 60.1.

Notes: If there is a "commencement day" (CD) (May 1997 or later), then child support (CS) is non-taxable and non-deductible. Given that CS is usually only to age 18, this now applies to virtually all CS (for recent litigation on varying pre-1997 child support see *Colucci*, 2021 SCC 24). Spousal/partner support is deductible and taxable whether or not there is a CD. See 56(1)(b), 60(b), 56.1(4)"child support amount" and Notes to 56.1(4)"support amount".

The joint election under (b)(i) can be made retroactively, even in 2011 to apply back to 1997: *Burke*, 2012 TCC 378.

Even a minor change to a pre-May/97 agreement or order, such as a change in the date on which CS will terminate years later, may create a CD and thus put the agreement into the non-inclusion non-deduction system.

For FCA interpretation see *Rosenberg*, 2003 FCA 363 (change must be in writing to be valid); *Dangerfield*, 2003 FCA 480 (court order pronounced in April 1997 but signed in May was held made in April, but since it specifically indicated a May 1 CD for part of the order, May 1 was the date for that part); *Kennedy*, 2004 FCA 437 (judgment on same terms as pre-May/97 minutes of settlement, so no CD); *Callwood*, 2006 FCA 188 (post-1997 variations provided in pre-1997 agreement did not create CD); *Whelan*, 2006 FCA 384 (revised amount awarded by court did not change total amount for 2 children, so no CD); *Holbrook*, 2007 FCA 145 (where old and new agreement require same payment, new agreement may be continuation of the old; but final CS order terminates interim order and so creates CD); *Callwood*, 2008 FCA 120 (obligation in agreement to pay certain expenses did not qualify under 56.1, so its deletion did not vary the support amount); *Warbinek*, 2008 FCA 276 (for (b)(iii), later order establishes CD for separation agreement only if it coexists with it and changes the amount); *Chadwick*, 2013 FCA 181 (divorce judgment incorporated existing child-support agreement and was not intended to vary or replace it).

Where a court order is made before May 1997 but varied on appeal, the date of the varied order should be considered to be pre-May 1997: *Dennis v. Wilson*, [1999] 2 C.T.C. 175 (Ont CA).

A post-April/97 Court order not changing the amount of support per child, but eliminating an order for arrears and so reducing the amount payable, created a CD in *Rivard*, 2004 TCC 777.

If either taxpayer is resident in Quebec, an election under (b)(i) must be copied to Revenu Québec: *Taxation Act* ss. 312.3, 21.4.6.

For TCC cases finding a CD see: *Kovarik*, [2001] 2 C.T.C. 2503; *O'Neill*, [2001] 3 C.T.C. 2644; *McNeil*, 2003 TCC 326; *McCarthy*, 2003 TCC 507, *Clermont*, 2003 TCC 752; *Lamaadar*, 2003 TCC 793; *Nowlan*, 2003 TCC 803; *Colbert*, 2004 TCC 571; *Poirier*, 2004 TCC 632; *Coughlin*, 2004 TCC 524; *McGeachy*, 2005 TCC 145; *Beach*, [2005] 5 C.T.C. 2303; *White*, 2005 TCC 656; *Strug*, 2006 TCC 596 (agreement changed previous obligations); *Parr*, 2007 TCC 134; *Stals*, 2007 TCC 77 (FCA appeal dismissed for delay A-126-07) (May 16/97 court order based on April 22/97 hearing); *Clement*, 2007 TCC 296 (new agreement changed CS amount); *Wheatley*, 2007 TCC 330 (variation of agreement); *Neal*, 2007 TCC 349; *Gray*, 2007 TCC 104 (on replacement of replacement of order, newest order date applies); *Troyer*, 2007 TCC 439 (CS varied); *Pooran*, 2007 TCC 584 (cancellation of arrears had effect of changing CS amounts); *Salvino*, 2008 TCC 100 (payments were under second agreement); *Gale*, 2008 TCC 226 (FCA appeal dismissed for delay A-240-08) (March/97 order with May 1/07 start date); *Gill*, 2008 TCC 473 (payment was under settlement agreement reached in 2005); *Elcich*, 2009 TCC 531 (order in June/98 retroactive to Jan. 12/98, which was the CD); *Hungerson*, 2010 TCC 299 (order increasing payments was not simply cost-of-living increase); *Roy*, 2010 TCC 412 (payment of arrears under original agreement was made under post-1997 agreement); *Burke*, 2012 TCC 378 (2009 court order applied back to 1997); *Gerrard*, 2013 TCC 114 (new separation agreement in 2000 changed total CS amounts); *Masson*, 2013 TCC 277 (reduction in support amount was not apparently intended to result in non-deductibility, but it did).

For cases finding no CD see: *Lack*, 2003 TCC 230; *Miller*, 2003 TCC 603; *Tape*, 2006 TCC 217 (Dec/97 judgment was not intended to change earlier settlement); *Westlake*, 2006 TCC 442 (revised amount awarded by court was combination of previous CS and spousal support); *McLaughlan*, 2007 TCC 209 (amendments recorded in 1999 reflected change made in Jan/97); *Cormier*, 2007 TCC 88 (oral variation did not change agreement); *Butters*, 2008 TCC 205 (agreement never varied, even though payments made 10 years late); *Bonin*, 2008 TCC 164 (oral agreement for non-taxability did not create CD); *McNeely*, 2008 TCC 450 (FCA appeal dismissed for delay A-502-08) (filing order with Family Responsibility Office to enforce payment did not create CD); *Gardin*, 2009 TCC 262 (cost-of-living increases under pre-1997 order did not create CD); *Cira*, 2009 TCC 439 (April/97 order made to start May 1/97 had no CD); *Woods*, 2010 TCC 48 (FCA appeal dismissed A-112-10, reasons not published) (correspondence and cheques did not vary separation agreement); *Guest*, 2010 TCC 102 (Sask. 2007 court order merely enforced pre-1997 Maine order under *Inter-jurisdictional Support Order Act*); *Paquette*, 2010 TCC 163 (1995 court order was not amended despite application to amend it); *Adat*, 2012 FCA 97 (2006 order stated that 1996 order was "to continue"); *Rankowicz-Timms*, 2011 TCC 445 (extension of time to appeal denied 2012 FCA 32) (temporary reduction of support by 1999 interim agreement while husband was seeking job did not refer to tax and there was no evidence parties intended to change tax status of payments); *Dehart*, 2011 TCC 512 (post-1997 order to pay arrears plus costs and appearance fees did not vary the amount of support); *Kerr*, 2011 TCC 551 (later separation agreement not filed with Court, and not enforced by the Family Responsibility Office, did not oust 1996 Court order).

See also VIEWS docs 9829185, 2004-0083521E5, 2004-009001117, 2006-021842117, 2008-027857117 (new cost-of-living adjustment clause creates CD); 2008-0294511E5; 2010-0367391E5 (2009 court order confirms arrears owing under 1988 judgment so no CD), 2010-0381601E5, 2012-0461011M4 and 2019-082043117 (post-1997 order for payment of arrears of amounts under earlier order does not change their tax status); 2010-0390751E5 (court order dated May/97 that states it applies from March/97 has CD); 2011-0415881E5. See Corbin, "Themes on a Variation", 21(1) *Money & Family Law* (Carswell) *[MFL]* 1-7 (Jan. 2006); "Commencement Day in the Federal Court of Appeal", 22(2) 9-11 (Feb. 2007); "Income Tax and Retroactive Child Support", 22(11) 83 (Nov. 2007); "Extinguished Arrears of 'Grandfathered' Child Support", p. 83;

"More on Interim Orders", 22(12) 89-91 (Dec. 2007); "Shred of Evidence?", 23(1) 1-2 (Jan. 2008); "Laundering Support Payments?", pp. 2-5; "The 'Hop-Scotch' Gambit", 23(12) 89-91 (Dec. 2008) [based on *Warbinek*, reduced payments can be left deductible/taxable by excusing payor from some payments].

A variation of an agreement or order does not cause the new regime to apply until the "first payment of the varied amount" (para. (b)). See doc 2000-0005877; Corbin, "Indivisibility of 'Grandfathered' Child Support Payments?" 16(5) *MFL* 33-35 (May 2001).

Definition added by 1996 Budget, for amounts received after 1996.

"support amount" means an amount payable or receivable as an allowance on a periodic basis for the maintenance of the recipient, children of the recipient or both the recipient and children of the recipient, if the recipient has discretion as to the use of the amount, and

    (a) the recipient is the spouse or common-law partner or former spouse or common-law partner of the payer, the recipient and payer are living separate and apart because of the breakdown of their marriage or common-law partnership and the amount is receivable under an order of a competent tribunal or under a written agreement; or

    (b) the payer is a legal parent of a child of the recipient and the amount is receivable under an order made by a competent tribunal in accordance with the laws of a province.

Related Provisions: 60.1(4) — Definition applies to ss. 60 and 60.1; 118(5) — No personal credit in respect of person to whom support amount payable; 248(1)"exempt income" — Support amount is not exempt income; 252(3) — Extended meaning of "spouse" and "former spouse".

Notes: A "support amount" is generally taxable to the recipient and deductible to the payer, but the taxability and deductibility do not depend on what happens on the other side. See Notes to 56(1)(b).

The parties must be separated due to breakdown in the relationship; separation because one spouse cannot immigrate to Canada does not qualify: *VanGhent*, 2012 TCC 245.

A provincial court's order that amounts be or not be taxable/deductible does not make them so, as only the ITA governs: *Sigglekow*, [1981] C.T.C. 2830 (TCC); *Bates*, [1998] 4 C.T.C. 2743 (TCC); *Parr*, 2007 TCC 134; *Stals*, 2007 TCC 77 (FCA appeal dismissed for delay A-126-07); *Leduc*, 2007 TCC 367; *Bayliss [Baylis]*, 2007 TCC 387; *Salzmann*, 2008 TCC 527; *Laboret*, 2009 TCC 283; *Welch*, 2012 TCC 350; *McBride*, 2015 TCC 31. However, "it is surely imperative to give effect to the expressly articulated intentions of an Order made by a Superior Court Judge where a reasonable construction of the terms of the Order allows it": *Stephenson*, 2007 TCC 559, para. 8. A provincial superior court can declare that payments under an agreement are support: *LeBlanc v. Young*, 2011 BCSC 1520, and see Notes to 169(1) re rectification. The parties' intentions alone cannot change deductibility or taxability: *Daigneault*, 2008 TCC 602; *Masson*, 2013 TCC 277, paras. 20-22.

For an amount to qualify as support it must be: (a) payable on a periodic basis; (b) limited and predetermined; (c) paid to enable the recipient to discharge a certain type of expense, for the recipient's maintenance; and (d) completely at the disposal of the recipient: *Gagnon*, [1986] 1 C.T.C. 410 (SCC); Income Tax Folio S1-F3-C3 ¶3.10. An amount can be "limited and predetermined" even if the agreement does not specify the exact dollar amount payable: *Pach (Rosenberg)*, 2003 FCA 363. *McKimmon*, [1990] 1 C.T.C. 109 (FCA), sets out 8 factors to consider: (1) payments made at intervals of more than 1 year are not normally support; (2) the amount of the payments relative to the parties' income and living standards; (3) whether they bear interest before the due date; (4) whether the amounts can be prepaid; (5) whether they allow significant capital accumulation by the recipient; (6) whether they are to continue indefinitely or are for a fixed term; (7) whether the payments can be assigned and whether the obligation to pay survives death; (8) whether they release the payer from future obligation to pay support. The payments required need not be regular, but must be more than one: *Tossell (Peterson)*, 2005 FCA 223; *Leduc*, 2007 TCC 367; *Stephenson*, 2007 TCC 559. The agreement need not call the payments "support" for them to be support: *Kelly*, 2011 TCC 242. In *Maheu*, 2013 TCC 279, payments were periodic but were held to be compensation for property division ("partition of the family patrimony", in Quebec), not support, and so were not deductible/taxable. In *Dicks*, 2018 TCC 197, a $200/month "contribution to an investment of the wife's choice", required by the agreement after explicit termination of support, was not support.

Lump sum payments: see Income Tax Folio S1-F3-C3 ¶3.44-3.47, and *Negin v. Fryers*, 2018 ONSC 4486. Payments need not actually be made on a periodic basis as long as the court order or written agreement *requires* they be. Lump-sum arrears payments were deductible/taxable in: *Sills*, [1985] 1 C.T.C. 49 (FCA); *Ostrowski*, 2002 FCA 299; *Butters*, 2008 TCC 205; *Laboret*, 2009 TCC 283; *Stuart*, 2009 TCC 265; *McLaren*, 2009 TCC 514; *Beninger*, 2010 TCC 301 (although amount payable was reduced, it was still the support originally ordered); *Dehart*, 2011 TCC 512. (See also Notes to 6(1)(f) on *Tsiaprailis* and the *surrogatum* principle.) Payments were support rather than property settlement or interest in: *Miller*, 2007 TCC 217 (honouring the parties' intention); *Sebag*, 2006 FCA 312; *Blue*, 2015 TCC 304; *Ross*, 2018 TCC 215 (payments over 2 years were in Nov-Dec because R's income was seasonal; transfer of car permitted as a payment).

Lump-sum payments were not deductible or taxable in: *Veliotis*, [1974] C.T.C. 237 (FCTD); *Gill*, 2008 TCC 473 (payment settled all arrears and its character was altered); *Warner*, 2009 TCC 151 (FCA appeal discontinued A-149-09) (payment was not linked to pre-existing obligation to pay regular support); *Scott*, 2009 TCC 115 (payment was not a "catch-up" because amount payable was reduced, and it released payer from further obligation); *Boittiaux*, 2008 TCC 608; *McDonough*, 2009 TCC 413; *Bennett*, 2010 FCA 249 (leave to appeal denied 2011 CarswellNat 1111 (SCC)) (one-time $50,000 payment made in lieu of spousal support); *Hamel*, 2010 TCC 514 ($50,000 payment was costs, not support); *Lachabi*, 2010 TCC 529 (if payments were made, they were for past expenses, not support); *Hurst*, 2011 TCC 549 (payment was not linked to any pre-existing obligation to pay support); *Bergeron*, 2012 TCC 143 (payment in 3 instalments was capital payment to be free of future support obligations); *Berty*, 2013 TCC 202 (payment of half the taxpayer's annual employment bonus was not "periodic" since the bonus varied and was not guaranteed [this seems incorrect, in the author's view]. In *Lam*, 2012 TCC 54, payments were periodic but were disallowed because they were for the release of the *future* obligation to pay support. In *Patenaude*, 2004 TCC 7, the court order required only 1 payment, and the recipient's agreement to accept instalments did not change that, so they were not "periodic".

In *Kuszka*, 2011 TCC 578, a court ordered a lump sum payment in 2006 for 2000-05 arrears, and the taxpayer paid in 2006, claiming the deduction for 2005. His 2005 appeal was dismissed and the judge suggested CRA reopen 2006 so he could appeal it, but CRA refused so he was unable to.

Re lump-sum payments, see also VIEWS docs 2005-0139191E5, 2008-029125117, 2010-0356151E5, 2010-0358951E5, 2010-0367391E5, 2010-037556117, 2010-0376821E5, 2010-038918117, 2010-0391461E5, 2011-039587117, 2011-0407661E5, 2011-0415191E5, 2012-0452401R3, 2013-048320117, 2014-0520191E5, 2014-0528041E5, 2014-0530261E5, 2014-0545611E5, 2016-064367117; 2016-0669271E5 (retroactive support covering periods before written agreement signed: non-deductible).

Conversely, payments that were periodic and described as support were taxable even though they compensated for the wife giving up equalization rights and were intended to be non-taxable: *McBride*, 2015 TCC 31.

Court-ordered retroactive payments were held not to be a "support amount" in *Tossell (Peterson)*, 2005 FCA 223, but were in: *Bayliss [Baylis]*, 2007 TCC 387 (the Court order created both a past obligation and a breach of it); *Salzmann*, 2008 TCC 527; *James*, 2013 TCC 164 [for criticism see Freedman, "Case Comment", 32(4) *Money & Family Law* (Carswell) 25-26 (April 2017)].

Interest paid on late support payments does not qualify, as its purpose is not maintenance but to compensate the recipient for late payment: *Cavanagh*, 2013 FCA 94.

Support need not be specified in the agreement or order as a dollar amount, as long as it can be calculated. Cost of living (inflation) adjustments are routine. Support can be based on future bonus or incentive payments: VIEWS doc 2011-0405131E5. If the support order is varied on consent for a specified period, payments under the original order after the period expires will qualify: 2011-0415191E5. See also Notes to 56.1(4)"child support amount".

The requirement that recipient R have discretion over use of the funds is met even if there is a legal obligation to use child support for the child's benefit: *McNeely*, 2008 TCC 450, para. 14 (FCA appeal dismissed for delay A-502-08); *Crone*, 2008 TCC 567 (FCA appeal discontinued A-564-08); and even where R directed the provincial Maintenance Enforcement office to deposit the payments to the child's account: *Gardin*, 2009 TCC 262. It was also met where R was obligated to use some of the funds to pay expenses such as mortgage, property taxes and utilities: *Larivière*, 2013 TCC 88; *Doucette*, 2013 TCC 112; *Lemieux*, 2013 TCC 304 (discusses the case law on "discretion" in detail). Where M had assigned her child support arrears to the provincial Family Responsibility Office (because the province paid her when her ex-spouse did not), her ex-spouse's arrears payments were not taxable because they were no longer available for her to use: *McAllister*, 2007 TCC 708. A payment required to be made directly to an adult child does not qualify: *Larouche*, 2011 TCC 326. Where payments are made to third parties, see Notes to 60.1(1) and (2).

Even if a lump-sum payment of arrears is non-deductible, the portion that is interest is still taxable to the recipient under 12(1)(c): VIEWS doc 2011-0407661E5.

Some CRA officials reportedly insist that the payor obtain receipts from the recipient for the amounts paid. However, this requirement is not in the legislation and payment can be proven in other ways (e.g., cancelled cheques).

A child is not required to be in the care of the recipient for child support to be deductible: *Wilson*, 2008 TCC 247. See Notes to 56.1(4)"child support amount" and "commencement day".

Payment made by the recipient spouse drawing on a joint line of credit does not qualify in CRA's view: doc 2014-0543931E5. This may be incorrect, since it is no different than the payor spouse writing a cheque on the same line of credit.

The deduction was allowed when payments were secured by purchasing an annuity in the spouse's name: *Pouzar*, [2007] 5 C.T.C. 2513 (TCC). However, in *Thorlakson*, [2008] 2 C.T.C. 2383 (TCC), the deduction was denied where there was no Court order that the husband purchase the annuity. See Barry Corbin, "Distinction With a Difference?", 23(9) *Money & Family Law* (Carswell) 65-67 (Sept. 2008).

See Notes to 118.8 for the meaning of "living separate and apart".

The payments must be required by, and made in accordance with, a court order or written agreement, so *ex gratia* payments, or payments not clearly made for support, do not qualify: *Palonek*, 2010 TCC 615; *Hurst*, 2011 TCC 549. Severed pension as court-ordered equalization of net family assets did not qualify in *Yourkin*, 2003 TCC 948, 2006 TCC 178, 2008 TCC 686, 2011 TCC 557, 2014 TCC 48, 2016 TCC 111 (he kept trying for different years on the same issue). See also VIEWS doc 2015-0599561E5 (garnishment order insufficient to demonstrate spousal support). In *Sigglekow*, [1985] 2 C.T.C. 251 (FCTD), a court order saying support was $20 weekly, "payable tax free", may have meant each payment should be grossed up to net to $20 after tax, but payments of $20 were still made under the order (even if less than the full payments) and were taxable. (If the payments were not taxable as the Tax Review Board had held, they then complied with the order and so paradoxically were taxable! See Gwyneth McGregor, "Kitten Chasing its Tail", 529 *Tax Topics* (CCH) 12 (1982), where David Sherman raised this issue.)

A signed standard minutes-of-settlement form was a "written agreement" for this definition: *Thomson*, 2004 TCC 772. So was an unsigned "Summary of Mediation Agreements" in *Hovasse*, 2011 TCC 143. Lawyers' correspondence created an agreement in *Ojo*, 2010 TCC 244. In *Lefebvre*, 2006 TCC 305, L claimed she received support under an oral agreement, not under a later record of it; the TCC ruled payment was under the written agreement and was taxable. The agreement need not be one document, but "may be constructed from separate but connected writings; signed and unsigned documents may be read together; and oral testimony may be admitted to show the connection between the documents": *Shaw*, 2007 TCC 148. However, receipts and cancelled cheques alone are insufficient: *Fortune*, 2007 TCC 20. An agreement that was operating but not signed for several years was not an agreement until it was signed, so earlier payments were not deductible: *Witzke*, 2008 TCC 596 (see 56.1(3) and 60.1(3) for going back 1 year). In *Danial*, 2013 TCC 182, an oral agreement, possibly reflected by an unsigned memo in Urdu, was insufficient. CRA accepts an exchange of correspondence (possibly including email) if there was an intention to create an enforceable contract and the terms are clear: Folio S1-F3-C3 ¶3.30-3.31; VIEWS doc 2009-0349901E5. Payments outside the scope of the written agreement are not deductible even if the other spouse has included them in income: *Ellis*, 2009 TCC 353. An arbitration award is not an order of a "competent tribunal" but may be a written agreement: 2009-0320481E5. Reconciliation does not necessarily terminate a separation agreement: in *Broad*, 2010 FCA 146 (overruling *Randall*, 2006 TCC 549), when the parties re-separated, restarted payments under the original agreement were deductible [Corbin, "Reconciling Differences", 25(12) *Money & Family Law* (Carswell) 89-90 (Dec. 2010)].

In *Syrek*, 2009 FCA 53 (reversing the TCC), payments under an interim agreement qualified, despite a clause saying "execution of this agreement shall not be construed as any indication that Syrek is able or liable to pay spousal support in the amount set out herein, or at all". That clause was held to mean only that his spouse could not rely on the interim agreement in seeking the same support in a final agreement.

A maintenance agreement filed with the Alberta Director of Maintenance Enforcement, and then filed with the Alberta Court of Queen's Bench under the province's *Maintenance Enforcement Act*, was held to be an "order made by a competent tribunal in accordance with the laws of a province" for para. (b): *Fraser*, [2004] 3 C.T.C. 1 (FCA).

An interdependent support payment under the Alberta *Interdependent Relationships Act* will be a "support amount" if it meets the definition: VIEWS doc 2014-0525691E5.

Proving deductibility may be difficult if the agreement was signed many years earlier and cannot be found: see Barry Corbin, "File Away For Future Reference", 21(12) *Money & Family Law* (Carswell) 95-96 (Dec. 2006).

Where either ex-spouse dies and payments continue from or to the deceased's estate, the amounts are not taxable or deductible as support: VIEWS docs 2003-0183665, 2005-0133301E5, 2005-0142401E5; but payments from an estate may be taxable under 104(13): *Zlot*, [1996] 1 C.T.C. 2998 (TCC).

A payment from the ex-spouse's corporation may not meet the definition, and may also be a non-deductible, 15(1)-taxable shareholder benefit: VIEWS doc 2007-0226001E5.

See also CRA guide P102, Barry Corbin's other articles in *Money & Family Law* [*MFL*], and Notes to 56.1(4) "commencement day", for more on support. See also Hilary Laidlaw & Sandra Mah, "Trust After Marriage: Using a Trust to Satisfy Support Obligations", 58(1) *Canadian Tax Journal* 145-63 (2010); Karen Yull, "What Support is Needed for Support Payments to be Deductible?", 7(12) *Tax Hyperion* (Carswell, Dec. 2010); Lorne Wolfson, "Settlement Sweeteners", 27(11) *MFL* 85-88 (Nov. 2012); Andrew Bateman, "Marriage Breakdown", 62(4) *CTJ* 1109 at 1109-17 (2014); Ranot, "Income Tax Issues in Matrimonial Settlements" [4 parts], 33(8) *MFL* 58-60 (Aug. 2018), 33(9) 66-68 (Sept.), 33(10) 74-75 (Oct.) and 33(11) 83-84 (Nov. 2018).

See also 56.1(1) (deemed payment), (2) (payment to third parties), (3) (prior payments).

Definition amended by 2005 same-sex marriage bill (effective July 20, 2005), 2000 same-sex partners bill. Added by 1996 Budget, effective 1997, but not applicable to certain pre-1997 agreements or orders on pre-1993 marriage breakdowns (see these Notes up to PITA 59th ed., and Notes at end of 56.1).

Forms: P102: Support payments [guide]; T1157: Election for child support payments; T1158: Registration of family support payments.

Notes [s. 56.1]: 56.1 amended by 1992 technical bill, for decrees, orders and judgments made after 1992 and agreements entered into after 1992, except where the marriage breakdown occurred before 1993 (this exception added by 1993 technical bill, s. 134). The changes were not substantive: they reflect the new definition of "spouse" in 252(4), the consolidation of 56(1)(b) and (c) into 56(1)(b) and the renumbering of 56(1)(c.1) as 56(1)(c). The descriptive formula in 56.1(2) was also redrafted in alge-

braic form. For decrees, orders and judgments made, and agreements entered into, before 1993, or where the marriage breakdown occurred before 1993, read:

56.1 (1) Maintenance — Where, after May 6, 1974, a decree, order, judgment or written agreement described in paragraph 56(1)(b), (c) or (c.1), or any variation thereof, has been made providing for the periodic payment of an amount

(a) to a taxpayer by a person who is

(i) the taxpayer's spouse or former spouse, or

(ii) where the amount is paid pursuant to an order made by a competent tribunal after February 10, 1988 in accordance with the laws of a province, an individual of the opposite sex who

(A) before the date of the order cohabited with the taxpayer in a conjugal relationship, or

(B) is the natural parent of a child of the taxpayer, or

(b) for the benefit of the taxpayer, children in the custody of the taxpayer or both the taxpayer and those children,

the amount or any part thereof, when paid, shall be deemed, for the purposes of paragraphs 56(1)(b), (c) and (c.1), to have been paid to and received by the taxpayer.

(2) Agreement — For the purposes of paragraphs 56(1)(b), (c) and (c.1), the amount, if any, by which

(a) the total of all amounts each of which is an amount (other than an amount to which paragraph 56(1)(b), (c) or (c.1) otherwise applies) paid by a person in a taxation year, pursuant to a decree, order or judgment of a competent tribunal or pursuant to a written agreement, in respect of an expense (other than an expenditure in respect of a self-contained domestic establishment in which the person resides or an expenditure for the acquisition of tangible property that is not an expenditure on account of a medical or educational expense or in respect of the acquisition, improvement or maintenance of a self-contained domestic establishment in which the taxpayer described in subparagraph (i) or (ii) resides) incurred in the year or the immediately preceding taxation year for maintenance of a taxpayer who is

(i) that person's spouse or former spouse, or

(ii) where the amount is paid pursuant to an order made by a competent tribunal after February 10, 1988 in accordance with the laws of a province, an individual of the opposite sex who

(A) before the date of the order cohabited with the person in a conjugal relationship, or

(B) is the natural parent of a child of the person,

or for the maintenance of children in the taxpayer's custody or both the taxpayer and those children if, at the time the expense was incurred and throughout the remainder of the year, the taxpayer was living apart from that person

exceeds

(b) the amount, if any, by which

(i) the total of all amounts each of which is an amount included in the aggregate determined under paragraph (a) in respect of the acquisition or improvement of a self-contained domestic establishment in which the taxpayer resides, including any payment of principal or interest in respect of a loan made or indebtedness incurred to finance, in any manner whatever, such acquisition or improvement

exceeds

(ii) the total of all amounts each of which is an amount equal to $\frac{1}{5}$ of the original principal amount of a loan or indebtedness described in subparagraph (i)

shall, where the decree, order, judgment or written agreement, as the case may be, provides that this subsection and subsection 60.1(2) shall apply to any payment made pursuant thereto, be deemed to be an amount paid by that person and received by the taxpayer as an allowance payable on a periodic basis.

(3) Prior payments — For the purposes of this section and section 56, where a decree, order or judgment of a competent tribunal or a written agreement made at any time in a taxation year provides that an amount received before that time and in the year or the immediately preceding taxation year is to be considered as having been paid and received pursuant thereto, the following rules apply:

(a) the amount shall be deemed to have been received pursuant thereto; and

(b) the person who made the payment shall be deemed to have been separated pursuant to a divorce, judicial separation or written separation agreement from that person's spouse or former spouse at the time the payment was made and throughout the remainder of the year.

56.1(1) amended by 1988 tax reform, except that for orders made after May 6, 1974 under the laws of Ontario, read "May 6, 1974" in place of "February 10, 1988" in 56.1(1)(a)(ii).

See also Notes to 56(1)(b) and 60.1(2).

Definitions [s. 56.1]: "amount" — 248(1); "child" — 252(1); "child support amount", "commencement day" — 56.1(4); "common-law partner", "common-law partnership" — 248(1); "corporation" — 248(1), *Interpretation Act* 35(1); "corporeal property" — Quebec *Civil Code* art. 899, 906; "employee benefit plan" — 248(1); "former spouse" — 252(3); "individual" — 248(1); "Minister" — 248(1); "parent" — 252(2)(a); "person", "prescribed", "principal amount", "property" — 248(1); "province" — *Interpretation Act* 35(1); "received" — 248(7); "self-contained domestic establishment", "share" — 248(1); "spouse" — 252(3); "superannuation or pension benefit" — 248(1); "support amount" — 56.1(4); "taxation year" — 249; "taxpayer" — 248(1); "written" — *Interpretation Act* 35(1) [writing].

56.2 Reserve claimed for debt forgiveness — There shall be included in computing an individual's income for a taxation year during which the individual was not a bankrupt the amount, if any, deducted under section 61.2 in computing the individual's income for the preceding taxation year.

Notes: 56.2 added by 1994 technical bill, effective for taxation years that end after February 21, 1994. See Notes to 61.2.

Definitions [s. 56.2]: "amount", "bankrupt", "individual" — 248(1); "taxation year" — 249.

56.3 Reserve claimed for debt forgiveness — There shall be included in computing a taxpayer's income for a taxation year during which the taxpayer was not a bankrupt the amount, if any, deducted under section 61.4 in computing the taxpayer's income for the preceding taxation year.

Related Provisions: 61.4(a)B(ii) — Effect on reserve for subsequent year; 87(2)(g) — Amalgamations — carryover of reserve; 115(1)(a)(iii.21) — Non-resident's taxable income earned in Canada.

Notes: 56.3 added by 1994 technical bill, effective for taxation years that end after February 21, 1994. See Notes to 61.4.

Definitions [s. 56.3]: "amount", "bankrupt" — 248(1); "taxation year" — 249; "taxpayer" — 248(1).

56.4 Restrictive covenants [Non-competition agreements] — (1) Definitions — The following definitions apply in this section.

Notes: See Notes at end of 56.4.

"eligible corporation", of a taxpayer, means a taxable Canadian corporation of which the taxpayer holds, directly or indirectly, shares of the capital stock.

"eligible individual", in respect of a vendor, at any time means an individual (other than a trust) who is related to the vendor and who has attained the age of 18 years at or before that time.

Notes: This was "eligible person" in the July 16/10 draft.

"eligible interest", of a taxpayer, means capital property of the taxpayer that is

(a) a partnership interest in a partnership that carries on a business;

(b) a share of the capital stock of a corporation that carries on a business; or

(c) a share of the capital stock of a corporation 90% or more of the fair market value of which is attributable to eligible interests in one other corporation.

Related Provisions: 56.4(4)(c) — Cost to purchaser of eligible interest.

Notes: (The definition "eligible person" in the July 16/10 draft has been changed to "eligible individual".)

"goodwill amount", of a taxpayer, is an amount the taxpayer has or may become entitled to receive that would, if this Act were read without reference to this section, be required to be included in the proceeds of disposition of a property included in Class 14.1 of Schedule II to the *Income Tax Regulations*, or is an amount to which subsection 13(38) applies, in respect of a business carried on by the taxpayer through a permanent establishment located in Canada.

Related Provisions: 56.4(7), (8) — Allocation of goodwill amount.

Notes: Definition amended by 2016 budget bill #2, effective 2017, as part of changing eligible capital property rules to CCA Class 14.1 (see Notes to 20(1)(b)). Before 2017, read:

"goodwill amount", of a taxpayer, is an amount the taxpayer has or may become entitled to receive that is required by the description of E in the definition "cumulative eligible capital" in subsection 14(5) to be included in computing the cumulative eligible capital of a business carried on by the taxpayer through a permanent establishment located in Canada.

"permanent establishment" means a permanent establishment as defined for the purpose of subsection 16.1(1).

Regulations: 8201 (meaning of permanent establishment).

"restrictive covenant", of a taxpayer, means an agreement entered into, an undertaking made, or a waiver of an advantage or right by the taxpayer, whether legally enforceable or not, that affects, or is intended to affect, in any way whatever, the acquisition or provision of property or services by the taxpayer or by another taxpayer that does not deal at arm's length with the taxpayer, other than an agreement or undertaking

(a) that disposes of the taxpayer's property; or

(b) that is in satisfaction of an obligation described in section 49.1 that is not a disposition except where the obligation being satisfied is in respect of a right to property or services that the taxpayer acquired for less than its fair market value.

Related Provisions: 68(c) — Allocation of amount to restrictive covenant must be reasonable.

Notes: This covers a non-competition agreement, and thus overrules *Manrell*, 2003 FCA 128. See Notes to 56.4(2).

See Notes at end of 56.4 for in-force rules; but for a restrictive covenant granted by a taxpayer before Nov. 9, 2006, read para. (b) as simply "that is in satisfaction of an obligation described in section 49.1 that is not a disposition".

"taxpayer" includes a partnership.

(2) Income — restrictive covenants [including non-competition agreements] — There is to be included in computing a taxpayer's income for a taxation year the total of all amounts each of which is an amount in respect of a restrictive covenant of the taxpayer that is received or receivable in the taxation year by the taxpayer or by a taxpayer with whom the taxpayer does not deal at arm's length (other than an amount that has been included in computing the taxpayer's income because of this subsection for a preceding taxation year or in the taxpayer's eligible corporation's income because of this subsection for the taxation year or a preceding taxation year).

Related Provisions: 6(3), (3.1) — Employment income inclusion from restrictive covenant; 12(1)(x)(v.1) — No income inclusion under 12(1)(x); 14(5.1) [before 2017] — Cumulative eligible capital — exclusion from calculation; 56.4(3) — Exceptions; 56.4(11) — Other person who receives the amount is not taxed on it; 60(f) — Deduction for bad debt; 68(c) — Allocation of amount to restrictive covenant must be reasonable; 212(1)(i), (13)(g) — Non-resident withholding tax.

Notes: 56.4(2) overrides *Manrell*, 2003 FCA 128, where entering into a non-competition agreement (NCA) was held not to be disposition of property (so the amount received was non-taxable). However, the definition 56.4(1)"restrictive covenant" (**RC**) is broad and covers more than NCAs.

In *Pangaea One*, 2020 FCA 21, non-resident shareholder X's shareholder-agreement right to veto a share sale was a RC, so 212(1)(i) applied to a payment to X to execute a sale agreement [Sherman & Kimiagar, "A Continental Divide", XXIII(2) *Corporate Finance* (Federated Press) 2-6 (2020)]. 56.4 is not limited to NCAs: paras. 11-16. In light of *Pangaea*, the CBA/CPA Canada Joint Committee wrote to Finance (Aug. 10, 2020) that 212(1) should exempt commitment fees, standby charges, consent fees and restructuring payments to lenders.

Pre-56.4, see also *RCI Environnement*, 2008 FCA 419 (leave to appeal denied 2009 CarswellNat 1832 (SCC)) (disposition of NCA right led to income inclusion under 14(1)); *Robert Glegg Investments*, 2008 FCA 332 (Court ruled no amount was paid for NCA since documentation did not support claim, so entire amount paid was proceeds of disposition of shares); *Wagner*, 2013 FCA 11 (NCA was valid and not a sham, but amount paid for it was zero because it had no value and entire value was attributable to proceeds of disposition of shares).

56.4 applies only to a RC granted by taxpayer T. An assignment of T's NCA (on sale of the business) is not subject to 56.4 or to *Manrell*, and is a sale of "property", since it is a right to compensation if X competes with the business (not a "right shared with everyone" per *Manrell*).

56.4 changed significantly from pre-2012 drafts. For discussion of the final version see Woltersdorf, "Restrictive Covenants", 2132 *Tax Topics [TT]* (CCH) 1-5 (Jan. 17, 2013) and 2135 1-7 (Feb. 7, 2013); Arkin, "Restrictive Covenants", 2013 Atlantic Provinces Tax Conf. 7B:1-17; Peters & Al-Shikarchy, "Restrictive Covenants and the Assumption of Liabilities in Purchase and Sale Transactions", 2013 Ontario Tax Conf. 6:1-48; Coburn, "Practical Strategies for Dealing with the Restrictive Covenant Provisions",

2014 Cdn Tax Foundation conference report, 8:1-29; Fenton, "The Taxation of Restrictive Covenants", 2570 *TT* 1-3 (June 8, 2021).

For planning see Keung & Mohamed, "Restrictive Covenants for Departing Executives", 24(4) *Taxation of Executive Compensation & Retirement* (Federated Press) 1604-08 (Nov. 2012); Ling & Wright, "Restrictive Covenants: Some Reminders", 7(1) *Canadian Tax Focus [CTFo]* (ctf.ca) 7 (Feb. 2017); Miazga, "Structuring a CCPC Shareholder's Exit with a Non-Compete", 7(3) *CTFo* 9-10 (Aug. 2017).

For CRA interpretation see VIEWS docs 2010-0373351C6 (CRA will not publish guidance on valuing a RC); 2013-0495691C6 [APFF q.19] (comments on 56.4(3) and (7)); 2014-053963117 (Canada-Luxembourg treaty does not reduce non-resident withholding tax on RC); 2015-0618601E5 (supplier loyalty inducement falls under 56.4(2)); 2017-070129117 (lump sum to non-resident for granting exclusive right to distribute product in Canada is RC, but no 212(1)(i) tax due to treaty Art. 7 [Wen, "Restrictive Covenant and Withholding Tax", 18(1) *Tax for the Owner-Manager* (ctf.ca) 10-11 (July 2018)]).

(3) Non-application of subsec. (2) — Subsection (2) does not apply to an amount received or receivable by a particular taxpayer in a taxation year in respect of a restrictive covenant granted by the particular taxpayer to another taxpayer (referred to in this subsection and subsection (4) as the "purchaser") with whom the particular taxpayer deals at arm's length (determined without reference to paragraph 251(5)(b)), if

(a) section 5 or 6 applied to include the amount in computing the particular taxpayer's income for the taxation year or would have so applied if the amount had been received in the taxation year;

(b) the amount would, if this Act were read without reference to this section, be required to be included in the proceeds of disposition of a property included in Class 14.1 of Schedule II to the *Income Tax Regulations*, or is an amount to which subsection 13(38) applies, in respect of the business to which the restrictive covenant relates, and the particular taxpayer elects (or if the amount is payable by the purchaser in respect of a business carried on in Canada by the purchaser, the particular taxpayer and the purchaser jointly elect) in prescribed form to apply this paragraph in respect of the amount; or

(c) subject to subsection (9), the amount directly relates to the particular taxpayer's disposition of property that is, at the time of the disposition, an eligible interest in the partnership or corporation that carries on the business to which the restrictive covenant relates, or that is at that time an eligible interest by virtue of paragraph (c) of the definition "eligible interest" in subsection (1) where the other corporation referred to in that paragraph carries on the business to which the restrictive covenant relates, and

(i) the disposition is to the purchaser (or to a person related to the purchaser),

(ii) the amount is consideration for an undertaking by the particular taxpayer not to provide, directly or indirectly, property or services in competition with the property or services provided or to be provided by the purchaser (or by a person related to the purchaser),

(iii) the restrictive covenant may reasonably be considered to have been granted to maintain or preserve the value of the eligible interest disposed of to the purchaser;

(iv) if the restrictive covenant is granted on or after July 18, 2005, subsection 84(3) does not apply to the disposition,

(v) the amount is added to the particular taxpayer's proceeds of disposition, as defined by section 54, for the purpose of applying this Act to the disposition of the particular taxpayer's eligible interest, and

(vi) the particular taxpayer and the purchaser elect in prescribed form to apply this paragraph in respect of the amount.

Related Provisions: 6(3), (3.1) — Employment income inclusion from restrictive covenant; 56.4(4) — Treatment of purchaser; 56.4(9) — Para. (c) does not apply to employment or business income; 56.4(13) — Filing of prescribed form for paras. (b) and (c); 220(3.2), Reg. 600(c) — Late filing or revocation of election under 56.4(3)(c); 257 — Formula cannot calculate to less than zero.

Notes: Relief under 56.4(3)(c) is lost if either the purchaser or the vendor files their tax return (with the election) even one day late (see 56.4(13)). However, an extension of time under 220(3) can extend the "filing-due date" (248(1)) and fix this problem.

For the meaning of "indirectly" in (c)(ii), see Notes to 17.1(1).

For a taxpayer filing a Quebec return, a 56.4(3)(b) or (c)(vi) election must be copied to Revenu Québec: *Taxation Act* ss. 333.6, 21.4.6.

56.4(3)(b) amended by 2016 budget bill #2, effective 2017, as part of changing eligible capital property rules to CCA Class 14.1 (see Notes to 20(1)(b)). Before 2017, read:

> (b) the amount would, if this Act were read without reference to this section, be required by the description of E in the definition "cumulative eligible capital" in subsection 14(5) to be included in computing the particular taxpayer's cumulative eligible capital in respect of the business to which the restrictive covenant relates, and the particular taxpayer elects (or if the amount is payable by the purchaser in respect of a business carried on in Canada by the purchaser, the particular taxpayer and the purchaser jointly elect) in prescribed form to apply this paragraph in respect of the amount; or

For a restrictive covenant granted by a taxpayer before Nov. 9, 2006, if the taxpayer elected by Dec. 23, 2013 by filing with the Minister an election in writing that para. 195(3)(b) of S.C. 2013, c. 34 [2002-2013 technical bill] apply, read 56.4(3)(c) in respect of the restrictive covenant as:

> (c) the amount directly relates to the particular taxpayer's disposition of property that is, at the time of the disposition, an eligible interest in the partnership or corporation that carries on the business to which the restrictive covenant relates, or that is at that time an eligible interest by virtue of paragraph (c) of the definition "eligible interest" where the other corporation referred to in that paragraph carries on the business to which the restrictive covenant relates, and
>
> (i) the disposition is to the purchaser (or to a person related to the purchaser),
>
> (ii) the amount is consideration for an undertaking by the particular taxpayer not to provide, directly or indirectly, property or services in competition with the property or services provided or to be provided by the purchaser (or by a person related to the purchaser),
>
> (iii) the amount does not exceed the amount determined by the formula
>
> $$A - B$$
>
> where
>
> A　is the amount that would be the fair market value of the particular taxpayer's eligible interest that is disposed of if all restrictive covenants that may reasonably be considered to relate to a disposition of an interest, or for civil law purposes a right, in the business by any taxpayer were provided for no consideration, and
>
> B　is the amount that would be the fair market value of the particular taxpayer's eligible interest that is disposed of if no covenant were granted by any taxpayer that held an interest, or for civil law purposes a right, in the business,
>
> (iv) if the restrictive covenant is granted on or after July 18, 2005, subsection 84(3) does not apply to the disposition,
>
> (v) the amount is added to the particular taxpayer's proceeds of disposition, as defined by section 54, for the purpose of applying this Act to the disposition of the particular taxpayer's eligible interest, and
>
> (vi) the particular taxpayer and the purchaser elect in prescribed form to apply this paragraph in respect of the amount.

(4) Treatment of purchaser — An amount paid or payable by a purchaser for a restrictive covenant is

(a) if the amount is required because of section 5 or 6 to be included in computing the income of an employee of the purchaser, to be considered to be wages paid or payable by the purchaser to the employee;

(b) if an election has been made under paragraph (3)(b) in respect of the amount, to be considered to be incurred by the purchaser on account of capital for the purpose of determining the cost of the property or for the purposes of subsection 13(35), as the case may be, and not to be an amount paid or payable for all other purposes of the Act; and

(c) if an election has been made under paragraph (3)(c), in respect of the amount and the amount relates to the purchaser's acquisition of property that is, immediately after the acquisition, an eligible interest of the purchaser, to be included in computing the cost to the purchaser of that eligible interest and considered not to be an amount paid or payable for all other purposes of the Act.

Related Provisions: 153(1)(a) — Tax to be withheld at source.

Notes: If an amount is deemed to be wages by 56.4(4)(a), the purchaser must withhold tax at source (153(1)(a)) and provide a T4 (Reg. 200).

56.4(4)(b) amended by 2016 budget bill #2, effective 2017, as part of changing eligible capital property rules to CCA Class 14.1 (see Notes to 20(1)(b)). Before 2017, read:

> (b) if an election has been made under paragraph (3)(b) in respect of the amount, to be considered to be incurred by the purchaser on account of capital for the

purpose of applying the definition "eligible capital expenditure" in subsection 14(5) and not to be an amount paid or payable for all other purposes of the Act; and

(5) Non-application of s. 68 — If this subsection applies to a restrictive covenant granted by a taxpayer, section 68 does not apply to deem consideration to be received or receivable by the taxpayer for the restrictive covenant.

Related Provisions: 56.4(6)–(8), (10) — Conditions for 56.4(5) to apply; 56.4(12) — Effect of 56.4(5) applying.

(6) Application of subsec. (5) — if employee provides covenant — Subsection (5) applies to a restrictive covenant if

(a) the restrictive covenant is granted by an individual to another taxpayer with whom the individual deals at arm's length (referred to in this subsection as the "purchaser");

(b) the restrictive covenant directly relates to the acquisition from one or more other persons (in this subsection and subsection (12) referred to as the "vendors") by the purchaser of an interest, or for civil law purposes a right, in the individual's employer, in a corporation related to that employer or in a business carried on by that employer;

(c) the individual deals at arm's length with the employer and with the vendors;

(d) the restrictive covenant is an undertaking by the individual not to provide, directly or indirectly, property or services in competition with property or services provided or to be provided by the purchaser (or by a person related to the purchaser) in the course of carrying on the business to which the restrictive covenant relates;

(e) no proceeds are received or receivable by the individual for granting the restrictive covenant; and

(f) the amount that can reasonably be regarded to be consideration for the restrictive covenant is received or receivable only by the vendors.

Related Provisions: 56.4(12)(a) — Effect of para. (f) applying.

Notes: CRA had said that "no proceeds" in para. (e) is not met if the agreement provides for even nominal consideration: VIEWS doc 2014-0522961C6 [2014 STEP q.15; Kakkar, "More Problems with Restrictive Covenants", 14(4) *Tax for the Owner-Manager* (ctf.ca) 8 (Oct. 2014)]. At the 2014 Cdn Tax Foundation conference q.3 [2014-0547251C6; conf. report p. 4:5], CRA changed its position, but only if the consideration is limited to $1. See also Notes to 69(1) on transfer vs gift.

For the meaning of "indirectly" in para. (d), see Notes to 17.1(1).

(7) Application of subsec. (5) — realization of goodwill amount and disposition of property — Subject to subsection (10), subsection (5) applies to a restrictive covenant granted by a taxpayer if

(a) the restrictive covenant is granted by the taxpayer (in this subsection and subsection (8) referred to as the "vendor") to

(i) another taxpayer (in this subsection referred to as the "purchaser") with whom the vendor deals at arm's length (determined without reference to paragraph 251(5)(b)) at the time of the grant of the restrictive covenant, or

(ii) another person who is an eligible individual in respect of the vendor at the time of the grant of the restrictive covenant;

(b) where subparagraph (a)(i) applies, the restrictive covenant is an undertaking of the vendor not to provide, directly or indirectly, property or services in competition with the property or services provided or to be provided by the purchaser (or by a person related to the purchaser) in the course of carrying on the business to which the restrictive covenant relates, and

(i) the amount that can reasonably be regarded as being consideration for the restrictive covenant is

(A) included by the vendor in computing a goodwill amount of the vendor, or

(B) received or receivable by a corporation that was an eligible corporation of the vendor when the restrictive

covenant was granted and included by the eligible corporation in computing a goodwill amount of the eligible corporation in respect of the business to which the restrictive covenant relates, or

(ii) it is reasonable to conclude that the restrictive covenant is integral to an agreement in writing,

(A) under which the vendor or the vendor's eligible corporation disposes of property (other than property described in clause (B) or subparagraph (i)) to the purchaser, or the purchaser's eligible corporation, for consideration that is received or receivable by the vendor, or the vendor's eligible corporation, as the case may be, or

(B) under which shares of the capital stock of a corporation (in this subsection and subsection (12) referred to as the "target corporation") are disposed of to the purchaser or to another person that is related to the purchaser and with whom the vendor deals at arm's length (determined without reference to paragraph 251(5)(b)),

(c) where subparagraph (a)(ii) applies, the restrictive covenant is an undertaking of the vendor not to provide, directly or indirectly, property or services in competition with the property or services provided or to be provided by the eligible individual (or by an eligible corporation of the eligible individual) in the course of carrying on the business to which the restrictive covenant relates, and

(i) either

(A) the amount that can reasonably be regarded as being consideration for the restrictive covenant is

(I) included by the vendor in computing a goodwill amount of the vendor, or

(II) received or receivable by a corporation that was an eligible corporation of the vendor when the restrictive covenant was granted and included by the eligible corporation in computing a goodwill amount of the eligible corporation in respect of the business to which the restrictive covenant relates, or

(B) it is reasonable to conclude that the restrictive covenant is integral to an agreement in writing

(I) under which the vendor or the vendor's eligible corporation disposes of property (other than property described in subclause (II) or clause (A)) to the eligible individual, or the eligible individual's corporation, for consideration that is received or receivable by the vendor, or the vendor's eligible corporation, as the case may be, or

(II) under which shares of the capital stock of the vendor's eligible corporation (in this subsection and subsection (12) referred to as the "family corporation") are disposed of to the eligible individual or the eligible individual's eligible corporation,

(ii) the vendor is resident in Canada at the time of the grant of the restrictive covenant and the disposition referred to in clause (i)(B), and

(iii) the vendor does not, at any time after the grant of the restrictive covenant and whether directly or indirectly in any manner whatever, have an interest, or for civil law a right, in the family corporation or in the eligible corporation of the eligible individual, as the case may be;

(d) no proceeds are received or receivable by the vendor for granting the restrictive covenant;

(e) subsection 84(3) does not apply in respect of the disposition of a share of the target corporation or family corporation, as the case may be;

(f) the restrictive covenant can reasonably be regarded to have been granted to maintain or preserve the fair market value of any of

(i) the benefit of the expenditure derived from the goodwill amount referred to in subparagraph (b)(i) or clause (c)(i)(A) and for which a joint election referred to in paragraph (g) was made,

(ii) the property referred to in clause (b)(ii)(A) or subclause (c)(i)(B)(I), or

(iii) the shares referred to in clause (b)(ii)(B) or subclause (c)(i)(B)(II); and

(g) a joint election in prescribed form to apply subsection (5) to the amount referred to in subparagraph (b)(i) or clause (c)(i)(A), if otherwise applicable, is made by

(i) in the case of subparagraph (b)(i), the vendor, or the vendor's eligible corporation, if it is required to include the goodwill amount in computing its income, and the purchaser, or the purchaser's eligible corporation, if it incurs the expenditure that is the goodwill amount to the vendor or the vendor's eligible corporation, as the case may be, or

(ii) in the case of clause (c)(i)(A), the vendor, or the vendor's eligible corporation, if it is required to include the goodwill amount in computing its income, and the eligible individual, or the eligible individual's eligible corporation, if it incurs the expenditure that is the goodwill amount to the vendor or the vendor's eligible corporation, as the case may be.

Related Provisions: 56.4(8), (10) — Application of subsec. (7); 56.4(13)(b) — Effect of (7)(b)(ii)(B) or (7)(c)(i)(B)(II) applying; 56.4(13) — Filing of prescribed form.

Notes: 56.4(7) and (8) replace (7), (8), (8.1) and (9) of the July 16/10 draft and were substantially rewritten. 56.4(7) revises rules introduced as 56.4(8.1) in the July16/10 draft, allowing succession planning by permitting a disposition to a related person, subject to certain conditions. For comment on former 56.4(8.1) see Fuller & Dolson, "The Amended Restricted (sic) Covenant Rules", 10(4) *Tax for the Owner-Manager* (ctf.ca) 13-14 (Oct. 2010).

See also Manu Kakkar, "Paragraph 56.4(7) and Holdco Sales", 14(1) *Tax for the Owner-Manager* (ctf.ca) 5 (Jan. 2014) and "Paragraph 56.4(7b) Related-Person Problem and Arm's-Length Minority Acquisitions", 14(2) 8-9 (April 2014).

For the meaning of "indirectly" in (b) and (c), see Notes to 17.1(1).

CRA considers that "no proceeds" in para. (d) is not met if the agreement provides for more than $1 nominal consideration: see Notes to 56.4(6).

For the meaning of "derived" in 56.4(7)(f)(i), see Notes to 18.1(12).

For a taxpayer filing a Quebec return, a para. (g) election must be copied to Revenu Québec: *Taxation Act* ss. 333.9, 21.4.6.

56.4(7) was considered to apply in VIEWS doc 2017-0688301I7 (non-solicitation clause was equivalent to non-compete) [Campbell, "CRA Releases Practical View on Restrictive Covenants", 15(1) *Tax Hyperion* (Carswell) 5-7 (Jan-Feb 2018)].

56.4(7) amended by 2017 budget bill #2, for restrictive covenants granted after Sept. 15, 2016, to add reference to subpara. (i) in (b)(ii)(A) and to cl. (A) in (c)(i)(B)(I), and to add commas before "if it is required" in both (g)(i) and (g)(ii).

See Notes at end of 56.4 for in-force rules; but for a restrictive covenant granted before July 17, 2010, read 56.4(7)(d) as:

(d) for the purpose of applying subparagraph (7)(b)(i) and paragraph (7)(c), no proceeds are received or receivable by the vendor for granting the restrictive covenant;

and for a restrictive covenant granted before Oct. 25, 2012, ignore 56.4(7)(g) and read 56.4(7)(f)(i) as:

(i) the benefit of the expenditure made by the taxpayer derived from the goodwill amount referred to in subparagraph (b)(i) or clause (c)(i)(A),

(8) Application of subsec. (7) and s. 69 — special rules — For the purpose

(a) of applying subsection (7), clause (7)(b)(ii)(A) and subclause (7)(c)(i)(B)(I) apply to a grant of a restrictive covenant only if

(i) the consideration that can reasonably be regarded as being in part the consideration for the restrictive covenant is received or receivable by the vendor or the vendor's eligible corporation, as the case may be, as consideration for the disposition of the property, and

(ii) if all or a part of the consideration can reasonably be regarded as being for a goodwill amount, subsection (2), para-

graph (3)(b), subparagraph (7)(b)(i) or clause (7)(c)(i)(A) applies to that consideration; and

(b) of determining if the conditions described in paragraph (7)(c) have been met, and for the purpose of applying section 69, in respect of a restrictive covenant granted by a vendor, the fair market value of a property is the amount that can reasonably be regarded as being the fair market value of the property if the restrictive covenant were part of the property.

Notes: See Notes to 56.4(7). See Notes at end of 56.4 for in-force rules; but for a restrictive covenant granted before July 17, 2010, read 56.4(8)(a) as:

(a) of applying subsection (7), clause (7)(b)(ii)(A) and subclause (7)(c)(i)(B)(I) do not apply to a grant of a restrictive covenant unless the consideration, that can reasonably be regarded as being in part the consideration for the restrictive covenant, is received or receivable by the vendor or the vendor's eligible corporation, as the case may be, as consideration for the disposition of the property;

(9) Anti-avoidance rule — non-application of para. (3)(c) — Paragraph (3)(c) does not apply to an amount that would, if this Act were read without reference to subsections (2) to (14), be included in computing a taxpayer's income from a source that is an office or employment or a business or property under paragraph 3(a).

Notes: This was 56.4(10) in the July 16/10 draft, and was not in the July 18/05 draft.

See Notes at end of 56.4 for in-force rules; but 56.4(9) does not apply to a restrictive covenant granted by a taxpayer before Nov. 9, 2006.

(10) Anti-avoidance — non-application of subsec. (7) — Subsection (7) does not apply in respect of a taxpayer's grant of a restrictive covenant if one of the results of not applying section 68 to the consideration received or receivable in respect of the taxpayer's grant of the restrictive covenant would be that paragraph 3(a) would not apply to consideration that would, if this Act were read without reference to subsections (2) to (14), be included in computing a taxpayer's income from a source that is an office or employment or a business or property.

Notes: This was 56.4(11) in the July 16/10 draft, and was not in the July 18/05 draft.

See Notes at end of 56.4 for in-force rules; but 56.4(10) does not apply to a restrictive covenant granted by a taxpayer before Nov. 9, 2006.

(11) Clarification if subsec. (2) applies — where another person receives the amount — For greater certainty, if subsection (2) applies to include in computing a taxpayer's income an amount received or receivable by another taxpayer, that amount is not to be included in computing the income of that other taxpayer.

Notes: This was 56.4(12) in the July 16/10 draft, and was not in the July 18/05 draft.

(12) Clarification if subsec. (5) applies — For greater certainty, if subsection (5) applies in respect of a restrictive covenant,

(a) the amount referred to in paragraph (6)(f) is to be added in computing the amount received or receivable by the vendors as consideration for the disposition of the interest or right referred to in paragraph (6)(b); and

(b) the amount that can reasonably be regarded as being in part consideration received or receivable for a restrictive covenant to which clause (7)(b)(ii)(B) or subclause (7)(c)(i)(B)(II) applies is to be added in computing the consideration that is received or receivable by each taxpayer who disposes of shares of the target corporation, or shares of the family corporation, as the case may be, to the extent of the portion of the consideration that is received or receivable by that taxpayer.

Notes: This was 56.4(13) in the July 16/10 draft, and 56.4(8) in the July 18/05 draft.

(13) Filing of prescribed form — For the purpose of paragraphs (3)(b) and (c) and subsection (7), an election in prescribed form filed under any of those provisions is to include a copy of the restrictive covenant and be filed

(a) if the person who granted the restrictive covenant was a person resident in Canada when the restrictive covenant was granted, by the person with the Minister on or before the person's filing-due date for the taxation year that includes the day on which the restrictive covenant was granted; and

(b) in any other case, with the Minister on or before the day that is six months after the day on which the restrictive covenant is granted.

Related Provisions: 220(3.2), Reg. 600(b) — Late filing or revocation of election.

Notes: This was 56.4(14) in the July 16/10 draft, and 56.4(9) in the July 18/05 draft. See Notes at end of 56.4 for in-force rules; a 56.4(13) election is deemed filed on time if it is filed by Dec. 23, 2013.

(14) Non-application of s. 42 — Section 42 does not apply to an amount received or receivable as consideration for a restrictive covenant.

Notes: This was 56.4(15) in the July 16/10 draft, and 56.4(10) in the July 18/05 draft.

Notes [s. 56.4]: See Notes to 56.4(2) for discussion of 56.4.

56.4 added by 2002-2013 technical bill (Part 5 — technical), effective [subject to various wording changes for pre-Oct. 24/12 restrictive covenants — see Notes to 56.4(1)"restrictive covenant", 56.4(3), (7), (8), (9) and (10)] for

(a) amounts received or receivable by a taxpayer after Oct. 7, 2003 other than amounts received by the taxpayer before 2005 under a grant of a restrictive covenant made in writing before Oct. 8, 2003 between the taxpayer and a purchaser with whom the taxpayer deals at arm's length; and

(b) amounts paid or payable by a purchaser after Oct. 7, 2003 other than amounts paid or payable by the purchaser before 2005 under a grant of a restrictive covenant made in writing before Oct. 8, 2003 between the purchaser and a taxpayer with whom the purchaser deals at arm's length.

Definitions [s. 56.4]: "amount" — 248(1); "arm's length" — 251(1); "business" — 248(1); "Canada" — 255, *Interpretation Act* 35(1); "capital gain" — 39(1)(a), 248(1); "capital property" — 54, 248(1); "corporation" — 248(1), *Interpretation Act* 35(1); "cumulative eligible capital" — 14(5), 248(1); "disposition" — 248(1); "eligible corporation", "eligible individual", "eligible interest" — 56.4(1); "employee", "employer", "employment" — 248(1); "fair market value" — see 69(1) Notes; "family corporation" — 56.4(7)(c)(i)(B)(II); "filing-due date" — 150(1), 248(1); "goodwill amount" — 56.4(1); "individual", "Minister" — 248(1); "month" — *Interpretation Act* 35(1); "office" — 248(1); "partnership" — see 96(1) Notes; "permanent establishment" — 56.4(1); "person", "prescribed", "property" — 248(1); "purchaser" — 56.4(7)(a)(i), (8)(a); "related" — 251(2)–(6); "resident in Canada" — 250; "restrictive covenant" — 56.4(1); "share" — 248(1); "target corporation" — 56.4(7)(b)(ii)(B); "taxable Canadian corporation" — 89(1), 248(1); "taxation year" — 249; "taxpayer" — 56.4(1), 248(1); "trust" — 104(1), 248(1), (3); "vendor" — 56.4(7)(a); "writing" — *Interpretation Act* 35(1).

57. (1) Certain superannuation or pension benefits — Notwithstanding subparagraph 56(1)(a)(i), there shall be included in computing the income of a taxpayer in respect of a payment received by the taxpayer out of or under a superannuation or pension fund or plan the investment income of which has at some time been exempt from taxation under the *Income War Tax Act* by reason of an election for such exemption by the trustees or corporation administering the fund or plan, only that part of the payment that remains after deducting the proportion thereof

(a) that the total of the amounts paid by the taxpayer into or under the fund or plan during the period when its income was exempt by reason of that election is of the total of all amounts paid by the taxpayer into or under the fund or plan, or

(b) that the total of the amounts paid by the taxpayer into or under the fund or plan during the period when its income was exempt by reason of that election together with simple interest on each amount so paid from the end of the year of payment thereof to the commencement of the superannuation allowance or pension at 3% per annum is of the total of all amounts paid by the taxpayer into or under the fund or plan together with simple interest, computed in the same manner, on each amount so paid,

whichever is the greater.

Related Provisions: 57(2)–(4) — Exceptions and limitations; 212(1)(h)(iv) — Parallel exemption from non-resident withholding tax.

(2) Exception — This section does not apply in respect of a payment received by a taxpayer out of or under a superannuation or pension fund or plan if the taxpayer made no payment into or under the fund or plan.

(3) Limitation — Where a payment, to which subsection (1) would otherwise be applicable, is received by a taxpayer out of or under a superannuation or pension fund or plan in respect of a period of service for part only of which the taxpayer made payments into or under the fund or plan, subsection (1) is applicable only to that part of the payment which may reasonably be regarded as having been received in respect of the period for which the taxpayer made payments into or under the fund or plan and any part of the payment which may reasonably be regarded as having been received in respect of a period for which the taxpayer made no payments into or under the fund or plan shall be included in computing the taxpayer's income for the year without any deduction whatever.

(4) Certain payments from pension plan — Where a taxpayer, during the period from August 15, 1944 to December 31, 1945, made a contribution in excess of $300 to or under a registered pension plan in respect of services rendered by the taxpayer before the taxpayer became a contributor, there shall be included in computing the taxpayer's income in respect of a payment received by the taxpayer out of or under the plan only that part of the payment that remains after deducting the proportion thereof that the contribution so made minus $300 is of the total of the amounts paid by the taxpayer to or under the plan.

Related Provisions: 212(1)(h)(iv) — Parallel benefits — non-residents.

(5) Payments to widow, etc., of contributor — Where, in respect of the death of a taxpayer who was a contributor to or under a superannuation or pension fund or plan described in subsection (1) or (4), a payment is received by a person in a taxation year out of or under the fund or plan, there shall be included in computing the income of that person for the year in respect thereof only that part of the payment that would, if the payment had been received by the taxpayer in the year out of or under the fund or plan, have been included by virtue of this section in computing the income of the taxpayer for the year.

Definitions [s. 57]: "amount" — 248(1); "corporation" — 248(1), *Interpretation Act* 35(1); "registered pension plan", "superannuation or pension benefit" — 248(1); "taxation year" — 249; "taxpayer" — 248(1).

Interpretation Bulletins [s. 57]: IT-499R: Superannuation or pension benefits.

58. [No longer relevant.]

Notes: S. 58 allows a deduction against annuity income received under annuity contracts entered into before June 25, 1940.

59. (1) Consideration for foreign resource property — Where a taxpayer has disposed of a foreign resource property, there shall be included in computing the taxpayer's income for a taxation year the amount, if any, by which

(a) the portion of the taxpayer's proceeds of disposition from the disposition of the property that becomes receivable in the year

exceeds

(b) the total of

(i) all amounts each of which is an outlay or expense made or incurred by the taxpayer for the purpose of making the disposition that was not otherwise deductible for the purposes of this Part, and

(ii) where the property is a foreign resource property in respect of a country, the amount designated under this subparagraph in prescribed form filed with the taxpayer's return of income for the year in respect of the disposition.

Related Provisions: 59(1.1) — Look-through rule for partnerships; 66.21(1)"cumulative foreign resource expense"F(a) — Amount under 59(1)(b)(ii); 72(2) — Election by legal representative and transferee re reserves; 87(2)(p) — Consideration for resource property disposition; 96(1)(d)(i) — Partnerships — no deduction for resource expenses; 104(5.2) — Trusts — 21-year deemed disposition; 248(1)"foreign resource property" — Meaning of foreign resource property in respect of a country.

Notes: 59(1) applies where X has disposed of a foreign resource property. The proceeds of disposition that become receivable in the year are included in income (net of outlays and expenses incurred for the purpose of making the disposition). Under 59(1)(b)(ii), to the extent X designates, there is no income inclusion from the disposition of a foreign resource property of X in respect of a country. Instead, the amount designated reduces cumulative FRE: see 66.21(1)"cumulative foreign resource expense"F(a).

59(1) amended by 2000 Budget, effective for taxation years that begin after 2000.

Interpretation Bulletins: IT-125R4: Dispositions of resource property.

(1.1) Partnerships [look-through rule] — Where a taxpayer is a member of a partnership in a fiscal period of the partnership, the taxpayer's share of the amount that would be included under subsection (1) in respect of a disposition of a foreign resource property in computing the partnership's income for a taxation year if the partnership were a person, the fiscal period were a taxation year, subsection (1) were read without reference to subparagraph (1)(b)(ii) and section 96 were read without reference to paragraph 96(1)(d) is deemed to be proceeds of disposition that become receivable by the taxpayer at the end of the fiscal period in respect of a disposition of the property by the taxpayer.

Related Provisions: 53(1)(e)(viii.1) — Addition to adjusted cost base; 66.2(6) — Parallel rule for CCDE; 66.4(6) — Parallel rule for CCOGPE.

Notes: 59(1.1) added by 2000 Budget, for fiscal periods that begin after 2000. It provides a look-through rule so that members of a partnership can avail themselves of a designation under 59(1). It is similar to the rules for partners in 66.2(6) and 66.4(6). A related amendment to 96(1)(d) provides that a member's share of partnership income is computed without reference to 59(1).

(2) Deduction under former section 64 in preceding year — There shall be included in computing a taxpayer's income for a taxation year any amount that has been deducted as a reserve under subsection 64(1), (1.1) or (1.2) of the *Income Tax Act*, chapter 148 of the Revised Statutes of Canada, 1952, in computing the taxpayer's income for the immediately preceding taxation year.

Related Provisions: 66(5) — Dealers; 85(1) — Transfer of property to corporation by shareholder; 85(2) — Transfer of property to corporation from partnership; 88 — Winding-up; 115(4) — Non-resident's income earned on Canadian resource property.

Notes: 59(2) refers to the s. 64 that was repealed by the 1981 Budget. See Notes to 64.

I.T. Application Rules: 69 (meaning of "chapter 148 of ...").

(3), (3.1) [Repealed under former Act]

Notes: 59(3) and (3.1), repealed by 1985 technical bill, dealt with disposition of a resource property acquired before 1972.

(3.2) Recovery of exploration and development expenses — There shall be included in computing a taxpayer's income for a taxation year

    (a) any amount referred to in paragraph 66(12.4)(b);

    (b) any amount referred to in subsection 66.1(1);

    (c) any amount referred to in subsection 66.2(1);

    (c.1) any amount referred to in subsection 66.21(3);

    (d) any amount referred to in subparagraph 66(10.4)(b)(ii); and

    (e) any amount referred to in paragraph 66(10.4)(c).

Related Provisions: 66(5) — Dealers; 66.21(1)"cumulative foreign resource expense"B — Amount under 59(3.2)(c.1); 66.21(3) — Amount to be included in income; 96(1)(d)(i) — Partnerships — no deduction for resource expenses; 104(5.2) — Trusts — 21-year deemed disposition; 110.6(1) — "investment income"; 115(1)(a)(iii.1) — Non-resident's taxable income earned in Canada; 125.11 — Resource rate reduction 2003-06.

Notes: For an example of 59(3.2)(c) applying see VIEWS doc 2016-0637221E5.

59(3.2)(c.1) added by 2000 Budget, for taxation years that begin after 2000.

I.T. Application Rules: 29(11)(b)(iv); 29(12)(b)(iv) (undeducted expenses incurred before 1972).

Interpretation Bulletins: IT-125R4: Dispositions of resource property.

(3.3) Amounts to be included in income — There shall be included in computing a taxpayer's income for a taxation year

    (a) 33⅓% of the total of all amounts, each of which is the stated percentage of

        (i) an amount that became receivable by the taxpayer after December 31, 1983 and in the year (other than an amount that would have been a Canadian oil and gas exploration expense if it had been an expense incurred by the taxpayer at the time it became receivable),

        (ii) an amount that became receivable by the taxpayer after December 31, 1983 and in the year that would have been a Canadian oil and gas exploration expense described in paragraph (c) or (d) of the definition "Canadian exploration expense" in subsection 66.1(6) in respect of a qualified tertiary

oil recovery project if it had been an expense incurred by the taxpayer at the time it became receivable, or

        (iii) 30% of an amount that became receivable by the taxpayer in the year and in 1984 that would have been a Canadian oil and gas exploration expense (other than an expense described in paragraph (c) or (d) of the definition "Canadian exploration expense" in subsection 66.1(6) in respect of a qualified tertiary oil recovery project) incurred in respect of non-conventional lands if it had been an expense incurred by the taxpayer at the time it became receivable

and in respect of which the consideration given by the taxpayer was a property (other than a share, depreciable property of a prescribed class or a Canadian resource property) or services the cost of which may reasonably be regarded as having been an expenditure that was added in computing the earned depletion base of the taxpayer or in computing the earned depletion base of a predecessor where the taxpayer is a successor corporation to the predecessor;

    (b) 33⅓% of the total of all amounts, each of which is the stated percentage of an amount in respect of a disposition of depreciable property of a prescribed class (other than a disposition of such property that had been used by the taxpayer to any person with whom the taxpayer was not dealing at arm's length) of the taxpayer after December 11, 1979 and in the year, the capital cost of which was added in computing the earned depletion base of the taxpayer or of a person with whom the taxpayer was not dealing at arm's length or in computing the earned depletion base of a predecessor where the taxpayer is a successor corporation to the predecessor, that is equal to the lesser of

        (i) the proceeds of disposition of the property, and

        (ii) the capital cost of the property to the taxpayer, the person with whom the taxpayer was not dealing at arm's length or the predecessor, as the case may be, computed as if no amount had been added thereto by virtue of paragraph 21(1)(b) or subsection 21(3);

    (c) 33⅓% of the total of all amounts, each of which is an amount in respect of a disposition of depreciable property of a prescribed class that is bituminous sands equipment (other than a disposition of such property that had been used by the taxpayer to any person with whom the taxpayer was not dealing at arm's length) of the taxpayer after December 11, 1979 and before 1990 and in the year, the capital cost of which was added in computing the supplementary depletion base of the taxpayer or of a person with whom the taxpayer was not dealing at arm's length or in computing the supplementary depletion base of a predecessor where the taxpayer is a successor corporation to the predecessor, that is equal to the lesser of

        (i) the proceeds of disposition of the property, and

        (ii) the capital cost of the property to the taxpayer, the person with whom the taxpayer was not dealing at arm's length or the predecessor, as the case may be, computed as if no amount had been added thereto by virtue of paragraph 21(1)(b) or subsection 21(3);

    (d) 50% of the total of all amounts, each of which is an amount in respect of a disposition of depreciable property of a prescribed class that is enhanced recovery equipment (other than a disposition of such property that had been used by the taxpayer to any person with whom the taxpayer was not dealing at arm's length) of the taxpayer after December 11, 1979 and before 1990 and in the year, the capital cost of which was added in computing the supplementary depletion base of the taxpayer or of a person with whom the taxpayer was not dealing at arm's length or in computing the supplementary depletion base of a predecessor where the taxpayer is a successor corporation to the predecessor, that is equal to the lesser of

        (i) the proceeds of disposition of the property, and

        (ii) the capital cost of the property to the taxpayer, the person with whom the taxpayer was not dealing at arm's length or the predecessor, as the case may be, computed as if no amount had been added thereto by virtue of paragraph 21(1)(b) or subsection 21(3);

(e) 66⅔% of the total of all amounts, each of which is an amount that became receivable by the taxpayer after December 11, 1979 and before 1990 and in the year and in respect of which the consideration given by the taxpayer was a property (other than a share or a Canadian resource property) or services the cost of which may reasonably be regarded as having been an expenditure in connection with an oil or gas well in respect of which an amount was included in computing the taxpayer's frontier exploration base or in computing the frontier exploration base of a predecessor where the taxpayer is a successor corporation to the predecessor; and

(f) 33⅓% of the total of all amounts, each of which is the stated percentage of an amount that became receivable by the taxpayer after April 19, 1983 and in the year and in respect of which the consideration given by the taxpayer was a property (other than a share, depreciable property of a prescribed class or a Canadian resource property) or services the cost of which may reasonably be regarded as having been an expenditure that was included in computing the mining exploration depletion base of the taxpayer or in computing the mining exploration depletion base of a specified predecessor of the taxpayer.

Related Provisions: 66(5) — Dealers; 66.1(2) — Deduction for principal business corporation; 87(1.2) — Amalgamation — continuing corporation; 88(1.5) — Winding-up — Parent deemed continuation of subsidiary.

Regulations: 1105 (classes in Schedule II are prescribed).

(3.4) Definitions — For the purposes of this subsection and subsection (3.3),

"specified predecessor" of a taxpayer means a person who is a predecessor of

(a) the taxpayer, or

(b) a person who is a specified predecessor of the taxpayer;

Notes: 59(3.4)"specified predecessor" was 59(3.4)(c) before RSC 1985 (5th Supp) consolidation for tax years ending after Nov. 1991.

"stated percentage" means

(a) in respect of an amount described in paragraph (3.3)(a) or (f) that became receivable by a taxpayer,

   (i) 100% where the amount became receivable before July, 1988,

   (ii) 50% where the amount became receivable after June, 1988 and before 1990, and

   (iii) 0% where the amount became receivable after 1989, and

(b) in respect of the disposition described in paragraph (3.3)(b) of a depreciable property of a taxpayer,

   (i) 100% where the property was disposed of before July, 1988,

   (ii) 50% where the property was disposed of after June, 1988 and before 1990, and

   (iii) 0% where the property was disposed of after 1989;

Related Provisions: 59(3.5) — Variation of stated percentage.

Notes: 59(3.4)"stated percentage" was 59(3.4)(b) before RSC 1985 (5th Supp) consolidation for tax years ending after Nov. 1991.

"successor corporation" means a corporation that has at any time after November 7, 1969 acquired, by purchase, amalgamation, merger, winding-up or otherwise (other than pursuant to an amalgamation that is described in subsection 87(1.2) or a winding-up to which the rules in subsection 88(1) apply), from another person (in this subsection and subsection (3.3) referred to as the "predecessor") all or substantially all of the Canadian resource properties of the predecessor in circumstances in which any of subsection 29(25) of the *Income Tax Application Rules* and subsections 66.7(1) and (3) to (5) apply to the corporation.

Notes: 59(3.4)"successor corporation" was 59(3.4)(a) before RSC 1985 (5th Supp) consolidation for tax years ending after Nov. 1991.

CRA considers that "substantially all" means 90% or more.

(3.5) Variation of stated percentage — Notwithstanding the definition "stated percentage" in subsection (3.4), where

(a) an amount became receivable by a taxpayer within 60 days after the end of 1989 in respect of a disposition of property or services, and

(b) the person to whom the disposition was made is a corporation that, before the end of 1989, had issued, or had undertaken to issue, a flow-through share and the corporation renounces under subsection 66(12.66), effective on December 31, 1989, an amount in respect of Canadian exploration expenses that includes an expenditure in respect of the amount referred to in paragraph (a),

the stated percentage in respect of the amount described in paragraph (a) shall be 50%.

(4) [Repealed under former Act]

Notes: 59(4), repealed by 1985 technical bill, defined "relevant percentage", a term no longer used.

(5) Definition of "proceeds of disposition" — In this section, "proceeds of disposition" has the meaning assigned by section 54.

Notes: 59(5) amended by 2001 technical bill for transactions/events after Dec. 23, 1998.

Interpretation Bulletins: IT-125R4: Dispositions of resource property.

(6) Definitions in regulations under section 65 — In this section, "bituminous sands equipment", "Canadian oil and gas exploration expense", "earned depletion base", "enhanced recovery equipment", "frontier exploration base", "mining exploration depletion base", "non-conventional lands", "qualified tertiary oil recovery project" and "supplementary depletion base" have the meanings assigned by regulations made for the purposes of section 65.

Regulations [subsec. 59(6)]: Part XII (Reg. 1206(1) and others).

Definitions [s. 59]: "amount" — 248(1); "bituminous sands equipment" — 59(6), Reg. 1206(1); "arm's length" — 251(1); "Canada" — 255; "Canadian exploration expense" — 66.1(6), 248(1); "Canadian oil and gas exploration expense" — 59(6), Reg. 1206(1); "Canadian resource property" — 66(15), 248(1); "corporation" — 248(1), *Interpretation Act* 35(1); "depreciable property" — 13(21), 248(1); "disposition" — 248(1); "earned depletion base" — 59(6), Reg. 1202(1), Reg. 1205(1); "enhanced recovery equipment" — 59(6), Reg. 1206(1); "fiscal period" — 249.1; "flow-through share", "foreign resource property" — 66(15), 248(1); "foreign resource property in respect of a country" — 248(1); "frontier exploration base" — 59(6), Reg. 1207(2); "mining exploration depletion base" — 59(6), Reg. 1203(2), (3); "non-conventional lands" — 59(6), Reg. 1206(1); "oil or gas well" — 248(1); "partnership" — see 96(1) Notes; "person", "prescribed" — 248(1); "proceeds of disposition" — 54, 59(5); "property", "share" — 248(1); "qualified tertiary oil recovery project" — 59(6), Reg. 1206(1); "specified predecessor" — 59(3.4); "stated percentage" — 59(3.4); "successor corporation" — 59(3.4); "supplementary depletion base" — 59(6), Reg. 1212(2)–(4); "taxation year" — 249; "taxpayer" — 248(1).

59.1 Involuntary disposition of resource property — Where in a particular taxation year an amount is deemed by subsection 44(2) to have become receivable by a taxpayer as proceeds of disposition described in paragraph (d) of the definition "proceeds of disposition" in section 54 of any Canadian resource property and the taxpayer elects, in the taxpayer's return of income under this Part for the year, to have this section apply to those proceeds of disposition,

(a) there shall be deducted in computing the taxpayer's income for the particular year such amount as the taxpayer may claim, not exceeding the least of,

   (i) the total of all those proceeds so becoming receivable in the particular year by the taxpayer to the extent that they have been included in the amount referred to in paragraph (a) of the description of F in the definition "cumulative Canadian development expense" in subsection 66.2(5) or in paragraph (a) of the description of F in the definition "cumulative Canadian oil and gas property expense" in subsection 66.4(5) in respect of the taxpayer,

(ii) the amount required to be included in computing the taxpayer's income for the particular year by virtue of paragraph 59(3.2)(c), and

(iii) the taxpayer's income for the particular year determined without reference to this section;

(b) the amount, if any, by which

(i) the amount deducted under paragraph (a)

exceeds

(ii) the total of such of the Canadian exploration expenses, Canadian development expenses and Canadian oil and gas property expenses made or incurred by the taxpayer in the taxpayer's ten taxation years immediately following the particular year as were designated by the taxpayer in the taxpayer's return of income for the year in which the expense was made or incurred,

shall be included in computing the taxpayer's income for the particular year and, notwithstanding subsections 152(4) and (5), such reassessment of the taxpayer's tax, interest or penalties for any year shall be made as is necessary to give effect to such inclusion; and

(c) any Canadian exploration expense, Canadian development expense or Canadian oil and gas property expense made or incurred by the taxpayer and designated in the taxpayer's return of income in accordance with subparagraph (b)(ii) shall (except for the purposes of subsections 66(12.1), (12.2), (12.3) and (12.5) and for the purpose of computing the taxpayer's earned depletion base within the meaning assigned by regulations made for the purposes of section 65) be deemed not to be a Canadian exploration expense, a Canadian development expense or a Canadian oil and gas property expense, as the case may be, of the taxpayer.

Related Provisions: 66(18) — Members of partnerships.

Notes: An election "in the taxpayer's return" is valid even if the return is filed late. See Notes to 7(1.31).

For a taxpayer filing Quebec returns, a 59.1 election and a 5.1(b)(ii) designation must be copied to Revenu Québec: *Taxation Act* ss. 333.1, 333.2, 21.4.6.

Definitions [s. 59.1]: "amount" — 248(1); "Canadian development expense" — 66.2(5), 248(1); "Canadian exploration expense" — 66.1(6), 248(1); "Canadian oil and gas property expense" — 66.4(5), 248(1); "Canadian resource property" — 66(15), 248(1); "earned depletion base" — Reg. 1202(1), Reg. 1205(1); "Minister", "property", "regulations" — 248(1); "taxation year" — 249; "taxpayer" — 248(1).

Interpretation Bulletins [s. 59.1]: IT-125R4: Dispositions of resource properties.

Subdivision E — Deductions in Computing Income

60. Other deductions — There may be deducted in computing a taxpayer's income for a taxation year such of the following amounts as are applicable:

Notes: 60 provides miscellaneous deductions in computing net income. For deductions against employment income, see 8; against income from business or property, see 9(1) and 20–37. For deductions from *net* income in computing *taxable* income, see 110–114.2.

Deductions under 60–66.8 cannot be taken if net income is already zero: VIEWS doc 2009-0350221I7.

(a) **capital element of annuity payments** — the capital element of each annuity payment included by virtue of paragraph 56(1)(d) in computing the taxpayer's income for the year, that is to say,

(i) if the annuity was paid under a contract, an amount equal to that part of the payment determined in prescribed manner to have been a return of capital, and

(ii) if the annuity was paid under a will or trust, such part of the payment as can be established by the recipient not to have been paid out of the income of the estate or trust;

Related Provisions: 110.6(1) — "investment income"; 148(9)"adjusted cost basis"K — Reduction in adjusted cost basis of insurance policy. See also at end of s. 60.

Regulations: 300 (prescribed manner).

Income Tax Folios: S3-F9-C1: Lottery winnings, miscellaneous receipts, and income (and losses) from crime [replaces IT-185R, IT-213R, IT-256R, IT-334R2].

Interpretation Bulletins: IT-415R2: Deregistration of registered retirement savings plans (cancelled).

I.T. Technical News: 25 (health and welfare trusts).

Advance Tax Rulings: ATR-68: Structured settlement.

(b) **[spousal or child] support** — the total of all amounts each of which is an amount determined by the formula

$$A - (B + C)$$

where

A   is the total of all amounts each of which is a support amount paid after 1996 and before the end of the year by the taxpayer to a particular person, where the taxpayer and the particular person were living separate and apart at the time the amount was paid,

B   is the total of all amounts each of which is a child support amount that became payable by the taxpayer to the particular person under an agreement or order on or after its commencement day and before the end of the year in respect of a period that began on or after its commencement day, and

C   is the total of all amounts each of which is a support amount paid by the taxpayer to the particular person after 1996 and deductible in computing the taxpayer's income for a preceding taxation year;

Related Provisions: 4(3) — Deductions applicable; 56(1)(b) — Parallel income inclusion for recipient; 56(1)(c.2) — Reimbursement of support payments; 56.1(4), 60.1(4) — Definitions of "commencement day", "support amount", "child support amount"; 60.1(1), (2) — Payments to third parties; 60.1(3) — Payments made before agreement signed or court order made; 118(5) — No personal credits in respect of person to whom support paid; 146(1)"earned income"(f) — 60(b) deduction reduces RRSP earned income; 212(1)(f) — No withholding tax on support paid to non-resident; 241(4)(e)(vii) — Disclosure of name and address for enforcement of support payments; 252(3) — Extended meaning of "spouse" and "former spouse"; 257 — Formula cannot calculate to less than zero; Canada-U.S. Tax Treaty:Art. XVIII:6 — Exemptions for cross-border alimony and support. See also at end of s. 60.

Notes: See Notes to 56(1)(b) and 56.1(4)"support amount".

60(b) rewritten by 1996 Budget, for amounts received after 1996, and amended on the same basis by 1995-97 technical bill. This overrides the previous version (reproduced here up to PITA 57th ed.), which had continued to apply to alimony or maintenance on a pre-1993 marriage breakdown. Earlier amendments by 1992 technical bill, 1981 and 1979 Budgets.

Regulations: 100(3)(d) (no source withholding on amount deductible under 60(b) where it is held back by employer).

Income Tax Folios: S1-F3-C3: Support payments [replaces IT-530R].

Interpretation Bulletins: IT-325R2: Property transfers after separation, divorce and annulment; IT-513R: Personal tax credits.

Forms: P102: Support payments (pamphlet); T1 General return, Line 22000 [former 220]; T1157: Election for child support payments; T1158: Registration of family support payments.

(c) **pension income reallocation** — where the taxpayer is a pensioner (as defined in subsection 60.03(1)), any amount that is a split-pension amount (as defined in that subsection) in respect of the pensioner for the taxation year;

Related Provisions: 60.03(2) — Effect of pension income splitting; 118(8)(d)(ii) — Effect on pension income credit; 153(2) — Source deductions deemed withheld on behalf of transferee.

Notes: 60(c) added by 2007 budget bill #1, for 2007 and later tax years. Together with 56(1)(a.2) and 60.03, it implements spousal pension income splitting.

Former 60(c) repealed by 1996 Budget, effective for amounts received after 1996. See Notes to 60(b).

(c.1) [Repealed]

Notes: 60(c.1) amended and renumbered 60(c) by 1992 technical bill, for orders made after 1992.

(c.2) **repayment of support payments** — an amount paid by the taxpayer in the year or one of the 2 preceding taxation years under a decree, order or judgment of a competent tribunal as a repayment of an amount included under paragraph 56(1)(b) or (c), or under paragraph 56(1)(c.1) (as it applies, in computing the taxpayer's income for the year or a preceding taxation year, to decrees, orders and judgments made before 1993) to the extent that it was not so deducted for a preceding taxation year;

Related Provisions: 56(1)(c.2) — Parallel rule for other taxpayer; 146(1)"earned income"(f) — Amount deducted under 60(c.2) reduces RRSP earned income.

Notes: *Cowan*, 2006 TCC 512, gave a broad interpretation to "repayment of a support amount", and allowed deduction of an amount that CRA considered arose from the division of a pension rather than being support.

60(c.2) added by 1992 technical bill, for payments made after 1990.

Income Tax Folios: S1-F3-C3: Support payments [replaces IT-530R].

(d) **interest on death duties** — an amount equal to annual interest accruing within the taxation year in respect of succession duties, inheritance taxes or estate taxes;

Related Provisions: 4(3) — Deductions applicable. See also at end of s. 60.

Notes: Neither Canada nor any province imposes succession duties, inheritance taxes or estate taxes, although the provinces impose probate fees, called estate administration tax in Ontario. This provision could apply to interest on US estate taxes, however.

Income Tax Folios: S3-F6-C1: Interest deductibility [replaces IT-533].

Interpretation Bulletins: IT-203: Interest on death duties (cancelled).

(e) **CPP/QPP contributions on self-employed earnings** — the total of

(i) ½ of the lesser of

(A) the total of all amounts each of which is an amount payable by the taxpayer in respect of self-employed earnings for the year as a contribution under subsection 10(1) of the *Canada Pension Plan* or as a like contribution under a "provincial pension plan", as defined in section 3 of that Act, and

(B) the maximum amount of such contributions payable by the taxpayer for the year under the plan, and

(ii) the lesser of

(A) the total of all amounts each of which is an amount payable by the taxpayer in respect of self-employed earnings for the year as a contribution under subsection 10(1.1) or (1.2) of the *Canada Pension Plan* or as a like contribution under a "provincial pension plan", as defined in section 3 of that Act, and

(B) the maximum amount of such contributions payable by the taxpayer for the year under the plan;

Related Provisions: 60(e.1) — Deduction for enhanced CPP contributions starting 2019; 118.7 — Credit for employee half of contributions.

Notes: 60(e) allows a deduction for CPP/QPP contributions payable on *self-employed* earnings, to the extent not allowed as a 15% credit. That credit is for ½ of the contributions at the 2018 level, plus annual inflation indexing, but without the increases due to enhancement of the CPP starting 2019: see Notes to 118.7. (For taxpayers not in the lowest bracket (see table at end of 117.1), deduction is worth more than a credit.)

The increased contributions on *employment* earnings after 2018 (beyond indexing) are deductible under 60(e.1).

60(e) amended by 2016 and 2018 budget bills #2, both effective 2019, to add subpara. (ii) to cover the increased contributions required after 2018 (see Notes to 118.7). Added by 2000 Budget, for 2001 and later tax years.

Former 60(e) repealed by 1988 tax reform. The deduction for tuition paid to a university outside Canada is now a credit under 118.5(1)(b).

Forms: T1 General return, Line 22200 [former 222].

(e.1) **enhanced CPP contributions** — the lesser of

(i) the total of all amounts each of which is an amount payable by the taxpayer for the year as an employee's contribution under subsection 8(1.1) or (1.2) of the *Canada Pension Plan* or as a like contribution under a "provincial pension plan", as defined in section 3 of that Act, and

(ii) the maximum amount of such contributions payable by the taxpayer for the year under the plan;

Notes: See Notes to 60(e). 60(e.1) added by 2016 budget bill #2 and amended by 2018 budget bill #2, both effective 2019.

Forms: T1 General return, Line 22215.

(f) **restrictive covenant — bad debt** — all debts owing to a taxpayer that are established by the taxpayer to have become bad debts in the taxation year and that are in respect of an amount included because of the operation of subsection 6(3.1) or 56.4(2)

in computing the taxpayer's income in a preceding taxation year;

Related Provisions: 56(1)(m) — Bad debt recovered — inclusion in income.

Notes: 60(f) added by 2002-2013 technical bill (Part 5 — technical), effective Oct. 8, 2003. See Notes to 56.4(2) re restrictive covenants.

Former 60(f) repealed by 1988 tax reform. The deduction for tuition paid in Canada is now a credit under 118.5(1)(a).

(g) **Quebec parental insurance plan — self-employed premiums** — the amount determined by the formula

$$A - B$$

where

A is the total of all amounts each of which is an amount payable by the taxpayer in respect of self-employed earnings for the taxation year as a premium under the *Act respecting parental insurance*, R.S.Q., c. A-29.011, and

B is the total of all amounts each of which is an amount that would be payable by the taxpayer as an employee's premium under the *Act respecting parental insurance*, R.S.Q., c. A-29.011, if those earnings were employment income of the taxpayer for the taxation year;

Related Provisions: 56(1)(a)(vii) — QPIP benefits — income inclusion; 118.7 — Credit for portion of QPIP premiums not deductible.

Notes: 60(g) added by 2002-2013 technical bill (Part 5 — technical), effective for 2006 and later taxation years (see Notes to 152(4.2) for late reassessment).

Former 60(g) repealed by 1988 tax reform. The deduction for tuition fees for commuting students is now a credit under 118.5(1)(c).

Forms: T1 General return, Line 22300 [former 223; on Quebec-residents form only].

(h) [Repealed under former Act]

Notes: Former 60(h) repealed by 1988 tax reform. The deduction for CPP contributions is now a 118.7 credit (and 60(e), (e.1) deductions).

(i) **premium or payment under RRSP or RRIF** — any amount that is deductible under section 146 or 146.3 or subsection 147.3(13.1) in computing the income of the taxpayer for the year;

Related Provisions: 4(3) — Deductions applicable; 146(5), (5.1), (6), (6.1), (8.2) — RRSP payments deductible; 152(6) — Reassessment. See also at end of s. 60.

Notes: 60(i) amended by 2008 budget bill #2 to add 146.3, effective where the last payment out of a RRIF is made after 2008. This allows a deduction for RRIF losses carried back to the deceased annuitant's estate under 146.3(6.3).

60(i) would have been amended to add reference to 146.1 by Bill C-253 (2008), a private member's bill sponsored by Liberal MP Dan McTeague, who got a majority in the Commons to approve it against the wishes of the minority Conservative government; but it never passed the Senate. (For the text, see PITA 34th-36th ed.) Bill C-253 added 146.1(2.01) to permit annual deduction of $5,000 of RESP contributions, and related amendments to 146.1(7.1) and (7.2). 2008 budget bill #1 repealed these changes so that they would not take effect even if C-253 were reintroduced and enacted. Since the Budget was a confidence measure, the Liberals chose not to vote against it and bring down the government, which would have forced an election. The Conservatives announced that this measure would have cost $900 million per year and was not acceptable. See Notes at end of 146.1 for the treatment of RESP contributions.

60(i) amended by 1992 technical bill, effective 1992, to add reference to 147.3(13.1).

Regulations: 100(3)(c) (payroll deduction of RRSP contribution reduces source withholding).

Interpretation Bulletins: IT-124R6: Contributions to registered retirement savings plans.

(j) **transfer of superannuation benefits [to RPP or RRSP]** — such part of the total of all amounts each of which is

(i) a superannuation or pension benefit (other than any amount in respect of the benefit that is deducted in computing the taxable income of the taxpayer for a taxation year because of subparagraph 110(1)(f)(i) or a benefit that is part of a series of periodic payments) payable out of or under a pension plan that is not a registered pension plan, attributable to services rendered by the taxpayer or a spouse or common-law partner or former spouse or common-law partner of the taxpayer in a period throughout which that person was not resident in Canada, and included in computing the income of the taxpayer for the year because of subparagraph 56(1)(a)(i), or

(ii) an eligible amount in respect of the taxpayer for the year under section 60.01, subsection 104(27) or (27.1) or paragraph 147(10.2)(d),

as

(iii) is designated by the taxpayer in the taxpayer's return of income under this Part for the year, and

(iv) does not exceed the total of all amounts each of which is an amount paid by the taxpayer in the year or within 60 days after the end of the year

(A) as a contribution to or under a registered pension plan for the taxpayer's benefit, other than the portion thereof deductible under paragraph 8(1)(m) in computing the taxpayer's income for the year, or

(B) as a premium (within the meaning assigned by subsection 146(1)) under a registered retirement savings plan under which the taxpayer is the annuitant (within the meaning assigned by subsection 146(1)), other than the portion thereof designated for a taxation year for the purposes of paragraph (l),

to the extent that the amount was not deducted in computing the taxpayer's income for a preceding taxation year;

Related Provisions: 60.2(1) — Refund of undeducted past service AVCs; 104(27) — Pension benefits; 104(27.1) — DPSP benefits; 146(5) — Amount of RRSP premiums deductible; 146(5.2) — Transfer of commuted RPP to RRSP when employer insolvent; 146(6.1) — Recontribution of certain withdrawals; 146(8.2) — Amount deductible; 146(16) — RRSP deduction on transfer of funds; 146(21.1) — Contribution to Saskatchewan Pension Plan deemed to be RRSP premium for purposes of 60(j); 147(10) — Amounts received taxable; 147(10.2) — Single payment on retirement etc.; 147(21) — Restriction re transfers; 147.1(3)(a) — Deemed registration; 147.3(12) — Restriction on transfer from RPP; 147.5(11) — Pooled registered pension plan contribution deemed to be RRSP premium; 204.2(1)(b)(i)(A) — Excess RRSP amount for a year; 212(1)(h)(iii.1) — Exclusion from non-resident withholding tax; 252(3) — Extended meaning of "spouse" and "former spouse". See also at end of s. 60.

Notes: Benefits from an RPP on death of a spouse can be transferred to an RRSP under 60(j): VIEWS doc 2005-0147221E5.

Lump-sum amounts (but not periodic benefits) from a US Individual Retirement Account (IRA) can be rolled into an RRSP under 60(j)(ii), if the IRA funds came from a US 401(k) plan, provided the taxpayer or spouse was the source of the contributions; see 56(1)(a)(i)(C.1), 56(12), 60.01, 248(1)"foreign retirement arrangement", VIEWS docs 2002-0125375, 2003-0182835 (which notes that the foreign tax credit under 126(1)(b)(i) is not reduced for the 60(j)(ii) deduction), and 2013-0493691C6 [APFF 2013 q.7]. See also Art. XVIII of the Canada-US tax treaty. Where the transfer to an RRSP was not made in time, it could not be done: *Barel*, 2009 TCC 156.

60(j) also allows transfer to an RPP or RRSP of a pension from Australia (VIEWS docs 2008-0293061E5, 2011-0409121E5), Hong Kong (2006-0168091E5), Malaysia, possibly (2015-0571591E5), Philippines (2011-0418171E5), Switzerland (2015-0566911E5) or the UK (IT-528 para. 26; 2005-0110431E5, 2012-0439641E5, 2012-0468271E5), but not a UK self-funded "personal pension scheme" (2014-0543091E5); nor an Isle of Man "retirement account": 2014-0555271E5; nor a Jersey "self-invested pension plan": 2017-0720721E5. See also Bullock, "Transfers From a Foreign Plan to an RRSP", 24(2) *Taxation of Executive Compensation & Retirement* (Federated Press) 1674-75 (Sept. 2012).

No tax-free transfer from an RRSP can be made to a UK pension: VIEWS doc 2009-0315041M4.

Benefits transferable to an RRSP under 60(j) can also be transferred to the Saskatchewan Pension Plan: 146(21.1).

A designation "in the taxpayer's return" is valid even if the return is filed late. See Notes to 7(1.31).

60(j) amended by 2000 same-sex partners bill (last change effective 2001), 1991 technical bill, 1990 pension bill.

Interpretation Bulletins: IT-124R6: Contributions to registered retirement savings plans; IT-528: Transfers of funds between registered plans.

Advance Tax Rulings: ATR-31: Funding of divorce settlement amount from DPSP.

(j.01) [No longer relevant]

Notes: 60(j.01) added by 1990 pension bill, effective for 1988 only. It allowed a rollover of an actuarial surplus under a defined benefit RPP to an RRSP.

(j.02) payment to registered pension plan [pre-April 1988 agreements] — [No longer relevant.]

Notes: 60(j.02), added by 1992 technical bill, allows a deduction for certain pension plan contributions made pursuant to an agreement or election made before March 28, 1988, in respect of pre-1990 service or amounts received before 1990.

(j.03) repayments of pre-1990 pension benefits — [No longer relevant]

Notes: 60(j.03) added by 1992 technical bill, effective 1991.

(j.04) repayments of post-1989 pension benefits — the total of all amounts each of which is an amount paid in the year by the taxpayer to a registered pension plan as

(i) a repayment under a prescribed statutory provision of an amount received from the plan that

(A) was included under subsection 56(1) in computing the taxpayer's income for a taxation year ending after 1989, and

(B) can reasonably be considered not to have been designated by the taxpayer for the purpose of paragraph (j.2), or

(ii) interest in respect of a repayment referred to in subparagraph (i),

except to the extent that the total was deductible under paragraph 8(1)(m) in computing the taxpayer's income for the year;

Notes: 60(j.04) added by 1992 technical bill, effective 1990.

Regulations: 6503 (prescribed statutory provisions for 60(j.04)(i)).

(j.1) transfer of retiring allowances [from pre-1996 employment to RRSP] — such part of the total of all amounts each of which is an amount paid to the taxpayer by an employer, or under a retirement compensation arrangement to which the employer has contributed, as a retiring allowance and included in computing the taxpayer's income for the year by virtue of subparagraph 56(1)(a)(ii) or paragraph 56(1)(x) as

(i) is designated by the taxpayer in the taxpayer's return of income under this Part for the year,

(ii) does not exceed the amount, if any, by which the total of

(A) $2,000 multiplied by the number of years before 1996 during which the employee or former employee in respect of whom the payment was made (in this paragraph referred to as the "retiree") was employed by the employer or a person related to the employer, and

(B) $1,500 multiplied by the number by which the number of years before 1989 described in clause (A) exceeds the number that can reasonably be regarded as the equivalent number of years before 1989 in respect of which employer contributions under either a pension plan or a deferred profit sharing plan of the employer or a person related to the employer had vested in the retiree at the time of the payment

exceeds the total of

(C) all amounts deducted under this paragraph in respect of amounts paid before the year in respect of the retiree

(I) by the employer or a person related to the employer, or

(II) under a retirement compensation arrangement to which the employer or a person related to the employer has contributed,

(C.1) all other amounts deducted under this paragraph for the year in respect of amounts paid in the year in respect of the retiree

(I) by a person related to the employer, or

(II) under a retirement compensation arrangement to which a person related to the employer has contributed, and

(D) all amounts deducted under paragraph (t) in computing the retiree's income for the year in respect of a retirement compensation arrangement to which the employer or a person related to the employer has contributed, and

(iii) does not exceed the total of all amounts each of which is an amount paid by the taxpayer in the year or within 60 days after the end of the year in respect of the amount so designated

(A) as a contribution to or under a registered pension plan, other than the portion thereof deductible under paragraph (j) or 8(1)(m) in computing the taxpayer's income for the year, or

(B) as a premium (within the meaning assigned by section 146) under a registered retirement savings plan under which the taxpayer is the annuitant (within the meaning assigned by section 146), other than the portion thereof that has been designated for the purposes of paragraph (j) or (l),

to the extent that it was not deducted in computing the taxpayer's income for a preceding taxation year

and for the purposes of this paragraph, "person related to the employer" includes

(iv) any person whose business was acquired or continued by the employer, and

(v) a previous employer of the retiree whose service therewith is recognized in determining the retiree's pension benefits;

Related Provisions: 127.52(1)(a) [repealed] — Limitation on add-back for minimum tax purposes; 146(5) — Amount of RRSP premiums deductible; 146(5.2) — Transfer of commuted RPP to RRSP when employer insolvent; 146(6.1) — Recontribution of certain withdrawals; 146(21.1) — Contribution to Saskatchewan Pension Plan deemed to be RRSP premium for purposes of 60(j.1); 147.3 — Transfer from RPP; 147.5(11) — Pooled registered pension plan contribution deemed to be RRSP premium; 204.2(1)(b)(i)(A) — Excess amount in respect of RRSP; *Interpretation Act* 27(5) — Meaning of "within 60 days". See also at end of s. 60.

Notes: In general, 60(j.1) allows a rollover to an RRSP [or the Saskatchewan Pension Plan: 146(21.1)], for long-time employees, of part of a "retiring allowance" (including a wrongful dismissal settlement or severance pay). See Income Tax Folio S2-F1-C2 (the interpretations in IT-337R4 remain valid: VIEWS doc 2016-0667811E5). The limit is $2,000 for each calendar year (or part year) of employment before 1996, plus $1,500 for each full year before 1989 for which the employer's pension or DPSP contributions (if any) have not vested. CRA interpretation of "vested" is in Folio S2-F1-C2 ¶2.31: "entitled to receive (or had previously received) their accrued benefits under the plan"; see also VIEWS docs 2008-0280831E5 (includes contributions paid out from a discontinued DPSP), 2014-0522681E5. The employer is not required to withhold tax on the portion transferred directly to the RRSP: Reg. 100(3)(c), Guide RC4157. (The taxpayer cannot double-dip by deducting the amount as an RRSP contribution: *Greene*, 2010 TCC 162 (FCA appeal discontinued A-191-10).) For amounts not transferred to the RRSP, Reg. 103(4) requires lump-sum withholding. There is no deduction for a transfer to an RCA: 2014-053534117. See also Notes to 248(1)"retiring allowance".

Employment before 1996 may have been with a "person related to the employer"; see extended definition in 60(j.1)(iv) and (v) (either condition is sufficient: VIEWS doc 2005-0130361E5). Thus, prior service with a different employer that was "bought back" for pension purposes qualifies: 2005-0156781E5, 2011-0425771E5, 2011-0431131E5. A foreign related employer qualifies: 2003-0047255. Employment by two federal departments (e.g. Canadian Armed Forces, then RCMP) is with a single employer (the Crown): 2009-0314971E5. Two employers controlled by the same provincial government are "related", but municipalities are not controlled by the province: 2003-0054211E5. Employment with a predecessor school board that amalgamated to form the current school board qualifies: 2010-0364291E5; but otherwise two school boards are not considered related: 2010-0358111E5. The periods of employment need not have been continuous: Income Tax Folio S2-F1-C2 ¶2.31, 2004-0077651E5. Where the employee's years of service are not transferred to the new employer, 60(j.1)(v) does not apply: 2006-0184711E5, 2008-0300801E5. See also 2013-0511791E5 (years with predecessors qualify). See also *GMAC Commercial Credit v. TCT*, 2006 SCC 35, and *Krishnamoorthy v. Olympus Canada*, 2017 ONCA 873, on whether employment by a successor employer is deemed continuous for non-tax purposes.

If the designation is not made in the taxpayer's return (60(j.1)(i)), the deduction is not available: *Haley*, 2006 TCC 464.

An amount paid by an employer after death to the employee's estate can be rolled to an RRSP, but only if it is a "retiring allowance" rather than a "death benefit" (248(1)): VIEWS doc 2008-0304261E5.

For a review of CRA positions on 60(j.1), see Jeffrey Sommers, "Recent Developments in the Taxation of Retiring Allowances", 12(8) *Taxation of Executive Compensation and Retirement* (Federated Press) 407-10 (April 2001). See also 2016-0632151E5.

Due to the repeal of 127.52(1)(a) effective 1998, RRSP rollovers under 60(j.1) are no longer added back into income for alternative minimum tax (AMT) purposes.

The words "before 1996" added to 60(j.1)(ii)(A) by 1995 Budget, effective 1996. This phases out the rollover of retiring allowances, as fewer departing employees have em-

ployment before 1996 as time passes. 60(j.1) earlier amended by 1991 technical bill, 1990 pension bill.

Regulations: 100(3)(c) (no source withholding where amount is paid by employer directly to RRSP).

Income Tax Folios: S2-F1-C2: Retiring allowances [replaces IT-337R4].

Interpretation Bulletins: IT-124R6: Contributions to registered retirement savings plans.

I.T. Technical News: 7 (retiring allowances); 19 (Retiring allowances — clarification to Interpretation Bulletin IT-337R3 — (d): Deductions at source); 20 (retiring allowances — effect of re-employment or employment with affiliate).

Advance Tax Rulings: ATR-12: Retiring allowance; ATR-48: Transfer of retiring allowance to an RRSP.

Forms: NRTA1: Authorization for non-resident tax exemption; RC4157: Deducting income tax on pension and other income, and filing the T4A slip and summary.

(j.2) **transfer to spousal RRSP [before 1995]** — [No longer relevant]

Notes: 60(j.2) applies to taxation years 1989-94 only.

(k) [Repealed under former Act]

Notes: 60(k) repealed by 1990 pension bill, effective 1990. It allowed transfers of amounts from one DPSP to another. See now 147(19)–(21).

(l) **transfer of refund of premium under RRSP [or other amount, on death]** — the total of all amounts each of which is an amount paid by or on behalf of the taxpayer in the year or within 60 days after the end of the year (or within such longer period after the end of the year as is acceptable to the Minister)

(i) as a premium under a registered retirement savings plan under which the taxpayer is the annuitant,

(ii) to acquire, from a person licensed or otherwise authorized under the laws of Canada or a province to carry on in Canada an annuities business, an annuity

(A) under which the taxpayer is the annuitant

(I) for the taxpayer's life, or for the lives jointly of the taxpayer and the taxpayer's spouse or common-law partner either without a guaranteed period, or with a guaranteed period that is not greater than 90 years minus the lesser of the age in whole years of the taxpayer and the age in whole years of the taxpayer's spouse or common-law partner at the time the annuity was acquired, or

(II) for a term equal to 90 years minus the age in whole years of the taxpayer or the age in whole years of the taxpayer's spouse or common-law partner, at the time the annuity was acquired, or

(B) under which the taxpayer is the annuitant for a term not exceeding 18 years minus the age in whole years of the taxpayer at the time the annuity was acquired

that does not provide for any payment thereunder except

(C) the single payment by or on behalf of the taxpayer,

(D) annual or more frequent periodic payments

(I) beginning not later than one year after the date of the payment referred to in clause (C), and

(II) each of which is equal to all other such payments or not equal to all other such payments solely because of an adjustment that would, if the annuity were an annuity under a retirement savings plan, be in accordance with subparagraphs 146(3)(b)(iii) to (v), and

(E) payments in full or partial commutation of the annuity and, where the commutation is partial,

(I) equal annual or more frequent periodic payments thereafter, or

(II) annual or more frequent periodic payments thereafter that are not equal solely because of an adjustment that would, if the annuity were an annuity under a retirement savings plan, be in accordance with subparagraphs 146(3)(b)(iii) to (v),

or

(iii) to a carrier as consideration for a registered retirement income fund under which the taxpayer is the annuitant

where that total

(iv) is designated by the taxpayer in the taxpayer's return of income under this Part for the year,

(v) does not exceed the total of

(A) the amount included in computing the taxpayer's income for the year as a refund of premiums out of or under a registered retirement savings plan under which the taxpayer's spouse or common-law partner was the annuitant,

(A.1) the amount included in computing the taxpayer's income for the year as a payment (other than a payment that is part of a series of periodic payments) received by the taxpayer out of or under a pooled registered pension plan as a consequence of the death of an individual who was, immediately before the death, a spouse or common-law partner of the taxpayer,

(A.2) the amount included by subsection 146.5(3) in computing the taxpayer's income for the year as a payment received by the taxpayer as a consequence of the death of an individual who was

(I) immediately before the death, the spouse or common-law partner of the taxpayer, or

(II) a parent or grandparent of the taxpayer, if, immediately before the death, the taxpayer was financially dependent on the individual for support because of mental or physical infirmity,

(B) the amount included in computing the taxpayer's income for the year as a refund of premiums out of or under a registered retirement savings plan where the taxpayer was dependent by reason of physical or mental infirmity on the annuitant under the plan,

(B.01) the amount included in computing the taxpayer's income for the year as a payment (other than a payment that is part of a series of periodic payments or that relates to an actuarial surplus) received by the taxpayer out of or under a pooled registered pension plan, a registered pension plan or a specified pension plan as a consequence of the death of an individual of whom the taxpayer was a child or grandchild, if the taxpayer was, immediately before the death, financially dependent on the individual for support because of mental or physical infirmity,

(B.1) the least of

(I) the amount paid by or on behalf of the taxpayer to acquire an annuity that would be described in subparagraph (ii) if that subparagraph were read without reference to clause (A) thereof,

(II) the amount (other than any portion of it that is included in the amount determined under clause (B), (B.01) or (B.2)) that is included in computing the taxpayer's income for the year as

1. a payment (other than a payment that is part of a series of periodic payments or that relates to an actuarial surplus) received by the taxpayer out of or under a pooled registered pension plan, a registered pension plan or a specified pension plan,

2. a refund of premiums out of or under a registered retirement savings plan, or

3. a designated benefit in respect of a registered retirement income fund (in this clause having the meaning assigned by subsection 146.3(1))

as a consequence of the death of an individual of whom the taxpayer is a child or grandchild, and

(III) the amount, if any, by which the amount determined for the year under subclause (II) in respect of the taxpayer exceeds the amount, if any, by which

1. the total of all designated benefits of the taxpayer for the year in respect of registered retirement income funds

exceeds

2. the total of all amounts that would be eligible amounts of the taxpayer for the year in respect of those funds (within the meaning that would be assigned by subsection 146.3(6.11) if the taxpayer were described in paragraph (b) thereof), and

(B.2) all eligible amounts of the taxpayer for the year in respect of registered retirement income funds (within the meaning assigned by subsection 146.3(6.11)),

and, where the amount is paid by a direct transfer from the issuer of a registered retirement savings plan or a carrier of a registered retirement income fund,

(C) the amount included in computing the taxpayer's income for the year as a consequence of a payment described in subparagraph 146(2)(b)(ii), and

(D) the amount, if any, by which

(I) the amount received by the taxpayer out of or under a registered retirement income fund under which the taxpayer is the annuitant and included because of subsection 146.3(5) in computing the taxpayer's income for the year

exceeds

(II) the amount, if any, by which the minimum amount (within the meaning assigned by subsection 146.3(1)) under the fund for the year exceeds the total of all amounts received out of or under the fund in the year by an individual who was an annuitant under the fund before the taxpayer became the annuitant under the fund and that were included because of subsection 146.3(5) in computing that individual's income for the year, and

(vi) was not deducted in computing the taxpayer's income for a preceding taxation year;

Related Provisions: 56(1)(d.2) — Income inclusion; 60(j) — Transfer of superannuation benefits; 60.011(3) — Application of 60(l)(ii) to qualifying trust annuity; 60.02(1)"eligible proceeds" — Amount deducted under 60(l) cannot also be rolled over to RDSP under 60.02; 60.022(1) — Reading of 60(l)(v)(B.2) for 2015; 70(3.1) — "Rights or things" treatment on death; 75.2 — Treatment of qualifying trust annuity payout or on death; 104(27)(e) — Where pension benefit paid to trust as a consequence of death; 146(1.1) — Where child presumed not financially dependent for 60(l)(v)(B.01); 146(2), (3) — Acceptance of plan for registration; 146(5) — Amount of RRSP premiums deductible; 146(6.1) — Recontribution of certain withdrawals; 146(8.1) — RRSP — deemed receipt of refund of premiums; 146(8.2) — RRSP — amount deductible; 146(16)(d) — RRSP — transfer of funds; 146(21) — Transfer from Sask. Pension Plan; 146(21.1) — Contribution to Sask. Pension Plan deemed to be RRSP premium for 60(l); 146.3(5.1) — Amount included in income; 146.3(6.11) — Transfer of designated benefit; 147.3 — Transfer from RPP; 147.5(11) — Pooled registered pension plan contribution deemed to be RRSP premium; 148(1)(e) — Amounts included in policyholder's income; 204.2(1)(b)(i)(A) — Excess amount for a year in respect of RRSP; 212(1)(q)(i)(B) — Exemption from non-resident withholding tax; 248(8) — Meaning of "consequence" of death; 252(3) — Extended meaning of "spouse"; *Interpretation Act* 27(5) — Meaning of "within 60 days". See also at end of s. 60.

Notes: A "refund of premiums", as defined in 146(1), is paid on the death of an RRSP annuitant. 60(l) allows it to be rolled into an RRSP or annuity of the deceased's spouse, child or grandchild, subject to conditions. See VIEWS doc 2005-0127821E5 and Notes to 146.3(1)"annuitant". No relief was available in *Maass-Howard*, 2013 FCA 234, where the taxpayer withdrew RRSP funds to pay for surgery unavailable in Canada. See also Notes to 146(8.8) re *Murphy Estate* case.

60(l)(v)(A.1) and (A.2) allow similar rollovers of proceeds on death, from a PRPP and an ALDA (advanced life deferred annuity).

See also Ann Elise Alexander, "RRSPs and RRIFs on Death", 2015 STEP Canada conference (contact memberservices@step.ca).

For CRA interpretation see docs 2011-0420781C6 (60(l)(v)(B.01)); 2012-0458231E5 (no rollover to non-RRSP trust for mentally competent spouse); 2014-0528551E5 (60(l)(v)(B.1)); 2014-0563261E5, 2015-0596781E5 (RRIF withdrawal may be rolled into life annuity); 2016-0627341R3 (ruling on purchase of annuity for deceased's grandson); 2016-0651711C6 [2016 APFF q.2] (designated benefit transferred to spouse's RRIF or RRSP is reduced by RRIF minimum amount if transfer is later than year of death); 2018-0758611E5 and 2019-0830781E5 (60(l)(ii) does not apply to charitable gift annuity, as the charity is not legally authorized to carry on annuities business, despite exemption from provincial insurance law).

For 60(l)(iv), a designation "in the taxpayer's return" is valid even if the return is filed late. See Notes to 7(1.31).

A 2005 Budget proposal, shown here up to PITA 57th ed., was enacted in 60.02.

60(l)(v)(A.2) added by 2021 budget bill #1, effective 2020.

60(l) amended by 2002-2013 technical bill (effective 1989), 2012 and 2011 budget bills #2, 2003 Budget, 2000 same-sex partners bill, 1999 Budget, 1995-97, 1993 and 1992 technical bills, 1990 pension bill.

Regulations: 7800 (Saskatchewan Pension Plan is specified pension plan, for 60(l)(v)(B.01) and (v)(B.1)(II)1).

Interpretation Bulletins: IT-124R6: Contributions to registered retirement savings plans; IT-307R4: Spousal or common-law partner registered retirement savings plans; IT-500R: RRSPs — death of an annuitant; IT-517R: Pension tax credit (cancelled); IT-528: Transfers of funds between registered plans.

Advance Tax Rulings: ATR-37: Refund of premiums transferred to spouse.

Forms: T2030: Direct transfer under subpara. 60(l)(v).

(m) such amount in respect of payments to a registered disability savings plan as is permitted under section 60.02;

Notes: 60(m) is not necessary, since the deductions allowed by 60.02 are already in the same subdivision. It was added for convenience since it is similar to 60(l).

60(m) replaced by 2010 budget bill #2, effective March 4, 2010. The previous version allowed a deduction for certain amounts paid under the *Estate Tax Act*, which was repealed as of 1972. Canada does not impose an estate tax, but see Notes to 70(5).

RDSP Bulletins: 3R1 (Bill C-38).

Forms: RC4625: Rollover to an RDSP under para. 60(m).

(m.1) **succession duties applicable to certain property** — that proportion of any superannuation or pension benefit, death benefit, benefit under a registered retirement savings plan, benefit under a deferred profit sharing plan or benefit that is a payment under an income-averaging annuity contract, received by the taxpayer in the year, on or after the death of a predecessor, in payment of or on account of property to which the taxpayer is the successor, that

(i) such part of any succession duties payable under a law of a province in respect of the death of the predecessor as may reasonably be regarded as attributable to the property in payment of or on account of which the benefit was so received,

is of

(ii) the value of the property in payment of or on account of which the benefit was so received, as computed for the purposes of the law referred to in subparagraph (i);

Notes: At present, none of the provinces imposes succession duties. They do impose probate fees (called estate administration tax in Ontario), but those do not appear to be covered by 60(m.1). See also Notes to 70(5).

(n) **repayment of pension or benefits** — any amount paid by the taxpayer in the year as a repayment (otherwise than because of Part VII of the *Unemployment Insurance Act*, chapter U-1 of the Revised Statutes of Canada, 1985, Part VII of the *Employment Insurance Act* or section 8 of the *Canada Recovery Benefits Act*) of any of the following amounts to the extent that the amount was included in computing the taxpayer's income, and not deducted in computing the taxpayer's taxable income, for the year or for a preceding taxation year, namely,

(i) a pension described in clause 56(1)(a)(i)(A),

(ii) a benefit described in clause 56(1)(a)(i)(B),

(iii) an amount described in subparagraph 56(1)(a)(ii),

(iv) a benefit described in subparagraph 56(1)(a)(iv),

(v) a benefit described in subparagraph 56(1)(a)(vi),

(v.1) a benefit described in subparagraph 56(1)(a)(vii), and

(vi) an amount described in paragraph 56(1)(r);

Related Provisions: 60(n.1) — Deduction for repayment of pension benefits received in error; 60(v.1) — Deduction for repayment under *EI Act* Part VII; 60(v.2) — Deduction for repayment of Canada Recovery Benefit; 60(v.3) — Deduction for other COVID-19 benefits repaid.

Notes: Since these amounts were included in income, repayment of them is deductible. (An example is repayment due to EI benefits overlapping with a wrongful dismissal settlement: *Court*, 2020 FCA 199, para. 24.)

The opening words exclude the Canada Recovery Benefit (CRB) because its repayment is deductible under 60(v.2) with more lenient timing. Repayment of the Canada Recovery Sickness Benefit (CRB) and Canada Recovery Caregiving Benefit (CRCB), paid under other CRBA sections, can be deducted under 60(n), as can the Canada Emergency Recovery Benefit (CERB) and Canada Emergency Student Benefit (CESB); all of these can alternatively be deducted in the year of the benefit (to cancel the income inclusion), under 60(v.3).

For the deduction on repayment of EI benefits by someone whose income is too high, see 60(v.1).

The 60(n) deduction applies only in the year the amount is repaid, not to retroactively cancel a 56(1)(a) inclusion: *Lessard*, 2007 FCA 9 (leave to appeal denied 2007 CarswellNat 1534 (SCC)); VIEWS doc 2015-0578071E5. It cannot be carried forward to a later year: 2009-0350221I7.

The words "and not deducted in computing the taxpayer's taxable income" prevent an amount deductible elsewhere (e.g., under 110(1)(f) or (g)) from being deducted again in computing net income. See *Grondin*, 2009 TCC 459.

Opening words amended to exclude CRBA s. 8 by 2020 COVID bill #4, effective Sept. 27, 2020.

60(n) amended by 2002-2013 technical bill (for 2006 and later tax years), 2001 Budget, 1995-97 technical bill, 1996 EI bill, 1993 and 1991 technical bills.

Remission Orders: *Clara Reid Remission Order*, P.C. 2006-372 (taxpayer paid tax on EI benefits and had no income against which to deduct later repayment); *Ronald Francoeur Remission Order*, P.C. 2006-503 (taxpayer paid tax on EI benefits and was unable to deduct later repayment; inequitable outcome was beyond his control).

Income Tax Folios: S1-F2-C3: Scholarships, research grants and other education assistance [replaces IT-340R].

Forms: PD24: Application for a refund of overdeducted CPP contributions or EI premiums; T1 General return, Line 23200 [former 232]: Other deductions; T2204: Employee overpayment of EI premiums.

(n.1) **repayment of pension benefits** — an amount paid by the taxpayer in the year to a pooled registered pension plan or registered pension plan if

(i) the taxpayer is an individual,

(ii) the amount is paid as

(A) a repayment of an amount received from the plan that was included in computing the taxpayer's income for the year or a preceding year, if

(I) it is reasonable to consider that the amount was paid under the plan as a consequence of an error and not as an entitlement to benefits, or

(II) it was subsequently determined that, as a consequence of a settlement of a dispute in respect of the taxpayer's employment, the taxpayer was not entitled to the amount, or

(B) interest in respect of a repayment described in clause (A), and

(iii) no portion of the amount is deductible under any of paragraph 8(1)(m) and subsections 146(5) to (5.2) in computing the taxpayer's income for the year;

Notes: 60(n.1) added by 2002-2013 technical bill, for 2009 and later tax years, but references to PRPP and 146(5)-(5.2) effective Dec. 14, 2012.

Registered Plans Directorate Newsletters: 18-1 (repayments to registered pension plans).

(o) **legal [or other] expenses [of objection or appeal]** — amounts paid by the taxpayer in the year in respect of fees or expenses incurred in preparing, instituting or prosecuting an objection to, or an appeal in relation to,

(i) an assessment of tax, interest or penalties under this Act or an Act of a province that imposes a tax similar to the tax imposed under this Act,

(ii) a decision of the Canada Employment Insurance Commission under the *Employment Insurance Act* or to an appeal of such a decision to the Social Security Tribunal,

(iii) an assessment of any income tax deductible by the taxpayer under section 126 or any interest or penalty with respect thereto, or

(iv) an assessment or a decision made under the *Canada Pension Plan* or a provincial pension plan as defined in section 3 of that Act;

Related Provisions: 20(1)(cc) — Deduction for representation expenses; 56(1)(l) — Reimbursed costs included in income; 152(1.2) — Rule applies to determination of losses as well as assessment. See also at end of s. 60.

Notes: *60(o)(i)* allows deduction of fees paid to object to (s. 165) or appeal (s. 169) an assessment, including an assessed penalty such as a 163(2) gross-negligence penalty. It does not apply to fees to defend against criminal charges for tax evasion (see 239(1) Notes). It applies to the costs of an action by a status Indian to have income declared exempt: VIEWS doc 2010-0374081I7; and to proceedings in the Tribunal administratif du Québec to obtain a personal tax credit: 2019-0812641C6 [2019 APFF q.5]. *Quaere* whether it applies to a non-arm's length transfer (160(1), (2)) or director-liability (227.1, 227(10)(a)) assessment (though CRA accepts this); these are not exactly assessments of "tax".

Audit disputes: CRA permits 60(o)(i) deduction for the cost of dealing with CRA auditors from the time one is told an audit has started: IT-99R5 para. 7; VIEWS doc 2019-0812641C6 [2019 APFF q.5]. This can include costs to obtain documents to respond to CRA enquiries: May 2011 ICAA roundtable (tinyurl.com/cra-abtax), q. 8.

Interest waiver applications (220(3.1)) do not qualify under 60(o)(i): VIEWS doc 2019-0812641C6 [2019 APFF q.5].

Voluntary disclosure costs (see Notes to 220(3.1)) do not qualify under 60(o)(i): docs 2012-0437831E5, 2014-0528451C6 (though 20(1)(cc) might apply if the disclosure relates to business income); deduction is allowed for further submissions if CRA proposes a different assessment than the disclosure: 921728, 2012-0434071E5, 2014-0532121E5, 2016-0625731C6 [CPA QC 2016 q.7]. For criticism see Morrison & Strawson, "Professional Fees Incurred for Voluntary Disclosure", 23(10) *Canadian Tax Highlights* (ctf.ca) 2-3 (Oct. 2015).

Contesting another person's assessment: 60(o)(i) does not say "an assessment of the taxpayer". Amounts X pays to contest Y's assessment are deductible, if X "has a pecuniary or other interest in the outcome that was not too remote": *Flood*, 2006 TCC 186 (executor-beneficiary contesting assessment of his mother's estate); *Sherman (Walbi Trust)*, [1976] C.T.C. 2207 (TRB) (shareholder contesting corporation's assessment). Thus, a tax shelter investor can deduct amounts paid towards another's appeal in a test case for the entire group. CRA initially refused to follow the above cases: Tataryn, "Deductibility of Legal Expenses", xxviii(14) *The Canadian Taxpayer* (Carswell) 110-11 (July 2006); but the Crown then conceded the point, in *Charles Haines*, TCC, 2006-1890(IT)G, with a Consent to Judgment that explicitly recognized a 60(o) deduction for amounts H paid for his mother's appeal; and in 2014, CRA Appeals accepted the author's submission and allowed fees X paid for her mother's objection.

What costs are deductible: Fees need not have been paid to a lawyer: VIEWS doc 2014-0524191I7. Deductible fees include sales tax paid on them, except, in effect, GST/HST or QST recoverable as input tax credit (it is deemed government assistance and included back in income to offset the deduction: 248(16), 12(1)(x)). (Whether such ITC is allowed under GST/HST depends on whether a TCC appeal is part of business activity, including winding it up: *Haggart*, 2003 FCA 446; *ONEnergy*, 2018 FCA 54; *614730 Ontario*, 2010 TCC 75, para. 42.) 60(o) applies to court costs awarded against the taxpayer: 2014-0524191I7, 2015-0578131I7.

60(o)(ii) and *(iv)* apply to EI and CPP dispute costs. *60(o)(iii)* applies to fees to contest another country's tax assessment that will affect Canadian foreign tax credit.

GST/HST assessment dispute fees (including director liability) are not deductible under 60(o): *Shapiro*, 2011 TCC 79; *Lacroix*, 2013 TCC 312. They may be deductible under ordinary business principles (see 9(1) Notes) if the business is still carried on or as part of winding it up. They may also be deductible under 20(1)(cc): see Notes thereto.

Legal fees (LF) generally may be deductible from business or property income, or capitalized as part of the cost of capital property, under ordinary accounting principles. See Notes to 9(1), 18(1)(a) and 18(1)(b); VIEWS docs 2005-0122544E5, 2012-0451331I7. For other provisions allowing deduction of (or credit for) specific LF, see 8(1)(b) (employee salary), 8(1)(f) (commission employee), 20(1)(e) (financing expenses), 20(1)(cc) (lobbying or representations), 60(o.1) (wrongful dismissal or pension), 62(3)(f) (moving expenses), 118.01(1)"eligible adoption expense"(b), 118.2(2)(l.1)(i) (transplant costs) and 152(1.2) (appealing a determination). See IT-99R5. LF relating to family law or spousal support; see 56(1)(b) Notes. LF to litigate rights under a shareholders' oppression remedy can be claimed in calculating the capital gain under 40(1)(a), and a portion can be allocated against interest received in the judgment: 2006-018119I17. LF to obtain workers' compensation benefits are not deductible: 2008-0289751E5, 2009-032473117, 2011-0393241E5. Nor are LF for action against a provincial health insurance plan for not paying for medical treatment: 2010-0389841E5. Nor are LF to settle an estate, but LF to secure the payment of dividends may be: 2010-0354711E5. Nor are LF to defend against a guarantee which itself is allowed as an ABIL: *Woloshyn*, 2011 TCC 306. LF may need to be apportioned between multiple purposes: *Mader* (originally reported as *Richards*), 2019 TCC 289, paras. 41-45.

Disclosing details of LF to a CRA auditor should not waive solicitor-client privilege: see Notes to 232(2).

60(o)(ii) amended by 2012 budget bill #1 (to apply to Social Security Tribunal), 1995-97 technical bill, 1996 Human Resources bill, 1996 EI bill.

Income Tax Folios: S4-F2-C1: Deductibility of fines and penalties [replaces IT-104R3].

Interpretation Bulletins: IT-99R5: Legal and accounting fees.

Forms: T1 General return, Line 23200 [former 232]: Other deductions.

(o.1) legal expenses [re job loss or pension benefit] — the amount, if any, by which the lesser of

(i) the total of all legal expenses (other than those relating to a division or settlement of property arising out of, or on a breakdown of, a marriage or common-law partnership) paid by the taxpayer in the year or in any of the 7 preceding taxation years to collect or establish a right to an amount of

(A) a benefit under a pension fund or plan (other than a benefit under the *Canada Pension Plan* or a provincial pension plan as defined in section 3 of that Act) in respect of the employment of the taxpayer or a deceased individual of whom the taxpayer was a dependant, relation or legal representative, or

(B) a retiring allowance of the taxpayer or a deceased individual of whom the taxpayer was a dependant, relation or legal representative, and

(ii) the amount, if any, by which the total of all amounts each of which is

(A) an amount described in clause (i)(A) or (B)

(I) that is received after 1985,

(II) in respect of which legal expenses described in subparagraph (i) were paid, and

(III) that is included in computing the income of the taxpayer for the year or a preceding taxation year, or

(B) an amount included in computing the income of the taxpayer under paragraph 56(1)(l.1) for the year or a preceding taxation year,

exceeds the total of all amounts each of which is an amount deducted under paragraph (j), (j.01), (j.1) or (j.2) in computing the income of the taxpayer for the year or a preceding taxation year, to the extent that the amount may reasonably be considered to have been deductible as a consequence of the receipt of an amount referred to in clause (A),

exceeds

(iii) the portion of the total described in subparagraph (i) in respect of the taxpayer that may reasonably be considered to have been deductible under this paragraph in computing the income of the taxpayer for a preceding taxation year;

Related Provisions: 8(1)(b) — Legal fees to obtain back pay; 56(1)(l.1) — Amounts included in income — award or reimbursement of legal expenses paid to collect or establish a right to retiring allowance, etc. See also at end of s. 60.

Notes: 60(o.1) allows a deduction for legal fees paid to obtain a "retiring allowance" (defined in 248(1) to include damages for wrongful dismissal: VIEWS doc 2012-043320117) or a pension benefit (other than a CPP/QPP benefit), but only against such income, with a 7-year carryforward. The limitation to income from that source is unfair but binding: *Bradley*, 2009 TCC 341 (this has been brought to Finance's attention). Carryforward past 7 years was denied in *Filion*, 2017 FCA 67.

In *Atkinson*, 2004 TCC 445, a police officer charged with criminal offences was allowed to deduct his legal fees because, had he been convicted, he would have lost his job and thus his right to a pension. *Contra*: in *Dalfort*, 2009 TCC 416 (FCA appeal dismissed for delay A-398-09), where D paid legal fees to defend claims from his ex-spouse, his investment portfolio was not a "pension plan" and no deduction was allowed; and in *Geick*, 2017 TCC 120, a police officer's pension was already vested and not at risk, so his fees to defend against criminal charges were not deductible. See also Notes to 8(1)(b).

"Legal expenses" means "services typically performed by a lawyer", and may include support services such as accounting fees to support a wrongful dismissal claim, but not other costs such as finding new employment: *Medynski*, 2009 TCC 216.

Legal expenses were disallowed as unproven in: *Naraine*, 2016 FCA 6, para. 3; *Barrett*, 2019 TCC 228.

Where a bankruptcy proposal is designed to allow the taxpayer to continue to collect his pension income, the CRA says the legal fees paid to file the proposal do not qualify: VIEWS doc 2004-0078001E5. Legal fees to make representations to OSFI against reduction in pension benefits qualify: 2013-0500911E5.

CRA says legal fees to obtain a Pension Division Order on marriage breakdown, and actuarial fees, are not deductible due to 18(1)(b) because they are capital expenses (VIEWS docs 2002-0177827, 2015-0614151E5). This is wrong in the author's view:

60(o.1) provides a standalone deduction, and 18(1)(b) restricts deductions only against income *from business or property* in s. 9.

See also IT-99R5 paras. 22-27, VIEWS doc 2008-0302451R5 and Notes to 60(o).

60(o.1) amended by 2000 same-sex partners bill (last change effective 2001) and 1992 technical bill; added by 1989 Budget.

See also Notes to 60(o).

Interpretation Bulletins: IT-99R5: Legal and accounting fees.

(p) **repayment of apprenticeship grants** — the total of all amounts each of which is an amount paid in the taxation year as a repayment under the Apprenticeship Incentive Grant program or the Apprenticeship Completion Grant program of an amount that was included under paragraph 56(1)(n.1) in computing the taxpayer's income for the taxation year or a preceding taxation year;

Related Provisions: 8(1)(r)(ii)B(B)(II)2 — Apprentice mechanics' tools deduction based on amount of repayment of Apprenticeship Incentive Grant.

Notes: 60(p) amended by 2002-2013 technical bill, for 2009 and later years.

60(p) added by 2006 budget bill #2, for 2007 and later tax years.

Former 60(p) repealed by 1992 Child Benefit bill effective 1995. It provided a deduction for repayment of an overpaid (pre-1993) family business.

(q) **refund of income payments** — where the taxpayer is an individual, an amount paid by the taxpayer in the year to a person with whom the taxpayer was dealing at arm's length (in this paragraph referred to as the "payer") if

(i) the amount has been included in computing the income of the taxpayer for the year or a preceding taxation year as an amount described in subparagraph 56(1)(n)(i) or paragraph 56(1)(o) paid to the taxpayer by the payer,

(ii) at the time the amount was paid by the payer to the taxpayer a condition was stipulated for the taxpayer to fulfil,

(iii) as a result of the failure of the taxpayer to fulfil the condition referred to in subparagraph (ii) the taxpayer was required to repay the amount to the payer,

(iv) during the period for which the amount referred to in subparagraph (i) was paid the taxpayer did not provide other than occasional services to the payer as an officer or under a contract of employment, and

(v) the amount was paid to the taxpayer for the purpose of enabling the taxpayer to further the taxpayer's education;

Related Provisions: 56(1)(p) — Income inclusion to recipient. See also at end of s. 60.

Notes: 60(q)(i) amended by 2013 budget bill #2, effective March 1994, to add "for the year or", so that a deduction is allowed for an amount repaid in the same year.

Income Tax Folios: S1-F2-C3: Scholarships, research grants and other education assistance [replaces IT-340R].

(r) **amounts included under subsec. 146.2(6) [RHOSP]** — [Obsolete]

Notes: 60(r) relates to registered home ownership savings plans (RHOSPs) under 146.2; they were eliminated in 1985.

(s) **repayment of policy loan** — the total of all repayments made by the taxpayer in the year in respect of a policy loan (within the meaning assigned by subsection 148(9) made under a life insurance policy, not exceeding the amount, if any, by which

(i) the total of all amounts required by subsection 148(1) to be included in computing the taxpayer's income for the year or a preceding taxation year from a disposition described in paragraph (b) of the definition "disposition" in subsection 148(9) in respect of that policy

exceeds

(ii) the total of all repayments made by the taxpayer in respect of the policy loan that were deductible in computing the taxpayer's income for a preceding taxation year;

Related Provisions: 148(4.01) — Repayment of policy loan on partial surrender; 148(9) — "value". See also at end of s. 60.

Notes: 60(s) does not apply to an amount that is not repaid by the taxpayer but is withheld by the insurer from the estate or heirs on the taxpayer's death: VIEWS docs 9909075, 2009-0327091C6.

Opening words of 60(s) amended by 1992 technical bill, effective for repayments made after Dec. 20, 1991, to change "payments" to "repayments", to clarify that the deductible portion will not include any amount in respect of interest paid on such a loan.

(t) **RCA distributions** — where an amount in respect of a particular retirement compensation arrangement is required by paragraph 56(1)(x) or (z) or subsection 70(2) to be included in computing the taxpayer's income for the year, an amount equal to the lesser of

(i) the total of all amounts in respect of the particular arrangement so required to be included in computing the taxpayer's income for the year, and

(ii) the amount, if any, by which the total of all amounts each of which is

(A) an amount (other than an amount deductible under paragraph 8(1)(m.2) or transferred to the particular arrangement under circumstances in which subsection 207.6(7) applies) contributed under the particular arrangement by the taxpayer while it was a retirement compensation arrangement and before the end of the year,

(A.1) an amount transferred in respect of the taxpayer before the end of the year to the particular arrangement from another retirement compensation arrangement under circumstances in which subsection 207.6(7) applies, to the extent that the amount would have been deductible under this paragraph in respect of the other arrangement in computing the taxpayer's income if it had been received by the taxpayer out of the other arrangement,

(B) an amount paid by the taxpayer before the end of the year and at a time when the taxpayer was resident in Canada to acquire an interest in the particular arrangement, or

(C) an amount that was received or became receivable by the taxpayer before the end of the year and at a time when the taxpayer was resident in Canada as proceeds from the disposition of an interest in the particular arrangement,

exceeds the total of all amounts each of which is

(D) an amount deducted under this paragraph or paragraph (u) in respect of the particular arrangement in computing the taxpayer's income for a preceding taxation year, or

(E) an amount transferred in respect of the taxpayer before the end of the year from the particular arrangement to another retirement compensation arrangement under circumstances in which subsection 207.6(7) applies, to the extent that the amount would have been deductible under this paragraph in respect of the particular arrangement in computing the taxpayer's income if it had been received by the taxpayer out of the particular arrangement;

Related Provisions: 107.2 — Distribution by retirement compensation arrangement. See also at end of s. 60.

Notes: In *Haley*, 2006 TCC 464, there was no 60(t) deduction to offset RCA benefits because H had not contributed directly to the RCA. His past contributions were made under the *Public Service Superannuation Act* and had been deducted when made.

60(t) amended by 1995-97 technical bill, effective for 1996 and later taxation years.

(u) **RCA dispositions** — where an amount in respect of a particular retirement compensation arrangement is required by paragraph 56(1)(y) to be included in computing the taxpayer's income for the year, an amount equal to the lesser of

(i) the total of all amounts in respect of the particular arrangement so required to be included in computing the taxpayer's income for the year, and

(ii) the amount, if any, by which the total of all amounts each of which is

(A) an amount (other than an amount deductible under paragraph 8(1)(m.2) or transferred to the particular arrangement under circumstances in which subsection 207.6(7) applies) contributed under the particular arrangement by the taxpayer while it was a retirement compensation arrangement and before the end of the year,

(A.1) an amount transferred in respect of the taxpayer before the end of the year to the particular arrangement from another retirement compensation arrangement under circumstances in which subsection 207.6(7) applies, to the extent that the amount would have been deductible under paragraph (t) in respect of the other arrangement in computing the taxpayer's income if it had been received by the taxpayer out of the other arrangement, or

(B) an amount paid by the taxpayer before the end of the year and at a time when the taxpayer was resident in Canada to acquire an interest in the particular arrangement

exceeds the total of all amounts each of which is

(C) an amount deducted under paragraph (t) in respect of the particular arrangement in computing the taxpayer's income for the year or a preceding taxation year,

(D) an amount deducted under this paragraph in respect of the particular arrangement in computing the taxpayer's income for a preceding taxation year, or

(E) an amount transferred in respect of the taxpayer before the end of the year from the particular arrangement to another retirement compensation arrangement under circumstances in which subsection 207.6(7) applies, to the extent that the amount would have been deductible under paragraph (t) in respect of the particular arrangement in computing the taxpayer's income if it had been received by the taxpayer out of the particular arrangement;

Related Provisions: 56(1)(y) — Retirement compensation arrangements; 107.2 — Distribution by a retirement compensation arrangement. See also at end of s. 60.

Notes: 60(u) amended by 1995-97 technical bill, for 1996 and later taxation years.

(v) **repayment — parents of victims of crime** — the total of all amounts each of which is an amount paid in the year as a repayment of a benefit that was included because of paragraph 56(1)(a.3) in computing the taxpayer's income for the year or a preceding taxation year;

Notes: 60(v) added by S.C. 2012, c. 27, effective 2013. See Notes to 56(1)(a.3).

Former 60(v) repealed by 2011 budget bill #2, for taxation years that begin after 2009. 146(21.1) now deems contributions to a "specified pension plan" (the Saskatchewan Pension Plan) to be RRSP contributions for certain purposes.

Former 60(v) amended by 2000 same-sex partners bill (last change effective 2001), 1998 Budget and 1990 pension bill.

(v.1) **UI and EI benefit repayment** — any benefit repayment payable by the taxpayer under Part VII of the *Unemployment Insurance Act* or Part VII of the *Employment Insurance Act* on or before April 30 of the following year, to the extent that the amount was not deductible in computing the taxpayer's income for any preceding taxation year;

Related Provisions: 56(1)(a)(iv) — Unemployment insurance/employment insurance benefits taxable; 56(9) — Meaning of "income for the year"; 60(n)(iv) — Deduction for repayment under other Parts of the UI/EI Act; 63(2) — Child care expenses — income exceeding income of supporting person; 180.01(3) — Stock option inclusion on elective adjustment for underwater shares not counted as income for EI Part VII.

Notes: Employment insurance benefits are partly repayable when net income exceeds $1.25 \times$ the maximum yearly insurable earnings: *Employment Insurance Act* s. 145(1). For 2020, $1.25 \times \$54,200 = \$67,750$; for 2021, $1.25 \times \$56,300 = \$70,375$. See Table I-8 in introductory pages for other years. The repayment is on the T1 return (line 23500). The repayment, reflecting income originally taxed under 56(1)(a)(iv), is deductible under 60(v.1) to prevent taxation of income not kept by the recipient. Before 1989, it was deductible in computing taxable income (rather than net income), under 110(1)(i).

For examples of this rule applying see *Henson*, 2014 TCC 43; *Meyer*, 2019 TCC 131 (RRSP withdrawal put M over the threshold). See 180.2(1) Notes re the legality of the EI benefit repayment requirement where the income threshold is exceeded due to income exempted under a tax treaty.

60(v.1) added by 1991 technical bill, effective 1989, and amended by 1996 EI bill and 1995-97 technical bill, both effective June 30, 1996.

Income Tax Folios: S1-F2-C3: Scholarships, research grants and other education assistance [replaces IT-340R]; S1-F3-C1: Child care expense deduction [replaces IT-495R3].

Remission Orders: *Micheline and Roch Malenfant Remission Order*, P.C. 2005-1732 (remission of tax on EI benefit where deduction under 60(v.1) was worthless in later year).

Forms: T1 General return, Line 23500 [former 235].

(v.2) **Canada Recovery Benefit repayment** — any benefit repayment payable by the taxpayer under section 8 of the *Canada Recovery Benefits Act* on or before the taxpayer's balance-due day for the taxation year, to the extent that the amount was not deductible in computing the taxpayer's income for any preceding taxation year;

Notes: The Canada Recovery Benefit (CRB) is included in income: 56(1)(r)(iv); tinyurl.com/cra-crb-tax. A repayment cannot be deducted under 60(n), as 60(v.2) is more flexible: it allows deduction for 2020 if repayment is due ("payable") by April 30, 2021. However, repayment of Canada Recovery Sickness Benefit and Canada Recovery Caregiving Benefit, which are paid under other CRBA sections, is deducted under 60(n).

The CRB is $500 per week for up to 26 weeks from Sept. 27, 2020 (on expiry of the Canada Emergency Response Benefit), for workers who are self-employed or ineligible for EI but still require income support due to COVID-19.

Repayment of at least part of the CRB is required if the person has net income (subject to certain adjustments) over $38,000: *Canada Recovery Benefits Act* s. 8(2)-(3). The repayment demand is treated as an income tax assessment, and the ITA objection and appeal provisions apply: *CRBA* s. 8(4).

Para. 60(v.2) added by 2020 COVID bill #4, effective Sept. 27, 2020.

(v.3) **COVID-19 — other benefit repayments** — any benefit repaid by the taxpayer before 2023 to the extent that the amount of the benefit was included in computing the taxpayer's income for the year under any of clauses 56(1)(r)(iv.1)(A) to (D), except to the extent that the amount is

(i) deducted in computing the taxpayer's income for any year under paragraph (n), or

(ii) deductible in computing the taxpayer's income for any year under paragraph (v.2);

Notes: 60(v.3), added by 2021 budget bill #1 retroactive to 2020, allows deduction for repayment of COVID-19 benefits, in the year of the *benefit* (i.e., reversing the income inclusion). One can instead choose to claim the deduction under 60(n) in the year of *repayment* (useful if one is in a higher bracket that later year), in which case no 60(v.3) deduction is available: (v.3)(i). The Canada Recovery Benefit is deductible only under 60(v.2). See tinyurl.com/covid-ben-tax.

(w) **tax under Part I.2** — the amount of the taxpayer's tax payable under Part I.2 for the year;

Related Provisions: 56(9) — Meaning of "income for the year"; 180.2 — OAS benefits clawback; 180.2(1)"adjusted income"(b) — Deduction does not reduce income for calculating clawback. See also at end of s. 60.

Notes: 60(w) added by 1989 Budget, effective 1989. Part I.2 (180.2) imposes a "clawback" tax on old age security payments received by high-income taxpayers. Where the clawback applies, the payment is partially or fully repaid under 180.2(1). Since it is also brought into income under 56(1)(a)(i), the amount repaid under 180.2 is deductible under 60(w) to avoid double tax.

Income Tax Folios: S1-F3-C1: Child care expense deduction [replaces IT-495R3].

(x) **repayment under *Canada Education Savings Act*** — the total of all amounts each of which is an amount paid by the taxpayer in the year as a repayment, under the *Canada Education Savings Act* or under a designated provincial program (as defined in subsection 146.1(1)), of an amount that was included because of subsection 146.1(7) in computing the taxpayer's income for the year or a preceding taxation year;

Related Provisions: 146.1(14)(a) — Reference to *Canada Education Savings Act* includes reference to earlier *DHRD Act*.

Notes: The *CES Act* (reproduced in Notes to 146.1) provides the Canada Education Student Grant (CESG), a 20% grant on the first $2,000 of annual contributions to a RESP (increased to 30% or 40% on the first $500 for low-income families). RESP trustees must limit CESG payments to $7,200 per beneficiary. If a person is a beneficiary under more than one RESP, the total grants could exceed this limit, and the person must repay the excess. Since the grants would have been included in income as educational assistance payments, 60(x) allows an offsetting deduction for the repayment.

60(x) amended by 2007 budget bill #2, effective for 2007 and later taxation years, effectively to extend the rule to Quebec education savings grants. Earlier amended by 2004 RESPs bill; added by 1998 Budget.

(y) **repayment of UCCB** — the total of all amounts each of which is an amount paid in the taxation year as a repayment, under the *Universal Child Care Benefit Act*, of a benefit that was

included because of subsection 56(6) in computing the taxpayer's income for the taxation year or a preceding taxation year;

Related Provisions: 122.5(1)"adjusted income"(b), 122.6"adjusted income"(b), 180.2(1)"adjusted income"(b) — Deduction does not affect entitlement to GST/HST Credit or Canada Child Benefit or clawback of Old Age Security.

Notes: See Notes to 56(6). 60(y) added by 2006 budget bill #1 (Part 6 — Universal Child Care Benefit), effective for repayments made after June 2006.

Forms: T1 General return, Line 21300 [former 213].

(z) repayment under the *Canada Disability Savings Act* — the total of all amounts each of which is an amount paid in the taxation year as a repayment, under or because of the *Canada Disability Savings Act* or a designated provincial program as defined in subsection 146.4(1), of an amount that was included because of section 146.4 in computing the taxpayer's income for the taxation year or a preceding taxation year; and

Related Provisions: 122.5(1)"adjusted income"(b), 122.6"adjusted income"(b), 180.2(1)"adjusted income"(b) — Deduction does not affect entitlement to GST/HST Credit or Canada Child Benefit or clawback of Old Age Security.

Notes: See Notes at end of 146.4 for the text of the CDSA.

60(z) amended by 2010 budget bill #1, for 2009 and later taxation years.

60(z) added by 2007 RDSPs bill, effective for 2008 and later taxation years.

(z.1) tax informant program — the total of all amounts each of which is an amount paid in the year as a repayment of an amount that was included, because of paragraph 56(1)(z.4), in computing the taxpayer's income for the year or a preceding taxation year.

Notes: See Notes to 56(1)(z.4). 60(z.1) added by 2014 budget bill #1, effective June 19, 2014.

Related Provisions [s. 60]: 4(2), (3) — Whether deductions under s. 60 are applicable to a particular source.

Definitions [s. 60]: "allowance" — 56(12); "amount" — 248(1); "annuitant" — 146(1), 146.3(1); "annuity" — 248(1); "beneficially interested" — 248(25); "benefit under a deferred profit sharing plan", "business" — 248(1); "Canada" — 255; "child" — 252(1); "child support amount", "commencement day" — 56.1(4), 60.1(4); "common-law partner", "common-law partnership" — 248(1); "consequence of the death" — 248(8); "death benefit" — 248(1); "deferred profit sharing plan" — 147(1), 248(1); "defined benefit provision" — 147.1(1); "designated benefit" — 146.3(1); "designated provincial program" — 146.1(1), 146.4(1); "eligible amount" — 60.01; "employee", "employee benefit plan", "employer", "employment" — 248(1); "estate" — 104(1), 248(1); "financially dependent" — 146(1.1); "former spouse" — 252(3); "income-averaging annuity contract" — 61(4), 248(1); "individual" — 248(1); "life insurance policy" — 138(12), 248(1); "minimum amount" — 146.3(1); "Minister" — 248(1); "parent" — 252(2)(a); "person" — 248(1); "policy loan" — 148(9); "pooled registered pension plan" — 147.5(1), 248(1); "prescribed", "property" — 248(1); "province" — *Interpretation Act* 35(1); "provincial pension plan" — *Canada Pension Plan* s. 3; "refund of premiums" — 146(1); "registered pension plan" — 248(1); "registered retirement income fund" — 146.3(1), 248(1); "registered retirement savings plan", "RRSP deduction limit" — 146(1), 248(1); "related" — 251(2); "resident in Canada" — 94(3)(a), 250; "retirement compensation arrangement", "retiring allowance" — 248(1); "series" — 248(10); "specified pension plan" — 248(1), Reg. 7800; "spouse" — 252(3); "superannuation or pension benefit" — 248(1); "support amount" — 56.1(4), 60.1(4); "taxable income" — 2(2), 248(1); "taxation year" — 249; "taxpayer" — 248(1); "trust" — 104(1), 248(1), (3); "writing" — *Interpretation Act* 35(1).

60.001 [Repealed]

Notes: 60.001 repealed by 2013 budget bill #2, for orders made after Dec. 12, 2013 (it was relevant only to orders made before 1993). It provided an alternate reading of former 60(c.1) for certain purposes. Added in the RSC 1985 (5th Supp) consolidation, this was originally in the application rule to the 1988 amendment to 60(c.1).

60.01 Eligible amount — For the purpose of paragraph 60(j), the amount, if any, by which

(a) the amount of any payment received by a taxpayer in a taxation year out of or under a foreign retirement arrangement and included in computing the taxpayer's income because of clause 56(1)(a)(i)(C.1) (other than any portion thereof that is included in respect of the taxpayer for the year under subparagraph 60(j)(i) or that is part of a series of periodic payments)

exceeds

(b) the portion, if any, of the payment included under paragraph (a) that can reasonably be considered to derive from contributions to the foreign retirement arrangement made by a person other than the taxpayer or the taxpayer's spouse or common-law partner or former spouse or common-law partner,

is an eligible amount in respect of the taxpayer for the year.

Notes: See Notes to 248(1)"foreign retirement arrangement" and 60(j); and Georgina Tollstam, "Periodic Payments Under a Foreign Retirement Arrangement", 22(1) *Canadian Tax Highlights* (ctf.ca) 7-8 (Jan. 2014).

60.01(b) amended by 2000 same-sex partners bill (last change effective 2001), 1992 technical bill. Added by 1991 technical bill.

Definitions [s. 60.01]: "amount", "common-law partner" — 248(1); "foreign retirement arrangement" — 248(1); "former spouse" — 252(3); "person" — 248(1); "series" — 248(10); "spouse" — 252(3); "taxation year" — 249; "taxpayer" — 248(1).

Interpretation Bulletins: IT-124R6: Contributions to registered retirement savings plans; IT-528: Transfers of funds between registered plans.

60.011 [Henson trust] — (1) Meaning of "lifetime benefit trust" — For the purpose of subsection (2), a trust is at any particular time a lifetime benefit trust with respect to a taxpayer and the estate of a deceased individual if

(a) immediately before the death of the deceased individual, the taxpayer

(i) was both a spouse or common-law partner of the deceased individual and mentally infirm, or

(ii) was both a child or grandchild of the deceased individual and dependent on the deceased individual for support because of mental infirmity; and

(b) the trust is, at the particular time, a personal trust under which

(i) no person other than the taxpayer may receive or otherwise obtain the use of, during the taxpayer's lifetime, any of the income or capital of the trust, and

(ii) the trustees

(A) are empowered to pay amounts from the trust to the taxpayer, and

(B) are required — in determining whether to pay, or not to pay, an amount to the taxpayer — to consider the needs of the taxpayer including, without limiting the generality of the foregoing, the comfort, care and maintenance of the taxpayer.

Related Provisions: 108(3) — Meaning of "income" of trust.

Notes: See Notes at end of 60.011.

(2) Meaning of "qualifying trust annuity" — Each of the following is a qualifying trust annuity with respect to a taxpayer:

(a) an annuity that meets the following conditions:

(i) it is acquired after 2005,

(ii) the annuitant under it is a trust that is, at the time the annuity is acquired, a lifetime benefit trust with respect to the taxpayer and the estate of a deceased individual,

(iii) it is for the life of the taxpayer (with or without a guaranteed period), or for a fixed term equal to 90 years minus the age in whole years of the taxpayer at the time it is acquired, and

(iv) if it is with a guaranteed period or for a fixed term, it requires that, in the event of the death of the taxpayer during the guaranteed period or fixed term, any amounts that would otherwise be payable after the death of the taxpayer be commuted into a single payment;

(b) an annuity that meets the following conditions:

(i) it is acquired after 1988,

(ii) the annuitant under it is a trust under which the taxpayer is the sole person beneficially interested (determined without regard to any right of a person to receive an amount from the trust only on or after the death of the taxpayer) in amounts payable under the annuity,

(iii) it is for a fixed term not exceeding 18 years minus the age in whole years of the taxpayer at the time it is acquired, and

(iv) if it is acquired after 2005, it requires that, in the event of the death of the taxpayer during the fixed term, any amounts that would otherwise be payable after the death of the taxpayer be commuted into a single payment; and

(c) an annuity that meets the following conditions:

(i) it is acquired

(A) after 2000 and before 2005 at a time at which the taxpayer was mentally or physically infirm, or

(B) in 2005 at a time at which the taxpayer was mentally infirm,

(ii) the annuitant under it is a trust under which the taxpayer is the sole person beneficially interested (determined without regard to any right of a person to receive an amount from the trust only on or after the death of the taxpayer) in amounts payable under the annuity, and

(iii) it is for the life of the taxpayer (with or without a guaranteed period), or for a fixed term equal to 90 years minus the age in whole years of the taxpayer at the time it is acquired.

Related Provisions: 60.011(3) — Lifetime benefit trust; 75.2 — Treatment of qualifying trust annuity payout or on death; 248(1)"qualifying trust annuity" — Definition applies to entire Act.

(3) Application of para. 60(l) to "qualifying trust annuity" — For the purpose of paragraph 60(l),

(a) in determining if a qualifying trust annuity with respect to a taxpayer is an annuity described in subparagraph 60(l)(ii), clauses 60(l)(ii)(A) and (B) are to be read without regard to their requirement that the taxpayer be the annuitant under the annuity; and

(b) if an amount paid to acquire a qualifying trust annuity with respect to a taxpayer would, if this Act were read without reference to this subsection, not be considered to have been paid by or on behalf of the taxpayer, the amount is deemed to have been paid on behalf of the taxpayer where

(i) it is paid

(A) by the estate of a deceased individual who was, immediately before death,

(I) a spouse or common-law partner of the taxpayer, or

(II) a parent or grandparent of the taxpayer on whom the taxpayer was dependent for support, or

(B) by the trust that is the annuitant under the qualifying trust annuity, and

(ii) it would, if it had been paid by the taxpayer, be deductible under paragraph 60(l) in computing the taxpayer's income for a taxation year and the taxpayer elects, in the taxpayer's return of income under this Part for that taxation year, to have this paragraph apply to the amount.

Related Provisions: 75.2 — Treatment of QTA payout or on death.

Notes: 60.011 can allow a rollover of an RRSP into a Henson trust (**HT**), which is a discretionary trust for a disabled child, designed so that the child does not lose entitlement to social assistance (*Ontario v. Henson*, 1987 CarswellOnt 654 (Ont. SCJ)). The Supreme Court of Canada held in *SA v. Metro Vancouver Housing*, 2019 SCC 4, that a HT need not be disclosed when applying for subsidized rent. However, not every HT qualifies under 60.011 (the one in *Henson* would not have qualified); it must be drafted to meet the conditions. In *1804-02565*, 2019 ONSBT 2071, the Social Benefits Tribunal found insufficient evidence to establish a HT.

See VIEWS docs 2005-0113721E5, 2005-0148641E5, 2019-0823751E5; Sklar, "The New Lifetime Benefit Trust", 162 *The Estate Planner* (CCH) 1-3 (July 2008); Baxter, "Trusts for Special Needs Family Members", 8(12) *Tax Hyperion [TH]* (Carswell, Dec. 2011); Watson, "RDSP or Henson Trust", 9(12) *TH* 4-6 (Dec. 2012); Donkor, "The Henson Trust", 27(10) *Money & Family Law* (Carswell) 75-76 (Oct. 2012); Golombek & Pearl-Weinberg, "Planning for Disabled Beneficiaries Using Life Insurance Trusts", XXIV(2) *Insurance Planning* (Federated Press) 2-6 (2019). A HT was approved in Quebec as excluded from the social assistance calculation in *Québec v. A.N.*, 2014 QCCS 616. In *Simms v. Simms*, 2017 ONSC 6624, a non-family member was appointed Special Trustee of a HT. Alberta excludes trust income (including from a HT) when determining provincial benefit eligibility: *Assured Income for the Severely Handicapped General Regulation*, Schedule 2 s. 2(2)(k). (Note also the RDSP rollover alternative in 60.02.)

For 60.011(3)(b)(ii), an election "in the taxpayer's return" is valid even if the return is filed late. See Notes to 7(1.31).

60.011 added by 2002-2013 technical bill, effective 1989, with an application rule deeming the election made for years before 2005 if a deduction was claimed.

Definitions [s. 60.011]: "amount", "annuity" — 248(1); "beneficially interested" — 248(25); "child" — 252(1); "common-law partner" — 248(1); "estate" — 104(1), 248(1); "grandparent" — 252(2)(d); "individual" — 248(1); "lifetime benefit trust" — 60.011(1); "parent" — 252(2)(a); "person", "personal trust" — 248(1); "qualifying trust annuity" — 60.011(2), 248(1); "taxation year" — 249; "taxpayer" — 248(1).

60.02 [Rollover from RRSP/RRIF/RPP to RDSP on death] — **(1) Definitions** — The definitions in this subsection apply in this section and section 146.4,

"eligible individual" means a child or grandchild of a deceased annuitant under a registered retirement savings plan or a registered retirement income fund, or of a deceased member of a pooled registered pension plan, a registered pension plan or a specified pension plan, who was financially dependent on the deceased for support, at the time of the deceased's death, by reason of mental or physical infirmity.

Related Provisions: 146(1.1) — Restriction on meaning of "financially dependent".

Notes: "Financially dependent" (see 146(1.1)) does not require the child to live with the parent: VIEWS doc 2019-0806541E5.

Definition amended by 2012 budget bill #2 (effective Dec. 14, 2012), 2011 budget bill #2.

"eligible proceeds" means an amount (other than an amount that was deducted under paragraph 60(l) in computing the eligible individual's income) received by an eligible individual as a consequence of the death after March 3, 2010 of a parent or grandparent of the eligible individual that is

(a) a refund of premiums (as defined in subsection 146(1));

(b) an eligible amount under subsection 146.3(6.11); or

(c) a payment (other than a payment that is part of a series of periodic payments or that relates to an actuarial surplus) out of or under a pooled registered pension plan, a registered pension plan or a specified pension plan.

Related Provisions: 60.02(2) — Rollover to RDSP on death.

Notes: Para. (c) amended by 2012 budget bill #2, effective Dec. 14, 2012, to refer to a PRPP.

60.02(1)"eligible proceeds"(c) amended by 2011 budget bill #2, effective March 4, 2010, to add "or a specified pension plan" (the Saskatchewan Pension Plan). See Notes to 248(1)"specified pension plan".

"specified RDSP payment" in respect of an eligible individual means a payment that

(a) is made to a registered disability savings plan under which the eligible individual is the beneficiary;

(b) complies with the conditions set out in paragraphs 146.4(4)(f) to (h);

(c) is made after June 2011;

(d) has been designated in prescribed form for a taxation year by the holder of the plan and the eligible individual at the time that the payment is made; and

(e) if the eligible individual is not a "DTC-eligible individual" (as defined in subsection 146.4(1)), is made not later than the end of the fourth taxation year following the first taxation year throughout which the beneficiary is not a DTC-eligible individual.

Related Provisions: 60.02(2) — Rollover to RDSP on death; 146.4(1)"contribution"(d) — Specified RDSP payment generally not counted as contribution.

Notes: Para (e) added by 2021 budget bill #1, effective March 19, 2019, to permit a tax-deferred rollover of proceeds from a deceased person's registered plan to an eligible beneficiary's RDSP by the end of the 5th year throughout which the beneficiary is DTC-ineligible.

"transitional eligible proceeds" of a taxpayer means

(a) any amount (other than an amount that is eligible proceeds or an amount that was deducted under paragraph 60(l) in computing the taxpayer's income) that is received by the taxpayer as a consequence of the death of an individual after 2007 and before 2011 out of or under

(i) a registered retirement savings plan or registered retirement income fund, or

(ii) a registered pension plan (other than an amount that is received as part of a series of periodic payments or that relates to an actuarial surplus); or

(b) an amount withdrawn from the taxpayer's registered retirement savings plan or a registered retirement income fund (in this subsection referred to as the "RRSP withdrawal") if

(i) the taxpayer previously deducted an amount under paragraph 60(l) in respect of an amount that would be described by paragraph (a) if it were read without reference to "other than an amount that is eligible proceeds or an amount that was deducted under paragraph 60(l) in computing the taxpayer's income",

(ii) the RRSP withdrawal is included in computing the taxpayer's income for the year of the withdrawal, and

(iii) the RRSP withdrawal does not exceed the amount deducted under subparagraph (i).

Related Provisions: 60.02(3)–(5) — Transitional rules.

(2) Rollover to RDSP on death — There may be deducted in computing the income for a taxation year of a taxpayer who is an eligible individual an amount that

(a) does not exceed the lesser of

(i) the total specified RDSP payments made in the year or within 60 days after the end of the year (or within any longer period after the end of the year that is acceptable to the Minister) in respect of the taxpayer; and

(ii) the total amount of eligible proceeds that is included in computing the taxpayer's income in the year; and

(b) was not deducted in computing the taxpayer's income for a preceding taxation year.

Related Provisions: 60(m) — Deductions under 60.02 allowed as deductions from income; 60.02(3)–(5) — Transitional rules; *Interpretation Act* 27(5) — Meaning of "within 60 days".

Notes: See Ruby Lim & Donald Carson, "RDSPs Enhanced", 18(5) *Canadian Tax Highlights* (ctf.ca) 7-8 (May 2010).

60.02(2) allows a deduction only where the benefit transferred to the financially dependent infirm child is paid from the deceased's RPP, not where it is paid from the estate: VIEWS doc 2016-0625061E5.

RDSP Bulletins: See under 60(m).

Forms: See under 60(m).

(3) Application of subsecs. (4) and (5) — Subsections (4) and (5) do not apply unless

(a) a taxpayer who was the annuitant under a registered retirement savings plan or a registered retirement income fund or was a member of a registered pension plan died after 2007 and before 2011;

(b) the taxpayer was, immediately before the taxpayer's death, the parent or grandparent of an eligible individual;

(c) transitional eligible proceeds were received from the plan or fund by

(i) an eligible individual in respect of the taxpayer,

(ii) a person who was the spouse or common- law partner of the taxpayer immediately before the taxpayer's death, or

(iii) a person who is a beneficiary of the taxpayer's estate or who directly received transitional eligible proceeds as a consequence of the death of the taxpayer; and

(d) the transitional eligible proceeds were included in computing the income of a person for a taxation year.

(4) Transitional rule — There may be deducted in computing the income of a taxpayer described in paragraph (3)(c) for a taxation year an amount approved by the Minister that does not exceed the lesser of

(a) the total specified RDSP payments made by the taxpayer before 2012, and

(b) the amount of transitional eligible proceeds included in computing the taxpayer's income for the year.

Related Provisions: 60(m) — Deductions under 60.02 allowed as deductions from income; 60.02(3) — Conditions for 60.02(4) to apply; 60.02(6) — Limitation.

(5) Transitional rule — deceased taxpayer — There may be deducted in computing the income of a taxpayer for the taxation year in which the taxpayer died an amount approved by the Minister that does not exceed the lesser of

(a) the total specified RDSP payments made before 2012 by an individual described in subparagraph (3)(c)(iii), and

(b) the amount by which the total of all amounts that were included in computing the taxpayer's income for the year under subsection 146(8.8) or 146.3(6) exceeds the total of all amounts, if any, that were deducted in computing the taxpayer's income for the year under subsection 146(8.92) or 146.3(6.3).

Related Provisions: 60(m) — Deductions under 60.02 allowed as deductions from income; 60.02(3) — Conditions for 60.02(5) to apply; 60.02(6) — Limitation.

(6) Limitation — The total amounts that may be deducted under subsections (4) and (5) in respect of transitional eligible proceeds received in respect of the death of a taxpayer shall not exceed the total transitional eligible proceeds received in respect of the deceased taxpayer.

Notes: 60.02 added by 2010 budget bill #2, effective March 4, 2010. (It addresses an issue raised in the 2005 Budget, reproduced as a Possible Future Amendment under 60(l)(ii)(A) up to PITA 57th ed.) It replaced a 60.02 (added in RSC 1985 (5th Supp) consolidation) which read "Subparagraph 60(v)(iii) is applicable to the 1991 and later taxation years."

Definitions [s. 60.02]: "amount" — 248(1); "beneficiary" — 248(25) [Notes]; "child" — 252(1); "common-law partner" — 248(1); "consequence" — 248(8); "DTC-eligible individual" — 146.4(1); "eligible amount" — 146.3(6.11); "eligible individual", "eligible proceeds" — 60.02(1); "estate" — 104(1), 248(1); "financially dependent" — 146(1.1); "grandparent" — 252(2)(d); "individual", "Minister" — 248(1); "parent" — 252(2)(a); "person" — 248(1); "pooled registered pension plan" — 147.5(1), 248(1); "prescribed" — 248(1); "registered disability savings plan" — 146.4(1), 248(1); "registered pension plan" — 248(1); "registered retirement income fund" — 146.3(1), 248(1); "registered retirement savings plan" — 146(1), 248(1); "specified RDSP payment" — 60.02(1); "specified pension plan" — 248(1), Reg. 7800; "taxation year" — 249; "taxpayer" — 248(1); "transitional eligible proceeds" — 60.02(1).

Information Circulars: 99-1R2: Registered disability savings plans.

Forms: RC4625: Rollover to an RDSP under para. 60(m).

60.021 [No longer relevant.]

Notes: 60.021 added by 2008 budget bill #2, effective March 12, 2009. It provides rules for the 25% reduction for 2008 in the minimum RRIF withdrawal (146.3(1.1)) and variable-benefit RPP payment (Reg. 8506(7)(b)), introduced due to the downturn in the economy.

60.022 (1) Additions to cl. 60(l)(v)(B.2) for 2015 [recontribution of above-minimum RRIF withdrawal] — In determining the amount that may be deducted because of paragraph 60(l) in computing a taxpayer's income for the 2015 taxation year, clause 60(l)(v)(B.2) is to be read as follows:

(B.2) the total of all amounts each of which is

(I) the taxpayer's eligible amount (within the meaning of subsection 146.3(6.11)) for the year in respect of a registered retirement income fund,

(II) the taxpayer's eligible RRIF withdrawal amount (within the meaning of subsection 60.022(2)) for the year in respect of a RRIF,

(III) the taxpayer's eligible variable benefit withdrawal amount (within the meaning of subsection 60.022(3)) for the year in respect of an account of the taxpayer under a money purchase provision of a registered pension plan, or

(IV) the taxpayer's eligible PRPP withdrawal amount (within the meaning of subsection 60.022(4)) for the year in respect of an account of the taxpayer under a PRPP,

Related Provisions: 60.022(2)–(5) — Interpretation.

Notes: 60.022(1) allows a deduction for recontribution of RRIF withdrawals taken in 2015 that exceed the reduced RRIF minimum amount for 2015 as set by the April 2015 Budget (see 2015 amendments to Reg. 7308(3), (4)). This is done by providing an alternate reading of 60(l)(v)(B.2) for 2015. The recontribution must be made by Feb. 29, 2016 (60(l) opening words: within 60 days after year-end). Similar recontribution is allowed for excessive payments from a defined-contribution RPP (Reg. 8506(11), (12)) and a PRPP (147.5(3)(b)(ii)). See tinyurl.com/rrif-min2015.

For CRA interpretation and policy see docs 2015-0587351E5, 2015-0596321E5.

(2) Eligible RRIF withdrawal amount — A taxpayer's eligible RRIF withdrawal amount for the taxation year in respect of a RRIF under which the taxpayer is the annuitant at the beginning of the taxation year is the amount determined by the formula

$$A - B$$

where

A is the lesser of

(a) the total of all amounts included, because of subsection 146.3(5), in computing the taxpayer's income for the taxation year in respect of amounts received out of or under the fund (other than an amount paid by direct transfer from the fund to another fund or to a registered retirement savings plan), and

(b) the amount that would be the minimum amount under the fund for the 2015 taxation year if it were determined using the prescribed factors under subsection 7308(3) or (4), as the case may be, of the *Income Tax Regulations* as they read on December 31, 2014; and

B is the minimum amount under the fund for the taxation year.

Related Provisions: 257 — Formula cannot calculate to less than zero.

(3) Eligible variable benefit withdrawal amount — A taxpayer's eligible variable benefit withdrawal amount for a taxation year in respect of an account of the taxpayer under a money purchase provision of a registered pension plan is the amount determined by the formula

$$A - B - C$$

where

A is the lesser of

(a) the total of all amounts each of which is the amount of a retirement benefit (other than a retirement benefit permissible under any of paragraphs 8506(1)(a) to (e) of the *Income Tax Regulations*) paid from the plan in the taxation year in respect of the account and included, because of paragraph 56(1)(a), in computing the taxpayer's income for the taxation year, and

(b) the amount that would be the minimum amount for the account for the 2015 taxation year if it were determined using the factor designated under subsection 7308(4) of the *Income Tax Regulations* as they read on December 31, 2014;

B is the minimum amount for the account for the taxation year; and

C is the total of all contributions made by the taxpayer under the provision and designated for the purposes of subsection 8506(12) of the *Income Tax Regulations*.

Related Provisions: 257 — Formula cannot calculate to less than zero.

(4) Eligible PRPP withdrawal amount — A taxpayer's eligible PRPP withdrawal amount for a taxation year in respect of an account of the taxpayer under a PRPP is the amount determined by the formula

$$A - B$$

where

A is the lesser of

(a) the total of all amounts each of which is the amount of a distribution made from the account in the taxation year and included, because of subsection 147.5(13), in computing the taxpayer's income for the taxation year, and

(b) the amount that would be the minimum amount for the account for the 2015 taxation year if it were determined using the factor designated under subsection 7308(4) of the *Income Tax Regulations* as they read on December 31, 2014, and

B is the minimum amount for the account for the taxation year.

Related Provisions: 257 — Formula cannot calculate to less than zero.

(5) Expressions used in this section — For the purposes of this section,

(a) **"money purchase provision"** has the same meaning as in subsection 147.1(1);

(b) **"retirement benefits"** has the same meaning as in subsection 8500(1) of the *Income Tax Regulations*;

(c) the minimum amount for an account of a taxpayer under a money purchase provision of a registered pension plan is the amount determined under subsection 8506(5) of the *Income Tax Regulations*; and

(d) the minimum amount for an account of a taxpayer under a PRPP is the amount that would be the minimum amount for the calendar year under subsection 8506(5) of the *Income Tax Regulations* if the taxpayer's account were an account under a money purchase provision of a registered pension plan.

Notes: 60.022 added by 2015 Budget bill, effective June 23, 2015. See Notes to 60.022(1).

Definitions [s. 60.022]: "amount" — 248(1); "calendar year" — *Interpretation Act* 37(1)(a); "eligible amount" — 146.3(6.11); "eligible PRPP withdrawal amount" — 60.022(4); "eligible RRIF withdrawal amount" — 60.022(2); "eligible variable benefit withdrawal amount" — 60.022(3); "minimum amount" — 60.022(5)(c), (d), 146.3(1); "money purchase provision" — 60.022(5)(a), 147.1(1); "prescribed" — 248(1); "PRPP" — 248(1)"pooled registered pension plan"; "RRIF" — 248(1)"registered retirement income fund"; "registered pension plan" — 248(1); "registered retirement income fund" — 146.3(1), 248(1); "registered retirement savings plan" — 146(1), 248(1); "retirement benefits" — 60.022(5)(b), Reg. 8500(1); "taxation year" — 249; "taxpayer" — 248(1).

60.03 [Pension income splitting] — **(1) Definitions** — The following definitions apply in this section.

"eligible pension income", of an individual for a taxation year, means the total of

(a) the eligible pension income (as defined in subsection 118(7)) of the individual for the year,

(b) if the individual has attained the age of 65 years before the end of the year, the lesser of

(i) the total of all amounts each of which is a payment made in the year to the individual

(A) out of or under a retirement compensation arrangement that provides benefits that supplement the benefits provided under a registered pension plan (other than an individual pension plan for the purposes of Part LXXXIII of the *Income Tax Regulations*), and

(B) in respect of a life annuity that is attributable to periods of employment for which benefits are also provided to the individual under the registered pension plan, and

(ii) the amount, if any, by which the defined benefit limit (as defined in subsection 8500(1) of the *Income Tax Regulations*) for the year multiplied by 35 exceeds the amount determined under paragraph (a), and

(c) the lesser of

(i) the total of all amounts received by the individual in the year on account of

(A) a retirement income security benefit payable to the individual under Part 2 of the *Veterans Well-being Act*, or

(B) an income replacement benefit payable to the individual under Part 2 of the *Veterans Well-being Act*, if the amount is determined under subsection 19.1(1), paragraph 23(1)(b) or subsection 26.1(1) of that Act (as modified, where applicable, under Part 5 of that Act), and

(ii) the amount, if any, by which the "defined benefit limit" (as defined in subsection 8500(1) of the *Income Tax Regulations*) for the year multiplied by 35 exceeds the total of the amounts determined under paragraphs (a) and (b).

Related Provisions: 118(3)B(b)(ii) — Pension income credit for such income.

Notes: See Notes at end of 60.03. For interpretation of "life annuity" from an RCA in (b), see VIEWS doc 2013-0515541E5.

Cl. (c)(i)(B) added by 2018 budget bill #1, effective April 2019. Before then, read:

(i) the total of all amounts received by the individual in the year on account of a retirement income security benefit payable to the individual under Part 2 of the *Veterans Well-being Act*, and

Subpara (c)(i) effectively amended by S.C. 2017, c. 20 (Bill C-44, Royal Assent June 22, 2017), subsec. 292(2), to change "*Canadian Forces Members and Veterans Re-establishment and Compensation Act*" (with all other such references in federal legislation) to "*Veterans Well-being Act*" effective April 2018.

Para. (c) added by 2017 budget bill #2, for 2015 and later tax years. It includes amounts received as a retirement income security benefit (RISB) under *VWA* Part 2. The RISB amount to be split is capped by (c)(ii). This allows couples to split RISB amounts, to the extent the total eligible pension income split does not exceed the defined benefit limit × 35 (for 2020, $27,830 / 9 × 35 = $108,228; for 2021, $29,210 / 9 × 35 = $113,594). This equals the maximum defined-benefit pension for a 35-year career.

Para. (b) added by 2012 budget bill #2, for 2013 and later taxation years. Before 2013, read " "eligible pension income" has the same meaning as in subsection 118(7)".

"joint election" in respect of a pensioner and a pension transferee for a taxation year means an election made jointly in prescribed form by the pensioner and the pension transferee and filed with the Minister with both the pensioner's and the pension transferee's returns of income for the taxation year in respect of which the election is made, on or before their respective filing-due dates for the taxation year.

Related Provisions: 60.03(2) — Effect of election; 60.03(3) — Only one election per taxation year; 60.03(4) — Election invalid if false declaration; 118(3) — Pension credit; 153(1.3)(a) — Election cannot reduce source withholdings; 153(2) — Source deductions deemed withheld on behalf of transferee; 160(1.3) — Spouses jointly liable for tax on split-pension amount; 220(3.201) — Extension of time to file or revoke election.

Notes: See Notes to 220(3.201) re late-filed elections.

"pension income" has the meaning assigned by section 118.

Related Provisions: 118(7), (8) — Definition of "pension income".

"pension transferee" for a taxation year means an individual who

(a) is resident in Canada,

(i) if the individual dies in the taxation year, at the time that is immediately before the individual's death, or

(ii) in any other case, at the end of the calendar year in which the taxation year ends; and

(b) at any time in the taxation year is married to, or in a common-law partnership with, a pensioner and is not, by reason of the breakdown of their marriage or common-law partnership, living separate and apart from the pensioner at the end of the taxation year and for a period of at least 90 days commencing in the taxation year.

Notes: If a taxpayer has a spouse in a nursing home (no breakdown of marriage?) as well as a common-law partner, both appear to qualify as "pension transferee", but CRA may disagree: VIEWS doc 2009-0330301C6.

See Notes to 118.8 for the meaning of "living separate and apart".

"pensioner" for a taxation year means an individual who

(a) receives eligible pension income in the taxation year; and

(b) is resident in Canada,

(i) if the individual dies in the taxation year, at the time that is immediately before the individual's death, or

(ii) in any other case, at the end of the calendar year in which the taxation year ends.

"qualified pension income" has the meaning assigned by section 118.

Related Provisions: 118(7), (8) — Definition of "qualified pension income".

"split-pension amount" for a taxation year is the amount elected by a pensioner and a pension transferee in a joint election for the taxation year not exceeding the amount determined by the formula

$$0.5A \times B/C$$

where

A is the eligible pension income of the pensioner for the taxation year;

B is the number of months in the pensioner's taxation year at any time during which the pensioner was married to, or was in a common-law partnership with, the pension transferee; and

C is the number of months in the pensioner's taxation year.

(2) Effect of pension income split — For the purpose of subsection 118(3), if a pensioner and a pension transferee have made a joint election in a taxation year,

(a) the pensioner is deemed not to have received the portion of the pensioner's pension income or qualified pension income, as the case may be, for the taxation year that is equal to the amount of the pensioner's split-pension amount for that taxation year; and

(b) the pension transferee is deemed to have received the split-pension amount

(i) as pension income, to the extent that the split-pension amount was pension income to the pensioner, and

(ii) as qualified pension income, to the extent that the split-pension amount was qualified pension income to the pensioner.

Related Provisions: See under 60.03(1)"joint election".

Notes: See Notes at end of 60.03.

Forms: T1032: Joint election to split pension income.

(3) Limitation — A pensioner may file only one joint election for a particular taxation year.

Notes: This rule prevents a person from splitting pension income with two persons (e.g., a still-married spouse and current common-law partner).

(4) False declaration — A joint election is invalid if the Minister establishes that a pensioner or a pension transferee has knowingly or under circumstances amounting to gross negligence made a false declaration in the joint election.

Notes [s. 60.03]: 60.03 (added by 2007 budget bill #1, for 2007 and later tax years) provides the rules for optional pension income splitting with the spouse. The actual deduction is in 60(c) and the income inclusion to the spouse is in 56(1)(a.2). See tinyurl.com/pension-splitting for details. The election can be revoked if CRA consents: 220(3.201). For what kinds of income qualify, see 60.03(1)"eligible pension income" and Notes to 118(7)"qualified pension income".

Both spouses are liable for the transferee's extra tax, with no reassessment limitation period: 160(1.3), (2).

Where foreign pension income is split, the foreign tax can also be split for foreign tax credit purposes: May 2008 ICAA roundtable (tinyurl.com/cra-abtax), q. 22.

60.03 splitting was disallowed in: *Létourneau*, 2009 TCC 614 (retired accountant's income from KPMG was deemed by 96(1.1) to be partnership (business) income, not pension income); *Talbot*, 2013 TCC 2 (Hydro-Québec lump sum pension payment during phased retirement was excluded by 118(8)(e); only life annuity income qualifies); *Tremblay*, 2013 TCC 186 (GIC bought with lump sum RRSP withdrawals [Golombek, "Problems with Pension Splitting", 2013(19) *Tax Times* (Carswell) 2 (Oct. 11, 2013)]); *Cantin*, 2014 TCC 20 (FC appeal dismissed on procedural grounds A-100-14) (long-term disability benefits).

The following can qualify for splitting: accrual income from a foreign annuity (VIEWS docs 2010-0371161E5, 2010-0375511E5); pension income received before spouse's death (2008-0275731E5); RCA distributions (2013-0497761E5, 2013-0515081I7 [shows calculations]); T4A-RCA amounts from a funded supplementary employee retirement plan (SERP) (2013-0501021E5); RRIF proceeds received on death, in some cases (2008-0284401C6, 2012-0453151C6); bankrupt spouse (2015-0589051E5).

The following do not qualify: payments from (or derived from) an RRSP or RRIF, for taxpayers under age 65 (doc 2008-0281261M4, 2009-0337451E5; this does not violate the *Charter of Rights*: *Hotte*, 2010 TCC 611); payments from an annuity to an under-65 spouse that are attributed to an over-65 spouse by 74.1(1) (2008-0284411C6); RRIF payment attributed to a spouse by 146.3(5.4): (2007-0257001E5); Individual Pension Plan minimum amount in excess of lifetime retirement benefits (2019-0799191C6 [CLHIA 2019 q.14]).

On the interaction of the election with the calculation of non-farming income for the capital gains exemption on farm property, see doc 2012-0439791E5.

If pension splitting results in lower marginal rates, it can be worth postponing discretionary claims, such as CCA (20(1)(a)) or loss carryforwards (111(1)(a)), to a later year when they are more useful.

Reverse splitting, from lower-income (LIS) to higher-income spouse, can be used to take the LIS out of OAS clawback range (see 180.2), or to reduce income-based nursing home fees: VIEWS doc 2020-0845211E5.

See also Nilson, "Understanding the New Pension Income Splitting Options", 1873 *Tax Topics* (CCH) 1-3 (Jan. 31, 2008); Cyna, "Splitting Pensions — Does the Payment Qualify?", 6(7) *Tax Hyperion* (Carswell, July 2009).

For a very different kind of income splitting for 2014-15 only, the "Family Tax Cut" for spouses with minor children, see 119.1.

See also 120.4(1.1)(c)(i), which provides that income-splitting tax does not apply to sprinkled income to a spouse of a person over 65 (e.g, by dividend) in certain cases.

Definitions [s. 60.03]: "amount", "annuity" — 248(1); "calendar year" — *Interpretation Act* 37(1)(a); "common-law partnership" — 248(1); "defined benefit limit" — Reg. 8500(1); "eligible pension income" — 60.03(1); "employment", "filing-due date", "individual" — 248(1); "individual pension plan" — Reg. 8300(1); "joint election" — 60.03(1); "Minister" — 248(1); "month" — *Interpretation Act* 35(1); "pension income" — 60.03(1), 118(7), (8); "pension transferee", "pensioner" — 60.03(1); "prescribed" — 248(1); "qualified pension income" — 60.03(1), 118(7), (8); "registered pension plan" — 248(1); "resident in Canada" — 250; "retirement compensation arrangement" — 248(1); "split-pension amount" — 60.03(1); "taxation year" — 249.

60.1 (1) Support [payment made to third party] — For the purposes of paragraph 60(b) and subsection 118(5), where an order or agreement, or any variation thereof, provides for the payment of an amount by a taxpayer to a person or for the benefit of the person, children in the person's custody or both the person and those children, the amount or any part thereof

(a) when payable, is deemed to be payable to and receivable by that person; and

(b) when paid, is deemed to have been paid to and received by that person.

Related Provisions: 56.1(1) — Parallel rule for recipient.

Notes: An amount paid to a third party at the recipient's direction can be considered paid to and received by the recipient either under 60.1(1) or because the recipient is considered to have discretion over the payment: *Arsenault*, [1999] 4 C.T.C. 174 (FCA); *Ojo*, 2010 TCC 244; VIEWS doc 2008-0302271I7. However, see also *Hinkelman*, [2001] 3 C.T.C. 2180 (TCC); *Sears*, 2004 TCC 751; *Hurst*, 2011 TCC 549, para. 11.

If child support is required to be paid directly to an adult child, the CRA considers it to fall within 56.1(1) and 60.1(1): VIEWS doc 2008-0279101E5. However, in *Larouche*, 2011 TCC 326, no deduction was allowed because the 20-year-old child was not in the ex-spouse's custody.

See also Notes at end of 60.1.

60.1(1) amended by 1996 Budget, effective for amounts received after 1996.

Income Tax Folios: S1-F3-C3: Support payments [replaces IT-530R].

(2) Agreement [to make third-party support payments] — For the purposes of section 60, this section and subsection 118(5), the amount determined by the formula

$$A - B$$

where

A   is the total of all amounts each of which is an amount (other than an amount that is otherwise a support amount) that became payable by a taxpayer in a taxation year, under an order of a competent tribunal or under a written agreement, in respect of an expense (other than an expenditure in respect of a self-contained domestic establishment in which the taxpayer resides or an expenditure for the acquisition of tangible property, or for civil law corporeal property, that is not an expenditure on account of a medical or education expense or in respect of the acquisition, improvement or maintenance of a self-contained domestic establishment in which the person described in paragraph (a) or (b) resides) incurred in the year or the preceding taxation year for

the maintenance of a person, children in the person's custody or both the person and those children, if the person is

(a) the taxpayer's spouse or common-law partner or former spouse or common-law partner, or

(b) where the amount became payable under an order made by a competent tribunal in accordance with the laws of a province, an individual who is a parent of a child of whom the taxpayer is a legal parent,

and

B   is the amount, if any, by which

(a) the total of all amounts each of which is an amount included in the total determined for A in respect of the acquisition or improvement of a self-contained domestic establishment in which that person resides, including any payment of principal or interest in respect of a loan made or indebtedness incurred to finance, in any manner whatever, such acquisition or improvement

exceeds

(b) the total of all amounts each of which is an amount equal to $\frac{1}{5}$ of the original principal amount of a loan or indebtedness described in paragraph (a),

is, where the order or written agreement, as the case may be, provides that this subsection and subsection 56.1(2) shall apply to any amount paid or payable thereunder, deemed to be an amount payable by the taxpayer to that person and receivable by that person as an allowance on a periodic basis, and that person is deemed to have discretion as to the use of that amount.

Related Provisions: 56.1(2) — Parallel rule for recipient; 252(3) — Extended meaning of "spouse" and "former spouse".

Notes: 60.1(2) permits a payment to a third party to qualify under 56.1(4)"support payment" if: it is paid under a decree, order or judgment of a competent tribunal or under a written agreement; the court order or agreement specifies the particular third-party expense (e.g., housekeeper, utilities, property taxes, mortgage); the expense is "incurred" in the year or the previous year; it is for maintenance of the spouse or former spouse (or common-law partner); it is not in respect of a home in which the payer resides; if it is for the acquisition of tangible property, it must be for medical or educational purposes; and if it relates to the acquisition or improvement of the other person's home, only $\frac{1}{5}$ of the original principal of the loan is deductible in any year. The amount deductible under 60.1(2) is included in the other spouse's income as support: 56.1(2).

For a careful review of the conditions in 60.1(2) see *Wrightson*, 2005 TCC 2. Car payments do not qualify because they are for the acquisition of tangible property: VIEWS doc 2008-026745117.

Although 60.1(2) purports to require the court order or agreement to explicitly refer to 56.1(2) and 60.1(2), the Courts may allow the reference to be implied, provided the parties' intention is clear: *Veilleux*, 2002 FCA 201; *Pelchat*, [1998] 1 C.T.C. 2741 (TCC); *Ferron*, [2001] 3 C.T.C. 2072 (TCC); *Wrightson*, 2005 TCC 2; *Ojo*, 2010 TCC 244; *Stewart*, 2018 TCC 210. However, some decisions have said the section numbers must be cited: *Armstrong*, [1996] 2 C.T.C. 266 (FCA); *Stohl*, 2006 FCA 162 (leave to appeal denied 2007 CarswellNat 343 (SCC)); *Paré*, [1994] 2 C.T.C. 2384 (TCC); *Minicozzi*, [1998] 2 C.T.C. 2618 (TCC); *Sanders*, [2002] 1 C.T.C. 2065 (TCC); *Hock*, 2003 TCC 691; *Bright*, 2005 TCC 146. CRA no longer requires specific reference to 56.1(2) and 60.1(2) as long as there is a "clear and unambiguous clause" saying the parties understand the payments will be taxable and deductible: Income Tax Folio S1-F3-C3 ¶3.58. Without such clause, provision of a vehicle by the husband's company to the wife was not "support": *J. Raymond Couvreur Inc.*, 2008 TCC 587; and where no intention for the payments to be deductible was in the agreement or correspondence, payment of house expenses was not deductible: *Poirier*, 2011 TCC 311. In *Kuch*, 2012 TCC 454, the parties had intended deductibility but since the Court Order did not refer to it, 60.1(2) did not apply.

As an alternative to payments to third parties qualifying under 60.1(2), a payment to a third party may be deductible if the payor is directed by the recipient to pay the third party, so that the recipient is still considered to have "discretion as to the use of the amount" (56.1(4)"support amount" and former 56(12)). See *Arsenault*, [1999] 4 C.T.C. 174 (FCA) and Notes to 60.1(1).

Where no deduction is available under 60.1(1) or (2), expenses paid for children's fitness or arts/cultural programs before 2017 may be eligible for credit under 118.031(2) or 122.8(2) [122.8 has replaced 118.03], as 122.8(1)"qualifying child" does not require that the child live with the parent claiming the credit (VIEWS doc 2011-0403581E5).

60.1(2)A opening words amended by 2002-2013 technical bill (Part 4 — bijuralism), effective June 26, 2013, to add "or for civil law corporeal property".

60.1(2)A(b) amended to change "natural parent" to "legal parent" by 2005 same-sex marriage bill, effective July 20, 2005. 60.1(2) earlier amended by 2000 same-sex partners bill, 1996 Budget. See also Notes at end of 60.1.

Income Tax Folios: S1-F3-C3: Support payments [replaces IT-530R].

(3) Prior payments — For the purposes of this section and section 60, where a written agreement or order of a competent tribunal made at any time in a taxation year provides that an amount paid before that time and in the year or the preceding taxation year is to be considered to have been paid and received thereunder,

(a) the amount is deemed to have been paid thereunder; and

(b) the agreement or order is deemed, except for the purpose of this subsection, to have been made on the day on which the first such amount was paid, except that, where the agreement or order is made after April 1997 and varies a child support amount payable to the recipient from the last such amount paid to the recipient before May 1997, each varied amount of child support paid under the agreement or order is deemed to have been payable under an agreement or order the commencement day of which is the day on which the first payment of the varied amount is required to be made.

Related Provisions: 56.1(3) — Parallel rule for recipient.

Notes: See Notes to the parallel income-inclusion rule in 56.1(3).

60.1(3) amended by 1996 Budget, effective for amounts received after 1996. The amended version of 60.1(3) has a very strange side effect. See Notes to 56.1(3).

Income Tax Folios: S1-F3-C3: Support payments [replaces IT-530R].

(4) Definitions — The definitions in subsection 56.1(4) apply in this section and section 60.

Notes [s. 60.1]: See Notes to 56.1.

60.1 amended by 1992 technical bill, for decrees, orders and judgments made after 1992 and agreements entered into after 1992, except where the marriage breakdown occurred before 1993 (this exception added by 1993 technical bill, s. 135). The changes were not substantive: they reflect the new definition of "spouse" in 252(4), the consolidation of 60(b) and (c) into 60(b), and the renumbering of 60(c.1) as 60(c). The descriptive formula in 60.1(2) was redrafted in algebraic form. For decrees, orders and judgments made, and agreements entered into, before 1993 or where the marriage breakdown occurred before 1993, read:

60.1 (1) Maintenance payments — Where, after May 6, 1974, a decree, order, judgment or written agreement described in paragraph 60(b), (c) or (c.1), or any variation thereof, has been made providing for the periodic payment of an amount by a taxpayer

(a) to a person who is

(i) the taxpayer's spouse or former spouse, or

(ii) where the amount is paid pursuant to an order made by a competent tribunal after February 10, 1988 in accordance with the laws of a province, an individual of the opposite sex who

(A) before the date of the order cohabited with the taxpayer in a conjugal relationship, or

(B) is the natural parent of a child of the taxpayer, or

(b) for the benefit of the person or children in the custody of the person, or both the person and those children,

the amount or any part thereof, when paid, shall be deemed, for the purposes of paragraphs 60(b), (c) and (c.1), to have been paid to and received by that person.

(2) Agreement — For the purposes of paragraphs 60(b), (c) and (c.1), the amount, if any, by which

(a) the total of all amounts each of which is an amount (other than an amount to which paragraph 60(b), (c) or (c.1) otherwise applies) paid by a taxpayer in a taxation year, pursuant to a decree, order or judgment of a competent tribunal or pursuant to a written agreement, in respect of an expense (other than an expenditure in respect of a self-contained domestic establishment in which the taxpayer resides or an expenditure for the acquisition of tangible property that is not an expenditure on account of a medical or educational expense or in respect of the acquisition, improvement or maintenance of a self-contained domestic establishment in which the person described in subparagraph (i) or (ii) resides) incurred in the year or the immediately preceding taxation year for maintenance of a person who is

(i) the taxpayer's spouse or former spouse, or

(ii) where the amount is paid pursuant to an order made by a competent tribunal after February 10, 1988 in accordance with the laws of a province, an individual of the opposite sex who

(A) before the date of the order cohabited with the taxpayer in a conjugal relationship, or

(B) is the natural parent of a child of the taxpayer,

or for the maintenance of children in the person's custody or both the person and those children if, at the time the expense was incurred and throughout the remainder of the year, the taxpayer was living apart from that person

exceeds

(b) the amount, if any, by which

(i) the total of all amounts each of which is an amount included in the total determined under paragraph (a) in respect of the acquisition or improvement of a self-contained domestic establishment in which that person resides, including any payment of principal or interest in respect of a loan made or indebtedness incurred to finance, in any manner whatever, the acquisition or improvement

exceeds

(ii) the total of all amounts each of which is an amount equal to $\frac{1}{5}$ of the original principal amount of a loan or indebtedness described in subparagraph (i)

shall, where the decree, order, judgment or written agreement, as the case may be, provides that this subsection and subsection 56.1(2) shall apply to any payment made pursuant thereto, be deemed to be an amount paid by the taxpayer and received by that person as an allowance payable on a periodic basis.

(3) Prior payments — For the purposes of this section and section 60, where a decree, order or judgment of a competent tribunal or a written agreement made at any time in a taxation year provides that an amount paid before that time and in the year or the immediately preceding taxation year is to be considered as having been paid and received pursuant thereto, the following rules apply:

(a) the amount shall be deemed to have been paid pursuant thereto; and

(b) the person who made the payment shall be deemed to have been separated pursuant to a divorce, judicial separation or written separation agreement from the person's spouse or former spouse at the time the payment was made and throughout the remainder of the year.

Definitions [s. 60.1]: "amount" — 248(1); "child" — 252(1); "child support amount", "commencement day" — 56.1(4), 60.1(4); "corporeal property" — Quebec Civil Code art. 899, 906; "former spouse" — 252(3); "housing unit" — 56.1(4); "individual" — 248(1); "parent" — 252(2)(a); "person", "prescribed", "principal amount", "property" — 248(1); "province" — Interpretation Act 35(1); "received" — 248(7); "self-contained domestic establishment" — 248(1); "spouse" — 252(3); "support amount" — 56.1(4), 60.1(4); "taxation year" — 249; "taxpayer" — 248(1); "written" — Interpretation Act 35(1) [writing].

60.11 [Repealed]

Notes: 60.11 repealed by 2013 budget bill #2, effective Dec. 12, 2013. It provided an interpretation rule for a version of 60.1(1) that applied before 1997. Added in the RSC 1985 (5th Supp) consolidation, this rule was formerly in the application rule in a 1988 amendment to 60.1(1).

60.2 (1) Refund of undeducted past service AVCs [pension contributions] — There may be deducted in computing a taxpayer's income for a taxation year an amount equal to the total of

(a) [applies only to years before 1991]; and

(b) the least of

(i) $3,500,

(ii) the total of all amounts each of which is an amount included after 1986 by reason of subparagraph 56(1)(a)(i) or paragraph 56(1)(d.2), (h) or (t) in computing the taxpayer's income for the year, and

(iii) the balance of the annuitized voluntary contributions of the taxpayer at the end of the year.

Related Provisions: 8(1)(m) — Employee's RRP contributions.

(2) Definition of "balance of the annuitized voluntary contributions" — For the purposes of subsection (1), "balance of the annuitized voluntary contributions" of a taxpayer at the end of a taxation year means the amount, if any, by which

(a) such part of the total of all amounts each of which is an additional voluntary contribution made by the taxpayer to a registered pension plan before October 9, 1986 in respect of services rendered by the taxpayer before the year in which the contribution was made, to the extent that the contribution was not deducted in computing the taxpayer's income for any taxation year, as may reasonably be considered as having been

(i) used before October 9, 1986 to acquire or provide an annuity for the taxpayer's benefit under a registered pension plan or registered retirement savings plan, or

(ii) transferred before October 9, 1986 to a registered retirement income fund under which the taxpayer was the annuitant (within the meaning assigned by subsection 146.3(1)) at the time of the transfer

exceeds

(b) the total of all amounts each of which is

(i) an amount deducted under paragraph (1)(b) in computing the taxpayer's income for a preceding taxation year, or

(ii) an amount deducted under paragraph (1)(a) in computing the taxpayer's income for the year or a preceding taxation year, to the extent that the amount can reasonably be considered to be in respect of a refund of additional voluntary contributions included in determining the total under paragraph (a).

Notes [s. 60.2]: 60.2 added by 1990 pension bill, effective 1986.

Definitions [s. 60.2]: "additional voluntary contribution", "amount", "annuity" — 248(1); "balance" — 60.2(2); "registered pension plan" — 248(1); "registered retirement income fund" — 146.3(1), 248(1); "registered retirement savings plan" — 146(1), 248(1); "taxation year" — 249; "taxpayer" — 248(1).

61. (1) [IAACs — No longer relevant]

Notes: 61(1) allowed a deduction for the purchase of an income-averaging annuity contract (IAAC), until 1981. See the definitions in 61(4). Amounts received from an IAAC by a taxpayer are included in income by 56(1)(e) and (f).

Taxpayers with large fluctuations in their income may be able to use RRSPs for income-averaging. See 146(5) and (8) and Notes to 146(10). See also Notes to 15(2). 110.2 provides a somewhat ineffective averaging for lump sum payments.

(2) [No longer relevant]

Notes: 61(2) provides rules for the deduction in 61(1), which is no longer available.

(3) [Repealed under former Act]

Notes: 61(3) moved to 61.1 in 1976.

(4) Definitions — In this section,

"annual annuity amount" of an individual in respect of an income-averaging annuity contract means the total of the equal payments described in paragraph (c) of the definition "income-averaging annuity contract" in this subsection that, under the contract, are receivable by the individual in the twelve month period commencing on the day that the first such payment under the contract becomes receivable by the individual;

"income-averaging annuity contract" of an individual means a contract between the individual and a person licensed or otherwise authorized under the laws of Canada or a province to carry on in Canada an annuities business or a corporation licensed or otherwise authorized under the laws of Canada or a province to carry on in Canada the business of offering to the public its services as trustee, under which

(a) in consideration of a qualifying payment as consideration under the contract, that person agrees to pay to the individual, commencing at a time not later than 10 months after the individual has made the qualifying payment,

(i) an annuity to the individual for the individual's life, with or without a guaranteed term not exceeding the number of years that is the lesser of

(A) 15, and

(B) 85 minus the age of the individual at the time the annuity payments commence, or

(ii) an annuity to the individual for a guaranteed term described in subparagraph (i), or

(b) in consideration of a single payment in respect of the individual's 1981 taxation year, other than a qualifying payment, made by the individual as consideration under the contract, that person makes all payments provided for under the contract to the individual before 1983

and under which no payments are provided except the single payment by the individual and,

(c) in respect of a contract referred to in paragraph (a), equal annuity payments that are to be made annually or at more frequent periodic intervals, or

(d) in respect of a contract referred to in paragraph (b), payments described therein to the individual;

Related Provisions: 128.1(10)"excluded right or interest"(f)(ii) — Emigration — no deemed disposition of right to IAAC.

"qualifying payment" means a single payment made before November 13, 1981 (or made on or after November 13, 1981 pursuant to an agreement in writing entered into before that date to make such a payment in respect of the individual's 1981 taxation year, or pursuant to an arrangement in writing made before that date to have funds withheld before 1982 from any of the individual's remuneration described in paragraph (1)(b) earned or received before November 13, 1981 and paid by or on behalf of the individual).

Notes: These three definitions were 61(4)(a)-(c) before RSC 1985 (5th Supp) consolidation for tax years ending after Nov. 1991.

Definitions [s. 61]: "allowable business investment loss" — 38(c), 248(1); "amount", "annuity", "business" — 248(1); "business investment loss" — 39(1)(c), 39(9), (10); "Canada" — 255; "corporation" — 248(1), *Interpretation Act* 35(1); "death benefit" — 248(1); "deferred profit sharing plan" — 147(1), 248(1); "employee" — 248(1); "employees profit sharing plan" — 144(1), 248(1); "employment", "individual", "office", "person" — 248(1); "province" — *Interpretation Act* 35(1); "registered retirement savings plan" — 146(1), 248(1); "resident in Canada" — 250; "taxation year" — 249; "taxpayer" — 248(1); "writing" — *Interpretation Act* 35(1).

61.1 (1) Where income-averaging annuity contract ceases to be such — Where a contract that was at any time an income-averaging annuity contract of an individual has, at a subsequent time, ceased to be an income-averaging annuity contract otherwise than by virtue of the surrender, cancellation, redemption, sale or the disposition thereof, the individual shall be deemed to have received at that subsequent time as proceeds of the disposition of an income-averaging annuity contract an amount equal to the fair market value of the contract at that subsequent time and to have acquired the contract, as another contract not being an income-averaging annuity contract, immediately thereafter at a cost to the individual equal to that fair market value.

Related Provisions: 56(1)(f) — Disposition of income-averaging annuity contracts; 61 — IAAC; 212(1)(n) — Withholding tax on payment to non-resident.

(2) Where annuitant dies and payments continued — Where an individual who was an annuitant under an income-averaging annuity contract has died and payments are subsequently made under that contract, the payments shall be deemed to be payments under an income-averaging annuity contract.

Interpretation Bulletins [subsec. 61.1(2)]: IT-212R3: Income of deceased persons — rights or things.

Definitions [s. 61.1]: "income-averaging annuity contract" — 61(4), 248(1); "fair market value" — see 69(1) Notes; "individual" — 248(1).

61.2 Reserve for debt forgiveness for resident individuals — There may be deducted in computing the income for a taxation year of an individual (other than a trust) resident in Canada throughout the year such amount as the individual claims not exceeding the amount determined by the formula

$$A + B - 0.2(C - \$40,000^2)$$

where

A is the amount, if any, by which

(a) the total of all amounts each of which is an amount that, because of the application of section 80 to an obligation payable by the individual (or a partnership of which the individual was a member) was included under subsection 80(13) in computing the income of the individual for the year or the income of the partnership for a fiscal period that ends in the

---

2 Not indexed for inflation — ed.

year (to the extent that, where the amount was included in computing income of a partnership, it relates to the individual's share of that income)

exceeds

(b) the total of all amounts deducted because of paragraph 80(15)(a) in computing the individual's income for the year,

B is the amount, if any, included under section 56.2 in computing the individual's income for the year, and

C is the greater of $40,000[2] and the individual's income for the year, determined without reference to this section, paragraph 20(1)(ww), section 56.2, paragraph 60(w), subsection 80(13) and paragraph 80(15)(a).

Related Provisions: 56.2 — Inclusion into income in following year; 61.3, 61.4 — Alternative deductions for corporations, non-residents and trusts; 80(16) — Designation by CRA to reduce reserve under 61.2; 114(a) — No deduction under 61.2 for part-year residents; 257 — Formula cannot calculate to less than zero.

Notes: 61.2 allows individuals with modest incomes a deferral of the income inclusion required by 80(13) on debt forgiveness. For individuals with net income not over $40,000/year, the income inclusion can be deferred indefinitely. Each year the amount deducted under 61.2 the previous year is included back into income under 56.2, but an offsetting reserve can be claimed again (see B in the formula) if the taxpayer qualifies. If the reserve is still being claimed by the year the taxpayer dies, the income will never be taxed. (For corporations, non-residents and trusts, see 61.3 and 61.4 instead.)

See also Mike Ehinger, "Relief from Debt-Forgiveness Inclusions: The Basics", 3(3) *Canadian Tax Focus* (ctf.ca) 6-7 (Aug. 2013) (re 61.2–61.4).

61.2:C amended by 1999 Budget, effective for 2000 and later taxation years, to add reference to 20(1)(ww). 61.2 added by 1994 technical bill.

Definitions [s. 61.2]: "amount" — 248(1); "fiscal period" — 249(2)(b), 249.1; "individual" — 248(1); "partnership" — see 96(1) Notes; "resident in Canada" — 250; "taxation year" — 249; "trust" — 104(1), 248(1), (3).

61.3 (1) Deduction for insolvency with respect to resident corporations — There shall be deducted in computing the income for a taxation year of a corporation resident in Canada throughout the year that is not exempt from tax under this Part on its taxable income, the lesser of

(a) the amount, if any, by which

(i) the total of all amounts each of which is an amount that, because of the application of section 80 to a commercial obligation (in this section having the meaning assigned by subsection 80(1)) issued by the corporation (or a partnership of which the corporation was a member) was included under subsection 80(13) in computing the income of the corporation for the year or the income of the partnership for a fiscal period that ends in the year (to the extent that the amount, where it was included in computing income of a partnership, relates to the corporation's share of that income)

exceeds

(ii) the total of all amounts deducted because of paragraph 80(15)(a) in computing the corporation's income for the year, and

(b) the amount determined by the formula

$$A - 2(B - C - D - E)$$

where

A is the amount determined under paragraph (a) in respect of the corporation for the year,

B is the total of

(i) the fair market value of the assets of the corporation at the end of the year,

(ii) the amounts paid before the end of the year on account of the corporation's tax payable under this Part or any of Parts I.3, II, VI and XIV for the year or on account of a similar tax payable for the year under an Act of a province, and

(iii) all amounts paid by the corporation in the 12-month period preceding the end of the year to a person with whom the corporation does not deal at arm's length

(A) as a dividend (other than a stock dividend),

(B) on a reduction of paid-up capital in respect of any class of shares of its capital stock,

(C) on a redemption, acquisition or cancellation of its shares, or

(D) as a distribution or appropriation in any manner whatever to or for the benefit of the shareholders of any class of its capital stock, to the extent that the distribution or appropriation cannot reasonably be considered to have resulted in a reduction in the amount otherwise determined for C in respect of the corporation for the year,

C is the total liabilities of the corporation at the end of the year (determined without reference to the corporation's liabilities for tax payable under this Part or any of Parts I.3, II, VI and XIV for the year or for a similar tax payable for the year under an Act of a province) and, for this purpose,

(i) the equity and consolidation methods of accounting shall not be used, and

(ii) subject to subparagraph (i) and except as otherwise provided in this description, the total liabilities of the corporation shall

(A) where the corporation is not an insurance corporation, a federal credit union or a bank to which clause (B) or (C) applies and the balance sheet as of the end of the year was presented to the shareholders of the corporation and was prepared in accordance with generally accepted accounting principles, be considered to be the total liabilities shown on that balance sheet,

(B) where the corporation is a bank, a federal credit union or an insurance corporation that is required to report to the Superintendent of Financial Institutions and the balance sheet as of the end of the year was accepted by the Superintendent, be considered to be the total liabilities shown on that balance sheet,

(C) where the corporation is an insurance corporation that is required to report to the superintendent of insurance or other similar officer or authority of the province under whose laws the corporation is incorporated and the balance sheet as of the end of the year was accepted by that officer or authority, be considered to be the total liabilities shown on that balance sheet, and

(D) in any other case, be considered to be the amount that would be shown as total liabilities of the corporation at the end of the year on a balance sheet prepared in accordance with generally accepted accounting principles,

D is the total of all amounts each of which is the principal amount at the end of the year of a distress preferred share (within the meaning assigned by subsection 80(1)) issued by the corporation, and

E is 50% of the amount, if any, by which

(i) the amount that would be the corporation's income for the year if that amount were determined without reference to this section and section 61.4

exceeds

(ii) the amount determined under paragraph (a) in respect of the corporation for the year.

Related Provisions: 37(1)(f.1) — Reduction in claim allowed for R&D expenditures; 61.2 — Reserve for individuals; 61.3(3) — Anti-avoidance; 61.4 — Additional reserve; 80(16) — Designation by CRA to reduce reserve under 61.3; 80.01(8), (9) — Deemed settlement on debt parking or debt becoming statute-barred; 80.04(4)(j) —

---

[2] Not indexed for inflation — ed.

Agreement to transfer forgiven amount; 87(2)(l.21) — Amalgamation — continuing corporation; 257 — Formula cannot calculate to less than zero.

Notes: 61.3(1) allows an offset (not a "reserve", as there is no later reinclusion) against an 80(13) income inclusion. The effect is that a corporation is required to recognize income under 80(13) only to the extent of twice its net assets, so if its combined federal/provincial tax rate does not exceed 50%, the income inclusion should not result in its liabilities exceeding the fair market value of its assets (which could make the corporation insolvent under corporate law). For interpretation see VIEWS doc 2011-0393561E5 and Notes to 61.2.

61.3(1)(b)C(i) is redundant. See 248(24).

References to federal credit union added to 61.3(1)(b)C(ii)(A) and (B) by 2010 budget bill #1, effective Dec. 19, 2012 (P.C. 2012-1623).

61.3(1) added by 1994 technical bill for tax years ending after Feb. 21, 1994, and amended retroactive to its introduction by 1995-97 technical bill.

(2) Reserve for insolvency with respect to non-resident corporations — There shall be deducted in computing the income for a taxation year of a corporation that is non-resident at any time in the year, the lesser of

(a) the amount, if any, by which

(i) the total of all amounts each of which is an amount that, because of the application of section 80 to a commercial obligation issued by the corporation (or a partnership of which the corporation was a member) was included under subsection 80(13) in computing the corporation's taxable income or taxable income earned in Canada for the year or the income of the partnership for a fiscal period that ends in the year (to the extent that, where the amount was included in computing income of a partnership, it relates to the corporation's share of the partnership's income added in computing the corporation's taxable income or taxable income earned in Canada for the year)

exceeds

(ii) the total of all amounts deducted because of paragraph 80(15)(a) in computing the corporation's taxable income or taxable income earned in Canada for the year, and

(b) the amount determined by the formula

$$A - 2(B - C - D - E)$$

where

A is the amount determined under paragraph (a) in respect of the corporation for the year,

B is the total of

(i) the fair market value of the assets of the corporation at the end of the year,

(ii) the amounts paid before the end of the year on account of the corporation's tax payable under this Part or any of Parts I.3, II, VI and XIV for the year or on account of a similar tax payable for the year under an Act of a province, and

(iii) all amounts paid in the 12-month period preceding the end of the year by the corporation to a person with whom the corporation does not deal at arm's length

(A) as a dividend (other than a stock dividend),

(B) on a reduction of paid-up capital in respect of any class of shares of its capital stock,

(C) on a redemption, acquisition or cancellation of its shares, or

(D) as a distribution or appropriation in any manner whatever to or for the benefit of the shareholders of any class of its capital stock, to the extent that the distribution or appropriation cannot reasonably be considered to have resulted in a reduction of the amount otherwise determined for C in respect of the corporation for the year,

C is the total liabilities of the corporation at the end of the year (determined without reference to the corporation's liabilities for tax payable under this Part or any of Parts I.3, II, VI and

XIV for the year or for a similar tax payable for the year under an Act of a province), determined in the manner described in the description of C in paragraph (1)(b),

D is the total of all amounts each of which is the principal amount at the end of the year of a distress preferred share (within the meaning assigned by subsection 80(1)) issued by the corporation, and

E is 50% of the amount, if any, by which

(i) the amount that would be the corporation's taxable income or taxable income earned in Canada for the year if that amount were determined without reference to this section and section 61.4

exceeds

(ii) the amount determined under paragraph (a) in respect of the corporation for the year.

Related Provisions: 37(1)(f.1) — Reduction in claim allowed for R&D expenditures; 61.3(3) — Anti-avoidance; 61.4 — Additional reserve; 80(16) — Designation by CRA to reduce reserve under 61.3; 80.01(8), (9) — Deemed settlement on debt parking or debt becoming statute-barred; 80.04(4)(j) — Agreement to transfer forgiven amount; 87(2)(l.21) — Amalgamation — continuing corporation; 257 — Formula cannot calculate to less than zero.

Notes: 61.3(2) added by 1994 technical bill, for taxation years that end after Feb. 21, 1994, and amended retroactive to its introduction by 1995-97 technical bill. It is similar to 61.3(1) but applies to non-resident corps. See Notes to 61.3(1).

(3) Anti-avoidance — Subsections (1) and (2) do not apply to a corporation for a taxation year where property was transferred in the 12-month period preceding the end of the year or the corporation became indebted in that period and it can reasonably be considered that one of the reasons for the transfer or the indebtedness was to increase the amount that the corporation would, but for this subsection, be entitled to deduct under subsection (1) or (2).

Related Provisions: 160.4 — Joint liability of transferee where property transferred so that 61.3(3) applies.

Notes: For CRA interpretation see VIEWS doc 2012-0468851E5.

61.3(3) added by 1994 technical bill, for taxation years that end after Feb. 21, 1994.

Definitions [s. 61.3]: "Act" — *Interpretation Act* 35(1); "amount" — 248(1); "arm's length" — 251(1); "bank" — 248(1); "class of shares" — 248(6); "commercial obligation" — 61.3(1)(a)(i), 80(1); "corporation" — 248(1), *Interpretation Act* 35(1); "distress preferred share" — 80(1); "dividend" — 248(1); "fair market value" — see 69(1) Notes; "federal credit union" — 248(1); "fiscal period" — 249(2)(b), 249.1; "insurance corporation", "non-resident" — 248(1); "officer" — 248(1)"office"; "paid-up capital" — 89(1), 248(1); "partnership" — see 96(1) Notes; "principal amount" — 248(1), (26); "property" — 248(1); "province" — *Interpretation Act* 35(1); "resident in Canada" — 250; "share", "shareholder", "stock dividend" — 248(1); "taxable income" — 2(2), 248(1); "taxable income earned in Canada" — 115(1), 248(1); "taxation year" — 249.

61.4 Reserve for debt forgiveness for corporations and others — There may be deducted as a reserve in computing the income for a taxation year of a taxpayer that is a corporation or trust resident in Canada throughout the year or a non-resident person who carried on business through a fixed placed of business in Canada at the end of the year such amount as the taxpayer claims not exceeding the least of

(a) the amount determined by the formula

$$A - B$$

where

A is the amount, if any, by which

(i) the total of all amounts each of which is an amount that, because of the application of section 80 to a commercial obligation (within the meaning assigned by subsection 80(1)) issued by the taxpayer (or a partnership of which the taxpayer was a member) was included under subsection 80(13) in computing the income of the taxpayer for the year or a preceding taxation year or of the partnership for a fiscal period that ends in that year or preceding year (to the extent that, where the amount was included in computing income of a partnership, it relates to the taxpayer's share of that income)

exceeds the total of

> (ii) all amounts each of which is an amount deducted under paragraph 80(15)(a) in computing the taxpayer's income for the year or a preceding taxation year, and
>
> (iii) all amounts deducted under section 61.3 in computing the taxpayer's income for the year or a preceding taxation year, and

B   is the amount, if any, by which the amount determined for A in respect of the taxpayer for the year exceeds the total of

> (i) the amount that would be determined for A in respect of the taxpayer for the year if that value did not take into account amounts included or deducted in computing the taxpayer's income for any preceding taxation year, and
>
> (ii) the amount, if any, included under section 56.3 in computing the taxpayer's income for the year,

(b) the total of

> (i) ⁴/₅ of the amount that would be determined for A in paragraph (a) in respect of the taxpayer for the year if that value did not take into account amounts included or deducted in computing the taxpayer's income for any preceding taxation year,
>
> (ii) ³/₅ of the amount that would be determined for A in paragraph (a) in respect of the taxpayer for the year if that value did not take into account amounts included or deducted in computing the taxpayer's income for the year or any preceding taxation year (other than the last preceding taxation year),
>
> (iii) ²/₅ of the amount that would be determined for A in paragraph (a) in respect of the taxpayer for the year if that value did not take into account amounts included or deducted in computing the taxpayer's income for the year or any preceding taxation year (other than the second last preceding taxation year), and
>
> (iv) ¹/₅ of the amount that would be determined for A in paragraph (a) in respect of the taxpayer for the year if that value did not take into account amounts included or deducted in computing the taxpayer's income for the year or any preceding taxation year (other than the third last preceding taxation year), and

(c) where the taxpayer is a corporation that commences to wind up in the year (otherwise than in circumstances to which the rules in subsection 88(1) apply), nil.

Related Provisions: 56.3 — Inclusion into income in following year; 61.2 — Reserve for resident individuals; 61.3 — Additional reserve for insolvent corporation; 80.04(4)(j) — Agreement to transfer forgiven amount; 87(2)(g), (h.1) — Amalgamation — carryover of reserve; 88(1)(e.1) — Subsidiary can claim reserve on windup; 250(6.1) — Trust that ceases to exist deemed resident throughout year.

Notes: 61.4 added by 1994 technical bill, for taxation years that end after Feb. 21, 1994. Together with 56.3 it allows the income inclusion required by the debt forgiveness rules in 80(13) to be spread over 5 years. The taxpayer must be a corporation or trust resident in Canada, or a non-resident carrying on business through a fixed place of business in Canada. No reserve is allowed for partnerships because of the special rules for partners in 80(15). No reserve is allowed for corporations that are winding up if 88(1) does not apply (see 61.4(c)). (Individuals resident in Canada can claim a reserve under 61.2. Some corporations may also claim a deduction under 61.3.)

Definitions [s. 61.4]: "amount", "business" — 248(1); "carrying on business in Canada" — 253; "commercial obligation" — 80(1); "corporation" — 248(1), *Interpretation Act* 35(1); "fiscal period" — 249(2)(b), 249.1; "non-resident" — 248(1); "partnership" — see 96(1) Notes; "resident in Canada" — 94(3)(a), 250; "taxation year" — 249; "taxpayer" — 248(1); "trust" — 104(1), 248(1), (3).

62. (1) Moving expenses — There may be deducted in computing a taxpayer's income for a taxation year amounts paid by the taxpayer as or on account of moving expenses incurred in respect of an eligible relocation, to the extent that

(a) they were not paid on the taxpayer's behalf in respect of, in the course of or because of, the taxpayer's office or employment;

(b) they were not deductible because of this section in computing the taxpayer's income for the preceding taxation year;

(c) the total of those amounts does not exceed

> (i) in any case described in subparagraph (a)(i) of the definition "eligible relocation" in subsection 248(1), the total of all amounts, each of which is an amount included in computing the taxpayer's income for the taxation year from the taxpayer's employment at a new work location or from carrying on the business at the new work location, or because of subparagraph 56(1)(r)(v) in respect of the taxpayer's employment at the new work location, and
>
> (ii) in any case described in subparagraph (a)(ii) of the definition "eligible relocation" in subsection 248(1), the total of amounts included in computing the taxpayer's income for the year because of paragraphs 56(1)(n) and (o); and

(d) all reimbursements and allowances received by the taxpayer in respect of those expenses are included in computing the taxpayer's income.

Related Provisions: 4(2) — Deductions under s. 62 not applicable to any particular source; 64.1 — Individuals absent from Canada; 115(2)(f) — Deduction for non-resident; 118.2(2)(l.5) — Medical expense credit for moving expenses.

Notes: See Notes to 248(1)"eligible relocation".

Moving expenses are deductible only if *paid*, not just incurred: *Zador*, 2007 FCA 175. CRA allows "some flexibility" in letting either spouse or common-law partner (CLP) claim the expenses, even if paid by only one, if they are spouses or CLPs at some point in the year: docs 2009-0313341E5, 2013-0476171E5. Moving expenses paid in years after the move (e.g. reimbursing an employer for amounts paid) are deductible in the year paid: 2010-0383551E5.

X's moving expenses that are non-deductible because X has no business or employment income in the new work location (or no job yet) can be carried forward and deducted against such income in a later year: *Moodie*, 2004 TCC 462; *Abrahamsen*, 2007 TCC 95; *Mazurkewich*, 2007 TCC 517; *Evangélist*, 2013 TCC 62; VIEWS docs 2008-0279271E5 (including after bankruptcy), 2009-0341571E5, 2009-0348011E5.

The income in the "new work location" (against which the deduction is taken) can include income from a different employer in the same city: *Dalisay*, 2004 TCC 126; doc 2009-0308461E5.

A student who earns employment income while at school may be able to deduct moving expenses against that income: VIEWS doc 2012-0440251E5. A student moving *solely* for studies can claim the deduction only against scholarship and research-grant income (62(1)(c)(ii), 2011-0421901E5); and due to the 56(3) exemption, often no deduction is possible. It cannot be claimed against a training allowance taxed under 56(1)(a)(i-iv) (2010-0388601E5), RESP income (2011-0405491E5), or employment income earned after completing studies (2007-0242721E5).

The value of frequent-flyer points used when moving was not proven, so no deduction was allowed: *Atsaidis*, [2000] 4 C.T.C. 2490 (TCC). See also Notes to 6(1)(a) under "Frequent-flyer points".

Claims that 62(1) was unconstitutional and discriminatory were struck out in *Konecny*, 2013 TCC 334.

See also Income Tax Folio S1-F3-C4; VIEWS doc 2004-0099541E5; *Joshi*, 2004 TCC 757; Drache, "Student Moving Expenses", xl(18) *The Canadian Taxpayer* (Carswell) 141-42 (Sept. 21, 2018).

62(1)(c)(i) amended by 2008 budget bill #2, for 2008 and later taxation years, to apply to multiple amounts of income and to 56(1)(r)(v).

62(1) amended by 1998 Budget, effective 1998.

I.T. Technical News: 6 (road distance to be used instead of "as the crow flies").

Forms: T1-M: Moving expenses deduction.

(2) Moving expenses of students — There may be deducted in computing a taxpayer's income for a taxation year the amount, if any, that the taxpayer would be entitled to deduct under subsection (1) if the definition "eligible relocation" in subsection 248(1) were read without reference to subparagraph (a)(i) of that definition and if the word "both" in paragraph (c) of that definition were read as "either or both".

Related Provisions: 64.1 — Individuals absent from Canada; 115(2) — Non-resident's taxable income earned in Canada.

Notes: 62(2) allows students to claim moving expenses for moves to or from outside Canada, but only against taxable scholarship and research grant income, due to 62(1)(c)(ii) (and most scholarship income under 56(1)(n) is now exempt due to 56(3)).

62(2) amended by 2017 budget bill #2, for tax years ending after Oct. 2011, to change "paragraph (b)" to "paragraph (c)".

62(2) amended by 1998 Budget, effective 1998.

(3) Definition of "moving expenses" — In subsection (1), "moving expenses" includes any expense incurred as or on account of

(a) travel costs (including a reasonable amount expended for meals and lodging), in the course of moving the taxpayer and members of the taxpayer's household from the old residence to the new residence,

(b) the cost to the taxpayer of transporting or storing household effects in the course of moving from the old residence to the new residence,

(c) the cost to the taxpayer of meals and lodging near the old residence or the new residence for the taxpayer and members of the taxpayer's household for a period not exceeding 15 days,

(d) the cost to the taxpayer of cancelling the lease by virtue of which the taxpayer was the lessee of the old residence,

(e) the taxpayer's selling costs in respect of the sale of the old residence,

(f) where the old residence is sold by the taxpayer or the taxpayer's spouse or common-law partner as a result of the move, the cost to the taxpayer of legal services in respect of the purchase of the new residence and of any tax, fee or duty (other than any goods and services tax or value-added tax) imposed on the transfer or registration of title to the new residence,

(g) interest, property taxes, insurance premiums and the cost of heating and utilities in respect of the old residence, to the extent of the lesser of $5,000 and the total of such expenses of the taxpayer for the period

(i) throughout which the old residence is neither ordinarily occupied by the taxpayer or by any other person who ordinarily resided with the taxpayer at the old residence immediately before the move nor rented by the taxpayer to any other person, and

(ii) in which reasonable efforts are made to sell the old residence, and

(h) the cost of revising legal documents to reflect the address of the taxpayer's new residence, of replacing drivers' licenses and non-commercial vehicle permits (excluding any cost for vehicle insurance) and of connecting or disconnecting utilities,

but, for greater certainty, does not include costs (other than costs referred to in paragraph (f)) incurred by the taxpayer in respect of the acquisition of the new residence.

Related Provisions: 56(1)(n) — Scholarships, bursaries, etc.; 56(1)(o) — Research grants; 64.1 — Individuals absent from Canada; 67.1(1) — Food and entertainment 50% restriction does not apply; 115(2) — Non-resident's taxable income earned in Canada; 118.2(2)(l.5) — Medical expense credit for moving expenses.

Notes: Per tinyurl.com/travel-cra, travel expenses for 62(3)(a) (also 110.7(1) northern residents' travel, 118.2(2) medical expense travel) can optionally be calculated without receipts: $23/meal or $69/day since 2020 ($17 and $51 for 2006-2019); and vehicle expenses (to cover both ownership and operating expenses) per qualifying km driven. Each year's rates are announced the *next* January. **For the 2020 tax year** the rates are: BC 52¢; Alta 47¢; Sask 49¢; Man. 49.5¢; Ont. 55¢; QC 52¢; NB 50.5¢; NS 51¢; PEI 49¢; Nfld&Lab 54.5¢; NWT 59.5¢; Nunavut 59¢; Yukon 58¢. CRA accepts these rates, set by the National Joint Council of the Public Service of Canada, as reasonable: docs 2013-0479951M4, 2013-0487151M4.

Although the list in 62(3) is not exhaustive, it applies only to costs of physically moving, not accessory costs or losses unrelated to the actual move: *Séguin*, [1998] 2 C.T.C. 13 (FCA). Deductions were denied for: replacement of property damaged in the move (*Fardeau*, [2002] 3 C.T.C. 2169 (TCC)); new furniture (*Nimis*, 2007 TCC 10); parking, and the costs of maintaining a second residence (*Lowe*, 2007 TCC 332); cartons, tape, phone cards, a table fan and lights for the new home (*Van Zant*, 2010 TCC 599); legal fees to contest ex-spouse's action to prevent children moving (*Vollmer*, 2011 TCC 174); central vacuum, inspection fees and CMHC mortgage fees for new home (*Nazih*, 2016 TCC 70, para. 11); cleaning and repairs of new home (*Sottile*, 2018 TCC 209). Reimbursement of unused school fees does not qualify: VIEWS doc 2009-0331701E5. See also 2014-0547981E5; and Notes to 188.1(5) re meaning of "includes".

The terms "old residence", "new residence" and "new work location" are all defined within 248(1)"eligible relocation". Expenses for moving from a home that the taxpayer has not yet lived in do not qualify: *Ménard*, 2008 TCC 376.

See VIEWS doc "May 1991-137" for a detailed discussion of moving and relocation expenses. Travel costs for a teacher on an international exchange program can include air tickets and trip cancellation insurance: doc 2004-0078551E5.

62(3)(a): does "meals and lodging" require the taxpayer to incur both kinds of expense? CRA allows someone not paying for lodging (e.g. travelling by RV or staying with friends) to claim meals *during* the move (62(3)(a)), but see re 62(3)(c) below.

Only the actual move qualifies. House-hunting travel costs were denied: *Nazih*, 2016 TCC 70, para. 9; even for a special-needs taxpayer: *Olney*, 2014 TCC 262, para. 29.

62(3)(b): "household effects" did not include a horse and horse trailer in *Yaeger*, [1986] 1 C.T.C. 2282; the TCC stated that the term does not include any animals. The CRA normally accepts moving expenses for household pets such as dogs, cats and birds. Household effects would include a motor boat, ski-doo or bicycle, and included a small hobby aircraft used for personal recreation, plus a ramp to move it: *Phillips*, 2009 TCC 163. It includes boats and trailers: Income Tax Folio S1-F3-C4 ¶4.22(b).

In *Christian*, 2010 TCC 458, para. 14, storage was allowed for only one month ("The decision to acquire a new residence which took more than a year to build was the Appellant's personal choice"); but 10 days to drive from Edmonton to southern Ontario was reasonable for someone with two children and health problems. In *Van Zant*, 2010 TCC 599, the taxpayer moved herself from Alberta to Manitoba in 3 trips by car, and was allowed motel stays for all 3 trips as well as storage for 3 months during this time, but was not allowed storage for 2 months before the move.

Renting a car qualified as a moving expense in *Phillips* (above) (while arranging to buy a car in the new city) and in *Trigg*, 2009 TCC 194 (when returning to previous city to complete sale of old home).

62(3)(c): CRA denies meals for 15 days around the move unless lodging costs are also incurred. The Court agreed with this in *Skrien*, 2015 TCC 322 (62(3)(c) applies only "when one is required to live in temporary accommodations" (para. 7), and also denied deduction because no expenses were actually incurred); and in *Sottile*, 2018 TCC 209. In *Vickers*, 2011 TCC 2, 15 days of meals and lodging were allowed on top of those under 62(3)(a), since (c) is independent of (a) [Carla Hanneman, "Moving Expenses: A Broadened Definition?", 1(2) *Canadian Tax Focus* (ctf.ca) 1-2 (Aug. 2011)]. In *Sirivar*, 2014 TCC 24, lodging was allowed for 20 weeks; there was no 15-day limit because 62(3) begins with "includes", and (c) "is meant to include things that might not otherwise be considered moving expenses" (para. 14).

62(3)(d): lease cancellation costs can still be claimed if the lessee was the taxpayer's spouse or common-law partner: VIEWS doc 2014-0527271E5. Such costs do not include "last month's rent" lost due to moving early: 2009-0324641E5 (this may be wrong in the author's view). Legal fees to contest eviction from the old home were disallowed in *Van Zant* (above). Mortgage cancellation penalty was denied in *Nazih*, 2016 TCC 70, para. 11.

62(3)(e): see doc 2003-0015765 for CRA's views on the length of time allowed between moving and selling the old home. Remedial work to remove mold from a home to sell it was not "selling costs": *Faibish*, 2008 TCC 241. Nor was painting to improve a house's salability, but a payment to the purchaser's mortgagee qualified: *Collin*, [1986] 1 C.T.C. 2603 (TCC). Asbestos removal costs qualified in *Trigg*, 2009 TCC 194, where an offer to buy the home was conditional on this being done.

62(3)(f): "where the old residence is sold" does not include a 45(1) deemed disposition on change in use of the property: *Renaud*, 2010 TCC 76. Nor does it apply when the house did not sell and the taxpayer had to rent it out at a loss: VIEWS doc 2011-0398301E5. Nor does it apply if the taxpayer rents for a year before buying a new home, as the second move does not qualify: *Calvano*, 2004 TCC 227; 2011-0406871E5.

CMHC (Canada Mortgage & Housing Corp.) fees do not fall within 62(3)(f) and are not deductible: *Knapik*, 2006 TCC 375. Nor did commission paid to a realtor on purchasing a new home, and due to 62(3) closing words it was not deductible: *Phillips* (above). Nor did the cost of permits in building a new home: *Christian* (above), para. 33. Nor do inspection fees for the new home: doc 2013-0486911E5.

See Notes to 60(o) re legal fees under 62(3)(f).

62(3)(f) denies deductibility for GST/HST and Quebec Sales Tax paid on purchase of a new home. This restriction, added in 1997 retroactive to the introduction of the GST in 1991, was described by Finance as "clarifying", but it overrides *Lachman*, [1995] 2 C.T.C. 2944D (TCC) and *Mann*, [1995] 2 C.T.C. 2049 (TCC) (but *contra* see *Harold Johnson*, [1995] 2 C.T.C. 2110 (TCC)). GST/HST and QST on legal fees and other expenses is allowed: VIEWS doc 2009-0322651E5.

The $5,000 limit in 62(3)(g) can be doubled by each spouse claiming it, if each one has an "eligible relocation": VIEWS doc 2010-0371141I7.

Costs of a lawsuit re mold in the old home did not qualify under 62(3)(g), in *Charbon*, 2010 TCC 504. Nor did the cost of paying off a writ filed against the old home, though its source was interest on a tax debt: *Christian*, 2010 TCC 458, para. 28.

Where R's son continued to live in the home after R moved, R was denied costs of maintaining the home due to 62(3)(g)(i): *Rosa*, 2005 TCC 206.

"Connecting utilities" in 62(3)(h) does not include buying a new satellite dish or antenna: *Cusson*, 2006 TCC 121.

See also Notes to 248(1)"eligible relocation".

62(3) amended by 2000 same-sex partners bill (last change effective 2001), 1998 Budget, 1995-97 technical bill.

Income Tax Folios: S1-F3-C4: Moving expenses [replaces IT-178R3].

Interpretation Bulletins [subsec. 62(3)]: IT-518R: Food, beverages and entertainment expenses.

Definitions [s. 62]: "amount", "business" — 248(1); "Canada" — 64.1, 255; "carrying on business" — 253; "common-law partner", "eligible relocation", "employed", "employer", "employment", "goods and services tax" — 248(1); "moving expenses" — 62(3); "new residence" — 248(1)"eligible relocation"(b); "new work location" — 248(1)"eligible relocation"(a); "office" — 248(1); "old residence" — 248(1)"eligible relocation"(b); "person", "property" — 248(1); "taxation year" — 249; "taxpayer" — 248(1).

Forms [s. 62]: T1-M: Moving expenses deduction.

63. (1) Child care expenses

— Subject to subsection (2), where a prescribed form containing prescribed information is filed with a taxpayer's return of income (other than a return filed under subsection 70(2) or 104(23), paragraph 128(2)(e) or subsection 150(4)) under this Part for a taxation year, there may be deducted in computing the taxpayer's income for the year such amount as the taxpayer claims not exceeding the total of all amounts each of which is an amount paid, as or on account of child care expenses incurred for services rendered in the year in respect of an eligible child of the taxpayer,

(a) by the taxpayer, where the taxpayer is described in subsection (2) and the supporting person of the child for the year is a person described in clause (i)(D) of the description of C in the formula in that subsection, or

(b) by the taxpayer or a supporting person of the child for the year, in any other case,

to the extent that

(c) the amount is not included in computing the amount deductible under this subsection by an individual (other than the taxpayer), and

(d) the amount is not an amount (other than an amount that is included in computing the taxpayer's income and that is not deductible in computing the taxpayer's taxable income) in respect of which any taxpayer is or was entitled to a reimbursement or any other form of assistance,

and the payment of which is proven by filing with the Minister one or more receipts each of which was issued by the payee and contains, where the payee is an individual, that individual's Social Insurance Number, but not exceeding the amount, if any, by which

(e) the lesser of

(i) ⅔ of the taxpayer's earned income for the year, and

(ii) the total of all amounts each of which is the annual child care expense amount in respect of an eligible child of the taxpayer for the year

exceeds

(f) the total of all amounts each of which is an amount that is deducted, in respect of the taxpayer's eligible children for the year, under this section in computing the income for the year of an individual (other than the taxpayer) to whom subsection (2) applies for the year.

Related Provisions: 4(2) — Deductions under s. 63 not applicable to any particular source; 56(6) — Universal Child Care Benefit is taxable to lower-income spouse; 63(2.2) — Deduction for person attending school or university; 64.1 — Individuals absent from Canada; 220(2.1) — Waiver of filing of documents.

Notes: 63(1) provides a deduction to the lower-income spouse (but see 63(2)) for child-care expenses, subject to a limit of ⅔ of "earned income" (63(3)), and to dollar limits based on the number of eligible children (63(3)"annual child care expense amount"): since 2015, $8,000 per child under 7 at year-end, $5,000 per child 7-16, and $11,000 per child eligible for the disability tax credit (118.3). See generally Income Tax Folio S1-F3-C1. The expenses do not need to be for each eligible child; if there is one 15-year-old ($5,000) needing no care and one 3-year-old ($8,000) needing care, $13,000 of day-care or nanny costs can be claimed. Where the parents are separated but both still live in the same house, whoever pays the child-care expenses can claim them: VIEWS doc 2010-0364841E5.

Provinces may offer further benefits, e.g. Ontario Child Tax Credit (since 2019: up to $6,000 per child under 7, $3,750 age 7-16, $8,250 per child with severe disability).

Although 63(1) requires receipts to be filed (see words after para. (d)), CRA does not request receipts with the return: Form T778, 220(2.1). The words requiring receipts are "directory" rather than "mandatory" (see also Notes to 166.1(2), 227.1(2)), so receipts need not be filed but payment must still be proven: *Senger-Hammond*, [1997] 1 C.T.C. 2728; *Wells*, [1997] 3 C.T.C. 2581; *Lachowski*, [1997] 3 C.T.C. 2924; *Dominguez*,

[1998] 4 C.T.C. 2222; *Burns*, [2001] 3 C.T.C. 2737 (all TCC); *Letarte*, 1997 Carswell-Que 358 (QCCA). In all of *Clarke*, 2013 TCC 191, *Abinah*, 2013 TCC 200, *Severinov*, 2013 TCC 292 (FCA appeal discontinued on settlement A-355-13), *Amyan*, 2014 TCC 175, *Amoako-Boatey*, 2016 TCC 282, *Phillip*, 2019 TCC 37 and *Mubenga*, 2019 QCCQ 4614, deduction was denied because receipts were unreliable and evidence of the expenses was unconvincing.

63(1)(d) reduces the child care deduction by any EI premium reduction (such as the Small Business Job Credit) received on the cost of a nanny: Folio S1-F3-C1 ¶1.29, VIEWS docs 2012-0459681I7, 2016-0654751I7; and by BC Temporary Parental Educational Support payments made to offset child-care costs resulting from the 2014 BC teacher strike: 2014-0542121I7. Entitlement to reimbursement from the other parent (P) reduces the deduction even if P does not pay: 2019-0829901E5, 2020-0837481E5.

The parent must reside with the child: 63(3)"child care expense"(a) opening words. CRA's view is that separated parents sharing custody of a child can each claim child care expenses relating to the period during which the child resided with that parent: docs 2003-0018815, 2011-0405961E5. Thus, in a 50-50 custody arrangement, each parent can claim half the child care costs. They need not each pay half to the caregiver, if one pays the full amount and the other reimburses half: 2009-0317671E5; but see also 2011-0409661E5.

No deduction is allowed for child-care expenses as business expenses, beyond the 63(1) dollar limits: *Symes*, [1994] 1 C.T.C. 40 (SCC). Before 2017, an excess might qualify for the Children's Fitness Tax Credit (122.8) or Children's Arts Tax Credit (118.031): VIEWS doc 2011-0428341E5.

For 1988-92 the dollar limits (now $8,000 and $5,000) were $4,000 and $2,000; for 1993-97, $5,000 and $3,000; for 1998-2014, $7,000 and $4,000.

63(1) amended by 2001 technical bill (for 1998 and later tax years), 2000 Budget, 1998 Budget, 1996 Budget, 1992 technical bill, 1992 Budget and 1991 technical bill.

Income Tax Folios: See list at end of s. 63.

Information Circulars: 82-2R2: SIN legislation that relates to the preparation of information slips.

Forms: T778: Child care expenses deduction.

(2) Income exceeding income of supporting person

— Where the income for a taxation year of a taxpayer who has an eligible child for the year exceeds the income for that year of a supporting person of that child (on the assumption that both incomes are computed without reference to this section and paragraphs 60(v.1) and (w)), the amount that may be deducted by the taxpayer under subsection (1) for the year as or on account of child care expenses shall not exceed the lesser of

(a) the amount that would, but for this subsection, be deductible by the taxpayer for the year under subsection (1); and

(b) the amount determined by the formula

$$A \times C$$

where

A   is the total of all amounts each of which is the periodic child care expense amount in respect of an eligible child of the taxpayer for the year, and

C   is the total of

(i) the number of weeks in the year during which the child care expenses were incurred and throughout which the supporting person was

(A) a student in attendance at a designated educational institution or a secondary school and enrolled in a program of the institution or school of not less than 3 consecutive weeks duration that provides that each student in the program spend not less than 10 hours per week on courses or work in the program,

(B) a person certified in writing by a medical doctor or a nurse practitioner to be a person who

(I) was incapable of caring for children because of the person's mental or physical infirmity and confinement throughout a period of not less than 2 weeks in the year to bed, to a wheelchair or as a patient in a hospital, an asylum or other similar institution, or

(II) was in the year, and is likely to be for a long, continuous and indefinite period, incapable of caring for children, because of the person's mental or physical infirmity,

(C) a person confined to a prison or similar institution throughout a period of not less than 2 weeks in the year, or

(D) a person who, because of a breakdown of the person's marriage or common-law partnership, was living separate and apart from the taxpayer at the end of the year and for a period of at least 90 days that began in the year, and

(ii) the number of months in the year (other than a month that includes all or part of a week included in the number of weeks referred to in subparagraph (i)), each of which is a month during which the child care expenses were incurred and the supporting person was a student in attendance at a designated educational institution or a secondary school and enrolled in a program of the institution or school that is not less than 3 consecutive weeks duration and that provides that each student in the program spend not less than 12 hours in the month on courses in the program.

Related Provisions: 3(f) — Nil income is deemed to be $0 income for comparative purposes; 118.4(2) — Reference to medical practitioners.

Notes: If X's spouse S's income is higher than X's, X cannot claim child-care expenses, even if S is a non-resident with no Canadian-source income: VIEWS doc 2005-0138441E5; even if the child is severely disabled and needs the care: *George*, 2010 TCC 496; and even if the two have contracted that only X pays for the child: *Macintosh*, 2019 TCC 155, paras. 14-23 (FCA appeal discontinued A-346-19). A status Indian whose income is exempt (see Notes to 81(1)(a)) is considered to have $0 income for s. 63: VIEWS doc 2007-0222641E5.

"Attendance" at an educational institution (63(2)(b)C(i)(A)) does not require physically being there: VIEWS doc 2012-0439101E5. (See also Notes to 118.5(1)(b) re Internet or correspondence courses.)

For "prison or similar institution" in 63(2)(b)C(i)(C), see Notes to 122.5(2). For "separate and apart" in 63(2)(b)C(i)(D), see Notes to 118.8.

The words "2 weeks" in 63(2)(b)C(i)(B)(I) and (i)(C) mean 2 consecutive weeks: VIEWS doc 2005-0109911I7.

63(2)(b)C(i)(B) opening words amended by 2017 budget bill #2 to add "or a nurse practitioner", for certifications made after Sept. 7, 2017.

63(2)(b)C(i)(B) opening words amended to add "in writing" by 2002-2013 technical bill (Part 5 — technical), for certifications made after Dec. 20, 2002.

63(2) earlier amended by 2000 Budget (effective for 2000 and later taxation years), 2000 same-sex partners bill, 1998 Budget, 1996 Budget, 1992 technical bill, 1991 technical bill and 1989 Budget.

Income Tax Folios: See list at end of s. 63.

(2.1) Taxpayer and supporting person with equal incomes

— For the purposes of this section, where in any taxation year the income of a taxpayer who has an eligible child for the year and the income of a supporting person of the child are equal (on the assumption that both incomes are computed without reference to this section and paragraphs 60(v.1) and (w)), no deduction shall be allowed under this section to the taxpayer and the supporting person in respect of the child unless they jointly elect to treat the income of one of them as exceeding the income of the other for the year.

Notes: 63(2.1) amended by 1989 Budget and 1991 technical bill, effective 1989.

Income Tax Folios: See list at end of s. 63.

(2.2) Expenses while at school

— There may be deducted in computing a taxpayer's income for a taxation year such part of the amount determined under subsection (2.3) as the taxpayer claims, where

(a) the taxpayer is, at any time in the year, a student in attendance at a designated educational institution or a secondary school and enrolled in a program of the institution or school of not less than 3 consecutive weeks duration that provides that each student in the program spend not less than

(i) 10 hours per week on courses or work in the program, or

(ii) 12 hours per month on courses in the program;

(b) there is no supporting person of an eligible child of the taxpayer for the year or the income of the taxpayer for the year

exceeds the income for the year of a supporting person of the child (on the assumption that both incomes are computed without reference to this section and paragraphs 60(v.1) and (w)); and

(c) a prescribed form containing prescribed information is filed with the taxpayer's return of income (other than a return filed under subsection 70(2) or 104(23), paragraph 128(2)(e) or subsection 150(4)) for the year.

Notes: 63(2.2) allows a deduction for child care expenses for periods during which a taxpayer is a student and is either the sole supporting person of an eligible child or, if there is another supporting person, is the supporting person with the higher income. See also 63(3)"child care expense"(a)(v).

63(2.2)(a)(ii) added by 1998 Budget. 63(2.2) added by 1996 Budget.

(2.3) Amount deductible [while at school]

— For the purpose of subsection (2.2), the amount determined in respect of a taxpayer for a taxation year is the least of

(a) the amount by which the total of all amounts, each of which is an amount paid as or on account of child care expenses incurred for services rendered in the year in respect of an eligible child of the taxpayer, exceeds the amount that is deductible under subsection (1) in computing the taxpayer's income for the year,

(b) ⅔ of the taxpayer's income for the year computed without reference to this section and paragraphs 60(v.1) and (w),

(c) the amount determined by the formula

$$A \times C$$

where

A is the total of all amounts each of which is the periodic child care expense amount in respect of an eligible child of the taxpayer for the year, and

C is

(i) if there is a supporting person of an eligible child of the taxpayer for the year,

(A) the number of weeks, in the year, in which both the taxpayer and the supporting person were students who would be described in paragraph (2.2)(a) if that paragraph were read without reference to subparagraph (ii), and

(B) the number of months in the year (other than a month that includes all or part of a week included in the number of weeks referred to in clause (A)), in which both the taxpayer and the supporting person were students described in paragraph (2.2)(a), and

(ii) in any other case,

(A) the number of weeks, in the year, in which the taxpayer was a student who would be described in paragraph (2.2)(a) if that paragraph were read without reference to subparagraph (ii), and

(B) the number of months in the year (other than a month that includes all or part of a week included in the number of weeks referred to in clause (A)), in which the taxpayer was a student described in paragraph (2.2)(a),

(d) the amount by which the total calculated under subparagraph (1)(e)(ii) in respect of eligible children of the taxpayer for the year exceeds the amount that is deductible under subsection (1) in computing the taxpayer's income for the year, and

(e) where there is a supporting person of an eligible child of the taxpayer for the year, the amount by which the amount calculated under paragraph (2)(b) for the year in respect of the taxpayer exceeds ⅔ of the taxpayer's earned income for the year.

Notes: See Notes to 63(3)"periodic child care expense amount". 63(2.3) amended by 2000 Budget (for 2000 and later taxation years), 1998 Budget; added by 1996 Budget.

(3) Definitions

— In this section,

"annual child care expense amount", in respect of an eligible child of a taxpayer for a taxation year, means

(a) $11,000, if the child is a person in respect of whom an amount may be deducted under section 118.3 in computing a taxpayer's tax payable under this Part for the year, and

(b) if the child is not a person referred to in paragraph (a),

(i) $8,000, if the child is under 7 years of age at the end of the year, and

(ii) $5,000, in any other case;

Notes: These numbers are not indexed for inflation. Definition amended by 2015 Budget bill, for 2015 and later tax years, to change $10,000 to $11,000, $7,000 to $8,000 and $4,000 to $5,000. These increases were first proposed in the Oct. 30, 2014 "benefits for families" news release that included the Family Tax Cut (119.1) and expanded Universal Child Care Benefit (see Notes to 56(6)) (both later reversed by the Liberals).

Definition "annual child care expense amount" added by 2000 Budget, for 2000 and later tax years. The dollar amounts were previously in 63(1)(e).

"child care expense" means an expense incurred in a taxation year for the purpose of providing in Canada, for an eligible child of a taxpayer, child care services including baby sitting services, day nursery services or services provided at a boarding school or camp if the services were provided

(a) *[for 2020-2021 see 63(3.1)(a) — ed.]* to enable the taxpayer, or the supporting person of the child for the year, who resided with the child at the time the expense was incurred,

(i) to perform the duties of an office or employment,

(ii) to carry on a business either alone or as a partner actively engaged in the business,

(iii) [Repealed]

(iv) to carry on research or any similar work in respect of which the taxpayer or supporting person received a grant, or

(v) to attend a designated educational institution or a secondary school, where the taxpayer is enrolled in a program of the institution or school of not less than three consecutive weeks duration that provides that each student in the program spend not less than

(A) 10 hours per week on courses or work in the program, or

(B) 12 hours per month on courses in the program, and

(b) by a resident of Canada other than a person

(i) who is the father or the mother of the child,

(ii) who is a supporting person of the child or is under 18 years of age and related to the taxpayer, or

(iii) in respect of whom an amount is deducted under section 118 in computing the tax payable under this Part for the year by the taxpayer or by a supporting person of the child,

except that

(c) any such expenses paid in the year for a child's attendance at a boarding school or camp to the extent that the total of those expenses exceeds the product obtained when the periodic child care expense amount in respect of the child for the year is multiplied by the number of weeks in the year during which the child attended the school or camp, and

(d) for greater certainty, any expenses described in subsection 118.2(2) and any other expenses that are paid for medical or hospital care, clothing, transportation or education or for board and lodging, except as otherwise expressly provided in this definition,

are not child care expenses;

Related Provisions: 63(1)(d) — Reduction for assistance received in respect of expenses; 63(3.1)(a) — Application of para. (a) in 2020-2021; 64.1 — Individuals absent from Canada; 67.1(1) — Food and entertainment 50% restriction does not apply.

Notes: See Notes to 63(1). The words "resided with the child" in para. (a) should be a much lower threshold than "cohabit in a conjugal relationship" (see Notes to 248(1)"common-law partner"). The "resided with" condition is not prohibited discrimi-

nation under the *Charter of Rights* or *Canadian Human Rights Act*: *Fannon*, 2013 FCA 99, 2017 FC 58.

The words "in Canada" in the opening words of the definition are effectively ignored for a resident of Canada while working outside Canada. See 64.1(a).

The expenses must be incurred for a purpose listed in para. (a), so child care to attend medical or workers' comp assessments was denied: *Phillip*, 2019 TCC 37, para. 27. For 2020-21, para. (a) does not apply to EI, QPIP and CERB recipients: 63(3.1)(a).

Employer-provided (or -paid) child care that is a taxable benefit under 6(1)(a) is considered paid by the employee for s. 63: VIEWS docs 2010-0390931E5, 2014-0528601C6.

The following all qualify: employer's portion of nanny's CPP contributions and EI premiums, excluding EI premium incentive refunds (VIEWS doc 2009-0317671E5, 2016-0654751I7); nanny transportation costs, medical insurance and Workers' Comp premiums (2011-0430351E5); Quebec's Additional Subsidized Childcare Contribution of $7.30/day (2015-0595651C6 [2015 APFF q.5], 2015-0614231E5). Any assistance for costs reduces the expense: 63(1)(d).

Camp fees including day camp fees and day sports schools qualify as child care expenses if they provide a "sufficient degree of child care services": Folio S1-F3-C1 ¶1.13, 1.17; VIEWS doc 2004-0086251E5. In *Wootton*, 2007 TCC 545, a day camp was held to provide child care for GST purposes, as the camp was responsible for the children's protection and care for the whole day. Accommodation at a host family does not qualify: 2012-0444581E5.

Parents can choose a school; thus, boarding for a teenager at a professional ballet school was allowed in *Lessard*, 2003 TCC 266. Similarly, in *Bailey*, 2005 TCC 305, the taxpayer needed child care and chose an academy that provided education (and was cheaper than child care); the deduction was allowed because her purpose was to obtain child care.

After school programs (e.g., gymnastics, dance lessons, riding lessons, hockey, music) have often been denied because they are recreational and the child care (even if needed so the parent can work) is merely incidental (all TCC): *Levine*, [1996] 2 C.T.C. 2147; *Keefer*, [2000] 2 C.T.C. 2622; *Bell*, [2001] 1 C.T.C. 2308; *Burlton*, [2001] 4 C.T.C. 2710; *Sykes*, [2005] 3 C.T.C. 2054; *Malecek*, 2007 TCC 271. However, in *Jones*, 2006 TCC 501, gym classes and summer gym camps were allowed; and in *Kwan*, 2018 TCC 184, chess, golf, math tutoring and Chinese language classes were allowed as enabling the parents to work. (See also *Bailey* in previous para.)

Education including full-day kindergarten does not qualify: para. (d); VIEWS doc 2012-0439601M4 ("a child in a typical child care setting is not expected to achieve any specific educational goals"). Pre-school fees qualify: 2010-0360281E5, 2012-0439101E5. Extended day fees for care at school outside school hours qualify: 2010-0366941E5, 2012-0439601M4.

A babysitter can qualify (*Allott*, 2010 TCC 232), but the expenses must be incurred to enable the taxpayer to work (or attend school). Paying a babysitter to go out for an evening would not normally qualify. However, in *Labrecque*, 2007 TCC 195, Saturday care for an autistic child (who required "constant attention and supervision") was allowed even though the parents were not working on those days, as it allowed them to go shopping and gave them respite so they could work during the week.

Payments to hold a daycare space open during parental leave can qualify: VIEWS docs 2010-0365202E5, 2011-0402001E5, 2011-0404311E5. Nanny pre-employment costs such as immigration lawyer fees can qualify: 2015-0580291E5.

Tuition to a private school to teach religion is partly a charitable donation: see Notes to 118.1(1)"total charitable gifts" under "Tuition". On allocation of private school fees between education and child care, see VIEWS doc 2004-0104911E5. A school can show both tuition and child care on one invoice: 2007-0232351E5.

For more on which expenses are deductible see VIEWS doc 2005-0114421E5.

Payments to the taxpayer's sister can qualify: VIEWS doc 2010-0357341E5; as can payments to the child's grandparents: 2011-0400631E5, and payments to the taxpayer's own company: 2011-0417371E5. See also Notes to 63(1) re expenses rejected as not credible.

For (a)(v), "attend" an educational institution does not require physically being there: VIEWS doc 2012-0439101E5. (See also Notes to 118.5(1)(b) re Internet or correspondence courses.)

Definition amended by 2000 Budget (for 2000 and later taxation years), 1998 and 1996 Budgets, 1992 and 1991 technical bills. 63(3)"child care expense" was 63(3)(a) before RSC 1985 (5th Supp) consolidation for tax years ending after Nov. 1991.

Income Tax Folios: See list at end of s. 63.

Interpretation Bulletins: IT-518R: Food, beverages and entertainment expenses.

"earned income" of a taxpayer means the total of

(a) all salaries, wages and other remuneration, including gratuities, received by the taxpayer in respect of, in the course of, or because of, offices and employments,

(b) all amounts that are included, or that would, but for paragraph 81(1)(a) or subsection 81(4), be included, because of section 6 or 7 or paragraph 56(1)(n), (n.1), (o) or (r) *[for 2020-21, also 56(1)(a)(iv) or (vii): see 63(3.1)(b) — ed.]*, in computing the taxpayer's income,

(c) all the taxpayer's incomes or the amounts that would, but for paragraph 81(1)(a), be the taxpayer's incomes from all businesses carried on either alone or as a partner actively engaged in the business, and

(d) all amounts received by the taxpayer as, on account of, in lieu of payment of or in satisfaction of, a disability pension under the *Canada Pension Plan* or a provincial pension plan as defined in section 3 of that Act;

Related Provisions: 110(2) — Definition applies to person who has taken vow of perpetual poverty.

Notes: Child care can be claimed only up to 2/3 of "earned income": 63(1)(e)(i).

Para. (a): "other remuneration" cannot include a dividend paid to a director: VIEWS doc 2019-0804961E5. (The letter's original summary suggested a dividend might be business income for para. (c) in some cases, but the text does not say this, and the summary was revised to remove it.)

Para. (b): exempt status-Indian income (see 81(1)(a) Notes) qualifies, creating room for child-care to be claimed against other income. EI, QPIP and CERB income (56(1)(a)(iv), (a)(vii) and (r)) all count as earned income for 2020-21: 63(3.1)(b) (VIEWS doc 2012-0452161I7 had noted QPIP does not qualify). Benefits under an *Unemployment Insurance Act* independent work program did not qualify: *Lambin*, [1998] 2 C.T.C. 2531 (TCC).

Definition amended by 2006 budget bill #2 (for 2007 and later tax years), 2001 and 1995-97 technical bills, 1997 Budget, 1992 Child Benefit bill. 63(3)"earned income" was 63(3)(b) before RSC 1985 (5th Supp) consolidation for tax years ending after Nov. 1991.

Interpretation Bulletins: IT-434R: Rental of real property by individual.

"eligible child" of a taxpayer for a taxation year means

(a) a child of the taxpayer or of the taxpayer's spouse or common-law partner, or

(b) a child dependent on the taxpayer or the taxpayer's spouse or common-law partner for support and whose income for the year does not exceed the amount determined for F in subsection 118(1.1) for the year

if, at any time during the year, the child

(c) is under 16 years of age, or

(d) is dependent on the taxpayer or on the taxpayer's spouse or common-law partner and has a mental or physical infirmity;

Notes: The 118(1.1)F basic personal amount (BPA) maximum is $13,229 for 2020, $13,808 for 2021.

Due to para. (c), 63(3)"annual child care expense amount" and 63(1)(e)(ii), $5,000 *per child* age 7-15 counts towards the expense limit. Thus, the $5,000 available for a 15-year old can be spent on care for any eligible child.

Grandparents can claim child care expenses if their daughter (going to school) and her children live with them: VIEWS doc 2005-0147101E5.

Para. (b) amended by 2021 budget bill #1, for 2020 and later tax years, to change the BPA reference from 118(1)B(c) to 118(1.1)F.

Definition amended by 2000 same-sex partners bill (effective 2001 or earlier), 1999, 1998 and 1996 Budgets, 1992 Child Benefit bill. 63(3)"eligible child" was 63(3)(c) before RSC 1985 (5th Supp) consolidation for tax years ending after Nov. 1991.

"periodic child care expense amount", in respect of an eligible child of a taxpayer for a taxation year, means $1/40$ of the annual child care expense amount in respect of the child for the year;

Notes: The periodic limits are:

- Disabled child ($11,000) — $275 per week
- Child under 7 ($8,000) — $200 per week
- Child over 7 ($5,000) — $125 per week

Before 2015, they were:

- Disabled child ($10,000) — $250 per week
- Child under 7 ($7,000) — $175 per week
- Child over 7 ($4,000) — $100 per week

Definition "periodic child care expense amount" added by 2000 Budget, effective for 2000 and later taxation years. The dollar amounts were previously in the formulas in 63(2) and (2.3) and in 63(3)"child care expense"(c).

"supporting person" of an eligible child of a taxpayer for a taxation year means a person, other than the taxpayer, who is

(a) a parent of the child,

(b) the taxpayer's spouse or common-law partner, or

(c) an individual who deducted an amount under section 118 for the year in respect of the child,

if the parent, spouse or common-law partner or individual, as the case may be, resided with the taxpayer at any time during the year and at any time within 60 days after the end of the year.

Notes: For this definition, it is irrelevant whether the person actually supports the child: *Macintosh*, 2019 TCC 155 (FCA appeal discontinued A-346-19), paras. 17-19. (See Notes to 248(1)"eligible relocation" under "New work location".)

For CRA interpretation of "resided with" see VIEWS docs 2015-0570791E5, 2015-0603711E5.

Definition amended by 2000 same-sex partners bill (effective 2001 or earlier), 1996 Budget bill. 63(3)"supporting person" was 63(3)(d) before RSC 1985 (5th Supp) consolidation for tax years ending after Nov. 1991.

(3.1) COVID-19 — child care expenses — For the purpose of applying this section in respect of a taxpayer for the 2020 or 2021 taxation year,

(a) the definition "child care expense" in subsection (3) is to be read without reference to its paragraph (a) if at any time in the year the taxpayer was entitled to an amount referred to in subparagraph 56(1)(a)(iv) or (vii) or paragraph 56(1)(r), in respect of the year; and

(b) paragraph (b) of the definition "earned income" in subsection (3) is to be read as follows:

"(b) all amounts that are included, or that would, but for paragraph 81(1)(a) or subsection 81(4), be included, because of section 6 or 7, subparagraph 56(1)(a)(iv) or (vii) or paragraph 56(1)(n), (n.1), (o) or (r), in computing the taxpayer's income,"

Related Provisions: 64.01 — Parallel rule for disability supports deduction.

Notes: 63(3.1) provides COVID-19 relief for 2020 and 2021, as announced by Finance news release Jan. 21, 2021. It allows Canadians receiving EI benefits to make the same claims for the child care expense claims as COVID-19 income support recipients. 64.01 does the same for the s. 64 Disability Supports Deduction.

Para. (a) says that, for 2020-21, if the taxpayer has any income from EI (56(1)(a)(iv)), Quebec Parental Insurance Plan (56(1)(a)(vii)) or CERB/CRB (56(1)(r)), then the 63(3)"child care expense"(a) requirement that the expense be incurred to earn income does not apply. Para. (b) says that EI and QPIP income count as "earned income" for 2020-21 (CERB/CRB income qualified already, as it is taxed under 56(1)(r)).

63(3.1) added by 2021 budget bill #1, effective 2020.

(4) Commuter's child care expense — Where in a taxation year a person resides in Canada near the boundary between Canada and the United States and while so resident incurs expenses for child care services that would be child care expenses if

(a) the definition "child care expense" in subsection (3) were read without reference to the words "in Canada", and

(b) the reference in paragraph (b) of the definition "child care expense" in subsection (3) to "resident of Canada" were read as "person",

those expenses (other than expenses paid for a child's attendance at a boarding school or camp outside Canada) shall be deemed to be child care expenses for the purpose of this section if the child care services are provided at a place that is closer to the person's principal place of residence by a reasonably accessible route, having regard to the circumstances, than any place in Canada where such child care services are available and, in respect of those expenses, subsection (1) shall be read without reference to the words "and contains, where the payee is an individual, that individual's Social Insurance Number".

Notes: 63(4) permits a deduction for child-care services provided in the US if all the conditions are met. It applies where there are no closer facilities in Canada; "such" does not refer to the same quality of child care as the taxpayer obtains in the US. No deduction was allowed for an "upscale private school" in Michigan where no comparable facility existed nearby: *Chan*, 2005 TCC 233.

63(4) added by 1993 technical bill, effective for 1992 and later taxation years.

Former 63(4), repealed by 1983 Budget, dealt with whether a child was in the custody of the taxpayer, a concept that no longer applies.

Definitions [s. 63]: "amount" — 248(1); "annual child care expense amount" — 63(3); "business" — 248(1); "Canada" — 64.1, 255; "child" — 252(1); "child care expense" — 63(3); "common-law partner", "common-law partnership" — 248(1); "designated educational institution" — 118.6(1); "earned income", "eligible child" — 63(3); "employment" — 248(1); "father" — 252(2)(a); "individual" — 248(1); "medical doctor" — 118.4(2)(a); "Minister" — 248(1); "month" — *Interpretation Act* 35(1); "mother" — 252(2)(a); "nurse practitioner" — 118.4(2); "office" — 248(1); "parent" — 252(2)(a); "periodic child care expense amount" — 63(3); "person", "prescribed" — 248(1); "provincial pension plan" — *Canada Pension Plan* s. 3; "resident of Canada" — 250; "supporting person" — 63(3); "taxable income" — 2(2), 248(1); "taxation year" — 249; "taxpayer" — 248(1); "United States" — *Interpretation Act* 35(1); "writing" — *Interpretation Act* 35(1).

Income Tax Folios [s. 63]: S1-F1-C1: Medical expense tax credit [replaces IT-519R2]; S1-F1-C2: Disability tax credit [replaces IT-519R2]; S1-F3-C1: Child care expense deduction [replaces IT-495R3].

63.1 [See s. 64.1]

64. Disability supports deduction — If a taxpayer files with the taxpayer's return of income (other than a return of income filed under subsection 70(2), paragraph 104(23)(d) or 128(2)(e) or subsection 150(4)) for the taxation year a prescribed form containing prescribed information, there may be deducted in computing the taxpayer's income for the year the lesser of

(a) the amount determined by the formula

$$A - B$$

where

A is the total of all amounts each of which is an amount paid by the taxpayer in the year and that

    (i) *[for 2020-2021 see 64.01 — ed.]* was paid to enable the taxpayer

        (A) to perform the duties of an office or employment,

        (B) to carry on a business either alone or as a partner actively engaged in the business,

        (C) to attend a designated educational institution or a secondary school at which the taxpayer is enrolled in an educational program, or

        (D) to carry on research or any similar work in respect of which the taxpayer received a grant,

    (ii) was paid

        (A) where the taxpayer has a speech or hearing impairment, for the cost of sign-language interpretation services or real time captioning services and to a person engaged in the business of providing such services,

        (B) where the taxpayer is deaf or mute, for the cost of a teletypewriter or similar device, including a telephone ringing indicator, prescribed by a medical practitioner, to enable the taxpayer to make and receive phone calls,

        (C) where the taxpayer is blind, for the cost of a device or equipment, including synthetic speech systems, Braille printers, and large print on-screen devices, prescribed by a medical practitioner, and designed to be used by blind individuals in the operation of a computer,

        (D) where the taxpayer is blind, for the cost of an optical scanner or similar device, prescribed by a medical practitioner, and designed to be used by blind individuals to enable them to read print,

        (E) where the taxpayer is mute, for the cost of an electronic speech synthesizer, prescribed by a medical practitioner, and designed to be used by mute individuals to enable them to communicate by use of a portable keyboard,

        (F) where the taxpayer has an impairment in physical or mental functions, for the cost of note-taking services and to a person engaged in the business of providing such services, if the taxpayer has been certified in writing by a medical practitioner to be a person who, because of that impairment, requires such services,

        (G) where the taxpayer has an impairment in physical functions, for the cost of voice recognition software, if the taxpayer has been certified in writing by a medical practitioner to be a person who, because of that impairment, requires that software,

        (H) where the taxpayer has a learning disability or an impairment in mental functions, for the cost of tutoring services that are rendered to, and supplementary to the primary education of, the taxpayer and to a person ordinarily engaged in the business of providing such services to individuals who are not related to the person, if the taxpayer has been certified in writing by a medical practitioner to be a person who, because of that disability or impairment, requires those services,

        (I) where the taxpayer has a perceptual disability, for the cost of talking textbooks used by the taxpayer in connection with the taxpayer's enrolment at a secondary school in Canada or at a designated educational institution, if the taxpayer has been certified in writing by a medical practitioner to be a person who, because of that disability, requires those textbooks,

        (J) where the taxpayer has an impairment in physical or mental functions, for the cost of attendant care services provided in Canada and to a person who is neither the taxpayer's spouse or common-law partner nor under 18 years of age, if the taxpayer is a taxpayer in respect of whom an amount may be deducted because of section 118.3, or if the taxpayer has been certified in writing by a medical practitioner to be a person who, because of that impairment is, and is likely to be indefinitely, dependent on others for their personal needs and care and who as a result requires a full-time attendant,

        (K) where the taxpayer has a severe and prolonged impairment in physical or mental functions, for the cost of job coaching services (not including job placement or career counselling services) and to a person engaged in the business of providing such services if the taxpayer has been certified in writing by a medical practitioner to be a person who, because of that impairment, requires such services,

        (L) where the taxpayer is blind or has a severe learning disability, for the cost of reading services and to a person engaged in the business of providing such services, if the taxpayer has been certified in writing by a medical practitioner to be a person who, because of that impairment or disability, requires those services,

        (M) where the taxpayer is blind and profoundly deaf, for the cost of deaf-blind intervening services and to a person engaged in the business of providing such services,

        (N) where the taxpayer has a speech impairment, for the cost of a device that is a Bliss symbol board, or a similar device, that is prescribed by a medical practitioner to help the taxpayer communicate by selecting the symbols or spelling out words,

        (O) where the taxpayer is blind, for the cost of a device that is a Braille note-taker, prescribed by a medical practitioner, to allow the taxpayer to take notes (that can, by the device, be read back to them or printed or displayed in Braille) with the help of a keyboard,

        (P) where the taxpayer has a severe and prolonged impairment in physical functions that markedly restricts their ability to use their arms or hands, for the cost of a device that is a page turner prescribed by a medical practitioner to help the taxpayer to turn the pages of a book or other bound document, and

(Q) where the taxpayer is blind, or has a severe learning disability, for the cost of a device or software that is prescribed by a medical practitioner and designed to enable the taxpayer to read print,

(iii) is evidenced by one or more receipts filed with the Minister each of which was issued by the payee and contains, where the payee is an individual who is a person referred to in clause (ii)(J), that individual's Social Insurance Number, and

(iv) is not included in computing a deduction under section 118.2 for any taxpayer for any taxation year, and

B is the total of all amounts each of which is the amount of a reimbursement or any other form of assistance (other than prescribed assistance or an amount that is included in computing a taxpayer's income and that is not deductible in computing the taxpayer's taxable income) that any taxpayer is or was entitled to receive in respect of an amount included in computing the value of A, and

(b) the total of

(i) the total of all amounts each of which is

(A) an amount included under section 5, 6 or 7 or paragraph 56(1)(n), (o) or (r) *[for 2020-21, also 56(1)(a)(iv) or (vii): see 64.01(b) — ed.]* in computing the taxpayer's income for the year, or

(B) the taxpayer's income for the year from a business carried on either alone or as a partner actively engaged in the business, and

(ii) where the taxpayer is in attendance at a designated educational institution or a secondary school at which the taxpayer is enrolled in an educational program, the least of

(A) $15,000,

(B) $375 times the number of weeks in the year during which the taxpayer is in attendance at the institution or school, and

(C) the amount, if any, by which the amount that would, if this Act were read without reference to this section, be the taxpayer's income for the year exceeds the total determined under subparagraph (i) in respect of the taxpayer for the year.

Related Provisions: 4(2) — Deductions under s. 64 not applicable to any particular source; 64.01 — Application of 64(a)A(i) and 64(b)(i)(A) in 2020-2021; 64.1 — Individuals absent from Canada; 118.2(2)(b), (b.1), (c) — Medical expense credit (MEC) — attendant care; 118.2(2)(l.4), (l.42), (l.91), Reg. 5700(k), (l), (o), (p), (w) — MEC for expenses listed in s. 64; 118.4(2) — Meaning of medical practitioner; 122.51(2)A(b)(ii) — 25% of s. 64 deduction available for refundable MEC; 257 — Formula cannot calculate to less than zero.

Notes: 64 allows a deduction for various disability-related costs, where a person with a disability earns business or employment income or attends school. For a taxpayer without sufficient income (or time in school) to qualify for the deduction due to 64(b), a medical expense credit claim can usually be made under 118.2(2). It can effectively offset taxable financial assistance provided to enable the person to work, as in *Simser*, 2004 FCA 414 (leave to appeal denied 2005 CarswellNat 1727 (SCC)).

For 2020-21: 64(a)A(i) does not apply to EI, QPIP and CERB/CRB recipients: 64.01(a); and EI, QPIP and CERB/CRB income (56(1)(a)(iv), (a)(vii) and (r)) all qualify under 64(b)(i)(A): 64.01(b).

The cost of an ASL sign language interpreter is deductible under 64: VIEWS doc 2006-0192141E5. No deduction is available to a deceased person's estate: 2006-0189561E5. For interpretation of "tutoring" in (H) and "job coaching" in (K) see 2015-0599661E5.

64(a)(ii)(J) refers to the "cost" of an attendant rather than "remuneration" (used in 118.2(2)(b.1), (c)), so should include related costs such as employer EI and CPP premiums.

64 amended by 2006 budget bills #1 and #2 (for 2005 and later tax years), 2004 and 2000 Budgets, 2000 same-sex partners bill, 1997 Budget, 1996 EI bill, 1991 technical bill. Added by 1989 Budget.

The previous s. 64, repealed by 1981 Budget but still referred to (as, in some but not all cases, s. 64 of R.S.C. 1952, c. 148) in 59(2), 61(1)(b)(iv.1), 66(5), 66(15)"reserve

amount"B, 66.4(1), 72(1)(d), (e), 72(2)(a)(iii)(D), 72(2)(c)(iii), 87(2)(p) and 88(1)(d)(i)(C) and Reg. 1204(1)(a)(i), (ii) and 5203(3)(b)(ii), was titled "Reserve in respect of consideration for disposition of resource property not receivable until subsequent year." It still applies to dispositions pursuant to the terms in existence on Nov. 12, 1981 of an offer or agreement in writing made or entered into by that date.

Definitions [s. 64]: "amount", "business" — 248(1); "Canada" — 255, *Interpretation Act* 35(1); "common-law partner", "employment", "individual" — 248(1); "medical practitioner" — 118.4(2); "Minister", "office", "person", "prescribed" — 248(1); "related" — 251(2)–(6); "taxable income" — 248(1); "taxation year" — 249; "taxpayer" — 248(1); "writing" — *Interpretation Act* 35(1).

Regulations: No assistance prescribed to date for 64(a)B.

Income Tax Folios: S1-F1-C1: Medical expense tax credit [replaces IT-519R2]; S1-F1-C2: Disability tax credit [replaces IT-519R2]; S1-F1-C3: Disability supports deduction [replaces IT-519R2].

Information Circulars: 82-2R2: SIN legislation that relates to the preparation of information slips.

Forms: RC4064: Medical and disability-related information [guide]; T929: Disability supports deduction.

64.01 COVID-19 — disability supports deduction — For the purpose of applying section 64 in respect of a taxpayer for the 2020 or 2021 taxation year,

(a) the description of A in paragraph 64(a) is to be read without reference to its subparagraph (i) if at any time in the year the taxpayer was entitled to an amount referred to in subparagraph 56(1)(a)(iv) or (vii) or paragraph 56(1)(r), in respect of the year; and

(b) clause 64(b)(i)(A) is to be read as follows:

"(A) an amount included under section 5, 6 or 7, subparagraph 56(1)(a)(iv) or (vii) or paragraph 56(1)(n), (o) or (r) in computing the taxpayer's income for the year, or"

Related Provisions: 63(3.1) — Parallel rule for child-care expenses.

Notes: See 63(3.1) Notes. 64.01 added by 2021 budget bill #1, effective 2020.

Definitions [s. 64.01]: "amount" — 248(1); "taxation year" — 249; "taxpayer" — 248(1).

64.1 Individuals absent from Canada — In applying sections 63 and 64 in respect of a taxpayer who is, throughout all or part of a taxation year, absent from but resident in Canada, the following rules apply for the year or that part of the year, as the case may be:

(a) the definition "child care expense" in subsection 63(3), and section 64, shall be read without reference to the words "in Canada";

(b) subsection 63(1) and section 64 shall be read without reference to the words "and contains, where the payee is an individual, that individual's Social Insurance Number", if the payment referred to in that subsection or section, as the case may be, is made to a person who is not resident in Canada; and

(c) paragraph (b) of the definition "child care expense" in subsection 63(3) shall be read as if the word "person" were substituted for the words "resident of Canada" where they appear therein.

Notes: 64.1 provides that while X is resident in Canada (see Notes to 250(1) — includes deemed residents such as diplomats abroad), but physically out of Canada, child care and disability expenses (ss. 63-64) can be incurred outside Canada. This does not apply while X is in Canada (due to "that part of the year"). Thus, if X takes her child C on a US business trip, a deduction for child care in the US can be allowed (subject to s. 63); but if X stays in Canada and sends C to a US summer camp, there is no deduction.

64.1 amended by 1998 Budget to delete references to s. 62, effective 1998. The rule still applies to moving expenses but is now in 248(1)"eligible relocation"(a)(i).

64.1 originally enacted as 63.1. Redrafted and renumbered by 1989 Budget, effective 1989, when 64 was enacted.

Definitions [s. 64.1]: "Canada" — 255; "person" — 248(1); "resident" — 250; "taxation year" — 249; "taxpayer" — 248(1).

Remission Orders: *Child Care Expense and Moving Expense Remission Order*, P.C. 1991-257 (same relief as section 64.1 for 1984-88).

Income Tax Folios: S1-F1-C3: Disability supports deduction [replaces IT-519R2]; S1-F3-C1: Child care expense deduction [replaces IT-495R3].

65. (1) Allowance for oil or gas well, mine or timber limit — There may be deducted in computing a taxpayer's income for a taxation year such amount as an allowance, if any, in respect of

(a) a natural accumulation of petroleum or natural gas, oil or gas well, mineral resource or timber limit,

(b) the processing of ore (other than iron ore or tar sands) from a mineral resource to any stage that is not beyond the prime metal stage or its equivalent,

(c) the processing of iron ore from a mineral resource to any stage that is not beyond the pellet stage or its equivalent, or

(d) the processing of tar sands from a mineral resource to any stage that is not beyond the crude oil stage or its equivalent

as is allowed to the taxpayer by regulation.

Related Provisions: 65(3) — Allocation of allowance for coal mine; 66(1) — Exploration and development expenses of principal-business corporations; 66.7 — Successor rules; 96(1)(d) — No deduction at partnership level; 127.52(1)(e) — Limitation on deduction for minimum tax purposes; 209 — Tax on carved-out income.

Notes: For the meaning of "timber limit", used in 65(1)(a), see 13(21)"timber resource property" Notes. For "prime metal stage or its equivalent" in 65(1)(b), see Reg. 1104(5) Notes.

Regulations: 1200.

I.T. Application Rules: 29(1)–(4), (11)–(14), (16), (24).

(2) Regulations — For greater certainty it is hereby declared that, in the case of a regulation made under subsection (1) allowing to a taxpayer an amount in respect of a natural accumulation of petroleum or natural gas, an oil or gas well or a mineral resource or in respect of the processing of ore,

(a) there may be allowed to the taxpayer by that regulation an amount in respect of any or all

(i) natural accumulations of petroleum or natural gas, oil or gas wells or mineral resources in which the taxpayer has any interest or, for civil law, right, or

(ii) processing operations described in any of paragraphs (1)(b), (c) or (d) that are carried on by the taxpayer; and

(b) notwithstanding any other provision contained in this Act, the Governor in Council may prescribe the formula by which the amount that may be allowed to the taxpayer by that regulation shall be determined.

Related Provisions: 66(1) — Exploration and development expenses of principal-business corporations; 66.7 — Successor rules; 221 — Rules applicable to regulations generally.

Notes: 65(2)(a)(i) amended by 2002-2013 technical bill (Part 4 — bijuralism), effective June 26, 2013, to add "or, for civil law, right".

Regulations: 1200–1209.

I.T. Application Rules: 29(1)–(4), (11)–(14), (16), (24).

(3) Lessee's share of allowance — Where a deduction is allowed under subsection (1) in respect of a coal mine operated by a lessee, the lessor and lessee may agree as to what portion of the allowance each may deduct and, in the event that they cannot agree, the Minister may fix the portions.

I.T. Application Rules: 29(1)–(4), (11)–(14), (16), (24).

Definitions [s. 65]: "amount", "mineral resource", "Minister", "oil or gas well", "regulation", "tar sands" — 248(1); "taxation year" — 249; "taxpayer" — 248(1).

66. (1) Exploration and development expenses of principal-business corporations — A principal-business corporation may deduct, in computing its income for a taxation year, the lesser of

(a) the total of such of its Canadian exploration and development expenses as were incurred by it before the end of the taxation year, to the extent that they were not deductible in computing income for a previous taxation year, and

(b) of that total, an amount equal to its income for the taxation year if no deduction were allowed under this subsection, section 65 or subsection 66.1(2), minus the deductions allowed for the year by sections 112 and 113.

Related Provisions: 87(6), (7) — Obligations of predecessor corporation. See also at end of s. 66.

(2) [No longer relevant]

Notes: 66(2) applies to expenses incurred before May 7, 1974.

(3) Expenses of other taxpayers — A taxpayer other than a principal-business corporation may deduct, in computing the taxpayer's income for a taxation year, the total of the taxpayer's Canadian exploration and development expenses to the extent that they were not deducted in computing the taxpayer's income for a preceding taxation year.

Related Provisions: 66(5) — Dealers.

(4) Foreign exploration and development expenses — A taxpayer who is resident throughout a taxation year in Canada may deduct, in computing the taxpayer's income for that taxation year, the lesser of

(a) the amount, if any, by which

(i) the total of the foreign exploration and development expenses incurred by the taxpayer

(A) before the end of the year,

(B) at a time at which the taxpayer was resident in Canada, and

(C) where the taxpayer became resident in Canada before the end of the year, after the last time (before the end of the year) that the taxpayer became resident in Canada,

exceeds the total of

(ii) such of the expenses described in subparagraph (i) as were deductible in computing the taxpayer's income for a preceding taxation year, and

(iii) all amounts by which the amount described in this paragraph in respect of the taxpayer is required because of subsection 80(8) to be reduced at or before the end of the year, and

(b) of that total, the greater of

(i) the amount, if any, claimed by the taxpayer not exceeding 10% of the amount determined under paragraph (a) in respect of the taxpayer for the year, and

(i.1) [Repealed]

(ii) the total of

(A) the part of the taxpayer's income for the year, determined without reference to this subsection and subsection 66.21(4), that can reasonably be regarded as attributable to

(I) the production of petroleum or natural gas from natural accumulations outside Canada or from oil or gas wells outside Canada, or

(II) the production of minerals from mines outside Canada,

(B) the taxpayer's income for the year from royalties in respect of a natural accumulation of petroleum or natural gas outside Canada, an oil or gas well outside Canada or a mine outside Canada, determined without reference to this subsection and subsection 66.21(4), and

(C) all amounts each of which is an amount, in respect of a foreign resource property that has been disposed of by the taxpayer, equal to the amount, if any, by which

(I) the amount included in computing the taxpayer's income for the year by reason of subsection 59(1) in respect of the disposition

exceeds

(II) the total of all amounts each of which is that portion of an amount deducted under subsection 66.7(2) in computing the taxpayer's income for the year that

1. can reasonably be considered to be in respect of the foreign resource property, and

2. cannot reasonably be considered to have reduced the amount otherwise determined under clause (A) or (B) in respect of the taxpayer for the year.

Related Provisions: 66(4.1) — Country-by-country FEDE allocations; 66(4.3) — Individuals who cease to be resident in Canada; 66(5) — Dealers; 66(11.4) — Change of control; 66(13.1) — Short taxation year; 66.21(1) "global foreign resource limit" — Determination of limit; 66.21(4) — Deduction for cumulative foreign resource expense; 66.7(2)(a) — Successor of foreign exploration and development expenses; 66.7(2.3) — Successor of foreign resource expenses; 80(8)(e) — Reduction of FEDE on debt forgiveness; 87(7) — Obligations of predecessor corporation; 104(5.2) — Trusts — 21-year deemed disposition; 110.6(1) "investment expense" (d) — effect of claim under 66(4) on capital gains exemption; 115(1)(e.1) — Deduction for unused FEDE balance against taxable income earned in Canada of non-resident; 115(4.1) — Taxable income earned in Canada — foreign resource pool expenses; 261(7)(a) — Functional currency reporting. See also at end of s. 66.

Notes: For interpretation of "income for the year" in 66(4)(b)(ii)(A) see VIEWS doc 2007-0226251I7.

66(4) amended by 2000 Budget/2001 technical bill (for tax years that begin after 2000), 1995-97 and 1994 technical bills.

(4.1) Country-by-country FEDE allocations — For greater certainty, the portion of an amount deducted under subsection (4) in computing a taxpayer's income for a taxation year that can reasonably be considered to be in respect of specified foreign exploration and development expenses of the taxpayer in respect of a country is considered to apply to a source in that country.

Related Provisions: 66(4.2) — Method of allocation; 66.7(2.1) — Parallel rule for successor corporation.

Notes: 66(4.1) added by 2000 Budget, effective for taxation years that begin after 1999, or earlier by designation (see Notes to 126(5)).

(4.2) Method of allocation — For the purpose of subsection (4.1), where a taxpayer has incurred specified foreign exploration and development expenses in respect of two or more countries, an allocation to each of those countries for a taxation year shall be determined in a manner that is

(a) reasonable having regard to all the circumstances, including the level and timing of

    (i) the taxpayer's specified foreign exploration and development expenses in respect of the country, and

    (ii) the profits or gains to which those expenses relate; and

(b) not inconsistent with the allocation made under subsection (4.1) for the preceding taxation year.

Related Provisions: 66.7(2.2) — Parallel rule for successor corporation.

Notes: 66(4.2) added by 2000 Budget, effective for taxation years that begin after 1999, or earlier by designation (see Notes to 126(5)).

(4.3) FEDE deductions where change of individual's residence — Where at any time in a taxation year an individual becomes or ceases to be resident in Canada,

(a) subsection (4) applies to the individual as if the year were the period or periods in the year throughout which the individual was resident in Canada; and

(b) for the purpose of applying subsection (4), subsection (13.1) does not apply to the individual for the year.

Notes: 66(4.3) added by 2000 Budget, effective for 1998 and later taxation years.

(5) Dealers — Subsections (3) and (4) and sections 59, 64, 66.1, 66.2, 66.21, 66.4 and 66.7 do not apply in computing the income for a taxation year of a taxpayer (other than a principal-business corporation) whose business includes trading or dealing in rights, licences or privileges to explore for, drill for or take minerals, petroleum, natural gas or other related hydrocarbons.

Related Provisions: 253 — Extended meaning of "carrying on business". See also at end of s. 66.

Notes: Whether someone is "trading or dealing" is a question of fact: VIEWS doc 2010-0357731E5. See the case law on "trader or dealer" in Notes to 39(5).

Reference to s. 64 in 66(5) should be to s. 64 of R.S.C. 1952, c. 148, meaning the version repealed by 1981 Budget. See Notes to 64.

66(5) amended by 2000 Budget, effective for taxation years that begin after 2000.

Income Tax Folios: S3-F8-C1: Principal-business corporations in the resource industries [replaces IT-400].

Interpretation Bulletins: IT-291R3: Transfer of property to a corporation under subsection 85(1); IT-314: Income of dealers in oil and gas leases (cancelled).

(6)–(9) [Repealed under former Act]

Notes: 66(6)–(9), repealed in 1987, permitted successor corporations to deduct certain expenses. These rules are now in 66.7.

(10)–(10.3) [Repealed]

Notes: 66(10)-(10.3), "Joint exploration corporation", were repealed by 1996 Budget, for renunciations made after March 5, 1996 (after 2006 in some cases). See Carr & Calverley, *Canadian Resource Taxation* (Carswell, looseleaf or *Taxnet Pro* Reference Centre), chap. 11.

66(10.1) earlier amended by 1992 Economic Statement, and 1991 technical bill.

(10.4) Idem [Joint exploration corporation] — [No longer relevant.]

Notes: 66(10.4) triggers ACB reduction or capital gain if taxpayer T makes a payment or loan to a joint exploration corp that has renounced expenses to T under 66(10.1)-(10.3). It can still apply, but those provisions were repealed many years ago.

(11) [No longer relevant]

Notes: 66(11) applies on certain acquisitions of control of a corporation before Nov. 13, 1981 (or, per 66(11.3), before 1983 under an agreement signed by Nov. 12, 1981).

(11.1), (11.2) [Repealed under former Act]

Notes: 66(11.1) and (11.2), repealed in 1987, dealt with the application of the successor rules on change in control or change in tax-exempt status of a corporation. This is now covered in 66.7(10) and (11).

(11.3) Control — For the purposes of subsections (11) and 66.7(10), where a corporation acquired control of another corporation after November 12, 1981 and before 1983 by reason of the acquisition of shares of the other corporation pursuant to an agreement in writing concluded on or before November 12, 1981, it shall be deemed to have acquired that control on or before November 12, 1981.

Related Provisions: See at end of s. 66.

(11.4) Loss restriction event [change in control] — If

(a) at any time a taxpayer is subject to a loss restriction event,

(b) within the 12-month period that ended immediately before that time, the taxpayer, a partnership of which the taxpayer was a majority-interest partner or a trust of which the taxpayer was a majority-interest beneficiary (as defined in subsection 251.1(3)) acquired a Canadian resource property or a foreign resource property (other than a property that was held, by the taxpayer, partnership or trust or by a person that would be affiliated with the taxpayer if section 251.1 were read without reference to the definition "controlled" in subsection 251.1(3), throughout the period that began immediately before the 12-month period began and ended at the time the property was acquired by the taxpayer, partnership or trust), and

(c) immediately before the 12-month period began the taxpayer, partnership or trust was not, or would not be if it were a corporation, a principal-business corporation,

for the purposes of subsection (4) and sections 66.2, 66.21 and 66.4, except as those provisions apply for the purposes of section 66.7, the property is deemed not to have been acquired by the taxpayer, partnership or trust, as the case may be, before that time, except that if the property has been disposed of by it before that time and not reacquired by it before that time, the property is deemed to have been acquired by the taxpayer, partnership or trust, as the case may be, immediately before it disposed of the property.

Related Provisions: 66(11.5) — Interpretation; 66(11.6) — Trust loss restriction event; 87(2)(j.6) — Amalgamation — continuing corporation; 251.2 — Loss restriction event. See also at end of s. 66.

Notes: 66(11.4) amended by 2013 budget bill #2 (this version effective Sept. 13, 2013), from referring to control of a corp being acquired to use "loss restriction event" so as to also apply to trusts (see Notes to 251.1(2)). Earlier amended by 2000 Budget, 1995-97 technical bill.

Income Tax Folios: S3-F8-C1: Principal-business corporations in the resource industries [replaces IT-400].

I.T. Technical News: 7 (control by a group — 50/50 arrangement).

(11.5) Affiliation — subsec. (11.4) — For the purposes of subsection (11.4), if the taxpayer referred to in that subsection was formed or created in the 12-month period referred to in that subsection, the taxpayer is deemed to have been, throughout the period that began immediately before the 12-month period and ended immediately after it was formed or created,

(a) in existence; and

(b) affiliated with every person with whom it was affiliated (otherwise than because of a right referred to in paragraph 251(5)(b)) throughout the period that began when it was formed or created and that ended immediately before the time at which the taxpayer was subject to the loss restriction event referred to in that subsection.

Related Provisions: 251.2 — Loss restriction event. See also at end of s. 66.

Notes: 66(11.5) amended by 2013 budget bill #2, effective March 21, 2013, to cover trusts as well as corporations (see 251.2(2)).

66(11.5) amended by 1995-97 technical bill, effective for acquisitions of control that occur after April 26, 1995.

(11.6) Trust loss restriction event — successor — If at any time a trust is subject to a loss restriction event,

(a) for the purposes of the provisions of this Act relating to deductions in respect of drilling and exploration expenses, prospecting, exploration and development expenses, Canadian exploration and development expenses, foreign resource pool expenses, Canadian exploration expenses, Canadian development expenses and Canadian oil and gas property expenses (in this subsection referred to as "resource expenses") incurred by the trust before that time, the following rules apply:

(i) the trust is (other than for purposes of this subsection and subsections (11.4), (11.5) and 66.7(10) to (11)) deemed to be a corporation that

(A) after that time is a successor (within the meaning assigned by any of subsections 66.7(1), (2) and (2.3) to (5)), and

(B) at that time, acquired all the properties held by the trust immediately before that time from an original owner of those properties,

(ii) if the trust did not hold a foreign resource property immediately before that time, the trust is deemed to have owned a foreign resource property immediately before that time,

(iii) a joint election is deemed to have been filed in accordance with subsections 66.7(7) and (8) in respect of the acquisition described in clause (i)(B),

(iv) the resource expenses incurred by the trust before that time are deemed to have been incurred by an original owner of the properties and not by the trust,

(v) the original owner is deemed to have been resident in Canada at every time before that time at which the trust was resident in Canada,

(vi) if at that time the trust is a member of a partnership and the property of the partnership includes a Canadian resource property or a foreign resource property,

(A) for the purposes of clause (i)(B), the trust is deemed to have held immediately before that time that portion of the partnership's property at that time that is equal to the trust's percentage share of the total of amounts that would be paid to all members of the partnership if it were wound up at that time, and

(B) for the purposes of clauses 66.7(1)(b)(i)(C) and (2)(b)(i)(B), subparagraph 66.7(2.3)(b)(i) and clauses 66.7(3)(b)(i)(C), (4)(b)(i)(B) and (5)(b)(i)(B) for a taxation year that ends after that time, the lesser of the following amounts is deemed to be income of the trust for the year that can reasonably be regarded as attributable to production from the property:

(I) the trust's share of the part of the income of the partnership for the fiscal period of the partnership that

ends in the year that can reasonably be regarded as attributable to the production from the property, and

(II) an amount that would be determined under subclause (I) for the year if the trust's share of the income of the partnership for the fiscal period of the partnership that ends in the year were determined on the basis of the percentage share referred to in clause (A), and

(vii) if after that time the trust disposes of property that was at that time held by the trust to another person, subsections 66.7(1) to (5) do not apply in respect of the acquisition by the other person of the property; and

(b) if before that time, the trust or a partnership of which the trust was a member acquired a property that is a Canadian resource property, a foreign resource property or an interest in a partnership and it can reasonably be considered that one of the main purposes of the acquisition is to avoid any limitation provided in any of subsections 66.7(1) to (5) on the deduction in respect of any expenses incurred by the trust, then the trust or the partnership, as the case may be, is deemed, for the purposes of applying those subsections to or in respect of the trust, not to have acquired the property.

Related Provisions: 251.2 — Loss restriction event.

Notes: For the meaning of "one of the main purposes" (para. (b)), see Notes to 83(2.1).

66(11.6) added by 2013 budget bill #2, effective March 21, 2013. See Notes to 251.2(2) re loss restriction events.

(12) Computation of exploration and development expenses — In computing a taxpayer's Canadian exploration and development expenses,

(a) there shall be deducted any amount paid to the taxpayer before May 7, 1974

(i) and after 1971 under the *Northern Mineral Exploration Assistance Regulations* made under an appropriation Act that provides for payments in respect of the Northern Mineral Grants Program, or

(ii) pursuant to any agreement entered into between the taxpayer and Her Majesty in right of Canada under the Northern Mineral Grants Program or the Development Program of the Department of Indian Affairs and Northern Development, to the extent that the amount has been expended by the taxpayer as or on account of Canadian exploration and development expenses incurred by the taxpayer; and

(b) there shall be included any amount, except an amount in respect of interest, paid by the taxpayer after 1971 and before May 7, 1974 under the Regulations referred to in subparagraph (a)(i) to Her Majesty in right of Canada.

Related Provisions: 66(12.1) — Limitations. See also at end of s. 66.

(12.1) Limitations of Canadian exploration and development expenses — Except as expressly otherwise provided in this Act,

(a) if as a result of a transaction occurring after May 6, 1974 an amount has become receivable by a taxpayer at a particular time in a taxation year and the consideration given by the taxpayer therefor was property (other than a share or a Canadian resource property, or an interest in or a right to — or, for civil law, a right in or to — the share or the property) or services, the original cost of which to the taxpayer may reasonably be regarded as having been primarily Canadian exploration and development expenses of the taxpayer (or would have been so regarded if they had been incurred by the taxpayer after 1971 and before May 7, 1974) or a Canadian exploration expense, there shall at that time be included in the amount determined for G in the definition "cumulative Canadian exploration expense" in subsection 66.1(6) in respect of the taxpayer the amount that became receivable by the taxpayer at that time; and

(b) if as a result of a transaction occurring after May 6, 1974 an amount has become receivable by a taxpayer at a particular time in a taxation year and the consideration given by the taxpayer therefor was property (other than a share or a Canadian resource property, or an interest in or a right to — or, for civil law, a right in or to — the share or the property) or services, the original cost of which to the taxpayer may reasonably be regarded as having been primarily a Canadian development expense, there shall at that time be included in the amount determined for G in the definition "cumulative Canadian development expense" in subsection 66.2(5) in respect of the taxpayer the amount that became receivable by the taxpayer at that time.

Related Provisions: 59(1) — Amounts received as consideration for disposition of resource property; 66(15) — Definitions. See also at end of s. 66.

Notes: For interpretation see VIEWS docs 2011-0420451E5, 2012-0446431C6, 2013-0489911E5.

66(12.1)(a), (b) amended by 2002-2013 technical bill (Part 4 — bijuralism), effective June 26, 2013, to change "or an interest therein or a right thereto" to "or an interest in or a right to — or, for civil law, a right in or to — the share or the property".

Interpretation Bulletins: IT-125R4: Dispositions of resource properties.

Advance Tax Rulings: ATR-59: Financing exploration and development through limited partnerships.

(12.2) Unitized oil or gas field in Canada

(12.2) Unitized oil or gas field in Canada — Where, pursuant to an agreement between a taxpayer and another person to unitize an oil or gas field in Canada, an amount has become receivable by the taxpayer at a particular time after May 6, 1974 from that other person in respect of Canadian exploration expense incurred by the taxpayer or Canadian exploration and development expenses incurred by the taxpayer (or expenses that would have been Canadian exploration and development expenses if they had been incurred by the taxpayer after 1971 and before May 7, 1974) in respect of that field or any part thereof, the following rules apply:

(a) there shall, at that time, be included by the taxpayer in the amount determined for G in the definition "cumulative Canadian exploration expense" in subsection 66.1(6) the amount that became receivable by the taxpayer; and

(b) there shall, at that time, be included by the other person in the amount referred to in paragraph (c) of the definition "Canadian exploration expense" in subsection 66.1(6) the amount that became payable by that person.

Related Provisions: 66(15) — Definitions. See also at end of s. 66.

Interpretation Bulletins: IT-273R2: Government assistance — general comments; IT-125R4: Dispositions of resource properties.

(12.3) Idem

(12.3) Idem — Where, pursuant to an agreement between a taxpayer and another person to unitize an oil or gas field in Canada, an amount has become receivable by the taxpayer at a particular time after May 6, 1974 from that other person in respect of Canadian development expense incurred by the taxpayer in respect of that field or any part thereof, the following rules apply:

(a) there shall, at that time, be included by the taxpayer in the amount determined for G in the definition "cumulative Canadian development expense" in subsection 66.2(5) the amount that became receivable by the taxpayer; and

(b) there shall, at that time, be included by the other person in the amount referred to in paragraph (a) of the definition "Canadian development expense" in subsection 66.2(5) the amount that became payable by that person.

Related Provisions: See at end of s. 66.

Interpretation Bulletins: IT-273R2: Government assistance — general comments; IT-125R4: Dispositions of resource properties.

(12.4) Limitation of FEDE

(12.4) Limitation of FEDE — Where, as a result of a transaction that occurs after May 6, 1974, an amount becomes receivable by a taxpayer at a particular time in a taxation year and the consideration given by the taxpayer for the amount receivable is property (other than a foreign resource property) or services, the original cost of which to the taxpayer can reasonably be regarded as having been primarily foreign exploration and development expenses of the taxpayer (or would have been so regarded if they had been incurred by the taxpayer after 1971 and the definition "foreign exploration and

development expenses" in subsection (15) were read without reference to paragraph (k) of that definition), the following rules apply:

(a) in computing the taxpayer's foreign exploration and development expenses at that time, there shall be deducted the amount receivable by the taxpayer;

(b) where the amount receivable exceeds the total of the taxpayer's foreign exploration and development expenses incurred before that time to the extent that those expenses were not deducted or deductible, as the case may be, in computing the taxpayer's income for a preceding taxation year, there shall be included in the amount referred to in paragraph 59(3.2)(a) the amount, if any, by which the amount receivable exceeds the total of

(i) the taxpayer's foreign exploration and development expenses incurred before that time to the extent that those expenses were not deducted or deductible, as the case may be, in computing the taxpayer's income for a preceding taxation year, and

(ii) the amount, designated by the taxpayer in prescribed form filed with the taxpayer's return of income for the year, not exceeding the portion of the amount receivable for which the consideration given by the taxpayer was property (other than a foreign resource property) or services, the original cost of which to the taxpayer can reasonably be regarded as having been primarily

(A) specified foreign exploration and development expenses in respect of a country, or

(B) foreign resource expenses in respect of a country; and

(c) where an amount is included in the amount referred to in paragraph 59(3.2)(a) by virtue of paragraph (b), the total of the taxpayer's foreign exploration and development expenses at that time shall be deemed to be nil.

Related Provisions: 59(3.2)(a) — Income inclusion; 66(12.41), (12.42) — Limitations of foreign resource expenses; 95(1) — "foreign affiliate". See also at end of s. 66.

Notes: Opening words of 66(12.4) and 66(12.4)(b) amended by 2000 Budget, effective for taxation years that begin after 2000.

(12.41) Limitations of foreign resource expenses

(12.41) Limitations of foreign resource expenses — Where a particular amount described in subsection (12.4) becomes receivable by a taxpayer at a particular time, there shall at that time be included in the value determined for G in the definition "cumulative foreign resource expense" in subsection 66.21(1) in respect of the taxpayer and a country the amount designated under subparagraph (12.4)(b)(ii) by the taxpayer in respect of the particular amount and the country.

Related Provisions: 66(12.42) — Partnerships; 66.21(1)"cumulative foreign resource expense"G.

Notes: 66(12.41) added by 2000 Budget, for taxation years that begin after 2000.

(12.42) Partnerships

(12.42) Partnerships — For the purposes of subsections (12.4) and (12.41), where a person or partnership is a member of a particular partnership and a particular amount described in subsection (12.4) becomes receivable by the particular partnership in a fiscal period of the particular partnership,

(a) the member's share of the particular amount is deemed to be an amount that became receivable by the member at the end of the fiscal period; and

(b) the amount deemed by paragraph (a) to be an amount receivable by the member is deemed to be an amount

(i) that is described in subsection (12.4) in respect of the member, and

(ii) that has the same attributes for the member as it did for the particular partnership.

Notes: 66(12.42) added by 2000 Budget, for fiscal periods that begin after 2000.

(12.5) Unitized oil or gas field in Canada

(12.5) Unitized oil or gas field in Canada — Where, pursuant to an agreement between a taxpayer and another person to unitize an oil or gas field in Canada, an amount has become receivable by the taxpayer at a particular time from that other person in respect of

Canadian oil and gas property expense incurred by the taxpayer in respect of that field or any part thereof, the following rules apply:

(a) there shall, at that time, be included by the taxpayer in the amount determined for G in the definition "cumulative Canadian oil and gas property expense" in subsection 66.4(5) the amount that became receivable by the taxpayer; and

(b) there shall, at that time, be included by the other person in the amount referred to in paragraph (a) of the definition "Canadian oil and gas property expense" in subsection 66.4(5) the amount that became payable by that person.

Related Provisions: See at end of s. 66.

Interpretation Bulletins: IT-125R4: Dispositions of resource properties.

(12.6) Canadian exploration expenses to flow-through shareholder — If a person gave consideration under an agreement to a corporation for the issue of a flow-through share of the corporation and, in the period that begins on the day on which the agreement was made and ends 24 months *[or 36 months per 66(12.6001) — ed.]* after the end of the month that includes that day, the corporation incurred Canadian exploration expenses (other than an expense deemed by subsection 66.1(9) to be a Canadian exploration expense of the corporation), the corporation may, after it complies with subsection (12.68) in respect of the share and before March of the first calendar year that begins after the period, renounce, effective on the day on which the renunciation is made or on an earlier day set out in the form prescribed for the purpose of subsection (12.7), to the person in respect of the share the amount, if any, by which the portion of those expenses that was incurred on or before the effective date of the renunciation (which portion is in this subsection referred to as the "specified expenses") exceeds the total of

(a) the assistance that the corporation has received, is entitled to receive or can reasonably be expected to receive at any time, and that can reasonably be related to the specified expenses or to Canadian exploration activities to which the specified expenses relate (other than assistance that can reasonably be related to expenses referred to in paragraph (b) or (b.1)),

(b) all specified expenses that are prescribed Canadian exploration and development overhead expenses of the corporation,

(b.1) all specified expenses each of which is a cost of, or for the use of, seismic data

(i) that had been acquired (otherwise than as a consequence of performing work that resulted in the creation of the data) by any other person before the cost was incurred,

(ii) in respect of which a right to use had been acquired by any other person before the cost was incurred, or

(iii) all or substantially all of which resulted from work performed more than one year before the cost was incurred, and

(c) the total of amounts that are renounced on or before the date on which the renunciation is made by any other renunciation under this subsection in respect of those expenses,

but not in any case

(d) exceeding the amount, if any, by which the consideration for the share exceeds the total of other amounts renounced under this subsection or subsection (12.601) or (12.62) in respect of the share on or before the day on which the renunciation is made, or

(e) exceeding the amount, if any, by which the cumulative Canadian exploration expense of the corporation on the effective date of the renunciation computed before taking into account any amounts renounced under this subsection on the date on which the renunciation is made, exceeds the total of all amounts renounced under this subsection in respect of any other share

(i) on the date on which the renunciation is made, and

(ii) effective on or before the effective date of the renunciation.

Related Provisions: 40(12), 54 "exemption threshold" — Deemed cost of flow-through share on donation to charity; 66(12.6001) — COVID-19 — 24 months is 36 months for agreement made March 2018–Dec. 2020; 66(12.601), (12.602) — Flow-through share rules for first $1 million of CDE before 2019; 66(12.61) — Effect of renunciation of CEE; 66(12.62)(d) — CDE to flow-through shareholder; 66(12.64)(c) — COGPE to flow-through shareholder; 66(12.66) — Expense in the first 60 days of the year; 66(12.67) — Restriction on renunciation; 66(12.68) — Filing selling instruments; 66(12.69) — Filing re partners; 66(12.7) — Filing; 66(12.71) — Restriction on renunciation; 66(12.73) — Adjustment in renunciation; 66(12.741) — Late renunciation; 66(16) — Partnership deemed to be a person; 66(19) — Renunciation by member of partnership, etc.; 66.3(3) — Cost of flow-through shares; 66.3(4)(a)(ii)(B) — Paid-up capital; 87(4.4) — Amalgamation — flow-through shares; 110.6(1) "investment expense" (d) — effect of renunciation on capital gains exemption; 127(9) "investment tax credit" (a.2), 127(9) "flow-through mining expenditure" (c), (d) — Investment tax credit; 127(9) "pre-production mining expenditure" (b) — Whether pre-production mining expenditures can be renounced; 163(2.2) — False statement or omissions — penalty; 211.91 — Tax on issuer using one-year look-back rule; 248(1) "specified future tax consequence" (b) — Reduction under 66(12.73) is a specified future tax consequence; 248(16), (16.1) — GST or QST input tax credit/refund and rebate deemed to be assistance; 248(18), (18.1) — GST or QST — repayment of input tax credit or refund. See also at end of s. 66.

Notes: 66(12.6), (12.601) and (12.66) allow flow-through shares (FTS) to work. A principal-business corporation (defined in 66(15)) that issues a FTS can "renounce" certain expenses it could otherwise claim, and pass them to shareholders. The shareholders then claim the expenses as if they had incurred them directly. This is particularly useful to obtain financing for corporations that are not yet profitable, as it allows the fast write-offs available for resource expenditures (e.g. CEE) to be used by the shareholders against their income. 66(12.601) allows some CDE to be converted to CEE for this purpose, and (12.66) allows retroactive renunciation if the investment is arm's length and paid for within certain time limits. What makes the share a FTS is the written agreement between the investor and the corporation, not any characteristic of the share itself; see 66(15) "flow-through share" (but note a Reg. 6202 or 6202.1 "prescribed share" is excluded). Investments may be structured as flow-through LPs, where investors become limited partners (see Notes to 96(1)) and the LP invests in FTS of junior resource companies. After two years, the LP units are typically rolled into a mutual fund corp under 85(2) and the LP is wound up under 85(3).

66(12.66) provides a "look-back" rule allowing a corp to renounce to arm's-length shareholders expenses incurred in the year or the next year (formerly up to 60 days after year-end), and extended for 2020 due to COVID-19 as per Proposed Amendments above. This triggers Part XII.6 tax on the corp under 211.91: *Tusk Exploration*, 2018 FCA 121, paras. 9-10 [D'Avignon, Case Comment, XII(3) *Resource Sector Taxation* (Federated Press) 2-4 (2018); Perry, "Flowthrough Shares: Beware Non-Arm's-Length Relationships", 8(3) *Canadian Tax Focus* (ctf.ca) 11-12 (Aug. 2018)].

FTS exist to recognize the "high risk and sizeable capital requirements" of the resource mining industry: *Mickleborough*, [1998] 4 C.T.C. 2584 (TCC), para. 52. In recent years they have also been issued for renewable energy projects.

Total flow-through share deductions were projected to cost the *federal* government $125 million (personal + corp income tax) in 2019, $115m in 2020, $110m in 2021 and $115m in 2022: *Report on Federal Tax Expenditures 2021*.

For discussion see Income Tax Folio S3-F8-C2 ¶2.49-2.53; tinyurl.com/cra-ftshares; CRA guide T100; Dept. of Finance, *Flow-Through Shares: An Evaluation Report* (Oct. 1994, 276 pp.); Gamble, *Taxation of Canadian Mining*, chap. 12 and Carr & Calverley, *Canadian Resource Taxation*, chap. 8 (both Carswell, looseleaf or Taxnet Pro Reference Centre); Toselli, "Flow-Through Shares: An Update", 10 *Canadian Petroleum Tax Journal [CPTJ]* (1997); Johnson, "A Practical Guide to the Flow-Through Share Rules", 15 *CPTJ* 19-50 (2002); Jodoin, "Federal and Quebec Incentives for Exploration", V(2) *Resource Sector Taxation [RST]* (Federated Press) 346-53 (2007); Gadbois & Jodoin, "A Flow-through Share or Is it?", VI(1) *RST* 398-403 (2008) (re *JES* case); Ross, "Revisiting Flow-through Shares", VI(4) *RST* 472-77 (2009); Nurmohamed, "Problems With Flow-through Shares", VII(2) *RST* 512-16 (2009); Johnson & Rousay, "Incurring Flow-through Share Expenditures", VIII(1) *RST* 555-58 (2010); Johnson & Winters, "The Companies' Creditors Arrangement Act and Flow-Through Shares", IX(1) *RST* 630-34 (2012); Jodoin, "Federal and Quebec Incentives for Exploration", 61(Supp.) *Canadian Tax Journal* 103-21 (2013); Sala, "Flowthrough Share Financing", 2015 Cdn Tax Foundation conference report, 10:1-32; Johnson & Novotny, "An Update on Flowthrough Shares in the Energy Sector", 2016 conference report, 12:1-39.

For descriptions of deals using FTS to renounce CRCE, see Richler, "Creststreet Income Fund Uses Flow-through Shares", IX(3) *Corporate Finance [CF]* (Federated Press) 1124-26 (2004); Horne, "Raising Capital for Resource Issuers" (NCE Flow-through (2004) LP), II(4) *Resource Sector Taxation* (Federated Press) 154-60 (2004); Richler, "Enhancement of Tax Rules Regarding Flow-Through Shares", IX(1) *CF* 802-805 (2001); ruling 2006-0212861R3.

Back-to-back renunciation is allowed for related corps (66(12.67)(a)), so a parent can renounce expenses that its sub renounced to it, subject to conditions: 2012-0455341E5.

Transferable flow-through warrants can qualify as FTS: VIEWS doc 2009-0336261R3. A warrant can be a "right to acquire a share" (66(15) "flow-through share") even if the underlying share to be acquired will not be a FTS: 2014-0534941E5.

If X buys FTS through a limited partnership and dies during the year, it is the estate that can deduct the CEE, since the renunciation of CEE is as of Dec. 31: VIEWS doc 2006-02016201E5. However, if X buys FTS directly and dies before the renunciation,

CRA's view is that no deduction is allowed to anyone because the person who acquired the shares no longer exists: 2013-0495271C6 [APFF 2013 q.8].

CCA cannot be renounced to investors, except for certain costs that constitute CRCE: VIEWS doc 2003-0045931E5. Canadian exploration expenses that are also prescribed Canadian exploration and development overhead expenses cannot be renounced: doc 2007-0246921E5.

CRA accepts that a sale of the shares for a pre-determined price below the actual issue price can be a capital gain (see Notes to 54"capital property") even though there is a tax gain because of the reduction in the shares' ACB: VIEWS doc 2012-0438651E5.

For more CRA interpretation see docs 9533295, 9601605, 9603955, 9604945, 2007-0254471E5, 2010-0384341C6 [2010 CTF Conf. p. 4:20, q.19], 2013-0472311E5.

For shares contracted for before the March 2011 Budget, FTS can be combined with the elimination of capital gains on donations to charity (see 38(a.1)), to allow donations that cost the taxpayer 0-10% of the amount the charity receives (the taxpayer gets a 100% deduction for the shares, plus some federal and possibly provincial investment tax credit, then a full donation credit under 118.1 for donating them once they can be donated). The Budget reduces this benefit by taxing the capital gain: see 40(12). A donation of a *private* company's FTS creates no tax credit, due to 66.3(3), 248(35) [248(37)(d) does not apply] and 248(31): 2012-0454451E5.

In *JES Investments*, 2007 FCA 337, the issuing corporation purported to renounce $100,000 of expenditures, but went out of business and did not incur any expenditures. The $100,000 was disallowed as a 66(12.6) deduction but was allowed as a capital loss. 66.3(3) did not reduce the shares' cost to nil because they were "prescribed shares" under Reg. 6202.1(1)(c)(i) and thus not FTS.

In *Fagan*, 2011 TCC 523, six investors incorporated Xco, which invested in Opco's FTS and then itself renounced the expenditures up another level to the investors. The Court ruled (para. 89) that CRA had no obligation to audit or assess Xco before denying the investors' expenditures on the ground that Opco's acquisition of seismic data had no business purpose.

Investors assessed to deny flow-through deductions can contest the underlying assessment disallowing the expenses to the corporation, even if the corporation did not appeal: *Fagan* (above), para. 82, citing *Gaucher*, [2001] 1 C.T.C. 125 (FCA) and *Forsberg*, 2005 TCC 591, paras. 8-9. (See also point 6 in Notes to 227.1(1).)

Claims under a company's indemnity if it fails to renounce expenses are in substance equity claims that rank behind creditor claims: *EarthFirst Canada*, 2009 ABQB 316.

For similar Quebec rules, see Claude Jodoin, "Quebec Incentives and Investment Expenses Deductions", III(4) *Resource Sector Taxation* 239-43 (2005).

66(12.6) amended by 2002-2013 technical bill (for renunciations made after Dec. 20, 2002), 1996 Budget, 1992 Economic Statement.

Income Tax Folios: S3-F8-C1: Principal-business corporations in the resource industries [replaces IT-400].

Interpretation Bulletins: IT-273R2: Government assistance — general comments.

Regulations: 228 (information return); 1206(1), (4.1), (4.2) (prescribed Canadian exploration and development overhead expenses, for 66(12.6)(b)).

I.T. Technical News: 41 (donation of flow-through shares).

Forms: T2 Sched. 12: Resource-related deductions; T100: Instructions for the flow-through share program [guide]; T101: Statement of resource expenses; T101A: Claim for renouncing CEEs and CDEs; T101B: Adjustments to CEEs and CDEs previously renonuced; T101C: Part XII.6 tax return; T101D: Summary of assistance; T1229: Statement of resource expenses and depletion allowance; T5013A: Statement of partnership income for tax shelters and renounced resource expenses.

(12.6001) COVID-19 — time extension to 36 months — The references to "24 months" in subsections (12.6) and (12.62) are to be read as references to "36 months" in respect of agreements entered into after February 2018 and before 2021.

Related Provisions: 66(12.731) — Extensions for agreements entered into in 2019-20; 211.91(2.1) — Part XII.6 tax — COVID-19 extension.

Notes: 66(12.6001) added by 2021 budget bill #1, for tax years that end after 2019. It, along with 66(12.731) and amendments to 211.91, provide COVID-19 relief by implementing a July 10, 2020 Finance news release, extending the deadline for companies to spend capital they raise via flow-through shares. The changes extend, by 12 months, the period to incur eligible flow-through share expenses under the general rule (66(12.6001)) and the look-back rule (66(12.731)), since 66(12.73)(a)(ii) applies where 66(12.66) applies).

CRA allowed taxpayers to file their returns, including Form T101C (Part XII.6 return), based on these rules before they were enacted: doc 2020-0874621E5.

(12.601) Flow-through share rules for first $1 million of Canadian development expenses [before 2019] — Where

(a) a person gave consideration under an agreement to a corporation for the issue of a flow-through share of the corporation,

(a.1) the corporation's taxable capital amount at the time the consideration was given was not more than $15,000,000, and

(b) during the period beginning on the particular day the agreement was entered into and ending on the earlier of December 31, 2018 and the day that is 24 months after the end of the month that included that particular day, the corporation incurred Canadian development expenses (excluding expenses that are deemed by subsection (12.66) to have been incurred on December 31, 2018) described in paragraph (a) or (b) of the definition "Canadian development expense" in subsection 66.2(5) or that would be described in paragraph (f) of that definition if the words "paragraphs (a) to (e)" in that paragraph were read as "paragraphs (a) and (b)",

the corporation may, after it complies with subsection (12.68) in respect of the share and before March of the first calendar year that begins after that period, renounce, effective on the day on which the renunciation is made or on an earlier day set out in the form prescribed for the purposes of subsection (12.7), to the person in respect of the share the amount, if any, by which the part of those expenses that was incurred on or before the effective date of the renunciation (which part is in this subsection referred to as the "specified expenses") exceeds the total of

(c) the assistance that the corporation has received, is entitled to receive, or can reasonably be expected to receive at any time, and that can reasonably be related to the specified expenses or Canadian development activities to which the specified expenses relate (other than assistance that can reasonably be related to expenses referred to in paragraph (d)),

(d) all specified expenses that are prescribed Canadian exploration and development overhead expenses of the corporation, and

(e) all amounts that are renounced on or before the day on which the renunciation is made by any other renunciation under this subsection or subsection (12.62) in respect of those expenses.

Related Provisions: 66(12.6011) — Meaning of "taxable capital amount" for 66(12.601)(a.1); 66(12.602) — Restriction; 66(12.62)(c), (d) — Canadian development expenses to flow-through shareholder; 66(12.64)(c) — Canadian oil and gas property expenses to flow-through shareholder; 66(12.66) — Expenses in first 60 days of following year; 66(12.67) — Restrictions on renunciation; 66(12.69) — Filing re partners; 66(12.7) — Filing; 66(12.71) — Restriction on renunciation; 66(12.73) — Adjustment in renunciation; 66(12.741) — Late renunciation; 66(16) — Partnership deemed to be a person; 66(19) — Renunciation by member of partnership, etc.; 66.1(6)"restricted expense"(c) — inclusion of renounced expenses; 66.3(4)(a)(ii)(B) — Paid-up capital; 87(4.4) — Amalgamations; 110.6(1)"investment expense"(d) — Effect of renunciation on capital gains exemption; 163(2.2) — False statements or omissions — penalty; 211.91 — Tax on issuer using one-year look-back rule; 248(1)"specified future tax consequence"(b) — Reduction under 66(12.73) is a specified future tax consequence.

Notes: See Notes to 66(12.6). For expenses incurred through 2018, 66(12.601) permits an eligible small oil and gas corp (taxable capital employed in Canada up to $15 million) to renounce up to $1 million (see 66(12.602)) of Canadian development expenses (CDE), normally claimed at 30% per year, to flow-through shareholders, who can then claim the renounced amount as Canadian exploration expenses (CEE), fully deductible in the year. The 2017 Budget eliminated this rule for expenses after 2018 (as part of the Liberals abandoning oil & gas in favour of "clean" energy), including expenses incurred in 2019 that could have been deemed to be incurred in 2018 because of the look-back rule in 66(12.66), except for expenses incurred after 2018 and before April 2019 that are renounced under a flow-through share agreement entered into after 2016 and before March 22, 2017.

2017 Budget Table 1 predicted this change will save the federal government $2 million in 2019-20 and 2020-21, and $1m in 2021-22. This change will affect the usefulness of flow-through shares for oil & gas in Western Canada: tinyurl.com/moodys-flow.

66(12.601)(b) amended by 2017 budget bill #2, effective Dec 14, 2017, except that, in its application in respect of agreements entered into after 2016 and before March 22, 2017, ignore the words "the earlier of December 31, 2018 and". Previously read:

(b) during the period beginning on the later of December 3, 1992 and the particular day the agreement was entered into and ending on the day that is 24 months after the end of the month that included that particular day, the corporation incurred Canadian development expenses described in paragraph (a) or (b) of the definition "Canadian development expense" in subsection 66.2(5) or that would be described in paragraph (f) of that definition if the words "paragraphs (a) to (e)" in that paragraph were read as "paragraphs (a) and (b)",

66(12.601) added by 1992 Economic Statement and amended by 1996 Budget.

Regulations: 1206(1), (4.1), (4.2) (prescribed Canadian exploration and development overhead expenses, for 66(12.601)(d)).

Income Tax Folios: S3-F8-C1: Principal-business corporations in the resource industries [replaces IT-400].

Forms: T2 Sched. 12: Resource-related deductions; T100: Instructions for the flow-through share program [guide]; T101: Statement of resource expenses; T101A: Claim for renouncing CEEs and CDEs; T101B: Adjustments to CEEs and CDEs previously renonouced; T101C: Part XII.6 tax return; T101D: Summary of assistance; T1229: Statement of resource expenses and depletion allowance; T5013A: Statement of partnership income for tax shelters and renounced resource expenses.

(12.6011) Taxable capital amount — For the purpose of subsection (12.601), a particular corporation's taxable capital amount at any time is the total of

(a) its taxable capital employed in Canada for its last taxation year that ended more than 30 days before that time, and

(b) the total of all amounts each of which is the taxable capital employed in Canada of another corporation associated at that time with the particular corporation for the other corporation's last taxation year that ended more than 30 days before that time.

Related Provisions: 66(12.6012) — Meaning of taxable capital employed in Canada; 66(12.6013) — Effect of amalgamation or merger; 256 — Associated corporations.

Notes: Where a corporation acquires all the shares of another corp and winds it up before issuing flow-through shares, the other corp's taxable capital will not be included in "taxable capital", since the corps were not associated when the shares were issued: VIEWS doc 2003-0047271E5.

66(12.6011) added by 1996 Budget, effective March 6, 1996, with certain grandfathering through 1998.

(12.6012) Taxable capital employed in Canada — For the purpose of determining a corporation's taxable capital amount at a particular time under subsection (12.6011) and for the purpose of subsection (12.6013), a particular corporation's taxable capital employed in Canada for a taxation year is the amount that would be its taxable capital employed in Canada for the year, determined in accordance with subsection 181.2(1) and without reference to the portion of its investment allowance (as determined under subsection 181.2(4)) that is attributable to shares of the capital stock of, dividends payable by, or indebtedness of, another corporation that

(a) was not associated with the particular corporation at the particular time; and

(b) was associated with the particular corporation at the end of the particular corporation's last taxation year that ended more than 30 days before that time.

Related Provisions: 256 — Associated corporations.

Notes: 66(12.6012) added by 1996 Budget, effective March 6, 1996.

(12.6013) Amalgamations and mergers — For the purpose of determining the taxable capital amount at a particular time under subsection (12.6011) of any corporation and for the purpose of this subsection, a particular corporation that was created as a consequence of an amalgamation or merger of other corporations (each of which is in this subsection referred to as a "predecessor corporation"), and that does not have a taxation year that ended more than 30 days before the particular time, is deemed to have taxable capital employed in Canada for a taxation year that ended more than 30 days before the particular time equal to the total of all amounts each of which is the taxable capital employed in Canada of a predecessor corporation for its last taxation year that ended more than 30 days before the particular time.

Notes: 66(12.6013) added by 1996 Budget, effective March 6, 1996.

(12.602) Idem [$1m limit for 66(12.601)] — A corporation shall be deemed not to have renounced any particular amount under subsection (12.601) in respect of a share where

(a) the particular amount exceeds the amount, if any, by which the consideration for the share exceeds the total of other amounts renounced in respect of the share under subsection (12.6), (12.601) or (12.62) on or before the day on which the renunciation is made;

(b) the particular amount exceeds the amount, if any, by which

(i) the cumulative Canadian development expense of the corporation on the effective date of the renunciation, computed before taking into account any amounts renounced under

subsection (12.601) on the day on which the renunciation is made,

exceeds

(ii) the total of all amounts renounced under subsection (12.601) by the corporation in respect of any other share

(A) on the day on which the renunciation is made, and

(B) effective on or before the effective date of the renunciation; or

(c) the particular amount relates to Canadian development expenses incurred by the corporation in a calendar year and the total amounts renounced, on or before the day on which the renunciation is made, under subsection (12.601) in respect of

(i) Canadian development expenses incurred by the corporation in that calendar year, or

(ii) Canadian development expenses incurred in that calendar year by another corporation associated with the corporation at the time the other corporation incurred such expenses

exceeds $1,000,000.

Related Provisions: 66(12.66) — Expenses in first 60 days of following year.

Notes: 66(12.602) added by 1992 Economic Statement, effective for expenses incurred after December 2, 1992. See Notes to 66(12.601).

66(12.602)(a) amended by 1996 Budget, for renunciations made in 1999 or later, to delete reference to 66(12.64).

Closing words of 66(12.602)(c) amended by 1996 Budget to change "$2 million" to "$1 million", effective for renunciations made after March 5, 1996, with certain grandfathering through 1998.

(12.61) Effect of renunciation — Subject to subsections (12.69) to (12.702), where under subsection (12.6) or (12.601) a corporation renounces an amount to a person,

(a) the Canadian exploration expenses or Canadian development expenses to which the amount relates shall be deemed to be Canadian exploration expenses incurred in that amount by the person on the effective date of the renunciation; and

(b) the Canadian exploration expenses or Canadian development expenses to which the amount relates shall, except for the purposes of that renunciation, be deemed on and after the effective date of the renunciation never to have been Canadian exploration expenses or Canadian development expenses incurred by the corporation.

Related Provisions: 66(16) — Partnership deemed to be a person; 66(17) — Non-arm's length partnerships; 127(9)"investment tax credit"(a.2), 127(9)"flow-through mining expenditure" — Investment tax credit. See also at end of s. 66.

Notes: 66(12.61) amended by 1996 Budget (for renunciations made after 1998), 1992 Economic Statement and 1991 technical bill.

(12.62) Canadian development expenses to flow-through shareholder — Where a person gave consideration under an agreement to a corporation for the issue of a flow-through share of the corporation and, in the period that begins on the day the agreement was made and ends 24 months after the end of the month that includes that day, the corporation incurred Canadian development expenses, the corporation may, after it complies with subsection (12.68) in respect of the share and before March of the first calendar year that begins after the period, renounce, effective on the day on which the renunciation is made or on an earlier day set out in the form prescribed for the purposes of subsection (12.7), to the person in respect of the share the amount, if any, by which the part of those expenses that was incurred on or before the effective date of the renunciation (which part is in this subsection referred to as the "specified expenses") exceeds the total of

(a) the assistance that the corporation has received, is entitled to receive, or can reasonably be expected to receive at any time, and that can reasonably be related to the specified expenses or to Canadian development activities to which the specified expenses relate (other than assistance that can reasonably be related to expenses referred to in paragraph (b) or (b.1)),

(b) all specified expenses that are prescribed Canadian exploration and development overhead expenses of the corporation,

337

(b.1) all specified expenses that are described in paragraph (e) of the definition "Canadian development expense" in subsection 66.2(5) or that are described in paragraph (f) of that definition because of the reference in the latter paragraph to paragraph (e), and

(c) the total of amounts that are renounced on or before the day on which the renunciation is made by any other renunciation under this subsection or subsection (12.601) in respect of those expenses,

but not in any case

(d) exceeding the amount, if any, by which the consideration for the share exceeds the total of other amounts renounced in respect of the share under this subsection or subsection (12.6) or (12.601) on or before the day on which the renunciation is made, or

(e) exceeding the amount, if any, by which the cumulative Canadian development expense of the corporation on the effective date of the renunciation computed before taking into account any amounts renounced under this subsection on the date on which the renunciation is made, exceeds the total of all amounts renounced under this subsection in respect of any other share

(i) on the date on which the renunciation is made, and

(ii) effective on or before the effective date of the renunciation.

Related Provisions: 66(12.6001) — COVID-19 — 24 months is 36 months for agreement March 2018–Dec. 2020; 66(12.601), (12.602) — Flow-through share rules for first $1 million of CDE before 2019; 66(12.63) — Effect of renunciation of CDE; 66(12.64)(c) — COGPE to flow-through shareholder; 66(12.67) — Restriction on renunciation; 66(12.68) — Filing selling instruments; 66(12.69) — Filing re partners; 66(12.7) — Filing; 66(12.71) — Restriction on renunciation; 66(12.73) — Adjustment in renunciation; 66(12.741) — Late renunciation; 66(16) — Partnership deemed to be a person; 66(19) — Renunciation by member of partnership, etc.; 66.1(6)"restricted expense"(c) — Inclusion of amount renounced; 66.2(5) — Definitions; 66.3(3) — Cost of flow-through shares; 66.3(4)(a)(ii)(B) — Paid-up capital; 87(4.4) — Flow-through shares; 110.6(1)"investment expense"(d) — effect of renunciation on capital gains exemption; 163(2.2) — False statement or omissions — penalty; 248(16), (16.1) — GST or QST input tax credit/refund and rebate deemed to be assistance; 248(18), (18.1) — GST or QST — repayment of input tax credit or refund. See also at end of s. 66.

Notes: 66(12.62) amended by 1996 Budget (last change effective for renunciations after 1998) and 1992 Economic Statement.

Income Tax Folios: S3-F8-C1: Principal-business corporations in the resource industries [replaces IT-400].

Interpretation Bulletins: IT-273R2: Government assistance — general comments.

Regulations: 228 (information return); 1206(1), (4.1), (4.2) (prescribed Canadian exploration and development overhead expenses, for 66(12.62)(b)).

Forms: T2 Sched. 12: Resource-related deductions; T100: Instructions for the flow-through share program [guide]; T101: Statement of resource expenses; T101A: Claim for renouncing CEEs and CDEs; T101B: Adjustments to CEEs and CDEs previously renonouced; T101C: Part XII.6 tax return; T101D: Summary of assistance; T1229: Statement of resource expenses and depletion allowance; T5013A: Statement of partnership income for tax shelters and renounced resource expenses.

(12.63) Effect of renunciation — Subject to subsections (12.69) to (12.702), if under subsection (12.62) a corporation renounces an amount to a person,

(a) the Canadian development expenses to which the amount relates shall be deemed to be Canadian development expenses incurred in that amount by the person on the effective date of the renunciation; and

(b) the Canadian development expenses to which the amount relates shall, except for the purposes of that renunciation, be deemed on and after the effective date of the renunciation never to have been Canadian development expenses incurred by the corporation.

Related Provisions: 66(16) — Partnership deemed to be a person; 66.2(5) — Definitions. See also at end of s. 66.

Notes: 66(12.63) opening words amended by 2002-2013 technical bill, for renunciations made after Dec. 20, 2002, to change "(12.691) to (12.702)" to "(12.69) to (12.702)".

66(12.63) amended by 1996 Budget (effective for renunciations made after 1998) and 1991 technical bill.

(12.64), (12.65) [Repealed]

Notes: 66(12.64), "Canadian oil and gas property expenses to flow-through shareholder", repealed by 1996 Budget, effective for renunciations made after March 5, 1996, with certain grandfathering through 1998. Thus, COGPE is no longer an eligible flow-through share expenditure. Previously amended by 1992 Economic Statement.

66(12.65) repealed by 1996 Budget, effective on the same basis as the repeal of 66(12.64). It dealt with the effect of renunciation under 66(12.64). Previously amended by 1991 technical bill.

(12.66) Expenses in the first 60 days of year [or throughout next calendar year] — Where

(a) a corporation that issues a flow-through share to a person under an agreement incurs, in a particular calendar year, Canadian exploration expenses or Canadian development expenses,

(a.1) the agreement was made in the preceding calendar year,

(b) the expenses

(i) are described in paragraph (a), (d), (f) or (g.1) of the definition "Canadian exploration expense" in subsection 66.1(6) or paragraph (a) or (b) of the definition "Canadian development expense" in subsection 66.2(5),

(ii) would be described in paragraph (h) of the definition "Canadian exploration expense" in subsection 66.1(6) if the reference to "paragraphs (a) to (d) and (f) to (g.4)" in that paragraph were read as "paragraphs (a), (d), (f) and (g.1)", or

(iii) would be described in paragraph (f) of the definition "Canadian development expense" in subsection 66.2(5) if the words "any of paragraphs (a) to (e)" were read as "paragraph (a) or (b)",

(c) before the end of that preceding year the person paid the consideration in money for the share to be issued,

(d) the corporation and the person deal with each other at arm's length throughout the particular year, and

(e) in January, February or March of the particular year, the corporation renounces an amount in respect of the expenses to the person in respect of the share in accordance with subsection (12.6) or (12.601) and the effective date of the renunciation is the last day of that preceding year,

the corporation is, for the purpose of subsection (12.6), or of subsection (12.601) and paragraph (12.602)(b), as the case may be, deemed to have incurred the expenses on the last day of that preceding year.

Related Provisions: 66(12.6) — Canadian exploration expenses to flow-through shareholder; 66(12.731), 211.91(2.1) — COVID-19 extensions for agreement made in 2019-20; 66(16) — Partnership deemed to be a person; 66(17) — Non-arm's length partnerships; 87(4.4) — Amalgamations; 127(9)"investment tax credit"(a.2), 127(9)"flow-through mining expenditure"(e) — Investment tax credit; 163(2.21), (2.22) — Penalty for false statement or omission; 211.91 — Tax on issuer using one-year look-back rule; 248(1)"specified future tax consequence"(b) — Reduction under 66(12.73) is a specified future tax consequence. See also at end of s. 66.

Notes: See Notes to 66(12.6) and (12.601).

66(12.66)(a.1) provides that, for the look-back rule to deem expenditures to be incurred at the end of a calendar year, the flow-through share agreement must have been made in that year.

66(12.66) amended by 2013 budget bill #2 (this version effective March 21, 2013), 2002-2013 technical bill (effective June 26, 2013), 2003 resource bill, 1995-97 technical bill, 1996 Budget and 1992 Economic Statement.

Income Tax Folios: S3-F8-C1: Principal-business corporations in the resource industries [replaces IT-400].

Forms: T100: Instructions for the flow-through share program [guide].

(12.67) Restrictions on renunciation — A corporation shall be deemed

(a) not to have renounced under any of subsections (12.6), (12.601) and (12.62) any expenses that are deemed to have been incurred by it because of a renunciation under this section by another corporation that is not related to it;

(b) not to have renounced under subsection (12.601) to a trust, corporation or partnership any Canadian development expenses (other than expenses renounced to another corporation that renounces under subsection (12.6) any Canadian exploration expense deemed to have been incurred by it because of the renunciation under subsection (12.601)) if, in respect of the renunciation under subsection (12.601), it has a prohibited relationship with the trust, corporation or partnership;

(c) not to have renounced under subsection (12.601) any Canadian development expenses deemed to have been incurred by it because of a renunciation under subsection (12.62); and

(d) not to have renounced under subsection (12.6) to a particular trust, corporation or partnership any Canadian exploration expenses (other than expenses ultimately renounced by another corporation under subsection (12.6) to an individual (other than a trust) or to a trust, corporation or partnership with which that other corporation does not have, in respect of that ultimate renunciation, a prohibited relationship) deemed to be incurred by it because of a renunciation under subsection (12.601) if, in respect of the renunciation under subsection (12.6), it has a prohibited relationship with the particular trust, corporation or partnership.

Related Provisions: 66(12.671) — Prohibited relationship. See also at end of s. 66.

Notes: See Notes to 66(12.6). 66(12.67)(a) amended by 1996 Budget (effective for renunciations after 1998) and 1992 Economic Statement.

(12.671) Prohibited relationship — For the purposes of subsection (12.67), where a trust, corporation (in paragraph (b) referred to as the "shareholder corporation") or partnership, as the case may be, gave consideration under a particular agreement for the issue of a flow-through share of a particular corporation, the particular corporation has, in respect of a renunciation under subsection (12.6) or (12.601) in respect of the share, a prohibited relationship

(a) with the trust if, at any time after the particular agreement was entered into and before the share is issued to the trust, the particular corporation or any corporation related to the particular corporation is beneficially interested in the trust;

(b) with the shareholder corporation if, immediately before the particular agreement was entered into, the shareholder corporation was related to the particular corporation; or

(c) with the partnership if any part of the amount renounced would, but for subsection (12.7001), be included, because of paragraph (h) of the definition "Canadian exploration expense" in subsection 66.1(6), in the Canadian exploration expense of

(i) the particular corporation, or

(ii) any other corporation that, at any time

(A) after the particular agreement was entered into, and

(B) before that part of the amount renounced would, but for this paragraph, be incurred,

would, if flow-through shares issued by the particular corporation under agreements entered into at the same time as or after the time the particular agreement was entered into were disregarded, be related to the particular corporation.

Notes: Opening words of 66(12.671)(c) amended by 1996 Budget, for renunciations made after 1998. 66(12.671) added by 1992 Economic Statement, for expenses incurred after Dec. 2, 1992.

(12.68) Filing selling instruments — A corporation that agrees to issue or prepares a selling instrument in respect of flow-through shares shall file with the Minister a prescribed form together with a copy of the selling instrument or agreement to issue the shares on or before the last day of the month following the earlier of

(a) the month in which the agreement to issue the shares is entered into, and

(b) the month in which the selling instrument is first delivered to a potential investor,

and the Minister shall thereupon assign an identification number to the form and notify the corporation of the number.

Related Provisions: 66(12.61) — Effect of renunciation; 66(12.74) — Late filed forms; 87(4.4) — Flow-through shares. See also at end of s. 66; 163.2(1)"excluded activity"(a)(i) — No good-faith reliance defence for advisor assessed third-party penalty; 237.3(14)(b), 237.3(16) — No information return required for reportable transaction if return filed under 237.1(7).

Forms: T100A: Flow-through share information — application for a selling instrument T100 identification number (SITIN); T100B: Flow-through share information — details of the flow-through shares (FTSs) and flow-through warrants (FTWs) subscribed; T100C: Flow-through share information — application for a T100 identification number (TIN) on the exercise of flow-through warrants (FTWs) and details of the FTWs exercised; T1221: Ontario focused flow-through share resource expenses; T1231: B.C. mining flow-through share tax credit.

(12.69) Filing re partners — Where, in a fiscal period of a partnership, an expense is incurred by the partnership as a consequence of a renunciation of an amount under subsection (12.6), (12.601) or (12.62), the partnership shall, before the end of the third month that begins after the end of the period, file with the Minister a prescribed form identifying the share of the expense attributable to each member of the partnership at the end of the period.

Related Provisions: 66(12.61), (12.63) — Effect of renunciation; 66(12.6901) — Consequences of partnership failing to file; 66(12.74) — Late filed forms; 66(15) — Definitions. See also at end of s. 66.

Notes: 66(12.69) amended by 1996 Budget (for renunciations made in 1999 or later), 1992 Economic Statement and 1991 technical bill.

(12.6901) Consequences of failure to file — Where a partnership fails to file a prescribed form as required under subsection (12.69) in respect of an expense, except for the purpose of subsection (12.69) the partnership is deemed not to have incurred the expense.

Notes: 66(12.6901) added by 1996 Budget, effective for renunciations made in 1999 or later (replacing a rule in 66(12.69)).

(12.691) Filing re assistance — Where a partnership receives or becomes entitled to receive assistance as an agent for its members or former members at a particular time in respect of any Canadian exploration expense or Canadian development expense that is or, but for paragraph (12.61)(b) or (12.63)(b), would be incurred by a corporation, the following rules apply:

(a) where the entitlement of any such member or former member to any part of the assistance is known by the partnership as of the end of the partnership's first fiscal period ending after the particular time and that part of the assistance was not required to be reported under paragraph (b) in respect of a calendar year ending before the end of that fiscal period, the partnership shall, on or before the last day of the third month following the end of that fiscal period, file with the Minister a prescribed form indicating the share of that part of the assistance paid to each of those members or former members before the end of that fiscal period or to which each of those members or former members is entitled at the end of that fiscal period;

(b) where the entitlement of any of those members or former members to any part of the assistance is known by the partnership as of the end of a calendar year that ends after the particular time and that part of the assistance was not required to be reported under paragraph (a) in respect of a fiscal period ending at or before the end of that calendar year, or under this paragraph in respect of a preceding calendar year, the partnership shall, on or before the last day of the third month following the end of that calendar year, file with the Minister a prescribed form indicating the share of that part of the assistance paid to each of those members or former members before the end of that fiscal period or to which each of those members or former members is entitled at the end of that calendar year; and

(c) where a prescribed form required to be filed under paragraph (a) or (b) is not so filed, the part of that expense relating to the assistance required to be reported in the prescribed form shall be deemed not to have been incurred by the partnership.

Related Provisions: 163(2.3) — False statement or omissions.

Notes: Opening words of 66(12.691) amended by 1996 Budget (effective for renunciations made in 1999 or later); added by 1991 technical bill.

(12.7) Filing re renunciation — Where a corporation renounces an amount in respect of Canadian exploration expenses or Canadian development expenses under subsection (12.6), (12.601) or (12.62), the corporation shall file a prescribed form in respect of the renunciation with the Minister before the end of the first month after the month in which the renunciation is made.

Related Provisions: 66(12.7001) — Consequences of corporation failing to file; 66(12.74) — Late filed forms. See also at end of s. 66.

Notes: 66(12.7) amended by 1996 Budget (for renunciations made in 1999 or later), 1992 Economic Statement and 1991 technical bill.

Forms: T2 Sched. 12: Resource-related deductions; T101: Statement of resource expenses; T101A: Claim for renouncing CEEs and CDEs; T101B: Adjustments to CEEs and CDEs previously renonouced; T101C: Part XII.6 tax return; T101D: Summary of assistance; T1229: Statement of resource expenses and depletion allowance; T5013A: Statement of partnership income for tax shelters and renounced resource expenses.

(12.7001) Consequences of failure to file — Where a corporation fails to file a prescribed form as required under subsection (12.7) in respect of a renunciation of an amount, subsections (12.61) and (12.63) do not apply in respect of the amount.

Notes: 66(12.7001) added by 1996 Budget, effective for renunciations made in 1999 or later (replacing a rule in 66(12.7)).

(12.701) Filing re assistance — Where a corporation receives or becomes entitled to receive assistance as an agent in respect of any Canadian exploration expense or Canadian development expense that is or, but for paragraph (12.61)(b) or (12.63)(b), would be incurred by the corporation, the corporation shall, before the end of the first month after the particular month in which it first becomes known to the corporation that a person that holds a flow-through share of the corporation is entitled to a share of any part of the assistance, file with the Minister a prescribed form identifying the share of the assistance to which each of those persons is entitled at the end of the particular month.

Related Provisions: 66(12.702) — Consequences of corporation failing to file; 66(16) — Partnership deemed to be a person; 163(2.3) — False statement or omissions.

Notes: 66(12.701) amended by 1996 Budget (effective for renunciations made in 1999 or later); added by 1991 technical bill.

Forms: T101D: Summary of assistance.

(12.702) Consequences of failure to file — Where a corporation fails to file a prescribed form as required under subsection (12.701) in respect of assistance, except for the purpose of subsection (12.701) the Canadian exploration expense or Canadian development expense to which the assistance relates is deemed not to have been incurred by the corporation.

Notes: 66(12.702) added by 1996 Budget, effective for renunciations made in 1999 or later. For earlier renunciations, the same rule applied in the last few words of 66(12.701), and effectively covered COGPE as well.

(12.71) Restriction on renunciation — A corporation may renounce an amount under subsection (12.6), (12.601) or (12.62) in respect of Canadian exploration expenses or Canadian development expenses incurred by it only to the extent that, but for the renunciation, it would be entitled to a deduction in respect of the expenses in computing its income.

Notes: 66(12.71) does not prevent a holding corporation from renouncing CEE incurred under a "farm-out" agreement: VIEWS doc 2007-0262881R3.

66(12.71) amended by 1996 Budget (for renunciations made in 1999 or later) and 1992 Economic Statement.

(12.72) [Repealed]

Notes: 66(12.72) repealed by 1996 Budget, effective April 25, 1997. It gave Revenue Canada authority to verify or ascertain various expenses. Given the authority provided by 231–231.3, it was unnecessary.

66(12.72) amended by 1992 Economic Statement, effective Dec. 3, 1992.

(12.73) Reductions in renunciations — Where an amount that a corporation purports to renounce to a person under subsection (12.6), (12.601) or (12.62) exceeds the amount that it can renounce to the person under that subsection,

(a) the corporation shall file a statement with the Minister in prescribed form where

(i) the Minister sends a notice in writing to the corporation demanding the statement, or

(ii) the excess arose as a consequence of a renunciation purported to be made in a calendar year under subsection (12.6)

or (12.601) because of the application of subsection (12.66) and, at the end of the year, the corporation knew or ought to have known of all or part of the excess;

(b) where subparagraph (a)(i) applies, the statement shall be filed not later than 30 days after the Minister sends a notice in writing to the corporation demanding the statement;

(c) where subparagraph (a)(ii) applies, the statement shall be filed before March of the calendar year following the calendar year in which the purported renunciation was made;

(d) except for the purpose of Part XII.6, any amount that is purported to have been so renounced to any person is deemed, after the statement is filed with the Minister, to have always been reduced by the portion of the excess identified in the statement in respect of that purported renunciation; and

(e) where a corporation fails in the statement to apply the excess fully to reduce one or more purported renunciations, the Minister may at any time reduce the total amount purported to be renounced by the corporation to one or more persons by the amount of the unapplied excess in which case, except for the purpose of Part XII.6, the amount purported to have been so renounced to a person is deemed, after that time, always to have been reduced by the portion of the unapplied excess allocated by the Minister in respect of that person.

Related Provisions: 66(12.731) — COVID-19 extension for agreement made in 2019-20; 66(16) — Partnership deemed to be a person; 152(4)(b)(v) — Three-year extension to normal reassessment period; 163(2.21), (2.22) — Penalty for false statement or omission; 248(1)"specified future tax consequence"(b) — Reduction is a specified future tax consequence. See also Related Provisions and Definitions at end of s. 66.

Notes: See 66(12.731) Notes. For an example of 66(12.73)(d) applying see VIEWS doc 2009-0307501E5.

66(12.73) amended by 1996 Budget, for purported renunciations made in 1997 or later, except that the reference to 66(12.64) in the opening words is only deleted for purported renunciations in 1999 or later. The amendments make 66(12.73) apply to excess renounced amounts on a renunciation-by-renunciation basis, in light of the special treatment of renunciations of anticipated expenditures under 66(12.66). This special treatment is necessary because there are expected to be cases where an issuing corporation fails to incur amounts that have been renounced by it under the new rules.

The amendments also deal explicitly with renunciations that can be made, under the look-back rule in 66(12.66), of expenditures that will be incurred after the renunciation is made. Where renunciations using the look-back rule are made, the issuing corporation must file the statement with the CRA without any demand for it. The statement must be filed before March of the year following the calendar year of the renunciation. Note that adjustments under 66(12.73) will not affect the issuing corporation's liability under new Part XII.6 (see 211.91).

66(12.73) amended by 1992 Economic Statement, effective for renunciations made after December 2, 1992, to add reference to 66(12.601).

(12.731) COVID-19 — agreements in 2019 or 2020 — If an agreement is entered into in 2019 or 2020 by a corporation to issue flow-through shares of the corporation,

(a) the reference in subparagraph (12.73)(a)(ii) to "at the end of the year" is to be read as a reference to "at the end of the subsequent year"; and

(b) the reference in paragraph (12.73)(c) to "before March of the calendar year" is to be read as a reference to "before March of the second calendar year".

Notes: See 66(12.6001) Notes. 66(12.731) effectively amends 66(12.73)(a)(ii), which applies where 66(12.6) (flow-through share renunciation) applies "because of the application of subsection (12.66)" (the look-back rule). Thus, Finance described this proposal (July 10, 2020 news release) as being: "Extend, by 12 months, the period to incur eligible flow-through share expenses under ... the look-back rule".

66(12.731) added by 2021 budget bill #1, for tax years that end after 2019.

(12.74) Late filed forms — A corporation or partnership may file with the Minister a document referred to in subsection (12.68), (12.69), (12.691), (12.7) or (12.701) after the particular day on or before which the document is required to be filed under the applicable subsection and the document shall, except for the purposes of this subsection and subsection (12.75), be deemed to have been filed on the day on or before which it was required to be filed if

(a) if it is filed

(i) on or before the day that is 90 days after the particular day, or

(ii) after that day that is 90 days after the particular day where, in the opinion of the Minister, the circumstances are such that it would be just and equitable to permit the document to be filed; and

(b) the corporation or partnership, as the case may be, pays to the Receiver General at the time of filing a penalty in respect of the late filing.

Related Provisions: 66(12.75) — Penalty.

Notes: For the meaning of "just and equitable" in (a)(ii), see Notes to 85(7.1).

66(12.74) amended by 1991 technical bill, effective July 14, 1990.

(12.741) Late renunciation — Where a corporation purports to renounce an amount under subsection (12.6), (12.601) or (12.62) after the period in which the corporation was entitled to renounce the amount, the amount is deemed, except for the purposes of this subsection and subsections (12.7) and (12.75), to have been renounced at the end of the period if

(a) the corporation purports to renounce the amount

(i) on or before the day that is 90 days after the end of that period, or

(ii) after the day that is 90 days after the end of that period where, in the opinion of the Minister, the circumstances are such that it would be just and equitable that the amount be renounced; and

(b) the corporation pays to the Receiver General a penalty in respect of the renunciation not more than 90 days after the renunciation.

Related Provisions: 66(12.75) — Penalty.

Notes: For the meaning of "just and equitable" in (a)(ii), see Notes to 85(7.1).

66(12.741) amended by 1996 Budget (effective for renunciations made in 1999 or later); added by 1992 Economic Statement.

(12.75) Penalty — For the purposes of subsections (12.74) and (12.741), the penalty in respect of the late filing of a document referred to in subsection (12.68), (12.69), (12.691), (12.7) or (12.701) or in respect of a renunciation referred to in subsection (12.741) is the lesser of $15,000 and

(a) where the penalty is in respect of the late filing of a document referred to in subsection (12.68), (12.69) or (12.7), the greater of

(i) $100, and

(ii) ¼ of 1% of the maximum amount in respect of the Canadian exploration expenses and Canadian development expenses renounced or attributed or to be renounced or attributed as set out in the document;

(b) where the penalty is in respect of the late filing of a document referred to in subsection (12.691) or (12.701), the greater of

(i) $100, and

(ii) ¼ of 1% of the assistance reported in the document; and

(c) where the penalty is in respect of a renunciation referred to in subsection (12.741), the greater of

(i) $100, and

(ii) ¼ of 1% of the amount of the renunciation.

Notes: 66(12.75)(a)(ii) amended by 1996 Budget, effective for renunciations made in 1999 or later, to delete reference to Canadian oil and gas property expenses.

Opening words of 66(12.75) amended to add reference to 66(12.741), and 66(12.75)(c) added, by 1992 Economic Statement, effective for renunciations purported to be made after February 1993. 66(12.75)(c) then amended retroactively by 1995-97 technical bill, retroactive to its introduction, to correct reference from (12.74) to (12.741).

66(12.75) amended by 1991 technical bill, effective December 18, 1991.

(13) Limitation — Where a taxpayer has incurred an outlay or expense in respect of which a deduction from income is authorized under more than one provision of this section or section 66.1, 66.2 or 66.4, the taxpayer is not entitled to make the deduction under more than one provision but is entitled to select the provision under which to make the deduction.

Related Provisions: See at end of s. 66.

(13.1) Short taxation year — If a taxpayer has a taxation year that is less than 51 weeks, the amount determined in respect of the year under each of subparagraph (4)(b)(i), paragraphs 66.2(2)(c) and (d), subparagraph (b)(i) of the definition "global foreign resource limit" in subsection 66.21(1), subparagraph 66.21(4)(a)(i), clause 66.21(4)(a)(ii)(B) and paragraphs 66.4(2)(b) and (c) and 66.7(2.3)(a), (4)(a) and (5)(a) shall not exceed that proportion of the amount otherwise determined that the number of days in the year is of 365.

Related Provisions: 20(1)(mm) — Deductions — injection substances; 66(4.3)(b), 66.21(5)(b) — No application to individual part-year resident. See also at end of s. 66.

Notes: 66(13.1) amended by 2021 budget bill #1, for tax years that end after July 30, 2019, to refer to 66.2(2)(d) and 66.4(2)(c). Earlier amended by 2000 Budget.

(14) Amounts deemed deductible under this Subdivision — For the purposes of section 3, any amount deductible under the *Income Tax Application Rules* in respect of this subsection shall be deemed to be deductible under this Subdivision.

Related Provisions: See at end of s. 66.

Notes: ITAR s. 29 provides deductions for various pre-1972 expenses.

I.T. Application Rules: 30(3).

(14.1)–(14.5) [No longer relevant.]

Notes: 66(14.1)–(14.5) allow non-taxable corps to designate CEE and CDE incurred before Oct. 1986 to obtain relief from their petroleum and gas revenue tax liability for the year.

(14.6) Deduction of carved-out income — A taxpayer may deduct in computing the taxpayer's income under this Part for a taxation year, an amount equal to the total of the taxpayer's carved-out incomes for the year within the meaning assigned by subsection 209(1).

Related Provisions: See at end of s. 66.

(15) Definitions — In this section,

Related Provisions: 66.1(6.1) — Application to 66.1; 66.2(5.1) — Application to 66.2; 66.21(2) — Application to 66.21; 66.4(5.1) — Application to 66.4; 66.7(18) — Application to 66.7.

Notes: Before RSC 1985 (5th Supp) consolidation for tax years ending after Nov. 1991, the opening words of 66(15) also referred to 66, 66.2, 66.4 and 66.7. That application is now provided by 66.1(6.1), 66.2(5.1), 66.4(5.1) and 66.7(18).

"agreed portion" in respect of a corporation that was a shareholder corporation of a joint exploration corporation means such amount as may be agreed on between the joint exploration corporation and the shareholder corporation not exceeding

(a) the total of all amounts each of which is a payment or loan referred to in paragraph (b) of the definition "shareholder corporation" in this subsection (except to the extent that the payment or loan was made by a shareholder corporation that was not a Canadian corporation and was used by the joint exploration corporation to acquire a Canadian resource property after December 11, 1979 from a shareholder corporation that was not a Canadian corporation) made by the shareholder corporation to the joint exploration corporation during the period it was a shareholder corporation of the joint exploration corporation,

minus

(b) the total of the amounts, if any, previously renounced by the joint exploration corporation under any of subsections (10) to (10.3) in favour of the shareholder corporation;

Related Provisions: 53(2)(f.1) — Deduction from ACB.

Notes: 66(15)"agreed portion" was 66(15)(a) before RSC 1985 (5th Supp) consolidation for tax years ending after Nov. 1991.

Advance Tax Rulings: ATR-60: Joint exploration corporations.

"assistance" means any amount, other than a prescribed amount, received or receivable at any time from a person or government, municipality or other public authority whether the amount is by way of a grant, subsidy, rebate, forgivable loan, deduction from royalty or tax, rebate of royalty or tax, investment allowance or any other form of assistance or benefit;

Related Provisions: 66(16) — Partnership deemed to be a person; 248(16), (16.1), (18), (18.1) — GST and QST input tax credit, refund and rebate deemed to be government assistance.

Notes: See 12(1)(x) Notes for interpretation. 66(15)"assistance" was 66(15)(a.1) before RSC 1985 (5th Supp) consolidation for tax years ending after Nov. 1991.

Interpretation Bulletins: IT-273R2: Government assistance — general comments.

"Canadian exploration and development expenses" incurred by a taxpayer means any expense incurred before May 7, 1974 that is

(a) any drilling or exploration expense, including any general geological or geophysical expense, incurred by the taxpayer after 1971 on or in respect of exploring or drilling for petroleum or natural gas in Canada,

(b) any prospecting, exploration or development expense incurred by the taxpayer after 1971 in searching for minerals in Canada,

(c) the cost to the taxpayer of any Canadian resource property acquired by the taxpayer after 1971,

(d) the taxpayer's share of the Canadian exploration and development expenses incurred after 1971 by any association, partnership or syndicate in a fiscal period thereof, if at the end of that fiscal period the taxpayer was a member or partner thereof,

(e) any expense incurred by the taxpayer after 1971 pursuant to an agreement with a corporation under which the taxpayer incurred the expense solely in consideration for shares of the capital stock of the corporation issued to the taxpayer by the corporation or any interest in such shares or right thereto, to the extent that the expense was incurred as or on account of the cost of

(i) drilling or exploration activities, including any general geological or geophysical activities, in or in respect of exploring or drilling for petroleum or natural gas in Canada,

(ii) prospecting, exploration or development activities in searching for minerals in Canada, or

(iii) acquiring a Canadian resource property, and

(f) any annual payment made by the taxpayer for the preservation of a Canadian resource property,

but, for greater certainty, does not include

(g) any consideration given by the taxpayer for any share or any interest therein or right thereto, except as provided by paragraph (e), or

(h) any expense described in paragraph (e) incurred by another taxpayer to the extent that the expense was, by virtue of that paragraph, a Canadian exploration and development expense of that other taxpayer;

Related Provisions: 49(2) — Where option expires; 53(2)(e)(i) — Deduction from ACB of shares; 66.7(1) — Deduction to successor corporation; 248(1)"Canadian exploration and development expenses" — Definition applies to entire Act. See also at end of s. 66.

Notes: For expenses incurred now, see the definitions of "Canadian exploration expense" (66.1(6) — 100% deductible); "Canadian development expense" (66.2(5) — 30% deductible); "Canadian oil and gas property expense" (66.4(5) — 10% deductible).

Para. (c) amended by 1995-97 technical bill, retroactive to taxation years that begin after 1984. 66(15)"Canadian exploration and development expenses" was 66(15)(b) before RSC 1985 (5th Supp) consolidation for tax years ending after Nov. 1991.

Interpretation Bulletins: IT-109R2: Unpaid amounts.

"Canadian resource property" of a taxpayer means any property of the taxpayer that is

(a) any right, licence or privilege to explore for, drill for or take petroleum, natural gas or related hydrocarbons in Canada,

(b) any right, licence or privilege to

(i) store underground petroleum, natural gas or related hydrocarbons in Canada, or

(ii) prospect, explore, drill or mine for minerals in a mineral resource in Canada other than a bituminous sands deposit or an oil shale deposit,

(c) any oil or gas well in Canada or any real property or immovable in Canada the principal value of which depends on its petroleum, natural gas or related hydrocarbon content (not including any depreciable property),

(d) any right to a rental or royalty computed by reference to the amount or value of production from an oil or a gas well in Canada, or from a natural accumulation of petroleum, natural gas or a related hydrocarbon in Canada, if the payer of the rental or royalty has an interest in, or for civil law a right in, the well or accumulation, as the case may be, and 90% or more of the rental or royalty is payable out of, or from the proceeds of, the production from the well or accumulation,

(e) any right to a rental or royalty computed by reference to the amount or value of production from a mineral resource in Canada, other than a bituminous sands deposit or an oil shale deposit, if the payer of the rental or royalty has an interest in, or for civil law a right in, the mineral resource and 90% or more of the rental or royalty is payable out of, or from the proceeds of, the production from the mineral resource,

(f) any real property or immovable in Canada (not including any depreciable property) the principal value of which depends on its mineral resource content other than where the mineral resource is a bituminous sands deposit or an oil shale deposit,

(g) any right to or interest in — or, for civil law, any right to or in — any property described in any of paragraphs (a) to (e), other than a right or an interest that the taxpayer has because the taxpayer is a beneficiary under a trust or a member of a partnership, or

(h) an interest in real property described in paragraph (f) or a real right in an immovable described in that paragraph, other than an interest or a right that the taxpayer has because the taxpayer is a beneficiary under a trust or a member of a partnership;

Related Provisions: 12(1)(x.2) — Crown charge rebate — income inclusion; 18.1(1)"right to receive production" — CRP excluded from matchable expenditure rules; 59(1) — Disposition of resource property; 66(5) — Dealers; 69 — Inadequate consideration and fair market value; 128.1(4)(b)(i) — CRP excluded from deemed disposition on emigration; 209 — Tax on carved-out income; 248(1)"Canadian resource property" — Definition applies to entire Act; 248(4.1) — Meaning of "real right in an immovable"; *Interpretation Act* 8(2.1), (2.2) — Application to exclusive economic zone and continental shelf. See also at end of s. 66.

Notes: For the meaning of "right, licence or privilege" in paras. (a)-(b), see *Alberta Energy*, [1995] 1 C.T.C. 2111 (TCC), para. 31 (aff'd [1998] 1 C.T.C. 305 (FCA)). For the meaning of "real property" see Notes to 248(4).

For CRA interpretation see VIEWS docs 2002-0174255 (patented mining claim is CRP), 2006-0174351R3 (royalty from partnership to partner is CRP), 2008-0297051E5 and 2013-0486901E5 (payments to landowner from oil & gas company for exploration rights are proceeds of disposition of CRP); 2011-0420451E5 and 2012-0446431C6 (farm-out position in IT-125R4 [Diep, "Expanding Farm-Outs to Royalties", XI(1) *Resource Sector Taxation* (Federated Press) 20-22 (2017)]); 2013-0480511I7 (para. (b) includes an amount paid to obtain license to explore for mineral resource); 2013-0509771E5 (treatment of oil & gas payments to US resident who owns CRP); 2017-0695131C6 [2017 CPTS q.2] ("interest" in para. (d) requires a right to take production).

See also Mar et al., "Basic Issues in Resource Taxation", 2008 Cdn Tax Foundation conference report, 10:1-32; Johnson & Mackey, "Inbound Investment in Canadian Oil and Gas Royalties", XIV(2) *Resource Sector Taxation* (Federated Press) 1-21 (2020); and articles below re 2011 amendments to (d) and (e).

Definition amended by 2011 budget bill #2, last change effective for properties and rights acquired after March 21, 2011, with grandfathering for acquisitions to end of 2011 in certain cases. The addition of "related hydrocarbon", "bituminous sands deposit" and "oil shale deposit" incorporates the July 16/10 draft technical changes [Carr, "Royalties and the Definition of Canadian Resource Property", I(3) *Resource Sector Taxation [RST]* (Federated Press) 47-51 (2003); Morphy & Eisenbraun, "The Taxation of Royalties Excluded from the Resource Property Regime", IX(1) *RST* 618-29 (2012)]. The amendments do not require that the rental or royalty be paid from a segregated source of funds that originates only from the proceeds of production of a particular well, accumulation or mineral resource: VIEWS doc 2003-004860A.

Definition earlier amended by 2003 resource bill, 2000 Budget. 66(15)"Canadian resource property" was 66(15)(c) before RSC 1985 (5th Supp) consolidation for tax years ending after Nov. 1991.

Interpretation Bulletins: IT-125R4: Dispositions of resource properties; IT-273R2: Government assistance — general comments; IT-291R3: Transfer of property to a corporation under subsection 85(1).

I.T. Technical News: 10 (net profits interests and proposed section 18.1).

"drilling or exploration expense" incurred on or in respect of exploring or drilling for petroleum or natural gas includes any expense incurred on or in respect of

(a) drilling or converting a well for the disposal of waste liquids from a petroleum or natural gas well,

(b) drilling for water or gas for injection into a petroleum or natural gas formation, or

(c) drilling or converting a well for the injection of water or gas to assist in the recovery of petroleum or natural gas from another well;

Related Provisions: 66(16) — Partnerships — person — taxation year; 87(4.4) — Flow-through shares.

Notes: 66(15)"drilling or exploration expense" was 66(15)(d) before RSC 1985 (5th Supp) consolidation for tax years ending after Nov. 1991.

Regulations: 6202, 6202.1 (prescribed share).

Income Tax Folios: S3-F8-C1: Principal-business corporations in the resource industries [replaces IT-400].

Interpretation Bulletins: IT-273R2: Government assistance — general comments.

"expense", incurred before a particular time by a taxpayer,

(a) includes an amount designated by the taxpayer at that time under paragraph 98(3)(d) or (5)(d) of the *Income Tax Act*, chapter 148 of the Revised Statutes of Canada, 1952, as a cost in respect of property that is a Canadian resource property or a foreign resource property,

but

(b) for greater certainty, does not include any amount paid or payable

(i) as consideration for services to be rendered after that time, or

(ii) as, on account or in lieu of payment of, or in satisfaction of, rent in respect of a period after that time;

Related Provisions: 66(15)"outlay" — same meaning as "expense".

Notes: 66(15)"expense" was 66(15)(g.2) and (g.3) before RSC 1985 (5th Supp) consolidation for tax years ending after Nov. 1991.

I.T. Application Rules: 69 (meaning of "chapter 148 of ...").

Interpretation Bulletins: IT-273R2: Government assistance — general comments; IT-503: Exploration and development shares (cancelled).

"flow-through share" means a share (other than a prescribed share) of the capital stock of a principal-business corporation, or a right (other than a prescribed right) to acquire a share of the capital stock of a principal-business corporation, issued to a person under an agreement in writing made between the person and the corporation under which the corporation, for consideration that does not include property to be exchanged or transferred by the person under the agreement in circumstances to which any of sections 51, 85, 85.1, 86 and 87 applies, agrees

(a) to incur, in the period that begins on the day on which the agreement was made and ends 24 months after the month that includes that day, Canadian exploration expenses or Canadian development expenses in an amount not less than the consideration for which the share or right is to be issued, and

(b) to renounce, in prescribed form and before March of the first calendar year that begins after that period, to the person in respect of the share or right, an amount in respect of the Canadian exploration expenses or Canadian development expenses so incurred by it not exceeding the consideration received by the corporation for the share or right;

Related Provisions: 40(12), 54"exemption threshold" — Deemed cost of flow-through share on donation to charity; 66(12.6), (12.601) — Flow-through of expenditures to shareholder; 66(16) — Partnership deemed to be a person; 127.52(1)(e), (e.1) — Minimum tax; 248(1)"flow-through share" — Definition applies to entire Act.

Notes: See Notes to 66(12.6) for discussion and interpretation.

Definition amended by 2002-2013 technical bill (for agreements made after Dec. 20, 2002), 1996 Budget, 1992 Economic Statement, 1991 technical bill. 66(15)"flow-through share" was 66(15)(d.1) before RSC 1985 (5th Supp) consolidation for tax years ending after Nov. 1991.

Regulations: 6202(1), (2) (prescribed share); 6202.1(1.1), (2.1) (prescribed right).

Income Tax Folios: S3-F8-C1: Principal-business corporations in the resource industries [replaces IT-400].

"foreign exploration and development expenses" incurred by a taxpayer means

(a) any drilling or exploration expense, including any general geological or geophysical expense, incurred by the taxpayer after 1971 on or in respect of exploring or drilling for petroleum or natural gas outside Canada,

(b) any expense incurred by the taxpayer for the purpose of determining the existence, location, extent or quality of a mineral resource outside Canada, including any expense incurred in the course of

(i) prospecting,

(ii) carrying out geological, geophysical or geochemical surveys,

(iii) drilling by rotary, diamond, percussion or other method, or

(iv) trenching, digging test pits and preliminary sampling,

(c) the cost to the taxpayer of any foreign resource property acquired by [the taxpayer],

(d) subject to section 66.8, the taxpayer's share of the foreign exploration and development expenses incurred after 1971 by a partnership in a fiscal period thereof, if at the end of that period the taxpayer was a member of the partnership, and

(e) any annual payment made by the taxpayer for the preservation of a foreign resource property,

but does not include

(f) any amount included at any time in the capital cost to the taxpayer of any depreciable property of a prescribed class,

(g) an expenditure incurred at any time after the commencement of production from a foreign resource property of the taxpayer in order to evaluate the feasibility of a method of recovery of petroleum, natural gas or related hydrocarbons from the portion of a natural reservoir to which the foreign resource property relates,

(h) an expenditure (other than a drilling expense) incurred at any time after the commencement of production from a foreign resource property of the taxpayer in order to assist in the recovery of petroleum, natural gas or related hydrocarbons from the portion of a natural reservoir to which the foreign resource property relates,

(i) an expenditure incurred at any time relating to the injection of any substance to assist in the recovery of petroleum, natural gas or related hydrocarbons from a natural reservoir,

(j) an expenditure that is the cost, or any part of the cost, to the taxpayer of any depreciable property of a prescribed class that was acquired after December 21, 2000,

(k) foreign resource expenses in respect of a country, or

(l) an expenditure made after February 27, 2000 by the taxpayer unless the expenditure was made

(i) pursuant to an agreement in writing made by the taxpayer before February 28, 2000,

(ii) for the acquisition of foreign resource property by the taxpayer, or

(iii) for the purpose of

(A) enhancing the value of foreign resource property that the taxpayer owned at the time the expenditure was incurred or that the taxpayer had a reasonable expectation of owning after that time, or

(B) assisting in evaluating whether a foreign resource property is to be acquired by the taxpayer;

Related Provisions: 66(4) — Deduction for FEDE; 66.7(2) — Deduction to successor corporation; 80(8)(e) — Reduction of FEDE on debt forgiveness; 248(1)"foreign exploration and development expenses" — Definition applies to entire Act.

Notes: See Ian Gamble, *Taxation of Canadian Mining*, chap. 16 and Carr & Calverley, *Canadian Resource Taxation* (both Carswell, looseleaf or *Taxnet Pro* Reference Centre), §4.4; Roch Martin, "Foreign Exploration and Development Expenditures — The New Rules", 14 *Canadian Petroleum Tax Journal* (2001).

Definition amended by 2000 Budget (last change effective for tax years that begin after 2000), 1996 Budget. 66(15)"foreign exploration and development expenses" was 66(15)(e) before RSC 1985 (5th Supp) consolidation for tax years ending after Nov. 1991.

Interpretation Bulletins: IT-109R2: Unpaid amounts; IT-273R2: Government assistance — general comments.

"foreign resource property" of a taxpayer means any property that would be a Canadian resource property of the taxpayer if the definition "Canadian resource property" in this subsection were read as if the references therein to "in Canada" were read as references to "outside Canada";

Related Provisions: 18.1(1)"right to receive production" — FRP excluded from matchable expenditure rules; 66.7(2.3) — Successor corporation rules; 248(1)"foreign resource property" — Definition applies to entire Act, and definition of FRP in respect of a country.

Notes: For a ruling that a net smelter return is FRP, see VIEWS doc 2008-0292141R3. 66(15)"foreign resource property" was 66(15)(f) before RSC 1985 (5th Supp) consolidation for tax years ending after Nov. 1991.

Interpretation Bulletins: IT-125R4: Dispositions of resource properties; IT-273R2: Government assistance — general comments.

"joint exploration corporation" means a principal-business corporation that has not at any time since its incorporation had more than 10 shareholders, not including any individual holding a share for the sole purpose of qualifying as a director;

Notes: See Notes to 66(10). 66(15)"joint exploration corporation" was 66(15)(g) before RSC 1985 (5th Supp) consolidation for tax years ending after Nov. 1991.

Income Tax Folios: S3-F8-C1: Principal-business corporations in the resource industries [replaces IT-400].

Interpretation Bulletins: IT-273R2: Government assistance — general comments.

Advance Tax Rulings: ATR-60: Joint exploration corporations.

"oil or gas well [para. 66(15)(g.1)]" — [Repealed under former Act]

Notes: 66(15)(g.1), repealed by 1985 technical bill, defined "oil or gas well". The definition was changed and moved to 248(1).

"original owner" of a Canadian resource property or a foreign resource property means a person

(a) who owned the property and disposed of it to a corporation that acquired it in circumstances in which subsection 29(25) of the *Income Tax Application Rules* or subsection 66.7(1), (2), (2.3), (3), (4) or (5) applies, or would apply if the corporation had continued to own the property, to the corporation in respect of the property, and

(b) who would, but for subsection 66.7(12), (13), (13.1) or (17), as the case may be, be entitled in computing that person's income for a taxation year that ends after that person disposed of the property to a deduction under section 29 of the *Income Tax Application Rules* or subsection (2), (3) or (4), 66.1(2) or (3), 66.2(2), 66.21(4) or 66.4(2) of this Act in respect of expenses described in subparagraph 29(25)(c)(i) or (ii) of that Act, Canadian exploration and development expenses, foreign resource pool expenses, Canadian exploration expenses, Canadian development expenses or Canadian oil and gas property expenses incurred by the person before the person disposed of the property;

Related Provisions: 66.7(10.1) — Amalgamation — partnership property.

Notes: Definition amended by 2000 Budget, effective for taxation years that begin after 2000. 66(15)"original owner" was 66(15)(g.11) before RSC 1985 (5th Supp) consolidation for tax years ending after Nov. 1991.

"outlay" made before a particular time by a taxpayer, has the meaning assigned to the expression "expense" by this subsection;

Notes: 66(15)"outlay" was included in the definitions of "expense" in 66(15)(g.2)-(g.3) before RSC 1985 (5th Supp) consolidation for tax years ending after Nov. 1991.

Interpretation Bulletins: IT-273R2: Government assistance — general comments; IT-503: Exploration and development shares (cancelled).

"predecessor owner" of a Canadian resource property or a foreign resource property means a corporation

(a) that acquired the property in circumstances in which subsection 29(25) of the *Income Tax Application Rules* or subsection 66.7(1), (2), (2.3), (3), (4) or (5) applies, or would apply if the corporation had continued to own the property, to the corporation in respect of the property,

(b) that disposed of the property to another corporation that acquired it in circumstances in which subsection 29(25) of the *Income Tax Application Rules* or subsection 66.7(1), (2), (2.3), (3), (4) or (5) applies, or would apply if the other corporation had continued to own the property, to the other corporation in respect of the property, and

(c) that would, but for subsection 66.7(14), (15), (15.1) or (17), as the case may be, be entitled in computing its income for a taxation year ending after it disposed of the property to a deduction under subsection 29(25) of the *Income Tax Application Rules* or subsection 66.7(1), (2), (2.3), (3), (4) or (5) in respect of expenses incurred by an original owner of the property;

Notes: Definition amended by 2000 Budget, effective for taxation years that begin after 2000. 66(15)"predecessor owner" was 66(15)(g.4) before RSC 1985 (5th Supp) consolidation for tax years ending after Nov. 1991.

"principal-business corporation" means a corporation the principal business of which is any of, or a combination of,

(a) the production, refining or marketing of petroleum, petroleum products or natural gas,

(a.1) exploring or drilling for petroleum or natural gas,

(b) mining or exploring for minerals,

(c) the processing of mineral ores for the purpose of recovering metals or minerals from the ores,

(d) the processing or marketing of metals or minerals that were recovered from mineral ores and that include metals or minerals recovered from mineral ores processed by the corporation,

(e) the fabrication of metals,

(f) the operation of a pipeline for the transmission of oil or gas,

(f.1) the production or marketing of calcium chloride, gypsum, kaolin, sodium chloride or potash,

(g) the manufacturing of products, where the manufacturing involves the processing of calcium chloride, gypsum, kaolin, sodium chloride or potash,

(h) the generation or distribution of energy, or the production of fuel, using property described in Class 43.1 or 43.2 of Schedule II to the *Income Tax Regulations*, and

(i) the development of projects for which it is reasonable to expect that at least 50% of the capital cost of the depreciable property to be used in each project would be the capital cost of property described in Class 43.1 or 43.2 of Schedule II to the *Income Tax Regulations*,

or a corporation all or substantially all of the assets of which are shares of the capital stock or indebtedness of one or more principal-business corporations that are related to the corporation (otherwise than because of a right referred to in paragraph 251(5)(b));

Related Provisions: 66.1(2) — Deduction for principal-business corporation; 66.1(3) — Deduction for corporation that is a principal-business corporation solely under paras. (h) and (i); 115(4) — Non-resident's income from Canadian resource property; 127(9)"pre-production mining expenditure"(b) — Pre-production mining expenditures renounced through a flow-through share agreement. See also at end of s. 66.

"production" from a Canadian resource property or a foreign resource property means

(a) petroleum, natural gas and related hydrocarbons produced from the property,

(b) heavy crude oil produced from the property processed to any stage that is not beyond the crude oil stage or its equivalent,

(c) ore (other than iron ore or tar sands) produced from the property processed to any stage that is not beyond the prime metal stage or its equivalent,

(d) iron ore produced from the property processed to any stage that is not beyond the pellet stage or its equivalent,

(e) tar sands produced from the property processed to any stage that is not beyond the crude oil stage or its equivalent, and

(f) any rental or royalty from the property computed by reference to the amount or value of the production of petroleum, natural gas or related hydrocarbons or ore;

"reserve amount" of a corporation for a taxation year in respect of an original owner or predecessor owner of a Canadian resource property means the amount determined by the formula

$$A - B$$

where

A is the total of all amounts that are

(a) required by subsection 59(2) to be included in computing the corporation's income for the year, and

(b) in respect of a reserve, deducted in computing the income of the original owner or predecessor owner and deemed by paragraph 87(2)(g) or by virtue of that paragraph and paragraph 88(1)(e.2) to have been deducted by the corporation as a reserve in computing its income for a preceding taxation year, and

B is the total of amounts deducted in computing the corporation's income for the year by virtue of subsection 64(1), (1.1) or (1.2) in respect of dispositions by the original owner or predecessor owner, as the case may be;

"selling instrument" in respect of flow-through shares means a prospectus, registration statement, offering memorandum, term sheet or other similar document that describes the terms of the offer (including the price and number of shares) pursuant to which a corporation offers to issue flow-through shares;

"shareholder corporation" of a joint exploration corporation means a corporation that for the period in respect of which the expression is being applied

(a) was a shareholder of the joint exploration corporation, and

(b) made a payment or loan to the joint exploration corporation in respect of Canadian exploration and development expenses, a Canadian exploration expense, a Canadian development expense or a Canadian oil and gas property expense incurred or to be incurred by the joint exploration corporation.

"specified foreign exploration and development expense" of a taxpayer in respect of a country (other than Canada) means an amount that is included in the taxpayer's foreign exploration and development expenses and that is

(a) a drilling or exploration expense, including any general geological or geophysical expense, incurred by the taxpayer on or in respect of exploring or drilling for petroleum or natural gas in that country,

(a.1) an expense incurred by the taxpayer after December 21, 2000 (otherwise than pursuant to an agreement in writing made before December 22, 2000) for the purpose of determining the existence, location, extent or quality of a mineral resource in that country, including any expense incurred in the course of

(i) prospecting,

(ii) carrying out geological, geophysical or geochemical surveys,

(iii) drilling by rotary, diamond, percussion or other methods, or

(iv) trenching, digging test pits and preliminary sampling,

(b) a prospecting, exploration or development expense incurred by the taxpayer before December 22, 2000 (or after December 21, 2000 pursuant to an agreement in writing made before December 22, 2000) in searching for minerals in that country,

(c) the cost to the taxpayer of the taxpayer's foreign resource property in respect of that country,

(d) an annual payment made by the taxpayer in a taxation year of the taxpayer for the preservation of a foreign resource property in respect of that country,

(e) an amount deemed by subsection 21(2) or (4) to be a foreign exploration and development expense incurred by the taxpayer, to the extent that it can reasonably be considered to relate to an amount that, without reference to this paragraph and paragraph (f), would be a specified foreign exploration and development expense in respect of that country, or

(f) subject to section 66.8, the taxpayer's share of the specified foreign exploration and development expenses of a partnership incurred in respect of that country in a fiscal period of the partnership if, at the end of that period, the taxpayer was a member of the partnership.

(15.1) Other definitions — The definitions in subsections 66.1(6), 66.2(5), 66.21(1), 66.4(5) and 66.5(2) apply in this section.

(16) Partnerships — For the purposes of subsections (12.6) to (12.73), the definitions "assistance" and "flow-through share" in subsection (15) and subsections (18), (19) and 66.3(3) and (4), a partnership is deemed to be a person and its taxation year is deemed to be its fiscal period.

Notes: Reference to 66(18) and (19) added by 1991 technical bill, retroactive to fiscal periods ending after February 1986. Reference to 66(12.6)–(12.66) changed to 66(12.6)–(12.73) by 1996 Budget, effective for fiscal periods that end after 1995.

(17) Non-arm's length partnerships — For the purpose of paragraph (12.66)(d), a partnership and a corporation are, at all times in a calendar year,

(a) deemed not to deal with each other at arm's length, if

(i) an expense is deemed by subsection (12.61) to be incurred by the partnership,

(ii) the expense would, if this Act were read without reference to paragraph (12.61)(b), be incurred in the calendar year by the corporation, and

(iii) a share of the expense is included, because of paragraph (h) of the definition "Canadian exploration expense" in subsection 66.1(6), in the Canadian exploration expense of the corporation or of a member of the partnership with whom the corporation, at any time in that calendar year, does not deal at arm's length; and

(b) deemed to deal with each other at arm's length, in any other case.

Notes: 66(17) amended by 2003 resource bill, effective for expenses incurred after Feb. 1997 at the latest. The subsec. was restructured, but the substance of the amendment was to change "during the first 60 days of a calendar year" to "in a calendar year", to be consistent with the lookback period in 66(12.66), which was changed in 1997 from 60 days to one year.

66(17) amended by 1991 technical bill, for fiscal periods ending after Feb. 1986.

(18) Members of partnerships — For the purposes of this section, subsection 21(2), sections 59.1 and 66.1 to 66.7, paragraph (d) of the definition "investment expense" in subsection 110.6(1), the definition "pre-production mining expenditure" in subsection 127(9) and the descriptions of C and D in subsection 211.91(1), where a person's share of an outlay or expense made or incurred by a partnership in a fiscal period of the partnership is included in respect of the person under paragraph (d) of the definition "foreign exploration and development expenses" in subsection (15), paragraph (h) of the definition "Canadian exploration expense" in subsection 66.1(6), paragraph (f) of the definition "Canadian development expense" in subsection 66.2(5), paragraph (e) of the definition "foreign resource expense" in subsection 66.21(1) or paragraph (b) of the definition "Canadian oil and gas property expense" in subsection 66.4(5), the portion of the outlay or expense so included is deemed, except for the purposes of applying the definitions "foreign exploration and development expenses", "Canadian exploration expense", "Canadian development expense", "foreign resource expense" and "Canadian oil and gas property expense" in respect of the person, to be made or incurred by the person at the end of that fiscal period.

Related Provisions: 54"exemption threshold"A(b)(ii) — Application of limitation on donations of flow-through shares; 66(16) — Partnership deemed to be a person; 66.1(7) — Canadian exploration expense — share of partner; 66.2(6) — Canadian development expense — share of partner; 66.4(6) — Canadian oil and gas property expense — share of partner; 96(1)(d) — Partnerships — no deduction at partnership level; 127(9)"investment tax credit"(a.2), 127(9)"flow-through mining expenditure" — Investment tax credit.

Notes: 66(18) amended by 2002-2013 technical bill (Part 5 — technical), effective for expenses incurred in fiscal periods that begin after 2001, to add reference to 127(9)"pre-production mining expenditure".

66(18) amended by 2000 Budget, effective for fiscal periods that begin after 2000. Earlier amended by 1996 Budget and 1991 technical bill.

(19) Renunciation by corporate partner, etc. — A corporation is not entitled to renounce under subsection (12.6), (12.601) or (12.62) to a person a specified amount in respect of the corporation where the corporation would not be entitled to so renounce the specified amount if

(a) the expression "end of that fiscal period" in subsection (18) were read as "time the outlay or expense was made or incurred by the partnership"; and

(b) the expression "on the effective date of the renunciation" in each of paragraphs (12.61)(a) and (12.63)(a) were read as "at the earliest time that any part of such expense was incurred by the corporation".

Related Provisions: 66(16) — Partnership deemed to be a person; 66(20) — Meaning of "specified amount".

Notes: 66(19) amended by 1996 Budget, effective for renunciations made in 1999 or later. Earlier amended by 1992 Economic Statement and 1991 technical bill.

(20) Specified amount — For the purpose of subsection (19), a specified amount in respect of a corporation is an amount that represents

(a) all or part of the corporation's share of an outlay or expense made or incurred by a partnership of which the corporation is a member or former member; or

(b) all or part of an amount renounced to the corporation under subsection (12.6), (12.601) or (12.62).

Notes: 66(20) added by 1996 Budget, effective for renunciations made in 1999 or later. This rule was formerly part of 66(19), where it also applied to COGPE (with references to 66(12.64) and 66(12.65)(b)).

Related Provisions [s. 66]: 35(1)(e) — Prospectors and grubstakers; 66.1(6), 66.2(5), 66.4(5) — Definitions; 66.7 — Successor rules; 66.8(1) — Resource expenses of limited partner; 87(1.2) — Amalgamations — new corporation deemed continuation of predecessor; 88(1.5) — Winding-up — parent deemed continuation of subsidiary; 127.52(1)(e) — Addition to adjusted taxable income for minimum tax purposes; 209 — Tax on carved-out income.

Definitions [s. 66]: "acquired" — 256(7)–(9); "adjusted cost base" — 54, 248(1); "adjusted cumulative Canadian development expense" — 66(14.3); "affiliated" — 66(11.5), 251.1; "agreed portion" — 66(15); "amount" — 248(1); "arm's length" — 66(17), 251(1); "assessment" — 248(1); "assistance" — 66(15), 79(4), 125.4(5), 248(16), (16.1), (18), (18.1); "associated" — 256; "beneficially interested" — 248(25); "beneficiary" — 248(25) [Notes]; "bituminous sands", "business" — 248(1); "calendar year" — *Interpretation Act* 37(1)(a); "Canada" — 255, *Interpretation Act* 8(2.1), (2.2); "Canadian corporation" — 89(1), 248(1); "Canadian development expense" — 66.2(5), 248(1); "Canadian exploration and development expenses" — 66(15), 248(1); "Canadian exploration and development overhead expense" — Reg. 1206(1); "Canadian exploration expense" — 66.1(6), 248(1); "Canadian oil and gas property expense" — 66.4(5), 248(1); "Canadian resource property" — 66(15), 248(1); "capital gain" — 39(1), 248(1); "capital property" — 54, 248(1); "control" — 256(6)–(9), 256.1(3); "corporation" — 248(1), *Interpretation Act* 35(1); "cumulative Canadian development expense" — 66(15.1), 66.2(5); "cumulative Canadian exploration expense" — 66(15.1), 66.1(6); "cumulative Canadian oil and gas property expense" — 66(15.1), 66.4; "cumulative foreign resource expense" — 66.21(1); "cumulative offset account" — 66(15.1), 66.5(2); "depreciable property" — 13(21), 248(1); "disposition" — 66.4(5), 248(1); "drilling or exploration expense", "expense" — 66(15); "fiscal period" — 66(16), 249(2), 249.1; "flow-through share" — 66(15); "foreign exploration and development expenses" — 66(15), 248(1); "foreign resource expense" — 66.21(1), 248(1); "foreign resource pool expense" — 248(1); "foreign resource property" — 66(15), 248(1); "global foreign resource limit" — 66.21(1); "Her Majesty" — *Interpretation Act* 35(1); "immovable" — Quebec *Civil Code* art. 900–907; "individual" — 248(1); "in respect of that country" — 248(1)"foreign resource property"; "interest in real property" — 248(4); "joint exploration corporation" — 66(15); "loss restriction event" — 251.2; "majority-interest beneficiary" — 251.1(3); "majority-interest partner", "mineral", "mineral resource", "Minister", "oil or gas well" — 248(1); "original owner", "outlay" — 66(15); "partnership" — see 96(1) Notes; "person" — 66(16), 248(1); "predecessor owner" — 66(15); "prescribed" — 248(1); "principal-business corporation", "production" — 66(15); "prohibited relationship" — 66(12.671); "property" — 248(1); "real right" — 248(4.1); "related" — 66(11.5), 251(2); "reserve amount" — 66(15); "resident in Canada" — 94(3)(a), 250; "restricted expense" — 66(15.1), 66.1(6); "selling instrument" — 66(15); "share", "shareholder" — 248(1); "shareholder corporation" — 66(15); "specified amount" — 66(20); "specified expenses" — 66(12.6), (12.601), (12.62); "specified foreign exploration and development expense" — 66(15); "specified purpose" — 66(15.1), 66.1(6); "substituted" — 248(5); "tar sands" — 248(1); "taxable capital amount" — 66(12.6011); "taxable capital employed in Canada" — 66(12.6012); "taxation year" — 66(16), 249; "taxpayer" — 248(1); "trust" — 104(1), 248(1), (3); "writing" — *Interpretation Act* 35(1).

I.T. Application Rules [s. 66]: 30.

66.1 [Canadian exploration expenses] — (1) Amount to be included in income — There shall be included in computing the amount referred to in paragraph 59(3.2)(b) in respect of a taxpayer for a taxation year the amount, if any, by which

(a) the total of all amounts referred to in the descriptions of F to M in the definition "cumulative Canadian exploration expense" in subsection (6) that are deducted in computing the taxpayer's cumulative Canadian exploration expense at the end of the year

exceeds the total of

(b) all amounts referred to in the descriptions of A to E.1 in the definition "cumulative Canadian exploration expense" in subsection (6) that are included in computing the taxpayer's cumulative Canadian exploration expense at the end of the year, and

(c) the total determined under subparagraph 66.7(12.1)(a)(i) in respect of the taxpayer for the year.

Related Provisions: 59(3.2)(b) — Income inclusion; 66.7(1) — Successor of Canadian exploration and development expenses; 87(1.3) — Amalgamations — shareholder corporation. See also at end of s. 66.1.

Notes: 66.1(1)(c) added by 1991 technical bill.

(2) Deduction for certain principal-business corporations — In computing the income for a taxation year of a principal-business corporation (other than a corporation that would not be a principal-business corporation if the definition "principal-business corporation" in subsection 66(15) were read without reference to paragraphs (h) and (i) of that definition), there may be deducted any amount that the corporation claims not exceeding the lesser of

(a) the total of

(i) the amount, if any, by which its cumulative Canadian exploration expense at the end of the year exceeds the amount, if any, designated by it for the year under subsection 66(14.1), and

(ii) the amount, if any, by which

(A) the total determined under subparagraph 66.7(12.1)(a)(i) in respect of the corporation for the year

exceeds

(B) the amount that would be determined under subsection (1) in respect of the corporation for the year, if that subsection were read without reference to paragraph (c) thereof, and

(b) the amount, if any, by which

(i) the amount that would be its income for the year if no deduction (other than a prescribed deduction) were allowed under this subsection or section 65

exceeds

(ii) the total of all amounts each of which is an amount deducted by the corporation under section 112 or 113 in computing its taxable income for the year.

Related Provisions: 20(1)(hh) — Repayments of inducements, etc.; 65 — Allowance for oil or gas well, mine or timber limit; 66 — Exploration and development expenses; 66.1(3) — Deduction for other taxpayers; 66.7(1) — Successor of Canadian exploration and development expenses; 127.52(1)(e) — Add-back of deduction for minimum tax purposes; 209 — Tax on carved-out income. See also at end of s. 66.1.

Notes: 66.1(2) generally limits the deduction of CEE of a principal-business corporation to the corporation's income for the year. Taxpayers that are not principal-business corporations may generally deduct their full CEE balances under 66.1(3).

Opening words of 66.1(2) amended by 1996 Budget to add the exclusion for a corporation described in 66(15)"principal-business corporation"(h) and (i), effective for taxation years that end after December 5, 1996. See 66.1(6)"Canadian renewable and conservation expense".

66.1(2) earlier amended by 1992 Economic Statement and 1991 technical bill.

Regulations: 1213 (prescribed deduction).

Income Tax Folios: S3-F8-C1: Principal-business corporations in the resource industries [replaces IT-400].

Advance Tax Rulings: ATR-59: Financing exploration and development through limited partnerships.

(3) Expenses of other taxpayer — In computing the income for a taxation year of a taxpayer that is not a principal-business corporation, or that is a corporation that would not be a principal-business corporation if the definition "principal-business corporation" in

subsection 66(15) were read without reference to paragraphs (h) and (i) of that definition, there may be deducted such amount as the taxpayer claims not exceeding the total of

(a) the amount, if any, by which the taxpayer's cumulative Canadian exploration expense at the end of the year exceeds the amount, if any, designated by the taxpayer for the year under subsection 66(14.1), and

(b) the amount, if any, by which

(i) the total determined under subparagraph 66.7(12.1)(a)(i) in respect of the taxpayer for the year

exceeds

(ii) the amount that would, but for paragraph (1)(c), be the amount determined under subsection (1) in respect of the taxpayer for the year.

Related Provisions: 66(11.6)(a) — Application of successor rules on change in control of trust; 66.1(2) — Deduction for principal-business corp; 110.6(1)"investment expense"(d) — effect of claim on capital gains exemption; 127.52(1)(e) — Add-back of deduction for minimum tax purposes. See also at end of s. 66.1.

Notes: CEE was denied due to lack of evidence in: *Bennett*, 2010 TCC 413; *Bonhomme*, 2016 TCC 152, paras. 83-99 (FCA appeal dismissed for delay A-321-16).

Opening words of 66.1(3) amended by 1996 Budget to add the reference to 66(15)"principal-business corporation"(h) and (i), effective for taxation years that end after December 5, 1996. See 66.1(6)"Canadian renewable and conservation expense".

66.1(3) earlier amended by 1991 technical bill.

Advance Tax Rulings: ATR-59: Financing exploration and development through limited partnerships.

Income Tax Folios: S3-F8-C1: Principal-business corporations in the resource industries [replaces IT-400].

Forms: T1 General return, Line 22400 [former 224]; T1229: Statement of resource expenses and depletion allowance.

(4), (5) [Repealed under former Act]

Notes: 66.1(4) and (5), repealed in 1987, dealt with a successor corporation's Canadian exploration expenses. See now 66.7.

(6) Definitions — In this section,

Notes: Before RSC 1985 (5th Supp) consolidation for tax years ending after Nov. 1991, the opening words also referred to 66, 66.2 and 66.4. This application rule is now in 66(15.1), 66.2(5.1) and 66.4(5.1).

"bitumen mine development project", of a taxpayer, means an undertaking for the sole purpose of developing a new mine to extract and process tar sands from a mineral resource of the taxpayer to produce bitumen or a similar product;

Notes: Definition "bitumen mine development project" added by 2011 budget bill #2, effective March 22, 2011.

"bitumen upgrading development project", of a taxpayer, means an undertaking for the sole purpose of constructing an upgrading facility to process bitumen or a similar feedstock (all or substantially all of which is from a mineral resource of the taxpayer) from a new mine to the crude oil stage or its equivalent;

Notes: Definition "bitumen upgrading development project" added by 2011 budget bill #2, effective March 22, 2011.

"Canadian exploration expense" of a taxpayer means any expense incurred after May 6, 1974 that is

(a) any expense incurred by the taxpayer (other than an expense incurred in drilling or completing an oil or gas well or in building a temporary access road to, or preparing a site in respect of, any such well) for the purpose of determining the existence, location, extent or quality of an accumulation of petroleum or natural gas (other than a mineral resource) in Canada, including such an expense that is

(i) a geological, geophysical or geochemical expense, or

(ii) an expense for environmental studies or community consultations (including studies or consultations that are undertaken to obtain a right, licence or privilege for the purpose of determining the existence, location, extent or quality of an accumulation of petroleum or natural gas),

(b) any expense (other than an expense incurred in drilling or completing an oil or gas well or in building a temporary access road to, or preparing a site in respect of, any such well) incurred by the taxpayer after March, 1985 for the purpose of bringing a natural accumulation of petroleum or natural gas (other than a mineral resource) in Canada into production and incurred prior to the commencement of the production (other than the production from an oil or gas well) in reasonable commercial quantities from such accumulation, including

(i) clearing, removing overburden and stripping, and

(ii) sinking a shaft or constructing an adit or other underground entry,

(c) any expense incurred before April, 1987 in drilling or completing an oil or gas well in Canada or in building a temporary access road to, or preparing a site in respect of, any such well,

(i) incurred by the taxpayer in the year, or

(ii) incurred by the taxpayer in any previous year and included by the taxpayer in computing the taxpayer's Canadian development expense for a previous taxation year,

if, within six months after the end of the year, the drilling of the well is completed and

(iii) it is determined that the well is the first well capable of production in commercial quantities from an accumulation of petroleum or natural gas (other than a mineral resource) not previously known to exist, or

(iv) it is reasonable to expect that the well will not come into production in commercial quantities within twelve months of its completion,

(d) any expense incurred by the taxpayer after March, 1987 and in a taxation year of the taxpayer in drilling or completing an oil or gas well in Canada or in building a temporary access road to, or preparing a site in respect of, any such well if

(i) the drilling or completing of the well resulted in the discovery that a natural underground reservoir contains petroleum or natural gas, where

(A) before the time of the discovery, no person or partnership had discovered that the reservoir contained either petroleum or natural gas,

(B) the discovery occurred at any time before six months after the end of the year, and

(C) the expense is incurred

(I) before 2021 (excluding an expense that is deemed by subsection 66(12.66) to have been incurred on December 31, 2020), if the expense is incurred in connection with an obligation that was committed to in writing (including a commitment to a government under the terms of a license or permit) by the taxpayer before March 22, 2017, or

(II) before 2019 (excluding an expense that is deemed by subsection 66(12.66) to have been incurred on December 31, 2018), in any other case,

(ii) the well is abandoned in the year or within six months after the end of the year without ever having produced otherwise than for specified purposes,

(iii) the period of 24 months commencing on the day of completion of the drilling of the well ends in the year, the expense was incurred within that period and in the year and the well has not within that period produced otherwise than for specified purposes, or

(iv) there has been filed with the Minister, on or before the day that is 6 months after the end of the taxation year of the taxpayer in which the drilling of the well was commenced, a certificate issued by the Minister of Natural Resources certi-

fying that, on the basis of evidence submitted to that Minister, that Minister is satisfied that

(A) the total of expenses incurred and to be incurred in drilling and completing the well, in building a temporary access road to the well and in preparing the site in respect of the well will exceed $5,000,000, and

(B) the well will not produce, otherwise than for a specified purpose, within the period of 24 months commencing on the day on which the drilling of the well is completed,

(e) any expense deemed by subsection (9) to be a Canadian exploration expense incurred by the taxpayer,

(f) any expense incurred by the taxpayer (other than an expense incurred in drilling or completing an oil or gas well or in building a temporary access road to, or preparing a site in respect of, any such well) for the purpose of determining the existence, location, extent or quality of a mineral resource in Canada including such an expense for environmental studies or community consultations (including, notwithstanding subparagraph (v), studies or consultations that are undertaken to obtain a right, licence or privilege for the purpose of determining the existence, location, extent or quality of a mineral resource in Canada) and any expense incurred in the course of

(i) prospecting,

(ii) carrying out geological, geophysical or geochemical surveys,

(iii) drilling by rotary, diamond, percussion or other methods, or

(iv) trenching, digging test pits and preliminary sampling,

but not including

(v) any Canadian development expense,

(v.1) any expense described in subparagraph (i), (iii) or (iv) in respect of the mineral resource, incurred before a new mine in the mineral resource comes into production in reasonable commercial quantities, that results in revenue or can reasonably be expected to result in revenue earned before the new mine comes into production in reasonable commercial quantities, except to the extent that the total of all such expenses exceeds the total of those revenues, or

(vi) any expense that may reasonably be considered to be related to a mine in the mineral resource that has come into production in reasonable commercial quantities or to be related to a potential or actual extension of the mine,

(g) any expense incurred by the taxpayer after November 16, 1978 and before March 21, 2013 for the purpose of bringing a new mine in a mineral resource in Canada, other than a bituminous sands deposit or an oil shale deposit, into production in reasonable commercial quantities and incurred before the new mine comes into production in such quantities, including an expense for clearing, removing overburden, stripping, sinking a mine shaft or constructing an adit or other underground entry, but not including any expense that results in revenue or can reasonably be expected to result in revenue earned before the new mine comes into production in reasonable commercial quantities, except to the extent that the total of all such expenses exceeds the total of those revenues,

(g.1) any Canadian renewable and conservation expense incurred by the taxpayer,

(g.2) any expense incurred by the taxpayer after March 21, 2011, that is

(i) a specified oil sands mine development expense, or

(ii) an eligible oil sands mine development expense,

(g.3) any expense incurred by the taxpayer that would be described in paragraph (g) if the reference to "March 21, 2013" in that paragraph were "2017" and that is incurred

(i) under an agreement in writing entered into by the taxpayer before March 21, 2013, or

(ii) as part of the development of a new mine, if

(A) the construction of the new mine was started by, or on behalf of, the taxpayer before March 21, 2013 (and for this purpose construction does not include obtaining permits or regulatory approvals, conducting environmental assessments, community consultations or impact benefit studies, and similar activities), or

(B) the engineering and design work for the construction of the new mine, as evidenced in writing, was started by, or on behalf of, the taxpayer before March 21, 2013 (and for this purpose engineering and design work does not include obtaining permits or regulatory approvals, conducting environmental assessments, community consultations or impact benefit studies, and similar activities),

(g.4) any expense incurred by the taxpayer, the amount of which is determined by the formula

$$A \times B$$

where

A is an expense that would be described in paragraph (g) if the reference to "March 21, 2013" in that paragraph were "2018" and that is not described in paragraph (g.3), and

B is

(i) 100% if the expense is incurred before 2015,

(ii) 80% if the expense is incurred in 2015,

(iii) 60% if the expense is incurred in 2016, and

(iv) 30% if the expense is incurred in 2017,

(h) subject to section 66.8, the taxpayer's share of any expense referred to in any of paragraphs (a) to (d) and (f) to (g.4) incurred by a partnership in a fiscal period of the partnership, if at the end of the period the taxpayer is a member of the partnership, or

(i) any expense referred to in any of paragraphs (a) to (g) incurred by the taxpayer pursuant to an agreement in writing with a corporation, entered into before 1987, under which the taxpayer incurred the expense solely as consideration for shares, other than prescribed shares, of the capital stock of the corporation issued to the taxpayer or any interest in or right to — or, for civil law, any right in or to — such shares,

but, for greater certainty, shall not include

(j) any consideration given by the taxpayer for any share or any interest in or right to — or, for civil law, any right in or to — a share, except as provided by paragraph (i),

(k) any expense described in paragraph (i) incurred by any other taxpayer to the extent that the expense was,

(i) by virtue of that paragraph, a Canadian exploration expense of that other taxpayer,

(ii) by virtue of paragraph (g) of the definition "Canadian development expense" in subsection 66.2(5), a Canadian development expense of that other taxpayer, or

(iii) by virtue of paragraph (c) of the definition "Canadian oil and gas property expense" in subsection 66.4(5), a Canadian oil and gas property expense of that other taxpayer,

(k.1) an expense that is the cost, or any part of the cost, to the taxpayer of any depreciable property of a prescribed class that was acquired after 1987,

(k.2) [Repealed]

(l) any amount (other than a Canadian renewable and conservation expense) included at any time in the capital cost to the taxpayer of any depreciable property of a prescribed class,

(m) an expenditure incurred at any time after the commencement of production from a Canadian resource property of the taxpayer in order to evaluate the feasibility of a method of recovery of, or to assist in the recovery of, petroleum, natural gas

or related hydrocarbons from the portion of a natural reservoir to which the Canadian resource property relates,

(n) an expenditure incurred at any time relating to the injection of any substance to assist in the recovery of petroleum, natural gas or related hydrocarbons from a natural reservoir, or

(o) the taxpayer's share of any consideration, expense, cost or expenditure referred to in any of paragraphs (j) to (n) given or incurred by a partnership,

but any assistance that a taxpayer has received or is entitled to receive after May 25, 1976 in respect of or related to the taxpayer's Canadian exploration expense shall not reduce the amount of any of the expenses described in any of paragraphs (a) to (i);

Possible Future Amendment — Documenting fossil fuel subsidies (precursor to elimination?)

Prime Minister's mandate letter to Minister of Finance, Dec. 2019: I will expect you to work with your colleagues and through established legislative, regulatory and Cabinet processes to deliver on your top priorities. In particular, you will: …

- Finalize a report, which will include a list of federal fossil fuel subsidies including the description of the subsidies, annual costs and analysis of the subsidies. This report will be made public once a peer review is finalized.

Notes: This appears to be a further step towards eliminating all tax (and other) assistance to Canada's oil and gas industry.

Related Provisions: 13(7.5) — Depreciable property treatment for costs associated with building roads and similar projects; 34.2(1)"qualified resource expense"(a), 34.2(6) — CEE qualifies for deduction from corporate accrual of partnership income; 66(15)"eligible oil sands mine development expense", "specified oil sands mine development expense" — Definitions; 66.1(6.2) — Certain amounts under paras. (f) and (g) deemed not to be capital expenditures; 66.1(8) — Expenses in first 60 days of year; 66.1(9)(a) — Past CDE deemed to be CEE; 66.1(10) — Certificate ceasing to be valid; 66.2(2) — Deduction — Canadian development expenses; 66.3 — Exploration and development shares; 127(9)"flow-through mining expenditure; 127(9)"investment tax credit"(a.2), (a.3), 127(9)"pre-production mining expenditure" — Investment tax credit; 127(9)"specified percentage"(k)(iii)(B) — Investment tax credit for 2015 based on para. (g.4); 248(1)"Canadian exploration expense" — Definition applies to entire Act; 248(16), (16.1) — GST or QST input tax credit/refund and rebate deemed to be assistance; 248(18), (18.1) — GST or QST — repayment of input tax credit or refund; Reg. 1102(1)(a) — Depreciable property takes priority over resource property; *Interpretation Act* 8(2.1), (2.2) — Application to exclusive economic zone and continental shelf. See also at end of s. 66.1.

Notes: CEE is fully deductible: 66.1(3); but not for a principal-business corp, and not if the taxpayer's business is "trading or dealing" in mineral or oil & gas rights: 66(5). See 66(12.6) Notes re flow-through shares for financing CEE. There are also provincial incentive "super"-deductions exceeding 100%, e.g., Revenu Québec Form CO-726.4.17.19-T.

See Gamble, *Taxation of Canadian Mining* (Carswell, looseleaf or *Taxnet Pro* Reference Centre), §3.3; Ladak, "Legislation Dealing with CEE ...", 16 *Canadian Petroleum Tax Journal* (2003); Mar et al., "Basic Issues in Resource Taxation", 2008 Cdn Tax Foundation conference report, 10:1-32; Colborne & Paton, "2013 Mining Update", 2013 conference report at 9:1-5; Morphy & Maguire, "An Update on the Taxation of Farm-Outs", IX(3) *Resource Sector Taxation* (Federated Press) 661-67 (2013); and articles in discussion of para. (f) below.

In *Petro-Canada*, 2004 FCA 158 (leave to appeal denied 2004 CarswellNat 4108 (SCC)), seismic data purchases were disallowed as CEE, as only a small percentage were actually used for locating oil or gas (para. (a)). Seismic data expenses were also disallowed in *Global Communications*, [1999] 3 C.T.C. 537 (FCA), where GC acquired the data solely for resale or licensing and was not exposed to financial loss; and *Rainforth*, 2007 TCC 132, where R was indifferent as to how the data was actually used. Such expenses were allowed in *McLarty*, 2008 SCC 104.

Per the FCA in *Gulf Canada*, [1992] 1 C.T.C. 183, for an expense to be incurred for the purpose of determining the existence of petroleum or natural gas on a property, there must be a connection between the expense and work actually done on the ground: "the purpose [of this rule] ... was to encourage actual exploration".

In *Forsberg*, 2005 TCC 591, expenses were denied as CEE for being Canadian Exploration and Development Overhead Expenses (Reg. 1206(1)), as they were paid to a "connected person".

Helium exploration does not qualify as CEE because helium is not a "mineral resource" and is not natural gas: VIEWS doc 2002-0141275.

Severance to an employee is not consideration for services and so cannot be CEE, in CRA's view: doc 2015-0616321E5.

Para. (a): For the meaning of "right, licence or privilege" in (a)(ii) and (f), see 66(15)"Canadian resource property" Notes.

Para. (a) amended by 2016 budget bill #1, for expenses incurred after Feb. 2015, effectively to add (a)(ii) allowing environmental studies and community consultations (as per March 1, 2015 Finance news release).

Para. (d) amended by 2017 budget bill #2, effective Dec. 14, 2017, to add (d)(i)(C), effectively dropping CEE eligibility for expenses of drilling for "discovery wells" as of 2019 (or 2021 for grandfathered expenses). Such expenses will be CDE under 66.2. The 2017 Budget eliminated this rule as part of the Liberals abandoning oil & gas in favour of "clean" energy. This effectively eliminates flow-through shares for oil & gas in Western Canada: tinyurl.com/moodys-flow. See VIEWS doc 2017-0735431E5.

Under (d)(iv), drilling expenditures can continue to be CEE if the well has been abandoned (or has not produced within 24 months) or the Minister of Natural Resources has certified that the costs associated with drilling the well are expected to exceed $5 million and it will not produce within 24 months. (In addition, CEE treatment continues to be available for other expenses such as early-stage geophysical and geochemical surveying: (f)(ii).)

Subpara. (d)(i) amended by 2001 technical bill, for expenses incurred after March 1987, to overrule *Resman Holdings (Dex Resources)*, [1998] 4 C.T.C. 2289 (TCC; overturned anyway at [2000] 3 C.T.C. 442 (FCA); leave to appeal denied 2001 CarswellNat 338 (SCC)). The TCC ruled that costs of a step-out well could qualify as CEE under former (d)(i), even though the well was being drilled merely to establish the extent of an already-known pool of oil.

Surface lease payments can fall within para. (d): VIEWS doc 2009-0345121E5.

Para. (f): CRA guidelines are in VIEWS docs 2016-0675902I7 (amending 2007-0252761E5) [Carr, "What is a Canadian Exploration Expense?", XIII(2) *Resource Sector Taxation [RST]* (Federated Press) 2-8 (2019)]; 2018-0762201E5 (Aboriginal community consultations, environmental studies); 2019-079679117 (detailed Mining Expenditure Review Table, 9pp). Lithium brine projects generally do not qualify: 2020-0858761E5. For rulings approving exploration programs under (f), see 2004-0088701R3, 2005-0133051R3, 2006-0206021R3, 2009-0350941R3 (new mines); 2005-0143221R3, 2005-0149001R3, 2008-0266211R3, 2008-0290331R3, 2009-0306061R3, 2019-0826011R3 (underground exploration); 2004-0103071R3, 2011-0422761R3 (surface drilling); 2007-0262881R3, 2010-0362481R3 (reactivating old mines), 2008-0293011R3, 2012-0441771R3, 2014-0534121R3; 2015-0614081R3 (farm-out agreement, flow-through shares); 2016-0639671R3 (new exploration at former mines); 2016-0649191R3 ((f)(vi) does not apply); 2016-0680761R3, 2018-0752291R3 (expenses not related to existing mine or potential extension of mine). The costs of making a site safe may qualify: 2005-0149651E5. Bulk sampling qualifies under (f), but revenues from selling samples reduce CEE under former (k.2), now (f)(v.1): 2002-0210261E5, 2006-0211941R3. (f)(v.1) excludes expenses that create pre-production revenue. (f)(vi) excludes a producing mine, but when a mine was exhausted and had been under "care and maintenance" for a year, using its shaft to drill elsewhere qualified as CEE under the parallel Quebec rule: *Wesdome Gold*, 2018 QCCA 518, para. 83 (leave to appeal denied 2019 CarswellQue 946 (SCC)) [Ho, "The Wesdome Decision", XII(3) *RST* 9-13 (2018)]. For what is a "mineral resource" see 248(1)"mineral resource" Notes. For more on para. (f) see Sala, "Flowthrough Share Financing", 2015 Cdn Tax Foundation conference report, 10:1-32.

A simple farm-out of an unproven resource property will not disqualify expenditures as being CEE of the farmee: IT-125R4 para. 14, VIEWS doc 2005-0119731E5.

Para. (f) amended by 2016 budget bill #1, for expenses incurred after Feb. 2015, to allow studies and consultations.

Para. (g): Building a permanent heavy-duty road to transport coal to market does not qualify: *Teck-Bullmoose*, [1998] 3 C.T.C. 195 (FCA). Environmental assessments and feasibility studies may be included in CEE under para. (g), if they are intended to bring a particular mine into production in reasonable commercial quantities: VIEWS doc 1999-001151117. In 2000-004407117, environmental expenses were considered part of the cost of obtaining a mining lease. Expenses "must be incurred after the decision has been made to proceed with bringing a new mine into production in reasonable commercial quantities": 2007-0246921E5, 2009-0350941R3. See also 2009-0306061R3, 2010-0355721R3, 2011-0408981R3, 2012-0453501R3, 2013-0507161R3, 2016-0635341R3 for more on "new mine", as well as rulings under para. (f) above.

Para. (g) amended by 2013 budget bill #2, effective March 21, 2013.

Paras. (g.3), (g.4) added by 2013 budget bill #2, effective March 21, 2013. They phased in from 2013-18 the change of pre-production mine expenses from CEE to CDE. See VIEWS doc 2017-071918117. "Development" of a mine (see (g.3)(ii)) was held for BC sales tax purposes to mean only "uncovering of a body or area which is to be the subject matter of the extraction process and preparation of the ... site for actual mining": *Flintstone Mining*, 2017 BCSC 1328, para. 54.

Para. (h) amended by 2013 budget bill #2, this version effective March 21, 2013.

Paras. (i), (j) amended by 2002-2013 technical bill, effective June 26, 2013, to refer to a civil law "right".

Para. (j): see VIEWS doc 2010-038925117 (buyer agrees to incur exploration expenses to acquire interest in unproven resource property; seller grants warrants for shares of its capital stock).

Para. (k.1), added by 2001 technical bill for 1988 and later tax years, overrules *Phénix*, [2001] 1 C.T.C. 74 (FCA), but see Carr & McIssac, "What is Depreciable Property?", XI(1) *Resource Sector Taxation* (Federated Press) 7-13 (2017). See also Reg. 1102(1)(a).

Para. (k.2) (added by 2003 resource bill, for expenses incurred after June 9, 2003; repealed by 2011 budget bill #2 for expenses incurred after Nov. 5, 2010) provided that production revenue earned before production begins in reasonable commercial quantities was to be netted out in computing CEE. It overruled *Mickleborough*, [1998] 4

C.T.C. 2584 (TCC) (Carr, "Recent Amendments to the Resource Tax Regime", 2003 Cdn Tax Foundation conference report at 34:24). See also under para. (f) above.

For a provincial mining tax case holding that expenses were "pre-production" and not "exploration" expenses, see *Tenacity v. Newfoundland*, 2021 NLSC 43.

Definition earlier amended by 2011 budget bill #2, 2003 resource bill, 1996 Budget. 66.1(6)"Canadian exploration expense" was 66.1(6)(a) before RSC 1985 (5th Supp) consolidation for tax years ending after Nov. 1991.

Regulations: 1215 (prescribed frontier exploration area); 6202 (prescribed share).

Income Tax Folios: S3-F8-C1: Principal-business corporations in the resource industries [replaces IT-400].

Interpretation Bulletins: IT-109R2: Unpaid amounts; IT-273R2: Government assistance — general comments; IT-476R: CCA — Equipment used in petroleum and natural gas activities; IT-503: Exploration and development shares (cancelled).

Advance Tax Rulings: ATR-59: Financing exploration and development through limited partnerships.

"Canadian renewable and conservation expense" has the meaning assigned by regulation, and for the purpose of determining whether an outlay or expense in respect of a prescribed energy conservation property is a Canadian renewable and conservation expense, the *Technical Guide to Canadian Renewable and Conservation Expenses (CRCE)*, as amended from time to time and published by the Department of Natural Resources, shall apply conclusively with respect to engineering and scientific matters;

Related Provisions: 66.1(6)"Canadian exploration expense"(g.1) — CRCE treated as CEE; 241(4)(d)(vi.1) — Communication with Dept. of Natural Resources permitted for purpose of determining whether an expense is a CRCE; Reg. 1102(1)(a.1) — CRCE ineligible for capital cost allowance.

Notes: For the *Technical Guide to Canadian Renewable and Conservation Expenses* (2012 ed., released Dec. 2014), see tinyurl.com/43-1guide.

In general terms, CRCE is certain intangible development costs associated with projects for which the required equipment is primarily Class 43.1 assets. See Reg. 1219. CRCE is fully deductible by being included in CEE: see 66.1(6)"Canadian exploration expense"(g.1) and 66.1(3). CRCE can be renounced under 66(12.6) by a PBC to investors in flow-through shares; see 66(15)"principal-business corporation"(h), (i). On the sale of CRCE see VIEWS doc 2014-0555071E5.

See also Hay, "Federal Income Tax Incentives for Independent Power Generation", VII(3) *Business Vehicles* (Federated Press) 342-50 (2001).

For discussion of photovoltaic systems / solar panels as CRCE see VIEWS docs 2006-0216881E5, 2013-0475491E5, 2013-0475931E5.

Definition amended by 2013 budget bill #2, effective Dec. 21, 2012. Added by 1996 Budget.

Regulations: 1219 (meaning of Canadian renewable and conservation expense); 8200.1 (prescribed energy conservation property).

Income Tax Folios: S3-F8-C1: Principal-business corporations in the resource industries [replaces IT-400].

"completion", of a specified oil sands mine development project, means the first attainment of a level of average output, measured over a 60-day period, equal to at least 60% of the planned level of average daily output (as determined in paragraph (b) of the definition "specified oil sands mine development project") for the specified oil sands mine development project;

Notes: Definition added by 2011 budget bill #2, effective March 22, 2011.

"cumulative Canadian exploration expense" of a taxpayer at any time in a taxation year means the amount determined by the formula

$$(A + B + C + D + E + E.1) -$$

$$(F + G + H + I + J + J.1 + K + L + M)$$

where

A is the total of all Canadian exploration expenses made or incurred by the taxpayer before that time,

B is the total of all amounts that were, because of subsection (1), included in computing the amount referred to in paragraph 59(3.2)(b) for the taxpayer's taxation years ending before that time,

C is the total of all amounts, except amounts in respect of interest, paid by the taxpayer after May 6, 1974 and before that time to Her Majesty in right of Canada in respect of amounts paid to the taxpayer before May 25, 1976 under the regulations referred to in paragraph (a) of the description of H,

D is the total of all amounts referred to in the description of G that are established by the taxpayer to have become bad debts before that time,

E is such part, if any, of the amount determined for J as has been repaid before that time by the taxpayer pursuant to a legal obligation to repay all or any part of that amount, and

E.1 is the total of all specified amounts determined under paragraph 66.7(12.1)(a) in respect of the taxpayer for taxation years ending before that time,

F is the total of all amounts deducted or required to be deducted in computing the taxpayer's income for a taxation year ending before that time in respect of the taxpayer's cumulative Canadian exploration expense,

G is the total of all amounts that became receivable by the taxpayer before that time that are to be included in the amount determined under this description by virtue of paragraph 66(12.1)(a) or (12.2)(a),

H is the total of all amounts paid to the taxpayer after May 6, 1974 and before May 25, 1976

   (a) under the *Northern Mineral Exploration Assistance Regulations* made under an appropriations Act that provides for payments in respect of the Northern Mineral Grants Program, or

   (b) pursuant to any agreement entered into between the taxpayer and Her Majesty in right of Canada under the Northern Mineral Grants Program or the Development Program of the Department of Indian Affairs and Northern Development,

to the extent that the amounts have been expended by the taxpayer as or on account of Canadian exploration and development expenses or Canadian exploration expense incurred by the taxpayer,

I is the total of all amounts each of which is an amount received before that time on account of any amount referred to in the description of D,

J is the total amount of assistance that the taxpayer has received or is entitled to receive in respect of any Canadian exploration expense incurred after 1980 or that can reasonably be related to Canadian exploration activities after 1980, to the extent that the assistance has not reduced the taxpayer's Canadian exploration expense by virtue of paragraph (9)(g),

J.1 is the total of all amounts by which the cumulative Canadian exploration expense of the taxpayer is required because of subsection 80(8) to be reduced at or before that time,

K is the total of all amounts that are required to be deducted before that time under subsection 66(14.1) in computing the taxpayer's cumulative Canadian exploration expense,

L is that portion of the total of all amounts each of which was deducted by the taxpayer under subsection 127(5) or (6) for a taxation year that ended before that time and that can reasonably be attributed to a qualified Canadian exploration expenditure, a pre-production mining expenditure or a flow-through mining expenditure (each expenditure within the meaning assigned by subsection 127(9)) made in a preceding taxation year, and

M is the total of all amounts that are required to be deducted before that time under paragraph 66.7(12)(b) in computing the taxpayer's cumulative Canadian exploration expense;

Related Provisions: 12(1)(t) — Investment tax credit; 20(1)(kk) — Exploration & development grants; 50(1)(a) — Deemed disposition where debt becomes bad debt; 59(3.2) — Recovery of exploration & development expenses; 66(12.1) — Limitations of Canadian exploration & development expenses; 66(12.2) — Unitized oil or gas field in Canada; 66(15) — Definitions; 66.1(1) — Amount to be included in income; 66.1(7) — Share of partner; 66.7(3) — Deduction to successor corporation; 79(4)(c) — Subsequent payment by debtor following surrender of property deemed to be repayment of assistance; 79.1(8) — No claim for principal amount of bad debt where property seized by creditor; 80(8)(b) — Reduction of CCEE on debt forgiveness; 87(2)(j.6) — Amalgamation — continuing corporation; 96(2.2)(d) — At-risk amount;

127(12.3) — Reduction of cumulative Canadian exploration expense of trust; 248(16), (16.1) — GST or QST input tax credit/refund and rebate deemed to be assistance; 248(18), (18.1) — GST or QST — repayment of input tax credit or refund; 257 — Formula cannot calculate to less than zero; 261(7)(d) — Functional currency reporting. See also at end of s. 66.1.

Notes: Because the investment tax credit calculation could become circular if the credit were to reduce CCEE in the same year in which the credit is claimed, the description of L requires a reduction of CCEE in the taxation year *following* the year in which the credit is claimed.

For meaning of "reasonably be attributed" in L, see *729658 Alberta*, 2004 TCC 474.

Definition amended by 2002-2013 technical bill (for tax years ending after Nov. 5, 2010), 2003 resource bill, 2000 Budget, 1994 technical bill, 1992 Economic Statement, 1991 technical bill, 1990 GST. 66.1(6)"cumulative Canadian exploration expense" was 66.1(6)(b) before RSC 1985 (5th Supp) consolidation for tax years ending after Nov. 1991.

"designated asset", in respect of an oil sands mine development project of a taxpayer, means a property that is a building, a structure, machinery or equipment and is, or is an integral and substantial part of,

   (a) in the case of a bitumen mine development project,

      (i) a crusher,

      (ii) a froth treatment plant,

      (iii) a primary separation unit,

      (iv) a steam generation plant,

      (v) a cogeneration plant, or

      (vi) a water treatment plant, or

   (b) in the case of a bitumen upgrading development project,

      (i) a gasifier unit,

      (ii) a vacuum distillation unit,

      (iii) a hydrocracker unit,

      (iv) a hydrotreater unit,

      (v) a hydroprocessor unit, or

      (vi) a coker;

Notes: Definition added by 2011 budget bill #2, effective March 22, 2011.

"eligible oil sands mine development expense", of a taxpayer, means an expense incurred by the taxpayer after March 21, 2011 and before 2016, the amount of which is determined by the formula

$$A \times B$$

where

A is an expense that would be a Canadian exploration expense of the taxpayer described in paragraph (g) of the definition "Canadian exploration expense" if that paragraph were read without reference to "and before March 21, 2013" and "other than a bituminous sands deposit or an oil shale deposit", but does not include an expense that is a specified oil sands mine development expense, and

B is

   (a) 100% if the expense is incurred before 2013,

   (b) 80% if the expense is incurred in 2013,

   (c) 60% if the expense is incurred in 2014, and

   (d) 30% if the expense is incurred in 2015;

Notes: Description of A amended by 2013 budget bill #2, effective March 21, 2013, to add " "and before March 21, 2013" and".

Definition added by 2011 budget bill #2, effective March 22, 2011.

"oil sands mine development project", of a taxpayer, means a bitumen mine development project or a bitumen upgrading development project of the taxpayer;

Notes: Definition "oil sands mine development project" added by 2011 budget bill #2, effective March 22, 2011.

"preliminary work activity", in respect of an oil sands mine development project, means activity that is preliminary to the acquisition, construction, fabrication or installation by or on behalf of a taxpayer of designated assets in respect of the taxpayer's oil sands mine development project including, without limiting the generality of the foregoing, the following activities:

(a) obtaining permits or regulatory approvals,

(b) performing design or engineering work,

(c) conducting feasibility studies,

(d) conducting environmental assessments, and

(e) entering into contracts;

Notes: Definition added by 2011 budget bill #2, effective March 22, 2011.

"restricted expense" of a taxpayer means an expense

(a) incurred by the taxpayer before April, 1987,

(b) that is deemed by paragraph 66(10.2)(c) to have been incurred by the taxpayer, or included by the taxpayer in the amount referred to in paragraph (a) of the definition "Canadian development expense" in subsection 66.2(5) by virtue of paragraph 66(12.3)(b), to the extent that the expense was originally incurred before April, 1987,

(c) that was renounced by the taxpayer under subsection 66(10.2), (12.601) or (12.62),

(d) in respect of which an amount referred to in subsection 66(12.3) becomes receivable by the taxpayer,

(e) deemed to be a Canadian exploration expense of the taxpayer or any other taxpayer by virtue of subsection (9), or

(f) where the taxpayer is a corporation, that was incurred by the corporation before the time control of the corporation was last acquired by a person or persons;

Related Provisions: 256(6)–(9) — Whether control acquired.

Notes: Reference to 66(12.601) in para. (c) added by 1992 Economic Statement, for expenses incurred after Dec. 2, 1992. 66.1(6)"restricted expense" was 66.1(6)(c) before RSC 1985 (5th Supp) consolidation for tax years ending after Nov. 1991.

"specified oil sands mine development expense", of a taxpayer, means an expense that

(a) would be a Canadian exploration expense described in paragraph (g) of the definition "Canadian exploration expense" if that paragraph were read without reference to "and before March 21, 2013" and "other than a bituminous sands deposit or an oil shale deposit",

(b) is incurred by the taxpayer after March 21, 2011 and before 2015, and

(c) is incurred by the taxpayer to achieve completion of a specified oil sands mine development project of the taxpayer;

Notes: Para. (a) amended by 2013 budget bill #2, effective March 21, 2013, to add " "and before March 21, 2013" and".

Definition "specified oil sands mine development expense" added by 2011 budget bill #2, effective March 22, 2011.

"specified oil sands mine development project", of a taxpayer, means an oil sands mine development project (not including any preliminary work activity) in respect of which

(a) one or more designated assets was, before March 22, 2011,

(i) acquired by the taxpayer, or

(ii) in the process of being constructed, fabricated or installed, by or on behalf of the taxpayer, and

(b) the planned level of average daily output (where that output is bitumen or a similar product in the case of a bitumen mine development project, or synthetic crude oil or a similar product in the case of a bitumen upgrading development project) that can reasonably be expected, is the lesser of

(i) the level that was the demonstrated intention of the taxpayer as of March 21, 2011 to produce from the oil sands mine development project, and

(ii) the maximum level of output associated with the design capacity, as of March 21, 2011, of the designated asset referred to in paragraph (a);

Notes: Definition added by 2011 budget bill #2, effective March 22, 2011.

"specified purpose" means

(a) the operation of an oil or gas well for the sole purpose of testing the well or the well head and related equipment, in accordance with generally accepted engineering practices,

(b) the burning of natural gas and related hydrocarbons to protect the environment, and

(c) prescribed purposes.

Notes: 66.1(6)"specified purpose" was 66.1(6)(d) before RSC 1985 (5th Supp) consolidation for tax years ending after Nov. 1991.

66.1(6)(d) (now "specified purpose") added by 1986 Budget, effective for expenses incurred after March 1987.

(6.1) Application of subsecs. 66(15), 66.2(5) and 66.4(5) — The definitions in subsections 66(15), 66.2(5) and 66.4(5) apply to this section.

Notes: 66.1(6.1) added in the RSC 1985 (5th Supp) consolidation, for tax years ending after Nov. 1991. This rule was formerly in the opening words of 66(15), 66.2(5) and 66.4(5).

(6.2) Deductible expense [deemed not capital expense] — An expense of a taxpayer that is not included in paragraph (f) or (g) of the definition "Canadian exploration expense" in subsection (6) because the taxpayer earned revenue from a mine in a mineral resource is deemed, for the purposes of this Part, not to be an outlay or payment described in paragraph 18(1)(b).

Notes: 66.1(6.2) added by 2002-2013 technical bill (Part 5 — technical), effective for expenses incurred after Nov. 5, 2010.

(7) Share of partner — Where a taxpayer is a member of a partnership, the taxpayer's share of any amount that would be an amount referred to in the description of E, G or J in the definition "cumulative Canadian exploration expense" in subsection (6) in respect of the partnership for a taxation year of the partnership if section 96 were read without reference to paragraph 96(1)(d) shall, for the purposes of this Act, be deemed to be an amount referred to in the description of E, G or J, as the case may be, in that definition in respect of the taxpayer for the taxation year of the taxpayer in which the partnership's taxation year ends.

Related Provisions: 87(1.2) — Amalgamations — new corporation deemed continuation of predecessor; 88(1.5) — Windup — parent corporation deemed to be continuation of subsidiary. See also at end of s. 66.1.

Notes: References to "cumulative Canadian exploration expense"E (formerly 66.1(6)(b)(iv.1)) added to 66.1(7) by 1991 technical bill, effective February 1990.

Interpretation Bulletins: IT-273R2: Government assistance — general comments; IT-353R2: Partnership interests — some adjustments to cost base (cancelled).

I.T. Technical News: 12 (adjusted cost base of partnership interest — subparagraph 53(1)(e)(viii)).

(8) [Repealed]

Notes: 66.1(8) repealed by 1996 Budget, effective March 7, 1996. See now 66(12.66).

(9) Canadian development expenses for preceding years — Where at any time in a taxpayer's taxation year

(a) the drilling or completing of an oil or gas well resulted in the discovery that a natural underground reservoir contains petroleum or natural gas and, before the time of the discovery, no person or partnership had discovered that the reservoir contained either petroleum or natural gas,

(b) the period of 24 months commencing on the day of completion of the drilling of an oil or gas well ends and the well has not, within that period, produced otherwise than for specified purposes, or

(c) an oil or gas well that has never produced, otherwise than for specified purposes, is abandoned,

the amount, if any, by which the total of

(d) all Canadian development expenses (other than restricted expenses) described in subparagraph (a)(ii) of the definition "Canadian development expense" in subsection 66.2(5) in respect of the well that are deemed by subsection 66(10.2) or (12.63) to have been incurred by the taxpayer in the year or a preceding taxation year,

(e) all Canadian development expenses (other than restricted expenses) described in subparagraph (a)(ii) of the definition "Canadian development expense" in subsection 66.2(5) in respect of the well that are required by paragraph 66(12.3)(b) to be included by the taxpayer in the amount referred to in paragraph (a) of that definition for the year or a preceding taxation year, and

(f) all Canadian development expenses (other than expenses referred to in paragraph (d) or (e) and restricted expenses) described in subparagraph (a)(ii) of the definition "Canadian development expense" in subsection 66.2(5) incurred by the taxpayer in respect of the well in a taxation year preceding the year,

exceeds

(g) any assistance that the taxpayer or a partnership of which the taxpayer is a member has received or is entitled to receive in respect of the expenses referred to in any of paragraphs (d) to (f),

shall, for the purposes of this Act, be deemed to be a Canadian exploration expense referred to in paragraph (e) of the definition "Canadian exploration expense" in subsection (6) incurred by the taxpayer at that time.

Related Provisions: 66(12.6) — Flow-through not available for reclassified expenses; 66.2(5)"cumulative Canadian development expense"I, M — Reduction in CCDE; 66.7(9) — CDE becoming CEE; 248(16), (16.1) — GST or QST input tax credit/refund and rebate deemed to be assistance; 248(18), (18.1) — GST or QST — repayment of input tax credit or refund. See also at end of s. 66.

Notes: For CRA interpretation see VIEWS doc 2013-0472311E5.

66.1(9) amended by 2001 technical bill, for expenses incurred after March 1987.

(10) Certificate ceasing to be valid — A certificate in respect of an oil or gas well issued by the Minister of Natural Resources for the purposes of paragraph (d)(iv) of the definition "Canadian exploration expense" in subsection (6) shall be deemed never to have been issued and never to have been filed with the Minister where

(a) the well produces, otherwise than for a specified purpose, within the period of 24 months commencing on the day on which the drilling of the well was completed; or

(b) in applying for the certificate, the applicant, in any material respect, provided any incorrect information or failed to provide information.

(11) [Repealed under former Act]

Notes: 66.1(11), repealed in 1987, dealt with successor corporations; see now 66.7.

Related Provisions [s. 66.1]: 66(5) — Dealers; 66(18) — Members of partnerships; 66.7 — Successor rules; 66.8(1) — Resource expenses of limited partner; 88(1.5) — Winding-up — parent deemed continuation of subsidiary.

Definitions [s. 66.1]: "acquired" — 256(7)–(9); "amount" — 248(1); "assistance" — 66(15), 66.1(6.1), 79(4), 125.4(5), 248(16), (16.1), (18), (18.1); "bitumen mine development project", "bitumen upgrading development project" — 66.1(6); "bituminous sands" — 248(1); "Canada" — 255, *Interpretation Act* 8(2.1), (2.2); "Canadian development expense" — 66.2(5), 248(1); "Canadian exploration expense" — 66.1(6), 248(1); "Canadian exploration and development expenses" — 66(15), 66.1(6.1); "Canadian oil and gas property expense" — 66.4(5), 248(1); "Canadian renewable and conservation expense", "completion" — 66.1(6); "control" — 256(6)–(9); "corporation" — 248(1), *Interpretation Act* 35(1); "cumulative Canadian development expense" — 66.1(6.1), 66.2(5); "depreciable property" — 13(21), 248(1); "designated asset", "eligible oil sands mine development expense" — 66.1(6); "expense" — 66(15), 66.1(6.1); "fiscal period" — 249(2), 249.1; "flow-through mining expenditure" — 127(9), (11.1)(c.2); "Her Majesty" — *Interpretation Act* 35(1); "mineral resource", "Minister" — 248(1); "Minister of Natural Resources" — *Department of Natural Resources Act* s. 3; "oil or gas well" — 248(1); "oil sands mine development project" — 66.1(6); "outlay" — 66(15), 66.1(6.1); "person" — 248(1); "preliminary work activity" — 66.1(6); "pre-production mining expenditure" — 127(9); "prescribed" — 248(1); "prescribed energy conservation property" — Reg. 8200.1; "principal-business corporation" — 66(15), 66.1(6.1); "property", "regulation", "share" — 248(1); "specified oil sands mine development expense", "specified oil sands mine development project", "specified purpose" — 66.1(6); "tar sands" — 248(1); "taxation year" — 249; "taxpayer" — 248(1); "writing" — *Interpretation Act* 35(1).

66.2 [Canadian development expenses] — (1) Amount to be included in income — There shall be included in computing

the amount referred to in paragraph 59(3.2)(c) in respect of a taxpayer for a taxation year the amount, if any, by which the total of

(a) all amounts referred to in the descriptions of E to O in the definition "cumulative Canadian development expense" in subsection (5) that are deducted in computing the taxpayer's cumulative Canadian development expense at the end of year, and

(b) the amount that is designated by the taxpayer for the year under subsection 66(14.2)

exceeds the total of

(c) all amounts referred to in the descriptions of A to D.1 in the definition "cumulative Canadian development expense" in subsection (5) that are included in computing the taxpayer's cumulative Canadian development expense at the end of the year, and

(d) the total determined under subparagraph 66.7(12.1)(b)(i) in respect of the taxpayer for the year.

Related Provisions: 59(3.2)(c) — Income inclusion; 66(11.4) — Change of control; 66.7(12) — Reduction of Canadian resource expenses; 104(5.2) — Trusts — 21-year deemed disposition; 115(1)(a)(iii.1) — Non-resident's taxable income earned in Canada. See also at end of s. 66.2.

Notes: See Notes to 66.2(2). For examples of 66.2(1) applying see VIEWS docs 2006-0172361I7, 2008-0297051E5, 2012-0452841E5, 2018-0739741E5.

66.2(1)(d) added by 1991 technical bill.

Interpretation Bulletins: IT-125R4: Dispositions of resource properties; IT-273R2: Government assistance — general comments.

(2) Deduction for cumulative Canadian development expenses — A taxpayer may deduct, in computing the taxpayer's income for a taxation year, such amount as the taxpayer may claim not exceeding the total of

(a) the lesser of

(i) the total of

(A) the taxpayer's cumulative Canadian development expense at the end of the year, and

(B) the amount, if any, by which

(I) the total determined under subparagraph 66.7(12.1)(b)(i) in respect of the taxpayer for the year

exceeds

(II) the amount that would, but for paragraph (1)(d), be determined under subsection (1) in respect of the taxpayer for the year, and

(ii) the amount, if any, by which the amount determined under subparagraph 66.4(2)(a)(ii) exceeds the amount determined under subparagraph 66.4(2)(a)(i),

(b) the lesser of

(i) the amount, if any, by which the amount determined under subparagraph (a)(i) exceeds the amount determined under subparagraph (a)(ii), and

(ii) the amount, if any, by which the total of all amounts each of which is

(A) an amount included in the taxpayer's income for the year by virtue of a disposition in the year of inventory described in section 66.3 that was a share or any interest in or right to — or, for civil law, any right in or to — a share, acquired by the taxpayer under circumstances described in paragraph (g) of the definition "Canadian development expense" in subsection (5) or paragraph (i) of the definition "Canadian exploration expense" in subsection 66.1(6), or

(B) an amount included by virtue of paragraph 12(1)(e) in computing the taxpayer's income for the year to the extent that it relates to inventory described in clause (A)

exceeds

(C) the total of all amounts deducted as a reserve by virtue of paragraph 20(1)(n) in computing the taxpayer's income for the year to the extent that the reserve relates to inventory described in clause (A),

(c) 30% of the amount, if any, by which the amount determined under subparagraph (b)(i) exceeds the amount determined under subparagraph (b)(ii), and

(d) the amount determined by the formula

$$A(B - C)$$

where

A is

(i) for taxation years that end before 2024, 15%,

(ii) for taxation years that begin before 2024 and end after 2023, the amount determined by the formula

$$0.15(I/J) + 0.075(K/J)$$

where

I is the total of all accelerated Canadian development expenses incurred by the taxpayer before 2024 and in the taxation year,

J is the total of all accelerated Canadian development expenses incurred by the taxpayer in the taxation year, and

K is the total of all accelerated Canadian development expenses incurred by the taxpayer after 2023 and in the taxation year, and

(iii) for taxation years that begin after 2023, 7.5%,

B is the total of all accelerated Canadian development expenses incurred by the taxpayer in the taxation year, and

C is the amount determined by the formula

$$(D - E) - (F - G - H)$$

where

D is the total of the amounts determined for E to O in the definition "cumulative Canadian development expense" in subsection (5) at the end of the taxation year,

E is the total of the amounts determined for E to O in the definition "cumulative Canadian development expense" in subsection (5) at the beginning of the taxation year,

F is the total of the amounts determined for A to D.1 in the definition "cumulative Canadian development expense" in subsection (5) at the end of the taxation year,

G is the total of the amounts determined for A to D.1 in the definition "cumulative Canadian development expense" in subsection (5) at the end of the preceding taxation year, and

H is the amount determined for B.

Related Provisions: 20(1)(hh) — Repayments of inducements, etc.; 66(13.1) — Short taxation year; 66(11.6)(a) — Application of successor rules on change in control of trust; 110.6(1)"investment expense"(d) — effect of claim under 66.2(2) on capital gains exemption; 127.52(1)(e) — Add-back of deduction for minimum tax purposes; 257 — Formula cannot calculate to less than zero. See also at end of s. 66.2.

Notes: 66.2(2) allows a deduction of 30% of CCDE at year-end; see 66.2(5)"cumulative Canadian development expense". 66.2(1) requires a taxpayer, in conjunction with 59(3.2)(c), to include in income any negative balance of CCDE at year-end.

Even after disposition of all Canadian resource property, there is no deduction other than the annual 30%: VIEWS doc 2012-0463841E5. On death, 30% of CCDE can be claimed for the year, but no further deduction is allowed for the unclaimed balance: 2005-0111431E5.

66.2(2)(d) (added by 2019 budget bill #1, effective June 21, 2019) provides additional first-year CDE for "accelerated Canadian development expense" (defined in 66.2(5)), as part of the Accelerated Investment Incentive (see Notes to Reg. 1100(2)). The additional deduction is 15% of expenses incurred from Nov. 21, 2018 through 2023 (i.e., total 45%), and 7.5% for 2024-2027.

66.2(2)(b)(ii)(A) amended by 2002-2013 technical bill (Part 4 — bijuralism), effective June 26, 2013, to change "share, any interest therein or right thereto" to "share or any interest in or right to — or, for civil law, any right in or to — a share".

66.2(2) amended by 1991 technical bill.

Interpretation Bulletins: IT-273R2: Government assistance — general comments; IT-438R2: Crown charges — resource properties in Canada.

Advance Tax Rulings: ATR-59: Financing exploration and development through limited partnerships.

(3), (4) [Repealed under former Act]

Notes: 66.2(3) and (4), repealed in 1987, dealt with a successor corporation's Canadian development expenses. See now 66.7.

(5) Definitions — In this section,

Related Provisions: 66(15.1) — Application to 66; 66.1(6.1) — Application to 66.1.

Notes: 66.2(5) applies to 66 and 66.1; see 66(15.1), 66.1(6.1) (this rule was in 66.2(5) opening words before RSC 1985 (5th Supp), for tax years ending before Dec. 1991).

"accelerated Canadian development expense", of a taxpayer, means any cost or expense incurred by the taxpayer during a taxation year if the cost or expense

(a) qualifies as a Canadian development expense at the time it is incurred, other than

(i) an expense in respect of which the taxpayer is a successor, within the meaning of subsection 66.7(4), and

(ii) a cost in respect of a Canadian resource property acquired by the taxpayer, or a partnership in which the taxpayer is a member, from a person or partnership with which the taxpayer does not deal at arm's length,

(b) is incurred after November 20, 2018 and before 2028, other than expenses deemed to have been incurred on December 31, 2027 because of subsection 66(12.66), and

(c) if the Canadian development expense is deemed to be a Canadian development expense incurred by the taxpayer because of paragraph 66(12.63)(a), is an amount renounced under an agreement entered into after November 20, 2018;

Notes: See Notes to 66.2(2) re 66.2(2)(d).

Despite (a)(ii) using the broad words "in respect of", the carveout does not catch drilling or completion expenses incurred on land acquired from a non-arm's-length person: VIEWS doc 2019-0816111C6 [2019 CPTS], q.6.

Definition added by 2019 budget bill #1, effective June 21, 2019.

"Canadian development expense" of a taxpayer means any cost or expense incurred after May 6, 1974 that is

(a) any expense incurred by the taxpayer in

(i) drilling or converting a well in Canada for the disposal of waste liquids from an oil or gas well,

(ii) drilling or completing an oil or gas well in Canada, building a temporary access road to the well or preparing a site in respect of the well, to the extent that the expense was not a Canadian exploration expense of the taxpayer in the taxation year in which it was incurred,

(iii) drilling or converting a well in Canada for the injection of water, gas or any other substance to assist in the recovery of petroleum or natural gas from another well,

(iv) drilling for water or gas in Canada for injection into a petroleum or natural gas formation, or

(v) drilling or converting a well in Canada for the purposes of monitoring fluid levels, pressure changes or other phenomena in an accumulation of petroleum or natural gas,

(b) any expense incurred by the taxpayer in drilling or recompleting an oil or gas well in Canada after the commencement of production from the well,

(c) any expense incurred by the taxpayer before November 17, 1978 for the purpose of bringing a mineral resource in Canada into production and incurred prior to the commencement of production from the resource in reasonable commercial quantities, including

(i) clearing, removing overburden and stripping, and

(ii) sinking a mine shaft, constructing an adit or other underground entry,

(c.1) any expense, or portion of any expense, that is not a Canadian exploration expense, incurred by the taxpayer for the purpose of bringing a new mine in a mineral resource in Canada that is a bituminous sands deposit or an oil shale deposit into production and incurred before the new mine comes into production in reasonable commercial quantities, including an expense for clearing the land, removing overburden and stripping, or building an entry ramp,

(c.2) any expense, or portion of any expense, that is not a Canadian exploration expense, incurred by the taxpayer after March 20, 2013 for the purpose of bringing a new mine in a mineral resource in Canada, other than a bituminous sands deposit or an oil shale deposit, into production in reasonable commercial quantities and incurred before the new mine comes into production in such quantities, including an expense for clearing, removing overburden, stripping, sinking a mine shaft or constructing an adit or other underground entry,

(d) any expense (other than an amount included in the capital cost of depreciable property) incurred by the taxpayer after 1987

(i) in sinking or excavating a mine shaft, main haulage way or similar underground work designed for continuing use, for a mine in a mineral resource in Canada built or excavated after the mine came into production, or

(ii) in extending any such shaft, haulage way or work,

(e) the cost to the taxpayer of, including any payment for the preservation of a taxpayer's rights in respect of, any property described in paragraph (b), (e) or (f) of the definition "Canadian resource property" in subsection 66(15), or any right to or interest in — or for civil law, any right in or to — the property (other than a right or an interest that the taxpayer has by reason of being a beneficiary under a trust or a member of a partnership),

(f) subject to section 66.8, the taxpayer's share of any expense referred to in any of paragraphs (a) to (e) incurred by a partnership in a fiscal period thereof at the end of which the taxpayer was a member of the partnership, unless the taxpayer elects in respect of the share in prescribed form and manner on or before the day that is 6 months after the taxpayer's taxation year in which that period ends, or

(g) any cost or expense referred to in any of paragraphs (a) to (e) incurred by the taxpayer pursuant to an agreement in writing with a corporation, entered into before 1987, under which the taxpayer incurred the cost or expense solely as consideration for shares, other than prescribed shares, of the capital stock of the corporation issued to the taxpayer or any interest in or right to — or, for civil law, any right in or to — such shares,

but, for greater certainty, shall not include

(h) any consideration given by the taxpayer for any share or any interest in or right to — or, for civil law, any right in or to — a share, except as provided by paragraph (g),

(i) any expense described in paragraph (g) incurred by any other taxpayer to the extent that the expense was,

(i) by virtue of that paragraph, a Canadian development expense of that other taxpayer,

(ii) by virtue of paragraph (i) of the definition "Canadian exploration expense" in subsection 66.1(6), a Canadian exploration expense of that other taxpayer, or

(iii) by virtue of paragraph (c) of the definition "Canadian oil and gas property expense" in subsection 66.4(5), a Canadian oil and gas property expense of that other taxpayer,

(i.1) an expense that is the cost, or any part of the cost, to the taxpayer of any depreciable property of a prescribed class that was acquired after 1987,

(j) any amount included at any time in the capital cost to the taxpayer of any depreciable property of a prescribed class, or

(k) the taxpayer's share of any consideration, expense, cost or expenditure referred to in any of paragraphs (h) to (j) given or incurred by a partnership,

but any assistance that a taxpayer has received or is entitled to receive after May 25, 1976 in respect of or related to the taxpayer's Canadian development expense shall not reduce the amount of any of the expenses described in any of paragraphs (a) to (g);

Related Provisions: 13(7.5) — Depreciable property treatment for costs associated with building roads and similar projects; 34.2(1)"qualified resource expense"(b), 34.2(6) — CDE qualifies for deduction from corporate accrual of partnership income; 53(1)(e)(vii.1) — Addition to ACB — partnership interest; 66.2(2) — Deduction for cumulative CDE; 66.2(8) — Presumption; 66.3 — Exploration and development shares; 248(1)"Canadian development expense" — Definition applies to entire Act; 248(16), (16.1) — GST or QST input tax credit/refund and rebate deemed to be assistance; 248(18), (18.1) — GST or QST — repayment of input tax credit or refund; Reg. 1102(1)(a) — Depreciable property takes priority over resource property; *Interpretation Act* 8(2.1), (2.2) — Application to exclusive economic zone and continental shelf. See also at end of s. 66.2.

Notes: See Ian Gamble, *Taxation of Canadian Mining* (Carswell, looseleaf or *Taxnet Pro* Reference Centre), §3.4; Mar, Rowe & Bereti, "Basic Issues in Resource Taxation", 2008 Cdn Tax Foundation conference report, 10:1-32.

An ongoing CDE appeal is *Boguski*, 2021 FCA 118 (procedural decision), re Royal Crown Gold Reserve mining rights.

Subpara. (a)(ii) can include surface lease payments (VIEWS doc 2009-0345121E5) and the costs of drilling and completing a shale natural gas well (2012-0459351E5).

Para. (c.1) added by 2011 budget bill #2, effective for expenses incurred after March 21, 2011.

Para. (c.2) added by 2013 budget bill #2, effective March 21, 2013 (pre-production expenses are phased over from CEE to CDE: 66.1(6)"Canadian exploration expense"(g), (g.3), (g.4)).

Para. (e) can include: an amount paid to obtain a license to explore for a mineral resource (VIEWS doc 2013-0480511I7); mineral subsurface rights (2016-0637221E5).

Para. (e) amended to change "such property" to "or for civil law, any right in or to — the property" by 2002-2013 technical bill (Part 5 — technical), this version for taxation years that begin after 2007.

Para. (e) amended by 2003 resource bill, effective for taxation years that begin after 2006 (consequential on the repeal of 18(1)(m)), to the version shown above.

Paras. (g), (h) amended by 2002-2013 technical bill (Part 4 — bijuralism), effective June 26, 2013, to change "interest in such shares or right thereto" to "interest in or right to — or, for civil law, any right in or to — such shares" (para. (g)) and "interest therein or right thereto" to "interests in or right to — or, for civil law, any right in or to — a share" (para. (h)).

Para. (i.1) added by 2001 technical bill, for 1988 and later taxation years. It overrules *Phénix*, [2001] 1 C.T.C. 74 (FCA). See also Reg. 1102(1)(a).

Paras. (j), (k) added by 1996 Budget, effective for taxation years that end after Dec. 5, 1996. They are parallel to 66.1(6)"Canadian exploration expense"(l) and (o).

66.2(5)"Canadian development expense" was 66.2(5)(a) before RSC 1985 (5th Supp) consolidation for tax years ending after Nov. 1991.

"Canadian development expense"(f) amended by 1992 technical bill, effective for partnership fiscal periods ending after 1990.

Regulations: 6202 (prescribed share).

Income Tax Folios: S3-F8-C1: Principal-business corporations in the resource industries [replaces IT-400].

Interpretation Bulletins: IT-109R2: Unpaid amounts; IT-273R2: Government assistance — general comments; IT-438R2: Crown charges — resource properties in Canada; IT-476R: CCA — Equipment used in petroleum and natural gas activities; IT-503: Exploration and development shares (cancelled).

Advance Tax Rulings: ATR-59: Financing exploration and development through limited partnerships.

Forms: T1086: Election by a partner waiving Canadian development expenses or oil and gas property expenses.

"cumulative Canadian development expense" of a taxpayer at any time in a taxation year means the amount determined by the formula

$$(A + B + C + D + D.1) - (E + F + G + H + I$$
$$+ J + K + L + M + M.1 + N + O)$$

where

A is the total of all Canadian development expenses made or incurred by the taxpayer before that time,

B is the total of all amounts that were, because of subsection (1), included in computing the amount referred to in paragraph 59(3.2)(c) for taxation years ending before that time,

C is the total of all amounts referred to in the description of F or G that are established by the taxpayer to have become a bad debt before that time,

D is such part, if any, of the amount determined for M as has been repaid before that time by the taxpayer pursuant to a legal obligation to repay all or any part of that amount,

D.1 is the total of all specified amounts determined under paragraph 66.7(12.1)(b) in respect of the taxpayer for taxation years ending before that time,

E is the total of all amounts deducted in computing the taxpayer's income for a taxation year ending before that time in respect of the taxpayer's cumulative Canadian development expense,

F is the total of all amounts each of which is an amount in respect of property described in paragraph (b), (e) or (f) of the definition "Canadian resource property" in subsection 66(15) or property disposed of after March 21, 2011 which was described in any of those paragraphs and the cost of which when acquired by the taxpayer was included in the Canadian development expense of the taxpayer, or any right to or interest in — or, for civil law, any right in or to — such a property, other than such a right or an interest that the taxpayer has by reason of being a beneficiary under a trust or a member of a partnership, (in this description referred to as "the particular property") disposed of by the taxpayer before that time equal to the amount, if any, by which

    (a) the amount, if any, by which the proceeds of disposition in respect of the particular property that became receivable by the taxpayer after May 6, 1974 and before that time exceed any outlays or expenses that were made or incurred by the taxpayer after May 6, 1974 and before that time for the purpose of making the disposition and that were not otherwise deductible for the purposes of this Part

exceeds

    (b) the amount, if any, by which

        (i) the total of all amounts that would be determined under paragraph 66.7(4)(a), immediately before the time (in this paragraph referred to as the "relevant time") when such proceeds of disposition became receivable, in respect of the taxpayer and an original owner of the particular property (or of any other property acquired by the taxpayer with the particular property in circumstances in which subsection 66.7(4) applied and in respect of which the proceeds of disposition became receivable by the taxpayer at the relevant time) if

            (A) amounts that became receivable at or after the relevant time were not taken into account,

            (B) each designation made under subparagraph 66.7(4)(a)(iii) in respect of an amount that became receivable before the relevant time were made before the relevant time,

            (C) paragraph 66.7(4)(a) were read without reference to "30% of", and

            (D) no reduction under subsection 80(8) at or after the relevant time were taken into account

        exceeds the total of

        (ii) all amounts that would be determined under paragraph 66.7(4)(a) at the relevant time in respect of the taxpayer and an original owner of the particular property (or of that other property) if

            (A) amounts that became receivable after the relevant time were not taken into account,

            (B) each designation made under subparagraph 66.7(4)(a)(iii) in respect of an amount that became receivable at or before the relevant time were made before the relevant time,

            (C) paragraph 66.7(4)(a) were read without reference to "30% of",

            (D) amounts described in subparagraph 66.7(4)(a)(iii) that became receivable at the relevant time were not taken into account, and

            (E) no reduction under subsection 80(8) at or after the relevant time were taken into account, and

    (iii) such portion of the amount otherwise determined under this paragraph as was otherwise applied to reduce the amount otherwise determined under this description,

G is the total of all amounts that became receivable by the taxpayer before that time that are to be included in the amount determined under this description by virtue of paragraph 66(12.1)(b) or (12.3)(a),

H is the total of all amounts each of which is an amount included by the taxpayer as an expense under paragraph (a) of the definition "Canadian development expense" in this subsection in computing the taxpayer's Canadian development expense for a previous taxation year that has become a Canadian exploration expense of the taxpayer by virtue of subparagraph (c)(ii) of the definition "Canadian exploration expense" in subsection 66.1(6),

I is the total of all amounts each of which is an amount that before that time has become a Canadian exploration expense of the taxpayer by virtue of subsection 66.1(9),

J is the total of all amounts each of which is an amount received before that time on account of any amount referred to in the description of C,

K is the total of all amounts paid to the taxpayer after May 6, 1974 and before May 25, 1976

    (a) under the *Northern Mineral Exploration Assistance Regulations* made under an appropriation Act that provides for payments in respect of the Northern Mineral Grants Program, or

    (b) pursuant to any agreement, entered into between the taxpayer and Her Majesty in right of Canada under the Northern Mineral Grants Program or the Development Program of the Department of Indian Affairs and Northern Development,

to the extent that the amounts have been expended by the taxpayer as or on account of Canadian development expense incurred by the taxpayer,

L is the amount by which the total of all amounts determined under subsection 66.4(1) in respect of a taxation year of the taxpayer ending at or before that time exceeds the total of all amounts each of which is the least of

    (a) the amount that would be determined under paragraph 66.7(4)(a), at a time (hereafter in this description referred to only as the "particular time") that is the end of the latest taxation year of the taxpayer ending at or before that time, in respect of the taxpayer as successor in respect of a disposition (in this description referred to as the "original disposition") of Canadian resource property by a person who is an original owner of the property because of the original disposition, if

        (i) that paragraph were read without reference to "30% of",

        (ii) where the taxpayer has disposed of all or part of the property in circumstances in which subsection 66.7(4) applied, that subsection continued to apply to the taxpayer in respect of the original disposition as if subsequent successors were the same person as the taxpayer, and

        (iii) each designation made under subparagraph 66.7(4)(a)(iii) in respect of an amount that became receivable before the particular time were made before the particular time,

    (b) the amount, if any, by which the total of all amounts each of which became receivable at or before the particular time and before 1993 by the taxpayer and is included in computing the amount determined under subparagraph 66.7(5)(a)(ii) in respect of the original disposition exceeds the amount, if any, by which

        (i) where the taxpayer disposed of all or part of the property before the particular time in circumstances in which subsection 66.7(5) applied, the amount that would be determined at the particular time under subparagraph 66.7(5)(a)(i) in respect of the original disposition if that subparagraph continued to apply to the taxpayer in respect of the original disposition as if subsequent successors were the same person as the taxpayer, and

(ii) in any other case, the amount determined at the particular time under subparagraph 66.7(5)(a)(i) in respect of the original disposition

exceeds

(iii) the amount that would be determined at the particular time under subparagraph 66.7(5)(a)(ii) in respect of the original disposition if that subparagraph were read without reference to the words "or the successor", wherever they appear therein, and if amounts that became receivable after 1992 were not taken into account, and

(c) where

(i) after the original disposition and at or before the particular time, the taxpayer disposed of all or part of the property in circumstances in which subsection 66.7(4) applied, otherwise than by way of an amalgamation or merger or solely because of the application of paragraph 66.7(10)(c), and

(ii) the winding-up of the taxpayer began at or before that time or the taxpayer's disposition referred to in subparagraph (i) (other than a disposition under an agreement in writing entered into before December 22, 1992) occurred after December 21, 1992,

nil,

M   is the total amount of assistance that the taxpayer has received or is entitled to receive in respect of any Canadian development expense (including an expense that has become a Canadian exploration expense of the taxpayer by virtue of subsection 66.1(9)) incurred after 1980 or that can reasonably be related to Canadian development activities after 1980,

M.1   is the total of all amounts by which the cumulative Canadian development expense of the taxpayer is required because of subsection 80(8) to be reduced at or before that time,

N   is the total of all amounts that are required to be deducted before that time under subsection 66(14.2) in computing the taxpayer's cumulative Canadian development expense, and

O   is the total of all amounts that are required to be deducted before that time under paragraph 66.7(12)(c) in computing the taxpayer's cumulative Canadian development expense.

Related Provisions: 35(1)(c) — Prospectors and grubstakers; 50(1)(a) — Deemed disposition where debt becomes bad debt; 59(3.2) — Recovery of exploration & development expenses; 66(12.1) — Limitations of Canadian exploration & development expenses; 66(12.3) — Unitized oil or gas field in Canada; 66.2(7) — Exception; 66.4(1) — Recovery of costs; 66.7(4) — Deduction to successor corp; 70(5.2) — Resource properties and land inventories of deceased; 79(4)(c) — Subsequent payment by debtor following surrender of property deemed to be repayment of assistance; 79.1(8) — No claim for principal amount of bad debt where property seized by creditor; 80(8)(c) — Reduction of CCDE on debt forgiveness; 96(2.2)(d) — at-risk amount; 104(5.2) — Trusts — 21-year deemed disposition; 248(16), (16.1) — GST or QST input tax credit/refund and rebate deemed to be assistance; 248(18), (18.1) — GST or QST — repayment of input tax credit or refund; 257 — Formula cannot calculate to less than zero; 261(7)(d) — Functional currency reporting. See also at end of s. 66.2; Reg. 1102(1)(a) — Deductible expenses.

Notes: If cumulative CDE goes negative, it is included in income: 66.2(1), 59(3.2)(c).

For interpretation of element F see VIEWS docs 2010-0389081I7, 2013-0505431R3.

Description of B amended by 2002-2013 technical bill (Part 5 — technical), for taxation years that end after Nov. 5, 2010, to apply to amounts included in income rather than those required to be included.

Description of F amended by 2011 budget bill #2 (effective March 22, 2011), 2003 resource bill, 1994 technical bill, 1993 and 1991 technical bills, 1990 GST. 66.2(5)"cumulative Canadian development expense" was 66.2(5)(b) before RSC 1985 (5th Supp) consolidation for tax years ending after Nov. 1991.

Interpretation Bulletins: IT-109R2: Unpaid amounts; IT-125R4: Dispositions of resource properties; IT-273R2: Government assistance — general comments.

(5.1) Application of subsecs. 66(15), 66.1(6) and 66.4(5) —
The definitions in subsections 66(15), 66.1(6) and 66.4(5) apply to this section.

Notes: 66.2(5.1) added in the RSC 1985 (5th Supp) consolidation, effective for tax years ending after Nov. 1991 (formerly in the opening words of subsecs. 66(15), 66.1(6) and 66.4(5)).

(6) Presumption [partner's share] — Except as provided in
subsection (7), where a taxpayer is a member of a partnership, the taxpayer's share of any amount that would be an amount referred to in the description of D in the definition "cumulative Canadian development expense" in subsection (5), in paragraph (a) of the description of F in that definition or in the description of G or M in that definition in respect of the partnership for a taxation year of the partnership if section 96 were read without reference to paragraph 96(1)(d) shall, for the purposes of this Act, be deemed to be an amount referred to in the description of D in the definition "cumulative Canadian development expense" in subsection (5), in paragraph (a) of the description of F in that definition or in the description of G or M in that definition, whichever is applicable, in respect of the taxpayer for the taxation year of the taxpayer in which the partnership's taxation year ends.

Related Provisions: 59(1.1) — Parallel rule for foreign resource property; 66.4(6) — Parallel rule for CCOGPE.

Notes: For a ruling applying 66.2(6) see VIEWS doc 2013-0505431R3.

References to "cumulative Canadian development expense"D (formerly 66.2(5)(b)(iii.1)) added to 66.2(6) by 1991 technical bill, effective February 1990.

Interpretation Bulletins: IT-125R4: Dispositions of resource properties; IT-273R2: Government assistance — general comments; IT-353R2: Partnership interest — some adjustments to cost base (cancelled).

I.T. Technical News: 12 (adjusted cost base of partnership interest — subparagraph 53(1)(e)(viii)).

(7) Exception — Where a non-resident person is a member of a
partnership that is deemed under paragraph 115(4)(b) to have disposed of any Canadian resource property, the person's share of any amount that would be an amount referred to in the description of D in the definition "cumulative Canadian development expense" in subsection (5), in paragraph (a) of the description of F in that definition or in the description of G or M in that definition in respect of the partnership for a taxation year of the partnership if section 96 were read without reference to paragraph 96(1)(d) shall, for the purposes of this Act, be deemed to be an amount referred to in the description of D in the definition "cumulative Canadian development expense" in subsection (5), in paragraph (a) of the description of F in that definition or in the description of G or M in that definition, whichever is applicable, in respect of the person for the taxation year of the person that is deemed under paragraph 115(4)(a) to have ended.

Notes: References to "cumulative Canadian development expense"D (formerly 66.2(5)(b)(iii.1)) added to 66.2(7) by 1991 technical bill, effective February 1990.

Interpretation Bulletins: IT-125R4: Dispositions of resource properties; IT-273R2: Government assistance — general comments.

(8) Presumption — Where pursuant to the terms of an arrange-
ment in writing entered into before December 12, 1979 a taxpayer acquired a property described in paragraph (a) of the definition "Canadian oil and gas property expense" in subsection 66.4(5), for the purposes of this Act, the cost of acquisition shall be deemed to be a Canadian development expense incurred at the time the taxpayer acquired the property.

Related Provisions [s. 66.2]: 66(5) — Dealers; 66(18) — Members of partnerships; 66.7 — Successor rules; 66.8(1) — Resource expenses of limited partner; 87(1.2) — New corporation deemed continuation of predecessor; 88(1.5) — Winding-up — parent deemed continuation of subsidiary.

Definitions [s. 66.2]: "accelerated Canadian development expense" — 66.2(5); "amount" — 248(1); "assistance" — 66(15), 66.1(6.1), 79(4), 125.4(5), 248(16), (16.1), (18), (18.1); "beneficiary" — 248(25) [Notes]; "bituminous sands" — 248(1); "Canada" — 255, Interpretation Act 8(2.1), (2.2); "Canadian development expense" — 66.2(5), (8), 248(1); "Canadian exploration expense" — 66.1(6), 248(1); "Canadian exploration and development expense" — 66(15), 66.2(5.1); "Canadian exploration expense" — 66.1(6), 248(1); "Canadian oil and gas property expense" — 66.4(5), 248(1); "Canadian resource property" — 66(15), 248(1); "corporation" — 248(1), Interpretation Act 35(1); "depreciable property" — 13(21), 248(1); "disposition" — 54, 66.2(5.1), 66.4(5); "expense" — 66(15), 66.2(5.1); "fiscal period" — 249(2)(b), 249.1; "Her Majesty" — Interpretation Act 35(1); "mineral resource", "non-resident", "oil or gas well" — 248(1); partnership — see 96(1) Notes; "person", "prescribed" — 248(1); "proceeds of disposition" — 54, 66.2(5.1), 66.4(5); "property", "share" — 248(1);

"successor" — 66.7(4); "taxation year" — 11(2), 249; "taxpayer" — 248(1); "trust" — 104(1), 248(1), (3); "writing" — *Interpretation Act* 35(1).

66.21 [Foreign resource expenses] — (1) Definitions — The definitions in this subsection apply in this section.

"adjusted cumulative foreign resource expense" of a taxpayer, in respect of a country, at the end of a taxation year means the total of

(a) the cumulative foreign resource expense of the taxpayer, in respect of that country, at the end of the year; and

(b) the amount, if any, by which

(i) the total determined under paragraph 66.7(13.2)(a) in respect of that country and the taxpayer for the year

exceeds

(ii) the amount that would, but for paragraph (3)(c), be determined under subsection (3) in respect of that country and the taxpayer for the year.

Notes: See Notes at end of 66.21.

"cumulative foreign resource expense" of a taxpayer, in respect of a country other than Canada at a particular time, means the amount determined by the formula

$$(A + A.1 + B + C + D) - (E + F + G + H + I + J)$$

where

A is the total of all foreign resource expenses, in respect of that country, made or incurred by the taxpayer

(a) before the particular time, and

(b) at a time (in this definition referred to as a "resident time")

(i) at which the taxpayer was resident in Canada, and

(ii) where the taxpayer became resident in Canada before the particular time, that is after the last time (before the particular time) that the taxpayer became resident in Canada;

A.1 is the total of all foreign resource expenses, in respect of that country, that is the cost to the taxpayer of any of the taxpayer's foreign resource property in respect of that country that is deemed to have been acquired by the taxpayer under paragraph 128.1(1)(c) at the last time (before the particular time) that the taxpayer became resident in Canada;

B is the total of all amounts included in computing the amount referred to in paragraph 59(3.2)(c.1) in respect of that country, for taxation years that ended before the particular time and at a resident time;

C is the total of all amounts referred to in the description of F or G that are established by the taxpayer to have become a bad debt before the particular time and at a resident time;

D is the total of all specified amounts determined under subsection 66.7(13.2), in respect of the taxpayer and that country, for taxation years that ended before the particular time and at a resident time;

E is the total of all amounts deducted, in computing the taxpayer's income for a taxation year that ended before the particular time and at a resident time, in respect of the taxpayer's cumulative foreign resource expense in respect of that country;

F is the total of all amounts each of which is an amount in respect of a foreign resource property, in respect of that country, (in this description referred to as the "particular property") disposed of by the taxpayer equal to the amount, if any, by which

(a) the amount designated under subparagraph 59(1)(b)(ii) by the taxpayer in respect of the portion of the proceeds of that disposition that became receivable before the particular time and at a resident time

exceeds

(b) the amount, if any, by which

(i) the total of all amounts that would be determined under paragraph 66.7(2.3)(a), immediately before the time (in this paragraph referred to as the "relevant time") when such proceeds of disposition became receivable, in respect of the taxpayer, that country and an original owner of the particular property (or of any other property acquired by the taxpayer with the particular property in circumstances to which subsection 66.7(2.3) applied and in respect of which the proceeds of disposition became receivable by the taxpayer at the relevant time) if

(A) amounts that became receivable at or after the relevant time were not taken into account,

(B) paragraph 66.7(2.3)(a) were read without reference to "30% of", and

(C) no reduction under subsection 80(8) at or after the relevant time were taken into account,

exceeds the total of

(ii) all amounts that would be determined under paragraph 66.7(2.3)(a) at the relevant time in respect of the taxpayer, that country and an original owner of the particular property (or of that other property) if

(A) amounts that became receivable after the relevant time were not taken into account,

(B) paragraph 66.7(2.3)(a) were read without reference to "30% of", and

(C) no reduction under subsection 80(8) at or after the relevant time were taken into account, and

(iii) the portion of the amount otherwise determined under this paragraph that was otherwise applied to reduce the amount otherwise determined under this description;

G is the total of all amounts, in respect of that country, each of which is an amount included in the amount determined under this description by reason of subsection 66(12.41) that became receivable by the taxpayer before the particular time and at a resident time;

H is the total of all amounts each of which is an amount received before the particular time and at a resident time on account of any amount referred to in the description of C;

I is the total of all amounts each of which is an amount by which the cumulative foreign resource expense of the taxpayer, in respect of that country, is required, by reason of subsection 80(8), to be reduced at or before the particular time and at a resident time; and

J is the total of all amounts each of which is an amount that is required to be deducted, before the particular time and at a resident time, under paragraph 66.7(13.1)(a) in computing the taxpayer's cumulative foreign resource expense.

Related Provisions: 66.21(5) — FRE on becoming resident; 104(5.2) — Trusts — 21-year deemed disposition; 248(1)"foreign resource property" — Meaning of foreign resource property in respect of a country; 257 — Formula cannot calculate to less than zero; 261(7)(d) — Functional currency reporting.

Notes: See Roch Martin, "Foreign Exploration and Development Expenditures — The New Rules", 14 *Canadian Petroleum Tax Journal* (2001).

Definition amended by 2002-2013 technical bill, last change effective for tax years ending after Nov. 5, 2010.

"foreign resource expense" of a taxpayer, in respect of a country other than Canada, means

(a) any drilling or exploration expense, including any general geological or geophysical expense, incurred by the taxpayer on or in respect of exploring or drilling for petroleum or natural gas in that country,

(b) any expense incurred by the taxpayer for the purpose of determining the existence, location, extent or quality of a mineral resource in that country, including any expense incurred in the course of

(i) prospecting,

(ii) carrying out geological, geophysical or geochemical surveys,

(iii) drilling by rotary, diamond, percussion or other methods, or

(iv) trenching, digging test pits and preliminary sampling,

(c) the cost to the taxpayer of any of the taxpayer's foreign resource property in respect of that country,

(d) any annual payment made by the taxpayer for the preservation of a foreign resource property in respect of that country, and

(e) subject to section 66.8, the taxpayer's share of an expense, cost or payment referred to in any of paragraphs (a) to (d) that is made or incurred by a partnership in a fiscal period of the partnership that begins after 2000 if, at the end of that period, the taxpayer was a member of the partnership

but does not include

(f) an expenditure that is the cost, or any part of the cost, to the taxpayer of any depreciable property of a prescribed class,

(g) an expenditure incurred at any time after the commencement of production from a foreign resource property of the taxpayer in order to evaluate the feasibility of a method of recovery of petroleum, natural gas or related hydrocarbons from the portion of a natural reservoir to which the foreign resource property relates,

(h) an expenditure (other than a drilling expense) incurred at any time after the commencement of production from a foreign resource property of the taxpayer in order to assist in the recovery of petroleum, natural gas or related hydrocarbons from the portion of a natural reservoir to which the foreign resource property relates,

(i) an expenditure, incurred at any time, that relates to the injection of any substance to assist in the recovery of petroleum, natural gas or related hydrocarbons from a natural reservoir,

(j) an expenditure incurred by the taxpayer, unless the expenditure was made

(i) for the acquisition of foreign resource property by the taxpayer, or

(ii) for the purpose of

(A) enhancing the value of foreign resource property that the taxpayer owned at the time the expenditure was incurred or that the taxpayer had a reasonable expectation of owning after that time, or

(B) assisting in evaluating whether a foreign resource property is to be acquired by the taxpayer, or

(k) the taxpayer's share of any cost or expenditure referred to in any of paragraphs (f) to (j) that is incurred by a partnership.

Related Provisions: 34.2(1)"qualified resource expense"(c), 34.2(6) — FRE qualifies for deduction from corporate accrual of partnership income; 66(18) — Expenses of partnerships; 66.7(2.3) — Successor of foreign resource expenses; 248(1)"foreign resource expense" — Definition applies to entire Act; 248(1)"foreign resource property" — Meaning of foreign resource property in respect of a country.

"foreign resource income" of a taxpayer for a taxation year, in respect of a country other than Canada, means the total of

(a) that part of the taxpayer's income for the year, determined without reference to subsections (4) and 66(4), that is reasonably attributable to

(i) the production of petroleum or natural gas from natural accumulations of petroleum or natural gas in that country or from oil or gas wells in that country, or

(ii) the production of minerals from mines in that country;

(b) the taxpayer's income for the year from royalties in respect of a natural accumulation of petroleum or natural gas in that country, an oil or gas well in that country or a mine in that coun-

try, determined without reference to subsections (4) and 66(4); and

(c) all amounts each of which is an amount, in respect of a foreign resource property in respect of that country that has been disposed of by the taxpayer, equal to the amount, if any, by which

(i) the amount included in computing the taxpayer's income for the year by reason of subsection 59(1) in respect of that disposition

exceeds

(ii) the total of all amounts each of which is that portion of an amount deducted under subsection 66.7(2) in computing the taxpayer's income for the year that

(A) can reasonably be considered to be in respect of the foreign resource property, and

(B) cannot reasonably be considered to have reduced the amount otherwise determined under paragraph (a) or (b) in respect of the taxpayer for the year.

Related Provisions: 248(1)"foreign resource property" — Meaning of foreign resource property in respect of a country.

"foreign resource loss" of a taxpayer for a taxation year in respect of a country other than Canada means the taxpayer's loss for the year in respect of the country determined in accordance with the definition "foreign resource income" with such modifications as the circumstances require.

"global foreign resource limit" of a taxpayer for a taxation year means the amount that is the lesser of

(a) the amount, if any, by which

(i) the amount determined under subparagraph 66(4)(b)(ii) in respect of the taxpayer for the year

exceeds the total of

(ii) the total of all amounts each of which is the maximum amount that the taxpayer would be permitted to deduct, in respect of a country, under subsection (4) in computing the taxpayer's income for the year if, in its application to the year, subsection (4) were read without reference to paragraph (4)(b), and

(iii) the amount deducted for the year under subsection 66(4) in computing the taxpayer's income for the year; and

(b) the amount, if any, by which

(i) 30% of the total of all amounts each of which is, at the end of the year, the taxpayer's adjusted cumulative foreign resource expense in respect of a country

exceeds

(ii) the total described in subparagraph (a)(ii).

Related Provisions: 66(13.1) — Short taxation year.

(2) Application of subsection 66(15) — The definitions in subsection 66(15) apply in this section.

(3) Amount to be included in income — For the purpose of paragraph 59(3.2)(c.1), the amount referred to in this subsection in respect of a taxpayer for a taxation year is the amount, if any, by which

(a) the total of all amounts referred to in the descriptions of E to J in the definition "cumulative foreign resource expense" in subsection (1) that are deducted in computing the taxpayer's cumulative foreign resource expense at the end of the year in respect of a country

exceeds the total of

(b) the total of all amounts referred to in the descriptions of A to D in the definition "cumulative foreign resource expense" in subsection (1) that are included in computing the taxpayer's cumulative foreign resource expense at the end of the year in respect of the country, and

(c) the total determined under paragraph 66.7(13.2)(a) for the year in respect of the taxpayer and the country.

Related Provisions: 59(3.2)(c.1) — Income inclusion; 66(5) — No application to certain dealers; 66(11.4)(c) — Change of control; 66.8(1) — Resource expenses of limited partner; 70(5.2)(a) — Death of taxpayer; 87(1.2) — Amalgamation — continuing corporation; 88(1.5) — Windup — parent continuation of subsidiary.

Notes: See Notes at end of 66.21.

(4) Deduction for cumulative foreign resource expense —
In computing a taxpayer's income for a taxation year throughout which the taxpayer is resident in Canada, the taxpayer may deduct the amount claimed by the taxpayer, in respect of a country other than Canada, not exceeding the total of

(a) the greater of

(i) 10% of a particular amount equal to the taxpayer's adjusted cumulative foreign resource expense in respect of the country at the end of the year, and

(ii) the least of

(A) if the taxpayer ceased to be resident in Canada immediately after the end of the year, the particular amount,

(B) if clause (A) does not apply, 30% of the particular amount,

(C) the amount, if any, by which the taxpayer's foreign resource income for the year in respect of the country exceeds the portion of the amount, deducted under subsection 66(4) in computing the taxpayer's income for the year, that applies to a source in the country, and

(D) the amount, if any, by which

(I) the total of all amounts each of which is the taxpayer's foreign resource income for the year in respect of a country

exceeds the total of

(II) all amounts each of which is the taxpayer's foreign resource loss for the year in respect of a country, and

(III) the amount deducted under subsection 66(4) in computing the taxpayer's income for the year, and

(b) the lesser of

(i) the amount, if any, by which the particular amount exceeds the amount determined for the year under paragraph (a) in respect of the taxpayer, and

(ii) that portion of the taxpayer's global foreign resource limit for the year that is designated for the year by the taxpayer, in respect of that country and no other country, in prescribed form filed with the Minister with the taxpayer's return of income for the year.

Related Provisions: 20(1)(hh) — Repayments of inducements; 66(5) — No application to certain dealers; 66(11.4)(c) — Change of control; 66(13.1) — Short taxation year; 66.8(1) — Resource expenses of limited partner; 70(5.2)(a) — Death of taxpayer; 87(1.2) — Amalgamation — continuing corporation; 88(1.5) — Windup — parent continuation of subsidiary; 96(1)(d)(ii) — Partnerships — no deduction for resource expenses; 110.6(1)"investment expense"(d) — Effect of claim under 66.21(4) on capital gains exemption; 115(4.1) — Taxable income earned in Canada — foreign resource pool expenses; 127.52(1)(e) — Add-back of deduction for minimum tax purposes.

Notes: See Notes at end of 66.21.

(5) Individual changing residence — Where at any time in a taxation year an individual becomes or ceases to be resident in Canada,

(a) subsection (4) applies to the individual as if the year were the period or periods in the year throughout which the individual was resident in Canada; and

(b) for the purpose of applying this section, subsection 66(13.1) does not apply to the individual for the year.

Related Provisions [subsec. 66.21(5)]: 66.21(1)"cumulative foreign resource expense"A.1 — FRP acquired when taxpayer becomes resident in Canada.

Notes: 66.21 contains the rules governing foreign resource expenses (FRE). FRE is defined in 66.21(1) essentially the same as FEDE, except that there are separate FRE accounts in respect of each country to which FRE relates. FRE is explicitly excluded

from 66(15)"foreign exploration and development expenses". 66.21(3), together with 59(3.2)(c.1), provides for an income inclusion for a "negative" FRE balance. 66.21(4) provides a deduction for the FRE balance (generally not exceeding 30% of the balance at the end of the year).

66.21 added by 2000 Budget, effective for taxation years that end after 2000.

Definitions [s. 66.21]: "adjusted cumulative foreign resource expense" — 66.21(1); "amount" — 248(1); "Canada" — 255, *Interpretation Act* 35(1); "commencement" — *Interpretation Act* 35(1); "cumulative foreign resource expense" — 66.21(1); "depreciable property" — 13(21), 248(1); "disposition" — 248(1); "drilling or exploration expense", "expense" — 66(15), 66.21(2); "fiscal period" — 249.1; "foreign resource expense" — 66.21(1), 248(1); "foreign resource income", "foreign resource loss" — 66.21(1); "foreign resource property" — 66(15), 248(1); "global foreign resource limit" — 66.21(1); "in respect of that country" — 248(1)"foreign resource property"; "individual", "mineral", "mineral resource", "Minister", "oil or gas well" — 248(1); "original owner" — 66(15), 66.21(2); "partnership" — see 96(1) Notes; "prescribed" — 248(1); "production" — 66(15), 66.21(2); "property" — 248(1); "related" — 251(2)–(6); "resident", "resident in Canada" — 250; "share" — 248(1); "taxation year" — 249; "taxpayer" — 248(1).

66.3 (1) Exploration and development shares — Any shares of the capital stock of a corporation or any interest in any such shares or right thereto acquired by a taxpayer under circumstances described in paragraph (i) of the definition "Canadian exploration expense" in subsection 66.1(6), paragraph (g) of the definition "Canadian development expense" in subsection 66.2(5) or paragraph (c) of the definition "Canadian oil and gas property expense" in subsection 66.4(5)

(a) shall, if acquired before November 13, 1981, be deemed

(i) not to be a capital property of the taxpayer,

(ii) subject to subsection 142.6(3), to be inventory of the taxpayer, and

(iii) to have been acquired by the taxpayer at a cost to the taxpayer of nil; and

(b) shall, if acquired after November 12, 1981, be deemed to have been acquired by the taxpayer at a cost to the taxpayer of nil.

Notes: Reference to 142.6(3) in 66.3(1)(a) added by 1994 technical bill, effective for taxation years that begin after Oct. 1994.

66.3(1) originally enacted as 66.3, effective for property acquired after July 1976. A later amendment to this provision by 1979 Budget, and its being changed to 66.3(1), have apparently not preserved this original date of application. It is therefore possible that 66.3(1)(a) applies for shares acquired before August 1976.

Interpretation Bulletins: IT-503: Exploration and development shares (cancelled).

(2) Deductions from paid-up capital — If, at any time after May 23, 1985, a corporation has issued a share of its capital stock under circumstances described in paragraph (i) of the definition "Canadian exploration expense" in subsection 66.1(6), paragraph (g) of the definition "Canadian development expense" in subsection 66.2(5) or paragraph (c) of the definition "Canadian oil and gas property expense" in subsection 66.4(5) or has issued a share of its capital stock on the exercise of an interest in or right to — or, for civil law, a right in or to — such a share granted under circumstances described in any of those paragraphs, in computing, at any particular time after that time, the paid-up capital in respect of the class of shares of the capital stock of the corporation that included that share

(a) there shall be deducted the amount, if any, by which

(i) the increase as a result of the issue of the share in the paid-up capital, determined without reference to this subsection as it applies to the share, in respect of all of the shares of that class

exceeds

(ii) the amount, if any, by which

(A) the total amount of consideration received by the corporation in respect of the share, including any consideration for the interest or right in respect of the share

exceeds

(B) 50% of the amount of the expense referred to in paragraph (i) of the definition "Canadian exploration expense" in subsection 66.1(6), paragraph (g) of the definition "Canadian development expense" in subsection 66.2(5) or paragraph (c) of the definition "Canadian oil and gas property expense" in subsection 66.4(5) that was incurred by a taxpayer who acquired the share or the interest or right on the exercise of which the share was issued, as the case may be, pursuant to an agreement with the corporation under which the taxpayer incurred the expense solely as consideration for the share, interest or right, as the case may be; and

(b) there shall be added an amount equal to the lesser of

(i) the amount, if any, by which

(A) the total of all amounts each of which is an amount deemed by subsection 84(3), (4) or (4.1) to be a dividend on shares of that class paid by the corporation after May 23, 1985 and before the particular time

exceeds

(B) the total that would be determined under clause (A) if this Act were read without reference to paragraph (a), and

(ii) the total of all amounts each of which is an amount required by paragraph (a) to be deducted in computing the paid-up capital in respect of that class of shares after May 22, 1985 and before the particular time.

Notes: 66.3(2) opening words amended by 2002-2013 technical bill (Part 4 — bijuralism), effective June 26, 2013, to add "or, for civil law, a right in or to".

(3) Cost of flow-through shares

— Any flow-through share (within the meaning assigned by subsection 66(15)) of a corporation acquired by a person who was a party to the agreement pursuant to which it was issued shall be deemed to have been acquired by the person at a cost to the person of nil.

Notes: See Notes to 66(12.6) re the *JES Investments* case and re donations of flow-through shares.

66.3(3) does not apply to shares received on a partnership windup where 85(3)(f) applies: VIEWS doc 2018-0751571E5.

(4) Paid-up capital

— Where, at any time after February, 1986, a corporation has issued a flow-through share (within the meaning assigned by subsection 66(15)), in computing, at any particular time after that time, the paid-up capital in respect of the class of shares of the capital stock of the corporation that included that share

(a) there shall be deducted the amount, if any, by which

(i) the increase as a result of the issue of the share in the paid-up capital, determined without reference to this subsection as it applies to the share, in respect of all of the shares of that class

exceeds

(ii) the amount, if any, by which

(A) the total amount of consideration received by the corporation in respect of the share

exceeds

(B) 50% of the total of the expenses that were renounced by the corporation under subsection 66(12.6), (12.601), (12.62) or (12.64) in respect of the share; and

(b) there shall be added an amount equal to the lesser of

(i) the amount, if any, by which

(A) the total of all amounts each of which is an amount deemed by subsection 84(3), (4) or (4.1) to be a dividend on shares of that class paid by the corporation after February, 1986 and before the particular time

exceeds

(B) the total that would be determined under clause (A) if this Act were read without reference to paragraph (a), and

(ii) the total of all amounts each of which is an amount required by paragraph (a) to be deducted in computing the paid-up capital in respect of that class of shares after February, 1986 and before the particular time.

Notes: Reference to 66(12.601) in 66.3(4)(a)(ii)(B) added by 1992 Economic Statement, effective December 3, 1992.

Related Provisions [s. 66.3]: 66(16) — Partnerships — person — taxation year; 66.4(2) — Deduction — COGPE; 66.7 — Successor rules.

Definitions [s. 66.3]: "amount" — 248(1); "capital property" — 54, 248(1); "class of shares" — 248(6); "corporation" — 248(1), *Interpretation Act* 35(1); "dividend", "inventory" — 248(1); "paid-up capital" — 89(1), 248(1); "person" — 66(16), 248(1); "share", "taxpayer" — 248(1).

66.4 [Canadian oil and gas property expenses] — (1) Recovery of costs

— For the purposes of the description of B in the definition "cumulative Canadian oil and gas property expense" in subsection (5) and the description of L in the definition "cumulative Canadian development expense" in subsection 66.2(5) and for the purpose of subparagraph 64(1.2)(a)(ii) of the *Income Tax Act*, chapter 148 of the Revised Statutes of Canada, 1952, as it applies to dispositions occurring before November 13, 1981, the amount determined under this subsection in respect of a taxpayer for a taxation year is the amount, if any, by which

(a) the total of all amounts referred to in the descriptions of E to J in the definition "cumulative Canadian oil and gas property expense" in subsection (5) that are deducted in computing the taxpayer's cumulative Canadian oil and gas property expense at the end of the year

exceeds the total of

(b) all amounts referred to in the descriptions of A to D.1 in the definition "cumulative Canadian oil and gas property expense" in subsection (5) that are included in computing the taxpayer's cumulative Canadian oil and gas property expense at the end of the year, and

(c) the total determined under subparagraph 66.7(12.1)(c)(i) in respect of the taxpayer for the year.

Related Provisions: 66(11.4) — Change of control; 66(13) — Limitation; 104(5.2) — Trusts — 21-year deemed disposition. See also at end of s. 66.4.

Notes: See Notes to 66.4(2).

66.4(1)(c) added by 1991 technical bill and amended by 1993 technical bill, effective for taxation years ending after February 17, 1987.

I.T. Application Rules: 69 (meaning of "chapter 148 of ...").

(2) Deduction for cumulative Canadian oil and gas property expense

— A taxpayer may deduct, in computing the taxpayer's income for a taxation year, such amount as the taxpayer may claim not exceeding the total of

(a) the lesser of

(i) the total of

(A) the taxpayer's cumulative Canadian oil and gas property expense at the end of the year, and

(B) the amount, if any, by which

(I) the total determined under subparagraph 66.7(12.1)(c)(i) in respect of the taxpayer for the year

exceeds

(II) the amount that would, but for paragraph (1)(c), be determined under subsection (1) in respect of the taxpayer for the year, and

(ii) the amount, if any, by which the total of all amounts each of which is

(A) an amount included in the taxpayer's income for the year by virtue of a disposition in the year of inventory described in section 66.3 that was a share or any interest in or right to — or, for civil law, any right in or to — a share acquired by the taxpayer under circumstances described in paragraph (c) of the definition "Canadian oil and gas property expense" in subsection (5), or

(B) an amount included by virtue of paragraph 12(1)(e) in computing the taxpayer's income for the year to the extent that it relates to inventory described in clause (A)

exceeds

    (C) the total of all amounts deducted as a reserve by virtue of paragraph 20(1)(n) in computing the taxpayer's income for the year to the extent that the reserve relates to inventory described in clause (A);

(b) 10% of the amount, if any, by which the amount determined under subparagraph (a)(i) exceeds the amount determined under subparagraph (a)(ii); and

(c) the amount determined by the formula

$$A(B - C)$$

where

A is

    (i) for taxation years that end before 2024, 5%,

    (ii) for taxation years that begin before 2024 and end after 2023, the amount determined by the formula

$$0.05(I/J) + 0.025(K/J)$$

    where

    I is the total of all accelerated Canadian oil and gas property expenses incurred by the taxpayer before 2024 and in the taxation year,

    J is the total of all accelerated Canadian oil and gas property expenses incurred by the taxpayer in the taxation year, and

    K is the total of all accelerated Canadian oil and gas property expenses incurred by the taxpayer after 2023 and in the taxation year, and

    (iii) for taxation years that begin after 2023, 2.5%,

B is the total of all accelerated Canadian oil and gas property expenses incurred by the taxpayer in the taxation year, and

C is the amount determined by the formula

$$(D - E) - (F - G - H)$$

where

D is the total of the amounts determined for E to J in the definition "cumulative Canadian oil and gas property expense" in subsection (5) at the end of the taxation year,

E is the total of the amounts determined for E to J in the definition "cumulative Canadian oil and gas property expense" in subsection (5) at the beginning of the taxation year,

F is the total of the amounts determined for A to D.1 in the definition "cumulative Canadian oil and gas property expense" in subsection (5) at the end of the taxation year,

G is the total of the amounts determined for A to D.1 in the definition "cumulative Canadian oil and gas property expense" in subsection (5) at the end of the preceding taxation year, and

H is the amount determined for B.

Related Provisions: 20(1)(hh) — Repayments of inducements, etc.; 66(11.6)(a) — Application of successor rules on change in control of trust; 66(13.1) — Short taxation year; 66.2(2) — Deduction for cumulative CDE; 110.6(1)"investment expense"(d) — effect of claim under 66.4(2) on capital gains exemption; 127.52(1)(e) — Add-back of deduction for minimum tax purposes; 257 — Formula cannot calculate to less than zero. See also at end of s. 66.4.

Notes: 66.4(2) allows a deduction of 10% of CCOGPE at the end of the year; see 66.4(5)"cumulative Canadian oil and gas property expense". 66.4(1), in conjunction with 66.2(5)"cumulative Canadian development expense"L, requires any negative balance in CCOGPE at the end of the year to reduce CCDE, which will result in an income inclusion under 66.2(1) and 59(3.2)(c) if a negative CCDE balance arises (e.g., VIEWS doc 2018-0739741E5).

66.4(2)(c) (added by 2019 budget bill #1, effective June 21, 2019) provides additional first-year COGPE for "accelerated Canadian oil and gas property expense" (defined in 66.4(5)), as part of the Accelerated Investment Incentive (see Notes to Reg. 1100(2)). The additional deduction is 5% of expenses incurred from Nov. 21, 2018 through 2023 (i.e., total 15%), and 2.5% for 2024-2027.

66.4(2)(a)(ii)(A) amended by 2002-2013 technical bill (Part 4 — bijuralism), effective June 26, 2013, to change "a share, any interest therein or right thereto" to "a share or any interest in or right to — or, for civil law, a right in or to — a share".

66.4(2) amended by 1991 technical bill, for taxation years ending after Feb. 17, 1987.

Interpretation Bulletins: IT-273R2: Government assistance — general comments; IT-438R2: Crown charges — resource properties in Canada.

(3), (4) [Repealed under former Act]

Notes: 66.4(3) and (4), repealed in 1987, dealt with a successor corporation's Canadian oil and gas property expenses. See now 66.7.

(5) Definitions — In this section

"accelerated Canadian oil and gas property expense", of a taxpayer, means any cost or expense incurred by the taxpayer during a taxation year, if the cost or expense

    (a) qualifies as a Canadian oil and gas property expense at the time it is incurred, other than

        (i) an expense in respect of which the taxpayer is a successor, within the meaning of subsection 66.7(5), and

        (ii) a cost in respect of a Canadian resource property acquired by the taxpayer, or a partnership in which the taxpayer is a member, from a person or partnership with which the taxpayer does not deal at arm's length, and

    (b) is incurred after November 20, 2018 and before 2028;

Notes: See Notes to 66.4(2). Definition added by 2019 budget bill #1, effective March 19, 2019.

Related Provisions: 66(15.1) — Application to s. 66; 66.1(6.1) — Application to s. 66.1; 66.2(5.1) — Application to s. 66.2.

Notes: Before RSC 1985 (5th Suppl) consolidation, the opening words of 66.4(5) referred to ss. 66, 66.1 and 66.2. See now 66(15.1), 66.1(6.1) and 66.2(5.1).

"Canadian oil and gas property expense" of a taxpayer means any cost or expense incurred after December 11, 1979 that is

    (a) the cost to the taxpayer of, including any payment for the preservation of a taxpayer's rights in respect of, any property described in paragraph (a), (c) or (d) of the definition "Canadian resource property" in subsection 66(15) or any right to or interest in — or, for civil law, any right in or to — the property (other than a right or an interest that the taxpayer has by reason of being a beneficiary under a trust or a member of a partnership), or an amount paid to Her Majesty in right of the Province of Saskatchewan as a net royalty payment pursuant to a net royalty petroleum and natural gas lease that was in effect on March 31, 1977 to the extent that it can reasonably be regarded as a cost of acquiring the lease,

    (b) subject to section 66.8, the taxpayer's share of any expense referred to in paragraph (a) incurred by a partnership in a fiscal period thereof at the end of which the taxpayer was a member of the partnership, unless the taxpayer elects in respect of the share in prescribed form and manner on or before the day that is 6 months after the taxpayer's taxation year in which that period ends, or

    (c) any cost or expense referred to in paragraph (a) incurred by the taxpayer pursuant to an agreement in writing with a corporation, entered into before 1987, under which the taxpayer incurred the cost or expense solely as consideration for shares, other than prescribed shares, of the capital stock of the corporation issued to the taxpayer or any interest in or right to — or, for civil law, any right in or to — such shares,

but, for greater certainty, shall not include

    (d) any consideration given by the taxpayer for any share or any interest therein or right thereto, except as provided by paragraph (c), or

    (e) any expense described in paragraph (c) incurred by any other taxpayer to the extent that the expense was,

        (i) by virtue of that paragraph, a Canadian oil and gas property expense of that other taxpayer,

(ii) by virtue of paragraph (i) of the definition "Canadian exploration expense" in subsection 66.1(6), a Canadian exploration expense of that other taxpayer, or

(iii) by virtue of paragraph (g) of the definition "Canadian development expense" in subsection 66.2(5), a Canadian development expense of that other taxpayer,

but any amount of assistance that a taxpayer has received or is entitled to receive in respect of or related to the taxpayer's Canadian oil and gas property expense shall not reduce the amount of any of the expenses described in any of paragraphs (a) to (c);

Related Provisions: 34.2(1)"qualified resource expense"(d), 34.2(6) — COGPE qualifies for deduction from corporate accrual of partnership income; 49(2) — Where option expires; 53(1)(e)(vii.1) — Addition to ACB — partnership interest; 66(12.5) — Unitized oil or gas field in Canada; 66.2(8) — Presumption; 66.3 — Exploration and development shares; 66.4(1) — Recovery of costs; 66.4(2) — Deduction for cumulative COGPE; 248(1)"Canadian oil and gas property expense" — Definition applies to entire Act; 248(16), (16.1) — GST or QST input tax credit/refund and rebate deemed to be assistance; 248(18), (18.1) — GST or QST — repayment of input tax credit or refund. See also at end of s. 66; *Interpretation Act* 8(2.1), (2.2) — Application to exclusive economic zone and continental shelf. See also at end of s. 66.4.

Notes: See Mar, Rowe & Bereti, "Basic Issues in Resource Taxation", 2008 Cdn Tax Foundation conference report, 10:1-32.

The cost of subsurface rights may be COGPE or CDE: VIEWS doc 2016-0637221E5.

Definition amended by 2002-2013 technical bill (last change effective June 26, 2013), 2003 resource bill, 1992 technical bill. 66.4(5)"Canadian oil and gas property expense" was 66.4(5)(a) before RSC 1985 (5th Supp) consolidation for tax years ending after Nov. 1991.

Regulations: 6202 (prescribed share).

Interpretation Bulletins: IT-109R2: Unpaid amounts; IT-273R2: Government assistance — general comments; IT-438R2: Crown charges — resource properties in Canada; IT-503: Exploration and development shares (cancelled).

Forms: T2 Sched. 12: Resource-related deductions; T1086: Election by a partner waiving Canadian development expenses or oil and gas property expenses.

"cumulative Canadian oil and gas property expense" of a taxpayer at any time in a taxation year means the amount determined by the formula

$$(A + B + C + D + D.1)$$
$$- (E + F + G + H + I + I.1 + J)$$

where

A   is the total of all Canadian oil and gas property expenses made or incurred by the taxpayer before that time,

B   is the total of all amounts determined under subsection (1) in respect of the taxpayer for taxation years ending before that time,

C   is the total of all amounts referred to in the description of F or G that are established by the taxpayer to have become bad debts before that time,

D   is such part, if any, of the amount determined for I as has been repaid before that time by the taxpayer pursuant to a legal obligation to repay all or any part of that amount,

D.1 is the total of all specified amounts, determined under paragraph 66.7(12.1)(c) in respect of the taxpayer for taxation years ending before that time,

E   is the total of all amounts deducted in computing the taxpayer's income for a taxation year ending before that time in respect of the taxpayer's cumulative Canadian oil and gas property expense,

F   is the total of all amounts each of which is an amount in respect of property described in paragraph (a), (c) or (d) of the definition "Canadian resource property" in subsection 66(15) or any right to or interest in — or, for civil law, any right in or to — such a property, other than such a right or interest that the taxpayer has by reason of being a beneficiary under a trust or a member of a partnership, (in this description referred to as "the particular property") disposed of by the taxpayer before that time equal to the amount, if any, by which

(a) the amount, if any, by which the proceeds of disposition in respect of the particular property that became receivable

by the taxpayer before that time exceed any outlays or expenses made or incurred by the taxpayer before that time for the purpose of making the disposition and that were not otherwise deductible for the purposes of this Part

exceeds the total of

(b) the amount, if any, by which

(i) the total of all amounts that would be determined under paragraph 66.7(5)(a), immediately before the time (in this paragraph and paragraph (c) referred to as the "relevant time") when such proceeds of disposition became receivable, in respect of the taxpayer and an original owner of the particular property (or of any other property acquired by the taxpayer with the particular property in circumstances in which subsection 66.7(5) applied and in respect of which the proceeds of disposition became receivable by the taxpayer at the relevant time) if

(A) amounts that became receivable at or after the relevant time were not taken into account,

(B) each designation made under subparagraph 66.7(4)(a)(iii) in respect of an amount that became receivable before the relevant time were made before the relevant time,

(C) paragraph 66.7(5)(a) were read without reference to "10% of", and

(D) no reduction under subsection 80(8) at or after the relevant time were taken into account

exceeds the total of

(ii) all amounts that would be determined under paragraph 66.7(5)(a) at the relevant time in respect of the taxpayer and an original owner of the particular property (or of that other property described in subparagraph (i)) if

(A) amounts that became receivable after the relevant time were not taken into account,

(B) each designation made under subparagraph 66.7(4)(a)(iii) in respect of an amount that became receivable at or before the relevant time were made before the relevant time,

(C) paragraph 66.7(5)(a) were read without reference to "10% of", and

(D) no reduction under subsection 80(8) at or after the relevant time were taken into account, and

(iii) such portion of the amount determined under this paragraph as was otherwise applied to reduce the amount otherwise determined under this description, and

(c) the amount, if any, by which

(i) the total of all amounts that would be determined under paragraph 66.7(4)(a), immediately before the relevant time, in respect of the taxpayer and an original owner of the particular property (or of any other property acquired by the taxpayer with the particular property in circumstances in which subsection 66.7(4) applied and in respect of which the proceeds of disposition became receivable by the taxpayer at the relevant time) if

(A) amounts that became receivable at or after the relevant time were not taken into account,

(B) each designation made under subparagraph 66.7(4)(a)(iii) in respect of an amount that became receivable before the relevant time were made before the relevant time,

(C) paragraph 66.7(4)(a) were read without reference to "30% of", and

(D) no reduction under subsection 80(8) at or after the relevant time were taken into account

exceeds the total of

(ii) all amounts that would be determined under paragraph 66.7(4)(a) at the relevant time in respect of the taxpayer and an original owner of the particular property (or of that other property described in subparagraph (i)) if

(A) amounts that became receivable after the relevant time were not taken into account,

(B) each designation made under subparagraph 66.7(4)(a)(iii) in respect of an amount that became receivable at or before the relevant time were made before the relevant time,

(C) paragraph 66.7(4)(a) were read without reference to "30% of",

(D) amounts described in subparagraph 66.7(4)(a)(ii) that became receivable at the relevant time were not taken into account, and

(E) no reduction under subsection 80(8) at or after the relevant time were taken into account, and

(iii) such portion of the amount otherwise determined under this paragraph as was otherwise applied to reduce the amount otherwise determined under this description,

G is the total of all amounts that became receivable by the taxpayer before that time that are to be included in the amount determined under this description by virtue of paragraph 66(12.5)(a),

H is the total of all amounts each of which is an amount received before that time on account of any amount referred to in the description of C,

I is the total amount of assistance that the taxpayer has received or is entitled to receive in respect of any Canadian oil and gas property expense incurred after 1980 or that can reasonably be related to any such expense after 1980,

I.1 is the total of all amounts by which the cumulative Canadian oil and gas property expense of the taxpayer is required because of subsection 80(8) to be reduced at or before that time, and

J is the total of all amounts that are required to be deducted before that time under paragraph 66.7(12)(d) in computing the taxpayer's cumulative Canadian oil and gas property expense;

Related Provisions: 20(1)(kk) — Exploration and development grants; 50(1)(a) — Deemed disposition where debt becomes bad debt; 66(12.5) — Unitized oil or gas field in Canada; 66.7(5) — Deduction to successor corporation; 70(5.2) — Resource properties and land inventories of deceased taxpayer; 79(4)(c) — Subsequent payment by debtor after surrender of property deemed to be repayment of assistance; 79.1(8) — No claim for principal amount of bad debt where property seized by creditor; 80(8)(d) — Reduction of CCOGPE on debt forgiveness; 96(2.2)(d) — At-risk amount; 104(5.2) — Trusts — 21-year deemed disposition; 248(16), (16.1) — GST or QST input tax credit/refund and rebate deemed to be assistance; 248(18), (18.1) — GST or QST repayment of input tax credit/refund; 257 — Formula cannot calculate to less than zero; 261(7)(d) — Functional currency reporting. See also at end of s. 66.4.

Notes: A payment on entering into a petroleum and natural gas lease is Canadian resource property (66(15)) that may be added to CCOGPE: VIEWS doc 2007-0227981E5. Granting such a lease is a disposition that reduces CCOGPE, and a negative balance is added to income: doc 2013-0486901E5.

Opening words of F amended by 2002-2013 technical bill (Part 4 — bijuralism), effective June 26, 2013, to add "or, for civil law, a right in or to".

Description of F amended by 2003 resource bill, effective for 2003 and later taxation years. 66.4(5)"cumulative Canadian oil and gas property expense" was 66.4(5)(b) before RSC 1985 (5th Supp) consolidation for tax years ending after Nov. 1991.

Interpretation Bulletins: IT-125R4: Dispositions of resource properties; IT-273R2: Government assistance — general comments.

"proceeds of disposition" has the meaning assigned by section 54.

Notes: Definition amended by 2001 technical bill, to delete definition of "disposition" (also referring to s. 54), effective for transactions and events that occur after December 23, 1998. See now 248(1)"disposition".

66.4(5)"disposition" and "proceeds of disposition" were 66.4(5)(c) before RSC 1985 (5th Supp) consolidation for tax years ending after Nov. 1991.

(5.1) Application of subsecs. 66(15) and 66.1(6) — The definitions in subsections 66(15) and 66.1(6) apply to this section.

Notes: 66.4(5.1) added in the RSC 1985 (5th Supp) consolidation, effective for tax years ending after Nov. 1991 (formerly contained in the opening words of subsecs. 66(15) and 66.1(6)).

(6) Share of partner — Except as provided in subsection (7), where a taxpayer is a member of a partnership, the taxpayer's share of any amount that would be an amount referred to in the description of D in the definition "cumulative Canadian oil and gas property expense" in subsection (5), in paragraph (a) of the description of F in that definition or in the description of G or I in that definition in respect of the partnership for a taxation year of the partnership if section 96 were read without reference to paragraph 96(1)(d) shall, for the purposes of this Act, be deemed to be an amount referred to in the description of D in the definition "cumulative Canadian oil and gas property expense" in subsection (5), in paragraph (a) of the description of F in that definition or in the description of G or I in that definition, whichever is applicable, in respect of the taxpayer for the taxation year of the taxpayer in which the partnership's taxation year ends.

Related Provisions: 59(1.1) — Parallel rule for foreign resource property; 66.2(6) — Parallel rule for CCDE.

Notes: For discussion of 66.4(6) see Greg Johnson, "Timing Issues on Allocating Resource Expenses and Resource Proceeds to Withdrawing Partners", V(2) *Resource Sector Taxation* (Federated Press) 338-45 (2007).

For a ruling applying 66.4(6), see VIEWS doc 2005-0147681R3.

66.4(6) amended by 1991 technical bill, effective February 1990.

Interpretation Bulletins: IT-125R4: Dispositions of resource properties; IT-273R2: Government assistance — general comments; IT-353R2: Partnership interests — some adjustments to cost base (cancelled).

I.T. Technical News: 12 (adjusted cost base of partnership interest — subparagraph 53(1)(e)(viii)).

(7) Exception — Where a non-resident person is a member of a partnership that is deemed under paragraph 115(4)(b) to have disposed of any Canadian resource property, the person's share of any amount that would be an amount referred to in the description of D in the definition "cumulative Canadian oil and gas property expense" in subsection (5), in paragraph (a) of the description of F in that definition or in the description of G or I in that definition in respect of the partnership for a taxation year of the partnership if section 96 were read without reference to paragraph 96(1)(d) shall, for the purposes of this Act, be deemed to be an amount referred to in the description of D in the definition "cumulative Canadian oil and gas property expense" in subsection (5), in paragraph (a) of the description of F in that definition or in the description of G or I in that definition, whichever is applicable, in respect of the person for the taxation year of the person that is deemed under paragraph 115(4)(a) to have ended.

Notes: References to "cumulative Canadian oil and gas property expense"D (formerly 66.4(5)(b)(iii.1)) added to 66.4(7) by 1991 technical bill, effective for partnerships' taxation years beginning after 1984.

Interpretation Bulletins: IT-125R4: Dispositions of resource properties; IT-273R2: Government assistance — general comments.

Related Provisions [s. 66.4]: 66(5) — Dealers; 66(18) — Members of partnerships; 66.7 — Successor rules; 66.8(1) — Resource expenses of limited partner; 87(1.2) — New corporation deemed continuation of predecessor.

Definitions [s. 66.4]: "accelerated Canadian oil and gas property expense" — 66.4(5); "amount" — 248(1); "arm's length" — 251(1); "assistance" — 66(15), 66.1(6.1), 79(4), 125.4(5), 248(16), (16.1), (18), (18.1); "Canada" — 255, *Interpretation Act* 8(2.1), (2.2); "Canadian exploration expense" — 66.1(6), 66.4(5.1), 248(1); "Canadian oil and gas property expense" — 66.4(5), 248(1); "Canadian resource property" — 66(15), 66.4(5.1), 248(1); "corporation" — 248(1), *Interpretation Act* 35(1); "disposition" — 248(1), 66.4(5.1); "expense" — 66(15), 66.4(5.1); "fiscal period" — 249.1; "Her Majesty" — *Interpretation Act* 35(1); "inventory", "mineral", "non-resident", "oil or gas well" — 248(1); "partnership" — see 96(1) Notes; "person", "prescribed" — 248(1); "proceeds of disposition" — 54, 66.4(5); "property", "share" — 248(1); "successor" — 66.7(5); "taxation year" — 11(2), 249; "taxpayer" — 248(1); "writing" — *Interpretation Act* 35(1).

Interpretation Bulletins [s. 66.4]: IT-273R2: Government assistance — general comments.

66.5 [No longer relevant]

Notes: 66.5 relates to payments under the *Petroleum and Gas Revenue Tax Act* and has not applied since 1986. See Carr & Calverley, *Canadian Resource Taxation* (Carswell, looseleaf or *Taxnet Pro* Reference Centre), chap. 12.

66.6 Acquisition from tax-exempt [person] — Where a corporation acquires, by purchase, amalgamation, merger, winding-up or otherwise, all or substantially all of the Canadian resource properties or foreign resource properties of a person whose taxable income is exempt from tax under this Part, subsection 29(25) of the *Income Tax Application Rules* and subsections 66.7(1) to (5) do not apply to the corporation in respect of the acquisition of the properties.

Related Provisions: 66.7 — Successor rules; 66.8(1) — Resource expenses of limited partner.

Notes: CRA considers that "substantially all" means 90% or more.

66.6 amended by 1995-97 technical bill, for acquisitions after April 26, 1995, with grandfathering to the end of 1995.

Definitions [s. 66.6]: "business" — 248(1); "corporation" — 248(1), *Interpretation Act* 35(1); "person", "property" — 248(1); "taxable income" — 2(2), 248(1); "writing" — *Interpretation Act* 35(1).

Interpretation Bulletins: IT-126R2: Meaning of "winding-up".

66.7 (1) Successor of Canadian exploration and development expenses — Subject to subsections (6) and (7), where after 1971 a corporation (in this subsection referred to as the "successor") acquired a particular Canadian resource property (whether by way of a purchase, amalgamation, merger, winding-up or otherwise), there may be deducted by the successor in computing its income for a taxation year an amount not exceeding the total of all amounts each of which is an amount determined in respect of an original owner of the particular property that is the lesser of

(a) the Canadian exploration and development expenses incurred by the original owner before the original owner disposed of the particular property to the extent that those expenses were not otherwise deducted in computing the income of the successor for the year, were not deducted in computing the income of the successor for a preceding taxation year and were not deductible under subsection 66(1) or deducted under subsection 66(2) or (3) by the original owner, or deducted by any predecessor owner of the particular property, in computing income for any taxation year, and

(b) the amount, if any, by which

(i) the part of the successor's income for the year that may reasonably be regarded as attributable to

(A) the amount included in computing its income for the year under paragraph 59(3.2)(c) that may reasonably be regarded as attributable to the disposition by it in the year or a preceding taxation year of any interest in or right to — or, for civil law, any right in or to — the particular property to the extent that the proceeds of the disposition have not been included in determining an amount under clause 29(25)(d)(i)(A) of the *Income Tax Application Rules*, this clause, clause (3)(b)(i)(A) or paragraph (10)(g) for a preceding taxation year,

(B) its reserve amount for the year in respect of the original owner and each predecessor owner, if any, of the particular property, or

(C) production from the particular property,

computed as if no deduction were allowed under section 29 of the *Income Tax Application Rules*, this section or any of sections 65 to 66.5,

exceeds the total of

(ii) all other amounts deducted under subsection 29(25) of the *Income Tax Application Rules*, this subsection and subsections (3), (4) and (5) for the year that can reasonably be regarded as attributable to the part of its income for the year described in subparagraph (i) in respect of the particular property, and

(iii) all amounts added because of subsection 80(13) in computing the amount determined under subparagraph (i).

Related Provisions: 66(1) — Exploration and development expenses; 66(11.6)(a) — Application of successor rules on change in control of trust; 66.7(2.3) — Income deemed not attributable to production from Canadian resource property; 66.7(6), (7) — Application rules; 66.7(10) — Change of control; 66.7(10.1) — Amalgamation — partnership property; 66.7(11) — Change of control — anti-avoidance rule; 66.7(12) — Reduction of Canadian resource expenses; 66.7(14) — Disposal of Canadian resource properties; 66.7(16) — Non-successor acquisitions; 66.7(17) — Restriction on deductions. See also at end of s. 66.7.

Notes: See Notes at end of 66.7. 66.7(1)(b)(i)(A) amended by 2002-2013 technical bill (Part 4 — bijuralism), effective June 26, 2013, to add "or, for civil law, any right in or to".

66.7(1) earlier amended by 1995-97 technical bill (for taxation years ending after Feb. 21, 1994), 1994 technical bill, 1991 technical bill.

Forms: T2010: Election to deduct resource expenses upon acquisition of resource property by a corporation.

(2) Successor of foreign exploration and development expenses — Subject to subsections (6) and (8), where after 1971 a corporation (in this subsection referred to as the "successor") acquired a particular foreign resource property (whether by way of a purchase, amalgamation, merger, winding-up or otherwise), there may be deducted by the successor in computing its income for a taxation year an amount not exceeding the total of all amounts each of which is an amount determined in respect of an original owner of the particular property that is the lesser of

(a) the amount, if any, by which

(i) the foreign exploration and development expenses incurred by the original owner before the original owner disposed of the particular property to the extent that those expenses were incurred when the original owner was resident in Canada, were not otherwise deducted in computing the successor's income for the year, were not deducted in computing the successor's income for a preceding taxation year and were not deductible by the original owner, nor deducted by any predecessor owner of the particular property, in computing income for any taxation year

exceeds

(ii) the total of all amounts each of which is an amount by which the amount described in this paragraph is required because of subsection 80(8) to be reduced at or before the end of the year, and

(b) the amount, if any, by which the total of

(i) the part of the successor's income for the year that can reasonably be regarded as attributable to

(A) the amount included under subsection 59(1) in computing its income for the year that can reasonably be regarded as attributable to the disposition by it of any interest in or right to — or, for civil law, any right in or to — the particular property, or

(B) production from the particular property,

computed as if no deduction were allowed under sections 65 to 66.5 and this section, and

(ii) the lesser of

(A) the total of all amounts each of which is the amount designated by the successor for the year in respect of a Canadian resource property owned by the original owner immediately before being acquired with the particular property by the successor or a predecessor owner of the particular property, not exceeding the amount included in the successor's income for the year, computed as if no deduction were allowed under section 29 of the *Income Tax Application Rules*, this section or any of sections 65 to 66.5, that can reasonably be regarded as being attributable to the production after 1988 from the Canadian resource property, and

(B) the amount, if any, by which 10% of the amount described in paragraph (a) for the year in respect of the original owner exceeds the total of all amounts each of which would, but for this subparagraph, clause (iii)(B) and subparagraph (10)(h)(vi), be determined under this paragraph for the year in respect of the particular property or other foreign resource property owned by the original owner immediately before being acquired with the particular property by the successor or a predecessor owner of the particular property

exceeds the total of

(iii) all other amounts deducted under this subsection for the year that can reasonably be regarded as attributable to

(A) the part of its income for the year described in subparagraph (i) in respect of the particular property, or

(B) a part of its income for the year described in clause (ii)(A) in respect of which an amount is designated by the successor under clause (ii)(A), and

(iv) all amounts added because of subsection 80(13) in computing the amount determined under subparagraph (i),

and income in respect of which an amount is designated under clause (b)(ii)(A) shall, for the purposes of clause 29(25)(d)(i)(B) of the *Income Tax Application Rules*, clauses (1)(b)(i)(C), (3)(b)(i)(C), (4)(b)(i)(B) and (5)(b)(i)(B) and subparagraph (10)(g)(iii), be deemed not to be attributable to production from a Canadian resource property.

Related Provisions: 66(4) — Foreign exploration and development expenses; 66(11.6)(a) — Application of successor rules on change in control of trust; 66.7(2.1), (2.2) — Country-by-country successor FEDE allocations; 66.7(2.3) — Income deemed not attributable to production from Canadian resource property; 66.7(6), (8) — Application rules; 66.7(10) — Change of control; 66.7(10.1) — Amalgamation — partnership property; 66.7(11) — Change of control — anti-avoidance rule; 66.7(13) — Reduction of foreign resource expenses; 66.7(15) — Disposal of foreign resource properties; 66.7(16) — Non-successor acquisitions; 66.7(17) — Restriction on deductions; 80(1)"successor pool" — Debt forgiveness; 80(8)(a) — Reduction of undeducted balances on debt forgiveness. See also at end of s. 66.7.

Notes: See Notes at end of 66.7. 66.7(2)(b)(i)(A) amended by 2002-2013 technical bill, effective June 26, 2013, to add "or, for civil law, any right in or to".

66.7(2) earlier amended by 2001 technical bill (for 1999 and later taxation years), 1995-97 technical bill, 1994 technical bill, 1993 and 1991 technical bills.

Forms: T2010: Election to deduct resource expenses upon acquisition of resource property by a corporation.

(2.1) Country-by-country successor FEDE allocations — For greater certainty, the portion of an amount deducted under subsection (2) in computing a taxpayer's income for a taxation year that can reasonably be considered to be in respect of specified foreign exploration and development expenses of the taxpayer in respect of a country is considered to apply to a source in that country.

Related Provisions: 66(4.1) — Parallel rule for predecessor; 66.7(2.2) — Method of allocation.

Notes: 66.7(2.1) added by 2000 Budget, effective for taxation years that begin after 1999, or earlier by designation (see Notes to 126(5)).

(2.2) Method of allocation — For the purpose of subsection (2.1), where a taxpayer has incurred specified foreign exploration and development expenses in respect of two or more countries, an allocation to each of those countries for a taxation year shall be determined in a manner that is

(a) reasonable having regard to all the circumstances, including the level and timing of

(i) the taxpayer's specified foreign exploration and development expenses in respect of the country, and

(ii) the profits or gains to which those expenses relate; and

(b) not inconsistent with the allocation made under subsection (2.1) for the preceding taxation year.

Related Provisions: 66(4.2) — Parallel rule for predecessor.

Notes: 66.7(2.2) added by 2000 Budget, for taxation years that begin after 1999, or earlier by designation (see Notes to 126(5)).

(2.3) Successor of foreign resource expenses — Subject to subsections (6) and (8), where a corporation (in this subsection referred to as the "successor") acquired a particular foreign resource property in respect of a country (whether by way of a purchase, amalgamation, merger, winding-up or otherwise), there may be deducted by the successor in computing its income for a taxation year an amount not exceeding the total of all amounts each of which is an amount determined in respect of an original owner of the particular property that is the lesser of

(a) 30% of the amount, if any, by which

(i) the cumulative foreign resource expense, in respect of the country, of the original owner determined immediately after the disposition of the particular property by the original owner to the extent that it has not been

(A) deducted by the original owner or any predecessor owner of the particular property in computing income for any taxation year,

(B) otherwise deducted in computing the income of the successor for the year, or

(C) deducted by the successor in computing its income for any preceding taxation year

exceeds the total of

(ii) all amounts each of which is an amount (other than any portion of the amount that can reasonably be considered to result in a reduction of the amount otherwise determined under this paragraph in respect of another original owner of a relevant resource property who is not a predecessor owner of a relevant resource property or who became a predecessor owner of a relevant resource property before the original owner became a predecessor owner of a relevant resource property) that became receivable by a predecessor owner of the particular property, or by the successor in the year or a preceding taxation year, and that

(A) was included by the predecessor owner or the successor in computing an amount determined under paragraph (a) of the description of F in the definition "cumulative foreign resource expense" in subsection 66.21(1) at the end of the year, and

(B) can reasonably be regarded as attributable to the disposition of a property (in this subparagraph referred to as a "relevant resource property") that is

(I) the particular property, or

(II) another foreign resource property in respect of the country that was acquired from the original owner with the particular property by the successor or a predecessor owner of the particular property, and

(iii) all amounts each of which is an amount by which the amount described in this paragraph is required by reason of subsection 80(8) to be reduced at or before the end of the year, and

(b) the amount, if any, by which the total of

(i) the part of the successor's income for the year that can reasonably be regarded as attributable to production from the particular property, computed as if no deduction were permitted under section 29 of the *Income Tax Application Rules*, this section or any of sections 65 to 66.5, except that, where the successor acquired the particular property from the original owner at any time in the year (otherwise than by way of an amalgamation or merger or solely by reason of the application of paragraph (10)(c)) and did not deal with the original owner at arm's length at that time, the amount determined under this subparagraph is deemed to be nil, and

(ii) unless the amount determined under subparagraph (i) is nil by reason of the exception provided under that subparagraph, the lesser of

(A) the total of all amounts each of which is the amount designated by the successor in respect of a Canadian resource property owned by the original owner immediately before being acquired with the particular property by the successor or a predecessor owner of the particular property, not exceeding the amount included in the successor's income for the year, computed as if no deduction were permitted under section 29 of the *Income Tax Application Rules*, this section or any of sections 65 to 66.5, that can reasonably be regarded as being attributable to the production from the Canadian resource property, and

(B) the amount, if any, by which 10% of the amount described in paragraph (a) for the year, in respect of the original owner, exceeds the total of all amounts each of which would, but for this subparagraph, clause (2)(b)(iii)(B) and subparagraph (10)(h)(vi), be determined under this paragraph for the year in respect of the particular property or other foreign resource property, in respect of the country, owned by the original owner immediately before being acquired with the particular property by the successor or by a predecessor owner of the particular property

exceeds the total of

(iii) all other amounts each of which is an amount deducted for the year under this subsection or subsection (2) that can reasonably be regarded as attributable to

(A) the part of its income for the year described in subparagraph (i) in respect of the particular property, or

(B) a part of its income for the year described in clause (ii)(A) in respect of which an amount is designated by the successor under clause (ii)(A), and

(iv) all amounts added by reason of subsection 80(13) in computing the amount determined under subparagraph (i),

and income in respect of which an amount is designated under clause (b)(ii)(A) is, for the purposes of clause 29(25)(d)(i)(B) of the *Income Tax Application Rules*, clauses (1)(b)(i)(C), (3)(b)(i)(C), (4)(b)(i)(B) and (5)(b)(i)(B) and subparagraph (10)(g)(iii), deemed not to be attributable to production from a Canadian resource property.

Related Provisions: 66(11.6)(a) — Application of successor rules on change in control of trust; 66(13.1) — Short taxation year; 66.21(1)"cumulative foreign resource expense"F(b)(i); 66.7(8) — Application; 66.7(10)(h)(v), (vi), 66.7(10)(j)(ii) — Change of control; 66.7(10.1) — Amalgamation — partnership property; 66.7(13.1) — Reduction of foreign resource expenses; 66.7(15.1) — Disposal of foreign resource properties; 80(8)(a) — Debt forgiveness; 248(1)"foreign resource property" — Meaning of foreign resource property in respect of a country.

Notes: 66.7(2.3) added by 2000 Budget, for tax years that begin after 2000. It provides for the transfer of an original owner's unused foreign resource expense (FRE) balance, on acquisition of foreign resource properties in circumstances where the successor rules apply. It is structured much like the 66.7(4) deduction for a successor of CDE, in that proceeds from disposition of such properties are generally applied to reduce the successor FRE balance. The amount by which a successor FRE balance is reduced offsets the reduction otherwise required under 66.21(1) to the successor's own cumulative FRE.

(3) Successor of Canadian exploration expense — Subject to subsections (6) and (7), where after May 6, 1974 a corporation (in this subsection referred to as the "successor") acquired a particular Canadian resource property (whether by way of a purchase, amalgamation, merger, winding-up or otherwise), there may be deducted by the successor in computing its income for a taxation year an amount not exceeding the total of all amounts each of which is an amount determined in respect of an original owner of the particular property that is the lesser of

(a) the amount, if any, by which

(i) the total of

(A) the cumulative Canadian exploration expense of the original owner determined immediately after the disposition of the particular property by the original owner, and

(B) all amounts required to be added under paragraph (9)(f) to the cumulative Canadian exploration expense of the original owner in respect of a predecessor owner of the particular property, or the successor, as the case may be, at any time after the disposition of the particular property by the original owner and before the end of the year,

to the extent that an amount in respect of that total was not

(C) deducted or required to be deducted under subsection 66.1(2) or (3) by the original owner or deducted by any predecessor owner of the particular property in computing income for any taxation year,

(D) otherwise deducted in computing the successor's income for the year,

(E) deducted in computing the successor's income for a preceding taxation year, or

(F) designated by the original owner pursuant to subsection 66(14.1) for any taxation year,

exceeds

(ii) the total of all amounts each of which is an amount by which the amount described in this paragraph is required because of subsection 80(8) to be reduced at or before the end of the year, and

(b) the amount, if any, by which

(i) the part of the successor's income for the year that may reasonably be regarded as attributable to

(A) the amount included in computing its income for the year under paragraph 59(3.2)(c) that may reasonably be regarded as being attributable to the disposition by it in the year or a preceding taxation year of any interest in or right to — or, for civil law, any right in or to — the particular property to the extent that the proceeds have not been included in determining an amount under clause 29(25)(d)(i)(A) of the *Income Tax Application Rules*, this clause, clause (1)(b)(i)(A) or paragraph (10)(g) for a preceding taxation year,

(B) its reserve amount for the year in respect of the original owner and each predecessor owner, if any, of the particular property, or

(C) production from the particular property,

computed as if no deduction were allowed under section 29 of the *Income Tax Application Rules*, this section or any of sections 65 to 66.5,

exceeds the total of

(ii) all other amounts deducted under subsection 29(25) of the *Income Tax Application Rules*, this subsection and subsections (1), (4) and (5) for the year that can reasonably be regarded as attributable to the part of its income for the year described in subparagraph (i) in respect of the particular property, and

(iii) all amounts added because of subsection 80(13) in computing the amount determined under subparagraph (i).

Related Provisions: 66(11.6)(a) — Application of successor rules on change in control of trust; 66.7(2.3) — Income deemed not attributable to production from Canadian resource property; 66.7(6), (7), (9) — Application rules; 66.7(10), (11) — Change of control; 66.7(10.1) — Amalgamation — partnership property; 66.7(12) — Reduction of Canadian resource expenses; 66.7(14) — Disposal of Canadian resource properties; 66.7(16) — Non-successor acquisitions; 66.7(17) — Restriction on deductions; 80(1)"successor pool" — Debt forgiveness; 80(8)(a) — Reduction of undeducted balances on debt forgiveness. See also at end of s. 66.7.

Notes: The successor pool need not be apportioned to each property based on whether the expenses in the pool relate to that property: VIEWS doc 2005-011467117. However, the 66.7(3)(b)(i)(C) allocation of indirect expenses to "income for the year" must be reasonable: 2007-022625117. See also Notes at end of 66.7.

66.7(3) amended by 2002-2013 technical bill (effective June 26, 2013), 1995-97 and 1994 technical bills, 1992 Economic Statement, 1991 technical bill.

Forms: T2010: Election to deduct resource expenses upon acquisition of resource property by a corporation.

(4) Successor of Canadian development expense — Subject to subsections (6) and (7), where after May 6, 1974 a corporation (in this subsection referred to as the "successor") acquired a particular Canadian resource property (whether by way of a purchase, amalgamation, merger, winding-up or otherwise), there may be deducted by the successor in computing its income for a taxation year an amount not exceeding the total of all amounts each of which is an amount determined in respect of an original owner of the particular property that is the lesser of

(a) 30% of the amount, if any, by which

(i) the amount, if any, by which

(A) the cumulative Canadian development expense of the original owner determined immediately after the disposition of the particular property by the original owner to the extent that it has not been

(I) deducted by the original owner or any predecessor owner of the particular property in computing income for any taxation year,

(I.1) otherwise deducted in computing the income of the successor for the year,

(II) deducted by the successor in computing its income for any preceding taxation year, or

(III) designated by the original owner pursuant to subsection 66(14.2) for any taxation year,

exceeds

(B) any amount required to be deducted under paragraph (9)(e) from the cumulative Canadian development expense of the original owner in respect of a predecessor owner of the particular property or the successor, as the case may be, at any time after the disposition of the particular property by the original owner and before the end of the year,

exceeds the total of

(ii) all amounts each of which is an amount (other than any portion thereof that can reasonably be considered to result in a reduction of the amount otherwise determined under this paragraph in respect of another original owner of a relevant mining property who is not a predecessor owner of a relevant mining property or who became a predecessor owner of a relevant mining property before the original owner became a predecessor owner of a relevant mining property) that became receivable by a predecessor owner of the particular property or the successor in the year or a preceding taxation year and that

(A) was included by the predecessor owner or the successor in computing an amount determined under paragraph (a) of the description of F in the definition "cumulative Canadian development expense" in subsection 66.2(5) at the end of the year, and

(B) can reasonably be regarded as attributable to the disposition of a property (in this subparagraph referred to as a "relevant mining property") that is the particular property or another Canadian resource property that was acquired from the original owner with the particular property by the successor or a predecessor owner of the particular property,

(iii) all amounts each of which is an amount (other than any portion thereof that can reasonably be considered to result in a reduction of the amount otherwise determined under paragraph (5)(a) in respect of the original owner or under this paragraph or paragraph (5)(a) in respect of another original owner of a relevant oil and gas property who is not a predecessor owner of a relevant oil and gas property or who became a predecessor owner of a relevant oil and gas property before the original owner became a predecessor owner of a relevant oil and gas property) that became receivable by a predecessor owner of the particular property or the successor after 1992 and in the year or a preceding taxation year and that

(A) is designated in respect of the original owner by the predecessor owner or the successor, as the case may be, in prescribed form filed with the Minister within 6 months after the end of the taxation year in which the amount became receivable,

(B) was included by the predecessor owner or the successor in computing an amount determined under paragraph (a) of the description of F in the definition "cumulative Canadian oil and gas property expense" in subsection 66.4(5) at the end of the year, and

(C) can reasonably be regarded as attributable to the disposition of a property (in this subparagraph referred to as a "relevant oil and gas property") that is the particular property or another Canadian resource property that was acquired from the original owner with the particular property by the successor or a predecessor owner of the particular property, and

(iv) all amounts each of which is an amount by which the amount described in this paragraph is required because of subsection 80(8) to be reduced at or before the end of the year, and

(b) the amount, if any, by which

(i) the part of the successor's income for the year that can reasonably be regarded as attributable to

(A) its reserve amount for the year in respect of the original owner and each predecessor owner of the particular property, or

(B) production from the particular property,

computed as if no deduction were allowed under section 29 of the *Income Tax Application Rules*, this section or any of sections 65 to 66.5, except that, where the successor acquired the particular property from the original owner at any time in the year (otherwise than by way of an amalgamation or merger or solely because of the application of paragraph (10)(c)) and did not deal with the original owner at arm's length at that time, the amount determined under this subparagraph shall be deemed to be nil,

exceeds the total of

(ii) all other amounts deducted under subsection 29(25) of the *Income Tax Application Rules*, this subsection and subsections (1), (3) and (5) for the year that can reasonably be regarded as attributable to the part of its income for the year described in subparagraph (i) in respect of the particular property, and

(iii) all amounts added because of subsection 80(13) in computing the amount determined under subparagraph (i).

Related Provisions: 66(11.6)(a) — Application of successor rules on change in control of trust; 66(13.1) — Short taxation year; 66.7(6), (7), (9) — Application rules; 66.7(10) — Change of control; 66.7(10.1) — Amalgamation — partnership property; 66.7(11) — Change of control — anti-avoidance rule; 66.7(12) — Reduction of Canadian resource expenses; 66.7(12.1) — Canadian resource properties — Specified amount; 66.7(14) — Disposal of Canadian resource properties; 66.7(16) — Non-successor acquisitions; 66.7(17) — Restriction on deductions; 80(1)"successor pool" — Debt forgiveness; 80(8)(a) — Reduction of undeducted balances on debt forgiveness; *Interpretation Act* 27(5) — Meaning of "within 6 months". See also at end of s. 66.7.

Notes: See Notes at end of 66.7.

66.7(4)(a)(ii) ensures that, in computing a successor CCDE balance of an original owner in respect of a particular property, there are deducted other proceeds of disposition with respect to other Canadian mining property owned by the original owner because of being acquired with the particular property by a successor; and where there is more than one original owner of a particular Canadian mining property, the proceeds of disposition are applied to reduce the successored CCDE balance of the first original owner before those of subsequent original owners.

The successor pool is not required to be apportioned to each property based on whether the expenses in the pool relate to that property: VIEWS doc 2005-0114671I7. For the ordering of reductions to resource pools on a 66.7(4)(a)(iii) designation see 2011-0429421I7.

66.7(4) amended by 1995-97 technical bill (for tax years that end after Feb. 21, 1994), 1994, 1993 and 1991 technical bills.

Forms: T2010: Election to deduct resource expenses upon acquisition of resource property by a corporation.

(5) Successor of Canadian oil and gas property expense — Subject to subsections (6) and (7), where after December 11, 1979 a corporation (in this subsection referred to as the "successor") acquired a particular Canadian resource property (whether by way of a purchase, amalgamation, merger, winding-up or otherwise), there may be deducted by the successor in computing its income for a taxation year an amount not exceeding the total of all amounts each of which is an amount determined in respect of an original owner of the particular property that is the lesser of

(a) 10% of the amount, if any, by which

(i) the cumulative Canadian oil and gas property expense of the original owner determined immediately after the disposition of the particular property by the original owner to the extent it has not been

(A) deducted by the original owner or any predecessor owner of the particular property in computing income for any taxation year,

(A.1) otherwise deducted in computing the income of the successor for the year, or

(B) deducted by the successor in computing its income for any preceding taxation year

exceeds the total of

(ii) the total of all amounts each of which is an amount (other than any portion thereof that can reasonably be considered to result in a reduction of the amount otherwise determined under this paragraph or paragraph (4)(a) in respect of another original owner of a relevant oil and gas property who is not a predecessor owner of a relevant oil and gas property or who became a predecessor owner of a relevant oil and gas property before the original owner became a predecessor owner of a relevant oil and gas property) that became receivable by a predecessor owner of the particular property or the successor in the year or a preceding taxation year and that

(A) was included by the predecessor owner or the successor in computing an amount determined under paragraph (a) of the description of F in the definition "cumulative Canadian oil and gas property expense" in subsection 66.4(5) at the end of the year, and

(B) can reasonably be regarded as attributable to the disposition of a property (in this subparagraph referred to as a "relevant oil and gas property") that is the particular property or another Canadian resource property that was acquired from the original owner with the particular property by the successor or a predecessor owner of the particular property, and

(iii) the total of all amounts each of which is an amount by which the amount described in this paragraph is required because of subsection 80(8) to be reduced at or before the end of the year, and

(b) the amount, if any, by which

(i) the part of the successor's income for the year that can reasonably be regarded as attributable to

(A) its reserve amount for the year in respect of the original owner and each predecessor owner of the particular property, or

(B) production from the particular property,

computed as if no deduction were allowed under section 29 of the *Income Tax Application Rules*, this section or any of sections 65 to 66.5, except that, where the successor acquired the particular property from the original owner at any time in the year (otherwise than by way of an amalgamation or merger or solely because of the application of paragraph (10)(c)) and did not deal with the original owner at arm's length at that time, the amount determined under this subparagraph shall be deemed to be nil,

exceeds the total of

(ii) all other amounts deducted under subsection 29(25) of the *Income Tax Application Rules*, this subsection and subsections (1), (3) and (4) for the year that can reasonably be regarded as attributable to the part of its income for the year

described in subparagraph (i) in respect of the particular property, and

(iii) all amounts added because of subsection 80(13) in computing the amount determined under subparagraph (i).

Related Provisions: 66(11.6)(a) — Application of successor rules on change in control of trust; 66(13.1) — Short taxation year; 66.7(2.3) — Income deemed not attributable to production from Canadian resource property; 66.7(6), (7) — Application rules; 66.7(10) — Change of control; 66.7(10.1) — Amalgamation — partnership property; 66.7(11) — Change of control — anti-avoidance rule; 66.7(12) — Reduction of Canadian resource expenses; 66.7(14) — Disposal of Canadian resource properties; 66.7(16) — Non-successor acquisitions; 66.7(17) — Restriction on deductions; 80(1)"successor pool" — Debt forgiveness; 80(8)(a) — Reduction of undeducted balances on debt forgiveness. See also at end of s. 66.7.

Notes: See Notes at end of 66.7. For CRA interpretation of 66.7(5) see VIEWS doc 2006-0169051I7.

66.7(5) amended by 1994 technical bill, effective for taxation years that end after Feb. 21, 1994; and by 1993 and 1991 technical bills.

Forms: T2010: Election to deduct resource expenses upon acquisition of resource property by a corporation.

(6) Where subsec. 29(25) of ITAR and subsecs. (1) to (5) do not apply — Subsection 29(25) of the *Income Tax Application Rules* and subsections (1) to (5) do not apply

(a) in respect of a Canadian resource property or a foreign resource property acquired by way of an amalgamation to which subsection 87(1.2) applies or a winding-up to which subsection 88(1.5) applies; or

(b) to permit, in respect of the acquisition by a corporation before February 18, 1987 of a Canadian resource property or a foreign resource property, a deduction by the corporation of an amount that the corporation would not have been entitled to deduct under section 29 of the *Income Tax Application Rules* or section 66, 66.1, 66.2 or 66.4 if those sections, as they read in their application to taxation years ending before February 18, 1987, applied to taxation years ending after February 17, 1987.

Related Provisions: See at end of s. 66.7.

(7) Application of subsec. 29(25) of ITAR and subsecs. (1), (3), (4) and (5) — Subsection 29(25) of the *Income Tax Application Rules* and subsections (1), (3), (4) and (5) apply only to a corporation that has acquired a particular Canadian resource property

(a) where it acquired the particular property in a taxation year commencing before 1985 and, at the time it acquired the particular property, the corporation acquired all or substantially all of the property used by the person from whom it acquired the particular property in carrying on in Canada such of the businesses described in paragraphs (a) to (g) of the definition "principal-business corporation" in subsection 66(15) as were carried on by the person;

(b) where it acquired the particular property in a taxation year commencing after 1984 and, at the time it acquired the particular property, the corporation acquired all or substantially all of the Canadian resource properties of the person from whom it acquired the particular property;

(c) where it acquired the particular property after June 5, 1987 by way of an amalgamation or winding-up and it has filed an election in prescribed form with the Minister on or before the day on or before which the corporation is required to file a return of income pursuant to section 150 for its taxation year in which it acquired the particular property;

(d) where it acquired the particular property after November 16, 1978 and in a taxation year ending before February 18, 1987 by any means other than by way of an amalgamation or winding-up and it and the person from whom it acquired the particular property, have filed with the Minister a joint election under and in accordance with any of subsection 29(25) of the *Income Tax Application Rules*, subsection 29(29) of the *Income Tax Application Rules, 1971*, Part III of chapter 63 of the Statutes of Canada, 1970-71-72, and subsections 66(6) and (7), 66.1(4) and (5), 66.2(3) and (4) and 66.4(3) and (4) of the *Income Tax Act*, chapter 148 of the Revised Statutes of Canada, 1952, as all of those subsections read in their application to that year; and

(e) where it acquired the particular property in a taxation year ending after February 17, 1987 by any means other than by way of an amalgamation or winding-up and it and the person from whom it acquired the particular property have filed a joint election in prescribed form with the Minister on or before the earlier of the days on or before which either of them is required to file a return of income pursuant to section 150 for its or the person's taxation year in which the corporation acquired the particular property.

Related Provisions: 66(11.6)(a)(iii) — Election deemed filed on change in control of trust; 220(3.2), Reg. 600(c) — Late filing or revocation of election under 66.7(7)(c), (d) or (e). See also at end of s. 66.7.

Notes: CRA considers that "substantially all", used in 66.7(7)(a) and (b), means 90% or more.

I.T. Application Rules: 69 (meaning of "chapter 148 of ..."; meaning of *Income Tax Application Rules, 1971*, Part III of chapter 63 of the Statutes of Canada, 1970-71-72").

Information Circulars: 07-1R1: Taxpayer relief provisions.

Forms: T2010: Election to deduct resource expenses upon acquisition of resource property by a corporation.

(8) Application of subsecs. (2) and (2.3) — Subsections (2) and (2.3) apply only to a corporation that has acquired a particular foreign resource property

(a) where it acquired the particular property in a taxation year commencing before 1985 and, at the time it acquired the particular property, the corporation acquired all or substantially all of the property used by the person from whom it acquired the particular property in carrying on outside Canada such of the businesses described in paragraphs (a) to (g) of the definition "principal-business corporation" in subsection 66(15) as were carried on by that person;

(b) where it acquired the particular property in a taxation year commencing after 1984 and, at the time it acquired the particular property, the corporation acquired all or substantially all of the foreign resource properties of the person from whom it acquired the particular property;

(c) where it acquired the particular property after June 5, 1987 by way of an amalgamation or winding-up and it has filed an election in prescribed form with the Minister on or before the day on or before which the corporation is required to file a return of income pursuant to section 150 for its taxation year in which it acquired the particular property;

(d) where it acquired the particular property after November 16, 1978 and in a taxation year ending before February 18, 1987 by any means other than by way of an amalgamation or winding-up and it and the person from whom it acquired the particular property, have filed with the Minister a joint election under and in accordance with subsection 66(6) or (7) (as modified by subsections 66(8) and (9), respectively) of the *Income Tax Act*, chapter 148 of the Revised Statutes of Canada, 1952, as those subsections read in their application to that year; and

(e) where it acquired the particular property in a taxation year ending after February 17, 1987 by any means other than by way of an amalgamation or winding-up and it and the person from whom it acquired the particular property have filed a joint election in prescribed form with the Minister on or before the earlier of the days on or before which either of them is required to file a return of income pursuant to section 150 for its or the person's taxation year in which the corporation acquired the particular property.

Related Provisions: 66(11.6)(a)(iii) — Election deemed filed on change in control of trust; 220(3.2), Reg. 600(c) — Late filing or revocation of election under 66.7(8)(c), (d) or (e). See also at end of s. 66.7.

Notes: CRA considers that "substantially all", used in 66.7(8)(a) and (b), means 90% or more.

Opening words of 66.7(8) amended by 2000 Budget to add reference to 66.7(2.3), effective for taxation years that begin after 2000.

I.T. Application Rules: 69 (meaning of "chapter 148 of ...").

Information Circulars: 07-1R1: Taxpayer relief provisions.

Forms: T2010: Election to deduct resource expenses upon acquisition of resource property by a corporation.

(9) Canadian development expense becoming Canadian exploration expense — Where

(a) a corporation acquires a Canadian resource property,

(b) subsection (4) applies in respect of the acquisition, and

(c) the cumulative Canadian development expense of an original owner of the property determined under clause (4)(a)(i)(A) in respect of the corporation includes a Canadian development expense incurred by the original owner in respect of an oil or gas well that would, but for this subsection, be deemed by subsection 66.1(9) to be a Canadian exploration expense incurred in respect of the well by the original owner at any particular time after the acquisition by the corporation and before it disposed of the property,

the following rules apply:

(d) subsection 66.1(9) does not apply in respect of the Canadian development expense incurred in respect of the well by the original owner,

(e) an amount equal to the lesser of

(i) the amount that would be deemed by subsection 66.1(9) to be a Canadian exploration expense incurred in respect of the well by the original owner at the particular time if that subsection applied in respect of the expense, and

(ii) the cumulative Canadian development expense of the original owner as determined under clause (4)(a)(i)(A) in respect of the corporation immediately before the particular time

shall be deducted at the particular time from the cumulative Canadian development expense of the original owner in respect of the corporation for the purposes of subparagraph (4)(a)(i), and

(f) the amount required by paragraph (e) to be deducted shall be added at the particular time to the cumulative Canadian exploration expense of the original owner in respect of the corporation for the purpose of paragraph (3)(a).

Related Provisions: See at end of s. 66.7.

Notes: 66.7(9)(f) amended by 1994 technical bill, for taxation years that end after Feb. 21, 1994, to change "subparagraph (3)(a)(ii)" to "paragraph (3)(a)".

(10) Change of control — Where at any time after November 12, 1981

(a) control of a corporation has been acquired by a person or group of persons, or

(b) a corporation ceased on or before April 26, 1995 to be exempt from tax under this Part on its taxable income,

for the purposes of the provisions of the *Income Tax Application Rules* and this Act (other than subsections 66(12.6), (12.601), (12.602), (12.62) and (12.71)) relating to deductions in respect of drilling and exploration expenses, prospecting, exploration and development expenses, Canadian exploration and development expenses, foreign resource pool expenses, Canadian exploration expenses, Canadian development expenses and Canadian oil and gas property expenses (in this subsection referred to as "resource expenses") incurred by the corporation before that time, the following rules apply:

(c) the corporation shall be deemed after that time to be a successor (within the meaning assigned by subsection 29(25) of the *Income Tax Application Rules* or any of subsections (1) to (5)) that had, at that time, acquired all the properties owned by the corporation immediately before that time from an original owner thereof,

(c.1) where the corporation did not own a foreign resource property immediately before that time, the corporation is deemed to have owned a foreign resource property immediately before that time,

(d) a joint election shall be deemed to have been filed in accordance with subsections (7) and (8) in respect of the acquisition,

(e) the resource expenses incurred by the corporation before that time shall be deemed to have been incurred by an original owner of the properties and not by the corporation,

(f) the original owner is deemed to have been resident in Canada before that time while the corporation was resident in Canada,

(g) where the corporation (in this paragraph referred to as the "transferee") was, immediately before and at that time,

(i) a parent corporation (within the meaning assigned by subsection 87(1.4)), or

(ii) a subsidiary wholly-owned corporation (within the meaning assigned by subsection 87(1.4))

of a particular corporation (in this paragraph referred to as the "transferor"), if both corporations agree to have this paragraph apply to them in respect of a taxation year of the transferor ending after that time and notify the Minister in writing of the agreement in the return of income under this Part of the transferor for that year, the transferor may, if throughout that year the transferee was such a parent corporation or subsidiary wholly-owned corporation of the transferor, designate in favour of the transferee, in respect of that year, for the purpose of making a deduction under subsection 29(25) of the *Income Tax Application Rules* or this section in respect of resource expenses incurred by the transferee before that time and when it was such a parent corporation or subsidiary wholly-owned corporation of the transferor, an amount not exceeding such portion of the amount that would be its income for the year, if no deductions were allowed under any of section 29 of the *Income Tax Application Rules*, this section and sections 65 to 66.5, that may reasonably be regarded as being attributable to

(iii) the production from Canadian resource properties owned by the transferor immediately before that time, and

(iv) the disposition in the year of any Canadian resource properties owned by the transferor immediately before that time,

to the extent that such portion of the amount so designated is not designated under this paragraph in favour of any other taxpayer, and the amount so designated shall be deemed, for the purposes of determining the amount under paragraph 29(25)(d) of the *Income Tax Application Rules* and paragraphs (1)(b), (3)(b), (4)(b) and (5)(b),

(v) to be income from the sources described in subparagraph (iii) or (iv), as the case may be, of the transferee for its taxation year in which that taxation year of the transferor ends, and

(vi) not to be income from the sources described in subparagraph (iii) or (iv), as the case may be, of the transferor for that year,

(h) where the corporation (in this paragraph referred to as the "transferee") was, immediately before and at that time,

(i) a parent corporation (within the meaning assigned by subsection 87(1.4)), or

(ii) a subsidiary wholly-owned corporation (within the meaning assigned by subsection 87(1.4))

of a particular corporation (in this paragraph referred to as the "transferor"), if both corporations agree to have this paragraph apply to them in respect of a taxation year of the transferor ending after that time and notify the Minister in writing of the agreement in the return of income under this Part of the transferor for that year, the transferor may, if throughout that year the transferee was such a parent corporation or subsidiary wholly-owned corporation of the transferor, designate in favour of the transferee, in respect of that year, for the purpose of making a deduction under this section in respect of resource expenses incurred by the transferee before that time and when it was such a parent corporation or subsidiary wholly-owned corporation of

the transferor, an amount not exceeding such portion of the amount that would be its income for the year, if no deductions were allowed under this section and sections 65 to 66.5, that may reasonably be regarded as being attributable to

(iii) the production from foreign resource properties owned by the transferor immediately before that time, and

(iv) the disposition of any foreign resource properties owned by the transferor immediately before that time,

to the extent that such portion of the amount so designated is not designated under this paragraph in favour of any other taxpayer, and the amount so designated shall be deemed,

(v) for the purposes of determining the amounts under paragraphs (2)(b) and (2.3)(b), to be income from the sources described in subparagraph (iii) or (iv), as the case may be, of the transferee for its taxation year in which that taxation year of the transferor ends, and

(vi) for the purposes of determining the amount under paragraphs (2)(b) and (2.3)(b), not to be income from the sources described in subparagraph (iii) or (iv), as the case may be, of the transferor for that year,

(i) where, immediately before and at that time, the corporation (in this paragraph referred to as the "transferee") and another corporation (in this paragraph referred to as the "transferor") were both subsidiary wholly-owned corporations (within the meaning assigned by subsection 87(1.4)) of a particular parent corporation (within the meaning assigned by subsection 87(1.4)), if the transferee and the transferor agree to have this paragraph apply to them in respect of a taxation year of the transferor ending after that time and notify the Minister in writing of the agreement in the return of income under this Part of the transferor for that year, paragraph (g) or (h), or both, as the agreement provides, shall apply for that year to the transferee and transferor as though one were the parent corporation (within the meaning of subsection 87(1.4)) of the other, and

(j) where that time is after January 15, 1987 and at that time the corporation was a member of a partnership that owned a Canadian resource property or a foreign resource property at that time

(i) for the purpose of paragraph (c), the corporation shall be deemed to have owned immediately before that time that portion of the property owned by the partnership at that time that is equal to its percentage share of the total of amounts that would be paid to all members of the partnership if it were wound up at that time, and

(ii) for the purposes of clause 29(25)(d)(i)(B) of the *Income Tax Application Rules*, clauses (1)(b)(i)(C) and (2)(b)(i)(B), subparagraph (2.3)(b)(i) and clauses (3)(b)(i)(C), (4)(b)(i)(B) and (5)(b)(i)(B) for a taxation year ending after that time, the lesser of

(A) its share of the part of the income of the partnership for the fiscal period of the partnership ending in the year that may reasonably be regarded as being attributable to the production from the property, and

(B) an amount that would be determined under clause (A) for the year if its share of the income of the partnership for the fiscal period of the partnership ending in the year were determined on the basis of the percentage share referred to in subparagraph (i),

shall be deemed to be income of the corporation for the year that may reasonably be attributable to production from the property.

Related Provisions: 66(11.3) — Control; 66.7(2.3) — Income deemed not attributable to production from Canadian resource property; 66.7(10.1) — Amalgamation — partnership property; 249(4) — Deemed year end on change of control; 256(6)–(9) — Whether control acquired; 256.1 — Deemed change in control if 75% FMV acquired. See also at end of s. 66.7.

Notes: For corporate partnerships see Warren Pahkowich, "The Application of the Successor Rules to Members of a Partnership", I(1) *Resource Sector Taxation [RST]* (Federated Press) 8-11 (2002); Brian Carr, "Partnerships and the Successor Corporation Rules", VI(2) *RST* 426-35 (2008). See also Notes at end of 66.7.

In *Devon Canada*, 2013 TCC 415 (FCA appeal discontinued A-431-13), the look-through rule in 66.7(10)(j) continued to apply where properties were dropped down to a second-tier partnership after change in control of a corporation holding an oil & gas partnership interest. Once a corporate partner is deemed to own partnership properties under 66.7(10)(j)(i), it is deemed continuously by 66.7(10)(c) to be the successor that acquired partnership properties from original owner: *Devon*, para. 32. See Diep & Kopstein case comment, 62(2) *Canadian Tax Journal* 483-90 (2014); Carr, "Devon Canada", IX(4) *Resource Sector Taxation* (Federated Press) 677-83 (2014).

66.7(10)(f) is consequential on an amendment to 66.7(2)(a)(i) affecting successor FEDE claims.

66.7(10)(j) deems ownership only of property of the partnership of which the corporation it itself is a member (not a lower-tier partnership): VIEWS doc 2012-0432931E5.

For corporations filing Quebec returns, notifications under (g)-(i) must be copied to Revenu Québec: *Taxation Act* ss. 418.26, 21.4.6.

66.7(10) amended by 2001 technical bill (for 1999 and later tax years), 2000 Budget (for tax years that begin after 2000), 1995-97 technical bill, 1996 Budget, 1992 Economic Statement and 1991 technical bill.

I.T. Technical News: 7 (control by a group — 50/50 arrangement).

Advance Tax Rulings: ATR-19: Earned depletion base and cumulative Canadian development expense.

(10.1) Amalgamation — partnership property

For the purposes of subsections (1) to (5) and the definition "original owner" in subsection 66(15), if at any particular time there has been an amalgamation within the meaning assigned by subsection 87(1), other than an amalgamation to which subsection 87(1.2) applies, of two or more corporations (each of which is referred to in this subsection as a "predecessor corporation") to form one corporate entity (referred to in this subsection as the "new corporation") and immediately before the particular time a predecessor corporation was a member of a partnership that owned a Canadian resource property or a foreign resource property,

(a) the predecessor corporation is deemed

(i) to have owned, immediately before the particular time, that portion of each Canadian resource property and of each foreign resource property owned by the partnership at the particular time that is equal to the predecessor corporation's percentage share of the total of the amounts that would be paid to all members of the partnership if the partnership were wound up immediately before the particular time, and

(ii) to have disposed of those portions to the new corporation at the particular time;

(b) the new corporation is deemed to have, by way of the amalgamation, acquired those portions at the particular time; and

(c) the income of the new corporation for a taxation year that ends after the particular time that can reasonably be attributable to production from those properties is deemed to be the lesser of

(i) the new corporation's share of the part of the income of the partnership for fiscal periods of the partnership that end in the year that can reasonably be regarded as being attributable to production from those properties, and

(ii) the amount that would be determined under subparagraph (i) for the year if the new corporation's share of the income of the partnership for the fiscal periods of the partnership that end in the year were determined on the basis of the percentage share referred to in paragraph (a).

Notes: 66.7(10.1) added by 2002-2013 technical bill (Part 5 — technical), effective for amalgamations that occur after 1996.

(11) Idem

Where, at any time,

(a) control of a taxpayer that is a corporation has been acquired by a person or group of persons, or

(b) a taxpayer has disposed of all or substantially all of the taxpayer's Canadian resource properties or foreign resource properties,

and, before that time, the taxpayer or a partnership of which the taxpayer was a member acquired a property that is a Canadian resource property, a foreign resource property or an interest in a partnership and it may reasonably be considered that one of the main purposes of the acquisition was to avoid any limitation provided in subsection 29(25) of the *Income Tax Application Rules* or any of subsections (1) to (5) on the deduction in respect of any expenses incurred by the taxpayer or a corporation referred to as a transferee in paragraph (10)(g) or (h), the taxpayer or the partnership, as the case may be, shall be deemed, for the purposes of applying those subsections to or in respect of the taxpayer, not to have acquired the property.

Related Provisions: 87(2)(j.6) — Amalgamation — continuing corporation; 249(4) — Deemed year end where change of control occurs; 256(6)–(9) — Whether control acquired; 256.1 — Deemed change in control if 75% FMV acquired. See also at end of s. 66.7.

Notes: CRA considers that "substantially all" means 90% or more. For the meaning of "one of the main purposes" see Notes to 83(2.1).

See also Notes at end of 66.7.

I.T. Technical News: 7 (control by a group — 50/50 arrangement).

(12) Reduction of Canadian resource expenses

Where in a taxation year an original owner of Canadian resource properties disposes of all or substantially all of the original owner's Canadian resource properties to a particular corporation in circumstances in which subsection 29(25) of the *Income Tax Application Rules* or subsection (1), (3), (4) or (5) applies,

(a) the Canadian exploration and development expenses incurred by the original owner before that owner so disposed of the properties shall, for the purposes of this Subdivision, be deemed after the disposition not to have been incurred by the original owner except for the purposes of making a deduction under subsection 66(1) or (2) for the year and of determining the amount that may be deducted under subsection (1) by the particular corporation or by any other corporation that subsequently acquires any of the properties;

(b) in determining the cumulative Canadian exploration expense of the original owner at any time after the time referred to in subparagraph (3)(a)(i), there shall be deducted the amount thereof determined immediately after the disposition;

(b.1) for the purposes of paragraph (3)(a), the cumulative Canadian exploration expenses of the original owner determined immediately after the disposition that was deducted or required to be deducted under subsection 66.1(2) or (3) in computing the original owner's income for the year shall be deemed to be equal to the lesser of

(i) the amount deducted under paragraph (b) in respect of the disposition, and

(ii) the amount, if any, by which

(A) the specified amount determined under paragraph (12.1)(a) in respect of the original owner for the year

exceeds

(B) the total of all amounts each of which is an amount determined under this paragraph in respect of any disposition made by the original owner before the disposition and in the year;

(b.2) for greater certainty, any amount (other than the amount determined under paragraph (b.1)) that was deducted or required to be deducted under subsection 66.1(2) or (3) by the original owner for the year or a subsequent taxation year shall, for the purposes of paragraph (3)(a), be deemed not to be in respect of the cumulative Canadian exploration expense of the original owner determined immediately after the disposition;

(c) in determining the cumulative Canadian development expense of the original owner at any time after the time referred to in clause (4)(a)(i)(A), there shall be deducted the amount thereof determined immediately after the disposition;

(c.1) for the purpose of paragraph (4)(a), the cumulative Canadian development expense of the original owner determined immediately after the disposition that was deducted under subsection 66.2(2) in computing the original owner's income for the year shall be deemed to be equal to the lesser of

(i) the amount deducted under paragraph (c) in respect of the disposition, and

(ii) the amount, if any, by which

(A) the specified amount determined under paragraph (12.1)(b) in respect of the original owner for the year

exceeds

(B) the total of all amounts determined under this paragraph in respect of any dispositions made by the original owner before the disposition and in the year;

(c.2) for greater certainty, any amount (other than the amount determined under paragraph (c.1)) that was deducted under subsection 66.2(2) by the original owner for the year or a subsequent taxation year shall, for the purpose of paragraph (4)(a), be deemed not to be in respect of the cumulative Canadian development expense of the original owner determined immediately after the disposition;

(d) in determining the cumulative Canadian oil and gas property expense of the original owner at any time after the time referred to in subparagraph (5)(a)(i), there shall be deducted the amount thereof determined immediately after the disposition;

(d.1) for the purpose of paragraph (5)(a), the cumulative Canadian oil and gas property expense of the original owner determined immediately after the disposition that was deducted under subsection 66.4(2) in computing the original owner's income for the year shall be deemed to be equal to the lesser of

(i) the amount deducted under paragraph (d) in respect of the disposition, and

(ii) the amount, if any, by which

(A) the specified amount determined under paragraph (12.1)(c) in respect of the original owner for the year

exceeds

(B) the total of all amounts determined under this paragraph in respect of any dispositions made by the original owner before the disposition and in the year;

(d.2) for greater certainty, any amount (other than the amount determined under paragraph (d.1)) that was deducted under subsection 66.4(2) by the original owner for the year or a subsequent taxation year shall, for the purpose of paragraph (5)(a), be deemed not to be in respect of the cumulative Canadian oil and gas property expense of the original owner determined immediately after the disposition; and

(e) the drilling and exploration expenses, including all general geological and geophysical expenses, incurred by the original owner before 1972 on or in respect of exploring or drilling for petroleum or natural gas in Canada and the prospecting, exploration and development expenses incurred by the original owner before 1972 in searching for minerals in Canada shall, for the purposes of section 29 of the *Income Tax Application Rules*, be deemed after the disposition not to have been incurred by the original owner except for the purposes of making a deduction under that section for the year and of determining the amount that may be deducted under subsection 29(25) of that Act by the particular corporation or any other corporation that subsequently acquires any of the properties.

Related Provisions: 66.1(6)"cumulative Canadian exploration expense"M — Reduction in CCEE; 66.2(5)"cumulative Canadian development expense"O — Reduction in CCDE; 66.4(5)"cumulative Canadian oil and gas property expense"J — Reduction in CCOGPE. See Related Provisions and Definitions at end of s. 66.7.

Notes: For interpretation see VIEWS doc 2012-0462511E5.

CRA considers that "substantially all", used in 66.7(12) opening words, means 90% or more.

66.7(12) amended by 1992 Economic Statement (effective for taxation years ending after December 2, 1992) and 1991 technical bill.

(12.1) Specified amount — Where in a taxation year an original owner of Canadian resource properties disposes of all or substan-tially all of the original owner's Canadian resource properties in circumstances in which subsection (3), (4) or (5) applies,

(a) the lesser of

(i) the total of all amounts each of which is the amount, if any, by which

(A) an amount deducted under paragraph (12)(b) in respect of a disposition in the year by the original owner

exceeds

(B) the amount, if any, designated by the original owner in prescribed form filed with the Minister within 6 months after the end of the year in respect of an amount determined under clause (A), and

(ii) the total of

(A) the amount claimed under subsection 66.1(2) or (3) by the original owner for the year, and

(B) the amount that would, but for paragraph 66.1(1)(c), be determined under subsection 66.1(1) in respect of the original owner for the year

is the specified amount in respect of the original owner for the year for the purposes of clause (12)(b.1)(ii)(A) and of determining the value of E.1 in the definition "cumulative Canadian exploration expense" in subsection 66.1(6);

(b) the lesser of

(i) the total of all amounts each of which is the amount, if any, by which

(A) an amount deducted under paragraph (12)(c) in respect of a disposition in the year by the original owner

exceeds

(B) the amount, if any, designated by the original owner in prescribed form filed with the Minister within 6 months after the end of the year in respect of an amount determined under clause (A), and

(ii) the total of

(A) the amount claimed under subsection 66.2(2) by the original owner for the year, and

(B) the amount that would, but for paragraph 66.2(1)(d), be determined under subsection 66.2(1) in respect of the original owner for the year

is the specified amount in respect of the original owner for the year for the purposes of clause (12)(c.1)(ii)(A) and of determining the value of D.1 in the definition "cumulative Canadian development expense" in subsection 66.2(5); and

(c) the lesser of

(i) the total of all amounts each of which is the amount, if any, by which

(A) an amount deducted under paragraph (12)(d) in respect of a disposition in the year by the original owner

exceeds

(B) the amount, if any, designated by the original owner in prescribed form filed with the Minister within 6 months after the end of the year in respect of an amount determined under clause (A), and

(ii) the total of

(A) the amount claimed under subsection 66.4(2) by the original owner for the year, and

(B) the amount that would, but for paragraph 66.4(1)(c), be determined under subsection 66.4(1) in respect of the original owner for the year

is the specified amount in respect of the original owner for the year for the purposes of clause (12)(d.1)(ii)(A) and of determining the value of D.1 in the definition "cumulative Canadian oil and gas property expense" in subsection 66.4(5).

Related Provisions: 66.1(1)(c) — Amount to be included in income; 66.1(2)(a)(ii)(A) — Deduction for principal-business corp; 66.1(3)(b)(i) — Expenses of other taxpayers; 66.1(6)"cumulative Canadian exploration expense"E.1 — addition to CCEE; 66.2(2)(a)(i)(B)(I) — Deduction for CCDE; 66.2(5)"cumulative Canadian development expense"D.1 — Addition to CCDE; 66.4(1)(c) — Recovery of costs; 66.4(2)(a)(i) — Deduction for CCOGPE; 66.4(5)"cumulative Canadian oil and gas property expense"D.1 — Addition to CCOGPE; *Interpretation Act* 27(5) — Meaning of "within 6 months".

Notes: For interpretation see VIEWS doc 2012-0462511E5.

CRA considers that "substantially all", used in the opening words of 66.7(12.1), means 90% or more.

66.7(12.1) added by 1991 technical bill.

Forms: T1046: Designation of resource amount by an original owner.

(13) Reduction of foreign resource expenses — Where after June 5, 1987 an original owner of foreign resource properties disposes of all or substantially all of the original owner's foreign resource properties to a particular corporation in circumstances in which subsection (2) applies, the foreign exploration and development expenses incurred by the original owner before that owner so disposed of the properties shall be deemed after the disposition not to have been incurred by the original owner except for the purposes of determining the amounts that may be deducted under that subsection by the particular corporation or any other corporation that subsequently acquires any of the properties.

Related Provisions: See at end of s. 66.7.

Notes: CRA considers that "substantially all" means 90% or more.

(13.1) Reduction of foreign resource expenses — Where in a taxation year an original owner of foreign resource properties in respect of a country disposes of all or substantially all of the original owner's foreign resource properties in circumstances to which subsection (2.3) applies,

(a) in determining the cumulative foreign resource expense of the original owner in respect of the country at any time after the time referred to in subparagraph (2.3)(a)(i), there shall be deducted the amount of that cumulative foreign resource expense determined immediately after the disposition; and

(b) for the purpose of paragraph (2.3)(a), the cumulative foreign resource expense of the original owner in respect of the country determined immediately after the disposition that was deducted under subsection 66.21(4) in computing the original owner's income for the year is deemed to be equal to the lesser of

(i) the amount deducted under paragraph (a) in respect of the disposition, and

(ii) the amount, if any, by which

(A) the specified amount determined under subsection (13.2) in respect of the original owner and the country for the year

exceeds

(B) the total of all amounts determined under this paragraph in respect of another disposition of foreign resource property in respect of the country made by the original owner before the disposition and in the year.

Related Provisions: 66.21(1)"cumulative foreign resource expense"J; 66.7(15.1) — Parallel rule for predecessor owner; 248(1)"foreign resource property" — Meaning of foreign resource property in respect of a country.

Notes: 66.7(13.1) added by 2000 Budget, effective for taxation years that begin after 2000. It sets out the tax consequences to an original owner of foreign resource properties who disposes of the properties in circumstances to which 66.7(2.3) applies. It is structured similarly to 66.7(12)(c) and (c.1), both of which relate to successor CDE.

(13.2) Specified amount — foreign resource expenses — Where in a taxation year an original owner of foreign resource properties in respect of a country disposes of all or substantially all of the original owner's foreign resource properties in circumstances to which subsection (2.3) applies, the specified amount in respect of the country and the original owner for the year for the purposes of clause (13.1)(b)(ii)(A) and of determining the value of D in the def-

inition "cumulative foreign resource expense" in subsection 66.21(1) is the lesser of

(a) the total of all amounts each of which is the amount, if any, by which

(i) an amount deducted under paragraph (13.1)(a) in respect of a disposition in the year by the original owner of foreign resource property in respect of the country

exceeds

(ii) the amount, if any, designated by the original owner in prescribed form filed with the Minister within six months after the end of the year in respect of an amount described under subparagraph (i), and

(b) the total of

(i) the amount claimed under subsection 66.21(4) by the original owner in respect of the country for the year, and

(ii) the amount that would, but for paragraph 66.21(3)(c), be determined under subsection 66.21(3) in respect of the country and the original owner for the year.

Related Provisions: 66.21(1)"adjusted cumulative foreign resource expense"; 66.21(1)"cumulative foreign resource expense"D; 66.21(3)(c) — Deduction; *Interpretation Act* 27(5) — Meaning of "within 6 months".

Notes: 66.7(13.2) added by 2000 Budget, for taxation years that begin after 2000.

(14) Disposal of Canadian resource properties — Where in a taxation year a predecessor owner of Canadian resource properties disposes of Canadian resource properties to a corporation in circumstances in which subsection 29(25) of the *Income Tax Application Rules* or subsection (1), (3), (4) or (5) applies,

(a) for the purposes of applying any of those subsections to the predecessor owner in respect of its acquisition of any Canadian resource property owned by it immediately before the disposition, it shall be deemed, after the disposition, never to have acquired any such properties except for the purposes of

(i) determining an amount deductible under subsection (1) or (3) for the year,

(ii) where the predecessor owner and the corporation dealt with each other at arm's length at the time of the disposition or the disposition was by way of an amalgamation or merger, determining an amount deductible under subsection (4) or (5) for the year, and

(iii) determining the amount for F in the definition "cumulative Canadian development expense" in subsection 66.2(5), the amounts for paragraphs (a) and (b) in the description of L in that definition and the amount for F in the definition "cumulative Canadian oil and gas property expense" in subsection 66.4(5); and

(b) where the corporation or another corporation acquires any of the properties on or after the disposition in circumstances in which subsection (4) or (5) applies, amounts that become receivable by the predecessor owner after the disposition in respect of Canadian resource properties retained by it at the time of the disposition shall, for the purposes of applying subsection (4) or (5) to the corporation or the other corporation in respect of the acquisition, be deemed not to have become receivable by the predecessor owner.

Related Provisions: See at end of s. 66.7.

Notes: 66.7(14) amended by 1991 technical bill and 1993 technical bill, both amendments retroactive to dispositions in taxation years that end after February 17, 1987.

CRA considers that "substantially all" means 90% or more.

(15) Disposal of foreign resource properties — Where after June 5, 1987 a predecessor owner of foreign resource properties disposes of all or substantially all of its foreign resource properties to a corporation in circumstances in which subsection (2) applies, for the purpose of applying that subsection to the predecessor owner in respect of its acquisition of any of those properties (or other foreign resource properties retained by it at the time of the disposition which were acquired by it in circumstances in which subsection (2)

applied), it shall be deemed, after the disposition, never to have acquired the properties.

Related Provisions: See at end of s. 66.7.

Notes: CRA considers that "substantially all" means 90% or more.

66.7(15) amended by 1993 technical bill, retroactive to taxation years that end after February 17, 1987.

(15.1) Disposal of foreign resource properties — subsec. (2.3) — Where in a taxation year a predecessor owner of foreign resource properties disposes of foreign resource properties to a corporation in circumstances to which subsection (2.3) applies,

(a) for the purpose of applying that subsection to the predecessor owner in respect of its acquisition of any foreign resource properties owned by it immediately before the disposition, it is deemed, after the disposition, never to have acquired any such properties except for the purposes of

(i) where the predecessor owner and the corporation dealt with each other at arm's length at the time of the disposition or the disposition was by way of an amalgamation or merger, determining an amount deductible under subsection (2.3) for the year, and

(ii) determining the value of F in the definition "cumulative foreign resource expense" in subsection 66.21(1); and

(b) where the corporation or another corporation acquires any of the properties on or after the disposition in circumstances to which subsection (2.3) applies, amounts that become receivable by the predecessor owner after the disposition in respect of foreign resource properties retained by it at the time of the disposition are, for the purposes of applying subsection (2.3) to the corporation or the other corporation in respect of the acquisition, deemed not to have become receivable by the predecessor owner.

Related Provisions: 66.7(13.1) — Parallel rule for original owner.

Notes: 66.7(15.1) added by 2000 Budget, effective for taxation years that begin after 2000. It provides rules for predecessor owners similar to those in 66.7(13.1) and (13.2) that apply to original owners. Under 66.7(15.1)(a), where a predecessor owner of foreign resource properties disposes of substantially all of them in circumstances where the successor rules apply, it is generally treated after the disposition as never having acquired the properties in respect of which the successor rule applied. As a consequence, the predecessor is generally precluded from claiming successor FRE deductions after the subsequent succession. 66.7(15.1) is structured similarly to 66.7(14).

(16) Non-successor acquisitions — If at any time a Canadian resource property or a foreign resource property is acquired by a person in circumstances in which none of subsections (1) to (5), nor subsection 29(25) of the *Income Tax Application Rules*, apply, every person who was an original owner or predecessor owner of the property before that time is, for the purpose of applying those subsections to or in respect of the person or any other person who after that time acquires the property, deemed after that time not to be an original owner or predecessor owner of the property before that time.

Related Provisions: See at end of s. 66.7.

Notes: For interpretation of 66.7(16) see VIEWS docs 2006-0168331E5, 2006-016905117; Mike Hegedus, "Subsection 66.7(16): Non-successor acquisitions", VII(4) *Resource Sector Taxation* (Federated Press) 534-39 (2010); and Notes at end of 66.7.

66.7(16) amended by 2002-2013 technical bill (Part 5 — technical), effective for property acquired after Nov. 5, 2010, to delete, after "owner of the property", the words "by reason of having disposed of the property before that time".

(17) Restriction on deductions — Where in a particular taxation year and before June 6, 1987 a person disposed of a Canadian resource property or a foreign resource property in circumstances in which any of subsection 29(25) of the *Income Tax Application Rules* and subsections (1) to (5) applies, no deduction in respect of an expense incurred before the property was disposed of may be made under this section or section 66, 66.1, 66.2 or 66.4 by the person in computing the person's income for a taxation year subsequent to the particular taxation year.

(18) Application of interpretation provisions — The definitions in subsection 66(15) and sections 66.1 to 66.4 apply in this section.

Notes: 66.7(18) amended by 2000 Budget to add reference to 66.1–66.4, effective for taxation years that end after 2000.

66.7(18) added in the RSC 1985 (5th Supp) consolidation, effective for tax years ending after Nov. 1991. This rule was formerly in the opening words to 66(15).

Related Provisions [s. 66.7]: 66(5) — Dealers; 66(18) — Members of partnerships; 66.1(6) — Canadian exploration expense; 66.6 — Acquisition from tax-exempt person; 66.8(1) — Resource expenses of limited partners; 87(1.2) — Amalgamation — new corporation deemed continuation of predecessor; 88(1.5) — Windup — parent continuation of subsidiary.

Notes [s. 66.7]: Starting with the 2021 tax year, CRA's position is that 66.7(3)-(5) deductions can preserve, but cannot create or increase, a non-capital loss to be used in another year: VIEWS doc 2018-0782181I7 [Ho, "CRA Announces a 'New' Assessing Position", XIV(4) *Resource Sector Taxation* (Federated Press) 9-13 (2020)].

For discussion of 66.7 see Gamble, *Taxation of Canadian Mining*, chap. 9 and Carr & Calverley, *Canadian Resource Taxation* (both Carswell, looseleaf or *Taxnet Pro* Reference Centre), chap. 7; Carr, "The Successor Corporation Rules Made Easy", 7(1) *Canadian Petroleum Tax Journal* (1994); Gratton & Wu, "Mergers & Acquisitions: Application of the Successor Rules", 11 *CPTJ* (1998); Moch & Pashkowich, "Advanced Issues in Resource Taxation", 2008 Cdn Tax Foundation conference report, 11:1-17. See also 66.7(10) Notes.

Definitions [s. 66.7]: "amount" — 248(1); "arm's length" — 251(1); "business" — 248(1); "Canada" — 255; "Canadian development expense" — 66.2(5), 248(1); "Canadian exploration and development expense" — 66(15), 248(1); "Canadian exploration expense" — 66.1(6), 248(1); "Canadian oil and gas property expense" — 66.4(5), 248(1); "Canadian resource property" — 66(15), 66.7(18), 248(1); "carrying on business" — 253; "control" — 256(6)–(9), 256.1(3); "corporation" — 248(1), *Interpretation Act* 35(1); "cumulative foreign resource expense" — 66.21(1), 66.7(18); "disposition" — 248(1); "expense" — 66(15), 66.7(18); "fiscal period" — 249(2), 249.1; "foreign exploration and development expenses" — 66(15), 248(1); "foreign resource expense" — 66.21(1), 248(1); "foreign resource pool expense" — 248(1); "foreign resource property" — 66(15), 248(1); "foreign resource property in respect of", "mineral", "Minister" — 248(1); "month" — *Interpretation Act* 35(1); "oil or gas well" — 248(1); "original owner" — 66(15), 66.7(18); "person", "prescribed" — 248(1); "predecessor owner" — 66(15), 66.7(18); "principal-business corporation" — 66(15); "property" — 248(1); "resident in Canada" — 250; "specified amount" — 66.7(12.1), (13.2); "specified foreign exploration and development expense" — 66(15), 66.7(18); "subsidiary wholly-owned corporation" — 248(1); "taxable income" — 2(2), 248(1); "taxation year" — 249; "taxpayer" — 248(1); "writing" — *Interpretation Act* 35(1).

Interpretation Bulletins [s. 66.7]: IT-126R2: Meaning of winding-up.

66.8 (1) Resource expenses of limited partner — Where a taxpayer is a limited partner of a partnership at the end of a fiscal period of the partnership, the following rules apply:

(a) determine the amount, if any, by which

(i) the total of all amounts each of which is the taxpayer's share of

(A) the Canadian oil and gas property expenses (in this subsection referred to as "property expenses"),

(B) the Canadian development expenses (in this subsection referred to as "development expenses"),

(C) the Canadian exploration expenses (in this subsection referred to as "exploration expenses"),

(D) the foreign resource expenses in respect of a country (in this subsection referred to as "country-specific foreign expenses"), or

(E) the foreign exploration and development expenses (in this subsection referred to as "global foreign expenses"),

incurred by the partnership in the fiscal period determined without reference to this subsection

exceeds

(ii) the amount, if any, by which

(A) the taxpayer's at-risk amount at the end of the fiscal period in respect of the partnership

exceeds

(B) the total of

(I) the amount required by subsection 127(8) in respect of the partnership to be added in computing the investment tax credit of the taxpayer in respect of the fiscal period, and

(II) the taxpayer's share of any losses of the partnership for the fiscal period from a farming business;

(b) the amount determined under paragraph (a) shall be applied

(i) first to reduce the taxpayer's share of property expenses,

(ii) if any remains unapplied, then to reduce the taxpayer's share of development expenses,

(iii) if any remains unapplied, then to reduce the taxpayer's share of exploration expenses,

(iv) if any remains unapplied, then to reduce (in the order specified by the taxpayer in writing filed with the Minister on or before the taxpayer's filing-due date for the taxpayer's taxation year in which the fiscal period ends or, where no such specification is made, in the order determined by the Minister) the taxpayer's share of country-specific foreign expenses, and

(v) if any remains unapplied, then to reduce the taxpayer's share of global foreign expenses,

incurred by the partnership in the fiscal period; and

(c) for the purposes of subparagraph 53(2)(c)(ii), sections 66 to 66.7, subsection 96(2.1) and section 111, the taxpayer's share of each class of expenses described in subparagraph (a)(i) incurred by the partnership in the fiscal period shall be deemed to be the amount by which the taxpayer's share of that class of expenses as determined under subparagraph (a)(i) exceeds the amount, if any, that was applied under paragraph (b) to reduce the taxpayer's share of that class of expenses.

Notes: 66.8(1) amended by 2000 Budget, for fiscal periods that begin after 2000.

(2) Expenses in following fiscal period — For the purposes of subparagraph (1)(a)(i), the amount by which a taxpayer's share of a class of expenses incurred by a partnership is reduced under paragraph (1)(b) in respect of a fiscal period of the partnership shall be added to the taxpayer's share, otherwise determined, of that class of expenses incurred by the partnership in the immediately following fiscal period of the partnership.

(3) Interpretation — In this section,

(a) the expression **"limited partner"** of a partnership has the meaning that would be assigned by subsection 96(2.4), if in subsection 96(2.5) each reference to

(i) "February 25, 1986" were a reference to "June 17, 1987",

(ii) "February 26, 1986" were a reference to "June 18, 1987",

(iii) "January 1, 1987" were a reference to "January 1, 1988",

(iv) "June 12, 1986" were a reference to "June 18, 1987", and

(v) "prospectus, preliminary prospectus or registration statement" were a reference to "prospectus, preliminary prospectus, registration statement, offering memorandum or notice that is required to be filed before any distribution of securities may commence";

(a.1) the expression **"at-risk amount"** of a taxpayer in respect of a partnership has the meaning that would be assigned by subsection 96(2.2) if paragraph 96(2.2)(c) read as follows:

(c) all amounts each of which is an amount owing at that time to the partnership, or to a person or partnership not dealing at arm's length with the partnership, by the taxpayer or by a person or partnership not dealing at arm's length with the taxpayer, other than any amount deducted under subparagraph 53(2)(c)(i.3) in computing the adjusted cost base, or under section 143.2 in computing the cost, to the taxpayer of the taxpayer's partnership interest at that time, or any amount owing by the taxpayer to a person in respect of which the taxpayer is a subsidiary wholly-owned corporation or where the taxpayer is a trust, to a person that is the sole beneficiary of the taxpayer, and;

(b) a reference to a taxpayer who is a member of a particular partnership shall include a reference to another partnership that is a member of the particular partnership; and

(c) a taxpayer's share of Canadian development expenses or Canadian oil and gas property expenses incurred by a partnership in a fiscal period in respect of which the taxpayer has elected in respect of the share under paragraph (f) of the definition "Canadian development expense" in subsection 66.2(5) or paragraph (b) of the definition "Canadian oil and gas property expense" in subsection 66.4(5), as the case may be, shall be deemed to be nil.

Notes: 66.8(3) amended by 2002-2013 technical bill, for fiscal periods that end after 2003.

Definitions [s. 66.8]: "amount" — 248(1); "at-risk amount" — 66.8(3)(a.1); "business" — 248(1); "Canadian development expense" — 66.2(5), 248(1); "Canadian exploration expense" — 66.1(6), 248(1); "Canadian oil and gas property expense" — 66.4(5), 248(1); "country-specific foreign expenses" — 66.8(1)(a)(i)(D); "farming", "filing-due date" — 248(1); "fiscal period" — 249(2), 249.1; "foreign exploration and development expenses" — 66(15), 248(1); "global foreign expenses" — 66.8(1)(a)(i)(E); "investment tax credit" — 127(9), 248(1); "limited partner" — 66.8(3)(a); "Minister", "share", "property" — 248(1); "taxation year" — 249; "taxpayer" — 248(1); "writing" — *Interpretation Act* 35(1).

Subdivision F — Rules Relating to Computation of Income

67. General limitation re expenses [must be reasonable] — In computing income, no deduction shall be made in respect of an outlay or expense in respect of which any amount is otherwise deductible under this Act, except to the extent that the outlay or expense was reasonable in the circumstances.

Related Provisions: 8(9) — Employee's aircraft costs must be reasonable; 18(1)(a) — Expense not deductible unless for purpose of earning income; 18(1)(h) — Personal or living expenses disallowed; 20(1)(c) closing words — Interest deduction limited to reasonable amount; 247(8) — Transfer pricing rules take priority over s. 67.

Notes [s. 67]: *Reasonableness generally*: See Raymond Adlington, "How Reasonable is Reasonable?", 14(5) *Tax Hyperion* (Carswell) 1-3 (Sept-Oct 2017). See also Notes to 9(2) under "Second-guessing business decisions"; to 20(1)(c) under "Reasonableness"; and VIEWS doc 9520875 (reasonableness must be examined at both individual and total expense level, and can be determined only on a case by case basis).

The governing principle for applying s. 67 is: "It is not a question of the Minister or this Court substituting its judgment for what is a reasonable amount to pay, but rather ... coming to the conclusion that no reasonable business man would have contracted to pay such an amount": *Gabco Ltd.*, [1968] C.T.C. 313 (Exch. Ct.), approved in *Petro-Canada*, 2004 FCA 158 (leave to appeal denied 2004 CarswellNat 4108 (SCC)); and cited in *Edison Transportation*, 2016 TCC 80, para. 18. For a good review of the principles see *Anderson*, 2016 TCC 106, paras. 21-26 (a $15,000 payment to a "sales celebrity" was unreasonable: para. 62). Arm's-length financing transaction fees were reasonable in *Banque Laurentienne*, 2020 TCC 73 (Crown had the onus of proof because CRA did not assume the fees were unreasonable when assessing: para. 92).

Unreasonable expenses should not simply be disallowed; the judge must allow the reasonable portion of each expense: *Peach*, 2016 FCA 173, para. 7 (specifics then determined at 2017 TCC 40) and 2020 TCC 12, para. 40.

Paying owners: A corporation can normally deduct unlimited salary or bonus payable to its owner-manager, on the principle that its profits are due to the owner's work: *Safety Boss*, [2000] 3 C.T.C. 2497 (TCC); *Technical News* 22; VIEWS doc 2004-0092931R3. The bonus can create a loss carried back to past years: 2004-0072741R3. CRA says that unlimited deduction is not allowed for payments to non-resident shareholders or for management fees to a personal services business company (2004-0070121E5), to a family trust (2002-0141115, 2010-0354671I7) or to a holding company (2001-0114993, 2006-0172051E5, 2009-0352801E5); but see *6051944 Canada Inc.*, 2015 TCC 180, allowing high fees to Holdcos for GST purposes. The author asked CRA Rulings to review its policy in light of this case, but CRA declined because it was a non-binding Informal Procedure decision: 2015-0622991E5. For management fees charged to a professional corp by a related company, see 2009-0343971E5. A one-time asset sale may fall outside the policy or may be allowed: *Technical News* 30; docs 2000-0016035, 2003-0046624, 2004-0060191R3, 2004-0101131R3, 2005-0146021R3, 2005-0146391R3, 2005-0157341R3, 2005-0163741R3, 2006-0168701R3, 2006-0168751R3, 2006-0189151R3, 2006-0201601R3, 2007-0246871R3. See also 2000-0013085, 2001-0064055, 2001-0074115, 2001-0092515, 2002-0128875, 2003-0054061I7, 2004-0086191R3, 2005-0156441E5, 2005-011580117, 2008-0305091R3 (farm corp paying couple bonus on retirement). CRA may reject bonusing income to a status Indian owner (see Notes to 81(1)(a)): 2004-0074171I7, 2010-0376541E5. In *Bell*, 2018 FCA 91 (leave to appeal denied 2019 CarswellNat 360 (SCC)), a company owned by a couple bonused out all its profits for years ($2m in one year) to wife W, a status Indian; CRA did not disallow the deduction via s. 67, but W's Indian exemption (see Notes to 81(1)(a)) did not apply (para. 25). See Notes to 78(4) if a bonus is accrued but not paid. On paying management fees rather than salary/bonus to an owner, see Notes to 248(1)"employee" and 125(7)"personal services business".

On balancing owner-manager remuneration see taxtemplates.ca spreadsheet "Salary vs Dividend"; Sanghera, "Owner-Manager Remuneration Update", 2012 BC Tax Conference (ctf.ca) 10:1-21; Carson, "Personal and Corporate Tax Rate Changes", 2012 Ontario Tax Conf. 10:1-35; Moody, "Owner Manager Remuneration", 2013 Prairie Provinces Tax Conf. (PPTC) 7:1-49; McMurtry, "Owner-Manager Remuneration", 2014 PPTC 11:1-22; De Rose, Di Maio & Szubzda, "Owner-Manager Year-End Tips", 27(10) Canadian Tax Highlights (ctf.ca) 7-10 (Oct. 2019) and 27(11) 2-3 (Nov. 2019); and Notes to 89(1)"eligible dividend". On documenting the mix see Wong, "End-of-Year Salary-Dividend Planning", 3(2) Canadian Tax Focus (ctf.ca) 1-2 (May 2013).

Pay of $50/hour to the owner-manager for SR&ED work on an adult tricycle was reasonable in Tri-O-cycles Concept, 2009 TCC 632.

Payment to a retired shareholder may be disallowed by CRA, other than a reasonable retiring allowance; see Notes to 248(1)"retiring allowance" and Bernstein, "Retiring Allowances for Owner-Managers", 200 The Estate Planner (CCH) 3-4 (Sept. 2011).

Due to the increased dividend tax credit on dividends from income not eligible for the small business deduction (see Notes to 89(1)"eligible dividend"), as well as reduced general corporate tax rates (see 123.4(2)), "bonusing down" to the small business limit is no longer always advisable. See Notes to 125(1).

Management fees paid to a related company are generally accepted up to a 15% markup over the expenses the company handles: Holmes, [1974] C.T.C. 156 (FCTD); Smith, [1987] 1 C.T.C. 2183 (TCC); Bertomeu, 2006 TCC 85; Revenue Canada Roundtable, 1985 Cdn Tax Foundation conference report, p. 49:10, q.18; VIEWS doc 2010-0373441C6. (Note that such fees bear GST/HST, so using such a management company may be inadvisable for a physician, dentist, vocational school or other business that cannot claim full input tax credits.) See also Nicolas Baass, "Are Management Fees a Useful Tool or Audit Time Bomb?", 22(8) Taxation of Executive Compensation & Retirement (Federated Press) 1391-95 (April 2011). The 2016 Budget amendments to s. 125 restrict the use of certain intercorporate management fees to multiply the small business deduction.

Management fees were disallowed as unreasonable in Agricultural & Industrial Corp., [1991] 2 C.T.C. 2721 (TCC); Pazner Scrap Metals, [1991] 2 C.T.C. 2295 (TCC); Bronson Homes, [1993] 2 C.T.C. 2060 (TCC); Burrows, 2006 TCC 463; Bessette v. Quebec, 2014 QCCQ 4329 [Thompson, "Deductibility of Corporate Management Fees Denied", 2(4) Arbitrary Assessment (Carswell) 20-22 (July 2014); Gosselin, "Quebec Finds Big Cavity in Dentist's Management Services Company", 14(4) Tax for the Owner-Manager (ctf.ca) 1 (Oct. 2014)].

Management fees paid to a subsidiary to use up its losses were disallowed where the subsidiary provided no management services: Entreprises Réjean Goyette, 2009 TCC 351; but see Notes to 111(5) re permissible loss consolidations.

Where management fees are disallowed, CRA will normally allow an offsetting deduction to the recipient to prevent double tax: "In the absence of special situations, such as abuses, it is the department's policy not to tax the same amount twice": 1986 Cdn Tax Foundation Conference Roundtable, q.39; VIEWS docs 2012-0440071E5, 2015-0595671C6 [2015 APFF q.10].

Management fees to family trusts were allowed in Costigane, 2003 TCC 67 (bookkeeping for dentist, but only 15% markup allowed); Ferrel, [1999] 2 C.T.C. 101 (FCA).

Management fees paid to a related non-resident: see 247(2) (transfer pricing).

Payments to wives were allowed in: Noel, 2011 TCC 27 (lawyer's payments for office work were reasonable, though made irregularly); Nithyanandan, 2011 TCC 160; Leaf, 2016 CarswellNat 5376 (TCC) (work was legitimate; no written contract needed). They were disallowed in: Jastrzebski, 2008 TCC 643 (lack of evidence of work done); Major, 2017 FCA 226 (no evidence of payment or contract). Payments to a wife's management company were allowed in: Aessie, 2004 TCC 421 (accountant with gross revenue of $55,000 paying fees of $34,500, even though tax planning was a reason for the fees: "many professionals and businessmen make less money from their businesses than their secretaries do" and the arrangement was "a common and reasonable business deal"); Nielsen Development, 2009 TCC 160 ($275,000-$300,000 annual fees to owner's wife's corp to manage hotel were reasonable in light of work she did); Sael Inspection, 2011 FCA 350 ($175,000 of annual fees of $250,000 to owner's wife's corp were allowed). See also VIEWS doc 2012-0473051E5. In Blott, 2018 TCC 1, para. 13, B's wife having access to a joint account where his salary went was not "payment" to her.

Meals shared with a spouse (allegedly to discuss business) were partly allowed in Phillips, 2012 TCC 337, paras. 3-6, and disallowed in Stevens, 2012 TCC 312, para. 39.

Payments to owners' spouses and children who do not work actively in the business may be taxed at the top marginal rate under 120.4, which was expanded in 2018 from a "kiddie tax" to a more general tax on split income.

Rent paid to related companies was partly disallowed as unreasonable in Produits pour Toitures Fransyl, 2006 FCA 112; and allowed in 8076958 Ontario, 2018 TCC 253.

Owners' children: It may be reasonable to pay more to a family member than an arm's-length employee due to the owner's trust in the employee's loyalty and commitment: Klyguine, "Income Splitting After the New Private Corporation Proposals: Salaries Paid to Family Members", 8(1) Canadian Tax Focus (ctf.ca) 1-2 (Feb. 2018). Salaries or bonuses were disallowed or reduced to nominal amounts in Mépalex Inc., [2004] 2 C.T.C. 2681 (TCC); Massicotte, 2009 TCC 602; Jastrzebski, 2008 TCC 643; Bitzanis,

2010 TCC 354; White, 2010 TCC 530, para. 15; Rail, 2011 TCC 130, para. 38; DiCosmo, 2015 TCC 325, para. 31 (aff'd 2017 FCA 60); but payments to teenage children were 75% allowed in Hokhold, 2013 FCA 86, and 50% allowed in Bruno, 2012 TCC 316 (payments made by purchasing luxury items for the children, but purchase documentation was lacking). Large bonuses to adult children or family members were allowed in: Gabco Ltd., [1968] C.T.C. 313 (Exch. Ct.) (19-year-old son being groomed to take over the business) [see second para. of these Notes]; Ambulances B.G.R., 2004 TCC 168 (fair pay for exceptional services, including in earlier years); Wedge, 2005 TCC 480 ("compensation for the many years in which they worked for no or substantially no pay"). $7,350 paid to a university-age son was allowed in Chaloux, 2015 TCC 284, para. 73 (FCA appeal discontinued A-540-15). Directors' fees to adult children were limited to $1,500/year for directors with minimal duties in Manchester Chivers Insurance Brokers, 2005 TCC 402. In Tiede, 2011 TCC 84, only some payments to adult children were allowed to offset rent they paid. (Owners' children may be independent contractors if the facts justify it, e.g. Bosveld, 2020 TCC 2.)

It was an error for the TCC to disallow expenses paid to children on the basis that, because the expenses far exceeded income, there was no business. Rather, the two-step approach in !@#Stewart must be used: determine whether there is a business, then apply s. 67 to specific expenses: Raghavan, 2007 FCA 27 (on rehearing, the expenses were denied anyway): 2009 FCA 63). See also Notes to 9(2).

For more on income splitting see Notes to 74.1(1).

Where children are paid with funds that are then circuited back to the parents or the business, the deduction may be disallowed: Slingerland, [1978] C.T.C. 2343 (TRB); Blake, [1981] C.T.C. 2020 (TRB); Clarke, [1984] C.T.C. 2944 (TCC); Muhammedi, 2004 TCC 408. Salaries paid to an account in trust for children age 8-13 were disallowed where the parent retained control of the account: Bradley, 2006 TCC 500.

Interest expenses exceeding a reasonable amount are disallowed explicitly by 20(1)(c); see Notes thereto.

Scammed taxpayers: Expenses were found unreasonable in: Hammill, 2005 FCA 252, para. 54 (leave to appeal denied 2006 CarswellNat 58 (SCC)) (victim of fraudulent scheme to profit from precious gems); Vankerk, 2006 FCA 96 (investors in fake partnerships, defrauded by promoters); Ruff, 2012 TCC 105 (lawyer's losses to Nigerian advance-fee scam); Garber, 2014 TCC 1, paras. 415-418 (FCA appeal discontinued A-83-14) (fraudulent purported luxury yacht chartering business).

Expenses were also unreasonable in: Lecerf, 2004 TCC 626 (rental property management fees of $57,000 paid without a management agreement to person who apparently lived with L, where the rent from the property was $5,000); Morris, 2006 TCC 502 (cottage expenses could only be 50% deducted where cottage was used personally for 24-35 days a year, rented out for 21-28 days, and vacant rest of year).

Expenses were found reasonable in: Ankrah, 2003 TCC 413 (Amway expenses: s. 67 should not deny expenses based on bad business judgment where they were incurred in the honest belief they would eventually lead to profits); Tannenbaum, 2005 TCC 13 (attempted gold trading business); Whitecap Ltd., 2005 TCC 480 (payments to shareholders as compensation for past services); Baxter, 2006 TCC 230 (rev'd on other grounds 2007 FCA 172, leave to appeal denied 2007 CarswellNat 3625 (SCC)) (software license was held to have the same value as what B paid).

For advertising and promotion expenses: see Notes to 18(1)(a).

The Supreme Court of Canada stated in Stewart, 2002 SCC 46 at para. 57: "if, in the circumstances, the expense is unreasonable in relation to the source of income, then s. 67 provides a mechanism to reduce or eliminate the amount of the expense. Again, however, excessive or unreasonable expenses have no bearing on the characterization of a particular activity as a source of income."

The fact expenses are undocumented does not make them unreasonable, and oral evidence of expenses can be accepted. See Notes to 9(1) under "Cash expenses".

Repayment of embezzled funds is deductible against income from criminal activity (Income Tax Folio S3-F9-C1 ¶1.32; see Notes to 9(1) under "Criminal activity"), but was disallowed as unreasonable in Humphrey, 2006 TCC 168, because H had never paid tax on the stolen funds due to bankruptcy.

CRA has stated that 67 cannot be used to disallow an expense to enforce an administrative obligation, e.g. if a construction contractor does not identify subcontractors as required by Reg. 238: VIEWS doc 2006-0181651I7.

Where unreasonable amounts are deducted for expenses paid to a related non-resident, see instead the transfer pricing rules in 247(2).

Definitions [s. 67]: "amount" — 248(1).

Income Tax Folios: S1-F2-C3: Scholarships, research grants and other education assistance [replaces IT-340R]; S1-F3-C4: Moving expenses [replaces IT-178R3].

Interpretation Bulletins: IT-131R2: Convention expenses; IT-357R2: Expenses of training; IT-467R2: Damages, settlements and similar payments; IT-468R: Management or administration fees paid to non-residents; IT-521R: Motor vehicle expenses claimed by self-employed individuals; IT-525R: Performing artists.

Information Circulars: 87-2R: International transfer pricing (archived); 06-1: Income tax transfer pricing and customs valuation.

I.T. Technical News: 12 (meals and beverages at golf clubs); 15 (Christmas parties and employer-paid special events); 16 (Shell case); 22 (shareholder-manager remuneration); 30 (reasonableness of shareholder/manager remuneration).

Advance Tax Rulings: ATR-12: Retiring allowance; ATR-45: Share appreciation rights plan.

67.1 (1) Expenses for food, etc. [or entertainment] — Subject to subsection (1.1), for the purposes of this Act, other than sections 62, 63, 118.01 and 118.2, an amount paid or payable in respect of the human consumption of food or beverages or the enjoyment of entertainment is deemed to be 50 per cent of the lesser of

(a) the amount actually paid or payable in respect thereof, and

(b) an amount in respect thereof that would be reasonable in the circumstances.

Related Provisions: 8(4) — Limitation on meals of employee.

Notes: 67.1 limits most meal and entertainment expenses to 50%, on the theory that some consumption is always personal (but see exceptions in 67.1(1.1)-(2)). It does not violate the *Charter of Rights*, even though federal government employees have a much larger meal allowance: *Smith*, 2006 BCCA 237 (leave to appeal denied 2006 CarswellBC 3007 (SCC)); *Stogrin*, 2011 TCC 532. The 50% applies to the "simplified" per-day amounts CRA allows (see Notes to 8(1)(g)): *King*, 2008 TCC 79.

Quebec has the same rule for its provincial tax, but also limits the expenses to 1.25%-2% of gross revenues, with different limits for sales agents: *Taxation Act* s. 175.6.1. The 50% limitation also applies to GST/HST input tax credits (ITCs), except for registered charities: *Excise Tax Act* s. 236. (Until June 2018 in Ontario and June 2021 in PEI, the ITC for large businesses is further reduced by ETA s. 236.01: see *Practitioner's Goods and Services Tax, Annotated*.) For the income tax and GST/HST calculations see Karen Yull, "M&E Expense Reporting for Income and Sales Tax Purposes", 7(9) *Tax Hyperion* (Carswell, Sept. 2010). A 50% limit also applies in the US: *Internal Revenue Code* §274(n)), though it is suspended for 2021-22 due to COVID-19: IRS Notice 2021-25.

For CRA interpretation see IT-518R (not updated to cover the long-haul trucker rule in 67.1(1.1)); VIEWS doc 2017-0714381E5 (67.1 applies to meal allowance, and to hockey tickets bought by hockey scout to watch games [this is wrong in the author's view: for the scout this is not "enjoyment of entertainment"]). Agreements between the CRA and each of the Canadian Construction Association and the Canadian Association of Oilwell Drilling Contractors set the portion of daily allowances in these industries considered to be for meals, where subsistence allowances paid by association members to crews working in the field. See Communiqué AD-98-24 (on *TaxPartner* and *Taxnet Pro*); 2006-0185471E5, 2013-049094117.

For discussion of what is "reasonable" for 67.1(1)(b), see Notes to 67.

"Entertainment" refers to activities, not purchases like electronic games and musical instruments: VIEWS doc 2009-033738117. It includes a Caribbean incentive trip: 2012-047221117.

In *Stapley*, 2006 FCA 36, a real estate broker was allowed only 50% deduction for vouchers for meals, drinks and entertainment he gave to clients, even though he did not participate in the consumption or enjoyment (the FCA commented that this is "unfair": para. 30). CRA's view is that gift cards usable at a supermarket, given to people who attend a marketing presentation, fall under 67.1 (doc 2014-0521211E5); this might be wrong in the author's view, depending on whether gift card costs are paid "in respect of consumption of food".

In *Caldwell*, 2003 TCC 232, the cost of doughnuts given as gifts to clients was allowed in full (not limited to 50%) as not equating to a "meal". However, CRA considers that gifts of food or wine fall within 67.1: VIEWS docs 2003-0000025, 2004-0088721E5. The same applies to coffee and water provided to clients and staff: 2004-0057101E5. This is likely correct in light of *Stapley*: see *Ngai*, 2018 TCC 26, paras. 46, 84, 92.

In *T. Evans Electric*, [2002] G.S.T.C. 115 (TCC), a corporation used its plane to take clients on fly-in fishing trips. The Court allowed full GST input tax credits for the plane operating costs, since "entertainment" does not include transportation: "Flying in a noisy little Cessna to get to the fishing may be enjoyable to some, but likely not to most... The fishing starts when you get to the lake." However, CRA generally considers travel to be included: VIEWS docs 2005-0152091I7, 2006-0181621E5.

In *Structures G.B. Ltée*, 1996 CarswellNat 2470 (TCC), meals provided in construction work camps were held to be subject to the 50% limitation, even though the expenditure was for business purposes. A truck driver's daily meal allowance is also caught by the rule: VIEWS docs 2004-0086611E5, 2005-011431117. However, where truck drivers' lodging and meal reimbursements were replaced by a per-km "lodging allowance" and the drivers had to buy their own meals, the allowance was fully deductible: *Transport Baie-Comeau Inc.*, 2006 TCC 108. CRA considers this case as specific to its facts and will not change its position: doc 2008-0285341C6.

The 50% limitation applies to a professional food critic's restaurant meals in the CRA's view: VIEWS doc 2009-0333481E5. It also applies to a golf club's restaurant and bar: see Notes to 18(1)(l).

See also Manu Kakkar, "Some Not So Obvious Exceptions to the 50% Meals and Entertainment Rules", 13(1) *Tax for the Owner-Manager* (ctf.ca) 3-4 (Jan. 2013).

67.1(1) amended by 2007 budget bill #2 (for amounts paid, or that become payable, after March 18, 2007); 2006 budget bill #1; 1994 Budget (to change "80%" to "50%" from March 1994).

Interpretation Bulletins: IT-504R2: Visual artists and writers; IT-518R: Food beverages and entertainment expenses; IT-525R: Performing artists.

Information Circulars: 73-21R9: Claims for meals and lodging expenses of transport employees.

I.T. Technical News: 12 (meals and beverages at golf clubs); 16 (*Scott* case).

(1.1) Meal expenses for long-haul truck drivers — An amount paid or payable in respect of the consumption of food or beverages by a long-haul truck driver during an eligible travel period of the driver is deemed to be the amount determined by multiplying the specified percentage in respect of the amount so paid or payable by the lesser of

(a) the amount so paid or payable, and

(b) a reasonable amount in the circumstances.

Related Provisions: 67.1(5) — Definitions.

Notes: 67.1(1.1) allows 80% rather than 50% of long-haul truck drivers' meal expenses, because such drivers have no choice about incurring meal expenses. See 67.1(5)"specified percentage", which phased in the increase from 2007-2011. The higher rate did not apply to years before 2007: *Dunn*, 2008 TCC 37.

For discussion of what is "reasonable", see Notes to 67 and VIEWS doc 2010-0364751E5. Note that self-employed truckers cannot use the simplified meals calculation allowed to employees for 8(1)(g): 2011-0392521E5, 2011-0392961E5.

67.1(1.1) added by 2007 budget bill #2, for amounts that are paid, or become payable, after March 18, 2007; and amended retroactive to its introduction by 2002-2013 technical bill, to ensure it applies regardless of whether the amount is paid *by* the driver.

(2) Exceptions — Subsection (1) does not apply to an amount paid or payable by a person in respect of the consumption of food or beverages or the enjoyment of entertainment where the amount

(a) is paid or payable for food, beverages or entertainment provided for, or in expectation of, compensation in the ordinary course of a business carried on by that person of providing the food, beverages or entertainment for compensation;

(b) relates to a fund-raising event the primary purpose of which is to benefit a registered charity;

(c) is an amount for which the person is compensated and the amount of the compensation is reasonable and specifically identified in writing to the person paying the compensation;

(d) is required to be included in computing any taxpayer's income because of the application of section 6 in respect of food or beverages consumed or entertainment enjoyed by the taxpayer or a person with whom the taxpayer does not deal at arm's length, or would be so required but for subparagraph 6(6)(a)(ii);

(e) is an amount that

(i) is not paid or payable in respect of a conference, convention, seminar or similar event,

(ii) would, but for subparagraph 6(6)(a)(i), be required to be included in computing any taxpayer's income for a taxation year because of the application of section 6 in respect of food or beverages consumed or entertainment enjoyed by the taxpayer or a person with whom the taxpayer does not deal at arm's length, and

(iii) is paid or payable in respect of the taxpayer's duties performed at a work site in Canada that is

(A) outside any population centre, as defined by the last Census Dictionary published by Statistics Canada before the year, that has a population of at least 40,000 individuals as determined in the last census published by Statistics Canada before the year, and

(B) at least 30 kilometres from the nearest point on the boundary of the nearest such population centre;

(e.1) is an amount that

(i) is not paid or payable in respect of entertainment or of a conference, convention, seminar or similar event,

(ii) would, if this Act were read without reference to subparagraph 6(6)(a)(i), be required to be included in computing a taxpayer's income for a taxation year because of the application of section 6 in respect of food or beverages consumed by the taxpayer or by a person with whom the taxpayer does not deal at arm's length,

(iii) is paid or payable in respect of the taxpayer's duties performed at a site in Canada at which the person carries on a construction activity or at a construction work camp referred to in subparagraph (iv) in respect of the site, and

(iv) is paid or payable for food or beverages provided at a construction work camp, at which the taxpayer is lodged, that was constructed or installed at or near the site to provide board and lodging to employees while they are engaged in construction services at the site; or

(f) is in respect of one of six or fewer special events held in a calendar year at which the food, beverages or entertainment is generally available to all individuals employed by the person at a particular place of business of the person and consumed or enjoyed by those individuals.

Notes: A meal eaten by a restaurant owner to check out a competing restaurant, or a theatre program attended by a theatre director in order to improve his own product, are still subject to the 50% limitation in CRA's view: doc 2010-0373331C6.

67.1(2)(a) requires compensation from a "paying customer", so providing meals to employees does not qualify (though para. (d) may apply): VIEWS doc 2014-0519051E5. Where food or entertainment is resold in promotional packages (e.g. store sells baking pan with food in it, or publisher provides free ticket to movie with purchase of book), 67.1(2)(a) applies so full deduction is allowed: 2004-0094761E5. The same applies to food provided in the course of a seminar, exposition or other event: *Pink Elephant*, 2011 TCC 395; docs 2012-0452491E5, 2014-0553081E5 (reversing 2006-0167861E5, 2010-0389131I7).

67.1(2)(b): The fund-raising expenses must still be deductible under 18(1)(a) or 110.1(1).

67.1(2)(c): If the charge is explicitly billed to a client as a disbursement, it is 100% deductible, but then the 50% rule applies to the client: doc 2004-0078521E5. If incorporated into charges to clients, see 67.1(2)(a).

In *Kelowna Flightcraft*, 2003 TCC 347, a *per diem* meal allowance paid by an air charter company to flight crews was fully deductible due to both 67.1(2)(c) and (e), as the company was reimbursed for these amounts, and because the crews were all the employees at the company's "place of business", which was the airplanes themselves.

67.1(2)(d) allows full deduction when meals are provided to employees (but not to self-employed contractors: VIEWS doc 2014-0519051E5), either as a taxable benefit or exempt only because of 6(6)(a)(ii). It includes meals for employees of a subcontractor, due to the words "any taxpayer's income".

67.1(2)(e): To determine if place X is within 30 km of a population centre of at least 40,000 for (iii)(B), see tinyurl.com/pop-centres and use maps.google.com to calculate normal road distance (see Notes to 248(1)"eligible relocation") from X. See also the *Kelowna Flightcraft* case above.

67.1(2)(e.1) allows full deductibility for meals provided to a taxpayer's employee at a work camp if certain conditions are met.

67.1(2)(f): The 6 special events are counted company-wide in a large organization, but simultaneous Christmas parties in different divisions will count as one: VIEWS doc 2005-0116071E5. The "special events" to which all employees must be invited may include clients, even if there are more clients than employees: 2003-0039975. However, *Francis*, 2014 TCC 137, rejected a para. (f) claim because a law firm did not show that its parties were only for staff, as they were partly for clients (para. 52), so the 50% limit applied.

67.1(2)(e)(iii) amended by 2013 budget bill #2, for 2013 and later tax years, to change "urban area" to "population centre". 67.1(2) earlier amended by 2001 and 1998 Budgets, 1991 technical bill.

I.T. Technical News: 15 (Christmas parties and employer-paid special events).

(3) Fees for convention, etc. — For the purposes of this section, where a fee paid or payable for a conference, convention, seminar or similar event entitles the participant to food, beverages or entertainment (other than incidental beverages and refreshments made available during the course of meetings or receptions at the event) and a reasonable part of the fee, determined on the basis of the cost of providing the food, beverages and entertainment, is not identified in the account for the fee as compensation for the food, beverages and entertainment, $50 or such other amount as may be prescribed shall be deemed to be the actual amount paid or payable in respect of food, beverages and entertainment for each day of the event on which food, beverages or entertainment is provided and, for the purposes of this Act, the fee for the event shall be deemed to be the actual amount of the fee minus the amount deemed by this subsection to be the actual amount paid or payable for the food, beverages and entertainment.

Related Provisions: 20(10) — Deduction for convention expenses.

Regulations: No amount other than $50 has been prescribed for purposes of 67.1(3).

Interpretation Bulletins: IT-131R2: Convention expenses.

(4) Interpretation — For the purposes of this section,

(a) no amount paid or payable for travel on an airplane, train or bus shall be considered to be in respect of food, beverages or entertainment consumed or enjoyed while travelling thereon; and

(b) **"entertainment"** includes amusement and recreation.

Notes: See Notes to 188.1(5) re meaning of "includes" in para. (b).

(5) Definitions — The following definitions apply for the purpose of this section.

"eligible travel period" in respect of a long-haul truck driver is a period during which the driver is away from the municipality or metropolitan area where the specified place in respect of the driver is located for a period of at least 24 continuous hours for the purpose of driving a long-haul truck that transports goods to, or from, a location that is beyond a radius of 160 kilometres from the specified place.

"long-haul truck" means a truck or a tractor that is designed for hauling freight and that has a gross vehicle weight rating (as that term is defined in subsection 2(1) of the *Motor Vehicle Safety Regulations*) that exceeds 11,788 kilograms.

Notes: The *Motor Vehicle Safety Regulations*, C.R.C., c. 1038, provide:

"gross vehicle weight rating" or "GVWR" means the value specified by the vehicle manufacturer as the loaded weight of a single vehicle;

Trailer weight is excluded; the GVWR is usually found on a sticker on the inside of the driver's side door: VIEWS doc 2014-0518911E5.

"long-haul truck driver" means an individual whose principal business or principal duty of employment is driving a long-haul truck that transports goods.

Notes: See VIEWS doc 2011-0399271E5 (general interpretation). For the meaning of "principal business" see Notes to 20(1)(bb).

"specified percentage" in respect of an amount paid or payable is

(a)-(d) [No longer relevant]

(e) 80 per cent, if the amount is paid or becomes payable after 2010.

Notes: See Notes to 67.1(1.1).

"specified place" means, in the case of an employee, the employer's establishment to which the employee ordinarily reports to work is located and, in the case of an individual whose principal business is to drive a long-haul truck to transport goods, the place where the individual resides.

Notes: For the meaning of "principal business" see Notes to 20(1)(bb).

67.1(5) added by 2007 budget bill #2, effective for amounts that are paid, or become payable, after March 18, 2007.

Definitions [s. 67.1]: "amount", "business" — 248(1); "calendar year" — *Interpretation Act* 37(1)(a); "eligible travel period" — 67.1(5); "employee", "employer", "employment" — 248(1); "entertainment" — 67.1(4)(b); "individual" — 248(1); "long-haul truck", "long-haul truck driver" — 67.1(5); "person", "prescribed", "registered charity" — 248(1); "specified percentage", "specified place" — 67.1(5); "writing" — *Interpretation Act* 35(1).

Income Tax Folios: S3-F6-C1: Interest deductibility [replaces IT-533].

Interpretation Bulletins: IT-518R: Food, beverages and entertainment expenses; IT-522R: Vehicle, travel and sales expenses of employees.

67.2 Interest on money borrowed for certain vehicles — For the purposes of this Act, if an amount is paid or payable for a period by a person in respect of interest on borrowed money used to acquire a passenger vehicle or zero-emission passenger vehicle, or on an amount paid or payable for the acquisition of such a vehicle, then in computing the person's income for a taxation year the amount of interest so paid or payable is deemed to be the lesser of the actual amount paid or payable and the amount determined by the formula

$$\frac{A}{30} \times B$$

where

A is $250 or such other amount as may be prescribed; and

B is the number of days in the period in respect of which the interest was paid or payable, as the case may be.

Related Provisions: 8(1)(j) — Automobile and aircraft costs; 20(1)(c) — Interest deductible; 20(1)(d) — Compound interest deductible; 67.4 — Where vehicle is jointly owned.

Notes: The limitation on deductible interest depends on the date of acquisition of the automobile; it is $300/month for acquisition in 2001-2021 (Reg. 7307(2)).

67.2 opening words amended by 2019 budget bill #1, effective March 19, 2019, to add "or zero-emission passenger vehicle" (and modernize the wording). This does not change the rule; 248(1)"passenger vehicle" was amended to exclude a ZEPV, so 67.2 was amended to apply to a ZEPV. Before March 19, 2019, read:

> 67.2 **Interest on money borrowed for passenger vehicle** — For the purposes of this Act, where an amount is paid or payable for a period by a person in respect of interest on borrowed money used to acquire a passenger vehicle or on an amount paid or payable for the acquisition of such a vehicle, in computing the person's income for a taxation year, the amount of interest so paid or payable shall be deemed to be the lesser of the actual amount paid or payable and the amount determined by the formula

67.2 amended by 1991 technical bill, retroactive to the introduction of the section (taxation years and fiscal periods commencing after June 17, 1987 that end after 1987). The new version deals with cash-basis taxpayers by using the words "paid or payable" rather than just "payable".

See also Notes to 13(7)(g).

Definitions [s. 67.2]: "amount", "borrowed money", "passenger vehicle", "person", "prescribed" — 248(1); "taxation year" — 11(2), 249; "zero-emission passenger vehicle" — 248(1).

Regulations: 7307(2) (prescribed amount).

Interpretation Bulletins: IT-355R2: Interest on loans to buy life insurance policies and annuity contracts, and interest on policy loans (cancelled); IT-521R: Motor vehicle expenses claimed by self-employed individuals; IT-522R: Vehicle, travel and sales expenses of employees; IT-525R: Performing artists.

I.T. Technical News: 10 (1997 deduction limits and benefit rates for automobiles).

67.3 Limitation re cost of leasing passenger vehicle — Notwithstanding any other section of this Act, where

(a) in a taxation year all or part of the actual lease charges in respect of a passenger vehicle are paid or payable, directly or indirectly, by a taxpayer, and

(b) in computing the taxpayer's income for the year an amount may be deducted in respect of those charges,

in determining the amount that may be so deducted, the total of those charges shall be deemed not to exceed the lesser of

(c) the amount determined by the formula

$$\left(A \times \frac{B}{30}\right) - C - D - E$$

where

A is $600 or such other amount as is prescribed,

B is the number of days in the period commencing at the beginning of the term of the lease and ending at the earlier of the end of the year and the end of the lease,

C is the total of all amounts deducted in computing the taxpayer's income for preceding taxation years in respect of the actual lease charges in respect of the vehicle,

D is the amount of interest that would be earned on the part of the total of all refundable amounts in respect of the lease that exceeds $1,000 if interest were

    (i) payable on the refundable amounts at the prescribed rate, and

    (ii) computed for the period before the end of the year during which the refundable amounts were outstanding, and

E is the total of all reimbursements that became receivable before the end of the year by the taxpayer in respect of the lease, and

(d) the amount determined by the formula

$$\left(\frac{A \times B}{0.85C}\right) - D - E$$

where

A is the total of the actual lease charges in respect of the lease incurred in respect of the year or the total of the actual lease charges in respect of the lease paid in the year (depending on the method regularly followed by the taxpayer in computing income),

B is $20,000 or such other amount as is prescribed,

C is the greater of $23,529 (or such other amount as is prescribed) and the manufacturer's list price for the vehicle,

D is the amount of interest that would be earned on that part of the total of all refundable amounts paid in respect of the lease that exceeds $1,000 if interest were

    (i) payable on the refundable amounts at the prescribed rate, and

    (ii) computed for the period in the year during which the refundable amounts are outstanding, and

E is the total of all reimbursements that became receivable during the year by the taxpayer in respect of the lease.

Related Provisions: 67.4 — Where vehicle is leased by more than one person; 257 — Formula cannot calculate to less than zero.

Notes: The limitation on deductible leasing cost for an automobile depends on the date of the lease; it is $800 per 30 days for a lease signed in 2001-2021 (Reg. 7307(3)). Where the lease runs the whole year, the limit in a non-leap year is $800 × 365 / 30 = $9,733.33. Note also the alternative limitation in 67.3(d).

The 2019 amendment to 248(1)"passenger vehicle" to exclude a "zero-emission passenger vehicle" (ZEPV), does not affect 67.3, because a ZEPV must be *owned* ("of the taxpayer" and included in Class 54). 67.3 thus continues to apply to a lease of an electric or hybrid car. (67.2 had to be amended to add reference to a ZEPV.) CRA agrees: "ZEPVs are subject to the leasing cost deduction rules" (in tinyurl.com/zepv-cra).

A lump-sum prepayment of a car lease can be either amortized over the term of the lease or currently deducted by a cash-basis taxpayer. See 18(9), IT-522R para. 9 and VIEWS docs 2003-0015675, 2003-0051791E5. The CRA considers lease cancellation fees that are deductible under 8(1)(h.1) to be subject to 67.3: 2004-0060021E5, 2008-0285361C6.

An over-mileage lease penalty is included in total lease costs when applying 67.3: VIEWS doc 2004-0072191E5.

In 67.3(a), payment "indirectly" of the lessor's lease charges would generally not include short-term daily car rentals, but could include a rental that stretches for weeks or months: VIEWS docs 2003-0032047, 2003-0032565. For more on "indirectly" see Notes to 17.1(1).

Element E includes GST/HST input tax credits and Quebec Sales Tax input tax refunds: VIEWS doc 2012-0473151E5.

67.3 amended by 1991 technical bill, last change effective for tax years that end after July 13, 1990; and for leases entered into before 1991, read (d)C differently.

See also Notes to 13(7)(g).

Definitions [s. 67.3]: "amount", "borrowed money", "motor vehicle", "passenger vehicle", "prescribed" — 248(1); "prescribed rate" — Reg. 4301; "taxation year" — 11(2), 249; "taxpayer" — 248(1); "trust" — 104(1), 248(1), (3).

Regulations: 4301(c) (prescribed rate of interest); 7307(1) (prescribed amount for 67.3(d)(b)); 7307(3) (for 67.3(c)A); 7307(4) (for 67.3(d)C).

Income Tax Folios: S4-F2-C1: Deductibility of fines and penalties [replaces IT-104R3].

Interpretation Bulletins: IT-521R: Motor vehicle expenses claimed by self-employed individuals; IT-522R: Vehicle, travel and sales expenses of employees; IT-525R: Performing artists.

I.T. Technical News: 10 (1997 deduction limits and benefit rates for automobiles); 12 (1998 deduction limits and benefit rates for automobiles).

67.4 More than one owner or lessor [lessee] — Where a person owns or leases a motor vehicle jointly with one or more other persons, the reference in paragraph 13(7)(g) to the amount of $20,000, in section 67.2 to the amount of $250 and in section 67.3 to the amounts of $600, $20,000 and $23,529 shall be read as a reference to that proportion of each of those amounts or such other amounts as may be prescribed for the purposes thereof that the fair market value of the first-mentioned person's interest in the vehicle

is of the fair market value of the interests in the vehicle of all those persons.

Notes: For interpretation see VIEWS doc 2006-0217551I7.

Definitions [s. 67.4]: "amount" — 248(1); "fair market value" — see 69(1) Notes; "motor vehicle", "person" — 248(1).

Regulations: 7307 (prescribed amounts).

Interpretation Bulletins: IT-521R: Motor vehicle expenses claimed by self-employed individuals; IT-522R: Vehicle, travel and sales expenses of employees; IT-525R: Performing artists.

I.T. Technical News: 10 (1997 deduction limits and benefit rates for automobiles).

67.41 More than one owner — If a person owns a zero-emission passenger vehicle jointly with one or more other persons, any reference in paragraph 13(7)(i) to the prescribed amount and in section 67.2 to the amount of $250 or such other amount as may be prescribed is to be read as a reference to that proportion of each of those amounts that the fair market value of the first-mentioned person's interest in the vehicle is of the fair market value of the interests in the vehicle of all those persons.

Notes: 67.41 (added by 2019 budget bill #1, effective March 19, 2019) maintains the rule in 67.4 for a "zero-emission passenger vehicle" (Class 54 electric or hybrid car), which is now excluded from 248(1)"passenger vehicle".

Definitions [s. 67.41]: "amount" — 248(1); "fair market value" — see 69(1) Notes; "person", "prescribed", "zero-emission passenger vehicle" — 248(1).

67.5 (1) Non-deductibility of illegal payments — In computing income, no deduction shall be made in respect of an outlay made or expense incurred for the purpose of doing anything that is an offence under section 3 of the *Corruption of Foreign Public Officials Act* or under any of sections 119 to 121, 123 to 125, 393 and 426 of the *Criminal Code*, or an offence under section 465 of the *Criminal Code* as it relates to an offence described in any of those sections.

Related Provisions: 67.6 — Non-deductibility of fines and penalties.

Notes: See Notes at end of 67.5.

(2) Reassessments — Notwithstanding subsections 152(4) to (5), the Minister may make such assessments, reassessments and additional assessments of tax, interest and penalties and such determinations and redeterminations as are necessary to give effect to subsection (1) for any taxation year.

Related Provisions: 165(1.1) — Limitation of right to object to assessment; 169(2)(a) — Limitation of right to appeal.

Notes [s. 67.5]: *Criminal Code* s. 119 deals with bribing judges, members of Parliament and members of a provincial or territorial legislature. S. 120: bribing officers involved in criminal law administration, such as police officers, justices and officers of a juvenile court. S. 121: paying government employees or officials to obtain contracts or other benefits. S. 123: attempts to influence municipal officials through bribery, threats, deceit, etc. S. 124: selling or paying for an appointment to an office. S. 125: influencing or negotiating appointments and dealing in offices. S. 393: paying off a collector who fails to collect a fare or admission fee. S. 426: secretly paying an agent a commission and deceiving the agent's principal. S. 465: conspiracy to commit an act that is an offence under the *Criminal Code*. S. 3 of the *Corruption of Foreign Public Officials Act* (CFPOA): bribing a foreign public official. See laws.justice.gc.ca.

Fines and penalties are generally non-deductible due to 67.6.

67.5 amended by the CFPOA, in force February 14, 1999, to refer to s. 3 of that Act. 67.5 added by 1991 technical bill, effective for outlays or expenses after July 13, 1990.

Definitions [s. 67.5]: "assessment", "Minister" — 248(1); "taxation year" — 249.

Income Tax Folios: S3-F6-C1: Interest deductibility [replaces IT-533]; S4-F2-C1: Deductibility of fines and penalties [replaces IT-104R3].

Interpretation Bulletins: IT-525R: Performing artists.

CRA Audit Manual: 13.10.0: Auditing bribes, kickbacks and similar payments.

67.6 Non-deductibility of fines and penalties — In computing income, no deduction shall be made in respect of any amount that is a fine or penalty (other than a prescribed fine or penalty) imposed under a law of a country or of a political subdivision of a country (including a state, province or territory) by any person or public body that has authority to impose the fine or penalty.

Related Provisions: 18(1)(t) — Non-deductibility of amounts paid under *Income Tax Act* and of GST interest; 67.5 — Non-deductibility of illegal payments.

Notes [s. 67.6]: 67.6 prohibits deductions for fines and penalties, including municipal parking tickets (although the Crown must show they were issued after March 22, 2004: *Li*, 2008 TCC 175). It overrules *65302 British Columbia (formerly Veekans Poultry) ["BC Eggs"]*, [2000] 1 C.T.C. 57 (SCC), and *Ferguson-Neudorf Glass*, 2008 TCC 684, which allowed such deduction; and see Notes to 9(1) under "Criminal activity". It does not cover late-payment penalties (which have been replaced with a higher interest rate for reporting periods since April 2007) under the GST (*Excise Tax Act*), the *Excise Act* and the *Air Travellers Security Charge Act*, but it does cover late-filing and gross-negligence penalties under those statutes: see Reg. 7309. "For administrative simplicity, we would permit a deduction in the year the amount is assessed or paid": *Income Tax Technical News* 38; 2007 Cdn Tax Foundation conference report at 4:5.

See Income Tax Folio S4-F2-C1 ¶1.4-1.7. CRA considers that 67.6 applies to: penalty imposed by the Investment Dealers Association or other self-regulating organization recognized by a provincial securities commission (VIEWS docs 2006-0185611I7, 2007-0256591M4); court-ordered payment to a charity on conviction under workplace safety legislation (2008-0294701E5); penalties under Ontario *Tobacco Tax Act* (but interest on the penalties may be deductible): 2012-0472261E5; administrative penalty under Alberta's *Climate Change and Emissions Management Act* (2012-04404715), but not contributions to the CCEM Fund to comply with that Act (2012-0462621E5). It does not apply to the surge mechanism under *Softwood Lumber Products Export Charge Act, 2006* s. 13: 2006-0212051E6.

67.6 does not prevent deduction of legal fees to defend against prosecutions that can lead to fines, if the fees are otherwise deductible (see 18(1)(a)): VIEWS docs 2008-027180117, 2008-0294701E5.

Proceeds of crime forfeited under *Criminal Code* s. 462.37 or the *Proceeds of Crime (Money Laundering) and Terrorist Financing Act*: 67.6 applied in *Chow*, 2011 TCC 263, para. 29: "Forfeiture of the proceeds of crime is a penalty for illegal activities". Before 67.6, such amounts were held non-deductible under 9(1) in: *Brizzi*, 2008 FCA 200; *Neeb*, 1997 CarswellNat 67 (TCC) (public policy denied deduction for seized marijuana); *Anjaria*, 2007 TCC 746; *Chan*, 2010 TCC 3 (aff'd on other grounds 2011 FCA 88); *Allan*, 2013 TCC 65 (FCA appeal discontinued A-115-13); were deductible in *Chronis*, 2010 TCC 218, para. 18; and the question was unresolved in *Toth*, 2004 TCC 56. General discussion of forfeiture: Peter German, *Proceeds of Crime and Money Laundering* (Carswell, 2 vols. looseleaf or ProView).

67.6 does not apply to interest, including interest on penalties: VIEWS doc 2004-0103901E5; or to interest on provincial capital tax: 2009-032694117. For discussion of deductibility of interest on GST, PST, source deductions and penalties for taxation years that begin after March 2007, see 2005-0119721E5. GST interest is non-deductible for taxation years that start after March 2007; 18(1)(t). See also Notes to Reg. 7309.

Penalties not restricted by 67.6 because they are prescribed are not necessarily deductible. A pre-2007 GST penalty due to non-remittance on the sale of capital property may be on account of capital: VIEWS doc 2005-0109721E5.

For the parallel Quebec income tax rules see Revenu Québec Interpretation Bulletin IMP.128-11/R2.

67.6 added by 2004 Budget, for fines and penalties imposed after March 22, 2004.

Regulations: 7309 (prescribed fines and penalties).

Income Tax Folios: S4-F2-C1: Deductibility of fines and penalties [replaces IT-104R3].

I.T. Technical News: 38 (income tax treatment of GST).

68. Allocation of amounts in consideration for property, services or restrictive covenants — If an amount received or receivable from a person can reasonably be regarded as being in part the consideration for the disposition of a particular property of a taxpayer, for the provision of particular services by a taxpayer or for a restrictive covenant as defined by subsection 56.4(1) granted by a taxpayer,

(a) the part of the amount that can reasonably be regarded as being the consideration for the disposition shall be deemed to be proceeds of disposition of the particular property irrespective of the form or legal effect of the contract or agreement, and the person to whom the property was disposed of shall be deemed to have acquired it for an amount equal to that part;

(b) the part of the amount that can reasonably be regarded as being consideration for the provision of particular services shall be deemed to be an amount received or receivable by the taxpayer in respect of those services irrespective of the form or legal effect of the contract or agreement, and that part shall be deemed to be an amount paid or payable to the taxpayer by the person to whom the services were rendered in respect of those services; and

(c) the part of the amount that can reasonably be regarded as being consideration for the restrictive covenant is deemed to be an amount received or receivable by the taxpayer in respect of the restrictive covenant irrespective of the form or legal effect of the contract or agreement, and that part is deemed to be an amount paid or payable to the taxpayer by the person to whom the restrictive covenant was granted.

Related Provisions: 12(1)(a) — Services, etc. to be rendered; 12(1)(b) — Amounts receivable in respect of services, etc, rendered; 13(33) — Consideration given for depreciable capital; 56.4(5)–(8) — Whether s. 68 applies to restrictive covenant (non-competition payment); 247(8) — Transfer pricing rules take priority over s. 68.

Notes: 68 can easily be misread. It does *not* say "If an amount ... can reasonably be regarded as being in part the consideration for the disposition of ... property *and as being in part* consideration for the provision of ... services ... or for a restrictive covenant". (That would allow it to apply only to a division between (1) property and (2) services or restrictive covenant.) There are three options for the "part of": property, services or restrictive covenant. Thus, s. 68 applies where what is received can be considered partly consideration for (a) disposition of property, (b) services provided by the taxpayer, or (c) a restrictive covenant, and partly something else (e.g., property and other property). It is the "something else" that can then be reallocated to proceeds of disposition (by 68(a)) or to income for services (by 68(b)) or to the restrictive covenant (by 68(c)). The pre-1988 wording, before s. 68 was expanded to services (and further expanded to restrictive covenants in 2013), was very clear: "in part the consideration for the disposition of any property of a taxpayer and as being in part consideration for something else". Note the "reasonably be regarded" test, which is quite broad.

Absent genuine bargaining between the parties, apportionments stated in a contract are not decisive: *Canadian Propane*, [1972] C.T.C. 566 (FCTD) (upheld CRA's reallocation of part of purchase price from depreciable assets to goodwill); *Wagner*, 2012 TCC 8 (aff'd as *Diaz*, 2013 FCA 11) (non-competition agreement valued at nil rather than $4m on $13m sale of shares). For more examples of allocations see *Golden*, [1986] 1 C.T.C. 274 (SCC) (parties' allocation between land and buildings was reasonable); *9075-5067 Québec*, 2004 TCC 692 (accepted taxpayer's allocation among land, buildings and equipment); *167849 Canada*, 2009 TCC 641 (allocation among leasehold improvements, franchise fees and equipment); *Sunrise Realty*, 2013 TCC 5 (allocation between land and building).

Transalta, 2012 FCA 20, held that on the $818m sale of an electricity transmission business, the arm's-length allocation of $190m to goodwill (based on industry practice) was reasonable, rejecting CRA's argument that a regulated business has no goodwill. Goodwill is the "residual" of sale price minus the value of the measurable assets [McCue, "The Section 68 Reasonableness Standard", 62(1) *Canadian Tax Journal* 43-67 (2014)]. It cannot be sold separately: para. 54; VIEWS doc 2020-0841791I7.

68(a) does not apply when the entire amount received can reasonably be regarded as consideration for disposition of 1 property: *Robert Glegg Investments*, 2008 FCA 332.

CRA will accept any method of allocation that is in compliance with GAAP and is "reasonable". (As a practical matter, it may accept an allocation on sale on the same basis as was done on purchase.) Legal fees on acquisition of business assets should be allocated proportionally to the various assets based on fair market value: 5(1) *Toronto West Tax Practitioners Consultation Group Newsletter* (CRA, Jan. 2004), p. 4.

CRA did not generally view a real estate purchaser as having bought pre-2017 eligible capital property (now Class 14.1) based solely on CICA *Handbook* accounting requirements to allocate part of the purchase price to intangible assets: May 2005 ICAA roundtable (tinyurl.com/cra-abtax), Supp. q. 1.

For discussion of para. (c) see CBA/CICA Joint Committee submission to Finance, Sept. 17, 2010, and articles cited in Notes to 56.4(2).

68 amended by 2002-2013 technical bill (Part 5 — technical), to add "or for a restrictive covenant as defined by subsection 56.4(1) granted by a taxpayer" and para. (c), effective Feb. 27, 2004 but the amendments do not apply to taxpayer X's grant of a restrictive covenant made in writing by X before Feb. 27, 2004 between X and a person with whom X deals at arm's length.

Definitions [s. 68]: "amount", "disposition", "person", "property" — 248(1); "received" — 248(7); "restrictive covenant" — 56.4(1); "taxpayer" — 248(1).

Income Tax Folios: S3-F4-C1: General discussion of CCA [replaces IT-220R2].

Interpretation Bulletins: IT-143R3: Meaning of eligible capital expenditure.

Transfer Pricing Memoranda: TPM-06: Bundled transactions.

69. (1) Inadequate considerations — Except as expressly otherwise provided in this Act,

(a) where a taxpayer has acquired anything from a person with whom the taxpayer was not dealing at arm's length at an amount in excess of the fair market value thereof at the time the taxpayer so acquired it, the taxpayer shall be deemed to have acquired it at that fair market value;

(b) where a taxpayer has disposed of anything

(i) to a person with whom the taxpayer was not dealing at arm's length for no proceeds or for proceeds less than the fair market value thereof at the time the taxpayer so disposed of it,

(ii) to any person by way of gift, or

(iii) to a trust because of a disposition of a property that does not result in a change in the beneficial ownership of the property;

the taxpayer shall be deemed to have received proceeds of disposition therefor equal to that fair market value; and

(c) where a taxpayer acquires a property by way of gift, bequest or inheritance or because of a disposition that does not result in a change in the beneficial ownership of the property, the taxpayer is deemed to acquire the property at its fair market value.

Related Provisions: 13(33) — Where depreciable property acquired for excessive price; 15(1) — Benefit conferred on shareholder; 28(1.1) — Farming or fishing business — acquisition of inventory; 38(a.1), (a.3) — Gift of publicly traded or exchangeable securities to charity; 53(5) — Recomputation of ACB on non-arm's length disposition; 56(11) — Parallel rule on disposition of property by RCA; 69(1.1) — Where 70(3) applies; 70(9.01), (9.11), (9.21), (9.31) — S. 69 does not apply on intergenerational rollover of farm or fishing property; 73(1) — Rollover at cost on transfer to spouse; 73(3.1)(d), (4.1)(d) — No application on family farm or fishing rollover; 79(3)E(a) — Where property surrendered to a creditor; 97(1) — Contribution of property by partner to partnership deemed to be at FMV; 107.4(3) — Tax consequences of qualifying disposition to a trust; 107.4(4) — FMV of vested interest in trust; 110.1(5), 118.1(10.1) — Determination of value on donation of cultural or ecological property; 127(11.8)(b) — Ignore 69(1)(c) for certain non-arm's length costs re investment tax credit; 142.7(4) — Deemed value of property on rollover from foreign bank subsidiary to branch; 146(9), 146.3(4) — Disposition or acquisition of property by RRSP or RRIF; 247(8) — Transfer pricing rules take priority over subsec. 69(1); 248(30) — Existence of advantage does not prevent there being a gift; 248(35)–(39) — Value of donation limited to cost if acquired within 3 years or as tax shelter; 251 — Arm's length; Canada-U.S. Tax Treaty:Art. IX — Adjustments for transactions between related persons.

Notes: 69(1) applies to gifts and non-arm's length transactions; see Notes to 251(1). It applies only to transfers of *property* (not services), but this can include a right to use property: VIEWS doc 1999-0009285. In *Ghaffari*, 2015 TCC 62, market-value rent was included in income because the lease called for it, even though the lease allowed it to be adjusted.

69(1)(b) applies to a donation of stock options, even though s. 7 provides specific rules: *Des Groseillers*, 2021 QCCA 906 (under the parallel Quebec rules).

CRA says (doc 2014-0532651E5) that 69(1)(a) can apply to a loan made at no interest, since the funds are being acquired at less than market value, triggering deemed interest under 12(4)! Making a loan payable on demand avoids this problem.

It is uncertain whether "*inter vivos*" in former 69(1)(b)(ii) (literally, "between living persons") refers only to individuals: VIEWS doc 2013-0484321E5. This was fixed as of 2016 by deleting those words.

Transfer vs gift: 69(1)(b)(ii) has a counterpart in (1)(c). However, 69(1)(a) and (1)(b)(i) are one-sided and have no counterpart. If X and Y are related and X sells Y a piece of land for $50, X is deemed to have sold the land for FMV but Y has acquired it for $50, leading to double tax when Y eventually sells it. To avoid this, X should *give* the land to Y. (Arguably, a "gift" is made of the excess value over the $50 paid. VIEWS docs 2013-0490711E5 and 2014-0538621C6 [2014 APFF q.8] imply it might be a gift under the Quebec *Civil Code*. See also 2018-0773301E5 and Notes to 56.4(6) on CRA willingness to ignore $1 nominal consideration.) See also Kakkar, "Business Migration: Is a Transfer for No Consideration a Gift?", 15(2) *Tax for the Owner-Manager* (ctf.ca) 8-9 (April 2015); Mancell, "Tax Treatment of Non-Arm's Length Transfer for $1", 2361 *Tax Topics* (CCH) 1-3 (June 8, 2017). Doc 2014-0519981E5 declined to say whether a gift of property with a charge on it is a "gift" in Quebec.

In addition to 69(1), non-arm's length transfers can trigger other provisions such as 15(1) (shareholder benefits), 56(2) (indirect payments), 74.1-74.4 (attribution rules), 160 (transferee liable for transferor's tax debts) and 246(1) (benefit conferred on a person). On transfer from a corp to a shareholder for less than market value, either 69(1)(b) or 69(4) may apply: *Boardman*, [1986] 1 C.T.C. 103 (FCTD); *Stan Wire*, 2009 TCC 425 (includes a "skip transfer" where transfer of real property made directly to vendor's purchaser).

Fair market value (FMV) is "the highest price an asset might reasonably be expected to bring if sold by the owner in the normal method applicable to the asset in question in the ordinary course of business in a market not exposed to any undue stresses and composed of willing buyers and sellers dealing at arm's length and under no compulsion to buy or sell": *Henderson*, [1973] C.T.C. 636 at 644 (FCTD); *Carr*, 2004 TCC 434; and "the highest price, expressed in terms of money or money's worth, obtainable in an open and unrestricted market between knowledgeable, informed and prudent parties acting at arm's length, neither party being under any compulsion to transact" (Information Circular 89-3 para. 3). Hindsight should not be used in determining FMV: *National System of Baking*, [1978] C.T.C. 30 (FCTD), para. 23 (aff'd [1980] C.T.C. 237 (FCA)). Where many taxpayers were defrauded, the amount paid was still FMV as it was thought to be the value: *Stewart*, 2019 TCC 22.

FMV determination is a question of fact, not law: *CIT Financial*, 2004 FCA 201; *Tremblay*, 2011 FCA 15; but *Nash (Tolley, Quinn)*, 2005 FCA 386 (leave to appeal denied 2006 CarswellNat 932 (SCC)) reversed a TCC finding of fact due to "palpable and overriding error". See also 248(35)-(39), which limit FMV to cost for many donations of property. FMV is determined at disposition date: VIEWS doc 2005-0147481E5.

A taxpayer's valuation figure that falls within the CRA appraiser's range of values is likely to be accepted: *Henco Industries*, 2014 TCC 192, para. 131.

Art: see Notes to 118.1(1)"total charitable gifts" re "art-flip" cases (*Klotz*, *Malette*, *Nash*, *Russell*, *Roher*).

Buildings: see "Real property" below.

Business assets: see *Dillon v. Dillon*, 2016 MBQB 238 (aircraft, backhoe, boat, debts, patents); *Lupien*, 2016 TCC 2; Barry Lipson, *The Art of the Corporate Deal* (Carswell, 2nd ed., 2015), chaps. 1-7; Line Racette, "Valuation Issues in High-Tech Businesses", 2000 Cdn Tax Foundation conference report, 3:1-29; H. Christopher Nobes, "Business Valuation in the Context of Estate Planning", 2009 Ontario Tax Conference (ctf.ca), 13:1-48. See also "Shares" below.

Client list or "book of business": see Aaron Franks, "Books of Business" [in 5 parts], 30(2) *Money & Family Law* (Carswell) 15 (Feb. 2015), 30(3) 21-23 (March), 30(4) 28-30 (April), 30(5) 38-39 (May), 30(6) 44-46 (June 2015).

Farm valuation including its assets: see *Ferme Koiris Inc.*, 2010 TCC 20.

Goodwill: see VIEWS doc 2008-0299651E5.

Horses: see *Teelucksingh*, [2011] 2 C.T.C. 2441 (TCC).

Land: see "Real property" below.

Life insurance policy: See Notes to 70(5.3).

Life interest or life estate in real property: see *Nauss*, 2005 TCC 488.

Non-competition agreement: Louis-Pierre Francoeur, "Intellectual Property and Restrictive Covenants — Valuation Overview", 2013 Atlantic Provinces Tax Conf. (ctf.ca), 7A:1-12.

Partnership interest: doc 2012-0471401E5 (professional partnership); Perry Truster, "Purchase of a Partnership Interest", 15(3) *Tax for the Owner-Manager* (ctf.ca) 2-3 (July 2015) (discount to reflect tax liability acquired).

Patents, copyright and other IP: Francoeur (above under "Non-competition").

Public dedicated-use property: In *Halifax*, 2012 SCC 29, the Supreme Court found it unreasonable for Canada to value the Halifax Citadel (a national historic site that could not be sold) at $0 for property tax purposes. (A federal panel later valued it at $41 million on Jan. 15, 2015: Canadian Press report.) For airports see *Gander v. Gander International Airport*, 2011 NLCA 65; *St. John's International*, 2015 NLTD(G) 175. See also Michael Crosbie, "Taxation of Public Infrastructure", 12(12) *Tax Hyperion* (Carswell) 1-4 (Dec. 2015).

Real property: see *Vine Estate*, 2014 TCC 64 (aff'd on other grounds 2015 FCA 125) (rental apartment building); *Colubriale*, 2005 FCA 329 (paper processing plant); *Bueti*, 2015 TCC 265, paras. 75-78 (old home); *Brassard*, 2017 FCA 205 (leave to appeal denied 2018 CarswellNat 8168 (SCC)) (mobile home lot); *Victory Motors*, 2017 BCCA 295 (effect of contamination of property); *Harvey*, 2018 TCC 67 (home); *Stellarbridge Management*, 2019 TCC 134 (land inventory); *Godcharles*, 2020 QCCQ 2219 (retirement home); Goodman, "Appropriate Level of Discounts for Undivided Interests in Real Estate", XI(4) *Goodman on Estate Planning* (Federated Press) 916-17 (2003); Weinstein, "Discounts to Consider in Valuing Partial Interests in Real Estate", II(2) *Personal Tax and Estate Planning* (Federated Press) 79-83 (2009); and 35+ cases listed in Cases annotation to 123(1)"fair market value" in the *Practitioner's Goods and Services Tax Annotated*. On allocation of value between land and buildings see Notes to s. 68 and 13(21.1). Where property is mortgaged and the purchaser or donee assumes the mortgage, the proceeds include that assumption: *Daishowa-Marubeni*, 2013 SCC 29, para. 26 and doc 2014-0519981E5. Real property includes "fixtures" attached to the land: see Notes to 248(4).

Shareholder loan valuation: *SRI Homes*, 2014 CarswellNat 2960 (TCC).

Shares of private company: see *Strachan*, 2013 TCC 362; *Montminy*, 2016 TCC 110, paras. 106-185 (rev'd on other grounds 2017 FCA 156); *Grimes (Ozerdinc Family Trust)*, 2016 TCC 280; *Mady*, 2017 TCC 112, para. 136 (dental practice corporation valued based on transaction with third party); *Mudronja v. Mudronja*, 2014 ONSC 6217, paras. 23-79; *Aquam Corp v. Coffey*, 2018 ONSC 6582 (dissenting shareholders' shares); *Prolink v. Jaitley*, 2019 ONSC 7577; Wise, *Guide to Canadian Business Valuations* (Carswell, looseleaf or *Taxnet Pro* Reference Centre); "Valuation Issues Relating to Shares of Private Corporations", 2004 Cdn Tax Foundation conference report, 13:1-40, "The Valuation of a 50% Shareholding", tinyurl.com/wise-50val; "Nuisance Value of Shares", 19(3) *Canadian Tax Highlights* (ctf.ca) 10 (April 2011); and "Current Challenges by the CRA Involving Fair Market Value", 2016 conference report, 30:1-39 (various issues including multiple share classes, discount for embedded taxes, minority discount, effect of a key person, inadmissibility of hindsight); Lawritsen & Wipf, "Valuation Considerations", 2015 Prairie Provinces Tax Conf. (ctf.ca), 12:1-9; Hodge, "Practical Issues in Current Challenges by the CRA Involving Fair Market Value", 2016 conference report, 31:1-15; Krofchick, "How Cash is Dealt With When Valuing a Business", 35(8) *Money & Family Law [MFL]* (Carswell) 60-61 (Aug. 2020) (unreported cash income); Freedman & Harris, "Impact of Unreported Income on Business Valuation", 36(1) *MFL* 3-4 (Jan. 2021). Embedded tax liabilities may be taken into account: *594710 B.C.*, 2016 TCC 288, paras. 139-144 (rev'd on other grounds 2018 FCA 166; leave to appeal denied 2019 CarswellNat 434 (SCC)). Preferred shares with voting control over a private company; see Notes to 86(1). Effect of a unanimous shareholder agreement on share values: *Kruger Wayagamack Inc.*, 2015 TCC 90, paras.

96-162; aff'd 2016 FCA 192. Shares that had not yet been issued and for which there was no market had $0 value in *Baribeau*, 2011 TCC 125. Effect of taxes (on accrued gains or distributions of assets) on share value: Welsh, "Latent Income Taxes", 2019 STEP Canada conference (contact memberservices@step.ca). See also VIEWS doc 2014-0538121C6 [2014 APFF q.12] (future recapture on corp's depreciable property does not affect shares' value); "Business assets" above.

Shares of public company: for large blocks, see *Shulkov*, [2013] 2 C.T.C. 2007 (TCC), paras. 41-130. *Dissenting shareholders' shares*: *Nixon v. Trace*, 2010 BCSC 175 [Wu, "Minority Dissent Proceedings", XIV(4) *Business Vehicles* (Federated Press) 766-72 (2012)]; *Carlock v. ExxonMobil*, 2020 YKCA 4; *Shanda Games v. Maso Capital*, [2020] UKPC 2 (Privy Council, Cayman Islands). Restricted shares: Ephraim Stulberg, "Valuing Restricted Shares and Restricted Share Units", 29(5) *Money & Family Law* (Carswell) 35-36 (May 2014) and 29(6) 43-45 (June 2014). Valuation of one company in a large international group: *Nortel Networks*, 2014 ONSC 6973, paras. 159-206.

Software licences in a donation shelter: *Mariano*, 2015 TCC 244, paras. 90-145.

Stock options: VIEWS doc 2016-0673331E5 ("appropriate" valuation method needed).

Trusts: in *Mudronja v. Mudronja*, 2014 ONSC 6217, para. 100, a husband who was sole trustee, non-fiduciary "protector" and a beneficiary was held to own the value of the trust assets for family-law purposes. An interest in a discretionary trust (with no right to payment) is arguably worthless since no-one would buy it, but CRA disagrees and may apply *Sagl v. Sagl*, 1997 CanLII 12248 (Ont. SCJ), para. 37, to consider that each beneficiary has a fractional interest: docs 2003-0181465, 2004-0062291E5. However, in *SA v. Metro Vancouver Housing*, 2019 SCC 4, the Supreme Court of Canada held that a Henson trust beneficiary (see Notes to 60.011), who was also a co-trustee, had only "a mere hope that the trustees will exercise their discretion in a manner favourable to her", and her interest was valued at nil for a rent subsidy application. See also Bernstein, "Discretionary Trust Interest", 11(5) *Canadian Tax Highlights* (ctf.ca) 1-2 (May 2003); Wise, "Current challenges by the CRA involving fair market value", 2016 Cdn Tax Foundation conference report at 30:11-16; Lee, "TOSI and Valuing a Discretionary Interest in a Trust", 9(1) *Canadian Tax Focus* (ctf.ca) 2 (Feb. 2019); McIntyre, "Trust Me, It's Property, But What's It Worth?", 34(10) *Money & Family Law* (Carswell) 74-77 (Oct. 2019). See also *Yared v. Karam*, 2019 SCC 62, where a "right to confer use" of property (for Quebec family law) included a settlor's right through a trust (where he could add himself as beneficiary).

Unique objects: see *Aikman*, 2002 FCA 114.

Wine donated to a charity was valued in *De Santis*, 2015 TCC 95 and *Balkwill*, 2018 TCC 99.

See Notes to 169(1) under "Expert evidence" re the valuator as expert witness.

See also David Sherman's *Canada GST Service* commentary to ETA 123(1)"fair market value" (also on *GST Partner* and *Taxnet Pro*); *Valuation Law Review — Taxation* (Cdn Institute of Chartered Business Valuators, cicbv.ca); Freedman & White, *Financial Principles of Family Law* (Carswell, 2 vols. looseleaf), Vol. 1, "Valuation"; Chow & Cadesky, *Taxation at Death: A Practitioner's Guide 2021* (Carswell), chap. 12; Wise, "The Effect of Special Interest Purchasers on Fair Market Value in Canada", 22(4) *Business Valuation Review* (bvreview.org) 196-203 (Dec. 2003); Harder, "Valuation and Tax Issues", 2004 BC Tax Conference (ctf.ca), 20:1-35; Muha, "The Valuator on the Clapham Omnibus", XIV(2) *Tax Litigation* (Federated Press) 877-80 (2006); Kroft & Turnbull, "Price and Fair Market Value in Tax Court Decisions", 21(10) & (11) *Money & Family Law* (Carswell) 78-80 & 86-87 (Oct. & Nov. 2006); Wise, "Valuation: Recent Developments", 2006 conference report, 33:1-28; Wise, "Critical Valuation Provisions of Buy-Sell Agreements", 2007 *Journal of Business Valuation* (2006 conference proceedings) 281-93; Wise, "The Admissibility of Hindsight in Tax-Purpose Valuations" 6 *Tax Profile* (CCH) 1-7 (June 2010); Bernstein & Wise, "Valuation and Tax Issues", 2011 Cdn Tax Foundation conference report, 17:1-31 and 18:1-32; Doody, "The Effect of Embedded Capital Gains on Fair Market Value", XVIII(2) *Tax Litigation* 1094-1100 (2011); Gentile, "Unsuspecting Applications of Fair Market Value in the Excise Tax Act", *2015 Commodity Tax Symposium* (CPA Canada); Smith, "Valuation Uncertainty and the Purchase and Sale Agreement", 65(3) *Canadian Tax Journal* 807-30 (2017) (planning around uncertainty); Brayley & McLeod, "Ballparks Rarely Never Work: A Primer on Valuations", 2017 BC Tax Conference (ctf.ca).

A transfer to joint tenancy (see Notes to 70(5)) with one's child, to avoid probate fees, may not be a disposition for tax purposes absent evidence the transferor intends to transfer beneficial ownership (due to presumption of resulting trust): *Pecore v. Pecore*, 2007 SCC 17, para. 70; *Mroz v. Mroz*, 2015 ONCA 171, paras. 70-73; *Kyle v. Kyle*, 2016 BCSC 855; *Coates v. Coates*, 2017 SKQB 303; *Petrick v. Petrick*, 2019 BCSC 1319 (no resulting trust since value given by co-signing mother's mortgage: para. 67); *Kent v. Kent*, 2020 ONCA 390; or may be a 50% disposition triggering capital gains: VIEWS docs 2005-0152011E5, 2008-0278801C6 q.5. However, if beneficial transfer to joint tenancy was intended, it cannot be undone unilaterally if the transferor changes his mind: *Griffith v. Davidson*, 2017 ONSC 187.

69(1) applies to a transfer to one's RRSP: VIEWS doc 2009-0312791I7.

In determining whether there is a "gift" for 69(1)(b)(ii) and 69(1)(c), see 248(30), which provides (albeit intended for charitable gifts) that a gift can exist even though the giver gets something back. See also Notes to 118.1(1)"total charitable gifts" on the meaning of "gift". Where a sole shareholder transfers property to a corporation for nothing (or for more shares), in theory there is no gift because the value of the corporate shares has increased, but CRA will accept that the corp has acquired the property at FMV if a reasonable attempt is made to determine FMV, and will apply a "quasi-price adjustment clause (CRA Roundtable q.15, 2009 Cdn Tax Foundation conference report, p. 3:15; *Income Tax Technical News* 44).

For transfer pricing (transactions with related non-residents) see 247(2) and François Vincent, "Subsection 247(2) Versus Subsection 69(1) of the Income Tax Act", XIII(3) *International Tax Planning* (Federated Press) 940-48 (2006).

GST or HST may be required to be calculated at FMV on a non-arm's length provision of property *or* services. See *Excise Tax Act* s. 155, in David M. Sherman, *Practitioner's Goods and Services Tax Annotated* (Carswell).

Price adjustment clause (PAC): If the price under a non-arm's length agreement is the FMV when the agreement is entered into, but is not FMV when the property is transferred, CRA said 69(1) applies to change the cost or proceeds of disposition: Revenue Canada Round Table, 1993 Cdn Tax Foundation conference report, 58:23-24, Q. 39. However, it can be argued that the agreement affects FMV, so that FMV is set by what is provided under PAC; see IT-140R3. On using a PAC to avoid s. 69 see also Income Tax Folio S4-F3-C1; VIEWS docs 2008-0285251C6, 2011-0429991E5, 2011-0426361C6, 2013-0507881E5; 2018-0768861C6 [2018 APFF q.15] (retroactive change does not reopen statute-barred year); May 2013 ICAA Roundtable q.11 (tiny-url.com/cra-abtax). In *Garron [St. Michael Trust]*, 2010 FCA 309 (aff'd on other grounds as *Fundy Settlement*, 2012 SCC 14), para. 38, the FCA said a PAC was never triggered because CRA had never determined the shares' value [Kakkar, "Passing comments on PACs", *CAmagazine*, Dec. 2011. pp. 44-46]. In *Boulet*, 2009 TCC 261, the FMV of property transferred by a corp to shareholders was reduced to the value set in a prior agreement they had made to acquire the land. In *Eyeball Networks*, 2021 FCA 17, para. 50, a PAC ensured 160(1) did not apply to an exchange. See also *Deragon*, 2015 TCC 294; Bernstein, "Price Adjustment Clauses", 18(2) *Canadian Tax Highlights* (ctf.ca) 3-4 (Feb. 2010); Jung, "Price Adjustment Clauses Under Attack?", 11(2) *Tax for the Owner-Manager* (ctf.ca) 1-3 (April 2011); Arkin, "Price Adjustment Clauses", 2012 Atlantic Provinces Tax Conference (ctf.ca), 3:1-15.

A transfer to a "bare trust" is not a disposition and will not trigger 69(1). See 69(1)(b)(iii) and Notes to 104(1).

A partnership is subject to 69(1)(a): *Deptuck*, 2003 FCA 177 (leave to appeal denied 2004 CarswellNat 86 (SCC)).

On death, the estate acquires the deceased's property at fair market value under 70(5)(b), not 69(1)(c); and 69(1)(c) also does not apply to a rollout from a trust to a beneficiary under 107(2): VIEWS doc 2002-0155735.

69(1) may apply where a trustee/beneficiary exercises a power to appoint more beneficiaries: VIEWS doc 2008-0281411I7.

69(1)(b)(ii) amended by 2014 budget bill #2, for 2016 and later taxation years, to change "gift *inter vivos*" to "gift" (in sync with generally replacing "testamentary trust" with "graduated rate estate").

69(1) amended by 2001 technical bill, for dispositions that occur after Dec. 23, 1998 (and corrected by 2002-2013 technical bill (Part 5 — technical), on the same basis, to delete an extraneous "and" at end of 69(1)(b)(iii)).

Regulations: 1102(14) — Class of depreciable property preserved on non-arm's length acquisition.

I.T. Application Rules: 20(1.3), 32.

Income Tax Folios: S3-F9-C1: Lottery winnings, miscellaneous receipts, and income (and losses) from crime [replaces IT-185R, IT-213R, IT-256R, IT-334R2]; S4-F3-C1: Price adjustment clauses [replaces IT-169]; S6-F2-C1: Disposition of an income interest in a trust [replaces IT-385R2]; S7-F1-C1: Split-receipting and deemed fair market value.

Interpretation Bulletins: IT-125R4: Dispositions of resource properties; IT-140R3: Buy-sell agreements; IT-143R3: Meaning of eligible capital expenditure; IT-188R: Sale of accounts receivable; IT-209R: *Inter vivos* gifts of capital property to individuals directly or through trusts; IT-212R3: Income of deceased persons — rights or things; IT-226R: Gift to a charity of a residual interest in real property or an equitable interest in a trust; IT-268R4: *Inter vivos* transfer of farm property to child; IT-288R2: Gifts of capital properties to a charity and others; IT-297R2: Gifts in kind to charity and others; IT-335R2: Indirect payments; IT-403R: Options on real estate; IT-405: Inadequate considerations — acquisitions and dispositions (cancelled); IT-427R: Livestock of farmers; IT-432R2: Benefits conferred on shareholders; IT-442R: Bad debts and reserves for doubtful debts; IT-490: Barter transactions; IT-504R2: Visual artists and writers.

Information Circulars: 87-2R: International transfer pricing (archived); 89-3: Policy statement on business equity valuations; 06-1: Income tax transfer pricing and customs valuation.

I.T. Technical News: 38 (value of company attributable to voting non-participating shares); 44 (cost of property acquired from a shareholder for no consideration).

CRA Audit Manual: 12.16.0: Requesting appraisal or valuation.

Advance Tax Rulings: ATR-1: Transfer of legal title in land to bare trustee corporation — mortgagee's requirements sole reason for transfer; ATR-9: Transfer of personal residence from corporation to its controlling shareholder; ATR-36: Estate freeze.

(1.1) Idem, where subsec. 70(3) applies — Where a taxpayer has acquired property that is a right or thing to which subsection 70(3) applies, the following rules apply:

(a) paragraph (1)(c) is not applicable to that property; and

(b) the taxpayer shall be deemed to have acquired the property at a cost equal to the total of

(i) such part, if any, of the cost thereof to the taxpayer who has died as had not been deducted by the taxpayer in computing the taxpayer's income for any year, and

(ii) any expenditures made or incurred by the taxpayer to acquire the property.

Interpretation Bulletins: IT-212R3: Income of deceased persons — rights or things; IT-427R: Livestock of farmers.

(1.2) Idem — Where, at any time,

(a) a taxpayer disposed of property for proceeds of disposition (determined without reference to this subsection) equal to or greater than the fair market value at that time of the property, and

(b) there existed at that time an agreement under which a person with whom the taxpayer was not dealing at arm's length agreed to pay as rent, royalty or other payment for the use of or the right to use the property an amount less than the amount that would have been reasonable in the circumstances if the taxpayer and the person had been dealing at arm's length at the time the agreement was entered into,

the taxpayer's proceeds of disposition of the property shall be deemed to be the greater of

(c) those proceeds determined without reference to this subsection, and

(d) the fair market value of the property at the time of the disposition, determined without reference to the existence of the agreement.

Related Provisions: See Related Provisions to 69(1).

Notes: 69(1.2) applies when selling a property at FMV or higher, but the FMV has been reduced artificially because of a non-arm's-length agreement that provides for lower than market rent. The proceeds, even on an arm's length sale, are bumped up to the "real" FMV (without the agreement). This prevents setting up such an agreement to deflate the value and reduce the gain on sale.

69(1.2) added by 1992 technical bill, effective for dispositions after Dec. 20, 1991.

(2), (3) [Repealed]

Notes: 69(2) and (3) repealed by 1995-97 technical bill, effective for taxation years that begin after 1997. They were replaced by a new transfer-pricing rule in 247(2).

69(2) and (3) addressed transfer pricing within multinational groups. 69(2) limited deductions for non-arm's length payments to non-residents to a reasonable amount. 69(3) required non-arm's length payments from non-residents to be at least a reasonable amount. See Notes to 247(2), including on the *GlaxoSmithKline* and *General Electric* cases under 69(2) and *Sundog* under 69(3). See also Canada-U.S. tax treaty: Art. IX.

69(3) amended by 1991 technical bill, effective July 14, 1990.

(4) Shareholder appropriations — Where at any time property of a corporation has been appropriated in any manner whatever to or for the benefit of a shareholder of the corporation for no consideration or for consideration that is less than the property's fair market value and a sale of the property at its fair market value would have increased the corporation's income or reduced a loss of the corporation, the corporation shall be deemed to have disposed of the property, and to have received proceeds of disposition therefor equal to its fair market value, at that time.

Related Provisions: 15(1) — Benefit conferred on shareholder; 142.7(4) — Deemed value of property on rollover from foreign bank subsidiary to branch.

Notes: In *Husky Oil*, 2010 FCA 125, 69(4) did not apply on an amalgamation because 87(4) took priority. See also Notes to 69(1).

69(4) does not apply to an "indirect" shareholder: VIEWS doc 2013-047862117. For determining the cost of property received as an in-kind return of capital from a corporation (to which 69(4) may apply), see 2013-050656117. See also 2016-0630761R3 and 2017-0693751R3 (69(4) did not apply to a rollover of foreign-affiliate shares to another FA followed by transfer to a related Cdn resident corp).

69(4) amended by 1993 technical bill, effective Dec. 22, 1992.

(5) Idem — Where in a taxation year of a corporation property of the corporation has been appropriated in any manner whatever to, or for the benefit of, a shareholder, on the winding-up of the corporation, the following rules apply:

(a) the corporation is deemed, for the purpose of computing its income for the year, to have disposed of the property immediately before the winding-up for proceeds equal to its fair market value at that time;

(b) the shareholder shall be deemed to have acquired the property at a cost equal to its fair market value immediately before the winding-up;

(c) subsections 52(1) and (2) do not apply for the purposes of determining the cost to the shareholder of the property; and

(d) subsections 13(21.2), 18(15) and 40(3.4) and (3.6) do not apply in respect of any property disposed of on the winding-up.

(e) [Repealed]

Related Provisions: 15(1) — Benefit conferred on shareholder; 54"superficial loss"(h) — Superficial loss rule inapplicable when 69(5) applies; 84(2) — Distribution on winding-up, etc; 88(3)–(3.5) — Liquidation or dissolution of foreign affiliate; 95(2)(e) — Liquidation and dissolution of foreign affiliate; 142.7(4) — Deemed value of property on rollover from foreign bank subsidiary to branch.

Notes: For CRA interpretation see VIEWS docs 2005-0137641E5 (69(5) applies where loan receivable is distributed to shareholder on dissolution); 2014-0560421I7 (69(5) does not apply on CFA windup because 88(3) applies); 2015-0573841C6 [2015 CLHIA q.4] and 2016-0651761C6 [2016 APFF q.3] (69(5) vs 148(7) on distribution of life insurance policy on 88(2) windup).

69(5)(d) amended to delete reference to 14(12) by 2016 budget bill #2, effective 2017, as part of changing eligible capital property rules to CCA Class 14.1 (see Notes to 20(1)(b)).

69(5) amended by 2001 technical bill (for dispositions after 1999), 1995-97 and 1991 technical bills.

Interpretation Bulletins: IT-444R: Corporations — involuntary dissolutions; IT-488R2: Winding-up of 90%-owned taxable Canadian corporations (cancelled).

Information Circulars: 89-3: Policy statement on business equity valuations.

(6)–(10) [Repealed]

Notes: 69(6)-(10) repealed by 2003 resource bill, effective for taxation years that begin after 2006 (consequential on repeal of 12(1)(o) and 18(1)(m)).

(11) Deemed proceeds of disposition — Where, at any particular time as part of a series of transactions or events, a taxpayer disposes of property for proceeds of disposition that are less than its fair market value and it can reasonably be considered that one of the main purposes of the series is

(a) to obtain the benefit of

(i) any deduction (other than a deduction under subsection 110.6(2.1) in respect of a capital gain from a disposition of a share acquired by the taxpayer in an acquisition to which subsection 85(3) or 98(3) applied) in computing income, taxable income, taxable income earned in Canada or tax payable under this Act, or

(ii) any balance of undeducted outlays, expenses or other amounts

available to a person (other than a person that would be affiliated with the taxpayer immediately before the series began, if section 251.1 were read without reference to the definition "controlled" in subsection 251.1(3)) in respect of a subsequent disposition of the property or property substituted for the property, or

(b) to obtain the benefit of an exemption available to any person from tax payable under this Act on any income arising on a subsequent disposition of the property or property substituted for the property,

notwithstanding any other provision of this Act, where the subsequent disposition occurs, or arrangements for the subsequent disposition are made, before the day that is 3 years after the particular time, the taxpayer is deemed to have disposed of the property at the particular time for proceeds of disposition equal to its fair market value at the particular time.

Related Provisions: 69(12) — No time limit on 69(11) reassessment; 69(13) — Amalgamation or merger; 69(14) — Where corporation incorporated during series of transactions; 73(3.1)(d), 73(4.1)(d) — Rule in 69(11) takes priority over 73(3)-(4.1); 87 — Amalgamations; 88(1) opening words — 69(11) takes priority over winding-up

rules; 160(1.1) — Joint liability; 248(5) — Substituted property; 256.1 — Deemed change in control if 75% FMV acquired.

Notes: 69(11) is an anti-avoidance rule that prevents a vendor from disposing of property on a tax-deferred basis so as to obtain the benefit of tax deductions or other entitlements available to a non-"affiliated" person (see 251.1) on a subsequent disposition of the property within 3 years. 69(11) denies the benefit of the rollover on the original disposition by deeming the vendor's proceeds of disposition to be equal to the fair market value (see Notes to 69(1)) of the property disposed of. For the meaning of "one of the main purposes" (in the opening words), see Notes to 83(2.1).

69(11) can apply to a rollover of farm or fishing property to a child under 70(9.01), 73(3.1) or 73(4.1): VIEWS docs 2002-0143635, 2010-0376451E5, 2010-0383601E5. On interaction with 44(1), see 2014-0551841E5; with 70(9.01), see 2014-0534681E5.

In *Oxford Properties*, 2018 FCA 30 (leave to appeal denied 2018 CarswellNat 7871 (SCC)), a combination of steps that took place after the three-year time limit in 69(11) triggered GAAR in 245(2). See Notes to 100(1).

See also Ton-That, "Unexpected Problems under Subsection 69(11)", V(3) *Corporate Structures & Groups* (Federated Press) 268-73 (1999); Williamson & Manly, "Subsection 69(11) — Unexpected Problems", V(4) *CS&G* 285-89 (1999); Truster, "Loss Trading and Subsection 69(11)", 17(2) *Tax for the Owner-Manager* (ctf.ca) 4-5 (April 2017) and "...The Sequel", 17(3) 3-4 (July 2017); docs 2006-0206351E5, 2008-0294051I7, 2012-0451421R3, 2013-050583117, 2019-0803691I7.

69(11) amended by 1995-97 technical bill, effective for each disposition that is part of a series of transactions or events that begins after April 26, 1995, with limited grandfathering for a disposition before 1996.

Income Tax Folios: S4-F7-C1: Amalgamations of Canadian corporations [replaces IT-474R2].

Interpretation Bulletins: IT-291R3: Transfer of property to a corporation under subsection 85(1); IT-488R2: Winding-up of 90%-owned taxable Canadian corporations (cancelled).

Information Circulars: 88-2, para. 9: General anti-avoidance rule — section 245 of the *Income Tax Act*.

I.T. Technical News: 9 (loss consolidation within a corporate group); 30 (corporate loss utilization transactions); 34 (loss consolidation — unanimous shareholder agreements).

CRA Audit Manual: 11.5.11: Joint liability assessments.

(12) Reassessments — Notwithstanding subsections 152(4) to (5), the Minister may at any time make such assessments or reassessments of the tax, interest and penalties payable by the taxpayer as are necessary to give effect to subsection (11).

Notes: 69(12) replaced by 1995-97 technical bill, effective on the same basis as the amendment to 69(11). It previously defined "specified person".

(12.1), (12.2) [Repealed]

Notes: 69(12.1), (12.2) repealed by 1995-97 technical bill, effective on the same basis as the amendment to 69(11). They were application rules for 69(11) and (12).

(13) Amalgamation or merger — Where there is an amalgamation or merger of a corporation with one or more other corporations to form one corporate entity (in this subsection referred to as the "new corporation"), each property of the corporation that becomes property of the new corporation as a result of the amalgamation or merger is deemed, for the purpose of determining whether subsection (11) applies to the amalgamation or merger, to have been disposed of by the corporation immediately before the amalgamation or merger for proceeds equal to

(a) in the case of a Canadian resource property or a foreign resource property, nil; and

(b) in the case of any other property, the cost amount to the corporation of the property immediately before the amalgamation or merger.

Related Provisions: 87(2)(e) — Rules applicable — capital property.

Notes: 69(13) amended by 1995-97 technical bill (for amalgamations and mergers after April 26, 1995), 1992 technical bill.

(14) New taxpayer — For the purpose of subsection (11), where a taxpayer is incorporated or otherwise comes into existence at a particular time during a series of transactions or events, the taxpayer is deemed

(a) to have existed at the time that was immediately before the series began; and

(b) to have been affiliated at that time with every person with whom the taxpayer is affiliated (otherwise than because of a right referred to in paragraph 251(5)(b)) at the particular time.

Notes: 69(14) is a relieving rule that prevents inappropriate effects where, because a taxpayer came into existence as part of the series of transactions described in 69(11), the taxpayer might not meet the affiliation test in 251.1 because it didn't exist immediately before the series began. The "taxpayer" may be the transferor or any other person in 69(11): VIEWS doc 2002-0156675.

69(14) added by 1995-97 technical bill, on the same basis as the amendment to 69(11).

Definitions [s. 69]: "amount" — 248(1); "affiliated" — 69(14), 251.1; "arm's length" — 251; "assessment" — 248(1); "beneficial ownership" — 248(3); "business" — 248(1); "Canada" — 255; "Canadian resource property" — 66(15), 248(1); "controlled" — 256(6)–(9), 256.1(3); "corporation" — 248(1), *Interpretation Act* 35(1); "eligible capital property" — 54, 248(1); "fair market value" — 248(35) and see 69(1) Notes; "foreign resource property" — 66(15), 248(1); "Her Majesty" — *Interpretation Act* 35(1); "non-resident", "oil or gas well", "person", "prescribed" — 248(1); "proceeds of disposition" — 54 [technically does not apply to s. 69]; "property" — 248(1); "province" — *Interpretation Act* 35(1); "series of transactions or events" — 248(10); "shareholder" — 248(1); "substituted" — 248(5); "tax payable" — 248(2); "taxable income" — 2(2), 248(1); "taxable income earned in Canada" — 115(1), 248(1); "taxation year" — 11(2), 249; "taxpayer" — 248(1).

70. (1) Death of a taxpayer

— In computing the income of a taxpayer for the taxation year in which the taxpayer died,

(a) an amount of interest, rent, royalty, annuity (other than an amount with respect to an interest in an annuity contract to which paragraph 148(2)(b) applies), remuneration from an office or employment, or other amount payable periodically, that was not paid before the taxpayer's death, shall be deemed to have accrued in equal daily amounts in the period for or in respect of which the amount was payable, and the value of the portion thereof so deemed to have accrued to the day of death shall be included in computing the taxpayer's income for the year in which the taxpayer died; and

(b) paragraph 12(1)(t) shall be read as follows:

"(t) the amount deducted under subsection 127(5) or (6) in computing the taxpayer's tax payable for the year or a preceding taxation year to the extent that it was not included in computing the taxpayer's income for a preceding taxation year under this paragraph or is not included in an amount determined under paragraph 13(7.1)(e) or 37(1)(e) or subparagraph 53(2)(c)(vi) or (h)(ii) or for I in the definition "undepreciated capital cost" in subsection 13(21) or L in the definition "cumulative Canadian exploration expense" in subsection 66.1(6);"

Related Provisions: 7(1)(e) — Stock option benefit where employee has died; 28(1) closing words — Farming or fishing business; 61.2 — Deduction of debt forgiveness reserve for year of death; 70(5) — Capital property of deceased; 72(1) — Reserves not allowed for year of death; 80(2)(p), (q) — Debt forgiveness rules — debt obligation settled by estate; 118.1(1)"total gifts"(a)(ii) — Charitable donation claim after death not limited to 75% of net income; 118.1(5), (5.1) — Donations by will or by the estate after death; 122.62(5)(a) — Notice to CRA required for Canada Child Benefit on death of spouse; 122.7(12) — Rule for Canada Workers Benefit on death; 135.2(8)(b)(ii) — Income inclusion on death of farmer owning eligible unit of Cdn Wheat Board Farmers' Trust; 146(8.8) — RRSP — effect of death; 146.01(6) — RRSP Home Buyers' Plan — income inclusion; 146.02(6) — RRSP Lifelong Learning Plan — income inclusions; 146.3(6) — RRIF — effect of death; 147.2(6) — Additional deductible pension contributions for year of death; 148.1(2)(b)(i) — No tax on provision of funeral or cemetary services from eligible funeral arrangement; 156.1(3) — Instalments not required after death; 164(6) — Election by executor to carry back losses of estate to year of death. See also Related Provisions to 70(5).

Notes: See Notes to 70(5).

For the scope of 70(1) and various interpretations see VIEWS doc 2012-0442941C6.

A retroactive pay increase or pay equity settlement to a deceased person may be nontaxable: VIEWS docs 2003-0018835, 2009-0324381E5. An undeclared periodic employment bonus is taxable: 2006-0168181E5. A payout of taxable (6(1)(f)) disability benefits after death is taxable: 2008-0293131E5 (but qualifies under 70(2)).

See also Edwin Harris, "Income Amounts Accruing at Death", 9(7) *Tax Hyperion* (Carswell) 1 (July 2012).

Interpretation Bulletins: IT-210R2: Income of deceased persons — periodic payments and investment tax credit; IT-212R3: Income of deceased persons — rights or things; IT-234: Income of deceased persons — farm crops; IT-396R: Interest income; IT-410R: Debt obligations — accrued interest on transfer (cancelled).

CRA Audit Manual: 16.2.2: Estate of a deceased person.

Forms: RC4111: What to do following a death [guide]; T4011: Preparing returns for deceased persons [guide].

(2) Amounts receivable ["rights or things" separate return]

— If a taxpayer who has died had at the time of death rights or things (other than any capital property or any amount included in computing the taxpayer's income by virtue of subsection (1)), the amount of which when realized or disposed of would have been included in computing the taxpayer's income, the value of the rights or things at the time of death shall be included in computing the taxpayer's income for the taxation year in which the taxpayer died, unless the taxpayer's legal representative has, not later than the later of the day that is one year after the date of death of the taxpayer and the day that is 90 days after the sending of any notice of assessment in respect of the tax of the taxpayer for the year of death, elected otherwise, in which case the legal representative shall file a separate return of income for the year under this Part and pay the tax for the year under this Part as if

(a) the taxpayer were another person;

(b) that other person's only income for the year were the value of the rights or things; and

(c) subject to sections 114.2 and 118.93, that other person were entitled to the deductions to which the taxpayer was entitled under sections 110, 118 to 118.7 and 118.9 for the year in computing the taxpayer's taxable income or tax payable under this Part, as the case may be, for the year.

Related Provisions: 28(1) — Farming or fishing business; 53(1)(e)(v) — Adjustments to cost base; 56(1)(z.2), 144.1(11) — Income from employee life and health trust; 60(t) — Deductions — amount included under 70(2); 70(3) — Rights or things transferred to beneficiaries; 70(4) — Revocation of election; 114.2 — Deductions in separate returns; 118.93 — Credits in separate returns; 120.2(4)(a) — No minimum tax carryover on special return; 127.1(1)(a) — No refundable investment tax credit on special return; 127.55 — Minimum tax not applicable; 150(1)(b) — Filing deadline for deceased's return; 159(5) — Election where certain provisions applicable; 244(14), (14.1) — Date when notice sent.

Notes: A "right or thing" is included in the deceased's income on death (unless distributed to a beneficiary before the election deadline: 70(3)), but by election it may be reported on a separate return on which low marginal rates apply. Due to 118.93, the basic and dependant personal credits (118(1)) and the age credit (118(2)) can be claimed on both this return and the regular return; so at a minimum, the first $12,298 of income in 2020 / $12,421 in 2021 (lowest basic personal amount) is effectively exempt. (See Notes to 70(5) for other "separate returns".)

Rights or things have been held to include: bonus (non-periodic) (VIEWS doc 2006-0168181E5); disability benefits payout (2008-0293131E5); dividend declared but unpaid (IT-212R3); employment equity retroactive salary adjustment (2006-0208561E5); farmer or fisher's inventory or debt receivable (if reporting on cash basis) (IT-212R3); grain marketed through Canadian Wheat Board, right to payment for (IT-212R3); lump-sum retroactive pension, GIS or CPP payment (2006-0192051I7, 2015-061520I17, 2017-0709461E5); old age security the deceased failed to apply for (9130825); partner's right to share of partnership income to date of death (2006-0177471E5); retirement compensation arrangement, right to (*Teitelbaum*, 2019 QCCA 1408 (leave to appeal denied 2020 CarswellQue 1736 (SCC)); trust promised income distribution (2012-0469761E5); US Individual Retirement Account, if owner dies before plan matures and plan property was not previously used to acquire an irrevocable annuity (9800545, 2003-0046111E5); vacation leave credits (IT-212R3); work in progress of a professional who elected under 34(a) (2011-0421801E5).

Rights or things do not include: accrued portion of periodic payments (IT-212R3); Canadian Forces disability-benefits class action settlement payments (2015-057485117); Canadian resource property (70(3.1)); dividend paid by cheque post-dated to date of death, as it was negotiable at time of death (2008-0300791E5); eligible capital property (pre-2017) (70(3.1)); foreign resource property (70(3.1)); land inventory (70(3.1)); life insurance policy interest, with certain exceptions (70(3.1)); NISA Fund No. 2 (IT-212R3); pension payment on death (see Notes to 56(1)(a)); prospector's mining claim (2008-0269451E5); RRSP (IT-212R3; *Baak Estate*, [2002] 2 C.T.C. 2317 (TCC) — 146(8.8) includes it in the terminal return); recaptured depreciation on deemed disposition of a rental property on death (*Mercure*, 2003 CarswellNat 5326 (TCC)); sick leave credits (considered a "death benefit" by IT-508R, and taxable to beneficiaries via 104(28) so they can claim the $10,000 exemption in 248(1)"death benefit").

Where a T4A(P) has been issued for a deceased's pension income and part of that income goes on the separate "rights or things" return, it is unclear whether the tax withheld at source should be split proportionately between the returns or all claimed on the main return (though the net effect will be the same).

The 70(2) income is not added to the deceased's income for OAS clawback (180.2): VIEWS doc 9304987.

When filing a "rights or things" return, write "70(2)" in the top right corner on page 1. See Guide T4011. It has been reported (in 2013) that if the income on such a return is less than $10,000, CRA will no longer issue a Notice of Assessment.

See also Heather Dawe, "Pension Lump-Sum Payment — A Right or Thing?", 9(7) *Tax Hyperion* (Carswell) 8-10 (July 2012); Barry Corbin, "Post-Mortem Claims for CPP and OAS", 34(1) *Money & Family Law* (Carswell) 3-4 (Jan. 2019).

70(2) opening words amended by 2010 budget bill #2, effective Dec. 15, 2010, to change "mailing" to "sending" to accommodate electronic notices under 244(14.1), and to make non-substantive wording changes.

Interpretation Bulletins: IT-210R2: Income of deceased persons — periodic payments and investment tax credit; IT-212R3: Income of deceased persons — rights or things; IT-234: Farm crops; IT-278R2: Death of a partner or of a retired person; IT-326R3: Returns of deceased persons as "another person"; IT-382: Debts bequeathed or forgiven on death (cancelled); IT-427R: Livestock of farmers; IT-457R: Election by professionals to exclude work in progress from income; IT-502: Employee benefit plans and employee trusts.

CRA Audit Manual: 16.2.2: Estate of a deceased person.

Forms: T4011: Preparing returns for deceased persons [guide].

(3) Rights or things transferred to beneficiaries — Where

before the time for making an election under subsection (2) has expired, a right or thing to which that subsection would otherwise apply has been transferred or distributed to beneficiaries or other persons beneficially interested in the estate or trust,

(a) subsection (2) is not applicable to that right or thing; and

(b) an amount received by one of the beneficiaries or persons on the realization or disposition of the right or thing shall be included in computing the income of the beneficiary or person for the taxation year in which the beneficiary or person received it.

Related Provisions: 44(3) — Where subsec. 70(3) not to apply; 69(1.1) — Deemed cost of property to beneficiary; 70(3.1) — Exception; 118.1(7), 118.1(7.1) — Donation of art or cultural property on death.

Notes: If a right is transferred to beneficiary B before the deadline for filing the 70(2) "rights or things" return, the income is taxed in B's hands. In *Teitelbaum*, 2019 QCCA 1408 (leave to appeal denied 2020 CarswellQue 1736 (SCC)), L's will designated T as beneficiary of L's pension plans. The Superior Court held this was a *Civil Code* "legacy by particular title", not a "designation of beneficiaries", so T did not need to include in income a right to a retirement compensation arrangement that was not transferred to her by the 1-year deadline; but the Court of Appeal held the right was transferred to her on L's death, so the Quebec equivalent of 70(3) applied.

For CRA interpretation see VIEWS docs 2011-0394961E5, 2011-0421801E5; 2016-0653921E5 (whether a testamentary trust is beneficially interested in the estate).

70(3)(b) amended by 1995-97 technical bill, for tax years ending after Nov. 1991.

Interpretation Bulletins: IT-210R2: Income of deceased persons — periodic payments and investment tax credit; IT-212R3: Income of deceased persons — rights or things; IT-278R2: Death of a partner or of a retired partner; IT-427R: Livestock of farmers.

(3.1) Exception — For the purposes of this section, "rights or

things" do not include an interest in a life insurance policy (other than an annuity contract of a taxpayer where the payment therefor was deductible in computing the taxpayer's income because of paragraph 60(l) or was made in circumstances in which subsection 146(21) applied), land included in the inventory of a business, a Canadian resource property or a foreign resource property.

Notes: "Land" includes buildings: see 70(5.2) Notes.

70(3.1) amended by 2016 budget bill #2, effective 2017, to delete "eligible capital property," before "land" (as part of changing ECP rules to CCA Class 14.1: see 20(1)(b) Notes).

70(3.1) amended by 1993 technical bill, for 1992 and later taxation years.

Interpretation Bulletins: IT-212R3: Income of deceased persons — rights or things; IT-313R2: Eligible capital property — rules where a taxpayer has ceased carrying on a business or has died.

(4) Revocation of election — An election made under subsec-

tion (2) may be revoked by a notice of revocation signed by the legal representative of the taxpayer and filed with the Minister within the time that an election under that subsection may be made.

Interpretation Bulletins: IT-212R3: Income of deceased persons — rights or things.

(5) Capital property of a deceased taxpayer — Where in a

taxation year a taxpayer dies,

(a) the taxpayer shall be deemed to have, immediately before the taxpayer's death, disposed of each capital property of the taxpayer and received proceeds of disposition therefor equal to the fair market value of the property immediately before the death;

(b) any person who as a consequence of the taxpayer's death acquires any property that is deemed by paragraph (a) to have been disposed of by the taxpayer shall be deemed to have acquired it at the time of the death at a cost equal to its fair market value immediately before the death;

(c) where any depreciable property of the taxpayer of a prescribed class that is deemed by paragraph (a) to have been disposed of is acquired by any person as a consequence of the taxpayer's death (other than where the taxpayer's proceeds of disposition of the property under paragraph (a) are redetermined under subsection 13(21.1)) and the amount that was the capital cost to the taxpayer of the property exceeds the amount determined under paragraph (b) to be the cost to the person thereof, for the purposes of sections 13 and 20 and any regulations made for the purpose of paragraph 20(1)(a),

(i) the capital cost to the person of the property shall be deemed to be the amount that was the capital cost to the taxpayer of the property, and

(ii) the excess shall be deemed to have been allowed to the person in respect of the property under regulations made for the purpose of paragraph 20(1)(a) in computing income for taxation years that ended before the person acquired the property; and

(d) where a property of the taxpayer that was deemed by paragraph (a) to have been disposed of is acquired by any person as a consequence of the taxpayer's death and the taxpayer's proceeds of disposition of the property under paragraph (a) are redetermined under subsection 13(21.1), notwithstanding paragraph (b),

(i) where the property was depreciable property of a prescribed class and the amount that was the capital cost to the taxpayer of the property exceeds the amount so redetermined under subsection 13(21.1), for the purposes of sections 13 and 20 and any regulations made for the purpose of paragraph 20(1)(a),

(A) its capital cost to the person shall be deemed to be the amount that was its capital cost to the taxpayer, and

(B) the excess shall be deemed to have been allowed to the person in respect of the property under regulations made for the purpose of paragraph 20(1)(a) in computing income for taxation years that ended before the person acquired the property, and

(ii) where the property is land (other than land to which subparagraph (i) applies), its cost to the person shall be deemed to be the amount that was the taxpayer's proceeds of disposition of the land as redetermined under subsection 13(21.1).

Related Provisions: 38(a.1)(ii) — No capital gain on bequest of publicly-traded securities to charity; 43.1(2) — Life estates in real property; 44(2) — Date of disposition for property stolen, destroyed or expropriated; 53(4) — Effect on ACB of share, partnership interest or trust interest; 54 "superficial loss" (c) — Superficial loss rule does not apply; 70(5.3) — Value of property that depends on life insurance policy; 70(5.31) — Leveraged insurance annuity — FMV rule; 70(6) — Rollover on transfer to spouse of spouse trust; 70(6.2) — Election; 70(9), (9.01), (9.2), (9.21) — Transfer of farm or fishing property to taxpayer's child, family corporation or partnership; 70(13) — Capital cost of certain depreciable property; 70(14) — Order of disposal of depreciable property; 75.2(b) — Qualifying trust annuity to be disregarded; 80(2)(p), (q) — Debt forgiveness rules — debt obligation settled by estate; 110.6(14)(g) — Related persons, etc.; 118.1(1) "total gifts" (a)(ii) — Charitable donation claim after death not limited to 75% of net income; 118.1(5), (5.1) — Donations by will or by the estate after death; 118.1(10.1) — Determination of value by Canadian Cultural Property Export Review Board; 120.4(1) "excluded amount" (c) — Income-splitting tax does not apply to capital gain under 70(5); 135.2(6) — Where Cdn Wheat Board Farmers' Trust (CWBFT) issues unit after farmer's death; 135.2(8) — Death of farmer owning eligible unit of CWBFT; 143.1(4) — Death of beneficiary of amateur athlete trust; 146(8.92)–(8.93), 146.3(6.3)–(6.4) — Carryback of post-death losses in RRSP or RRIF; 159(5) — Election where certain provisions applicable; 164(6) — Election by executor to carry back losses of estate to year of death; 248(8) — Meaning of "consequence" of death; 256(7)(a)(i)(D) — Control of corporation deemed not acquired due to death; Canada-U.S. Tax Treaty: Art. XXIX-B:6, 7 — Credit for U.S. estate taxes.

Notes: On death, 70(5) generally triggers deemed disposition of property at fair market value (FMV — see Notes to 69(1)), taxing accrued gains in the deceased's final return. (It is thus known informally as a "death tax".) For capital property, the resulting capital gain under 39(1)(a) is half included in income as taxable capital gain under 38(a). For depreciable property, there may also be recapture; see the ordering rule in 70(14), and Notes to 13(1). Donations made by will can reduce the liability: see sub-heading "Charitable donations" below.

Accrued capital losses are also triggered by 70(5), and the superficial loss rule does not apply: 54"superficial loss"(c). Allowable capital losses can be applied against all income, not just taxable capital gains: 111(2)(b).

The 2015 Conservative Budget proposed that, starting 2017, the capital gain on private company shares and real estate would be reduced by donations made by the estate (38(a.4), 38.3, 38.4), but this proposal was cancelled in the 2016 Liberal Budget.

The main exception to 70(5) is in 70(6), if property is left to the deceased's spouse (or common-law partner) or a "spousal trust" meeting certain conditions. Other ways to reduce the tax cost of the deemed gain: farm/fishing property rollover to children and grandchildren (70(9)-(9.31)); capital gains exemption for small business shares does not require 2-year holding period (110.6(14)(g)); apply capital loss carryforwards (111(2)(b)); spread out payment of the tax over 10 years with interest (159(5), (7)); elect to carry estate losses back to the terminal return (164(6)); sell home or cottage soon after death for a capital loss equal to real estate commission and legal fees (see Notes to 54"personal use property").

Non-residents are not subject to 70(5) according to *McKenzie*, 2017 TCC 56 (Informal Procedure), but CRA disagrees: VIEWS doc 2018-0742141C6 [STEP 2018 q.8].

Worthless shares held at death are deemed sold at nil and create a capital loss, but not if the corporation had been dissolved (since the loss would have been triggered earlier): VIEWS doc 2012-0442961C6.

If a corporation's articles provide that its shares are automatically redeemed for a nominal amount on the holder's death, the CRA states that this does not reduce the value for 70(5): VIEWS doc 2001-0094085, citing *Nussey Estate*, [2001] 2 C.T.C. 222 (FCA).

If the deceased held only legal title rather than beneficial ownership, 70(5) may not apply to the property: VIEWS doc 2010-0387181I7, and see Notes to 54"capital property" and 104(1) re nominee owners and bare trusts.

Joint tenants (JTs) legally each own 100% of the property subject to the rights of the other JT, so a JT's interest vanishes on death and is not part of his/her estate. The JTcy can be broken and made a 50%-each tenancy-in-common by unilateral action, mutual agreement, or a "course of dealing" showing that all parties treated it as such: *Hansen Estate*, 2012 ONCA 112; *Zeligs v. Janes*, 2016 BCCA 280 (unilaterally withdrawing all of a bank account severed it); *Marley v. Salga*, 2020 ONCA 104 (course of dealing); *Thompson v. Elliott*, 2020 ONSC 1004 (unilateral action before death). On a JT's death, CRA's view is that 70(5) applies to the deceased's interest in the property and the remaining owner acquires that interest at FMV, even though at common law the deceased's interest simply vanishes: doc 2003-0013735. See also Notes to 69(1) re *Pecore* case; Flannery, "Joint Tenancy", XXI(4) *Insurance Planning* (Federated Press) 1370-75 (2015); Spenceley, "Joint Tenancy Review", 260 *The Estate Planner* (CCH) 1-3 (Sept. 2016).

A reference in a will to "capital gains tax" to be paid by the estate referred to tax under 70(5): *Fournie v. Cromarty*, 2011 ONSC 6587. Unless all beneficiaries agree or the will provides otherwise, the estate must bear the burden of the 70(5) tax, and beneficiaries cannot be forced to use part of their capital gains exemption to reduce the tax: *Podulsky Estate*, 2015 ABQB 509, paras. 91-126.

70(5)(b): The estate, as well as each heir (248(8)), acquires property from the deceased at FMV: *MacDonald*, 2012 TCC 123, para. 73 (rev'd on other grounds 2013 FCA 110); VIEWS docs 2008-0269451E5, 2010-0359311I7, 2010-0368141E5, 2010-0388591R3. See planning tip under Notes to 54"personal-use property". However, in *Bueti*, 2015 TCC 265 (TCC), a house not specifically left to B (who was a residual beneficiary and an estate trustee) was found to have been purchased by B for $50,000 rather than received as beneficiary, so that was her cost. Where the will *provides* that a person may purchase property at a price below FMV, the transfer to the purchaser is a rollout under 107(2): 2007-0232421R3.

70(5)(b) can apply to an interest in a trust: VIEWS doc 2013-0511391E5.

Tax consequences of death (aside from 70(5))

For CRA "What to do when someone has died": canada.ca/taxes-deceased. See also *Income Tax Audit Manual* chap. 17.

The estate exists as a separate person until all property is distributed and it is wound up, and is treated as a testamentary trust (starting 2016, a "graduated rate estate" for 36 months). See 104(1) and 248(1)"trust", and Notes to 248(1)"graduated rate estate" about actions to take within 36 months before losing GRE status.

A recipient pays no tax on a bequest or inheritance, as it is not income from a "source" under s. 3; VIEWS doc 2014-0525991M4. In *Bui*, 2013 TCC 326, a beneficiary could not deduct rental losses on properties that had not yet been transferred to him.

Neither Canada nor any province has estate taxes or succession duties, but the provinces impose probate fees or estate administration tax on probating a deceased's will, of up to 1.5% of the estate value. See tinyurl.com/can-probate for rates; Doobay & David, "Amended Ontario Estate Tax", 21(3) *Canadian Tax Highlights* (ctf.ca) 4-6 (March 2013); Notes to 248(1)"alter ego trust" re using an AET to avoid probate fees. Note that in Ontario, the estate trustee must file an Estate Information Return with the Ministry of Finance by 90 days after the Certificate of Estate Trustee is issued. See Corbin, "Minister of Finance's Regulation Regarding Estate Administration Tax", 30(1) *Money & Family Law* (Carswell) 1-2 (Jan. 2015); Lund, "Ontario's New Estate

Information Return", V(2) *Personal Tax and Estate Planning* (Federated Press) 222-25 (2015); Ontario Forms 9955E (estate information return) and 9955E_Guide.

Alternative minimum tax does not apply for the year of death: 127.55(c).

CRA authorizations are no longer cancelled on death, so the deceased's accountant can continue to deal with CRA: see Notes to 241(5).

Capital loss carryforwards can be used against any income for the year of death and the previous year, not just taxable capital gains: 111(2)(b). If the will forgives a debt, the estate may be denied a capital loss due to 40(2)(g)(ii): VIEWS doc 2012-0442951C6 [2012 STEP q.3].

Change in control of a corporation is not triggered by death or by transfer from the estate to a related beneficiary: 256(7)(a)(i)(C), (D).

Charitable donations made by will up to 5 years after death can be claimed by either the estate or the deceased (and carried back to the year before death): see 118.1(1)"total charitable gifts"(c)(i)(C) and 118.1(4)-(5.1).

Death benefit ($10,000 tax-free): see 56(1)(a)(iii), 104(28) and 248(1)"death benefit". A CPP death benefit (*Canada Pension Plan* s. 71) is payable and taxable to the estate, not the deceased: 56(1)(a)(i)(F), 56(1)(a.1).

Debt forgiven by bequest or inheritance does not trigger the usual debt-forgiveness consequences to the debtor: 80(2)(a).

Depreciable property on death: see Notes to 13(1).

Employer payments for vacation pay are taxable but can go on a separate "rights or things" 70(2) return (IT-212R3); sick leave credits are a "death benefit" (IT-508R), and taxable to beneficiaries via 104(28) so they can claim the $10,000 exemption in 248(1)"death benefit". See also VIEWS doc 2018-0746971E5 (bonus received after death: timing of T4 reporting vs income inclusion [Tollstam, "CRA Recognizes Potential Reporting Mismatch for Amounts Paid After Death", 27(7) *Canadian Tax Highlights* (ctf.ca) 8-9 (July 2019)].

Estate taxes of other countries: see "US tax" below, and Catherine Brown, "Death as a Taxable Event — Impact of Jurisdictions Levying Tax", III(3) *Personal Tax and Estate Planning* (Federated Press) 147-48 (2010).

Executor obligations: The executor (estate trustee) can be liable for distributing estate assets without a clearance certificate: see Notes to 159(3). See Notes to 150(1)(a) re whether an executor must file a deceased sole shareholder's corporate return.

Executor's expenses: Estate administration costs are generally non-deductible: see Notes to 18(1)(a). However, see Notes to 8(1)(b) re an executor deducting the cost of passing of accounts. CRA's view is that "outlays and expenses" in 40(1)(a)(i) does not include the estate's costs relating to the 70(5) deemed disposition: VIEWS doc 2006-0185591C6; however, such costs were allowed in *Brosamler Estate*, 2012 TCC 204. CRA does not accept *Brosamler*: see Notes to 164(6).

Family home, if left to the estate and sold, can create a capital loss equal to the real estate commission and legal fees. See "Planning tip" in 54"personal-use property" Notes.

Farm and fishing property rollovers: see 70(9)-(9.31), (9.8).

Filing and payment deadline: The return deadline is extended to 6 months after a November-December death: 150(1)(b). The payment deadline is also extended: 248(1)"balance-due day"(b), For the cohabiting spouse or common-law partner, the filing (but not payment) deadline is also extended: 150(1)(d)(iii).

Flow-through shares bought by a deceased who died before the renunciation: no deduction is available to either the deceased or the estate in the CRA's view: 2013-0495271C6.

Foreign property reporting: A deceased person does not own property at year-end, so the terminal return may need a T1135 but the foreign property cost to report will be $0: VIEWS doc 2014-0527611E5.

France: inheritance tax can be offset against the 70(5) tax on capital gains, per Canada-France tax treaty Art. 23:1(c), 23:2(c).

GST/HST: Excise Tax Act s. 267 (see David M. Sherman, *Practitioner's Goods and Services Tax, Annotated*) provides that, on X's death, GST/HST applies as if X had not died. Thus, the estate is considered a continuation of X. The executor or administrator "steps into X's shoes" and continues with X's GST/HST registration number and status. Obligations (such as to remit past net tax) continue; and a sale by the estate is a "taxable supply" only if that sale by X would have been. Exceptions to this rule: ETA 267(a)-(b) (new reporting period starts the day after X dies); 267.1, 268 and 270 (rules for trusts); 279 (who may sign documents). A transfer under X's will to beneficiary B may be taxable, requiring B to pay GST/HST on the property's value to receive it: *Lamont Estate*, 2017 SKQB 67. If B is a registrant, business assets can transfer tax-free under ETA 167(2). Otherwise, ETA 269 deems the distribution to be a sale for consideration equal to the ITA proceeds of distribution. ITA 70(5)(a) deems X to have received proceeds equal to FMV, and 70(5)(b) deems the estate to have acquired the property for the same FMV. ITA 107(2) then deems the estate, as a "personal trust", to have disposed of the property for proceeds equal to its cost to the estate, which is the same FMV, so this amount applies for ETA 269.

Income-splitting tax may not apply to property acquired on a death: 120.4(1)"excluded amount"(a), (c); 120.4(1.1)(b), (c)(ii).

Instalments are not required after death: 156.1(3).

Life estate and remainder interest bequests: VIEWS docs 2011-0409961C6, 2011-0401401C6, 2012-0442871C6; May 2011 ICAA roundtable (tinyurl.com/cra-abtax), q.20.

Life insurance policy: see 70(5.3); Wark, "Life Insurance Bequests on Death", XX(2) *Insurance Planning [IP]* (Federated Press) 1270-72 (2014); and other issues of *IP*. See Notes to 118.1(5.2) on the use of life insurance, with a charity designated as beneficiary, to shelter the 70(5) gain. Insurance proceeds designations can be used to avoid probate: Niedermayer, "Insurance Trusts", 2012 Atlantic Provinces Tax Conference (ctf.ca), 7B:1-7; Ideias, "Separate Insurance Trusts: What a Tax Planner Needs to Know", Tax Planner Guide 6 (*Taxnet Pro*, July 2018, 6pp.); Botsford, "Insurance Trusts", VIII(1) *Personal Tax & Estate Planning* (Federated Press) 17-41 (2019).

Medical expenses can be claimed for a 24-month period ending in the year of death, instead of the usual 12 months: 118.2(1)B(d); and the attendant care limit is doubled to $20,000 for that year: 118.2(2)(b.1) closing words.

Online mail: CRA registration is cancelled on death: May 2016 Alberta CPA Roundtable (tinyurl.com/cra-abtax), q. 19(b).

Pay equity settlement or retroactive pay increase to a deceased taxpayer, under an agreement signed after death, is not taxable: VIEWS docs 2003-0018835, 2009-0324381E5.

Pipeline planning to extract corporate surplus after death: see Notes to 84(2).

RRSPs: see 146(8.8).

RRIFs: see 146.3(6).

Rights or things: The deceased can file a "separate return", multiplying the personal credits and low brackets, for "rights or things" (see Notes to 70(2)); for business income after the fiscal year-end in the year of death, if using a non-calendar year (34.1(9)); and for income received before death from an estate or testamentary trust after its year-end (104(23)(d)).

Stock options on death: see 7(1) Notes.

TFSAs: see Notes to 146.2(1)"survivor".

US tax: Non-US executors must obtain IRS transfer certificates before selling US securities in an estate of a non-US citizen (US financial institutions may require this before taking funds out of the account): see tinyurl.com/irs-xfr-cert. US estate tax may apply to US assets held on death, even in a Canadian brokerage account and even where held through a corporation. US estate tax applies to non-resident non-citizens only on property situated in the US: *Internal Revenue Code* (IRC) §2103 (including stock issued by a US corp: §2104(a)). The IRS administratively considers American Depository Receipts (ADRs) not to be US-situated even if traded on US exchanges: private letter ruling 200243031. The status of Exchange Traded Funds (ETFs) that do not hold US assets is uncertain. If setting up a trust to hold assets to avoid estate tax, note that in the US, under "substance over form", the trust may be treated as something else for US tax law (see Reg. 301.7701-4). The estate tax top marginal rate is now 40%, with a credit on the first $11.7m (2021, indexed for inflation), twice that for a married couple if both spouses are US persons; this exemption has been doubled for 2018-25. One can use a deceased spouse's unused credit if both spouses are US citizens (IRC §2010(c)(4)). A couple holding US property may benefit from owning the property as tenants in common rather than as joint owners, as each fraction can benefit from the pro-rated estate tax exemption under the Canada-US tax treaty. Some US states have death taxes as well. An estate tax return is required if the deceased had more than $60,000 in US assets, even if a fully offsetting credit is available (see Canada-US treaty Art. XXIX-B). If an estate tax return is not filed, the beneficiaries may be deemed to inherit property at nil cost: Berg, "Canadian Decedents with US Real Estate", 24(5) *CTH* 13-14 (May 2016). US citizens receiving funds from an estate may also need to file Form 3520 (on irs.gov: IRC §6039F): see Notes to 233.3(3).

US estate tax detailed discussion: Chaho, "Death and Taxes in the United States: A Canadian's Guide to Navigating US Estate Taxation", 54(1) *Canadian Tax Journal* 263-86 (2006); Yager & Carey, "Dynasty Trusts for American Beneficiaries of Canadians", 2008 Cdn Tax Foundation conference report, 33:1-31; Campbell, Churchill & King, "Estate Planning for US Citizens Resident in Canada", 2009 Atlantic Provinces Tax Conference (ctf.ca), 5B:1-17; Carey, "US Estate Tax", 2010 Prairie Provinces Tax Conf. 14:1-12; Fitzsimmons, "Death and Taxes", 2011 Atlantic Provinces Tax Conf. 4C:1-20; Dumont & Evans, "Trust and Estate Planning for US Beneficiaries", 2011 Ontario Tax Conf. 6:1-32; Ibrahim, Piontnica & Stephens, "Canadians Purchasing US Real Estate", Cdn Tax Foundation 2012 conference report, 39:1-33; Gluc, "US Estate Tax Update", 2012 Atlantic Provinces Tax Conf. 4:1-15; Ouellette & Warner, "Estate Planning: US-Resident Beneficiaries of a Canadian Estate", 62(1) *CTJ* 197-219 and 62(3) 835-56 (2014); Loughlin & Reynolds, "US Tax Considerations in Canadian Estate Planning", 2013 BC Tax Conf. 11:1-30; Ideias, "US Estate Tax: What a Tax Planner Needs to Know" (*Taxnet Pro* Tax & Estate Planning Centre, 2020, 13pp); Hanson et al., *Death of a Taxpayer* (CCH, 12th ed., 2020), pp. 321-44.

US estate tax shorter articles: Eberl, "US Estate Planning", 21(7) *Canadian Tax Highlights [CTH]* (ctf.ca) 9-10 (July 2013) and "US Estate Tax Returns", 22(9) 9 (Sept. 2014); Bernstein & Atsaidis, "Cross-Border Estate Planning Traps", 22(7) *CTH* 12-14 (July 2014); Joseffer, "Liability for a Decedent's US Tax", 23(4) *CTH* (ctf.ca) 9 (April 2015); Pereira & Hsu, "The Determination of a Person's US Residency Status under US Estate and Gift Tax Law", 9(3) *BorderCrossings* (Carswell) 1-6 (Sept. 2016); Choudhury, "US Estate Tax: Partnership Investing in US Realty", 24(10) *CTH* 5-6 (Oct. 2016); Reed, "Protecting Canadians from the US Estate Tax", *The Tax Advocate* (*Taxnet Pro* Tax Disputes Centre), July 2017; McKenna, "US Tax Reform and Estate Tax", 26(2) *CTH* 3 (Feb. 2018); Gluc, "Refresher on US Estate Tax Filing for Canadi-

ans", 27(11) *CTH* 14-15 (Nov. 2019); Fitzsimmons, "US Federal Estate Tax and Gift Tax Update", 27(12) *CTH* 2 (Dec. 2019); Kirkpatrick, "US Estate and Gift Tax Planning Update for Canadian Residents", XXV(1) *Insurance Planning* (Federated Press) 13-16 (2020).

Zombies, vampires, other undead, and persons frozen cryogenically for future resuscitation: Adam Chodorow, "Death and Taxes and Zombies", ssrn.com/abstract=2045255.

See also CRA Guide T4011 and pamphlet RC4111; Brown, *Taxation and Estate Planning* (Carswell, looseleaf or *Taxnet Pro* Reference Centre), chap. 2; Chow & Cadesky, *Taxation at Death: A Practitioner's Guide 2021* (Carswell, 475 pp.); Stevens, "Passage of Shares of a Private Corporation on Death", *Taxation of Private Corporations and their Shareholders* (ctf.ca, 5th ed., 2020), 19:1-68; Hanson et al., *Death of a Taxpayer* (CCH, 12th ed., 2020, 378pp); Rintoul, *The Practitioner's Guide to Estate Practice in Ontario* (LexisNexis, 7th ed., 2019); Stephan & van der Wissel, "Advising the Personal Representative", 2004 Cdn Tax Foundation conference report, 36:1-56; Riggin, "Death of a Taxpayer", 2005 Ontario Tax Conference (ctf.ca), 9:1-34; Christian, "Post-Mortem Tax Planning", 2007 conference report, 37:1-29; Choran & Farina, "Canadian Estate's Executor", 21(5) *Canadian Tax Highlights* (ctf.ca) 7-8 (May 2013); Ideias, "Post-Mortem Tax Planning... What a Tax Planner Needs to Know" (*Taxnet Pro* Tax & Estate Planning Centre, 2020, 9pp); "Death of a Taxpayer Checklist" (*ibid.*, 7pp); "Executor's Duties Checklist" (*ibid.*, 9pp); Goldberg, "Post-Mortem Planning for Private Companies", 2559 *Tax Topics* (CCH) 1-4 (March 23, 2021), 2561:1-4 (April 6, 2021) or 315 *The Estate Planner* 1-4 (April 2021), 316:1-4 (May 2021).

Planning before death: see references in David M. Sherman, *The Lawyer's Guide to Income Tax and GST/HST* (Carswell, 2017), chapter "Wills and Estates"; *Miller Thomson on Estate Planning* (Carswell, 2 vols., looseleaf or ProView); Duncan & Duncan, *When I Die* (Carswell, 9th ed., 2020, 150pp); and Notes to 86(1) re estate freezing. See also Donahue & Crummey, "Tax Issues in Will Planning", 48(4) & (5) *Canadian Tax Journal* 1299-1320 & 1674-97 (2000); Deighan, "Death of a Businessman", 2003 Cdn Tax Foundation conference report, 14:1-41; Rideout, "Grasping at Straws — Tax Planning on Intestacy", 10(2) *Tax Hyperion* (Carswell) 2-3 (Feb. 2013); Citrome & Wong, "Voluntary Disclosure — Do it Before You Die", 65(4) *Canadian Tax Journal* 1021-46 (2017); and planning tip in 54"personal-use property" Notes. See also 248(1)"alter ego trust" Notes.

For non-tax issues see Hull & Popovic-Montag, *Probate Practice* (Carswell, 5th ed., 2016, 1,122pp). Under the common-law "rule of convenience", the executor normally has one year (the "executor's year") to wind up an estate, after which interest is owed to beneficiaries: *Rivard v. Morris*, 2018 ONCA 181.

70(5) amended and restructured by 1992 and 1993 technical bills, effective 1993.

I.T. Application Rules: 20(1.2) (where depreciable property owned since before 1972 is transferred on death).

Interpretation Bulletins: IT-140R3: Buy-sell agreements; IT-242R: Retired partners; IT-217R: Depreciable property owned on December 31, 1971 (cancelled); IT-259R4: Exchanges of property; IT-278R2: Death of a partner or of a retired partner; IT-288R2: Gifts of capital properties to a charity and others; IT-305R4: Testamentary spouse trusts; IT-325R2: Property transfers after separation, divorce and annulment; IT-382: Debts bequeathed or forgiven on death (cancelled); IT-349R3: Intergenerational transfers of farm property on death; IT-416R3: Valuation of shares of a corporation receiving life insurance proceeds on death of a shareholder; IT-504R2: Visual artists and writers; IT-522R: Vehicle, travel and sales expenses of employees.

Information Circulars: 89-3: Policy statement on business equity valuations.

CRA Audit Manual: 16.2.2: Estate of a deceased person.

Forms: RC549–RC561: Affidavit for intestate succession for [each province]; RC4111: What to do following a death [guide]; T4011: Preparing returns for deceased persons [guide].

(5.1) Transfer or distribution — Class 14.1 — Notwithstanding subsection (6), if property included in Class 14.1 of Schedule II to the *Income Tax Regulations* of the taxpayer in respect of a business carried on by the taxpayer immediately before the taxpayer's death that is a property to which subsection (5) would otherwise apply is, as a consequence of the death, transferred or distributed (otherwise than by way of a distribution of property by a trust that claimed a deduction under paragraph 20(1)(a) or (b) in respect of the property or in circumstances to which subsection 24(2) applies) to any person (in this subsection referred to as the "beneficiary"), the following rules apply:

(a) paragraphs (5)(a) and (b) do not apply in respect of the property;

(b) the taxpayer is deemed to have, immediately before the taxpayer's death, disposed of the property and received proceeds of disposition equal to the lesser of the capital cost and the cost amount to the taxpayer of the property immediately before the death;

(c) the beneficiary is deemed to have acquired the property at the time of the death at a cost equal to those proceeds; and

(d) paragraph (5)(c) applies as if the references to "paragraph (a)" were read as references to "paragraph (5.1)(b)" and the reference to "paragraph (b)" were read as reference to "paragraph (5.1)(c)".

Related Provisions: 24(2) — Where business carried on by spouse or controlled corporation; 110.6(1)"qualified farm property"(d), "qualified fishing property"(d) — Capital gains exemption; 248(8) — Meaning of "consequence" of death.

Notes: 70(5.1) amended by 2016 budget bill #2, effective 2017, as part of changing eligible capital property rules to CCA Class 14.1 (see Notes to 20(1)(b)). Before 2017, read:

(5.1) **Eligible capital property of deceased** — Notwithstanding subsection 24(1), where at any time a taxpayer dies and any person (in this subsection referred to as the beneficiary), as a consequence of the taxpayer's death, acquires an eligible capital property of the taxpayer in respect of a business carried on by the taxpayer immediately before that time (otherwise than by way of a distribution of property by a trust that claimed a deduction under paragraph 20(1)(b) in respect of the property or in circumstances to which subsection 24(2) applies),

(a) the taxpayer shall be deemed to have disposed of the property, immediately before the taxpayer's death, for proceeds equal to $^4/_3$ of that proportion of the cumulative eligible capital of the taxpayer in respect of the business that the fair market value immediately before that time of the property is of the fair market value immediately before that time of all of the eligible capital property of the taxpayer in respect of the business;

(b) subject to paragraph (c), the beneficiary shall be deemed to have acquired a capital property at the time of the taxpayer's death at a cost equal to the proceeds referred to in paragraph (a);

(c) where the beneficiary continues to carry on the business previously carried on by the taxpayer, the beneficiary shall be deemed to have, at the time of the taxpayer's death, acquired an eligible capital property and made an eligible capital property expenditure at a cost equal to the total of

(i) the proceeds referred to in paragraph (a), and

(ii) $^4/_3$ of that proportion of the amount, if any, determined for F in the definition "cumulative eligible capital" in subsection 14(5) in respect of the business of the taxpayer at that time that the fair market value immediately before that time of the particular property is of the fair market value immediately before that time of all eligible capital property of the taxpayer in respect of the business,

and, for the purposes of determining at any time the beneficiary's cumulative eligible capital in respect of the business, an amount equal to $^3/_4$ of the amount determined under subparagraph (ii) shall be added to the amount otherwise determined, in respect of the business, for P in the definition "cumulative eligible capital" in subsection 14(5); and

(d) for the purpose of determining, after that time, the amount required by paragraph 14(1)(b) to be included in computing the income of the beneficiary in respect of any subsequent disposition of the property of the business, there shall be added to the amount determined for Q in the definition "cumulative eligible capital" in subsection 14(5) the amount determined by the formula

$$A \times B/C$$

where

A   is the amount, if any, determined for Q in that definition in respect of the business of the taxpayer immediately before that time,

B   is the fair market value immediately before that time of the particular property, and

C   is the fair market value immediately before that time of all eligible capital property of the taxpayer in respect of the business.

See VIEWS doc 2010-0384701E5 on interaction of pre-2017 70(5.1) with the 40(1)(a)(iii) capital gains reserve.

70(5.1)(d) amended by 2000 Budget (effective for taxation years that end after Feb. 27, 2000), 1994 Budget, 1993, 1992 and 1991 technical bills.

Interpretation Bulletins: IT-313R2: Eligible capital property — rules where a taxpayer has ceased carrying on a business or has died.

(5.2) Resource property and land inventory — If in a taxation year a taxpayer dies,

(a) the taxpayer is deemed

(i) to have disposed, at the time that is immediately before the taxpayer's death, of each

(A) Canadian resource property of the taxpayer,

(B) foreign resource property of the taxpayer, and

(C) property that was land included in the inventory of a business of the taxpayer, and

(ii) subject to paragraph (c), to have received at that time proceeds of disposition for each such property equal to its fair market value at that time;

(b) any person who, as a consequence of the taxpayer's death, acquires a property that is deemed by paragraph (a) to have been disposed of by the taxpayer is, subject to paragraph (c), deemed to have acquired the property at the time of the death at a cost equal to its fair market value at the time that is immediately before the death; and

(c) where the taxpayer was resident in Canada at the time that is immediately before the taxpayer's death, a particular property described in clause (a)(i)(A), (B) or (C) is, on or after the death and as a consequence of the death, transferred or distributed to a spouse or common-law partner of the taxpayer described in paragraph (6)(a) or a trust described in paragraph (6)(b), and it can be shown within the period that ends 36 months after the death (or, where written application has been made to the Minister by the taxpayer's legal representative within that period, within any longer period that the Minister considers reasonable in the circumstances) that the particular property has, within that period, vested indefeasibly in the spouse, common-law partner or trust, as the case may be,

(i) the taxpayer is deemed to have received, at the time that is immediately before the taxpayer's death, proceeds of disposition of the particular property equal to

(A) if the particular property is Canadian resource property of the taxpayer or foreign resource property of the taxpayer, the amount specified by the taxpayer's legal representative in the taxpayer's return of income filed under paragraph 150(1)(b), not exceeding its fair market value at that time, and

(B) if the particular property was land included in the inventory of a business of the taxpayer, its cost amount to the taxpayer at that time, and

(ii) the spouse, common-law partner or trust, as the case may be, is deemed to have acquired at the time of the death the particular property at a cost equal to the amount determined under subparagraph (i) in respect of the disposition of it under paragraph (a).

Related Provisions: 104(4)(a)(i.1) — Deemed disposition of trust property; 159(5) — Election where certain provisions applicable; 248(8) — Meaning of "consequence" of death; 248(9.2) — Meaning of "vested indefeasibly"; Canada-U.S. Tax Treaty:Art. XXIX-B:5 — US resident deemed resident in Canada before death.

Notes: For examples of 70(5.2) see VIEWS docs 2014-0532221E5, 2018-0739741E5.

"Land" includes buildings for purposes of 70(5.2) (and likely other provisions aside from 18(2), for which 18(3) excludes buildings): VIEWS doc 2017-0728051E5. (Note also that 70(5)(d)(ii), 70(9.01)(a)(ii)(B)(II), Reg. 808(2)(a)(ii) and other rules apply to land "other than" depreciable property, implying that "land" normally includes buildings; and Reg. 2300 refers to land as already "including" a home on it.)

70(5.2) amended by 2002-2013 technical bill (Part 5 — technical), for tax years beginning after 2006. (The draft "foreign investment entities" rules (proposed 94.1-94.4), which were dropped in 2010, had proposed to add references to 94.2.)

70(5.2) amended by 2001 technical bill (effective for taxation years that begin after 2000), 2000 Budget, 2000 same-sex partners bill and 1993 technical bill.

Interpretation Bulletins: IT-125R4: Dispositions of resource properties; IT-212R3: Income of deceased persons — rights or things; IT-449R: Meaning of "vested indefeasibly" (cancelled).

(5.3) Fair market value [of life insurance policy] — For the purposes of subsections (5) and 104(4) and section 128.1, the fair market value at any time of any property deemed to have been disposed of at that time as a consequence of a particular individual's death or as a consequence of the particular individual becoming or ceasing to be resident in Canada shall be determined as though the fair market value at that time of any life insurance policy, under which the particular individual (or any other individual not dealing at arm's length with the particular individual at that time or at the time the policy was issued) was a person whose life was insured, were the cash surrender value (as defined in subsection 148(9)) of the policy immediately before the particular individual died or became or ceased to be resident in Canada, as the case may be.

Related Provisions: 139.1(5) — Value of ownership rights in insurer during demutualization; 248(8) — Meaning of "consequence" of death; 251 — Arm's length.

Notes: 70(5.3) provides that for purposes of deemed dispositions (of any property, often shares) on death, emigration and the 21-year trust deemed disposition, the value of a life insurance policy is its cash surrender value. However, CRA Information Circular 89-3, paras. 17-31, indicates that a buy-sell agreement can take priority in determining value of shares on death.

70(5.3) can apply to multiple-life policies, due to the words "(or any other individual..." added in 2001, overriding former CRA policy in doc 2000-0014245.

For CRA's views on how to distribute the cash surrender value of a policy between categories of shares, see docs 2005-0138111C6, 2005-0138361C6, 2006-0197111C6 [2006 APFF q.7]. See also 2010-0390911E5 (interaction with 104(4)).

VIEWS doc 2003-0004335 states that an outstanding policy loan is not considered in valuing the policy as a corporate asset, but ordinary valuation principles apply in determining whether the policy loan is otherwise considered in valuing the deceased's shares for purposes of 70(5).

Valuing a life insurance policy where 70(5.3) does not apply: Information Circular 89-3 paras. 40-41; VIEWS docs 2008-0270401C6, 2013-0473981E5 (for certain purposes, use cash surrender value due to 110.6(15)); 2020-0842191C6 [2020 CALU q.5] (jointly-owned policy). On transfer by a corp to its shareholder, 148(7) may take priority over 69(1): 2016-0651761C6 [2016 APFF q.3]. See also Marino & Natale, *Canadian Taxation of Life Insurance* (Carswell, 10th ed., 2020), §3.3; Friedlan, "Revised Valuation Rules for Life Insurance", VIII(1) *Insurance Planning [IP]* (Federated Press) 492-95 (2000); Wark, "Valuing a Charitable Gift of Insurance", XII(4) *IP* 804-06 (2006) and "Fair Market Value of 'Special' Insurance Shares", XV(2) *IP* 959-60 (2009) [re VIEWS doc 2008-0286151C6]; Girouard, "Description of the Methodology Used to Determine the FMV of a Life Insurance Policy", 2013 STEP Canada conference (contact memberservices@step.ca); Debresser & Ranot, "Exercise Caution When Valuing Life Insurance Policies", 33(4) *Money & Family Law* (Carswell) 26 (April 2018); Korenblum, "Valuation Issues for Life Insurance", XXV(1) *IP* 7-12 (2020). See also Notes to 118.1(1)"total charitable gifts" re valuing a policy donated to a charity.

70(5.3) amended by 2001 technical bill, for dispositions after Oct. 1, 1996.

I.T. Application Rules: 69 (meaning of "chapter 148 of ...").

Interpretation Bulletins: IT-416R3: Valuation of shares of a corporation receiving life insurance proceeds on death of a shareholder.

Information Circulars: 89-3: Policy statement on business equity valuations.

(5.31) Fair market value [leveraged insurance annuity] —
For the purposes of subsections (5) and 104(4), the fair market value at any time of any property deemed to have been disposed of at that time as a consequence of a particular individual's death is to be determined as though the fair market value at that time of any annuity contract were the total of all amounts each of which is the amount of a premium paid on or before that time under the contract if

(a) the contract is, in respect of an LIA policy, a contract referred to in subparagraph (b)(ii) of the definition "LIA policy" in subsection 248(1); and

(b) the particular individual is the individual, in respect of the LIA policy, referred to in that subparagraph.

Related Provisions: 248(8) — Meaning of "consequence" of death.

Notes: See Notes to 248(1)"LIA policy". 70(5.31) added by 2013 budget bill #2, effective for taxation years ending after March 20, 2013.

(5.4) NISA on death —
Where a taxpayer who dies has at the time of death a net income stabilization account, all amounts held for or on behalf of the taxpayer in the taxpayer's NISA Fund No. 2 shall be deemed to have been paid out of that fund to the taxpayer immediately before that time.

Related Provisions: 12(10.2) — NISA receipts; 248(9.1) — Whether trust created by taxpayer's will.

Notes: 70(5.4) added by 1992 technical bill, effective 1991. See Notes to 70(2) and to 248(1)"net income stabilization account".

Interpretation Bulletins: IT-212R3: Income of deceased persons — rights or things; IT-305R4: Testamentary spouse trusts.

(6) Where transfer or distribution to spouse [or common-law partner] or spouse trust —
Where any property of a taxpayer who was resident in Canada immediately before the taxpayer's death that is a property to which subsection (5) would otherwise apply is, as a consequence of the death, transferred or distributed to

(a) the taxpayer's spouse or common-law partner who was resident in Canada immediately before the taxpayer's death, or

(b) a trust, created by the taxpayer's will, that was resident in Canada immediately after the time the property vested indefeasibly in the trust and under which

(i) the taxpayer's spouse or common-law partner is entitled to receive all of the income of the trust that arises before the spouse's or common-law partner's death, and

(ii) no person except the spouse or common-law partner may, before the spouse's or common-law partner's death, receive or otherwise obtain the use of any of the income or capital of the trust,

if it can be shown, within the period ending 36 months after the death of the taxpayer or, where written application therefor has been made to the Minister by the taxpayer's legal representative within that period, within such longer period as the Minister considers reasonable in the circumstances, that the property has become vested indefeasibly in the spouse or common-law partner or trust, as the case may be, the following rules apply:

(c) paragraphs (5)(a) and (b) do not apply in respect of the property,

(d) subject to paragraph (d.1), the taxpayer shall be deemed to have, immediately before the taxpayer's death, disposed of the property and received proceeds of disposition therefor equal to

(i) where the property was depreciable property of a prescribed class, the lesser of the capital cost and the cost amount to the taxpayer of the property immediately before the death, and

(ii) in any other case, its adjusted cost base to the taxpayer immediately before the death,

and the spouse or common-law partner or trust, as the case may be, shall be deemed to have acquired the property at the time of the death at a cost equal to those proceeds,

(d.1) where the property is an interest in a partnership (other than an interest in a partnership to which subsection 100(3) applies),

(i) the taxpayer shall, except for the purposes of paragraph 98(5)(g), be deemed not to have disposed of the property as a consequence of the taxpayer's death,

(ii) the spouse or common-law partner or the trust, as the case may be, shall be deemed to have acquired the property at the time of the death at a cost equal to its cost to the taxpayer, and

(iii) each amount added or deducted in computing the adjusted cost base to the taxpayer of the property shall be deemed to be required by subsection 53(1) or (2) to be added or deducted, as the case may be, in computing the adjusted cost base to the spouse or common-law partner or the trust, as the case may be, of the property; and

(e) where the property was depreciable property of the taxpayer of a prescribed class, paragraph (5)(c) applies as if the references therein to "paragraph (a)" and to "paragraph (b)" were read as references to "paragraph (6)(d)".

Related Provisions: 40(3.18)(a) — Grandfathering of partnership interest transferred under 70(6)(d.1); 40(4) — Where principal residence disposed of to spouse or spouse trust; 44.1(4) — Treatment of small business investment rollover on death; 70(6.2) — Election; 70(7) — Special rules applicable re spouse trust; 70(9.1), (9.11), (9.3), (9.31) — Transfer of farm or fishing property from spouse trust to settlor's children; 72(2) — Election by legal representative and transferee re reserves; 73(1.01) — *Inter vivos* transfer of property; 94(4)(b) — Deeming non-resident trust to be resident in Canada does not apply; 104(4)(a)(i.1) — Trust — deemed disposition on death of spouse; 108(3) — Income of trust; 108(4) — Trust not disqualified by reason only of payment of certain duties and taxes; 148(8.2) — Rollover of life insurance policy to spouse on death; 248(8) — Meaning of "consequence" of death; 248(9.1) — Whether trust created by taxpayer's will; 248(9.2) — Meaning of "vested indefeasibly"; 248(23.1) — Transfer under provincial family law after death; 248(37)(g) — Rule limiting value of donated property does not apply where 70(6) applied; 252(3) — Extended meaning of "spouse"; 256(7)(a)(i)(D) — Control of corporation deemed not acquired; Canada-U.S. Tax Treaty:Art. XXVI:3(g) — Relief from double taxation; Canada-U.S. Tax Treaty:Art. XXIX-B:5, 6 — Credit for U.S. estate taxes.

Notes: The deemed disposition on death under 70(5) can be deferred by leaving property to a spouse (70(6)(a)); or by will (see 248(9.1)) or by provincial family law (see

248(23.1)) to a "spouse trust" (70(6)(b)) where the spouse will get all the income and no-one else can get any of the capital as long as the spouse is alive. (The spouse may be entitled to none, some or all of the capital.) Provided the property "vests indefeasibly" (see 248(9.2)) in the spouse or trust within 36 months of death, the deceased's cost base in the property then rolls over to the spouse or trust (70(5)(d)). The executor can elect out of the rollover with respect to any particular property (70(6.2)) or to pay debts of the estate (70(7)). The gain is triggered on the spouse's death: 104(4)(a).

For discussion see *Miller Thomson on Estate Planning* (Carswell, 2 vols. looseleaf or ProView); Schusheim, "Spouse Trusts: Tips and Traps — Part 1", 47(6) *Canadian Tax Journal* 1525-44 (1999), and Bratz, "...Part 2", 48(2) *CTJ* 477-97 (2000) (Part 2 deals with cases where one spouse is a US citizen); Adlington, "Spousal Trust Terms", 8(11) *Tax Hyperion* (Carswell, Nov. 2011); Corbin, "Electing on Fractional Shares", 28(9) *Money & Family Law* (Carswell) 65-66 (Sept. 2013); Ma, "Spouse Trust: Problems and Solutions", 4(3) *Canadian Tax Focus [CTFo]* (ctf.ca) 11-12 (Aug. 2014); ZoBell, "Spousal Trusts Have Limited CGD Access", 8(1) *CTFo* 15 (Feb. 2018).

In *Husel Estate*, [1995] 1 C.T.C. 2298 (TCC), shares transferred to the executor to settle the deceased's debt to her did not qualify because they were not transferred to her *qua* beneficiary.

See also Notes to 108(1)"testamentary trust".

"Entitled" in 70(6)(b)(i) means that the spouse has the legal right to enforce payment in the year in which the income is realized, according to the CRA: VIEWS doc 2003-0008285. A spouse's renunciation of the entitlement under the Quebec *Civil Code*, or election for relief under s. 5 of the Ontario *Family Law Act*, does not prevent 70(6) from applying: docs 2006-0189931E5, 2006-0202871E5 (see 248(23.1)).

A taxpayer can have both a spouse and a common-law spouse, and 70(6) can apply to bequests to both: docs 2010-0373901I7, 2014-0523091C6 [2014 STEP q.1].

A trust's ability to lend funds on non-commercial terms may "taint" the trust so that it is not a spousal trust: VIEWS doc 2003-0019235. A trust that retains income at the discretion of the spouse beneficiary is not tainted, since the beneficiary has the legal right to enforce payment: 2003-0014515. Distributing a capital dividend to a person other than the spouse does not disqualify the trust: 2004-0060161E5. A beneficiary paying a trust's tax that is payable due to a 104(13.1) designation does not taint the trust: 2012-0432201E5.

A term requiring the trust to pay for life insurance on the surviving spouse or the residual-beneficiary children, with the trust as the beneficiary, will taint the trust, but making the trust the beneficiary of a policy will not: VIEWS docs 2006-0174041C6, 2006-0185551C6, 2010-0358461E5, 2012-0435681C6 [2012 CALU q.2], 2018-0761511C6 [2018 APFF Financial q.7]; Wark, "Insurance Taints Spousal Trust", XII(1) *Insurance Planning [IP]* (Federated Press) 785 (2006) and "Life Insurance in Spousal Trusts", XVIII(1) 1122-24 (2011); Stephens, "Testamentary Spousal Trusts: Life Insurance Planning Issues", XXI(4) *IP* 15-18 (2017). See also 2012-0435681C6 (trust owning policy on surviving spouse); 2012-0435701C6 [2012 CALU q.2], 2012-0453121C6 [2012 APFF Financial q.1] (joint last-to-die policy held by trust).

If a trust is "tainted" by terms that prevent it from being a spouse trust, consider a variation of the will or of the trust (provincial Variation of Trusts legislation), a disclaimer by other beneficiaries (248(8)(b)); or that there are actually two trusts (*Kamichik Estate*, [1973] C.T.C. 2208 (TRB); *MacNeil Estate*, [1973] C.T.C. 2248 (TRB)). Such rectification was granted in *Balaz*, 2009 CarswellOnt 2007 (Ont. SCJ), but see Notes to 169(1) re rectification; due to *Fairmont Hotels* it would no longer be.

Note that for US property, a 70(6) election will lose the ability to claim a foreign tax credit (FTC) for US tax on the gain. A 70(6.2) election may be preferable, to trigger Canadian tax that can be offset by a FTC, and increase the cost base. See Jack Bernstein, "Cross-Border Nightmare", 187 *The Estate Planner* (CCH) 7 (Aug. 2010).

For CRA interpretation see docs 2005-0132351C6, 2008-0287541E5; 2010-0370511C6 (charitable donations by trust); 2010-0371911C6 (property left to the spouse but sold by the estate trustee to pay the estate's debts does not fall within 70(6)); 2011-0391911E5 ("vested indefeasibly" where spouse dies before probate); May 2013 ICAA Roundtable q.13 (tinyurl.com/cra-abtax) (effect of variation of spousal trust); 2015-0596611C6 [2015 APFF q.9] (property transferred can be in the residue of the estate, but must be same property that was owned by deceased). See also Notes to 73(1); 2015-0601141E5 (spousal trust may have final distribution date 3 years after death); 2016-0632631C6 [2016 CALU q.4] and 2016-0645821C6 [2016 STEP q.11] (per IT-305R4 para. 8, once a trust qualifies it remains a spousal trust even if its terms are varied, but other provisions may be triggered); 2016-0641511C6 [2016 STEP q.15] (70(6) does not apply where executor transfers property to spousal trust created by deceased's will); 2016-0672501E5 (usufruct as spousal trust); 2017-0693331C6 [2017 STEP q.11] (substituted property, e.g. on conversion of a class of shares to another, does not qualify); 2019-0812781C6 [2019 APFF q.9] (change in trustees taints trust if they have discretion to encroach on capital).

For the parallel *inter vivos* spouse trust created during the taxpayer's life, see 73(1.01)(c).

70(6) amended by 2000 same-sex partners bill (last change effective 2001) and by 1993, 1992 and 1991 technical bills.

I.T. Application Rules: 20(1.1)(a) (property owned since before 1972).

Income Tax Folios: S7-F1-C1: Split-receipting and deemed fair market value.

Interpretation Bulletins: IT-125R4: Dispositions of resource properties; IT-236R4: Reserves — disposition of capital property (cancelled); IT-242R: Retired partners; IT-

259R4: Exchange of property; IT-278R2: Death of a partner or of a retired partner; IT-305R4: Testamentary spouse trusts; IT-321R: Insurance agents and brokers — unearned commissions (cancelled); IT-325R2: Property transfers after separation, divorce and annulment; IT-382: Debts bequeathed or forgiven on death (cancelled); IT-449R: Meaning of "vested indefeasibly" (cancelled); IT-522R: Vehicle, travel and sales expenses of employees.

Advance Tax Rulings: ATR-37: Refund of premiums transferred to spouse.

Forms: T4011: Preparing returns for deceased persons [guide].

(6.1) Transfer or distribution of NISA to spouse [or common-law partner] or trust — Where a property that is a net income stabilization account of a taxpayer is, on or after the taxpayer's death and as a consequence thereof, transferred or distributed to

(a) the taxpayer's spouse or common-law partner, or

(b) a trust, created by the taxpayer's will, under which

(i) the taxpayer's spouse or common-law partner is entitled to receive all of the income of the trust that arises before the spouse's or common-law partner's death, and

(ii) no person except the spouse or common-law partner may, before the spouse's or common-law partner's death, receive or otherwise obtain the use of any of the income or capital of the trust,

subsections (5.4) and 73(5) do not apply in respect of the taxpayer's NISA Fund No. 2 if it can be shown, within the period ending 36 months after the death of the taxpayer or, where written application therefor has been made to the Minister by the taxpayer's legal representative within that period, within such longer period as the Minister considers reasonable in the circumstances, that the property has vested indefeasibly in the spouse or common-law partner or trust, as the case may be.

Related Provisions: 12(10.2) — NISA receipts; 70(6.2) — Election; 70(7) — Special rules applicable re spouse trust; 104(5.1) — NISA Fund No. 2 held by spousal trust; 104(6) — Deduction in computing income of trust; 104(14.1) — NISA election; 108(3) — Meaning of "income" of trust; 108(4) — Trust not disqualified by reason only of payment of certain duties and taxes; 248(8) — Meaning of "consequence" of death; 248(9.1) — Whether trust created by taxpayer's will; 248(9.2) — Meaning of "vested indefeasibly"; 252(3) — Extended meaning of "spouse".

Notes: 70(6.1) amended by 2000 same-sex partners bill to refer to "common-law partner", effective as per Notes to 248(1)"common-law partner".

70(6.1) added by 1992 technical bill, effective 1991.

Former 70(6.1), repealed by 1992 technical bill, provided the rule now in 248(9.1).

Interpretation Bulletins: IT-212R3: Income of deceased persons — rights or things; IT-305R4: Testamentary spouse trusts.

(6.2) Election — Subsection (5.1), (6) or (6.1) does not apply to any property of a deceased taxpayer in respect of which the taxpayer's legal representative elects, in the taxpayer's return of income under this Part (other than a return of income filed under subsection (2) or 104(23), paragraph 128(2)(e) or subsection 150(4)) for the year in which the taxpayer died, to have subsection (5) or (5.4), as the case may be, apply.

Related Provisions: 220(3.2), Reg. 600(b) — Late filing or revocation of election.

Notes: The election under 70(6.2) is typically made to use up the deceased's capital losses or capital gains exemption. It applies on a property-by-property basis, and can be made on a portion of a block of shares, but not on only part of a share or part of a partnership interest: VIEWS docs 2006-0206391E5, 2012-0442921C6.

Whether to elect is at the executor's discretion, so the surviving spouse had no claim when the executor declined to elect and the spouse ended up with a lower cost base than he wanted: *Picard v. Lagotte*, 2017 QCCS 330, para. 42 (motion to summarily dismiss appeal denied 2017 QCCA 782).

An election "in the taxpayer's return" is valid even if the return is filed late. See Notes to 7(1.31).

70(6.2) amended by 2016 budget bill #2, effective 2017, to refer to 70(5.1).

70(6.2) amended by 1992 technical bill, effective 1991.

Interpretation Bulletins: IT-305R4: Testamentary spouse trusts.

Information Circulars: 07-1R1: Taxpayer relief provisions.

(7) Special rules applicable in respect of trust for benefit of spouse [or common-law partner] — Where a trust created by a taxpayer's will would, but for the payment of, or provision for payment of, any particular testamentary debts in respect of the taxpayer, be a trust to which subsection (6) or (6.1) applies,

(a) for the purpose of determining the day on or before which a return (in this subsection referred to as the "taxpayer's return") of the taxpayer's income for the taxation year in which the taxpayer died is required to be filed by the taxpayer's legal representatives, subsection 150(1) shall be read without reference to paragraph 150(1)(b) and as if paragraph 150(1)(d) read as follows:

"(d) in the case of any other person, by the person's legal representative within 18 months after the person's death; or"; and

(b) where the taxpayer's legal representative so elects in the taxpayer's return (other than a return of income filed under subsection (2) or 104(23), paragraph 128(2)(e) or subsection 150(4)) and lists therein one or more properties (other than a net income stabilization account) that were, on or after the taxpayer's death and as a consequence thereof, transferred or distributed to the trust, the total fair market value of which properties immediately after the taxpayer's death was not less than the total of the non-qualifying debts in respect of the taxpayer,

(i) subsection (6) does not apply in respect of the properties so listed, and

(ii) notwithstanding the payment of, or provision for payment of, any such particular testamentary debts, the trust shall be deemed to be a trust described in subsection (6),

except that, where the fair market value, immediately after the taxpayer's death, of all of the properties so listed exceeds the total of the non-qualifying debts in respect of the taxpayer (the amount of which excess is referred to in this subsection as the "listed value excess") and the taxpayer's legal representative designates in the taxpayer's return one property so listed (other than money) that is capital property other than depreciable property,

(iii) the amount of the taxpayer's capital gain or capital loss, as the case may be, from the disposition of that property deemed by subsection (5) to have been made by the taxpayer is that proportion of that capital gain or capital loss otherwise determined that

(A) the amount, if any, by which the fair market value of that property immediately after the taxpayer's death exceeds the listed value excess,

is of

(B) the fair market value of that property immediately after the taxpayer's death, and

(iv) the cost to the trust of that property is

(A) where the taxpayer has a capital gain from the disposition of that property deemed by subsection (5) to have been made by the taxpayer, the total of

(I) its adjusted cost base to the taxpayer immediately before the taxpayer's death, and

(II) the amount determined under subparagraph (iii) to be the taxpayer's capital gain from the disposition of that property, or

(B) where the taxpayer has a capital loss from the disposition of that property deemed by subsection (5) to have been made by the taxpayer, the amount by which

(I) its adjusted cost base to the taxpayer immediately before the taxpayer's death

exceeds

(II) the amount determined under subparagraph (iii) to be the taxpayer's capital loss from the disposition of that property.

Related Provisions: 70(8) — Meaning of certain expressions; 248(8) — Meaning of "consequence" of death; 248(9.1) — Whether trust created by taxpayer's will; *Interpretation Act* 27(5) — Meaning of "within 18 months".

Notes: 70(7) allows a "tainted" spousal trust to qualify as a spousal trust for the rollover in 70(6), if the trust is tainted by provision for payment of certain testamentary debts. It provides a mechanism by which such debts may be applied against certain property of the trust listed by the executor. 70(7)(a) allows the deceased's terminal return to be filed up to 18 months after death. (However, if the surviving spouse elects under provincial family law to take an equalization entitlement and thus forfeits his/her entitlement under the trust, the trust will no longer qualify as a spousal trust, and the extension of time will not apply!) See also VIEWS doc 2002-016643A.

A will can presumably give the executor the extended filing deadline by deliberately tainting the spouse trust with a direction to pay a small testamentary debt.

An election or designation "in the taxpayer's return" is valid even if the return is filed late. See Notes to 7(1.31).

70(7) amended by 1995 Budget (effective 1995), 1992 and 1991 technical bills.

Interpretation Bulletins: IT-305R4: Testamentary spouse trusts.

(8) Meaning of certain expressions in subsec. (7) — In subsection (7),

(a) the "fair market value" at any time of any property subject to a mortgage or hypothec is the amount, if any, by which the fair market value at that time of the property otherwise determined exceeds the amount outstanding at that time of the debt secured by the mortgage or hypothec, as the case may be;

(b) "non-qualifying debt" in respect of a taxpayer who has died and by whose will any trust has been created that would, but for the payment of, or provision for payment of, any particular testamentary debts in respect of the taxpayer, be a trust described in subsection (6), means any such particular testamentary debt in respect of the taxpayer other than

(i) any estate, legacy, succession or inheritance duty payable, in consequence of the taxpayer's death, in respect of any property of, or interest in, the trust, or

(ii) any debt secured by a mortgage or hypothec on property owned by the taxpayer immediately before the taxpayer's death; and

(c) "testamentary debt", in respect of a taxpayer who has died, means

(i) any debt owing by the taxpayer, or any other obligation of the taxpayer to pay an amount, that was outstanding immediately before the taxpayer's death, and

(ii) any amount payable (other than any amount payable to any person as a beneficiary of the taxpayer's estate) by the taxpayer's estate in consequence of the taxpayer's death,

including any income or profits tax payable by or in respect of the taxpayer for the taxation year in which the taxpayer died or for any previous taxation year, and any estate, legacy, succession or inheritance duty payable in consequence of the taxpayer's death.

Related Provisions: 248(8) — Meaning of "consequence" of death.

Notes: References to "hypothec" added to 70(8)(a) and (b)(ii) by 2001 *Civil Code* harmonization bill, effective June 14, 2001. The change is non-substantive; see *Interpretation Act* s. 8.2.

Interpretation Bulletins: IT-305R4: Testamentary spouse trusts.

(9) When subsec. (9.01) applies — Subsection (9.01) applies to a taxpayer and a child of the taxpayer in respect of land in Canada or depreciable property in Canada of a prescribed class of the taxpayer in respect of which subsection (5) would, if this Act were read without reference to this subsection, apply if

(a) the property was, before the death of the taxpayer, used principally in a farming or fishing business carried on in Canada in which the taxpayer, the spouse or common-law partner of the taxpayer or a child or a parent of the taxpayer was actively engaged on a regular and continuous basis (or, in the case of property used in the operation of a woodlot, was engaged to the extent required by a prescribed forest management plan in respect of that woodlot);

(b) the child of the taxpayer was resident in Canada immediately before the day on which the taxpayer died; and

(c) as a consequence of the death of the taxpayer, the property is transferred to and becomes vested indefeasibly in the child within the period ending 36 months after the death of the taxpayer or, if written application has been made to the Minister by the taxpayer's legal representative within that period, within any longer period that the Minister considers reasonable in the circumstances.

Possible Future Amendments — 70(9)–(9.31)

Federal Budget, March 19, 2019, Chapter 4, Part 7: *Intergenerational Business Transfers*

The Government understands the importance Canadian farmers, fishers and other business owners place on being able to pass their businesses on to their children. The Government will continue its outreach to farmers, fishers and other business owners throughout 2019 to develop new proposals to better accommodate intergenerational transfers of businesses while protecting the integrity and fairness of the tax system.

Prime Minister's mandate letter to Minister of Finance, Dec. 2019: I will expect you to work with your colleagues and through established legislative, regulatory and Cabinet processes to deliver on your top priorities. In particular, you will: . . .

- Work with the Minister of Agriculture and Agri-Food on tax measures to facilitate the intergenerational transfer of farms.

Liberal.ca election platform, Oct. 2019: We will also continue to work with farmers on tax measures to facilitate the intergenerational transfer of farms, making it easier for farmers to transfer or sell family farms to family members or others.

Related Provisions: 70(10) — Definitions; 248(9.2) — Meaning of "vested indefeasibly"; 248(29) — Property used in a combination of farming and fishing; 250 — Resident in Canada.

Notes: Generally, 70(9) and (9.01) allow a rollover at cost of a deceased's farming or fishing property left to a child, grandchild or great-grandchild [see 70(10)"child"], including [grand]children-in-law and step-[grand]children [see 252(1)]. 70(9.1) and (9.11) provide a similar rollover on a transfer by a trust for the deceased. 70(9.2) and (9.21) provide a rollover on transfer of shares of a family farm/fishing corporation, or an interest in a family farm/fishing partnership. 70(9.3) and (9.31) do the same for a transfer by a trust for the deceased. In each case numerous conditions must be met.

See VIEWS docs 2007-0240321E5 (property need not have been used in farming/fishing immediately before death); 2008-0271421E5 (prescribed forest management plan (PFMP)); 2008-0303071E5 (woodlot used in farming business can qualify even if no PFMP); 2009-0316191E5 (general discussion); 2008-0303761E5 and 2016-0670841E5 (owning multiple farms does not preclude working on a "regular and continuous basis" on all of them); 2010-0376451E5 (70(9.01) may apply); 2010-0381321E5 (70(9.01) may apply); 2010-0389561E5 ("in-law" relationships do not continue after death of the connecting person, for 70(9)); 2011-0401401C6 (issues re life estates); May 2011 ICAA roundtable (tinyurl.com/cra-abtax), q. 20 (bequests of life and remainder interests); 2013-0474461E5 (use test applies separately to each legal parcel of land); 2014-0551841E5 (interaction with 69(11)). For the meaning of "used principally" see Notes to 73(3).

See also Purse, "How to Give Away the Farm When You've Bought the Farm", 7(5) *Taxes & Wealth Management* (Carswell) 4-6 (Nov. 2014); Johnson, "Intergenerational Transfers of Woodlots", 16(4) *Tax Hyperion* (Carswell) 5-8 (July-Aug. 2019).

70(9)(a) amended by 2014 budget bill #2, effective 2014, to change "fishing or farming business" to "farming or fishing business" (to fit the wording of 248(29)).

70(9) amended by 2006 budget bill #2, for dispositions after May 1, 2006, with grandfathering for dispositions before 2007. (The main purpose of the amendments was to extend 70(9)-(9.3) to fishing property. 70(9) was split into 70(9) and (9.01).)

70(9)(a) amended by 2001 Budget, for transfers of property as a consequence of deaths after Dec. 10, 2001, to add the rule for woodlots. This was a budget proposal to promote sustainable woodlot management. See Regulations annotation below.

70(9) earlier amended by 2000 same-sex partners bill (last change effective 2001), 1993 and 1992 technical bills.

Regulations: 7400 (prescribed forest management plan).

I.T. Application Rules: 26(18) (farmland owned since before 1972).

Income Tax Folios: S7-F1-C1: Split-receipting and deemed fair market value.

Interpretation Bulletins: IT-349R3: Intergenerational transfers of farm property on death; IT-382: Debts bequeathed or forgiven on death (cancelled); IT-449R: Meaning of "vested indefeasibly" (cancelled).

Forms: RC4060 (for PE, ON, AB): Farming income and the AgriStability and AgriInvest programs guide; RC4408 (for BC, SK, MB, NS, NL, YK): Farming income and the AgriStability and AgriInvest programs harmonized guide — joint forms and guide; T4003: Farming and fishing income [guide].

(9.01) Transfer of farming and fishing property to child —
If, because of subsection (9), this subsection applies to the taxpayer and a child of the taxpayer in respect of a property of the taxpayer that has been transferred to the child as a consequence of the death of the taxpayer, the following rules apply:

(a) where the taxpayer's legal representative does not elect in the taxpayer's return of income under this Part for the year in which the taxpayer died, to have paragraph (b) apply to the taxpayer and the child in respect of the property,

(i) paragraphs (5)(a) and (b) and section 69 do not apply to the taxpayer and the child in respect of the property,

(ii) the taxpayer is deemed to have

(A) disposed of the property immediately before the taxpayer's death, and

(B) received, at the time of the disposition of the property, proceeds of disposition in respect of that disposition of the property equal to

(I) where the property was depreciable property of a prescribed class, the lesser of

1. the capital cost to the taxpayer of the property, and

2. the amount, determined immediately before the time of the disposition of the property, that is that proportion of the undepreciated capital cost of property of that class to the taxpayer that the capital cost to the taxpayer of the property is of the capital cost to the taxpayer of all property of that class that had not, at or before that time, been disposed of, and

(II) where the property is land (other than land to which subclause (I) applies), the adjusted cost base to the taxpayer of the property immediately before the time of the disposition of the property,

(iii) the child is, immediately after the time of the disposition of the property, deemed to have acquired the property at a cost equal to the taxpayer's proceeds of disposition in respect of the disposition of the property determined under subparagraph (ii), and

(iv) where the property was depreciable property of a prescribed class, paragraphs (5)(c) and (d) apply to the taxpayer and the child in respect of the property as if the references in those paragraphs to "paragraph (a)" and "paragraph (b)" were read as "subparagraph (9.01)(a)(ii)" and "subparagraph (9.01)(a)(iii)", respectively; and

(b) where the taxpayer's legal representative elects, in the taxpayer's return of income under this Part for the taxation year in which the taxpayer died, to have this paragraph apply to the taxpayer in respect of the property,

(i) paragraphs (5)(a) and (b) and section 69 do not apply to the taxpayer and the child in respect of the property,

(ii) the taxpayer is deemed to have

(A) disposed of the property immediately before the taxpayer's death, and

(B) received, at the time of the disposition of the property, proceeds of disposition in respect of that disposition of the property equal to

(I) where the property was depreciable property of a prescribed class, the amount that the legal representative designates, which must not be greater than the greater of nor less than the lesser of

1. the fair market value of the property immediately before the time of the disposition of the property, and

2. the lesser of the capital cost to the taxpayer of the property and the amount, determined immediately before the time of the disposition of the property, that is that proportion of the undepreciated capital cost of property of that class to the taxpayer that the capital cost to the taxpayer of the property is of the capital cost to the taxpayer of all property

of that class that had not, at or before that time, been disposed of, and

(II) where the property is land (other than land to which subclause (I) applies), the amount that the legal representative designates, which must not be greater than the greater of nor less than the lesser of

1. the fair market value of the property immediately before the time of the disposition of the property, and

2. the adjusted cost base to the taxpayer of the property immediately before the time of the disposition of the property,

(iii) the child is, immediately after the time of the disposition of the property, deemed to have acquired the property at a cost equal to the taxpayer's proceeds of disposition in respect of the disposition of the property determined under subparagraph (ii),

(iv) where the property was depreciable property of a prescribed class, paragraphs (5)(c) and (d) apply to the taxpayer in respect of the property as if the references in those paragraphs to "paragraph (a)" and "paragraph (b)" were read as "subparagraph (9.01)(b)(ii)" and "subparagraph (9.01)(b)(iii)", respectively,

(v) except for the purpose of this subparagraph,

(A) where the amount designated by the taxpayer's legal representative under subclause (ii)(B)(I), exceeds the greater of the amounts determined under sub-subclauses (ii)(B)(I)1 and 2 in respect of the property, the amount designated is deemed to be equal to the greater of those amounts, and

(B) where the amount designated by the taxpayer's legal representative under subclause (ii)(B)(II) exceeds the greater of the amounts determined under sub-subclauses (ii)(B)(II)1 and 2 in respect of the property, the amount designated is deemed to be equal to the greater of those amounts, and

(vi) except for the purpose of this subparagraph,

(A) where the amount designated by the taxpayer's legal representative under subclause (ii)(B)(I) is less than the lesser of the amounts determined under sub-subclauses (ii)(B)(I)1 and 2 in respect of the property, the amount designated is deemed to be equal to the lesser of those amounts, and

(B) where the amount designated by the taxpayer's legal representative under subclause (ii)(B)(II) is less than the lesser of the amounts determined under sub-subclauses (ii)(B)(II)1 and 2 in respect of the property, the amount designated is deemed to be equal to the lesser of those amounts.

Related Provisions: 70(9.6) — Transfer to parent; 70(9.8) — Farm or fishing property used by corporation or partnership; 70(10) — Definitions; 70(13) — Capital cost of certain depreciable property; 73(3), (3.1) — *Inter vivos* transfer of farm or fishing property to child; 220(3.2), Reg. 600(b) — Late filing or revocation of election; 248(8) — Meaning of "consequence" of death.

Notes: See Notes to 70(9). 70(9.01) added by 2006 budget bill #2, effective on the same basis as the amendment to 70(9).

For 70(9.01)(b), an election "in the taxpayer's return" is valid even if the return is filed late. See Notes to 7(1.31).

Interpretation Bulletins: IT-349R3: Intergenerational transfers of farm property on death.

Information Circulars: 07-1R1: Taxpayer relief provisions.

Forms: RC4060 (for PE, ON, AB): Farming income and the AgriStability and AgriInvest programs guide; RC4408 (for BC, SK, MB, NS, NL, YK): Farming income and the AgriStability and AgriInvest programs harmonized guide — joint forms and guide; T4003: Farming and fishing income [guide].

(9.1) When subsec. (9.11) applies — Subsection (9.11) applies to a trust and a child of the settlor of the trust in respect of a property in respect of which subsection 104(4) or (5) would, if this Act

were read without reference to this subsection, apply to the trust as a consequence of the death of the beneficiary under the trust who was a spouse or a common-law partner of the settlor if

(a) the property (or property for which the property was substituted) was transferred to the trust by the settlor;

(b) subsection (6), subsection 73(1) (as that subsection applied to transfers before 2000) or subparagraph 73(1.01)(c)(i) applied to the settlor and the trust in respect of the transfer referred to in paragraph (a);

(c) the property is, immediately before the beneficiary's death, land or a depreciable property of a prescribed class of the trust that was used in a farming or fishing business carried on in Canada;

(d) the child of the settlor is, immediately before the beneficiary's death, resident in Canada; and

(e) as a consequence of the beneficiary's death, the property is transferred to and becomes vested indefeasibly in the child of the settlor within the period ending 36 months after that beneficiary's death or, if written application has been made to the Minister by the taxpayer's legal representative within that period, within any longer period that the Minister considers reasonable in the circumstances.

Related Provisions: 70(10) — Definitions; 248(9.2) — Meaning of "vested indefeasibly"; 250 — Resident in Canada.

Notes: For interpretation see Notes to 70(9).

70(9.1)(c) amended by 2014 budget bill #2, effective 2014, to change "fishing or farming business" to "farming or fishing business" (to fit the wording of 248(29)).

70(9.1) amended by 2006 budget bill #2 (split into 70(9.1) and (9.11)), effective on the same basis as the amendment to 70(9). Earlier amended by 2001 technical bill, 2000 same-sex partners bill, 1993 and 1992 technical bills.

Interpretation Bulletins: IT-349R3: Intergenerational transfers of farm property on death; IT-382: Debts bequeathed or forgiven on death (cancelled); IT-449R: Meaning of "vested indefeasibly" (cancelled).

Forms: RC4060 (for PE, ON, AB): Farming income and the AgriStability and AgriInvest programs guide; RC4408 (for BC, SK, MB, NS, NL, YK): Farming income and the AgriStability and AgriInvest programs harmonized guide — joint forms and guide; T4003: Farming and fishing income [guide].

(9.11) Transfer of farming and fishing property from trust to settlor's children — If, because of subsection (9.1), this subsection applies to the trust and a child of the settlor of the trust in respect of a property of the trust that has been distributed to the child as a consequence of the death of the beneficiary under the trust who was the spouse or common-law partner of the settlor, the following rules apply:

(a) where the trust does not elect, in its return of income under this Part for the taxation year in which the beneficiary died, to have paragraph (b) apply to the trust in respect of the property,

(i) subsections 104(4) and (5) and section 69 do not apply to the trust and the child in respect of the property,

(ii) the trust is deemed to have

(A) disposed of the property immediately before that beneficiary's death, and

(B) received, at the time of the disposition, proceeds of disposition in respect of that disposition of the property equal to

(I) where the property was depreciable property of a prescribed class, the lesser of

1. the capital cost to the trust of the property, and

2. the amount, determined immediately before the time of the disposition of the property, that is that proportion of the undepreciated capital cost of property of that class to the trust that the capital cost to the trust of the property is of the capital cost to the trust of all property of that class that had not, at or before that time, been disposed of, and

(II) where the property is land (other than land to which subclause (I) applies), the adjusted cost base to the trust of the property immediately before the time of the disposition of the property, and

(iii) the child is, immediately after the time of the disposition of the property, deemed to have acquired the property at a cost equal to the trust's proceeds of disposition in respect of the disposition of the property determined under subparagraph (ii);

(b) where the trust elects, in the trust's return of income under this Part for the taxation year in which the beneficiary died, to have this paragraph apply to the trust in respect of the property,

(i) subsections 104(4) and (5) do not apply to the trust in respect of the property,

(ii) the trust is deemed to have

(A) disposed of the property immediately before that beneficiary's death, and

(B) received, at the time of the disposition of the property, proceeds of disposition in respect of the disposition of the property equal to

(I) where the property was depreciable property of a prescribed class, the amount that the trust designates, which must not be greater than the greater of nor less than the lesser of

1. the fair market value of the property immediately before the time of the disposition of the property, and

2. the lesser of the capital cost to the trust of the property and the amount, determined immediately before the time of the disposition of the property, that is that proportion of the undepreciated capital cost of property of that class to the trust that the capital cost to the trust of the property is of the capital cost to the trust of all property of that class that had not, at or before that time, been disposed of, and

(II) where the property is land (other than land to which subclause (I) applies), the amount that the trust designates, which must not be greater than the greater of nor less than the lesser of

1. the fair market value of the property immediately before the time of the disposition of the property, and

2. the adjusted cost base to the trust of the property immediately before the time of the disposition of the property,

(iii) the child is, immediately after the time of the disposition of the property, deemed to have acquired the property at a cost equal to the trust's proceeds of disposition in respect of the disposition of the property determined under subparagraph (ii),

(iv) except for the purpose of this subparagraph,

(A) where the amount designated by the trust under subclause (ii)(B)(I) exceeds the greater of the amounts determined under sub-subclauses (ii)(B)(I)1 and 2 in respect of the property, the amount designated is deemed to be equal to the greater of those amounts, and

(B) where the amount designated by the trust under subclause (ii)(B)(II) exceeds the greater of the amounts determined under sub-subclauses (ii)(B)(II)1 and 2 in respect of the property, the amount designated is deemed to be equal to the greater of those amounts, and

(v) except for the purpose of this subparagraph,

(A) where the amount designated by the trust under subclause (ii)(B)(I) is less than the lesser of the amounts determined under sub-subclauses (ii)(B)(I)1 and 2 in respect of the property, the amount designated is deemed to be equal to the lesser of those amounts, and

(B) where the amount designated by the trust under subclause (ii)(B)(II), is less than the lesser of the amounts determined under sub-subclauses (ii)(B)(II)1 and 2 in respect of the property, the amount designated is deemed to be equal to the lesser of those amounts;

(c) where paragraph (a) or (b) (each of which is referred to in this subsection as the "relevant provision") applied to the trust in respect of a property that was depreciable property of a prescribed class (other than where the trust's proceeds of disposition of the property under the relevant provision are redetermined under subsection 13(21.1)),

(i) the capital cost to the child of the property, immediately after the time of the disposition, is deemed to be the amount that was the capital cost to the trust of the property, immediately before the time of the disposition, and

(ii) the amount, if any, by which the capital cost to the trust of the property, immediately before the time of the disposition, exceeds the amount determined under the relevant provision to be the cost of the property to the child, immediately after the time of the disposition, is, for the purposes of sections 13 and 20 and any regulations made for the purpose of paragraph 20(1)(a), deemed to have been allowed to the child in respect of the property under regulations made for the purpose of paragraph 20(1)(a) in computing income for taxation years that ended before the child acquired the property; and

(d) where the relevant provision applied to the trust in respect of a property and the trust's proceeds of disposition in respect of the disposition of the property determined under the relevant provision are redetermined under subsection 13(21.1), notwithstanding the relevant provision,

(i) where the capital cost to the trust of the property, immediately before the time of the disposition, exceeds the amount redetermined under subsection 13(21.1), for the purposes of sections 13 and 20 and any regulations made for the purpose of paragraph 20(1)(a),

(A) the capital cost to the child of the property, immediately after the time of the disposition, is deemed to be the amount that was the capital cost to the trust of the property, immediately before the time of the disposition, and

(B) the amount, if any, by which the capital cost to the trust of the property, immediately before the time of the disposition, exceeds the amount redetermined under subsection 13(21.1) is deemed to have been allowed to the child in respect of the property under regulations made for the purpose of paragraph 20(1)(a) in computing income for taxation years that ended before the child acquired the property, and

(ii) where the property is land, the cost to the child of the property is deemed to be the amount that was the trust's proceeds of disposition as redetermined under subsection 13(21.1).

Related Provisions: 70(9.6) — Transfer to parent; 70(10) — Definitions; 70(13) — Capital cost of certain depreciable property; 70(14) — Order of disposal of depreciable property; 73(4), (4.1) — *Inter vivos* transfer of family farm or fishing corporations and partnerships; 220(3.2), Reg. 600(b) — Late filing or revocation of election; 248(8) — Meaning of "consequence" of death.

Notes: 70(9.11) added by 2006 budget bill #2, effective on the same basis as the amendment to 70(9).

Interpretation Bulletins: IT-349R3: Intergenerational transfers of farm property on death.

Information Circulars: 07-1R1: Taxpayer relief provisions.

(9.2) When subsec. (9.21) applies — Subsection (9.21) applies to a taxpayer and a child of the taxpayer in respect of a property of the taxpayer in respect of which subsection (5) would, if this Act were read without reference to this subsection, apply to the taxpayer and the child if

(a) the property was, immediately before the death of the taxpayer, a share of the capital stock of a family farm or fishing corporation of the taxpayer or an interest in a family farm or fishing partnership of the taxpayer;

(b) the child of the taxpayer was resident in Canada immediately before the day on which taxpayer died; and

(c) as a consequence of the death of the taxpayer, the property is transferred to and becomes vested indefeasibly in the child within the period ending 36 months after the death of the taxpayer or, if written application has been made to the Minister by the taxpayer's legal representative within that period, within any longer period that the Minister considers reasonable in the circumstances.

Related Provisions: 40(3.18)(b) — Grandfathering of partnership interest transferred under 70(9.2)(c); 44.1(4) — Treatment of small business investment rollover on death; 70(10) — Definitions; 248(9.2) — Meaning of "vested indefeasibly"; 250 — Resident in Canada.

Notes: A contractual right to acquire shares following a parent's death, when exercised, is not a transfer in consequence of death for 70(9.2): VIEWS doc 2006-0197151C6. See also 2012-0457891E5 (transfer by will may qualify under para. (c)).

For more interpretation see Notes to 70(9).

70(9.2)(a) amended by 2014 budget bill #2, effective 2014, to use "family farm or fishing" terms instead of "family farm" and "family fishing".

70(9.2) amended by 2006 budget bill #2 (split into 70(9.2) and (9.21)), effective on the same basis as the amendment to 70(9). Earlier amended by 1993, 1992 and 1991 technical bills.

Interpretation Bulletins: IT-349R3: Intergenerational transfers of farm property on death; IT-382: Debts bequeathed or forgiven on death (cancelled); IT-449R: Meaning of "vested indefeasibly" (cancelled).

Forms: RC4060 (for PE, ON, AB): Farming income and the AgriStability and AgriInvest programs guide; RC4408 (for BC, SK, MB, NS, NL, YK): Farming income and the AgriStability and AgriInvest programs harmonized guide — joint forms and guide; T4003: Farming and fishing income [guide].

(9.21) Transfer of family farm and fishing corporations and partnerships — If, because of subsection (9.2), this subsection applies to the taxpayer and a child of the taxpayer in respect of a property of the taxpayer that has been transferred to the child as a consequence of the death of the taxpayer, the following rules apply:

(a) where the taxpayer's legal representative does not elect, in the taxpayer's return of income under this Part for the taxation year in which the taxpayer died, to have paragraph (b) apply to the taxpayer in respect of the property,

(i) paragraphs (5)(a) and (b) and section 69 do not apply to the taxpayer and the child in respect of the property,

(ii) where the property is, immediately before the death of the taxpayer, a share of the capital stock of a family farm or fishing corporation of the taxpayer,

(A) the taxpayer is deemed to have

(I) disposed of the property immediately before the taxpayer's death, and

(II) received proceeds of disposition in respect of that disposition equal to the adjusted cost base to the taxpayer, immediately before the time of that disposition, of the property, and

(B) the child is, immediately after the time of the disposition, deemed to have acquired the property at a cost equal to the taxpayer's proceeds of disposition in respect of that disposition determined under clause (A), and

(iii) where the property is, immediately before the death of the taxpayer, a partnership interest described in paragraph (9.2)(a) (other than a partnership interest to which subsection 100(3) applies),

(A) the taxpayer is, except for the purpose of paragraph 98(5)(g), deemed not to have disposed of the property as a consequence of the taxpayer's death,

(B) the child is deemed to have acquired the property at the time of the taxpayer's death at a cost equal to the cost to the taxpayer of the interest immediately before the time that is immediately before the time of the taxpayer's death, and

(C) each amount required by subsection 53(1) or (2) to be added or deducted in computing the adjusted cost base to the taxpayer, immediately before the time of the taxpayer's death, of the property is deemed to be an amount required by subsection 53(1) or (2) to be added or deducted in computing, at any time at or after the time of the taxpayer's death, the adjusted cost base to the child of the property; and

(b) where the taxpayer's legal representative elects, in the taxpayer's return of income under this Part for the taxation year in which the taxpayer died, to have this paragraph apply to the taxpayer in respect of the property,

(i) paragraphs (5)(a) and (b) and section 69 do not apply to the taxpayer and the child in respect of the property,

(ii) subject to subparagraph (iii), where the property is, immediately before the taxpayer's death, a share of the capital stock of a family farm or fishing corporation of the taxpayer or an interest in a family farm or fishing partnership of the taxpayer,

(A) the taxpayer is deemed to have

(I) disposed of the property immediately before the taxpayer's death, and

(II) received, at the time of the disposition of the property, proceeds of disposition in respect of the disposition of the property equal to the amount that the taxpayer's legal representative designates, which must not be greater than the greater of nor less than the lesser of

1. the fair market value of the property immediately before the taxpayer's death, and

2. the adjusted cost base to the taxpayer of the property immediately before the time of the disposition,

(B) the child is, immediately after the time of the disposition, deemed to have acquired the property at a cost equal to the taxpayer's proceeds of disposition in respect of the disposition of the property determined under clause (A),

(C) except for the purpose of this clause, where the amount designated by the taxpayer's legal representative under subclause (A)(II) exceeds the greater of the amounts determined under sub-subclauses (A)(II)1 and 2 in respect of the property, the amount designated is deemed to be equal to the greater of those amounts, and

(D) except for the purpose of this clause, where the amount designated by the taxpayer's legal representative under subclause (A)(II) is less than the lesser of the amounts determined under sub-subclauses (A)(II)1 and 2 in respect of the property, the amount designated is deemed to be equal to the lesser of those amounts, and

(iii) where the property is, immediately before the death of the taxpayer, a partnership interest described in paragraph (9.2)(a) (other than a partnership interest to which subsection 100(3) applies), and the taxpayer's legal representative further elects, in the taxpayer's return of income under this Part for the taxation year in which the taxpayer died, to have this subparagraph apply to the taxpayer in respect of the property,

(A) the taxpayer is, except for the purpose of paragraph 98(5)(g), deemed not to have disposed of the property as a consequence of the taxpayer's death,

(B) the child is deemed to have acquired the property at the time of the taxpayer's death at a cost equal to the cost to the taxpayer of the interest immediately before the time that is immediately before the death of the taxpayer, and

(C) each amount required by subsection 53(1) or (2) to be added or deducted in computing the adjusted cost base to the taxpayer, immediately before the time of the taxpayer's death, of the property is deemed to be an amount required by subsection 53(1) or (2) to be added or deducted in computing, at any time at or after the taxpayer's death, the adjusted cost base to the child of the property.

Related Provisions: 44.1(4) — Treatment of small business investment rollover on death; 70(9.6) — Transfer to parent; 70(10) — Definitions; 70(13) — Capital cost of certain depreciable property; 220(3.2), Reg. 600(b) — Late filing or revocation of election; 248(8) — Meaning of "consequence" of death.

Notes: For 70(9.21)(b), an election "in the taxpayer's return" is valid even if the return is filed late. See Notes to 7(1.31).

70(9.21)(a)(ii) opening words and (b)(ii) opening words amended by 2014 budget bill #2, effective 2014, to use the "family farm or fishing" terms instead of "family farm" and "family fishing".

70(9.21) added by 2006 budget bill #2, effective on the same basis as the amendment to 70(9).

Interpretation Bulletins: IT-349R3: Intergenerational transfers of farm property on death.

Information Circulars: 07-1R1: Taxpayer relief provisions.

(9.3) When subsec. (9.31) applies — Subsection (9.31) applies to a trust and a child of the settlor of the trust in respect of a property in respect of which subsection 104(4) would, if this Act were read without reference to this subsection, apply to the trust as a consequence of the death of the beneficiary under the trust who was a spouse or a common-law partner of the settlor of the trust if

(a) the property (or property for which the property was substituted) was transferred to the trust by the settlor and was, immediately before that transfer, a share of the capital stock of a family farm or fishing corporation of the settlor or an interest in a family farm or fishing partnership of the settlor;

(b) subsection (6), subsection 73(1) (as that subsection applied to transfers before 2000) or subparagraph 73(1.01)(c)(i) applied to the settlor and the trust in respect of the transfer referred to in paragraph (a);

(c) the property is, immediately before the beneficiary's death,

(i) a share of the capital stock of a Canadian corporation that would, immediately before that beneficiary's death, be a share of the capital stock of a family farm or fishing corporation of the settlor, if the settlor owned the share at that time and paragraph (a) of the definition "share of the capital stock of a family farm or fishing corporation" in subsection (10) were read without the words "in which the individual, the individual's spouse or common-law partner, a child of the individual or a parent of the individual was actively engaged on a regular and continuous basis (or, in the case of property used in the operation of a woodlot, was engaged to the extent required by a prescribed forest management plan in respect of that woodlot)", or

(ii) [Repealed]

(iii) a partnership interest in a partnership that carried on in Canada a farming or fishing business in which it used all or substantially all of the property;

(d) the child of the settlor was, immediately before that beneficiary's death, resident in Canada; and

(e) as a consequence of that beneficiary's death, the property is transferred to and becomes vested indefeasibly in the child within the period ending 36 months after that beneficiary's death or, if written application has been made to the Minister by the taxpayer's legal representative within that period, within any longer period that the Minister considers reasonable in the circumstances.

Related Provisions: 40(3.18)(c) — Grandfathering of partnership interest transferred under 70(9.3)(e); 70(10) — Definitions; 248(9.2) — Meaning of "vested indefeasibly"; 250 — Resident in Canada.

Notes: For interpretation see Notes to 70(9).

70(9.3)(a) and (c) amended by 2014 budget bill #2, effective 2014, to use the "family farm or fishing" terms instead of "family farm" and "family fishing".

70(9.3) amended by 2006 budget bill #2 (split into 70(9.3) and (9.31)), effective on the same basis as the amendment to 70(9). Earlier amended by 2001 technical bill and 2001 Budget, 2000 same-sex partners bill, and 1992 and 1991 technical bills.

Regulations: 7400 (prescribed forest management plan).

Interpretation Bulletins: IT-349R3: Intergenerational transfers of farm property on death; IT-382: Debts bequeathed or forgiven on death (cancelled); IT-449R: Meaning of "vested indefeasibly" (cancelled).

Forms: RC4060 (for PE, ON, AB): Farming income and the AgriStability and AgriInvest programs guide; RC4408 (for BC, SK, MB, NS, NL, YK): Farming income and the AgriStability and AgriInvest programs harmonized guide — joint forms and guide; T4003: Farming and fishing income [guide].

(9.31) Transfer of family farm or fishing corporation or family farm or fishing partnership from trust to children of settlor — If, because of subsection (9.3), this subsection applies to the trust and a child of the settlor of the trust in respect of a property of the trust that has been distributed to the child as a consequence of the death of the beneficiary under the trust who was a spouse or common-law partner of the settlor of the trust, the following rules apply:

(a) where the trust does not elect, in its return of income under this Part for the taxation year in which the beneficiary died, to have paragraph (b) apply to the trust in respect of the property

(i) section 69 and subsection 104(4) do not apply to the trust and the child in respect of the property,

(ii) where the property is, immediately before the beneficiary's death, a share described in subparagraph (9.3)(c)(i),

(A) the trust is deemed to have

(I) disposed of the property immediately before the beneficiary's death, and

(II) received proceeds of disposition in respect of that disposition equal to the adjusted cost base to the trust of the property immediately before the time of that disposition, and

(B) the child is, immediately after the time of the disposition, deemed to have acquired the property at a cost equal to the trust's proceeds of disposition in respect of that disposition of the property determined under clause (A), and

(iii) where the property is, immediately before the beneficiary's death, a partnership interest described in subparagraph (9.3)(c)(iii) (other than a partnership interest to which subsection 100(3) applies),

(A) the trust is, except for the purpose of paragraph 98(5)(g), deemed not to have disposed of the property as a consequence of the beneficiary's death,

(B) the child is deemed to have acquired the property, at the time of the beneficiary's death, at a cost equal to the cost to the trust of the interest immediately before the time that is immediately before the time of the beneficiary's death, and

(C) each amount required by subsection 53(1) or (2) to be added or deducted in computing the adjusted cost base to the trust, immediately before the beneficiary's death, of the property is deemed to be an amount required by subsection 53(1) or (2) to be added or deducted in computing, at or after the time of the beneficiary's death, the adjusted cost base to the child of the property; and

(b) where the trust elects, in its return of income under this Part for the taxation year in which the beneficiary died, to have this paragraph apply to the trust in respect of the property

(i) subsection 104(4) does not apply to the trust in respect of the property and section 69 does not apply to the trust or the child in respect of the transfer of the property,

(ii) subject to subparagraph (iii), where the property is, immediately before the beneficiary's death, a share described in subparagraph (9.3)(c)(i) or a partnership interest described in subparagraph (9.3)(c)(iii),

(A) the trust is deemed to have

(I) disposed of the property immediately before the beneficiary's death, and

(II) received, at the time of the disposition of property, proceeds of disposition in respect of the disposition of the property equal to the amount that the trust designates, which must not be greater than the greater of nor less than the lesser of

1. the fair market value of the property immediately before the beneficiary's death, and

2. the adjusted cost base to the trust of the property immediately before the beneficiary's death, and

(B) the child is, immediately after the time of the disposition of the property, deemed to have acquired the property at a cost equal to the trust's proceeds of disposition in respect of that disposition of the property determined under clause (A),

(iii) where the property is, immediately before that beneficiary's death, a partnership interest described in subparagraph (9.3)(c)(iii) (other than a partnership interest to which subsection 100(3) applies), and the trust further elects, in its return of income under this Part for the taxation year in which the beneficiary died, to have this subparagraph apply to the trust in respect of the property,

(A) the trust is, except for the purpose of paragraph 98(5)(g), deemed not to have disposed of the property as a consequence of the beneficiary's death,

(B) the child is deemed to have acquired the property, at the time of the beneficiary's death, at a cost equal to the cost to the trust of the property immediately before the time that is immediately before the beneficiary's death, and

(C) each amount required by subsection 53(1) or (2) to be added or deducted in computing, immediately before the beneficiary's death, the adjusted cost base to the trust of the property is deemed to be an amount required by subsection 53(1) or (2) to be added or deducted in computing, at or after the time of the beneficiary's death, the adjusted cost base to the child of the property,

(iv) except for the purpose of this subparagraph, where the amount designated by the trust under subclause (ii)(A)(II) exceeds the greater of the amounts determined under sub-subclauses (ii)(A)(II)1 and 2 in respect of the property, the amount designated is deemed to be equal to the greater of those amounts, and

(v) except for the purpose of this subparagraph, where the amount designated by the trust under subclause (ii)(A)(II) is less than the lesser of the amounts determined under sub-subclauses (ii)(A)(II)1 and 2 in respect of the property, the amount designated is deemed to be equal to the lesser of those amounts.

Related Provisions: 70(9.6) — Transfer to parent; 70(10) — Definitions; 220(3.2), Reg. 600(b) — Late filing or revocation of election; 248(8) — Meaning of "consequence" of death.

Notes: 70(9.31)(a)(ii) opening words and (b)(ii) opening words amended by 2014 budget bill #2, effective 2014 [non-substantive changes].

70(9.31) added by 2006 budget bill #2, effective on same basis as amendment to 70(9).

Interpretation Bulletins: IT-349R3: Intergenerational transfers of farm property on death.

Information Circulars: 07-1R1: Taxpayer relief provisions.

(9.4), (9.5) [Repealed under former Act]

Notes: 70(9.4)-(9.5), repealed by 1985 Budget (on introduction of the capital gains exemption in 110.6), provided rollovers on transfer of small business corporation shares to the taxpayer's child and from a spousal trust to the settlor's children.

(9.6) Transfer to a parent — Subsection (9.01) or (9.21), as the case may be, applies in respect of a transfer of a property as if the references in those subsections to "child" were read as references to "parent" if

(a) the property was acquired by a taxpayer in circumstances where any of subsections (9.01), (9.11), (9.21), (9.31) and 73(3.1) and (4.1) applied in respect of the acquisition;

(b) as a consequence of the death of the taxpayer the property is transferred to a parent of the taxpayer; and

(c) the taxpayer's legal representative has elected, in the taxpayer's return of income under this Part for the taxation year in which the taxpayer died, that this subsection apply in respect of the transfer.

Related Provisions: 248(8) — Meaning of "consequence" of death.

Notes: For 70(9.6)(c), an election "in the taxpayer's return" is valid even if the return is filed late. See Notes to 7(1.31).

70(9.6) amended by 2006 budget bill #2, effective on same basis as amendment to 70(9).

Interpretation Bulletins: IT-268R4: *Inter vivos* transfer of farm property to child.

(9.7) [Repealed under former Act]

Notes: 70(9.7), repealed by 1985 Budget (on introduction of the capital gains exemption in 110.6), dealt with retransfer to a parent, on a child's death, of small business corporation shares that had been rolled over to the child under 70(9.4)-(9.5) or 73(5).

(9.8) Leased farm or fishing property — For the purposes of subsections (9) and 73(3) and paragraph (d) of the definition "qualified farm or fishing property" in subsection 110.6(1), a property of an individual is, at a particular time, deemed to be used by the individual in a farming or fishing business carried on in Canada if, at that particular time, the property is being used, principally in the course of carrying on a farming or fishing business in Canada, by

(a) a corporation, a share of the capital stock of which is a share of the capital stock of a family farm or fishing corporation of the individual, the individual's spouse or common-law partner, a child of the individual or a parent of the individual; or

(b) a partnership, a partnership interest in which is an interest in a family farm or fishing partnership of the individual, the individual's spouse or common-law partner, a child of the individual or a parent of the individual.

Related Provisions: 248(29) — Property used in a combination of farming and fishing.

Notes: For the meaning of used "principally", see Notes to 73(3). For an example of 70(9.8) applying see VIEWS doc 2011-0430031E5.

Ownership can be a combination of direct ownership and through a Holdco: VIEWS doc 2011-0403741E5.

70(9.8) opening words amended by 2016 budget bill #2, effective 2017, to delete references to 14(1) and 20(1)(b) (as part of changing eligible capital property rules to CCA Class 14.1: see Notes to 20(1)(b)).

70(9.8) amended by 2014 budget bill #2, for dispositions and transfers in the 2014 and later taxation years, to use the "farm or fishing" terms instead of separate terms.

70(9.8) amended by 2006 budget bill #2, effective on the same basis as the amendment to 70(9). Earlier amended by 2000 same-sex partners bill and 1991 technical bill.

Interpretation Bulletins: IT-268R4: *Inter vivos* transfer of farm property to child.

(10) Definitions — In this section,

Related Provisions: 40(8), 44(8), 73(6) — Definitions in 70(10) apply to ss. 40, 44 and 73.

Notes: Before RSC 1985 (5th Supp) consolidation, the opening words of 70(10) also referred to 40, 44, 73, 146(5.3) and 146(5.4). These rules of application are now in 40(8), 44(8) and 73(6); 146(5.3) and (5.4) have been repealed.

Opening words of 70(10) amended by 1990 pension bill, effective 1989.

"child" of a taxpayer includes

(a) a child of the taxpayer's child,

(b) a child of the taxpayer's child's child,

(b.1) a person who was a child of the taxpayer immediately before the death of the person's spouse or common-law partner, and

(c) a person who, at any time before the person attained the age of 19 years, was wholly dependent on the taxpayer for support and of whom the taxpayer had, at that time, in law or in fact, the custody and control;

Related Provisions: 84.1(2.2)(a)(i), 212.1(3)(b)(i) — Extended meaning of "child" applies for dividend stripping rules; 110.6(1)"child" — Extended meaning applies for capital gains exemption; 148(9)"child" — Extended meaning applies for life insurance policy rules; 252(1) — Additional extended meaning of "child".

Notes: Since this definition uses "includes" rather than "means", the definition of "child" in 252(1)(b) applies as well (see Notes to 188.1(5)).

Due to this definition, "parent" (in 252(2)(a) as applied to ss. 70 and 110.6) can refer to a grandparent or great-grandparent: VIEWS doc 2012-0454701I7.

Para. (b.1) added by 2014 budget bill #2, effective 2014. See Notes to 252(2) for implications of para (b.1).

70(10)"child" was 70(10)(a) before RSC 1985 (5th Supp) consolidation for tax years ending after Nov. 1991.

Interpretation Bulletins: IT-489R: Non-arm's length sale of shares to a corporation.

"interest in a family farm or fishing partnership", of an individual at any time, means a partnership interest owned by the individual at that time if, at that time, all or substantially all of the fair market value of the property of the partnership was attributable to

(a) property that has been used principally in the course of carrying on a farming or fishing business in Canada in which the individual, the individual's spouse or common-law partner, a child of the individual or a parent of the individual was actively engaged on a regular and continuous basis (or, in the case of property used in the operation of a woodlot, was engaged to the extent required by a prescribed forest management plan in respect of that woodlot), by

(i) the partnership,

(ii) a corporation, a share of the capital stock of which was a share of the capital stock of a family farm or fishing corporation of the individual, the individual's spouse or common-law partner, a child of the individual or a parent of the individual,

(iii) a partnership, a partnership interest in which was an interest in a family farm or fishing partnership of the individual, the individual's spouse or common-law partner, a child of the individual or a parent of the individual, or

(iv) the individual, the individual's spouse or common-law partner, a child of the individual or a parent of the individual,

(b) shares of the capital stock or indebtedness of one or more corporations of which all or substantially all of the fair market value of the property was attributable to property described in paragraph (d),

(c) partnership interests or indebtedness of one or more partnerships of which all or substantially all of the fair market value of the property was attributable to property described in paragraph (d), or

(d) properties described in any of paragraphs (a) to (c);

Related Provisions: 70(12) — Value of NISA deemed nil; 248(29) — Property used in a combination of farming and fishing; 256(6), (6.1) — Meaning of "controlled".

Notes: For the meaning of "used principally" in para. (a), see Notes to 73(3).

Definition added by 2014 budget bill #2, effective 2014 (replacing "interest in a family farm partnership" and "interest in a family fishing partnership").

Regulations: 7400 (prescribed forest management plan).

I.T. Application Rules: 20(1.11), 26(20).

Interpretation Bulletins: IT-236R4: Reserves — disposition of capital property (cancelled); IT-349R3: Intergenerational transfers of farm property on death.

Advance Tax Rulings: ATR-28: Redemption of capital stock of family farm corporation; ATR-56: Purification of a family farm corporation.

"interest in a family farm partnership" — [Repealed]

Notes: Definition repealed by 2014 budget bill #2, effective 2014, and replaced with "interest in a family farm or fishing partnership".

For the meaning of "used principally" in para. (a), see Notes to 73(3).

Definition amended by 2006 budget bill #2 (last change effective for dispositions before 2007), 2001 Budget, 2000 same-sex partners bill. 70(10)"interest in a family farm partnership" was 70(10)(c) before RSC 1985 (5th Supp) consolidation for tax years ending after Nov. 1991.

Regulations: 7400 (prescribed forest management plan).

I.T. Application Rules: 20(1.11), 26(20).

Interpretation Bulletins: IT-236R4: Reserves — disposition of capital property (cancelled); IT-349R3: Intergenerational transfers of farm property on death.

Advance Tax Rulings: ATR-28: Redemption of capital stock of family farm corporation; ATR-56: Purification of a family farm corporation.

"interest in a family fishing partnership" — [Repealed]

Notes: Definition repealed by 2014 budget bill #2, effective 2014, and replaced with "interest in a family farm or fishing partnership".

For the meaning of "used principally" in para. (a), see Notes to 73(3).

70(10)"interest in a family fishing partnership" added by 2006 budget bill #2, effective on the same basis as the amendment to 70(9).

"share of the capital stock of a family farm corporation" — [Repealed]

Notes: Definition repealed by 2014 budget bill #2, effective 2014; replaced with "share of the capital stock of a family farm or fishing corporation". Earlier amended by 2001 Budget, 2000 same-sex partners bill, 1995-97 technical bill. 70(10)"share of the capital stock of a family farm corporation" was 70(10)(b) before RSC 1985 (5th Supp) consolidation for tax years ending after Nov. 1991.

Regulations: 7400 (prescribed forest management plan).

I.T. Application Rules: 20(1.11), 26(20).

Interpretation Bulletins: IT-236R4: Reserves — disposition of capital property (cancelled); IT-349R3: Intergenerational transfers of farm property on death.

Advance Tax Rulings: ATR-28: Redemption of capital stock of family farm corporation; ATR-56: Purification of a family farm corporation.

"share of the capital stock of a family farm or fishing corporation", of an individual at any time, means a share of the capital stock of a corporation owned by the individual at that time if, at that time, all or substantially all of the fair market value of the property owned by the corporation was attributable to

(a) property that has been used principally in the course of carrying on a farming or fishing business in Canada in which the individual, the individual's spouse or common-law partner, a child of the individual or a parent of the individual was actively engaged on a regular and continuous basis (or, in the case of property used in the operation of a woodlot, was engaged to the extent required by a prescribed forest management plan in respect of that woodlot), by

(i) the corporation,

(ii) a corporation, a share of the capital stock of which was a share of the capital stock of a family farm or fishing corporation of the individual, the individual's spouse or common-law partner, a child of the individual or a parent of the individual,

(iii) a corporation controlled by a corporation described in subparagraph (i) or (ii),

(iv) a partnership, a partnership interest in which was an interest in a family farm or fishing partnership of the individual, the individual's spouse or common-law partner, a child of the individual or a parent of the individual, or

(v) the individual, the individual's spouse or common-law partner, a child of the individual or a parent of the individual,

(b) shares of the capital stock or indebtedness of one or more corporations of which all or substantially all of the fair market value of the property was attributable to property described in paragraph (d),

(c) partnership interests or indebtedness of one or more partnerships of which all or substantially all of the fair market value of the property was attributable to property described in paragraph (d), or

(d) properties described in any of paragraphs (a) to (c).

Related Provisions: 70(12) — Value of NISA deemed nil; 110.6(15) — Value of assets of corporations; 248(29) — Property used in a combination of farming and fishing; 256(6), (6.1) — Meaning of "controlled".

Notes: For the meaning of "used principally" in para. (a), see Notes to 73(3). CRA considers that "substantially all" means 90% or more.

For CRA interpretation of the previous "...farm corporation" definition, see VIEWS docs 2005-0154931E5 (shares qualify); 2012-0440061E5 (grazing co-op shares do not); 2012-0457891E5 (question of fact); 2012-0457881E5 (use of property includes period before corporation acquired it); 2014-0517611E5 (shares of holding company may qualify).

Definition added by 2014 budget bill #2, effective 2014 (replacing "share ... of a family farm corporation" and "... of a family fishing corporation").

Regulations: 7400 (prescribed forest management plan).

I.T. Application Rules: 20(1.11), 26(20).

Interpretation Bulletins: IT-236R4: Reserves — disposition of capital property (cancelled); IT-349R3: Intergenerational transfers of farm property on death.

Advance Tax Rulings: ATR-28: Redemption of capital stock of family farm corporation; ATR-56: Purification of a family farm corporation.

"share of the capital stock of a family fishing corporation" — [Repealed]

Notes: Definition repealed by 2014 budget bill #2, effective 2014; replaced with "share of the capital stock of a family farm or fishing corporation". 70(10)"share of the capital stock of a family fishing corporation" added by 2006 budget bill #2, effective on the same basis as the amendment to 70(9).

Notes [subsec. 70(10)]: "interest in a family farm partnership" and "share of the capital stock of a family farm corporation" amended by 1992 technical bill.

Interpretation Bulletins [subsec. 70(10)]: IT-268R4: *Inter vivos* transfer of farm property to child.

(11) Application of subsec. 138(12) — The definitions in subsection 138(12) apply to this section.

Notes: 70(11) added in the RSC 1985 (5th Supp) consolidation, for tax years ending after Nov. 1991. This was formerly in the opening words of 138(12).

Former 70(11), repealed by 1985 Budget, provided definitions for "cumulative small business gains account" (no longer necessary, owing to the repeal of other provisions) and "small business corporation" (moved to 248(1)).

(12) Value of NISA — For the purpose of the definition "share of the capital stock of a family farm or fishing corporation" in subsection (10), the fair market value of a net income stabilization account is deemed to be nil.

Notes: 70(12) amended by 2014 budget bill #2, effective 2014, to change "family farm" to "family farm or fishing".

70(12) added by 1992 technical bill, effective 1992.

(13) Capital cost of certain depreciable property — For the purposes of this section and, where a provision of this section (other than this subsection) applies, for the purposes of sections 13 and 20 (but not for the purposes of any regulation made for the purpose of paragraph 20(1)(a)),

(a) the capital cost to a taxpayer of depreciable property of a prescribed class disposed of immediately before the taxpayer's death, or

(b) the capital cost to a trust, to which subsection (9.1) applies, of depreciable property of a prescribed class disposed of immediately before the death of the spouse or common-law partner described in that subsection,

shall, in respect of property that was not disposed of by the taxpayer or the trust before that time, be the amount that it would be if subsection 13(7) were read without reference to

(c) the expression "the lesser of" in paragraph (b) and clause (d)(i)(A) thereof, and

(d) subparagraph (b)(ii), subclause (d)(i)(A)(II), clause (d)(i)(B) and paragraph (e) thereof.

Related Provisions: 13(7) — Change in use of depreciable property.

Notes: 70(13)(b) amended by 2000 same-sex partners bill to refer to "common-law partner", effective as per Notes to 248(1)"common-law partner".

70(13) added by 1993 technical bill, effective for dispositions and acquisitions in 1993 or later. It readjusts the capital cost of depreciable property for purposes of 70(6)(d), 70(9)(b) and 70(9.1)(b). The readjusted capital cost is used for determining undepreciated capital cost (UCC) and the amount by which UCC is reduced on a disposition, but does not affect CCA claims under 20(1)(a).

Interpretation Bulletins: IT-349R3: Intergenerational transfers of farm property on death.

(14) Order of disposal of depreciable property — Where 2 or more depreciable properties of a prescribed class are disposed of at the same time as a consequence of a taxpayer's death, this section and paragraph (a) of the definition "cost amount" in subsection 248(1) apply as if each property so disposed of were separately disposed of in the order designated by the taxpayer's legal representative or, in the case of a trust described in subsection (9.1), by the trust and, where the taxpayer's legal representative or the trust, as the case may be, does not designate an order, in the order designated by the Minister.

Notes: 70(14) added by 1993 technical bill, effective 1993.

Interpretation Bulletins: IT-349R3: Intergenerational transfers of farm property on death.

Definitions [s. 70]: "active business" — 248(1); "adjusted cost base" — 54, 248(1); "amount", "annuity" — 248(1); "arm's length" — 251; "assessment" — 248(1); "beneficiary" — 248(25) [Notes]; "business" — 248(1); "Canada" — 255, *Interpretation Act* 35(1); "Canadian corporation" — 89(1), 248(1); "Canadian resource property" — 66(15), 248(1); "capital cost" — 70(13); "capital gain", "capital loss" — 39(1), 248(1); "capital property" — 54, 248(1); "carrying on business" — 253; "child" — 70(10), 252(1); "common-law partner" — 248(1); "consequence" — 248(8); "controlled" — 256(6), (6.1); "corporation" — 248(1), *Interpretation Act* 35(1); "cost amount" — 248(1); "created by the taxpayer's will" — 248(9.1); "cumulative eligible capital" — 14(5), 248(1); "depreciable property" — 13(21), 248(1); "disposition" — 248(1); "eligible capital expenditure" — 14(5), 248(1); "eligible capital property" — 54, 248(1); "employment" — 248(1); "estate" — 104(1), 248(1); "fair market value" — 70(8), 70(12), 139.1(5) and see 69(1) Notes; "family farm or fishing corporation", "family farm or fishing partnership" — 70(10); "farming", "fishing" — 248(1); "foreign resource property" — 66(15), 248(1); "income" — of trust 108(3); "individual" — 248(1); "interest in a family farm or fishing partnership" — 70(10); "inventory", "LIA policy" — 248(1); "land" — see 70(5.2) Notes; "legal representative" — 248(1); "life insurance policy" — 138(12), 248(1); "Minister" — 248(1); "month" — *Interpretation Act* 35(1); "NISA Fund No. 2", "net income stabilization account", "office" — 248(1); "non-qualifying debt" — 70(8); "parent" — 252(2)(a); "partnership" — see 96(1) Notes; "person", "prescribed", "property" — 248(1); "qualified farm or fishing property" — 110.6(1); "regulation" — 248(1); "related" — 251(2); "relevant provision" — 70(9.11)(c); "resident in Canada" — 250; "right or thing", "rights or things" — 70(3.1); "share" — 248(1); "share of the capital stock of a family farm or fishing corporation" — 70(10); "specified investment business" — 125(7); "spouse" — 252(3); "substituted" — 248(5); "tax payable" — 248(2); "taxable income" — 2(2), 248(1); "taxation year" — 11(2), 249; "taxpayer" — 248(1); "testamentary debt" — 70(8); "trust" — 104(1), 248(1), (3); "undepreciated capital cost" — 13(21), 248(1); "vested indefeasibly" — 248(9.2); "written" — *Interpretation Act* 35(1)"writing".

Interpretation Bulletins [s. 70]: IT-226R: Gift to a charity of a residual interest in real property or an equitable interest in a trust.

71. [Repealed under former Act]

Notes: 71, repealed by 1985 Budget, allowed unlimited use of previous years' allowable capital losses to offset income in the year of death. It was replaced by 111(2).

72. (1) Reserves, etc., for year of death — Where in a taxation year a taxpayer has died,

(a) paragraph 20(1)(n) does not apply to allow, in computing the income of the taxpayer for the year from a business, the deduction of any amount as a reserve in respect of property sold in the course of the business;

(b) no amount is deductible under subsection 32(1) as a reserve in respect of unearned commissions in computing the taxpayer's income for the year;

(c) no amount may be claimed under subparagraph 40(1)(a)(iii), paragraph 40(1.01)(c) or subparagraph 44(1)(e)(iii) in computing any gain of the taxpayer for the year;

(d), (e) [No longer relevant.]

Related Provisions: 61.2 — Deduction of debt forgiveness reserve for year of death; 72(2) — Election by legal representative and transferee re reserves.

Notes: 72(1)(c) amended by 1997 Budget and 1991 technical bill.

72(1)(d) and (e) provide rules for a version of s. 64 that was repealed in 1981.

Interpretation Bulletins: IT-152R3: Special reserves — sale of land; IT-154R: Special reserves; IT-236R4: Reserves — disposition of capital property (cancelled); IT-321R: Insurance agents and brokers — unearned commissions (cancelled).

(2) Election by legal representative and transferee re reserves — Where property of a taxpayer that is a right to receive any amount has, on or after the death of the taxpayer and as a consequence thereof, been transferred or distributed to the taxpayer's spouse or common-law partner described in paragraph 70(6)(a) or to a trust described in paragraph 70(6)(b) (in this subsection referred to as the "transferee"), if the taxpayer was resident in Canada immediately before the taxpayer's death and the taxpayer's legal representative and the transferee have executed jointly an election in respect of the property in prescribed form,

(a) any amount in respect of the property that would, but for paragraph (1)(a), (b), (d) or (e), as the case may be, have been deductible as a reserve in computing the taxpayer's income for the taxation year in which the taxpayer died shall,

(i) notwithstanding subsection (1), be deducted in computing the taxpayer's income for the taxation year in which the taxpayer died,

(ii) be included in computing the transferee's income for the transferee's first taxation year ending after the death of the taxpayer, and

(iii) be deemed to be

(A) an amount that has been included in computing the transferee's income from a business for a previous year in respect of property sold in the course of the business,

(B) an amount that has been included in computing the transferee's income for a previous year as a commission in respect of an insurance contract, other than a life insurance contract,

(C) an amount that by virtue of subsection 59(1) has been included in computing the transferee's income for a preceding taxation year, or

(D) for the purposes of subsection 64(1.1)[5], an amount that by virtue of paragraph 59(3.2)(c) has been included in computing the transferee's income for a preceding taxation year and to be an amount deducted by the transferee pursuant to paragraph 64(1.1)(a)[5] in computing the transferee's income for the transferee's last taxation year ending before the death,

as the case may be;

(b) any amount in respect of the property that could, but for paragraph (1)(c), have been claimed under subparagraph 40(1)(a)(iii) or 44(1)(e)(iii) in computing the amount of any gain of the taxpayer for the year shall,

(i) notwithstanding paragraph (1)(c), be deemed to have been so claimed, and

(ii) for the purpose of computing the transferee's income for the transferee's first taxation year ending after the death of the taxpayer and any subsequent taxation year, be deemed to have been

(A) proceeds of the disposition of capital property disposed of by the transferee in that first taxation year, and

(B) the amount determined under subparagraph 40(1)(a)(i) or 44(1)(e)(i), as the case may be, in respect of the capital property referred to in clause (A); and

(c) notwithstanding paragraphs (a) and (b), where any property had been disposed of by the taxpayer, in computing the income of the transferee for any taxation year ending after the death of the taxpayer,

(i) the amount of the transferee's deduction under paragraph 20(1)(n) as a reserve in respect of the property sold in the course of business,

(ii) the amount of the transferee's claim under subparagraph 40(1)(a)(iii) or 44(1)(e)(iii) in respect of the disposition of the property, and

(iii) the amount of the transferee's deduction under section 64[5] as a reserve in respect of the disposition of the property

shall be computed as if the transferee were the taxpayer who had disposed of the property and as if the property were disposed of by the transferee at the time it was disposed of by the taxpayer.

Related Provisions: 220(3.2), Reg. 600(b) — Late filing or revocation of election; 248(8) — Meaning of "consequence" of death.

Notes: For an example of 72(2) applying see VIEWS doc 2006-0217341I7.

For a taxpayer filing Quebec returns, a 72(2) election must be copied to Revenu Québec: *Taxation Act* ss. 453, 21.4.6.

72(2) amended by 2000 same-sex partners bill (effective 2001), 1991 technical bill.

The references in 72(2)(a)(iii)(D) and (c)(iii) to 64(1.1) are to a version of 64 that has been repealed. See Notes to 64.

Interpretation Bulletins [subsec. 72(2)]: IT-152R3: Special reserves — sale of land; IT-236R4: Reserves — disposition of capital property (cancelled).

Information Circulars [subsec. 72(2)]: 07-1R1: Taxpayer relief provisions.

Forms [subsec. 72(2)]: T2069: Election in respect of amounts not deductible as reserves for the year of death; T4011: Preparing returns for deceased persons [guide].

Definitions [s. 72]: "amount", "business" — 248(1); "Canada" — 255; "capital property", "common-law partner" — 54, 248(1); "consequence" — 248(8); "prescribed", "property" — 248(1); "resident in Canada" — 250; "taxation year" — 11(2), 249; "taxpayer" — 248(1); "trust" — 104(1), 248(1), (3).

73. (1) *Inter vivos* **transfers by individuals** — For the purposes of this Part, where at any time any particular capital property of an individual (other than a trust) has been transferred in circumstances to which subsection (1.01) applies and both the individual and the transferee are resident in Canada at that time, unless the individual elects in the individual's return of income under this Part for the taxation year in which the particular property was transferred that the provisions of this subsection not apply, the particular property is deemed

(a) to have been disposed of at that time by the individual for proceeds equal to,

(i) where the particular property is depreciable property of a prescribed class, that proportion of the undepreciated capital cost to the individual immediately before that time of all property of that class that the fair market value immediately before that time of the particular property is of the fair market value immediately before that time of all of that property of that class, and

(ii) in any other case, the adjusted cost base to the individual of the particular property immediately before that time; and

(b) to have been acquired at that time by the transferee for an amount equal to those proceeds.

Related Provisions: 40(4) — Where principal residence disposed of to a spouse; 44.1(5) — Small business investment rollover on breakdown of relationship; 53(4) — Effect on ACB of share, partnership interest or trust interest; 70(6)(a) — Where transfer or distribution to spouse or trust; 73(1.1) — Interpretation; 73(2) — Transfer of depreciable property; 74.1(1) — Attribution of income or loss on property transferred to spouse; 74.2(1) — Gain or loss deemed that of lender or transferor; 94(4)(b) — Deeming non-resident trust to be resident in Canada does not apply; 104(4)(a), (a.3), (a.4) — Deemed disposition by trust following transfer under 73(1); 107.4 — Qualifying disposition to a trust; 108(3) — Meaning of "income" of trust; 108(4) — Trust not disqualified by reason only of payment of certain taxes; 148(8) — Disposition at non-arm's length and similar cases; 148(8.1) — *Inter vivos* transfer to spouse; 220(3.2), Reg. 600(b) — Late filing or revocation of election; 248(37)(g) — Rule limiting value of donated property does not apply if 73(1) applies; 252(3) — Extended meaning of "spouse" and "former spouse".

Notes: Under the opening words, the transferor can "elect out" of the application of 73(1). There is no specific form required for the election. Note, however, that the election must be made "in" the return, not merely by the due date for the return. (This also means that if the return is filed late, the election can still be made "in" the return.) If either spouse has died, 73(1) cannot apply in CRA's view: doc 2016-0651721C6 [2016 APFF q.5] (see 70(6) on the transferor's death). [However, see *Kuchta*, 2015 TCC 289 (appeal to FCA discontinued A-551-15 but the decision may be a nullity due to *Birchcliff Energy* — see Notes to 169(1) under "Replacement by the Chief Justice").]

After a spousal transfer, whether or not the transferor has elected out of 73(1), future income or gains from the property will be attributed back to the transferor under 74.1(1) or 74.2(1), unless one of the exceptions in 74.5(1)–(3) applies. See VIEWS doc 2008-0302831E5.

See Notes to 54"superficial loss" on using 73(1) to transfer a capital loss to a spouse.

For planning see Addison & Korn, "Interspousal Property Transfers", 50(2) *Canadian Tax Journal* 728-57 (2002). In *Antle*, 2010 FCA 280 (leave to appeal denied 2011 CarswellNat 1491 (SCC); motion for reconsideration dismissed 2012 CarswellNat 172), a rollover to a spousal trust resident in Barbados was intended to step up the cost base of capital property, but failed because the trust was not validly formed and was a sham (the TCC had also applied GAAR). In *Gervais*, 2018 FCA 3, 73(1) was used to transfer half of a capital gain between spouses so the wife could claim the capital gains exemption: this was held to violate GAAR (245(2)) by avoiding 74.2(1) attribution.

For examples of 73(1) applying on transfers to a trust see VIEWS docs 2005-0139651R3, 2005-0150821E5, 2010-0363461R3, 2013-0493801R3. See Notes to 248(1)"alter ego trust" for transfers to an AE trust.

---

[5] The section 64 meant to be referred to is s. 64 of R.S.C. 1952, c. 148. See Notes to 64 — ed.

73(1) applies only to capital property, so an artist cannot transfer inventory to his spouse tax-free: VIEWS doc 2008-0304871E5.

For more on 73(1) and (1.01) see docs 2010-0376171E5 (spouse is entitled to receive all income from trust where she has discretion not to receive it, or where she directs the income be retained in the trust to be paid later); 2010-0367401R3 (variation of testamentary trust terms does not cause 73(1) to apply on later transfer); 2011-0400951E5 and 2012-0469571E5 (test in 70(1.01)(b) is met); 2011-0418291E5 (interaction with 74.2 on divorce); 2011-0427871E5 (interaction with 98(3) and (5)); 2012-0435691C6 (trust duty to fund life insurance can taint trust); 2012-0469331E5 (blind trust for politician can fall under 73(1.01)(c)(ii)); 2014-0523031C6 [2014 STEP q.2] (interpretation of 73(1.01)(c)(iii)); 2014-0527261E5 (settlor is sole beneficiary of Quebec trust, but trustees have discretion to retain income so 73(1) does not apply); 2014-0529361E5 (allowing trust to pay life insurance premiums on spouse's life taints trust, even though payout comes after spouse's death); 2017-0705221C6 [2017 APFF q.1] (73(1) can apply on common-law partners' separation even though Quebec law gives no property rights). See also Notes to 70(6).

See also Barry Corbin, "Electing on Fractional Shares", 28(9) *Money & Family Law* (Carswell) 65-66 (Sept. 2013); Andrew Bateman, "Marriage Breakdown", 62(4) *Canadian Tax Journal* 1109 at 1118-31 (2014).

73(1) amended by 2001 technical bill (for transfers after 1999 with a transitional rule for those in 2000-06), 2000 same-sex partners bill, 1992 and 1991 technical bills.

I.T. Application Rules: 20(1.1) (where property owned since before 1972).

Income Tax Folios: S7-F1-C1: Split-receipting and deemed fair market value.

Interpretation Bulletins: IT-209R: *Inter vivos* gifts of capital property to individuals directly or through trusts; IT-325R2: Property transfers after separation, divorce and annulment.

Information Circulars: 07-1R1: Taxpayer relief provisions.

(1.01) Qualifying transfers — Subject to subsection (1.02), property is transferred by an individual in circumstances to which this subsection applies where it is transferred to

(a) the individual's spouse or common-law partner;

(b) a former spouse or common-law partner of the individual in settlement of rights arising out of their marriage or common-law partnership; or

(c) a trust created by the individual under which

(i) the individual's spouse or common-law partner is entitled to receive all of the income of the trust that arises before the spouse's or common-law partner's death and no person except the spouse or common-law partner may, before the spouse's or common-law partner's death, receive or otherwise obtain the use of any of the income or capital of the trust,

(ii) the individual is entitled to receive all of the income of the trust that arises before the individual's death and no person except the individual may, before the individual's death, receive or otherwise obtain the use of any of the income or capital of the trust, or

(iii) either

(A) the individual or the individual's spouse is, in combination with the other, entitled to receive all of the income of the trust that arises before the later of the death of the individual and the death of the spouse and no other person may, before the later of those deaths, receive or otherwise obtain the use of any of the income or capital of the trust, or

(B) the individual or the individual's common-law partner is, in combination with the other, entitled to receive all of the income of the trust that arises before the later of the death of the individual and the death of the common-law partner and no other person may, before the later of those deaths, receive or otherwise obtain the use of any of the income or capital of the trust.

Related Provisions: 73(1.02) — Limitation on transfers to trusts; 108(3) — Calculation of trust income; 108(4) — Trust not disqualified by reason only of payment of certain duties and taxes; 248(1)"alter ego trust" — Trust for individual during own lifetime.

Notes: See Notes to 73(1). A trust under (c)(i) is a spouse trust (spousal trust); under (c)(ii) is an "*alter ego* trust" or self-benefit trust (see Notes to 248(1)"alter ego trust"); under (c)(iii) is a "joint spousal or common-law partner trust" (248(1)). For a spousal trust created on death by the taxpayer's will, see 70(6). See also conditions in 73(1.02).

A spouse trust continues to be a spouse trust after divorce: IT-325R2 para. 11.

73(1.01) added by 2001 technical bill, last change effective for transfers after 2000.

(1.02) Exception for transfers — Subsection (1.01) applies to a transfer of property by an individual to a trust the terms of which satisfy the conditions in subparagraph (1.01)(c)(ii) or (iii) only where

(a) the trust was created after 1999;

(b) either

(i) the individual had attained 65 years of age at the time the trust was created, or

(ii) the transfer does not result in a change in beneficial ownership of the property and there is immediately after the transfer no absolute or contingent right of a person (other than the individual) or partnership as a beneficiary (determined with reference to subsection 104(1.1)) under the trust; and

(c) in the case of a trust the terms of which satisfy the conditions in subparagraph (1.01)(c)(ii), the trust does not make an election under subparagraph 104(4)(a)(ii.1).

Related Provisions: 104(1.1) — Restricted meaning of "beneficiary".

Notes: For CRA interpretation see VIEWS doc 2012-0453911C6 [2012 APFF q.2] (transfer results in change in beneficial ownership).

73(1.02) added by 2001 technical bill, this version effective for transfers after March 15, 2001.

(1.1) Interpretation — For greater certainty, a property is, for the purposes of subsections (1) and (1.01), deemed to be property of the individual referred to in subsection (1) that has been transferred to a particular transferee where,

(a) under the laws of a province or because of a decree, order or judgment of a competent tribunal made in accordance with those laws, the property

(i) is acquired or is deemed to have been acquired by the particular transferee,

(ii) is deemed or declared to be property of, or is awarded to, the particular transferee, or

(iii) has vested in the particular transferee; and

(b) the property was or would, but for those laws, have been a capital property of the individual referred to in subsection (1).

Related Provisions: 70(9.1), (9.11), (9.3), (9.31) — Transfer of farm or fishing property from spouse trust to settlor's children.

Notes: 73(1.1) amended by 2001 technical bill (for transfers after 1999) and 1993 technical bill.

Regulations: 6500(2) (prescribed provisions; no longer needed).

I.T. Application Rules: 20(1.1).

Interpretation Bulletins: IT-325R2: Property transfers after separation, divorce and annulment.

(1.2) [Repealed under former Act]

Notes: The rule in 73(1.2), extending the meaning of "spouse" and "former spouse" to include a party to a void or voidable marriage, was moved to 252(3) effective 1982.

(2) Capital cost and amount deemed allowed to spouse, etc., or trust — If a transferee is deemed by subsection (1) to have acquired any particular depreciable property of a prescribed class of a taxpayer for an amount determined under paragraph (1)(b) and the capital cost to the taxpayer of the particular property exceeds the amount determined under that paragraph, in applying sections 13 and 20 and any regulations made under paragraph 20(1)(a)

(a) the capital cost to the transferee of the particular property is deemed to be the amount that was the capital cost to the taxpayer of the particular property; and

(b) the excess is deemed to have been allowed to the transferee in respect of the particular property under regulations made under paragraph 20(1)(a) in computing income for taxation years before the acquisition of the particular property.

Notes: 73(2) amended by 2002-2013 technical bill for transfers after 1999.

I.T. Application Rules: 20(1.1) (where property owned since before 1972).

Interpretation Bulletins: IT-209R: *Inter vivos* gifts of capital property to individuals directly or through trusts; IT-325R2: Property transfers after separation, divorce and annulment.

(3) When subsec. (3.1) applies — Subsection (3.1) applies to a taxpayer and a child of the taxpayer in respect of property that has been transferred, at any time, by the taxpayer to the child, where

(a) the property was, before the transfer, land in Canada or depreciable property in Canada of a prescribed class, of the taxpayer;

(b) the child of the taxpayer was resident in Canada immediately before the transfer; and

(c) the property has been used principally in a farming or fishing business in which the taxpayer, the taxpayer's spouse or common-law partner, a child of the taxpayer or a parent of the taxpayer was actively engaged on a regular and continuous basis (or in the case of property used in the operation of a woodlot, was engaged to the extent required by a prescribed forest management plan in respect of that woodlot).

> **Possible Future Amendments — 73(3)–(4.1)**
> **Prime Minister's mandate letter to Minister of Finance, Dec. 2019 and Liberal.ca election platform, Oct. 2019**: See under 70(9).

Related Provisions: 248(29) — Property used in a combination of farming and fishing; 250 — Resident in Canada.

Notes: 73(3) provides a rollover of farm or fishing property to a child, grandchild, etc. (see extended definitions in 70(10)"child" and 252(1)). CRA considers that the "use" test applies separately to each legal parcel of land: VIEWS doc 2013-0474461E5; and that "land" includes buildings: see 70(5.2) Notes. The parent is generally deemed to dispose of the property at an amount between cost and fair market value (depending on the amount paid). There is no election out of the rollover: 2012-0435361E5. The taxpayer (or spouse or children) must have used the property in the business of farming (2005-0115811E5, 2005-0154271E5), but not necessarily immediately before the transfer: 2007-0240321E5. A transfer from parent to corporation as bare trustee for children will qualify: 2006-0167011I7. A deceased spouse's use qualifies: 2008-0294051I7. A transfer to a trust for a minor child qualifies if certain conditions are satisfied: IT-286R4 para. 13, 2005-0152241E5. If the property is sold within 3 years, 69(11) may retroactively deny the rollover: 2002-0143635, 2005-0154271E5, 2012-0435361E5. A transfer of an existing life interest may qualify: doc 2006-0216421E5. If the property does not qualify for the rollover but the transfer has been completed, the capital gain must be recognized: 2006-0165321E5. See also 2008-0271421E5, 2014-0536851E5 (woodlot and prescribed forest management plan). For favourable rulings see 2014-0535661R3, 2015-0576961R3.

See Henkelman, "Farm Succession Planning", 2010 Prairie Provinces Tax Conference (ctf.ca), 13:1-22; ZoBell, "Nuances in Farm Rollover Rules", 7(2) *Canadian Tax Focus* (ctf.ca) 11 (May 2017).

"Principally" (or "primarily"), in para. (c) or elsewhere, means more than 50% of the years in CRA's view (doc 2007-0240321E5), but the phrase may mean "first in importance" if a qualitative test provides a clear answer: *Mother's Pizza*, [1988] 2 C.T.C. 197 (FCA); *Burger King*, [2000] 2 C.T.C. 1 (FCA); *McDonald's v. West Edmonton Mall*, 1994 CanLII 9040 (Alta QB), para. 61 [aff'd on other ground 1995 ABCA 503]; *McDonnell Douglas Canada*, 1996 CarswellNat 2096 (FCTD), para. 14; *Seaspan International*, 2002 FCT 675; *Grove Acceptance*, [2003] 1 C.T.C. 2377 (TCC); *Colleges of Applied Arts*, 2003 TCC 618; *Fleming School of Dance*, 2007 TCC 651; *Gestions Calce*, 2019 QCCQ 7377 (and see also *Coles Book Stores*, 1972 CanLII 176 (SCC)). For detailed discussion see David Sherman's *Canada GST Service* analysis of *Excise Tax Act* s. 199(2) (also on *Taxnet Pro*). Property leased out is not "used" in farming (IT-268R4 para. 25), but see 70(9.8) exception.

If the property is sold within 3 years, 69(11) may retroactively deny the rollover.

If the property is held in partnership or through a corporation, see 73(4)-(4.1).

73(3)(a) amended by 2016 budget bill #2, effective 2017, to delete from the end "or any eligible capital property in respect of a farming or fishing business carried on in Canada by the taxpayer" (as part of changing ECP to CCA Class 14.1: see Notes to 20(1)(b)).

73(3) amended by 2014 budget bill #2 (for 2014 and later tax years), 2002-2013 technical bill, 2006 budget bill #2 (splitting 73(3) into (3)-(3.1) and extending 73(3)-(4) to fishing property), 2001 Budget, 2000 same-sex partners bill, 1994 Budget, 1992 technical bill.

Regulations: 7400 (prescribed forest management plan).

I.T. Application Rules: 26(19) (property owned since before 1972).

Income Tax Folios: S7-F1-C1: Split-receipting and deemed fair market value.

Interpretation Bulletins: IT-268R4: *Inter vivos* transfer of farm property to child.

(3.1) *Inter vivos* transfer of farm or fishing property to child — If, because of subsection (3), this subsection applies to the

---

taxpayer and a child of the taxpayer in respect of a property transferred by the taxpayer to the child of the taxpayer, the following rules apply:

(a) where, immediately before the transfer, the property was depreciable property of a prescribed class, the taxpayer is deemed to have disposed of the property, at the time of the transfer, for proceeds of disposition equal to

(i) in any case to which neither subparagraph (ii) nor (iii) applies, the taxpayer's proceeds of disposition otherwise determined,

(ii) the greater of the amounts referred to in clauses (A) and (B), if the taxpayer's proceeds of disposition otherwise determined exceed the greater of

(A) the fair market value of the property immediately before the time of the transfer, and

(B) the lesser of

(I) the capital cost to the taxpayer of the property, and

(II) the amount, determined immediately before the time of the disposition of the property, that is that proportion of the undepreciated capital cost of property of that class to the taxpayer that the capital cost to the taxpayer of the property is of the capital cost to the taxpayer of all property of that class that had not, at or before that time, been disposed of, or

(iii) if the taxpayer's proceeds of disposition otherwise determined are less than the lesser of the amounts referred to in clauses (ii)(A) and (B), the lesser of those amounts;

(b) where the property transferred was land, the taxpayer is deemed to have disposed of the property at the time of the transfer for proceeds of disposition equal to,

(i) in any case to which neither subparagraph (ii) nor (iii) applies, the taxpayer's proceeds of disposition otherwise determined,

(ii) the greater of the amounts referred to in clauses (A) and (B), if the taxpayer's proceeds of disposition otherwise determined exceed the greater of

(A) the fair market value of the land immediately before the time of the transfer, and

(B) the adjusted cost base to the taxpayer of the land immediately before the time of the transfer, or

(iii) if the taxpayer's proceeds of disposition otherwise determined are less than the lesser of the amounts referred to in clauses (ii)(A) and (B), the lesser of those amounts;

(c) [Repealed]

(d) subsection 69(1) does not apply to the taxpayer and the child in respect of the property;

(e) the child is deemed to have acquired the property at a cost equal to the taxpayer's proceeds of disposition in respect of the disposition of the property determined under

(i) where the property is depreciable property of the taxpayer, paragraph (a), and

(ii) where the property is land of the taxpayer, paragraph (b); and

(f), (g) [Repealed]

(h) where the property is depreciable property of a prescribed class of the taxpayer and the capital cost to the taxpayer of the property exceeds the cost to the child of the property, for the purposes of sections 13 and 20 and any regulations made under paragraph 20(1)(a),

(i) the capital cost to the child of the property is deemed to be the amount that was the capital cost to the taxpayer of the property immediately before the transfer, and

(ii) the excess is deemed to have been allowed to the child in respect of the property under regulations made under paragraph 20(1)(a) in computing income for taxation years that ended before the the the child acquired the property.

Related Provisions: 44(1.1) — Farm or fishing property (FFP) disposed of to child; 69(11) — Anti-avoidance rule where property sold after rollover; 70(9), (9.01) — Transfer of FFP to child; 70(9.6) — Transfer to parent; 70(9.8) — FFP used by corporation or partnership; 75.1 — Gain or loss deemed that of transferor; 104(4)(a.4) — Deemed disposition by trust following transfer; 110.6(1)"qualified farm property"(d), "qualified fishing property"(d) — Property to which 73(3)(d.1) applies eligible for capital gains exemption; 110.6(2) — Capital gains exemption on farm or fishing property; 257 — Formula cannot calculate to less than zero.

Notes: See Notes to 73(3).

73(3.1)(c), (f) and (g) repealed by 2016 budget bill #2, effective 2017, as part of changing eligible capital property rules to CCA Class 14.1 (see Notes to 20(1)(b)). They read:

(c) where, immediately before the transfer, the property was eligible capital property, the taxpayer is deemed to have disposed of the property, at the time of the transfer, for proceeds of disposition equal to,

(i) in any case to which neither subparagraph (ii) nor (iii) applies, the taxpayer's proceeds of disposition otherwise determined,

(ii) the greater of the amounts referred to in clauses (A) and (B), if the taxpayer's proceeds of disposition otherwise determined exceed the greater of

(A) the fair market value of the property immediately before the time of the transfer, and

(B) the amount determined by the formula

$$4/3\ (A \times B/C)$$

where

A   is the taxpayer's cumulative eligible capital in respect of the business,

B   is the fair market value of the property immediately before the transfer, and

C   is the fair market value immediately before the transfer of all the taxpayer's eligible capital property in respect of the business, or

(iii) if the taxpayer's proceeds of disposition otherwise determined are less than the lesser of the amounts referred to in clauses (ii)(A) and (B), the lesser of those amounts;

. . . . .

(f) if the property was, immediately before the transfer, an eligible capital property of the taxpayer in respect of a business, the child is deemed to have acquired

(i) where the child does not continue to carry on the business, a capital property, immediately after the transfer, at a cost equal to the taxpayer's proceeds of disposition in respect of the disposition of the property determined under paragraph (c),

(ii) where the child continues to carry on the business, an eligible capital property and to have made an eligible capital expenditure at a cost equal to the total of

(A) the taxpayer's proceeds of disposition referred to in paragraph (c), and

(B) ⁴/₃ of the amount determined by the formula

$$(A \times B/C) - D$$

where

A   is the amount, if any, determined for F in the definition "cumulative eligible capital" in subsection 14(5) in respect of the business immediately before the transfer,

B   is the fair market value of the property immediately before the transfer,

C   is the fair market value immediately before the transfer of all the taxpayer's eligible capital property in respect of the business, and

D   is the amount, if any, included under paragraph 14(1)(a) in computing the taxpayer's income as a result of the disposition, and

(iii) for the purpose of determining at any subsequent time the child's cumulative eligible capital in respect of the business, an amount equal to ³/₄ of the amount determined under subparagraph (ii) is to be added to the amount otherwise determined for P in the definition "cumulative eligible capital" in subsection 14(5);

(g) for the purpose of determining, in respect of any disposition of the property, after the time of the transfer, the amount deemed to be the child's taxable capital gain, and the amount to be included in computing the child's income, there shall be added to the amount otherwise determined for Q in respect of the business in the definition "cumulative eligible capital" in subsection 14(5), the amount determined by the formula,

$$A \times B/C$$

where

A   is the amount, if any, determined for Q in that definition in respect of the business immediately before the time of the transfer,

B   is the fair market value, immediately before that time, of the transferred property, and

C   is the fair market value immediately before that time of all the taxpayer's eligible capital property in respect of the business; and

73(3.1) added by 2006 budget bill #2, effective on the same basis as the amendment to 73(3).

Interpretation Bulletins: IT-268R4: *Inter vivos* transfer of farm property to child.

(4) When subsec. (4.1) applies — Subsection (4.1) applies to a taxpayer and a child of the taxpayer in respect of property that has been transferred, at any time, to the child if

(a) the child was resident in Canada immediately before the transfer; and

(b) the property was, immediately before the transfer, a share of the capital stock of a family farm or fishing corporation of the taxpayer or an interest in a family farm or fishing partnership of the taxpayer (as defined in subsection 70(10)).

Related Provisions: 69(11) — Anti-avoidance rule where property sold after rollover; 250 — Resident in Canada.

Notes: 73(4) amended by 2014 budget bill #2 (for 2014 and later tax years), 2006 budget bill #2.

I.T. Application Rules: 20(1.1) (where depreciable property disposed of to spouse, common-law partner, trust or child).

Income Tax Folios: S7-F1-C1: Split-receipting and deemed fair market value.

Interpretation Bulletins: IT-268R4: *Inter vivos* transfer of farm property to child.

Advance Tax Rulings: ATR-56: Purification of a family farm corporation.

(4.1) *Inter vivos* **transfer of family farm or fishing corporations and partnerships** — If, because of subsection (4), this subsection applies to the taxpayer and the taxpayer's child in respect of the transfer of the property by the taxpayer to the child,

(a) subject to paragraph (c), where the property was, immediately before the transfer, a share of the capital stock of a family farm or fishing corporation of the taxpayer or an interest in a family farm or fishing partnership of the taxpayer, the taxpayer is deemed to have disposed of the property at the time of the transfer for proceeds of disposition equal to,

(i) in any case to which neither subparagraph (ii) nor (iii) applies, the taxpayer's proceeds of disposition otherwise determined,

(ii) the greater of the amounts referred to in clauses (A) and (B), if the taxpayer's proceeds of disposition otherwise determined exceed the greater of

(A) the fair market value of the property immediately before the time of the transfer, and

(B) the adjusted cost base to the taxpayer of the property immediately before the time of the transfer, or

(iii) if the taxpayer's proceeds of disposition otherwise determined are less than the lesser of the amounts referred to in clauses (ii)(A) and (B), the lesser of those amounts;

(b) subject to paragraph (c), where the property is, immediately before the transfer, a share of the capital stock of a family farm or fishing corporation of the taxpayer or an interest in a family farm or fishing partnership of the taxpayer, the child is deemed to have acquired the property for an amount equal to the taxpayer's proceeds of disposition in respect of the disposition of the property determined under paragraph (a);

(c) where the property is, immediately before the transfer, an interest in a family farm or fishing partnership of the taxpayer (other than a partnership interest to which subsection 100(3) applies), the taxpayer receives no consideration in respect of the transfer of the property and the taxpayer elects, in the taxpayer's return of income under this Part for the taxation year which includes the time of the transfer, to have this paragraph apply in respect of the transfer of the property,

(i) the taxpayer is, except for the purpose of paragraph 98(5)(g), deemed not to have disposed of the property at the time of the transfer,

(ii) the child is deemed to have acquired the property at the time of the transfer at a cost equal to the cost to the taxpayer of the interest immediately before the transfer, and

(iii) each amount required by subsection 53(1) or (2) to be added or deducted in computing the adjusted cost base to the taxpayer, immediately before the transfer, of the property is deemed to be an amount required by subsection 53(1) or (2) to be added or deducted in computing at any time at or after the time of the transfer, the adjusted cost base to the child of the property; and

(d) subsection 69(1) does not apply to the taxpayer and the child in respect of the property.

Related Provisions: 53(4) — Effect on ACB of share or partnership interest; 70(9.2), (9.21) — Transfer of family farm and fishing corporations and partnerships; 70(9.6) — Transfer to parent; 70(10) — "child"; 75.1 — Gain or loss deemed that of transferor; 104(4)(a.4) — Deemed disposition by trust following transfer.

Notes: For 73(4.1)(c), an election "in the taxpayer's return" is valid even if the return is filed late. See Notes to 7(1.31).

On transfer by a non-resident, a s. 116 certificate or waiver may be needed: VIEWS doc 2015-0602781E5. On making the 73(4.1)(c) election for a partnership interest whose ACB is negative, see 2018-0747761E5.

For rulings that 73(4.1) applies see VIEWS docs 2009-0327951R3 (butterfly); 2012-0472721R3 (rollover of Farmco to two children).

73(4.1)(a) opening words, (b), and (c) opening words amended by 2014 budget bill #2, for 2014 and later taxation years, to use the "family farm or fishing" terms instead of "family farm" and "family fishing".

73(4.1) added by 2006 budget bill #2, effective on the same basis as the amendment to 73(3).

Interpretation Bulletins: IT-268R4: *Inter vivos* transfer of farm property to child.

(5) Disposition of a NISA — Where at any time a taxpayer disposes of an interest in the taxpayer's NISA Fund No. 2, an amount equal to the balance in the fund so disposed of shall be deemed to have been paid out of the fund at that time to the taxpayer except that,

(a) where the interest is disposed of to the taxpayer's spouse or common-law partner, former spouse or common-law partner or an individual referred to in paragraph (1)(d) (as it applies to transfers of property that occurred before 1993) in settlement of rights arising out of their marriage or common-law partnership, on or after the breakdown of the marriage or common-law partnership, that amount shall not be deemed to have been paid to the taxpayer if

(i) the disposition is made under a decree, order or judgment of a competent tribunal or, in the case of a spouse or common-law partner or former spouse or common-law partner, a written separation agreement, and

(ii) the taxpayer elects in the taxpayer's return of income under this Part for the taxation year in which the property was disposed of to have this paragraph apply to the disposition; and

(b) where the interest is disposed of to a taxable Canadian corporation in a transaction in respect of which an election is made under section 85, an amount equal to the proceeds of disposition in respect of that interest shall be deemed to be paid, at that time, to the taxpayer out of the taxpayer's NISA Fund No. 2.

Related Provisions: 252(3) — Extended meaning of "spouse" and "former spouse".

Notes: For 73(5)(a)(ii), an election "in the taxpayer's return" is valid even if the return is filed late. See Notes to 7(1.31).

73(5)(a) amended by 2000 same-sex partners bill to refer to "common-law partner" and "common-law partnership", effective as per Notes to 248(1)"common-law partner".

73(5) added by 1992 technical bill, effective for dispositions after 1990.

Former 73(5), repealed by 1985 Budget (due to the introduction of the capital gains exemption in 110.6), provided a limited rollover of shares of a small business corporation to a taxpayer's child.

Interpretation Bulletins: IT-268R3: *Inter vivos* transfer of farm property to child.

(6) Application of subsec. 70(10) — The definitions in subsection 70(10) apply to this section.

Notes: 73(6) added in the RSC 1985 (5th Supp) consolidation, effective for tax years ending after Nov. 1991. This rule was formerly in the opening words of 70(10).

Interpretation Bulletins: IT-268R4: *Inter vivos* transfer of farm property to child.

Definitions [s. 73]: "adjusted cost base" — 54, 248(1); "amount" — 248(1); "beneficial ownership" — 248(3); "beneficiary" — 104(1.1); "business" — 248(1); "Canada" — 255; "capital property" — 54, 73(1.1), 248(1); "carrying on business" — 253; "child" — 70(10), 73(6), 252(1); "common-law partner", "common-law partnership" — 248(1); "cumulative eligible capital" — 14(5), 248(1); "depreciable property" — 13(21), 248(1); "eligible capital property" — 54, 248(1); "fair market value" — see 69(1) Notes; "farming", "fishing" — 248(1); "former spouse" — 252(3); "income" — of trust 108(3); "individual" — 248(1); "interest in a family farm or fishing partnership" — 70(10), 73(6); "land" — see 70(5.2) Notes; "NISA Fund No. 2" — 248(1); "partnership" — see 96(1) Notes; "person", "prescribed" — 248(1); "proceeds of disposition" — 54; "property" — 248(1); "province" — *Interpretation Act* 35(1); "regulation" — 248(1); "resident in Canada" — 250; "separation agreement" — 248(1); "share of the capital stock of a family farm or fishing corporation" — 70(10), 73(6); "specified participating interest" — 248(1); "spouse" — 252(3); "taxable Canadian corporation" — 89(1), 248(1); "taxation year" — 11(2), 249; "taxpayer" — 248(1); "transfer" — 73(1.1); "trust" — 104(1), 248(1), (3); "undepreciated capital cost" — 13(21), 248(1).

74. [Repealed under former Act]

Notes: 74 repealed by 1985 Budget, generally for transfers after May 22, 1985, with the introduction of new attribution rules in 74.1–74.5. It still applies to income from property transferred before May 23, 1985. For the text of s. 74 see PITA 1st-38th ed.

74.1 (1) [Attribution rule —] Transfers and loans to spouse or common-law partner — If an individual has transferred or lent property (otherwise than by an assignment of any portion of a retirement pension under section 65.1 of the *Canada Pension Plan* or a comparable provision of a provincial pension plan as defined in section 3 of that Act), either directly or indirectly, by means of a trust or by any other means whatever, to or for the benefit of a person who is the individual's spouse or common-law partner or who has since become the individual's spouse or common-law partner, any income or loss, as the case may be, of that person for a taxation year from the property or from property substituted therefor, that relates to the period in the year throughout which the individual is resident in Canada and that person is the individual's spouse or common-law partner, is deemed to be income or a loss, as the case may be, of the individual for the year and not of that person.

Related Provisions: 56(2) — Indirect payments; 56(4.1) — Interest free or low interest loans; 73(1) — Transfer to spouse deemed at cost; 74.1(3) — Repayment of existing indebtedness; 74.2(1) — Gain or loss deemed that of lender or transferor; 74.3 — Transfer or loan to a trust; 74.4(4) — Benefit not granted to designated person; 74.5(1) — Transfer for fair market value consideration; 74.5(2) — Loan for value; 74.5(3) — Spouses living apart; 74.5(6) — Back-to-back loans or transfers; 74.5(7) — Guarantees; 74.5(9) — Transfer or loan to a trust; 74.5(11) — Artificial transactions; 74.5(12) — Attribution rules — exemption; 74.5(13) — No attribution of split income subject to income-splitting tax; 82(2) — Attributed dividends deemed received by taxpayer; 96(1.8) — Transfer or loan of partnership interest; 119.1 — Income splitting effectively permitted for 2014-15 between spouses with children under 18; 160(1)(d) — Transferee jointly liable for transferor's tax on the attributed income; 212(12) — No non-resident withholding tax where income attributed; 248(5) — Substituted property.

Notes: 74.1 to 74.5 are known as the "attribution" rules: they attribute income of a transferee or borrower back to the transferor or lender of property, so as to prevent income splitting aimed at multiplying the use of the low rates of tax that apply to lower levels of taxable income (see 117(2)). These rules apply to transfers done "directly or indirectly"; see Notes to 17.1(1) for the meaning of "indirectly". They apply to transfers made and loans outstanding after May 22, 1985. (For earlier transfers (but not loans), see repealed s. 74, which still applies to attribute income from such transferred property.) The transferee is not required to repay the transferor for the transferor's tax resulting from attribution: VIEWS docs 2015-0595781C6 [2015 APFF q.13]; 2016-0655841C6 [2016 APFF q.19] (though this would be for a Court to rule on; it is not for the CRA to decide).

74.1(1) attributes income (or loss) and 74.2(1) attributes capital gain (or loss), to a spouse or common-law partner. 74.1(2) attributes income (or loss) from a child under 18. 74.3 and 74.5(9) cover transfers and loans to or through a trust, and 74.4 covers those to a corporation (but not a "small business corporation"). See also 56(4.1) (loan for income-splitting purpose); 120.4 (tax on split income (TOSI), greatly expanded in 2018); 146(8.3) (attribution of spousal RRSP contribution).

74.5 provides various exceptions and anti-avoidance rules. Exceptions include: transfer for fair market value (74.5(1)); loan on which enough interest is paid (74.5(2)); marriage or relationship breakdown (74.5(3)-(4)); spousal RRSP (74.5(12)(a)); RDSP (74.5(12)(a.2)); TFSA (74.5(12)(c)); amounts deductible and included in the other's income (74.5(12)(b)); where TOSI applies (74.5(13)). Anti-avoidance rules include: back-to-back loans or transfers (74.5(6)), guarantees (74.5(7)); using the rules to reduce tax (74.5(11)).

Note that the attribution rules apply to income on the property transferred, but not to income on *that* income ("secondary" income). They also do not apply to income earned with business assets transferred or loaned, since such income is not income from property (see Notes to 9(1) under "Business income vs property income").

See also 160(1)(d), which makes the transferee jointly liable for the transferor's tax on the attributed income.

74.1(1) and 74.2(1) applied to investments where the taxpayer's spouse had minimal income over the years: *Muio*, 2007 TCC 536. Providing collateral to secure a joint line of credit is not a transfer, but 74.5(7) will apply to trigger 74.1(1): VIEWS doc 2009-0317041E5. If spouse A puts funds into a joint account and spouse B uses the funds to buy property, that is a transfer from A to B: 2016-0642811E5.

Where the loan or indebtedness is repaid with property other than the property loaned or property substituted therefor, the CRA takes the position that the attribution of income under 74.1 continues. See Revenue Canada Round Table, 1993 Cdn Tax Foundation conference report, pp. 58:21-22, Q. 36.

Other income-splitting strategies include: pension income splitting (60.03); pay salary or consulting fee to spouse or children (67 Notes); invest Canada Child Benefit payments for children (74.1(2)); transfer property to children for capital gain (74.2(1) Notes); use small business corp (74.4(2)(c)); transfer for FMV (74.5(1)); loan with interest paid by Jan. 30 (74.5(2)); spousal RRSP (146(5.1), (8.3)); RESP for child (146.1); earn interest on interest; higher-income spouse pays non-deductible household expenses and lower-income spouse's tax; lower-income spouse claims donations (118.1(3) Notes) and medical expenses; get gift or loan from a non-resident.

For more on income splitting see Notes to: 9(1) (at "Diverting income"), 56(2), 67, 78(4), 120.4; Bernstein & Brent, "What's Left in Income Splitting?", 316 *The Estate Planner* (CCH) 6-10 (May 2021).

See *Miller Thomson on Estate Planning* (Carswell, 2 vols. looseleaf or ProView), chap. 11; Munro, "The Attribution Rules", 1999 Ontario Tax Conference (ctf.ca), 13:1-29; Luvisotto, "Owner Manager Remuneration", 2010 Ontario Tax Conf. 9A:1-9; Jacob & Lee, "Income Splitting Strategies", 58(4) *Canadian Tax Journal [CTJ]* 1005-23 (2010); Brown & Wiener, "A Practical Look at the Attribution Rules", 2011 Cdn Tax Foundation conference report, 38:1-60; Hoffstein & Lee, "Revisiting the Attribution Rules", 2012 Ontario Tax Conf. 9:1-40; Goldberg, "The Effective Use of Trusts in Connection With Income Splitting", 242 *The Estate Planner* (CCH) 1-3 (March 2015), 243:1-3 (April), 244:4-8 (May), 245:3-5 (June 2015); Desmarais et al., "The Attribution Rules", 2017 STEP Canada conference (97 slides; contact memberservices@step.ca); Grant-Young & Rogers, "Income-Splitting Update", 67(1) *CTJ* 209-34 (2019); Ideias, "Tax on Split Income and the Attribution Rules", Tax Planner Guide 9 (*Taxnet Pro*, 2019, 10pp); McBey, "Attribution Rules", 2485 *Tax Topics* (CCH) 1-6 (Oct. 24, 2019). For policy see Policy Forum articles, 61(3) *CTJ* 677-721 (2013). See also under "Splitting" in Topical Index.

There is no general policy against income splitting in the Act: see *Neuman* (SCC), discussed in Notes to 56(2), and *Hall v. Quebec*, [1998] 2 C.T.C. 133 (SCC), para. 49: "income splitting is integral to the scheme of taxation of estates and is not in any way reprehensible per se".

Lipson, 2009 SCC 1, held 4-3 that using 74.1(1) to allow a husband to claim his wife's interest deduction, as part of a scheme to make mortgage interest deductible, triggered GAAR (245(2)): "a specific anti-avoidance rule is being used to facilitate abusive tax avoidance" (para. 42). This may override *Overs*, 2006 TCC 26, where using 74.1(1) to allow O to claim losses from an investment transferred to his wife did not trigger GAAR, and *Evans*, 2005 TCC 684, where relying on an exception in the attribution rules did not trigger GAAR. See also Notes to 74.5(11).

See also 56(4.1) (alternative attribution rule for loans), and Notes at end of 74.1.

As between the spouses, the spouse who receives the property may be liable to the transferring spouse to pay the attributed tax: *Zeitler v. Zeitler Estate*, 2010 BCCA 216.

74.1(1) amended by 2011 budget bill #2, effective for transfers and loans made after 2010, to delete "or of a prescribed provincial pension plan" within the parentheses. (Saskatchewan Pension Plan income is now treated as RRSP income for purposes of 74.5(12), which prevents 74.1 from applying: see 146(21.1).)

74.1(1) amended by 2000 same-sex partners bill to refer to "common-law partner", effective as per Notes to 248(1)"common-law partner".

Income Tax Folios: S4-F3-C1: Price adjustment clauses [replaces IT-169]; S6-F2-C1: Disposition of an income interest in a trust [replaces IT-385R2].

Interpretation Bulletins: IT-295R4: Taxable dividends received after 1987 by a spouse; IT-325R2: Property transfers after separation, divorce and annulment; IT-394R2: Preferred beneficiary election; IT-434R: Rental of real property by individual; IT-511R: Interspousal and certain other transfers and loans of property; IT-531: Eligible funeral arrangements.

CRA Audit Manual: 15.7.13: Application of attribution rules to trusts.

(2) [Attribution rule —] Transfers and loans to minors — If an individual has transferred or lent property, either directly or indirectly, by means of a trust or by any other means whatever, to or for the benefit of a person who was under 18 years of age (other than an amount received in respect of that person either as a consequence of the operation of subsection 122.61(1) or under section 4 of the *Universal Child Care Benefit Act*) and who

(a) does not deal with the individual at arm's length, or

(b) is the niece or nephew of the individual,

any income or loss, as the case may be, of that person for a taxation year from the property or from property substituted for that property, that relates to the period in the taxation year throughout which the individual is resident in Canada, is deemed to be income or a loss, as the case may be, of the individual and not of that person unless that person has, before the end of the taxation year, attained the age of 18 years.

Related Provisions: 56(2) — Indirect payments; 56(4.1) — Interest free or low interest loans; 69(1)(b) — Transfer not at arm's length deemed to be disposition at fair market value; 74.1(3) — Repayment of existing indebtedness; 74.3 — Transfer or loan to a trust; 74.4(4) — Benefit not granted to designated person; 74.5(1) — Transfer for fair market value consideration; 74.5(2) — Loan for value; 74.5(3) — Spouses living apart; 74.5(6) — Back-to-back loans or transfers; 74.5(7) — Guarantees; 74.5(9) — Transfer or loan to a trust; 74.5(11) — Artificial transactions; 74.5(12) — Attribution rules — exemption; 74.5(13) — No attribution of split income subject to income-splitting tax; 75(1) — Transfer before May 23, 1985; 82(2) — Attributed dividends deemed received by taxpayer; 96(1.8) — Transfer or loan of partnership interest; 120.4 — Income-splitting tax; 160(1)(d) — Transferee jointly liable for transferor's tax on attributed income; 212(12) — No non-resident withholding tax where income attributed; 248(5) — Substituted property.

Notes: See Notes to 74.1(1). 74.1(2) attributes income on property transferred or loaned to minors. There is no attribution of capital gains, however, so "growth" shares (or mutual fund units) can be given to children (directly or through a trust) for income-splitting purposes as well as to multiply the capital gains exemption under 110.6(2.1) (but if private corp shares, see the tax on split income in 120.4).

74.1(2) does not apply to Canada Child Benefit payments or (pre-July 2016) Universal Child Care Benefit payments placed on account for the child, but this exclusion does not extend to the Quebec child tax benefit: VIEWS doc 2007-0219801E5. 74.1(2) does not apply to educational assistance payments from a RESP, due to 74.3(1)(a), since they are taxed under 146.1(17) rather than 12(1)(m): VIEWS doc 2004-0064551E5.

74.1(2) may apply if a taxpayer pays income taxes owing by a trust for his children: VIEWS doc 2006-0173711E5 (this view may be incorrect).

The application of 74.1(2) does not require that the parent's Social Insurance Number be shown on the T5 slip: doc 2007-0233801C6.

In *Romkey*, [2000] 1 C.T.C. 390 (FCA); leave to appeal denied 2000 CarswellNat 2423 (SCC), a company was inactive. The owners caused the company to issue shares to a trust for their children. The Court held that the owners were forgoing the right to receive future dividends, and this was a "transfer of property" to which 74.1(2) applied to later dividends, even though the company had no value at the time. This extends the principle of *Kieboom*, [1992] 2 C.T.C. 59 (FCA), where share issuance by an active company, giving the children instant value, was held to be a transfer of property to the children. CRA indicates (VIEWS doc 2001-0072705) that it will not change its assessing practice due to *Romkey* to apply 74.1(2) to estate freezes; but see also 75(2) Notes on *Garron* and on doc 2010-0366301I7. In *Krauss*, 2009 TCC 597 [aff'd on other grounds 2010 FCA 284], 74.1(2) applied to an arrangement that was not a conventional estate freeze, to attribute income of a family trust earned through a partnership.

Opening words of 74.1(2) amended by 2006 budget bill #2, effective for amounts received after June 2006, to add reference to *UCCB Act* s. 4 and make non-substantive wording changes.

Parenthetical exclusion in opening words of 74.1(2) added by 1992 Child Benefit bill, effective 1993. It provides that Canada Child Benefit payments may be given to the children in respect of whom they were paid, and allowed to earn income that will not be attributed back to the parents. This was already Revenue Canada's long-standing policy for pre-1993 family allowances (Information Circular 79-9R para. 16).

Income Tax Folios: S4-F3-C1: Price adjustment clauses [replaces IT-169]; S6-F2-C1: Disposition of an income interest in a trust [replaces IT-385R2].

Interpretation Bulletins: IT-268R4: *Inter vivos* transfer of farm property to child; IT-325R2: Property transfers after separation, divorce and annulment; IT-394R2: Preferred beneficiary election; IT-434R: Rental of real property by individual; IT-510: Transfers and loans of property made after May 22, 1985 to a related minor; IT-531: Eligible funeral arrangements.

CRA Audit Manual: 15.7.13: Application of attribution rules to trusts.

(3) Repayment of existing indebtedness — For the purposes of subsections (1) and (2), where, at any time, an individual has lent or transferred property (in this subsection referred to as the "lent or transferred property") either directly or indirectly, by means of a trust or by any other means whatever, to or for the benefit of a person, and the lent or transferred property or property substituted therefor is used

(a) to repay, in whole or in part, borrowed money with which other property was acquired, or

(b) to reduce an amount payable for other property,

there shall be included in computing the income from the lent or transferred property, or from property substituted therefor, that is so used, that proportion of the income or loss, as the case may be, derived after that time from the other property or from property substituted therefor that the fair market value at that time of the lent or transferred property, or property substituted therefor, that is so used is of the cost to that person of the other property at the time of its acquisition, but for greater certainty nothing in this subsection shall affect the application of subsections (1) and (2) to any income or loss derived from the other property or from property substituted therefor.

Notes: For the meaning of "derived", see Notes to 18.1(12).

Where a loan at prescribed interest rate is refinanced, 74.1(3) may apply; see Notes to 74.5(2). See also Notes to 74.1(1).

Interpretation Bulletins [subsec. 74.1(3)]: IT-325R2: Property transfers after separation, divorce and annulment; IT-394R2: Preferred beneficiary election; IT-510: Transfers and loans of property made after May 22, 1985 to a related minor.

Notes [s. 74.1]: 74.1 added by 1985 Budget, for property transferred after May 22, 1985 and (after 1987) for all loans. For earlier transfers, see former 74 and 75(1).

Definitions [s. 74.1]: "amount" — 248(1); "arm's length" — 251(1); "borrowed money" — 248(1); "Canada" — 255, *Interpretation Act* 35(1); "common-law partner" — 248(1); "fair market value" — see 69(1) Notes; "individual" — 248(1); "nephew", "niece" — 252(2)(g); "person", "prescribed", "property" — 248(1); "provincial pension plan" — *Canada Pension Plan* s. 3; "resident in Canada" — 250; "substituted" — 248(5); "taxation year" — 249; "trust" — 104(1), 248(1), (3).

74.2 (1) [Spousal attribution —] Gain or loss deemed that of lender or transferor

— Where an individual has lent or transferred property (in this section referred to as "lent or transferred property"), either directly or indirectly, by means of a trust or by any other means whatever, to or for the benefit of a person (in this subsection referred to as the "recipient") who is the individual's spouse or common-law partner or who has since become the individual's spouse or common-law partner, the following rules apply for the purposes of computing the income of the individual and the recipient for a taxation year:

(a) the amount, if any, by which

(i) the total of the recipient's taxable capital gains for the year from dispositions of property (other than listed personal property) that is lent or transferred property or property substituted therefor occurring in the period (in this subsection referred to as the "attribution period") throughout which the individual is resident in Canada and the recipient is the individual's spouse or common-law partner

exceeds

(ii) the total of the recipient's allowable capital losses for the year from dispositions occurring in the attribution period of property (other than listed personal property) that is lent or transferred property or property substituted therefor

shall be deemed to be a taxable capital gain of the individual for the year from the disposition of property other than listed personal property;

(b) the amount, if any, by which the total determined under subparagraph (a)(ii) exceeds the total determined under subparagraph (a)(i) shall be deemed to be an allowable capital loss of the individual for the year from the disposition of property other than listed personal property;

(c) the amount, if any, by which

(i) the amount that the total of the recipient's gains for the year from dispositions occurring in the attribution period of listed personal property that is lent or transferred property or property substituted therefor would be if the recipient had at

no time owned listed personal property other than listed personal property that was lent or transferred property or property substituted therefor

exceeds

(ii) the amount that the total of the recipient's losses for the year from dispositions of listed personal property that is lent or transferred property or property substituted therefor would be if the recipient had at no time owned listed personal property other than listed personal property that was lent or transferred property or property substituted therefor,

shall be deemed to be a gain of the individual for the year from the disposition of listed personal property;

(d) the amount, if any, by which the total determined under subparagraph (c)(ii) exceeds the total determined under subparagraph (c)(i) shall be deemed to be a loss of the individual for the year from the disposition of listed personal property; and

(e) any taxable capital gain or allowable capital loss or any gain or loss taken into account in computing an amount described in paragraph (a), (b), (c) or (d) shall, except for the purposes of those paragraphs and to the extent that the amount so described is deemed by virtue of this subsection to be a taxable capital gain or an allowable capital loss or a gain or loss of the individual, be deemed not to be a taxable capital gain or an allowable capital loss or a gain or loss, as the case may be, of the recipient.

Related Provisions: 73(1) — Transfer to spouse deemed at cost; 74.1(1) — Transfer or loan to spouse; 74.2(3) — Application to disposition on emigration; 74.3 — Transfer or loan to a trust; 74.4(4) — Benefit not granted to a designated person; 74.5(1) — Transfer for fair market consideration; 74.5(2) — Loans for value; 74.5(3) — Spouses living apart; 74.5(6) — Back-to-back loans and transfers; 74.5(7) — Guarantees; 74.5(12) — Attribution rules — exemption; 119.1 — Income splitting effectively permitted for 2014-15 between spouses with children under 18; 160(1)(d) — Transferee jointly liable for transferor's tax on attributed income; 248(5) — Substituted property.

Notes: See Notes to 74.1(1). On transfer of capital property to a spouse, there is normally no capital gain (73(1)), but future capital gains are attributed back to the transferor. See VIEWS doc 2006-0198071E5 for an example. See also 2011-0405071E5.

On a transfer to a trust for self, spouse and children, and the interaction with 74.5 and 75(2), see VIEWS doc 2010-0365581E5.

There is no attribution of capital gains on property transferred to one's children. See Notes to 74.1(2).

The attribution rules do not apply after divorce: 74.5(3), VIEWS doc 2012-0465711E5.

74.2(1) applied in *Lafontaine*, 2007 TCC 89 and *St-Pierre*, 2007 TCC 90, both aff'd 2008 FCA 204 (the 248(10) "series of transactions" concept does not apply to 74.2(1)).

In *Gervais*, 2018 FCA 3, half of a capital gain was transferred by the husband so the wife could claim the capital gains exemption: this was held to violate GAAR (245(2)) by avoiding 74.2(1).

74.2(1) amended by 2000 same-sex partners bill to refer to "common-law partner", effective as per Notes to 248(1)"common-law partner".

74.2(1) added by 1985 Budget, effective for property transferred after May 22, 1985 and (after 1987) for all loans. For earlier transfers, see former 74. For transfers to minor children, see Notes to 74.1(2).

Income Tax Folios: S4-F3-C1: Price adjustment clauses [replaces IT-169].

Interpretation Bulletins: IT-325R2: Property transfers after separation, divorce and annulment; IT-394R2: Preferred beneficiary election; IT-511R: Interspousal and certain other transfers and loans of property; IT-531: Eligible funeral arrangements.

(2) Deemed gain or loss

— Where an amount is deemed by subsection (1) or 75(2) or section 75.1 of this Act, or subsection 74(2) of the *Income Tax Act*, chapter 148 of the Revised Statutes of Canada, 1952, to be a taxable capital gain or an allowable capital loss of an individual for a taxation year,

(a) for the purposes of sections 3 and 111, as they apply for the purposes of section 110.6, such portion of the gain or loss as may reasonably be considered to relate to the disposition of a property by another person in the year shall be deemed to arise from the disposition of that property by the individual in the year; and

(b) for the purposes of section 110.6, that property shall be deemed to have been disposed of by the individual on the day on which it was disposed of by the other person.

Notes: In *Kaiser*, 2008 TCC 84, 74.2(2) did not apply to journal entries made retroactively to honour a spouse's matrimonial rights to a company.

74.2(2) amended by 1994 Budget (effective 1994) and 1991 technical bill.

I.T. Application Rules: 69 (meaning of "chapter 148 of ...").

Income Tax Folios: S4-F3-C1: Price adjustment clauses [replaces IT-169].

Interpretation Bulletins: IT-369R: Attribution of trust income to settlor; IT-394R2: Preferred beneficiary election.

(3) Election for subsection (1) to apply — Subsection (1) does not apply to a disposition at any particular time (in this subsection referred to as the "emigration disposition") under paragraph 128.1(4)(b), by a taxpayer who is a recipient referred to in subsection (1), unless the recipient and the individual referred to in that subsection, in their returns of income for the taxation year that includes the first time, after the particular time, at which the recipient disposes of the property, jointly elect that subsection (1) apply to the emigration disposition.

Related Provisions: 74.2(4) — Application rule.

Notes: If either taxpayer is resident in Quebec, the election must be copied to Revenu Québec: *Taxation Act* ss. 462.6.1, 21.4.6.

74.2(3) added by 2001 technical bill, effective October 2, 1996.

(4) Application of subsection (3) — For the purpose of applying subsection (3) and notwithstanding subsections 152(4) to (5), any assessment of tax payable under this Act by the recipient or the individual referred to in subsection (1) shall be made that is necessary to take an election under subsection (3) into account except that no such assessment shall affect the computation of

(a) interest payable under this Act to or by a taxpayer in respect of any period that is before the taxpayer's filing-due date for the taxation year that includes the first time, after the particular time referred to in subsection (3), at which the recipient disposes of the property referred to in that subsection; or

(b) any penalty payable under this Act.

Notes: 74.2(4) added by 2001 technical bill, effective Oct. 2, 1996.

Definitions [s. 74.2]: "allowable capital loss" — 38(b), 248(1); "amount", "assessment" — 248(1); "Canada" — 255; "common-law partner", "disposition", "filing-due date", "individual" — 248(1); "lent or transferred property" — 74.2(1); "listed personal property" — 54, 248(1); "person", "property" — 248(1); "resident in Canada" — 250; "substituted" — 248(5); "taxable capital gain" — 38(a), 248(1); "taxation year" — 249; "taxpayer" — 248(1); "trust" — 104(1), 248(1), (3).

74.3 (1) [Attribution rule —] Transfers or loans to a trust — Where an individual has lent or transferred property (in this section referred to as "lent or transferred property"), either directly or indirectly, by means of a trust or by any other means whatever, to a trust in which another individual who is at any time a designated person in respect of the individual is beneficially interested at any time, the following rules apply:

(a) for the purposes of section 74.1, the income of the designated person for a taxation year from the lent or transferred property shall be deemed to be an amount equal to the lesser of

(i) the amount in respect of the trust that was included by virtue of paragraph 12(1)(m) in computing the income for the year of the designated person, and

(ii) that proportion of the amount that would be the income of the trust for the year from the lent or transferred property or from property substituted therefor if no deduction were made under subsections 104(6) or (12) that

(A) the amount determined under subparagraph (i) in respect of the designated person for the year

is of

(B) the total of all amounts each of which is an amount determined under subparagraph (i) for the year in respect of the designated person or any other person who is throughout the year a designated person in respect of the individual; and

(b) for the purposes of section 74.2, an amount equal to the lesser of

(i) the amount that was designated under subsection 104(21) in respect of the designated person in the trust's return of income for the year, and

(ii) the amount, if any, by which

(A) the total of all amounts each of which is a taxable capital gain for the year from the disposition by the trust of the lent or transferred property or property substituted therefor

exceeds

(B) the total of all amounts each of which is an allowable capital loss for the year from the disposition by the trust of the lent or transferred property or property substituted therefor,

shall be deemed to be a taxable capital gain of the designated person for the year from the disposition of property (other than listed personal property) that is lent or transferred property.

Related Provisions: 56(4.1) — Interest free or low-interest loans; 74.4(4) — Benefit not granted to a designated person; 74.5(5) — "Designated person"; 74.5(6) — Back to back loans and transfers; 74.5(7) — Guarantees; 74.5(9) — Transfer or loan to a trust; 74.5(12) — Attribution rules — exemption; 74.5(13) — No attribution of split income subject to income-splitting tax; 75(2) — Reversionary trusts — attribution rules; 82(2) — Attributed dividends deemed received by individual; 96(1.8) — Transfer or loan of partnership interest; 212(12) — No non-resident withholding tax where income attributed; 248(5) — Substituted property; 248(25) — Beneficially interested.

Notes: See Notes to 74.1(1). See also 74.5(9), which overlaps with 74.3.

74.3(1) may apply if a taxpayer pays income taxes owing by a trust for his children: VIEWS doc 2006-0173711E5.

Income Tax Folios: S4-F3-C1: Price adjustment clauses [replaces IT-169].

Interpretation Bulletins: IT-394R2: Preferred beneficiary election; IT-510: Transfers and loans of property made after May 22, 1985 to a related minor; IT-511R: Interspousal and certain other transfers and loans of property.

CRA Audit Manual: 15.7.13: Application of attribution rules to trusts.

(2) Definition of "designated person" — In this section, "designated person", in respect of an individual, has the meaning assigned by subsection 74.5(5).

Notes: 74.3(2) added in the RSC 1985 (5th Supp) consolidation, effective for tax years ending after Nov. 1991. This rule was formerly contained within 74.5(5).

Notes [s. 74.3]: 74.3 added by 1985 Budget, for property transferred after May 22, 1985 and (after 1987) for all loans. For earlier transfers, see former 74 and 75.

Definitions [s. 74.3]: "allowable capital loss" — 38(b), 248(1); "amount" — 248(1); "beneficially interested" — 248(25); "designated person" — 74.3(2), 74.5(5); "individual" — 248(1); "lent or transferred property" — 74.3(1); "listed personal property" — 54, 248(1); "property" — 248(1); "substituted" — 248(5); "taxable capital gain" — 38(a), 248(1); "taxation year" — 249; "trust" — 104(1), 248(1), (3).

74.4 (1) Definitions — In this section,

"designated person", in respect of an individual, has the meaning assigned by subsection 74.5(5);

Notes: 74.4(1)"designated person" added in the RSC 1985 (5th Supp) consolidation, effective for tax years ending after Nov. 1991. This rule of application was formerly contained within 74.5(5).

"excluded consideration", at any time, means consideration received by an individual that is

(a) indebtedness,

(b) a share of the capital stock of a corporation, or

(c) a right to receive indebtedness or a share of the capital stock of a corporation.

(2) [Attribution rule —] Transfers and loans to corporations — Where an individual has transferred or lent property, either directly or indirectly, by means of a trust or by any other means whatever, to a corporation and one of the main purposes of the transfer or loan may reasonably be considered to be to reduce the income of the individual and to benefit, either directly or indirectly, by means of a trust or by any other means whatever, a person who is a designated person in respect of the individual, in computing the income of the individual for any taxation year that includes a period after the loan or transfer throughout which

(a) the person is a designated person in respect of the individual and would have been a specified shareholder of the corporation if the definition "specified shareholder" in subsection 248(1) were read without reference to paragraphs (a) and (d) of that definition and if the reference therein to "any other corporation that is related to the corporation" were read as a reference to "any other corporation (other than a small business corporation) that is related to the corporation",

(b) the individual was resident in Canada, and

(c) the corporation was not a small business corporation,

the individual shall be deemed to have received as interest in the year the amount, if any, by which

(d) the amount that would be interest on the outstanding amount of the loan or transferred property for such periods in the year if the interest were computed thereon at the prescribed rate of interest for such periods

exceeds the total of

(e) any interest received in the year by the individual in respect of the transfer or loan (other than amounts deemed by this subsection to be interest),

(f) all amounts included in the individual's income for the taxation year pursuant to subsection 82(1) or 90(1) in respect of taxable dividends received (other than dividends deemed by section 84 to have been received) by the individual in the year on shares that were received from the corporation as consideration for the transfer or as repayment for the loan that were excluded consideration at the time the dividends were received or on shares substituted therefor that were excluded consideration at that time, and

(g) where the designated person is a specified individual in relation to the year, the amount required to be included in computing the designated person's income for the year in respect of all taxable dividends received by the designated person that

(i) can reasonably be considered to be part of the benefit sought to be conferred, and

(ii) are included in computing the designated person's split income for any taxation year.

Related Provisions: 56(4.1) — Interest free or low interest loan to individual; 74.4(4) — Benefit not granted to a designated person; 82(2) — Attributed dividends deemed received by individual; 120.4 — Income-splitting tax; 160(1)(d) — Transferee jointly liable for transferor's tax on attributed income; 248(5) — Substituted property. See also at end of s. 74.4.

Notes: When reading a VIEWS doc or article in French about 74.2(2), note that the paragraph numbering is totally different than in English.

Where a person transfers or loans property (including money) to a corporation, 74.4(2) may include in the person's income annual interest on the property at the prescribed rate in Reg. 4301(c). It applies if one of the main purposes of the transfer or loan is to reduce the person's income and benefit a "designated person" (74.5(5): e.g., a spouse or related child under 18). If the person later becomes non-resident the annual attribution stops (74.4(2)(b)). For the meaning of "one of the main purposes" see 74.4(4) and Notes to 83(2.1).

The "period" in the opening words of 74.4(2) can be any period throughout which the conditions are satisfied (e.g. one day or 6 months); the deemed interest under para. (d) then applies to that "period".

Because of 74.4(2)(c), the shares of a small business corporation (as defined in 248(1)) will not trigger 74.4 if used for income splitting (through a trust or otherwise) with a spouse or children. However, the tax on split income in 120.4 (as expanded in 2018) will generally apply.

For interpretation see VIEWS docs 2001-0067725 (74.4(2) applies in typical estate freeze, where trust for minor child acquires common shares of freezor's Holdco); 2005-0162181E5; 2007-0243191C6 (rejects 3 methods used to avoid 74.4(2); 2008-0285091C6 (considers two scenarios); 2011-0410411E5 (74.4(2) does not apply); 2012-0449871E5 (74.4(2) applies); 2013-0504261E5 (purpose test is a question of fact); 2014-0538041C6 [2014 APFF q.19] (74.4(2) does not apply); 2015-0570071E5 (application to a trust doing a freeze); 2015-0601561E5 (application in 2 scenarios); 2015-0613401E5 (application in 2 scenarios); 2016 Alberta CPA (tinyurl.com/cra-abtax), q. 9 (interpretation of "one of the main purposes"); 2017-0709071C6 [2017 APFF q.9] (trust exchanging Opco shares in second freeze: 74.4(2) may apply); 2019-0812751C6 [2019 APFF q.16] (purpose test can be met even if expanded TOSI in

120.4 applies to prevent income-splitting); 2020-0852271C6 [2020 APFF q.15] (s. 51 estate freeze by spouses creating discretionary trusts that benefit both of them: 74.4(2) may apply). See also 74.4(3) Notes.

See also Yager, "Corporate Attribution Derails Estate Freeze", 16(10) *Canadian Tax Highlights* (ctf.ca) 4-5 (Oct. 2008)); Festeryga, "Corporate Attribution: The 'Anti-Freeze' Rule", 58(3) *Canadian Tax Journal* 675-96 (2010); Goldberg, "The Corporate Attribution Rules", 220 *The Estate Planner* (CCH) 1-3 (May 2013). CRA declined to provide data on how much 74.4 is used or to say how it applies to various fact patterns: May 2009 ICAA roundtable (tinyurl.com/cra-abtax) q.18. See also Notes to 74.4(4).

See also Notes to 56(2) regarding attempts to apply that provision to counter income-splitting that is done through corporations.

74.4(2)(a) amended by 1991 technical bill, effective (since 1988) for loans and transfers made after October 27, 1986.

74.4(2)(g) added by 1999 Budget, for 2000 and later tax years. (It applies to "split income" taxed under 120.4.)

Regulations: 4301(c) (prescribed rate of interest for 74.4(2)(d)).

Income Tax Folios: S4-F3-C1: Price adjustment clauses [replaces IT-169].

Interpretation Bulletins: IT-394R2: Preferred beneficiary election.

Information Circulars: 88-2, para. 10: General anti-avoidance rule — section 245 of the *Income Tax Act*.

I.T. Technical News: 16 (*Neuman* case).

Advance Tax Rulings: ATR-25: Estate freeze; ATR-36: Estate freeze; ATR-47: Transfer of assets to Realtyco.

(3) Outstanding amount — For the purposes of subsection (2), the outstanding amount of a transferred property or loan at a particular time is

(a) in the case of a transfer of property to a corporation, the amount, if any, by which the fair market value of the property at the time of the transfer exceeds the total of

(i) the fair market value, at the time of the transfer, of the consideration (other than consideration that is excluded consideration at the particular time) received by the transferor for the property, and

(ii) the fair market value, at the time of receipt, of any consideration (other than consideration that is excluded consideration at the particular time) received by the transferor at or before the particular time from the corporation or from a person with whom the transferor deals at arm's length, in exchange for excluded consideration previously received by the transferor as consideration for the property or for excluded consideration substituted for such consideration;

(b) in the case of a loan of money or property to a corporation, the amount, if any, by which

(i) the principal amount of the loan of money at the time the loan was made, or

(ii) the fair market value of the property lent at the time the loan was made,

as the case may be, exceeds the fair market value, at the time the repayment is received by the lender, of any repayment of the loan (other than a repayment that is excluded consideration at the particular time).

Notes: For examples of 74.4(3) calculations see VIEWS docs 2001-0063305, 2012-0449871E5.

See also Kakkar, Ghani & Volfovsky, "Corporate Attribution: Refreeze May Cause Unsolvable Corporate Attribution Problem", 18(3) *Tax for the Owner-Manager* (ctf.ca) 6-7 (July 2018); VIEWS doc 2020-0860961C6 [2020 CTF q.10] (CRA agrees).

(4) Benefit not granted to a designated person — For the purposes of subsection (2), one of the main purposes of a transfer or loan by an individual to a corporation shall not be considered to be to benefit, either directly or indirectly, a designated person in respect of the individual, where

(a) the only interest that the designated person has in the corporation is a beneficial interest in shares of the corporation held by a trust;

(b) by the terms of the trust, the designated person may not receive or otherwise obtain the use of any of the income or capital of the trust while being a designated person in respect of the individual; and

(c) the designated person has not received or otherwise obtained the use of any of the income or capital of the trust, and no deduction has been made by the trust in computing its income under subsection 104(6) or (12) in respect of amounts paid or payable to, or included in the income of, that person while being a designated person in respect of the individual.

Notes: For interpretation of 74.4(4) see VIEWS docs 2007-0254311E5 (two trusts); 2008-0267251R3 (74.4(4) applies); 2014-0549571E5 (trust with indirect interest in corp: para. (a) does not apply) [Gosselin, "Estate Freeze Plan Trips over Corporate Attribution Rules", 15(2) *Tax for the Owner-Manager* (ctf.ca) 1-2 (April 2015)]; 2014-0552321R3 (indefeasible vesting of interests in trusts does not prevent para. (b) from applying).

Related Provisions [s. 74.4]: 51(1)(e) — Exchange deemed transfer of convertible property by taxpayer to corporation; 74.5(4) — Exemption where spouses are living separate and apart; 74.5(5) — "Meaning of designated person"; 74.5(6) — Back-to-back loans and transfers; 74.5(7) — Guarantees; 74.5(9) — Transfers or loans to a trust; 74.5(11) — Artificial transactions; 82(2) — Dividends deemed received; 87(2)(j.7) — Amalgamation — continuing corporation; 212(12) — No non-resident withholding tax where income attributed; 248(25) — Meaning of "beneficial interest".

Notes [s. 74.4]: 74.4 added in 1986, effective (since 1988) for loans and transfers made after Oct. 27, 1986. For those made from Nov. 22, 1985 through Oct. 27, 1986, a different version applies (see Notes up to the 28th ed.). For earlier transfers, see repealed 74 and 75(1).

Definitions [s. 74.4]: "amount" — 248(1); "arm's length" — 251(1); "Canada" — 255; "corporation" — 248(1), *Interpretation Act* 35(1); "designated person" — 74.4(1), 74.5(5); "dividend" — 248(1); "excluded consideration" — 74.4(1); "fair market value" — see 69(1) Notes; "individual" — 248(1); "outstanding amount" — 74.4(3); "person", "prescribed" — 248(1); "prescribed rate" — Reg. 4301; "principal amount" — 248(1), (26); "property" — 248(1); "received" — 248(7); "resident in Canada" — 250; "share", "small business corporation" — 248(1); "specified individual" — 120.4(1), 248(1); "specified shareholder" — 248(1); "split income" — 120.4(1), 248(1); "substituted" — 248(5); "taxable dividend" — 89(1), 248(1); "taxation year" — 249; "trust" — 104(1), 248(1), (3).

74.5 (1) Transfers for fair market consideration — Notwithstanding any other provision of this Act, subsections 74.1(1) and (2) and section 74.2 do not apply to any income, gain or loss derived in a particular taxation year from transferred property or from property substituted therefor if

(a) at the time of the transfer the fair market value of the transferred property did not exceed the fair market value of the property received by the transferor as consideration for the transferred property;

(b) where the consideration received by the transferor included indebtedness,

(i) interest was charged on the indebtedness at a rate equal to or greater than the lesser of

(A) the prescribed rate that was in effect at the time the indebtedness was incurred, and

(B) the rate that would, having regard to all the circumstances, have been agreed on, at the time the indebtedness was incurred, between parties dealing with each other at arm's length,

(ii) the amount of interest that was payable in respect of the particular year in respect of the indebtedness was paid not later than 30 days after the end of the particular year, and

(iii) the amount of interest that was payable in respect of each taxation year preceding the particular year in respect of the indebtedness was paid not later than 30 days after the end of each such taxation year; and

(c) where the property was transferred to or for the benefit of the transferor's spouse or common-law partner, the transferor elected in the transferor's return of income under this Part for the taxation year in which the property was transferred not to have the provisions of subsection 73(1) apply.

Related Provisions: 74.5(6) — Back-to-back loans and transfers. See also at end of s. 74.5.

Notes: 74.5(1) prevents the attribution rules from applying when there is fair market value (FMV) consideration (see Notes to 69(1)), but does not have any impact on a later 85(1) rollover of the property because it does not contain a deeming rule with respect to FMV of the property: VIEWS doc 2005-0140581E5.

On the requirement in 74.5(1)(b) to pay fair-market interest by January 30, see Notes to 74.5(2), which contains the same requirement.

Note that under 74.5(1)(c), spouses who wish to use this rule must elect out of 73(1), thus paying tax on any capital gain on the transfer.

For the meaning of "derived" in opening words, see Notes to 18.1(12).

74.5(1)(c) amended by 2000 same-sex partners bill to refer to "common-law partner", effective as per Notes to 248(1)"common-law partner".

Regulations: 4301(c) (prescribed rate of interest for 74.5(1)(b)(i)(A)).

Interpretation Bulletins: IT-394R2: Preferred beneficiary election; IT-510: Transfers and loans of property made after May 22, 1985 to a related minor; IT-511R: Interspousal and certain other transfers and loans of property.

(2) Loans for value — Notwithstanding any other provision of this Act, subsections 74.1(1) and (2) and section 74.2 do not apply to any income, gain or loss derived in a particular taxation year from lent property or from property substituted therefor if

(a) interest was charged on the loan at a rate equal to or greater than the lesser of

(i) the prescribed rate that was in effect at the time the loan was made, and

(ii) the rate that would, having regard to all the circumstances, have been agreed on, at the time the loan was made, between parties dealing with each other at arm's length;

(b) the amount of interest that was payable in respect of the particular year in respect of the loan was paid not later than 30 days after the end of the particular year; and

(c) the amount of interest that was payable in respect of each taxation year preceding the particular year in respect of the loan was paid not later than 30 days after the end of each such taxation year.

Related Provisions: 74.5(7) — Guarantees. See also at end of s. 74.5.

Notes: The attribution rules do not apply if a loan is made for at least the current prescribed rate of interest (Reg. 4301(c)), and the interest is paid by January 30 each year. There is no limit to the term of such loan (e..g, made when the rate is only 1%): VIEWS doc 2013-0480271C6 [2013 STEP q.2]. Later refinancing at a lower prescribed rate might constitute a "novation", lose 74.5(2) protection and trigger the attribution rules due to 74.1(3): 2002-0143985; but refinancing after paying off the loan with appreciated securities bought with the borrowed money is OK: 2020-0860981C6 [2020 CTF q.11]. See also Notes to pre-2008 212(1)(b) re "novation"; Drache, "Non-Arm's Length Loan Renegotiation Dicey", xxxi(20) *The Canadian Taxpayer* (Carswell) 157-58 (Oct. 6, 2009); Goldberg & Didkovsky, "Refinancing Prescribed-Rate Loans", 10(3) *Canadian Tax Focus* (ctf.ca) 2-3 (Aug. 2020).

The loan strategy is particularly attractive during periods when the prescribed interest rate (Reg. 4301(c)) is 1%. However, it may not be a good strategy if one of the taxpayers is a US citizen: tinyurl.com/moody-loan-us.

Beware also the new tax on split income in 120.4: Austin del Rio, "Prescribed-Rate Loan Planning with a Trust Under the New Rules", 18(2) *Tax for the Owner-Manager* (ctf.ca) 3-5 (April 2018).

Note that paying interest within one year of incurring the debt will not suffice, as interest must be paid within 30 days of the end of the taxation year: VIEWS docs 2008-0274221I7, 2009-0330081C6. See also Cy Fien letter, 30(11) *The Canadian Taxpayer* (Carswell) 88 (May 27, 2008). In CRA's view, a loan created by unpaid interest is not payment of interest, and a later catch-up payment will not undo the failure to pay interest by January 30: May 2008 ICAA roundtable (tinyurl.com/cra-abtax), q. 8. Similarly, interest cannot be paid by promissory note in CRA's view (despite *Banner Pharmacaps*, 2003 FCA 367, paras. 6-7): 2018-0761551C6 [2018 APFF Financial q.10].

For the meaning of "derived" in opening words, see Notes to 18.1(12).

Regulations: 4301(c) (prescribed rate of interest for 74.5(2)(a)(i)).

Interpretation Bulletins: IT-394R2: Preferred beneficiary election; IT-510: Transfers and loans of property made after May 22, 1985 to a related minor; IT-511R: Interspousal and certain other transfers and loans of property.

(3) Spouses [or common-law partners] living apart — Notwithstanding subsection 74.1(1) and section 74.2, where an individual has lent or transferred property, either directly or indirectly, by means of a trust or by any other means whatever, to or for the benefit of a person who is the individual's spouse or common-law partner or who has since become the individual's spouse or common-law partner,

(a) subsection 74.1(1) does not apply to any income or loss from the property, or property substituted therefor, that relates to the period throughout which the individual is living separate and apart from that person because of a breakdown of their marriage or common-law partnership; and

(b) section 74.2 does not apply to a disposition of the property, or property substituted therefor, occurring at any time while the individual is living separate and apart from that person because of a breakdown of their marriage or common-law partnership, if an election completed jointly with that person not to have that section apply is filed with the individual's return of income under this Part for the taxation year that includes that time or for any preceding taxation year.

Notes: See Notes to 118.8 for the meaning of "living separate and apart".

The attribution rules do not apply after divorce: VIEWS doc 2012-0465711E5.

For examples of elections under 74.5(3) see VIEWS docs 2007-0234521E5, 2008-0302831E5. CRA believes that living apart due to breakdown of a common-law partnership does not require the 90-day separation period in 248(1)"common-law partner": 2012-0438021E5, 2012-0453201C6 [2012 APFF q.22].

If either spouse is resident in Quebec, an election under 74.5(3)(b) must be copied to Revenu Québec: *Taxation Act* ss. 462.16, 21.4.6.

See also Manu Kakkar, "The Attribution Rules and Living Separate and Apart", 9(3) *Tax for the Owner-Manager* (ctf.ca) 9-10 (July 2009).

74.5(3) amended by 2000 same-sex partners bill (last change effective 2001), 1991 technical bill.

Interpretation Bulletins: IT-394R2: Preferred beneficiary election; IT-434R: Rental of real property by individual; IT-511R: Interspousal and certain other transfers and loans of property.

(4) Idem — No amount shall be included in computing the income of an individual under subsection 74.4(2) in respect of a designated person in respect of the individual who is the spouse or common-law partner of the individual for any period throughout which the individual is living separate and apart from the designated person by reason of a breakdown of their marriage or common-law partnership.

Related Provisions: See at end of s. 74.5.

Notes: See Notes to 118.8 for the meaning of "living separate and apart".

74.5(4) amended by 2000 same-sex partners bill, effective as per Notes to 248(1)"common-law partner".

(5) Definition of "designated person" — For the purposes of this section, "designated person" in respect of an individual, means a person

(a) who is the spouse or common-law partner of the individual; or

(b) who is under 18 years of age and who

(i) does not deal with the individual at arm's length, or

(ii) is the niece or nephew of the individual.

Notes: For CRA interpretation see VIEWS doc 2017-0709071C6 [2017 APFF q.9].

Before RSC 1985 (5th Supp) consolidation, 74.5(5) explicitly applied for purposes of 74.3 and 74.4. Those application rules are now in 74.3(2) and 74.4(1).

74.5(5)(a) amended by 2000 same-sex partners bill to refer to "common-law partner", effective as per Notes to 248(1)"common-law partner".

Interpretation Bulletins: IT-394R2: Preferred beneficiary election; IT-511R: Interspousal and certain other transfers and loans of property.

(6) Back to back loans and transfers — Where an individual has lent or transferred property

(a) to another person and that property, or property substituted therefor, is lent or transferred by any person (in this subsection referred to as a "third party") directly or indirectly to or for the benefit of a specified person with respect to the individual, or

(b) to another person on condition that property be lent or transferred by any person (in this subsection referred to as a "third party") directly or indirectly to or for the benefit of a specified person with respect to the individual,

the following rules apply:

(c) for the purposes of sections 74.1, 74.2, 74.3 and 74.4, the property lent or transferred by the third party shall be deemed to have been lent or transferred, as the case may be, by the individual to or for the benefit of the specified person, and

(d) for the purposes of subsection (1), the consideration received by the third party for the transfer of the property shall be deemed to have been received by the individual.

Related Provisions: 74.5(8) — "Specified person". See also at end of s. 74.5.

Notes: 74.5(6) applied in *Lafontaine*, 2007 CarswellNat 492 (TCC) and *St-Pierre*, [2008] 5 C.T.C. 2706 (TCC); aff'd [2008] 5 C.T.C. 271 (FCA) (the "series of transactions" concept from 248(10) does not apply to 74.5(6)).

Interpretation Bulletins: IT-394R2: Preferred beneficiary election; IT-510: Transfers and loans of property made after May 22, 1985 to a related minor; IT-511R: Interspousal and certain other transfers and loans of property.

(7) Guarantees — Where an individual is obligated, either absolutely or contingently, to effect any undertaking including any guarantee, covenant or agreement given to ensure the repayment, in whole or in part, of a loan made by any person (in this subsection referred to as the "third party") directly or indirectly to or for the benefit of a specified person with respect to the individual or the payment, in whole or in part, of any interest payable in respect of the loan, the following rules apply:

(a) for the purposes of sections 74.1, 74.2, 74.3 and 74.4, the property lent by the third party shall be deemed to have been lent by the individual to or for the benefit of the specified person; and

(b) for the purposes of paragraphs (2)(b) and (c), the amount of interest that is paid in respect of the loan shall be deemed not to include any amount paid by the individual to the third party as interest on the loan.

Related Provisions: 74.5(8) — "Specified person". See also at end of s. 74.5.

Notes: 74.5(7) can apply to a joint spousal line of credit, so the taxpayer may be considered to have lent funds to the spouse: VIEWS doc 2009-0317041E5.

Interpretation Bulletins: IT-394R2: Preferred beneficiary election; IT-510: Transfers and loans of property made after May 22, 1985 to a related minor; IT-511R: Interspousal and certain other transfers and loans of property.

(8) Definition of "specified person" — For the purposes of subsections (6) and (7), "specified person", with respect to an individual, means

(a) a designated person in respect of the individual; or

(b) a corporation, other than a small business corporation, of which a designated person in respect of the individual would have been a specified shareholder if the definition "specified shareholder" in subsection 248(1) were read without reference to paragraphs (a) and (d) of that definition.

Interpretation Bulletins: IT-394R2: Preferred beneficiary election; IT-510: Transfers and loans of property made after May 22, 1985 to a related minor; IT-511R: Interspousal and certain other transfers and loans of property.

(9) Transfers or loans to a trust — Where a taxpayer has lent or transferred property, either directly or indirectly, by means of a trust or by any other means whatever, to a trust in which another taxpayer is beneficially interested, the taxpayer shall, for the purposes of this section and sections 74.1 to 74.4, be deemed to have lent or transferred the property, as the case may be, to or for the benefit of the other taxpayer.

Related Provisions: 74.3(1) — Transfer or loan to a trust; 248(25) — Beneficially interested.

Interpretation Bulletins: IT-394R2: Preferred beneficiary election; IT-510: Transfers and loans of property made after May 22, 1985 to a related minor; IT-511R: Interspousal and certain other transfers and loans of property.

(10) [Repealed]

Notes: 74.5(10), repealed by 1992 technical bill, defined "beneficially interested" (in a trust), for purposes of 74.1–74.5. The definition was moved to 248(25), effective 1991.

(11) Artificial transactions — Notwithstanding any other provision of this Act, sections 74.1 to 74.4 do not apply to a transfer or loan of property where it may reasonably be concluded that one of the main reasons for the transfer or loan was to reduce the amount of tax that would, but for this subsection, be payable under this Part on the income and gains derived from the property or from property substituted therefor.

Notes: 74.5(11) prevents "reverse attribution" — using the attribution rules backwards with the intent of having them apply to reduce tax. In *Lipson*, 2009 SCC 1, 6 of 7 judges held that 74.5(11) did not apply to a scheme that did this because the Crown had conceded that it did not apply (4 ruled that GAAR applied instead); Rothstein J. ruled that 74.5(11) "was engaged by operation of law" (para. 120).

74.5(11) applied in *Mady*, 2017 TCC 112, paras. 105-121 (shares in dentist's professional corp transferred from a trust to his wife first, then him, so dividends would be attributed to her). See Nancy Lum, "Reverse Attribution and LCGE", 7(4) *Canadian Tax Focus* (ctf.ca) 9 (Nov. 2017).

74.5(11) did not apply in *Swirsky*, 2013 TCC 73 (aff'd on other grounds 2014 FCA 36), but only because the onus of proof was reversed since 74.5(11) was first raised in the Crown's Reply.

For the meaning of "one of the main reasons" see Notes to 83(2.1). For the meaning of "derived" see Notes to 18.1(12).

See also VIEWS doc 2014-0519661E5 (74.5(11) may apply where professional's spouse transfers shares of professional corporation to him, supposedly to meet regulatory requirements but really as part of a scheme to split income).

Interpretation Bulletins: IT-394R2: Preferred beneficiary election; IT-510: Transfers and loans of property made after May 22, 1985 to a related minor; IT-511R: Interspousal and certain other transfers and loans of property.

(12) Where sections 74.1 to 74.3 do not apply — Sections 74.1, 74.2 and 74.3 do not apply in respect of a transfer by an individual of property

(a) as a payment of a premium under a registered retirement savings plan under which the individual's spouse or common-law partner is, immediately after the transfer, the annuitant (within the meaning of subsection 146(1)) to the extent that the premium is deductible in computing the income of the individual for a taxation year;

(a.1) [Repealed]

(a.2) as a payment of a contribution under a registered disability savings plan;

(b) as or on account of an amount paid by the individual to another individual who is the individual's spouse or common-law partner or a person who was under 18 years of age in a taxation year and who

(i) does not deal with the individual at arm's length, or

(ii) is the niece or nephew of the individual,

that is deductible in computing the individual's income for the year and is required to be included in computing the income of the other individual; or

(c) to the individual's spouse or common-law partner,

(i) while the property, or property substituted for it, is held under a TFSA of which the spouse or common-law partner is the holder, and

(ii) to the extent that the spouse or common-law partner does not, at the time of the contribution of the property under the TFSA, have an excess TFSA amount (as defined in subsection 207.01(1)).

Related Provisions: 146(5.1) — Amount of spousal RRSP premiums deductible; 146(8.3) — Attribution on spousal RRSP payments if withdrawn soon; 146(21.1) — Contribution to Saskatchewan Pension Plan deemed to be RRSP premium for purposes of 74.5(12)(a).

Notes: For interpretation of 74.5(12)(c) see VIEWS doc 2008-0301491I7. Although 74.5(12)(c) prevents attribution of income from a TFSA, it does not prevent future attribution if funds are transferred to a spouse's TFSA and then withdrawn by the spouse: 2010-0354491E5.

74.5(12)(a.1) repealed by 2011 budget bill #2, effective for transfers made after 2010. Saskatchewan Pension Plan income is now treated as RRSP income for purposes of 74.5(12): see 146(21.1).

74.5(12) earlier amended by 2008 budget bill #1 (for 2009 and later years), 2007 RDSPs bill, 2001 technical bill.

Interpretation Bulletins [subsec. 74.5(12)]: IT-394R2: Preferred beneficiary election; IT-510: Transfers and loans of property made after May 22, 1985 to a related minor; IT-511R: Interspousal and certain other transfers and loans of property.

(13) Exception from attribution rules [tax on split income] — Subsections 74.1(1) and (2), 74.3(1) and 75(2) of this Act and section 74 of the *Income Tax Act*, chapter 148 of the Revised Statutes of Canada, 1952, do not apply to any amount that is included in computing a specified individual's split income for a taxation year.

Notes: 74.5(13) added by 1999 Budget, for 2000 and later tax years. It provides that the attribution rules do not apply to "split income" taxed at a high rate under 120.4.

Related Provisions [s. 74.5]: 51(1)(c) — Exchange deemed transfer of convertible property by taxpayer to corporation; 87(2)(j.7) — Amalgamation — continuing corporation; 248(5) — Substituted property.

Notes [s. 74.5]: 74.5 added by 1985 Budget, effective for transfers of property after May 22, 1985 and (after 1987) for all loans.

Definitions [s. 74.5]: "amount" — 248(1); "arm's length" — 251(1); "beneficially interested" — 248(25); "capital gain" — 39(1)(a), 248(1); "common-law partner", "common-law partnership" — 248(1); "corporation" — 248(1), *Interpretation Act* 35(1); "designated person" — 74.5(5); "fair market value" — see 69(1) Notes; "individual" — 248(1); "nephew", "niece" — 252(2)(g); "person", "prescribed" — 248(1); "prescribed rate" — Reg. 4301; "property" — 248(1); "registered disability savings plan" — 146.4(1), 248(1); "registered retirement savings plan" — 146(1), 248(1); "shareholder", "small business corporation" — 248(1); "specified individual" — 120.4(1), 248(1); "specified person" — 74.5(8); "specified shareholder" — 248(1); "split income" — 120.4(1), 248(1); "substituted" — 248(5); "TFSA" — 146.2(5), 248(1); "taxable dividend" — 89(1), 248(1); "taxation year" — 249; "taxpayer" — 248(1); "trust" — 104(1), 248(1), (3).

75. (1) [Repealed under former Act]

Notes: 75(1), "Transfers to minors", repealed by 1985 Budget (on the introduction of new attribution rules in 74.1-74.5), for property transfers after May 22, 1985. See now 74.1(2). For earlier transfers, it is reproduced in PITA 1st-38th ed.

(2) Trusts [revocable or reversionary] — If a trust, that is resident in Canada and that was created in any manner whatever since 1934, holds property on condition

(a) that it or property substituted therefor may

(i) revert to the person from whom the property or property for which it was substituted was directly or indirectly received (in this subsection referred to as "the person"), or

(ii) pass to persons to be determined by the person at a time subsequent to the creation of the trust, or

(b) that, during the existence of the person, the property shall not be disposed of except with the person's consent or in accordance with the person's direction,

any income or loss from the property or from property substituted for the property, and any taxable capital gain or allowable capital loss from the disposition of the property or of property substituted for the property, shall, during the existence of the person while the person is resident in Canada, be deemed to be income or a loss, as the case may be, or a taxable capital gain or allowable capital loss, as the case may be, of the person.

Related Provisions: 56(4.1) — Interest free or low interest loans; 73(1) — Rollover of capital property to revocable living trust; 74.2(2) — Deemed gain or loss; 74.5(13) — No attribution of split income subject to income-splitting tax; 75(3) — Exceptions; 82(2) — Dividends deemed received; 94(4)(h) — Deeming non-resident trust to be resident in Canada does not apply to 75(2); 94(8.1), (8.2) — Application to non-resident trust; 107(4.1) — Denial of 107(2) rollover; 107.4(1)(e) — No qualifying disposition where settlor can change beneficiaries of trust; 135.2(3)(d) — No application to Cdn Wheat Board Farmers' Trust; 160(1) — Tax liability — non-arm's length property transfer; 212(12) — Deemed payments to spouse, etc; 248(5) — Substituted property; 256(1.2)(f)(iv) — Associated corporations — where shares owned by 75(2) trust.

Notes: 75(2) is an attribution rule (see also Notes to 74.1(1)) that applies to a "reversionary" or "revocable" trust (75(2)(a)), and attributes the income from the property back to the settlor (so it is not income of the trust: IT-369R para. 10; *Fiducie Financière Satoma*, 2018 FCA 74, para. 36) (leave to appeal denied 2019 CarswellNat 898 (SCC)). When 75(2) applies, 107(4.1) generally prevents a rollout of trust property to beneficiaries other than the settlor or spouse.

75(2) does not apply to a person who sells property to a trust at fair market value: *Sommerer*, 2012 FCA 207; *Brent Kern Family Trust*, 2014 CarswellNat 4166 (FCA) (leave to appeal denied 2015 CarswellNat 854 (SCC)). The CRA accepts *Sommerer*, with some qualifications: VIEWS docs 2013-0480351C6 [2013 STEP q.9], 2013-0495721C6 [2013 APFF q.7]. In *Pallen Trust*, 2015 BCCA 222, rescission was granted of dividends that were expected to be attributed by 75(2) but were not because of *Sommerer*. Due to *Fairmont Hotels* (see 169(1) Notes under Rectification), rescission was no longer expected to be granted in such a case, but surprisingly *was* granted in *Collins Family Trust*, 2019 BCSC 1030, aff'd 2020 BCCA 196 (leave to appeal granted to Crown March 25/21, file 39383), on essentially the same facts as *Pallen*.

75(2) applies only to income or loss from property, not from business (including through a limited partnership): VIEWS docs 2013-0476871E5, 2013-050884117. For the distinction see Notes to 9(1) under "Business income vs property income". It does not apply to "secondary" income earned on income that was attributed to the contributor. It applies only while the contributor is still alive and resident in Canada.

Avoidance of 75(2) may trigger GAAR, but the specific anti-avoidance rule in 74.5(11) does not apply to 75(2).

75(2) did not apply to a unit trust in *Fraser*, [1991] 1 C.T.C. 314 (FCTD): "75(2) anticipates a situation in which the whole corpus of the trust is capable of reverting to the settlor (75(2)(a)) or where the corpus during the life of the trust remains under the control of the settlor (75(2)(b))".

In *Garron*, 2009 TCC 450 (aff'd on other grounds as *St. Michael Trust*, 2010 FCA 309, aff'd as *Fundy Settlement*, 2012 SCC 14), the TCC held that 75(2) did not apply to Barbados trusts used to realize capital gains on shares, because "was directly or indirectly received" applied only to the manner in which a transfer was effected, and not to indirect shareholdings through holding companies. However, the FCA, though it did not discuss 75(2), held that similar language in former 94(1) did apply. The TCC also held that the exemption for capital gains in Canada-Barbados treaty Art. XIV took precedence over 75(2). For more on "indirectly" see Notes to 17.1(1).

In *Labow*, 2011 FCA 305, para. 35, an offshore group sickness insurance trust for specific employees fell under 75(2) because it provided that residual amounts reverted to the employer, and did not fall under 75(3)(b) because it was not really intended to provide employment benefits.

In *Sommerer*, 2011 TCC 212 the TCC held that an Austrian Privatstiftung (foundation) was not a trust, but a trustee of a trust. The FCA (2012 FCA 207) doubted this was correct (para. 43), but did not resolve the issue.

Note that there is no exception to 75(2) where the settlor's right to acquire is at fair market value: VIEWS doc 5M08340 [1994 APFF], q.24.

Rectification of a trust deed to avoid 75(2) was allowed in *McPeake*, 2012 BCSC 132 [though due to *Sommerer* it was not needed: *McPeake v. Cadesky*, 2018 ONCA 554], and denied in *Kanji*, 2013 ONSC 781. (See Notes to 169(1) re rectification; due to *Fairmont Hotels* these would no longer be granted.)

For discussion of 75(2) see Roth et al., *Canadian Taxation of Trusts* (ctf.ca, 2016), pp. 423-95; Saunders, "Inter Vivos Discretionary Family Trusts", 1993 Cdn Tax Foundation conference report, 37:6-14; Crockett, "Subsection 75(2)", 53(3) *Canadian Tax Journal* 806-30 (2005); Spenceley, "Reversionary Trust Review", 131 *The Estate Planner* (CCH) 1-7 (Dec. 2005); Blom, "Subsection 75(2) and Corporate Beneficiaries of a Trust", 4(5) *Tax Hyperion [TH]* (Carswell, May 2007); Newcombe, "What are the Filing Requirements if Subsection 75(2) Applies to a Trust?", 5(10) *TH* (Oct. 2008); Louis, "Is a Family Trust Vulnerable to the CRA?", 186 *The Estate Planner* 1-3 (July 2010); Roth & Youdan, "Subsection 75(2): Is the CRA's Interpretation Appropriate?", 2010 conference report, 34:1-57; Léger & Gombita, "Family Trusts and the Reversionary Rules", 12(1) *Tax for the Owner-Manager* (ctf.ca) 7-9 (Jan. 2012); Brown, "The Strange Case of Subsection 75(2)", 4(3) *Personal Tax and Estate Planning* (Federated Press) 192-96 (2013); Thompson, "Revisiting the Attribution Rules", 2013 BC Tax Conf. (ctf.ca), 12:1-24; Bernstein & Atsaidis, "Subsection 75(2) and the 21-Year Rule", 23(1) *Canadian Tax Highlights* (ctf.ca) 4-5 (Oct. 2015); Ideias, "Subsection 75(2): What a Tax Planner Needs to Know" (*Taxnet Pro* Tax & Estate Planning Centre, 2021, 10pp; includes table summarizing all CRA interpretations)..

In *Howson*, 2006 TCC 644, funds deposited to a family trust were held to be a loan, so 75(2) did not apply since a loan is "not subject to reversion by the terms of the Trust. It returns to the lender by operation of the loan itself" (para. 15). See Stacey, "Lending to Trusts", 15(1) *Canadian Tax Highlights* (ctf.ca) 1-2 (Jan. 2007). The CRA accepts this concept: VIEWS docs 2007-0240421C6, 2008-0300401E5, 2009-0330251C6.

In *Ho*, 2010 TCC 325, a 91(1) FAPI inclusion imputed to a beneficiary under 75(2) was not a "transaction" to extend the 152(4)(b)(iii) reassessment deadline, but this was overruled by 152(4)(b)(iii)(B), added in 2018.

Deliberate use of 75(2) and 104(19) to attribute a dividend to a corporation that paid no tax on it triggered GAAR (245(2)): *Fiducie Financière Satoma*, 2018 FCA 74 (leave to appeal denied 2019 CarswellNat 898 (SCC)).

CRA will challenge dividend-stripping schemes that attempt to use 75(2) to avoid tax: VIEWS doc 2011-0401951C6.

For CRA views that 75(2) may apply, see docs 9407905 (settlor can replace trustees); 1999-0013055 (settlor is sole trustee); 2000-0023997 (settlor's letter of wishes may effectively be binding on trustees); 2002-0162855 (trust indenture gives settlor's spouse power to appoint capital beneficiary); 2004-0080731I7 (non-resident trust deemed resident in Canada and trustees have discretion); 2004-0086941C6 (freeze shares acquired by trust for nominal FMV and settlor is a beneficiary); 2005-0126261R3 (property can revert on termination of trust); 2005-0127351E5 (75(2) does not require a "loan" or "transfer"); 2005-0140951C6 (corporation is beneficiary of trust that holds shares in the corporation); 2006-0185571C6 (loan of income-producing property); 2006-0185671C6 (attribution of FAPI under 75(2); "revert" has its ordinary meaning, not legal meaning); 2008-0268121E5 (loan to trust falls within *Howson*); 2008-0292061E5 (settlor is co-trustee — question of fact); 2008-0301241E5 (application to unit trust in Quebec); 2009-0352711E5 (settlor can become a beneficiary by marrying a named person); 2010-036630117 (transfer of growth shares to trust with price adjustment clause; may now be overridden by *Sommerer*); 2010-0372531E5, 2011-0391831R3 and 2014-052851117 (First Nations land claim settlement trusts, but 75(2) does not apply to secondary income); 2011-0428661E5 (funds payable to child are left in the trust and reinvested); 2013-049921117 (particular trust transaction); 2016-066988117 (settlor was 1 of 2 trustees with power to remove the other); 2017-071802117 (TFSA that loses its status because it borrows money; but 75(2) does not apply to second-generation income).

For CRA views that 75(2) does not apply, see docs 2001-0067955 (transfer from 75(2) trust to second trust); 2002-0118255 (settlor has right to live in building bought by trust; and effect of renouncing right to reacquire); 2002-0123843 (trustees are directors of corporation that settles trust); 2002-0139205 (transfer of spouse trust assets after spouse's death); 2003-0050671E5 (settlor is trustee but cannot add beneficiaries, but 75(2) applies if settlor's spouse has power to appoint settlor as capital beneficiary); 2004-0086921C6 (settlor is co-trustee without control); 2004-0086951C6 (settlor's spouse has power to allocate among beneficiaries but cannot add settlor); 2006-0191431R3 (merging of 3 identical family trusts); 2006-0218501E5 and 2009-0317641E5 (company issues shares to a trust of which it can become a beneficiary); 2006-0185571C6 (loan of cash); 2007-0243241C6 and 2010-038855117 (where trust buys shares of corporate beneficiary for FMV); 2011-042434117 (technical analysis of particular Quebec trust); 2013-048165117; 2013-0500711E5 (executor E transferring estate property, under the will, to family trust of which E is a beneficiary); 2015-0610391R3 (ruling on specific trust).

For more CRA interpretation see docs 2006-0196231C6, 2014-0523001C6 [2014 STEP q.5] (using 75(2) intentionally may trigger GAAR); 2006-0201361R3 and 2008-0282491R3 (75(2) attributes income to tax-exempt Indian bands); 2006-0216491E5 and 2008-0278801C6 q.4 (CCA limitations on rental property when 75(2) applies); 2007-0233701C6 (no foreign tax credit on trust's foreign income attributed under 75(2)); 2007-0239951E5 (rental property transferred to trust; whether Reg. 1100(11) applies); 2011-0401831C6 (rollout from 75(2) trust to avoid 21-year rule); 2012-0453591C6 (what constitutes a genuine loan to a trust); 2012-0453891C6 (price adjustment clause will be considered in determining whether 75(2) applies); 2014-0538241C6 [2014 APFF q.5] (attributed income retains its nature, so rental income qualifies as RRSP earned income; interaction with 40(3.6)); 2014-0560361E5 (treatment of US revocable living trust); 2018-0744161C6 [STEP 2018 q.13] (*alter ego* trust with foreign dividends — foreign tax credit); 2018-0748341C6 [STEP 2018 q.11] (*alter ego* trust and post-1971 spousal trust).

See also Notes to 150(1)(c) re a trust whose income is attributed elsewhere by 75(2) needing to file a T3 return.

75(2) opening words amended by 2013 budget bill #2, for taxation years ending after March 20, 2013, to be limited to trusts resident in Canada (see now 94(8.1)–(8.2) for non-resident trusts).

75(2) amended by 2001 technical bill, effective for years that begin after 2000.

Income Tax Folios: S4-F3-C1: Price adjustment clauses [replaces IT-169]; S6-F1-C1: Residence of a trust or estate [replaces IT-447].

Interpretation Bulletins: IT-325R2: Property transfers after separation, divorce and annulment; IT-394R2: Preferred beneficiary election; IT-369R: Attribution of trust income to settlor; IT-531: Eligible funeral arrangements.

I.T. Technical News: 7 (revocable living trusts; protective trusts).

CRA Audit Manual: 15.7.13: Application of attribution rules to trusts.

(3) Exceptions — Subsection (2) does not apply to property held in a taxation year

(a) by a trust governed by a deferred profit sharing plan, an employee benefit plan, an employees profit sharing plan, a pooled registered pension plan, a registered disability savings plan, a registered education savings plan, a registered pension plan, a registered retirement income fund, a registered retirement savings plan, a registered supplementary unemployment benefit plan, a retirement compensation arrangement or a TFSA;

(b) by an employee life and health trust, an employee trust, a private foundation that is a registered charity, a related segregated fund trust (within the meaning assigned by paragraph 138.1(1)(a)), a trust described by paragraph (a.1) of the definition "trust" in subsection 108(1), or a trust described by paragraph 149(1)(y);

(c) by a qualifying environmental trust; or

(d) by a trust if

(i) the trust acquired the property, or other property for which the property is a substitute, from a particular individual,

(ii) the particular individual acquired the property or the other property, as the case may be, in respect of another individual as a consequence of the operation of subsection 122.61(1) or under section 4 of the *Universal Child Care Benefit Act*, and

(iii) the trust has no "beneficiaries" (as defined in subsection 108(1)) who may for any reason receive directly from the trust any of the income or capital of the trust other than individuals in respect of whom the particular individual acquired property as a consequence of the operation of a provision described in subparagraph (ii).

Notes: 75(3) does not apply to a charitable trust. It may not apply to a non-resident health and welfare trust: VIEWS doc 2004-0057511I7. See also Notes to 75(2).

75(3)(a): If a TFSA loses its status, 75(2) applies: VIEWS doc 2017-0718021I7.

75(3)(d) can prevent attribution under 75(2) from applying to Canada Child Benefit (former Child Tax Benefit) payments (122.61), as well as to pre-July 2016 UCCB payments (see Notes to 56(6)).

75(3)(d) changed from "by a prescribed trust" [no trusts had been prescribed] by 2017 budget bill #2, for taxation years ending after Sept. 15, 2016.

75(3)(c)-(c.3) replaced with (c) by 2013 budget bill #2, for taxation years ending after March 20, 2013. References to non-resident trusts were deleted because amended 75(2) no longer applies to them (see now 94(8.1)–(8.2)). For CRA policy on 75(3)(c.2) while it was pending, see VIEWS docs 2007-0233811C6, 2007-0259271E5. It applied to a US revocable trust that is an immigration trust: 2012-0442891C6.

75(3) earlier amended by 2002-2013 technical bill (last change effective for tax years that begin after Oct. 2011), 2012 and 2010 budget bills #2, 2008 budget bill #1, 2007 RDSPs bill, 2001 technical bill, 1994 Budget.

Definitions [s. 75]: "allowable capital loss" — 38(b), 248(1); "beneficiary" — 248(25) [Notes]; "Canada" — 255; "capital gain", "capital loss" — 39(1), 248(1); "contributor" — 94(1); "deferred profit sharing plan" — 147(1), 248(1); "employee benefit plan" — 248(1); "employee life and health trust" — 144.1(2), 248(1); "employee trust" — 248(1); "employees profit sharing plan" — 144(1), 248(1); "individual", "non-resident", "person" — 248(1); "private foundation" — 149.1(1), 248(1); "property" — 248(1); qualifying environmental trust" — 211.6(1), 248(1); "registered charity" — 248(1); "registered disability savings plan" — 146.4(1), 248(1); "registered education savings plan" — 146.1(1), 248(1); "registered pension plan" — 248(1); "registered retirement income fund" — 146.3(1), 248(1); "registered retirement savings plan" — 146(1), 248(1); "registered supplementary unemployment benefit plan" — 145(1), 248(1); "related segregated fund trust" — 138.1(1)(a); "resident contributor" — 94(1); "resident in Canada" — 94(3)(a), 250; "retirement compensation arrangement" — 248(1); "substituted" — 248(5); "TFSA" — 146.2(5), 248(1); "taxable capital gain" — 38(a), 248(1); "taxation year" — 249; "taxpayer" — 248(1); "trust" — 104(1), 248(1), (3).

Interpretation Bulletins [s. 75]: IT-268R3: *Inter vivos* transfer of farm property to child; IT-369R: Attribution of trust income to settlor.

75.1 (1) Gain or loss deemed that of transferor — Where

(a) subsection 73(3) or (4) applied to the transfer of property (in this subsection referred to as "transferred property") by a taxpayer to a child of the taxpayer,

(b) the transfer was made at less than the fair market value of the transferred property immediately before the time of the transfer, and

(c) in a taxation year, the transferee disposed of the transferred property and did not, before the end of that year, attain the age of 18 years,

the following rules apply:

(d) the amount, if any, by which

(i) the total of the transferee's taxable capital gains for the year from dispositions of transferred property

exceeds

(ii) the total of the transferee's allowable capital losses for the year from dispositions of transferred property,

shall, during the lifetime of the transferor while the transferor is resident in Canada, be deemed to be a taxable capital gain of the transferor for the year from the disposition of property,

(e) the amount, if any, by which the total determined under subparagraph (d)(ii) exceeds the total determined under subparagraph (d)(i) shall, during the lifetime of the transferor while the transferor is resident in Canada, be deemed to be an allowable capital loss of the transferor for the year from the disposition of property, and

(f) any taxable capital gain or allowable capital loss taken into account in computing an amount described in paragraph (d) or the amount described in paragraph (e) shall, except for the purposes of those paragraphs, to the extent that the amount so described is deemed by virtue of this subsection to be a taxable capital gain or an allowable capital loss of the transferor, be deemed not to be a taxable capital gain or an allowable capital loss, as the case may be, of the transferee.

Related Provisions: 74.2(2) — Deemed gain or loss.

Notes: 75.1(1)(a) amended by 1991 technical bill, effective for property transferred after 1989, to add reference to 73(4).

(2) Definition of "child" — For the purposes of this section, "child" of a taxpayer includes a child of the taxpayer's child and a child of the taxpayer's child's child.

Related Provisions: 70(10) — Parallel definition for other purposes; 252(1) — Further extended meaning of "child".

Definitions [s. 75.1]: "allowable capital loss" — 38(b), 248(1); "amount" — 248(1); "Canada" — 255; "child" — 75.1(2), 252(1); "fair market value" — see 69(1) Notes; "property" — 248(1); "resident in Canada" — 250; "taxable capital gain" — 38(a), 248(1); "taxation year" — 249; "taxpayer" — 248(1); "transferred property" — 75.1(1)(a).

Interpretation Bulletins [s. 75.1]: IT-268R4: *Inter vivos* transfer of farm property to child.

75.2 Rules applicable with respect to "qualifying trust annuity" — If an amount paid to acquire a qualifying trust annuity with respect to a taxpayer was deductible under paragraph 60(l) in computing the taxpayer's income,

(a) any amount that is paid out of or under the annuity at any particular time after 2005 and before the death of the taxpayer is deemed to have been received out of or under the annuity at the particular time by the taxpayer, and not to have been received by any other taxpayer; and

(b) if the taxpayer dies after 2005

(i) an amount equal to the fair market value of the annuity at the time of the taxpayer's death is deemed to have been received, immediately before the taxpayer's death, by the taxpayer out of or under the annuity, and

(ii) for the purpose of subsection 70(5), the annuity is to be disregarded in determining the fair market value (immediately before the taxpayer's death) of the taxpayer's interest in the trust that is the annuitant under the annuity.

Related Provisions: 60.011(2) — Qualifying trust annuity; 160.2(2.1), (2.2) — Joint and several liability for tax under 75.2.

Notes: See Notes to 60.011. 75.2 provides attribution rules for a "qualifying trust annuity" (QTA) with respect to a taxpayer (see 60.011(2)), the purchase price of which is deductible by the taxpayer under 60(l). The annuitant of a QTA is a qualifying trust of which the taxpayer is a beneficiary.

75.2(a) deems any amount paid from a QTA before the taxpayer's death to have been received by the taxpayer; this amount is taxed by 56(1)(d.2) in that year, as would be the case if the taxpayer were the annuitant. 75.2(a) also deems the amount not to have been received by any other taxpayer, thus ensuring that the amount, although payable to the trust that is the annuitant under the QTA, is disregarded in determining the trust's income for tax purposes.

75.2(b) contains special provisions that apply on the death of a taxpayer who was entitled to a deduction under 60(l) for the purchase price of a QTA. 75.2(b)(i) deems the taxpayer to have received the full value of the annuity immediately before death; this amount is included in the deceased's income by 56(1)(d.2).

75.2(b)(ii) provides for the QTA to be disregarded in determining, for 70(5), the fair market value (FMV) of the taxpayer's interest in the trust that is the annuitant under the QTA. 70(5) deems a deceased taxpayer to have disposed of each capital property they owned for FMV proceeds. To the extent 70(5) deems a taxpayer who dies to have disposed of an interest in a trust that is the annuitant under a QTA, 75.2(b)(ii) avoids double tax, by disregarding the QTA in determining the value of the taxpayer's interest in the trust.

75.2 added by 2002-2013 technical bill (Part 5 — technical), effective 2006.

Definitions [s. 75.2]: "amount" — 248(1); "fair market value" — see 69(1) Notes; "qualifying trust annuity" — 60.011(2), 248(1); "taxpayer" — 248(1); "trust" — 104(1), 248(1), (3).

76. (1) Security in satisfaction of income debt — Where a person receives a security or other right or a certificate of indebtedness or other evidence of indebtedness wholly or partially as payment of, in lieu of payment of or in satisfaction of, a debt that is then payable, the amount of which debt would be included in computing the person's income if it were paid, the value of the security, right or indebtedness or the applicable portion thereof shall, notwithstanding the form or legal effect of the transaction, be included in computing the person's income for the taxation year in which it is received.

Related Provisions: 214(4) — Non-resident — securities.

Notes: 76(1) can apply to a security received as absolute payment for a debt if the debt would be included in income when paid (e.g. for a farmer using the cash method): VIEWS doc 2004-0073061I7. On amalgamation of two farming corps, see 2011-0429071E5.

Advance Tax Rulings: ATR-6: Vendor reacquires business assets following default by purchaser.

(2) Idem — Where a security or other right or a certificate of indebtedness or other evidence of indebtedness is received by a person wholly or partially as payment of, in lieu of payment of or in satisfaction of, a debt before the debt is payable, but is not itself payable or redeemable before the day on which the debt is payable, it shall, for the purpose of subsection (1), be deemed to be received by the person holding it at that time when the debt becomes payable.

Interpretation Bulletins: IT-77R: Securities in satisfaction of an income debt (cancelled).

(3) Section enacted for greater certainty — This section is enacted for greater certainty and shall not be construed as limiting the generality of the other provisions of this Part by which amounts are required to be included in computing income.

(4) [Grain] Debt deemed not to be income debt — Where a cash purchase ticket or other form of settlement prescribed pursuant to the *Canada Grain Act* or by the Minister is issued to a taxpayer in respect of grain delivered in a taxation year of a taxpayer to a primary elevator or process elevator and the ticket or other form of settlement entitles the holder thereof to payment by the operator of the elevator of the purchase price, without interest, stated in the ticket for the grain at a date that is after the end of that taxation year, the amount of the purchase price stated in the ticket or other form of settlement shall, notwithstanding any other provision of this section, be included in computing the income of the taxpayer to whom the ticket or other form of settlement was issued for the taxpayer's taxation year immediately following the taxation year in which the grain was delivered and not for the taxation year in which the grain was delivered.

Related Provisions: 76(5) — Meaning of certain expressions; 135.2 — Effect of privatization of Canadian Wheat Board.

Notes: When farmer F delivers a listed grain (wheat, oats, barley, rye, flaxseed, rapeseed or canola) to operator O of a licensed elevator, O may issue a cash purchase ticket (CPT) or other prescribed form of payment to F. If the CPT is payable in the next year (a "deferred CPT"), F includes the CPT amount in income in that next year. See Kiefer & Miazga, "Section 76 and the Taxation of Cash Purchase Tickets", 18(4) *Tax for the Owner-Manager* (ctf.ca) 4-5 (Oct. 2018).

The March 2017 Budget launched a consultation on possibly eliminating the 76(4) deferral. Finance announced on Nov. 6, 2017 that it will maintain the current rules.

In *Dixon*, 2003 TCC 102, the taxpayers were not taxed on proceeds of grain sales tickets realized through a partnership, as it was not a "taxpayer" for 76(4) [this might be wrong but was not appealed].

CPTs under 76(4) are not inventory for purposes of the 28(1)(b) and (c) inventory adjustments: VIEWS doc 2010-0381741E5.

See also Notes to 76(1).

Interpretation Bulletins: IT-184R: Deferred cash purchase tickets issued for grain.

CRA Audit Manual: 27.12.4: Farming and fishing income — income tax implications — deferred cash purchase tickets.

(5) Definitions of certain expressions — In subsection (4), the expressions **"cash purchase ticket"**, **"operator"**, **"primary elevator"** and **"process elevator"** have the meanings assigned by the *Canada Grain Act*, and **"grain"** means wheat, oats, barley, rye, flaxseed, rapeseed and canola produced in Canada.

Related Provisions: 24 — Ceasing to carry on business; 214(4) — Non-resident's tax on securities income.

Notes: 76(5) amended by 2012 budget bill #1, for cash purchase tickets and other forms of settlement issued after Dec. 14, 2011, to change "rapeseed produced in the designated area defined by the *Canadian Wheat Board Act*" to "rapeseed and canola produced in Canada" (consequential on the *Marketing Freedom for Grain Farmers Act*; see Notes to 135.2).

Definitions [s. 76]: "amount" — 248(1); "cash purchase ticket", "grain" — 76(5); "Minister" — 248(1); "operator" — 76(5); "person" — 248(1); "primary elevator", "process elevator" — 76(5); "taxpayer" — 248(1); "taxation year" — 249.

76.1 (1) Non-resident moving debt from Canadian business — If at any time a debt obligation of a non-resident taxpayer that is denominated in a foreign currency ceases to be an obligation of the taxpayer in respect of a business or part of a business carried on by the taxpayer in Canada immediately before that time (other than an obligation in respect of which the taxpayer ceased to be indebted at that time), for the purpose of determining the amount of any income, loss, capital gain or capital loss due to the fluctuation in the value of the foreign currency relative to Canadian currency, the taxpayer is deemed to have settled the debt obligation immediately before that time at the amount outstanding on account of its principal amount.

(2) Non-resident assuming debt — If at any time a debt obligation of a non-resident taxpayer that is denominated in a foreign currency becomes an obligation of the taxpayer in respect of a business or part of a business that the taxpayer carries on in Canada after that time (other than an obligation in respect of which the taxpayer became indebted at that time), the amount of any income, loss, capital gain or capital loss in respect of the obligation due to the fluctuation in the value of the foreign currency relative to Canadian currency shall be determined based on the amount of the obligation in Canadian currency at that time.

Related Provisions: 261 — Functional currency reporting.

Notes: 76.1 does not apply to a "loan" between a Canadian branch and its US head office, since they are the same person: VIEWS doc 2010-038357117.

76.1 added by 2001 technical bill, effective June 28, 1999 for an authorized foreign bank, and August 9, 2000 in any other case.

Definitions [s. 76.1]: "amount", "business" — 248(1); "Canada" — 255, *Interpretation Act* 35(1); "Canadian currency" — 261(5)(f)(i); "capital gain" — 39(1)(a), 248(1); "capital loss" — 39(1)(b), 248(1); "foreign currency", "non-resident", "principal amount" — 248(1); "resident in Canada" — 94(3)(a), 250; "taxpayer" — 248(1).

Interpretation Bulletins [s. 76.1]: IT-77R: Securities in satisfaction of an income debt.

77. [Repealed]

Notes: 77, "Bond conversion", repealed by 1994 technical bill, effective for exchanges occurring after October 1994. See now 51.1 instead.

78. (1) Unpaid amounts — Where an amount in respect of a deductible outlay or expense that was owing by a taxpayer to a person with whom the taxpayer was not dealing at arm's length at the time the outlay or expense was incurred and at the end of the second taxation year following the taxation year in which the outlay or expense was incurred, is unpaid at the end of that second taxation year, either

(a) the amount so unpaid shall be included in computing the taxpayer's income for the third taxation year following the taxation year in which the outlay or expense was incurred, or

(b) where the taxpayer and that person have filed an agreement in prescribed form on or before the day on or before which the taxpayer is required by section 150 to file the taxpayer's return of income for the third succeeding taxation year, for the purposes of this Act the following rules apply:

(i) the amount so unpaid shall be deemed to have been paid by the taxpayer and received by that person on the first day of that third taxation year, and section 153, except subsection 153(3), is applicable to the extent that it would apply if that amount were being paid to that person by the taxpayer, and

(ii) that person shall be deemed to have made a loan to the taxpayer on the first day of that third taxation year in an amount equal to the amount so unpaid minus the amount, if any, deducted or withheld therefrom by the taxpayer on account of that person's tax for that third taxation year.

Related Provisions: 12(1)(b) — Income inclusion for certain amounts not received until after end of year; 78(3) — Late filing; 78(4), (5) — Unpaid remuneration; 80(1)"excluded obligation"(c) — Obligation not subject to debt forgiveness rules; 127(26) — Parallel rule for unpaid amounts re investment tax credit; 248(1)"salary deferral arrangement"(k) — No SDA where bonus paid within 3 years.

Notes: 78(1) provides that an expense deducted on the accrual basis in year 1, and still unpaid to a non-arm's length person at the end of year 3, must be reincluded in income in year 4, unless the parties file an agreement to treat it as paid and loaned back (if this is filed late, see 78(3)). The non-arm's length test must be met both when the expense is incurred and at the end of year 3: IT-109R2 para. 1(b). (If the amount is salary or bonus, see 78(4) instead.)

CRA will generally not apply 78(1) if both taxpayers use the accrual basis: IT-109R2 para. 15(a); VIEWS doc 2011-0401241I7 (but did apply it in *Redclay Holdings*, [1996] 2 C.T.C. 2347 (TCC), despite this policy). 78(1) does not apply to inventory or capital property: IT-109R2 para. 3(c), or to capitalized loan interest: doc 9520115.

CRA does not consider that "deductible outlay or expense" includes an amount payable by a trust to a beneficiary: VIEWS doc 2012-0449791C6.

See also docs 2002-0170145 (78(1) does not apply to an amount forgiven under s. 80, since it is not "unpaid"); 2009-0339191E5, 2010-0366521C6 and 2010-0366531C6 (application of 78(1)(b) to LLC or ULC where Canada-US tax treaty Art. IV:6 or 7 applies); 2010-0374881E5 (timing of deemed interest under 78(1)(b) for non-resident withholding tax); 2011-040124117 (income inclusion can be made where original deduction year is statute-barred); 2019-0798721C6 [2019 IFA q.4] (effect of deemed interest on thin-capitalization rules).

In *Dow Chemical*, 2008 FCA 231, leave to appeal denied 2008 CarswellNat 4683 (SCC), 78(1) applied to an amalgamated corp, where the years were accelerated due to change in control followed by amalgamation. The "taxation years" need not be 12-month years.

The debt forgiveness rules apply in the following order: s. 78; 6(15) for employee indebtedness; 15(1.2) for shareholder indebtedness; 9(1); s. 79 for foreclosures and repossessions; s. 80. See Notes to 80(2)(c).

78(1) applies to an expense incurred *by* a partnership (IT-109R2 para. 8) but arguably not to amounts owing to a partnership: Greg Johnson, "Selected Tax Issues Relating to Capitalizing Private Equity Investments in the Oil and Gas Industry", VI(4) *Resource Sector Taxation* (Federated Press) 466 at 471 (2009).

Where the amount is owing to a foreign affiliate, 90(6) may also apply (unless 248(28) applies): Clara Pham, "An Unpaid Amount Could Be an Upstream Loan", 5(3) *Canadian Tax Focus* (ctf.ca) 5-6 (Aug. 2015).

Interpretation Bulletins: IT-109R2: Unpaid amounts; IT-152R3: Special reserves — sale of land.

Information Circulars: 88-2, para. 16: General anti-avoidance rule — section 245 of the *Income Tax Act*.

Forms: T2047: Agreement in respect of unpaid amounts.

(2) Idem — Where an amount in respect of a deductible outlay or expense that was owing by a taxpayer that is a corporation to a person with whom the taxpayer was not dealing at arm's length is unpaid at the time when the taxpayer is wound up, and the taxpayer is wound up before the end of the second taxation year following the taxation year in which the outlay or expense was incurred, the amount so unpaid shall be included in computing the taxpayer's income for the taxation year in which it is wound up.

Related Provisions: 80(1)"excluded obligation"(c) — Obligation not subject to debt forgiveness rules.

Notes: CRA will apply 78(2) even before formal dissolution of the corporation is complete (VIEWS doc 2001-0067105, applying the policy in IT-126R2).

Interpretation Bulletins: IT-109R2: Unpaid amounts; IT-126R2: Meaning of "Winding-up".

(3) Late filing — Where, in respect of an amount described in subsection (1) that was owing by a taxpayer to a person, an agreement in a form prescribed for the purposes of this section is filed after the day on or before which the agreement is required to be filed for the purposes of paragraph (1)(b), both paragraphs (1)(a) and (b) apply in respect of the said amount, except that paragraph (1)(a) shall be read and construed as requiring 25% only of the said amount to be included in computing the taxpayer's income.

Interpretation Bulletins: IT-109R2: Unpaid amounts.

(4) Unpaid remuneration and other amounts — Where an amount in respect of a taxpayer's expense that is a superannuation or pension benefit, a retiring allowance, salary, wages or other remuneration (other than reasonable vacation or holiday pay or a deferred amount under a salary deferral arrangement) in respect of an office or employment is unpaid on the day that is 180 days after the end of the taxation year in which the expense was incurred, for the purposes of this Act other than this subsection, the amount shall be deemed not to have been incurred as an expense in the year and shall be deemed to be incurred as an expense in the taxation year in which the amount is paid.

Related Provisions: 37(11) — SR&ED expense must be claimed as such even if not deductible due to 78(4); 78(5) — 78(4) takes priority over 78(1); 80(1)"excluded obli-

gation"(c) — Obligation not subject to debt forgiveness rules; 127(9)"investment tax credit"(m) — investment tax credit must be claimed as such even if not deductible due to 78(4); 127(26) — Unpaid amounts re investment tax credit; 248(1)"salary deferral arrangement"(k) — No SDA where bonus paid within 3 years.

Notes: Under 78(4), a bonus declared by an employer in a fiscal year must be paid by 180 days (technically 179 days but administratively 180 *per* IT-109R2 para. 10 and VIEWS doc 2012-0446671E5, though some rulings require 179 days, e.g. 2006-0189151R3) after the end of the year to be deductible. The employee pays tax on employment income only when received (see 5(1)); so a one-year deferral is possible if the employer corporation's fiscal year-end is July 6 or later and the payment is correctly timed. (The employer normally still has to withhold tax at source under 153(1).) See also Notes to s. 67 re large bonuses to owner-managers, to 144(1) for the alternative of using an EPSP, and to 248(1)"salary deferral arrangement" if the purpose is to postpone taxing the salary.

In *WPH Mechanical Services*, 2006 TCC 677, a bonus was "paid" by being recorded as loaned back to the corporation under a loan agreement.

The "best evidence of payment is that the payroll withholdings were remitted on time": Revenue Canada Round Table, 1987 Cdn Tax Foundation conference report, Q.32, p. 47:23; VIEWS doc 2012-0452531E5 (also says that a demand note can constitute payment). CRA will not apply 78(4) to unpaid wages if the employer remits source deductions and issues a T4 and the employee reports the income: 2004-0060641E5.

78(4) amended by 1991 technical bill, effective for expenses incurred after July 1990, to extend to unfunded obligations in respect of pension benefits and retiring allowances (which include severance payments).

Interpretation Bulletins: IT-109R2: Unpaid amounts.

I.T. Technical News: 38 (subsec. 78(4) — liability assumed by third party).

(5) Where subsec. (1) does not apply — Subsection (1) does not apply in any case where subsection (4) applies.

Definitions [s. 78]: "amount" — 248(1); "arm's length" — 251(1); "corporation" — 248(1), *Interpretation Act* 35(1); "deferred amount", "employment", "office", "person", "prescribed", "retiring allowance" — 248(1); "salary, wages" — 248(1)"salary or wages"; "salary deferral arrangement", "superannuation or pension benefit" — 248(1); "taxation year" — 11(2), 249; "taxpayer" — 248(1).

Interpretation Bulletins [s. 78]: IT-109R2: Unpaid amounts; IT-152R3: Special reserves — sale of land.

79. [Surrender of property — debtor] — (1) Definitions — In this section,

"creditor" of a particular person includes a person to whom the particular person is obligated to pay an amount under a mortgage, hypothecary claim or similar obligation and, where property was sold to the particular person under a conditional sales agreement, the seller of the property (or any assignee with respect to the agreement) is deemed to be a creditor of the particular person in respect of that property;

Related Provisions: 79.1(1)"creditor" — Definition applies to s. 79.1.

Notes: See Notes to 188.1(5) re meaning of "includes".

Reference to "hypothecary claim" added by 2001 *Civil Code* harmonization bill, effective June 14, 2001 (non-substantive change: see *Interpretation Act* s. 8.2).

"debt" includes an obligation to pay an amount under a mortgage, hypothecary claim or similar obligation or under a conditional sales agreement;

Related Provisions: 79.1(1)"debt" — Definition applies to s. 79.1.

Notes: See Notes to 188.1(5) re meaning of "includes".

This definition is relevant beyond s. 79 "because it sets out basic and relevant aspects of the concept of indebtedness": *1200757 Ontario*, 2011 ONSC 4959, para. 38.

For the meaning of "debt", see *Barejo Holdings*, 2015 TCC 274 [FCA refused to hear appeal, saying the TCC appeal did not turn on that issue: 2016 FCA 304; leave to appeal denied 2017 CarswellNat 2765 (SCC)] and 2018 TCC 200, aff'd 2020 FCA 47 (leave to appeal denied 2020 CarswellNat 4099) (notes with undefined principal were debt for 94.1(1)(a)). [Barejo was tied in with Ludmer: see *Ludmer*, 2020 QCCA 697, para. 75, footnote 47 (leave to appeal denied 2021 CarswellQue 2160 (SCC)).] See also Friedlander, *Taxation of Corporate Finance* (Carswell, looseleaf or *Taxnet Pro* Reference Centre), chap. 1; Samuel & Beswick, "Selected Issues in Transactions Involving Debt", 2019 Cdn Tax Foundation conference report, 19:1-27.

Reference to "hypothecary claim" added by 2001 *Civil Code* harmonization bill, effective June 14, 2001 (non-substantive change: see *Interpretation Act* s. 8.2).

"person" includes a partnership;

Related Provisions: 79.1(1)"person" — Definition applies to s. 79.1.

"property" does not include

   (a) money, or

(b) indebtedness owed by or guaranteed by the government of a country, or a province, state, or other political subdivision of that country;

Related Provisions: 79.1(1)"property" — Definition applies to s. 79.1.

"specified amount" at any time of a debt owed or assumed by a person means

(a) the unpaid principal amount of the debt at that time, and

(b) unpaid interest accrued to that time on the debt.

Related Provisions: 79.1(1)"specified amount" — Definition applies to s. 79.1.

(2) Surrender of property — For the purposes of this section, a property is surrendered at any time by a person to another person where the beneficial ownership of the property is acquired or reacquired at that time from the person by the other person and the acquisition or reacquisition of the property was in consequence of the person's failure to pay all or part of one or more specified amounts of debts owed by the person to the other person immediately before that time.

Related Provisions: 79.1(2) — Seizure of property by creditor; 180.2(1)"adjusted income" — No OAS clawback on gain to which 79(2) applies.

(3) Proceeds of disposition for debtor — Where a particular property is surrendered at any time by a person (in this subsection referred to as the "debtor") to a creditor of the debtor, the debtor's proceeds of disposition of the particular property shall be deemed to be the amount determined by the formula

$$(A + B + C + D + E - F) \times \frac{G}{H}$$

where

A is the total of all specified amounts of debts of the debtor that are in respect of properties surrendered at that time by the debtor to the creditor and that are owing immediately before that time to the creditor;

B is the total of all amounts each of which is a specified amount of a debt that is owed by the debtor immediately before that time to a person (other than the creditor), to the extent that the amount ceases to be owing by the debtor as a consequence of properties being surrendered at that time by the debtor to the creditor;

C is the total of all amounts each of which is a specified amount of a particular debt that is owed by the debtor immediately before that time to a person (other than a specified amount included in the amount determined for A or B as a consequence of properties being surrendered at that time by the debtor to the creditor), where

(a) any property surrendered at that time by the debtor to the creditor was security for

(i) the particular debt, and

(ii) another debt that is owed by the debtor immediately before that time to the creditor, and

(b) the other debt is subordinate to the particular debt in respect of that property;

D is

(a) where a specified amount of a debt owed by the debtor immediately before that time to a person (other than the creditor) ceases, as a consequence of the surrender at that time of properties by the debtor to the creditor, to be secured by all properties owned by the debtor immediately before that time, the lesser of

(i) the amount, if any, by which the total of all such specified amounts exceeds the portion of that total included in any of the amounts determined for B or C as a consequence of properties being surrendered at that time by the debtor to the creditor, and

(ii) the amount, if any, by which the total cost amount to the debtor of all properties surrendered at that time by the debtor to the creditor exceeds the total amount that would, but for this description and the description of F, be deter-

mined under this subsection as a consequence of the surrender, and

(b) in any other case, nil;

E is

(a) where the particular property is surrendered at that time by the debtor in circumstances in which paragraph 69(1)(b) would, but for this subsection, apply and the fair market value of all properties surrendered at that time by the debtor to the creditor exceeds the amount that would, but for this description and the description of F, be determined under this subsection as a consequence of the surrender, that excess, and

(b) in any other case, nil;

F is the total of all amounts each of which is the lesser of

(a) the portion of a particular specified amount of a particular debt included in the amount determined for A, B, C or D in computing the debtor's proceeds of disposition of the particular property, and

(b) the total of

(i) all amounts included under paragraph 6(1)(a) or subsection 15(1) in computing the income of any person because the particular debt was settled, or deemed by subsection 80.01(8) to have been settled, at or before the end of the taxation year that includes that time,

(ii) all amounts renounced under subsection 66(10), (10.1), (10.2) or (10.3) by the debtor in respect of the particular debt,

(iii) all amounts each of which is a forgiven amount (within the meaning assigned by subsection 80(1)) in respect of the debt at a previous time that the particular debt was deemed by subsection 80.01(8) to have been settled,

(iv) where the particular debt is an excluded obligation (within the meaning assigned by subsection 80(1)), the particular specified amount, and

(v) the lesser of

(A) the unpaid interest accrued to that time on the particular debt, and

(B) the total of

(I) the amount, if any, by which the total of all amounts included because of section 80.4 in computing the debtor's income for the taxation year that includes that time or for a preceding taxation year in respect of interest on the particular debt exceeds the total of all amounts paid before that time on account of interest on the particular debt, and

(II) such portion of that unpaid interest as would, if it were paid, be included in the amount determined under paragraph 28(1)(e) in respect of the debtor;

G is the fair market value at that time of the particular property; and

H is the fair market value at that time of all properties surrendered by the debtor to the creditor at that time.

Related Provisions: 13(21)"proceeds of disposition"(h) — Inclusion for depreciable property rules; 15(1.21)(b) — 79(3) inclusion ignored for calculating shareholder benefit from forgiven amount; 18(9.3) — Rule where debtor previously prepaid interest; 79(2) — Meaning of "surrendered"; 79(4) — Subsequent payment by debtor; 79(5) — Where amount included due to properties being surrendered before the year; 79(7) — Where debt denominated in foreign currency; 80(1)"forgiven amount"B(f) — Debt forgiveness rules do not apply; 87(2)(h.1) — Amalgamation — continuing corp; 118(2)B — Inclusion under s. 79 ignored for old age credit threshold; 122.5(1)"adjusted income"(a)(ii), 122.6"adjusted income"(a)(ii), 122.7(1)"adjusted net income"(b), 180.2(1)"adjusted income"(a)(ii) — Inclusion under s. 79 ignored for GST/HST credit, Canada Child Benefit, Canada Workers Benefit and Old Age Security clawback thresholds; 257 — Formula cannot calculate to less than zero.

Notes: See Notes at end of s. 79.

Interpretation Bulletins: IT-505: Mortgage foreclosures and conditional sales repossessions (cancelled).

(4) Subsequent payment by debtor — An amount paid at any time by a person as, on account of or in satisfaction of, a specified amount of a debt that can reasonably be considered to have been included in the amount determined for A, C or D in subsection (3) in respect of a property surrendered before that time by the person shall be deemed to be a repayment of assistance, at that time in respect of the property, to which

(a) subsection 39(13) applies, where the property was capital property (other than depreciable property) of the person immediately before its surrender;

(b) paragraph 20(1)(hh.1) applies, where the cost of the property to the person was an eligible capital expenditure at the time the property was acquired;

(c) the description of E in the definition "cumulative Canadian exploration expense" in subsection 66.1(6), the description of D in the definition "cumulative Canadian development expense" in subsection 66.2(5) or the description of D in the definition "cumulative Canadian oil and gas property expense" in subsection 66.4(5), as the case may be, applies, where the cost of the property to the person was a Canadian exploration expense, a Canadian development expense or a Canadian oil and gas property expense; or

(d) paragraph 20(1)(hh) applies, in any other case.

Notes: 79(4)(b) amended by 2016 budget bill #2, effective 2017, as part of changing eligible capital property rules to CCA Class 14.1 (see Notes to 20(1)(b)), to add "at the time the property was acquired".

(5) Subsequent application with respect to employee or shareholder debt — Any amount included under paragraph 6(1)(a) or subsection 15(1) in computing a person's income for a taxation year that can reasonably be considered to have been included in the amount determined for A, C or D in subsection (3) as a consequence of properties being surrendered before the year by the person shall be deemed to be a repayment by the person, immediately before the end of the year, of assistance to which subsection (4) applies.

Forms: T2 Sched. 11: Transactions with shareholders, officers, or employees.

(6) Surrender of property not payment or repayment by debtor — Where a specified amount of a debt is included in the amount determined at any time for A, B, C or D in subsection (3) in respect of a property surrendered at that time by a person to a creditor of the person, for the purpose of computing the person's income, no amount shall be considered to have been paid or repaid by the person as a consequence of the acquisition or reacquisition of the surrendered property by the creditor.

Advance Tax Rulings: ATR-6: Vendor reacquires business assets following default by purchaser.

(7) Foreign exchange — Where a debt is denominated in a currency (other than Canadian currency), any amount determined for A, B, C or D in subsection (3) in respect of the debt shall be determined with reference to the relative value of that currency and Canadian currency at the time the debt was issued.

Related Provisions: 261(2)(b) — 79(7) overrides general currency conversion rules; 261(5)(c), (f)(i) — Functional currency reporting.

Notes [s. 79]: 79 provides rules for debtors on foreclosures, conditional sale repossessions and similar transactions. For the effects on creditors, see 79.1. See Bernstein, "Update on Debt Forgiveness and Mortgage Foreclosure Proposals", 1995 *Corporate Management Tax Conference* (ctf.ca) at 21:30-34; Morry, "Revised Section 79", 1995 *Prairie Provinces Tax Conference* (ctf.ca), 1:1-151; Shillinger & Ulmer, "Advanced Topics in Real Estate Tax Planning", 2009 Cdn Tax Foundation conference report, 33:27-33; Wong, "Cross Border Issues Related to the Foreclosure or Abandonment of Real Estate", 5(4) *BorderCrossings* (Carswell) 1-6 (Nov. 2012); Qubti, "Economic Downturn", 20(4) *Tax for the Owner-Manager* (ctf.ca) 11 (Oct. 2020) (using 79 vs s. 80). For CRA interpretation see VIEWS doc 2009-0305751E5.

79 applies only if the transfer is to the creditor, not where to someone else who pays off the creditor: *Pigeau*, 2009 TCC 582, para. 14.

Note that special GST/HST rules apply to the repossession and subsequent use or sale of the property by the creditor. See ss. 183 and 266 of the *Excise Tax Act*, reproduced in the *Practitioner's Goods and Services Tax Annotated* and the *Canada GST Service*.

79 completely replaced by 1994 technical bill, effective for property acquired or reacquired after Feb. 21, 1994, other than property acquired or reacquired pursuant to a court order made before Feb. 22, 1994.

Former 79 amended by 1991 technical bill.

Definitions [s. 79]: "amount" — 248(1); "assistance" — 79(4), 125.4(5), 248(16), (16.1), (18), (18.1); "beneficial ownership" — 248(3); "Canadian currency" — 261(5)(f)(i); "Canadian exploration expense" — 66.1(6), 248(1); "Canadian development expense" — 66.2(5), 248(1); "Canadian oil and gas property expense" — 66.4(5), 248(1); "creditor", "debt" — 79(1); "debtor" — 79(3); "depreciable property" — 13(21), 248(1); "eligible capital expenditure" — 14(5), 248(1); "excluded obligation" — 80(1); "fair market value" — see 69(1) Notes; "partnership" — see 96(1) Notes; "person" — 79(1), 248(1); "principal amount" — 248(1), (26); "property" — 79(1), 248(1); "province" — *Interpretation Act* 35(1); "specified amount" — 79(1); "surrendered" — 79(2); "taxation year" — 249.

79.1 [Seizure of property — creditor] — (1) Definitions — In this section,

"creditor" has the meaning assigned by subsection 79(1);

Notes: See Notes at end of 79.

"debt" has the meaning assigned by subsection 79(1);

"person" has the meaning assigned by subsection 79(1);

"property" has the meaning assigned by subsection 79(1);

"specified amount" has the meaning assigned by subsection 79(1);

"specified cost" to a person of a debt owing to the person means

(a) where the debt is capital property of the person, the adjusted cost base to the person of the debt, and

(b) in any other case, the amount, if any, by which

(i) the cost amount to the person of the debt

exceeds

(ii) such portion of that cost amount as would be deductible in computing the person's income (otherwise than in respect of the principal amount of the debt) if the debt were established by the person to have become a bad debt or to have become uncollectable.

Related Provisions: 20(1)(p), 20(4)–(4.2), 50(1) — Provisions allowing deductions for bad debts.

(2) Seizure of property — Subject to subsection (2.1) and for the purpose of this section, a property is seized at any time by a person in respect of a debt where

(a) the beneficial ownership of the property is acquired or reacquired at that time by the person; and

(b) the acquisition or reacquisition of the property is in consequence of another person's failure to pay to the person all or part of the specified amount of the debt.

Related Provisions: 50(1) — Deemed disposition of debt on bad debt, windup, insolvency or bankruptcy; 79(2) — Surrender of property by debtor; 79.1(2.1) — Exception — foreign resource property; 138(11.93)(a) — 79.1 does not apply to insurer.

Notes: 79.1(2) amended by 2000 Budget, for property acquired or reacquired after Feb. 27, 2000, to make it subject to 79.1(2.1).

See also Notes at end of 79.1.

(2.1) Exception — For the purpose of this section, foreign resource property is deemed not to be seized at any time from

(a) an individual or a corporation, if the individual or corporation is non-resident at that time; or

(b) a partnership (other than a partnership each member of which is resident in Canada at that time).

Notes: 79.1(2.1) added by 2000 Budget, effective for property acquired or reacquired after February 27, 2000.

(3) Creditor's capital gains reserves — Where a property is seized at any time in a particular taxation year by a creditor in respect of a debt, for the purpose of computing the income of the creditor for the particular year, the amount claimed by the creditor under subparagraph 40(1)(a)(iii) or 44(1)(e)(iii) in computing the creditor's gain for the preceding taxation year from any disposition before the particular year of the property shall be deemed to be the amount, if any, by which the amount so claimed exceeds the total of all amounts each of which is an amount determined under paragraph (6)(a) or (b) in respect of the seizure.

(4) Creditor's inventory reserves — Where a property is seized at any time in a particular taxation year by a creditor in respect of a debt, for the purpose of computing the income of the creditor for the particular year, the amount deducted under paragraph 20(1)(n) in computing the income of the creditor for the preceding taxation year in respect of any disposition of the property before the particular year shall be deemed to be the amount, if any, by which the amount so deducted exceeds the total of all amounts each of which is an amount determined under paragraph (6)(a) or (b) in respect of the seizure.

(5) Adjustment where disposition and reacquisition of capital property in same year — Where a property is seized at any time in a taxation year by a creditor in respect of one or more debts and the property was capital property of the creditor that was disposed of by the creditor at a previous time in the year, the proceeds of disposition of the property to the creditor at the previous time shall be deemed to be the lesser of the amount of the proceeds (determined without reference to this subsection) and the amount that is the greater of

(a) the amount, if any, by which the amount of such proceeds (determined without reference to this subsection) exceeds such portion of the proceeds as is represented by the specified amounts of those debts immediately before that time, and

(b) the cost amount to the creditor of the property immediately before the previous time.

(6) Cost of seized properties for creditor — Where a particular property is seized at any time in a taxation year by a creditor in respect of one or more debts, the cost to the creditor of the particular property shall be deemed to be the amount, if any, by which the total of

(a) that proportion of the total specified costs immediately before that time to the creditor of those debts that

(i) the fair market value of the particular property immediately before that time

is of

(ii) the fair market value of all properties immediately before that time that were seized by the creditor at that time in respect of those debts, and

(b) all amounts each of which is an outlay or expense made or incurred, or a specified amount at that time of a debt that is assumed, by the creditor at or before that time to protect the creditor's interest, or for civil law the creditor's right, in the particular property, except to the extent the outlay or expense

(i) was included in the cost to the creditor of property other than the particular property,

(ii) was included before that time in computing, for the purposes of this Act, any balance of undeducted outlays, expenses or other amounts of the creditor, or

(iii) was deductible in computing the creditor's income for the year or a preceding taxation year

exceeds

(c) the amount, if any, claimed or deducted under paragraph 20(1)(n) or subparagraph 40(1)(a)(iii) or 44(1)(e)(iii), as the case may be, in respect of the particular property in computing the creditor's income or capital gain for the preceding taxation year or the amount by which the proceeds of disposition of the creditor of the particular property are reduced because of subsection (5) in respect of a disposition of the particular property by the creditor occurring before that time and in the year.

Related Provisions: 79.1(3) — Capital gains reserve; 79.1(4) — Inventory reserve.

Notes: For examples of 79.1(6) applying see *Saskatchewan Wheat Pool*, 2008 TCC 8 and *568864 B.C.*, 2014 TCC 373. See also VIEWS doc 2014-0560961E5.

79.1(6)(b) opening words amended by 2002-2013 technical bill (Part 4 — bijuralism), effective June 26, 2013, to add "or for civil law the creditor's right".

(7) Treatment of debt — Where a property is seized at any time in a taxation year by a creditor in respect of a particular debt,

(a) the creditor shall be deemed to have disposed of the particular debt at that time;

(b) the amount received on account of the particular debt as a consequence of the seizure shall be deemed

(i) to be received at that time, and

(ii) to be equal to

(A) where the particular debt is capital property, the adjusted cost base to the creditor of the particular debt, and

(B) in any other case, the cost amount to the creditor of the particular debt;

(c) where any portion of the particular debt is outstanding immediately after that time, the creditor shall be deemed to have reacquired that portion immediately after that time at a cost equal to

(i) where the particular debt is capital property, nil, and

(ii) in any other case, the amount, if any, by which

(A) the cost amount to the creditor of the particular debt

exceeds

(B) the specified cost to the creditor of the particular debt; and

(d) where no portion of the particular debt is outstanding immediately after that time and the particular debt is not capital property, the creditor may deduct as a bad debt in computing the creditor's income for the year the amount described in subparagraph (c)(ii) in respect of the seizure.

Related Provisions: 79.1(8) — No deduction for principal amount of bad debt; 142.4(3)(a) — Disposition of specified debt obligation.

(8) Claims for debts — Where a property is seized at any time in a taxation year by a creditor in respect of a debt, no amount in respect of the debt

(a) is deductible in computing the creditor's income for the year or a subsequent taxation year as a bad, doubtful or impaired debt; or

(b) shall be included after that time in computing, for the purposes of this Act, any balance of undeducted outlays, expenses or other amounts of the creditor as a bad, doubtful or impaired debt.

Related Provisions: 50(1)(a) — Deemed disposition of bad debt; 79.1(7)(d) — Deduction by creditor for bad debt.

Notes: 79.1(8) amended by 1995-97 technical bill, effective for taxation years that end after September 1997, or earlier by election for amended 20(1)(l) to apply.

Notes [s. 79.1]: 79.1 provides the rules for creditors on foreclosures, conditional sale repossessions and similar transactions. (79 provides the rules for debtors.) See Jack Bernstein, "Update on Debt Forgiveness and Mortgage Foreclosure Proposals", 1995 *Corporate Management Tax Conference* (ctf.ca) at 21:34-36; Lorne Shillinger & John Ulmer, "Advanced Topics in Real Estate Tax Planning", 2009 Cdn Tax Foundation conference report, 33:27-33. See also VIEWS doc 2011-0427101C6 (79.1 does not apply when creditor seizes a share of (or partnership interest in) the debtor).

Note that special GST/HST rules apply to repossession and subsequent use or sale of the property by the creditor. See ss. 183 and 266 of the *Excise Tax Act*, reproduced in *Practitioner's Goods and Services Tax Annotated*.

79.1 added by 1994 technical bill, for property acquired or reacquired after Feb. 21, 1994, other than pursuant to a court order made before Feb. 22, 1994.

Definitions [s. 79.1]: "adjusted cost base" — 54, 248(1); "amount" — 248(1); "beneficial ownership" — 248(3); "capital gain" — 39(1), 248(1); "capital property" — 54, 248(1); "corporation" — 248(1), *Interpretation Act* 35(1); "cost" — 79.1(6); "cost amount" — 248(1); "creditor", "debt" — 79(1), 79.1(1); "disposition" — 248(1); "foreign resource property" — 66(15), 248(1); "individual", "non-resident" — 248(1); "partnership" — see 96(1) Notes; "person" — 79(1), 79.1(1), 248(1); "principal amount" — 248(1), (26); "proceeds of disposition" — 54; "property" — 79(1), 79.1(1), 248(1); "resident in Canada" — 94(3)(a), 250; "seized" — 79.1(2); "specified amount" — 79(1), 79.1(1); "specified cost" — 79.1(1); "taxation year" — 249.

80. [Debt forgiveness] — **(1) Definitions** — In this section,

"commercial debt obligation" issued by a debtor means a debt obligation issued by the debtor

(a) where interest was paid or payable by the debtor in respect of it pursuant to a legal obligation, or

(b) if interest had been paid or payable by the debtor in respect of it pursuant to a legal obligation,

an amount in respect of the interest was or would have been deductible in computing the debtor's income, taxable income or taxable income earned in Canada, as the case may be, if this Act were read without reference to subsections 15.1(2) and 15.2(2), paragraph 18(1)(g), subsections 18(2), (3.1) and (4) and section 21;

Related Provisions: 6(15) — Income inclusion on forgiveness of debt owing by employee; 80.01(1)"commercial debt obligation" — Definition applies to s. 80.01; 80.02(1) — Definition applies to s. 80.02; 80.03(1) — Definition applies to s. 80.03; 80.03(7)(b)(i) — Commercial debt obligation deemed issued where amount designated; 80.04(1) — Definition applies to s. 80.04; 80.04(4)(e) — Commercial debt obligation deemed issued on agreement to transfer forgiven amount; 95(2)(g.1)(i) — Application to FAPI; 248(26) — Liability deemed to be obligation issued by debtor; 248(27) — Partial settlement of debt obligation.

Notes: See Notes at end of 80, and VIEWS doc 2008-0293901E5.

As is clear from the English wording, a debt can be a "commercial debt obligation" even without a legal obligation to pay interest: *Genex Communications*, 2009 FCA 353.

On the meaning of "debt", see Notes to 79(1)"debt".

"commercial obligation" issued by a debtor means

(a) a commercial debt obligation issued by the debtor, or

(b) a distress preferred share issued by the debtor;

Related Provisions: 40(2)(e.2) — Disposition of commercial obligation in exchange for another obligation issued by same person; 80(2)(b) — Obligation to pay interest deemed to be a debt obligation; 80.01(1)"commercial obligation" — Definition applies to s. 80.01; 80.02(1) — Definition applies to s. 80.02; 80.03(1) — Definition applies to s. 80.03; 80.04(1) — Definition applies to s. 80.04.

Notes: See Notes at end of s. 80, and VIEWS doc 2008-0293901E5.

"debtor" includes any corporation that has issued a distress preferred share and any partnership;

Related Provisions: 80.01(1)"debtor" — Definition applies to s. 80.01; 80.04(1) — Definition applies to s. 80.04.

"directed person" at any time in respect of a debtor means

(a) a taxable Canadian corporation or an eligible Canadian partnership by which the debtor is controlled at that time, or

(b) a taxable Canadian corporation or an eligible Canadian partnership that is controlled at that time by

(i) the debtor,

(ii) the debtor and one or more persons related to the debtor, or

(iii) a person or group of persons by which the debtor is controlled at that time;

Related Provisions: 80(2)(j) — Extended meaning of "related" and "controlled"; 80.04(1) — Definition applies to s. 80.04; 256(6), (6.1) — Meaning of "controlled".

"distress preferred share" issued by a corporation means, at any time, a share issued after February 21, 1994 (other than a share issued pursuant to an agreement in writing entered into on or before that date) by the corporation that is a share described in paragraph (e) of the definition "term preferred share" in subsection 248(1) that would be a term preferred share at that time if that definition were read without reference to paragraphs (e) and (f);

Related Provisions: 61.3(1)(b)D, 61.3(2)(b)D — Deduction of principal amount of distress preferred share in determining debt forgiveness reserve; 80.01(1)"distress preferred share" — Definition applies to s. 80.01; 80.02(1) — Definition applies to s. 80.02; 80.03(1) — Definition applies to s. 80.03.

Notes: See Notes to 80.02(2). The reference to para. (e) of 248(1)"term preferred share" (TPS) is to an *exclusion* in that definition. A distress preferred share (DPS) is defined as a share falling in para. (e), and (because it says "would be a TPS") that also meets the conditions to be a TPS. If the definition stopped there, no share could ever be a DPS, because TPS para. (e) would exclude it. Hence the wording at the end, to ignore para. (e) (as well as (f)).

"eligible Canadian partnership" at any time means a Canadian partnership none of the members of which is, at that time,

(a) a non-resident owned investment corporation,

(b) a person exempt, because of subsection 149(1), from tax under this Part on all or part of the person's taxable income,

(c) a partnership, other than an eligible Canadian partnership, or

(d) a trust, other than a trust in which no non-resident person and no person described in paragraph (a), (b) or (c) is beneficially interested;

Related Provisions: 80.04(1) — Definition applies to s. 80.04; 102(1) — Canadian partnership.

"excluded obligation" means an obligation issued by a debtor where

(a) the proceeds from the issue of the obligation

(i) were included in computing the debtor's income or, but for the expression "other than a prescribed amount" in paragraph 12(1)(x), would have been so included,

(ii) were deducted in computing, for the purposes of this Act, any balance of undeducted outlays, expenses or other amounts, or

(iii) were deducted in computing the capital cost or cost amount to the debtor of any property of the debtor,

(b) an amount paid by the debtor in satisfaction of the entire principal amount of the obligation would be included in the amount determined under paragraph 28(1)(e) or section 30 in respect of the debtor,

(c) section 78 applies to the obligation, or

(d) the principal amount of the obligation would, if this Act were read without reference to sections 79 and 80 and the obligation were settled without any amount being paid in satisfaction of its principal amount, be included in computing the debtor's income because of the settlement of the obligation;

Related Provisions: 79(3)F(b)(iv) — Proceeds of disposition for debtor; 80(1)"forgiven amount"B(j) — Debt forgiveness rules do not apply to principal amount of excluded obligation; 80(2)(a) — Debt forgiveness rules do not apply to obligation settled as consideration for share described in para. (c).

Notes: For CRA interpretation see docs 2014-0538151C6 [2014 APFF q.15] (para. (a) applies); 2014-0541921E5 (143.4(1) contingent amount falls under (a)(ii) and (iii)); 2014-0545591E5 (upstream loan included in income by 90(6) is excluded obligation).

"excluded property" means property of a non-resident debtor that is treaty-protected property or that is not taxable Canadian property;

Related Provisions: 111(9) — Losses ignored while taxpayer is non-resident.

Notes: Definition amended by 1998 Budget, effective for 1998 and later taxation years. See also Notes at end of s. 80.

"excluded security" issued by a corporation to a person as consideration for the settlement of a debt means

(a) a distress preferred share issued by the corporation to the person, or

(b) a share issued by the corporation to the person under the terms of the debt, where the debt was a bond, debenture or note listed on a designated stock exchange in Canada and the terms for the conversion to the share were not established or substantially modified after the later of February 22, 1994 and the time that the bond, debenture or note was issued;

Notes: 80(1)"excluded security"(b) amended by 2007 budget bill #2 to change "prescribed stock exchange" to "designated stock exchange", effective Dec. 14, 2007.

"forgiven amount" at any time in respect of a commercial obligation issued by a debtor is the amount determined by the formula

$$A - B$$

where

A is the lesser of the amount for which the obligation was issued and the principal amount of the obligation, and

B is the total of

(a) the amount, if any, paid at that time in satisfaction of the principal amount of the obligation,

(b) the amount, if any, included under paragraph 6(1)(a) or subsection 15(1) in computing the income of any person because of the settlement of the obligation at that time,

(c) the amount, if any, deducted at that time under paragraph 18(9.3)(f) in computing the forgiven amount in respect of the obligation,

(d) the capital gain, if any, of the debtor resulting from the application of subsection 39(3) to the purchase at that time of the obligation by the debtor,

(e) such portion of the principal amount of the obligation as relates to an amount renounced under subsection 66(10), (10.1), (10.2) or (10.3) by the debtor,

(f) any portion of the principal amount of the obligation that is included in the amount determined for A, B, C or D in subsection 79(3) in respect of the debtor for the taxation year of the debtor that includes that time or for a preceding taxation year,

(g) the total of all amounts each of which is a forgiven amount at a previous time that the obligation was deemed by subsection 80.01(8) or (9) to have been settled,

(h) such portion of the principal amount of the obligation as can reasonably be considered to have been included under section 80.4 in computing the debtor's income for a taxation year that includes that time or for a preceding taxation year,

(i) where the debtor is a bankrupt at that time, the principal amount of the obligation,

(j) such portion of the principal amount of the obligation as represents the principal amount of an excluded obligation,

(k) where the debtor is a partnership and the obligation was, since the later of the creation of the partnership or the issue of the obligation, always payable to a member of the partnership actively engaged, on a regular, continuous and substantial basis, in those activities of the partnership that are other than the financing of the partnership business, the principal amount of the obligation, and

(l) the amount, if any, given at or before that time by the debtor to another person as consideration for the assumption by the other person of the obligation;

Related Provisions: 6(15.1) — Meaning of "forgiven amount" for employee benefits; 15(1.21) — Meaning of "forgiven amount" for shareholder benefits; 80(2)(k) — Determination of forgiven amount where obligation denominated in foreign currency; 80.01(1)"forgiven amount" — Application of definition to s. 80.01; 80.01(8)(b) — Determination of forgiven amount on debt parking; 80.02(3)-(6) — Distress preferred share — determination of amount paid in satisfaction of principal; 80.03(1) — Definition applies to s. 80.03; 80.03(7)(b)(ii) — Deemed forgiven amount where amount designated after debt forgiveness; 80.04(1) — Definition applies to s. 80.04; 80.04(4)(f) — Agreement to transfer forgiven amount; 87(2)(h.1) — Amalgamation — continuing corporation; 137.1(10) — Settlement of debts by deposit insurance corporation; 248(26) — Liability deemed to be obligation issued by debtor; 248(27) — Partial settlement of debt obligation; 257 — Formula cannot calculate to less than zero.

Notes: 80(3)-(14) set out a scheme of rules for using up the forgiven amount. See Notes at end of 80.

A forgiven amount arises when a settlement agreement is signed, not when an amount is paid under the agreement: *Richer*, 2009 TCC 394.

In *Genex Communications*, 2010 FCA 353, the FCA refused to consider how "forgiven amount" (FA) should be calculated because this had not been raised at trial.

For CRA interpretation re FA see VIEWS docs 2003-0002485 (gift of funds from creditor to debtor to allow repayment of debt is indirect forgiveness and subject to GAAR); 2010-0387451C6 [2010 CTF conf report q.1, p.4:1-3] (if bankruptcy is annulled, para. (i) does not continue to apply); 2011-0426051R3 (debt restructuring). See also Notes to 80(1)"excluded obligation".

For rulings that there is no FA see 2006-0177541R3 (converting debt obligation to common shares of same value); 2008-0302511I7 (market repurchase of Liquid Yield Options Notes); 2009-0343201R3 (trust conversion to corporation); 2009-0350481R3 (REIT reorg); 2009-0350711R3 (80.01(4) election); 2010-0366651R3 (spinoff butterfly (bf)); 2010-0376681R3 (set-off and cancellation of promissory notes); 2010-0379741R3 (reorg); 2011-0416001R3 (split-up bf); 2012-0450391R3 (restructuring to consolidate profits and losses in corporate group); 2012-0452821R3 and 2012-0462141R3 (recapitalization with debt forgiveness); 2012-0459781R3 (cross-border bf); 2013-0514191R3 and 2014-0547871R3 (debt restructuring); 2013-0516121E5 (GST/HST forgiven under *Bankruptcy and Insolvency Act* compromise: 12(1)(x) could apply to the interest/penalty portion); 2014-0519231I7 (forgiveness of guarantee); 2014-0528291R3, 2014-0539031R3, 2015-0582421R3, 2018-0745061R3 (bf); 2016-0675881R3, 2017-0704351R3 (55(3)(a) reorg).

I.T. Application Rules: 26(1.1) (debt outstanding since before 1972).

Advance Tax Rulings: ATR-27: Exchange and acquisition of interests in capital properties through rollovers and winding-up ("butterfly").

I.T. Technical News: 15 (tax consequences of the adoption of the "euro" currency).

"person" includes a partnership;

Related Provisions: 80(15)(c) — Where commercial debt obligation issued by partnership; 80.01(1)"person" — Definition applies to s. 80.01; 80.02(1) — Definition applies to s. 80.02; 80.03(1) — Definition applies to s. 80.03; 80.04(1) — Definition applies to s. 80.04.

"relevant loss balance", at a particular time for a commercial obligation and in respect of a debtor's non-capital loss, farm loss, restricted farm loss or net capital loss, as the case may be, for a particular taxation year, is

(a) subject to paragraph (b), the amount of such loss that would be deductible in computing the debtor's taxable income or taxable income earned in Canada, as the case may be, for the taxation year that includes that time if

(i) the debtor had sufficient incomes from all sources and sufficient taxable capital gains,

(ii) subsections (3) and (4) did not apply to reduce such loss at or after that time, and

(iii) paragraph 111(4)(a) and subsection 111(5) did not apply to the debtor, and

(b) nil if the debtor is a taxpayer that was at a previous time subject to a loss restriction event and the particular year ended before the previous time, unless

(i) the obligation was issued by the debtor before, and not in contemplation of, the loss restriction event, or

(ii) all or substantially all of the proceeds from the issue of the obligation were used to satisfy the principal amount of another obligation to which subparagraph (i) or this subparagraph would apply if the other obligation were still outstanding;

Related Provisions: 80(15)(c)(iv)(B) — Application of para. (e) of definition where obligation issued by partnership; 80.04(4)(h)(ii) — Application of para. (e) of definition on agreement to transfer forgiven amount; 251.2 — Loss restriction event.

Notes: For interpretation see VIEWS doc 2011-0418071I7. CRA considers that "substantially all", used in para. (e), means 90% or more.

Definition amended by 2013 budget bill #2, effective March 21, 2013, to extend the change-in-control rule to trusts by referring to a "loss restriction event" (see Notes to 251.2(2)).

I.T. Technical News: 7 (control by a group — 50/50 arrangement).

"successor pool" at any time for a commercial obligation and in respect of an amount determined in relation to a debtor means the portion of that amount that would be deductible under subsection 66.7(2), (2.3), (3), (4) or (5), as the case may be, in computing the debtor's income for the taxation year that includes that time, if

(a) the debtor had sufficient incomes from all sources,

(b) subsection (8) did not apply to reduce the amount so determined at that time,

(c) the year ended immediately after that time, and

(d) paragraphs 66.7(2.3)(a), (4)(a) and (5)(a) were read without reference to the expressions "30% of", "30% of" and "10% of", respectively,

except that the successor pool at that time for the obligation is deemed to be nil unless

(e) the obligation was issued by the debtor before, and not in contemplation of, the event described in paragraph (8)(a) that gives rise to the deductibility under subsection 66.7(2), (2.3),

(3), (4) or (5), as the case may be, of all or part of that amount in computing the debtor's income, or

(f) all or substantially all of the proceeds from the issue of the obligation were used to satisfy the principal amount of another obligation to which paragraph (e) or this paragraph would apply if the other obligation were still outstanding;

Related Provisions: 80(15)(c)(iv)(B) — Application of para. (f) of definition where obligation issued by partnership; 80.04(4)(h)(ii) — Application of para. (f) of definition on agreement to transfer forgiven amount; 256(8) — Deemed acquisition of shares.

Notes: CRA considers that "substantially all", used in para. (f), means 90% or more.

80(1)"successor pool" amended by 2000 Budget, effective for taxation years that begin after 2000, to add references to 66.7(2.3). See also Notes at end of s. 80.

"unrecognized loss", at a particular time, in respect of an obligation issued by a debtor, from the disposition of a property, is the amount that would, but for subparagraph 40(2)(g)(ii), be a capital loss from the disposition by the debtor at or before the particular time of a debt or other right to receive an amount, except that if the debtor is a taxpayer that is subject to a loss restriction event before the particular time and after the time of the disposition, the unrecognized loss at the particular time in respect of the obligation is nil unless

(a) the obligation was issued by the debtor before, and not in contemplation of, the loss restriction event, or

(b) all or substantially all of the proceeds from the issue of the obligation were used to satisfy the principal amount of another obligation to which paragraph (a) or this paragraph would apply if the other obligation were still outstanding.

Related Provisions: 80(15)(c)(iv)(B) — Application of para. (b) of definition where obligation issued by partnership; 80.04(4)(h)(ii) — Application of para. (b) of definition on agreement to transfer forgiven amount; 87(2)(l.21) — Amalgamation — continuing corporation; 251.2 — Loss restriction event.

Notes: Opening words and para. (a) of definition amended by 2013 budget bill #2, effective March 21, 2013, to extend the change-in-control rule to trusts by referring to a "loss restriction event" (see Notes to 251.2(2)).

Definition earlier amended by 1995-97 technical bill.

CRA considers that "substantially all", used in para. (b), means 90% or more.

(2) Application of debt forgiveness rules — For the purposes of this section,

(a) **[when obligation settled]** — an obligation issued by a debtor is settled at any time where the obligation is settled or extinguished at that time (otherwise than by way of a bequest or inheritance or as consideration for the issue of a share described in paragraph (b) of the definition "excluded security" in subsection (1));

Related Provisions: 6(15) — Forgiveness of debt owing by employee — taxable benefit; 15(1.2) — Forgiveness of debt owing by shareholder — taxable benefit; 80.01(2)(a) — Application to s. 80.01; 80.01(3)–(9) — Deemed settlement of debts; 80.02(2)(c) — Meaning of "settled" for distress preferred share; 80.02(7)(a) — Deemed settlement where share ceases to be distress preferred share; 80.03(7)(b)(i) — Deemed settlement where amount designated; 80.04(3) — Application to s. 80.04; 80.04(4)(e) — Deemed settlement on agreement to transfer forgiven amount.

Notes: See VIEWS docs 2012-0433941E5 (bequest/inheritance exception does not apply); 2012-0454081C6 (application depends on the facts and civil law); 2014-0535361E5 ("settle" connotes a final and legal resolution of an obligation so that it is reduced or brought to an end).

A debt might not be "extinguished" when it goes statute-barred (e.g., under a province's *Limitations Act*): *Temple*, 2012 ONSC 376, para. 19 (and see 80.01(9), which contemplates a limitation period applying without extinguishing the debt). However, a real property mortgage may be extinguished, depending on the wording of the legislation: *Shook v. Munro*, 1947 CanLII 211 (Ont CA); *McVan v. Arthur*, 2002 CanLII 45035 (Ont. SCJ).

A limitation period can expire as early as 2 years from when a promissory note is signed: *Hare v. Hare*, 2006 CanLII 4160 (Ont CA); Jakolev & Turner, "Demand Loan Statute-Barred", 16(5) *Canadian Tax Highlights* (ctf.ca) 3-4 (May 2008). For Ontario, this was fixed in *Limitations Act, 2002* s. 5(3), providing that the 2-year clock starts only when *demand* for payment is made and not honoured.

(b) **[interest deemed to be obligation]** — an amount of interest payable by a debtor in respect of an obligation issued by

the debtor shall be deemed to be an obligation issued by the debtor that

(i) has a principal amount, and

(ii) was issued by the debtor for an amount,

equal to the portion of the amount of such interest that was deductible or would, but for subsection 18(2) or (3.1) or section 21, have been deductible in computing the debtor's income for a taxation year;

Related Provisions: 6(15.1)(d), 15(1.21)(d) — 80(2)(b) ignored for employee and shareholder benefit purposes; 80.01(2)(a) — Application to s. 80.01; 80.04(3) — Application to s. 80.04.

Notes: For interpretation of 80(2)(b) see VIEWS docs 2007-0259531R3, 2008-0289731E5 (where creditor waives right to interest), 2011-0426051R3.

For interest accruing before July 14, 1990, read "was deductible" in 80(2)(b) as "was deducted" (1994 technical bill, para. 27(2)(b).) See also Notes at end of 80.

(c) **[ordering of rules]** — subsections (3) to (5) and (8) to (13) apply in numerical order to the forgiven amount in respect of a commercial obligation;

Related Provisions: 80(15) — Deduction by member of partnership; 80.04(4)(b) — Transfer of forgiven amount to related person after maximum designations; 248(27)(b), (c) — Partial settlement of debt deemed to be proportional to entire amount.

Notes: The rules for debt forgiveness apply in the following order:

- 78 [see 79(3)F, 80(1)"excluded obligation"(c)]
- 6(1), 6(15) [see 79(3)F, 79(5), 80(1)"forgiven amount"B(b)]
- 15(1), (1.2) [see 79(3)F, 79(5), 80(1)"forgiven amount"B(b)]
- 9(1) [see 79(3)F, 80(1)"excluded obligation", 4(4), 248(28)]
- 79 [see 80(1)"forgiven amount"B(f)]
- 80 [per 80(2)(c); the unstated assumption is that the rules apply in *ascending* numerical order]

80(2)(c) amended to delete reference to 80(7) by 2016 budget bill #2, effective 2017.

(d) **[applicable fraction]** — the applicable fraction of the unapplied portion of a forgiven amount at any time in respect of an obligation issued by the debtor is in respect of a loss for any other taxation year[6], the fraction required to be used under section 38 for that year;

Notes: 80(2)(d) amended by 2000 Budget, effective for taxation years that end after Feb. 27, 2000, due to the change in capital gains taxation rates.

(e) **[where applicable fraction reduces loss]** — where an applicable fraction (as determined under paragraph (d)) of the unapplied portion of a forgiven amount is applied under subsection (4) to reduce at any time a loss for a taxation year, the portion of the forgiven amount so applied shall, except for the purpose of reducing the loss, be deemed to be the quotient obtained when the amount of the reduction is divided by the applicable fraction;

(f) [Repealed]

Notes: 80(2)(f) repealed by 2016 budget bill #2, effective 2017, as part of changing eligible capital property to CCA Class 14.1 (see Notes to 20(1)(b)). It read:

(f) [cumulative eligible capital] — where $3/4$ of the unapplied portion of a forgiven amount is applied under subsection (7) to reduce cumulative eligible capital, except for the purpose of reducing the cumulative eligible capital, the portion of the forgiven amount so applied shall be deemed to be $4/3$ of the amount of the reduction;

(g) **[amount paid in satisfaction of debt]** — where a corporation issues a share (other than an excluded security) to a person as consideration for the settlement of a debt issued by the corporation and payable to the person, the amount paid in satisfaction of the debt because of the issue of the share is deemed to be equal to the fair market value of the share at the time it was issued;

Related Provisions: 51(1) — Conversion of convertible debt into shares.

Notes: See Thomas Bauer, "Restructuring Debt Obligations", 2008 Cdn Tax Foundation conference report at 37:10-14.

In *Corner Brook Pulp*, 2006 TCC 70, shares issued in exchange for $20 million of debt were held to be at least equal in value to the debt, so s. 80 did not apply.

---

[6] *Sic.* The word "other" was inadvertently left over from an earlier draft and should be ignored — ed.

In *Pièces Automobiles Lecavalier*, 2013 TCC 310, GAAR (245(2)) applied to a transaction that circumvented 80(2)(g) and 80.01(6)–(8). Paras. 115-120 discuss the object, spirit and purpose of 80(2)(g).

80(2)(g) amended by 1995-97 technical bill, retroactive to its introduction (see Notes at end of s. 80). It was split into paras. (g) and (g.1). The main difference is that new (g) and (g.1) do not limit the amount considered to have been paid in satisfaction of a debt because of any non-share consideration that is given by a debtor.

(g.1) **[amount paid in satisfaction of debt]** — where a debt issued by a corporation and payable to a person is settled at any time, the amount, if any, that can reasonably be considered to be the increase, as a consequence of the settlement of the debt, in the fair market value of shares of the capital stock of the corporation owned by the person (other than any shares acquired by the person as consideration for the settlement of the debt) is deemed to be an amount paid at that time in satisfaction of the debt;

Notes: 80(2)(g.1) added by 1995-97 technical bill, effective for taxation years ending after February 21, 1994. See Notes to 80(2)(g).

(h) **[debt replaced with debt]** — where any part of the consideration given by a debtor to another person for the settlement at any time of a particular commercial debt obligation issued by the debtor and payable to the other person consists of a new commercial debt obligation issued by the debtor to the other person

(i) an amount equal to the principal amount of the new obligation shall be deemed to be paid by the debtor at that time, because of the issue of the new obligation, in satisfaction of the principal amount of the particular obligation, and

(ii) the new obligation shall be deemed to have been issued for an amount equal to the amount, if any, by which

(A) the principal amount of the new obligation

exceeds

(B) the amount, if any, by which the principal amount of the new obligation exceeds the amount for which the particular obligation was issued;

Related Provisions: 40(2)(e.2) — Limitation on capital loss; 80(2)(l) — Where debt replaced with debt to third party; 248(1)"principal amount" — Principal amount excludes amounts payable on account of interest.

Notes: See Thomas Bauer, "Restructuring Debt Obligations", 2008 Cdn Tax Foundation conference report at 37:14-18.

I.T. Technical News: 15 (tax consequences of the adoption of the "euro" currency).

(i) **[multiple debts settled]** — where 2 or more commercial obligations issued by a debtor are settled at the same time, those obligations shall be treated as if they were settled at different times in the order designated by the debtor in a prescribed form filed with the debtor's return of income under this Part for the debtor's taxation year that includes that time or, if the debtor does not so designate any such order, in the order designated by the Minister;

Related Provisions: 220(3.21)(a) — Late filing, amendment or revocation of designation.

Notes: The prescribed form for 1994 could be filed with Revenue Canada up to the end of 1995. (1994 technical bill, para. 27(2)(c).)

Forms: T2153: Designation under para. 80(2)(i) when two or more commercial obligations are settled at the same time.

(j) **["related" and "controlled"]** — for the purpose of determining, at any time, whether 2 persons are related to each other or whether any person is controlled by any other person, it shall be assumed that

(i) each partnership and each trust is a corporation having a capital stock of a single class of voting shares divided into 100 issued shares,

(ii) each member of a partnership and each beneficiary under a trust owned at that time the number of issued shares of that class that is equal to the proportion of 100 that

(A) the fair market value at that time of the member's interest in the partnership or the beneficiary's interest in the trust, as the case may be

is of

(B) the fair market value at that time of all members' interests in the partnership or all beneficiaries' interests in the trust, as the case may be, and

(iii) where a beneficiary's share of the income or capital of a trust depends on the exercise by any person of, or the failure by any person to exercise, any discretionary power, the fair market value at any time of the beneficiary's interest in the trust is equal to

(A) where the beneficiary is not entitled to receive or otherwise obtain the use of any of the income or capital of the trust before the death after that time of one or more other beneficiaries under the trust, nil, and

(B) in any other case, the total fair market value at that time of all beneficiaries' interests under the trust;

Related Provisions: 39(2.03) — Application to foreign-currency debt-parking rules; 40(2)(e.1) — Application to stop-loss rule; 80.01(2)(a) — Application to s. 80.01; 80.04(3) — Application to s. 80.04.

(k) **[foreign currency obligation]** — where an obligation is denominated in a currency (other than Canadian currency), the forgiven amount at any time in respect of the obligation shall be determined with reference to the relative value of that currency and Canadian currency at the time the obligation was issued;

Related Provisions: 79(7) — Parallel rule re proceeds of disposition where property surrendered to creditor; 80.01(11) — Debt parking and statute-barred debt rules ignored where currency fluctuates; 261(2)(b) — 80(2)(k) overrides general currency conversion rules; 261(5)(c), (f)(i), 261(9)(b), 261(13)(b) — Effect of functional currency reporting.

Notes: See Bauer, "Restructuring Debt Obligations", 2008 Cdn Tax Foundation conference report at 37:18-21; Smit, "Debt Restructuring and the Falling Canadian Dollar", 86 *International Tax* (CCH) 3-4 (Feb. 2016); VIEWS doc 2010-0386881E5.

Where a foreign currency loan is deemed settled on amalgamation of debtor and creditor, see Notes to 80.01(3). On the application of 80(2)(k) to 80.01 see Notes to 80.01(3), (4) and (8).

(l) **[debt replaced with debt to third party]** — where an amount is paid in satisfaction of the principal amount of a particular commercial obligation issued by a debtor and, as a consequence of the payment, the debtor is legally obliged to pay that amount to another person, the obligation to pay that amount to the other person shall be deemed to be a commercial obligation that was issued by the debtor at the same time and in the same circumstances as the particular obligation;

Related Provisions: 80(2)(h) — Where debt replaced with new debt; 80.01(2)(a) — Application to s. 80.01.

(m) **[amount reducible only to zero]** — for greater certainty, the amount that can be applied under this section to reduce another amount may not exceed that other amount;

Related Provisions: 257 — Formulas cannot calculate to less than zero.

(n) **[where debt owed by partnership]** — except for the purposes of this paragraph, where

(i) a commercial debt obligation issued by a debtor is settled at any time,

(ii) the debtor is at that time a member of a partnership, and

(iii) the obligation was, under the agreement governing the obligation, treated immediately before that time as a debt owed by the partnership,

the obligation shall be considered to have been issued by the partnership and not by the debtor;

Related Provisions: 80(2)(o) — Override rule where debtor jointly liable with others; 80(15) — Commercial debt obligation issued by partnership; 80.01(2)(a) — Application to s. 80.01; 80.04(3) — Application to s. 80.04.

(o) **[where joint liability for debt]** — notwithstanding paragraph (n), if a commercial debt obligation, for which a particular person is liable with one or more other persons, is settled at any time in respect of the particular person but not in respect of all of the other persons, the portion of the obligation that can reasonably be considered to be the particular person's share of the obligation shall be considered to have been issued by the particular person and settled at that time and not at any subsequent time;

Notes: 80(2)(o) amended by 2002-2013 technical bill, effective June 26, 2013.

(p) **[death of debtor]** — a commercial debt obligation issued by an individual that is outstanding at the time of the individual's death and settled at a subsequent time shall, if the estate of the individual was liable for the obligation immediately before the subsequent time, be deemed to have been issued by the estate at the same time and in the same circumstances as the obligation was issued by the individual; and

Related Provisions: 80(2)(q) — Where debt settled within 6 months of death.

(q) **[death of debtor]** — where a commercial debt obligation issued by an individual would, but for this paragraph, be settled at any time in the period ending 6 months after the death of an individual (or within such longer period as is acceptable to the Minister and the estate of the individual) and the estate of the individual was liable immediately before that time for the obligation

(i) the obligation shall be deemed to have been settled at the beginning of the day on which the individual died and not at that time,

(ii) any amount paid at that time by the estate in satisfaction of the principal amount of the obligation shall be deemed to have been paid at the beginning of the day on which the individual died,

(iii) any amount given by the estate at or before that time to another person as consideration for assumption by the other person of the obligation shall be deemed to have been given at the beginning of the day on which the individual died, and

(iv) paragraph (b) shall not apply in respect of the settlement to interest that accrues within that period,

except that this paragraph does not apply in circumstances in which any amount is because of the settlement included under paragraph 6(1)(a) or subsection 15(1) in computing the income of any person or in which section 79 applies in respect of the obligation.

Related Provisions: 6(15.1)(d), 15(1.21)(d) — 80(2)(q) ignored for employee and shareholder benefit purposes; 80(2)(p) — If debt not settled within 6 months of death.

(3) Reductions of non-capital losses — Where a commercial obligation issued by a debtor is settled at any time, the forgiven amount at that time in respect of the obligation shall be applied to reduce at that time, in the following order,

(a) the debtor's non-capital loss for each taxation year that ended before that time to the extent that the amount so applied

(i) does not exceed the amount (in subsection (4) referred to as the debtor's "ordinary non-capital loss at that time for the year") that would be the relevant loss balance at that time for the obligation and in respect of the debtor's non-capital loss for the year if the description of E in the definition "non-capital loss" in subsection 111(8) were read without reference to the expression "the taxpayer's allowable business investment loss for the year", and

(ii) does not, because of this subsection, reduce the debtor's non-capital loss for a preceding taxation year;

(b) the debtor's farm loss for each taxation year that ended before that time, to the extent that the amount so applied

(i) does not exceed the amount that is the relevant loss balance at that time for the obligation and in respect of the debtor's farm loss for the year, and

(ii) does not, because of this subsection, reduce the debtor's farm loss for a preceding taxation year; and

(c) the debtor's restricted farm loss for each taxation year that ended before that time, to the extent that the amount so applied

(i) does not exceed the amount that is the relevant loss balance at that time for the obligation and in respect of the debtor's restricted farm loss for the year, and

(ii) does not, because of this subsection, reduce the debtor's restricted farm loss for a preceding taxation year.

Related Provisions: 31(1.1)(b) — Reduction in restricted farm loss; 80(2)(c) — Order of application of rules; 80(2)(m) — Reduction cannot exceed the amount of losses; 80(4)(a) — Reduction of allowable business investment loss carryforward; 111(8)"farm loss"C — Reduction in farm loss; 111(8)"non-capital loss"D.2 — Reduction in non-capital loss.

Notes: 80(3)–(14) set out a scheme of rules for using up the "forgiven amount" as defined in 80(1). See Notes at end of 80.

80(3) applied in *Ridge Run Developments*, 2007 TCC 68.

For CRA interpretation see VIEWS docs 2007-0259531R3, 2011-0418071I7.

(4) Reductions of capital losses — Where a commercial obligation issued by a debtor is settled at any time, the applicable fraction of the remaining unapplied portion of a forgiven amount at that time in respect of the obligation shall be applied to reduce at that time, in the following order,

(a) the debtor's non-capital loss for each taxation year that ended before that time to the extent that the amount so applied

(i) does not exceed the amount, if any, by which

(A) the relevant loss balance at that time for the obligation and in respect of the debtor's non-capital loss for the year

exceeds

(B) the debtor's ordinary non-capital loss (within the meaning assigned by subparagraph (3)(a)(i)) at that time for the year, and

(ii) does not, because of this subsection, reduce the debtor's non-capital loss for a preceding taxation year; and

(b) the debtor's net capital loss for each taxation year that ended before that time, to the extent that the amount so applied

(i) does not exceed the relevant loss balance at that time for the obligation and in respect of the debtor's net capital loss for the year, and

(ii) does not, because of this subsection, reduce the debtor's net capital loss for a preceding taxation year.

Related Provisions: 80(2)(c) — Order of application of rules; 80(2)(e) — Determination of applicable fraction; 80(2)(m) — Reduction cannot exceed the amount of losses; 111(8)"net capital loss"D — Reduction in net capital loss; 111(8)"non-capital loss"D.2 — Reduction in non-capital loss.

Notes: Reductions under 80(4) do not affect the capital dividend account: VIEWS doc 2006-020290I7.

(5) Reductions with respect to depreciable property — Where a commercial obligation issued by a debtor is settled at any time, the remaining unapplied portion of the forgiven amount at that time in respect of the obligation shall be applied, in such manner as is designated by the debtor in a prescribed form filed with the debtor's return of income under this Part for the taxation year that includes that time, to reduce immediately after that time the following amounts:

(a) the capital cost to the debtor of a depreciable property that is owned by the debtor immediately after that time; and

(b) the undepreciated capital cost to the debtor of depreciable property of a prescribed class immediately after that time.

Related Provisions: 13(7.1)(g) — Reduction in capital cost of depreciable property; 13(21)"undepreciated capital cost"E.1 — Reduction in undepreciated capital cost; 80(2)(c) — Order of application of rules; 80(2)(m) — Reduction cannot exceed the capital cost or UCC; 80(6) — Restriction with respect to depreciable property; 80(13)D(a) — Income inclusion of remaining balance; 80(16) — Designation by CRA where debtor fails to designate; 80.04(4)(b) — Transfer of forgiven amount after maximum designations; 96(3) — Designation by members of partnership; 220(3.21)(a) — Late filing, amendment or revocation of designation.

Notes: For an example of 80(5) applying see *Bisson*, 2007 TCC 178.

Regulations: 1105 (prescribed classes of depreciable property).

Forms: T2153: Designation under para. 80(2)(i) when two or more commercial obligations are settled at the same time; T2154: Designation of forgiven amount by the debtor — subsecs. 80(5) to 80(11).

(6) Restriction with respect to depreciable property — Where a commercial obligation issued by a debtor is settled at any time,

(a) an amount may be applied under subsection (5) to reduce, immediately after that time, the capital cost to the debtor of a depreciable property of a prescribed class only to the extent that

(i) the undepreciated capital cost to the debtor of depreciable property of that class at that time

exceeds

(ii) the total of all other reductions immediately after that time to that undepreciated capital cost; and

(b) an amount may be applied under subsection (5) to reduce, immediately after that time, the capital cost to the debtor of a depreciable property (other than a depreciable property of a prescribed class) only to the extent that

(i) the capital cost to the debtor of the property at that time

exceeds

(ii) the amount that was allowed to the debtor before that time under Part XVII of the *Income Tax Regulations* in respect of the property.

Regulations: 1105 (prescribed classes of depreciable property).

(7) [Repealed]

Notes: 80(7) repealed by 2016 budget bill #2, effective 2017, as part of changing eligible capital property rules to CCA Class 14.1 (see Notes to 20(1)(b)). Before 2017, read:

(7) Reductions of cumulative eligible capital — Where a commercial obligation issued by a debtor is settled at any time, ¾ of the remaining unapplied portion of the forgiven amount at that time in respect of the obligation shall be applied (to the extent designated in a prescribed form filed with the debtor's return of income under this Part for the taxation year that includes that time) to reduce immediately after that time the cumulative eligible capital of the debtor in respect of each business of the debtor (or, where the debtor is at that time non-resident, in respect of each business carried on in Canada by the debtor).

(8) Reductions of resource expenditures — Where a commercial obligation issued by a debtor is settled at any time, the remaining unapplied portion of the forgiven amount at that time in respect of the obligation shall be applied (to the extent designated in a prescribed form filed with the debtor's return of income under this Part for the taxation year that includes that time) to reduce immediately after that time the following amounts:

(a) where the debtor is a corporation resident in Canada throughout that year, each particular amount that would be determined in respect of the debtor under paragraph 66.7(2)(a), (2.3)(a), (3)(a), (4)(a) or (5)(a) if paragraphs 66.7(2.3)(a), (4)(a) and (5)(a) were read without reference to the expressions "30% of", "30% of" and "10% of", respectively, as a consequence of the acquisition of control of the debtor by a person or group of persons, the debtor ceasing to be exempt from tax under this Part on its taxable income or the acquisition of properties by the debtor by way of an amalgamation or merger, where the amount so applied does not exceed the successor pool immediately after that time for the obligation and in respect of the particular amount;

(b) the cumulative Canadian exploration expense (within the meaning assigned by subsection 66.1(6)) of the debtor;

(c) the cumulative Canadian development expense (within the meaning assigned by subsection 66.2(5)) of the debtor;

(d) the cumulative Canadian oil and gas property expense (within the meaning assigned by subsection 66.4(5)) of the debtor;

(e) the total determined under paragraph 66(4)(a) in respect of the debtor, where

(i) the debtor is resident in Canada throughout that year, and

(ii) the amount so applied does not exceed such portion of the total of the debtor's foreign exploration and development expenses (within the meaning assigned by subsection 66(15)) as were incurred by the debtor before that time and would be deductible under subsection 66(4) in computing the debtor's

income for that year if the debtor had sufficient income described in subparagraph 66(4)(b)(ii) and if that year ended at that time; and

(f) the cumulative foreign resource expense (within the meaning assigned by subsection 66.21(1)) of the debtor in respect of a country.

Related Provisions: 66(4)(a)(iii) — Reduction in claim for FEDE; 66.1(6)"cumulative Canadian exploration expense"J.1 — Reduction in CCEE; 66.2(5)"cumulative Canadian development expense"M.1 — Reduction in CCDE; 66.21(1)"cumulative foreign resource expense"I; 66.4(5)"cumulative Canadian oil and gas property expense"I.1 — Reduction in CCOGPE; 66.7(2)(a)(ii), 66.7(3)(a)(ii), 66.7(4)(a)(iv), 66.7(5)(a)(iii) — Reductions in successor pools; 80(2)(c) — Order of application of rules; 80(2)(m) — Reduction cannot exceed resource expenditures reduced; 80(13)D(a) — Income inclusion of remaining balance; 80(16) — Designation by CRA where debtor fails to designate; 80.04(4)(b) — Transfer of forgiven amount after maximum designations; 220(3.21)(a) — Late filing, amendment or revocation of designation; 256(6)–(9) — Whether control acquired.

Notes: 80(8) amended by 2000 Budget, for tax years that begin after 2000.

Forms: T2153: Designation under para. 80(2)(i) when two or more commercial obligations are settled at the same time; T2154: Designation of forgiven amount by the debtor — subsecs. 80(5) to 80(11).

(9) Reductions of adjusted cost bases of capital properties — If a commercial obligation issued by a debtor is settled at any time and amounts have been designated under subsections (5) and (8) to the maximum extent permitted in respect of the settlement, subject to subsection (18)

(a) the remaining unapplied portion of the forgiven amount at that time in respect of the obligation shall be applied (to the extent designated in a prescribed form filed with the debtor's return of income under this Part for the taxation year that includes that time) to reduce immediately after that time the adjusted cost bases to the debtor of capital properties (other than shares of the capital stock of corporations of which the debtor is a specified shareholder at that time, debts issued by corporations of which the debtor is a specified shareholder at that time, interests in partnerships that are related to the debtor at that time, depreciable property that is not of a prescribed class, personal-use properties and excluded properties) that are owned by the debtor immediately after that time;

(b) an amount may be applied under this subsection to reduce, immediately after that time, the capital cost to the debtor of a depreciable property of a prescribed class only to the extent that

(i) the capital cost immediately after that time to the debtor of the property (determined without reference to the settlement of the obligation at that time)

exceeds

(ii) its capital cost immediately after that time to the debtor for the purposes of paragraphs 8(1)(j) and (p), sections 13 and 20 and any regulations made for the purpose of paragraph 20(1)(a) (determined without reference to the settlement of the obligation at that time); and

(c) for the purposes of paragraphs 8(1)(j) and (p), sections 13 and 20 and any regulations made for the purpose of paragraph 20(1)(a), no amount shall be considered to have been applied under this subsection.

Related Provisions: 53(2)(g.1) — Reduction in ACB; 80(2)(c) — Order of application of rules; 80(2)(j) — Extended meaning of "related"; 80(2)(m) — Reduction cannot exceed the ACB; 80(10), (11) — Reduction of ACB of certain shares, debt and partnership interests; 80(13)D(a) — Income inclusion of remaining balance; 80(16) — Designation by CRA where debtor fails to designate; 80(18) — Limitation on designation by partnership; 80.04(4)(b) — Transfer of forgiven amount after maximum designations; 96(3) — Designation by partners; 220(3.21)(a) — Late filing, amendment or revocation of designation.

Notes: A debtor can use 80(9)(a) to reduce the ACB of a debt issued by a related partnership: VIEWS doc 2010-0371021E5.

80(9) opening words amended to delete reference to 80(7) by 2016 budget bill #2, effective 2017.

Regulations: 1105 (prescribed classes of depreciable property).

Forms: T2153: Designation under para. 80(2)(i) when two or more commercial obligations are settled at the same time; T2154: Designation of forgiven amount by the debtor — subsecs. 80(5) to 80(11).

(10) Reduction of adjusted cost bases of certain shares and debts — If a commercial obligation issued by a debtor is settled at any time in a taxation year and amounts have been designated by the debtor under subsections (5), (8) and (9) to the maximum extent permitted in respect of the settlement, subject to subsection (18) the remaining unapplied portion of that forgiven amount shall be applied (to the extent that it is designated in a prescribed form filed with the debtor's return of income under this Part for the year) to reduce immediately after that time the adjusted cost bases to the debtor of capital properties, owned by the debtor immediately after that time, that are shares of the capital stock of corporations of which the debtor is a specified shareholder at that time and debts issued by corporations of which the debtor is a specified shareholder at that time (other than shares of the capital stock of corporations related to the debtor at that time, debts issued by corporations related to the debtor at that time and excluded properties).

Related Provisions: 53(2)(g.1) — Reduction in ACB; 80(2)(c) — Order of application of rules; 80(2)(j) — Extended meaning of "related"; 80(2)(m) — Reduction cannot exceed the ACB; 80(11) — Reduction of ACB of certain shares, debt and partnership interests; 80(13)D(a) — Income inclusion of remaining balance; 80(16) — Designation by CRA where debtor fails to designate; 80(18) — Limitation on designation by partnership; 80.04(4)(b) — Transfer of forgiven amount after maximum designations; 96(3) — Designation by partners; 220(3.21)(a) — Late filing, amendment or revocation of designation.

Notes: 80(10) amended to delete reference to 80(7) by 2016 budget bill #2, effective 2017.

Forms: T2153: Designation under para. 80(2)(i) when two or more commercial obligations are settled at the same time; T2154: Designation of forgiven amount by the debtor — subsecs. 80(5) to 80(11).

(11) Reduction of adjusted cost bases of certain shares, debts and partnership interests — If a commercial obligation issued by a debtor is settled at any time in a taxation year and amounts have been designated by the debtor under subsections (5), (8), (9) and (10) to the maximum extent permitted in respect of the settlement, subject to subsection (18) the remaining unapplied portion of that forgiven amount shall be applied (to the extent that it is designated in a prescribed form filed with the debtor's return of income under this Part for the year) to reduce immediately after that time the adjusted cost bases to the debtor of

(a) shares and debts that are capital properties (other than excluded properties and properties the adjusted cost bases of which are reduced at that time under subsection (9) or (10)) of the debtor immediately after that time; and

(b) interests in partnerships that are related to the debtor at that time that are capital properties (other than excluded properties) of the debtor immediately after that time.

Related Provisions: 53(2)(g.1) — Reduction in ACB; 80(2)(c) — Order of application of rules; 80(2)(j) — Extended meaning of "related"; 80(2)(m) — Reduction cannot exceed the ACB; 80(13)B(a) — Income inclusion where reductions in ACB are excessive; 80(16) — Designation by CRA where debtor fails to designate; 80(18) — Limitation on designation by partnership; 80.03 — Gains on subsequent dispositions; 96(3) — Designation by partners; 220(3.21)(a) — Late filing, amendment or revocation of designation.

Notes: For an example of 80(11) applying see VIEWS doc 2012-0433941E5.

80(11) opening words amended to delete reference to 80(7) by 2016 budget bill #2, effective 2017.

Forms: T2153: Designation under para. 80(2)(i) when two or more commercial obligations are settled at the same time; T2154: Designation of forgiven amount by the debtor — subsecs. 80(5) to 80(11).

(12) Capital gain where current year capital loss — If a commercial obligation issued by a debtor (other than a partnership) is settled at any time in a taxation year and amounts have been designated by the debtor under subsections (5), (8) and (9) to the maximum extent permitted in respect of the settlement,

(a) the debtor shall be deemed to have a capital gain for the year from the disposition of capital property (or, where the debtor is non-resident at the end of the year, taxable Canadian property), equal to the lesser of

(i) the remaining unapplied portion of the forgiven amount at that time in respect of the obligation, and

(ii) the amount, if any, by which the total of

(A) all of the debtor's capital losses for the year from the dispositions of properties (other than listed personal properties and excluded properties), and

(B) twice the amount that would, because of subsection 88(1.2), be deductible under paragraph 111(1)(b) in computing the debtor's taxable income for the year, if the debtor had sufficient income and taxable capital gains for the year,

exceeds the total of

(C) all of the debtor's capital gains for the year from the dispositions of such properties (determined without reference to this subsection), and

(D) all amounts each of which is an amount deemed by this subsection to be a capital gain of the debtor for the year as a consequence of the application of this subsection to other commercial obligations settled before that time; and

(b) the forgiven amount at that time in respect of the obligation shall be considered to have been applied under this subsection to the extent of the amount deemed by this subsection to be a capital gain of the debtor for the year as a consequence of the application of this subsection to the settlement of the obligation at that time.

Related Provisions: 80(2)(c) — Order of application of rules.

Notes: 80(12) applied in *Jones Development*, 2009 TCC 397. For CRA interpretation see VIEWS docs 2009-032925117; 2011-0412541E5 (deemed capital gain is included in capital dividend account).

80(12) opening words amended to delete reference to 80(7) by 2016 budget bill #2, effective 2017.

80(12)(a)(ii)(B) amended by 2000 Budget to change "⁴/₃ of" to "twice", effective for taxation years that end after Feb. 27, 2000, with transitional rules for 2000.

(13) Income inclusion — Where a commercial obligation issued by a debtor is settled at any time in a taxation year, there shall be added, in computing the debtor's income for the year from the source in connection with which the obligation was issued, the amount determined by the formula

$$(A + B - C - D) \times E$$

where

A is the remaining unapplied portion of the forgiven amount at that time in respect of the obligation,

B is the lesser of

(a) the total of all amounts designated under subsection (11) by the debtor in respect of the settlement of the obligation at that time, and

(b) the residual balance at that time in respect of the settlement of the obligation,

C is the total of all amounts each of which is an amount specified in an agreement filed under section 80.04 in respect of the settlement of the obligation at that time,

D is

(a) if the debtor has designated amounts under subsections (5), (8), (9) and (10) to the maximum extent permitted in respect of the settlement, the amount, if any, by which

(i) the total of all amounts each of which is an unrecognized loss at that time, in respect of the obligation, from the disposition of a property

exceeds

(ii) twice the total of all amounts each of which is an amount by which the amount determined before that time under this subsection in respect of a settlement of an obligation issued by the debtor has been reduced because of an amount determined under this paragraph, and

(b) in any other case, nil, and

E is

    (a) where the debtor is a partnership, 1, and

    (b) in any other case, $1/2$.

Related Provisions: 4(1) — Income from a source; 6(15) — Income inclusion on forgiveness of debt owing by employee; 12(1)(z.3) — Inclusion into income from business or property; 28(1)(d) — Inclusion in farming or fishing income when using cash method; 61.2–61.4 — Reserves to offset amount included under 80(13); 66.7(1)(b)(iii), 66.7(2)(b)(iv), 66.7(3)(b)(iii), 66.7(4)(b)(iii), 66.7(5)(b)(iii) — Resource expenditures — reduction in successor pools; 80(2)(c) — Order of application of rules; 80(14) — Determination of residual balance; 80(16) — Designation by CRA to reduce reserve under 61.2; 80.04(8) — Where corporations become related in order to transfer forgiven amount; 95(1)"foreign accrual property income"A.1 — $4/3$ inclusion in FAPI; 137.1(10) — Settlement of debts by deposit insurance corporation; 257 — Formula cannot calculate to less than zero.

Notes: See Notes at end of s. 80. If after applying the "forgiven amount" (defined in 80(1)) as set out in 80(3)-(12) there is still a residual balance (defined in 80(14)), it is included into income under 80(13) unless it can be transferred to another taxpayer under 80.04. See Notes at end of 80. However, there may be an offsetting deduction under 61.3 and/or a deferral of the income to later years under 61.2 and 61.4.

80(13) applied in *Komutel Inc.*, 2010 TCC 284.

80(13)D(a) opening words amended to delete reference to 80(7) by 2016 budget bill #2, effective 2017.

80(13) amended by 2000 Budget (for tax years ending after Oct. 17, 2000), 1995-97 technical bill.

Interpretation Bulletins: See list at end of s. 80.

Information Circulars: See list at end of s. 80.

Advance Tax Rulings: ATR-27: Exchange and acquisition of interests in capital properties through rollovers and winding-up ("butterfly").

(14) Residual balance — For the purpose of subsection (13), the residual balance at any time in a taxation year in respect of the settlement of a particular commercial obligation issued by a debtor is the amount, if any, by which

    (a) the gross tax attributes of directed persons at that time in respect of the debtor

exceeds the total of

    (b) the value of A in subsection (13) in respect of the settlement of the particular obligation at that time,

    (c) all amounts each of which is

        (i) the amount, if any, by which the value of A in subsection (13) in respect of a settlement before that time and in the year of a commercial obligation issued by the debtor exceeds the value of C in that subsection in respect of the settlement,

        (ii) the value of A in subsection (13) in respect of a settlement of a commercial obligation that is deemed by paragraph 80.04(4)(e) to have been issued by a directed person in respect of the debtor because of the filing of an agreement under section 80.04 in respect of a settlement before that time and in the year of a commercial obligation issued by the debtor, or

        (iii) the amount specified in an agreement (other than an agreement with a directed person in respect of the debtor) filed under section 80.04 in respect of the settlement before that time and in the year of a commercial obligation issued by the debtor, and

    (d) all amounts each of which is an amount in respect of a settlement at a particular time before that time and in the year of a commercial obligation issued by the debtor equal to the least of

        (i) the total of all amounts designated under subsection (11) in respect of the settlement,

        (ii) the residual balance of the debtor at the particular time, and

        (iii) the amount, if any, by which the sum of the values of A and B in subsection (13) in respect of the settlement exceeds the value of C in that subsection in respect of the settlement.

Related Provisions: 80(14.1) — Meaning of "gross tax attributes".

Notes: 80(14) amended by 1995-97 technical bill, retroactive to its introduction (see Notes at end of s. 80).

(14.1) Gross tax attributes — The gross tax attributes of directed persons at any time in respect of a debtor means the total of all amounts each of which is an amount that would be applied under any of subsections (3) to (10) and (12) in respect of a settlement of a separate commercial obligation (in this subsection referred to as a "notional obligation") issued by directed persons at that time in respect of the debtor if the following assumptions were made:

    (a) a notional obligation was issued immediately before that time by each of those directed persons and was settled at that time;

    (b) the forgiven amount at that time in respect of each of those notional obligations was equal to the total of all amounts each of which is a forgiven amount at or before that time and in the year in respect of a commercial obligation issued by the debtor;

    (c) amounts were designated under subsections (5), (8), (9) and (10) by each of those directed persons to the maximum extent permitted in respect of the settlement of each of those notional obligations; and

    (d) no amounts were designated under subsection (11) by any of those directed persons in respect of the settlement of any of the notional obligations.

Notes: 80(14.1)(c) amended to delete reference to 80(7) by 2016 budget bill #2, effective 2017.

80(14.1) added by 1995-97 technical bill, for tax years ending after Feb. 21, 1994.

(15) Members of partnerships — Where a commercial debt obligation issued by a partnership (in this subsection referred to as the "partnership obligation") is settled at any time in a fiscal period of the partnership that ends in a taxation year of a member of the partnership,

    (a) the member may deduct, in computing the member's income for the year, such amount as the member claims not exceeding the relevant limit in respect of the partnership obligation;

    (b) for the purpose of paragraph (a), the relevant limit in respect of the partnership obligation is the amount that would be included in computing the member's income for the year as a consequence of the application of subsection (13) and section 96 to the settlement of the partnership obligation if the partnership had designated amounts under subsections (5), (8), (9) and (10) to the maximum extent permitted in respect of each obligation settled in that fiscal period and if income arising from the application of subsection (13) were from a source of income separate from any other sources of partnership income; and

    (c) for the purposes of this section and section 80.04,

        (i) the member shall be deemed to have issued a commercial debt obligation that was settled at the end of that fiscal period,

        (ii) the amount deducted under paragraph (a) in respect of the partnership obligation in computing the member's income shall be treated as if it were the forgiven amount at the end of that fiscal period in respect of the obligation referred to in subparagraph (i),

        (iii) subject to subparagraph (iv), the obligation referred to in subparagraph (i) shall be deemed to have been issued at the same time at which, and in the same circumstances in which, the partnership obligation was issued,

        (iv) if the member is a taxpayer that was subject to a loss restriction event at a particular time that is before the end of that fiscal period and before the taxpayer became a member of the partnership, and the partnership obligation was issued before the particular time,

            (A) subject to the application of this subparagraph to the taxpayer after the particular time and before the end of that fiscal period, the obligation referred to in subparagraph (i) is deemed to have been issued by the member after the particular time, and

            (B) subparagraph (b)(ii) of the definition "relevant loss balance" in subsection (1), paragraph (f) of the definition "successor pool" in that subsection and paragraph (b) of the definition "unrecognized loss" in that subsection do not apply in respect of the loss restriction event, and

(v) the source in connection with which the obligation referred to in subparagraph (i) was issued shall be deemed to be the source in connection with which the partnership obligation was issued.

Related Provisions: 4(1) — Income from a source; 20(1)(uu) — Deduction for amount allowed under para. 80(15)(a); 61.2:A(b) — Effect of para. 80(15)(a) on reserve for individuals; 61.2:A(b), 61.3(1)(a)(ii), 61.3(2)(a)(ii), 61.4(a)A(ii) — Reserve in respect of debt forgiven; 80(1) — "Person" includes a partnership; 80(2)(n) — Commercial debt obligation issued by partner — deemed issued by partnership; 80(13)E(a) — Income inclusion where debtor is partnership; 80(14)(b) — Residual balance where debtor is partnership; 80(18) — Limitation on designation by partnership; 96(3) — Designation by partners; 251.2 — Loss restriction event.

Notes: 80(15) provides relief for members of a partnership, since a partner may have undeducted loss carryforwards and resource expenditure pools that are attributable to partnership activities. Forgiveness of an obligation that is deemed to arise for a partner is treated the same as a forgiven amount in respect of an obligation issued by the debtor. Further relief for certain partnership obligations is provided under 80(1)"forgiven amount"B(k). Special rules for partnership obligations are also provided under 80(2)(n) and (o) and 80(18). See also Notes at end of 80.

See also VIEWS docs 2005-0120341I7 (interaction of 80(15)(c)(ii) and 80(9)(a)); 2010-0358091E5 (80(15) has no effect on ACB of partnership interest); 2016-0666481E5 (80(15) applies in a tiered partnership structure).

80(15)(b) amended to delete reference to 80(7) by 2016 budget bill #2, effective 2017.

80(15)(c)(iv) amended by 2013 budget bill #2, effective March 21, 2013, to change references from control of a corporation being acquired to a "loss restriction event", to extend the rule to trusts (see Notes to 251.2(2)).

(16) Designations by Minister — Where a commercial obligation issued by a debtor is settled at any time in a taxation year and, as a consequence of the settlement an amount would, but for this subsection, be deducted under section 61.2 or 61.3 in computing the debtor's income for the year and the debtor has not designated amounts under subsections (5) to (11) to the maximum extent possible in respect of the settlement,

(a) the Minister may designate amounts under subsections (5) to (11) to the extent that the debtor would have been permitted to designate those amounts; and

(b) the amounts designated by the Minister shall, except for the purpose of this subsection, be deemed to have been designated by the debtor as required by subsections (5) to (11).

Notes: 80(16) allows the CRA to designate amounts under any of 80(5)–(11), to the extent the debtor would have been permitted to have designated those amounts. However, this is only where an amount would otherwise be deducted under 61.2 or 61.3. Note that, in these circumstances, the CRA can designate an amount under 80(11) even where that increase also results in an increase in the amount added in computing the debtor's income under 80(13) and, therefore, an increase in an offsetting amount deducted under section 61.3. For CRA interpretation see VIEWS docs 2009-0329251I7, 2012-0468851E5. See also Notes at end of 80.

(17) [Repealed]

Notes: 80(17) repealed by 1995-97 technical bill, retroactive to its introduction (see Notes at end of s. 80). It was repealed to reduce the complexity of the debt forgiveness rules. It was titled "Income inclusion where residual balance a positive amount".

(18) Partnership designations — Where a commercial obligation issued by a partnership is settled at any time after December 20, 1994, the amount designated under subsection (9), (10) or (11) in respect of the settlement by the partnership to reduce the adjusted cost base of a capital property acquired shall not exceed the amount, if any, by which the adjusted cost base at that time to the partnership of the property exceeds the fair market value at that time of the property.

Notes [subsec. 80(18)]: The purpose of 80(18) is to prevent partnerships from acquiring capital properties in order to minimize the impact of s. 80. It is limited to partnerships because many tax attributes (e.g. loss carryforwards and resource expenditures) are allocated to partnership members and the forgiveness of a commercial obligation considered to have been issued by a partnership does not result in a reduction of those attributes, subject to the application of 80(15).

Notes [s. 80]: 80 sets out a series of rules for a debtor to apply the "forgiven amount" (defined in 80(1)) where a commercial debt is forgiven. Simplified, the balance is applied first to non-capital losses and farm losses (80(3)), then ABILs and net capital losses (80(4)), then [the rest are all optional: *Richer*, 2009 TCC 394, para. 110] depre-

ciable property capital cost and UCC balances (80(5), (6)), resource expenditure balances (80(8)), ACB of certain capital property (80(9)–(11)), then current year net capital losses (80(12)). Any remaining balance may be transferable to another taxpayer under 80.04. If there is still a "residual balance" (80(14)), half of it (all of it for a partnership) is included in income by 80(13), possibly offset by a deduction or reserve under 61.2–61.4. See also the special rules in 80.01–80.04, and 80(15)–(18) Notes.

The debt forgiveness rules apply in the following order: 78 [see 80(1)"excluded obligation"(c)]; 6(1) and (15) [see 80(1)"forgiven amount"B(b)]; 15(1), (1.2), 9(1) [e.g. if a trade account payable is settled]; 79 [see 80(1)"forgiven amount"(f)]; finally, s. 80.

For the context and purpose of the s. 80 scheme, see *Pièces Automobiles Lecavalier*, 2013 TCC 310, paras. 87-103.

See also Pickford & Tunney, "The Tax Treatment of Forgiveness of Debt and Foreclosures", 1994 Cdn Tax Foundation conference report, 3:1-62; Felesky & Sykora, "The Debt Forgiveness and Foreclosure Rules", 43(5) *Canadian Tax Journal* 1316-42 (1995) (policy discussion); Bernstein, "Update on Debt Forgiveness", 1995 *Corporate Management Tax Conference* (ctf.ca) 21:1-43; Nimchuk, "Revised Section 80", 1995 Prairie Provinces Tax Conference [PPTC] (ctf.ca), 2:1-22; Ahmed & Silverson, "The New Debt-Forgiveness Rules", 1996 conference report, 21:1-38; Glass, "Section 80", 2002 BC Tax Conf. 16:1-37; Baek, "Tax Planning for Recessionary Times", 2003 conference report, 53:1-34; Courage, "Utilization of Tax Losses and Debt Restructuring" 2006 Ontario Tax Conf., 9:1 at 9:74-86; Bauer, "Restructuring Debt Obligations", 2008 conference report, 37:1-35; Boehmer et al., "Insolvency", 2009 conference report, 7:1-40; Hurowitz et al., "Debt Restructuring", *ibid.*, 14:1-44; Cruickshank, "Understanding the Boundaries of Section 80", 2009 Atlantic Provinces Tax Conf. 4B:1-33; Vantil, "Corporate Debt Settlement and Forgiveness", 2009 B.C. Tax Conf. 6:1-38; Dale, "Debt Forgiveness", 2009 Ontario Tax Conf. 3:1-11; Hegedus, "Fond Memories of Section 80", 2009 PPTC 9:1-40; D'Avignon, "Tax Planning for Economic Downturns", 22(1) *Canadian Petroleum Tax Journal* 31-52 (2009); Beaudry & Kraus, "Selected Income Tax Considerations in Court-Approved Debt Restructuring", 2015 conference report, 13:1-44; Aiken & Tai, "Debt-Restructuring Transactions", 2016 conference report, 14:1-24; Friedlander, *Taxation of Corporate Finance* (Carswell, looseleaf or *Taxnet Pro* Reference Centre), §4.4.3; Choudhury, "Debt Restructuring During and After COVID-19", 2518 *Tax Topics* (CCH) 7-11 (June 9, 2020); Bodie & Haughey, "Introduction to Debt Forgiveness", *YP Focus Virtual Conference* (ctf.ca, Sept. 2020), 2:1-56; Hosanna, "Debt Restructuring in the Resource Sector", XXVIII(3) *Taxation of Executive Compensation & Retirement* (Federated Press) 2-14 (2020).

For application of the debt forgiveness rules under FAPI see 95(2)(g.1).

Where the debt is partnership debt, see Mah and Vantil, "Debt Forgiveness — Opportunities and Pitfalls of Restructuring Partnership Debt", VIII(4) *Corporate Structures & Groups* (Federated Press) 447-49 (2003); Montes, "Debt Forgiveness in a Partnership Context", 11(2) *Tax for the Owner-Manager* (ctf.ca) 11-12 (April 2011).

For CRA views that s. 80 does not apply see docs 2010-0389651R3 (ELHT's assumption of employer's obligation to provide post-retirement benefits); 2013-0498551R3, 2014-0543911R3 (loss consolidations); 2014-0529981I7 (debt of limited partnership to partner corp's parent; s. 80 avoided); 2015-0568411E5 (release of tax debts under consumer proposal).

On interaction with 143.4 see Notes to 143.4(2).

See also docs 2009-0338911E5 (s. 80 applies where creditor-shareholders of a CCPC consent to dissolve it); 2009-0343601I7 (tax pools reduced before 80(13) income inclusion); 2010-0370991E5 (debt forgiveness between corps owned 50/50 by the same two individuals); 2010-0371941C6 (application on amalgamation or windup); 2011-0392171R3 (GAAR applies to pre-amalgamation debt capitalization transactions that misuse s. 80); 2011-0393561E5 (general discussion); 2015-0595481E5 (debt forgiveness added to income under GAAP can trigger Ontario corporate minimum tax).

S. 80 applies only to commercial debts (see 80(1)"commercial debt obligation" and "forgiven amount"). Where debt of an employee is settled or forgiven, see 6(15).

A bankruptcy proposal to exempt the bankrupt from all claims by the CRA arising out of the bankruptcy, including the future application of s. 80, is illegal because a proposal is a contract between debtor and creditors and the CRA cannot contract out of its duty to assess tax under the Act: *Beach*, [2002] 1 C.T.C. 89 (BCCA).

80 completely replaced by 1994 technical bill, for taxation years ending after Feb. 21, 1994, with grandfathering for an obligation settled or extinguished under an agreement in writing entered into by Feb. 21, 1994, or under certain amendments (to such agreement) entered into by July 11, 1994 (see up to 51st ed. for details).

For the former version of s. 80, see these Notes in any edition up to the 28th.

Definitions [s. 80]: "adjusted cost base" — 54, 248(1); "allowable business investment loss" — 38(c), 248(1); "amount" — 248(1); "applicable fraction" — 80(2)(d); "bankrupt" — 248(1); "beneficially interested" — 248(25); "business" — 80.03(7)(b)(iii), 248(1); "Canada" — 255; "Canadian currency" — 261(5)(f)(i); "Canadian partnership" — 102(1), 248(1); "capital gain", "capital loss" — 39(1), 248(1); "capital property" — 54, 248(1); "carried on in Canada" — 253; "class" — 248(6); "commercial debt obligation" — 80(1); "control", "controlled" — 80(2)(j), 256(6)–(9); "controlled directly or indirectly" — 256(5.1)–(6); "corporation" — 248(1), *Interpretation Act* 35(1); "cost amount" — 248(1); "cumulative eligible capital" — 14(5), 248(1); "cumulative foreign resource expense" — 66.21(1); "debtor" — 80(1); "depreciable property" — 13(21), 248(1); "designated stock exchange" — 248(1), 262; "directed person" — 80(1); "distress preferred share", "eligible Canadian partnership", "excluded obligation", "excluded property", "excluded security" — 80(1); "fair market value" — see 69(1) Notes; "farm loss" — 111(8), 248(1); "fiscal period" — 249(2)(b),

249.1; "foreign exploration and development expenses" — 66(15); "forgiven amount" — 80(1), 80.01(8)(b), 80.03(7)(b)(ii); "gross tax attributes" — 80(14.1) "listed personal property" — 54, 248(1); "loss restriction event" — 251.2; "Minister" — 248(1); "net capital loss", "non-capital loss" — 111(8), 248(1); "non-resident" — 248(1); "non-resident-owned investment corporation" — 133(8), 248(1); "ordinary non-capital loss" — 80(3)(a)(i); "partnership" — see 96(1) Notes; "partnership obligation" — 80(15); "person" — 80(1), 248(1); "personal-use property" — 54, 248(1); "prescribed" — 248(1); "principal amount" — 248(1), (26); "property", "regulation" — 248(1); "related" — 80(2)(j), 251(2); "relevant limit" — 80(15)(b); "relevant loss balance" — 80(1); "residual balance" — 80(14); "resident in Canada" — 94(3)(a), 250; "restricted farm loss" — 31, 248(1); "settled" — 80(2)(a), 80.01(3)–(9), 80.02(2)(c), 80.02(7)(a), 80.03(7)(b)(i); "share" — 248(1); "source" — 4(1), 80.03(7)(b)(iv); "specified shareholder" — 248(1); "successor pool" — 80(1); "taxable Canadian corporation" — 89(1), 248(1); "taxable Canadian property" — 248(1); "taxable capital gain" — 38(a), 248(1); "taxable income" — 2(2), 248(1); "taxable income earned in Canada" — 115(1), 248(1); "taxation year" — 11(2), 249; "taxpayer", "treaty-protected property" — 248(1); "trust" — 104(1), 248(1), (3); "undepreciated capital cost" — 13(21), 248(1); "unrecognized loss" — 80(1); "writing" — *Interpretation Act* 35(1).

I.T. Application Rules [s. 80]: 26(1.1) (debt outstanding since before 1972.).

Interpretation Bulletins [s. 80]: IT-109R2: Unpaid amounts; IT-142R3: Settlement of debts on the winding-up of a corporation; IT-232R3: Losses — their deductibility in the loss year or in other years; IT-262R2: Losses of non-residents and part-year residents; IT-268R3: *Inter vivos* transfer of farm property to child; IT-293R: Debtor's gain on settlement of debt; IT-382: Debts bequeathed or forgiven on death (cancelled); IT-430R3: Life insurance proceeds received by a private corporation or a partnership as a consequence of death; IT-488R2: Winding-up of 90%-owned taxable Canadian corporations (cancelled).

Information Circulars [s. 80]: 88-2, para. 23: General anti-avoidance rule — section 245 of the *Income Tax Act*; 88-2 Supplement, para. 6: General anti-avoidance rule — section 245 of the *Income Tax Act*.

80.01 [Debt parking] — (1) Definitions — In this section,

"**commercial debt obligation**" has the meaning assigned by subsection 80(1);

Notes: See Notes at end of 80.01.

"**commercial obligation**" has the meaning assigned by subsection 80(1);

"**debtor**" has the meaning assigned by subsection 80(1);

"**distress preferred share**" has the meaning assigned by subsection 80(1);

"**forgiven amount**" has the meaning assigned by subsection 80(1) except that, where an amount would be included in computing a person's income under paragraph 6(1)(a) or subsection 15(1) as a consequence of the settlement of an obligation if the obligation were settled without any payment being made in satisfaction of its principal amount, "forgiven amount" in respect of that obligation has the meaning assigned by subsection 6(15.1) or 15(1.21), as the case may be;

"**person**" has the meaning assigned by subsection 80(1);

"**specified cost**" at any time to a person of an obligation means,

(a) where the obligation is capital property of the person at that time, the adjusted cost base at that time to the person of the obligation, and

(b) in any other case, the cost amount to the person of the obligation.

(2) Application — For the purposes of this section,

(a) paragraphs 80(2)(a), (b), (j), (l) and (n) apply; and

(b) a person has a significant interest in a corporation at any time if the person owned at that time

(i) shares of the capital stock of the corporation that would give the person 25% or more of the votes that could be cast under all circumstances at an annual meeting of shareholders of the corporation, or

(ii) shares of the capital stock of the corporation having a fair market value of 25% or more of the fair market value of all the issued shares of the capital stock of the corporation

and, for the purposes of this paragraph, a person shall be deemed to own at any time each share of the capital stock of a corporation that is owned, otherwise than because of this paragraph, at that time by another person with whom the person does not deal at arm's length.

(3) Deemed settlement on amalgamation — Where a commercial obligation or another obligation (in this subsection referred to as the "indebtedness") of a debtor that is a corporation to pay an amount to another corporation (in this subsection referred to as the "creditor") is settled on an amalgamation of the debtor and the creditor, the indebtedness shall be deemed to have been settled immediately before the time that is immediately before the amalgamation by a payment made by the debtor and received by the creditor of an amount equal to the amount that would have been the creditor's cost amount of the indebtedness at that time if

(a) the definition "cost amount" in subsection 248(1) were read without reference to paragraph (e) of that definition; and

(b) that cost amount included amounts added in computing the creditor's income in respect of the portion of the indebtedness representing unpaid interest, to the extent those amounts have not been deducted in computing the creditor's income as bad debts in respect of that unpaid interest.

Related Provisions: 39(2.01)–(2.03) — Debt parking to avoid foreign exchange gains; 80(3)–(13) — Treatment of obligation deemed to have been settled.

Notes: See VIEWS docs 2008-0267831E5 (no FX loss where foreign currency loan is deemed settled on debtor-creditor amalgamation, due to 80(2)(k)); 2009-0330881R3 (foreign mergers were "amalgamations"); 2010-0376681R3 (80.01(3) applies); 2011-0429071E5 (amalgamation of farming corps that both use the cash method); 2014-0544941E5 (deemed loss under 111(12) does not affect 80.01(3)).

Income Tax Folios: S4-F7-C1: Amalgamations of Canadian corporations [replaces IT-474R2].

(4) Deemed settlement on winding-up — Where there is a winding-up of a subsidiary to which the rules in subsection 88(1) apply and

(a) a debt or other obligation (in this subsection referred to as the "subsidiary's obligation") of the subsidiary to pay an amount to the parent, or

(b) a debt or other obligation (in this subsection referred to as the "parent's obligation") of the parent to pay an amount to the subsidiary

is, as a consequence of the winding-up, settled at a particular time without any payment of an amount or by the payment of an amount that is less than the principal amount of the subsidiary's obligation or the parent's obligation, as the case may be,

(c) where that payment is less than the amount that would have been the cost amount to the parent or subsidiary of the subsidiary's obligation or the parent's obligation immediately before the particular time if the definition "cost amount" in subsection 248(1) were read without reference to paragraph (e) of that definition and the parent so elects in a prescribed form on or before the day on or before which the parent is required to file a return of income pursuant to section 150 for the taxation year that includes the particular time, the amount paid at that time in satisfaction of the principal amount of the subsidiary's obligation or the parent's obligation shall be deemed to be equal to the amount that would be the cost amount to the parent or the subsidiary, as the case may be, of the subsidiary's obligation or the parent's obligation immediately before the particular time if

(i) the definition "cost amount" in subsection 248(1) were read without reference to paragraph (e) of that definition, and

(ii) that cost amount included amounts added in computing the parent's income or the subsidiary's income in respect of the portion of the indebtedness representing unpaid interest, to the extent that the parent or the subsidiary has not deducted any amounts as bad debts in respect of that unpaid interest, and

(d) for the purposes of applying section 80 to the subsidiary's obligation, where property is distributed at any time in circumstances to which paragraph 88(1)(a) or (b) applies and the subsidiary's obligation is settled as a consequence of the distribution, the subsidiary's obligation shall be deemed to have been settled immediately before the time that is immediately before the time of the distribution and not at any later time.

Related Provisions: 39(2.01)–(2.03) — Debt parking to avoid foreign exchange gains; 50(1)(b)(ii) — Deemed disposition of debt or shares on winding-up; 80(3)–(13) — Treatment of obligation deemed to have been settled; 80.01(5) — Where distress preferred share issued; 220(3.2), Reg. 600(b) — Late filing or revocation of election under 80.01(4)(c).

Notes: For interpretation of 80.01(4) see VIEWS docs 2009-0313921R3 (subsidiary creditor wound up into debtor); 2009-0343201R3 (trust conversion to corporation); 2009-0347661C6 (application of 80(2)(k)); 2009-0350711R3 (no "forgiven amount" if election made); 2011-0426051R3 (debt restructuring).

On whether the election is valid if it is not filed, see Notes to 80.1(4).

For a taxpayer filing Quebec returns, an election under 80.01(4)(c) must be copied to Revenu Québec: *Taxation Act* ss. 485.21, 21.4.6.

Advance Tax Rulings: ATR-66: Non-arm's length transfer of debt followed by a winding-up and a sale of shares.

Forms: T2027: Election to deem amount of settlement of a debt or obligation.

(5) Deemed settlement on winding-up — Where there is a winding-up of a subsidiary to which the rules in subsection 88(1) apply and, as a consequence of the winding-up, a distress preferred share issued by the subsidiary and owned by the parent (or a distress preferred share issued by the parent and owned by the subsidiary) is settled at any time without any payment of an amount or by the payment of an amount that is less than the principal amount of the share,

(a) where the payment was less than the adjusted cost base of the share to the parent or the subsidiary, as the case may be, immediately before that time, for the purposes of applying the provisions of this Act to the issuer of the share, the amount paid at that time in satisfaction of the principal amount of the share shall be deemed to be equal to its adjusted cost base to the parent or to the subsidiary, as the case may be; and

(b) for the purposes of applying section 80 to the share, where property is distributed at any time in circumstances to which paragraph 88(1)(a) or (b) applies and the share is settled as a consequence of the distribution, the share shall be deemed to have been settled immediately before the time that is immediately before the time of the distribution and not at any later time.

Related Provisions: 39(2.01)–(2.03) — Debt parking to avoid foreign exchange gains; 50(1)(b)(ii) — Deemed disposition of debt or shares on winding-up; 80(3)–(13) — Treatment of obligation deemed to have been settled; 80.02(2)(c) — Meaning of "settled" for distress preferred shares; 88(1)(b) — Determination of proceeds of disposition to parent.

(5.1) Deemed settlement on SIFT trust wind-up event — If a trust that is a SIFT wind-up entity is the only beneficiary under another trust (in this subsection referred to as the "subsidiary trust"), and a capital property that is a debt or other obligation (in this subsection referred to as the "subsidiary trust's obligation") of the subsidiary trust to pay an amount to the SIFT wind-up entity is, as a consequence of a distribution from the subsidiary trust that is a SIFT trust wind-up event, settled at a particular time without any payment of an amount or by the payment of an amount that is less than the principal amount of the subsidiary trust's obligation

(a) paragraph (b) applies if

(i) the payment is less than the amount that would have been the adjusted cost base to the SIFT wind-up entity of the subsidiary trust's obligation immediately before the particular time, and

(ii) the SIFT wind-up entity elects, in prescribed form on or before the SIFT wind-up entity's filing-due date for the taxation year that includes the particular time, to have paragraph (b) apply;

(b) if this paragraph applies, the amount paid at the particular time in satisfaction of the principal amount of the subsidiary trust's obligation is deemed to be equal to the amount that would be the adjusted cost base to the SIFT wind-up entity of the sub-

sidiary trust's obligation immediately before the particular time if that adjusted cost base included amounts added in computing the SIFT wind-up entity's income in respect of the portion of the indebtedness representing unpaid interest, to the extent that the SIFT wind-up entity has not deducted any amounts as bad debts in respect of that unpaid interest; and

(c) for the purposes of applying section 80 to the subsidiary trust's obligation, the subsidiary trust's obligation is deemed to have been settled immediately before the time that is immediately before the distribution.

Notes: 80.01(5.1) added by 2008 budget bill #2, effective July 15, 2008. See Notes to 85.1(8) re SIFT windups. For an entity filing a Quebec return, an (a)(ii) election must be copied to Revenu Québec: *Taxation Act* ss. 485.22.1, 21.4.6.

(6) Specified obligation in relation to debt parking — For the purpose of subsection (7), an obligation issued by a debtor is, at a particular time, a specified obligation of the debtor where

(a) at any previous time (other than a time before the last time, if any, the obligation became a parked obligation before the particular time),

(i) a person who owned the obligation

(A) dealt at arm's length with the debtor, and

(B) where the debtor is a corporation, did not have a significant interest in the debtor, or

(ii) the obligation was acquired by the holder of the obligation from another person who was, at the time of that acquisition, not related to the holder or related to the holder only because of paragraph 251(5)(b); or

(b) the obligation is deemed by subsection 50(1) to be reacquired at the particular time.

Related Provisions: 80(2)(j), 80.01(2)(a) — Special rules for determining the meaning of "related" and "arm's length"; 80.01(7) — Meaning of "parked obligation".

Notes: See Notes to 80.01(8). For discussion of *when* the "significant interest" is determined, see VIEWS doc 2005-0141111C6.

(7) Parked obligation — For the purposes of this subsection and subsections (6), (8) and (10),

(a) an obligation issued by a debtor is a "parked obligation" at any time where at that time

(i) the obligation is a specified obligation of the debtor, and

(ii) the holder of the obligation

(A) does not deal at arm's length with the debtor, or

(B) where the debtor is a corporation and the holder acquired the obligation after July 12, 1994 (otherwise than pursuant to an agreement in writing entered into on or before July 12, 1994), has a significant interest in the debtor; and

(b) an obligation that is, at any time, acquired or reacquired in circumstances to which subparagraph (6)(a)(ii) or paragraph (6)(b) applies shall, if the obligation is a parked obligation immediately after that time, be deemed to have become a parked obligation at that time.

Related Provisions: 80(2)(j), 80.01(2)(a) — Special rules for determining the meaning of "related" and thence "arm's length"; 80.01(6) — Meaning of "specified obligation".

(8) Deemed settlement after debt parking — Where at any particular time after February 21, 1994 a commercial debt obligation that was issued by a debtor becomes a parked obligation (otherwise than pursuant to an agreement in writing entered into before February 22, 1994) and the specified cost at the particular time to the holder of the obligation is less than 80% of the principal amount of the obligation, for the purpose of applying the provisions of this Act to the debtor

(a) the obligation shall be deemed to have been settled at the particular time; and

(b) the forgiven amount at the particular time in respect of the obligation shall be determined as if the debtor had paid an amount at the particular time in satisfaction of the principal amount of the obligation equal to that specified cost.

Related Provisions: 40(2)(e.1), (e.2), (g)(ii) — Stop-loss rules on disposition of debt; 50(1)(a) — Deemed disposition of bad debt; 79(3)F(b)(i), (iii) — Where property surrendered to creditor; 80(1)"forgiven amount"B(g) — Debt forgiveness rules do not apply if parked obligation subsequently forgiven; 80(3)–(13) — Treatment of obligation deemed settled; 80.01(7) — Meaning of "parked obligation"; 80.01(10) — Subsequent payments; 80.01(11) — Foreign currency fluctuation to be ignored.

Notes: 80.01(6)-(8) deal with debt parking, which was found not to violate GAAR (245(2)) in *Jabin Investments*, 2002 FCA 520. Since 80.01(8) deems the debt to be settled, s. 80 applies.

In *Pièces Automobiles Lecavalier*, 2013 TCC 310, GAAR applied to a transaction that circumvented 80(2)(g) and 80.01(6)-(8). Paras. 107-114 discuss the context and purpose of 80.01(6)-(8).

A shareholder loan written off is considered a parked debt: VIEWS doc 2005-0113051E5. On receipt of partial payment of a debt, see 2008-0299771E5. On the application of 80(2)(k) see 2009-0347661C6. On interaction with 50(1) see 2009-0338911E5, 2014-0524951E5; with 40(2)(e.1) and 53(1)(f.1): 2014-0524391E5.

See also Wortsman et al., "Recent Transactions in Corporate Finance", 2008 Cdn Tax Foundation conference report, at 9:58-64; Bauer, "Restructuring Debt", *ibid.* at 37:21-35; Aiken & Tai, "Debt-Restructuring Transactions", 2016 conference report at 14:12-17.

(9) Statute-barred debt — Where at any particular time after February 21, 1994 a commercial debt obligation issued by a debtor that is payable to a person (other than a person with whom the debtor is related at the particular time) becomes unenforceable in a court of competent jurisdiction because of a statutory limitation period and the obligation would, but for this subsection, not have been settled or extinguished at the particular time, for the purpose of applying the provisions of this Act to the debtor, the obligation shall be deemed to have been settled at the particular time.

Related Provisions: 80(1)"forgiven amount"B(g) — Debt forgiveness rules do not apply; 80(2)(j), 80.01(2)(a) — Special rules for determining the meaning of "related"; 80(3)–(13) — Treatment of obligation deemed to have been settled; 80.01(10) — Subsequent payments; 80.01(11) — Foreign currency fluctuation to be ignored.

Notes: For CRA interpretation see doc 2012-0454081C6. See also 80(2)(a) Notes.

(10) Subsequent payments in satisfaction of debt — Where a commercial debt obligation issued by a debtor is first deemed by subsection (8) or (9) to have been settled at a particular time, at a subsequent time a payment is made by the debtor of an amount in satisfaction of the principal amount of the obligation and it cannot reasonably be considered that one of the reasons the obligation became a parked obligation or became unenforceable, as the case may be, before the subsequent time was to have this subsection apply to the payment, in computing the debtor's income for the taxation year (in this subsection referred to as the "subsequent year") that includes the subsequent time from the source in connection with which the obligation was issued, there may be deducted the amount determined by the formula

$$0.5(A - B) - C$$

where

A   is the amount of the payment,

B   is the amount, if any, by which

    (a) the principal amount of the obligation

  exceeds the total of

    (b) all amounts each of which is a forgiven amount at any time

      (i) in the period that began at the particular time and ended immediately before the subsequent time, and

      (ii) at which a particular portion of the obligation is deemed by subsection (8) or (9) to be settled

  in respect of the particular portion, and

    (c) all amounts paid in satisfaction of the principal amount of the obligation in the period that began at the particular time and ended immediately before the subsequent time, and

C   is the amount, if any, by which the total of

    (a) all amounts deducted under section 61.3 in computing the debtor's income for the subsequent year or a preceding taxation year,

    (b) all amounts added because of subsection 80(13) in computing the debtor's income for the subsequent year or a preceding taxation year in respect of a settlement under subsection (8) or (9) in a period during which the debtor was exempt from tax under this Part on its taxable income, and

    (c) all amounts added because of subsection 80(13) in computing the debtor's income for the subsequent year or a preceding taxation year in respect of a settlement under subsection (8) or (9) in a period during which the debtor was non-resident (other than any of those amounts added in computing the debtor's taxable income or taxable income earned in Canada)

  exceeds the total of

    (d) the amount, if any, deducted because of paragraph 37(1)(f.1) in determining the balance determined under subsection 37(1) in respect of the debtor immediately after the subsequent year, and

    (e) all amounts by which the amount deductible under this subsection in respect of a payment made by the debtor before the subsequent time in computing the debtor's income for the subsequent year or a preceding year has been reduced because of this description.

Related Provisions: 3, 4(1) — Income from a source; 20(1)(uu) — Deduction for amount allowed under subsec. 80.01(10); 80.01(7) — Meaning of "parked obligation"; 87(2)(l.21) — Amalgamation — continuing corporation; 257 — Formula cannot calculate to less than zero.

Notes: On receipt of partial payment of a debt, see doc 2008-0299771E5.

80.01(10) amended by 2000 Budget to change "0.75" to "0.5", this version effective for taxation years that end after Oct. 17, 2000, with transitional rules for 2000 (which were corrected by 2002-2013 technical bill, s. 372).

(11) Foreign currency gains and losses — Where an obligation issued by a debtor is denominated in a currency (other than the Canadian currency) and the obligation is deemed by subsection (8) or (9) to have been settled, those subsections do not apply for the purpose of determining any gain or loss of the debtor on the settlement that is attributable to a fluctuation in the value of the currency relative to the value of Canadian currency.

Related Provisions: 39(1.1), (2) — Gain or loss on fluctuation of foreign currency; 79(7) — Currency fluctuation where property surrendered to creditor; 80(2)(k) — Determination of forgiven amount where obligation denominated in foreign currency; 261(5)(c), (f)(i) — Functional currency reporting.

I.T. Technical News: 15 (tax consequences of the adoption of the "euro" currency).

Notes [s. 80.01]: 80.01 deems debts to be settled in a number of specific situations, leading to the s. 80 debt forgiveness rules applying. See Notes to 80.01(8) re debt parking.

80.01 added by 1994 technical bill, for taxation years that end after Feb. 21, 1994, with certain grandfathering (see Notes to end of s. 80).

Definitions [s. 80.01]: "adjusted cost base" — 54, 248(1); "amount" — 248(1); "arm's length" — 80(2)(j), 80.01(2)(a), 251(1); "Canadian currency" — 261(5)(f)(i); "capital property" — 54, 248(1); "commercial debt obligation", "commercial obligation" — 80(1), 80.01(1); "corporation" — 248(1), *Interpretation Act* 35(1); "cost amount" — 248(1); "creditor" — 80.01(3); "debtor", "distress preferred share" — 80(1), 80.01(1); "fair market value" — see 69(1) Notes; "filing-due date" — 248(1); "forgiven amount" — 80(1), 80.01(1), 80.01(8)(b); "non-resident" — 248(1); "parent" — 88(1); "parked obligation" — 80.01(7); "person" — 80(1), 80.01(1), 248(1); "prescribed" — 248(1); "principal amount" — 248(1), (26); "related" — 80(2)(j), 80.01(2)(a), 251(2); "SIFT trust wind-up event", "SIFT wind-up entity" — 248(1); "settled" — 80(2)(a), 80.01(3)–(9), 80.02(2)(c), 80.02(7)(a); "significant interest" — 80.01(2)(b); "source" — 4(1); "specified cost" — 80.01(1); "specified obligation" — 80.01(6); "specified shareholder" — 248(1); "subsidiary" — 88(1); "taxation year" — 249; "trust" — 104(1), 248(1), (3); "writing" — *Interpretation Act* 35(1).

80.02 [Distress preferred shares] — **(1) Definitions** — In this section, "commercial debt obligation", "commercial obligation", "distress preferred share" and "person" have the meanings assigned by subsection 80(1).

(2) General rules for distress preferred shares — For the purpose of applying the provisions of this Act to an issuer of a distress preferred share,

(a) the principal amount, at any time, of the share shall be deemed to be the amount (determined at that time) for which the share was issued;

(b) the amount for which the share was issued shall, at any time, be deemed to be the amount, if any, by which the total of

(i) the amount for which the share was issued, determined without reference to this paragraph, and

(ii) all amounts by which the paid-up capital in respect of the share increased after the share was issued and before that time

exceeds

(iii) the total of all amounts each of which is an amount paid before that time on a reduction of the paid-up capital in respect of the share, except to the extent that the amount is deemed by section 84 to have been paid as a dividend;

(c) the share shall be deemed to be settled at such time as it is redeemed, acquired or cancelled by the issuer; and

(d) a payment in satisfaction of the principal amount of the share is any payment made on a reduction of the paid-up capital in respect of the share to the extent that the payment would be proceeds of disposition of the share within the meaning that would be assigned by the definition "proceeds of disposition" in section 54 if that definition were read without reference to paragraph (j).

Related Provisions: 80.02(3)(b), 80.02(5)(b) — Deemed amounts for purposes of subpara. 80.02(2)(b)(i).

Notes: A distress preferred share (defined in 80(1)) is an option for a corp in financial difficulty to convert debt to pref shares (paying a lower return) for up to 5 years (248(1)"term preferred share"(e)); if the lender agrees, the borrower gets cash-flow relief and the lender's interest income becomes tax-free intercorporate dividends (see 113(1)). See Bernstein & Choudhury, "Distress Preferred Shares", 16(12) *Canadian Tax Highlights* (ctf.ca) 4-5 (Dec. 2008); Bennett & Tkachenko, "Tax for Troubled Times", XI(1) *Corporate Structures & Groups* (Federated Press) 602-05 (2008); Tkachenko & Bennett, "Reducing Financing Costs Through Distress Preferred Shares", XV(4) *Corporate Finance* (Federated Press) 1712-14 (2009); Elsaghir & Jankovic, "Distress Preferred Shares", *COVID-19 and Canadian Tax* (ctf.ca) 7-8 (July 2020).

(3) Substitution of distress preferred share for debt — Where any part of the consideration given by a corporation to another person for the settlement or extinguishment at any time of a commercial debt obligation that was issued by the corporation and owned immediately before that time by the other person consists of a distress preferred share issued by the corporation to the other person,

(a) for the purposes of section 80, the amount paid at that time in satisfaction of the principal amount of the obligation because of the issue of that share shall be deemed to be equal to the lesser of

(i) the principal amount of the obligation, and

(ii) the amount by which the paid-up capital in respect of the class of shares that include that share increases because of the issue of that share; and

(b) for the purpose of subparagraph (2)(b)(i), the amount for which the share was issued shall be deemed to be equal to the amount deemed by paragraph (a) to have been paid at that time.

Related Provisions: 80.02(2) — General rules.

(4) Substitution of commercial debt obligation for distress preferred share — Where any part of the consideration given by a corporation to another person for the settlement at any time of a distress preferred share that was issued by the corporation and owned immediately before that time by the other person consists of a commercial debt obligation issued by the corporation to the other person, for the purposes of section 80

(a) the amount paid at that time in satisfaction of the principal amount of the share because of the issue of that obligation shall be deemed to be equal to the principal amount of the obligation; and

(b) the amount for which the obligation was issued shall be deemed to be equal to its principal amount.

(5) Substitution of distress preferred share for other distress preferred share — Where any part of the consideration given by a corporation to another person for the settlement at any time of a particular distress preferred share that was issued by the corporation and owned immediately before that time by the other person consists of another distress preferred share issued by the corporation to the other person, for the purposes of section 80

(a) the amount paid at that time in satisfaction of the principal amount of the particular share because of the issue of the other share shall be deemed to be equal to the amount by which the paid-up capital in respect of the class of shares that includes the other share increases because of the issue of the other share; and

(b) for the purpose of subparagraph (2)(b)(i), the amount for which the other share was issued shall be deemed to be equal to the amount deemed by paragraph (a) to have been paid at that time.

(6) Substitution of non-commercial obligation for distress preferred share — Where any part of the consideration given by a corporation to another person for the settlement at any time of a distress preferred share that was issued by the corporation and owned immediately before that time by the other person consists of another share (other than a distress preferred share) or an obligation (other than a commercial obligation) issued by the corporation to the other person, for the purposes of section 80, the amount paid at that time in satisfaction of the principal amount of the distress preferred share because of the issue of the other share or obligation shall be deemed to be equal to the fair market value of the other share or obligation, as the case may be, at that time.

Related Provisions: 80.02(2) — General rules.

(7) Deemed settlement on expiry of term — Where at any time a distress preferred share becomes a share that is not a distress preferred share, for the purposes of section 80

(a) the share shall be deemed to have been settled immediately before that time; and

(b) a payment equal to the fair market value of the share at that time shall be deemed to have been made immediately before that time in satisfaction of the principal amount of the share.

Related Provisions: 80(1)"distress preferred share", 248(1)"term preferred share"(e) — Maximum term of distress preferred share is 5 years.

Notes [s. 80.02]: See Notes to 80.02(2). 80.02 added by 1994 technical bill, for tax years ending after Feb. 21, 1994, except where grandfathered (see Notes at end of s. 80).

Definitions [s. 80.02]: "amount" — 80.02(2)(b), 248(1); "class of shares" — 248(6); "commercial debt obligation", "commercial obligation" — 80(1), 80.02(1); "corporation" — 248(1), *Interpretation Act* 35(1); "distress preferred share" — 80(1), 80.02(1); "dividend" — 248(1); "fair market value" — see 69(1) Notes; "paid-up capital" — 89(1), 248(1); "payment in satisfaction" — 80.02(2)(d); "person" — 80(1), 80.02(1), 248(1); "principal amount" — 80.02(2)(a), 248(1), (26); "settled" — 80(2)(a), 80.01(5), 80.02(2)(c), 80.02(7)(a); "share" — 248(1).

80.03 (1) Definitions — In this section, "commercial debt obligation", "commercial obligation", "distress preferred share", "forgiven amount" and "person" have the meanings assigned by subsection 80(1).

Notes: 80.03(1) restored by 2017 budget bill #2, for taxation years ending after Feb. 21, 1994. These definitions were accidentally deleted from the English version on 3rd Reading of the 1995-97 technical bill (S.C. 1998, c. 19), when only "taxable dividend" should have been repealed (that term is no longer used in 80.03).

(2) Deferred recognition of debtor's gain on settlement of debt — Where at any time in a taxation year a person (in this subsection referred to as the "transferor") surrenders a particular capital property (other than a distress preferred share) that is a share, a capital interest in a trust or an interest in a partnership, the person shall be deemed to have a capital gain from the disposition at that time of another capital property (or, where the particular property is a taxable Canadian property, another taxable Canadian property) equal to the amount, if any, by which

(a) the total of all amounts deducted under paragraph 53(2)(g.1) in computing the adjusted cost base to the transferor of the particular property immediately before that time

exceeds the total of

(b) the amount that would be the transferor's capital gain for the year from the disposition of the particular property if this Act were read without reference to subsection 100(2), and

(c) where, at the end of the year, the transferor is resident in Canada or is a non-resident person who carries on business in Canada through a fixed place of business, the amount designated under subsection (7) by the transferor in respect of the disposition, at that time or immediately after that time, of the particular property.

Related Provisions: 80.03(3) — Meaning of "surrender"; 253 — Extended meaning of carrying on business in Canada.

Notes: 80.03(2) applies on a share-by-share basis: VIEWS doc 2002-0176625.

See also Notes at end of 80.03.

(3) Surrender of capital property — For the purpose of subsection (2), a person shall be considered to have surrendered a property at any time only where

(a) in the case of a share of the capital stock of a particular corporation,

(i) the person is a corporation that disposed of the share at that time and the proceeds of disposition of the share are determined under paragraph 88(1)(b), or

(ii) the person is a corporation that owned the share at that time and, immediately after that time, amalgamates or merges with the particular corporation;

(b) in the case of a capital interest in a trust, the person disposed of the interest at that time and the proceeds of disposition are determined under paragraph 107(2)(c); and

(c) in the case of an interest in a partnership, the person disposed of the interest at that time and the proceeds of disposition are determined under paragraph 98(3)(a) or (5)(a).

(4)–(6) [Repealed]

Notes: 80.03(4), (5) and (6) repealed by 1995-97 technical bill, retroactive to their introduction (taxation years ending after Feb. 21, 1994 — see Notes at end of 80.03). These rules applied where a corporation disposed of capital property that was a share, or partnership or trust interest. In certain cases, there were tax consequences based on ACB adjustments arising because of s. 80 and dividends received by the corporation. They were repealed to reduce the complexity of the debt forgiveness rules, although the GAAR in 245(2) may apply to some of the cases where 80.03(4) applied.

(7) Alternative treatment — Where at any time in a taxation year a person disposes of a property, for the purposes of subsection (2) and section 80

(a) the person may designate an amount in a prescribed form filed with the person's return of income under this Part for the year; and

(b) where an amount is designated by the person under paragraph (a) in respect of the disposition,

(i) the person shall be deemed to have issued a commercial debt obligation at that time that is settled immediately after that time,

(ii) the lesser of the amount so designated and the amount that would, but for this subsection, be a capital gain determined in respect of the disposition because of subsection (2) shall be treated as if it were the forgiven amount at the time of the settlement in respect of the obligation referred to in subparagraph (i),

(iii) the source in connection with which the obligation referred to in subparagraph (i) was issued shall be deemed to be the business, if any, carried on by the person at the end of the year, and

(iv) where the person does not carry on a business at the end of the year, the person shall be deemed to carry on an active business at the end of the year and the source in connection with which the obligation referred to in subparagraph (i) was issued shall be deemed to be the business deemed by this subparagraph to be carried on.

Related Provisions: 87(2)(h.1) — Amalgamation — continuing corporation; 220(3.21)(a) — Late filing, amendment or revocation of designation.

Notes: Opening words of 80.03(7) and 80.03(7)(b)(ii) both amended to delete reference to 80.03(4) (after "subsection (2)" in both cases), by 1995-97 technical bill, retroactive to their introduction (taxation years ending after February 21, 1994 — see Notes at end of 80.03). This was consequential on the repeal of 80.03(4).

Forms: T2155: Alternative treatment of capital gains arising under s. 80.03 on settlement of debt.

(8) Lifetime capital gains exemption — If, as a consequence of the disposition at any time by an individual of a property that is a qualified farm or fishing property of the individual or a qualified small business corporation share of the individual (as defined in subsection 110.6(1)), the individual is deemed by subsection (2) to have a capital gain at that time from the disposition of another property, for the purposes of sections 3, 74.3 and 111, as they apply for the purposes of section 110.6, the other property is deemed to be a qualified farm or fishing property of the individual or a qualified small business corporation share of the individual, as the case may be.

Notes: 80.03(8) amended by 2014 budget bill #2, for dispositions in the 2014 and later tax years.

Notes [s. 80.03]: 80.03 is designed to preserve the effectiveness of the debt forgiveness rules in 80, where 80 has resulted in a reduction of ACB of a share, partnership interest or trust interest (see 80(10) and (11)).

80.03 added by 1994 technical bill, effective for taxation years that end after Feb. 21, 1994, except where grandfathering applies (see Notes to end of s. 80).

Definitions [s. 80.03]: "active business" — 248(1); "adjusted cost base" — 54, 248(1); "amount" — 248(1); "business" — 248(1); "capital dividend" — 83(2), 248(1); "capital gain" — 39(1)(a), 248(1); "capital interest" — in a trust 108(1), 248(1); "capital property" — 54, 248(1); "carries on business in Canada" — 253; "commercial debt obligation" — 80(1), 80.03(1), 80.03(7)(b)(i); "commercial obligation" — 80(1), 80.03(1); "corporation" — 248(1), *Interpretation Act* 35(1); "directed person" — 80(1), 80.04(1); "distress preferred share" — 80(1), 80.03(1); "fiscal period" — 249(2)(b), 249.1; "forgiven amount" — 80(1), 80.03(1), 80.03(7)(b)(ii); "individual", "non-resident" — 248(1); "partnership" — see 96(1) Notes; "person" — 80(1), 80.03(1), 248(1); "prescribed" — 248(1); "proceeds of disposition" — 54; "property" — 248(1); "qualified farm or fishing property", "qualified small business corporation share" — 110.6(1); "resident in Canada" — 94(3)(a), 250; "settled" — 80.03(7)(b)(i); "share" — 248(1); "source" — 4(1), 80.03(7)(b)(iv); "surrender" — 80.03(3); "taxable Canadian property" — 248(1); "taxable income" — 2(2), 248(1); "taxation year" — 249; "transferor" — 80.03(2); "trust" — 104(1), 248(1), (3); "vendor" — 80.03(4).

80.04 [Transfer of forgiven amount to other taxpayer] —
(1) Definitions — In this section, "commercial debt obligation", "commercial obligation", "debtor", "directed person", "eligible Canadian partnership", "forgiven amount" and "person" have the meanings assigned by subsection 80(1).

Notes: See Notes at end of 80.04.

(2) Eligible transferee — For the purpose of this section, an "eligible transferee" of a debtor at any time is a directed person at that time in respect of the debtor or a taxable Canadian corporation or eligible Canadian partnership related (otherwise than because of a right referred to in paragraph 251(5)(b)) at that time to the debtor.

Related Provisions: 87(2)(h.1) — Amalgamation — continuing corporation.

(3) Application — Paragraphs 80(2)(a), (b), (j), (l) and (n) apply for the purpose of this section.

(4) Agreement respecting transfer of forgiven amount — Where

(a) a particular commercial obligation (other than an obligation deemed by paragraph (e) to have been issued) issued by a debtor is settled at a particular time,

(b) amounts have been designated by the debtor under subsections 80(5) to (10) to the maximum extent permitted in respect of the settlement of the particular obligation at the particular time,

(c) the debtor and an eligible transferee of the debtor at the particular time file under this section an agreement between them in respect of that settlement, and

(d) an amount is specified in that agreement

the following rules apply:

(e) except for the purposes of subsection 80(11), the transferee shall be deemed to have issued a commercial debt obligation that was settled at the particular time,

(f) the specified amount shall be deemed to be the forgiven amount at the particular time in respect of the obligation referred to in paragraph (e),

(g) subject to paragraph (h), the obligation referred to in paragraph (e) shall be deemed to have been issued at the same time (in paragraph (h) referred to as the "time of issue") at which, and in the same circumstances in which, the particular obligation was issued,

(h) if the transferee is a taxpayer that is subject to a loss restriction event after the time of issue and the transferee and the debtor were, if the transferee is a corporation, not related to each other — or, if the transferee is a trust, not affiliated with each other — immediately before the loss restriction event,

(i) the obligation referred to in paragraph (e) is deemed to have been issued after the loss restriction event, and

(ii) subparagraph (b)(ii) of the definition "relevant loss balance" in subsection 80(1), paragraph (f) of the definition "successor pool" in that subsection and paragraph (b) of the definition "unrecognized loss" in that subsection do not apply in respect of the loss restriction event,

(i) the source in connection with which the obligation referred to in paragraph (e) was issued shall be deemed to be the source in connection with which the particular obligation was issued, and

(j) for the purposes of sections 61.3 and 61.4, the amount included under subsection 80(13) in computing the income of the eligible transferee in respect of the settlement of the obligation referred to in paragraph (e) or deducted under paragraph 80(15)(a) in respect of such income shall be deemed to be nil.

Related Provisions: 80(13)C — Amount specified in agreement reduces income inclusion; 80(14)(c) — Calculation of residual balance for income inclusion; 80(15)(c) — Where commercial debt obligation issued by partnership; 80.04(5) — Where consideration given for entering into agreement; 80.04(6) — How and when agreement to be filed with CRA; 87(2)(h.1) — Amalgamation — continuing corporation; 251.2 — Loss restriction event; 256(8) — Deemed acquisition of shares.

Notes: See Notes at end of 80.04. 80.04(4)(h) amended by 2013 budget bill #2, effective March 21, 2013, to change references from control of a corporation being acquired to a "loss restriction event", so as to extend the rule to trusts (see Notes to 251.2(2)).

(5) Consideration for agreement — For the purposes of this Part, where property is acquired at any time by an eligible transferee as consideration for entering into an agreement with a debtor that is filed under this section

(a) where the property was owned by the debtor immediately before that time,

(i) the debtor shall be deemed to have disposed of the property at that time for proceeds equal to the fair market value of the property at that time, and

(ii) no amount may be deducted in computing the debtor's income as a consequence of the transfer of the property, except any amount arising as a consequence of the application of subparagraph (i);

(b) the cost at which the property was acquired by the eligible transferee at that time shall be deemed to be equal to the fair market value of the property at that time; and

(c) the eligible transferee shall not be required to add an amount in computing income solely because of the acquisition at that time of the property.

(d) [Repealed]

Related Provisions: 80.04(5.1) — No benefit conferred on debtor as a consequence of the agreement; 191.3(1.1) — Similar rule for purposes of Part VI.1 tax.

Notes: 80.04(5)(d) repealed by 1995-97 technical bill, retroactive to its introduction (taxation years ending after February 21, 1994 — see Notes at end of 80.03). A more general rule is now in 80.04(5.1).

(5.1) No benefit conferred — For the purposes of this Part, where a debtor and an eligible transferee enter into an agreement that is filed under this section, no benefit shall be considered to have been conferred on the debtor as a consequence of the agreement.

Notes: 80.04(5.1) added by 1995-97 technical bill, effective for taxation years ending after February 21, 1994 (i.e., retroactive to the introduction of 80.04). This rule was formerly in 80.04(5)(d), but the new rule applies whether or not property is acquired by an eligible transferee as consideration for entering into an agreement filed under 80.04.

(6) Manner of filing agreement — Subject to subsection (7), a particular agreement between a debtor and an eligible transferee in respect of an obligation issued by the debtor that was settled at any time shall be deemed not to have been filed under this section

(a) where it is not filed with the Minister in a prescribed form

(i) on or before the later of

(A) the day on or before which the debtor's return of income under this Part is required to be filed for the taxation year or fiscal period, as the case may be, that includes that time (or would be required to be filed if tax under this Part were payable by the debtor for the year), and

(B) the day on or before which the transferee's return of income under this Part is required to be filed for the taxation year or fiscal period, as the case may be, that includes that time, or

(ii) on or before the later of

(A) the expiry of the 90-day period commencing on the day of mailing of an assessment of tax payable under this Part or a notification that no tax is payable under this Part, as the case may be, for a taxation year or fiscal period described in clause (i)(A) or (B), as the case may be, and

(B) if the debtor is an individual (other than a trust) or a graduated rate estate, the day that is one year after the taxpayer's filing-due date for the year;

(b) where it is not accompanied by,

(i) where the debtor is a corporation and its directors are legally entitled to administer its affairs, a certified copy of their resolution authorizing the agreement to be made,

(ii) where the debtor is a corporation and its directors are not legally entitled to administer its affairs, a certified copy of the document by which the person legally entitled to administer its affairs authorized the agreement to be made,

(iii) where the transferee is a corporation and its directors are legally entitled to administer its affairs, a certified copy of their resolution authorizing the agreement to be made, and

(iv) where the transferee is a corporation and its directors are not legally entitled to administer its affairs, a certified copy of the document by which the person legally entitled to administer its affairs authorized the agreement to be made; or

(c) if an agreement amending the particular agreement has been filed in accordance with this section, except where subsection (8) applies to the particular agreement.

Related Provisions: 80.04(7) — Deemed due dates for partnership to file return and service notice of objection; 96(3) — Agreement of members of partnership; 150(1) — Due date for return; 165(1) — Deadline for serving notice of objection.

Notes: 80.04(6)(a)(ii)(B) amended by 2014 budget bill #2, for 2016 and later taxation years, to change "testamentary trust" to "graduated rate estate". (See Notes to 122(1).)

80.04(6)(a)(ii) amended by 2002-2013 technical bill (Part 5 — technical), retroactive to the introduction of 80.04 (taxation years that end after Feb. 21, 1994).

Forms: T2156: Agreement to transfer a forgiven amount under s. 80.04.

(7) Filing by partnership — For the purpose of subsection (6), where an obligation is settled at any time in a fiscal period of a partnership, it shall be assumed that

(a) the partnership is required to file a return of income under this Part for the fiscal period on or before the latest day on or before which any member of the partnership during the fiscal period is required to file a return of income under this Part for the taxation year in which that fiscal period ends (or would be required to file such a return of income if tax under this Part were payable by the member for that year); and

(b) the partnership may serve a notice of objection described in subparagraph (6)(a)(ii) within each period within which any member of the partnership during the fiscal period may serve a notice of objection to tax payable under this Part for a taxation year in which that fiscal period ends.

(8) Related corporations — Where at any time a corporation becomes related to another corporation and it can reasonably be considered that the main purpose of the corporation becoming related to the other corporation is to enable the corporations to file an agreement under this section, the amount specified in the agreement shall be deemed to be nil for the purpose of the description of C in subsection 80(13).

(9) Assessment of taxpayers in respect of agreement — The Minister shall, notwithstanding subsections 152(4) to (5), assess or reassess the tax, interest and penalties payable under this Act by any taxpayer in order to take into account an agreement filed under this section.

(10) Liability of debtor — Without affecting the liability of any person under any other provision of this Act, where a debtor and an eligible transferee file an agreement between them under this section in respect of an obligation issued by the debtor that was settled at any time, the debtor is, to the extent of 30% of the amount specified in the agreement, liable to pay

(a) where the transferee is a corporation, all taxes payable under this Act by it for taxation years that end in the period that begins at that time and ends 4 calendar years after that time;

(b) where the transferee is a partnership, the total of all amounts each of which is the tax payable under this Act by a person for a taxation year

(i) that begins or ends in that period, and

(ii) that includes the end of a fiscal period of the partnership during which the person was a member of the partnership; and

(c) interest and penalties in respect of such taxes.

Related Provisions: 80.04(11) — Joint and several liability; 80.04(12) — Assessment; 80.04(14) — Where partnership is a member of a partnership; 87(2)(h.1) — Amalgamation — continuing corporation.

Notes: 80.04(10)(a) amended to change "10 years" to "4 years" by 1995-97 technical bill, retroactive to its introduction (taxation years ending after Feb. 21, 1994).

(11) Joint and several, or solidary, liability — If taxes, interest and penalties are payable under this Act by a person for a taxation year and those taxes, interest and penalties are payable by a debtor because of subsection (10), the debtor and the person are jointly and severally, or solidarily, liable to pay those amounts.

Related Provisions: 87(2)(h.1) — Amalgamation — continuing corporation.

Notes: 80.04(11) amended by 2002-2013 technical bill (Part 4 — bijuralism), effective June 26, 2013, to add "or solidarily".

(12) Assessments in respect of liability — Where a debtor and an eligible transferee file an agreement between them under this section in respect of an obligation issued by the debtor that was settled at a particular time,

(a) where the debtor is an individual or a corporation, the Minister may at any subsequent time assess the debtor in respect of taxes, interest and penalties for which the debtor is liable because of subsection (10); and

(b) where the debtor is a partnership, the Minister may at any subsequent time assess any person who has been a member of the partnership in respect of taxes, interest and penalties for which the partnership is liable because of subsection (10), to the extent that those amounts relate to taxation years of the transferee (or, where the transferee is another partnership, members of the other partnership) that end at or after

(i) where the person was not a member of the partnership at the particular time, the first subsequent time the person becomes a member of the partnership, and

(ii) in any other case, the particular time.

Related Provisions: 80.04(13) — Provisions applicable to assessment; 80.04(14) — Where partnership is a member of a partnership; 87(2)(h.1) — Amalgamation — continuing corporation.

(13) Application of Division I — The provisions of Division I apply to an assessment under subsection (12) as though it had been made under section 152.

(14) Partnership members — For the purposes of paragraphs (10)(b) and (12)(b) and this subsection, where at any time a member of a particular partnership is another partnership, each member of the other partnership shall be deemed to be a member of the particular partnership at that time.

Notes [s. 80.04]: 80.04 applies where a commercial debt obligation has been settled, but the "forgiven amount" (as defined in 80(1)) has not all been used up under 80(3)–(12). The remaining balance may be transferred, in certain cases, to another taxpayer to prevent it from being included in income under 80(13) or (17). The mechanism is similar to that under 191.3 for Part VI.1 tax.

80.04 added by 1994 technical bill, effective for taxation years that end after Feb. 21, 1994, except where grandfathering applies (see Notes to end of s. 80).

Definitions [s. 80.04]: "amount" — 80.04(5), 248(1); "assessment" — 248(1); "benefit" — 80.04(5.1); "commercial debt obligation" — 80(1), 80.04(1), (4)(e); "commercial obligation" — 80(1), 80.04(1); "control" — 256(5)–(9); "corporation" — 248(1), *Interpretation Act* s. 35(1); "debtor", "directed person", "eligible Canadian partnership" — 80(1), 80.04(1); "eligible transferee" — 80.04(2); "fair market value" — see 69(1) Notes; "filing-due date" — 150(1), 248(1); "fiscal period" — 249(2)(b), 249.1; "forgiven amount" — 80(1), 80.01(8)(b), 80.04(1); "graduated rate estate", "individual" — 248(1); "loss restriction event" — 251.2; "Minister" — 248(1); "partnership" — see 96(1) Notes; "person" — 80(1), 80.04(1), 248(1); "prescribed" — 248(1); "related" — 80(2)(j), 80.04(3), (8), 251(2); "settled" — 80(2)(a), 80.01(3)–(9), 80.02(2)(c), 80.02(7)(a), 80.04(4)(e); "specified amount" — 80.04(4)(d); "taxable Canadian corporation" — 89(1), 248(1); "taxation year" — 249; "taxpayer" — 248(1); "time of issue" — 80.04(4)(g); "trust" — 104(1), 248(1), (3).

80.1 (1) Expropriation assets acquired as compensation for, or as consideration for sale of, foreign property taken by or sold to foreign issuer — Where in a taxation year ending coincidentally with or after December 31, 1971 a taxpayer resident in Canada has acquired any bonds, debentures, mortgages, hypothecary claims, notes or similar obligations (in this section referred to as "expropriation assets") issued by the government of a country other than Canada or issued by a person resident in a country other than Canada and guaranteed by the government of that country,

(a) as compensation for

(i) shares owned by the taxpayer of the capital stock of a foreign affiliate of the taxpayer that carried on business in that country, or

(ii) all or substantially all of the property used by the taxpayer in carrying on business in that country,

(which shares or property, as the case may be, are referred to in this section as "foreign property"), taken, after June 18, 1971, from the taxpayer by the issuer under the authority of a law of that country, or

(b) as consideration for the sale of foreign property sold, after June 18, 1971, by the taxpayer to the issuer, if

(i) the sale was, by a law of that country, expressly required to be made, or

(ii) the sale was made after notice or other manifestation of an intention to take the foreign property, if the taxpayer has so elected, in prescribed form and within pre-scribed time, in respect of all of the expropriation assets so acquired by the taxpayer, the following rule applies, namely, an amount in respect of each such expropriation asset, equal to

(c) the principal amount of the asset, or

(d) where the taxpayer has designated in the taxpayer's election an amount in respect of the asset that is less than the principal amount thereof, the amount so designated,

shall be deemed to be

(e) the cost to the taxpayer of the asset, and

(f) for the purpose of computing the taxpayer's proceeds of dis-position of the foreign property so taken or sold, the amount re-ceived by the taxpayer by virtue of the taxpayer's acquisition of the asset,

except that in no case may the taxpayer designate an amount in re-spect of any expropriation asset so that the taxpayer's proceeds of disposition of the foreign property so taken or sold (computed hav-ing regard to the provisions of paragraph (f)) are less than the cost amount to the taxpayer of the foreign property immediately before it was so taken or sold.

Related Provisions: 53(1)(k), 53(2)(n) — Adjustments to cost base; 90–95 — Shareholders of corporations not resident in Canada; 220(3.2), Reg. 600 — Late filing or revocation of election.

Notes: CRA considers that "substantially all", used in 80.1(1)(a)(ii), means 90% or more.

For a taxpayer filing Quebec returns, this election must be copied to Revenu Québec: *Taxation Act* ss. 470, 21.4.6.

Reference to "hypothecary claims" added to 80.1(1) opening words by 2001 *Civil Code* harmonization bill, effective June 14, 2001. The change is non-substantive; see *Inter-pretation Act* s. 8.2.

Regulations: 4500 (prescribed time).

Forms: T2079: Election re: expropriation assets acquired as compensation for or a consideration for sale of foreign property taken by or sold to foreign issuer.

(2) Election re interest received or to be received on expropriation assets acquired by taxpayer — Where a tax-payer has elected in prescribed form and within prescribed time in respect of all amounts (each of which is referred to in this subsec-tion as an "interest amount") received or to be received by the tax-payer as or on account of interest on all expropriation assets ac-quired by the taxpayer as compensation for, or as consideration for the sale of, foreign property taken by or sold to any particular issuer as described in subsection (1), the following rules apply in respect of each such asset so acquired by the taxpayer:

(a) in computing the taxpayer's income for a taxation year from the asset, there may be deducted, in respect of each interest amount received by the taxpayer in the year on the asset, the lesser of the interest amount and the total of

(i) the amount required by paragraph (b) to be added, by vir-tue of the receipt by the taxpayer of the interest amount, in computing the adjusted cost base to the taxpayer of the asset, and

(ii) the greater of

(A) the adjusted cost base to the taxpayer of the asset im-mediately before the interest amount was so received by the taxpayer, and

(B) the adjusted principal amount to the taxpayer of the asset immediately before the interest amount was so re-ceived by the taxpayer,

and there shall be included, in respect of each amount (in this paragraph referred to as a "capital amount") received by the tax-payer in the year as, on account or in lieu of payment of, or in satisfaction of,

(iii) any proceeds of disposition of the asset, or

(iv) the principal amount of the asset,

the amount, if any, by which the capital amount exceeds the greater of the adjusted cost base to the taxpayer of the asset im-mediately before the capital amount was received by the tax-

payer and its adjusted principal amount to the taxpayer at that time;

(b) in computing, at any particular time, the adjusted cost base to the taxpayer of the asset, there shall be added, in respect of each interest amount received by the taxpayer on the asset before the particular time, an amount equal to the lesser of

(i) any income or profits tax paid by the taxpayer to the gov-ernment of a country other than Canada in respect of the in-terest amount, and

(ii) that proportion of the tax referred to in subparagraph (i) that the adjusted cost base to the taxpayer of the asset imme-diately before the interest amount was received by the tax-payer is of the amount, if any, by which the interest amount exceeds the tax referred to in that subparagraph,

and there shall be deducted

(iii) each interest amount received by the taxpayer on the as-set before the particular time, and

(iv) each amount received by the taxpayer before the particu-lar time on account of the principal amount of the asset;

(c) the receipt by the taxpayer of an amount described in subpar-agraph (b)(iv) in respect of the asset shall be deemed not to be a partial disposition thereof; and

(d) for the purposes of section 126, notwithstanding the defini-tion "non-business-income tax" in subsection 126(7), the "non-business-income tax" paid by a taxpayer does not include any tax, or any portion thereof, the amount of which is required by paragraph (b) to be added in computing the adjusted cost base to the taxpayer of the asset.

Related Provisions: 53(1)(k), 53(2)(n) — Adjustments to cost base.

Notes: For the meaning of "income or profits tax" in (b)(i), see Notes to 126(4).

For a taxpayer filing Quebec returns, this election must be copied to Revenu Québec: *Taxation Act* ss. 471, 21.4.6.

Regulations: 4500 (prescribed time).

Forms: T2079: Election re: expropriation assets acquired as compensation for or a consideration for sale of foreign property taken by or sold to foreign issuer.

(3) Where interest amount and capital amount received at same time — For the purposes of subsection (2), where an interest amount on an expropriation asset and a capital amount with respect to that asset are received by a taxpayer at the same time, the interest amount shall be deemed to have been received by the taxpayer im-mediately before the capital amount.

(4) Assets acquired from foreign affiliate of taxpayer as dividend in kind or as benefit to shareholder — Where a foreign affiliate of a taxpayer resident in Canada would, on the as-sumption that the foreign affiliate were resident in Canada and its only foreign affiliates were corporations that were foreign affiliates of the taxpayer, be entitled to make an election under subsection (1) in respect of assets acquired by it that would, on that assumption, be expropriation assets of the foreign affiliate, and all or any of those assets are subsequently acquired by the taxpayer from the foreign affiliate as a dividend payable in kind, or as a benefit received from the foreign affiliate that would otherwise be required by subsection 15(1) to be included in computing the income of the taxpayer, if the taxpayer has so elected, in prescribed form and within prescribed time, in respect of all of the assets so acquired by the taxpayer from the foreign affiliate, the following rules apply in respect of each such asset so acquired by the taxpayer:

(a) an amount equal to

(i) the principal amount of the asset, or

(ii) where the taxpayer has designated in the taxpayer's elec-tion an amount in respect of the asset that is less than the principal amount thereof, the amount so designated,

shall be deemed to be,

(iii) notwithstanding subsection 52(2), the cost to the tax-payer of the asset, and

(iv) the amount of the dividend or benefit, as the case may be, received by the taxpayer by virtue of the acquisition by the taxpayer of the asset;

(b) where the asset was so acquired as such a benefit and the taxpayer has designated in the election a class of shares as described in this paragraph in respect of the asset, the amount of the benefit shall be deemed

(i) to have been received by the taxpayer as a dividend from the foreign affiliate in respect of such class of shares of the capital stock thereof as the taxpayer has designated in the election, and

(ii) not to be an amount required by subsection 15(1) to be included in computing the taxpayer's income;

(c) in computing the taxable income of the taxpayer for the taxation year in which the taxpayer acquired the asset, there may be deducted from the taxpayer's income for the year the amount, if any, by which the amount received by the taxpayer as a dividend by virtue of the acquisition by the taxpayer of the asset exceeds the total of amounts deductible in respect of the dividend under sections 91 and 113 in computing the taxpayer's income or taxable income, as the case may be, for the year;

(d) there shall be deducted in computing the adjusted cost base to the taxpayer of each share of the capital stock of the foreign affiliate that is a share of a class in respect of which an amount was received by the taxpayer as a dividend by virtue of the acquisition by the taxpayer of the asset, the quotient obtained by dividing the amount, if any, deducted by the taxpayer under paragraph (c) in respect of the dividend by the number of shares of that class owned by the taxpayer immediately before that amount was received by the taxpayer as a dividend;

(e) any capital loss of the taxpayer from the disposition, after that time when the asset was so acquired by the taxpayer, of a share of the capital stock of the foreign affiliate shall be deemed to be nil; and

(f) where the taxpayer has so elected in prescribed form and within prescribed time, subsection (2) applies as if the asset were an expropriation asset acquired by the taxpayer as compensation for foreign property taken by a particular issuer as described in subsection (1).

Related Provisions: 53(2)(b) — Reduction in ACB.

Notes: For a taxpayer filing Quebec returns, an 80.1(4) election must be copied to Revenu Québec: *Taxation Act* ss. 477, 21.4.6.

80.1(4) requires the taxpayer to have "elected" in prescribed form but does not require the form to be filed with the Minister. The *Excise Tax Act* (GST/HST legislation) was amended in 1993 in numerous places (e.g., 167(2)(d), 191(7), 233(2), 233(3), V-III-6, V-VI-17) to change wording from "files an election" to "elects", specifically so that elections could be made and kept in taxpayers' records without needing to be filed with CRA. Arguably the same applies to 80.01(4) and 80.1(4).

Regulations: 4500 (prescribed time).

Forms: T2079: Election re: expropriation assets acquired as compensation for or a consideration for sale of foreign property taken by or sold to foreign issuer.

(5) Assets acquired from foreign affiliate of taxpayer as consideration for settlement, etc., of debt — Where a foreign affiliate of a taxpayer resident in Canada would, on the assumption that the foreign affiliate were resident in Canada and its only foreign affiliates were corporations that were foreign affiliates of the taxpayer, be entitled to make an election under subsection (1) in respect of assets acquired by it that would, on that assumption, be expropriation assets of the foreign affiliate, and all or any of those assets are subsequently acquired by the taxpayer from the foreign affiliate as consideration for the settlement or extinguishment of a capital property of the taxpayer that was a debt payable by the foreign affiliate to the taxpayer or any other obligation of the foreign affiliate to pay an amount to the taxpayer (which debt or other obligation is referred to in this subsection as the "obligation"), if the taxpayer has so elected, in prescribed form and within prescribed

time, in respect of all of the assets so acquired by the taxpayer from the foreign affiliate, the following rules apply in respect of each such asset so acquired by the taxpayer,

(a) paragraph (4)(a) applies in respect of the asset as if subparagraph (4)(a)(iv) were read as follows:

"(iv) the taxpayer's proceeds of the disposition of the obligation settled or extinguished by virtue of the acquisition by the taxpayer of the asset;";

(b) where the taxpayer has designated in the taxpayer's election a class of shares as described in this paragraph in respect of the asset,

(i) the amount, if any, by which the cost to the taxpayer of the asset (computed having regard to paragraph (a) and paragraph (4)(a)) exceeds the amount of the obligation settled or extinguished by virtue of the acquisition by the taxpayer of the asset shall be deemed to have been received by the taxpayer as a dividend from the foreign affiliate in respect of such class of shares of the capital stock thereof as the taxpayer has designated in the election, and

(ii) the taxpayer's gain, if any, from the disposition of the obligation shall be deemed to be nil;

(c) the taxpayer's loss, if any, from the disposition of the obligation shall be deemed to be nil; and

(d) paragraphs (4)(c) to (f) apply in respect of the asset.

Notes: For a taxpayer filing Quebec returns, an 80.1(5) election must be copied to Revenu Québec: *Taxation Act* ss. 478, 21.4.6.

Regulations: 4500 (prescribed time).

Forms: T2079: Election re: expropriation assets acquired as compensation for or a consideration for sale of foreign property taken by or sold to foreign issuer.

(6) Assets acquired from foreign affiliate of taxpayer on winding-up, etc. — Where a foreign affiliate of a taxpayer resident in Canada would, on the assumption that the foreign affiliate were resident in Canada and its only foreign affiliates were corporations that were foreign affiliates of the taxpayer, be entitled to make an election under subsection (1) in respect of assets acquired by it that would, on that assumption, be expropriation assets of the foreign affiliate, and all or any of those assets are subsequently acquired by the taxpayer from the foreign affiliate,

(a) on the winding-up, discontinuance or reorganization of the business of the foreign affiliate, or

(b) as consideration for the redemption, cancellation or acquisition by the foreign affiliate of shares of its capital stock,

if the taxpayer has so elected, in prescribed form and within prescribed time,

(c) in respect of all of the assets so acquired by the taxpayer from the foreign affiliate, subsection (1) applies in respect of each such asset, or

(d) in respect of all amounts received or to be received by the taxpayer as or on account of interest on all of the assets so acquired by the taxpayer from the foreign affiliate, subsection (2) applies in respect of each such asset,

as if the assets were expropriation assets acquired by the taxpayer as consideration for the sale of foreign property that consisted of shares of the capital stock of the foreign affiliate owned by the taxpayer immediately before the assets were so acquired and that was sold to a particular issuer as described in subsection (1).

Notes: For the meaning of "winding-up, discontinuance or reorganization" in 80.1(6)(a), see Notes to 84(2).

For a taxpayer filing Quebec returns, an 80.1(6) election must be copied to Revenu Québec: *Taxation Act* ss. 479, 21.4.6.

Regulations: 4500 (prescribed time).

Forms: T2079: Election re: expropriation assets acquired as compensation for or a consideration for sale of foreign property taken by or sold to foreign issuer.

(7) Definition of "adjusted principal amount" — In this section, "adjusted principal amount" to a taxpayer of an expropriation asset at any particular time means the amount, if any, by which

(a) the total of the principal amount of the asset and, in respect of each interest amount received by the taxpayer on the asset before the particular time, the lesser of the tax referred to in subparagraph (2)(b)(i) in respect of that interest amount and the proportion determined under subparagraph (2)(b)(ii) in respect thereof,

exceeds

(b) the total of each amount received by the taxpayer before the particular time as an interest amount on the asset and each amount received by the taxpayer before the particular time as, on account or in lieu of payment of, or in satisfaction of, the principal amount of the asset.

(8) Currency in which adjusted principal amount to be computed or expressed — For the purposes of this section, the adjusted principal amount, at any particular time, of an expropriation asset or of any asset assumed for the purposes of this section to be an expropriation asset shall be computed in the currency in which the principal amount of the asset is, under the terms thereof, payable, except that for greater certainty, for the purposes of paragraph (2)(a), the adjusted principal amount at any particular time of such an asset is its adjusted principal amount at that time computed as provided in this subsection but expressed in Canadian currency.

Related Provisions: 261(5)(c), (f)(i) — Functional currency reporting.

(9) Election in respect of two or more expropriation assets acquired by taxpayer — For the purposes of Subdivision C and subsection (2), and in applying subsections (7) and (8) for those purposes, where two or more expropriation assets that were

(a) issued by the government of a country other than Canada, or

(b) issued by a person resident in a country other than Canada and guaranteed by the government of that country

at the same time, or as compensation for, or consideration for the sale of, the same foreign property, have been acquired by a taxpayer and the taxpayer has so elected, in prescribed form and within prescribed time, in respect of all of the expropriation assets that were so issued or guaranteed by the government of that country and acquired by the taxpayer before the making of the election, all of those expropriation assets shall be considered to be a single expropriation asset that was issued or guaranteed by the government of that country and acquired by the taxpayer.

Notes: Subdivision c deals with taxable capital gains and allowable capital losses (38–55).

For a taxpayer filing Quebec returns, an 80.1(9) election must be copied to Revenu Québec: *Taxation Act* ss. 475, 21.4.6.

Regulations: 4500 (prescribed time).

Forms: T2079: Election re: expropriation assets acquired as compensation for or a consideration for sale of foreign property taken by or sold to foreign issuer.

Definitions [s. 80.1]: "adjusted cost base" — 54, 248(1); "adjusted principal amount" — 80.1(7); "amount", "business" — 248(1); "Canada" — 255; "Canadian currency" — 261(5)(f)(i); "capital loss" — 39(1)(b), 248(1); "capital property" — 54, 248(1); "class of shares" — 248(6); "corporation" — 248(1), *Interpretation Act* 35(1); "cost amount", "dividend" — 248(1); "expropriation assets" — 80.1(1); "foreign affiliate" — 95(1), 248(1); "foreign property" — 80.1(1)(a); "income or profits tax" — 126(4); "person", "prescribed", "principal amount", "property" — 248(1); "resident in Canada" — 94(3)(a), 250; "share" — 248(1); "taxable income" — 2(2), 248(1); "taxation year" — 11(2), 249; "taxpayer" — 248(1).

80.2 [Resource royalty reimbursement] — [No longer relevant.]

Notes: 80.2, added by 2002-2013 technical bill effective 2002 to replace a similar rule repealed in 2003, applies to reimbursement of resource royalties that fell within former 12(1)(o) or 18(1)(m). Due to 80.2(2), it effectively does not apply to a tax year that begins after 2007. For the text, in-force rules and commentary, see up to PITA 47th ed.

80.3 [Income deferrals — livestock] — **(1) Definitions** — In this section,

"**breeding animals**" means deer, elk and other similar grazing ungulates, bovine cattle, bison, goats, sheep and horses that are over 12 months of age and are kept for breeding;

Notes: Bees are not "breeding animals": VIEWS doc 2010-0364901M4, but see now 80.3(1)"breeding bees".

Definition amended by 2014 budget bill #2, for 2014 and later taxation years, to change, for horses, "kept for breeding in a commercial production of pregnant mares' urine" to "kept for breeding".

Definition earlier amended by 1992 technical bill.

"**breeding bee stock**", of a taxpayer at any time, means a reasonable estimate of the quantity of a taxpayer's breeding bees held at that time in the course of carrying on a farming business using a unit of measurement that is accepted as an industry standard;

Related Provisions: 80.3(7) — Bee stock to be measured consistently for year.

Notes: Definition added by 2014 budget bill #2, effective for the 2014 and later taxation years.

"**breeding bees**" means bees that are not used principally to pollinate plants in greenhouses and larvae of those bees;

Notes: Definition added by 2014 budget bill #2, effective for the 2014 and later taxation years.

"**breeding herd**" of a taxpayer at any time means the number determined by the formula

$$A - (B - C)$$

where

A   is the total number of the taxpayer's breeding animals held in the course of carrying on a farming business at that time,

B   is the total number of the taxpayer's breeding animals held in the business at that time that are female bovine cattle that have not given birth to calves, and

C   is the lesser of the number determined as the value of B and one-half the total number of the taxpayer's breeding animals held in the business at that time that are female bovine cattle that have given birth to calves.

(2) Income deferral from the destruction of livestock — Where a particular amount in respect of the forced destruction of livestock under statutory authority in a taxation year of a taxpayer is included in computing the income of the taxpayer for the year from a farming business, there may be deducted in computing that income such amount as the taxpayer claims not exceeding the particular amount.

Related Provisions: 28(1)(g) — Deduction for farming business using cash method; 80.3(3) — Inclusion of deferred amount; 80.3(6) — Where subsecs. (2) and (4) not to apply.

Notes: Government assistance for loss of farming income due to forced destruction of livestock is taxable, but under 80.3(2) can be deducted and included in income the next year (80.3(3)). Thus, farmers using the cash method (28(1)) who replace the livestock by year-end suffer no tax cost, since the replacement cost offsets the income inclusion. This applies to assistance received by poultry farmers in B.C. due to Avian flu: VIEWS doc 2004-0096621M4.

Interpretation Bulletins: IT-425: Miscellaneous farm income.

(3) Inclusion of deferred amount — The amount deducted under subsection (2) in computing the income of a taxpayer from a farming business for a taxation year shall be deemed to be income of the taxpayer from the business for the taxpayer's immediately following taxation year.

Proposed Addition — Deferral for bovine tuberculosis

Agriculture and Agri-Food Canada news release, Nov. 6, 2017: *Additional Tax Support for Canadian Farmers*

...

Agriculture and Agri-Food Minister, Lawrence MacAulay, on behalf of Finance Minister, Bill Morneau, today announced tax relief to help farmers by:

• Providing tax relief for farmers who receive compensation under the *Health of Animals Act* as a consequence of the forced destruction of their livestock because of the bovine tuberculosis (TB) outbreak in 2016 and 2017 in Alberta and Saskatchewan [see below — ed.].

• Designating the regions for 2017 in which farmers qualify for a livestock tax deferral to help them replenish their herds after flood or drought conditions cease, allowing livestock producers in these prescribed regions to defer a portion of their 2017 sale proceeds of breeding livestock to 2018 [see under Reg. 7305.01(1) — ed.].

The Government also announced it will maintain the current tax treatment of cash purchase tickets for deliveries of listed grains [see under 76(4) — ed.].

Contacts: Guy Gallant, Director of Communications, Office of the Honourable Lawrence MacAulay, 613-773-1059; Media Relations, Agriculture and Agri-Food Canada, Ottawa, Ontario, 613-773-7972, 1-866-345-7972.

Backgrounder: *Tax Relief for Ranchers Affected by Bovine Tuberculosis*

The Government has announced further tax relief for taxpayers who receive compensation under the *Health of Animals Act* due to the 2016 and 2017 bovine tuberculosis (TB) outbreak in Alberta and Saskatchewan that forced the destruction of livestock.

Current income tax rules provide a tax deferral [80.3(2) — ed.] that allows a taxpayer to defer paying tax on the amount received in a tax year as compensation for the forced destruction of livestock from the current tax year to the following tax year [80.3(3) — ed.].

The objective of the deferral is to allow farmers who would otherwise realize a large income inclusion in the year they receive compensation to have the option to defer the income inclusion to the following year, when that income inclusion may be partially, or fully, offset by the cost of acquiring new livestock.

The Government recognizes that taxpayers affected by bovine TB may be unable to fully replenish their herds within a year and that replacement purchases are expected to extend over several years.

Accordingly, the Government intends to extend the existing tax deferral to better correspond to the repopulation plans and replacement purchases schedule, as determined in consultation with the industry.

As a result, taxpayers who received amounts as compensation in 2016 or 2017 under the *Health of Animals Act* as a consequence of the forced destruction of their livestock because of the bovine TB outbreak will effectively have the option of including those amounts in income for tax purposes, as follows:

- 2016 and 2017 tax year: no amount of compensation received will be included in income;
- 2018 tax year: 83% of compensation received will be included in income;
- 2019 tax year: 11% of compensation received will be included in income; and
- 2020 tax year: 6% of compensation received will be included in income.

Related Provisions: 28(1)(d) — Inclusion in farming income when using cash method; 87(2)(tt) — Amalgamations — deferral of amounts received; 88(1)(e.2) — Winding-up — rules applicable.

Interpretation Bulletins: IT-425: Miscellaneous farm income.

(4) Income deferral for regions of drought, flood or excessive moisture

— If in a taxation year a taxpayer carries on a farming business in a region that is at any time in the year a prescribed drought region or a prescribed region of flood or excessive moisture and the taxpayer's breeding herd at the end of the year in respect of the business does not exceed 85% of the taxpayer's breeding herd at the beginning of the year in respect of the business, there may be deducted in computing the taxpayer's income from the business for the year the amount that the taxpayer claims, not exceeding the amount, if any, determined by the formula

$$(A - B) \times C$$

where

A is the amount by which

(a) the total of all amounts included in computing the taxpayer's income for the year from the business in respect of the sale of breeding animals in the year

exceeds

(b) the total of all amounts deducted under paragraph 20(1)(n) in computing the taxpayer's income from the business for the year in respect of an amount referred to in paragraph (a) of this description;

B is the total of all amounts deducted in computing the taxpayer's income from the business for the year in respect of the acquisition of breeding animals; and

C is

(a) 30% where the taxpayer's breeding herd at the end of the year in respect of the business exceeds 70% of the taxpayer's breeding herd at the beginning of the year in respect of the business, and

(b) 90% where the taxpayer's breeding herd at the end of the year in respect of the business does not exceed 70% of the taxpayer's breeding herd at the beginning of the year in respect of the business.

Related Provisions: 28(1)(g) — Deduction for farming business using cash method; 80.3(4.1) — Deferral for bees; 80.3(5) — Inclusion of deferred amount; 80.3(6) — Where subsecs. (2) and (4) not to apply; 257 — Formula cannot calculate to less than zero.

Regulations: 7305.01(1) (prescribed regions for drought, flood, excessive moisture).

Notes: 80.3(4) opening words amended by 2009 budget bill #2, effective for 2008 and later taxation years, to add "prescribed region of flood or excessive moisture". This implements a March 5/09 Finance and Agriculture Canada announcement, to provide relief for flooding in Manitoba's Interlake region (see Reg. 7305.02).

(4.1) Income deferral [for bees]

— If in a taxation year a taxpayer carries on a farming business in a region that is at any time in the year a prescribed drought region or a prescribed region of flood or excessive moisture and the taxpayer's breeding bee stock at the end of the year in respect of the business does not exceed 85% of the taxpayer's breeding bee stock at the beginning of the year in respect of the business, there may be deducted in computing the taxpayer's income from the business for the year the amount that the taxpayer claims, not exceeding the amount, if any, determined by the formula

$$(A - B) \times C$$

where

A is the amount by which

(a) the total of all amounts included in computing the taxpayer's income from the business for the year in respect of the sale of breeding bees in the year

exceeds

(b) the total of all amounts deducted under paragraph 20(1)(n) in computing the taxpayer's income from the business for the year in respect of an amount referred to in paragraph (a);

B is the total of all amounts deducted in computing the taxpayer's income from the business for the year in respect of the acquisition of breeding bees; and

C is

(a) 30% if the taxpayer's breeding bee stock in respect of the business at the end of the year exceeds 70% of the taxpayer's breeding bee stock in respect of the business at the beginning of the year, and

(b) 90% if the taxpayer's breeding bee stock in respect of the business at the end of the year does not exceed 70% of the taxpayer's breeding bee stock in respect of the business at the beginning of the year.

Related Provisions: 28(1)(g) — Deduction for farming business using cash method; 80.3(4) — Deferral for livestock; 80.3(5) — Inclusion of deferred amount; 80.3(6) — Where subsec. (4.1) not to apply; 80.3(7) — Bee stock to be measured consistently for year; 257 — Formula cannot calculate to less than zero.

Notes: 80.3(4.1) added by 2014 budget bill #2, effective for the 2014 and later taxation years.

(5) Inclusion of deferred amount

— An amount deducted under subsection (4) or (4.1) in computing the income of a taxpayer for a particular taxation year from a farming business carried on in a region prescribed under those subsections may, to the extent that the taxpayer so elects, be included in computing the taxpayer's income from the business for a taxation year ending after the particular taxation year, and is, except to the extent that the amount has been included under this subsection in computing the taxpayer's income from the business for a preceding taxation year after the particular year, deemed to be income of the taxpayer from the business for the taxation year of the taxpayer that is the earliest of

(a) the first taxation year beginning after the end of the period or series of continuous periods, as the case may be, for which the region is prescribed under those subsections,

(b) the first taxation year, following the particular taxation year, at the end of which the taxpayer is

(i) non-resident, and

(ii) not carrying on business through a fixed place of business in Canada, and

(c) the taxation year in which the taxpayer dies.

Related Provisions: 28(1)(d) — Amount under 80.3(5) to be added to income of farming business using cash method.

Notes: For a taxpayer filing a Quebec return, an 80.3(5) election must be copied to Revenu Québec: *Taxation Act* ss. 487.0.3, 21.4.6.

80.3(5) amended by 2014 budget bill #2 (for 2014 and later tax years, to refer to 80.3(4.1)), 2009 budget bill #2, 1991 technical bill.

Regulations: 7305, 7305.01 (prescribed drought regions for each year).

(6) Subsecs. (2), (4) and (4.1) not applicable — Subsections (2), (4) and (4.1) do not apply to a taxpayer in respect of a farming business for a taxation year

(a) in which the taxpayer died; or

(b) where at the end of the year the taxpayer is non-resident and not carrying on the business through a fixed place of business in Canada.

Notes: 80.3(6) opening words amended by 2014 budget bill #2, for 2014 and later taxation years, to add reference to 80.3(4.1).

80.3(6)(b) amended by 1991 technical bill, for fiscal periods and tax years ending after 1987.

(7) Measuring breeding bee stock — In applying subsection (4.1) in respect of a taxation year, the unit of measurement used for estimating the quantity of a taxpayer's breeding bee stock held in the course of carrying on a farming business at the end of the year is to be the same as that used for the beginning of the year.

Notes: 80.3(7) added by 2014 budget bill #2, for the 2014 and later tax years.

Notes [s. 80.3]: 80.3 completely revised by 1989 Budget, effective for fiscal periods and taxation years ending after 1987.

Definitions [s. 80.3]: "amount" — 248(1); "breeding animals", "breeding bee stock", "breeding bees", "breeding herd" — 80.3(1); "business" — 248(1); "Canada" — 255; "farming" — 248(1); "month" — *Interpretation Act* 35(1); "prescribed" — 248(1); "taxation year" — 11(2), 249; "taxpayer" — 248(1); "year" — 11(2).

80.4 (1) Loans [to employees — deemed interest] — Where a person or partnership receives a loan or otherwise incurs a debt because of or as a consequence of a previous, the current or an intended office or employment of an individual, or because of the services performed or to be performed by a corporation carrying on a personal services business, the individual or corporation, as the case may be, shall be deemed to have received a benefit in a taxation year equal to the amount, if any, by which the total of

(a) all interest on all such loans and debts computed at the prescribed rate on each such loan and debt for the period in the year during which it was outstanding, and

(b) the total of all amounts each of which is an amount of interest that was paid or payable in respect of the year on such a loan or debt by

(i) a person or partnership (in this paragraph referred to as the "employer") that employed or intended to employ the individual,

(ii) a person (other than the debtor) related to the employer, or

(iii) a person or partnership to or for whom or which the services were or were to be provided or performed by the corporation or a person (other than the debtor) that does not deal at arm's length with that person or any member of such partnership,

exceeds the total of

(c) the amount of interest for the year paid on all such loans and debts not later than 30 days after the end of the year, and

(d) any portion of the total determined in respect of the year under paragraph (b) that is reimbursed in the year or within 30

days after the end of the year by the debtor to the person or entity who made the payment referred to in that paragraph.

Related Provisions: 6(9) — Inclusion as income from employment; 6(23) — Employer-provided mortgage subsidy is taxable; 12(1)(w) — Benefit from carrying on personal services business; 15(2) — Shareholder debt; 79(3)F(b)(v)(B)(I) — Where property surrendered to creditor; 80(1)"forgiven amount"B(h) — Debt forgiveness rules do not apply; 80.4(1.1) — Interpretation; 80.4(3) — Loans — exceptions; 80.4(4) — Interest on loans for home purchase or relocation; 80.5 — Interest deemed paid; 110(1)(j) — Home relocation loan — deduction before 2018; 248(1)"home relocation loan"(c) — Definition based on application of 80.4(1); *Interpretation Act* 27(5) — Meaning of "within 30 days."

Notes: See CRA Guide T4130. For examples of calculating the 80.4(1) benefit, see IT-421R2, VIEWS doc 2009-0331661E5. Note that an interest subsidy (including via credit card) to an employee may be taxable under 6(1)(a) or 6(23) if 80.4 does not apply: 2004-0058061E5, 2005-0154531E5, 2012-0463501E5.

The deemed interest inclusion under 80.4(1) (taxable as employment income under 6(9)) can be offset by a deduction under 80.5 in some cases. See Notes to 80.5. However, a loan to the taxpayer in his/her capacity as a shareholder rather than as an employee may also lead to full inclusion of the loan into income under 15(2), in which case 80.4(1) does not apply: see 80.4(3)(b).

An employer's loan to an employee in advance of an expected workers' compensation award does not generate deemed interest: VIEWS doc 2013-0496251E5.

For CRA interpretation that 80.4(1) applies see 2008-0290481R3, 2010-0384201E5.

Opening words of 80.4(1) amended by 1992 technical bill, effective for taxation years that begin after 1991.

Regulations: 4301(c) (prescribed rate of interest for 80.4(1)(a)); but see also ITA 80.4(7)"prescribed rate".

Interpretation Bulletins: IT-171R2: Non-resident individuals — computation of taxable income earned in Canada and non-refundable tax credits (cancelled); IT-421R2: Benefits to individuals, corporations and shareholders from loans or debt.

I.T. Technical News: 6 (payment of mortgage interest subsidy by employer).

CRA Audit Manual: 24.12.4: Subsection 15(2) — audit issues — indirect benefit calculation (section 80.4); 24.12.5: Section 80.4 — benefit on interest-free or low-interest loans.

(1.1) Interpretation — A loan or debt is deemed to have been received or incurred because of an individual's office or employment, or because of services performed by a corporation that carries on a personal services business, as the case may be, if it is reasonable to conclude that, but for an individual's previous, current or intended office or employment, or the services performed or to be performed by the corporation,

(a) the terms of the loan or debt would have been different; or

(b) the loan would not have been received or the debt would not have been incurred.

Related Provisions: 6(23) — Employer-provided mortgage subsidy is taxable; 248(1)"home relocation loan"(c) — Definition based on application of 80.4(1).

Notes: 80.4(1.1) is a response to *Siwik*, [1996] 2 C.T.C. 2417 (TCC). It was added by 1998 Budget, effective for loans received and debts incurred after February 23, 1998 except that, where the loan or debt is in respect of an eligible relocation in connection with which the individual begins employment at the new work location by September 30, 1998, it does not apply to taxation years that end before 2001.

(2) Idem [loan to shareholder — deemed interest] — Where a person (other than a corporation resident in Canada) or a partnership (other than a partnership each member of which is a corporation resident in Canada) was

(a) a shareholder of a corporation,

(b) connected with a shareholder of a corporation, or

(c) a member of a partnership, or a beneficiary of a trust, that was a shareholder of a corporation,

and by virtue of such shareholding that person or partnership received a loan from, or otherwise incurred a debt to, that corporation, any other corporation related thereto or a partnership of which that corporation or any corporation related thereto was a member, the person or partnership shall be deemed to have received a benefit in a taxation year equal to the amount, if any, by which

(d) all interest on all such loans and debts computed at the prescribed rate on each such loan and debt for the period in the year during which it was outstanding

exceeds

    (e) the total of

        (i) the amount of interest for the year paid on all such loans and debts (other than loans deemed to have been made under subsection 15(2.17)) not later than 30 days after the end of the year, and

        (ii) the specified interest amounts, for the year, in respect of all such loans that are deemed to have been made under subsection 15(2.17).

Related Provisions: 15(2) — Income inclusion for amount of loan; 15(2.16)–(2.192) — Back-to-back loans; 15(9) — Deemed benefit to shareholder; 79(3)F(b)(v)(B)(I) — Where property surrendered to creditor; 80(1)"forgiven amount"B(h) — Debt forgiveness rules do not apply; 80.4(3) — Exceptions; 80.4(7) — Definitions; 80.4(8) — Meaning of "connected"; 80.5 — Deemed interest; 95(1)"foreign accrual property income"A(d) — Definitions — "foreign accrual property income".

Notes: See 15(9). The deemed interest inclusion under 80.4(2) can be offset by a deduction under 80.5 in some cases. See Notes to 80.5. If the loan is fully included in income as a shareholder loan under 15(2), 80.4 will not apply: see 80.4(3)(b). See also *Income Tax Audit Manual* §24.12.6.

An 80.4(2) benefit to a non-resident shareholder is subject to withholding tax as a deemed dividend via 15(9), 15(1), 214(3) and 212(2). See VIEWS docs 2007-0241991R3, 2008-0280041R3, 2010-0353141R3, 2011-0418711R3; 2015-0622751I7 [Kandev, "NIB Loan to Non-FA-Related Non-Resident", 26(4) *Canadian Tax Highlights* (ctf.ca) 5-6 (April 2018)].

In *Bolduc*, 2005 TCC 675, 80.4(2) applied to debts owing by B which B had arranged to have transferred to a corp of which B was a shareholder; 80.5 did not provide an offsetting deduction as its conditions were not met.

In *Robertson*, 2009 TCC 183, a shareholder who took advances through the year, and cancelled them with bonus or dividends by the following March 31, was subject to 80.4(2) interest benefit. 80.4(2) similarly applied in: *Bibby*, 2009 TCC 588; *Hansen*, 2011 TCC 194 (even if there was a loan outstanding from the shareholder, there was no evidence of set-off against the advance from the corp [see Notes to 15(1)]); *Desgagné*, 2012 TCC 63 (lawyer owed money to law firm's management company).

In *St-Pierre*, 2018 FCA 144, a capital dividend was overpaid due to miscalculation of the capital dividend account; after the Quebec Superior Court nullified the dividend, the TCC held that 80.4(2) applied to the cash paid to S, but the FCA overruled this.

"Year" in 80.4(2)(d) and (e) refers to the borrower's tax year: VIEWS doc 2006-0187061E5.

80.4(2)(e) amended by 2016 budget bill #2, effective for

    (a) loans received and indebtedness incurred after March 21, 2016; and

    (b) any portion of a particular loan received or indebtedness incurred before March 22, 2016 that remains outstanding on that day, as if that portion were a separate loan or indebtedness that was received or incurred, as the case may be, on March 22, 2016 in the same manner and on the same terms as the particular loan or indebtedness.

Before the amendment, read:

    (e) the amount of interest for the year paid on all such loans and debts not later than 30 days after the later of the end of the year and December 31, 1982.

Regulations: 4301(c) (prescribed rate of interest for 80.4(2)(d)); but see also ITA 80.4(7)"prescribed rate".

Interpretation Bulletins: IT-421R2: Benefits to individuals, corporations and shareholders from loans or debt.

CRA Audit Manual: 24.12.4: Subsection 15(2) — audit issues — indirect benefit calculation (section 80.4); 24.12.5: Section 80.4 — benefit on interest-free or low-interest loans; 24.12.6: Subsection 80.4(2) — audit issues.

(3) Where subsecs. (1) and (2) do not apply — Subsections (1) and (2) do not apply in respect of any loan or debt, or any part thereof,

    (a) on which the rate of interest was equal to or greater than the rate that would, having regard to all the circumstances (including the terms and conditions of the loan or debt), have been agreed on, at the time the loan was received or the debt was incurred, between parties dealing with each other at arm's length if

        (i) none of the parties received the loan or incurred the debt by virtue of an office or employment or by virtue of the shareholding of a person or partnership, and

        (ii) the ordinary business of the creditor included the lending of money,

except where an amount is paid or payable in any taxation year to the creditor in respect of interest on the loan or debt by a party other than the debtor; or

    (b) that was included in computing the income of a person or partnership under this Part.

Notes: For interpretation of "ordinary business included the lending of money" in 80.4(3)(a)(ii), see Notes to 15(2.3).

80.4(3)(b) excludes 80.4 from applying if the amount was already fully included in income as a shareholder loan under 15(2) or a forgiven employee loan under 6(15). In *Tardif*, 2006 TCC 314, there was no 80.4(2) benefit because the loan itself had been included in T's income under 15(2). In *Robertson*, 2009 TCC 183, dividends or bonus declared the next year to offset shareholder draws did not fall within 80.4(3)(b). See also VIEWS doc 2011-039792I7.

CRA Audit Manual: 24.12.5: Section 80.4 — benefit on interest-free or low-interest loans.

(4) Interest on loans for home purchase or relocation — For the purpose of computing the benefit under subsection (1) in a taxation year in respect of a home purchase loan or a home relocation loan, the amount of interest determined under paragraph (1)(a) shall not exceed the amount of interest that would have been determined thereunder if it had been computed at the prescribed rate in effect at the time the loan was received or the debt was incurred, as the case may be.

Related Provisions: 80(14)(d) — Residual balance; 80.4(6) — Interest rate cap reset every 5 years; 110(1.4) — Replacement of home relocation loan.

Notes: 80.4(4) amended by 2017 budget bill #1, effective 2018, to delete "and for the purpose of paragraph 110(1)(j)" after "home relocation loan". (The 110(1)(j) home relocation loan deduction was repealed.)

Regulations: 4301(c) (prescribed rate of interest); but see also ITA 80.4(7)"prescribed rate".

Interpretation Bulletins: IT-421R2: Benefits to individuals, corporations and shareholders from loans or debt.

(5) [No longer relevant]

Notes: 80.4(5) affects the 1982 and 1983 taxation years.

(6) Deemed new home purchase loans — For the purposes of this section, other than paragraph (3)(a) and subsection (5), where a home purchase loan or a home relocation loan of an individual has a term for repayment exceeding five years, the balance outstanding on the loan on the date that is five years from the day the loan was received or was last deemed by this subsection to have been received shall be deemed to be a new home purchase loan received by the individual on that date.

Related Provisions: 110(1)(j) — Home relocation loan; 110(1.4) — Replacement of home relocation loan.

Interpretation Bulletins: IT-421R2: Benefits to individuals, corporations and shareholders from loans or debt.

(7) Definitions — In this section,

"home purchase loan" means that portion of any loan received or debt otherwise incurred by an individual in the circumstances described in subsection (1) that is used to acquire, or to repay a loan or debt that was received or incurred to acquire, a dwelling, or a share of the capital stock of a cooperative housing corporation acquired for the sole purpose of acquiring the right to inhabit a dwelling owned by the corporation, where the dwelling is for the habitation of

    (a) the individual by virtue of whose office or employment the loan is received or the debt is incurred,

    (b) a specified shareholder of the corporation by virtue of whose services the loan is received or the debt is incurred, or

    (c) a person related to a person described in paragraph (a) or (b),

or that is used to repay a home purchase loan;

Notes: On refinancing to pay an existing mortgage plus penalties, only the original borrowed amount qualifies, not the amount covering the penalties: VIEWS doc 2009-0328311E5.

Definition amended by 1991 technical bill, retroactive to 1985. 80.4(7)"home purchase loan" was 80.4(7)(a) before RSC 1985 (5th Supp) consolidation for tax years ending after Nov. 1991.

Interpretation Bulletins: IT-421R2: Benefits to individuals, corporations and shareholders from loans or debt.

"prescribed rate" of interest means

(a), (b) [apply to years before 1979 — ed.]

(c) for any year, or part thereof, after 1978, such rate of interest as is prescribed therefor except that, for the purpose of computing the benefit under subsection (1) in a taxation year on a home purchase loan received after November 12, 1981 and before 1982, the prescribed rate of interest at the time the loan was received shall be deemed to be 16% per annum.

Notes: 80.4(7)"prescribed rate" was 80.4(7)(b) before RSC 1985 (5th Supp) consolidation for tax years ending after Nov. 1991.

Regulations: 4301(c) (prescribed rate of interest for para. (c)).

"specified interest amount", for a year, in respect of a loan (referred to in this definition as the "deemed loan") deemed to have been made under subsection 15(2.17) by an "ultimate funder" (as defined in subsection 15(2.192)), means the amount determined by the formula

$$A \times (B/C)$$

where

A is the amount of interest for the year paid not later than 30 days after the end of the year on all debts — owing by one or more "funders" (as defined in subsection 15(2.192), but excluding any funders that are "ultimate funders" as defined in subsection 15(2.192)) under one or more "funding arrangements" (as defined in subsection 15(2.192)) to the ultimate funder — that gave rise to the deemed loan;

B is the average amount outstanding for the year in respect of the deemed loan; and

C is the total of all amounts each of which is the average amount outstanding in the year as or on account of an amount owing under a debt described in A.

Notes: Definition added by 2016 budget bill #2, effective on the same basis as the amendment to 80.4(2)(e).

(8) Meaning of connected — For the purposes of subsection (2), a person or partnership is connected with a shareholder of a corporation if that person or partnership does not deal at arm's length with, or is affiliated with, the shareholder, unless, in the case of a person, that person is

(a) a foreign affiliate of the corporation; or

(b) a foreign affiliate of a person resident in Canada with which the corporation does not deal at arm's length.

Notes: 80.4(8) opening words amended by 2002-2013 technical bill (Part 5 — technical), effective for loans made and indebtedness arising after Oct. 2011, essentially to add references to a partnership. Before the amendment, read:

(8) Persons connected with a shareholder — For the purposes of subsection (2), a person is connected with a shareholder of a corporation if that person does not deal at arm's length with the shareholder and if that person is a person other than

Definitions [s. 80.4]: "affiliated" — 251.1; "amount" — 248(1); "arm's length" — 251(1); "because of" — 80.4(1.1); "Canada" — 255; "carrying on business" — 253; "common-law partner" — 248(1); "connected" — 80.4(8); "corporation" — 248(1), *Interpretation Act* 35(1); "employee" — 248(1); "employer" — 80.4(1)(b)(i); "employment" — 248(1); "foreign affiliate" — 95(1), 248(1); "funder", "funding arrangement" — 15(2.192); "home purchase loan" — 80.4(7); "home relocation loan", "individual", "office", "officer" — 248(1); "partnership" — see 96(1) Notes; "person" — 248(1); "personal services business" — 125(7), 248(1); "prescribed" — 80.4(7), 248(1); "prescribed rate" — Reg. 4301; "related" — 251(2); "resident in Canada" — 94(3)(a), 250; "share", "shareholder" — 248(1); "specified interest amount" — 80.4(7); "specified shareholder" — 248(1); "taxation year" — 249; "ultimate funder" — 15(2.192); "writing" — *Interpretation Act* 35(1).

80.5 Deemed interest — Where a benefit is deemed by section 80.4 to have been received in a taxation year by

(a) an individual or corporation under subsection 80.4(1), or

(b) a person or partnership under subsection 80.4(2),

the amount of the benefit shall, for the purposes of subparagraph 8(1)(j)(i) and paragraph 20(1)(c), be deemed to be interest paid in,

and payable in respect of, the year by the debtor pursuant to a legal obligation to pay interest on borrowed money.

Notes: If the purpose for which the loan was used entitles the taxpayer to a deduction for interest expense under 20(1)(c) or 8(1)(j), 80.5 will negate the effect of the income inclusion under 80.4 by allowing an offsetting deduction. Thus, for example, an interest-free loan to enable the taxpayer to acquire common shares will normally have no net tax cost to the taxpayer. However, there may be an income inclusion under 15(2) of the amount of the loan, with a deduction under 20(1)(j) when it is repaid.

Definitions [s. 80.5]: "amount" — 248(1); "corporation" — 248(1), *Interpretation Act* 35(1); "individual", "person" — 248(1); "taxation year" — 249.

Interpretation Bulletins: IT-421R2: Benefits to individuals, corporations and shareholders from loans or debt.

CRA Audit Manual: 24.12.5: Section 80.4 — benefit on interest-free or low-interest loans.

80.6 (1) Synthetic disposition — If a synthetic disposition arrangement is entered into in respect of a property owned by a taxpayer and the synthetic disposition period of the arrangement is one year or more, the taxpayer is deemed

(a) to have disposed of the property immediately before the beginning of the synthetic disposition period for proceeds equal to its fair market value at the beginning of the synthetic disposition period; and

(b) to have reacquired the property at the beginning of the synthetic disposition period at a cost equal to that fair market value.

(2) Exception — Subsection (1) does not apply in respect of a property owned by a taxpayer if

(a) the disposition referred to in subsection (1) would not result in the realization of a capital gain or income;

(b) the property is a mark-to-market property (as defined in subsection 142.2(1)) of the taxpayer;

(c) the synthetic disposition arrangement referred to in subsection (1) is a lease of tangible property or, for civil law, corporeal property;

(d) the arrangement is an exchange of property to which subsection 51(1) applies; or

(e) the property is disposed of as part of the arrangement, within one year after the day on which the synthetic disposition period of the arrangement begins.

Related Provisions: See under 248(1)"synthetic disposition arrangement".

Notes: See Notes to 248(1)"synthetic disposition arrangement".

Note that the exception in 80.6(2)(e), where the property is sold within 1 year, applies only if the disposition was planned, so that it is "part of the arrangement". This exception appears to permit a deliberate deferral of 1 year of capital gains via an SDA.

80.6 added by 2013 budget bill #2, for agreements and arrangements entered into after March 20, 2013; and for an earlier agreement or arrangement whose terms are extended after March 20, 2013, as if it were entered into at the time of the extension.

Definitions [s. 80.6]: "capital gain" — 39(1)(a), 248(1); "disposition" — 248(1); "fair market value" — see 69(1) Notes; "mark-to-market property" — 142.2(1); "property", "synthetic disposition arrangement", "synthetic disposition period", "taxpayer" — 248(1).

Subdivision G — Amounts Not Included in Computing Income

81. (1) Amounts not included in income — There shall not be included in computing the income of a taxpayer for a taxation year,

Notes: Traditionally, an exemption was construed narrowly, so it applied only if it was clear: *Toronto General Trusts*, 1935 CarswellOnt 116 (SCC), para. 13; *Gustavson Drilling*, 1975 CarswellNat 376 (SCC), para. 7; *Beatrice Foods* (1991), 4 T.C.T. 6175 (Ont. SCJ); *London Jewish v. MPAC*, 2020 ONSC 6794, para. 19. However, per *Notre-Dame de Bon-Secours*, 1994 CanLII 58 (SCC), para. 34: "adhering to the principle that taxation is clearly the rule and exemption the exception no longer corresponds to the reality of present-day tax law". The "text, context and purpose" rule of *Canada Trustco*, 2005 SCC 54, para. 10 may thus apply.

See also s. 3 Notes re payments that are non-taxable as not from a "source".

(a) **statutory exemptions [including Indians]** — an amount that is declared to be exempt from income tax by any other enactment of Parliament, other than an amount received or receivable by an individual that is exempt by virtue of a provision contained in a tax convention or agreement with another country that has the force of law in Canada;

Proposed Amendment — Aboriginal income taxation

Federal Budget, March 19, 2019, Chapter 3, Part 2: *Tax Agreements with Indigenous Governments*

The Government has been engaging with Indigenous groups and organizations to hear their perspectives on tax matters and the role of tax powers and tax arrangements in the new fiscal relationship. Discussions are ongoing with, among others, self-governing Indigenous governments, Indigenous groups in self-government negotiations and the Assembly of First Nations.

The Government is assessing the proposals advanced by Indigenous groups and organizations to date and will continue to work collaboratively with Indigenous partners on charting the path forward.

The Government also confirms its continued willingness to negotiate agreements with interested Indigenous governments to enable the implementation of First Nations Goods and Services Tax within their settlement lands or reserves, and with interested self-governing Indigenous governments to enable them to implement a personal income tax within their settlement lands. The Government also supports and encourages direct taxation arrangements between interested provinces or territories and Indigenous governments and will continue to facilitate such arrangements. The Government recognizes the important role that tax powers and tax arrangements could play in establishing a new fiscal relationship and in supporting self-sufficiency and self-determination for Indigenous governments.

Federal Budget, Chapter 8, April 19, 2021: *Supporting Self-determination Through Tax Agreements*

Tax arrangements between the Crown and Indigenous governments support self-determination and social and economic development by creating opportunities for Indigenous governments to raise tax revenues within their reserve or settlement lands in support of community priorities.

The federal government continues to be committed to negotiating agreements with interested Indigenous governments that enable them to implement a First Nations Goods and Services Tax within their reserves or settlement lands and with interested self-governing Indigenous governments to enable them to implement a personal income tax within their lands. The federal government also remains committed to facilitating similar arrangements between interested provincial and territorial governments and Indigenous governments.

Budget 2021 announces the Government of Canada's intention to engage with interested Indigenous governments and organizations on a framework for the negotiation of agreements that would enable interested Indigenous governments to implement a fuel, alcohol, tobacco, and cannabis sales tax within their reserves or settlement lands.

Notes: See guides RC4072, *First Nations Tax*, and RC4365, *First Nations Goods and Services Tax*. For the annotated *First Nations Goods and Services Tax Act* see David M. Sherman, *Practitioner's Goods and Services Tax Annotated* (Carswell).

Related Provisions: 110(1)(f)(i) — Deduction for amount exempted by treaty; 120(2.2) — Credit for persons subject to First Nations Tax; 126(3)(c) — Employees of international organizations; 147.5(31)"exempt earned income"(a), 147.5(31) — Income exempt under *Indian Act* is eligible for PRPP contribution; 150(1)(a)(ii) — Non-resident claiming treaty exemption must file tax return; 212(1)(h)(iii) — Exemption from non-resident withholding tax.

Notes: *Indian Act* s. 87 exempts status Indians from taxation of their "personal property situated on a reserve", and income is personal property: *Nowegijick*, [1983] C.T.C. 20 (SCC). There are no fixed rules for determining when income is "situated on a reserve"; there must be "sufficient connecting factors" to the reserve: *Williams*, [1992] 1 C.T.C. 225 (SCC). *Bastien*, 2011 SCC 38, para. 18, states that the *Williams* connecting factors include the payor's and payee's residence, place of payment, and the location of the work generating the income; but depending on the context, different factors may be given differen weight. Whether the income is integral to the life of the reserve or preservation of the Indian way of life is irrelevant: para. 28.

The reserve on which the income is located need not be the reserve where the Indian lives for the exemption to apply: *Dubé*, 2011 SCC 39, para. 15. As to whether land is a "reserve" see *Ross River*, 2002 SCC 54 (Indian village in Yukon not a reserve because no clear Crown intention); *Jeddore*, 2003 FCA 323 (Nfld. land that belonged to colonial government before Confederation was not reserve); *Veitch Holdings*, 2010 TCC 98 (land title not determinative; the land must be set aside for use by Indians); VIEWS doc 2014-0531421E5 (traditional lands not a reserve). An Indian living off-reserve, working for a band located on a lot "that was not yet a reserve, but was going to become a reserve in the future", was not entitled to the exemption: *McKay*, 2009 FCA 43. An Indian Settlement under various remission orders is treated as a reserve, so an Indian who sells land on such a settlement pays no tax: 2008-0301581117.

Who qualifies for exemption: Most Indians in Yukon no longer qualify, due to a treaty with the federal government: full details in VIEWS doc 2015-0586673I7 (also 9821446, 9806857, 2006-020218117). Nisga'a citizens do not qualify, due to the Nisga'a Final Agreement: 2014-0539641E5. An Indian who was entitled to be registered can be refunded the tax paid for years before being registered: 2007-0223911E5.

Descendants of aboriginals who signed Treaty 8 in 1899 do not qualify: *Benoit*, 2003 FCA 236 (leave to appeal denied 2004 CarswellNat 1209 (SCC)); *Dumont*, 2008 FCA 32; *Laboucan*, 2013 TCC 357 (appeal to FCA dismissed for delay A-423-13); in *Tuccaro*, 2014 FCA 184 and 2016 FCA 259, an appeal of this issue was able to proceed; but TCC appeal withdrawn June 5/18, file 2013-188(IT)G. A similar claim by Métis was rejected in *Gauthier (Gisborn)*, 2006 TCC 290; and a status Indian could not escape conviction of failing to file returns by claiming exemption under Treaty 4: *Campeau*, 2007 SKPC 110. Descent from Indians does not qualify without obtaining an Indian status card: *Girard*, 2014 TCC 107. In *Daniels*, 2016 SCC 12, the Supreme Court of Canada held that Métis and non-status Indians are "Indians" for *Constitution Act, 1867* s. 91(24) and thus under federal jurisdiction. This does not make them "Indians" under the *Indian Act*: 2016-0656851E5, 2016-06663811E5. Govt. of Saskatchewan Information Notice 2016-01 (April 2016) states: "Since the federal government has authority over the *Indian Act* (Canada), the Province will wait for their direction to determine whether this legislation will be impacted before considering any changes to the manner in which the current tax exemptions are administered." See also Dolson, "Daniels: Tax Changes for Non-Status Aboriginals?", 24(5) *Canadian Tax Highlights* (ctf.ca) 4-5 (May 2016). A tax protester's claim that her Métis heritage made her exempt from Canadian criminal courts was rejected in *Anderson*, 2016 BCSC 2170 (appeal quashed 2017 BCCA 153), 2021 BCCA 101.

Employment income: CRA has developed the *Indian Act Exemption for Employment Income Guidelines* (1994): tinyurl.com/cra-ind-guide; and Form TD1-IN for an employee to provide to an employer, showing why the employee qualifies. During the COVID-19 pandemic, see *Guidance on the application of the 'Indian Act Exemption for Employment Income Guidelines' to issues raised by the COVID-19 crisis*, tinyurl.com/covid-indian.

Guideline (GL) 1 (90% of employment duties on reserve means income is exempt; prorate exemption if <90%): see VIEWS docs 2008-0296171E5 (reserve not yet created); 2010-0361631E5 (vacation and sick days); 2010-0380481E5 (prorating for on-reserve duties); 2012-0462251E5; 2012-047037117; 2014-0523531E5; 2014-0544241E5. Being forced to work off-reserve due to COVID-19 will not lose the exemption: tinyurl.com/cra-indig; 2020-0864651E5, 2020-0874991E5, 2021-0876571E5.

For GL 1 and 3, travel time getting to work is generally excluded from the calculation of duties: 2009-0344911E5; but may be counted for a truck driver: 2009-0348641E5. An employee on sabbatical is not performing "duties of employment": 2010-037836117. Telework done by an Indian on a reserve is generally exempt: 2002-0153867, 2003-004770117, 2012-0437531E5.

GL 2 (if employer resident on reserve and Indian lives on reserve, income is exempt): 2008-0302001E5; 2012-0434151E5; 2015-0585751E5; 2013-0489791E5 (where corporate income paid out to owner as salary); 2015-0603891E5; 2015-0615931E5 (corporation's head office and strategic decision-making is off-reserve); 2016-0629491E5.

GL 3 (if either employer is resident or Indian lives on reserve, and >50% duties on reserve, income is exempt): 2012-0443291E5; 2014-0544241E5; 2020-0864811E5 and 2020-0875231E5 (working at on-reserve home office during COVID-19 qualifies).

GL 4 (if employer is resident on reserve, and is Indian band or certain Indian organizations dedicated to certain non-commercial activities): 2007-0233931E5; 2008-026706117; 2009-0352661M4; 2010-0355071E5; 2011-042509117; 2011-042824117; 2013-047431117; 2014-0521931E5; 2014-053336117; 2015-0568081E5 (effect of employer moving office off reserve); 2018-0781651E5; 2018-0784991E5 (teacher: GL 4 does not apply but likely exempt anyway).

CRA findings that no GL applies (so income not exempt): 2005-015507117; 2009-031660117; 2009-032728117 (employment outside Canada); 2009-0329681E5 (same); 2012-0466691E5; 2013-0484341E5; 2014-0530711E5 (volunteer firefighters); 2010-035844117 (advance of salary not exempt); 2015-0569171E5 and 2016-0663231E5 (most work off-reserve); 2015-0601891E5; 2019-0832681E5 (benefiting a reserve is not enough); 2020-0840271E5 (helping Indigenous women who live off-reserve).

General comments: 2007-0234591M4; 2007-0260311E5; 2009-0318031E5 (pilot flying to remote areas); 2009-0341211M4; 2010-0364891M4; 2011-0410881E5; 2011-0425781E5; 2012-0465231E5; 2013-050790117; 2014-0537591E5; 2014-0518771E5 (effect of company relocating off-reserve); 2014-0539231E5 (CRA will not issue rulings); 2016-0649601M4; 2016-0659651E5 (effect of change in circumstances); 2016-0617871E5; 2019-080003117 (insufficient information to answer). Employee leasing: see para. "NLS" below.

On employment income, aside from *Bastien* and *Dubé* under "Interest" below, see *Clarke*, [1997] 3 C.T.C. 157 (FCA); *Monias*, 2001 FCA 239 (leave to appeal denied 2002 CarswellNat 504 (SCC)); *Akiwenzie*, 2003 FCA 469; *Tsuruda*, 2006 TCC 288; *Wyse*, 2007 FC 535; *Picard*, 2009 FCA 370; *Morrisseau*, 2020 TCC 5 (working in Winnipeg for company owned by tribal councils — taxable). In *Bell*, 2018 FCA 91 (leave to appeal denied 2019 CarswellNat 360 (SCC)), a construction company owned by a couple, doing projects off-reserve (but with head office on a reserve), bonused out all profits to the wife, a status Indian; the exemption did not apply, as the connecting factors for business rather than employment income applied. CRA may reject a corporation bonusing down its income to its Indian owner as exempt: docs 2004-007417117, 2010-0376541E5.

NLS/employee leasing: Many cases held that employees of two related on-reserve employee leasing services (Native Leasing Services / OI Employee Leasing / Roger Obonsawin) did not have sufficient "connecting factors", so their earnings from working off-reserve were taxable: *Shilling*, 2001 FCA 178 (leave to appeal denied 2002 CarswellNat 502 (SCC)); *Horn (Williams)*, 2008 FCA 352 (leave to appeal denied 2009 CarswellNat 851); *Zoccole*, 2015 FCA 258 (leave to appeal denied as *Forsythe*, 2016

CarswellNat 1183); *Roe*, 2008 TCC 667 (FCA appeal dismissed for delay A-22-09); *Googoo*, 2008 TCC 589 (FCA appeal dismissed for delay A-121-09); *McIvor*, 2009 TCC 469; *LaFontaine*, 2010 TCC 433; *Pigeon*, 2010 TCC 643; *Johnston*, 2010 TCC 627; *Hester*, 2010 TCC 647 (FCA appeal discontinued A-33-11); *Robinson*, 2010 TCC 649 (FCA appeal discontinued A-47-11); *Davad*, 2011 TCC 162; *Dale*, 2011 TCC 206; *Baptiste*, 2011 TCC 295; *Nahwegahbow*, 2011 TCC 296; *Dreaver*, 2011 TCC 443; *Marcinyshyn*, 2011 TCC 516; *Vincent*, 2011 TCC 430; *Assinewe*, 2012 TCC 24; *Verreault*, 2012 TCC 293; *Ozawagosh*, 2013 TCC 311; *Baldwin*, 2014 TCC 284. In some of these, the appellants merely read statements claiming they were not Canadian citizens but First Nation citizens, while others deal with the legal issues. Irrelevant claims (how CRA treated other taxpayers, and NLS's own status) were struck from notices of appeal in *Baldwin*, 2013 TCC 363. Attempts by NLS or OI employees to file late appeals failed in *Johnston*, 2009 TCC 327 (FCA appeal dismissed for delay A-293-09), as the *Indian Act* did not extend their appeal rights, and *Keshane*, 2010 TCC 651 (FCA appeal (as *Toulouse*) discontinued A-31-11); *Sampson*, 2012 TCC 156. The only substantive success in a written decision was in *Dugan*, 2011 TCC 269 where 3 of 6 appeals were allowed on the basis of sufficient connecting factors; and in *Clarkson*, an unreported case cited in *Dugan*. (The Tax Court faced 1,100 NLS appeals and got through the backlog in 13 months by devoting resources specifically to hearing them: Rossiter ACJ, speaking to CRA Toronto Centre tax professionals group Nov. 2, 2011.) For CRA interpretation see tinyurl.com/cra-ee-leasing; VIEWS docs 2010-0371781E5, 2018-0750821I7.

Employment at a mill on land that had previously been a reserve qualified in *Boubard*, 2008 FCA 392. (Despite *Boubard*, it was not unreasonable for CRA to reject claims for late reassessment under 152(4.2) by other members of the same band: *Abraham*, 2012 FCA 266 (leave to appeal denied 2013 CarswellNat 729 (SCC)).) Traditional territory that is not a reserve does not qualify: VIEWS doc 2012-0441791E5. Nor does employment on the US side of a reserve: doc 9528647.

Deductions from exempt employment income (such as 8(1)(m) pension contributions) apply to that income, so cannot be used against other sources: *Smith*, 2018 TCC 61.

COVID-19 benefits: Canada Emergency Response Benefit (CERB) income is generally exempt (and also exempt from repayment under the *Canada Recovery Benefits Act* for income being too high), to the extent the income it replaces was exempt: tinyurl.com/cra-cerb-tax; VIEWS docs 2020-0864791E5, 2020-0866491I7, 2020-0867841I7. So are Canada Recovery Benefit (CRB): tinyurl.com/cra-crb-tax; Canada Recovery Sickness Benefit (CRSB): tinyurl.com/cra-crsb-tax; and Canada Recovery Caregiving Benefit (CRCB): tinyurl.com/cra-crcb-tax. Canada Emergency Student Benefit (CESB) is not exempt: tinyurl.com/cra-cesb, 2020-0867851I7.

Fishing income: both *Robertson*, 2012 FCA 94 (leave to appeal denied 2012 CarswellNat 4075 (SCC)) and *Ballantyne*, 2012 FCA 95 (leave to appeal denied 2012 CarswellNat 4073) applied *Bastien* and ruled fishing income exempt even though the fish were caught and sold off-reserve, where other factors (including residence, fish cleaning and packing, and the Co-op handling fish purchases) were on-reserve. These decisions (also *McDonald*, 2011 TCC 437; Crown's FCA appeal discontinued A-388-11) overrule *Roberts*, 2010 TCC 52 and CRA docs 2004-0068451M4, 2009-0343511E5, 2011-0397651I7, 2015-0585231E5. In *Pilfold*, 2014 FCA 97, fishing income was taxable because the planning, preparation, fishing and post-fishing processing were all off-reserve, although P lived part-time on-reserve and kept the business records there. CRA now accepts *Ballantyne* and *Robertson* for "similar situations" (which it interprets narrowly): 2012-0473421E5.

Other business income: A self-employed consultant to First Nations, teaching and interpreting traditional law, might be exempt in light of *Bastien* even though his work was mostly off-reserve: *Kelly*, [2013] 5 C.T.C. 194 (FCA, sending the matter back to the TCC for new evidence): "the focus of the analysis is whether the income earned by the taxpayer can be said to be situated on a reserve in light of the type of property, the nature of the taxation of the property and the purposes behind section 87" (para. 52). Post-*Bastien* and *Dubé*, clearing off-reserve trees for oil companies was exempt where the business administration, sales, contract signing and equipment storage were on-reserve: *Dickie*, 2014 CarswellNat 255 (FCA); a "commercial mainstream" test is no longer relevant (TCC, para. 67). In *Murray*, 2013 CarswellNat 3016 (TCC), management fees from Murray's off-reserve companies, for work done mostly off-reserve, were taxable; billing for only on-reserve time was an "economic fiction" (para. 75). Farming on a reserve is exempt, as are related AgriInvest or AgriStability payments and crop insurance proceeds: 2011-0396431E5. A logging contractor's income was not exempt where his customers (and the trees) were off-reserve: *Pelletier*, [2011] 1 C.T.C. 172 (FCA, 2-1). For more on self-employment income see docs 2009-0313071E5, 2009-0332711E5, 2010-0367591I7, 2010-0390201E5, 2010-0395841E5, 2012-0444561E5, 2012-0466041E5, 2012-0466691E5, 2012-0472781E5, 2013-0505711E5, 2014-0553331E5. E-commerce income selling goods made on a reserve is likely exempt: 2007-0258701E5. Conversely, accessing a server on the reserve is not working on the reserve: 2008-0271391E5. Payments to an Indian for services provided to other Indians in a prison that is not on a reserve are likely taxable: 2008-0296021I7. An honorarium for ceremonial services performed off-reserve, received from an off-reserve payer, is likely taxable: 2008-0299381E5. Partnership income is taxed based on the "connecting factors" tests for business income: 2008-0296711E5.

Old Age Security benefits are never exempt in CRA's view, because they are available to all Canadians and have insufficient "connecting factors": docs 932789A, 9411598, 2013-0509161E5. The same applies to the Canada Child Benefit: 2009-0307981I7.

Pension income and CPP benefits are exempt to the extent the employment income was exempt: 2002-0148995, 2008-0286141E5, 2009-0310221E5, 2009-0335761I7, 2013-0500501E5, 2013-0509161E5, 2014-0523581E5; 2015-0601081I7 and 2016-0668851E5 (pension transferred on divorce); 2018-0741061M4. (An Indian can elect under *Canada Pension Plan Regulations* s. 29.1 to make CPP contributions on exempt income: Form CPT20; or the employer can elect on Form CPT124.) On return of registered pension plan (RPP) contributions to an employer, see 2008-0300991E5. RPP contributions in respect of past years' exempt income can be deducted: 2007-0240681I7. Monthly payments by a First Nation to its elders may be taxable under 56(1)(a), or exempt: 2015-0574241E5. See also next para. re transfer of an RPP to an RRSP.

RRSPs, RRIFs, DPSPs, PRPPs: An Indian's exempt income does not create RRSP contribution room, and if contributed can be withdrawn tax-free (but the penalty tax in 204.1(2.1) applies): docs 2003-0016735, 2005-0125561E5. RRSP/RRIF income is normally taxable since exempt income is ineligible for RRSP contribution, but is exempt if it was transferred from an RPP and the original income was exempt: 2004-0070161I7, 2013-0485331I7, 2014-0540461I7 (the T4RSP/T4RIF will not show the exempt amount, as the financial institution cannot determine it: 2014-0547711E5). DPSP payments are exempt if the original employment income was exempt: 2005-0125561E5. Withholding is required from PRPP payments unless CRA provides a 153(1.1) waiver: 2015-0564171E5.

Interest and other investment income earned by a status Indian is exempt based primarily on the following connecting factors: location of the financial institution; place where payment is required to be made; location of the term deposits; contract entered into on the reserve: *Bastien*, 2011 SCC 38, paras. 44-45. Additional relevant factors are the residence of the Indian on a reserve and the source of the capital giving rise to the interest (para. 47; but in *Dubé*, 2011 SCC 39, the fact the source was not income earned on a reserve was not enough to undo the exemption). Whether the investment income is integral to the life of the reserve or preservation of the Indian way of life is irrelevant: *Bastien*, para. 28. The fact the institution invests the Indian's term deposit in the commercial mainstream is irrelevant: *Bastien*, paras. 52-64. See now VIEWS docs 2012-0443661E5; 2014-0540051E5 (interest from life annuity); 2016-0632951I7 (mutual funds purchased at bank branch on reserve). (*Bastien* likely overturns earlier cases giving weight to how the institution used the funds: *Recalma*, [1998] 2 C.T.C. 403 (FCA); *Sero*, 2004 FCA 6 (leave to appeal denied 2004 CarswellNat 2127 (SCC)); *Large*, 2007 FCA 360; *Vachon*, 2007 TCC 641; *Gros-Louis*, 2007 TCC 628, 652 and 725; *Boivin*, 2007 TCC 722; *Stigen*, 2008 TCC 405; 2006-0202991M4.) Pre-*Bastien*, CRA considered interest income exempt in docs 2006-0198111R3, 2006-0200321R3. See West & McMechan, "Metaphysics for Tax Practitioners: The SCC in Dubé and Bastien Estate", 19(8) *Canadian Tax Highlights* (ctf.ca) 3 (Aug. 2011). Gold investments: VIEWS doc 2013-0473751I7 (may be business income so those rules would apply). Interest on Common Experience Payments: 2016-0675631I7.

Dividend income is exempt if the corporation's head office, management *and* principal "income-generating activities" are all on a reserve: VIEWS doc 2016-0663541E5.

Rental income is exempt only if the property is on a reserve: doc 2015-0579831E5.

Capital gains on sale of an investment are exempt to the extent the income from that investment would be exempt: doc 2014-0520721I7; and for shares in a family business corporation, that in turn is based on the "business income" test above.

Other types of income: Cree Hunters and Trappers Income Security Board benefits are taxable/deductible under 56(1)(u)/110(1)(f) rather than exempt under the *Indian Act*: 9505637. Death benefits: 2009-0348631E5. EI benefits are exempt if the underlying income was exempt: VIEWS docs 2003-0012285, 2014-0526471E5. EI Part II (training) benefits are exempt if sufficiently connected to the reserve (e.g. training takes place on reserve: 2005-0140431M4), otherwise taxable but may be eligible for 110(1)(g) deduction: 2003-0013475, 2003-0053541M4, 2005-0163311E5. Federal land settlement payments from a First Nation to its members are not taxable, but trust income distributions may be: 2014-0528511I7, 2014-0534251I7. RDSP payments sourced from taxable investment income are taxable: 2010-0377331E5. Rental assistance paid by a band so members can temporarily live near the reserve (due to a housing shortage on reserve) is exempt: 2014-0554111I7 (otherwise it may be social assistance for 56(1)(u) and 110(1)(f)). Severance benefits are exempt if the employment was exempt: 2012-0462411I7. Social assistance payments (normally deductible under 110(1)(f) anyway) are exempt if received in the person's capacity as an Indian residing on the reserve: 932789A, 2015-0615021I7, 2015-0622871I7. Wage loss replacement income is exempt if it replaces exempt employment income: 2011-0394921E5. Workers' Compensation benefits are exempt if the employment income to which they relate was exempt: doc 932789A. Residential school and Indian Day School settlement payments (for abuse) are tax-free: 2006-0199251I7, 2019-0827981E5.

Post-secondary education assistance to a status Indian, paid through Indian and Northern Affairs Canada's Post-Secondary Student Support Program or University and College Entrance Preparation Program, is exempt as a scholarship under 56(3): VIEWS docs 2010-0370681E5 (also discusses tuition and education credits), 2010-0377351E5, 2011-0405821E5, 2014-0523371M4. (Before 56(3), such assistance was to have been taxable beginning 2006 [2005-0128501M4 and others], but after review it continued exempt [2005-0109621M4, 2005-0140431M4, 2005-0148481M4].)

Indian Act s. 90, which exempts certain property received from the federal government, does not apply to income funded by a government program: *Kakfwi*, [1999] 4 C.T.C. 264 (FCA, leave to appeal to SCC denied); VIEWS doc 2011-0416141M4.

Income-tested benefits: an Indian's exempt income usually does not count towards income thresholds: 2015-0622871I7. But see 63(3)"earned income"(b) (it increases the claim for child care expenses), and 122.7(1.1) (special rule for Canada Workers Benefit).

Tax credits: The GST/HST Credit is calculated excluding an Indian's exempt income: 122.5"adjusted income", VIEWS doc 2016-0645991M4. The medical expense credit (118.2(1)) can be claimed by the spouse of an Indian whose income is exempt, including expenses for the Indian: 2011-0397631E5.

First Nation bands are usually exempt; see Notes to 149(1)(c). A corporation owned by an Indian band does not have *Indian Act* protection: *Tron Power*, 2013 SKQB 179. The CRA has an administrative policy not to impose penalties on a First Nation for failing to withhold taxes, but the policy "can be revoked if the First Nation abuses the exemption privilege": VIEWS doc 2014-053309117.

CRA does not provide clear information on determining exempt income. The Ombudsman is reviewing this issue: *Taxpayers' Ombudsman Annual Report 2019-2020*, p. 25.

See also tinyurl.com/cra-aboriginal; Alexander, *Taxation and Financing of Aboriginal Businesses in Canada* (Carswell, 2 vols. looseleaf or *Taxnet Pro* Reference Centre); *Aboriginal Law Handbook* (Carswell, 5th ed., 2018), chap. 20; Morry & Ranson, "The Taxation of First Nations and Their Members", 2011 Prairie Provinces Tax Conference (ctf.ca), 10:1-49; Michael Welters, "First Nations: Business Structures", 2011 BC Tax Conf. 4:1-32; MacKinnon & Welters, "First Nations: Taxation and Business Structures", 2014 Cdn Tax Foundation conference report, 39:1-29; Decembrini, *Annotated Aboriginal Law* (Carswell, annual), annotations to *Indian Act* s. 87 (20pp).

The *Gender Equity in Indian Registration Act* took effect Jan. 31, 2011 for purposes of determining who is an Indian: VIEWS doc 2012-0442201M4. It provides exemption only for periods since that date: 2011-0420371M4, 2013-0514531M4.

Canada has personal income tax administration agreements with the Nunatsiavut Government and the Tåîchô Government, co-ordinating the *Nunatsiavut Personal Income Tax Act* and the *Tåîchô Income Tax Law* with the ITA. See tinyurl.com/t1-NL01 and tinyurl.com/t1-nt12. Individuals residing on Labrador Inuit Lands or in the Inuit Communities of Rigolet, Nain, Hopedale, Makkovik, or Postville must tick "Yes" in the "Residency information for tax administration agreements" box on p. 1 of the Newfoundland & Labrador return. Individuals who reside on Tåîchô lands or in the Tåîchô communities of Behchokö (Rae-Edzo), Whatì (Lac La Martre), Gamètì (Rae Lakes), or Wekweètì (Snare Lake) must tick "Yes" in the same box on the Northwest Territories return. CRA uses this information to administer its agreements with the Nunatsiavut and Tåîchô Governments.

Ambiguity in treaties and statutes relating to aboriginals is resolved in favour of the aboriginals (*Nowegijick*, [1983] C.T.C. 20 (SCC) para. 25), but this does not apply to interpreting other ITA provisions: *Bellrose*, 2012 FCA 67, para. 17. In *Sackaney*, 2013 TCC 303, arguments that First Nation members had "inherent rights" to immunity from taxation were struck out.

GST/HST is not payable by a status Indian on property or services delivered to the Indian on a reserve, but Indians must collect and remit GST/HST on sales to non-Indians: see CRA GST/HST Technical Information Bulletin B-039 and David Sherman's *Canada GST Service* commentary to *Excise Tax Act* s. 165 (also on *GST Partner* or *Taxnet Pro*).

Several Indian (First Nation) bands now impose tax either on liquor and tobacco products (First Nations Tax), or on all goods and services to parallel the GST (First Nations GST), and this tax is administered by the Canada Revenue Agency so that it effectively operates as though the GST applied on the reserve. See the *First Nations Goods and Services Tax Act*, reproduced in David M. Sherman, *Practitioner's Goods and Services Tax Annotated*; the commentary to *Excise Tax Act* s. 165 in the *Canada GST Service* or on *Taxnet Pro*; and Guides RC4072 and RC4365.

Amounts exempted by tax treaty are included in income and then granted an offsetting deduction under 110(1)(f)(i): VIEWS doc 2015-0571591E5. The effect is to increase net income without affecting taxable income. This can have a number of side effects, including losing the Canada Child Benefit (122.61) and GST/HST Credit (122.5), paying OAS clawback (180.2), eliminating another person's credits for the taxpayer as a dependent spouse (118(1)B(a)), increasing the taxpayer's threshold for medical expenses (118.2(1)C) and increasing the taxpayer's ability to claim charitable donations (118.1(1)"total gifts"(a)(iii)). Where the increase in net income results in increased tax, the treaty overrides the increased tax if it is a real tax, but not if it is a clawback of social benefits. See *Peter*, [1997] 2 C.T.C. 2504 (TCC); *Swantje*, [1996] 1 C.T.C. 355 (SCC), aff'g [1994] 2 C.T.C. 382 (FCA); and Canada-U.S. tax treaty, Art. XXIV:10.

Certain income of members of *armed forces of other countries* in Canada may be exempt. See subsec. 22(2) of the *Visiting Forces Act*, reproduced in the Notes to 250(1).

Foreign diplomats are usually exempt from tax due to 149(1)(a) and/or the *Foreign Missions and International Organizations Act*: VIEWS doc 2004-008653117. Canadian resident citizens working for foreign organizations are not exempt, due to FMIOA s. 5(3): docs 2007-0222831E5, 2011-0414091E5. In *Lapierre*, 2019 TCC 18, an International Security Assistance Force employee did not qualify for exemption under the *Privileges and Immunities (North Atlantic Treaty Organisation) Act*.

Other federal legislation can exempt income, e.g. *Airport Transfer (Miscellaneous Matters) Act* s. 8(1) (designated airport authorities: VIEWS doc 2016-0651841E5); *Regional Development Incentives Act* s. 12.

See also s. 149, which exempts entities rather than specific kinds of income, and s. 3 Notes re non-taxable payments.

Remission Orders: *Indian Settlements Remission Order*, P.C. 2000-1112 (certain settlements treated as reserves); *Indian Income Tax Remission Order (Yukon Territory Lands)*, P.C. 1995-197 (certain lands in Yukon treated as reserves); *Indian Income Tax Remission Order*, P.C. 1993-523, P.C. 1993-1649 (remission of tax on income from an employer that resides on a reserve); *Indians and Bands on Certain Indian Settlements Remission Orders*, P.C. 1992-1052 (certain settlements treated as reserves); *Indians and Bands on Certain Indian Settlements Remission Orders (1997)*, P.C. 1997-1529 (certain settlements treated as reserves); *McIntyre Lands Income Tax Remission Order*, P.C. 2005-2230 (lands in the Hillcrest McIntyre subdivision of Whitehorse treated as a reserve); *Saskatchewan Indian Federal College Remission Order, 2003*, P.C. 2003-910 (college campus treated as a reserve); *Remission Order in Respect of a Transfer of a Sahtu Dene and Metis Settlement Corporation's assets under the Self-Government Agreement*, P.C. 2015-637 (no tax when settlement corp transfers all its assets to a SD&M first nation government).

Income Tax Folios: S1-F3-C1: Child care expense deduction [replaces IT-495R3].

Interpretation Bulletins: IT-62: Indians [withdrawn — under revision: see Notes]; IT-397R: Amounts excluded from income — statutory exemptions and certain service or RCMP pensions, allowances and compensation.

I.T. Technical News: 2 (tax exemption for Indians); 5 (statutory exemptions — *Indian Act*); 7 (Indians: interest income — situs of savings accounts); 9 (taxation of Indians' investment income).

Forms: CPT20: Election to pay *Canada Pension Plan* contributions; T1-BC10, T1-NL01, T1-NT12: Residency information for tax administration agreements; TD1-IN: Determination of exemption of an Indian's employment income.

(b) **War Savings Certificate** — an amount received under a War Savings Certificate issued by His Majesty in right of Canada or under a similar savings certificate issued by His Majesty in right of Newfoundland before April 1, 1949;

Related Provisions: 212(1)(h)(iii) — Exemption from non-resident withholding tax.

(c) **ship or aircraft of non-residents** — the income for the year of a non-resident person earned in Canada from international shipping or from the operation of aircraft in international traffic, if the country in which the person is resident grants substantially similar relief for the year to persons resident in Canada;

Related Provisions: 248(1)"taxable Canadian property"(b)(ii) — Exclusion of ship or aircraft from taxable Canadian property; 250(6) — Residence of international shipping corporation; 250(6.02), (6.03) — Service provider deemed to have international shipping as principal business; Canada-U.S. Tax Treaty:Art. VIII — Operation of ships or aircraft in international traffic.

Notes: See 248(1)"international shipping" and "international traffic", and 250(6)–(6.04) for rules deeming a foreign corporation engaged in international shipping to be non-resident. For the meaning of "aircraft" see Notes to 8(1)(j).

Profits earned by the Canadian office of a foreign airline are normally exempt under 81(1)(c) or under Article 8 of Canada's tax treaties: VIEWS doc 2003-0004605. A non-resident airline subcontracted to transport Canadian passengers qualifies: 2013-0515431E5.

See Notes to Reg. 105 re withholding on payments to international shipping companies.

81(1)(c) amended by 2014 budget bill #2, effective for taxation years that begin after July 12, 2013.

For the meaning of "operation of ships" in the former version see VIEWS docs 9611145, 2009-0342101E5.

Interpretation Bulletins: IT-494: Hire of ships and aircraft from non-residents.

(d) **service pension, allowance or compensation** — a pension payment, an allowance or compensation that is received under or is subject to the *Pension Act*, the *Civilian War-related Benefits Act* or the *War Veterans Allowance Act*, an amount received under the *Gallantry Awards Order* or compensation received under the regulations made under section 9 of the *Aeronautics Act*;

Related Provisions: 81(1)(d.1) — Exemption for certain Canadian Forces members and veterans benefits; 212(1)(h)(iii) — Exemption from non-resident withholding tax.

Notes: 81(1)(d) covers a bursary paid under the *Children of Deceased Veterans Education Assistance Act*: VIEWS doc 2003-0040151E5, and Veteran Independence Program payments: 2013-0489561M4. It does not apply to an RCMP pension: 2008-0286341E5 (but see 81(1)(i)). Regular (non-disability) Canadian Forces pensions are taxable, and this is not a *Charter* violation: *Chiasson*, 2010 TCC 202.

81(1)(d) amended by S.C. 1999, c. 10, effective May 1, 1999 (P.C. 1999-738), and by 1991 technical bill, effective 1986.

(d.1) **Canadian Forces members and veterans amounts** — the total of all amounts received by the taxpayer in the year on account of

(i) a Canadian Forces income support benefit payable to the taxpayer under Part 2 of the *Veterans Well-being Act*,

(ii) pain and suffering compensation, additional pain and suffering compensation or a critical injury benefit, disability award, death benefit, clothing allowance or detention benefit payable to the taxpayer under Part 3 of the *Veterans Well-being Act*,

(iii) a caregiver recognition benefit payable to the taxpayer under Part 3.1 of the *Veterans Well-being Act*, or

(iv) an amount payable to the taxpayer under subsection 132(1) of the *Veterans Well-being Act*;

Related Provisions: 6(1)(f.1) — Income inclusion for certain payments under CFMVRCA; 81(1)(d) — Exemption for other service pensions.

Notes: For details on the Critical Injury Benefit in (d.1)(ii) see tinyurl.com/critical-inj. For the Caregiver Recognition Benefit in (iii) see tinyurl.com/care-recog.

A regular (non-disability) Canadian Forces pension is taxable, and this is not a *Charter* violation: *Chiasson*, 2010 TCC 202.

81(1)(d.1)(iii) amended by 2018 budget bill #1, for 2020 and later tax years, to delete initial words "a family caregiver relief benefit or".

81(1)(d.1) amended by 2018 budget bill #1, effective April 2019, effectively to add subpara. (iv). Before then, read:

> (d.1) the total of all amounts received by the taxpayer in the year on account of a Canadian Forces income support benefit payable to the taxpayer under Part 2 of the *Veterans Well-being Act*, on account of a critical injury benefit, disability award, death benefit, clothing allowance or detention benefit payable to the taxpayer under Part 3 of that Act or on account of a family caregiver relief benefit or a caregiver recognition benefit payable to the taxpayer under Part 3.1 of that Act;

81(1)(d.1) amended by 2017 budget bill #1, effective April 2018, to change "*Canadian Forces Members and Veterans Re-establishment and Compensation Act*" to "*Veterans Well-being Act*" and to add "or a caregiver recognition benefit". A further amendment by the same bill (s. 6(2), (5)), which would have taken effect as of 2020, was repealed and replaced by 2018 budget bill #1.

81(1)(d.1) amended by 2015 Budget bill, for 2015 and later taxation years, to add "critical injury benefit" and "on account of a family caregiver relief benefit...".

81(1)(d.1) added by S.C. 2005, c. 21, effective April 2006 (P.C. 2006-136).

(e) **war pensions** — a pension payment received on account of disability or death arising out of a war from a country that was an ally of Canada at the time of the war, if that country grants substantially similar relief for the year to a person receiving a pension referred to in paragraph (d);

Related Provisions: 212(1)(h)(iii) — Exemption from non-resident withholding tax.

Notes: On war veteran pensions from Australia, see VIEWS doc 2004-0080131E5; Hong Kong, 9308451, 9308457, 9334105, 2011-0429881E5 and 2014-0529791E5; Netherlands, 9325267 and ("Wuv" benefit for injuries from wartime imprisonment) 2011-0404251E5; Norway, 2004-010585117 and 2011-0403951E5; South Africa, 2007-0251041E5; UK (war widow's pension), 2009-0342951E5; USA, 2000-0037447.

81(1)(e) amended by 1991 technical bill, effective 1988, to delete the phrase "war service" and thus exempt pensions paid to qualifying civilian war casualties.

(f) **Halifax disaster pensions, grants or allowances** — a pension payment, a grant or an allowance in respect of death or injury sustained in the explosion at Halifax in 1917 and received from the Halifax Relief Commission the incorporation of which was confirmed by *An Act respecting the Halifax Relief Commission*, chapter 24 of the Statutes of Canada, 1918, or received pursuant to the *Halifax Relief Commission Pension Continuation Act*, chapter 88 of the Statutes of Canada, 1974-75-76;

Related Provisions: 212(1)(h)(iii) — Exemption from non-resident withholding tax.

Notes: It appears the last survivor has died: tinyurl.com/hal-exp.

(g) **compensation by Federal Republic of Germany** — a payment made by the Federal Republic of Germany or by a public body performing a function of government within that country as compensation to a victim of National Socialist persecu-

tion, where no tax is payable in respect of that payment under a law of the Federal Republic of Germany that imposes an income tax;

Notes: 81(1)(g) exempts payments to Holocaust survivors made by Germany as compensation for persecution by Nazi Germany from 1933-45. It was enacted in 1964 to override *Koller* (1963), 34 Tax A.B.C. 93. It applies to payments by a foundation ("Remembrance, Responsibility and Future") created by Germany to compensate Holocaust survivors: VIEWS doc 2000-0051495. Swiss bank Holocaust settlements may qualify: 2002-0176265. So may payments under the 2002 Gesetz zur Zahlbarmachung von Renten aus Beschäftigungen in einem Ghetto (ZRBG — Law re Pensions Payable from Employment in a Ghetto): 2005-0128051E5. Restitution negotiated by the Claims Conference: 2009-0348971E5. Widergutmachungs rente (BEG): 2012-03442561E5.

Where property seized by the Nazis is returned by the German government to a Canadian resident, VIEWS docs 2003-0015117, 2006-0188911E5 said it was deemed reacquired at current value and 81(1)(g) may exempt retroactive rental payments. However, 2011-040427117 says that if the property was never legally transferred to a foreign government and was looted or stolen, the accrued gains are taxable to the owner when it is re-obtained and sold [but only since 1972: see ITAR 26(3)].

For the meaning of "public body performing a function of government", see Notes to 149(1)(c).

(g.1) **income from personal injury award property** — the income for the year from any property acquired by or on behalf of a person as an award of, or pursuant to an action for, damages in respect of physical or mental injury to that person, or from any property substituted therefor and any taxable capital gain for the year from the disposition of any such property,

(i) where the income was income from the property, if the income was earned in respect of a period before the end of the taxation year in which the person attained the age of 21 years, and

(ii) in any other case, if the person was less than 21 years of age during any part of the year;

Related Provisions: 81(1)(g.2) — Income from income exempt under paragraph (g.1); 81(5) — Election to increase ACB of capital property at age 21; 212(1)(h)(iii) — Exemption from non-resident holding tax; 248(5) — Substituted property.

Notes: In *Fiducie Chantale Naud*, 2007 TCC 649, a trust was created to administer money paid by the SAAQ (Quebec auto insurance) to two children due to their father's death in a car accident. 81(1)(g.1) and (g.2) did not apply because the payment was not in respect of injury to the children.

In *Saunders*, 2020 TCC 114, damages for failing to pay CRA employees overtime were taxable, as they replaced income that would have been taxable (note that 81(1)(g.1) is aimed at *income from* a personal injury award, not the award itself).

See also VIEWS docs 2014-0520401E5 (amount paid to parents to care for injured child is not taxable); 2015-0620311E5, 2015-0628941E5 ((g.1) and (g.2) as alternative to structured settlement).

(g.2) **income from income exempt under para. (g.1)** — any income for the year from any income that is by virtue of this paragraph or paragraph (g.1) not required to be included in computing the taxpayer's income (other than any income attributable to any period after the end of the taxation year in which the person on whose behalf the income was earned attained the age of 21 years);

Related Provisions: 212(1)(h)(iii) — Exemption from non-resident withholding tax.

Notes: See Notes to 81(1)(g.1).

(g.3) **certain government funded trusts** — the amount that, but for this paragraph, would be the income of the taxpayer for the year if

(i) the taxpayer is the trust established under

(A) the 1986-1990 Hepatitis C Settlement Agreement entered into by Her Majesty in right of Canada and Her Majesty in right of each of the provinces,

(B) the Pre-1986/Post-1990 Hepatitis C Settlement Agreement entered into by Her Majesty in right of Canada, or

(C) the Indian Residential Schools Settlement Agreement entered into by Her Majesty in right of Canada on May 8, 2006, and

(ii) the only contributions made to the taxpayer before the end of the year are those provided for under the relevant Agreement described in subparagraph (i);

Notes: 81(1)(g.3) amended by 2002-2013 technical bill (last change effective for 2007 and later tax years). Added by 1999 Budget. Former 81(1)(g.3), repealed in 1985, dealt with property acquired as an award and held for the benefit of an injured person under 21. This is now covered by 81(1)(g.1).

(g.4) **relief for increased heating expenses** — an amount received pursuant to the *Order Authorizing Ex Gratia Payments for Increased Heating Expenses*;

Notes: The heating expenses credit, of $125/person or $250/family eligible for the GST credit (in 122.5), was announced in the Oct. 18/00 Economic Statement and passed by P.C. 2000-1760 (Dec. 12, 2000). 81(1)(g.4) ensures the payments are non-taxable (probably not necessary; see 56(1)(s)). See also 81(1)(g.5).

81(1)(g.4) added by 2000 Budget bill, effective for amounts received after 2000.

(g.5) **energy cost relief** — an amount received pursuant to Part 1 of the *Energy Costs Assistance Measures Act*;

Related Provisions: 241(4)(d)(vii.2) — Disclosure of taxpayer information to permit payment of benefit.

Notes: 81(1)(g.5) added by *Energy Costs Assistance Measures Act*, S.C. 2005, c. 49. It provided payments in Jan. 2006 to low-income Canadians for high energy costs due to rising oil prices (Finance news release 2005-066, Oct. 6, 2005).

(g.6) **Ontario Electricity Support Program** — an amount of rate assistance received under section 79.2 of the *Ontario Energy Board Act, 1998*, S.O. 1998, c.15, Sch B, as amended from time to time;

Notes: The Ontario Electricity Support Program is an Ont. government program that assists low-income households with electricity costs, via a credit on the monthly electricity bill. The credit would normally be included in income by 56(1)(u) with offsetting deduction under 110(1)(f), and so could reduce income-tested benefits (see Notes to 56(1)(u)). 81(1)(g.6), announced in the 2016 Budget and added by 2016 budget bill #1 for 2016 and later tax years, fixes this by exempting the credit.

(h) **social assistance [and foster care]** — where the taxpayer is an individual (other than a trust), a social assistance payment (other than a prescribed payment) ordinarily made on the basis of a means, needs or income test under a program provided for by an Act of Parliament or a law of a province, to the extent that it is received directly or indirectly by the taxpayer for the benefit of another individual (other than the taxpayer's spouse or common-law partner or a person who is related to the taxpayer or to the taxpayer's spouse or common-law partner), if

(i) no family allowance under the *Family Allowances Act* or any similar allowance under a law of a province that provides for payment of an allowance similar to the family allowance provided under that Act is payable in respect of the other individual for the period in respect of which the social assistance payment is made, and

(ii) the other individual resides in the taxpayer's principal place of residence, or the taxpayer's principal place of residence is maintained for use as the residence of that other individual, throughout the period referred to in subparagraph (i);

Related Provisions: 18(1)(c) — Foster parents cannot deduct expenses laid out to earn exempt income; 56(1)(u) — Income inclusion and deduction — social assistance payments; 81(1)(h.1) — Kinship care assistance is exempt; 110(1)(f) — Income inclusion and deduction — social assistance payments; 212(1)(h)(iii) — Exemption from non-resident holding tax.

Notes: 81(1)(h) exempts social assistance payments related to foster children (not related to the taxpayer — if they are related, see 81(1)(h.1) instead) in the taxpayer's care, if the conditions are met, even if the quantum is large: VIEWS doc 2011-0396551E5. Such payments could otherwise be taxable under 56(1)(u), with an offsetting deduction under 110(1)(f), and thus would increase "net income" (see Notes to 56(1)(u)). No T4A reporting is required if 81(1)(h) applies: 2011-0407071E5. For detailed administrative interpretation see *Income Tax Technical News* No. 31R2. See also *Income Tax Audit Manual* §§27.11.3, 4.

Foster care payments can be flowed through a for-profit entity and still be exempt under 81(1)(h) to the foster parents as received "indirectly" under a federal or provincial program: VIEWS docs 2003-0030745, 2004-0103001E5, 2011-0422881E5, 2019-0808371E5. For more CRA policy on exempting foster care income, see docs 9204925, 9419595, 9431726, 9519285, 9623985, 9824935, 9831245, 2000-0040544, 2000-0047285, 2001-0100045, 2003-0004625, 2003-0050841E5, 2004-0061721E5, 2005-0114371E5, 2005-0131341E5, 2005-0146891E5, 2006-0175271E5, 2006-0213501E5, 2007-0219471E5, 2007-0241611E5, 2007-0263591E5, 2007-0267351M4, 2008-

0275181E5, 2009-0310441E5, 2009-032736117, 2010-0359971M4, 2010-0369811E5, 2011-0394641E5, 2012-0440351E5, 2014-0552031E5, 2014-0548121E5, 2014-0559421E5, 2015-0564201E5. For more on "indirectly" see Notes to 17.1(1).

A foster child could be deemed "related" to the taxpayer and thus not qualify: see 251(2)(a), 251(6)(a), 252(1)(b), VIEWS doc 2003-0007497. However, 81(1)(h.1) may now exempt the payment.

Foster care fees received in the course of a business are taxable, even if the foster children qualify for subsidy: *Income Tax Technical News* 17; *Anderson*, [2001] 4 C.T.C. 2837 (TCC) (costs of care were deductible against the fees); *Gallant*, 2010 FCA 138; *Lessard*, 2012 TCC 361.

In *Webster v. BC*, 2010 BCSC 888, CRA assessed W on the basis that fees for foster home services were taxable, but later withdrew the assessment. W lost his suit against the BC government for his costs of contesting the assessment, as the Ministry of Children and Families had not told him his income would not be taxable and there was no implied contractual term that BC would cover his legal fees.

81(1)(h) can apply, if the conditions are met, to adult care: VIEWS docs 2003-0024075 (home for seniors); 2010-0357481E5 (taxpayer rents room to unrelated adult); 2016-0677071E5 (provincial home-sharing plan).

Payments for respite care (e.g., Alberta's Persons with Developmental Disabilities Program, BC's HomeShare program), are exempt if the patient lives in the caregiver's home (81(1)(h)(ii)) and taxable if not: VIEWS docs 2005-0135291E5, 2010-0366631E5, 2010-0389151E5, 2011-0421581E5. (Where the patient is related to the payee, see 2010-0359971M4.)

81(1)(h) amended by 2000 same-sex partners bill (last change effective 2001), 1992 and 1991 technical bills.

Former 81(1)(h), repealed effective 1982, exempted workers' compensation payments from tax. They are now taxed under 56(1)(v) but subject to an offsetting deduction under 110(1)(f).

Regulations: No prescribed payments to date.

I.T. Technical News: 17 (application of para. 81(1)(h) to employment income); 31R2 (application of para. 81(1)(h)).

CRA Audit Manual: 27.34.0: Social assistance payments.

(h.1) **social assistance for informal care programs** — if the taxpayer is an individual (other than a trust), a social assistance payment ordinarily made on the basis of a means, needs or income test provided for under a program of the Government of Canada or the government of a province, to the extent that it is received directly or indirectly by the taxpayer for the benefit of a particular individual, if

(i) payments to recipients under the program are made for the care and upbringing, on a temporary basis, of another individual in need of protection,

(ii) the particular individual is a child of the taxpayer because of paragraph 252(1)(b) (or would be a child of the taxpayer because of that paragraph if the taxpayer did not receive payments under the program), and

(iii) no special allowance under the *Children's Special Allowances Act* is payable in respect of the particular individual for the period in respect of which the social assistance payment is made;

Related Provisions: 122.61(1) [Proposed Amendment] — Payments do not reduce Canada Child Benefit; 122.7(1.2) — Payments do not prevent Canada Workers Benefit single-parent status.

Notes: Some provinces offer "kinship care programs", such as the PEI Grandparents and Care Providers program, as alternatives to foster care for children who need temporary out-of-home care. If the care provider receives financial assistance to help defray the costs, such payments may be tax-free due to 56(1)(u) and 110(1)(f), but the increased *net* income can reduce income-tested benefits such as the GST/HST Credit and Canada Child Benefit (see Notes to 56(1)(v)). 81(1)(h.1) exempts such income to avoid this problem. Nothing in 81(1)(h.1) requires the care provider to be related to the child, but if they are not related, 81(1)(h) exempts the payment anyway.

81(1)(h.1) added by 2019 budget bill #1, retroactive to 2009.

(i) **RCMP pension or compensation** — a pension payment or compensation received under section 5, 31 or 45 of the *Royal Canadian Mounted Police Pension Continuation Act*, chapter R-10 of the Revised Statutes of Canada, 1970, or section 32 or 33 of the *Royal Canadian Mounted Police Superannuation Act*, in respect of an injury, disability or death;

Related Provisions: 212(1)(h)(iii) — Exemption from non-resident withholding tax.

Notes: In *Gingras*, [1998] 2 C.T.C. 2557 (TCC), a disabled officer received an annuity under s. 11 of the *RCMP Superannuation Act*, as well as a disability pension exempted under 81(1)(i). The annuity was taxable. Similarly, in *Laquerre*, 2007 FCA 229, a supplementary allowance under s. 35 of that Act was taxable.

Where an RCMP employee settled grievances related to a work injury by accepting payment and medical discharge, 81(1)(i) did not apply: VIEWS doc 2011-0398651E5.

Interpretation Bulletins: IT-397R: Amounts excluded from income — statutory exemptions and certain service or RCMP pensions, allowances and compensation.

(j) memorial grant [first responders] — an amount received under the Memorial Grant Program for First Responders established under the authority of the *Department of Public Safety and Emergency Preparedness Act* in respect of individuals who die in the course of, or as a result of, their duties or as a result of an occupational illness or psychological impairment;

Notes: 81(1)(j) added by 2018 budget bill #1, for amounts received after March 2018. The Memorial Grant for First Responders implements a 2017 Budget proposal "to provide $80 million over five years, starting in 2018-19, and $20 million thereafter, to support the establishment of a tax-free Community Heroes benefit to be implemented in cooperation with provinces, territories and municipalities. This benefit will support the families of public safety officers who have fallen in the line of duty." The Oct. 2019 Liberal election platform stated: "We will expand the Memorial Grant Program to include correctional workers by the end of 2020, and will continue to consult with other public safety workers to further broaden the program as appropriate." (The Liberals were elected as a minority government.)

Former 81(1)(j), repealed effective 1982, exempted social assistance payments (such as welfare) from tax. They are now taxed under 56(1)(u) but subject to an offsetting deduction under 110(1)(f).

(k) employees profit sharing plan — a payment or part of a payment from an employees profit sharing plan that section 144 provides is not to be included;

Related Provisions: 212(1)(h)(iii) — Exemption from non-resident withholding tax.

(l) prospecting — an amount in respect of the receipt of a share that section 35 provides is not to be included;

Related Provisions: 212(1)(h)(iii) — Exemption from non-resident withholding tax.

(m) interest on certain obligations — [No longer relevant]

Notes: 81(1)(m) exempts, under certain conditions, interest on a bond or note received on disposition before June 18, 1971 of a public utility outside Canada.

(n) Governor General — income from the office of Governor General of Canada, other than salary under the *Governor General's Act*;

Notes: Para. (n) amended by 2012 budget bill #1, for 2013 and later tax years, to add "other than salary under the *Governor General's Act*". Historically the GG was not taxed because he/she is the Queen's representative in Canada, and it would be tantamount to Her Majesty taxing herself. The GG's salary was increased to offset this change (amendment to *Governor General's Act* s. 4), so there is no change other than making the salary cost transparent.

(o), (p) [Repealed]

Notes: 81(1)(o) and (p) repealed by 1997 Budget, for 1998 and later tax years. They listed RESP refunds of payments and educational assistance payments (146.1(1)). 81(1)(o) was unnecessary, since nothing would otherwise include a "refund of payments" in income. 81(1)(p) was repealed because 146.1(14) was repealed, and no amount is included in a subscriber's income on revocation of a RESP (146.1(13)).

(q) provincial indemnities — an amount paid to an individual as an indemnity under a prescribed provision of the law of a province;

Notes: A workers' compensation award to a prison guard for injuries suffered from inmates was not a Criminal Injuries Compensation Board payment and thus fell under 56(1)(v), not 81(1)(q): *Sveinson*, 2011 TCC 34 (see also *Dupuis*, 2011 TCC 485).

Regulations: 6501 (prescribed provisions — criminal injuries compensation and motor vehicle accident claims).

(r) foreign retirement arrangements — an amount that is credited or added to a deposit or account governed by a foreign retirement arrangement as interest or other income in respect of the deposit or account, where the amount would, but for this paragraph, be included in the taxpayer's income solely because of that crediting or adding; or

Related Provisions: 56(1)(a)(i)(C.1), 56(12) — Inclusion in income of payment from foreign retirement arrangement; 146(20) — Where amount credited or added deemed not received.

Notes: 81(1)(r) added by 1991 technical bill, effective 1990. It ensures that amounts accruing in a foreign retirement arrangement (a U.S. Individual Retirement Account, or

IRA) are not taxed until they are paid out. See however 56(12) and Notes to 248(1)"foreign retirement arrangement".

(s) salary deferral leave plans [amounts previously taxed] — an amount paid to the taxpayer in the year under an arrangement described in paragraph 6801(a) of the *Income Tax Regulations* to the extent that the amount may reasonably be considered to be attributable to amounts that

(i) were included in the taxpayer's income for a preceding taxation year and were income, interest or other additional amounts, described in subparagraph 6801(a)(iv) of the *Income Tax Regulations*, and

(ii) were re-contributed by the taxpayer under the arrangement in a preceding taxation year.

Notes: See Notes to Reg. 6801 re "sabbatical" arrangements in 6801(a). Under 81(1)(s), if the income is taxed but recontributed to the plan, a later distribution of this amount is exempt.

81(1)(s) added by 2002-2013 technical bill (Part 5 — technical), for 2000 and later taxation years.

Notes [subsec. 81(1)]: See Notes to 81(1) opening words.

(1.1) [Repealed under former Act]

Notes: 81(1.1), repealed in 1986, defined terms for former 81(1)(s).

(2) [Repealed]

Notes: 81(2) repealed by 2017 budget bill #1, effective 2019. From 1972-2018, read:

> (2) M.L.A.'s expense allowance — Where an elected member of a provincial legislative assembly has, under an Act of the provincial legislature, been paid an allowance in a taxation year for expenses incident to the discharge of the member's duties in that capacity, the allowance shall not be included in computing the member's income for the year unless it exceeds ½ of the maximum fixed amount provided by law as payable to the member by way of salary, indemnity and other remuneration as a member in respect of attendance at a session of the legislature, in which event there shall be included in computing the member's income for the year only the amount by which the allowance exceeds ½ of that maximum fixed amount.

"MLA" stands for Member of a Legislative Assembly. Ontario members are called Members of Provincial Parliament; those in Quebec are Members of the National Assembly (Assemblée Nationale).

81(2) allowed ⅓ of an MLA's remuneration to be tax-free until 2018 as an unaccountable "allowance". There was no requirement that the MLA prove expenses equal to the allowance: VIEWS doc 9520875. (Reimbursements for actual expenses are also non-taxable.) Where an allowance was non-taxable due to 81(2), travel expenses for employment were not deductible under 8(1)(h.1): 2017-0693671I7.

The 81(2) rule applied to territorial as well as provincial legislatures. See *Interpretation Act* 35(1)"Act", "legislative assembly" and "province", near the end of the book.

Despite repeal of 81(2), 6(1)(b)(vii) exempts a temporary residence allowance for an apartment in the capital far from the home constituency office: doc 2019-0820401E5.

The parallel rule for federal Members of Parliament (MPs) is 6(1)(b)(i)(A). See Notes to 6(1)(b). For municipal officials (before 2019), see 81(3).

(3) [Repealed]

Notes: 81(3) repealed by 2017 budget bill #1, effective 2019. From 1974-2018, read:

> (3) Municipal officers' expense allowance — Where a person who is
>
> (a) an elected officer of an incorporated municipality,
>
> (b) an officer of a municipal utilities board, commission or corporation or any other similar body, the incumbent of whose office as such an officer is elected by popular vote, or
>
> (c) a member of a public or separate school board or similar body governing a school district,
>
> has been paid by the municipal corporation or the body of which the person was such an officer or member (in this subsection referred to as the person's "employer") an amount as an allowance in a taxation year for expenses incident to the discharge of the person's duties as such an officer or member, the allowance shall not be included in computing the person's income for the year unless it exceeds ½ of the amount that was paid to the person in the year by the person's employer as salary or other remuneration as such an officer or member, in which event there shall be included in computing the person's income for the year only the amount by which the allowance exceeds ½ of the amount so paid to the person by way of salary or remuneration.

See IT-292 and Notes to (repealed) 81(2). In some provinces, ⅓ of municipal officers' remuneration is deemed by legislation to be an allowance so as to qualify under 81(3) (e.g., former Ontario *Municipal Act* s. 255). CRA accepts the ⅓ fraction: VIEWS docs 2006-0212631E5, 2011-039878117. On whether payments from a Discretionary Fund qualified under 81(3), see 2012-0433121E5. A reimbursement (as opposed to an allowance) is included in income: 2012-0433441M4; one taxable under 6(1)(a) created additional ⅓ tax-free allowance room: 2014-0518901E5, 2014-0521201E5.

81(3) could apply to a municipal official receiving remuneration from a municipal utilities board, commission or corporation, but not from a taxable, for-profit corp: doc 2005-0160561E5; nor from a 149(1)(c) "public body performing a function of government": 2008-0266831E5. See also 2011-0395041E5 (general discussion); 2012-0468051E5 (claiming expenses against taxable portion of allowance).

Members of a municipal commission had to be "elected by popular vote" to qualify for 81(3): doc 2007-0223881E5. The Métis Regional Council did not qualify because it had no powers of self-government and did not provide typical municipal services: *Bellrose*, 2012 FCA 67.

(3.1) Travel expenses — There shall not be included in computing an individual's income for a taxation year an amount (not in excess of a reasonable amount) received by the individual from an employer with whom the individual was dealing at arm's length as an allowance for, or reimbursement of, travel expenses incurred by the individual in the year in respect of the individual's part-time employment in the year with the employer (other than expenses incurred in the performance of the duties of the individual's part-time employment) if

(a) throughout the period in which the expenses were incurred,

(i) the individual had other employment or was carrying on a business, or

(ii) where the employer is a designated educational institution (as within the meaning assigned by subsection 118.6(1)), the duties of the individual's part-time employment were the provision in Canada of a service to the employer in the individual's capacity as a professor or teacher; and

(b) the duties of the individual's part-time employment were performed at a location not less than 80 kilometres from,

(i) where subparagraph (a)(i) applies, both the individual's ordinary place of residence and the place of the other employment or business referred to in that subparagraph, and

(ii) where subparagraph (a)(ii) applies, the individual's ordinary place of residence.

Notes: 81(3.1) exempts reasonable allowances to part-time teachers or professors who travel at least 80km to work (based on normal road distance: see Notes to 248(1)"eligible relocation"), provided the employer is arm's length and the teacher has other employment (not at a post-secondary educational institution) or business: VIEWS docs 2006-0200171E5, 2010-037077117. See also 2008-0273351E5, 2009-0330331C6, 2009-034550117, 2011-0423851E5.

81(3.1) amended by 2001 technical bill, for 1995 and later taxation years.

Interpretation Bulletins: IT-522R: Vehicle, travel and sales expenses of employees.

(4) Payments for volunteer [emergency] services — Where

(a) an individual was employed or otherwise engaged in a taxation year by a government, municipality or public authority (in this subsection referred to as "the employer") and received in the year from the employer one or more amounts for the performance, as a volunteer, of the individual's duties as

(i) an ambulance technician,

(ii) a firefighter, or

(iii) a person who assists in the search or rescue of individuals or in other emergency situations, and

(b) if the Minister so demands, the employer has certified in writing that

(i) the individual was in the year a person described in paragraph (a), and

(ii) the individual was at no time in the year employed or otherwise engaged by the employer, otherwise than as a volunteer, in connection with the performance of any of the duties referred to in paragraph (a) or of similar duties,

there shall not be included in computing the individual's income derived from the performance of those duties the lesser of $1,000 and the total of those amounts, unless the individual makes a claim under section 118.06 or 118.07 for the year.

Related Provisions: 118.06 — Volunteer firefighter tax credit.

Notes: The exemption applies once for each employer of the taxpayer: VIEWS doc 2017-069025117.

The certification requirement in 81(4)(b) is similar to that in 8(10) for many employment expenses, but applies only if CRA asks for it.

For the meaning of "derived" in closing words, see Notes to 18.1(12).

The Act does not define "volunteer"; CRA uses several factors in determining whether a person is one. The amount paid to a volunteer is "usually nominal in comparison to what it would have cost in the same circumstances to have the same duties performed by a regular full-time or part-time individual": VIEWS doc 2003-0052601E5. The CRA once said that firefighters can receive substantial amounts and still be "volunteers", and that the municipality or public authority can determine "volunteer" status (2008-0267941E5, 2008-0276851E5, 2011-0421551E5), but now says that if the hourly rate is similar to a paid firefighter, the person is not a volunteer: 2012-0442321E5, 2012-0444461E5, 2015-0602671E5 (and continues this view despite *Bourgeois*, 2015 QCCQ 1962 holding otherwise for Quebec tax purposes). An employed firefighter cannot also qualify as a volunteer for the same employer, due to 81(4)(b)(ii): 2014-0548701E5.

See 118.06 and 118.07 for tax credits for volunteer firefighters and search-and-rescue personnel, as an alternative to this exemption.

81(4) amended by 2014 Budget bill #1 (for 2014 and later tax years), 2011 Budget bill #2. Added by 2001 technical bill. The allowance exemption for volunteer firemen was $300 in 1961 and became $500 in 1980 and $1,000 in 1998. See 8(1)(a) Notes re why it is now an exemption rather than a deduction.

Income Tax Folios: S1-F3-C1: Child care expense deduction [replaces IT-495R3].

(5) Election — Where a taxpayer or a person described in paragraph (1)(g.1) has acquired capital property under the circumstances described in that paragraph, the taxpayer or the person may, in the return of income of the taxpayer for the taxation year in which the taxpayer attains the age of 21 years, elect to treat any such capital property held by the taxpayer or person as having been disposed of on the day immediately preceding the day on which the taxpayer attained the age of 21 years for proceeds of disposition equal to the fair market value of the property on that day and the person or taxpayer making the election shall be deemed to have reacquired that property immediately thereafter at a cost equal to those proceeds.

Notes: If the individual is resident in Quebec, the election must be copied to Revenu Québec: *Taxation Act* ss. 496, 21.4.6.

Definitions [s. 81]: "Act" — *Interpretation Act* 35(1); "amount" — 248(1); "arm's length" — 251(1); "business" — 248(1); "Canada" — 255, *Interpretation Act* 35(1); "capital property" — 54, 248(1); "child" — 252(1); "common-law partner" — 248(1); "corporation" — 248(1), *Interpretation Act* 35(1); "designated educational institution" — 118.6(1); "employees profit sharing plan" — 144(1), 248(1); "employed" — 248(1); "employer" — 81(4)(a), 248(1); "employment" — 248(1); "fair market value" — see 69(1) Notes; "foreign retirement arrangement" — 248(1); "Her Majesty" — *Interpretation Act* 35(1); "His Majesty" — *Interpretation Act* 35(1)"Her Majesty"; "individual", "international shipping", "international traffic" — 248(1); "legislative assembly", "legislature" — *Interpretation Act* 35(1)"legislative assembly"; "Minister", "non-resident", "office" — 248(1); "Parliament" — *Interpretation Act* 35(1); "person", "prescribed", "property" — 248(1); "province" — *Interpretation Act* 35(1); "provincial" — *Interpretation Act* 33(3), 35(1)"province"; "regulation" — 248(1); "related" — 251(2); "resident" — 250; "resident in Canada" — 94(3)(a), 250; "share" — 248(1); "substituted" — 248(5); "taxable capital gain" — 38(a), 248(1); "taxation year" — 249; "taxpayer" — 248(1); "trust" — 104(1), 248(1), (3); "writing" — *Interpretation Act* 35(1).

Subdivision H — Corporations Resident in Canada and Their Shareholders

82. (1) Taxable dividends received — In computing the income of a taxpayer for a taxation year, there shall be included the total of the following amounts:

(a) the amount, if any, by which

(i) the total of all amounts, other than eligible dividends and amounts described in paragraph (c), (d) or (e), received by the taxpayer in the taxation year from corporations resident in Canada as, on account of, in lieu of payment of or in satisfaction of, taxable dividends,

exceeds

(ii) if the taxpayer is an individual, the total of all amounts each of which is, or is deemed by paragraph 260(12)(b) to have been, paid by the taxpayer in the taxation year and deemed by subsection 260(5.1) to have been received by another person as a taxable dividend (other than an eligible dividend);

(a.1) the amount, if any, by which

(i) the total of all amounts, other than amounts included in computing the income of the taxpayer because of paragraph (c), (d) or (e), received by the taxpayer in the taxation year from corporations resident in Canada as, on account of, in lieu of payment of or in satisfaction of, eligible dividends,

exceeds

(ii) if the taxpayer is an individual, the total of all amounts each of which is, or is deemed by paragraph 260(12)(b) to have been, paid by the taxpayer in the taxation year and deemed by subsection 260(5.1) to have been received by another person as an eligible dividend;

(b) if the taxpayer is an individual, other than a trust that is a registered charity, the total of

(i) the product of the amount determined under paragraph (a) in respect of the taxpayer for the taxation year multiplied by

(A) for the 2018 taxation year, 16%, and

(B) for taxation years after 2018, 15%, and

(ii) the product of the amount determined under paragraph (a.1) in respect of the taxpayer for the taxation year multiplied by

(A) for taxation years that end after 2005 and before 2010, 45%,

(B) for the 2010 taxation year, 44%,

(C) for the 2011 taxation year, 41%, and

(D) for taxation years that end after 2011, 38%;

(c) all taxable dividends received by the taxpayer in the taxation year, from corporations resident in Canada, under dividend rental arrangements of the taxpayer;

(d) all taxable dividends (other than taxable dividends described in paragraph (c)) received by the taxpayer in the taxation year from corporations resident in Canada that are not taxable Canadian corporations; and

(e) if the taxpayer is a trust, all amounts each of which is all or part of a taxable dividend (other than a taxable dividend described in paragraph (c) or (d)) that was received by the trust in the taxation year on a share of the capital stock of a taxable Canadian corporation and that can reasonably be considered to have been included in computing the income of a beneficiary under the trust who was non-resident at the end of the taxation year.

Related Provisions: 12(1)(j) — Inclusion into income from business or property; 52(3) — Cost of stock dividend; 82(1.1) — Application of 82(1)(a)(i); 82(2) — Dividends included in income by attribution rules; 82(3) — Dividends received by spouse; 84 — Deemed dividends; 86.1 — Election to avoid income inclusion when shares received on foreign spin-off; 89(1)"eligible dividend", "excessive eligible dividend designation" — Eligible dividends; 89(14) — Designation of eligible dividend; 90 — Dividends received from non-resident corporation; 104(19) — Taxable dividend received by trust; 112(3)(b)(i) — Reduction in loss on subsequent disposition of share by corporate shareholder; 112(4)–(4.3) — Loss on share held as inventory; 120.4(1)"split income" — Certain capital gains deemed to be dividends; 121 — Dividend tax credit; 127.52(1)(f) — Exclusion of gross-up for minimum tax purposes; 137(4.2) — Credit unions — deemed interest deemed not to be a dividend; 139.1(4)(f), (g) — Deemed dividend on demutualization of insurance corporation; 139.2 — Deemed dividend on distribution by mutual holding corporation; 146.2(7) — No tax on dividend income received within TFSA; 187.2, 187.3 — Tax on corporation receiving dividend on taxable preferred shares or taxable RFI shares; 191.1 — Tax on corporation paying dividend on taxable preferred shares; 248(7)(a) — Dividend payment deemed received when mailed; Canada-U.S. Tax Treaty:Art. X — Taxation of dividends; Canada-U.S. Tax Treaty:Art. XXIX:5(d) — No income inclusion from share of U.S. "S" corporation.

Notes: 82(1) is simpler than it looks, in most cases. Where there is no dividend rental arrangement, securities lending arrangement or trust receiving dividends for a non-resident beneficiary, read only 82(1)(a)(i) and 82(1)(b). The income inclusion is the actual dividend plus, *for individuals*, a gross-up of 38% for eligible dividends (89(1)"eligible dividend": generally from public corporations) and 15% (starting 2019) for other dividends (generally from CCPCs on income eligible for the small business deduction under 125(1)). The higher tax resulting from the gross-up is more than offset by the dividend tax credit (DTC) in s. 121. The gross-up brings the income inclusion up to the

theoretical pre-tax corporate income, assuming a particular corporate federal+provincial income tax (e.g., 15% gross-up presumes a rate of 13.04% (15/115ths: $86.96 is left of $100 after paying 13.04% corporate tax, and 15% of $86.96 is $13.04)). The DTC then offsets the federal portion of the 13.04% corporate tax theoretically paid on that corporate income, so the net result is that the shareholder pays tax at the same rate as if they had earned the income the corporation earned. This is called "integration". See also Notes to 121 for further detail.

For 2018, the gross-up was 16%, presuming a federal+provincial rate of 13.79% (16/116ths: $86.21 is left of $100 after paying 13.79% corporate tax, and 16% of $86.21 is $13.79).

For 82(1)(a.1)(ii), see Notes to 260(1)"securities lending arrangement".

Although the DTC more than offsets the gross-up, net income is higher than actual income, which can adversely impact the Guaranteed Income Supplement (*Gaisford*, 2011 FCA 28), Old Age Security clawback (180.2), medical expense credit (118.2(1)C), GST/HST Credit (122.5), Canada Child Benefit (122.61), etc.; and Ontario surtax, as the DTC comes after the surtax calculation: VIEWS doc 2017-0692261M4. There is no option to not report the gross-up: 2012-0458321M4.

For calculating the effects of earning income through a corp or personally see taxtemplates.ca spreadsheet "Integration". For provincial DTC rates, marginal rates of tax on dividends and examples, see Di Maio & Lim, "Eligible Dividend Rates", 22(11) *Canadian Tax Highlights [CTH]* (ctf.ca) 6-8 (Nov. 2014); "Dividend Rates and Investment Income Update", 23(1) 7-9 (Jan. 2015) and "Non-Eligible Dividend Rates Update", 25(12) 8-10 (Dec. 2017); Moody & Keung, "Alberta Provincial Dividend Tax Rates" (June 17, 2019), tinyurl.com/moody-abrates. Earlier years: 16(6) *CTH* 6-7, 17(7) 8-9, 19(1) 6-7, 19(8) 8-9, 19(9) 7-8, 19(12) 7-9, 21(1) 8-9, 21(3) 7-9, 22(2) 7-9, 21(9) 5-7, 22(12) 5-7; *Tax for the Owner-Manager* (ctf.ca) 11(4) 7, 12(4) 4-6 and 13(4) 9-10; Bleiwas & Ball, "Current Issues for Private Companies", 2013 Cdn Tax Foundation conference report, 6:1-32. See also Tables I-6, I-7 at beginning of this book; and Notes to 67 and 125(1).

For corporations, the full dividend is included in income under 82(1)(a)(ii)(A), but an offsetting deduction in computing taxable income is generally allowed under 112(1), so there is no net tax cost. However, the deduction can be denied by several anti-avoidance rules (112(2.1)–(2.9)); and the dividend may be subject to Part IV tax (186(1)) even where the deduction is allowed; and if the dividend's purpose is to reduce the value of the shares or the capital gain realized on their sale, 55(2) may deem it to be a capital gain. Also, a loss on the share may be denied after the deduction has been claimed: 112(3)–(4.22).

Received: A dividend is taxable only when *received* (82(1)(a)(i)), not when receivable, but can be paid by way of promissory note: *Banner Pharmacaps*, 2003 FCA 367, paras. 6-7. See Notes to 5(1) for the meaning of "received".

For the meaning of "dividend" see Notes to 248(1)"dividend".

A dividend not properly declared may be included in the shareholder's income under 15(1) or 15(2), with no DTC. CRA is often flexible about how a dividend is declared, but something more than a mere journal entry is needed: VIEWS docs 9823175, 2007-0229311I7, 2013-0515761E5; *Harland*, 2010 TCC 105. A dividend declared retroactively after year-end may be invalid: *Wood*, [1988] 1 C.T.C. 2312 (TCC) (see Notes to 169(1) under "If there is no rectification").

82(1)(e) provides that the gross-up does not apply to taxable dividends received by a trust in the year from a taxable Canadian corporation, to the extent such dividends are included in the income of a non-resident beneficiary (NRB). The trust's DTC will thus not be affected by whether or not the trust designates amounts under 104(19) in respect of NRBs. The reason for this is that the DTC is aimed at Canadian residents, whose tax rates are generally higher than the withholding rates for non-residents. 82(1)(e) prevents trusts with NRBs from obtaining access to the DTC on income allocated to the NRBs that has not been flowed-out to them under 104(19).

A dividend is a transfer of property, so if the corporation paying the dividend is unable to pay its debts to the CRA, a non-arm's length shareholder can be assessed for the amount of the dividend. See Notes to 160(1). Liability may also arise under 159(2) if the corporation is insolvent when it pays the dividend and no clearance certificate is issued; see *L'Écuyer v. Québec*, [1993] R.D.F.Q. 110 (Que. Ct.).

82(1)(b)(i) amended by 2018 budget bill #1 to change the rate from 17%, for 2018 and later tax years.

82(1)(b)(i) amended by 2015 Budget bill and 2016 budget bill #1, for 2016 and later tax years. For 2014-2015, read "18% of the amount determined under paragraph (a) in respect of the taxpayer for the taxation year". 82(1) previously amended by 2013 budget bill #1 (for dividends paid after 2013, to change "25%" to "18%"), 2002-2013 technical bill, 2008 budget bill #1, 2006 budget bill #2, 1989 Budget.

Regulations: 201(1)(a) (information return).

Interpretation Bulletins: IT-67R3: Taxable dividends from corporations resident in Canada; IT-379R: Employees profit sharing plans — allocations to beneficiaries; IT-432R2: Benefits conferred on shareholders; IT-524: Trusts — flow-through of taxable dividends to a beneficiary — after 1987.

I.T. Technical News: 11 (U.S. spin-offs (divestitures) — dividends in kind).

Forms: RC257: Request for an information return program account (RZ); T1 General return, Lines 12000, 12010; T3 Sched. 8: Investment income, carrying charges and gross-up amount of dividends retained by trust; T5: Statement of investment income; T5 Summ: Return of investment income.

(1.1) Limitation as to para. (1)(c) — An amount shall be included in the amounts described in paragraph (1)(c) in respect of a taxable dividend received at any time as part of a dividend rental arrangement only if that dividend was received on a share acquired before that time and after April, 1989.

Notes: 82(1.1) amended by 2002-2013 technical bill (Part 5 — technical) to change "subparagraph (1)(a)(i)" to "paragraph (1)(c)", effective for amounts received or paid after 2005.

82(1.1) added in RSC 1985 (5th Supp) consolidation. Formerly an application rule in the 1989 Budget bill.

(2) Certain dividends [deemed] received by taxpayer — Where by reason of subsection 56(4) or (4.1) or sections 74.1 to 75 of this Act or section 74 of the *Income Tax Act*, chapter 148 of the Revised Statutes of Canada, 1952, there is included in computing a taxpayer's income for a taxation year a dividend received by another person, for the purposes of this Act, the dividend shall be deemed to have been received by the taxpayer.

Notes: This rule ensures that the gross-up (82(1)(b)) dividend tax credit (s. 121) and other consequences of receiving a dividend all apply when dividend income is subject to the attribution rules.

I.T. Application Rules: 69 (meaning of "chapter 148 of ...").

Interpretation Bulletins: IT-440R2: Transfer of rights to income.

(3) Dividends received by spouse or common-law partner — Where the amount that would, but for this subsection, be deductible under subsection 118(1) by reason of paragraph 118(1)(a) in computing a taxpayer's tax payable under this Part for a taxation year that is less than the amount that would be so deductible if no amount were required by subsection (1) to be included in computing the income for the year of the taxpayer's spouse or common-law partner and the taxpayer so elects in the taxpayer's return of income for the year under this Part, all amounts described in paragraph (1)(a) or (a.1) received in the year from taxable Canadian corporations by the taxpayer's spouse or common-law partner are deemed to have been so received by that taxpayer and not by the spouse or common-law partner.

Related Provisions: 60.03 — Pension income splitting with spouse; 220(3.2), Reg. 600(b) — Late filing or revocation of election.

Notes: The word "that" after "for a taxation year" is extraneous and should be deleted. This has been pointed out to Finance.

82(3) exists because of the gross-up and dividend tax credit (DTC); see Notes to 82(1) and 121. If lower-income spouse L has dividends but is not paying enough tax to use the DTC, 82(3) allows all L's dividends and DTC to be transferred to higher-income spouse H, if this increases the 118(1)B(a) spousal tax credit. The increased spousal credit, plus allowing H the DTC, can more than offset the taxation of the dividend in H's hands.

As per the T1 General Income Tax Guide, a spouse or common-law partner's dividends are simply reported on Lines 12000 and 12010 [former 120] of the T1, along with other dividends. No special form is required.

An election "in the taxpayer's return" is valid even if the return is filed late. See Notes to 7(1.31).

See also Lee & Kakkar, "Subsection 82(3): Possible Exclusion from TOSI", 19(3) *Tax for the Owner-Manager* (ctf.ca) 7-8 (July 2019).

82(3) amended by 2006 budget bill #2 (for amounts received or paid after 2005), 2000 same-sex partners bill.

Interpretation Bulletins [subsec. 82(3)]: IT-295R4: Taxable dividends received after 1987 by a spouse; IT-513R: Personal tax credits.

Definitions [s. 82]: "amount" — 248(1); "Canada" — 255; "Canadian corporation" — 89(1), 248(1); "common-law partner" — 248(1); "corporation" — 248(1), *Interpretation Act* 35(1); "dividend", "dividend rental arrangement" — 248(1); "eligible dividend" — 89(1), 248(1); "individual" — 248(1); "non-resident" — 248(1); "person" — 248(1); "received" — 248(7)(a); "registered charity" — 248(1); "resident in Canada" — 250; "series of transactions" — 248(10); "share" — 248(1); "tax payable" — 248(2); "taxable Canadian corporation", "taxable dividend" — 89(1), 248(1); "taxation year" — 249; "taxpayer" — 248(1); "trust" — 104(1), 248(1), (3).

83. (1) Qualifying dividends — [No longer relevant]

Notes: Tax-free "qualifying dividends" as defined in 83(6) had to be paid before 1991. Before 1979, 83(1) applied to dividends paid out of "tax-paid undistributed surplus" or "1971 capital surplus on hand", concepts that have been eliminated.

(2) Capital dividend [not taxable] — Where at any particular time after 1971 a dividend becomes payable by a private corporation to shareholders of any class of shares of its capital stock and the corporation so elects in respect of the full amount of the dividend, in prescribed manner and prescribed form and at or before the particular time or the first day on which any part of the dividend was paid if that day is earlier than the particular time, the following rules apply:

(a) the dividend shall be deemed to be a capital dividend to the extent of the corporation's capital dividend account immediately before the particular time; and

(b) no part of the dividend shall be included in computing the income of any shareholder of the corporation.

Related Provisions: 83(2.1) — Capital dividend on certain shares disallowed; 83(3) — Late filed elections; 87(2)(z.1) — Amalgamations — capital dividend account; 88(2)(b)(i) — Deemed separate dividend on certain windups; 89(1) — Capital dividend account; 89(1)"taxable dividend"(a) — Taxable dividend excludes capital dividend; 89(3) — Simultaneous dividends; 104(20) — Flow-through of capital dividend through trust; 108(3)(a) — "Income" of a trust; 112(3)(a), 112(3)(b)(ii) — Reduction in loss on disposition of share on which capital dividend paid; 112(3.1)(a), 112(3.1)(b)(ii) — Reduction in loss of partner on disposition of share by partnership; 112(3.2)(b) — Reduction in loss on disposition of share by trust; 112(5.2)B(b)(iv) — Adjustment for dividends received on mark-to-market property; 184, 185 — Tax on excessive elections; 212(1)(c)(ii) — Tax on payments to non-residents — estate or trust income derived from capital dividend; 212(2)(b) — Tax on capital dividend paid to non-resident; 220(3.2), Reg. 600(b) — Late filing or revocation of election; 248(1)"capital dividend" — Definition applies to entire Act.

Notes: The "capital dividend" mechanism allows the untaxed ½ of any capital gain realized by a private corporation (or 100% for donations of publicly-traded securities to charities; see 38(a.1)) to be flowed out tax-free to the shareholders, either directly or through intermediate holding corporations, so that it remains untaxed. See 89(1)"capital dividend" Notes, Income Tax Folio S3-F2-C1 and Keey, *Checklist 3 — Capital Dividend Election*, *Taxnet Pro* Corporate Tax Centre (2021, 24pp). (A capital dividend to a non-resident is subject to withholding tax, like a regular dividend: 212(2)(b).) A capital dividend can be declared on a series (not just a class) of shares, due to 248(6) (subject to 83(2.1)): VIEWS doc 2020-0852191C6 [2020 APFF q.7].

The election procedure in Reg. 2101 must be carefully followed, and Form T2054 must be filed on time, with a certified copy of the directors' resolution. The CRA will not accept the *original* resolution: Brian Wilson, "Capital Dividends: Practice Update", 3(3) *Tax for the Owner-Manager* (ctf.ca) 3-4 (July 2003). For more on CRA procedures see May 2006 ICAA roundtable (tinyurl.com/cra-abtax), q. 17. Note that a provincial election may need to be filed as well, e.g. in Quebec (if the corporation has a permanent establishment in Quebec or Quebec resident shareholders).

CRA says (doc 2020-0852211C6 [2020 APFF q.9]) that the directors' resolution cannot express the dividend amount using a mathematical formula. In the author's view, this is wrong if the dividend is valid under corporate law; 83(2) and Reg. 2101 do not require an "amount". (Cf. using a price-adjustment clause (69(1) Notes), or limiting a capital dividend on windup to the CDA, allowed by 2017-0709021C6 [2017 APFF q.4].) [See also 89(14) Notes on this issue.]

An accounting journal entry recording a dividend as payable to a shareholder is not sufficient to consider it received by the shareholder: VIEWS docs 2007-0229311I7, 2007-0229431I7; May 2009 ICAA roundtable q.2 (tinyurl.com/cra-abtax). Once a dividend is declared it cannot be modified before becoming payable: 2011-0412071C6 (but see Notes to 169(1) on rectification).

It is important to pay out a capital dividend before triggering capital losses, since the losses reduce the capital dividend account. Before 2017, a timing problem could arise with eligible capital property under 14(1), or if the dividend recipient was no longer a shareholder when the dividend was received. See VIEWS doc 2002-0143945 and discussion of 14(1.01) in Notes to repealed s. 14. In *Non Corp Holdings*, 2016 ONSC 2737, a capital dividend (likely from sale of goodwill) was mistakenly paid on the last day of the taxation year; the Court rectified to deem it paid one day later. (See Notes to 169(1) re rectification; due to *Fairmont Hotels* this might no longer be granted.) In *St-Pierre*, 2018 FCA 144, after the Quebec Superior Court nullified (instead of rectifying) a dividend, the TCC held the cash paid out was taxed under 15(2) and 80.4, but the FCA overruled this. A capital loss in the next year after paying a capital dividend causes no problem: 2019-0791631E5.

If the dividend exceeds the capital dividend account, the corporation pays 60% tax on the excess under 184(2), unless an election is made under 184(3). See VIEWS doc 2002-0118665. (An excess dividend on which the tax is paid does not reduce the CDA: 2011-0417511E5.) In *Felix & Norton International*, 2009 QCCS 919, a capital dividend was nullified by the Court where an excess dividend was paid. See also Notes to 184(3). (Again, due to *Fairmont Hotels* this would no longer be granted.)

CRA's view is that an 84.1 deemed dividend (84.1DD) cannot be a capital dividend, unless the transferor was already a shareholder of the transferee corp: docs 2002-0128955, 2006-0183851E5, 2011-0414731E5; Atsaidis & Jakolev, "The Scope of Fiction", 10(11) *Canadian Tax Highlights* (ctf.ca) 83 (Nov. 2002). However, at 2019-0819401C6 [2019 APFF q.1] and 2019-0824521C6 [2019 CTF q.4], CRA said that 2002-0128955 is no longer correct in saying that an 84.1DD cannot trigger a *129(1) dividend refund*, but Rulings later advised the author (email, Dec. 23/19) that this position does not affect CRA's view on an 84.1DD not necessarily being a capital dividend.

Where a capital dividend is paid to a trust, see Wolfe Goodman, "Capital Dividends and Trust Law", XIII(4) *Goodman on Estate Planning* 1094-96 (2005).

In *Faraggi* (*2529-1915 Québec, 2530-1284 Québec*), 2008 FCA 398; leave to appeal denied 2009 CarswellNat 1152 (SCC), a complex scheme to create capital dividends was held to be a sham and thus ineffective.

For favourable rulings on capital dividends see VIEWS docs 2008-0270081R3, 2014-0528291R3, 2014-0539031R3.

Note that 112(3) reduces a loss on selling shares on which a capital dividend was paid.

Regulations: 2101 (prescribed manner, prescribed form).

Income Tax Folios: S3-F2-C1: Capital Dividends [replaces IT-66R6].

Interpretation Bulletins: IT-67R3: Taxable dividends from corporations resident in Canada; IT-146R4: Shares entitling shareholders to choose taxable or capital dividends; IT-149R4: Winding-up dividend; IT-430R3: Life insurance proceeds received by a private corporation or a partnership as a consequence of death.

Information Circulars: 07-1R1: Taxpayer relief provisions.

I.T. Technical News: 9 (life insurance policy used as security for indebtedness).

CRA Audit Manual: 28.6.2: Late filed capital dividends election.

Advance Tax Rulings: ATR-54: Reduction of paid-up capital.

Forms: T2 Sched. 89: Request for capital dividend account balance verification; T2054: Election for a capital dividend under subsec. 83(2).

(2.1) Idem [anti-avoidance] — Notwithstanding subsection (2), where a dividend that, but for this subsection, would be a capital dividend is paid on a share of the capital stock of a corporation and the share (or another share for which the share was substituted) was acquired by its holder in a transaction or as part of a series of transactions one of the main purposes of which was to receive the dividend,

(a) the dividend shall, for the purposes of this Act (other than for the purposes of Part III and computing the capital dividend account of the corporation), be deemed to be received by the shareholder and paid by the corporation as a taxable dividend and not as a capital dividend; and

(b) paragraph (2)(b) does not apply in respect of the dividend.

Related Provisions: 83(2.2)-(2.4) — Exceptions; 87(2)(z.1) — Amalgamations — capital dividend account; 112(3)(a)(i), 112(3)(b)(ii), 112(3.1)(a), 112(3.1)(b)(ii), 112(3.2)(b) — Taxable dividend under 83(2.1) excluded from stop-loss rule on disposition of share; 248(1)"life insurance capital dividend" — Definition applies to entire Act; 248(10) — Series of transactions.

Notes: Note the exceptions in 83(2.2)-(2.4). See Truster, "Subsection 83(2.1): The Capital Dividend Anti-Avoidance Provision", 11(1) *Tax for the Owner-Manager* (ctf.ca) 5-6 (Jan. 2011); VIEWS docs 2008-0296371E5; 2015-0624611R3 (83(2.1) does not apply).

83(2.1) applied in *Groupe Honco*, 2013 FCA 128, where Aco agreed to acquire shares of Bco for several valid business reasons, but was unable to show there was not another "main purpose" of eventually accessing Bco's CDA (given that Bco held life insurance on BCo's owner who had terminal pancreatic cancer). (However, *Honco* did not consider 83(2.3). See Glenn Stephens, "Capital Dividend Account Anti-Avoidance Provisions and Life Insurance", XXIII(1) *Insurance Planning* (Federated Press) 2-5 (2018).) See Income Tax Folio S3-F2-C1 ¶1.95. Nat Boidman, "One of the Main Purposes Test", 22(5) *Canadian Tax Highlights* (ctf.ca) 9 (May 2014), suggests following UK case law so that "one of the main purposes" (or "reasons") means a transaction's "driving purpose" rather than, as in *Honco*, "one of the purposes". See also *Lenco Fibre*, [1979] C.T.C. 374 (FCTD), para. 4 (effect of there being "other main reasons" aside from tax reduction); other cases in Notes to 256(2.1); and Nikolakakis, "Purpose", 2019 Cdn Tax Foundation conference report, 21:1-33.

Cases where 83(2.1) is not normally triggered: IT-146R4 para. 6 (designation or reclassification of shares); docs 2000-0026615 (purpose is to pay capital dividends to existing shareholders); 2017-0704221E5 (sale of shares to third party; GAAR may apply); 2020-0852201C6 [2020 APFF q.8] (streaming of capital dividend to original shareholder). For a ruling that 83(2.1) will not apply on an arrangement transferring an unused charitable donation to a related corp, see 2012-0439121R3, 2013-0497001R3.

This version of 83(2.1) added by 1988 tax reform, effective for dividends paid after 4pm EDST, September 25, 1987. Former 83(2.1), repealed effective for dividends paid after May 23, 1985, permitted a corporation to elect for a dividend to be a "life insurance capital dividend". The normal capital dividend rules now apply to proceeds of disposition from life insurance: see 89(1)"capital dividend account"(d) and (e). However, life insurance capital dividends paid before May 24, 1985 are still taken into account for adjusted cost base purposes (see 53(1)(e)(ii)) and for limiting capital losses (112(3)–(3.2)), and are tracked through amalgamations (87(2)(x)) and windups (88(1)(d)(i.1)(B)). "Life insurance capital dividend" is still (erroneously) defined for the Act in 248(1) by reference to 83(2.1), even though it has been repealed.

Income Tax Folios: S3-F2-C1: Capital Dividends [replaces IT-66R6].

Advance Tax Rulings: ATR-54: Reduction of paid-up capital.

(2.2) Where subsec. (2.1) does not apply — Subsection (2.1) does not apply in respect of a particular dividend, in respect of which an election is made under subsection (2), paid on a share of the capital stock of a particular corporation to an individual where it is reasonable to consider that all or substantially all of the capital dividend account of the particular corporation immediately before the particular dividend became payable consisted of amounts other than any amount

(a) added to that capital dividend account under paragraph (b) of the definition "capital dividend account" in subsection 89(1) in respect of a dividend received on a share of the capital stock of another corporation, which share (or another share for which the share was substituted) was acquired by the particular corporation in a transaction or as part of a series of transactions one of the main purposes of which was that the particular corporation receive the dividend, but not in respect of a dividend where it is reasonable to consider that the purpose of paying the dividend was to distribute an amount that was received by the other corporation and included in computing the other corporation's capital dividend account by reason of paragraph (d) of that definition;

(b) added to that capital dividend account under paragraph 87(2)(z.1) as a result of an amalgamation or winding-up or a series of transactions including the amalgamation or winding-up that would not have been so added had the amalgamation or winding-up occurred or the series of transactions been commenced after 4:00 p.m. Eastern Daylight Saving Time, September 25, 1987;

(c) added to that capital dividend account at a time when the particular corporation was controlled, directly or indirectly, in any manner whatever, by one or more non-resident persons; or

(d) in respect of a capital gain from a disposition of a property by the particular corporation or another corporation that may reasonably be considered as having accrued while the property (or another property for which it was substituted) was a property of a corporation that was controlled, directly or indirectly, in any manner whatever, by one or more non-resident persons.

Related Provisions: 248(5) — Substituted property; 248(10) — Series of transactions; 256(5.1), (6.2) — Controlled directly or indirectly.

Notes: For CRA interpretation see VIEWS doc 2008-0296371E5.

CRA considers that "substantially all", used in the opening words of 83(2.2), means 90% or more.

Income Tax Folios: S3-F2-C1: Capital Dividends [replaces IT-66R6].

I.T. Technical News: 25 (*Silicon Graphics* case — dispersed control is not control).

(2.3) Idem — Subsection (2.1) does not apply in respect of a dividend, in respect of which an election is made under subsection (2), paid on a share of the capital stock of a corporation where it is reasonable to consider that the purpose of paying the dividend was to distribute an amount that was received by the corporation and included in computing its capital dividend account by reason of paragraph (d) of the definition "capital dividend account" in subsection 89(1).

Notes: 83(2.3) might have applied in *Groupe Honco*, 2013 CarswellNat 1476 (FCA) (see Notes to 83(2.1)), but it was not properly raised and argued in time.

Income Tax Folios: S3-F2-C1: Capital Dividends [replaces IT-66R6].

(2.4) Idem — Subsection (2.1) does not apply in respect of a particular dividend, in respect of which an election is made under subsection (2), paid on a share of the capital stock of a particular corporation to a corporation (in this subsection referred to as the "related corporation") related (otherwise than by reason of a right referred to in paragraph 251(5)(b)) to the particular corporation where it is reasonable to consider that all or substantially all of the capital dividend account of the particular corporation immediately before the particular dividend became payable consisted of amounts other than any amount

(a) added to that capital dividend account under paragraph (b) of the definition "capital dividend account" in subsection 89(1) in respect of a dividend received on a share of the capital stock of another corporation if it is reasonable to consider that any portion of the capital dividend account of that other corporation immediately before that dividend became payable consisted of amounts added to that account under paragraph 87(2)(z.1) or paragraph (b) of that definition as a result of a transaction or a series of transactions that would not have been so added had the transaction occurred or the series of transactions been commenced after 4:00 p.m. Eastern Daylight Saving Time, September 25, 1987;

(b) that represented the capital dividend account of a corporation before it became related to the related corporation;

(c) added to the capital dividend account of the particular corporation at a time when that corporation was controlled, directly or indirectly, in any manner whatever, by one or more non-resident persons;

(d) in respect of a capital gain from a disposition of a property by the particular corporation or another corporation that may reasonably be considered as having accrued while the property (or another property for which it was substituted) was a property of a corporation that was controlled, directly or indirectly, in any manner whatever, by one or more non-resident persons; or

(e) in respect of a capital gain from a disposition of a property (or another property for which it was substituted) that may reasonably be considered as having accrued while the property or the other property was a property of a person that was not related to the related corporation.

Related Provisions: 248(5) — Substituted property; 248(10) — Series of transactions; 256(5.1), (6.2) — Controlled directly or indirectly.

Notes: For CRA interpretation see VIEWS doc 2008-0296371E5.

CRA considers that "substantially all", used in the opening words of 83(2.4), means 90% or more.

Income Tax Folios: S3-F2-C1: Capital Dividends [replaces IT-66R6].

I.T. Technical News: 25 (*Silicon Graphics* case — dispersed control is not control).

(3) Late filed elections — Where at any particular time after 1974 a dividend has become payable by a corporation to shareholders of any class of shares of its capital stock, and subsection (1) or (2) would have applied to the dividend except that the election referred to therein was not made on or before the day on or before which the election was required by that subsection to be made, the election shall be deemed to have been made at the particular time or on the first day on which any part of the dividend was paid, whichever is the earlier, if

(a) the election is made in prescribed manner and prescribed form;

(b) an estimate of the penalty in respect of that election is paid by the corporation when that election is made; and

(c) the directors or other person or persons legally entitled to administer the affairs of the corporation have, before the time the election is made, authorized the election to be made.

Related Provisions: 83(3.1) — Request for late filed election; 83(4) — Penalty for late filed election; 83(5) — Unpaid balance of penalty.

Notes: See Income Tax Folio S3-F2-C1 ¶1.21-1.23. See VIEWS docs 2017-0718311E5 (when 83(3) applies, dividend goes into receiving corp's CDA when received); 2019-0812721C6 [2019 APFF q.13] (directors must authorize election before it is made, not necessarily before dividend is declared).

Regulations: 2101(e) (prescribed manner, prescribed form).

Income Tax Folios: S3-F2-C1: Capital Dividends [replaces IT-66R6].

CRA Audit Manual: 28.6.2: Late filed capital dividends election.

Forms: T2054: Election for a capital dividend under subsec. 83(2).

(3.1) Request for election — The Minister may at any time, by written request served personally or by registered mail, request that an election referred to in subsection (3) be made by a taxpayer, and where the taxpayer on whom such a request is served does not comply therewith within 90 days of service thereof on the taxpayer, subsection (3) does not apply to such an election made by the taxpayer.

Related Provisions: 244(5), (6) — Proof of service; 248(7) — Mail deemed received on day mailed; *Interpretation Act* 27(5) — Meaning of "within 90 days".

CRA Audit Manual: 28.6.2: Late filed capital dividends election.

(4) Penalty for late filed election — For the purposes of this section, the penalty in respect of an election referred to in paragraph (3)(a) is an amount equal to the lesser of

(a) 1% per annum of the amount of the dividend referred to in the election for each month or part of a month during the period commencing with the time that the dividend became payable, or the first day on which any part of the dividend was paid if that day is earlier, and ending with the day on which that election was made, and

(b) the product obtained when $500 is multiplied by the proportion that the number of months or parts of months during the period referred to in paragraph (a) bears to 12.

Related Provisions: 83(5) — Unpaid balance of penalty.

CRA Audit Manual: 28.6.2: Late filed capital dividends election.

(5) Unpaid balance of penalty — The Minister shall, with all due dispatch, examine each election referred to in paragraph (3)(a), assess the penalty payable and send a notice of assessment to the corporation and the corporation shall pay, forthwith to the Receiver General, the amount, if any, by which the penalty so assessed exceeds the total of all amounts previously paid on account of that penalty.

(6) [No longer relevant]

Notes: A "qualifying dividend", tax-free under 83(1), had to be paid before 1991.

(7) Amalgamation where there are tax-deferred preferred shares — For the purposes of this section, where, after March 31, 1977, there has been an amalgamation within the meaning of section 87 and one or more of the predecessor corporations had a series of shares outstanding on March 31, 1977 that was prescribed to be a tax-deferred preferred series, the following rules apply:

(a) the series of shares of the capital stock of the predecessor corporation that was prescribed to be a tax-deferred preferred series shall be deemed to have been continued in existence in the form of the new shares; and

(b) the new corporation shall be deemed to be the same corporation as, and a continuation of, each such predecessor corporation.

Regulations: 2107 (tax-deferred preferred series).

Definitions [s. 83]: "adjusted cost base" — 54, 248(1); "amount", "assessment" — 248(1); "Canadian corporation" — 89(1), 248(1); "capital dividend" — 83(2), 248(1); "capital dividend account" — 89(1); "capital gain" — 39(1)(a), 248(1); "class", "class of shares" — 248(6); "controlled directly or indirectly" — 256(5.1)–(6); "corporation" — 248(1), *Interpretation Act* 35(1); "dividend", "individual", "Minister", "non-resident" — 248(1); "payable" — 84(7), 89(3); "person", "preferred share", "prescribed" — 248(1); "private corporation" — 89(1), 248(1); "property" — 248(1); "qualifying dividend" — 83(6); "received" — 248(7); "series of transactions" — 248(10); "share", "shareholder" — 248(1); "substituted" — 248(5); "taxable dividend" — 89(1), 248(1).

84. (1) Deemed dividend — Where a corporation resident in Canada has at any time after 1971 increased the paid-up capital in respect of the shares of any particular class of its capital stock, otherwise than by

(a) payment of a stock dividend,

(b) a transaction by which

(i) the value of its assets less its liabilities has been increased, or

(ii) its liabilities less the value of its assets have been decreased,

by an amount not less than the amount of the increase in the paid-up capital in respect of the shares of the particular class,

(c) a transaction by which the paid-up capital in respect of the shares of all other classes of its capital stock has been reduced by an amount not less than the amount of the increase in the paid-up capital in respect of the shares of the particular class,

(c.1) if the corporation is an insurance corporation, any action by which it converts contributed surplus related to its insurance business (other than any portion of that contributed surplus that arose at a time when it was non-resident, or that arose in connection with a disposition to which subsection 212.1(1.1) applies or an "investment", as defined in subsection 212.3(10), to which subsection 212.3(2) applies) into paid-up capital in respect of the shares of its capital stock,

(c.2) if the corporation is a bank, any action by which it converts any of its contributed surplus that arose on the issuance of shares of its capital stock (other than any portion of that contributed surplus that arose at a time when it was non-resident, or that arose in connection with a disposition to which subsection 212.1(1.1) applies or an "investment", as defined in subsection 212.3(10), to which subsection 212.3(2) applies) into paid-up capital in respect of shares of its capital stock, or

(c.3) if the corporation is neither an insurance corporation nor a bank, any action by which it converts into paid-up capital in respect of a class of shares of its capital stock any of its contributed surplus that arose after March 31, 1977 (other than any portion of that contributed surplus that arose at a time when it was non-resident, or that arose in connection with a disposition to which subsection 212.1(1.1) applies or an "investment", as defined in subsection 212.3(10), to which subsection 212.3(2) applies)

(i) on the issuance of shares of that class or shares of another class for which the shares of that class were substituted (other than an issuance to which section 51, 66.3, 84.1, 85, 85.1, 86 or 87 or subsection 192(4.1) or 194(4.1) applied),

(ii) on the acquisition of property by the corporation from a person who at the time of the acquisition held any of the issued shares of that class or shares of another class for which shares of that class were substituted for no consideration or for consideration that did not include shares of the capital stock of the corporation, or

(iii) as a result of any action by which the paid-up capital in respect of that class of shares or in respect of shares of another class for which shares of that class were substituted was reduced by the corporation, to the extent of the reduction in paid-up capital that resulted from the action,

the corporation shall be deemed to have paid at that time a dividend on the issued shares of the particular class equal to the amount, if any, by which the amount of the increase in the paid-up capital exceeds the total of

(d) the amount, if any, of the increase referred to in subparagraph (b)(i) or the decrease referred to in subparagraph (b)(ii), as the case may be,

(e) the amount, if any, of the reduction referred to in paragraph (c), and

(f) the amount, if any, of the increase in the paid-up capital that resulted from a conversion referred to in paragraph (c.1), (c.2) or (c.3),

and a dividend shall be deemed to have been received at that time by each person who held any of the issued shares of the particular class immediately after that time equal to that proportion of the dividend so deemed to have been paid by the corporation that the number of the shares of the particular class held by the person immediately after that time is of the number of the issued shares of that class outstanding immediately after that time.

Related Provisions: 15(1) — Benefit conferred on shareholder — income inclusion; 53(1)(b) — Addition to ACB; 82(1) — Income inclusion of dividend deemed received; 84(8) — Application; 84(10) — Reduction of contributed surplus; 84(11) — Computation of contributed surplus; 85(2.1) — Reduction in paid-up capital to prevent deemed dividend on s. 85 rollover; 86(2.1) — Adjustment to paid-up capital on internal reorganization; 87(2)(y) — Amalgamations — contributed surplus; 89(3) — Simultaneous dividends; 131(4) — S. 84 does not apply to mutual fund corporation; 131(11)(c) — Rules re prescribed labour-sponsored venture capital corporations; 138(11.9) — Computation of contributed surplus.

Notes: See Notes to 53(1)(b) and 84(3).

84(1)(c.3)(i), (ii) and (iii) seem to apply differently in English and French. The words "shares of another class for which shares of that class were substituted" refer to a *pred-*

ecessor class, but "actions d'une autre catégorie ayant remplacé les actions de la catégorie donnée" refer to a *successor* class. This has been pointed out to Finance.

In *Faraggi (2529-1915 Québec, 2530-1284 Québec)*, 2008 FCA 398 (leave to appeal denied 2009 CarswellNat 1152 (SCC)), a complex scheme to create capital dividends was held to be a sham and thus ineffective.

On the interaction of the PUC reductions in 51(3), 85(2.1) and 86(2.1) with 84(1), see VIEWS doc 2008-0293401E5.

For rulings on 84(1) see VIEWS docs 2006-0173771R3 and 2015-0584151R3 (84(1)(c.3)); 2008-0284591R3 (split-up butterfly); 2010-0359981R3, 2010-0360501R3, 2010-0364531R3, 2011-0399121R3 and 2012-0471921R3 (interactions with Canada-US tax treaty). See also 2016-0625001E5 (transaction using 84(1) and a trust is considered surplus stripping and GAAR would apply).

84(1)(c.1)-(c.2), and (c.3) before (ii), amended by 2018 budget bill #2, for transactions or events after Feb. 26, 2018, effectively to exclude any portion of a corporation's contributed surplus that arose when it was non-resident. Before the amendment, read:

(c.1) if the corporation is an insurance corporation, any action by which it converts contributed surplus related to its insurance business (other than any portion of that contributed surplus that arose in connection with an investment, as defined in subsection 212.3(10), to which subsection 212.3(2) applies) into paid-up capital in respect of the shares of its capital stock,

(c.2) if the corporation is a bank, any action by which it converts any of its contributed surplus that arose on the issuance of shares of its capital stock (other than any portion of that contributed surplus that arose in connection with an investment, as defined in subsection 212.3(10), to which subsection 212.3(2) applies) into paid-up capital in respect of shares of its capital stock, or

(c.3) if the corporation is neither an insurance corporation nor a bank, any action by which it converts into paid-up capital in respect of a class of shares of its capital stock any of its contributed surplus that arose after March 31, 1977 (other than any portion of that contributed surplus that arose in connection with an investment, as defined in subsection 212.3(10), to which subsection 212.3(2) applies)

(i) on the issuance of shares of that class or shares of another class for which the shares of that class were substituted (other than an issuance to which section 51, 66.3, 84.1, 85, 85.1, 86 or 87 or subsection 192(4.1), 194(4.1) or 212.1(1.1) applied),

84(1)(c.3)(i) amended by 2016 budget bill #2 to change "212.1" to "212.1(1.1)", effective March 22, 2016.

84(1)(c.1), (c.2), and (c.3) opening words amended by 2012 budget bill #2, effective March 29, 2012, to add parenthesized exclusions re 212.3.

84(1)(c.3)(iii) amended by 1993 technical bill, this version effective for actions occurring after Dec. 21, 1992. 84(1) earlier amended by 1991 technical bill.

Regulations: 201(1)(a) (information return).

Interpretation Bulletins: IT-67R3: Taxable dividends from corporations resident in Canada; IT-243R4: Dividend refund to private corporations; IT-291R3: Transfer of property to a corporation under subsection 85(1); IT-432R2: Benefits conferred on shareholders; IT-463R2: Paid-up capital.

Information Circulars: 76-19R3: Transfer of property to a corporation under s. 85.

Advance Tax Rulings: ATR-33: Exchange of shares.

Forms: RC257: Request for an information return program account (RZ); T5: Statement of investment income; T5 Summ: Return of investment income.

(2) Distribution on winding-up, etc.

(2) Distribution on winding-up, etc. — Where funds or property of a corporation resident in Canada have at any time after March 31, 1977 been distributed or otherwise appropriated in any manner whatever to or for the benefit of the shareholders of any class of shares in its capital stock, on the winding-up, discontinuance or reorganization of its business, the corporation shall be deemed to have paid at that time a dividend on the shares of that class equal to the amount, if any, by which,

(a) the amount or value of the funds or property distributed or appropriated, as the case may be,

exceeds

(b) the amount, if any, by which the paid-up capital in respect of the shares of that class is reduced on the distribution or appropriation, as the case may be,

and a dividend shall be deemed to have been received at that time by each person who held any of the issued shares at that time equal to that proportion of the amount of the excess that the number of the shares of that class held by the person immediately before that time is of the number of the issued shares of that class outstanding immediately before that time.

Related Provisions: 15(1)(a)(ii), 15(1)(a.1)(iii) — No shareholder-benefit income inclusion; 54"proceeds of disposition"(j) — exclusion of deemed dividend; 55(1) —

"Permitted redemption" for butterfly purposes; 69(5) — Unreasonable consideration; 84(5) — Amount distributed or paid where a share; 84(6), (8) — Application rules; 88(1) — Winding-up; 88(2)(b) — Winding up of a Canadian corporation; 89(3) — Simultaneous dividends; 131(4) — S. 84 does not apply to mutual fund corporation; 135.1(7), (8) — Rules for agricultural co-op's tax deferred cooperative shares; 135.2(3)(e) — No application to Canadian Wheat Board shares; 137(4.2) — No application to credit union.

Notes: See Notes to 84(3).

"Winding-up, discontinuance or reorganization" (WDR): if there is no true WDR of the business, 84(2) does not apply, but 15(1) applies to appropriation of the corporation's property by shareholders, leading to income inclusion without the beneficial treatment given to dividend income (112(1), 121): *Felray Inc.*, [1998] 2 C.T.C. 4 (FCTD). There was WDR in: *MacDonald*, 2013 FCA 110 (converting medical professional corp to holding company). There was no WDR in: *Kennedy*, [1973] C.T.C. 437 (FCA), para. 8 (car dealership sold building, then leased it back); *McMullen*, 2007 TCC 16 (series of transactions to enable shareholders to sever their relationship [Anderson et al., "Breaking Up a Business or Surplus Stripping?", XV(1) *Tax Litigation* (Federated Press) 910-17 (2007)]; *Kvas*, 2016 TCC 199, para. 23 (corp involuntarily dissolved). See also VIEWS docs 2007-0243221C6 (business need not cease for there to be "reorganization"); 2012-0445341C6 [2012 Prairie Conf. q.14] (in CRA's view, even investment assets are a "business" for 84(2)).

Leveraged buyout: see VIEWS docs 2013-0479651E5, 2016-0655911C6 [2016 APFF q.12] (leveraged buyout is not likely WDR); 2019-0809581R3 (leveraged buyout of Carmanah [Nitikman, "Missing the Forest", 2519 *Tax Topics* (CCH) 5-10 (June 16, 2020); Willson & O'Connor, "Carmanah Technologies", XXIII(3) *Corporate Finance* (Federated Press) 20-25 (2020)); Kabouchi & Lang, "The Application of 84(2) to Leveraged Buy-Out", *ibid*, 26-31]).

Surplus stripping by converting a taxable dividend into proceeds of disposition triggers 84(2): doc 2007-0224151E5. 84(2) applied to a share sale that in substance was extraction of corporate surplus, in *RMM Canadian Enterprises (Equilease)*, [1998] 1 C.T.C. 2300 (TCC). However, in *Tremblay*, 2010 FCA 119, (2-1 decision), 84(2) did not apply where a corp was sold via 85.1 share exchange with no distribution or appropriation of assets [Osborne, "Tax Court Reins in CRA's Views on Subsection 84(2)", XVI(1) *Corporate Finance* (Federated Press) 1755-58 (2009); Brender, "The Queen v. Tremblay", XII(1) *Corporate Structures & Groups* (Federated Press) 644-47 (2010); Kiefer, "Tuck-Under Transactions", XIV(4) *Business Vehicles* (Federated Press) 773-78 (2012)]. CRA noted the dissent in the FCA and will continue to challenge certain "tuck under" transactions: docs 2010-0370551E5, 2010-0373291C6.

In *Geransky*, [2001] 2 C.T.C. 2147 (TCC), 84(2) did not apply to a series of transactions whereby shareholders extracted corporate surplus and claimed the capital gains exemption on a share sale. The CRA accepts this result with qualifications: 2002-0156695, 2003-0029955, 2004-0086771C6, but may restrict it to a partial sale of a business: Jean-François Drouin, "Selling a Business: Selling Shares, Assets or... Both", 1(1) *It's Personal* (Carswell) 4 (Nov. 2007). See also Clark, Proulx & Pandher, "Hybrid Sales", 25(5) *Canadian Tax Highlights* (ctf.ca) 4-5 (May 2017).

In *MacDonald*, 2013 FCA 110, 84(2) applied due to the words "in any manner whatever", where at the end of a planned series of transactions, the taxpayer ended up with his company's funds. The FCA ruled that 84(2) applies to a person who was a shareholder at the beginning of an arrangement, even if the person was not a shareholder when receiving the funds: para. 29. See Falk & Morand, "Federal Court of Appeal Strikes Down Inter Vivos Surplus Strip", 2150 *Tax Topics* (CCH) 1-9 (May 23, 2013) and 222 *The Estate Planner* (CCH) 3-10 (July 2013); Haney case comment, 61(3) *Canadian Tax Journal* 739-45 (2013); Sommerfeldt, "The Queen v. MacDonald", XIX(1) *Tax Litigation* (Federated Press) 1134-40 (2013). In *Descarries*, 2014 TCC 75, a dividend stripping plan using an internal rollover to offset a capital loss against a deemed dividend was held not to fall within 84(2) or abuse 84(2) for GAAR, but was abuse of 84.1(1) so GAAR applied. For 84(2) to apply, the WDR must happen at the same time as the distribution: *Descarries*, para. 29. CRA could not appeal *Descarries* on 84(2) because it won under GAAR, but disagrees with it and will pursue this issue in another case: doc 2014-0538091C6 [2014 APFF q.21].

In *Latham*, 2015 TCC 75, CRA presumed that retained earnings on a company's books were distributed to the shareholders when it ceased operating, but the Court held the books were incorrect and nothing had been distributed.

Pipeline: 84(2) can apply to a post-mortem "pipeline", where a corp's surplus is extracted by selling the corp to a Holdco for a capital gain, taking back a note, then having the corp pay a tax-free intercorporate dividend to the Holdco, which repays the note. However, if the estate waits 1 year to wind up the corp into Holdco, and it is not an inactive corp whose underlying assets are cash, CRA permits the pipeline and will not apply GAAR: docs 2002-0154223, 2005-0142111R3, 2009-0326961C6, 2009-0346351R3, 2010-0377601R3, 2010-0388591R3, 2010-0386001C6 [2010 CTF q.6, conf. report p. 4:7-8], 2011-0403031R3 2011-0401861C6, 2011-0401811R3, 2011-0426371C6 [2011 CTF q.23, conf. report p. 4:16-17], 2012-0435131R3, 2012-0456221R3, 2012-0464501R3, 2013-0503611R3, 2013-0509251R3, 2014-0526361R3, 2014-0526431R3, 2014-0540861R3, 2014-0541261R3, 2014-0545531R3, 2014-0548621R3, 2014-0552071R3, 2014-0559481R3, 2014-0563081R3; 2015-0569891R3 (pipeline with US beneficiary); 2015-0588551R3, 2015-0604851R3, 2015-0606721R3; 2015-0617601E5, 2016-0646891R3 (pipeline followed by butterfly); 2015-0602831R3; 2016-0629511R3 (allows extraction of "hard ACB"); 2016-0634371R3, 2016-0677751R3, 2016-0670871R3, 2016-0675861R3; 2018-0754531R3; 2018-0765411R3 (avoiding 104(4))) [Hamelin, "Pipeline Transactions and the 21-Year Rule", 19(2) *Tax*

for the Owner-Manager (ctf.ca) 1-2 (April 2019)]; 2018-0767431R3 (business of investing in securities); 2018-0777441R3, 2018-0780201R3 [2019-0796351R3]; 2018-0789911R3 [Hamelin, "Post Mortem Pipeline: The CRA Relaxes Its Position", 20(3) *Tax for the Owner-Manager* (ctf.ca) 6-7 (July 2020)]; 2019-0790001R3; 2019-0832601R3, 2019-0835131R3, 2020-0839401R3; 2019-0793281R3, 2019-0819191R3, 2019-0822951R3, 2019-0824211R3 (hybrid pipelines); 2020-0838951R3 (pipeline implemented by beneficiaries, not the estate); 2020-0842241C6 [2020 CALU q.6] (gradual repayment of note), 2020-0858741R3; 2020-0860231R3 (pipeline and bump). 2010-0389551R3 is a withdrawn ruling request on the pipeline strategy (inactive company with only liquid assets), where the ruling would have been negative. CRA's views have been questioned, though the FCA decision in *MacDonald* seems to support them: see the TCC's *obiter* comments in *MacDonald*, 2012 TCC 123, paras. 70-82 (although *MacDonald* was reversed and 84(2) broadened, the FCA did not discuss the pipeline). A normal pipeline does not trigger 55(2): 2017-0693421C6 [2017 STEP q.7]. Where there are non-resident heirs, a pipeline triggers withholding tax, but this will be fixed by Finance in most cases: see Notes to 212.1(6).

For discussion of the pipeline since the FCA decision see Bernstein & Gucciardo, "Surplus Stripping in MacDonald", 21(6) *Canadian Tax Highlights [CTH]* (ctf.ca) 9-11 (June 2013); Welch, "Subsection 84(2) and Pipeline Planning", XX(4) *Insurance Planning [IP]* (Federated Press) 1294-1300 (2014) (discusses *Descarries*); Harding, "Post Mortem Planning", XXII(2) *IP* 7-12 (2017); Haughey, "Pipelines and Non-Resident Beneficiaries", 27(3) *CTH* 7-8 (March 2019); Miller, "The Status of Post-Mortem Pipeline", XXIV(3) *IP* 2-6 (2019); Pham, "Post-mortem pipeline transactions", tinyurl.com/rsm-pipeline (Sept. 4, 2019).

The July 18, 2017 proposed amendments (84.1 and 246.1) might have curtailed use of the pipeline, but these were dropped: Manu Kakkar, "The Pipeline Comes Back to Life (But for How Long?)", 18(1) *Tax for the Owner-Manager* (ctf.ca) 2-3 (Jan. 2018) and 18(2) 2-3 (April 2018). CRA has confirmed it will continue to issue favourable rulings: 2018-0748381C6 [STEP 2018 q.10].

See also VIEWS docs 2002-0168603 (public corp (PCo) spin-off using tax-free return of PUC [Fedchun, "New Ruling", XI(1) *Corporate Finance* (Federated Press) 1033-35 (2003)]; 2005-0163191R3 (PCo exchanges LP units for units of mutual fund trust holding interest in LP, followed by distribution of trust units as reduction of capital); 2006-0169591R3, 2006-0184821R3, 2006-0210741R3, 2008-0289331R3, 2008-0297681R3, 2011-0417351R3, 2011-0425211R3, 2011-0432431R3, 2012-0435291R3, 2012-0470281R3, 2017-0731971R3 (PUC reduction by PCo); 2014-0537161R3 (same; shares or warrants distributed under 84(2) have cost equal to their FMV); 2008-0270081R3 (84(2) does not apply on sale of business); 2019-0811641R3 (84(2) applies as part of a butterfly).

On discontinuance of business, payments to shareholders actively involved in the business can be bonuses (deductible to the corp), while payments to others are treated as dividends by 84(2): VIEWS doc 2004-010695117. Liquidation of an agricultural cooperative under 135.1: 2010-0375361E5.

When a business is discontinued, any annual information returns (not the tax return) must be filed within 30 days: Reg. 205(2).

If a corp winds up with unpaid tax of $N or more, and shareholder S gets $N from the corp, S can be assessed for $N under 160(1) (or pursued via other legislation, e.g. Ontario *Business Corporations Act* s. 243), even if 84(2) also includes $N in S's income (but not if it was dissolved involuntarily: *Kvas*, 2016 TCC 199). See Notes to 160(1); VIEWS doc 2010-035875117. CRA also claims it can assess S under s. 159 even if S got no funds: 2011-039919117 [Chong, "Parent Company: Sub's Legal Representative", 19(10) *Canadian Tax Highlights* (ctf.ca) 6-7 (Oct. 2011)].

Regulations: 201(1)(a) (information return).

Interpretation Bulletins: IT-67R3: Taxable dividends from corporations resident in Canada; IT-126R2: Meaning of "winding-up"; IT-149R4: Winding-up dividend; IT-243R4: Dividend refund to private corporations; IT-409: Winding-up of a non-profit organization (cancelled); IT-444R: Corporations — involuntary dissolutions; IT-488R2: Winding-up of 90%-owned taxable Canadian corporations (cancelled).

(3) Redemption, etc. — Where at any time after December 31, 1977 a corporation resident in Canada has redeemed, acquired or cancelled in any manner whatever (otherwise than by way of a transaction described in subsection (2)) any of the shares of any class of its capital stock,

(a) the corporation shall be deemed to have paid at that time a dividend on a separate class of shares comprising the shares so redeemed, acquired or cancelled equal to the amount, if any, by which the amount paid by the corporation on the redemption, acquisition or cancellation, as the case may be, of those shares exceeds the paid-up capital in respect of those shares immediately before that time; and

(b) a dividend shall be deemed to have been received at that time by each person who held any of the shares of that separate class at that time equal to that portion of the amount of the excess determined under paragraph (a) that the number of those shares held by the person immediately before that time is of the total number of shares of that separate class that the corporation has redeemed, acquired or cancelled, at that time.

Related Provisions: 8(12) — Return of employee shares by trustee; 15(1)(a.1)(ii) — No shareholder-benefit income inclusion if corporation not resident in Canada; 40(3.6) — Stop-loss rule on disposition of share of corporation to the corporation; 54"proceeds of disposition"(j) — exclusion of deemed dividend; 55(1) — "Permitted redemption" for butterfly purposes; 55(2) — Deemed proceeds or capital gain on capital gains strip; 55(3)(a) — Butterfly; 84(5) — Amount distributed or paid where a share; 84(6), (8) — Application rules; 84(9) — Shares disposed of on redemption; 89(3) — Simultaneous dividends; 112(5.2)B(a) — Stop-loss rule on share repurchase; 128.1(3) — Addition to PUC of corporation that previously became resident in Canada; 131(4) — S. 84 does not apply to mutual fund corporation; 135.1(7), (8) — Rules for agricultural co-op's tax deferred cooperative shares; 135.2(3)(e) — No application to Canadian Wheat Board shares; 137(4.1) — Deemed interest on certain reductions of capital by credit union; 137(4.2) — No application to credit union; 191.1(1) — Application of Part VI.1 tax to corporation; 212.3(8)(a)(i) — Effect of foreign affiliate dumping on PUC.

Notes: On a share redemption, 84(3) provides for a deemed dividend to the extent the amount paid on redemption exceeds the paid-up capital (PUC) of the shares. If the shareholder is a corporation, the deemed dividend will normally pass tax-free due to 82(1)(a) and 112(1); but 55(2) may deem the dividend to be a capital gain if the effect is to strip capital gains from the value of the redeeming corp's shares; or the stop-loss rules in s. 112 or Part IV tax in 186(1) may apply. If the shares are preferred shares, Part VI.1 tax may apply to the corp. If the shareholder is non-resident, the deemed dividend is subject to withholding tax under 212(2): VIEWS doc 2005-0159711E5 (and Canada-US Treaty Art. X:2 reduces the withholding tax rate: 2011-0424211R3). If the shares are taxable Canadian property, the corp is liable under 116(5) if it does not obtain a s. 116 certificate: 2008-0301701E5.

The amount "paid by the corporation" on redemption includes unpaid amounts owing on the purchase: *Cabezuelo*, [1983] C.T.C. 2775; *Belair*, [1989] 2 C.T.C. 2186; 1984 CTF conference Round Table q. 45 (p. 818); VIEWS doc 2005-0145891E5. It also includes an amount payable later due to a price adjustment clause: 2011-0422191E5 (the extra tax is payable in the year of receipt of the additional payment: 2013-0507881E5). Where shares owned by a partnership were cancelled for no consideration on transfer of the partnership interests to the corp, 84(3) did not apply: 2018-0745681E5.

Like the rest of s. 84, 84(3) ensures that PUC can be returned to the shareholder free of tax but that any excess is treated as a dividend. 84.1, 85(2.1), 87(3) and other provisions ensure that PUC cannot be artificially increased through corporate reorganizations. "Simply because PUC was validly created does not mean that it may be validly preserved": *Copthorne Holdings*, 2011 SCC 63, para. 99 (so a restructuring to avoid the cancellation of PUC under 87(3) violated GAAR under 245(2)).

On interaction with 55(2) and surplus stripping, see VIEWS doc 2012-0434501E5. On application of 40(3.6) to deem a loss from an 84(3) deemed dividend to be nil, see 2011-0427461E5. On interaction with 261 (functional currency rules) see 2016-0642111C6 [2016 IFA q.3] [Wach, "Paid-up Capital of Shares held by a Functional-Currency Reporter: How Do we Resolve the Conflicts?", 65(4) *Canadian Tax Journal* 1001-20 (2017)]. Capital loss consolidation: 2018-0772921R3.

84(3) did not apply in *McClarty Family Trust*, 2012 TCC 80, to transactions that resulted in the conversion of dividend income to capital gains in the hands of trust beneficiaries: "The manner in which each person who holds the redeemed, acquired or cancelled shares came to be in possession of the shares is not what needs to be determined under subsection 84(3)" (para. 63).

PUC is calculated under 89(1) by class, not by individual shareholder, so issuance of new shares can change existing shareholders' PUC. However, artificial averaging "up" of PUC using this technique might contravene the general anti-avoidance rule: *Nadeau*, [1999] 3 C.T.C. 2235 (TCC).

A deemed dividend on a share redemption can trigger Part IV tax. See Notes to 186(1).

84(3) can apply where an employee sells stock-option shares back to the employer corporation. See Notes to 7(1).

When 84(3) applies, the corporation must report the dividend by issuing a T5, unless 84(8) applied (Reg. 201(1)(a)).

On the redemption of shares held by a non-resident where the shares are taxable Canadian property (value primarily attributable to Canadian real estate), withholding applies under *both* 212(2) and 116(5); the International TSO would have to be contacted for any administrative relief: VIEWS doc 2010-0387151E5.

On the redemption of publicly listed shares held by a specified financial institution, the deemed "separate class" poses a potential problem. See Notes to Reg. 6201(2).

Where 69(1)(b) applies because the shares' FMV exceeds the redemption amount, the excess is not considered "paid" for purposes of 84(3) so as to increase the deemed dividend, so it is capital gain: VIEWS docs 2004-009178I17, 2004-0086821C6, 2012-045082I17.

84(3) does not apply to a redemption by a non-resident corporation (including one non-resident due to 250(5)), which is treated as an ordinary disposition.

Regulations: 201(1)(a) (information return).

Income Tax Folios: S4-F5-C1: Share for share exchange [replaces IT-450R]; S4-F7-C1: Amalgamations of Canadian corporations [replaces IT-474R2].

Interpretation Bulletins: IT-146R4: Shares entitling shareholders to choose taxable or capital dividends; IT-243R4: Dividend refund to private corporations; IT-291R3: Transfer of property to a corporation under subsection 85(1); IT-489R: Non-arm's length sale of shares to a corporation.

Advance Tax Rulings: ATR-28: Redemption of capital stock of family farm corporation; ATR-35: Partitioning of assets to get specific ownership — "butterfly"; ATR-54: Reduction of paid-up capital; ATR-57: Transfer of property for estate planning purposes; ATR-58: Divisive reorganization.

(4) Reduction of paid-up capital — Where at any time after March 31, 1977 a corporation resident in Canada has reduced the paid-up capital in respect of any class of shares of its capital stock otherwise than by way of a redemption, acquisition or cancellation of any shares of that class or a transaction described in subsection (2) or (4.1),

    (a) the corporation shall be deemed to have paid at that time a dividend on shares of that class equal to the amount, if any, by which the amount paid by it on the reduction of the paid-up capital, exceeds the amount by which the paid-up capital in respect of that class of shares of the corporation has been so reduced; and

    (b) a dividend shall be deemed to have been received at that time by each person who held any of the issued shares at that time equal to that proportion of the amount of the excess referred to in paragraph (a) that the number of the shares of that class held by the person immediately before that time is of the number of the issued shares of that class outstanding immediately before that time.

Related Provisions: 53(2)(a)(ii) — Reduction in ACB; 84(5) — Amount distributed or paid where a share; 84(8) — Application; 89(3) — Simultaneous dividends; 128.1(3) — Addition to PUC of corporation that previously became resident in Canada; 131(4) — S. 84 does not apply to mutual fund corporation; 137(4.1) — Deemed interest on certain reductions of capital by credit union; 137(4.2) — No application to credit union; 212.3(8)(a)(i) — Effect of foreign affiliate dumping on PUC.

Notes: See Notes to 84(3). 84(4) allows a shareholder to receive a tax-free return of capital from a corporation provided the payment does not exceed the reduction in the PUC of the shares. However, for a public corporation, 84(4.1) may deem a dividend.

In *Collins & Aikman Products*, 2010 FCA 251, GAAR (245(2)) did not apply to a reorganization followed by a return of capital to the non-resident shareholder, as 84(4) was not misused (today it would be caught by 212.3).

In a June 9, 1997 letter to the chair of the CICA Taxation Committee, Revenue Canada's Assistant Deputy Minister, VECR (Barry Lacombe) pointed out that 84(4) may apply when a corporation returns part of its share capital to shareholders after a comprehensive revaluation of its assets and liabilities under *CICA Handbook* §1625. Such revaluation occurs following a financial reorganization where there has been substantial realignment of the equity and non-equity interest of an enterprise, or where its assets and liabilities are revised after its purchase.

Where a corporation overpays, in error, on a reduction of PUC, 84(4) applies but CRA may grant administrative relief: VIEWS doc 2008-0266181I7. On the interaction of 84(4) and s. 261, see 2016-0642111C6 (see Notes to 84(3)).

See also Marie-Emmanuelle Vaillancourt, "Negative Paid-Up Capital and Subsection 84(4) Reduction", 1894 *Tax Topics* (CCH) 1-3 (June 26, 2008).

Regulations: 201(1)(a) (information return).

Income Tax Folios: S4-F5-C1: Share for share exchange [replaces IT-450R].

Interpretation Bulletins: IT-67R3: Taxable dividends from corporations resident in Canada; IT-243R4: Dividend refund to private corporations.

(4.1) Deemed dividend on reduction of paid-up capital —

Any amount paid by a public corporation on the reduction of the paid-up capital in respect of any class of shares of its capital stock, otherwise than by way of a redemption, acquisition or cancellation of any shares of that class or by way of a transaction described in subsection (2) or section 86, is deemed to have been paid by the corporation and received by the person to whom it was paid, as a dividend, unless

    (a) the amount may reasonably be considered to be derived from proceeds of disposition realized by the public corporation, or by a person or partnership in which the public corporation had a direct or indirect interest at the time that the proceeds were realized, from a transaction that occurred

        (i) outside the ordinary course of the business of the corporation, or of the person or partnership that realized the proceeds, and

(ii) within the period that commenced 24 months before the payment; and

(b) no amount that may reasonably be considered to be derived from those proceeds was paid by the public corporation on a previous reduction of the paid-up capital in respect of any class of shares of its capital stock.

Related Provisions: 53(2)(a) — Reduction in ACB; 84(4) — Reduction of paid-up capital; 89(3) — Simultaneous dividends; 128.1(3) — Addition to PUC of corporation that previously became resident in Canada; 131(4) — S. 84 does not apply to mutual fund corporation; 212.3(8)(a)(i) — Effect of foreign affiliate dumping on PUC.

Notes: 84(4.1), which limits the ability of a public corporation to return capital to shareholders on a tax-deferred basis, can be circumvented: see VIEWS doc 9626163 and Daniel Lang, "Using 84(2) to Effect a Return of Capital for a Public Corporation", VI(2) *Corporate Structures & Groups* (Federated Press) 316-19 (2000).

For CRA statements and rulings on 84(4.1) see VIEWS docs 9833526, 1999-0014315, 2004-0088951R3, 2005-0137101R3, 2005-0140981C6, 2005-0149751R3, 2005-0163191R3, 2005-0165091R3, 2006-0169591R3, 2006-0184821R3, 2006-0201051R3, 2006-0201052R3, 2006-0210741R3, 2008-0289331R3, 2008-0297681R3, 2010-0355001R3, 2011-0417351R3, 2011-0432431R3, 2011-0425211R3, 2011-0426151C6, 2012-0435291R3, 2012-0470281R3, 2014-0537161R3, 2016-0679281R3, 2017-0731971R3.

For the meaning of "derived" in (a) and (b), see Notes to 18.1(12).

84(4.1) amended (effectively to add paras. (a) and (b)) by 2002-2013 technical bill (Part 5 — technical), this version effective for amounts paid after Feb. 26, 2004. For amounts paid from 1997 to Feb. 26, 2004, a broader rule applies (see 45th ed.). The reason for the broader rule is that a 1998 comfort letter (reproduced here up to the 43rd ed.) proposed to substantially gut 84(4.1). The amendment released in 2004 (and enacted in 2013) is not as broad. See Juneja, "Analysis of Proposed Amendments Limiting Distributions of Paid-up Capital by Public Corporations", IX(2) *Corporate Structures & Groups* (Federated Press) 472-77 (2004); Scott & Elawny, "The Provision That Never Arrived", 1937 *Tax Topics* (CCH) 1-4 (April 23, 2009). Grandfathering was thus provided for taxpayers that may have relied on the comfort letter.

Income Tax Folios: S3-F6-C1: Interest deductibility [replaces IT-533]; S4-F5-C1: Share for share exchange [replaces IT-450R].

Interpretation Bulletins: IT-243R4: Dividend refund to private corporations.

(4.2) Deemed dividend on term preferred share — Where, at any time after November 16, 1978, the paid-up capital in respect of a term preferred share owned by a shareholder that is

(a) a specified financial institution, or

(b) a partnership or trust of which a specified financial institution or a person related to such an institution was a member or a beneficiary,

was reduced otherwise than by way of a redemption, acquisition or cancellation of the share or of a transaction described in subsection (2) or (4.1), the amount received by the shareholder on the reduction of the paid-up capital in respect of the share shall be deemed to be a dividend received by the shareholder at that time unless the share was not acquired in the ordinary course of the business carried on by the shareholder.

Related Provisions: 89(3) — Simultaneous dividends; 131(4) — S. 84 does not apply to mutual fund corporation; 248(13) — Interests in trusts or partnerships.

(4.3) Deemed dividend on guaranteed share — Where at any time after 1987 the paid-up capital in respect of a share of the capital stock of a particular corporation owned

(a) by a shareholder that is another corporation to which subsection 112(2.2) or (2.4) would, if the particular corporation were a taxable Canadian corporation, apply to deny the deduction under subsection 112(1) or (2) or 138(6) of a dividend received on the share, or

(b) by a partnership or trust of which such other corporation is a member or beneficiary, as the case may be,

was reduced otherwise than by way of a redemption, acquisition or cancellation of the share or of a transaction described in subsection (2) or (4.1), the amount received by the shareholder on the reduction of the paid-up capital in respect of the share shall be deemed to be a dividend received by the shareholder at that time.

Related Provisions: 89(3) — Simultaneous dividends; 131(4) — S. 84 does not apply to mutual fund corporation; 248(13) — Interests in trusts or partnerships.

(5) Amount distributed or paid where a share — Where

(a) the amount of property distributed by a corporation or otherwise appropriated to or for the benefit of its shareholders as described in paragraph (2)(a), or

(b) the amount paid by a corporation as described in paragraph (3)(a) or (4)(a),

includes a share of the capital stock of the corporation, for the purposes of subsections (2) to (4) the following rules apply:

(c) in computing the amount referred to in paragraph (a) at any time, the share shall be valued at an amount equal to its paid-up capital at that time, and

(d) in computing the amount referred to in paragraph (b) at any time, the share shall be valued at an amount equal to the amount by which the paid-up capital in respect of the class of shares to which it belongs has increased by virtue of its issue.

Related Provisions: 51(3), 86(2.1) — Computation of paid-up capital after share exchange.

Interpretation Bulletins: IT-291R3: Transfer of property to a corporation under subsection 85(1).

(6) Where subsec. (2) or (3) does not apply — Subsection (2) or (3), as the case may be, is not applicable

(a) in respect of any transaction or event, to the extent that subsection (1) is applicable in respect of that transaction or event; and

(b) in respect of any purchase by a corporation of any of its shares in the open market, if the corporation acquired those shares in the manner in which shares would normally be purchased by any member of the public in the open market.

(7) When dividend payable — A dividend that is deemed by this section or section 84.1, 128.1 or 212.1 to have been paid at a particular time is deemed, for the purposes of this Subdivision and sections 131 and 133, to have become payable at that time.

Related Provisions: 15(1) — Appropriation of property to a shareholder.

Notes: 84(7) amended by 1998 Budget, and "this section" corrected to "this subsection" by 2002-2013 technical bill (Part 5 — technical), both effective for dividends deemed paid after Feb. 23, 1998. Earlier amended by 1991 technical bill.

(8) Where subsec. (3) does not apply — Subsection (3) does not apply to deem a dividend to have been received by a shareholder of a public corporation where the shareholder is an individual resident in Canada who deals at arm's length with the corporation and the shares redeemed, acquired or cancelled are prescribed shares of the capital stock of the corporation.

Regulations: 6206 (prescribed shares — Class I shares of Reed Stenhouse).

(9) Shares disposed of on redemptions, etc. — For greater certainty it is declared that where a shareholder of a corporation has disposed of a share of the capital stock of the corporation as a result of the redemption, acquisition or cancellation of the share by the corporation, the shareholder shall, for the purposes of this Act, be deemed to have disposed of the share to the corporation.

Income Tax Folios: S4-F8-C1: Business investment losses [replaces IT-484R2].

Interpretation Bulletins: IT-243R4: Dividend refund to private corporations; IT-444R: Corporations — involuntary dissolutions.

(10) Reduction of contributed surplus — For the purpose of paragraph (1)(c.3), there shall be deducted in determining at any time a corporation's contributed surplus that arose after March 31, 1977 in any manner described in that paragraph the lesser of

(a) the amount, if any, by which the amount of a dividend paid by the corporation at or before that time and after March 31, 1977 and when it was a public corporation exceeded its retained earnings immediately before the payment of the dividend, and

(b) the amount of its contributed surplus immediately before the payment of the dividend referred to in paragraph (a) that arose after March 31, 1977.

Related Provisions: 84(11) — Computation of contributed surplus; 87(2)(y) — Amalgamations — contributed surplus.

Notes: 84(10) added by 1991 technical bill, effective July 14, 1990.

Interpretation Bulletins: IT-463R2: Paid-up capital.

(11) Computation of contributed surplus

For the purpose of subparagraph (1)(c.3)(ii), where the property acquired by the corporation (in this subsection referred to as the "acquiring corporation") consists of shares (in this subsection referred to as the "subject shares") of any class of the capital stock of another corporation resident in Canada (in this subsection referred to as the "subject corporation") and, immediately after the acquisition of the subject shares, the subject corporation would be connected (within the meaning that would be assigned by subsection 186(4) if the references in that subsection to "payer corporation" and "particular corporation" were read as "subject corporation" and "acquiring corporation", respectively) with the acquiring corporation, the contributed surplus of the acquiring corporation that arose on the acquisition of the subject shares shall be deemed to be the lesser of

(a) the amount added to the contributed surplus of the acquiring corporation on the acquisition of the subject shares, and

(b) the amount, if any, by which the paid-up capital in respect of the subject shares at the time of the acquisition exceeded the fair market value of any consideration given by the acquiring corporation for the subject shares.

Related Provisions: 84(10) — Reduction of contributed surplus; 186(7) — Interpretation of "connected".

Notes: 84(11) is intended to prevent circumvention of the anti-surplus-stripping rules in 84.1 and 212.1. Added by 1993 technical bill.

Interpretation Bulletins: IT-463R2: Paid-up capital.

Definitions [s. 84]: "amount" — 248(1); "arm's length" — 251(1); "bank", "business" — 248(1); "Canada" — 255; "class", "class of shares" — 248(6); "connected" — 186(4), (7); "contributed surplus" — 84(10), (11); "corporation" — 248(1), *Interpretation Act* 35(1); "dividend" — 248(1); "fair market value" — see 69(1) Notes; "insurance corporation" — 248(1); "investment" — 212.3(10); "month" — *Interpretation Act* 28, 35(1); "non-resident" — 248(1); "paid-up capital" — 89(1), 248(1); "particular corporation" — 186(4); "partnership" — see 96(1) Notes; "payable" — 84(7), 89(3); "payer corporation" — 186(4); "person", "prescribed" — 248(1); "private corporation", "public corporation" — 89(1), 248(1); "property" — 248(1); "received" — 248(7); "resident in Canada" — 94(3)(a), 250; "share", "shareholder", "specified financial institution" — 248(1); "subject corporation" — 84(11); "substituted" — 248(5); "taxable Canadian corporation" — 89(1), 248(1); "taxable income" — 2(2), 248(1); "term preferred share" — 248(1); "trust" — 104(1), 248(1), (3).

84.1 (1) Non-arm's length sale of shares

Where after May 22, 1985 a taxpayer resident in Canada (other than a corporation) disposes of shares that are capital property of the taxpayer (in this section referred to as the "subject shares") of any class of the capital stock of a corporation resident in Canada (in this section referred to as the "subject corporation") to another corporation (in this section referred to as the "purchaser corporation") with which the taxpayer does not deal at arm's length and, immediately after the disposition, the subject corporation would be connected (within the meaning assigned by subsection 186(4) if the references therein to "payer corporation" and to "particular corporation" were read as "subject corporation" and "purchaser corporation" respectively) with the purchaser corporation,

(a) where shares (in this section referred to as the "new shares") of the purchaser corporation have been issued as consideration for the subject shares, in computing the paid-up capital, at any particular time after the issue of the new shares, in respect of any particular class of shares of the capital stock of the purchaser corporation, there shall be deducted an amount determined by the formula

$$(A - B) \times \frac{C}{A}$$

where

A is the increase, if any, determined without reference to this section as it applies to the acquisition of the subject shares, in the paid-up capital in respect of all shares of the capital stock of the purchaser corporation as a result of the issue of the new shares,

B is the amount, if any, by which the greater of

(i) the paid-up capital, immediately before the disposition, in respect of the subject shares, and

(ii) subject to paragraphs (2)(a) and (a.1), the adjusted cost base to the taxpayer, immediately before the disposition, of the subject shares,

exceeds the fair market value, immediately after the disposition, of any consideration (other than the new shares) received by the taxpayer from the purchaser corporation for the subject shares, and

C is the increase, if any, determined without reference to this section as it applies to the acquisition of the subject shares, in the paid-up capital in respect of the particular class of shares as a result of the issue of the new shares; and

(b) for the purposes of this Act, a dividend shall be deemed to be paid to the taxpayer by the purchaser corporation and received by the taxpayer from the purchaser corporation at the time of the disposition in an amount determined by the formula

$$(A + D) - (E + F)$$

where

A is the increase, if any, determined without reference to this section as it applies to the acquisition of the subject shares, in the paid-up capital in respect of all shares of the capital stock of the purchaser corporation as a result of the issue of the new shares,

D is the fair market value, immediately after the disposition, of any consideration (other than the new shares) received by the taxpayer from the purchaser corporation for the subject shares,

E is the greater of

(i) the paid-up capital, immediately before the disposition, in respect of the subject shares, and

(ii) subject to paragraphs (2)(a) and (a.1), the adjusted cost base to the taxpayer, immediately before the disposition, of the subject shares, and

F is the total of all amounts each of which is an amount required to be deducted by the purchaser corporation under paragraph (a) in computing the paid-up capital in respect of any class of shares of its capital stock by virtue of the acquisition of the subject shares.

Abandoned Proposed Amendment — Converting private corporation's income to capital gains

Notes: Dept. of Finance consultation paper *Tax Planning Using Private Corporations*, July 18, 2017 (reproduced here in the 53rd ed.), proposed amendments to 84.1, and new 246.1, to catch "surplus stripping" that converts dividends to capital gains. The government abandoned these proposals, as announced in Finance news release and Backgrounder, Oct. 19, 2017 (also reproduced here in the 53rd ed.). (CRA will still apply GAAR to surplus stripping it considers abusive: see Notes to 84.1(1) below.) Related changes announced in July 2017 to extend the tax on income splitting (120.4) have proceeded with revisions; changes re passive income of private corporations (reproduced under 123.3 in the 53rd ed.) have been replaced by limitations on the small business deduction (125(5.1)(b)) and dividend refund (s. 129); changes to limit the capital gains exemption (110.6(12), (12.1), (17.1)-(18.1), (24)-(30.1)) have been dropped.

Related Provisions: 53(2)(a)(iii), 53(2)(p) — Reductions in adjusted cost base; 54"proceeds of disposition"(k) — Exclusion of deemed dividend from proceeds; 84(7) — When dividend payable; 84.1(2) — Non-arm's length sale of shares; 85(2.1) — Alternative reduction in paid-up capital of new shares; 89(1) — Definitions; 186(7) — Interpretation of "connected"; 212.1 — Similar rule for non-residents; 257 — Formula amounts cannot calculate to less than zero.

Notes: 84.1(1) is designed to prevent "surplus stripping" (extracting profits as tax-free return of capital rather than as taxable dividends). 84.1(1)(a) ensures that where shares with low paid-up capital (PUC) are transferred to a corporation (whether under s. 85 or not), the PUC of the acquiring corporation is not increased beyond the PUC of the shares transferred (except to the extent the adjusted cost base exceeds that PUC). This is consistent with the general scheme of the Act to permit PUC, which is essentially corporate "stated capital", to be extracted as return of capital. 85(2.1) and other provisions listed in 89(1)"paid-up capital"(b)(iii) have the same objective. See Notes to 84(3). 84.1(1)(b) creates a deemed dividend out of any "boot" (non-share consideration) that exceeds both PUC and ACB (double tax is avoided by 54"proceeds of disposition"(k)).

The Act has no general policy against surplus stripping, but in a given case it may violate GAAR: *Copthorne Holdings*, 2011 SCC 63, paras. 96, 118; *1245989 Alberta (Wild)*, 2018 FCA 114 (no GAAR, as benefit not yet realized); *Gwartz*, 2013 TCC 86, paras. 49-51. CRA disagrees and intends to show the Courts there is an "overall scheme against surplus stripping": docs 2012-0433261E5, 2014-0538091C6 [2014 APFF q.21]; 2013 Cdn Tax Foundation conference Roundtable (Mark Symes, noting that 75(2) strips as in *Brent Kern Family Trust* are "abusive"). See also Meredith and Fehr, "Surplus Stripping", 2013 British Columbia Tax Conf. (ctf.ca), 14:1-29; Demner & Lamothe, "The Future of Surplus Stripping", 2019 Ontario Tax Conference (ctf.ca), 99pp; Dishy & Anderson, "The Permissibility of Surplus Stripping", 69(1) *Canadian Tax Journal [CTJ]* 1-33 (2021). Proposed and then abandoned 246.1 (July 18, 2017 draft) would have largely resolved this issue for CRA; its withdrawal on Oct. 19, 2017 implies that the *Copthorne* SCC statement is still correct. For history of surplus stripping back to 1917, see Stikeman & Couzin, "Surplus Stripping", 43(5) *CTJ* 1844-60 (1995).

The reference in the opening words of 84.1(1) to "connected" as defined in 186(4) incorporates the meaning of "control" in 186(2). See 186(7).

84.1(1)(b) deems a dividend "to be paid", but not "on a share", so CRA's view *was* that this deemed dividend (84.1DD) is not eligible for the 129(1) dividend refund (VIEWS doc 2002-0128955, reversing 9729855); however, at 2019-0819401C6 [2019 APFF q.1] and 2019-0824521C6 [2019 CTF q.4], CRA reversed this and said that granting a dividend refund on an 84.1DD "is more in accordance with the integration principle" [Hirji & Keung, "Planning Possibilities Resulting from CRA Policy Reversal", 20(1) *Tax for the Owner-Manager* (ctf.ca) 8-9 (Jan. 2020)]. 2002-0128955 also says an 84.1DD cannot be a capital dividend unless the transferor was already a shareholder of the transferee corp; CRA has confirmed that this view is unchanged (see Notes to 83(2)). An 84.1DD can be an "eligible dividend" under 89(1): 2012-0454091C6. An 84.1DD is deemed paid and so cannot become a bad debt: see Notes to 20(1)(p) re *Mills* case.

84.1(1) applied in *Fiducie Famille Gauthier*, 2012 FCA 76, *Létourneau*, 2007 TCC 91 and *Emory*, 2010 TCC 71; and was held not to apply in *Brouillette*, 2005 TCC 203 and *McMullen*, 2007 TCC 16. GAAR (245(2)) applied to avoidance of 84.1(1) in both *Descarries*, 2014 TCC 75 (capital loss reduced deemed dividend) and *Pomerleau*, 2018 FCA 129 (loss shifted using 40(3.6)) [Hamelin, "Surplus Stripping", 18(4) *Tax for the Owner-Manager* (ctf.ca) 7-8 (Oct. 2018)]. In *Poulin*, 2016 TCC 154 (aff'd as *Turgeon*, 2017 FCA 103), 84.1(1) applied to one shareholder (held to be acting in concert with the corp) but not to another (at arm's length with it); for CRA comment see 2016-0669661C6 [2016 CTF q.6]; doc 2016-0655831C6 [2016 APFF q.20]. In light of *Descarries*, CRA will now apply GAAR in cases similar to 2005-0134731R3 (step up ACB via capital gains exemption, then redeem shares for deemed dividend and capital loss): 2015-0595631C6 [2015 APFF q.14], 2015-0610711C6 [2015 CTF q.11], even on intergenerational transfer of a family business: 2016-0633351E5.

See Lamarre et al., *Taxation of Corporate Reorganizations* (Carswell, 3rd ed., 2019), §5.1; Schweitzer & Nurmohamed, "Accommodating Employees and Section 84.1: a Trap for the Unwary Employer", 17(2) *Taxation of Executive Compensation & Retirement* (Federated Press) 579-82 (Sept. 2005); Diksic, "Selected Issues in Purchase and Sale Transactions", 2005 Cdn Tax Foundation conference report, at 43:1-6; Richard Kirby, "Section 84.1 Again: *Brouillette*", 6(1) *Tax for the Owner-Manager* (ctf.ca) 8-9 (Jan. 2006); Kraft & Kraft, "The Application of Section 84.1", 60(2) *Canadian Tax Journal* 449-70 (2012); Blucher, "Non-Arm's Length Share Sales", 9(6) *Tax Hyperion* (Carswell) 4-5 (June 2012); Dergousoff, "Employee Buyco Transactions", 3(4) *Canadian Tax Focus* (ctf.ca) 2-3 (Nov. 2013); Engel, "A Review of Common Mistakes and Errors", 2015 Prairie Provinces Tax Conf. (ctf.ca) at 7:1-13; Moody, "Inter-Generational Business Transfers", XXIV(3) *Insurance Planning* (Federated Press) 14-16 (2019).

For non-residents, the parallel rule is 212.1. See 212.1(1) Notes.

84.1(1) does not apply to arm's-length transactions: *McMullen* (above), but CRA will apply it if the purchaser corp acts as facilitator to avoid 84.1: May 2008 ICAA roundtable (tinyurl.com/cra-abtax), q. 7. Surplus stripping via an arm's-length sale may not violate GAAR: see *Evans*, 2005 TCC 684 and *Brouillette* (above) (superseding *McNichol* and *RMM Canadian*); but see also *Desmarais*, 2006 TCC 44, where setting up a 9.8% holding in a company to avoid being "connected" (see 84.1(1) opening words) violated GAAR. See Taylor, "Surplus Stripping and GAAR Revisited", XIII(4) *Tax Litigation* (Federated Press) 834-38 (2006); Crosbie, "*Copthorne* and Collins & Aikman", XVI(1) *Corporate Finance* (Federated Press) 1759-66 (2009); Durand & Gwyer, "Surplus Stripping and Domestic Private Corporations", 2012 Cdn Tax Foundation conference report, 13:1-20.

See also VIEWS docs 2005-0163621E5, 2006-0170641E5, 2006-0178061R3, 2006-0198561R3, 2007-0228281E5; 2007-0237511R3 (84.1(1)(b) deemed dividend not affected by 69(1)(b)(i)); 2007-0243171C6 (interpretation of arm's length test); 2008-0287611E5 (84.1(1) applies to dividend strip); 2008-0288221R3 (post-mortem bump: no 84.1(1)); 2010-0378681E5 (84.1(1) applies); 2010-0382651E5 (84.1(1) applies); 2010-0370611E5 and 2010-0373221C6 (whether GAAR applies to share exchange that increases PUC [see Ryan Keey, "PUC Enhancement Transactions", 8(4) *Tax Hyperion* (Carswell, April 2011]); 2010-0384371R3, 2010-0388591R3 (84.1(1) will not apply); 2010-0387211R3 (same); 2011-0412121C6 (interaction with 85(2.1)); 2012-0443421E5 (individual transfers shares to partnership P, then sells interest in P to holdco and P winds up); 2013-0479402C6 [2012 CTF conf.] (employee buyco); 2015-

0602751E5 (interaction with capital gains exemption); 2020-0852281R3 (55(3)(a) reorg: 84.1(1)(b) will not apply); 2020-0854401R3 (internal reorg); 2020-0868661R3 (leveraged buyout approved). See Notes to 84(2) re post-mortem pipeline.

In doc 2010-0374211R3, the CRA refused a ruling on "abusive dividend stripping", saying it would apply GAAR as well as 84.1.

Juliar, [2001] 4 C.T.C. 45 (Ont CA) (leave to appeal denied 2001 CarswellOnt 1805 (SCC)), allowed rectification to implement intended tax savings and avoid 84.1(1). *Juliar* was overruled in *Fairmont Hotels* (see Notes to 169(1) under "Rectification"); but in *Crean*, 2019 BCSC 146, rectification was again allowed to avoid 84.1 because the parties explicitly sought a capital gain.

84.1(1) amended by 1991 technical bill, effective for dispositions after May 22, 1985.

Interpretation Bulletins: IT-67R3: Taxable dividends from corporations resident in Canada; IT-489R: Non-arm's length sale of shares to a corporation.

Information Circulars: 88-2 Supplement, paras. 4, 9: General anti-avoidance rule — section 245 of the *Income Tax Act*.

Advance Tax Rulings: ATR-27: Exchange and acquisition of interests in capital properties through rollovers and winding-up ("butterfly"); ATR-32: Rollover of fixed assets from Opco into Holdco; ATR-35: Partitioning of assets to get specific ownership — "butterfly"; ATR-36: Estate freeze; ATR-42: Transfer of shares; ATR-55: Amalgamation followed by sale of shares; ATR-57: Transfer of property for estate planning purposes.

(2) Idem — For the purposes of this section,

(a) where a share disposed of by a taxpayer was acquired by the taxpayer before 1972, the adjusted cost base to the taxpayer of the share at any time shall be deemed to be the total of

(i) the amount that would be its adjusted cost base to the taxpayer if the *Income Tax Application Rules* were read without reference to subsections 26(3) and (7) of that Act, and

(ii) the total of all amounts each of which is an amount received by the taxpayer after 1971 and before that time as a dividend on the share and in respect of which the corporation that paid the dividend has made an election under subsection 83(1);

(a.1) where a share disposed of by a taxpayer was acquired by the taxpayer after 1971 from a person with whom the taxpayer was not dealing at arm's length, was a share substituted for such a share or was a share substituted for a share owned by the taxpayer at the end of 1971, the adjusted cost base to the taxpayer of the share at any time shall be deemed to be the amount, if any, by which its adjusted cost base to the taxpayer, otherwise determined, exceeds the total of

(i) where the share or a share for which the share was substituted was owned at the end of 1971 by the taxpayer or a person with whom the taxpayer did not deal at arm's length, the amount in respect of that share equal to the amount, if any, by which

(A) the fair market value of the share or the share for which it was substituted, as the case may be, on valuation day (within the meaning assigned by section 24 of the *Income Tax Application Rules*)

exceeds the total of

(B) the actual cost (within the meaning assigned by subsection 26(13) of that Act) of the share or the share for which it was substituted, as the case may be, on January 1, 1972, to the taxpayer or the person with whom the taxpayer did not deal at arm's length, and

(C) the total of all amounts each of which is an amount received by the taxpayer or the person with whom the taxpayer did not deal at arm's length after 1971 and before that time as a dividend on the share or the share for which it was substituted and in respect of which the corporation that paid the dividend has made an election under subsection 83(1), and

(ii) the total of all amounts each of which is an amount determined after 1984 under subparagraph 40(1)(a)(i) in respect of a previous disposition of the share or a share for which the share was substituted (or such lesser amount as is established by the taxpayer to be the amount in respect of which a deduction under section 110.6 was claimed) by the taxpayer or an individual with whom the taxpayer did not deal at arm's length;

(a.2) [Repealed]

(b) in respect of any disposition described in subsection (1) by a taxpayer of shares of the capital stock of a subject corporation to a purchaser corporation, the taxpayer shall, for greater certainty, be deemed not to deal at arm's length with the purchaser corporation if the taxpayer

    (i) was, immediately before the disposition, one of a group of fewer than 6 persons that controlled the subject corporation, and

    (ii) was, immediately after the disposition, one of a group of fewer than 6 persons that controlled the purchaser corporation, each member of which was a member of the group referred to in subparagraph (i);

(c) [Repealed]

(d) a trust and a beneficiary of the trust or a person related to a beneficiary of the trust shall be deemed not to deal with each other at arm's length; and

(e) if the subject shares are qualified small business corporation shares or "shares of the capital stock of a family farm or fishing corporation" within the meaning of subsection 110.6(1), the taxpayer and the purchaser corporation are deemed to be dealing at arm's length if the purchaser corporation is controlled by one or more children or grandchildren of the taxpayer who are 18 years of age or older and if the purchaser corporation does not dispose of the subject shares within 60 months of their purchase.

Proposed Amendment — 84.1(2)(e), 84.1(2.3) and 55(5)(e) — Application date

Dept. of Finance news release, June 30, 2021: *Government of Canada provides details on next steps for Private Member's Bill C-208*

Private Member's Bill C-208 has passed in both Houses of Parliament and received Royal Assent. Bill C-208 makes amendments to the *Income Tax Act* but does not include an application date.

The federal government is committed to facilitating genuine intergenerational share transfers, while preventing tax avoidance that undermines the equity of Canada's tax system.

The government proposes to introduce legislation to clarify that these amendments would apply at the beginning of the next taxation year, starting on January 1, 2022.

Contacts

Media may contact: Media Relations, Department of Finance Canada, mediare@fin.gc.ca, 613-369-4000. General enquiries: 1-833-712-2292, financepublic-financepublique@fin.gc.ca

Notes: This does not "clarify" the Bill C-208 amendments; rather, it *changes* them by delaying their application. Amendments that do not specify an application date take effect on Royal Assent — June 29, 2021 in this case. Finance is doing what it can to undermine the effect of this Private Member's Bill, which it opposed.

Related Provisions: 84.1(2.01) — Rules for 84.1(2)(a.1); 84.1(2.1) — Where capital gains reserve claimed; 84.1(2.2) — Rules for 84.1(2)(b); 84.1(2.3) — Limitations on rule in 84.1(2)(e); 256(6), (6.1) — Meaning of "controlled".

Notes: The effect of the reduction in (a.1) is to allow the adjusted cost base of a share to be increased on a non-arm's length transfer only to the extent that any capital gain arising on that transfer was taxed (and, for 84.1(2)(a.1)(ii), see 53(2)(a)(iii)). For interpretation of 84.1(2)(a.1) see VIEWS docs 2005-0163621E5, 2015-0595561C6 [2015 APFF q.7]; of 84.1(2)(b), see 2010-0368161I7.

84.1(2)(e) added by 2021 family business transfers bill, effective June 29, 2021. This was a **private Member's bill** (C-208), which amended 55(5)(e)(i) and added 84.1(2)(e) and 84.1(2.3). It is rare for a private Member's bill to be enacted, and extraordinarily rare for one to be enacted with technical ITA amendments that overrule Finance's wishes. The official Parliamentary summary to the bill reads:

> This enactment amends the *Income Tax Act* in order to provide that, in the case of qualified small business corporation shares and shares of the capital stock of a family farm or fishing corporation, siblings are deemed not to be dealing at arm's length and to be related *[55(5)(e)(i) — ed.]* and that, under certain conditions, the transfer of those shares by a taxpayer to the taxpayer's child or grandchild who is 18 years of age or older is to be excluded from the anti-avoidance rule of section 84.1 *[84.1(2)(e), 84.1(2.3) — ed.]*.

The bill was sponsored by Larry Maguire, the Conservative MP for Brandon-Souris, Manitoba. He stated in Parliament on May 12, 2021:

> Mr. Speaker, later this afternoon we will have the final vote on my private member's bill, Bill C-208. The purpose of this bill is straightforward. It will level the playing field by giving families the exact same tax treatment when they transfer their businesses or operations to their children as when they transfer it to a stranger. It would result in more locally owned and operated businesses, the type of businesses that are deeply involved in their communities and provide steady employment for countless individuals.

> Bill C-208 sends a message of hope to young farmers who want to carry on what their families started. No longer will parents be given the false choice of having to choose between a larger retirement package after selling to a stranger, or a massive tax bill after selling to a family member, their own child or grandchild.

> I urge all members to vote in favour of Bill C-208 and bring tax fairness to the *Income Tax Act* for all qualifying small businesses.

Wayne Easter, Liberal MP for Malpeque, PEI and Chair of the Commons Finance Committee, stated in Parliament on May 5, 2021:

> Bill C-208 has a long history, and it criss-crosses the political landscape. It was first introduced by the current member of Parliament for Bourassa, a Liberal, two parliaments ago. In the last Parliament, the same bill was brought forward by Guy Caron, an NDP member. Now, in this current Parliament, it is sponsored by the member for Brandon-Souris, a Conservative member.

> This long history, across all major political parties in the House, certainly shows that there is a need to bring fairness and equity from a taxation perspective to the transfer of family farm corporations, fisheries enterprises and small family businesses. Quite honestly, it is long past time that this problem was fixed.

> During an earlier discussion at third reading, it was suggested by the government spokesman that just maybe the bill could provide opportunities for tax avoidance. I would agree that tax avoidance is a legitimate concern. However, I must point out that at the finance committee we heard from 17 witnesses, and every opportunity was given to address the concern of tax avoidance. We called on the public and Finance Canada to provide witnesses and propose amendments, to anybody who had those kinds of concerns.

> I certainly appreciate that the assistant deputy minister of the tax policy branch and the senior director of the tax legislation division in the tax policy branch appeared and answered questions, and their comments appear in the transcript for the finance committee for anybody who wants to see it. To be fair, they did outline some concerns, especially as it relates to what is called "surplus stripping" for the purpose of tax avoidance.

> ..... [an] example was a father wanting to sell his farm to his son to fund his retirement. If the father were to sell his farm to a stranger, he could use his capital gains exemption on the sale, resulting in an effective tax rate of 13.39%. However, if the farmer sold his farm to his son, that sale would be recorded as a dividend rather than a capital gain, and the farmer would pay 47.4% in tax. That is a huge difference, and I think we can all agree that it is completely unfair.

> ..... this is an issue of equity and fairness. Business owners should not be penalized for selling their business to a family member. Tax implications should never be a consideration when making the decision to sell a business to a family member.

(For more detail, see the full Hansard quote in *Department of Finance Technical Notes*, or in the "Technical Notes" section on Taxnet Pro.) See also Fong & Loney, "Bill C-208: Long-Awaited Relief For Family Businesses And Intergenerational Transfers" (June 2021), tinyurl.com/fong-loney; Sweeney, Fowlis & Brayley, "New taxation rules impacting transfers of family businesses to the next generation; Everything you thought you knew about intergenerational transfers is now wrong", tinyurl.com/c208-miller; and the Proposed Amendment above.

84.1(2) amended by 1995-97 technical bill (last change effective June 18, 1998), 1992 and 1991 technical bills. (84.1(2)(a.2) was moved to 84.1(2.01)(a).)

Interpretation Bulletins: IT-67R3: Taxable dividends from corporations resident in Canada; IT-489R: Non-arm's length sale of shares to a corporation.

Advance Tax Rulings: ATR-42: Transfer of shares; ATR-55: Amalgamation followed by sale of shares.

(2.01) Rules for para. 84.1(2)(a.1) — For the purpose of paragraph (2)(a.1),

(a) where at any time a corporation issues a share of its capital stock to a taxpayer, the taxpayer and the corporation are deemed not to be dealing with each other at arm's length at that time;

(b) where a taxpayer is deemed by paragraph 110.6(19)(a) to have reacquired a share, the taxpayer is deemed to have acquired the share at the beginning of February 23, 1994 from a person with whom the taxpayer was not dealing at arm's length; and

(c) where a share owned by a particular person, or a share substituted for that share, has by one or more transactions or events between persons not dealing at arm's length become vested in another person, the particular person and the other person are deemed at all times not to be dealing at arm's length with each other whether or not the particular person and the other person coexisted.

Notes: 84.1(2.01) added by 1995-97 technical bill, last change effective for determination of a share's ACB after June 20, 1996. Para. (a) was previously in 84.1(2)(a.1).

(2.1) Idem — For the purposes of subparagraph (2)(a.1)(ii), where the taxpayer or an individual with whom the taxpayer did not deal at arm's length (in this subsection referred to as the "transferor") disposes of a share in a taxation year and claims an amount under subparagraph 40(1)(a)(iii) in computing the gain for the year from the disposition, the amount in respect of which a deduction under section 110.6 was claimed in respect of the transferor's gain from the disposition shall be deemed to be equal to the lesser of

(a) the total of

(i) the amount claimed under subparagraph 40(1)(a)(iii) by the transferor for the year in respect of the disposition, and

(ii) twice the amount deducted under section 110.6 in computing the taxable income of the transferor for the year in respect of the taxable capital gain from the disposition, and

(b) twice the maximum amount that could have been deducted under section 110.6 in computing the taxable income of the transferor for the year in respect of the taxable capital gain from the disposition if

(i) no amount had been claimed by the transferor under subparagraph 40(1)(a)(iii) in computing the gain for the year from the disposition, and

(ii) all amounts deducted under section 110.6 in computing the taxable income of the transferor for the year in respect of taxable capital gains from dispositions of property to which this subsection does not apply were deducted before determining the maximum amount that could have been deducted under section 110.6 in respect of the taxable capital gain from the disposition,

and, for the purposes of subparagraph (ii), ½ of the total of all amounts determined under this subsection for the year in respect of other property disposed of before the disposition of the share shall be deemed to have been deducted under section 110.6 in computing the taxable income of the transferor for the year in respect of the taxable capital gain from the disposition of property to which this subsection does not apply,

and, for the purposes of this subsection, where more than one share to which this subsection applies is disposed of in the year, each such share shall be deemed to have been separately disposed of in the order designated by the taxpayer in the taxpayer's return of income under this Part for the year.

Notes: For CRA interpretation see docs 2015-0594461E5 and 2018-0744141C6 [STEP 2018 q.17] (84.1(2.1) applies to deem capital gains exemption claimed even if not claimed due to 40(1)(a)(iii) reserve).

For the closing words of 84.1(2.1), an election "in the taxpayer's return" is valid even if the return is filed late. See Notes to 7(1.31).

See also Jin Wen & Michelle Dickinson, "Are Shares Tainted Forever Under Subsection 84.1(2.1)?", 8(4) *Canadian Tax Focus* (ctf.ca) 15 (Nov. 2018).

For a taxpayer filing Quebec returns, a designation under the closing words of 84.1(2.1) must be copied to Revenu Québec: *Taxation Act* ss. 517.4.5, 21.4.6.

84.1(2.1) amended by 2000 Budget, for taxation years ending after Oct. 17, 2000. Added by 1991 technical bill, effective for dispositions after July 13, 1990.

(2.2) Rules for para. 84.1(2)(b) — For the purpose of paragraph (2)(b),

(a) in determining whether or not a taxpayer referred to in that paragraph was a member of a group of fewer than 6 persons that controlled a corporation at any time, any shares of the capital stock of that corporation owned at that time by

(i) the taxpayer's child (as defined in subsection 70(10)), who is under 18 years of age, or the taxpayer's spouse or common-law partner,

(ii) a trust of which the taxpayer, a person described in subparagraph (i) or a corporation described in subparagraph (iii), is a beneficiary, or

(iii) a corporation controlled by the taxpayer, by a person described in subparagraph (i) or (ii) or by any combination of those persons or trusts

are deemed to be owned at that time by the taxpayer and not by the person who actually owned the shares at that time;

(b) a group of persons in respect of a corporation means any 2 or more persons each of whom owns shares of the capital stock of the corporation;

(c) a corporation that is controlled by one or more members of a particular group of persons in respect of that corporation is considered to be controlled by that group of persons; and

(d) a corporation may be controlled by a person or a particular group of persons even though the corporation is also controlled or deemed to be controlled by another person or group of persons.

Related Provisions: 256(6), (6.1) — Extended meaning of "controlled".

Notes: For interpretation of "group" in 84.1(2.2)(b) see VIEWS docs 9305575, 9406355, 2010-0368161I7 (shares do not have to be voting shares).

84.1(2.2)(a)(i) amended by 2000 same-sex partners bill to refer to "common-law partner", effective 2001 (or earlier).

84.1(2.2) added by 1995-97 technical bill, effective June 18, 1998. These rules were formerly in 84.1(2)(c) and (e).

(2.3) Rules for para. 84.1(2)(e) — For the purposes of paragraph (2)(e),

(a) if, otherwise than by reason of death, the purchaser corporation disposes of the subject shares within 60 months of their purchase:

(i) paragraph (2)(e) is deemed never to have applied,

(ii) the taxpayer is deemed, for the purposes of this section, to have disposed of the subject shares to the person who acquired them from the purchaser corporation, and

(iii) the period of 60 months applicable to the operation that is deemed to have taken place under subparagraph (ii) is deemed to have begun when the taxpayer disposed of the subject shares to the purchaser corporation;

(b) the deduction referred to in subsection 110.6(2) or (2.1) is, for a particular taxation year, the amount, if any, by which that deduction exceeds the amount determined by the formula:

$$A \times B / \$11,250$$

where

A is the amount that would, but for this subsection, be the capital gains deduction referred to in subsection 110.6(2) or (2.1) for the particular taxation year; and

B is the amount determined by the formula

$$0.00225 \times (D - \$10 \text{ million})$$

where

D is

(a) if, in both the particular taxation year and the preceding taxation year, the corporation is not associated with any corporation, the taxable capital employed in Canada (within the meaning assigned by subsection 181.2(1) or 181.3(1) or section 181.4, as the case may be) of the corporation for the preceding taxation year,

(b) if, in the particular taxation year, the corporation is not associated with any corporation but was associated with one or more corporations in the preceding taxation year, the taxable capital employed in Canada (within the meaning assigned by subsection 181.2(1) or 181.3(1) or section 181.4, as the case may be) of the corporation for the particular taxation year, or

(c) if, in the particular taxation year, the corporation is associated with one or more particular corporations, the total of all amounts each of which is the taxable capital employed in Canada (within the meaning assigned by subsection 181.2(1) or 181.3(1) or section 181.4, as the case may be) of the corporation or of any of the particular corporations for its last taxation year that ended in the preceding calendar year; and

(c) the taxpayer must provide the Minister with an independent assessment of the fair market value of the subject shares and an affidavit signed by the taxpayer and by a third party attesting to the disposal of the shares.

(3) Addition to paid-up capital — In computing the paid-up capital at any time after May 22, 1985 in respect of any class of shares of the capital stock of a corporation, there shall be added an amount equal to the lesser of

(a) the amount, if any, by which

(i) the total of all amounts each of which is an amount deemed by subsection 84(3), (4) or (4.1) to be a dividend on shares of the class paid after May 22, 1985 and before that time by the corporation

exceeds

(ii) the total of such dividends that would be determined under subparagraph (i) if this Act were read without reference to paragraph (1)(a), and

(b) the total of all amounts required by paragraph (1)(a) to be deducted in computing the paid-up capital in respect of that class of shares after May 22, 1985 and before that time.

Interpretation Bulletins: IT-67R3: Taxable dividends from corporations resident in Canada; IT-489R: Non-arm's length sale of shares to a corporation.

Definitions [s. 84.1]: "adjusted cost base" — 54, 248(1); "amount" — 248(1); "arm's length" — 84.1(2)(b), (d), 84.1(2.01)(a), (c), 251(1); "associated" — 256; "calendar year" — *Interpretation Act* 37(1)(a); "child" — 70(10), 252(1); "class of shares" — 248(6); "common-law partner" — 248(1); "connected" — 186(4), (7); "control" — 84.1(2.2)(c), (d); "controlled" — 256(6), (6.1); "corporation" — 248(1), *Interpretation Act* 35(1); "dividend", "fishing" — 248(1); "group" — 84.1(2.2)(a), (b); "fair market value" — see 69(1) Notes; "individual", "Minister" — 248(1); "month" — *Interpretation Act* 35(1); "new shares" — 84.1(1)(a); "paid-up capital" — 84.1(3), 89(1), 248(1); "particular corporation", "payer corporation" — 186(4); "person" — 248(1); "private corporation" — 89(1), 248(1); "purchaser corporation" — 84.1(1); "resident in Canada" — 94(3)(a), 250; "share" — 248(1); "shares of the capital stock of a family farm or fishing corporation" — 110.6(1); "small business corporation" — 248(1); "subject corporation", "subject shares" — 84.1(1); "substituted" — 248(5); "taxable capital employed in Canada" — 181.2(1), 181.3(1), 181.4; "taxable income" — 2(2), 248(1); "taxation year" — 249; "taxpayer" — 248(1); "trust" — 104(1), 248(1), (3).

84.2 (1) Computation of paid-up capital in respect of particular class of shares — In computing the paid-up capital in respect of any particular class of shares of the capital stock of a corporation at any particular time after March 31, 1977,

(a) there shall be deducted that proportion of the amount, if any, by which the paid-up capital in respect of all of the issued shares of the capital stock of the corporation on April 1, 1977, determined without reference to this section, exceeds the greater of

(i) the amount that the paid-up capital limit of the corporation would have been on March 31, 1977 if paragraph 89(1)(d) of the *Income Tax Act*, chapter 148 of the Revised Statutes of Canada, 1952, as it read at that date, were read without reference to clause 89(1)(d)(iv.1)(F) of that Act and without reference to all subparagraphs of paragraph 89(1)(d) of that Act except subparagraphs 89(1)(d)(iv.1) and (vii) of that Act, and

(ii) the paid-up capital limit of the corporation on March 31, 1977,

that the paid-up capital on April 1, 1977, determined without reference to this section, in respect of the particular class of shares is of the paid-up capital on April 1, 1977, determined without reference to this section, in respect of all of the issued and outstanding shares of the capital stock of the corporation; and

(b) there shall be added an amount equal to the lesser of

(i) the amount, if any, by which

(A) the total of all amounts each of which is an amount deemed by subsection 84(3) or (4) to be a dividend on shares of the particular class paid by the corporation after March 31, 1977 and before the particular time

exceeds

(B) the total that would be determined under clause (A) if this Act were read without reference to paragraph (a), and

(ii) the amount required by paragraph (a) to be deducted in computing the paid-up capital of shares of the particular class.

Related Provisions: 84.1 — Non-arm's length sale of shares.

I.T. Application Rules: 69 (meaning of "chapter 148 of ...").

(2) Debt deficiency — In computing, after March 31, 1977, the adjusted cost base to an individual of a debt that was owing to the individual by a corporation on March 31, 1977, there shall be deducted the amount of any dividend that would have been deemed to have been received by the individual on that day if the corporation had paid the debt in full on that day.

Related Provisions: 53(2)(p) — Deduction from ACB; 84.2(3) — Where debt converted to shares.

(3) Idem — Where, after March 31, 1977 and before 1979, any debt referred to in subsection (2) owing by a corporation and held by an individual on March 31, 1977 and continuously after that date until conversion, is converted into shares of a particular class of the capital stock of the corporation,

(a) subsection (2) shall not apply in respect of the debt; and

(b) in computing the paid-up capital in respect of the shares of the particular class at any particular time after the conversion,

(i) there shall be deducted the amount by which the adjusted cost base to the taxpayer of the debt would, but for paragraph (a), have been reduced by virtue of subsection (2), and

(ii) there shall be added an amount equal to the lesser of

(A) the amount, if any, by which

(I) the total of all amounts deemed by subsection 84(3), (4) or (4.1) to be a dividend on shares of the particular class paid by the corporation after the conversion and before the particular time,

exceeds

(II) the total that would be determined under subclause (I) if this Act were read without reference to subparagraph (i), and

(B) the amount required by subparagraph (i) to be deducted in computing the paid-up capital of shares of the particular class.

Definitions [s. 84.2]: "adjusted cost base" — 54, 248(1); "amount" — 248(1); "class of shares" — 248(6); "corporation" — 248(1), *Interpretation Act* 35(1); "dividend" — 248(1); "paid-up capital" — 89(1), 248(1); "share" — 248(1); "taxation year" — 249; "taxpayer" — 248(1).

85. (1) Transfer of property to corporation by shareholders [rollover] — Where a taxpayer has, in a taxation year, disposed of any of the taxpayer's property that was eligible property to a taxable Canadian corporation for consideration that includes shares of the capital stock of the corporation, if the taxpayer and the corporation have jointly elected in prescribed form and in accordance with subsection (6), the following rules apply:

(a) **[elected amount deemed to be proceeds and cost]** — the amount that the taxpayer and the corporation have agreed on in their election in respect of the property shall be deemed to be the taxpayer's proceeds of disposition of the property and the corporation's cost of the property;

(b) **[elected amount not less than boot]** — subject to paragraph (c), where the amount that the taxpayer and the corporation have agreed on in their election in respect of the property is less than the fair market value, at the time of the disposition, of the consideration therefor (other than any shares of the capital stock of the corporation or a right to receive any such shares) received by the taxpayer, the amount so agreed on shall, irrespective of the amount actually so agreed on by them, be deemed to be an amount equal to that fair market value;

(c) **[elected amount not more than FMV of property transferred]** — where the amount that the taxpayer and the corporation have agreed on in their election in respect of the property is greater than the fair market value, at the time of the disposition, of the property so disposed of, the amount so agreed on shall, irrespective of the amount actually so agreed on, be deemed to be an amount equal to that fair market value;

(c.1) **[elected amount minimum — most property]** — where the property was inventory, capital property (other than depreciable property of a prescribed class), a NISA Fund No. 2 or a property that is eligible property because of paragraph (1.1)(g) or (g.1), and the amount that the taxpayer and corporation have agreed on in their election in respect of the property is less than the lesser of

(i) the fair market value of the property at the time of the disposition, and

(ii) the cost amount to the taxpayer of the property at the time of the disposition,

the amount so agreed on shall, irrespective of the amount actually so agreed on by them, be deemed to be an amount equal to the lesser of the amounts described in subparagraphs (i) and (ii);

(c.2) **[elected amount — farm inventory]** — subject to paragraphs (b) and (c) and notwithstanding paragraph (c.1), where the taxpayer carries on a farming business the income from which is computed in accordance with the cash method and the property was inventory owned in connection with that business immediately before the particular time the property was disposed of to the corporation,

(i) the amount that the taxpayer and the corporation agreed on in their election in respect of inventory purchased by the taxpayer shall be deemed to be equal to the amount determined by the formula

$$\left(A \times \frac{B}{C} \right) + D$$

where

A   is the amount that would be included because of paragraph 28(1)(c) in computing the taxpayer's income for the taxpayer's last taxation year beginning before the particular time if that year had ended immediately before the particular time,

B   is the value (determined in accordance with subsection 28(1.2)) to the taxpayer immediately before the particular time of the purchased inventory in respect of which the election is made,

C   is the value (determined in accordance with subsection 28(1.2)) of all of the inventory purchased by the taxpayer that was owned by the taxpayer in connection with that business immediately before the particular time, and

D   is such additional amount as the taxpayer and the corporation designate in respect of the property,

(ii) for the purpose of subparagraph 28(1)(a)(i), the disposition of the property and the receipt of proceeds of disposition therefor shall be deemed to have occurred at the particular time and in the course of carrying on the business, and

(iii) where the property is owned by the corporation in connection with a farming business and the income from that business is computed in accordance with the cash method, for the purposes of section 28,

(A) an amount equal to the cost to the corporation of the property shall be deemed to have been paid by the corporation, and

(B) the corporation shall be deemed to have purchased the property for an amount equal to that cost,

at the particular time and in the course of carrying on that business;

(d)–(d.12) [eligible capital property — repealed]

(e) **[elected amount minimum — depreciable property]** — where the property was depreciable property of a prescribed class of the taxpayer and the amount that, but for this paragraph, would be the proceeds of disposition thereof is less than the least of

(i) the undepreciated capital cost to the taxpayer of all property of that class immediately before the disposition,

(ii) the cost to the taxpayer of the property, and

(iii) the fair market value of the property at the time of the disposition,

the amount agreed on by the taxpayer and the corporation in their election in respect of the property shall, irrespective of the amount actually so agreed on by them, be deemed to be the least of the amounts described in subparagraphs (i) to (iii);

(e.1) **[order of dispositions]** — where two or more properties, each of which is a property described in paragraph (e), are disposed of at the same time, paragraph (e) applies as if each property so disposed of had been separately disposed of in the order designated by the taxpayer before the time referred to in subsection (6) for the filing of an election in respect of those properties or, if the taxpayer does not so designate any such order, in the order designated by the Minister;

(e.2) **[where excess is benefit to related person]** — where the fair market value of the property immediately before the disposition exceeds the greater of

(i) the fair market value, immediately after the disposition, of the consideration received by the taxpayer for the property disposed of by the taxpayer, and

(ii) the amount that the taxpayer and the corporation have agreed on in their election in respect of the property, determined without reference to this paragraph,

and it is reasonable to regard any part of the excess as a benefit that the taxpayer desired to have conferred on a person related to the taxpayer (other than a corporation that was a wholly owned corporation of the taxpayer immediately after the disposition), the amount that the taxpayer and the corporation agreed on in their election in respect of the property shall, regardless of the amount actually so agreed on by them, be deemed (except for the purposes of paragraphs (g) and (h)) to be an amount equal to the total of the amount referred to in subparagraph (ii) and that part of the excess;

(e.3) **[conflict between deeming rules and para. (b)]** — where, under any of paragraphs (c.1) and (e), the amount that the taxpayer and the corporation have agreed on in their election in respect of the property (in this paragraph referred to as the "elected amount") would be deemed to be an amount that is greater or less than the amount that would be deemed, subject to paragraph (c), to be the elected amount under paragraph (b), the elected amount is deemed to be the greater of

(i) the amount deemed by paragraph (c.1) or (e), as the case may be, to be the elected amount, and

(ii) the amount deemed by paragraph (b) to be the elected amount;

(e.4) **[transfer of automobile costing over $30,000]** — where

(i) the property is depreciable property of a prescribed class of the taxpayer and is a passenger vehicle the cost to the taxpayer of which was more than $20,000 or such other amount as may be prescribed, and

(ii) the taxpayer and the corporation do not deal at arm's length,

the amount that the taxpayer and the corporation have agreed on in their election in respect of the property shall be deemed to be an amount equal to the undepreciated capital cost to the taxpayer of the class immediately before the disposition, except that, for the purposes of subsection 6(2), the cost to the corporation of the vehicle shall be deemed to be an amount equal to its fair market value immediately before the disposition;

(e.5) **[transfer of zero-emission automobile costing over $55,000]** — if the property is depreciable property of a prescribed class of the taxpayer that is a zero-emission passenger vehicle to which paragraph 13(7)(i) applies and the taxpayer and the corporation do not deal at arm's length,

(i) the amount that the taxpayer and the corporation have agreed on in their election in respect of the vehicle is deemed to be an amount equal to the cost amount to the taxpayer of the vehicle immediately before the disposition, and

(ii) for the purposes of subsection 6(2), the cost to the corporation of the vehicle is deemed to be an amount equal to its fair market value immediately before the disposition;

(f) **[deemed cost of boot]** — the cost to the taxpayer of any particular property (other than shares of the capital stock of the corporation or a right to receive any such shares) received by the taxpayer as consideration for the disposition shall be deemed to be an amount equal to the lesser of

(i) the fair market value of the particular property at the time of the disposition, and

(ii) that proportion of the fair market value, at the time of the disposition, of the property disposed of by the taxpayer to the corporation that

(A) the amount determined under subparagraph (i)

is of

(B) the fair market value, at the time of the disposition, of all properties (other than shares of the capital stock of the corporation or a right to receive any such shares) received by the taxpayer as consideration for the disposition;

(g) **[deemed cost of preferred shares]** — the cost to the taxpayer of any preferred shares of any class of the capital stock of the corporation receivable by the taxpayer as consideration for the disposition shall be deemed to be the lesser of the fair market value of those shares immediately after the disposition and that proportion of the amount, if any, by which the proceeds of the disposition exceed the fair market value of the consideration (other than shares of the capital stock of the corporation or a right to receive any such shares) received by the taxpayer for the disposition, that

(i) the fair market value, immediately after the disposition, of those preferred shares of that class,

is of

(ii) the fair market value, immediately after the disposition, of all preferred shares of the capital stock of the corporation receivable by the taxpayer as consideration for the disposition;

(h) **[deemed cost of common shares]** — the cost to the taxpayer of any common shares of any class of the capital stock of the corporation receivable by the taxpayer as consideration for the disposition shall be deemed to be that proportion of the amount, if any, by which the proceeds of the disposition exceed the total of the fair market value, at the time of the disposition,

of the consideration (other than shares of the capital stock of the corporation or a right to receive any such shares) received by the taxpayer for the disposition and the cost to the taxpayer of all preferred shares of the capital stock of the corporation receivable by the taxpayer as consideration for the disposition, that

(i) the fair market value, immediately after the disposition, of those common shares of that class,

is of

(ii) the fair market value, immediately after the disposition, of all common shares of the capital stock of the corporation receivable by the taxpayer as consideration for the disposition; and

(i) **[transfer of taxable Canadian property]** — where the property so disposed of is taxable Canadian property of the taxpayer, all of the shares of the capital stock of the Canadian corporation received by the taxpayer as consideration for the property are deemed to be, at any time that is within 60 months after the disposition, taxable Canadian property of the taxpayer.

Related Provisions: 13(7)(e) — Deemed maximum capital cost on non-arm's length transfer; 13(21.2)(d) — No election allowed on certain transfers of depreciable property where UCC exceeds fair market value; 40(3.3), (3.4) — Limitation on loss where share acquired by affiliated person; 44.1(6), (7) — Small business investment rollover on exchange of shares; 51(4) — Application of 85(1) to exchange of convertible property; 53(4) — Effect on ACB of share, partnership interest or trust interest; 54.2 — Certain shares deemed to be capital property; 55(1) — "Permitted redemption" for butterfly purposes; 55(3.1)(b) — Rules where foreign vendor's capital gain exempted by treaty; 69(11) — Where corp later sells transferred property and shelters gain; 85(1.1) — "Eligible property"; 85(2) — Rollover of property to corp from partnership; 85(5) — Rules on transfers of depreciable property; 85(6) — Time for election; 86(3)(a) — 85(1) takes precedence over s. 86; 97(2)(a) — Rollover of property to a partnership; 107.4(3)(f) — Deemed taxable Canadian property retains status when rolled out of trust or into trust; 131(4.1) — Mutual fund switch-fund shares — no rollover; 135.2(3)(e) — No application to Canadian Wheat Board shares; 138(11.5) — Transfer of insurance business by non-resident insurer; 142.5(9) — Transitional rule — mark-to-market property acquired by financial institution on rollover; 142.7(3) — Application on conversion of foreign bank affiliate to branch; 248(25.1) — Deemed taxable Canadian property retains status through trust-to-trust transfer; 248(37)(f) — Rule limiting value of donated property does not apply to certain 85(1) rollovers; 256(7)(c)–(d) — Whether control of corp acquired on rollover; 257 — Formula cannot calculate to less than zero; Reg. 5301(8) — Effect of transfer on instalment base of transferee; Canada-U.S. Tax Treaty:Art. XIII:8 — Deferral of tax for U.S. resident transferor.

Notes: The "section 85 rollover" allows the transfer of assets to a corporation at cost in exchange for shares of the corporation. It can be used if the opening words of 85(1) are satisfied and the property being transferred to a corporation is "eligible property" (85(1.1)). The amount elected will become the deemed proceeds of disposition of the property as well as its deemed cost to the corporation. However, the elected amount cannot be less than the non-share consideration or "boot" (85(1)(b)); nor can it exceed the value of the property transferred (85(1)(c)); nor can it be less than both the cost and the value of the property transferred (85(1)(c.1), (d), (e)). The amount elected is then allocated for cost purposes, first to boot, then to preferred shares and finally (if anything is left) to common shares (85(1)(f), (g), (h)). (The above explanation is simplified.) See IT-291R3. Note that 84.1 may apply on a non-arm's length sale of shares (or 212.1 on a sale by a non-resident).

Form T2057 is used for the election. It is extremely important, when both a lawyer and an accountant are involved in a transaction, that it be well documented who has the responsibility for filing the 85(1) election under 85(6). If the deadline is missed, see 85(7)–(9). If the form is not filed, the Court can possibly still consider whether the conditions for the election have been satisfied: *Vachon*, 2006 TCC 669. Recording property in a wrong category (see 85(1.1)) on the form does not invalidate the election: VIEWS doc 2014-0544651I7. A party making the election can later dispute facts stated in the election form, as a back-door to amending the form: see Notes to 97(2). If the transferor and the corp report in different currencies (s. 261), 2 forms should be filed (and note 261(18)): 2020 IFA Roundtable q.1.

Where an Ontario corp acquires real property in Ontario, see Notes to 248(4).

For practical discussion see Carlin & Jason, *Section 85 Rollovers* (CCH, 2001, 140pp); Lamarre et al., *Taxation of Corporate Reorganizations* (Carswell, 3rd ed., 2019), chap. 3; Cohen, *Taxation of Private Corporations* (ctf.ca, 5th ed., 2020), chap. 11; Keey, *Checklist 6 — Rollovers (Section 85)*, Taxnet Pro Corporate Tax Centre (2020, 30pp). For valuation, see 69(1) Notes. For common traps see Wilkenfeld, "Section 85 Rollovers", 1(3) *Tax for the Owner-Manager* (ctf.ca) 17-18 (July 2001). For GST/HST issues see Visser, "Commodity Tax Issues in Corporate Reorganizations", *2011 CICA Commodity Tax Symposium* (58 slides). For general discussion by CRA see VIEWS doc 2011-0395501E5. For software that assists in applying 85(1) see *T2057: Section 85 Election Eligibility Classifier* at bluejlegal.com.

For rulings that 85(1) applies see the rulings listed in Notes to 55(3), and 2013-0488291R3 (spinout of assets). For some public transactions using 85(1) see Smit,

"Cross-Border Exchangeable Shares", XIV(1) *Corporate Structures and Groups* (Federated Press) 12-16 (2017).

Be alert for GST/HST possibly applying when transferring property to a corporation, and whether the corp is GST/HST-registered so as to be able to claim input tax credits for any GST or HST it must pay. *Excise Tax Act* s. 167 allows no tax to apply on transfer of a business, but only if its conditions are met (see David M. Sherman, *Practitioner's Goods and Services Tax Annotated*). On a transfer of land, provincial land transfer tax normally applies (an exemption for transactions between related corporations may be available).

If a rollover puts assets out of creditors' hands, it may be void under fraudulent preferences legislation. See end of Notes to 160(1). A rollover may result in the taxpayer, on separation, losing credit for the pre-marriage value of the transferred shares: *Dillon v. Dillon*, 2015 MBQB 138, para. 19.

If the rollover is to a non-"affiliated" person and the property is sold within 3 years, 69(11) may retroactively deny the rollover.

When incorporating a business with expected high cash flow (e.g. a professional practice), it may be advisable to not elect under 85(1) for goodwill, pay relatively low tax up front, and get the value of the goodwill into the corporation as capital that can be returned tax-free (see Notes to 84(3)).

Where capital property (see 54"capital property" Notes) is rolled into a corp, it remains capital property even if the corp sells it immediately: *Income Tax Technical News* 7; Revenue Canada's statements at the 1983, 1984 and 1995 Cdn Tax Foundation conference round tables; VIEWS doc 2013-0500891I7 [Koh & Bernstein, "Derivative Still Capital After Rollover", 22(9) *Canadian Tax Highlights* (ctf.ca) 6-8 (Sept. 2014); *Hickman Motors*, [1998] 1 C.T.C. 213 (SCC); *Mara Properties*, [1996] 2 C.T.C. 54 (SCC). The same could apply to pre-2017 eligible capital property: 2008-0285151C6.

Where the corporation fails to issue or to authorize the shares when the property is transferred but does so before the election filing deadline, the rollover is still valid, according to a Nov. 20, 2002 CCRA letter cited in Paul Hickey, "Pre-Budget Recommendations", 11(1) *Canadian Tax Highlights* (ctf.ca) 1 (Jan. 2003); and VIEWS doc 2010-0373231C6 (the shares need not be issued simultaneously with the transfer of property, unlike 51(1)). If the transaction is not done properly, rectification is often no longer possible: see Notes to 169(1).

A transfer of shares done through the public market rather than directly (where required by Universal Market Integrity Rules) does not qualify for 85(1): doc 2012-0451291C6.

CRA states (2000 Cdn Tax Foundation conference report, 36:17-19) that *85(1)(b)* applies to a transfer of property with liabilities in excess of cost, if the excess is assumed by the transferor in exchange for a promissory note issued by the corporation. The obligation assumed is considered consideration (boot) for the transfer of property.

85(1)(b) will not apply where a corporation pays an amount owing to a shareholder by assuming a debt owing by the shareholder, even if the effect of the assumption is to reduce the debt that must be assumed by the corporation on a transfer of property to it: VIEWS doc 2002-0170485. Assumption of debt as co-obligor was not "boot" for 85(1)(b) in 2003-0054013, 2005-0119481R3; but it will be boot if the joint debt exceeds the tax cost of the assets rolled in: McLaren, "Assumption as Co-Obligor", 13(11) *Canadian Tax Highlights* (ctf.ca) 4 (Nov. 2005). Otherwise, assumption of debt is boot to which 85(1)(b) applies: 2013-0501831E5.

85(1)(d.1) prevents an overstatement of the corporation's income under 14(1)(b) resulting from a later disposition of eligible property.

85(1)(e.2) applies when the rollover is intended to confer a benefit on a person related to the transferor. For some VIEWS docs that 85(1)(e.2) does not apply see 2003-0004835 (97(2) rollover by majority interest partner); 2004-0081531R3 (internal restructuring); 2005-0141921R3 (public company spinoff); 2005-0158461R3 (single-wing butterfly); 2005-0158841R3 (butterfly distribution); 2006-0171291R3, 2019-0819971R3 (loss consolidations); 2006-0188371R3, 2008-0267251R3 (estate freezes); 2006-0191591R3 (sequential butterfly reorg); 2011-0404641C6 (shareholders agreement and freeze shares); 2011-0415811R3, 2014-0544221R3, 2015-0565151R3, 2015-0601411R3 (consolidation of foreign affiliates); 2011-0416001R3 (split-up butterfly); 2013-0503531E5 (rollover of discretionary-dividend shares); 2015-0582431R3 (standard butterfly). See also *Husky Oil* case in 87(4) Notes, interpreting the "confer a benefit" rule on an amalgamation; and Perry Truster, "A Closer Look at Paragraph 85(1)(e.2)", 13(2) *Tax for the Owner-Manager* (ctf.ca) 5-6 (April 2013).

85(1)(i) applies to taxable Canadian property (TCP) even while the taxpayer is resident in Canada. See also VIEWS doc 2002-0127987.

Checking "yes" on Form T2057 to the existence of a price adjustment clause eliminates the need to file a letter with the return as stated in former IT-169 [Income Tax Folio S4-F3-C1 no longer has this requirement]: Information Circular 01-1 para. 71; VIEWS docs 2004-0081631E5, 2007-0243251C6 (Bulletin IMP. 28-4/R1 para. 7 for Quebec tax). For more on price adjustment clauses see Notes to 69(1).

85(1)(e.5) added by 2019 budget bill #1, effective March 19, 2019.

85(1)(d)–(d.12) repealed, and (e.1) and (e.3) amended, by 2016 budget bill #2, effective 2017, as part of changing the eligible capital property rules to CCA Class 14.1 (see Notes to 20(1)(b)). Before 2017, read:

> (d) [elected amount minimum — eligible capital property] — where the property was eligible capital property in respect of a business of the taxpayer and

the amount that, but for this paragraph, would be the proceeds of disposition of the property is less than the least of

> (i) 4/3 of the taxpayer's cumulative eligible capital in respect of the business immediately before the disposition,

> (ii) the cost to the taxpayer of the property, and

> (iii) the fair market value of the property at the time of the disposition,

the amount agreed on by the taxpayer and the corporation in their election in respect of the property shall, irrespective of the amount actually so agreed on by them, be deemed to be the least of the amounts described in subparagraphs (i) to (iii);

(d.1) [eligible capital property] — for the purpose of determining after the disposition time the amount to be included under paragraph 14(1)(b) in computing the corporation's income, there shall be added to the amount otherwise determined for C in that paragraph the amount determined by the formula

$$1/2 \times [(A \times B/C) - 2(D - E)] + F + G$$

where

A   is the amount, if any, determined for Q in the definition "cumulative eligible capital" in subsection 14(5) in respect of the taxpayer's business immediately before the disposition time,

B   is the fair market value immediately before the disposition time of the eligible capital property disposed of to the corporation by the taxpayer,

C   is the total of the fair market value immediately before the disposition time of all eligible capital property of the taxpayer in respect of the business and each amount that was described in B in respect of an earlier disposition made after the taxpayer's adjustment time,

D   is the amount, if any, that would be included under subsection 14(1) in computing the taxpayer's income as a result of the disposition if the values determined for C and D in paragraph 14(1)(b) were zero,

E   is the amount, if any, that would be included under subsection 14(1) in computing the taxpayer's income as a result of the disposition if the value determined for D in paragraph 14(1)(b) were zero,

F   is the total of all amounts, each of which is an amount determined under this paragraph as it applied to the taxpayer in respect of a disposition to the corporation on or before the disposition time, and

G   is the total of all amounts, each of which is an amount determined under subparagraph 88(1)(c.1)(ii) as it applied to the taxpayer in respect of a winding-up before the disposition time;

(d.11) [eligible capital property] — for the purpose of determining after the time of the disposition (referred to in this paragraph and in paragraphs (d.1) and (d.12) as the "disposition time") the amount to be included under paragraph 14(1)(a) or (b) in computing the corporation's income, there shall be added to the amount otherwise determined for each of A and F in the definition "cumulative eligible capital" in subsection 14(5) the amount, if any, determined by the formula

$$(A \times B/C) + D + E$$

where

A   is the amount, if any, that would be determined for F in that definition in respect of the taxpayer's business at the beginning of the taxpayer's following taxation year if the taxpayer's taxation year that includes the disposition time had ended immediately after the disposition time and if, in respect of the disposition, this Act were read without reference to paragraph (d.12),

B   is the fair market value immediately before the disposition time of the eligible capital property disposed of to the corporation by the taxpayer,

C   is the fair market value immediately before the disposition time of all eligible capital property of the taxpayer in respect of the business and each amount that was described in B in respect of an earlier disposition made after the taxpayer's adjustment time,

D   is the total of all amounts, each of which is an amount determined under this paragraph as it applied to the taxpayer in respect of a disposition to the corporation on or before the disposition time, and

E   is the total of all amounts, each of which is an amount determined under subparagraph 88(1)(c.1)(i) as it applied to the taxpayer in respect of a winding-up before the disposition time;

(d.12) [eligible capital property] — for the purpose of determining after the disposition time the amount to be included under paragraph 14(1)(a) or (b) in computing the taxpayer's income, the amount, if any, determined by the formula in paragraph (d.11) in respect of the disposition is to be deducted from each of the amounts otherwise determined

> (i) by subparagraph 14(1)(a)(ii), and

> (ii) for the description of B in paragraph 14(1)(b);

. . . . .

(e.1) where two or more properties, each of which is a property described in paragraph (d) or each of which is a property described in paragraph (e), are disposed of at the same time, paragraph (d) or (e), as the case may be, applies as if each property so disposed of had been separately disposed of in the order designated by the taxpayer before the time referred to in subsection (6) for the filing of an election in respect of those properties or, if the taxpayer does not so designate any such order, in the order designated by the Minister;

. . . . .

(e.3) where, under any of paragraphs (c.1), (d) and (e), the amount that the taxpayer and the corporation have agreed on in their election in respect of the property (in this paragraph referred to as "the elected amount") would be deemed to be an amount that is greater or less than the amount that would be deemed, subject to paragraph (c), to be the elected amount under paragraph (b), the elected amount shall be deemed to be the greater of

(i) the amount deemed by paragraph (c.1), (d) or (e), as the case may be, to be the elected amount, and

(ii) the amount deemed by paragraph (b) to be the elected amount;

85(1) amended by 2002-2013 technical bill (last change effective June 8, 2007), 2010 budget bill #1 (effective March 5, 2010), 2000 and 1994 Budgets, 1994 technical bill, 1992 and 1991 technical bills.

Regulations: 7307(1) (prescribed amount for 85(1)(e.4)(i)).

I.T. Application Rules: 20(1.2) (transfer of depreciable property by person who owned it before 1972).

Income Tax Folios: S4-F3-C1: Price adjustment clauses [replaces IT-169]; S7-F1-C1: Split-receipting and deemed fair market value.

Interpretation Bulletins: IT-188R: Sale of accounts receivable; IT-217R: Depreciable property owned on December 31, 1971 (cancelled); IT-243R4: Dividend refund to private corporations; IT-291R3: Transfer of property to a corporation under subsection 85(1); IT-427R: Livestock of farmers; IT-457R: Election by professionals to exclude work in progress from income; IT-489R: Non-arm's length sale of shares to a corporation; IT-521R: Motor vehicle expenses claimed by self-employed individuals; IT-522R: Vehicle, travel and sales expenses of employees.

Information Circulars: 76-19R3: Transfer of property to a corporation under s. 85; 88-2, paras. 9, 10, 13, 14, 22: General anti-avoidance rule — section 245 of the *Income Tax Act*; 88-2 Supplement, paras. 3, 8: General anti-avoidance rule — section 245 of the *Income Tax Act*; 89-3: Policy statement on business equity valuations.

I.T. Technical News: 3 (section 85 — *Dale* case); 7 (rollovers of capital property — *Mara Properties*); 10 (1997 limits for automobiles (for 85(1)(e.4)(i)).

Advance Tax Rulings: ATR-6: Vendor reacquires business assets following default by purchaser; ATR-7: Amalgamation involving losses and control; ATR-19: Earned depletion base and cumulative Canadian development expense; ATR-25: Estate freeze; ATR-27: Exchange and acquisition of interests in capital properties through rollovers and winding-up ("butterfly"); ATR-28: Redemption of capital stock of family farm corporation; ATR-32: Rollover of fixed assets from Opco into Holdco; ATR-35: Partitioning of assets to get specific ownership — "butterfly"; ATR-36: Estate freeze; ATR-42: Transfer of shares; ATR-55: Amalgamation followed by sale of shares; ATR-57: Transfer of property for estate planning purposes; ATR-58: Divisive reorganization; ATR-70: Distribution of taxable Canadian property by a trust to a non-resident.

Forms: T2 Sched. 44: Non-arm's length transactions; T2057: Election on disposition of property by a taxpayer to a taxable Canadian corporation.

(1.1) Definition of "eligible property" — For the purposes of subsection (1), "eligible property" means

(a) a capital property (other than real or immovable property, an option in respect of such property, or an interest in real property or a real right in an immovable, owned by a non-resident person);

(b) a capital property that is real or immovable property, an option in respect of such property, or an interest in real property or a real right in an immovable, owned by a non-resident insurer if that property and the property received as consideration for that property are designated insurance property for the year;

(c) a Canadian resource property;

(d) a foreign resource property;

(e) [Repealed]

(f) an inventory (other than real or immovable property, an option in respect of such property, or an interest in real property or a real right in an immovable);

(g) a property that is a security or debt obligation used by the taxpayer in the year in, or held by it in the year in the course of, carrying on the business of insurance or lending money, other than

(i) a capital property,

(ii) inventory, or

(iii) where the taxpayer is a financial institution in the year, a mark-to-market property for the year;

(g.1) where the taxpayer is a financial institution in the year, a specified debt obligation (other than a mark-to-market property of the taxpayer for the year);

(h) a capital property that is real or immovable property, an option in respect of such property, or an interest in real property or a real right in an immovable, owned by a non-resident person (other than a non-resident insurer) and used in the year in a business carried on in Canada by that person; or

(i) a NISA Fund No. 2, if that property is owned by an individual.

Related Provisions: 85(1.11) — Exception — foreign resource property or interest in FIE; 85(1.12) — Derivative is not eligible property if mark-to-market election made; 85(1.2) — Limitation on 85(1.1)(h); 131(4.1) — Mutual fund switch-fund shares not eligible; 248(4) — Interest in real property includes a leasehold interest but not a security interest; 248(4.1) — Meaning of "real right in an immovable",

Notes: Eligible property can include: Canadian resource property that is real property (IT-291R3 para. 6); capital interest in a personal trust (VIEWS docs 2012-0459541E5, 2014-0526561C6 [2014 STEP q.17]); copyright (2002-0149781R3, 2007-0238221E5); derivatives [possibly, despite 85(1.12)] (Marcovitz & Tam, "Derivatives: Eligible Property?", 26(2) *Canadian Tax Highlights* (ctf.ca) 2-3 (Feb. 2018)); farm inventory (IT-291R3 para. 5); franchise agreement rights and goodwill (2004-0091531R3); milk quota (2011-0394231E5); mineral subsurface rights (2016-0637221E5); partnership interest (2006-0215891E5), or part of one (2014-0543751E5); related segregated fund trust interest (2020-0842171C6 [2020 CALU q.4]); right to use a patent, possibly (2011-0412581E5); stock option (2020-0836991E5); swap contract that is inventory (2014-0544651I7).

Eligible property does not include: eligible derivatives where mark-to-market election made (85(1.12)); foreign resource property, or a partnership interest that includes FRP (85(1.11)); intangible expenditures on electricity generation projects, as such amounts reduce Canadian renewable and conservation expense and are thus not (pre-2017) eligible capital property (VIEWS doc 2013-0489911E5); land inventory (85(1.1)(f); *Dalron Construction*, 2008 TCC 476; *984274 Alberta*, 2020 FCA 125, para. 13 (leave to appeal denied 2021 CarswellNat 1167 (SCC))); lessee's interest in an equipment lease (2015-0576831E5).

Fishing licence (FL): CRA's view was that a FL could not be transferred to a corp (doc 9726477), but *Haché*, 2011 FCA 104, held that a FL is property, and *Buston*, [1993] 2 C.T.C. 2720 (TCC) held that beneficial ownership can be transferred. From 2011 see Power, "Atlantic Canada Fishing Licences", 1(1) *Canadian Tax Focus* (ctf.ca) 4-5 (May 2011) and 2(1) 6-7 (Feb. 2012), describing new CRA guidelines; Visser, "Fishing for Answers", 8(8) & 8(9) *Tax Hyperion [TH]* (Carswell, Aug. & Sept. 2011). But from April 2021, new rules prohibit many transfers: Campbell, "Fisheries Act Regulations Making Waves in Atlantic Canada", 18(2) *TH* 5-8 (March-April 2021).

In *Loyens*, 2003 TCC 214, 85(1.1)(f) was avoided by transferring real property inventory to an existing partnership and rolling the partnership into a corporation. GAAR did not apply since the object of the transaction was to use loss carryforwards, not to convert income to capital gains.

The restriction in 85(1.1)(i) to an individual prevents trading in NISA funds. See Notes to 12(10.4).

85(1.1)(e) ["an eligible capital property"] repealed by 2016 budget bill #2, effective 2017, as part of changing the ECP rules to CCA Class 14.1 (see Notes to 20(1)(b)).

85(1.1)(a), (b), (f) and (h) amended by 2002-2013 technical bill (Part 4 — bijuralism), effective June 26, 2013.

85(1.1) earlier amended by 2007 budget bill #2 (effective 2008), 1996 Budget, 1994 technical bill, 1992 and 1991 technical bills.

Interpretation Bulletins: IT-291R3: Transfer of property to a corporation under subsection 85(1).

(1.11) Exception — Notwithstanding subsection (1.1), a foreign resource property, or an interest in a partnership that derives all or part of its value from one or more foreign resource properties, is not an eligible property of a taxpayer in respect of a disposition by the taxpayer to a corporation where

(a) the taxpayer and the corporation do not deal with each other at arm's length; and

(b) it is reasonable to conclude that one of the purposes of the disposition, or a series of transactions or events of which the disposition is a part, is to increase the extent to which any person may claim a deduction under section 126.

Related Provisions: 251(1) — Arm's length.

Notes: 85(1.11) is intended to counter the avoidance of income-based limits on the foreign tax credit in s. 126 that might be achieved through the sale of direct or indirect interests in foreign resource property at less than fair market value. In general terms, under 126(2) the FTC in respect of a business carried on in a foreign country cannot exceed a specified percentage of the taxpayer's Canadian income tax. The specified percentage is essentially the percentage that the taxpayer's "qualifying income" from that business is of the taxpayer's world-wide income.

85(1.11) added by 2000 Budget, for dispositions after Dec. 21, 2000 other than pursuant to an agreement in writing made by the taxpayer by that date.

Interpretation Bulletins: IT-291R3: Transfer of property to a corporation under subsection 85(1).

(1.12) Eligible derivatives [where mark-to-market election made] — Notwithstanding subsection (1.1), an "eligible derivative" (as defined in subsection 10.1(5)) of a taxpayer to which subsection 10.1(6) applies is not an eligible property of the taxpayer in respect of a disposition by the taxpayer to a corporation.

Notes: 85(1.12) added by 2017 budget bill #2, for taxation years that begin after March 21, 2017.

(1.2) Application of subsec. (1) [to non-resident vendor] — Subsection (1) does not apply to a disposition by a taxpayer to a corporation of a property referred to in paragraph (1.1)(h) unless

(a) immediately after the disposition, the corporation is controlled by the taxpayer, a person or persons related (otherwise than because of a right referred to in paragraph 251(5)(b)) to the taxpayer or the taxpayer and a person or persons so related to the taxpayer;

(b) the disposition is part of a transaction or series of transactions in which all or substantially all of the property used in the business referred to in paragraph (1.1)(h) is disposed of by the taxpayer to the corporation; and

(c) the disposition is not part of a series of transactions that result in control of the corporation being acquired by a person or group of persons after the time that is immediately after the disposition.

Related Provisions: 256(6)–(9) — Whether control acquired.

Notes: 85(1.2) added by 1991 technical bill, effective for dispositions after 1989 (after 1984 for U.S. and Netherlands residents).

CRA considers that "substantially all", used in 85(1.2)(b), means 90% or more.

Interpretation Bulletins: IT-291R3: Transfer of property to a corporation under subsection 85(1).

(1.3) Meaning of "wholly owned corporation" — For the purposes of this subsection and paragraph (1)(e.2), "wholly owned corporation" of a taxpayer means a corporation all the issued and outstanding shares of the capital stock of which (except directors' qualifying shares) belong to

(a) the taxpayer;

(b) a corporation that is a wholly owned corporation of the taxpayer; or

(c) any combination of persons described in paragraph (a) or (b).

Notes: "Directors' qualifying shares" are shares (sometimes just one) that a director must legally own to qualify as a director. Federal and provincial business corporations acts no longer require this, but some companies' articles or bylaws still may.

85(1.3) added by 1991 technical bill, effective for dispositions after June 1988.

Interpretation Bulletins: IT-291R3: Transfer of property to a corporation under subsection 85(1).

(1.4) Definitions — For the purpose of subsection (1.1), "financial institution", "mark-to-market property" and "specified debt obligation" have the meanings assigned by subsection 142.2(1).

Notes: 85(1.4) added by 1994 technical bill, effective for dispositions occurring after February 22, 1994.

(2) Transfer of property to corporation from partnership — Where

(a) a partnership has disposed, to a taxable Canadian corporation for consideration that includes shares of the corporation's capital stock, of any partnership property (other than an "eligible derivative", as defined in subsection 10.1(5), of the partnership if subsection 10.1(6) applies to the partnership) that was

(i) a capital property (other than real or immovable property, an option in respect of such property, or an interest in real

property or a real right in an immovable, if the partnership was not a Canadian partnership at the time of the disposition),

(ii) a property described in any of paragraphs (1.1)(c) to (f), or

(iii) a property that would be described in paragraph (1.1)(g) or (g.1) if the references in those paragraphs to "taxpayer" were read as "partnership", and

(b) the corporation and all the members of the partnership have jointly so elected, in prescribed form and within the time referred to in subsection (6),

paragraphs (1)(a) to (i) are applicable, with such modifications as the circumstances require, in respect of the disposition as if the partnership were a taxpayer resident in Canada who had disposed of the property to the corporation.

Related Provisions: 13(21.2)(d) — No election allowed on certain transfers of depreciable property where UCC exceeds fair market value; 40(3.3), (3.4) — Limitation on loss where share acquired by affiliated person; 51(4) — Application of 85(2) to exchange of convertible property; 54.2 — Certain shares deemed to be capital property; 69(11) — Where corporation later sells transferred property and shelters gain; 85(3) — Where partnership wound up; 85(5) — Rules on transfers of depreciable property; 85(6) — Time for election; 86(3)(a) — Section 86 does not apply where 85(2) applies; 131(4.1) — Mutual fund switch-fund shares — no rollover; 139.1(4)(c) — No election allowed re ownership rights on demutualization of insurer; 248(4) — Interest in real property; 248(4.1) — Meaning of "real right in an immovable"; 248(37)(f) — Rule limiting value of donated property does not apply to certain 85(2) rollovers; Reg. 5301(8) — Effect of transfer on instalment base of transferee; Canada-U.S. Tax Treaty:Art. XIII:8 — Deferral of tax for U.S. resident transferor.

Notes: 85(2) allows rollovers from a partnership to a corporation. For rollovers from an individual to a partnership, see 97(2).

For some rulings approving 85(2) rollovers see VIEWS docs 2010-0365371R3, 2010-0387211R3, 2013-0505431R3. For software that assists in applying 85(2) see *T2058: Section 85 Election Eligibility Classifier* at bluejlegal.com.

Corporations in Alberta electing under 85(2) were required to file a copy of the federal form with Alberta, under 2001 amendments to the *Alberta Corporate Tax Act*, but this requirement was repealed in 2002 retroactive to its introduction (*ACTA* s. 14.2).

85(2)(a) opening words amended by 2017 budget bill #2 to exclude an eligible derivative, for taxation years that begin after March 21, 2017.

85(2)(a)(i) amended by 2002-2013 technical bill (Part 4 — bijuralism), effective June 26, 2013, effectively to add references to "immovable" and a "real right".

85(2)(a) amended by 1995-97 technical bill, for dispositions after June 20, 1996.

I.T. Application Rules: 20(1.2) (transfer of depreciable property by person who owned it before 1972).

Income Tax Folios: S7-F1-C1: Split-receipting and deemed fair market value.

Interpretation Bulletins: IT-217R: Depreciable property owned on December 31, 1971 (cancelled); IT-378R: Winding-up of a partnership; IT-457R: Election by professionals to exclude work in progress from income.

Information Circulars: 76-19R3: Transfer of property to a corporation under s. 85.

Forms: T2 Sched. 44: Non-arm's length transactions; T2058: Election on disposition of property by a partnership to a taxable Canadian corporation.

(2.1) Computing paid-up capital — Where subsection (1) or (2) applies to a disposition of property (other than a disposition of property to which section 84.1 or 212.1 applies) to a corporation by a person or partnership (in this subsection referred to as the "taxpayer"),

(a) in computing the paid-up capital in respect of any particular class of shares of the capital stock of the corporation at the time of, and at any time after, the issue of shares of the capital stock of the corporation in consideration for the disposition of the property, there shall be deducted an amount determined by the formula

$$(A - B) \times \frac{C}{A}$$

where

A is the increase, if any, determined without reference to this section as it applies to the disposition of the property, in the paid-up capital in respect of all the shares of the capital stock of the corporation as a result of the acquisition by the corporation of the property,

B is the amount, if any, by which the corporation's cost of the property, immediately after the acquisition, determined under subsection (1) or (2), as the case may be, exceeds the fair market value, immediately after the acquisition, of any consideration (other than shares of the capital stock of the corporation) received by the taxpayer from the corporation for the property, and

C is the increase, if any, determined without reference to this section as it applies to the disposition of the property, in the paid-up capital in respect of the particular class of shares as a result of the acquisition by the corporation of the property; and

(b) in computing the paid-up capital, at any time after November 21, 1985, in respect of any class of shares of the capital stock of a corporation, there shall be added an amount equal to the lesser of

(i) the amount, if any, by which

(A) the total of all amounts each of which is an amount deemed by subsection 84(3), (4) or (4.1) to be a dividend on shares of that class paid after November 21, 1985 and before that time by the corporation

exceeds

(B) the total of such dividends that would be determined under clause (A) if the Act were read without reference to paragraph (a), and

(ii) the total of all amounts required by paragraph (a) to be deducted in computing the paid-up capital in respect of that class of shares after November 21, 1985 and before that time.

Related Provisions: 257 — Formula cannot calculate to less than zero.

Notes: See Notes to 84(3).

For CRA interpretation see VIEWS docs 2008-0293401E5 (interaction with 84(1)); 2011-0412121C6 (interaction with 84.1); 2013-0475621I7 (PUC reduced where CRA determines that property transferred in statute-barred year had lower value).

Opening words of 85(2.1) and of (a) amended by 1993 technical bill, effective for dispositions occurring after Nov. 21, 1985. Notwithstanding 152(4) and (5), such assessments and determinations in respect of any taxation year may be made as are consequential on the application of this amendment to dispositions occurring before 1993.

Interpretation Bulletins: IT-291R3: Transfer of property to a corporation under subsection 85(1).

Advance Tax Rulings: ATR-28: Redemption of capital stock of family farm corporation; ATR-32: Rollover of fixed assets from Opco into Holdco; ATR-35: Partitioning of assets to get specific ownership — "butterfly"; ATR-36: Estate freeze.

(3) Where partnership wound up — Where,

(a) in respect of any disposition of partnership property of a partnership to a corporation, subsection (2) applies,

(b) the affairs of the partnership were wound up within 60 days after the disposition, and

(c) immediately before the winding-up there was no partnership property other than money or property received from the corporation as consideration for the disposition,

the following rules apply:

(d) the cost to any member of the partnership of any property (other than shares of the capital stock of the corporation or a right to receive any such shares) received by the member as consideration for the disposition of the member's partnership interest on the winding-up shall be deemed to be the fair market value of the property at the time of the winding-up,

(e) the cost to any member of the partnership of any preferred shares of any class of the capital stock of the corporation receivable by the member as consideration for the disposition of the member's partnership interest on the winding-up shall be deemed to be

(i) where any common shares of the capital stock of the corporation were also receivable by the member as consideration for the disposition of the interest, the lesser of

(A) the fair market value, immediately after the winding-up, of the preferred shares of that class so receivable by the member, and

(B) that proportion of the amount, if any, by which the adjusted cost base to the member of the member's partnership interest immediately before the winding-up exceeds the total of the fair market value, at the time of the winding-up, of the consideration (other than shares of the capital stock of the corporation or a right to receive any such shares) received by the member for the disposition of the interest, that

(I) the fair market value, immediately after the winding-up, of the preferred shares of that class so receivable by the member,

is of

(II) the fair market value, immediately after the winding-up, of all preferred shares of the capital stock of the corporation receivable by the member as consideration for the disposition, and

(ii) in any other case, the amount determined under clause (i)(B),

(f) the cost to any member of the partnership of any common shares of any class of the capital stock of the corporation receivable by the member as consideration for the disposition of the member's partnership interest on the winding-up shall be deemed to be that proportion of the amount, if any, by which the adjusted cost base to the member of the member's partnership interest immediately before the winding-up exceeds the total of the fair market value, at the time of the winding-up, of the consideration (other than shares of the capital stock of the corporation or a right to receive any such shares) received by the member for the disposition of the interest and the cost to the member of all preferred shares of the capital stock of the corporation receivable by the member as consideration for the disposition of the interest, that

(i) the fair market value, immediately after the winding-up, of the common shares of that class so receivable by the member,

is of

(ii) the fair market value, immediately after the winding-up, of all common shares of the capital stock of the corporation so receivable by the member as consideration for the disposition,

(g) the proceeds of disposition of the partnership interest of any member of the partnership shall be deemed to be the cost to the member of all shares and property receivable or received by the member as consideration for the disposition of the interest plus the amount of any money received by the member as consideration for the disposition, and

(h) where the partnership has distributed partnership property referred to in paragraph (c) to a member of the partnership, the partnership shall be deemed to have disposed of that property for proceeds equal to the cost amount to the partnership of the property immediately before its distribution.

Related Provisions: 69(11)(a)(i) — Exception to rule deeming proceeds at FMV where capital gains exemption claimed after incorporation of partnership; 98(2) — Deemed proceeds; 98(4) — Winding-up of partnership.

Notes: See IT-378R. Where a partnership is wound up and 85(3) applies, there is a disposition of the partnership interest and a general partner with negative ACB will have a gain under 100(2): VIEWS doc 2013-0501831E5. If the partnership has wound up its affairs but cannot transfer legal title to property within 60 days, 85(3) can still apply if the transfer is done as soon as practical: 2014-0559731E5. 85(3)(f) overrides 66.3(3): 2018-0751571E5.

I.T. Application Rules: 20(1.2) (transfer of depreciable property by person who owned it before 1972).

Interpretation Bulletins: IT-217R: Depreciable property owned on December 31, 1971 (cancelled); IT-242R: Retired partners; IT-338R2: Partnership interests — effects on adjusted cost base resulting from the admission or retirement of a partner (cancelled); IT-378R: Winding-up of a partnership; IT-457R: Election by professionals to exclude work in progress from income.

(4) [Repealed]

Notes: 85(4) repealed by 1995-97 technical bill, effective (subject to grandfathering) for dispositions of property after April 26, 1995. See Notes to 13(21.2) and 40(3.4) re the "accrued loss" regime, and 40(3.6) for the loss denial rule that has replaced it.

85(4)(b)(ii) amended before its repeal by 1995-97 technical bill, retroactive to 1988. 85(4) earlier amended by 1994 technical bill, 1993 and 1991 technical bills.

(5) Rules on transfers of depreciable property — Where

subsection (1) or (2) has applied to a disposition at any time of depreciable property to a person (in this subsection referred to as the "transferee") and the capital cost to the transferor of the property exceeds the transferor's proceeds of disposition of the property, for the purposes of sections 13 and 20 and any regulations made for the purpose of paragraph 20(1)(a),

(a) the capital cost to the transferee of the property is deemed to be the amount that was its capital cost to the transferor; and

(b) the excess is deemed to have been deducted by the transferee under paragraph 20(1)(a) in respect of the property in computing income for taxation years that ended before that time.

Related Provisions: 13(7)(e) — Similar rule on non-arm's length transfer of depreciable property; 132.2(5)(d) — Parallel rule on mutual fund reorganization.

Notes: 85(5) amended by 1995-97 technical bill, on the same basis as the repeal of former 85(5.1), to delete reference to (5.1) at the beginning. (Other wording changes were cosmetic.)

Interpretation Bulletins: IT-291R3: Transfer of property to a corporation under subsection 85(1).

(5.1) Acquisition of certain tools — capital cost and deemed depreciation — If subsection (1) has applied in respect

of the acquisition at any particular time of any depreciable property by a corporation from an individual, the cost of the property to the individual was included in computing an amount under paragraph 8(1)(r) or (s) in respect of the individual, and the amount that would be the cost of the property to the individual immediately before the transfer if this Act were read without reference to subsection 8(7) (which amount is in this subsection referred to as the "individual's original cost") exceeds the individual's proceeds of disposition of the property,

(a) the capital cost to the corporation of the property is deemed to be equal to the individual's original cost; and

(b) the amount by which the individual's original cost exceeds the individual's proceeds of disposition in respect of the property is deemed to have been deducted by the corporation under paragraph 20(1)(a) in respect of the property in computing income for taxation years that ended before that particular time.

Related Provisions: 56(1)(k) — Income inclusion where tools disposed of without rollover; 97(5) — Parallel rule for rollover to partnership.

Notes: 85(5.1) applies on a rollover of tools by a tradesperson or apprentice mechanic who claimed an 8(1)(r) or (s) deduction. It applies where the individual's cost of the property was reduced under 8(7) and the property is depreciable property of the corporation. The corporation's capital cost is deemed to be the original cost of the property to the individual, and the amount by which the cost was reduced under 8(7) is deemed to have been deducted by the corporation as CCA. The difference may be recaptured under 13(1) on a later disposition by the corporation (a capital gain can also arise to the extent the proceeds exceed the tool's deemed ACB). See also Notes to 8(1)(r).

85(5.1) amended by 2006 budget bill #2, for 2006 and later taxation years. 85(5.1) added by 2001 Budget, effective for dispositions after 2001.

Former 85(5.1) repealed by 1995-97 technical bill, effective (subject to grandfathering) for dispositions after April 26, 1995. See Notes to 13(21.2) and 40(3.4) re the "accrued loss" regime that replaced it.

Interpretation Bulletins: IT-291R3: Transfer of property to a corporation under subsection 85(1).

(6) Time for election — Any election under subsection (1) or (2)

shall be made on or before the day that is the earliest of the days on or before which any taxpayer making the election is required to file a return of income pursuant to section 150 for the taxation year in which the transaction to which the election relates occurred.

Related Provisions: 85(7)–(9) — Late-filed election.

(7) Late filed election — Where the election referred to in sub-

section (6) was not made on or before the day on or before which the election was required by that subsection to be made and that day is after May 6, 1974, the election shall be deemed to have been made on that day if, on or before the day that is 3 years after that day,

(a) the election is made in prescribed form; and

(b) an estimate of the penalty in respect of that election is paid by the taxpayer or the partnership, as the case may be, when that election is made.

Related Provisions: 85(8), (9) — Penalty for late-filed election.

Notes: CRA will not accept a late-filed election based on a contract modified after-the-fact by the parties to include share consideration: VIEWS doc 2008-0296721E5. This can no longer be fixed by court order: see Notes to 169(1) re rectification.

In *Construction PCA*, 2019 QCCQ 8876 (on the parallel Quebec rule), Revenu Québec's accepting the election and assessing the 85(8)-equivalent penalty did not prevent it later finding the election invalid because the shares had not been issued.

Information Circulars: 76-19R3: Transfer of property to a corporation under s. 85.

CRA Audit Manual: 28.6.1: Penalties for late filed/amended elections — section 85 rollovers.

(7.1) Special cases — Where, in the opinion of the Minister, the

circumstances of a case are such that it would be just and equitable

(a) to permit an election under subsection (1) or (2) to be made after the day that is 3 years after the day on or before which the election was required by subsection (6) to be made, or

(b) to permit an election made under subsection (1) or (2) to be amended,

the election or amended election shall be deemed to have been made on the day on or before which the election was so required to be made if

(c) the election or amended election is made in prescribed form, and

(d) an estimate of the penalty in respect of the election or amended election is paid by the taxpayer or partnership, as the case may be, when the election or amended election is made,

and where this subsection applies to the amendment of an election, that election shall be deemed not to have been effective.

Related Provisions: 85(8), (9) — Penalty for late-filed election.

Notes: For CRA guidelines on "just and equitable" (including cases where no amended election is required), see Information Circular 76-19R3 paras. 16-19. See also Carla Hanneman, "What is 'Just and Equitable'?", 3(4) *Canadian Tax Focus* (ctf.ca) 8 (Nov. 2013); and *Patterson Dental*, 2014 TCC 62, para. 31.

A CRA decision under 85(7.1) cannot be appealed (*Govender*, 2010 TCC 486) but is subject to Federal Court judicial review (JR): see Notes to 220(3.1) and 171(1). JR was **denied** in: *Bugera*, 2003 FCT 392 (retroactive tax planning not allowed; Court also noted [para. 24] that requiring the taxpayer to make the election and pay the estimated penalties pending CRA decision is consistent with the wording of 85(7.1)); *S. Cunard & Co.*, 2012 FC 683 (FCA appeal discontinued A-378-12) (CRA's decision was reasonable); *Masson*, 2019 FC 887 (no evidence of intention to do rollover at time of transaction). JR was **allowed** in *Brent Carlson Family Trust*, 2021 FC 506 (capital gain exemption claims triggered 120.4(5): CRA did not explain why late amendment to election should not be allowed to avoid kiddie tax by increasing gain up-front, or why CRA was not following its guidelines (para. 61); test for amendment is not the same as for rectification (para. 53)). The auditor on the file should not be the person who considers the late-filing request: *Brent Carlson*, para. 65.

CRA cannot require an 85(7.1) election to recognize a price adjustment clause so as not to apply 85(1)(e.2): docs 2007-0243251C6, 2011-0412111C6, 2011-043700117.

Information Circulars: 76-19R3: Transfer of property to a corporation under s. 85; 07-1R1: Taxpayer relief provisions.

CRA Audit Manual: 28.6.1: Penalties for late filed/amended elections — section 85 rollovers.

(8) Penalty for late filed election — For the purposes of this

section, the penalty in respect of an election or an amended election referred to in paragraph (7)(a) or (7.1)(c) is an amount equal to the lesser of

(a) ¼ of 1% of the amount, if any, by which

(i) the fair market value of the property in respect of which that election or amended election was made, at the time the property was disposed of,

exceeds

(ii) the amount agreed on in the election or amended election by the taxpayer or partnership, as the case may be, and the corporation,

for each month or part of a month during the period commencing with the day on or before which the election is required by subsection (6) to be made and ending on the day the election or amended election is made, and

(b) an amount, not exceeding $8,000, equal to the product obtained by multiplying $100 by the number of months each of which is a month all or part of which is during the period referred to in paragraph (a).

Related Provisions: 220(3.1) — Waiver of penalty by CRA.

Notes: The penalty applies per form, not per property: VIEWS doc 2016-0652951C6 [2016 APFF q.1A].

CRA Audit Manual: 28.6.1: Penalties for late filed/amended elections — section 85 rollovers.

(9) Unpaid balance of penalty — The Minister shall, with all due dispatch, examine each election and amended election referred to in paragraph (7)(a) or (7.1)(c), assess the penalty payable and send a notice of assessment to the taxpayer or partnership, as the case may be, and the taxpayer or partnership, as the case may be, shall pay forthwith to the Receiver General the amount, if any, by which the penalty so assessed exceeds the total of all amounts previously paid on account of that penalty.

Notes: See Notes to 152(1) on the meaning of "all due dispatch".

Definitions [s. 85]: "acquired" — 256(7)–(9); "adjusted cost base" — 54, 248(1); "amount" — 248(1); "arm's length" — 251(1); "assessment", "business" — 248(1); "Canada" — 255; "Canadian corporation" — 89(1), 248(1); "Canadian partnership" — 102(1), 248(1); "Canadian resource property" — 66(15), 248(1); "capital loss" — 39(1)(b), 248(1); "capital property" — 54, 248(1); "cash method" — 28(1), 248(1); "class of shares" — 248(6); "common share" — 248(1); "control" — 256(6)–(9); "controlled" — 256(6), (6.1); "corporation" — 248(1), *Interpretation Act* 35(1); "cost amount" — 248(1); "cumulative eligible capital" — 14(5), 248(1); "depreciable property" — 13(21), 248(1); "designated insurance property" — 138(12), 248(1); "disposition" — 248(1); "eligible capital property" — 54, 248(1); "eligible derivative" — 10.1(5); "eligible property" — 85(1.1), (1.11), (1.12); "fair market value" — see 69(1) Notes; "farming" — 248(1); "financial institution" — 85(1.4), 142.2(1); "foreign affiliate" — 95(1), 248(1); "foreign resource property" — 66(15), 248(1); "immovable" — Quebec *Civil Code* art. 900–907; "individual", "insurer" — 248(1); "interest in real property" — 248(4); "inventory" — 248(1); "mark-to-market property" — 85(1.4), 142.2(1); "Minister", "NISA Fund No. 2", "non-resident" — 248(1); "partnership" — see 96(1) Notes; "paid-up capital" — 89(1), 248(1); "passenger vehicle", "person", "preferred share", "prescribed", "property" — 248(1); "qualifying share" — 192(6), 248(1) [*not intended to apply to s. 85*]; "real right in an immovable" — 248(4.1); "regulation" — 248(1); "related" — 251(2); "resident in Canada" — 94(3)(a), 250; "series of transactions" — 248(10); "share", "shareholder" — 248(1); "specified debt obligation" — 85(1.4), 142.2(1); "taxable Canadian corporation" — 89(1), 248(1); "taxable Canadian property" — 248(1); "taxable dividend" — 89(1), 248(1); "taxation year" — 249; "taxpayer" — 248(1); "undepreciated capital cost" — 13(21), 248(1); "wholly owned corporation" — 85(1.3); "zero-emission passenger vehicle" — 248(1).

Income Tax Folios [s. 85]: S4-F7-C1; Amalgamations of Canadian corporations [replaces IT-474R2].

Interpretation Bulletins [s. 85]: IT-188R: Sale of accounts receivable.

Information Circulars [s. 85]: 76-19R3: Transfer of property to a corporation under s. 85.

85.1 (1) Share for share exchange — Where shares of any particular class of the capital stock of a Canadian corporation (in this section referred to as the "purchaser") are issued to a taxpayer (in this section referred to as the "vendor") by the purchaser in exchange for a capital property that is shares of any particular class of the capital stock (in this section referred to as the "exchanged shares") of another corporation that is a taxable Cana-

dian corporation (in this section referred to as the "acquired corporation"), subject to subsection (2),

(a) except where the vendor has, in the vendor's return of income for the taxation year in which the exchange occurred, included in computing the vendor's income for that year any portion of the gain or loss, otherwise determined, from the disposition of the exchanged shares, the vendor shall be deemed

(i) to have disposed of the exchanged shares for proceeds of disposition equal to the adjusted cost base to the vendor of those shares immediately before the exchange, and

(ii) to have acquired the shares of the purchaser at a cost to the vendor equal to the adjusted cost base to the vendor of the exchanged shares immediately before the exchange,

and where the exchanged shares were taxable Canadian property of the vendor, the shares of the purchaser so acquired by the vendor are deemed to be, at any time that is within 60 months after the exchange, taxable Canadian property of the vendor; and

(b) the cost to the purchaser of each exchanged share, at any time up to and including the time the purchaser disposed of the share, shall be deemed to be the lesser of

(i) its fair market value immediately before the exchange, and

(ii) its paid-up capital immediately before the exchange.

Related Provisions: 7(1.5) — Shares acquired through employee stock option; 40(3.5)(b)(ii) — Application of loss deferral rules on share exchange; 85.1(2) — Where rollover not to apply; 85.1(2.2) — Issuance to trust under court-approved plan; 85.1(3)–(6) — Exchange of foreign shares; 85.1(6.1) — Issuance to trust under court-approved plan; 107.4(3)(f) — Deemed taxable Canadian property retains status when rolled out of trust or into trust; 112(7) — Application of stop-loss rule where shares exchanged; 128.3 — Deferral applies to post-emigration disposition for certain purposes; 131(4.1) — Mutual fund switch-fund shares — no rollover; 219.1(1) — Corporate emigration; 248(25.1) — Deemed taxable Canadian property retains status through trust-to-trust transfer; 256(7)(c)–(d) — Whether control of corporation acquired on rollover; Canada-U.S. Tax Treaty:Art. XIII:8 — Deferral of tax for U.S. resident transferor.

Notes: For discussion of 85.1 see Income Tax Folio S4-F5-C1; Lamarre et al., *Taxation of Corporate Reorganizations* (Carswell, 3rd ed., 2019), chap. 6; Green et al., *Taxation of Private Corporations and their Shareholders* (ctf.ca, 5th ed., 2020), pp. 12:6-9; Cobb, "Share-for-Share Exchanges", 43(6) *Canadian Tax Journal* 2230-42 (1995); Snider, "Share for Share Exchanges", 114 *International Tax* (CCH) 4-8 (Oct. 2020).

For an example of 85.1 flexibility see the Encana Nov. 2009 spinoff. A s. 86 rollover split Encana common shares into common and special shares; the special shares were then exchanged for Cenovus common shares under 85.1. Shareholders wanting a loss or a full gain to current value on the 85.1 exchange needed to simply report it (see 85.1(1)(a) opening words); those wanting a partial gain could contact Encana to file a joint 85(1) election (see 85.1(2)(c)).

See also VIEWS docs 2010-0366651R3 and 2014-0533601R3 (85.1(1) applying to spinoff butterflies); 2014-0530371R3 (combination of credit unions).

85.1(1)(a) amended by 2010 budget bill #1, effective in determining after March 4, 2010 whether a property is taxable Canadian property of a taxpayer, to add "at any time that is within 60 months after the exchange". See Notes to 44.1(2).

85.1(1) earlier amended by 1992 technical bill.

I.T. Application Rules: 26(26), (28).

Income Tax Folios: S4-F5-C1: Share for share exchange [replaces IT-450R].

Interpretation Bulletins: IT-243R4: Dividend refund to private corporations; IT-291R3: Transfer of property to a corporation under subsection 85(1).

Advance Tax Rulings: ATR-26: Share exchange.

(2) Where subsec. (1) does not apply — Subsection (1) does not apply where

(a) the vendor and purchaser were, immediately before the exchange, not dealing with each other at arm's length (otherwise than because of a right referred to in paragraph 251(5)(b) that is a right of the purchaser to acquire the exchanged shares);

(b) the vendor or persons with whom the vendor did not deal at arm's length, or the vendor together with persons with whom the vendor did not deal at arm's length,

(i) controlled the purchaser, or

(ii) beneficially owned shares of the capital stock of the purchaser having a fair market value of more than 50% of the fair market value of all of the outstanding shares of the capital stock of the purchaser,

immediately after the exchange;

(c) the vendor and the purchaser have filed an election under subsection 85(1) or (2) with respect to the exchanged shares;

(d) consideration other than shares of the particular class of the capital stock of the purchaser was received by the vendor for the exchanged shares, notwithstanding that the vendor may have disposed of shares of the capital stock of the acquired corporation (other than the exchanged shares) to the purchaser for consideration other than shares of one class of the capital stock of the purchaser; or

(e) the vendor

(i) is a foreign affiliate of a taxpayer resident in Canada at the end of the taxation year of the vendor in which the exchange occurred, and

(ii) has included any portion of the gain or loss, otherwise determined, from the disposition of the exchanged shares in computing its foreign accrual property income for the taxation year of the vendor in which the exchange occurred.

Related Provisions: 256(6), (6.1) — Meaning of "controlled".

Notes: 85.1(2) amended by 2001 technical bill (exchanges after 1995), 1993 technical bill.

Income Tax Folios: S4-F5-C1: Share for share exchange [replaces IT-450R].

Interpretation Bulletins: IT-243R4: Dividend refund to private corporations; IT-291R3: Transfer of property to a corporation under subsection 85(1).

Advance Tax Rulings: ATR-26: Share exchange.

(2.1) Computation of paid-up capital — Where, at any time, a purchaser has issued shares of its capital stock as a result of an exchange to which subsection (1) applied, in computing the paid-up capital in respect of any particular class of shares of its capital stock at any particular time after that time

(a) there shall be deducted that proportion of the amount, if any, by which

(i) the increase, if any, as a result of the issue, in the paid-up capital in respect of all the shares of the capital stock of the purchaser, computed without reference to this subsection as it applies to the issue,

exceeds

(ii) the paid-up capital in respect of all of the exchanged shares received as a result of the exchange

that

(iii) the increase, if any, as a result of the issue, in the paid-up capital in respect of the particular class of shares, computed without reference to this subsection as it applies to the issue,

is of

(iv) the amount, if any, determined in subparagraph (i) in respect of the issue; and

(b) there shall be added an amount equal to the lesser of

(i) the amount, if any, by which

(A) the total of all amounts each of which is an amount deemed by subsection 84(3), (4) or (4.1) to be a dividend on shares of that class paid by the purchaser before the particular time

exceeds

(B) the total that would be determined under clause (A) if this Act were read without reference to paragraph (a), and

(ii) the total of all amounts required by paragraph (a) to be deducted in respect of that particular class of shares before the particular time.

Related Provisions: 219.1(1) — Corporate emigration; 256(6), (6.1) — Meaning of "controlled".

Notes: 85.1(2.1) added in 1987, for shares exchanged after June 5, 1987, with grandfathering for shares issued pursuant to an earlier agreement or prospectus.

Income Tax Folios: S4-F5-C1: Share for share exchange [replaces IT-450R].

Interpretation Bulletins: IT-243R4: Dividend refund to private corporations; IT-291R3: Transfer of property to a corporation under subsection 85(1).

(2.2) Issuance deemed made to vendor — For the purposes of subsection (1), if a purchaser issues shares of a class of its capital stock (in this subsection referred to as "purchaser shares") to a trust under a court-approved plan or scheme of arrangement in consideration for which a vendor disposes of exchanged shares that trade on a designated stock exchange to the purchaser solely for purchaser shares that are widely traded on a designated stock exchange immediately after and as part of completion of the plan or scheme of arrangement, the issuance to the trust is deemed to be an issuance to the vendor.

Notes: 85.1(2.2) was evidently added for consistency with 85.1(6.1) for foreign reorganizations, which was introduced to solve a specific problem. See Notes to 85.1(6.1).

85.1(2.2) added by 2002-2013 technical bill, for share exchanges made after June 2005, with an election to have it not apply to a share exchange before Nov. 5, 2010.

Income Tax Folios: S4-F5-C1: Share for share exchange [replaces IT-450R].

(3) Disposition of shares of foreign affiliate — Where a taxpayer has disposed of capital property that was shares of the capital stock of a foreign affiliate of the taxpayer to any corporation that was, immediately following the disposition, a foreign affiliate of the taxpayer (in this subsection referred to as the "acquiring affiliate") for consideration including shares of the capital stock of the acquiring affiliate,

(a) the cost to the taxpayer of any property (other than shares of the capital stock of the acquiring affiliate) receivable by the taxpayer as consideration for the disposition shall be deemed to be the fair market value of the property at the time of the disposition;

(b) the cost to the taxpayer of any shares of any class of the capital stock of the acquiring affiliate receivable by the taxpayer as consideration for the disposition shall be deemed to be that proportion of the amount, if any, by which the total of the adjusted cost bases to the taxpayer, immediately before the disposition, of the shares disposed of exceeds the fair market value at that time of the consideration receivable for the disposition (other than shares of the capital stock of the acquiring affiliate) that

(i) the fair market value, immediately after the disposition, of those shares of the acquiring affiliate of that class

is of

(ii) the fair market value, immediately after the disposition, of all shares of the capital stock of the acquiring affiliate receivable by the taxpayer as consideration for the disposition;

(c) the taxpayer's proceeds of disposition of the shares shall be deemed to be an amount equal to the cost to the taxpayer of all shares and other property receivable by the taxpayer from the acquiring affiliate as consideration for the disposition; and

(d) the cost to the acquiring affiliate of the shares acquired from the taxpayer shall be deemed to be an amount equal to the taxpayer's proceeds of disposition referred to in paragraph (c).

Related Provisions: 44.1(6), (7) — Small business investment rollover on exchange of shares; 53(1)(c) — Addition to ACB of share; 85.1(4) — Exception; 93.2(3) — Application to non-resident corp without share capital; 95(2)(c) — Rollover for FAPI purposes.

Notes: For VIEWS docs using 85.1(3) see 2004-0085771R3 (public company spinoff); 2006-0196691R3 (no 85.1(3)); 2007-0226091R3, 2007-0242911R3, 2007-0255061R3, 2007-0259331R3 (estate freezes of non-resident corp), 2007-0243721E5, 2008-0264671R3, 2010-0373801R3; 2016-0648991R3 (internal spinoff; shares remain capital property); 2016-0630761R3, 2017-0693751R3 (transfer of FA shares to another FA followed by transfer to related Cdn resident corp).

See also Heather O'Hagan & Ken Buttenham, "Foreign Affiliate Reorganizations: Where Are We Now?", 2013 Cdn Tax Foundation conference report at 20:2-12.

(4) Exception — Subsection (3) does not apply in respect of a disposition at any time by a taxpayer of a share of the capital stock of a particular foreign affiliate of the taxpayer to another foreign affiliate of the taxpayer if

(a) both

(i) all or substantially all of the property of the particular affiliate was, immediately before that time, excluded property (within the meaning assigned by subsection 95(1)) of the particular affiliate, and

(ii) the disposition is part of a transaction or event or a series of transactions or events for the purpose of disposing of the share to a person or partnership that, immediately after the transaction, event or series, was a person or partnership (other than a foreign affiliate of the taxpayer in respect of which the taxpayer has a qualifying interest (within the meaning assigned by paragraph 95(2)(m)) at the time of the transaction or event or throughout the series, as the case may be) with whom the taxpayer was dealing at arm's length; or

(b) the adjusted cost base to the taxpayer of the share at that time is greater than the amount that would, in the absence of subsection (3), be the taxpayer's proceeds of disposition of the share in respect of the disposition.

Related Provisions: 87(8.3) — Anti-avoidance — using foreign affiliate merger to avoid 85.1(4); 248(10) — Series of transactions.

Notes: CRA considers that "substantially all" means 90% or more.

CRA may use 95(6) if shares are issued to avoid 85.1(4). See Notes to 95(6).

85.1(4) amended by 2002-2013 technical bill (Part 3 — FA reorganizations), effective for dispositions that occur after Aug. 19, 2011.

Interpretation Bulletins: IT-243R4: Dividend refund to private corporations; IT-291R3: Transfer of property to a corporation under subsection 85(1).

(5) Foreign share for foreign share exchange — Subject to subsections (3) and (6) and 95(2), where a corporation resident in a country other than Canada (in this section referred to as the "foreign purchaser") issues shares of its capital stock (in this section referred to as the "issued foreign shares") to a vendor in exchange for shares of the capital stock of another corporation resident in a country other than Canada (in this section referred to as the "exchanged foreign shares") that were immediately before the exchange capital property of the vendor, except where the vendor has, in the vendor's return of income for the taxation year in which the exchange occurred, included in computing the vendor's income for that year any portion of the gain or loss, otherwise determined, from the disposition of the exchanged foreign shares, the vendor is deemed

(a) to have disposed of the exchanged foreign shares for proceeds of disposition equal to the adjusted cost base to the vendor of those shares immediately before the exchange, and

(b) to have acquired the issued foreign shares at a cost to the vendor equal to the adjusted cost base to the vendor of the exchanged foreign shares immediately before the exchange,

and where the exchanged foreign shares were taxable Canadian property of the vendor, the issued foreign shares so acquired by the vendor are deemed to be, at any time that is within 60 months after the exchange, taxable Canadian property of the vendor.

Related Provisions: 85.1(6) — Where rollover does not apply; 85.1(6.1) — Issuance to trust under court-approved plan; 86.1(1) — Foreign spinoff; 107.4(3)(f), 248(25.1) — Deemed taxable Canadian property retains status when rolled out of or into trust or between trusts.

Notes: 85.1(5) implements a proposal announced by Finance news release, April 15, 1999, to allow a rollover on a foreign share-for-share exchange. For foreign spinoffs see 86.1. See also Steeves, "Foreign Share Exchanges", 49(4) *Canadian Tax Journal* 1066-75 (2001); VIEWS docs 2010-0373801R3, 2011-039289117 (IT-450R para. 6 [now Folio S4-F5-C1 ¶1.7] policy on cash in lieu of fractional shares applies to 85.1(6)(c)); 2015-0614981E5 (policy on cash does not apply unless *purchaser's offer* specifies the fraction of each share exchanged for cash) [Cepparo, "Cash Consideration", 25(2) *Canadian Tax Highlights* (ctf.ca) 8-9 (Feb. 2017)].

85.1(5) closing words amended by 2010 budget bill #1, effective in determining after March 4, 2010 whether a property is taxable Canadian property of a taxpayer, to add "at any time that is within 60 months after the exchange". See Notes to 44.1(2).

85.1(5) added by 2001 technical bill, effective for exchanges that occur after 1995.

(6) Where subsection (5) does not apply — Subsection (5) does not apply where

(a) the vendor and foreign purchaser were, immediately before the exchange, not dealing with each other at arm's length (otherwise than because of a right referred to in paragraph 251(5)(b) that is a right of the foreign purchaser to acquire the exchanged foreign shares);

(b) immediately after the exchange the vendor, persons with whom the vendor did not deal at arm's length or the vendor together with persons with whom the vendor did not deal at arm's length

(i) controlled the foreign purchaser, or

(ii) beneficially owned shares of the capital stock of the foreign purchaser having a fair market value of more than 50% of the fair market value of all of the outstanding shares of the capital stock of the foreign purchaser;

(c) consideration other than issued foreign shares was received by the vendor for the exchanged foreign shares, notwithstanding that the vendor may have disposed of shares of the capital stock of the other corporation referred to in subsection (5) (other than the exchanged foreign shares) to the foreign purchaser for consideration other than shares of the capital stock of the foreign purchaser;

(d) the vendor

(i) is a foreign affiliate of a taxpayer resident in Canada at the end of the taxation year of the vendor in which the exchange occurred, and

(ii) has included any portion of the gain or loss, otherwise determined, from the disposition of the exchanged foreign shares in computing its foreign accrual property income for the taxation year of the vendor in which the exchange occurred; or

(e) the vendor is a foreign affiliate of a taxpayer resident in Canada at the end of the taxation year of the vendor in which the exchange occurred and the exchanged foreign shares are excluded property (within the meaning assigned by subsection 95(1)) of the vendor.

Notes: See Notes to 85.1(5). 85.1(6) added by 2001 technical bill, for exchanges that occur after 1995.

(6.1) Issuance deemed made to vendor — For the purposes of subsection (5), if a foreign purchaser issues shares of a class of its capital stock (in this subsection referred to as "foreign purchaser shares") to a trust under a court-approved plan or scheme of arrangement in consideration for which a vendor disposes of exchanged foreign shares that trade on a designated stock exchange to the purchaser solely for foreign purchaser shares that are widely traded on a designated stock exchange immediately after and as part of completion of the plan or scheme of arrangement, the issuance to the trust is deemed to be an issuance to the vendor.

Notes: 85.1(6.1) addresses a problem described in a Dec. 16, 2005 Finance comfort letter (reproduced here up to the 43rd ed., and in *Dept. of Finance Technical Notes*). 85.1(6.1) added by 2002-2013 technical bill, effective on the same basis as 85.1(2.2).

(7) Application of subsec. (8) — Subsection (8) applies in respect of the disposition before 2013 by a taxpayer of SIFT wind-up entity equity (referred to in subsection (8) as the "particular unit") to a taxable Canadian corporation if

(a) the disposition occurs during a period (referred to in this subsection and subsection (8) as the "exchange period") of no more than 60 days at the end of which all of the equity in the SIFT wind-up entity is owned by the corporation;

(b) the taxpayer receives no consideration for the disposition other than a share (referred to in this subsection and subsection (8) as the "exchange share") of the capital stock of the corporation that is issued during the exchange period to the taxpayer by the corporation;

(c) neither of subsections 85(1) and (2) applies to the disposition; and

(d) all of the exchange shares issued to holders of equity in the SIFT wind-up entity are shares of a single class of the capital stock of the corporation.

Notes: 85.1(7) opening words corrected to change "referred to" to "referred to in" by 2002-2013 technical bill (Part 5 — technical), effective June 26, 2013.

85.1(7) added by 2008 budget bill #2, on the same basis as 85.1(8).

(8) Rollover on SIFT unit for share exchange — If this subsection applies in respect of a disposition by a taxpayer of a particular unit of a SIFT wind-up entity to a corporation for consideration that is an exchange share, the following rules apply:

(a) the taxpayer's proceeds of disposition of the particular unit, and cost of the exchange share, are deemed to be equal to the cost amount to the taxpayer of the particular unit immediately before the disposition;

(b) if the particular unit was immediately before the disposition taxable Canadian property of the taxpayer, the exchange share is deemed to be, at any time that is within 60 months after the disposition, taxable Canadian property of the taxpayer;

(c) if the exchange share's fair market value immediately after the disposition exceeds the particular unit's fair market value at the time of the disposition, the excess is deemed to be an amount that section 15 requires to be included in computing the taxpayer's income for the taxpayer's taxation year in which the disposition occurs;

(d) if the particular unit's fair market value at the time of the disposition exceeds the exchange share's fair market value immediately after the disposition, and it is reasonable to regard any part of the excess as a benefit that the taxpayer desired to have conferred on a person, or partnership, with whom the taxpayer does not deal at arm's length, the excess is deemed to be an amount that section 15 requires to be included in computing the taxpayer's income for the taxpayer's taxation year in which the disposition occurs;

(e) the cost to the corporation of the particular unit is deemed to be the lesser of

(i) the fair market value of the particular unit immediately before the disposition, and

(ii) the amount determined for B in the formula in paragraph

(f) in respect of the particular unit; and

(f) in computing the paid-up capital in respect of each class of shares of the capital stock of the corporation at any time after the disposition there shall be deducted the amount determined by the formula

$$(A - B) \times C/A$$

where

A is the increase, if any, as a result of the disposition, in the paid-up capital in respect of all the shares of the capital stock of the corporation, computed without reference to this paragraph as it applies to the disposition,

B is the amount determined by the formula

$$D - E$$

where

D is

(i) unless subparagraph (ii) applies, the total of all amounts each of which is

(A) if the SIFT wind-up entity is a trust, the fair market value of property received by the SIFT wind-up entity on the issuance of the particular unit, or

(B) if the SIFT wind-up entity is a partnership,

(I) an amount that has at any time been added, in computing the adjusted cost base to any taxpayer of the particular unit on or before the disposition, because of subparagraph 53(1)(e)(iv) or (x), or

(II) an amount that would at any time have been added, in computing the adjusted cost base to any taxpayer of the particular unit on or before the disposition, because of subparagraph 53(1)(e)(i) if subsection 96(1) were read without reference to its paragraph (d) and the partnership deducted all amounts otherwise deductible because of that paragraph, and

(ii) if the SIFT wind-up entity has on or after the end of the exchange period issued a unit, nil, and

E is the total of all amounts each of which

(i) if the SIFT wind-up entity is a trust, has become payable by the SIFT wind-up entity, in respect of the particular unit, to any holder of the unit on or before the disposition, other than an amount that has become payable out of its income (determined without reference to subsection 104(6)) or capital gains, and

(ii) if the SIFT wind-up entity is a partnership,

(A) has at any time been deducted, in computing the adjusted cost base to any taxpayer of the particular unit on or before the disposition, because of subparagraph 53(2)(c)(iv) or (v), or

(B) would have at any time been deducted, in computing the adjusted cost base to any taxpayer of the particular unit on or before the disposition, because of subparagraph 53(2)(c)(i) if subsection 96(1) were read without reference to its paragraph (d) and the partnership deducted all amounts otherwise deductible because of that paragraph, and

C is the increase, if any, as a result of the disposition, in the paid-up capital in respect of the class of shares, computed without reference to this paragraph as it applies to the disposition.

Related Provisions: 40(3.5)(b.1) — SIFT wind-up corporation deemed identical property for 40(3.3)–(3.4); 85.1(7) — Conditions for 85.1(8) to apply; 88.1(2), 107(3.1) — Alternative mechanism of wind-up of SIFT trust; 107.4(3)(f) — Deemed taxable Canadian property retains status on rollover; 128.3 — Deferral applies to post-emigration disposition for certain purposes; 248(25.1) — Deemed TCP retains status through trust-to-trust transfer; 257 — Formula cannot calculate to less than zero.

Notes: 85.1(8) allowed a rollover of SIFT trust or partnership units to a corporation before 2013. This allowed a SIFT trust to convert back to corporate form (unwind), in advance of the tax on SIFT trust distributions applying in 2011 (see 122.1(2) and Notes to 104(16)). For an alternate mechanism permitting a SIFT trust to roll out its assets on a tax-free basis, see 88.1(2) and 107(3.1).

For a list of SIFTs that unwound or were unwinding in 2009 see Derek Alty & John Owen, "Recent Transactions of Interest", 2009 Cdn Tax Foundation conference, slides 4-5 (paper not written for conference report); Marie-Emmanuelle Vaillancourt, "Exchangeable Structures in the Context of Income Fund Conversions", XII(1) *Corporate Structures & Groups* (Federated Press) 648-50 (2010). For a ruling approving a reorganization without using 85.1(7)-(8) see VIEWS doc 2010-0358731R3. For 2010 transactions see Cannon, Pashkowich & Thompson, "Recent Transactions of Interest", 2010 Cdn Tax Foundation conference report, 6:1-34.

For discussion see Bauer, "The New Income Trust Conversion Proposals", XII(1) *Business Vehicles* (Federated Press) 610-17 (2008); Fyfe, Holmes & Powrie, "Canada Facilitates Conversions of Income Trusts to Corporations", XV(1) *Corporate Finance* (Federated Press) 1591-95 (2008); Newcombe, "Conversion of a SIFT to a Corporation", 5(12) *Tax Hyperion* (Carswell, Dec. 2008); Juneja, "The SIFT Conversion Rules in the Takeover Context", XI(1) *Corporate Structures & Groups* (Federated Press) 592-98 (2008); Perry, "Income Trusts: Reorganizations and Planning for 2011", 2008 Cdn Tax Foundation conference report, 8:1-38. For discussion of the Nov. 2008 changes see Sherman, "SIFT Update — Conversions and Normal Growth", XV(3) *Corporate Finance* 1678-82 (2009); Nearing & Jamal, "Trust Conversions", 22(1) *Canadian Petroleum Tax Journal* 1-30 (2009). As to whether the costs are deductible or capital see Hanna & Morin, "Reorganization Costs", VI(1) *Resource Sector Taxation* (Federated Press) 410-16 (2008). For suggested amendments see Hickey, "Joint Committee: SIFT Legislation", 16(11) *Canadian Tax Highlights* (ctf.ca) 7-8 (Nov. 2008).

Many income trusts merged with tax-loss companies to absorb income, as the "change in control" rules (see Notes to 111(5)) did not apply to trusts (see now 251.2(2)) and GAAR might not apply. See Jim Middlemiss, "Ottawa faces tax loss in trusts", *National Post*, Jan. 27, 2010, giving examples of Superior Plus Income Fund (merging with Ballard Power Systems Inc. [though this was not done via merger: *Superior Plus*, 2015 TCC 132, para. 7 (aff'd 2015 FCA 241; see also 2016 TCC 217)]), Total Energy Services Trust (Biomerge Industries Ltd.), Exchange Industry Income Fund (HMY Airways), Premium Brands Income Fund (Thallion Pharmaceuticals Inc.), Algonquin

Power Income Fund (Hydrogenics Corp.), Colabor Income Fund (Conjuchem Biotechnologies Inc.), and Cervus LP (Vasogen Inc.). The 2010 amendments to 256(7) were introduced to prevent this.

85.1(8)(f) corrected to change "paid up capital" to "paid-up capital" by 2002-2013 technical bill (Part 5 — technical), effective June 26, 2013.

85.1(8)(b) amended by 2010 budget bill #1, effective in determining after March 4, 2010 whether a property is taxable Canadian property of a taxpayer, to add "at any time that is within 60 months after the disposition". See Notes to 44.1(2).

85.1(8) added by 2008 budget bill #2, effective for dispositions after July 13, 2008 (or after Dec. 19, 2007 by election — see up to PITA 48th ed. for details).

Proposed Amendment — Canadian/foreign (cross-border) share-for-share exchange

Supplementary Information, Economic Statement, Oct. 18, 2000; Federal budget Supplementary Information, Feb. 18, 2003, March 23, 2004 and Feb. 23, 2005: See after 86.1.

Definitions [s. 85.1]: "acquired corporation" — 85.1(1); "adjusted cost base" — 54, 248(1); "amount" — 248(1); "arm's length" — 251(1); "beneficially owned" — 248(3); "Canadian corporation" — 89(1), 248(1); "capital gain" — 39(1)(a), 248(1); "capital property" — 54, 248(1); "class of shares" — 248(6); "controlled" — 256(6), (6.1); "corporation" — 248(1), *Interpretation Act* 35(1); "cost amount" — 248(1); "designated stock exchange" — 248(1), 262; "disposition" — 248(1); "dividend" — 248(1); "exchange period" — 85.1(7)(a); "exchange share" — 85.1(7)(b); "exchanged foreign shares" — 85.1(5); "exchanged property" — 85.1(1); "excluded property" — 95(1); "fair market value" — see 69(1) Notes; "filing-due date" — 248(1); "foreign accrual property income" — 95(1); "foreign affiliate" — 95(1), 248(1); "foreign purchaser", "issued foreign shares" — 85.1(5); "Minister" — 248(1); "paid-up capital" — 89(1), 248(1); "particular unit" — 85.1(7); "partnership" — see 96(1) Notes; "person", "property" — 248(1); "purchaser" — 85.1(1); "purchaser shares" — 85.1(2.2); "qualifying interest" — 95(2)(m); "resident" — 250; "resident in Canada" — 94(3)(a), 250; "SIFT wind-up entity", "SIFT wind-up entity equity" — 248(1); "series", "series of transactions" — 248(10); "share" — 248(1); "taxable Canadian corporation" — 89(1), 248(1); "taxable Canadian property" — 248(1); "taxation year" — 249; "taxpayer" — 248(1); "trust" — 104(1), 248(1), (3); "vendor" — 85.1(1); "writing" — *Interpretation Act* 35(1).

86. (1) Exchange of shares by a shareholder in course of reorganization of capital
— Where, at a particular time after May 6, 1974, in the course of a reorganization of the capital of a corporation, a taxpayer has disposed of capital property that was all the shares of any particular class of the capital stock of the corporation that were owned by the taxpayer at the particular time (in this section referred to as the "old shares"), and property is receivable from the corporation therefor that includes other shares of the capital stock of the corporation (in this section referred to as the "new shares"), the following rules apply:

(a) the cost to the taxpayer of any property (other than new shares) receivable by the taxpayer for the old shares shall be deemed to be its fair market value at the time of the disposition;

(b) the cost to the taxpayer of any new shares of any class of the capital stock of the corporation receivable by the taxpayer for the old shares shall be deemed to be that proportion of the amount, if any, by which the total of the adjusted cost bases to the taxpayer, immediately before the disposition, of the old shares exceeds the fair market value at that time of the consideration receivable for the old shares (other than new shares) that

(i) the fair market value, immediately after the disposition, of those new shares of that class,

is of

(ii) the fair market value, immediately after the disposition, of all new shares of the capital stock of the corporation receivable by the taxpayer for the old shares; and

(c) the taxpayer shall be deemed to have disposed of the old shares for proceeds of disposition equal to the cost to the taxpayer of all new shares and other property receivable by the taxpayer for the old shares.

Related Provisions: 7(1.5) — Exchange of shares; 51(1), (2) — Conversion of debt to shares; 51(4) — Application of s. 86 to exchange of convertible property; 55(1) — "Permitted redemption" for butterfly purposes; 85(1)-(3) — Transfer of property to corporation; 86(2.1) — Computation of paid-up capital; 86(3) — No application if 85(1) election made; 86(4) — Debt forgiveness — reduction in adjusted cost base of new shares; 93.2(3) — Application to non-resident corp without share capital; 112(7) — Application of stop-loss rule where shares exchanged; 128.3 — Deferral ap-

plies to post-emigration disposition for certain purposes; 131(4.1) — Mutual fund switch-fund shares — no rollover; Canada-U.S. Tax Treaty:Art. XIII:8 — Deferral of tax for U.S. resident transferor.

Notes: 86(1) allows an "internal reorganization" — exchange of all the shares of a class for another class — with no tax effect, with the cost of the old shares rolling over to the new shares. It applies automatically if its conditions are met, but does not apply if a s. 85 election is made: 86(3). See Fenton, "Exchange of shares", 2554 *Tax Topics* (CCH) 1-4 (Feb. 16, 2021). For planning ideas see Tabuchi, "Share Capital Reorganizations for Private Corporations", 51(3) *Canadian Tax Journal* 1340-78 (2003). If not all shares of a class are exchanged, 51(1) applies instead.

CRA states that a "reorganization" for 86(1) requires that the corporation's articles be amended: VIEWS docs 2010-0373271C6, 2020-0860971C6 [2020 CTF q.14]. Thus, if the corp was set up ahead of time with multiple classes of shares to permit 86(1) exchanges, the exchange may not qualify! (CRA may be wrong, as issuing new shares should constitute a "reorganization". See also Lang, "Linkage Required for Section 86 Reorganization", XVII(1) *Corporate Finance* (Federated Press) 1944-46 (2011).) Similarly, CRA states that a conversion under Quebec *Business Corporations Act* s. 91 is not a "reorganization" but falls under s. 51: 2011-0412191C6.

86(1) is often used for an "**estate freeze**", where a business owner converts all common shares to retractable preferred voting shares (keeping control and having a fixed value equal to the retraction value) while the children subscribe to new common shares, for future growth and capital gain (this simplest form is called a "wasting freeze"). For the attributes CRA requires for estate freeze pref shares, see 1980 Cdn Tax Foundation conference report, round table q. 13 (p. 602); VIEWS doc 2008-0285241C6. If there are children not involved in the business, and the parents' voting pref shares may go to them on death, a shareholder agreement may help ensure those children do not demand redemption and ruin the company financially. (If the family has other corps, note that an estate freeze can inadvertently cause them to become associated (e.g., 256(1.2), (1.3)) and required to share the small business deduction.) (Retractable shares may need to be classified as debt for accounting purposes, effective 2021: Hirji, Keung & Moody, tinyurl.com/moodys-retract.)

Owners planning an estate freeze may have several goals, including limiting tax on death; multiplying the capital gains exemption; income splitting; giving children an incentive to work in the business; protection from creditors (and from children's spouses on marriage breakdown); and providing retirement income for the owners. Possible pitfalls include: capital gain on transfer; income-splitting tax (120.4); shareholder benefit triggered by freezor extracting too much (15(1)); valuation of freeze shares (see Notes to 69(1)); attribution rules (e.g. 74.4(2)). A "reverse freeze" can undo future growth of an estate freeze, but an artificial capital loss created in a reverse freeze was denied under GAAR: *Triad Gestco*, 2012 FCA 258.

Family law impact: an estate freeze may be challenged by a separating spouse or other family member. See *McNamee v. McNamee*, 2011 ONCA 533 (transfer of common shares to son was "gift", exempt from Ontario *Family Law Act* property division); *Reisman v. Reisman*, 2014 ONCA 109 (freeze was not fraudulent conveyance under *Fraudulent Conveyances Act* [see end of Notes to 160(1) for discussion of that Act]); *Hamm v. Hamm*, 2014 MBQB 14 ("risky" to undertake freeze without informing spouse and arranging for spouse to get independent legal advice); *Hui v. Hoa*, 2015 BCCA 128 (mother's expected retirement income from freeze taken away by son); *Shinder v. Shinder*, 2017 ONSC 4177 (impact of freeze unresolved); *Leitch v. Novac*, 2017 ONSC 6888 (unresolved). See also Corbin, "The Estate Freeze — A Fraudulent Conveyance?", 29(4) *Money & Family Law* (Carswell) 25-27 (April 2014); Rocchi, "Pre-Separation Estate Planning — Asking for Trouble?", 10(4) *Taxes & Wealth Management* (Carswell) 1-5 (Dec. 2017).

For more on estate freezing see Roth et al., *Canadian Taxation of Trusts* (ctf.ca, 2016), pp. 1010-33; *Miller Thomson on Estate Planning*, chap. 13 and Brown, *Taxation and Estate Planning*, chap. 7 (both Carswell, looseleaf or *Taxnet Pro* Reference Centre); Louis, *Implementing Estate Freezes* (3rd ed., CCH, 2011); Rochwerg & Ng-A-Mann, "Freezing, Thawing, and Refreezing", 2009 Ontario Tax Conf. (ctf.ca), 12:1-29; Kirby & Gilbert, "Fundamentals of Estate Freezing", 2009 Prairie Provinces Tax Conf. 6:1-71; Yager, "Estate Freeze and Reversionary Trust Rule", 19(6) *Canadian Tax Highlights [CTH]* (ctf.ca) 11-12 (June 2011); Goldberg series "Selected Tax Issues and Traps Associated with Estate Freezes", 217-221 The *Estate Planner [TEP]* (Feb.-June 2013); Brodlieb, "Wasting Freezes Now Less Attractive in Ontario", 3(3) *Canadian Tax Focus [CTFo]* (ctf.ca) 1-2 (Aug. 2013); Ehinger, "Implementing an Estate Freeze Through a Stock Dividend", 4(2) *CTFo* 4-5 (May 2014); Roth, "Including or Adding the Freezor as a Discretionary Trust Beneficiary", 2013 Ontario Tax Conf. 14C:1-25; Bernstein, "Estate Freezing", 23(9) *CTH* 9-10 (Sept. 2015) and 256 *TEP* 3-6 (May 2016); Estate Freeze from Hell (case study, 190pp), 2019 STEP Canada conference; Cheng, "Estate Freezes and Practical Planning", 20(2) *Tax for the Owner-Manager [TfOM]* 11-12 (April 2020); Ideias, "Estate Freezes: What a Tax Planner Needs to Know" (*Taxnet Pro* Tax & Estate Planning Centre, 2021, 8pp); "Estate Freeze Checklist" (*ibid.*, 6pp).

Estate freezing and specific issues: Family law: Bales, "Estate Freezes and Family Law", 2013 Ontario Tax Conf. 14A:1-13; papers "Avoiding Family Law Fiascos in Estate Freezes" by Low (BC, Alberta), Marquis (Quebec), Van Cauwenberghe (all provinces), 2013 STEP Canada conf (contact memberservices@step.ca). Using a partnership for an estate freeze: see 97(2) Notes. Price adjustment clauses (PACs) in an estate freeze: see 69(1) Notes (amount payable due to a PAC on redeeming freeze shares may be a deemed dividend: 2011-0422191E5). US citizens: Bernstein, "Estate Freezes: US Beneficiaries", 21(12) *CTH* 5-6 (Dec. 2013) and "Canadian Estate Freezes in Favor of US Citizens", 241 *TEP* 1-12 (Feb. 2015); Turkovich, "US Tax Reform Error Affects Canadian Estate Freezes", 27(2) *CTH* 10-11 (Feb. 2019). Thawing an estate freeze: May 2009 ICAA roundtable (tinyurl.com/cra-abtax) q.19. Refreeze: Bernstein, "Time to Refreeze?", 17(8) *CTH* 1-2 (Aug. 2009); Newcombe, "Reconfirming the Tax Consequences of a Refreeze", 7(12) *Tax Hyperion* (Carswell, Dec. 2010); MacDonald, "When Does an Estate Refreeze Trigger a Shareholder Benefit?", 11(1) *TfOM* 7-8 (Jan. 2011); del Rio, "Part VI.1 Tax on Dividend Paid Through Family Trust", 19(3) *TfOM* 9-10 (July 2019); Demner & McIsaac, "Freezes and Refreezes", *COVID-19 and Canadian Tax* (ctf.ca) 5-7 (July 2020); MacInnis, "Estate Freeze or Re-Freeze of Real Estate Holdings", 311 *TEP* 1-2 (Dec. 2020); Hennessey, "Potential Application of Part VI.1 and Subsection 104(2) in Estate Freezes", 21(1) *TfOM* 9-9 (Jan. 2021); and 74.4(3) Notes.

The votes attached to the pref shares may give them a premium value: *Income Tax Technical News* 38 [2007 Cdn Tax Foundation conference report at 4:21-22]; and see VIEWS doc 2020-0842251C6 [2020 CALU q.7]. CRA stated at the 2009 Cdn Tax Foundation conf Roundtable q.1 (conference report p. 3;1; *Technical News* 44) that CRA will accept a nil value for estate freeze purposes, "provided the owners of all the shares act in a manner consistent with the assumption that no value attaches to the voting rights". However, if later facts show a value, such as in an offer to purchase them, the CRA will assess based on those facts. (Phil Jolie, in presenting this answer, referred to the Wizard of Oz line "Pay no attention to the man behind the curtain!": don't show CRA facts that give the shares a value. If the shares don't disappear quietly and CRA sees this, they will take the value into account.) See also 2009-0330211C6; 2013-0487431C6 [2010 CTF conf. report q.17, p. 4:16-18]; May 2009 ICAA round-table (tinyurl.com/cra-abtax) q.20; *Laflamme*, 2008 CarswellNat 3050 (TCC). For discussion see Yull, "What's the 'Skinny' on Voting, Non-Participating Shares?", 5(11) *Tax Hyperion* (Carswell, Nov. 2008); Funt, "Closely-held Corporations and the Valuation of Voting Shares", XII(3) *Business Vehicles* (Federated Press) 642-45; Louis, "A Note Re Control Premiums", 177 *The Estate Planner* (CCH) 1-2 (Oct. 2009), "Control Premium", 1960 *Tax Topics* (CCH) 1-2 (Oct. 1, 2009) and "The Control Premium Issue", 2009 STEP Canada conference (contact memberservices@step.ca); Yager, "Freeze Share Valuation", 17(10) *Canadian Tax Highlights* (ctf.ca) 3-4 (Oct. 2009); Morand, "Common sense? The valuation of shares of family-held private corporations", 1919 *Tax Topics* 9-11 (Dec. 18, 2008) (also in 168 *The Estate Planner* 1-4 (Jan. 2009)); Brown, "Estate Freezes Under Fire", II(3) *Personal Tax and Estate Planning* (Federated Press) 98-100 (2009).

A stock split or consolidation also has no tax effect: IT-65; *Brulotte*, 2003 TCC 467; VIEWS doc 2019-0799981R3 (US corp).

For CRA interpretation see VIEWS doc 2008-0300391C6 (if common shares with nil value exchanged for pref shares, the pref shares will have $0 ACB due to 86(1)(b)).

See also Lamarre et al., *Taxation of Corporate Reorganizations* (Carswell, 3rd ed., 2019), §4.1; Pamela Earle, "Restrictions on the Reorganization of Capital", 8(10) *Tax Hyperion* (Carswell, Oct. 2011); Ian Crosbie & Raj Juneja, "Canadian Spinco Acquisition Transactions", *Mergers & Acquisitions Newsletter* (Taxnet Pro Corporate Tax Centre), Nov. 2011.

Regulations: 230(3) (no information return required if no other consideration).

I.T. Application Rules: 26(27), (28).

Interpretation Bulletins: IT-65: Stock splits and consolidations; IT-146R4: Shares entitling shareholders to choose taxable or capital dividends.

I.T. Technical News: 44 (valuation of special voting shares).

Advance Tax Rulings: ATR-22R: Estate freeze using share exchange; ATR-33: Exchange of shares.

(2) Idem — Notwithstanding paragraphs (1)(b) and (c), where a taxpayer has disposed of old shares in circumstances described in subsection (1) and the fair market value of the old shares immediately before the disposition exceeds the total of

(a) the cost to the taxpayer of the property (other than new shares) receivable by the taxpayer for the old shares as determined under paragraph (1)(a), and

(b) the fair market value of the new shares, immediately after the disposition,

and it is reasonable to regard any portion of the excess (in this subsection referred to as the "gift portion") as a benefit that the taxpayer desired to have conferred on a person related to the taxpayer, the following rules apply:

(c) the taxpayer shall be deemed to have disposed of the old shares for proceeds of disposition equal to the lesser of

(i) the total of the cost to the taxpayer of the property as determined under paragraph (1)(a) and the gift portion

and

(ii) the fair market value of the old shares immediately before the disposition,

(d) the taxpayer's capital loss from the disposition of the old shares shall be deemed to be nil, and

(e) the cost to the taxpayer of any new shares of any class of the capital stock of the corporation receivable by the taxpayer for the old shares shall be deemed to be that proportion of the amount, if any, by which the total of the adjusted cost bases to the taxpayer, immediately before the disposition, of the old shares exceeds the total determined under subparagraph (c)(i) that

(i) the fair market value, immediately after the disposition, of the new shares of that class,

is of

(ii) the fair market value, immediately after the disposition, of all new shares of the capital stock of the corporation receivable by the taxpayer for the old shares.

Related Provisions: 85(1)(e.2) — Parallel rule for s. 85 rollover; 86(3) — Application.

Notes: 86(2) did not apply in VIEWS doc 2010-0369661R3 (reorganization of incestuous shareholdings of Western Coal: Carrie Smit, "Recent Transactions of Interest", 2011 Cdn Tax Foundation conference report at 10:5-10). Nor did it apply in *Mady*, 2017 TCC 112, paras. 122-133 (sole shareholder remained sole shareholder after transaction; family members' intention to acquire shares in prearranged steps did not give them a beneficial interest) [Lum, "Reverse Attribution and LCGE", 7(4) *Canadian Tax Focus* (ctf.ca) 9 (Nov. 2017)].

I.T. Application Rules: 26(27), (28) (where shares or property owned since before 1972).

Income Tax Folios: S4-F3-C1: Price adjustment clauses [replaces IT-169]; S4-F7-C1: Amalgamations of Canadian corporations [replaces IT-474R2].

Advance Tax Rulings: ATR-22R: Estate freeze using share exchange; ATR-33: Exchange of shares.

(2.1) Computation of paid-up capital — Where subsection (1) applies to a disposition of shares of the capital stock of a corporation (in this subsection referred to as the "exchange"), in computing the paid-up capital in respect of a particular class of shares of the capital stock of the corporation at any particular time that is the time of, or any time after, the exchange,

(a) there shall be deducted the amount determined by the formula

$$(A - B) \times C / A$$

where

A is the total of all amounts each of which is the increase, if any, as a result of the exchange, in the paid-up capital in respect of a class of shares of the capital stock of the corporation, computed without reference to this subsection as it applies to the exchange,

B is the amount, if any, by which the paid-up capital in respect of the old shares exceeds the fair market value of the consideration (other than shares of the capital stock of the corporation) given by the corporation for the old shares on the exchange, and

C is the increase, if any, as a result of the exchange, in the paid-up capital in respect of the particular class of shares, computed without reference to this subsection as it applies to the exchange; and

(b) there shall be added an amount equal to the lesser of

(i) the amount, if any, by which

(A) the total of all amounts deemed by subsection 84(3), (4) or (4.1) to be a dividend on shares of that class paid by the corporation before the particular time

exceeds

(B) the total that would be determined under clause (A) if this Act were read without reference to paragraph (a), and

(ii) the total of all amounts required by paragraph (a) to be deducted in respect of that particular class of shares before the particular time.

Related Provisions: 257 — Formula cannot calculate to less than zero.

Notes: The effect of 86(2.1), which reduces the paid-up capital (PUC) of the new shares, is to permit a PUC deficiency on the old shares (such as may have arisen where 85(2.1) applied to reduce PUC following a rollover under 85(1)) to flow through to the new shares. Thus, the 86(1) exchange will not result in an increase in PUC to which 84(1) would apply; and the amount received for the old shares for purposes of 84(3) will be equal to the PUC of the old shares (see 84(5)). 51(3) applies the same rule to share exchanges that fall under s. 51.

See VIEWS docs 2008-0293401E5 (interaction of 86(2.1) and 84(1)); 2013-0505431R3 (transfer of resource royalty within related group).

86(2.1) added by 1993 technical bill.

(3) Application [s. 85 takes priority] — Subsections (1) and (2) do not apply in any case where subsection 85(1) or (2) applies.

Related Provisions: 51(4) — Application of section 51.

Notes: 86(3) amended by 1993 technical bill, effective for reorganizations that begin after Dec. 21, 1992, to remove reference to s. 51. Under the old rules 86 did not apply if 51 applied. Now 86 takes precedence, and 51 does not apply if 86 can (see 51(4)).

(4) Computation of adjusted cost base — Where a taxpayer has disposed of old shares in circumstances described in subsection (1),

(a) there shall be deducted after the disposition in computing the adjusted cost base to the taxpayer of each new share the amount determined by the formula

$$A \times B/C$$

where

A is the amount, if any, by which

(i) the total of all amounts deducted under paragraph 53(2)(g.1) in computing the adjusted cost base to the taxpayer of the old shares immediately before the disposition

exceeds

(ii) the amount that would be the taxpayer's capital gain for the taxation year that includes the time of the disposition from the disposition of the old shares if paragraph 40(1)(a) were read without reference to subparagraph (iii) of that paragraph,

B is the fair market value of the new share at the time it was acquired by the taxpayer in consideration for the disposition of the old shares, and

C is the total of all amounts each of which is the fair market value of a new share at the time it was acquired by the taxpayer in consideration for the disposition of the old shares; and

(b) the amount determined under paragraph (a) in respect of the acquisition shall be added in computing the adjusted cost base to the taxpayer of the new share after the disposition.

Related Provisions: 53(1)(q) — Addition to ACB for amount under 86(4)(b); 53(2)(g.1) — Reduction in ACB under 86(4)(a); 80.03(2)(a) — Deemed gain on disposition following debt forgiveness.

Notes: 86(4) added by 1994 technical bill, effective for taxation years that end after February 21, 1994. See Notes to 47(1).

Definitions [s. 86]: "adjusted cost base" — 54, 248(1); "amount" — 248(1); "capital loss" — 39(1)(b), 248(1); "capital property" — 54, 248(1); "class of shares" — 248(6); "common share" — 248(1); "corporation" — 248(1), *Interpretation Act* 35(1); "designated stock exchange" — 248(1), 262; "fair market value" — see 69(1) Notes; "new shares", "old shares" — 86(1); "person", "preferred share", "property", "share" "taxpayer" — 248(1).

I.T. Application Rules [s. 86]: 26(27) (where old shares owned since before 1972).

Interpretation Bulletins [s. 86]: IT-146R4: Shares entitling shareholders to choose taxable or capital dividends; IT-243R4: Dividend refund to private corporations.

86.1 Foreign spin-offs — (1) Eligible distribution not included in income — Notwithstanding any other provision of this Part,

(a) the amount of an eligible distribution received by a taxpayer shall not be included in computing the income of the taxpayer; and

(b) subsection 52(2) does not apply to the eligible distribution received by the taxpayer.

Related Provisions: 15(1)(a.1)(i) — No shareholder-benefit income inclusion if corporation not resident in Canada; 85.1(5) — Foreign share-for-share exchange; 86.1(2) — Eligible distribution.

Notes: See Notes at end of 86.1.

(2) Eligible distribution — For the purpose of this section, a distribution by a particular corporation that is received by a taxpayer is an eligible distribution if

(a) the distribution is with respect to all of the taxpayer's common shares of the capital stock of the particular corporation (in this section referred to as the "original shares");

(b) the distribution consists solely of common shares of the capital stock of another corporation that were owned by the particular corporation immediately before their distribution to the taxpayer (in this section referred to as the "spin-off shares");

(c) in the case of a distribution that is not prescribed,

(i) at the time of the distribution, both corporations are resident in the United States and were never resident in Canada,

(ii) at the time of the distribution, the shares of the class that includes the original shares are widely held and

(A) are actively traded on a designated stock exchange in the United States, or

(B) are required, under the *Securities Exchange Act of 1934* of the United States, as amended from time to time, to be registered with the Securities and Exchange Commission of the United States and are so registered, and

(iii) under the provisions of the *Internal Revenue Code of 1986* of the United States, as amended from time to time, that apply to the distribution, the shareholders of the particular corporation who are resident in the United States are not taxable in respect of the distribution;

(d) in the case of a distribution that is prescribed,

(i) at the time of the distribution, both corporations are resident in the same country, other than the United States, with which Canada has a tax treaty (in this section referred to as the "foreign country") and were never resident in Canada,

(ii) at the time of the distribution, the shares of the class that includes the original shares are widely held and actively traded on a designated stock exchange,

(iii) under the law of the foreign country, those shareholders of the particular corporation who are resident in that country are not taxable in respect of the distribution, and

(iv) the distribution is prescribed subject to such terms and conditions as are considered appropriate in the circumstances;

(e) before the end of the sixth month following the day on which the particular corporation first distributes a spin-off share in respect of the distribution, the particular corporation provides to the Minister information satisfactory to the Minister establishing

(i) that, at the time of the distribution, the shares of the class that includes the original shares are shares described in subparagraph (c)(ii) or (d)(ii),

(ii) that the particular corporation and the other corporation referred to in paragraph (b) were never resident in Canada,

(iii) the date of the distribution,

(iv) the type and fair market value of each property distributed to residents of Canada,

(v) the name and address of each resident of Canada that received property with respect to the distribution,

(vi) in the case of a distribution that is not prescribed, that the distribution is not taxable under the provisions of the *Internal Revenue Code of 1986* of the United States, as amended from time to time, that apply to the distribution,

(vii) in the case of a distribution that is prescribed, that the distribution is not taxable under the law of the foreign country, and

(viii) such other matters that are required, in prescribed form; and

(f) the taxpayer elects in writing filed with the taxpayer's return of income for the taxation year in which the distribution occurs that this section apply to the distribution and provides information satisfactory to the Minister

(i) of the number, cost amount (determined without reference to this section) and the fair market value of the taxpayer's original shares immediately before the distribution,

(ii) of the number, and fair market value, of the taxpayer's original shares and the spin-off shares immediately after the distribution of the spin-off shares to the taxpayer,

(iii) except where the election is filed with the taxpayer's return of income for the year in which the distribution occurs, concerning the amount of the distribution, the manner in which the distribution was reported by the taxpayer and the details of any subsequent disposition of original shares or spin-off shares for the purpose of determining any gains or losses from those dispositions, and

(iv) of such other matters that are required, in prescribed form.

Related Provisions: 86.1(5) — Reassessments beyond limitation period; 95(2)(g.2) — Foreign accrual property income; 96(3) — Election by members of partnership; 220(3.2), Reg. 600(c) — Late filing of election under 86.1(2)(f).

Notes: See Notes at end of 86.1, and Reg. 5600. In 86.1(2)(c)(i), "central management and control" (see 250(5) Notes) applies in determining "resident": VIEWS doc 2018-0785991I7.

In *Coster*, 2003 TCC 112, the election deadline was missed but the Court strongly recommended that CRA extend time under 220(3.2). If the election is filed late, CRA will consider delay in issuing approval as a factor in waiving the late-filing penalty: doc 2020-0848761C6 [2020 APFF Financial q.3].

86.1(2) amended by 2002-2013 technical bill, for distributions after 1999, including adding 86.1(2)(c)(ii)(B) (as proposed in a June 11, 2001 Finance comfort letter). Earlier amended by 2007 budget bill #2, 2005 budget bill #1.

Regulations: 5600 (prescribed distribution).

I.T. Technical News: 28 (foreign spin-offs with "poison pill" shareholder rights plans).

(3) Cost adjustments — Where a spin-off share is distributed by a corporation to a taxpayer pursuant to an eligible distribution with respect to an original share of the taxpayer,

(a) there shall be deducted for the purpose of computing the cost amount to the taxpayer of the original share at any time the amount determined by the formula

$$A \times (B/C)$$

where

A   is the cost amount, determined without reference to this section, to the taxpayer of the original share at the time that is immediately before the distribution or, if the original share is disposed of by the taxpayer, before the distribution, at the time that is immediately before its disposition,

B   is the fair market value of the spin-off share immediately after its distribution to the taxpayer, and

C   is the total of

(i) the fair market value of the original share immediately after the distribution of the spin-off share to the taxpayer, and

(ii) the fair market value of the spin-off share immediately after its distribution to the taxpayer; and

(b) the cost to the taxpayer of the spin-off share is the amount by which the cost amount of the taxpayer's original share was reduced as a result of paragraph (a).

Notes: The reference to "the spin-off share" in B and C should take the distribution ratio into account rather than meaning a whole share, where the shares are not exchanged on a 1:1 basis: VIEWS doc 2002-0134537.

See also Notes at end of 86.1.

(4) Inventory — For the purpose of calculating the value of the property described in an inventory of a taxpayer's business,

(a) an eligible distribution to the taxpayer of a spin-off share that is included in the inventory is deemed not to be an acquisition of property in the fiscal period of the business in which the distribution occurs; and

(b) for greater certainty, the value of the spin-off share is to be included in computing the value of the inventory at the end of that fiscal period.

(5) Reassessments — Notwithstanding subsections 152(4) to (5), the Minister may make at any time such assessments, reassessments, determinations and redeterminations that are necessary where information is obtained that the conditions in subparagraph (2)(c)(iii) or (d)(iii) are not, or are no longer, satisfied.

Notes [s. 86.1]: 86.1 allows for a tax deferral, generally on an elective basis, in respect of certain foreign distributions of spin-off shares by a foreign corporation that are received by its Canadian resident shareholders. The jurisdiction of the foreign corporation must not impose tax on shareholders resident in that jurisdiction (e.g., U.S. *Internal Revenue Code* §355). Without 86.1, such shares would be treated as foreign dividends. See also 85.1(5), which applies to foreign share-for-share exchanges.

The election can be filed late under 220(3.2) with payment of the 220(3.5) penalty, which will not be waived merely because the taxpayer was unaware of the election: VIEWS doc 2014-0534831C6 [2014 APFF q.4].

For details on the eligibility criteria, see the May 13, IFA 2002 Government Roundtable at www.ifacanada.org, Question 2.

CRA may apply 86.1 to "poison pill" plans, despite VIEWS docs 2002-0135575 [IFA 2002], 2002-0168455: Mitchell Thaw, "Poison Pills on Foreign Spinoffs", 11(4) *Canadian Tax Highlights* (ctf.ca) 3 (April 2003).

See tinyurl.com/cra-spinoffs for CRA's current list of announced approved spinoffs. CRA will not disclose whether any other spinoff qualifies without the corp's consent, due to the s. 241 confidentiality rules: VIEWS doc 2002-0149644. Particular spinoffs were approved in 2006-0178941I7, 2007-0225221I7, 2014-0530961R3, 2018-0785991I7, 2019-0794571R3 [2019-0833091R3]; and rejected in 2007-0259051E5, 2008-0271141E5, 2008-0285911E5, 2009-0326271E5 (no tax treaty with country). See also Reg. 5600 for prescribed spinoffs.

In *Morasse*, 2004 TCC 239, a Mexico *escisión* of América Móvil did not fall within 86.1, but no tax was payable, as there was no profit distribution and the reorganization was more like a stock split than a stock dividend. Similarly, in *Capancini*, 2010 TCC 581, a non-qualifying Bermuda spinoff of Tyco International was held not to pay "dividends" when the taxpayer received shares of new companies for his Tyco shares. However, in all of *Hamley*, 2010 TCC 459, *Yang*, 2011 TCC 187, *Rezayat*, 2011 TCC 286, *Marshall*, 2012 TCC 497 and *Ahmad*, 2013 TCC 127, this argument was rejected for the same Tyco-Covidien spinoff, and tax applied. See now 15(1)(a.1)(i) and 15(1.5), the latter specifically aimed at Mexico *escisión* and similar spinoffs.

In *Allen*, 2006 TCC 598, there was insufficient evidence that a spinoff of First National Bankshares by FNB Corp. (U.S.) qualified, so the distribution was taxable.

See also Christopher Steeves, "Foreign Share Exchanges and Foreign Spinoffs", 49(4) *Canadian Tax Journal* 1066-1075 (2001); Daniel Lyons, "Foreign Reorganizations and Canadian Shareholders", 2047 *Tax Topics* (CCH) 1-4 (June 2, 2011).

See Notes to 85.1(1) for a Canadian spinoff using 86 and 85.1.

86.1 added by 2000 Budget, effective for distributions received after 1997; the first deadlines under 86.1(2)(e) and (f) were Sept. 11, 2001.

Definitions [s. 86.1]: "amount", "assessment", "business" — 248(1); "Canada" — 255, *Interpretation Act* 35(1); "common share" — 248(1); "corporation" — 248(1), *Interpretation Act* 35(1); "cost amount" — 248(1); "designated stock exchange" — 248(1), 262; "disposition" — 248(1); "eligible distribution" — 86.1(2); "fair market value" — see 69(1) Notes; "fiscal period" — 249.1; "foreign country" — 86.1(2)(d); "inventory", "Minister" — 248(1); "month" — *Interpretation Act* 35(1); "original shares" — 86.1(2)(a); "prescribed", "property" — 248(1); "resident", "resident in Canada" — 250; "share", "shareholder" — 248(1); "spin-off shares" — 86.1(2)(b); "tax treaty" — 248(1); "taxation year" — 249; "taxpayer" — 248(1); "United States", "writing" — *Interpretation Act* 35(1).

Proposed Amendment — Cross-border share-for-share exchanges

Supplementary information, Economic Statement, Oct. 18, 2000: *Canadian/Foreign Share-for-Share Exchanges*

Under the *Income Tax Act*, certain share-for-share exchanges can be effected on a tax-deferred basis where the corporations involved are all resident in Canada or are all non-residents. These rules do not apply, however, to a Canadian resident shareholder who exchanges shares of a domestic corporation for shares of a foreign corporation (or vice versa).

It is intended that a share-for-share exchange rollover rule be developed in consultation with the private sector to apply to cross-border share-for-share exchanges where a Canadian resident shareholder receives only share consideration on the exchange. To ensure the preservation of the Canadian income tax base, rules must be developed to provide for, among other things, cost base adjustments, paid-up capital adjustments, the preservation of taxable Canadian property status, and adjustments for tax benefits that could potentially arise because of the conversion of capital gains into dividends (or vice versa). Any such rollover rule would not take effect before the release of draft legislation for public discussion.

Federal budget, Supplementary Information, Feb. 18, 2003: *Cross-Border Share-For-Share Exchanges*

Under the *Income Tax Act*, certain share-for-share exchanges can be undertaken on a tax-deferred basis where the corporations involved are all resident in Canada or are all non-residents. These rules do not apply, however, to a Canadian resident shareholder who exchanges shares of a domestic corporation for shares of a foreign corporation. While there may be other indirect means of accomplishing such an exchange on a tax-deferred basis, the resulting transactions can be complex and costly.

In the October 2000 Economic Statement and Budget Update, the Government undertook to consult with interested parties on a tax deferral provision that specifically address tax-deferred cross-border share-for-share exchanges. At the same time, the Government noted that a basic requirement for such a mechanism is that it protect Canada's tax base.

A draft of legislative proposals, designed to balance these objectives, will be released in the near future for public review and comment.

Federal budget, Supplementary Information, March 23, 2004: *Cross-Border Share-For-Share Exchanges*

Under the *Income Tax Act*, certain share-for-share exchanges can be undertaken on a tax-deferred basis where the corporations involved are all resident in Canada or are all non-residents. These rules do not apply, however, to a Canadian resident shareholder who exchanges shares of a domestic corporation for shares of a foreign corporation. While there may be other indirect means of accomplishing such an exchange on a tax-deferred basis, the resulting transactions can be complex and costly.

In the October 2000 Economic Statement and Budget Update, the Government undertook to consult with interested parties on the merits and technical design of a tax deferral provision that would, if implemented, apply in respect of cross-border share-for-share exchanges. Budget 2003 reiterated this plan.

It is intended that a detailed proposal be released for public comment in the coming months.

Federal budget, Supplementary Information, Feb. 23, 2005: *Cross-Border Share-for-Share Exchanges*

The 2000 Economic Statement and Budget Update and subsequent budgets indicated the Government's intention to develop rules that would provide an explicit rollover for cross-border share-for-share exchanges while ensuring that the Canadian tax base is protected. A discussion draft of proposed income tax amendments to implement this initiative will be released in the near future.

Notes: See Monica Biringer, "The Much Anticipated Share-For-Share Exchange Rules", XIII(3) *Corporate Finance* (Federated Press) 1361-63 (2006). Brian Ernewein of the Dept. of Finance indicated at the Cdn Tax Foundation annual conference on Nov. 28, 2006 that Finance has had difficulty in designing legislation that preserves Canada's tax rights. They are considering differentiating between small and large shareholders, as the US rules do. No timetable has been set for release of draft legislation. Ernewein advised on Nov. 27, 2007 that this measure has "not been a priority in the past year" and that "work on it has not advanced". Nothing further has been announced since then, but as of Nov. 2014 this proposal was still formally pending.

87. (1) Amalgamations — In this section, an amalgamation means a merger of two or more corporations each of which was, immediately before the merger, a taxable Canadian corporation (each of which corporations is referred to in this section as a "predecessor corporation") to form one corporate entity (in this section referred to as the "new corporation") in such a manner that

(a) all of the property (except amounts receivable from any predecessor corporation or shares of the capital stock of any predecessor corporation) of the predecessor corporations immediately before the merger becomes property of the new corporation by virtue of the merger,

(b) all of the liabilities (except amounts payable to any predecessor corporation) of the predecessor corporations immediately before the merger become liabilities of the new corporation by virtue of the merger, and

(c) all of the shareholders (except any predecessor corporation), who owned shares of the capital stock of any predecessor corporation immediately before the merger, receive shares of the capital stock of the new corporation because of the merger,

otherwise than as a result of the acquisition of property of one corporation by another corporation, pursuant to the purchase of that property by the other corporation or as a result of the distribution of that property to the other corporation on the winding-up of the corporation.

Related Provisions: 53(6) — Effect of amalgamation or merger on ACB of share, partnership interest or trust interest; 69(13) — Amalgamation or merger — deemed proceeds of disposition; 80.03(1), (3)(a)(ii) — Capital gain on amalgamation after debt forgiveness; 87(1.1) — Shares deemed received on merger; 87(8) — Foreign mergers; 87(9) — Triangular amalgamations; 89(1)"Canadian corporation" — Whether amalgamated corp is Canadian corp; 89(1)"taxable Canadian corporation"(b) — Farmers' or fishermen's insurer — amalgamation rules; 89(2) — Where corporation is beneficiary under life insurance policy; 112(7) — Application of stop-loss rule following amalgamation; 128.2 — Predecessor corps take on residence status of amalgamated corp; 131(4.1) — Mutual fund switch-fund shares — no rollover; 137(4.3) — Determination of preferred-rate amount; 139.1(3)(g) — Where insurance corp merges causing demutualization; 204.85(3) — Rules on amalgamation of LSVCCs; 248(1)"disposition"(n) — Cancellation of shares on foreign amalgamation deemed not to be a disposition; 251(3.1), (3.2) — Amalgamated corp deemed related to predecessor; 261(17)–(19) — Effect of functional currency reporting. See also at end of s. 87.

Notes: 87(2) provides extensive rules for rollovers and carryforwards on an amalgamation. See Income Tax Folio S4-F7-C1. See Notes to 248(1)"business number" re whether a new BN must be obtained. The amalgamated company is liable for the tax debts of the predecessors: VIEWS doc 2008-0289321I7, and can prepare T5 information slips for the predecessors: 2011-0397221E5. An authorized representative of *all* the predecessors will be accepted as authorized for the new company: 2011-0404651I7.

Although a new corporation is created, the old corps do not cease to exist and can still be assessed: *Guaranty Properties*, [1990] 2 C.T.C. 94 (FCA). The new corp does not "acquire" the old corps' assets, which simply "become" the new corp's property: *Pan Ocean Oil*, [1994] 2 C.T.C. 143 (FCA). Retained earnings from the old corps carry through to the new: doc 2005-0121941E5. See all the 87(2) paras. for more detail.

See Tobias, *Taxation of Corporations, Partnerships and Trusts* (Carswell, 5th ed., 2017), chap. 13; Lamarre et al., *Taxation of Corporate Reorganizations* (Carswell, 3rd ed., 2019), chap. 7; Green et al., *Taxation of Private Corporations and their Shareholders* (ctf.ca, 5th ed., 2020), pp. 12:9-20; Keey, *Checklist 2 — Amalgamations, Taxnet Pro* Corporate Tax Centre (2020, 26pp); Brayley, "Merging Companies: A Practical Checklist for Amalgamations and Windups", 2000 Cdn Tax Foundation conference report, 6:1-62; Heine & Legge, "Merger Building Blocks: Amalgamations and Windups", 2004 conference report, 37:1-60; Davies Ward LLP, "Key Canadian Federal Tax Considerations in Corporate Merger and Acquisition Transactions", *Mergers and Acquisitions Executive Brief* (*Taxnet Pro* Corporate Tax), July 2013, 33pp; Nijhawan & Richards, "Corporate Combinations", 2013 conference report, 8:1-87 (includes detailed checklist); Mackey & Johnson, "Dissenting Shareholders in Amalgamations", XIII(4) *Corporate Structures & Groups* (Federated Press) 744-53 (2015); Choudhury & Saxe, "Issues in Amalgamations", 2019 Ontario Tax Conference 13 (ctf.ca, 70pp).

Although 87(1) provides that nothing but shares can be received on the amalgamation, CRA permits cash to be received by dissenting shareholders or for fractional shares (Folio S4-F7-C1 ¶1.5, 1.70); also issuing preferred shares that are immediately redeemed for cash does not violate GAAR (Information Circular 88-2 para. 28). Non-share consideration received is otherwise treated as proceeds of disposition: VIEWS docs 2017-0696821E5, 2018-0785921E5.

Where a predecessor's shares are cancelled on amalgamation, their ACB is added to the cost of the common shares of the new corp: 87(4), Folio S4-F7-C1 ¶1.68-1.76.

In *Envision Credit Union*, 2013 SCC 48, two amalgamating credit unions (CUs) tried to create a "non-87(1)" merger (or "broken amalgamation") by transferring some property to another company at the same instant as the merger, so that 87(1)(a) would not be satisfied. The Supreme Court held that the CUs could not contract out of BC *Credit Union Incorporation Act* s. 23, which provided that the amalgamated CU "is seized of and holds" all the property of the predecessors. Therefore, 87(1) applied, and CCA and other balances carried through to the new CU. See Joel Scheuerman case comment, 62(1) *Canadian Tax Journal* 175-83 (2014).

For application of 87(1) to a "Delaware" style merger by absorption, where the parent corp. survives the merger and the subsidiary disappears (which can take place in Canada under a plan of arrangement — for a foreign merger see 87(8.2)), see VIEWS docs 2006-0178571R3, 2010-0355941R3; Richards, "U.S. Delaware Merger Imported to Canada", X(2) *Corporate Structures & Groups* (Federated Press) 552-53 (2006); Ruby, "Recent Transactions of Interest", 2007 Cdn Tax Foundation conference report at 3:13-17 (re merger of Chesapeake Gold Corp. and American Gold Capital Corp.: see 87(9)); Chong, "Amalgamation Fictions", 20(6) *Canadian Tax Highlights* (ctf.ca) 10-11 (June 2012).

See also Ton-That & Chan, "Is a Foreign Merger an Amalgamation?", XII(2) *Corporate Structures & Groups* (Federated Press) 666-69 (2010); Bernstein & Gucciardo, "Canada-US Mergers and Acquisitions", 23(11) *Canadian Tax Highlights* (ctf.ca) 9-10 (Nov. 2015). VIEWS doc 2010-038796I17 said that a kyushu gappei (absorptive merger) under the Japan Commercial Code is not considered an amalgamation, but CRA requested on April 5, 2012 that this doc be removed from all databases.

For charity and non-profit amalgamations see Registered Charities Newsletters 16, 21; Drache, "Charity Amalgamations, Mergers and Consolidations", 21(10) *Canadian Not-for-Profit News* (Carswell) 78-79 (Oct. 2013); VIEWS docs 2008-0300741R3 (amalgamation of NPOs), 2018-0750471R3 (NPO and public foundation). Amalg of mutual funds: 2014-0523221R3. Cross-statute amalg: 2015-0564981R3.

87(1)(c) amended by 1992 technical bill, for amalgamations after 1989, to add "who owned shares of the capital stock". Thus, shareholders who did not actually own shares (such as a policyholder of a mutual insurance corporation) do not have to receive shares of the new corporation for the merger to qualify as an amalgamation.

Regulations: 230(3) (no information return required on cancellation of predecessor's shares).

I.T. Application Rules: 26(28).

Income Tax Folios: S4-F7-C1: Amalgamations of Canadian corporations [replaces IT-474R2].

Interpretation Bulletins: IT-302R3: Losses of a corporation — the effect that acquisitions of control, amalgamations, and windings-up have on their deductibility. See also at end of s. 87.

Information Circulars: 88-2, paras. 20, 28: General anti-avoidance rule — section 245 of the *Income Tax Act*; 88-2 Supplement, para. 9: General anti-avoidance rule — section 245 of the *Income Tax Act*.

Advance Tax Rulings: ATR-29: Amalgamation of social clubs; ATR-55: Amalgamation followed by sale of shares; ATR-59: Financing exploration and development through limited partnerships.

Registered Charities Newsletters: 16 (issues; amalgamations, mergers, and consolidations); 21 (when is an amalgamation not an amalgamation?).

(1.1) Shares deemed to have been received by virtue of merger

— For the purposes of paragraph (1)(c) and the *Income Tax Application Rules*, where there is a merger of

(a) a corporation and one or more of its subsidiary wholly-owned corporations, or

(b) two or more corporations each of which is a subsidiary wholly-owned corporation of the same corporation,

any shares of the capital stock of a predecessor corporation owned by a shareholder (except any predecessor corporation) immediately before the merger that were not cancelled on the merger shall be deemed to be shares of the capital stock of the new corporation received by the shareholder by virtue of the merger as consideration for the disposition of the shares of the capital stock of the predecessor corporations.

Related Provisions: 87(1.4) — Subsidiary wholly-owned corporation. See also at end of s. 87.

Notes: For an example of 87(1.1) applying see VIEWS doc 2010-0376681R3.

On a horizontal short-form amalgamation, where shares of a predecessor corp are cancelled for no consideration, their ACB is added to the cost of the new shares: Income Tax Folio S4-F7-C1 ¶1.74, VIEWS doc 2018-074993117.

Income Tax Folios: S4-F7-C1: Amalgamations of Canadian corporations [replaces IT-474R2].

Interpretation Bulletins: See list at end of s. 87.

(1.2) New corporation continuation of a predecessor

— Where there has been an amalgamation of corporations described in paragraph (1.1)(a) or of two or more corporations each of which is a subsidiary wholly-owned corporation of the same person, the new corporation is, for the purposes of section 29 of the *Income Tax Application Rules*, subsection 59(3.3) and sections 66, 66.1, 66.2, 66.21, 66.4 and 66.7, deemed to be the same corporation as, and a continuation of, each predecessor corporation, except that this subsection does not affect the determination of any predecessor corporation's fiscal period, taxable income or tax payable.

Related Provisions: 87(1.4) — Subsidiary wholly-owned corporation. See also at end of s. 87.

Notes: 87(1.2) amended by 2000 Budget, effective for amalgamations that occur after 2000, to add reference to 66.21.

87(1.2) amended by 1993 technical bill, for amalgamations after Dec. 21, 1992.

Regulations: 1214 (resource and processing allowances — purposes for which amalgamated corporation deemed to be continuation of predecessors).

Income Tax Folios: S4-F7-C1: Amalgamations of Canadian corporations [replaces IT-474R2].

Interpretation Bulletins: IT-125R4: Dispositions of resource properties. See also at end of s. 87.

(1.3) [Repealed under former Act]

Notes: 87(1.3), repealed in 1985, dealt with an amalgamation of a "shareholder corporation" (under the joint exploration corporation rules) with its subsidiary. This case is now covered by 87(1.2).

(1.4) Definition of "subsidiary wholly-owned corporation"

— Notwithstanding subsection 248(1), for the purposes of this subsection and subsections (1.1), (1.2) and (2.11), "subsidiary wholly-owned corporation" of a person (in this subsection referred to as the "parent") means a corporation all the issued and outstanding shares of the capital stock of which belong to

(a) the parent;

(b) a corporation that is a subsidiary wholly-owned corporation of the parent; or

(c) any combination of persons each of which is a person described in paragraph (a) or (b).

Related Provisions: See Related Provisions at end of s. 87.

Notes: 87(1.4) amended by 1993 technical bill (for amalgamations occurring after Dec. 21, 1992), 1992 technical bill.

Income Tax Folios: S4-F7-C1: Amalgamations of Canadian corporations [replaces IT-474R2].

Interpretation Bulletins: See list at end of s. 87.

(1.5) Definitions

— For the purpose of this section, "financial institution", "mark-to-market property" and "specified debt obligation" have the meanings assigned by subsection 142.2(1).

Notes: 87(1.5) added by 1994 technical bill, effective for taxation years that end after February 22, 1994.

(2) Rules applicable

— Where there has been an amalgamation of two or more corporations after 1971 the following rules apply:

Notes: See Notes to 87(1).

(a) **[deemed new corporation —] taxation year** — for the purposes of this Act, the corporate entity formed as a result of the amalgamation shall be deemed to be a new corporation the first taxation year of which shall be deemed to have commenced at the time of the amalgamation, and a taxation year of a predecessor corporation that would otherwise have ended after the amalgamation shall be deemed to have ended immediately before the amalgamation;

Notes: This rule can cause loss carryforwards (see 87(2.1)) to expire a year earlier than they otherwise would, even where they are still deductible after the amalgamation.

For some other effects of the deemed year-end, see Notes to 249(4), and Topical Index under "Short taxation year". See also Notes to 256(9) re amalgamation on the same day as acquisition of control.

87(2)(a), 249(3.1) and 249(4) can trigger multiple year-ends from the same amalgamation: see Notes to 249(4).

87(2)(a) applies for all purposes of the Act, not just for computing income: *CGU Holdings*, 2009 FCA 20; and see Richard Bennett, "Amalgamations in Tax Law", XI(2) *Corporate Structures & Groups* (Federated Press) 608-13 (2009).

See also Aimee Hass, "Amalgamations Revisited: Paragraph 87(2)(a)", 58(1) *Canadian Tax Journal* 187-207 (2010); Sarah Chiu, "Half-Year Rule and Amalgamations", IX(2) *Resource Sector Taxation* (Federated Press) 638-42 (2013).

Income Tax Folios: S4-F7-C1: Amalgamations of Canadian corporations [replaces IT-474R2].

Interpretation Bulletins: IT-179R: Change of fiscal period. See also at end of s. 87.

Information Circulars: 88-2, para. 21: General anti-avoidance rule — section 245 of the *Income Tax Act*.

(b) **inventory** — for the purpose of computing the income of the new corporation, where the property described in the inventory, if any, of the new corporation at the beginning of its first taxation year includes property that was described in the inventory of a predecessor corporation at the end of the taxation year of the predecessor corporation that ended immediately before the amalgamation (which taxation year of a predecessor corporation is referred to in this section as its "last taxation year"), the property so included shall be deemed to have been acquired by the new corporation at the beginning of its first taxation year for an amount determined in accordance with section 10 as the value thereof for the purpose of computing the income of the predecessor corporation for its last taxation year, except that where the income of the predecessor corporation for its last taxation year from a farming business was computed in accordance with the cash method, the amount so determined in respect of inventory owned in connection with that business shall be deemed to be the total of all amounts each of which is an amount included because of paragraph 28(1)(b) or (c) in computing that income for that year and, where the income of the new corporation from a farming business is computed in accordance with the cash method, for the purpose of section 28,

(i) an amount equal to that total shall be deemed to have been paid by the new corporation, and

(ii) the new corporation shall be deemed to have purchased the property for an amount equal to that total,

in its first taxation year and in the course of carrying on that business;

Notes: 87(2)(b) last amended by 1991 technical bill.

Income Tax Folios: S4-F7-C1: Amalgamations of Canadian corporations [replaces IT-474R2].

Interpretation Bulletins: IT-427R: Livestock of farmers. See also at end of s. 87.

(c) **method adopted for computing income** — in computing the income of the new corporation for a taxation year from a business or property

(i) there shall be included any amount received or receivable (depending on the method followed by the new corporation in computing its income for that year) by it in that year that would, if it had been received or receivable (depending on the method followed by the predecessor corporation in computing its income for its last taxation year) by the predecessor corporation in its last taxation year, have been included in computing the income of the predecessor corporation for that year, and

(ii) there may be deducted any amount paid or payable (depending on the method followed by the new corporation in computing its income for that year) by it in that year that would, if it had been paid or payable (depending on the method followed by the predecessor corporation in computing its income for its last taxation year) by the predecessor corporation in its last taxation year, have been deductible in computing the income of the predecessor corporation for that year;

Related Provisions: 87(2)(b) — Meaning of "last taxation year"; 88(1)(e.2) — Winding-up. See also at end of s. 87.

Interpretation Bulletins: See list at end of s. 87.

(d) **depreciable property** — for the purposes of sections 13 and 20 and any regulations made under paragraph 20(1)(a),

(i) where depreciable property of a prescribed class has been acquired by the new corporation from a predecessor corporation, the capital cost of the property to the new corporation shall be deemed to be the amount that was the capital cost of the property to the predecessor corporation, and

(ii) in determining the undepreciated capital cost to the new corporation of depreciable property of a prescribed class at any time,

(A) there shall be added to the capital cost to the new corporation of depreciable property of the class acquired before that time the cost amount, immediately before the amalgamation, to a predecessor corporation of each property included in that class by the new corporation,

(B) there shall be subtracted from the capital cost to the new corporation of depreciable property of that class acquired before that time the capital cost to the new corporation of property of that class acquired by virtue of the amalgamation,

(C) a reference in subparagraph 13(5)(b)(ii) to amounts that would have been deducted in respect of property in computing a taxpayer's income shall be construed as including a reference to amounts that would have been deducted in respect of that property in computing a predecessor corporation's income, and

(D) where depreciable property that is deemed by subsection 37(6) to be a separate prescribed class has been acquired by the new corporation from a predecessor corporation, the property shall continue to be deemed to be of that same separate prescribed class;

Notes: UCC of a predecessor to be added to the pool of the new corporation is net of CCA claimed by the predecessor: VIEWS doc 2009-0314801E5.

87(2)(d)(ii)(C) amended by 1991 technical bill and by 1996 Budget, effective for taxation years that begin after 1996.

I.T. Application Rules: 20(1.2) (transfer of depreciable property by person who owned it before 1972).

Income Tax Folios: S4-F7-C1: Amalgamations of Canadian corporations [replaces IT-474R2].

Interpretation Bulletins: See list at end of s. 87.

(d.1) **depreciable property acquired from predecessor corporation** — for the purposes of this Act, where depreciable property (other than property of a prescribed class) has been acquired by the new corporation from a predecessor corporation, the new corporation shall be deemed to have acquired the property before 1972 at an actual cost equal to the actual cost of the property to the predecessor corporation, and the new corporation shall be deemed to have been allowed the total of all amounts allowed to the predecessor corporation in respect of the property, under regulations made under paragraph 20(1)(a), in computing the income of the predecessor corporation;

Related Provisions: 88(1)(e.2) — Winding-up. See also at end of s. 87.

I.T. Application Rules: 20(1.2) (transfer of depreciable property by person who owned it before 1972).

Income Tax Folios: S4-F7-C1: Amalgamations of Canadian corporations [replaces IT-474R2].

Interpretation Bulletins: See list at end of s. 87.

(e) **capital property** — subject to paragraph (e.4) and subsection 142.6(5), where a capital property (other than depreciable property or an interest in a partnership) has been acquired by the new corporation from a predecessor corporation, the cost of the property to the new corporation shall be deemed to be the amount that was the adjusted cost base of the property to the predecessor corporation immediately before the amalgamation;

Related Provisions: 53(6) — Effect of amalgamation on ACB of share, partnership interest or trust interest; 69(13) — Amalgamation or merger. See also at end of s. 87.

Notes: References to 87(2)(e.4) and 142.6(5) added to 87(2)(e) by 1994 technical bill, effective for taxation years that end after February 22, 1994.

Interpretation Bulletins: See list at end of s. 87.

(e.1) **partnership interest** — where a partnership interest that is capital property has been acquired from a predecessor corporation to which the new corporation was related, for the purposes of this Act, the cost of that partnership interest to the new corporation shall be deemed to be the amount that was the cost of that interest to the predecessor corporation and, in respect of that partnership interest, the new corporation shall be deemed to be the same corporation as and a continuation of the predecessor corporation;

Related Provisions: 53(1)(e), 53(2)(c) — ACB — partnership interest; 88(1)(c), 88(1)(e.2) — Winding-up; 100(2.1) — Gain from disposition of partnership interest on amalgamation. See also at end of s. 87.

Notes: See VIEWS doc 2009-0317211E5 (87(2)(e.1) determines cost of partnership interest acquired on 88.1 windup).

Income Tax Folios: S4-F7-C1: Amalgamations of Canadian corporations [replaces IT-474R2].

Interpretation Bulletins: See list at end of s. 87.

(e.2) **security or debt obligation** — subject to paragraphs (e.3) and (e.4) and subsection 142.6(5), where a property that is a security or debt obligation (other than a capital property or an inventory) of a predecessor corporation used by it in the year in, or held by it in the year in the course of, carrying on the business of insurance or lending money in the taxation year ending immediately before the amalgamation has been acquired by the new corporation from the predecessor corporation, the cost of the property to the new corporation shall be deemed to be the amount that was the cost amount of the property to the predecessor corporation immediately before the amalgamation;

Notes: 87(2)(e.2) amended by 1994 technical bill, for tax years that end after Feb. 22, 1994.

Interpretation Bulletins: See list at end of s. 87.

(e.3) **financial institutions — specified debt obligation** — where the new corporation is a financial institution in its first taxation year, it shall be deemed, in respect of a specified debt obligation (other than a mark-to-market property) acquired from a predecessor corporation that was a financial institution in its last taxation year, to be the same corporation as, and a continuation of, the predecessor corporation;

Related Provisions: 87(1.5) — Interpretation; 87(2)(b) — Meaning of "last taxation year"; 88(1)(e.2) — Winding-up; 142.6(5) — Parallel rule for rollover transactions generally. See also at end of s. 87.

Notes: 87(2)(e.3) added by 1994 technical bill, effective for amalgamations occurring, and windups beginning, after Feb. 22, 1994.

(e.4) **financial institutions — mark-to-market property** — where

(i) the new corporation is a financial institution in its first taxation year and a property acquired by the new corporation from a predecessor corporation is a mark-to-market property of the new corporation for the year, or

(ii) a predecessor corporation was a financial institution in its last taxation year and a property acquired by the new corporation from the predecessor corporation was a mark-to-market property of the predecessor corporation for the year,

the cost of the property to the new corporation shall be deemed to be the amount that was the fair market value of the property immediately before the amalgamation;

Related Provisions: 87(1.5) — Interpretation; 87(2)(b) — Meaning of "last taxation year"; 87(2)(e), (e.2) — Rule overrides normal rules for capital property, securities and debt obligations; 87(2)(g.2), 142.6(1)(b) — Predecessor non-FI deemed to have disposed of property before amalgamation; 142.5(2) — Predecessor FI deemed to have disposed of property before amalgamation; 142.6(5), (6) — Acquisition of specified debt obligation by FI in rollover transaction. See also at end of s. 87.

Notes: 87(2)(e.4) added by 1994 technical bill, effective for amalgamations occurring after October 1994.

(e.41) **[mark-to-market election for derivatives]** — if subsection 10.1(6) applied to a predecessor corporation in its last taxation year, each "eligible derivative" (as defined in subsection 10.1(5)) of the predecessor corporation immediately before the end of its last taxation year is deemed to have been reacquired, or reissued or renewed, as the case may be, by the new corporation at its fair market value immediately before the amalgamation;

Notes: 87(2)(e.41) added by 2017 budget bill #2, for taxation years that begin after March 21, 2017.

(e.42) **[mark-to-market election for derivatives — first year]** — for the purposes of subsection 10.1(7), the new corporation is deemed to be the same corporation as, and a continuation of, each predecessor corporation;

Related Provisions: 88(1)(e.2) — Winding-up.

Notes: 87(2)(e.42) added by 2017 budget bill #2, for taxation years that begin after March 21, 2017.

(e.5) **financial institutions — mark-to-market property** — for the purposes of subsections 112(5) to (5.2) and (5.4) and the definition "mark-to-market property" in subsection 142.2(1), the new corporation shall be deemed to be the same corporation as, and a continuation of, each predecessor corporation;

Related Provisions: 87(1.5) — Interpretation; 88(1)(h) — Parallel rule on windup; 142.7(6)(a) — Parallel rule on conversion of foreign bank affiliate to branch. See also at end of s. 87.

Notes: 87(2)(e.5) added by 1994 technical bill, effective for amalgamations occurring at any time.

(f) [Repealed]

Notes: 87(2)(f) repealed by 2016 budget bill #2, effective 2017, as part of changing the eligible capital property rules to CCA Class 14.1 (see Notes to 20(1)(b)). It read:

(f) eligible capital property — for the purposes of determining under this Act any amount relating to cumulative eligible capital, an eligible capital amount, an eligible capital expenditure or eligible capital property, the new corporation shall be deemed to be the same corporation as, and a continuation of, each predecessor corporation;

87(2)(f) amended by 1992 technical bill, for amalgamations after June 1988.

Interpretation Bulletins: See list at end of s. 87.

(f.1) [Repealed]

Notes: 87(2)(f.1) repealed by 1992 technical bill, retroactive to its introduction, in conjunction with the amendment to 87(2)(f) above.

(g) **reserves** — for the purpose of computing the income of the new corporation for a taxation year,

(i) any amount that has been deducted as a reserve in computing the income of a predecessor corporation for its last taxation year shall be deemed to have been deducted as a reserve in computing the income of the new corporation for a taxation year immediately preceding its first taxation year, and

(ii) any amount deducted under paragraph 20(1)(p) in computing the income of a predecessor corporation for its last taxation year or a previous taxation year shall be deemed to have been deducted under that paragraph in computing the income of the new corporation for a taxation year immediately preceding its first taxation year;

Related Provisions: 87(2)(b) — Meaning of "last taxation year"; 88(1)(e.2) — Winding-up.

(g.1) **continuation** — for the purposes of sections 12.4 and 26, subsection 97(3) and section 256.1, the new corporation is deemed to be the same corporation as, and a continuation of, each predecessor corporation;

Related Provisions: 88(1)(e.2) — Winding-up. See also at end of s. 87.

Notes: 87(2)(g.1) amended by 2013 budget bill #2, effective March 21, 2013, to add reference to 256.1.

87(2)(g.1) amended by 2012 budget bill #2, effective for amalgamations that occur and windups that begin after March 28, 2012, to delete 12.3 and 20(26) (originally proposed in technical package of Oct. 31/11) and add 97(3).

Interpretation Bulletins: See list at end of s. 87.

(g.2) **financial institution rules** — for the purposes of paragraphs 142.4(4)(c) and (d) and subsections 142.51(11) and 142.6(1), the new corporation is deemed to be the same corporation as, and a continuation of, each predecessor corporation;

Related Provisions: 88(1)(e.2) — Winding-up; 142.6(1)(b) — Deemed disposition of specified debt obligations and mark-to-market properties on becoming a financial institution. See also list at end of s. 87.

Notes: 87(2)(g.2) amended to delete reference to 142.5(5) and (7) by 2002-2013 technical bill (Part 5 — technical), for taxation years that begin after Oct. 2011. Earlier amended by 2008 budget bill #2 (for taxation years that begin after Sept. 2006), 1994 technical bill.

(g.3) **superficial losses** — for the purposes of applying subsections 13(21.2), 18(15) and 40(3.4) to any property that was disposed of by a predecessor corporation before the amalgamation, the new corporation is deemed to be the same corporation as, and a continuation of, each predecessor corporation;

Related Provisions: 88(1)(e.2) — Winding-up. See also at end of s. 87.

Notes: 87(2)(g.3) amended to delete reference to 14(12) by 2016 budget bill #2, effective 2017.

87(2)(g.3) added by 1995-97 technical bill, effective for amalgamations occurring (and, by 88(1)(e.2), for windups beginning) after April 26, 1995.

(g.4) **superficial losses — capital property** — for the purpose of applying paragraph 40(3.5)(c) in respect of any share that was acquired by a predecessor corporation, the new corporation is deemed to be the same corporation as, and a continuation of, each predecessor corporation;

Related Provisions: 88(1)(e.2) — Winding-up. See also at end of s. 87.

Notes: 87(2)(g.4) added by 1995-97 technical bill, effective for amalgamations occurring (and, by 88(1)(e.2), for windups beginning) after April 26, 1995.

(g.5) **patronage dividends** — for the purposes of section 135, the new corporation is deemed to be the same corporation as, and a continuation of, each predecessor corporation;

Related Provisions: 88(1)(e.2) — Winding-up. See also at end of s. 87.

Notes: 87(2)(g.5) added by 2002-2013 technical bill (Part 5 — technical), effective for amalgamations that occur (and, per 88(1)(e.2), windups that begin) after 1997.

(g.6) COVID-19 — emergency subsidies — for the purposes of section 125.7, the new corporation is deemed to be the same corporation as, and a continuation of, each predecessor corporation unless it is reasonable to consider that one of the main purposes of the amalgamation is to cause the new corporation to qualify for the deemed overpayment under any of subsections 125.7(2) to (2.2) or to increase the amount of that deemed overpayment;

Related Provisions: 88(1)(e.2) — Winding-up. See also at end of s. 87.

Notes: 87(2)(g.6) amended by 2021 budget bill #1, effective June 29, 2021, to refer to 125.7(2.2); by 2020 COVID bill #5, effective Sept. 27, 2020, to refer to 125.7(2.1). Added by 2020 COVID bill #3, effective April 11, 2020.

(g.7) COVID-19 — automobile benefits — for the purposes of subsections 6(2.2) and (2.3), the new corporation is deemed to be the same corporation as, and a continuation of, each predecessor corporation;

Related Provisions: 88(1)(e.2) — Winding-up. See also at end of s. 87.

Notes: 87(2)(g.7) added by 2021 budget bill #1, effective 2020.

(h) debts — for the purpose of computing a deduction from the income of the new corporation for a taxation year under paragraph 20(1)(l), (l.1) or (p)

(i) any debt owing to a predecessor corporation that was included in computing the income of the predecessor corporation for its last taxation year or a preceding taxation year,

(ii) where a predecessor corporation was an insurer or a corporation the ordinary business of which included the lending of money, any loan or lending asset made or acquired by the predecessor corporation in the ordinary course of its business of insurance or the lending of money, or

(iii) where a predecessor corporation was an insurer or a corporation the ordinary business of which included the lending of money, any instrument or commitment described in paragraph 20(1)(l.1) that was issued, made or assumed by the predecessor corporation in the ordinary course of its business of insurance or the lending of money,

and that by reason of the amalgamation, has been acquired by the new corporation, shall be deemed to be a debt owing to the new corporation that was included in computing its income for a preceding taxation year, a loan or lending asset made or acquired or an instrument or commitment that was issued, made or assumed by the new corporation in a preceding taxation year in the ordinary course of its business of insurance or the lending of money, as the case may be;

Related Provisions: 80(2) — Deemed settlement on amalgamation; 87(2)(b) — Meaning of "last taxation year"; 88(1)(e.2) — Winding-up. See also at end of s. 87.

Notes: For interpretation of "ordinary business includes the lending of money", see Notes to 15(2.3).

Interpretation Bulletins: See list at end of s. 87.

(h.1) debts — for the purposes of section 61.4, the description of F in subsection 79(3), the definition "forgiven amount" in subsection 80(1), subsection 80.03(7) and section 80.04, the new corporation shall be deemed to be the same corporation as, and a continuation of, each predecessor corporation;

Related Provisions: 88(1)(e.2) — Winding-up. See also at end of s. 87.

Notes: 87(2)(h.1) added by 1994 technical bill, effective for taxation years that end after February 21, 1994. It covers various rules relating to debt forgiveness (see also 87(2)(l.21) for others). It does not refer to 56.3 because 87(2)(g) provides for reserves claimed by a predecessor (including reserves under 61.4) to be added back to the amalgamated corporation's income.

Interpretation Bulletins: See list at end of s. 87.

(i) special reserve — for the purpose of computing a deduction from the income of the new corporation for a taxation year under paragraph 20(1)(n), any amount included in computing the income of a predecessor corporation from a business for its last taxation year or a previous taxation year in respect of property sold in the course of the business shall be deemed to have

been included in computing the income of the new corporation from the business for a previous year in respect of that property;

Related Provisions: 87(2)(b) — Meaning of "last taxation year"; 88(1)(e.2) — Winding-up. See also at end of s. 87.

Interpretation Bulletins: IT-154R: Special reserves. See also at end of s. 87.

(j) special reserves — for the purposes of paragraphs 20(1)(m), (m.1) and (m.2), subsection 20(24) and section 34.2, the new corporation is deemed to be the same corporation as, and a continuation of, each predecessor corporation;

Related Provisions: 88(1)(e.2) — Winding-up. See also at end of s. 87.

Notes: 87(2)(j) reworded by 1992 technical bill, effective for amalgamations occurring (and, by 88(1)(e.2), for windings-up beginning) after 1990.

Reference to 34.2 added to 87(2)(j) by 1995 Budget, effective for amalgamations that occur, and (per 88(1)(e.2)) windups that begin, after 1994.

Interpretation Bulletins: IT-154R: Special reserves. See also at end of s. 87.

(j.1) inventory adjustment — for the purposes of paragraph 20(1)(ii), an amount required by paragraph 12(1)(r) to be included in computing the income of a predecessor corporation for its last taxation year shall be deemed to be an amount required by paragraph 12(1)(r) to be included in computing the income of the new corporation for a taxation year immediately preceding its first taxation year;

Related Provisions: 87(2)(b) — Meaning of "last taxation year"; 88(1)(e.2) — Winding-up. See also list at end of s. 87.

Interpretation Bulletins: See list at end of s. 87.

(j.2) prepaid expenses and matchable expenditures — for the purposes of subsections 18(9) and (9.01), section 18.1 and paragraph 20(1)(mm), the new corporation is deemed to be the same corporation as, and a continuation of, each predecessor corporation;

Related Provisions: 88(1)(e.2) — Winding-up. See also at end of s. 87.

Notes: Reference in 87(2)(j.2) to 18(9.01) added by 1994 Budget, effective 1994. Reference to 18.1 added by 1995-97 technical bill, effective November 18, 1996.

Interpretation Bulletins: See list at end of s. 87.

(j.3) employee benefit plans, etc. [SDAs, RCAs] — for the purposes of paragraphs 12(1)(n.1) to (n.3) and 20(1)(r), (s), (oo) and (pp), section 32.1, paragraph 104(13)(b), subsections 144.1(4) to (7) and Part X1.3, the new corporation is deemed to be the same corporation as, and a continuation of, each predecessor corporation;

Related Provisions: 88(1)(e.2) — Winding-up. See also at end of s. 87.

Notes: 87(2)(j.3) amended by 2010 budget bill #2, effective 2010, to refer to 20(1)(s) and 144.1(4)-(7). Earlier amended by 1993 and 1991 technical bills.

Interpretation Bulletins: IT-502: Employee benefit plans and employee trusts. See also list at end of s. 87.

(j.4) accrual rules — for the purposes of subsections 12(3) and (9), section 12.2, subsection 20(19) and the definition "adjusted cost basis" in subsection 148(9) of this Act, and subsections 12(5) and (6) and paragraph 56(1)(d.1) of the *Income Tax Act*, chapter 148 of the Revised Statutes of Canada, 1952, the new corporation shall be deemed to be the same corporation as, and a continuation of, each predecessor corporation;

Related Provisions: 88(1)(e.2) — Winding-up. See also at end of s. 87.

I.T. Application Rules: 69 (meaning of "chapter 148 of ...").

Interpretation Bulletins: See list at end of s. 87.

(j.5) cancellation of lease — for the purposes of paragraphs 20(1)(z) and (z.1), the new corporation shall be deemed to be the same corporation as, and a continuation of, each predecessor corporation;

Related Provisions: 88(1)(e.2) — Winding-up. See also at end of s. 87.

Interpretation Bulletins: See list at end of s. 87.

(j.6) continuing corporation — for the purposes of paragraphs 12(1)(t) and (x), subsections 12(2.2) and 13(7.1), (7.4) and (24), paragraphs 13(27)(b) and (28)(c), subsections 13(29) and 18(9.1), paragraphs 20(1)(e), (e.1) and (hh), sections 20.1 and 32, paragraph 37(1)(c), subsection 39(13), subparagraphs 53(2)(c)(vi) and (h)(ii), paragraph 53(2)(s), subsections 53(2.1), 66(11.4), 66.7(11) and 127(10.2), section 139.1, subsection 152(4.3), the determination of D in the definition "undepreciated capital cost" in subsection 13(21) and the determination of L in the definition "cumulative Canadian exploration expense" in subsection 66.1(6), the new corporation is deemed to be the same corporation as, and a continuation of, each predecessor corporation;

Related Provisions: 55(3.2)(b) — Continuation for purposes of butterfly reorganizations and capital gains stripping; 88(1)(e.2) — Winding-up. See also at end of s. 87.

Notes: Undepreciated capital cost balances are effectively carried through to the new corp, even if the amalgamation does not fall within 87(1): *Envision Credit Union*, 2010 TCC 576, para. 88 (aff'd on basis the amalgamation fell within 87(1): 2011 FCA 321 and 2013 SCC 48).

Reference to 127(10.2) added by 2019 budget bill #1, for tax years that end after March 18, 2019. (For earlier years, see 87(2)(oo).)

87(2)(j.6) earlier amended by 1999 Budget, 1993, 1992 and 1991 technical bills.

Income Tax Folios: S4-F7-C1: Amalgamations of Canadian corporations [replaces IT-474R2].

Interpretation Bulletins: See list at end of s. 87.

(j.7) **certain transfers and loans [attribution rules]** — for the purposes of sections 74.4 and 74.5, the new corporation shall be deemed to be the same corporation as, and a continuation of, each predecessor corporation;

Related Provisions: 88(1)(e.2) — Winding-up. See also at end of s. 87.

Interpretation Bulletins: See list at end of s. 87.

(j.8) [Repealed]

Notes: 87(2)(j.8) repealed by 2013 budget bill #1, effective for taxation years that begin after March 20, 2013. For earlier years, read:

(j.8) international banking centre business — for the purposes of section 33.1, the new corporation shall be deemed to be the same corporation as, and a continuation of, each predecessor corporation;

(j.9) **Part I.3 tax** — for the purpose of determining the amount deductible by the new corporation for any taxation year under section 125.3, the new corporation is deemed to be the same corporation as, and a continuation of, each predecessor corporation;

Related Provisions: 88(1)(e.2) — Winding-up. See also at end of s. 87.

Notes: 87(2)(j.9) amended to delete reference to 125.2 by 2002-2013 technical bill (Part 5 — technical), effective for taxation years that begin after Oct. 2011.

Interpretation Bulletins: See list at end of s. 87.

(j.91) **Part I.3 and Part VI tax** — for the purpose of determining the amount deductible under subsection 181.1(4) or 190.1(3) by the new corporation for any taxation year, the new corporation is deemed to be the same corporation as, and a continuation of, each predecessor corporation, except that this paragraph does not affect the determination of the fiscal period of any corporation or the tax payable by any corporation for any taxation year that ends before the amalgamation;

Related Provisions: 88(1)(e.2) — Winding-up. See also at end of s. 87.

Notes: For application of 87(2)(j.91) after the 2013 amendment below, see VIEWS doc 2006-0181631E5 (reversing 2001-0064973).

87(2)(j.91) amended by 2002-2013 technical bill (Part 5 — technical), for amalgamations that occur (and, per 88(1)(e.2), windups that begin) after Dec. 20, 2002. Earlier amended by 1995-97, 1992 technical bills.

(j.92) **subsections 125(5.1) and 157.1(1) [small business deduction and instalment deferral]** — for the purposes of subsection 125(5.1) and the definition "eligible corporation" in subsection 157.1(1), the new corporation is deemed to be the same corporation as, and a continuation of, each predecessor corporation;

Related Provisions: 88(1)(e.2) — Winding-up. See also at end of s. 87.

Notes: 87(2)(j.92) amended to add reference to 157.1(1)"eligible corporation" by 2001 Budget, effective for 2002 and later taxation years.

87(2)(j.92) added by 1994 Budget, effective for taxation years that end after June 1994.

(j.93) **mining reclamation trusts [now qualifying environmental trusts]** — for the purposes of paragraphs 12(1)(z.1) and (z.2) and 20(1)(ss) and (tt) and sections 107.3 and 127.41, the new corporation shall be deemed to be the same corporation as, and a continuation of, each predecessor corporation;

Related Provisions: 88(1)(e.2) — Winding-up. See also at end of s. 87.

Notes: 87(2)(j.93) added by 1994 Budget, effective for amalgamations that occur and windups (by 88(1)(e.2)) that begin after February 22, 1994.

(j.94) **film or video productions** — for the purposes of sections 125.4 and 125.5, the new corporation is deemed to be the same corporation as, and a continuation of, each predecessor corporation;

Related Provisions: 88(1)(e.2) — Winding-up. See also at end of s. 87.

Notes: See VIEWS doc 2012-0449101E5 (application of 25-year copyright rule).

87(2)(j.94) amended by 1995-97 technical bill, for amalgamations occurring (and, by 88(1)(e.2), windups beginning) after Oct. 1997. Added by 1995 Budget.

(j.95) **non-resident entities** — for the purposes of sections 94 to 94.2, the new corporation is deemed to be the same corporation as, and a continuation of, each predecessor corporation;

Related Provisions: 88(1)(e.2) — Winding-up. See also at end of s. 87.

Notes: 87(2)(j.95) added by 2002-2013 technical bill, for tax years that end after 2000.

(j.96) **journalism organizations** — for the purposes of section 125.6, the new corporation is deemed to be the same corporation as, and a continuation of, each predecessor corporation;

Notes: 125.6 is the labour credit for journalism organizations. 87(2)(j.96) added by 2019 budget bill #1, effective 2019.

(j.97) **continuing corporation** — for the purposes of subsection 110(0.1), paragraph 110(1)(e) and subsection 110(1.31), the new corporation is deemed to be the same corporation as, and a continuation of, each predecessor corporation;

Related Provisions: 88(1)(e.2) — Winding-up. See also at end of s. 87.

Notes: 87(2)(j.97) added by 2021 budget bill #1, effective July 2021.

(k) **certain payments to employees** — for the purpose of subsection 6(3), any amount received by a person from the new corporation that would, if received by the person from a predecessor corporation, be deemed for the purpose of section 5 to be remuneration for that person's services rendered as an officer or during a period of employment, shall be deemed for the purposes of section 5 to be remuneration for services so rendered by the person;

Related Provisions: 88(1)(e.2) — Winding-up. See also at end of s. 87.

(l) **scientific research and experimental development** — for the purposes of section 37 and Part VIII, the new corporation shall be deemed to be the same corporation as, and a continuation of, each predecessor corporation;

Related Provisions: 88(1)(e.2) — Winding-up. See also at end of s. 87.

Interpretation Bulletins: See list at end of s. 87.

(l.1), (l.2) [No longer relevant]

Notes: 87(2)(l.1) and (l.2) provide rules for purposes of the additional R&D allowance in 37.1, which was generally eliminated in 1983.

(l.21) **[debt forgiveness rules]** — for the purposes of section 61.3, the definition "unrecognized loss" in subsection 80(1) and subsection 80.01(10), the new corporation is deemed to be the same corporation as, and a continuation of, each predecessor corporation;

Related Provisions: 88(1)(e.2) — Winding-up. See also at end of s. 87.

Notes: 87(2)(l.21) added by 1994 technical bill, for tax years that end after Feb. 21, 1994; and amended by 1995-97 technical bill retroactive to its introduction to add reference to 80(1)"unrecognized loss". It covers various rules relating to debt forgiveness (see also 87(2)(h.1) for others).

(l.3) **replacement property** — where before the amalgamation property of a predecessor corporation was unlawfully taken, lost, destroyed or taken under statutory authority, or was a former business property of the predecessor corporation, for the purposes of applying sections 13 and 44 and the definition "former business property" in subsection 248(1) to the new corporation in respect of the property and any replacement property acquired therefor, the new corporation shall be deemed to be the same corporation as, and a continuation of, the predecessor corporation;

Related Provisions: 88(1)(e.2) — Winding-up. See also at end of s. 87.

Notes: 87(2)(l.3) reworded by 1992 technical bill, for amalgamations occurring (and, by 88(1)(e.2), for windings-up beginning) after 1989.

(l.4) **subsec. 13(4.2) election** — for the purposes of subsection 13(4.3) and paragraph 20(16.1)(b), the new corporation is deemed to be the same corporation as, and a continuation of, each predecessor corporation;

Related Provisions: 88(1)(e.2) — Winding-up. See also at end of s. 87.

Notes: 87(2)(l.4) added by 2002-2013 technical bill (Part 5 — technical), effective for amalgamations that occur (and, per 88(1)(e.2), windups that begin) after Dec. 20, 2002.

(l.5) **contingent amount — s. 143.4** — for the purposes of section 143.4, the new corporation is deemed to be the same corporation as, and a continuation of, each predecessor corporation;

Related Provisions: 88(1)(e.2) — Winding-up. See also at end of s. 87.

Notes: 87(2)(l.5) added by 2002-2013 technical bill (Part 5 — technical), effective for taxation years that end after March 15, 2011.

(m) **reserves** — for the purpose of computing the income of the new corporation for a taxation year, any amount claimed under subparagraph 40(1)(a)(iii) or 44(1)(e)(iii) in computing a predecessor corporation's gain for its last taxation year from the disposition of any property shall be deemed

(i) to have been claimed under subparagraph 40(1)(a)(iii) or 44(1)(e)(iii), as the case may be, in computing the new corporation's gain for a taxation year immediately preceding its first taxation year from the disposition of that property by it before its first taxation year, and

(ii) to be the amount determined under subparagraph 40(1)(a)(i) or 44(1)(e)(i), as the case may be, in respect of that property;

Related Provisions: 87(2)(b) — Meaning of "last taxation year"; 88(1)(e.2) — Winding-up. See also at end of s. 87.

Notes: 87(2)(m) amended by 1991 technical bill, effective 1990.

(m.1) **[charitable] gift of non-qualifying security** — for the purpose of computing the new corporation's gain under subsection 40(1.01) for any taxation year from the disposition of a property, the new corporation is deemed to be the same corporation as, and a continuation of, each predecessor corporation;

Related Provisions: 88(1)(e.2) — Winding-up. See also at end of s. 87.

Notes: 87(2)(m.1) added by 1997 Budget, effective for 1997 and later taxation years.

(m.2) **[charitable] gift of predecessor's property** — for the purpose of computing the fair market value of property under subsection 248(35), the new corporation is deemed to be the same corporation as, and a continuation of, each predecessor corporation;

Related Provisions: 88(1)(e.2) — Winding-up. See also at end of s. 87.

Notes: 87(2)(m.2) added by 2002-2013 technical bill (Part 5 — technical), effective for gifts of property made after 6pm EST on Dec. 4, 2003 (24 hours before 248(35) came into effect, though it is not clear why that was needed).

(n) **outlays made pursuant to warranty** — for the purpose of section 42, any outlay or expense made or incurred by the new corporation in a taxation year, pursuant to or by virtue of an obligation described in that section incurred by a predecessor corporation, that would, if the outlay or expense had been made or incurred by the predecessor corporation in that year, have been deemed to be a loss of the predecessor corporation for that year from the disposition of a capital property shall be deemed to be a loss of the new corporation for that year from the disposition of a capital property;

Related Provisions: 88(1)(e.2) — Winding-up. See also at end of s. 87.

Interpretation Bulletins: IT-330R: Disposition of capital property subject to warranty, covenant, etc. (cancelled). See also at end of s. 87.

(o) **expiration of options previously granted** — for the purpose of subsection 49(2),

(i) any option granted by a predecessor corporation that expires after the amalgamation is deemed to have been granted by the new corporation, and any proceeds received by the predecessor corporation for the granting of the option is deemed to have been received by the new corporation,

(ii) any person to whom the option was granted who was not dealing at arm's length with the predecessor corporation at the time that the option was granted is deemed to have been dealing with the new corporation not at arm's length at the time that the option was granted, and

(iii) any person to whom the option was granted who was dealing at arm's length with the predecessor corporation at the time that the option was granted is deemed to have been dealing with the new corporation at arm's length at the time that the option was granted;

Related Provisions: 88(1)(e.2) — Winding-up. See also at end of s. 87.

Notes: 87(2)(o)(ii) and (iii) added by 2002-2013 technical bill, for options issued after Oct. 24, 2012. For earlier options read:

(o) for the purpose of subsection 49(2), any option granted by a predecessor corporation that expires after the amalgamation shall be deemed to have been granted by the new corporation, and any proceeds received by the predecessor corporation for the granting of the option shall be deemed to have been received by the new corporation therefor;

Income Tax Folios: S4-F7-C1: Amalgamations of Canadian corporations [replaces IT-474R2].

(p) **consideration for resource property disposition** — for the purpose of computing a deduction from the income of the new corporation for a taxation year under section 64 of the *Income Tax Act*, chapter 148 of the Revised Statutes of Canada, 1952, any amount that has been included in computing the income of a predecessor corporation for its last taxation year or a previous taxation year by virtue of subsection 59(1) or paragraph 59(3.2)(c) of this Act, of subsection 59(3) of the *Income Tax Act*, chapter 148 of the Revised Statutes of Canada, 1952, or of subsection 83A(5ba) or (5c) of that Act as it read in its application to a taxation year before the 1972 taxation year, shall be deemed to have been included in computing the income of the new corporation for a previous year by virtue thereof;

Related Provisions: 87(2)(b) — Meaning of "last taxation year"; 88(1)(e.2) — Winding-up. See also at end of s. 87.

Notes: The version of s. 64 referred to was repealed in 1981. See Notes to s. 64.

I.T. Application Rules: 69 (meaning of "chapter 148 of ...").

(q) **registered [pension] plans [and DPSPs]** — for the purposes of sections 147, 147.1 and 147.2 and any regulations made under subsection 147.1(18), the new corporation shall be deemed to be the same corporation as, and a continuation of, each predecessor corporation;

Related Provisions: 88(1)(e.2) — Winding-up. See also at end of s. 87.

Notes: For CRA interpretation see VIEWS docs 2009-0326971C6, 2009-0326981C6.

Income Tax Folios: S4-F7-C1: Amalgamations of Canadian corporations [replaces IT-474R2].

Interpretation Bulletins: See list at end of s. 87.

(r) **employees profit sharing plan** — an election made under subsection 144(10) by a predecessor corporation is deemed to be an election made by the new corporation;

Related Provisions: 88(1)(e.2) — Winding-up. See also at end of s. 87.

Notes: 87(2)(r) added by 2002-2013 technical bill (Part 5 — technical), effective for amalgamations that occur (and, per 88(1)(e.2), windups that begin) after 1994.

(s) **tax deferred cooperative shares** — for the purpose of section 135.1, if the new corporation is, at the beginning of its first taxation year, an agricultural cooperative corporation (within the meaning assigned by subsection 135.1(1)),

(i) the new corporation is deemed to be the same corporation as, and a continuation of, each predecessor corporation that was an agricultural cooperative corporation at the end of the predecessor corporation's last taxation year, and

(ii) if, on the amalgamation, the new corporation issues a share (in this subparagraph and subsection 135.1(10) referred to as the "new share") that is described in all of paragraphs (b) to (d) of the definition "tax deferred cooperative share" in subsection 135.1(1) to a taxpayer in exchange for a share of a predecessor corporation (in this subparagraph and subsection 135.1(10) referred to as the "old share") that was, at the end of the predecessor corporation's last taxation year, a tax deferred cooperative share within the meaning assigned by that definition, and the amount of paid-up capital, and the amount, if any, that the taxpayer is entitled to receive on a redemption, acquisition or cancellation, of the new share are equal to those amounts, respectively, in respect of the old share, subsection 135.1(10) applies in respect of the exchange;

> **Proposed Amendment — Triangular amalgamation of cooperative corps**
>
> **Letter from Dept. of Finance, June 17, 2019**: See under 87(9).

Related Provisions: 88(1)(e.2) — Winding-up. See also at end of s. 87.

Notes: On a triangular amalgamation, see VIEWS doc 2019-0793911E5; this will be fixed as per the June 17, 2019 comfort letter reproduced at 87(9).

87(2)(s)(ii) amended by 2002-2013 technical bill (Part 5 — technical), effective Sept. 29, 2009, effectively to move former (s)(ii)(A) and (B) to new 135.1(10) and cross-reference to them.

87(2)(s) added by 2006 budget bill #1, effective 2006.

(s.1) **deemed SIFT wind-up corporation** — if a predecessor corporation was a SIFT wind-up corporation immediately before the amalgamation, the new corporation is deemed to be a SIFT wind-up corporation;

Related Provisions: 88(1)(e.2) — Winding-up. See also at end of s. 87.

Notes: 87(2)((s.1) added by 2008 budget bill #2, effective Dec. 20, 2007. See Notes to 85.1(8) re SIFT windups.

(t) **pre-1972 capital surplus on hand** — for the purpose of subsection 88(2.1), any capital property owned by a predecessor corporation on December 31, 1971 that was acquired by the new corporation by virtue of the amalgamation shall be deemed to have been acquired by the new corporation before 1972 at an actual cost to it equal to the actual cost of the property to the predecessor corporation;

Related Provisions: 88(1)(e.2) — Winding-up. See also at end of s. 87.

Interpretation Bulletins: See list at end of s. 87.

(u) **shares of foreign affiliate** — where one or more shares of the capital stock of a foreign affiliate of a predecessor corporation have, by virtue of the amalgamation, been acquired by the new corporation and as a result of the acquisition the affiliate has become a foreign affiliate of the new corporation,

(i) for the purposes of subsection 91(5) and paragraph 92(1)(b), any amount required by section 92 to be added or deducted, as the case may be, in computing the adjusted cost base of any such share to the predecessor corporation before the amalgamation shall be deemed to have been so required to be added or deducted, as the case may be, in computing the adjusted cost base of the share to the new corporation, and

(ii) for the purposes of subsections 93(2.01), (2.11), (2.21) and (2.31), any exempt dividend received by the predecessor corporation on any such share is deemed to be an exempt dividend received by the new corporation on the share;

Related Provisions: 88(1)(e.2) — Winding-up; Reg. 5905(5.1) — Effect on FAPI accounts. See also at end of s. 87.

Notes: 87(2)(u)(ii) amended by 2002-2013 technical bill to change "subsections 93(2) to (2.3)" to "subsections 93(2.01), (2.11), (2.21) and (2.31)", effective if 93(2.01) applies; but if 93(2.01) applies and 93(2.11) does not, read as "subsection 93(2.01)".

87(2)(u)(ii) amended by 2001 technical bill, effective December 1999.

Interpretation Bulletins: See also list at end of s. 87.

(v) **gifts [donations]** — for the purposes of section 110.1, the new corporation shall be deemed to be the same corporation as, and a continuation of, each predecessor corporation with respect to gifts;

Interpretation Bulletins: See list at end of s. 87.

(w) [Repealed under former Act]

Notes: 87(2)(w), repealed in 1983, prevented restricted farm losses from being carried through an amalgamation. See now 87(2.1).

(x) **taxable dividends** — for the purposes of subsections 112(3) to (4.22),

(i) any taxable dividend received on a share that was deductible from the predecessor corporation's income for a taxation year under section 112 or subsection 138(6) is deemed to be a taxable dividend received on the share by the new corporation that was deductible from the new corporation's income under section 112 or subsection 138(6), as the case may be,

(ii) any dividend (other than a taxable dividend) received on a share by the predecessor corporation is deemed to have been received on the share by the new corporation, and

(iii) a share acquired by the new corporation from a predecessor corporation is deemed to have been owned by the new corporation throughout any period of time throughout which it was owned by a predecessor corporation;

Related Provisions: 88(1)(e.2) — Winding-up. See also at end of s. 87.

Notes: 87(2)(x) amended by 1995-97 technical bill, this version effective for dispositions of shares after April 26, 1995.

Interpretation Bulletins: See list at end of s. 87.

(y) **contributed surplus** — for the purposes of subsections 84(1) and (10), the new corporation shall be deemed to be the same corporation as, and a continuation of, each predecessor corporation;

Notes: 87(2)(y) added by 1991 technical bill, effective July 14, 1990.

(y.1) [Repealed]

Notes: 87(2)(y.1) repealed by 1995-97 technical bill, effective for taxes payable for taxation years that begin after 1986. It provided a rule for computing the "preferred-earnings amount" under former 181(2). These rules were eliminated with the repeal of former Part II, which imposed a special 12.5% tax from 1982-86 on dividends paid by corporations out of income subject to the small business deduction.

Interpretation Bulletins: See list at end of s. 87.

(z) **foreign tax carryover** — for the purposes of determining the new corporation's unused foreign tax credit (within the meaning of subsection 126(7)) in respect of a country for any taxation year and determining the extent to which subsection 126(2.3) applies to reduce the amount that may be claimed by the new corporation under paragraph 126(2)(a) in respect of an unused foreign tax credit in respect of a country for a taxation year, the new corporation shall be deemed to be the same corporation as, and a continuation of, each predecessor corporation, except that this paragraph shall in no respect affect the determination of

(i) the fiscal period of the new corporation or any of its predecessor corporations, or

(ii) the tax payable under this Act by any predecessor corporation;

Income Tax Folios: S5-F2-C1: Foreign tax credit [replaces IT-270R3, IT-395R2, IT-520].

(z.1) **capital dividend account** — for the purposes of computing the capital dividend account of the new corporation, it shall be deemed to be the same corporation as, and a continuation of, each predecessor corporation, other than a predecessor corporation to which subsection 83(2.1) would, if a dividend were paid immediately before the amalgamation and an election were made under subsection 83(2) in respect of the full amount of that dividend, apply to deem any portion of the dividend to be paid by the predecessor corporation as a taxable dividend;

Related Provisions: 88(1)(e.2) — Winding-up. See also at end of s. 87.

Notes: On a windup of a wholly-owned subsidiary, its CDA is incorporated into that of the parent: VIEWS doc 2007-0223381I7; and the IT-126R2 para. 5 policy, accepting a windup before formal dissolution is complete, applies: 2019-0812651C6 [2019 APFF q.6].

87(2)(z.1) was applied in *Groupe Honco*, 2012 TCC 305 (aff'd 2013 FCA 128 without discussing 87(2)(z.1)).

87(2)(z.1) amended by 1991 technical bill, for amalgamations that occur, and (per 88(1)(e.2)) windups that begin, after July 13, 1990, to ensure that a negative balance in a predecessor's CDA effectively flows through to the new corporation.

Income Tax Folios: S3-F2-C1: Capital Dividends [replaces IT-66R6].

(z.2) application of Parts III and III.1 — for the purposes of Parts III and III.1, the new corporation is deemed to be the same corporation as, and a continuation of, each predecessor corporation;

Related Provisions: 88(1)(e.2) — Winding-up. See also at end of s. 87.

Notes: Under 87(2)(z.2) and 88(1)(e.2), if a subsidiary makes an excessive capital dividend election and then winds up, the parent can make the 184(3) election.

87(2)(z.2) amended to add reference to Part III.1 by 2006 budget bill #2 (Part 2 — eligible dividends), effective for amalgamations that occur and (per 88(1)(e.2)) wind-ups that begin after 2005.

Interpretation Bulletins: See list at end of s. 87.

(aa) refundable dividend tax on hand — if the new corporation was a private corporation immediately after the amalgamation, the following rules apply:

(i) for the purpose of computing the "eligible refundable dividend tax on hand" and "non-eligible refundable dividend tax on hand" (as defined in subsection 129(4)) of the new corporation at the end of its first taxation year there shall be added to the total determined under those definitions in respect of the new corporation for the year

(A) in respect of the new corporation's eligible refundable dividend tax on hand, the total of all amounts each of which is the amount, if any, by which the eligible refundable dividend tax on hand of a predecessor corporation at the end of its last taxation year exceeds the total of all amounts each of which is the portion, if any, of its dividend refund for its last taxation year from its eligible refundable dividend tax on hand determined under subparagraph 129(1)(a)(i) or clause 129(1)(a)(ii)(B), and

(B) in respect of the new corporation's non-eligible refundable dividend tax on hand, the total of all amounts each of which is the amount, if any, by which the non-eligible refundable dividend tax on hand of a predecessor corporation at the end of its last taxation year exceeds the portion, if any, of its dividend refund for its last taxation year from its non-eligible refundable dividend tax on hand determined under clause 129(1)(a)(ii)(A), and

(ii) no amount shall be added under this paragraph in respect of a predecessor corporation

(A) that was not a private corporation at the end of its last taxation year, or

(B) where subsection 129(1.2) would have applied to deem a dividend paid by the predecessor corporation immediately before the amalgamation not to be a taxable dividend for the purpose of subsection 129(1);

Related Provisions: 87(2)(b) — Meaning of "last taxation year"; 88(1)(e.2) — Winding-up; 129(5.1) — 2019 transitional RDTOH; 131(5) — Dividend refund to mutual fund corporation; 186(5) — Deemed private corporation. See also at end of s. 87.

Notes: 87(2)(aa) amended by 2018 budget bill #1 to apply to ERDTOH and NERDTOH instead of the former RDTOH, for taxation years that begin after 2018. However, all the bill's amendments to 87(2)(aa), 125(5.1), 125(5.2), 129, 131 and 186(5) also apply to a corporation's taxation year that begins before 2019 and ends after 2018 if

(a) the corp's preceding taxation year was, because of a transaction or event or a series of transactions or events, shorter than it would have been in the absence of that transaction, event or series; and

(b) one of the reasons for the transaction, event or series was to defer the amendments to 125(5.1), 125(5.2) or 129 to the corp.

(In other words, these amendments apply earlier if planning was used to try to trigger a year-end before new 125(5.1)(b) kicked in.) Before the amendment, read:

(aa) where the new corporation was a private corporation immediately after the amalgamation, for the purpose of computing the refundable dividend tax on hand (within the meaning assigned by subsection 129(3)) of the new corporation at the end of its first taxation year there shall be added to the total determined under subsection 129(3) in respect of the new corporation for the year the total of all amounts each of which is the amount, if any, by which the refundable dividend tax on hand of a predecessor corporation at the end of its last taxation year exceeds its dividend refund (within the meaning assigned by subsection 129(1)) for

its last taxation year, except that no amount shall be added under this paragraph in respect of a predecessor corporation

(i) that was not a private corporation at the end of its last taxation year, or

(ii) where subsection 129(1.2) would have applied to deem a dividend paid by the predecessor corporation immediately before the amalgamation not to be a taxable dividend for the purpose of subsection 129(1);

87(2)(aa) amended by 1995 Budget, for amalgamations that occur, and (per 88(1)(e.2)) windups that begin, after June 1995. (Earlier windups were dealt with by 88(1)(e.5).) The amendment reflects changes in the RDTOH calculation under 129(3).

Interpretation Bulletins: See list at end of s. 87.

(bb) mutual fund and investment corporations — where the new corporation is a mutual fund corporation or an investment corporation, there shall be added to

(i) the amount determined under each of paragraphs (a) and (b) of the definition "capital gains dividend account" in subsection 131(6), and

(ii) the values of A and B in the definition "refundable capital gains tax on hand" in that subsection

in respect of the new corporation at any time the amounts so determined and the values of those factors immediately before the amalgamation in respect of each predecessor corporation that was, immediately before the amalgamation, a mutual fund corporation or an investment corporation;

Notes: 87(2)(bb) amended by 1995-97 technical bill, this version for amalgamations that occur after Feb. 22, 1994. Earlier amended by 1991 technical bill.

(bb.1) flow-through entities — where a predecessor corporation was, immediately before the amalgamation, an investment corporation, a mortgage investment corporation or a mutual fund corporation and the new corporation is an investment corporation, a mortgage investment corporation or a mutual fund corporation, as the case may be, for the purpose of section 39.1, the new corporation is deemed to be the same corporation as, and a continuation of, the predecessor corporation;

Notes: 87(2)(bb.1) added by 1995-97 technical bill, for amalgamations after 1993.

(cc) non-resident-owned investment corporation — in the case of a new corporation that is a non-resident-owned investment corporation,

(i) for the purpose of computing its allowable refundable tax on hand (within the meaning assigned by subsection 133(9)) at any time, where a predecessor corporation had allowable refundable tax on hand immediately before the amalgamation, the amount thereof shall be added to the total determined for A in the definition "allowable refundable tax on hand" in subsection 133(9),

(ii) for the purpose of computing its capital gains dividend account (within the meaning assigned by subsection 133(8)) at any time, where a predecessor corporation had an amount in its capital gains dividend account immediately before the amalgamation, that amount shall be added to the amount determined under paragraph (a) of the description of A in the definition "capital gains dividend account" in subsection 133(8), and

(iii) for the purpose of computing its cumulative taxable income (within the meaning assigned by subsection 133(9)) at any time, where a predecessor corporation had cumulative taxable income immediately before the amalgamation, the amount thereof shall be added to the total determined for A in the definition "cumulative taxable income" in subsection 133(9);

Related Provisions: 88(1)(e.2) — Winding-up. See also at end of s. 87.

Interpretation Bulletins: See list at end of s. 87.

(dd)–(hh) [Repealed under former Act]

(ii) public corporation — where a predecessor corporation was a public corporation immediately before the amalgamation, the new corporation shall be deemed to have been a public corporation at the commencement of its first taxation year;

Interpretation Bulletins: See list at end of s. 87.

(jj) **interest on certain obligations** — for the purposes of paragraph 81(1)(m), the new corporation shall be deemed to be the same corporation as, and a continuation of, each predecessor corporation;

Interpretation Bulletins: See list at end of s. 87.

(kk) **disposition of shares of controlled corporation** — for the purposes of paragraph 40(2)(h),

(i) where a corporation was controlled, directly or indirectly in any manner whatever, by a predecessor corporation immediately before the amalgamation and has, by reason of the amalgamation, become controlled, directly or indirectly in any manner whatever, by the new corporation, the new corporation shall be deemed to have acquired control of the corporation so controlled at the time control thereof was acquired by the predecessor corporation, and

(ii) where a predecessor corporation was immediately before the amalgamation controlled, directly or indirectly in any manner whatever, by a corporation that, immediately after the amalgamation, controlled, directly or indirectly in any manner whatever, the new corporation, the new corporation shall be deemed to be the same corporation as, and a continuation of, each predecessor corporation;

Related Provisions: 256(5.1), (6.2) — Controlled directly or indirectly. See also at end of s. 87.

Interpretation Bulletins: See list at end of s. 87.

(ll) **para. 20(1)(n) and subpara. 40(1)(a)(iii) amounts** — notwithstanding any other provision of this Act, where any property was disposed of by a predecessor corporation, the new corporation shall, in computing

(i) the amount of any deduction under paragraph 20(1)(n) as a reserve in respect of the property sold in the course of business, and

(ii) the amount of its claim under subparagraph 40(1)(a)(iii) or 44(1)(e)(iii) in respect of the disposition of the property,

be deemed to be the same corporation as, and a continuation of, the predecessor corporation;

Related Provisions: 88(1)(e.2) — Winding-up. See also at end of s. 87.

Notes: 87(2)(ll) amended by 1991 technical bill, for amalgamations after 1989.

(mm) [Repealed]

Notes: 87(2)(mm) repealed by 2002-2013 technical bill, for amalgamations after March 20, 2003. It related to 126.1, which gave a credit to employers for 1993 to offset increases in Unemployment Insurance premiums. Added by 1992 Economic Statement.

(nn) **refundable Part VII tax on hand** — [no longer relevant]

Notes: 87(2)(nn) relates to s. 192, which effectively expired in 1986.

(oo) [Repealed]

Notes: 87(2)(oo) repealed by 2019 budget bill #1, for tax years that end after March 18, 2019. (With 127(10.2) now simplified, a reference to 127(10.2) was added to 87(2)(j.6) instead.) It read:

(oo) investment tax credit — for the purpose of applying subsection 127(10.2) to any corporation, the new corporation is deemed to have had

(i) a particular taxation year that

(A) where it was associated with another corporation in the new corporation's first taxation year, ended in the calendar year that precedes the calendar year in which that first year ends, and

(B) in any other case, immediately precedes that first year, and

(ii) taxable income for the particular year (determined before taking into consideration the specified future tax consequences for the particular year) equal to the total of all amounts each of which is a predecessor corporation's taxable income for its taxation year that ended immediately before the amalgamation (determined before taking into consideration the specified future tax consequences for that year);

Earlier amended by 1996 Budget, last change effective for amalgamations after 1996.

Interpretation Bulletins: See list at end of s. 87.

(oo.1) **refundable investment tax credit and balance-due day** — for the purpose of applying the definition "qualifying corporation" in subsection 127.1(2), and subparagraph (d)(i)

of the definition "balance-due day" in subsection 248(1), to any corporation, the new corporation is deemed to have had

(i) a particular taxation year that

(A) where it was associated with another corporation in the new corporation's first taxation year, ended in the calendar year that precedes the calendar year in which that first year ends, and

(B) where clause (A) does not apply, immediately precedes that first year,

(ii) taxable income for the particular year (determined before taking into consideration the specified future tax consequences for the particular year) equal to the total of all amounts each of which is a predecessor corporation's taxable income for its taxation year that ended immediately before the amalgamation (determined before taking into consideration the specified future tax consequences for that year),

(iii) a business limit for the particular year equal to the total of all amounts each of which is a predecessor corporation's business limit for its taxation year that ended immediately before the amalgamation, and

(iv) a qualifying income limit for the particular year equal to the total of all amounts each of which is a predecessor corporation's qualifying income limit for its taxation year that ended immediately before the amalgamation;

Notes: 87(2)(oo.1)(iv) added by 2013 budget bill #2, effective for amalgamations that occur after Feb. 25, 2008.

87(2)(oo.1) amended by 2001 Budget, for 2002 and later taxation years. Added by 1996 Budget.

(pp) **cumulative offset account computation** — for the purpose of computing the cumulative offset account (within the meaning assigned by subsection 66.5(2)) of the new corporation at any time, there shall be added to the total otherwise determined under paragraph 66.5(2)(a) the total of all amounts each of which is the amount, if any, by which

(i) a predecessor corporation's cumulative offset account at the end of its last taxation year

exceeds

(ii) the amount deducted under subsection 66.5(1) in computing the predecessor corporation's income for its last taxation year;

Related Provisions: 87(2)(b) — Meaning of "last taxation year"; 88(1)(e.2) — Winding-up. See also list at end of s. 87.

Interpretation Bulletins: See list at end of s. 87.

(qq) **continuation of corporation [investment tax credit]** — for the purpose of computing the new corporation's investment tax credit at the end of any taxation year, the new corporation is deemed to be the same corporation as, and a continuation of, each predecessor corporation, except that this paragraph does not affect the determination of the fiscal period of any corporation or the tax payable by any predecessor corporation;

Related Provisions: See Related Provisions at end of s. 87.

Notes: 87(2)(qq) amended by 1995-97 technical bill, effective for amalgamations occurring after April 26, 1995.

Interpretation Bulletins: See list at end of s. 87.

(rr) **tax on taxable preferred shares** — for the purposes of subsections 112(2.9), 191(4), and 191.1(2) and (4), the new corporation shall be deemed to be the same corporation as, and a continuation of, each predecessor corporation;

Related Provisions: 88(1)(e.2) — Winding-up. See also at end of s. 87.

(ss) **transferred liability for Part VI.1 tax** — for the purposes of section 191.3, the new corporation shall be deemed to be the same corporation as, and a continuation of, each predecessor corporation;

(tt) **livestock — inclusion of deferred amount** — for the purposes of subsections 80.3(3) and (5), the new corporation shall be deemed to be the same corporation as, and a continuation of, each predecessor corporation;

Related Provisions: 88(1)(e.2) — Winding-up. See also at end of s. 87.

(uu) **fuel tax rebates** — [No longer relevant]

Notes: 87(2)(uu) tracks fuel tax rebates and the use of the 1992 Loss Offset Program, and the 1997-2000 aviation fuel rebate. See Notes to 12(1)(x.1).

87(2)(uu) added by 1992 transportation support bill, for amalgamations after 1991, and amended by 1997 Budget (bill #1), for 1997 and later taxation years.

(vv) **general rate income pool** — if the new corporation is a Canadian-controlled private corporation or a deposit insurance corporation in its first taxation year, in computing its general rate income pool at the end of that first taxation year there shall be added the total of all amounts determined under subsection 89(5) in respect of the corporation for that first taxation year; and

Related Provisions: 88(1)(e.2)(ix), 89(6) — Winding-up; 89(15) — Meaning of "deposit insurance corporation"; 125(7)"Canadian-controlled private corporation"(d) — Election not to be CCPC for purposes of 87(2)(vv). See also at end of s. 87.

Notes: 87(2)(vv) added by 2006 budget bill #2 (Part 2 — eligible dividends), effective for amalgamations that occur and (per 88(1)(e.2) windups that begin after 2005.

Forms: T2 Sched. 53: General rate income pool (GRIP) calculation.

(ww) **low rate income pool** — if the new corporation is neither a Canadian-controlled private corporation nor a deposit insurance corporation in its first taxation year, there shall be added in computing its low rate income pool at any time in that first taxation year the total of all amounts determined under subsection 89(9) in respect of the corporation for that first taxation year.

Related Provisions: 88(1)(e.2)(ix), 89(10) — Winding-up; 89(15) — Meaning of "deposit insurance corporation"; 125(7)"Canadian-controlled private corporation"(d) — Election not to be CCPC for 87(2)(ww). See also at end of s. 87.

Notes: 87(2)(ww) added by 2006 budget bill #2 (Part 2 — eligible dividends), for amalgamations that occur and (per 88(1)(e.2) windups that begin after 2005.

Forms: T2 Sched. 54: Low rate income pool (LRIP) calculation.

(2.01) Application of subsec. 37.1(5) — The definitions in subsection 37.1(5) apply to subsection (2).

Notes: 87(2.01) added in the RSC 1985 (5th Supp) consolidation, for tax years ending after Nov. 1991. This rule was formerly in the opening words of 37.1(5). S. 37.1, which provided an additional R&D allowance, has been repealed.

(2.1) Non-capital losses, etc., of predecessor corporations — Where there has been an amalgamation of two or more corporations, for the purposes only of

(a) determining the new corporation's non-capital loss, net capital loss, restricted farm loss, farm loss or limited partnership loss, as the case may be, for any taxation year, and

(b) determining the extent to which subsections 111(3) to (5.4) and paragraph 149(10)(c) apply to restrict the deductibility by the new corporation of any non-capital loss, net capital loss, restricted farm loss, farm loss or limited partnership loss, as the case may be,

the new corporation shall be deemed to be the same corporation as, and a continuation of, each predecessor corporation, except that this subsection shall in no respect affect the determination of

(c) the fiscal period of the new corporation or any of its predecessors,

(d) the income of the new corporation or any of its predecessors, or

(e) the taxable income of, or the tax payable under this Act by, any predecessor corporation.

Related Provisions: 87(2)(a) — Taxation year-end; 87(2.11) — Losses, etc., on amalgamation with subsidiary wholly-owned corporation; 256(7) — Where control deemed not acquired. See also at end of s. 87.

Notes: See Notes to 87(2)(a). 87(2.1)(d)-(e) allow losses to be carried forward through an amalgamation (subject to 87(2)(a) and the change-of-control rule in 111(4) and (5)), since they are deducted in computing the *taxable* income of the new corporation. Losses cannot be carried back: 87(2.1)(e), VIEWS doc 2016-0651951E5 (except on vertical amalgamation: 87(2.11)).

For rulings on 87(2.1) see docs 2005-0163141R3, 2005-0165201R3, 2010-0376681R3, 2019-0819871R3. See also Kabouchi & Klyguine, "Loss Utilization in Amalgamations and Wind-Ups", XX(2) *Corporate Finance* (Federated Press) 32-35 (2016).

87(2.1)(b) amended by 1995-97 technical bill.

Income Tax Folios: S4-F7-C1: Amalgamations of Canadian corporations [replaces IT-474R2].

Interpretation Bulletins: IT-302R3: Losses of a corporation — the effect that acquisitions of control, amalgamations, and windings-up have on their deductibility. See also at end of s. 87.

(2.11) Vertical amalgamations — Where a new corporation is formed by the amalgamation of a particular corporation and one or more of its subsidiary wholly-owned corporations, the new corporation is deemed to be the same corporation as, and a continuation of, the particular corporation for the purposes of applying sections 111 and 126, subsections 127(5) to (26) and 181.1(4) to (7), Part IV and subsections 190.1(3) to (6) in respect of the particular corporation.

Related Provisions: 87(1.4) — Definition of "subsidiary wholly-owned corporation"; 87(2.1) — Non-capital losses, etc., of predecessor corporations; 87(11) — Vertical amalgamation — effects; 256(7) — Where control deemed not acquired.

Notes: 87(2.11) effectively permits losses of the amalgamated corporation to be carried back to the predecessor parent (under the rules in 111) on a vertical short-form amalgamation or other amalgamation of a corporation with a subsidiary wholly-owned corporation (see 87(1.4))

Revenue Canada indicated, at the 1994 Cdn Tax Foundation conference, that the purpose of 87(2.11) is to put vertical amalgamations on an equal footing with 88(1) windups re the ability to carry back losses to the parent. 87(2.11) does not permit an application of a subsidiary's prior year losses to be carried back against the parent's prior year's income. This is consistent with the rules in 88(1.1).

On the interaction with 87(2.1) see VIEWS doc 2006-0170341E5. On the interaction with SR&ED investment tax credits see 9833526. For rulings that 87(2.11) applies see 9633803, 980576B, 2004-0096661R3, 2010-0371661R3, 2011-0411821R3. See also 9336226, 9410360 and 9429010 (all: sub's losses cannot be used against parent's income); 9509195 (carryback to parent); 9802725 (whether 87(2.11) applies); 9825705 (no carryback of losses to sub).

87(2.11) added by 1992 technical bill and amended by 1995-97 technical bill, effective for amalgamations that occur after April 26, 1995.

Income Tax Folios: S4-F7-C1: Amalgamations of Canadian corporations [replaces IT-474R2].

I.T. Technical News: 3 (subsection 87(2.11)).

(2.2) Amalgamation of insurers — Where there has been an amalgamation and one or more of the predecessor corporations was an insurer, the new corporation is, notwithstanding subsection (2), deemed, for the purposes of paragraphs 12(1)(d), (e), (e.1), (i) and (s), subsection 12.5(8), paragraphs 20(1)(l), (l.1), (p) and (jj) and 20(7)(c), subsections 20(22) and 20.4(4), sections 138, 138.1, 140, 142 and 148 and Part XII.3, to be the same corporation as, and a continuation of, each of those predecessor corporations.

Related Provisions: 139.1(3)(g) — Where merger causes demutualization of insurer. See also at end of s. 87.

Notes: 87(2.2) amended by 2008 budget bill #2 to refer to 12.5(8) and 20.4(4), effective for taxation years that begin after September 2006.

87(2.2) amended by 1996 Budget, for amalgamations that occur after 1995.

I.T. Application Rules: 69 (meaning of "chapter 148 of ...").

Interpretation Bulletins: See list at end of s. 87.

(2.3) Quebec credit unions — For the purpose of applying this section to an amalgamation governed by section 689 of *An Act respecting financial services cooperatives*, R.S.Q., c. C-67.3, an investment deposit of a credit union is deemed to be a share of a separate class of the capital stock of a predecessor corporation in respect of the amalgamation the adjusted cost base and paid up capital of which to the credit union is equal to the adjusted cost base to the credit union of the investment deposit immediately before the amalgamation if

(a) immediately before the amalgamation, the investment deposit is an investment deposit to which section 425 of the *Savings and Credit Unions Act*, R.S.Q., c. C-4.1, applies to the investment fund of that predecessor corporation; and

(b) on the amalgamation the credit union disposes of the investment deposit for consideration that consists solely of shares of a class of the capital stock of the new corporation.

Notes: 87(2.3) added by 2002-2013 technical bill (Part 5 — technical), for amalgamations after June 2001. It implements a Dec. 5, 2000 Finance comfort letter.

(3) Computation of paid-up capital [limitation after amalgamation] — Subject to subsection (3.1), where there is an amalgamation or a merger of 2 or more Canadian corporations, in computing at any particular time the paid-up capital in respect of any particular class of shares of the capital stock of the new corporation,

(a) there shall be deducted that proportion of the amount, if any, by which the paid-up capital, determined without reference to this subsection, in respect of all the shares of the capital stock of the new corporation immediately after the amalgamation or merger exceeds the total of all amounts each of which is the paid-up capital in respect of a share (except a share held by any other predecessor corporation) of the capital stock of a predecessor corporation immediately before the amalgamation or merger, that

(i) the paid-up capital, determined without reference to this subsection, of the particular class of shares of the capital stock of the new corporation immediately after the amalgamation or merger

is of

(ii) the paid-up capital, determined without reference to this subsection, in respect of all of the issued and outstanding shares of the capital stock of the new corporation immediately after the amalgamation or merger; and

(b) there shall be added an amount equal to the lesser of

(i) the amount, if any, by which

(A) the total of all amounts each of which is an amount deemed by subsection 84(3), (4) or (4.1) to be a dividend on shares of the particular class paid by the new corporation before the particular time

exceeds

(B) the total that would be determined under clause (A) if this Act were read without reference to paragraph (a), and

(ii) the amount required by paragraph (a) to be deducted in computing the paid-up capital of shares of the particular class.

Related Provisions: 87(3.1) — Election for 87(3) not to apply. See also at end of s. 87.

Notes: See Notes to 84(3).

"As a general rule, when two corporations amalgamate, the PUC of the shares of both amalgamating corporations are aggregated to form the PUC of the shares of the amalgamated corporation. However, where the relationship between the amalgamating corporations is parent and subsidiary — a so-called 'vertical' amalgamation — the PUC of the shares of both corporations are not aggregated. Rather the PUC of the shares of the subsidiary corporation which are owned by the parent is cancelled": *Copthorne Holdings*, 2011 SCC 63, para. 2. In *Copthorne*, avoidance of 87(3) by changing a vertical structure to a sister-corp structure before amalgamation violated GAAR (see 245(2)).

Opening words of 87(3) amended by 1992 technical bill, effective for amalgamations after 1990, to make it subject to 87(3.1).

Income Tax Folios: S4-F7-C1: Amalgamations of Canadian corporations [replaces IT-474R2].

Interpretation Bulletins: See list at end of s. 87.

(3.1) Election for non-application of subsec. (3) — Where,

(a) there is an amalgamation of 2 or more corporations,

(b) all of the issued shares, immediately before the amalgamation, of each class of shares (other than a class of shares all of the issued shares of which were cancelled on the amalgamation) of the capital stock of each predecessor corporation (in this subsection referred to as the "exchanged class") are converted into all of the issued shares, immediately after the amalgamation, of a separate class of shares of the capital stock of the new corporation (in this subsection referred to as the "substituted class"),

(c) immediately after the amalgamation, the number of shareholders of each substituted class, the number of shares of each substituted class owned by each shareholder, the number of issued shares of each substituted class, the terms and conditions of

each share of a substituted class, and the paid-up capital of each substituted class determined without reference to the provisions of this Act are identical to the number of shareholders of the exchanged class from which the substituted class was converted, the number of shares of each such exchanged class owned by each shareholder, the number of issued shares of each such exchanged class, the terms and conditions of each share of such exchanged class, and the paid-up capital of each such exchanged class determined without reference to the provisions of this Act, respectively, immediately before the amalgamation, and

(d) the new corporation elects in its return of income filed in accordance with section 150 for its first taxation year to have the provisions of this subsection apply,

for the purpose of computing at any particular time the paid-up capital in respect of any particular class of shares of the capital stock of the new corporation,

(e) subsection (3) does not apply in respect of the amalgamation, and

(f) each substituted class shall be deemed to be the same as, and a continuation of, the exchanged class from which it was converted.

Notes: See Yahui Zhu, "Amalgamations: Avoiding PUC Shifts", 9(1) *Canadian Tax Focus* (ctf.ca) 9-10 (Feb. 2019).

87(3.1) added by 1992 technical bill, for amalgamations after 1990.

Income Tax Folios: S4-F7-C1: Amalgamations of Canadian corporations [replaces IT-474R2].

(4) Shares of predecessor corporation — Where there has been an amalgamation of two or more corporations after May 6, 1974, each shareholder (except any predecessor corporation) who, immediately before the amalgamation, owned shares of the capital stock of a predecessor corporation (in this subsection referred to as the "old shares") that were capital property to the shareholder and who received no consideration for the disposition of those shares on the amalgamation, other than shares of the capital stock of the new corporation (in this subsection referred to as the "new shares"), shall be deemed

(a) to have disposed of the old shares for proceeds equal to the total of the adjusted cost bases to the shareholder of those shares immediately before the amalgamation, and

(b) to have acquired the new shares of any particular class of the capital stock of the new corporation at a cost to the shareholder equal to that proportion of the proceeds described in paragraph (a) that

(i) the fair market value, immediately after the amalgamation, of all new shares of that particular class so acquired by the shareholder,

is of

(ii) the fair market value, immediately after the amalgamation, of all new shares so acquired by the shareholder,

except that, where the fair market value of the old shares immediately before the amalgamation exceeds the fair market value of the new shares immediately after the amalgamation and it is reasonable to regard any portion of the excess (in this subsection referred to as the "gift portion") as a benefit that the shareholder desired to have conferred on a person related to the shareholder, the following rules apply:

(c) the shareholder shall be deemed to have disposed of the old shares for proceeds of disposition equal to the lesser of

(i) the total of the adjusted cost bases to the shareholder, immediately before the amalgamation, of the old shares and the gift portion, and

(ii) the fair market value of the old shares immediately before the amalgamation,

(d) the shareholder's capital loss from the disposition of the old shares shall be deemed to be nil,

(e) the cost to the shareholder of any new shares of any class of the capital stock of the new corporation acquired by the shareholder on the amalgamation shall be deemed to be that proportion of the lesser of

(i) the total of the adjusted cost bases to the shareholder, immediately before the amalgamation, of the old shares, and

(ii) the total of the fair market value, immediately after the amalgamation, of all new shares so acquired by the shareholder and the amount that, but for paragraph (d), would have been the shareholder's capital loss from the disposition of the old shares

that

(iii) the fair market value, immediately after the amalgamation, of the new shares of that class so acquired by the shareholder

is of

(iv) the fair market value, immediately after the amalgamation, of all new shares so acquired by the shareholder,

and where the old shares were taxable Canadian property of the shareholder, the new shares are deemed to be, at any time that is within 60 months after the amalgamation, taxable Canadian property of the shareholder.

Related Provisions: 44.1(6), (7) — Small business investment rollover on exchange of shares; 7(1.5) — Shares acquired through employee stock option; 53(4) — Effect on ACB of shares; 87(5) — Option to acquire share of predecessor corporation; 87(8) — Merger of foreign affiliate; 87(9)(a), (c) — Effect of triangular amalgamation; 95(2)(d) — Merger of foreign affiliate; 107.4(3)(f) — Deemed taxable Canadian property retains status when rolled out of or into trust; 248(1)"disposition"(n) — Cancellation of shares on foreign amalgamation deemed not to be disposition; 248(25.1) — Deemed taxable Canadian property retains status through trust-to-trust transfer. See also at end of s. 87.

Notes: See Income Tax Folio S4-F7-C1 ¶1.69-1.76.

In *Husky Oil*, 2010 FCA 125, one shareholder received worthless preferred shares on an amalgamation as part of an arrangement to reduce capital gains on a takeover; the 87(4) rollover took priority over 69(4). The 87(4)(c)-(e) exception did not apply: it "is intended to deter a taxpayer from using the device of a corporate amalgamation to shift part or all of the value of a predecessor corporation to the amalgamated corporation if, but only if, a person related to the taxpayer has a direct or indirect interest in the amalgamated corporation that will be enhanced by the shift in value" (para. 58).

For rulings that no benefit is conferred in a butterfly or other reorganization, see VIEWS docs 2007-0221331R3, 2007-0226931R3, 2007-0227501R3, 2007-0232261R3, 2007-0240881R3, 2009-0330511R3, 2010-0376681R3 and many others.

For other rulings applying 87(4) see 2002-0177163 (shareholder rights plan), 2002-0167465 (shares acquired under stock option agreement), 2003-0031790 (amalgamation of mutual insurers), 2005-0152611R3 (foreign merger), 2011-0402571R3 (debt settlement on amalgamating Profitco and Lossco).

Income Tax Folio S4-F7-C1 ¶1.82 and VIEWS doc 2011-0429021E5 state that a non-resident holder of shares that fall under 87(4) and that are taxable Canadian property need not obtain a s. 116 certificate.

A taxpayer who receives cash of less than $200 in lieu of fractional shares can still use the 87(4) rollover: Folio S4-F7-C1 ¶1.70. Beyond that amount, 87(4) does not apply: VIEWS doc 2017-0696821E5.

87(4) closing words amended by 2010 budget bill #1, effective in determining after March 4, 2010 whether a property is taxable Canadian property of the taxpayer, to add "at any time that is within 60 months after the amalgamation". See Notes to 44.1(2).

Income Tax Folios: S4-F7-C1: Amalgamations of Canadian corporations [replaces IT-474R2].

Interpretation Bulletins: IT-113R: Benefits to employees — stock options. See also list at end of s. 87.

(4.1) Exchanged shares — For the purposes of the definition "term preferred share" in subsection 248(1), where there has been an amalgamation of two or more corporations after November 16, 1978 and a share of any class of the capital stock of the new corporation (in this subsection referred to as the "new share") was issued in consideration for the disposition of a share of any class of the capital stock of a predecessor corporation (in this subsection referred to as the "exchanged share") and the terms and conditions of the new share were the same as, or substantially the same as, the terms and conditions of the exchanged share,

(a) the new share shall be deemed to have been issued at the time the exchanged share was issued;

(b) if the exchanged share was issued under an agreement in writing, the new share shall be deemed to have been issued under that agreement; and

(c) the new corporation shall be deemed to be the same corporation as, and a continuation of, each such predecessor corporation.

Related Provisions: 87(9)(a.1) — Effect of triangular amalgamation. See also at end of s. 87.

Interpretation Bulletins: See list at end of s. 87.

(4.2) Idem — Where there has been an amalgamation or merger of two or more corporations after November 27, 1986 and a share of any class of the capital stock of the new corporation (in this subsection referred to as the "new share") was issued to a shareholder in consideration for the disposition of a share by that shareholder of any class of the capital stock of a predecessor corporation (in this subsection referred to as the "exchanged share") and the terms and conditions of the new share were the same as, or substantially the same as, the terms and conditions of the exchanged share, for the purposes of applying the provisions of this subsection, subsections 112(2.2) and (2.4), Parts IV.1 and VI.1, section 258 and the definitions "grandfathered share", "short-term preferred share", "taxable preferred share" and "taxable RFI share" in subsection 248(1) to the new share, the following rules apply:

(a) the new share shall be deemed to have been issued at the time the exchanged share was issued;

(b) where the exchanged share was a share described in paragraph (a), (b), (c) or (d) of the definition "grandfathered share" in subsection 248(1), the new share shall be deemed to be the same share as the exchanged share for the purposes of that definition;

(c) the new share shall be deemed to have been acquired by the shareholder at the time the exchanged share was acquired by the shareholder;

(d) the new corporation shall be deemed to be the same corporation as, and a continuation of, each predecessor corporation;

(e) an election made under subsection 191.2(1) by a predecessor corporation with respect to the class of shares of its capital stock to which the exchanged share belonged shall be deemed to be an election made by the new corporation with respect to the class of shares of its capital stock to which the new share belongs; and

(f) where the terms or conditions of the exchanged share or an agreement in respect of the exchanged share specify an amount in respect of the exchanged share for the purposes of subsection 191(4) and an amount equal to the amount so specified in respect of the exchanged share is specified in respect of the new share for the purposes of subsection 191(4),

(i) for the purposes of subparagraphs 191(4)(d)(i) and (e)(i), the new share shall be deemed to have been issued for the same consideration as that for which the exchanged share was issued and to have been issued for the purpose for which the exchanged share was issued,

(ii) for the purposes of subparagraphs 191(4)(d)(ii) and (e)(ii), the new share shall be deemed to be the same share as the exchanged share and to have been issued for the purpose for which the exchanged share was issued, and

(iii) where the shareholder received no consideration for the disposition of the exchanged share other than the new share, for the purposes of subsection 191(4),

(A) in the case of an exchanged share to which subsection 191(4) applies because of paragraph 191(4)(a), the new share shall be deemed to have been issued for consideration having a fair market value equal to the consideration for which the exchanged share was issued, and

(B) in the case of an exchanged share to which subsection 191(4) applies because of an event described in paragraph 191(4)(b) or (c), the consideration for which the new share was issued shall be deemed to have a fair market value equal to the fair market value of the exchanged share immediately before the time that event occurred.

Related Provisions: 87(9)(a.1) — Effect of triangular amalgamation.

Notes: 87(4.2)(f) added by 1991 technical bill, effective 1988.

Interpretation Bulletins: See list at end of s. 87.

(4.3) Exchanged rights — Where there has been an amalgamation or merger of two or more corporations after June 18, 1987 and a right listed on a designated stock exchange to acquire a share of any class of the capital stock of the new corporation (in this subsection referred to as the "new right") was acquired by a shareholder in consideration for the disposition of a right described in paragraph (d) of the definition "grandfathered share" in subsection 248(1) to acquire a share of any class of the capital stock of a predecessor corporation (in this subsection referred to as the "exchanged right"), the new right shall be deemed to be the same right as the exchanged right for the purposes of paragraph (d) of the definition "grandfathered share" in subsection 248(1) where the terms and conditions of the new right were the same as, or substantially the same as, the terms and conditions of the exchanged right and the terms and conditions of the share receivable on an exercise of the new right were the same as, or substantially the same as, the terms and conditions of the share that would have been received on an exercise of the exchanged right.

Related Provisions: 87(9)(a.2) — Effect of triangular amalgamation. See also at end of s. 87.

Notes: 87(4.3) amended by 2007 budget bill #2, effective Dec. 14, 2007, to change "prescribed stock exchange" to "designated stock exchange".

Interpretation Bulletins: See list at end of s. 87.

(4.4) Flow-through shares — Where

(a) there is an amalgamation of two or more corporations each of which is a principal-business corporation (within the meaning assigned by subsection 66(15)) or a corporation that at no time carried on business,

(b) a predecessor corporation entered into an agreement with a person at a particular time for consideration given by the person to the predecessor corporation,

(c) for the consideration under the agreement

(i) a share (in this subsection referred to as the "old share") of the predecessor corporation that was a flow-through share (other than a right to acquire a share) was issued to the person before the amalgamation, or

(ii) a right was issued to the person before the amalgamation to acquire a share that would, if it were issued, be a flow-through share, and

(d) the new corporation

(i) issues, on the amalgamation and in consideration for the disposition of the old share, a share (in this subsection referred to as a "new share") of any class of its capital stock to the person (or to any person or partnership that subsequently acquired the old share) and the terms and conditions of the new share are the same as, or substantially the same as, the terms and conditions of the old share, or

(ii) is, because of the right referred to in subparagraph (c)(ii), obliged after the amalgamation to issue to the person a share of any class of the new corporation's capital stock that would, if it were issued, be a flow-through share,

for the purposes of subsection 66(12.66) and Part XII.6 and for the purposes of renouncing an amount under subsection 66(12.6), (12.601) or (12.62) in respect of Canadian exploration expenses or Canadian development expenses that would, but for the renunciation, be incurred by the new corporation after the amalgamation,

(e) the person shall be deemed to have given the consideration under the agreement to the new corporation for the issue of the new share,

(f) the agreement shall be deemed to have been entered into between the new corporation and the person at the particular time,

(g) the new share shall be deemed to be a flow-through share of the new corporation, and

(h) the new corporation shall be deemed to be the same corporation as, and a continuation of, the predecessor corporation.

Related Provisions: 87(9)(a.21) — Effect of triangular amalgamation. See also at end of s. 87.

Notes: 87(4.4)(c) and (d) amended by 2002-2013 technical bill (Part 5 — technical), effective for amalgamations after 1997.

87(4.4) amended by 1996 Budget (in-force rule corrected by 1995-97 technical bill) and 1992 Economic Statement. Added by 1991 technical bill.

(5) Options to acquire shares of predecessor corporation — Where there has been an amalgamation of two or more corporations after May 6, 1974, each taxpayer (except any predecessor corporation) who immediately before the amalgamation owned a capital property that was an option to acquire shares of the capital stock of a predecessor corporation (in this subsection referred to as the "old option") and who received no consideration for the disposition of that option on the amalgamation, other than an option to acquire shares of the capital stock of the new corporation (in this subsection referred to as the "new option"), shall be deemed

(a) to have disposed of the old option for proceeds equal to the adjusted cost base to the taxpayer of that option immediately before the amalgamation, and

(b) to have acquired the new option at a cost to the taxpayer equal to the proceeds described in paragraph (a),

and where the old option was taxable Canadian property of the taxpayer, the new option is deemed to be, at any time that is within 60 months after the amalgamation, taxable Canadian property of the taxpayer.

Related Provisions: 7(1.4) — Employee stock options; 87(5.1) — ACB of option; 87(8) — Merger of foreign affiliate; 87(9)(a.3) — Rules applicable in respect of certain mergers; 107.4(3)(f) — Deemed taxable Canadian property retains status when rolled out of or into trust; 248(25.1) — Deemed taxable Canadian property retains status through trust-to-trust transfer. See also at end of s. 87.

Notes: See Notes to 87(4).

87(5) closing words amended by 2010 budget bill #1, effective in determining after March 4, 2010 whether a property is taxable Canadian property of a taxpayer, to add "at any time that is within 60 months after the amalgamation". See Notes to 44.1(2).

Income Tax Folios: S4-F7-C1: Amalgamations of Canadian corporations [replaces IT-474R2].

Interpretation Bulletins: See list at end of s. 87.

(5.1) Adjusted cost base of option — Where the cost to a taxpayer of a new option is determined at any time under subsection (5),

(a) there shall be deducted after that time in computing the adjusted cost base to the taxpayer of the new option the total of all amounts deducted under paragraph 53(2)(g.1) in computing, immediately before that time, the adjusted cost base to the taxpayer of the old option; and

(b) the amount determined under paragraph (a) shall be added after that time in computing the adjusted cost base to the taxpayer of the new option.

Related Provisions: 53(1)(q) — Addition to ACB for amount under 87(5.1)(b); 53(2)(g.1) — Reduction in ACB under 87(5.1)(a); 80.03(2)(a) — Deemed gain on disposition following debt forgiveness. See also at end of s. 87.

Notes: 87(5.1) added by 1994 technical bill, effective for taxation years that end after February 21, 1994. See Notes to 47(1).

(6) Obligations of predecessor corporation — Notwithstanding subsection (7), where there has been an amalgamation of two or more corporations after May 6, 1974, each taxpayer (except any predecessor corporation) who, immediately before the amalgamation, owned a capital property that was a bond, debenture, mortgage, hypothecary claim, note or other similar obligation of a predecessor corporation (in this subsection referred to as the "old property") and who received no consideration for the disposition of the old property on the amalgamation other than a bond, debenture, mortgage, hypothecary claim, note or other similar obligation respectively, of the new corporation (in this subsection referred to as the "new property") is, if the amount payable to the holder of the new property on its maturity is the same as the amount that would have been payable to the holder of the old property on its maturity, deemed

(a) to have disposed of the old property for proceeds equal to the adjusted cost base to the taxpayer of that property immediately before the amalgamation; and

(b) to have acquired the new property at a cost to the taxpayer equal to the proceeds described in paragraph (a).

Related Provisions: 80(2) — Deemed settlement on amalgamation; 87(6.1) — ACB of property; 88(1)(e.2) — Application to winding-up. See also at end of s. 87.

Notes: The term "bond, debenture, mortgage, hypothecary claim, note or other similar obligation" may not include bankers' acceptances: *Federated Co-operatives*, 2001 FCA 217; leave to appeal denied 2001 CarswellNat 1788 (SCC).

Reference to "hypothecary claims" added to 87(6) opening words by 2001 *Civil Code* harmonization bill, effective June 14, 2001. The change is non-substantive; see *Interpretation Act* s. 8.2.

I.T. Application Rules: 26(23) (where taxpayer acquired the old property before 1972).

Interpretation Bulletins: See list at end of s. 87.

(6.1) Adjusted cost base

— Where the cost to a taxpayer of a particular property that is a bond, debenture or note is determined at any time under subsection (6) and the terms of the bond, debenture or note conferred upon the holder the right to exchange that bond, debenture or note for shares,

(a) there shall be deducted after that time in computing the adjusted cost base to the taxpayer of the bond, debenture or note the total of all amounts deducted under paragraph 53(2)(g.1) in computing, immediately before that time, the adjusted cost base to the taxpayer of the property for which the particular property was exchanged at that time; and

(b) the amount determined under paragraph (a) in respect of the particular property shall be added after that time in computing the adjusted cost base to the taxpayer of the particular property.

Related Provisions: 53(1)(q) — Addition to ACB for amount under 87(6.1)(b); 53(2)(g.1) — Reduction in ACB under 87(6.1)(a); 80.03(2)(a) — Deemed gain on disposition following debt forgiveness. See also at end of s. 87.

Notes: 87(6.1) added by 1994 technical bill, effective for taxation years that end after February 21, 1994. See Notes to 47(1).

(7) [Obligations of predecessor corporation]

— Where there has been an amalgamation of two or more corporations after May 6, 1974 and

(a) a debt or other obligation of a predecessor corporation that was outstanding immediately before the amalgamation became a debt or other obligation of the new corporation on the amalgamation, and

(b) the amount payable by the new corporation on the maturity of the debt or other obligation, as the case may be, is the same as the amount that would have been payable by the predecessor corporation on its maturity,

the provisions of this Act

(c) shall not apply in respect of the transfer of the debt or other obligation to the new corporation, and

(d) shall apply as if the new corporation had incurred or issued the debt or other obligation at the time it was incurred or issued by the predecessor corporation under the agreement made on the day on which the predecessor corporation made an agreement under which the debt or other obligation was issued,

except that, for the purposes of the definition "income bond" or "income debenture" in subsection 248(1), paragraph (d) shall not apply to any debt or other obligation of the new corporation unless the terms and conditions thereof immediately after the amalgamation are the same as, or substantially the same as, the terms and conditions of the debt or obligation that was an income bond or income debenture of the predecessor corporation immediately before the amalgamation.

Related Provisions: 87(6) — Obligations of predecessor corporation; 88(1)(e.2) — Application to winding-up. See also at end of s. 87.

Notes: In *Dow Chemical*, 2008 FCA 231, leave to appeal denied 2008 CarswellNat 4683 (SCC), 87(7) was held to cause 78(1) to require an amalgamated corporation to include in income an unpaid amount deducted by a predecessor.

For CRA interpretation see VIEWS docs 2009-0344721E5, 2010-0387601E5.

87(7)(a) amended by 1992 technical bill, effective June 10, 1993.

Income Tax Folios: S3-F6-C1: Interest deductibility [replaces IT-533]; S4-F7-C1: Amalgamations of Canadian corporations [replaces IT-474R2].

Interpretation Bulletins: See list at end of s. 87.

(8) Foreign merger

— Subject to subsection 95(2), where there has been a foreign merger in which a taxpayer's shares or options to acquire shares of the capital stock of a corporation that was a predecessor foreign corporation immediately before the merger were exchanged for or became shares or options to acquire shares of the capital stock of the new foreign corporation or the foreign parent corporation, unless the taxpayer elects in the taxpayer's return of income for the taxation year in which the foreign merger took place not to have this subsection apply, subsections (4) and (5) apply to the taxpayer as if the references in those subsections to

(a) "amalgamation" were read as "foreign merger";

(b) "predecessor corporation" were read as "predecessor foreign corporation"; and

(c) "new corporation" were read as "new foreign corporation or the foreign parent corporation".

Related Provisions: 87(8.1) — Definition of "foreign merger"; 87(8.3) — Anti-avoidance; 95(2)(d) — Effect of foreign merger on FAPI; Reg. 5905(3) — Effect of foreign merger on FAPI accounts. See also at end of s. 87.

Notes: For CRA approval of mergers as qualifying under 87(8) and (8.1) see VIEWS docs 2005-0152611R3, 2007-0225221I7, 2009-0330881R3, 2014-0550641E5. For the effect of not electing under 87(8) see 2009-033772117.

An election "in the taxpayer's return" is valid even if the return is filed late. See Notes to 7(1.31).

A taxpayer who receives cash of less than $200 in lieu of fractional shares can still use the 87(8) rollover: VIEWS doc 2003-0013315.

See also Gordon Zittlau, "Corporate Reorganizations Involving Taxable Canadian Property — Foreign Merger Considerations", XX(3) *International Tax Planning* (Federated Press) 6-9 (2016).

87(8) amended by 2001 technical bill (for mergers and combinations after 1995), 1998 Budget (for mergers and combinations after Feb. 24, 1998).

Interpretation Bulletins: See list at end of s. 87.

(8.1) Definition of "foreign merger"

— For the purposes of this section, "foreign merger" means a merger or combination of two or more corporations each of which was, immediately before the merger or combination, resident in a country other than Canada (each of which is in this section referred to as a **"predecessor foreign corporation"**) to form one corporate entity resident in a country other than Canada (in this section referred to as the **"new foreign corporation"**) in such a manner that, and otherwise than as a result of the distribution of property to one corporation on the winding-up of another corporation,

(a) all or substantially all the property (except amounts receivable from any predecessor foreign corporation or shares of the capital stock of any predecessor foreign corporation) of the predecessor foreign corporations immediately before the merger or combination becomes property of the new foreign corporation as a consequence of the merger or combination;

(b) all or substantially all the liabilities (except amounts payable to any predecessor foreign corporation) of the predecessor foreign corporations immediately before the merger or combination become liabilities of the new foreign corporation as a consequence of the merger or combination; and

(c) all or substantially all of the shares of the capital stock of the predecessor foreign corporations (except any shares or options owned by any predecessor foreign corporation) are exchanged for or become, because of the merger or combination,

(i) shares of the capital stock of the new foreign corporation, or

(ii) if, immediately after the merger, the new foreign corporation was controlled by another corporation (in this section referred to as the "foreign parent corporation") that was resident in a country other than Canada, shares of the capital stock of the foreign parent corporation.

Proposed Amendment — 87(8.1)

Letter from Dept. of Finance, July 28, 2016:

Dear [xxx]:

SUBJECT: Foreign merger — tax-deferred rollover

I am writing in response to your correspondence to the Tax Legislation Division, and your various related communications, concerning your request for comfort in respect of a disposition, resulting from a foreign merger transaction, of shares of a corporation resident in Canada that are taxable Canadian property ("TCP") owned by one of the merging foreign corporations. It is your view that, in policy terms, this disposition should occur on a tax-deferred basis, but the *Income Tax Act* (the "Act") currently does not provide for this result.

The issue you have raised arises from the following contemplated transaction, described in your letter. As part of a series of transactions designed to simplify the [xxx] group's corporate structure, the two principal [xxx] parent corporations of its Canadian operating subsidiaries ([xxx] Co 1 and [xxx] Co 2) will merge. You have indicated that this merger will, under the governing corporate law of [xxx], necessarily result in one (but not both) of [xxx] Co 1 and [xxx] Co 2 ceasing to exist, and consequently, for purposes of the Act, the discontinuing [xxx] corporation will be considered to dispose of the shares of one or more corporations resident in Canada (the "Canco shares") owned by it. The Canco shares are TCP, and are not treaty-protected property, both as defined in subsection 248(1) of the Act. Accordingly, although you indicate that the merger will occur on a tax-deferred basis under [xxx] tax law, any gain realized by the discontinuing [xxx] corporation on the disposition of the Canco shares would be taxable in Canada, absent an applicable provision in the Act providing tax-deferred ("rollover") treatment in respect of the merger.

The Act currently does not contain a provision that would allow the disposition of the Canco shares by the discontinuing [xxx] corporation in the above-described circumstances to occur on a tax-deferred basis. First, you have submitted to us that the transaction in question may not qualify as an absorptive merger described in subsection 87(8.2) of the Act, due to the exclusion in subsections 87(8.1) and (8.2) for cases involving "the distribution of property to one corporation on the winding-up of another corporation." (Since [xxx] Co 1 is the parent corporation of [xxx] Co 2, if the transaction is structured such that [xxx] Co 1 is the surviving corporation, the transaction will constitute a winding-up of [xxx] Co 2 into [xxx] Co 1.) Second, even if the transaction were to qualify as an absorptive merger described in subsection 87(8.2), and a foreign merger for purposes of subsection 87(8) (as defined in subsection 87(8.1)) — and none of the shareholders of the merging corporations received consideration (other than shares of the surviving corporation) for the disposition of shares of the merging corporations on the foreign merger — subsection 87(4) would generally apply, with the result that the merger could occur on a tax-deferred basis to the shareholders; however, neither subsection 87(4), nor any other provision in the Act, provides for the disposition of property by the merging corporations (in this case, [xxx] Co 1 and [xxx] Co 2) to occur on a tax-deferred basis. You submit that, in the circumstances, this result is inappropriate in policy terms, since economically the foreign merger does not result in a realization event, and is inconsistent with the tax-deferred treatment of other economically equivalent transactions under the Act.

Our Comments:

We agree that, in policy terms, it would be appropriate, in the circumstances described above, for the disposition of the Canco shares by either [xxx] Co 1 or [xxx] Co 2 to occur on a tax-deferred basis. We are therefore prepared to recommend to the Minister of Finance that the Act be amended to deem shares of a corporation resident in Canada that are TCP (other than treaty-protected property) to be disposed of by a "predecessor foreign corporation" to a "new foreign corporation" (both as defined in subsection 87(8.1)) for proceeds of disposition equal to the adjusted cost base of the shares to the disposing predecessor foreign corporation immediately before the disposition, and the cost of the shares to the new foreign corporation to be equal to these deemed proceeds of disposition, where the following conditions are satisfied:

- The disposition is because of a "foreign merger" of the disposing "predecessor foreign corporation" and one or more other "predecessor foreign corporations" to form the "new foreign corporation" (within the meanings assigned by subsection 87(8.1), read without reference to the phrase "otherwise than as a result of the distribution of property to one corporation on the winding-up of another corporation").

- The predecessor foreign corporations are, immediately prior to the foreign merger, related and resident in the same country.

- None of the shareholders of any of the predecessor foreign corporations receives consideration (other than shares of the new foreign corporation) in connection with the merger.

- The corporation resident in Canada is not, at any time in the 24-month period beginning at the time of disposition, subject to a loss restriction event, as part of a transaction or event, or series of transactions or events, including the foreign merger.

While we cannot offer any assurance that either the Minister of Finance or Parliament will agree with our recommendations in respect of this matter, we hope that this statement of our intentions is helpful.

Yours sincerely,

　Brian Ernewein, General Director — Legislation, Tax Policy Branch

Related Provisions: 87(8.2) — Absorptive merger of foreign corps; 95(2)(d.1) — Foreign merger (for FAPI); 95(4.1) — Application to FAPI; 142.7(1)"qualifying foreign merger" — Merger of foreign bank affiliates; 248(1)"disposition"(n) — Cancellation of shares on foreign merger deemed not to be disposition; 256(6), (6.1) — Meaning of "controlled". See also Related Provisions at end of s. 87.

Notes: See Notes to 87(8). In VIEWS doc 2006-0178941I7, a merger was considered not to qualify because the test in 87(8.1)(a) was not met.

See Marc Ton-That & Rebecca Chan, "Is a Foreign Merger an Amalgamation?", XII(2) *Corporate Structures & Groups* (Federated Press) 666-69 (2010).

87(8.1) amended by 2001 technical bill, for mergers and combinations after 1995. Known as the "Chrysler amendment", this accommodated the merger of (US) Chrysler with (German) Daimler-Benz in 1998, and allowed Canadian shareholders of either pre-merger company to defer gains the merger would have triggered. The replacement-property rule in 44(1) was also amended to not apply to shares.

87(8.1) appears to apply to the 2015 Kraft-Heinz merger: tinyurl.com/kraft-s87.

87(8.1)(c) amended by 1998 Budget to add "or options" and subpara. (ii), effective on same basis as the amendments to 87(8).

Before re-enactment in RSC 1985 (5th Supp), 87(8.1) explicitly applied for purposes of section 95. This rule of application is now in 95(4.1).

CRA considers that "substantially all" means 90% or more.

Interpretation Bulletins: See list at end of s. 87.

(8.2) Absorptive mergers — For the purposes of the definition "foreign merger" in subsection (8.1), if there is a merger or combination, otherwise than as a result of the distribution of property to one corporation on the winding-up of another corporation, of two or more non-resident corporations (each of which is referred to in this subsection as a "predecessor foreign corporation"), as a result of which one or more predecessor foreign corporations ceases to exist and, immediately after the merger or combination, another predecessor foreign corporation (referred to in this subsection as the "survivor corporation") owns properties (except amounts receivable from, or shares of the capital stock of, any predecessor foreign corporation) representing all or substantially all of the fair market value of all such properties owned by each predecessor foreign corporation immediately before the merger or combination, then

(a) the merger or combination is deemed to be a merger or combination of the predecessor foreign corporations to form one non-resident corporation;

(b) the survivor corporation is deemed to be the non-resident corporation so formed;

(c) all of the properties of the survivor corporation immediately before the merger or combination that are properties of the survivor corporation immediately after the merger or combination are deemed to become properties of the survivor corporation as a consequence of the merger or combination;

(d) all of the liabilities of the survivor corporation immediately before the merger or combination that are liabilities of the survivor corporation immediately after the merger or combination are deemed to become liabilities of the survivor corporation as a consequence of the merger or combination;

(e) all of the shares of the capital stock of the survivor corporation that were outstanding immediately before the merger or combination that are shares of the capital stock of the survivor corporation immediately after the merger or combination are deemed to become shares of the capital stock of the survivor corporation as a consequence of the merger or combination; and

(f) all of the shares of the capital stock of each predecessor foreign corporation (other than the survivor corporation) that were outstanding immediately before the merger or combination and that cease to exist as a consequence of the merger or combination are deemed to be exchanged by the shareholders of each such predecessor corporation for shares of the survivor corporation as a consequence of the merger or combination.

Notes: For discussion of 87(8.2) see Marley & Slaats, "Foreign Affiliate Reorganizations", 2012 Cdn Tax Foundation conference report, at 27:2-5. For CRA applying 87(8.2) see VIEWS docs 2012-0449371I7 (foreign downstream absorptive merger); 2014-0550641E5 (87(8.2) applies for 87(8) and thus 87(4)); 2017-0709331E5 (vertical absorptive foreign merger: cancellation of shares is a disposition).

87(8.2) added by 2002-2013 technical bill, for mergers or combinations after 1994, or after Aug. 19, 2011 by election. It was 95(4.2) in the Aug. 19/11 draft, where it was to apply only for s. 95.

(8.3) Anti-avoidance — Subsection (8) does not apply in respect of a taxpayer's shares of the capital stock of a predecessor foreign corporation that are exchanged for or become, on a foreign merger, shares of the capital stock of the new foreign corporation or the foreign parent corporation, if

(a) the new foreign corporation is, at the time that is immediately after the foreign merger, a foreign affiliate of the taxpayer;

(b) shares of the capital stock of the new foreign corporation are, at that time, excluded property (as defined in subsection 95(1)) of another foreign affiliate of the taxpayer; and

(c) the foreign merger is part of a transaction or event or a series of transactions or events that includes a disposition of shares of the capital stock of the new foreign corporation, or property substituted for the shares, to

(i) a person (other than a foreign affiliate of the taxpayer in respect of which the taxpayer has a qualifying interest (within the meaning assigned by paragraph 95(2)(m)) at the time of the transaction or event or throughout the series, as the case may be) with whom the taxpayer was dealing at arm's length immediately after the transaction, event or series, or

(ii) a partnership a member of which is, immediately after the transaction, event or series, a person described in subparagraph (i).

Related Provisions: 93.1(3)(c) — Tiered partnership — look-through rule.

Notes: 87(8.3) prevents certain structures aimed at circumventing the anti-avoidance rule in 85.1(4), which provides that 85.1(3) does not apply if substantially all the property of the transferred foreign affiliate (FA) is "excluded property" under 95(1), and the transfer is part of a series of transactions or events for the purpose of disposing of the shares to an arm's length person or partnership. 87(8.3) is intended to ensure that certain foreign merger transactions cannot be used to effectively transfer shares of a FA (substantially all of whose property is excluded property) to an arm's length person in a manner inconsistent with 85.1(4). (Finance Technical Notes)

87(8.3) added by 2014 budget bill #2, for foreign mergers that occur after July 12, 2013.

(8.4) Taxable Canadian property — conditions for rollover — Subsection (8.5) applies at any time if

(a) there is at that time a foreign merger of two or more predecessor foreign corporations (within the meaning assigned by subsection (8.1), if that subsection and subsection (8.2) were read without reference to the expression "otherwise than as a result of the distribution of property to one corporation on the winding-up of another corporation") that were, immediately before that time,

(i) resident in the same country, and

(ii) related to each other (determined without reference to paragraph 251(5)(b));

(b) because of the foreign merger,

(i) a predecessor foreign corporation (referred to in this subsection and subsection (8.5) as the **"disposing predecessor foreign corporation"**) disposes of a property (referred to in this subsection and subsection (8.5) as the **"subject property"**) that is, at that time,

(A) a taxable Canadian property (other than treaty-protected property) of the disposing predecessor foreign corporation, and

(B) any of the following:

(I) a share of the capital stock of a corporation,

(II) an interest in a partnership, and

(III) an interest in a trust, and

(ii) the subject property becomes property of a corporation that is a new foreign corporation for the purposes of subsection (8.1);

(c) no shareholder (except any predecessor foreign corporation) that owned shares of the capital stock of a predecessor foreign corporation immediately before the foreign merger received consideration for the disposition of those shares on the foreign merger, other than shares of the capital stock of the new foreign corporation;

(d) if the subject property is a share of the capital stock of a corporation or an interest in a trust, the corporation or trust is not, at any time in the 24-month period beginning at that time, as part of a transaction or event, or series of transactions or events including the foreign merger, subject to a loss restriction event; and

(e) the new foreign corporation and the disposing predecessor foreign corporation jointly elect in writing under this paragraph in respect of the foreign merger and file the election with the Minister on or before the filing-due date of the disposing predecessor foreign corporation (or the date that would be its filing-due date, if subsection (8.5) did not apply in respect of the disposition of the subject property) for the taxation year that includes that time.

Notes: See Notes to 87(8.5). 87(8.4) added by 2017 budget bill #2, for foreign mergers after Sept. 15, 2016, and a para. (e) election filed by June 14, 2018 is deemed filed on time.

(8.5) Foreign merger — taxable Canadian property rollover — If this subsection applies at any time,

(a) if the subject property is an interest in a partnership,

(i) the disposing predecessor foreign corporation is deemed not to dispose of the subject property (other than for the purposes of subsection (8.4)), and

(ii) the new foreign corporation is deemed

(A) to have acquired the subject property at a cost equal to the cost of the subject property to the disposing predecessor foreign corporation, and

(B) to be the same corporation as, and a continuation of, the disposing predecessor foreign corporation in respect of the subject property; and

(b) if the subject property is a share of the capital stock of a corporation or an interest in a trust,

(i) the subject property is deemed to have been disposed of at that time by the disposing predecessor foreign corporation to the new foreign corporation (that is referred to in subparagraph (8.4)(b)(ii)) for proceeds of disposition equal to the adjusted cost base of the subject property to the disposing predecessor foreign corporation immediately before that time, and

(ii) the cost of the subject property to the new foreign corporation is deemed to be the amount that is deemed by subparagraph (i) to be the proceeds of disposition of the subject property.

Related Provisions: 87(8.4) — Conditions for 87(8.5) to apply.

Notes: 87(8.4)-(8.5) allow an election for rollover on disposition of taxable Canadian property (defined in 248(1)) that is shares of a Canadian-resident corp, where the disposition results from a foreign merger that meets certain conditions. (A disposition by a merging foreign corp on a foreign merger otherwise triggers tax; 87(4) and (8) provide a rollover on disposition of *shares* of a merging foreign corp, but not for disposition of *property owned* by the merging foreign corps.) On application of s. 116 see VIEWS docs 2017-0724241C6 [2017 CTF q.14], 2017-0734841C6 [2017 TEI q.E3].

There is no prescribed form for 87(8.4)(e): the election should be in a letter, and could be filed before (8.4)-(8.5) were enacted: Cdn Tax Foundation 2017 conference roundtable q.14 (also says these rules will not be extended to exempt share dispositions from s. 116 notification).

87(8.5) added by 2017 budget bill #2, for foreign mergers after Sept. 15, 2016.

(9) Rules applicable in respect of certain mergers [triangular amalgamation] — Where there has been a merger of two or more taxable Canadian corporations to form a new corporation that was controlled, immediately after the merger, by a taxable Canadian corporation (in this subsection referred to as the "parent") and, on the merger, shares of the capital stock of the parent (in this subsection referred to as "parent shares") were issued by the parent to persons who were, immediately before the merger, shareholders of a predecessor corporation, the following rules apply:

(a) for the purposes of paragraph (1)(c), subsection (4) and the *Income Tax Application Rules*, any parent shares received by a shareholder of a predecessor corporation shall be deemed to be shares of the capital stock of the new corporation received by the shareholder by virtue of the merger;

(a.1) for the purposes of subsections (4.1) and (4.2), a parent share issued to a shareholder in consideration for the disposition of a share of a class of the capital stock of a predecessor corporation shall be deemed to be a share of a class of the capital stock of the new corporation that was issued in consideration for the disposition of a share of a class of the capital stock of a predecessor corporation by that shareholder;

(a.2) for the purposes of subsection (4.3), a right listed on a designated stock exchange to acquire a share of a class of the capital stock of the parent shall be deemed to be a right listed on a designated stock exchange to acquire a share of a class of the capital stock of the new corporation;

(a.21) for the purpose of paragraph (4.4)(d)

(i) each parent share received by a shareholder of a predecessor corporation is deemed to be a share of the capital stock of the new corporation issued to the shareholder by the new corporation on the merger, and

(ii) any obligation of the parent to issue a share of any class of its capital stock to a person in circumstances described in subparagraph (4.4)(d)(ii) is deemed to be an obligation of the new corporation to issue a share to the person;

(a.3) for the purpose of applying subsection (5) in respect of the merger, the reference in that subsection to "the new corporation" shall be read as a reference to "the parent";

(a.4) for the purpose of paragraph (c), any shares of the new corporation acquired by the parent on the merger shall be deemed to be new shares;

(a.5) for the purpose of applying subsection (10) in respect of the merger,

(i) the reference in paragraph (10)(b) to "the new corporation" shall be read as a reference to "the new corporation or the parent, within the meaning assigned by subsection (9)", and

(ii) the references in paragraphs (10)(c) and (f) to "the new corporation" shall be read as references to "the public corporation described in paragraph (b)".

(b) in computing, at any particular time, the paid-up capital in respect of any particular class of shares of the capital stock of the parent that included parent shares immediately after the merger

(i) there shall be deducted that proportion of the amount, if any, by which the paid-up capital, determined without reference to this paragraph, in respect of all the shares of the capital stock of the parent immediately after the merger exceeds the total of all amounts each of which is the paid-up capital in respect of a share of the capital stock of the parent or a predecessor corporation (other than any share of a predecessor corporation owned by the parent or by another predecessor corporation and any share of a predecessor corporation owned by a shareholder other than the parent or another predecessor corporation that was not exchanged on the merger for parent shares) immediately before the merger that

(A) the paid-up capital, determined without reference to this paragraph, in respect of that particular class of shares

of the capital stock of the parent immediately after the merger

is of

(B) the paid-up capital, determined without reference to this paragraph, in respect of all the issued and outstanding shares of the classes of the capital stock of the parent that included parent shares immediately after the merger, and

(ii) there shall be added an amount equal to the lesser of

(A) the amount, if any, by which

(I) the total of all amounts each of which is an amount deemed by subsection 84(3), (4) or (4.1) to be a dividend on shares of the particular class paid by the parent before the particular time

exceeds

(II) the total that would be determined under subclause (I) if this Act were read without reference to subparagraph (i), and

(B) the amount required by subparagraph (i) to be deducted in computing the paid-up capital of shares of the particular class; and

(c) notwithstanding paragraph (4)(b), the parent shall be deemed to have acquired the new shares of any particular class of the capital stock of the new corporation at a cost equal to the total of

(i) the amount otherwise determined under paragraph (4)(b) to be the cost of those shares, and

(ii) in any case where the parent owned, immediately after the merger, all of the issued shares of the capital stock of the new corporation, such portion of

(A) the amount, if any, by which

(I) the amount by which the total of the money on hand of the new corporation and all amounts each of which is the cost amount to the new corporation of a property owned by it, immediately after the merger, exceeds the total of all amounts each of which is the amount of any debt owing by the new corporation, or of any other obligation of the new corporation to pay any amount, that was outstanding immediately after the merger,

exceeds

(II) the total of the adjusted cost bases to the parent of all shares of the capital stock of each predecessor corporation beneficially owned by it immediately before the merger

as is designated by the parent in respect of the shares of that particular class in its return of income under this Part for its taxation year in which the merger occurred, except that

(B) in no case shall the amount so designated in respect of the shares of a particular class exceed the amount, if any, by which the total fair market value, immediately after the merger, of the shares of that particular class issued by virtue of the merger exceeds the cost of those shares to the parent determined without reference to this paragraph, and

(C) in no case shall the total of the amounts so designated in respect of the shares of each class of the capital stock of the new corporation exceed the amount determined under clause (A).

Proposed Amendment — Triangular amalgamation of cooperative corps

Letter from Dept. of Finance, June 17, 2019: Mr. Christian Jacques, Exceldor Cooperative, Lévis, QC

Dear Mr. Jacques:

Triangular amalgamation of cooperative corporations

I am writing in response to your correspondence and discussions with the Tax Legislation Division regarding the rules relating to tax deferred cooperative shares in the *In-*

come Tax Act (the "Act") and how they apply in the context of a "triangular amalgamation" involving agricultural cooperative corporations.

In general terms, the rules in section 135.1 of the Act allow agricultural cooperative corporations to make patronage payments in the form of qualifying shares of their capital stock rather than cash. The benefit of doing so is that the cooperative can deduct the patronage payment in computing its income while the members that receive the shares can defer the inclusion of these payments in the computation of their income until the shares are disposed of. Qualifying shares are referred to as "tax deferred cooperative shares" and the conditions for qualification are set out in the definition of that term in subsection 135.1(1) of the Act, including the requirement that the shares be issued after 2005 and before 2021.

The Act currently addresses two situations where tax deferred cooperative shares are disposed of but are allowed to maintain their tax deferral. One involves reorganizations of a cooperative's share capital, the other involves amalgamations of cooperative corporations. The latter rule currently contemplates only a situation where an agricultural cooperative corporation amalgamates with another corporation and the new corporation formed on the amalgamation issues new shares that qualify as tax deferred cooperative shares. Such a "linear amalgamation" is the type of amalgamation generally contemplated in subsection 87(1) of the Act.

You advise us that your agricultural cooperative corporation wishes to undertake a triangular amalgamation with another agricultural cooperative corporation that has tax deferred cooperative shares outstanding. More specifically, your corporation would incorporate a wholly-owned subsidiary that would amalgamate with the other agricultural cooperative corporation and members of the other corporation would receive tax deferred cooperative shares of your corporation (the "parent"), rather than shares of the new corporation formed on the amalgamation, in exchange for their tax deferred cooperative shares of the other corporation that are cancelled on the amalgamation.

You assert that, under the current rules of the Act, such a cancellation of tax deferred cooperative shares would cause the tax deferral to cease. As such, members would have to include the deferred patronage payment in their income and there would be a requirement to withhold and remit tax equal to 15% of these amounts, pursuant to subsection 135.1(7) of the Act.

You submit that this is not an appropriate result, particularly in light of the fact that these types of triangular amalgamations are generally accommodated in subsection 87(9) of the Act. Accordingly, you have requested an amendment to the Act to allow for the continued deferral of tax of a member of an agricultural cooperative corporation that exchanges its tax deferred cooperative shares for similar shares of a parent agricultural cooperative corporation in a triangular amalgamation. You submit that the conditions and results in respect of such a rule should be similar to those that currently apply in respect of linear amalgamations of agricultural cooperative corporations, under the combined application of paragraph 87(2)(s) and subsection 135.1(10) of the Act.

Our comments

We agree that it would be appropriate to extend the current rules that allow for the continued deferral of tax to a member of an agricultural cooperative corporation on the exchange of tax deferred cooperative shares on a linear amalgamation of agricultural cooperative corporations to a triangular amalgamation of such cooperative corporations such as the one you have described.

Accordingly, we will recommend to the Minister of Finance that the necessary amendments be made to the Act to provide for such a result, effective for amalgamations that occur after 2018.

While we cannot offer any assurance that either the Minister of Finance or Parliament will agree with our recommendations in respect of this matter, we hope that this statement of our intentions is helpful.

Yours sincerely,

Brian Ernewein, Assistant Deputy Minister — Legislation, Tax Policy Branch

Notes: For CRA interpretation of this situation before this proposed amendment, saying the tax deferral would cease, see VIEWS doc 2019-0793911E5.

Related Provisions: 88(4) — Amalgamation deemed not to be acquisition of control; 256(6), (6.1) — Meaning of "controlled". See also at end of s. 87.

Notes: The merger described in 87(9) is generally called a "triangular amalgamation". See Lamarre et al., *Taxation of Corporate Reorganizations* (Carswell, 3rd ed., 2019), pp. 324-328; Trossman, "Triangular Amalgamations", 2001 Cdn Tax Foundation conference report, pp. 22:1-25; Xiao & Juneja, "Recent Transactions of Interest", 2017 conference report at 5:17-25 (Metro acquiring Jean Coutu Group).

For application of 87(9)(a.4) and (c) where Mergeco and Targetco amalgamate to form Amalco, and the former Targetco shareholders receive shares of Parentco, VIEWS doc 2019-0824491C6 [2019 CTF conf q.13].

Interest on a loan taken to redeem pref shares issued by Targetco is deductible up to a point: VIEWS doc 2018-0779991C6 [2018 CTF q.13].

87(9)(a.21) added by 2002-2013 technical bill (Part 5 — technical), effective for amalgamations that occur after 1997.

87(9)(a.2) amended by 2007 budget bill #2, effective Dec. 14, 2007, to change "prescribed stock exchange" to "designated stock exchange".

87(9) earlier amended by 1995-97, 1992 and 1991 technical bills.

Income Tax Folios: S4-F7-C1: Amalgamations of Canadian corporations [replaces IT-474R2].

(10) Share deemed listed — Where

(a) a new corporation is formed as a result of an amalgamation,

(b) the new corporation is a public corporation,

(c) the new corporation issues a share (in this subsection referred to as the "new share") of its capital stock,

(d) the new share is issued in exchange for a share (in this subsection referred to as the "old share") of the capital stock of a predecessor corporation,

(e) immediately before the amalgamation, the old share was listed on a designated stock exchange, and

(f) the new share is redeemed, acquired or cancelled by the new corporation within 60 days after the amalgamation,

the new share is deemed, for the purposes of subsection 116(6), the definitions "qualified investment" in subsections 146(1), 146.1(1), 146.3(1) and 146.4(1), in section 204 and in subsection 207.01(1), and the definition "taxable Canadian property" in subsection 248(1), to be listed on the exchange until the earliest time at which it is so redeemed, acquired or cancelled.

Related Provisions: 87(9)(a.5) — Effect of triangular amalgamation; *Interpretation Act* 27(5) — Meaning of "within 60 days". See also at end of s. 87.

Notes: For the list of designated stock exchanges for para. (e), see Notes to 262.

87(10) closing words amended by 2017 budget bill #2, effective March 23, 2017, to refer to 146.4(1) instead of 205(1). 87(10) earlier amended by 2008 budget bill #1 (for 2009 and later taxation years), 2007 RDSPs bill, 2007 budget bill #2, 2001 technical bill, 1998 Budget, 1995-97 technical bill.

Income Tax Folios: S4-F7-C1: Amalgamations of Canadian corporations [replaces IT-474R2].

(11) Vertical amalgamations — Where at any time there is an amalgamation of a corporation (in this subsection referred to as the "parent") and one or more other corporations (each of which in this subsection is referred to as the "subsidiary") each of which is a subsidiary wholly-owned corporation of the parent,

(a) the shares of the subsidiary are deemed to have been disposed of by the parent immediately before the amalgamation for proceeds equal to the proceeds that would be determined under paragraph 88(1)(b) if subsections 88(1) and (1.7) applied, with any modifications that the circumstances require, to the amalgamation; and

(b) the cost to the new corporation of each capital property of the subsidiary acquired on the amalgamation is deemed to be the amount that would have been the cost to the parent of the property if the property had been distributed at that time to the parent on a winding-up of the subsidiary and subsections 88(1) and (1.7) had applied to the winding-up.

Related Provisions: 87(2.11) — Vertical amalgamation — carryback of losses; 87(9)(a.5) — Application on triangular amalgamation; 212.3(22) — Application to foreign affiliate dumping rules; 248(1)"disposition"(n) — Cancellation of shares on foreign amalgamation deemed not to be a disposition; Reg. 5905(5.1) — FAPI — amalgamation of corporation holding foreign affiliate. See also at end of s. 87.

Notes: PUC can be reduced without consideration to avoid a capital gain on a vertical amalgamation (or windup: see 88(1)(b)): VIEWS doc 2006-0196011C6; but since 2019, CRA will apply GAAR if the transaction is abusive: 2018-0780041C6 [2018 CTF q.5; Finn, "CRA Upsets PUC Applecart", XXII(1) *Corporate Finance* (Federated Press) 9-12 (2019); Dolson & Ross, "Windings-Up, PUC Reductions and the GAAR", XV(1) *Corporate Structures & Groups* (Federated Press) 2-9 (2019) and 19(4) *Tax for the Owner-Manager* (ctf.ca) 5-6 (Oct. 2019)].

For more CRA interpretations and rulings on 87(11) see VIEWS docs 9633813, 9701005, 9706125, 9706705, 9827430, 9909265, 2002-0130715, 2005-0125982R3, 2005-0163131R3, 2006-0205771R3, 2007-0227521R3, 2007-0231331R3, 2007-0237481R3, 2007-0237482R3, 2007-0240271R3, 2008-0268041R3, 2008-0275441R3, 2008-0286111E5, 2009-0335251R3, 2010-0355941R3 [Chong, "Amalgamation Fictions", 20(6) *Canadian Tax Highlights* (ctf.ca) 10-11 (June 2012)], 2010-0376681R3, 2011-0428071E5, 2012-0451421R3, 2013-0483341R3, 2016-0643931R3, 2019-080676117, 2020-0858741R3.

87(11) added by 1995-97 technical bill, effective for amalgamations after 1994 (with grandfathering for a designation under 88(1)(d) filed by Sept. 30, 1998 and for amalgamation before June 20, 1996).

Income Tax Folios: S4-F7-C1: Amalgamations of Canadian corporations [replaces IT-474R2].

Related Provisions [s. 87]: 66.7 — Resource taxation — successor corporation rules; 89(1)"Canadian corporation" — Whether amalgamated corp is a Canadian corporation; 128.2 — Predecessor corporations take on residence status of amalgamated corp; 128.3 — Deferral applies to post-emigration disposition for certain purposes; 131(4.1) — Mutual fund switch-fund shares — s. 87 does not apply; 142.6(5), (6) — Acquisition of specified debt obligation by financial institution in rollover transaction; 251(3.1), (3.2) — Amalgamated corp — whether related to predecessor; 261(17)–(19) — Effect of functional currency reporting.

Definitions [s. 87]: "adjusted cost base" — 54, 248(1); "agricultural cooperative corporation" — 135.1(1); "amalgamation" — 87(1); "amount", "balance-due day" — 248(1); "arm's length" — 251(1); "beneficially owned" — 248(3); "business" — 248(1); "business limit" — 125(2)–(5.1), 248(1); "calendar year" — *Interpretation Act* 37(1)(a); "Canada" — 255; "Canadian-controlled private corporation" — 125(7), 248(1); "Canadian corporation" — 89(1), 248(1); "Canadian development expense" — 66.2(5), 248(1); "Canadian exploration expense" — 66.1(6), 248(1); "Canadian oil and gas property expense" — 66.4(5), 248(1); "capital dividend" — 83(2), 248(1); "capital gain", "capital loss" — 39(1), 248(1); "capital property" — 54, 248(1); "carrying on business" — 253; "cash method" — 248(1); "class", "class of shares" — 248(6); "common share" — 248(1); "controlled directly or indirectly" — 256(5.1)–(6); "corporation" — 248(1), *Interpretation Act* 35(1); "cost amount" — 248(1); "credit union" — 137(6), 248(1); "cumulative eligible capital" — 14(5), 248(1); "deposit insurance corporation" — 89(15); "depreciable property" — 13(21), 248(1); "designated stock exchange" — 248(1), 262; "disposing predecessor foreign corporation" — 87(8.4)(b)(i); "disposition", "dividend" — 248(1); "eligible capital expenditure" — 14(5), 248(1); "eligible capital property" — 54, 248(1); "eligible derivative" — 10.1(5); "eligible refundable dividend tax on hand" — 129(4); "employment" — 248(1); "excluded property" — 95(1); "fair market value" — see 69(1) Notes; "farming" — 248(1); "farm loss" — 111(8), 248(1); "filing-due date" — 150(1), 248(1); "financial institution" — 87(1.5), 142.2(1); "fiscal period" — 249(2)(b), 249.1; "flow-through share" — 66(15), 87(4.4), 248(1); "foreign affiliate" — 95(1), 248(1); "foreign merger" — 87(8.1), (8.2); "foreign parent corporation" — 87(8.1)(c); "former business property" — 248(1); "general rate income pool" — 89(1), 248(1); "grandfathered share", "income bond", "insurance corporation", "insurer", "inventory" — 248(1); "investment corporation" — 130(3), 248(1); "investment tax credit" — 127(9), 248(1); "last taxation year" — 87(2)(b); "lending asset" — 248(1); "life insurance capital dividend" — 83(2.1), 248(1); "life insurance corporation", "limited partnership loss" — 248(1); "loss restriction event" — 251.2; "low rate income pool" — 89(1), 248(1); "mark-to-market property" — 87(1.5), 142.2(1); "mineral" — 248(1); "mutual fund corporation" — 131(8), 248(1); "net capital loss" — 111(8), 248(1); "new corporation" — 87(1); "new foreign corporation" — 87(8.1); "non-capital loss" — 111(8), 248(1); "non-eligible refundable dividend tax on hand" — 129(4); "non-resident" — 248(1); "non-resident-owned investment corporation" — 133(8), 248(1); "paid-up capital" — 89(1), 248(1); "partnership" — see 96(1) Notes; "person" — 248(1); "predecessor corporation" — 87(1); "predecessor foreign corporation" — 87(8.1); "preferred share", "prescribed" — 248(1); "principal-business corporation" — 66(15); "private corporation" — 89(1), 248(1); "property" — 248(1); "public corporation" — 89(1), 248(1); "qualified expenditure" — 87(2.01); "qualifying income limit" — 127.1(2); "regulation" — 248(1); "related" — 251(2)–(6); "research property" — 37.1(5), 87(2.01); "resident" — 250; "restricted farm loss" — 31, 248(1); "SIFT wind-up corporation" — 248(1); "series of transactions" — 248(10); "share", "shareholder", "short-term preferred share" — 248(1); "specified debt obligation" — 87(1.5), 142.2(1); "specified future tax consequence" — 248(1); "subject property" — 87(8.4)(b)(i); "subsidiary wholly-owned corporation" — 87(1.4), 248(1); "substituted" — 248(5); "substituted class" — 87(3.1)(b); "tax payable" — 248(2); "taxable Canadian corporation" — 89(1), 248(1); "taxable Canadian property" — 248(1); "taxable dividend" — 89(1), 248(1); "taxable income" — 2(2), 248(1); "taxable preferred share", "taxable RFI share" — 248(1); "taxation year" — 87(2)(a), 249; "taxpayer" — 248(1); "term preferred share", "treaty-protected property" — 248(1); "writing" — *Interpretation Act* 35(1).

I.T. Application Rules [s. 87]: 20(1.2), 26(21)–(23), 34(4), (7), 58(3.3).

Interpretation Bulletins [s. 87]: IT-52R4: Income bonds and income debentures (cancelled); IT-121R3: Election to capitalize cost of borrowed money (cancelled); IT-243R4: Dividend refund to private corporations; IT-315: Interest expense incurred for the purpose of winding-up or amalgamation (cancelled); IT-488R2: Winding-up of 90%-owned taxable Canadian corporations (cancelled).

Information Circulars [s. 87]: 88-2, para. 20: General anti-avoidance rule — section 245 of the *Income Tax Act*.

88. (1) Winding-up [of subsidiary] — Where a taxable Canadian corporation (in this subsection referred to as the "subsidiary") has been wound up after May 6, 1974 and not less than 90% of the issued shares of each class of the capital stock of the subsidiary were, immediately before the winding-up, owned by another taxable Canadian corporation (in this subsection referred to as the "parent") and all of the shares of the subsidiary that were not owned by the parent immediately before the winding-up were owned at that time by persons with whom the parent was dealing at arm's length, notwithstanding any other provision of this Act other than subsection 69(11), the following rules apply:

Related Provisions: See at end of subsec. 88(1).

Notes: See Notes to 111(5), which applies the same principle on change in control of a corporation.

The shareholder can be assessed for a dissolved corp's tax: see Notes to 152(1).

Where the conditions in the opening words of 88(1) are satisfied (an "88(1) windup"), there is a general rollover of most properties and tax accounts, as set out in the rest of 88(1) (see especially 88(1)(e.2)). (This also applies to a SIFT trust windup before 2013: 88.1(2).) Otherwise, 88(2) applies. See also 84(2) and 69(5).

CRA applies 88(1) before formal dissolution is complete: IT-126R2 para. 5.

See Tobias, *Taxation of Corporations, Partnerships & Trusts* (Carswell, 5th ed., 2017), chap. 13; Lamarre et al., *Taxation of Corporate Reorganizations* (Carswell, 3rd ed., 2019), chap. 9; Green et al., *Taxation of Private Corporations* (ctf.ca, 5th ed., 2020), pp. 12:9-20; Keey, *Checklist 8 — Wind-Up/Liquidation*, Taxnet Pro Corporate Tax Centre (2018, 22pp) and *Checklist 13 — Dissolving a Corporation* (2021, 4pp); Brayley, "Merging Companies: A Practical Checklist for Amalgamations and Windups", 2000 Cdn Tax Foundation conference report, 6:1-62; Heine & Legge, "Merger Building Blocks", 2004 conference report, 37:1-60; Kirby & Montes, "Practical Issues Encountered When Winding-Up a Corp", 2011 Prairie Provinces Tax Conf. (ctf.ca), 11:1-37; Frajman, "Non-Profit Corporate Wind-Ups", xxxv(9) *The Canadian Taxpayer* (Carswell) 70-72 (May 3, 2013).

A dissolved corp cannot make an election: *S. Cunard & Co.*, 2012 FC 683 (FCA appeal discontinued A-378-12); or bring a motion in Court: *GMC Distribution*, 2012 TCC 262. See also Notes to 150(1)(a), 152(1), 169(1) and 227.1(4) re dissolved corps.

If a corp winds up with unpaid tax, the shareholders may be liable. See Notes to 84(2).

A corp dissolved involuntarily (e.g., for not filing provincial information returns) may forfeit its property to the provincial government. In Ontario, see the *Forfeited Corporate Property Act, 2015* and *Escheats Act, 2015*; the corp can recover its assets only if revived within 3 years of dissolution.

Forms: RC145: Request to close Business Number (BN) program accounts.

(a) [property of subsidiary — deemed disposition] — subject to paragraphs (a.1) and (a.3), each property (other than an interest in a partnership) of the subsidiary that was distributed to the parent on the winding-up shall be deemed to have been disposed of by the subsidiary for proceeds equal to

> (i) in the case of a Canadian resource property, a foreign resource property or a right to receive production (as defined in subsection 18.1(1)) to which a matchable expenditure (as defined in subsection 18.1(1)) relates, nil, and

> (ii) [Repealed]

> (iii) in the case of any other property, the cost amount to the subsidiary of the property immediately before the winding-up;

Related Provisions: 53(4) — Effect on ACB of share or trust interest; 84(2) — Deemed dividend on distribution of assets; 88(2) — Windup of other corporation; 261(11), (12), (15)(a), (16) — Effect of functional currency reporting.

Notes: The subsidiary's property may keep its character in the parent's hands: VIEWS doc 2005-0157321E5. For a ruling that 88(1)(a) applies on windup of a credit union immediately after an 85.1(1) exchange see 2014-0530371R3.

88(1)(a) amended by 1997-97 technical bill (effective Nov. 18, 1996), 1994 technical bill, 1992 and 1991 technical bills.

Interpretation Bulletins: IT-259R4: Exchanges of property.

Advance Tax Rulings: ATR-67: Increase in the cost of property on the winding-up of a wholly-owned subsidiary.

(a.1) [pre-1972 capital surplus on hand] — each property of the subsidiary that was distributed to the parent on the winding-up shall, for the purpose of paragraph (2.1)(b) or (e), be deemed not to have been disposed of;

(a.2) [partnership interest] — each interest of the subsidiary in a partnership that was distributed to the parent on the winding-up shall, except for the purpose of paragraph 98(5)(g), be deemed not to have been disposed of by the subsidiary;

Notes: 88(1)(a.2) amended by 1991 technical bill, effective for windups beginning after Jan. 15, 1987, so as not to apply for purposes of 98(5)(g).

(a.3) [specified debt obligation] — where

> (i) the subsidiary was a financial institution in its taxation year in which its assets were distributed to the parent on the winding up, and

> (ii) the parent was a financial institution in its taxation year in which it received the assets of the subsidiary on the winding up,

each specified debt obligation (other than a mark-to-market property) of the subsidiary that was distributed to the parent on the winding-up shall, except for the purpose of subsection 69(11), be deemed not to have been disposed of, and for the purpose of this paragraph, "financial institution", "mark-to-market property" and "specified debt obligation" have the meanings assigned by subsection 142.2(1);

Related Provisions: Reg. 9204(2) — Residual portion of specified debt obligation.

Notes: 88(1)(a.3) added by 1994 technical bill, effective for windups that begin after February 22, 1994.

(b) **[shares of subsidiary]** — the shares of the capital stock of the subsidiary owned by the parent immediately before the winding-up shall be deemed to have been disposed of by the parent on the winding-up for proceeds equal to the greater of

(i) the lesser of the paid-up capital in respect of those shares immediately before the winding-up and the amount determined under subparagraph (d)(i), and

(ii) the total of all amounts each of which is an amount in respect of any share of the capital stock of the subsidiary so disposed of by the parent on the winding-up, equal to the adjusted cost base to the parent of the share immediately before the winding-up;

Related Provisions: 80.01(5) — Determination of proceeds of disposition of distress preferred share to subsidiary; 80.03(1), (3)(a)(i) — Capital gain where para. 88(1)(b) applies to share on disposition following debt forgiveness; 87(11) — Application to vertical amalgamation. See also at end of 88(1).

Notes: PUC can be reduced without consideration to avoid capital gain on windup, but CRA will now apply GAAR if the transaction is abusive: see Notes to 87(11).

(c) **[cost to parent]** — subject to paragraph 87(2)(e.3) (as modified by paragraph (e.2)), and notwithstanding paragraph 87(2)(e.1) (as modified by paragraph (e.2)), the cost to the parent of each property of the subsidiary distributed to the parent on the winding-up shall be deemed to be

(i) in the case of a property that is an interest in a partnership, the amount that but for this paragraph would be the cost to the parent of the property, and

(ii) in any other case, the amount, if any, by which

(A) the amount that would, but for subsection 69(11), be deemed by paragraph (a) to be the proceeds of disposition of the property

exceeds

(B) any reduction of the cost amount to the subsidiary of the property made because of section 80 on the winding-up,

plus, where the property was a capital property (other than an ineligible property) of the subsidiary at the time that the parent last acquired control of the subsidiary and was owned by the subsidiary thereafter without interruption until such time as it was distributed to the parent on the winding-up, the amount determined under paragraph (d) in respect of the property and, for the purposes of this paragraph, "ineligible property" means

(iii) depreciable property,

(iv) property transferred to the parent on the winding-up where the transfer is part of a distribution (within the meaning assigned by subsection 55(1)) made in the course of a reorganization in which a dividend was received to which subsection 55(2) would, but for paragraph 55(3)(b), apply,

(v) property acquired by the subsidiary from the parent or from any person or partnership that was not (otherwise than because of a right referred to in paragraph 251(5)(b)) dealing at arm's length with the parent, or any other property acquired by the subsidiary in substitution for it, where the acquisition was part of the series of transactions or events in which the parent last acquired control of the subsidiary, and

(vi) property distributed to the parent on the winding-up where, as part of the series of transactions or events that includes the winding-up,

(A) the parent acquired control of the subsidiary, and

(B) any property distributed to the parent on the winding-up or any other property acquired by any person in substitution therefor is acquired by

(I) a particular person (other than a specified person) that, at any time during the course of the series and before control of the subsidiary was last acquired by the parent, was a specified shareholder of the subsidiary,

(II) 2 or more persons (other than specified persons), if a particular person would have been, at any time during the course of the series and before control of the subsidiary was last acquired by the parent, a specified shareholder of the subsidiary if all the shares that were then owned by those 2 or more persons were owned at that time by the particular person, or

(III) a corporation (other than a specified person or the subsidiary)

1. of which a particular person referred to in subclause (I) is, at any time during the course of the series and after control of the subsidiary was last acquired by the parent, a specified shareholder, or

2. of which a particular person would be, at any time during the course of the series and after control of the subsidiary was last acquired by the parent, a specified shareholder if all the shares then owned by persons (other than specified persons) referred to in subclause (II) and acquired by those persons as part of the series were owned at that time by the particular person;

Related Provisions: 87(11) — Application to vertical amalgamation; 88(1)(c.2) — Specified person for 88(1)(c)(vi); 88(1)(c.3) — Property acquired in substitution, for purpose of 88(1)(c)(vi)(B); 88(1)(c.7) — Extended meaning of depreciable property; 88(1)(d.2) — When taxpayer last acquired control; 88(1)(d.3) — Where control acquired because of death; 88(1.7) — Where parent did not deal at arm's length; 88(4) — Amalgamation deemed not to be acquisition of control; 248(10) — Series of transactions or events; 256(6)–(9) — Whether control acquired. See also at end of 88(1).

Notes: 88(1)(c) implements a "bump"; see Notes to 88(1)(d).

See Singh, "An Introduction to the 'Bump' Rules", 2003 Cdn Tax Foundation conference report, 51:1-31; Truster, "The Windup Bump", 6(2) *Tax for the Owner-Manager* (ctf.ca) 1-2 (April 2006); Brady, "Using a Target's Cash as a Source of Funds", X(4) *Corporate Structures & Groups* (Federated Press) 587-90 (2008); Richardson & Weekes, "Recent Developments in Corporate Reorganizations", 2008 conference report at 38:7-17.

For post-mortem use of the bump see Brender, "Combining the Bump and the Butterfly in Post-mortem Reorganization", IX(4) *CS&G* 504-10 (2005); Ireland, "Selected Developments in Post-Mortem Planning", 2005 conference report, 13:6-22. On the interaction with the functional currency rules see Notes at end of 261.

88(1)(c)(vi) prevents a "back-door butterfly" in most cases. See Woods, "The Bump Denial Rule in Subparagraph 88(1)(c)(vi)", 1998 Cdn Tax Foundation conference report, 14:1-40; Ton-That, "The Bump Denial Rules", 2000 conference report, 27:1-66; Turner, "Another Bump on the Road — the Subclause 88(1)(c)(vi)(B)(III) Anomaly", X(1) *Corporate Structures & Groups* 531-37 (2006); Carr & Colden, "The Bump Denial Rules Revisited", 62(1) *Canadian Tax Journal* 273-99 (2014). See also Notes to 88(1)(c.3) and (c.4).

For more on 88(1)(c) see VIEWS docs 2006-0205771R3, 2006-0212691R3, 2007-0227521R3, 2007-0234481R3, 2007-0237481R3, 2007-0237482R3, 2007-0243261C6, 2008-0268041R3, 2008-0275441R3, 2008-0279781R3, 2008-0288221R3, 2009-0320211R3, 2010-0386041C6 [2010 CTF conf p.4:15-16, q.15: meaning of "all of the shares" in 88(1)(c)(vi)(B)(II)], 2011-0397081R3, 2011-0422981E5, 2011-0423921R3, 2011-0428561E5, 2012-0451421R3, 2013-0483341R3, 2018-0772921R3, 2018-0782751R3.

88(1)(c)(vi)(B)(III) amended by 2001 technical bill to add "or the subsidiary", effective for windings-up that begin after November 1994. Finance had issued several comfort letters in 1997-98 promising this amendment.

88(1)(c) earlier amended by 1995-97 technical bill (effective for windups that begin after 1996, and for windups that begin after June 20, 1996 other than as part of an arrangement that was substantially advanced, as evidenced in writing, before June 21, 1996), 1994 technical bill, 1994 Budget, 1992 and 1991 technical bills.

Advance Tax Rulings: ATR-67: Increase in the cost of property on the winding-up of a wholly-owned subsidiary.

I.T. Technical News: 9 (the backdoor butterfly rule).

(c.1) [Repealed]

Notes: 88(1)(c.1) repealed by 2016 budget bill #2, effective 2017, as part of changing the eligible capital property rules to CCA Class 14.1 (see Notes to 20(1)(b)). Before 2017, read:

(c.1) [eligible capital property] — for the purpose of determining after the winding-up the amount to be included under subsection 14(1) in computing the parent's income in respect of the business carried on by the subsidiary immediately before the winding-up

(i) there shall be added to the amount otherwise determined for each of the descriptions of A and F in the definition "cumulative eligible capital" in subsection 14(5), the total of all amounts, each of which is the amount, if any,

(A) determined for the description of F in that definition in respect of that business immediately before the winding up,

(B) determined under this subparagraph as it applied to the subsidiary in respect of a winding-up before that time, or

(C) determined under paragraph 85(1)(d.11) as it applied to the subsidiary in respect of a disposition to the subsidiary before that time, and

(ii) there shall be added to the amount determined for the description of C in the formula in paragraph 14(1)(b), the total of all amounts, each of which is an amount that is

(A) one-half of the amount, if any, determined for the description of Q in that definition in respect of that business immediately before the winding up,

(B) determined under this subparagraph as it applied to the subsidiary in respect of a winding-up before that time, or

(C) determined under paragraph 85(1)(d.1) as it applied to the subsidiary in respect of a disposition to the subsidiary before that time;

88(1)(c.1) amended by 2002-2013 technical bill (Part 5 — technical), effective for the disposition of an eligible capital property by a subsidiary to a parent after Dec. 20, 2002 (Nov. 8, 2006 in certain cases). Added by 1992 technical bill.

(c.2) **["specified person" and "specified shareholder"]** — for the purposes of this paragraph and subparagraph (c)(vi),

(i) "specified person", at any time, means

(A) the parent,

(B) each person who would be related to the parent at that time if

(I) this Act were read without reference to paragraph 251(5)(b), and

(II) each person who is the child of a deceased individual were related to each brother or sister of the individual and to each child of a deceased brother or sister of the individual, and

(C) if the time is before the incorporation of the parent, each person who is described in clause (B) throughout the period that begins at the time the parent is incorporated and ends at the time that is immediately before the beginning of the winding-up,

(i.1) a person described in clause (i)(B) or (C) is deemed not to be a specified person if it can reasonably be considered that one of the main purposes of one or more transactions or events is to cause the person to be a specified person so as to prevent a property that is distributed to the parent on the winding-up from being an ineligible property for the purposes of paragraph (c),

(ii) where at any time a property is owned or acquired by a partnership or a trust,

(A) the partnership or the trust, as the case may be, shall be deemed to be a person that is a corporation having one class of issued shares, which shares have full voting rights under all circumstances,

(B) each member of the partnership or beneficiary under the trust, as the case may be, shall be deemed to own at that time the proportion of the number of issued shares of the capital stock of the corporation that

(I) the fair market value at that time of that member's interest in the partnership or that beneficiary's interest in the trust, as the case may be,

is of

(II) the fair market value at that time of all the members' interests in the partnership or beneficiaries' interests in the trust, as the case may be, and

(C) the property shall be deemed to have been owned or acquired at that time by the corporation,

(iii) in determining whether a person is a specified shareholder of a corporation,

(A) the reference in the definition "specified shareholder" in subsection 248(1) to "the issued shares of any class of the capital stock of the corporation or of any other corporation that is related to the corporation" shall be read as "the issued shares of any class (other than a specified class) of the capital stock of the corporation or of any other corporation that is related to the corporation and that has a significant direct or indirect interest in any issued shares of the capital stock of the corporation",

(A.1) a corporation controlled by another corporation is, at any time, deemed not to own any shares of the capital stock of the other corporation if, at that time, the corporation does not have a direct or an indirect interest in any of the shares of the capital stock of the other corporation,

(A.2) the definition "specified shareholder" in subsection 248(1) is to be read without reference to its paragraph (a) in respect of any share of the capital stock of the subsidiary that the person would, but for this clause, be deemed to own solely because the person has a right described in paragraph 251(5)(b) to acquire shares of the capital stock of a corporation that

(I) is controlled by the subsidiary, and

(II) does not have a direct or an indirect interest in any of the shares of the capital stock of the subsidiary, and

(B) a corporation is deemed not to be a specified shareholder of itself; and

(iv) property that is distributed to the parent on the winding-up is deemed not to be acquired by a person if the person acquired the property before the acquisition of control referred to in clause (c)(vi)(A) and the property is not owned by the person at any time after that acquisition of control;

Related Provisions: 88(1)(c.8) — Meaning of "specified class" for 88(1)(c.2)(iii)(A); 88(4) — Amalgamation deemed not to be acquisition of control.

Notes: See Paul Stepak & Eric Xiao, "The Paragraph 88(1)(d) Bump", 2013 Cdn Tax Foundation conference report at 13:20-26.

For the meaning of "one of the main purposes" in (c.2)(i.1), see Notes to 83(2.1).

88(1)(c.2) amended by 2013 budget bill #2, for windups that begin, and amalgamations that occur, after 2001. Subpara (i) was replaced with (i)-(i.1) as per Feb. 23, 2007 Finance comfort letter [see also VIEWS doc 2009-0335251R3]. Cl. (iii)(A.1) was added as per Aug. 13, 2007 comfort letter [Suarez, "New 88(1) Comfort Letter Addresses Bump Anomaly", 18(1) *Canadian Current Tax* (LexisNexis) 1-5 (Oct. 2007)]. Cl. (iii)(A.2) was added as per Aug. 13, 2004 comfort letter. Subpara. (iv) was added as per Sept. 1, 2006 comfort letter.

For interpretation see VIEWS docs 2009-0350491R3, 2011-0428561E5.

88(1)(c.2) amended by 2001 technical bill (for windups beginning after Nov. 1994), 1995-97 technical bill, 1994 Budget.

(c.3) **[substituted property]** — for the purpose of clause (c)(vi)(B), property acquired by any person in substitution for particular property or properties distributed to the parent on the winding-up includes

(i) property (other than a specified property) owned by the person at any time after the acquisition of control referred to in clause (c)(vi)(A) more than 10% of the fair market value of which is, at that time, attributable to the particular property or properties, and

(ii) property owned by the person at any time after the acquisition of control referred to in clause (c)(vi)(A) the fair market value of which is, at that time, determinable primarily by reference to the fair market value of, or to any proceeds from a disposition of, the particular property or properties

but does not include

(iii) money,

(iv) property that was not owned by the person at any time after the acquisition of control referred to in clause (c)(vi)(A),

(v) property described in subparagraph (i) if the only reason the property is described in that subparagraph is because a specified property described in any of subparagraphs (c.4)(i) to (iv) was received as consideration for the acquisition of a share of the capital stock of the subsidiary in the circumstances described in subparagraphs (c.4)(i) to (iv);

(vi) a share of the capital stock of the subsidiary or a debt owing by it, if the share or debt, as the case may be, was owned by the parent immediately before the winding-up, or

(vii) a share of the capital stock of a corporation or a debt owing by a corporation, if the fair market value of the share or debt, as the case may be, was not, at any time after the beginning of the winding-up, wholly or partly attributable to property distributed to the parent on the winding-up;

Related Provisions: 88(1)(c.4) — Meaning of specified property; 88(1)(c.6) — Where control acquired by way of articles of arrangement; 88(1)(c.7) — Extended meaning of depreciable property; 88(4) — Amalgamation deemed not to be acquisition of control; 248(5) — Substituted property; 256(6)–(9) — Whether control acquired.

Notes: For discussion see James Yaskowich, "A Case of Substituted Property and Specified Property — the 'Bump Denial' Rules", X(1) *Business Vehicles* (Federated Press) 495-503 (2004); Stepak & Xiao, "The Paragraph 88(1)(d) Bump", 2013 Cdn Tax Foundation conference report at 13:9-16 (re 2013 amendment); McLean & Oldewening, "Allocation of Debt under the Safe Harbour in 88(1)(c.3)(i)", XIV(2) *Corporate Structures & Groups* (Federated Press) 2-12 (2017).

For CRA interpretation on 88(1)(c.3)(vi) see VIEWS docs 2007-0231331R3, 2009-0335251R3; on (c.3)(vii), see 2004-0091771E5, 2009-0311331E5. See also 2004-0064821E5 (88(1)(c.2)(ii) did not apply); 2006-0196031C6; 2006-0205771R3; 2007-0243261C6; 2009-0320211R3 and 2009-0340351R3 (guarantee rights are not substituted property); 2011-0428561E5 (money is excluded from "substituted property" but not from "distributed property"); 2012-0451421R3, 2013-0483341R3.

88(1)(c.3)(i) amended by 2013 budget bill #2, for windups that begin, and amalgamations that occur, after Dec. 20, 2012, to change "the fair market value of which is, at that time, wholly or partly attributable" to "more than 10% of the fair market value of which is, at that time, attributable". (Adding a 10% threshold reduced the need for an exhaustive list of acceptable properties in 88(1)(c.4).)

88(1)(c.3)(vi), (vii) added by 2002-2013 technical bill (Part 5 — technical), for windups that begin, and amalgamations that occur, after 1997.

88(1)(c.3) added by 1995-97 technical bill, last change effective for windups that begin after June 20, 1996 (except where part of an arrangement that was substantially advanced, as evidenced in writing, by that date).

I.T. Technical News: 9 (the backdoor butterfly rule).

(c.4) ["specified property"] — for the purposes of subparagraphs (c.3)(i) and (v), a specified property is

(i) a share of the capital stock of the parent that was

(A) received as consideration for the acquisition of a share of the capital stock of the subsidiary by the parent or by a corporation that was a specified subsidiary corporation of the parent immediately before the acquisition, or

(B) issued for consideration that consists solely of money,

(ii) an indebtedness that was issued

(A) by the parent as consideration for the acquisition of a share of the capital stock of the subsidiary by the parent, or

(B) for consideration that consists solely of money,

(iii) a share of the capital stock of a taxable Canadian corporation that was received as consideration for the acquisition of a share of the capital stock of the subsidiary by the taxable Canadian corporation or by the parent where the parent was a

specified subsidiary corporation of the taxable Canadian corporation immediately before the acquisition,

(iv) an indebtedness of a taxable Canadian corporation that was issued by it as consideration for the acquisition of a share of the capital stock of the subsidiary by the taxable Canadian corporation or by the parent where the parent was a specified subsidiary corporation of the taxable Canadian corporation immediately before the acquisition, and

(v) if the subsidiary was formed on the amalgamation of two or more predecessor corporations at least one of which was a subsidiary wholly-owned corporation of the parent,

(A) a share of the capital stock of the subsidiary that was issued on the amalgamation and that is, before the beginning of the winding-up,

(I) redeemed, acquired or cancelled by the subsidiary for consideration that consists solely of money or shares of the capital stock of the parent, or of any combination of the two, or

(II) exchanged for shares of the capital stock of the parent, or

(B) a share of the capital stock of the parent issued on the amalgamation in exchange for a share of the capital stock of a predecessor corporation.

(vi) [Repealed]

Related Provisions: 88(1)(c.5) — Meaning of specified subsidiary corporation; 88(1)(c.9) — Reference to "share" in (c.4) includes option, warrant or other right; 88(4) — Amalgamation deemed not to be acquisition of control.

Notes: See Turner, "Bumps on the Road to the Bump: Deficiencies in the Specified Property Exception", IX(4) *Corporate Structures & Groups* (Federated Press) 511-21 (2005). For discussion of the 2013 amendments see Stepak & Xiao, "The Paragraph 88(1)(d) Bump", 2013 Cdn Tax Foundation conference report at 13:16-20, 13:26-28.

For CRA interpretation see VIEWS docs 2007-0196031C6, 2011-0428561E5.

88(1)(c.4) amended by 2013 budget bill #2, for windups that begin, and amalgamations that occur, after 2001.

88(1)(c.4) amended by 2002-2013 technical bill, for windups that begin, and amalgamations that occur, after 1997.

88(1)(c.4) added by 1995-97 technical bill, for windups that begin after Feb. 21, 1994.

(c.5) ["specified subsidiary corporation"] — for the purpose of paragraph (c.4), a corporation is a specified subsidiary corporation of another corporation, at any time, where the other corporation holds, at that time, shares of the corporation

(i) that give the shareholder 90% or more of the votes that could be cast under all circumstances at an annual meeting of shareholders of the corporation, and

(ii) having a fair market value of 90% or more of the fair market value of all the issued shares of the capital stock of the corporation;

Related Provisions: 88(4) — Amalgamation deemed not to be acquisition of control.

Notes: 88(1)(c.5) added by 1995-97 technical bill, for windups that begin after Feb. 21, 1994.

(c.6) [control acquired by way of articles of arrangement] — for the purpose of paragraph (c.3) and notwithstanding subsection 256(9), where control of a corporation is acquired by way of articles of arrangement, that control is deemed to have been acquired at the end of the day on which the arrangement becomes effective;

Related Provisions: 88(4) — Amalgamation deemed not to be acquisition of control.

Notes: 88(1)(c.6) added by 1995-97 technical bill, for windups that begin after Feb. 21, 1994.

(c.7) [depreciable property] — for the purpose of subparagraph (c)(iii), a leasehold interest in a depreciable property and an option to acquire a depreciable property are depreciable properties;

Related Provisions: 88(4) — Amalgamation deemed not to be acquisition of control.

Notes: 88(1)(c.7) added by 1995-97 technical bill, for windups that begin after June 20, 1996.

(c.8) **["specified class"]** — for the purpose of clause (c.2)(iii)(A), a specified class of the capital stock of a corporation is a class of shares of the capital stock of the corporation where

(i) the paid-up capital in respect of the class was not, at any time, less than the fair market value of the consideration for which the shares of that class then outstanding were issued,

(ii) the shares are non-voting in respect of the election of the board of directors of the corporation, except in the event of a failure or default under the terms or conditions of the shares,

(iii) under neither the terms and conditions of the shares nor any agreement in respect of the shares are the shares convertible into or exchangeable for shares other than shares of a specified class of the capital stock of the corporation, and

(iv) under neither the terms and conditions of the shares nor any agreement in respect of the shares is any holder of the shares entitled to receive on the redemption, cancellation or acquisition of the shares by the corporation or by any person with whom the corporation does not deal at arm's length an amount (excluding any premium for early redemption) greater than the total of the fair market value of the consideration for which the shares were issued and the amount of any unpaid dividends on the shares;

Related Provisions: 88(4) — Amalgamation deemed not to be acquisition of control.

Notes: 88(1)(c.8) added by 2001 technical bill, for windups that begin after November 1994. It applies for the divisive reorganization commonly known as a "backdoor butterfly", described in 88(1)(c)(vi).

(c.9) **["share" in (c.4)]** — for the purposes of paragraph (c.4), a reference to a share of the capital stock of a corporation includes a right to acquire a share of the capital stock of the corporation;

Notes: For discussion of 88(1)(c.9) see CICA/CBA Joint Committee letter to Finance, Feb. 15, 2013, pp. 10-12; Paul Stepak & Eric Xiao, "The Paragraph 88(1)(d) Bump", 2013 Cdn Tax Foundation conference report at 13:28-29.

88(1)(c.9) added by 2013 budget bill #2, effective for windups that begin, and amalgamations that occur, after 2001 (implementing Finance comfort letters of April 22, 2002, June 24, 2003 and April 15, 2005).

(d) **[increase in cost amounts (bump)]** — the amount determined under this paragraph in respect of each property of the subsidiary distributed to the parent on the winding-up is such portion of the amount, if any, by which the total determined under subparagraph (b)(ii) exceeds the total of

(i) the amount, if any, by which

(A) the total of all amounts each of which is an amount in respect of any property owned by the subsidiary immediately before the winding-up, equal to the cost amount to the subsidiary of the property immediately before the winding-up, plus the amount of any money of the subsidiary on hand immediately before the winding-up,

exceeds the total of

(B) all amounts each of which is the amount of any debt owing by the subsidiary, or of any other obligation of the subsidiary to pay any amount, that was outstanding immediately before the winding-up, and

(C) the amount of any reserve (other than a reserve referred to in paragraph 20(1)(n), subparagraph 40(1)(a)(iii) or 44(1)(e)(iii) of this Act or in subsection 64(1) or (1.1) of the *Income Tax Act*, chapter 148 of the Revised Statutes of Canada, 1952, as those two provisions read immediately before November 3,[7] 1981) deducted in computing the subsidiary's income for its taxation year during which its assets were distributed to the parent on the winding-up, and

(i.1) the total of all amounts each of which is an amount in respect of any share of the capital stock of the subsidiary disposed of by the parent on the winding-up or in contemplation of the winding-up, equal to the total of all amounts received by the parent or by a corporation with which the parent was not dealing at arm's length (otherwise than because of a right referred to in paragraph 251(5)(b) in respect of the subsidiary) in respect of

(A) taxable dividends on the share or on any share (in this subparagraph referred to as a "replaced share") for which the share or a replaced share was substituted or exchanged to the extent that the amounts thereof were deductible from the recipient's income for any taxation year by virtue of section 112 or subsection 138(6) and were not amounts on which the recipient was required to pay tax under Part VII of the *Income Tax Act*, chapter 148 of the Revised Statutes of Canada, 1952, as it read on March 31, 1977, or

(B) capital dividends and life insurance capital dividends on the share or on any share (in this subparagraph referred to as a "replaced share") for which a share or a replaced share was substituted or exchanged,

as is designated by the parent in respect of that capital property in its return of income under this Part for its taxation year in which the subsidiary was so wound up, except that

(ii) the amount designated in respect of any such capital property may not exceed the amount determined by the formula

$$A - (B + C)$$

where

A is the fair market value of the property at the time the parent last acquired control of the subsidiary,

B is the greater of the cost amount to the subsidiary of the property at the time the parent last acquired control of the subsidiary and the cost amount to the subsidiary of the property immediately before the winding-up, and

C is the prescribed amount, and

(ii.1) for the purpose of calculating the amount in subparagraph (ii) in respect of an interest of the subsidiary in a partnership, the fair market value of the interest at the time the parent last acquired control of the subsidiary is deemed to be the amount determined by the formula

$$A - B$$

where

A is the fair market value (determined without reference to this subparagraph) of the interest at that time, and

B is the portion of the amount by which the fair market value (determined without reference to this subparagraph) of the interest at that time exceeds its cost amount at that time as may reasonably be regarded as being attributable at that time to the total of all amounts each of which is

(A) in the case of a depreciable property held directly by the partnership or held indirectly by the partnership through one or more other partnerships, the amount by which the fair market value (determined without reference to liabilities) of the property exceeds its cost amount,

(B) in the case of a Canadian resource property or a foreign resource property held directly by the partnership or held indirectly by the partnership through one or more other partnerships, the fair market value (determined without reference to liabilities) of the property, or

---

[7] *Sic.* The date should be November 13, although in practice it makes no difference. See Notes to s. 64 — ed.

(C) in the case of a property that is not a capital property, a Canadian resource property or a foreign resource property and that is held directly by the partnership or held indirectly through one or more other partnerships, the amount by which the fair market value (determined without reference to liabilities) of the property exceeds its cost amount, and

(iii) in no case shall the total of amounts so designated in respect of all such capital properties exceed the amount, if any, by which the total determined under subparagraph (b)(ii) exceeds the total of the amounts determined under subparagraphs (i) and (i.1).

Related Provisions: 88(1)(d.2) — When taxpayer last acquired control; 88(1)(d.3) — Where control acquired because of death; 88(1)(d.4) — Share in foreign affiliate of subsidiary; 88(1)(e) — Interpretation for 88(1)(d)(ii.1)A; 88(1.7) — Where parent did not deal at arm's length; 88(1.8), (1.9) — Amended designation re tax-free surplus balance; 88(4) — Amalgamation deemed not to be acquisition of control; 97(3) — Transactions excluded from partnership rollover to corporation; 256(6)–(9) — Whether control acquired; 257 — Formula amount cannot calculate to less than zero; Reg. 5905(5.1) — FAPI — windup of corporation holding foreign affiliate. See also at end of 88(1).

Notes: The increase in cost amounts of assets under 88(1)(d) is called a "bump". It is implemented by 88(1)(c), between subparas. (ii) and (iii). See Notes to 88(1)(c). See Notes to 125(7)"Canadian-controlled private corporation" re the meaning of "control".

The designation must be made "in" the return; see Notes to 150.1 to do this in an electronic return. For a corporation filing Quebec returns, a designation under 88(1)(d) must be copied to Revenu Québec: *Taxation Act* ss. 569, 21.4.6.

A late designation under 88(1)(d) (including for an 87(11) amalgamation) is allowed administratively in certain cases: VIEWS doc 2009-0323661E5. It will be allowed where audit action increases the bump room during the 152(4)(b)(iii) extended reassessment period (despite Income Tax Folio S4-F7-C1 ¶1.40): 2019-080676I17.

In *Slate Management*, 2016 ONSC 4216, a 3-corp amalgamation was intended to obtain the bump, but was done in 1 step instead of 2; the Court granted rectification to fix this retroactively. (See Notes to 169(1) re rectification; due to *Fairmont Hotels* this would no longer be granted.)

In *Oxford Properties*, 2018 FCA 30 (leave to appeal denied 2018 CarswellNat 7871 (SCC)), a combination of steps that included an 88(1)(d) bump (before (d)(ii.1) was added) triggered GAAR in 245(2). See Notes to 100(1).

See also Stepak & Wilkie, "Relieving and Clarifying Changes to Canadian Basis Bump Rules", XVIII(3) *Corporate Finance* (Federated Press) 2130-33 (2012); Blanchet, "The Impact of the 2012 Budget on Transactions Involving Interests in Partnerships", 2012 Cdn Tax Foundation conference report, at 10:13-17; Yip, "Recent Legislation Affecting Partnerships and Foreign Affiliates", 61(1) *Canadian Tax Journal* 229-256 (2013); Peters, "The Bump", 2(3) *The Newsletter* (Tax Executives Institute, Toronto Chapter) 4-7 (March 2013); Stepak & Xiao, "The Paragraph 88(1)(d) Bump", 2013 conference report, 13:1-60; Frydberg, "Top Technical Bill Issues for Owner-Managers", 2013 Prairie Provinces Tax Conference (ctf.ca), 11:1, §10; Suarez, "Canada's 88(1)(d) Tax Cost Bump: A Guide for Foreign Purchasers", 72(1) *Tax Notes International* (taxnotes.com) 935-55 (Dec. 9, 2013); Alty & Ranasinghe, "Tax Basis Bump — Post-Acquisition Mergers and Earn-Outs", XIV(1) *Corporate Structures & Groups* (Federated Press) 5-11 (2017); Notes to 88(1)(c).

For rulings and interpretations on 88(1)(d) see VIEWS docs 2002-0118695, 2002-0118705, 2002-0148283, 2003-0047281R3, 2004-0060271R3, 2004-0064461R3, 2005-0125982R3, 2005-0155371R3, 2005-0161681R3, 2005-0163131R3, 2006-0178571R3, 2006-0194321R3, 2006-0205771R3, 2006-0212691R3, 2006-0217481R3, 2007-0231331R3, 2007-0234481R3, 2007-0237481R3, 2007-0237482R3, 2007-0243261C6, 2007-0240271R3, 2008-0268041R3, 2008-0275441R3, 2008-0286111E5 (late-filed designation), 2008-0288221R3, 2008-0302421E5, 2009-0335251R3, 2009-0350491R3, 2010-0379741R3, 2011-0397081R3; 2011-0404521C6 (position on 88(1)(d)(ii)(B)); 2011-0416881E5 (late-filed designation); 2011-0423921R3, 2012-0451421R3, 2012-0461741E5, 2013-0483341R3; 2015-0617771E5 (88(1)(d)(i)(B)); 2016-0629701E5 (bump to cost of land that is capital property of sub, even though it will be inventory to parent); 2016-0643931R3 [Wang & Lee, "Buy, Bump and Emigrate?", 26(8) *Canadian Tax Highlights* (ctf.ca) 8-9 (Aug. 2018)].

88(1)(d)(ii) amended by 2013 budget bill #2, effective for windups that begin, and amalgamations that occur, after Dec. 20, 2012, with certain grandfathering for amalgamations and windups begun before July 2013.

88(1)(d)(ii)(B) added by 2002-2013 technical bill (Part 2 — FA surplus rules), effective for windups that begin, and amalgamations that occur, after Feb. 27, 2004.

88(1)(d)(ii.1) added by 2012 budget bill #2, with certain grandfathering for amalgamations and windups begun before July 2013.

Closing words of 88(1)(d) repealed by 1995-97 technical bill, effective for windups that begin after Feb. 21, 1994 (interpretation provision moved to 88(1.7)). 88(1)(d) earlier amended by 1994 Budget, 1991 technical bill.

Regulations: 5905(5.4) (prescribed amount for 88(1)(d)(ii)C).

I.T. Application Rules: 26(5)(c)(i)(C) (where property owned since before 1972); 69 (meaning of "chapter 148 of ...").

I.T. Technical News: 16 (*Parthenon Investments* case).

Advance Tax Rulings: ATR-67: Increase in the cost of property on the winding-up of a wholly-owned subsidiary.

(d.1) [rules not applicable] — subsection 84(2) and section 21 of the *Income Tax Application Rules* do not apply to the winding-up of the subsidiary, and subsection 13(21.2) does not apply to the winding-up of the subsidiary with respect to property acquired by the parent on the winding-up;

Notes: 88(1)(d.1) amended to delete reference to 14(12) (after 13(21.2)) by 2016 budget bill #2, effective 2017, as part of changing the eligible capital property rules to CCA Class 14.1 (see Notes to 20(1)(b)).

88(1)(d.1) amended by 1995-97 technical bill to add references to 13(21.2) and 14(12) effective for windups that begin after April 26, 1995; and to delete a reference to 85(5.1), effective for windups that begin after 1995.

(d.2) [when control acquired] — in determining, for the purposes of this paragraph and paragraphs (c) and (d), the time at which a person or group of persons (in this paragraph and paragraph (d.3) referred to as the "acquirer") last acquired control of the subsidiary, where control of the subsidiary was acquired from another person or group of persons (in this paragraph referred to as the "vendor") with whom the acquirer was not (otherwise than solely because of a right referred to in paragraph 251(5)(b)) dealing at arm's length, the acquirer is deemed to have last acquired control of the subsidiary at the earlier of

(i) the time at which the vendor last acquired control (within the meaning that would be assigned by subsection 186(2) if the reference in that subsection to "another corporation" were read as "a person" and the references in that subsection to "the other corporation" were read as "the person") of the subsidiary, and

(ii) the time at which the vendor was deemed for the purpose of this paragraph to have last acquired control of the subsidiary;

Related Provisions: 88(1)(d.3) — Where control acquired because of death; 88(4) — Amalgamation deemed not to be acquisition of control; 256(6)–(9) — Whether control acquired. See also at end of 88(1).

Notes: For interpretation of 88(1)(d.2) see VIEWS docs 2007-0227521R3, 2008-0288221R3; 2011-0391821E5 (interaction with (d.3)); 2011-0422981E5, 2011-0428561E5, 2020-0858741R3.

88(1)(d.2) amended by 1992, 1993 and 1995-97 technical bills, all effective for windups that begin after Dec. 20, 1991.

(d.3) [control acquired due to death] — for the purposes of paragraphs (c), (d) and (d.2), where at any time control of a corporation is last acquired by an acquirer because of an acquisition of shares of the capital stock of the corporation as a consequence of the death of an individual, the acquirer is deemed to have last acquired control of the corporation immediately after the death from a person who dealt at arm's length with the acquirer;

Related Provisions: 88(4) — Amalgamation deemed not to be acquisition of control; 256(6)–(9) — Whether control acquired. See also at end of 88(1).

Notes: For discussion of 88(1)(d.3) see Rhonda Rudick, "Bump Denial Rules: Time of Acquisition of Control in the Context of Post-Mortem Estate Planning", VII(1) *Corporate Structures & Groups* (Federated Press) 355-58 (2001); VIEWS docs 2001-0093363, 2006-0174021C6 (CRA will provide rulings on post-mortem bumps), 2007-0227521R3, 2009-0350491R3, 2011-0391821E5 (interaction with 88(1)(d.2)), 2011-0428561E5, 2020-0858741R3. See also Notes to 88(1)(c).

88(1)(d.3) added by 1995-97 technical bill, for windups that begin after Dec. 20, 1991.

Proposed **88(1)(d.4)** in the Feb. 27, 2004 foreign-affiliate proposals was dropped.

(e) for the purposes of the description of A in subparagraph (d)(ii.1), the fair market value of an interest in a particular partnership held by the subsidiary at the time the parent last acquired control of the subsidiary is deemed not to include the amount that is the total of each amount that is the fair market value of a property that would otherwise be included in the fair market value of the interest, if

(i) as part of the transaction or event or series of transactions or events in which control of the subsidiary is last acquired by the parent and on or before the acquisition of control,

(A) the subsidiary disposes of the property to the particular partnership or any other partnership and subsection 97(2) applies to the disposition, or

(B) where the property is an interest in a partnership, the subsidiary acquires the interest in the particular partnership or any other partnership from a person or partnership with whom the subsidiary does not deal at arm's length (otherwise than because of a right referred to in paragraph 251(5)(b)) and section 85 applies in respect of the acquisition of the interest, and

(ii) at the time of the acquisition of control, the particular partnership holds directly, or indirectly through one or more other partnerships, property described in clauses (A) to (C) of the description of B in subparagraph (d)(ii.1);

Notes: 88(1)(e) is an anti-avoidance rule that reduces the FMV of a subsidiary's partnership interest for 88(1)(d)(ii.1)A. It is meant to address rollovers to a partnership under 97(2), or of a partnership interest under s. 85, before the parent acquires control of the subsidiary (during the series of transactions in which control is acquired) in circumstances where transfers are made to change the factors that may be relevant when applying 88(1)(d)(ii.1).

88(1)(e) added by 2012 budget bill #2, effective for dispositions made after Aug. 13, 2012, with certain grandfathering to end of 2012.

(e.1) **[reserves]** — the subsidiary may, for the purposes of computing its income for its taxation year during which its assets were transferred to, and its obligations were assumed by, the parent on the winding-up, claim any reserve that would have been allowed under this Part if its assets had not been transferred to, or its obligations had not been assumed by, the parent on the winding-up and notwithstanding any other provision of this Part, no amount shall be included in respect of any reserve so claimed in computing the income of the subsidiary for its taxation year, if any, following the year in which its assets were transferred to or its obligations were assumed by the parent;

(e.2) **[application of amalgamation rules]** — paragraphs 87(2)(c), (d.1), (e.1), (e.3), (e.42), (g) to (l), (l.21) to (u), (x), (z.1), (z.2), (aa), (cc), (ll), (nn), (pp), (rr) and (tt) to (ww), subsection 87(6) and, subject to section 78, subsection 87(7) apply to the winding-up as if the references in those provisions to

(i) "amalgamation" were read as "winding-up",

(ii) "predecessor corporation" were read as "subsidiary",

(iii) "new corporation" were read as "parent",

(iv) "its first taxation year" were read as "its taxation year during which it received the assets of the subsidiary on the winding-up",

(v) "its last taxation year" were read as "its taxation year during which its assets were distributed to the parent on the winding-up",

(vi) "predecessor corporation's gain" were read as "subsidiary's gain",

(vii) "predecessor corporation's income" were read as "subsidiary's income",

(viii) "new corporation's income" were read as "parent's income",

(ix) "subsection 89(5)" and "subsection 89(9)" were read as "subsection 89(6)" and "subsection 89(10)", respectively,

(x) "any predecessor private corporation" were read as "the subsidiary (if it was a private corporation at the time of the winding-up)",

(xi), (xii) [Repealed]

(xiii) "two or more corporations" were read as "a subsidiary",

(xiv), (xv) [Repealed]

(xvi) "the life insurance capital dividend account of any predecessor corporation immediately before the amalgamation" were read as "the life insurance capital dividend account of the subsidiary at the time the subsidiary was wound-up",

(xvii) "predecessor corporation's refundable Part VII tax on hand" were read as "subsidiary's refundable Part VII tax on hand",

(xviii) "predecessor corporation's Part VII refund" were read as "subsidiary's Part VII refund",

(xix) "predecessor corporation's refundable Part VIII tax on hand" were read as "subsidiary's refundable Part VIII tax on hand",

(xx) "predecessor corporation's Part VIII refund" were read as "subsidiary's Part VIII refund", and

(xxi) "predecessor corporation's cumulative offset account" were read as "subsidiary's cumulative offset account";

Related Provisions: 88(1)(g) — Where subsidiary was insurance corporation. See also at end of 88(1).

Notes: 88(1)(e.2) opening words amended by 2017 budget bill #2 to apply to 87(2)(e.42) for taxation years that end after 2001, and to 87(2)(l.21) for years that begin after March 21, 2017.

88(1)(e.2) earlier amended by 2006 budget bill #2 (effective 2006), 1995-97 technical bill, 1995 Budget, 1994 technical bill, 1992 transportation support bill, 1991 technical bill, 1989 Budget. Subparas. (xiv)-(xv) dealt with the "preferred-earnings amount", used in 87(2)(y.1) and old Part II and repealed in 1986.

Income Tax Folios: S3-F2-C1: Capital Dividends [replaces IT-66R6].

Interpretation Bulletins: IT-330R: Dispositions of capital property subject to warranty, covenant, etc. (cancelled); IT-502: Employee benefit plans and employee trusts. See also lists at end of subsec. 88(1) and s. 88.

(e.3) **[investment tax credit]** — for the purpose of computing the parent's investment tax credit at the end of any particular taxation year ending after the subsidiary was wound up,

(i) property acquired or expenditures made by the subsidiary or an amount included in the investment tax credit of the subsidiary by virtue of paragraph (b) of the definition "investment tax credit" in subsection 127(9) in a taxation year (in this paragraph referred to as the "expenditure year") shall be deemed to have been acquired, made or included, as the case may be, by the parent in its taxation year in which the expenditure year of the subsidiary ended, and

(ii) there shall be added to the amounts otherwise determined for the purposes of paragraphs (f) to (k) of the definition "investment tax credit" in subsection 127(9) in respect of the parent for the particular year

(A) the amounts that would have been determined in respect of the subsidiary for the purposes of paragraph (f) of the definition "investment tax credit" in subsection 127(9) for its taxation year in which it was wound up if the reference therein to "a preceding taxation year" were read as a reference to "the year or a preceding taxation year",

(B) the amounts determined in respect of the subsidiary for the purposes of paragraphs (g) to (i) and (k) of the definition "investment tax credit" in subsection 127(9) for its taxation year in which it was wound up, and

(C) the amount determined in respect of the subsidiary for the purposes of paragraph (j) of the definition "investment tax credit" in subsection 127(9) for its taxation year in which it was wound up except that, for the purpose of the calculation in this clause, where control of the subsidiary has been acquired by a person or group of persons (each of whom is referred to in this clause as the "purchaser") at any time (in this clause referred to as "that time") before the end of the taxation year in which the subsidiary was wound up, there may be added to the amount determined under subparagraph 127(9.1)(d)(i) in respect of the subsidiary the amount, if any, by which that proportion of the amount that, but for subsections 127(3) and (5) and sections 126, 127.2 and 127.3, would be the parent's tax payable under this Part for the particular year, that,

(I) where the subsidiary carried on a particular business in the course of which a property was acquired, or an expenditure was made, before that time in respect of which an amount was included in computing the subsidiary's investment tax credit for its taxation year in which it was wound up, and the parent carried on the particular business throughout the particular year, the amount, if any, by which the total of all amounts each of which is the parent's income for the particular year from the particular business, or the parent's income for the particular year from any other business substantially all the income of which was derived from the sale, leasing, rental or development of properties or the rendering of services similar to the properties sold, leased, rented or developed, or the services rendered, as the case may be, by the subsidiary in carrying on the particular business before that time, exceeds the total of the amounts, if any, deducted for the particular year under paragraph 111(1)(a) or (d) by the parent in respect of a non-capital loss or a farm loss, as the case may be, for a taxation year in respect of the particular business

is of the greater of

(II) the amount determined under subclause (I), and

(III) the parent's taxable income for the particular year

exceeds the amount, if any, calculated under subparagraph 127(9.1)(d)(i) in respect of the particular business or the other business, as the case may be, in respect of the parent at the end of the particular year

to the extent that such amounts determined in respect of the subsidiary may reasonably be considered to have been included in computing the parent's investment tax credit at the end of the particular year by virtue of subparagraph (i),

and, for the purposes of the definitions "first term shared-use-equipment" and "second term shared-use-equipment" in subsection 127(9), the parent shall be deemed to be the same corporation as, and a continuation of, the subsidiary;

Related Provisions: 88(1.3) — Rules relating to computation of income and tax of parent; 256(6)–(9) — Whether control acquired. See also at end of 88(1).

Notes: For CRA interpretation on R&D expenses and ITCs after a windup, see VIEWS docs 932113A, 2004-0078161I7, 2010-0391291E5.

CRA considers that "substantially all", used in 88(1)(e.3)(ii)(C)(I), means 90% or more. For "derived" in (e.3)(ii)(C)(I), see Notes to 18.1(12).

88(1)(e.3)(ii)(C)(I) amended by 1993 technical bill, for windups that begin after Dec. 21, 1992, to add "and the parent carried on the particular business throughout the particular year". Thus, the flow-through of ITCs restricted by the change-of-control rules (127(9.1)) on an 88(1) windup is conditional on the parent carrying on the business of the subsidiary throughout the year in which the flowed-through ITC is claimed.

88(1)(e.3) earlier amended by 1992 Economic Statement.

(e.4) **[employment tax credit]** — [No longer relevant]

Notes: The employment tax credit (former 127(13)-(16)) was repealed effective 1989.

(e.5) **[refundable dividend tax on hand]** — [Repealed]

Notes: 88(1)(e.5) repealed by 1995 Budget, effective for windups that begin after June 1995. RDTOH is now dealt with by reference to 87(2)(aa) in 88(1)(e.2).

(e.6) **[charitable donations]** — if a subsidiary has made a gift in a taxation year (in this section referred to as the "gift year"), for the purposes of computing the amount deductible under section 110.1 by the parent for its taxation years that end after the subsidiary was wound up, the parent is deemed to have made a gift, in each of its taxation years in which a gift year of the subsidiary ended, equal to the amount, if any, by which the total of all amounts, each of which is the amount of a gift or, in the case of a gift made after December 20, 2002, the eligible amount of the gift, made by the subsidiary in the gift year exceeds the total of all amounts deducted under section 110.1 by the subsidiary in respect of those gifts;

Related Provisions: 110.1(1.2) — No carryforward of donations after change in control; 248(30)–(33) — Determination of eligible amount of gift.

Notes: *Dominion Nickel*, 2015 TCC 14 (preliminary decision) was an appeal involving 88(1)(e.6), claiming $65 million in donations by the acquired corporation to the Banyan Tree Foundation. The appeal was withdrawn in Oct. 2015.

88(1)(e.6) amended by 2002-2013 technical bill (Part 5 — technical), effective for windups that begin, and amalgamations that occur, after Dec. 20, 2002.

I.T. Application Rules: 69 (meaning of "chapter 148 of ...").

(e.61) **[donation of non-qualifying securities]** — the parent is deemed for the purpose of section 110.1 to have made any gift deemed by subsection 118.1(13) to have been made by the subsidiary after the subsidiary ceased to exist;

Notes: 88(1)(e.61) added by 1997 Budget, effective August 1997.

(e.7) **[foreign tax credit]** — for the purposes of

(i) determining the amount deductible by the parent under subsection 126(2) for any taxation year commencing after the commencement of the winding-up, and

(ii) determining the extent to which subsection 126(2.3) applies to reduce the amount that may be claimed by the parent under paragraph 126(2)(a),

any unused foreign tax credit (within the meaning of subsection 126(7)) of the subsidiary in respect of a country for a particular taxation year (in this section referred to as the "foreign tax year"), to the extent that it exceeds the total of all amounts each of which is claimed in respect thereof under paragraph 126(2)(a) in computing the tax payable by the subsidiary under this Part for any taxation year, shall be deemed to be an unused foreign tax credit of the parent for its taxation year in which the subsidiary's foreign tax year ended;

Related Provisions: 88(1.3) — Rules relating to computation of income and tax of parent. See also at end of 88(1).

Income Tax Folios: S5-F2-C1: Foreign tax credit [replaces IT-270R3, IT-395R2, IT-520].

(e.8) [Repealed]

Notes: 88(1)(e.8) repealed by 2019 budget bill #1, for tax years that end after March 18, 2019, due to 127(10.2) being simplified. (For later years, see 87(2)(j.6) and 88(1)(e.2).) It read:

(e.8) [investment tax credit — expenditure limit] — for the purpose of applying subsection 127(10.2) to any corporation (other than the subsidiary)

(i) where the parent is associated with another corporation in a taxation year (in this paragraph referred to as the "current year") of the parent that begins after the parent received an asset of the subsidiary on the winding-up and that ends in a calendar year,

(A) the parent's taxable income for its last taxation year that ended in the preceding calendar year (determined before taking into consideration the specified future tax consequences for that last year) is deemed to be the total of

(I) its taxable income for that last year (determined before applying this paragraph to the winding-up and before taking into consideration the specified future tax consequences for that last year), and

(II) the total of the subsidiary's taxable incomes for its taxation years that ended in that preceding calendar year (determined without reference to clause (B) and before taking into consideration the specified future tax consequences for those years), and

(B) the subsidiary's taxable income for each of its taxation years that ends after the first time that the parent receives an asset of the subsidiary on the winding-up of the subsidiary is deemed to be nil, and

(ii) where the parent received an asset of the subsidiary on the winding-up before the current year and is not associated with any corporation in the current year, the parent's taxable income for its immediately preceding taxation year (determined before taking into consideration the specified future tax consequences for that preceding year) is deemed to be the total of

(A) its taxable income for that preceding taxation year (determined before applying this paragraph to the winding-up and before taking into consideration the specified future tax consequences for that preceding taxation year), and

(B) the total of the subsidiary's taxable incomes for its taxation years that ended in the calendar year in which that preceding taxation year ended (determined before taking into consideration the specified future tax consequences for those years);

Earlier amended by 1996 Budget, last change effective for applying 127(10.1)-(10.2) to tax years that begin after 1996. For 127.1(2)"qualifying corporation" and 157(1)(b)(i), covered by 88(1)(e.8) until that amendment, see now 88(1)(e.9).

(e.9) [refundable ITC and balance-due day] — for the purpose of applying the definition "qualifying corporation" in subsection 127.1(2), and subparagraph (d)(i) of the definition "balance-due day" in subsection 248(1), to any corporation (other than the subsidiary)

(i) where the parent is associated with another corporation in a taxation year (in this paragraph referred to as the "current year") of the parent that begins after the parent received an asset of the subsidiary on the winding-up and ends in a calendar year,

(A) the parent's taxable income for its last taxation year that ended in the preceding calendar year (determined before taking into consideration the specified future tax consequences for that last year) is deemed to be the total of

(I) its taxable income for that last year (determined before applying this paragraph to the winding-up and before taking into consideration the specified future tax consequences for that last year), and

(II) the total of the subsidiary's taxable incomes for its taxation years that ended in that preceding calendar year (determined without reference to subparagraph (iii) and before taking into consideration the specified future tax consequences for those years),

(B) the parent's business limit for that last year is deemed to be the total of

(I) its business limit (determined before applying this paragraph to the winding-up) for that last year, and

(II) the total of the subsidiary's business limits (determined without reference to subparagraph (iii)) for its taxation years that ended in that preceding calendar year, and

(C) the parent's qualifying income limit for that last year is deemed to be the total of

(I) its qualifying income limit (determined before applying this paragraph to the winding-up) for that last year, and

(II) the total of the subsidiary's qualifying income limits (determined without reference to subparagraph (iii)) for its taxation years that ended in that preceding calendar year,

(ii) where the parent received an asset of the subsidiary on the winding-up before the current year and subparagraph (i) does not apply,

(A) the parent's taxable income for its immediately preceding taxation year (determined before taking into consideration the specified future tax consequences for that preceding year) is deemed to be the total of

(I) its taxable income for that preceding taxation year (determined before applying this paragraph to the winding-up and before taking into consideration the specified future tax consequences for that preceding taxation year), and

(II) the total of the subsidiary's taxable incomes for the subsidiary's taxation years that end in the calendar year in which that preceding taxation year ended (determined before taking into consideration the specified future tax consequences for those years),

(B) the parent's business limit for that preceding taxation year is deemed to be the total of

(I) its business limit (determined before applying this paragraph to the winding-up) for that preceding taxation year, and

(II) the total of the subsidiary's business limits (determined without reference to subparagraph (iii)) for the subsidiary's taxation years that end in the calendar year in which that preceding taxation year ended, and

(C) the parent's qualifying income limit for that preceding taxation year is deemed to be the total of

(I) its qualifying income limit (determined before applying this paragraph to the winding-up) for that preceding taxation year, and

(II) the total of the subsidiary's qualifying income limits (determined without reference to subparagraph (iii)) for the subsidiary's taxation years that end in the calendar year in which that preceding taxation year ended, and

(iii) where the parent and the subsidiary are associated with each other in the current year, the subsidiary's taxable income, the subsidiary's business limit and the subsidiary's qualifying income limit for each taxation year that ends after the first time that the parent receives an asset of the subsidiary on the winding-up are deemed to be nil;

Notes: 88(1)(e.9) amended by 2013 budget bill #2 (for windups that begin after Feb. 25, 2008), 2001 and 1996 Budgets.

(f) [depreciable property] — where property that was depreciable property of a prescribed class of the subsidiary has been distributed to the parent on the winding-up and the capital cost to the subsidiary of the property exceeds the amount deemed by paragraph (a) to be the subsidiary's proceeds of disposition of the property, for the purposes of sections 13 and 20 and any regulations made under paragraph 20(1)(a),

(i) notwithstanding paragraph (c), the capital cost to the parent of the property shall be deemed to be the amount that was the capital cost of the property to the subsidiary, and

(ii) the excess shall be deemed to have been allowed to the parent in respect of the property under regulations made under paragraph 20(1)(a) in computing income for taxation years before the acquisition by the parent of the property;

Notes: For a ruling applying 88(1)(f) see VIEWS doc 2015-0582421E5.

I.T. Application Rules: 20(1.2) (transfer of depreciable property by person who owned it before 1972).

(g) [insurance corporation] — where the subsidiary was an insurance corporation,

(i) for the purposes of paragraphs 12(1)(d), (e), (e.1), (i) and (s), subsection 12.5(8), paragraphs 20(1)(l), (l.1), (p) and (jj) and 20(7)(c), subsections 20(22) and 20.4(4), sections 138, 138.1, 140, 142 and 148 and Part XII.3, the parent is deemed to be the same corporation as, and a continuation of, the subsidiary, and

(ii) for the purpose of determining the amount of the gross investment revenue required to be included under subsection 138(9) in the income of the subsidiary and the parent and the amount of gains and losses of the subsidiary and the parent from property used by them in the year or held by them in the year in the course of carrying on an insurance business in Canada

(A) the subsidiary and the parent shall, in addition to their normal taxation years, be deemed to have had a taxation year ending immediately before the time when the property of the subsidiary was transferred to, and the obligations of the subsidiary were assumed by, the parent on the winding-up, and

(B) for the taxation years of the subsidiary and the parent following the time referred to in clause (A), the property transferred to, and the obligations assumed by, the parent on the winding-up shall be deemed to have been transferred or assumed, as the case may be, on the last day of the taxation year ending immediately before that time and the parent shall be deemed to be the same corporation as and a continuation of the subsidiary with respect to that property, those obligations and the insurance businesses carried on by the subsidiary;

Notes: 88(1)(g)(i) amended by 2008 budget bill #2 to refer to 12.5(8) and 20.4(4), effective for taxation years that begin after September 2006. Earlier amended by 1996 Budget, effective for windups that begin after 1995.

I.T. Application Rules: 69 (meaning of "chapter 148 of ...").

(h) [financial institution — mark-to-market property] — for the purposes of subsections 112(5) to (5.2) and (5.4) and the definition "mark-to-market property" in subsection 142.2(1), the parent shall be deemed, in respect of each property distributed to it on the winding-up, to be the same corporation as, and a continuation of, the subsidiary;

Notes: 88(1)(h) added by 1994 technical bill, effective for windups that begin at any time.

(i) [financial institution — mark-to-market property] — for the purpose of subsection 142.5(2), the subsidiary's taxation year in which its assets were distributed to the parent on the winding-up shall be deemed to have ended immediately before the time when the assets were distributed; and

Notes: 88(1)(i) added by 1994 technical bill, effective for windups that begin after October 1994.

(j) [mark-to-market election for derivatives] — for the purposes of subsection 10.1(6), the subsidiary's taxation year in which an "eligible derivative" (as defined in subsection 10.1(5)) was distributed to, or assumed by, the parent on the winding-up is deemed to have ended immediately before the time when the eligible derivative was distributed or assumed.

Notes: 88(1)(j) added by 2017 budget bill #2, for taxation years that begin after March 21, 2017. This was 88(1)(i.1) in the March 22, 2017 draft legislation.

Related Provisions [subsec. 88(1)]: 12.5(4), 138(20), 142.51(6) — Financial institutions and insurers — transitional rules for accounting changes; 15(1)(a)(iv), 15(1)(a.1)(iv) — No shareholder-benefit income inclusion; 69(5) — Deemed distribution of corporation's property before windup; 69(11)–(13) — Anti-avoidance rule where property sold after rollover; 80.01(4) — Deemed settlement of debt on winding-up; 80.01(5) — Deemed settlement of distress preferred share on winding-up; 84(2) — Distribution on winding-up, etc.; 87(11) — Application to vertical amalgamation; 88.1(2) — Windup of SIFT trust into corporation before 2013; 89(3) — Ordering of simultaneous dividends; 98(5)(a)(i) — Where partnership business carried on as sole proprietorship; 137(4.3) — Determination of preferred-rate amount; 142.6(5), (6) — Acquisition of specified debt obligation by financial institution in rollover transaction; 159(2) — Clearance certificate; 186(5) — Presumption; 212.3(22) — Application to foreign affiliate dumping rules; 261(16) — Effect of functional currency reporting.

Notes [subsec. 88(1)]: See Notes to opening words of 88(1).

Interpretation Bulletins [subsec. 88(1)]: IT-109R2: Unpaid amounts; IT-121R3: Election to capitalize cost of borrowed money (cancelled); IT-126R2: Meaning of "winding-up"; IT-142R3: Settlement of debts on the winding-up of a corporation; IT-154R: Special reserves; IT-321R: Insurance agents and brokers — unearned commissions (cancelled); IT-488R2: Winding-up of 90%-owned taxable Canadian corporations (cancelled). See also at end of s. 88.

Information Circulars [subsec. 88(1)]: 88-2 Supplement, para. 8: General anti-avoidance rule — section 245 of the *Income Tax Act*.

I.T. Technical News [subsec. 88(1)]: 16 (*Continental Bank* case).

CRA Audit Manual [subsec. 88(1)]: 16.1.3: Clearance certificates — corporations with leave to surrender charter.

Forms [subsec. 88(1)]: T2 Sched. 24: First time filer after incorporation, amalgamation or winding-up of a subsidiary into a parent.

(1.1) Non-capital losses, etc., of subsidiary — Where a Canadian corporation (in this subsection referred to as the "subsidiary") has been wound up and not less than 90% of the issued shares of each class of the capital stock of the subsidiary were, immediately before the winding-up, owned by another Canadian corporation (in this subsection referred to as the "parent") and all the shares of the subsidiary that were not owned by the parent immediately before the winding-up were owned at that time by a person or persons with whom the parent was dealing at arm's length, for the purpose of computing the taxable income of the parent under this Part and the tax payable under Part IV by the parent for any taxation year commencing after the commencement of the winding-up, such portion of any non-capital loss, restricted farm loss, farm loss or limited partnership loss of the subsidiary as may reasonably be regarded as its loss from carrying on a particular business (in this subsection referred to as the "subsidiary's loss business") and any other

portion of any non-capital loss or limited partnership loss of the subsidiary as may reasonably be regarded as being derived from any other source or being in respect of a claim made under section 110.5 for any particular taxation year of the subsidiary (in this subsection referred to as "the subsidiary's loss year"), to the extent that it

(a) was not deducted in computing the taxable income of the subsidiary for any taxation year of the subsidiary, and

(b) would have been deductible in computing the taxable income of the subsidiary for any taxation year beginning after the commencement of the winding-up, on the assumption that it had such a taxation year and that it had sufficient income for that year,

shall, for the purposes of this subsection, paragraphs 111(1)(a), (c), (d) and (e), subsection 111(3) and Part IV,

(c) in the case of such portion of any non-capital loss, restricted farm loss, farm loss or limited partnership loss of the subsidiary as may reasonably be regarded as its loss from carrying on the subsidiary's loss business, be deemed, for the taxation year of the parent in which the subsidiary's loss year ended, to be a non-capital loss, restricted farm loss, farm loss or limited partnership loss, respectively, of the parent from carrying on the subsidiary's loss business, that was not deductible by the parent in computing its taxable income for any taxation year that commenced before the commencement of the winding-up,

(d) in the case of any other portion of any non-capital loss or limited partnership loss of the subsidiary as may reasonably be regarded as being derived from any other source, be deemed, for the taxation year of the parent in which the subsidiary's loss year ended, to be a non-capital loss or a limited partnership loss, respectively, of the parent that was derived from the source from which the subsidiary derived the loss and that was not deductible by the parent in computing its taxable income for any taxation year that commenced before the commencement of the winding-up, and

(d.1) in the case of any other portion of any non-capital loss of the subsidiary as may reasonably be regarded as being in respect of a claim made under section 110.5, be deemed, for the taxation year of the parent in which the subsidiary's loss year ended, to be a non-capital loss of the parent in respect of a claim made under section 110.5 that was not deductible by the parent in computing its taxable income for any taxation year that commenced before the commencement of the winding-up,

except that

(e) if control of the parent has been acquired by a person or group of persons at any time after the commencement of the winding-up, or control of the subsidiary has been acquired by a person or group of persons at any time whatever, no amount in respect of the subsidiary's non-capital loss or farm loss for a taxation year ending before that time is deductible in computing the taxable income of the parent for a particular taxation year ending after that time, except that such portion of the subsidiary's non-capital loss or farm loss as may reasonably be regarded as its loss from carrying on a business and, where a business was carried on by the subsidiary in that year, such portion of the non-capital loss as may reasonably be regarded as being in respect of an amount deductible under paragraph 110(1)(k) in computing its taxable income for the year is deductible only

(i) if that business is carried on by the subsidiary or the parent for profit or with a reasonable expectation of profit throughout the particular year, and

(ii) to the extent of the total of the parent's income for the particular year from that business and, where properties were sold, leased, rented or developed or services rendered in the course of carrying on that business before that time, from any other business substantially all of the income of which was derived from the sale, leasing, rental or development, as the case may be, of similar properties or the rendering of similar services,

and, for the purpose of this paragraph, where this subsection applied to the winding-up of another corporation in respect of which the subsidiary was the parent and this paragraph applied in respect of losses of that other corporation, the subsidiary shall be deemed to be the same corporation as, and a continuation of, that other corporation with respect to those losses, and

(f) any portion of a loss of the subsidiary that would otherwise be deemed by paragraph (c), (d) or (d.1) to be a loss of the parent for a particular taxation year beginning after the commencement of the winding-up shall be deemed, for the purpose of computing the parent's taxable income for taxation years beginning after the commencement of the winding-up, to be such a loss of the parent for its immediately preceding taxation year and not for the particular year, where the parent so elects in its return of income under this Part for the particular year.

Related Provisions: 10(11) — Adventure in the nature of trade deemed to be business carried on by corporation; 88(1.3) — Rules relating to computation of income and tax of parent; 256(6)–(9) — Whether control acquired; 256.1 — Deemed change in control if 75% FMV acquired.

Notes: See Notes to 111(5), which applies the same principle on change in control of a corporation. For examples of rulings that 88(1.1) will apply on loss utilization transactions, see VIEWS docs 2009-0347041R3, 2010-0353911R3, 2011-0416921R3, 2011-0425461R3, 2013-0511991R3, 2014-0563151R3, 2014-0536651R5, 2017-0711911R3, 2018-0741691R3, 2020-0865971R3.

In *S.T.B. Holdings*, 2011 TCC 144, a non-capital loss was allowed despite 88(1.1)(e), as STB was held to carry on the "same business" (land development) as its wound-up subsidiary (land speculation).

CRA states that for 88(1.1) to apply, formal dissolution of the corporation must be complete (VIEWS docs 2001-0067105, 2001-0093395, 2013-0496351R3, 2013-0511991R3). The policy in IT-126R2 para. 5, accepting a windup before formal dissolution is complete, does not apply to 88(1.1). The sub's losses can be deducted by the parent in the same year the sub is dissolved: 2015-0618211E5.

See VIEWS docs 2004-0064951E5 and 2005-0144591E5 for the timing of expiry of losses where 88(1.1) applies. Losses from property cannot be carried forward: 2011-0401721I7. On the election under 88(1.1)(f): 2012-0447961E5. Losses can be claimed after a 2-step acquisition of the sub's business and then its shares: 2017-0711071R3.

Saipem UK, 2011 FCA 243, rejected the argument that the "non-discrimination" clause in the Canada-UK tax treaty should permit a non-resident corporation to be treated as a "Canadian corporation" for purposes of 88(1.1). The same would apply under the Canada-US treaty: VIEWS doc 2017-0685651E5.

CRA considers that "substantially all", used in 88(1.1)(e)(ii), means 90% or more. For the meaning of "derived" see Notes to 18.1(12).

88(1.1)(e) opening words amended by 2002-2013 technical bill (Part 5 — technical), effective for windups that begin after May 1996.

88(1.1) earlier amended by 1991 technical bill, effective 1990.

Interpretation Bulletins: IT-302R3: Losses of a corporation — the effect that acquisitions of control, amalgamations, and windings-up have on their deductibility. See also at end of s. 88.

(1.2) Net capital losses of subsidiary — Where the winding-up of a Canadian corporation (in this subsection referred to as the "subsidiary") commenced after March 31, 1977 and not less than 90% of the issued shares of each class of the capital stock of the subsidiary were, immediately before the winding-up, owned by another Canadian corporation (in this subsection referred to as the "parent") and all of the shares of the subsidiary that were not owned by the parent immediately before the winding-up were owned at that time by persons with whom the parent was dealing at arm's length, for the purposes of computing the taxable income of the parent for any taxation year commencing after the commencement of the winding-up, any net capital loss of the subsidiary for any particular taxation year of the subsidiary (in this subsection referred to as the "subsidiary's loss year"), to the extent that it

(a) was not deducted in computing the taxable income of the subsidiary for any taxation year of the subsidiary, and

(b) would have been deductible in computing the taxable income of the subsidiary for any taxation year beginning after the commencement of the winding-up, on the assumption that it had such a taxation year and that it had sufficient income and taxable capital gains for that year,

shall, for the purposes of this subsection, paragraph 111(1)(b) and subsection 111(3), be deemed to be a net capital loss of the parent for its taxation year in which the particular taxation year of the subsidiary ended, except that

(c) where at any time control of the parent or subsidiary has been acquired by a person or group of persons, no amount in respect of the subsidiary's net capital loss for a taxation year ending before that time is deductible in computing the parent's taxable income for a taxation year ending after that time, and

(d) any portion of a net capital loss of the subsidiary that would otherwise be deemed by this subsection to be a loss of the parent for a particular taxation year beginning after the commencement of the winding-up shall be deemed, for the purposes of computing its taxable income for taxation years beginning after the commencement of the winding-up, to be a net capital loss of the parent for its immediately preceding taxation year and not for the particular year, where the parent so elects in its return of income under this Part for the particular year.

Related Provisions: 80(12)(a)(ii)(B) — Application of sub's capital losses against capital gain from forgiveness of debt; 88(1.3) — Computation of income and tax of parent; 111(5.4) — Non-capital loss; 256(6)–(9) — Whether control acquired; 256.1 — Deemed change in control if 75% FMV acquired.

Notes: The sub's losses can be deducted by the parent in the same year the sub is dissolved: VIEWS doc 2015-0618211E5.

88(1.2) amended by 1991 technical bill, for parents' 1985 and later tax years (or, by election, a later year up to 1992).

Interpretation Bulletins: IT-302R3: Losses of a corporation — the effect that acquisitions of control, amalgamations, and windings-up have on their deductibility. See also at end of s. 88.

(1.3) Computation of income and tax of parent — For the purpose of paragraphs (1)(e.3), (e.6) and (e.7), subsections (1.1) and (1.2), section 110.1, subsections 111(1) and (3) and Part IV, where a parent corporation has been incorporated or otherwise formed after the end of an expenditure year, gift year, foreign tax year or loss year, as the case may be, of a subsidiary of the parent, for the purpose of computing the taxable income of, and the tax payable under this Part and Part IV by, the parent for any taxation year,

(a) it shall be deemed to have been in existence during the particular period beginning immediately before the end of the subsidiary's first expenditure year, gift year, foreign tax year or loss year, as the case may be, and ending immediately after it was incorporated or otherwise formed;

(b) it shall be deemed to have had, throughout the particular period, fiscal periods ending on the day of the year on which its first fiscal period ended; and

(c) it shall be deemed to have been controlled, throughout the particular period, by the person or persons who controlled it immediately after it was incorporated or otherwise formed.

Related Provisions: 88(1)(e.6) — Meaning of "gift year"; 256(6), (6.1) — Meaning of "controlled".

Notes: 88(1.3)(a) amended by 1992 technical bill, effective for windings-up that begin after 1988, to add reference to "expenditure year".

Interpretation Bulletins: IT-302R3: Losses of a corporation — the effect that acquisitions of control, amalgamations, and windings-up have on their deductibility.

(1.4) Qualified expenditure of subsidiary — For the purposes of this subsection and section 37.1, where the rules in subsection (1) applied to the winding-up of a subsidiary, for the purpose of computing the income of its parent for any taxation year commencing after the subsidiary has been wound up, the following rules apply:

(a) where the parent's base period consists of fewer than three taxation years, its base period shall be determined on the assumption that it had taxation years in each of the calendar years preceding the year in which it was incorporated, each of which commenced on the same day of the year as the day of its incorporation;

(b) the qualified expenditure made by the parent in a particular taxation year in its base period shall be deemed to be the total of the amount thereof otherwise determined and the qualified expenditure made by the subsidiary in its taxation year ending in the same calendar year as the particular year;

(c) the total of the amounts paid to the parent by persons referred to in subparagraphs (b)(i) to (iii) of the definition "expenditure base" in subsection 37.1(5) in a particular taxation year in its base period shall be deemed to be the total otherwise determined and all those amounts paid to the subsidiary by a person referred to in those subparagraphs in the subsidiary's taxation year ending in the same calendar year as the particular year; and

(d) there shall be added to the total of the amounts otherwise determined in respect of the parent under subparagraphs 37.1(3)(b)(i) and (iii) respectively, the total of the amounts determined under those subparagraphs in respect of the subsidiary.

(1.41) Application of subsec. 37.1(5) — The definitions in subsection 37.1(5) apply to subsection (1.4).

Notes: 88(1.41) added in the RSC 1985 (5th Supp) consolidation, for tax years ending after Nov. 1991. This rule was formerly in the opening words of 37.1(5). S. 37.1, which provided an additional R&D allowance, has been repealed.

(1.5) Parent continuation of subsidiary — For the purposes of section 29 of the *Income Tax Application Rules*, subsection 59(3.3) and sections 66, 66.1, 66.2, 66.21, 66.4 and 66.7, where the rules in subsection (1) applied to the winding-up of a subsidiary, its parent is deemed to be the same corporation as, and a continuation of, the subsidiary.

Notes: See Mike Hegedus & Andrew Bateman, "A Closer Look at Subsection 88(1.5)", VIII(3) *Resource Sector Taxation* (Federated Press) 591-95 (2011).

88(1.5) amended by 2000 technical bill, effective for windings-up that occur after 2000, to add reference to 66.21.

Interpretation Bulletins: IT-125R4: Dispositions of resource properties; IT-488R2: Winding-up of 90%-owned taxable Canadian corporations (cancelled).

(1.6) Idem — Where a corporation that carries on a farming business and computes its income from that business in accordance with the cash method is wound up in circumstances to which subsection (1) applies and, at the time that is immediately before the winding-up of the corporation, owned inventory that was used in connection with that business,

(a) for the purposes of subparagraph (1)(a)(iii), the cost amount to the corporation at that time of property purchased by it that is included in that inventory shall be deemed to be the amount determined by the formula

$$(A \times B / C) + D$$

where

A is the amount, if any, that would be included under paragraph 28(1)(c) in computing the corporation's income for its last taxation year beginning before that time if that year had ended at that time,

B is the value (determined in accordance with subsection 28(1.2)) to the corporation at that time of the purchased inventory that is distributed to the parent on the winding-up,

C is the value (determined in accordance with subsection 28(1.2)) of all of the inventory purchased by the corporation that was owned by it in connection with that business at that time, and

D is the lesser of

(i) such additional amount as the corporation designates in respect of the property, and

(ii) the amount, if any, by which the fair market value of the property at that time exceeds the amount determined for A in respect of the property;

(b) for the purpose of subparagraph 28(1)(a)(i), the disposition of the inventory and the receipt of the proceeds of disposition therefor shall be deemed to have occurred at that time and in the course of carrying on the business; and

(c) where the parent carries on a farming business and computes its income therefrom in accordance with the cash method, for the purposes of section 28,

(i) an amount equal to the cost to the parent of the inventory shall be deemed to have been paid by it, and

(ii) the parent shall be deemed to have purchased the inventory for an amount equal to that cost,

in the course of carrying on that business and at the time it acquired the inventory.

Notes: 88(1.6) added by 1991 technical bill, for windups commencing after July 13, 1990.

Interpretation Bulletins: IT-427R: Livestock of farmers.

(1.7) Interpretation — For the purposes of paragraphs (1)(c) and (d), where a parent of a subsidiary did not deal at arm's length with another person (other than a corporation the control of which was acquired by the parent from a person with whom the parent dealt at arm's length) at any time before the winding-up of the subsidiary, the parent and the other person are deemed never to have dealt with each other at arm's length, whether or not the parent and the other person coexisted.

Related Provisions: 87(11) — Application to vertical amalgamation; 256(6)–(9) — Whether control acquired.

Notes: The words "another person" are considered not to include a partnership: VIEWS doc 2006-0212691R3. Acquisition of a public corp may qualify for the parenthesized exception even if it is not controlled by any person or group: 2011-0418971E5.

88(1.7) added by 1995-97 technical bill, for windups that begin after Feb. 21, 1994. This rule was formerly in 88(1)(d) closing words.

(1.8) Application of subsec. (1.9) — Subsection (1.9) applies if

(a) a corporation has made a designation (referred to in this subsection and subsection (1.9) as the "initial designation") under paragraph (1)(d) in respect of a share of the capital stock of a foreign affiliate of the corporation, or an interest in a partnership that, based on the assumptions contained in paragraph 96(1)(c), owns a share of the capital stock of a foreign affiliate of the corporation, on or before the filing-due date for its return of income under this Part for the taxation year in which a disposition of the share or the partnership interest, as the case may be, occurred in the course of a winding-up referred to in subsection (1) or an amalgamation referred to in subsection 87(11);

(b) the corporation made reasonable efforts to determine the foreign affiliate's tax-free surplus balance (within the meaning assigned by subsection 5905(5.5) of the *Income Tax Regulations*), in respect of the corporation, that was relevant in the computation of the maximum amount available under subparagraph (1)(d)(ii) to be designated in respect of that disposition; and

(c) the corporation amends the initial designation on or before the day that is 10 years after the filing-due date referred to in paragraph (a).

Notes: 88(1.8) added by 2002-2013 technical bill (Part 2 — FA surplus rules), effective Dec. 19, 2009. Rules permitting late reassessment for numerous amendments made by the same Part 2 are discussed in these Notes up to the 58th ed.

(1.9) Amended designation — If this subsection applies and, in the opinion of the Minister, the circumstances are such that it would be just and equitable to permit the initial designation to be amended, the amended designation under paragraph (1.8)(c) is deemed to have been made on the day on which the initial designation was made and the initial designation is deemed not to have been made.

Related Provisions: 88(1.8) — Conditions for 88(1.9) to apply.

Notes: For the meaning of "just and equitable", see Notes to 85(7.1).

88(1.9) added by 2002-2013 technical bill (Part 2 — FA surplus rules), effective Dec. 19, 2009.

(2) Winding-up of [other] Canadian corporation — Where a Canadian corporation (other than a subsidiary to the winding-up of which the rules in subsection (1) applied) has been wound up after 1978 and, at a particular time in the course of the winding-up, all or substantially all of the property owned by the corporation immediately before that time was distributed to the shareholders of the corporation,

(a) for the purposes of computing the corporation's

(i) capital dividend account,

(i.1) capital gains dividend account (within the meaning assigned by subsection 131(6)), where the corporation is an investment corporation,

(ii) capital gains dividend account (within the meaning assigned by section 133), and

(iii) pre-1972 capital surplus on hand,

at the time (in this paragraph referred to as the "time of computation") immediately before the particular time,

(iv) the taxation year of the corporation that otherwise would have included the particular time shall be deemed to have ended immediately before the time of computation, and a new taxation year shall be deemed to have commenced at that time, and

(v) each property of the corporation that was so distributed at the particular time shall be deemed to have been disposed of by the corporation immediately before the end of the taxation year so deemed to have ended for proceeds equal to the fair market value of the property immediately before the particular time;

(vi) [Repealed]

(b) where the corporation is, by virtue of subsection 84(2), deemed to have paid at the particular time a dividend (in this paragraph referred to as the "winding-up dividend") on shares of any class of its capital stock, the following rules apply:

(i) such portion of the winding-up dividend as does not exceed the corporation's capital dividend account immediately before that time or capital gains dividend account immediately before that time, as the case may be, shall be deemed, for the purposes of an election in respect thereof under subsection 83(2), 131(1) (as that subsection applies for the purposes of section 130) or 133(7.1), as the case may be, and where the corporation has so elected, for all other purposes, to be the full amount of a separate dividend,

(i.1) [Repealed under former Act]

(ii) the portion of the winding-up dividend equal to the lesser of the corporation's pre-1972 capital surplus on hand immediately before that time and the amount by which the winding-up dividend exceeds

(A) the portion thereof in respect of which the corporation has made an election under subsection 83(2), or

(B) the portion thereof in respect of which the corporation has made an election under subsection 133(7.1),

as the case may be, shall be deemed not to be a dividend,

(iii) notwithstanding the definition "taxable dividend" in subsection 89(1), the winding-up dividend, to the extent that it exceeds the total of the portion thereof deemed by subparagraph (i) to be a separate dividend for all purposes and the portion deemed by subparagraph (ii) not to be a dividend, shall be deemed to be a separate dividend that is a taxable dividend, and

(iv) each person who held any of the issued shares of that class at the particular time shall be deemed to have received that proportion of any separate dividend determined under subparagraph (i) or (iii) that the number of shares of that class held by the person immediately before the particular time is of the number of issued shares of that class outstanding immediately before that time; and

(c) for the purpose of computing the income of the corporation for its taxation year that includes the particular time, paragraph 12(1)(t) shall be read as follows:

"(t) the amount deducted under subsection 127(5) or (6) in computing the taxpayer's tax payable for the year or a preceding taxation year to the extent that it was not included under this paragraph in computing the taxpayer's income for a preceding taxation year or is not included in an amount determined under paragraph 13(7.1)(e) or 37(1)(e) or subparagraph 53(2)(c)(vi) or (h)(ii) or the amount determined for I in the definition "undepreciated capital cost" in subsection 13(21) or L in the definition "cumulative Canadian exploration expense" in subsection 66.1(6);".

Related Provisions: 15(1)(a)(iv), 15(1)(a.1)(iv) — No shareholder-benefit income inclusion; 44(2) — Date of disposition for property stolen, destroyed or expropriated; 69(5) — Property appropriated by shareholder on winding-up of corporation; 84(2) — Distribution of property on winding-up of corporation; 88(2.1) — "Pre-1972 capital surplus on hand" defined; 89(3) — Ordering of simultaneous dividends; 159(2) — Clearance certificate.

Notes: The deemed year-end in 88(2)(a)(iv) is only for the limited purposes stated, so no return need be filed for the deemed year: VIEWS doc 2013-0480771E5.

Where a corporation's charter is cancelled but the business continues, the owners are considered to carry on the business directly, as sole proprietor, partners or joint venture: VIEWS docs 2009-0331481I7, 2009-0331531I7; *Dello*, 2003 TCC 392; *Amerey*, 2005 FCA 428.

If a corp winds up with unpaid tax, the shareholders may be liable. See Notes to 84(2).

Where the corp owns a life insurance policy, CRA's view is that 69(5) (transfer at FMV) applies rather than 148(7) (cash surrender value): doc 2015-0573841C6 [2015 CLHIA q.4]. This may be wrong: "Distributing an Interest in a Life Insurance Policy on a Corporate Wind-Up", tinyurl.com/rochwerg-sharma.

CRA considers that "substantially all", used in 88(2) opening words, means 90% or more. 88(2) can apply before formal dissolution is complete: IT-126R2 para. 5.

For some rulings applying 88(2)(b) see VIEWS docs 2012-0443081R3, 2013-0512531R3, 2015-0582431R3, 2019-0816991R3, 2019-0811641R3. For an 88(2)(b)(i) capital dividend election, CRA permits an estimate of the CDA balance that cannot be determined, to be adjusted later: 2017-0709021C6 [2017 APFF q.4] [Ross, "Taxable Windup: A Practical Approach to Capital Dividends", 18(3) *Tax for the Owner-Manager* (ctf.ca) 3-4 (July 2018)].

See Lamarre et al., *Taxation of Corporate Reorganizations* (Carswell, 3rd ed., 2019), §9.3; Dalsin, "ECP-Related CDA Dividend 'In the Course of a Winding-Up' Pre-2017", 27(8) *Canadian Tax Highlights* (ctf.ca) 1-2 (Aug. 2019).

88(2) amended by 1991 technical bill, for windups beginning after 1987 or 1988.

Interpretation Bulletins: IT-126R2: Meaning of "winding-up"; IT-149R4: Winding-up dividend. See also at end of s. 88.

CRA Audit Manual: 16.1.3: Clearance certificates — corporations with leave to surrender charter.

Forms: RC145: Request to close Business Number (BN) program accounts.

(2.1) Definition of "pre-1972 capital surplus on hand" — For the purposes of subsection (2), "pre-1972 capital surplus on hand" of a particular corporation at a particular time means the amount, if any, by which the total of

(a) the corporation's 1971 capital surplus on hand on December 31, 1978 within the meaning of the *Income Tax Act*, chapter 148 of the Revised Statutes of Canada, 1952, as it read on that date,

(b) the total of all amounts each of which is an amount in respect of a capital property of the corporation owned by it on December 31, 1971 and disposed of by it after 1978 and before the particular time, equal to the amount, if any, by which the lesser of its fair market value on valuation day (within the meaning assigned by section 24 of the *Income Tax Application Rules*) and the corporation's proceeds of disposition of that capital property exceeds its actual cost to the corporation determined without reference to the *Income Tax Application Rules* other than subsections 26(15), (17) and (21) to (27) of that Act,

(c) where before the particular time a subsidiary (to the winding-up of which the rules in subsection (1) applied) of the particular corporation has been wound up after 1978, an amount equal to the pre-1972 capital surplus on hand of the subsidiary immediately before the commencement of the winding-up, and

(d) where the particular corporation is a new corporation formed as a result of an amalgamation (within the meaning of section

87) after 1978 and before the particular time, the total of all amounts each of which is an amount in respect of a predecessor corporation, equal to the predecessor corporation's pre-1972 capital surplus on hand immediately before the amalgamation

exceeds

(e) the total of all amounts each of which is an amount in respect of a capital property (other than depreciable property) of the corporation owned by it on December 31, 1971 and disposed of by it after 1978 and before the particular time equal to the amount, if any, by which its actual cost to the corporation determined without reference to the *Income Tax Application Rules*, other than subsections 26(15), (17) and (21) to (27) of that Act, exceeds the greater of the fair market value of the property on valuation day (within the meaning assigned by section 24 of that Act) and the corporation's proceeds of disposition of the property.

Related Provisions: 84(2) — Distribution on winding-up, etc.; 87(2)(t) — Deemed date of acquisition; 88(2.2) — Determination of pre-1972 CSOH; 88(2.3) — Actual cost of certain depreciable property.

Notes: For rulings applying 88(2.1)(b), see docs 2012-0443081R3, 2013-0512531R3.

I.T. Application Rules: 26(15), (17), (21)–(27); 69 (meaning of "chapter 148 of ...").

Interpretation Bulletins: IT-488R2: Winding-up of 90%-owned taxable Canadian corporations (cancelled). See also at end of s. 88.

(2.2) Determination of pre-1972 capital surplus on hand — For the purposes of determining the pre-1972 capital surplus on hand of any corporation at a particular time after 1978, the following rules apply:

(a) an amount referred to in paragraphs (2.1)(b) and (e) in respect of the corporation shall be deemed to be nil, where the property disposed of is

(i) a share of the capital stock of a subsidiary, within the meaning of subsection (1), that was disposed of on the winding-up of the subsidiary where that winding-up commenced after 1978,

(ii) a share of the capital stock of another Canadian corporation that was controlled, within the meaning assigned by subsection 186(2), by the corporation immediately before the disposition and that was disposed of by the corporation after 1978 to a person with whom the corporation was not dealing at arm's length immediately after the disposition, other than by a disposition referred to in paragraph (b), or

(iii) subject to subsection 26(21) of the *Income Tax Application Rules*, a share of the capital stock of a particular corporation that was disposed of by the corporation after 1978, on an amalgamation, within the meaning assigned by subsection 87(1), where the corporation controlled, within the meaning assigned by subsection 186(2), both the particular corporation immediately before the amalgamation and the new corporation immediately after the amalgamation; and

(b) where another corporation that is a Canadian corporation owned a capital property on December 31, 1971 and subsequently disposed of it to the corporation in a transaction to which section 85 applied, the other corporation shall be deemed not to have disposed of that property in the transaction and the corporation shall be deemed to have owned that property on December 31, 1971 and to have acquired it at an actual cost equal to the actual cost of that property to the other corporation.

Notes: For a ruling applying 88(2.2)(b), see VIEWS docs 2012-0443081R3, 2013-0512531R3.

Interpretation Bulletins: IT-488R2: Winding-up of 90%-owned taxable Canadian corporations (cancelled). See also at end of s. 88.

(2.3) Actual cost of certain depreciable property — For the purpose of subsection (2.1), the actual cost of the depreciable property that was acquired by a corporation before the commencement of its 1949 taxation year that is capital property referred to in that subsection shall be deemed to be the capital cost of that property to the corporation (within the meaning assigned by section 144 of the

Income Tax Act, chapter 148 of the Revised Statutes of Canada, 1952, as it read in its application to the 1971 taxation year).

I.T. Application Rules: 69 (meaning of "chapter 148 of ...").

(3) Liquidation and dissolution of foreign affiliate — Notwithstanding subsection 69(5), if at any time a taxpayer receives a property (referred to in this subsection as the "distributed property") from a foreign affiliate (referred to in this subsection as the "disposing affiliate") of the taxpayer on a liquidation and dissolution of the disposing affiliate and the distributed property is received in respect of shares of the capital stock of the disposing affiliate that are disposed of on the liquidation and dissolution,

(a) subject to subsections (3.3) and (3.5), the distributed property is deemed to have been disposed of at that time by the disposing affiliate to the taxpayer for proceeds of disposition equal to the relevant cost base (within the meaning assigned by subsection 95(4)) to the disposing affiliate of the distributed property in respect of the taxpayer, immediately before that time, if

(i) the liquidation and dissolution is a qualifying liquidation and dissolution of the disposing affiliate, or

(ii) the distributed property is a share of the capital stock of another foreign affiliate of the taxpayer that was, immediately before that time, excluded property (within the meaning assigned by subsection 95(1)) of the disposing affiliate;

(b) if paragraph (a) does not apply to the distributed property, the distributed property is deemed to have been disposed of at that time by the disposing affiliate to the taxpayer for proceeds of disposition equal to the distributed property's fair market value at that time;

(c) the distributed property is deemed to have been acquired, at that time, by the taxpayer at a cost equal to the amount determined under paragraph (a) or (b) to be the disposing affiliate's proceeds of disposition of the distributed property;

(d) each share (referred to in paragraph (e) and subsections (3.3) and (3.4) as a "disposed share") of a class of the capital stock of the disposing affiliate that is disposed of by the taxpayer on the liquidation and dissolution is deemed to be disposed of for proceeds of disposition equal to the amount determined by the formula

$$A/B$$

where

A is the total of all amounts each of which is the net distribution amount in respect of a distribution of distributed property made, at any time, in respect of the class, and

B is the total number of issued and outstanding shares of the class that are owned by the taxpayer during the liquidation and dissolution; and

(e) if the liquidation and dissolution is a qualifying liquidation and dissolution of the disposing affiliate, any loss of the taxpayer in respect of the disposition of a disposed share is deemed to be nil.

Related Provisions: 88(3.1) — Qualifying liquidation and dissolution; 88(3.2) — Net distribution amount; 88(3.3)–(3.4) — Suppression election; 88(3.5) — Where distributed property is taxable Canadian property; 95(1)"foreign accrual property income"B(b) — Inclusion in FAPI; 95(2)(e) — Rules where liquidation results in distribution to another foreign affiliate (lower tier liquidation).

Notes: The effect of a windup depends on whether it is a qualifying liquidation and dissolution (QLAD) under 88(3.1).

If 88(3) applies to a CFA windup, 69(5) does not: VIEWS doc 2014-0560421I7.

For discussion of 88(3) and the then-proposed amendments see Turner, "Foreign Affiliate Liquidation and Merger Rollovers", 53(3) *Canadian Tax Journal* 640 (2005), at 649-657; Jack et al, "The February 27, 2004 Draft Proposals", 2004 Cdn Tax Foundation conference report, at 20:43-54; Woolford, "Winding Up a Foreign Affiliate", XIII(2) *International Tax Planning* (Federated Press) 930-38 (2006); Barnicke, "Subsection 88(3)", 14(8) *Canadian Tax Highlights* (ctf.ca) 7-8 (Aug. 2006); Meister, "Foreign Affiliate Update" 19 *Canadian Petroleum Tax Journal* (2006) §3; Lockwood & Lopes, "Subsection 88(3)", 61(1) *Canadian Tax Journal* 209-228 (2013).

For discussion since the 2013 amendments see Discepola & Nearing, "Subsection 88(3)", *International Tax* newsletter (*Taxnet Pro* Corporate Tax Centre), Nov. 2013, pp. 1-3; O'Hagan & Buttenham, "Foreign Affiliate Reorganizations", 2013 Cdn Tax Foundation conference report at 20:19-28.

88(3) amended by 2002-2013 technical bill (for liquidations and foreign affiliate dissolutions that begin after Feb. 27, 2004, with an election to apply differently up to Aug. 18, 2011), 1991 technical bill.

Regulations: 5907(2.01) (FAPI — determining earnings derived from disposition).

(3.1) Qualifying liquidation and dissolution — For the purposes of subsections (3), (3.3) and (3.5), a "qualifying liquidation and dissolution" of a foreign affiliate (referred to in this subsection as the "disposing affiliate") of a taxpayer means a liquidation and dissolution of the disposing affiliate in respect of which the taxpayer elects in accordance with prescribed rules and

(a) the taxpayer owns not less than 90% of the issued and outstanding shares of each class of the capital stock of the disposing affiliate throughout the liquidation and dissolution; or

(b) both

(i) the percentage determined by the following formula is greater than or equal to 90%:

$$A/B$$

where

A is the amount, if any, by which

(A) the total of all amounts each of which is the fair market value, at the time at which it is distributed, of a property that is distributed by the disposing affiliate to the taxpayer in the course of the liquidation and dissolution in respect of shares of the capital stock of the disposing affiliate

exceeds

(B) the total of all amounts each of which is an amount owing (other than an unpaid dividend) by, or an obligation of, the disposing affiliate that was assumed or cancelled by the taxpayer in consideration for a property referred to in clause (A), and

B is the amount, if any, by which

(A) the total of all amounts each of which is the fair market value, at the time at which it is distributed, of a property that is distributed by the disposing affiliate to a shareholder of the disposing affiliate in the course of the liquidation and dissolution in respect of shares of the capital stock of the disposing affiliate

exceeds

(B) the total of all amounts each of which is an amount owing (other than an unpaid dividend) by, or an obligation of, the disposing affiliate that was assumed or cancelled by a shareholder of the disposing affiliate in consideration for a property referred to in clause (A), and

(ii) at the time of each distribution of property by the disposing affiliate in the course of the liquidation and dissolution in respect of shares of the capital stock of the disposing affiliate, the taxpayer holds shares of that capital stock that would, if an annual general meeting of the shareholders of the disposing affiliate were held at that time, entitle it to 90% or more of the votes that could be cast under all circumstances at the meeting.

Related Provisions: 13(21.2)(e)(iii)(E)(I)1, 18(15)(b)(iv)(A)(I), 40(3.4)(b)(v)(A)(I), 40(3.5)(c)(iii) — QLAD excluded from pregnant-loss rules; 96(3) — Election by members of partnership.

Notes: For a taxpayer filing a Quebec return, an 88(3.1) election must be copied to Revenu Québec: *Taxation Act* ss. 569.0.0.1, 21.4.6.

88(3.1) added by 2002-2013 technical bill (Part 3 — FA reorganizations), effective on the same basis as amended 88(3).

Regulations: 5911(1) (prescribed rules for election).

(3.2) Net distribution amount — For the purposes of the description of A in paragraph (3)(d), "net distribution amount" in

respect of a distribution of distributed property means the amount determined by the formula

$$A - B$$

where

A is the cost to the taxpayer of the distributed property as determined under paragraph (3)(c), and

B is the total of all amounts each of which is an amount owing (other than an unpaid dividend) by, or an obligation of, the disposing affiliate that was assumed or cancelled by the taxpayer in consideration for the distribution of the distributed property.

Related Provisions: 257 — Formula cannot calculate to less than zero.

Notes: 88(3.2) added by 2002-2013 technical bill (Part 3 — FA reorganizations), effective on the same basis as amended 88(3).

(3.3) Suppression election — For the purposes of paragraph (3)(a), if the liquidation and dissolution is a qualifying liquidation and dissolution of the disposing affiliate and the taxpayer would, in the absence of this subsection and, for greater certainty, after taking into account any election under subsection 93(1), realize a capital gain (the amount of which is referred to in subsection (3.4) as the "capital gain amount") from the disposition of a disposed share, the taxpayer may elect, in accordance with prescribed rules, that distributed property that was, immediately before the disposition, capital property of the disposing affiliate be deemed to have been disposed of by the disposing affiliate to the taxpayer for proceeds of disposition equal to the amount claimed (referred to in subsection (3.4) as the "claimed amount") by the taxpayer in the election.

Related Provisions: 88(3.4) — Conditions for election; 95(1)"foreign accrual property income"E(a) — Property subject to election excluded from FAPI; 96(3) — Election by members of partnership; 257 — Formula cannot calculate to less than zero.

Notes: See Clara Pham & Alex Feness, "CFA Suppression Election: Potential Risks", 3(3) *Canadian Tax Focus* (ctf.ca) 2 (Aug. 2013).

For a taxpayer filing a Quebec return, an 88(3.3) election must be copied to Revenu Québec: *Taxation Act* ss. 569.0.0.3, 21.4.6.

88(3.3) added by 2002-2013 technical bill (Part 3 — FA reorganizations), effective on the same basis as amended 88(3).

Regulations: 5911(1) (prescribed rules for election).

(3.4) Conditions for subsec. (3.3) election — An election under subsection (3.3) in respect of distributed property disposed of in the course of the liquidation and dissolution is not valid unless

(a) the claimed amount in respect of each distributed property does not exceed the amount that would, in the absence of subsection (3.3), be determined under paragraph (3)(a) in respect of the distributed property; and

(b) the amount determined by the following formula does not exceed the total of all amounts each of which is the capital gain amount in respect of a disposed share:

$$A - B$$

where

A is the total of all amounts that would, in the absence of subsection (3.3), be determined under paragraph (3)(a) to be the proceeds of disposition of a distributed property in respect of which an election under subsection (3.3) is made by the taxpayer, and

B is the total of all amounts each of which is the claimed amount in respect of a distributed property referred to in the description of A.

Notes: 88(3.4) added by 2002-2013 technical bill (Part 3 — FA reorganizations), effective on the same basis as amended 88(3).

(3.5) Taxable Canadian property — For the purposes of paragraph (3)(a), the distributed property is deemed to have been disposed of by the disposing affiliate to the taxpayer for proceeds of disposition equal to the adjusted cost base of the distributed property to the disposing affiliate immediately before the time of its disposition, if

(a) the liquidation and dissolution is a qualifying liquidation and dissolution of the disposing affiliate;

(b) the distributed property is, at the time of its disposition, taxable Canadian property (other than treaty-protected property) of the disposing affiliate that is a share of the capital stock of a corporation resident in Canada; and

(c) the taxpayer and the disposing affiliate have jointly elected in accordance with prescribed rules.

Related Provisions: 96(3) — Election by members of partnership.

Notes: For a taxpayer filing a Quebec return, an 88(3.5)(c) election must be copied to Revenu Québec: *Taxation Act* ss. 569.0.0.4, 21.4.6.

88(3.5) added by 2002-2013 technical bill (Part 3 — FA reorganizations), effective on the same basis as amended 88(3).

Regulations: 5911(1) (prescribed rules for 88(3.5)(c)).

(4) Amalgamation deemed not to be acquisition of control — For the purposes of paragraphs (1)(c), (c.2), (d) and (d.2) and, for greater certainty, paragraphs (c.3) to (c.8) and (d.3),

(a) subject to paragraph (c), control of any corporation shall be deemed not to have been acquired because of an amalgamation;

(b) any corporation formed as a result of an amalgamation shall be deemed to be the same corporation as, and a continuation of, each predecessor corporation; and

(c) in the case of an amalgamation described in subsection 87(9), control of a predecessor corporation that was not controlled by the parent before the amalgamation shall be deemed to have been acquired by the parent immediately before the amalgamation.

Notes: For the application of 88(4)(b) to multiple amalgamations, see VIEWS doc 2001-0110363.

88(4) amended by 2001 technical bill (for windings-up that begin after Nov. 1994), 1991 technical bill.

Interpretation Bulletins: IT-488R2: Winding-up of 90%-owned taxable Canadian corporations (cancelled).

Definitions [s. 88]: "acquired" — 88(1)(c.6), (d.2), 88(4), 256(7)–(9); "acquirer" — 88(1)(d.2); "adjusted cost base" — 54, 248(1); "allowable business investment loss", "allowable capital loss" — 38, 248(1); "amount" — 248(1); "arm's length" — 88(1.7), 251(1); "assessment" — 248(1); "associated" — 256; "brother" — 252(2)(b); "business" — 248(1); "business limit" — 125(2)–(5.1), 248(1); "calendar year" — *Interpretation Act* 37(1)(a); "Canadian corporation" — 89(1), 248(1); "Canadian resource property" — 66(15), 248(1); "capital gain" — 39(1)(a), 248(1); "capital gain amount" — 88(3.3); "capital property" — 54, 248(1); "carrying on business" — 253; "cash method" — 28(1), 248(1); "child" — 252(1); "claimed amount" — 88(3.3); "class", "class of shares" — 248(6); "consequence of the death" — 248(8); "control" — 256(6)–(9), 256.1(3); "controlled" — 88(1)(c.6), (d.2), 88(4), 256(6)–(9), 256.1(3); "controlled foreign affiliate" — 95(1), 248(1); "corporation" — 248(1), *Interpretation Act* 35(1); "cost amount" — 248(1); "depreciable property" — 13(21), 88(1)(c.7), 248(1); "disposed share" — 88(3)(d); "disposing affiliate" — 88(3), (3.1); "disposition", "dividend" — 248(1); "distributed property" — 88(3); "eligible amount" — 248(31), (41); "eligible derivative" — 10.1(5); "excluded property" — 95(1); "expenditure year" — 88(1)(e.3); "fair market value — see 69(1) Notes; "farm loss" — 111(8); "farming" — 248(1); "financial institution" — 142.2(1); "filing-due date" — 248(1); "fiscal period" — 249(2)(b), 249.1; "foreign affiliate" — 95(1), 248(1); "foreign resource property" — 66(15), 248(1); "foreign tax year" — 88(1)(e.7); "gift year" — 88(1)(e.6); "individual" — 248(1); "ineligible property" — 88(1)(c) [before (iii)]; "initial designation" — 88(1.8); "investment tax credit" — 127(9), 248(1); "life insurance capital dividend" — 83(2.1), 248(1); "limited partnership loss" — 248(1); "mark-to-market property" — 142.2(1); "Minister" — 248(1); "net capital loss" — 111(8), 248(1); "net distribution amount" — 88(3.2); "non-capital loss" — 111(8), 248(1); "paid-up capital" — 89(1), 248(1); "parent" — 88(1), (1.1), (1.2); "partnership" — see 96(1) Notes; "payable" — 84(7), 89(3); "person" — 248(1); "pre-1972 capital surplus on hand" — 88(2.1), (2.2); "prescribed", "property" — 248(1); "qualified expenditure" — 37.1(5), 88(1.41); "qualifying income limit" — 127.1(2); "qualifying liquidation and dissolution" — 88(3.1); "related" — 251(2)–(6); "relevant cost base" — 95(4); "resident in Canada" — 250; "restricted farm loss" — 31, 248(1); "series of transactions" — 248(10); "share" — 88(1)(c.9), 248(1); "shareholder" — 248(1); "sister" — 252(2)(c); "specified class" — 88(1)(c.8); "specified debt obligation" — 142.2(1); "specified future tax consequence" — 248(1); "specified person" — 88(1)(c.2)(i); "specified property" — 88(1)(c.4); "specified shareholder" — 88(1)(c.2)(iii), 248(1); "specified subsidiary corporation" — 88(1)(c.5); "subsidiary" — 88(1), (1.1), (1.2); "subsidiary wholly-owned corporation" — 248(1); "substituted" — 248(5); "substitution" — 88(1)(c.3); "tax-free surplus balance" — Reg. 5905(5.5); "tax payable" — 248(2); "taxable Canadian corporation" — 89(1), 248(1); "taxable Canadian property" — 248(1); "taxable capital gain" — 38, 248(1); "taxable dividend" — 89(1), 248(1); "taxable income" — 2(2), 248(1); "taxation year" — 249; "taxpayer", "treaty-protected property" — 248(1); "trust" — 104(1), 108(1); "writing" — *Interpretation Act* 35(1).

I.T. Application Rules [s. 88]: 20(1.2).

Income Tax Folios [s. 88]: S4-F7-C1: Amalgamations of Canadian corporations [replaces IT-474R2].

Interpretation Bulletins [s. 88]: IT-188R: Sale of accounts receivable; IT-243R4: Dividend refund to private corporations.

88.1 (1) [SIFT wind-up —] Application — Subsection (2) applies to a trust's distribution of property to a taxpayer if

(a) the distribution is a SIFT trust wind-up event;

(b) the trust is

(i) a SIFT wind-up entity whose only beneficiary, at all times at which the trust makes a distribution that is a SIFT trust wind-up event, is a taxable Canadian corporation, or

(ii) a trust whose only beneficiary, at all times at which the trust makes a distribution that is a SIFT trust wind-up event, is another trust described by subparagraph (i);

(c) where the trust is a SIFT wind-up entity, the distribution occurs no more than 60 days after the earlier of

(i) the first SIFT trust wind-up event of the trust, and

(ii) the first distribution to the trust that is a SIFT trust wind-up event of another trust; and

(d) if the property is shares of the capital stock of a taxable Canadian corporation,

(i) the property was not acquired by the trust on a distribution to which subsection 107(3.1) applies, and

(ii) the trust elects in writing, filed with the Minister on or before the trust's filing-due date for its taxation year that includes the time of the distribution, that this section apply to the distribution.

Notes: See Notes at end of 88.1.

(2) SIFT trust wind-up event — If this subsection applies to a trust's distribution of property to a taxpayer, subsections 88(1) to (1.7), and section 87 and paragraphs 256(7)(a) to (e) as they apply for the purposes of those subsections, apply, with any modifications that the circumstances require, as if

(a) the trust were a taxable Canadian corporation (in this subsection referred to as the "subsidiary") that is not a private corporation;

(b) where the taxpayer is a SIFT wind-up entity, the taxpayer were a taxable Canadian corporation that is not a private corporation;

(c) the distribution were a winding-up of the subsidiary;

(d) the taxpayer's interest as a beneficiary under the trust were shares of a single class of shares of the capital stock of the subsidiary owned by the taxpayer;

(e) paragraph 88(1)(b) deemed the taxpayer's proceeds of disposition of the shares described in paragraph (d) and owned by the taxpayer immediately before the distribution to be equal to the adjusted cost base to the taxpayer of the taxpayer's interest as a beneficiary under the trust immediately before the distribution;

(f) each trust, a majority-interest beneficiary (in this subsection, within the meaning assigned by section 251.1) of which is another trust that is by operation of this subsection treated as if it were a corporation, were a corporation; and

(g) except for the purposes of subsections 88(1.1) and (1.2), the taxpayer last acquired control of the subsidiary and of each corporation (including a trust that is by operation of this subsection treated as if it were a corporation) controlled by the subsidiary at the time, if any, at which the taxpayer last became a majority-interest beneficiary of the trust.

Related Provisions: 80.01(5.1) — Debt settlement on wind-up event; 85.1(7), (8) — Alternate mechanism for rollover of SIFT units to corporation; 88.1(1) — Conditions for 88.1(2) to apply; 107(2) — Regular trust rollout rules do not apply; 107(3), (3.1) — Rollout of SIFT trust assets to beneficiaries.

Notes: 88.1(2) allows a rollout of a SIFT trust's assets to a beneficiary corporation as though it were a windup into a parent corporation under 88(1), if done before 2013 (see 248(1)"SIFT trust wind-up event"(a)). This allowed a SIFT trust to convert back to corporate form, in advance of the tax on SIFT trust distributions applying in 2011 (see

122.1(2) and Notes to 104(16)). Where the beneficiaries are multiple taxpayers, see the rollout in 107(3)–(3.1). For a different mechanism permitting a beneficiary to roll the trust units into a corporation, see 85.1(7), (8).

For a trust filing a Quebec return, an 88.1(1)(d)(ii) election must be copied to Revenu Québec: *Taxation Act* ss. 569.0.1, 21.4.6.

For articles discussing these rules see Notes to 85.1(8).

When transferring assets out of a trust under 88.1, consider GST, HST, provincial sales tax and land transfer tax on asset transfers.

Where a trust transferred its assets under 88.1 and wound up, Rule 29 of the *Tax Court of Canada Rules* permitted another entity (such as the corp that received the assets and would be liable for the trust's tax debt under 160(1)) to continue the appeal at the TCC's discretion: *Clearwater Seafoods*, 2013 FCA 180.

See also VIEWS docs 2009-0317211E5 (cost of partnership interest acquired on windup is determined under 87(2)(e.1)); 2011-0394271I7 (filing-due date is not affected by Reg. 205(2) information return deadline).

88.1 added by 2008 budget bill #2, effective July 15, 2008, but ignore 88.1(1)(c) in its application to a trust's distribution of property before May 12, 2009.

Definitions [s. 88.1]: "adjusted cost base" — 54, 248(1); "class of shares" — 248(6); "corporation" — 248(1), *Interpretation Act* 35(1); "disposition", "filing-due date, "Minister"" — 248(1); "private corporation" — 89(1), 248(1); "property", "share", "SIFT trust wind-up event", "SIFT wind-up entity" — 248(1); "taxable Canadian corporation" — 89(1), 248(1); "taxation year" — 249; "taxpayer" — 248(1); "trust" — 104(1), 248(1), (3); "writing" — *Interpretation Act* 35(1).

89. (1) Definitions — In this Subdivision,

"adjusted taxable income" of a corporation for a taxation year is the amount determined by the formula

$$A - B - C$$

where

A is

(a) unless paragraph (b) applies, the corporation's taxable income for the taxation year, and

(b) if the corporation is a deposit insurance corporation in the taxation year, nil,

B is the amount determined by multiplying the amount, if any, deducted by the corporation under subsection 125(1) for the taxation year by the quotient obtained by dividing 100 by the rate of the deduction provided under that subsection for the taxation year, and

C is

(a) if the corporation is a Canadian-controlled private corporation in the taxation year, the lesser of the corporation's aggregate investment income for the taxation year and the corporation's taxable income for the taxation year, and

(b) in any other case, nil;

Related Provisions: 89(1)"general rate income pool"A:D — Application of adjusted taxable income; 257 — Formula cannot calculate to less than zero.

Notes: 89(1)"adjusted taxable income" added by 2008 budget bill #2, effective for 2006 and later taxation years. It replaces the former "D-E-F" in the formula in 89(1)"general rate income pool".

"Canadian corporation" at any time means a corporation that is resident in Canada at that time and was

(a) incorporated in Canada, or

(b) resident in Canada throughout the period that began on June 18, 1971 and that ends at that time,

and, for greater certainty, a corporation formed at any particular time by the amalgamation or merger of, or by a plan of arrangement or other corporate reorganization in respect of, 2 or more corporations (otherwise than as a result of the acquisition of property of one corporation by another corporation, pursuant to the purchase of the property by the other corporation or as a result of the distribution of the property to the other corporation on the winding-up of the corporation) is a Canadian corporation because of paragraph (a) only if

(c) that reorganization took place under the laws of Canada or a province, and

(d) each of those corporations was, immediately before the particular time, a Canadian corporation;

Related Provisions: 219.1(1) — Tax when corporation ceases to be Canadian corporation; 248(1)"Canadian corporation" — Definition applies to entire Act; 248(1)"corporation" — meaning of "incorporated in Canada"; 250 — Resident in Canada.

Notes: Definition "Canadian corporation" amended by 1993 technical bill to add everything after para. (b), effective June 15, 1994.

Income Tax Folios: S4-F7-C1: Amalgamations of Canadian corporations [replaces IT-474R2].

Interpretation Bulletins: IT-98R2: Investment corporations (cancelled); IT-291R3: Transfer of property to a corporation under subsection 85(1); IT-458R2: Canadian-controlled private corporation.

"capital dividend account" of a corporation at any particular time means the amount, if any, by which the total of

(a) the amount, if any, by which the total of

(i) the total of all amounts each of which is the amount if any, by which

(A) the amount of the corporation's capital gain — computed without reference to subclause 52(3)(a)(ii)(A)(II) and subparagraph 53(1)(b)(ii) — from the disposition (other than a disposition under paragraph 40(3.1)(a) or subsection 40(12) or a disposition that is the making of a gift after December 8, 1997 that is not a gift described in subsection 110.1(1)) of a property in the period beginning at the beginning of its first taxation year that began after the corporation last became a private corporation and that ended after 1971 and ending immediately before the particular time (in this definition referred to as "the period")

exceeds the total of

(B) the portion of the capital gain referred to in clause (A) that is the corporation's taxable capital gain,

(B.1) the corporation's taxable capital gain from a disposition in the period under subsection 40(12), and

(C) the portion of the amount, if any, by which the amount determined under clause (A) exceeds the amount determined under clause (B) from the disposition by it of a property that can reasonably be regarded as having accrued while the property, or a property for which it was substituted,

(I) except in the case of a disposition of a designated property, was a property of a corporation (other than a private corporation, an investment corporation, a mortgage investment corporation or a mutual fund corporation),

(II) where, after November 26, 1987, the property became a property of a Canadian-controlled private corporation (otherwise than by reason of a change in the residence of one or more shareholders of the corporation), was a property of a corporation controlled directly or indirectly in any manner whatever by one or more non-resident persons, or

(III) where, after November 26, 1987, the property became a property of a private corporation that was not exempt from tax under this Part on its taxable income, was a property of a corporation exempt from tax under this Part on its taxable income, and

(i.1) all amounts each of which is an amount in respect of a distribution made, in the period and after September 15, 2016, by a trust to the corporation in respect of capital gains of the trust equal to the lesser of

(A) the amount, if any, by which

(I) the amount of the distribution

exceeds

(II) the amount designated under subsection 104(21) by the trust in respect of the net taxable capital gains of the trust attributable to those capital gains, and

(B) the amount determined by the formula

$$A \times B$$

where

A is the fraction or whole number determined when 1 is subtracted from the reciprocal of the fraction under paragraph 38(a) applicable to the trust for the year, and

B is the amount referred to in subclause (A)(II),

exceeds

(ii) the total of all amounts each of which is the amount, if any, by which

(A) the amount of the corporation's capital loss — computed without reference to subclause 52(3)(a)(ii)(A)(II) and subparagraph 53(1)(b)(ii) — from the disposition (other than a disposition under subsection 40(3.12) or a disposition that is the making of a gift after December 8, 1997 that is not a gift described in subsection 110.1(1)) of a property in the period

exceeds the total of

(B) the part of the capital loss referred to in clause (A) that is the corporation's allowable capital loss, and

(C) the portion of the amount, if any, by which the amount determined under clause (A) exceeds the amount determined under clause (B) from the disposition by it of a property that can reasonably be regarded as having accrued while the property, or a property for which it was substituted,

(I) except in the case of a disposition of a designated property, was a property of a corporation (other than a private corporation, an investment corporation, a mortgage investment corporation or a mutual fund corporation),

(II) where, after November 26, 1987, the property became a property of a Canadian-controlled private corporation (otherwise than by reason of a change in the residence of one or more shareholders of the corporation), was a property of a corporation controlled directly or indirectly in any manner whatever by one or more non-resident persons, or

(III) where, after November 26, 1987, the property became a property of a private corporation that was not exempt from tax under this Part on its taxable income, was a property of a corporation exempt from tax under this Part on its taxable income,

(b) all amounts each of which is an amount in respect of a dividend received by the corporation on a share of the capital stock of another corporation in the period, which amount was, by virtue of subsection 83(2), not included in computing the income of the corporation,

(c) the total of all amounts each of which is an amount required to have been included under this paragraph as it read in its application to a taxation year that ended before February 28, 2000,

(c.1) the amount, if any, by which

(i) ½ of the total of all amounts each of which is an amount required by paragraph 14(1)(b) (as it read before 2017) to be included in computing the corporation's income in respect of a business carried on by the corporation for a taxation year that is included in the period and that ended after February 27, 2000 and before October 18, 2000,

exceeds

(ii) where the corporation has deducted an amount under subsection 20(4.2) in respect of a debt established by it to have become a bad debt in a taxation year that is included in the period and that ended after February 27, 2000 and before October 18, 2000, or has an allowable capital loss for such a year because of the application of subsection 20(4.3), the amount determined by the formula

$$V + W$$

where

V is ½ of the value determined for A under subsection 20(4.2) in respect of the corporation for the last such taxation year that ended in the period, and

W is ⅓ of the value determined for B under subsection 20(4.2) in respect of the corporation for the last such taxation year that ended in the period, and

(iii) in any other case, nil,

(c.2) the amount, if any, by which

(i) the total of all amounts each of which is an amount required by paragraph 14(1)(b) (as it read before 2017) or subparagraph 13(38)(d)(iii) to be included in computing the corporation's income in respect of a business carried on by the corporation for a taxation year that is included in the period and that ends after October 17, 2000,

exceeds

(ii) where the corporation has deducted an amount under subsection 20(4.2) in respect of a debt established by it to have become a bad debt in a taxation year that is included in the period and that ends after October 17, 2000, or has an allowable capital loss for such a year because of the application of subsection 20(4.3), the amount determined by the formula

$$X + Y$$

where

X is the value determined for A under subsection 20(4.2) in respect of the corporation for the last such taxation year that ended in the period, and

Y is ⅓ of the value determined for B under subsection 20(4.2) in respect of the corporation for the last such taxation year that ended in the period, and

(iii) in any other case, nil,

(d) the amount, if any, by which the total of

(i) all amounts each of which is the proceeds of a life insurance policy of which the corporation was a beneficiary on or before June 28, 1982 received by the corporation in the period and after 1971 in consequence of the death of any person, and

(ii) all amounts each of which is the proceeds of a life insurance policy (other than an LIA policy) of which the corporation was not a beneficiary on or before June 28, 1982 received by the corporation in the period and after May 23, 1985 in consequence of the death of any person

exceeds the total of all amounts each of which is

(iii) the "adjusted cost basis" (in this paragraph as defined in subsection 148(9)), immediately before the death, of

(A) if the death occurs before March 22, 2016, a policy referred to in subparagraph (i) or (ii) to the corporation, and

(B) if the death occurs after March 21, 2016, a policyholder's interest in a policy referred to in subparagraph (i) or (ii),

(iv) if the policy is a 10/8 policy immediately before the death and the death occurs after 2013, the amount outstanding, immediately before the death, of the borrowing that is described in subparagraph (a)(i) of the definition "10/8 policy" in subsection 248(1) in respect of the policy,

(v) if the death occurs after March 21, 2016, an interest in the policy was disposed of by a policyholder (other than a taxable Canadian corporation) after 1999 and before March 22,

2016 and subsection 148(7) applied to the disposition, the total of

(A) the amount, if any, by which the fair market value of consideration given in respect of the disposition exceeds the total of

(I) the greater of the amount determined under subparagraph 148(7)(a)(i) in respect of the disposition and the adjusted cost basis to the policyholder of the interest immediately before the disposition, and

(II) the amount by which the paid-up capital of any class of the capital stock of a corporation resulting from the disposition is reduced at the beginning of March 22, 2016 because of the application of paragraphs 148(7)(c) and (f) in respect of the disposition, and

(B) if the paid-up capital in respect of a class of shares of the capital stock of a corporation was increased before March 22, 2016 as described in subparagraph 148(7)(f)(iii) in respect of the disposition, the amount, if any, by which the total reduction in the paid-up capital in respect of that class — not exceeding the amount of that increase — after that increase and before March 22, 2016 (except to the extent that the amount of the reduction was deemed by subsection 84(4) or (4.1) to be a dividend received by a taxpayer) exceeds the amount determined under subparagraph 148(7)(a)(i) in respect of the disposition, or

(vi) if the death occurs after March 21, 2016, an interest in the policy was disposed of by a policyholder (other than a taxable Canadian corporation) after 1999 and before March 22, 2016 and subsection 148(7) applied to the disposition, the amount, if any, determined by the formula

$$A - B$$

where

A is the amount, if any, by which the lesser of the adjusted cost basis to the policyholder of the interest immediately before the disposition and the fair market value of consideration given in respect of the disposition exceeds the amount determined under subparagraph 148(7)(a)(i) in respect of the disposition, and

B is the absolute value of the negative amount, if any, that would be, in the absence of section 257, the adjusted cost basis, immediately before the death, of the interest in the policy,

(e) the amount of the corporation's life insurance capital dividend account immediately before May 24, 1985,

(f) all amounts each of which is an amount in respect of a distribution made, in the period and before September 16, 2016, by a trust to the corporation in respect of capital gains of the trust equal to the lesser of

(i) the amount, if any, by which

(A) the amount of the distribution,

exceeds

(B) the amount designated under subsection 104(21) by the trust (other than a designation to which subsection 104(21.4), as it read in its application to the corporation's last taxation year that began before November 2011, applied) in respect of the net taxable capital gains of the trust attributable to those capital gains, and

(ii) the amount determined by the formula

$$A \times B$$

where

A is the fraction or whole number determined when 1 is subtracted from the reciprocal of the fraction under paragraph 38(a) applicable to the trust for the year, and

B is the amount referred to in clause (i)(B), and

(g) all amounts each of which is an amount in respect of a distribution made by a trust to the corporation in the period in respect of a dividend (other than a taxable dividend) paid on a share of the capital stock of another corporation resident in Canada to the trust during a taxation year of the trust throughout which the trust was resident in Canada equal to the lesser of

(i) the amount of the distribution, and

(ii) the amount designated under subsection 104(20) by the trust in respect of the corporation in respect of that dividend,

exceeds the total of all capital dividends that became payable by the corporation after the commencement of the period and before the particular time;

Related Provisions: 34.2(5) — CDA determined without reference to 34.2; 83(2) — Election to pay capital dividend out of capital dividend account; 83(2.3) — Life insurance proceeds included under 89(1)"capital dividend account"(d); 87(2)(z.1) — Amalgamations; 88(2)(a) — Winding-up of a Canadian corp; 89(1.1) — CDA where control acquired; 89(1.2) — CDA where corp ceases to be exempt; 89(2) — Where corporation is beneficiary; 104(20) — Flow-through of capital dividend through trust; 131(11)(e) — Rules re prescribed labour-sponsored venture capital corps; 141.1 — Insurance corporation deemed not to be private corp; 248(5) — Substituted property; 248(8) — Meaning of "consequence" of death; 256(5.1), (6.2) — Controlled directly or indirectly; 257 — Formula cannot calculate to less than zero.

Notes: The capital dividend account (CDA) is used to pay out tax-free capital dividends under 83(2). Although the definition is horrendously complex, the CDA is basically the "untaxed ½" (¼ before Feb. 28, 2000, ⅓ from then through Oct. 17, 2000) of capital gains (see cls. (a)(i)(A) and (B) of the definition). Capital dividends paid out to a corporation go into the recipient corporation's CDA to preserve the flow-through of the "untaxed ½" of capital gains; para. (b). See Income Tax Folio S3-F2-C1. For a spreadsheet to calculate CDA see taxtemplates.ca "Capital Dividend Account".

Note that where 38(a.1) or (a.2) applies so that none (instead of 1/2) of a gain is taxed (donation of publicly listed securities, ecological property), the effect of (a)(i) is that the CDA is the "untaxed full amount", rather than the "untaxed 1/2"! This offers an extra bonus to corporations to make such donations. See VIEWS doc 2015-0613761E5; Drache. "Donations of Shares from Holding Companies", xxxvi(18) *The Canadian Taxpayer* (Carswell) 142-43 (Sept. 26, 2014). (This does not apply to flow-through shares where (a)(i)(B.1) applies: see 2012-0441151E5.)

Where a capital dividend is paid to a spousal trust, see VIEWS doc 2004-0060161E5; where one is paid to a trust of which a corporation is beneficiary, see 2010-0358471E5, 2012-0469591E5.

A credit to the CDA will occur on share redemption where a corporation redeems shares held by another corporation, triggering 84(3) and 55(2), but makes a 55(5)(f) designation: VIEWS doc 2009-0310251E5.

Para. (a): A deemed capital gain under 80(12) is included under (a)(i)(A): doc 2011-0412541E5. A 40(3.1) gain is not: 2016-0678361E5. Where 40(3.6) or 112(3) deems a loss to be nil, the 39(1)(b) capital loss is nil, so the CDA is not reduced under (a)(ii)(A): 2014-0540361E5.

Para. (b) does not apply to amounts the corporation received when it was a public corporation, per the definition of "the period" in (a)(i)(A): VIEWS doc 2002-0156545.

Para. (c.2) allows an addition for eligible capital property income inclusion under pre-2017 14(1)(b), but 14(1)(b) applied only at year-end: see Notes to 83(2). For a corporate partner, see VIEWS doc 2006-0215001E5 and Jon Gilbert, "Capital Dividend Timing Following a Sale of Partnership Goodwill", XI(3) *Business Vehicles* (Federated Press) 592-93 (2007).

Para. (d) adds life insurance proceeds, minus the adjusted cost basis, to the CDA. See Income Tax Folio S3-F2-C1 ¶1.59-1.72; VIEWS doc 2011-0407291C6; *Rogers Enterprises*, 2020 TCC 92. The insurer can be non-resident: 2005-0132331C6.

On whether a corp has "received" the proceeds see 2012-0435641C6. In (d)(ii), the corp is not the beneficiary of the policy, so a CDA increase was allowed where insurance proceeds paid off a bank loan owing by the corp: *Innovative Installation*, 2010 FCA 285. See Peters, "Creditor Insurance", 1975 *Tax Topics* (CCH) 1-3 (Jan. 14, 2010); Wark & Stephens, "Creditor Insurance Revisited", XVI(1) *Insurance Planning [IP]* (Federated Press) 994-95 (2009); Friedlan, "Insurance Proceeds", XVII(2) *IP* 1078-80 (2011) [also in 2011 STEP Canada conference, contact memberservices@step.ca]. CRA accepts *Innovative Installation* for "similar or identical" facts (not insurance proceeds paid through a trust: 2011-0399771C6): 2011-0401431C6, 2011-0401991E5, 2012-0447171E5, 2012-0453231C6 [2012 APFF q.19]; 2014-0555581E5 (policy assigned to bank as collateral for loan); May 2011 ICAA roundtable (tinyurl.com/cra-abtax), q. 7, and will revise IT-430R3 para. 6 (but will issue no Folio beyond S3-F2-C1: 2020-0842281C6 [2020 CALU q.8]).

For a ruling on unexpected proceeds from a policy payable to a predecessor corp, see doc 2015-0624611R3. On the "fund value" portion of a payment from a universal life policy: 2020-0842151C6 [2020 CALU q.3]. Return of premiums due to death from an excluded activity: 2020-0842141C6 [2020 CALU q.2]. Multiple beneficiaries cannot prorate the ACB: 2017-0690311C6 [2017 CLHIA q.1], 2018-0745811C6 [2018 CALU q.2]; Finance stated at 2017 APFF that this will be addressed. In *Ribeiro Estate v.*

Braun Nursery, 2009 CarswellOnt 171 (Ont. SCJ), a corp that received this increase and was repurchasing the deceased employee's shares (per a shareholders' agreement) was not required to elect that the resulting deemed dividend be treated as a capital dividend; it used the CDA to pay capital dividends to other shareholders. See also Stephens, "The Denille Case", XVIII(3) *Insurance Planning* (Federated Press) 1160-62 (2012); and Reg. 306(1) Notes.

After assignment of corporate-owned life insurance so that the corp has deducted premiums under 20(1)(e.2), can insurance proceeds increase the CDA? See IT-430R3 para. 6; docs 2004-006814E5, 2008-0289441C6; Wark, "Collateral Insurance and the Capital Dividend Account", XI(1) *Insurance Planning [IP]* (Federated Press) 690-91 (2004); Flannery, "Creditor Insurance", XVI(1) *IP* 946-47 (2008).

Before (d)(iii)(B) was added in 2016, CDA was increased by the full proceeds, without deducting ACB if the policy was held by a different corp: *Rogers Enterprises*, 2020 TCC 92, para. 86; and profiting from this rule did not violate GAAR.

Subparas. (d)(v)-(vi) are an anti-avoidance measure announced in the 2016 Budget under "Distributions Involving Life Insurance Policies".

Under *para. (g)*, a capital dividend received by a trust, paid out to a corporate beneficiary and designated under 104(20) is added to the CDA only at the trust's year-end: VIEWS doc 2010-0363191C6.

A capital gains reserve under 40(1)(a)(iii) is brought in to the CDA on the first day of the next taxation year: VIEWS doc 2004-0090461E5.

Capital gains of a foreign affiliate, taxed in Canada as FAPI, cannot be included in the CDA: VIEWS doc 2007-0228301E5.

Where a non-profit corporation ceases to be exempt, 89(1.2) reduces its CDA to zero: VIEWS doc 2012-0463361R3.

In *Sutherland v. Birks*, 2003 CanLII 39961 (Ont CA), a minority shareholder oppression claim, the Court ordered the CDA to be allocated *pro rata* to the minority [Sohmer, "The Tax Expert", xxvi(13) *The Canadian Taxpayer* (Carswell) 102-04 (June 29, 2004)].

To request verification of the CDA balance use T2 Schedule 89, providing the corp's calculations; CRA will verify as a "courtesy", and only once every 3 years unless it is filed with a T2054 electing a capital dividend: tinyurl.com/t2sch89. As of 2017, after the balance is verified, it is recorded on My Business Account (see May 2016 Alberta CPA (tinyurl.com/cra-abtax), q.1).

For more on the CDA see Hoegner, "The Best Things in Life are (Tax-)Free", 50(4) *Canadian Tax Journal* 1426-63 (2002); Barrett, "Capital Dividend 101", 29(10) *Money & Family Law* (Carswell) 79-80 (Oct. 2014) [effect on spousal support and division of assets]; Hamelin, "CDAs and Surplus Stripping", 19(3) *Tax for the Owner-Manager* (ctf.ca) 3-4 (July 2019); Stevens, "Effective Use of the Capital Dividend Account", 2019 Ontario Tax Conference 4 (ctf.ca, 95pp); Goldberg, "Unlocking Liquidity in Corporate Capital Losses — Planning to Maximize the [CDA]" (3 parts), 2522 *Tax Topics* (CCH) 4-7 (July 7, 2020), 2524 1-4 (July 20) and 2527 1-4 (Aug. 11).

Para. (a) opening words amended to add "the total of"; (a)(i.1) added; and (f) opening words amended to add "and before September 16, 2016"; all by 2017 budget bill #2, effective Dec. 14, 2017.

Subparas. (c.1)(i) and (c.2)(i) amended by 2016 budget bill #2, effective 2017 (as part of changing the eligible capital property rules to CCA Class 14.1: see Notes to 20(1)(b)), to add "(as it read before 2017)" to both and refer to 13(38)(d)(iii) in (c.2)(i).

Subpara. (d)(iii) amended and (d)(v), (vi) added by 2016 budget bill #2, effective Dec. 15, 2016. Before that date, read:

> (d)(iii) the adjusted cost basis (within the meaning assigned by subsection 148(9)) of a policy referred to in subparagraph (i) or (ii) to the corporation immediately before the death, or

Cls. (a)(i)(A) and (a)(ii)(A) amended by 2016 budget bill #1, for dispositions after April 20, 2015, to change 52(3)(a)(ii) references to 52(3)(a)(ii)(A)(II).

Para. (d) amended by 2013 budget bill #2, for taxation years that end after March 20, 2013, to add LIA policy and 10/8 policy exclusions (see Notes to 248(1)"LIA policy" and "10/8 policy").

Cl. (a)(i)(A) amended by 2002-2013 technical bill (Part 5 — technical). The reference to 40(3.1)(a) was added for dispositions under 40(3.1)(a) that occur after Oct. 2011. The words "computed without reference to subparagraphs 52(3)(a)(ii) and 53(1)(b)(ii)" were added for dispositions after Nov. 8, 2006 (on this amendment, see VIEWS docs 2011-0421141E5, 2011-0423861E5); and the amendment below by 2011 budget bill #2 was re-done.

Cl. (a)(i)(A) amended to refer to 40(12), and (a)(i)(B.1) added, by 2011 budget bill #2, for dispositions that occur after March 21, 2011.

Cl. (a)(ii)(A) amended by 2002-2013 technical bill. The reference to 40(3.12) was added for 40(3.12) dispositions after Oct. 2011, other than those relating to amounts deemed by 40(3.1) to have been a gain from a pre-Nov. 2011 disposition. (In *Gladwin Realty*, 2020 FCA 142, using 40(3.12) before this amendment violated GAAR; paras. 56-66 discuss the object and spirit of the CDA regime.) The exclusion of 52(3)(a)(ii) and 53(1)(b)(ii) was added for dispositions after Nov. 8, 2006.

Cl. (f)(i)(B) amended by 2002-2013 technical bill (Part 5 — technical), effective for taxation years that begin after Oct. 2011, to change "subsection 104(21.4) applies" to

"subsection 104(21.4), as it read in its application to the corporation's last taxation year that began before Nov. 2011, applied". 104(21.4), now repealed, read:

> (21.4) Deemed gains [transitional for 2000] — Where an amount is designated in respect of a beneficiary by a trust for a particular taxation year of the trust that includes February 28, 2000 or October 17, 2000 and that amount is, because of subsection (21), deemed to be a taxable capital gain of the beneficiary from the disposition of capital property for the taxation year of the beneficiary in which the particular taxation year of the trust ends (in this subsection referred to as the "allocated gain"),
>
> (a) the beneficiary is deemed to have realized capital gains (in this subsection referred to as the "deemed gains") from the disposition of capital property in the beneficiary's taxation year in which the particular taxation year ends equal to the amount, if any, by which
>
> > (i) the amount determined when the amount of the allocated gain is divided by the fraction in paragraph 38(a) that applies to the trust for the particular taxation year
>
> exceeds
>
> > (ii) the amount claimed by the beneficiary not exceeding the beneficiary's exempt capital gains balance for the year in respect of the trust;
>
> (b) notwithstanding subsection (21) and except as a consequence of the application of paragraph (a), the amount of the allocated gain shall not be included in computing the beneficiary's income for the beneficiary's taxation year in which the particular taxation year ends;
>
> (c) the trust shall disclose to the beneficiary in prescribed form the portion of the deemed gains that are in respect of capital gains realized on dispositions of property that occurred before February 28, 2000, after February 27, 2000 and before October 18, 2000, and after October 17, 2000 and, if it does not do so, the deemed gains are deemed to be in respect of capital gains realized on dispositions of property that occurred before February 28, 2000; and
>
> (d) where a trust so elects under this paragraph in its return of income for the year,
>
> > (i) the portion of the deemed gains that are in respect of capital gains from dispositions of property that occurred before February 28, 2000 is deemed to be that proportion of the deemed gains that the number of days that are in the particular year and before February 28, 2000 is of the number of days that are in the particular year,
>
> > (ii) the portion of the deemed gains that are in respect of capital gains from dispositions of property that occurred in the year and in the period that began at the beginning of February 28, 2000 and ended at the end of October 17, 2000, is deemed to be that proportion of the deemed gains that the number of days that are in the year and in that period is of the number of days that are in the particular year, and
>
> > (iii) the portion of the deemed gains that are in respect of capital gains from dispositions of property that occurred in the year and in the period that begins at the beginning of October 18, 2000 and ends at the end of the particular year, is deemed to be that proportion of the deemed gains that the number of days that are in the year and in that period is of the number of days that are in the particular year; and
>
> (e) no amount may be claimed by the beneficiary under subsection 39.1(3) in respect of the allocated gain.

Paras. (f) and (g) added by 2001 technical bill, effective for elections for capital dividends that become payable after 1997.

Para. (c) amended and (c.1), (c.2) added by 2000 Budget, for taxation years that end after Feb. 27, 2000. For earlier years (needed for current para. (c)), read:

> (c) all amounts each of which is an amount in respect of a business carried on by the corporation at any time in the period, equal to the amount, if any, by which the total of
>
> > (i) where the period commenced before the corporation's adjustment time, the amount, if any, by which
>
> > > (A) the total of the amounts in respect of the business required to be included in the calculation of the corporation's cumulative eligible capital by reason of the description of E in the definition "cumulative eligible capital" in subsection 14(5) with respect to that portion of the period preceding its adjustment time
>
> > exceeds the total of
>
> > > (B) the cumulative eligible capital of the corporation in respect of the business at the commencement of the period, and
>
> > > (C) ½ of the total of the eligible capital expenditures in respect of the business that were made or incurred by the corporation during that portion of the period preceding its adjustment time,
>
> > (ii) ⅓ of the total of the amounts in respect of the business required to be included in the calculation of the corporation's cumulative eligible capital by reason of the description of E in the definition "cumulative eligible capital" in subsection 14(5) with respect to that portion of the period following its adjustment time, and

(iii) ⅓ of all amounts received in the period that were required to be included in the corporation's income by reason of paragraph 12(1)(i.1)

exceeds the total of

(iv) where the period commenced after the corporation's adjustment time, ⅓ of its cumulative eligible capital in respect of the business at the commencement of the period,

(v) ¼ of the total of the eligible capital expenditures in respect of the business made or incurred by the corporation with respect to that portion of the period after its adjustment time,

(vi) where the period commenced before the corporation's adjustment time, ½ of the amount, if any, by which the total of the amounts determined in respect of the corporation under clauses (i)(B) and (C) exceeds the amount determined in respect of the corporation under clause (i)(A), and

(vii) ⅓ of all amounts deducted by the corporation under subsection 20(4.2) in respect of debts established by it to have become bad debts during the period,

Definition earlier amended by 1997 Budget bill (for dispositions made after Dec. 8, 1997, other than a disposition made under a written agreement made by that date), 1991 technical bill. 89(1)"capital dividend account" was 89(1)(b) before RSC 1985 (5th Supp) consolidation for tax years ending after Nov. 1991.

I.T. Application Rules: 32.1(4) (where dividend paid or payable before May 7, 1974).

Income Tax Folios: S3-F2-C1: Capital Dividends [replaces IT-66R6]; S4-F8-C1: Business investment losses [replaces IT-484R2].

Interpretation Bulletins: IT-123R4: Disposition of eligible capital property; IT-123R6: Transactions involving eligible capital property; IT-149R4: Winding-up dividend; IT-430R3: Life insurance proceeds received by a private corporation or a partnership as a consequence of death.

I.T. Technical News: 10 (life insurance policy used as security for indebtedness); 25 (*Silicon Graphics* case — dispersed control is not control).

Advance Tax Rulings: ATR-54: Reduction of paid-up capital.

Forms: T2 Sched. 89: Request for capital dividend account balance verification.

"designated property" means

(a) any property of a private corporation that last became a private corporation before November 13, 1981 and that was acquired by it

(i) before November 13, 1981, or

(ii) after November 12, 1981 pursuant to an agreement in writing entered into on or before that date,

(b) any property of a private corporation that was acquired by it from another private corporation with whom the private corporation was not dealing at arm's length (otherwise than by virtue of a right referred to in paragraph 251(5)(b)) at the time the property was acquired, where the property was a designated property of the other private corporation,

(c) a share acquired by a private corporation in a transaction to which section 51, subsection 85(1) or section 85.1, 86 or 87 applied in exchange for another share that was a designated property of the corporation, or

(d) a replacement property (within the meaning assigned by section 44) for a designated property disposed of by virtue of an event referred to in paragraph (b), (c) or (d) of the definition "proceeds of disposition" in section 54;

Related Provisions: 89(1)"capital dividend account"(a)(i)(C)(I), 89(1)"capital dividend account"(a)(ii)(C)(I) — Application to capital dividend account.

Notes: Designated property is essentially property owned by a corp since before Nov. 13, 1981; its status carries through transfers within a group and corporate reorgs. The term is used in 89(1)"capital dividend account"(a)(i)(C)(I), (a)(ii)(C)(I) and 129(4)"eligible portion".

89(1)"designated property" was 89(1)(b.1) before RSC 1985 (5th Supp) consolidation for tax years ending after Nov. 1991.

Income Tax Folios: S3-F2-C1: Capital Dividends [replaces IT-66R6].

Interpretation Bulletins: IT-243R4: Dividend refund to private corporations.

"eligible dividend" means

(a) an amount that is equal to the portion of a taxable dividend that is received by a person resident in Canada, paid by a corporation resident in Canada and designated under subsection (14) to be an eligible dividend, and

(b) in respect of a person resident in Canada, an amount that is deemed by subsection 96(1.11) or 104(16) to be a taxable dividend that is received by the person;

Related Provisions: 82(1)(a.1), 82(1)(b)(ii) — 45% gross-up for eligible dividend; 89(14) — Designation of eligible dividend; 89(14.1) — Late designation; 96(1.11)(b) — Publicly-traded partnership distribution deemed to be eligible dividend; 104(16) — Income trust distribution deemed to be eligible dividend; 121 — 11/18ths dividend tax credit for eligible dividend; 185.1 — Penalty tax on excessive eligible dividend designation; 248(1)"eligible dividend" — Definition applies to entire Act; 260(1.1), (5) — Dividend compensation payment deemed to be eligible dividend.

Notes: An "eligible dividend" is taxed at a lower rate in an individual's hands, due to the 38% gross-up (82(1)(b)(ii)) and resulting higher dividend tax credit (121(b)) instead of a lower gross-up (82(1)(b)(i)) and lower dividend tax credit (121(a)). See Notes to 82(1). An eligible dividend is essentially a dividend paid out of GRIP (89(1)"general rate income pool"), which is income that was taxed at the high corporate rate (not eligible for the 125(1) small business deduction, and not investment income of a CCPC: see 89(1)"adjusted taxable income"C). It also includes a distribution from an income trust or publicly traded partnership: 104(16), 96(1.11)(b).

Despite the higher dividend tax credit, an eligible dividend can cost the taxpayer more than an ordinary dividend because the higher gross-up bumps up "net income", affecting the old age security clawback (180.2), medical expenses (118.2(1)), GST credit (122.5), Canada Child Benefit (122.61), dependent spouse (118(1)B(a)(ii)C), etc.

The 2012 Budget amendments to this definition and 89(14) allow any portion of a dividend to be designated as an eligible dividend, rather than the entire dividend.

A CCPC can pay an eligible dividend only to the extent it has GRIP *at year-end*. A non-CCPC can pay an eligible dividend as long as it has no LRIP (89(1)"low rate income pool") *at the time the dividend is paid*. See Notes to 89(1)"excessive eligible dividend designation".

An eligible dividend can include a stock dividend and a deemed dividend, but not a capital dividend or capital gains dividend. If it is not received by a Canadian resident it is not an eligible dividend, so if an 89(14)-designated dividend is paid to both resident and non-resident shareholders, only the portion received by residents is an eligible dividend: VIEWS doc 2010-0363851C6. Each such dividend must be designated under 89(14). The recipient need not be a shareholder, so an 84.1(1) deemed dividend can be an eligible dividend: 2012-0454091C6.

An eligible dividend received by a trust can be flowed out as such via 104(19) to a beneficiary. An eligible dividend received by a partnership is flowed out as such to partners under 96(1)(f).

See also Lamarre et al., *Taxation of Corporate Reorganizations* (Carswell, 3rd ed., 2019), chap. 12; Woo & Friedley, *Taxation of Private Corporations and their Shareholders* (ctf.ca, 5th ed., 2020), chap. 9; Keey, *Checklist 5 — Eligible Dividend, Taxnet Pro* Corporate Tax Centre (2020, 11pp); Ireland, "Owner-manager Compensation and the Eligible Dividend Rules", 18(4) *Taxation of Executive Compensation & Retirement* (Federated Press) 747-52 (Nov. 2006); Cuperfain, "The New Dividend Rules and Succession Planning", XIII(1) *Insurance Planning* (Federated Press) 810-13 (2006); Evans & Schusheim, "Dividend Taxation: The New Regime", 2006 Cdn Tax Foundation conference report, 1:1-28; Stack, "Getting a Grip on the New Dividend Rules", V(1) *Resource Sector Taxation* (Federated Press) 330-34 (2007); Stubbing & Foreman, "The Eligible Dividend Rules", 2007 BC Tax Conference (ctf.ca), 15:1-36; Lewin, "Structuring the Sale of a Private Corp in the Context of the New Dividend Rules", 2007 conference report, 30:1-25; Schusheim, "The New Eligible Dividend Rules and Private Corporations", 55(4) *Canadian Tax Journal* 894-912 (2007); Marino, "Federal Changes to the Preferential Tax Treatment of Eligible Dividends", XIV(3) *Insurance Planning* 907-11 (2008), corrected in "Eligible Dividends Revisited", XIV(4) 921-23 (2008); Ball, "Owner Manager Remuneration", 2010 Ontario Tax Conference 9B:1-31. See also Notes to s. 67.

For CRA interpretation see VIEWS docs 2007-0223561M4, 2007-02315231R3, 2007-0243111C6 (prescribed forms T2 Sched. 53-55), 2007-0243131C6 (mechanism for directing eligible dividend to a particular shareholder); 2010-0361381E5 (eligible dividend and other dividend can be paid in same cheque); 2014-0539951E5 (US dollar dividend qualifies); May 2010 ICAA roundtable (tinyurl.com/cra-abtax), q.14 (effect on LRIP of dividends to non-resident shareholders). The CRA stated at the 2008 Cdn Tax Foundation conference (conference report at 3:3-4): (1) where some shareholders are non-resident, reorganization into two classes of shares is unnecessary; (2) an eligible dividend maintains its character when flowed out through a trust under 104(19).

Para. (a) amended by 2012 budget bill #1, for dividends paid after March 28, 2012, to allow a portion of a dividend to be designated.

Para. (b) added by 2007 budget bill #1, effective Oct. 31, 2006.

89(1)"eligible dividend" added by 2006 budget bill #2 (Part 2 — eligible dividends), effective for 2006 and later taxation years.

I.T. Technical News: 41 (eligible dividend designation).

"excessive eligible dividend designation", made by a corporation in respect of an eligible dividend paid by the corporation at any time in a taxation year, means

(a) unless paragraph (c) applies to the dividend, if the corporation is in the taxation year a Canadian-controlled private corporation or a deposit insurance corporation, the amount, if any, determined by the formula

$$(A - B) \times \frac{C}{A}$$

where

A   is the total of all amounts each of which is the amount of an eligible dividend paid by the corporation in the taxation year,

B   is the greater of nil and the corporation's general rate income pool at the end of the taxation year, and

C   is the amount of the eligible dividend,

(b) unless paragraph (c) applies to the dividend, if the corporation is not a corporation described in paragraph (a), the amount, if any, determined by the formula

$$A \times \frac{B}{C}$$

where

A   is the lesser of

    (i) the total of all amounts each of which is an eligible dividend paid by the corporation at that time, and

    (ii) the corporation's low rate income pool at that time,

B   is the amount of the eligible dividend, and

C   is the amount determined under subparagraph (i) of the description of A, and,

(c) an amount equal to the amount of the eligible dividend, if it is reasonable to consider that the eligible dividend was paid in a transaction, or as part of a series of transactions, one of the main purposes of which was to artificially maintain or increase the corporation's general rate income pool, or to artificially maintain or decrease the corporation's low rate income pool;

Related Provisions: 125(7)"Canadian-controlled private corporation"(d) — Election not to be CCPC for purposes of definition; 185.1 — Penalty tax on excessive designation; 248(1)"excessive eligible dividend designation" — Definition applies to entire Act; 248(10) — Series of transactions; 257 — Formula cannot calculate to less than zero.

Notes: See 185.1 (Part III.1), which imposes tax on a excessive eligible dividend designation (EEDD). See also Notes to 89(1)"eligible dividend".

Whether a corporation has made an EEDD depends partly on whether it is a CCPC or deposit insurance corp (DIC) and to what extent the corporation has a balance in its GRIP or LRIP (see 89(1)"general rate income pool", "low rate income pool").

Unless para. (c) applies, para. (a) applies to eligible dividends paid by CCPCs and DICs. The EEDD made by a CCPC or DIC is determined by a formula, which has two parts: A – B identifies any amount by which the total eligible dividends paid in the year exceeds the corporation's GRIP at year-end (or exceeds nil, if the corporation had a negative GRIP); and C/A prorates any excess on a dividend by dividend basis. Thus, the ability of CCPCs and DICs to pay eligible dividends in a year without making an EEDD is limited to the GRIP they have at the end of the year (and to the extent para. (c) does not apply). However, this also means that a CCPC or DIC can pay an eligible dividend at a time when it has no GRIP, provided it has enough GRIP by year-end.

Unless para. (c) applies, para. (b) applies to eligible dividends paid by other corporations, including public corporations. Although the EEDD formula is similar to para. (a), there are two major distinctions. First, LRIP is calculated at any time in the corporation's taxation year (not just year-end). Second, the formula in (b), unlike (a), effectively introduces an ordering rule by requiring a corporation to first pay non-eligible dividends to the extent of its LRIP when it pays taxable dividends (to avoid tax on the EEDD under 185.1). This also means that (subject to para. (c) below) corporations described in (b) that at any given time have no LRIP can pay eligible dividends.

Para. (c) is an anti-avoidance provision. It applies if it is reasonable to consider that the eligible dividend was paid in a transaction, or as part of a series of transactions, one of the main purposes of which was to artificially manipulate the corporation's GRIP or LRIP. Finance intends that a corporation be considered to have artificially maintained or increased GRIP if the transaction or series produces GRIP that is unreflective of income retained after payment of Part I tax (including of another corporation) at a rate not less than applies to full rate taxable income (see 123.4(1)). Likewise, a corporation is generally considered to have artificially maintained or decreased LRIP if the transaction or series produces LRIP that is unreflective of income retained after payment of Part I tax (including of another corporation) at a rate less than applies to full rate taxable income. If para. (c) applies, the excessive designation is the full amount of the eligible dividend. For the meaning of "one of the main purposes" see Notes to 83(2.1).

For a ruling on para. (c) see VIEWS doc 2007-0231521R3 and Tom Stack, "Canada Revenue Agency Ruling on Eligible Dividend Anti-Avoidance Rule", V(4) *Resource*

Sector Taxation (Federated Press) 393-96 (2008). For an example of para. (c) applying see doc 2011-0395121E5 (LRIP parking). See also 2013-0495781C6 [2013 APFF q.15] (para. (c) would not apply; uncertain whether GAAR would).

89(1)"excessive eligible dividend designation" added by 2006 budget bill #2 (Part 2 — eligible dividends), for 2006 and later taxation years.

"general rate factor" of a corporation for a taxation year is the total of

    (a) that proportion of 0.68 that the number of days in the taxation year that are before 2010 is of the number of days in the taxation year,

    (b) that proportion of 0.69 that the number of days in the taxation year that are in 2010 is of the number of days in the taxation year,

    (c) that proportion of 0.70 that the number of days in the taxation year that are in 2011 is of the number of days in the taxation year, and

    (d) that proportion of 0.72 that the number of days in the taxation year that are after 2011 is of the number of days in the taxation year;

Related Provisions: 89(1)"general rate income pool"A:D — Application of factor.

Notes: 89(1)"general rate factor" added by 2008 budget bill #2, effective for 2006 and later taxation years. It is used in 89(1)"general rate income pool".

"general rate income pool" at the end of a particular taxation year, of a taxable Canadian corporation that is a Canadian-controlled private corporation or a deposit insurance corporation in the particular taxation year, is the positive or negative amount determined by the formula

$$A - B$$

where

A   is the positive or negative amount that would, before taking into consideration the specified future tax consequences for the particular taxation year, be determined by the formula

$$C + D + E + F - G$$

  where

    C   is the corporation's general rate income pool at the end of its preceding taxation year,

    D   is the amount, if any, that is the product of the corporation's general rate factor for the particular taxation year multiplied by its adjusted taxable income for the particular taxation year,

    E   is the total of all amounts each of which is

        (a) an eligible dividend received by the corporation in the particular taxation year, or

        (b) an amount deductible under section 113 in computing the taxable income of the corporation for the particular taxation year,

    F   is the total of all amounts determined under subsections (4) to (6) in respect of the corporation for the particular taxation year, and

    G   is

        (a) unless paragraph (b) applies, the amount, if any, by which

            (i) the total of all amounts each of which is the amount of an eligible dividend paid by the corporation in its preceding taxation year

        exceeds

            (ii) the total of all amounts each of which is an excessive eligible dividend designation made by the corporation in its preceding taxation year, or

        (b) if subsection (4) applies to the corporation in the particular taxation year, nil, and

B   is the amount determined by the formula

$$H \times (I - J)$$

where

H   is the corporation's general rate factor for the particular taxation year,

I   is the total of the corporation's full rate taxable incomes (as would be defined in the definition "full rate taxable income" in subsection 123.4(1), if that definition were read without reference to its subparagraphs (a)(i) to (iii)) for the corporation's preceding three taxation years, determined without taking into consideration the specified future tax consequences, for those preceding taxation years, that arise in respect of the particular taxation year, and

J   is the total of the corporation's full rate taxable incomes (as would be defined in the definition "full rate taxable income" in subsection 123.4(1), if that definition were read without reference to its subparagraphs (a)(i) to (iii)) for those preceding taxation years;

Related Provisions: 82(1)(b)(ii) — Dividend paid out of general rate income pool eligible for high dividend tax credit; 89(1)"low rate income pool" — Other income; 89(4) — GRIP addition on becoming CCPC; 89(5), 87(2)(vv) — GRIP addition on amalgamation; 89(6), 87(2)(vv), 88(1)(e.2)(ix) — GRIP addition on windup; 89(7) — GRIP addition for 2006; 125(7)"Canadian-controlled private corporation"(d) — Election not to be CCPC for purposes of definition; 248(1)"general rate income pool" — Definition applies to entire Act; 257 — Formula cannot calculate to less than zero unless stated otherwise.

Notes: See Notes to 89(1)"eligible dividend" and "excessive eligible dividend designation". GRIP is, essentially, income taxed at the full rate (not small business deduction and not a CCPC's investment income: 89(1)"adjusted taxable income"C), after applying notional 28% corporate tax (89(1)"general rate factor"), plus eligible dividends received, minus eligible dividends paid out. For the starting balance in 2006, see 89(7).

GRIP is "good" in that is allows eligible dividends to be paid out and taxed at a lower rate (82(1)(a.1)(i), 82(1)(b)(ii), 121). If the federal+provincial corporate tax rate is less than 28%, retained earnings will exceed GRIP and if it is all paid out, some dividends will be non-eligible.

The two formula references to "positive or negative amount" override s. 257.

A T2 Sch. 53 GRIP calculation is normally required from a CCPC, but not a credit union: see Notes to 137(7).

For CRA interpretation see VIEWS docs 2007-0257721E5 (why T2 Sched. 53 Line 300 does not count dividends paid in current year); 2007-0243091C6 (impact of losses on GRIP calculation); 2008-0284951C6 (the portion of an eligible dividend paid to a non-resident does not reduce GRIP); 2009-0330151C6 (formula element E must be calculated using the taxation year, not the calendar year); 2013-0477771E5 (calculation where corp becomes CCPC during year); 2016-0648481E5 (corp can choose not to claim 125(1) small business deduction so as to maximize GRIP [but the general rate reduction is lost: see Notes to 123.4(2)]); May 2008 ICAA roundtable (tinyurl.com/cra-abtax), q. 3 (whether GRIP adjustment can be negative due to charitable donations); May 2011 ICAA roundtable, q. 14 (calculation when losses carried back).

Where 55(2) applies, GRIP is permanently reduced, but the recipient corporation may add the safe income portion of the dividend to its GRIP: VIEWS doc 2007-0233771C6 (for more details see 2008-0271401E5, 2008-0284961C6). The excess over safe income, although deemed by 55(2)(a) not to be *received* as a dividend, is still a dividend *paid* for purposes of G(a)(i) in the CRA's view: 2010-0385991C6 [CTF conf report p.4:5-6, q.5]. Also, safe income can be consolidated in a corporate group but GRIP cannot. See Jon Gilbert, "GRIP Tips: Subsec. 55(2) and Safe Income", 8(1) *Tax for the Owner-Manager* (ctf.ca) 1-2 (Jan. 2008).

See also Yull, "Another GRIPping Saga", 5(5) *Tax Hyperion* (Carswell, May 2008) and "GRIP and LRIP", 6(6) *TH* (June 2009); Carreiro & Crosbie, "Update on GRIP/LRIP Calculations", 2009 Cdn Tax Foundation conference report, 12:1-38; Granelli, "Getting a Handle on GRIP", 2252 *Tax Topics* (CCH) 1-5 (May 7, 2015).

Although Quebec has a more restrictive small business deduction, Quebec's GRIP is based on the ITA, so the rules do not work well: Shah & Kakkar, "Coming to Grips with Quebec's Lack of GRIP", 17(2) *Tax for the Owner-Manager* (ctf.ca) 6-7 (April 2017).

Definition amended by 2008 budget bill #2, for 2006 and later tax years. The substantive changes were to introduce a new "general rate factor" (increased from 68%) after 2009, and to ensure that the former formula amount "0.68(D-E-F)" cannot be negative.

89(1)"general rate income pool" added by 2006 budget bill #2, for 2006 and later tax years.

Forms: T2 Sched. 53: General rate income pool (GRIP) calculation.

"life insurance capital dividend account [para. 89(1)(b.2)]" — [Repealed under former Act]

Notes: 89(1)(b.2), repealed by 1985 Budget, defined "life insurance capital dividend account". The proceeds of life insurance are now dealt with in 89(1)"capital dividend account"(d) and (e). See Notes to 83(2.1).

"low rate income pool", at any particular time in a particular taxation year, of a corporation (in this definition referred to as the "non-CCPC") that is resident in Canada and is in the particular taxation year neither a Canadian-controlled private corporation nor a deposit insurance corporation, is the amount determined by the formula

$$(A + B + C + D + E + F) - (G + H)$$

where

A   is the non-CCPC's low rate income pool at the end of its preceding taxation year,

B   is the total of all amounts each of which is an amount deductible under section 112 in computing the non-CCPC's taxable income for the year in respect of a taxable dividend (other than an eligible dividend) that became payable, in the particular taxation year but before the particular time, to the non-CCPC by a corporation resident in Canada,

C   is the total of all amounts determined under subsections (8) to (10) in respect of the non-CCPC for the particular taxation year,

D   is

(a) if the non-CCPC would, but for paragraph (d) of the definition "Canadian-controlled private corporation" in subsection 125(7), be a Canadian-controlled private corporation in its preceding taxation year, 80% of its aggregate investment income for its preceding taxation year, and

(b) in any other case, nil,

E   is

(a) if the non-CCPC was not a Canadian-controlled private corporation in its preceding taxation year, 80% of the amount determined by multiplying the amount, if any, deducted by the corporation under subsection 125(1) for that preceding taxation year by the quotient obtained by dividing 100 by the rate of the deduction provided under that subsection for that preceding taxation year, and

(b) in any other case, nil,

F   is

(a) if the non-CCPC was an investment corporation in its preceding taxation year, four times the amount, if any, deducted by it under subsection 130(1) for its preceding taxation year, and

(b) in any other case, nil,

G   is the total of all amounts each of which is a taxable dividend (other than an eligible dividend, a capital gains dividend within the meaning assigned by subsection 130.1(4) or 131(1) or a taxable dividend deductible by the non-CCPC under subsection 130.1(1) in computing its income for the particular taxation year or for its preceding taxation year) that became payable, in the particular taxation year but before the particular time, by the non-CCPC, and

H   is the total of all amounts each of which is an excessive eligible dividend designation made by the non-CCPC in the particular taxation year but before the particular time;

Related Provisions: 82(1)(b)(ii) — Dividend paid out of general rate income pool eligible for high dividend tax credit; 89(1)"general rate income pool" — Other income; 89(8) — LRIP addition on ceasing to be CCPC; 89(9), 87(2)(ww) — LRIP addition on amalgamation; 89(10), 87(2)(ww), 88(1)(e.2)(ix) — LRIP addition on windup; 125(7)"Canadian-controlled private corporation"(d) — Election not to be CCPC for purposes of definition; 248(1)"low rate income pool" — Definition applies to entire Act; 257 — Formula cannot calculate to less than zero.

Notes: See Notes to 89(1)"eligible dividend" and "excessive eligible dividend designation". LRIP is, essentially, income that benefited from the small business deduction (125(1)), plus non-eligible dividends received from other corporations. For CRA interpretation see docs 2008-0284981C6 (timing of addition for non-eligible dividends received from mutual fund trusts: unresolved); 2009-0308511E5 (dividend paid to non-residents reduces LRIP; see Hickey, "LRIP Eliminated: Non-Resident Shareholders", 17(10) *Canadian Tax Highlights* (ctf.ca) 4-5 (Oct. 2009)); 2010-0363851C6 (effect on LRIP of designated dividend paid to both resident and non-resident shareholders); 2011-0395121E5 (LRIP parking — anti-avoidance); 2011-0425501E5 (CRA can adjust LRIP of statute-barred year); May 2010 ICAA roundtable (tinyurl.com/cra-abtax), q.14 (effect on LRIP of dividends to non-resident shareholders).

See also Yull, "GRIP and LRIP — Ongoing Issues", 6(6) *Tax Hyperion* (Carswell, June 2009); Carreiro & Crosbie, "Update on GRIP/LRIP Calculations", 2009 Cdn Tax Foundation conference report, 12:1-38; Biderman, "Recent Low Rate Income Pool Issues", XVI(2) *Corporate Finance* (Federated Press) 1798-1801 (2009).

89(1)"low rate income pool" added by 2006 budget bill #2, for 2006 and later tax years, but (as amended before Third Reading by Commons Finance Committee) for such years that began before 2006, in formula element B read "in the particular taxation year" as "in the particular taxation year and after 2005". Formula element A is $0 before 2006; this is the only sensible interpretation, and is confirmed by CRA's Form T2 Schedule 54 heading ("2006 and later tax years") and Line 100 ("enter 0 for first tax year ending in 2006").

I.T. Technical News: 44 (calculating LRIP for cash-basis taxpayers).

Forms: T2 Sched. 54: Low rate income pool (LRIP) calculation.

"paid-up capital" at any particular time means,

(a) in respect of a share of any class of the capital stock of a corporation, an amount equal to the paid-up capital at that time, in respect of the class of shares of the capital stock of the corporation to which that share belongs, divided by the number of issued shares of that class outstanding at that time,

(b) in respect of a class of shares of the capital stock of a corporation,

(i) where the particular time is before May 7, 1974, an amount equal to the paid-up capital in respect of that class of shares at the particular time, computed without reference to the provisions of this Act,

(ii) where the particular time is after May 6, 1974, and before April 1, 1977, an amount equal to the paid-up capital in respect of that class of shares at the particular time, computed in accordance with the *Income Tax Act*, chapter 148 of the Revised Statutes of Canada, 1952, as it read on March 31, 1977, and

(iii) if the particular time is after March 31, 1977, an amount equal to the paid-up capital in respect of that class of shares at the particular time, computed without reference to the provisions of this Act except subsections 51(3) and 66.3(2) and (4), sections 84.1 and 84.2, subsections 85(2.1), 85.1(2.1) and (8), 86(2.1), 87(3) and (9), paragraph 128.1(1)(c.3), subsections 128.1(2) and (3), section 135.2, subsections 138(11.7), 139.1(6) and (7), 148(7), 192(4.1) and 194(4.1) and sections 212.1 and 212.3,

except that, where the corporation is a cooperative corporation (within the meaning assigned by subsection 136(2)) or a credit union and the statute by or under which it was incorporated does not provide for paid-up capital in respect of a class of shares, the paid-up capital in respect of that class of shares at the particular time, computed without reference to the provisions of this Act, shall be deemed to be the amount, if any, by which

(iv) the total of the amounts received by the corporation in respect of shares of that class issued and outstanding at that time

exceeds

(v) the total of all amounts each of which is an amount or part thereof described in subparagraph (iv) repaid by the corporation to persons who held any of the issued shares of that class before that time, and

(c) in respect of all the shares of the capital stock of a corporation, an amount equal to the total of all amounts each of which is an amount equal to the paid-up capital in respect of any class of shares of the capital stock of the corporation at the particular time;

Related Provisions

Provisions referenced in (b)(iii): 51(3) — Exchange of convertible property; 66.3(2) — Exploration and development shares — deductions from PUC; 66.3(4) — PUC of flow-through share; 84.1 — Grind of PUC on non-arm's length sales of shares; 84.2 — Computation of PUC in respect of particular class of shares; 85(2.1) — Transfer of property to corporation by shareholders — computation of PUC; 85.1(2.1) — Share for share exchange — computation of PUC; 86(2.1) — Internal reorganization; 87(3), (3.1) — Amalgamation — computation of PUC; 87(9)(b) — PUC following triangular amalgamation; 128.1(1)(c.3) — Foreign affiliate dumping — corporate immi-

gration; 128.1(2), (3) — Corporation becoming resident in Canada; 135.2(3)(c), 135.2(12) — Canadian Wheat Board PUC determination; 138(11,7) — Insurance corporations — computation of PUC; 139.1(6), (7) — PUC after demutualization of insurer; 192(4.1), 194(4.1) — Computing PUC after SPTC or SRTC designation; 212.1 — Non-arm's length sale of shares by non-resident; 212.3(2)(b), 212.3(7)(b), (8), (9) — Foreign affiliate dumping — adjustments to PUC.

Other provisions: 219.1(2) — PUC of emigrating corporation deemed nil for departure tax purposes (foreign affiliate dumping); 248(1)"paid-up capital" — Definition applies to entire Act; 248(6) — Series of shares; 261(7)(g) — Functional currency reporting.

Notes: The definition of paid-up capital (PUC) in terms of PUC, in subpara. (b)(iii), is a reference to PUC (or "stated capital") as determined for corporate law purposes under the applicable business corporations legislation (federal or provincial); *Copthorne Holdings*, 2011 SCC 63, paras. 75-77. See ss. 26, 38 and 39 of the *Canada Business Corporations Act* federally. From there, PUC is modified for tax purposes by the specific provisions listed in subpara. (b)(iii). See Richard Lewin, "Tax Attributes", 1998 Cdn Tax Foundation conference report, at 8:17-40; VIEWS doc 2010-0373301C6 (PUC of separate classes with identical characteristics should be computed separately) .

CRA's practice is to determine PUC by taking into account all relevant documents as well as applicable corporate law and GAAP: VIEWS doc 2004-0094131E5.

PUC can generally be extracted by a shareholder tax-free, while increases in PUC trigger a deemed dividend. See 84(1) and Notes to 84(3); Corrado Cardarelli, "Transactions Involving Paid-Up Capital", 2004 Cdn Tax Foundation conference report, 26:1-25. Artificial inflation of PUC can trigger GAAR: *Copthorne* (above); VIEWS doc 2010-0373221C6. See also Notes to 248(1)"dividend" re distribution of share premium from a foreign corporation; and Notes to 87(11) re reducing PUC on a windup or vertical amalgamation to avoid a capital gain.

Para. (a) requires averaging of PUC among all shares of a class. Misuse of this rule to avoid 84.1 did not trigger GAAR (245(2)) in *1245989 Alberta Ltd. (Wild)*, 2018 FCA 114, as the surplus had not yet been extracted.

See Smith & Devan, "Paid-Up Capital Planning", 51(6) *Canadian Tax Journal [CTJ]* 2296-2319 (2003); Morin, "Pre- and Post-Acquisition PUC Planning; GAARable?", 23(2) *Canadian Tax Highlights* (ctf.ca) 8-9 (Feb. 2015); Nobrega, "Paid-Up Capital Planning", 63(1) *CTJ* 315-36 (2015); Oldewening, "Duality of Paid-up Capital", XXI(2) *International Tax Planning* (Federated Press) 7-19 (2017) (interaction with s. 261); D'Iorio, "Additions to PUC for Share Compensation", XXV(3) *Taxation of Executive Compensation & Retirement* (Federated Press) 2-10 (2018).

Where a payment in reduction of PUC results in a reduction of adjusted cost base (53(2)(a)(ii)) below zero, a capital gain will be triggered under 40(3): VIEWS doc 2002-0168815.

Subpara. (b)(iii) amended to refer to: 148(7) by 2016 budget bill #2 (effective Dec. 15, 2016); 135.2 by 2016 budget bill #1 (effective July 2015); 128.1(1)(c.3) and 212.3 by 2012 budget bill #2 (effective March 29, 2012).

Definition earlier amended by 2008 budget bill #2 (effective Dec. 20, 2007), 1999 Budget, 1993 and 1991 technical bills. 89(1)"paid-up capital" was 89(1)(c) before RSC 1985 (5th Supp) consolidation for tax years ending after Nov. 1991.

I.T. Application Rules: 69 (meaning of "chapter 148 of ...").

Interpretation Bulletins: IT-88R2: Stock dividends; IT-463R2: Paid-up capital; IT-489R: Non-arm's length sale of shares to a corporation.

Advance Tax Rulings: ATR-27: Exchange and acquisition of interests in capital properties through rollovers and winding-up ("butterfly"); ATR-28: Redemption of capital stock of family farm corporation; ATR-35: Partitioning of assets to get specific ownership — "butterfly"; ATR-54: Reduction of paid-up capital.

"paid-up capital deficiency [para. 89(1)(d)]" and "paid-up capital limit [para. 89(1)(e)]" — [Repealed under former Act]

Notes: 89(1)(d) and (e), repealed in 1977, defined "paid-up capital deficiency" and "paid-up capital limit", terms no longer used.

"private corporation" at any particular time means a corporation that, at the particular time, is resident in Canada, is not a public corporation and is not controlled by one or more public corporations (other than prescribed venture capital corporations) or prescribed federal Crown corporations or by any combination thereof and, for greater certainty, for the purposes of determining at any particular time when a corporation last became a private corporation,

(a) a corporation that was a private corporation at the commencement of its 1972 taxation year and thereafter without interruption until the particular time shall be deemed to have last become a private corporation at the end of its 1971 taxation year, and

(b) a corporation incorporated after 1971 that was a private corporation at the time of its incorporation and thereafter without interruption until the particular time shall be deemed to have last become a private corporation immediately before the time of its incorporation;

Related Provisions: 27(2) — Crown corporations; 136(1) — Cooperative corporation not private corporation; 137(7) — Credit union not private corporation; 137.1(6) — Deposit insurance corporation not private corporation; 141.1 — Insurance corporation not private corporation for certain purposes; 186(5) — Subject corporation deemed private corporation for certain purposes; 227(16) — Municipal or provincial corporation deemed not private corporation for Part IV tax; 248(1)"private corporation" — Definition applies to entire Act; 250 — Resident in Canada; 256(6), (6.1) — Meaning of "controlled".

Notes: A corporation controlled by a public corporation is not a private corp, although it is not a public corp either. For most purposes it is treated similarly to a public corp. A Crown corporation is neither public nor private: VIEWS doc 2014-0527341E5. Note also that to be *either* a private or a public corp, a corporation must first be resident in Canada (see 250(4), (5)).

See generally *Taxation of Private Corporations* (ctf.ca, 5th ed., 2020).

89(1)"private corporation" was 89(1)(f) before RSC 1985 (5th Supp) consolidation for tax years ending after Nov. 1991. Definition amended by 1991 technical bill, effective July 14, 1990.

Regulations: 6700 (prescribed venture capital corporation); 7100 (prescribed federal Crown corporation).

I.T. Application Rules: 50(1) (status of corporation in 1972 taxation year).

Interpretation Bulletins: IT-243R4: Dividend refund to private corporations; IT-391R: Status of corporations; IT-458R2: Canadian-controlled private corporation.

I.T. Technical News: 25 (*Silicon Graphics* case — dispersed control is not control).

"public corporation" at any particular time means

(a) a corporation that is resident in Canada at the particular time if at that time a class of shares of the capital stock of the corporation is listed on a designated stock exchange in Canada,

(b) a corporation (other than a prescribed labour-sponsored venture capital corporation) that is resident in Canada at the particular time if at any time after June 18, 1971 and

(i) before the particular time, it elected in prescribed manner to be a public corporation, and at the time of the election it complied with prescribed conditions relating to the number of its shareholders, the dispersal of ownership of its shares and the public trading of its shares, or

(ii) before the day that is 30 days before the day that includes the particular time it was, by notice in writing to the corporation, designated by the Minister to be a public corporation and at the time it was so designated it complied with the conditions referred to in subparagraph (i),

unless, after the election or designation, as the case may be, was made and before the particular time, it ceased to be a public corporation because of an election or designation under paragraph (c), or

(c) a corporation (other than a prescribed labour-sponsored venture capital corporation) that is resident in Canada at the particular time if, at any time after June 18, 1971 and before the particular time it was a public corporation, unless after the time it last became a public corporation and

(i) before the particular time, it elected in prescribed manner not to be a public corporation, and at the time it so elected it complied with prescribed conditions relating to the number of its shareholders, the dispersal of ownership of its shares and the public trading of its shares, or

(ii) before the day that is 30 days before the day that includes the particular time, it was, by notice in writing to the corporation, designated by the Minister not to be a public corporation and at the time it was so designated it complied with the conditions referred to in subparagraph (i),

and where a corporation has, on or before its filing-due date for its first taxation year, become a public corporation, it is, if it so elects in its return of income for the year, deemed to have been a public corporation from the beginning of the year until the time when it so became a public corporation;

Related Provisions: 13(27)(f) — Restriction on deduction before available for use; 87(2)(ii) — Amalgamations — public corporation; 130.1(5) — Mortgage investment

corporation deemed to be public corporation; 141(2) — Life insurance corporation deemed to be public corporation; 141(3) — Life insurance holding corporation deemed to be public corporation; 248(1)"public corporation" — Definition applies to entire Act; 250 — Resident in Canada.

Notes: See Notes to 262 re "designated stock exchange".

A capital pool company is a public corporation from the time it completes its initial offering and is listed on TSX Venture Exchange Tier 2: VIEWS doc 2010-0377411E5.

A corporation controlled by a public corp is not a "private corporation" but is also not a public corp: VIEWS doc 2012-0455231E5.

Elections under (c)(i) *not to be* a public corp are allowed after an amalgamation if the delisted shares no longer exist: VIEWS docs 2008-0268962R3, 2010-0355001R3, 2015-0577141R3, 2017-0723771C6 [2017 CTF q.12], 2018-0752531R3. (See also 2010-0377251E5 on the interaction of this election with 89(11).) An election under the closing words *to be* a public corporation was allowed in 2009-0343201R3 (trust conversion to corporation) and 2010-0366651R3 (spinoff butterfly). The retroactivity of the election to become a public corporation allows its shares to retroactively be "qualified investments" for RRSP etc. purposes: 9610015, 9733475, 2010-0355281E5.

See CBA/CPA Canada Joint Committee letter to Finance, March 4, 2019, seeking to have the definition cease to apply as soon as an M&A "going private" share acquisition is completed.

See also Notes to 89(1)"private corporation".

89(1)"public corporation"(a) amended by 2007 budget bill #2 to change "prescribed stock exchange" to "designated stock exchange", effective Dec. 14, 2007.

Definition earlier amended by 1997 Budget, effective for 1995 and later taxation years. 89(1)"public corporation" was 89(1)(g) before RSC 1985 (5th Supp) consolidation for tax years ending after Nov. 1991.

Regulations: 4800, 4803 (prescribed conditions); 6701 (prescribed labour-sponsored venture capital corporation).

I.T. Application Rules: 50 (status of corporation in 1972 taxation year).

Interpretation Bulletins: IT-98R2: Investment corporations (cancelled); IT-176R2: Taxable Canadian property — interests in and options on real property and shares; IT-391R: Status of corporations; IT-458R2: Canadian-controlled private corporation.

Forms: T2067: Election not to be a public corporation; T2073: Election to be a public corporation.

"tax equity [para. 89(1)(h)]" — [Repealed under former Act]

Notes: 89(1)(h), repealed effective 1979, defined the "tax equity" of a corporation at the end of its 1971 taxation year, a concept no longer used.

"taxable Canadian corporation" means a corporation that, at the time the expression is relevant,

(a) was a Canadian corporation, and

(b) was not, by reason of a statutory provision, exempt from tax under this Part;

Related Provisions: 149 — Statutory provisions exempting taxpayers from tax under this Part; 248(1)"taxable Canadian corporation" — Definition applies to entire Act.

Notes: Para. (b) amended by 2017 budget bill #1, for tax years that begin after 2018, to change "a statutory provision other than paragraph 149(1)(t)" to "a statutory provision" (due to repeal of 149(1)(t)).

Para. (b) amended by 2002-2013 technical bill (Part 5 — technical), for tax years that end after 1999, to add 149(1)(t) exclusion, so 87(1) could apply to an amalgamation of farming or fishing insurers (Finance comfort letter, Feb. 21, 2000).

Interpretation Bulletins: IT-291R3: Transfer of property to a corporation under subsection 85(1).

"taxable dividend" means a dividend other than

(a) a dividend in respect of which the corporation paying the dividend has elected in accordance with subsection 83(1) as it read prior to 1979 or in accordance with subsection 83(2), and

(b) a qualifying dividend paid by a public corporation to shareholders of a prescribed class of tax-deferred preferred shares of the corporation within the meaning of subsection 83(1).

Related Provisions: 82(1) — Inclusion of taxable dividend in income; 88(2) — Winding-up of a Canadian corporation; 96(1.11)(b) — Publicly-traded partnership distribution deemed to be dividend; 104(16) — Income trust distribution deemed to be taxable dividend; 120.4(4), (5) — Certain capital gains deemed to be taxable dividends for split-income rules; 129(1.2) — Dividends paid to create dividend refund deemed not to be taxable dividends for purposes of s. 129; 129(7) — Capital gains dividend is not a taxable dividend for purposes of dividend refund; 142.7(10)(a) — Branch-establishment dividend to foreign entrant bank deemed not to be taxable dividend; 248(1)"taxable dividend" — Definition applies to entire Act; 260(5) — Deemed taxable dividend on securities lending arrangement.

Notes: In effect, a taxable dividend means a dividend other than a capital dividend. Note that "dividend", defined in 248(1), includes some stock dividends. See also Notes to 82(1).

89(1)"taxable dividend" was 89(1)(j) before RSC 1985 (5th Supp) consolidation for tax years ending after Nov. 1991.

Regulations: 2107 (tax-deferred preferred series).

Interpretation Bulletins: IT-52R4: Income bonds and income debentures (cancelled); IT-67R3: Taxable dividends from corporations resident in Canada; IT-146R4: Shares entitling shareholders to choose taxable or capital dividends.

"tax-paid undistributed surplus on hand [para. 89(1)(k)]" — [Repealed under former Act]

"1971 capital surplus on hand [para. 89(1)(l)]" — [Repealed under former Act]

Notes: 89(1)(k) and (l), repealed effective 1979, defined "tax-paid undistributed surplus on hand" and "1971 capital surplus on hand", terms no longer used. From 1972 through 1978 these represented amounts that pre-dated the introduction of capital gains tax and could be extracted from a corporation tax-free in certain circumstances.

(1.01) Application of subsec. 138(12) — The definitions in subsection 138(12) apply to this section.

Notes: 89(1.01) added in the RSC 1985 (5th Supp) consolidation, effective for tax years ending after Nov. 1991. This rule was formerly in the opening words of 138(12).

(1.1) Capital dividend account where control acquired — Where at any particular time after March 31, 1977 a corporation that was, at a previous time, a private corporation controlled directly or indirectly in any manner whatever by one or more non-resident persons becomes a Canadian-controlled private corporation (otherwise than by reason of a change in the residence of one or more of its shareholders), in computing the corporation's capital dividend account at and after the particular time there shall be deducted the amount of the corporation's capital dividend account immediately before the particular time.

Related Provisions: 256(5.1), (6.2) — Controlled directly or indirectly; 256(7) — Where control deemed not acquired.

Income Tax Folios: S3-F2-C1: Capital Dividends [replaces IT-66R6].

(1.2) Capital dividend account of tax-exempt corporation — Where at any particular time after November 26, 1987 a corporation ceases to be exempt from tax under this Part on its taxable income, in computing the corporation's capital dividend account at and after the particular time there shall be deducted the amount of the corporation's capital dividend account (computed without reference to this subsection) immediately after the particular time.

Notes: Due to 89(1.2), an NPO that ceases to be an NPO cannot later pay a capital dividend: VIEWS doc 2012-0463361R3.

Income Tax Folios: S3-F2-C1: Capital Dividends [replaces IT-66R6].

(2) Where corporation is beneficiary — For the purposes of this section,

(a) where a corporation was a beneficiary under a life insurance policy on June 28, 1982, it shall be deemed not to have been a beneficiary under such a policy on or before June 28, 1982 where at any time after December 1, 1982 a prescribed premium has been paid under the policy or there has been a prescribed increase in any benefit on death under the policy; and

(b) where a corporation becomes a beneficiary under a life insurance policy by virtue of an amalgamation or a winding-up to which subsection 87(1) or 88(1) applies, it shall be deemed to have been a beneficiary under the policy throughout the period during which its predecessor or subsidiary, as the case may be, was a beneficiary under the policy.

Regulations: 309 (prescribed increase, prescribed premium).

(3) Simultaneous dividends — Where a dividend becomes payable at the same time on more than one class of shares of the capital stock of a corporation, for the purposes of sections 83, 84 and 88, the dividend on any such class of shares shall be deemed to become

payable at a different time than the dividend on the other class or classes of shares and to become payable in the order designated

(a) by the corporation on or before the day on or before which its return of income for its taxation year in which such dividends become payable is required to be filed; or

(b) in any other case, by the Minister.

Notes: For a corporation filing Quebec returns, an 89(3) designation must be copied to Revenu Québec: *Taxation Act* ss. 500, 21.4.6.

(4) GRIP addition — becoming CCPC — If, in a particular taxation year, a corporation is a Canadian-controlled private corporation or a deposit insurance corporation but was, in its preceding taxation year, a corporation resident in Canada other than a Canadian-controlled private corporation or a deposit insurance corporation, there may be included in computing the corporation's general rate income pool at the end of the particular taxation year, the amount determined by the formula

$$A + B + C - D - E - F - G - H$$

where

A is the total of all amounts each of which is the cost amount to the corporation of a property immediately before the end of its preceding taxation year;

B is the amount of any money of the corporation on hand immediately before the end of its preceding taxation year;

C is the amount, if any, by which

(a) the total of all amounts that, if the corporation had had unlimited income for its preceding taxation year from each business carried on, and from each property held, by it in that preceding taxation year and had realized an unlimited amount of capital gains for that preceding taxation year, would have been deductible under subsection 111(1) in computing its taxable income for that preceding taxation year

exceeds

(b) the total of all amounts deducted under subsection 111(1) in computing the corporation's taxable income for that preceding taxation year;

D is the total of all amounts each of which is the amount of any debt owing by the corporation, or of any other obligation of the corporation to pay any amount, that was outstanding immediately before the end of its preceding taxation year;

E is the paid up capital, immediately before the end of its preceding taxation year, of all of the issued and outstanding shares of the capital stock of the corporation;

F is the total of all amounts each of which is a reserve deducted in computing the corporation's income for its preceding taxation year;

G is the corporation's capital dividend account, if any, immediately before the end of its preceding taxation year; and

H is the corporation's low rate income pool immediately before the end of its preceding taxation year.

Related Provisions: 125(7)"Canadian-controlled private corporation"(d) — Election not to be CCPC for purposes of 89(4); 249(3.1) — Deemed year-end on becoming CCPC; 257 — Formula cannot calculate to less than zero.

Notes: 89(4) added by 2006 budget bill #2 (Part 2 — eligible dividends), effective for 2006 and later taxation years.

Former 89(4)–(6), repealed in 1977, provided rules for the definitions in 89(1) of paid-up capital deficiency and 1971 capital surplus on hand, concepts that no longer exist.

(5) GRIP addition — post-amalgamation — If a Canadian-controlled private corporation or a deposit insurance corporation (in this subsection referred to as the "new corporation") is formed as a result of an amalgamation (within the meaning assigned by subsection 87(1)), there shall be included in computing the new corporation's general rate income pool at the end of its first taxation year the total of all amounts each of which is

(a) in respect of a predecessor corporation that was, in its taxation year that ended immediately before the amalgamation (in this paragraph referred to as its "last taxation year"), a Canadian-controlled private corporation or a deposit insurance corporation, the positive or negative amount determined in respect of the predecessor corporation by the formula

$$A - B$$

where

A is the predecessor corporation's general rate income pool at the end of its last taxation year, and

B is the amount, if any, by which

(i) the total of all amounts each of which is an eligible dividend paid by the predecessor corporation in its last taxation year

exceeds

(ii) the total of all amounts each of which is an excessive eligible dividend designation made by the predecessor corporation in its last taxation year; or

(b) in respect of a predecessor corporation (in this paragraph referred to as the "non-CCPC predecessor") that was, in its taxation year that ended immediately before the amalgamation (in this paragraph referred to as its "last taxation year"), not a Canadian-controlled private corporation or a deposit insurance corporation, the amount determined by the formula

$$A + B + C - D - E - F - G - H$$

where

A is the total of all amounts each of which is the cost amount to the non-CCPC predecessor of a property immediately before the end of its last taxation year,

B is the amount of any money of the non-CCPC predecessor on hand immediately before the end of its last taxation year,

C is the amount, if any, by which

(i) the total of all amounts that, if the non-CCPC predecessor had had unlimited income for its last taxation year from each business carried on, and from each property held, by it in that last taxation year and had realized an unlimited amount of capital gains for that last taxation year, would have been deductible under subsection 111(1) in computing its taxable income for that last taxation year

exceeds

(ii) the total of all amounts deducted under subsection 111(1) in computing the non-CCPC predecessor's taxable income for its last taxation year,

D is the total of all amounts each of which is the amount of any debt owing by the non-CCPC predecessor, or of any other obligation of the non-CCPC predecessor to pay any amount, that was outstanding immediately before the end of its last taxation year,

E is the paid up capital, immediately before the end of its last taxation year, of all of the issued and outstanding shares of the capital stock of the non-CCPC predecessor,

F is the total of all amounts each of which is a reserve deducted in computing the non-CCPC predecessor's income for its last taxation year,

G is the non-CCPC predecessor's capital dividend account, if any, immediately before the end of its last taxation year, and

H is the non-CCPC predecessor's low rate income pool immediately before the end of its last taxation year.

Related Provisions: 87(2)(vv) — Application on amalgamation; 88(1)(e.2)(ix) — Application on windup; 125(7)"Canadian-controlled private corporation"(d) — Election not to be CCPC for purposes of 89(5); 257 — Formula in para. (b) cannot calculate to less than zero.

Notes: The para. (a) reference to "positive or negative amount" overrides s. 257.

89(5) added by 2006 budget bill #2, for 2006 and later tax years.

(6) GRIP addition — post-winding-up — If subsection 88(1) applies to the winding-up of a subsidiary into a parent (within the meanings assigned by that subsection) that is a Canadian-controlled private corporation or a deposit insurance corporation, there shall be included in computing the parent's general rate income pool at the end of its taxation year that immediately follows the taxation year during which it receives the assets of the subsidiary on the winding-up

(a) if the subsidiary was, in its taxation year during which its assets were distributed to the parent on the winding-up (in this paragraph referred to as its "last taxation year"), a Canadian-controlled private corporation or a deposit insurance corporation, the positive or negative amount determined by the formula

$$A - B$$

where

A is the subsidiary's general rate income pool at the end of its last taxation year, and

B is the amount, if any, by which

(i) the total of all amounts each of which is an eligible dividend paid by the subsidiary in its last taxation year

exceeds

(ii) the total of all amounts each of which is an excessive eligible dividend designation made by the subsidiary in its last taxation year; and

(b) in any other case, the amount determined by the formula

$$A + B + C - D - E - F - G - H$$

where

A is the total of all amounts each of which is the cost amount to the subsidiary of a property immediately before the end of its taxation year during which its assets were distributed to the parent on the winding-up (in this paragraph referred to as its "last taxation year"),

B is the amount of any money of the subsidiary on hand immediately before the end of its last taxation year,

C is the amount, if any, by which

(i) the total of all amounts that, if the subsidiary had had unlimited income for its last taxation year from each business carried on, and from each property held, by it in that last taxation year and had realized an unlimited amount of capital gains for that last taxation year, would have been deductible under subsection 111(1) in computing its taxable income for that last taxation year

exceeds

(ii) the total of all amounts deducted under subsection 111(1) in computing the subsidiary's taxable income for its last taxation year,

D is the total of all amounts each of which is the amount of any debt owing by the subsidiary, or of any other obligation of the subsidiary to pay any amount, that was outstanding immediately before the end of its last taxation year,

E is the paid up capital, immediately before the end of its last taxation year, of all of the issued and outstanding shares of the capital stock of the subsidiary,

F is the total of all amounts each of which is a reserve deducted in computing the subsidiary's income for its last taxation year,

G is the subsidiary's capital dividend account, if any, immediately before the end of its last taxation year, and

H is the subsidiary's low rate income pool immediately before the end of its last taxation year.

Related Provisions: 87(2)(vv), 88(1)(e.2)(ix) — Application on windup; 125(7)"Canadian-controlled private corporation"(d) — Election not to be CCPC for purposes of 89(6); 257 — Formula in para. (b) cannot calculate to less than zero.

Notes: The first formula reference to "positive or negative amount" overrides s. 257.

89(6) added by 2006 budget bill #2, for 2006 and later tax years.

(7) GRIP addition for 2006 — If a corporation was (or, but for an election under subsection (11), would have been), throughout its first taxation year that includes any part of January 1, 2006, a Canadian-controlled private corporation, its general rate income pool at the end of its immediately preceding taxation year is deemed to be the greater of nil and the amount determined by the formula

$$A - B$$

where

A is the total of

(a) 63% of the total of all amounts each of which is the corporation's full rate taxable income (as defined in subsection 123.4(1)), for a taxation year of the corporation that ended after 2000 and before 2004, determined before taking into consideration the specified future tax consequences for that taxation year,

(b) 63% of the total of all amounts each of which is the corporation's full rate taxable income (as would be defined in subsection 123.4(1), if that definition were read without reference to its subparagraphs (a)(i) and (ii)), for a taxation year of the corporation that ended after 2003 and before 2006, determined before taking into consideration the specified future tax consequences for that taxation year, and

(c) all amounts each of which was deductible under subsection 112(1) in computing the corporation's taxable income for a taxation year of the corporation (in this paragraph referred to as the "particular corporation") that ended after 2000 and before 2006, and is in respect of a dividend received from a corporation (in this paragraph referred to as the "payer corporation") that was, at the time it paid the dividend, connected (within the meaning assigned by subsection 186(4)) with the particular corporation, to the extent that it is reasonable to consider, having regard to all the circumstances (including but not limited to other shareholders having received dividends from the payer corporation), that the dividend was attributable to an amount that is, or if this subsection applied to the payer corporation would be, described in this paragraph or in paragraph (a) or (b) in respect of the payer corporation; and

B is the total of all amounts each of which is a taxable dividend paid by the corporation in those taxation years.

Related Provisions: 257 — Formula cannot calculate to less than zero.

Notes: This is a "rough justice" relieving rule designed to approximate GRIP for the transition into the system in 2006, by measuring a corporation's full-rate taxable income for the previous five years minus dividends paid out. Although it could be adjusted and refined, Finance has indicated that it will not be modified (Evans & Schusheim, Cdn Tax Foundation 2006 conference report, p. 1:19). Effectively, an opening GRIP balance is available to high-income CCPCs which retained income in the corporation rather than bonusing down to the small business limit (125(2)).

CRA has stated (APFF Congrès, Oct./07) that the condition in 89(7)(c) may apply on a cumulative basis: Ernst & Young Commentary N-85-07 (CICA) Dec. 3/07.

For more interpretation see VIEWS docs 2007-0225481E5, 2007-0227071E5, 2007-0227531E5, 2007-0243051C6, 2007-0243091C6, 2007-0250841E5, 2007-0257721E5, 2007-0263001E5, 2008-0264561E5, 2008-0264691E5, 2008-0294111E5, 2008-0284941C6, 2009-0340831E5, 2009-0340841E5, 2010-0390111I7, 2012-0468511E5, 2013-0476901E5; May 2008 ICAA roundtable (tinyurl.com/cra-abtax), q. 2.

89(7) added by 2006 budget bill #2 (Part 2 — eligible dividends), effective only for the first taxation year of a corporation that includes any part of January 1, 2006.

Forms: T2 Sched. 53: General rate income pool (GRIP) calculation.

(8) LRIP addition — ceasing to be CCPC — If, in a particular taxation year, a corporation is neither a Canadian-controlled private corporation nor a deposit insurance corporation but was, in its preceding taxation year, a Canadian-controlled private corporation or a deposit insurance corporation, there shall be included in computing the corporation's low rate income pool at any time in the particular taxation year the amount determined by the formula

$$A + B + C - D - E - F - G - H$$

where

A is the total of all amounts each of which is the cost amount to the corporation of a property immediately before the end of its preceding taxation year;

B is the amount of any money of the corporation on hand immediately before the end of its preceding taxation year;

C is the amount, if any, by which

(a) the total of all amounts that, if the corporation had had unlimited income for its preceding taxation year from each business carried on, and from each property held, by it in that preceding taxation year and had realized an unlimited amount of capital gains for that preceding taxation year, would have been deductible under subsection 111(1) in computing its taxable income for that preceding taxation year

exceeds

(b) the total of all amounts deducted under subsection 111(1) in computing the corporation's taxable income for its preceding taxation year;

D is the total of all amounts each of which is the amount of any debt owing by the corporation, or of any other obligation of the corporation to pay any amount, that was outstanding immediately before the end of its preceding taxation year;

E is the paid up capital, immediately before the end of its preceding taxation year, of all of the issued and outstanding shares of the capital stock of the corporation;

F is the total of all amounts each of which is a reserve deducted in computing the corporation's income for its preceding taxation year;

G is

(a) if the corporation is not a private corporation in the particular taxation year, the corporation's capital dividend account, if any, immediately before the end of its preceding taxation year, and

(b) in any other case, nil; and

H is the positive or negative amount determined by the formula

$$I - J$$

where

I is the corporation's general rate income pool at the end of its preceding taxation year, and

J is the amount, if any, by which

(a) the total of all amounts each of which is an eligible dividend paid by the corporation in its preceding taxation year

exceeds

(b) the total of all amounts each of which is an excessive eligible dividend designation made by the corporation in its preceding taxation year.

Related Provisions: 125(7)"Canadian-controlled private corporation"(d) — Election not to be CCPC for purposes of 89(8); 249(3.1) — Deemed year-end on ceasing to be CCPC; 257 — First formula cannot calculate to less than zero.

Notes: The reference to "positive or negative amount" in H overrides s. 257.

The cost amount of a declared but unpaid dividend is included under A and valued as per 248(1)"cost amount"(e): VIEWS doc 2012-0437271E5.

For examples of 89(8) applying see May 2008 ICAA roundtable (tinyurl.com/cra-abtax), q. 5; VIEWS docs 2009-0325881E5, 2010-0390831E5, 2011-0395121E5.

89(8) added by 2006 budget bill #2, for 2006 and later tax years.

I.T. Technical News: 44 (calculating LRIP for cash-basis taxpayers).

(9) LRIP addition — amalgamation — If a corporation that is resident in Canada and that is neither a Canadian-controlled private corporation nor a deposit insurance corporation (in this subsection referred to as the "new corporation") is formed as a result of the amalgamation or merger of two or more corporations one or more of which is a taxable Canadian corporation, there shall be included in computing the new corporation's low rate income pool at any time in its first taxation year the total of all amounts each of which is

(a) in respect of a predecessor corporation that was, in its taxation year that ended immediately before the amalgamation, neither a Canadian-controlled private corporation nor a deposit insurance corporation, the predecessor corporation's low rate income pool at the end of that taxation year; and

(b) in respect of a predecessor corporation (in this paragraph referred to as the "CCPC predecessor") that was, throughout its taxation year that ended immediately before the amalgamation (in this paragraph referred to as its "last taxation year"), a Canadian-controlled private corporation or a deposit insurance corporation, the amount determined by the formula

$$A + B + C - D - E - F - G - H$$

where

A   is the total of all amounts each of which is the cost amount to the CCPC predecessor of a property immediately before the end of its last taxation year,

B   is the amount of any money of the CCPC predecessor on hand immediately before the end of its last taxation year,

C   is the amount, if any, by which

(i) the total of all amounts that, if the CCPC predecessor had had unlimited income for its last taxation year from each business carried on, and from each property held, by it in that last taxation year and had realized an unlimited amount of capital gains for that last taxation year, would have been deductible under subsection 111(1) in computing its taxable income for that last taxation year

exceeds

(ii) the total of all amounts deducted under subsection 111(1) in computing the CCPC predecessor's taxable income for its last taxation year,

D   is the total of all amounts each of which is the amount of any debt owing by the CCPC predecessor, or of any other obligation of the CCPC predecessor to pay any amount, that was outstanding immediately before the end of its last taxation year,

E   is the paid up capital, immediately before the end of its last taxation year, of all of the issued and outstanding shares of the capital stock of the CCPC predecessor,

F   is the total of all amounts each of which is a reserve deducted in computing the CCPC predecessor's income for its last taxation year,

G   is

(i) if the new corporation is not a private corporation in its first taxation year, the CCPC predecessor's capital dividend account, if any, immediately before the end of its last taxation year, and

(ii) in any other case, nil, and

H   is the positive or negative amount determined by the formula

$$I - J$$

where

I   is the CCPC predecessor's general rate income pool at the end of its last taxation year, and

J   is the amount, if any, by which

(i) the total of all amounts each of which is an eligible dividend paid by the CCPC predecessor in its last taxation year

exceeds

(ii) the total of all amounts each of which is an excessive eligible dividend designation made by the CCPC predecessor in its last taxation year.

Related Provisions: 87(2)(ww) — Application on amalgamation; 88(1)(e.2)(ix) — Application on winding-up; 125(7)"Canadian-controlled private corporation"(d) —

Election not to be CCPC for purposes of 89(9); 257 — Formulas cannot calculate to less than zero.

Notes: 89(9) added by 2006 budget bill #2, for 2006 and later tax years.

(10) LRIP addition — winding-up — If, in a particular taxation year, a corporation (in this subsection referred to as the "parent") is neither a Canadian-controlled private corporation nor a deposit insurance corporation and in the particular taxation year all or substantially all of the assets of another corporation (in this subsection referred to as the "subsidiary") were distributed to the parent on a dissolution or winding-up of the subsidiary, there shall be included in computing the parent's low rate income pool at any time in the particular taxation year that is at or after the end of the subsidiary's taxation year (in this subsection referred to as the subsidiary's "last taxation year") during which its assets were distributed to the parent on the winding-up,

(a) if the subsidiary was, in its last taxation year, neither a Canadian-controlled private corporation nor a deposit insurance corporation, the subsidiary's low rate income pool immediately before the end of that taxation year; and

(b) in any other case, the amount determined by the formula

$$A + B + C - D - E - F - G - H$$

where

A   is the total of all amounts each of which is the cost amount to the subsidiary of a property immediately before the end of its last taxation year,

B   is the amount of any money of the subsidiary on hand immediately before the end of its last taxation year,

C   is the amount, if any, by which

(i) the total of all amounts that, if the subsidiary had had unlimited income for its last taxation year from each business carried on, and from each property held, by it in that last taxation year and had realized an unlimited amount of capital gains for that last taxation year, would have been deductible under subsection 111(1) in computing its taxable income for that last taxation year

exceeds

(ii) the total of all amounts deducted under subsection 111(1) in computing the subsidiary's taxable income for its last taxation year,

D   is the total of all amounts each of which is the amount of any debt owing by the subsidiary, or of any other obligation of the subsidiary to pay any amount, that was outstanding immediately before the end of its last taxation year,

E   is the paid up capital, immediately before the end of its last taxation year, of all of the issued and outstanding shares of the capital stock of the subsidiary,

F   is the total of all amounts each of which is a reserve deducted in computing the subsidiary's income for its last taxation year,

G   is

(i) if the parent is not a private corporation in the particular taxation year, the subsidiary's capital dividend account, if any, immediately before the end of its last taxation year, and

(ii) in any other case, nil, and

H   is the positive or negative amount determined by the formula

$$I - J$$

where

I   is the subsidiary's general rate income pool at the end of its last taxation year, and

J   is the amount, if any, by which

(i) the total of all amounts each of which is an eligible dividend paid by the subsidiary in its last taxation year

exceeds

(ii) the total of all amounts each of which is an excessive eligible dividend designation made by the subsidiary in its last taxation year.

Related Provisions: 87(2)(ww), 88(1)(e.2)(ix) — Application on winding-up; 125(7)"Canadian-controlled private corporation"(d) — Election not to be CCPC for purposes of 89(10); 257 — Formula in para. (b) cannot calculate to less than zero.

Notes: The second formula (for H) reference to "positive or negative amount" overrides s. 257.

89(10) added by 2006 budget bill #2, for 2006 and later tax years.

(11) Election: non-CCPC — Subject to subsection (12), a corporation that files with the Minister on or before its filing-due date for a particular taxation year an election in prescribed form to have this subsection apply is deemed for the purposes described in paragraph (d) of the definition "Canadian-controlled private corporation" in subsection 125(7) not to be a Canadian-controlled private corporation at any time in or after the particular taxation year.

Related Provisions: 89(12) — Revocation of election; 220(2.1) — Extension of time for filing election.

Notes: When this election is made, the corporation loses the small business deduction under 125(1), but its dividends are eligible for increased dividend tax credit (82(1)(b)(ii), 121(b)). See 125(7)"Canadian-controlled private corporation"(d). The refundable tax on investment income (123.3) is still payable. A corporation making this election will no longer need to track GRIP (but will have LRIP). The election does not trigger a 249(3.1) year-end because it applies from the beginning of the year: VIEWS doc 2014-0550191I7.

When a corporation makes an 89(11) election, the amount under 125.1(1)(a) for the M&P deduction is nil, but the corporation can still determine a business limit under 125(2) (e.g., for pre-2008 127(10.2): VIEWS docs 2007-026234117, 2008-0281921E5; May 2013 ICAA Roundtable q.24 (tinyurl.com/cra-abtax)).

See also VIEWS doc 2008-0285011C6 (whether 89(11) continues to apply after acquisition or amalgamation); 2010-0377251E5 (interaction with election under 89(1)"public corporation"(c)(i) not to be a public corp).

See also Stephan, "Electing Out of CCPC Status in Share Sale Planning", 7(3) *Tax For the Owner-Manager* (ctf.ca) 3-4 (July 2007); Baass, "Planning Strategies Involving the Subsection 89(11) Election", 20(10) *Taxation of Executive Compensation & Retirement* (Federated Press) 1155-62 (June 2009); Thivierge, "Income Tax Due Diligence Considerations in Mergers and Acquisitions", 2015 Cdn Tax Foundation conference report at 18:18-19 (election can reduce multiple year-ends on non-resident's acquisition of a CCPC).

For a corporation filing Quebec returns, an election under 89(11) (and any revocation under 89(12)) must be copied to Revenu Québec: *Taxation Act* ss. 21.19, 21.4.6.

89(11) added by 2006 budget bill #2, for 2006 and later tax years.

Forms: T2002: Election, or revocation of an election, not to be a CCPC.

(12) Revoking election — If a corporation files with the Minister on or before its filing-due date for a particular taxation year a notice in prescribed form revoking, as of the end of the particular taxation year, an election described in subsection (11), the election ceases to apply to the corporation at the end of the particular taxation year.

Related Provisions: 89(13) — Consent required for re-election.

Notes: The revocation does not trigger a 249(3.1) year-end because it applies from the beginning of the next year: VIEWS doc 2014-0550191I7.

89(12) added by 2006 budget bill #2, for 2006 and later tax years.

Forms: T2002: Election, or revocation of an election, not to be a CCPC.

(13) Repeated elections — consent required — If a corporation has, under subsection (12), revoked an election, any subsequent election under subsection (11) or subsequent revocation under subsection (12) is invalid unless

(a) the Minister consents in writing to the subsequent election or the subsequent revocation, as the case may be; and

(b) the corporation complies with any conditions imposed by the Minister.

Notes: 89(13) added by 2006 budget bill #2, for 2006 and later tax years.

(14) Dividend designation — A corporation designates a portion of a dividend it pays at any time to be an eligible dividend by notifying in writing at that time each person or partnership to whom the dividend is paid that the portion of the dividend is an eligible dividend.

Related Provisions: 89(14.1) — Late designation; 185.1 — Penalty tax on excessive eligible dividend designation; 248(7)(a) — Notification deemed received once it is mailed.

Notes: For CRA policy on how a corporation can notify shareholders of designation of eligible dividends, see tinyurl.com/cra-elig-des. For a public corp, CRA accepts a statement that "all dividends are eligible dividends unless indicated otherwise" on the corp's website, in quarterly or annual reports or in shareholder publications. "A notice posted on a corporate website is notification that an eligible dividend is paid to shareholders until the notice is removed. Similarly, a notice in an annual or quarterly report that an eligible dividend has been paid is considered valid for that year or quarter, respectively." A statement in a press release announcing the declaration of a dividend will also do. For private corps, examples of notification include letters to shareholders, dividend cheque stubs and (if all shareholders are directors) a notation in the minutes. See also VIEWS doc 2006-0217891Z0 (Dec. 26, 2006 news release).

This position applies to the designation of part of a dividend: doc 2012-0449821E5. Note that all shareholders must be notified. A partial designation of a dividend was allowed administratively for 2006 only (2007-0227531E5, 2007-0243141C6), but was not possible from 2007 until the 2012 Budget amendment (2008-0284961C6, 2010-0387541E5), even though the dividend would not be an eligible dividend for non-resident shareholders (see 89(1)"eligible dividend"). However, an excessive dividend (see 89(1)"excessive eligible dividend designation") can be cured by 185.1(2). For late designation, see 89(14.1). See also 2006-0207651E5.

CRA says (doc 2020-0852231C6 [2020 APFF q.11]) that a corp cannot designate the eligible portion of a dividend as being the GRIP balance, but must specify an amount. In the author's view, this is wrong; see 83(2) Notes on the same issue.

If a dividend is paid only to non-resident shareholders, there is no point in making a designation, and if no designation is made, the dividend cannot be an excessive eligible dividend designation.

For more on 89(14) see VIEWS docs 2007-0244111I7 and 2007-0260221E5 (no late filing allowed where excess portion of capital dividend designated under 184(3)); 2007-0249941E5 (for CCPC, notification must state amount of dividend rather than advising how to calculate it); 2008-0300381C6, 2019-0824471C6 [2019 CTF q.16] (administrative relief for public corps will not be extended to CCPCs; for a CCPC, director's resolution is enough if all shareholders are directors); 2009-0309111E5 (notification on T3 and T5 slips is not acceptable); 2009-0330141C6 (dividend designation and partnership); 2009-0347491C6 (where parent and sub have same directors, resolution of sub's directors is considered delivered when signed); 2010-0363851C6 (if designated dividend is paid to both resident and non-res shareholders, only the portion received by residents is an eligible dividend); 2010-0373281C6 (where designation made on 84(3) deemed dividend and PUC was miscalculated); 2013-0512041E5 (designation of entire dividend still permitted after 2012 amendment); 2017-0720731E5 (notice can be given by email, and should be given after dividend declared and before it is paid).

CRA also provided several interpretations at the 2008 Cdn Tax Foundation conference (conference report at 3:2-4, updated in *Income Tax Technical News* 41), including: where registered holder is a nominee; where some shareholders are non-resident; handwritten notification on information slips will be extended to 2008 taxation year; notification at time dividend is paid.

See also Notes to 89(1)"eligible dividend".

89(14) amended by 2012 budget bill #1, for dividends paid after March 28, 2012, to allow a portion of a dividend to be designated.

89(14) added by 2006 budget bill #2, for 2006 and later tax years.

I.T. Technical News: 41 (eligible dividend designation).

(14.1) Late designation — If, in the opinion of the Minister, the circumstances are such that it would be just and equitable to permit a designation under subsection (14) to be made before the day that is three years after the day on which the designation was required to be made, the designation is deemed to have been made at the time the designation was required to be made.

Notes: For the meaning of "just and equitable", see Notes to 85(7.1).

For discussion of the criteria for accepting a late designation see VIEWS doc 2013-0495771C6 [2013 APFF q.14]. CRA will not accept a late designation done deliberately, on a regular basis for retroactive tax planning purposes (and Reg. 600 will not be amended to allow late designations): 2012-0445661C6; nor will CRA accept and hold in abeyance a designation conditional on failure of an appeal of a small business deduction denial, which failure would increase GRIP: 2014-0541991E5 [Daniel Gosselin, "Late-Filed Eligible-Dividend Designations", 15(3) *Tax for the Owner-Manager* (ctf.ca) 4-5 (July 2015)]. For a case where late designation would be allowed, see 2013-0475261E5.

A CRA refusal to accept a late designation is subject to judicial review by the Federal Court if it is unreasonable. See Notes to 220(3.1).

89(14.1) added by 2012 budget bill #1, for dividends paid after March 28, 2012.

(15) Meaning of expression "deposit insurance corporation" — For the purposes of paragraphs 87(2)(vv) and (ww) (including, for greater certainty, in applying those paragraphs as pro-

vided under paragraph 88(1)(e.2)), the definitions "excessive eligible dividend designation", "general rate income pool", and "low rate income pool" in subsection (1) and subsections (4) to (6) and (8) to (10), a corporation is a deposit insurance corporation if it would be a deposit insurance corporation as defined in the definition "deposit insurance corporation" in subsection 137.1(5) were that definition read without reference to its paragraph (b) and were this Act read without reference to subsection 137.1(5.1).

Notes: 89(15) added by 2006 budget bill #2, for 2006 and later tax years.

Definitions [s. 89]: "adjusted cost basis" — 148(9); "adjusted taxable income" — 89(1); "aggregate investment income" — 129(4), 248(1); "allowable capital loss" — 38(b), 248(1); "amalgamation" — 87(1); "amount" — 248(1); "arm's length" — 251(1); "beneficiary" — 248(25) [Notes]; "business" — 248(1); "Canada" — 255; "Canadian-controlled private corporation" — 125(7), 248(1); "Canadian corporation" — 89(1), 248(1); "capital dividend" — 83(2)–(2.4), 248(1); "capital gain" — 39(1)(a), 248(1); "capital loss" — 39(1)(b), 248(1); "capital property" — 54, 248(1); "class", "class of shares" — 248(6); "connected" — 186(4); "consequence of the death" — 248(8); "controlled" — 256(6), (6.1); "controlled directly or indirectly" — 256(5.1)–(6); "cooperative corporation" — 136(2); "corporation" — 248(1), *Interpretation Act* 35(1); "cost amount" — 248(1); "credit union" — 137(6), 248(1); "cumulative eligible capital" — 14(5), 248(1); "deposit insurance corporation" — 89(15); "depreciable property" — 13(21), 248(1); "designated property" — 89(1); "designated stock exchange" — 248(1), 262; "disposition", "dividend" — 248(1); "eligible capital expenditure" — 14(5), 248(1); "eligible dividend" — 89(1), 248(1), 260(5); "excessive eligible dividend designation" — 89(1), 248(1); "fair market value" — see 69(1) Notes; "filing-due date" — 248(1); "foreign affiliate" — 95(1); "full rate taxable income" — 123.4(1); "general rate factor" — 89(1); "general rate income pool" — 89(1), 248(1); "incorporated in Canada" — 248(1)"corporation incorporated in Canada"; "insurance corporation", "inventory" — 248(1); "investment corporation" — 130(3), 248(1); "LIA policy", "life insurance corporation" — 248(1); "life insurance policy" — 138(12), 248(1); "low rate income pool" — 89(1), 248(1); "Minister" — 248(1); "mortgage investment corporation" — 130.1(6), 248(1); "mutual fund corporation" — 131(8), 248(1); "non-resident" — 248(1); "paid-up capital" — 89(1), 248(1); "parent" — 88(1); "partnership" — see 96(1) Notes; "payable" — 84(7); "period" — 89(1)"capital dividend account"(a)(i)(A); "person", "prescribed" — 248(1); "prescribed increase" — Reg. 309(2); "prescribed labour-sponsored venture capital corporation" — Reg. 6701; "prescribed premium" — Reg. 309(1); "prescribed venture capital corporation" — Reg. 6700; "private corporation" — 89(1), 248(1); "property" — 248(1); "province" — *Interpretation Act* 35(1); "public corporation" — 89(1), 248(1); "resident in Canada" — 94(3)(a), 250; "series of transactions" — 248(10); "share", "shareholder", "specified future tax consequence" — 248(1); "subsidiary" — 88(1); "substituted" — 248(5); "taxable Canadian corporation" — 89(1), 248(1); "taxable capital gain" — 38(a), (a.1), 248(1); "taxable dividend" — 89(1); "taxable income" — 2(2), 248(1); "taxation year" — 249; "taxpayer" — 248(1); "trust" — 104(1), 248(1), (3); "writing" — *Interpretation Act* 35(1); "10/8 policy" — 248(1).

89.1 [Repealed under former Act]

Notes: 89.1, repealed in 1977, provided rules for determining PUC under 89(1)(c), which defined "paid-up capital".

Subdivision I — Shareholders of Corporations Not Resident in Canada

90. (1) Dividend from non-resident corporation — In computing the income for a taxation year of a taxpayer resident in Canada, there is to be included any amount received by the taxpayer at any time in the year as, on account or in lieu of payment of, or in satisfaction of, a dividend on a share owned by the taxpayer of the capital stock of a non-resident corporation.

Related Provisions: 82(1) — Dividends received from corporation resident in Canada; 90(2) — Deemed dividend from foreign affiliate; 90(5) — No amount is dividend from foreign affiliate unless deemed; 93.1(1) — Shares owned by partnership deemed owned by partners; 113(1) — Deduction to corporation for dividend received from foreign affiliate.

Notes: See Notes to 248(1)"dividend" on the meaning of "dividend". See Notes to 248(1)"amount" on the "amount" of a stock dividend to be included.

The inclusion in income of dividends from non-resident corporations can be offset by a deduction under 113(1), depending on the country of source (see Reg. 5907(11)) and whether the dividend is paid out of a foreign affiliate's taxable surplus, exempt surplus or pre-acquisition surplus. See Notes to 113(1).

See Sandra Slaats, "Repatriations from Foreign Affiliates: Selected Issues", 53 *Canadian Tax Journal* 858-84 (2005). For FAPI, see Notes to 91(1).

In *Moyes*, 2010 FCA 18, US-source amounts on a T5 under "code 5" were held taxable as likely foreign-source dividends, rather than capital gains.

90 renumbered as 90(1) and amended (non-substantively) by 2002-2013 technical bill (Part 3 — FA reorganizations), effective Aug. 20, 2011 (or earlier by election).

(2) [Deemed] Dividend from foreign affiliate — For the purposes of this Act, an amount is deemed to be a dividend paid or received, as the case may be, at any time on a share of a class of the capital stock of a non-resident corporation that is a foreign affiliate of a taxpayer if the amount is the share's portion of a pro rata distribution (other than a distribution made in the course of a liquidation and dissolution of the corporation, on a redemption, acquisition or cancellation of the share by the corporation, or on a qualifying return of capital in respect of the share) made at that time by the corporation in respect of all the shares of that class.

Related Provisions: 90(3) — Qualifying return of capital; 93.1(1) — Shares owned by partnership deemed owned by partners; 113(1) — Deductions against dividend from foreign affiliate; Reg. 5901(2)(b) — Election for dividend to come out of pre-acquisition surplus.

Notes: For discussion of 90(2) see Elaine Buzzell, "Distributions of Share Premium by Foreign Affiliates", XVII(2) *Corporate Finance* (Federated Press) 1962-68 (2011); Marley & Slaats, "Foreign Affiliate Reorganizations", 2012 Cdn Tax Foundation conference report, at 27:8-13; Michael Gemmiti, "FA Dividends Must Be Pro Rata", 3(3) *Canadian Tax Focus* (ctf.ca) 7 (Aug. 2013). See also Notes to Reg. 5901(2).

See also VIEWS docs 2013-0483741C6 [2013 IFA q.2] (no shareholder benefit on foreign spinoff); 2013-0506731E5 (distribution is made when dividend is paid, so dividend declared and payable while taxpayer non-resident, but paid once taxpayer is resident in Canada, is taxed under 90(2)); 2014-0527961R3 (shares denominated in different currencies are different classes for 90(2)); 2016-0642081C6 [2016 IFA q.6] (90(2) can apply to payment under "profit transfer agreement" by German sub to German parent [Huynh & Barnicke, "German Organschafts", 24(6) *Canadian Tax Highlights* (ctf.ca) 5-6 (June 2016)]); 2015-0617351R3 (payments under German profit transfer agreement fall under 90(2)); 2016-0670541I7 (foreign affiliate share redemption).

90(2) added by 2002-2013 technical bill (Part 3 — FA reorganizations), effective Aug. 20, 2011 (or earlier by election).

(3) Qualifying return of capital — For the purposes of subsection (2), a distribution made at any time by a foreign affiliate of a taxpayer in respect of a share of the capital stock of the affiliate that is a reduction of the paid-up capital of the affiliate in respect of the share and that would, in the absence of this subsection, be deemed under subsection (2) to be a dividend paid or received, at that time, on the share is a qualifying return of capital, at that time, in respect of the share if an election is made under this subsection, in respect of the distribution and in accordance with prescribed rules,

(a) by the taxpayer, where there is no person or partnership that meets the conditions in subparagraphs (b)(i) and (ii); or

(b) jointly by the taxpayer and each person or partnership that is, at that time,

(i) a connected person or partnership in respect of the taxpayer, and

(ii) a person or partnership of which the affiliate would, at that time, be a foreign affiliate if paragraph (b) of the definition "equity percentage" in subsection 95(4) were read as if the reference in that paragraph to "any corporation" were a reference to "any corporation other than a corporation resident in Canada".

Related Provisions: 53(2)(b)(i)(B)(II) — Reduction in ACB for qualifying return of capital; 90(4) — Connected person or partnership; 96(3) — Election by members of partnership.

Notes: See Turner, "New Foreign Affiliate Capital Distribution Elections", 2133 *Tax Topics* (CCH) 1-4 (Jan. 24, 2013); VIEWS doc 2014-0535971E5 (meaning of PUC). For a taxpayer filing a Quebec return, a 90(3) election must be copied to Revenu Québec: *Taxation Act* ss. 577.3, 21.4.6.

90(3) added by 2002-2013 technical bill (effective Aug. 20, 2011).

Regulations: 5911(6) (prescribed rules for election).

(4) Connected person or partnership — For the purposes of subsection (3), a "connected person or partnership" in respect of a taxpayer, at any time, is

(a) a person that is, at that time, related to the taxpayer, and

(b) a partnership a member of which is, at that time,

(i) the taxpayer, or

(ii) a person that is related to the taxpayer.

Notes: 90(4) added by 2002-2013 technical bill (Part 3 — FA reorganizations), effective Aug. 20, 2011 (or earlier by election).

(5) Exclusion — No amount paid or received at any time is, for the purposes of this Act, a dividend paid or received on a share of the capital stock of a non-resident corporation that is a foreign affiliate of a taxpayer unless it is so deemed under this Part.

Related Provisions: 90(2) — Deemed dividend from foreign affiliate; 93.1(1) — Shares owned by partnership deemed owned by partners.

Notes: 90(5) added by 2002-2013 technical bill (Part 3 — FA reorganizations), effective Aug. 20, 2011 (or earlier by election).

(6) Loan from foreign affiliate — Except where subsection 15(2) applies, if a person or partnership receives at any time a loan from, or becomes at that time indebted to, a creditor that is at that time a foreign affiliate (referred to in subsections (9), (11) and (15) as the "creditor affiliate") of a taxpayer resident in Canada or that is at that time a partnership (referred to in subsections (9), (11) and (15) as the "creditor partnership") of which such an affiliate is a member and the person or partnership is at that time a specified debtor in respect of the taxpayer, then the specified amount in respect of the loan or indebtedness is to be included in computing the income of the taxpayer for the taxpayer's taxation year that includes that time.

Related Provisions: 15(1)(a.1), 15(1.5) — Benefit from non-resident corporation included in shareholder's income; 39(2.1)–(2.3), 95(2)(g.04) — Foreign currency adjustment where loan is repaid; 90(6.1), (6.11) — Continuity of upstream loan on reorganization; 90(7) — Back-to-back loans; 90(8) — Exceptions to subsec. (6); 90(8)(d), 90(8.1) — Treatment of upstream deposit of eligible bank affiliate; 90(9) — Offsetting deduction if conditions satisfied; 90(14) — Deduction on repayment of loan; 93.1(1) — Shares owned by partnership deemed owned by partners.

Notes: 90(6) includes "upstream loans" from foreign affiliates (FAs) in income, with an offsetting deduction under 90(14) when the loan is repaid, and an annual deduction/postponement under 90(9) if the FA could have paid the Canadian parent a tax-free dividend. It is similar to 15(2), which applies only to non-corporate shareholders, and includes exceptions in 90(8) similar to the exceptions to 15(2).

Note that "specified debtor" in 90(15) includes the taxpayer (shareholder).

The effect of the in-force rule below, combined with 90(8)(a), is that grandfathering is provided until Aug. 19, 2016 for loans existing on Aug. 19, 2011. (This replaces the 2-year grandfathering when the rules were first announced on Aug. 19, 2011.)

This subsection was 90(4) in the Aug. 19/11 draft. For discussion and criticism of the 2011 draft of s. 90 see these Notes up to the 54th ed. For CRA interpretation of that draft see VIEWS doc 2011-0414431R3 (the rule applies).

For comment on the current (Oct. 2012) version see McDowell et al., "Upstream Loans", 2012 Cdn Tax Foundation conference report, 21:1-29; Barnicke & Huynh, "Revised Upstream Loan Rules", 20(12) *Canadian Tax Highlights* (ctf.ca) 4-5 (Dec. 2012) and "Upstream Loans", 21(12) 3-4 (Dec. 2013); Buttenham, "Are You Ready for the Upstream Loan Rules?", 61(3) *Canadian Tax Journal* 747-68 (2013); Bradley et al., "Recommended Amendments to the Upstream Loan Rules", 63(1) *CTJ* 245-67 (2015); Turner, "Upstream Loans and Dispositions of Foreign Affiliate Shares", 85 *International Tax* (CCH) 1-6 (Dec. 2015); Spinelli & Ariyakumaran, "Upstream Loans Disadvantage Corporate Members of a Partnership", 8(1) *Canadian Tax Focus* (ctf.ca) 4-5 (Nov. 2018).

For CRA interpretation see VIEWS docs 2013-0483791C6 [2013 IFA q.5] (various scenarios); 2013-0488881E5 (various scenarios); 2013-0499121E5 (relief from double tax via 248(28) where loan from FA2 to Canco is transferred to FA1 on windup of FA2; no double tax where FAs amalgamate); 2013-0510551R3 (90(6) does not apply); 2014-0526731C6 [2014 IFA q.3(b)] (90(6) applies to accrued interest not yet payable); 2014-0545591E5 (forgiveness of loan is not "repayment" under 90(8) or (14)); 2015-0610621C6 [2015 CTF q.8] (on FA windup, loan is not considered "repaid" [at the conference it was stated that this has been brought to Finance's attention and may be fixed]); 2016-0645521I7 (90(6) and 90(14) do not depend on whether the FA remains a creditor affiliate); 2016-0673661I7 (FIFO used to determine which loans repaid); 2017-0670971R3 (applying 90(8) and (14) to particular facts).

90(6)-(15) added by 2002-2013 technical bill, for loans received and indebtedness incurred after Aug. 19, 2011, and for any portion of an earlier loan that remained outstanding on Aug. 19, 2014. An election could be filed in 2014 to ignore 90(7) in respect of all loans received and indebtedness incurred by Oct. 24, 2012.

(6.1) Upstream loan continuity — reorganizations — Subsection (6.11) applies at any time if

(a) immediately before that time, a person or partnership (referred to in this subsection and subsection (6.11) as the "**original debtor**") owes an amount in respect of a loan or indebtedness (referred to in this subsection and subsection (6.11) as the "**pre-transaction loan**") to another person or partnership (referred to in this subsection and subsection (6.11) as the "**original creditor**");

(b) the pre-transaction loan was, at the time it was made or entered into, a loan or indebtedness that is described in subsection (6); and

(c) in the course of an amalgamation, a merger, a winding-up or a liquidation and dissolution,

(i) the amount owing in respect of the pre-transaction loan becomes owing at that time by another person or partnership (the amount owing after that time and the other person or partnership are referred to in subsection (6.11) as the "**post-transaction loan payable**" and the "**new debtor**", respectively),

(ii) the amount owing in respect of the pre-transaction loan becomes owing at that time to another person or partnership (the amount owing after that time and the other person or partnership are referred to in subsection (6.11) as the "**post-transaction loan receivable**" and the "**new creditor**", respectively), or

(iii) the taxpayer in respect of which the original debtor was a specified debtor at the time referred to in paragraph (b)

(A) ceases to exist, or

(B) merges with one or more corporations to form one corporate entity (referred to in subsection (6.11) as the "new corporation").

Notes: See Notes to 90(6.11).

(6.11) Upstream loan continuity — reorganizations — If this subsection applies at any time, for the purposes of subsections (6) and (7) to (15) and 39(2.1) and (2.2) and paragraph 95(2)(g.04),

(a) if the condition in subparagraph (6.1)(c)(i) is met,

(i) the post-transaction loan payable is deemed to be the same loan or indebtedness as the pre-transaction loan, and

(ii) the new debtor is deemed to be same debtor as, and a continuation of, the original debtor;

(b) if the condition in subparagraph (6.1)(c)(ii) is met,

(i) the post-transaction loan receivable is deemed to be the same loan or indebtedness as the pretransaction loan, and

(ii) the new creditor is deemed to be same creditor as, and a continuation of, the original creditor;

(c) if the condition in clause (6.1)(c)(iii)(A) is met,

(i) subject to subparagraph (ii), each entity that held an equity interest in the taxpayer immediately before the winding-up (referred to in this paragraph as a "successor entity") is deemed to be the same entity as, and a continuation of, the taxpayer, and

(ii) for the purposes of applying subsection (13) and the description of A in subsection (14), an amount is deemed, in respect of a loan or indebtedness, to have been included under subsection (6) in computing the income of each successor entity equal to

(A) if the taxpayer is a partnership, the amount that may reasonably be considered to be the successor entity's share (determined in a manner consistent with the determination of the successor entity's share of the income of the partnership under subsection 96(1) for the taxpayer's final fiscal period) of the specified amount that was required to be included in computing the income of the taxpayer under subsection (6) in respect of the loan or indebtedness, and

(B) in any other case, the proportion of the specified amount included in computing the taxpayer's income under subsection (6), in respect of the loan or indebtedness, that the fair market value of the successor entity's equity interest in the taxpayer, immediately before the distribution of the taxpayer's assets on the winding-up, is of the total fair market value of all equity interests in the taxpayer at that time; and

(d) if the condition in clause (6.1)(c)(iii)(B) is met, the new corporation is deemed to be the same corporation as, and a continuation of, the taxpayer.

Related Provisions: 90(6.1) — Conditions for 90(6.11) to apply.

Notes: There is no reason for this to be numbered (6.11). It should be (6.2).

90(6.1) and (6.11) provide "continuity" rules for the upstream loan (UL) rules in subsections 90(6) and (7)-(15), where there has been a reorganization of a corporation or partnership. They are intended to ensure that the UL rules continue to apply, and cannot be avoided, where a reorg occurs after making a UL. They are also intended to ensure that a reorg does not result in double tax, either by causing the UL rules to apply multiple times to what is in substance the same debt, or by preventing a debt repayment from being effective for the rules.

These rules are designed to ensure, *inter alia*, that (consistent with the policy intent) the annual 90(12) and (9) inclusions and deductions continue after a reorg, even if a taxpayer has ceased to exist. They are also intended to ensure that a reorg does not cause a new 90(6) income inclusion from an upstream loan for which there has already been one inclusion, or inappropriately interfere with the ability to qualify for relief under 90(8) or (14) on subsequent repayment of a UL.

90(6.1) and (6.11) added by 2017 budget bill #2, for transactions and events that occur after Sept. 15, 2016, but if a taxpayer filed an election with the Minister before 2017, they apply in respect of the taxpayer as of Aug. 20, 2011.

(7) Back-to-back loans — For the purposes of this subsection and subsections (6), (8) to (15) and 39(2.1) and (2.2) and paragraph 95(2)(g.04), if at any time a person or partnership (referred to in this subsection as the "intermediate lender") makes a loan to another person or partnership (in this subsection referred to as the "intended borrower") because the intermediate lender received a loan from another person or partnership (in this subsection referred to as the "initial lender")

(a) the loan made by the intermediate lender to the intended borrower is deemed, at that time, to have been made by the initial lender to the intended borrower (to the extent of the lesser of the amount of the loan made by the initial lender to the intermediate lender and the amount of the loan made by the intermediate lender to the intended borrower) under the same terms and conditions and at the same time as it was made by the intermediate lender; and

(b) the loan made by the initial lender to the intermediate lender and the loan made by the intermediate lender to the intended borrower are deemed not to have been made to the extent of the amount of the loan deemed to have been made under paragraph (a).

Proposed Amendment — Repayment deemed by 90(7) allowed for 90(8)(a) and 90(14)

Letter from Dept. of Finance, May 1, 2018: See under 90(8)(a).

Notes: See Notes to 90(6). This rule was not in the Aug. 19/11 draft.

The 2016 Budget extended the domestic shareholder-loan rule in 15(2) to apply to back-to-back loans: 15(2.16)-(2.192). There is no current proposal to extend those rules to 90(7), though that might happen in the future.

CRA considers the deemed loan repaid when the specified debtor repays the intermediary, or it is reasonable to consider that it is no longer funded by the foreign affiliate: VIEWS doc 2013-0508151C6 [2013 CTF q. 2.2.2].

See also docs 2014-0526741C6 [2014 IFA q.3(c)] (cash pooling arrangement: no position on how 90(7) applies); 2016-0642091C6 [2016 IFA q.5] (application in 2 scenarios).

90(7) opening words amended by 2017 budget bill #2 to refer to 39(2.1)-(2.2) and 95(2)(g.04), for loans received and indebtedness incurred after Aug. 19, 2011; also in respect of any portion of a particular loan received or a particular indebtedness incurred earlier that remained outstanding on Aug. 19, 2014 as if that portion were a separate loan or indebtedness that was received or incurred, as the case may be, on Aug. 20, 2014 in the same manner and on the same terms as the particular loan or indebtedness.

(8) Exceptions to subsec. (6) — Subsection (6) does not apply to

(a) a loan or indebtedness that is repaid, other than as part of a series of loans or other transactions and repayments, within two years of the day the loan was made or the indebtedness arose;

Proposed Amendment — 90(8)(a) — Repayment of loan deemed by 90(7)

Letter from Dept. of Finance, May 1, 2018: Dear [xxx]:

I am writing in response to your recent letter to, and subsequent discussions with, officials of the Tax Legislation Division concerning an issue you have identified in respect of the "upstream loan" rules in subsections 90(6) to (15) of the *Income Tax Act* (the "Act"). This issue arises in the context of impending refinancing transactions involving a Bermuda-resident foreign affiliate ("FA 1") of your client, [xxx] ("Canco").

You have described the following financing structure involving FA 1 and other members of Canco's [xxx]-parented group. FA 1 has made loans (the "FA 1 Loans") to [xxx] ("Forco 1"), which, in turn, has made loans (the "Forco 1 Loans") to [xxx] ("Forco 2"). Forco 1 and Forco 2 are specified debtors, as defined in subsection 90(15), in respect of Canco and are not foreign affiliates of Canco. The FA 1 Loans and the Forco 1 Loans are back-to-back loans described in subsection 90(7), with the result that, for the purposes of subsections 90(6) to (15), paragraph 90(7)(a) has deemed the Forco 1 Loans to have been made by FA 1 to Forco 2 (each a "Deemed Loan"), and paragraph 90(7)(b) has deemed each actual FA 1 Loan and Forco 1 Loan not to have been made.

For each taxation year in which a Deemed Loan has been deemed to be made, subsection 90(6) has applied to include a specified amount in respect of the Deemed Loan in Canco's income and Canco has claimed an offsetting deduction under subsection 90(9) in respect of FA 1's exempt surplus. In each subsequent year, the amount so deducted has been brought back into Canco's income under subsection 90(12) and another offsetting deduction has been claimed under subsection 90(9).

As part of the impending refinancing transactions, Forco 1 will repay the FA 1 Loans and FA 1 will use the proceeds of such repayments to make loans to another specified debtor in respect of Canco (the "FA 1-New Specified Debtor Loans").

You note that there are no provisions in the Act that provide, for the purposes of paragraph 90(8)(a) and subsection 90(14), for the repayment of a loan that is deemed to have been made under subsection 90(7). You are therefore concerned that the repayment of the FA 1 Loans as part of the refinancing transactions may not be considered to result in the repayment of the Deemed Loans. In that case, the repayment, combined with the subsequent redeployment of the proceeds in the FA 1-New Specified Debtor Loans, could result in a double income inclusion to Canco for the year, with subsection 90(12) applying to bring into income the amount claimed in the previous year as a deduction in respect of each Deemed Loan under subsection 90(9), and subsection 90(6) applying to bring the amount of each FA 1-New Specified Debtor Loan into Canco's income for the year. This would be an adverse result since FA 1 does not have sufficient exempt surplus to support a deduction by Canco under subsection 90(9) equal to the amount of the two income inclusions.

Our Comments

We agree that, in policy terms, the transactions described above ought not to give rise to two concurrent upstream loans, and two related income inclusions under the upstream loan rules. We are therefore prepared to recommend to the Minister of Finance that the Act be amended to introduce rules — similar to the deemed repayment rules in subsections 15(2.18) and (2.19) (which apply for the purposes of the back-to-back shareholder loan rules in subsections 15(2.16) and (2.17)), but with such modifications as are required by the context of the upstream loan rules — that would deem all or a portion of a loan that is deemed to be made under subsection 90(7) to be repaid for the purposes of paragraph 90(8)(a) and subsection 90(14) if certain conditions are met.

These conditions would be similar to those in subsection 15(2.18). In general terms, a loan deemed to have been made under subsection 90(7) would be deemed to be repaid, in whole or in part, as a result of certain repayments, in whole or in part, of one or both of the loans between the "initial lender" and the "intermediate lender", and the "intermediate lender" and the "intended borrower" (as those terms are defined in subsection 90(7)).

As in the case of a deemed repayment under subsection 15(2.19), the determination whether a deemed repayment is part of a series of loans or other transactions or repayments for purposes of paragraph 90(8)(a) and subsection 90(14) would need to be made on a case-by-case basis, having regard to all of the facts and circumstances.

We will recommend that this proposed amendment apply to repayments occurring after April 10, 2018.

While we cannot offer any assurance that either the Minister of Finance or Parliament will agree with our recommendations in respect of this matter, we hope that this statement of our intentions is helpful.

Yours sincerely,

Brian Ernewein, General Director — Legislation, Tax Policy Branch

(b) indebtedness that arose in the ordinary course of the business of the creditor or a loan made in the ordinary course of the creditor's ordinary business of lending money if, at the time the indebtedness arose or the loan was made, *bona fide* arrangements were made for repayment of the indebtedness or loan within a reasonable time;

(c) a loan that was made, or indebtedness that arose, in the ordinary course of carrying on a life insurance business outside Canada if

(i) the loan or indebtedness is owed by the taxpayer or by a subsidiary wholly-owned corporation of the taxpayer,

(ii) the taxpayer, or the subsidiary wholly-owned corporation, as the case may be, is a life insurance corporation resident in Canada,

(iii) the loan or indebtedness directly relates to a business of the taxpayer, or of the subsidiary wholly-owned corporation, that is carried on outside Canada, and

(iv) the interest on the loan or indebtedness is, or would be if it were otherwise income from property, included in the active business income of the creditor, or if the creditor is a partnership, a member of the partnership, under clause 95(2)(a)(ii)(A); and

(d) subject to subsection (8.1), an upstream deposit owing to an eligible bank affiliate.

Related Provisions: 15(2.3) — Parallel rule to 90(8)(b) for domestic loans; 15(2.6) — Similar rule to 90(8)(a) for domestic loans; 90(7) — Back-to-back loans; 90(8.1) — Treatment of upstream deposit of eligible bank affiliate; 90(15) — Definitions of "upstream deposit" and "eligible bank affiliate"; *Interpretation Act* 27(5) — Meaning of "within two years".

Notes: See Notes to 90(6). 90(8)(a) and (b) are similar to the exceptions in 15(2.6) and (2.3) for domestic loans. See Notes to those provisions for interpretation. The CRA applies the same interpretation as under s. 15, so "repaid" includes by set-off against another obligation (the parties' intention is relevant, as are the accounting records): VIEWS doc 2013-0508141C6 [2013 CTF q. 2.2.1].

Loans outstanding on Aug. 19, 2011 are deemed made on Aug. 20, 2014, starting the 2-year clock for 90(8)(a).

For examples of 90(8)(a) applying see VIEWS docs 2013-0491061R3, 2016-0642151C6 [2016 IFA q.4], 2016-0670971R3. 90(8)(a) requires repayment of the debt and does not apply on sale of the creditor affiliate: 2016-0645521I7.

See also Turner, "Transitional Tax Treatment of Grandfathered Upstream Loans", 88 *International Tax* (CCH) 5-8 (June 2016) and 2318 *Tax Topics* 4-8 (Aug. 11, 2016).

Para. (d) added by 2014 budget bill #2, for taxation years of a taxpayer's foreign affiliate that begin after Feb. 27, 2014.

90(8)(a)-(b) were 90(5) in the Aug. 19/11 draft. 90(8)(c) was first released on Oct. 24/12.

(8.1) Upstream deposit — eligible bank affiliate — For the purposes of this section, if a taxpayer is an eligible Canadian bank and an eligible bank affiliate of the taxpayer is owed, at any time in a particular taxation year of the affiliate or the immediately preceding taxation year, an upstream deposit,

(a) the affiliate is deemed to make a loan to the taxpayer immediately before the end of the particular year equal to the amount determined by the following formula, where all amounts referred to in the formula are to be determined using Canadian currency:

$$A - B - C$$

where

A is 90% of the average of all amounts each of which is, in respect of a calendar month that ends in the particular year, the greatest total amount at any time in the month of the upstream deposits owing to the affiliate,

B is the lesser of

(i) the amount, if any, by which the affiliate's excess liquidity for the particular year exceeds the average of all amounts each of which is, in respect of a calendar month that ends in the particular year, the greatest total amount at any time in the month of eligible Canadian indebtedness owing to the affiliate, and

(ii) the amount determined for A, and

C is the amount, if any, by which the amount determined for A for the immediately preceding year exceeds the amount determined for B for the immediately preceding year; and

(b) if the formula in paragraph (a) would, in the absence of section 257, result in a negative amount for the particular year,

(i) the taxpayer is deemed to repay immediately before the end of the particular year — in an amount equal to the absolute value of the negative amount and in the order in which they arose — loans made by the affiliate under paragraph (a) in a prior taxation year and not previously repaid, and

(ii) the repayment is deemed to not be part of a series of loans or other transactions and repayments.

Related Provisions: 90(8)(d) — Upstream deposit excluded from upstream loan income inclusion; 257 — Formula cannot calculate to less than zero.

Notes: For purposes of the upstream loan rules in 90(6)–(15), 90(8.1) deems an eligible bank affiliate (EBA) of an eligible Canadian bank (ECB) to make an upstream loan to the bank when the EBA's upstream deposits with the bank exceed the difference between the EBA's excess liquidity and all eligible Canadian indebtedness owing to the EBA. In combination, 90(8) and (8.1) result in 90(6) not applying to loans made by an EBA to an ECB if 90% of all upstream deposits the bank owes to the affiliate does not exceed the affiliate's available excess liquidity for the year. This is consistent with the policy of the excess liquidity rules in 95(2.43)–(2.45). (Finance Technical Notes)

90(8.1) added by 2014 budget bill #2, effective for taxation years of a taxpayer's foreign affiliate that begin after Feb. 27, 2014.

(9) Corporations: deduction for amounts included under subsec. (6) or (12) — There may be deducted in computing the income for a taxation year of a corporation resident in Canada a particular amount, in respect of a specified amount included under subsection (6), or an amount included under subsection (12), in computing the corporation's income for the taxation year in respect of a particular loan or indebtedness, if

(a) the corporation demonstrates that the particular amount is the total of all amounts (not to exceed the amount so included) each of which would — if the specified amount in respect of the particular loan or indebtedness were, at the time (referred to in subparagraph (i) and subsection (11) as the "lending time") the particular loan was made or the particular indebtedness was incurred, instead paid by the creditor affiliate, or the creditor partnership, as the case may be, to the corporation directly as part of one dividend, or indirectly as part of one or more dividends and, if applicable, partnership distributions — reasonably be considered to have been deductible, in respect of the payment, for the corporation's taxation year in which the specified amount was included in its income under subsection (6), in computing

(i) the taxable income of the corporation under any of

(A) paragraph 113(1)(a), in respect of the exempt surplus — at the lending time, in respect of the corporation — of a foreign affiliate of the corporation,

(B) paragraph 113(1)(a.1), in respect of the hybrid surplus — at the lending time, in respect of the corporation — of a foreign affiliate of the corporation, if the amount of that hybrid surplus is less than or equal to the amount determined by the formula

$$[A \times (B - 0.5)] + (C \times 0.5)$$

where

A is the affiliate's hybrid underlying tax in respect of the corporation at the lending time,

B is the corporation's relevant tax factor (within the meaning assigned by subsection 95(1)) for the corporation's taxation year that includes the lending time, and

C is the affiliate's hybrid surplus in respect of the corporation at the lending time,

(C) paragraph 113(1)(b), in respect of the taxable surplus — at the lending time, in respect of the corporation — of a foreign affiliate of the corporation, and

(D) paragraph 113(1)(d), in respect of the pre-acquisition surplus — at the lending time, in respect of the corporation — of a foreign affiliate of the corporation to the extent of the adjusted cost base to the corporation, at the lending time, of the shares of the capital stock of the affiliate, and except if the specified debtor is

(I) a non-resident person with which the corporation does not deal at arm's length, or

(II) a partnership any member of which is a person described in subclause (I), or

(ii) the income of the corporation under subsection 91(5), in respect of the taxable surplus of a foreign affiliate of the corporation, unless the specified debtor is a person or partnership described in subclause (i)(D)(I) or (II);

(b) that exempt surplus, hybrid surplus, taxable surplus, or adjusted cost base is not relevant in applying this subsection in respect of any other loan made or indebtedness incurred, or in respect of any deduction claimed under subsection 91(5) or 113(1) in respect of a dividend paid, during the period in which the particular loan or indebtedness is outstanding; and

(c) that adjusted cost base is not relevant in determining the taxability of any other distribution made during the period in which the particular loan or indebtedness is outstanding.

Related Provisions: 90(7) — Back-to-back loans; 90(10) — Application to corporate partners; 90(11) — Downstream surplus; 90(12) — Amount deducted added back the next year; 90(13) — No double deduction once amount repaid.

Notes: If the foreign affiliate could have paid the Canadian parent a tax-free dividend (deductible under 113(1)), then 90(9) allows a deduction to postpone the income inclusion under 90(6), but the amount is re-included the next year under 90(12) so the test must be reapplied each year (the next year, the deduction here is of "an amount included under subsection (12)" in 90(9) opening words). Once the loan is repaid and deducted under 90(14), it can no longer be deducted here: see 90(13).

For relief for the affiliate's ability to pay pre-acquisition surplus dividends (113(1)(d)), see 90(9)(a)(i)(D). For dividends on previously-taxed FAPI (deductible under 91(5)), if the loan is to a non-resident see 90(9)(a)(ii), and if to a Canadian resident see VIEWS doc 2013-0483791C6 [2013 IFA q.5] (amount added to Canco's ACB of shares of FA can be deducted under (a)(i)(D)). There is no relief for repayment of existing loans from the Canadian parent.

See also VIEWS docs 2013-0488881E5 (various questions); 2014-0526721C6 [2014 IFA q.3(a)] (application of Reg. 5901(2)(a) does not change 90(9)(a)(i)(A)-(C) amounts); 2015-0581501C6 [2015 IFA q.4] (90(9) applies in 3 scenarios); Yuri Revenko & Gordon Zittlau, "Subsection 90(9) Deductions and the '90-Day Rule' ", XIX(4) *International Tax Planning* (Federated Press) 1353-56 (2014).

See also Notes to 90(6). This rule was 90(6) in the Aug. 19/11 draft.

90(9)(a)(ii) amended to change "if" to "unless" by 2017 budget bill #2, for loans received and indebtedness incurred after Aug. 19, 2011; also in respect of any portion of a particular loan received or a particular indebtedness incurred before Aug. 20, 2011 that remains outstanding on Aug. 19, 2014 as if that portion were a separate loan or indebtedness that was received or incurred, as the case may be, on Aug. 20, 2014 in the same manner and on the same terms as the particular loan or indebtedness. In respect of loans received and indebtedness incurred before Sept. 16, 2016, ignore "unless the specified debtor is a person or partnership described in subclause (i)(D)(I) or (II)".

Before this amendment, previously-taxed FAPI was an element of the 90(9) deduction, but only where the specified debtor (SD: 90(15)) was a non-resident not dealing at arm's length with the taxpayer (or was a partnership of which such a non-resident was a member). 90(9)(a)(ii) was amended to instead include previously-taxed FAPI in the 90(9) deduction only in the converse case: where the SD is a person or partnership *other than* a non-resident not at arm's length with the taxpayer (or is a partnership of which such a non-resident is a member). This ensures that the rules apply as intended, to include previously-taxed FAPI in the 90(9) deduction where the SD is either the Canadian-resident taxpayer, a person resident in Canada not at arm's length with the taxpayer (or a partnership no member of which is non-resident not at arm's length with the taxpayer). It also ensures that the 90(9) deduction does not include previously-taxed FAPI in cases where a foreign multinational corporate group may otherwise synthetically repatriate the FAPI free of withholding tax. (Finance Technical Notes)

(10) Corporate partners: application of subsec. (9) — In applying subsection (9) to a corporation resident in Canada that is a member of a partnership at the end of a fiscal period of the partnership,

(a) each amount that may reasonably be considered to be the corporation's share (determined in a manner consistent with the determination of the corporation's share of the income of the partnership under subsection 96(1)) of each specified amount that is required to be included in computing the income of the partnership for that fiscal period under subsection (6), in respect of a particular loan or indebtedness, is deemed to be a specified amount in respect of the particular loan or indebtedness that was included in the corporation's income, for its taxation year that includes the last day of that fiscal period, under subsection (6);

(b) subparagraph (9)(a)(i) is to be read without reference to its clause (D);

(c) subparagraph (9)(a)(ii) is to be read as follows:

(ii) the income of the partnership, referred to in subsection (10), under subsection 91(5), in respect of the taxable surplus of a foreign affiliate of the partnership, to the extent of the amount that may reasonably be considered to be the corporation's share of that deduction (determined in a manner consistent with the determination of the corporation's share of the income of the partnership under subsection 96(1));

(d) paragraph (9)(b) is to be read as follows:

(b) that exempt surplus, hybrid surplus, or taxable surplus is not relevant in applying this subsection in respect of any other loan made or indebtedness incurred, or in respect of any deduction claimed under subsection 91(5) or 113(1) in respect of a dividend paid, during the period in which the particular loan or indebtedness is outstanding; and

(e) subsection (9) is to be read without reference to its paragraph (c).

Related Provisions: 90(7) — Back-to-back loans.

Notes: See Notes to 90(6). This provision was not in the Aug. 19/11 draft.

(11) Downstream surplus — For the purposes of subparagraph (9)(a)(i), the amounts of exempt surplus or exempt deficit, hybrid surplus or hybrid deficit, hybrid underlying tax, taxable surplus or taxable deficit, and underlying foreign tax of the creditor affiliate, or of each foreign affiliate of the corporation that is a member of the creditor partnership, as the case may be, in respect of the corporation, at the lending time are deemed to be the amounts that would be determined, at the lending time, under subparagraph 5902(1)(a)(i) of the *Income Tax Regulations* if that subparagraph were applicable at the lending time and the references in that subparagraph to "the dividend time" were references to the lending time.

Related Provisions: 90(7) — Back-to-back loans.

Notes: See Notes to 90(6). This provision was not in the Aug. 19/11 draft.

(12) Add-back for subsec. (9) deduction — There is to be included in computing the income of a corporation resident in Canada for a particular taxation year any amount deducted by the corporation under subsection (9) in computing the corporation's income for the taxation year that immediately precedes the particular year.

Related Provisions: 90(9) — Offsetting deduction if conditions satisfied.

Notes: See Notes to 90(6) and (9). This was 90(7) in the Aug. 19/11 draft.

(13) No double deduction — A corporation may not claim a deduction for a taxation year under subsection (9) in respect of the same portion of the specified amount in respect of a loan or indebtedness for which a deduction is claimed for that year or a preceding year by the corporation, or by a partnership of which the corporation is a member, under subsection (14).

Notes: See Notes to 90(6). This was 90(8) in the Aug. 19/11 draft.

(14) Repayment of loan — There may be deducted in computing the income of a taxpayer for a particular taxation year the amount determined by the formula

$$A \times B/C$$

where

A is the specified amount, in respect of a loan or indebtedness, that is included under subsection (6) in computing the taxpayer's income for a preceding taxation year,

B is the portion of the loan or indebtedness that was repaid in the particular year, to the extent it is established, by subsequent events or otherwise, that the repayment was not part of a series of loans or other transactions and repayments, and

C is the amount, in respect of the loan or indebtedness, that is referred to in the description of A in the definition "specified amount" in subsection (15).

Proposed Amendment — 90(14) — Repayment of loan deemed by 90(7)	

Letter from Dept. of Finance, May 1, 2018: See under 90(8)(a).

Related Provisions: 39(2.1)–(2.3), 95(2)(g.04) — Foreign currency adjustment where loan is repaid; 90(7) — Back-to-back loans; 90(13) — No deduction under 90(9) if loan repayment deducted under 90(14); 90(15) — Definition of "specified amount".

Notes: See Notes to 90(6). This was 90(9) in the Aug. 19/11 draft.

(15) Definitions — The following definitions apply in this section.

"eligible bank affiliate" has the same meaning as in subsection 95(2.43).

Notes: Definition added by 2014 budget bill #2, effective for taxation years of a taxpayer's foreign affiliate that begin after Feb. 27, 2014.

"eligible Canadian bank" has the same meaning as in subsection 95(2.43).

Notes: Definition added by 2014 budget bill #2, effective for taxation years of a taxpayer's foreign affiliate that begin after Feb. 27, 2014.

"eligible Canadian indebtedness" has the same meaning as in subsection 95(2.43).

Notes: Definition added by 2014 budget bill #2, effective for taxation years of a taxpayer's foreign affiliate that begin after Feb. 27, 2014.

"excess liquidity" has the same meaning as in subsection 95(2.43).

Notes: Definition added by 2014 budget bill #2, effective for taxation years of a taxpayer's foreign affiliate that begin after Feb. 27, 2014.

"specified amount", in respect of a loan or indebtedness that is required by subsection (6) to be included in computing the income of a taxpayer for a taxation year, means the amount determined by the formula

$$A \times (B - C)$$

where

A is the amount of the loan or indebtedness, and

B is, in the case of

(a) a creditor affiliate of the taxpayer, the percentage that is or would be, if the taxpayer referred to in subsection (6) were a corporation resident in Canada, the taxpayer's surplus entitlement percentage (in this definition determined without reference to subsection 5908(1) of the *Income Tax Regulations*) in respect of the creditor affiliate at the time (referred to in this definition as the "determination time") referred to in subsection (6), or

(b) a creditor partnership of which a foreign affiliate of the taxpayer is a member, the total of each percentage determined, in respect of a member (referred to in this paragraph as a "member affiliate") of the creditor partnership that is a foreign affiliate of the taxpayer, by the formula

$$D \times E/F$$

where

D is the percentage that is or would be, if the taxpayer were a corporation resident in Canada, the taxpayer's surplus entitlement percentage in respect of a particular member affiliate at the determination time,

E is the fair market value, at the determination time, of the particular member affiliate's direct or indirect interest in the creditor partnership, and

F is the fair market value, at the determination time, of all interests in the creditor partnership, and

C is,

(a) if the debtor under the loan or indebtedness is

(i) another foreign affiliate of the taxpayer, the percentage that is or would be, if the taxpayer were a corporation resident in Canada, the taxpayer's surplus entitlement percentage in respect of the other affiliate at the determination time, or

(ii) a partnership (referred to in this paragraph as the "borrower partnership") of which one or more other foreign affiliates of the taxpayer are members, the total of each percentage that is determined by the following formula in respect of each such member

$$G \times H/I$$

where

G is the percentage that is or would be, if the taxpayer were a corporation resident in Canada, the taxpayer's surplus entitlement percentage in respect of a particular member of the borrower partnership at the determination time,

H is the fair market value, at the determination time, of the particular member's direct or indirect interest in the borrower partnership, and

I is the fair market value, at the determination time, of all interests in the borrower partnership, and

(b) in any other case, nil.

Related Provisions: 90(6) — Specified amount included in income; 90(7) — Back-to-back loans; 93.1(1) — Shares owned by partnership deemed owned by partners; 257 — Formula cannot calculate to less than zero.

Notes: See Notes to 90(6). This definition was in 90(10) in the Aug. 19/11 draft.

"specified debtor", in respect of a taxpayer resident in Canada, at any time, means

(a) the taxpayer;

(b) a person with which the taxpayer does not, at that time, deal at arm's length, other than

(i) a non-resident corporation that is at that time a "controlled foreign affiliate", within the meaning assigned by section 17, of the taxpayer, or

(ii) a non-resident corporation (other than a corporation that is described in subparagraph (i)) that is, at that time, a foreign affiliate of the taxpayer, if each share of the capital stock of the affiliate is owned at that time by any of

(A) the taxpayer,

(B) persons resident in Canada,

(C) non-resident persons that deal at arm's length with the taxpayer,

(D) persons described in subparagraph (i),

(E) partnerships, each member of which is described in any of clauses (A) to (F), and

(F) a corporation each shareholder of which is described in any of clauses (A) to (F);

(c) a partnership a member of which is at that time a person or partnership that is a specified debtor in respect of the taxpayer because of paragraph (a) or (b); and

(d) if the taxpayer is a partnership,

(i) any member of the partnership that is a corporation resident in Canada if the creditor affiliate, or member of the creditor partnership, as the case may be, is, at that time, a foreign affiliate of the corporation,

(ii) a person with which a corporation referred to in subparagraph (i) does not, at that time, deal at arm's length, other than a controlled foreign affiliate, within the meaning assigned by section 17, of the partnership or of a member of the partnership that owns, directly or indirectly, an interest in the partnership representing at least 90% of the fair market value of all such interests, or

(iii) a partnership a member of which is at that time a person that is a specified debtor in respect of the taxpayer because of subparagraph (i) or (ii).

Related Provisions: 90(6) — Inclusion of loan from foreign affiliate in specified debtor's income; 90(7) — Back-to-back loans.

Notes: See Notes to 90(6). This definition was in 90(10) in the Aug. 19/11 draft.

See Paul Barnicke & Melanie Huynh, "Upstream Loan Comfort Letter", 23(8) *Canadian Tax Highlights* (ctf.ca) 7-8 (Aug. 2015).

Subpara. (b)(ii) added by 2017 budget bill #2, for loans received and indebtedness incurred after Aug. 19, 2011 and in respect of any portion of a particular loan received or indebtedness incurred earlier that remained outstanding on Aug. 19, 2014.

"upstream deposit" has the same meaning as in subsection 95(2.43).

Notes: Definition added by 2014 budget bill #2, effective for taxation years of a taxpayer's foreign affiliate that begin after Feb. 27, 2014.

Related Provisions [s. 90]: 82(1) — Dividends received from corporation resident in Canada; 113(1) — Deduction to corporation for dividend received from foreign affiliate; 139.1(4)(f), (g) — Deemed dividend on demutualization of insurance corporation; 139.2 — Deemed dividend on distribution by mutual holding corporation.

Notes [s. 90]: For possible future international tax amendments as a result of BEPS recommendations, see at end of s. 95.

Definitions [s. 90]: "active business" — 95(1); "adjusted cost base" — 54, 248(1); "amount" — 248(1); "arm's length" — 251(1); "business" — 248(1); "Canada" — 255, *Interpretation Act* 35(1); "connected person or partnership" — 90(4); "controlled foreign affiliate" — 95(1), 248(1); "corporation" — 248(1), *Interpretation Act* 35(1); "creditor affiliate" — 90(6); "creditor partnership" — 90(6); "dividend" — 248(1); "eligible Canadian bank", "eligible Canadian indebtedness", "excess liquidity" — 90(15), 95(2.43); "exempt deficit" — Reg. 5907(1); "exempt surplus" — 113(1)(a), Reg. 5907(1), (1.01); "fair market value" — see 69(1) Notes; "fiscal period" — 249.1; "foreign affiliate" — 95(1), 248(1); "hybrid deficit" — Reg. 5907(1); "hybrid surplus" — 113(1)(a.1)(i), Reg. 5907(1), (1.01); "hybrid underlying tax" — Reg. 5907(1); "income from property" — 9(1), 95(1); "lending time" — 90(9)(a); "life insurance business", "life insurance corporation" — 248(1); "month" — *Interpretation Act* 35(1); "new corporation" — 90(6.1)(c)(iii)(B); "new creditor" — 90(6.1)(c)(ii); "new debtor" — 90(6.1)(c)(i); "non-resident" — 248(1); "original creditor", "original debtor" — 90(6.1)(a); "paid-up capital" — 89(1), 248(1); "partnership" — see 96(1) Notes; "person" — 248(1); "post-transaction loan payable" — 90(6.1)(c)(i); "post-transaction loan receivable" — 90(6.1)(c)(ii); "pre-transaction loan" — 90(6.1)(a); "prescribed" — 248(1); "qualifying return of capital" — 90(3); "related" — 251(2)–(6); "relevant tax factor" — 95(1); "resident in Canada" — 94(3)(a), 250; "share", "shareholder" — 248(1); "specified amount", "specified debtor" — 90(15); "subsidiary wholly-owned corporation" — 248(1); "surplus entitlement percentage" — 95(1); "taxable deficit" — Reg. 5907(1); "taxable income" — 2(2), 248(1); "taxable surplus" — 113(1)(b)(i), Reg. 5907(1), (1.01); "taxation year" — 95(1), 249; "taxpayer" — 248(1); "upstream deposit" — 90(15), 95(2.43).

Interpretation Bulletins: IT-451R: Deemed disposition and acquisition on ceasing to be or becoming resident in Canada.

91. (1) Amounts to be included in respect of share of foreign affiliate

— In computing the income for a taxation year of a taxpayer resident in Canada, there shall be included, in respect of each share owned by the taxpayer of the capital stock of a controlled foreign affiliate of the taxpayer, as income from the share, the percentage of the foreign accrual property income of any controlled foreign affiliate of the taxpayer, for each taxation year of the affiliate ending in the taxation year of the taxpayer, equal to that share's participating percentage in respect of the affiliate, determined at the end of each such taxation year of the affiliate.

Related Provisions: 17(1)B(c) — Amount included as FAPI not taxed under rule for loan to non-resident; 18(8) — Exception to thin-capitalization rule; 53(1)(d.1) — Increase in ACB of capital interest in non-resident trust; 91(1.1)–(1.5) — Deemed year-end to trigger FAPI on reduction in surplus entitlement percentage; 91(4) — Deduction to reflect foreign tax paid; 92(1) — Addition to ACB; 94.2 — Non-resident trust deemed to be controlled foreign affiliate for FAPI; 95(11) — Deemed separate corporation for tracked property; 113(1) — Deduction for dividend received from foreign affiliate; 152(6.1) — Reassessment to apply FAPI loss carryback; 161(7)(a)(xii), 161(7)(b)(iii), 164(5)(h.4), (k) — Interest calculation on carryback of FAPL; 233.2–233.5 — Disclosure of foreign property.

Notes: The FAPI (foreign accrual property income) rules seek to prevent Canadian resident taxpayers from avoiding tax by earning passive (investment) income in foreign holding companies and not bringing the funds back to Canada. The rules "impute" the foreign passive income to the Canadian taxpayer. The US has similar rules in Subpart F (§951-965) of the *Internal Revenue Code*.

For any resident taxpayer, FAPI (defined in 95(1)) of a controlled foreign affiliate (CFA, defined in 95(1)) is brought into income by 91(1) on a current basis. If the foreign jurisdiction imposes tax on the CFA, an offsetting deduction is usually available under 91(4) for such "foreign accrual tax" to prevent double tax.

Although the concept is straightforward, the rules are staggeringly complex. See 95 and Reg. 5900–5911.

FAPI catches [95(1)"foreign accrual property income"A, C]: (1) 95(1)"income from property", which includes income from an adventure in the nature of trade and from a

95(1)"investment business"; (2) 95(1)"non-qualifying business" income, which is income earned from a permanent establishment in a non-treaty, non-TIEA country; (3) income from a business other than a 95(1)"active business"; and (4) taxable capital gains. Income from an "active business" is taxed by Canada only under s. 90 when paid to the shareholder as a dividend.

Various rules move income from one category to another. For example: certain payments made by a Canadian resident to its CFA for services are FAPI (95(2)(b)); most real estate income is FAPI unless the affiliate has 6 or more employees (95(1)"active business", "investment business"); and the sale of goods acquired non-arm's length can be FAPI (95(2)(a.1)).

A foreign accrual property loss (FAPL) can be carried forward 20 years or back 3 years to apply against FAPI: Reg. 5903.

CRA can now choose to assess FAPI either under 91(1) or by denying a 113(1) deduction on a later dividend: Allan Lanthier, "FAPI or Taxable Surplus Dividend", 23(2) *Canadian Tax Highlights* (ctf.ca) 4-5 (Feb. 2015).

Texts on FAPI: Nikolakakis, *Taxation of Foreign Affiliates* (Carswell, looseleaf or *Taxnet Pro* Reference Centre); Li & Cockfield, *International Taxation in Canada*, 4th ed. (LexisNexis, 2018), chap. 13; Vidal, *Introduction to International Tax in Canada* (Carswell, 8th ed., 2020), chaps. 15, 17-19; *McCarthy Tétrault's Canada Tax Service Foreign Affiliates Guide, 2nd ed.* (Carswell, 2015, 480pp.) [commentary from *Canada Tax Service*].

Articles on FAPI: Parts of the pre-2012 articles here are no longer relevant, due to various changes from the 1995, 2004, 2010 and 2011 drafts to what was enacted in 2013 by 2002-2013 technical bill Parts 2 and 3. See Jack, "The Foreign Affiliate Rules: The 1995 Amendments", 43(2) *Canadian Tax Journal* 347-400 (1995), and especially the flowcharts on pp. 396-98 for characterizing income as FAPI or not; Lockwood et al., "Foreign Affiliates and FAPI", 46(2) *CTJ* 377-414 (1998); Huynh & Lockwood, "Foreign Accrual Property Income", 48(3) *CTJ* 752-77 (2000); Jack et al, "International Taxation: The Feb. 27, 2004 Draft Proposals", 2004 Cdn Tax Foundation conference report, 20:1-105; Talakshi, "The Foreign Affiliate Proposals", 2005 conference report, 14:1-22; Goguen & Jack, "Selected Recent ... Developments", 2007 conference report, 19:1-65; Nikolakakis, "The Taxation of Foreign Affiliates in the Resource Sectors", 2008 conference report, 29:1-70; Ton-That & Huynh, "Inconsistent Treatment of Partnerships in the Foreign Affiliate Rules", 2009 conference report, 24:1-66; Samuel, "Stopping the Losses: The Application of Stop-Loss Rules to Transactions Involving Foreign Affiliates", 58(4) *CTJ* 897-925 (2010); Brade, "International Tax Update — FAPI Traps", 2012 Prairie Provinces Tax Conf. (ctf.ca), 11:1-24; Marley & Slaats, "Foreign Affiliate Reorganizations", 2012 conference report, 27:1-29; Morier & Juneja, "Foreign Affiliates: An Updated Primer", *ibid.*, 28:1-58; Nikolakakis, "Outbound Foreign Direct Investment", 61(Supp.) *CTJ* 311-43 (2013); Dhesi & Fehrmann, "Integration Across Borders", 63(4) *CTJ* 1049-72 (2015) (re private corps); Kandev & Slaats, "Recent Developments in the Foreign Affiliate Area", 2015 conference report, 31:1-43; Bidner, "An Individual's Direct Ownership of a CFA", 6(4) *Canadian Tax Focus* (ctf.ca) 12-13 (Nov. 2016) (re high total tax rate on repatriating income); Shadrin, Kakkar & Ghani, "FAPI and TOSI Overlap: 107% Tax Is Not Fair", 20(1) *Tax for the Owner-Manager* (ctf.ca) 5-6 (Jan. 2020); Duval & Kandev, "Foreign Affiliate Issues in Troubled Times", 112 *International Tax* (CCH, June 2020).

In *Canwest Mediaworks*, 2008 FCA 5 (leave to appeal denied 2008 CarswellNat 1642 (SCC)), 91(1) applied despite a limitation period in the Canada-Barbados tax treaty, because another treaty provision unreservedly permitted Canada to tax FAPI.

In *Ho*, 2010 TCC 325, a 91(1) FAPI inclusion imputed to a beneficiary under 75(2) was not a "transaction" to extend the reassessment deadline under 152(4)(b)(iii), but this was overruled by 152(4)(b)(iii)(B), added in 2018.

See Notes to 94(1)"resident contributor" on the use of an immigration trust for new immigrants, which could potentially avoid FAPI for 5 years before the 2014 Budget eliminated this rule.

Interpretation Bulletins: IT-392: Meaning of the term "share"; IT-451R: Deemed disposition and acquisition on ceasing to be or becoming resident in Canada.

I.T. Application Rules: 35(1) (ITAR 26 does not apply to gains and losses of foreign affiliates for FAPI purposes).

Information Circulars: 77-9R: Books, records and other requirements for taxpayers having foreign affiliates.

CRA Audit Manual: 15.12.2: Foreign accrual property income (FAPI) and foreign affiliates.

(1.1) Conditions for application of subsec. (1.2)

— Subsection (1.2) applies at a particular time in respect of a particular foreign affiliate of a taxpayer resident in Canada if

(a) an amount would be included under subsection (1) in computing the income of the taxpayer, in respect of a share of the particular affiliate or another foreign affiliate of the taxpayer that has an "equity percentage" (as defined in subsection 95(4)) in the particular affiliate, for the taxation year of the particular affiliate (determined without reference to subsection (1.2)) that includes the particular time (referred to in this subsection and subsection (1.3) as the **"ordinary taxation year"** of the particular affiliate), if the ordinary taxation year of the particular affiliate ended at the particular time;

(b) immediately after the particular time, there is

(i) an acquisition of control of the taxpayer, or

(ii) a triggering event that can reasonably be considered to result in a change in the aggregate participating percentage of the taxpayer in respect of the particular affiliate for the ordinary taxation year of the particular affiliate;

(c) if subparagraph (b)(i) applies, all or a portion of an amount described in paragraph 95(2)(f) that accrued to the particular affiliate during the portion of the ordinary taxation year of the particular affiliate before the particular time is excluded in computing the income of another taxpayer because paragraph 95(2)(f.1) applies as a result of the taxpayer being, at a time before the acquisition of control, a designated acquired corporation of the other taxpayer; and

(d) if subparagraph (b)(ii) applies, none of the following is the case:

(i) the change referred to in that subparagraph

(A) is a decrease, and

(B) is equal to the total of all amounts each of which is the increase — that can reasonably be considered to result from the triggering event — in the aggregate participating percentage of another taxpayer, in respect of the particular affiliate for the ordinary taxation year of the particular affiliate, if the other taxpayer

(I) is a person resident in Canada, other than a person that is — or a trust, any of the beneficiaries under which is — by reason of a statutory provision, exempt from tax under this Part, and

(II) is related to the taxpayer,

1 if the triggering event results from a winding-up of the taxpayer to which subsection 88(1) applies, at the particular time, and

2 in any other case, immediately after the particular time,

(ii) the triggering event is on an "amalgamation" as defined in subsection 87(1),

(iii) the triggering event is an excluded acquisition or disposition, in respect of the ordinary taxation year of the particular affiliate, and

(iv) if one or more triggering events — all of which are described in subparagraph (b)(ii) and in respect of which none of the conditions in subparagraphs (i) to (iii) are satisfied — occur in the ordinary taxation year of the particular affiliate, the percentage determined by the following formula is not greater than 5%:

$$A - B$$

where

A is the total of all amounts each of which is the decrease — which can reasonably be considered to result from a triggering event described in subparagraph (b)(ii) (other than a triggering event that satisfies the conditions in subparagraph (i) or (ii)) — in the aggregate participating percentage of the taxpayer in respect of the particular affiliate for the ordinary taxation year of the particular affiliate, and

B is the total of all amounts each of which is the increase — which can reasonably be considered to result from a triggering event described in subparagraph (b)(ii) (other than a triggering event that satisfies the conditions in subparagraph (i) or (ii)) — in the aggregate participating percentage of the taxpayer in respect of the particular affiliate for the ordinary taxation year of the particular affiliate.

Related Provisions: 91(1.3) — Definitions; 257 — Formula cannot calculate to less than zero; Reg. 5905(13) — Surplus entitlement percentage.

Notes: 91(1.1)-(1.4) ensure that the correct amount of FAPI is included in taxpayer T's income by 91(1) if: T is subject to an acquisition of control and FAPI previously earned by a foreign affiliate (FA) is not included in another taxpayer's income because of 95(2)(f.1); or T's interest in a FA is reduced in certain circumstances. Absent 91(1.2) in such cases, T would generally not be required to include in income the "stub-period FAPI" earned by the FA in the portion of the FA's taxation year before the acquisition of control or reduction of T's interest. See also Reg. 5907(8) and (8.1).

For discussion of 91(1.1)-(1.5) see Barnicke & Huynh, "Revised Stub-Period FAPI", 25(10) *Canadian Tax Highlights [CTH]* (ctf.ca) 3-4 (Oct. 2017); Cheang & Fehrmann, "The New Stub-Period FAPI Rules", 66(1) *Canadian Tax Journal* 135-57 (2018); Alty & Sandler article cited in 95(9) Notes.

91(1.1)-(1.5) added by 2017 budget bill #2, effective July 12, 2013, except that

(a) a 91(1.4) election is deemed filed on time by the particular taxpayer and all specified corporations referred to in 91(1.4) if it is filed by the earliest filing-due date, for all taxpayers making the election, for the respective taxation year that includes Dec. 14, 2017;

(b) a 91(1.5) election is deemed filed on time by the particular taxpayer T referred to in 91(1.5) if it is filed by T's filing-due date for its taxation year that includes Dec. 14, 2017;

(c) subject to (d) below, if the particular time referred to in 91(1.1) is before Sept. 8, 2017, read 91(1.1)-(1.4) as:

(1.1) Conditions for application of subsec. (1.2) — Subsection (1.2) applies at a particular time in respect of a particular foreign affiliate of a taxpayer resident in Canada if

(a) an amount would be included under subsection (1) in computing the income of the taxpayer, in respect of a share of the particular affiliate or another foreign affiliate of the taxpayer that has an "equity percentage" (as defined in subsection 95(4)) in the particular affiliate, for the taxation year of the particular affiliate (determined without reference to subsection (1.2)) that includes the particular time, if that taxation year ended at the particular time; and

(b) immediately after the particular time, there is an acquisition or disposition of shares of the capital stock of a foreign affiliate of the taxpayer that results in a change to the surplus entitlement percentage of the taxpayer in respect of the particular affiliate (determined as if the taxpayer were a corporation resident in Canada), unless

(i) the change is a decrease in the surplus entitlement percentage of the taxpayer (determined as if the taxpayer were a corporation resident in Canada) in respect of the particular affiliate and, as a result of the acquisition or disposition, one or more taxpayers, each of which is a taxable Canadian corporation that does not deal at arm's length with the taxpayer immediately after the particular time, have increases to their surplus entitlement percentages in respect of the particular affiliate that are, in total, equal to the reduction in the taxpayer's surplus entitlement percentage in respect of the particular affiliate immediately after the particular time,

(ii) the acquisition or disposition is on an "amalgamation" as defined in subsection 87(1), or

(iii) if one or more such acquisitions or dispositions in respect of which the conditions in subparagraphs (i) and (ii) are not satisfied occur in a particular taxation year of the particular affiliate (determined without reference to this subsection and subsection (1.2)), the percentage determined by the following formula is not greater than 5%:

$$A - B$$

where

A is the total of all amounts each of which is the decrease in the surplus entitlement percentage of the taxpayer in respect of the particular affiliate resulting from such acquisition or disposition in the particular year (other than an acquisition or disposition described in subparagraph (i) or (ii)), and

B is the total of all amounts each of which is the increase in the surplus entitlement percentage of the taxpayer in respect of the particular affiliate resulting from such acquisition or disposition in the particular year (other than an acquisition from a person that does not deal at arm's length with the taxpayer).

(1.2) Deemed year-end — If this subsection applies at a particular time in respect of a foreign affiliate of a particular taxpayer resident in Canada, then for the purposes of this section and section 92,

(a) in respect of the particular taxpayer and each corporation or partnership that is connected to the particular taxpayer, the affiliate's taxation year that would, in the absence of this subsection, have included the particular time is deemed to have ended at the time (referred to in this section as the "stub-period end time") that is immediately before the particular time;

Non-Resident Corps/Trusts

(b) if the affiliate is, immediately after the particular time, a foreign affiliate of the particular taxpayer or a corporation or partnership that is connected to the particular taxpayer, the affiliate's next taxation year after the stub-period end time is deemed, in respect of the taxpayer or the connected corporation or partnership, as the case may be, to begin immediately after the particular time; and

(c) in determining the foreign accrual property income of the affiliate for that taxation year in respect of the particular taxpayer or a corporation or partnership that is connected to the particular taxpayer, all transactions or events that occur at the particular time are deemed to occur at the stub-period end time.

(1.3) Connected — meaning — For the purposes of subsection (1.2),

(a) a corporation is connected to the particular taxpayer if, at or immediately after the particular time, it is resident in Canada and does not deal at arm's length with the taxpayer; and

(b) a partnership is connected to the particular taxpayer if, at or immediately after the particular time, the particular taxpayer or a corporation described in paragraph (a) is, directly or indirectly through one or more partnerships, a member of the partnership.

(1.4) Election for application of subsec. (1.2) — If the conditions in subsection (1.1) are not met at a particular time in respect of a particular foreign affiliate of a taxpayer resident in Canada, subsection (1.2) applies in respect of the particular affiliate at that time if

(a) the conditions in paragraph (1.1)(a) are met in respect of the particular affiliate at the particular time;

(b) immediately after the particular time there is a disposition of shares of the capital stock of the particular affiliate or another foreign affiliate of the taxpayer that had an "equity percentage" (as defined in subsection 95(4)) in the particular affiliate by

(i) the taxpayer, or

(ii) a controlled foreign affiliate of the taxpayer, if the shares are not excluded property of the controlled foreign affiliate immediately after the particular time; and

(c) the taxpayer and all specified corporations jointly elect, by filing with the Minister in prescribed manner a form containing prescribed information on or before the day that is the earliest filing-due date for all taxpayers making the election in respect of the taxation year in which the transaction to which the election relates occurred, and for this purpose, a "specified corporation" means a corporation that at or immediately after the particular time meets the following conditions:

(i) the corporation is resident in Canada,

(ii) the corporation does not deal at arm's length with the taxpayer, and

(iii) the particular affiliate is a foreign affiliate of the corporation, or of a partnership of which the corporation is, directly or indirectly through one or more partnerships, a member.

(d) para. (c) above does not apply in respect of taxpayer T if

(i) T and all connected persons and connected partnerships (as those are defined in 91(1.3)) in respect of T jointly elect in writing, and

(ii) the election is filed with the Minister by the later of June 14, 2018 and T's filing-due date for its taxation year that includes Sept. 8, 2017;

(e) if para. (c) does not apply in respect of taxpayer T because of para, (d), then:

(i) ignore 91(1.5), and

(ii) ignore 91(1.1)(b)(i) and 91(1.1)(c) in respect of any acquisition of control of T that occurred before Sept. 8, 2017.

(1.2) Deemed year-end — If this subsection applies at a particular time in respect of a foreign affiliate of a particular taxpayer resident in Canada, then for the purposes of this section and section 92,

(a) in respect of the particular taxpayer and each connected person, or connected partnership, in respect of the particular taxpayer, the affiliate's taxation year that would, in the absence of this subsection, have included the particular time is deemed to have ended at the time (referred to in this section as the "stub-period end time") that is immediately before the particular time;

(b) if the affiliate is, immediately after the particular time, a foreign affiliate of the particular taxpayer or a connected person, or connected partnership, in respect of the particular taxpayer, the affiliate's next taxation year after the stub-period end time is deemed, in respect of the particular taxpayer or the connected person or connected partnership, as the case may be, to begin immediately after the particular time; and

(c) in determining the foreign accrual property income of the affiliate for the taxation year referred to in paragraph (a) in respect of the particular taxpayer or a connected person or connected partnership, in respect of the particular taxpayer, all transactions or events that occur at the particular time are deemed to occur at the stub-period end time.

Related Provisions: 91(1.1) — Conditions for 91(1.2) to apply; 91(1.3) — Definitions; 91(1.4) — Elections for application of 91(1.2); Reg. 5907(8)(b) — Calculation of various amounts for stub period.

Notes: See Notes to 91(1.1).

(1.3) Definitions — The following definitions apply in this subsection and subsections (1.1) and (1.2).

"aggregate participating percentage", of a taxpayer in respect of a foreign affiliate of the taxpayer for a taxation year of the affiliate, means the total of all amounts, each of which is the participating percentage, in respect of the affiliate, of a share of the capital stock of a corporation that is owned by the taxpayer at the end of the taxation year.

"connected partnership", in respect of a particular taxpayer, means a partnership if, at or immediately after the particular time at which subsection (1.2) applies in respect of a foreign affiliate of the particular taxpayer,

(a) the particular taxpayer or a connected person in respect of the particular taxpayer is, directly or indirectly through one or more partnerships, a member of the partnership; or

(b) if paragraph (a) does not apply,

(i) the foreign affiliate is a foreign affiliate of the partnership at the particular time, and

(ii) the aggregate participating percentage of the partnership in respect of the foreign affiliate for the affiliate's ordinary taxation year may reasonably be considered to have increased as a result of the triggering event that gave rise to the application of subsection (1.2).

"connected person", in respect of a particular taxpayer, means a person that — at or immediately after the particular time at which subsection (1.2) applies in respect of a foreign affiliate of the particular taxpayer — is resident in Canada and

(a) does not deal at arm's length with the particular taxpayer; or

(b) deals at arm's length with the particular taxpayer, if

(i) the foreign affiliate is a foreign affiliate of the person at the particular time, and

(ii) the aggregate participating percentage of the person in respect of the foreign affiliate for the affiliate's ordinary taxation year may reasonably be considered to have increased as a result of the triggering event that gave rise to the application of subsection (1.2).

"excluded acquisition or disposition", in respect of a taxation year of a foreign affiliate of a taxpayer, means an acquisition or disposition of an equity interest in a corporation, partnership or trust that can reasonably be considered to result in a change in the aggregate participating percentage of the taxpayer in respect of the affiliate for the taxation year of the affiliate, if

(a) the change is less than 1%; and

(b) it cannot reasonably be considered that one of the main reasons the acquisition or disposition occurs as a separate acquisition or disposition from one or more other acquisitions or dispositions is to avoid the application of subsection (1.2).

"triggering event" means

(a) an acquisition or disposition of an equity interest in a corporation, partnership or trust;

(b) a change in the terms or conditions of a share of the capital stock of a corporation or the rights as a member of a partnership or as a beneficiary under a trust; and

(c) a disposition or change of a right referred to in paragraph 95(6)(a).

Related Provisions: 251(1) — Arm's length.

Notes: See Notes to 91(1.1).

(1.4) Election for application of subsec. (1.2) — If the conditions in subsection (1.1) are not met at a particular time in respect of a particular foreign affiliate of a taxpayer resident in Canada, subsection (1.2) applies in respect of the particular affiliate at that time if

(a) the conditions in paragraph (1.1)(a) are met in respect of the particular affiliate at the particular time;

(b) immediately after the particular time there is a disposition of shares of the capital stock of the particular affiliate or another foreign affiliate of the taxpayer that had an "equity percentage" (as defined in subsection 95(4)) in the particular affiliate by

(i) the taxpayer, or

(ii) a controlled foreign affiliate of the taxpayer; and

(c) the taxpayer and all specified corporations jointly elect in writing to apply subsection (1.2) in respect of the disposition and file the election with the Minister on or before the day that is the earliest filing-due date for all taxpayers making the election in respect of the taxation year in which the transaction to which the election relates occurred, and for this purpose, a **"specified corporation"** means a corporation that at or immediately after the particular time meets the following conditions:

(i) the corporation is resident in Canada,

(ii) the corporation does not deal at arm's length with the taxpayer, and

(iii) the particular affiliate is a foreign affiliate of the corporation, or of a partnership of which the corporation is, directly or indirectly through one or more partnerships, a member.

Related Provisions: 220(3.2), Reg. 600(b) — Late filing or revocation of election.

Notes: See Notes to 91(1.1).

(1.5) [Repealed]

Notes: See Notes to 91(1.1) for enactment of 91(1.5), which was repealed by 2017 budget bill #2 (the same bill that enacted it) for taxation years that begin after Sept. 7, 2017. It read:

(1.5) Election for application of subsec. (1.2) — A particular taxpayer resident in Canada may elect, by filing with the Minister in prescribed manner a form containing prescribed information on or before the particular taxpayer's filing-due date for its taxation year that includes a particular time, to have subsection (1.2) apply at the particular time in respect of a particular foreign affiliate of the particular taxpayer if

(a) immediately after the particular time, there is an acquisition or disposition of shares of the capital stock of a foreign affiliate of another taxpayer that results in a decrease to the surplus entitlement percentage of the other taxpayer in respect of the particular affiliate;

(b) as a result of the acquisition or disposition described in paragraph (a), subsection (1.2) applies to the other taxpayer resident in Canada in respect of the particular affiliate;

(c) the surplus entitlement percentage of the particular taxpayer in respect of the particular affiliate increases as a result of the acquisition or disposition described in paragraph (a);

(d) subsection (1.2) does not apply, in the absence of this subsection, to the particular taxpayer in respect of the acquisition or disposition; and

(e) the particular affiliate is a foreign affiliate of the particular taxpayer at the particular time.

91(1.5) was repealed because 91(1.2) applies automatically in the circumstances described in 91(1.5), since 91(1.3)"connected person"(b) now incorporates such circumstances.

(2) Reserve where foreign exchange restriction — Where an amount in respect of a share has been included in computing the income of a taxpayer for a taxation year by virtue of subsection (1) or (3) and the Minister is satisfied that, by reason of the operation of monetary or exchange restrictions of a country other than Canada, the inclusion of the whole amount with no deduction for a reserve in respect thereof would impose undue hardship on the taxpayer,

there may be deducted in computing the taxpayer's income for the year such amount as a reserve in respect of the amount so included as the Minister deems reasonable in the circumstances.

Related Provisions: 53(2)(b.1) — Decrease in ACB of capital interest in non-resident trust; 91(3) — Reserve included in income following year; 94.2 — Non-resident trust deemed to be controlled foreign affiliate for FAPI.

Interpretation Bulletins: IT-392: Meaning of the term "share".

(3) Reserve for preceding year to be included — In computing the income of a taxpayer for a taxation year, there shall be included each amount in respect of a share that was deducted by virtue of subsection (2) in computing the taxpayer's income for the immediately preceding year.

Related Provisions: 53(1)(d.1) — Increase in ACB of capital interest in non-resident trust; 92(1) — Addition to ACB; 94.2 — Non-resident trust deemed to be controlled foreign affiliate for FAPI.

(4) Amounts deductible in respect of foreign taxes — Where, by virtue of subsection (1), an amount in respect of a share has been included in computing the income of a taxpayer for a taxation year or for any of the 5 immediately preceding taxation years (in this subsection referred to as the "income amount"), there may be deducted in computing the taxpayer's income for the year the lesser of

(a) the product obtained when

(i) the portion of the foreign accrual tax applicable to the income amount that was not deductible under this subsection in any previous year

is multiplied by

(ii) the taxpayer's relevant tax factor for the year, and

(b) the amount, if any, by which the income amount exceeds the total of the amounts in respect of that share deductible under this subsection in any of the 5 immediately preceding taxation years in respect of the income amount.

Related Provisions: 53(2)(b.1) — Decrease in ACB of capital interest in non-resident trust; 94.2 — Application of FAPI to non-resident trust; 95(11) — Deemed separate corporation for tracked property.

Notes: The deduction under 91(4) is claimed for the year in which the taxation year of the foreign affiliate for which it is paid ends: VIEWS doc 2002-013420117 (includes various other interpretations for 91(4)). See also 2010-0386661E5 (general comments).

See Bronstetter & Christie, "The Fickle Finger of FAT: An Analysis of Foreign Accrual Tax", 51(3) *Canadian Tax Journal* 1317-39 (2003); Barnicke & Huynh, "Losing the FAT", 21(2) *Canadian Tax Highlights* (ctf.ca) 1-2 (Feb. 2013). See also Notes to Reg. 5907(1.3).

91(4)(a)(ii) changed from "the relevant tax factor, and" by 2002-2013 technical bill (Part 5 — technical), effective for 2002 and later taxation years. See 95(1)"relevant tax factor".

(4.1) Denial of foreign accrual tax — For the purposes of the definition "foreign accrual tax" in subsection 95(1), foreign accrual tax applicable to a particular amount included in computing a taxpayer's income under subsection (1) for a taxation year of the taxpayer in respect of a particular foreign affiliate of the taxpayer is not to include the amount that would, in the absence of this subsection, be foreign accrual tax applicable to the particular amount if, at any time in the taxation year (referred to in this subsection as the "affiliate year") of the particular affiliate that ends in the taxation year of the taxpayer,

(a) a specified owner in respect of the taxpayer is considered,

(i) under the income tax laws (referred to in subsections (4.5) and (4.6) as the "relevant foreign tax law") of any country other than Canada under the laws of which any income of a particular corporation — that is, at any time in the affiliate year, a pertinent person or partnership in respect of the particular affiliate — is subject to income taxation, to own less than all of the shares of the capital stock of the particular corporation that are considered to be owned by the specified owner for the purposes of this Act, or

(ii) under the income tax laws (referred to in subsections (4.5) and (4.6) as the "relevant foreign tax law") of any country other than Canada under the laws of which any income of a particular partnership — that is, at any time in the affiliate year, a pertinent person or partnership in respect of the particular affiliate — is subject to income taxation, to have a lesser direct or indirect share of the income of the particular partnership than the specified owner is considered to have for the purposes of this Act; or

(b) where the taxpayer is a partnership, the direct or indirect share of the income of the partnership of any member of the partnership that is, at any time in the affiliate year, a person resident in Canada or a foreign affiliate of such a person is, under the income tax laws (referred to in subsection (4.6) as the "relevant foreign tax law") of any country other than Canada under the laws of which any income of the partnership is subject to income taxation, less than the member's direct or indirect share of that income for the purposes of this Act.

Related Provisions: 91(4.2) — Specified owner; 91(4.3) — Pertinent person or partnership; 91(4.5) — Exception — hybrid entities; 91(4.6) — Exception — partnerships; 91(4.7) — Deemed ownership; 93.1(3) — Look-through rule for tiered partnerships; 126(4.11), Reg. 5907(1.03) — Parallel rules to 91(4.1).

Notes: 91(4.1)–(4.7) are part of the "foreign tax credit generator" rules, along with 126(4.11)–(4.13) and Reg. 5907(1.03)–(1.09). For discussion see Notes to 126(4.11); and Montillaud & Russell, "Foreign Accrual Tax and Flow-through Entities", XVIII(4) *International Tax Planning* (Federated Press) 1280-82 (2013). See also VIEWS doc 2017-0691121C6 [2017 IFA q.5] (application to Brazilian "interest on equity" distribution).

91(4.1)–(4.7) added by 2002-2013 technical bill, this version effective for the computation of foreign accrual tax applicable to an amount included in computing a taxpayer's income under 91(1), for a taxpayer's taxation year that ends after Oct. 24, 2012.

(4.2) Specified owner — For the purposes of subsections (4.1) and (4.5), a "specified owner", at any time, in respect of a taxpayer means the taxpayer or a person or partnership that is, at that time,

(a) a partnership of which the taxpayer is a member;

(b) a foreign affiliate of the taxpayer;

(c) a partnership a member of which is a foreign affiliate of the taxpayer; or

(d) a person or partnership referred to in any of subparagraphs (4.4)(a)(i) to (iii).

Related Provisions: 91(4.4) — Interpretation; Reg. 5907(1.04) — Parallel rule.

Notes: See Notes to 91(4.1).

(4.3) Pertinent person or partnership — For the purposes of this subsection and subsection (4.1), a "pertinent person or partnership", at any time, in respect of a particular foreign affiliate of a taxpayer means the particular affiliate or a person or partnership that is, at that time,

(a) another foreign affiliate of the taxpayer

(i) in which the particular affiliate has an equity percentage, or

(ii) that has an equity percentage in the particular affiliate;

(b) a partnership a member of which is at that time a pertinent person or partnership in respect of the particular affiliate under this subsection; or

(c) a person or partnership referred to in any of subparagraphs (4.4)(b)(i) to (iii).

Related Provisions: 91(4.4) — Interpretation; 93.1(3) — Look-through rule for tiered partnerships.

Notes: See Notes to 91(4.1). This was 91(4.5) in the Aug. 27/10 draft.

(4.4) Series of transactions — For the purposes of subsections (4.2) and (4.3), if, as part of a series of transactions or events that includes the earning of the foreign accrual property income that gave rise to the particular amount referred to in subsection (4.1), a foreign affiliate (referred to in this subsection as the "funding affiliate") of the taxpayer or of a person (referred to in this subsection as the "related person") resident in Canada that is related to the taxpayer, or a partnership (referred to in this subsection as the "funding partnership") of which such an affiliate is a member, directly or indirectly provided funding to the particular affiliate, or a partnership of which the particular affiliate is a member, otherwise than by way

of loans or other indebtedness that are subject to terms or conditions made or imposed, in respect of the loans or other indebtedness, that do not differ from those that would be made or imposed between persons dealing at arm's length or by way of an acquisition of shares of the capital stock of any corporation, then

(a) if the funding affiliate is, or the funding partnership has a member that is, a foreign affiliate of the related person, the following persons and partnerships are deemed, at all times during which the foreign accrual property income is earned by the particular affiliate, to be specified owners in respect of the taxpayer:

(i) the related person,

(ii) each foreign affiliate of the related person, and

(iii) each partnership a member of which is a person referred to in subparagraph (i) or (ii); and

(b) the following persons and partnerships are deemed, at all times during which the foreign accrual property income is earned by the particular affiliate, to be pertinent persons or partnerships in respect of the particular affiliate:

(i) the funding affiliate or the funding partnership,

(ii) a non-resident corporation

(A) in which the funding affiliate has an equity percentage, or

(B) that has an equity percentage in the funding affiliate, and

(iii) a partnership a member of which is a person or partnership referred to in subparagraph (i) or (ii).

Notes: See Notes to 91(4.1). For the meaning of "indirectly" in the opening words, see Notes to 17.1(1).

(4.5) Exception — hybrid entities — For the purposes of subparagraph (4.1)(a)(i), a specified owner in respect of the taxpayer is not to be considered, under the relevant foreign tax law, to own less than all of the shares of the capital stock of a corporation that are considered to be owned for the purposes of this Act solely because the specified owner or the corporation is not treated as a corporation under the relevant foreign tax law.

Notes: See Notes to 91(4.1). This was 91(4.2) in the Aug. 27/10 draft.

91(4.5) amended by 2017 budget bill #2 to add "or the corporation", for computation of foreign accrual tax applicable to an amount included in computing a taxpayer T's income under 91(1), for a taxation year of T that ends after Oct. 24, 2012, in respect of a foreign affiliate of T. This implements a March 1, 2016 Finance comfort letter.

(4.6) Exceptions — partnerships — For the purposes of subparagraph (4.1)(a)(ii) and paragraph (4.1)(b), a member of a partnership is not to be considered to have a lesser direct or indirect share of the income of the partnership under the relevant foreign tax law than for the purposes of this Act solely because of one or more of the following:

(a) a difference between the relevant foreign tax law and this Act in the manner of

(i) computing the income of the partnership, or

(ii) allocating the income of the partnership because of the admission to, or withdrawal from, the partnership of any of its members;

(b) the treatment of the partnership as a corporation under the relevant foreign tax law; or

(c) the fact that the member is not treated as a corporation under the relevant foreign tax law.

Related Provisions: 126(4.12), Reg. 5907(1.08) — Parallel rules.

Notes: See Notes to 91(4.1). This was 91(4.3) in the Aug. 27/10 draft.

(4.7) Deemed ownership — For the purposes of subsection (4.1), if a specified owner owns, for the purposes of this Act, shares of the capital stock of a corporation and the dividends, or similar amounts, in respect of those shares are treated under the income tax laws of any country other than Canada under the laws of which any income of the corporation is subject to income taxation as interest or another form of deductible payment, the specified owner is deemed to be considered, under those tax laws, to own less than all of the shares of the capital stock of the corporation that are considered to be owned by the specified owner for the purposes of this Act.

Notes: See Notes to 91(4.1).

(5) Amounts deductible in respect of dividends received — Where in a taxation year a taxpayer resident in Canada has received a dividend on a share of the capital stock of a corporation that was at any time a controlled foreign affiliate of the taxpayer, there may be deducted, in respect of such portion of the dividend as is prescribed to have been paid out of the taxable surplus of the affiliate, in computing the taxpayer's income for the year, the lesser of

(a) the amount by which that portion of the dividend exceeds the amount, if any, deductible in respect thereof under paragraph 113(1)(b), and

(b) the amount, if any, by which

(i) the total of all amounts required by paragraph 92(1)(a) to be added in computing the adjusted cost base to the taxpayer of the share before the dividend was so received by the taxpayer

exceeds

(ii) the total of all amounts required by paragraph 92(1)(b) to be deducted in computing the adjusted cost base to the taxpayer of the share before the dividend was so received by the taxpayer.

Related Provisions: 20(13) — Deduction for dividend; 80.1(4)(c) — Assets acquired from foreign affiliate as dividend in kind or benefit to shareholder; 87(2)(u) — Effect of amalgamation; 91(6) — Amounts deductible re dividends received; 91(7) — Where share acquired by partner from partnership; 113(1) — Deduction for dividend received from foreign affiliate.

Notes: A trust deemed resident by 94(3) in 2007, which had FAPI inclusion under pre-2007 94(1)(c)(i)(C), could claim a 91(5) deduction: VIEWS doc 2015-0598491I7.

Regulations: 5900(1)(b), 5900(3) (portion of dividend prescribed to be paid out of taxable surplus).

Interpretation Bulletins: IT-392: Meaning of the term "share".

Information Circulars: 77-9R: Books, records and other requirements for taxpayers having foreign affiliates.

(5.1)–(5.3) [Repealed]

Notes: 91(5.1)-(5.3) added by 2007 budget bill #2 but repealed by 2009 budget bill #1, both effective 2012, in conjunction with the introduction and repeal of 18.2. See Notes to 18.2. For their text, see PITA 33rd-36th ed.

(6) Idem — Where a share of the capital stock of a foreign affiliate of a taxpayer that is a taxable Canadian corporation is acquired by the taxpayer from another corporation resident in Canada with which the taxpayer is not dealing at arm's length, for the purpose of subsection (5), any amount required by section 92 to be added or deducted, as the case may be, in computing the adjusted cost base to the other corporation of the share shall be deemed to have been so required to be added or deducted, as the case may be, in computing the adjusted cost base to the taxpayer of the share.

Notes: 91(6) added by 1991 technical bill, effective 1990.

Interpretation Bulletins: IT-392: Meaning of the term "share".

(7) Shares acquired from a partnership — For the purpose of subsection (5), where a taxpayer resident in Canada acquires a share of the capital stock of a corporation that is immediately after the acquisition a foreign affiliate of the taxpayer from a partnership of which the taxpayer, or a corporation resident in Canada with which the taxpayer was not dealing at arm's length at the time the share was acquired, was a member (each such person referred to in this subsection as the "member") at any time during any fiscal period of the partnership that began before the acquisition,

(a) that portion of any amount required by subsection 92(1) to be added to the adjusted cost base to the partnership of the share of the capital stock of the foreign affiliate equal to the amount included in the income of the member because of subsection 96(1)

in respect of the amount that was included in the income of the partnership because of subsection (1) or (3) in respect of the foreign affiliate and added to that adjusted cost base, and

(b) that portion of any amount required by subsection 92(1) to be deducted from the adjusted cost base to the partnership of the share of the capital stock of the foreign affiliate equal to the amount by which the income of the member from the partnership under subsection 96(1) was reduced because of the amount deducted in computing the income of the partnership under subsection (2), (4) or (5) and deducted from that adjusted cost base

is deemed to be an amount required by subsection 92(1) to be added or deducted, as the case may be, in computing the adjusted cost base to the taxpayer of the share.

Notes: 91(7) added by 2001 technical bill, for shares acquired after Nov. 1999.

Interpretation Bulletins: IT-392: Meaning of the term "share".

Definitions [s. 91]: "adjusted cost base" — 54, 248(1); "affiliate year" — 91(4.1); "aggregate participating percentage" — 91(1.3); "amalgamation" — 87(1); "amount" — 248(1); "arm's length" — 251(1); "beneficiary" — 248(25) [Notes]; "Canada" — 255, *Interpretation Act* 35(1); "capital gain" — 39(1)(a), 248(1); "class of shares" — 248(6); "connected partnership", "connected person" — 91(1.3); "control" — 256(5)-(9), 256.1(3); "controlled foreign affiliate" — 95(1), 248(1); "corporation" — 248(1), *Interpretation Act* 35(1); "designated acquired corporation" — 95(1); "disposition", "dividend" — 248(1); "equity percentage" — 95(4); "excluded acquisition or disposition" — 91(1.3); "excluded property" — 95(1); "filing-due date" — 150(1), 248(1); "fiscal period" — 249.1; "foreign accrual property income" — 95(1), (2), 248(1); "foreign accrual tax" — 95(1); "foreign affiliate" — 95(1), 248(1); "Minister", "non-resident" — 248(1); "ordinary taxation year" — 91(1.1)(a); "participating percentage" — 95(1); "partnership" — see 96(1) Notes; "person" — 248(1); "pertinent person or partnership" — 91(4.3); "prescribed" — 248(1); "related" — 251(2)-(6); "relevant foreign tax law" — 91(4.1)(a)(i), (ii); "relevant tax factor" — 95(1); "resident in Canada" — 94(3)(a), 250; "series of transactions" — 248(10); "share", "shareholder" — 248(1); "specified owner" — 91(4.2); "specified proportion" — 248(1); "stub-period end time" — 91(1.2)(a); "surplus entitlement percentage" — 95(1), Reg. 5905(13); "taxable Canadian corporation" — 89(1), 248(1); "taxable surplus" — 113(1)(b)(i), Reg. 5907(1); "taxation year" — 95(1) (for foreign affiliate only), 249; "taxpayer" — 248(1); "triggering event" — 91(1.3); "trust" — 104(1), 248(1), (3); "writing" — *Interpretation Act* 35(1).

92. (1) Adjusted cost base of share of foreign affiliate — In computing, at any time in a taxation year, the adjusted cost base to a taxpayer resident in Canada of any share owned by the taxpayer of the capital stock of a foreign affiliate of the taxpayer,

(a) there shall be added in respect of that share any amount included in respect of that share under subsection 91(1) or (3) in computing the taxpayer's income for the year or any preceding taxation year (or that would have been required to have been so included in computing the taxpayer's income but for subsection 56(4.1) and sections 74.1 to 75 of this Act and section 74 of the *Income Tax Act*, chapter 148 of the Revised Statutes of Canada, 1952); and

(b) there shall be deducted in respect of that share

(i) any amount deducted by the taxpayer under subsection 91(2) or (4), and

(ii) any dividend received by the taxpayer before that time, to the extent of the amount deducted by the taxpayer, in respect of the dividend, under subsection 91(5)

in computing the taxpayer's income for the year or any preceding taxation year (or that would have been deductible by the taxpayer but for subsection 56(4.1) and sections 74.1 to 75 of this Act and section 74 of the *Income Tax Act*, chapter 148 of the Revised Statutes of Canada, 1952).

Related Provisions: 53(1)(d) — ACB additions; 53(2)(b) — ACB deductions; 87(2)(u) — Shares of foreign affiliate; 91(6) — Amounts deductible re dividends received; 92(1.1) — Addition to ACB of share of FA owned by another FA; 92(1.3) [transitional] — Whether 93(1) election is a specified section 93 election.

Notes: For an example of 92(1) applying see VIEWS doc 2007-0247551E5.

92(1) amended by 2009 budget bill #1, effective 2012.

I.T. Application Rules: 69 (meaning of "chapter 148 of ...").

Interpretation Bulletins: IT-392: Meaning of the term "share".

(1.1) Adjustment for prescribed amount — The prescribed amount shall be added in computing the adjusted cost base of a

share of the capital stock of a foreign affiliate of a corporation resident in Canada to

(a) another foreign affiliate of the corporation; or

(b) a partnership of which another foreign affiliate of the corporation is a member.

Related Provisions: 53(1)(d) — ACB additions.

Notes: 92(1.1) added by 2002-2013 technical bill (Part 2 — FA surplus rules), effective Dec. 19, 2009.

Former proposed 92(1.1)-(1.4) in the Feb. 27, 2004 draft legislation will not be permanently enacted, but are available transitionally as 92(1.2)-(1.5) for those that used them before they were withdrawn in 2009. See Notes to 92(1.2).

Regulations: 5905(7.6), (7.7), 5908(11), (12) (prescribed amount).

(1.2) Adjustment re adjusted cost base — There is to be added in computing the adjusted cost base to a taxpayer of a share of the capital stock of a foreign affiliate of the taxpayer any amount required by paragraph 93(4)(b) to be so added.

Related Provisions: 53(1)(c) — ACB additions.

Notes: 92(1.2) added by 2002-2013 technical bill (Part 3 — FA reorganizations), effective Feb. 28, 2004.

Consolidated net surplus rules: Former proposed 92(1.1)-(1.4) in the Feb. 27, 2004 draft legislation are available transitionally as 92(1.2)-(1.5), for those that used them before they were withdrawn in the Dec 18/09 draft legislation. These were part of the Feb. 27/04 "consolidated net surplus" regime, in parts of proposed Reg. 5902 and 5905, which has been abandoned (Dept. of Finance Technical Notes to Reg. 5900-5919 (Sept. 10, 2010), #6). Sections 51-52 of the 2002-2013 technical bill provide these transitional 92(1.1)-(1.5), which apply to a disposition of shares from Dec. 21, 2002 through Dec. 18, 2009. For the text, see PITA 44th-47th ed. See also Notes to Reg. 5905(1).

(2) Deduction in computing adjusted cost base — In computing, at any time in a taxation year,

(a) the adjusted cost base to a corporation resident in Canada (in this subsection referred to as an "owner") of any share of the capital stock of a foreign affiliate of the corporation, or

(b) the adjusted cost base to a foreign affiliate (in this subsection referred to as an "owner") of a person resident in Canada of any share of the capital stock of another foreign affiliate of that person,

there shall be deducted, in respect of any dividend received on the share before that time by the owner of the share, an amount equal to the amount, if any, by which

(c) such portion of the amount of the dividend so received as was deductible by virtue of paragraph 113(1)(d) from the income of the owner for the year in computing the owner's taxable income for the year or as would have been so deductible if the owner had been a corporation resident in Canada,

exceeds

(d) such portion of any income or profits tax paid by the owner to the government of a country other than Canada as may reasonably be regarded as having been paid in respect of the portion described in paragraph (c).

Related Provisions: 53(2)(b) — ACB deductions; 91(6) — Amounts deductible re dividends received.

Notes: For the meaning of "income or profits tax" in 92(2)(d), see Notes to 126(4).

Interpretation Bulletins: IT-392: Meaning of the term "share".

(3) Idem — In computing, at any time in a taxation year, the adjusted cost base to a corporation resident in Canada of any share of the capital stock of a foreign affiliate of the corporation, there shall be deducted an amount in respect of any dividend received on the share by the corporation before that time equal to such portion of the amount so received as was deducted under subsection 113(2) from the income of the corporation for the year or any preceding year in computing its taxable income.

Related Provisions: 53(2)(b) — ACB deductions.

Interpretation Bulletins: IT-392: Meaning of the term "share".

(4) Disposition of a partnership interest — Where a corporation resident in Canada or a foreign affiliate of a corporation resident in Canada has at any time disposed of all or a portion of an interest in a partnership of which it was a member, there shall be

added, in computing the proceeds of disposition of that interest, the amount determined by the formula

$$(A - B) \times (C/D)$$

where

A is the amount, if any, by which

(a) the total of all amounts each of which is an amount that was deductible under paragraph 113(1)(d) by the member from its income in computing its taxable income for any taxation year of the member that began before that time in respect of any portion of a dividend received by the partnership, or would have been so deductible if the member were a corporation resident in Canada,

exceeds

(b) the total of all amounts each of which is the portion of any income or profits tax paid by the partnership or the member of the partnership to a government of a country other than Canada that can reasonably be considered as having been paid in respect of the member's share of the dividend described in paragraph (a);

B is the total of

(a) the total of all amounts each of which was an amount added under this subsection in computing the member's proceeds of a disposition before that time of another interest in the partnership, and

(b) the total of all amounts each of which was an amount deemed by subsection (5) to be a gain of the member from a disposition before that time of a share by the partnership;

C is the adjusted cost base, immediately before that time, of the portion of the member's interest in the partnership disposed of by the member at that time; and

D is the adjusted cost base, immediately before that time, of the member's interest in the partnership immediately before that time.

Related Provisions: 257 — Formula cannot calculate to less than zero.

Notes: For the meaning of "income or profits tax" in A(b), see Notes to 126(4).

For discussion of 92(4)-(6) see Barnicke & Huynh, "FA Shares Held in Partnership", 22(6) *Canadian Tax Highlights* (ctf.ca) 8-9 (June 2014); Turner, "ACB Adjustments for Foreign Affiliate Shares Held Through Partnerships", 79 *International Tax* (CCH) 1-6 (Dec. 2014); Cen, "Planning for FA Distributions Paid Through a Partnership", 10(2) *Canadian Tax Focus* (ctf.ca) 6-7 (May 2020). See also VIEWS docs 2012-043373117 (effect of 92(5)-(6) where shares of foreign corp held by partnership with Canadian corporate partner are rolled into another corp owned by the partnership); 2014-0526751C6 [2014 IFA q.5] (no administrative relief from 92(4)-(6): effect of extracting pre-acquisition surplus from FA held through a partnership).

92(4) added by 2001 technical bill, for dispositions that occur after Nov. 1999.

(5) Deemed gain from the disposition of a share — Where a partnership has, at any time in a fiscal period of the partnership at the end of which a corporation resident in Canada or a foreign affiliate of a corporation resident in Canada was a member, disposed of a share of the capital stock of a corporation, the amount determined under subsection (6) in respect of such a member is deemed to be a gain of the member from the disposition of the share by the partnership for the member's taxation year in which the fiscal period of the partnership ends.

Notes: See Notes to 92(4). 92(5) added by 2001 technical bill, effective for dispositions that occur after November 1999.

(6) Formula — The amount determined for the purposes of subsection (5) is the amount determined by the formula

$$A - B$$

where

A is the amount, if any, by which

(a) the total of all amounts each of which is an amount that was deductible under paragraph 113(1)(d) by the member from its income in computing its taxable income for a taxation year in respect of any portion of a dividend received by the partnership on the share in a fiscal period of the partnership that began before the time referred to in subsection (5) and ends in the member's taxation year, or would have been so deductible if the member were a corporation resident in Canada,

exceeds

(b) the total of all amounts each of which is the portion of any income or profits tax paid by the partnership or the member to a government of a country other than Canada that can reasonably be considered as having been paid in respect of the member's share of the dividend described in paragraph (a); and

B is the total of all amounts each of which is an amount that was added under subsection (4) in computing the member's proceeds of a disposition before the time referred to in subsection (5) of an interest in the partnership.

Related Provisions: 257 — Formula cannot calculate to less than zero.

Notes: See Notes to 92(4). For the meaning of "income or profits tax" in A(b), see Notes to 126(4).

92(6) added by 2001 technical bill, effective for dispositions after Nov. 1999.

Definitions [s. 92]: "adjusted cost base" — 54, 248(1); "amount" — 248(1); "arm's length" — 251(1); "Canada" — 255; "computation time" — 92(1.2) [transitional]; "corporation" — 248(1), *Interpretation Act* 35(1); "designated person" — 92(1.5) [transitional]; "disposition", "dividend" — 248(1); "election time" — 92(1.3) [transitional]; "equity percentage" — 95(4); "excluded property" — 95(1); "exempt surplus" — 113(1)(a); "fiscal period" — 249.1; "foreign affiliate" — 95(1), 248(1); "income or profits tax" — 126(4); "partnership" — see 96(1) Notes; "person", "prescribed" — 248(1); "related" — 251(2)–(6); "relevant foreign affiliate", "relevant share" — 92(1.2) [transitional]; "resident in Canada" — 94(3)(a), 250; "share" — 248(1); "specified section 93 election" — 92(1.3) [transitional]; "taxable income" — 2(2), 248(1); "taxation year" — 95(1) (for foreign affiliate only), 249; "taxpayer" — 248(1).

93. (1) Election re disposition of share of foreign affiliate

— For the purposes of this Act, if a corporation resident in Canada elects, in accordance with prescribed rules, in respect of any share of the capital stock of a particular foreign affiliate of the corporation that is disposed of, at any time, by the corporation (referred to in this subsection as the "disposing corporation") or by another foreign affiliate (referred to in this subsection as the "disposing affiliate") of the corporation,

(a) the amount (referred to in this subsection as the "elected amount") designated by the corporation in its election not exceeding the amount that would, in the absence of this subsection, be the gain of the disposing corporation or disposing affiliate, as the case may be, from the disposition of the share, is deemed

(i) to have been a dividend received on the share from the particular affiliate by the disposing corporation or disposing affiliate, as the case may be, immediately before that time, and

(ii) not to have been received by the disposing corporation or disposing affiliate, as the case may be, as proceeds of disposition in respect of the disposition of the share; and

(b) if subsection 40(3) applies to the disposing corporation or disposing affiliate, as the case may be, in respect of the share, the amount deemed by that subsection to be the gain of the disposing corporation or disposing affiliate, as the case may be, from the disposition of the share is, except for the purposes of paragraph 53(1)(a), deemed to be equal to the amount, if any, by which

(i) the amount deemed by that subsection to be the gain from the disposition of the share determined without reference to this paragraph

exceeds

(ii) the elected amount.

Related Provisions: 40(3) — Deemed gain where ACB goes negative; 93(1.1), (1.11) — Deemed election where foreign affiliate disposes of share or on election for dividend out of pre-acquisition surplus; 93(5) — Late filed elections; 93(5.2) — Amended election; 93.1(1) — Where shares are owned by partnership; 95(2)(f) — Determination of certain components of foreign accrual property income; Reg. 5900(2) —

No election for dividend to have been paid out of taxable surplus; Reg. 5902(1)(b) — Reductions to surplus accounts of foreign affiliate.

Notes: 93(1) allows a corporation disposing of shares of an FA to elect to treat the gain as a dividend, which can possibly be offset by a 113(1) deduction. Also, if the corp has an FA disposing of shares of another FA, 93(1) allows the corp to elect to treat its FA's gain as a dividend, so it will not be FAPI: 95(1)"foreign accrual property income"A(b).

See Kotecha, "The Subsection 93(1) Election", XI(3) *International Tax Planning* (Federated Press) 792-800 (2003); Jack et al, "The February 27, 2004 Draft Proposals on Foreign Affiliates", 2004 Cdn Tax Foundation conference report, at 20:26-35; Colborne & McLaren, "Section 93 Elections", 55(4) *Canadian Tax Journal* 856-93 (2007), and 58(2) *CTJ* 357-91 (2010); Woolford & Favre, "The Latest Foreign Affiliate Proposals", 58(4) *CTJ* 791 at 796-822 (2010).

In the absence of a 93(1) election, a redemption premium on mandatory redeemable pref shares is proceeds of disposition, not a dividend: doc 2014-0528361E5 (cancelling 2012-043974I17). See also VIEWS docs 2007-0242871R3, 2008-0290361R3, 2010-038763117.

A deemed dividend under 93(1), offset by a dividend deduction under 112 or 113, cannot create a bad debt deduction. See Notes to 20(1)(p).

For a taxpayer filing Quebec returns, a 93(1) election must be copied to Revenu Québec: *Taxation Act* ss. 589, 21.4.6.

93(1) amended by 2002-2013 technical bill (last change effective for elections for dispositions after Aug. 19, 2011, but not effective for determining income earned or realized by a corp's foreign affiliate under 55(5)(d) unless amended 55(5)(d) applies to that determination), 2001 and 1991 technical bills.

Regulations: 5902 (prescribed manner, prescribed time).

Interpretation Bulletins: IT-392: Meaning of the term "share"; IT-451R: Deemed disposition and acquisition on ceasing to be or becoming resident in Canada.

Information Circulars: 76-19R3: Transfer of property to a corporation under s. 85; 77-9R: Books, records and other requirements for taxpayers having foreign affiliates.

Forms: T2107: Election for a disposition of shares in a foreign affiliate.

(1.1) Application of subsec. (1.11)

— Subsection (1.11) applies if

(a) a particular foreign affiliate of a corporation resident in Canada disposes at any time of a share (referred to in this paragraph and subsection (1.11) as the "disposed share") of the capital stock of another foreign affiliate of the corporation and the particular affiliate would, in the absence of subsections (1) and (1.11), have a capital gain from the disposition of the disposed share; or

(b) a corporation resident in Canada would, in the absence of subsections (1) and (1.11), be deemed under subsection 40(3), because of an election under subsection 90(3) or subparagraph 5901(2)(b)(i) of the *Income Tax Regulations*, to have realized a gain from a disposition at any time of a share (referred to in subsection (1.11) as the "disposed share") of the capital stock of a foreign affiliate of the corporation.

Related Provisions: 40(3) — Deemed gain where ACB goes negative; 95(2)(f) — Determination of certain components of foreign accrual property income; Reg. 5902(6) — Effect of election deemed by 93(1.11).

Notes: 93(1.1) results in a deemed 93(1) election when the pre-acquisition surplus election amount (Reg. 5901(2)(b)) exceeds ACB, resulting in a deemed gain under 40(3). This ensures hybrid and taxable surplus are not effectively converted to capital gains. See also VIEWS docs 2016-0630761R3, 2017-0693751R3.

93(1.1) amended and 93(1.11) added by 2002-2013 technical bill, for dispositions of shares of a corp's foreign affiliate after Aug. 19, 2011 (or earlier by election). For an example applying pre-2011 93(1.1), see doc 2007-0242871R3.

Regulations: 5902(6) (prescribed amount).

(1.11) Deemed election

— If this subsection applies, the corporation resident in Canada referred to in subsection (1.1) is deemed

(a) to have made an election, at the time referred to in subsection (1.1), under subsection (1) in respect of the disposition of the disposed share; and

(b) to have designated, in the election, the prescribed amount in respect of the disposition of the disposed share.

Related Provisions: 93(1.1) — Conditions for 93(1.11) to apply.

Notes: See 93(1.1) Notes.

(1.2) Disposition of a share of a foreign affiliate held by a partnership

— Where a particular corporation resident in Canada or a foreign affiliate of the particular corporation (each of which is referred to in this subsection as the "disposing corporation") would, but for this subsection, have a taxable capital gain from a disposition by a partnership, at any time, of shares of a class of the capital stock of a foreign affiliate of the particular corporation and the particular corporation so elects in prescribed manner in respect of the disposition,

(a) twice

(i) the amount designated by the particular corporation (which amount shall not exceed the amount that is equal to the proportion of the taxable capital gain of the partnership that the number of shares of that class of the capital stock of the foreign affiliate, determined as the amount, if any, by which the number of those shares that were deemed to have been owned by the disposing corporation for the purposes of subsection 93.1(1) immediately before the disposition exceeds the number of those shares that were deemed to have been owned for those purposes by the disposing corporation immediately after the disposition, is of the number of those shares of the foreign affiliate that were owned by the partnership immediately before the disposition), or

(ii) if subsection (1.3) applies, the prescribed amount

in respect of those shares is deemed to have been a dividend received immediately before that time on the number of those shares of the foreign affiliate which shall be determined as the amount, if any, by which the number of those shares that the disposing corporation was deemed to own for the purpose of subsection 93.1(1) immediately before the disposition exceeds the number of those shares of the foreign affiliate that the disposing corporation was deemed to own for the purposes of subsection 93.1 (1) immediately after the disposition;

(b) notwithstanding section 96, the disposing corporation's taxable capital gain from the disposition of those shares is deemed to be the amount, if any, by which the disposing corporation's taxable capital gain from the disposition of the shares otherwise determined exceeds the amount designated by the particular corporation in respect of the shares;

(c) for the purpose of any regulation made under this subsection, the disposing corporation is deemed to have disposed of the number of those shares of the foreign affiliate which shall be determined as the amount, if any, by which the number of those shares that the disposing corporation was deemed to own for the purposes of subsection 93.1(1) immediately before the disposition exceeds the number of those shares that the disposing corporation was deemed to own for those purposes immediately after the disposition;

(d) for the purposes of section 113 in respect of the dividend referred to in paragraph (a), the disposing corporation is deemed to have owned the shares on which that dividend was received; and

(e) where the disposing corporation has a taxable capital gain from the partnership because of the application of subsection 40(3) to the partnership in respect of those shares, for the purposes of this subsection, the shares are deemed to have been disposed of by the partnership.

Related Provisions: 40(3) — Deemed gain where ACB goes negative; 93(1.3) — Deemed election; 93.1(1) — Where shares are owned by partnership; Reg. 5900(2) — No election for dividend to have been paid out of taxable surplus.

Notes: See Colborne & McLaren, "Section 93 Elections", 55(4) *Canadian Tax Journal* 856-93 (2007), and 58(2) *CTJ* 357-91 (2010).

For a corporation filing a Quebec return, a 93(1.2) election must be copied to Revenu Québec: *Taxation Act* ss. 589.2, 21.4.6.

93(1.2) amended by 2002-2013 technical bill (for elections in respect of dispositions after Nov. 1999). Added by 2001 technical bill.

Regulations: 5902 (prescribed manner, prescribed time); 5908(8)(b) (how and when election made); 5908(8)(c) (prescribed amount for 93(1.2)(a)(ii)).

(1.3) Deemed election — Where a foreign affiliate of a particular corporation resident in Canada has a gain from the disposition by a partnership at any time of shares of a class of the capital stock of a foreign affiliate of the particular corporation that are excluded property, the particular corporation is deemed to have made an election under subsection (1.2) in respect of the number of shares of the foreign affiliate which shall be determined as the amount, if any, by which the number of those shares that the disposing corporation was deemed to own for the purposes of subsection 93.1(1) immediately before the disposition exceeds the number of those shares that the disposing corporation was deemed to own for those purposes immediately after the disposition.

Notes: See Colborne & McLaren, "Section 93 Elections", 58(2) *Canadian Tax Journal* 357 at 385-87 (2010). 93(1.3) added by 2001 technical bill, for dispositions after Nov. 1999.

Proposed **93(1.4)** in the Feb. 27, 2004 draft legislation was dropped.

(2) Application of subsec. (2.01) — Subsection (2.01) applies if

(a) a particular corporation (referred to in subparagraph (2.01)(b)(ii) as the **"vendor"**, as the context requires) resident in Canada has a particular loss, determined without reference to this section, from the disposition by it at any time (referred to in subsection (2.01) as the "disposition time") of a share (referred to in subsection (2.01) as the "affiliate share") of the capital stock of a foreign affiliate of the particular corporation; or

(b) a foreign affiliate (referred to in subparagraph (2.01)(b)(ii) as the **"vendor"**) of a particular corporation resident in Canada has a particular loss, determined without reference to this section, from the disposition by it at any time (referred to in subsection (2.01) as the **"disposition time"**) of a share (referred to in subsection (2.01) as the **"affiliate share"**) of the capital stock of another foreign affiliate of the particular corporation that is not excluded property.

Notes: 93(2)–(2.32) contain stop-loss rules similar to 112(3). A loss on disposition of shares of a foreign affiliate (FA) is reduced by any exempt dividends received on the shares (such as a dividend paid out of exempt surplus: 93(3)).

For discussion of 93(2) before the 2013 amendments, see Kopstein & Pantry, "Foreign Exchange Issues", 2003 Cdn Tax Foundation conference report, 27:39-42. For rulings that previous 93(2) applied see VIEWS docs 2006-0196691R3, 2009-0328141I7.

For CRA interpretation see docs 2012-046490117, 2013-047631117 (shares not considered substituted for 93(2.01)(a)B); 2013-0486741C6 [2013 IFA q.3], 2013-0508161C6 [2013 CTF] (GAAR applies to transactions that avoid 93(2) or (2.01): 93(2.01)(b)(ii) specifies which gains are acceptable; same conditions apply as under 112(3)); 2014-053859117 [Cepparo, "Foreign Exchange Losses on CFA Windup", 23(3) *Canadian Tax Highlights* (ctf.ca) 10 (March 2015)]; 2016-063282117, 2016-0642121C6 [2016 IFA q.7] ("substituted" shares in 93(2.01)(a)C can include shares of FA1 to which taxpayer contributed shares of FA2).

93(2), (2.1), (2.2), (2.3) and (3) amended; and (2.01), (2.02), (2.11), (2.12), (2.21), (2.22), (2.31) and (2.32) added; by 2002-2013 technical bill, for losses of a corporation resident in Canada, or of FAs of such a corp, in respect of dispositions of shares and partnership interests after Feb. 27, 2004; but various provisions read differently and various elections were available for dispositions before Aug. 19, 2012 (see up to PITA 51st ed.). 93(2) earlier amended by 2001 and 1991 technical bills.

Interpretation Bulletins: IT-392: Meaning of the term "share"; IT-451R: Deemed disposition and acquisition on ceasing to be or becoming resident in Canada.

Related Provisions: 93(2.1), (2.2), (2.3) — Parallel rules for disposition by partnership.

(2.01) Loss limitation on disposition of share of foreign affiliate — If this subsection applies, the amount of the particular loss referred to in paragraph (2)(a) or (b) is deemed to be the greater of

(a) the amount determined by the formula

$$A - (B - C)$$

where

A is the amount of the particular loss determined without reference to this section,

B is the total of all amounts each of which is an amount received before the disposition time, in respect of an exempt dividend on the affiliate share or on a share for which the affiliate share was substituted, by

(i) the particular corporation referred to in subsection (2),

(ii) another corporation that is related to the particular corporation,

(iii) a foreign affiliate of the particular corporation, or

(iv) a foreign affiliate of another corporation that is related to the particular corporation, and

C is the total of

(i) the total of all amounts each of which is the amount by which a loss (determined without reference to this section), from a previous disposition by a corporation, or a foreign affiliate described in the description of B, of the affiliate share or a share for which the affiliate share was substituted, was reduced under this paragraph in respect of the exempt dividends referred to in the description of B,

(ii) the total of all amounts each of which is twice the amount by which an allowable capital loss (determined without reference to this section), of a corporation or a foreign affiliate described in the description of B, from a previous disposition by a partnership of the affiliate share or a share for which the affiliate share was substituted, was reduced under paragraph (2.11)(a) in respect of the exempt dividends referred to in the description of B,

(iii) the total of all amounts each of which is the amount by which a loss (determined without reference to this section), from a previous disposition by a corporation, or a foreign affiliate described in the description of B, of an interest in a partnership, was reduced under paragraph (2.21)(a) in respect of the exempt dividends referred to in the description of B, and

(iv) the total of all amounts each of which is twice the amount by which an allowable capital loss (determined without reference to this section), of a corporation, or a foreign affiliate described in the description of B, from a previous disposition by a partnership of an interest in another partnership, was reduced under paragraph (2.31)(a) in respect of the exempt dividends referred to in the description of B, and

(b) the lesser of

(i) the portion of the particular loss, determined without reference to this section, that can reasonably be considered to be attributable to a fluctuation in the value of a currency other than Canadian currency relative to Canadian currency, and

(ii) the amount determined in respect of the vendor that is

(A) if the particular loss is a capital loss, the amount of a gain (other than a specified gain) that

(I) was made within 30 days before or after the disposition time by the vendor and that

1. is deemed under subsection 39(2) to be a capital gain of the vendor for the taxation year that includes the time the gain was made from the disposition of currency other than Canadian currency, and

2. is in respect of the settlement or extinguishment of a foreign currency debt that was issued or incurred by the vendor within 30 days before or after the acquisition of the affiliate share by the vendor and that was, at all times at which it was a debt obligation of the vendor owing to a person or partnership that dealt, at all times during which the foreign currency debt was outstanding, at arm's length with the particular corporation and can reasonably be considered to have been issued or incurred in relation to the acquisition of the affiliate share, or

(II) is a capital gain realized within 30 days before or after the disposition time by the vendor under an agreement that

1. was entered into by the vendor within 30 days before or after the acquisition of the affiliate share by the vendor with a person or partnership that

dealt, at all times during which the agreement was in force, at arm's length with the particular corporation,

2. provides for the purchase, sale or exchange of currency, and

3. can reasonably be considered to have been entered into by the vendor for the principal purpose of hedging the foreign exchange exposure arising in connection with the acquisition of the affiliate share, or

(B) in any other case, the amount of a gain (other than a specified gain or a capital gain) that was realized within 30 days before or after the disposition time by the vendor that is included in computing the income of the vendor for the taxation year that includes the time the gain was realized and

(I) that is in respect of the settlement or extinguishment of a foreign currency debt that

1. was issued or incurred by the vendor within 30 days before or after the acquisition of the affiliate share by the vendor,

2. was, at all times at which it was a debt obligation of the vendor owing to a person or partnership that dealt, at all times during which the foreign currency debt was outstanding, at arm's length with the particular corporation, and

3. can reasonably be considered to have been issued or incurred in relation to the acquisition of the affiliate share, or

(II) under an agreement that

1. was entered into by the vendor within 30 days before or after the acquisition of the affiliate share by the vendor with a person or partnership that dealt, at all times during which the agreement was in force, at arm's length with the particular corporation,

2. provides for the purchase, sale or exchange of currency, and

3. can reasonably be considered to have been entered into by the vendor for the principal purpose of hedging the foreign exchange exposure arising in connection with the acquisition of the affiliate share.

Related Provisions: 40(3) — Deemed gain where ACB goes negative; 40(3.3), (3.4) — Limitation on loss where share acquired by affiliated person; 87(2)(u)(ii) — Amalgamation; 93(2) — Conditions for 93(2.01) to apply; 93(2.02) — Meaning of "specified gain"; 93(2.11), (2.21), (2.31) — Parallel rules for disposition by partnership; 93(3) — Exempt dividends; 93(4) — Loss on disposition of shares of foreign affiliate; 93.1(1) — Where shares are owned by partnership; 93.1(2) — Dividend on shares of foreign affiliate held by partnership; 261(5)(f)(i) — Functional currency reporting — meaning of "Canadian currency"; 257 — Formula amounts cannot calculate to less than zero; *Interpretation Act* 27(5) — Meaning of "within 30 days".

Notes: See 93(2) Notes for application of 93(2.01).

(2.02) Specified gain — For the purposes of clauses (2.01)(b)(ii)(A) and (B), a "specified gain" means a gain in respect of the settlement or extinguishment of a foreign currency debt referred to in sub-subclause (2.01)(b)(ii)(A)(I)2 or subclause (2.01)(b)(ii)(B)(I), as the case may be, or that arises under a particular agreement referred to in subclause (2.01)(b)(ii)(A)(II) or (B)(II), if the particular corporation, or any person or partnership with which the particular corporation was not — at any time during which the foreign currency debt was outstanding or the particular agreement was in force, as the case may be — dealing at arm's length, entered into an agreement that may reasonably be considered to have been entered into for the principal purpose of hedging any foreign exchange exposure arising in connection with the foreign currency debt or the particular agreement.

Notes: See 93(2) Notes for application of 93(2.02). For the meaning of "extinguishment", see 80(2)(a) Notes.

(2.1) Application of subsec. (2.11) — Subsection (2.11) applies if

(a) a particular corporation resident in Canada has a particular allowable capital loss, determined without reference to this section, from the disposition at any time (referred to in subsection (2.11) as the **"disposition time"**) by a partnership (referred to in subsections (2.11) and (2.12) as the **"disposing partnership"**) of a share (referred to in subsection (2.11) as the **"affiliate share"**) of the capital stock of a foreign affiliate of the particular corporation; or

(b) a foreign affiliate of a particular corporation resident in Canada has a particular allowable capital loss, determined without reference to this section, from the disposition at any time (referred to in subsection (2.11) as the **"disposition time"**) by a partnership (referred to in subsections (2.11) and (2.12) as the **"disposing partnership"**) of a share (referred to in subsection (2.11) as the **"affiliate share"**) of the capital stock of another foreign affiliate of the particular corporation that would not be excluded property of the affiliate if the affiliate had owned the share immediately before the disposition time.

Related Provisions: 93(2.2), (2.3) — Parallel rules for disposition by partnership with FA shares.

Notes: See 93(2) Notes for application of 2013 amendment. 93(2.1) added by 2001 technical bill, last change effective for tax years ending after Oct. 17, 2000.

(2.11) Loss limitation on disposition of foreign affiliate share by a partnership — If this subsection applies, the amount of the particular allowable capital loss referred to in paragraph (2.1)(a) or (b) is deemed to be the greater of

(a) the amount determined by the formula

$$A - (B - C)$$

where

A   is the amount of the particular allowable capital loss determined without reference to this section,

B   is ½ of the total of all amounts each of which is an amount received before the disposition time, in respect of an exempt dividend on the affiliate share or on a share for which the affiliate share was substituted, by

(i) the particular corporation referred to in subsection (2.1),

(ii) another corporation that is related to the particular corporation,

(iii) a foreign affiliate of the particular corporation, or

(iv) a foreign affiliate of another corporation that is related to the particular corporation, and

C   is the total of

(i) the total of all amounts each of which is ½ of the amount by which a loss (determined without reference to this section), from a previous disposition by a corporation, or a foreign affiliate described in the description of B, of the affiliate share or a share for which the affiliate share was substituted, was reduced under paragraph (2.01)(a) in respect of the exempt dividends referred to in the description of B,

(ii) the total of all amounts each of which is the amount by which an allowable capital loss (determined without reference to this section), of a corporation or a foreign affiliate described in the description of B, from a previous disposition by a partnership of the affiliate share or a share for which the affiliate share was substituted, was reduced under this paragraph in respect of the exempt dividends referred to in the description of B,

(iii) the total of all amounts each of which is ½ of the amount by which a loss (determined without reference to this section), from a previous disposition by a corpora-

tion, or a foreign affiliate described in the description of B, of an interest in a partnership, was reduced under paragraph (2.21)(a) in respect of the exempt dividends referred to in the description of B, and

(iv) the total of all amounts each of which is the amount by which an allowable capital loss (determined without reference to this section), of a corporation, or a foreign affiliate described in the description of B, from a previous disposition by a partnership of an interest in another partnership, was reduced under paragraph (2.31)(a) in respect of the exempt dividends referred to in the description of B, and

(b) the lesser of

(i) the portion of the particular allowable capital loss, determined without reference to this section, that can reasonably be considered to be attributable to a fluctuation in the value of a currency other than Canadian currency relative to Canadian currency, and

(ii) ½ of the amount determined in respect of the particular corporation, or the foreign affiliate (that is referred to in paragraph (2.1)(b)) of the particular corporation, that is the amount of a gain (other than a specified gain) that

(A) was made within 30 days before or after the disposition time by the disposing partnership to the extent that the gain is reasonably attributable to the particular corporation or the foreign affiliate, as the case may be, and that

(I) is deemed under subsection 39(2) to be a capital gain of the disposing partnership for the taxation year that includes the time the gain was made from the disposition of currency other than Canadian currency, and

(II) is in respect of the settlement or extinguishment of a foreign currency debt that

1. was issued or incurred by the disposing partnership within 30 days before or after the acquisition of the affiliate share by the disposing partnership,

2. was, at all times at which it was a debt obligation of the disposing partnership, owing to a person or partnership that dealt, at all times during which the foreign currency debt was outstanding, at arm's length with the particular corporation, and

3. can reasonably be considered to have been issued or incurred in relation to the acquisition of the affiliate share, or

(B) is a capital gain (to the extent that the capital gain is reasonably attributable to the particular corporation or the foreign affiliate, as the case may be) realized within 30 days before or after the disposition time by the disposing partnership under an agreement that

(I) was entered into by the disposing partnership, within 30 days before or after the acquisition of the affiliate share by the disposing partnership, with a person or partnership that dealt, at all times during which the agreement was in force, at arm's length with the particular corporation,

(II) provides for the purchase, sale or exchange of currency, and

(III) can reasonably be considered to have been entered into by the disposing partnership for the principal purpose of hedging the foreign exchange exposure arising in connection with the acquisition of the affiliate share.

Related Provisions: 40(3) — Deemed gain where ACB goes negative; 87(2)(u)(ii) — Amalgamation; 93(2.1) — Conditions for 93(2.11) to apply; 93(2.12) — Meaning of "specified gain"; 93(2.21), (2.31) — Parallel rules for disposition by partnership with FA shares; 93(3) — Exempt dividends; 93.1(2) — Dividend on shares of foreign affiliate held by partnership; 261(5)(f)(i) — Functional currency reporting —

meaning of "Canadian currency"; 257 — Formula amounts cannot calculate to less than zero; *Interpretation Act* 27(5) — Meaning of "within 30 days".

Notes: See 93(2) Notes for application of 93(2.11).

(2.12) Specified gain — For the purposes of subparagraph (2.11)(b)(ii), a "specified gain" means a gain in respect of the settlement or extinguishment of a foreign currency debt referred to in subclause (2.11)(b)(ii)(A)(II), or that arises under a particular agreement referred to in clause (2.11)(b)(ii)(B), if the disposing partnership, or any person or partnership with which the particular corporation was not — at any time during which the foreign currency debt was outstanding or the particular agreement was in force, as the case may be — dealing at arm's length, entered into an agreement that may reasonably be considered to have been entered into for the principal purpose of hedging any foreign exchange exposure arising in connection with the foreign currency debt or the particular agreement.

Notes: See 93(2) Notes for application of 93(2.12).

(2.2) Application of subsec. (2.21) — Subsection (2.21) applies if

(a) a particular corporation (referred to in subparagraph (2.21)(b)(ii) as the **"vendor"**, as the context requires) resident in Canada has a particular loss, determined without reference to this section, from the disposition by it at any time (referred to in subsection (2.21) as the **"disposition time"**) of an interest (referred to in subsection (2.21) as the **"partnership interest"**) in a partnership that has a direct or indirect interest, or, for civil law, a direct or indirect right, in shares (referred to in subsection (2.21) as the **"affiliate shares"**) of the capital stock of a foreign affiliate of the particular corporation; or

(b) a foreign affiliate (referred to in subparagraph (2.21)(b)(ii) as the **"vendor"**) of a particular corporation resident in Canada has a particular loss, determined without reference to this section, from the disposition by it at any time (referred to in subsection (2.21) as the **"disposition time"**) of an interest (referred to in subsection (2.21) as the **"partnership interest"**) in a partnership that has a direct or indirect interest, or, for civil law, a direct or indirect right, in shares (referred to in subsection (2.21) as the **"affiliate shares"**) of the capital stock of another foreign affiliate of the particular corporation that would not be excluded property of the affiliate if the affiliate had owned the shares immediately before the disposition time.

Related Provisions: 93(3) — Exempt dividends; 93.1(1) — Where shares are owned by partnership; 93.1(2) — Dividend on shares of foreign affiliate held by partnership; 257 — Formula amounts cannot calculate to less than zero.

Notes: See 93(2) Notes for application of 2013 amendment. 93(2.2) added by 2001 technical bill, last change effective for tax years ending after Oct. 17, 2000.

(2.21) Loss limitation on disposition of partnership that has foreign affiliate shares — If this subsection applies, the amount of the particular loss referred to in paragraph (2.2)(a) or (b) is deemed to be the greater of

(a) the amount determined by the formula

$$A - (B - C)$$

where

A   is the amount of the particular loss determined without reference to this section,

B   is the total of all amounts each of which is an amount received before the disposition time, in respect of an exempt dividend on affiliate shares or on shares for which affiliate shares were substituted, by

    (i) the particular corporation referred to in subsection (2.2),

    (ii) another corporation that is related to the particular corporation,

    (iii) a foreign affiliate of the particular corporation, or

    (iv) a foreign affiliate of another corporation that is related to the particular corporation, and

C   is the total of

    (i) the total of all amounts each of which is the amount by which a loss (determined without reference to this section), from a previous disposition by a corporation, or a foreign affiliate described in the description of B, of the affiliate shares or shares for which the affiliate shares were substituted, was reduced under paragraph (2.01)(a) in respect of the exempt dividends referred to in the description of B,

    (ii) the total of all amounts each of which is twice the amount by which an allowable capital loss (determined without reference to this section), of a corporation or a foreign affiliate described in the description of B, from a previous disposition by a partnership of the affiliate shares or shares for which the affiliate shares were substituted, was reduced under paragraph (2.11)(a) in respect of the exempt dividends referred to in the description of B,

    (iii) the total of all amounts each of which is the amount by which a loss (determined without reference to this section), from a previous disposition by a corporation, or a foreign affiliate described in the description of B, of an interest in a partnership, was reduced under this paragraph in respect of the exempt dividends referred to in the description of B, and

    (iv) the total of all amounts each of which is twice the amount by which an allowable capital loss (determined without reference to this section), of a corporation, or a foreign affiliate described in the description of B, from a previous disposition by a partnership of an interest in another partnership, was reduced under paragraph (2.31)(a) in respect of the exempt dividends referred to in the description of B, and

(b) the lesser of

    (i) the portion of the particular loss, determined without reference to this section, that can reasonably be considered to be attributable to a fluctuation in the value of a currency other than Canadian currency relative to Canadian currency, and

    (ii) the amount determined in respect of the vendor that is

      (A) if the particular loss is a capital loss, the amount of a gain (other than a specified gain) that

        (I) was made within 30 days before or after the disposition time by the vendor and that

          1. is deemed under subsection 39(2) to be a capital gain of the vendor for the taxation year that includes the time the gain was made from the disposition of currency other than Canadian currency, and

          2. is in respect of the settlement or extinguishment of a foreign currency debt that was issued or incurred by the vendor within 30 days before or after the acquisition of the partnership interest by the vendor and that was, at all times at which it was a debt obligation of the vendor owing to a person or partnership that dealt, at all times during which the foreign currency debt was outstanding, at arm's length with the particular corporation and can reasonably be considered to have been issued or incurred in relation to the acquisition of the partnership interest, or

        (II) is a capital gain realized within 30 days before or after the disposition time by the vendor under an agreement that

          1. was entered into by the vendor within 30 days before or after the acquisition of the partnership interest by the vendor with a person or partnership that dealt, at all times during which the agreement was in force, at arm's length with the particular corporation,

2. provides for the purchase, sale or exchange of currency, and

3. can reasonably be considered to have been entered into by the vendor for the principal purpose of hedging the foreign exchange exposure arising in connection with the acquisition of the partnership interest, or

(B) in any other case, the amount of a gain (other than a specified gain or a capital gain) that was realized within 30 days before or after the disposition time by the vendor that is included in computing the income of the vendor for the taxation year that includes the time the gain was realized and

(I) that is in respect of the settlement or extinguishment of a foreign currency debt that

1. was issued or incurred by the vendor within 30 days before or after the acquisition of the partnership interest by the vendor,

2. was, at all times at which it was a debt obligation of the vendor owing to a person or partnership that dealt, at all times during which the foreign currency debt was outstanding, at arm's length with the particular corporation, and

3. can reasonably be considered to have been issued or incurred in relation to the acquisition of the partnership interest, or

(II) under an agreement that

1. was entered into by the vendor within 30 days before or after the acquisition of the partnership interest by the vendor with a person or partnership that dealt, at all times during which the agreement was in force, at arm's length with the particular corporation,

2. provides for the purchase, sale or exchange of currency, and

3. can reasonably be considered to have been entered into by the vendor for the principal purpose of hedging the foreign exchange exposure arising in connection with the acquisition of the partnership interest.

Related Provisions: 40(3) — Deemed gain where ACB goes negative; 87(2)(u)(ii) — Amalgamation; 93(2.2) — Conditions for 93(2.21) to apply; 93(2.22) — Meaning of "specified gain"; 93(2.31) — Parallel rules for disposition by partnership with indirect interest in FA shares; 93(3) — Exempt dividends; 93.1(1) — Where shares are owned by partnership; 93.1(2) — Dividend on shares of foreign affiliate held by partnership; 257 — Formula amounts cannot calculate to less than zero; 261(5)(f)(i) — Functional currency reporting — meaning of "Canadian currency"; *Interpretation Act* 27(5) — Meaning of "within 30 days".

Notes: See 93(2) Notes for application of 93(2.21).

(2.22) Specified gain — For the purposes of clauses (2.21)(b)(ii)(A) and (B), a "specified gain" means a gain in respect of the settlement or extinguishment of a foreign currency debt referred to in sub-subclause (2.21)(b)(ii)(A)(I)2 or subclause (2.21)(b)(ii)(B)(I), as the case may be, or that arises under a particular agreement referred to in subclause (2.21)(b)(ii)(A)(II) or (B)(II), if the particular corporation, or any person or partnership with which the particular corporation was not — at any time during which the foreign currency debt was outstanding or the particular agreement was in force, as the case may be — dealing at arm's length, entered into an agreement that may reasonably be considered to have been entered into for the principal purpose of hedging any foreign exchange exposure arising in connection with the foreign currency debt or the particular agreement.

Notes: See 93(2) Notes for application of 93(2.22).

(2.3) Application of subsec. (2.31) — Subsection (2.31) applies if

(a) a particular corporation resident in Canada has a particular allowable capital loss, determined without reference to this sec-

tion, from the disposition at any time (referred to in subsection (2.31) as the **"disposition time"**) by a particular partnership of an interest (referred to in subsection (2.31) as the **"partnership interest"**) in another partnership that has a direct or indirect interest, or, for civil law, a direct or indirect right, in shares (referred to in subsection (2.31) as the **"affiliate shares"**) of the capital stock of a foreign affiliate of the particular corporation; or

(b) a foreign affiliate of a particular corporation resident in Canada has a particular allowable capital loss, determined without reference to this section, from the disposition at any time (referred to in subsection (2.31) as the **"disposition time"**) by a particular partnership of an interest (referred to in subsection (2.31) as the **"partnership interest"**) in another partnership that has a direct or indirect interest, or, for civil law, a direct or indirect right, in shares (referred to in subsection (2.31) as the **"affiliate shares"**) of the capital stock of a foreign affiliate of the particular corporation that would not be excluded property of the affiliate if the affiliate had owned the shares immediately before the disposition time.

Related Provisions: 93(3) — Exempt dividends; 93.1(1) — Where shares are owned by partnership; 93.1(2) — Dividend on shares of foreign affiliate held by partnership.

Notes: See 93(2) Notes for application of 2013 amendment. 93(2.3) added by 2001 technical bill, last change effective for tax years ending after Oct. 17, 2000.

(2.31) Loss limitation on disposition by a partnership of an indirect interest in foreign affiliate shares — If this subsection applies, the amount of the particular allowable capital loss referred to in paragraph (2.3)(a) or (b) is deemed to be the greater of

(a) the amount determined by the formula

$$A - (B - C)$$

where

A is the amount of the particular allowable capital loss determined without reference to this section,

B is ½ of the total of all amounts each of which is an amount received before the disposition time, in respect of an exempt dividend on the affiliate shares or on shares for which the affiliate shares were substituted, by

(i) the particular corporation referred to in subsection (2.3),

(ii) another corporation that is related to the particular corporation,

(iii) a foreign affiliate of the particular corporation, or

(iv) a foreign affiliate of another corporation that is related to the particular corporation, and

C is the total of

(i) the total of all amounts each of which is ½ of the amount by which a loss (determined without reference to this section), from a previous disposition by a corporation, or a foreign affiliate described in the description of B, of the affiliate shares or shares for which the affiliate shares were substituted, was reduced under paragraph (2.01)(a) in respect of the exempt dividends referred to in the description of B,

(ii) the total of all amounts each of which is the amount by which an allowable capital loss (determined without reference to this section), of a corporation or a foreign affiliate described in the description of B, from a previous disposition by a partnership of the affiliate shares or shares for which the affiliate shares were substituted, was reduced under paragraph (2.11)(a) in respect of the exempt dividends referred to in the description of B,

(iii) the total of all amounts each of which is ½ of the amount by which a loss (determined without reference to this section), from a previous disposition by a corporation, or a foreign affiliate described in the description of

B, of an interest in a partnership, was reduced under paragraph (2.21)(a) in respect of the exempt dividends referred to in the description of B, and

(iv) the total of all amounts each of which is the amount by which an allowable capital loss (determined without reference to this section), of a corporation, or a foreign affiliate described in the description of B, from a previous disposition by a partnership of an interest in another partnership, was reduced under this paragraph in respect of the exempt dividends referred to in the description of B, and

(b) the lesser of

(i) the portion of the particular allowable capital loss, determined without reference to this section, that can reasonably be considered to be attributable to a fluctuation in the value of a currency other than Canadian currency relative to Canadian currency, and

(ii) ½ of the amount determined in respect of the particular corporation, or the foreign affiliate (that is referred to in paragraph (2.3)(b)), of the particular corporation, that is the amount of a gain (other than a specified gain) that

(A) was made within 30 days before or after the disposition time by the particular partnership to the extent that the gain is reasonably attributable to the particular corporation or the foreign affiliate, as the case may be, and that

(I) is deemed under subsection 39(2) to be a capital gain of the particular partnership for the taxation year that includes the time the gain was made from the disposition of currency other than Canadian currency, and

(II) is in respect of the settlement or extinguishment of a foreign currency debt that

1. was issued or incurred by the particular partnership within 30 days before or after the acquisition of the partnership interest by the particular partnership,

2. was, at all times at which it was a debt obligation of the particular partnership, owing to a person or partnership that dealt, at all times during which the foreign currency debt was outstanding, at arm's length with the particular corporation, and

3. can reasonably be considered to have been issued or incurred in relation to the acquisition of the partnership interest, or

(B) is a capital gain (to the extent that the capital gain is reasonably attributable to the particular corporation or the foreign affiliate, as the case may be) realized within 30 days before or after the disposition time by the particular partnership under an agreement that

(I) was entered into by the particular partnership, within 30 days before or after the acquisition of the partnership interest by the particular partnership, with a person or partnership that dealt, at all times during which the agreement was in force, at arm's length with the particular corporation,

(II) provides for the purchase, sale or exchange of currency, and

(III) can reasonably be considered to have been entered into by the particular partnership for the principal purpose of hedging the foreign exchange exposure arising in connection with the acquisition of the partnership interest.

Related Provisions: 40(3) — Deemed gain where ACB goes negative; 87(2)(u)(ii) — Amalgamation; 93(2.3) — Conditions for 93(2.31) to apply; 93(2.32) — Meaning of "specified gain"; 93(3) — Exempt dividends; 93.1(1) — Where shares are owned by partnership; 93.1(2) — Dividend on shares of foreign affiliate held by partnership; 257 — Formula amounts cannot calculate to less than zero; 261(5)(f)(i) —

Functional currency reporting — meaning of "Canadian currency"; *Interpretation Act* 27(5) — Meaning of "within 30 days".

Notes: See 93(2) Notes for application of 93(2.31).

(2.32) Specified gain — For the purposes of subparagraph (2.31)(b)(ii), a "specified gain" means a gain in respect of the settlement or extinguishment of a foreign currency debt referred to in subclause (2.31)(b)(ii)(A)(II), or that arises under a particular agreement referred to in clause (2.31)(b)(ii)(B), if the particular partnership, or any person or partnership with which the particular corporation was not — at any time during which the foreign currency debt was outstanding or the particular agreement was in force, as the case may be — dealing at arm's length, entered into an agreement that may reasonably be considered to have been entered into for the principal purpose of hedging any foreign exchange exposure arising in connection with the foreign currency debt or the particular agreement.

Notes: See 93(2) Notes for application of 93(2.32).

(3) Exempt dividends — For the purposes of subsections (2.01), (2.11), (2.21) and (2.31),

(a) a dividend received by a corporation resident in Canada is an exempt dividend to the extent of the amount in respect of the dividend that is deductible from the income of the corporation for the purpose of computing the taxable income of the corporation because of any of paragraphs 113(1)(a) to (c);

(b) a dividend received by a particular foreign affiliate of a corporation resident in Canada from another foreign affiliate of the corporation is an exempt dividend to the extent of the amount, if any, by which the portion of the dividend that was not prescribed to have been paid out of the pre-acquisition surplus of the other affiliate exceeds the total of such portion of the income or profits tax that can reasonably be considered to have been paid in respect of that portion of the dividend by the particular affiliate or by a partnership in which the particular affiliate had, at the time of the payment of the income or profits tax, a partnership interest, either directly or indirectly; and

(c) the prescribed amount is deemed to be an amount that is received, at the adjustment time referred to in subsection 5905(7.7) of the *Income Tax Regulations*, by a particular foreign affiliate of a corporation resident in Canada from another foreign affiliate of the corporation and that is in respect of an exempt dividend on a share of the capital stock of the other affiliate.

Notes: For the meaning of "income or profits tax" in para. (b), see 126(4) Notes. 93(3) amended by 2002-2013 technical bill (see 93(2) Notes), 2001 technical bill.

Regulations: 5900(1)(c) (amount prescribed to have been paid out of pre-acquisition surplus); 5905(7.7) (prescribed amount for 93(3)(c)).

(4) Loss on disposition of shares of foreign affiliate [stop-loss rule] — If a taxpayer resident in Canada or a foreign affiliate (which taxpayer or foreign affiliate is referred to in this subsection as the "transferee") of the taxpayer has acquired shares of the capital stock of one or more foreign affiliates (each referred to in this subsection as an "acquired affiliate") of the taxpayer on a disposition of shares (such shares disposed of being referred to in this subsection as the "disposed shares") of the capital stock of any other foreign affiliate of the taxpayer (other than, where the transferee is a foreign affiliate of the taxpayer, a disposition of shares that are, immediately before the acquisition, excluded property of the transferee or a disposition to which subsection 40(3.4) applies), the following rules apply:

(a) the capital loss, if any, of the transferee from the disposition, is deemed to be nil; and

(b) in computing the adjusted cost base to the transferee of a share of a particular class of the capital stock of an acquired affiliate that is owned by the transferee immediately after the disposition, there is to be added the amount determined by the formula

$$[(A - B) \times C/D] / E$$

where

A is the total of all amounts each of which is the cost amount to the transferee, immediately before the disposition, of a disposed share,

B is the total of

(i) the total of all amounts each of which is the proceeds of disposition of a disposed share, and

(ii) the total of all amounts in respect of the computation of losses of the transferee from the dispositions of the disposed shares, each of which is, in respect of the disposition of a disposed share, the amount by which the amount for A in the formula in paragraph (2.01)(a) exceeds the amount determined by that formula,

C is the fair market value, immediately after the disposition, of all shares of the particular class owned, immediately after the disposition, by the transferee,

D is the fair market value, immediately after the disposition, of all shares owned, immediately after the disposition, by the transferee of the capital stock of all acquired affiliates, and

E is the number of shares of the particular class that are owned by the transferee immediately after the disposition.

Related Provisions: 92(1.2) — Addition to ACB of share of foreign affiliate; 93(2)–(2.31) — Loss limitation on disposition of share; 93.1(1) — Where shares are owned by partnership; 257 — Formula cannot calculate to less than zero.

Notes: CRA considers that 93(4) applies to foreign-affiliate shares received on dissolution of another FA: VIEWS doc 2017-069824I7.

93(4) amended by 2002-2013 technical bill (last change effective for share acquisitions after Aug. 19, 2011), 1995-97 technical bill, 1991 technical bill.

Interpretation Bulletins: See at end of s. 93.

(5) Late filed elections — Where the election referred to in subsection (1) was not made on or before the day on or before which the election was required by that subsection to be made, the election shall be deemed to have been made on that day if, on or before the day that is 3 years after that day,

(a) the election is made in prescribed manner; and

(b) an estimate of the penalty in respect of that election is paid by the corporation when that election is made.

Regulations: 5902 (prescribed manner).

CRA Audit Manual: 28.6.1: Penalties for late filed/amended elections — disposition of shares in a foreign affiliate.

Forms: T2107: Election for a disposition of shares in a foreign affiliate.

(5.1) Special cases — Where, in the opinion of the Minister, the circumstances of a case are such that it would be just and equitable

(a) to permit an election under subsection (1) to be made after the day that is 3 years after the day on or before which the election was required by that subsection to be made, or

(b) to permit an election made under subsection (1) to be amended,

the election or amended election shall be deemed to have been made on the day on or before which the election was so required to be made if

(c) the election or amended election is made in prescribed form, and

(d) an estimate of the penalty in respect of the election or amended election is paid by the corporation when the election or amended election is made,

and where this subsection applies to the amendment of an election, that election shall be deemed not to have been effective.

Notes: For the meaning of "just and equitable", see 85(7.1) Notes.

CRA Audit Manual: 28.6.1: Penalties for late filed/amended elections.

Forms: T2107: Election for a disposition of shares in a foreign affiliate.

(5.2) Amended election — An election (referred to in this subsection as the "amended election") by a taxpayer under subsection (1) in respect of a disposition of shares of the capital stock of a foreign affiliate of the taxpayer is deemed to have been made on the day on or before which the election was required to be made and any previous election (referred to in this subsection as the "old election") under subsection (1) in respect of that disposition is deemed not to have been made if

(a) the taxpayer has not elected under section 51 of the *Technical Tax Amendments Act, 2012* [for transitional 92(1.2)–(1.5) and various amendments to the Regulations to apply; see Notes to 92(1.2) — ed.];

(b) the taxpayer made the old election on or before December 18, 2009;

(c) in the opinion of the Minister, the circumstances are such that it would be just and equitable to permit the old election to be amended; and

(d) the amended election is made in prescribed form on or before December 31, 2013.

Notes: For para. (c), Finance's Technical Notes state: "it is generally expected that the 'just and equitable' standard would be met where the original 93(1) election was filed on the basis of the 'consolidated net surplus' rules and the taxpayer simply wishes to amend the election to reflect their non-application". For more on "just and equitable" see 85(7.1) Notes.

93(5.2) added by 2002-2013 technical bill, effective Dec. 19, 2009.

(6) Penalty for late filed election — For the purposes of this section, the penalty in respect of an election or amended election referred to in paragraph (5)(a) or (5.1)(c) is an amount equal to the lesser of

(a) ¼ of 1% of the amount designated in the election or amended election for each month or part of a month during the period commencing with the day on or before which the election is required by subsection (1) to be made and ending on the day the election is made, and

(b) an amount, not exceeding $8,000, equal to the product obtained by multiplying $100 by the number of months each of which is a month all or part of which is during the period referred to in paragraph (a).

Related Provisions: 93(7) — Assessment of penalty; 220(3.1) — Waiver of penalty by CRA.

CRA Audit Manual: 28.6.1: Penalties for late filed/amended elections — disposition of shares in a foreign affiliate.

(7) Unpaid balance of penalty — The Minister shall, with all due dispatch, examine each election and amended election referred to in paragraph (5)(a) or (5.1)(c), assess the penalty payable and send a notice of assessment to the corporation, and the corporation shall pay forthwith to the Receiver General the amount, if any, by which the penalty so assessed exceeds the total of all amounts previously paid on account of that penalty.

Definitions [s. 93]: "acquired affiliate" — 93(4); "adjusted cost base" — 54, 248(1); "affiliate share" — 93(2)(a), (b), 93(2.1)(a), (b), 93(2.2)(a), (b), 93(2.3)(a), (b); "allowable capital loss" — 38(b), 248(1); "amount" — 248(1); "arm's length" — 251(1); "assessment" — 248(1); "Canada" — 255; "Canadian currency" — 261(5)(f)(i); "capital gain" — 39(1)(a), 248(1); "capital loss" — 39(1)(b), 248(1); "class" — of shares 248(6); "corporation" — 248(1), *Interpretation Act* 35(1); "cost amount" — 248(1); "disposed share" — 93(1.1)(a), (b), 93(4); "disposing affiliate", "disposing corporation" — 93(1); "disposing partnership" — 93(2.1)(a), (b); "disposition" — 248(1); "disposition time" — 93(2)(a), (b), 93(2.1)(a), (b), 93(2.2)(a), (b), 93(2.3)(a), (b); "dividend" — 248(1); "elected amount" — 93(1)(a); "excluded property" — 95(1); "exempt dividend" — 93(3); "exempt surplus" — 113(1)(a), Reg. 5907(1)(d); "fair market value" — see 69(1) Notes; "foreign affiliate" — 93.1(1), 95(1), 248(1); "foreign currency debt" — 111(8), 248(1); "income or profits tax" — 126(4); "Minister" — 248(1); "partnership" — see 96(1) Notes; "partnership interest" — 93(2.2)(a), (b), 93(2.3)(a), (b); "person" — 248(1); "pre-acquisition surplus" — Reg. 5900(1)(c); "prescribed" — 248(1); "proceeds of disposition" — 54; "property", "regulation" — 248(1); "related" — 251(2)–(6); "resident in Canada" — 250; "share" — 248(1); "specified gain" — 93(2.02), (2.12), (2.22), (2.32); "substituted" — 248(5); "taxable capital gain" — 38(a), 248(1); "taxable income" — 2(1), 248(1); "taxable surplus" — 113(1)(b)(i), Reg. 5907(1)(k); "taxation year" — 95(1) (for foreign affiliate only), 249; "taxpayer" — 248(1); "transferee" — 93(4); "vendor" — 93(2)(a), (b), 93(2.2)(a), (b).

93.1 (1) Shares held by a partnership — For the purpose of determining whether a non-resident corporation is a foreign affiliate of a corporation resident in Canada for the purposes of a specified provision, if, based on the assumptions contained in paragraph

96(1)(c), at any time shares of a class of the capital stock of a corporation are owned by a partnership or are deemed under this subsection to be owned by a partnership, then each member of the partnership is deemed to own at that time the number of those shares that is equal to the proportion of all those shares that

(a) the fair market value of the member's interest in the partnership at that time

is of

(b) the fair market value of all members' interests in the partnership at that time.

Related Provisions: 93.1(1.1) — Specified provisions; 93.1(3)(a) — Tiered partnership — look-through rule; Reg. 5908 — Shares owned through partnership.

Notes: Under 93.1, shares of a non-resident corp that are owned by a partnership are deemed owned by the partners when determining whether the corp is a foreign affiliate of the Canadian partners for purposes of the provisions listed in 93.1(1.1). (Note that a partnership that is a member of another partnership is not intended to compute income: *Green*, 2017 FCA 107, para. 29.)

See Lockwood et al., "Proposed Technical Amendments to the FAPI", 48(2) *Canadian Tax Journal* 456-476 (2000); Baker, "FAs Owned by Partnerships", 12(9) *Canadian Tax Highlights [CTH]* (ctf.ca) 7 (Sept. 2004); Barnicke, "Faulty Tower Structure", 13(4) *CTH* 1 (April 2005) (discusses doc 2004-0073101E5); Ton-That & Huynh, "Inconsistent Treatment of Partnerships in the Foreign Affiliate Rules", 2009 Cdn Tax Foundation conference report, 24:1-66; Ariyakumaran & Spinelli, "Holding a Foreign Affiliate Through a Partnership", 8(1) *Canadian Tax Focus* (ctf.ca) 14-15 (Feb. 2018); VIEWS docs 2007-0247551E5, 2011-0394631I7.

93.1(1) amended by 2014 budget bill #2 (last change effective July 12, 2013), 2002-2013 technical bill, 2012 budget bill #2. Added by 2001 technical bill.

(1.1) Specified provisions for subsec. (1) — For the purposes of subsection (1), the specified provisions are

(a) subsections (2), (5), 20(12) and 39(2.1), sections 90, 93, 93.3 and 113, paragraphs 128.1(1)(c.3) and (d), section 212.3, subsection 219.1(2) and section 233.4;

(b) section 95 to the extent that section is applied for the purposes of the provisions referred to in paragraph (a);

(c) any regulations made for the purposes of the provisions referred to in paragraph (a); and

(d) paragraph 95(2)(g.04), subsections 95(2.2) and (8) to (12) and section 126.

Notes: 93.1(1.1)(d) amended by 2018 budget bill #2 to refer to 95(8)-(12), effective Feb. 27, 2018 (to ensure FA status can flow through a partnership for purpose of those tracking-interest rules).

93.1(1.1) added by 2014 budget bill #2, last change effective July 12, 2013.

(2) Where dividends received by a partnership — Where, based on the assumptions contained in paragraph 96(1)(c), at any time shares of a class of the capital stock of a foreign affiliate of a corporation resident in Canada (in this subsection referred to as "affiliate shares") are owned by a partnership and at that time the affiliate pays a dividend on affiliate shares to the partnership (in this subsection referred to as the "partnership dividend"),

(a) for the purposes of sections 93 and 113 and any regulations made for the purposes of those sections, each member of the partnership (other than another partnership) is deemed to have received the proportion of the partnership dividend that

(i) the fair market value of the member's interest held, directly or indirectly through one or more other partnerships, in the partnership at that time

is of

(ii) the fair market value of all the interests in the partnership held directly by members of the partnership at that time;

(b) for the purposes of sections 93 and 113 and any regulations made for the purposes of those sections, the proportion of the partnership dividend deemed by paragraph (a) to have been received by a member of the partnership at that time is deemed to have been received by the member in equal proportions on each affiliate share that is property of the partnership at that time;

(c) for the purpose of applying section 113, in respect of the dividend referred to in paragraph (a), each affiliate share referred to

in paragraph (b) is deemed to be owned by each member of the partnership; and

(d) notwithstanding paragraphs (a) to (c),

(i) where the corporation resident in Canada is a member of the partnership, the amount deductible by it under section 113 in respect of the dividend referred to in paragraph (a) shall not exceed the portion of the amount of the dividend included in its income pursuant to subsection 96(1), and

(ii) where another foreign affiliate of the corporation resident in Canada is a member of the partnership, the amount included in that other affiliate's income in respect of the dividend referred to in paragraph (a) shall not exceed the amount that would be included in its income pursuant to subsection 96(1) in respect of the partnership dividend received by the partnership if the value for H in the definition "foreign accrual property income" in subsection 95(1) were nil and this Act were read without reference to this subsection.

Related Provisions: 92(4)–(6) — Dividend from pre-acquisition surplus; 93.1(1) — Where shares are owned by partnership; 93.1(3)(a) — Tiered partnership — look-through rule; 95(1)"foreign accrual property income"H — Exclusion from FAPI.

Notes: See 93.1(1) Notes. 93.1(2) applies where a partnership receives a dividend from a foreign affiliate. In applying 93.1(2)(d)(i), a 91(5) deduction is taken into account: VIEWS docs 2016-0658171I7, 2018-0749171C6 [2018 IFA q.3]. 93.1(2)(d)(ii) permits the partner a deduction equal to their share of the gross amount of the dividends received by the partnership: 2001-0111675, 2003-0048251E5.

93.1(2)(a) added by 2001 technical bill and amended by 2014 budget bill #2, both for dividends received after Nov. 1999.

(3) Tiered partnerships — A person or partnership that is (or is deemed by this subsection to be) a member of a particular partnership that is a member of another partnership is deemed to be a member of the other partnership, and the person or partnership is deemed to have, directly, rights to the income or capital of the other partnership to the extent of the person or partnership's direct and indirect rights to that income or capital, for the purposes of applying

(a) except to the extent that the context otherwise requires, a provision of this Subdivision;

(b) any of paragraphs 13(21.2)(a), 14(12)(a), 18(13)(a), 40(2)(e.1), (e.3) and (g) and (3.3)(a); and

(c) subsections 39(2.1), 40(3.6) and 87(8.3).

Notes: A March 2012 Budget proposal to add 93.1(3)(d) referring to section 212.3 was replaced by 212.3(25)(f), which applies the look-through rule to 212.3.

93.1(3)(c) amended by 2014 budget bill #2, for foreign affiliate tax years ending after July 12, 2013. Added by 2002-2013 technical bill.

(4) Partnership deemed to be corporation — For the purpose of applying clause 95(2)(a)(ii)(D) in respect of an amount paid or payable by a partnership to a foreign affiliate, of a taxpayer, that is a member of the partnership or to another foreign affiliate of the taxpayer,

(a) if, at any time, all the members (in this subsection referred to as "member affiliates") of the partnership are foreign affiliates of the taxpayer,

(i) the partnership is deemed to be, at that time in respect of the taxpayer and the member affiliates, a non-resident corporation without share capital, and

(ii) all the membership interests in the partnership are deemed to be, at that time, equity interests in the corporation held by the member affiliates; and

(b) if, at any time, all the member affiliates are resident in a particular country and the partnership does not carry on business outside the particular country, the partnership is deemed to be, at that time, resident in the particular country,

Notes: 93.1(4) added by 2014 budget bill #2, for foreign affiliate tax years ending after July 12, 2013.

(5) Computing FAPI in respect of partnership — For the purpose of applying a relevant provision in respect of a foreign affiliate of a taxpayer resident in Canada, if at any time the taxpayer is a partnership of which a particular corporation resident in Canada, or a foreign affiliate of the particular corporation, is a member and if, based on the relevant assumptions, the particular corporation and the taxpayer would be related, then

(a) a non-resident corporation that is, at that time, a foreign affiliate of the particular corporation is deemed to be, at that time, a foreign affiliate of the taxpayer; and

(b) the taxpayer is deemed to have, at that time, a qualifying interest in respect of that foreign affiliate if the particular corporation has, at that time, a qualifying interest in respect of the non-resident corporation.

Related Provisions: 93.1(1) — Shares owned by partnership deemed owned proportionately by partners; 93.1(6) — Relevant provisions and relevant assumptions; 95(2)(n) — Qualifying interest.

Notes: 93.1(5) added by 2014 budget bill #2, for foreign affiliate tax years ending after July 12, 2013 (or earlier by election).

(6) Relevant provisions and assumptions — For the purposes of subsection (5),

(a) the relevant provisions are

(i) paragraph (b) of the description of A in the definition "foreign accrual property income" in subsection 95(1),

(ii) in determining whether a property of a foreign affiliate of a taxpayer is excluded property of the affiliate, the description of B in the definition "foreign accrual property income" in subsection 95(1),

(iii) paragraphs 95(2)(a) and (g), and

(iv) subsections 95(2.2) and (2.21); and

(b) the relevant assumptions are that

(i) the partnership is a non-resident corporation having capital stock of a single class divided into 100 issued shares that each have full voting rights, and

(ii) each member of the partnership (other than another partnership) owns, at any time, the proportion of the issued shares of that class that

(A) the fair market value of the member's interest held, directly or indirectly through one or more partnerships, in the partnership at that time

is of

(B) the fair market value of all the interests in the partnership held directly by members of the partnership at that time.

Notes: 93.1(6) added by 2014 budget bill #2, effective on the same basis as 93.1(5).

Definitions [s. 93.1]: "amount", "business" — 248(1); "corporation" — 248(1), *Interpretation Act* 35(1); "dividend" — 248(1); "excluded property" — 95(1); "fair market value" — see 69(1) Notes; "foreign accrual property income" — 95(1), (2), 248(1); "foreign affiliate" — 93.1(1), 95(1), 248(1); "member affiliate" — 93.1(4)(a); "non-resident" — 248(1); "partnership" — see 96(1) Notes; "person", "property", "regulation" — 248(1); "related" — 251(2)–(6); "relevant assumption" — 93.1(6)(b); "relevant provision" — 93.1(6)(a); "resident", "resident in Canada" — 250; "share" — 248(1); "specified provision" — 93.1(1.1); "taxpayer" — 248(1).

93.2 (1) Definitions — The definitions in this subsection apply in this section.

"equity interest", in a non-resident corporation without share capital, means any right, whether absolute or contingent, conferred by the non-resident corporation to receive, either immediately or in the future, an amount that can reasonably be regarded as all or any part of the capital, revenue or income of the non-resident corporation, but does not include a right as creditor.

Notes: See Notes at end of 93.2.

"non-resident corporation without share capital" means a non-resident corporation that, determined without reference to this section, does not have capital divided into shares.

Notes: A common example is a U.S. limited liability company (LLC).

(2) Non-resident corporation without share capital — For the purposes of this Act,

(a) equity interests in a non-resident corporation without share capital that have identical rights and obligations, determined without reference to proportionate differences in all of those rights and obligations, are deemed to be shares of a separate class of the capital stock of the corporation;

(b) the corporation is deemed to have 100 issued and outstanding shares of each class of its capital stock;

(c) each person or partnership that holds, at any time, an equity interest in a particular class of the capital stock of the corporation is deemed to own, at that time, that number of shares of the particular class that is equal to the proportion of 100 that

(i) the fair market value, at that time, of all the equity interests of the particular class held by the person or partnership

is of

(ii) the fair market value, at that time, of all the equity interests of the particular class; and

(d) shares of a particular class of the capital stock of the corporation are deemed to have rights and obligations that are the same as those of the corresponding equity interests.

Related Provisions: 93.2(1) — Definitions; 93.2(3) — Rollovers.

Notes: For CRA interpretation see VIEWS doc 2014-0522971C6 [2014 STEP q.3] (how equity interests are divided into deemed classes of stock) [Barnicke & Huynh, "Deemed Shares in a US LLC", 22(8) *Canadian Tax Highlights* (ctf.ca) 8-9 (Aug. 2014)]; 2015-0571441R3 (Dutch cooperative falls within 93.2);.

(3) Non-resident corporation without share capital — For the purposes of section 51, subsection 85.1(3), section 86 and paragraph 95(2)(c),

(a) subject to paragraph (b), if at any time a taxpayer resident in Canada or a foreign affiliate of the taxpayer (in this subsection referred to as the "vendor") disposes of capital property that is shares of the capital stock of a foreign affiliate of the taxpayer, or a debt obligation owing to the taxpayer by the affiliate, to — or exchanges the shares or debt for shares of the capital stock of — a non-resident corporation without share capital, that is immediately after that time a foreign affiliate of the taxpayer, in a manner that increases the fair market value of a class of shares of the capital stock of the non-resident corporation, the non-resident corporation is deemed to have issued, and the vendor is deemed to have received, new shares of the class as consideration in respect of the disposition or exchange; and

(b) if the taxpayer elects under this paragraph and files the election in writing with the Minister on or before its filing-due date for the taxation year that includes the day on which the disposition or exchange occurs, paragraph (a) does not apply to the disposition or exchange.

Notes: For an example of 93.2(3) applying to 95(2)(c), see VIEWS doc 2016-0642101C6 [2016 IFA q.10].

For a taxpayer filing a Quebec return, a 93.2(3)(b) election must be copied to Revenu Québec: *Taxation Act* ss. 592.6, 21.4.6.

Notes [s. 93.2]: This was 93.3 in the July 12/13 draft legislation but was renumbered 93.2 because it comes into force earlier than former proposed 93.2, which is now 93.3.

93.2 added by 2014 budget bill #2, for tax years of non-resident corps that end after 1994 (or, by election, that end after July 12, 2013).

Definitions [s. 93.2]: "amount" — 248(1); "capital property" — 54, 248(1); "class of shares" — 248(6); "corporation" — 248(1), *Interpretation Act* 35(1); "disposition" — 248(1); "equity interest" — 93.2(1); "fair market value" — see 69(1) Notes; "filing-due date" — 150(1), 248(1); "foreign affiliate" — 95(1), 248(1); "identical" — 248(12); "Minister", "non-resident" — 248(1); "non-resident corporation without share capital" — 93.2(1); "partnership" — see 96(1) Notes; "person" — 248(1); "resident in Canada" — 94(3)(a), 250; "share" — 248(1); "taxation year" — 95(1), 249; "taxpayer" — 248(1); "writing" — *Interpretation Act* 35(1).

93.3 (1) Definition of "Australian trust" — In this section, "Australian trust", at any time, means a trust in respect of which the following apply at that time:

(a) in the absence of subsection (3), the trust would be described in paragraph (h) of the definition "exempt foreign trust" in subsection 94(1);

(b) the trust is resident in Australia;

(c) the interest of each beneficiary under the trust is described by reference to units of the trust; and

(d) the liability of each beneficiary under the trust is limited by the operation of any law governing the trust.

Notes: See Notes at end of 93.3.

(2) Conditions for subsec. (3) — Subsection (3) applies at any time to a taxpayer resident in Canada in respect of a trust if

(a) a non-resident corporation is at that time beneficially interested in the trust;

(b) the non-resident corporation is at that time a foreign affiliate of the taxpayer in respect of which the taxpayer has a qualifying interest;

(c) the trust is at that time an Australian trust;

(d) the total fair market value at that time of all fixed interests (in this section as defined in subsection 94(1)) of a class in the trust held by the non-resident corporation, or persons or partnerships that do not deal at arm's length with the non-resident corporation, is at least 10% of the total fair market value at that time of all fixed interests of the class; and

(e) unless the non-resident corporation first acquires a beneficial interest in the trust at that time, immediately before that time (referred to in this paragraph as the "preceding time") subsection (3) applied

(i) to the taxpayer in respect of the trust, or

(ii) to a corporation resident in Canada, that at the preceding time did not deal at arm's length with the taxpayer, in respect of the trust.

Related Provisions: 93.3(1) — Definition of "Australian trust".

(3) Australian trusts — If this subsection applies at any time to a taxpayer resident in Canada in respect of a trust, the following rules apply at that time for the specified purposes:

(a) the trust is deemed to be a non-resident corporation that is resident in Australia and not to be a trust;

(b) each particular class of fixed interests in the trust is deemed to be a separate class of 100 issued shares, of the capital stock of the non-resident corporation, that have the same attributes as the interests of the particular class;

(c) each beneficiary under the trust is deemed to hold the number of shares of each separate class described in paragraph (b) equal to the proportion of 100 that the fair market value at that time of that beneficiary's fixed interests in the corresponding particular class of fixed interests in the trust is of the fair market value at that time of all fixed interests in the particular class;

(d) the non-resident corporation is deemed to be controlled by the taxpayer resident in Canada — a foreign affiliate of which is referred to in paragraph (2)(b) and is beneficially interested in the trust — that has the greatest equity percentage in the non-resident corporation;

(e) a particular foreign affiliate of the taxpayer in which the taxpayer has a direct equity percentage (as defined in subsection 95(4)) at a particular time, and that is not a controlled foreign affiliate of the taxpayer at that time, is deemed to be a controlled foreign affiliate of the taxpayer at that time if, at that time,

(i) the particular affiliate has an equity percentage (as defined in subsection 95(4)) in the foreign affiliate referred to in paragraph (2)(b), or

(ii) the particular affiliate is the foreign affiliate referred to in paragraph (2)(b); and

(f) section 94.2 does not apply to the taxpayer in respect of the trust.

Related Provisions: 93.3(2) — Conditions for 93.3(3) to apply; 93.3(4) — Specified purposes; 93.3(5) — Effect of amalgamation or windup.

(4) Specified purposes — For the purposes of subsection (3), the specified purposes are

(a) the determination, in respect of an interest in an Australian trust, of the Canadian tax results (as defined in subsection 261(1)) of the taxpayer resident in Canada referred to in subsection (3) for a taxation year in respect of shares of the capital stock of a foreign affiliate of the taxpayer;

(b) the filing obligations of the taxpayer under section 233.4; and

(c) if the taxpayer is a corporation resident in Canada, the application of section 212.3 in respect of an investment (as defined in subsection 212.3(10)) by the taxpayer.

(5) Mergers — For the purposes of this section,

(a) if there has been an amalgamation to which subsection 87(1) applies, the new corporation referred to in that subsection is deemed to be the same corporation as, and a continuation of, each predecessor corporation referred to in that subsection; and

(b) if there has been a winding-up to which subsection 88(1) applies, the parent referred to in that subsection is deemed to be the same corporation as, and a continuation of, the subsidiary referred to in that subsection.

Notes: 93.3 provides a special regime for an Australia-resident trust in which a taxpayer's foreign affiliate (FA) has a beneficial interest. Where 93.3's conditions are met, the trust is deemed for certain purposes to be a non-resident corporation, not a trust. Where this results in the trust being treated as a FA, distributions from the trust to the FA can be treated as inter-affiliate dividends. Absent this regime, distributions from the trust would be included in the FA's FAPI even if the underlying earnings were active business profits. However, 93.3 can also result in the trust being a controlled FA of the taxpayer, so the trust's FAPI is generally attributed to the taxpayer under 91(1).

This regime is limited to Australian trusts, as Australia has unique tax and commercial law rules that make commercial trusts the preferred entity to carry on certain types of active business activities. (Finance Technical Notes)

This was 93.2 in the July 12/13 draft legislation, but was renumbered 93.3 because it came into force later than former proposed 93.3, which is now 93.2.

93.3 added by 2014 budget bill #2, effective July 12, 2013 (or, by election, effective 2006).

Definitions [s. 93.3]: "arm's length" — 251(1); "Australian trust" — 93.3(1); "beneficially interested" — 248(25); "beneficiary" — 248(25) [Notes]; "controlled foreign affiliate" — 95(1), 248(1); "corporation" — 248(1), *Interpretation Act* 35(1); "direct equity percentage", "equity percentage" — 95(4); "fair market value" — see 69(1) Notes; "foreign affiliate" — 95(1), 248(1); "new corporation" — 87(1) opening words; "non-resident" — 248(1); "parent" — 88(1) opening words; "partnership" — see 96(1) Notes; "person" — 248(1); "resident" — 250; "resident in Canada" — 94(3)(a), 250; "share" — 248(1); "taxation year" — 95(1), 249; "taxpayer" — 248(1); "trust" — 104(1), 248(1), (3).

94. [Non-resident trusts deemed resident in Canada] — (1) Definitions — The definitions in this subsection apply in this section and in section 94.2.

Notes: See Notes at end of 94 for in-force rules.

"arm's length transfer", at any time by a person or partnership (referred to in this definition as the "transferor") means a transfer or loan (which transfer or loan is referred to in this definition as the "transfer") of property (other than restricted property) that is made at that time (referred to in this definition as the "transfer time") by the transferor to a particular person or partnership (referred to in this definition as the "recipient") if

(a) it is reasonable to conclude that none of the reasons (determined by reference to all the circumstances including the terms of a trust, an intention, the laws of a country or the existence of an agreement, a memorandum, a letter of wishes or any other arrangement) for the transfer is the acquisition at any time by any person or partnership of an interest as a beneficiary under a non-resident trust; and

Non-Resident Corps/Trusts

(b) the transfer is

(i) a payment of interest, of a dividend, of rent, of a royalty or of any other return on investment, or any substitute for such a return on investment, in respect of a particular property held by the recipient, if the amount of the payment is not more than the amount that the transferor would have paid if the transferor dealt at arm's length with the recipient,

(ii) a payment made by a corporation on a reduction of the paid-up capital in respect of shares of a class of its capital stock held by the recipient, if the amount of the payment is not more than the lesser of the amount of the reduction in the paid-up capital and the consideration for which the shares were issued,

(iii) a transfer in exchange for which the recipient transfers or loans property to the transferor, or becomes obligated to transfer or loan property to the transferor, and for which it is reasonable to conclude

(A) having regard only to the transfer and the exchange, that the transferor would have been willing to make the transfer if the transferor dealt at arm's length with the recipient, and

(B) that the terms and conditions, and circumstances, under which the transfer was made would have been acceptable to the transferor if the transferor dealt at arm's length with the recipient,

(iv) a transfer made in satisfaction of an obligation referred to in subparagraph (iii) and for which it is reasonable to conclude

(A) having regard only to the transfer and the obligation, that the transferor would have been willing to make the transfer if the transferor dealt at arm's length with the recipient, and

(B) that the terms and conditions, and circumstances, under which the transfer was made would have been acceptable to the transferor if the transferor dealt at arm's length with the recipient,

(v) a payment of an amount owing by the transferor under a written agreement the terms and conditions of which, when entered into, were terms and conditions that, having regard only to the amount owing and the agreement, would have been acceptable to the transferor if the transferor dealt at arm's length with the recipient of the payment,

(vi) a payment made before 2002 to a trust, to a corporation controlled by a trust or to a partnership of which a trust is a majority-interest partner in repayment of or otherwise in respect of a loan made by a trust, corporation or partnership to the transferor, or

(vii) a payment made after 2001 to a trust, to a corporation controlled by the trust or to a partnership of which the trust is a majority-interest partner, in repayment of or otherwise in respect of a particular loan made by the trust, corporation or partnership to the transferor and either

(A) the payment is made before 2011 and they would have been willing to enter into the particular loan if they dealt at arm's length with each other, or

(B) the payment is made before 2005 in accordance with fixed repayment terms agreed to before June 23, 2000.

Related Provisions: 87(2)(j.95) — Amalgamation — continuing corporation; 94(4)(a) — Deeming non-resident trust to be resident in Canada does not apply.

Notes: For para. (a), it may not be clear whose "reasons" are to be considered in "none of the reasons ... for the transfer" — presumably the transferor's.

See Notes at end of 94 for in-force rule.

Subparas. (b)(vi), (vii) amended by 2013 budget bill #2, effective Dec. 12, 2013, to change "majority interest partner" to "majority-interest partner" (with a hyphen).

"beneficiary" under a trust includes

(a) a person or partnership that is beneficially interested in the trust; and

(b) a person or partnership that would be beneficially interested in the trust if the reference in subparagraph 248(25)(b)(ii) to

(i) "any arrangement in respect of the particular trust" were read as a reference to "any arrangement (including, for greater certainty, the terms or conditions of a share, or any arrangement in respect of a share, of the capital stock of a corporation that is beneficially interested in the particular trust) in respect of the particular trust", and

(ii) "the particular person or partnership might" were read as a reference to "the particular person or partnership becomes (or could become on the exercise of any discretion by any person or partnership), directly or indirectly, entitled to any amount derived, directly or indirectly, from the income or capital of the particular trust or might".

Related Provisions: 248(25) — Meaning of "beneficially interested".

Notes: For the meaning of "includes" in the opening words, see Notes to 188.1(5). For the meaning of "derived" in (b)(ii), see Notes to 18.1(12).

"closely held corporation" at any time means a corporation, other than a corporation in respect of which

(a) there is at least one class of shares of its capital stock that includes shares prescribed for the purpose of paragraph 110(1)(d);

(b) it is reasonable to conclude that at that time, in respect of each class of shares described in paragraph (a), shares of the class are held by at least 150 shareholders each of whom holds shares of the class that have a total fair market value of at least $500; and

(c) it is reasonable to conclude that at that time in no case does a particular shareholder (or particular shareholder together with any other shareholder with whom the particular shareholder does not deal at arm's length) hold shares of the corporation

(i) that would give the particular shareholder (or the particular shareholder together with those other shareholders referred to in this paragraph) 10% or more of the votes that could be cast under any circumstance at an annual meeting of shareholders of the corporation if the meeting were held at that time, or

(ii) that have a fair market value of 10% or more of the fair market value of all of the issued and outstanding shares of the corporation.

Related Provisions: 94(15)(a)(i) — Anti-avoidance rule re conditions in para. (b).

Notes: Counting shareholders for para. (b): see 130.1(6) Notes re 130.1(6)(d).

"connected contributor", to a trust at a particular time, means a contributor to the trust at the particular time, other than a person all of whose contributions to the trust made at or before the particular time were made at a non-resident time of the person.

Related Provisions: 87(2)(j.95) — Amalgamation — continuing corporation; 94(1)"contributor" — Exempt person excluded; 94(10) — Where contributor becomes resident in Canada within 60 months; 94(13)(a) — Deemed connected contributor if trust transfers property to another trust.

Notes: Definition amended by 2014 budget bill #2 to delete the 60-month immigration trust rule in para. (a) [see 94(1)"resident contributor" Notes], for tax years that end after Feb. 10, 2014 (or after 2014 if certain conditions are satisfied).

"contribution" to a trust by a particular person or partnership means

(a) a transfer or loan (other than an arm's length transfer) of property to the trust by the particular person or partnership;

(b) if a particular transfer or loan (other than an arm's length transfer) of property is made by the particular person or partnership as part of a series of transactions that includes another transfer or loan (other than an arm's length transfer) of property to the trust by another person or partnership, that other transfer or loan to the extent that it can reasonably be considered to have been made in respect of the particular transfer or loan; and

(c) if the particular person or partnership becomes obligated to make a particular transfer or loan (other than a transfer or loan that would, if it were made, be an arm's length transfer) of property as part of a series of transactions that includes another transfer or loan (other than an arm's length transfer) of property to the trust by another person or partnership, that other transfer or loan to the extent that it can reasonably be considered to have been made in respect of the obligation.

Related Provisions: 94(2)(g) — Deemed transfers; 94(2)(s)–(v) — Certain transfers deemed not to be contribution; 94(9) — Determination of contribution amount.

"contributor" to a trust at any time means a person (other than an exempt person but including a person that has ceased to exist) that, at or before that time, has made a contribution to the trust.

Related Provisions: 94(13)(a) — Deemed connected contributor where trust transfers property to another trust; 233.2(4) — Annual information return required by contributor to non-resident trust.

Notes: In CRA's view, if a deceased leaves a non-discretionary bequest to a foreign trust, the deceased's estate is a "contributor" and a "resident contributor" to the trust, so 94(3) applies to the trust until the estate is wound up: VIEWS docs 2013-0514771E5, 2014-0523071C6 [2014 STEP q.12]. This is wrong in the author's view, as the real contributor is the deceased, who cannot be a "resident contributor" when dead (due to the words "at that time resident in Canada"), and the estate is merely the vehicle through which the deceased leaves the bequest, with no discretion to the estate trustee. CRA was asked to reconsider this issue and confirmed in Oct. 2014 that its view is firm. The author has asked Finance to consider an amendment, though 94(5) will apply anyway to deem the trust non-resident. For more criticism of CRA's position see David Fox, "Deemed Resident Trust Rules", V(2) *Personal Tax and Estate Planning* (Federated Press) 230-32 (2015).

"electing contributor" at any time in respect of a trust means a resident contributor, to the trust, who has elected to have subsection (16) apply in respect of the contributor and the trust for a taxation year of the contributor that includes that time or that ends before that time and for all subsequent taxation years, if

(a) the election was in writing filed with the Minister on or before the contributor's filing-due date for the first taxation year of the contributor for which the election was to take effect (referred to in this definition as the "initial year"); and

(b) the election included both the trust's account number as assigned by the Minister and evidence that the contributor notified, no later than 30 days after the end of the trust's taxation year that ends in the initial year, the trust that the election would be made.

Related Provisions: 94(16) — Election to limit liability from trust; 94(17) — Liability for joint contribution.

Notes: An electing contributor is required to attribute a portion of the trust's income back to the contributor (like 75(2)), but then has limited liability for the trust's tax. See 94(16) and (17).

For a contributor filing a Quebec return, the election must be copied to Revenu Québec: *Taxation Act* ss. 593 (last para.), 21.4.6.

"electing trust" in respect of a trust's particular taxation year means the trust, if the trust

(a) holds at any time in the particular taxation year, or in a prior taxation year of the trust throughout which it was deemed by subsection (3) to be resident in Canada for the purpose of computing its income, property that is at that time part of its non-resident portion;

(b) elects to have paragraph (3)(f) apply to it for

(i) its first taxation year

(A) throughout which it is deemed by subsection (3) to be resident in Canada for the purpose of computing its income, and

(B) in which it holds property that is at a time in the year part of its non-resident portion, and

(ii) all of its taxation years that end after its taxation year described in subparagraph (i); and

(c) files the election described in paragraph (b) in writing filed with the Minister with the trust's return of income for its taxation year described in subparagraph (b)(i).

Related Provisions: 94(3)(f) — Rules for electing trust.

Notes: For a trust filing a Quebec return, the election must be copied to Revenu Québec: *Taxation Act* ss. 593 (last para.), 21.4.6.

"exempt amount" in respect of a trust's particular taxation year means an amount that is

(a) paid or credited (in this definition within the meaning assigned by Part XIII) by the trust before 2004;

(b) paid or credited by the trust and referred to in paragraph 104(7.01)(b) in respect of the trust for the particular taxation year; or

(c) paid in the particular taxation year (or within 60 days after the end of the particular taxation year) by the trust directly to a beneficiary (determined without reference to subsection 248(25)) under the trust if

(i) the beneficiary is a natural person none of whose interests as a beneficiary under the trust was ever acquired for consideration,

(ii) the amount is described in subparagraph 212(1)(c)(i) and is not included in computing an exempt amount in respect of any other taxation year of the trust,

(iii) the trust was created before October 30, 2003, and

(iv) no contribution has been made to the trust on or after July 18, 2005.

Related Provisions: 108(7) — Meaning of "acquired for consideration" in para. (c)(i); *Interpretation Act* 27(5) — Meaning of "within 60 days".

Notes: For CRA interpretation see VIEWS doc 2007-0250731E5 (issuance of shares of US corporation to deemed-resident trust for cash; payment of trust expense by beneficiary).

"exempt foreign trust" at a particular time means

(a) a non-resident trust if

(i) each beneficiary under the trust at the particular time is

(A) an individual who, at the time that the trust was created, was, because of mental or physical infirmity, dependent on an individual who is a contributor to the trust or on an individual related to such a contributor (which beneficiary is referred to in this paragraph as an "infirm beneficiary"), or

(B) a person who is entitled, only after the particular time, to receive or otherwise obtain the use of any of the trust's income or capital,

(ii) at the particular time there is at least one infirm beneficiary who suffers from a mental or physical infirmity that causes the beneficiary to be dependent on a person,

(iii) each infirm beneficiary is, at all times that the infirm beneficiary is a beneficiary under the trust during the trust's taxation year that includes the particular time, non-resident, and

(iv) each contribution to the trust made at or before the particular time can reasonably be considered to have been, at the time that the contribution was made, made to provide for the maintenance of an infirm beneficiary during the expected period of the beneficiary's infirmity;

(b) a non-resident trust if

(i) the trust was created as a consequence of the breakdown of a marriage or common-law partnership of two particular individuals to provide for the maintenance of a beneficiary under the trust who was, during that marriage or common-law partnership,

(A) a child of both of those particular individuals (which beneficiary is referred to in this paragraph as a "child beneficiary"), or

(B) one of those particular individuals (which beneficiary is referred to in this paragraph as the "adult beneficiary"),

(ii) each beneficiary under the trust at the particular time is

(A) a child beneficiary under 21 years of age,

(B) a child beneficiary under 31 years of age who is enrolled at any time in the trust's taxation year that includes

Non-Resident Corps/Trusts

the particular time at an educational institution that is described in subclause (iv)(B)(I) or (II),

(C) the adult beneficiary, or

(D) a person who is entitled, only after the particular time, to receive or otherwise obtain the use of any of the trust's income or capital,

(iii) each beneficiary described in any of clauses (ii)(A) to (C) is, at all times that the beneficiary is a beneficiary under the trust during the trust's taxation year that includes the particular time, non-resident, and

(iv) each contribution to the trust, at the time that the contribution was made, was

(A) an amount paid by the particular individual other than the adult beneficiary that would be a support amount as defined in subsection 56.1(4) if it had been paid by that particular individual directly to the adult beneficiary, or

(B) made by one of those particular individuals or a person related to one of those particular individuals to provide for the maintenance of a child beneficiary while the child was either under 21 years of age or was under 31 years of age and enrolled at an educational institution located outside Canada that is

(I) a university, college or other educational institution that provides courses at a post-secondary school level, or

(II) an educational institution that provides courses designed to furnish a person with skills for, or improve a person's skills in, an occupation;

(c) a non-resident trust if

(i) at the particular time the trust is an agency of the United Nations,

(ii) at the particular time the trust owns and administers a university described in subparagraph (a)(iv) of the definition "qualified donee" in subsection 149.1(1),

(iii) at any time in the trust's taxation year that includes the particular time or at any time in the preceding calendar year Her Majesty in right of Canada has made a gift to the trust, or

(iv) the trust is established under the *International Convention on the Establishment of an International Fund for Compensation for Oil Pollution Damage, 1992*, or any protocol to it that has been ratified by the Government of Canada;

(d) a non-resident trust

(i) that throughout the particular period that began at the time it was created and ends at the particular time would be non-resident if this Act were read without reference to subsection (1) as that subsection read in its application to taxation years that include December 31, 2000,

(ii) that was created exclusively for charitable purposes and has been operated throughout the particular period exclusively for charitable purposes,

(iii) if the particular time is more than 24 months after the day on which the trust was created, in respect of which, there are at the particular time at least 20 persons (other than trusts) each of whom at the particular time

(A) is a contributor to the trust,

(B) exists, and

(C) deals at arm's length with at least 19 other contributors to the trust,

(iv) the income of which (determined in accordance with the laws described in subparagraph (v)) for each of its taxation years that ends at or before the particular time would, if the income were not distributed and the laws described in subparagraph (v) did not apply, be subject to an income or profits tax in the country in which it was resident in each of those taxation years, and

(v) that was, for each of its taxation years that ends at or before the particular time, exempt under the laws of the country in which it was resident from the payment of income or profits tax to the government of that country in recognition of the charitable purposes for which the trust is operated;

(e) a non-resident trust that throughout the trust's taxation year that includes the particular time is a trust governed by an employees profit sharing plan, a retirement compensation arrangement or a foreign retirement arrangement;

(f) a non-resident trust if

(i) throughout the particular period that began when it was created and ends at the particular time it has been operated exclusively for the purpose of administering or providing employee benefits in respect of employees or former employees, and

(ii) throughout the trust's taxation year that includes the particular time

(A) the trust is a trust governed by an employee benefit plan or is a trust described in paragraph (a.1) of the definition "trust" in subsection 108(1),

(B) the trust is maintained for the benefit of natural persons the majority of whom are non-resident, and

(C) no benefits are provided under the trust other than benefits in respect of qualifying services;

(g) a non-resident trust (other than a prescribed trust or a trust described in paragraph (a.1) of the definition "trust" in subsection 108(1)) that throughout the particular period that began when it was created and ends at the particular time

(i) has been resident in a particular country (other than Canada) the laws of which have, throughout the particular period,

(A) imposed an income or profits tax, and

(B) exempted the trust from the payment of all income tax, and all profits tax, to the government of that particular country in recognition of the purposes for which the trust is operated, and

(ii) has been operated exclusively for the purpose of administering or providing superannuation or pension benefits that are primarily in respect of services rendered in the particular country by natural persons who were non-resident at the time those services were rendered;

(h) a non-resident trust (other than a trust that elects, in writing filed with the Minister on or before the trust's filing-due date for the trust's taxation year that includes the particular time, not to be an exempt foreign trust under this paragraph for the taxation year in which the election is made and for each subsequent taxation year), if at the particular time

(i) the only beneficiaries who may for any reason receive, at or after the particular time and directly from the trust, any of the income or capital of the trust are beneficiaries that hold fixed interests in the trust, and

(ii) any of the following applies:

(A) there are at least 150 beneficiaries described in subparagraph (i) under the trust each of whose fixed interests in the trust have at the particular time a total fair market value of at least $500,

(B) all fixed interests in the trust are listed on a designated stock exchange and in the 30 days immediately preceding the particular time fixed interests in the trust were traded on a designated stock exchange on at least 10 days,

(C) each outstanding fixed interest in the trust

(I) was issued by the trust in exchange for consideration that was not less than 90% of the interest's proportionate share of the net asset value of the trust's property at the time of its issuance, or

(II) was acquired in exchange for consideration equal to the fair market value of the interest at the time of its acquisition, or

(D) the trust is governed by

(I) a Roth IRA, within the meaning of section 408A of the *Internal Revenue Code* of the United States, or

(II) a plan or arrangement that was created after September 21, 2007, that is subject to that Code and that the Minister agrees is substantially similar to a Roth IRA; or

(i) a trust that is at the particular time a prescribed trust.

Related Provisions: 93.3(1)(a) — Special regime for certain Australian trusts; 94(2)(s) — Where trust manager required by securities law to acquire interest in commercial investment trust; 94(4)(a) — Deeming non-resident trust to be resident in Canada does not apply; 94(5.1) — Becoming an EFT — deemed resident status ends; 94(6) — Ceasing to be an EFT; 94(15)(a)(ii) — Anti-avoidance rule re conditions in cl. (h)(ii)(A); 94(15)(b) — Anti-avoidance rule re para. (f); 94(15)(c) — Anti-avoidance rule re para. (h); 94.1(2)"non-resident entity"(c) — Whether 94.1 applies to EFT; 94.2(1) — EFT under para. (h) or (i) may be subject to FAPI rules; 108(3) — Meaning of "income" of trust; 233.2(4) — Exclusion from reporting requirements.

Notes: *(b)(iv)(B)(I)*: for the meaning of "post-secondary" see Notes to 118.5(1)(a).

(c)(iii): for the foreign charities that qualify because Canada has donated to them recently, see Notes to 149.1(1)"qualified donee".

(d)(ii): for CRA interpretation see VIEWS doc 2016-0647951E5.

(d)(iv)-(v) and (g)(i): for the meaning of "income or profits tax" see Notes to 126(4).

(e)-(g) (pre-2010 draft): see Elizabeth Boyd, "Implications of the Proposed Non-resident Trust for Cross-Border Employee Share Ownership Plans", 17(1) *Taxation of Executive Compensation & Retirement* (Federated Press) 567-71 (July/August 2005).

(h) is the exception for a "commercial" trust. For a ruling that two US trusts qualified under the pre-2010 draft, see doc 2006-0217281R3. A Roth IRA generally qualifies: Income Tax Folio S5-F3.C1 ¶1.6. For a trust filing a Quebec return, a para. (h) election must be copied to Revenu Québec: *Taxation Act* ss. 593 (last para.), 21.4.6.

Regulations: 3503 (prescribed universities outside Canada, for subpara. (c)(ii)). No prescribed trusts proposed for para. (i).

Income Tax Folios: S5-F3-C1: Taxation of a Roth IRA.

Information Circulars: 84-3R6: Gifts to certain charitable organizations outside Canada.

I.T. Technical News: 43 (taxation of Roth IRAs).

"exempt person" at any time means

(a) Her Majesty in right of Canada or a province;

(b) a person whose taxable income for the taxation year that includes that time is exempt from tax under this Part because of subsection 149(1);

(c) a trust resident in Canada or a Canadian corporation

(i) that was established by or arises under an Act of Parliament or of the legislature of a province, and

(ii) the principal activities of which at that time are to administer, manage or invest the monies of one or more pension funds or plans established under an Act of Parliament or of the legislature of a province;

(d) a trust or corporation established by or arising by reason of an Act of Parliament or the legislature of a province in connection with a scheme or program for the compensation of workers injured in an accident arising out of or in the course of their employment;

(e) a trust resident in Canada all the beneficiaries under which are at that time exempt persons;

(f) a Canadian corporation all the shares, or rights to shares, of which are held at that time by exempt persons;

(g) a Canadian corporation without share capital all the property of which is held at that time exclusively for the benefit of exempt persons;

(h) a partnership all the members of which are at that time exempt persons; and

(i) a trust or corporation that is at that time a mutual fund.

Related Provisions: 94(1)"contributor" — Exempt person excluded from being contributor (and thus also from "resident contributor" and "connected contributor");

94(1)"resident beneficiary" — Exempt person excluded from being resident beneficiary.

"exempt service" means a service rendered at any time by a person or partnership (referred to in this definition as the "service provider") to, for or on behalf of, another person or partnership (referred to in this definition as the "recipient") if

(a) the recipient is a trust and the service relates to the administration of the trust; or

(b) the following conditions apply in respect of the service, namely,

(i) the service is rendered in the service provider's capacity at that time as an employee or agent of the recipient,

(ii) in exchange for the service, the recipient transfers or loans property or becomes obligated to transfer or loan property, and

(iii) it is reasonable to conclude

(A) having regard only to the service and the exchange, that the service provider would be willing to carry out the service if the service provider were dealing at arm's length with the recipient, and

(B) that the terms, conditions and circumstances under which the service is provided would be acceptable to the service provider if the service provider were dealing at arm's length with the recipient.

Related Provisions: 94(2)(f) — Exempt service excluded from rule deeming service to be transfer of property.

Notes: For CRA policy on when a person is an "agent" (for (b)(i)), see GST/HST Policy P-182R.

"fixed interest" at any time of a person or partnership in a trust means an interest of the person or partnership as a beneficiary (in this definition, determined without reference to subsection 248(25)) under the trust provided that no amount of the income or capital of the trust to be distributed at any time in respect of any interest in the trust depends on the exercise by any person or partnership of, or the failure by any person or partnership to exercise, any discretionary power, other than a power in respect of which it is reasonable to conclude that

(a) the power is consistent with normal commercial practice;

(b) the power is consistent with terms that would be acceptable to the beneficiaries under the trust if the beneficiaries were dealing with each other at arm's length; and

(c) the exercise of, or failure to exercise, the power will not materially affect the value of an interest as a beneficiary under the trust relative to the value of other such interests under the trust.

Notes: The term **"indirect contributor"**, which appeared in pre-2010 drafts, was deleted as of the Aug. 27/10 draft (see Notes at end of s. 94).

"joint contributor" at any time in respect of a contribution to a trust means, if more than one contributor has made the contribution, each of those contributors that is at that time a resident contributor to the trust.

Related Provisions: 94(16)(a)A(ii) — Attribution of trust's income to electing contributors; 94(17) — Liability of joint contributor.

"mutual fund" at a particular time means a mutual fund trust or mutual fund corporation (referred to in this definition as the "fund"), but does not include a fund in respect of which statements or representations have been made at or before the particular time — by the fund, or by a promoter or other representative of the fund, in respect of the acquisition or offering of an interest in the fund — that the taxes, if any, under this Part on the income, profit or gains for any particular year — in respect of property that is held by the fund and that is, or derives its value from, an interest in a trust — are less than, or are expected to be less than, the tax that would have been applicable under this Part if the income, profits or gains from the property had been earned directly by a person who acquires an interest in the fund.

Non-Resident Corps/Trusts

Related Provisions: 94(1)"promoter"(b) — Extended meaning of "promoter" for this definition.

"non-resident portion" of a trust at any time means all property held by the trust to the extent that it is not at that time part of the resident portion of the trust.

Notes: See 94(1)"resident portion".

"non-resident time" of a person in respect of a contribution to a trust and a particular time means a time (referred to in this definition as the "contribution time") at which the person made a contribution to a trust that is before the particular time and at which the person was non-resident (or, if the person is not in existence at the contribution time, the person was non-resident throughout the 18 months before ceasing to exist), if the person was non-resident or not in existence throughout the period that began 60 months before the contribution time (or, if the person is an individual and the trust arose on and as a consequence of the death of the individual, 18 months before the contribution time) and ends at the earlier of

(a) the time that is 60 months after the contribution time, and

(b) the particular time.

Related Provisions: 94(2)(j) — Where trust acquires property as a consequence of death of individual; 94(10) — Where contributor becomes resident in Canada within 60 months; 248(8) — Meaning of "consequence" of death.

Notes: See Notes at end of 94 for in-force rule.

"promoter" of a trust or corporation at any time means

(a) a person or partnership that at or before that time establishes, organizes or substantially reorganizes the undertakings of the trust or corporation, as the case may be; and

(b) for the purposes of the definition "mutual fund" in this subsection, a person or partnership described by paragraph (a) and a person or partnership who in the course of a business

(i) sells or issues, or promotes the sale, issuance or acquisition of, an interest in a mutual fund corporation or mutual fund trust,

(ii) acts as an agent or advisor in respect of the sale or issuance, or the promotion of the sale, issuance or acquisition of, an interest in a mutual fund corporation or mutual fund trust, or

(iii) accepts, whether as a principal or agent, consideration in respect of an interest in a mutual fund corporation or mutual fund trust.

Related Provisions: 94(2)(s) — Where promoter required by securities law to acquire interest in commercial investment trust.

Notes: This definition was new in the Oct. 24/12 draft (see Notes at end of s. 94).

"qualifying services" means services that are

(a) rendered to an employer by an employee of the employer, which employee was non-resident throughout the period during which the services were rendered;

(b) rendered to an employer by an employee of the employer, other than services that were

(i) rendered primarily in Canada,

(ii) rendered primarily in connection with a business carried on by the employer in Canada, or

(iii) a combination of services described in subparagraphs (i) and (ii);

(c) rendered in a particular calendar month to an employer by an employee of the employer, which employee

(i) was resident in Canada throughout no more than 60 months during the 72-month period that ends at the end of the particular month, and

(ii) became a member of, or a beneficiary under, the plan or trust under which benefits in respect of the services may be provided (or a similar plan or trust for which the plan or trust was substituted) before the end of the calendar month following the month in which the employee became resident in Canada; or

(d) any combination of services that are qualifying services determined without reference to this paragraph.

Related Provisions: 94(1)"exempt foreign trust"(f)(ii)(C) — Providing benefits in respect of qualifying services does not disqualify trust.

"resident beneficiary" under a trust at any time means a person (other than a person that is at that time a successor beneficiary under the trust or an exempt person) that is, at that time, a beneficiary under the trust if, at that time,

(a) the person is resident in Canada; and

(b) there is a connected contributor to the trust.

Related Provisions: 94(1)"beneficiary" — Extended meaning of "beneficiary"; 94(3)(a) — Trust with resident beneficiary deemed resident in Canada for certain purposes; 94(3)(d), 94(7) — Liability of resident beneficiary for trust's tax.

Notes: A Canadian resident whose beneficial interest in a trust is only as a successor beneficiary to a non-resident beneficiary is not a "resident beneficiary" who would make the trust resident under 94(3): VIEWS doc 2007-0235241C6.

"resident contributor", to a trust at any time, means a person that is, at that time, resident in Canada and a contributor to the trust, but — if the trust was created before 1960 by a person who was non-resident when the trust was created — does not include an individual (other than a trust) who has not, after 1959, made a contribution to the trust.

Related Provisions: 94(1)"connected contributor"(a) — 60-month limit; 94(1)"contributor" — Exempt person excluded; 94.1(2)"non-resident entity"(c) — Offshore investment property rules do not apply to immigration trust; 94(3)(a) — Trust with resident beneficiary deemed resident in Canada for certain purposes; 94(3)(d)(i) — Liability of resident contributor for trust's tax; 94(5) — Trust ceases to be resident in Canada once there is no resident contributor.

Notes: See Notes to 94(3).

Note that the definition of "contributor" in 94(1) excludes an "exempt person" (defined in 94(1)) but includes a dead person.

Definition amended by 2014 budget bill #2 to delete the 60-month immigration trust rule in para. (a), effective for taxation years that end after Feb. 10, 2014, subject to grandfathering to the end of 2014. (For examples of the timing of this amendment, see VIEWS docs 2014-0529821C6 [2014 STEP q.10]; 2014-0529831C6 [2014 STEP q.11] (whether trust will be deemed resident from beginning of year).)

Former para. (a) and 94(1)"connected contributor"(a) effectively gave non-residents moving to Canada up to 5 years to keep assets in a properly structured trust (often called an "immigration trust") in a tax haven. (A similar rule was in 94(1)(b)(i)(A)(III) for decades, before new s. 94 was enacted in 2013.) The trust had to be non-resident (see Notes to 250(1)). Once it qualified, income and capital gains (except on taxable Canadian property) were exempt and added to the trust's capital, and could be distributed later tax-free to beneficiaries (which could include the immigrant's spouse and children). To have maximum time for the trust to escape Canadian tax, it had to be set up before the person became resident in Canada. Aside from 94.1, concerns when setting up an immigration trust included 75(2) (reversionary trust); 74.1–74.4 (attribution rules); 56(4.1) (attribution on loan); 120.4 (tax on split income); US grantor trust rules; and UK gift and inheritance taxes. For an example of a successful immigration trust see *Howson*, 2006 TCC 644. See VIEWS doc 2005-0115671E5 for compliance issues; Kester, "Stepping Up Asset Values Upon Immigration to Canada", 1(4) *BorderCrossings* (Carswell) 3-4 (Nov. 2008). The 60 months in para. (a) included residence in Canada before becoming non-resident: 2009-0327911E5.

"resident portion" of a trust at a particular time means all of the trust's property that is

(a) property in respect of which a contribution has been made at or before the particular time to the trust by a contributor that is at the particular time a resident contributor, or if there is at the particular time a resident beneficiary under the trust a connected contributor, to the trust and, for the purposes of this paragraph,

(i) if a property is held by a contributor in common or in partnership immediately before the property is contributed to the trust, it is contributed by the contributor only to the extent that the contributor so held the property, and

(ii) if the contribution is a transfer described by any of paragraphs (2)(a), (c), (d) or (f), the property in respect of which the contribution has been made is deemed to be

(A) in respect of a transfer under paragraph (2)(a), property

(I) if clause (2)(a)(ii)(A) applies, the fair market value of which has increased because of a transfer or loan described by subparagraph (2)(a)(i), or

(II) if clause (2)(a)(ii)(B) applies, that would not otherwise be included in the resident portion of the trust, that is selected by the trust (or, failing which, is selected by the Minister) and that has a fair market value at least equal to the absolute value of a decrease in a liability or potential liability of the trust that arose because of a transfer or loan described by subparagraph (2)(a)(i),

(B) in respect of a transfer under paragraph (2)(c), property described by subparagraph (2)(c)(ii),

(C) in respect of a transfer under paragraph (2)(d), property acquired as a result of any undertaking including a guarantee, covenant or agreement given by a person or partnership other than the trust to ensure the repayment, in whole or in part, of a loan or other indebtedness incurred by the trust as described by paragraph (2)(d), and

(D) in respect of a transfer under paragraph (2)(f), property selected by the trust (or, failing which, is selected by the Minister) that has a fair market value at least equal to the fair market value of property deemed to be transferred to the trust as described by paragraph (2)(f);

(b) property that is acquired, at or before the particular time, by way of indebtedness incurred by the trust (referred to in this paragraph as the "subject property"), if

(i) all or part of the indebtedness is secured on property (other than the subject property) that is held in the trust's resident portion,

(ii) it was reasonable to conclude, at the time that the indebtedness was incurred, that the indebtedness would be repaid with recourse to any property (other than the subject property) held at any time in the trust's resident portion, or

(iii) a person resident in Canada or partnership of which a person resident in Canada is a member has become obligated, either absolutely or contingently, to effect any undertaking including a guarantee, covenant or agreement given to ensure the repayment, in whole or in part, of the indebtedness, or provided any other financial assistance in respect of the indebtedness;

(c) property to the extent that it is derived, directly or indirectly, in any manner whatever, from property described by any of paragraphs (a), (b) and (d), and, without limiting the generality of the foregoing, including property derived from the income (computed without reference to paragraph (16)(f) and subsections 104(6) and (12)) of the trust for a taxation year of the trust that ends at or before the particular time and property in respect of which an amount would be described at the particular time in respect of the trust by the definition "capital dividend account" in subsection 89(1) if the trust were at the particular time a corporation; and

(d) property to the extent that it is at the particular time substituted for a property described by any of paragraphs (a) to (c).

Related Provisions: 94(1)"non-resident portion" — Trust property that is not the resident portion; 94(3)(f) — Only resident portion included in trust's income.

Notes: Only the income from the "resident portion" of a deemed-resident trust's assets is included in income subject to tax: 94(3)(f). This addresses concerns raised where a small Canadian contribution is made to a large foreign trust. Under 94(3)(g), withholding tax may be payable (and not recovered by the trust) on the non-resident portion.

For a trust filing a Quebec return, a "selecting" of property under (a)(ii)(A)(II) or (a)(ii)(D) must be copied to Revenu Québec: *Taxation Act* ss. 593 (last para.), 21.4.6.

For the meaning of "derived" in para. (c), see Notes to 18.1(12).

"restricted property" of a person or partnership means property that the person or partnership holds and that is

(a) a share (or a right to acquire a share) of the capital stock of a closely held corporation if the share or right, or a property for which the share or right was substituted, was at any time ac-

quired by the person or partnership as part of a transaction or series of transactions under which

(i) a specified share of the capital stock of a closely held corporation was acquired by any person or partnership in exchange for, as consideration for or upon the conversion of any property and the cost of the specified share to the person who acquired it was less than the fair market value of the specified share at the time of the acquisition, or

(ii) a share (other than a specified share) of the capital stock of a closely held corporation becomes a specified share of the capital stock of the corporation;

(b) an indebtedness or other obligation, or a right to acquire an indebtedness or other obligation, of a closely held corporation if

(i) the indebtedness, obligation or right, or property for which the indebtedness, obligation or right was substituted, became property of the person or partnership as part of a transaction or series of transactions under which

(A) a specified share of the capital stock of a closely held corporation was acquired by any person or partnership in exchange for, as consideration for or upon the conversion of any property and the cost of the specified share to the person who acquired it was less than the fair market value of the specified share at the time of the acquisition, or

(B) a share (other than a specified share) of a closely held corporation becomes a specified share of the capital stock of the corporation, and

(ii) the amount of any payment under the indebtedness, obligation or right (whether the right to the amount is immediate or future, absolute or contingent or conditional on or subject to the exercise of any discretion by any person or partnership) is, directly or indirectly, determined primarily by one or more of the following criteria:

(A) the fair market value of, production from or use of any of the property of the closely held corporation,

(B) gains or profits from the disposition of any of the property of the closely held corporation,

(C) income, profits, revenue or cash flow of the closely held corporation, or

(D) any other criterion similar to a criterion referred to in any of clauses (A) to (C); and

(c) property

(i) that the person or partnership acquired as part of a series of transactions described in paragraph (a) or (b) in respect of another property, and

(ii) the fair market value of which is derived in whole or in part, directly or indirectly, from that other property.

Related Provisions: 87(2)(j.95) — Amalgamation — continuing corporation; 94(2)(b), (c.1) — Deemed restricted property on indirect transfer to trust; 94(9) — Determination of contribution amount when restricted property contributed to trust; 94(14) — Restricted property — exception; 94(15)(b) — Anti-avoidance; 94.2(1)(b)(ii) — FAPI treatment on contribution of restricted property to certain trusts.

Notes: For the meaning of "derived" in (c)(ii), see Notes to 18.1(12).

The definition **"specified fixed interest"** in the Aug. 27/10 draft has been replaced by "fixed interest".

"specified party" in respect of a particular person at any time means

(a) the particular person's spouse or common-law partner at that time;

(b) a corporation that at that time

(i) is a controlled foreign affiliate of the particular person or their spouse or common-law partner, or

(ii) would be a controlled foreign affiliate of a partnership, of which the particular person is a majority-interest partner, if the partnership were a person resident in Canada at that time;

(c) a person, or a partnership of which the particular person is a majority-interest partner, for which it is reasonable to conclude that the benefit referred to in subparagraph (8)(a)(iv) was conferred

(i) in contemplation of the person becoming after that time a corporation described by paragraph (b), or

(ii) to avoid or minimize a liability that arose, or that would otherwise have arisen, under this Part with respect to the particular person; or

(d) a corporation in which the particular person, or partnership of which the particular person is a majority-interest partner, is a shareholder if

(i) the corporation is at or before that time a beneficiary under a trust, and

(ii) the particular person or the partnership is a beneficiary under the trust solely because of the application of paragraph (b) of the definition "beneficiary" in this subsection to the particular person or the partnership in respect of the corporation.

Related Provisions: 87(2)(j.95) — Amalgamation — continuing corporation.

Notes: Paras. (b)-(d) amended by 2013 budget bill #2, effective Dec. 12, 2013, to change "majority interest partner" to "majority-interest partner" (with a hyphen).

"specified share" means a share of the capital stock of a corporation other than a share that is a prescribed share for the purpose of paragraph 110(1)(d).

"specified time" in respect of a trust for a taxation year of the trust means

(a) if the trust exists at the end of the taxation year, the time that is the end of that taxation year; and

(b) in any other case, the time in that taxation year that is immediately before the time at which the trust ceases to exist.

"successor beneficiary" at any time under a trust means a person that is a beneficiary under the trust solely because of a right of the person to receive any of the trust's income or capital, if under that right the person may so receive that income or capital only on or after the death after that time of an individual who, at that time, is alive and

(a) is a contributor to the trust;

(b) is related to (in this definition including an uncle, aunt, niece or nephew of) a contributor to the trust; or

(c) would have been related to a contributor to the trust if every individual who was alive before that time were alive at that time.

Notes: An example of a successor beneficiary is where a Canadian resident puts funds into a U.S. trust for a U.S. resident child, where a Canadian resident child is the residual beneficiary if the U.S. child dies first: VIEWS doc 2007-0235241C6.

"transaction" includes an arrangement or event.

Notes: See Notes to 245(1)"transaction", which is the same definition for GAAR.

"trust" includes, for greater certainty, an estate.

Related Provisions: 94(3)(f) — Deemed separate trust for non-resident portion of electing trust; 108(1) — Definition of "testamentary trust".

Notes: Because this definition uses "includes" rather than "means", the general definition of "trust" in 104(1), applicable due to 248(1), also applies (see Notes to 188.1(5)).

Regulations: 5909 (prescribed circumstances for 94(1)(b)(i)).

Income Tax Folios: S6-F1-C1: Residence of a trust or estate [replaces IT-447].

Interpretation Bulletins: IT-451R: Deemed disposition and acquisition on ceasing to be or becoming resident in Canada.

Information Circulars: 77-9R: Books, records and other requirements for taxpayers having foreign affiliates.

I.T. Technical News: 38 (Canada-US treaty's competent authority provision); 43 (taxation of Roth IRAs).

CRA Audit Manual: 15.7.12: Application of FAPI rules to trusts.

Forms: T2 Sched. 22: Non-resident discretionary trust.

(2) Rules of application — In this section and section 94.2,

(a) **[indirect transfer increasing value of trust property]** — a person or partnership is deemed to have transferred, at any time, a property to a trust if

(i) at that time the person or partnership transfers or loans property (other than by way of an arm's length transfer) to another person or partnership, and

(ii) because of that transfer or loan

(A) the fair market value of one or more properties held by the trust increases at that time, or

(B) a liability or potential liability of the trust decreases at that time;

(b) **[value of transfer under (a)]** — the fair market value, at any time, of a property deemed by paragraph (a) to be transferred at that time by a person or partnership is deemed to be the amount of the absolute value of the increase or decrease, as the case may be, referred to in subparagraph (a)(ii) in respect of the property, and if that time is after August 27, 2010, and the property that the person or partnership transfers or loans at that time is restricted property of the person or partnership, the property deemed by paragraph (a) to be transferred at that time to a trust is deemed to be restricted property transferred at that time to the trust;

(c) **[anti-avoidance — deemed transfer to trust]** — a person or partnership is deemed to have transferred, at any time, property to a trust if

(i) at that time the person or partnership transfers restricted property, or loans property other than by way of an arm's length transfer, to another person (referred to in this paragraph and paragraph (c.1) as the "intermediary"),

(ii) at or after that time, the trust holds property (other than property described by paragraph (14)(b)) the fair market value of which is derived in whole or in part, directly or indirectly, from property held by the intermediary, and

(iii) it is reasonable to conclude that one of the reasons the transfer or loan is made is to avoid or minimize a liability under this Part;

(c.1) **[value of transfer under (c)]** — the fair market value, at any time, of a property deemed by paragraph (c) to be transferred at that time by a person or partnership is deemed to be the fair market value of the property referred to in subparagraph (c)(i), and if that time is after October 24, 2012 and the property that the person or partnership transfers or loans to the intermediary is restricted property of the intermediary, the property deemed by paragraph (c) to be transferred at that time by the person or partnership to a trust is deemed to be restricted property transferred at that time to the trust throughout the period in which the intermediary holds the restricted property;

(d) **[guarantee of repayment deemed a transfer]** — if, at any time, a particular person or partnership becomes obligated, either absolutely or contingently, to effect any undertaking including a guarantee, covenant or agreement given to ensure the repayment, in whole or in part, of a loan or other indebtedness incurred by another person or partnership, or has provided any other financial assistance to another person or partnership,

(i) the particular person or partnership is deemed to have transferred, at that time, property to that other person or partnership, and

(ii) the property, if any, transferred to the particular person or partnership from the other person or partnership in exchange for the guarantee or other financial assistance is deemed to have been transferred to the particular person or partnership in exchange for the property deemed by subparagraph (i) to have been transferred;

(e) **[value of transfer under (d)]** — the fair market value at any time of a property deemed by subparagraph (d)(i) to have been transferred at that time to another person or partnership is deemed to be the amount at that time of the loan or indebtedness incurred by the other person or partnership to which the property relates;

(f) **[service deemed to be transfer of property]** — if, at any time after June 22, 2000, a particular person or partnership renders any service (other than an exempt service) to, for or on behalf of another person or partnership,

(i) the particular person or partnership is deemed to have transferred, at that time, property to that other person or partnership, and

(ii) the property, if any, transferred to the particular person or partnership from the other person or partnership in exchange for the service is deemed to have been transferred to the particular person or partnership in exchange for the property deemed by subparagraph (i) to have been transferred;

(g) **[acquisition deemed to be transfer]** — each of the following acquisitions of property by a particular person or partnership is deemed to be a transfer of the property, at the time of the acquisition of the property, to the particular person or partnership from the person or partnership from which the property was acquired, namely, the acquisition by the particular person or partnership of

(i) a share of a corporation from the corporation,

(ii) an interest as a beneficiary under a trust (otherwise than from a beneficiary under the trust),

(iii) an interest in a partnership (otherwise than from a member of the partnership),

(iv) a debt owing by a person or partnership from the person or partnership, and

(v) a right (granted after June 22, 2000, by the person or partnership from which the right was acquired) to acquire or to be loaned property;

(h) **[value of transfer under (f)(i)]** — the fair market value at any time of a property deemed by subparagraph (f)(i) to have been transferred at that time is deemed to be the fair market value at that time of the service to which the property relates;

(i) **[obligation to do act that would be transfer or loan]** — a person or partnership that at any time becomes obligated to do an act that would, if done, constitute the transfer or loan of a property to another person or partnership is deemed to have become obligated at that time to transfer or loan, as the case may be, property to that other person or partnership;

(j) **[transfer as consequence of death]** — in applying at any time the definition "non-resident time" in subsection (1), if a trust acquires property of an individual as a consequence of the death of the individual and the individual was immediately before death resident in Canada, the individual is deemed to have transferred the property to the trust immediately before the individual's death;

(k) **[anti-avoidance — transfer at direction of other person]** — a transfer or loan of property at any time is deemed to be made at that time jointly by a particular person or partnership and a second person or partnership (referred to in this paragraph as the "specified person") if

(i) the particular person or partnership transfers or loans property at that time to another person or partnership,

(ii) the transfer or loan is made at the direction, or with the acquiescence, of the specified person, and

(iii) it is reasonable to conclude that one of the reasons the transfer or loan is made is to avoid or minimize the liability, of any person or partnership, under this Part that arose, or that would otherwise have arisen, because of the application of this section;

(k.1) **[employee benefits — deemed transfer of property]** — a transfer or loan of property made at any time on or after November 9, 2006, is deemed to be made at that time

jointly by a particular person or partnership and a second person or partnership (referred to in this paragraph as the "specified person") if

(i) the particular person or partnership transfers or loans property at that time to another person or partnership, and

(ii) a purpose or effect of the transfer or loan may reasonably be considered to be to provide benefits in respect of services rendered by a person as an employee of the specified person (whether the provision of the benefits is because of a right that is immediate or future, absolute or contingent, or conditional on or subject to the exercise of any discretion by any person or partnership);

(l) **[transfer deemed made jointly by corporation and specified person]** — a transfer or loan of property at any time is deemed to be made at that time jointly by a corporation and a person or partnership (referred to in this paragraph as the "specified person") if

(i) the corporation transfers or loans property at that time to another person or partnership,

(ii) the transfer or loan is made at the direction, or with the acquiescence, of the specified person,

(iii) that time is not, or would not be if the transfer or loan were a contribution of the specified person,

(A) a non-resident time of the specified person, or

(B) if the specified person is a partnership, a non-resident time of one or more members of the partnership, and

(iv) either

(A) the corporation is, at that time, a controlled foreign affiliate of the specified person, or would at that time be a controlled foreign affiliate of the specified person if the specified person were at that time resident in Canada, or

(B) it is reasonable to conclude that the transfer or loan was made in contemplation of the corporation becoming after that time a corporation described in clause (A);

(m) **[exchange of shares or property]** — a particular person or partnership is deemed to have transferred, at a particular time, a particular property or particular part of it, as the case may be, to a corporation described in subparagraph (i) or a second person or partnership described in subparagraph (ii) if

(i) the particular property is a share of the capital stock of a corporation held at the particular time by the particular person or partnership, and as consideration for the disposition at or before the particular time of the share, the particular person or partnership received at the particular time (or became entitled at the particular time to receive) from the corporation a share of the capital stock of the corporation, or

(ii) the particular property (or property for which the particular property is substituted) was acquired, before the particular time, from the second person or partnership by any person or partnership, in circumstances that are described by any of subparagraphs (g)(i) to (v) (or would be so described if it applied at the time of that acquisition) and at the particular time,

(A) the terms or conditions of the particular property change,

(B) the second person or partnership redeems, acquires or cancels the particular property or the particular part of it,

(C) if the particular property is a debt owing by the second person or partnership, the debt or the particular part of it is settled or cancelled, or

(D) if the particular property is a right to acquire or to be loaned property, the particular person or partnership exercises the right;

(n) **[contribution by trust deemed contribution by its contributors]** — a contribution made at any time by a particular trust to another trust is deemed to have been made at that time jointly by the particular trust and by each person or partnership that is at that time a contributor to the particular trust;

(o) **[contribution by partnership deemed contribution by its partners]** — a contribution made at any time by a particular partnership to a trust is deemed to have been made at that time jointly by the particular partnership and by each person or partnership that is at that time a member of the particular partnership;

(p) **[amount of contribution is FMV of property contributed]** — subject to paragraph (q) and subsection (9), the amount of a contribution to a trust at the time it was made is deemed to be the fair market value, at that time, of the property that was the subject of the contribution;

(q) **[acquisition of specified fixed interest deemed to be contribution]** — a person or partnership that at any time acquires a fixed interest in a trust (or a right, issued by the trust, to acquire a fixed interest in the trust) from another person or partnership (other than from the trust that issued the interest or the right) is deemed to have made at that time a contribution to the trust and the amount of the contribution is deemed to be equal to the fair market value at that time of the interest or right, as the case may be;

(r) **[exception to (q)]** — a particular person or partnership that has acquired a fixed interest in a trust as a consequence of making a contribution to the trust — or that has made a contribution to the trust as a consequence of having acquired a fixed interest in the trust or a right described in paragraph (q) — is, for the purpose of applying this section at any time after the time that the particular person or partnership transfers the fixed interest or the right, as the case may be, to another person or partnership (which transfer is referred to in this paragraph as the "sale"), deemed not to have made the contribution in respect of the fixed interest, or right, that is the subject of the sale if

(i) in exchange for the sale, the other person or partnership transfers or loans, or becomes obligated to transfer or loan, property (which property is referred to in subparagraph (ii) as the "consideration") to the particular person or partnership, and

(ii) it is reasonable to conclude

(A) having regard only to the sale and the consideration that the particular person or partnership would be willing to make the sale if the particular person or partnership were dealing at arm's length with the other person or partnership, and

(B) that the terms and conditions made or imposed in respect of the exchange would be acceptable to the particular person or partnership if the particular person or partnership were dealing at arm's length with the other person or partnership;

(s) **[certain transfers required by securities law deemed not to be contributions]** — a transfer to a trust by a particular person or partnership is deemed not to be, at a particular time, a contribution to the trust if

(i) the particular person or partnership has transferred, at or before the particular time and in the ordinary course of business of the particular person or partnership, property to the trust,

(ii) the transfer is not an arm's length transfer, but would be an arm's length transfer if the definition "arm's length transfer" were read without reference to paragraph (a) and subparagraphs (b)(i), (ii) and (iv) to (vii) of that definition,

(iii) it is reasonable to conclude that the particular person or partnership was the only person or partnership that acquired, in respect of the transfer, an interest as a beneficiary under the trust,

(iv) the particular person or partnership was required, under the securities law of a country or of a political subdivision of

the country in respect of the issuance by the trust of interests as a beneficiary under the trust, to acquire an interest because of the particular person or partnership's status at the time of the transfer as a manager or promoter of the trust,

(v) at the particular time the trust is not an exempt foreign trust, but would be at that time an exempt foreign trust if it had not made an election under paragraph (h) of the definition "exempt foreign trust", and

(vi) the particular time is before the earliest of

(A) the first time at which the trust becomes an exempt foreign trust,

(B) the first time at which the particular person or partnership ceases to be a manager or promoter of the trust, and

(C) the time that is 24 months after the first time at which the total fair market value of consideration received by the trust in exchange for interests as a beneficiary (other than the particular person or partnership's interest referred to in subparagraph (iii)) under the trust is greater than $500,000;

(t) **[certain transfers deemed not to be contributions]** — a transfer, by a Canadian corporation of particular property, that is at a particular time a contribution by the Canadian corporation to a trust, is deemed not to be, after the particular time, a contribution by the Canadian corporation to the trust if

(i) the trust acquired the property before the particular time from the Canadian corporation in circumstances described in subparagraph (g)(i) or (iv),

(ii) as a result of a transfer (which transfer is referred to in this paragraph as the "sale") at the particular time by any person or partnership (referred to in this paragraph as the "seller") to another person or partnership (referred to in this paragraph as the "buyer") the trust

(A) no longer holds any property that is shares of the capital stock of, or debt issued by, the Canadian corporation, and

(B) no longer holds any property that is property the fair market value of which is derived in whole or in part, directly or indirectly, from shares of the capital stock of, or debt issued by, the Canadian corporation,

(iii) the buyer deals at arm's length immediately before the particular time with the Canadian corporation, the trust and the seller,

(iv) in exchange for the sale, the buyer transfers or becomes obligated to transfer property (which property is referred to in this paragraph as the "consideration") to the seller, and

(v) it is reasonable to conclude

(A) having regard only to the sale and the consideration that the seller would be willing to make the sale if the seller were dealing at arm's length with the buyer,

(B) that the terms and conditions made or imposed in respect of the exchange would be acceptable to the seller if the seller were dealing at arm's length with the buyer, and

(C) that the value of the consideration is not, at or after the particular time, determined in whole or in part, directly or indirectly, by reference to shares of the capital stock of, or debt issued by, the Canadian corporation;

(u) **[transfer to personal trust before Oct. 11/02]** — a transfer, before October 11, 2002, to a personal trust by an individual (other than a trust) of particular property is deemed not to be a contribution of the particular property by the individual to the trust if

(i) the individual identifies the trust in prescribed form filed with the Minister on or before the individual's filing-due date for the individual's 2003 taxation year (or a later date that is acceptable to the Minister), and

(ii) the Minister is satisfied that

(A) the individual (and any person or partnership not dealing at any time at arm's length with the individual) has never loaned or transferred, directly or indirectly, restricted property to the trust,

(B) in respect of each contribution (determined without reference to this paragraph) made before October 11, 2002, by the individual to the trust, none of the reasons (determined by reference to all the circumstances including the terms of the trust, an intention, the laws of a country or the existence of an agreement, a memorandum, a letter of wishes or any other arrangement) for the contribution was to permit or facilitate, directly or indirectly, the conferral at any time of a benefit (for greater certainty, including an interest as a beneficiary under the trust) on

(I) the individual,

(II) a descendant of the individual, or

(III) any person or partnership with whom the individual or descendant does not, at any time, deal at arm's length, and

(C) the total of all amounts each of which is the amount of a contribution (determined without reference to this paragraph) made before October 11, 2002, by the individual to the trust does not exceed the greater of

(I) 1% of the total of all amounts each of which is the amount of a contribution (determined without reference to this paragraph) made to the trust before October 11, 2002, and

(II) $500; and

(v) **[loan by financial institution not a contribution]** — a loan made by a particular specified financial institution to a trust is deemed not to be a contribution to the trust if

(i) the loan is made on terms and conditions that would have been agreed to by persons dealing at arm's length, and

(ii) the loan is made by the specified financial institution in the ordinary course of the business carried on by it.

Related Provisions: 51(1)(c) — Exchange of convertible property is disposition for purposes of 94(2)(m); 87(2)(j.95) — Amalgamation — continuing corporation; 94(9) — Determination of contribution amount — restricted property.

Notes: For an example of 94(2)(a) and (f) applying see VIEWS doc 2018-0772971I7.

For the meaning of "derived" in 94(2)(c)(ii) and 94(2)(t)(ii)(B), see Notes to 18.1(12).

94(2)(g)(i) can catch a non-resident trust that acquires additional shares of its own wholly-owned corporation, since that is deemed to be a contribution to the trust!

On the effect of 94(2)(t) on 94(2)(g) see VIEWS docs 2013-0509111E5, 2018-0781041I7, 2019-0798621C6 [2019 STEP q.1].

See Notes at end of 94 for in-force rule. 94(2)(c)-(c.1) were not in the Aug. 27/10 draft. Proposed 94(2)(c) of that draft is now 94(2)(v). (A pre-2010 proposed 94(2)(c), deeming certain transfers or loans to a third party to be transfers to the trust, was dropped.)

(3) Liabilities of non-resident trusts [deemed resident in Canada] and others — If at a specified time in a trust's particular taxation year (other than a trust that is, at that time, an exempt foreign trust) the trust is non-resident (determined without reference to this subsection) and, at that time, there is a resident contributor to the trust or a resident beneficiary under the trust,

(a) **[trust deemed resident in Canada for many purposes]** — the trust is deemed to be resident in Canada throughout the particular taxation year for the purposes of

(i) section 2,

(ii) computing the trust's income for the particular taxation year,

(iii) applying subsections 104(13.1) to (28) and 107(2.1), in respect of the trust and a beneficiary under the trust,

(iv) applying clause 53(2)(h)(i.1)(B), the definition "non-resident entity" in subsection 94.1(2), subsection 107(2.002) and section 115, in respect of a beneficiary under the trust,

(v) paragraph (c) and subsection 111(9),

(vi) determining an obligation of the trust to file a return under section 233.3 or 233.4,

(vii) determining the rights and obligations of the trust under Divisions I and J,

(viii) determining the liability of the trust for tax under Part I, and under Part XIII on amounts paid or credited (in this paragraph having the meaning assigned by Part XIII) to the trust,

(ix) applying Part XIII in respect of an amount (other than an exempt amount) paid or credited by the trust to any person, and

(x) determining whether a foreign affiliate of a taxpayer (other than the trust) is a controlled foreign affiliate of the taxpayer;

(b) **[foreign tax credit]** — no deduction shall be made under subsection 20(11) by the trust in computing its income for the particular taxation year, and for the purposes of applying subsection 20(12) and section 126 to the trust for the particular taxation year

(i) in determining the non-business-income tax (in this paragraph as defined by subsection 126(7)) paid by the trust for the particular taxation year, paragraph (b) of the definition "non-business-income tax" does not apply, and

(ii) if, at that specified time, the trust is resident in a country other than Canada,

(A) the trust's income for the particular taxation year (other than income — not including dividends or interest — from sources in Canada) is deemed to be from sources in that country and not to be from any other source, and

(B) the business-income tax (in this paragraph as defined by subsection 126(7)), and the non-business-income tax, paid by the trust for the particular taxation year are deemed to have been paid by the trust to the government of that country and not to any other government;

(c) **[bump of asset costs to FMV]** — if the trust was non-resident throughout its taxation year (referred to in this paragraph as the "preceding year") immediately preceding the particular taxation year, the trust is deemed to have

(i) immediately before the end of the preceding year, disposed of each property (other than property described in any of subparagraphs 128.1(1)(b)(i) to (iv)) held by the trust at that time for proceeds of disposition equal to its fair market value at that time, and

(ii) at the beginning of the particular taxation year, acquired each of those properties so disposed of at a cost equal to its proceeds of disposition;

(d) **[resident contributor and resident beneficiary liable for trust's income tax]** — each person that at any time in the particular taxation year is a resident contributor to the trust (other than an electing contributor in respect of the trust at the specified time) or a resident beneficiary under the trust

(i) has jointly and severally, or solidarily, with the trust and with each other such person, the rights and obligations of the trust in respect of the particular taxation year under Divisions I and J, and

(ii) is subject to Part XV in respect of those rights and obligations;

(e) **[liability of pre-2007 beneficiary]** — each person that at any time in the particular taxation year is a beneficiary under the trust and was a person from whom an amount would be recoverable at the end of the trust's 2006 taxation year under subsection (2) (as it read in its application to taxation years that end before 2007) in respect of the trust if the person had received before the trust's 2007 taxation year amounts described under paragraph

(2)(a) or (b) in respect of the trust (as those paragraphs read in their application to taxation years that end before 2007)

(i) has, to the extent of the person's recovery limit for the year, jointly and severally, or solidarily, with the trust and with each other such person, the rights and obligations of the trust in respect of the taxation years, of the trust, that end before 2007 under Divisions I and J, and

(ii) is, to the extent of the person's recovery limit for the year, subject to Part XV in respect of those rights and obligations;

(f) **[election to calculate trust's income on resident portion of assets]** — if the trust (referred to in this paragraph as the "particular trust") is an electing trust in respect of the particular taxation year,

(i) an *inter vivos* trust (in this paragraph referred to as the "non-resident portion trust") is deemed for the purposes of this Act (other than for the purposes of subsection 104(2))

(A) to be created at the first time at which the particular trust exists in its first taxation year in respect of which the particular trust is an electing trust, and

(B) to continue in existence until the earliest of

(I) the time at which the particular trust ceases to be resident in Canada because of subsection (5) or (5.1),

(II) the time at which the particular trust ceases to exist, and

(III) the time at which the particular trust becomes resident in Canada otherwise than because of this subsection,

(ii) all of the particular trust's property that is part of the particular trust's non-resident portion is deemed to be the property of the non-resident portion trust and not to be, except for the purposes of this paragraph and the definition "electing trust" in subsection (1), the particular trust's property,

(iii) the terms and conditions of, and rights and obligations of beneficiaries under, the particular trust (determined by reference to all the circumstances including the terms of a trust, an intention, the laws of a country or the existence of an agreement, a memorandum, a letter of wishes or any other arrangement) are deemed to be the terms and conditions of, and rights and obligations of beneficiaries under, the non-resident portion trust,

(iv) for greater certainty

(A) the trustees of the particular trust are deemed to be the trustees of the non-resident portion trust,

(B) the beneficiaries under the particular trust are deemed to be the beneficiaries under the non-resident portion trust, and

(C) the non-resident portion trust is deemed not to have a resident contributor or connected contributor to it,

(v) the non-resident portion trust is deemed to be, without affecting the liability of its trustees for their own income tax, in respect of its property an individual,

(vi) if all or part of a property becomes at a particular time part of the particular trust's non-resident portion and immediately before that time the property or that part, as the case may be, was part of its resident portion, the particular trust is deemed to have transferred at the particular time the property or that part, as the case may be, to the non-resident portion trust,

(vii) if all or part of a property becomes at a particular time part of the particular trust's resident portion and immediately before that time the property or that part, as the case may be, was part of its non-resident portion, the non-resident portion trust is deemed to have transferred at the particular time the property or that part, as the case may be, to the particular trust,

(viii) the particular trust and the non-resident portion trust are deemed at all times to be affiliated with each other and to not deal with each other at arm's length,

(ix) the particular trust

(A) has jointly and severally, or solidarily, with the non-resident portion trust, the rights and obligations of the non-resident portion trust in respect of any taxation year under Divisions I and J, and

(B) is subject to Part XV in respect of those rights and obligations, and

(x) if the non-resident portion trust ceases to exist at a particular time (for greater certainty, as determined by clause (i)(B))

(A) the non-resident portion trust is deemed, at the time (referred to in this subparagraph as the "disposition time") that is immediately before the time that is immediately before the particular time, to have

(I) in the case of each property of the non-resident portion trust that is property described in any of subparagraphs 128.1(1)(b)(i) to (iv), disposed of the property for proceeds of disposition equal to the cost amount to it of the property at the disposition time, and

(II) in the case of each other property of the non-resident portion trust, disposed of the property for proceeds of disposition equal to its fair market value of the property at the disposition time,

(B) the particular trust is deemed to have acquired, at the time that is immediately before the particular time, each property described in subclause (A)(I) or (II) at a cost equal to the proceeds determined under that subclause in respect of the property, and

(C) each person or partnership that is at the time immediately before the particular time a beneficiary under the non-resident portion trust is deemed

(I) at the disposition time to have disposed of the beneficiary's interest as a beneficiary under the non-resident portion trust for proceeds equal to the beneficiary's cost amount in the interest at the disposition time, and

(II) at the disposition time, to have ceased to be, other than for purposes of this clause, a beneficiary under the non-resident portion trust; and

(g) **[withholding tax deemed paid by trust on account]** — if a person deducts or withholds any amount (referred to in this paragraph as the "withholding amount") as required by section 215 from a particular amount paid or credited or deemed to have been paid or credited to the trust, and the particular amount has been included in the trust's income for the particular taxation year, the withholding amount is deemed to have been paid on account of the trust's tax under this Part for the particular taxation year.

Related Provisions: 94(4) — Excluded provisions for 94(3)(a); 94(5), (5.1) — Trust deemed to cease being resident in Canada; 94(7) — Limit to amount recoverable under 94(3)(d); 94(8) — "Recovery limit" for 94(3)(e); 94(11)–(13) — Where property transferred by trust to another trust to avoid tax; 94(16) — Attribution of income to electing contributors; 104(7.01) — Limit to trust's deduction under 104(6); 128.1(1.1) — No deemed disposition/acquisition on immigration of trust; 152(4)(b)(vii) — Three-year extension to reassessment deadline; 160(2.1) — Assessment of amount payable because of 94(3)(d) or (e); 160(3) — Discharge of liability under 94(3)(d) or (e); 216(4.1) — Where trust receives rental income from property in Canada; 233.2(4) — Annual information return by contributor; 233.3(3) — Annual information return by person owning interest in trust; Reg. 202(6.1) — Trust deemed resident for non-resident withholding tax filing obligations; *Income Tax Conventions Interpretation Act* 4,3 — Deemed residence under 94(3) overrides treaties.

Notes: See Notes at end of s. 94; note that some pre-2013 commentary is inaccurate due to changes in the Aug. 27/10 and Oct. 24/12 versions. Much of 94(3) was modified in the 2010 draft, but paras. (a)-(e) were mostly the same; (f)-(g) were new. In the 2012 (final) draft, 94(3)(b)(i) of the 2010 draft was dropped (and (ii)-(iii) renumbered (i)-(ii)), and para. (f) was totally changed.

94(3)(a) deems a non-resident trust to be resident in Canada *throughout* its tax year for many purposes, if it has a 94(1)"resident contributor" or "resident beneficiary" at year-end (the "specified time"). In turn, 94(1)"resident beneficiary" requires a "connected contributor", which excludes a non-resident, so a "granny trust" (contributions from a non-resident relative) can avoid 94(3), provided it is not resident in Canada and is run by non-resident trustees who genuinely make the decisions (for trusts that failed, see *Garron [St. Michael Trust Corp., Fundy Settlement]*, 2012 SCC 14, and *Antle*, 2010 FCA 280 (leave to appeal denied 2011 CarswellNat 1491 (SCC); motion for reconsideration dismissed 2012 CarswellNat 183)).

However, if the non-resident contributor immigrates to Canada within 5 years of making the contribution (and the trust has a resident beneficiary), 94(3) applies retroactive to the year of contribution: 94(10), VIEWS docs 2015-0572141C6 [STEP 2015 q.7], 2018-0744091C6 [STEP 2018 q.14].

A genuinely non-resident trust that escapes 94(3) and 94.1 can keep its income and gains offshore and pay tax-free capital to Canadian beneficiaries.

Where a deceased Canadian resident leaves a bequest to a foreign trust with only non-resident beneficiaries, CRA's view is that 94(3) applies to the trust as long as the estate is not wound up. The author believes this is incorrect, but even if CRA is right, 94(5) deems the trust to become non-resident as soon as it is deemed resident! See Notes to 94(1)"contributor".

See also VIEWS docs 2006-0211121E5, 2008-0285961E5; 2011-0430841E5 (application to US grantor trust); 2016-0634911C6 [2016 STEP q.7] (94(3)(a) does not affect CCPC status of corporation controlled by the trust); 2012-0437211I7, 2012-0448681E5 (application to estate with non-resident executors, Canadian beneficiaries); 2008-0278801C6 q.9 (interpretation of 94(3)(a)(x)).

For CRA views that 94(3) does *not* apply see 2009-0334021E5 (family trust); 2009-0335281R3, 2009-0347891R3, 2009-0347901R3 (all: Dutch closed FGRs); 2015-0581681E5 (no resident contributor or resident beneficiary).

A deemed-resident trust is limited in deductions for amounts paid to non-resident beneficiaries: see 104(7.01); and can be subject to Part XII.2 tax: VIEWS doc 2016-0657531E5.

94(3) overrides tax treaties: *Income Tax Conventions Interpretation Act* s. 4.3.

Because 94(3) is an anti-avoidance rule, CRA is unlikely to agree to competent authority determination of residence under Canada-US tax treaty Art. IV:4: *Income Tax Technical News* 38; 2007 Cdn Tax Foundation conference report at 4:7-11; VIEWS doc 2013-0492821C6 [2013 APFF q.3]. For an example see *Perry [Julien Family Delaware Dynasty Trust]*, 2008 FCA 260 (Court refused to order competent authority consideration of 94(3) before it was enacted) [Fitzsimmons, "Too Late and Too Early: No Relief for NRTs", 1915 *Tax Topics* (CCH) 1-4 (Nov. 20, 2008)].

Although 94(3)(a)(viii) deems the trust resident in Canada for Part XIII (thus not liable for non-resident withholding tax), the payor must still withhold due to 215(1), and that amount becomes a credit on the trust's T3 return: 94(3)(g) (see below). See also 94(4)(c) and 216(4.1).

94(3)(b) allows a foreign tax credit to the trust, similar to pre-2007 94(1)(c)(ii). See VIEWS doc 2013-047638I17 (credit reflects full US tax paid on capital gains that are half-taxed in Canada).

94(3)(c) triggers a bump of the trust's asset values to current value, if the trust was "non-resident" in the preceding year. (See Notes to 128.1(1.1) for its interaction with 128.1(1).) Due to 94(3)(a)(v), once 94(3)(a) deems a trust resident, that deeming applies to 94(3)(c) for the next year.

94(3)(d): on liability of exempt entities see VIEWS doc 2008-0285491C6.

94(3)(f) was introduced in the Oct. 24/12 draft (the version enacted); instead of the "resident portion" and "non-resident portion" being split automatically, an election is required (94(1)"electing trust") and the NR portion is deemed to be a separate trust: 94(3)(f)(i). Neither trust need file a T1135 to report foreign property: VIEWS doc 2014-0532601E5. One cannot amend, revoke or late-file the election, as it is not listed in Reg. 600; Finance advises that this is not an oversight.

94(3)(g) provides that Canadian withholding tax (see 94(4)(c)) is credited back to the trust on filing its return, so it is not a tax, only an advance payment (like instalments). For CRA interpretation see docs 2013-0485651E5, 2013-051364I17 (Part XIII tax withheld is on account of trust's Part I tax liability); 2014-0517511E5 (Part XIII tax withheld on capital dividend can be refunded only via 227(6)).

94(3) does not deem the trust to be resident in Canada for s. 116, so a s. 116 certificate is needed by an estate with US resident executors that transfers Canadian real property to Canadian resident beneficiaries: VIEWS docs 2012-0448681E5, 2013-0485651E5 (and see Notes to 116(1)).

Quebec has a parallel rule imposing provincial tax: "Non-resident trusts in Québec", 2(1) *Arbitrary Assessment* (Carswell) 3-4 (Jan. 2014). However, it might not be constitutionally valid: Bradley Thompson, "Non-Resident Trusts in Quebec", 2(6) *Provincial & Territorial Tax News* (Carswell) 1-2 (Nov. 2013); "Lessons from the US: is tax the next Québec constitutional challenge?", 2(1) *Arbitrary Assessment* 5-6 (Jan. 2014).

94(3)(b)(ii)(A) amended by 2017 budget bill #2, for taxation years that end after Sept. 15, 2016, to add "(other than income ... from sources in Canada)".

(4) Excluded provisions — For greater certainty, paragraph (3)(a) does not deem a trust to be resident in Canada for the purposes of

(a) the definitions "arm's length transfer" and "exempt foreign trust" in subsection (1);

(b) subsections (8.1) and (8.2), paragraph (14)(a), subsections 70(6) and 73(1), the definition "Canadian partnership" in subsection 102(1), paragraph 107.4(1)(c), the definition "qualified disability trust" in subsection 122(3), paragraph (a) of the definition "mutual fund trust" in subsection 132(6), the definition "eligible trust" in subsection 135.2(1) and subparagraph (b)(i) of the definition "investment fund" in subsection 251.2(1);

(c) determining the liability of a person (other than the trust) that would arise under section 215;

(d) determining whether, in applying subsection 128.1(1), the trust becomes resident in Canada at a particular time;

(e) determining whether, in applying subsection 128.1(4), the trust ceases to be resident in Canada at a particular time;

(f) subparagraph (f)(i) of the definition "disposition" in subsection 248(1);

(g) determining whether subsection 107(5) applies to a distribution on or after July 18, 2005, of property to the trust; and

(h) determining whether subsection 75(2) applies.

Notes: For interaction between 94 and 128.1(1), see Notes to 128.1(1.1). For 94(4)(c) see VIEWS docs 2013-0485651E5, 2013-051364I17 and Notes to 94(3) re 94(3)(g).

See Notes at end of 94 for in-force rules.

94(4) amended by 2016 budget bill #2 (effective March 21, 2013), 2016 budget bill #1 (effective July 2015), 2014 budget bill #2 (for 2016 and later tax years, to add reference to 122(3)"qualified disability trust"), 2013 budget bill #2.

Interpretation Bulletins: IT-342R: Trusts — income payable to beneficiaries; IT-451R: Deemed disposition and acquisition on ceasing to be or becoming resident in Canada.

(5) Deemed cessation of residence — loss of resident contributor or resident beneficiary — A trust is deemed to cease to be resident in Canada at the earliest time at which there is neither a resident contributor to the trust nor a resident beneficiary under the trust in a taxation year (determined without reference to subsection 128.1(4)) of the trust

(a) that immediately follows a taxation year of the trust throughout which it was deemed by subsection (3) to be resident in Canada for the purpose of computing its income; and

(b) at a specified time in which the trust

(i) is non-resident,

(ii) is not an exempt foreign trust, and

(iii) has no resident contributor to it or resident beneficiary under it.

Related Provisions: 94(3)(a) — Trust deemed resident in Canada; 94(5.2) — Rules on ceasing to be resident.

Notes: See Notes at end of 94 for in-force rule.

(5.1) Deemed cessation of residence — becoming an exempt foreign trust — A trust is deemed to cease to be resident in Canada at the earliest time at which the trust becomes an exempt foreign trust in a taxation year (determined without reference to subsection 128.1(4)) of the trust

(a) that immediately follows a taxation year of the trust throughout which it was deemed by subsection (3) to be resident in Canada for the purpose of computing its income; and

(b) at a specified time in which

(i) there is a resident contributor to the trust or a resident beneficiary under the trust, and

(ii) the trust is an exempt foreign trust.

Related Provisions: 94(5.2) — Rules on ceasing to be resident.

(5.2) Administrative relief — changes in status — If a trust is deemed by subsection (5) or (5.1) to cease to be resident in Canada at a particular time, the following rules apply to the trust in

Non-Resident Corps/Trusts

respect of the particular taxation year that is, as a result of that cessation of residence, deemed by subparagraph 128.1(4)(a)(i) to end immediately before the particular time:

(a) the trust's return of income for the particular taxation year is deemed to be filed with the Minister on a timely basis if it is filed with the Minister within 90 days from the end of the trust's taxation year that is deemed by subparagraph 128.1(4)(a)(i) to start at the particular time; and

(b) an amount that is included in the trust's income (determined without reference to subsections 104(6) and (12)) for the particular taxation year but that became payable (determined without regard to this paragraph) by the trust in the period after the particular taxation year and before the end of the trust's taxation year that is deemed by subparagraph 128.1(4)(a)(i) to start at the particular time, is deemed to have become payable by the trust immediately before the end of the particular taxation year and not at any other time.

Related Provisions: 104(24) — Whether amount payable to beneficiary.

(6) Ceasing to be an exempt foreign trust — If at a specified time in a trust's taxation year it is an exempt foreign trust, at a particular time in the immediately following taxation year (determined without reference to this subsection) the trust ceases to be an exempt foreign trust (otherwise than because of becoming resident in Canada), and at the particular time there is a resident contributor to, or resident beneficiary under, the trust,

(a) the trust's taxation year (determined without reference to this subsection) that includes the particular time is deemed to have ended immediately before the particular time and a new taxation year of the trust is deemed to begin at the particular time; and

(b) for the purpose of determining the trust's fiscal period after the particular time, the trust is deemed not to have established a fiscal period before the particular time.

(7) Limit to amount recoverable — The maximum amount recoverable under the provisions referred to in paragraph (3)(d) at any particular time from a person in respect of a trust (other than a person that is deemed, under subsection (12) or (13), to be a contributor or a resident contributor to the trust) and a particular taxation year of the trust is the person's recovery limit at the particular time in respect of the trust and the particular year if

(a) either

(i) the person is liable under a provision referred to in paragraph (3)(d) in respect of the trust and the particular year solely because the person was a resident beneficiary under the trust at a specified time in respect of the trust in the particular year, or

(ii) at a specified time in respect of the trust in the particular year, the total of all amounts each of which is the amount, at the time it was made, of a contribution to the trust made before the specified time by the person or by another person or partnership not dealing at arm's length with the person, is not more than the greater of

(A) $10,000, and

(B) 10% of the total of all amounts each of which was the amount, at the time it was made, of a contribution made to the trust before the specified time;

(b) except if the total determined in subparagraph (a)(ii) in respect of the person and all persons or partnerships not dealing at arm's length with the person is $10,000 or less, the person has filed on a timely basis under section 233.2 all information returns required to be filed by the person before the particular time in respect of the trust (or on any later day that is acceptable to the Minister); and

(c) it is reasonable to conclude that for each transaction that occurred before the end of the particular year at the direction of, or with the acquiescence of, the person

(i) none of the purposes of the transaction was to enable the person to avoid or minimize any liability under a provision referred to in paragraph (3)(d) in respect of the trust, and

(ii) the transaction was not part of a series of transactions any of the purposes of which was to enable the person to avoid or minimize any liability under a provision referred to in paragraph (3)(d) in respect of the trust.

Related Provisions: 94(8) — Recovery limit; 94(9) — Determination of contribution amount.

(8) Recovery limit — The recovery limit referred to in paragraph (3)(e) and subsection (7) at a particular time of a particular person in respect of a trust and a particular taxation year of the trust is the amount, if any, by which the greater of

(a) the total of all amounts each of which is

(i) an amount received or receivable after 2000 and before the particular time

(A) by the particular person on the disposition of all or part of the person's interest as a beneficiary under the trust, or

(B) by a person or partnership (that was, when the amount became receivable, a specified party in respect of the particular person) on the disposition of all or part of the specified party's interest as a beneficiary under the trust,

(ii) an amount (other than an amount described in subparagraph (i)) made payable by the trust after 2000 and before the particular time to

(A) the particular person because of the interest of the particular person as a beneficiary under the trust, or

(B) a person or partnership (that was, when the amount became payable, a specified party in respect of the particular person) because of the interest of the specified party as a beneficiary under the trust,

(iii) an amount received after August 27, 2010, by the particular person, or a person or partnership (that was, when the amount was received, a specified party in respect of the particular person), as a loan from the trust to the extent that the amount has not been repaid,

(iv) an amount (other than an amount described in any of subparagraphs (i) to (iii)) that is the fair market value of a benefit received or enjoyed, after 2000 and before the particular time, from or under the trust by

(A) the particular person, or

(B) a person or partnership that was, when the benefit was received or enjoyed, a specified party in respect of the particular person, or

(v) the maximum amount that would be recoverable from the particular person at the end of the trust's 2006 taxation year under subsection (2) (as it read in its application to taxation years that end before 2007) if the trust had tax payable under this Part at the end of the trust's 2006 taxation year and that tax payable exceeded the total of the amounts described in respect of the particular person under paragraphs (2)(a) and (b) (as they read in their application to taxation years that end before 2007), except to the extent that the amount so recoverable is in respect of an amount that is included in the particular person's recovery limit because of subparagraph (i) or (ii), and

(b) the total of all amounts each of which is the amount, when made, of a contribution to the trust before the particular time by the particular person,

exceeds the total of all amounts each of which is

(c) an amount recovered before the particular time from the particular person in connection with a liability of the particular person (in respect of the trust and the particular year or a preceding taxation year of the trust) that arose because of the application of subsection (3) (or the application of this section as it read in its application to taxation years that end before 2007),

(d) an amount (other than an amount in respect of which this paragraph has applied in respect of any other person) recovered before the particular time from a specified party in respect of the particular person in connection with a liability of the particular person (in respect of the trust and the particular year or a preceding taxation year of the trust) that arose because of the application of subsection (3) (or the application of this section as it read in its application to taxation years that end before 2007), or

(e) the amount, if any, by which the particular person's tax payable under this Part for any taxation year in which an amount described in any of subparagraphs (a)(i) to (iv) was paid, became payable, was received, became receivable or was enjoyed by the particular person exceeds the amount that would have been the particular person's tax payable under this Part for that taxation year if no such amount were paid, became payable, were received, became receivable or were enjoyed by the particular person in that taxation year.

Related Provisions: 94(9) — Determination of contribution amount; 104(24) — Whether amount payable to beneficiary.

(8.1) Application of subsec. (8.2) — Subsection (8.2) applies at any time to a particular person, and to a particular property, in respect of a non-resident trust, if at that time

(a) the particular person is resident in Canada; and

(b) the trust holds the particular property on condition that the particular property or property substituted for the particular property

   (i) may

      (A) revert to the particular person, or

      (B) pass to one or more persons or partnerships to be determined by the particular person, or

   (ii) shall not be disposed of by the trust during the existence of the particular person, except with the particular person's consent or in accordance with the particular person's direction.

Related Provisions: 94(4)(b) — Deeming non-resident trust to be resident in Canada does not apply to 94(8.1).

Notes: See Notes to 94(8.2).

(8.2) Deemed transfer of restricted property [reversionary trust] — If this subsection applies at any time to a particular person, and to a particular property, in respect of a non-resident trust, then in applying this section in respect of the trust for a taxation year of the trust that includes that time

(a) every transfer or loan made at or before that time by the particular person (or by a trust or partnership of which the particular person was a beneficiary or member, as the case may be) of the particular property, of another property for which the particular property is a substitute, or of property from which the particular property derives, or the other property derived, its value in whole or in part, directly or indirectly, is deemed to be a transfer or loan, as the case may be, by the particular person

   (i) that is not an arm's length transfer, and

   (ii) that is, for the purposes of paragraph (2)(c) and subsection (9), a transfer or loan of restricted property; and

(b) paragraph (2)(c) is to be read without reference to subparagraph (2)(c)(iii) in its application to each transfer and loan described in paragraph (a).

Related Provisions: 94(4)(b) — Deeming non-resident trust to be resident in Canada does not apply to 94(8.2); 94(8.1) — Conditions for 94(8.2) to apply; 107(4.1)(b) — Denial of 107(2) rollover.

Notes: 94(8.1) and (8.2) replace 75(2) for non-resident trusts. They trigger the 94(3) deemed-residence rule for a non-resident trust that holds property on conditions that grant effective ownership to a Canadian resident. See Christopher Montes, "The 2013 Budget and Sommerer", 21(5) *Canadian Tax Highlights* (ctf.ca) 3-4 (May 2013).

For CRA interpretation see docs 2013-0480351C6 [2013 STEP q.9], 2015-0581681E5. 94(8.1), (8.2) added by 2013 budget bill #2, for tax years ending after March 20, 2013.

(9) Determination of contribution amount — restricted property — If a person or partnership contributes at any time restricted property to a trust, the amount of the contribution at that time is deemed, for the purposes of this section, to be the greater of

(a) the amount, determined without reference to this subsection, of the contribution at that time, and

(b) the amount that is the greatest fair market value of the restricted property, or property substituted for it, in the period that begins immediately after that time and ends at the end of the third calendar year that ends after that time.

Related Provisions: 152(4)(b)(vi) — Three-year extension to reassessment period.

(10) Contributor — resident in Canada within 60 months after contribution — In applying this section at each specified time, in respect of a trust's taxation year, that is before the particular time at which a contributor to the trust becomes resident in Canada within 60 months after making a contribution to the trust, the contribution is deemed to have been made at a time other than a non-resident time of the contributor if

(a) in applying the definition "non-resident time" in subsection (1) at each of those specified times, the contribution was made at a non-resident time of the contributor; and

(b) in applying the definition "non-resident time" in subsection (1) immediately after the particular time, the contribution is made at a time other than a non-resident time of the contributor.

Related Provisions: 152(4)(b)(vi) — Three-year extension to reassessment period.

Notes: For CRA interpretation see doc 2015-0572141C6 [2015 STEP q.7].

(11) Application of subsecs. (12) and (13) — Subsections (12) and (13) apply to a trust or a person in respect of a trust if

(a) at any time property of a trust (referred to in this subsection and subsections (12) and (13) as the "original trust") is transferred or loaned, directly or indirectly, in any manner, to another trust (referred to in this subsection and subsections (12) and (13) as the "transferee trust");

(b) the original trust

   (i) is deemed to be resident in Canada immediately before that time because of paragraph (3)(a),

   (ii) would be deemed to be resident in Canada immediately before that time because of paragraph (3)(a) if this section, as it read in its application to the 2013 taxation year, were read without reference to paragraph (a) of the definition "connected contributor" in subsection (1) and paragraph (a) of the definition "resident contributor" in that subsection,

   (iii) was deemed to be resident in Canada immediately before that time because of subsection (1) as it read in its application to taxation years that end before 2007, or

   (iv) would have been deemed to be resident in Canada immediately before that time because of subsection (1) as it read in its application to taxation years that end before 2007 if that subsection were read in that application without reference to subclause (b)(i)(A)(III) of that subsection; and

(c) it is reasonable to conclude that one of the reasons the transfer or loan is made is to avoid or minimize a liability under this Part that arose, or that would otherwise have arisen, because of the application of this section (or the application of this section as it read in its application to taxation years that end before 2007).

Notes: 94(11)(b)(ii) amended by 2014 budget bill #2, effective on the same basis as the amendment to 94(1)"connected contributor".

(12) Deemed resident contributor — The original trust described in subsection (11) (including a trust that has ceased to exist) is deemed to be, at and after the time of the transfer or loan referred to in that subsection, a resident contributor to the transferee trust for the purpose of applying this section in respect of the transferee trust.

Related Provisions: 94(11) — Application of 94(12).

(13) Deemed contributor — A person (including any person that has ceased to exist) that is, at the time of the transfer or loan referred to in subsection (11), a contributor to the original trust, is deemed to be at and after that time

(a) a contributor to the transferee trust; and

(b) a connected contributor to the transferee trust, if at that time the person is a connected contributor to the original trust.

Related Provisions: 94(11) — Application of 94(13).

(14) Restricted property — exception — A particular property that is, or will be, at any time held, loaned or transferred, as the case may be, by a particular person or partnership is not restricted property held, loaned or transferred, as the case may be, at that time by the particular person or partnership if

(a) the following conditions are met:

(i) the particular property (and property, if any, for which it is, or is to be, substituted) was not, and will not be, at any time acquired, held, loaned or transferred by the particular person or partnership (or any person or partnership with whom the particular person or partnership does not at any time deal at arm's length) in whole or in part for the purpose of permitting any change in the value of the property of a corporation (that is, at any time, a closely held corporation) to accrue directly or indirectly in any manner whatever to the value of property held by a non-resident trust,

(ii) the Minister is satisfied that the particular property (and property, if any, for which it is, or is to be, substituted) is described by subparagraph (i), and

(iii) the particular property is identified in prescribed form, containing prescribed information, filed, by or on behalf of the particular person or partnership, with the Minister on or before

(A) in the case of a person, the particular person's filing-due date for the particular person's taxation year that includes that time,

(B) in the case of a partnership, the day on or before which a return is required by section 229 of the *Income Tax Regulations* to be filed in respect of the fiscal period of the particular partnership or would be required to be so filed if that section applied to the partnership, or

(C) another date that is acceptable to the Minister; or

(b) at that time

(i) the particular property is

(A) a share of the capital stock of a corporation,

(B) a fixed interest in a trust, or

(C) an interest, as a member of a partnership, under which, by operation of any law governing the arrangement in respect of the partnership, the liability of the member as a member of the partnership is limited,

(ii) there are at least 150 persons each of whom holds at that time property that at that time

(A) is identical to the particular property, and

(B) has a total fair market value of at least $500,

(iii) the total of all amounts each of which is the fair market value, at that time, of the particular property (or of identical property that is held, at that time, by the particular person or partnership or a person or partnership with whom the particular person or partnership does not deal at arm's length) does not exceed 10% of the total of all amounts each of which is the fair market value, at that time, of the particular property or of identical property held by any person or partnership,

(iv) property that is identical to the particular property can normally be acquired by and sold by members of the public in the open market, and

(v) the particular property, or identical property, is listed on a designated stock exchange.

Related Provisions: 94(4)(b) — Deeming non-resident trust to be resident in Canada does not apply to para. (a); 94(15)(a)(iii) — Anti-avoidance rule re condition in 94(14)(b)(ii); 248(12) — Identical properties.

Notes: For a person or partnership filing a Quebec return, a filing under 94(14)(a)(iii) must be copied to Revenu Québec: *Taxation Act* ss. 597.0.12, 21.4.6.

(15) Anti-avoidance — In applying this section,

(a) **[150-investor rule]** — if it can reasonably be considered that one of the main reasons that a person or partnership

(i) is at any time a shareholder of a corporation is to cause the condition in paragraph (b) of the definition "closely held corporation" in subsection (1) to be satisfied in respect of the corporation, the condition is deemed not to have been satisfied at that time in respect of the corporation,

(ii) holds at any time an interest in a trust is to cause the condition in clause (h)(ii)(A) of the definition "exempt foreign trust" in subsection (1) to be satisfied in respect of the trust, the condition is deemed not to have been satisfied at that time in respect of the trust, and

(iii) holds at any time a property is to cause the condition described in subparagraph (14)(b)(ii) to be satisfied in respect of the property or an identical property held by any person, the condition is deemed not to have been satisfied at that time in respect of the property or the identical property;

(b) **[para. 94(1)"exempt foreign trust"(f)]** — if at any time at or before a specified time in a trust's taxation year, a resident contributor to the trust contributes to the trust property that is restricted property of the trust, or property for which restricted property of the trust is substituted, and the trust is at that specified time an exempt foreign trust by reason of paragraph (f) of the definition "exempt foreign trust" in subsection (1), the amount of the trust's income for the taxation year from the restricted property, and the amount of any taxable capital gain from the disposition in the taxation year by the trust of the restricted property, shall be included in computing the income of the resident contributor for its taxation year in which that taxation year of the trust ends and not in computing the income of the trust for that taxation year of the trust; and

(c) **[para. 94(1)"exempt foreign trust"(h)]** — if at a specified time in a trust's taxation year it is an exempt foreign trust by reason of paragraph (h) of the definition "exempt foreign trust" in subsection (1), at a time immediately before a particular time in the immediately following taxation year (determined without reference to subsection (6)) there is a resident contributor to, or resident beneficiary under, the trust, at the time that is immediately before the particular time a beneficiary holds a fixed interest in the trust, and at the particular time the interest ceases to be a fixed interest in the trust,

(i) the trust is deemed, other than for purposes of subsection (6), not to be an exempt foreign trust at any time in the trust's taxation year (referred to in this paragraph as its "assessment year") that ends (for greater certainty as determined under paragraph (6)(a)) at the time that is immediately before the particular time,

(ii) the trust shall include in computing its income for its assessment year an amount equal to the amount determined by the formula

$$A - B - C$$

where

A is the amount by which the total of all amounts each of which is the fair market value of a property held by the trust at the end of its assessment year exceeds the total of all amounts each of which is the principal amount outstanding at the end of its assessment year of a liability of the trust,

B   is the amount by which the total of all amounts each of which is the fair market value of a property held by the trust at the earliest time at which there is a resident contributor to, or resident beneficiary under, the trust and at which the trust is an exempt foreign trust (referred to in this paragraph as the "initial time") exceeds the total of all amounts each of which is the principal amount outstanding at the initial time of a liability of the trust, and

C   is the total of all amounts each of which is the amount of a contribution made to the trust in the period that begins at the initial time and ends at the end of its assessment year (in this paragraph referred to as the "interest gross-up period"), and

(iii) if the trust is liable for tax for its assessment year, then throughout the period that begins at the trust's balance-due day for each taxation year that ends in the interest gross-up period and ends at the balance-due day for its assessment year, the trust is (in addition to any excess otherwise determined in respect of the trust under that subsection) deemed to have an excess for the purposes of subsection 161(1) equal to the amount determined by the formula

$$A/B \times 42.92\%$$

where

A   is the amount determined under subparagraph (ii) in respect of the trust for the particular taxation year, and

B   is the number of the trust's taxation years that end in the interest gross-up period.

Related Provisions: 248(12) — Identical properties; 257 — Formula cannot calculate to less than zero.

Notes: For the meaning of "one of the main reasons" in para. (a), see Notes to 83(2.1).

(16) Attribution to electing contributors — If at a specified time in respect of a trust for a taxation year of the trust (referred to in this subsection as the "trust's year"), there is an electing contributor in respect of the trust, the following rules apply:

(a) the electing contributor is required to include in computing their income for their taxation year (referred to in this subsection as the "contributor's year") in which the trust's year ends, the amount determined by the formula

$$A/B \times (C - D)$$

where

A   is the total of all amounts each of which is

(i) if at or before the specified time the electing contributor has made a contribution to the trust and is not a joint contributor in respect of the trust and the contribution, the amount of the contribution, or

(ii) if at or before the specified time the electing contributor has made a contribution to the trust and is a joint contributor in respect of the trust and the contribution, the amount obtained when the amount of the contribution is divided by the number of joint contributors in respect of the contribution,

B   is the total of all amounts each of which is the amount that would be determined under A for each resident contributor, or connected contributor, to the trust at the specified time if all of those contributors were electing contributors in respect of the trust,

C   is the trust's income, computed without reference to paragraph (f), for the trust's year, and

D   is the amount deducted by the trust under section 111 in computing its taxable income for the trust's year;

(b) subject to paragraph (c), the amount, if any, required by paragraph (a) to be included in the electing contributor's income for

the contributor's year is deemed to be income from property from a source in Canada;

(c) for the purposes of this paragraph, paragraph (d) and section 126, an amount in respect of the trust's income for the trust's year from a source in a country other than Canada is deemed to be income of the electing contributor for the contributor's year from that source if

(i) the amount is designated by the trust, in respect of the electing contributor, in the trust's return of income under this Part for the trust's year,

(ii) the amount may reasonably be considered (having regard to all the circumstances including the terms and conditions of the trust) to be part of the amount that because of paragraph (a) was included in computing the income of the electing contributor for the contributor's year, and

(iii) the total of all amounts designated by the trust, under this paragraph or subsection 104(22) in respect of that source, in the trust's return of income under this Part for the trust's year is not greater than the trust's income for the trust's year from that source;

(d) for the purposes of this paragraph and section 126, the electing contributor is deemed to have paid as business-income tax (in this subsection as defined by subsection 126(7)) or non-business-income tax (in this subsection as defined by subsection 126(7)), as the case may be, for the contributor's year in respect of a source the amount determined by the formula

$$A \times B/C$$

where

A   is the amount that, in the absence of subparagraph (e)(i), would be the businessincome tax or non-business-income tax, as the case may be, paid by the trust in respect of that source for the trust's year,

B   is the total of all amounts each of which is an amount designated under paragraph (c) in respect of that source by the trust in respect of the electing contributor in the trust's return of income under this Part for the trust's year, and

C   is the trust's income for the trust's year from that source;

(e) in applying subsection 20(12) and section 126 in respect of the trust's year there shall be deducted

(i) in computing the trust's income from a source for the trust's year the total of all amounts each of which is an amount deemed by paragraph (c) to be income from that source of the electing contributor for the contributor's year, and

(ii) in computing the business-income tax or non-business-income tax paid by the trust for the trust's year in respect of a source the total of all amounts in respect of that source each of which is an amount deemed by paragraph (d) to be paid by the electing contributor as business-income tax or non-business-income tax, as the case may be, in respect of that source;

(f) in computing the trust's income for the trust's year there may be deducted the amount that does not exceed the amount included by reason of paragraph (a) in the electing contributor's income for the contributor's year; and

(g) if before the specified time the electing contributor made a contribution to the trust as part of a series of transactions in which another person made the same contribution, in applying paragraphs (a) to (f) in respect of the electing contributor and the other person, the other person is deemed not to be a joint contributor in respect of the contribution if it can reasonably be considered that one of the main purposes of the series was to obtain the benefit of any deduction in computing income, taxable income or tax payable under this Act or any balance of undeducted outlays, expenses or other amounts available to the other person or any exemption available to the other person from tax payable under this Act.

Related Provisions: 257 — Formula cannot calculate to less than zero.

Notes: For meaning of "one of the main purposes" in para. (g), see Notes to 83(2.1).

(17) Liability for joint contribution — If, at or before a specified time in a trust's taxation year (referred to in this subsection as the "trust's year"), there is an electing contributor in respect of the trust who is a joint contributor in respect of a contribution to the trust,

(a) each person who is a joint contributor in respect of the contribution

(i) has, in respect of the contribution, jointly and severally, or solidarily, the rights and obligations under Divisions I and J of each other person (referred to in this subsection as the "specified person") who is, at or before the specified time, a joint contributor in respect of that contribution, for the specified person's taxation year in which the trust's year ends, and

(ii) is subject to Part XV in respect of those rights and obligations; and

(b) the maximum amount recoverable under the provisions referred to in paragraph (a) at a particular time from the person in respect of the contribution and a taxation year, of another person who is the specified person, in which the trust's year ends is the amount determined by the formula

$$A - B - C$$

where

A is the total of the amounts payable by the specified person under this Part for the specified person's taxation year in which the trust's year ends,

B is the amount that would be determined for A if the total of the amounts payable by the specified person under this Part for the particular specified person's taxation year in which the trust's year ends were computed without reference to the contribution, and

C is the amount recovered before the particular time from the specified person, and any other joint contributor in respect of the trust and the contribution, in connection with the liability of the specified person in respect of the contribution.

Related Provisions: 160(2.1) — Assessment of amount payable because of 94(7); 160(3) — Discharge of liability under 94(17); 257 — Formula cannot calculate to less than zero; *Interpretation Act* 27(5) — Meaning of "within 365 days".

Notes [s. 94]: See Notes to 94(3) for an overview of the Non-Resident Trust (NRT) rules. These rules went through 7 drafts: June 22/00, Aug. 2/01, Oct. 11/02, Oct. 30/03, July 18/05, Nov. 9/06 (Bills C-33, C-10), Aug. 27/10 and finally the Oct. 24/12 version enacted by Bill C-48, the 2002-2013 technical bill, on June 26, 2013.

For discussion see Roth et al., *Canadian Taxation of Trusts* (ctf.ca, 2016), pp. 745-838; Rusak & Charron, "Taxation of Non-Resident Trusts", chap. 25 of Vidal, *Introduction to International Tax in Canada* (Carswell, 8th ed., 2020); Murdoch, "Inbound Trusts", 2011 STEP Canada conference (contact memberservices@step.ca); Webster & Wong, "Commercial NRTs and Canadian Mutual Funds Investing in NRTs", XVIII(4) *Corporate Finance* (Federated Press) 2174-78 (2013); Schweitzer & Brodlieb, "Canadian Taxation of Income Earned and Distributed by a Subsection 94(3) Trust", 61(2) *Canadian Tax Journal [CTJ]* 461-78 (2013); Harris et al., "The Long and Winding Road", 2013 Cdn Tax Foundation conference report at 23:2-46; Megoudis, "The Canadian Non-resident Trust Rules and Global Employee Benefit Plan Trusts", 24(3) *Taxation of Executive Compensation & Retirement* (Federated Press) 1583-90 (Oct. 2012); Roth & Brown, "Non-Resident Trusts", 64(2) *CTJ* 487-508 (2016); Goldberg, "NRT Tax Traps and the Non-Specialist Advisor", 638 and 640-642 *Tax Notes* (CCH) 1-3 (March, May, June, July 2016); Perron, "Difficulties with the Quebec Non-Resident Trust Rules", 6(2) *Canadian Tax Focus* (ctf.ca) 6-7 (May 2016); Doobay, "Dual-Resident Estate", 25(10) *Canadian Tax Highlights* (ctf.ca) 4-5 (Oct. 2017); McBey, "Taxation of Non-Resident Trusts", 2480 *Tax Topics* (CCH) 1-5 (Sept. 19, 2019); Wen, "Non-Resident Trust Deemed Resident in Canada", 9(4) *Canadian Tax Focus* (ctf.ca) 11-12 (Nov. 2019).

94 replaced by 2002-2013 technical bill for tax years that end after 2006, with various in-force rules and elections to have provisions of s. 94 read differently, the last one being for trust tax years that ended before Oct. 25, 2012; as well as an election, filed by June 26, 2014, to have s. 94 apply to 2001-06 (see up to 51st ed. for all these). For the former version of 94 effective at the latest through 2006, see up to the 45th ed. However, the following portions of the in-force rules still apply to current years:

(f) in 94(1)"non-resident time", read "if the person is an individual and the trust arose on and as a consequence of the death of the individual, 18 months before the contribution time", in respect of contributions made before June 23, 2000, as

"if the contribution time is before June 23, 2000, 18 months before the end of the trust's taxation year that includes the contribution time" [this rule applied in VIEWS doc 2018-0768281I7];

. . .

(i) read 94(4)(b) in its application to a transfer by a trust that occurred before Feb. 28, 2004 as:

(b) subsections 70(6) and 73(1), paragraph 107.4(1)(c) other than subparagraph (i) of that paragraph and paragraph (a) of the definition "mutual fund trust" in subsection 132(6);

(j) read 94(4)(f) in its application to a transfer by a trust that occurred before Feb. 28, 2004 as:

(f) determining the residency of the transferee in applying subparagraph (f)(ii) of the definition "disposition" in subsection 248(1);

(k) read 94(2)(o) in its application to a transfer that occurred before Aug. 27, 2010 as:

(o) a contribution made at any time by a particular partnership to a trust is deemed to have been made at that time jointly by the particular partnership and by each person or partnership that is at that time a member of the particular partnership (other than a member of the particular partnership if the liability of the member as a member of the particular partnership is limited by operation of any law governing the partnership arrangement).

Former 94(1) applied to Barbados trusts in *Garron [St. Michael Trust]*, 2010 FCA 309 (aff'd on other grounds as *Fundy Settlement*, 2012 SCC 14), paras. 79-80: the words "acquired property directly or indirectly in any manner whatever" in 94(1)(b) apply to indirect shareholdings through holding companies; but the Canada-Barbados treaty (CBBT) exemption overrode s. 94 (para. 81). In *Morris (RCI Trust)*, 2009 FCA 373 (leave to appeal denied 2010 CarswellNat 1311 (SCC)), the FC had held that 94(1) did not apply because the CBBT took precedence, but the FCA ruled that the FC had no jurisdiction to address the issue (really about s. 116 liability), which should be brought to the Tax Court.

Deductions for contributions to an offshore "health and welfare" trust for select employees were denied in *Labow*, 2011 FCA 305; see Notes to 18(1)(a).

94(1) amended by 2001 technical bill, 1996 Budget and 1991 technical bill.

Definitions [s. 94]: "acquired for consideration" — 108(7); "adult beneficiary" — 94(1)"exempt foreign trust"(b)(i)(B); "affiliated" — 251.1; "allowable capital loss" — 38(b), 248(1); "amount" — 248(1); "arm's length" — 251(1); "arm's length transfer" — 94(1); "aunt" — 252(2)(e); "beneficially interested" — 248(25); "beneficiary" — 94(1), 248(25) [Notes]; "business" — 248(1); "business-income tax" — 126(7); "calendar year" — *Interpretation Act* 37(1)(a); "Canada" — 255, *Interpretation Act* 35(1); "Canadian corporation" — 89(1), 248(1); "child" — 252(1); "child beneficiary" — 94(1)"exempt foreign trust"(b)(i)(A); "class of shares" — 248(6); "closely held corporation" — 94(1); "common-law partner", "common-law partnership" — 248(1); "connected contributor" — 94(1), 94(13)(b); "consequence of the death" — 248(8); "contribution" — 94(1); "contributor" — 94(1), 94(13)(a); "controlled foreign affiliate" — 95(1), 248(1); "corporation" — 248(1), *Interpretation Act* 35(1); "cost amount" — 248(1); "designated stock exchange" — 248(1), 262; "disposition", "dividend" — 248(1); "electing contributor", "electing trust" — 94(1); "employee", "employee benefit plan" — 248(1); "employees profit sharing plan" — 144(1), 248(1); "employer", "employment" — 248(1); "estate" — 104(1), 248(1); "exempt amount", "exempt foreign trust", "exempt person", "exempt service" — 94(1); "fair market value" — see 69(1) Notes; "filing-due date" — 248(1); "fiscal period" — 249.1; "fixed interest" — 94(1); "foreign affiliate" — 95(1), 248(1); "foreign retirement arrangement" — 248(1), Reg 6803; "Her Majesty" — *Interpretation Act* 35(1); "identical" — 248(12); "income from property" — 95(1); "individual" — 248(1); "inter vivos trust" — 108(1), 248(1); "interest gross-up period" — 94(15)(c)(ii)C; "joint contributor" — 94(1); "majority-interest partner", "Minister" — 248(1); "month" — *Interpretation Act* 35(1); "mutual fund" — 94(1); "mutual fund corporation" — 131(8), 248(1); "mutual fund trust" — 132(6)–(7), 132.2(3)(n), 248(1); "nephew", "niece" — 252(2)(g); "non-business-income tax" — 126(7); "non-resident" — 248(1); "non-resident portion" — 94(1); "non-resident portion trust" — 94(3)(f)(i); "non-resident time" — 94(1); "original trust" — 94(11)(a); "paid-up capital" — 89(1), 248(1); "Parliament" — *Interpretation Act* 35(1); "partnership" — see 96(1) Notes; "person", "personal trust", "prescribed" — 248(1); "principal amount" — 248(1), (26); "promoter" — 94(1); "property" — 248(1); "province" — *Interpretation Act* 35(1); "qualified disability trust" — 122(3); "qualifying services" — 94(1); "recipient" — 94(1)"arm's length transfer", 94(1)"exempt service"; "recovery limit" — 94(8); "regulation" — 248(1); "related" — 251(2)–(6); "resident" — 250; "resident beneficiary", "resident contributor" — 94(1); "resident in Canada" — 94(3)(a), 250; "resident portion" — 94(1); "restricted property" — 94(1), (14); "retirement compensation arrangement" — 248(1); "series of transactions" — 248(10); "share", "shareholder", "specified financial institution" — 248(1); "specified party", "specified share", "specified time" — 94(1); "substituted" — 248(5); "successor beneficiary" — 94(1); "superannuation or pension benefit" — 248(1); "taxable capital gain" — 38(a), 248(1); "taxable income", "taxable income earned in Canada" — 248(1); "taxation year" — 95(1), 249; "taxpayer" — 248(1); "transaction" — 94(1); "transfer time" — 94(1)"arm's length transfer"; "transferee trust"; "transferor" — 94(11)(a); "transferor" — 94(1)"arm's length transfer"; "trust" — 94(1); "uncle" — 252(2)(e); "United States" — *Interpretation Act* 35(1); "writing", "written" — *Interpretation Act* 35(1)"writing".

Interpretation Bulletins [s. 94]: IT-451R: Deemed disposition and acquisition on ceasing to be or becoming resident in Canada.

94.1 (1) Offshore investment fund property — If in a taxation year a taxpayer holds or has an interest in property (referred to in this section as an "offshore investment fund property")

(a) that is a share of the capital stock of, an interest in, or a debt of, a non-resident entity (other than a controlled foreign affiliate of the taxpayer or a prescribed non-resident entity) or an interest in or a right or option to acquire such a share, interest or debt, and

(b) that may reasonably be considered to derive its value, directly or indirectly, primarily from portfolio investments of that or any other non-resident entity in

(i) shares of the capital stock of one or more corporations,

(ii) indebtedness or annuities,

(iii) interests in one or more corporations, trusts, partnerships, organizations, funds or entities,

(iv) commodities,

(v) real estate,

(vi) Canadian or foreign resource properties,

(vii) currency of a country other than Canada,

(viii) rights or options to acquire or dispose of any of the foregoing, or

(ix) any combination of the foregoing,

and it may reasonably be concluded, having regard to all the circumstances, including

(c) the nature, organization and operation of any non-resident entity and the form of, and the terms and conditions governing, the taxpayer's interest in, or connection with, any non-resident entity,

(d) the extent to which any income, profits and gains that may reasonably be considered to be earned or accrued, whether directly or indirectly, for the benefit of any non-resident entity are subject to an income or profits tax that is significantly less than the income tax that would be applicable to such income, profits and gains if they were earned directly by the taxpayer, and

(e) the extent to which the income, profits and gains of any non-resident entity for any fiscal period are distributed in that or the immediately following fiscal period,

that one of the main reasons for the taxpayer acquiring, holding or having the interest in such property was to derive a benefit from portfolio investments in assets described in any of subparagraphs (b)(i) to (ix) in such a manner that the taxes, if any, on the income, profits and gains from such assets for any particular year are significantly less than the tax that would have been applicable under this Part if the income, profits and gains had been earned directly by the taxpayer, there shall be included in computing the taxpayer's income for the year the amount, if any, by which

(f) the total of all amounts each of which is the product obtained when

(i) the designated cost to the taxpayer of the offshore investment fund property at the end of a month in the year

is multiplied by

(ii) $\frac{1}{12}$ of the total of

(A) the prescribed rate of interest for the period that includes that month, and

(B) two per cent

exceeds

(g) the taxpayer's income for the year (other than a capital gain) from the offshore investment fund property determined without reference to this subsection.

Related Provisions: 53(1)(m) — Addition to ACB; 87(2)(j.95) — Amalgamation — continuing corporation; 94(3)(a) — Certain non-resident trusts treated as resident in Canada for certain purposes; 94.2(2) — Trust deemed to be corporation for purposes of

94.1(1)(a) so 94.2 takes priority if both apply; 95(1)"foreign accrual property income"C — Application to determination of FAPI; 152(4)(b)(vii) — Three-year extension to reassessment deadline; 261(5)(f)(ii) — Functional currency reporting — meaning of "currency of a country other than Canada".

Notes: With the abandonment of the "Foreign Investment Entity" (FIE) rules in former proposed 94.1–94.4 (proposed and revised from 2000-2010 — see transitional rules at end of 94.2), existing 94.1 remains. See Roth et al., *Canadian Taxation of Trusts* (ctf.ca, 2016), pp. 838-852; Wiener, "Foreign Investment Entities: Unresolved Issues", 1987 *Tax Topics* (CCH) 1-8 (April 8, 2010); Tamaki, "Section 94.1 and Non-Resident Trusts", 2010 Cdn Tax Foundation conference report, 17:1-27; Harris, "Offshore Investment Fund Property", 9(2) *Tax Hyperion* (Carswell, Feb. 2012); Harris & Webel, "Offshore Funds and Non-Resident Trusts", 2013 STEP Canada conference (contact memberservices@step.ca), slides 2-11; Harris, Munro & Ross, "The Long and Winding Road; Sections 94, 94.1 and 94.2", 2013 conference report at 23:48-50; Raveendran & Navkar, "The Rise of Crypto Funds and the Offshore Investment Rules", 27(12) *Canadian Tax Highlights* (ctf.ca) 13-15 (Dec. 2019).

In *Walton*, [1999] 1 C.T.C. 2105 (TCC), 94.1(1) applied to funds placed in a Bermuda investment company pending use in a business venture which did not materialize.

In *Barejo Holdings*, 2015 TCC 274, foreign equity-linked notes with undefined principal were held to be "debt", but 2016 FCA 304 (leave to appeal denied 2017 CarswellNat 2765 (SCC)) held that the TCC's general discussion of "debt" did not apply to 94.1(1), and refused to hear an appeal, saying it was irrelevant. 2018 TCC 200, aff'd 2020 FCA 47 (leave to appeal denied 2020 CarswellNat 4099), gave the same answer for purposes of 94.1(1)(a). It was reasonable for CRA to apply 94.1 to the same notes in *Ludmer*, 2018 QCCS 3381, paras. 71, 218, 358-385; aff'd 2020 QCCA 697, paras. 75-81 (leave to appeal denied 2021 CarswellQue 2160 (SCC)). (The same dispute included *3488063 Canada*, 2016 FCA 233 (procedural issues).) See also Gurmukh & Davis, "Guidance on What is a Debt", XXIV(2) *International Tax Planning* (Federated Press) 2-9 (2020).

In *Gerbro Holdings*, 2018 FCA 197, 94.1(1) did not apply because tax deferral was not "one of the main reasons" for choosing offshore hedge fund investments: "the business reasons overshadowed any tax benefit obtained incidentally" (TCC para. 199). See Carl Irvine case comment, 64(4) *Canadian Tax Journal* 825-31 (2016).

See also VIEWS docs 2009-034286I7 (whether investment in foreign affiliate that carries on active business can be portfolio investment); 2013-0485311C6 [2013 IFA q.1] (94.1 can apply to offshore mutual fund).

For the meaning of "income or profits tax" in para. (d), see Notes to 126(4). For "indirectly" in para. (d), see Notes to 17.1(1). For "one of the main reasons" after para. (e), see Notes to 83(2.1).

The Aug. 27/10 draft proposed to amend 94.1(1)(a) to exclude a trust under 94.2. This was dropped in the amendments introduced on Oct. 24/12 and enacted in 2013.

Note also the reporting rules in 233.2–233.7.

94.1(1) amended by 2002-2013 technical bill: "other than a non-resident-owned investment corporation" deleted from opening words (after "a taxpayer"); and (f)(ii) changed from "the quotient obtained when the prescribed rate of interest for the period including that month is divided by 12"; both changes effective for tax years that end after March 4, 2010, and also for each tax year of a beneficiary under a trust that ends before March 5, 2010, if amended 94(1) (see Notes at end of s. 94) applies to the trust for a tax year of the trust that ends in that earlier taxation year of the beneficiary.

See Notes at end of 94.2 for transitional rules for taxpayers who followed the Foreign Investment Entity (FIE) rules in proposed 94.1-94.4 that were never enacted.

Regulations: 4301(c) (prescribed rate of interest for 94.1(1)(f)(ii)); to date, no prescribed non-resident entities prescribed for 94.1(1)(a).

Interpretation Bulletins: IT-451R: Deemed disposition and acquisition on ceasing to be or becoming resident in Canada.

(2) Definitions — In this section,

"designated cost" to a taxpayer at any time in a taxation year of an offshore investment fund property that the taxpayer holds or has an interest in means the amount determined by the formula

$$A + B + C + D$$

where

A is the cost amount to the taxpayer of the property at that time (determined without reference to paragraphs 53(1)(m) and (q), subparagraph 53(2)(c)(i.3), paragraphs 53(2)(g) and (g.1) and section 143.2),

B is, where an additional amount has been made available by a person to another person after 1984 and before that time, whether by way of gift, loan, payment for a share, transfer of property at less than its fair market value or otherwise, in circumstances such that it may reasonably be concluded that one of the main reasons for so making the additional amount available to the other person was to increase the value of the property, the total of all amounts each of which is the amount, if any, by which such an additional amount exceeds any increase in the cost amount to the taxpayer of the property by virtue of that additional amount,

C   is the total of all amounts each of which is an amount included in respect of the offshore investment fund property by virtue of this section in computing the taxpayer's income for a preceding taxation year, and

D   is

(a) where the taxpayer has held or has had the interest in the property at all times since the end of 1984, the amount, if any, by which the fair market value of the property at the end of 1984 exceeds the cost amount to the taxpayer of the property at the end of 1984, or

(b) in any other case, the total of

(i) the amount, if any, by which the fair market value of the property at the particular time the taxpayer acquired the property exceeds the cost amount to the taxpayer of the property at the particular time, and

(ii) the amount, if any, by which

(A) the total of all amounts each of which is an amount that would have been included in respect of the property because of this section in computing the taxpayer's income for a taxation year that began before June 20, 1996 if the cost to the taxpayer of the property were equal to the fair market value of the property at the particular time

exceeds

(B) the total of all amounts each of which is an amount that was included in respect of the property because of this section in computing the taxpayer's income for a taxation year that began before June 20, 1996,

except that the designated cost of an offshore investment fund property that is a prescribed offshore investment fund property is nil;

Related Provisions: 94.1(3) — Pre-Feb. 15/84 property.

Notes: For the meaning of "one of the main reasons" in B, see Notes to 83(2.1).

Definition amended by 1995-97 technical bill, last change effective for tax years that begin after June 20, 1996. 94.1(2)"designated cost" was 94.1(2)(a) before RSC 1985 (5th Supp) consolidation for tax years ending after Nov. 1991.

Regulations: 6900 (prescribed offshore investment fund property).

"non-resident entity" at any time means

(a) a corporation that is at that time non-resident,

(b) a partnership, organization, fund or entity that is at that time non-resident or is not at that time situated in Canada, or

(c) an exempt foreign trust (other than a trust described in any of paragraphs (a) to (g) of the definition "exempt foreign trust" in subsection 94(1)).

Notes: This version is different from the Aug. 27/10 draft (see Notes at end of s. 94), which neglected to exclude immigration trusts and various other exempt foreign trusts.

Definition amended by 2002-2013 technical bill, effective on same basis as the amendments to 94.1(1). 94.1(2)"non-resident entity" was 94.1(2)(b) before RSC 1985 (5th Supp) consolidation for tax years ending after Nov. 1991.

(3) Interpretation — Where subsection (1) is applied with respect to an offshore investment fund property that was

(a) held by the taxpayer on February 15, 1984,

(b) received as a stock dividend in respect of a share of the capital stock of a non-resident entity held by the taxpayer on February 15, 1984,

(c) received as a stock dividend in respect of a share of the capital stock of a non-resident entity that the taxpayer had previously received as described in paragraph (b), or

(d) substituted for a property held by the taxpayer on February 15, 1984 pursuant to an arrangement that existed on that date,

the reference to "1984" in the descriptions of B and D in the definition "designated cost" in subsection (2) shall be read as a reference to "1985".

Definitions [s. 94.1]: "amount", "annuity" — 248(1); "Canada" — 255, *Interpretation Act* 35(1); "capital gain" — 39(1)(a), 248(1); "controlled foreign affiliate" — 95(1), 248(1); "corporation" — 248(1), *Interpretation Act* 35(1); "cost amount" — 248(1); "currency of a country other than Canada" — 261(5)(f)(ii); "designated cost" — 94.1(2); "exempt foreign trust" — 94(1); "fair market value" — see 69(1) Notes; "fiscal period" — 249(2), 249.1; "foreign affiliate" — 95(1), 248(1); "foreign resource property" — 66(15), 248(1); "immovable" — Quebec *Civil Code* art. 900–907; "income or profits tax" — 126(4); "investment corporation" — 130(3), 248(1); "month" — *Interpretation Act* 35(1); "non-resident" — 248(1); "non-resident entity" — 94.1(2); "offshore investment fund property" — 94.1(1); "partnership" — see 96(1) Notes; "prescribed" — 248(1); "prescribed rate" — Reg. 4301; "property" — 248(1); "qualifying interest" — 95(2)(m); "resident", "resident in Canada" — 250; "share" — 248(1); "substituted" — 248(5); "taxation year" — 95(1), 249; "taxpayer" — 248(1); "trust" — 104(1), 248(1), (3).

94.2 (1) Investments in non-resident commercial trusts — Subsection (2) applies to a beneficiary under a trust, and to any particular person of which any such beneficiary is a controlled foreign affiliate, at any time if

(a) the trust is at that time an exempt foreign trust (other than a trust described in any of paragraphs (a) to (g) of the definition "exempt foreign trust" in subsection 94(1));

(b) either

(i) the total fair market value at that time of all fixed interests of a particular class in the trust held by the beneficiary, persons or partnerships not dealing at arm's length with the beneficiary, or persons or partnerships that acquired their interests in the trust in exchange for consideration given to the trust by the beneficiary, is at least 10% of the total fair market value at that time of all fixed interests of the particular class, or

(ii) the beneficiary or the particular person has at or before that time contributed restricted property to the trust; and

(c) the beneficiary is at that time a

(i) resident beneficiary,

(ii) mutual fund,

(iii) controlled foreign affiliate of the particular person, or

(iv) partnership of which a person described in any of subparagraphs (i) to (iii) is a member.

Related Provisions: 87(2)(j.95) — Amalgamation — continuing corporation; 93.3(1)(b), 93.3(3)(e) — Special regime for certain Australian trusts; 94(1) — Definitions apply to 94.2; 94(2) — Rules of application apply to 94.2.

Notes: See Notes to 94.2(2).

94.2(1) opening words amended by 2014 budget bill #2, effective on the same basis as the amendment to 94(1)"connected contributor", to delete "(other than an individual described in paragraph (a) of the definition "connected contributor" in subsection 94(1))" after "particular person".

Income Tax Folios: S5-F3-C1: Taxation of a Roth IRA.

(2) Deemed corporation — If this subsection applies at any time to a beneficiary under, or a particular person in respect of, a trust, then for the purposes of applying this section, subsections 91(1) to (4), paragraph 94.1(1)(a) and sections 95 and 233.4 to the beneficiary under, and, if applicable, to the particular person in respect of, the trust

(a) the trust is deemed to be at that time a non-resident corporation

(i) controlled by each of the beneficiary and the particular person, and

(ii) having, for each particular class of fixed interests in the trust, a separate class of capital stock of 100 issued shares that have the same attributes as the interests of the particular class; and

(b) each beneficiary under the trust is deemed to hold at that time the number of shares of each separate class described in subparagraph (a)(ii) equal to the proportion of 100 that the fair market value at that time of that beneficiary's fixed interests in the corresponding particular class of fixed interests in the trust is of the fair market value at that time of all fixed interests in the particular class.

Related Provisions: 87(2)(j.95) — Amalgamation — continuing corporation; 94(1) — Definitions apply to 94.2 94(2) — Rules of application apply to 94.2; 94.1(1)(a) — Offshore investment fund rules do not apply if 94.2 applies; 94.2(1) — Conditions for 94.2(2) to apply; 94.2(3) — Relief from double tax; 94.2(4) — Effect of not providing information to CRA; 152(4)(b)(vii) — Three-year extension to reassessment deadline.

Notes: 94.2(1) and (2) are totally changed from the Aug. 27/10 draft (see Notes at end of s. 94), but have the same general effect of triggering FAPI on the trust's income.

If the deemed corporation is deemed controlled by a financial institution, it is subject to the mark-to-market and related rules in 142.2-142.6 and required by 95(2)(f.14) to determine FAPI using Canadian currency: VIEWS doc 2013-0475421E5.

See Harris, Munro & Ross, "The Long and Winding Road; Sections 94, 94.1 and 94.2", 2013 Cdn Tax Foundation conference report at 23:47-48.

(3) Relief from double tax — For the purposes of applying subsection 91(1) to the beneficiary, and, if applicable, to the particular person, to whom subsection (2) applies

(a) there may be deducted in computing the foreign accrual property income of the trust referred to in paragraph (2)(a) (in this subsection referred to as the "entity") for a particular taxation year of the entity the amount that would, in the absence of this paragraph, be the portion of the entity's foreign accrual property income that would reasonably be considered to have been if this Part were applicable to all beneficiaries of the entity, included under subsection 104(13) in computing the income of any beneficiary of the entity for the taxation year in which the particular taxation year of the entity ends; and

(b) subsection 5904(2) of the *Income Tax Regulations* is to be read without reference to its paragraph (a) in determining the distribution entitlement of all the shares of a class of the capital stock of the entity at the end of the particular taxation year.

Related Provisions: 87(2)(j.95) — Amalgamation — continuing corporation; 94.2(4) — Effect of not providing information to Minister.

(4) Request for information — If the Minister sends a written request, served personally or by registered mail, to a taxpayer requesting additional information for the purpose of enabling the Minister to determine the fair market value of interests in a trust for the purpose of determining the application of subsections (1) to (3) for a taxation year to the taxpayer, and information that may reasonably be considered to be sufficient to make the determination is not received by the Minister within 120 days (or within any longer period that is acceptable to the Minister) after the Minister sends the request, then in applying this section for the taxation year to the taxpayer the fair market value of those interests is deemed to be the fair market value as reasonably determined by the Minister based on the information received by the Minister within 120 days (or within any longer period that is acceptable to the Minister) after the Minister sends the request and any other information the Minister considers reasonable.

Related Provisions: *Interpretation Act* 27(5) — Meaning of "within 120 days".

Notes [s. 94.2]: 94.2 added by 2002-2013 technical bill (Part 1 — NRTs), effective for taxation years that end after March 4, 2010, except that for taxation years that end before Oct. 24, 2012, read 94.2(1)(c) as "the beneficiary is at that time a resident beneficiary or a mutual fund"; and if amended 94(1) applies to a trust for a taxation year that ends before March 5, 2010 (see Notes at end of s. 94), then 94.2 applies to each beneficiary under the trust, and to each person of which a beneficiary under the trust is a controlled foreign affiliate, for a taxation year of the beneficiary or person in which the earlier taxation year of the trust ends and reads differently for those pre-March 5, 2010 years (for that version see PITA 44th-47th ed.).

Transitional rules for taxpayers that complied with former proposed 94.1-94.4

Proposed 94.1 to 94.4 would have introduced a complex set of rules for Foreign Investment Entities (FIEs), released together with the first five drafts of the non-resident trust rules (see Notes at end of s. 94). The FIE rules originally would have been in force from 2001. They were dropped on March 4, 2010 after extensive objections to their complexity. Transitional rules are provided for taxpayers who voluntary complied with these never-enacted rules. Clauses 8(5)-(10) of the 2002-2013 technical bill provide these rules, which apply (by election) to taxation years that ended before March 5, 2010. They are reproduced in PITA 44th-47th ed.

In *Ludmer*, 2018 QCCS 3381, paras. 227, 466-516, 702; aff'd 2020 QCCA 697, CRA gave the taxpayers the benefit of the transitional rules, but only after years of proposing

not to, and was liable for damages as a result (leave to appeal denied 2021 Carswell-Que 2160 (SCC)).

Definitions [s. 94.2]: "amount" — 248(1); "arm's length" — 251(1); "beneficiary" — 248(25) [Notes]; "connected contributor" — 94(1); "controlled foreign affiliate" — 95(1), 248(1); "corporation" — 94.2(2), 248(1), *Interpretation Act* 35(1); "entity" — 94.2(3); "exempt foreign trust" — 94(1); "fair market value" — see 69(1) Notes; "fixed interest" — 94(1); "foreign accrual property income" — 95(1); "individual", "Minister" — 248(1); "mutual fund" — 94(1); "non-resident" — 248(1); "partnership" — see 96(1) Notes; "person", "property" — 248(1); "resident" — 250; "resident beneficiary", "restricted property" — 94(1); "share" — 248(1); "taxation year" — 95(1), 249; "taxpayer" — 248(1); "trust" — 104(1), 248(1), (3); "written" — *Interpretation Act* 35(1)"writing".

95. (1) Definitions for this Subdivision — In this Subdivision,

Notes: This subdivision is sections 90-95.

"active business" of a foreign affiliate of a taxpayer means any business carried on by the foreign affiliate other than

(a) an investment business carried on by the foreign affiliate,

(b) a business that is deemed by subsection (2) to be a business other than an active business carried on by the foreign affiliate, or

(c) a non-qualifying business of the foreign affiliate;

Related Provisions: 95(1)"income from an active business" — What income included; 248(1) — Meanings of "active business" and "business".

Notes: Definition amended by 2007 budget bill #2 (for foreign affiliates' tax years that begin after 2008), 1994 technical bill.

"antecedent corporation" of a particular corporation means

(a) a predecessor corporation (within the meaning assigned by subsection 87(1)) in respect of an amalgamation to which subsection 87(11) applied and by which the particular corporation was formed,

(b) a predecessor corporation (within the meaning of subsection 87(1)) of the corporation (referred to in this definition as the "first amalco") that was formed on an amalgamation of the predecessor corporation and another corporation, where

(i) shares of the capital stock of the predecessor corporation that were not owned by the other corporation, or by a corporation of which the other corporation is a subsidiary wholly-owned corporation, were exchanged on the amalgamation for shares of the capital stock of the first amalco that were, during the series of transactions or events that includes the amalgamation, redeemed, acquired or cancelled by the first amalco for money,

(ii) the first amalco was a predecessor corporation (within the meaning assigned by subsection 87(1)) in respect of an amalgamation to which subsection 87(11) applied and by which the particular corporation was formed, and

(iii) the amalgamation referred to in subparagraph (i) occurred in a series of transactions or events that included the amalgamation referred to in subparagraph (ii),

(c) a corporation that was wound-up into the particular corporation in a winding-up to which subsection 88(1) applied, or

(d) an antecedent corporation of an antecedent corporation of the particular corporation;

Related Provisions: 248(10) — Series of transactions or events.

Notes: Para. (b) was not in the Nov. 28/08 draft; paras. (c)-(d) were (b)-(c) there.

95(1)"antecedent corporation" added by 2008 budget bill #2, last change effective for foreign affiliates' tax years that begin after Oct. 2, 2007.

"calculating currency" for a taxation year of a foreign affiliate of a taxpayer means

(a) the currency of the country in which the foreign affiliate is resident at the end of the taxation year, or

(b) any currency that the taxpayer demonstrates to be reasonable in the circumstances;

Related Provisions: 261 — Functional currency reporting.

Notes: 95(1)"calculating currency" added by 2008 budget bill #2, last change effective for foreign affiliates' tax years that begin after Oct. 2, 2007.

Definitions **"calculating currency exchange rate"** and **"Canadian currency exchange rate"** were proposed in Oct. 2/07 draft legislation, but deleted when it became 2007 budget bill #2. The Nov. 21/07 Technical Notes say this was due to withdrawal of 95(2)(f)-(f.2) "for further consideration in response to submissions received". The 2008 legislation replacing them with 95(2)(f)-(f.15) did not include these terms.

"controlled foreign affiliate", at any time, of a taxpayer resident in Canada, means

(a) a foreign affiliate of the taxpayer that is, at that time, controlled by the taxpayer, or

(b) a foreign affiliate of the taxpayer that would, at that time, be controlled by the taxpayer if the taxpayer owned

(i) all of the shares of the capital stock of the foreign affiliate that are owned at that time by the taxpayer,

(ii) all of the shares of the capital stock of the foreign affiliate that are owned at that time by persons who do not deal at arm's length with the taxpayer,

(iii) all of the shares of the capital stock of the foreign affiliate that are owned at that time by the persons (each of whom is referred to in this definition as a "relevant Canadian shareholder"), in any set of persons not exceeding four (which set of persons shall be determined without reference to the existence of or the absence of any relationship, connection or action in concert between those persons), who

(A) are resident in Canada,

(B) are not the taxpayer or a person described in subparagraph (ii), and

(C) own, at that time, shares of the capital stock of the foreign affiliate, and

(iv) all of the shares of the capital stock of the foreign affiliate that are owned at that time by persons who do not deal at arm's length with any relevant Canadian shareholder;

Related Provisions: 17(15)"controlled foreign affiliate" — Application of definition to loan by corp to non-resident; 94.2(2) — Non-resident trust deemed to be CFA for certain purposes; 94(3)(a)(x) — Application to trust deemed resident in Canada; 95(2.01), (2.02) — Shares held through holding companies, partnerships and trusts; 95(12) — Deemed CFA where tracking arrangement used; 128.1(1)(d) — Foreign affiliate becoming resident in Canada deemed to have been CFA; 233.4(4) — Reporting requirements; 248(1)"controlled foreign affiliate" — Definition applies to entire Act; 256(6), (6.1) — Meaning of "controlled"; Canada-U.S. Tax Treaty:Art. XXIX:5(a) — US "S" corp may be deemed to be CFA.

Notes: Para. (b) overrides *Silicon Graphics*, 2002 FCA 260, where dispersed non-resident ownership was not "control" for 125(7)"Canadian-controlled private corporation".

For interpretation see VIEWS doc 2007-0247551E5.

Definition amended by 2007 budget bill #2, last change effective for foreign affiliates' tax years that begin after Feb. 27, 2004. Earlier amended by 1991 technical bill. 95(1)"controlled foreign affiliate" was 95(1)(a) before RSC 1985 (5th Supp) consolidation for tax years ending after Nov. 1991.

"designated acquired corporation" of a taxpayer means a particular antecedent corporation of the taxpayer if

(a) the taxpayer or another antecedent corporation of the taxpayer acquired control of

(i) the particular antecedent corporation, or

(ii) a corporation (referred to in this definition as a "successor corporation") of which the particular antecedent corporation is an antecedent corporation, and

(b) immediately before the acquisition of control or a series of transactions or events that includes the acquisition of control, the taxpayer, the other antecedent corporation or a corporation resident in Canada of which the taxpayer or the other antecedent corporation is a subsidiary wholly-owned corporation, as the case may be, dealt at arm's length (otherwise than because of a right referred to in paragraph 251(5)(b)) with the particular antecedent corporation or the successor corporation, as the case may be;

Related Provisions: 248(10) — Series of transactions or events.

Notes: Definition added by 2008 budget bill #2, last change effective for foreign affiliates' tax years that begin after Oct. 2, 2007.

"designated liquidation and dissolution", of a foreign affiliate (referred to in this definition as the "disposing affiliate") of a taxpayer, means a liquidation and dissolution of the disposing affiliate in respect of which

(a) the taxpayer had, immediately before the time of the earliest distribution of property by the disposing affiliate in the course of the liquidation and dissolution, a surplus entitlement percentage in respect of the disposing affiliate of not less than 90%,

(b) both

(i) the percentage determined by the following formula is greater than or equal to 90%:

$$A/B$$

where

A is the amount, if any, by which

(A) the total of all amounts each of which is the fair market value, at the time at which it is distributed, of a property that is distributed by the disposing affiliate, in respect of shares of the capital stock of the disposing affiliate, in the course of the liquidation and dissolution to one particular shareholder of the disposing affiliate that was, immediately before the time of the distribution, a foreign affiliate of the taxpayer

exceeds

(B) the total of all amounts each of which is an amount owing (other than an unpaid dividend) by, or an obligation of, the disposing affiliate that was assumed or cancelled by the particular shareholder in consideration for a property referred to in clause (A), and

B is the amount, if any, by which

(A) the total of all amounts each of which is the fair market value, at the time at which it is distributed, of a property that is distributed by the disposing affiliate, in respect of shares of the capital stock of the disposing affiliate, to a shareholder of the disposing affiliate in the course of the liquidation and dissolution

exceeds

(B) the total of all amounts each of which is an amount owing (other than an unpaid dividend) by, or an obligation of, the disposing affiliate that was assumed or cancelled by a shareholder of the disposing affiliate in consideration for a property referred to in clause (A), and

(ii) at the time of each distribution of property by the disposing affiliate in the course of the liquidation and dissolution in respect of shares of the capital stock of the disposing affiliate, the particular shareholder holds shares of that capital stock that would, if an annual general meeting of the shareholders of the disposing affiliate were held at that time, entitle it to 90% or more of the votes that could be cast under all circumstances at the meeting, or

(c) one particular shareholder of the disposing affiliate that was, throughout the liquidation and dissolution, a foreign affiliate of the taxpayer owns not less than 90% of the issued shares of each class of the capital stock of the disposing affiliate throughout the liquidation and dissolution;

Related Provisions: 13(21.2)(e)(iii)(E)(I)2, 18(15)(b)(iv)(A)(II), 40(3.4)(b)(v)(A)(II), 40(3.5)(c)(iii) — DLAD excluded from pregnant-loss rules; 95(2)(e) — Liquidation and dissolution of foreign affiliate.

Notes: Definition added by 2002-2013 technical bill, effective (with amended 95(2)(e) and repeal of 95(2)(e.1)) for foreign affiliate liquidations and dissolutions that begin after Aug. 19, 2011, with an election to apply earlier.

A definition **"designated taxable Canadian property"** was proposed in Oct. 2/07 draft legislation, but deleted when it became 2007 budget bill #2. The Nov. 21/07 Technical Notes say this was due to withdrawal of 95(2)(f)-(f.2) "for further consideration in response to submissions received". The 2008 legislation replacing them with 95(2)(f)-(f.15) did not include the term.

"eligible trust", at any time, means a trust, other than a trust

(a) created or maintained for charitable purposes,

(b) governed by an employee benefit plan,

(c) described in paragraph (a.1) of the definition "trust" in subsection 108(1),

(d) governed by a salary deferral arrangement,

(e) operated for the purpose of administering or providing superannuation, pension, retirement or employee benefits, or

(f) where the amount of income or capital that any entity may receive directly from the trust at any time as a beneficiary under the trust depends on the exercise by any entity of, or the failure by any entity to exercise, a discretionary power;

Notes: Definition added by 2007 budget bill #2, effective Feb. 28, 2004.

"entity" includes an association, a corporation, a fund, a natural person, a joint venture, an organization, a partnership, a syndicate and a trust;

Notes: See Notes to 188.1(5) re meaning of "includes".

95(1)"entity" added by 2007 budget bill #2, for foreign affiliates' tax years that begin after 1994.

"excluded property", at a particular time, of a foreign affiliate of a taxpayer means any property of the foreign affiliate that is

(a) used or held by the foreign affiliate principally for the purpose of gaining or producing income from an active business carried on by it,

(b) shares of the capital stock of another foreign affiliate of the taxpayer where all or substantially all of the fair market value of the property of the other foreign affiliate is attributable to property, of that other foreign affiliate, that is excluded property,

(c) property all or substantially all of the income from which is, or would be, if there were income from the property, income from an active business (which, for this purpose, includes income that would be deemed to be income from an active business by paragraph (2)(a) if that paragraph were read without reference to subparagraph (v)), or

(c.1) property arising under or as a result of an agreement that

(i) provides for the purchase, sale or exchange of currency, and

(ii) either

(A) can reasonably be considered to have been made by the affiliate to reduce its risk, with respect to an amount that was receivable under an agreement that relates to the sale of excluded property or with respect to an amount that was receivable and was a property described in paragraph (c), of fluctuations in the value of the currency in which the amount receivable was denominated, or

(B) can reasonably be considered to have been made by the affiliate to reduce its risk, with respect to any of the following amounts, of fluctuations in the value of the currency in which that amount was denominated:

(I) an amount that was payable under an agreement that relates to the purchase of property that (at all times between the time of the acquisition of the property and the particular time) is excluded property of the affiliate,

(II) an amount of indebtedness, to the extent that the proceeds derived from the issuance or incurring of the indebtedness can reasonably be considered to have been used to acquire property that (at all times between the time of the acquisition of that property and the particular time) is excluded property of the affiliate, or

(III) an amount of indebtedness, to the extent that the proceeds derived from the issuance or incurring of the indebtedness can reasonably be considered to have been used to repay the outstanding balance of

1. an amount that, immediately before the time of that repayment, is described by subclause (I),

2. an amount of indebtedness of the affiliate that, immediately before the time of that repayment, is described by subclause (II), or

3. an amount of indebtedness of the affiliate that, immediately before the time of that repayment, is described by this subclause,

and, for the purposes of the definitions "foreign affiliate" in this subsection and "direct equity percentage" in subsection (4) as they apply to this definition, where at any time a foreign affiliate of a taxpayer has an interest in a partnership,

(d) the partnership shall be deemed to be a non-resident corporation having capital stock of a single class divided into 100 issued shares, and

(e) the affiliate shall be deemed to own at that time that proportion of the issued shares of that class that

(i) the fair market value of the affiliate's interest in the partnership at that time

is of

(ii) the fair market value of all interests in the partnership at that time;

Related Provisions: 85.1(4)(a) — Exception to share-for-share exchange rules where foreign affiliate's property is substantially all excluded property; 95(2.45)(b) — Banks — treatment of upstream deposit by eligible bank affiliate where election made under 95(2.44); Reg. 5907(5.1) — Rules on disposition of excluded property by FA.

Notes: "Excluded property" (EP) is relevant in computing FAPI and tax surpluses and deficits of a foreign affiliate (FA). Under 95(1)"foreign accrual property income", capital gains and losses from disposition of EP are disregarded in computing FAPI except as per formula element B.

CRA considers that "substantially all", in paras. (b) and (c), means 90% or more. For "derived" in (c.1)(ii)(B)(II), see Notes to 18.1(12).

See VIEWS docs 2007-0251651E5, 2008-0288021E5 (partnership **[pship]** interest is EP); 2006-0168571E5 (deeming in (d)-(e) does not treat pship as corp for purposes of determining if pship and corp are related); 2007-0242871R3 (purifying FA so shares are EP); 2010-0373531C6 (whether license is EP); 2014-0546581E5 ((e) does not deem non-FA to hold shares of deemed non-resident corp [Barchichat, "Quirk in Definition of FA", 5(3) *Canadian Tax Focus* (ctf.ca) 4 (Aug. 2015)]); 2014-0536331E5 (property deemed disposed of by 88(3)(b) can be EP); 2014-0546581E5 (pship interest is not EP [Barnicke & Huynh, "FA's LP Interest: Excluded Property?", 23(4) *Canadian Tax Highlights [CTH]* (ctf.ca) 4-5 (April 2015)]); 2014-0549761I7 (FA's internally generated goodwill is counted in determining whether its shares are EP); 2015-059255117 (pship interest on dissolution is not EP [Wang, "A Foreign Partnership's Dissolution", 26(11) *CTH* 10-11 (Nov. 2018)]).

See also Porter & Bunn, "Excluded Property and Foreign Rollovers", XV(3) *International Tax Planning* (Federated Press) 1060-65 (2010).

Definition amended by 2007 budget bill #2 (for FAs' tax years that begin after Dec. 20, 2002, or earlier by election), 1991 technical bill. 95(1)"excluded property" was 95(1)(a.1) before RSC 1985 (5th Supp) consolidation for tax years ending after Nov. 1991.

"exempt trust", at a particular time in respect of a taxpayer resident in Canada, means a trust that, at that time, is a trust under which the interest of each beneficiary under the trust is, at all times that the interest exists during the trust's taxation year that includes the particular time, a specified fixed interest of the beneficiary in the trust, if at the particular time

(a) the trust is an eligible trust,

(b) there are at least 150 beneficiaries each of whom holds a specified fixed interest, in the trust, that has a fair market value of at least $500, and

(c) the total of all amounts each of which is the fair market value of an interest as a beneficiary under the trust held by a specified purchaser in respect of the taxpayer is not more than 10% of the total fair market value of all interests as a beneficiary under the trust;

Notes: Definition added by 2007 budget bill #2, effective Feb. 28, 2004.

"foreign accrual property income" of a foreign affiliate of a taxpayer, for any taxation year of the affiliate, means the amount determined by the formula

$$(A + A.1 + A.2 + B + C) - (D + E + F + F.1 + G + H)$$

where

A is the amount that would, if section 80 did not apply to the affiliate for the year or a preceding taxation year, be the total of all amounts, each of which is the affiliate's income for the year from property, the affiliate's income for the year from a business other than an active business or the affiliate's income for the year from a non-qualifying business of the affiliate, in each case that amount being determined as if each amount described in clause $(2)(a)(ii)(D)$ that was paid or payable, directly or indirectly, by the affiliate to another foreign affiliate of the taxpayer or of a person with whom the taxpayer does not deal at arm's length were nil where an amount in respect of the income derived by the other foreign affiliate from that amount that was paid or payable to it by the affiliate was added in computing its income from an active business, other than

    (a) interest that would, by virtue of paragraph $81(1)(m)$, not be included in computing the income of the affiliate if it were resident in Canada,

    (b) a dividend from another foreign affiliate of the taxpayer,

    (c) a taxable dividend to the extent that the amount thereof would, if the dividend were received by the taxpayer, be deductible by the taxpayer under section 112, or

    (d) any amount included because of subsection $80.4(2)$ in the affiliate's income in respect of indebtedness to another corporation that is a foreign affiliate of the taxpayer or of a person resident in Canada with whom the taxpayer does not deal at arm's length,

A.1 is twice the total of all amounts included in computing the affiliate's income from property or businesses (other than active businesses) for the year because of subsection $80(13)$,

A.2 is the amount determined for G in respect of the affiliate for the preceding taxation year,

B is the total of all amounts each of which is the portion of the affiliate's income (to the extent that the income is not included under the description of A) for the year, or of the affiliate's taxable capital gain for the year that can reasonably be considered to have accrued after its 1975 taxation year, from a disposition of property

    (a) that is not, at the time of disposition, excluded property of the affiliate, or

    (b) that is, at the time of disposition, excluded property of the affiliate, if any of paragraphs $(2)(c)$, (d) and $(d.1)$, subparagraph $(2)(e)(i)$ and paragraph $88(3)(a)$ applies to the disposition,

C is, where the affiliate is a controlled foreign affiliate of the taxpayer, the amount that would be required to be included in computing its income for the year if

    (a) subsection $94.1(1)$ were applicable in computing that income,

    (b) the words "earned directly by the taxpayer" in that subsection were replaced by the words "earned by the person resident in Canada in respect of whom the taxpayer is a foreign affiliate",

    (c) the words "other than a controlled foreign affiliate of the taxpayer or a prescribed non-resident entity" in paragraph $94.1(1)(a)$ were replaced by the words "other than a prescribed non-resident entity or a controlled foreign affiliate of a person resident in Canada of whom the taxpayer is a controlled foreign affiliate", and

    (d) the words "other than a capital gain" in paragraph $94.1(1)(g)$ were replaced by the words "other than any income that would not be included in the taxpayer's foreign accrual property income for the year if the value of C in the definition "foreign accrual property income" in subsection $95(1)$ were nil and other than a capital gain",

D is the total of all amounts, each of which is the affiliate's loss for the year from property, the affiliate's loss for the year from a business other than an active business of the affiliate or the affiliate's loss for the year from a non-qualifying business of the affiliate, in each case that amount being determined as if there were not included in the affiliate's income any amount described in any of paragraphs (a) to (d) of the description of A and as if each amount described in clause $(2)(a)(ii)(D)$ that was paid or payable, directly or indirectly, by the affiliate to another foreign affiliate of the taxpayer or of a person with whom the taxpayer does not deal at arm's length were nil where an amount in respect of the income derived by the other foreign affiliate from that amount that was paid or payable to it by the affiliate was added in computing its income from an active business,

E is the lesser of

    (a) the amount of the affiliate's allowable capital losses for the year from dispositions of property (other than excluded property and property in respect of which an election is made by the taxpayer under subsection $88(3.3)$) that can reasonably be considered to have accrued after its 1975 taxation year, and

    (b) the total of all amounts each of which is the portion of a taxable capital gain of the affiliate that is included in the amount determined for B in respect of the affiliate for the year,

F is the prescribed amount for the year,

F.1 is the lesser of

    (a) the prescribed amount for the year, and

    (b) the amount, if any, by which

        (i) the total of all amounts each of which is the portion of a taxable capital gain of the affiliate that is included in the amount determined for B in respect of the affiliate for the year

    exceeds

        (ii) the amount determined for E in respect of the affiliate for the year,

G is the amount, if any, by which

    (a) the total of amounts determined for A.1 and A.2 in respect of the affiliate for the year

    exceeds

    (b) the total of all amounts determined for D to F.1 in respect of the affiliate for the year, and

H is

    (a) if the affiliate was a member of a partnership at the end of the fiscal period of the partnership that ended in the year and the partnership received a dividend at a particular time in that fiscal period from a corporation that would be, if the reference in subsection $93.1(1)$ to "corporation resident in Canada" were a reference to "taxpayer resident in Canada", a foreign affiliate of the taxpayer for the purposes of sections 93 and 113 at that particular time, then the portion of the amount of that dividend that is included in the value determined for A in respect of the affiliate for the year and that would be, if the reference in subsection $93.1(2)$ to "corporation resident in Canada" were a reference to "taxpayer resident in Canada", deemed by paragraph $93.1(2)(a)$ to have been received by the affiliate for the purposes of sections 93 and 113, and

    (b) in any other case, nil;

Related Provisions: $34.2(8)(a)$ — Corporate partner stub-period accrual does not apply to FAPI; $40(3)(d)$ — Deemed gain where ACB would become negative; $53(1)(m)$ — ACB of offshore investment fund property; $93.1(5)$, $(6)(a)$ — FAPI of a partnership, for A(b) and B; 94.2 — Non-resident trust deemed to be controlled foreign affiliate for FAPI; $95(2)$ — Determination of certain components of FAPI; $95(2)(e)(v)(A)(I)$, $95(2)(e)(v)(B)$ — Designated liquidation and dissolution of foreign affiliate; $152(6.1)$ — Reassessment to apply FAPI loss carryback; $248(1)$"foreign accrual property income" — Definition applies to entire Act; 257 — Formula cannot calculate to less than zero; 261(6.1), (7)(a)(i) — Application when functional currency election made; Canada-U.S. Tax Treaty:Art. XXIX:5(b) — U.S. "S" corporation income may be deemed to be FAPI.

Notes: See Notes to 91(1) for overview of FAPI. See 95(2) for detailed rules affecting the calculation.

For the meaning of "indirectly" in A and D, see Notes to 17.1(1). For "derived" in D, see Notes to 18.1(12).

Element F, before amendment in 2001, provided a 5-year carryforward of deductible losses. A 20-year carryforward and 3-year carryback is now allowed by Reg. 5903(1).

For some rulings that amounts will not be FAPI see VIEWS docs 2008-0290361R3, 2010-0359731R3, 2010-0374301R3; 2012-0463611R3 (foreign divisive reorg); 2014-0536661R3 (disposition of excluded property by foreign LP).

Definition amended by 2014 budget bill #2 (for foreign affiliates' (FA) tax years that end after 2006), 2002-2013 technical bill (for FAs' tax years that end after Aug. 19, 2011, or earlier by election), 2007 budget bill #2, 2001 technical bill, 2000 Budget, 1995-97, 1994 and 1991 technical bills. 95(1)"foreign accrual property income" was 95(1)(b) before RSC 1985 (5th Supp) consolidation for tax years ending after Nov. 1991.

Regulations: 5903 (prescribed amount); 5903.1 (prescribed amount for F.1(a)).

Income Tax Folios: S5-F3-C1: Taxation of a Roth IRA.

I.T. Application Rules: 35(1) (ITAR 26 does not apply in determining gains and losses of foreign affiliates; 35(4) (where corporation deemed to be foreign affiliate before May 7, 1974 because of election).

Interpretation Bulletins: IT-451R: Deemed disposition and acquisition on ceasing to be or becoming resident in Canada.

CRA Audit Manual: 15.12.2: Foreign accrual property income (FAPI) and foreign affiliates.

"foreign accrual tax" applicable to any amount included under subsection 91(1) in computing a taxpayer's income for a taxation year of the taxpayer in respect of a particular foreign affiliate of the taxpayer means, subject to subsection 91(4.1),

(a) the portion of any income or profits tax that may reasonably be regarded as applicable to that amount and that is paid by

(i) the particular affiliate,

(ii) another foreign affiliate (in paragraph (b) referred to as the "shareholder affiliate") of the taxpayer where

(A) the other affiliate has an equity percentage in the particular affiliate,

(B) the income or profits tax is paid to a country other than Canada, and

(C) the other affiliate, and not the particular affiliate, is liable for that tax under the laws of that country, or

(iii) another foreign affiliate of the taxpayer in respect of a dividend received, directly or indirectly, from the particular affiliate, if that other affiliate has an equity percentage in the particular affiliate, and

(b) any amount prescribed in respect of the particular affiliate or the shareholder affiliate, as the case may be, to be foreign accrual tax applicable to that amount;

Related Provisions: 91(4.1)–(4.7) — Limitation — artificial foreign tax credit generators.

Notes: See Notes to 91(4).

For the meaning of "income or profits tax" in (a), see Notes to 126(4). For "indirectly" in (a)(iii) see Notes to 17.1(1).

For (a)(i), the foreign affiliate (FA) that realizes FAPI must be the same FA that pays the foreign tax: VIEWS doc 2004-0078921E5. US tax on a US LLC's income paid by the owners is not FAT: 2013-0480321C6. Example of FAT: see 2007-0247551E5.

Definition amended by 2014 budget bill #2 (for FAs' tax years that end after 2010), 2002-2013 technical bill (for taxpayer's tax years that end after March 4, 2010). 95(1)"foreign accrual tax" was 95(1)(c) before RSC 1985 (5th Supp) consolidation for tax years ending after Nov. 1991.

Regulations: 5907(1.3)–(1.7) (prescribed foreign accrual tax).

"foreign affiliate", at any time, of a taxpayer resident in Canada means a non-resident corporation in which, at that time,

(a) the taxpayer's equity percentage is not less than 1%, and

(b) the total of the equity percentages in the corporation of the taxpayer and of each person related to the taxpayer (where each such equity percentage is determined as if the determinations under paragraph (b) of the definition "equity percentage" in sub-

section (4) were made without reference to the equity percentage of any person in the taxpayer or in any person related to the taxpayer) is not less than 10%,

except that a corporation is not a foreign affiliate of a non-resident-owned investment corporation;

Related Provisions: 87(8) — Merger of FA; 93.1 — Look-through rules for shares held by a partnership; 95(4) — Equity percentage; 128.1(1)(d) — FA becoming resident in Canada; 233.4(4) — Reporting requirements; 248(1)"foreign affiliate" — Definition applies to entire Act.

Notes: See Notes to 91(1). For interpretation see VIEWS docs 2007-0247551E5, 2012-0467121E5. Only a corp can be a FA: see Notes to 248(1)"corporation".

Definition amended by 1994 technical bill, last change effective for FAs' tax years that end after 1994. 95(1)"foreign affiliate" was 95(1)(d) before RSC 1985 (5th Supp) consolidation for tax years ending after Nov. 1991.

I.T. Application Rules: 35(4) (where corporation deemed to be foreign affiliate due to election made before May 6, 1974).

Interpretation Bulletins: IT-343R: Meaning of the term "corporation"; IT-451R: Deemed disposition and acquisition on ceasing to be or becoming resident in Canada.

Information Circulars: 77-9R: Books, records and other requirements for taxpayers having foreign affiliates.

Forms: T2 Sched. 25: Investment in foreign affiliates.

"foreign bank" means an entity that would be a foreign bank within the meaning assigned by the definition of that expression in section 2 of the *Bank Act* if

(a) that definition were read without reference to the portion thereof after paragraph (g) thereof, and

(b) the entity had not been exempt under section 12 of that Act from being a foreign bank;

Notes: For interpretation of "foreign bank" see Notes to 95(2)(l).

Section 2 of the *Bank Act*, S.C. 1991, c. 46 (as amended), defines "foreign bank":

"foreign bank", subject to section 12, means an entity incorporated or formed by or under the laws of a country other than Canada that

(a) is a bank according to the laws of any foreign country where it carries on business,

(b) carries on a business in any foreign country that, if carried on in Canada, would be, wholly or to a significant extent, the business of banking,

(c) engages, directly or indirectly, in the business of providing financial services and employs, to identify or describe its business, a name that includes the word "bank", "banque", "banking" or "bancaire", either alone or in combination with other words, or any word or words in any language other than English or French corresponding generally thereto,

(d) engages in the business of lending money and accepting deposit liabilities transferable by cheque or other instrument,

(e) engages, directly or indirectly, in the business of providing financial services and is affiliated with another foreign bank,

(f) controls another foreign bank, or

(g) is a foreign institution, other than a foreign bank within the meaning of any of paragraphs (a) to (f), that controls a bank incorporated or formed under this Act,

but does not include a subsidiary of a bank named in Schedule I as that Schedule read immediately before the day section 184 of the *Financial Consumer Agency of Canada Act* comes into force, unless the Minister has specified that subsection 378(1) no longer applies to the bank;

Note that the closing words do not apply for this definition, so a subsidiary of a Schedule I bank (Canadian bank) can be a foreign bank for FAPI. *Bank Act* s. 12, which also does not apply for FAPI, provides that the Minister of Finance may exempt an entity from being a foreign bank.

Definition added by 1994 technical bill, last change effective for foreign affiliates' tax years that end after 1994.

"income from a non-qualifying business" of a foreign affiliate of a taxpayer resident in Canada for a taxation year includes the foreign affiliate's income for the taxation year that pertains to or is incident to that non-qualifying business, but does not include

(a) the foreign affiliate's income from property for the taxation year, or

(b) the foreign affiliate's income for the taxation year from a business that is deemed by subsection (2) to be a business other than an active business of the foreign affiliate;

Notes: Definition added by 2007 budget bill #2, for foreign affiliates' tax years that begin after 2008.

"income from an active business" of a foreign affiliate of a taxpayer for a taxation year includes the foreign affiliate's income for the taxation year that pertains to or is incident to that active business but does not include

 (a) the foreign affiliate's income from property for the taxation year,

 (b) the foreign affiliate's income for the taxation year from a business that is deemed by subsection (2) to be a business other than an active business of the foreign affiliate, or

 (c) the foreign affiliate's income from a non-qualifying business of the foreign affiliate for the taxation year;

Related Provisions: 17(8)(a)(i) — 17(1) does not apply to loan used for earning income from an active business; 95(1)"active business" — Businesses excluded; 95(1)"income from property" — Extended meaning of income from property.

Notes: Definition amended by 2007 budget bill #2, for foreign affiliates' tax years that begin after 2008. Added by 1994 technical bill.

"income from property" of a foreign affiliate of a taxpayer for a taxation year includes the foreign affiliate's income for the taxation year from an investment business and the foreign affiliate's income for the taxation year from an adventure or concern in the nature of trade, but does not include

 (a) the foreign affiliate's income for the taxation year from a business that is deemed by subsection (2) to be a business other than an active business of the foreign affiliate, or

 (b) the foreign affiliate's income for the taxation year that pertains to or is incident to

  (i) an active business of the foreign affiliate, or

  (ii) a non-qualifying business of the foreign affiliate;

Related Provisions: 9(1) — Determination of income from property; 95(1)"investment business" — Meaning of investment business; 95(2)(l) — Income from trading or dealing in indebtedness.

Notes: For a ruling that an amount is not IFP see VIEWS doc 2009-0308961R3.

Definition amended by 2007 budget bill #2, for foreign affiliates' tax years that begin after 2008. Added by 1994 technical bill.

"investment business" of a foreign affiliate of a taxpayer means a business carried on by the foreign affiliate in a taxation year (other than a business deemed by subsection (2) to be a business other than an active business carried on by the foreign affiliate and other than a non-qualifying business of the foreign affiliate) the principal purpose of which is to derive income from property (including interest, dividends, rents, royalties or any similar returns or substitutes for such interest, dividends, rents, royalties or returns), income from the insurance or reinsurance of risks, income from the factoring of trade accounts receivable, or profits from the disposition of investment property, unless it is established by the taxpayer or the foreign affiliate that, throughout the period in the taxation year during which the business was carried on by the foreign affiliate,

 (a) the business (other than any business conducted principally with persons with whom the affiliate does not deal at arm's length) is

  (i) a business carried on by it as a foreign bank, a trust company, a credit union, an insurance corporation or a trader or dealer in securities or commodities, the activities of which are regulated under the laws

   (A) of each country in which the business is carried on through a permanent establishment in that country and of the country under whose laws the affiliate is governed and any of exists, was (unless the affiliate was continued in any jurisdiction) formed or organized, or was last continued,

   (B) of the country in which the business is principally carried on, or

   (C) if the affiliate is related to a non-resident corporation, of the country under whose laws that non-resident corporation is governed and any of exists, was (unless that non-resident corporation was continued in any jurisdiction) formed or organized, or was last continued, if those regu-

lating laws are recognized under the laws of the country in which the business is principally carried on and all of those countries are members of the European Union, or

  (ii) the development of real property or immovables for sale, the lending of money, the leasing or licensing of property or the insurance or reinsurance of risks,

 (b) either

  (i) the affiliate (otherwise than as a member of a partnership) carries on the business (the affiliate being, in respect of those times, in that period of the year, that it so carries on the business, referred to in paragraph (c) as the "operator"), or

  (ii) the affiliate carries on the business as a qualifying member of a partnership (the partnership being, in respect of those times, in that period of the year, that the affiliate so carries on the business, referred to in paragraph (c) as the "operator"), and

 (c) the operator employs

  (i) more than five employees full time in the active conduct of the business, or

  (ii) the equivalent of more than five employees full time in the active conduct of the business taking into consideration only

   (A) the services provided by employees of the operator, and

   (B) the services provided outside Canada to the operator by any one or more persons each of whom is, during the time at which the services were performed by the person, an employee of

    (I) a corporation related to the affiliate (otherwise than because of a right referred to in paragraph 251(5)(b)),

    (II) in the case where the operator is the affiliate,

     1. a corporation (referred to in this subparagraph as a "providing shareholder") that is a qualifying shareholder of the affiliate,

     2. a designated corporation in respect of the affiliate, or

     3. a designated partnership in respect of the affiliate, and

    (III) in the case where the operator is the partnership described in subparagraph (b)(ii),

     1. any person (referred to in this subparagraph as a "providing member") who is a qualifying member of that partnership,

     2. a designated corporation in respect of the affiliate, or

     3. a designated partnership in respect of the affiliate,

if the corporations referred to in subclause (B)(I) and the designated corporations, designated partnerships, providing shareholders or providing members referred to in subclauses (B)(II) and (III) receive compensation from the operator for the services provided to the operator by those employees the value of which is not less than the cost to those corporations, partnerships, shareholders or members of the compensation paid or accruing to the benefit of those employees that performed the services during the time at which the services were performed by those employees;

Related Provisions: 95(1)"active business"(a) — Investment business excluded from active business; 95(2)(a.2) — Income from insurance business; 95(2)(o)–(r) — Qualifying member, qualifying shareholder; 95(2)(s) — Designated corporation; 95(2)(t) — Designated partnership; 95(2.1) — Whether dealing with foreign affiliate at arm's length; 95(2.11) — Offshore regulated banks — conditions for subpara. (a)(i); 95(2.45)(a) — Canadian bank and affiliate deemed to deal at arm's length if conditions met; 95(9) — Deemed investment business where tracking arrangement used; 125(7) — Analogous definition of "specified investment business" for small business deduction purposes.

Notes: A controlled foreign affiliate's "investment business" (IB) is excluded by 95(1)"active business"(a); its profits are 95(1)"income from property" and 95(1)"foreign accrual property income"A, taxed as FAPI by 91(1).

Since 2015, 95(2.11) limits the "foreign bank" exception in (a)(i) to subsidiaries of Canadian financial institutions. Before, in *Loblaw Financial*, 2018 TCC 182, rev'd 2020 FCA 79 (SCC appeal heard May 13/21), a Barbados bank owned by Loblaw qualified as a regulated foreign bank (TCC paras. 169, 202-205, 250) and as having equivalent of more than 5 full-time employees (TCC paras. 251-270); the FCA (reversing the TCC on this point only) held the bank's profits were not FAPI because it conducted business principally with arm's-length persons, despite "support and oversight" from Loblaw (para. 73) [Haughey & Page, "Loblaw Financial", XXIV(2) *International Tax Planning* (Federated Press) 17-25 (2020)]. (TCC paras. 206-249 have a lengthy discussion of the history of 95(1)"investment business".)

CRA considers shrink-wrap software to be tangible goods, so its sale is active business income (ABI), not IB income: VIEWS doc 2003-0016791E5. But see also docs 9507915, 9520295 and 9722915 on whether royalty income is ABI.

For "more than 5 full-time employees", see Notes to 125(7)"specified investment business". CRA accepts that case law for 95(1)"investment business": doc 2008-0299161I7.

See also Jack et al, "International Taxation: The February 27, 2004 Draft Proposals", 2004 Cdn Tax Foundation conference report, at 20:67-70; Holms & Shields, "The Effect of the Investment Business Definition on Real Estate Developers", 54(4) *Canadian Tax Journal* 937-67 (2006); VIEWS doc 2009-0308961R3.

The words "any of exists..." in (a)(i)(A), (C) should be read "any of {(1) exists, (2) was formed or organized, or (3) was last continued}", though this is not correct English.

Definition amended by 2002-2013 technical bill (last change effective June 26, 2013), 2007 budget bill #2. Added by 1994 technical bill.

Regulations: 5906(2)(b) (permanent establishment).

I.T. Technical News: 41 (the "more than five full-time employees" test).

"investment property" of a foreign affiliate of a taxpayer includes

(a) a share of the capital stock of a corporation other than a share of another foreign affiliate of the taxpayer that is excluded property of the affiliate,

(b) an interest in a partnership other than an interest in a partnership that is excluded property of the affiliate,

(c) an interest in a trust other than an interest in a trust that is excluded property of the affiliate,

(d) indebtedness or annuities,

(e) commodities or commodities futures purchased or sold, directly or indirectly in any manner whatever, on a commodities or commodities futures exchange (except commodities manufactured, produced, grown, extracted or processed by the affiliate or a person to whom the affiliate is related (otherwise than because of a right referred to in paragraph 251(5)(b)) or commodities futures in respect of such commodities),

(f) currency,

(g) real property or immovables,

(h) Canadian and foreign resource properties,

(i) interests in funds or entities other than corporations, partnerships and trusts, and

(j) interests in, or for civil law rights in, or options in respect of, property that is included in any of paragraphs (a) to (i);

Notes: For meaning of "includes" in opening words, see Notes to 188.1(5). For "indirectly" in (e) see Notes to 17.1(1). For "real property" in (g) see Notes to 248(4).

Definition amended by 2002-2013 technical bill, effective June 26, 2013. Added by 1994 technical bill.

"lease obligation" of a person includes an obligation under an agreement that authorizes the use of or the production or reproduction of property including information or any other thing;

Notes: Definition added by 1994 technical bill, last change effective for foreign affiliates' tax years that end after 1994.

"lending of money" by a person (for the purpose of this definition referred to as the "lender") includes

(a) the acquisition by the lender of trade accounts receivable (other than trade accounts receivable owing by a person with whom the lender does not deal at arm's length) from another person or the acquisition by the lender of any interest in any such accounts receivable,

(b) the acquisition by the lender of loans made by and lending assets (other than loans or lending assets owing by a person with whom the lender does not deal at arm's length) of another person or the acquisition by the lender of any interest in such a loan or lending asset,

(c) the acquisition by the lender of a foreign resource property (other than a foreign resource property that is a rental or royalty payable by a person with whom the lender does not deal at arm's length) of another person, and

(d) the sale by the lender of loans or lending assets (other than loans or lending assets owing by a person with whom the lender does not deal at arm's length) or the sale by the lender of any interest in such loans or lending assets;

and for the purpose of this definition, the definition "lending asset" in subsection 248(1) shall be read without the words "but does not include a prescribed property";

Notes: Definition amended by 1995-97 technical bill, last change effective for foreign affiliates' tax years that end after Sept. 1997. Added by 1994 technical bill.

"licensing of property" includes authorizing the use of or the production or reproduction of property including information or any other thing;

Notes: Definition added by 1994 technical bill, last change effective for foreign affiliates' tax years that end after 1994.

"non-qualifying business" of a foreign affiliate of a taxpayer at any time means a business carried on by the foreign affiliate through a permanent establishment in a jurisdiction that, at the end of the foreign affiliate's taxation year that includes that time, is a non-qualifying country, other than

(a) an investment business of the foreign affiliate, or

(b) a business that is deemed by subsection (2) to be a business other than an active business of the foreign affiliate;

Related Provisions: 95(1)"foreign accrual property income"A — Income from non-qualifying business is FAPI; 95(1)"income from a non-qualifying business" — Extended definition.

Notes: See Notes to 95(1)"non-qualifying country". Definition added by 2007 budget bill #2, for foreign affiliates' tax years that begin after 2008.

"non-qualifying country", at any time, means a country or other jurisdiction

(a) with which Canada neither has a tax treaty at that time nor has, before that time, signed an agreement that will, on coming into effect, be a tax treaty,

(a.1) for which, if the time is after February 2014, the Convention on Mutual Administrative Assistance in Tax Matters — concluded at Strasbourg on January 25, 1988, as amended from time to time by a protocol, or other international instrument, as ratified by Canada — is at that time not in force and does not have effect,

(b) with which Canada does not have a comprehensive tax information exchange agreement that is in force and has effect at that time, and

(c) with which Canada has, more than 60 months before that time, either

(i) begun negotiations for a comprehensive tax information exchange agreement (unless that time is before 2014 and Canada was, on March 19, 2007, in the course of negotiating a comprehensive tax information exchange agreement with that jurisdiction), or

(ii) sought, by written invitation, to enter into negotiations for a comprehensive tax information exchange agreement (unless that time is before 2014 and Canada was, on March 19, 2007, in the course of negotiating a comprehensive tax information exchange agreement with that jurisdiction);

Related Provisions: 95(1)"non-qualifying business" — Business carried on in non-qualifying country may be non-qualifying business; 95(1.1) — BVI deemed to have TIEA effective 2014.

Notes: Income earned from a PE in a non-qualifying country (95(1)"non-qualifying business") is FAPI: 95(1)"foreign accrual property income"A.

A TIEA is a "listed international agreement" (248(1)). Canada has signed TIEAs with Anguilla, Antigua & Barbuda (Oct. 31, 2017; not yet in force), Aruba, Bahamas, Bahrain, Bermuda, British Virgin Islands [deemed by 95(1.1) anyway], Brunei, Cayman Islands, Cook Islands, Costa Rica, Dominica, Grenada, Guernsey, Isle of Man, Jersey, Liechtenstein, Netherlands Antilles, Panama, San Marino, Saint Lucia, St. Kitts & Nevis, St. Vincent & the Grenadines, Turks & Caicos, Uruguay. TIEAs are under negotiation with Belize, Gibraltar, Liberia, Montserrat, Vanuatu. See tinyurl.com/fintiea. The TIEA with the US is completely different, and requires CRA to collect and share with the IRS information on US citizens' and other US persons' accounts at Canadian financial institutions. It is reproduced after the Canada-US tax treaty (see also ss. 263-269 and Notes to 269). A TIEA (other than the one with the US) does not provide automatic information exchange, but only on specific request. However, more than 100 countries have implemented automatic exchange of financial account information: see 270-281.

See also *Global Forum on Transparency and Exchange of Information for Tax Purposes*, oecd.org/tax/transparency; Nanji & Virani, "The Possible Future of TIEAs", 8(2) *Canadian Tax Focus* (ctf.ca) 9-10 (May 2018).

See tinyurl.com/oecd-mutu > "See chart of participating jurisdictions" for countries for which the Convention in (a.1) is in force (including Belize, Gibraltar, Montserrat, Vanuatu). As of 2020, only Liberia has not ratified the Convention and so is non-qualifying under para. (c) due to 5 years passing.

In *Ludmer*, 2018 QCCS 3381, paras. 554-571, 702, 750-760; aff'd 2020 QCCA 697, paras. 18, 22 (leave to appeal denied 2021 CarswellQue 2160 (SCC)), CRA requesting information from Bermuda under the TIEA and saying it was for a "criminal tax matter", when it was not, justified damages against CRA. (See 171(1) Notes under "Lawsuits in Quebec".)

Definition amended by 2014 budget bill #2, effective 2014. Added by 2007 budget bill #2.

"participating percentage" of a particular share owned by a taxpayer of the capital stock of a corporation in respect of any foreign affiliate of the taxpayer that was, at the end of its taxation year, a controlled foreign affiliate of the taxpayer is

(a) where the foreign accrual property income of the affiliate for that year is $5,000 or less, nil, and

(b) where the foreign accrual property income of the affiliate for that year exceeds $5,000,

(i) the percentage that would be the taxpayer's equity percentage in the affiliate at the end of that taxation year on the assumption that the taxpayer owned no shares other than the particular share (but in no case shall that assumption be made for the purpose of determining whether or not a corporation is a foreign affiliate of the taxpayer) if

(A) the affiliate and each corporation that is relevant to the determination of the taxpayer's equity percentage in the affiliate have, at that time, only one class of issued shares, and

(B) no foreign affiliate (referred to in this clause as the "upper-tier affiliate") of the taxpayer that is relevant to the determination of the taxpayer's equity percentage in the affiliate has, at that time, an equity percentage in a foreign affiliate (including, for greater certainty, the affiliate) of the taxpayer that has an equity percentage in the upper-tier affiliate, and

(ii) in any other case, the percentage determined in prescribed manner;

Related Provisions: 95(4) — Equity percentage.

Notes: Subpara. (b)(i) amended by 2002-2013 technical bill, for foreign affiliates' tax years that begin after Aug. 19, 2011. 95(1)"participating percentage" was 95(1)(e) before RSC 1985 (5th Supp) consolidation for tax years ending after Nov. 1991.

Regulations: 5904 (prescribed manner).

"permanent establishment" has the meaning assigned by regulation;

Notes: Definition added by 2002-2013 technical bill, for foreign affiliates' tax years that begin after 1999.

A definition **"relevant non-arm's length entity"** was proposed in Oct. 2/07 draft legislation, but deleted when that became 2007 budget bill #2. The Technical Notes of Nov. 21/07 state that it was deleted due to withdrawal of 95(2)(f)-(f.2) "for further consideration in response to submissions received". The 2008 legislation that replaced those provisions with 95(2)(f)-(f.15) did not include this term.

Regulations: 5906(2)(b) (meaning of permanent establishment).

"relevant tax factor", of a person or partnership for a taxation year, means

(a) in the case of a corporation, or of a partnership all the members of which, other than non-resident persons, are corporations, the quotient obtained by the formula

$$1/(A - B)$$

where

A is the percentage set out in paragraph 123(1)(a), and

B is

(i) in the case of a corporation, the percentage that is the corporation's general rate reduction percentage (as defined by section 123.4) for the taxation year, and

(ii) in the case of a partnership, the percentage that would be determined under subparagraph (i) in respect of the partnership if the partnership were a corporation whose taxation year is the partnership's fiscal period, and

(b) in any other case, 1.9;

Notes: For a corporation, the relevant tax factor since 2012 is 1/(.38–.13) = 4; see Notes to 123.4(2). (See also 248(1)"relevant factor".)

Para. (b) amended by 2016 budget bill #1, for 2016 and later tax years, to change "2.2" to "1.9" (to reflect the 117(2) top rate increase to 33%). Definition earlier amended by 2002-2013 technical bill, for 2002 and later tax years. 95(1)"relevant tax factor" was 95(1)(f) before RSC 1985 (5th Supp) consolidation for tax years ending after Nov. 1991.

"specified fixed interest", at any time, of an entity in a trust, means an interest of the entity as a beneficiary under the trust if

(a) the interest includes, at that time, rights of the entity as a beneficiary under the trust to receive, at or after that time and directly from the trust, income and capital of the trust,

(b) the interest was issued by the trust, at or before that time, to an entity, in exchange for consideration and the fair market value, at the time at which the interest was issued, of that consideration was equal to the fair market value, at the time at which it was issued, of the interest,

(c) the only manner in which any part of the interest may cease to be the entity's is by way of a disposition (determined without reference to paragraph (i) of the definition "disposition" in subsection 248(1) and paragraph 248(8)(c)) by the entity of that part, and

(d) no amount of income or capital of the trust that any entity may receive directly from the trust at any time as a beneficiary under the trust depends on the exercise by any entity of, or the failure by any entity to exercise, a discretionary power;

Notes: Definition added by 2007 budget bill #2, effective Feb. 28, 2004.

"specified person or partnership", in respect of a taxpayer, at any time means the taxpayer or a person (other than a designated acquired corporation of the taxpayer), or a partnership, that is at that time

(a) a person (other than a partnership) that is resident in Canada and does not, at that time, deal at arm's length with the taxpayer,

(b) a specified predecessor corporation of the taxpayer or of a specified person or partnership in respect of the taxpayer,

(c) a foreign affiliate of

(i) the taxpayer,

(ii) a person that is at that time a specified person or partnership in respect of the taxpayer under this definition because of paragraph (a) or (b), or

(iii) a partnership that is at that time a specified person or partnership in respect of the taxpayer under this definition because of paragraph (d), or

(d) a partnership a member of which is at that time a specified person or partnership in respect of the taxpayer under this definition;

Related Provisions: 95(2.6) — Interpretation rule for definition.

Notes: Definition added by 2008 budget bill #2, last change effective for foreign affiliates' tax years that begin after Oct. 2, 2007.

"specified predecessor corporation" of a particular corporation means

(a) an antecedent corporation of the particular corporation,

(b) a predecessor corporation (within the meaning assigned by subsection 87(1)) in respect of an amalgamation by which the particular corporation was formed, or

(c) a specified predecessor corporation of a specified predecessor corporation of the particular corporation;

Notes: Definition added by 2008 budget bill #2, last change effective for foreign affiliates' tax years that begin after Oct. 2, 2007.

"specified purchaser", at any time, in respect of a particular taxpayer resident in Canada, means an entity that is, at that time,

(a) the particular taxpayer,

(b) an entity resident in Canada with which the particular taxpayer does not deal at arm's length,

(c) a foreign affiliate of an entity described in any of paragraphs (a) and (b) and (d) to (f),

(d) a trust (other than an exempt trust) in which an entity described in any of paragraphs (a) to (c) and (e) and (f) is beneficially interested,

(e) a partnership of which an entity described in any of paragraphs (a) to (d) and (f) is a member, or

(f) an entity (other than an entity described in any of paragraphs (a) to (e)) with which an entity described in any of paragraphs (a) to (e) does not deal at arm's length;

Notes: Definition added by 2007 budget bill #2, last change effective Oct. 2, 2007.

"surplus entitlement percentage", at any time, of a taxpayer in respect of a foreign affiliate has the meaning assigned by regulation;

Related Provisions: 91(1.1) — Deemed year-end to trigger FAPI when SEP reduced.

Notes: 95(1)"surplus entitlement percentage" was 95(1)(f.1) before RSC 1985 (5th Supp) consolidation for tax years ending after Nov. 1991.

Regulations: 5905(13) ("surplus entitlement percentage").

"taxable Canadian business", at any time, of a foreign affiliate of a taxpayer resident in Canada or of a partnership of which a foreign affiliate of a taxpayer resident in Canada is a member (which foreign affiliate or partnership is referred to in this definition as the "operator"), means a business the income from which

(a) is, or would be if there were income from the business for the operator's taxation year or fiscal period that includes that time, included in computing the foreign affiliate's taxable income earned in Canada for a taxation year under subparagraph 115(1)(a)(ii), and

(b) is not, or would not be if there were income from the business for the operator's taxation year or fiscal period that includes that time, exempt, because of a tax treaty with a country, from tax under this Part;

Related Provisions: 95(2)(j.1), (k), (k.2) — Application to FAPI rules.

Notes: Definition added by 2002-2013 technical bill, generally for years that begin after Dec. 20, 2002.

"taxation year" in relation to a foreign affiliate of a taxpayer means the period for which the accounts of the foreign affiliate have been ordinarily made up, but no such period may exceed 53 weeks.

Related Provisions: 95(1) — Foreign affiliate; 249 — Taxation year.

Notes: See Eric Lockwood, "Taxation Year of a Foreign Affiliate", 1889 *Tax Topics* (CCH) 1-4 (May 22, 2008); VIEWS doc 2012-0449941R3.

95(1)"taxation year" was 95(1)(g) before RSC 1985 (5th Supp) consolidation for tax years ending after Nov. 1991.

A definition **"transitional exchange rate"** was proposed in Oct. 2/07 draft legislation, but deleted when that became 2007 budget bill #2. The Nov. 21/07 Technical Notes say this was due to withdrawal of 95(2)(f)-(f.2) "for further consideration in response to submissions received". The 2008 legislation replacing them with 95(2)(f)-(f.15) did not include the term.

"trust company" includes a corporation that is resident in Canada and that is a "loan company" as defined in subsection 2(1) of the *Canadian Payments Act*.

Notes: See Notes to 188.1(5) re meaning of "includes".

Canadian Payments Act s. 2(1) defines "loan company":

"loan company" means a body corporate that accepts deposits transferable by order to a third party and that

(a) is a company to which the *Trust and Loan Companies Act* applies and that is not a trust company pursuant to subsection 57(2) of that Act, or

(b) carries on, under an Act of the legislature of a province or a constating instrument issued under provincial jurisdiction, a business substantially similar to the business of a company referred to in paragraph (a);

Legislative cross-reference amended by 2017 budget bill #2, effective Oct. 24, 2001. Definition added by 1995-97 technical bill, last change effective for foreign affiliates' tax years that end after 1994.

(1.1) British Virgin Islands — For the purposes of paragraph (b) of the definition "non-qualifying country" in subsection (1), the British Overseas Territory of the British Virgin Islands is deemed to have a comprehensive tax information exchange agreement with Canada that is in force and has effect after 2013 and before March 11, 2014.

Notes: 95(1.1) added by 2014 budget bill #2, effective 2014.

(2) Determination of certain components of foreign accrual property income — For the purposes of this Subdivision,

(a) **[income related to active business]** — in computing the income or loss from an active business for a taxation year of a particular foreign affiliate of a taxpayer in respect of which the taxpayer has a qualifying interest throughout the year or that is a controlled foreign affiliate of the taxpayer throughout the year, there shall be included any income or loss of the particular foreign affiliate for the year from sources in a country other than Canada that would otherwise be income or loss from property of the particular foreign affiliate for the year to the extent that

(i) the income or loss

(A) is derived by the particular foreign affiliate from activities of the particular foreign affiliate, or of a particular partnership of which the particular foreign affiliate is a member, to the extent that the activities occur while the particular affiliate is a qualifying member of the particular partnership that can reasonably be considered to be directly related to active business activities carried on in a country other than Canada by

(I) another foreign affiliate of the taxpayer in respect of which the taxpayer has a qualifying interest throughout the year,

(II) a life insurance corporation that is resident in Canada throughout the year and that is

1. the taxpayer,

2. a person who controls the taxpayer,

3. a person controlled by the taxpayer, or

4. a person controlled by a person who controls the taxpayer,

(III) the particular foreign affiliate or a partnership of which the particular foreign affiliate is a member, to the extent that the activities occur while the particular affiliate is a qualifying member of the partnership, or

(IV) a partnership of which another foreign affiliate of the taxpayer, in respect of which the taxpayer has a qualifying interest throughout the year, is a member, to the extent that the activities occur while the other affiliate is a qualifying member of the partnership, and

(B) if any of subclauses (A)(I), (II) and (IV) applies, would be included in computing the amount prescribed to be the earnings or loss, from an active business carried on in a country other than Canada, of

(I) that other foreign affiliate referred to in subclause (A)(I) or (IV), if the income were earned by it, or

(II) the life insurance corporation referred to in subclause (A)(II), if that life insurance corporation were a foreign affiliate of the taxpayer and the income were earned by it,

(ii) the income or loss is derived from amounts that were paid or payable, directly or indirectly, to the particular foreign affiliate or a partnership of which the particular foreign affiliate was a member

(A) by a life insurance corporation that is resident in Canada and that is the taxpayer, a person who controls the taxpayer, a person controlled by the taxpayer or a person controlled by a person who controls the taxpayer, to the extent that those amounts that were paid or payable were for expenditures that are deductible in a taxation year of the life insurance corporation by the life insurance corporation in computing its income or loss for a taxation year from carrying on its life insurance business outside Canada and are not deductible in computing its income or loss for a taxation year from carrying on its life insurance business in Canada,

(B) by

(I) another foreign affiliate of the taxpayer in respect of which the taxpayer has a qualifying interest throughout the year, to the extent that those amounts that were paid or payable are for expenditures that were deductible by that other foreign affiliate in computing the amounts prescribed to be its earnings or loss for a taxation year from an active business (other than an active business carried on in Canada), or

(II) a partnership of which another foreign affiliate of the taxpayer (in respect of which other foreign affiliate the taxpayer has a qualifying interest throughout the year) is a qualifying member throughout each period, in the fiscal period of the partnership that ends in the year, in which that other foreign affiliate was a member of the partnership, to the extent that those amounts that were paid or payable are for expenditures that are deductible by the partnership in computing that other foreign affiliate's share of any income or loss of the partnership, for a fiscal period, that is included in computing the amounts prescribed to be that other foreign affiliate's earnings or loss for a taxation year from an active business (other than an active business carried on in Canada),

(C) by a partnership of which the particular foreign affiliate is a qualifying member throughout each period, in the fiscal period of the partnership that ends in the year, in which the particular foreign affiliate was a member of the partnership, to the extent that those amounts that were paid or payable are for expenditures that are deductible by the partnership in computing the particular foreign affiliate's share of any income or loss of the partnership, for a fiscal period, that is included in computing the amounts prescribed to be the particular foreign affiliate's earnings or loss for a taxation year from an active business (other than an active business carried on in Canada), or

(D) by another foreign affiliate (referred to in this clause as the "second affiliate") of the taxpayer — in respect of which the taxpayer has a qualifying interest throughout the year — to the extent that the amounts are paid or pay-

able by the second affiliate, in respect of any particular period in the year,

(I) under a legal obligation to pay interest on borrowed money used for the purpose of earning income from property, or

(II) on an amount payable for property acquired for the purpose of gaining or producing income from property

where

(III) the property is, throughout the particular period, excluded property of the second affiliate that is shares of the capital stock of a corporation (referred to in this clause as the "third affiliate") which is, throughout the particular period, a foreign affiliate (other than the particular foreign affiliate) of the taxpayer in respect of which the taxpayer has a qualifying interest, and

(IV) in respect of each of the second affiliate and the third affiliate, for each of their taxation years (each of which is referred to in this subclause as a "relevant taxation year") that end in the year, either

1. that affiliate is subject to income taxation in a country other than Canada in that relevant taxation year, or

2. the members or shareholders of that affiliate (which, for the purposes of this sub-subclause, includes a person that has, directly or indirectly, an interest, or for civil law a right, in a share of the capital stock of, or in an equity interest in, the affiliate) at the end of that relevant taxation year are subject to income taxation in a country other than Canada on, in aggregate, all or substantially all of the income of that affiliate for that relevant taxation year in their taxation years in which that relevant taxation year ends,

(V) [Repealed]

(iii) the income or loss is derived by the particular foreign affiliate from the factoring of trade accounts receivable acquired by the particular foreign affiliate, or a partnership of which the particular foreign affiliate was a member, from another foreign affiliate of the taxpayer in respect of which the taxpayer has a qualifying interest throughout the year to the extent that the accounts receivable arose in the course of an active business carried on in a country other than Canada by that other foreign affiliate,

(iv) the income or loss is derived by the particular foreign affiliate from loans or lending assets acquired by the particular foreign affiliate, or a partnership of which the particular foreign affiliate was a member, from another foreign affiliate of the taxpayer in respect of which the taxpayer has a qualifying interest throughout the year, to the extent that the loans or lending assets arose in the course of an active business carried on in a country other than Canada by that other foreign affiliate,

(v) the income or loss is derived by the particular foreign affiliate from the disposition of excluded property that is not capital property, or

(vi) the income or loss is derived by the particular foreign affiliate under or as a result of an agreement that provides for the purchase, sale or exchange of currency and that can reasonably be considered to have been made by the particular foreign affiliate to reduce

(A) its risk — with respect to an amount that increases the amount required by this paragraph to be included in computing the particular foreign affiliate's income for a taxation year from an active business or that decreases the amount required by this paragraph to be included in computing the particular foreign affiliate's loss for a taxation year from an active business — of fluctuations in the value of the currency in which the amount was denominated, or

(B) its risk — with respect to an amount that decreases the amount required by this paragraph to be included in computing the particular foreign affiliate's income for a taxation year from an active business or that increases the amount required by this paragraph to be included in computing the particular foreign affiliate's loss for a taxation year from an active business — of fluctuations in the value of the currency in which the amount was denominated;

Related Provisions: 20(3) — Purpose for which borrowed money deemed to have been used; 93.1(4) — Partnership deemed to be corporation for 95(2)(a)(ii)(D); 93.1(5), (6)(a)(iii) — FAPI of a partnership; 95(2)(n) — Deemed FA and deemed qualifying interest; 95(2)(o), (q), (r) — Qualifying member; 95(2)(y), (z) — Look-through rules for partnerships; 95(2.2) — Interpretation rules; 95(2.201) — Deemed controlled foreign affiliate throughout year; 95(2.21) — Interpretation rules; 95(6) — Anti-avoidance rules; 212.3(24) — Foreign affiliate dumping rules — indirect funding; 253 — Whether business carried on in Canada.

Notes: 95(2)(a) characterizes certain property income as active business income (ABI) and thus not FAPI; see Notes to 91(1). For its origin (Arnold Sherman's work), see Brian Arnold, "The Grand Old Man of Canadian Tax", 75 *The Arnold Report* (ctf.ca, Feb. 5, 2015).

For the meaning of "derived", see Notes to 18.1(12).

95(2)(a)(i): see VIEWS docs 2000-0044387 (FA's real estate development income did not qualify under (B) [this may change since the 2014 amendment]); 2005-0125801C6 (where FA insurer reinsures risk with second FA); 2007-0229841C6 (income from investments used to support risks in reinsurance business is ABI); 2011-0400531R3; 2012-0439661I7 (income on funds earmarked for future projects at other FAs is FAPI); 2012-0452291R3 (double-dip financing structure [Bernstein, "Shares Not Debt in Luxembourgco", 21(4) *Canadian Tax Highlights* (ctf.ca) 7-8 (April 2013)]); 2015-0573141R3; 2015-0604451R3. See also Holms & Shields, "Foreign Affiliate Rules: The Effect of the Investment Business Definition on Real Estate Developers", 54(4) *Canadian Tax Journal* 937 at 949-54 (2006); Russell, " 'Mothership' Revisited", XV(4) *International Tax Planning* (Federated Press) 1076-80 (2010).

95(2)(a)(ii) opening words — "indirectly": VIEWS docs 2004-0073431E5; 2007-0257241R3 [2009-0332861R3] (income derived from payments from another FA's ABI); 2012-044160I17; and Notes to 17.1(1). On "payable": 2005-013046I17.

95(2)(A)(ii)(A): see Bernstein & Gucciardo, "Canada-US Hybrid Financing", 83(13) *Tax Notes International* (taxnotes.com) 1151-59 (Sept. 26, 2016).

95(2)(a)(ii)(B)(I) preserves a FA's ABI when paid as property income to another FA, similar to 129(6) in Canada. See also Huynh et al., "Foreign Affiliates: Tracing the Purpose and Use of Funds", 59(3) *Canadian Tax Journal* 571-89 (2011); Tang & Wong, "Cross-Charges for Real Estate in the International Context", 9(4) *Canadian Tax Focus* (ctf.ca) 10-11 (Nov. 2019).

95(2)(a)(ii)(B) — rulings that it applies: 2008-0273471R3; 2008-0287701R3; 2010-0363361R3 and 2010-0375111R3 [Sikham, "CRA Confirms Luxco Financing Structure", 1(2) *Canadian Tax Focus [CTFo]* (ctf.ca) 3-4 (Aug. 2011)]; 2010-0386201R3 (tower structure); 2012-0452291R3 (double-dip financing structure). More on (a)(ii)(B): 2012-044160I17 (it does not apply to interest payments); 2015-0581571C6 [2015 IFA q.11]; 2016-0642041C6 [2016 IFA q.8] (borrowing to return capital); 2016-068080I17 (interpretation of (B)(II) [Khazam, "CRA Confirms Interpretation of Cap B in Partnership Context", 8(1) *CTFo* 6 (Feb. 2018); Barnicke & Huynh, "Cap B Loan to Partnership", 26(2) *Canadian Tax Highlights* (ctf.ca) 9 (Feb. 2018)]). See also Keey, "Transfer Payments under Foreign Tax Laws", 2010(22) *Tax Times* (Carswell) 1-2 (Nov. 19, 2010); Pham, "FAPI Recharacterization and LLCs", 3(1) *CTFo* 9-10 (Feb. 2013).

German Organschaft and other profit-transfer agreements: 2008-0290091R3, 2009-0347881C6; 2016-0642081C6 [2016 IFA q.6] (90(2) can apply [Huynh & Barnicke, "German Organschafts", 24(6) *Canadian Tax Highlights [CTH]* (ctf.ca) 5-6 (June 2016)]); 2017-0682291E5 (95(2)(a)(ii) applies [Cepparo, "FA Profit Transfer Payments", 25(5) *CTH* 11 (May 2017)]).

95(2)(a)(ii)(D) recharacterizes as ABI "any related-party interest and royalties deducted by an FA from ABI, and thus enables a Canco to have a financing FA (e.g., in Luxembourg) that lends to an opco in a higher-tax jurisdiction (for example, the US) and allows the corporate group to benefit from reduction in corporate taxes. Interest is deducted at a US corporate tax rate of 35% plus state tax; it is taxed at a minimal rate (such as 1%) in Luxembourg; and it is not taxed upon repatriation to Canada as a tax-free dividend out of exempt surplus": Bernstein, "Transfer Pricing May Be EC State Aid", 23(12) *Canadian Tax Highlights* (ctf.ca) 2-4 (Dec. 2015).

CRA considers that "substantially all", in 95(2)(a)(ii)(D)(IV)2, means 90% or more.

95(2)(a)(ii)(D) — rulings that it applies: 2008-0287701R3; 2010-0386201R3 (tower structure). More on (a)(ii)(D): 2009-0317191C6 (affiliate must be resident and subject to income tax in the same jurisdiction for it to apply); 2014-0519801I7 (reverses 2013-049684117 [Barnicke & Huynh, "TI Denies Cap D Rule", 22(2) *Canadian Tax Highlights [CTH]* (ctf.ca) 12-13 (Feb. 2014)] and says (D)(II) applies); 2015-0581601C6 [2015 IFA q.6] (explains this reversal [Bian, "Clause 95(2)(a)(ii)(D) Recharacteriza-

tion", 6(1) *Canadian Tax Focus* (ctf.ca) 5 (Feb. 2016)]); 2015-0610561C6 [2015 CTF q.9] (re (D)(IV)2); 2013-0482351E5 [Jan. 2017] (inter-CFA loan prepayment penalty qualifies [Barnicke & Huynh, "Cap D and Make-Whole Payment", 24(4) *CTH* 9-10 (April 2017)]); 2017-0691221C6 [2017 IFA q.7] (re (D)(IV)2 "substantially all" test).

95(2)(a)(ii)(D): see also Porter & Bunn, "The Same-Country Requirement in Clause 95(2)(a)(ii)(D)", XVI(2) *International Tax Planning* (Federated Press) 1105-11 (2010) and "Is it Time to Simplify the Holding Company Rule?", XIX(2) 1304-10 (2014); Huynh et al., "Foreign Affiliates: Tracing the Purpose and Use of Funds", 59(3) *Canadian Tax Journal* 571-89 (2011); Kandev, "Putting on our Thinking Cap about "Cap D" ", 94 *International Tax* (CCH) 5-10 (June 2017).

95(2)(a)(ii) generally: see also Boidman & Kandev, "BEPS Cash Box Inconsistent with Canadian Tax Rules", 24(10) *CTH* 1-2 (Oct. 2016);

95(2)(a) generally: Tremblay & Wilkie, "... Uneasy Interaction of Subsection 15(2), Section 17 and Subsection 95(2)", 2002 Cdn Tax Foundation conference report at 18:1-17; Ton-That & Huynh, "Inconsistent Treatment of Partnerships in the Foreign Affiliate Rules", 2009 conference report, at 24:24-35; Korovilas & Morier, "Non-Corporate Vehicles in the Foreign Affiliate Context", 2018 conference report, at 20:25-27, 59-78. See also Notes to 91(1). A TCC appeal, *Honeywell Ltd.* (procedural decision 2007 FCA 22), was settled: 2005-2502(IT)G. See also VIEWS doc 2005-0151751R3 (95(2)(a) income or loss is included in Reg. 5907(1)"earnings", "loss").

95(2)(a) amended by 2014 budget bill #2 (last change effective for foreign affiliates' tax years that begin after July 12, 2013), 2007 budget bill #2, 1994 and 1991 technical bills. For detail, including the 2007 "Global Section 95 Election", see up to PITA 56th ed.

Regulations: 5907(1)"earnings"(b) (increase in earnings from an active business); 5907(1)"exempt earnings"(d) (inclusion in exempt earnings); 5907(1)"exempt loss"(c) (inclusion in exempt loss); 5907(1)"loss"(b) (increase in loss from an active business); 5907(2.7), (2.8) (where amount included in 95(2)(a)(i) or (ii)).

Interpretation Bulletins: IT-392: Meaning of term "share".

Information Circulars: 77-9R: Books, records and other requirements for taxpayers having foreign affiliates.

(a.1) [income from sale of property] — in computing the income from a business other than an active business for a taxation year of a foreign affiliate of a taxpayer there shall be included the income of the affiliate for the year from the sale of property (which, for the purposes of this paragraph, includes the income of the affiliate for the year from the performance of services as an agent in relation to a purchase or sale of property) where

(i) it is reasonable to conclude that the cost to any person of the property (other than property that is designated property) is relevant in computing the income from a business carried on by the taxpayer or by a person resident in Canada with whom the taxpayer does not deal at arm's length or is relevant in computing the income from a business carried on in Canada by a non-resident person with whom the taxpayer does not deal at arm's length, and

(ii) the property was not

(A) manufactured, produced, grown, extracted or processed in the country

(I) under whose laws the affiliate is governed and any of exists, was (unless the affiliate was continued in any jurisdiction) formed or organized, or was last continued, and

(II) in which the affiliate's business is principally carried on,

(B) an interest in real property, or a real right in an immovable, located in, or a foreign resource property in respect of, the country

(I) under whose laws the affiliate is governed and any of exists, was (unless the affiliate was continued in any jurisdiction) formed or organized, or was last continued, and

(II) in which the affiliate's business is principally carried on, or

(C) an indebtedness, or a lease obligation, of a person resident in Canada or in respect of a business carried on in Canada, that was purchased and sold by the affiliate on its own account,

unless more than 90% of the gross revenue of the affiliate for the year from the sale of property (other than a property the income

Non-Resident Corps/Trusts

from the sale of which is not included in computing the income from a business other than an active business of the affiliate under this paragraph because of subsection (2.31)) is derived from the sale of such property (other than a property described in subparagraph (ii) the cost of which to any person is a cost referred to in subparagraph (i)) to persons with whom the affiliate deals at arm's length (which, for this purpose, includes a sale of property to a non-resident corporation with which the affiliate does not deal at arm's length for sale to persons with whom the affiliate deals at arm's length) and, where this paragraph applies to include income of the affiliate from the sale of property in the income of the affiliate from a business other than an active business,

    (iii) the sale of such property shall be deemed to be a separate business, other than an active business, carried on by the affiliate, and

    (iv) any income of the affiliate that pertains to or is incident to that business shall be deemed to be income from a business other than an active business;

Related Provisions: 95(2)(n) — Deemed FA and deemed qualifying interest; 95(2.3) — Application of 95(2)(a.1); 95(2.31) — Application to eligible Canadian bank; 95(3.1) — Designated property; 95(3.2) — Contract manufacturing (for 95(2)(a.1)(ii)(A)); 253 — Whether business carried on in Canada.

Notes: See Notes to 91(1).

95(2)(a.1) was introduced to counter *Spur Oil*, [1981] C.T.C. 336 (FCA), and *Irving Oil*, [1991] 1 C.T.C. 350 (FCA). Its object is to treat income as FAPI where a Canadian parent establishes a subsidiary in a low-tax jurisdiction for the purchase of goods in a third country and their sale at a profit for use in the Canadian business. See also Nelson Ong, "Sale of Property and Paragraph 95(2)(a.1)", 60(3) *Canadian Tax Journal* 679-99 (2012); VIEWS doc 2015-0573801C6 [2015 CLHIA q.2].

If goods are to be manufactured in China, a Hong Kong (HK) or Macao company can be used to pay tax on the markup (up to fair market value: see 247(2)) at a lower rate than in China or Canada. Because HK and Macao are part of China, the condition in (a.1)(ii)(A) will not be satisfied.

For the meaning of "derived", see Notes to 18.1(12).

The words "any of exists..." in (ii)(A)(I) and (ii)(B)(I) should be read "any of {(1) exists, (2) was formed or organized, or (3) was last continued}", though this is not correct English.

95(2)(a.1)(iv) does not apply to a capital gain: VIEWS doc 2016-0658241I7.

95(2)(a.1) amended by 2017 and 2014 budget bills #2 (both for FAs' tax years that end after Oct. 2012), 2007 budget bill #2. Added by 1994 technical bill.

(a.2) [income from insurance] — in computing the income from a business other than an active business for a taxation year of a foreign affiliate of a taxpayer

    (i) there shall be included the income of the affiliate for the year from the insurance of specified Canadian risks (which, for the purposes of this paragraph, includes income for the year from the reinsurance of specified Canadian risks), unless more than 90% of the gross premium revenue of the affiliate for the year from the insurance of risks (net of reinsurance ceded) was in respect of the insurance of risks (other than specified Canadian risks) of persons with whom the affiliate deals at arm's length,

    (ii) if subparagraph (i) applies to include income of the affiliate from the insurance of specified Canadian risks,

        (A) the insurance of those risks is deemed to be a separate business, other than an active business, carried on by the affiliate, and

        (B) any income of the affiliate that pertains to or is incident to that business is deemed to be income from a business other than an active business,

    (iii) there shall be included the income of the affiliate for the year in respect of the ceding of specified Canadian risks — except to the extent that the income is included because of subparagraph (i) or (ii) — which, for the purposes of this paragraph, includes

        (A) income of the affiliate from services in respect of the ceding of specified Canadian risks, and

        (B) except to the extent the amount is included under clause (A), the amount, if any, by which the fair market value of the consideration provided in respect of the ceding of the specified Canadian risks exceeds the affiliate's cost in respect of those specified Canadian risks, and

    (iv) if subparagraph (iii) applies to include income of the affiliate in respect of the ceding of specified Canadian risks,

        (A) the ceding of those risks is deemed to be a separate business, other than an active business, carried on by the affiliate, and

        (B) any income of the affiliate that pertains to or is incident to that business is deemed to be income from a business other than an active business;

Related Provisions: 95(2)(a.21), (a.22) — Insurance swap arrangements; 95(2)(a.23) — Meaning of "specified Canadian risk"; 95(2)(a.24) — Anti-avoidance; 95(2)(n) — Deemed FA and deemed qualifying interest; 138(2.1) — Parallel rule for life insurer's branch outside Canada; 253 — Whether business carried on in Canada.

Notes: FAPI under 95(2)(a.2) can be offset with mark-to-market losses resulting from currency fluctuations: VIEWS doc 2010-0354421I7.

95(2)(a.2) amended by 2016 budget bill #1, for tax years that begin after April 20, 2015. (See Notes to 95(2)(a.21).) For earlier years, read:

    (a.2) in computing the income from a business other than an active business for a taxation year of a foreign affiliate of a taxpayer there shall be included the income of the affiliate for the year from the insurance of a risk (which, for the purposes of this paragraph, includes income of the affiliate for the year from the reinsurance of a risk) where the risk was in respect of

        (i) a person resident in Canada,

        (ii) a property situated in Canada, or

        (iii) a business carried on in Canada

    unless more than 90% of the gross premium revenue of the affiliate for the year from the insurance of risks (net of reinsurance ceded) was in respect of the insurance of risks (other than risks in respect of a person, a property or a business described in subparagraphs (i) to (iii)) of persons with whom the affiliate deals at arm's length and, where this paragraph applies to include income of the affiliate from the insurance of risks in the income of the affiliate from a business other than an active business,

        (iv) the insurance of those risks shall be deemed to be a separate business, other than an active business, carried on by the affiliate, and

        (v) any income of the affiliate that pertains to or is incident to that business shall be deemed to be income from a business other than an active business;

95(2)(a.2) added by 1994 technical bill, last change effective for foreign affiliates' tax years that end after 1994.

(a.21) [insurance swaps] — for the purposes of paragraph (a.2), one or more risks insured by a foreign affiliate of a taxpayer that, if this Act were read without reference to this paragraph, would not be specified Canadian risks (in this paragraph referred to as the "foreign policy pool") are deemed to be specified Canadian risks if

    (i) the affiliate, or a person or partnership that does not deal at arm's length with the affiliate, enters into one or more agreements or arrangements in respect of the foreign policy pool,

    (ii) the affiliate's risk of loss or opportunity for gain or profit in respect of the foreign policy pool, in combination with its risk of loss or opportunity for gain in respect of the agreements or arrangements, can reasonably be considered to be — or could reasonably be considered to be if the affiliate had entered into the agreements or arrangements entered into by the person or partnership — determined, in whole or in part, by reference to one or more criteria in respect of one or more risks insured by another person or partnership (in this paragraph referred to as the "tracked policy pool"), which criteria are

        (A) the fair market value of the tracked policy pool,

        (B) the revenue, income, loss or cash flow from the tracked policy pool, or

        (C) any other similar criteria, and

    (iii) 10% or more of the tracked policy pool consists of specified Canadian risks;

Related Provisions: 95(2)(a.22) — Additional rules for insurance swaps; 95(2)(a.23) — Meaning of "specified Canadian risk"; 95(2)(a.24) — Anti-avoidance; 138(2.2), (2.3) — Parallel rule for life insurer's branch outside Canada.

Notes: 95(2)(a.21) and (a.22) target insurance swaps circumventing 95(2)(a.2), which aims to prevent Canadian financial institutions from shifting income from insuring Canadian risks to a foreign affiliate (FA).

The 2016 amendments to 95(2)(a.2)-(a.21) target arrangements where the FA receives consideration with an embedded profit component (based on the expected return on the pool of Canadian risks) in exchange for ceding its Canadian risks. See Discepola, "FAPI and Offshore Captive Insurance Arrangements", *International Tax Newsletter* (Taxnet Pro), July 2015, pp. 1-2.

95(2)(a.21) opening words and subpara. (iii) amended by 2016 budget bill #1, for tax years that begin after April 20, 2015. For earlier years, read:

> (a.21) for the purposes of paragraph (a.2), one or more risks insured by a foreign affiliate of a taxpayer that, if this Act were read without reference to this paragraph, would not be risks in respect of a person, property or business described in any of subparagraphs (a.2)(i) to (iii) (in this paragraph referred to as the "foreign policy pool") are deemed to be risks in respect of a person resident in Canada if
>
>> (i) the affiliate, or a person or partnership that does not deal at arm's length with the affiliate, enters into one or more agreements or arrangements in respect of the foreign policy pool,
>>
>> (ii) the affiliate's risk of loss or opportunity for gain or profit in respect of the foreign policy pool, in combination with its risk of loss or opportunity for gain or profit in respect of the agreements or arrangements, can reasonably be considered to be — or could reasonably be considered to be if the affiliate had entered into the agreements or arrangements entered into by the person or partnership — determined, in whole or in part, by reference to one or more criteria in respect of one or more risks insured by another person or partnership (in this paragraph referred to as the "tracked policy pool"), which criteria are
>>
>>> (A) the fair market value of the tracked policy pool,
>>>
>>> (B) the revenue, income, loss or cash flow from the tracked policy pool, or
>>>
>>> (C) any other similar criteria, and
>>
>> (iii) 10% or more of the tracked policy pool consists of risks in respect of a person, property or business described in any of subparagraphs (a.2)(i) to (iii);

95(2)(a.21) and (a.22) added by 2014 budget bill #2, for tax years that begin after Feb. 10, 2014.

(a.22) [insurance swaps] — if the conditions in paragraph (a.21) are satisfied in respect of a foreign affiliate of a taxpayer, or a foreign affiliate of another taxpayer if that other taxpayer does not deal at arm's length with the taxpayer, and a particular foreign affiliate of the taxpayer, or a partnership of which the particular affiliate is a member, has entered into one or more agreements or arrangements described in that paragraph,

(i) activities performed in connection with those agreements or arrangements are deemed to be a separate business, other than an active business, carried on by the particular affiliate to the extent that those activities can reasonably be considered to be performed for the purpose of obtaining the result described in subparagraph (a.21)(ii), and

(ii) any income of the particular affiliate from the business (including income that pertains to or is incident to the business) is deemed to be income from a business other than an active business;

Related Provisions: 95(2)(a.24) — Anti-avoidance; 138(2.4) — Parallel rule for life insurer's branch outside Canada.

Notes: See Notes to 95(2)(a.21).

(a.23) ["specified Canadian risk"] — for the purposes of paragraphs (a.2), (a.21) and (a.24),"specified Canadian risk" means a risk in respect of

(i) a person resident in Canada,

(ii) a property situated in Canada, or

(iii) a business carried on in Canada;

Related Provisions: 95(2)(a.24) — Anti-avoidance.

Notes: 95(2)(a.23) amended to refer to (a.24) by 2017 budget bill #2, for transactions after March 21, 2017. Added by 2016 budget bill #1, for tax years that begin after April 20, 2015. These risks were listed in 95(2)(a.2)(i)-(iii).

(a.24) [insurance — anti-avoidance] — for the purposes of paragraph (a.2),

(i) a risk is deemed to be a specified Canadian risk of a particular foreign affiliate of a taxpayer if

(A) as part of a transaction or series of transactions, the particular affiliate insured or reinsured the risk,

(B) the risk would not be a specified Canadian risk if this Act were read without reference to this paragraph, and

(C) it can reasonably be concluded that one of the purposes of the transaction or series of transactions was to avoid the application of any of paragraphs (a.2) to (a.22), and

(ii) if the particular affiliate — or a foreign affiliate of another taxpayer, if that other taxpayer or affiliate, or a partnership of which that other taxpayer or affiliate is a member, does not deal at arm's length with the particular affiliate — enters into one or more agreements or arrangements in respect of the risk,

(A) activities performed in connection with those agreements or arrangements are deemed to be a separate business, other than an active business, carried on by the particular affiliate or other affiliate, as the case may be, and

(B) any income of the particular affiliate or other affiliate, as the case may be, from the business (including income that pertains to or is incident to the business) is deemed to be income from a business other than an active business;

Notes: 95(2)(a.24) implements a Dec. 23, 2016 Finance comfort letter to Brookfield Asset Management. Added by 2017 budget bill #2, for transactions after March 21, 2017.

(a.3) [income from Canadian debt and lease obligations] — in computing the income from a business other than an active business for a taxation year of a foreign affiliate of a taxpayer there shall be included the income of the affiliate for the year derived directly or indirectly from indebtedness and lease obligations (which, for the purposes of this paragraph, includes the income of the affiliate for the year from the purchase and sale of indebtedness and lease obligations on its own account, but does not include excluded income)

(i) of persons resident in Canada, or

(ii) in respect of businesses carried on in Canada

unless more than 90% of the gross revenue of the affiliate derived directly or indirectly from indebtedness and lease obligations (other than excluded revenue or revenue that is not included in computing the income from a business other than an active business of the affiliate under this paragraph because of subsection (2.31)) was derived directly or indirectly from indebtedness and lease obligations of non-resident persons with whom the affiliate deals at arm's length and, where this paragraph applies to include income of the affiliate for the year in the income of the affiliate from a business other than an active business,

(iii) those activities carried out to earn such income shall be deemed to be a separate business, other than an active business, carried on by the affiliate, and

(iv) any income of the affiliate that pertains to or is incident to that business shall be deemed to be income from a business other than an active business;

Related Provisions: 95(2)(n) — Deemed FA and deemed qualifying interest; 95(2.4)–(2.42) — Application of 95(2)(a.3); 95(2.5) — Definitions for 95(2)(a.3).

Notes: For the meaning of "derived", see Notes to 18.1(12). For "indirectly" see Notes to 17.1(1).

For a ruling applying the 95(2.4) exception see VIEWS doc 2006-0212871R3.

A July 17, 2006 comfort letter, shown here up to PITA 57th ed., was implemented in 95(2.5)"excluded income"(d).

95(2)(a.3) amended by 2014 budget bill #2 (for foreign affiliates' tax years that begin after Oct. 2012), 2001 technical bill. Added by 1994 technical bill.

Regulations: 7900 (prescribed financial institutions).

(a.4) [income from partnership debt and lease obligations] — in computing the income from a business other than an active business for a taxation year of a foreign affiliate of a taxpayer there shall be included (to the extent not included under paragraph (a.3) in such income of the affiliate for the year) that proportion of the income of the affiliate for the year derived directly or indirectly from indebtedness and lease obligations (which, for the purposes of this paragraph, includes the income of the affiliate for the year from the purchase and sale of indebtedness and lease obligations on its own account) in respect of a business carried on outside Canada by a partnership (any portion of the income or loss of which for fiscal periods of the partnership that end in the year is included or would, if the partnership had an income or loss for such fiscal periods, be included directly or indirectly in computing the income or loss of the taxpayer or a person resident in Canada with whom the taxpayer does not deal at arm's length) that

(i) the total of all amounts each of which is the income or loss of the partnership for fiscal periods of the partnership that end in the year that are included directly or indirectly in computing the income or loss of the taxpayer or a person resident in Canada with whom the taxpayer does not deal at arm's length

is of

(ii) the total of all amounts each of which is the income or loss of the partnership for fiscal periods of the partnership that end in the year

unless more than 90% of the gross revenue of the affiliate derived directly or indirectly from indebtedness and lease obligations was derived directly or indirectly from indebtedness and lease obligations of non-resident persons with whom the affiliate deals at arm's length (other than indebtedness and lease obligations of a partnership described in this paragraph) and where this paragraph applies to include a proportion of the income of the affiliate for the year in the income of the affiliate from a business other than an active business

(iii) those activities carried out to earn such income of the affiliate for the year shall be deemed to be a separate business, other than an active business, carried on by the affiliate, and

(iv) any income of the affiliate that pertains to or is incident to that business shall be deemed to be income from a business other than an active business

and for the purpose of this paragraph, where the income or loss of a partnership for a fiscal period that ends in the year is nil, the proportion of the income of the affiliate that is to be included in the income of the affiliate for the year from a business other than an active business shall be determined as if the partnership had income of $1,000,000 for that fiscal period;

Related Provisions: 95(2)(n) — Deemed FA and deemed qualifying interest; 253 — Whether business carried on in Canada.

Notes: For the meaning of "derived", see Notes to 18.1(12). For "indirectly" see Notes to 17.1(1).

95(2)(a.4) added by 1994 technical bill, last change effective for foreign affiliates' tax years that end after 1994.

(b) [services deemed not active business] — the provision, by a foreign affiliate of a taxpayer, of services or of an undertaking to provide services

(i) is deemed to be a separate business, other than an active business, carried on by the affiliate, and any income from that business or that pertains to or is incident to that business is deemed to be income from a business other than an active business, to the extent that the amounts paid or payable in consideration for those services or for the undertaking to provide services

(A) are deductible, or can reasonably be considered to relate to amounts that are deductible, in computing the income from a business carried on in Canada, by

(I) any taxpayer of whom the affiliate is a foreign affiliate, or

(II) another taxpayer who does not deal at arm's length with

1. the affiliate, or

2. any taxpayer of whom the affiliate is a foreign affiliate, or

(B) are deductible, or can reasonably be considered to relate to an amount that is deductible, in computing the foreign accrual property income of a foreign affiliate of

(I) any taxpayer of whom the affiliate is a foreign affiliate, or

Proposed Amendments — 95(2)(b)(i)(B)(I)

Letter from Dept. of Finance, Dec. 23, 2016: Mr. David Grosman, Senior Vice President, Taxation, Brookfield Asset Management Inc., Toronto

Dear Mr. Grosman:

SUBJECT: Foreign accrual property income resulting from the application of paragraph 95(2)(b) of the Income Tax Act to inter-affiliate payments for services

I am writing in response to your correspondence to the Tax Legislation Division, and your various related communications, concerning your request for an amendment to the *Income Tax Act* (the "Act") to ensure that paragraph 95(2)(b) of the Act does not apply to certain services fees paid by one foreign affiliate of Brookfield Asset Management Inc. ("Brookfield") to another foreign affiliate of Brookfield.

Paragraph 95(2)(b) is one of the "base erosion" rules in the Act. Your request relates, in particular, to subclause 95(2)(b)(i)(B)(I). That subclause provides that, if a particular foreign affiliate of a taxpayer provides services to another foreign affiliate of the taxpayer, then, to the extent that amounts paid by the other foreign affiliate in consideration for the services are deductible in computing its foreign accrual property income ("FAPI") (as defined in subsection 95(1) of the Act), these amounts are deemed to be income of the particular foreign affiliate from a business other than an active business – and are therefore included in the particular foreign affiliate's FAPI.

The issue that you have raised arises from the application of subclause 95(2)(b)(i)(B)(I) in the following factual situation, described in your letter. Brookfield, a corporation resident in Canada, and its subsidiaries establish and invest in certain investment funds. In structuring such investments, a non-resident holding corporation ("Holdco") is formed to acquire shares of a non-resident operating company ("Opco") that carries on an active business (as defined in subsection 95(1) of the Act). Brookfield (or a controlled foreign affiliate of Brookfield) and a group of arm's length investors contribute capital to Holdco to fund the acquisition of Opco. A wholly-owned, non-resident subsidiary corporation of Brookfield ("Manager") provides asset management and investment advisory services in respect of Opco in consideration for a management fee. Holdco, rather than Opco, pays the management fee to Manager because (among other reasons) Holdco is not the sole shareholder of Opco and Opco's other shareholders are unwilling to bear the fee.

In the investment structure described above, Holdco, Opco and Manager are all "foreign affiliates" of Brookfield (as defined in subsection 95(1)). You note that, since Holdco does not carry on an active business (its sole activity being the holding of shares of Opco), the services fees paid by Holdco to Manager are deductible in computing Holdco's FAPI, resulting in a foreign accrual property loss ("FAPL"). Accordingly, subclause 95(2)(b)(i)(B)(I) applies with the result that the services income is included in Manager's FAPI.

You have submitted to us that this result is inappropriate in policy terms. In this regard, you note that neither Opco nor Holdco earns FAPL. In addition, Manager's services are provided in respect of Opco, a subsidiary of Holdco that carries on an active business and the shares of which are "excluded property" of Holdco (as defined in subsection 95(1)); if the services fees were paid by Opco out of its active business income, instead of by Holdco, paragraph 95(2)(b) would not apply.

Our Comments:

We agree that, in policy terms, paragraph 95(2)(b) ought not to apply to cause the services fees received by Manager from Holdco to be FAPI in the circumstances described above.

We are therefore prepared to recommend to the Minister of Finance that the Act be amended to provide that, effective for taxation years of foreign affiliates ending after 2016, subclause 95(2)(b)(i)(B)(I) does not apply in respect of income of a foreign affiliate ("FA1") of a taxpayer from the provision of services, to the extent that conditions generally analogous to those in clause 95(2)(a)(ii)(D) are satisfied, including in particular the following conditions:

- The income derives from amounts paid or payable by another foreign affiliate ("FA2") of the taxpayer in consideration for the services;

- The amounts paid or payable are for expenditures incurred by FA2 for the purpose of gaining or producing income from property;

- The property is shares of another foreign affiliate ("FA3") that are "excluded property" of FA2 (as defined in subsection 95(1)); and

- The Canadian taxpayer has a "qualifying interest" (as defined in paragraph 95(2)(m) of the Act) in FA1, FA2 and FA3.

We will also recommend that, to the extent that subclause 95(2)(b)(i)(B)(I) does not apply in respect of FA1's income from services because of the above recommended amendment, any FAPL of FA2 otherwise resulting from its corresponding expenditures for those services be eliminated.

While we cannot offer any assurance that either the Minister of Finance or Parliament will agree with our recommendations in respect of this matter, we hope that this statement of our intentions is helpful.

Yours sincerely,

    Brian Ernewein, General Director–Legislation, Tax Policy Branch

Letter from Dept. of Finance, June 12, 2017:

Dear [xxx]:

SUBJECT: Foreign accrual property income resulting from the application of paragraph 95(2)(b) of the Income Tax Act to inter-affiliate payments for services

I am writing in response to your correspondence to the Tax Legislation Division, and various related communications, concerning your request for an amendment to the *Income Tax Act* (the "Act") to ensure that paragraph 95(2)(b) of the Act applies appropriately to certain services fees paid by one foreign affiliate of the [xxx] ("Canco") to another foreign affiliate of Canco.

Paragraph 95(2)(b) is one of the "base erosion" rules in the Act. Your request relates, in particular, to clause 95(2)(b)(i)(B). In general terms, that clause deems the provision of services by a particular foreign affiliate of a taxpayer to be a separate business, other than an active business, of the particular foreign affiliate — and includes any income from that business in the particular foreign affiliate's foreign accrual property income ("FAPI") (as defined in subsection 95(1) of the Act) — to the extent that amounts paid or payable in consideration for those services are deductible in computing the FAPI of:

- another foreign affiliate of the taxpayer,

- a foreign affiliate of any other taxpayer of which the particular foreign affiliate is a foreign affiliate, or

- a foreign affiliate of another taxpayer that does not deal at arm's length with either the particular foreign affiliate, or a taxpayer of which the particular foreign affiliate is a foreign affiliate.

The issue that you have raised arises from the application of sub-clause 95(2)(b)(i)(B)(I) in the following factual situation, described in your letter. Canco, a corporation resident in Canada, carries on a foreign asset management business through its foreign subsidiaries. Typically, in the course of this business, an investment fund (the "Fund") is established in the form of a non-resident corporation, and equity interests in the Fund are marketed and sold to arm's length investors. A non-resident wholly-owned subsidiary of Canco ("Manager") provides asset management services in respect of the Fund in consideration for a fee that is payable by the Fund. We understand that Canco and Manager each have a taxation year-end of [xxx] and typically the Fund will have a taxation year-end of [xxx].

Although the Fund is generally owned primarily by arm's length non-resident investors, Manager or a related Canco group entity may hold a small equity interest in the Fund. For example, Manager may make an initial "seed capital" investment when the Fund is established, which may subsequently be redeemed once the Fund has attracted sufficient investment from arm's length investors.

In the investment structure described above, Manager is a "foreign affiliate" of Canco (as defined in subsection 95(1)). If Canco's "equity percentage" (as defined in subsection 95(4)) in the Fund is not less than 10%, the Fund is also a foreign affiliate of Canco. Assuming the services fees paid or payable by the Fund to Manager are deductible in computing the Fund's FAPI (e.g., in computing its income from carrying on an "investment business", as defined in subsection 95(1)), then sub-clause 95(2)(b)(i)(B)(I) applies with the result that 100% of the services fees paid by the Fund is included in computing Manager's FAPI.

You have submitted to us that this is a disproportionate result. In your view, if paragraph 95(2)(b) is to apply in these circumstances, clause 95(2)(b)(i)(B) should be amended such that the services fees are included in computing Manager's FAPI only in proportion to Canco's economic interest in the Fund's FAPI.

Our Comments:

We agree that, in policy terms, the application of paragraph 95(2)(b) in the circumstances described above can be refined so that less than 100% of the services fees paid or payable to Manager by the Fund is included in computing Manager's FAPI. It would be consistent with the policy intent of paragraph 95(2)(b) that the proportion of the services fees so included be determined having regard to Canco's economic interest in the Fund's FAPI.

We are therefore prepared to recommend to the Minister of Finance that, effective for taxation years of foreign affiliates beginning after 2015, the Act be amended such that clause 95(2)(b)(i)(B) deems the provision of services (or an undertaking to provide services) by a foreign affiliate of a taxpayer (the "first affiliate") to be a separate business, other than an active business, of the first affiliate — and includes any income from that business in the first affiliate's FAPI — to the extent of the portion of the amounts paid or payable in consideration for the services (or for the undertaking) determined by the formula A × B, where:

A   is an amount paid or payable in consideration for the services or for the undertaking that is deductible, or can reasonably be considered to relate to an amount that is deductible, in computing the FAPI of a foreign affiliate of any of the taxpayers described in sub-clause 95(2)(b)(i)(B)(I) or (II) (the "second affiliate"); and

B   is the total of the participating percentages (as defined in subsection 95(1)), in respect of the second affiliate of shares of corporations that are owned by any taxpayer resident in Canada of which the second affiliate is a foreign affiliate, at the end of the second affiliate's tax year in which that amount is deductible. For this purpose, the definition of "participating percentage" is to be read as though it applies to all foreign affiliates, and not only controlled foreign affiliates.

While we cannot offer any assurance that either the Minister of Finance or Parliament will agree with our recommendations in respect of this matter, we hope that this statement of our intentions is helpful.

Yours sincerely,

    Brian Ernewein, General Director–Legislation, Tax Policy Branch

        (II) another taxpayer who does not deal at arm's length with

           1. the affiliate, or

           2. any taxpayer of whom the affiliate is a foreign affiliate, and

(ii) is deemed to be a separate business, other than an active business, carried on by the affiliate, and any income from that business or that pertains to or is incident to that business is deemed to be income from a business other than an active business, to the extent that the services are, or are to be, performed by

      (A) any taxpayer of whom the affiliate is a foreign affiliate,

      (B) a relevant person who does not deal at arm's length with

        (I) the affiliate, or

        (II) any taxpayer of whom the affiliate is a foreign affiliate,

      (C) a partnership any member of which is a person described in clause (A) or (B), or

      (D) a partnership in which any person or partnership described in any of clauses (A) to (C) has, directly or indirectly, a partnership interest;

Related Provisions: 95(2)(n) — Deemed FA and deemed qualifying interest; 95(2.2) — Interpretation rules; 95(3) — "Services" defined; 95(3.01) — Application to eligible Canadian bank; 95(3.02) — "Relevant person", and separate businesses; 253 — Whether business carried on in Canada.

Notes: Provision of services is normally active business, but service revenues can be deemed FAPI by 95(2)(b) if the Canadian parent or a related entity is paying for the services, or the services are performed by a Canadian member of the group. This can apply to R&D services even if an arm's-length fee is paid: VIEWS doc 2016-067192I7.

See Halvorson, "Tax Policy and Subparagraph 95(2)(b)(ii)", 18(3) *Canadian Tax Highlights* (ctf.ca) 4-5 (March 2010); Brady & Roy, "Paragraph 95(2)(b)", XIX(2) *International Tax Planning* (Federated Press) 1311-14 (2014). See also Notes to 95(3).

In 95(2)(b)(ii)(B), the reference to "relevant person" (see 95(3.02)) implements a March 23, 2010 Finance comfort letter.

In *Loblaw Financial*, 2018 TCC 182 (rev'd on other grounds 2020 FCA 79; SCC appeal heard May 13/21), para. 278, 95(2)(b) applied to fees for managing assets of related companies.

If Canco charges its FA a markup for seconding employees to the FA, 95(2)(b) will apply to part of the FA's income: VIEWS docs 2013-0474431E5, 2014-0550511C6 [2014 CTF q.8]; Tollstam, "Seconded Employees", 22(3) *Canadian Tax Highlights* (ctf.ca) 13-14 (March 2014).

95(2)(b) amended by 2014 budget bill #2 (for FAs' tax years that begin after July 12, 2013, or earlier by election), 2007 budget bill #2, 1991 technical bill.

  (c) [rollover of FA shares to another FA] — if a foreign affiliate (referred to in this paragraph as the "disposing affiliate") of a taxpayer has, at any time, disposed of capital property (other than property the adjusted cost base of which, at that time, is greater than the amount that would, in the absence of this paragraph, be the disposing affiliate's proceeds of disposition of the property in respect of the disposition) that was shares (referred to in this paragraph as the "shares disposed of") of the capital stock of another foreign affiliate of the taxpayer to any other corporation that was, immediately after that time, a foreign affiliate (referred to in this paragraph as the "acquiring affiliate") of the taxpayer for consideration that includes shares of the capital stock of the acquiring affiliate,

(i) the cost to the disposing affiliate of any property (other than shares of the capital stock of the acquiring affiliate) receivable by the disposing affiliate as consideration for the disposition is deemed to be the fair market value of the property at that time,

(ii) the cost to the disposing affiliate of each share of a class of the capital stock of the acquiring affiliate that is receivable by the disposing affiliate as consideration for the disposition is deemed to be the amount determined by the formula

$$(A - B) \times C/D$$

where

A   is the total of all amounts each of which is the relevant cost base to the disposing affiliate at that time, in respect of the taxpayer, of a share disposed of,

B   is the fair market value at that time of the consideration receivable for the disposition (other than shares of the capital stock of the acquiring affiliate),

C   is the fair market value, immediately after that time, of the share, and

D   is the fair market value, immediately after that time, of all shares of the capital stock of the acquiring affiliate receivable by the disposing affiliate as consideration for the disposition,

(iii) the disposing affiliate's proceeds of disposition of the shares are deemed to be an amount equal to the cost to it of all shares and other property receivable by it from the acquiring affiliate as consideration for the disposition, and

(iv) the cost to the acquiring affiliate of the shares acquired from the disposing affiliate is deemed to be an amount equal to the disposing affiliate's proceeds of disposition referred to in subparagraph (iii);

Related Provisions: 53(1)(c) — Addition to ACB of share; 85.1(3) — Rollover for Canadian tax purposes; 93.2(3) — Application to non-resident corp without share capital; 95(1)"foreign accrual property income"B(b) — Inclusion in FAPI; 95(2)(n) — Deemed FA and deemed qualifying interest; 95(6) — Anti-avoidance rules; 257 — Formula cannot calculate to less than zero.

Notes: See O'Hagan & Buttenham, "Foreign Affiliate Reorganizations — Where Are We Now?", 2013 Cdn Tax Foundation conference report at 20:12-19. See also VIEWS doc 2015-0571441R3 (rollover of shares to Dutch cooperative).

See Notes to 93.2(3) re foreign corp without share capital.

95(2)(c) amended by 2002-2013 technical bill, for dispositions after Aug. 19, 2011.

Proposed **95(2)(c.1)-(c.6)** in the Feb. 27, 2004 draft legislation (reproduced in PITA 26th-40th ed.) will not be enacted. They were intended to suspend the recognition of capital gain on a foreign affiliate (FA)'s internal disposition of a Canadian resident corp (or a partnership of which the FA was a member) of a share of another FA of a Canadian resident corp that was excluded property to the vendor (or would be if the vendor were a FA of the taxpayer). On these proposals (which replaced Dec. 20, 2002 draft 93(1.4)-(1.6)), see Jack et al, "The February 27, 2004 Draft Proposals on Foreign Affiliates", 2004 Cdn Tax Foundation conference report, at 20:10-19; Meister, "Foreign Affiliate Update", 19 *Canadian Petroleum Tax Journal* (2006).

Regulations: 5907(1)"net earnings"(d)(i), "net loss"(d)(i), "taxable earnings"(b)(v), "taxable loss"(b)(v) (exclusions from reduction); 5907(5.3)(b) (Reg. 5907(5.1) does not apply to disposition).

Interpretation Bulletins: IT-392: Meaning of term "share".

(d) **[foreign merger]** — where there has been a foreign merger in which the shares owned by a foreign affiliate of a taxpayer of the capital stock of a corporation that was a predecessor foreign corporation immediately before the merger were exchanged for

or became shares of the capital stock of the new foreign corporation or the foreign parent corporation, subsection 87(4) applies to the foreign affiliate as if the references in that subsection to

(i) "amalgamation" were read as "foreign merger",

(ii) "predecessor corporation" were read as "predecessor foreign corporation",

(iii) "new corporation" were read as "new foreign corporation or the foreign parent corporation", and

(iv) "adjusted cost bases" were read as "relevant cost bases, in respect of the taxpayer,";

Related Provisions: 87(8.1) — Foreign merger; 95(1)"foreign accrual property income"B(b) — Inclusion in FAPI; 95(2)(n) — Deemed FA and deemed qualifying interest.

Notes: For discussion of 95(2)(d)-(d.1) and an earlier draft of the 2013 amendments see Turner, "Foreign Affiliate Liquidation and Merger Rollovers", 53(3) *Canadian Tax Journal* 640 (2005), at 666-74.

See also VIEWS doc 2009-0330881R3 (95(2)(d) and (d.1) applied).

95(2)(d)(iv) amended by 2002-2013 technical bill (for mergers or combinations in respect of a foreign affiliate after Aug. 19, 2011), 1998 Budget.

Regulations: 5907(1)"net earnings"(d)(i), "net loss"(d)(i), "taxable earnings"(b)(v), "taxable loss"(b)(v) (exclusions from reduction); 5907(2.01) (determining earnings derived from disposition); 5907(5.3)(b) (Reg. 5907(5.1) does not apply to disposition).

Interpretation Bulletins: IT-392: Meaning of term "share".

(d.1) **[foreign merger]** — if there has been a foreign merger of two or more predecessor foreign corporations to form a new foreign corporation that is, immediately after the merger, a foreign affiliate of a taxpayer and one or more of the predecessor foreign corporations (each being referred to in this paragraph as a "foreign affiliate predecessor") was, immediately before the merger, a foreign affiliate of the taxpayer,

(i) each property of the new foreign corporation that was a property of a foreign affiliate predecessor immediately before the merger is deemed to have been

(A) disposed of by the foreign affiliate predecessor immediately before the merger for proceeds of disposition equal to the relevant cost base of the property to the foreign affiliate predecessor, in respect of the taxpayer, at that time, and

(B) acquired by the new foreign corporation, at that time, at a cost equal to the amount determined under clause (A),

(ii) the new foreign corporation is deemed to be the same corporation as, and a continuation of, each foreign affiliate predecessor for the purposes of applying

(A) this subsection and the definition "foreign accrual property income" in subsection (1) with respect to any disposition by the new foreign corporation of any property to which subparagraph (i) applied,

(B) subsections 13(21.2), 18(15) and 40(3.4) in respect of any property that was disposed of, at any time before the merger, by a foreign affiliate predecessor, and

(C) paragraph 40(3.5)(c) in respect of any share that was deemed under that paragraph to be owned, at any time before the merger, by a foreign affiliate predecessor, and

(iii) for the purposes of the description of A.2 in the definition "foreign accrual property income" in subsection (1), the total of all amounts each of which is the amount determined for G in respect of a foreign affiliate predecessor for its last taxation year that ends on or before the time of the merger is deemed to be the amount determined for G in respect of the new foreign corporation for its taxation year that immediately precedes its first taxation year;

Related Provisions: 87(8.1) — Foreign merger; 95(1)"foreign accrual property income"B(b) — Inclusion in FAPI; 95(2)(n) — Deemed FA and deemed qualifying interest; Reg. 5903(5)(a) — Effect of 95(2)(d.1) on FAPL.

Notes: See Notes to 95(2)(d). For discussion see O'Hagan & Buttenham, "Foreign Affiliate Reorganizations", 2013 Cdn Tax Foundation conference report at 20:44-50.

95(2)(d.1)(ii)(B) amended to delete reference to 14(12) by 2016 budget bill #2, effective 2017 (as part of changing the eligible capital property rules to CCA Class 14.1: see Notes to 20(1)(b)).

95(2)(d.1) earlier amended by 2002-2013 technical bill (for a foreign affiliate merger or combination after Aug. 19, 2011, with an election for different rules for the taxpayer's tax year that includes June 26, 2013: see up to PITA 46th ed.), 1991 technical bill.

Regulations: 5907(2.01) (determining earnings derived from disposition).

Interpretation Bulletins: IT-392: Meaning of term "share".

(e) **[windup of foreign affiliate]** — notwithstanding subsection 69(5), if at any time a foreign affiliate (referred to in this paragraph as the "shareholder affiliate") of a taxpayer receives a property (referred to in this paragraph as the "distributed property") from another foreign affiliate (referred to in this paragraph as the "disposing affiliate") of the taxpayer on a liquidation and dissolution of the disposing affiliate and the distributed property is received in respect of shares of the capital stock of the disposing affiliate that are disposed of on the liquidation and dissolution,

(i) the distributed property is deemed to have been disposed of at that time by the disposing affiliate to the shareholder affiliate for proceeds of disposition equal to the relevant cost base to the disposing affiliate of the distributed property in respect of the taxpayer, immediately before that time, if

(A) the liquidation and dissolution is a designated liquidation and dissolution of the disposing affiliate, or

(B) the distributed property is a share of the capital stock of another foreign affiliate of the taxpayer that was, immediately before that time, excluded property of the disposing affiliate,

(ii) if subparagraph (i) does not apply to the distributed property, the distributed property is deemed to have been disposed of at that time by the disposing affiliate to the shareholder affiliate for proceeds of disposition equal to the distributed property's fair market value at that time,

(iii) the distributed property is deemed to have been acquired, at that time, by the shareholder affiliate at a cost equal to the amount determined under subparagraph (i) or (ii) to be the disposing affiliate's proceeds of disposition of the distributed property,

(iv) each share of a class of the capital stock of the disposing affiliate that is disposed of by the shareholder affiliate on the liquidation and dissolution of the disposing affiliate is deemed to be disposed of for proceeds of disposition equal to

(A) if the liquidation and dissolution is a designated liquidation and dissolution of the disposing affiliate

(I) where the amount that would, if clause (B) applied, be determined under that clause in respect of the share is greater than or equal to the adjusted cost base of the share to the shareholder affiliate immediately before the disposition, that adjusted cost base, or

(II) where the adjusted cost base of the share to the shareholder affiliate immediately before the disposition exceeds the amount that would, if clause (B) applied, be determined under that clause in respect of the share

1. if the share is not excluded property of the shareholder affiliate, that adjusted cost base, and

2. in any other case, the amount that would be determined under clause (B), and

(B) in any other case, the amount determined by the formula

$$(A - B)/C$$

where

A is the total of all amounts each of which is the cost to the shareholder affiliate of a distributed property, as determined under subparagraph (iii), received, at any time, in respect of the class,

B is the total of all amounts each of which is an amount owing (other than an unpaid dividend) by, or an obligation of, the disposing affiliate that was assumed or cancelled by the shareholder affiliate in consideration for the distribution of a distributed property referred to in the description of A, and

C is the total number of issued and outstanding shares of the class that are owned by the shareholder affiliate during the liquidation and dissolution, and

(v) if the liquidation and dissolution is a designated liquidation and dissolution of the disposing affiliate,

(A) the shareholder affiliate is deemed to be the same corporation as, and a continuation of, the disposing affiliate for the purposes of applying

(I) this subsection and the definition "foreign accrual property income" in subsection (1) with respect to any disposition by the shareholder affiliate of any property to which clause (i)(A) applied,

(II) subsections 13(21.2), 18(15) and 40(3.4) in respect of any property that was disposed of, at any time before the liquidation and dissolution, by the disposing affiliate, and

(III) paragraph 40(3.5)(c) in respect of any share that was deemed under that paragraph to be owned, at any time before the liquidation and dissolution, by the disposing affiliate, and

(B) for the purposes of the description of A.2 in the definition "foreign accrual property income" in subsection (1), the amount, if any, determined for G in respect of the disposing affiliate for its first taxation year that ends after the beginning of the liquidation and dissolution is to be added to the amount otherwise determined for G in respect of the shareholder affiliate for its taxation year that immediately precedes its taxation year that includes the time at which the liquidation and dissolution began;

Related Provisions: 88(3)–(3.5) — Rules where liquidation results in distribution to Canadian parent; 95(1)"foreign accrual property income"B(b) — Inclusion in FAPI; 95(2)(n) — Deemed FA and deemed qualifying interest; 257 — Formula amount cannot calculate to less than zero; Reg. 5903(5)(b) — Effect of 95(2)(e) on FAPL; Reg. 5905(7) — Effect of liquidation and dissolution on surplus computations.

Notes: For discussion of 95(2)(e)-(e.1) and an earlier draft of the 2013 amendments see Turner, "Foreign Affiliate Liquidation and Merger Rollovers", 53(3) *Canadian Tax Journal* 640 at 657-65 (2005). For discussion since those amendments see O'Hagan & Buttenham, "Foreign Affiliate Reorganizations", 2013 Cdn Tax Foundation conference report at 20:33-43.

CRA's view (doc 2003-0034311E5) is that a liquidation requires all contractual relationships to be terminated, all property sold, and all obligations and liabilities settled and satisfied. The company must then be deleted from the Commercial Register.

95(2)(e)(v)(A)(II) amended to delete reference to 14(12) by 2016 budget bill #2, effective 2017 (as part of changing the eligible capital property rules to CCA Class 14.1: see Notes to 20(1)(b)).

95(2)(e) earlier amended by 2002-2013 technical bill, for foreign affiliate liquidations and dissolutions that begin after Aug. 19, 2011, with an election to apply earlier.

Regulations: 5905(7) (computation of balances where 95(2)(e) applies); 5907(1)"net earnings"(d)(i), "net loss"(d)(i), "taxable earnings"(b)(v), "taxable loss"(b)(v) (exclusions from reduction); 5907(2.01) (determining earnings derived from disposition); 5907(5.3)(b) (Reg. 5907(5.1) does not apply to disposition); 5907(9) (dissolution).

Interpretation Bulletins: IT-392: Meaning of term "share".

(e.1) [Repealed]

Notes: See Notes to 95(2)(e). 95(2)(e.1) repealed by 2002-2013 technical bill, for foreign affiliate liquidations and dissolutions that begin after Aug. 19, 2011, with an election to apply earlier. Earlier amended by 1991 technical bill.

Proposed **95(2)(e.2)-(e.6)**, in the Feb. 27, 2004 draft legislation, will not be enacted.

Regulations: 5905(7) (computation of balances where 95(2)(e.1) applies); 5907(2.01) (determining earnings derived from disposition); 5907(9) (dissolution where 95(2)(e.1) does not apply).

Interpretation Bulletins: IT-392: Meaning of term "share".

(f) **[rules for calculating income of foreign affiliate]** — except as otherwise provided in this Subdivision and except to the extent that the context otherwise requires, a foreign affiliate of a taxpayer is deemed to be at all times resident in Canada for the purposes of determining, in respect of the taxpayer for a taxation year of the foreign affiliate, each amount that is the foreign affiliate's

(i) capital gain, capital loss, taxable capital gain or allowable capital loss from a disposition of a property, or

(ii) income or loss from a property, from a business other than an active business or from a non-qualifying business;

Related Provisions: 95(2)(f.1), (f.11) — Additional rules; 95(2)(f.12)–(f.15) — Currency to be used in calculations; 95(2)(n) — Deemed FA and deemed qualifying interest; 248(10) — Series of transactions or events; 261 — Functional currency reporting.

Notes: See Maikawa & Martin, "Foreign Exchange and Foreign Affiliates", 54(1) *Canadian Tax Journal [CTJ]* 241-61 (2006); Huynh & Lockwood, "Foreign Affiliates and Adjusted Cost Base", 55(1) *CTJ* 141-59 (2007); Ancimer & Beswick, "Foreign Exchange Legislation", 2017 Cdn Tax Foundation conference report, at 17:5-11.

In *Loblaw Financial*, 2018 TCC 182 (rev'd on other grounds 2020 FCA 79; SCC appeal heard May 13/21), paras. 272-277, investment in short-term securities was on income account.

For CRA interpretation see VIEWS docs 2006-0207391R3 and 2006-0217481R3 (gains excluded by what is now 95(2)(f.1)); 2017-0738081E5 (20(1)(c) deduction for FA need not be claimed, but cannot be saved and claimed later).

95(2)(f) amended by 2008 budget bill #2 (last change effective for foreign affiliates' tax years that begin after 2008), 1991 technical bill.

Regulations: 5903(1), (3) (deductible loss); 5907(5) (capital gain rules to be used).

(f.1) **[calculating income of foreign affiliate]** — in computing an amount described in paragraph (f) in respect of a property or a business, there is not to be included any portion of that amount that can reasonably be considered to have accrued, in respect of the property (including for the purposes of this paragraph any property for which the property was substituted) or the business, while no person or partnership that held the property or carried on the business was a specified person or partnership in respect of the taxpayer referred to in paragraph (f);

Related Provisions: 95(4)"relevant cost base" — Effect on cost base.

Notes: See Porter & Slaats, "The Carve-out Rule in Proposed Para. 95(2)(f.1)", XV(1) *International Tax Planning* (Federated Press) 1024-29 (2009); Turner, "The New 95(2)(f.1) Carve-Out Rule", 1974 *Tax Topics* (CCH) 1-6 (Jan. 7, 2010); VIEWS docs 2008-0290351E5, 2009-0349701R3, 2010-0365861R3.

See also Notes to 95(2)(f). 95(2)(f.1) added by 2008 budget bill #2, last change effective for foreign affiliates' tax years that begin after Oct. 2, 2007.

(f.11) **[calculating income of foreign affiliate]** — in determining an amount described in paragraph (f) for a taxation year of a foreign affiliate of a taxpayer,

(i) if the amount is described in subparagraph (f)(i), this Act is to be

(A) read without reference to section 26 of the *Income Tax Application Rules*, and

(B) applied as if, in respect of any debt obligation owing by the foreign affiliate or a partnership of which the foreign affiliate is a member (which foreign affiliate or partnership is referred to in this clause as the "debtor"), each capital gain or loss of the debtor that is deemed to arise under subsection 39(2) or (3) in respect of the debt obligation were from a disposition of property that was held by the debtor throughout the period during which the debt obligation was owed by the debtor and, for greater certainty, at the time of the disposition,

(ii) if the amount is described in subparagraph (f)(ii),

(A) this Act is to be read without reference to subsections 17(1) and 18(4) and section 91, except that, where the foreign affiliate is a member of a partnership, section 91 is to be applied to determine the income or loss of the partnership and for that purpose subsection 96(1) is to be applied to determine the foreign affiliate's share of that income or loss of the partnership,

(B) if the foreign affiliate has, in the taxation year, disposed of a foreign resource property in respect of a country, it is deemed to have designated, in respect of the dis-

position and in accordance with subparagraph 59(1)(b)(ii) for the taxation year, the amount, if any, by which

(I) the amount determined under paragraph 59(1)(a) in respect of the disposition

exceeds

(II) the amount determined under subparagraph 59(1)(b)(i) in respect of the disposition, and

(C) this Act is to be applied as if, in respect of any debt obligation owing by the foreign affiliate or a partnership of which the foreign affiliate is a member (which foreign affiliate or partnership is referred to in this clause as the "debtor"), each amount of income or loss of the debtor — from a property, from a business other than an active business or from a non-qualifying business — in respect of the debt obligation were from such a property that was held, or such a business that was carried on, as the case may be, by the debtor throughout the period during which the debt obligation was owed by the debtor and at the time at which the debt obligation was settled or extinguished;

Related Provisions: 95(2)(f.12)–(f.15) — Currency to be used in calculations; 95(2)(n) — Deemed FA and deemed qualifying interest; 261 — Functional currency reporting.

Notes: 247(2) can apply in computing FAPI, but CRA will not normally challenge transfer pricing accepted by a foreign tax authority if its guidelines use the arm's-length principle: VIEWS doc 2017-0691191C6 [2017 IFA q.2].

95(2)(f.11)(ii)(A) amended to delete reference to 14(1.01)-(1.03) by 2016 budget bill #2, effective 2017 (as part of changing the eligible capital property rules to CCA Class 14.1: see Notes to 20(1)(b)).

95(2)(f.11) amended by 2002-2013 technical bill (for foreign affiliates' tax years that end after Aug. 19, 2011, or earlier by election). Added by 2008 budget bill #2.

(f.12) **[currency to be used for foreign affiliate]** — a foreign affiliate of a taxpayer shall determine each of the following amounts using its calculating currency for a taxation year:

(i) subject to paragraph (f.13), each capital gain, capital loss, taxable capital gain and allowable capital loss (other than a gain or loss in respect of a debt referred to in subparagraph (i)(i) or (ii)) of the foreign affiliate for the taxation year from the disposition, at any time, of a property that, at that time, was an excluded property of the foreign affiliate,

(ii) its income or loss for the taxation year from each active business carried on by it in the taxation year in a country, and

(iii) its income or loss that is included in computing its income or loss from an active business for the taxation year because of paragraph (a);

Related Provisions: 95(2)(f.13)-(f.15) — Rules; 261(5)(e), 261(5)(h)(i) — Functional currency reporting.

Notes: 95(2)(f.12) amended by 2002-2013 technical bill, for foreign affiliates' tax years that end after Aug. 19, 2011, or earlier by election. Added by 2008 budget bill #2.

(f.13) **[currency to be used for foreign affiliate]** — where the calculating currency of a foreign affiliate of a taxpayer is a currency other than Canadian currency, the foreign affiliate shall determine the amount included in computing its foreign accrual property income, in respect of the taxpayer for a taxation year of the foreign affiliate, attributable to its capital gain or taxable capital gain, from the disposition of an excluded property in the taxation year, in Canadian currency by converting the amount of the capital gain, or taxable capital gain, otherwise determined under subparagraph (f.12)(i) using its calculating currency for the taxation year into Canadian currency using the rate of exchange quoted by the Bank of Canada on the day on which the disposition was made, or another rate of exchange that is acceptable to the Minister;

Related Provisions: 261(5)(h) — Functional currency reporting.

Notes: 95(2)(f.13) amended by 2017 budget bill #2, effective March 2017, to change "at noon on the day" to "on the day" (since Bank of Canada [BoC] now publishes only 1 rate daily), and to add "or another rate of exchange that is acceptable to the Minister". Finance Technical Notes say that a rate other than that published by BoC will be allowed only if BoC does not publish an exchange rate for the currency.

95(2)(f.13) added by 2009 budget bill #1, last change effective for foreign affiliates' tax years that begin after Oct. 2, 2007.

(f.14) [currency to be used for foreign affiliate] — a foreign affiliate of a taxpayer is to determine using Canadian currency each amount of its income, loss, capital gain, capital loss, taxable capital gain or allowable capital loss for a taxation year, other than an amount to which paragraph (f.12), (f.13) or (f.15) applies;

Related Provisions: 261(5)(h)(i)(A) — Functional currency reporting — meaning of "Canadian currency".

Notes: See Mark Dumalski, "Non-Canadian-Dollar Loans Involving FAs", 2(1) *Canadian Tax Focus* (ctf.ca) 1 (Feb. 2012).

95(2)(f.14) amended by 2002-2013 technical bill, for foreign affiliates' tax years that end after Aug. 19, 2011, or earlier by election. Added by 2009 budget bill #1.

(f.15) [currency to be used for foreign affiliate] — for the purposes of applying subparagraph (f)(i), the references in subsection 39(2) to "Canadian currency" are to be read as "the taxpayer's calculating currency"

(i) in respect of a debt obligation owing by a foreign affiliate of a taxpayer, or a partnership of which the foreign affiliate is a member, that is a debt referred to in subparagraph (i)(i) or (ii), and

(ii) in respect of an agreement described in subparagraph (i)(iii) entered into by a foreign affiliate of a taxpayer, or a partnership of which the foreign affiliate is a member;

Related Provisions: 261(5)(e), (5)(h)(i) — Functional currency reporting.

Notes: 95(2)(f.15)(ii) added by 2017 budget bill #2, for foreign affiliates' tax years that begin after Oct. 2, 2007. 95(2)(f.15) earlier amended by 2002-2013 technical bill, for FAs' tax years that end after Aug. 19, 2011, or earlier by election. Added by 2009 budget bill #1.

Proposed **95(2)(f.3)-(f.94)** in the Feb. 27, 2004 draft legislation (reproduced in PITA 26th-40th ed.) will not be enacted. They were intended to suspend the recognition of income or capital gain that would otherwise arise on an internal disposition of an excluded property: see Jack et al, "The February 27, 2004 Draft Proposals on Foreign Affiliates", 2004 Cdn Tax Foundation conference report, at 20:19-23.

(g) [currency fluctuation] — income earned, a loss incurred or a capital gain or capital loss realized, as the case may be, in a taxation year by a particular foreign affiliate of a taxpayer in respect of which the taxpayer has a qualifying interest throughout the taxation year or a particular foreign affiliate of a taxpayer that is a controlled foreign affiliate of the taxpayer throughout the taxation year, because of a fluctuation in the value of the currency of a country other than Canada relative to the value of Canadian currency, is deemed to be nil if it is earned, incurred or realized in reference to any of the following sources:

(i) a debt obligation that was owing to

(A) another foreign affiliate of the taxpayer in respect of which the taxpayer has a qualifying interest throughout the year (which other foreign affiliate is referred to in this paragraph as a "qualified foreign affiliate") by the particular affiliate, or

(B) the particular affiliate by a qualified foreign affiliate,

(ii) the redemption, acquisition or cancellation of, or a qualifying return of capital (within the meaning assigned by subsection 90(3)) in respect of, a share of the capital stock of a qualified foreign affiliate by the qualified foreign affiliate, or

(iii) the disposition to a qualified foreign affiliate of a share of the capital stock of another qualified foreign affiliate;

Related Provisions: 93.1(5), (6)(a)(iv) — FAPI of a partnership; 95(2)(g.01) — Currency hedging; 95(2)(g.03) — Application of 95(2)(g) to partners; 95(2)(n) — Deemed FA and deemed qualifying interest; 95(2.201) — Deemed controlled foreign affiliate throughout year; 261(5)(h)(i) — Meaning of "Canadian currency" and "currency of a country other than Canada".

Notes: See Notes to 95(2)(f).

95(2)(g) amended by 2002-2013 technical bill (for FAs' tax years that end after Aug. 19, 2011, or earlier by election), 2007 budget bill #2, 2001 technical bill.

Interpretation Bulletins: IT-392: Meaning of term "share".

I.T. Technical News: 15 (tax consequences of the adoption of the "euro" currency).

(g.01) [currency hedging] — any income, loss, capital gain or capital loss, derived by a foreign affiliate of a taxpayer under or as a result of an agreement that provides for the purchase, sale or exchange of currency and that can reasonably be considered to have been made by the foreign affiliate to reduce its risk (with respect to any source, any particular income, gain or loss determined in reference to which is deemed by paragraph (g) to be nil) of fluctuations in the value of currency, is, to the extent of the absolute value of the particular income, gain or loss, deemed to be nil;

Notes: For the meaning of "derived", see Notes to 18.1(12).

95(2)(g.01) added by 2007 budget bill #2, for foreign affiliates' tax years that begin after Dec. 20, 2002.

(g.02) [Repealed]

Notes: 95(2)(g.02) provided that in applying 39(2) for FAPI purposes, gains and losses of excluded property were computed separately. Repealed by 2002-2013 technical bill for foreign affiliates' tax years that end after Aug. 19, 2011, or earlier by election. Added by 2007 budget bill #2.

(g.03) [application of 95(2)(g) to partners] — if at any time a particular foreign affiliate referred to in paragraph (g) is a member of a partnership or a qualified foreign affiliate referred to in that paragraph is a member of a partnership,

(i) in applying this paragraph, where a debt obligation is owing at that time by a debtor to the partnership of which the particular foreign affiliate is a member, the debt obligation is deemed to be owing at that time by the debtor to the particular foreign affiliate in the proportion that the particular foreign affiliate shared in any income earned, loss incurred or capital gain or capital loss realized by the partnership in respect of the debt obligation,

(ii) in applying this paragraph, where a debt obligation is owing at that time to a creditor by the partnership of which the particular foreign affiliate is a member, the debt obligation is deemed to be owing at that time to the creditor by the particular foreign affiliate in the proportion that the particular foreign affiliate shared in any income earned, loss incurred or capital gain or capital loss realized by the partnership in respect of the debt obligation,

(iii) in applying paragraph (g) and this paragraph, where a debt obligation is owing at that time by a debtor to the partnership of which the qualified foreign affiliate is a member, the debt obligation is deemed to be owing at that time by the debtor to the qualified foreign affiliate in the proportion that the qualified foreign affiliate shared in any income earned, loss incurred or capital gain or capital loss realized by the partnership in respect of the debt obligation,

(iv) in applying paragraph (g) and this paragraph, where a debt obligation is owing at that time to a creditor by the partnership of which the qualified foreign affiliate is a member, the debt obligation is deemed to be owing at that time to the creditor by the qualified foreign affiliate in the proportion that the qualified foreign affiliate shared in any income earned, loss incurred or capital gain or capital loss realized by the partnership in respect of the debt obligation, and

(v) in computing the particular foreign affiliate's income or loss from a partnership, any income earned, loss incurred or capital gain or capital loss realized, as the case may be, by the partnership — in respect of the portion of a debt obligation owing to or owing by the partnership that is deemed by any of subparagraphs (i) to (iv) to be a debt obligation owing to or owing by the particular foreign affiliate (referred to in this subparagraph as the "allocated debt obligation") — because of a fluctuation in the value of the currency of a country other than Canada relative to the value of Canadian currency, that is attributable to the allocated debt obligation is deemed to be nil to the extent that paragraph (g) would, if the rules in subparagraphs (i) to (iv) were applied, have applied to the particular foreign affiliate, to deem to be nil the in-

Non-Resident Corps/Trusts

come earned, loss incurred or capital gain or capital loss realized, as the case may be, by the particular foreign affiliate in respect of the allocated debt obligation, because of a fluctuation in the value of the currency of a country other than Canada relative to the value of Canadian currency;

Related Provisions: 95(2)(i) — Look-through rule for partnerships; 261(5)(h)(i) — Meaning of "Canadian currency" and "currency of a country other than Canada".

Notes: 95(2)(g.03) added by 2007 budget bill #2, last change effective (as per 2002-2013 technical bill) for foreign affiliates' tax years that begin after 2008.

(g.04) **[where loan received from foreign affiliate]** — if at any time a corporation resident in Canada or a partnership of which such a corporation is a member (such corporation or partnership referred to in this paragraph as the "borrowing party") has received a loan from, or become indebted to, a creditor that is a foreign affiliate (referred to in this paragraph as a "creditor affiliate") of a "qualifying entity" (in this paragraph within the meaning assigned by subsection 39(2.2)), or that is a partnership (referred to in this paragraph as a "creditor partnership") of which such an affiliate is a member, and the loan or indebtedness is at a later time repaid, in whole or in part, then the amount of the creditor affiliate's or creditor partnership's capital gain or capital loss, as the case may be, determined in the absence of this paragraph, in respect of the repayment, is to be reduced

(i) in the case of a capital loss

(A) if the creditor is a creditor affiliate, by an amount, not exceeding the amount of that capital loss so determined, that is determined by the formula

$$A/B$$

where

A   is the amount by which the borrowing party's capital gain is reduced under paragraph 39(2.1)(a) in respect of that repayment, and

B   is the total of all participating percentages, determined at the end of the taxation year of the creditor affiliate that includes the later time, of shares of the capital stock of a foreign affiliate that are owned by qualifying entities and on which an amount would be included under subsection 91(1), on the assumptions that

(I) the capital loss of the creditor affiliate, determined in the absence of this paragraph, in respect of the repayment of the loan or indebtedness were a capital gain of the creditor affiliate, and

(II) neither the creditor affiliate nor any other foreign affiliate of a qualifying entity had any other income, gain or loss for any taxation year, and

(B) if the creditor is a creditor partnership, by an amount, not exceeding the capital loss so determined, that is equal to the amount determined by the formula

$$A/(B \times C)$$

where

A   is the amount by which the borrowing party's capital gain is reduced under paragraph 39(2.1)(a) in respect of that repayment,

B   is the proportion that the amount of the capital loss of the creditor partnership in respect of the repayment of the loan or indebtedness, determined in the absence of this paragraph, that would be included in the determination of the income, gain or loss of the members of the creditor partnership that are foreign affiliates of qualifying entities is of the amount of the capital loss so determined, and

C   is the total of all participating percentages, each of which is the participating percentage in respect of a share of the capital stock of a foreign affiliate of a

qualifying entity, and that is owned by a qualifying entity, that is relevant in determining the amount that would be included in computing a qualifying entity's income under subsection 91(1), on the assumptions that

(I) the capital loss of the creditor partnership, determined in the absence of this paragraph, in respect of the repayment of the loan or indebtedness were a capital gain of the creditor partnership, and

(II) neither the creditor partnership nor any foreign affiliate of a qualifying entity had any other income, gain or loss for any taxation year, and

(ii) in the case of a capital gain,

(A) if the creditor is a creditor affiliate, by an amount, not exceeding that capital gain so determined, that is equal to the amount determined by the formula

$$A/B$$

where

A   is the amount by which the borrowing party is required to reduce its capital loss under paragraph 39(2.1)(b) in respect of that repayment, and

B   is the total of all participating percentages, determined at the end of the taxation year of the creditor affiliate that includes the later time, of shares of the capital stock of a foreign affiliate that are owned by qualifying entities and on which an amount would be included under subsection 91(1), on the assumption that neither the creditor affiliate nor any foreign affiliate of a qualifying entity had any other income, gain or loss for any taxation year other than its capital gain, determined in the absence of this paragraph, in respect of the repayment of the loan or indebtedness, and

(B) if the creditor is a creditor partnership, by an amount, not exceeding the capital loss so determined, that is equal to the amount determined by the following formula

$$A/(B \times C)$$

where

A   is the amount by which the borrowing party is required to reduce its capital loss under paragraph 39(2.1)(b) in respect of that repayment,

B   is the proportion that the amount of the capital gain of the creditor partnership in respect of the repayment of the loan or indebtedness, determined in the absence of this paragraph, that would be included in the determination of the income, gain or loss of the members of the creditor partnership that are foreign affiliates of qualifying entities is of the amount of the capital gain so determined, and

C   is the total of all participating percentages, each of which is the participating percentage in respect of a share of the capital stock of a foreign affiliate of a qualifying entity, and that is owned by a qualifying entity, that is relevant in determining the amount that would be included in computing a qualifying entity's income under subsection 91(1), on the assumption that neither the creditor partnership nor any foreign affiliate of a qualifying entity had any other income, gain or loss for any taxation year;

Related Provisions: 39(2.1)–(2.3) — Upstream loans — transitional foreign currency adjustment until 2016; 90(6)–(15) — Income inclusion on upstream loan; 93.1(1) — Shares owned by partnership deemed owned by partners.

Notes: See Notes to 39(2.1).

95(2)(g.04) amended by 2017 budget bill #2, retroactive to its introduction. Added by 2002-2013 technical bill, effective for the portions of loans received and indebtedness incurred before Aug. 20, 2011 that remained outstanding on Aug. 19, 2011 and that were repaid, in whole or in part, by Aug. 19, 2016.

(g.1) [debt forgiveness rules] — in computing the foreign accrual property income of a foreign affiliate of a taxpayer the Act shall be read

(i) as if the expression "income, taxable income or taxable income earned in Canada, as the case may be" in the definition "commercial debt obligation" in subsection 80(1) were read as "foreign accrual property income (within the meaning assigned by subsection 95(1))", and

(ii) without reference to subsections 80(3) to (12) and (15) and 80.01(5) to (11) and sections 80.02 to 80.04;

Notes: See Coleman & Bellefontaine, "Forgiveness, Foreign Affiliates and FAPI", X(1) *Resource Sector Taxation* (Federated Press) 694-700 (2015). See VIEWS doc 2002-0165195 for application of 95(2)(g.1) in a particular case; and Funt & Nitikman, "FAPI and Debt Forgiveness", 1724 *Tax Topics* (CCH) 1-4 (March 24, 2005), re debt forgiveness on windup of one controlled FA into another.

95(2)(g.1) added by 1994 technical bill and amended by 1995-97 technical bill, both for tax years that end after Feb. 21, 1994.

(g.2) [foreign spin-off election] — for the purpose of computing the foreign accrual property income of a foreign affiliate of any taxpayer resident in Canada for a taxation year of the affiliate, an election made pursuant to paragraph 86.1(2)(f) in respect of a distribution received by the affiliate in a particular taxation year of the affiliate is deemed to have been filed under that paragraph by the affiliate if

(i) where there is only one taxpayer resident in Canada in respect of whom the affiliate is a controlled foreign affiliate, the election is filed by the taxpayer with the taxpayer's return of income for the taxpayer's taxation year in which the particular year of the affiliate ends, and

(ii) where there is more than one taxpayer resident in Canada in respect of whom the affiliate is a controlled foreign affiliate, all of those taxpayers jointly elect in writing and each of them files the joint election with the Minister with their return of income for their taxation year in which the particular year of the affiliate ends;

Notes: 95(2)(g.2) added by 2001 technical bill, for distributions received after 1997.

(h) [Repealed]

Notes: 95(2)(h), dealing with currency fluctuation on foreign affiliate shares, repealed by 2001 technical bill. Earlier amended by 1993 technical bill.

Proposed **95(2)(h)-(h.5)** in the Feb. 27, 2004 draft legislation (reproduced in PITA 26th-40th ed.) will not be enacted. They would have suspended loss recognition on an internal disposition of property that was not excluded property, depreciable property or eligible capital property: see Jack et al, "The February 27, 2004 Draft Proposals on Foreign Affiliates", 2004 Cdn Tax Foundation conference report, at 20:23-26; Meister, "Foreign Affiliate Update" 19 *Canadian Petroleum Tax Journal* (2006).

(i) [settlement of debt relating to excluded property] — any income, gain or loss of a foreign affiliate of a taxpayer or of a partnership of which a foreign affiliate of a taxpayer is a member (which foreign affiliate or partnership is referred to in this paragraph as the "debtor"), for a taxation year or fiscal period of the debtor, as the case may be, is deemed to be income, a gain or a loss, as the case may be, from the disposition of an excluded property of the debtor, if the income, gain or loss is

(i) derived from the settlement or extinguishment of a debt of the debtor all or substantially all of the proceeds from which

(A) were used to acquire property, if at all times after the time at which the debt became debt of the debtor and before the time of that settlement or extinguishment, the property (or property substituted for the property) was property of the debtor and was, or would if the debtor were a foreign affiliate of the taxpayer be, excluded property of the debtor,

(B) were used at all times to earn income from an active business carried on by the debtor, or

(C) were used by the debtor for a combination of the uses described in clause (A) or (B),

(ii) derived from the settlement or extinguishment of a debt of the debtor all or substantially all of the proceeds from which were used to settle or extinguish a debt referred to in subparagraph (i) or in this subparagraph, or

(iii) derived under or as a result of an agreement that provides for the purchase, sale or exchange of currency and that can reasonably be considered to have been made by the debtor to reduce its risk, with respect to a debt referred to in subparagraph (i) or (ii), of fluctuations in the value of the currency in which the debt was denominated;

Notes: See Huynh, Lockwood & Maikawa, "Foreign Affiliates: Tracing the Purpose and Use of Funds", 59(3) *Canadian Tax Journal* 571-89 (2011) at 580-82. For CRA interpretation see VIEWS docs 2009-0337801R3, 2010-0386201R3, 2014-0526771C6, 2014-054664117; 2015-0581581C6 [2015 IFA q.9].

For the meaning of "derived", see Notes to 18.1(12). CRA considers that "substantially all", used in (i)(i), means 90% or more.

95(2)(i) amended by 2007 budget bill #2, last change effective for settlements and extinguishments after Oct. 1, 2007 of debt held by a foreign affiliate.

(j) [ACB of partnership interest] — the adjusted cost base to a foreign affiliate of a taxpayer of an interest in a partnership at any time shall be such amount as is prescribed by regulation;

Notes: See Ton-That & Huynh, "Inconsistent Treatment of Partnerships in the Foreign Affiliate Rules", 2009 Cdn Tax Foundation conference report, 24:1-66.

Regulations: 5907(12) [repealed], 5908(10).

(j.1) [conditions for para. (j.2) to apply] — paragraph (j.2) applies if, in a particular taxation year of a foreign affiliate of a taxpayer or in a particular fiscal period of a partnership (which foreign affiliate or partnership is referred to in this paragraph and paragraph (j.2) as the "operator" and which particular taxation year or particular fiscal period is referred to in this paragraph and paragraph (j.2) as the "specified taxation year") a member of which is, at the end of the period, a foreign affiliate of a taxpayer,

(i) the operator carries on a business,

(ii) the business includes the insuring of risks,

(iii) the business is not, at any time, a taxable Canadian business,

(iv) the business is

(A) an investment business,

(B) a non-qualifying business, or

(C) a business whose activities include activities deemed by paragraph (a.2) or (b) to be a separate business, other than an active business, carried on by the affiliate, and

(v) in respect of the investment business, non-qualifying business or separate business (each of these businesses being referred to in this subparagraph and paragraph (j.2) as a "foreign business"), as the case may be, the operator would, if it were a corporation carrying on the foreign business in Canada, be required by law to report to, and be subject to the supervision of, a regulatory authority that is the Superintendent of Financial Institutions or is a similar authority of a province;

Related Provisions: 95(2)(k.2) — Portion of business carried on in Canada deemed separate business.

Notes: 95(2)(j.1), (j.2), (k.1) and (k.2) added, (k) amended and 95(1)"taxable Canadian business" added, all by 2002-2013 technical bill, last change effective for foreign affiliates' tax years that begin after Aug. 18, 2011.

(j.2) [policy reserves in respect of insurance business] — if this paragraph applies, in computing the operator's income or loss from the foreign business for the specified taxation year and each subsequent taxation year or fiscal period in which the foreign business is carried on by the operator

(i) the operator is deemed to carry on the foreign business in Canada throughout that part of the specified taxation year, and of each of those subsequent taxation years or fiscal periods, in which the foreign business is carried on by the operator, and

(ii) for the purposes of Part XIV of the *Income Tax Regulations*,

(A) the operator is deemed to be required by law to report to, and to be subject to the supervision of, the regulatory authority referred to in subparagraph (j.1)(v), and

(B) if the operator is a life insurer and the foreign business is part of a life insurance business, the life insurance policies issued in the conduct of the foreign business are deemed to be life insurance policies in Canada;

Related Provisions: 95(2)(j.1) — Condition for para. (j.2) to apply, and meaning of "operator" and "specified taxation year".

Notes: See Notes to 95(2)(j.1) for effective date of 95(2)(j.2).

(k) **[conditions for para. (k.1) to apply]** — paragraph (k.1) applies if

(i) in a particular taxation year of a foreign affiliate of a taxpayer or in a particular fiscal period of a partnership (which foreign affiliate or partnership is referred to in this paragraph and paragraph (k.1) as the "operator" and which particular taxation year or particular fiscal period is referred to in this paragraph and paragraph (k.1) as the "specified taxation year") a member of which is, at the end of the period, a foreign affiliate of a taxpayer,

(A) the operator carries on a business,

(B) the business is not, at any time, a taxable Canadian business, and

(C) the business is

(I) an investment business,

(II) a non-qualifying business,

(III) a business whose activities include activities deemed by any of paragraphs (a.1) to (b) to be a separate business, other than an active business, carried on by the affiliate, or

(IV) a business the income from which is included by paragraph (l) in computing the affiliate's income from property for the specified taxation year, and

(ii) in the taxation year of the affiliate or the fiscal period of the partnership that includes the day that is immediately before the beginning of the specified taxation year,

(A) the affiliate or partnership carried on the business, or the activities so deemed to be a separate business, as the case may be,

(B) the business was not, or the activities were not, as the case may be, at any time, part of a taxable Canadian business, and

(C) the business was not described in any of subclauses (i)(C)(I), (II) and (IV), or the activities were not described in subclause (i)(C)(III), as the case may be;

Related Provisions: 95(2)(k.2) — Portion of business carried on in Canada deemed separate business; 253 — Whether business carried on in Canada.

Notes: CRA says 95(2)(k) can apply to a foreign corp. acquired by a Canco, that was not an FA in the preceding year, despite 95(2)(k)(ii)(A): VIEWS doc 2014-0536581I7. This does not change despite the interpretation of similar wording in 138(11.3) in *Standard Life*, 2015 TCC 97 (aff'd as *SCDA*, 2017 FCA 177): 2015-0585381I7.

95(2)(k) amended by 2002-2013 technical bill (see Notes to 95(2)(j.1)). Added by 1994 technical bill.

Regulations: 5907(2.9) (computation of earnings for preceding taxation year).

(k.1) **[change in business — fresh start rule]** — if this paragraph applies, in computing the operator's income or loss from the investment business, non-qualifying business, separate business or business described in paragraph (l) (each of these businesses being referred to in this paragraph as a "foreign business"), as the case may be, and the operator's capital gain or capital loss from the disposition of property used or held in the course of carrying on the foreign business, for the specified tax-

ation year and each subsequent taxation year or fiscal period in which the foreign business is carried on by the operator

(i) the operator is deemed

(A) to begin to carry on the foreign business in Canada at the beginning of the specified taxation year, and

(B) to carry on the foreign business in Canada throughout that part of the specified taxation year, and of each of those subsequent taxation years or fiscal periods, in which the foreign business is carried on by the operator,

(ii) where, in respect of the foreign business, the operator would, if it were a corporation carrying on the foreign business in Canada, be required by law to report to, and be subject to the supervision of, a regulatory authority that is the Superintendent of Financial Institutions or a similar authority of a province,

(A) the operator is deemed to be required by law to report to, and to be subject to the supervision of, the regulatory authority, and

(B) if the operator is a life insurer and the foreign business is part of a life insurance business, the life insurance policies issued in the conduct of the foreign business are deemed to be life insurance policies in Canada, and

(iii) paragraphs 138(11.91)(c) to (e) apply to the operator for the specified taxation year in respect of the foreign business as if

(A) the operator were the insurer referred to in subsection 138(11.91),

(B) the specified taxation year of the operator were the particular taxation year of the insurer referred to in that subsection,

(C) the foreign business of the operator were the business of the insurer referred to in that subsection, and

(D) the reference in paragraph 138(11.91)(e) to "property owned by it at that time that is designated insurance property in respect of the business" were read as a reference to "property owned or held by it at that time that is used or held by it in the particular taxation year in the course of carrying on the insurance business";

Related Provisions: 95(2)(k) — Conditions for para. (k.1) to apply, and meaning of "operator" and "specified taxation year"; 95(2)(k.2) — Portion of business carried on in Canada deemed separate business.

Notes: See Barnicke & Huynh, "Fresh-Start FA Rules", 22(12) *Canadian Tax Highlights* (ctf.ca) 7-9 (Dec. 2014); Russell & Montillaud, "Fresh Start Rules on Becoming an Affiliate", XX(2) *International Tax Planning* (Federated Press) 1392-95 (2015).

See Notes to 95(2)(j.1) for effective date of 95(2)(k.1).

Regulations: 5907(2.9) (computation of earnings for preceding taxation year).

(k.2) **[fresh start rule — portion of business in Canada deemed separate]** — for the purposes of paragraphs (j.1) to (k.1) and the definition "taxable Canadian business" in subsection (1), any portion of a business carried on by a person or partnership that is carried on in Canada is deemed to be a business that is separate from any other portion of the business carried on by the person or partnership;

Notes: See Notes to 95(2)(j.1) for effective date of 95(2)(k.2).

Proposed **95(2)(k.2)-(k.6)** of the Feb. 27, 2004 draft legislation (reproduced in PITA 26th-40th ed.) will not be enacted. (k.2)-(k.3) would have implemented a "reverse fresh start" rule. (k.4)-(k.6) are superseded by a simpler (k.2) deeming the portion of the business carried on in Canada to be a separate business. For discussion of the proposals see Jack et al, "The February 27, 2004 Draft Proposals on Foreign Affiliates", 2004 Cdn Tax Foundation conference report, at 20:70-72; Mahnger & McKilligan, "The Foreign Affiliate Fresh Start Rules", 57(2) *Canadian Tax Journal* 319-37 (2009).

Proposed **95(2)(k.7)** was enacted as 95(2)(u) (now repealed).

(l) **[trading or dealing in debt]** — in computing the income from property for a taxation year of a foreign affiliate of a taxpayer there shall be included the income of the affiliate for the year from a business (other than an investment business of the affiliate) the principal purpose of which is to derive income from trading or dealing in indebtedness (which for the purpose of this paragraph includes the earning of interest on indebtedness) other than

(i) indebtedness owing by persons with whom the affiliate deals at arm's length who are resident in the country in which the affiliate was formed or continued and exists and is governed and in which the business is principally carried on, or

(ii) trade accounts receivable owing by persons with whom the affiliate deals at arm's length,

unless it is established by the taxpayer or the foreign affiliate that, throughout the period in the taxation year during which the business was carried on by the affiliate,

(iii) the business (other than any business conducted principally with persons with whom the affiliate does not deal at arm's length) is carried on by the affiliate as a foreign bank, a trust company, a credit union, an insurance corporation or a trader or dealer in securities or commodities, the activities of which are regulated under the laws

(A) of each country in which the business is carried on through a permanent establishment in that country and of the country under whose laws the affiliate is governed and any of exists, was (unless the affiliate was continued in any jurisdiction) formed or organized, or was last continued,

(B) of the country in which the business is principally carried on, or

(C) if the affiliate is related to a non-resident corporation, of the country under whose laws that non-resident corporation is governed and any of exists, was (unless that non-resident corporation was continued in any jurisdiction) formed or organized, or was last continued, if those regulating laws are recognized under the laws of the country in which the business is principally carried on and all of those countries are members of the European Union;

(iv) [Repealed]

Related Provisions: 95(2.11) — Offshore regulated banks — conditions for 95(2)(l)(iii); 253 — Whether business carried on in Canada.

Notes: See Jayme Yeung, "Trading or Dealing in Indebtedness Offshore: Paragraph 95(2)(l) Revisited", 59(1) *Canadian Tax Journal* 85-101 (2011).

In *CIT Group*, 2016 TCC 163, a Barbados affiliate met the opening words as "trading or dealing in indebtedness", but fell under 95(2)(l)(iii) as a "foreign bank" because it was regulated as one, though it was not a conventional bank.

For CRA interpretation of 95(2)(l) see VIEWS doc 2004-0093111E5.

The words "any of exists..." in 95(2)(l)(iii)(A) and (C) should be read "any of {(1) exists, (2) was formed or organized, or (3) was last continued}", though this is not correct English.

95(2)(l) amended by 2018 budget bill #2, for foreign affiliates' tax years that begin after Feb. 26, 2018, to add everything after "unless" between (ii) and (iii) and "(other than ... arm's length)" in (iii), and to repeal (iv). For earlier years, read (iv) as:

(iv) the taxpayer is

(A) a bank, a trust company, a credit union, an insurance corporation or a trader or dealer in securities or commodities resident in Canada, the business activities of which are subject by law to the supervision of a regulating authority such as the Superintendent of Financial Institutions or a similar authority of a province,

(B) a subsidiary wholly-owned corporation of a corporation described in clause (A),

(C) a corporation of which a corporation described in clause (A) is a subsidiary wholly-owned corporation, or

(D) a partnership each member of which is a corporation described in any of clauses (A) to (C);

95(2)(l) earlier amended by 2014 budget bill #2 (for tax years that begin after 2014), 2002-2013 technical bill, 2007 budget bill #2.

Regulations: 5906(2)(b) (permanent establishment, for 95(2)(l)(iii)(A)).

(m) **["qualifying interest"]** — a taxpayer has a qualifying interest in respect of a foreign affiliate of the taxpayer at any time if, at that time, the taxpayer owned

(i) not less than 10% of the issued and outstanding shares (having full voting rights under all circumstances) of the affiliate, and

(ii) shares of the affiliate having a fair market value of not less than 10% of the fair market value of all the issued and outstanding shares of the affiliate

and for the purpose of this paragraph

(iii) where, at any time, shares of a corporation are owned or are deemed for the purposes of this paragraph to be owned by another corporation (in this paragraph referred to as the "holding corporation"), those shares shall be deemed to be owned at that time by each shareholder of the holding corporation in a proportion equal to the proportion of all such shares that

(A) the fair market value of the shares of the holding corporation owned at that time by the shareholder

is of

(B) the fair market value of all the issued shares of the holding corporation outstanding at that time,

(iv) where, at any time, shares of a corporation are property of a partnership or are deemed for the purposes of this paragraph to be property of a partnership, those shares shall be deemed to be owned at that time by each member of the partnership in a proportion equal to the proportion of all such shares that

(A) the member's share of the income or loss of the partnership for its fiscal period that includes that time

is of

(B) the income or loss of the partnership for its fiscal period that includes that time

and for the purpose of this subparagraph, where the income and loss of the partnership for its fiscal period that includes that time are nil, that proportion shall be computed as if the partnership had income for the period in the amount of $1,000,000, and

(v) where, at any time, a person is a holder of convertible property issued by the affiliate before June 23, 1994 the terms of which confer on the holder the right to exchange the convertible property for shares of the affiliate and the taxpayer elects in its return of income for its first taxation year that ends after 1994 to have the provisions of this subparagraph apply to the taxpayer in respect of all the convertible property issued by the affiliate and outstanding at that time, each holder shall, in respect of the convertible property held by it at that time, be deemed to have, immediately before that time,

(A) exchanged the convertible property for shares of the affiliate, and

(B) acquired shares of the affiliate in accordance with the terms and conditions of the convertible property;

Notes: See VIEWS doc 2011-0415911E5 (95(2)(y) does not prevent partnership from having "qualifying interest" in FA under 95(2)(m)).

Regulations: 5907(1)"exempt loss"(c)(ii)(H)(IV) (exempt loss).

Interpretation Bulletins: IT-392: Meaning of term "share".

(n) **["qualifying interest"]** — in applying paragraphs (a) and (g), paragraph (b) of the description of A in the formula in the definition "foreign accrual property income" in subsection (1), subsections (2.2), (2.21) and 93.1(5) and paragraph (d) of the definition "exempt earnings", and paragraph (c) of the definition "exempt loss", in subsection 5907(1) of the *Income Tax Regulations*, a non-resident corporation is deemed to be, at any time, a foreign affiliate of a particular corporation resident in Canada, and a foreign affiliate of the particular corporation in respect of which the particular corporation has a qualifying interest, if at that time

    (i) the non-resident corporation is a foreign affiliate of another corporation that is resident in Canada and that is related (otherwise than because of a right referred to in paragraph 251(5)(b)) to the particular corporation, and

    (ii) that other corporation has a qualifying interest in respect of the non-resident corporation;

Notes: For a ruling interpreting 95(2)(n) see VIEWS doc 2003-0016811R3.

95(2)(n) amended by 2014 budget bill #2, for foreign affiliates' tax years that end after July 12, 2013. Added by 2007 budget bill #2.

(o) **["qualifying member"]** — a particular person is a qualifying member of a partnership at a particular time if, at that time, the particular person is a member of the partnership and

    (i) throughout the period, in the fiscal period of the partnership that includes the particular time, during which the member was a member of the partnership, the particular person is, on a regular, continuous and substantial basis

        (A) actively engaged in those activities, of the principal business of the partnership carried on in that fiscal period by the partnership, that are other than activities connected with the provision of or the acquisition of funds required for the operation of that principal business, or

        (B) actively engaged in those activities, of a particular business carried on in that fiscal period by the particular person (otherwise than as a member of a partnership) that is similar to the principal business carried on in that fiscal period by the partnership, that are other than activities connected with the provision of or the acquisition of funds required for the operation of the particular business, or

    (ii) throughout the period, in the fiscal period of the partnership that includes the particular time, during which the particular person was a member of the partnership

        (A) the total of the fair market value of all partnership interests in the partnership owned by the particular person was equal to or greater than 1% of the total of the fair market value of all partnership interests in the partnership owned by all members of the partnership, and

        (B) the total of the fair market value of all partnership interests in the partnership owned by the particular person or persons (other than trusts) related to the particular person was equal to or greater than 10% of the total of the fair market value of all partnership interests in the partnership owned by all members of the partnership;

Notes: "Qualifying member" is used in 95(1)"investment business", 95(2)(a)(i)-(ii), (r), (t).

For the meaning of "principal business" see Notes to 20(1)(bb).

95(2)(o) added by 2007 budget bill #2, for tax years that end after 1999.

Regulations: 5907(1)"exempt earnings"(a.1) (exempt earnings).

(p) **["qualifying shareholder"]** — a particular person is a qualifying shareholder of a corporation at any time if throughout the period, in the taxation year of the corporation that includes that time, during which the particular person was a shareholder of the corporation

    (i) the particular person owned 1% or more of the issued and outstanding shares (having full voting rights under all circumstances) of the capital stock of the corporation,

    (ii) the particular person, or the particular person and persons (other than trusts) related to the particular person, owned 10% or more of the issued and outstanding shares (having full voting rights under all circumstances) of the capital stock of the corporation,

    (iii) the total of the fair market value of all the issued and outstanding shares of the capital stock of the corporation

owned by the particular person is 1% or more of the total fair market value of all the issued and outstanding shares of the capital stock of the corporation, and

    (iv) the total of the fair market value of all the issued and outstanding shares of the capital stock of the corporation owned by the particular person or by persons (other than trusts) related to the particular person is 10% or more of the total fair market value of all the issued and outstanding shares of the capital stock of the corporation;

Related Provisions: 95(2)(v) — Shares held through holding corporation.

Notes: "Qualifying shareholder" is used in 95(1)"investment business".

95(2)(p) added by 2007 budget bill #2, for FAs' tax years that end after 1999.

Interpretation Bulletins: IT-392: Meaning of term "share".

(q) **[look-through rules for paras. (o) and (p)]** — in applying paragraphs (o) and (p),

    (i) where interests in any partnership or shares of the capital stock of any corporation (which interests or shares are referred to in this subparagraph as "equity interests") are, at any time, property of a particular partnership or are deemed under this paragraph to be, at any time, property of the particular partnership, the equity interests are deemed to be owned at that time by each member of the particular partnership in a proportion equal to the proportion of the equity interests that

        (A) the fair market value, at that time, of the member's partnership interest in the particular partnership

is of

        (B) the fair market value, at that time, of all members' partnership interests in the particular partnership, and

    (ii) where interests in a partnership or shares of the capital stock of a corporation (which interests or shares are referred to in this subparagraph as "equity interests") are, at any time, property of a non-discretionary trust (within the meaning assigned by subsection 17(15)) or are deemed under this paragraph to be, at any time, property of such a non-discretionary trust, the equity interests are deemed to be owned at that time by each beneficiary under that trust in a proportion equal to that proportion of the equity interests that

        (A) the fair market value, at that time, of the beneficiary's beneficial interest in the trust

is of

        (B) the fair market value, at that time, of all beneficial interests in the trust;

Notes: 95(2)(q) added by 2007 budget bill #2, for tax years that end after 1999.

Interpretation Bulletins: IT-392: Meaning of term "share".

(r) **["qualifying member"]** — in applying paragraph (a) and in applying paragraph (d) of the definition "exempt earnings", and paragraph (c) of the definition "exempt loss", in subsection 5907(1) of the Regulations, a partnership is deemed to be, at any time, a partnership of which a foreign affiliate — of a particular corporation resident in Canada and in respect of which foreign affiliate the particular corporation has a qualifying interest — is a qualifying member, if at that time

    (i) a particular foreign affiliate — of another corporation that is resident in Canada and that is related (otherwise than because of a right referred to in paragraph 251(5)(b)) to the particular corporation — is a member of the partnership,

    (ii) that other corporation has a qualifying interest in respect of the particular foreign affiliate, and

    (iii) the particular foreign affiliate is a qualifying member of the partnership;

Notes: 95(2)(r) added by 2007 budget bill #2, for FAs' tax years that end after 1999.

(s) **["designated corporation"]** — in applying the definition "investment business" in subsection (1), a particular corporation is, at any time, a designated corporation in respect of a foreign affiliate of a taxpayer, if at that time

(i) a qualifying shareholder of the foreign affiliate or a person related to such a qualifying shareholder is a qualifying shareholder of the particular corporation,

(ii) the particular corporation

(A) is controlled by a qualifying shareholder of the foreign affiliate, or

(B) would be controlled by a particular qualifying shareholder of the foreign affiliate if the particular qualifying shareholder of the foreign affiliate owned each share of the capital stock of the particular corporation that is owned by a qualifying shareholder of the foreign affiliate or by a person related to a qualifying shareholder of the foreign affiliate, and

(iii) the total of all amounts each of which is the fair market value of a share of the capital stock of the particular corporation owned by a qualifying shareholder of the foreign affiliate or by a person related to a qualifying shareholder of the foreign affiliate is greater than 50% of the total fair market value of all the issued and outstanding shares of the capital stock of the particular corporation;

Notes: 95(2)(s) added by 2007 budget bill #2, for FAs' tax years that end after 1999.

(t) **["designated partnership"]** — in applying the definition "investment business" in subsection (1) in respect of a business carried on by a foreign affiliate of a taxpayer in a taxation year, a particular partnership is, at any time, a designated partnership in respect of the foreign affiliate of the taxpayer, if at that time

(i) the foreign affiliate or a person related to the foreign affiliate is a qualifying member of the particular partnership, and

(ii) the total of all amounts — each of which is the fair market value of a partnership interest in the particular partnership held by the foreign affiliate, by a person related to the foreign affiliate or (where the foreign affiliate carries on, at that time, the business as a qualifying member of another partnership) by a qualifying member of the other partnership — is greater than 50% of the total fair market value of all partnership interests in the particular partnership owned by all members of the particular partnership;

Notes: 95(2)(t) added by 2007 budget bill #2, for FAs' tax years that end after 1999.

(u) [Repealed]

Notes: 95(2)(u) provided a look-through rule for partnerships for many paras. of 95(2) (see now 95(2)(y)-(z).) Repealed by 2002-2013 technical bill (and re-repealed, after being amended, by 2014 budget bill #2), for foreign affiliates' tax years that end after Aug. 19, 2011. Earlier amended by 2002-2013 technical bill, for FAs' tax years that begin after Dec. 20, 2002. Added by 2007 budget bill #2, replacing proposed 95(2)(k.7) in the Feb. 27/04 draft legislation.

(v) **[shares held through holding corporation]** — in applying paragraph (p),

(i) where shares of the capital stock of any corporation (referred to in this paragraph as the "issuing corporation") are, at any time, owned by a corporation (referred to in this paragraph as the "holding corporation") or are deemed under this paragraph to be, at any time, owned by a corporation (referred to in this paragraph as the "holding corporation"), those shares are deemed to be owned at that time by each shareholder of the holding corporation in a proportion equal to the proportion of those shares that

(A) the fair market value, at that time, of the shares of the capital stock of the issuing corporation that are owned by the shareholder

is of

(B) the fair market value, at that time, of all the issued and outstanding shares of the capital stock of the issuing corporation, and

(ii) a person who is deemed by subparagraph (i) to own, at any time, shares of the capital stock of a corporation is deemed to be, at that time, a shareholder of the corporation;

Notes: 95(2)(v) added by 2007 budget bill #2, for FAs' tax years that end after 1999.

(w) **[where FA active in more than one country]** — where a foreign affiliate of a corporation resident in Canada carries on an active business in more than one country,

(i) where the business is carried on in a country other than Canada, it is deemed to carry on that business in that country only to the extent that the profit or loss from that business can reasonably be attributed to a permanent establishment situated in that country, and

(ii) where the business is carried on in Canada, it is deemed to carry on that business in Canada only to the extent that the income from the active business is subject to tax under this Part;

Notes: 95(2)(w) added by 2007 budget bill #2, for FAs' tax years beginning after 2008.

(x) **[losses of FA]** — the loss from an active business, from a non-qualifying business or from property (as the case may be) of a foreign affiliate of a taxpayer resident in Canada for a taxation year is the amount of that loss, if any, that is computed by applying the provisions in this Subdivision with respect to the computation of income from the active business, from the non-qualifying business or from property (as the case may be) of the foreign affiliate for the taxation year with any modifications that the circumstances require;

Notes: 95(2)(x) added by 2007 budget bill #2, for FAs' tax years that begin after 2008.

(y) **[look-through rule for partnerships]** — in determining — for the purpose of paragraph (a) and for the purpose of applying subsections (2.2) and (2.21) for the purpose of applying that paragraph — whether a non-resident corporation is, at any time, a foreign affiliate of a taxpayer in respect of which the taxpayer has a qualifying interest, where interests in any partnership or shares of the capital stock of any corporation (which interests or shares are referred to in this paragraph as "equity interests") are, at that time, property of a particular partnership or are deemed under this paragraph to be, at any time, property of the particular partnership, the equity interests are deemed to be owned at that time by each member of the particular partnership in a proportion equal to the proportion of the equity interests that

(i) the fair market value, at that time, of the member's partnership interest in the particular partnership

is of

(ii) the fair market value, at that time, of all members' partnership interests in the particular partnership; and

Notes: See Ton-That & Huynh, "Inconsistent Treatment of Partnerships in the Foreign Affiliate Rules", 2009 Cdn Tax Foundation conference report, 24:1-66.

For CRA interpretation see VIEWS doc 2011-0415911E5 (95(2)(y) does not prevent partnership from having "qualifying interest" in FA under 95(2)(m)).

95(2)(y) added by 2007 budget bill #2, for FAs' tax years that end after 1999.

(z) **[where FA is a partner]** — where a particular foreign affiliate of a taxpayer — in respect of which the taxpayer has a qualifying interest or that is a controlled foreign affiliate of the taxpayer — is a member of a partnership, the particular foreign affiliate's foreign accrual property income or loss in respect of the taxpayer for a taxation year shall not include any income or loss of the partnership to the extent that the income or loss

(i) is attributable to the foreign accrual property income or loss of a foreign affiliate of the partnership that is also a foreign affiliate of the taxpayer (referred to in this paragraph as the "second foreign affiliate") in respect of which the taxpayer has a qualifying interest or that is a controlled foreign affiliate of the taxpayer, and

(ii) is, because of paragraph (a) as applied in respect of the taxpayer, included in computing the income or loss from an active business of the second foreign affiliate for a taxation year.

Notes: See Notes to 95(2)(y). 95(2)(z) added by 2007 budget bill #2, for foreign affiliates' tax years that end after 1999.

(2.01) Rules for the definition "controlled foreign affiliate" — In applying paragraph (b) of the definition "controlled foreign affiliate" in subsection (1) and in applying this subsection,

(a) shares of the capital stock of a corporation that are at any time owned by, or that are deemed by this subsection to be at any time owned by, another corporation are deemed to be, at that time, owned by, or property of, as the case may be, each shareholder of the other corporation in the proportion that

(i) the fair market value at that time of the shares of the capital stock of the other corporation that, at that time, are owned by, or are property of, the shareholder

is of

(ii) the fair market value at that time of all the issued and outstanding shares of the capital stock of the other corporation;

(b) shares of the capital stock of a corporation that are, or are deemed by this subsection to be, at any time, property of a partnership, are deemed to be, at that time, owned by, or property of, as the case may be, each member of the partnership in the proportion that

(i) the fair market value at that time of the member's partnership interest in the partnership

is of

(ii) the fair market value at that time of all partnership interests in the partnership;

(c) shares of the capital stock of a corporation that are at any time owned by, or that are deemed by this subsection to be at any time owned by, a non-discretionary trust (within the meaning assigned by subsection 17(15)) other than an exempt trust (within the meaning assigned by subsection (1)) are deemed to be, at that time, owned by, or property of, as the case may be, each beneficiary of the trust in the proportion that

(i) the fair market value at that time of the beneficiary's beneficial interest in the trust

is of

(ii) the fair market value at that time of all beneficial interests in the trust; and

(d) all of the shares of the capital stock of a corporation that are at any time owned by, or that are deemed by this subsection to be at any time owned by, a particular trust (other than an exempt trust within the meaning assigned by subsection (1) or a non-discretionary trust within the meaning assigned by subsection 17(15)) are deemed to be, at that time, owned by, or property of, as the case may be,

(i) each beneficiary of the particular trust at that time, and

(ii) each settlor (within the meaning assigned by subsection 17(15)) in respect of the particular trust at that time.

Related Provisions: 95(2.02) — No double counting.

Notes: 95(2.01) added by 2007 budget bill #2, for foreign affiliates' tax years that begin after Feb. 27, 2004.

(2.02) Rule against double-counting — In applying the assumption in paragraph (b) of the definition "controlled foreign affiliate" in subsection (1) in respect of a taxpayer resident in Canada to determine whether a foreign affiliate of the taxpayer is at any time a controlled foreign affiliate of the taxpayer, nothing in that paragraph or in subsection (2.01) is to be read or construed as requiring an interest, or for civil law a right, in a share of the capital stock of the foreign affiliate of the taxpayer owned at that time by the taxpayer to be taken into account more than once.

Notes: 95(2.02) added by 2007 budget bill #2, for foreign affiliates' tax years that begin after Feb. 27, 2004.

(2.1) Rule for definition "investment business" — For the purposes of the definition "investment business" in subsection (1), a foreign affiliate of a taxpayer, the taxpayer and, where the taxpayer is a corporation all the issued shares of which are owned by a corporation described in subparagraph (a)(i), such corporation described in subparagraph (a)(i) shall be considered to be dealing with each other at arm's length in respect of the entering into of agreements that provide for the purchase, sale or exchange of currency and the execution of such agreements where

(a) the taxpayer is

(i) a bank, a trust company, a credit union, an insurance corporation or a trader or dealer in securities or commodities resident in Canada, the business activities of which are subject by law to the supervision of a regulating authority such as the Superintendent of Financial Institutions or a similar authority of a province, or

(ii) a subsidiary wholly-owned corporation of a corporation described in subparagraph (i);

(b) the agreements are swap agreements, forward purchase or sale agreements, forward rate agreements, futures agreements, options or rights agreements or similar agreements;

(c) the affiliate entered into the agreements in the course of a business carried on by the affiliate, if

(i) the business is carried on by the affiliate principally in a country (other than Canada) and principally with persons with whom the affiliate deals at arm's length, and

(ii) the business activities of the affiliate are regulated in that country; and

(d) the terms and conditions of such agreements are substantially the same as the terms and conditions of similar agreements made by persons dealing at arm's length.

Related Provisions: 95(2.41) — Foreign affiliate of life insurer.

Notes: 95(2.1) amended by 2007 budget bill #2, for foreign affiliates' tax years that begin after 1999. Added by 1994 technical bill.

(2.11) Rule for "investment business" definition and para. (2)(l) — A taxpayer or a foreign affiliate of the taxpayer, as the case may be, is deemed not to have established that the conditions in subparagraph (a)(i) of the definition "investment business" in subsection (1), or in subparagraph (2)(l)(iii), have been satisfied throughout a period in a particular taxation year of the affiliate unless

(a) throughout the period the taxpayer is

(i) a particular corporation resident in Canada

(A) that is a bank listed in Schedule I to the *Bank Act*, a trust company, a credit union, an insurance corporation or a trader or dealer in securities or commodities that is a registered securities dealer, the business activities of which are subject to the supervision of a regulating authority such as the Superintendent of Financial Institutions, a similar regulating authority of a province or an authority of, or approved by, a province to regulate traders or dealers in securities or commodities, and

(B) that is not a corporation the fair market value of any share of the capital stock of which is determined primarily by reference to one or more of the fair market value of, any revenue, income or cash flow from, any profits or gains from the disposition of, or any other similar criteria in respect of, property the fair market value of which is less than 90% of the fair market value of all of the property of the corporation,

(ii) a corporation resident in Canada

(A) of which

(I) the particular corporation described in subparagraph (i) is a subsidiary controlled corporation, or

(II) a corporation described in this subparagraph is a subsidiary wholly-owned corporation, and

(B) that is not a corporation the fair market value of any share of the capital stock of which is determined primarily by reference to one or more of the fair market value of, any revenue, income or cash flow from, any profits or gains from the disposition of, or any other similar criteria in respect of, property the fair market value of which is less than 90% of the fair market value of all of the property of the corporation,

(iii) a corporation resident in Canada each of the shares of the capital stock of which is owned by a corporation that is described in this subparagraph or in subparagraph (i) or (ii), or

(iv) a partnership

(A) each member of which is a corporation described in any of subparagraphs (i) to (iii), or another partnership described in this subparagraph, or

(B) in respect of which the following conditions are satisfied:

(I) the partnership is a registered securities dealer, the business activities of which are subject to the supervision of a regulating authority described in clause (a)(i)(A), and

(II) the share of the total income or loss of the partnership of a majority-interest partner of the partnership that is either a corporation resident in Canada or a Canadian partnership — together with the share of each corporation resident in Canada that is affiliated with the majority-interest partner — is equal to all or substantially all of the total income or loss of the partnership; and

(b) either

(i) throughout the period the particular corporation described in subparagraph (a)(i) has, or is deemed for certain purposes to have, $2 billion or more of equity

(A) if the particular corporation is a bank, under the *Bank Act*,

(B) if the particular corporation is a trust company, under the *Trust and Loan Companies Act*, or

(C) if the particular corporation is an insurance corporation, under the *Insurance Companies Act*, or

(ii) more than 50% of the total of all amounts each of which is an amount of taxable capital employed in Canada (within the meaning assigned by Part I.3) of the taxpayer — or of a corporation resident in Canada that is affiliated with the taxpayer — for the taxation year of the taxpayer or of the affiliated corporation, as the case may be, that ends in the particular year is attributable to a business carried on in Canada, the activities of which are subject to the supervision of a regulating authority such as the Superintendent of Financial Institutions, a similar regulating authority of a province or an authority of, or approved by, a province to regulate traders or dealers in securities or commodities.

Notes: 95(2.11) targets the following (2014 Budget papers): "Certain Canadian taxpayers that are not financial institutions purport to qualify for the regulated foreign financial institution exception [95(1)"investment business"(a)(i)] (and thus avoid Canadian tax) by establishing foreign affiliates and electing to subject those affiliates to regulation under foreign banking and financial laws. However, the main purpose of these affiliates is often to engage in proprietary activities — that is, to invest or trade in securities on their own account — and not to facilitate financial transactions for customers. It is not intended that the exception be satisfied in these circumstances." For an example, see *Loblaw Financial*, 2020 FCA 79 (SCC appeal heard May 13/21), para. 86 (see 95(1)"investment business" Notes).

Opening words amended by 2018 budget bill #2 to add "or in subparagraph (2)(l)(iii)", for foreign affiliates' tax years that begin after Feb. 26, 2018.

95(2.11) added by 2014 budget bill #2, for a taxpayer's tax years that begin after 2014.

(2.2) Qualifying interest throughout year — For the purposes of paragraphs (2)(a) and (g), a non-resident corporation that is not a foreign affiliate of a taxpayer in respect of which the taxpayer has a qualifying interest throughout a particular taxation year is deemed to be a foreign affiliate of the taxpayer in respect of which the tax-

payer has a qualifying interest throughout that particular taxation year if

(a) a person or partnership has, in that particular taxation year, acquired or disposed of shares of the capital stock of that non-resident corporation or of any other corporation and, because of that acquisition or disposition, that non-resident corporation becomes or ceases to be a foreign affiliate of the taxpayer in respect of which the taxpayer has a qualifying interest, and

(b) at the beginning of that particular taxation year or at the end of that particular taxation year, the non-resident corporation is a foreign affiliate of the taxpayer in respect of which the taxpayer has a qualifying interest.

Related Provisions: 93.1(1) — Shares owned by partnership deemed owned proportionately by partners; 93.1(5), (6)(a)(iv) — FAPI of a partnership; 95(2)(n) — Deemed FA and deemed qualifying interest; 95(2)(y) — Look-through rule for partnerships; 95(2.21) — Application of 95(2.2).

Notes: CRA's view is that 95(2.2) can apply when the non-resident corp's shares are acquired through a partnership: doc 2004-0073101E5.

95(2.2) amended by 2008 budget bill #2 (last change effective for foreign affiliates' tax years that begin after 2008), 2007 budget bill #2, 2001 technical bill. Added by 1994 technical bill; it was 95(2)(s) in the Jan. 23, 1995 draft legislation.

(2.201) Controlled foreign affiliate throughout year — For the purposes of paragraphs (2)(a) and (g), a non-resident corporation is deemed to be a controlled foreign affiliate of a taxpayer throughout a taxation year of the non-resident corporation if

(a) in the taxation year, a person or partnership acquires or disposes of shares of the capital stock of a corporation and, because of the acquisition or disposition, the non-resident corporation becomes or ceases to be a controlled foreign affiliate of the taxpayer; and

(b) at either or both of the beginning and end of the taxation year, the non-resident corporation is a controlled foreign affiliate of the taxpayer.

Notes: 95(2.201) added by 2008 budget bill #2, last change effective for foreign affiliates' tax years that begin after Dec. 20, 2002.

(2.21) Rule re subsec. (2.2) — Subsection (2.2) does not apply for the purpose of paragraph (2)(a) in respect of any income or loss referred to in that paragraph, of a particular foreign affiliate of the taxpayer, to the extent that that income or loss can reasonably be considered to have been realized or to have accrued before the earlier of

(a) the time at which the particular affiliate became, as determined without reference to subsection (2.2), a foreign affiliate of the taxpayer in respect of which the taxpayer had a qualifying interest, and

(b) the time at which the particular affiliate became, as determined without reference to subsection (2.2), a foreign affiliate of another person resident in Canada in respect of which the other person resident in Canada had a qualifying interest, where

(i) the taxpayer is a corporation,

(ii) the taxpayer did not exist at the beginning of the taxation year,

(iii) the particular affiliate became a foreign affiliate of the taxpayer in the taxation year because of a disposition, in the taxation year, of shares of the capital stock of the particular affiliate to the taxpayer by the other person resident in Canada, and

(iv) the other person resident in Canada was, immediately before that disposition, related to the taxpayer.

Related Provisions: 93.1(5), (6)(a)(iv) — FAPI of a partnership; 95(2)(n) — Deemed FA and deemed qualifying interest; 95(2)(y) — Look-through rule for partnerships.

Notes: 95(2.21) added by 2007 budget bill #2, last change effective for foreign affiliates' tax years that begin after 2008.

(2.3) Application of para. (2)(a.1) — Paragraph (2)(a.1) does not apply to a foreign affiliate of a taxpayer in respect of a sale or exchange of property that is currency or a right to purchase, sell or exchange currency where

(a) the taxpayer is

(i) a bank, a trust company, a credit union, an insurance corporation or a trader or dealer in securities or commodities resident in Canada, the business activities of which are subject by law to the supervision of a regulating authority such as the Superintendent of Financial Institutions or a similar authority of a province, or

(ii) a subsidiary wholly-owned corporation of a corporation described in subparagraph (i);

(b) the sale or exchange was made by the affiliate in the course of a business conducted principally with persons with whom the affiliate deals at arm's length, if

(i) the business is principally carried on in the country (other than Canada) under whose laws the affiliate is governed and any of exists, was (unless the affiliate was continued in any jurisdiction) formed or organized, or was last continued, or

(ii) the affiliate is a foreign bank, a trust company, a credit union, an insurance corporation or a trader or dealer in securities or commodities and the activities of the business are regulated

(A) under the laws of the country under whose laws the affiliate is governed and any of exists, was (unless the affiliate was continued in any jurisdiction) formed or organized, or was last continued, and under the laws of each country in which the business is carried on through a permanent establishment in that country,

(B) under the laws of the country (other than Canada) in which the business is principally carried on, or

(C) if the affiliate is related to a corporation, under the laws of the country under the laws of which that related corporation is governed and any of exists, was (unless that related corporation was continued in any jurisdiction) formed or organized, or was last continued, if those regulating laws are recognized under the laws of the country in which the business is principally carried on and all of those countries are members of the European Union; and

(c) the terms and conditions of the sale or exchange of such property are substantially the same as the terms and conditions of similar sales or exchanges of such property by persons dealing at arm's length.

Notes: The words "any of exists..." in 95(2.3)(b)(i) and (ii)(A) and (C) should be read "any of {(1) exists, (2) was formed or organized, or (3) was last continued}", though this is not correct English.

95(2.3) amended by 2002-2013 technical bill (for foreign affiliates' tax years that begin after 1999), 2007 budget bill #2. Added by 1994 technical bill.

Regulations: 5906(2)(b) (permanent establishment, for 95(2.3)(b)(i)(A)).

(2.31) Application of paras. (2)(a.1) and (a.3) — Paragraphs (2)(a.1) and (a.3) do not apply to a controlled foreign affiliate (for the purposes of section 17) of an eligible Canadian bank (as defined in subsection (2.43)) in respect of activities carried out to earn income from a property, other than a specified property of the affiliate, if

(a) the affiliate sells the property, or performs services as an agent in relation to a purchase or sale of the property, and it is reasonable to conclude that the cost to any person of the property is relevant in computing the income from

(i) a business carried on by the bank or a person resident in Canada with whom the bank does not deal at arm's length, or

(ii) a business carried on in Canada by a non-resident person with whom the bank does not deal at arm's length;

(b) the property has a readily available fair market value and

(i) is listed on a recognized stock exchange,

(ii) would be a mark-to-market property (as defined in subsection 142.2(1)) of the bank if it were owned by the bank, or

(iii) is a debt obligation owing by the bank that would be a mark-to-market property (as defined in subsection 142.2(1)) of the affiliate if

(A) the affiliate were the taxpayer referred to in that definition, and

(B) the definition "specified debt obligation" in subsection 142.2(1) were read without reference to its paragraph (d);

(c) the purchase and sale of the property by the affiliate, or services performed by the affiliate as agent in respect of the purchase or sale, are made

(i) on terms and conditions that are substantially the same as the terms and conditions of similar purchases or sales of, or services performed in respect of the purchase or sale of, such property by persons dealing at arm's length,

(ii) in the course of a business

(A) that regularly includes trading or dealing in securities principally with persons with whom the affiliate deals at arm's length, and

(B) that is principally carried on through a permanent establishment in a country other than Canada, and

(iii) for the purpose of enabling the purchase or sale of the property by a particular person who deals at arm's length with the affiliate and the bank; and

(d) the affiliate is a foreign bank or a trader or dealer in securities and the activities of the business are regulated

(i) under the laws of the country under whose laws the affiliate is governed and any of exists, was (unless the affiliate was continued in any jurisdiction) formed or organized, or was last continued, and under the laws of each country in which the business is carried on through a permanent establishment in that country,

(ii) under the laws of the country (other than Canada) in which the business is principally carried on, or

(iii) if the affiliate is related to a corporation, under the laws of the country under whose laws that related corporation is governed and any of exists, was (unless that related corporation was continued in any jurisdiction) formed or organized, or was last continued, if those regulating laws are recognized under the laws of the country in which the business is principally carried on and all those countries are members of the European Union.

Related Provisions: 95(2.32) — Definition of specified property; 95(2.43)–(2.45) — Rules for eligible bank affiliate; 95(3.01) — Parallel rule for 95(2)(b).

Notes: 95(2.31)–(2.32) and (3.01) are intended to "ensure that certain securities transactions undertaken in the course of a bank's business of facilitating trades for arm's length customers are not inappropriately caught by the base erosion rules": 2012 Budget papers.

The words "any of exists..." in (d)(i) and (d)(iii) should be read "any of {(1) exists, (2) was ... formed or organized, or (3) was last continued}", though this is not correct English.

95(2.31)–(2.32) added by 2014 budget bill #2, for foreign affiliates' tax years that begin after Oct. 2012.

(2.32) Definition of "specified property" — For the purposes of subsection (2.31), "specified property", of a foreign affiliate, means a property that is owned by the affiliate for more than 10 days and that is

(a) a share of the capital stock of a corporation resident in Canada;

(b) a property traded on a stock exchange located in Canada and not traded on a stock exchange located in the jurisdiction in which the affiliate is resident; or

(c) a debt obligation

(i) of a corporation resident in Canada,

(ii) of a trust or partnership, units of which are traded on a stock exchange located in Canada, or

(iii) of, or guaranteed by, the Government of Canada, the government of a province, an agent of a province, a municipality in Canada or a municipal or public body performing a function of government in Canada.

Notes: See Notes to 95(2.31). For the meaning of "municipal or public body..." in (c)(iii), see Notes to 149(1)(c).

(2.4) Application of para. (2)(a.3) — Paragraph (2)(a.3) does not apply to a foreign affiliate of a taxpayer in respect of its income derived directly or indirectly from indebtedness to the extent that

(a) the income is derived by the affiliate in the course of a business conducted principally with persons with whom the affiliate deals at arm's length carried on by it as a foreign bank, a trust company, a credit union, an insurance corporation or a trader or dealer in securities or commodities, the activities of which are regulated under the laws

(i) of the country under whose laws the affiliate is governed and any of exists, was (unless the affiliate was continued in any jurisdiction) formed or organized, or was last continued and of each country in which the business is carried on through a permanent establishment in that country,

(ii) of the country in which the business is principally carried on, or

(iii) if the affiliate is related to a corporation, of the country under the laws of which that related corporation is governed and any of exists, was (unless that related corporation was continued in any jurisdiction) formed or organized, or was last continued, if those regulating laws are recognized under the laws of the country in which the business is principally carried on and all of those countries are members of the European Union, and

(b) all the following conditions are satisfied:

(i) the income is derived by the affiliate from trading or dealing in the indebtedness (which, for this purpose, consists of income from the actual trading or dealing in the indebtedness and interest earned by the affiliate during a short term holding period on indebtedness acquired by it for the purpose of the trading or dealing) directly or indirectly with persons (in this subsection referred to as "regular customers") that

(A) deal at arm's length with the affiliate, and

(B) are resident, or carry on business through a permanent establishment, in a country other than Canada,

(ii) the affiliate has a substantial market presence in the country, and

(iii) one or more persons that deal at arm's length with the affiliate and are resident, or carry on business through a permanent establishment, in the country

(A) carry on a business

(I) that competes in the country with the business of the affiliate, and

(II) the activities of which are regulated under the laws of the country or, where the country is a member of the European Union, any country that is a member of the European Union, in the same manner as are the activities of the business of the affiliate, and

(B) have a substantial market presence in the country,

and, for the purpose of this subsection, an acquisition of indebtedness from the taxpayer shall be deemed to be part of the trading or dealing in indebtedness described in paragraph (b) where the indebtedness is acquired by the affiliate and sold to regular customers and the terms and conditions of the acquisition and the sale are substantially the same as the terms and conditions of similar acquisitions and sales made by the affiliate in transactions with persons with whom it deals at arm's length.

Notes: The words "any of exists..." in (a)(i) and (iii) should be read "any of {(1) exists, (2) was ... formed or organized, or (3) was last continued}", though this is not correct English.

For the meaning of "derived", see Notes to 18.1(12). For "indirectly" see Notes to 17.1(1). The term "substantial market presence", used in (b)(ii), is not defined.

For a ruling applying 95(2.4) see VIEWS doc 2006-0212871R3.

95(2.4) amended by 2014 budget bill #2 (for foreign affiliates' tax years that begin after Oct. 2012), 2002-2013 technical bill (for FAs' tax years that begin after 1999), 2007 budget bill #2. Added by 1994 technical bill.

Regulations: 5906(2)(b) (permanent establishment, for 95(2.4)(a)(i)).

(2.41) Application of para. (2)(a.3) — Paragraph (2)(a.3) does not apply to a foreign affiliate of a taxpayer resident in Canada in respect of the foreign affiliate's income for a taxation year derived, directly or indirectly, from indebtedness of persons resident in Canada or from indebtedness in respect of businesses carried on in Canada (referred to in this subsection as the "Canadian indebtedness") if

(a) the taxpayer is, at the end of the foreign affiliate's taxation year

(i) a life insurance corporation resident in Canada, the business activities of which are subject by law to the supervision of the Superintendent of Financial Institutions or a similar authority of a province, or

(ii) a corporation resident in Canada that is a subsidiary controlled corporation of a corporation described in subparagraph (i);

(b) the Canadian indebtedness is used or held by the foreign affiliate, throughout the period in the taxation year that that Canadian indebtedness was used or held by the foreign affiliate, in the course of carrying on a business (referred to in this subsection as the "foreign life insurance business") that is a life insurance business carried on outside Canada (other than a business deemed by paragraph (2)(a.2) to be a separate business other than an active business), the activities of which are regulated

(i) under the laws of the country under whose laws the foreign affiliate is governed and any of exists, was (unless the foreign affiliate was continued in any jurisdiction) formed or organized, or was last continued, and

(ii) under the laws of the country, if any, in which the business is principally carried on;

(c) more than 90% of the gross premium revenue of the foreign affiliate for the taxation year in respect of the foreign life insurance business was derived from the insurance or reinsurance of risks (net of reinsurance ceded) in respect of persons

(i) that were non-resident at the time at which the policies in respect of those risks were issued or effected, and

(ii) that were at that time dealing at arm's length with the foreign affiliate, the taxpayer and all persons that were related at that time to the foreign affiliate or the taxpayer; and

(d) it is reasonable to conclude that the foreign affiliate used or held the Canadian indebtedness

(i) to fund a liability or reserve of the foreign life insurance business, or

(ii) as capital that can reasonably be considered to have been required for the foreign life insurance business.

Related Provisions: 95(2.1)(c) — Rule for definition of "investment business".

Notes: For the meaning of "derived", see Notes to 18.1(12). For "indirectly" see Notes to 17.1(1).

The words "any of exists..." in (b)(i) should be read "any of {(1) exists, (2) was formed or organized, or (3) was last continued}", though this is not correct English.

95(2.41) added by 2007 budget bill #2, for FAs' tax years that begin after 1999.

(2.42) Exception re para. (2)(a.3) — If, at any time in a taxation year of a foreign affiliate of a taxpayer referred to in paragraph (2)(a.3), a life insurance corporation resident in Canada is the taxpayer referred to in paragraph (2)(a.3) or is a person who controls, or is controlled by, such a taxpayer, a particular indebtedness or a particular lease obligation of the life insurance corporation is, for

Non-Resident Corps/Trusts

the purposes of that paragraph, deemed, at that time, not to be an indebtedness or a lease obligation of a person resident in Canada, to the extent of the portion of the particular indebtedness or lease obligation that can reasonably be considered to have been issued by the life insurance corporation to the foreign affiliate

(a) in respect of the life insurance corporation's life insurance business carried on outside Canada; and

(b) not in respect of

(i) the life insurance corporation's life insurance business carried on in Canada, or

(ii) any other use.

Notes: 95(2.42) added by 2007 budget bill #2, for FAs' tax years that begin after 1999.

(2.43) Definitions — subsecs. (2.43) to (2.45) — The following definitions apply in this subsection and subsections (2.44) and (2.45).

"Canadian indebtedness" means indebtedness (other than upstream deposits) owed by persons resident in Canada or in respect of businesses carried on in Canada.

Notes: See Notes to 95(2.44).

"eligible bank affiliate", of an eligible Canadian bank at any time, means a foreign bank that, at that time, is a controlled foreign affiliate (for the purposes of section 17) of the eligible Canadian bank and is described in subparagraph (a)(i) of the definition "investment business" in subsection (1).

Related Provisions: 90(15)"eligible bank affiliate" — Definition applies to s. 90.

"eligible Canadian bank" means a bank listed in Schedule I to the *Bank Act*.

Related Provisions: 90(15)"eligible Canadian bank" — Definition applies to s. 90; 95(2.31), (3.01) — Exceptions to FAPI rules for certain securities transactions; 125.21 — Credit to offset Part XIII withholding tax.

Notes: The Schedule I banks (June 2021) are: ADS Canadian Bank, B2B Bank, Bank of Montreal, Bank of Nova Scotia, Bridgewater Bank, CS Alterna Bank, Caisse populaire acadienne ltée, Canadian Imperial Bank of Commerce, Canadian Tire Bank, Canadian Western Bank, Coast Capital Savings Federal Credit Union, Concentra Bank, Digital Commerce Bank, Duo Bank of Canada, Equitable Bank, Exchange Bank of Canada, First Nations Bank of Canada, General Bank of Canada, Haventree Bank, Home Bank, HomeEquity Bank, Laurentian Bank of Canada, Manulife Bank of Canada, Motus Bank, National Bank of Canada, People's Bank of Canada, President's Choice Bank, RFA Bank of Canada, Rogers Bank, Royal Bank of Canada, Tangerine Bank, Toronto-Dominion Bank, VanCity Community Investment Bank, VersaBank, Wealth One Bank of Canada.

"eligible Canadian indebtedness", owing to an eligible bank affiliate of an eligible Canadian bank, means bonds, debentures, notes or similar obligations of the Government of Canada, the government of a province, an agent of a province, a municipality in Canada or a municipal or public body performing a function of government in Canada, that are owing to the affiliate, other than property in respect of which paragraph (2)(a.3) does not apply because of subsection (2.31).

Related Provisions: 90(15)"eligible Canadian indebtedness" — Definition applies to s. 90.

Notes: For the meaning of "municipal or public body...", see Notes to 149(1)(c).

"eligible currency hedge", of an eligible bank affiliate of an eligible Canadian bank, means an agreement that provides for the purchase, sale or exchange of currency and that

(a) can reasonably be considered to have been made by the affiliate to reduce its risk of fluctuations in the value of currency with respect to eligible Canadian indebtedness and upstream deposits owing to the affiliate; and

(b) cannot reasonably be considered to have been made by the affiliate to reduce its risk with respect to property other than eligible Canadian indebtedness and upstream deposits owing to the affiliate.

"excess liquidity", of an eligible bank affiliate of an eligible Canadian bank for a taxation year of the affiliate, means the amount, if any, by which

(a) the average of all amounts each of which is, in respect of a month that ends in the 12-month period that begins 60 days prior to the beginning of the year — or, if the affiliate was formed after the beginning of the period, in respect of a month that ends in the year — the amount of the affiliate's relationship deposits for the month, expressed in the affiliate's calculating currency for the year unless the context requires otherwise,

exceeds

(b) the average of all amounts each of which is, in respect of a month that ends in the period — or, if the affiliate was formed after the beginning of the period, in respect of a month that ends in the year — the amount of the affiliate's organic assets for the month, expressed in the affiliate's calculating currency for the year unless the context requires otherwise.

Related Provisions: 90(15)"excess liquidity" — Definition applies to s. 90.

"organic assets", of an eligible bank affiliate of an eligible Canadian bank for a month, means the total of all amounts in respect of the affiliate each of which is

(a) included in the amounts reported as loans in the assets section of the consolidated monthly balance sheet accepted by the Superintendent of Financial Institutions that is filed for the month by the bank, or another corporation resident in Canada that is related to the bank at the end of the month, or

(b) an amount owing to the affiliate by a person that is related to the affiliate (other than an amount described in paragraph (a))

but does not include the amount of an eligible Canadian indebtedness or upstream deposit owing to the affiliate.

"qualifying indebtedness", owing to an eligible bank affiliate of an eligible Canadian bank, means an upstream deposit owing to, or an eligible Canadian indebtedness of, the affiliate, to the extent that it can reasonably be considered that

(a) the upstream deposit or the acquisition of eligible Canadian indebtedness, as the case may be, is funded by

(i) property transferred or lent by a person other than the bank or a person resident in Canada that was not, at the time of the transfer or loan, dealing at arm's length with the bank,

(ii) a repayment of all or part of an upstream deposit owing to the affiliate, or

(iii) the purchase of eligible Canadian indebtedness by the bank or a person resident in Canada that was not, at the time of the transfer or loan, dealing at arm's length with the bank; and

(b) the proceeds of the upstream deposit or the proceeds received by the vendor of the eligible Canadian indebtedness, as the case may be, are used for a purpose other than to fund a transfer or loan of property by the bank — or another person resident in Canada that was not, at the time of the transfer or loan, dealing at arm's length with the bank — to the affiliate or another foreign affiliate of the bank or of the other person.

"relationship deposits", of an eligible bank affiliate of an eligible Canadian bank for a month, means the total of all amounts included in the amounts reported as demand and notice deposits, and fixed-term deposits in the liabilities section of the consolidated monthly balance sheet accepted by the Superintendent of Financial Institutions that is filed for the month by the bank, or another corporation resident in Canada that is related to the bank at the end of the month, that are deposits (other than of a temporary nature) of the affiliate made by a person who at the end of the month

(a) deals at arm's length with the affiliate; and

(b) is not resident in Canada.

"total specified indebtedness", owing to an eligible bank affiliate of an eligible Canadian bank for a taxation year of the affiliate, means the average of all amounts each of which is, in respect of a month that ends in the year, the greatest total amount at any time in the month that is the total of all amounts each of which is

(a) the amount of an upstream deposit owing to the affiliate;

(b) the amount of an eligible Canadian indebtedness owing to the affiliate; or

(c) the positive or negative fair market value of an eligible currency hedge of the affiliate.

"upstream deposit", owing to an eligible bank affiliate of an eligible Canadian bank, means indebtedness owing by the bank to the affiliate.

Related Provisions: 90(8)(d), 90(8.1) — Treatment of upstream deposit for upstream loan rules; 90(15)"upstream deposit" — Definition applies to s. 90; 125.21 — Credit to offset Part XIII withholding tax on upstream deposits.

Notes: See Notes to 95(2.44).

(2.44) FAPI adjustment — eligible bank affiliate — If a non-resident corporation (in this subsection referred to as the "affiliate") is, throughout a taxation year of the affiliate, an eligible bank affiliate of an eligible Canadian bank, and the bank elects in writing under this subsection, in respect of the affiliate for the year, and files the election with the Minister on or before the filing-due date of the bank for the particular taxation year of the bank in which the year ends,

(a) there is to be deducted in computing the amount determined for A in the definition "foreign accrual property income" in subsection (1) in respect of the affiliate for the year, the lesser of

(i) the amount determined, without reference to this paragraph, for A in that definition in respect of the affiliate for the year, and

(ii) the amount determined by the following formula, where each amount referred to in the formula is to be determined using Canadian currency:

$$A - B - C - D$$

where

A is the total of all amounts each of which is the affiliate's income for the year that is from a qualifying indebtedness owing to, or an eligible currency hedge of, the affiliate and that would, in the absence of this subsection, be included in computing the income of the affiliate from a business other than an active business of the affiliate,

B is the total of all amounts each of which is the affiliate's loss for the year that is from a qualifying indebtedness owing to, or an eligible currency hedge of, the affiliate and that would, in the absence of this subsection, be deducted in computing the income of the affiliate from a business other than an active business of the affiliate,

C is the total of all amounts each of which is the amount, if any, by which an amount included in computing the amount determined for A or B in respect of an upstream deposit exceeds the amount that would be the affiliate's income, or is less than the amount that would be the affiliate's loss, as the case may be, for the year from the upstream deposit if the interest received or receivable by the affiliate in respect of the upstream deposit were computed at an interest rate equal to the lesser of

(A) the rate of interest in respect of the upstream deposit, and

(B) the benchmark rate of interest, acceptable to the Minister, that is

(I) if the upstream deposit is denominated in a qualifying currency (as defined in subsection 261(1)), the average, for the year, of a daily interbank offered rate for loans denominated in that currency with a term to maturity of three months, or

(II) in any other case, the average, for the year, of a daily rate for Canadian dollar denominated bankers' acceptances with a term to maturity of three months, and

D is the amount determined by the formula

$$E \times F/G$$

where

E is the amount, if any, by which the amount determined for A exceeds the total of the amounts determined for B and C,

F is the amount, if any, by which the total specified indebtedness owing to the affiliate for the year exceeds the affiliate's excess liquidity for the year, and

G is the total specified indebtedness owing to the affiliate for the year; and

(b) there is to be included, in computing the income of the affiliate from an active business for the year, an amount equal to the proportion of the amount computed under the formula in subparagraph (a)(ii), computed as if each amount referred to in that formula were determined using the affiliate's calculating currency, that the amount that is required to be deducted under paragraph (a) for the year is of the amount described in subparagraph (a)(ii).

Related Provisions: 95(2.31) — Rules for eligible Canadian bank; 95(2.43) — Definitions; 257 — Formula cannot calculate to less than zero; Reg. 5907(1)"earnings"(b), "exempt earnings"(d)(ii)(J) — Inclusion of 95(2.44) amount.

Notes: 95(2.43)–(2.45), intended to "alleviate the tax cost to Canadian banks of using excess liquidity of their foreign affiliates in their Canadian operations" (2012 Budget papers), all added by 2014 budget bill #2, for FAs' tax years that begin after Oct. 2012.

(2.45) Investment business and excluded property — If an election is made under subsection (2.44) in respect of an eligible bank affiliate of an eligible Canadian bank for a taxation year of the affiliate,

(a) for the purposes of the definition "investment business" in subsection (1), the bank, and any other person resident in Canada that does not deal at arm's length with the bank, are deemed to deal at arm's length with the affiliate in respect of the making of upstream deposits, and acquisitions of Canadian indebtedness from the bank or the other person, by the affiliate in the course of a business carried on by the affiliate in the year if the affiliate's excess liquidity for the year is at least 90% of the total specified indebtedness owing to the affiliate for the year; and

(b) for the purposes of paragraph (b) of the definition "excluded property" in subsection (1),

(i) the fair market value of each upstream deposit and Canadian indebtedness owing to, and eligible currency hedge of, the affiliate is deemed to be nil,

(ii) at any particular time, the lesser of the following amounts is deemed to be the fair market value of a property of the affiliate that is excluded property at that particular time:

(A) the total of all amounts each of which is the fair market value of an upstream deposit or Canadian indebtedness owing to, or an eligible currency hedge of, the affiliate, and

(B) the amount, if any, by which

(I) the affiliate's relationship deposits for the calendar month that is two months prior to the particular time (or if the affiliate was formed less than two months prior to the particular time, for the calendar month that includes the particular time)

exceeds

(II) the amount of the affiliate's organic assets for the calendar month that is two months prior to the particular time (or if the affiliate was formed less than two months prior to the particular time, for the calendar month that includes the particular time), and

(iii) the amount, if any, by which the amount in clause (ii)(A) exceeds the amount in subparagraph (ii) is deemed to be the fair market value of a property of the eligible bank affiliate that is not excluded property at that time.

Related Provisions: 95(2.43) — Definitions.

Notes: See Notes to 95(2.44).

Proposed **95(2.46)** in the Nov. 27, 2012 draft legislation was dropped.

(2.5) Definitions for para. (2)(a.3) — For the purpose of paragraph (2)(a.3),

"excluded income" and **"excluded revenue"** for a taxation year in respect of a foreign affiliate of a taxpayer mean, respectively, income or revenue, that is

(a) derived directly or indirectly from a specified deposit with a prescribed financial institution,

(b) derived directly or indirectly from a lease obligation of a person (other than the taxpayer or a person that does not deal at arm's length with the taxpayer) resident in Canada relating to property used by the person in the course of carrying on a business through a permanent establishment outside Canada,

(c) included in computing the affiliate's income for the year from carrying on a business through a permanent establishment in Canada, or

(d) included in computing the affiliate's income or loss from an active business for the year because of subparagraph (2)(a)(ii);

Notes: For the meaning of "derived", see Notes to 18.1(12). For "indirectly" see Notes to 17.1(1).

Para. (b) amended (to refer to a PE) and para. (d) added by 2014 budget bill #2 (implementing two July 17, 2006 Finance comfort letters), last change effective for FAs' tax years that begin after July 12, 2013. Definition added by 2001 technical bill.

Regulations: 5906(2)(b).

"indebtedness" does not include obligations of a particular person under agreements with non-resident corporations providing for the purchase, sale or exchange of currency where

(a) the agreements are swap agreements, forward purchase or sale agreements, forward rate agreements, futures agreements, options or rights agreements, or similar agreements,

(b) the particular person is a bank, a trust company, a credit union, an insurance corporation or a trader or dealer in securities or commodities resident in Canada, the business activities of which are subject by law to the supervision of a regulating authority in Canada such as the Superintendent of Financial Institutions or a similar authority of a province,

(c) the agreements are entered into by the non-resident corporation in the course of a business conducted principally with persons with whom the non-resident corporation deals at arm's length, if

(i) the business is principally carried on in the country (other than Canada) under whose laws the non-resident corporation is governed and any of exists, was (unless the non-resident corporation was continued in any jurisdiction) formed or organized, or was last continued, or

(ii) the non-resident corporation is a foreign affiliate of the particular person, or of a person related to the particular person, and

(A) the non-resident corporation is a foreign bank, a trust company, a credit union, an insurance corporation or a trader or dealer in securities or commodities, and

(B) the activities of the business are regulated

(I) under the laws of the country under whose laws the non-resident corporation is governed and any of exists, was (unless the non-resident corporation was continued in any jurisdiction) formed or organized, or was last continued and under the laws of each country in

which the business is carried on through a permanent establishment in that country,

(II) under the laws of the country (other than Canada) in which the business is principally carried[8], or

(III) if the affiliate is related to a corporation, under the laws of the country under the laws of which a corporation related to the non-resident corporation is governed and any of exists, was (unless that related corporation was continued in any jurisdiction) formed or organized, or was last continued, if those regulating laws are recognized under the laws of the country in which the business is principally carried on and all of those countries are members of the European Union, and

(d) the terms and conditions of such agreements are substantially the same as the terms and conditions of similar agreements made by persons dealings at arm's length;

Notes: The words "any of exists..." in (c)(i) and (c)(ii)(B)(I) and (III) should be read "any of {(1) exists, (2) was formed or organized, or (3) was last continued}", though this is not correct English.

Definition amended by 2002-2013 technical bill (for foreign affiliates' tax years that begin after 1999), 2007 budget bill #2.

Regulations: 5906(2)(b) (permanent establishment, for (c)(ii)(B)(I)).

"specified deposit", of a foreign affiliate of a taxpayer, means a deposit of the affiliate made with a permanent establishment in a country other than Canada of a prescribed financial institution resident in Canada if the income from the deposit is income of the affiliate for the year that would, in the absence of paragraph (2)(a.3), be income from an active business carried on by the affiliate in a country other than Canada, other than a business the principal purpose of which is to derive income from property (including any interest, dividends, rents, royalties or similar returns, or any substitutes for any of those) or profits from the disposition of investment property.

Notes: Definition amended by 2014 budget bill #2, for foreign affiliates' tax years that begin after Oct. 2012.

Regulations: 5906(2)(b) (permanent establishment); 7900 (prescribed financial institution).

Notes: 95(2.5) added by 1994 technical bill, last change effective for foreign affiliates' tax years that end after 1994.

(2.6) Rule for the definition "specified person or partnership" — For the purposes of paragraphs (a) to (d) of the definition "specified person or partnership" in subsection (1), if a person or partnership (referred to in this subsection as the "taxpayer") is not dealing at arm's length with another person or partnership (referred to in this subsection as the "particular person") at a particular time, the taxpayer is deemed to have existed and not to have dealt at arm's length with the particular person, nor with each specified predecessor corporation of the particular person, throughout the period that began when the particular person or the specified predecessor corporation, as the case may be, came into existence and that ends at the particular time.

Notes: 95(2.6) added by 2008 budget bill #2, last change effective for foreign affiliates' tax years that begin after July 13, 2008.

(3) Definition of "services" — For the purposes of paragraph (2)(b), "services" includes the insurance of Canadian risks but does not include

(a) the transportation of persons or goods;

(b) services performed in connection with the purchase or sale of goods;

(c) the transmission of electronic signals or electricity along a transmission system located outside Canada; or

(d) the manufacturing or processing outside Canada, in accordance with the taxpayer's specifications and under a contract between the taxpayer and the affiliate, of tangible property, or for civil law corporeal property, that is owned by the taxpayer if the

---

[8] *Sic.* Should be "carried on" — ed.

property resulting from the manufacturing or processing is used or held by the taxpayer in the ordinary course of the taxpayer's business carried on in Canada.

Notes: *Para. (b)*: only services "directly related to the sales function" qualify, so prototype testing and R&D do not: VIEWS docs 9729770, 2002-0123755, 2013-049736I7, 2016-067192I7.

Para. (d): R&D is not "manufacturing and processing": doc 2016-067192I7. See also 125.1(3)"manufacturing or processing" Notes.

95(3) amended by 2007 budget bill #2, last change effective for foreign affiliates' 2001 and later tax years.

(3.01) Application of para. (2)(b) — eligible Canadian bank — Paragraph (2)(b) does not apply to a controlled foreign affiliate (for the purposes of section 17) of an eligible Canadian bank (as defined in subsection (2.43)) in respect of services performed in connection with the purchase or sale of a property described in paragraph (2.31)(b) if

(a) the services have been performed by the affiliate

(i) under terms and conditions that are substantially the same as the terms and conditions that would have been made between persons who deal at arm's length with each other,

(ii) in the course of a business

(A) that regularly includes trading or dealing in securities principally with persons with whom the affiliate deals at arm's length, and

(B) that is principally carried on through a permanent establishment in a country other than Canada, and

(iii) for the purpose of enabling the acquisition or disposition of the property by a person who, at the time of the acquisition or disposition, deals at arm's length with the affiliate and the eligible Canadian bank; and

(b) the affiliate is a foreign bank or a trader or dealer in securities and the activities of the business are regulated

(i) under the laws of the country under whose laws the affiliate is governed and any of exists, was (unless the affiliate was continued in any jurisdiction) formed or organized, or was last continued, and under the laws of each country in which the business is carried on through a permanent establishment in that country,

(ii) under the laws of the country (other than Canada) in which the business is principally carried on, or

(iii) if the affiliate is related to a corporation, under the laws of the country under whose laws that related corporation is governed and any of exists, was (unless that related corporation was continued in any jurisdiction) formed or organized, or was last continued, if those regulating laws are recognized under the laws of the country in which the business is principally carried on and all those countries are members of the European Union.

Related Provisions: 95(2.31) — Parallel rule for 95(2)(a); 95(2.43)–(2.46) — Rules for eligible bank affiliate.

Notes: See Notes to 95(2.31).

The words "any of exists..." in (b)(i) and (iii) should be read "any of {(1) exists, (2) was ... formed or organized, or (3) was last continued}", though this is not correct English.

95(3.01) added by 2014 budget bill #2, for FAs' tax years that begin after Oct. 2012.

(3.02) Rules for cl. (2)(b)(ii)(B) ["relevant person", separate business] — For the purposes of clause (2)(b)(ii)(B),

(a) a relevant person is

(i) a person resident in Canada, or

(ii) a non-resident person if the non-resident person performs the services referred to in subparagraph (2)(b)(ii) in the course of a business (other than a treaty-protected business) carried on in Canada; and

(b) any portion of a business carried on by a non-resident person that is carried on in Canada is deemed to be a business that is separate from any other portion of the business carried on by the person.

Notes: 95(3.02) added by 2014 budget bill #2, for foreign affiliates' tax years that begin after July 12, 2013 (or earlier by election).

(3.1) Designated property — subpara. (2)(a.1)(i) — Designated property referred to in subparagraph (2)(a.1)(i) is property that is described in the portion of paragraph (2)(a.1) that is before subparagraph (i) that is

(a) property that was sold to non-resident persons other than the affiliate, or sold to the affiliate for sale to non-resident persons, and

(i) that

(A) was — in the course of carrying on a business in Canada — manufactured, produced, grown, extracted or processed in Canada by the taxpayer, or by a person with whom the taxpayer does not deal at arm's length, or

(B) was — in the course of a business carried on by a foreign affiliate of the taxpayer outside Canada — manufactured or processed from tangible property, or for civil law corporeal property, that, at the time of the manufacturing or processing, was owned by the taxpayer or by a person related to the taxpayer and used or held by the owner in the course of carrying on a business in Canada, if the manufacturing or processing was in accordance with the specifications of the owner of that tangible or corporeal property and under a contract between that owner and that foreign affiliate,

(ii) that was acquired, in the course of carrying on a business in Canada, by a purchaser from a vendor, if

(A) the purchaser is the taxpayer or is a person resident in Canada with whom the taxpayer does not deal at arm's length, and

(B) the vendor is a person

(I) with whom the taxpayer deals at arm's length,

(II) who is not a foreign affiliate of the taxpayer, and

(III) who is not a foreign affiliate of a person resident in Canada with whom the taxpayer does not deal at arm's length, or

(iii) that was acquired by a purchaser from a vendor, if

(A) the purchaser is the taxpayer or is a person resident in Canada with whom the taxpayer does not deal at arm's length,

(B) the vendor is a foreign affiliate of

(I) the taxpayer, or

(II) a person resident in Canada with whom the taxpayer does not deal at arm's length, and

(C) that property was manufactured, produced, grown, extracted or processed in the country

(I) under whose laws the vendor is governed and any of exists, was (unless the vendor was continued in any jurisdiction) formed or organized, or was last continued, and

(II) in which the vendor's business is principally carried on; or

(b) property that is an interest in real property, or a real right in an immovable, located in, or a foreign resource property in respect of, the country

(i) under whose laws the affiliate is governed and any of exists, was (unless the affiliate was continued in any jurisdiction) formed or organized, or was last continued, and

(ii) in which the affiliate's business is principally carried on.

Notes: For (a)(i)(B): see 125.1(3)"manufacturing or processing" Notes.

The words "any of exists..." in (a)(iii)(C)(I) and (b)(i) should be read "any of {(1) exists, (2) was formed or organized, or (3) was last continued}", though this is not correct English.

Non-Resident Corps/Trusts

95(3.1) added by 2007 budget bill #2, for foreign affiliates' tax years that begin after Dec. 20, 2002, or earlier by election.

Proposed **95(3.2)-(3.8)** in the Feb. 27, 2004 draft legislation were withdrawn. They provided rules for proposed 95(2)(c.1)-(c.6), (e.2)-(e.5) and (f.3)-(f.7), all of which were also withdrawn with the Aug. 19, 2011 draft.

(3.2) Contract manufacturing — For the purposes of clause (2)(a.1)(ii)(A), property of a particular foreign affiliate of a taxpayer is deemed to have been manufactured by the particular affiliate in a particular country if the property is

(a) developed and designed by the particular affiliate in the particular country in the course of an active business carried on by the particular affiliate in the particular country; and

(b) manufactured, produced or processed outside the particular country by another foreign affiliate of the taxpayer, during a period throughout which the taxpayer has a qualifying interest in the other affiliate,

(i) under a contract between the particular affiliate and the other affiliate, and

(ii) in accordance with specifications provided by the particular affiliate.

Notes: 95(3.2) added by 2014 budget bill #2, for FAs' tax years that end after 2008.

(4) Definitions — In this section,

"direct equity percentage" at any time of any person in a corporation is the percentage determined by the following rules:

(a) for each class of the issued shares of the capital stock of the corporation, determine the proportion of 100 that the number of shares of that class owned by that person at that time is of the total number of issued shares of that class at that time, and

(b) select the proportion determined under paragraph (a) for that person in respect of the corporation that is not less than any other proportion so determined for that person in respect of the corporation at that time,

and the proportion selected under paragraph (b), when expressed as a percentage, is that person's direct equity percentage in the corporation at that time;

Notes: See "equity percentage" below. On "owned by" in para. (a), see Sala, "The Impact of a European Usufruct on the FA Status of a Non-Resident Corp Held by a Quebec Resident Taxpayer", 2354 *Tax Topics* (CCH) 1-4 (April 20, 2017).

95(4)"direct equity percentage" was 95(4)(a) before RSC 1985 (5th Supp) consolidation for tax years ending after Nov. 1991.

Interpretation Bulletins: IT-392: Meaning of term "share".

"eligible controlled foreign affiliate", of a taxpayer, at any time, means a foreign affiliate at that time of the taxpayer in respect of which the following conditions are met:

(a) the affiliate is a controlled foreign affiliate of the taxpayer at that time and at the end of the affiliate's taxation year that includes that time, and

(b) the total of all amounts each of which would be, if this definition were read without reference to this paragraph, the participating percentage (determined at the end of the taxation year) of a share owned by the taxpayer of the capital stock of a corporation, in respect of the affiliate, is not less than 90%;

Notes: Under para. (b), the participating percentage is nil if FAPI for the year is under $5,000, due to a drafting error which Finance is reviewing.

Definition added by 2002-2013 technical bill, last change effective for determinations made after Aug. 19, 2011.

"equity percentage" at any time of a person, in any particular corporation, is the total of

(a) the person's direct equity percentage at that time in the particular corporation, and

(b) all percentages each of which is the product obtained when the person's equity percentage at that time in any corporation is multiplied by that corporation's direct equity percentage at that time in the particular corporation

except that for the purposes of the definition "participating percentage" in subsection (1), paragraph (b) shall be read as if the reference to "any corporation" were a reference to "any corporation other than a corporation resident in Canada";

Related Provisions: 149.1(1)"equity percentage" — Meaning of term for private foundation corporate-holding rules.

Notes: See 95(1)"foreign affiliate". 95(4)"equity percentage" was 95(4)(b) before RSC 1985 (5th Supp) consolidation for tax years ending after Nov. 1991.

"relevant cost base", of a property at any time to a foreign affiliate of a taxpayer, in respect of the taxpayer, means the greater of

(a) the amount determined — or, if the taxpayer is not a corporation, the amount that would be determined if the taxpayer were a corporation resident in Canada — by the formula

$$A + B - C$$

where

A   is the amount for which the property could be disposed of at that time that would not, in the absence of paragraph (2)(f.1), result in any amount being added to, or deducted from, any of the affiliate's

(i) exempt earnings, exempt loss, taxable earnings and taxable loss (all within the meaning of subsection 5907(1) of the *Income Tax Regulations*), in respect of the taxpayer, for the taxation year of the affiliate that includes that time, and

(ii) hybrid surplus and hybrid deficit, in respect of the taxpayer, at that time,

B   is the amount, if any, by which any income or gain from a disposition of the property would, if the property were disposed of at that time for proceeds of disposition equal to its fair market value at that time be reduced under paragraph (2)(f.1), and

C   is the amount, if any, by which any loss from a disposition of the property would, if the property were disposed of at that time for proceeds of disposition equal to its fair market value at that time be reduced under paragraph (2)(f.1), and

(b) either

(i) if the affiliate is an eligible controlled foreign affiliate of the taxpayer at that time, the amount that the taxpayer elects, in accordance with prescribed rules, in respect of the property not exceeding the fair market value at that time of the property, or

(ii) in any other case, nil.

Related Provisions: 96(3) — Election by members of partnership; 257 — Formula cannot calculate to less than zero.

Notes: Definition amended by 2002-2013 technical bill, generally for determinations made after Feb. 27, 2004.

95(4)"relevant cost base" was 95(4)(c) before RSC 1985 (5th Supp) consolidation for tax years ending after Nov. 1991.

Regulations: 5911(5) (prescribed rules for election).

(4.1) Application of subsec. 87(8.1) — In this section, the expressions "foreign merger", "predecessor foreign corporation", "new foreign corporation" and "foreign parent corporation" have the meanings assigned by subsection 87(8.1).

Notes: 95(4.1) amended by 1998 Budget, for mergers or combinations of foreign corporations after Feb. 24, 1998 (earlier in some cases). Added in the RSC 1985 (5th Supp) consolidation, for tax years ending after Nov. 1991; the rule was formerly in 87(8.1) opening words.

Proposed **95(4.2)** in the Aug. 19/11 draft legislation, "Absorptive mergers", was replaced by a more general rule for such mergers in 87(8.2).

(5) Income bonds or debentures issued by foreign affiliates — For the purposes of this Subdivision, an income bond or income debenture issued by a corporation (other than a corporation resident in Canada) shall be deemed to be a share of the capital stock of the corporation unless any interest or other similar periodic amount paid by the corporation on or in respect of the bond or debenture was, under the laws of the country in which the corporation was resident, deductible in computing the amount for the year on which the corporation was liable to pay income or profits tax imposed by the government of that country.

Notes: For the meaning of "income or profits tax", see Notes to 126(4).

Interpretation Bulletins: IT-388: Income bonds issued by foreign corporations (cancelled).

(6) Where rights or shares issued, acquired or disposed of to avoid tax — For the purposes of this Subdivision (other than section 90),

(a) where any person or partnership has a right under a contract, in equity or otherwise, either immediately or in the future and either absolutely or contingently, to, or to acquire, shares of the capital stock of a corporation or interests in a partnership and

(i) it can reasonably be considered that the principal purpose for the existence of the right is to cause 2 or more corporations to be related for the purpose of paragraph (2)(a), those corporations shall be deemed not to be related for that purpose, or

(ii) it can reasonably be considered that the principal purpose for the existence of the right is to permit any person to avoid, reduce or defer the payment of tax or any other amount that would otherwise be payable under this Act, those shares or partnership interests, as the case may be, are deemed to be owned by that person or partnership; and

(b) where a person or partnership acquires or disposes of shares of the capital stock of a corporation or interests in a partnership, either directly or indirectly, and it can reasonably be considered that the principal purpose for the acquisition or disposition is to permit a person to avoid, reduce or defer the payment of tax or any other amount that would otherwise be payable under this Act, that acquisition or disposition is deemed not to have taken place, and where the shares or partnership interests were unissued by the corporation or partnership immediately before the acquisition, those shares or partnership interests, as the case may be, are deemed not to have been issued.

Related Provisions: 17(14) — Similar rule re loans to non-residents; 256(5.1) — Controlled directly or indirectly.

Notes: Using a second-tier financing structure with a Barbados company to avoid 95(6)(b) did not trigger GAAR, in *Univar Canada*, 2005 TCC 723. This may override CRA policy extending 95(6) to various second-tier financing structures including double-dip "tower" structures, artificial arrangements to bypass 85.1(4), FAPI arrangements and duplication of surplus accounts.

Following review of *Univar* (VIEWS doc 2005-0158741C6), CRA issued *Income Tax Technical News* No. 36 (July 27, 2007), which includes several examples and notes that all proposed 95(6)(b) reassessments will be reviewed at HQ. For an earlier Q&A see 2005-0155331E5. For rulings that 95(6) will not apply to restructurings see 2006-0207391R3, 2007-0219291R3, 2008-0264671R3; 2008-0273471R3 (structure to use expected startup losses); 2009-0347271R3 (foreign affiliate restructuring financing); 2010-0373801R3 (conversion from Dutch BV to Dutch cooperative); 2012-0452291R3 (double-dip financing structure [Bernstein, "Shares Not Debt in Luxembourgco", 21(4) *Canadian Tax Highlights* (ctf.ca) 7-8 (April 2013)]); 2012-0463611R3 (foreign divisive reorg). In 2006-0217481, CRA says that 95(6)(b) may apply. See Johnson et al., "A Reasoned Response to the CRA's Views on ... Para. 95(6)(b)", 54(3) *Canadian Tax Journal* 571-632 (2006); Deloitte commentary, 2007(17) *Tax Times* (Carswell) 1-2 (Sept. 14/07); Sinclair & Richardson, "Financing Foreign Affiliates", XIV(3) *Corporate Finance* (Federated Press) 1518-21 (2007). However, CRA stated at the 2007 conference (*Income Tax Technical News* 38; conference report, 4:16-17) that 95(6) will be applied only if the principal purpose is to avoid, reduce or defer tax, and that in any given case CRA must look at all the facts. See also Bunn, "Debt Dumping", 2(2) *Canadian Tax Focus* (ctf.ca) 2 (May 2012).

Per *Lehigh Cement*, 2014 FCA 103, 95(6) is not a broad anti-avoidance rule and must be interpreted narrowly. The purpose to be considered is that of the acquisition or disposition of the shares, not of the series of transactions (para. 46). 95(6) applies only to a transaction "for the purpose of affecting the status of a nonresident corporation" (para. 47) via "manipulation of share ownership of the nonresident corporation to meet or fail the relevant tests for foreign affiliate, controlled foreign affiliate or related-corporation" (para. 56). See Baker & Slaats, "Lehigh: Paragraph 95(6)(b) Restricted", 22(5) *Canadian Tax Highlights* (ctf.ca) 1-2 (May 2014). CRA accepts *Lehigh* but believes 95(6)(b) can still apply in other contexts such as manipulation of the participating percentage in a controlled foreign affiliate; and the 95(6) Committee will continue to review cases (GAAR will also be considered for pre-212.3 cases): doc 2014-0550441C6 [2014 CTF q.9; Crosbie & Anderson, "Paragraph 95(6)(b) Post-Lehigh Position", XIX(3) *Corporate Finance* (Federated Press) 2549-55 (2014)].

Imperial Tobacco was a 95(6)(b) appeal [Hanna, "Subsection 95(6) Foreign Debt Dumping at the Tax Court", XVIII(1) *International Tax Planning* (Federated Press) 1233-35 (2012)], with procedural decisions at 2012 TCC 135 (principal-purpose test in 95(6)(b) is objective, so notice of appeal need not state taxpayer's purpose in acquiring shares); 2013 TCC 144 (document disclosure). The appeal was withdrawn in 2015.

As of fall 2020, the 95(6) Committee members are: Chantal Tuble [Acting Chair, 613-670-7366] (Senior Technical Field Advisor, Intl & Large Business Directorate); Nicholas Bilodeau, Manager, Income Tax Rulings Directorate; Suzanne Saydeh, Manager, Tax Avoidance Divn; Venetia Putureanu (Director, Intl Ta Divn); Jim Randall (Manager, Tax Avoidance Divn); plus "invited guests from functional areas". As of Oct. 2020, the Committee had considered 58 cases and recommended 95(6) be applied in 21 of them. (*Access to Information Act* disclosure) See also VIEWS doc 2014-0526761C6 [IFA 2014 q.6].

95(6) amended by 2001 technical bill (effective Dec. 1999), 1994 technical bill.

I.T. Technical News: 32 (subsec. 95(6): scope of application); 34 (update on subsection 95(6)); 36 (paragraph 95(6)(b)); 38 (application of para. 95(6)(b)).

(7) Stock dividends from foreign affiliates — For the purposes of this Subdivision and subsection 52(3), the amount of any stock dividend paid by a foreign affiliate of a corporation resident in Canada shall, in respect of the corporation, be deemed to be nil.

Notes: For a ruling applying 95(7) see VIEWS doc 2010-0374141R3.

Interpretation Bulletins [subsec. 95(7)]: IT-88R2: Stock dividends.

(8) Tracking interests — interpretation — For the purposes of subsections (9) to (12), a particular property is a tracking interest in respect of a person or partnership (referred to in this subsection as the "tracked entity") if

(a) all or part of the fair market value of the particular property — or of any payment or right to receive an amount in respect of the particular property — can reasonably be considered to be determined, directly or indirectly, by reference to one or more of the following criteria in respect of property or activities of the tracked entity (referred to in this subsection and subsections (9) to (11) as the **"tracked property and activities"**):

(i) the fair market value of property of the tracked entity,

(ii) any revenue, income or cash flow from property or activities of the tracked entity,

(iii) any profits or gains from the disposition of property of the tracked entity, and

(iv) any similar criteria in respect of property or activities of the tracked entity; and

(b) the tracked property and activities in respect of the particular property represent less than all of the property and activities of the tracked entity.

Proposed Amendment — 95(8)

Letter from Dept. of Finance, March 25, 2019: See under 95(11).

Notes: See Notes to 95(9). For the meaning of "indirectly" in para. (a), see Notes to 17.1(1).

95(8)-(12) added by 2018 budget bill #2, for a foreign affiliate's tax years that begin after Feb. 26, 2018, except that, despite 95(10), 95(11) does not apply to the FA's tax years that begin before Oct. 25, 2018, if the taxpayer

(a) elects in writing under s. 7(7) of 2018 budget bill #2 in respect of all its FAs; and

(b) files the election with CRA by the later of June 13, 2019 and the taxpayer's filing-due date for its tax year that includes Oct. 25, 2018.

(9) Tracking interests — "investment business" definition — For the purposes of the definition "investment business" in subsection (1), if, at any time in a taxation year of a foreign affiliate of a taxpayer, a person or partnership holds a tracking interest in respect of the affiliate or a partnership of which the affiliate is a member, the tracked property and activities in respect of the tracking interest are, to the extent they would not otherwise be part of an investment business of the affiliate, deemed, in respect of the taxpayer,

(a) to be a separate business carried on by the affiliate throughout the year; and

(b) not to be part of any other business of the affiliate.

Related Provisions: 95(8) — Tracking interests — interpretation.

Notes: For discussion of 95(8)-(12) see Boidman, "Canada Targets Conduits and Tracking Shares", 91(12) *Tax Notes International* (taxnotes.com) 1223-26 (Sept. 18, 2018); Lee & Wang, "The Tracking Interest Rules", 103 *International Tax* (CCH) 5-10 (Dec. 2018); Alty & Sandler, "The Interaction of the Tracking Interest Rules and the Stub-Period FAPI Rules", XVI(2) *Corporate Structures & Groups* (Federated Press) 12-18 (2020).

See Notes to 95(8) re enactment of 95(9).

(10) Conditions for subsec. (11) [deemed separate corp] — Subsection (11) applies in respect of a foreign affiliate of a taxpayer for a taxation year of the affiliate if, at any time in the year,

(a) the taxpayer holds a property that is a tracking interest in respect of the affiliate; and

(b) shares of a class of the capital stock of the affiliate the fair market value of which can reasonably be considered to be determined by reference to the tracked property and activities in respect of the tracking interest (referred to in subsection (11) as a "tracking class") are held by the taxpayer or a foreign affiliate of the taxpayer.

Related Provisions: 95(8) — Tracking interests — interpretation.

Notes: This was 95(11) in the July 27, 2018 draft legislation. See Notes to 95(8) re enactment of 95(10); and Notes to 95(9).

(11) Tracking class — separate corporation — If this subsection applies in respect of a foreign affiliate (referred to in this subsection as the "actual affiliate") of a taxpayer for a taxation year of the actual affiliate, the following rules apply for the purpose of determining the amounts, if any, to be included under subsection 91(1), and to be deducted under subsection 91(4), by the taxpayer in respect of the year and for the purpose of applying section 233.4 in respect of the year:

(a) the tracked property and activities of the actual affiliate are deemed to be property and activities of a non-resident corporation (referred to in this subsection as the "separate corporation") that is separate from the actual affiliate and not to be property or activities of the actual affiliate;

(b) any income, losses or gains for the year in respect of the property and activities described in paragraph (a) are deemed to be income, losses or gains of the separate corporation and not of the actual affiliate;

(c) all rights and obligations of the actual affiliate in respect of the property and activities described in paragraph (a) are deemed to be rights and obligations of the separate corporation and not of the actual affiliate;

(d) the separate corporation is deemed to have, at the end of the year, 100 issued and outstanding shares of a single class (referred to in this subsection as the "single class") of its capital stock, having full voting rights under all circumstances;

(e) each shareholder of the actual affiliate is deemed to own, at the end of the year, that number of shares of the single class that is equal to the product of 100 and the amount that would be the "aggregate participating percentage" (as defined in subsection 91(1.3)) of that shareholder in respect of the actual affiliate for the year if

(i) the actual affiliate were a controlled foreign affiliate of that shareholder at the end of the year,

(ii) the only shares of the capital stock of the actual affiliate issued and outstanding at the end of the year were shares of tracking classes in respect of the tracked properties and activities, and

(iii) the only income, losses and gains of the actual affiliate for the year were those referred to in paragraph (b); and

(f) any amounts included under subsection 91(1), or deducted under subsection 91(4), by the taxpayer in respect of shares of the separate corporation are deemed to be amounts included under subsection 91(1), or deducted under subsection 91(4), as the case may be, by the taxpayer in respect of shares of tracking classes held by the taxpayer or a foreign affiliate of the taxpayer, as the case may be.

Proposed Amendment — 95(11)

Letter from Dept. of Finance, March 25, 2019: Mr. James Carman, Senior Policy Advisor, Taxation, The Investment Funds Institute of Canada, Toronto, ON

Dear Mr. Carman:

SUBJECT: Application of the foreign affiliate "tracking arrangement" rules in subsections 95(8) to (12) of the *Income Tax Act*

I am writing in response to the various communications of The Investment Funds Institute of Canada ("IFIC") with the Tax Legislation Division concerning DFIC's request for an amendment to ensure that neither of subsections 95(11) and (12) of the *Income Tax Act* (the "Act") applies to cause certain investment funds that are structured as non-resident "umbrella corporations" to be treated as controlled foreign affiliates of Canadian investors. Those provisions are among the foreign affiliate "tracking arrangement" rules, in subsections 95(8) to (12) of the Act, that were contained in Bill C-86, which received Royal Assent on December 13, 2018. Those rules apply in respect of taxation years of foreign affiliates beginning after February 26, 2018.

IFIC observes that it is common in the asset management context for non-resident investment funds holding portfolio investments to be structured as umbrella corporations. An umbrella corporation is a single corporation comprising several sub-funds that are traded as individual investment funds, with the assets and liabilities of each sub-fund being separate from those of each other sub-fund. Umbrella corporations typically issue multiple classes of participating shares, each of which provides shareholders with exposure to the returns on assets of a particular sub-fund and not assets of other sub-funds of the umbrella corporation.

Shares of an umbrella corporation generally constitute a tracking interest in respect of the umbrella corporation, within the meaning of subsection 95(8), since the fair market value of those shares is determined by reference to the assets of the corresponding sub-fund and not the assets of other sub-funds of the umbrella corporation. If a taxpayer owns 10 per cent or more of a class (or series) of shares of a non-resident umbrella corporation, the umbrella corporation is a foreign affiliate of the taxpayer. Accordingly, the conditions set out in subsection 95(10) are met, with the result that subsection 95(11) will apply in respect of the umbrella corporation. In some cases, the application of subsection 95(11) could, in effect, cause the sub-fund in which the taxpayer is invested to be deemed to be a separate non-resident corporation that is a controlled foreign affiliate of the taxpayer for the purposes set out in subsection 95(11). Notably, these purposes include the purpose of determining the amounts, if any, to be included under subsection 91(1) in computing the taxpayer's income.

IFIC asserts that foreign asset managers, dealing at arm's length with investors, often structure investment funds as non-resident umbrella corporations — rather than housing each investment fund within a separate non-resident corporation — for reasons such as to allow greater flexibility and reduce non-tax costs, and not to assist any Canadian taxpayer in avoiding the foreign accrual property income ("FAPI") rules in the Act. Similarly, for reasons that do not include avoidance of the FAPI rules, Canadian-resident investors, including Canadian-resident investment funds, commonly seek to gain exposure in their investment portfolios to the returns on the foreign assets within a sub-fund of a non-resident umbrella corporation that is managed by an arm's length foreign asset manager by acquiring shares of the corresponding class. Another example is that Canadian asset management companies with a global focus and global customer base sometimes launch or manage sub-funds within non-resident umbrella corporations, and often make "seed capital" investments in a sub-fund (either directly or through a foreign subsidiary) to cover start-up costs and allow the fund to establish a track record during the initial, seeding stage. IFIC is of the view that, in all of these cases, it is not appropriate in policy terms to apply the tracking arrangement rules, and by extension the FAPI rules.

IFIC also notes that non-resident investment funds often issue separate classes (or series) of shares to investors resident in different countries and enter into currency hedging contracts to hedge investors' foreign currency exposure back to the currency of their country of residence. Under the tracking arrangement rules, these currency hedging contracts may in certain cases cause

(i) Canadian investors to be considered to have a tracking interest in respect of a fund, or

(ii) a sub-fund of a foreign umbrella corporation to be a controlled foreign affiliate of Canadian investors under subsection 95(11), by differentiating the tracked property and activities in respect of the class (or series) of shares held by Canadians from those in respect of classes (or series) held by investors resident in other countries.

IFIC is of the view that these results are also inappropriate in policy terms.

Our Comments:

The rules in subsections 95(10) to (12) of the Act are intended to prevent taxpayers from avoiding accrual-based taxation of FAPI by using a tracking arrangement in respect of a foreign affiliate to avoid controlled foreign affiliate status. In a recent submission to the Department, one of IFIC's members recommended an amendment to the Act that would, in effect, provide an exception from subsections 95(11) and (12) where it cannot reasonably be considered that one of the purposes for the creation or issuance of a tracking interest in respect of an umbrella corporation, or the acquisition of the interest by a taxpayer, is to avoid the corporation being a controlled foreign affiliate of the taxpayer.

We agree that an acquisition, or holding, by a taxpayer (or a foreign affiliate of the taxpayer) of shares of a non-resident umbrella corporation that constitute a tracking interest in respect of portfolio investments in a sub-fund of the umbrella corporation is beyond the intended scope of this 2018 budget measure if it cannot reasonably be considered that one of the purposes for the acquisition or holding, or for the taxpayer's investment being made through an umbrella corporation rather than a non-resident corporation housing only the sub-fund, is to permit a taxpayer to avoid an income inclusion under subsection 91(1). We are therefore prepared to recommend to the Minister of Finance that the Act be amended in a manner that ensures that neither subsection 95(11) nor (12) applies to cause an umbrella corporation to be a controlled foreign affiliate of a taxpayer in those circumstances.

We are also prepared to recommend amendments to ensure that where a non-resident investment fund enters into currency hedging contracts in the circumstances described above, this fact will not cause

(i) a taxpayer to be considered to have a tracking interest in respect of the fund, or

(ii) if a taxpayer otherwise has a tracking interest in respect of the fund (e.g., an umbrella corporation), the tracked property and activities in respect of that tracking interest to be considered distinct from the tracked property and activities in respect of tracking interests of other investors in the corporation for the purposes of subsection 95(11).

We will recommend that the above-noted amendments be effective for taxation years of foreign affiliates beginning after February 26, 2018.

While we cannot offer any assurance that either the Minister of Finance or Parliament will agree with our recommendations in respect of this matter, we hope that this statement of our intentions is helpful.

Yours sincerely,

Brian Ernewein, Assistant Deputy Minister — Tax Legislation, Tax Policy Branch

Related Provisions: 95(8) — Tracking interests — interpretation; 95(10) — Conditions for 95(11) to apply.

Notes: This was 95(12) in the July 27, 2018 draft legislation, and required an election to apply instead of applying automatically. See Notes to 95(8) re enactment of 95(11), including election to defer its application; and Notes to 95(9).

(12) Tracking interests — controlled foreign affiliate — If subsection (11) does not apply in respect of a foreign affiliate of the taxpayer for a taxation year of the affiliate, the affiliate is deemed to be a controlled foreign affiliate of the taxpayer throughout the taxation year if, at any time in the year, a tracking interest in respect of the affiliate, or a partnership of which the affiliate is a member, is held by

(a) the taxpayer; or

(b) a person or partnership (each referred to in this paragraph as a "holder"), if

(i) the holder does not deal at arm's length with the taxpayer at that time,

(ii) where either the taxpayer or the holder is a partnership and the other party is not, any member of the partnership does not deal at arm's length, at that time, with the other party, or

(iii) where both the taxpayer and the holder are partnerships, the taxpayer or any member of the taxpayer does not deal at arm's length, at that time, with the holder or any member of the holder.

Proposed Amendment — 95(12)

Letter from Dept. of Finance, March 25, 2019: See under 95(11).

Related Provisions: 95(8) — Tracking interests — interpretation; 95(10), (11) — Tracking class deemed to be separate corporation.

Notes: This was 95(10) in the July 27, 2018 draft legislation. See Notes to 95(8) re enactment of 95(12); and Notes to 95(9).

Proposed Amendments and Ongoing Developments — OECD BEPS Action Plan

Federal Budget, Supplementary Information, April 19, 2021. *Base Erosion and Profit Shifting*

The government is committed to safeguarding Canada's tax system and to that end continues to be an active participant in multilateral efforts to address base erosion and profit shifting (BEPS). BEPS primarily refers to international tax planning arrangements used by multinational enterprises to reduce their taxes by exploiting the interaction between domestic and international tax rules — for example, through shifting profits earned in Canada to other jurisdictions. (Some BEPS issues also have implications for domestic tax avoidance arrangements, and need not focus exclusively upon planning arrangements used by multinational enterprises.) The government has already implemented the measures agreed to as minimum standards under the action plan developed by the Organisation for Economic Co-operation and Development (OECD) and

the Group of 20 (G20) to address BEPS (the BEPS Action Plan). These minimum standards address:

- the exchange of information on confidential tax rulings to counter harmful tax practices;
- the adoption of treaty rules to address treaty shopping and other forms of abuse of Canada's tax treaties;
- the exchange of country-by-country reports on the global distribution of income, taxes and business activities of multinational enterprises; and
- making dispute resolution mechanisms in tax treaties more effective.

Canada has followed through on other BEPS recommendations by accepting the new transfer pricing guidance developed under the BEPS project [see 247(2) Notes — ed.], continuing to strengthen its robust foreign affiliate regime, and ratifying the Multilateral Convention to Implement Tax Treaty Related Measures to Prevent Base Erosion and Profit Shifting [MLI — reproduced before the Canada-US Treaty — ed.] (which allows countries to modify the application of their existing tax treaties to put in place anti-BEPS measures without having to individually renegotiate those treaties).

Budget 2021 builds on this work by proposing to implement the best practices recommended by the BEPS Action Plan on interest deductibility [see Proposed Amendments under 20(1)(c) — ed.] and hybrid mismatch arrangements [see Proposed Amendments under 248(1)"corporation" — ed.]. More details on the interest deductibility and hybrid mismatch arrangements measures are set out [under those proposals — ed.]. In addition, the government is proposing consultations on enhancements to Canada's transfer pricing and mandatory disclosure rules [see Proposed Amendments under 247(2) and at end of 237.3 — ed.]. The transfer pricing and mandatory disclosure measures are discussed elsewhere in these budget documents.

Federal Budget, Chapter 4, "Tax Fairness for the Middle Class", March 22, 2017: *Combatting International Tax Avoidance and Evasion*

Canada has worked together with the other members of the Group of 20 (G20) and the Organisation for Economic Co-operation and Development (OECD) to develop recommendations that will address base erosion and profit shifting (BEPS). BEPS refers to international tax planning arrangements used by multinational enterprises to unfairly minimize their taxes. For example, some enterprises will shift their taxable profits away from the jurisdiction where the underlying economic activity has taken place in order to avoid paying their fair share.

The Government remains firmly committed to protecting Canada's tax system, and has implemented — or is in the process of implementing — the measures agreed to as minimum standards under the BEPS project:

- Legislation was enacted in December 2016 [233.8 — ed.] that requires large multinational enterprises to file country-by-country reports. These reports provide information about the international distribution of the activities of a corporate group. This information will give tax authorities in each country a clearer picture of where the operations of the group in their particular jurisdiction fit into the group's global operations. This will enable them to better assess high-level avoidance risks such as the potential for mispricing of transactions between entities of the group in different jurisdictions.

- Canada participated in the development of a multilateral instrument [MLI — see before the Canada-US tax treaty — ed.] to streamline the implementation of tax treaty-related BEPS recommendations, including those addressing treaty abuse. The multilateral instrument is a tax treaty that many countries could sign modifying certain provisions of existing bilateral tax treaties without the need for separate bilateral negotiations. The Government is pursuing signature of the multilateral instrument and is undertaking the necessary domestic processes to do so.

- Canada has committed to the effective and timely resolution of tax treaty-related disputes by improving the mutual agreement procedure in Canada's tax treaties.

- The CRA has begun the spontaneous exchange with other tax administrations of tax rulings that could otherwise give rise to BEPS concerns. As part of the effort to counter harmful tax practices, this helps ensure that revenue authorities are not granting to taxpayers non-transparent "private" rulings that guarantee favourable tax treatment with respect to a transaction.

With respect to other BEPS recommendations:

- Canada has robust "controlled foreign corporation" rules in the form of our foreign accrual property income regime [ss. 91-95 — ed.], which helps prevent taxpayers from avoiding Canadian income tax by shifting income into foreign subsidiaries.

- Canada has implemented requirements for taxpayers, as well as promoters and advisors, to disclose specified tax avoidance transactions to the CRA [237.1, 237.3 — ed.].

- The CRA is applying revised international guidance on transfer pricing by multinational enterprises [see Actions 8-10 above, and Notes to 247(2) — ed.]. These guidelines provide an improved interpretation of the requirement in the tax laws of Canada and most other countries that transactions between entities of a corporate group in different jurisdictions should be priced as if they were arm's length transactions.

The Government will continue to work with its international partners to ensure a coherent and consistent response to fight tax avoidance through BEPS.

The Government is also strengthening its efforts to combat international tax evasion through enhanced sharing of information between tax authorities. The automatic exchange of information with respect to financial accounts held by non-residents —

Non-Resident Corps/Trusts

under the framework of the Common Reporting Standard developed by the OECD — is an important tool to promote compliance, combat international tax evasion, and ensure that taxpayers are reporting their income from all sources. To date, more than 100 jurisdictions have committed to implement the new standard. Canada recently enacted legislation [ss. 270-280 — ed.] to implement the standard starting on July 1, 2017, which will allow for first exchanges of information with other countries in 2018.

Notes: The Organisation for Economic Cooperation and Development (OECD), together with the G-20 (total 62 countries representing 90% of the world economy), engaged in an ambitious project from 2013-2015 to address Base Erosion and Profit Shifting (BEPS), which refers to multinationals using different tax rules in different countries, along with tax treaties, to shift profits to low- or zero-tax jurisdictions and to "erode" the income base on which countries impose tax.

Although the BEPS project is directed at multinationals, if these proposals are implemented in Canada they will to some degree affect every Canadian corporation doing business outside Canada.

The project produced final reports in 2015 on **15 "Action Items"** (tinyurl.com/oecd-beps2015). If all the countries implement the recommended changes in sync, it is thought that BEPS, which might be costing governments collectively $240 billion per year in lost corporate income tax, will be significantly reduced.

"With the adoption of the BEPS package, OECD and G20 countries, as well as all developing countries that have participated in its development, will lay the foundations of a modern international tax framework under which profits are taxed where economic activity and value creation occurs ... consistent implementation and application [of these changes] are key". (OECD Explanatory Statement, Introduction)

See also Vidal et al., *Introduction to International Tax in Canada* (Carswell, 8th ed., 2020), chap. 2; Baker & Trossman, "BEPS Final Reports Released", 23(11) *Canadian Tax Highlights* (ctf.ca) 5-7 (Nov. 2015); Chaudhury, "Final BEPS Report — Canadian Tax Considerations", 2287 *Tax Topics* 1-6 (Jan. 7, 2016); Boidman & Kandev, "BEPS: A Spent Force or Radical Change?", 80(10) *Tax Notes International* (taxnotes.com) 837-46 (Dec. 7, 2015) and "Canada Takes First BEPS Steps", 82(4) 371-78 (April 25, 2016); Lagerberg et al., "BEPS Goes Global", 2016(16) *Tax Times* (Carswell) 1-3 (Aug. 19, 2016).

(For the proposals of Canada's 2008 Advisory Panel on International Taxation and followup, see "Possible Future Amendment" box at end of s. 90 up to the 48th ed.; Pantaleo, "Advisory Panel on Canada's System of International Taxation", 2009 Prairie Provinces Tax Conf. (ctf.ca), 4:1-19; Mustard et al., "Why Not Kenora? Reflections on What Canada's Approach to Taxing Foreign Business Income Is and Could Be", 2009 Cdn Tax Foundation conference report, 6:1-48; Mustard, "Canada's System of International Taxation", 61(Supp.) *Canadian Tax Journal* 257-70 (2013).)

See Finance Quebec, *Tax Havens: Tax Fairness Action Plan* (Nov. 10, 2017, 256pp., www.finances.gouv.qc.ca), discussing Quebec's plans to implement many of the BEPS measures, and to take other actions to protect its tax base.

Below are David Sherman's brief summaries of each report and its implications for Canada. **Actions 5, 6, 13 and 14 are "minimum standards" that all countries are to follow**, considered fundamental to solving BEPS. Actions 7-10 are "reinforced international standards". Actions 2-4 and 12 are non-mandatory "common approaches and best practices"; Actions 1, 11 and 15 are "analytical" reports (though Action 1 contains specific recommendations).

Canada's specific responses to date, in the March 2016 federal Budget, appear under some of the Action Items below. See also Proposed Amendments to 212.1 re cross-border surplus stripping, and to 212(3.2) re back-to-back loans.

Action 1: Digital Economy [290 pages]:

David Sherman summary: The list of exceptions to the definition of "permanent establishment" (PE) in the OECD Model Treaty will be modified, so that each exception is restricted to activities that are otherwise of a "preparatory or auxiliary" character, and to introduce a new anti-fragmentation rule to address splitting up business activities to different entities in a group. For example, under the new standard, if an online seller of physical goods relies on quick delivery to customers, maintaining a large local warehouse with many employees to deliver goods sold online would create a PE.

The definition of PE will also be modified to address "artificial arrangements" whereby sales of one company in a multinational group "effectively result in the conclusion of contracts" (e.g., parent sells goods or services online, and a subsidiary's sales force plays the main role in concluding contracts).

The transfer pricing guidelines have been amended to clarify that legal ownership of an intangible does not of itself create a right to a return on the intangible. Instead, the guidelines will look to which companies in the group perform the important functions, contribute the important assets and control the risks. As well, transfer pricing analysis should not be "weakened by information asymmetries between the tax administration and the taxpayer in relation to hard-to-value intangibles, or by using special contractual relationships, such as a cost contribution arrangement".

Action 1 also discusses broader tax challenges raised by the digital economy, especially with respect to VAT/GST.

See also Dale Pinto, "Options to Address the Direct Tax Challenges Raised by the Digital Economy", 65(2) *Canadian Tax Journal* 291-331 (2017).

2021 update: The OECD, after identifying a "Programme of Work to Develop a Consensus Solution to the Tax Challenges Arising from the Digitalisation of the Economy" (May 2019, tinyurl.com/oecd-pow), produced detailed blueprints Oct. 12, 2020 (for

consultation) on **"Pillar One"** (tinyurl.com/oecd-pillar1, 234pp), changing the allocation of profits (and taxing rights) to countries, and **"Pillar Two"** (tinyurl.com/oecd-pillar2, 249pp), imposing a global minimum business tax rate. Both Pillars are extraordinarily complex, even though many details are still to be resolved.

Pillar One would (for certain industries) replace the tax treaty "permanent establishment" concept, to determine which jurisdiction can tax (see Canada-US Treaty Art. VII:1, and Art. V for the PE definition). The OECD seeks to prevent proliferation of unilateral "digital services taxes" aimed at profits earned by offshore digital companies (e.g. Netflix), including the one announced in Canada's Nov. 30, 2020 Economic Statement and April 2021 Budget (see Proposed Amendment under 115(1)). Highly simplified: market jurisdictions (where customers are, with a minimum revenue threshold) would be given a share of a multinational's residual profits, after a fixed return is allocated to countries where certain marketing and distribution activities are physically performed. Pillar One would apply to automated digital services and certain businesses aimed at consumers. It might apply only to companies with over €750 million in revenues.

Pillar Two, or Global Anti-Base Erosion ("GloBE"), would be a global minimum tax of 10%-12.5% to prevent profits being shifted to low-tax jurisdictions, for multinationals with at least €750 million in revenues. Highly simplified: a "top-up tax" would apply where a country's effective tax rate is below the minimum rate, but exempting income calculated as a fixed return from substantive activity in the country. The top-up tax would be payable on an additional income inclusion by the parent company of the group, to its home jurisdiction (like a FAPI on active business income).

On June 5, 2021, the G-7 (US, UK, France, Germany, Italy, Japan, Canada) agreed to Pillar One for corps with at least 10% profit margin, and Pillar Two with a minimum 15% tax rate: tinyurl.com/g7-beps, tinyurl.com/cbc-g7-beps. Agreement from the G20 will be sought next, followed by other countries.

See Marley et al., "OECD releases blueprint reports on international tax reform" (Oct. 14, 2020), tinyurl.com/osler-pillars; Nikolakakis, "BEPS 2.0", 114 *International Tax* (CCH) 1-4 (Oct. 2020); TEI comments to OECD (Dec. 13, 2020, 32pp), tinyurl.com/tei-pillars; Woolford, "Pillar One and Two", XXIII(4) *Corporate Finance* (Federated Press) 7-12 (2020).

Canada has proposed a 3% Digital Services Tax to take effect Jan. 1, 2022, pending a multilateral solution to Action 1. See Proposed Amendment under 115(1).

Action 2: Hybrid Mismatch Arrangements [458 pages]:

David Sherman summary: Hybrid mismatch arrangements — e.g., an entity such as a limited liability corporation (LLC) that is considered a corporation in some jurisdictions and not others — exploit differences in the tax treatment of an entity or instrument in different jurisdictions. This can result in long-term deferral or double non-taxation. These types of arrangements are widespread and result in substantial erosion of the tax base. They have an overall negative impact on competition, efficiency, transparency and fairness.

Part I of the report recommends specific rules to address such mismatches in the tax treatment of payments made under a hybrid financial instrument and payments made to or by a hybrid entity. It also recommends rules to address "indirect" mismatches, where the effects of a hybrid mismatch arrangement are imported into a third country. The recommendations take the form of "linking rules" to align the tax treatment in the different jurisdictions without disturbing the commercial effect. The rules will apply automatically, and there will be an "ordering" of rules, to prevent more than one country applying a rule to the same arrangement, and also to prevent double taxation.

The primary rule will deny a deduction for a payment to the extent it is not included in the recipient's taxable income in the other country, or is also deductible in that country. If this rule does not apply, the other country will be able to generally apply a "defensive" rule, requiring the deductible payment to be included in income or denying the deduction.

The report recognizes the importance of co-ordination in the implementation of these rules, to ensure they work properly and to minimize compliance and administration costs for taxpayers and tax administrations. It sets out common design principles and defined terms, so that the new rules will be applied consistently.

Part II of Action 2 addresses the use of hybrid instruments and entities, as well as dual resident entities, to obtain inappropriate treaty benefits, as well as ensuring that treaties cannot be used to avoid the recommendations in Part I.

Canada has addressed hybrids in Art. IV:6 and IV:7 of the Canada-US tax treaty. For CRA policy on classifying a foreign entity, see 248(1)"corporation" Notes. The April 2021 Budget announced new rules that will apply from July 2022. See Proposed Amendments under 248(1)"corporation". The MLI (multi-lateral instrument, reproduced before the Canada-US treaty), in its Art. 3, addresses hybrid mismatches, but Canada has not signed on to that Article.

Action 3: Controlled Foreign Company Rules [75 pages]:

David Sherman summary: This report addresses controlled foreign companies (CFCs) being used to shift income to low-tax countries or tax havens. Currently, 30 of the countries participating in the BEPS project have CFC rules, and many others are interested in implementing them. However, even existing rules have often not kept pace with changes in the international business environment, and many of them do not address BEPS effectively.

The report recommends six "building blocks" to prevent income being shifted to foreign subsidiaries: definition of a CFC; CFC exemptions and de minimis thresholds; the definition of "income"; computation of income (using the parent jurisdiction's rules, and offsetting losses against only profits of the same CFC or others in the same jurisdiction); attribution of income (based on the proportion of ownership); and preventing double taxation (a very important consideration).

(These issues are generally covered by Canada's existing FAPI rules, in ss. 91-95.)

Action 4: Interest Deductions and Other Financial Payments [120 pages]:

David Sherman summary: Multinational groups can achieve tax advantages by adjusting the level of debt in a group entity, and can multiply debt via intra-group financing. As well, financial instruments can be structured with payments that are economically equivalent to interest but have a different legal form. Specific BEPS concerns include: (a) high levels of debt in high tax countries; (b) intragroup loans that generate interest deductions exceeding actual third-party interest expense; (c) using financing with deductible interest to generate tax-exempt income.

Action 4 recommends addressing the above risks with a fixed ratio rule that limits net deductions for interest (and economically equivalent payments) to a percentage of EBITDA. To ensure that countries apply a fixed ratio that is low enough to address BEPS, while recognizing that not all countries are in the same position, a ratio of 10%-30% will be permitted. The report includes factors that countries should consider in fixing their ratio within this range. The report further proposes a worldwide group ratio rule, which would allow an entity with net interest expense exceeding a country's fixed ratio to deduct interest up to the level of the net interest/EBITDA ratio of its worldwide group. A country may also choose not to introduce any group ratio rule, in which case the fixed ratio would apply to both domestic and multinational entities.

The recommendation also allows countries to supplement these ratios with other provisions, such as: a de minimis threshold; an exclusion for interest paid to third-party lenders on loans used to fund public-benefit projects; and carryforward of disallowed interest expense. Anti-avoidance rules are also recommended. The report also recognizes that special rules are needed to address BEPS in the banking and insurance sectors.

Further technical work, including the details of the worldwide group ratio rule and the specific rules for banking and insurance, is expected to be completed in 2016.

Canada has thin-capitalization rules in 18(4)-(8) and "Kiwi loan" rules in 20.3, but was not successful before 2021 in finding other ways to restrict interest deductibility. See 18.2 (repealed in 2009 before coming into force), proposed 3.1 (2003, later abandoned) and proposed 20.1 and 20.2 (1991) (abandoned), and 20(1)(c) Notes. The April 2021 Budget introduces limitations on interest expense exceeding 30% of tax EBITDA.

See also David Duff, "Interest Deductibility and International Taxation in Canada After BEPS Action 4", 2018 Cdn Tax Foundation conference report, 23:1-26.

Action 5: Harmful Tax Practices [85 pages]:

David Sherman summary: This report addresses "preferential regimes" that can be used for artificial profit shifting, as well as the "lack of transparency" with respect to certain rulings. The priorities in this area are requiring "substantial activity" for any preferential regime, and improving transparency, including "compulsory spontaneous exchange on rulings related to preferential regimes". The report includes a review identifying 43 "preferential regimes". The only one in Canada is its "life insurance business regime" (see Notes to 138(2)), which is described as "Potentially harmful but not actually harmful". (Canada has addressed the exchange of rulings issue, immediately below.) See also OECD, *Harmful Tax Practices — 2018 Progress Report* (Nov. 2020, 67pp).

Federal Budget, Supplementary Information, March 22, 2016: Spontaneous Exchange of Tax Rulings

The lack of transparency in connection with certain tax rulings provided by tax administrations was identified as an area of concern by the BEPS project. This lack of transparency can give rise to mismatches in tax treatment and instances of double non-taxation.

The BEPS project developed a framework for the spontaneous exchange of certain tax rulings that could give rise to BEPS concerns in the absence of such exchanges. The framework covers six categories of rulings: (i) rulings related to preferential regimes; (ii) cross-border unilateral advance pricing arrangements; (iii) rulings giving a downward adjustment to profits; (iv) permanent establishment rulings; (v) conduit rulings; and (vi) any other type of ruling agreed to in the future.

The Canada Revenue Agency has an established exchange of information program and exchanges information under Canada's tax treaties, tax information exchange agreements and the multilateral Convention on Mutual Administrative Assistance in Tax Matters. These agreements include provisions to restrict the use of the exchanged information, typically limiting its use to the enforcement of tax laws, and to ensure the confidentiality of the information. Any information exchanged with respect to the targeted tax rulings will be subject to the confidentiality provisions in the relevant agreement and therefore protected in the same manner as taxpayer information.

Budget 2016 confirms the Government's intention to implement the BEPS minimum standard for the spontaneous exchange of certain tax rulings. The Canada Revenue Agency will commence exchanging tax rulings in 2016 with other jurisdictions that have committed to the minimum standard. [See also VIEWS doc 2016-0632941I7, explaining the process including the types of ruling that will be exchanged — ed.]

Action 6: Inappropriate Treaty Benefits [106 pages]:

David Sherman summary: Action 6 addresses treaty shopping and other treaty abuse to obtain unintended treaty benefits. Countries have agreed to include anti-abuse provisions in treaties, including a minimum standard to counter treaty shopping (with some

flexibility to accommodate each country's specific needs and its relationship to its treaty partners).

Section A of this report provides new rules addressing treaty shopping. This will include: a clear statement in treaties that the countries intend to avoid creating opportunities for non-taxation or reduced taxation through avoidance (including treaty shopping); and including both a limitation-on-benefits (LOB) rule and a general anti-abuse rule in the OECD Model Treaty.

Section A also includes new rules to be included in treaties to address other forms of treaty abuse, such as (a) dividend transfer transactions intended to avoid withholding tax on dividends; (b) transactions that circumvent the treaty rule permitting source taxation of shares of companies that derive their value primarily from real property; (c) dual-resident situations; (d) planning using PEs in third countries and transferring certain assets to PEs in countries that tax certain kinds of income preferentially.

Section B addresses the use of treaties to create double non-taxation.

Section C discusses tax policies that countries should consider before deciding to enter into a tax treaty with another country. This will help countries justify why not to enter into a treaty with a low or no-tax jurisdictions, as well as whether to terminate any given treaty.

See also Watson, "Treaty Shopping and Base Erosion and Profit Shifting Action 6", 62(4) *Canadian Tax Journal* 1085-1108 (2014). The Canada-US treaty is Canada's only treaty that currently includes a "limitation on benefits" provision (Art. XXIX-A). For Canada's response, see immediately below. OECD update, in *Third Peer Review Report on Treaty Shopping* (tinyurl.com/action6-3, May 2021, 302pp) at p. 69: "No jurisdiction has raised any concerns about their agreements with Canada."

[Part III of the multilateral instrument published in Nov. 2016 (see Action 15 below) addresses treaty abuse.]

Federal Budget, Supplementary Information, March 22, 2016: Treaty Abuse

The BEPS project identifies treaty abuse, and in particular treaty shopping, as one of the most important sources of BEPS concerns. Treaty shopping occurs, for example, where a third-country resident creates an intermediary holding company in a treaty country for purposes of channelling, through the company, income and gains sourced in Canada to access benefits granted under a tax treaty that would not otherwise have been available to them.

Treaty shopping effectively extends tax treaty benefits to third-country residents in circumstances that were not contemplated when the tax treaty was entered into and without any reciprocal benefits accruing to Canadian investors or to Canada. This practice undermines the bilateral nature of tax treaties and the balance of compromise reached between Canada and its treaty partners.

The BEPS treaty abuse minimum standard requires countries to include in their tax treaties an express statement that their common intention is to eliminate double taxation without creating opportunities for non-taxation or reduced taxation through tax evasion or avoidance, including through treaty shopping arrangements. In addition, the treaty abuse minimum standard requires countries to implement this common intention by adopting in their tax treaties one of two approaches to treaty anti-abuse rules. The first of these is a general anti-abuse rule that uses the criterion of whether one of the principal purposes of an arrangement or transaction was to obtain treaty benefits in a way that is not in accordance with the object and purpose of the relevant treaty provisions (a principal purpose test). The second approach is the use of a more mechanical and specific anti-abuse rule that requires satisfaction of a series of tests in order to qualify for treaty benefits (a limitation on benefits rule).

Budget 2016 confirms the Government's commitment to address treaty abuse in accordance with the minimum standard. Canada currently has one treaty that has adopted a limitation-on-benefits approach as well as several treaties that have adopted a limited principal purpose test. Going forward, Canada will consider either minimum standard approach, depending on the particular circumstances and discussions with Canada's tax treaty partners. Amendments to Canada's tax treaties to include a treaty anti-abuse rule could be achieved through bilateral negotiations, the multilateral instrument that will be developed in 2016, or a combination of the two. The multilateral instrument is a tax treaty that many countries could sign modifying certain provisions of existing bilateral treaties. Canada is actively participating in international work to develop the multilateral instrument, which would streamline the implementation of treaty-related BEPS recommendations, including treaty abuse.

Extension of the Back-to-Back Rules

[See now rules enacted at 212(3.1)-(3.94) — ed.]

Action 7: Artificial Avoidance of PE Status [51 pages]:

David Sherman summary: Tax treaties generally provide that business profits are taxable in a foreign country only where they are attributable to a PE in that country. This report revises the definition of PE, to prevent certain tax avoidance strategies that circumvent the existing definition. Changes are also needed to prevent misuse of the exceptions in Art. 5(4) of the OECD Model Treaty, an issue particularly relevant in the digital economy.

This report discusses various strategies currently used to avoid the PE definition, and includes changes to be made to the definition of PE in the Model Treaty, which is widely used as the basis for negotiating tax treaties. These changes will be proposed for inclusion in the "multilateral instrument" discussed in Action 15 below. Follow-up work on attribution of profits will continue, with a view to providing a report by the end of 2016.

If these changes are implemented in Canada's treaties (through the "multilateral instrument" in Action 15), that would have a significant impact on Canadian businesses.

[Part IV of the multilateral instrument published in Nov. 2016 (see Action 15 below) addresses avoidance of PE status.]

Actions 8, 9, 10: Transfer Pricing [190 pages]:

David Sherman summary: Action 8 looks at transfer pricing issues relating to intangibles. Action 9 considers the contractual allocation of risks, and the resulting allocation of profits to those risks, and addresses the level of returns to funding provided by a capital-rich multinational group member. Action 10 examines other high-risk areas, including re-characterizing profit allocations resulting from transactions that are not "commercially rational" for the individual entities, and neutralizing the use of certain types of payments (e.g., management fees, head office expenses) to inappropriately erode the tax base.

The work under Actions 8-10 is intended to have transfer pricing outcomes better align with "value creation" in the multinational group. The object is to make capital-rich, low-functioning entities less useful in BEPS planning. All of this is intended to function as part of the arm's length principle.

Further work will be undertaken on profit splits and financial transactions. The report specifically addresses the needs of developing countries.

The OECD says the amendments to the Guidelines are "clarifying", so they may effectively be retroactive; from the March 2016 announcement immediately below, it appears that the CRA will apply them retroactively, as being "consistent with current practices". See also Notes to 247(2).

See also Nikolakakis, "Transfer Pricing — Aligning Transfer Pricing Outcomes With Value Creation", XX(3) *International Tax Planning* (Federated Press) 1-6 (2016).

Federal Budget, Supplementary Information, March 22, 2016: Revised Transfer Pricing Guidance

The principle discussed above that transfer prices on intra-group transactions by an MNE should reflect arm's length terms is the basis of Article 9 of the OECD and United Nations Model Tax Conventions. This principle is included in most bilateral tax treaties, including all of Canada's tax treaties. Many countries also include the arm's length principle in their legislation. In Canada, the arm's length principle is mandated by section 247 of the *Income Tax Act*.

As noted above, the OECD's Transfer Pricing Guidelines for Multinational Enterprises and Tax Administrations provide guidance on the application of the arm's length principle. Although the Transfer Pricing Guidelines are not explicitly incorporated into Canada's legislation, they are used by taxpayers, the Canada Revenue Agency and the courts for interpreting and applying section 247. Consistent application of the arm's length principle across jurisdictions, through application of the Transfer Pricing Guidelines, helps to ensure the proper measurement of taxable income in each jurisdiction, avoid double taxation, minimize inter-jurisdictional conflict between tax administrations and promote international trade and investment.

The recommendations arising from the BEPS project include revisions to the Transfer Pricing Guidelines. These revisions provide an improved interpretation of the arm's length principle, and are intended to better ensure alignment of the profits of MNEs with the economic activities generating those profits. The clarifications provided in the revisions generally support the Canada Revenue Agency's current interpretation and application of the arm's length principle, as reflected in its audit and assessing practices. These revisions are thus being applied by the Canada Revenue Agency as they are consistent with current practices.

In two areas, however, where the revisions to the Transfer Pricing Guidelines are not yet complete, the Canada Revenue Agency will not be adjusting its administrative practices at this time. The BEPS project participants are still engaged in follow-up work on the development of a threshold for the proposed simplified approach to low value-adding services. Work is also continuing to clarify the definition of risk-free and risk-adjusted returns for minimally functional entities (often referred to as "cash boxes"). Canada will decide on a course of action with regards to these measures after the outstanding work is complete.

Action 11: Measuring and Monitoring BEPS [272 pages]:

David Sherman summary: This report discusses the significant costs of BEPS, and six indicators that highlight the existence of BEPS, such as that multinationals' profit rates in lower-tax countries are (on average) twice as high as their group's worldwide profit rate. The effective tax rates paid by large MNEs are estimated to be 4 to 8.5 percentage points lower than similar enterprises with only domestic operations. It also discusses ways to improve the "tools and data available to measure BEPS".

Action 12: Mandatory Disclosure Rules [102 pages]:

David Sherman summary: This report discusses mandatory disclosure of aggressive tax planning strategies. See 237.1 and 237.3, which already require this in Canada, though those rules do not really address BEPS issues. The report suggests that companies that enter into "intra-group transactions with material tax consequences" should be required to "make reasonable enquiries" to identify reportable cross-border transactions. Canada's rules could be extended to implement this change. The report also recommends that "Countries develop hallmarks that focus on the type of cross-border BEPS outcomes that cause them concern", and describes enhanced information sharing among countries via the Joint International Tax Shelter Information and Collaboration (JITSIC) Network.

Canada, in its April 2021 Budget, has introduced new "mandatory disclosure" rules to strengthen its reporting requirements. See Proposed Amendments at end of 237.3.

Action 13: Transfer Pricing Documentation and Country-by-Country Reporting [74 pages]:

David Sherman summary: Transfer pricing documentation will require multinationals to provide all relevant tax administrations with information regarding their global business operations and transfer pricing policies.

See now ITA 233.8, which implements "country-by-country" reporting for large multinationals (consolidated group revenue over €750 million) and is thought to apply to 100-300 companies in Canada.

Action 14: Dispute Resolution Mechanisms [50 pages]:

David Sherman summary: Countries agree that the BEPS changes should not lead to unnecessary uncertainty for compliant taxpayers, or to unintended double taxation. Improving dispute resolution mechanisms is considered an integral component of the BEPS work.

Action 14 seeks to strengthen the effectiveness and efficiency of the mutual agreement procedure (MAP) in OECD Model Treaty Art. 25. There is a "strong political commitment to the effective and timely resolution of disputes" through MAP. Countries have agreed to important changes in their approach to dispute resolution, in particular by implementing a minimum standard for resolution of treaty-related disputes, with a "robust peer-based monitoring mechanism" that will report to the G20. As well as the minimum standard, the report recommends "best practices".

[Parts V and VI of the multilateral instrument published in Nov. 2016 (see Action 15 below) address dispute resolution and arbitration.]

OECD "peer review and monitoring" of Action 14 progress in Canada (Stage 2, August 2019): tinyurl.com/action14-canada. See also *BEPS Action 14: Making Dispute Mechanisms More Effective — 2020 Review* (OECD, Nov. 2020).

Action 15: Multilateral Instrument to Modify Treaties [50 pages]:

David Sherman summary: This report recommended an innovative "multilateral instrument", to allow bilateral tax treaties to be amended to incorporate the above Action items. Currently it takes years to renegotiate any one treaty, and very few are amended by any one country each year, so any wholesale change takes decades to implement.

The resulting **Multilateral Instrument (MLI)** was approved by the OECD, was signed by Canada on June 7, 2017, and was ratified by Canada on June 21, 2019 (Bill C-82, S.C. 2019, c. 12). See near the end of this book, after the *Income Tax Conventions Interpretation Act* and before the Canada-US tax treaty, for the MLI.

Definitions [s. 95]: "active business" — 95(1); "adjusted cost base" — 54, 248(1); "affiliated" — 251.1; "aggregate participating percentage" — 91(1.3); "allowable capital loss" — 38(b), 248(1); "amount" — 95(7), 248(1); "annuity" — 248(1); "antecedent corporation" — 95(1); "arm's length" — 95(2.45), 95(2.6), 251(1); "bank" — 248(1); "beneficially interested" — 248(25); "borrowed money", "business" — 248(1); "business carried on in Canada" — 253; "calculating currency" — 95(1); "Canada" — 255, *Interpretation Act* 35(1); "Canadian currency" — 261(5)(h)(i)(A); "Canadian indebtedness" — 95(2.43); "Canadian resource property" — 66(15), 248(1); "capital gain" — 39(1)(a), 248(1); "capital interest" — 108(1), 248(1); "capital loss" — 39(1)(b), 248(1); "capital property" — 54, 248(1); "carrying on a business in Canada" — 253; "class" — of shares 248(6); "controlled" — 256(6), (6.1); "controlled directly or indirectly" — 256(5.1)–(6); "corporation" — 248(1), *Interpretation Act* 35(1); "cost amount" — 248(1); "credit union" — 137(6), 248(1); "cumulative eligible capital" — 14(5), 248(1); "currency of a country other than Canada" — 261(5)(h)(i)(B); "depreciable property" — 13(21), 248(1); "designated acquired corporation" — 95(1); "designated corporation" — 95(2)(s); "designated insurance property" — 138(12), 248(1); "designated liquidation and dissolution" — 95(1); "designated partnership" — 95(2)(t); "designated property" — 95(3.1); "direct equity percentage" — 95(4); "disposition", "dividend" — 248(1); "eligible bank affiliate", "eligible Canadian bank", "eligible Canadian indebtedness" — 95(2.43); "eligible capital expenditure" — 14(5), 248(1); "eligible capital property" — 54, 248(1); "eligible controlled foreign affiliate" — 95(4); "eligible currency hedge" — 95(2.43); "eligible trust" — 95(1); "employee" — 248(1); "employee benefit plan" — 248(1); "entity" — 95(1); "equity percentage" — 95(4); "excess liquidity" — 95(2.43); "excluded income" — 95(2.5); "excluded property" — 95(1); "excluded revenue" — 95(2.5); "exempt surplus" — 113(1)(a); "exempt trust" — 95(1); "fair market value" — see 69(1) Notes; "filing-due date" — 150(1), 248(1); "first amalco" — 95(1)"antecedent corporation"(b); "fiscal period" — 249(2)(b), 249.1; "foreign accrual property income" — 95(1), 95(2), 248(1); "foreign accrual tax" — 95(1); "foreign affiliate" — 93.1(1), 95(1), 248(1); "foreign bank" — 95(1); "foreign business" — 95(2)(j.1)(v), 95(2)(k); "foreign merger", "foreign parent corporation" — 87(8.1), 95(4.1); "foreign resource property" — 66(15), 248(1); "general rate reduction percentage" — 123.4(1); "government of a country" — 95(2)(y); "gross revenue" — 248(1); "holding corporation" — 95(2)(m)(iii); "hybrid deficit" — Reg. 5907(1); "hybrid surplus" — 113(1)(a.1)(i), Reg. 5900(1)(a.1), 5907(1), (1.01); "immovable" — Quebec *Civil Code* art. 900–907; "income bond", "income debenture" — 248(1); "income from a non-qualifying business", "income from an active business" — 95(1); "income from property" — 9(1), 95(1); "income or profits tax" — 126(4); "indebtedness" — 95(2.5); "ineligible Canadian indebtedness" — 95(2.43); "insurance corporation", "insurer" — 248(1); "interest in real property" — 248(4); "investment business" — 95(1), (9); "investment property", "lease obligation" — 95(1); "lending asset" — 95(1)"lending of money", 248(1); "lending of money", "licensing of property" — 95(1); "life insurance business", "life insurance corporation" — 248(1); "life insurance policy" — 138(12), 248(1); "life insurer", "majority-interest partner" — 248(1); "mark-to-market property" — 142.2(1); "Minister" — 248(1); "month" — *Interpretation Act* 35(1); "new foreign corporation" — 87(8.1), 95(4.1); "non-discretionary trust" — 17(15); "non-qualifying business", "non-qualifying country" — 95(1); "non-resident" — 248(1); "non-resident-owned investment corporation" — 133(8), 248(1); "operating partnership" — 95(1)"investment business"(b); "operator" — 95(1)"taxable Canadian business", 95(2)(j.1), (k); "organic assets" — 95(2.43); "partnership" — see 96(1) Notes; "permanent establishment" — 95(1), Reg. 5906(2)(b); "person", "personal trust" — 248(1); "predecessor corporation" — 87(1); "predecessor foreign corporation" — 87(8.1), 95(4.1); "prescribed" — 248(1); "prescribed financial institution" — Reg. 7900; "property" — 248(1); "province" — *Interpretation Act* 35(1); "qualified foreign affiliate" — 95(2)(g); "qualifying entity" — 39(2.2); "qualifying indebtedness" — 95(2.43); "qualifying interest" — 95(2)(m), (n), 95(2.2); "qualifying member" — 95(2)(o)–(r), 248(1); "qualifying shareholder" — 95(2)(p), (q); "rate of exchange quoted" — 261(5)(h)(ii); "real right" — 248(4.1); "recognized stock exchange", "registered securities dealer", "regulation" — 248(1); "related" — 95(2.2)(b), 95(6)(a)(i), 251(2); "related group" — 251(4); "relationship deposits" — 95(2.43); "relevant cost base" — 95(4); "relevant non-arm's length entity" — 95(1); "relevant person" — 95(3.02); "resident", "resident in Canada" — 94(3)(a), 250; "salary deferral arrangement" — 248(1); "series of transactions", "series of transactions or events" — 248(10); "services" — 95(3); "settlor" — 17(15); "share", "shareholder" — 248(1); "specified Canadian risk" — 95(2)(a.23), (a.24); "specified deposit" — 95(2.5); "specified fixed interest" — 95(1); "specified member" — 248(1); "specified person or partnership", "specified predecessor corporation" — 95(1); "specified property" — 95(2.32); "specified purchaser" — 95(1); "specified taxation year" — 95(2)(j), (k); "subsidiary controlled corporation", "subsidiary wholly-owned corporation" — 248(1); "substituted" — 248(5); "successor corporation" — 95(1)"designated acquired corporation"(a)(ii); "surplus entitlement percentage" — 95(1), Reg. 5905(13); "tax treaty" — 248(1); "taxable Canadian business" — 95(1); "taxable Canadian property" — 248(1); "taxable capital employed in Canada" — 181.2(1), 181.3(1), 181.4; "taxable capital gain" — 38(a), 248(1); "taxable dividend" — 89(1), 248(1); "taxable income earned in Canada" — 248(1); "taxation year" — 95(1), 249; "taxpayer" — 248(1); "total specified indebtedness" — 95(2.43); "tracked entity" — 95(8); "tracked property and activities" — 95(8)(a); "tracking class" — 95(10)(b); "tracking interest" — 95(8); "treaty-protected business" — 248(1); "trust" — 104(1), 248(1), (3); "trust company" — 95(1); "undepreciated capital cost" — 13(21), 248(1); "upper-tier affiliate" — 95(1)"participating percentage"(b)(i)(B); "upstream deposit" — 95(2.43); "writing", "written" — *Interpretation Act* 35(1)"writing".

Subdivision J — Partnerships and Their Members

96. (1) General rules — Where a taxpayer is a member of a partnership, the taxpayer's income, non-capital loss, net capital loss, restricted farm loss and farm loss, if any, for a taxation year, or the taxpayer's taxable income earned in Canada for a taxation year, as the case may be, shall be computed as if

(a) the partnership were a separate person resident in Canada;

(b) the taxation year of the partnership were its fiscal period;

(c) each partnership activity (including the ownership of property) were carried on by the partnership as a separate person, and a computation were made of the amount of

(i) each taxable capital gain and allowable capital loss of the partnership from the disposition of property, and

(ii) each income and loss of the partnership from each other source or from sources in a particular place,

for each taxation year of the partnership;

(d) each income or loss of the partnership for a taxation year were computed as if

(i) this Act were read without reference to sections 34.1 and 34.2, subsection 59(1), paragraph 59(3.2)(c.1) and subsections 66.1(1), 66.2(1) and 66.4(1), and

(ii) no deduction were permitted under any of section 29 of the *Income Tax Application Rules*, subsection 65(1) and sections 66, 66.1, 66.2, 66.21 and 66.4;

(e) each gain of the partnership from the disposition of land used in a farming business of the partnership were computed as if this Act were read without reference to paragraph 53(1)(i);

(e.1) the amount, if any, by which

(i) the total of all amounts determined under paragraphs 37(1)(a) to (c.1) in respect of the partnership at the end of the taxation year

exceeds

(ii) the total of all amounts determined under paragraphs 37(1)(d) to (g) in respect of the partnership at the end of the year

were deducted under subsection 37(1) by the partnership in computing its income for the year;

(f) the amount of the income of the partnership for a taxation year from any source or from sources in a particular place were the income of the taxpayer from that source or from sources in that particular place, as the case may be, for the taxation year of the taxpayer in which the partnership's taxation year ends, to the extent of the taxpayer's share thereof; and

(g) the amount, if any, by which

(i) the loss of the partnership for a taxation year from any source or sources in a particular place,

exceeds

(ii) in the case of a specified member (within the meaning of the definition "specified member" in subsection 248(1) if that definition were read without reference to paragraph (b) thereof) of the partnership in the year, the amount, if any, deducted by the partnership by virtue of section 37 in calculating its income for the taxation year from that source or sources in the particular place, as the case may be, and

(iii) in any other case, nil

were the loss of the taxpayer from that source or from sources in that particular place, as the case may be, for the taxation year of the taxpayer in which the partnership's taxation year ends, to the extent of the taxpayer's share thereof.

Related Provisions

"Person" (P) or "taxpayer" (TP) includes a partnership for certain purposes: 18.1(1) — matchable-expenditure rules (TP); 56.4(1) — restrictive-covenant rules (TP); 66(16) — flow-through share rules (P); 79(1), 79.1(1) — seizure of property by creditor (P); 80(1), 80.01(1) — debt forgiveness rules (P); 96(2.01) — at-risk rules (TP); 125.7(2) — Canada Emergency Wage Subsidy (TP); 135.2(1) — Cdn Wheat Board Farmers' Trust rules (P); 139.1(1) — insurance demutualization (P); 143.2(1), 143.3(1), 143.4(1) — expenditure-limitation rules (TP); 163.2(1) — third-party civil penalties (P); 187.4(c) — Part IV.1 tax (P); 209(6) — tax on carved-out income (P); 227(5.2), (15) — withholding tax (P); 233.4(2)(b) — foreign-affiliate reporting (P); 237.1(1) — tax shelter identification rules (P); 237.3(1) — reportable-transaction rules (P); 251.1(4)(b) — definition of affiliated persons (P); 251.2(1) — trust loss trading rules (P); 256.1(1) — attribute trading restrictions on change in control (P).

Other Related Provisions: 12(1)(l) — Inclusion of partnership income; 12(1)(y) — Auto provided to partner; 18(7) — Partners deemed to owe proportion of partnership debt for thin-capitalization rules; 34.2, 34.3 — Corporate partner — inclusion of stub-period income in corporation's income; 53(1)(e), 53(2)(c) — ACB of partnership interest; 66(18) — Resource expenditures claimed by members of partnerships; 66.1(7), 66.2(6), (7), 66.4(6), (7), 66.7(11) — Resource expenses; 80(1)"forgiven amount"B(k) — Debt forgiveness rules do not apply to debt forgiven by partnership to active partner; 80(15) — Application of debt forgiveness rules to partners; 87(2)(e.1) — Amalgamation — partnership interest; 93(1.2) — Disposition of share of foreign affiliate; 93.1 — Shares of foreign affiliate held by partnership; 96(1.01)(a) — Income allocation to former partner; 96(1.1) — Allocation of income share to retiring partner; 96(1.11) — Allocation of non-portfolio earnings of SIFT partnership; 96(1.7) — Gains and losses; 96(2.1) — Limited partnership losses; 100(2.1) — Disposition of interest in partnership; 107(1)(d) — Stop-loss rule on disposition by partnership of interest in trust that flowed out dividends; 112(3.1) — Stop-loss rule for partner on disposition by partnership of share on which dividends paid; 118.1(8) — Donation made by partnership; 120.4(1)"split income"(b) — Income-splitting tax on partnership income of children; 127(8), (8.1) — Investment tax credit of partnership or limited partner; 127.52(1)(c.1) — Minimum tax — no deduction for losses of limited partner; 127.52(2) — Application of partnership income and loss for minimum tax purposes; 152(1.4)–(1.8) — Determination by CRA of partnership income or loss; 162(8.1) — Rules where partnership liable to penalty; 197 — Tax equivalent to corporate tax on SIFT partnership; 212(13.1) — Non-resident withholding tax where payer or payee is a partnership; 212.1(5)–(7) — Cross-border surplus stripping using partnerships; 227(5.2) — Partnership liable for obligations re withholding tax; 227(15) — Assessment of partnership for Part XIII tax; 244(20) — Notice to members of partnerships; 249.1(1)(b)(ii), (1)(c), (8)–(11) — Fiscal year of partnership; 261(6) — Effect of functional currency election; *Income Tax Conventions Interpretation Act* 6.2 — Partnership with Canadian resident partner cannot be resident in another country.

Notes: Under 96(1), a partnership is not a person, but partnership income is calculated as though it were, and allocated to the partners for tax purposes. The partners report this income (or loss) regardless of actual distributions from the partnership. Distributions (draws) are counted as adjustments to the cost base of the partnership interest under 53(1)(e) and 53(2)(c) (see Notes to 53(2)(c)). (Income and distributions from a publicly-traded partnership that is a SIFT are taxed as though it were a corporation: 96(1.11).) Where distributions take the ACB of a limited or passive partner below zero, there is a deemed capital gain: see Notes to 40(3) and (3.1)

A partnership does not file a tax return, but may have to file an information return under Reg. 229 (note new filing requirements effective 2011). Partnership income or loss can effectively be assessed by the CRA under 152(1.4)–(1.8).

Income from a partnership retains its character in the hands of the partner, e.g., as business income or dividends. See 96(1)(f) and 4(1). This is in contrast to a trust, where the character of the income disappears (see 108(5)), except for certain designations made by the trust under s. 104 (e.g., 104(19) and (21)).

Business expenses, CCA (VIEWS doc 2010-0379751E5) and reserves are claimed at the partnership level. However, some items are allocated to and claimed by the partner, including investment tax credits (127(8)), resource expenditures (96(1)(d), 20(1)(v.1), Reg. 1210), charitable donations (118.1(8), 110.1(4)) and political contributions (127(4.2)). (See Nancy Diep, "History of the Resource Taxation Rules and Partnerships", XII(1) *Resource Sector Taxation* (Federated Press) 12-17 (2018).) Capital gains and losses are allocated separately to partners, and netted at the partner level: 96(1)(c), doc 2013-0495891C6 [2013 APFF q.21]; but a 40(1)(a)(iii) capital gains reserve is claimed at the partnership level: 2015-0595471E5. Treatment under tax treaties varies, but Canada usually looks through a partnership to allow each partner to claim treaty relief. In *Keus*, 2010 TCC 294, para. 19 [aff'd on other grounds 2010 FCA 303], interest paid by a fishing partnership on a truck owned by one of the partners was allowed to that partner rather than to the partnership.

Auray-Blais, 2005 CarswellNat 4085 (TCC), held that a partnership's SR&ED expenses must be claimed in the year incurred, and cannot be carried over. Even though 37(1)(a)–(c.1) "pool" such expenses, to be claimed whenever the taxpayer wants, the closing words of 96(1)(e.1) require claiming the maximum each year. See also VIEWS doc 2010-0389611E5 on the interaction of ss. 37 and 96.

Partnership losses for a limited partner (note extended definition in 96(2.4)) are limited to the "at-risk" amount (typically the cash invested) by 96(2.1)–(2.7), and R&D deductions are limited by 96(1)(g)(ii): *Ménard*, 2009 TCC 363. See also Notes to 248(1)"corporation" re limited liability partnerships.

Other than 12(1)(y) (automobile standby fee), a partner is not taxed on benefits received from the partnership: VIEWS doc 2006-0209341E5.

A partnership cannot pay a partner a "salary": *Income Tax Technical News* 25; VIEWS doc 2002-0132797; *Blais (Auray-Blais)*, 2005 TCC 818 and 2010 TCC 195; *McCormick v. Fasken Martineau*, 2014 SCC 39 (for human-rights discrimination purposes, a partner at a large law firm was not an employee, though the Supreme Court noted (para. 46) that this would change if "the powers, rights and protections normally associated with a partnership were greatly diminished"). If the result of allocating partnership income among partners is unreasonable, 103(1) or (1.1) will apply. In *Archbold*, [1995] 1 C.T.C. 2872 (TCC), a "salary" paid by a husband-wife partnership to the wife was allowed as a deduction in computing the partnership loss, but 103(1.1) applied to require a 50-50 allocation of the loss. See also Bowman CJ's musings in *Mazurkewich*, 2007 TCC 517, paras. 11-18. CRA does not accept *Archbold* and usually disallows deductions for amounts paid to a partner: Round Table, Cdn Tax Foundation 2003 conference report, 8A:7-10; 2010-0372191I7. A partner acting outside the capacity of partner (e.g. a lawyer who happens to be a partner, or a partner who agrees with the partnership to provide management services to it) can charge the partnership fees that are deductible: *Technical News* 30, q. 4; doc 9711923 (limited partnership can deduct management fee paid to general partner, unrelated to GP's ownership of partnership units). See also Tamaki, "Salaried Partners and Old Interpretation Bulletin IT-138R", VIII(4) *Business Vehicles* (Federated Press) 416-18 (2002); Skingle & Jankovic, "Can a Partner Enter into a Contract with a Partnership of Which the Partner is a Member?", 13(4) *Tax for the Owner-Manager* (ctf.ca) 8 (Oct. 2013).

Wolfe Goodman, in "Can Nil Partnership Income Be Allocated So as to Show a Profit for One Partner and a Loss for Another?", IX(3) *Goodman on Estate Planning* (Federated Press) 731 (2000), suggested that a partnership with nil income could allocate $100,000 loss to one partner and $100,000 income to another! (But see 103(1).) The allocation must be based on the partnership agreement, however: *Mazurkewich*, [2008] 2 C.T.C. 2132 (TCC). The CRA says that nil income cannot be allocated because of 96(1)(f) and (g): VIEWS docs 2008-0288561E5, 2011-0431171E5; and that streaming of different types of income to different partners is not allowed under 103(1): Cdn Tax Foundation 2014 conference roundtable q.5 [2014-0547311C6].

If a partnership is carrying on business, each partner is considered to be carrying on business: *Robinson*, [1998] 1 C.T.C. 272 (FCA); however, 253.1(1) overrides this rule for limited partners for certain specific purposes. A limited partner's income is allocated to provinces based on where the partnership earned the income: VIEWS doc 2010-0367621E5.

The effect of 96(1)(a) and (c) is that a partnership is subject to the arm's-length fair market value rule in 69(1)(a): *Deptuck*, [2003] 3 C.T.C. 287 (FCA) (leave to appeal denied 2004 CarswellNat 84 (SCC)).

For 96(1)(e), "land" can include buildings: see 70(5.2) Notes.

In *Landrus*, 2009 FCA 113, GAAR (245(2)) did not apply to a disposition from a partnership to a related partnership to trigger a terminal loss early. The tax benefit was the interaction of 96(1) and 20(16), but no policy objective was being frustrated. However, in *594710 B.C.*, 2018 FCA 166 (leave to appeal denied 2019 CarswellNat 434 (SCC)), GAAR applied to abuse of 96(1)(f) and 103(1) by selling shares of corporate partners to shift income to an unrelated public company with unused losses.

A reference to a partnership by its firm name is deemed to be a reference to all the partners: see 244(20)(a).

A partner can be an "officer" of the partnership: *9098-9005 Quebec*, 2012 TCC 324.

See generally Tobias, *Taxation of Corporations, Partnerships and Trusts* (Carswell, 5th ed., 2017), chap. 2; Magee, *Insight into Canadian Income Tax* (Carswell, 2017-2018 ed.), chap. 14; Thomas & Johnson, *Understanding the Taxation of Partnerships* (CCH, 5th ed., 2006, 458pp.); Krahn, "Taxation of Partners", 2001 British Columbia Tax Conference (ctf.ca), 7:1-27; Maclagan, "Partnerships: An Update", 2005 Cdn Tax Foundation conference report, 37:1-46; Beiles, "Partnerships: A Review of Tax Planning Strategies", 2006 BC Tax Conf. 11:1-31; Misutka, "Partnership Planning", 2009 Prairie Provinces Tax Conf. 11:1-15; Baxter & MacIntyre, "Business Planning With Partnerships", 2010 Atlantic Provinces Tax Conf. 3:1-42; Lille & Johnson, "Partnerships", 2010 conference report, 36:1-68; Bernstein, "Non-Residents and Partnerships", 20(2) *Canadian Tax Highlights [CTH]* (ctf.ca) 10-12 (Feb. 2012); Copeland, "Use of Partnerships for Investment Purposes", 2011 conference report, 41:1-16; Gamble, *Taxation of Canadian Mining* (Carswell, looseleaf or *Taxnet Pro* Reference Centre), chap. 11; Carr & Calverley, *Canadian Resource Taxation* (Carswell, looseleaf or *Taxnet Pro* Reference Centre), chap. 10; Bernstein, "Canada-US Partnerships", 22(12) *CTH* 9-10 (Dec. 2014) [planning points]; Blanchet et al., "Partnership Law and Intersections with Tax", 2018 Ontario Tax Conf. (ctf.ca), 12:1-11; Diep, "Taxation of Partnerships: Then and Now", 2018 Cdn Tax Foundation conference report, 8:1-34; Korkh & Sulaiman, "Outbound Partnerships: FAPI in Unexpected Places", 27(12) *CTH* 10-11 (Dec. 2019).

Meaning of "partnership": The term is not defined; refer to provincial law (both common-law and legislation such as the provincial *Partnerships Act*). Partnership is a *relationship*, not an entity. The standard test is "carrying on business in common with a view to profit". See Income Tax Folio S4-F16-C1 [replaces IT-90]; *Continental Bank of Canada*, [1998] 4 C.T.C. 119 (SCC); *McEwen Brothers*, [1999] 3 C.T.C. 373 (FCA) (purported partners who did not contribute "capital, property, effort, knowledge, skill and assets to a joint undertaking" were not partners); *Backman*, 2001 FCA 53; *Spire Freezers*, 2001 SCC 11; *Witkin*, 2002 FCA 174; *Hayes (Rezek)*, 2005 TCC 390; *Caissy*, 2006 CarswellNat 2544 (TCC); *Makuz*, 2006 TCC 263 (there must be a genuine intention to carry on business, not simply buy into tax losses); *177795 Canada*, 2009 FCA 19 (leave to appeal denied 2009 CarswellNat 1758 (SCC)) (no intention to carry on business); *Stow*, 2010 TCC 406 (joining partnership just before year-end to claim losses did not stop it being a partnership). There must be contractual agreement: *Blue Line Hockey v. Orca Bay*, 2009 BCCA 34; *Roy*, 2011 TCC 299. The expected "profit" can include profits to be earned after the business is incorporated, so preordained arrangements that guarantee losses to partners do not invalidate a partnership: *Teelucksingh*, 2011 TCC 22. A purported partnership based on fraud was not a partnership because there was no "business carried on" or "view to profit": *Garber*, 2014 TCC 1, paras. 382-385 (FCA appeal discontinued A-83-14); see also Notes to 9(2). Reporting partnership income in income tax returns can create a partnership for purposes of liability to third parties: *Prince Albert Co-op v. Rybka*, 2010 SKCA 144. See also 98(6) re continuation of predecessor partnership as new partnership.

Spouses were held to be partners in *Loewen*, [1998] G.S.T.C. 6 (TCC) (builder, wife and third person selling a new home); *DenHaan*, 2008 TCC 126; *Stefanson Farms*, 2008 TCC 682, *Neufeld*, 2009 TCC 352; *Duivenvoorde*, 2011 TCC 525. Spouses were not partners in *Bains*, 2005 FCA 378 (rental property was held in co-ownership); *Marks*, 2007 TCC 113; *Scott-Trask*, 2008 TCC 638 (despite signed partnership agreement). See also VIEWS doc 2015-0564641E5.

In Quebec, see *Civil Code* s. 2186; Bouchard, "Report on the Legal Nature of Partnership", *The Harmonization of Federal Legislation with Quebec Civil Law: Collection of Studies in Tax Law* (APFF, 2002), 6:1-63 and "The issue of Collection from a Partnership as a Function of the Permeability of its Patrimony", *The Harmonization ... Second Collection of Studies* (2005, apff.org), 3:1-74; *Ménard*, 2009 TCC 363 (tax shelter was not true partnership); *Raposo*, 2019 FCA 208 (partnership to carry on illegal acts (selling drugs) was a nullity under the *Civil Code*); *Iberville Developments*, 2018 TCC 102, paras. 22-36 (contract created partnership before transfer of property to it) (aff'd on other grounds 2020 FCA 115 [see para. 21]; leave to appeal denied 2021 CarswellNat 863 (SCC)); VIEWS doc 2011-0411911C6 (partnership need not carry on business).

If the only partners are placeholders for future "real" partners, *quaere* whether a partnership is actually formed, since the "partners" are not carrying on business: *Samarkand Film*, [2017] EWCA Civ 77 (England Court of Appeal), paras. 67-68.

On the meaning of "partnership" see also Schieman, "Establishing a Partnership", VIII(4) *Business Vehicles [BV]* (Federated Press) 410-15 (2002); Horne, "Partnerships: Necessary Ingredients", III(2) *Resource Sector Taxation* (Federated Press) 186-92 (2005); Leopardi & Zimka, "Determining Whether an Association is a Partnership", X(3) *BV* 522-27 (2005); Calverley & Kurrant, "Tax Planning with Partnerships", 20 *Canadian Petroleum Tax Journal* (2007); Jenny Mboutsiadis, "The 'In Common' Ingredient of the Partnership Test", OBA Taxation Law, Jan. 2015, tinyurl.com/mboupart. For limited partnerships see Galeski & Pitcher, "The Liability Protection Afforded a Limited Partner", XIV(3) *BV* 753-58 (2012); *Canadian Home Publishers v. Parker*, 2019 ONCA 314 (leave to appeal denied 2019 CarswellOnt 18739 (SCC)) (on dissolution due to limited partner's death, only his capital contribution returned to his estate).

For foreign partnerships see Darmo, "Characterization of Foreign Business Associations", 53(2) *Canadian Tax Journal* 481-505 (2005). For foreign arrangements considered corps or trusts rather than partnerships, see Notes to 248(1)"corporation" and 104(1).

Joint venture differs from partnership in that each party normally owns part of the property and shares in the gross revenues, not profits. See GST/HST Policy P-171R; Cherniawsky, "Use of Partnerships and Joint Ventures", 2005 Prairie Provinces Tax Conf., Appendix A (37pp.); DiGregorio & Vandale, "Commercial Vehicles", 2016 Cdn Tax Foundation conference report at 9:7-17; Geldenhuys, "Revisiting the partnership and joint venture debate", XIII(1) *Resource Sector Taxation* (Federated Press) 2-10 (2019); VIEWS docs 2008-026972117, 2010-0388771E5; 2015-0606141R3 (fund management contractual arrangement is co-ownership).

Where a partnership interest is purchased in order to obtain tax losses, see 96(8) and Notes to 96(8) re the *Backman* and *Spire Freezers* cases; and *Stow*, [2011] 1 C.T.C. 2434 (TCC), where the losses were allowed.

Partners may or may not be considered to own the partnership's property under the common law: *Seven Mile Dam Contractors*, 1980 CanLII 451 (BCCA) (yes); *Kucor Construction v. Canada Life*, 1998 CanLII 4236 (Ont CA) (no); *Fengate Developments*, [2004] EWHC 165 (England & Wales High Court) (no); *Edenvale Restoration*, 2013 BCCA 85 (yes, but taking back units in limited partnership did not reduce tax on a sale); *Rojoda*, [2020] HCA 7 (Australia), para. 21 (no); Barnett & Wang, "If the Partners Do Not Own the Assets — Who Does?", VII(3) *Sales and Use Tax* (Federated Press) 379-81 (2004); Nitikman, "Who has De Jure Control of a Corporation When Its Shares Are Held by a Limited Partnership?", 59(4) *Canadian Tax Journal* 765-82 (2011); Welters, "Limited Partner's Interest in Partnership Property", 21(7) *Canadian Tax Highlights* (ctf.ca) 3-4 (July 2013). See also VIEWS doc 2010-0364021E5 (person renting home from their own partnership cannot use RRSP Home Buyer's Plan [for first-time buyers], since they have an ownership interest in the partnership property).

Tiered partnerships: "Parliament did not intend for a partnership that is a member of another partnership to compute income": *Green*, 2017 FCA 107, para. 29 (see Notes to 96(2.1)); but this has been reversed by 96(2.01).

Death of a partner: see 70(2), 70(5)(a), 53(1)(e)(v), 100(3) and VIEWS doc 2006-0177471E5.

The inclusion is for the partnership's income for the partnership year *ending* in the partner's fiscal year, so a capital gain realized before X became a partner, or while X was non-resident, can be taxed in X's hands: VIEWS doc 2016-064716117. Deferral of income is prevented by a "stub period" income inclusion for individuals in 34.1, and for corporations in 34.2 and 34.3 (introduced in 2011). See Notes at end of 34.2. Before 34.2, one year (but not two) of corporate income deferral through tiered partnerships was accepted by the CRA, based on *Fredette*, [2001] 3 C.T.C. 2468 (TCC).

For CRA policy on joint venture fiscal periods, see Notes to 249.1(1).

On using a partnership for an estate freeze see Notes to 97(2).

If a partnership acquisition is a "tax shelter" under 237.1(1), the partner must file a T5004 to claim losses: 237.1(6).

A partnership receiving income from a US source may need to file a Form W-8IMY (see irs.gov) with the IRS.

For more CRA interpretation see docs 2008-0302851E5 (foreign affiliate partner is allocated its share of the partnership's capital gains); 2010-0365421E5 (how partner should show no income for purposes of EI self-employed benefits when on maternity leave); 2010-0384691E5 (reporting income or loss from a US partnership); 2010-038593117 (interaction of 96(1) with 115(1) and 116); 2011-039409117 (allocation to provinces of corporate income earned through partnership); 2011-0421971R3 (incorporation of professional partner); 2013-0477571E5 (reporting of financing fees on T5013, and provincial income allocation); 2013-047851117 (determining nature of amount distributed by limited partnership). See also Notes to 125(7)"personal services business".

US citizens and dual residents in Canada may have to file IRS Forms 926 and 8865 on contributing to or selling a non-US partnership (see Notes to 233.3(3) for more on US reporting).

96(1)(d)(i) amended to add reference to 34.2, and (d)(ii) amended to delete reference to (former) 34.2(4), by 2011 budget bill #2, for 2011 and later taxation years.

96(1)(d) amended by 2003 resource bill, for taxation years that begin after 2006, to delete references to 12(1)(z.5) and 20(1)(v.1). 96(1)(d) earlier amended by 2000 Budget, 1996 and 1995 Budgets, 1992 technical bill.

Regulations: 229 (partnership information return); 1101(1ab), 1102(1a) (depreciable property of partnership).

I.T. Application Rules: 20(3) (depreciable property of partnership held since before 1972).

Income Tax Folios: S4-F16-C1: What is a partnership? [replaces IT-90].

Interpretation Bulletins: IT-123R6: Transactions involving eligible capital property; IT-259R4: Exchanges of property; IT-278R2: Death of a partner or of a retired partner; IT-346R: Commodity futures and certain commodities; IT-353R2: Partnership interests — some adjustments to cost base (cancelled); IT-406R2: Tax payable by an *inter vivos* trust. See also list at end of s. 96.

Information Circulars: 73-13: Investment clubs; 89-5R: Partnership information return.

I.T. Technical News: 3 (use of a partner's assets by a partnership); 6 (expenses paid personally by partner where fiscal years do not coincide — policy in para. 14 of IT-138R reversed); 25 (partnership issues); 30 (computation/allocation of partnership income and losses).

Advance Tax Rulings: ATR-59: Financing exploration and development through limited partnerships; ATR-62: Mutual fund distribution limited partnership — amortization of selling commissions.

Application Policies: SR&ED 2004-02R5: Filing requirements for claiming SR&ED.

Forms: RC257: Request for an information return program account (RZ); T1229: Statement of resource expenses and depletion allowance; T2121: Statement of fishing activities; T2125: Statement of business or professional activities; T4068: Guide for the partnership information return; T5013 Sched. 9: List of partnerships; T5013 Summ: Summary of partnership income; T5013-Inst: Statement of partnership income — instructions for recipient; T5013A: Statement of partnership income for tax shelters and renounced resource expenses.

(1.01) Income allocation to former member — If, at any time in a fiscal period of a partnership, a taxpayer ceases to be a member of the partnership

(a) for the purposes of subsection (1), sections 34.1, 101 and 103 and paragraph 249.1(1)(b), and notwithstanding paragraph 98.1(1)(d), the taxpayer is deemed to be a member of the partnership at the end of the fiscal period; and

(b) for the purposes of the application of paragraph (2.1)(b), subsection 40(3.12) and subparagraphs 53(1)(e)(i) and (viii) and (2)(c)(i) to the taxpayer, the fiscal period of the partnership is deemed to end

(i) immediately before the time at which the taxpayer is deemed by subsection 70(5) to have disposed of the interest in the partnership, where the taxpayer ceased to be a member of the partnership because of the taxpayer's death, and

(ii) immediately before the time that is immediately before the time that the taxpayer ceased to be a member of the partnership, in any other case.

Related Provisions: 96(3) — Election by members of partnership.

Notes: 96(1.01) clarifies that, although a person may have ceased to be a partner before the end of the partnership's fiscal period, a portion of the partnership's income or loss is allocable to the person under 96(1).

For discussion of 96(1.01) see Northup, "Seeking a Safe Exit", 13(3) *Taxation Law* (Ontario Bar Assn. oba.org) 12-17 (March 2003); Tamaki, "Draft Technical Amendments — ACB of a Partnership Interest", IX(3) *Business Vehicles* (Federated Press) 461-63 (2004); Johnson, "Timing Issues on Allocating Resource Expenses and Resource Proceeds to Withdrawing Partners", V(2) *Resource Sector Taxation* (Federated Press) 338 at 343-45 (2007). See also VIEWS docs 2006-0214411E5 (acquisition of other partner's interest); 2007-0251001E5 (amalgamation of corporate partners); 2008-0297011E5 (amending partnership agreement to split income and capital interests); 2009-0334031E5 (where partner retains 0.1% interest in partnership, 96(1.01) does not apply); 2012-0433281E5 (no need to change partnership year-end in light of 96(1.01)); 2014-052998117 (allocation of partnership loss to former partner).

96(1.01) added by 2002-2013 technical bill, last change effective for tax years that end after Oct. 2011.

Income Tax Folios: S4-F7-C1: Amalgamations of Canadian corporations [replaces IT-474R2].

(1.1) Allocation of share of income to retiring partner — For the purposes of subsection (1) and sections 34.1, 34.2, 101, 103 and 249.1,

(a) where the principal activity of a partnership is carrying on a business in Canada and its members have entered into an agreement to allocate a share of the income or loss of the partnership from any source or from sources in a particular place, as the case may be, to any taxpayer who at any time ceased to be a member of

(i) the partnership, or

(ii) a partnership that at any time has ceased to exist or would, but for subsection 98(1), have ceased to exist, and either

(A) the members of that partnership, or

(B) the members of another partnership in which, immediately after that time, any of the members referred to in clause (A) became members

have agreed to make such an allocation

or to the taxpayer's spouse, common-law partner, estate or heirs or to any person referred to in subsection (1.3), the taxpayer, spouse, common-law partner, estate, heirs or person, as the case may be, shall be deemed to be a member of the partnership; and

(b) all amounts each of which is an amount equal to the share of the income or loss referred to in this subsection allocated to a taxpayer from a partnership in respect of a particular fiscal period of the partnership shall, notwithstanding any other provision of this Act, be included in computing the taxpayer's income for the taxation year in which that fiscal period of the partnership ends.

Related Provisions: 53(2)(c) — ACB of partnership interest; 96(1.2) — Disposal of right to share in income; 96(1.3) — Deductions; 96(1.4) — Right deemed not to be capital property; 96(1.5) — Disposition by virtue of death of taxpayer; 96(1.6) — Deemed members of partnership are deemed to carry on business.

Notes: 96(1.1) permits a retired partner to direct some or all of the allocation of partnership income to his or her spouse, but 56(2) or (4) may include the allocation back into the retired partner's income: VIEWS doc 2003-0006465. The agreement can be effective retroactive to the retirement date: 2014-0522551E5. The income cannot be split under 60.03 because it is deemed to be partnership income, not pension income: *Létourneau*, 2009 TCC 614. Similarly, it would not be "specified partnership income" under 125(7) or "aggregate investment income" under 129(4): 2012-0438241E5, or small business income for 125(1): 9531565. The "retired partner" may itself be a partnership, due to 102(2): 2002-0178335. Payments made to the US-resident widow of a retired partner are taxed as business profits, not as pension under the Canada-US tax treaty: 2005-0140621E5. If the partnership has nil income, no amount can be allocated under 96(1.1): 2008-0288561E5. The source of income (such as dividends) can be preserved on the allocation: 2015-0595811C6 [2015 APFF q.17]. See also 2005-0160581E5, 2008-0297011E5, 2009-0313121E5.

In *Dunne*, 2007 SCC 19, a retired Ontario accountant who had never worked or lived in Quebec was subject to Quebec tax on his pension because the partnership carried on business in Quebec.

In *Freitas*, 2018 FCA 110, para. 30, a retired accountant's 96(1.1) income was not business income, as 96(1.1) did not deem F to be a partner or to be carrying on business (so no CPP contributions were required).

96(1.1)(a) amended by 2000 same-sex partners bill, effective as per Notes to 248(1)"common-law partner". 96(1.1) earlier amended by 1995 Budget, effective 1995.

Interpretation Bulletins: IT-278R2: Death of a partner or of a retired partner; IT-338R2: Partnership interests — effects on adjusted cost base resulting from the admission or retirement of a partner (cancelled). See also at end of s. 96.

(1.11) Deemed dividend of SIFT partnership — If a SIFT partnership is liable to tax for a taxation year under Part IX.1,

(a) paragraph (1)(f) is to be read as if the expression "the amount of the income of the partnership for a taxation year from any source or from sources in a particular place" were read as "the amount, if any, by which the income of the partnership for a taxation year from any source or from sources in a particular place exceeds, in respect of each such source, the portion of the partnership's taxable non-portfolio earnings for the taxation year that is applicable to that source"; and

(b) the partnership is deemed to have received a dividend in the taxation year from a taxable Canadian corporation equal to the amount by which the partnership's taxable non-portfolio earnings for the taxation year exceeds the tax payable by the partnership for the taxation year under Part IX.1.

Related Provisions: 89(1)"eligible dividend"(b) — Dividend under 96(1.11) eligible for 45% gross-up and high dividend tax credit; 126(8) — Foreign tax credit where income arises outside Canada; 197(2) — Part IX.1 tax on partnership distributions; 197(3) — Part IX.1 tax calculated without reference to 96(1.11).

Notes: 96(1.11) added by 2007 budget bill #1, effective Oct. 31, 2006. It is part of the SIFT rules that impose a distributions tax on publicly-traded income trusts and partnerships (see Notes to 104(16)) effective 2011, or earlier in some cases (see 122.1(2) and 197(8)). It effectively provides that Part IX.1 tax payable by a SIFT partnership reduces the "taxable non-portfolio earnings" (197(1)) that will be subject to tax in the partners' hands under s. 96. More specifically, 96(1.11)(a) amends 96(1)(f) when Part IX.1 tax is payable, to reduce the allocation of partnership income to a partner by an amount representing the partner's share of taxable non-portfolio earnings. Part of that allocation is deemed by 96(1.11)(b) to be a dividend received by the partnership, allocated to the partners in the same proportion as the taxable non-portfolio earnings. The deemed dividend is the amount by which the taxable non-portfolio earnings of the partnership exceed the tax payable under Part IX.1 for the year.

(1.2) Disposal of right to share in income, etc — Where in a taxation year a taxpayer who has a right to a share of the income or

loss of a partnership under an agreement referred to in subsection (1.1) disposes of that right,

(a) there shall be included in computing the taxpayer's income for the year the proceeds of the disposition; and

(b) for greater certainty, the cost to the taxpayer of each property received by the taxpayer as consideration for the disposition is the fair market value of the property at the time of the disposition.

Related Provisions: 96(1.3) — Deductions.

Interpretation Bulletins: See list at end of s. 96.

(1.3) Deductions — Where, by virtue of subsection (1.1) or (1.2), an amount has been included in computing a taxpayer's income for a taxation year, there may be deducted in computing the taxpayer's income for the year the lesser of

(a) the amount so included in computing the taxpayer's income for the year, and

(b) the amount, if any, by which the cost to the taxpayer of the right to a share of the income or loss of a partnership under an agreement referred to in subsection (1.1) exceeds the total of all amounts in respect of that right that were deductible by virtue of this subsection in computing the taxpayer's income for previous taxation years.

Interpretation Bulletins: IT-278R2: Death of a partner or of a retired partner; IT-338R2: Partnership interests — effects on adjusted cost base resulting from the admission or retirement of a partner (cancelled). See also at end of s. 96.

(1.4) Right deemed not to be capital property — For the purposes of this Act, a right to a share of the income or loss of a partnership under an agreement referred to in subsection (1.1) shall be deemed not to be capital property.

Interpretation Bulletins: IT-338R2: Partnership interests — effects on adjusted cost base resulting from the admission or retirement of a partner (cancelled).

(1.5) Disposition by virtue of death of taxpayer — Where, at the time of a taxpayer's death, the taxpayer has a right to a share of the income or loss of a partnership under an agreement referred to in subsection (1.1), subsections 70(2) to (4) apply.

Related Provisions: 53(1)(e)(v) — Adjustments to cost base.

Interpretation Bulletins: IT-212R3: Income of deceased persons — rights or things; IT-278R2: Death of a partner or of a retired partner. See also list at end of s. 96.

(1.6) Members deemed carrying on business — If a partnership carries on a business in Canada at any time, each taxpayer who is deemed by paragraph (1.1)(a) to be a member of the partnership at that time is deemed to carry on the business in Canada at that time for the purposes of subsection 2(3), sections 34.1 and 150 and (subject to subsection 34.2(18)) section 34.2.

Notes: 96(1.6) amended by 2013 budget bill #2, for taxation years that end after March 22, 2011, to change reference from 34.2(7) to 34.2(18).

96(1.6) amended by 1995 Budget, effective 1994.

Interpretation Bulletins: See list at end of s. 96.

(1.7) Gains and losses — Notwithstanding subsection (1) or section 38, if in a particular taxation year of a taxpayer, the taxpayer is a member of a partnership with a fiscal period that ends in the particular year, the amount of a taxable capital gain, allowable capital loss or allowable business investment loss of the taxpayer for the particular year determined in respect of the partnership is the amount determined by the formula

$$A \times B/C$$

where

A is the amount of the taxpayer's taxable capital gain, allowable capital loss or allowable business investment loss, as the case may be, for the particular year otherwise determined under this section in respect of the partnership;

B is the relevant fraction that applies under paragraph 38(a), (a.1), (a.2), (b) or (c) for the particular year in respect of the taxpayer; and

C is the fraction that was used under section 38 for the fiscal period of the partnership.

Notes: For interpretation of "reasonably be attributed", see *729658 Alberta*, 2004 TCC 474.

96(1.7) opening words and A amended by 2016 budget bill #2, effective 2017, as part of changing the eligible capital property rules to CCA Class 14.1 (see Notes to 20(1)(b)). Before 2017, read:

> (1.7) Notwithstanding subsection (1) or section 38, where in a particular taxation year of a taxpayer, the taxpayer is a member of a partnership with a fiscal period that ends in the particular year, the amount of a taxable capital gain (other than that part of the amount that can reasonably be attributed to an amount deemed under subsection 14(1.1) to be a taxable capital gain of the partnership), allowable capital loss or allowable business investment loss of the taxpayer for the particular year determined in respect of the partnership is the amount determined by the formula
>
> . . . . .
>
> A is the amount of the taxpayer's taxable capital gain (other than that part of the amount that can be attributed to an amount deemed under subsection 14(1.1) to be a taxable capital gain of the partnership), allowable capital loss or allowable business investment loss, as the case may be, for the particular year otherwise determined under this section in respect of the partnership;

96(1.7) amended by 2000 Budget: opening words effective for taxation years that end after Feb. 27, 2000; and amended A and B effective for fiscal periods that begin after 2000. Per 2002-2013 technical bill (Part 5 — technical), s. 228(11), if a taxpayer, who is a member of a partnership at the end of a particular fiscal period (of the partnership) that ends in the taxpayer's 2000 taxation year, elects in writing and files the election with the Minister by the taxpayer's filing-due date for the taxpayer's taxation year that includes June 26, 2013, then various rules apply to the 2000 year (see PITA 44th to 47th ed.).

Interpretation Bulletins: See list at end of s. 96.

(1.71) Application — Where the fraction referred to in the description of C in subsection (1.7) cannot be determined by a taxpayer in respect of a fiscal period of a partnership that ended before February 28, 2000, or includes February 28, 2000 or October 17, 2000, for the purposes of subsection (1.7), the fraction is deemed to be

(a) where the fiscal period ended before or began before February 28, 2000, ³/₄;

(b) where the fiscal period began after February 27, 2000 and before October 18, 2000, ²/₃; and

(c) in any other case, ¹/₂.

Notes: 96(1.71) added by 2000 Budget, effective for fiscal periods that begin after 2000. See Notes to 38(a).

(1.8) Loan of property — For the purposes of subsection 56(4.1) and sections 74.1 and 74.3, where an individual has transferred or lent property, either directly or indirectly, by means of a trust or by any other means whatever, to a person and the property or property substituted therefor is an interest in a partnership, the person's share of the amount of any income or loss of the partnership for a fiscal period in which the person was a specified member of the partnership shall be deemed to be income or loss, as the case may be, from the property or substituted property.

Related Provisions: 248(5) — Substituted property.

Notes: For the meaning of "indirectly", see Notes to 17.1(1).

Proposed **96(1.9)**, in the foreign investment entity rules dropped in 2010, will not be enacted.

Interpretation Bulletins: IT-511R: Interspousal and certain other transfers and loans of property. See also at end of s. 96.

(2) Construction — The provisions of this Subdivision shall be read and construed as if each of the assumptions in paragraphs (1)(a) to (g) were made.

(2.01) Tiered partnerships [meaning of "taxpayer"] — For the purposes of this section, a taxpayer includes a partnership.

Notes: 96(2.01) added by 2018 budget bill #2, for taxation years that end after Feb. 26, 2018. It reverses *Green*, 2017 FCA 107, which held that certain portions of s. 96 do not apply to partnerships that are members of other partnerships.

(2.1) Limited partnership losses [at-risk rule] — Notwithstanding subsection (1), where a taxpayer is, at any time in a taxa-

tion year, a limited partner of a partnership, the amount, if any, by which

(a) the total of all amounts each of which is the taxpayer's share of the amount of any loss of the partnership, determined in accordance with subsection (1), for a fiscal period of the partnership ending in the taxation year from a business (other than a farming business) or from property

exceeds

(b) the amount, if any, by which

(i) the taxpayer's at-risk amount in respect of the partnership at the end of the fiscal period

exceeds the total of

(ii) the amount required by subsection 127(8) in respect of the partnership to be added in computing the investment tax credit of the taxpayer for the taxation year,

(iii) the taxpayer's share of any losses of the partnership for the fiscal period from a farming business, and

(iv) the taxpayer's share of

(A) the foreign resource pool expenses, if any, incurred by the partnership in the fiscal period,

(B) the Canadian exploration expense, if any, incurred by the partnership in the fiscal period,

(C) the Canadian development expense, if any, incurred by the partnership in the fiscal period, and

(D) the Canadian oil and gas property expense, if any, incurred by the partnership in the fiscal period,

shall

(c) not be deducted in computing the taxpayer's income for the year,

(d) not be included in computing the taxpayer's non-capital loss for the year,

(e) if the taxpayer is not a partnership, be deemed to be the taxpayer's limited partnership loss in respect of the partnership for the year, and

(f) if the taxpayer is a partnership, reduce the taxpayer's share of any loss of the partnership for a fiscal period of the partnership ending in the taxation year of the taxpayer from a business (other than a farming business) or from property.

Related Provisions: 66.8(1) — Resource expenses of limited partner; 87(2.1)(a) — Amalgamation — limited partnership loss carried forward; 96(1.01)(b) — Deemed end of fiscal period when taxpayer ceases to be partner; 96(2.2) — At-risk amount; 102(2) — Look-through rule for tiered partnerships; 111(1)(e) — Carryforward of non-deductible limited partnership losses; 111(9) — Limited partnership loss where taxpayer not resident in Canada; 127.52(1)(i)(ii)(B) — Calculation of previous year's limited partnership loss for minimum tax purposes; 152(1.1)–(1.3) — Determination of losses; 248(1)"limited partnership loss" — Definition applies to entire Act.

Notes: The essence of the "at-risk rules" is in 96(2.1)(b)(i) and 96(2.2)(a) — losses from a limited partnership (LP) can be claimed against other income (i.e., used as a tax shelter) only to the extent of the taxpayer's investment in the LP that is "at risk" of being lost if the LP fails — typically the cash actually invested, plus income earned from the LP (96(2.2)). The rest of the rules in 96(2.1)-(2.7) implement this rule and protect it from avoidance. LP losses (96(2.1)(e)) cannot be deducted against other sources of income (96(2.1)(c)), but can be carried forward indefinitely and claimed under 111(1)(e) against income from the same LP or additional capital contributed (and such claims reduce the partnership interest ACB: 53(2)(c)(i.1)). They cannot be deducted on dissolution of the LP: 2013-0477711E5. The portion of the loss corresponding to the at-risk amount is treated as a regular non-capital loss: VIEWS doc 2013-0495901C6.

See also 143.2 and 237.1 re partnerships that are tax shelters, and Notes to 96(2.2).

Revenue Canada took the position that the at-risk rules applied even without being enacted, on general principles. However, the FCA disagreed, in *Signum Communications*, [1992] 2 C.T.C. 31.

LP losses in a multi-tier partnership arrangement: CRA said such losses are not deductible at the top tier and simply evaporate (docs 2004-0062801E5, 2004-0107981E5, 2012-0436521E5). *Green*, 2017 FCA 107, held that 96(2.1)(c)-(e) do not apply to a top-tier partnership because "Parliament did not intend for a partnership that is a member of another partnership to compute income" (para. 29); instead, each source of income was kept separate, so business losses flowed through to the ultimate partners. However, *Green* was reversed by new 96(2.01) and 96(2.1)(f). See Sala, "Treatment of

Limited Partnership Losses in Multi-Tier Partnership Structures Post-*Canada v. Green*", 2418 *Tax Topics* (CCH) 1-4 (July 12, 2018).

LP losses cannot be claimed after the LP winds up: 2010-0379901I7.

See also CRA news release "Warning: Watch Out for Real Estate Investment Schemes", tinyurl.com/cra-warn-re (June 7, 2019).

96(2.1)(e) amended to add "if the taxpayer is not a partnership" and para. (f) added by 2018 budget bill #2, for tax years that end after Feb. 26, 2018. (See above re *Green*.)

96(2.1)(b)(iv)(A) amended by 2000 Budget, for fiscal periods that begin after 2000.

Interpretation Bulletins: IT-232R3: Losses — their deductibility in the loss year or in other years; IT-262R2: Losses of non-residents and part-year residents; IT-302R3: Losses of a corporation — the effect that acquisitions of control, amalgamations, and windings-up have on their deductibility. See also at end of s. 96.

I.T. Technical News: 5 (adjusted cost base of partnership interest).

Advance Tax Rulings: ATR-51: Limited partner at-risk rules; ATR-59: Financing exploration and development through limited partnerships.

(2.11) Tiered partnerships — adjustments — The following rules apply to taxation years of a taxpayer that end after February 26, 2018:

(a) for the purpose of applying section 111, the taxpayer's non-capital loss, or limited partnership loss in respect of a partnership, for a preceding taxation year shall be determined as if subsection (2.01) and paragraph (2.1)(f) applied in respect of taxation years that end before February 27, 2018; and

(b) in computing the adjusted cost base to the taxpayer of the taxpayer's interest in a partnership after February 26, 2018, there shall be added an amount equal to the portion of the amount of any reduction because of paragraph (a) in a non-capital loss of the taxpayer that can reasonably be considered to relate to the amount of a loss deducted under subparagraph 53(2)(c)(i) in computing the adjusted cost base of that interest.

Notes: 96(2.11) added by 2018 budget bill #2, effective Dec. 13, 2018 (but opening words limit it to applying to tax years that end after Feb. 26, 2018). It is intended "to preclude retrospective planning to carry forward losses arising in taxation years that ended before Feb. 27, 2018". (Finance Technical Notes) See Notes to 96(2.1).

(2.2) At-risk amount — For the purposes of this section and sections 111 and 127, the at-risk amount of a taxpayer, in respect of a partnership of which the taxpayer is a limited partner, at any particular time is the amount, if any, by which the total of

(a) the adjusted cost base to the taxpayer of the taxpayer's partnership interest at that time, computed in accordance with subsection (2.3) where applicable,

(b) where the particular time is the end of the fiscal period of the partnership, the taxpayer's share of the income of the partnership from a source for that fiscal period computed under the method described in subparagraph 53(1)(e)(i), and

(b.1) where the particular time is the end of the fiscal period of the partnership, the amount referred to in subparagraph 53(1)(e)(viii) in respect of the taxpayer for that fiscal period

exceeds the total of

(c) all amounts each of which is an amount owing at that time to the partnership, or to a person or partnership not dealing at arm's length with the partnership, by the taxpayer or by a person or partnership not dealing at arm's length with the taxpayer, other than any amount deducted under subparagraph 53(2)(c)(i.3) in computing the adjusted cost base, or under section 143.2 in computing the cost, to the taxpayer of the taxpayer's partnership interest at that time, and

(d) any amount or benefit that the taxpayer or a person not dealing at arm's length with the taxpayer is entitled, either immediately or in the future and either absolutely or contingently, to receive or to obtain, whether by way of reimbursement, compensation, revenue guarantee, proceeds of disposition, loan or any other form of indebtedness or in any other form or manner whatever, granted or to be granted for the purpose of reducing the impact, in whole or in part, of any loss that the taxpayer may sustain because the taxpayer is a member of the partnership or holds or disposes of an interest in the partnership, except to the extent that the amount or benefit is included in the determination

of the value of J in the definition "cumulative Canadian exploration expense" in subsection 66.1(6), of M in the definition "cumulative Canadian development expense" in subsection 66.2(5) or of I in the definition "cumulative Canadian oil and gas property expense" in subsection 66.4(5) in respect of the taxpayer, or the entitlement arises

(i) by virtue of a contract of insurance with an insurance corporation dealing at arm's length with each member of the partnership under which the taxpayer is insured against any claim arising as a result of a liability incurred in the ordinary course of carrying on the partnership business,

(ii) [Repealed]

(iii) as a consequence of the death of the taxpayer,

(iv), (v) [Repealed]

(vi) in respect of an amount not included in the at-risk amount of the taxpayer determined without reference to this paragraph, or

(vii) because of an excluded obligation (as defined in subsection 6202.1(5) of the *Income Tax Regulations*) in relation to a share issued to the partnership by a corporation,

and, for the purposes of this subsection,

(e) where the amount or benefit to which the taxpayer or the person is entitled at any time is provided by way of an agreement or other arrangement under which the taxpayer or the person has a right, either immediately or in the future and either absolutely or contingently (otherwise than as a consequence of the death of the taxpayer), to acquire other property in exchange for all or any part of the partnership interest, for greater certainty the amount or benefit to which the taxpayer or the person is entitled under the agreement or arrangement is considered to be not less than the fair market value of the other property at that time, and

(f) where the amount or benefit to which the taxpayer or the person is entitled at any time is provided by way of a guarantee, security or similar indemnity or covenant in respect of any loan or other obligation of the taxpayer or the person, for greater certainty the amount or benefit to which the taxpayer or the person is entitled under the guarantee or indemnity at any particular time is considered to be not less than the total of the unpaid amount of the loan or obligation at that time and all other amounts outstanding in respect of the loan or obligation at that time.

Related Provisions: 40(3.14)(b) — Meaning of "limited partner" re negative ACB of partnership interest; 66.8 — Resource expenses of limited partner; 96(2.3) — Computation of at-risk amount; 96(2.6) — Artificial transactions; 96(2.7) — Non-arm's length contribution of capital to partnership; 143.2(2), (6) — At-risk adjustment to tax shelter investment; 248(8) — Meaning of "consequence" of death.

Notes: See Notes to 96(2.1). In *Howe*, 2004 TCC 719, 96(2.2)(d) did not apply to a liquidity option on a partnership investment. See Ebel & Gnanakumar, "Liquidity Options Do Not Reduce 'At-Risk Amount' ", IX(2) *Corporate Structures & Groups* (Federated Press) 483-85 (2004).

The at-risk amount was reduced in *O'Dea*, 2009 TCC 295, due to 143.2(7).

For CRA interpretation see VIEWS docs 2008-0296131I7 (96(2.2)(c) does not apply); 2011-0421491I7 (effect of bump in partnership interest ACB under 111(4)); 2012-0440191R3 (no ruling on limited partnership financing arrangement, as result depended on future intentions of the parties); 2015-0595801C6 [2015 APFF q.16] (at-risk amount reduced on partial disposition where 96(1.01) does not apply).

For a detailed ruling that 96(2.2)(d) does not apply on a two-tier partnership tax shelter structure designed to flow-out CDE, CEE and COGPE incurred by farming-in to Canadian resource properties, see doc 2003-0016563. CRA will no longer rule on 96(2.2) for tax shelters: 2017-0706671R3, 2017-0724291C6 [2017 CTF q.10].

96(2.2) amended by 1995-97 technical bill (last change effective for partnership interests acquired after April 26, 1995, with grandfathering for deals underway by then), 1995 and 1994 Budgets, 1991 technical bill. The 1995 change removed a film-production exclusion from the at-risk rules, thus eliminating films as tax shelters (replaced with the 125.4 production credit). See also 18.1(17) Notes.

Interpretation Bulletins: IT-232R3: Losses — their deductibility in the loss year or in other years. See also at end of s. 96.

I.T. Technical News: 5 (adjusted cost base of partnership interest); 12 (adjusted cost base of partnership interest).

(2.3) Idem — For the purposes of subsection (2.2), where a taxpayer has acquired the taxpayer's partnership interest at any time from a transferor other than the partnership, the adjusted cost base to the taxpayer of that interest shall be computed as if the cost to the taxpayer of the interest were the lesser of

(a) the taxpayer's cost otherwise determined, and

(b) the greater of

(i) the adjusted cost base of that interest to the transferor immediately before that time, and

(ii) nil,

and where the adjusted cost base of the transferor cannot be determined, it shall be deemed to be equal to the total of the amounts determined in respect of the taxpayer under paragraphs (2.2)(c) and (d) immediately after that time.

Notes: See VIEWS doc 2011-0421491I7 (effect of bump in partnership interest ACB under 111(4)).

(2.4) Limited partner — For the purposes of this section and sections 111 and 127, a taxpayer who is a member of a partnership at a particular time is a limited partner of the partnership at that time if the member's partnership interest is not an exempt interest (within the meaning assigned by subsection (2.5)) at that time and if, at that time or within 3 years after that time,

(a) by operation of any law governing the partnership arrangement, the liability of the member as a member of the partnership is limited (except by operation of a provision of a statute of Canada or a province that limits the member's liability only for debts, obligations and liabilities of the partnership, or any member of the partnership, arising from negligent acts or omissions, from misconduct or from fault of another member of the partnership or an employee, an agent or a representative of the partnership in the course of the partnership business while the partnership is a limited liability partnership);

(b) the member or a person not dealing at arm's length with the member is entitled, either immediately or in the future and either absolutely or contingently, to receive an amount or to obtain a benefit that would be described in paragraph (2.2)(d) if that paragraph were read without reference to subparagraphs (ii) and (vi);

(c) one of the reasons for the existence of the member who owns the interest

(i) can reasonably be considered to be to limit the liability of any person with respect to that interest, and

(ii) cannot reasonably be considered to be to permit any person who has an interest in the member to carry on that person's business (other than an investment business) in the most effective manner; or

(d) there is an agreement or other arrangement for the disposition of an interest in the partnership and one of the main reasons for the agreement or arrangement can reasonably be considered to be to attempt to avoid the application of this subsection to the member.

Related Provisions: 40(3.14) — Definition of limited partner for purposes of negative ACB rules; 66.8 — Resource expenses of limited partner; 96(2.5) — Exempt interest in a partnership; 127.52(3) — Definition for minimum tax purposes; 143.2(1)"tax shelter investment"(b) — Whether limited partnership interest is tax shelter investment.

Notes: The 3 years in the opening words of 96(2.4) refer to a taxpayer's entitlement to a benefit, rather than actual receipt of the benefit; and 96(2.4)(b) applies retroactively: *Brown*, 2003 FCA 192 (leave to appeal denied 2004 CarswellNat 84 (SCC)).

In *Foley*, 2003 TCC 680, partners were held to be "at risk" and thus not limited partners (LPns). In *Docherty*, 2005 FCA 93, two general partners were LPns because under the partnership agreement they were not liable for operating losses from the project for 15 years, even though this clause was never invoked. In *Vinet*, 2019 QCCA 574, on the parallel Quebec rule, V claimed his involvement in the business made him not a LPn due to the *Civil Code*, but he may have been acting as agent or manager, and also he was bound by the LP structure he had chosen to use. Taxpayers were also found to be LPns in: *Amar*, 2006 TCC 420; *Ménard*, 2009 TCC 363 (due to 96(2.4)(b)). See also VIEWS docs 2010-0388771E5, 2010-0391271R3.

For the meaning of "one of the main reasons" in para. (d), see Notes to 83(2.1).

96(2.4)(a) amended by 2002-2013 technical bill (Part 5 — technical), effective June 21, 2001, to add reference to "fault" (for Quebec civil law).

96(2.4)(a) amended by 2001 technical bill, effective 1998, to add the parenthesized exception for limited liability partnerships (LLPs). See also 40(3.14)(a). This amendment was promised by Finance in late 1998 as a result of new provincial legislation permitting accounting and law firms to form LLPs, whereby partners are not liable for negligence of other partners. Most law and accounting partnerships are now LLPs.

96(2.4) amended by 1995-97 technical bill, for fiscal periods ending after Nov. 1994.

Interpretation Bulletins: IT-232R3: Losses — their deductibility in the loss year or in other years. See also at end of s. 96.

(2.5) Exempt interest — For the purposes of subsection (2.4), an exempt interest in a partnership at any time means a prescribed partnership interest or an interest in a partnership that was actively carrying on business on a regular and a continuous basis immediately before February 26, 1986 and continuously thereafter until that time or that was earning income from the rental or leasing of property immediately before February 26, 1986 and continuously thereafter until that time, where there has not after February 25, 1986 and before that time been a substantial contribution of capital to the partnership or a substantial increase in the indebtedness of the partnership and, for this purpose, an amount will not be considered to be substantial where

(a) the amount was used by the partnership to make an expenditure required to be made pursuant to the terms of a written agreement entered into by it before February 26, 1986, or to repay a loan, debt or contribution of capital that had been received or incurred in respect of any such expenditure,

(b) the amount was raised pursuant to the terms of a prospectus, preliminary prospectus or registration statement filed before February 26, 1986 with a public authority in Canada pursuant to and in accordance with the securities legislation of Canada or of any province, and, where required by law, accepted for filing by that public authority, or

(c) the amount was used for the activity that was carried on by the partnership on February 25, 1986 but was not used for a significant expansion of the activity

and, for the purposes of this subsection,

(d) a partnership in respect of which paragraph (b) applies shall be considered to have been actively carrying on a business on a regular and a continuous basis immediately before February 26, 1986 and continuously thereafter until the earlier of the closing date, if any, stipulated in the document referred to that paragraph and January 1, 1987, and

(e) an expenditure shall not be considered to have been required to be made pursuant to the terms of an agreement where the obligation to make the expenditure is conditional in any way on the consequences under this Act relating to the expenditure and the condition has not been satisfied or waived before June 12, 1986.

Regulations: No prescribed partnership interests to date.

(2.6) Artificial transactions — For the purposes of paragraph (2.2)(c), where at any time an amount owing by a taxpayer or a person with whom the taxpayer does not deal at arm's length is repaid and it is established, by subsequent events or otherwise, that the repayment was made as part of a series of loans or other transactions and repayments, the amount owing shall be deemed not to have been repaid.

Related Provisions: 248(10) — Series of transactions.

(2.7) Idem — For the purposes of paragraph (2.2)(a), where at any time a taxpayer makes a contribution of capital to a partnership and the partnership or a person or partnership with whom or which the partnership does not deal at arm's length makes a loan to the taxpayer or to a person with whom the taxpayer does not deal at arm's length or repays the contribution of capital, and it is established, by subsequent events or otherwise, that the loan or repayment, as the case may be, was made as part of a series of loans or other transactions and repayments, the contribution of capital shall be deemed not to have been made to the extent of the loan or repayment, as the case may be.

Related Provisions: 248(10) — Series of transactions.

Interpretation Bulletins: See list at end of s. 96.

(3) Agreement or election of partnership members — If a taxpayer who was a member of a partnership at any time in a fiscal period has, for any purpose relevant to the computation of the taxpayer's income from the partnership for the fiscal period, made or executed an agreement, designation or election under or in respect of the application of any of subsections 10.1(1), 13(4), (4.2) and (16), section 15.2, subsections 20(9) and 21(1) to (4), section 22, subsection 29(1), section 34, clause 37(8)(a)(ii)(B), subsections 44(1) and (6), 50(1) and 80(5) and (9) to (11), section 80.04, subsections 86.1(2), 88(3.1), (3.3) and (3.5) and 90(3), the definition "relevant cost base" in subsection 95(4) and subsections 97(2), 139.1(16) and (17) and 249.1(4) and (6) that, if this Act were read without reference to this subsection, would be a valid agreement, designation or election,

    (a) the agreement, designation or election is not valid unless

        (i) it was made or executed on behalf of the taxpayer and each other person who was a member of the partnership during the fiscal period, and

        (ii) the taxpayer had authority to act for the partnership;

    (b) unless the agreement, designation or election is invalid because of paragraph (a), each other person who was a member of the partnership during the fiscal period shall be deemed to have made or executed the agreement, designation or election; and

    (c) notwithstanding paragraph (a), any agreement, designation or election deemed by paragraph (b) to have been made or executed by any person shall be deemed to be a valid agreement, designation or election made or executed by that person.

Related Provisions: 244(20) — Members of partnerships; Reg. 229.1(4) — Parallel rule for publicly-traded partnership information disclosure.

Notes: A partnership can make a s. 22 election: VIEWS doc 2011-0426271C6 [2011 CTF conf p.4:15, q.20].

96(3) opening words amended by 2017 budget bill #2 to add reference to 10.1(1), for taxation years that begin after March 21, 2017.

96(3) opening words amended by 2016 budget bill #2, effective 2017, to delete references to 14(1.01), (1.02) and (6) (as part of changing the eligible capital property rules to CCA Class 14.1: see Notes to 20(1)(b)).

96(3) earlier amended by 2002-2013 technical bill (last change effective for agreements, designations and elections made or executed after Aug. 19, 2011), 2001 technical bill, 1999 and 1995 Budgets, 1994 technical bill, 1992 Economic Statement, 1992 and 1991 technical bills.

Interpretation Bulletins: IT-278R2: Death of a partner or of a retired partner; IT-413R: Election by members of a partnership under subsection 97(2); IT-457R: Election by professionals to exclude work in progress from income. See also at end of s. 96.

CRA Audit Manual: 27.25.0: Income of professionals and fiscal period issues.

(4) Election — Any election under subsection 97(2) or 98(3) shall be made on or before the day that is the earliest of the days on or before which any taxpayer making the election is required to file a return of income pursuant to section 150 for the taxpayer's taxation year in which the transaction to which the election relates occurred.

Related Provisions: 96(5) — Late filing; 96(6) — Penalty for late filing; 96(7) — Unpaid balance of penalty.

Interpretation Bulletins: IT-413R: Election by members of a partnership under subsection 97(2). See also at end of s. 96.

Forms: T2060: Election for disposition of property upon cessation of partnership.

(5) Late filing — Where an election referred to in subsection (4) was not made on or before the day on or before which the election was required by that subsection to be made and that day was after May 6, 1974, the election shall be deemed to have been made on that day if, on or before the day that is 3 years after that day,

    (a) the election is made in prescribed form; and

    (b) an estimate of the penalty in respect of that election is paid by the taxpayer referred to in subsection 97(2) or by the persons referred to in subsection 98(3), as the case may be, when that election is made.

Interpretation Bulletins: IT-413R: Election by members of a partnership under subsection 97(2). See also at end of s. 96.

CRA Audit Manual: 28.6.1: Penalties for late filed/amended elections — disposition of property to a partnership.

(5.1) Special cases — Where, in the opinion of the Minister, the circumstances of a case are such that it would be just and equitable

    (a) to permit an election under subsection 97(2) or 98(3) to be made after the day that is 3 years after the day on or before which the election was required by subsection (4) to be made, or

    (b) to permit an election made under subsection 97(2) to be amended,

the election or amended election shall be deemed to have been made on the day on or before which the election was so required to be made if

    (c) the election or amended election is made in prescribed form, and

    (d) an estimate of the penalty in respect of the election or amended election is paid by the taxpayer referred to in subsection 97(2) or by the persons referred to in subsection 98(3), as the case may be, when the election or amended election is made,

and where this subsection applies to the amendment of an election, that election shall be deemed not to have been effective.

Notes: For the meaning of "just and equitable", see Notes to 85(7.1). In *R & S Industries*, 2016 FC 275, judicial review of a refusal to extend time was denied as the application was filed too late, and in any event CRA's decision was reasonable.

Interpretation Bulletins: IT-413R: Election by members of a partnership under subsection 97(2). See also at end of s. 96.

CRA Audit Manual: 28.6.1: Penalties for late filed/amended elections — disposition of property to a partnership.

(6) Penalty for late-filed election — For the purposes of this section, the penalty in respect of an election or an amended election referred to in paragraph (5)(a) or (5.1)(c) is

    (a) where the election or amended election is made under subsection 97(2), an amount equal to the lesser of

        (i) $\frac{1}{4}$ of 1% of the amount by which the fair market value of the property disposed of by the taxpayer referred to therein at the time of disposition exceeds the amount agreed on by the taxpayer and the members of the partnership in the election or amended election, for each month or part of a month during the period commencing with the day on or before which the election is required by subsection (4) to be made and ending on the day the election or amended election is made, and

        (ii) an amount, not exceeding $8,000, equal to the product obtained by multiplying $100 by the number of months each of which is a month all or part of which is during the period referred to in subparagraph (i); and

    (b) where the election is made under subsection 98(3), an amount equal to the lesser of

        (i) $\frac{1}{4}$ of 1% of the amount by which

            (A) the total of all amounts of money and the fair market value of partnership property received by the persons referred to therein as consideration for their interests in the partnership at the time that the partnership ceased to exist

exceeds

            (B) the total of each such person's proceeds of disposition of that person's interest in the partnership as determined under paragraph 98(3)(a),

for each month or part of a month during the period commencing with the day on or before which the election is required by subsection (4) to be made and ending on the day the election or amended election is made, and

        (ii) an amount, not exceeding $8,000, equal to the product obtained by multiplying $100 by the number of months each of which is a month all or part of which is during the period referred to in subparagraph (i).

Related Provisions: 96(7) — Assessment of penalty; 220(3.1) — Waiver of penalty.

Interpretation Bulletins: IT-413R: Election by members of a partnership under subsection 97(2). See also at end of s. 96.

CRA Audit Manual: 28.6.1: Penalties for late filed/amended elections — disposition of property to a partnership.

(7) Unpaid balance of penalty — The Minister shall, with all due dispatch, examine each election and amended election referred to in paragraph (5)(a) or (5.1)(c), assess the penalty payable and send a notice of assessment to the taxpayer or persons, as the case may be, and the taxpayer or persons, as the case may be, shall pay forthwith to the Receiver General the amount, if any, by which the penalty so assessed exceeds the total of all amounts previously paid on account of that penalty.

(8) Foreign partnerships — For the purposes of this Act, where at a particular time a person resident in Canada becomes a member of a partnership, or a person who is a member of a partnership becomes resident in Canada, and immediately before the particular time no member of the partnership is resident in Canada, the following rules apply for the purpose of computing the partnership's income for fiscal periods ending after the particular time:

(a) where, at or before the particular time, the partnership held depreciable property of a prescribed class (other than taxable Canadian property),

(i) no amount shall be included in determining the amounts for any of A, C, D and F to I in the definition "undepreciated capital cost" in subsection 13(21) in respect of the acquisition or disposition before the particular time of the property, and

(ii) where the property is the partnership's property at the particular time, the property shall be deemed to have been acquired, immediately after the particular time, by the partnership at a capital cost equal to the lesser of its fair market value and its capital cost to the partnership otherwise determined;

(b) in the case of the partnership's property that is inventory (other than inventory of a business carried on in Canada) or non-depreciable capital property (other than taxable Canadian property) of the partnership at the particular time, its cost to the partnership shall be deemed to be, immediately after the particular time, equal to the lesser of its fair market value and its cost to the partnership otherwise determined; and

(c) any loss in respect of the disposition of a property (other than inventory of a business carried on in Canada or taxable Canadian property) by the partnership before the particular time shall be deemed to be nil;

(d) [Repealed]

Related Provisions: 96(9) — Anti-avoidance.

Notes: 96(8)(a) ensures that CCA on a foreign partnership's depreciable property is based on capital costs that do not exceed the lesser of the value of the partnership's property and its capital cost at the time when the property becomes relevant for purposes of the Canadian tax system. See also Notes to Reg. 1100(2.2) and (2.21).

96(8)(b) ensures that a partnership that previously had no Canadian resident partners cannot import and allocate an unrealized loss to a Canadian partner.

96(8)(c) ensures that a loss on a disposition by the partnership before it acquires a Canadian resident partner is deemed to be nil, even if it is incurred in the same fiscal period in which 96(8) applies. There is no parallel rule for a gain, so a capital gain triggered before the person became a partner is taxed: VIEWS doc 2016-0647161I7.

Where Canadian partner C joined foreign partnership FP, former 96(8)(d) provided that if ⅓ of the cumulative eligible capital (CEC) of FP's foreign business was greater than the value of all eligible capital property (ECP) of that business, FP was deemed to have disposed of an ECP for proceeds equal to the excess. CEC was reduced to the lower of CEC and ¾ of the business's ECP. Later claims under 20(1)(b) were thus limited to being based on the ECP's value at the time C joined.

CRA considers that 96(8) is largely clarifying, and that the same rules should apply without 96(8). In *Backman*, 2001 SCC 10, the Supreme Court of Canada denied the losses on the basis that there was no real partnership since there was no intention to carry on business in common with a view to profit after making the investment. But in *Spire Freezers*, 2001 SCC 11, released at the same time, the Court allowed the losses on the basis that there was a side business (not just window-dressing) that was still carried on, and thus a partnership existed.

96(8)(d) repealed by 2016 budget bill #2, effective 2017, as part of changing the eligible capital property rules to CCA Class 14.1 (see Notes to 20(1)(b)). It read:

(d) where ⁴⁄₃ of the cumulative eligible capital in respect of a business carried on at the particular time outside Canada by the partnership exceeds the total of the fair market value of each eligible capital property in respect of the business at that time, the partnership shall be deemed to have, immediately after that time, disposed of an eligible capital property in respect of the business for proceeds equal to the excess and to have received those proceeds.

96(8) added by 1993 technical bill, effective for a particular partnership where a person or partnership becomes a member of the particular partnership after December 21, 1992, or where a member of the particular partnership becomes resident in Canada after August 30, 1993. However, before May 1994, ignore 96(8)(d).

Income Tax Folios: S4-F16-C1: What is a partnership? [replaces IT-90].

(9) Application of foreign partnership rule — For the purposes of applying subsection (8) and this subsection,

(a) where it can reasonably be considered that one of the main reasons that a member of a partnership is resident in Canada is to avoid the application of subsection (8), the member is deemed not to be resident in Canada; and

(b) where at any time a particular partnership is a member of another partnership,

(i) each person or partnership that is, at that time, a member of the particular partnership is deemed to be a member of the other partnership at that time,

(ii) each person or partnership that becomes a member of the particular partnership at that time is deemed to become a member of the other partnership at that time, and

(iii) each person or partnership that ceases to be a member of the particular partnership at that time is deemed to cease to be a member of the other partnership at that time.

Related Provisions: 93.1(3) — Look-through of tiered partnerships for FAPI purposes.

Notes: For the meaning of "one of the main reasons" in para. (a), see Notes to 83(2.1).

96(9) amended for fiscal periods that begin after June 22, 2000 by 2002-2013 technical bill (Part 5 — technical), effectively to add para. (b) and to add "and this subsection" to the opening words.

96(9) added by 1993 technical bill, effective on same basis as 96(8).

Definitions [s. 96]: "adjusted cost base" — 54, 248(1); "allowable business investment loss" — 38(c), 248(1); "allowable capital loss" — 38, 248(1); "amount" — 248(1); "arm's length" — 251(1); "assessment" — 248(1); "at-risk amount" — 96(2.2); "business" — 248(1); "Canada" — 250, 255; "Canadian development expense" — 66.2(5), 248(1); "Canadian exploration expense" — 66.1(6), 248(1); "Canadian oil and gas property expense" — 66.4(5), 248(1); "Canadian partnership" — 102(1), 248(1); "capital cost" — of depreciable property 13(7); "capital property" — 54, 248(1); "carried on in Canada", "carries on a business in Canada", "carrying on a business in Canada" — 253; "common-law partner" — 248(1); "consequence of the death" — 248(8); "controlled foreign affiliate" — 95(1), 248(1); "cost" — 96(8); "cumulative eligible capital" — 14(5), 248(1); "depreciable property" — 13(21), 248(1); "disposition" — 13(21), 248(1); "dividend" — 248(1); "eligible capital property" — 54, 248(1); "employee" — 248(1); "excluded obligation" — Reg. 6202.1(5); "fair market value" — see 69(1) Notes; "farm loss" — 111(8), 248(1); "farming", "filing-due date" — 248(1); "fiscal period" — 249(2)(b), 249.1; "foreign accrual property income" — 95(1), 248(1); "foreign affiliate" — 95(1), 248(1); "foreign resource pool expense", "gross revenue", "insurance corporation", "inventory" — 248(1); "investment tax credit" — 127(9), 248(1); "land" — see 70(5.2) Notes; "limited partner" — 96(2.4); "limited partnership loss" — 96(2.1), 248(1); "member" — 102(2); "Minister" — 248(1); "net capital loss", "non-capital loss" — 111(8), 248(1); "non-resident" — 248(1); "partnership" — see 96(1) Notes; "person", "prescribed", "property" — 248(1); "province" — *Interpretation Act* 35(1); "resident in Canada" — 250; "restricted farm loss" — 31, 248(1); "SIFT partnership" — 197(1), (8), 248(1); "series of loans", "series of transactions" — 248(10); "share", "specified member" — 248(1); "substituted" — 248(5); "taxable Canadian corporation", "taxable Canadian property" — 248(1); "taxable capital gain" — 38(a), 248(1); "taxable income earned in Canada" — 115(1), 248(1); "taxable non-portfolio earnings" — 197; "taxation year" — 11(2), 96(1)(b), 249; "taxpayer" — 96(2.01), 248(1); "trust" — 104(1), 248(1), (3); "written" — *Interpretation Act* 35(1)"writing".

Interpretation Bulletins [s. 96]: IT-81R: Partnerships — income of non-resident partners; IT-242R: Retired partners.

97. (1) Contribution of property to partnership [deemed at FMV] — Where at any time after 1971 a partnership has acquired property from a taxpayer who was, immediately after that time, a member of the partnership, the partnership shall be deemed to have acquired the property at an amount equal to its fair market value at that time and the taxpayer shall be deemed to have disposed of the property for proceeds equal to that fair market value.

Related Provisions: 13(21.2)(d) — No application on certain transfers of depreciable property where UCC exceeds fair market value; 96(2) — Construction; 97(2) — Election for rollover on transfer of property to partnership.

Notes: For the meaning of "fair market value" see Notes to 69(1).

97(1) applied in *Jones Development Corp.*, 2009 TCC 397.

Interpretation Bulletins: IT-457R: Election by professionals to exclude work in progress from income; IT-471R: Merger of partnerships.

I.T. Technical News: 3 (use of a partner's assets by a partnership).

(2) Rules if election by partners [rollover to partnership] —
Notwithstanding any other provision of this Act other than subsections (3) and 13(21.2), where a taxpayer at any time disposes of any property (other than an "eligible derivative", as defined in subsection 10.1(5), of the taxpayer if subsection 10.1(6) applies to the taxpayer) that is a capital property, Canadian resource property, foreign resource property or inventory of the taxpayer to a partnership that immediately after that time is a Canadian partnership of which the taxpayer is a member, if the taxpayer and all the other members of the partnership jointly so elect in prescribed form within the time referred to in subsection 96(4),

(a) the provisions of paragraphs 85(1)(a) to (f) apply to the disposition as if

   (i) the reference therein to "corporation's cost" were read as a reference to "partnership's cost",

   (ii) the references therein to "other than any shares of the capital stock of the corporation or a right to receive any such shares" and to "other than shares of the capital stock of the corporation or a right to receive any such shares" were read as references to "other than an interest in the partnership",

   (iii) the references therein to "shareholder of the corporation" were read as references to "member of the partnership",

   (iv) the references therein to "the corporation" were read as references to "all the other members of the partnership", and

   (v) the references therein to "to the corporation" were read as references to "to the partnership";

(b) in computing, at any time after the disposition, the adjusted cost base to the taxpayer of the taxpayer's interest in the partnership immediately after the disposition,

   (i) there shall be added the amount, if any, by which the taxpayer's proceeds of disposition of the property exceed the fair market value, at the time of the disposition, of the consideration (other than an interest in the partnership) received by the taxpayer for the property, and

   (ii) there shall be deducted the amount, if any, by which the fair market value, at the time of the disposition, of the consideration (other than an interest in the partnership) received by the taxpayer for the property so disposed of by the taxpayer exceeds the fair market value of the property at the time of the disposition; and

(c) where the property so disposed of by the taxpayer to the partnership is taxable Canadian property of the taxpayer, the interest in the partnership received by the taxpayer as consideration for the property is deemed to be, at any time that is within 60 months after the disposition, taxable Canadian property of the taxpayer.

Related Provisions: 13(21.2)(d) — No election allowed on certain transfers of depreciable property where UCC exceeds fair market value; 40(3.3), (3.4) — Limitation on loss where share acquired by affiliated person; 53(4) — Effect on ACB of share, partnership interest or trust interest; 69(11) — Anti-avoidance rule where property sold after rollover; 96(2) — Construction; 96(3) — Election by members; 96(4)–(7) — Elections; 97(3) — Election not available on certain windups; 97(4) — Where capital cost to partner exceeds proceeds of disposition; 98.1(2) — Continuation of original partnership; 107.4(3)(f), 248(25.1) — Deemed taxable Canadian property retains status when rolled out of or into trust or between trusts; Canada-U.S. Tax Treaty:Art. XIII:8 — Deferral of tax for U.S. resident transferor.

Notes: 97(2) provides a rollover of property into a Canadian partnership (see 102(1)) that parallels the rollover under 85(1) for transfers to a corporation. Without this rol-

lover, 97(1) deems the transfer to take place at fair market value. For rollovers from a partnership to a corporation, see 85(2).

The election (Form T2059) must be filed by the earliest return due date of any of the taxpayers: 96(4), but can be filed up to 3 years late with a penalty: 96(5). Further extension is at CRA's discretion: 96(5.1). A party making the election can later dispute facts stated in the election form (to effectively amend the election without CRA consent), and while this would be an "uphill battle" the Tax Court has jurisdiction to hear the dispute: *R & S Industries*, 2017 TCC 75, para. 13 (after R & S had been denied judicial review of the CRA's refusal to allow it to amend the election: 2016 FC 275) [Gill, "Backdoor Amendment of the Elected Amount in Rollovers", 7(3) *Canadian Tax Focus* (ctf.ca) 1-2 (Aug. 2017)].

See Keey, *Checklist 4 — Property transferred to a Canadian Partnership*, Taxnet Pro Corporate Tax Centre (2021, 13pp). On using 97(2) in partnership estate freezes, see *Krauss*, 2009 TCC 597 (aff'd on other grounds 2010 FCA 284); Kirby, "Estate Freezes: Not Just for Corporations", XIII(1) *Business Vehicles* (Federated Press) 672-74 (2009); Elawny & Iorio, "Krauss", 1984 *Tax Topics* (CCH) 1-4 (March 18, 2010). Note that CRA can apply 103(1) or (1.1) to reallocate partnership income: VIEWS doc 2010-0373361C6.

97(2) increases the partnership interest ACB by the elected amount, but the actual value transferred is not *also* added, as that would be absurd: *Iberville Developments*, 2020 FCA 115, paras. 38, 40 (leave to appeal denied 2021 CarswellNat 863 (SCC)).

In *Bodine*, 2011 FCA 157, rolling long-held farmland into a partnership so as to sell it caused it to be inventory when sold (the partnership by definition was carrying on business with a view to profit). See Notes to 54"capital property".

97(2) was used to bypass the prohibition on rolling real estate inventory into a corporation in 85(1.1)(f), in *Loyens*, [2003] 3 C.T.C. 2381 (TCC).

In *Ceco Operations*, 2006 TCC 256 (FCA appeal discontinued), extraction of the "boot" on a 97(2) rollover was held to violate GAAR in 245(2).

If no 97(2) election is made, 97(1) applies instead: *Jones Development*, 2009 TCC 397.

In *Oxford Properties*, 2018 FCA 30 (leave to appeal denied 2018 CarswellNat 7871 (SCC)), a combination of steps that included a 97(2) rollover triggered GAAR in 245(2). See Notes to 100(1).

If a non-resident joins the partnership immediately after the rollover (so it is no longer a Canadian partnership), the CRA will apply GAAR: VIEWS doc 2014-0547321C6 [2014 CTF q.6].

If 97(2) is used for income splitting, the CRA may apply s. 103 to reallocate income: VIEWS doc 2004-0079171E5.

Retired partners are not considered partners for purposes of 97(2): VIEWS doc 2004-0073351E5. See also doc 2008-0297011E5; Joanne Golden, "Conversion of Partnership Interests into Income and Capital Components", 1967 *Tax Topics* (CCH) 1-3 (Nov. 19, 2009).

See Notes to 96(1) for the meaning of "partnership". A partnership is a "taxpayer" for this rollover, and can likely use 97(2) together with 98(3): VIEWS doc 2011-0429601E5. 97(2) cannot be used to roll property to an investment club, even though CRA administratively (IC 73-13) may tax such a club as a partnership: 2007-0242461C6.

Corporations in Alberta electing under 97(2) were required to file a copy of the federal form with Alberta, under 2001 amendments to the *Alberta Corporate Tax Act*, effective May 30, 2001. However, this requirement was repealed in 2002 retroactive to its introduction (*ACTA* s. 16.1).

97(2) opening words amended by 2017 budget bill #2 to exclude an eligible derivative, for taxation years that begin after March 21, 2017.

97(2) opening words amended by 2016 budget bill #2 to delete "eligible capital property" before "or inventory" effective 2017, as part of changing the ECP rules to CCA Class 14.1 (see Notes to 20(1)(b)).

97(2) earlier amended by 2012 budget bill #2 (for dispositions after March 28, 2012), 2010 budget bill #1, 1995-97 technical bill.

I.T. Application Rules: 20(1.2) (where transferred depreciable property was owned by the transferor since before 1972).

Income Tax Folios: S4-F7-C1: Amalgamations of Canadian corporations [replaces IT-474R2].

Interpretation Bulletins: IT-188R: Sale of accounts receivable; IT-338R2: Partnership interests — effects on adjusted cost base resulting from the admission or retirement of a partner (cancelled); IT-413R: Election by members of a partnership under subsection 97(2); IT-457R: Election by professionals to exclude work in progress from income; IT-471R: Merger of partnerships.

Information Circulars: 76-19R3: Transfer of property to a corporation under s. 85; 88-2, paras. 12, 22: General anti-avoidance rule — section 245 of the *Income Tax Act*.

I.T. Technical News: 16 (*Continental Bank* case).

Forms: T2059: Election on disposition of property by a taxpayer to a Canadian partnership.

(3) Election not available — s. 88 [windup] — Subsection (2) does not apply to a disposition of a property by a taxpayer to a particular partnership if

(a) as part of a transaction or event or series of transactions or events that includes the disposition

(i) control of a taxable Canadian corporation (in this subsection referred to as the "subsidiary") is acquired by another taxable Canadian corporation (in this paragraph referred to as the "parent"),

(ii) the subsidiary is wound up under subsection 88(1) or amalgamated with one or more other corporations under subsection 87(11), and

(iii) the parent makes a designation under paragraph 88(1)(d) in respect of an interest in a partnership;

(b) the disposition occurs after the acquisition of control of the subsidiary;

(c) the property

(i) is referred to in clauses (A) to (C) of the description of B in subparagraph 88(1)(d)(ii.1), or

(ii) is an interest in a partnership that holds, directly or indirectly through one or more partnerships, property referred to in clauses (A) to (C) of the description of B in subparagraph 88(1)(d)(ii.1); and

(d) the subsidiary is the taxpayer or has, before the disposition of the property, directly or indirectly in any manner whatever, an interest in the taxpayer.

Related Provisions: 87(2)(g.1) — Amalgamation — continuing corporation.

Notes: 97(3) added by 2012 budget bill #2, for dispositions after March 28, 2012.

Former 97(3) repealed by 1995-97 technical bill, effective (subject to grandfathering) for dispositions after April 26, 1995 (earlier amended by 1994 technical bill). Under 40(3.4), a loss arising on transfer of property to a partnership of which the transferor is a majority interest partner is still denied, but is no longer added to the partnership interest ACB, and is deferred until the property is sold out of the affiliated group. See Notes to 40(3.4).

(3.1) [Repealed]

Notes: 97(3.1) repealed by 1995-97 technical bill, effective (subject to grandfathering) for dispositions after April 26, 1995. The definition "majority interest partner" now appears in 248(1).

(4) Where capital cost to partner exceeds proceeds of disposition — Where subsection (2) has been applicable in respect of the acquisition of any depreciable property by a partnership from a taxpayer who was, immediately after the taxpayer disposed of the property, a member of the partnership and the capital cost to the taxpayer of the property exceeds the taxpayer's proceeds of the disposition, for the purposes of sections 13 and 20 and any regulations made under paragraph 20(1)(a)

(a) the capital cost to the partnership of the property shall be deemed to be the amount that was the capital cost thereof to the taxpayer; and

(b) the excess shall be deemed to have been allowed to the partnership in respect of the property under regulations made under paragraph 20(1)(a) in computing income for taxation years before the acquisition by the partnership of the property.

Related Provisions: 13(7)(e) — Non-arm's length transfer of depreciable property.

(5) Acquisition of certain tools — capital cost and deemed depreciation — If subsection (2) has applied in respect of the acquisition at any particular time of any depreciable property by a partnership from an individual, the cost of the property to the individual was included in computing an amount under paragraph 8(1)(r) or (s) in respect of the individual, and the amount that would be the cost of the property to the individual immediately before the transfer if this Act were read without reference to subsection 8(7) (which amount is in this subsection referred to as the "individual's

original cost") exceeds the individual's proceeds of disposition of the property,

(a) the capital cost to the partnership of the property is deemed to be equal to the individual's original cost; and

(b) the amount by which the individual's original cost exceeds the individual's proceeds of disposition in respect of the property is deemed to have been deducted by the partnership under paragraph 20(1)(a) in respect of the property in computing income for taxation years that ended before that particular time.

Related Provisions: 56(1)(k) — Income inclusion where tools disposed of without rollover; 85(5.1) — Parallel rule for rollover to corporation.

Notes: See Notes to the parallel rule in 85(5.1).

97(5) opening words amended to refer to 8(1)(s) by 2006 budget bill #2, for 2006 and later taxation years. 97(5) added by 2001 Budget, for dispositions after 2001.

Definitions [s. 97]: "adjusted cost base" — 54, 248(1); "amount" — 248(1); "Canadian partnership" — 102(1), 248(1); "Canadian resource property" — 66(15), 248(1); "capital property" — 54, 248(1); "control" — 256(6)–(9); "corporation" — 248(1), *Interpretation Act* 35(1); "depreciable property" — 13(21), 248(1); "disposition" — 248(1); "eligible capital property" — 54, 248(1); "eligible derivative" — 10.1(5); "fair market value" — see 69(1) Notes; "fiscal period" — 249(2)(b), 249.1; "foreign resource property" — 66(15), 248(1); "inventory", "majority-interest partner" — 248(1); "member" — 102(2); "net capital loss", "non-capital loss" — 111(8), 248(1); "parent" — 97(3); "partnership" — see 96(1) Notes; "person", "prescribed", "property", "regulation" — 248(1); "restricted farm loss" — 31, 248(1); "series of transactions" — 248(10); "taxable Canadian corporation" — 89(1), 248(1); "taxable Canadian property" — 248(1); "taxation year" — 249; "taxpayer" — 248(1).

98. (1) Disposition of partnership property — For the purposes of this Act, where, but for this subsection, at any time after 1971 a partnership would be regarded as having ceased to exist, the following rules apply:

(a) until such time as all the partnership property and any property substituted therefor has been distributed to the persons entitled by law to receive it, the partnership shall be deemed not to have ceased to exist, and each person who was a partner shall be deemed not to have ceased to be a partner,

(b) the right of each such person to share in that property shall be deemed to be an interest in the partnership, and

(c) notwithstanding subsection 40(3), where at the end of a fiscal period of the partnership, in respect of an interest in the partnership,

(i) the total of all amounts required by subsection 53(2) to be deducted in computing the adjusted cost base to the taxpayer of the interest at that time

exceeds

(ii) the total of the cost to the taxpayer of the interest determined for the purpose of computing the adjusted cost base to the taxpayer of that interest at that time and all amounts required by subsection 53(1) to be added to the cost to the taxpayer of the interest in computing the adjusted cost base to the taxpayer of that interest at that time,

the amount of the excess shall be deemed to be a gain of the taxpayer for the taxpayer's taxation year that includes that time from a disposition at that time of that interest.

Related Provisions: 20(1)(e)(vi) — Expenses re financing; 40(3.2) — Para. 98(1)(c) takes precedence over subsec. 40(3.1); 98(3) — Rules where partnership ceases to exist; 98.1(2) — Continuation of original partnership; 99(1) — Fiscal period of terminated partnership; 99(2) — Fiscal period for individual member of terminated partnership; 248(5) — Substituted property.

Notes: 98(1) recognizes that, for ITA purposes, "an event giving rise to dissolution does not automatically result in the distribution of the partnership property to the partners": *Bow River Pipe Lines*, [2001] 1 C.T.C. 194 (FCA), para. 19.

See R. Daren Baxter, "Termination of Partnerships", 11(1) *Tax Hyperion* (Carswell) 1-3 (Dec. 2014). See also Notes to 96(1) on the meaning of "partnership".

For CRA interpretation see VIEWS docs 2011-0403001E5 (partnership can claim CCA before continuing as sole proprietorship); 2011-0423191E5 (capital loss claim by partner); 2013-0482081E5 (whether limited partnership has ceased to exist); 2014-0522771E5 (whether partnership has ceased to exist); 2014-0545051E5 (98(1)(a) does not apply to a former partner who left before the partnership ceased to exist).

Closing words of 98(1)(c) amended by 1994 Budget, this version effective 1996. Previously amended by 1991 technical bill.

I.T. Application Rules: 23(4.1)(a) (where professional business carried on in partnership since before 1972).

Interpretation Bulletins: IT-338R2: Partnership interests — effects on ACB resulting from admission or retirement of a partner (cancelled).

(2) Deemed proceeds — Subject to subsections (3) and (5) and 85(3), where at any time after 1971 a partnership has disposed of property to a taxpayer who was, immediately before that time, a member of the partnership, the partnership shall be deemed to have disposed of the property for proceeds equal to its fair market value at that time and the taxpayer shall be deemed to have acquired the property at an amount equal to that fair market value.

Related Provisions: 53(4) — Effect on ACB of share, partnership interest or trust interest.

Notes: For a ruling applying 98(2) see VIEWS doc 2013-0505431R3.

Interpretation Bulletins: IT-338R2: Partnership interests — effects on ACB resulting from admission or retirement of a partner (cancelled); IT-457R: Election by professionals to exclude work in progress from income.

(3) Rules applicable where partnership ceases to exist [rollout] — If at any particular time after 1971 a Canadian partnership has ceased to exist and all the partnership property has been distributed to persons who were members of the partnership immediately before that time so that immediately after that time each such person has, in each such property, an undivided interest, or for civil law an undivided right (which undivided interest or undivided right is referred to in this subsection as an "undivided interest or right", as the case may be) that, when expressed as a percentage (referred to in this subsection as that person's "percentage") of all undivided interests or rights in the property, is equal to the person's undivided interest or right, when so expressed, in each other such property, if each such person has jointly so elected in respect of the property in prescribed form and within the time referred to in subsection 96(4), the following rules apply:

(a) each such person's proceeds of the disposition of the person's interest in the partnership shall be deemed to be an amount equal to the greater of

(i) the adjusted cost base to the person, immediately before the particular time, of the person's interest in the partnership, and

(ii) the amount of any money received by the person on the cessation of the partnership's existence, plus the person's percentage of the total of amounts each of which is the cost amount to the partnership of each such property immediately before its distribution;

(b) the cost to each such person of that person's undivided interest or right in each such property is deemed to be an amount equal to the total of

(i) that person's percentage of the cost amount to the partnership of the property immediately before its distribution, and

(i.1) [Repealed]

(ii) where the amount determined under subparagraph (a)(i) exceeds the amount determined under subparagraph (a)(ii), the amount determined under paragraph (c) in respect of the person's undivided interest or right in the property;

(c) the amount determined under this paragraph in respect of each such person's undivided interest or right in each such property that was a capital property (other than depreciable property) of the partnership is such portion of the excess, if any, described in subparagraph (b)(ii) as is designated by the person in respect of the property, except that

(i) in no case shall the amount so designated in respect of the person's undivided interest or right in any such property exceed the amount, if any, by which the person's percentage of the fair market value of the property immediately after its distribution exceeds the person's percentage of the cost amount to the partnership of the property immediately before its distribution, and

(ii) in no case shall the total of amounts so designated in respect of the person's undivided interest or right in all such

capital properties (other than depreciable property) exceed the excess, if any, described in subparagraph (b)(ii);

(d) [Repealed under former Act]

(e) if the property so distributed by the partnership was depreciable property of the partnership of a prescribed class and any such person's percentage of the amount that was the capital cost to the partnership of that property exceeds the amount determined under paragraph (b) to be the cost to the person of the person's undivided interest or right in the property, for the purposes of sections 13 and 20 and any regulations made under paragraph 20(1)(a)

(i) the capital cost to the person of the person's undivided interest or right in the property is deemed to be the person's percentage of the amount that was the capital cost to the partnership of the property, and

(ii) the excess is deemed to have been allowed to the person in respect of the property under regulations made under paragraph 20(1)(a) in computing income for taxation years before the acquisition by the person of the undivided interest or right; and

(f) the partnership shall be deemed to have disposed of each such property for proceeds equal to the cost amount to the partnership of the property immediately before its distribution;

(g) [Repealed]

Related Provisions: 53(4) — Effect on ACB of partnership interest; 69(11)(a)(i) — Exception to rule deeming proceeds at FMV where capital gains exemption claimed after dissolution of partnership; 80.03(1), (3)(c) — Capital gain where para. 98(3)(a) applies to partnership interest on disposition following debt forgiveness; 85(3) — Alternative provision where partnership wound up; 96(4) — Election; 96(6) — Penalty for late filed election; 98(7) — Leasehold interest in or option on depreciable property is depreciable property for (3)(c); 98(2) — Deemed proceeds; 98(4) — Application.

Notes: A 98(3) election cannot be revoked or amended: VIEWS docs 2005-0141981E5, 2014-0540611E5. See also 2006-0174191I7 (renounced resource expenditures on partnership windup); 2007-0225151R3, 2007-0245281R3 (rulings that 98(3) applies); 2009-0317591E5 (partnership must recognize FX gains/losses when foreign debt is assumed by partners); 2011-0427871E5 (interaction with 73(1)); 2002-0147315 and 2011-0429601E5 (use by partnership that is partner); 2014-0540611E5 (election must apply to all the partnership property); 2014-0538171C6 [2014 APFF q.23] (98(3) does not apply when partnership dissolves by one partner acquiring remaining partnership interests); 2016-0660321R3 (REIT reorganization).

On a 98(3) election, the undivided interests in real property of the partnership can qualify as 248(1)"former business property", so the partners can exchange their interests via 44(6) rollover: Income Tax Folio S3-F3-C1, ¶1.55.

In *Oxford Properties*, 2018 FCA 30 (leave to appeal denied 2018 CarswellNat 7871 (SCC)), a combination of steps that included a 98(3) partnership windup triggered GAAR in 245(2). See Notes to 100(1).

See also Nick Fabiano, "Wind Ups and Mergers of Partnerships", 2005 Ontario Tax Conference (ctf.ca), 4A:1-22; Mike Dolson, "Death of a Partner — Consequences of an Unwritten Partnership Agreement", XIV(2) *Business Vehicles* (Federated Press) 739-42 (2011); Kim Maguire, "Partnership Dissolutions: The Undivided Interest Condition", 4(4) *Canadian Tax Focus* (ctf.ca) 4-5 (Nov. 2014); Cormack & Pantry, "Partnership Reorganizations", 26(6) *Canadian Tax Highlights* (ctf.ca) 5-6 (June 2018).

98(3)(b)(i.1) and (g) repealed by 2016 budget bill #2, effective 2017, as part of changing the eligible capital property rules to CCA Class 14.1 (see Notes to 20(1)(b)). They read:

(b)(i.1) where the property is eligible capital property, that person's percentage of ⁴/₃ of the amount, if any, determined for F in the definition "cumulative eligible capital" in subsection 14(5) in respect of the partnership's business immediately before the particular time, and

. . . . .

(g) where the property so distributed by the partnership was eligible capital property in respect of the business,

(i) for the purposes of determining under this Act any amount relating to cumulative eligible capital, an eligible capital amount, an eligible capital expenditure or eligible capital property, each such person is deemed to have continued to carry on the business, in respect of which the property was eligible capital property and that was previously carried on by the partnership, until the time that the person disposes of the person's undivided interest or right in the property,

(ii) for the purposes of determining the person's cumulative eligible capital in respect of the business, an amount equal to ³/₄ of the amount determined under subparagraph (b)(i.1) in respect of the business shall be added to the amount otherwise determined in respect thereof for P in the definition "cumulative eligible capital" in subsection 14(5), and

(iii) for the purpose of determining after the particular time the amount required by paragraph 14(1)(b) to be included in computing the person's income in respect of any subsequent disposition of property of the business, the value determined for Q in the definition "cumulative eligible capital" in subsection 14(5) is deemed to be the amount, if any, of that person's percentage of the value determined for Q in that definition in respect of the partnership's business immediately before the particular time.

98(3) amended by 2002-2013 technical bill (adding "or right" effective June 26, 2013), 2000 and 1994 Budgets, 2001, 1992 and 1991 technical bills. Grandfathering still available on the 1985 repeal of 98(3)(d): see VIEWS doc 2009-0350571E5.

Regulations: 230(3) (no information return required).

I.T. Application Rules: 20(1.2) (where transferred depreciable property was owned by transferor since before 1972).

Interpretation Bulletins: IT-338R2: Partnership interests — effects on ACB resulting from admission or retirement of a partner (cancelled); IT-442R: Bad debts and reserves for doubtful debts; IT-457R: Election by professionals to exclude work in progress from income; IT-471R: Merger of partnerships.

I.T. Technical News: 12 (adjusted cost base of partnership interest).

Information Circulars: 76-19R3: Transfer of property to a corporation under s. 85.

Forms: T2060: Election for disposition of property upon cessation of partnership.

(4) Where subsec. (3) does not apply — Subsection (3) is not applicable in any case in which subsection (5) or 85(3) is applicable.

(5) Where partnership business carried on as sole proprietorship — Where at any particular time after 1971 a Canadian partnership has ceased to exist and within 3 months after the particular time one, but not more than one, of the persons who were, immediately before the particular time, members of the partnership (which person is in this subsection referred to as the "proprietor", whether an individual, a trust or a corporation) carries on alone the business that was the business of the partnership and continues to use, in the course of the business, any property that was, immediately before the particular time, partnership property and that was received by the proprietor as proceeds of disposition of the proprietor's interest in the partnership, the following rules apply:

(a) the proprietor's proceeds of disposition of the proprietor's interest in the partnership shall be deemed to be an amount equal to the greater of

(i) the total of the adjusted cost base to the proprietor, immediately before the particular time, of the proprietor's interest in the partnership, and the adjusted cost base to the proprietor of each other interest in the partnership deemed by paragraph (g) to have been acquired by the proprietor at the particular time, and

(ii) the total of

(A) the cost amount to the partnership, immediately before the particular time, of each such property so received by the proprietor, and

(B) the amount of any other proceeds of the disposition of the proprietor's interest in the partnership received by the proprietor;

(b) the cost to the proprietor of each such property shall be deemed to be an amount equal to the total of

(i) the cost amount to the partnership of the property immediately before that time, and

(i.1) [Repealed]

(ii) where the amount determined under subparagraph (a)(i) exceeds the amount determined under subparagraph (a)(ii), the amount determined under paragraph (c) in respect of the property;

(c) the amount determined under this paragraph in respect of each such property so received by the proprietor that is a capital property (other than depreciable property) of the proprietor is such portion of the excess, if any, described in subparagraph

(b)(ii) as is designated by the proprietor in respect of the property, except that

(i) in no case shall the amount so designated in respect of any such property exceed the amount, if any, by which the fair market value of the property immediately after the particular time exceeds the cost amount to the partnership of the property immediately before that time, and

(ii) in no case shall the total of amounts so designated in respect of all such capital properties (other than depreciable property) exceed the excess, if any, described in subparagraph (b)(ii);

(d) [Repealed under former Act]

(e) where any such property so received by the proprietor was depreciable property of a prescribed class of the partnership and the amount that was the capital cost to the partnership of that property exceeds the amount determined under paragraph (b) to be the cost to the proprietor of the property, for the purposes of sections 13 and 20 and any regulations made under paragraph 20(1)(a)

(i) the capital cost to the proprietor of the property shall be deemed to be the amount that was the capital cost to the partnership of the property, and

(ii) the excess shall be deemed to have been allowed to the proprietor in respect of the property under regulations made under paragraph 20(1)(a) in computing income for taxation years before the acquisition by the proprietor of the property;

(f) the partnership shall be deemed to have disposed of each such property for proceeds equal to the cost amount to the partnership of the property immediately before the particular time; and

(g) where, at the particular time, all other persons who were members of the partnership immediately before that time have disposed of their interests in the partnership to the proprietor, the proprietor shall be deemed at that time to have acquired partnership interests from those other persons and not to have acquired any property that was property of the partnership;

(h) [Repealed]

Related Provisions: 53(4) — Effect on ACB of partnership interest; 80.03(1), (3)(c) — Capital gain where para. 98(5)(a) applies to partnership interest on disposition following debt forgiveness; 88(1)(a.2) — Winding-up; 98(2) — Deemed proceeds; 98(4) — Subsec. 98(3) does not apply; 98(7) — Leasehold interest in or option on depreciable property is depreciable property for (5)(c); *Interpretation Act* 27(5) — Meaning of "within 3 months".

Notes: 98(5) can apply where a partner's retirement results in the partnership's dissolution and the business continues as a sole proprietorship: IT-338R2 para. 12, VIEWS doc 2007-0230671E5. For interpretation of the "business continuity test", see 2008-0275151E5 (where partnership's only asset is shares or a partnership interest); 2011-0422551E5 (partnership was tenant and remaining partner becomes owner of property). On the interaction with 13(21.2) see 2009-0347301R3. On interaction with 20(1)(c) and s. 80 see 2016-0651621R3. On the proprietor carrying forward 20(1)(c), (m) and (n) deductions, see 2015-0601441R3 (and 2015-0623731R3, same file, re 55(3)(a)). On interaction with 73(1) see 2011-0427871E5. On interaction of 98(5)(f) with 99(1) see 2011-0403001E5. On interaction with 116(5) see 2015-0709351E5 (116(5) does not apply). Where a partnership holds a leasehold interest and a partner is the lessor, see 2011-0426091E5. On transfer of depreciable property see 2014-0529231E5. 98(5) did not apply in 2017-0722961E5 (amalgamation of former partner with former subsidiary of partnership). Rollover on internal reorg: 2020-0844991R3. Where Opco shares owned by a partnership are cancelled on transfer of the partnership interests to Opco, 98(5) does not apply: 2018-0745681E5. See also Dolson article in Notes to 98(3).

CRA says that the 98(5)(c) designation must be filed with the return (there is no prescribed form) and can be accepted late at CRA's discretion: doc 2012-0452411E5.

98(5) applied to grind down the cost of assets in *Stefanson Farms*, 2008 TCC 682; the Court rejected the 99%-partner's claim that he had not really been in partnership with his mother.

In *Canada Life*, 2015 ONSC 281, rectification was initially granted to avoid an unintended 98(5) rollover, but due to *Fairmont* (see Notes to 169(1) re rectification) this was reversed at 2018 ONCA 562 (leave to appeal denied 2019 CarswellOnt 3325 (SCC)).

See also Peter McQuillan, "A Quarter Century in Partnerships", 43(5) *Canadian Tax Journal* 1465 at 1483-85 (1995); Perry Truster, "Windup-Bump Comparison: Subsections 98(3) and (5)", 15(1) *Tax for the Owner-Manager* (ctf.ca) 8-9 (Jan. 2015).

98(5)(b)(i.1) and (h) repealed by 2016 budget bill #2, effective 2017, as part of changing the eligible capital property rules to CCA Class 14.1 (see Notes to 20(1)(b)). They read:

(b)(i.1) where the property is eligible capital property, ⁴/₃ of the amount, if any, determined for F in the definition "cumulative eligible capital" in subsection 14(5) in respect of the partnership's business immediately before the particular time, and

. . . . .

(h) where the property so received by the proprietor is eligible capital property in respect of the business,

(i) for the purpose of determining the proprietor's cumulative eligible capital in respect of the business, an amount equal to ¾ of the amount determined under subparagraph (b)(i.1) in respect of the business shall be added to the amount otherwise determined in respect thereof for P in the definition "cumulative eligible capital" in subsection 14(5), and

(ii) for the purpose of determining after the particular time the amount required by paragraph 14(1)(b) to be included in computing the proprietor's income in respect of any subsequent disposition of property of the business, the value determined for Q in the definition "cumulative eligible capital" in subsection 14(5) is deemed to be the value, if any, determined for Q in that definition in respect of the partnership's business immediately before the particular time.

98(5)(h)(ii) amended by 2000 Budget (effective for taxation years that end after Feb. 27, 2000), 1994 Budget and 1992 and 1991 technical bills.

I.T. Application Rules: 20(1.2) (where transferred depreciable property was owned by transferor since before 1972).

Income Tax Folios: S4-F7-C1: Amalgamations of Canadian corporations [replaces IT-474R2].

Interpretation Bulletins: IT-338R2: Partnership interests — effects on ACB resulting from admission or retirement of a partner (cancelled); IT-457R: Election by professionals to exclude work in progress from income.

Information Circulars: 88-2, para. 22: General anti-avoidance rule — section 245 of the *Income Tax Act*.

(6) Continuation of predecessor partnership by new partnership

— Where a Canadian partnership (in this subsection referred to as the "predecessor partnership") has ceased to exist at any particular time after 1971 and, at or before that time, all of the property of the predecessor partnership has been transferred to another Canadian partnership (in this subsection referred to as the "new partnership") the only members of which were members of the predecessor partnership, the new partnership shall be deemed to be a continuation of the predecessor partnership and any member's partnership interest in the new partnership shall be deemed to be a continuation of the member's partnership interest in the predecessor partnership.

Related Provisions: 53(4) — Effect on ACB of share, partnership interest or trust interest; 142.51(10) — Accounting changes — transitional rules for financial institutions; Reg. 9204(4) — Residual portion of specified debt obligation.

Notes: See VIEWS doc 2014-0522181E5 (98(6) applies when LP becomes GP on dissolution of sole general partner; 98(6) can apply even though payment made to withdrawing partner).

Regulations: 230(3) (no information return required).

Income Tax Folios: S4-F7-C1: Amalgamations of Canadian corporations [replaces IT-474R2].

Interpretation Bulletins [subsec. 98(6)]: IT-338R2: Partnership interests — effects on ACB resulting from admission or retirement of a partner (cancelled); IT-457R: Election by professionals to exclude work in progress from income.

(7) Depreciable property — leasehold interests and options

— For the purposes of paragraphs (3)(c) and (5)(c), a leasehold interest in a depreciable property and an option to acquire a depreciable property are depreciable properties.

Notes: 98(7) ensures that the cost base of a leasehold interest in a depreciable property, and an option to acquire a depreciable property, cannot be "bumped" under the rules that apply when a partnership ceases to exist. Added by 2017 budget bill #2, for partnerships that cease to exist after Sept. 15, 2016.

A former proposed 98(7), in the foreign investment entity rules (proposed 94.1) that were dropped in 2010, will not be enacted.

Definitions [s. 98]: "adjusted cost base" — 54, 248(1); "amount", "business" — 248(1); "Canadian partnership" — 102(1), 248(1); "capital property" — 54, 248(1); "cost amount" — 248(1); "cumulative eligible capital" — 14(5), 248(1); "depreciable property" — 13(21), 98(7), 248(1); "eligible capital expenditure" — 14(5), 248(1); "eligible capital property" — 54, 248(1); "fair market value" — see 69(1) Notes; "member" — 102(2); "partnership" — see 96(1) Notes; "person", "property", "regulation" — 248(1); "substituted" — 248(5); "taxation year" — 11(2), 249; "taxpayer" — 248(1).

98.1 (1) Residual interest in partnership

— Where, but for this subsection, at any time after 1971 a taxpayer has ceased to be a member of a partnership of which the taxpayer was a member immediately before that time, the following rules apply:

(a) until such time as all the taxpayer's rights (other than a right to a share of the income or loss of the partnership under an agreement referred to in subsection 96(1.1)) to receive any property of or from the partnership in satisfaction of the taxpayer's interest in the partnership immediately before the time at which the taxpayer ceased to be a member of the partnership are satisfied in full, that interest (in this section referred to as a "residual interest") is, subject to sections 70, 110.6 and 128.1 but notwithstanding any other section of this Act, deemed not to have been disposed of by the taxpayer and to continue to be an interest in the partnership;

(b) where all of the taxpayer's rights described in paragraph (a) are satisfied in full before the end of the fiscal period of the partnership in which the taxpayer ceased to be a member thereof, the taxpayer shall, notwithstanding paragraph (a), be deemed not to have disposed of the taxpayer's residual interest until the end of that fiscal period;

(c) notwithstanding subsection 40(3), where at the end of a fiscal period of the partnership, in respect of a residual interest in the partnership,

(i) the total of all amounts required by subsection 53(2) to be deducted in computing the adjusted cost base to the taxpayer of the residual interest at that time

exceeds

(ii) the total of the cost to the taxpayer of the residual interest determined for the purpose of computing the adjusted cost base to the taxpayer of that interest at that time and all amounts required by subsection 53(1) to be added to the cost to the taxpayer of the residual interest in computing the adjusted cost base to the taxpayer of that interest at that time

the amount of the excess shall be deemed to be a gain of the taxpayer, for the taxpayer's taxation year that includes that time, from a disposition at that time of that residual interest; and

(d) where a taxpayer has a residual interest

(i) by reason of paragraph (b), the taxpayer shall, except for the purposes of subsections 110.1(4) and 118.1(8), be deemed not to be a member of the partnership, and

(ii) in any other case, the taxpayer shall, except for the purposes of subsection 85(3), be deemed not to be a member of the partnership.

Related Provisions: 40(3.2) — Para. 98.1(1)(c) takes precedence over subsec. 40(3.1); 96(1.01)(a) — Income allocation to former partner; 98.1(2) — Continuation of original partnership; 98.2 — Transfer of interest on death.

Notes: 98.1(1)(d)(i) amended by *Federal Accountability Act* (S.C. 2006, c. 9), effective 2007, to delete reference to 127(4.2).

The sale of a partnership interest may be fully taxable if the proceeds are based on future income. See Notes to 12(1)(g).

A retiring partner's interest in the partnership continues as a residual interest under 98.1(1). Since partnership income is not added to the adjusted cost base (ACB) of the partnership interest under 53(1)(e) until the beginning of the next year, ACB in the retirement year may be negative, triggering a capital gain under 40(3.1): VIEWS doc 2002-0146335. See also 2014-0545051E5 (where former partner withdrew before partnership dissolution).

98.1(1) earlier amended by 1995-97 technical bill (effective 1994 and later taxation years), 1994 Budget (effective 1996), 1993 technical bill and 1991 technical bill.

I.T. Application Rules: 23(4.1)(b) (where professional practice carried on in partnership since before 1972).

Interpretation Bulletins: IT-242R: Retired partners; IT-278R2: Death of a partner or of a retired partner.

(2) Continuation of original partnership

— Where a partnership (in this subsection referred to as the "original partnership") has or would but for subsection 98(1) have ceased to exist at a time when a taxpayer had rights described in paragraph (1)(a) in respect of that partnership and the members of another partnership agree to satisfy all or part of those rights, that other partnership shall, for the purposes of that paragraph, be deemed to be a continuation of the original partnership.

Interpretation Bulletins: IT-278R2: Death of a partner or of a retired partner.

Definitions [s. 98.1]: "amount" — 248(1); "partnership" — see 96(1) Notes; "property" — 248(1); "residual interest" — 98.1(1)(a); "taxpayer" — 248(1).

98.2 Transfer of interest on death — Where by virtue of the
death of an individual a taxpayer has acquired a property that was an interest in a partnership to which, immediately before the individual's death, section 98.1 applied,

(a) the taxpayer shall be deemed to have acquired a right to receive partnership property and not to have acquired an interest in a partnership;

(b) the taxpayer shall be deemed to have acquired the right referred to in paragraph (a) at a cost equal to the amount determined to be the proceeds of disposition of the interest in the partnership to the deceased individual by virtue of paragraph 70(5)(a) or (6)(d), as the case may be; and

(c) section 43 is not applicable to the right.

Related Provisions: 53(2)(o) — Deductions from ACB; 248(8) — Meaning of "consequence" of death.

Definitions [s. 98.2]: "amount", "individual" — 248(1); "partnership" — see 96(1) Notes; "property", "taxpayer" — 248(1).

Interpretation Bulletins [s. 98.2]: IT-242R: Retired partners; IT-278R2: Death of a partner or of a retired partner; IT-349R3: Intergenerational transfers of farm property on death.

99. (1) Fiscal period of terminated partnership — Subject to
subsection (2), if, at any particular time in a fiscal period of a partnership, the partnership would, if this Act were read without reference to subsection 98(1), have ceased to exist, the fiscal period is deemed to have ended immediately before the time that is immediately before that particular time.

Related Provisions: 127.52(1)(c.1), (c.2) — Exclusion from minimum tax.

Notes: The deeming rule in pre-2013 99(1) applied before 98(5)(f) for purposes of 98(1): VIEWS doc 2011-0403001E5. See also 2013-0477711E5 (windup of LP); 2014-0525441R3 (loss consolidation ruling); 2015-0617101R3 (partner's share of partnership final-period income or loss included in ACB of partnership interest before disposition [Papale, "No Double Taxation When a Partnership Ceases to Exist", 8(1) *Canadian Tax Focus* (ctf.ca) 9 (Feb. 2018)]).

99(1) amended by 2002-2013 technical bill, effective June 26, 2013, essentially to add the second "immediately before" [Tamaki, "Draft Technical Amendments", X(3) *Business Vehicles* (Federated Press) 531-32 (2005)].

(2) Fiscal period of terminated partnership for individual
member — Where an individual was a member of a partnership that, at any time in a fiscal period of a partnership, has or would have, but for subsection 98(1), ceased to exist, for the purposes of computing the individual's income for a taxation year the partnership's fiscal period may, if the individual so elects and subsection 249.1(4) does not apply in respect of the partnership, be deemed to have ended immediately before the time when the fiscal period of the partnership would have ended if the partnership had not so ceased to exist.

Related Provisions: 25(1) — Parallel rule for individuals; 99(3), (4) — Validity of election.

Notes: If the individual is resident in Quebec, the 99(2) election must be copied to Revenu Québec: *Taxation Act* ss. 601, 21.4.6.

99(2) amended by 1995 Budget, for fiscal periods that begin after 1994.

I.T. Technical News: 9 (calculation of the adjusted cost base of a partnership interest).

Interpretation Bulletins: IT-179R: Change of fiscal period.

Information Circulars: 76-19R3: Transfer of property to a corporation under s. 85.

(3) Validity of election — An election under subsection (2) is not
valid unless the individual was resident in Canada at the time when the fiscal period of the partnership would, if the election were valid, be deemed to have ended.

Related Provisions: 96(4)–(7) — Elections.

(4) Idem — An election under subsection (2) is not valid if, for the
individual's taxation year in which a fiscal period of the partnership would not, if the election were valid, be deemed to have ended but in which it would otherwise have ended, the individual elects to have applicable the rules set out in the *Income Tax Application Rules* that apply when two or more fiscal periods of a partnership end in the same taxation year.

Definitions [s. 99]: "Canada" — 255; "fiscal period" — 99(1), (2), 249.1; "individual" — 248(1); "member" — 102(2); "partnership" — see 96(1) Notes; "resident in Canada" — 94(3)(a), 250; "taxation year" — 11(2), 249; "taxpayer" — 248(1).

100. (1) Disposition of interest in a partnership — If, as part
of a transaction or event or series of transactions or events, a taxpayer disposes of an interest in a partnership and an interest in the partnership is acquired by a person or partnership described in any of paragraphs (1.1)(a) to (d), then notwithstanding paragraph 38(a), the taxpayer's taxable capital gain for a taxation year from the disposition of the interest is deemed to be the total of

(a) $\frac{1}{2}$ of such portion of the taxpayer's capital gain for the year from the disposition as may reasonably be regarded as attributable to increases in the value of any partnership property of the partnership that is capital property (other than depreciable property) held directly by the partnership or held indirectly by the partnership through one or more other partnerships, and

(b) the whole of the remaining portion of that capital gain.

Related Provisions: 100(1.3) — Exception — disposition to non-resident; 100(1.4), (1.5) — Anti-avoidance rule; 100(5) — Deemed capital loss on amount paid following disposition of partnership interest; 248(10) — Series of transactions.

Notes: 100(1)–(1.5) prevent transferring a partnership interest to a tax-exempt person to then trigger accrued gains on partnership property without paying tax. See Blanchet, "The Impact of the 2012 Budget", 2012 Cdn Tax Foundation conference report at 10:1-13; Doucette, "Partnerships: Anti-avoidance Rules", 2(2) *The Newsletter* (Tax Executives Institute, Toronto Chapter) 9-11 (Dec. 2012); Sherman & Saddington, "100 1 Damnations!", XVIII(3) *Corporate Finance* (Federated Press) 2126-29 (2012); Yip, "Recent Legislation Affecting Partnerships", 61(1) *Canadian Tax Journal* 229-256 (2013); Fabbro, "Dispositions of Partnership Interests", 2162 *Tax Topics* (CCH) 1-4 (Aug. 15, 2013).

In *Oxford Properties*, 2018 FCA 30 (leave to appeal denied 2018 CarswellNat 7871 (SCC)), paras. 111-116, the combination of a 97(2) rollover, 88(1)(d) bump, 98(3) partnership windup and a sale to a tax-exempt entity — after the 3-year time limit in 69(11) — frustrated the object of 100(1)(b) so as to trigger GAAR in 245(2). See Crosbie, "Oxford Properties", XXI(2) *Corporate Finance* (Federated Press) 2-8 (2018); Stirling, "Partnership Bump Flattened by GAAR", 66(2) *Canadian Tax Journal* 408-20 (2018).

For CRA interpretation see VIEWS doc 2013-0482431E5 (100(1) and RRSP trusts).

100(1) amended by 2012 budget bill #2, last change effective for dispositions after Aug. 13, 2012, and amended retroactively by 2017 budget bill #2 to parenthesize "other than depreciable property". Earlier amended by 2000 Budget.

(1.1) Acquisition by certain persons or partnerships —
Subject to subsection (1.2), subsection (1) applies in respect of a disposition of a partnership interest by a taxpayer if the interest is acquired by

(a) a person exempt from tax under section 149;

(b) a non-resident person;

(c) another partnership to the extent that the interest can reasonably be considered to be held, at the time of its acquisition by the other partnership, indirectly through one or more partnerships, by a person that is

(i) exempt from tax under section 149,

(ii) a non-resident, or

(iii) a trust resident in Canada (other than a mutual fund trust) if

(A) an interest as a beneficiary (in this subsection and subsection (1.2) having the meaning assigned by subsection 108(1)) under the trust is held, directly or indirectly through one or more other partnerships, by a person that is exempt from tax under section 149 or that is a trust (other than a mutual fund trust), and

(B) the total fair market value of the interests as beneficiaries under the trust held by persons referred to in clause (A) exceeds 10% of the fair market value of all the interests as beneficiaries under the trust; or

(d) a trust resident in Canada (other than a mutual fund trust) to the extent that the trust can reasonably be considered to have a beneficiary that is

(i) exempt from tax under section 149,

(ii) a partnership, if

(A) an interest in the partnership is held, whether directly or indirectly through one or more other partnerships, by one or more persons that are exempt from tax under section 149 or are trusts (other than mutual fund trusts), and

(B) the total fair market value of the interests held by persons referred to in clause (A) exceeds 10% of the fair market value of all the interests in the partnership, or

(iii) another trust (other than a mutual fund trust), if

(A) one or more beneficiaries under the other trust are a person exempt from tax under section 149, a partnership or a trust (other than a mutual fund trust), and

(B) the total fair market value of the interests as beneficiaries under the other trust held by the beneficiaries referred to in clause (A) exceeds 10% of the fair market value of all the interests as beneficiaries under the other trust.

Related Provisions: 100(1.2) — *De minimis* exception.

Notes: See Notes to 100(1) for discussion of 100(1.1)–(1.5).

100(1.1) added by 2012 budget bill #2, effective Aug. 14, 2012, with certain grandfathering to end of 2012.

(1.2) *De minimis* — Subsection (1) does not apply to a taxpayer's disposition of a partnership interest to a partnership or trust described in paragraph (1.1)(c) or (d) — other than a trust under which the amount of the income or capital to be distributed at any time in respect of any interest as a beneficiary under the trust depends on the exercise by any person or partnership of, or the failure by any person or partnership to exercise, any discretionary power — if the extent to which subsection (1) would, but for this subsection, apply to the taxpayer's disposition of the interest because of subsection (1.1) does not exceed 10% of the taxpayer's interest.

Notes: 100(1.2) added by 2012 budget bill #2, on the same basis as 100(1.1).

(1.3) Exception — non-resident person — Subsection (1) does not apply in respect of a disposition of an interest in a partnership by a taxpayer to a person referred to in paragraph (1.1)(b) if

(a) property of the partnership is used, immediately before and immediately after the acquisition of the interest by the non-resident person, in carrying on business through one or more permanent establishments in Canada; and

(b) the total fair market value of the property referred to in paragraph (a) equals at least 90% of the total fair market value of all property of the partnership.

Notes: 100(1.3) added by 2012 budget bill #2, effective March 29, 2012.

Regulations: 8201 (permanent establishment).

(1.4) Anti-avoidance — dilution — Subsection (1.5) applies in respect of a taxpayer's interest in a partnership if

(a) it is reasonable to conclude that one of the purposes of a dilution, reduction or alteration of the interest was to avoid the application of subsection (1) in respect of the interest; and

(b) as part of a transaction or event or series of transactions or events that includes the dilution, reduction or alteration, there is

(i) an acquisition of an interest in the partnership by a person or partnership described in any of paragraphs (1.1)(a) to (d), or

(ii) an increase in, or alteration of, an interest in the partnership held by a person or partnership described in any of paragraphs (1.1)(a) to (d).

Notes: See Notes to 100(1). 100(1.4) added by 2012 budget bill #2, effective on the same basis as 100(1.1).

(1.5) Deemed gain — dilution — If this subsection applies in respect of a particular interest in a partnership of a taxpayer, then for the purposes of subsection (1),

(a) the taxpayer is deemed to have disposed of an interest in the partnership at the time of the dilution, reduction or alteration;

(b) the taxpayer is deemed to have a capital gain from the disposition equal to the amount by which the fair market value of the particular interest immediately before the dilution, reduction or alteration exceeds its fair market value immediately thereafter; and

(c) the person or partnership referred to in paragraph (1.4)(b) is deemed to have acquired an interest in the partnership as part of the transaction or event or series of transactions or events that includes the disposition referred to in paragraph (a).

Related Provisions: 100(1.4) — Conditions for 100(1.5) to apply.

Notes: 100(1.5) added by 2012 budget bill #2, effective on the same basis as 100(1.1).

(2) Gain from disposition of interest in partnership — In computing a taxpayer's gain for a taxation year from the disposition of an interest in a partnership, there shall be included, in addition to the amount thereof determined under subsection 40(1), the amount, if any, by which

(a) the total of all amounts required by subsection 53(2) to be deducted in computing the adjusted cost base to the taxpayer, immediately before the disposition, of the interest in the partnership,

exceeds

(b) the total of

(i) the cost to the taxpayer of the interest in the partnership determined for the purpose of computing the adjusted cost base to the taxpayer of that interest at that time, and

(ii) all amounts required by subsection 53(1) to be added to the cost to the taxpayer of that interest in computing the adjusted cost base to the taxpayer of that interest at that time.

Related Provisions: 100(5) — Deemed capital loss on amount paid following disposition of partnership interest.

Interpretation Bulletins: IT-268R4: *Inter vivos* transfer of farm property to child; IT-278R2: Death of a partner or of a retired partner.

(2.1) Idem — Where, as a result of an amalgamation or merger, an interest in a partnership owned by a predecessor corporation has become property of the new corporation formed as a result of the amalgamation or merger and the predecessor corporation was not related to the new corporation, the predecessor corporation shall be deemed to have disposed of the interest in the partnership to the new corporation immediately before the amalgamation or merger for proceeds of disposition equal to the adjusted cost base to the predecessor corporation of the interest in the partnership at the time of the disposition and the new corporation shall be deemed to have acquired the interest in the partnership from the predecessor corporation immediately after that time at a cost equal to the proceeds of disposition.

Related Provisions: 87(2)(e.1) — Partnership interest.

Notes: For an example of 100(2.1) applying see VIEWS doc 2007-0251001E5.

Income Tax Folios: S4-F7-C1: Amalgamations of Canadian corporations [replaces IT-474R2].

(3) Transfer of interest on death — Where by virtue of the death of an individual a taxpayer has acquired a property that was an interest in a partnership immediately before the individual's death (other than an interest to which, immediately before the individual's death, section 98.1 applied) and the taxpayer is not a member of the partnership and does not become a member of the partnership by reason of that acquisition,

(a) the taxpayer shall be deemed to have acquired a right to receive partnership property and not to have acquired an interest in a partnership;

(b) the taxpayer shall be deemed to have acquired the right referred to in paragraph (a) at a cost equal to the amount determined to be the proceeds of disposition of the interest in the partnership to the deceased individual by virtue of paragraph 70(5)(a) or (6)(d), as the case may be; and

(c) section 43 is not applicable to the right.

Related Provisions: 53(2)(o) — Deduction from ACB; 248(8) — Meaning of "consequence" of death.

Interpretation Bulletins: IT-278R2: Death of a partner or of a retired partner; IT-349R3: Intergenerational transfers of farm property on death.

(4) Loss re interest in partnership — Notwithstanding paragraph 39(1)(b), the capital loss of a taxpayer from the disposition at any time of an interest in a partnership is deemed to be the amount of the loss otherwise determined minus the total of all amounts each of which is the amount by which the taxpayer's share of the partnership's loss, in respect of a share of the capital stock of a corporation that was property of a particular partnership at that time, would have been reduced under subsection 112(3.1) if the fiscal period of every partnership that includes that time had ended immediately before that time and the particular partnership had disposed of the share immediately before the end of that fiscal period for proceeds equal to its fair market value at that time.

Related Provisions: 40(3.7) — Application to non-resident individual; 53(2)(c)(i)(C) — Rule ignored in determining reduction in ACB; 100(5) — Deemed capital loss on amount paid following disposition of partnership interest; 107.4(3)(b)(ii) — Application of stop-loss rule to qualifying disposition.

Notes: For CRA interpretation see doc 2009-0315431I7 (interaction with 40(3.4)).

100(4) amended by 1995-97 technical bill, for dispositions after April 26, 1995.

(5) Replacement of partnership capital — A taxpayer who pays an amount at any time in a taxation year is deemed to have a capital loss from a disposition of property for the year if

(a) the taxpayer disposed of an interest in a partnership before that time or, because of subsection (3), acquired before that time a right to receive property of a partnership;

(b) that time is after the disposition or acquisition, as the case may be;

(c) the amount would have been described in subparagraph 53(1)(e)(iv) had the taxpayer been a member of the partnership at that time; and

(d) the amount is paid pursuant to a legal obligation of the taxpayer to pay the amount.

Notes: 100(5) added by 2002-2013 technical bill (Part 5 — technical), effective for 1995 and later taxation years.

Definitions [s. 100]: "adjusted cost base" — 54, 248(1); "amount" — 248(1); "arm's length" — 251(1); "beneficiary" — 108(1); "business" — 248(1); "Canada" — 255, *Interpretation Act* 35(1); "capital gain" — 39(1)(a), 248(1); "capital loss" — 39(1)(b), 248(1); "capital property" — 54, 248(1); "corporation" — 248(1), *Interpretation Act* 35(1); "depreciable property" — 13(21), 248(1); "disposition" — 248(1); "fair market value" — see 69(1) Notes; "fiscal period" — 249(2)(b), 249.1; "member" — 102(2); "mutual fund trust" — 132(6)-(7), 132.2(3)(n), 248(1); "non-resident" — 248(1); "partnership" — see 96(1) Notes; "permanent establishment" — Reg. 8201; "person", "property" — 248(1); "resident in Canada" — 94(3)(a), 250; "series of transactions" — 248(10); "share" — 248(1); "taxable capital gain" — 38(a), 248(1); "taxation year" — 249; "taxpayer" — 248(1); "trust" — 104(1), 248(1), (3); "written" — *Interpretation Act* 35(1)"writing".

101. Disposition of farmland by partnership — Where a taxpayer was a member of a partnership at the end of a taxation year of the partnership in which the partnership disposed of land used in a farming business of the partnership, there may be deducted in computing the taxpayer's income for the taxpayer's taxation year in which the taxation year of the partnership ended, ½ of the total of all amounts each of which is an amount in respect of that taxation year of the taxpayer or any preceding taxation year of the taxpayer

ending after 1971, equal to the taxpayer's loss, if any, for the year from the farming business, to the extent that the loss

(a) was, by virtue of section 31, not deductible in computing the taxpayer's income for the year;

(b) was not deducted for the purpose of computing the taxpayer's taxable income for the taxpayer's taxation year in which the partnership's taxation year in which the land was disposed of ended, or for any preceding taxation year of the taxpayer;

(c) did not exceed that proportion of the total of

(i) taxes (other than income or profits taxes or taxes imposed by reference to the transfer of the property) paid by the partnership in its taxation year ending in the year or payable by it in respect of that taxation year to a province or a Canadian municipality in respect of the property, and

(ii) interest paid by the partnership in its taxation year ending in the year or payable by it in respect of that taxation year, pursuant to a legal obligation to pay interest on borrowed money used to acquire the property or on any amount as consideration payable for the property,

(to the extent that the taxes and interest were included in computing the loss of the partnership for that taxation year from the farming business), that

(iii) the taxpayer's loss from the farming business for the year

is of

(iv) the partnership's loss from the farming business for its taxation year ending in the year; and

(d) did not exceed the remainder obtained when

(i) the total of each of the taxpayer's losses from the farming business for taxation years preceding the year (to the extent that those losses are included in computing the amount determined under this section in respect of the taxpayer)

is deducted from

(ii) twice the amount of the taxpayer's taxable capital gain from the disposition of the land.

Related Provisions: 53(1)(i) — Corresponding rule for non-partnerships — addition to ACB; 96(1.01)(a) — Income allocation to former partner; 96(1.1) — Allocation of share of income to retiring partner; 111(7) — Limitation on loss carryforward.

Notes: "Land" can include buildings: see 70(5.2) Notes.

101 amended by 2000 Budget, for tax years that end after Oct. 17, 2000.

Definitions [s. 101]: "amount", "borrowed money", "business", "farming" — 248(1); "land" — see 70(5.2) Notes; "member" — 102(2); "partnership" — see 96(1) Notes; "property" — 248(1); "province" — *Interpretation Act* 35(1); "taxable capital gain" — 38(a), 248(1); "taxable income" — 2(2), 248(1); "taxation year" — 249; "taxpayer" — 248(1).

102. (1) Definition of "Canadian partnership" — In this Subdivision, "Canadian partnership" means a partnership all of the members of which were, at any time in respect of which the expression is relevant, resident in Canada.

Related Provisions: 80(1) — "Eligible Canadian partnership"; 94(4)(b) — Deeming non-resident trust to be resident in Canada does not apply to para. (b); 96(8) — Anti-avoidance rules; 212(13.1)(b) — Non-Canadian partnership deemed non-resident for withholding tax purposes; 248(1)"Canadian partnership" — Definition applies to entire Act; *Income Tax Conventions Interpretation Act* 6.2 — Partnership with Canadian resident partner cannot be resident in another country.

Notes: CRA will issue a Certificate of Residency for tax-treaty purposes to confirm a partnership is a Canadian partnership and all partners are Canadian resident: see Notes to 250(1).

A partnership that has a Canadian partnership as a member can still be a Canadian partnership: VIEWS doc 9121825.

(2) Member of a partnership — In this Subdivision, a reference to a person or a taxpayer who is a member of a particular partnership shall include a reference to another partnership that is a member of the particular partnership.

Notes: 102(2) applies to tiered partnerships, to ensure that a partnership can be a partner without needing to consider the ultimate partners. For parallel rules in other contexts see 93.1(3) and Topical Index under Tiers of partnerships. For an example of

102(2) applying see VIEWS doc 2012-0436521E5. The source and location of income is preserved through each level of a tiered partnership: *Devon Canada*, 2013 TCC 415, para. 45 (FCA appeal discontinued A-431-13).

102(1) and (2) were 102(a) and (b) before RSC 1985 (5th Supp) consolidation for tax years ending after Nov. 1991.

Definitions [s. 102]: "Canada" — 255; "partnership" — see 96(1) Notes; "person" — 248(1); "resident in Canada" — 250; "taxpayer" — 248(1).

Interpretation Bulletins [s. 102]: IT-123R6: Transactions involving eligible capital property; IT-338R2: Partnership interests — effects on adjusted cost base resulting from the admission or retirement of a partner (cancelled); IT-413R: Election by members of a partnership under subsection 97(2); IT-417R: Merger of partnerships.

103. (1) Agreement to share income, etc., so as to reduce or postpone tax otherwise payable

— Where the members of a partnership have agreed to share, in a specified proportion, any income or loss of the partnership from any source or from sources in a particular place, as the case may be, or any other amount in respect of any activity of the partnership that is relevant to the computation of the income or taxable income of any of the members thereof, and the principal reason for the agreement may reasonably be considered to be the reduction or postponement of the tax that might otherwise have been or become payable under this Act, the share of each member of the partnership in the income or loss, as the case may be, or in that other amount, is the amount that is reasonable having regard to all the circumstances including the proportions in which the members have agreed to share profits and losses of the partnership from other sources or from sources in other places.

Related Provisions: 96(1.01)(a) — Income allocation to former partner; 103(1.1) — Unreasonable allocation of income; 103(2) — Meaning of "losses"; 248(1) — Definition of "specified proportion".

Notes: In *XCO Investments (West Topaz)*, 2007 FCA 53, a partnership held real estate with accrued capital gains. An unrelated company (Woodwards) with unused business losses took an 80% interest in the partnership. The partnership sold the property, allocating 80% of the gain to Woodwards to be sheltered by its losses. 103(1) applied to reallocate most of the gain back to the original partners.

Similarly, in *594710 B.C.*, 2018 FCA 166, corporate partners nearing the end of a profitable partnership year were sold to an unrelated public corp with unused losses, and wound up so that all the income was allocated to it; this was held to either trigger 103(1), or violate GAAR by abusing 96(1)(f) and 103(1).

103(1) applied in *Penn West Petroleum*, 2007 TCC 190 (FCA appeal discontinued A-236-07), to undo a disproportionate allocation to one partner of proceeds of disposition. The Court doubted that partners can contractually set the division of partnership income for tax purposes without that applying for civil purposes. See Edward Rowe, "Penn-West", V(1) *Resource Sector Taxation* (Federated Press) 322-29 (2007).

103(1) also applied in *Aquilini*, 2019 TCC 132 (FCA appeal heard June 23/21) (partnership allocations of income to corporations and losses to individuals provided distorted returns relative to capital invested and work done).

103(1) and (1.1) did not apply in *Stow*, 2010 TCC 406: the taxpayer's 80% investment in a partnership (shortly before its year-end with losses) was a real investment.

103(1) may apply to "preference units" in a partnership: *Income Tax Technical News* 30; VIEWS doc 2007-0227191E5. 103(1) would also likely apply if a partnership were used for an estate freeze: doc 2004-0070001C6; or based on partners' need for CCA: 2011-0431171E5. 103(1) can apply to a limited partnership: 2006-0170071E5; 2007 STEP Conference Roundtable q.18 (www.step.ca). The CRA may refuse to issue an advance ruling on 103(1) and (1.1), leaving it to Audit to determine the facts (e.g. 2008-0272731R3, 2010-0367231E5), but did rule in 2011-0421261R3, 2012-0447491R3 (incorporation of professional partner), and 2011-0421971R3 (same).

Partners' income allocation should recognize both capital and non-monetary contributions to prevent 103(1) or (1.1) from applying: Revenue Canada Round Table, 1992 Cdn Tax Foundation conference report, Q. 13, p. 54:9.

See also Notes to 96(1), para. "Wolfe Goodman...", re streaming of income.

See also Demchenko & Somayaji, "The Taxation of Partnerships: Selected Issues", 63(3) *Canadian Tax Journal* 851 (2015), at 858-65; Morphy, "Reasonable Allocations in Resource Partnerships", XI(2) *Resource Sector Taxation [RST]* (Federated Press) 24-28 (2017); Morphy & Biggar, "The Mineral Tax Act (British Columbia) and Partnerships", XV(1) *RST* 6-8 (2021); and s. 67 Notes re "reasonable".

I.T. Technical News: 30 (computation/allocation of partnership income and losses).

(1.1) Agreement to share income, etc., in unreasonable proportions

— Where two or more members of a partnership who are not dealing with each other at arm's length agree to share any income or loss of the partnership or any other amount in respect of any activity of the partnership that is relevant to the computation of the income or taxable income of those members and the share of

any such member of that income, loss or other amount is not reasonable in the circumstances having regard to the capital invested in or work performed for the partnership by the members thereof or such other factors as may be relevant, that share shall, notwithstanding any agreement, be deemed to be the amount that is reasonable in the circumstances.

Related Provisions: 96(1.01)(a) — Income allocation to former partner.

Notes: See Notes to 103(1) re "reasonable". 103(1.1) applied in: *Spencer*, 2003 TCC 343 (husband/wife partnership loss allocation changed from 90/10 to 75/25); *Krauss*, 2010 FCA 284 ($125,000 annual income for $100 partnership contribution was unreasonable); *Aquilini*, 2019 TCC 132 (FCA appeal heard June 23/21) (partnership allocations provided distorted returns [103(1.1) does not need a tax avoidance purpose to apply: para. 65]). It did not apply in *Stow* (see Notes to 103(1)) or *Paajanen*, 2011 TCC 310 (legitimate reason for sisters to share income unequally).

In a farming partnership or when one partner is on maternity leave, 100% allocation to the partner who provides all the labour for a period is reasonable: VIEWS docs 2010-0365421E5, 2010-0369581E5, 2011-0399411C6. Allocation based on ownership of units was ruled reasonable in 2011-0421261R3. The amount of a partner's work, time and expertise level are all factors considered: 2012-0454001C6 [2012 APFF q.7], 2013-0493971I7. See also 2002-0132797 (103(1.1) applies); 2015-0595821C6 [2015 APFF q.18] (general comments).

Interpretation Bulletins: IT-231R2: Partnerships — partners not dealing at arm's length.

(2) Definition of "losses"

— For the purposes of this section, the word "losses" when used in the expression "profits and losses" means losses determined without reference to other provisions of this Act.

Related Provisions: 96(1.1) — Allocation of share of income to retiring partner.

Definitions [s. 103]: "amount" — 248(1); "arm's length" — 251(1); "assessment" — 248(1); "losses" — 103(2); "member" — 102(2); "partnership" — see 96(1) Notes; "specified proportion" — 248(1); "taxable income" — 2(2), 248(1).

Interpretation Bulletins: IT-338R2: Partnership interests — effects on adjusted cost base resulting from the admission or retirement of a partner (cancelled).

Subdivision K — Trusts and Their Beneficiaries

104. (1) Reference to trust or estate

— In this Act, a reference to a trust or estate (in this Subdivision referred to as a "trust") shall, unless the context otherwise requires, be read to include a reference to the trustee, executor, administrator, liquidator of a succession, heir or other legal representative having ownership or control of the trust property, but, except for the purposes of this subsection, subsection (1.1), subparagraph (b)(v) of the definition "disposition" in subsection 248(1) and paragraph (k) of that definition, a trust is deemed not to include an arrangement under which the trust can reasonably be considered to act as agent for all the beneficiaries under the trust with respect to all dealings with all of the trust's property unless the trust is described in any of paragraphs (a) to (e.1) of the definition "trust" in subsection 108(1).

> **Possible Future Amendment — Employee ownership trusts**
>
> **Federal Budget, Chapter 3, April 19, 2021**: See under 7(1).

Related Provisions: 75(2) — Revocable or reversionary trust; 94(3)(a) — Non-resident trust deemed resident in Canada; 94(3)(f) — Deemed separate trust for non-resident portion of non-resident trust that is deemed resident in Canada; 104(1.1) — Restricted meaning of "beneficiary"; 108(1) — Meaning of "trust"; 122(1) — High rate of tax for most trusts; 128(1)(b), 128(2)(b) — Estate of bankrupt deemed not to be a trust; 146.1(1)"trust" — RESPs — meaning of "trust"; 212.1(5)–(7) — Cross-border surplus stripping using trusts; 233.2(4) — Reporting requirement re transfers to foreign trust; 233.6(1) — Reporting requirement re distributions from foreign trust; 248(1)"disposition"(b)(v) — Where trustee ceasing to act as agent of beneficiary; 248(1)"estate" — Definition applies to entire Act; 248(1)"trust" — Definition applies to entire Act; 248(3) — Deemed trusts in Quebec; 251(1)(b) — Personal trust and beneficiary deemed not to deal at arm's length.

Notes: A trust is deemed to be an individual (104(2)), files a return (T3; see 150(1)(c)) and pays tax as a separate person, normally at the top marginal rate: 122(1)(a). When a person dies, the person's estate (represented by the executor or administrator) is treated as a trust (248(1)"trust") until the deceased's affairs are wound up and all assets are distributed to beneficiaries: VIEWS docs 2006-0184741E5, 2011-0411841C6 (and opening words of 104(1)). For the first 36 months it can qualify under 248(1)"graduated rate estate" as a GRE, and get various benefits including low marginal tax rates (122(1) opening words, 117(2)).

If the deceased's will creates a trust, that is a "testamentary trust" under 108(1), separate from the estate: *Hess*, 2011 TCC 360. It can survive long beyond the estate's windup and must file its own annual T3, but it gets no special benefits and pays tax at the top rate (unless it is a "qualified disability trust" under 122(3)). At common law, an estate is not a trust: *Homer*, 2009 TCC 219, paras. 13-17; *Milne Estate*, 2019 ONSC 579 (saying a will is not a trust); but 248(1)"trust" and "estate" now make an estate a trust for ITA purposes, overruling *Lipson*, 2012 TCC 20. See 2009-0330271C6 on the relationship between the trustee and the trust property.

Generally, trust T can deduct income paid out to beneficiary B (104(6)), and B includes it in income (104(13)). The character of dividends, capital gains and foreign income (earned by T) can be preserved in B's hands by electing under 104(19)-(22.4). T's losses cannot be flowed out to B: 108(5)(b). Unrealized gains on T's property can sometimes be deferred by rolling out property to B under 107(2).

A trust's (or estate's) income from business or property is calculated under the normal rules in 9(1), and trustee (or executor) fees are deductible to the extent they are incurred for purposes of earning income: VIEWS doc 2008-0278801C6.

Once a trust's income has been capitalized — normally by being reported and taxed — the capital can be received tax-free: VIEWS doc 2004-0105141E5. This leads to obvious tax planning ideas for receiving capital from a non-resident trust (NRT) whose income has been capitalized but was not taxed in Canada. See s. 94 for detailed anti-avoidance rules that deem certain NRTs to be resident in Canada; and Notes to 250(1) re where a trust is resident.

Where a trust has non-resident or exempt beneficiaries, Part XII.2 tax may apply. See Notes to 210(1)"designated beneficiary". A trust with any beneficiaries in California may be subject to California tax: Cardinal Point, "How California Taxes a Canadian Trust", tinyurl.com/calif-can-tax.

Audits: Starting 2022, new rules requiring disclosure of beneficial interests (see proposed 150(1.2) and Reg. 204.2) will enhance CRA's ability to audit trusts. Per 2012 Ont. Tax Conf (ctf.ca) roundtable, Q3, frequent audit concerns include: eligibility of shares for capital gains exemption; large dividends, gains or carrying charges; trust income allocated to non-beneficiaries; circular dividends between related entities; using a series of trusts to move income to a lower-rate province; the 21-year rule (104(4)); aggressive use of 164(6); active business reported in a trust. Per VIEWS doc 2014-0523061C6 [2014 STEP q.6], issues Rulings has addressed for Audit include: carrying charges; gifts by will; 75(2) attribution; late or amended 104(21) designations; 105(1) benefits; 112(3.2) stop-loss rule. See also 2011-0398351C6 [2011 CLHIA q.1]; May 2011 ICAA roundtable (tinyurl.com/cra-abtax), q.12; Jeanne Cheng, "The CRA's Audit Crackdown on Family Trusts", 19(4) *Tax for the Owner-Manager* (ctf.ca) 3-4 (Oct. 2019). An auditor may find a non-resident trust to be resident in Canada under 94(3), or based on "central management and control" (see Notes to 250(1)).

Definition of "trust": a relationship whereby a *settlor* contributes *property*, to be held (legal title) by a *trustee*, for benefit of a *beneficiary*. There must be "three certainties" of intention, subject matter and object: *Century Services [Leroy Trucking]*, 2010 SCC 60, para. 83; Waters, *Waters' Law of Trusts in Canada* (Carswell, 4th ed., 2012), chap. 5; Oosterhoff et al., *Oosterhoff on Trusts* (Carswell, 9th ed., 2019), chap. 4; Thaw, *Taxation of Mutual Fund Trusts and Corporations* (Carswell, looseleaf or *Taxnet Pro* Reference Centre), chap. 2; Pavlich, *Trusts in Common-Law Canada* (LexisNexis, 3rd ed., 2019), chap. 4; *Davis*, 2008 TCC 31. As well, delivery of the trust property to the trustee needs to be legally completed. For certainty of intention, it is advisable to ensure the settlor has read and understands the trust document. In *Duca Financial v. Bozzo*, 2011 ONCA 455, where B declared that he held shares in trust for his wife, the Court ruled he did not because he retained control of them, so there was no certainty of intention. In *Mason*, 2014 TCC 297, para. 17 (aff'd 2016 FCA 15), the certainties were not met. 104(1) does not assist in determining whether a trust exists, and provincial law must be applied: VIEWS doc 2008-0264381E5 (see also Notes to *Interpretation Act* s. 8.1). A trust in common-law provinces (if not in respect of land) need not be in writing: *Hartstein v. Ricottone*, 2016 ONCA 913; *Goldman*, 2021 TCC 13, para. 32. (In Quebec, see *Civil Code* ss. 1262, 1824.) A statutory trust is not always a real trust: *British Columbia Investment Management Corp*, 2019 SCC 63, para. 62. A trustee has fiduciary obligations to the beneficiaries and may be liable for delegating his or her duties: *Penman v. Penman*, 2014 ONCA 83. BC and New Brunswick have a *Conflict of Laws Rules for Trusts Act* to determine what province's law governs a trust. In Quebec, see 248(3) Notes. There can also be a "secret trust", created orally; in *Bergler v. Odenthal*, 2020 BCCA 175, testamentary instructions a deceased gave her common-law spouse created such a trust; and see *Gefen v. Gaertner*, 2019 ONSC 6015, paras. 147-148.

The common-law "rule against perpetuities" prevents a trust from lasting beyond a certain number of years, except where overridden by provincial legislation, e.g. Nova Scotia *Perpetuities Act* [Niedermayer, "Dynastic Dynamism", xl(9) *The Canadian Taxpayer* (Carswell) 65-67 (May 4, 2018)]. However, a trust must recognize accrued gains every 21 years: 104(4).

An escrow arrangement may be set up as a trust: Hennel, "Escrow Arrangements in Acquisition Agreements", 2176 *Tax Topics* (CCH) 1-4 (Nov. 21, 2013). If there are multiple settlors, 75(2) may deem income earned on the funds to be taxed in the wrong hands. It can be preferable to avoid a trust, and instead create a bare trust, agency or bailment: Lang & Woltersdorf, "A Fresh Look at Tax Clauses in Acquisition Agreements", 2013 Cdn Tax Foundation conference report at 12:36-38.

In *Antle*, 2010 FCA 280 (leave to appeal denied 2011 CarswellNat 1491 (SCC); motion for reconsideration dismissed 2012 CarswellNat 183), an attempted capital property step-up through a Barbados spousal trust failed because the trust was not validly constituted as a trust (there was no real intention to settle shares in a discretionary trust and the shares were not properly transferred to the trustee) and was a sham.

In *Sommerer*, 2011 TCC 212, the TCC held that an Austrian Privatstiftung (foundation) was not a trust, but a trustee of a trust. The FCA doubted this was correct (2012 FCA 207, para. 43), but did not resolve the issue. See also Donovan Waters, "Private Foundations (Civil Law) Versus Trusts (Common Law)", 21(4) *Estates, Pensions & Trusts Journal* 281-330 (Oct. 2002) for detail on private foundations (privatstiftung) in Liechtenstein, Austria, Panama, Netherlands Antilles and Luxembourg.

Foreign arrangements: CRA has said the following are trusts: German investment fund (fiduziarische Treuhand) (VIEWS docs 2004-0106101R3, 2005-0135761R3, 2007-0235881R3); Liechtenstein foundation (stiftung) (2008-0266251I7, 2008-0278801C6 q.10, 2010-0388611I7, 2015-0581681E5 [apparently overruling 2003-0018027]); Liechtenstein Trust Enterprise (2010-0353701I7, 2011-0392131I7); Netherlands Antilles private foundation (2008-0289461I7); a particular Pennsylvania business trust even though it had no settlor, was a purpose trust, had perpetual existence and was a legal entity (2007-0236981I7). See also 2008-0284241C6 (CRA review of an Austrian foundation, a Liechtenstein foundation and some German investment funds concluded that they were trusts). The following are considered co-ownership arrangements, not trusts (see 248(1)"corporation" Notes): Irish or other Common Contractual Fund; Luxembourg fonds commun de placement; Dutch closed FGR. The CRA does not have a list of foreign entities that it considers to be trusts: 2015-0581961C6 [2015 STEP q.8]. See also Notes to 248(1)"corporation". *Yu*, 2018 FCA 68, rejected a claim that funds transferred were not subject to 160(1) because they were held in trust under Chinese custom: "If a trust is to be established in Canada, it must be established in accordance with the laws of Canada" (para. 22). See also Kandev & Milet, "Foreign Trusts", 2017 Cdn Tax Foundation conference report, 29:1-36; Gvelesiani, *Trusts and Trust-Like Devices* (LexisNexis, 2021, 140pp).

See generally Chow & Pryor, *Taxation of Trusts and Estates 2021* (Carswell, 681pp); *Miller Thomson on Estate Planning* (Carswell, looseleaf or ProView), chap. 3 "Trusts and their Taxation" and chap. 7 "Administration of Estates and Trusts"; Roth et al., *Canadian Taxation of Trusts* (ctf.ca, 2016, 1185pp); Tobias, *Taxation of Corporations, Partnerships and Trusts* (Carswell, 5th ed., 2017), chaps. 4-5; Kessler & Hunter, *Drafting Trusts and Will Trusts* (LexisNexis, 2020, 640pp); Kerr & Sorensen, "Use of Special Purpose Trusts", 2007 Cdn Tax Foundation conference report, 35:1-48; Radu & Matthews, "Trust Administration — Best Practices", 2010 Atlantic Provinces Tax Conference (ctf.ca), 4A:1-20; Worland, "Constant and Current Issues in the Taxation of Domestic Trusts", 2010 BC Tax Conf 4:1-54; Caruk, "Trust Principles", 2010 Prairie Provinces Tax Conf [PPTC] 3:1-33; Brown, "The Use of 'Regular' Corporations as Trustees", IV(1) *Personal Tax and Estate Planning* (Federated Press) 162-66 (2011); Truster, "Corporate Beneficiaries of Discretionary Family Trusts: The Part IV Tax Trap", 12(2) *Tax for the Owner-Manager [TfOM]* (ctf.ca) 4 (April 2012); MacKnight, "Using a Trust as a Unilateral Marriage Contract", 12(4) *TfOM* 6-8 (Oct. 2012); Bonora, "Trusts: Drafting with Intention", 2013 PPTC 3A:1-9; Eberl, "Canadian Trust Subject to US Tax", 27(6) *Canadian Tax Highlights* (ctf.ca) 8-9 (June 2019); Marples, "The Intersection of Trust Law and Tax", 2019 BC Tax Conf 4:1-49; Angelini, "Sham trusts and how to expose them", 34(1) *Money & Family Law* (Carswell) 84-85 (Nov. 2019); Hoffstein, "The Intersection of Trust Law and Tax Law", 2019 Ont. Tax Conf 3 (154pp).

A sole trustee cannot be removed unless a replacement can be appointed, at least in some jurisdictions: *Novak v. McDougall*, 2019 SKQB 261, para. 16.

On having a power to change beneficiaries see Goldberg, "Not Quite Chicken Soup", 2174 & 2175 *Tax Topics* (CCH) 1-3 (Nov. 7 & 14, 2013) or 227 & 228 *The Estate Planner* (CCH) 1-3 (Dec. 2013, Jan. 2014); Roth & Goldberg, "Powers to Add and Remove Trust Beneficiaries", 30(1) *Money & Family Law* (Carswell) 76-80 (Oct. 2015), 30(11) 82-85 (Nov. 2015) and 30(12) 90-92 (Dec. 2015).

A *constructive trust* or *resulting trust* is one deemed by the common law for equity (fairness) purposes, such as where a common-law spouse has provided services to the other for years (*Peter v. Beblow*, [1993] 1 S.C.R. 980 (SCC); *Darte*, 2008 TCC 66; *McInerney v. Laass*, 2015 BCSC 1708); or where ex-husband breached agreement to keep ex-wife as beneficiary of his life insurance: *Moore v. Sweet*, 2018 SCC 52, paras. 91-95. See Donovan Waters, *Waters' Law of Trusts in Canada* (Carswell, 4th ed., 2012), chaps. 10-11 "The Resulting Trust" and "The Constructive Trust"; Oosterhoff et al., *Oosterhoff on Trusts* (Carswell, 9th ed., 2019), chaps. 9-12; Thomas Bauer, "Constructively Yours", 3(5) *Canadian Tax Highlights* (ctf.ca) 33-34 (May 1995); Brown & Rajan, "Constructive and Resulting Trusts", 45(4) *Canadian Tax Journal* 659-89 (1997); Nathens & Schwartz, "Trust Me — This Property is Mine", 33(10) *Money & Family Law* (Carswell) 76-78 (Nov. 2018). Quebec law differs, as the *Civil Code* does not recognize a constructive trust or implied trust: *Groupe Sutton-Royal*, 2015 QCCA 1069, para. 90 (leave to appeal denied 2016 CarswellQue 3452 (SCC)).

Revocable living trust and protective trust: CRA considers these to be trusts: *Income Tax Technical News* 7; VIEWS docs 2013-0490891I7, 2016-0645781C6 [2016 STEP q10]; but see also 2014-0560361E5 (might be agency, not trust). (Some call a so-called protective trust a "blind trust".) See also Hassan article in next para.; and Notes to 248(1)"alter ego trust".

A *bare trust* is a non-entity for tax purposes: the beneficiary is considered to deal directly with the property through the bare trustee as agent or nominee. See the "agent" exception in 104(1); IT-216; Income Tax Folio S1-F3-C2 ¶2.79-2.82; VIEWS docs 2008-0280771E5, 2010-0357491E5. There is no disposition on distribution of a bare trust's property to the contributor-beneficiary: 2006-0185601C6. See also end of Notes to 54"capital property"; Notes to 248(1)"disposition" where there is a transfer of title with no change in beneficial ownership; Hassan, "Impact of Canadian Bijuralism on the Taxation of Certain Types of Trusts", *The Harmonization of Federal Legislation with Quebec Civil Law: Second Collection of Studies in Tax Law* (2005, apff.org), 5:1-30; Donald Bowman, "Bare Trusts and Nominee Corporations", 2318 *Tax Topics* (CCH) 1-4 (Aug. 11, 2016) (bare trustee is an agent, not a trustee); Canis, "Why Are Bare Trustees So Prevalent in Real Estate Structures?", 8(3) *Canadian Tax Focus* (ctf.ca) 5-6 (Aug. 2018). In Quebec, a nominee (bare trust) agreement must be disclosed to Revenu Québec: see end of Notes to 54"capital property". In BC, beneficial ownership of real property will need to be disclosed under the *Land Owner Transparency Act*: see Notes to 40(2)(b). Federally and increasingly in the provinces, beneficial ownership of corporations must be disclosed: see Notes to 150(1)(a).

Cases looking through a bare trust as a conduit or agent: *Brookview Investments*, [1963] C.T.C. 316 (Exch.); *Leowski*, [1996] G.S.T.C. 55 (TCC); *La Guercia Investments*, [1996] G.S.T.C. 87; *Cherny*, [1998] G.S.T.C. 97; *De Mond*, [1999] 4 C.T.C. 2007 (TCC), paras. 30-31; *Carnelian Investments*, [1999] G.S.T.C. 92; *Szirtes*, [2000] G.S.T.C. 96; *Coburn Realty*, 2006 TCC 245; *507582 B.C.*, 2008 TCC 447; *Fourney*, 2011 TCC 520; *Peragine*, 2012 TCC 348. See David Sherman's *Canada GST Service* Analysis to ETA 123(1)"person" (also on *GST Partner* and *Taxnet Pro*). *Contra*, in *Moxsom*, 2006 TCC 541, a daughter who received her late father's pension benefits was taxable on them despite sharing them with her siblings as per her father's wishes. Under the GST/HST, a bare trustee may be a "recipient" (person liable to pay for a supply), so a bare trust is not always ignored: *Cheema*, 2018 FCA 45 (leave to appeal to SCC requested). A self-directed RRSP is not a bare trust: *Olympia Trust*, 2015 FCA 279, para. 76. See also R. Daren Baxter, "The Tax Effect of Bare Trust and Agency", 10(12) *Tax Hyperion* (Carswell) 1-3 (Dec. 2013).

For CRA policy on "in trust for" (ITF) accounts see VIEWS docs 9427115, 2002-017676A (detailed review of case law), 2007-0233761C6, 2010-0367571E5; Notes to 54"capital property" re legal title without beneficial ownership; Murray & Chiu, "Bare Trusts: the Bare Bones", XIII(3) *Business Vehicles* (Federated Press) 698-700 (2010).

For an overview of the many different kinds of trust under the Act (*alter ego*, bare, blind, charitable purpose, commercial, discretionary, Henson, health & welfare, immigration, *inter vivos*, joint spousal, mutual fund, non-discretionary, non-resident, personal, pre-1971 *inter vivos*, post-1971 spousal, pre-1972 spousal, real estate investment, resident, revocable, tainted spousal, testamentary and unit trust), see Bernstein & Nicholls, "A Trust Menagerie", 8(3) *Canadian Tax Highlights* (ctf.ca) 21-22 (March 2000). See also Michael Cadesky, "Canadian Taxation of Trusts and Non-Resident Beneficiaries", 2014 STEP Canada conference (contact memberservices@step.ca).

Employee benefits paid via a trust are taxed under s. 6; 104-108 did not apply in *Scott*, 2017 TCC 224, para. 68.

Resettlement of a trust (so it was no longer the same trust and could not carry forward losses) happened in CRA's view where a commercial trust's settlors sold their interests ("the intention of the two original settlors was completely set aside"): VIEWS doc 2014-0526171I7.

Residence of a trust: see Notes to 250(1), and to 111(5) re the dangers of changing trustees of a trust that controls a corporation.

Variation or amendment of trusts: see discussion of rectification in Notes to 169(1); Nitikman, "Life is Change: Using Powers of Amendment in a ... Trust", 65(3) *Canadian Tax Journal* 559-632 (2017); and Notes to 248(1)"disposition" re amendments that do not cause a disposition.

For more CRA interpretations on trusts see VIEWS docs 2010-0367401R3 (effect of variation of testamentary trust); 2010-0373401C6 (consequences of discretionary trust getting Court variation to add a beneficiary); 2010-0373621C6 (general comments on abusive uses of family trusts).

104(1) amended by 2001 technical bill, last change effective for 1999 and later tax years.

Income Tax Folios: S6-F1-C1: Residence of a trust or estate [replaces IT-447].

Interpretation Bulletins: IT-216: Corporation holding property as agent for shareholder (cancelled).

I.T. Technical News: 7 (revocable living trusts, protective trusts, bare trusts); 38 (control of corporation owned by income trust — impact of change in trustees).

CRA Audit Manual: 16.2.0: Estates and trusts program; 16.2.5: Bare trusts.

Charities Guidance: CG-009: Trust document.

(1.1) Restricted meaning of "beneficiary" — Notwithstanding subsection 248(25), for the purposes of subsection (1), paragraph (4)(a.4), subparagraph 73(1.02)(b)(ii) and paragraph 107.4(1)(e), a person or partnership is deemed not to be a beneficiary under a trust at a particular time if the person or partnership is beneficially interested in the trust at the particular time solely because of

(a) a right that may arise as a consequence of the terms of the will or other testamentary instrument of an individual who, at the particular time, is a beneficiary under the trust;

(b) a right that may arise as a consequence of the law governing the intestacy of an individual who, at that time, is a beneficiary under the trust;

(c) a right as a shareholder under the terms of the shares of the capital stock of a corporation that, at the particular time, is a beneficiary under the trust;

(d) a right as a member of a partnership under the terms of the partnership agreement, where, at the particular time, the partnership is a beneficiary under the trust; or

(e) any combination of rights described in paragraphs (a) to (d).

Notes: 104(1.1) opening words amended by 2002-2013 technical bill (Part 5 — technical), effective for 1998 and later taxation years, to change "248(25.1)" to "248(25)".

104(1.1) added by 2001 technical bill, for 1998 and later taxation years.

(2) Taxed as individual — A trust shall, for the purposes of this Act, and without affecting the liability of the trustee or legal representative for that person's own income tax, be deemed to be in respect of the trust property an individual, but where there is more than one trust and

(a) substantially all of the property of the various trusts has been received from one person, and

(b) the various trusts are conditioned so that the income thereof accrues or will ultimately accrue to the same beneficiary, or group or class of beneficiaries,

such of the trustees as the Minister may designate shall, for the purposes of this Act, be deemed to be in respect of all the trusts an individual whose property is the property of all the trusts and whose income is the income of all the trusts.

Related Provisions: 127.53(2), (3) — Multiple trusts must share minimum tax exemption; 248(1)"individual" — Trust is an individual.

Notes: 104(2) prevents creation of multiple testamentary trusts (TTs) with the same beneficiaries in order to take advantage of the low rates of tax before 2016 (see Notes to 122(1)(a)) on low amounts of income. Everything from "but where..." is now not needed for that purpose, since the only trusts that get low marginal rates — 248(1)"graduated rate estate" and 122(3)"qualified disability trust" — have definitions that prevent multiple trusts for the same person. However, CRA might still use 104(2) to "consolidate" trusts' income such as for provincial income-shifting plans.

CRA's view is that since a trust is deemed by 104(2) to be an individual, a trust is related to a beneficiary who is related to the trustee: doc 2009-0311891I7. See also 2009-0330271C6.

Pre-2016: 104(2) does not apply to separate TTs set up by the same will, each of which has a different beneficiary: *Mitchell* (1956), 16 Tax A.B.C. 99; VIEWS doc 2013-0486211E5. Nor does it apply to multiple TTs with the same income beneficiary (deceased's spouse) but different residual beneficiaries (children), as the test must be met over the life of the trust, not annually: *Evoy Estate*, 2016 TCC 263. Nevertheless, the CRA considers that "the same group or class of beneficiaries" can apply to trusts for overlapping family beneficiaries: 2002-0162865, 2011-0430261E5, 2013-0486211E5, although CRA may accept valid non-tax reasons for multiple trusts: 2004-0090941E5. Where a will creates trusts for the deceased's children, plus a spousal trust with the residue (on the spouse's death) divided into trusts for the same children, 104(2) could apply: 2006-0178031E5. See also May 2013 ICAA q.14 (tinyurl.com/cra-abtax). Where the deceased made two wills, one to be probated and one not (to save probate fees or Ontario estate administration tax), each creating a spousal trust under 70(6), 104(2) would apply to the trusts, but that should not prevent them from both qualifying under 70(6), and each trust still needs to file a T3: 2010-0358461E5. CRA considers that "substantially all" in para. (a) means 90% or more.

Regulations: 204 (information return).

Income Tax Folios: S6-F1-C1: Residence of a trust or estate [replaces IT-447].

Interpretation Bulletins: IT-406R2: Tax payable by an *inter vivos* trust.

Forms: T3: Statement of trust income allocations and designations; T3-ADJ: T3 adjustment request; T3 Sched. 9: Income allocations and designations to beneficiaries.

(3) [Repealed under former Act]

Notes: 104(3), repealed by 1988 tax reform, prohibited deductions for personal exemptions under 109, also repealed. Personal credits under 118 are now prohibited to trusts by 122(1.1).

(4) Deemed disposition by trust [every 21 years or on death] — Every trust is, at the end of each of the following days, deemed to have disposed of each property of the trust (other than exempt property) that was capital property (other than depreciable property) or land included in the inventory of a business of the trust for proceeds equal to its fair market value (determined with reference to subsection 70(5.3)) at the end of that day and to have reacquired the property immediately after that day for an amount equal

to that fair market value, and for the purposes of this Act those days are

(a) where the trust

(i) is a trust that was created by the will of a taxpayer who died after 1971 and that, at the time it was created, was a trust,

(i.1) is a trust that was created by the will of a taxpayer who died after 1971 to which property was transferred in circumstances to which paragraph 70(5.2)(c) (or, in the case of a transfer that occurred in a taxation year before 2007, (b) or (d), as those paragraphs read in their application to that taxation year) or (6)(d) applied, and that, immediately after any such property vested indefeasibly in the trust as a consequence of the death of the taxpayer, was a trust,

(ii) is a trust that was created after June 17, 1971 by a taxpayer during the taxpayer's lifetime that, at any time after 1971, was a trust, or

(ii.1) is a trust (other than a trust the terms of which are described in clause (iv)(A) that elects in its return of income under this Part for its first taxation year that this subparagraph not apply) that was created after 1999 by a taxpayer during the taxpayer's lifetime and that, at any time after 1999, was a trust

under which

(iii) the taxpayer's spouse or common-law partner was entitled to receive all of the income of the trust that arose before the spouse's or common-law partner's death and no person except the spouse or common-law partner could, before the spouse's or common-law partner's death, receive or otherwise obtain the use of any of the income or capital of the trust, or

(iv) in the case of a trust described in subparagraph (ii.1) created by a taxpayer who had attained 65 years of age at the time the trust was created,

(A) the taxpayer was entitled to receive all of the income of the trust that arose before the taxpayer's death and no person except the taxpayer could, before the taxpayer's death, receive or otherwise obtain the use of any of the income or capital of the trust,

(B) the taxpayer or the taxpayer's spouse was, in combination with the spouse or the taxpayer, as the case may be, entitled to receive all of the income of the trust that arose before the later of the death of the taxpayer and the death of the spouse and no other person could, before the later of those deaths, receive or otherwise obtain the use of any of the income or capital of the trust, or

(C) the taxpayer or the taxpayer's common-law partner was, in combination with the common-law partner or the taxpayer, as the case may be, entitled to receive all of the income of the trust that arose before the later of the death of the taxpayer and the death of the common-law partner and no other person could, before the later of those deaths, receive or otherwise obtain the use of any of the income or capital of the trust,

the day on which the death or the later death, as the case may be, occurs;

(a.1) where the trust is a pre-1972 spousal trust on January 1, 1993 and the spouse or common-law partner referred to in the definition "pre-1972 spousal trust" in subsection 108(1) in respect of the trust was

(i) in the case of a trust created by the will of a taxpayer, alive on January 1, 1976, and

(ii) in the case of a trust created by a taxpayer during the taxpayer's lifetime, alive on May 26, 1976,

the day that is the later of

(iii) the day on which that spouse or common-law partner dies, and

(iv) January 1, 1993;

(a.2) where the trust makes a distribution to a beneficiary in respect of the beneficiary's capital interest in the trust, it is reasonable to conclude that the distribution was financed by a liability of the trust and one of the purposes of incurring the liability was to avoid taxes otherwise payable under this Part as a consequence of the death of any individual, the day on which the distribution is made (determined as if a day ends for the trust immediately after the time at which each distribution is made by the trust to a beneficiary in respect of the beneficiary's capital interest in the trust);

(a.3) where property (other than property described in any of subparagraphs 128.1(4)(b)(i) to (iii)) has been transferred by a taxpayer after December 17, 1999 to the trust in circumstances to which subsection 73(1) applied, it is reasonable to conclude that the property was so transferred in anticipation that the taxpayer would subsequently cease to reside in Canada and the taxpayer subsequently ceases to reside in Canada, the first day after that transfer during which the taxpayer ceases to reside in Canada (determined as if a day ends for the trust immediately after each time at which the taxpayer ceases to be resident in Canada);

(a.4) where the trust is a trust to which property was transferred by a taxpayer who is an individual (other than a trust) in circumstances in which section 73 or subsection 107.4(3) applied, the transfer did not result in a change in beneficial ownership of that property and no person (other than the taxpayer) or partnership has any absolute or contingent right as a beneficiary under the trust (determined with reference to subsection (1.1)), the day on which the death of the taxpayer occurs;

(b) the day that is 21 years after the latest of

(i) January 1, 1972,

(ii) the day on which the trust was created, and

(iii) where applicable, the day determined under paragraph (a), (a.1) or (a.4) as those paragraphs applied from time to time after 1971; and

(c) the day that is 21 years after any day (other than a day determined under any of paragraphs (a) to (a.4)) that is, because of this subsection, a day on which the trust is deemed to have disposed of each such property.

Related Provisions: 53(4) — Effect on ACB of share, partnership interest or trust interest; 54"principal residence"(c.1)(iii.1)(A) — Principal residence exemption; 54"superficial loss"(c) — Superficial loss rule does not apply; 70(5.3) — Value of property that depends on life insurance policy; 70(5.31) — Leveraged insurance annuity — FMV rule; 70(6)(a) — Where transfer or distribution to spouse or trust; 70(9.1), (9.11) — Transfer of farm or fishing property from spouse trust to settlor's children; 73(1.01) — *Inter vivos* transfer of property to spouse trust; 94 — Certain non-resident trusts deemed resident; 104(1.1) — Restricted meaning of "beneficiary" for 104(4)(a.4); 104(5) — Deemed disposition of depreciable property; 104(5.8) — Trust transfers; 104(6) — Deduction in computing income of trust; 104(13.4) — Death of beneficiary — spousal and similar trusts; 104(15)(a) — Allocable amount for preferred beneficiary election; 107(4) — Distributions from trust; 107.4(3)(h) — Qualifying disposition to a trust; 108(1) — "accumulating income"; 108(1)"cost amount"(a.1) — Cost amount before death of taxpayer; 108(1)"trust" — Exclusions to meaning of "trust"; 108(3) — Meaning of "income" of trust; 108(4) — Trust payment of duties and taxes; 108(6) — Where terms of trust are varied; 127.55(e) — Application of minimum tax; 132.11(4) — Amounts paid from December 16-31 by mutual fund trust to beneficiary; 138.1(1) — Rules re segregated funds; 139.1(5) — Value of ownership rights in insurer during demutualization; 159(6.1) — Election to postpone payment of tax on deemed disposition; 248(1)"*alter ego*" trust" — Name for trust described in 104(4)(a)(iv)(A); 248(1)"joint spousal or common-law partner trust" — Name for trust described in 104(4)(a)(iv)(B); 248(8) — Meaning of "consequence" of death; 248(9.1) — Whether trust created by taxpayer's will; 248(9.2) — Meaning of "vested indefeasibly"; 252(3) — Extended meaning of "spouse".

Notes: 104(4) is the "21-year deemed disposition rule", forcing trusts (except those listed in 108(1)"trust"(g)) to recognize and pay tax on their accrued capital gains every 21 years. (A similar rule for depreciable property applies under 104(5), and for resource property under 104(5.2).) For the meaning of "fair market value" see Notes to 69(1). The tax can be paid over 10 years (with interest); see 159(6.1). Under 104(5.3) the first disposition could be deferred until Jan. 1, 1999 in certain cases. The deemed disposition does not apply to "exempt property" or "excluded property", both as defined in 108(1), so for non-residents it applies only to taxable Canadian property that is not treaty-protected property. Nor does it apply to a unit trust, or a trust in which all interests have vested indefeasibly: 108(1)"trust"(f), (g) (see Notes to 248(9.2) for meaning of "vested indefeasibly"). The 21 years start running on day of death for a testamentary trust in CRA's view: see Notes to 108(1)"testamentary trust".

For a life insurance policy, or shares whose value is in part based on a life insurance policy, see 70(5.3) for a special rule.

104(4) also applies to a spousal trust [70(6)(b), 73(1.01)(c)] on the day the spouse dies: 104(4)(a). (The deferred gain cannot be flowed out to a beneficiary: *Levatte Estate*, 2019 TCC 177, para. 4.) The deemed disposition is "at the end of" that day (104(4) opening words). It was arguably avoidable with a 107(2) rollout of property after death and before midnight that day, but no longer, due to the 2013 amendment to 107(4): 107(4)(a) will apply as the spouse has died, and 107(4)(b) will apply as the distribution is before the deemed "reacquired the property immediately after that day" in 104(4) opening words.

One way to avoid the 21-year rule is to roll the property out under 107(2). In *Kanji*, 2013 ONSC 781, where the trust was subject to 75(2) so 107(4.1) prevented the rollout, the Court refused to rectify the trust deed to allow 107(2) to apply. However, in *Fishleigh-Eaton v. Eaton-Kent*, 2013 ONSC 7985, the Court ordered non-retroactive variation of a trust to allow encroachment on capital, so that 107(2) could be used to avoid tax that would be triggered by 104(4). (See Notes to 169(1) on rectification.)

Anti-avoidance: Rolling property into a new trust (e.g., under 107.4) does not postpone the deemed disposition, as under 104(5.8)(a)(i)(A) the new trust inherits the old trust's "disposition day"; and see Notes to 104(5.8). CRA will apply GAAR to schemes that avoid 104(4), such as a 107(2) distribution to a Canco where the beneficiaries are non-resident: 2017-0720321C6 [2017 APFF q.4], 2017-0724301C6 [2017 CTF q.1]; or to a Canco whose shares are held by a new trust: 2017-0693321C6 [2017 STEP q.2]. See also Notes to 104(19) re 2017-0683021I7 (transfer of capital interests to a ULC).

See Roth et al., *Canadian Taxation of Trusts* (ctf.ca, 2016), pp. 544-85; Goodman, "Some Methods of Dealing with the 21-Year Deemed Disposition", VIII(3) *Goodman on Estate Planning* (Federated Press) 623-26 (1999); "Coping with Deemed Realization of Trust Property", IX(4) 740-49 (2001); Youdan, "Planning to Deal with the 21-Year Deemed Disposition Rule", 2008 Ontario Tax Conference (ctf.ca), 4:1-16; Stephan, "Understanding and Dealing With the 21-Year Deemed Disposition Rules", 2008 Prairie Provinces Tax Conf. 14:1-35; Rudick, "New TCP Definition: 21-year Trust Rule", 18(7) *Canadian Tax Highlights* (ctf.ca) 7-8 (July 2010); Bernstein, "21-year Rule: US Beneficiary", 19(4) *CTH* 8-9 (April 2011); Burns, Prior & Roth, "21-Year Deemed Disposition Planning" (62 slides), 2012 STEP Canada conference (contact memberservices@step.ca); Brown, "Planning for the 21-Year Rule and Trusts for Minors", 4(3) *Personal Tax and Estate Planning* (Federated Press) 186-91 (2013); Baxter and Miedema, "Trusts — The 21-Year Rule", 2013 Atlantic Provinces Tax Conf. 4:1-20; Blucher, "21-Year Deemed Disposition Rule Planning With Non-Resident Beneficiaries", 11(6) *TH* 5-6 (June 2014); Shannon & Baxter, "21 Year Deemed Disposition Rule", 2014 STEP Canada conference; Balsara, "GAAR and Trust 21-Year Planning", XXII(3) *Insurance Planning* (Federated Press) 8-12 (2017); Ward, "Twenty-One Years is Not Enough: Avoiding Canada's 21-Year Rule with Trusts for US Beneficiaries", 46(11) *Tax Management International Journal* (Bloomberg) 710-12 (Nov. 10, 2017); Ideias, "The 21-year Rule: What a Tax Planner Needs to Know" (*Taxnet Pro* Tax & Estate Planning Centre, 2021, 9pp); Hamelin, "Pipeline Transactions and the 21-Year Rule", 19(2) *Tax for the Owner-Manager* (ctf.ca) 1-2 (April 2019) (re doc 2018-0765411R3).

In *Green*, 2012 TCC 10, a trust failed to report and pay tax on the capital gain, and later transferred the property to a beneficiary, who was held to have acquired it at the trust's original cost due to 107(2). (This seems wrong since 104(4) deems the trust to have reacquired the property at FMV, whether or not it pays the tax.)

"Land" in 104(4) opening words can include buildings: see 70(5.2) Notes.

For a trust under 104(4)(a)(iv)(A), see Notes to 248(1)"alter ego trust".

For CRA interpretation of 104(4) see VIEWS docs 2006-0187741E5, 2006-0196501R3, 2007-0243581R3, 2010-0371031E5, 2010-0379431E5; 2010-0390911E5 (interaction with 70(5.3); 2011-0399501E5 (non-resident trust is subject to 104(4)(b)); 2011-0401831C6 (104(4) applies to a 75(2) trust); 2011-0411851C6; 2012-0453971C6 (successive testamentary trusts in Quebec); 2012-0459531E5 (104(4) applies to gross royalty trust certificates held by estate); 2013-0486001C6 (deemed disposition day of transferee trust where 104(5.8) applies); 2016-0645821C6 [2016 STEP q.11] (application to spouse trust whose terms are changed).

104(4) opening words amended by 2017 budget bill #2, for taxation years that begin after 2016, to delete "excluded property or" before "depreciable property". (108(1)"excluded property" now defines the term for a different purpose.)

104(4) earlier amended by 2002-2013 technical bill (for trust tax years that begin after 2006), 2001 technical bill, 2000 same-sex partners bill, 1995-97 technical bill, 1995 Budget, 1992 technical bill.

The draft non-resident trusts legislation of 2002-2009 (eventually enacted by 2002-2013 technical bill) proposed a 104(4)(a.5) which would have applied the 21-year rule with a new start date to a trust deemed resident by 94(3). This was dropped as of the Aug. 27, 2010 draft, as it did not work properly in the situation where some contributors with unlimited liability elected under 94(16) and others did not. The normal 21-year rule in 104(4) still applies.

104(4.1), proposed in the Foreign Investment Entity rules dropped in 2010, was withdrawn and will not be enacted.

Income Tax Folios: S1-F3-C2: Principal residence [replaces IT-120R6, IT-437R]; S2-F1-C1: Health and welfare trusts [replaces IT-85R2].

Interpretation Bulletins: IT-286R2: Trusts — amounts payable; IT-325R2: Property transfers after separation, divorce and annulment; IT-349R3: Intergenerational transfers of farm property on death; IT-370: Trusts — capital property owned on December 31, 1971 (cancelled); IT-381R3: Trusts — capital gains and losses and the flow-through of taxable capital gains to beneficiaries; IT-394R2: Preferred beneficiary election; IT-449R: Meaning of "vested indefeasibly" (cancelled); IT-465R — Non-resident beneficiaries of trusts.

Advance Tax Rulings: ATR-38: Distribution of all of the property of an estate.

Forms: T1055: Summary of deemed dispositions.

(5) Depreciable property [deemed disposition] — Every trust is, at the end of each day determined under subsection (4) in respect of the trust, deemed to have disposed of each property of the trust (other than exempt property) that was a depreciable property of a prescribed class of the trust for proceeds equal to its fair market value at the end of that day and to have reacquired the property immediately after that day at a capital cost (in this subsection referred to as the "deemed capital cost") equal to that fair market value, except that

(a) where the amount that was the capital cost to the trust of the property immediately before the end of the day (in this paragraph referred to as the "actual capital cost") exceeds the deemed capital cost to the trust of the property, for the purpose of sections 13 and 20 and any regulations made for the purpose of paragraph 20(1)(a) as they apply in respect of the property at any subsequent time,

(i) the capital cost to the trust of the property on its reacquisition shall be deemed to be the amount that was the actual capital cost to the trust of the property, and

(ii) the excess shall be deemed to have been allowed under paragraph 20(1)(a) to the trust in respect of the property in computing its income for taxation years that ended before the trust reacquired the property;

(b) for the purposes of this subsection, the reference to "at the end of a taxation year" in subsection 13(1) shall be read as a reference to "at the particular time a trust is deemed by subsection 104(5) to have disposed of depreciable property of a prescribed class"; and

(c) for the purpose of computing the excess, if any, referred to in subsection 13(1) at the end of the taxation year of a trust that included a day on which the trust is deemed by this subsection to have disposed of a depreciable property of a prescribed class, any amount that, on that day, was included in the trust's income for the year under subsection 13(1) as it reads because of paragraph (b), shall be deemed to be an amount included under section 13 in the trust's income for a preceding taxation year.

Related Provisions: 70(9.1), (9.11) — Transfer of farm or fishing property from spouse trust to settlor's children; 104(5.8) — Trust transfers; 104(6) — Deduction in computing income of trust; 108(1) — "accumulating income"; 108(1)"cost amount"(a.1) — Cost amount before death of taxpayer; 108(1)"trust" — Exclusions to meaning of "trust"; 108(6) — Where terms of trust are varied.

Notes: The deemed disposition of depreciable property may lead to recapture under 13(1) (where the undepreciated capital cost of the class goes negative) and/or a capital gain under 39(1) (where current fair market value exceeds the adjusted cost base). If the deemed disposition takes place on the last day of the taxation year (Dec. 31 for an *inter vivos* trust, or the day first picked under 104(23)(a) for a testamentary trust), then since the deemed reacquisition is not until the next day, there can be a terminal loss under 20(16) (where UCC is positive and no assets are left in the class at year-end). Thus, creating a trust on Dec. 31 is a planning strategy that could entitle the trust to a terminal loss 21 years later!

Where a person transfers depreciable property used in a business carried on in Canada to a trust under 73(1), and then emigrates, 104(5) will not apply due to the exception in 104(4)(a.3) for property described in 128.1(4)(b)(i)-(iii): VIEWS doc 2004-0104951E5.

Opening words of 104(5) amended by 2001 technical bill, to add "(other than exempt property), effective for days after December 23, 1998 that are determined under 104(4). Exempt property is defined in 108(1). Earlier amended by 1993 technical bill and 1992 technical bill.

Interpretation Bulletins: IT-286R2: Trusts — amount payable; IT-349R3: Intergenerational transfers of farm property on death; IT-381R3: Trusts — capital gains and losses and the flow-through of taxable capital gains to beneficiaries; IT-394R2: Preferred beneficiary election; IT-465R: Non-resident beneficiaries of trusts.

Forms: T1055: Summary of deemed dispositions.

(5.1) NISA Fund No. 2 [deemed disposition] — Every trust that holds an interest in a NISA Fund No. 2 that was transferred to it in circumstances to which paragraph 70(6.1)(b) applied is deemed, at the end of the day on which the spouse or common-law partner referred to in that paragraph dies, to have been paid an amount out of the fund equal to the balance at the end of that day in the fund so transferred.

Related Provisions: 104(5.8) — Trust transfers; 104(6) — Deduction in computing income of trust; 252(3) — Extended meaning of "spouse".

Notes: 104(5.1) amended by 2014 budget bill #2, for 2016 and later taxation years, due to the repeal of 104(14.1).

104(5.1) amended by 2000 same-sex partners bill to refer to "common-law partner", effective as per Notes to 248(1)"common-law partner". 104(5.1) added by 1992 technical bill, effective 1991.

Forms: T1055: Summary of deemed dispositions.

(5.2) Resource property [deemed disposition] — Where at the end of a day determined under subsection (4) in respect of a trust, the trust owns a Canadian resource property (other than an exempt property) or a foreign resource property (other than an exempt property),

(a) for the purposes of determining the amounts under subsection 59(1), paragraphs 59(3.2)(c) and (c.1), subsections 66(4) and 66.2(1), the definition "cumulative Canadian development expense" in subsection 66.2(5), the definition "cumulative foreign resource expense" in subsection 66.21(1), subsection 66.4(1) and the definition "cumulative Canadian oil and gas property expense" in subsection 66.4(5), the trust is deemed

(i) to have a taxation year (in this subsection referred to as the "old taxation year") that ended at the end of that day and a new taxation year that begins immediately after that day, and

(ii) to have disposed, immediately before the end of the old taxation year, of each of those properties for proceeds that became receivable at that time equal to its fair market value at that time and to have reacquired, at the beginning of the new taxation year, each such property for an amount equal to that fair market value; and

(b) for the particular taxation year of the trust that included that day, the trust shall

(i) include in computing its income for the particular taxation year the amount, if any, determined under paragraph 59(3.2)(c) in respect of the old taxation year and the amount so included shall, for the purposes of the determination of B in the definition "cumulative Canadian development expense" in subsection 66.2(5), be deemed to have been included in computing its income for a preceding taxation year,

(i.1) include in computing its income for the particular taxation year the amount, if any, determined under paragraph 59(3.2)(c.1) in respect of the old taxation year and the amount so included is, for the purpose of determining the value of B in the definition "cumulative foreign resource expense" in subsection 66.21(1), deemed to have been included in computing its income for a preceding taxation year, and

(ii) deduct in computing its income for the particular taxation year the amount, if any, determined under subsection 66(4) in respect of the old taxation year and the amount so deducted shall, for the purposes of paragraph 66(4)(a), be deemed to have been deducted for a preceding taxation year.

Related Provisions: 104(5.8) — Trust transfers; 104(6) — Deduction in computing income of trust; 108(1) — "accumulating income"; 108(1) — "trust"; 108(6) — Where terms of trust are varied; 159(6.1) — Election to postpone payment of tax.

Notes: 104(5.2) opening words and para. (a) amended by 2000 Budget/2001 technical bill (effective for days after December 23, 1998) that are determined under amended 104(4) and 2000 Budget (effective for taxation years that begin after 2000).

Interpretation Bulletins: IT-394R2: Preferred beneficiary election.

(5.3)–(5.7) [Repealed]

Notes: 104(5.3)-(5.7) allowed deferral of the 21-year deemed disposition rule (104(4)) for certain family trusts. They were added by 1992 technical bill, effective Feb. 12, 1991. The impetus for their enactment was the existence of pre-1972 trusts (from the era before capital gains were taxed) that would have had to recognize and pay tax on their accrued capital gains due to a deemed disposition under 104(4)(b)(i) on Jan. 1, 1993. The deferral was eliminated as part of a political response to concerns about tax deferral through family trusts. This was done by the 1995 Budget, retroactive to Feb. 12, 1991, adding "before 1999" in the opening words of 104(5.3) and adding 104(5.3)(a)(i). Thus, the election was not available after 1998, and if it had been made, the deemed disposition occurred on Jan. 1, 1999.

Note that a "roll-out" of the trust assets to the beneficiaries under 107(2) can still defer recognition of gains on the assets.

As 104(5.3)-(5.7) had expired, they were repealed by 2002-2013 technical bill, for tax years that begin after Oct. 2011. Earlier amended by 2001 technical bill, 2000 same-sex partners bill, 1995 Budget.

(5.8) Trust transfers — Where capital property, land included in inventory, Canadian resource property or foreign resource property is transferred at a particular time by a trust (in this subsection referred to as the "transferor trust") to another trust (in this subsection referred to as the "transferee trust") in circumstances in which subsection 107(2) or 107.4(3) or paragraph (f) of the definition "disposition" in subsection 248(1) applies,

(a) for the purposes of applying subsections (4) to (5.2) after the particular time,

(i) subject to paragraphs (b) to (b.3), the first day (in this subsection referred to as the "disposition day") that ends at or after the particular time that would, if this section were read without reference to paragraph (4)(a.2) and (a.3), be determined in respect of the transferee trust is deemed to be the earliest of

(A) the first day ending at or after the particular time that would be determined under subsection (4) in respect of the transferor trust without regard to the transfer and any transaction or event occurring after the particular time,

(B) the first day ending at or after the particular time that would otherwise be determined under subsection (4) in respect of the transferee trust without regard to any transaction or event occurring after the particular time,

(C) the first day that ends at or after the particular time, where

(I) the transferor trust is a joint spousal or common-law partner trust, a post-1971 spousal or common-law partner trust or a trust described in the definition "pre-1972 spousal trust" in subsection 108(1), and

(II) the spouse or common-law partner referred to in paragraph (4)(a) or in the definition "pre-1972 spousal trust" in subsection 108(1) is alive at the particular time,

(C.1) the first day that ends at or after the particular time, where

(I) the transferor trust is an *alter ego* trust, a trust to which paragraph (4)(a.4) applies or a joint spousal or common-law partner trust; and

(II) the taxpayer referred to in paragraph (4)(a) or (a.4), as the case may be, is alive at the particular time, and

(D) where

(I) the disposition day would, but for the application of this subsection to the transfer, be determined under paragraph (5.3)(a) in respect of the transferee trust, and

(II) the particular time is after the day that would, but for subsection (5.3), be determined under paragraph (4)(b) in respect of the transferee trust,

the first day ending at or after the particular time, and

(ii) where the disposition day determined in respect of the transferee trust under subparagraph (i) is earlier than the day referred to in clause (i)(B) in respect of the transferee trust, subsections (4) to (5.2) do not apply to the transferee trust on the day referred to in clause (i)(B) in respect of the transferee trust;

(b) paragraph (a) does not apply in respect of the transfer where

(i) the transferor trust is a post-1971 spousal or common-law partner trust or a trust described in the definition "pre-1972 spousal trust" in subsection 108(1),

(ii) the spouse or common-law partner referred to in paragraph (4)(a) or in the definition "pre-1972 spousal trust" in subsection 108(1) is alive at the particular time, and

(iii) the transferee trust is a post-1971 spousal or common-law partner trust or a trust described in the definition "pre-1972 spousal trust" in subsection 108(1);

(b.1) paragraph (a) does not apply in respect of the transfer where

(i) the transferor trust is an *alter ego* trust,

(ii) the taxpayer referred to in paragraph (4)(a) is alive at the particular time, and

(iii) the transferee trust is an *alter ego* trust;

(b.2) paragraph (a) does not apply in respect of the transfer where

(i) the transferor trust is a joint spousal or common-law partner trust,

(ii) either the taxpayer referred to in paragraph (4)(a), or the spouse or common-law partner referred to in that paragraph, is alive at the particular time, and

(iii) the transferee trust is a joint spousal or common-law partner trust;

(b.3) paragraph (a) does not apply in respect of the transfer where

(i) the transferor trust is a trust to which paragraph (4)(a.4) applies,

(ii) the taxpayer referred to in paragraph (4)(a.4) is alive at the particular time, and

(iii) the transferee trust is a trust to which paragraph (4)(a.4) applies; and

(c) for the purposes of subsection (5.3), unless a day ending before the particular time has been determined under paragraph (4)(a.1) or (b) or would, but for subsection (5.3), have been so determined, a day determined under subparagraph (a)(i) shall be deemed to be a day determined under paragraph (4)(a.1) or (b), as the case may be, in respect of the transferee trust.

Related Provisions: 248(25.1) — Trust-to-trust transfers.

Notes: 104(5.8) prevents avoidance of the 21-year deemed realization rule by trust transfers. See VIEWS docs 2004-0089251R3 (allows indirect transfer via a corporation, to freeze the value of property of a testamentary spousal trust); 2005-0143361R3 (transfer of assets from 3 trusts into 5 new trusts); 2012-0459621E5 (deemed disposition day where election made under 104(5.3) before 1999); 2013-0486001C6 (same); 2016-0669301C6 [2016 CTF q.1] (getting property to a new trust in a way that bypasses 104(5.8) triggers GAAR). "Land" in 104(5.8) opening words can include buildings: see 70(5.2) Notes.

In *Ozerdinc Family Trust v. Gowling Lafleur*, 2017 ONSC 6, a lawyer set up a family trust in 1990, then rolled its assets into a new trust in 2007 to prevent the children getting the assets too early; he failed to advise the trustees about the 21-year rule applying to the trusts, and was liable in negligence.

104(5.8) opening words amended by 2017 budget bill #2, to delete "(other than excluded property)" after "Where capital property", for taxation years that begin after 2016. (108(1)"excluded property" now defines the term for a different purpose.)

104(5.8) amended by 2001 technical bill (last change effective for transfers after 1999), 2000 same-sex partners bill (effective 2001) and 1992 technical bill.

(6) Deduction in computing income of trust — Subject to subsections (7) to (7.1), for the purposes of this Part, there may be deducted in computing the income of a trust for a taxation year

(a) in the case of an employee trust, the amount by which the amount that would, but for this subsection, be its income for the year exceeds the amount, if any, by which

(i) the total of all amounts each of which is its income for the year from a business

exceeds

(ii) the total of all amounts each of which is its loss for the year from a business;

(a.1) in the case of a trust governed by an employee benefit plan, such part of the amount that would, but for this subsection, be its income for the year as was paid in the year to a beneficiary;

(a.2) where the taxable income of the trust for the year is subject to tax under this Part because of paragraph 146(4)(c) or subsection 146.3(3.1), the part of the amount that, but for this subsection, would be the income of the trust for the year that was paid in the year to a beneficiary;

(a.3) in the case of a trust deemed by subsection 143(1) to exist in respect of a congregation that is a constituent part of a religious organization, such part of its income for the year as became payable in the year to a beneficiary;

(a.4) in the case of an employee life and health trust, an amount that became payable by the trust in the year as a designated employee benefit (as defined in subsection 144.1(1)); and

(b) in any other case, the amount that the trust claims not exceeding the amount, if any, determined by the formula

$$A - B$$

where

A is the part of its income (determined without reference to this subsection and subsection (12)) for the year that became payable in the year to, or that was included under subsection 105(2) in computing the income of, a beneficiary, and

B is

(i) if the trust is a trust for which a day is to be determined under paragraph (4)(a) or (a.4) by reference to a death or later death, as the case may be, that has not occurred before the beginning of the year, the total of

(A) the part of its income (determined without reference to this subsection and subsection (12)) for the year that became payable in the year to, or that was included under subsection 105(2) in computing the income of, a beneficiary (other than an individual whose death is that death or later death, as the case may be), and

(B) the total of all amounts each of which

(I) is included in its income (determined without reference to this subsection and subsection (12)) for the year — if the year is the year in which that death or later death, as the case may be, occurs and paragraph (13.4)(b) does not apply in respect of the trust for the year — because of the application of subsection (4), (5), (5.1) or (5.2) or 12(10.2), and

(II) is not included in the amount determined for clause (A) for the year, and

(ii) if the trust is a SIFT trust for the year, the amount, if any, by which

(A) the amount determined for A for the trust for the year

exceeds

(B) the amount, if any, by which the amount determined for A for the trust for the year exceeds its non-portfolio earnings for the year.

Related Provisions: 4(3)(b) — Whether deductions under 104(6) are applicable to a particular source; 18(5.4) — Trust can designate thin-cap interest paid to non-resident as being payment to beneficiary instead; 104(7) — Non-resident beneficiary; 104(7.01) — Limitation where non-resident trust deemed resident in Canada; 104(7.02) — No deduction for amount claimed as charitable donation; 104(7.1) — Deduction denied — capital interest greater than income interest; 104(13) — Income inclusion to beneficiary; 104(13.1), (13.2) — Designation of income distributed to beneficiary; 104(16) — SIFT distribution deemed to be dividend; 104(18) — Trust for minor; 104(24) — Whether amount payable; 107(2.11) — Election to not flow out gain on distribution to beneficiaries; 107.1 — Deemed disposition where employee trust or employee benefit plan distributes property; 108(5) — Restriction on deduction for beneficiary; 111(8)"non-capital loss"(a.1) — Amount under 104(6)(a.4) included in calculation of ELHT's non-capital loss; 120.4 — Income-splitting tax on beneficiary's income; 132.11(6) — Additional income of mutual fund trust electing for December 15 year-end; 135.2(4)(a) — Limitation on deduction for Cdn Wheat Board Farmers' Trust; 138.1(1) — Rules re segregated funds; 144.1(3)(b) — No deduction to employee life and health trust if operated primarily for benefit of key employees; 146.2(6)(c) — No deduction under 104(6) for TFSA that is required to pay Part I tax; 149.1(12) — Rules — charities; 210.2(1) — Part XII.2 tax where trust has non-resident or exempt beneficiaries; 257 — Formula cannot calculate to less than zero.

Notes: The essence of 104(6) for ordinary trusts is 104(6)(b)A — a trust can deduct amounts payable (including paid — but see 104(24)) to beneficiaries, who include such income under 104(13). (By making a preferred beneficiary election under 104(14), a trust can also deduct under 104(12) amounts allocated to disabled "preferred beneficiaries" that are included in those beneficiaries' income without actually being paid.) Once either the trust or the beneficiary has paid tax on the trust's income, that income is "capitalized" and can be paid to beneficiaries free of tax (just as a beneficiary can receive capital of the trust — see Notes to 104(1)). Note that in certain cases the income-splitting tax in 120.4 may apply to the income.

For an unpaid amount to be "payable" and thus deductible, the trust may need to issue a demand promissory note to the beneficiary, in the CRA's view. See Notes to 104(24).

If an amount cannot legally be paid under the trust's terms, it is not "payable" and cannot fall under 104(6) and (13), even if paid (104(24) does not actually deem an amount to be "payable"): VIEWS doc 2016-066397117 [Hamelin, "Trusts and Double Taxation", 17(3) *Tax for the Owner-Manager* (ctf.ca) 11-12 (July 2017); Rodrigo, "Interpretation of Deeming Rules", 7(3) *Canadian Tax Focus* (ctf.ca) 3-4 (Aug. 2017)].

If an amount is deducted but not paid for 3 years, it might have to be reincluded in the trust's income under 78(1), though this is uncertain.

The deduction under 104(6)(b) is for "the amount that the trust claims". A trust might claim less than the maximum in order to keep income taxed at the trust level (e.g., to use up loss carryforwards). It can then make a tax-free distribution of capital to beneficiaries under 104(13.1) or (13.2). This can also allow a graduated rate estate to split income with a beneficiary, using the estate's tax-free or low-tax brackets of income.

104(6)(b)B(ii) limits the deduction that a SIFT trust (see Notes to 104(16)) can claim. It prevents a SIFT trust from deducting under 104(6) any "non-portfolio earnings" (NPE — see 122.1(1)) payable to a beneficiary. Effectively, NPE is the last income to be considered distributed; this is beneficial to the SIFT trust, as it can use non-capital loss carryovers to reduce NPE that are subject to tax.

Payments to third parties on a beneficiary's behalf may not be deductible: *Langer Family Trust*, [1992] 1 C.T.C. 2119 (TCC). CRA allows deduction in some cases: *Income Tax Technical News* 11, but for minor beneficiaries, this is under review: VIEWS doc 2017-0693351C6 [2017 STEP q.10]. See also *Cockeram*, 2004 TCC 307 (aff'd 2005 FCA 372), suggesting third-party payments should be deductible despite *Langer*.

In *Turcotte*, 2015 QCCA 396 (leave to appeal denied 2015 CarswellQue 7382 (SCC)), a donation by will created a credit and could not also be a 104(6) deduction to the estate as an amount paid to a beneficiary.

Where a trust pays income to non-resident or exempt beneficiaries, Part XII.2 or XIII tax may apply. See Notes to 210(1)"designated beneficiary" and 212(1)(c).

See also VIEWS docs 2007-0245281R3 (deduction for capital gains paid out on windup of income trust), 2009-0317641E5 (deduction for corporate dividend flowed out to new corp), 2011-0401851C6 (testamentary spouse trust after spouse's death); 2016-0669871C6 [2016 CTF q.14] (whether an estate can pay income to a residual beneficiary and use 104(6)); 2017-0716451E5 (deduction cannot exceed trust's income net of losses; excess distribution could be taxable under 105(1)); 2018-0768901C6 [2018 APFF q.2] (deduction for 84(2) deemed dividend made payable to beneficiary).

104(6)(a.4) permits an ELHT to deduct "designated employee benefits" (DEB). The deduction is available for DEB that are *payable*, even if not paid out by year-end. If an amount payable is not DEB, the trust will normally be offside and no longer an ELHT for the year, due to 144.1(2)(a) and (g).

104(6) amended by 2016 budget bill #2 (for 2016 and later tax years, adding (b)B(i)(B)), 2014 budget bill #2 (for 2016 and later tax years), 2002-2013 technical bill, 2010 budget bill #2, 2007 budget bill #1, 2001 technical bill, 2000 same-sex partners bill, 1995-97 technical bill, 1995 Budget, 1992 technical bill.

Interpretation Bulletins: IT-286R2: Trusts — amount payable; IT-342R: Trusts — income payable to beneficiaries; IT-381R3: Trusts — capital gains and losses and the flow-through of taxable capital gains to beneficiaries; IT-394R2: Preferred beneficiary election; IT-465R — Non-resident beneficiaries of trusts; IT-493: Agency cooperative corporations; IT-500R: RRSPs — death of annuitant; IT-502: Employee benefit plans and employee trusts.

I.T. Technical News: 11 (payments made by a trust for the benefit of a minor beneficiary); 25 (health and welfare trusts).

CRA Audit Manual: 16.2.3: Income allocated and designated to beneficiaries.

Advance Tax Rulings: ATR-65: Reduction to management fees for large investments in a mutual fund.

(7) Non-resident beneficiary — No deduction may be made under subsection (6) in computing the income for a taxation year of a trust in respect of such part of an amount that would otherwise be its income for the year as became payable in the year to a beneficiary who was, at any time in the year, a designated beneficiary of the trust (as that expression applies for the purposes of section 210.3) unless, throughout the year, the trust was resident in Canada.

Related Provisions: 104(7.01) — Where trust deemed resident in Canada by 94(3); 104(24) — Whether amount payable; 210.2(1) — Part XII.2 tax on trust; 212(1)(c) — Withholding tax on payment to non-resident beneficiary; 250(6.1) — Trust that ceases to exist deemed resident throughout year.

Notes: See Notes to 210(1)"designated beneficiary".

Interpretation Bulletins: IT-393R2: Election re tax on rents and timber royalties — non-residents.

(7.01) Trusts deemed to be resident in Canada [— limitation on deduction] — If a trust is deemed by subsection 94(3) to be resident in Canada for a taxation year for the purpose of computing the trust's income for the year, the maximum amount deductible under subsection (6) in computing its income for the year is the amount, if any, by which

(a) the maximum amount that, if this Act were read without reference to this subsection, would be deductible under subsection (6) in computing its income for the year,

exceeds

(b) the total of

(i) the portion of the trust's designated income for the year (within the meaning assigned by section 210) that became payable in the year to a non-resident beneficiary under the trust in respect of an interest of the non-resident as a beneficiary under the trust, and

(ii) all amounts each of which is determined by the formula

$$A \times B$$

where

A is an amount (other than an amount described in subparagraph (i)) that

(A) is paid or credited (having the meaning assigned by Part XIII) in the year to the trust,

(B) would, if this Act were read without reference to subparagraph 94(3)(a)(viii), paragraph 212(2)(b) and sections 216 and 217, be an amount as a consequence of the payment or crediting of which the trust would have been liable to tax under Part XIII, and

(C) becomes payable in the year by the trust to a non-resident beneficiary under the trust in respect of an interest of the non-resident as a beneficiary under the trust, and

B is

(A) 0.35, if the trust can establish to the satisfaction of the Minister that the non-resident beneficiary to whom the amount described in the description of A is payable is resident in a country with which Canada has a tax treaty under which the income tax that Canada may impose on the beneficiary in respect of the amount is limited, and

(B) 0.6, in any other case.

Related Provisions: 94(1)"exempt amount"(b) — Amount under 104(7.01)(b) is exempt amount for non-resident trust rules; 104(24) — Whether amount payable to beneficiary.

Notes: For interpretation of 104(7.01) see VIEWS docs 2008-0285481C6, 2013-051364117.

104(7.01) added by 2002-2013 technical bill (Part 1 — NRTs), effective for taxation years that end after 2006, and also for each earlier taxation year of a trust to which amended 94(1) applies (see Notes at end of s. 94) and each taxation year of a beneficiary under the trust in which one of those earlier taxation years of the trust ends.

(7.02) Limitation — amount claimed as gift — No deduction may be made under subsection (6) in computing the income for a taxation year of an estate that arose on and as a consequence of an individual's death in respect of a payment to the extent that the payment is a gift in respect of which an amount is deducted under section 118.1 for any taxation year in computing the individual's tax payable under this Part.

Notes: 104(7.02) provides that if a charitable donation credit is claimed on the deceased's terminal return for a gift, then the gift cannot be deducted as a trust income distribution.

104(7.02) added by 2014 budget bill #2, effective for taxation years that end after Aug. 28, 2014.

(7.1) Capital interest greater than income interest — Where it is reasonable to consider that one of the main purposes for the existence of any term, condition, right or other attribute of an interest in a trust (other than a personal trust) is to give a beneficiary a percentage interest in the property of the trust that is greater than the beneficiary's percentage interest in the income of the trust, no amount may be deducted under paragraph (6)(b) in computing the income of the trust.

Related Provisions: 104(7.2) — Anti-avoidance rule.

Notes: For rulings that 104(7.1) does not apply see docs 2002-0159043, 2003-0014473, 2003-0016433, 2005-0126801R3, 2005-0128301R43, 2006-0171431R3, 2006-0181051R3, 2007-0234061R3, 2007-0257551R3, 2010-0361771R3 [RioCan REIT: Smit, "Recent Transactions of Interest", 2011 Cdn Tax Foundation conference report, 10:1-5], 2010-0389921R3, 2011-0410181R3, 2011-0429611R3, 2014-0518521R3, 2015-0578051R3. See also 2012-0448351E5 (mutual fund rebate paid to investor).

For the meaning of "one of the main purposes" see Notes to 83(2.1).

104(7.1) does not apply to a trust created before Nov. 26, 1985 in which no beneficial interest is issued after 5pm EST that day (other than on account of a distribution of the trust's income in accordance with the terms of the trust in effect on that day).

Interpretation Bulletins: IT-381R3: Trusts — capital gains and losses and the flow-through of taxable capital gains to beneficiaries.

Advance Tax Rulings: ATR-65: Reduction to management fees for large investments in a mutual fund.

(7.2) Avoidance of subsec. (7.1) — Notwithstanding any other provision of this Act, where

(a) a taxpayer has acquired a right to or to acquire an interest in a trust, or a right to or to acquire a property of a trust, and

(b) it is reasonable to consider that one of the main purposes of the acquisition was to avoid the application of subsection (7.1) in respect of the trust,

on a disposition of the right (other than pursuant to the exercise thereof), the interest or the property, there shall be included in computing the income of the taxpayer for the taxation year in which the disposition occurs the amount, if any, by which

(c) the proceeds of disposition of the right, interest or property, as the case may be,

exceed

(d) the cost amount to the taxpayer of the right, interest or property, as the case may be.

Notes: For the meaning of "one of the main purposes" in (b), see Notes to 83(2.1).

(8), (9) [Repealed under former Act]

Notes: 104(8), repealed by 1988 tax reform (effective 1988), denied a deduction under 104(6) for distributions to designated beneficiaries. See now the tax in Part XII.2 (210-210.2). 104(9) repealed effective 1974.

(10), (11) [Repealed]

Notes: 104(10), (11) repealed by 2002-2013 technical bill (Part 5 — technical), for 2005 and later tax years. They applied to income a trust received from a non-resident-owned investment corporation. NROs were eliminated after 2003: see Notes to s. 133.

(12) Deduction of amounts included in preferred beneficiaries' incomes — There may be deducted in computing the income of a trust for a taxation year the lesser of

(a) the total of all amounts designated under subsection (14) by the trust in respect of the year, and

(b) the accumulating income of the trust for the year.

Related Provisions: 4(3)(b) — Whether deductions under 104(12) are applicable to a particular source; 104(6) — Deduction in computing trust income; 104(13) — Income payable to beneficiary; 108(1) — Accumulating income defined; 108(5) — Restriction on deduction for beneficiary; 149.1(12) — Rules — charities.

Notes: See Notes to 104(6) and 104(14).

104(12) amended by 1995 Budget, for trust taxation years that begin after 1995.

Interpretation Bulletins: IT-381R3: Trusts — capital gains and losses and the flow-through of taxable capital gains to beneficiaries; IT-394R2: Preferred beneficiary election; IT-465R: Non-resident beneficiaries of trusts; IT-500R: RRSPs — death of an annuitant.

Advance Tax Rulings: ATR-34: Preferred beneficiary's election.

(13) Income of beneficiary — There shall be included in computing the income for a particular taxation year of a beneficiary under a trust such of the following amounts as are applicable:

(a) in the case of a trust (other than a trust referred to in paragraph (a) of the definition "trust" in subsection 108(1)), such part of the amount that, but for subsections (6) and (12), would be the trust's income for the trust's taxation year that ended in the particular year as became payable in the trust's year to the beneficiary; and

(b) in the case of a trust governed by an employee benefit plan to which the beneficiary has contributed as an employer, such part of the amount that, but for subsections (6) and (12), would be the trust's income for the trust's taxation year that ended in the particular year as was paid in the trust's year to the beneficiary.

Related Provisions: 6(1)(h) — Income from employee trust; 12(1)(m) — Income inclusion — benefits from trusts; 18(5.4) — Trust can designate thin-cap interest paid to non-resident as being payment to beneficiary instead; 53(2)(h) — Reduction of ACB of beneficiary's interest re amount paid or payable by trust; 104(13.1), (13.2) — Designation of distributed income by trust; 104(16)(c) — SIFT distribution deemed not to be payable to beneficiary; 104(18) — Trust for minor; 104(19) — Portion of taxable dividends deemed received by beneficiary; 104(21) — Portion of taxable capital gains deemed gain of beneficiary; 104(22)–(22.4) — Foreign tax credit allocation to beneficiary; 104(24) — Whether amount payable; 104(27) — Pension benefits flowed through estate; 104(30), (31) — Deduction for Part XII.2 tax; 106(1) — Income interest in trust; 106(2)(a)(ii) — Reduction of income inclusion on disposition of income interest; 107(2.11) — Election to not flow out gain to beneficiaries on distribution; 107.1 — Deemed cost to beneficiary where employee trust or employee benefit plan distributes property; 107.3(4) — No application to qualifying environmental trusts; 108(5) — Amount deemed to be income from trust; 120.4(5) — Certain capital gains earned through trust deemed to be dividends for income-splitting tax; 120.4 — Income-splitting tax; 132.11(4) — Amounts paid from Dec. 16-31 by mutual fund trust to beneficiary; 132.11(6) — Additional income of MFT electing for Dec. 15 year-end; 146(8.1) — RRSP — deemed receipt of refund of premiums; 210.2(1) — Part XII.2 tax where trust has non-resident or exempt beneficiaries; 212(1)(c) — Non-resident withholding tax; 214(3)(f) — Non-resident withholding tax — deemed payments; 250(6.1) — Trust that ceases to exist deemed resident throughout year; 250.1(b) — Non-resident trust deemed to have income calculated under the Act.

Notes: See Notes to 104(6). The trustee can normally choose whether a payment to beneficiary B is from the trust's income (deductible under 104(6) and taxable to B under 104(13)) or from its capital, to the extent there are both income and capital: VIEWS docs 2002-0183437, 2003-005173I7. An estate can allocate amounts differently to beneficiaries, if the will permits: 2005-0116041E5; but amounts may be "payable" to a residual beneficiary once the "executor's year" has passed: 2017-0703921C6 [2017 CPA Alberta q.25]. A mutual fund trust management fee reimbursed to a unitholder from trust income is taxable: 2012-0459061E5. Money from the capital of an estate is not taxable: 2004-0105141E5 (see Notes to 104(1)). A capital gain distribution by a non-resident trust is only half taxable, due to 250.1: 2012-0448021E5. See also 2010-0376171E5 (income is "payable" and thus taxable if beneficiary can enforce payment, even if it is not paid out); 2013-047550I7 (104(13) applied to income paid to children as agent of taxpayer).

The form of a corporate distribution determines whether a trust can allocate it to beneficiaries as "income" or "capital": Figliomeni, "It's Hard to Break the Form Rule", IX(3) *Personal Tax & Estate Planning* (Federated Press) 2-10 (2020). For the character of the income in the beneficiary's hands, see Notes to 108(5).

Income is taxed in the beneficiary's taxation year in which the trust taxation year ends. For examples see VIEWS docs 2005-0159081I7, 2012-0453041E5. For timing of income recognition from income trusts see 2004-0107751E5; 2011-0403561E5 (on death there is no deemed year-end; pre-death distributions would seem to be included in the terminal return but CRA is unclear). Where a corporation sells all its trust units after receiving an income distribution in the same year, the amount included under 104(13) is excluded from the capital gain: 2008-0264181E5.

Income Tax Folios: S1-F2-C3: Scholarships, research grants and other education assistance [replaces IT-340R]; S6-F2-C1: Disposition of an income interest in a trust [replaces IT-385R2].

Interpretation Bulletins: IT-201R2: Foreign tax credit — trust and beneficiaries; IT-243R4: Dividend refund to private corporations; IT-286R2: Trusts — amount payable; IT-342R: Trusts — income payable to beneficiaries; IT-381R3: Trusts — capital gains and losses and the flow-through of taxable capital gains to beneficiaries; IT-465R: Non-resident beneficiaries of trusts; IT-500R: RRSPs — death of an annuitant; IT-502: Employee benefit plans and employee trusts; IT-524: Trusts — flow-through of taxable dividends to a beneficiary — after 1987; IT-531: Eligible funeral arrangements.

I.T. Technical News: 11 (payments made by a trust for the benefit of a minor beneficiary).

CRA Audit Manual: 16.2.3: Income allocated and designated to beneficiaries.

Forms: T1 General return, Line 13000 [former 130]: Other income; T4011: Preparing returns for deceased persons [guide].

(13.1) Amounts deemed not paid

(13.1) Amounts deemed not paid — Where a trust, in its return of income under this Part for a taxation year throughout which it was resident in Canada and not exempt from tax under Part I by reason of subsection 149(1), designates an amount in respect of a beneficiary under the trust, not exceeding the amount determined by the formula

$$\frac{A}{B} \times (C - D - E)$$

where

A   is the beneficiary's share of the income of the trust for the year computed without reference to this Act,

B   is the total of all amounts each of which is a beneficiary's share of the income of the trust for the year computed without reference to this Act,

C   is the total of all amounts each of which is an amount that, but for this subsection or subsection (13.2), would be included in computing the income of a beneficiary under the trust by reason of subsection (13) or 105(2) for the year,

D   is the amount deducted under subsection (6) in computing the income of the trust for the year, and

E   is equal to the amount determined by the trust for the year and used as the value of C for the purposes of the formula in subsection (13.2) or, if no amount is so determined, nil,

the amount so designated shall be deemed, for the purposes of subsections (13) and 105(2), not to have been paid or to have become payable in the year to or for the benefit of the beneficiary or out of income of the trust.

Related Provisions: 94(3)(a)(iii) — Application to trust deemed resident in Canada; 104(13.3) — Designation valid only to use up trust losses; 108(1) — "trust"; 250(6.1) — Trust that ceases to exist deemed resident throughout year; 257 — Formula cannot calculate to less than zero.

Notes: 104(13.1) and (13.2) allow a trust to choose to have distributed income and capital gains taxed in the trust rather than in the beneficiary's hands, to use up trust losses or loss carryovers. Before 2016 they could be used by a testamentary trust that paid low marginal rates (see 122(1)); now, due to 104(13.3), they cannot be used if the trust has any taxable income. When this election is made, it applies for Quebec purposes also: *Taxation Act* s. 657.1.0.1.

See VIEWS docs 2008-0300401E5 (interaction of 104(13.1) and 75(2)); 2009-0330181C6 (using 104(13.1) where income was taxed to the beneficiaries but trust did not claim deduction under 104(6)); 2010-0371921C6 (pension or DPSP payment received by estate can be taxed at the estate level); 2012-0437171E5 (designation must be made separately for each beneficiary); 2015-0565951E5 (application to Quebec "legatee by particular"); 2016-0630781E5 (application to CPP or QPP death benefit).

Late designation: In *Lussier*, [2000] 2 C.T.C. 2147 (TCC), the Court allowed a letter from the taxpayer's accountant after the fact to designate an amount, ruling that 104(13.1) did not prescribe any time period in which the designation had to be made. CRA accepts this, provided the trustee can establish that an honest mistake was made: 2000 Cdn Tax Foundation conference report, pp. 36:13-14; VIEWS docs 2009-0330181C6; 2016-0634901C6 [2016 STEP q.5] (procedure for late designation).

Interpretation Bulletins: IT-342R: Trusts — income payable to beneficiaries; IT-381R3: Trusts — capital gains and losses and the flow-through of taxable capital gains to beneficiaries; IT-394R2: Preferred beneficiary election.

(13.2) Idem — Where a trust, in its return of income under this Part for a taxation year throughout which it was resident in Canada and not exempt from tax under Part I by reason of subsection 149(1), designates an amount in respect of a beneficiary under the trust, not exceeding the amount determined by the formula

$$\frac{A}{B} \times C$$

where

A   is the amount designated by the trust for the year in respect of the beneficiary under subsection (21),

B   is the total of all amounts each of which has been designated for the year in respect of a beneficiary of the trust under subsection (21), and

C   is the amount determined by the trust and used in computing all amounts each of which is designated by the trust for the year under this subsection, not exceeding the amount by which

> (i) the total of all amounts each of which is an amount that, but for this subsection or subsection (13.1), would be included in computing the income of a beneficiary under the trust by reason of subsection (13) or 105(2) for the year

exceeds

> (ii) the amount deducted under subsection (6) in computing the income of the trust for the year,

the amount so designated shall

(a) for the purposes of subsections (13) and 105(2) (except in the application of subsection (13) for the purposes of subsection (21)), be deemed not to have been paid or to have become payable in the year to or for the benefit of the beneficiary or out of income of the trust; and

(b) except for the purposes of subsection (21) as it applies for the purposes of subsections (21.1) and (21.2), reduce the amount of the taxable capital gains of the beneficiary otherwise included in computing the beneficiary's income for the year by reason of subsection (21).

Related Provisions: 94(3)(a)(iii) — Application to trust deemed resident in Canada; 104(13.3) — Designation valid only to use up trust losses; 250(6.1) — Trust that ceases to exist deemed resident throughout year.

Notes: See Notes to 104(13.1).

104(13.2)(a) amended to change "beneficiaries" to "beneficiary" by 2002-2013 technical bill (Part 5 — technical), effective June 26, 2013. This corrected an error which did not appear in the French text (see also *Interpretation Act* s. 33(2)).

Interpretation Bulletins: IT-342R: Trusts — income payable to beneficiaries; IT-381R3: Trusts — capital gains and losses and the flow-through of taxable capital gains to beneficiaries.

(13.3) Invalid designation

(13.3) Invalid designation — Any designation made under subsection (13.1) or (13.2) by a trust in its return of income under this Part for a taxation year is invalid if the trust's taxable income for the year, determined without reference to this subsection, is greater than nil.

Notes: 104(13.3) added by 2014 budget bill #2, for 2016 and later taxation years.

(13.4) Death of beneficiary — spousal and similar trusts

(13.4) Death of beneficiary — spousal and similar trusts — If an individual's death occurs on a day in a particular taxation year of a trust and the death is the death or later death, as the case may be, referred to in paragraph (4)(a), (a.1) or (a.4) in respect of the trust,

(a) the particular year is deemed to end at the end of that day, a new taxation year of the trust is deemed to begin immediately after that day and, for the purpose of determining the trust's fiscal period after the new taxation year began, the trust is deemed not to have established a fiscal period before the new taxation year began;

(b) subject to paragraph (b.1), the trust's income (determined without reference to subsections (6) and (12)) for the particular year is, notwithstanding subsection (24), deemed

> (i) to have become payable in the year to the individual, and

(ii) not

(A) to have become payable to another beneficiary, or

(B) to be included under subsection 105(2) in computing the individual's income;

(b.1) paragraph (b) does not apply in respect of the trust for the particular year, unless

(i) the individual is resident in Canada immediately before the death,

(ii) the trust is, immediately before the death, a testamentary trust that

(A) is a post-1971 spousal or common-law partner trust, and

(B) was created by the will of a taxpayer who died before 2017, and

(iii) an election — made jointly between the trust and the legal representative administering the individual's graduated rate estate in prescribed form — that paragraph (b) applies is filed with

(A) the individual's return of income under this Part for the individual's year, and

(B) the trust's return of income under this Part for the particular year; and

(c) in respect of the particular year

(i) the references in paragraph 150(1)(c) to "year" and in subparagraph (a)(ii) of the definition "balance-due day" in subsection 248(1) to "taxation year" are to be read as "calendar year in which the taxation year ends", and

(ii) the reference in subsection 204(2) of the *Income Tax Regulations* to "end of the taxation year" is to be read as "end of the calendar year in which the taxation year ends".

Related Provisions: 160(1.4) — Individual and trust jointly liable for trust's tax on 104(13.4) amount.

Notes: 104(13.4)'s requirement as first enacted in 2014, that the spouse (not the spousal trust) pay the tax on capital gains realized by the trust on the spouse's death, "separates the tax liability from the ownership of the property that created the tax obligation"; this was raised with Finance as inappropriate (see articles cited here up to the 54th ed). A Nov. 16, 2015 Finance comfort letter promised relief, and 104(13.4)(b.1) provides it, as para. (b) now applies only by election and only for death before 2017. See also Brown & Ma, "Draft legislation on Spouse and Other Trusts", 24(2) *Canadian Tax Highlights* (ctf.ca) 5 (Feb. 2016). For CRA interpretation before the amendment see VIEWS docs 2015-0572101C6, 2015-0572121C6 [2015 STEP qq. 5-6].

See also VIEWS docs 2018-0742431E5 (election can only be made for all of the trust's income, but 104(13.1) or (13.2) designation may be available); 2018-0748241C6 [STEP 2018 q.11] (application to *alter ego* trust subject to 75(2)); 2019-0824501C6 [2019 CTF q.15] (2nd deemed year's capital loss carryback cannot be claimed directly on 1st deemed-year return even if known by return due date; T3A must be filed); 2020-0840001C6 [2020 STEP q.2] (CRA must process loss on 2nd year's T3A before applying it to 1st year, so interest appears on 1st year's assessment and is reversed later).

For a trust or estate filing a Quebec return, the (b.1)(iii) election must be copied to Revenu Québec: *Taxation Act* ss. 663.0.1, 21.4.6.

104(13.4)(b.1) added, and (b) and (c)(i) amended, by 2016 budget bill #2, for 2016 and later tax years. 104(13.4) added by 2014 budget bill #2, for 2016 and later tax years.

(14) Election by trust and preferred beneficiary — Where a trust and a preferred beneficiary under the trust for a particular taxation year of the trust jointly so elect in respect of the particular year in prescribed manner, such part of the accumulating income of the trust for the particular year as is designated in the election, not exceeding the allocable amount for the preferred beneficiary in respect of the trust for the particular year, shall be included in computing the income of the preferred beneficiary for the beneficiary's taxation year in which the particular year ended and shall not be included in computing the income of any beneficiary of the trust for a subsequent taxation year.

Related Provisions: 12(1)(m) — Income inclusion — benefits from trusts; 94(3)(a)(iii) — Application to trust deemed resident in Canada; 104(12) — Deduction for amount included in preferred beneficiary's income; 104(15) — Allocable amount; 104(19) — Portion of net taxable dividends deemed received by beneficiary; 104(21) — Portion of taxable capital gains deemed gain of beneficiary; 108(5) — In-

terpretation; 146(8.1) — RRSP — deemed receipt of refund premiums; 220(3.2), Reg. 600(b) — Late filing or revocation of election.

Notes: The preferred beneficiary election (PBE) was, before 1996, a useful mechanism for splitting income by allocating income of a trust to certain beneficiaries. (The attribution rules in 74.1–74.5 must be considered, however.) Since 1996 only a disabled person may be a "preferred beneficiary", although the 1997 Budget relaxed slightly the persons who qualify (see 108(1)"preferred beneficiary"). Note also that if a person other than the settlor (including a beneficiary) contributes capital to the trust, the settlor may cease to be the "settlor" as defined in 108(1) and beneficiaries may thus cease to be "preferred beneficiaries" under 108(1). Multiple PBEs may be set up for the same beneficiary (unlike a qualified disability trust): VIEWS doc 2016-0645801C6 [2016 STEP q.4].

220(3.2) and Reg. 600(b) permit late filing of a PBE at CRA's discretion, but Agency officials do not often allow it.

A qualified disability trust (see 122(3)) can make a PBE: VIEWS docs 2015-0605111E5, 2016-0645801C6 [2016 STEP q.4].

Income allocated under 104(14) is not caught by 120.4(1)"split income"(c); but if a 104(19) designation is made, 120.4(1)"split income"(a) triggers TOSI: VIEWS docs 2018-0759521E5, 2019-0798501C6 [2019 STEP q.13], 2019-0798511C6 [2019 STEP q.14]. Showing the amount in Box 26 ("Other income") on the T3 avoids the designation.

104(14) amended by 1995 Budget, for trust taxation years that begin after 1995. The essence of the amendment was to change the reference to "preferred beneficiary's share" to "allocable amount" (see 104(15) for both terms). The total allocable amounts for multiple preferred beneficiaries will typically exceed the trust's accumulating income. However, because of 104(12), there is no advantage to making elections under 104(14) in excess of the trust's accumulating income for the taxation year.

Regulations: 2800(1), (2) (prescribed manner, prescribed time).

Interpretation Bulletins: IT-201R2: Foreign tax credit — trust and beneficiaries; IT-243R4: Dividend refund to private corporations; IT-381R3: Trusts — capital gains and losses and the flow-through of taxable capital gains to beneficiaries; IT-394R2: Preferred beneficiary election; IT-500R: RRSPs — death of an annuitant; IT-524: Trusts — flow-through of taxable dividends to a beneficiary — after 1987.

Information Circulars: 07-1R1: Taxpayer relief provisions.

CRA Audit Manual: 16.2.4: Preferred beneficiaries.

Advance Tax Rulings: ATR-30: Preferred beneficiary election on accumulating income of estate; ATR-34: Preferred beneficiary's election.

(14.01), (14.02) [Repealed]

Notes: 104(14.01) and (14.02) repealed by 2014 budget bill #2, for 2016 and later taxation years. They applied only to the taxation year that includes Feb. 22, 1994. They related to the 110.6(19)-(30) election to crystallize the capital gains exemption in 1994.

(14.1) [Repealed]

Notes: 104(14.1) repealed by 2014 budget bill #2, for 2016 and later tax years, due to amendments made to 104(5.1) and (13.4). It addressed amounts deemed paid on death to a spousal trust from a NISA Fund No. 2 (farm income stabilization). Added by 1992 technical bill.

(15) Allocable amount for preferred beneficiary — For the purpose of subsection (14), the allocable amount for a preferred beneficiary under a trust in respect of the trust for a taxation year is

(a) where the trust is an *alter ego* trust, a joint spousal or common-law partner trust, a post-1971 spousal or common-law partner trust or a trust described in the definition "pre-1972 spousal trust" in subsection 108(1) at the end of the year and a beneficiary, referred to in paragraph (4)(a) or in that definition, is alive at the end of the year, an amount equal to

(i) if the preferred beneficiary is a beneficiary so referred to, the trust's accumulating income for the year, and

(ii) in any other case, nil;

(b) where paragraph (a) does not apply and the preferred beneficiary's interest in the trust is not solely contingent on the death of another beneficiary who has a capital interest in the trust and who does not have an income interest in the trust, the trust's accumulating income for the year; and

(c) in any other case, nil.

Related Provisions: 94(3)(a)(iii) — Application to trust deemed resident in Canada; 108(1) — Trust defined; 138.1(1) — Rules re segregated funds; 250(6.1) — Trust that ceases to exist deemed resident throughout year.

Notes: See Notes to 104(14). 104(15) amended by 2001 technical bill (for 2000 and later taxation years), 2000 same-sex partners bill, 1995 Budget and 1992 technical bill.

Regulations: 2800(3), (4) (prescribed manner for 104(15)(c)).

Interpretation Bulletins: IT-394R2: Preferred beneficiary election.

Advance Tax Rulings: ATR-30: Preferred beneficiary election on accumulating income of estate; ATR-34: Preferred beneficiary's election.

(16) SIFT deemed dividend — If an amount (in this subsection and section 122 referred to as the trust's "non-deductible distributions amount" for the taxation year) is determined under subparagraph (ii) of the description of B in paragraph (6)(b) in respect of a SIFT trust for a taxation year

(a) each beneficiary under the SIFT trust to whom at any time in the taxation year an amount became payable by the trust is deemed to have received at that time a taxable dividend that was paid at that time by a taxable Canadian corporation;

(b) the amount of a dividend described in paragraph (a) as having been received by a beneficiary at any time in a taxation year is equal to the amount determined by the formula

$$A/B \times C$$

where

A is the amount that became payable at that time by the SIFT trust to the beneficiary,

B is the total of all amounts, each of which became payable in the taxation year by the SIFT trust to a beneficiary under the SIFT trust, and

C is the SIFT trust's non-deductible distributions amount for the taxation year;

(c) the amount of a dividend described in paragraph (a) in respect of a beneficiary under the SIFT trust is deemed for the purpose of subsection (13) not to be an amount payable to the beneficiary; and

(d) for the purposes of applying Part XIII in respect of each dividend described in paragraph (a), the SIFT trust is deemed to be a corporation resident in Canada that paid the dividend.

Related Provisions: 53(2)(h)(i.1)(A.1) — Reduction in ACB excludes dividend deemed received; 82(1) — Taxable dividend included in income with gross-up; 89(1)"eligible dividend"(b) — Dividend under 104(16) eligible for 45% gross-up and high dividend tax credit; 104(24) — Whether amount payable; 122(1)(b) — SIFT trust pays corporate tax on distributed income; 157(2) — SIFT trust pays same instalments as a corporation; 197(2) — Taxation of SIFT partnership distributions.

Notes: 104(16) is part of the "SIFT" (specified investment flow-through) rules that apply to publicly-traded income trusts and partnerships. The rules took effect in 2011, or earlier for new entities or those that exceeded "normal growth" guidelines: see 122.1(2) and 197(8), and 122.1(1)"SIFT trust". These rules responded to extensive conversions of major corporations to income trusts, which were distorting the economy (since income trusts must distribute virtually all their profits each year to remain tax-effective). (For more of the story see *Edwin*, 2010 TCC 362. See also Notes to 89(1)"eligible dividend" and 132(5.1).) Under 104(16), amounts distributed to beneficiaries are deemed to be taxable dividends. Instead of being deductible to the trust under 104(6), they are excluded by 104(6)(b)(iv), and are taxed to the trust under 122(1)(b) at the same rate as public corporations. This eliminates the incentive for corporations to convert to income trusts. 197(2) and 96(1.11) apply the same tax to publicly-traded partnerships.

Where a corporation converted to an income trust before these rules, the conversion triggered a capital gain on the corporate shares: *Roud Estate*, 2013 TCC 36.

104(13.1) cannot be used to reduce the trust's non-deductible distributions amount, as it does not apply for purposes of 104(16).

See Roth et al., *Canadian Taxation of Trusts* (ctf.ca, 2016), pp. 1130-66; Cardarelli, "Income Trust and Mutual Fund Trust Developments", 2006 Cdn Tax Foundation conference report, 10:1-19; Bodie & Vandale, "Sifting Through the Wreckage", 2007 Prairie Provinces Tax Conference (ctf.ca), 9:1-44; Sherman and Freeman, "The Gift of SIFT", 2007 conference report, 14:1-37; Hegedus, "The SIFT Rules", 20 *Canadian Petroleum Tax Journal* (2007); VIEWS doc 2008-0301681E5.

On acquisitions of income trusts (examples being Canada Cartage and Norcast), see Stephen Ruby, "Recent Transactions of Interest", 2007 Cdn Tax Foundation conference report at 3:30-41.

Annex B to the Fifth Protocol to the Canada-US Tax Treaty (reproduced after the treaty), para. 3, provides that "distributions from Canadian income trusts and royalty trusts that are treated as dividends under the taxation laws of Canada shall be considered dividends" for purposes of the reduced withholding tax on dividends.

When the SIFT rules were announced, Canada had about 170 publicly traded income trusts structured to avoid taxation on business profits: Bernstein, "Income Trusts for Sale", 15(5) *Canadian Tax Highlights* (ctf.ca) 9-10 (May 2007). Income trusts generally reverted to corporate form because of the SIFT rules. This could be done before 2013 by a rollover of trust units to a corp (85.1(7), (8)) or by a rollout of the trust property to beneficiaries (107(3), (3.1)) or to a single corp (88.1(2)). See 85.1(8) Notes.

See also Trossman, "IPOs: The Old Alternative to Income Trusts", 2009 Cdn Tax Foundation conference report, 13:1-23. Another alternative to income trusts may be a US master limited partnership: Van Dyke & Pearson, "Coming to Canada", *CAmagazine* (cica.ca) Jan/Feb 2009, 52-53. A further option is an *unlisted* income trust — not tradeable on the market, but usually set up as an "open-ended" trust that can be called on to redeem units. Another is a foreign asset income trust (FAIT), also known as a cross-border income trust (CBIT), carrying on business outside Canada to fall outside 122.1(1)"SIFT trust", e.g. Eagle Energy Trust (2010), Parallel Energy Trust (2011), Argent Energy Trust (2012), Crius Energy Trust (2012); Johnson et al., "Current Transactions", 2012 conference report, 8:1-39; Kearl & Friess, "Will Cross-border Income Trusts Be Next?", XVII(4) *International Tax Planning* (Federated Press) 1204-08 (2012). (The underlying Opco pays US corporate tax but reduces it with arm's length interest payments, depletion and depreciation.)

See Notes to 104(17)-(17.2) for former 104(16).

104(16) opening words amended by 2014 budget bill #2, for 2016 and later taxation years, to change reference from 104(6)(b)(iv) to 104(6)(b)B(ii).

104(16) added by 2007 budget bill #1, effective Oct. 31, 2006.

(17)–(17.2) [Repealed under former Act]

Notes: Former 104(16)-(17.2), repealed by 1988 tax reform, allowed a beneficiary to claim CCA, terminal losses and depletion allowances, now claimed only at the trust level under 104(13).

(18) Trust for minor [under 21] — Where any part of the amount that, but for subsections (6) and (12), would be the income of a trust for a taxation year throughout which it was resident in Canada

(a) has not become payable in the year,

(b) was held in trust for an individual who did not attain 21 years of age before the end of the year,

(c) the right to which vested at or before the end of the year otherwise than because of the exercise by any person of, or the failure of any person to exercise, any discretionary power, and

(d) the right to which is not subject to any future condition (other than a condition that the individual survive to an age not exceeding 40 years),

notwithstanding subsection (24), that part of the amount is, for the purposes of subsections (6) and (13), deemed to have become payable to the individual in the year.

Related Provisions: 94(3)(a)(iii) — Application to trust deemed resident in Canada; 250(6.1) — Trust that ceases to exist deemed resident throughout year.

Notes: 104(18) amended by 1995 Budget, effective for trust taxation years that begin after 1995. The amendment makes it more difficult to make amounts "payable" to a minor beneficiary of a discretionary trust so as to put the income in that minor's hands (under 104(6)) for income-splitting purposes. See also the tax on split income in 120.4.

For interpretation of 104(18) in various situations see VIEWS docs 2004-0093601E5, 2004-0093661E5, 2004-0100001E5, 2013-0500561E5. See also Notes to 104(24).

See also Perry Truster, "Income Allocated by a Family Trust to Beneficiaries", 16(3) *Tax for the Owner-Manager* (ctf.ca) 7-8 (July 2016).

Interpretation Bulletins: IT-286R2: Trusts — amount payable; IT-342R: Trusts — income payable to beneficiaries; IT-381R3: Trusts — capital gains and losses and the flow-through of taxable capital gains to beneficiaries; IT-394R2: Preferred beneficiary election.

I.T. Technical News: 11 (payments made by a trust for the benefit of a minor beneficiary).

(19) Designation in respect of taxable dividends — A portion of a taxable dividend received by a trust, in a particular taxation year of the trust, on a share of the capital stock of a taxable Canadian corporation is, for the purposes of this Act other than Part XIII, deemed to be a taxable dividend on the share received by a taxpayer, in the taxpayer's taxation year in which the particular taxation year ends, and is, for the purposes of paragraphs 82(1)(b) and 107(1)(c) and (d) and section 112, deemed not to have been received by the trust, if

(a) an amount equal to that portion

(i) is designated by the trust, in respect of the taxpayer, in the trust's return of income under this Part for the particular taxation year, and

(ii) may reasonably be considered (having regard to all the circumstances including the terms and conditions of the trust) to be part of the amount that, because of paragraph (13)(a), subsection (14) or section 105, was included in computing the income for that taxation year of the taxpayer;

(b) the taxpayer is in the particular taxation year a beneficiary under the trust;

(c) the trust is, throughout the particular taxation year, resident in Canada; and

(d) the total of all amounts each of which is an amount designated, under this subsection, by the trust in respect of a beneficiary under the trust in the trust's return of income under this Part for the particular taxation year is not greater than the total of all amounts each of which is the amount of a taxable dividend, received by the trust in the particular taxation year, on a share of the capital stock of a taxable Canadian corporation.

Related Provisions: 82(1) — Taxable dividends received; 94(3)(a)(iii) — Application to trust deemed resident in Canada; 107(1)(c), (d) — Loss on disposition of capital interest in trust; 112(3.12) — Exclusion from stop-loss rule where beneficiary is partnership or trust; 112(3.2) — Stop-loss rule; 112(5.2)B(b)(iii) — Adjustment for dividends received on mark-to-market property; 250(6.1) — Trust that ceases to exist deemed resident throughout year.

Notes: See Notes to 108(5) and 104(13). 104(19) allows the character of dividend income to be preserved when flowed through to a beneficiary (B). Thus, B, if an individual, benefits from the gross-up and dividend tax credit (82(1)(b) and 121), and if a corp, benefits from the intercorporate dividend deduction (112(1)). Where the Bs include a corp, the trust must allocate "safe income" (see 55(2) Notes) *pro rata*: VIEWS doc 2019-0833061E5 [Wen, "Discretionary Trusts and Safe Income", 10(2) *Canadian Tax Focus* (ctf.ca) 1-2 (May 2020); Hamelin, "Trusts and Safe-Income Allocation", 20(4) *Tax for the Owner-Manager* (ctf.ca) 6-7 (Oct. 2020)].

CRA stated at the 2008 Cdn Tax Foundation conference (*Income Tax Technical News* 41) that an 89(1)"eligible dividend" maintains its character when flowed out under 104(19). See also VIEWS docs 2011-0392661E5, 2013-0495801C6 [2013 APFF q.9] (reporting procedures where designation made [Tremblay, "Deemed Timing of a Dividend Receipt by a Trust Beneficiary", 4(1) *Canadian Tax Focus* (ctf.ca) 5 (Feb. 2014)]); 2012-0465131E5, 2016-0647621E5, 2018-0757591I7, 2020-0845821C6 [2020 APFF q.17] (timing: dividend is received at end of trust's tax year, so if the shares have been sold, Part IV tax can still apply [Kakkar & Halil, "Are Dividend Allocations to a Corporate Beneficiary Subject to Part IV Tax?", 16(4) *Tax for the Owner-Manager* (ctf.ca) 2-3 (Oct. 2016); Campbell, "CRA Doubles Down on Part IV Tax and Trust Issue", 16(5) *Tax Hyperion* (Carswell) 1-3 (Sept-Oct 2019) (CRA may be wrong)]); 2020-0839891C6 [2020 STEP q.11] (same issue re end of year, but if B dies during the year, dividend is included in B's final return, as tax year-end is still Dec. 31 [Carolin & Kakkar, "Estate Plans", 21(2) *Tax for the Owner-Manager* (ctf.ca) 2 (April 2021), and see 186(4) Notes]).

In *Fiducie Financière Satoma*, 2018 FCA 74 (leave to appeal denied 2019 CarswellNat 898 (SCC)), deliberately using 75(2) and 104(19) to attribute a dividend to a corporation that paid no tax on it triggered GAAR (245(2)).

104(19) cannot apply to a dividend received by an employee trust and paid out to the employer, because such amount is taxable not under 104(13) but rather under 12(1)(n): VIEWS doc 2013-0495741C6 [2013 APFF q.8]. It also did not apply where beneficiaries assigned their capital interests in the trust to a ULC, because the ULC did not become a beneficiary: 2017-0683021I7 [Rudick & Abitbol, "Risks of Assigning a Trust Interest", 27(6) *Canadian Tax Highlights* (ctf.ca) 9-10 (June 2019)].

A designation of a 104(14) preferred-beneficiary amount can trigger TOSI: see Notes to 104(14).

104(19) amended by 2002-2013 technical bill, last change effective for tax years that end after July 18, 2005.

Closing words of 104(19) amended by 2001 technical bill, effective for taxation years that end after 2000.

Interpretation Bulletins: IT-328R3: Losses on shares on which dividends have been received; IT-524: Trusts — flow-through of taxable dividends to a beneficiary — after 1987.

I.T. Technical News: 41 (eligible dividend designation).

(20) Designation in respect of non-taxable dividends —
The portion of the total of all amounts, each of which is the amount of a dividend (other than a taxable dividend) paid on a share of the capital stock of a corporation resident in Canada to a trust during a taxation year of the trust throughout which the trust was resident in Canada, that can reasonably be considered (having regard to all the circumstances including the terms and conditions of the trust arrangement) to be part of an amount that became payable in the year to a particular beneficiary under the trust shall be designated by the trust in respect of the particular beneficiary in the return of the trust's income for the year for the purposes of subclause 53(2)(h)(i.1)(B)(II), paragraphs 107(1)(c) and (d) and subsections 112(3.1), (3.2), (3.31) and (4.2).

Related Provisions: 83(2) — Capital dividends; 89(1)"capital dividend account"(g) — Amount designated can increase CDA; 94(3)(a)(iii) — Application to trust deemed resident in Canada; 107(1)(c) — Stop-loss rule where beneficiary is corporation; 104(24) — Whether amount payable; 112(3.2) — Stop-loss rule; 112(4.3) — Limitation on loss on disposition of share by trust; 132(3) — Application to a mutual fund trust; 248(1)"disposition"(i)(ii) — Payment in respect of capital interest in a trust; 250(6.1) — Trust that ceases to exist deemed resident throughout year.

Notes: 104(20) deals with capital dividends (see 83(2)), but applies only for the specific purposes stated. It does not provide for a general flow-through of the exemption to the beneficiary. However, 105(1)(b) provides, in effect, that capital dividends are not included in the income of a beneficiary of a commercial trust, since they are allowed as a deduction from the beneficiary's ACB under 53(2)(h). Also, for a personal trust, a capital dividend paid out to a beneficiary will not be included in income, since the income inclusion in 104(13)(a) applies only to amounts that would otherwise be income *of the trust*, and a capital dividend is not income of the trust in the first place.

The amount designated can be added to the corporation's CDA due to 89(1)"capital dividend account"(g): VIEWS doc 2010-0358471E5, but not if the dividend is not actually paid out: 2012-0469591E5 [Tollstam, "CDA Trapped in Trust", 21(8) *Canadian Tax Highlights* (ctf.ca) 12 (Aug, 2013)].

Note that 104(20) uses "shall", so the designation is mandatory.

104(20) amended by 1995-97 technical bill, effective April 27, 1995.

Income Tax Folios: S3-F2-C1: Capital Dividends [replaces IT-66R6].

Interpretation Bulletins: IT-328R3: Losses on shares on which dividends have been received.

(21) Designation in respect of taxable capital gains — For the purposes of sections 3 and 111, except as they apply for the purposes of section 110.6, and subject to paragraph 132(5.1)(b), an amount in respect of a trust's net taxable capital gains for a particular taxation year of the trust is deemed to be a taxable capital gain, for the taxation year of a taxpayer in which the particular taxation year ends, from the disposition by the taxpayer of capital property if

(a) the amount

(i) is designated by the trust, in respect of the taxpayer, in the trust's return of income under this Part for the particular taxation year, and

(ii) may reasonably be considered (having regard to all the circumstances including the terms and conditions of the trust) to be part of the amount that, because of paragraph (13)(a), subsection (14) or section 105, was included in computing the income for that taxation year of the taxpayer;

(b) the taxpayer is

(i) in the particular taxation year, a beneficiary under the trust, and

(ii) resident in Canada, unless the trust is, throughout the particular taxation year, a mutual fund trust;

(c) the trust is, throughout the particular taxation year, resident in Canada; and

(d) the total of all amounts each of which is an amount designated, under this subsection, by the trust in respect of a beneficiary under the trust in the trust's return of income under this Part for the particular taxation year is not greater than the trust's net taxable capital gains for the particular taxation year.

Related Provisions: 89(1)"capital dividend account"(f) — Addition to CDA for capital gains allocated by trust to corporate beneficiary; 94(3)(a)(iii) — Application to trust deemed resident in Canada; 104(13.2) — Designation of amount by trust; 104(21.2) — Beneficiary's taxable capital gain; 104(21.3) — Determination of net taxable capital gains; 120.4(5) — Certain capital gains earned through trust deemed to be dividends for income-splitting tax; 127.52(1)(d)(ii), (1)(g)(ii) — Adjusted taxable income (for minimum tax); 131(6)"capital gains dividend account"(a)(ii)B — Flow-out through mutual fund corp; 132(5.1), (5.2) — Mutual fund trust — distribution of gain on taxable Canadian property; 212(1)(c) — Estate or trust income — non-residents; 250(6.1) — Trust that ceases to exist deemed resident throughout year.

Notes: 104(21) allows capital gains realized by the trust to be preserved as such when flowed through to a beneficiary (B). Thus, capital gains of the trust will only be ½ taxed in B's hands (see 38(a)) and can be offset by B's capital losses (see 3(b)(ii) and 111(1)(b)). However, they are not eligible for the capital gains exemption under 110.6 (see the closing words of 104(21)) unless a further designation is made by the trust under 104(21.2). Late designation cannot be made: 2014-0517191I7 (also discusses what happens if designation is not made); but see Notes to 220(3.2). A designation can be made for a B added later in the year than the disposition: 2015-0571801E5.

Only the taxable half of a capital gain need be paid (or made payable) to a B for the designation to be available: VIEWS doc 2020-0839881C6 [2020 STEP q.3].

104(21) does not apply to a trust not resident in Canada (see Notes to 250(1)), so capital gains from a US mutual fund trust are income under 108(5)(a): VIEWS doc 2011-0405261C6.

When Fording Canadian Coal Trust made no 104(21) designation on payment it made on being taken over, the amount was fully taxable under 104(13) rather than capital gain to the beneficiary: *Joseph*, 2010 CarswellNat 1797 (TCC); *Gros*, 2012 CarswellNat 120 (TCC). See however *Burchat*, 2011 CarswellNat 1859 (TCC) (CRA pleadings deficient re Fording Canadian Coal Trust and Teck Cominco).

Where taxable capital gains are designated by a mutual fund trust to a corporate beneficiary, the non-taxable portion is added to the corporation's capital dividend account: 89(1)"capital dividend account"(a)(i.1) [(f), before Sept. 16, 2016]. For rulings approving flow-out of capital gains to redeeming unitholders see VIEWS docs 2007-0224201R3, 2007-0257551R3. For the flow-out on windup of an income trust see 2007-0245281R3. Flow-out through a mutual fund corporation is allowed by 131(6)"capital gains dividend account"(a)(ii)B.

104(21) amended by 2002-2013 technical bill (last change effective for tax years ending after July 18, 2005), 2004 Budget.

Interpretation Bulletins: IT-123R6: Transactions involving eligible capital property; IT-342R: Trusts — income payable to beneficiaries; IT-381R3: Trusts — capital gains and losses and the flow-through of taxable capital gains to beneficiaries; IT-394R2: Preferred beneficiary election; IT-465R: Non-resident beneficiaries of trusts; IT-493: Agency cooperative corporations.

Advance Tax Rulings: ATR-34: Preferred beneficiary's election.

Forms: RC4169: Tax treatment of mutual funds for individuals [guide]; T3 Sched. 3: Eligible taxable capital gains.

(21.01), (21.02), (21.03) [No longer relevant.]

Notes: 104(21.01) to (21.03), added by 1995-97 technical bill, apply only to the taxation year that includes Feb. 22, 1994. They provide for a late, amended or revoked election or designation under 110.6(19)-(30) to crystallize the capital gains exemption.

(21.1) [Repealed]

Notes: 104(21.1) repealed by 2002-2013 technical bill, for tax years that begin after Oct. 2011. It was a transitional provision to deal with the change in capital gains inclusion rates under 38(a) from ½ (before 1988) to ⅔ (1988 and 1989) to ¾ (1990-Feb. 27, 2000) to ⅔ (Feb. 28-Oct. 17, 2000) to ½ (since Oct. 18, 2000). It applied where a trust allocated capital gains to beneficiary B under 104(21) but the trust and B had different tax years.

(21.2) Beneficiaries' taxable capital gain — Where, for the purposes of subsection (21), a personal trust or a trust referred to in subsection 7(2) designates an amount in respect of a beneficiary in respect of its net taxable capital gains for a taxation year (in this subsection referred to as the "designation year"),

(a) the trust shall in its return of income under this Part for the designation year designate an amount in respect of its eligible taxable capital gains, if any, for the designation year in respect of the beneficiary equal to the amount determined in respect of the beneficiary under each of subparagraphs (b)(i) and (ii); and

(b) the beneficiary is, for the purposes of section 120.4 and for the purposes of sections 3, 74.3 and 111 as they apply for the purposes of section 110.6,

(i) deemed to have disposed of the capital property referred to in clause (ii)(A), (B) or (C) if a taxable capital gain is determined in respect of the beneficiary for the beneficiary's taxation year in which the designation year ends under those clauses, and

(ii) deemed to have a taxable capital gain for the beneficiary's taxation year in which the designation year ends

(A) from a disposition of a capital property that is qualified farm or fishing property (as defined for the purpose of section 110.6) of the beneficiary equal to the amount determined by the formula

$$(A \times B \times C)/(D \times E)$$

and

(B) from a disposition of a capital property that is a qualified small business corporation share (as defined for the purpose of section 110.6) of the beneficiary equal to the amount determined by the formula

$$(A \times B \times F)/(D \times E)$$

(C) [Repealed]

where

A is the lesser of

(I) the amount determined by the formula

$$G - H$$

where

G is the total of amounts designated under subsection (21) for the designation year by the trust, and

H is the total of amounts designated under subsection (13.2) for the designation year by the trust, and

(II) the trust's eligible taxable capital gains for the designation year,

B is the amount, if any, by which the amount designated under subsection (21) for the designation year by the trust in respect of the beneficiary exceeds the amount designated under subsection (13.2) for the year by the trust in respect of the beneficiary for the taxation year,

C is the amount, if any, that would be determined under paragraph 3(b) for the designation year in respect of the trust's capital gains and capital losses if the only properties referred to in that paragraph were properties that, at the time they were disposed of, were qualified farm properties, qualified fishing properties or qualified farm or fishing properties of the trust,

D is the total of all amounts each of which is the amount determined for B for the designation year in respect of a beneficiary under the trust,

E is the total of the amounts determined for C and F for the designation year in respect of the beneficiary, and

F is the amount, if any, that would be determined under paragraph 3(b) for the designation year in respect of the trust's capital gains and capital losses if the only properties referred to in that paragraph were properties that, at the time they were disposed of, were qualified small business corporation shares of the trust, other than qualified farm property, qualified fishing property or qualified farm or fishing property,

I [Repealed]

and for the purposes of section 110.6, those capital properties shall be deemed to have been disposed of by the beneficiary in that taxation year of the beneficiary.

Related Provisions: 39(10) — Reduction of business investment loss; 94(3)(a)(iii) — Application to trust deemed resident in Canada; 104(21.3) — Determination of net taxable capital gains; 110.6(11) — No capital gains exemption allowed in certain cases; 110.6(12) — Spousal trust deduction; 110.6(14)(c) — Related persons, etc.; 110.6(20) — Election to trigger capital gains exemption; 257 — Formula amount cannot calculate to less than zero.

Notes: 104(21.2) permits a beneficiary (B) to claim the capital gains exemption under 110.6 in respect of a portion of the capital gains of a trust allocated to B. See Notes to 104(21). Designations can be structured to maximize use of Bs' available exemptions: VIEWS doc 2004-0086971C6. For further interpretation and examples see 2009-0330241C6, 2009-0341711E5, 2012-0439271E5, 2014-0518951E5, 2015-0571801E5 (individual can become B of trust before or after disposition of the shares, and gain can be allocated over 4 years if IT-426 cost recovery method is used).

104(21.2) can be used by a trust that receives capital gains designated under 104(21) by another trust: VIEWS docs 2018-0738271E5, 2019-081830117, 2020-0837001C6 [2020 STEP q.17], 2020-0852761C6 [2020 APFF Financial q.1] (reversing 2016-0667361E5).

See Notes to 104(24) re requirements in the trust indenture to make the deemed capital gain under 104(21.2) payable to the beneficiary.

104(21.2)(b) amended by 2018 budget bill #1 to refer to 120.4, for 2018 and later tax years.

104(21.2) amended by 2014 budget bill #2, for dispositions in the 2014 and later tax years, to use the "farm or fishing" terms instead of "farm" and "fishing" separately. Earlier amended by 2006 budget bill #2 (for a trust's taxation years ending after May 1, 2006), 2001 technical bill, 1994 Budget, 1992 and 1991 technical bills.

Interpretation Bulletins: IT-123R6: Transactions involving eligible capital property; IT-381R3: Trusts — capital gains and losses and the flow-through of taxable capital gains to beneficiaries.

Advance Tax Rulings: ATR-34: Preferred beneficiary's election.

Forms: T3 Sched. 3: Eligible taxable capital gains; T3 Sched. 4: Cumulative net investment loss; T3 Sched. 9: Income allocations and designations to beneficiaries.

(21.21) Beneficiaries QFFP taxable capital gain — If clause (21.2)(b)(ii)(A) applies to deem, for the purposes of section 110.6, the beneficiary under a trust to have a taxable capital gain (referred to in this subsection as the "QFFP taxable capital gain") from a disposition of capital property that is qualified farm or fishing property of the beneficiary, for the beneficiary's taxation year that ends on or after April 21, 2015, and in which the designation year of the trust ends, for the purposes of subsection 110.6(2.2), the beneficiary is, if the trust complies with the requirements of subsection (21.22), deemed to have a taxable capital gain from the disposition of qualified farm or fishing property of the beneficiary on or after April 21, 2015 equal to the amount determined by the formula

$$A \times B/C$$

where

A   is the amount of the QFFP taxable capital gain;

B   is, if the designation year of the trust ends on or after April 21, 2015, the amount that would be determined in respect of the trust for the designation year under paragraph 3(b) in respect of capital gains and capital losses if the only properties referred to in that paragraph were qualified farm or fishing properties of the trust that were disposed of by the trust on or after April 21, 2015; and

C   is, if the designation year of the trust ends on or after April 21, 2015, the amount that would be determined in respect of the trust for the designation year under paragraph 3(b) in respect of capital gains and capital losses if the only properties referred to in that paragraph were qualified farm or fishing properties.

Related Provisions: 104(21.22) — Determination and designation of amount.

Notes: 104(21.21) and (21.22) are consequential on 110.6(2.2), which increases the capital gains deduction on sale of qualified farm or fishing property (QFFP) after April 20, 2015 to $1 million. In determining entitlement to the additional deduction, one must establish the extent to which taxable capital gains arose from dispositions of QFFP after that date. 104(21.21) and (21.22) assist an individual to whom a personal trust has designated QFFP taxable capital gains under 104(21.2). It provides a formula to prorate the "QFFP taxable capital gain" between dispositions before and after the cutoff. 104(21.22) requires a trust to determine and designate the beneficiary's QFFP taxable capital gains in its return.

104(21.21) and (21.22) added by 2015 Budget bill, for tax years that end after April 20, 2015.

Former 104(21.21)–(21.24) repealed by 2014 budget bill #2, effective for dispositions in the 2014 and later taxation years. They related to the 2007 increase in the capital gains exemption from $500,000 to $750,000, and applied only to dispositions of property in years that included March 19, 2007. Added by 2007 budget bill #2.

(21.22) Trusts to designate amounts [for (21.21)] — A trust shall determine and designate, in its return of income under this Part for a designation year of the trust, the amount that is determined under subsection (21.21) to be the beneficiary's taxable capital gain from the disposition on or after April 21, 2015 of qualified farm or fishing property of the beneficiary.

Notes: See Notes to 104(21.21).

(21.23), (21.24) [Repealed]

(21.3) Net taxable capital gains of trust determined — For the purposes of this section, the net taxable capital gains of a trust for a taxation year is the amount, if any, determined by the formula

$$A + B - C - D$$

where

A   is the total of all amounts each of which is a taxable capital gain of the trust for the year from the disposition of a capital property that was held by the trust immediately before the disposition,

B   is the total of all amounts each of which is deemed by subsection (21) to be a taxable capital gain of the trust for the year,

C   is the total of all amounts each of which is an allowable capital loss (other than an allowable business investment loss) of the trust for the year from the disposition of a capital property, and

D   is the amount, if any, deducted under paragraph 111(1)(b) in computing the trust's taxable income for the year.

Related Provisions: 257 — Formula cannot calculate to less than zero.

Notes: The exclusion of ABILs in C, originally added effective 2001 (to 104(21.3)(a)) as per below, means that ABILs do not reduce taxable capital gains that can be flowed through the beneficiaries and against which allowable capital losses can be claimed.

104(21.3) amended by 2002-2013 technical bill (Part 5 — technical), effective for taxation years that begin after Oct. 2011.

104(21.3)(a) changed from "its allowable capital losses for the year" by 2002-2013 technical bill, for trust tax years that begin after 2000.

Interpretation Bulletins: IT-381R3: Trusts — capital gains and losses and the flow-through of taxable capital gains to beneficiaries.

Forms: T3 Sched. 3: Eligible taxable capital gains.

(21.4)–(21.7) [Repealed]

Notes: 104(21.4)-(21.7) repealed (after amending 104(21.6)) by 2002-2013 technical bill, for tax years that begin after Oct. 2011. They were transitional rules for 2000, added by 2000 Budget.

For the text of 104(21.4), see Notes to 89(1)"capital dividend account" (it is still relevant for cl. (f)(i)(B) of that definition).

(22) Designation in respect of foreign source income — For the purposes of this subsection, subsection (22.1) and section 126, an amount in respect of a trust's income for a particular taxation year of the trust from a source in a country other than Canada is deemed to be income of a taxpayer, for the taxation year of the taxpayer in which the particular taxation year ends, from that source if

(a) the amount

(i) is designated by the trust, in respect of the taxpayer, in the trust's return of income under this Part for the particular taxation year, and

(ii) may reasonably be considered (having regard to all the circumstances including the terms and conditions of the trust) to be part of the amount that, because of paragraph (13)(a) or subsection (14), was included in computing the income for that taxation year of the taxpayer;

(b) the taxpayer is in the particular taxation year a beneficiary under the trust;

(c) the trust is, throughout the particular taxation year, resident in Canada; and

(d) the total of all amounts each of which is an amount designated, under this subsection in respect of that source, by the trust in respect of a beneficiary under the trust in the trust's return of income under this Part for the particular taxation year is not greater than the trust's income for the particular taxation year from that source.

Related Provisions: 4(3) — Whether deductions are applicable to a particular source; 94(3)(a)(iii) — Application to trust deemed resident in Canada; 104(22.2), (22.3) — Recalculation of trust's foreign-source income and foreign tax; 250(6.1) — Trust that ceases to exist deemed resident throughout year.

Notes: 104(22)–(22.4) allow a trust to flow out to a beneficiary the foreign-source income of the trust, and to treat the beneficiary as having paid foreign tax paid by the trust on that income, so that the beneficiary can claim the foreign tax credit under 126 to offset Canadian taxes payable on the income of the beneficiary from the trust.

104(22) amended by 2002-2013 technical bill (Part 5 — technical), this version effective for taxation years that end after July 18, 2005.

104(22) earlier amended by 1993 technical bill.

Interpretation Bulletins: IT-201R2: Foreign tax credit — trust and beneficiaries; IT-506: Foreign income taxes as a deduction from income.

(22.1) Foreign tax deemed paid by beneficiary — Where a taxpayer is a beneficiary under a trust, for the purposes of this subsection and section 126, the taxpayer shall be deemed to have paid as business-income tax or non-business-income tax, as the case may be, for a particular taxation year in respect of a source the amount determined by the formula

$$A \times B / C$$

where

A   is the amount that, but for subsection (22.3), would be the business-income tax or non-business-income tax, as the case may be, paid by the trust in respect of the source for a taxation year (in this subsection referred to as "that year") of the trust that ends in the particular year;

B   is the amount deemed, because of a designation under subsection (22) for that year by the trust, to be the taxpayer's income from the source; and

C   is the trust's income for that year from the source.

Related Provisions: 4(3) — Whether deductions are applicable to a particular source; 94(3)(a)(iii) — Application to trust deemed resident in Canada; 126(2.22) — Foreign tax credit to trust on disposition of property by non-resident beneficiary.

Notes: 104(22.1) added by 1993 technical bill, effective for taxation years ending after November 12, 1981. It replaces former 104(22)(b). See Notes to 104(22).

Interpretation Bulletins: IT-201R2: Foreign tax credit — trust and beneficiaries.

(22.2) Recalculation of trust's foreign source income —
For the purpose of section 126, there shall be deducted in computing a trust's income from a source for a taxation year the total of all amounts deemed, because of designations under subsection (22) by the trust for the year, to be income of beneficiaries under the trust from that source.

Related Provisions: 94(3)(a)(iii) — Application to trust deemed resident in Canada.

Notes: 104(22.2) added by 1993 technical bill, effective for taxation years ending after November 12, 1981. It replaces former 104(22)(c).

Interpretation Bulletins: IT-201R2: Foreign tax credit — trust and beneficiaries.

(22.3) Recalculation of trust's foreign tax —
For the purpose of section 126, there shall be deducted in computing the business-income tax or non-business-income tax paid by a trust for a taxation year in respect of a source the total of all amounts deemed, because of designations under subsection (22) by the trust for the year, to be paid by beneficiaries under the trust as business-income tax or non-business-income tax, as the case may be, in respect of the source.

Related Provisions: 94(3)(a)(iii) — Application to trust deemed resident in Canada; 126(7)"non-business-income tax"(c.1) — Amount deducted under 104(22.3) from business-income tax excluded from non-business-income tax.

Notes: 104(22.3) added by 1993 technical bill, effective for taxation years ending after November 12, 1981. It replaces former 104(22)(d).

Interpretation Bulletins: IT-201R2: Foreign tax credit — trust and beneficiaries.

(22.4) Definitions —
For the purposes of subsections (22) to (22.3), the expressions "business-income tax" and "non-business-income tax" have the meanings assigned by subsection 126(7).

Notes: 104(22.4) added by 1993 technical bill, effective for taxation years ending after November 12, 1981. See Notes to 104(22).

Interpretation Bulletins: IT-201R2: Foreign tax credit — trust and beneficiaries.

(23) Deceased beneficiary of graduated rate estate —
In the case of a trust that is a graduated rate estate,

(a) [Repealed]

(b) [Repealed]

(c) the income of a person for a taxation year from the trust shall be deemed to be the person's benefits from or under the trust for the taxation year or years of the trust that ended in the year determined as provided by this section and section 105; and

(d) where an individual having income from the trust died after the end of a taxation year of the trust but before the end of the calendar year in which the taxation year ended, the individual's income from the trust for the period commencing immediately after the end of the taxation year and ending at the time of death shall be included in computing the individual's income for the individual's taxation year in which the individual died unless the individual's legal representative has elected otherwise, in which case the legal representative shall file a separate return of income for the period under this Part and pay the tax for the period under this Part as if

(i) the individual were another person,

(ii) the period were a taxation year,

(iii) that other person's only income for the period were the individual's income from the trust for that period, and

(iv) subject to sections 114.2 and 118.93, that other person were entitled to the deductions to which the individual was entitled under sections 110, 118 to 118.7 and 118.9 for the period in computing the individual's taxable income or tax payable under this Part, as the case may be, for the period.

(e) [Repealed]

Related Provisions: 94(3)(a)(iii) — Application to trust deemed resident in Canada; 114.2 — Deductions in separate returns; 118.93 — Credits in separate returns; 120.2(4)(a) — No minimum tax carryover on special return under 104(23)(d); 127.1(1)(a) — No refundable investment tax credit on special return; 127.55 — Minimum tax not applicable; 249(1)(c), (5), (6) — Taxation year of testamentary trust; *Interpretation Act* 27(5) — Meaning of "within 90 days".

Notes: Before 2016, 104(23) and 122(1) provided numerous benefits to a testamentary trust (TT), including low marginal tax rates. These have been eliminated other than for a graduated rate estate or qualified disability trust: see Notes to 122(1). See also Notes to 104(1), 70(5) re testamentary insurance trusts and 248(1)"graduated rate estate".

104(23) opening words amended and (e) repealed by 2014 budget bill #2, for 2016 and later taxation years.

104(23)(a)-(b) repealed by 2002-2013 technical bill (Part 5 — technical) effective Dec. 21, 2002. Instead of 104(23)(a), a TT's taxation year was determined under 249(1)(c) and 249(5), (6), and as of 2016, only 249(1)(c). The rule in 104(23)(b) is now in 249(1.1). For CRA policy on when a change in year-end was permitted under 104(23)(a), see Notes to 249.1(7), which provides the same rule for corporations. 104(23)(a) amended by 1995 Budget, 1993 Budget.

Interpretation Bulletins: IT-179R: Change of fiscal period; IT-326R3: Returns of deceased persons as "another person".

Forms: T4011: Preparing returns for deceased persons [guide].

(24) Amount payable —
For the purposes of subsections (6), (7), (7.01), (13), (16) and (20), subparagraph 53(2)(h)(i.1) and subsections 94(5.2) and (8), an amount is deemed not to have become payable to a beneficiary in a taxation year unless it was paid in the year to the beneficiary or the beneficiary was entitled in the year to enforce payment of it.

Related Provisions: 94(3)(a)(iii) — Application to trust deemed resident in Canada; 104(13.4)(b) — Death of beneficiary — spousal and similar trusts; 104(18) — Trust for person under age 21; 135.2(8)(d)(iii) — Override where Cdn Wheat Board Farmers' Trust unit bequeathed to spouse or common-law partner and election made.

Notes: 104(24) deems an amount *not* to be payable, but does not deem any amount to *be* payable. See Notes to 104(6) re an amount that cannot legally be paid.

CRA considers that a deemed capital gain (such as under 104(21.2)) is a "nothing" for trust law purposes (VIEWS docs 9529647, 9816425, 2010-0363071C6, 2010-0373431C6, 2015-0604971E5 [Greg Leslie, "Trusts — Be Mindful of Allocating Deemed Income!", 13(11) *Tax Hyperion* (Carswell) 7-8 (Nov. 2016)]). A general power to encroach on capital is insufficient to make a deemed capital gain payable. For it to be considered payable under 104(24), the terms of the trust must specifically give the trustees the discretion to pay out or make payable an amount equivalent to the deemed capital gain or the discretion to pay out or make payable amounts that are defined as income under the Act. Also, the trustees must be required to exercise their discretion before the end of the trust's taxation year and the exercise of discretion must be irrevocable with no conditions attached to the beneficiaries' entitlement to enforce payment of the amount in the year. The apportionment of the trust's income to each beneficiary must also be established. Also, the beneficiaries must be advised before the end of the trust's taxation year of the trustees' decision. The trustees' exercise of discretion and notification to the beneficiaries of their decision should be in writing (e.g., resolution signed by the trustees, minutes of trustees' meeting).

The first 12 months after death are the "executor's year", during which, at common law, the beneficiaries cannot enforce payment. Despite this, CRA may consider the trust's income during this period to be "payable" to the beneficiaries: IT-286R2 para. 6; VIEWS docs 2005-0116041E5, 2016-0669871C6 [2016 CTF q.14], 2020-0839931C6 [2020 STEP q.1]. See also 104(13) Notes.

Exchanging cheques with beneficiary B (loaning back the funds to the trust), where there are otherwise not enough funds to cover the cheque to B, might or might not constitute payment: VIEWS doc 9703437, citing *Cox Estate*, [1971] C.T.C. 2271 (SCC); *Produits L.D.G.*, [1973] C.T.C. 273 (FCTD); *W. Vézina et Fils Ltée*, [1973] C.T.C. 2197 (TRB); *Distillers Corp.*, [1974] C.T.C. 2258 (TRB); *Orenstein & Partners Inc.*, [1996] 2 C.T.C. 105 (FCTD).

On "payment" by issuing a promissory note, see docs 2010-0363071C6, 2012-0444891C6 [2012 Prairie Tax Conf. q.12], 2012-0462931C6 [2012 Ontario Tax Conf. q.20]; May 2010 ICAA roundtable (tinyurl.com/cra-abtax), q.21.

For more on 104(24) see VIEWS docs 2004-0100001E5; 2006-0185631 (104(24) does not determine beneficiary's income); 2011-0401851C6 (meaning of "payable"); 2011-0424341I7 (amounts designated to beneficiaries were not payable to them); 2012-0453581C6 [2012 APFF q.17]; 2013-047550117 (trust income paid to children not theirs because they received it as agent of father); 2015-0595111E5 (transfer of property constitutes "paid"); 2015-0595851C6 [2015 APFF q.6] (difference between tax income and accounting income is not "payable"); 2017-0703921C6 [2017 CPA Alberta q.25] (application to residual beneficiary of estate).

104(24) amended by 2002-2013 technical bill (generally effective 2007), 2007 budget bill #1.

Interpretation Bulletins: IT-286R2: Trusts — amount payable; IT-342R: Trusts — income payable to beneficiaries; IT-381R3: Trusts — capital gains and losses and the flow-through of taxable capital gains to beneficiaries.

I.T. Technical News: 11 (payments made by a trust for the benefit of a minor beneficiary).

(25), (25.1), (26) [Repealed under former Act]

Notes: 104(25) and (25.1), repealed by 1988 tax reform, provided rules to prevent the same income from being taxed in both the trust's and the beneficiaries' hands. Because of other amendments, these rules are no longer needed. 104(26), repealed by 1988 tax reform, preserved the character of a trust's interest income in a beneficiary's hands for purposes of the $1,000 investment income deduction under former 110.1, repealed at the same time.

(27) Pension benefits [flowed through estate] — If a trust, in a taxation year in which it is resident in Canada and is the graduated rate estate of an individual, receives a superannuation or pension benefit or a benefit out of or under a foreign retirement arrangement and designates, in its return of income for the year under this Part, an amount in respect of a beneficiary under the trust equal to the portion (in this subsection referred to as the "beneficiary's share") of the benefit that

(a) may reasonably be considered (having regard to all the circumstances including the terms and conditions of the trust arrangement) to be part of the amount that, by reason of subsection (13), was included in computing the income for a particular taxation year of the beneficiary, and

(b) was not designated by the trust in respect of any other beneficiary under the trust,

the following rules apply:

(c) where

(i) the benefit is an amount described in subparagraph (a)(i) of the definition "pension income" in subsection 118(7), and

(ii) the beneficiary was a spouse or common-law partner of the individual,

the beneficiary's share of the benefit shall be deemed, for the purposes of subsections 118(3) and (7), to be a payment described in subparagraph (a)(i) of the definition "pension income" in subsection 118(7) that is included in computing the beneficiary's income for the particular year,

(d) where the benefit

(i) is a single amount (as defined in subsection 147.1(1)), other than an amount that relates to an actuarial surplus, paid by a registered pension plan to the trust as a consequence of the individual's death and the individual was, at the time of death, a spouse or common-law partner of the beneficiary, or

(ii) would be an amount included in the total determined under paragraph 60(j) in respect of the beneficiary for the taxation year of the beneficiary in which the benefit was received by the trust if the benefit had been received by the beneficiary at the time it was received by the trust,

the beneficiary's share of the benefit is, for the purposes of paragraph 60(j), an eligible amount in respect of the beneficiary for the particular year, and

(e) where the benefit is a single amount (as defined in subsection 147.1(1)) paid by a registered pension plan to the trust as a consequence of the individual's death,

(i) if the beneficiary was, immediately before the death, a child or grandchild of the individual who, because of mental or physical infirmity, was financially dependent on the individual for support, the beneficiary's share of the benefit (other than any portion of it that relates to an actuarial surplus) is deemed, for the purposes of paragraph 60(l), to be an

amount from a registered pension plan included in computing the beneficiary's income for the particular year as a payment described in clause 60(l)(v)(B.01), and

(ii) if the beneficiary was, at the time of the death, under 18 years of age and a child or grandchild of the individual, the beneficiary's share of the benefit (other than any portion of it that relates to an actuarial surplus) is deemed, for the purposes of paragraph 60(l), to be an amount from a registered pension plan included in computing the beneficiary's income for the particular year as a payment described in subclause 60(l)(v)(B.1)(II).

Related Provisions: 60(l)(v)(B.1) — Rollover of RRSP/RRIF designated benefits to child or grandchild on death; 94(3)(a)(iii) — Application to trust deemed resident in Canada; 146(1.1) — Where child presumed not financially dependent for 104(27)(e)(i); 248(8) — Meaning of "consequence" of death; 250(6.1) — Trust that ceases to exist deemed resident throughout year.

Notes: 104(27) permits a trust to flow pension benefits out to a beneficiary, so that the beneficiary's trust income has the status of pension income for purposes of the 118(3) pension credit, the 60(j) RRSP rollover and the 60(l) deduction. Starting 2016, 104(27) can be used only by a GRE: see Notes to 248(1)"graduated rate estate".

For CRA interpretation of 104(27)(d)(ii) see VIEWS doc 2013-0506671I7.

104(27)(e)(i) is consequential on the rollover in 60(l)(v)(B.01) for certain lump sum pension benefits. It makes the rollover available where the benefit is paid to a testamentary trust and included in the child's income.

104(27) amended by 2014 budget bill #2 (for 2016 and later tax years), 2003 Budget, 2000 same-sex partners bill, 1992 and 1991 technical bills, 1990 pension bill.

Interpretation Bulletins: IT-124R6: Contributions to registered retirement savings plans; IT-528: Transfers of funds between registered plans.

Forms: T3 Sched. 7: Pension income allocations or designations; T3 Sched. 9: Income allocations and designations to beneficiaries.

(27.1) DPSP benefits [flowed through estate] — Where

(a) a trust, in a taxation year (in this subsection referred to as the "trust year") in which it is resident in Canada and is the graduated rate estate of an individual, receives an amount from a deferred profit sharing plan as a consequence of the individual's death,

(b) the individual was an employee of an employer who participated in the plan on behalf of the individual, and

(c) the amount is not part of a series of periodic payments,

such portion of the amount as

(d) is included under subsection 147(10) in computing the income of the trust for the trust year,

(e) can reasonably be considered (having regard to all the circumstances including the terms and conditions of the trust arrangement) to be part of the amount that was included under subsection (13) in computing the income for a particular taxation year of a beneficiary under the trust who was, at the time of the death, the individual's spouse or common-law partner, and

(f) is designated by the trust in respect of the beneficiary in the trust's return of income under this Part for the trust year

is, for the purposes of paragraph 60(j), an eligible amount in respect of the beneficiary for the particular year.

Related Provisions: 94(3)(a)(iii) — Application to trust deemed resident in Canada; 248(8) — Meaning of "consequence" of death; 250(6.1) — Trust that ceases to exist deemed resident throughout year.

Notes: Since 2016, 104(27.1) can be used only by a GRE: see Notes to 248(1)"graduated rate estate".

104(27.1) amended by 2014 budget bill #2 (for 2016 and later tax years), 2000 same-sex partners bill, 1992 technical bill, 1990 pension bill.

Interpretation Bulletins: IT-124R6: Contributions to registered retirement savings plans; IT-528: Transfers of funds between registered plans.

(28) Death benefit [flowed through estate] — If the graduated rate estate of an individual receives an amount on or after the individual's death in recognition of the individual's service in an office or employment, the portion of the amount that can reasonably be considered (having regard to all the circumstances including the

terms and conditions of the trust arrangement) to be paid or payable at any time to a beneficiary under the estate is deemed

(a) to be an amount received by the beneficiary at that time on or after the death in recognition of the individual's service in an office or employment; and

(b) except for purposes of this subsection, not to have been received by the estate.

Related Provisions: 56(1)(a)(iii) — Death benefit included in income; 94(3)(a)(iii) — Application to trust deemed resident in Canada; 250(6.1) — Trust that ceases to exist deemed resident throughout year.

Notes: 104(28) allows a death benefit to flow through an estate, so that the first $10,000 remains non-taxable in the beneficiary's hands. See the definition of "death benefit" in 248(1), and 56(1)(a)(iii). Starting 2016, 104(28) can be used only by a GRE: see Notes to 248(1)"graduated rate estate".

104(28) amended by 2014 budget bill #2, for 2016 and later taxation years, effectively to change "testamentary trust" to "graduated rate estate".

Interpretation Bulletins: IT-508R: Death benefits.

(29) [Repealed]

Notes: 104(29) amended by 2003 resource bill, for trust taxation years that end after Dec. 20, 2002, and repealed for taxation years that begin after 2006 (consequential on the repeal of 12(1)(o) and 18(1)(m)). 104(29) earlier amended by 1992 technical bill.

(30) Tax under Part XII.2 — For the purposes of this Part, there shall be deducted in computing the income of a trust for a taxation year the tax paid by the trust for the year under Part XII.2.

Related Provisions: 18(1)(t) — Tax under Part XII.2 is deductible.

(31) Idem — The amount in respect of a taxation year of a trust that is deemed under subsection 210.2(3) to have been paid by a beneficiary under the trust on account of the beneficiary's tax under this Part shall, for the purposes of subsection (13), be deemed to be an amount in respect of the income of the trust for the year that has become payable by the trust to the beneficiary at the end of the year.

Interpretation Bulletins: IT-342R: Trusts — income payable to beneficiaries.

Definitions [s. 104]: "accumulating income" — 108(1); "allocable amount" — 104(15); "allowable business investment loss" — 38(c), 248(1); "allowable capital loss" — 38(b), 248(1); "*alter ego* trust", "amount", "assessment" — 248(1); "aunt" — 252(2)(e); "beneficial ownership" — 248(3); "beneficially interested" — 248(25); "beneficiary" — 104(1.1), (5.5), 108(1); "brother" — 252(2); "business" — 248(1); "business-income tax" — 104(22.4), 126(7); "calendar year" — *Interpretation Act* 37(1)(a); "Canada" — 255, *Interpretation Act* 35(1); "Canadian resource property" — 66(15), 248(1); "capital gain" — 39(1)(a), 248(1); "capital interest" — 108(1), 248(1); "capital loss" — 39(1)(b), 248(1); "capital property" — 54, 248(1); "child" — 252(1); "common-law partner" — 248(1); "consequence" — 248(8); "contributor" — 94(1); "controlled" — 256(6), (6.1); "corporation" — 248(1), *Interpretation Act* 35(1); "cost amount" — 107(1)(e), 108(1); "created by the taxpayer's will" — 248(9.1); "deemed capital cost" — 104(5); "deferred profit sharing plan" — 147(1), 248(1); "depreciable property" — 13(21), 248(1); "designated beneficiary" — 210(1); "designated contributor" — 104(5.6), (5.7)(c); "designated employee benefit" — 144.1(1); "designated income" — 210(1); "designation year" — 104(21.2); "disposition" — 248(1); "disposition day" — 104(5.8); "dividend" — 248(1); "eligible taxable capital gains" — 108(1); "employee", "employee benefit plan" — 248(1); "employee life and health trust" — 144.1(2), 248(1); "employee trust", "employer", "employment" — 248(1); "estate" — 104(1), 248(1); "exempt beneficiary" — 104(5.4); "exempt property" — 108(1); "fair market value" — see 69(1) Notes; "financially dependent" — 146(1.1); "fiscal period" — 249.1; "foreign resource property" — 66(15), 248(1); "foreign retirement arrangement" — 248(1), Reg. 6803; "former spouse" — 252(3); "graduated rate estate" — 248(1); "grandparent" — 252(2); "great-aunt", "great-uncle" — 252(2)(f); "income" — of trust 108(3); "income interest" — 108(1), 248(1); "individual" — 248(1); "*inter vivos* trust" — 108(1), 248(1); "inventory" — 248(1); "investment tax credit" — 127(9), 248(1); "joint spousal or common-law partner trust" — 248(1); "land" — see 70(5.2) Notes; "legal representative", "Minister" — 248(1); "mutual fund trust" — 132(6)–(7), 132.2(3)(n), 248(1); "net taxable capital gains" — 104(21.3); "NISA Fund No. 2" — 248(1); "non-business-income tax" — 104(22.4), 126(7); "non-deductible distributions amount" — 104(16); "non-portfolio earnings" — 122.1(1); "non-resident" — 248(1); "non-resident-owned investment corporation" — 133(8), 248(1); "office" — 248(1); "parent" — 252(2)(a); "partnership" — see 96(1) Notes; "payable" — 104(24); "person", "personal trust", "post-1971 spousal or common-law partner trust" — 248(1); "pre-1972 spousal trust", "preferred beneficiary" — 108(1); "preferred beneficiary's share" — 104(15); "prescribed", "property" — 248(1); "qualified farm or fishing property" — 110.6(1); "received" — 248(7); "registered charity", "registered pension plan" — 248(1); "related" — 104(5.7)(b), 251(2); "relevant period" — 104(5.7); "resident contributor" — 94(1); "resident in Canada" — 94(3)(a), 250; "SIFT trust" — 122.1(1), (2), 248(1); "series" — 248(10); "settlor" — 108(1); "share", "shareholder" — 248(1); "single amount" — 147.1(1); "sister" — 252(2); "small business corporation" — 248(1); "spouse" — 252(3); "substituted" — 248(5);

"superannuation or pension benefit" — 248(1); "tax treaty" — 248(1); "taxable Canadian corporation" — 89(1), 248(1); "taxable capital gain" — 38(a), 248(1); "taxable dividend" — 89(1), 248(1); "taxable income" — 2(2), 248(1); "taxation year" — 249; "taxpayer" — 248(1); "trust" — 104(1), (3), 108(1), 248(1), (3); "uncle" — 252(2)(e); "vested indefeasibly" — 248(9.2).

Income Tax Folios [s. 104]: S1-F5-C1: Related persons and dealing at arm's length [replaces IT-419R2].

105. (1) Benefits under trust — The value of all benefits to a taxpayer during a taxation year from or under a trust, irrespective of when created, shall, subject to subsection (2), be included in computing the taxpayer's income for the year except to the extent that the value

(a) is otherwise required to be included in computing the taxpayer's income for a taxation year; or

(b) has been deducted under paragraph 53(2)(h) in computing the adjusted cost base of the taxpayer's interest in the trust or would be so deducted if that paragraph

(i) applied in respect of the taxpayer's interest in the trust, and

(ii) were read without reference to clause 53(2)(h)(i.1)(B).

Related Provisions: 104(19) — Portion of dividends deemed received by beneficiary; 104(21) — Portion of capital gains deemed gain of beneficiary; 107.3(4) — No application to qualifying environmental trusts; 108(5) — Interpretation.

Notes: 105(1) is not interpreted as broadly as it reads. VIEWS doc 9707317 states: "although it is the Department's position that the use of trust property by a beneficiary of the trust constitutes a benefit for the purposes of subsection 105(1), in the case of personal-use property owned by a trust, the Department will generally not assess a benefit for the use of that property. In this regard, personal-use property of a trust will, in accordance with the definition in section 54, include property (such as homes, cottages, boats, cars, etc.) owned primarily for the personal use or enjoyment of a beneficiary of the trust or any person related to the beneficiary." (See also 1988 and 1989 Cdn Tax Foundation conference Round Tables, qq. 69 and 31 respectively; *Income Tax Technical News* 11; 2006-0173711E5, 2012-0470951E5, 2020-0861041C6 [2020 CTF q.7].)

An interest-free loan is not a 105(1) "benefit": *Cooper*, [1989] C.T.C. 66 (F.C.T.D.).

For more on 105(1) see VIEWS docs 2006-017326117, 2008-0301881E5; 2012-0469481E5 (condition in 105(1)(a) not met), 2013-047550117, 2017-0716451E5.

Income Tax Folios: S1-F2-C3: Scholarships, research grants and other education assistance [replaces IT-340R].

Interpretation Bulletins: IT-243R4: Dividend refund to private corporations; IT-524: Trusts — flow-through of taxable dividends to a beneficiary — after 1987.

I.T. Technical News: 11 (payments made by a trust for the benefit of a minor beneficiary; taxable benefit for use of personal-use property).

(2) Upkeep, etc. — Such part of an amount paid by a trust out of income of the trust for the upkeep, maintenance or taxes of or in respect of property that, under the terms of the trust arrangement, is required to be maintained for the use of a tenant for life or a beneficiary as is reasonable in the circumstances shall be included in computing the income of the tenant for life or other beneficiary from the trust for the taxation year for which it was paid.

Related Provisions: 104(6) — Deduction in computing trust income; 104(13.1), (13.2) — Designation of distributed income by trust; 104(13.4)(b)(ii)(B) — Death of beneficiary — spousal and similar trusts; 108(5) — Interpretation; 120.4(1)"split income"(c), 120.4(5) — Income-splitting tax.

Notes: For interpretation of 105(2) see VIEWS docs 2005-0141481E5 (upkeep of a residence owned by an estate), 2006-017326117 (various situations).

Interpretation Bulletins: IT-243R4: Dividend refund to private corporations; IT-342R: Trusts — income payable to beneficiaries; IT-381R3: Trusts — capital gains and losses and the flow-through of taxable capital gains to beneficiaries; IT-465R: Non-resident beneficiaries of trusts; IT-524: Trusts — flow-through of taxable dividends to a beneficiary — after 1987.

I.T. Technical News: 11 (taxable benefit for use of personal-use property).

Definitions [s. 105]: "adjusted cost base" — 54, 248(1); "amount" — 248(1); "beneficiary" — 108(1); "property" — 248(1); "taxation year" — 249; "taxpayer" — 248(1); "trust" — 104(1), 108(1), 248(1), (3).

106. (1) Income interest in trust — Where an amount in respect of a taxpayer's income interest in a trust has been included in computing the taxpayer's income for a taxation year by reason of subsection (2) or 104(13), except to the extent that an amount in respect of that income interest has been deducted in computing the taxpayer's taxable income pursuant to subsection 112(1) or 138(6), there may be deducted in computing the taxpayer's income for the year the lesser of

(a) the amount so included in computing the taxpayer's income for the year, and

(b) the amount, if any, by which the cost to the taxpayer of the income interest exceeds the total of all amounts in respect of the interest that were deductible under this subsection in computing the taxpayer's income for previous taxation years.

Related Provisions: 106(1.1) — Cost of income interest; 108(1) — Exclusions from definition of "trust"; 115(1)(a)(iv) — Non-residents' taxable income earned in Canada; 128.1(10)"excluded right or interest"(j), (k) — Emigration — whether a deemed disposition of income interest.

Income Tax Folios: S6-F2-C1: Disposition of an income interest in a trust [replaces IT-385R2].

(1.1) Cost of income interest in a trust — The cost to a taxpayer of an income interest of the taxpayer in a trust is deemed to be nil unless

(a) any part of the interest was acquired by the taxpayer from a person who was the beneficiary in respect of the interest immediately before that acquisition; or

(b) the cost of any part of the interest would otherwise be determined not to be nil under paragraph 128.1(1)(c) or (4)(c).

Related Provisions: 108(1) — Exclusions from definition of "trust".

Notes: 106(1.1) amended by 2001 technical bill, for 2000 and later taxation years.

Income Tax Folios: S6-F2-C1: Disposition of an income interest in a trust [replaces IT-385R2].

(2) Disposition by taxpayer of income interest — Where in a taxation year a taxpayer disposes of an income interest in a trust,

(a) except where subsection (3) applies to the disposition, there shall be included in computing the taxpayer's income for the year the amount, if any, by which

(i) the proceeds of disposition

exceed

(ii) where that interest includes a right to enforce payment of an amount by the trust, the amount in respect of that right that has been included in computing the taxpayer's income for a taxation year because of subsection 104(13);

(b) any taxable capital gain or allowable capital loss of the taxpayer from the disposition shall be deemed to be nil; and

(c) for greater certainty, the cost to the taxpayer of each property received by the taxpayer as consideration for the disposition is the fair market value of the property at the time of the disposition.

Related Provisions: 107.3(4) — No application to qualifying environmental trusts; 107.4(3)(n) — No disposition of income interest in trust on qualifying disposition; 108(1) — Exclusions from definition of "trust"; 115(1)(a)(iv) — Non-residents' taxable income earned in Canada.

Notes: See Income Tax Folio S6-F2-C1. In *McKenzie*, 2011 TCC 289, a disposition by an income beneficiary to the trust itself, of a life interest in a bequest of company shares (given to encourage her to stay as a key employee after the owner's death), was not taxable under 106(2) because 106(3) applied. "A plain reading of 106(2) and (3) makes it clear that the Act generally does not seek to tax an income beneficiary whose rights are disposed of to the trust itself, but will tax any economic gain the income beneficiary may be able to realize on a disposition to a third party" (para. 29).

See also Roth et al., *Canadian Taxation of Trusts* (ctf.ca, 2016), pp. 336-51; Kay Gray, "Tax Implications of Distributing Property from a Personal Trust", 2005 BC Tax Conference (ctf.ca), 8:1-23.

See also Notes to 248(1)"disposition".

106(2)(a)(ii) added by 2001 technical bill, for 2000 and later taxation years.

Proposed amendments to 106(2) and (3) in the original version of the 1995-97 technical bill (Bill C-69) were not included when that bill was enacted (1998, c. 19). See instead the amendments to 108(1)"trust" enacted in 2001.

Income Tax Folios: S6-F2-C1: Disposition of an income interest in a trust [replaces IT-385R2].

Advance Tax Rulings: ATR-3: Winding-up of an estate.

(3) Proceeds of disposition of income interest — For greater certainty, where at any time any property of a trust has been distributed by the trust to a taxpayer who was a beneficiary under the trust in satisfaction of all or any part of the taxpayer's income interest in the trust, the trust shall be deemed to have disposed of the property for proceeds of disposition equal to the fair market value of the property at that time.

Notes: See Notes to 106(2).

Income Tax Folios: S6-F2-C1: Disposition of an income interest in a trust [replaces IT-385R2].

Definitions [s. 106]: "allowable capital loss" — 38(b), 248(1); "amount" — 248(1); "beneficiary" — 108(1); "cost" — 106(1.1); "fair market value" — see 69(1) Notes; "income interest" — 108(1), 248(1); "person" — 248(1); "proceeds of disposition" — 54, 106(3); "property" — 248(1); "taxable capital gain" — 38(a), 248(1); "taxable income" — 2(2), 248(1); "taxation year" — 249; "taxpayer" — 248(1); "trust" — 104(1), 108(1), 248(1), (3).

107. (1) Disposition by taxpayer of capital interest — Where a taxpayer has disposed of all or any part of the taxpayer's capital interest in a trust,

(a) where the trust is a personal trust or a prescribed trust, for the purpose of computing the taxpayer's capital gain, if any, from the disposition, the adjusted cost base to the taxpayer of the interest or the part of the interest, as the case may be, immediately before the disposition is, unless any part of the interest has ever been acquired for consideration and, at the time of the disposition, the trust is non-resident, deemed to be the greater of

(i) its adjusted cost base, otherwise determined, to the taxpayer immediately before the disposition, and

(ii) the amount, if any, by which

(A) its cost amount to the taxpayer immediately before the disposition

exceeds

(B) the total of all amounts deducted under paragraph 53(2)(g.1) in computing its adjusted cost base to the taxpayer immediately before the disposition;

(b) [Repealed]

(c) where the taxpayer is not a mutual fund trust, the taxpayer's loss from the disposition is deemed to be the amount, if any, by which the amount of that loss otherwise determined exceeds the amount, if any, by which

(i) the total of all amounts each of which was received or would, but for subsection 104(19), have been received by the trust on a share of the capital stock of a corporation before the disposition (and, where the trust is a unit trust, after 1987) and

(A) where the taxpayer is a corporation,

(I) was a taxable dividend designated under subsection 104(19) by the trust in respect of the taxpayer, to the extent of the amount of the dividend that was deductible under section 112 or subsection 115(1) or 138(6) in computing the taxpayer's taxable income or taxable income earned in Canada for any taxation year, or

(II) was an amount designated under subsection 104(20) by the trust in respect of the taxpayer,

(B) where the taxpayer is another trust, was an amount designated under subsection 104(19) or (20) by the trust in respect of the taxpayer, and

(C) where the taxpayer is not a corporation, trust or partnership, was an amount designated under subsection 104(20) by the trust in respect of the taxpayer

exceeds

(ii) the portion of the total determined under subparagraph (i) that can reasonably be considered to have resulted in a reduction, under this paragraph, of the taxpayer's loss otherwise determined from a previous disposition of an interest in the trust,

(d) where the taxpayer is a partnership, the share of a person (other than another partnership or a mutual fund trust) of any loss of the partnership from the disposition is deemed to be the amount, if any, by which that loss otherwise determined exceeds the amount, if any, by which

(i) the total of all amounts each of which is a dividend that was received or would, but for subsection 104(19), have been received by the trust on a share of the capital stock of a corporation before the disposition (and, where the trust is a unit trust, after 1987) and

(A) where the person is a corporation,

(I) was a taxable dividend that was designated under subsection 104(19) by the trust in respect of the taxpayer, to the extent of the amount of the dividend that was deductible under section 112 or subsection 115(1) or 138(6) in computing the person's taxable income or taxable income earned in Canada for any taxation year, or

(II) was a dividend designated under subsection 104(20) by the trust in respect of the taxpayer and was an amount received by the person,

(B) where the person is an individual other than a trust, was a dividend designated under subsection 104(20) by the trust in respect of the taxpayer and was an amount received by the person, and

(C) where the person is another trust, was a dividend designated under subsection 104(19) or (20) by the trust in respect of the taxpayer and was an amount received by the person (or that would have been received by the person if this Act were read without reference to subsection 104(19)),

exceeds

(ii) the portion of the total determined under subparagraph (i) that can reasonably be considered to have resulted in a reduction, under this paragraph, of the person's loss otherwise determined from a previous disposition of an interest in the trust; and

(e) if the capital interest is not a capital property of the taxpayer, notwithstanding the definition "cost amount" in subsection 108(1), its cost amount is deemed to be the amount, if any, by which

(i) the amount that would, if this Act were read without reference to this paragraph and the definition "cost amount" in subsection 108(1), be its cost amount

exceeds

(ii) the total of all amounts, each of which is an amount in respect of the capital interest that has become payable to the taxpayer before the disposition and that would be described in subparagraph 53(2)(h)(i.1) if that subparagraph were read without reference to its subclause (B)(I).

Related Provisions: 40(3.7) — Application to non-resident individual; 104(19) — Taxable dividends flowed through trust; 106 — Disposition of income interest; 107(1.1) — Cost of capital interest; 107.3(4) — No application to qualifying environmental trusts; 107.4(3)(b)(ii) — Application of stop-loss rule to qualifying disposition; 108(6) — Where terms of trust are varied; 108(7) — Meaning of "acquired for consideration"; 128.1(10)"excluded right or interest"(j), (k) — Emigration — whether a deemed disposition of capital interest; 248(1)"disposition"(d), (h) — Whether transfer by trust is a disposition of capital interest; 248(25.4) — Addition to cost of capital interest in trust.

Notes: On a distribution of capital to a non-resident beneficiary, CRA may require a s. 116 certificate; but new 116(5.01) provides some relief.

See VIEWS docs 2006-0169371E5 (107(1)(a)); 2007-0245281R3 (107(1)(c) does not apply); 2014-0538261C6 [2014 APFF q.9] (distribution by way of promissory note does not count). See also Notes to 248(1)"disposition".

107(1)(e) and 107(1.2) added by 2002-2013 technical bill for dispositions that occur, and valuations made, after Feb. 27, 2004 or earlier (extended to end of 2004 in some cases).

107(1) amended by 2001 technical bill (last change effective 2007); 1995-97, 1994, 1993 and 1991 technical bills.

Regulations: 4800.1 (prescribed trust).

Advance Tax Rulings: ATR-38: Distribution of all of the property of an estate.

(1.1) Cost of capital interest in a trust — The cost to a taxpayer of a capital interest of the taxpayer in a personal trust or a prescribed trust is deemed to be,

(a) where the taxpayer elected under subsection 110.6(19) in respect of the interest and the trust does not elect under that subsection in respect of any property of the trust, the taxpayer's cost of the interest determined under paragraph 110.6(19)(a); and

(b) in any other case, nil, unless

(i) any part of the interest was acquired by the taxpayer from a person who was the beneficiary in respect of the interest immediately before that acquisition, or

(ii) the cost of any part of the interest would otherwise be determined not to be nil under section 48 as it read in its application before 1993 or under paragraph 111(4)(e) or 128.1(1)(c) or (4)(c).

Related Provisions: 107.4(3)(k)–(m) — Cost of capital interest in trust following qualifying disposition; 107.4(4) — Fair market value of capital interest in trust; 248(25.4) — Addition to cost of capital interest in trust.

Notes: 107(1.1) amended by 2001 technical bill (for 2000 and later tax years), 1995-97 technical bill.

Regulations: 4800.1 (prescribed trust).

(1.2) Deemed fair market value — non-capital property — For the purpose of section 10, the fair market value at any time of a capital interest in a trust is deemed to be equal to the amount that is the total of

(a) the amount that would, if this Act were read without reference to this subsection, be its fair market value at that time, and

(b) the total of all amounts, each of which is an amount that would be described, in respect of the capital interest, in subparagraph 53(2)(h)(i.1) if that subparagraph were read without reference to its subclause (B)(I), that has become payable to the taxpayer before that time.

Related Provisions: 107.4(4) — Fair market value of vested capital interest.

Notes: See Notes to 107(1) for enactment of 107(1.2) and in-force rules.

(2) Distribution [rollout] by personal trust — Subject to subsections (2.001), (2.002) and (4) to (5), if at any time a property of a personal trust or a prescribed trust is distributed (otherwise than as a SIFT trust wind-up event) by the trust to a taxpayer who was a beneficiary under the trust and there is a resulting disposition of all or any part of the taxpayer's capital interest in the trust,

(a) the trust shall be deemed to have disposed of the property for proceeds of disposition equal to its cost amount to the trust immediately before that time;

(b) subject to subsection (2.2), the taxpayer is deemed to have acquired the property at a cost equal to the total of its cost amount to the trust immediately before that time and the specified percentage of the amount, if any, by which

(i) the adjusted cost base to the taxpayer of the capital interest or part of it, as the case may be, immediately before that time (determined without reference to paragraph (1)(a))

exceeds

(ii) the cost amount to the taxpayer of the capital interest or part of it, as the case may be, immediately before that time;

(b.1) for the purpose of paragraph (b), the specified percentage is,

(i) where the property is capital property (other than depreciable property), 100%, and

(ii) [Repealed]

(iii) in any other case, 50%;

(c) the taxpayer's proceeds of disposition of the capital interest in the trust (or of the part of it) disposed of by the taxpayer on the distribution are deemed to be equal to the amount, if any, by which

> (i) the cost at which the taxpayer would be deemed by paragraph (b) to have acquired the property if the specified percentage referred to in that paragraph were 100%

exceeds

> (ii) the total of all amounts each of which is an eligible offset at that time of the taxpayer in respect of the capital interest or the part of it;

(d) where the property so distributed was depreciable property of a prescribed class of the trust and the amount that was the capital cost to the trust of that property exceeds the cost at which the taxpayer is deemed by this section to have acquired the property, for the purposes of sections 13 and 20 and any regulations made under paragraph 20(1)(a)

> (i) the capital cost to the taxpayer of the property shall be deemed to be the amount that was the capital cost of the property to the trust, and

> (ii) the excess shall be deemed to have been allowed to the taxpayer in respect of the property under regulations made under paragraph 20(1)(a) in computing income for taxation years before the acquisition by the taxpayer of the property;

(d.1), (e), (f) [Repealed]

Related Provisions: 43(3) — No capital loss on payment out of trust's income or gains; 53(4) — Effect on ACB of trust interest; 69(11) — Deemed proceeds of disposition; 80.03(1), (3)(b) — Capital gain where subsec. 107(2) applies to trust interest on disposition following debt forgiveness; 104(4)(a.2) — Anti-avoidance rule where trust distributes property before death; 104(5.8) — Trust transfers; 107(2.01) — Principal residence distribution by personal trust; 107(2.1) — Application where trust elects out of 107(2); 107(4) — Where trust in favour of spouse or self; 107(4.1) — Where subsec. 75(2) applicable to trust; 107(4.2) — Application of subsec. (2.1) instead of subsec. (2); 107(5) — Distribution to non-resident; 107.4(3) — Rollover of property to trust where no change in beneficial ownership; 107.4(4) — Fair market value of capital interest in trust; 126(2.22) — Foreign tax credit to trust on disposition of property by non-resident beneficiary; 220(4.6)–(4.63) — Security for tax on distribution of taxable Canadian property to non-resident beneficiary; 248(1)"disposition"(d), (h) — Whether transfer by trust is a disposition of capital interest; 248(25.1) — Deemed taxable Canadian property retains status through trust-to-trust transfer.

Notes: 107(2) allows a "rollout" of a personal trust's property to the beneficiaries at cost in many cases. See, however, 107(2.001), (2.002), (4), (4.1), (4.2) and (5) for various restrictions, including a capital distribution to a non-resident (107(5)). See also Notes to 107(2.1).

107(2) can apply where a personal trust distributes property to a beneficiary whose capital interest in the trust is subject to the exercise of discretion by the trustee: VIEWS doc 2004-0069901C6.

107(2) can be used to roll out property to avoid the 21-year deemed disposition in 104(4); but if the beneficiary is non-resident, 107(5) stops 107(2) from applying. A rollout to a corp whose shares are owned by a non-resident or a new trust may trigger GAAR (other than for property in 128.1(4)(b)(i)-(iii)): 2017-0693321C6 [2017 STEP q.2], 2017-0720321C6 [2017 APFF q.4], 2017-0724301C6 [2017 CTF q.1]; 2019-0823581C6 [2019 CTF q.6], 2020-0839991C6 [2020 STEP q.12]. See also Sweeney, "The Perils of an Assignment by a Non-Resident Beneficiary of a Capital Interest in a Trust to a Canadian Corp", VIII(1) *Personal Tax & Estate Planning* (Federated Press) 2-16 (2019).

For more CRA interpretation see VIEWS docs 2004-0062121E5 (Cdn resident estate with non-resident [NR] beneficiaries [Bs], and NR estate with resident Bs); 2007-0224131R3, 2007-0232421R3 (X entitled under deceased's will to buy property from estate); 2010-0367401R3 (107(2) applies after variation of testamentary trust), 2010-0376681R3 (107(2) applies); 2011-0391781E5 (distribution of life insurance policy); 2011-0399501E5 (NR trust distributing TCP to NR B); 2012-0442741E5 (distribution by NR trust to NR B); 2012-0464321E5 (distribution to multiple Bs); 2012-0464841R3 (various matters); 2012-0465081I7 (107(2)(a) determines proceeds of disposition but does not create new disposition or change timing of disposition for s. 116); 2013-0488061E5 and 2013-0488381E5 (property transfer is part 107(2) rollout, part debt payment); 2013-0499021I7, 2013-0503481E5 and 2014-0526551C6 [2014 STEP q.8] (transfer cannot be both 107(2) distribution and debt settlement); 2013-0511391E5 (property acquired from trust by deceased B's estate: cost stepped up to FMV); 2014-0538261C6 [2014 APFF q.9] (distribution by promissory note does not qualify for 107(2)); 2015-0593091C6 [2015 APFF q.8] (distribution of property subject to mortgage held by B); 2015-0606771R3 (107(2) applies in situation involving disclaimer); 2016-0635051R3 (107(2) applies on rollout to NR trust whose settlor no longer exists); 2019-0795761R3 (107(2) applies on rollout to daughters); 2020-0839991C6 [2020 STEP q.6] (examples, including where B assumes 108(1)"eligible offset" debt as condition of trust distribution); 2020-0847201C6 [2020 STEP q.13] (107(2) can apply to real property distributed by a NR estate to NR Bs).

See also Roth et al., *Canadian Taxation of Trusts* (ctf.ca, 2016), pp. 271-336; Kay Gray, "Tax Implications of Distributing Property from a Personal Trust", 2005 BC Tax Conference (ctf.ca), 8:1-23.

107(2)(b.1)(ii) and (f) repealed by 2016 budget bill #2, effective 2017, as part of changing the eligible capital property rules to CCA Class 14.1 (see Notes to 20(1)(b)). Before 2017, read:

> (b.1)(ii) where the property is eligible capital property in respect of a business of the trust, 100%, and

>   . . . . .

> (f) where the property so distributed was eligible capital property of the trust in respect of a business of the trust,

>> (i) where the eligible capital expenditure of the trust in respect of the property exceeds the cost at which the taxpayer is deemed by this subsection to have acquired the property, for the purposes of sections 14, 20 and 24,

>>> (A) the eligible capital expenditure of the taxpayer in respect of the property shall be deemed to be the amount that was the eligible capital expenditure of the trust in respect of the property, and

>>> (B) ¾ of the excess shall be deemed to have been allowed under paragraph 20(1)(b) to the taxpayer in respect of the property in computing income for taxation years ending

>>>> (I) before the acquisition by the taxpayer of the property, and

>>>> (II) after the adjustment time of the taxpayer in respect of the business, and

>> (ii) for the purpose of determining after that time the amount required by paragraph 14(1)(b) to be included in computing the taxpayer's income in respect of any subsequent disposition of property of the business, there shall be added to the value otherwise determined for Q in the definition "cumulative eligible capital" in subsection 14(5) the amount determined by the formula

$$A \times B/C$$

> where

> A   is the amount, if any, determined for Q in that definition in respect of the business of the trust immediately before the distribution,

> B   is the fair market value of the property so distributed immediately before the distribution, and

> C   is the fair market value immediately before the distribution of all eligible capital property of the trust in respect of the business.

107(2) amended by 2002-2013 technical bill (last change effective for distributions after Dec. 20, 2002), 2010 budget bill #1 (effective March 5, 2010), 2008 budget bill #2, 2001 technical bill, 2000 Budget, 1995-97 technical bill, 1994 Budget, 1991 technical bill.

Regulations: 4800.1 (prescribed trust).

Income Tax Folios: S1-F3-C2: Principal residence [replaces IT-120R6, IT-437R].

Interpretation Bulletins: IT-209R: *Inter vivos* gifts of capital property to individuals directly or through trusts; IT-349R3: Intergenerational transfers of farm property on death; IT-393R2: Election re tax on rents and timber royalties — non-residents.

Advance Tax Rulings: ATR-38: Distribution of all of the property of an estate; ATR-70: Distribution of taxable Canadian property by a trust to a non-resident.

(2.001) No rollover on election by a trust — Where a trust makes a distribution of a property to a beneficiary of the trust in full or partial satisfaction of the beneficiary's capital interest in the trust and so elects in prescribed form filed with the Minister with the trust's return of income for its taxation year in which the distribution occurred, subsection (2) does not apply to the distribution if

(a) the trust is resident in Canada at the time of the distribution;

(b) the property is taxable Canadian property; or

(c) the property is capital property used in, or property described in the inventory of, a business carried on by the trust through a "permanent establishment" (as defined by regulation) in Canada immediately before the time of the distribution.

Related Provisions: 107(2.002) — Election by beneficiary; 107(2.1) — Scheme that applies when election made; 220(3.2), Reg. 600(b) — Late filing or revocation of election; 248(1)"taxable Canadian property"(m)–(q) — Extended meaning of TCP.

Notes: Once the election is made, the distribution falls under 107(2.1) instead of 107(2), and a 107(2.11) election may be appropriate.

If the trust is resident in Quebec, the election must be copied to Revenu Québec: *Taxation Act* ss. 688.0.0.1, 21.4.6.

For CRA interpretation see VIEWS docs 2009-0349411I7; 2012-0470391E5 (election can be made on fewer than all shares); 2012-0471061E5 (election can apply on a property-by-property basis, and should be by letter attached to T3 return); 2014-

0526581C6 [2014 STEP q.18] (election can be made on 1 property; send letter to CRA separately when filing electronically; lists information required in the letter).

If no election is filed, the rollover is automatic and the beneficiary inherits the low cost base: *Green*, 2012 CarswellNat 106 (TCC).

See also Barry Corbin, "Electing on Fractional Shares", 28(9) *Money & Family Law* (Carswell) 65-66 (Sept. 2013).

107(2.001)(c) amended by 2016 budget bill #2, effective 2017, to delete "eligible capital property in respect of," after "used in" (as part of changing the ECP rules to CCA Class 14.1: see Notes to 20(1)(b)).

107(2.001) added by 2001 technical bill, for distributions after Oct. 1, 1996.

Regulations: No regulation defining "permanent establishment" as yet (though Reg. 8201 would be the logical choice).

(2.002) No rollover on election by a beneficiary — Where a non-resident trust makes a distribution of a property (other than a property described in paragraph (2.001)(b) or (c)) to a beneficiary of the trust in full or partial satisfaction of the beneficiary's capital interest in the trust and the beneficiary makes an election under this subsection in prescribed form filed with the Minister with the beneficiary's return of income for the beneficiary's taxation year in which the distribution occurred,

(a) subsection (2) does not apply to the distribution; and

(b) for the purpose of subparagraph (1)(a)(ii), the cost amount of the interest to the beneficiary is deemed to be nil.

Related Provisions: 94(3)(a)(iv) — Application to trust deemed resident in Canada; 107(2.001) — Election by trust; 107(2.1) — Scheme that applies when election made.

Notes: For CRA interpretation see VIEWS doc 2015-0582701E5.

For a beneficiary filing Quebec returns, the election must be copied to Revenu Québec: *Taxation Act* ss. 688.0.0.2, 21.4.6.

The election should be made by letter attached to the T3 return, or sent to CRA separately when filing electronically: VIEWS docs 2013-0496431E5, 2014-0526581C6 [lists the information required in the letter].

An election "filed with the ... return" is valid even if the return is filed late. See Notes to 7(1.31).

107(2.002) added by 2001 technical bill, for distributions made after 1999.

(2.01) Distribution of principal residence — Where property that would, if a personal trust had designated the property under paragraph (c.1) of the definition "principal residence" in section 54, be a principal residence (within the meaning of that definition) of the trust for a taxation year, is at any time (in this subsection referred to as "that time") distributed by the trust to a taxpayer in circumstances to which subsection (2) applies and the trust so elects in its return of income for the taxation year that includes that time,

(a) the trust shall be deemed to have disposed of the property immediately before the particular time that is immediately before that time for proceeds of disposition equal to the fair market value of the property at that time; and

(b) the trust shall be deemed to have reacquired the property at the particular time at a cost equal to that fair market value.

Notes: 107(2.01) allows a trust to "bump up" the cost of a principal residence where the gain is exempt due to 54"principal residence"(c.1) and 40(2)(b) (see Notes thereto).

For CRA interpretation see VIEWS doc 2012-0464321E5 (election on distribution to multiple beneficiaries).

If the trust is resident in Quebec, the election must be copied to Revenu Québec: *Taxation Act* ss. 688.0.1, 21.4.6.

107(2.01) amended by 2001 technical bill (for distributions after 1999), 1992 technical bill. Added by 1991 technical bill.

Income Tax Folios: S1-F3-C2: Principal residence [replaces IT-120R6, IT-437R].

(2.1) Other distributions — Where at any time a property of a trust is distributed by the trust to a beneficiary under the trust, there would, if this Act were read without reference to paragraphs (h) and (i) of the definition "disposition" in subsection 248(1), be a resulting disposition of all or any part of the beneficiary's capital interest in the trust (which interest or part, as the case may be, is in this subsection referred to as the "former interest") and the rules in subsections (2) and (3.1) and sections 88.1 and 132.2 do not apply in respect of the distribution,

(a) the trust is deemed to have disposed of the property for proceeds equal to its fair market value at that time;

(b) the beneficiary is deemed to have acquired the property at a cost equal to the proceeds determined under paragraph (a);

(c) subject to paragraph (e), the beneficiary's proceeds of disposition of the portion of the former interest disposed of by the beneficiary on the distribution are deemed to be equal to the amount, if any, by which

(i) the proceeds determined under paragraph (a) (other than the portion, if any, of the proceeds that is a payment to which paragraph (h) or (i) of the definition "disposition" in subsection 248(1) applies),

exceed the total of

(ii) where the property is not a Canadian resource property or foreign resource property, the amount, if any, by which

(A) the fair market value of the property at that time

exceeds the total of

(B) the cost amount to the trust of the property immediately before that time, and

(C) the portion, if any, of the excess that would be determined under this subparagraph if this subparagraph were read without reference to this clause that represents a payment to which paragraph (h) or (i) of the definition "disposition" in subsection 248(1) applies, and

(iii) all amounts each of which is an eligible offset at that time of the taxpayer in respect of the former interest;

(d) notwithstanding paragraphs (a) to (c), where the trust is non-resident at that time, the property is not described in paragraph (2.001)(b) or (c) and, if this Act were read without reference to this paragraph, there would be no income, loss, taxable capital gain or allowable capital loss of a taxpayer in respect of the property because of the application of subsection 75(2) to the disposition at that time of the property,

(i) the trust is deemed to have disposed of the property for proceeds equal to the cost amount of the property,

(ii) the beneficiary is deemed to have acquired the property at a cost equal to the fair market value of the property, and

(iii) the beneficiary's proceeds of disposition of the portion of the former interest disposed of by the beneficiary on the distribution are deemed to be equal to the amount, if any, by which

(A) the fair market value of the property

exceeds the total of

(B) the portion, if any, of the amount of the distribution that is a payment to which paragraph (h) or (i) of the definition "disposition" in subsection 248(1) applies, and

(C) all amounts each of which is an eligible offset at that time of the taxpayer in respect of the former interest; and

(e) where the trust is a mutual fund trust, the distribution occurs in a taxation year of the trust before its 2003 taxation year, the trust has elected under subsection (2.11) in respect of the year and the trust so elects in respect of the distribution in prescribed form filed with the trust's return of income for the year,

(i) this subsection shall be read without reference to paragraph (c), and

(ii) the beneficiary's proceeds of disposition of the portion of the former interest disposed of by the beneficiary on the distribution are deemed to be equal to the amount determined under paragraph (a).

Related Provisions: 43(3) — No capital loss on payment out of trust's income or gains; 53(2)(h) — Reduction in ACB of interest in trust; 53(4) — Effect on ACB of trust interest; 94(3)(a)(iii) — Application to trust deemed resident in Canada; 107(2.11) — Election not to flow out gains to beneficiaries; 107(4.2) — Application of subsec. (2.1); 107(5) — 107(2.1) applies to capital distribution to non-resident beneficiary; 107.4(4) — Fair market value of capital interest in trust; 135.2(10)(a) — 107(2.1 does not apply to Canadian Wheat Board Farmers' Trust windup; 248(1)"disposition"(d), (h) — Whether transfer by trust is a disposition of capital interest.

Notes: For CRA interpretation on 107(2.1) see VIEWS docs 2007-0237011R3, 2009-0330901R3, 2010-0371391E5; 2015-0576751E5 (13(7)(e) can apply to a 107(2.1) distribution).

107(2.1) amended by 2008 budget bill #2 (effective July 15, 2008), 2001 and 1995-97 technical bills.

(2.11) Gains not distributed to beneficiaries

— If a trust that is resident in Canada for a taxation year makes in the taxation year one or more distributions to which subsection (2.1) applies and the trust elects in prescribed form filed with the trust's return for the year or a preceding taxation year to have one of the following paragraphs apply, the income of the trust for the year (determined without reference to subsection 104(6)) shall, for the purposes of subsections 104(6) and (13), be computed without regard

(a) if the election is to have this paragraph apply, to all of those distributions (other than distributions of cash denominated in Canadian dollars) to non-resident persons (including a partnership other than a Canadian partnership); and

(b) if the election is to have this paragraph apply, to all of those distributions (other than distributions of cash denominated in Canadian dollars).

Related Provisions: 43(3) — No capital loss on payment out of trust's income or gains; 107(2.12) — Whether election applies for 2003 and later years.

Notes: In the absence of an election under 107(2.11), the accrued gain realized by a trust on distribution of property to a non-resident beneficiary is considered payable to that beneficiary: VIEWS doc 2003-0000695.

If the trust is resident in Quebec, the election must be copied to Revenu Québec: *Taxation Act* ss. 688.1.1, 21.4.6.

107(2.11) amended by 2002-2013 technical bill (for 2002 and later tax years, or earlier by election), 2001 technical bill.

(2.12) Election — subsec. (2.11)

— An election made under subsection (2.11) by a mutual fund trust is deemed, for the trust's 2003 and subsequent taxation years, not to have been made if

(a) the election is made after December 20, 2000 and applies to any taxation year that ends before 2003; and

(b) the proceeds of disposition of a beneficiary's interest in the trust have been determined under paragraph (2.1)(e).

Notes: 107(2.12) added by 2001 technical bill [per Commons Finance Committee report, May 2001], in force June 14, 2001 (Royal Assent).

(2.2) Flow-through entity

— Where at any time before 2005 a beneficiary under a trust described in paragraph (h), (i) or (j) of the definition "flow-through entity" in subsection 39.1(1) received a distribution of property from the trust in satisfaction of all or a portion of the beneficiary's interests in the trust and the beneficiary files with the Minister on or before the beneficiary's filing-due date for the taxation year that includes that time an election in respect of the property in prescribed form, there shall be included in the cost to the beneficiary of a particular property (other than money) received by the beneficiary as part of the distribution of property the least of

(a) the amount, if any, by which the beneficiary's exempt capital gains balance (as defined in subsection 39.1(1)) in respect of the trust for the beneficiary's taxation year that includes that time exceeds the total of all amounts each of which is

(i) an amount by which a capital gain is reduced under section 39.1 in the year because of the beneficiary's exempt capital gains balance in respect of the trust,

(ii) twice an amount by which a taxable capital gain is reduced under section 39.1 in the year because of the beneficiary's exempt capital gains balance in respect of the trust, or

(iii) an amount included in the cost to the beneficiary of another property received by the beneficiary at or before that time in the year because of this subsection,

(b) the amount by which the fair market value of the particular property at that time exceeds the adjusted cost base to the trust of the particular property immediately before that time, and

(c) the amount designated in respect of the particular property in the election.

Related Provisions: 39.1(1)"exempt capital gains balance"F(a) — Exempt capital gains balance of flow-through entity.

Notes: 107(2.2)(a)(ii) amended by 2000 Budget to change "⅓ of" to "twice", effective for taxation years that end after Oct. 17, 2000, with a transitional rule to track the reduction in capital gains rate in 2000 from ¾ to ⅔ to ½.

107(2.2) added by 1995-97 technical bill, effective for dispositions made after 1993; the prescribed form could be filed until the end of 1998.

(3) Application of subsec. (3.1)

— Subsection (3.1) applies to a trust's distribution of property to a taxpayer if

(a) the distribution is a SIFT trust wind-up event to which section 88.1 does not apply;

(b) the property is a share and the only shares distributed on any SIFT trust wind-up event of the trust are of a single class of the capital stock of a taxable Canadian corporation; and

(c) where the trust is a SIFT wind-up entity, the distribution occurs no more than 60 days after the earlier of

(i) the first SIFT trust wind-up event of the trust, and

(ii) the first distribution to the trust that is a SIFT trust wind-up event of another trust.

Notes: 107(3) added by 2008 budget bill #2, this version effective for a trust's distribution of property after May 11, 2009.

Former 107(3) repealed by 2001 technical bill, for distributions made after 1999.

(3.1) SIFT trust wind-up event

— If this subsection applies to a trust's distribution of property, the following rules apply:

(a) the trust is deemed to have disposed of the property for proceeds of disposition equal to the adjusted cost base to the trust of the property immediately before the distribution;

(b) the taxpayer is deemed to have disposed of the taxpayer's interest as a beneficiary under the trust for proceeds of disposition equal to the cost amount to the taxpayer of the interest immediately before the distribution;

(c) the taxpayer is deemed to have acquired the property at a cost equal to

(i) if, at all times at which the trust makes a distribution that is a SIFT trust wind-up event, the taxpayer is the only beneficiary under the trust and is a SIFT wind-up entity or a taxable Canadian corporation, the adjusted cost base to the trust of the property immediately before the distribution, and

(ii) in any other case, the cost amount to the taxpayer of the taxpayer's interest as a beneficiary under the trust immediately before the distribution;

(d) if the taxpayer's interest as a beneficiary under the trust was immediately before the disposition taxable Canadian property of the taxpayer, the property is deemed to be, at any time that is within 60 months after the distribution, taxable Canadian property of the taxpayer; and

(e) if a liability of the trust becomes as a consequence of the distribution a liability of the corporation described in paragraph (3)(b) in respect of the distribution, and the amount payable by the corporation on the maturity of the liability is the same as the amount that would have been payable by the trust on its maturity,

(i) the transfer of the liability by the trust to the corporation is deemed not to have occurred, and

(ii) the liability is deemed

(A) to have been incurred or issued by the corporation at the time at which, and under the agreement under which, it was incurred or issued by the trust, and

(B) not to have been incurred or issued by the trust.

Related Provisions: 80.01(5.1) — Debt settlement on wind-up event; 85.1(7), (8) — Alternate mechanism for rollover of SIFT units to corporation; 88.1(2) — Wind-up of SIFT trust to single corporation; 107(2), (2.1) — Regular rollout rules do not apply; 107(3) — Conditions for 107(3.1) to apply; 107.4(3)(f) — Deemed taxable Canadian property retains status on rollover; 108(1)"cost amount" — Definition does not apply to 107(3.1); 248(25.1) — Deemed taxable Canadian property retains status through trust-to-trust transfer.

Notes: 107(3.1) allows a tax-free rollout of a SIFT trust's assets to a beneficiary at cost, if done before 2013 (see 248(1)"SIFT trust wind-up event"(a)). This allows a SIFT trust to convert back to corporate form, in advance of the tax on SIFT trust distributions applying in 2011 (see 122.1(2) and Notes to 104(16)). Where the beneficiary is a single corporation, see the "windup rollout" in 88.1(2). For a different mechanism permitting a beneficiary to roll the trust units into a corporation, see 85.1(7), (8). See Notes to 85.1(8) and 88.1(2).

107(3.1)(d) amended by 2010 budget bill #1, effective in determining after March 4, 2010 whether a property is taxable Canadian property of a taxpayer, to add "at any time that is within 60 months after the distribution". See Notes to 44.1(2).

107(3.1) added by 2008 budget bill #2, effective July 15, 2008.

(4) Trusts in favour of spouse, common-law partner or self — Subsection (2.1) applies (and subsection (2) does not apply) at any time to property distributed to a beneficiary by a trust described in paragraph 104(4)(a) where

(a) the beneficiary is not

(i) in the case of a post-1971 spousal or common-law partner trust, the spouse or common-law partner referred to in paragraph 104(4)(a),

(ii) in the case of an *alter ego* trust, the taxpayer referred to in paragraph 104(4)(a), and

(iii) in the case of a joint spousal or common-law partner trust, the taxpayer, spouse or common-law partner referred to in paragraph 104(4)(a); and

(b) the distribution of the property occurs on or before the earlier of

(i) a reacquisition, in respect of any property of the trust, that occurs immediately after the day described by paragraph 104(4)(a), and

(ii) the cessation of the trust's existence.

Related Provisions: 104(6) — Deduction in computing income of trust; 107(5) — Distribution to non-resident beneficiary; 108(1) — "accumulating income".

Notes: 107(4)(b) amended by 2002-2013 technical bill (Part 5 — technical) effective for distributions made after Oct. 2011. 107(4) earlier amended by 2000 same-sex partners bill, 2001 and 1992 technical bills.

Income Tax Folios: S1-F3-C2: Principal residence [replaces IT-120R6, IT-437R].

Interpretation Bulletins: IT-286R2: Trusts — amount payable; IT-381R3: Trusts — capital gains and losses and the flow-through of taxable capital gains to beneficiaries; IT-465R: Non-resident beneficiaries of trusts.

(4.1) Where subsec. 75(2) applicable to trust — Subsection (2.1) applies (and subsection (2) does not apply) in respect of a distribution of any property of a particular personal trust or prescribed trust (other than an excluded property of the particular trust) by the particular trust to a taxpayer who was a beneficiary under the particular trust where

(a) the distribution was in satisfaction of all or any part of the taxpayer's capital interest in the particular trust;

(b) subsection 75(2) was applicable (determined without its reference to "while the person is resident in Canada" and as if subsection 75(3) as it read before March 21, 2013 were read without reference to its paragraph (c.2)), or subsection 94(8.2) was applicable (determined without reference to paragraph 94(8.1)(a)), at a particular time in respect of any property of

(i) the particular trust, or

(ii) a trust the property of which included a property that, through one or more dispositions to which subsection 107.4(3) applied, became a property of the particular trust, and the property was not, at any time after the particular time and before the distribution, the subject of a disposition for proceeds of disposition equal to the fair market value of the property at the time of the disposition;

(c) the taxpayer was neither

(i) the person (other than a trust described in subparagraph (b)(ii)) from whom the particular trust directly or indirectly received the property, or property for which the property was substituted, nor

(ii) an individual in respect of whom subsection 73(1) would be applicable on the transfer of capital property from the person described in subparagraph (i); and

(d) the person described in subparagraph (c)(i) was in existence at the time the property was distributed.

Related Provisions: 248(5) — Substituted property.

Notes: 107(4.1) provides that a trust to which 75(2) applies cannot roll out property under 107(2) to any beneficiary other than the person from whom it was received (or that person's spouse or former spouse or common-law partner). For examples of 107(4.1) applying see VIEWS docs 2010-0376681R3, 2011-0423141E5.

For discussion see David Louis, "Is a Family Trust Vulnerable to the CRA?", 186 *The Estate Planner* (CCH) 1-3 (July 2010); Manu Kakkar, "Trust Rollouts", 13(2) *Tax for the Owner-Manager* (ctf.ca) 1 (April 2013).

For the meaning of "indirectly" in (c)(i), see Notes to 17.1(1).

Rectification of a trust deed to avoid 107(4.1) was denied in *Kanji*, 2013 ONSC 781. (See Notes to 169(1) on rectification.)

To interpret "75(2) was applicable", see VIEWS docs 2005-0118181E5, 2011-0401831C6. For rulings that 107(4.1) does not apply see 2007-0224201R3, 2007-0226101R3. 107(4.1) ceases to apply when the beneficiary who contributed the 75(2)-tainted property dies: 2014-0552341E5.

107(4.1) opening words amended by 2017 budget bill #2, for taxation years that begin after 2016, to add the exclusion of "excluded property". This is a rewording of proposed 107(4.1)(a.1) in the Oct. 3, 2016 draft legislation (re principal residences).

107(4.1) amended by 2013 budget bill #2 (for tax years that end after March 20, 2013), 2002-2013 and 2001 technical bills. For explanation of the grandfathering for a pre-1989 trust, see Oct. 19, 2007 Finance comfort letter, reproduced here up to PITA 43rd ed. and in *Dept. of Finance Technical Notes*.

Regulations: 4800.1 (prescribed trust).

(4.2) Distribution of property received on qualifying disposition — Subsection (2.1) applies (and subsection (2) does not apply) at any time to property distributed after December 20, 2002 to a beneficiary by a personal trust or a trust prescribed for the purpose of subsection (2), if

(a) at a particular time before December 21, 2002 there was a qualifying disposition (within the meaning assigned by subsection 107.4(1)) of the property, or of other property for which the property is substituted, by a particular partnership or a particular corporation, as the case may be, to a trust; and

(b) the beneficiary is neither the particular partnership nor the particular corporation.

Related Provisions: 248(5) — Substituted property.

Notes: 107(4.2) added by 2002-2013 technical bill (Part 5 — technical) for distributions made after Dec. 20, 2002.

(5) Distribution to non-resident — Subsection (2.1) applies (and subsection (2) does not apply) in respect of a distribution of a property (other than a share of the capital stock of a non-resident-owned investment corporation or property described in any of subparagraphs 128.1(4)(b)(i) to (iii)) by a trust to a non-resident taxpayer (including a partnership other than a Canadian partnership) in satisfaction of all or part of the taxpayer's capital interest in the trust.

Related Provisions: 94(4)(g) — Deeming non-resident trust to be resident in Canada does not apply to 107(5); 107(2.11) — Election for gain not to be flowed out to beneficiary; 107(5.1) — Gain does not increase instalment requirements; 126(2.22) — Foreign tax credit to trust on disposition of property by non-resident beneficiary; 212(11) — Payment to non-resident beneficiary deemed paid as income of trust for withholding tax purposes; 220(4.6)–(4.63) — Security for tax on distribution of taxable Canadian property to non-resident beneficiary.

Notes: See Notes to 107(2). If a non-resident beneficiary disposes of an interest in a trust resident in Canada whose underlying value is primarily Canadian real property or certain resource property, s. 116 will apply since the interest falls under 248(1)"taxable Canadian property"(d).

CRA interprets the "(other than...)" exclusion to mean that distribution by a non-resident trust to a non-resident beneficiary of shares of an NRO or of property described in 128.1(4)(b)(i)-(iii) is eligible for the 107(2) rollover: VIEWS doc 2012-0442741E5.

107(5) amended by 2002-2013 technical bill (Part 5 — technical) for distributions made after Feb. 27, 2004, to change "by a trust resident in Canada" to "by a trust", so that the rule applies to non-resident trusts.

107(5) earlier amended by 2001 and 1992 technical bills.

Advance Tax Rulings: ATR-70: Distribution of taxable Canadian property by a trust to a non-resident.

(5.1) Instalment interest — If, solely because of the application of subsection (5), paragraphs (2)(a) to (c) do not apply to a distribution in a taxation year of taxable Canadian property by a trust, in applying sections 155 and 156 and subsections 156.1(1) to (3) and 161(2), (4) and (4.01) and any regulations made for the purposes of those provisions, the trust's tax payable under this Part for the year is deemed to be the lesser of

(a) the trust's tax payable under this Part for the year, determined before taking into consideration the specified future tax consequences for the year, and

(b) the amount that would be determined under paragraph (a) if subsection (5) did not apply to each distribution in the year of taxable Canadian property to which the rules in subsection (2) do not apply solely because of the application of subsection (5).

Notes: 107(5.1) opening words and para. (a) amended by 2002-2013 technical bill (Part 5 — technical), for distributions made after Oct. 2011, to change reference from 156.1 to 156.1(1)-(3) (thus excluding 156.1(4), which is the obligation to pay the remaining balance by the balance-due day), and to change (twice) "total taxes payable under this Part and Part I.1" to "tax payable under this Part".

107(5.1) added by 2001 technical bill, for distributions made after Oct. 1, 1996. It was 107(5.2) in the Dec. 23, 1998 draft legislation. Former proposed 107(5.1) was revised and enacted as 107(2.11).

(6) Loss reduction — Notwithstanding any other provision of this Act, where a person or partnership (in this subsection referred to as the "vendor") has disposed of property and would, but for this subsection, have had a loss from the disposition, the vendor's loss otherwise determined in respect of the disposition shall be reduced by such portion of that loss as may reasonably be considered to have accrued during a period in which

(a) the property or property for which it was substituted was held by a trust; and

(b) either

(i) the trust was non-resident and the property (or property for which it was substituted) was not taxable Canadian property of the trust, or

(ii) neither the vendor — nor a person that would, if section 251.1 were read without reference to the definition "controlled" in subsection 251.1(3), be affiliated with the vendor — had a capital interest in the trust.

Related Provisions: 248(5) — Substituted property.

Notes: 107(6) is an anti-avoidance rule designed to deal with acquisition of a capital interest in a trust that has a property (P) with an accrued loss. Where P is distributed to beneficiary B in satisfaction of that interest, any loss realized on a later disposition of P by B is denied to the extent it can reasonably be considered to have accrued when P was owned by the trust and either (i) the trust was non-resident (and P was not taxable Canadian property), or (ii) neither B nor certain affiliated persons had a capital interest in the trust. See also 251.2 re trust loss trading.

107(6) amended by 2002-2013 technical bill (Part 5 — technical), for dispositions made after Oct. 2011, to change "owned" to "held" in para. (a) and add subpara. (b)(i).

107(6)(b) amended by 1995-97 technical bill, effective April 27, 1995, to use the new "affiliated person" concept in 251.1.

Definitions [s. 107]: "acquired for consideration" — 108(7); "adjusted cost base" — 54, 248(1); "affiliated" — 251.1; "*alter ego* trust" — 248(1); "allowable capital loss" — 38(b), 248(1); "amount" — 248(1); "beneficiary" — 108(1); "business" — 248(1); "Canada" — 255; "Canadian partnership" — 102(1), 248(1); "Canadian resource property" — 66(15), 248(1); "capital gain" — 39(1), 248(1); "capital interest" — 108(1), 248(1); "capital loss" — 39(1)(b), 107(1)(c), 248(1); "capital property" — 54, 248(1); "common-law partner" — 248(1); "corporation" — 248(1), *Interpretation Act* 35(1); "cost" — 107(1.1); "cost amount" — 107(1)(e), 108(1); "depreciable property" — 13(21), 248(1); "disposition" — 248(1); "eligible capital expenditure" — 14(5), 248(1); "eligible capital property" — 54, 248(1); "eligible offset" — 108(1); "fair market value" — 107.4(4) and see 69(1) Notes; "foreign resource property" — 66(15), 248(1); "insurance corporation" — 248(1); "*inter vivos* trust" — 108(1), 248(1); "inventory" — 248(1); "joint spousal or common-law partner trust", "Minister" — 248(1); "mutual fund trust" — 132(6)–(7), 132.2(3)(n), 248(1); "non-resident" — 248(1); "non-resident-owned investment corporation" — 133(8), 248(1); "partnership" — see 96(1) Notes; "person", "personal trust", "post-1971 spousal or common-law partner trust", "prescribed" — 248(1); "prescribed trust" — Reg. 4800.1; "principal residence" — 54; "property" — 248(1); "qualifying disposition" — 107.4(1); "regulation" — 248(1); "related" — 251(2); "resident in Canada" — 94(3)(a), 250; "SIFT trust wind-up event", "SIFT wind-up entity", "share", "specified

future tax consequence" — 248(1); "specified percentage" — 107(2)(b.1); "substituted" — 248(5); "taxable Canadian corporation" — 89(1), 248(1); "taxable Canadian property" — 248(1); "taxable capital gain" — 38(a), 248(1); "taxation year" — 249; "taxpayer" — 248(1); "trust" — 104(1), 108(1), 248(1), (3); "unit trust" — 108(2), 248(1).

107.1 Distribution by certain employment-related trusts — If at any time any property of an employee life and health trust, an employee trust, a trust governed by an employee benefit plan or a trust described in paragraph (a.1) of the definition "trust" in subsection 108(1) has been distributed by the trust to a taxpayer who was a beneficiary under the trust in satisfaction of all or any part of the taxpayer's interest in the trust, the following rules apply:

(a) in the case of an employee life and health trust, an employee trust or a trust described in paragraph (a.1) of the definition "trust" in subsection 108(1),

(i) the trust shall be deemed to have disposed of the property immediately before that time for proceeds of disposition equal to its fair market value at that time, and

(ii) the taxpayer shall be deemed to have acquired the property at a cost equal to its fair market value at that time;

(b) in the case of a trust governed by an employee benefit plan,

(i) the trust shall be deemed to have disposed of the property for proceeds of disposition equal to its cost amount to the trust immediately before that time, and

(ii) the taxpayer shall be deemed to have acquired the property at a cost equal to the greater of

(A) its fair market value at that time, and

(B) the adjusted cost base to the taxpayer of the taxpayer's interest or part thereof, as the case may be, immediately before that time;

(c) the taxpayer shall be deemed to have disposed of the taxpayer's interest or part thereof, as the case may be, for proceeds of disposition equal to the adjusted cost base to the taxpayer of that interest or part thereof immediately before that time; and

(d) where the property was depreciable property of a prescribed class of the trust and the amount that was the capital cost to the trust of that property exceeds the cost at which the taxpayer is deemed by this section to have acquired the property, for the purposes of sections 13 and 20 and any regulations made under paragraph 20(1)(a),

(i) the capital cost to the taxpayer of the property shall be deemed to be the amount that was the capital cost of the property to the trust, and

(ii) the excess shall be deemed to have been allowed to the taxpayer in respect of the property under regulations made under paragraph 20(1)(a) in computing income for taxation years before the acquisition by the taxpayer of the property.

Related Provisions: 6(1)(g) — Income from employee benefit plan; 6(1)(h) — Income from employee trust; 18(1)(o) — No deduction for employee benefit plan contributions; 32.1 — Employee benefit plan deductions; 104(6) — Deduction in computing income of trust; 104(13) — Income payable to beneficiary.

Notes: 107.1(b) does not apply to a plan taxed under s. 7: VIEWS doc 2010-0373561C6.

107.1 amended by 2010 budget bill #2 (effective 2010), 2001 technical bill.

Definitions [s. 107.1]: "adjusted cost base" — 54, 248(1); "amount" — 108(1), 248(1); "cost amount" — 107(1)(e), 108(1); "depreciable property" — 13(21), 248(1); "employee benefit plan" — 248(1); "employee life and health trust" — 144.1(2), 248(1); "employee trust" — 248(1); "fair market value" — see 69(1) Notes; "property", "regulation" — 248(1); "taxation year" — 249; "taxpayer" — 248(1); "trust" — 104(1), 108(1), 248(1), (3).

Interpretation Bulletins: IT-502: Employee benefit plans and employee trusts.

107.2 Distribution by a retirement compensation arrangement — Where, at any time, any property of a trust governed by a retirement compensation arrangement has been distributed by the trust to a taxpayer who was a beneficiary under the trust in satisfaction of all or any part of the taxpayer's interest in the trust, for the purposes of this Part and Part XI.3, the following rules apply:

(a) the trust shall be deemed to have disposed of the property for proceeds of disposition equal to its fair market value at that time;

(b) the trust shall be deemed to have paid to the taxpayer as a distribution an amount equal to that fair market value;

(c) the taxpayer shall be deemed to have acquired the property at a cost equal to that fair market value;

(d) the taxpayer shall be deemed to have disposed of the taxpayer's interest or part thereof, as the case may be, for proceeds of disposition equal to the adjusted cost base to the taxpayer of that interest or part thereof immediately before that time; and

(e) where the property was depreciable property of a prescribed class of the trust and the amount that was the capital cost to the trust of that property exceeds the cost at which the taxpayer is deemed by this section to have acquired the property, for the purposes of sections 13 and 20 and any regulations made under paragraph 20(1)(a),

(i) the capital cost to the taxpayer of the property shall be deemed to be the amount that was the capital cost of the property to the trust, and

(ii) the excess shall be deemed to have been allowed to the taxpayer in respect of the property under regulations made under paragraph 20(1)(a) in computing the taxpayer's income for taxation years before the acquisition by the taxpayer of the property.

Related Provisions: 56(1)(x)–(z) — Benefits from RCA; 60(t) — Amount included under para. 56(1)(x) or (z) or subsec. 70(2); 60(u) — Amount included under para. 56(1)(y); 153(1)(q) — Withholding required on distribution by RCA; Part XI.3 — Tax in respect of retirement compensation arrangements.

Definitions [s. 107.2]: "adjusted cost base" — 54, 248(1); "depreciable property" — 13(21), 248(1); "fair market value" — see 69(1) Notes; "prescribed", "property", "regulation", "retirement compensation arrangement" — 248(1); "taxation year" — 249; "taxpayer" — 248(1); "trust" — 104(1), 108(1), 248(1), (3).

107.3 (1) Treatment of beneficiaries under qualifying environmental trusts — Where a taxpayer is a beneficiary under a qualifying environmental trust in a taxation year of the trust (in this subsection referred to as the "trust's year") that ends in a particular taxation year of the taxpayer,

(a) subject to paragraph (b), the taxpayer's income, non-capital loss and net capital loss for the particular year shall be computed as if the amount of the income or loss of the trust for the trust's year from any source or from sources in a particular place were the income or loss of the taxpayer from that source or from sources in that particular place for the particular year, to the extent of the portion thereof that can reasonably be considered to be the taxpayer's share of such income or loss; and

(b) if the taxpayer is non-resident at any time in the particular year and an income or loss described in paragraph (a) or an amount to which paragraph 12(1)(z.1) or (z.2) applies would not otherwise be included in computing the taxpayer's taxable income or taxable income earned in Canada, as the case may be, notwithstanding any other provision of this Act, the income, the loss or the amount shall be attributed to the carrying on of business in Canada by the taxpayer through a fixed place of business located in the province in which the site to which the trust relates is situated.

Related Provisions: 12(1)(z.1) — Inclusion in income of amount received from trust; 87(2)(j.93) — Amalgamation — continuing corporation; 107.3(2) — Where property transferred to beneficiary; 127.41 — Tax credit to beneficiary of QET.

Notes: See Notes to 248(1)"qualifying environmental trust".

107.3(1) added by 1994 Budget, for taxation years that end after Feb. 22, 1994; and amended by 1997 Budget, for taxation years that end after Feb. 18, 1997.

(2) Transfers to beneficiaries — Where property of a qualifying environmental trust is transferred at any time to a beneficiary

under the trust in satisfaction of all or any part of the beneficiary's interest as a beneficiary under the trust,

(a) the trust shall be deemed to have disposed of the property at that time for proceeds of disposition equal to its fair market value at that time; and

(b) the beneficiary shall be deemed to have acquired the property at that time at a cost equal to its fair market value at that time.

Related Provisions: 87(2)(j.93) — Amalgamation — continuing corporation; 107.3(1) — Income or loss flowed through to beneficiaries.

Notes: Any income or loss resulting from this rule is flowed through to the beneficiaries under 107.3(1).

107.3(2) added by 1994 Budget, for taxation years that end after Feb. 22, 1994; and amended by 1997 Budget, effective for taxation years that end after Feb. 18, 1997.

(3) Ceasing to be a qualifying environmental trust — If at any time a trust ceases to be a qualifying environmental trust,

(a) for the purposes of subsections 111(5.5) and 149(10), the trust is deemed to cease at that time to be exempt from tax under this Part on its taxable income;

(b) each beneficiary under the trust immediately before that time is deemed to receive at that time from the trust an amount equal to the percentage of the fair market value of the properties of the trust immediately after that time that can reasonably be considered to be the beneficiary's interest in the trust; and

(c) each beneficiary under the trust is deemed to acquire immediately after that time an interest in the trust at a cost equal to the amount deemed by paragraph (b) to be received by the beneficiary from the trust.

Related Provisions: 87(2)(j.93) — Amalgamation — continuing corporation.

Notes: 107.3(3) amended by 2013 budget bill #2, effective March 21, 2013 (consequential on an amendment extending 149(10) to trusts).

107.3(3) added by 1994 Budget, for tax years that end after Feb. 22, 1994; and amended by 1997 Budget, for tax years that end after Feb. 18, 1997.

(4) Application — Subsection 104(13) and sections 105 to 107 do not apply to a trust with respect to a taxation year during which it is a qualifying environmental trust.

Related Provisions: 12(1)(z.1) — Income inclusion in lieu of application of 104(13).

Notes: 107.3(4) added by 1994 Budget, for taxation years that end after Feb. 22, 1994.

Definitions [s. 107.3]: "business" — 248(1), 253; "fair market value" — see 69(1) Notes; "net capital loss", "non-capital loss" — 111(8), 248(1); "non-resident" — 248(1); "property" — 248(1); "province" — Interpretation Act 35(1); "qualifying environmental trust" — 211.6(1), 248(1); "resident in Canada" — 94(3)(a), 250; "taxable income" — 2(2), 248(1); "taxable income earned in Canada" — 248(1); "taxation year" — 11(2), 107.3(3)(a), 249; "taxpayer" — 248(1); "trust's year" — 107.3(1).

107.4 (1) Qualifying disposition — In this section, a "qualifying disposition" of a property means a disposition of the property before December 21, 2002 by a person or partnership, and a disposition of property after December 20, 2002 by an individual, (which person, partnership or individual is referred to in this subsection as the "contributor") as a result of a transfer of the property to a particular trust where

(a) the disposition does not result in a change in the beneficial ownership of the property;

(b) the proceeds of disposition would, if this Act were read without reference to this section and sections 69 and 73, not be determined under any provision of this Act;

(c) the particular trust is resident in Canada at the time of the transfer;

(d) [Repealed]

(e) unless the contributor is a trust, there is immediately after the disposition no absolute or contingent right of a person or partnership (other than the contributor or, where the property was co-owned, each of the joint contributors) as a beneficiary (determined with reference to subsection 104(1.1)) under the particular trust;

(f) the contributor is not an individual (other than a trust described in any of paragraphs (a) to (e.1) of the definition "trust" in subsection 108(1)), if the particular trust is described in any of paragraphs (a) to (e.1) of the definition "trust" in subsection 108(1);

(g) the disposition is not part of a series of transactions or events

(i) that begins after December 17, 1999 and that includes the subsequent acquisition, for consideration given to a personal trust, of a capital interest or an income interest in the trust,

(ii) that begins after December 17, 1999 and that includes the disposition of all or part of a capital interest or an income interest in a personal trust, other than a disposition solely as a consequence of a distribution from a trust to a person or partnership in satisfaction of all or part of that interest, or

(iii) that begins after June 5, 2000 and that includes the transfer to the particular trust of particular property as consideration for the acquisition of a capital interest in the particular trust, if the particular property can reasonably be considered to have been received by the particular trust in order to fund a distribution (other than a distribution that is proceeds of disposition of a capital interest in the particular trust);

(h) the disposition is not, and is not part of, a transaction

(i) that occurs after December 17, 1999, and

(ii) that includes the giving to the contributor, for the disposition, of any consideration (other than consideration that is an interest of the contributor as a beneficiary under the particular trust or that is the assumption by the particular trust of debt for which the property can, at the time of the disposition, reasonably be considered to be security);

(i) subsection 73(1) does not apply to the disposition and would not apply to the disposition if

(i) no election had been made under that subsection, and

(ii) section 73 were read without reference to subsection 73(1.02); and

(j) if the contributor is an amateur athlete trust, a cemetery care trust, an employee life and health trust, an employee trust, a trust deemed by subsection 143(1) to exist in respect of a congregation that is a constituent part of a religious organization, a related segregated fund trust (within the meaning assigned by paragraph 138.1(1)(a)), a trust described in paragraph 149(1)(o.4) or a trust governed by an eligible funeral arrangement, an employees profit sharing plan, a registered disability savings plan, a registered education savings plan, a registered supplementary unemployment benefit plan or a TFSA, the particular trust is the same type of trust.

Related Provisions: 75(2) — Revocable or reversionary trust; 94(4)(b) — Application of rule deeming non-resident trust to be resident in Canada; 104(1.1) — Restricted meaning of "beneficiary"; 107(4.2) — Application of subsec. 107(2.1); 107.4(2) — Application of para. (1)(a); 107.4(3) — Tax consequences of qualifying dispositions; 248(1)"disposition" — Whether transfer to a trust is a disposition; 248(10) — Series of transactions or events.

Notes: See Notes to 107.4(3).

107.4(1)(j) amended by 2014 budget bill #2, for 2016 and later taxation years, to change "an *inter vivos* trust" to "a trust" (in sync with generally replacing "testamentary trust" with "graduated rate estate").

107.4(1) earlier amended by 2002-2013 technical bill (last change effective for dispositions after Feb. 27, 2004), 2010 budget bill #2, 2008 budget bill #1, 2007 RDSPs bill. Added by 2001 technical bill.

(2) Application of paragraph (1)(a) — For the purpose of paragraph (1)(a),

(a) except where paragraph (b) applies, where a trust (in this paragraph and subsection (2.1) referred to as the "transferor trust"), in a period that does not exceed one day, disposes of one or more properties in the period to one or more other trusts, there is deemed to be no resulting change in the beneficial ownership of those properties if

(i) the transferor trust receives no consideration for the disposition, and

(ii) as a consequence of the disposition, the value of each beneficiary's beneficial ownership at the beginning of the period under the transferor trust in each particular property of the transferor trust (or group of two or more properties of the transferor trust that are identical to each other) is the same as the value of the beneficiary's beneficial ownership at the end of the period under the transferor trust and the other trust or trusts in each particular property (or in property that was immediately before the disposition included in the group of identical properties referred to above); and

(b) where a trust (in this paragraph referred to as the "transferor") governed by a registered retirement savings plan or by a registered retirement income fund transfers a property to a trust (in this paragraph referred to as the "transferee") governed by a registered retirement savings plan or by a registered retirement income fund, the transfer is deemed not to result in a change in the beneficial ownership of the property if the annuitant of the plan or fund that governs the transferor is also the annuitant of the plan or fund that governs the transferee.

Related Provisions: 107.4(2.1) — Fractional interest in a share.

Notes: 107.4(2) added by 2001 technical bill, for dispositions after Dec. 23, 1998.

(2.1) Fractional interests — For the purpose of applying paragraph (2)(a) in respect of a transfer by a transferor trust of property that includes a share and money, the other trust or trusts referred to in that paragraph may receive, in lieu of a transfer of a fractional interest in a share that would otherwise be required, a disproportionate amount of money or interest in the share (the value of which does not exceed the lesser of $200 and the fair market value of the fractional interest).

Notes: For a ruling applying 107.4(2.1) see VIEWS doc 2019-0792771R3.

107.4(2.1) added by 2001 technical bill, effective for dispositions after Dec. 23, 1998. It overrides a technical interpretation in VIEWS doc 2000-0032685.

(3) Tax consequences of qualifying dispositions — Where at a particular time there is a qualifying disposition of a property by a person or partnership (in this subsection referred to as the "transferor") to a trust (in this subsection referred to as the "transferee trust"),

(a) the transferor's proceeds of disposition of the property are deemed to be

(i) where the transferor so elects in writing and files the election with the Minister on or before the transferor's filing-due date for its taxation year that includes the particular time, or at any later time that is acceptable to the Minister, the amount specified in the election that is not less than the cost amount to the transferor of the property immediately before the particular time and not more than the fair market value of the property at the particular time, and

(ii) in any other case, the cost amount to the transferor of the property immediately before the particular time;

(b) the transferee trust's cost of the property is deemed to be the amount, if any, by which

(i) the proceeds determined under paragraph (a) in respect of the qualifying disposition

exceed

(ii) the amount by which the transferor's loss otherwise determined from the qualifying disposition would be reduced because of subsection 100(4), paragraph 107(1)(c) or (d) or any of subsections 112(3) to (4.2), if the proceeds determined under paragraph (a) were equal to the fair market value of the property at the particular time;

(c) [Repealed]

(d) if the property was depreciable property of a prescribed class of the transferor and its capital cost to the transferor exceeds the cost at which the transferee trust is deemed by this subsection to have acquired the property, for the purposes of sections 13 and

20 and any regulations made for the purpose of paragraph 20(1)(a),

(i) the capital cost of the property to the transferee trust is deemed to be the amount that was the capital cost of the property to the transferor, and

(ii) the excess is deemed to have been allowed to the transferee trust in respect of the property under regulations made for the purpose of paragraph 20(1)(a) in computing income for taxation years that ended before the particular time;

(e) [Repealed]

(f) if, as a result of a transaction or event, the property was deemed to be taxable Canadian property of the transferor by this paragraph or any of paragraphs 44.1(2)(c), 51(1)(f), 85(1)(i) and 85.1(1)(a), subsection 85.1(5), paragraph 85.1(8)(b), subsections 87(4) and (5) and paragraphs 97(2)(c) and 107(3.1)(d), the property is also deemed to be, at any time that is within 60 months after the transaction or event, taxable Canadian property of the transferee trust;

(g) where the transferor is a related segregated fund trust (in this paragraph having the meaning assigned by section 138.1),

(i) paragraph 138.1(1)(i) does not apply in respect of a disposition of an interest in the transferor that occurs in connection with the qualifying disposition, and

(ii) in computing the amount determined under paragraph 138.1(1)(i) in respect of a subsequent disposition of an interest in the transferee trust where the interest is deemed to exist in connection with a particular life insurance policy, the acquisition fee (as defined by subsection 138.1(6)) in respect of the particular policy shall be determined as if each amount determined under any of paragraphs 138.1(6)(a) to (d) in respect of the policyholder's interest in the transferor had been determined in respect of the policyholder's interest in the transferee trust;

(h) if the transferor is a trust to which property had been transferred by an individual (other than a trust),

(i) where subsection 73(1) applied in respect of the property so transferred and it is reasonable to consider that the property was so transferred in anticipation of the individual ceasing to be resident in Canada, for the purposes of paragraph 104(4)(a.3) and the application of this paragraph to a disposition by the transferee trust after the particular time, the transferee trust is deemed after the particular time to be a trust to which the individual had transferred property in anticipation of the individual ceasing to reside in Canada and in circumstances to which subsection 73(1) applied, and

(ii) for the purposes of paragraph (j) of the definition "excluded right or interest" in subsection 128.1(10) and the application of this paragraph to a disposition by the transferee trust after the particular time, where the property so transferred was transferred in circumstances to which this subsection would apply if subsection (1) were read without reference to paragraphs (1)(h) and (i), the transferee trust is deemed after the particular time to be a trust an interest in which was acquired by the individual as a consequence of a qualifying disposition;

(i) if the transferor is a trust (other than a personal trust or a trust prescribed for the purposes of subsection 107(2)), the transferee trust is deemed to be neither a personal trust nor a trust prescribed for the purposes of subsection 107(2);

(j) if the transferor is a trust and a taxpayer disposes of all or part of a capital interest in the transferor because of the qualifying disposition and, as a consequence, acquires a capital interest or part of it in the transferee trust

(i) the taxpayer is deemed to dispose of the capital interest or part of it in the transferor for proceeds equal to the cost amount to the taxpayer of that interest or part of it immediately before the particular time, and

(ii) the taxpayer is deemed to acquire the capital interest or part of it in the transferee trust at a cost equal to the amount, if any, by which

(A) that cost amount

exceeds

(B) the amount by which the taxpayer's loss otherwise determined from the disposition referred to in subparagraph (i) would be reduced because of paragraph 107(1)(c) or (d) if the proceeds under that subparagraph were equal to the fair market value of the capital interest or part of it in the transferor immediately before the particular time;

(k) where the transferor is a trust, a taxpayer's beneficial ownership in the property ceases to be derived from the taxpayer's capital interest in the transferor because of the qualifying disposition and no part of the taxpayer's capital interest in the transferor was disposed of because of the qualifying disposition, there shall, immediately after the particular time, be added to the cost otherwise determined of the taxpayer's capital interest in the transferee trust, the amount determined by the formula

$$A \times [(B - C)/B] - D$$

where

A is the cost amount to the taxpayer of the taxpayer's capital interest in the transferor immediately before the particular time,

B is the fair market value immediately before the particular time of the taxpayer's capital interest in the transferor,

C is the fair market value at the particular time of the taxpayer's capital interest in the transferor (determined as if the only property disposed of at the particular time were the particular property), and

D is the lesser of

(i) the amount, if any, by which the cost amount to the taxpayer of the taxpayer's capital interest in the transferor immediately before the particular time exceeds the fair market value of the taxpayer's capital interest in the transferor immediately before the particular time, and

(ii) the maximum amount by which the taxpayer's loss from a disposition of a capital interest otherwise determined could have been reduced because of paragraph 107(1)(c) or (d) if the taxpayer's capital interest in the transferor had been disposed of immediately before the particular time;

(l) where paragraph (k) applies to the qualifying disposition in respect of a taxpayer, the amount that would be determined under that paragraph in respect of the qualifying disposition if the amount determined for D in that paragraph were nil shall, immediately after the particular time, be deducted in computing the cost otherwise determined of the taxpayer's capital interest in the transferor;

(m) where paragraphs (j) and (k) do not apply in respect of the qualifying disposition, the transferor is deemed to acquire the capital interest or part of it in the transferee trust that is acquired as a consequence of the qualifying disposition

(i) where the transferee trust is a personal trust, at a cost equal to nil, and

(ii) in any other case, at a cost equal to the excess determined under paragraph (b) in respect of the qualifying disposition; and

(n) if the transferor is a trust and a taxpayer disposes of all or part of an income interest in the transferor because of the qualifying disposition and, as a consequence, acquires an income interest or a part of an income interest in the transferee trust, for the purpose of subsection 106(2), the taxpayer is deemed not to dispose of any part of the income interest in the transferor at the particular time.

Related Provisions: 53(4) — Effect on ACB of trust interest; 104(4)(a.4) — Deemed disposition by trust after 107.4(3) applied; 104(5.8) — Where property transferred from one trust to another; 107(4.1)(b)(ii) — Application to subsequent distribution by trust; 107.4(4) — Fair market value of capital interest in trust; 257 — Formula cannot calculate to less than zero.

Notes: 107.4(3) provides a rollover on certain transfers of property ("qualifying disposition" in 107.4(1)) that involve no change in beneficial ownership of the property.

For the meaning of "derived" in 107.4(3)(k), see Notes to 18.1(12).

107.4 applied in VIEWS docs 2005-0143361R3 (3 trusts split into 5 new trusts); 2007-0229731C6 (mergers and partitions of seg funds); 2007-0244691R3 and 2016-0660321R3 (REIT reorganizations); 2011-0428321R3 (transfer of assets by class of unitholders to new pooled fund); 2013-0492731R3 and 2014-0518511R3 (MFT reorg to eliminate subtrust); 2014-0527261E5 (settlor is sole beneficiary of Quebec trust and trustees have discretion to retain income: 107.4 applies); 2016-0625301R3 (merger of related segregated fund trusts); 2017-0720591R3, 2018-0752811R3 (reorgs of stapled commercial trust structures); 2018-0778961R3 (split-up of mutual fund trusts). It did not apply in 2011-0423291E5 (conditions not met).

There is no prescribed form for the election. A letter should be attached to the T3 return: VIEWS doc 2013-0474861E5.

For a transferor filing Quebec returns, an election under subpara. (a)(i) must be copied to Revenu Québec: *Taxation Act* ss. 692.8, 21.4.6.

107.4(3)(e) repealed by 2016 budget bill #2, effective 2017, as part of changing the eligible capital property rules to CCA Class 14.1 (see Notes to 20(1)(b)). It read:

(e) if the property was eligible capital property of the transferor in respect of a business of the transferor,

(i) where the eligible capital expenditure of the transferor in respect of the property exceeds the cost at which the transferee trust is deemed by this subsection to have acquired the property, for the purposes of sections 14, 20 and 24,

(A) the eligible capital expenditure of the transferee trust in respect of the property is deemed to be the amount that was the eligible capital expenditure of the transferor in respect of the property, and

(B) ¾ of the excess is deemed to have been allowed under paragraph 20(1)(b) to the transferee trust in respect of the property in computing income for taxation years that ended

(I) before the particular time, and

(II) after the adjustment time of the transferee trust in respect of the business, and

(ii) for the purpose of determining after the particular time the amount required by paragraph 14(1)(b) to be included in computing the transferee trust's income in respect of any subsequent disposition of the property of the business, there shall be added to the value otherwise determined for Q in the definition "cumulative eligible capital" in subsection 14(5) the amount determined by the formula

$$A \times (B/C)$$

where

A is the amount, if any, determined for Q in that definition in respect of the business of the transferor immediately before the particular time,

B is the fair market value of the property immediately before the particular time, and

C is the fair market value immediately before the particular time of all eligible capital property of the transferor in respect of the business;

107.4(3)(f) amended by 2010 budget bill #1, effective in determining after March 4, 2010 whether a property is taxable Canadian property, effectively to delete reference to (repealed) 107(2)(d.1) and add the 60-month limitation (see Notes to 44.1(2)).

107.4(3) earlier amended by 2008 budget bill #2 (for dispositions after Dec. 23, 1998) and 2005 budget bill #1 (for dispositions after 2004). Added by 2000 Budget.

(4) Fair market value of vested interest in trust — Where

(a) a particular capital interest in a trust is held by a beneficiary at any time,

(b) the particular interest is vested indefeasibly at that time,

(c) the trust is not described in any of paragraphs (a) to (e.1) of the definition "trust" in subsection 108(1), and

(d) interests under the trust are not ordinarily disposed of for consideration that reflects the fair market value of the net assets of the trust,

the fair market value of the particular interest at that time is deemed to be not less than the amount determined by the formula

$$(A - B) \times (C/D)$$

where

A is the total fair market value at that time of all properties of the trust,

B is the total of all amounts each of which is the amount of a debt owing by the trust at that time or the amount of any other obligation of the trust to pay any amount that is outstanding at that time,

C is the fair market value at that time of the particular interest (determined without reference to this subsection), and

D is the total fair market value at that time of all interests as beneficiaries under the trust (determined without reference to this subsection).

Related Provisions: 107(1.2) — Fair market value of capital interest in trust for purposes of valuation as inventory; 248(9.2) — Meaning of "vested indefeasibly"; 257 — Formula cannot calculate to less than zero.

Notes: 107.4(4) added by 2001 technical bill, for dispositions after Dec. 23, 1998.

Definitions [s. 107.4]: "amateur athlete trust" — 143.1(1.2)(a), 248(1); "amount" — 248(1); "beneficial ownership" — 248(3); "beneficiary" — 104(1.1), 108(1); "business" — 248(1); "Canada" — 255, *Interpretation Act* 35(1); "capital interest" — 108(1), 248(1); "capital property" — 54, 248(1); "cemetery care trust" — 148.1(1), 248(1); "contributor" — 107.4(1); "cost amount" — 107(1)(e), 248(1); "depreciable property" — 13(21), 248(1); "disposition" — 248(1); "eligible capital expenditure" — 14(5), 248(1); "eligible capital property" — 54, 248(1); "eligible funeral arrangement" — 148.1(1), 248(1); "employee life and health trust" — 144.1(2), 248(1); "employee trust" — 248(1); "employees profit sharing plan" — 144(1), 248(1); "fair market value" — 107.4(4) and see 69(1) Notes; "filing-due date" — 248(1); "income interest" — 108(1), 248(1); "individual" — 248(1); "*inter vivos* trust" — 108(1), 248(1); "life insurance policy" — 138(12), 248(1); "Minister", "non-resident" — 248(1); "partnership" — see 96(1) Notes; "person", "personal trust", "prescribed", "property" — 248(1); "qualifying disposition" — 107.4(1); "registered disability savings plan" — 146.4(1), 248(1); "registered education savings plan" — 146.1(1), 248(1); "registered supplementary unemployment benefit plan" — 145(1), 248(1); "regulation" — 248(1); "related" — 251(2)–(6); "related segregated fund trust" — 138.1(1)(a); "resident in Canada" — 94(3)(a), 250; "series of transactions" — 248(10); "security" — *Interpretation Act* 35(1); "taxable Canadian property" — 248(1); "TFSA" — 146.2(5), 248(1); "taxation year" — 249; "taxpayer" — 248(1); "transferor trust" — 107.4(2)(a); "trust" — 104(1), (3), 108(1), 248(1); "vested indefeasibly" — 248(9.2); "writing" — *Interpretation Act* 35(1).

108. (1) Definitions — In this Subdivision,

Notes: "This subdivision" (subdivision k) is ss. 104-108.

"accumulating income" of a trust for a taxation year means the amount that would be the income of the trust for the year if that amount were computed

(a) without reference to paragraphs 104(4)(a) and (a.1) and subsections 104(5.1), (5.2) and (12) and 107(4),

(b) as if the greatest amount that the trust was entitled to claim under subsection 104(6) in computing its income for the year were so claimed, and

(c) without reference to subsection 12(10.2), except to the extent that that subsection applies to amounts paid to a trust to which paragraph 70(6.1)(b) applies and before the death of the spouse or common-law partner referred to in that paragraph;

Notes: Para. (b) ensures that, if a trust fails to claim the maximum deduction under 104(6), "accumulating income" is computed as if the maximum claim had been made. (It may be advantageous not to claim the maximum under 104(6) in order to allow for a tax-free distribution to a beneficiary under 104(13.1) or (13.2).)

Definition amended by 2001 technical bill (for 2000 and later tax years), 2000 same-sex partners bill (effective 2001 or earlier), 1995 Budget, 1992 technical bill. 108(1)"accumulating income" was 108(1)(a) before RSC 1985 (5th Supp) consolidation for tax years ending after Nov. 1991.

Interpretation Bulletins: IT-381R3: Trusts — capital gains and losses and the flow-through of taxable capital gains to beneficiaries; IT-394R2: Preferred beneficiary election.

Advance Tax Rulings: ATR-34: Preferred beneficiary's election.

"beneficiary" under a trust includes a person beneficially interested therein;

Related Provisions: 104(1.1) — Restricted meaning of "beneficiary" for certain purposes; 104(5.5) — Meaning of "beneficiary" for purposes of election to postpone deemed disposition; 143.1(1.2)(e) — Deemed beneficiary of amateur athletes' reserve fund; 248(3) — Rules applicable in Quebec; 248(13) — Deemed beneficiary for certain purposes; 248(25) — Meaning of "beneficially interested".

Notes: Even though this definition applies only to 104-108, it was effectively extended to the entire Act in *Propep Inc.*, 2009 FCA 274 (leave to appeal denied 2010 CarswellNat 506 (SCC)), ruling that 248(25) applied to "beneficiary" in 256(1.2)(f)(ii).

See Notes to 188.1(5) re meaning of "includes".

108(1)"beneficiary" was 108(1)(b) before RSC 1985 (5th Supp) consolidation for tax years ending after Nov. 1991.

Income Tax Folios: S3-F10-C2: Prohibited investments — RRSPs, RRIFs and TFSAs.

"capital interest" of a taxpayer in a trust means all rights of the taxpayer as a beneficiary under the trust, and after 1999 includes a right (other than a right acquired before 2000 and disposed of before March 2000) to enforce payment of an amount by the trust that arises as a consequence of any such right, but does not include an income interest in the trust;

Related Provisions: 53(2)(h), (i) — Reduction in ACB of capital interest; 248(1)"capital interest" — Definition applies to entire Act; 248(1)"disposition"(d), (h) — Whether transfer by trust is a disposition of capital interest.

Notes: "Capital interest" amended by 2001 technical bill, effective 2000. 108(1)"capital interest" was 108(1)(c) before RSC 1985 (5th Supp) consolidation for tax years ending after Nov. 1991.

"cost amount" to a taxpayer at any time of a capital interest or part of it, as the case may be, in a trust, means (notwithstanding subsection 248(1) and except for the purposes of subsection 107(3.1) and section 107.4 and except in respect of a capital interest in a trust that is at that time a foreign affiliate of the taxpayer),

(a) where any money or other property of the trust has been distributed by the trust to the taxpayer in satisfaction of all or part of the taxpayer's capital interest (whether on the winding-up of the trust or otherwise), the total of

(i) the money so distributed, and

(ii) all amounts each of which is the cost amount to the trust, immediately before the distribution, of each such other property,

(iii) [Repealed]

(a.1) where that time (in this paragraph referred to as the "particular time") is immediately before the time that is immediately before the time of the death of the taxpayer and subsection 104(4) or (5) deems the trust to dispose of property at the end of the day that includes the particular time, the amount that would be determined under paragraph (b) if the taxpayer had died on a day that ended immediately before the time that is immediately before the particular time, and

(b) in any other case, the amount determined by the formula

$$(A - B) \times \frac{C}{D}$$

where

A is the total of

(i) all money of the trust on hand immediately before that time, and

(ii) all amounts each of which is the cost amount to the trust, immediately before that time, of each other property of the trust,

B is the total of all amounts each of which is the amount of any debt owing by the trust, or of any other obligation of the trust to pay any amount, that was outstanding immediately before that time,

C is the fair market value at that time of the capital interest or part thereof, as the case may be, in the trust, and

D is the fair market value at that time of all capital interests in the trust;

Related Provisions: 107(1)(e) — Cost amount of capital interest in trust that is not capital property; 248(1)"cost amount" — Definition for other purposes; 248(25.3) — Deemed cost of trust units; 257 — Formula cannot calculate to less than zero.

Notes: Definition amended by 2002-2013 technical bill (effective June 26, 2013), 2008 budget bill #2; 2001, 1993 and 1991 technical bills. 108(1)"cost amount" was 108(1)(d) before RSC 1985 (5th Supp) consolidation for tax years ending after Nov. 1991.

Advance Tax Rulings: ATR-38: Distribution of all of the property of an estate.

"designated income [para. 108(1)(d.1)]" — [Repealed under former Act]

Notes: Former 108(1)(d.1), which defined "designated income", repealed by 1988 tax reform effective 1988. The term is no longer used.

"eligible offset" at any time of a taxpayer in respect of all or part of the taxpayer's capital interest in a trust is the portion of any debt or obligation that is assumed by the taxpayer and that can reasonably be considered to be applicable to property distributed at that time in satisfaction of the interest or part of the interest, as the case may be, if the distribution is conditional upon the assumption by the taxpayer of the portion of the debt or obligation;

Notes: For an example of an EO see VIEWS doc 2020-0839991C6 [2020 STEP q.6]. "Eligible offset" added by 2001 technical bill, effective 2000.

"eligible real property gain", **"eligible real property loss"** — [Repealed]

Notes: "Eligible real property gain" and "eligible real property loss" (originally 108(1)(d.1) and (d.11)) added by 1992 technical bill, amended by 1993 technical bill, and repealed by 1994 Budget, effective for taxation years that begin after Feb. 22, 1994, as a result of the elimination of the $100,000 capital gains exemption in 110.6(3).

"eligible taxable capital gains", of a trust for a taxation year, means the lesser of

(a) its annual gains limit (within the meaning assigned by subsection 110.6(1)) for the year, and

(b) the amount determined by the formula

$$A - B$$

where

A is its cumulative gains limit (within the meaning assigned by subsection 110.6(1)) at the end of the year, and

B is the total of all amounts designated under subsection 104(21.2) by the trust in respect of beneficiaries for taxation years before that year;

Related Provisions: 257 — Formula cannot calculate to less than zero.

Notes: Opening words amended by 2017 budget bill #2, effective Dec. 14, 2017, to change "personal trust" to "trust" and add the commas. "Eligible taxable capital gains" (originally 108(1)(d.2)) added by 1992 technical bill, amended by 1993 technical bill, 1994 Budget.

Interpretation Bulletins: IT-381R3: Trusts — capital gains and losses and the flow-through of taxable capital gains to beneficiaries.

Forms: T3 Sched. 3: Eligible taxable capital gains.

"excluded property", of a trust, means property owned by the trust at, and distributed by the trust after, the end of 2016, if

(a) the trust is not in its first taxation year that begins after 2016 a trust described in subparagraph (c.1)(iii.1) of the definition "principal residence" in section 54, and

(b) the property is a property that would be the trust's "principal residence" (as defined in section 54) for the taxation year in which the distribution occurs if

(i) that definition were read without reference to its subparagraph (c.1)(iii.1), and

(ii) the trust designated the property under that definition as its principal residence for the taxation year;

Notes: Definition replaced by 2017 budget bill #2, for taxation years that begin after 2016. See 107(4.1). (The previous definition, long irrelevant, was "means a share of the capital stock of a non-resident-owned investment corporation that is not taxable Canadian property". See Notes to 133.)

108(1)"excluded property" amended by 1995-97 technical bill, effective April 27, 1995. Added by 1992 technical bill, effective February 12, 1991. Before redrafting to fit the RSC 1985 (5th Supp), it was para. 108(1)(d.12).

"exempt property" of a taxpayer at any time means property any income or gain from the disposition of which by the taxpayer at that time would, because the taxpayer is non-resident or because of a provision contained in a tax treaty, not cause an increase in the taxpayer's tax payable under this Part;

Related Provisions: 104(4), (5), (5.2) — Exempt property excluded from 21-year deemed disposition.

Notes: 108(1)"exempt property" added by 2001 technical bill, effective 1993 except that, before 1999, read "tax treaty" (now in 248(1)) as "convention or agreement with another country that has the force of law in Canada".

"income interest" of a taxpayer in a trust means a right (whether immediate or future and whether absolute or contingent) of the taxpayer as a beneficiary under a personal trust to, or to receive, all or any part of the income of the trust and, after 1999, includes a right (other than a right acquired before 2000 and disposed of before March 2000) to enforce payment of an amount by the trust that arises as a consequence of any such right;

Related Provisions: 108(3) — Meaning of "income" of trust; 248(1)"income interest" — Definition applies to entire Act.

Notes: 108(1)"income interest" amended by 2001 technical bill to add everything from "and, after 1999, includes a right ...".

"Income interest" amended in 1987, effective for interests created or materially altered after January 1987 that were acquired after 10pm EST, February 6, 1987. For earlier interests, read "under the trust" in place of "under a personal trust".

108(1)"income interest" was 108(1)(e) before RSC 1985 (5th Supp) consolidation for tax years ending after Nov. 1991.

Income Tax Folios: S6-F2-C1: Disposition of an income interest in a trust [replaces IT-385R2].

"inter vivos trust" means a trust other than a testamentary trust;

Related Provisions: 248(1)"*inter vivos* trust" — Definition applies to entire Act.

Notes: 108(1)"*inter vivos* trust" was 108(1)(f) before RSC 1985 (5th Supp) consolidation for tax years ending after Nov. 1991.

"non-qualifying real property" — [Repealed]

Notes: "Non-qualifying real property" added by 1992 technical bill, for 1992 and later taxation years. Before the RSC 1985 (5th Supp) consolidation, it was para. 108(1)(f.1). Definition repealed by 1994 Budget, for taxation years that begin after Feb. 22, 1994.

"pre-1972 spousal trust" at a particular time means a trust that was

(a) created by the will of a taxpayer who died before 1972, or

(b) created before June 18, 1971 by a taxpayer during the taxpayer's lifetime

that, throughout the period beginning at the time it was created and ending at the earliest of January 1, 1993, the day on which the taxpayer's spouse or common-law partner died and the particular time, was a trust under which the taxpayer's spouse or common-law partner was entitled to receive all of the income of the trust that arose before the spouse's or common-law partner's death, unless a person other than the spouse or common-law partner received or otherwise obtained the use of any of the income or capital of the trust before the end of that period;

Related Provisions: 104(4)(a.1) — Deemed disposition by a trust; 104(15) — Preferred beneficiary's share; 104(15)(a) — Allocable amount for preferred beneficiary election; 108(3) — Meaning of "income" of trust; 108(4) — Trust not disqualified by reason only of payment of certain duties and taxes; 248(9.1) — Whether trust created by taxpayer's will; 252(3) — Extended meaning of "spouse".

Notes: 108(1)"pre-1972 spousal trust" amended by 2000 same-sex partners bill (effective 2001, or earlier by election). Added by 1992 technical bill, originally as 108(1)(f.2).

Interpretation Bulletins: IT-381R3: Trusts — capital gains and losses and the flow-through of taxable capital gain to beneficiaries.

"preferred beneficiary" under a trust for a particular taxation year of the trust means a beneficiary under the trust at the end of the particular year who is resident in Canada at that time if

(a) the beneficiary is

(i) an individual in respect of whom paragraphs 118.3(1)(a) to (b) apply for the individual's taxation year (in this definition referred to as the "beneficiary's year") that ends in the particular year, or

(ii) an individual

(A) who attained the age of 18 years before the end of the beneficiary's year, was a dependant (within the meaning assigned by subsection 118(6)) of another individual for

the beneficiary's year and was dependent on the other individual because of mental or physical infirmity, and

(B) whose income (computed without reference to subsection 104(14)) for the beneficiary's year does not exceed the amount determined for F in subsection 118(1.1) for the year, and

(b) the beneficiary is

(i) the settlor of the trust,

(ii) the spouse or common-law partner or former spouse or common-law partner of the settlor of the trust, or

(iii) a child, grandchild or great grandchild of the settlor of the trust or the spouse or common-law partner of any such person;

Related Provisions: 104(14) — Preferred beneficiary election.

Notes: See Notes to 104(14). Note that the "settlor" of a trust, defined below, can lose such status due to another person's contribution of more property. Thus, a preferred beneficiary can cease to be one even though the trust's terms are unchanged.

Before 1996, PBs did not need to be disabled. See Notes to 104(14) and 118.3(1).

Cl. (a)(ii)(B) amended by 2021 budget bill #1, for 2020 and later tax years, to reflect the "basic personal amount" moving from 118(1)B(c) to 118(1.1)F.

Definition amended by 2000 same-sex partners bill (last change effective 2001), 1999, 1997 and 1995 Budgets. 108(1)"preferred beneficiary" was 108(1)(g) before RSC 1985 (5th Supp.) consolidation for tax years ending after Nov. 1991.

Interpretation Bulletins: IT-374: Meaning of "settlor" (cancelled); IT-381R3: Trusts — capital gains and losses and the flow-through of taxable gains to beneficiaries; IT-394R2: Preferred beneficiary election.

"qualified farm property", "qualified fishing property", "qualified small business corporation share" — [Repealed]

Notes: "Qualified farm property" (QFaP), "qualified fishing property" (QFiP) and "qualified small business corporation share" (QSBCS) repealed by 2014 budget bill #2, for dispositions in the 2014 and later taxation years. (They cross-referenced to the definitions in 110.6(1).) QFaP and QSBCS were 108(1)(g.1) and (g.2) before RSC 1985 (5th Supp) consolidation for tax years ending after Nov. 1991. QFiP added by 2006 budget bill #2 effective May 2, 2006.

"settlor",

(a) in relation to a testamentary trust, means the individual referred to in the definition "testamentary trust" in this subsection, and

(b) in relation to an *inter vivos* trust,

(i) if the trust was created by the transfer, assignment or other disposition of property thereto (in this paragraph referred to as property "contributed") by not more than one individual and the fair market value of such of the property of the trust as was contributed by the individual at the time of the creation of the trust or at any subsequent time exceeds the fair market value of such of the property of the trust as was contributed by any other person or persons at any subsequent time (such fair market values being determined at the time of the making of any such contribution), means that individual, and

(ii) if the trust was created by the contribution of property thereto jointly by an individual and the individual's spouse or common-law partner and by no other person and the fair market value of such of the property of the trust as was contributed by them at the time of the creation of the trust or at any subsequent time exceeds the fair market value of such of the property of the trust as was contributed by any other person or persons at any subsequent time (such fair market values being determined at the time of the making of any such contribution), means that individual and the spouse or common-law partner;

Related Provisions: 17(15)"settlor" — Alternate definition for purposes of loan by corporation to non-resident.

Notes: This definition applies only for ss. 104-108, and thus only to 108(1)"preferred beneficiary" (see Notes thereto). Note that X losing settlor status due to contributions by Y does not make Y a "settlor".

The Aug. 29/14 draft legislation proposed to repeal this definition, as many of the provisions that referred to it no longer do. However, it is still used in some provisions, and the proposed repeal was not included in 2014 budget bill #2.

108(1)"settlor"(b)(ii) amended by 2000 same-sex partners bill to refer to "common-law partner", effective as per Notes to 248(1)"common-law partner".

108(1)"settlor" was 108(1)(h) before RSC 1985 (5th Supp) consolidation for tax years ending after Nov. 1991.

Interpretation Bulletins: IT-374: Meaning of "settlor" (cancelled); IT-394R2: Preferred beneficiary election.

"testamentary trust", in a taxation year, means a trust that arose on and as a consequence of the death of an individual (including a trust referred to in subsection 248(9.1)), other than

(a) a trust created by a person other than the individual,

(b) a trust created after November 12, 1981 if, before the end of the taxation year, property has been contributed to the trust otherwise than by an individual on or after the individual's death and as a consequence thereof,

(c) a trust created before November 13, 1981 if

(i) after June 28, 1982 property has been contributed to the trust otherwise than by an individual on or after the individual's death and as a consequence thereof, or

(ii) before the end of the taxation year, the total fair market value of the property owned by the trust that was contributed to the trust otherwise than by an individual on or after the individual's death and as a consequence thereof and the property owned by the trust that was substituted for such property exceeds the total fair market value of the property owned by the trust that was contributed by an individual on or after the individual's death and as a consequence thereof and the property owned by the trust that was substituted for such property, and for the purposes of this paragraph the fair market value of any property shall be determined as at the time it was acquired by the trust; and

(d) a trust that, at any time after December 20, 2002 and before the end of the taxation year, incurs a debt or any other obligation owed to, or guaranteed by, a beneficiary or any other person or partnership (which beneficiary, person or partnership is referred to in this paragraph as the "specified party") with whom any beneficiary of the trust does not deal at arm's length, other than a debt or other obligation

(i) incurred by the trust in satisfaction of the specified party's right as a beneficiary under the trust

(A) to enforce payment of an amount of the trust's income or capital gains payable at or before that time by the trust to the specified party, or

(B) to otherwise receive any part of the capital of the trust,

(ii) owed to the specified party, if the debt or other obligation arose because of a service (for greater certainty, not including any transfer or loan of property) rendered by the specified party to, for or on behalf of the trust,

(iii) owed to the specified party, if

(A) the debt or other obligation arose because of a payment made by the specified party for or on behalf of the trust,

(B) in exchange for the payment (and in full settlement of the debt or other obligation), the trust transfers property, the fair market value of which is not less than the principal amount of the debt or other obligation, to the specified party within 12 months after the payment was made (or, if written application has been made to the Minister by the trust within that 12-month period, within any longer period that the Minister considers reasonable in the circumstances), and

(C) it is reasonable to conclude that the specified party would have been willing to make the payment if the specified party dealt at arm's length with the trust, except where the trust is the individual's estate and that payment was made within the first 12 months after the individual's death (or, if written application has been made to the

Minister by the estate within that 12-month period, within any longer period that the Minister considers reasonable in the circumstances), or

(iv) incurred by the trust before October 24, 2012 if, in full settlement of the debt or other obligation the trust transfers property, the fair market value of which is not less than the principal amount of the debt or other obligation, to the person or partnership to whom the debt or other obligation is owed within 12 months after the day on which the *Technical Tax Amendments Act, 2012* receives royal assent (or if written application has been made to the Minister by the trust within that 12-month period, within any longer period that the Minister considers reasonable in the circumstances);

Related Provisions: 94(1)"trust" — Non-resident trust rules apply to estates; 108(1.1) — Home renovation expenditure by beneficiary, and certain trust transfers, do not put trust offside; 248(1)"testamentary trust" — Definition applies to entire Act; 248(3) — Trusts in Quebec; 248(8) — Meaning of "consequence" of death; *Interpretation Act* 27(5) — Meaning of "within 12 months".

Notes: Since 2016, most references to "testamentary trust" (TT) in the Act are changed to "graduated rate estate", which must be a TT under this definition but has additional limitations. See Notes to 122(1) and 248(1)"graduated rate estate".

Life insurance proceeds are not "property contributed to the trust" under para. (b): VIEWS doc 2005-0132271C6. However, a trust settled with proceeds of a joint last-to-die life insurance policy is a TT: 2008-0270421C6, 2008-0278801C6 q.2 (but see 2012-0435701C6); and a trust funded from proceeds of a policy available on an individual's death is considered a TT, if the individual establishes the terms during his lifetime (within or outside his will): 2009-0350811E5.

Dividends are not "property contributed to the trust" under para. (b): 2008-0285431C6. Para. (b) refers to a "voluntary payment into the estate, made for no consideration, and for the purpose of increasing the capital of the estate": *Greenberg Estate*, [1997] 3 C.T.C. 2859 (TCC), para. 10.

A trust funded from the proceeds of an RRSP or RRIF on death qualifies as a TT if the RRSP/RRIF designation is a testamentary instrument under provincial legislation: doc 2003-0007365. A spouse's waiver of income earned by the trust would disqualify it as a TT, based on *Greenberg Estate* (above): 2005-0141181C6; see Nathan Wright, "Spousal Trust Trap: Waiving Entitlement to Income", 3(1) *Canadian Tax Focus* (ctf.ca) 7 (Feb. 2013). On whether a TT is created in Quebec: 2009-0328441E5, 2011-0417391E5, 2013-0493671C6 [2013 APFF q.5]. A TT can be designated as an RRSP beneficiary: 2005-0116491E5. An asset protection trust set up before death cannot transfer the assets to a TT: 2011-0411851C6. A TT can receive property from another TT (pursuant to the same deceased's will) without losing its status: 2014-0539841E5.

CRA states that a TT is "created" on the day of death even if it is formed later (docs 2000-0052935, 2007-0233721C6, 2012-0442931C6, 2018-0744101C6 [STEP 2018 q.2]), but see Wolfe Goodman, "Is a Testamentary Trust Created When the Testator Dies?", XI(1) *Goodman on Estate Planning* (Federated Press) 852 (2002).

Para. (d) will not apply where a beneficiary pays tax owed by a trust on income taxed due to a designation under 104(13.1) or (13.2), since the trust would not normally be indebted to the beneficiary: VIEWS doc 2003-000552A.

Definition amended by 2002-2013 technical bill (for tax years ending after June 25, 2013), 1993 technical bill. 108(1)"testamentary trust" was 108(1)(i) before RSC 1985 (5th Supp) consolidation for tax years ending after Nov. 1991.

Interpretation Bulletins: IT-381R3: Trusts — capital gains and losses and the flow-through of taxable capital gains to beneficiaries.

"trust" includes an *inter vivos* trust and a testamentary trust but in subsections 104(4), (5), (5.2), (12), (13.1), (13.2), (14) and (15) and sections 105 to 107 does not include

(a) an amateur athlete trust, an employee life and health trust, an employee trust, a trust described in paragraph 149(1)(o.4) or a trust governed by a deferred profit sharing plan, an employee benefit plan, an employees profit sharing plan, a foreign retirement arrangement, a pooled registered pension plan, a registered disability savings plan, a registered education savings plan, a registered pension plan, a registered retirement income fund, a registered retirement savings plan, a registered supplementary unemployment benefit plan or a TFSA,

(a.1) a trust (other than a trust described in paragraph (a) or (d), a trust to which subsection 7(2) or (6) applies or a trust prescribed for the purpose of subsection 107(2)) all or substantially all of the property of which is held for the purpose of providing benefits to individuals each of whom is provided with benefits in respect of, or because of, an office or employment or former office or employment of any individual,

(b) a related segregated fund trust (within the meaning assigned by section 138.1),

(c) a trust deemed by subsection 143(1) to exist in respect of a congregation that is a constituent part of a religious organization,

(d) an RCA trust (within the meaning assigned by subsection 207.5(1)),

(e) a trust each of the beneficiaries under which was at all times after it was created a trust referred to in paragraph (a), (b) or (d) or a person who is a beneficiary of the trust only because of being a beneficiary under a trust referred to in any of those paragraphs, or

(e.1) a cemetery care trust or a trust governed by an eligible funeral arrangement,

and, in applying subsections 104(4), (5), (5.2), (12), (14) and (15) at any time, does not include

(f) a trust that, at that time, is a unit trust, or

(g) a trust all interests in which, at that time, have vested indefeasibly, other than

(i) an *alter ego* trust, a joint spousal or common-law partner trust, a post-1971 spousal or common-law partner trust or a trust to which paragraph 104(4)(a.4) applies,

(ii) [Repealed]

(iii) a trust that has, in its return of income under this Part for its first taxation year that ends after 1992, elected that this paragraph not apply,

(iv) a trust that is at that time resident in Canada where the total fair market value at that time of all interests in the trust held at that time by beneficiaries under the trust who at that time are non-resident is more than 20% of the total fair market value at that time of all interests in the trust held at that time by beneficiaries under the trust,

(v) a trust under the terms of which, at that time, all or part of a person's interest in the trust is to be terminated with reference to a period of time (including a period of time determined with reference to the person's death), otherwise than as a consequence of terms of the trust under which an interest in the trust is to be terminated as a consequence of a distribution to the person (or the person's estate) of property of the trust if the fair market value of the property to be distributed is required to be commensurate with the fair market value of that interest immediately before the distribution, or

(vi) a trust that, before that time and after December 17, 1999, has made a distribution to a beneficiary in respect of the beneficiary's capital interest in the trust, if the distribution can reasonably be considered to have been financed by a liability of the trust and one of the purposes of incurring the liability was to avoid taxes otherwise payable under this Part as a consequence of the death of any individual;

Related Provisions: 75(2) — Revocable or reversionary trust; 94(1)"exempt foreign trust"(f) — Trust under (a.1) excluded from non-resident trust rules; 94(3) — Non-resident trust deemed resident in Canada; 104(1) — Reference to trust or estate; 107.4(4) — Fair market value of capital interest in trust; 146.1(1)"trust" — Meaning of "trust" for RESP; 210(2)(d) — Certain trusts not subject to Part XII.2 tax; 233.2(4) — Reporting requirement re transfers to foreign trust; 233.6(1) — Reporting requirement re distributions from foreign trust; 248(1)"disposition"(b)(v) — Where trustee ceasing to act as agent of beneficiary; 248(1)"trust" — Definition outside subdiv. k is that in 104(1); 248(3) — Deemed trusts in Quebec; 248(9.2) — Meaning of "vested indefeasibly"; 248(25.1) — Trust-to-trust transfers — deemed same trust; 251(1)(b) — Personal trust and beneficiary deemed not to deal at arm's length.

Notes: See Notes to 104(1) re trusts generally. See Notes to 188.1(5) re meaning of "includes".

Para. (a.1) is aimed at trusts that escape the definitions of "employee trust" and "employee benefit plan" in 248(1). See also 107.1 re distributions from such a trust.

See VIEWS doc 2008-0285051C6 re subpara. (g)(v).

For interpretation of para. (g) see VIEWS doc 2011-0414841E5 (where discretionary trust becomes non-discretionary).

Para. (c) amended by 2014 budget bill #2, for 2016 and later taxation years, to change "an *inter vivos* trust" to "a trust" (in sync with generally replacing "testamentary trust" with "graduated rate estate").

Definition amended by 2002-2013 technical bill (last change effective for tax years that begin after Oct. 2011), 2012 budget bill #2 (effective Dec. 14, 2012, to refer to PRPPs), 2010 budget bill #2, 2008 budget bill #1, 2007 RDSPs bill, 2001, 1995-97, 1994 and 1992 technical bills. 108(1)"trust" was 108(1)(j) before RSC 1985 (5th Supp) consolidation for tax years ending after Nov. 1991. The provisions' order was changed; paras. (a)-(e) were formerly 108(1)(j)(ii)-(vi), and (f)-(g) were formerly (j)(i)-(i.1).

Income Tax Folios: S2-F1-C1: Health and welfare trusts [replaces IT-85R2].

Interpretation Bulletins [subsec. 108(1)"trust"]: IT-394R2: Preferred beneficiary election; IT-449R: Meaning of "vested indefeasibly" (cancelled); IT-502: Employee benefit plans and employee trusts; IT-531: Eligible funeral arrangements.

Related Provisions [subsec. 108(1)]: 104(4), (5), (5.2) — Exempt property excluded from 21-year deemed disposition.

(1.1) Testamentary trust not disqualified — For the purpose of the definition "testamentary trust" in subsection (1), a contribution to a particular trust does not include

(a) a "qualifying expenditure" (within the meaning of section 118.04 or 118.041) of a beneficiary under the trust; or

(b) an amount paid to, or on behalf of, the trust by another trust if

(i) the trust is an individual's graduated rate estate (determined without regard to the payment and this subsection),

(ii) paragraph 104(13.4)(b) applies to the other trust, for a taxation year that ends at a time determined by reference to the individual's death, because of a joint election made under subparagraph 104(13.4)(b.1)(iii) by the other trust and the legal representative administering the estate,

(iii) the payment is on account of the tax payable by the individual, for the individual's taxation year that includes the day on which the individual dies, under

(A) this Part, or

(B) the law of the province, in which the individual was resident immediately before the individual's death, that imposes a tax on the taxable income of individuals resident in that province, and

(iv) the amount of the payment does not exceed the amount by which that tax payable is greater than it would have been if paragraph 104(13.4)(b) did not apply to the other trust in respect of the taxation year referred to in subparagraph (ii).

Notes: 108(1.1)(a) provides that a renovation qualifying for the home accessibility credit in 118.041, when paid for by beneficiary B for a property owned by a testamentary trust (TT), does not count as a "contribution" that would disqualify the trust as a TT (see 108(1)"testamentary trust"(b)) and thus as a GRE (see 248(1)"graduated rate estate"(b)). This allows the credit to be claimed for a home a deceased has left in trust for use of B (see 118.041(1)"eligible dwelling"(a)), without impacting the estate.

108(1.1)(b) added by 2016 budget bill #2, for 2016 and later taxation years.

108(1.1) amended by 2015 Budget bill to add reference to 118.041 for 2016 and later taxation years. Added by 2009 budget bill #2, for 2009 and later years.

(2) Where trust is a unit trust — For the purposes of this Act, a trust is a unit trust at any particular time if, at that time, it was an *inter vivos* trust the interest of each beneficiary under which was described by reference to units of the trust, and

(a) the issued units of the trust included

(i) units having conditions attached thereto that included conditions requiring the trust to accept, at the demand of the holder thereof and at prices determined and payable in accordance with the conditions, the surrender of the units, or fractions or parts thereof, that are fully paid, or

(ii) units qualified in accordance with prescribed conditions relating to the redemption of the units by the trust,

and the fair market value of such of the units as had conditions attached thereto that included such conditions or as were so qualified, as the case may be, was not less than 95% of the fair market value of all of the issued units of the trust (such fair market values being determined without regard to any voting rights attaching to units of the trust),

(b) each of the following conditions was satisfied:

(i) throughout the taxation year that includes the particular time (in this paragraph referred to as the "current year"), the trust was resident in Canada,

(ii) throughout the period or periods (in this paragraph referred to as the "relevant periods") that are in the current year and throughout which the conditions in paragraph (a) are not satisfied in respect of the trust, its only undertaking was

(A) the investing of its funds in property (other than real property or an interest in real property or an immovable or a real right in an immovable),

(B) the acquiring, holding, maintaining, improving, leasing or managing of any real property or an interest in real property, or of any immovable or a real right in immovables, that is capital property of the trust, or

(C) any combination of the activities described in clauses (A) and (B),

(iii) throughout the relevant periods at least 80% of its property consisted of any combination of

(A) shares,

(B) any property that, under the terms or conditions of which or under an agreement, is convertible into, is exchangeable for or confers a right to acquire, shares,

(C) cash,

(D) bonds, debentures, mortgages, hypothecary claims, notes and other similar obligations,

(E) marketable securities,

(F) real property situated in Canada, and interests in such real property, or immovables situated in Canada and real rights in such immovables, and

(G) rights to and interests in — or, for civil law, rights in or to — any rental or royalty computed by reference to the amount or value of production from a natural accumulation of petroleum or natural gas in Canada, from an oil or gas well in Canada or from a mineral resource in Canada,

(iv) either

(A) not less than 95% of its income for the current year (computed without regard to subsections 39(2), 49(2.1) and 104(6)) was derived from, or from the disposition of, investments described in subparagraph (iii), or

(B) not less than 95% of its income for each of the relevant periods (computed without regard to subsections 39(2), 49(2.1) and 104(6) and as though each of those periods were a taxation year) was derived from, or from the disposition of, investments described in subparagraph (iii),

(v) throughout the relevant periods, not more than 10% of its property consisted of bonds, securities or shares in the capital stock of any one corporation or debtor other than Her Majesty in right of Canada or a province or a Canadian municipality, and

(vi) where the trust would not be a unit trust at the particular time if this paragraph were read without reference to this subparagraph and subparagraph (iii) were read without reference to clause (F), the units of the trust are listed at any time in the current year or in the following taxation year on a designated stock exchange in Canada, or

(c) the fair market value of the property of the trust at the end of 1993 was primarily attributable to real property or an interest in real property — or to immovables or a real right in immovables — and the trust was a unit trust throughout any calendar year that ended before 1994 and the fair market value of the property of the trust at the particular time is primarily attributable to property described in paragraph (a) or (b) of the definition "qualified investment" in section 204, real property or an inter-

est in real property — or immovables or a real right in immovables — or any combination of those properties.

Related Provisions: 20(1)(e)(i) — Deduction for expenses relating to sale of units; 53(1)(d.2), 53(2)(h), (j) — ACB of units; 108(1)"trust"(f) — Unit trusts excluded from many trust rules; 132(6) — Meaning of "mutual fund trust"; 132(6.2) — Mutual fund trust — retention of status; 135.2(4)(e)(ii) — Cdn Wheat Board Farmers' Trust deemed not to be unit trust; 248(1)"unit trust" — Definition applies to entire Act; 248(4.1) — Meaning of "real right in an immovable"; 250(6.1) — Trust that ceases to exist deemed resident throughout year; 253.1(1) — Limited partner not considered to carry on partnership business.

Notes: 108(2)(a) describes an open-end trust (at least 95% of units redeemable by holder), and 108(2)(b) a closed-end trust that is resident in Canada, has at least 80% "good basket" assets (subpara. (iii)), at least 95% of income from such assets ((iv)), and no more than 10% holdings of any one corporation or debtor ((v)).

108(2)(a)(i) is satisfied if the units meet the provincial securities commission's definition of "redeemable on demand", e.g. at least twice annually: VIEWS doc 2015-0595041E5; and in 2017-0723421R3, redemptions could be suspended for up to 1 year.

For CRA VIEWS on 108(2) see docs 2001-0095675 (effect of unit trusts investing in a limited partnership); 2004-0071451E5 (income from writing covered call options is considered derived from the underlying security for 108(2)(b)(iv)); 2006-0177231R3 and 2007-0226101R3 (REITs qualify as open-ended unit trusts); 2006-0213721R3 (after amendment to trust indenture deleting all references to units, trust is no longer a unit trust); 2006-0217441R3 (trust is a unit trust).

For the meaning of "derived" in 108(2)(b)(iv)(A), see Notes to 18.1(12).

108(2) amended by 2002-2013 technical bill (last change effective June 26, 2013), 2007 budget bill #2, 2001, 1995-97, 1994 and 1991 technical bills.

Income Tax Folios: S6-F2-C1: Disposition of an income interest in a trust [replaces IT-385R2].

I.T. Technical News: 6 (mutual funds trading — meaning of "investing its funds in property" in 108(2)(b)(ii)(A)).

(3) Income of a trust in certain provisions — For the purposes of the definitions "income interest" in subsection (1), "lifetime benefit trust" in subsection 60.011(1) and "exempt foreign trust" in subsection 94(1), the income of a trust is its income computed without reference to the provisions of this Act and, for the purposes of the definition "pre-1972 spousal trust" in subsection (1) and paragraphs 70(6)(b) and (6.1)(b), 73(1.01)(c) and 104(4)(a), the income of a trust is its income computed without reference to the provisions of this Act, minus any dividends included in that income

(a) that are amounts not included by reason of section 83 in computing the income of the trust for the purposes of the other provisions of this Act;

(b) that are described in subsection 131(1); or

(c) to which subsection 131(1) applies by reason of subsection 130(2).

Related Provisions: 108(5) — Interpretation.

Notes: Under Quebec civil law, cash dividends paid to a trust from a corporation's retained earnings are considered income under 108(3): VIEWS doc 2001-0076845.

"Income" of a trust for trust law purposes can be different from that under the ITA; see VIEWS doc 2004-0060161E5 for discussion.

108(3) opening words amended by 2002-2013 technical bill (Part 1 — NRTs), for trust taxation years that begin after 2000, to apply to 60.011(1)"lifetime benefit trust" and 94(1)"exempt foreign trust".

108(3) amended by 2001 technical bill (effective for 2000 and later taxation years) and 1992 technical bill.

Income Tax Folios: S6-F2-C1: Disposition of an income interest in a trust [replaces IT-385R2].

Interpretation Bulletins: IT-305R4: Testamentary spouse trusts.

(4) Trust not disqualified — For the purposes of the definition "pre-1972 spousal trust" in subsection (1), subparagraphs 70(6)(b)(ii) and (6.1)(b)(ii) and paragraphs 73(1.01)(c) and 104(4)(a), if a trust was created by a taxpayer whether by the taxpayer's will or otherwise, no person is deemed to have received or otherwise obtained or to be entitled to receive or otherwise obtain the use of any income or capital of the trust solely because of

(a) the payment, or provision for payment, as the case may be, by the trust of

(i) any estate, legacy, succession or inheritance duty payable, in consequence of the death of the taxpayer, or a spouse or common-law partner of the taxpayer who is a beneficiary under the trust, in respect of any property of, or interest in, the trust, or

(ii) any income or profits tax payable by the trust in respect of any income of the trust; or

(b) the inhabiting at any time by an individual of a housing unit that is, or is in respect of, property that is owned at that time by the trust, if

(i) the property is described in the definition "principal residence" in section 54 in respect of the trust for the trust's taxation year that includes that time, and

(ii) the individual is

(A) the taxpayer, or

(B) the taxpayer's

(I) spouse or common-law partner,

(II) former spouse or common-law partner, or

(III) child.

Related Provisions: 248(8) — Meaning of "consequence" of death; 248(9.1) — Whether trust created by taxpayer's will.

Notes: 108(4) amended by 2017 budget bill #2, for taxation years that begin after 2016, effectively to add para. (b) (former (a), (b) are now (a)(i), (ii)).

108(4) earlier amended by 2001 technical bill (for 2000 and later taxation years), 2000 same-sex partners bill, 1992 technical bill.

Interpretation Bulletins: IT-305R4: Testamentary spouse trusts.

(5) Interpretation — Except as otherwise provided in this Part,

(a) an amount included in computing the income for a taxation year of a beneficiary of a trust under subsection 104(13) or (14) or section 105 shall be deemed to be income of the beneficiary for the year from a property that is an interest in the trust and not from any other source, and

(b) an amount deductible in computing the amount that would, but for subsections 104(6) and (12), be the income of a trust for a taxation year shall not be deducted by a beneficiary of the trust in computing the beneficiary's income for a taxation year,

but, for greater certainty, nothing in this subsection shall affect the application of subsection 56(4.1), sections 74.1 to 75 and 120.4 and subsection 160(1.2) of this Act and section 74 of the *Income Tax Act*, chapter 148 of the Revised Statutes of Canada, 1952.

Related Provisions: 3 — Calculation of income; 129(4) — "Canadian investment income" and "foreign investment income" defined.

Notes: 108(5) means that, in effect, income loses its character and becomes property income when flowed out to a beneficiary under 104(6) and (13). As a result, no provincial allocation of business income is needed for beneficiaries: VIEWS doc 2011-0415181I7; and dividend income allocated by a US trust to a Canadian resident loses its character: 2016-0634191I7. See 4(1) regarding the source of income. Note that certain kinds of distributions can be designated to retain their character in the beneficiary's hands — e.g., dividends under 104(19), capital gains under 104(21), pension benefits under 104(27), DPSP benefits under 104(27.1) and death benefits under 104(28). See Notes to 96(1) re income flowed through a partnership.

108(5) was enacted in 1983. Wolfe Goodman wrote to the author in 1999 that it was introduced because of a planned limited partnership that would engage in active mortgage lending. Based on *Robins*, [1963] C.T.C. 27 (Ex. Ct.), Goodman's firm had advised that if a trust for minor children bought the LP units, the resulting income would be business income and not attributed back to the contributor of the funds. (TOSI in 120.4 would apply now.)

108(5) amended by 1999 Budget, effective for 2000 and later taxation years, to add reference to 120.4 and 160(1.2).

I.T. Application Rules: 69 (meaning of "chapter 148 of ...").

Interpretation Bulletins: IT-243R4: Dividend refund to private corporations.

I.T. Technical News: 38 (SIFT entities — definition of REIT).

(6) Variation of trusts — Where at any time the terms of a trust are varied

(a) for the purposes of subsections 104(4), (5) and (5.2) and subject to paragraph (b), the trust is, at and after that time, deemed to be the same trust as, and a continuation of, the trust immediately before that time;

(b) for greater certainty, paragraph (a) does not affect the application of paragraph 104(4)(a.1); and

(c) for the purposes of paragraph 53(2)(h), subsection 107(1), paragraph (j) of the definition "excluded right or interest" in subsection 128.1(10) and the definition "personal trust" in subsection 248(1), no interest of a beneficiary under the trust before it was varied is considered to be consideration for the interest of the beneficiary in the trust as varied.

Notes: 108(6) amended, effectively to add para. (c), by 2001 technical bill, for 2000 and later taxation years. 108(6) added by 1992 technical bill, effective Feb. 12, 1991.

(7) Interests acquired for consideration — For the purposes of paragraph 53(2)(h), subparagraph (c)(i) of the definition "exempt amount" in subsection 94(1), subsection 107(1), paragraph (j) of the definition "excluded right or interest" in subsection 128.1(10) and paragraph (b) of the definition "personal trust" in subsection 248(1),

(a) an interest in a trust is deemed not to be acquired for consideration solely because it was acquired in satisfaction of any right as a beneficiary under the trust to enforce payment of an amount by the trust; and

(b) if all the beneficial interests in a particular trust acquired by way of the transfer, assignment or other disposition of property to the particular trust were acquired by

(i) one person, or

(ii) two or more persons who would be related to each other if

(A) a trust and another person were related to each other, where the other person is a beneficiary under the trust or is related to a beneficiary under the trust, and

(B) a trust and another trust were related to each other, where a beneficiary under the trust is a beneficiary under the other trust or is related to a beneficiary under the other trust,

any beneficial interest in the particular trust acquired by such a person is deemed to have been acquired for no consideration.

Notes: For CRA interpretation see VIEWS doc 2015-0522641E5 (108(7) does not apply to usufruct created for consideration).

108(7) amended by 2014 budget bill #2 (for 2016 and later tax years, to change "a particular *inter vivos* trust" to "a particular trust", in sync with generally replacing "testamentary trust" with "graduated rate estate"), 2002-2013 technical bill. Added by 2001 technical bill, effective Dec. 24, 1998.

Income Tax Folios: S1-F5-C1: Related persons and dealing at arm's length [replaces IT-419R2].

Definitions [s. 108]: "*alter ego* trust" — 143.1(1.2)(a), 248(1); "amateur athlete trust" — 143.1(1.2)(a), 248(1); "amount" — 248(1); "arm's length" — 251(1); "beneficially interested" — 248(25); "beneficiary" — 108(1); "calendar year" — *Interpretation Act* 37(1)(a); "Canada" — 255, *Interpretation Act* 35(1); "capital gain" — 39(1)(a), 248(1); "capital interest" — 108(1), 248(1); "capital property" — 54, 248(1); "cemetery care trust" — 248(1); "child" — 252(1); "common-law partner" — 248(1); "consequence" — 248(8); "corporation" — 248(1), *Interpretation Act* 35(1); "cost amount" — 107(1)(e), 108(1); "created by the taxpayer's will" — 248(9.1); "deferred profit sharing plan" — 147(1), 248(1); "designated stock exchange" — 248(1), 262; "disposition" — 248(1); "dividend" — 248(1); "eligible capital property" — 54, 248(1); "eligible funeral arrangement" — 148.1(1), 248(1); "employee benefit plan" — 248(1); "employee life and health trust" — 144.1(2), 248(1); "employee trust", "employment" — 248(1); "estate" — 104(1), 248(1); "employees profit sharing plan" — 144(1), 248(1); "fair market value" — 107.4(4) and see 69(1) Notes; "foreign affiliate" — 95(1), 248(1); "foreign retirement arrangement" — 248(1); "Her Majesty" — *Interpretation Act* 35(1); "immovable" — Quebec *Civil Code* art. 900–907; "income of beneficiary" — 108(5); "income of trust" — 108(3); "income interest" — 108(1), 248(1); "individual" — 248(1); "interest in real property", "interests in such real property" — 248(4); "*inter vivos* trust" — 108(1), 248(1); "joint spousal or common-law partner trust", "mineral resource", "Minister" — 248(1); "month" — *Interpretation Act* 28, 35(1); "non-resident" — 248(1); "non-resident-owned investment corporation" — 133(8), 248(1); "office", "oil or gas well" — 248(1); "partnership" — see 96(1) Notes; "person", "personal trust" — 248(1); "pooled registered pension plan" — 147.5(1), 248(1); "post-1971 spousal or common-law partner trust" — 248(1); "pre-1972 spousal trust" — 108(1); "prescribed" — 248(1); "prescribed trust" — Reg. 4800.1; "principal amount", "property" — 248(1); "province" — *Interpretation Act* 35(1); "qualifying expenditure" — 118.04(1), 118.041(1); "real right" — 248(4.1); "registered disability savings plan" — 146.4(1), 248(1); "registered education savings plan" — 146.1(1), 248(1); "registered pension plan" — 248(1); "registered retirement income fund" — 146.3(1), 248(1); "registered retirement savings plan" — 146(1), 248(1); "registered supplementary unemployment benefit plan" — 145(1), 248(1); "related" — 251(2)–(6); "related segregated fund trust" — 138.1(1)(a); "relevant periods" — 108(2)(b)(ii); "resident in Canada" — 94(3)(a), 250; "retirement compensation arrangement" — 248(1); "settlor" — 108(1); "share" — 248(1); "spouse" — 252(3); "substituted" — 248(5); "TFSA" — 146.2(5), 248(1); "tax treaty" — 248(1); "taxation year" — 249; "taxpayer" — 248(1); "testamentary trust" — 108(1), 248(1); "trust" — 104(1), 108(1), 248(1), (3); "unit trust" — 108(2), 248(1); "vested indefeasibly" — 248(9.2); "written" — *Interpretation Act* 35(1)"writing".

DIVISION C — COMPUTATION OF TAXABLE INCOME

109. [Repealed under former Act]

Notes: 109, repealed by 1988 tax reform effective 1988, provided exemptions (deductions in calculating taxable income) for an individual's personal status and for dependants. These were replaced by the "non-refundable credits" in 118.

110. (0.1) Definitions — The following definitions apply in this section.

"consolidated financial statements" has the same meaning as in subsection 233.8(1).

Notes: Definition added by 2021 budget bill #1, effective July 2021.

"specified person", at any time, means a qualifying person that meets the following conditions:

(a) it is not a Canadian-controlled private corporation;

(b) if the qualifying person is a member of a group that annually prepares consolidated financial statements, the total consolidated group revenue reflected in the last consolidated financial statements of the group presented to shareholders or unitholders — of the member of the group that would be the "ultimate parent entity", as defined in subsection 233.8(1), of the group if the group were a "multinational enterprise group", as defined in subsection 233.8(1) — before that time exceeds $500 million; and

(c) if paragraph (b) does not apply, it has gross revenue in excess of $500 million based on

(i) the amounts reflected in the financial statements of the qualifying person presented to the shareholders or unitholders of the qualifying person for the last fiscal period of the qualifying person that ended before that time,

(ii) if subparagraph (i) does not apply, the amounts reflected in the financial statements of the qualifying person presented to the shareholders or unitholders of the qualifying person for the last fiscal period of the qualifying person that ended before the end of the last fiscal period referred to in subparagraph (i), and

(iii) if subparagraph (i) does not apply and financial statements were not presented as described in subparagraph (ii), the amounts that would have been reflected in the annual financial statements of the qualifying person for the last fiscal period of the qualifying person that ended before that time, if such statements had been prepared in accordance with generally accepted accounting principles.

Related Provisions: 7(7) — Definitions; 87(2)(j.97) — Amalgamation — continuing corporation.

Notes: Definition added by 2021 budget bill #1, effective July 2021.

Regulations: No prescribed conditions yet. Finance accepted comments as to what the conditions should be until Sept. 16, 2019 at fin.EDO-OAAE.fin@canada.ca. An option the author has suggested is any corp that was a CCPC within the past (say) five years.

"vesting year", of a security to be acquired under an agreement, means

(a) if the agreement specifies the calendar year in which the taxpayer's right to acquire the security first becomes exercisable (otherwise than as a consequence of an event that is not reasonably foreseeable at the time the agreement is entered into), that calendar year; and

(b) in any other case, the calendar year in which the right to acquire the security would become exercisable if the agreement

had specified that all identical rights to acquire securities become exercisable on a pro rata basis over the period that

(i) begins on the day that the agreement was entered into, and

(ii) ends on the day that is the earlier of

(A) the day that is 60 months after the day the agreement is entered into, and

(B) the last day that the right to acquire the security could become exercisable under the agreement.

Related Provisions: 7(7) — Definitions.

Notes: Definition added by 2021 budget bill #1, effective July 2021.

(1) Deductions permitted — For the purpose of computing the taxable income of a taxpayer for a taxation year, there may be deducted such of the following amounts as are applicable:

(a)–(c) [Repealed under former Act]

Notes: 110(1)(a), (b) and (b.1), repealed by 1988 tax reform, provided deductions for charitable and similar donations. These were moved to 118.1 (credit for individuals) and 110.1 (deduction for corporations). 110(1)(c), repealed by the same bill, provided a deduction for medical expenses, now a credit under 118.2.

(d) **employee [stock] options** — an amount equal to ½ of the amount of the benefit deemed by subsection 7(1) to have been received by the taxpayer in the year in respect of a security (other than a security that is a non-qualified security) that a particular qualifying person has agreed after February 15, 1984 to sell or issue under an agreement, in respect of the transfer or other disposition of rights under the agreement or as a result of the death of the taxpayer because the taxpayer immediately before death owned a right to acquire the security under the agreement, if

(i) the security was acquired under the agreement

(A) by the taxpayer or a person not dealing at arm's length with the taxpayer in circumstances described in paragraph 7(1)(c), or

(B) in the case of a benefit deemed by paragraph 7(1)(e) to have been received by the taxpayer, within the first taxation year of the graduated rate estate of the taxpayer, by

(I) the graduated rate estate of the taxpayer,

(II) a person who is a "beneficiary" (as defined in subsection 108(1)) under the graduated rate estate of the taxpayer, or

(III) a person in whom the rights of the taxpayer under the agreement have vested as a result of the death,

(i.1) the security

(A) is a prescribed share at the time of its sale or issue, as the case may be,

(B) would have been a prescribed share if it were issued or sold to the taxpayer at the time the taxpayer disposed of rights under the agreement,

(B.1) in the case of a benefit deemed by paragraph 7(1)(e) to have been received by the taxpayer, would have been a prescribed share if it were issued or sold to the taxpayer immediately before the death of the taxpayer,

(C) would have been a unit of a mutual fund trust at the time of its sale or issue if those units issued by the trust that were not identical to the security had not been issued,

(D) would have been a unit of a mutual fund trust if

(I) it were issued or sold to the taxpayer at the time the taxpayer disposed of rights under the agreement, and

(II) those units issued by the trust that were not identical to the security had not been issued, or

(E) in the case of a benefit deemed by paragraph 7(1)(e) to have been received by the taxpayer, would have been a unit of a mutual fund trust if

(I) it were issued or sold to the taxpayer immediately before the death of the taxpayer, and

(II) those units issued by the trust that were not identical to the security had not been issued,

(ii) where rights under the agreement were not acquired by the taxpayer as a result of a disposition of rights to which subsection 7(1.4) applied,

(A) the amount payable by the taxpayer to acquire the security under the agreement is not less than the amount by which

(I) the fair market value of the security at the time the agreement was made

exceeds

(II) the amount, if any, paid by the taxpayer to acquire the right to acquire the security, and

(B) at the time immediately after the agreement was made, the taxpayer was dealing at arm's length with

(I) the particular qualifying person,

(II) each other qualifying person that, at the time, was an employer of the taxpayer and was not dealing at arm's length with the particular qualifying person, and

(III) the qualifying person of which the taxpayer had, under the agreement, a right to acquire a security, and

(iii) where rights under the agreement were acquired by the taxpayer as a result of one or more dispositions to which subsection 7(1.4) applied,

(A) the amount payable by the taxpayer to acquire the security under the agreement is not less than the amount that was included, in respect of the security, in the amount determined under subparagraph 7(1.4)(c)(ii) with respect to the most recent of those dispositions,

(B) at the time immediately after the agreement the rights under which were the subject of the first of those dispositions (in this subparagraph referred to as the "original agreement") was made, the taxpayer was dealing at arm's length with

(I) the qualifying person that made the original agreement,

(II) each other qualifying person that, at the time, was an employer of the taxpayer and was not dealing at arm's length with the qualifying person that made the original agreement, and

(III) the qualifying person of which the taxpayer had, under the original agreement, a right to acquire a security,

(C) the amount that was included, in respect of each particular security that the taxpayer had a right to acquire under the original agreement, in the amount determined under subparagraph 7(1.4)(c)(iv) with respect to the first of those dispositions was not less than the amount by which

(I) the fair market value of the particular security at the time the original agreement was made

exceeded

(II) the amount, if any, paid by the taxpayer to acquire the right to acquire the security, and

(D) for the purpose of determining if the condition in paragraph 7(1.4)(c) was satisfied with respect to each of the particular dispositions following the first of those dispositions,

(I) the amount that was included, in respect of each particular security that could be acquired under the agreement the rights under which were the subject of the particular disposition, in the amount determined under subparagraph 7(1.4)(c)(iv) with respect to the particular disposition

was not less than

(II) the amount that was included, in respect of the particular security, in the amount determined under subparagraph 7(1.4)(c)(ii) with respect to the last of those dispositions preceding the particular disposition;

Related Provisions: 7(1.4) — Rules where options exchanged; 7(1.5) — Rules where securities exchanged; 7(1.7) — Deemed disposition where rights cease to be exercisable; 7(2) — Securities held by trustee; 7(6)(a) — Sale to trustee for employees; 7(7) — Definitions; 7(14) — Deferral deemed valid at CRA's discretion; 110(1)(d.01) — Deduction on donating employee stock-option shares to charity; 110(1)(d.1) — Alternative deduction; 110(1.1), (1.2) — Election by employer to forgo deduction for cash-out payment; 110(1.3)–(1.44) — Determination of non-qualified securities; 110(1.43), (1.44) — Cash-out — securities not designated as non-qualified; 110(1.5) — Determination of amounts; 110(1.7), (1.8) — Reduction in exercise price of stock option; 110.1(3)(b)(i) — Reduced recapture on donation of property to charity; 111(8)"non-capital loss"A:E — Amount included in non-capital loss; 111.1 — Order of applying provisions; 114.2 — Deductions in separate returns; 127.52(1)(h)(ii) — Deduction partly allowed for minimum tax purposes; 153(1.01) — Withholding tax on stock option benefits; 164(6.1) — Exercise or disposition of employee stock option by legal representative of deceased employee; 180.01 — Election to reduce tax on shares that have dropped in value.

Notes: See Notes to 7(1) re inclusion of income from stock option benefit. This offsetting ½ deduction is available in two ways. Simplified, if the share is a prescribed share (a "vanilla" common share — see Notes to Reg. 6204(1)), the value of the share *when the stock option agreement was entered into* did not exceed the exercise price of the option, and the corporation was dealing at arm's length with the employee at that time [110(1)(d)(ii)(B), (iii)(B)], the deduction is available. Otherwise, if the corporation was a CCPC dealing at arm's length with the employee when the agreement was entered into, the deduction is available under 110(1)(d.1) provided the employee holds the share (or a share it was exchanged for — see 7(1.5)) for at least two years. In both cases, the deduction leaves the "gain" on the shares taxed at the same rate as a capital gain (see 38(a)), but ineligible for special capital gains rules such as the lifetime capital gains exemption under 110.6(2) or (2.1) and the ability to offset the gain with capital losses under 3(b).

For options granted after June 2021, if the employer has annual group revenues over $500 million and is not a CCPC (110(0.1)"specified person"), this benefit is limited to $200,000 annually of options that have vested (i.e., are exercisable), based on the value of the underlying shares when the option is granted. See 110(1.3)-(1.44), and Notes to 110(1.31). The excess (options on "non-qualified securities") is deductible to the employer (110(1)(e)), so the net economic effect is the same as paying salary (fully taxable to the employee).

110(1)(d) also applies to mutual fund trust units (see Notes to 7(1)). (While shares must be "prescribed shares", trust units are instead required by 110(1)(d)(i.1)(C) or (D) to be of a "mutual fund trust": see conditions in 132(6) and Reg. 4801.)

Where an employer reduces the exercise price to reflect reductions in market value of the stock, the deduction may be lost, but see 110(1.7) and (1.8), which preserve the deduction if certain conditions are met. See VIEWS doc 9724275 and Colin Smith, "Re-Pricing Employee Stock Options", 13(5) *Taxation of Executive Compensation and Retirement* (Federated Press) 63-66 (Dec-Jan. 2002), and "...: An Update", 13(7) *TECR* 111-112 (March 2002).

2010 budget bill #2 added 110(1)(d)(i), preventing an employee exercising a "cash-out right" (or "stock appreciation right": getting cash in lieu of the excess of stock price over option exercise price) from using 110(1)(d), unless the employer files a 110(1.1) election to forgo the deduction (see 18(1)(m)). Before this amendment, the employee could claim the deduction: *Income Tax Technical News* 7, 9; VIEWS doc 2006-0213941R3; Holmes, "CCRA Positions Relating to Cash-Out Rights", 12(4) *Taxation of Executive Compensation & Retirement* (Federated Press) 356-7 (Nov. 2000).

In *Montminy*, 2017 FCA 156, Cco issued options to 7 employees in 2001, exercisable if Cco went public; it unexpectedly got an offer in 2007 to buy its assets rather than shares. The stock option agreement was amended to allow the employees to exercise the option and immediately sell their shares to Cco's parent. On a detailed analysis of Reg. 6204(1) and (2), the FCA allowed the 110(1)(d) deduction because the employees carried the risk from 2001-07. See Goguen, "Montminy", XIV(4) *Corporate Structures & Groups* (Federated Press) 8-12 (2018).

110(1)(d)(i) prevents the deduction where the benefit arises under 7(1)(e) on the employee's death, in CRA's view: docs 2009-0327221I7, 2011-0423441E5 [but 2013-0484181E5 now says a 110(1.1) election can be made to allow 110(1)(d) to apply]; but see Lee, "Death of a Taxpayer", 13(2) *Tax for the Owner-Manager* (ctf.ca) 6-7 (April 2013); Fournier & Arnould, "Paragraphs 110(1)(d) and 7(1)(e)", 24(1) *Taxation of Executive Compensation & Retirement* (Federated Press) 1562-64 (July/Aug. 2012).

In 110(1)(d)(ii)(A), the "amount payable ... under the agreement" is under the amended agreement if the exercise price is reduced, not the original agreement: *Fettes*, 2015 TCC 198.

See also Sidhu, "The Effect of Restrictions on the Exercise of Stock Options", 16(7) *Taxation of Executive Compensation & Retirement* (Federated Press) 522-24 (March 2005); Moses, "Foreign-Based Equity Compensation Plans", XXVIII(1) *TECR* 12-15 (2020).

See also VIEWS docs 2005-0120771R3 (110(1)(d) applies); 2005-0149841I7 (no 110(1)(d) on "reload" stock option because shares are not prescribed shares); 2013-0502761E5 (no 110(1)(d) on proceeds of shares acquired under option); 2015-0572381E5 (no 110(1)(d) or (d.1) if corp issues shares equal to in-the-money value of option).

110(1)(d) applies where the option is issued at a price at or above FMV of the shares on the date the option is issued. See VIEWS docs 9321835 and 9619933. In *McAnulty*, [2002] 1 C.T.C. 2035 (TCC), advice from Bre-X's president that the taxpayer would receive options was held to fix this date even though the company's directors' resolution authorizing the shares was not passed until a month later.

Since 110(1)(d) applies only to an employee, it is better to be an employee than an independent contractor for this purpose (see *Andersen*, 2006 TCC 522).

110(1)(d) amended by 2021 budget bill #1, effective July 2021, to add exclusion for a non-qualified security.

110(1)(d) before (ii) amended by 2017 budget bill #2, for acquisitions of securities and transfers or dispositions of rights occurring after 4:00 pm EST, March 4, 2010, but for taxation years ending before 2016, read "graduated rate estate" as "estate".

110(1)(d)(i) added (and former (i) renumbered (i.1)) by 2010 budget bill #2, for acquisitions of securities and transfers or dispositions of rights occurring after 4pm EST, March 4, 2010.

110(1)(d) earlier amended by 2000 and 1998 Budgets, 1993 and 1991 technical bills.

Regulations: 6204 (prescribed share for 110(1)(d)(i.1)).

Interpretation Bulletins: IT-113R4: Benefits to employees — stock options.

I.T. Technical News: 7 (stock options plans — receipt of cash in lieu of shares); 19 (Securities option plan — disposal of securities option rights for shares).

(d.01) **charitable donation of employee option securities** — subject to subsection (2.1), if the taxpayer disposes of a security acquired in the year by the taxpayer under an agreement referred to in subsection 7(1) by making a gift of the security to a qualified donee, an amount in respect of the disposition of the security equal to ½ of the lesser of the benefit deemed by paragraph 7(1)(a) to have been received by the taxpayer in the year in respect of the acquisition of the security and the amount that would have been that benefit had the value of the security at the time of its acquisition by the taxpayer been equal to the value of the security at the time of the disposition, if

(i) the security is a security described in subparagraph 38(a.1)(i),

(ii) [Repealed]

(iii) the gift is made in the year and on or before the day that is 30 days after the day on which the taxpayer acquired the security, and

(iv) the taxpayer is entitled to a deduction under paragraph (d) in respect of the acquisition of the security;

Related Provisions: 7(1.3) — Order of disposition of securities; 7(2) — Securities held by trustee; 7(6)(a) — Sale to trustee for employees; 7(7) — Definitions; 38(a.1), (a.3) — Parallel inclusion rate for capital gains on donated shares or exchangeable partnership interests; 110(2.1) — Donation made with proceeds of sale; 111(8)"non-capital loss"A:E — Amount included in non-capital loss; 127.52(1)(h)(iii) — Deduction allowed for minimum tax purposes; 153(1.01) — Withholding tax on stock option benefits.

Notes: 110(1)(d.01) parallels 38(a.1), which provides that on donation of publicly listed securities to a charity, the capital gains inclusion is zero. 110(1)(d.01) applies to employee stock options, where a deduction was available under 110(1)(d) to bring the effective tax rate on the employee benefit (under 7(1)) down to the capital gains rate [normally ½]. If the stock-option shares are donated to a charity, 110(1)(d.01) provides a further ½ deduction, thus reducing the effective taxable benefit from ½ (after 110(1)(d)) to 0% (the rate under 38(a.1)). See also 110(2.1) if the broker is directed to pay the proceeds directly to the charity. An election under 7(1.31) may be needed to get 110(1)(d.01) to work: VIEWS doc 2010-0370501C6. On hedging with a short-sale to protect the value of the gift, see 2010-0370481C6. 110(1)(d.01) and (d.1) cannot both apply to the same shares: 2011-0407951C6. 110(1)(d.01) cannot apply to a 7(1)(e) deemed benefit on death: 2020-0851631C6 [2020 APFF Financial q.6].

See also Dov Begun, "Donation of Shares Acquired Under an Employee Stock Option", XXV(1) *Taxation of Executive Compensation & Retirement* (Federated Press) 7-9 (2017); Adam Aptowitzer, "Keeping the Options Open", xli(15) *The Canadian Taxpayer* (Carswell) 118-19 (July 26, 2019) and 27(8) *Canadian Not-for-Profit News* (Carswell) 61-62 (Aug. 2019) [effect of proposed amendments to 110(1)(d)].

110(1)(d.01) amended by 2007 budget bill #2 (for gifts after March 18, 2007), 2006 budget bill #1, 2001 Budget. Added by 2000 Budget.

(d.1) **idem [employee stock options]** — where the taxpayer

(i) is deemed, under paragraph 7(1)(a) by virtue of subsection 7(1.1), to have received a benefit in the year in respect of a share acquired by the taxpayer after May 22, 1985,

(ii) has not disposed of the share (otherwise than as a consequence of the taxpayer's death) or exchanged the share within two years after the date the taxpayer acquired it, and

(iii) has not deducted an amount under paragraph (d) in respect of the benefit in computing the taxpayer's taxable income for the year,

an amount equal to ½ of the amount of the benefit;

Related Provisions: 7(1.3) — Order of disposition of securities; 7(1.5) — Rules where securities exchanged; 7(1.6) — Emigration does not trigger disposition for purposes of 110(1)(d.1); 7(2) — Securities held by trustee; 7(6)(a) — Sale to trustee for employees; 110(1)(d) — Alternative deduction; 111(8)"non-capital loss"A:E — Amount included in non-capital loss; 111.1 — Order of applying provisions; 114.2 — Deductions in separate returns; 127.52(1)(h)(iv) — Deduction partly allowed for minimum tax purposes; 248(8) — Meaning of "consequence" of death.

Notes: See Notes to 110(1)(d).

110(1)(d.1) amended by 2000 Budget to change "¼" to "½", effective for dispositions and exchanges that occur after Oct. 17, 2000. For those that occurred from Feb. 28, 2000 through Oct. 17, 2000, read "½" as "⅓".

Interpretation Bulletins: IT-113R4: Benefits to employees — stock options.

(d.2) **prospector's and grubstaker's shares** — where the taxpayer has, under paragraph 35(1)(d), included an amount in the taxpayer's income for the year in respect of a share received after May 22, 1985, an amount equal to ½ of that amount unless that amount is exempt from income tax in Canada by reason of a provision contained in a tax convention or agreement with another country that has the force of law in Canada;

Related Provisions: 111(8)"non-capital loss"A:E — Amount included in non-capital loss; 111.1 — Order of applying provisions; 114.2 — Deductions in separate returns; 127.52(1)(h)(iv) — Deduction partly allowed for minimum tax purposes.

Notes: 110(1)(d.2) amended by 2000 Budget to change "¼" to "½", effective for dispositions and exchanges that occur after Oct. 17, 2000. For those from Feb. 28, 2000 through Oct. 17, 2000, read "½" as "⅓".

(d.3) **employer's shares [where election made re DPSP]** — where the taxpayer has, under subsection 147(10.4), included an amount in computing the taxpayer's income for the year, an amount equal to ½ of that amount;

Related Provisions: 111(8)"non-capital loss"A:E — Amount included in non-capital loss; 111.1 — Order of applying provisions; 114.2 — Deductions in separate returns; 127.52(1)(h)(iv) — Deduction partly allowed for minimum tax purposes.

Notes: 110(1)(d.3) amended by 2000 Budget to change "¼" to "½", effective for dispositions and exchanges that occur after Oct. 17, 2000. For those from Feb. 28, 2000 through Oct. 17, 2000, read "½" as "⅓".

Interpretation Bulletins: IT-281R2: Elections on single payments from a deferred profit-sharing plan (cancelled).

(e) **employer deduction — non-qualified securities** — an amount equal to the amount of the benefit in respect of employment with the taxpayer deemed by subsection 7(1) to have been received by an individual in the year in respect of a non-qualified security that the taxpayer (or a qualifying person that does not deal at arm's length with the taxpayer) has agreed to sell or issue under an agreement with the individual, if

(i) the taxpayer is a qualifying person,

(ii) at the time the agreement was entered into, the individual was an employee of the taxpayer,

(iii) the amount is not claimed as a deduction in computing the taxable income of another qualifying person,

(iv) an amount would have been deductible in computing the taxable income of the individual under paragraph (d) if the security were not a non-qualified security,

(v) in the case of an individual who is not resident in Canada throughout the year, the benefit deemed by subsection 7(1) to have been received by the individual was included in computing the taxable income earned in Canada of the individual for the year, and

(vi) the notification requirements in subsection (1.9) are met in respect of the security;

Related Provisions: 7(7) — Definitions; 87(2)(j.97) — Amalgamation — continuing corporation; 110(1.9) — Notification to employee and CRA of status of security; 111(8)"non-capital loss"A:E — Amount included in non-capital loss; 143.3(5) — Deduction under 110(1)(e) overrides 143.3.

Notes: This deduction makes the tax treatment of the benefit from the non-qualified security (where no 110(1)(d) is allowed) effectively identical to salary: deductible to the employer (110(1)(e)) and taxable to the employee (7(1)(a)). See 110(1)(d) Notes.

Due to 7(3)(b) and 143.3, no deduction is normally available for the "cost" of issuing shares. 143.3(5) ensures that 110(1)(e) overrides 143.3; and 7(3)(b) applies in calculating "income" (net income), while 110(1)(e) provides a deduction in calculating *taxable* income, so 7(3)(b) does not restrict 110(1)(e).

110(1)(e) added by 2021 budget bill #1, effective in respect of agreements to sell or issue securities entered into after June 2021. However, it does not apply in respect of rights under an agreement to which 7(1.4) applies that are "new options" (under 7(1.4)) in respect of which an "exchanged option" (on the assumption that 7(1.4)(e) applies) was issued before July 2021.

(e.1), (e.2) [Repealed under former Act]

Notes: 110(1)(e.1)-(e.2), repealed by 1988 tax reform, provided deductions for dependants with disabilities. See now 118.3(2)-(4).

(f) **deductions for payments** — any social assistance payment made on the basis of a means, needs or income test and included because of clause 56(1)(a)(i)(A) or paragraph 56(1)(u) in computing the taxpayer's income for the year or any amount that is

(i) an amount exempt from income tax in Canada because of a provision contained in a tax convention or agreement with another country that has the force of law in Canada,

(ii) compensation received under an employees' or workers' compensation law of Canada or a province in respect of an injury, disability or death, except any such compensation received by a person as the employer or former employer of the person in respect of whose injury, disability or death the compensation was paid,

(iii) income from employment with a prescribed international organization,

(iv) the taxpayer's income from employment with a prescribed international non-governmental organization, where the taxpayer

(A) was not, at any time in the year, a Canadian citizen,

(B) was a non-resident person immediately before beginning that employment in Canada, and

(C) if the taxpayer is resident in Canada, became resident in Canada solely for the purpose of that employment, or

(v) the lesser of

(A) the employment income earned by the taxpayer as a member of the Canadian Forces, or as a police officer, while serving on a deployed international operational mission (as determined by the Minister of National Defence, the Minister of Public Safety and Emergency Preparedness or by a person designated by either Minister), and

(B) the employment income that would have been so earned by the taxpayer if the taxpayer had been paid at the maximum rate of pay that applied, from time to time during the mission, to a Lieutenant-Colonel (General Service Officers) of the Canadian Forces;

to the extent that it is included in computing the taxpayer's income for the year;

Related Provisions: 56(1)(u) — Social assistance payments; 56(1)(v) — Workers' compensation; 81(1)(a) — Amounts not included in income; 111(8)"non-capital loss"A:E — Amount included in non-capital loss; 111.1 — Order of applying provisions; 114.2 — Deductions in separate returns; 126(7)"tax-exempt income" — Income exempted by tax treaty; 127.52(1)(h)(v) — Application of deduction for minimum tax

purposes; 146(1)"earned income"(c) — Income exempted by tax treaty is not earned income of a non-resident for RRSP purposes; 150(1)(a)(ii) — Non-resident corp claiming treaty exemption must file return; 153(1.1) — Application for reduced source withholding where amount exempt under treaty; 248(1)"treaty-protected business", "treaty-protected property" — Amounts exempted by treaty.

Notes: *Opening words*: see Notes to 56(1)(u).

110(1)(f)(i): Amounts exempted by treaty cannot be simply not reported; they must be included in net income and an offsetting deduction claimed: VIEWS doc 2015-0571591E5. For deductions based on the Canada-US and Canada-UK treaties, see Notes to those treaties (e.g., *Korfage* in Notes to Canada-US treaty Art. XVIII:1). 50% of German social security is deductible under 110(1)(f)(i) due to the Canada-Germany treaty: *Hahn*, 2011 FCA 282 (leave to appeal denied 2012 CarswellNat 1508 (SCC)). "Country" includes Hong Kong and Taiwan: see Notes to 219.2.

110(1)(f)(ii): see Notes to 56(1)(v).

110(1)(f)(iii)-(v) apply only to employment income, not business income, using the usual distinction between the two: VIEWS docs 2004-0096371E6, 2012-0446871I7 (see Notes to 248(1)"employee"). "Employment income" does not include income originating or derived from such income (such as a pension): *Granaas*, 2009 TCC 547; doc 2004-0101881E5.

For *110(1)(f)(iii)*, the UN and certain UN agencies are prescribed under Reg. 8900(1). Employment must be directly by the UN. Thus, the deduction was denied in: *Creagh*, [1997] 1 C.T.C. 2392 (TCC) (employees of Cdn Helicopter working on a UN peacekeeping mission were not employed directly by the UN or the agency: VIEWS doc 2012-0454881E5); *Godin*, [1998] 2 C.T.C. 2853 (TCC) (employee of Cdn Commercial Corp working on UNPROFOR mission in former Yugoslavia); *Lalancette*, 2002 FCA 335 (RCMP employee assigned to UNCIVPOL mission in Haiti); *Smyth*, 2007 TCC 366 (FCA appeal dismissed for delay A-118-07) (Edmonton police officer serving in Kosovo); *Herchak*, 2009 TCC 486 (employee of US company under contract with USAID for UN Interim Administration Mission in Kosovo); *Nightingale*, 2010 TCC 1 (employee of Vietnam Veterans of America Foundation, under contract to the UN in Iraq); *Lapierre*, 2019 TCC 18 (International Security Assistance Force employee: authorized by UN but separate from the UN). See also Notes to Reg. 8900(1).

110(1)(f)(iv): See Reg. 8900(2). Employees of the World Anti-Doping Agency qualify, and should report the income and claim the offsetting deduction: VIEWS docs 2017-0717801E5, 2017-0729751E5.

110(1)(f)(v), before 2017, effectively exempted employment income for Canadian Forces members and police serving in high-risk locations such as Afghanistan, Bosnia and Haiti. See former 110(1.3) for the list of missions. (For missions initiated before Oct. 2012, see former version below and Reg. 7500; also Reg. 102(6), and VIEWS docs 2010-0375241E5, 2010-0379321E5, 2010-0387281I7, 2011-0411921E5.) The exemption does not apply to civilian members of the RCMP: 2006-0215221E5, 2007-0221651E5. For its application to a lump sum paid in lieu of severance, see 2013-047441117.

Since 2017, 110(1)(f)(v) applies to all "deployed international operational missions" (for the list see tinyurl.com/forces-ops). See National Defence news release, May 18, 2017 (reproduced here in PITA 52nd-53rd ed.).

110(1)(f)(v) covers all pay up to the level of Lieutenant-Colonel. A more senior officer still has salary exempted up to that pay level: 110(1)(f)(v)(B).

110(1)(f)(v)(A) amended by 2018 budget bill #2, superseding amendments by 2018 budget bill #1 (which also amended (B)) and 2013 budget bill #1. The current version is effective for 2017 and later tax years. For earlier years, for missions initiated after Sept. 2012 and for other missions that were not prescribed under Reg. 7500 as of Feb. 28, 2013, read (as amended by 2018 budget bill #2):

(A) the employment income earned by the taxpayer as a member of the Canadian Forces, or as a police officer, while serving on a deployed operational mission (as determined by the Department of National Defence or the Department of Public Safety and Emergency Preparedness) that is

(I) assessed for risk allowance at level 3 or higher (as determined by the Department of National Defence), or

(II) assessed at a risk score greater than 1.99 and less than 2.50 (as determined by the Department of National Defence) and designated by the Minister of Finance, and

110(1)(f)(v)(A) amended by 2013 budget bill #1, for missions initiated after Sept. 2012, and for other missions not prescribed under Reg. 7500 as of Feb. 28, 2013.

110(1)(f)(v) added by 2004 Budget, for 2004 and later taxation years. 110(1)(f) earlier amended by 1993, 1992 and 1991 technical bills.

Regulations: 102(6) (no source withholding on 110(1)(f)(v)(iii)–(v) amounts); 232, 233 (information return); 7500 (prescribed missions begun before Oct. 2012, for 110(1)(f)(v)(A)(II)); 8900(1) (prescribed international organization for 110(1)(f)(iii)); 8900(2) (prescribed international non-governmental organization for 110(1)(f)(iv)).

Interpretation Bulletins: IT-202R2: Employees' or workers' compensation; IT-499R: Superannuation or pension benefits; IT-528: Transfers of funds between registered plans.

CRA Audit Manual: 27.34.0: Social assistance payments.

Forms: T1 General return, Line 25600 [former 256]: Additional deductions.

(g) financial assistance [adult basic education] — any amount that

(i) is received by the taxpayer in the year under a program referred to in subparagraph 56(1)(r)(ii) or (iii), a program established under the authority of the *Department of Employment and Social Development Act* or a prescribed program,

(ii) is financial assistance for the payment of tuition fees of the taxpayer that are not included in computing an amount deductible under subsection 118.5(1) in computing the taxpayer's tax payable under this Part for any taxation year,

(iii) is included in computing the taxpayer's income for the year, and

(iv) is not otherwise deductible in computing the taxpayer's taxable income for the year;

Related Provisions: 60(n) — No second deduction if amount repaid; 111(8)"non-capital loss"A:E — Amount included in non-capital loss; 127.52(1)(h)(vi) — Deduction allowed for minimum tax purposes.

Notes: 110(1)(g) provides a deduction for tuition assistance received for basic adult education. Generally, it is available for tuition assistance received under a program established under the *Department of Human Resources and Skills Development Act* or a similar provincial program under a labour-market agreement. The deduction is allowed only where the assistance is included in the student's income and the student cannot claim a tuition fee credit for the program. It applies only to tuition assistance and not to other assistance a student may receive in connection with training.

CCRA published a detailed Q&A on Feb. 14, 2002, entitled "Tax deduction for tuition assistance received for adult basic education (ABE)". See (2002)5 *Tax Times* (Carswell, March 8, 2002). See also VIEWS doc 2016-0644171E5 (various questions).

110(1)(g) amended by 2013 budget bill #2 (effective Dec. 12, 2013), S.C. 2005, c. 34. Added by 2001 Budget. Former 110(1)(g), repealed by 1988 tax reform, provided a $50/month student exemption, replaced by the 118.6 education credit (repealed as of 2017).

Income Tax Folios: S1-F2-C3: Scholarships, research grants and other education assistance [replaces IT-340R].

Forms: T1 General return, Line 25600 [former 256]: Additional deductions.

(h) [grandfathering half-taxation of pre-1996 US social security] — 35 per cent of the total of all benefits (in this paragraph referred to as "U.S. social security benefits") that are received by the taxpayer in the taxation year and to which paragraph 5 of Article XVIII of the *Convention between Canada and the United States of America with respect to Taxes on Income and on Capital* as set out in Schedule I to the *Canada-United States Tax Convention Act, 1984*, S.C. 1984, c. 20, applies, if

(i) the taxpayer has continuously during a period that begins before 1996 and ends in the taxation year, been resident in Canada, and has received U.S. social security benefits in each taxation year that ends in that period, or

(ii) in the case where the benefits are payable to the taxpayer in respect of a deceased individual,

(A) the taxpayer was, immediately before the deceased individual's death, the deceased individual's spouse or common-law partner,

(B) the taxpayer has continuously during a period that begins at the time of the deceased individual's death and ends in the taxation year, been resident in Canada,

(C) the deceased individual was, in respect of the taxation year in which the deceased individual died, a taxpayer described in subparagraph (i), and

(D) in each taxation year that ends in a period that begins before 1996 and that ends in the taxation year, the taxpayer, the deceased individual, or both of them, received U.S. social security benefits.

Notes: 110(1)(h), added by 2010 budget bill #1, for 2010 and later tax years, fulfills a 2008 Conservative election promise: "Starting in 1997, the Liberal government began to tax 85% of U.S. Social Security payments received by Canadian seniors [by negotiating an amendment to Canada-US tax treaty Art. XVIII:5 — ed.]. A re-elected Conservative Government will restore the 50% inclusion rate that applied before the Liberals took office. The restored, lower rate will apply to Canadians who were receiving U.S. Social Security payments prior to 1996."

Former 110(1)(h), repealed by 1988 tax reform, provided for a deduction for a dependant who was a full-time student, replaced by rules in 118.8 and 118.9 permitting the transfer of education credits.

(i) [Repealed under former Act]

Notes: 110(1)(i) repealed by 1991 technical bill, effective 1989. Employment Insurance (formerly UI) benefits may be partially repayable when the taxpayer's net income exceeds a given threshold. The repayment is administered through the T1 income tax return. Such repayments, which reflect income that was originally taxed under 56(1)(a)(iv), were formerly deductible under 110(1)(i). They are now deductible in computing net income (rather than taxable income), under 60(v.1).

(j) [Repealed]

Related Provisions: 80.4(4) — Interest on home relocation loan; 110(1.4) — Replacement of home relocation loan; 111(8)"non-capital loss"A:E — Amount included in non-capital loss; 111.1 — Order of applying provisions; 114.2 — Deductions in separate returns; 127.52(1)(h) — Deduction disallowed for minimum tax purposes.

Notes: 110(1)(j) repealed by 2017 budget bill #1, effective 2018. It provided a deduction reducing the employee benefit from an 80.4(4) interest-free or low-interest loan to an employee, if the loan was a "home relocation loan". The benefit was capped at the prescribed interest rate on a $25,000 loan that was limited to 5 years. The 2017 Budget papers state: "Evidence suggests that this deduction disproportionately benefits the wealthy, and does little to help the middle class and those working hard to join it." 110(1)(j) read:

(j) home relocation loan — where the taxpayer has, by virtue of section 80.4, included an amount in the taxpayer's income for the year in respect of a benefit received by the taxpayer in respect of a home relocation loan, the least of

(i) the amount of the benefit that would have been deemed to have been received by the taxpayer under section 80.4 in the year if that section had applied only in respect of the home relocation loan,

(ii) the amount of interest for the year that would be computed under paragraph 80.4(1)(a) in respect of the home relocation loan if that loan were in the amount of $25,000 and were extinguished on the earlier of

(A) the day that is five years after the day on which the home relocation loan was made, and

(B) the day on which the home relocation loan was extinguished, and

(iii) the amount of the benefit deemed to have been received by the taxpayer under section 80.4 in the year; and

Interpretation Bulletins: IT-421R2: Benefits to individuals, corporations and shareholders from loans or debt.

I.T. Technical News: 6 (payment of mortgage interest subsidy by employer).

(k) Part VI.1 tax — the amount determined by multiplying the taxpayer's tax payable under subsection 191.1(1) for the year by

(i) if the taxation year ends before 2010, 3,

(ii) if the taxation year ends after 2009 and before 2012, 3.2, and

(iii) if the taxation year ends after 2011, 3.5.

Related Provisions: 111(5) — Change in control of corporation; 111(8)"non-capital loss"A:E — Amount included in non-capital loss; 191.3(4) — Related corporations.

Notes: Tax Executives Institute (TEI) has asked Finance to raise the factor to 3.8, to properly offset Part VI.1 tax (Dec. 5/12, Nov. 19/14 and Dec. 6/17 submissions). However, Finance is unwilling to make this change, given that provincial corporate tax rates are generally "on an upward trend" (Dec. 2017 response).

110(1)(k) changed from "9/4 of the tax payable under subsection 191.1(1) by the taxpayer for the year" by 2002-2013 technical bill, for 2003 and later tax years. Earlier amended by 1989 Budget, last change effective for 1990 and later tax years.

Interpretation Bulletins: IT-302R3: Losses of a corporation — the effect that acquisitions of control, amalgamations, and windings-up have on their deductibility.

Forms: T2 Sched. 43: Calculation of Parts IV.1 and VI.1 taxes.

(1.1) Election by particular qualifying person — For the purpose of computing the taxable income of a taxpayer for a taxation year, paragraph (1)(d) shall be read without reference to its subparagraph (i) in respect of a right granted to the taxpayer under an agreement to sell or issue securities referred to in subsection 7(1) if

(a) the particular qualifying person elects in prescribed form that neither the particular qualifying person nor any person not dealing at arm's length with the particular qualifying person will deduct in computing its income for a taxation year any amount (other than a designated amount described in subsection (1.2)) in respect of a payment to or for the benefit of a taxpayer for the taxpayer's transfer or disposition of that right;

(b) the particular qualifying person files the election with the Minister;

(c) the particular qualifying person provides the taxpayer or, if the taxpayer is deceased, the graduated rate estate of the taxpayer, with evidence in writing of the election; and

(d) the taxpayer or, if the taxpayer is deceased, the graduated rate estate of the taxpayer, files the evidence with the Minister with the taxpayer's return of income for the year in which a deduction under paragraph (1)(d) is claimed.

Related Provisions: 18(1)(m) — No deduction for amount in respect of which election made; 110(1.2) — Designated amount; 110(1.4)(b) — Election not allowed on right to acquire securities designated as non-qualified securities.

Notes: 110(1.1) and (1.2) provide an election by an employer to forgo (see 18(1)(m)) a deduction for a cash-out payment in respect of a stock option (see 7(1)(b), (b.1), (d.1)), in which case the employee can claim the 110(1)(d) deduction. See Paul Carenza, "Proper Interpretation of the 110(1.1) Election", XXV(1) *Taxation of Executive Compensation & Retirement* (Federated Press) 2-6 (2017).

CRA administratively accepts a 110(1.1) election if 7(1)(e) applies and the other 110(1)(d) conditions are met: VIEWS docs 2013-0484181E5, 2013-0483471E5 [Morreale, "Stock Option Deduction is Available on Death", 5(3) *Canadian Tax Focus* (ctf.ca) 13 (Aug. 2015)]. CRA accepts 110(1.1) where the employer would get no deduction anyway due to 7(3)(b): 2016-0674411E5, 2016-0672931E5, 2017-0724191C6 [2017 CTF q.9]. CRA will not permit the election to an arm's-length purchaser who is also buying the employee's options: 2015-0585171E5 [Wen, "Stock Options in Merger and Acquisition Transactions", 6(2) *Canadian Tax Focus* (ctf.ca) 9 (May 2016)].

110(1.1) opening words amended to change "all rights" to "a right", and para. (a) amended to change "rights under the agreement" to "that right", by 2021 budget bill #1, effective on the same basis as 110(1)(e) (generally, stock options granted after June 2021). (110(1.3)-(1.44) apply on a "right by right" basis.)

110(1.1)(c) and (d) both amended by 2017 budget bill #2 to add "or, if the taxpayer is deceased, the graduated rate estate of the taxpayer", effective on the same basis as the 2010 amendment below (except that for taxation years ending before 2016, read "graduated rate estate" as "estate").

110(1.1) added by 2010 budget bill #2, effective in respect of acquisitions of securities and transfers or dispositions of rights occurring after 4pm EST, March 4, 2010.

(1.2) Designated amount — For the purposes of subsections (1.1) and (1.44), an amount is a designated amount if the following conditions are met:

(a) the amount would otherwise be deductible in computing the income of the particular qualifying person in the absence of subsections (1.1) and (1.44);

(b) the amount is payable to a person

(i) with whom the particular qualifying person deals at arm's length, and

(ii) who is neither an employee of the particular qualifying person nor of any person not dealing at arm's length with the particular qualifying person; and

(c) the amount is payable in respect of an arrangement entered into for the purpose of managing the particular qualifying person's financial risk associated with a potential increase in value of the securities under the agreement described in subsection (1.1) or (1.44).

Notes: 110(1.2) amended to refer to 110(1.44) by 2021 budget bill #1, effective on the same basis as 110(1)(e) (generally, stock options granted after June 2021).

110(1.2) added by 2010 budget bill #2, effective in respect of acquisitions of securities and transfers or dispositions of rights after 4pm EST, March 4, 2010.

(1.3) Determination of non-qualified securities — Subsection (1.31) applies to a taxpayer in respect of an agreement if

(a) a particular qualifying person agrees to sell or issue securities of the particular qualifying person (or another qualifying person that does not deal at arm's length with the particular qualifying person) to the taxpayer under the agreement;

(b) at the time the agreement is entered into (in this subsection and subsection (1.31) referred to as the **"relevant time"**), the taxpayer is an employee of the particular qualifying person or of a qualifying person that does not deal at arm's length with the particular qualifying person; and

(c) at the relevant time, any of the following persons is a specified person:

(i) the particular qualifying person,

(ii) the other qualifying person, if any, referred to in paragraph (a), or

(iii) the other qualifying person, if any, referred to in paragraph (b).

Notes: See Notes to 110(1)(d) and 110(1.31). 110(1.3) added by 2021 budget bill #1, effective on the same basis as 110(1)(e) (generally, stock options granted after June 2021).

Pre-2018 110(1.3)

Former 110(1.3) repealed by 2018 budget bill #1, for 2017 and later tax years. Before 2017, it allowed designation by the Minister of Finance for 110(1)(f)(v) (exemption for salaries of deployed Armed Forces personnel and police), replacing prescribed missions previously listed in Reg. 7500. It read:

(1.3) **Designated mission** — The Minister of Finance may, on the recommendation of the Minister of National Defence (in respect of members of the Canadian Forces) or the Minister of Public Safety (in respect of police officers), designate a deployed operational mission for the purposes of subclause (1)(f)(v)(A)(II). The designation shall specify the day on which it comes into effect, which may precede the day on which the designation is made.

Since 2017, *all* deployed international operational missions qualify: 110(1)(f)(v)(A).

110(1.3) added by 2013 budget bill #1, for missions initiated after Sept. 2012, and those initiated earlier that were not prescribed under Reg. 7500 as of Feb. 28, 2013.

Finance news release "Tax Relief for Personnel Deployed on Designated International Operational Missions", June 12, 2015, states:

The Government of Canada provides tax relief to members of the Canadian Armed Forces (CAF) and police officers deployed on international high- and moderate-risk operational missions. This tax relief recognizes the special contribution that CAF members and police officers make to international peace and stability while serving their country abroad.

Eligible CAF members and police officers may claim a deduction against taxable income in respect of income earned while deployed on such missions. The maximum amount that an individual may deduct in a taxation year cannot exceed the highest level of pay earned by a non-commissioned member of the CAF.

For personnel deployed on high-risk missions — i.e., missions assessed by the Department of National Defence as carrying a risk score between 2.50 and 4.00 — tax relief is automatically provided for the period over which the mission is assessed as being high-risk.

For moderate-risk missions — i.e., missions carrying a risk score between 2.00 and 2.49 — tax relief is provided when the mission has been designated by the Minister of Finance, and for the period over which the mission is assessed as being moderate-risk.

On May 1, 2015, the Minister of Finance designated the following moderate-risk missions for tax relief:

Designated International Operational Missions

Mission name	Beginning of the applicable period	End of the applicable period
Op CROCODILE [Congo — ed.]	July 1, 2015	Ongoing
Op FOUNDATION (Qatar) [counter-terrorism — ed.]	April 1, 2010	May 31, 2015
Op ATHENA / ISAF Headquarters Detachment Qatar [Afghanistan — ed.]	April 1, 2010	December 31, 2011
Op RENAISSANCE [Philippines typhoon relief — ed.]	November 12, 2013	December 27, 2013
Op HERRICK (Camp Bastion, Helmand, Afghanistan)	June 1, 2012	November 30, 2012
Op AFGHAN ASSIST (Mazar-e-Sharif, Afghanistan)	June 1, 2012	February 24, 2014
Op HERRICK (Kandahar Airfield, Afghanistan)	July 31, 2013	August 31, 2013
Op HERRICK (Kandahar Airfield, Afghanistan)	January 23, 2014	May 3, 2014

For national security reasons, classified missions that are designated are not listed. For such missions, the Department of National Defence and/or Public Safety Canada are responsible for contacting eligible CAF members and police officers.

Prior to legislative amendments enacted in June 2013, moderate-risk missions qualified for tax relief when prescribed in the *Income Tax Regulations*. Prescribed missions are listed in Section 7500 of the *Income Tax Regulations*.

Previous 110(1.3), repealed by 1988 tax reform, provided rules relating to disabled persons; these were moved to 118.4(1).

(1.31) Annual vesting limit — If this subsection applies to a taxpayer in respect of an agreement, the securities to be sold or issued under the agreement, for each vesting year of those securities, are deemed to be non-qualified securities for the purposes of this section in the proportion determined by the formula

$$A/B$$

where

A is the amount determined by the formula

$$C + D - \$200,000$$

where

C is the total of all amounts each of which is the fair market value at the relevant time of each security under the agreement that has that same vesting year, and

D is the lesser of

(a) $200,000, and

(b) the total of all amounts each of which is an amount determined for C in respect of securities that have that same vesting year under agreements (other than the agreement) entered into at or before the relevant time with the particular qualifying person referred to in subsection (1.3) (or another qualifying person that does not deal at arm's length with the particular qualifying person), other than

(i) securities designated under subsection (1,4),

(ii) old securities (within the meaning of subsection 7(1.4)),

(iii) securities where the right to acquire those securities is an old right (within the meaning of subsection (1.7)), and

(iv) securities in respect of which

(A) the right to acquire those securities has expired, or has been cancelled, before the relevant time, and

(B) no amount is deductible under paragraph (1)(d) in computing the taxable income of the taxpayer for any year; and

B is the amount determined for C.

Related Provisions: 87(2)(j.97) — Amalgamation — continuing corporation; 110(1.3) — Conditions for 110(1.31) to apply; 110(1.4) — Designation of non-qualified security; 110(1.41) — Ordering rule; 110(1.42) — Ordering of simultaneous agreements; 110(1.43), (1.44) — Cash-out — securities not designated as non-qualified; 110(1.9) — Notification to employee and CRA of status of security; 257 — Formula cannot calculate to less than zero.

Notes: 110(1.3)–(1.44), with 110(1)(d) amended to exclude a "non-qualified security", implement rules limiting the 110(1)(d) deduction to $200,000 worth of stock option grants per year, based on the share value at the time the options are granted. The limit is not affected by the value of the stock option benefit once exercised, and there is no lifetime limit. CCPCs and other growing companies (not yet defined) are exempt from these rules: see 110(0.1)"specified person", 110(1.3). Amounts disallowed under these rules are deductible to the employer: 110(1)(e).

The Liberals originally proposed capping the stock option deduction in their 2015 election platform, and when they were elected with a majority on Oct. 19, 2015, this was expected to happen. However, it was not in the Prime Minister's Nov. 2015 "mandate letter" telling the Finance Minister what to work on during the 4-year mandate, nor in the 2016 Budget. See "Tech bosses get Liberals to drop limit on stock options", *Financial Post*, March 23, 2016, p. FP5: "The plan to place a limit was met by industry blowback, particularly from Canada's tech sector, which relies on stock options to attract talent."

The March 2019 Budget revived the proposal, addressing the high-tech issue by applying a $200,000 grant limit only to "employees of large, long-established, mature firms", later determined to be non-CCPCs with group revenue over $500 million. More detail followed in a June 17, 2019 news release and Backgrounder, inviting input from the public. Postponement to July 2021 from the original Jan. 1, 2020 in-force date was announced on Dec. 10, 2019, and final details were included in the Nov. 30, 2020 Economic Statement.

The Finance Technical Notes gives this example:

Mckayla is an employee of Xco, which is a specified person. In 2022, Xco agrees to grant her 70,000 employee stock options to acquire 70,000 shares of Xco, each with a strike price of $2 (the fair market value of the underlying securi-

ities at the time the options are granted). The first year Mckayla will be able to acquire those securities is in the 2024 calendar year.

The proportion of those securities that are deemed to be non-qualified securities is:

$$A/B$$

$$A = C + D - \$200,000$$

where

C = $140,000 (i.e., 70,000 × $2)

D = is the lesser of

(i) $200,000; and

(ii) 0

A = 0 (i.e., $140,000 + 0 – $200,000)

B = $140,000

A/B = $0/$140,000

As a result, none of the securities in respect of which options are granted in 2022 are non-qualified securities.

In 2023, Xco agrees to grant Mckayla another 50,000 options to acquire 50,000 shares of Xco with a strike price of $2 (the fair market value of the underlying securities at the time the options are granted) with a vesting year of 2024.

The proportion of those securities that are deemed to be non-qualified securities is:

$$A/B$$

$$A = C + D - \$200,000$$

where

C = $100,000 (i.e., 50,000 × $2)

D = is the lesser

(i) of $200,000; and

(ii) $140,000 (i.e., the amount for C for the previous options with the same vesting year)

A = $40,000 (i.e., $100,000 + $140,000 – $200,000)

B = $100,000

A/B = $40,000/$100,000

As a result, 20,000 (i.e., 50,000 × ($40,000/$100,000)) of the 50,000 securities in respect of which options are granted in 2023 are non-qualified securities.

See Pitch, "The New Stock Option Regime", XXVIII(3) *Taxation of Executive Compensation & Retirement* (Federated Press) 8-12 (2020); Singh & Kamboj, "Proposed Limits on Employee Stock Option Deductions", 2021(2) *Tax Times* (Carswell) 1-3 (Jan. 29, 2021).

For discussion of the 2019 draft (mostly the same as the enacted version), see Choudhury, "Proposed Stock Option Changes in Budget 2019", 2458 *Tax Topics [TT]* (CCH) 1-2 (April 18, 2019); Frankovic, "The Taxation of Employee Stock Options", 2475 *TT* 1-4 (Aug. 15, 2019); Himelfarb, "Proposed Amendments to Stock Option Rules", 27(7) *Canadian Tax Highlights* (ctf.ca) 7-8 (July 2019); Keey, "Proposed Stock Option Rules", *Taxnet Pro* Corporate Tax Centre (July 2019, 3pp); Begun & Lacoursière, "Recent Canadian Stock Option Proposals: A Comparison to the US Rules", XXVIII(1) *Taxation of Executive Compensation & Retirement* (Federated Press) 8-11 (2020).

Table 1 of the Supplementary Information to the Nov. 2020 Economic Statement forecasts that this measure will bring in almost no revenue until 2025-26, when the extra revenue will be $55 million.

110(1.31) added by 2021 budget bill #1, effective on the same basis as 110(1)(e) (generally, stock options granted after June 2021).

(1.4) Non-qualified security designation — If subsection (1.31) applies to a taxpayer in respect of an agreement and the particular qualifying person referred to in paragraph (1.3)(a) designates one or more securities to be sold or issued under the agreement as non-qualified securities, the following rules apply:

(a) those securities are deemed to be non-qualified securities for the purposes of this section; and

(b) the particular qualifying person may not elect under subsection (1.1) in respect of a right to acquire those securities.

Notes: 110(1.4) added by 2021 budget bill #1, effective on the same basis as 110(1)(e) (generally, stock options granted after June 2021).

Former 110(1.4) repealed by 2017 budget bill #1, effective 2018 (consequential on repeal of 110(1)(j)). It read:

(1.4) Replacement of home relocation loan — For the purposes of paragraph (1)(j), a loan received by a taxpayer that is used to repay a home relocation loan shall be deemed to be the same loan as the relocation loan and to have been made on the same day as the relocation loan.

Interpretation Bulletins: IT-421R2: Benefits to individuals, corporations and shareholders from loans or debt.

(1.41) Ordering of acquisition of securities — If a taxpayer acquires a security under an agreement and the acquired security could be a security that is not a non-qualified security, the security is to be considered a security that is not a non-qualified security for the purposes of this section.

Related Provisions: 110(1.9) — Notification to employee and CRA of status of security.

Notes: 110(1.41) added by 2021 budget bill #1, effective on the same basis as 110(1)(e) (generally, stock options granted after June 2021).

(1.42) Ordering of simultaneous agreements — subsec. (1.31) — If two or more agreements to sell or issue options are entered into at the same time and the particular qualifying person referred to in subsection (1.3) designates the order of the agreements, then the agreements are deemed to have been entered into in that order for the purposes of paragraph (b) of the description of D in subsection (1.31).

Notes: 110(1.42) added by 2021 budget bill #1, effective on the same basis as 110(1)(e) (generally, stock options granted after June 2021).

(1.43) Application of subsec. (1.44) — Subsection (1.44) applies in respect of a taxpayer's right to acquire a security under an agreement if

(a) subsection (1.31) applies to the taxpayer in respect of the agreement;

(b) the security is not a non-qualified security; and

(c) a payment is made to or for the benefit of the taxpayer for the taxpayer's transfer or disposition of the right.

Notes: 110(1.43) added by 2021 budget bill #1, effective on the same basis as 110(1)(e) (generally, stock options granted after June 2021).

(1.44) Cash-out — securities not designated as non-qualified — If this subsection applies in respect of a taxpayer's right to acquire a security under an agreement

(a) no qualifying person may deduct, in computing its income for a taxation year, an amount (other than a designated amount described in subsection (1.2)) in respect of the payment referred to in paragraph (1.43)(c); and

(b) paragraph (1)(d) shall, in respect of the right, be read without reference to its subparagraph (i).

Related Provisions: 110(1.2) — Designated amount; 110(1.43) — Conditions for 110(1.44) to apply.

Notes: 110(1.44) added by 2021 budget bill #1, effective on the same basis as 110(1)(e) (generally, stock options granted after June 2021).

(1.5) Determination of amounts relating to employee security [stock] options — For the purpose of paragraph (1)(d),

(a) the amount payable by a taxpayer to acquire a security under an agreement referred to in subsection 7(1) shall be determined without reference to any change in the value of a currency of a country other than Canada, relative to Canadian currency, occurring after the agreement was made;

(b) the fair market value of a security at the time an agreement in respect of the security was made shall be determined on the assumption that all specified events associated with the security that occurred after the agreement was made and before the sale or issue of the security or the disposition of the taxpayer's rights under the agreement in respect of the security, as the case may be, had occurred immediately before the agreement was made; and

(c) in determining the amount that was included, in respect of a security that a qualifying person has agreed to sell or issue to a taxpayer, in the amount determined under subparagraph 7(1.4)(c)(ii) for the purpose of determining if the condition in paragraph 7(1.4)(c) was satisfied with respect to a particular disposition, an assumption shall be made that all specified events associated with the security that occurred after the particular disposition and before the sale or issue of the security or the taxpayer's subsequent disposition of rights under the agreement in respect of the security, as the case may be, had occurred immediately before the particular disposition.

Related Provisions: 110(1.6) — Meaning of "specified event"; 110(1.7) — Definitions in 7(7) apply.

Notes: 110(1.5)(a) applies only for 110(1)(d); in *Ferlaino*, 2017 FCA 105, US$ stock options were taxed using the exchange rate on the day they were exercised.

110(1.5) amended by 2000 Budget, effective for 1998 and later taxation years. Added by 1991 technical bill, effective 1988.

Interpretation Bulletins: IT-113R4: Benefits to employees — stock options.

(1.6) Meaning of "specified event" — For the purpose of subsection (1.5), a specified event associated with a security is,

(a) where the security is a share of the capital stock of a corporation,

(i) a subdivision or consolidation of shares of the capital stock of the corporation,

(ii) a reorganization of share capital of the corporation, and

(iii) a stock dividend of the corporation; and

(b) where the security is a unit of a mutual fund trust,

(i) a subdivision or consolidation of the units of the trust, and

(ii) an issuance of units of the trust as payment, or in satisfaction of a person's right to enforce payment, out of the trust's income (determined before the application of subsection 104(6)) or out of the trust's capital gains.

Related Provisions: 110(1.7) — Definitions in 7(7) apply.

Notes: 110(1.6) added by 2000 Budget, effective for 1998 and later taxation years.

(1.7) Reduction in exercise price — If the amount payable by a taxpayer to acquire securities under an agreement referred to in subsection 7(1) is reduced at any particular time and the conditions in subsection (1.8) are satisfied in respect of the reduction,

(a) the rights (referred to in this subsection and subsection (1.8) as the **"old rights"**) that the taxpayer had under the agreement immediately before the particular time are deemed to have been disposed of by the taxpayer immediately before the particular time;

(b) the rights (referred to in this subsection and subsection (1.8) as the **"new rights"**) that the taxpayer has under the agreement at the particular time are deemed to be acquired by the taxpayer at the particular time; and

(c) the taxpayer is deemed to receive the new rights as consideration for the disposition of the old rights.

Notes: For discussion of 110(1.7) and (1.8) see Monaghan, "Tax Planners' Notebook", VIII(4) *Corporate Structures & Groups* (Federated Press) 440-44 (2003).

For CRA comment on determining value see *Income Tax Technical News* 38. 110(1.7) and (1.8) do not restrict the number of times the exercise price under an option can be reduced: VIEWS doc 2004-0093241E5.

110(1.7) added (technically amended) by 2002-2013 technical bill, effective for reductions that occur after 1998. (The former 110(1.7) it replaced provided that the definitions in 7(7) apply to 110(1.5) and (1.6); that rule is in 7(7) anyway.) Former 110(1.7) added by 2000 Budget, for 1998 and later tax years.

(1.8) Conditions for subsec. (1.7) to apply — The following are the conditions in respect of the reduction:

(a) that the taxpayer would not be entitled to a deduction under paragraph (1)(d) if the taxpayer acquired securities under the agreement immediately after the particular time and this section were read without reference to subsection (1.7); and

(b) that the taxpayer would be entitled to a deduction under paragraph (1)(d) if the taxpayer

(i) disposed of the old rights immediately before the particular time,

(ii) acquired the new rights at the particular time as consideration for the disposition, and

(iii) acquired securities under the agreement immediately after the particular time.

Notes: See Notes to 110(1.7). 110(1.8) added by 2002-2013 technical bill (Part 5 — technical), effective for reductions that occur after 1998.

(1.9) Notification — non-qualified security — If a security to be issued or sold under an agreement between an employee and a qualifying person is a non-qualified security, the employer of the employee shall

(a) notify the employee in writing that the security is a non-qualified security no later than 30 days after the day that the agreement is entered into; and

(b) notify the Minister in prescribed form that the security is a non-qualified security on or before the filing-due date for the taxation year of the qualifying person that includes the time that the agreement is entered into.

Notes: 110(1.9) added by 2021 budget bill #1, effective on the same basis as 110(1)(e) (generally, stock options granted after June 2021).

(2) Charitable gifts [vow of perpetual poverty] — Where an individual is, during a taxation year, a member of a religious order and has, as such, taken a vow of perpetual poverty, the individual may deduct in computing the individual's taxable income for the year an amount equal to the total of the individual's superannuation or pension benefits and the individual's earned income for the year (within the meaning assigned by section 63) if, of the individual's income, that amount is paid in the year to the order.

Related Provisions: 118.1(1)"total charitable gifts"(b) — No donation credit allowed; 127.52(1)(h)(i) — Deduction allowed for minimum tax purposes; 143(2)(c) — Hutterites taxed under s. 143 cannot use 110(2).

Notes: 110(2) effectively exempts the income of monks, nuns, friars and other members of Christian religious orders (Augustinians, Benedictines, Carmelites, Dominicans, Franciscans, Jesuits and others) who have taken a vow of perpetual poverty ("a life of labour lived in moderation and foreign to earthly riches"), and whose income and assets are turned over to the order. Due to 110(2) they pay no tax on their earned income and pension benefits, and cannot claim charitable donations [118.1(1)"total charitable gifts"(b)]; however, they should still file tax returns to obtain the GST/HST credit (122.5), Climate Action Incentive (122.8) and other refundable credits. They must also report and pay tax on any investment income, if they do have any assets invested. (Hutterites whose communities use the 143(2) election cannot claim the 110(2) exemption.) 110(2) apparently does not apply to Buddhist monks: VIEWS doc 2011-0399551M4. Where a nun leaves her Order and the Order gives her money due to her age and illness, without expectation and not as compensation for her service, it is non-taxable: 2011-0399461I7.

For a fascinating discussion of the links between income tax law and the religious obligation to tithe, see Adam Chodorow, "God's Income Tax: What Jewish Tithing Practices Can Teach Us About Tax Reform" (2006), ssrn.com/abstract=889960.

"Religious order" in 110(2) is interpreted as per IT-141R para. 9: VIEWS doc 2002-0145447.

Interpretation Bulletins: IT-86R: Vow of perpetual poverty; IT-141R: Clergy residence deduction.

Information Circulars: 78-5R3: Communal organizations.

Forms: T1 General return, Line 25600 [former 256]: Additional deductions.

(2.1) Charitable donation — proceeds of disposition of employee option securities — Where a taxpayer, in exercising a right to acquire a security that a particular qualifying person has agreed to sell or issue to the taxpayer under an agreement referred to in subsection 7(1), directs a broker or dealer appointed or approved by the particular qualifying person (or by a qualifying person that does not deal at arm's length with the particular qualifying person) to immediately dispose of the security and pay all or a portion of the proceeds of disposition of the security to a qualified donee,

(a) if the payment is a gift, the taxpayer is deemed, for the purpose of paragraph (1)(d.01), to have disposed of the security by making a gift of the security to the qualified donee at the time the payment is made; and

(b) the amount deductible under paragraph (1)(d.01) by the taxpayer in respect of the disposition of the security is the amount determined by the formula

$$A \times B / C$$

where

A is the amount that would be deductible under paragraph (1)(d.01)in respect of the disposition of the security if this subsection were read without reference to this paragraph,

B is the amount of the payment, and

C is the amount of the proceeds of disposition of the security.

Related Provisions: 7(1.3) — Order of disposition of securities; 153(1.01) — Withholding tax on stock option benefits.

Notes: See VIEWS doc 2015-0605971E5: (1) directing broker to sell shares and then donating personally does not work; (2) "immediately" applies to both selling the shares and making the donation; (3) 7(1.31) election may be needed.

110(2.1) added by 2000 Budget, effective for 2000 and later taxation years.

(2.2)–(9) [Repealed under former Act]

Notes: Former 110(2.1)–(9), repealed by 1988 tax reform, provided special rules re charitable donations, medical expenses and the disability deduction. These have been integrated into the rules for credits in 118.1-118.4.

Definitions [s. 110]: "amount" — 248(1); "arm's length" — 251(1); "associated" — 256; "beneficiary" — 108(1); "calendar year" — *Interpretation Act* 37(1)(a); "Canada" — 255; "Canadian-controlled private corporation" — 125(7), 248(1); "capital gain" — 39(1)(a), 248(1); "common-law partner" — 248(1); "consequence of the taxpayer's death" — 248(8); "consolidated financial statements" — 233.8(1); "corporation" — 248(1), *Interpretation Act* 35(1); "designated amount" — 110(1.2); "disposition", "employee", "employer", "employment" — 248(1); "exchanged option" — 7(1.4)(a); "fair market value" — see 69(1) Notes; "filing-due date" — 150(1), 248(1); "fiscal period" — 249.1; "graduated rate estate", "gross revenue" — 248(1); "home relocation loan" — 110(1.4), 248(1); "identical" — 248(12); "individual", "Minister" — 248(1); "Minister of Finance" — *Financial Administration Act* 14; "month" — *Interpretation Act* 35(1); "multinational enterprise group" — 233.8(1); "mutual fund trust" — 132(6)–(7), 132.2(3)(n), 248(1); "new option" — 7(1.4); "new right" — 110(1.7)(b); "new share" — 7(1.4); "non-qualified security" — 110(1.3)–(1.42); "non-resident" — 248(1); "old right" — 7(1.4), 110(1.7)(a); "old securities" — 7(1.4); "old share" — 7(1.4)(a); "person", "prescribed" — 248(1); "prescribed international organization" — Reg. 8900(1); "private foundation" — 149.1(1), 248(1); "province" — *Interpretation Act* 35(1); "qualified donee" — 149.1(1), 248(1); "qualifying person" — 7(7); "relevant time" — 110(1.3)(b); "resident in Canada" — 94(3)(a), 250; "security" — 7(7); "share", "shareholder" — 248(1); "specified event" — 110(1.6); "specified person" — 110(0.1); "stock dividend" — 248(1); "taxable income" — 2(2), 248(1); "taxable income earned in Canada" — 248(1); "taxation year" — 249; "taxpayer" — 248(1); "trust" — 104(1), 248(1), (3); "ultimate parent entity" — 233.8(1); "vesting year" — 110(0.1); "writing" — *Interpretation Act* 35(1).

Interpretation Bulletins: IT-326R3: Returns of deceased persons as "another person".

110.1 (1) Deduction for [charitable] gifts [by corporation] — For the purpose of computing the taxable income of a corporation for a taxation year, there may be deducted such of the following amounts as the corporation claims:

(a) **charitable gifts** — the total of all amounts each of which is the eligible amount of a gift (other than a gift described in paragraph (c) or (d)) made by the corporation in the year or in any of the five preceding taxation years to a qualified donee, not exceeding the lesser of the corporation's income for the year and the amount determined by the formula

$$0.75A + 0.25 (B + C + D)$$

where

A is the corporation's income for the year computed without reference to subsection 137(2),

B is the total of all amounts, each of which is that proportion of the corporation's taxable capital gain for the taxation year in respect of a gift made by the corporation in the taxation year (in respect of which gift an eligible amount is described in this paragraph for the taxation year) that the eligible amount of the gift is of the corporation's proceeds of disposition in respect of the gift,

C is the total of all amounts each of which is a taxable capital gain of the corporation for the year, because of subsection 40(1.01), from a disposition of a property in a preceding taxation year, and

D   is the total of all amounts each of which is determined in respect of the corporation's depreciable property of a prescribed class and equal to the lesser of

(A) the amount included under subsection 13(1) in respect of the class in computing the corporation's income for the year, and

(B) the total of all amounts each of which is determined in respect of a disposition that is the making of a gift of property of the class by the corporation in the year (in respect of which gift an eligible amount is described in this paragraph for the taxation year) equal to the lesser of

(I) that proportion, of the amount by which the proceeds of disposition of the property exceeds any outlays and expenses, to the extent that they were made or incurred by the corporation for the purpose of making the disposition, that the eligible amount of the gift is of the corporation's proceeds of disposition in respect of the gift, and

(II) that proportion, of the capital cost to the corporation of the property, that the eligible amount of the gift is of the corporation's proceeds of disposition in respect of the gift;

(a.1) [Repealed]

(b) **gifts to Her Majesty** — [Repealed]

(c) **gifts to institutions** — the total of all amounts each of which is the eligible amount of a gift (other than a gift described in paragraph (d)) of an object that the Canadian Cultural Property Export Review Board has determined meets the criterion set out in paragraph 29(3)(b) of the *Cultural Property Export and Import Act*, which gift was made by the corporation in the year or in any of the five preceding taxation years to an institution or a public authority in Canada that was, at the time the gift was made, designated under subsection 32(2) of that Act either generally or for a specified purpose related to that object; and

(d) **ecological gifts** — the total of all amounts each of which is the eligible amount of a gift of land (including a covenant or an easement to which land is subject or, in the case of land in the Province of Quebec, a personal servitude (the rights to which the land is subject and which has a term of not less than 100 years) or a real servitude) if

(i) the fair market value of the gift is certified by the Minister of the Environment,

(ii) the land is certified by that Minister, or by a person designated by that Minister, to be ecologically sensitive land, the conservation and protection of which is, in the opinion of that Minister or the designated person, important to the preservation of Canada's environmental heritage, and

(iii) the gift was made by the corporation in the year or in any of the 10 preceding taxation years to a qualified donee that is

(A) Her Majesty in right of Canada or of a province,

(B) a municipality in Canada that is approved by that Minister or the designated person in respect of the gift,

(C) a municipal or public body performing a function of government in Canada that is approved by that Minister or the designated person in respect of the gift, or

(D) a registered charity (other than a private foundation) one of the main purposes of which is, in the opinion of that Minister, the conservation and protection of Canada's environmental heritage, and that is approved by that Minister or the designated person in respect of the gift.

Related Provisions: 37(5) — R&D expenditures not deductible under 110.1; 46(1), (5) — Capital gain on certain donations of art and other property; 87(2)(v) — Amalgamations — gifts; 88(1)(e.6), 88(1.3) — Effect of winding-up; 110.1(1.1)(a) — Gifts not deductible if previously deducted; 110.1(1.2) — No carryforward of deduction after change in control of corporation; 110.1(3) — Election for reduced proceeds on donation of capital property; 110.1(5) — Fair market value of ecological servitude, cove-

nant or easement; 110.1(10)–(13) — Effect of corp granting option to charity; 110.1(14)–(17) — Donation denied where property returned to corp; 118.1(1) — Parallel rules for donations by individuals; 118.1(10)–(10.5) — Determination of value of ecological or cultural property; 149.1(6.4) — Donation to registered national arts service org; 188.2(3)(a) — Effect of suspension of charity's receipting privileges; 207.3, 207.31 — Tax on donee that disposes of cultural or ecologcal property; 225.1(7) — Donation shelter assessment can be half-collected while under appeal; 230(2) — Records of donations; 237.1(1)"gifting arrangement", "tax shelter" — Tax shelter registration requirement; 248(30)–(33) — Determination of eligible amount; 248(35)–(39) — Value of gift limited to cost if acquired within 3 years or as tax shelter; 248(41) — Donation value deemed nil if taxpayer does not inform donee of circumstances requiring reduction; 261(7)(a) — Functional currency reporting; Canada-U.S. Tax Treaty:Art. XXI:7 — Donations to U.S. charities.

Notes: 110.1 applies only to corporations. Charitable donations by individuals and trusts are eligible for a credit under 118.1, whose rules are generally parallel to 110.1. See Notes to 118.1(1)"total charitable gifts" and "total gifts". Donations by partnerships are deemed to have been made by the partners: 110.1(4), 118.1(8).

On which way to donate, see Chloe Man, "Charitable Donations: Personally or Through a Corporation?", tinyurl.com/donate-which.

See Notes to 149.1(1)"qualified donee" for discussion of various non-charity donees such as municipalities and foreign universities.

As an alternative to a receipted donation under 110.1, a corporation may be able to deduct a donation as an advertising expense or sponsorship, especially if public recognition is given. (If something else of value is received, see 248(32) and VIEWS doc 2010-0388751E5.) See Drache, "Corporate Donations to U.S. Charities", 19(4) *Canadian Not-for-Profit News* (Carswell) 31-32 (April 2011) and "Payments from Businesses to Charities", 25(10) 79-80 (Oct. 2017). However, in *Emballages Starflex*, 2016 QCCA 1856, a company that claimed a donation was not allowed to argue in the alternative that the payment was a business expense (for Quebec tax purposes), when this argument was raised only at trial and the company sought different treatment depending on whether donations were made in the US or Canada. If the donation is advertised to encourage sales ("cause-related marketing"), no tax receipt can be issued but an advertising expense may be allowed: tinyurl.com/cra-cause.

A stock option granted by a corporation to a charity is not a transfer of property as there is no "impoverishment" of the donor (*Boisselle*, [1989] 1 C.T.C. 2385 (TCC)). Thus, it is not a gift and no 110.1 credit is available: VIEWS doc 2003-0014695. Similarly, issuing shares does not constitute a transfer of property: *Algoa Trust*, [1993] 1 C.T.C. 2294 (TCC); aff'd without reasons 1998 CarswellNat 3211 (FCA). For criticism of this view see Drache, "CCRA Nixes Stock Option Gifts", 12(6) *Canadian Not-for-Profit News* (Carswell) 47 (June 2004).

See also VIEWS docs 2007-0247091R3 (donation of ecologically sensitive land qualifies); 2012-0439121R3; 2012-0446631E5 (consequences of donating depreciable property); 2013-0497001R3 (ruling approving transfer of gift deduction to related corp).

For 110.1(1)(d), if the donee ever disposes of the land without authorization from the Minister of the Environment, a special 50% tax applies under 207.31.

110.1(1)(c) amended by 2019 budget bill #1, effective March 19, 2019, to change "criteria set out in paragraphs 29(3)(b) and (c)" to "criterion set out in paragraph 29(3)(b)".

110.1(1)(d) opening words and (d)(iii)(B)-(D) amended by 2017 budget bill #2, for gifts made after March 21, 2017, For earlier gifts, read:

(d) the total of all amounts each of which is the eligible amount of a gift of land (including a covenant or an easement to which land is subject or, in the case of land in the Province of Quebec, a real servitude) if

. . . . .

(B) a municipality in Canada,

(C) a municipal or public body performing a function of government in Canada, or

(D) a registered charity one of the main purposes of which is, in the opinion of that Minister, the conservation and protection of Canada's environmental heritage, and that is approved by that Minister or the designated person in respect of the gift.

110.1(1)(a.1) repealed by 2017 budget bill #1, for gifts made after March 21, 2017. It and 110.1(8)-(9) (and Reg. 3505) implemented a 2007 budget proposal allowing an extra deduction for donations of pharmaceuticals in inventory, to specific charities working in developing countries. (For a similar Ontario credit of 25% of the value of a farmer's donation of agricultural products to certain charities, see *Taxation Act, 2007*, s. 103.1.2.) Originally added by 2007 budget bill #2, for gifts made after March 18, 2007, and amended retroactively by 2002-2013 technical bill. It read:

(a.1) **gifts of medicine** — the total of all amounts each of which is an amount, in respect of property that is the subject of an eligible medical gift made by the corporation in the taxation year or in any of the five preceding taxation years, determined by the formula

$$A \times B/C$$

where

A   is the lesser of

(a) the cost to the corporation of the property, and

(b) 50 per cent of the amount, if any, by which the corporation's proceeds of disposition of the property in respect of the gift exceeds the cost to the corporation of the property;

B   is the eligible amount of the gift; and

C   is the corporation's proceeds of disposition of the property in respect of the gift.

110.1(1) amended by 2014 budget bill #2 (for 2016 and later tax years, to repeal para. (b) for gifts to the Crown, which still count as regular donations), 2014 budget bills #1 and #2, 2002-2013 technical bill, 2011 budget bill #2, 2000, 1997, 1996 and 1995 Budgets, 1991 technical bill.

Regulations: 3503, Sch. VIII (prescribed universities outside Canada [since 2012, prescribed for 149.1(1)"qualified donee"(a)(iv)]).

Income Tax Folios: S3-F2-C1: Capital Dividends [replaces IT-66R6]; S7-F1-C1: Split-receipting and deemed fair market value [replaces IT-110R3].

Interpretation Bulletins: IT-226R: Gift to a charity of a residual interest in real property or an equitable interest in a trust; IT-244R3: Gifts of life insurance policies as charitable donations; IT-288R2: Gifts of capital properties to a charity and others; IT-297R2: Gifts in kind to charity and others; IT-407R4: Dispositions of cultural property to designated Canadian institutions.

Information Circulars: 84-3R6: Gifts to certain charitable organizations outside Canada.

Advance Tax Rulings: ATR-63: Donations to agents of the Crown.

I.T. Technical News: 17 (loan of property as a gift).

Registered Charities Newsletters: See under 118.1(1)"total charitable gifts".

Charities Guidance: CG-007: Donation of gift certificates or gift cards; CG-010: Qualified donees.

Forms: RC4142: Tax advantages of donating to a charity [guide]; T2 Sched. 2: Charitable donations and gifts; T1236: Qualified donees worksheet/amounts provided to other organizations.

(1.1) Limitation on deductibility

— For the purpose of determining the amount deductible under subsection (1) in computing a corporation's taxable income for a taxation year,

(a) an amount in respect of a gift is deductible only to the extent that it exceeds amounts in respect of the gift deducted under that subsection in computing the corporation's taxable income for preceding taxation years; and

(b) no amount in respect of a gift made in a particular taxation year is deductible under any of paragraphs (1)(a) to (d) until amounts deductible under that paragraph in respect of gifts made in taxation years preceding the particular year have been deducted.

Related Provisions: 118.1(2.1) — Ordering rule parallel to 110.1(1.1)(b).

Notes: 110.1(1.1) added by 1997 Budget, effective for taxation years that begin after 1996. Its "first-in, first-out" assumption reflects Revenue Canada's previous assessing policy and is the assumption most favourable to taxpayers, since it allows the largest carryforward of unused donations.

(1.2) Where control acquired

— Notwithstanding paragraph 88(1)(e.6), if control of a particular corporation is acquired at any time by a person or group of persons,

(a) no amount is deductible under any of paragraphs (1)(a) to (d) in computing any corporation's taxable income for a taxation year that ends on or after that time in respect of a gift made by the particular corporation before that time; and

(b) no amount is deductible under any of paragraphs (1)(a) to (d) in computing any corporation's taxable income for a taxation year that ends on or after that time in respect of a gift made by any corporation on or after that time if the property that is the subject of the gift was acquired by the particular corporation under an arrangement under which it was expected that control of the particular corporation would be so acquired by a person or group of persons, other than a qualified donee that received the gift, and the gift would be so made.

Related Provisions: 111(4), (5) — Change of control rules for losses; 256(6)–(9) — Whether control acquired.

Notes: 110.1(1.2) added by 2004 Budget, effective for gifts made after March 22, 2004. It prevents "trading" in charitable donation deductions by disallowing them after a change in control. See Notes to 111(5).

(2) Proof of gift

— An eligible amount of a gift shall not be included for the purpose of determining a deduction under subsection

(1) unless the making of the gift is evidenced by filing with the Minister

(a) a receipt for the gift that contains prescribed information;

(b) in the case of a gift described in paragraph (1)(c), the certificate issued under subsection 33(1) of the *Cultural Property Export and Import Act*; and

(c) in the case of a gift described in paragraph (1)(d), both certificates referred to in that paragraph.

Related Provisions: 118.1(2) — Parallel rule for individuals; 188 — Revocation tax where registration of charity is revoked; 248(30)–(33) — Determination of eligible amount; 248(41) — Donation value deemed nil if taxpayer does not inform donee of circumstances requiring reduction.

Notes: In *9228-2987 Québec*, 2019 TCC 281, a corporation could not deduct donations where the cheques came from its shareholder (under a nominee agreement), and the charity refused to issue receipts in the corp's name.

110.1(2) amended by 2002-2013 technical bill (for gifts made after Dec. 20, 2002), 2000 Budget.

Regulations: 3500–3502 (prescribed information).

Advance Tax Rulings: ATR-63: Donations to agents of the Crown.

Forms: T2 Sched. 2: Charitable donations and gifts.

(2.1) Where subsec. (3) applies

— Subsection (3) applies in circumstances where

(a) a corporation makes a gift at any time of

(i) capital property to a qualified donee, or

(ii) in the case of a corporation not resident in Canada, real or immovable property situated in Canada to a prescribed donee who provides an undertaking, in a form satisfactory to the Minister, to the effect that the property will be held for use in the public interest; and

(b) the fair market value of the property otherwise determined at that time exceeds

(i) in the case of depreciable property of a prescribed class, the lesser of the undepreciated capital cost of that class at the end of the taxation year of the corporation that includes that time (determined without reference to the proceeds of disposition designated in respect of the property under subsection (3)) and the adjusted cost base to the corporation of the property immediately before that time, and

(ii) in any other case, the adjusted cost base to the corporation of the property immediately before that time.

Related Provisions: 118.1(5.4) — Parallel rule for individuals; 248(35)–(39) — Value of gift limited to cost if acquired within 3 years or as tax shelter.

Notes: 110.1(2.1) added by 2002-2013 technical bill, last change effective 2012.

Regulations: 3504 (prescribed donee for 110.1(2.1)(a)(ii)).

Income Tax Folios: S7-F1-C1: Split-receipting and deemed fair market value [replaces IT-110R3].

(3) Gifts of capital property

— If this subsection applies in respect of a gift by a corporation of property, and the corporation designates an amount in respect of the gift in its return of income under section 150 for the year in which the gift is made, the amount so designated is deemed to be its proceeds of disposition of the property and, for the purpose of subsection 248(31), the fair market value of the gift, but the amount so designated may not exceed the fair market value of the property otherwise determined and may not be less than the greater of

(a) in the case of a gift made after December 20, 2002, the amount of the advantage, if any, in respect of the gift, and

(b) the amount determined under subparagraph (2.1)(b)(i) or (ii), as the case may be, in respect of the property.

Related Provisions: 38(a.1) — Donation of listed securities; 118.1(5.4), (6) — Parallel rule for individuals; 248(32) — Determination of amount of advantage; 248(35)–(37) — Value of gift limited to cost if acquired within 3 years or as tax shelter.

Notes: See Notes to the parallel rule in 118.1(6). For a corporation filing Quebec returns, the designation must be copied to Revenu Québec: *Taxation Act* ss. 716, 21.4.6.

110.1(3) replaced by 2002-2013 technical bill (last change effective for gifts made after Dec. 20, 2002), 2011 budget bill #2, 2001 technical bill, 1995 Budget, 1992 technical bill.

Income Tax Folios: S7-F1-C1: Split-receipting and deemed fair market value [replaces IT-110R3].

Interpretation Bulletins: IT-288R2: Gifts of capital properties to a charity and others.

(4) Gifts made by partnership — If at the end of a fiscal period of a partnership a corporation is a member of the partnership, its share of any amount that would, if the partnership were a person, be the eligible amount of a gift made by the partnership to any donee is, for the purpose of this section, deemed to be the eligible amount of a gift made to that donee by the corporation in its taxation year in which the fiscal period of the partnership ends.

Related Provisions: 53(2)(c)(iii) — Deduction from ACB of partnership interest; 118.1(8) — Parallel rule for individuals; 248(30)–(33) — Determination of eligible amount.

Notes: 110.1(4) amended by 2002-2013 technical bill (Part 5 — technical) effective for gifts made after Dec. 20, 2002, to add "the eligible amount of" twice.

(5) Ecological gifts — For the purposes of applying subparagraph 69(1)(b)(ii), this section and section 207.31 in respect of a gift described in paragraph (1)(d) that is made by a taxpayer, the amount that is the fair market value (or, for the purpose of subsection (3), the fair market value otherwise determined) of the gift at the time the gift was made and, subject to subsection (3), the taxpayer's proceeds of disposition of the gift, is deemed to be the amount determined by the Minister of the Environment to be

(a) where the gift is land, the fair market value of the gift; or

(b) where the gift is a covenant or an easement to which land is subject or, in the case of land in the Province of Quebec, a real or personal servitude, the greater of

(i) the fair market value otherwise determined of the gift, and

(ii) the amount by which the fair market value of the land is reduced as a result of the making of the gift.

Related Provisions: 43(2) — calculation for 110.1(5) also applies for determining capital gain or loss on disposition; 118.1(12) — Parallel rule for individuals.

Notes: "Land" can include buildings: see 70(5.2) Notes.

110.1(5) amended by 2017 budget bill #2 (for gifts made after March 21, 2017, to add "or personal" to (b)), 2002-2013 technical bill, 2000 and 1997 Budgets.

(6) Non-qualifying securities — Subsections 118.1(13) to (14) and (16) to (20) apply to a corporation as if the references in those subsections to an individual were read as references to a corporation and as if a non-qualifying security of a corporation included a share (other than a share listed on a designated stock exchange) of the capital stock of the corporation.

Related Provisions: 40(1.01) — Capital gains reserve on disposition of non-qualifying security; 88(1)(e.61) — Winding-up of subsidiary — gift deemed made by parent corporation; 110.1(7) — Where corporation ceases to exist after making donation of non-qualifying securities; 118.1(18) — Definition of non-qualifying security.

Notes: 110.1(6) amended by 2011 budget bill #2 (effective March 22, 2011), 2007 budget bill #2. Added by 1997 Budget.

(7) Corporation ceasing to exist — If, but for this subsection, a corporation (other than a corporation that was a predecessor corporation in an amalgamation to which subsection 87(1) applied or a corporation that was wound up in a winding-up to which subsection 88(1) applied) would be deemed by subsection 118.1(13) to have made a gift after the corporation ceased to exist, for the purpose of this section, the corporation is deemed to have made the gift in its last taxation year, except that the amount of interest payable under any provision of this Act is the amount that it would be if this subsection did not apply to the gift.

Notes: 110.1(7) added by 1997 Budget, effective August 1997.

(8), (9) [Repealed]

Notes: 110.1(8), (9) repealed by 2017 budget bill #1, for gifts made after March 21, 2017. (See Notes to 110.1(1) re 110.1(1)(a.1).) They read:

(8) Eligible medical gift — For the purpose of paragraph (1)(a.1), a gift referred to in paragraph (1)(a) is an eligible medical gift of a corporation if

(a) the corporation has directed the donee to apply the gift to charitable activities outside of Canada;

(b) the property that is the subject of the gift is a medicine that is available for the donee's use at least six months prior to its expiration date, within the meaning of the *Food and Drug Regulations*;

(c) the medicine qualifies as a drug, within the meaning of the *Food and Drugs Act*, and the drug

(i) meets the requirements of that Act, or would meet those requirements if that Act were read without reference to its subsection 37(1), and

(ii) is not a food, cosmetic or device (as those terms are defined in that Act), a natural health product (as defined in the *Natural Health Products Regulations*) or a veterinary drug;

(d) the property was, immediately before the making of the gift, described in an inventory in respect of a business of the corporation; and

(e) the donee is a registered charity that, in the opinion of the Minister for International Development (or, if there is no such Minister, the Minister of Foreign Affairs) meets conditions prescribed by regulation.

(9) Rules governing international medical charities — For the purpose of paragraph (8)(e),

(a) for greater certainty, nothing in paragraph (8)(b) modifies the application to a registered charity of the prescribed conditions referred to in paragraph (8)(e);

(b) if, in respect of a registered charity, the Minister referred to in paragraph (8)(e) is of the opinion described in that paragraph

(i) that Minister may also designate a period of time during which that opinion is valid, and

(ii) notwithstanding subparagraph (i), the opinion may be revoked at any time by that Minister if

(A) that Minister is of the opinion that the registered charity no longer meets prescribed conditions referred to in paragraph (8)(e), or

(B) any person has made any misrepresentation that is attributable to neglect, carelessness or wilful default for the purpose of obtaining the opinion; and

(c) a revocation referred to in subparagraph (b)(ii) is effective as of the time that notice, in writing, of the revocation is issued by that Minister to the registered charity.

For the *Food and Drugs Act* and *Food and Drug Regulations*, see canlii.org.

110.1(8) earlier amended by 2013 budget bill #1 (effective June 26, 2013, to change the name of the relevant Minister), 2008 budget bills #1 and #2. Added by 2007 budget bill #2.

110.1(9) added by 2008 budget bill #2, for gifts made after June 2008. See Finance news release 2008-038 (May 16, 2008).

(10) Options [granted by corporation to qualified donee] — Subject to subsections (12) and (13), if a corporation has granted an option to a qualified donee in a taxation year, no amount in respect of the option is to be included in computing an amount under any of paragraphs (1)(a) to (d) in respect of the corporation for any year.

Related Provisions: 118.1(21) — Parallel rule for individuals.

Notes: 110.1(10) added by 2011 budget bill #2, effective for options granted after March 21, 2011.

(11) Application of subsec. (12) — Subsection (12) applies if

(a) an option to acquire a property of a corporation is granted to a qualified donee;

(b) the option is exercised so that the property is disposed of by the corporation and acquired by the qualified donee at a particular time; and

(c) either

(i) the amount that is 80% of the fair market value of the property at the particular time is greater than or equal to the total of

(A) the consideration received by the corporation from the qualified donee for the property, and

(B) the consideration received by the corporation from the qualified donee for the option, or

(ii) the corporation establishes to the satisfaction of the Minister that the granting of the option or the disposition of the property was made by the corporation with the intention to make a gift to the qualified donee.

Related Provisions: 118.1(22) — Parallel rule for individuals.

Notes: 110.1(11) added by 2011 budget bill #2, for options granted after March 21, 2011.

(12) Granting of an option — If this subsection applies, notwithstanding subsection 49(3),

(a) the corporation is deemed to have received proceeds of disposition of the property equal to the property's fair market value at the particular time; and

(b) there shall be included in the total referred to in paragraph (1)(a), for the corporation's taxation year that includes the particular time, the amount by which the property's fair market value exceeds the total described in subparagraph (11)(c)(i).

Related Provisions: 110.1(11) — Conditions for 110.1(12) to apply; 118.1(23) — Parallel rule for individuals.

Notes: See Notes to 118.1(21). 110.1(12) added by 2011 budget bill #2, effective for options granted after March 21, 2011.

(13) Disposition of an option — If an option to acquire a particular property of a corporation is granted to a qualified donee and the option is disposed of by the qualified donee (otherwise than by the exercise of the option) at a particular time

(a) the corporation is deemed to have disposed of a property at the particular time

(i) the adjusted cost base of which to the corporation immediately before the particular time is equal to the consideration, if any, paid by the qualified donee for the option, and

(ii) the proceeds of disposition of which are equal to the lesser of the fair market value of the particular property at the particular time and the fair market value of any consideration (other than a non-qualifying security of any person) received by the qualified donee for the option; and

(b) there shall be included in the total referred to in paragraph (1)(a) for the corporation's taxation year that includes the particular time the amount, if any, by which the proceeds of disposition as determined by paragraph (a) exceed the consideration, if any, paid by the qualified donee for the option.

Related Provisions: 118.1(24) — Parallel rule for individuals.

Notes: 110.1(13) added by 2011 budget bill #2, effective for options granted after March 21, 2011.

(14) Returned property — Subsection (15) applies if a qualified donee has issued to a corporation a receipt referred to in subsection (2) in respect of a transfer of a property (in this subsection and subsection (15) referred to as the "original property") and a particular property that is

(a) the original property is later transferred to the corporation (unless that later transfer is reasonable consideration or remuneration for property acquired by or services rendered to a person); or

(b) any other property that may reasonably be considered compensation for or a substitute for, in whole or in part, the original property, is later transferred to the corporation.

Related Provisions: 118.1(25) — Parallel rule for individuals.

Notes: 110.1(14) added by 2011 budget bill #2, effective for transfers of property made after March 21, 2011.

Charities Guidance: CG-016: Qualified donees — Consequences of returning donated property.

(15) Returned property — If this subsection applies, then

(a) irrespective of whether the transfer of the original property by the corporation to the qualified donee referred to in subsection (14) was a gift, the corporation is deemed not to have disposed of the original property at the time of that transfer nor to have made a gift;

(b) if the particular property is identical to the original property, the particular property is deemed to be the original property; and

(c) if the particular property is not the original property, then

(i) the corporation is deemed to have disposed of the original property at the time that the particular property is transferred to the corporation for proceeds of disposition equal to the greater of the fair market value of the particular property at that time and the fair market value of the original property at the time that it was transferred by the corporation to the donee, and

(ii) if the transfer of the original property by the corporation would be a gift if this section were read without reference to paragraph (a), the corporation is deemed to have, at the time of that transfer, transferred to the donee a property that is the subject of a gift having a fair market value equal to the amount, if any, by which the fair market value of the original property at the time of that transfer exceeds the fair market value of the particular property at the time that it is transferred to the corporation.

Related Provisions: 110.1(14) — Conditions for 110.1(15) to apply; 110.1(16) — Information return required; 110.1(17) — Reassessment to undo donation deduction; 118.1(26) — Parallel rule for individuals.

Notes: See Notes to 118.1(26). 110.1(15) added by 2011 budget bill #2, effective for transfers of property made after March 21, 2011.

Charities Guidance: CG-016: Qualified donees — Consequences of returning donated property.

(16) Information return — If subsection (15) applies in respect of a transfer of property to a corporation and that property has a fair market value greater than $50, the transferor must file an information return containing prescribed information with the Minister not later than 90 days after the day on which the property was transferred and provide a copy of the return to the corporation.

Related Provisions: 118.1(27) — Parallel rule for individuals.

Notes: See Notes to 118.1(26). 110.1(16) added by 2011 budget bill #2, effective for transfers of property made after March 21, 2011, and an information return filed by Nov. 15, 2011 is deemed filed on time.

Regulations: 3501.1 (contents of information return).

Charities Guidance: CG-016: Qualified donees — Consequences of returning donated property.

(17) Reassessment — If subsection (15) applies in respect of a transfer of property to a corporation, the Minister may reassess a return of income of any person to the extent that the reassessment can reasonably be regarded as relating to the transfer.

Related Provisions: 118.1(28) — Parallel rule for individuals.

Notes: 110.1(17) added by 2011 budget bill #2, for transfers of property made after March 21, 2011. 110.1(14)-(17) were not in the June 6, 2011 Budget draft legislation.

Former 110.1, which provided a deduction for individuals offsetting the first $1,000 of interest and dividend income from Canadian sources, was repealed in 1988 when the personal deductions in 109-110 were changed to credits in 118.

Definitions [s. 110.1]: "adjusted cost base" — 54, 248(1); "advantage" — 248(32); "amount", "business" — 248(1); "Canada" — 255, *Interpretation Act* 35(1); "capital property" — 54, 248(1); "corporation" — 248(1), *Interpretation Act* 35(1); "depreciable property" — 13(21), 248(1); "designated stock exchange" — 248(1), 262; "disposition" — 248(1); "eligible amount" — 248(31), (41); "fair market value" — 110.1(5), 118.1(10), 248(35) and see 69(1) Notes; "fiscal period" — 249(2)(b), 249.1; "Her Majesty" — *Interpretation Act* 35(1); "identical" — 248(12); "immovable" — Quebec *Civil Code* art. 900–907; "individual", "inventory" — 248(1); "land" — see 70(5.2) Notes; "Minister" — 248(1); "original property" — 110.1(14); "partnership" — see 96(1) Notes; "person", "prescribed", "property" — 248(1); "province" — *Interpretation Act* 35(1); "qualified donee" — 149.1(1), 188.2(3)(a), 248(1); "real servitude" — Quebec *Civil Code* art. 1177; "registered Canadian amateur athletic association", "registered charity", "regulation" — 248(1); "resident in Canada" — 250; "share" — 248(1); "taxable income" — 2(2), 248(1); "taxation year" — 249; "undepreciated capital cost" — 13(21), 248(1); "writing", "written" — *Interpretation Act* 35(1) "writing".

110.2 [Lump-sum averaging] — **(1) Definitions** — The definitions in this subsection apply in this section and section 120.31.

"eligible taxation year", in respect of a qualifying amount received by an individual, means a taxation year

(a) that ended after 1977 and before the year in which the individual received the qualifying amount;

(b) throughout which the individual was resident in Canada;

(c) that did not end in a calendar year in which the individual became a bankrupt; and

(d) that was not included in an averaging period, within the meaning assigned by section 119 (as it read in its application to the 1987 taxation year), pursuant to an election that was made and not revoked by the individual under that section.

Notes: See Notes at end of 110.2.

"qualifying amount" received by an individual in a taxation year means an amount (other than the portion of the amount that can reasonably be considered to be received as, on account of, in lieu of payment of or in satisfaction of, interest) that is included in computing the individual's income for the year and is

(a) an amount

(i) that is received pursuant to an order or judgment of a competent tribunal, an arbitration award or a contract by which the payor and the individual terminate a legal proceeding, and

(ii) that is

(A) included in computing the individual's income from an office or employment, or

(B) received as, on account of, in lieu of payment of or in satisfaction of, damages in respect of the individual's loss of an office or employment,

(b) a superannuation or pension benefit (other than a benefit referred to in clause 56(1)(a)(i)(B)) received on account of, in lieu of payment of or in satisfaction of, a series of periodic payments (other than payments that would have otherwise been made in the year or in a subsequent taxation year),

(c) an amount described in paragraphs 6(1)(f) or (f.1), subparagraph 56(1)(a)(iv) or paragraph 56(1)(b), or

(d) a prescribed amount or benefit,

except to the extent that the individual may deduct for the year an amount under paragraph 8(1)(b), (n) or (n.1), 60(n) or (o.1) or 110(1)(f) in respect of the amount so included.

Notes: In *Park*, 2012 TCC 306, the Canadian Forces Recruiting Group was held to be a "competent tribunal" for subpara. (a)(i), and a formal request for review that was not a grievance qualified as a "legal proceeding".

For CRA VIEWS finding a "qualifying amount" (QA) see docs 2006-0165501R3 (past wages paid to settle employment dispute); 2004-0063421E5 (class action lawsuit settlement); 2008-0264231E5 (interest arbitration award); 2005-0153051E5 (fixed sum paid by pension plan); 2006-020464117 (payment of prior years' pension benefits after the annuitant's death); 2006-0166891E5 (pension benefits even where paid by former employer); 2012-045794117 (severance pay under collective agreement); 2013-0479451E5 (unspecified retroactive lump sum amount); 2013-048832117 (retroactive lump sum payment of pension benefits); 2014-0547271E5 (lump sum in satisfaction of periodic payments from a SERP [see 248(1)"salary deferral arrangement" Notes]); 2019-0796871E5, 2019-083491117 (collective bargaining arbitration award).

For docs finding no QA see 2007-0239411E5, 2007-0261081E5 and 2008-026566117 (collective bargaining settlement where no legal proceeding terminated); 2002-0143295 and 2008-0300251E5 (grievance settlement), 2006-018478117 (workers' compensation payment).

The QA need not be the gross payment where part of it had been repaid to an insurer: *Laframboise*, 2004 TCC 639.

See also Notes at end of 110.2.

Para. (c) amended to add reference to 6(1)(f.1) by 2002-2013 technical bill (Part 5 — technical), effective April 2006.

"specified portion", in relation to an eligible taxation year, of a qualifying amount received by an individual means the portion of the qualifying amount that relates to the year, to the extent that the individual's eligibility to receive the portion existed in the year.

Related Provisions: 120.31(1) — Definitions apply to 120.31.

(2) Deduction for lump-sum payments — There may be deducted in computing the taxable income of an individual (other than a trust) for a particular taxation year the total of all amounts each of which is a specified portion of a qualifying amount received by the individual in the particular year, if that total is $3,000 or more.

Related Provisions: 120.31 — Tax payable for other years.

Forms: T1198: Statement of qualifying retroactive lump-sum payment.

Notes [s. 110.2]: 110.2 provides limited retroactive averaging of certain kinds of income (see 110.2(1)"qualifying amount"). It was introduced primarily to accommodate federal government pay equity settlements. It addresses taxpayers who are pushed into a higher bracket as a result of having all the income lumped into the year in which it is received (see 5(1)). The deduction under 110.2(2) is offset by tax payable for the other years under 120.31. Note however that under 120.31(3)(b) an amount in lieu of interest must be paid for the earlier years. Where possible, CRA's computer will calculate and process the adjustment automatically. For lump-sum arrears of spousal or child support, the taxpayer must request relief on Form T1198: VIEWS doc 2012-0461011M4. Although it "would seem appropriate" for the payor to complete a T1198 so the recipient can use 110.2, there is no legal obligation to do so: 2008-0264231E5. For an example of 110.2 and 120.31 applying see *Robson*, 2005 TCC 287, para. 9.

An amount deducted under 110.2 is still in net income, and so can cause Old Age Security clawback under 180.2: *Parisée*, 2009 TCC 132; *Burchill*, 2010 FCA 145; or losing the Guaranteed Income Supplement: *Vincent*, 2017 TCC 254. It does not affect RRSP earned income: VIEWS doc 2009-0345111E5.

Because of the interest component, 110.2 is useless if the spread covers more than 4 years: *Milliken*, [2002] 2 C.T.C. 2783 (TCC), *Burchill*, 2010 FCA 145; Drache, "The Promise and the Reality", xxiv(11) *The Canadian Taxpayer* (Carswell) 86-88 (May 28/02). In *Public Service Alliance*, 2012 FCA 7 (leave to appeal denied 2012 CarswellNat 4342 (SCC)), the Canadian Human Rights Tribunal had rejected a complaint that this interest component results in discrimination against taxpayers receiving pay equity settlements; the Courts refused judicial review of this decision.

For the application of 110.2 and 120.31 following bankruptcy see *Guy Lessard*, 2002 CarswellNat 4348 (TCC).

CRA's calculations were also upheld in *Jackson*, 2013 TCC 195.

See also Frankovic, "The Taxation of Retroactive Lump-Sum Payments", 58(1) *Canadian Tax Journal* 1-23 (2010); CRA, "Income Tax Information About Pay Equity" (Nov. 1, 2000), on *Taxnet Pro* under "Guides" (document 10-2000); VIEWS docs 2008-0269311E5 (retroactive salary adjustment); 2010-0381851E5 (pay equity adjustments); 2008-0292081R3 (pay equity payments to settle human rights complaint: nontaxable); 2012-0472351M4 (lump-sum pay equity settlement taxable, eligible for 110.2).

Quebec offers income averaging for professional artists, an "eligible income-averaging annuity" that can spread income over a period of up to 7 years: tinyurl.com/rq-arts. The cost of the annuity is deductible in the year for provincial tax purposes if acquired in the year or within 60 days after year-end.

For other forms of averaging see Notes to 15(2) and 146(10).

110.2 added by 1999 Budget, for amounts received by an individual after 1994 (other than an amount in respect of which tax has been remitted to the individual [by remission order] under *Financial Administration Act* 23(2)) and, notwithstanding 152(4)-(5), any assessment of the individual's tax payable for any taxation year that ended before 1999 shall be made as is necessary to take its introduction into account.

Former 110.2, repealed by 1988 tax reform, provided for a pension income deduction, replaced by a credit in 118(3).

Definitions [s. 110.2]: "amount", "bankrupt" — 248(1); "calendar year" — *Interpretation Act* 37(1)(a); "eligible taxation year" — 110.2(1); "employment", "individual", "non-resident", "office", "prescribed" — 248(1); "qualifying amount" — 110.2(1); "resident in Canada" — 250; "specified portion" — 110.2(1); "superannuation or pension benefit", "taxable income" — 248(1); "taxation year" — 249; "trust" — 104(1), 248(1), 248(3).

110.3 [Repealed under former Act]

Notes: 110.3, repealed by 1988 tax reform, provided for a transfer to a spouse of certain unused deductions, replaced by a transfer of the pension credit under 118.8.

110.4 [Repealed]

Notes: 110.4 repealed by 1999 Budget, effective for 1998 and later taxation years. Until 1987, 110.4(1) permitted "forward averaging", under which a certain amount of income could be deferred to a later year, provided that the taxpayer prepaid a special amount under 120.1(2). Recovery of amounts prepaid before 1988 was available until 1997 under 110.4(2), with an income inclusion (useful for a taxpayer now in a lower bracket) for the forward-averaged amount.

Retroactive averaging of certain lump-sum payments is now available under 110.2 and 120.31. For taxpayers with fluctuating incomes, some income averaging is possible through the use of RRSPs: see section 146. See Notes to 15(2) for another method.

110.5 Additions for foreign tax deductions — There shall be added to a corporation's taxable income otherwise determined for a taxation year such amount as the corporation may claim to the extent that the addition thereof

(a) increases any amount deductible by the corporation under subsection 126(1) or (2) for the year; and

(b) does not increase an amount deductible by the corporation under any of sections 125, 125.1, 127, 127.2 and 127.3 for the year.

Related Provisions: 111(8)"non-capital loss"B — Carryover of amount determined under 110.5; 115(1)(a)(vii) — Parallel rule for authorized foreign bank; 126(1)(b)(ii)(B), 126(2.1)(a)(ii)(B) — Increase in denominator for FTC calculation.

Notes: Under 110.5, a corporation can choose to add an amount to taxable income to avoid wasting foreign tax credit (FTC) on income taxed by a foreign jurisdiction (see Notes to 126(1)). The extra income becomes a loss carryforward (or carryback) under 111(8)"non-capital-loss"B, so it can be deducted in a later (or earlier) year under 111(1)(a). This cannot be done if the additional income will increase the corporation's small business deduction (125), M&P credit (125.1) or investment tax credit (127).

This adjustment should be made when the return is filed, but can apparently be considered if requested later: VIEWS docs 2010-0379801I7, 2013-0512601I7. It qualifies for the 3-year reassessment deadline extension under 152(4)(b)(iv): 2016-0641721I7. The addition is not "safe income" for 55(2): 2011-0415071E5. A loss-consolidation structure using 110.5 to prevent wasting FTCs was acceptable: 2012-0461651I7. The income inclusion is not limited by a provincial FTC, but increased federal FTC may reduce the provincial FTC: 2014-0522861E5.

As an alternative to 110.5, consider forgoing claims for discretionary deductions (such as CCA) to increase taxable income and thus increase the FTC: Manjit Singh & Andrew Spiro, "The Canadian Income Tax Treatment of Foreign Taxes", 2014 Cdn Tax Foundation conference report at 22:22-23.

Definitions [s. 110.5]: "amount" — 248(1); "corporation" — 248(1), *Interpretation Act* 35(1); "taxable income" — 2(2), 248(1); "taxation year" — 249.

Income Tax Folios [s. 110.5]: S5-F2-C1: Foreign tax credit [replaces IT-270R3, IT-395R2, IT-520].

Interpretation Bulletins [s. 110.5]: IT-232R3: Losses — their deductibility in the loss year or in other years; IT-302R3: Losses of a corporation — the effect that acquisitions of control, amalgamations, and windings-up have on their deductibility.

110.6 (1) [Capital gains exemption —] Definitions — For the purposes of this section,

"annual gains limit" of an individual for a taxation year means the amount determined by the formula

$$A - B$$

where

A   is the lesser of

(a) the amount determined in respect of the individual for the year under paragraph 3(b) in respect of capital gains and capital losses, and

(b) the amount that would be determined in respect of the individual for the year under paragraph 3(b) in respect of capital gains and losses if the only properties referred to in that paragraph were properties that, at the time they were disposed of, were qualified farm properties, qualified fishing properties, qualified farm or fishing properties and qualified small business corporation shares, and

B   is the total of

(a) the amount, if any, by which

(i) the individual's net capital losses for other taxation years deducted under paragraph 111(1)(b) in computing the individual's taxable income for the year

exceeds

(ii) the amount, if any, by which the amount determined in respect of the individual for the year under paragraph 3(b) in respect of capital gains and capital losses exceeds the amount determined for A in respect of the individual for the year, and

(b) all of the individual's allowable business investment losses for the year;

Related Provisions: 110.6(13) — Meaning of "amount determined under para. 3(b)"; 257 — Formula cannot calculate to less than zero. See also at end of s. 110.6.

Notes: In calculating B(a)(i), 104(21) applies: VIEWS doc 2010-0358541I7.

Para. B(b) prevents "double-dipping" by claiming both an ABIL (against other income) and the capital gains exemption. See Notes to 39(9).

Para. A(b) amended by 2014 budget bill #2, for dispositions and transfers in the 2014 and later taxation years, to add reference to qualified farm and fishing properties.

Para. A(b) amended by 2006 budget bill #2, effective for dispositions of property after May 1, 2006, to add reference to qualified fishing property. Para. A(b) earlier amended by 1994 Budget, 1993 technical bill and 1992 technical bill.

Interpretation Bulletins: IT-236R4: Reserves — disposition of capital property (cancelled).

Forms: See list at end of s. 110.6.

"child" has the meaning assigned by subsection 70(10);

"cumulative gains limit" of an individual at the end of a taxation year means the amount, if any, by which

(a) the total of all amounts determined in respect of the individual for the year or preceding taxation years that end after 1984 for A in the definition "annual gains limit"

exceeds the total of

(b) all amounts determined in respect of the individual for the year or preceding taxation years that end after 1984 for B in the definition "annual gains limit",

(c) the amount, if any, deducted under paragraph 3(e) in computing the individual's income for the 1985 taxation year,

(d) all amounts deducted under this section in computing the individual's taxable incomes for preceding taxation years, and

(e) the individual's cumulative net investment loss at the end of the year;

Notes: The cumulative gains limit (CGL) limits the lifetime capital gains deduction: 110.6(2)(b), (2.1)(b), (2.2)(b). Note that due to para. (b), past ABILs (see Notes to 39(9)) and certain capital loss claims reduce the CGL: see 110.6(1)"annual gains limit"B(a)(i) and B(b).

Definition "cumulative gains limit" amended by 1992 technical bill and 1993 technical bill, this version effective 1985.

"cumulative net investment loss" of an individual at the end of a taxation year means the amount, if any, by which

(a) the total of all amounts each of which is the investment expense of the individual for the year or a preceding taxation year ending after 1987

exceeds

(b) the total of all amounts each of which is the investment income of the individual for the year or a preceding taxation year ending after 1987;

Notes: Cumulative net investment loss (CNIL, pronounced "senile") is used to limit the ability of a taxpayer to claim interest expense and other investment expenses that are deductible against income from other sources, while at the same time enjoying tax-free capital gains (possibly from the same investments) by virtue of the capital gains exemption. (The policy reason for this is less relevant since the 1994 repeal of the general $100,000 exemption in 110.6(3).)

All investment expenses since 1988 are pooled, and to the extent the total exceeds all investment income since 1988, there is a CNIL balance. The CNIL is used in para. (e) of the definition "cumulative gains limit" above, and effectively denies the exemption to the extent of the CNIL account. A CNIL account can be eliminated by earning sufficient investment income (which is, of course, taxed) in subsequent years.

Definitions **"eligible employee beneficiary"** and **"eligible LCGE trust"**, proposed in July 18, 2017 draft legislation, will not be enacted. See Abandoned Proposed Addition under 110.6(12), (12.1)

Forms: T936: Calculation of cumulative net investment loss.

"eligible real property gain", "eligible real property loss" — [Repealed]

Notes: "Eligible real property gain" (ERPG) and "eligible real property loss" (ERPL) added by 1992 Budget, effective 1992, and repealed by 1994 Budget effective 1996. ERPG restricted the exemption for capital gains on most real estate investments (see repealed "non-qualifying real property") to months in which the property was owned before March 1992 (and since 1972), divided by the total months in which it was owned (since 1972). ERPL did the same with losses. They were repealed when the general exemption in 110.6(3) was eliminated as of Feb. 22, 1994.

"interest in a family farm or fishing partnership", of an individual (other than a trust that is not a personal trust) at any time, means a partnership interest owned by the individual at that time if

(a) throughout any 24-month period ending before that time, more than 50% of the fair market value of the property of the partnership was attributable to

(i) property that was used principally in the course of carrying on a farming or fishing business in Canada in which the individual, a beneficiary referred to in clause (C) or a spouse, common-law partner, child or parent of the individual or of a beneficiary referred to in clause (C) was actively engaged on a regular and continuous basis, by

(A) the partnership,

(B) the individual,

(C) if the individual is a personal trust, a beneficiary of the trust,

(D) a spouse, common-law partner, child or parent of the individual or of a beneficiary referred to in clause (C),

(E) a corporation, a share of the capital stock of which was a share of the capital stock of a family farm or fishing corporation of the individual, a beneficiary referred to in clause (C) or a spouse, common-law partner, child or parent of the individual or of a beneficiary referred to in clause (C), or

(F) a partnership, a partnership interest in which was an interest in a family farm or fishing partnership of the individual, a beneficiary referred to in clause (C) or a spouse, common-law partner, child or parent of the individual or of a beneficiary referred to in clause (C),

(ii) shares of the capital stock or indebtedness of one or more corporations of which all or substantially all of the fair market value of the property was attributable to properties described in subparagraph (iv),

(iii) a partnership interest in or indebtedness of one or more partnerships of which all or substantially all of the fair market value of the property was attributable to properties described in subparagraph (iv), or

(iv) properties described in any of subparagraphs (i) to (iii), and

(b) at that time, all or substantially all of the fair market value of the property of the partnership was attributable to property described in subparagraph (a)(iv);

Related Provisions: 248(29) — Property used in a combination of farming and fishing. See also at end of s. 110.6.

Notes: This term has replaced "interest in a family farm partnership" and "interest in a family fishing partnership", and allows farming and fishing activities to be combined: see 248(29). It is used in 110.6(1) "qualified farm or fishing property" and (1.3), as well as 40(1.1), 70(9.2)-(9.8), 73(4)-(4.1).

The definition was met in *Otteson*, 2014 TCC 250 (taxpayers' appeal to FCA discontinued A-417-14), where two spouses were held to be partners in a tree farming business on their property.

CRA's view is that the partnership must have been in existence for 24 months to qualify: VIEWS doc 2004-0075041E5. However, the interest in the partnership need not have been held for 24 months: doc 2006-0217861E5. Where the partnership interest was a share that qualified, the underlying land need not have been used by the corporation at time of disposition: 2013-0478961E5.

"Principally" in (a)(i) refers to use over the entire period of ownership, so the property need not be used in farming/fishing at the time of disposition: VIEWS doc 2004-0063481E5. "Property" in (a)(i) includes both land and home: 2017-0709161C6 [2017 APFF q.16].

The "all or substantially all" test, in para. (b), applies only at the time of the disposition. CRA considers that "substantially all" means 90% or more.

See Zuhair Ladha, "Capital Gains Deduction Planning for Family Farm Partnerships", 1(2) *Canadian Tax Focus* (ctf.ca) 2-3 (Aug. 2011).

Definition added by 2014 budget bill #2, effective for dispositions and transfers in the 2014 and later taxation years.

Interpretation Bulletins: See at end of 110.6.

"interest in a family farm partnership" — [Repealed]

Notes: Definition replaced with "interest in a family farm *or fishing* partnership" by 2014 budget bill #2, for dispositions/transfers in the 2014 and later tax years. For interpretation see Notes to the new definition. Earlier amended by 2006 budget bill #2, 2001 technical bill, 2000 same-sex partners bill, 1992 and 1991 technical bills.

"interest in a family fishing partnership" — [Repealed]

Notes: Definition replaced with "interest in a family *farm or* fishing partnership" by 2014 budget bill #2, for dispositions/transfers in the 2014 and later tax years. For interpretation see Notes to the new definition. Added by 2006 budget bill #2, for dispositions after May 1, 2006.

"investment expense" of an individual for a taxation year means the total of

(a) all amounts deducted in computing the individual's income for the year from property (except to the extent that the amounts were otherwise taken into account in computing the individual's investment expense or investment income for the year) other than any amounts deducted under

(i) paragraph 20(1)(c), (d), (e), or (e.1) of this Act or paragraph 20(1)(k) of the *Income Tax Act*, chapter 148 of the Revised Statutes of Canada, 1952, in respect of borrowed money that was used by the individual, or that was used to acquire property that was used by the individual,

(A) to make a payment as consideration for an income-averaging annuity contract,

(B) to pay a premium under a registered retirement savings plan, or

(C) to make a contribution to a pooled registered pension plan, registered pension plan or deferred profit sharing plan, or

(ii) paragraph 20(1)(j) or subsection 65(1), 66(4), 66.1(3), 66.2(2), 66.21(4) or 66.4(2),

(b) the total of

(i) all amounts deducted under paragraph 20(1)(c), (d), (e), (e.1), (f) or (bb) of this Act or paragraph 20(1)(k) of the *Income Tax Act*, chapter 148 of the Revised Statutes of Canada, 1952, in computing the individual's income for the year from a partnership of which the individual was a specified member in the fiscal period of the partnership ending in the year, and

(ii) all amounts deducted under subparagraph 20(1)(e)(vi) in computing the individual's income for the year in respect of an expense incurred by a partnership of which the individual was a specified member in the fiscal period of the partnership ending immediately before it ceased to exist,

(c) the total of

(i) all amounts (other than allowable capital losses) deducted in computing the individual's income for the year in respect of the individual's share of the amount of any loss of a partnership of which the individual was a specified member in the partnership's fiscal period ending in the year, and

(ii) all amounts each of which is an amount deducted under paragraph 111(1)(e) in computing the individual's taxable income for the year,

(d) 50% of the total of all amounts each of which is an amount deducted under subsection 66(4), 66.1(3), 66.2(2), 66.21(4) or 66.4(2) in computing the individual's income for the year in respect of expenses

(i) incurred and renounced under subsection 66(12.6), (12.601), (12.62) or (12.64) by a corporation, or

(ii) incurred by a partnership of which the individual was a specified member in the fiscal period of the partnership in which the expense was incurred, and

(e) the total of all amounts each of which is the amount of the individual's loss for the year from

(i) property, or

(ii) renting or leasing a rental property (within the meaning assigned by subsection 1100(14) of the *Income Tax Regula-*

tions) or a property described in Class 31 or 32 of Schedule II to the *Income Tax Regulations*

owned by the individual or by a partnership of which the individual was a member, other than a partnership of which the individual was a specified member in the partnership's fiscal period ending in the year, and

(f) the amount, if any, by which the total of the individual's net capital losses for other taxation years deducted under paragraph 111(1)(b) in computing the individual's taxable income for the year exceeds the amount determined in respect of the individual for the year under paragraph (a) of the description of B in the definition "annual gains limit";

Related Provisions: 66(18) — Expenses of partnerships (re para. (d)). See also at end of s. 110.6.

Notes: See Notes to 110.6(1)"cumulative net investment loss".

Cl. (a)(i)(C) amended by 2012 budget bill #2, effective Dec. 14, 2012, to add reference to a PRPP.

110.6.(1)"investment expense" amended by 2000 Budget (effective for taxation years that begin after 2000), 1992 Economic Statement and 1992 and 1991 technical bills.

I.T. Application Rules: 69 (meaning of "chapter 148 of ...").

"investment income" of an individual for a taxation year means the total of

(a) all amounts included in computing the individual's income for the year from property (other than an amount included under subsection 15(2) or paragraph 56(1)(d) of this Act or paragraph 56(1)(d.1) of the *Income Tax Act*, chapter 148 of the Revised Statutes of Canada, 1952), including, for greater certainty, any amount so included under subsection 13(1) in respect of a property any income from which would be income from property (except to the extent that the amount was otherwise taken into account in computing the individual's investment income or investment expense for the year),

(b) all amounts (other than taxable capital gains) included in computing the individual's income for the year in respect of the individual's share of the income of a partnership of which the individual was a specified member in the partnership's fiscal period ending in the year, including, for greater certainty, the individual's share of all amounts included under subsection 13(1) in computing the income of the partnership,

(c) 50% of all amounts included under subsection 59(3.2) in computing the individual's income for the year,

(d) all amounts each of which is the amount of the individual's income for the year from

(i) a property, or

(ii) renting or leasing a rental property (within the meaning assigned by subsection 1100(14) of the *Income Tax Regulations*) or a property described in Class 31 or 32 of Schedule II to the *Income Tax Regulations*

owned by the individual or by a partnership of which the individual was a member (other than a partnership of which the individual was a specified member in the partnership's fiscal period ending in the year), including, for greater certainty, any amount included under subsection 13(1) in computing the individual's income for the year in respect of a rental property of the individual or the partnership or in respect of a property any income from which would be income from property,

(e) the amount, if any, by which

(i) the total of all amounts (other than amounts in respect of income-averaging annuity contracts or annuity contracts purchased under deferred profit sharing plans or plans referred to in subsection 147(15) as revoked plans) included under paragraph 56(1)(d) of this Act or paragraph 56(1)(d.1) of the *Income Tax Act*, chapter 148 of the Revised Statutes of Canada, 1952, in computing the individual's income for the year

exceeds

(ii) the total of all amounts deducted under paragraph 60(a) in computing the individual's income for the year, and

(f) the amount, if any, by which the total of all amounts included under paragraph 3(b) in respect of capital gains and capital losses in computing the individual's income for the year exceeds the amount determined in respect of the individual for the year for A in the definition "annual gains limit";

Notes: See Notes to 110.6(1)"cumulative net investment loss".

Para. (f) added to "investment income" by 1992 technical bill, effective 1992. Definition earlier amended by 1991 technical bill.

I.T. Application Rules: 69 (meaning of "chapter 148 of ...").

"non-qualifying real property" — [Repealed]

Notes: Definition "non-qualifying real property" added by 1992 Budget and amended by 1993 technical bill, effective 1992, then repealed by 1994 Budget effective 1996. The exemption under 110.6(3) for gains on such property was restricted to the proportion of the gain that accrued in months before March 1992. It was repealed because the general exemption under 110.6(3) was eliminated effective February 22, 1994.

"qualified farm or fishing property", of an individual (other than a trust that is not a personal trust) at any time, means a property that is owned at that time by the individual, the spouse or common-law partner of the individual or a partnership, an interest in which is an interest in a family farm or fishing partnership of the individual or the individual's spouse or common-law partner and that is

(a) real or immovable property or a fishing vessel that was used in the course of carrying on a farming or fishing business in Canada by,

(i) the individual,

(ii) if the individual is a personal trust, a beneficiary of the trust that is entitled to receive directly from the trust any income or capital of the trust,

(iii) a spouse, common-law partner, child or parent of an individual referred to in subparagraph (i) or (ii),

(iv) a corporation, a share of the capital stock of which is a share of the capital stock of a family farm or fishing corporation of an individual referred to in any of subparagraphs (i) to (iii), or

(v) a partnership, an interest in which is an interest in a family farm or fishing partnership of an individual referred to in any of subparagraphs (i) to (iii),

(b) a share of the capital stock of a family farm or fishing corporation of the individual or the individual's spouse or common-law partner,

(c) an interest in a family farm or fishing partnership of the individual or the individual's spouse or common-law partner, or

(d) a property included in Class 14.1 of Schedule II to the *Income Tax Regulations*, used by a person or partnership referred to in any of subparagraphs (a)(i) to (v), or by a personal trust from which the individual acquired the property, in the course of carrying on a farming or fishing business in Canada;

Related Provisions: 70(9.8) — Farm or fishing property used by corporation or partnership; 80.03(8) — Deemed qualified farm or fishing property where capital gain deemed on disposition following debt forgiveness; 110.6(1.3) — Interpretation — property used in a farming or fishing business; 120.4(1)"excluded amount"(d) — No income-splitting tax on most dispositions of QFFP; 248(5) — Substituted property. See also at end of s. 110.6.

Notes: Qualified farm or fishing property (QFFP) is eligible for the $1 million lifetime capital gains exemption under 110.6(2), as topped up by 110.6(2.2). This term has replaced "qualified farm property" and "qualified fishing property", and allows farming and fishing to be combined: see 248(29). The pre-2015 cases and interpretation below relate to the previous definitions (mostly farming).

Quotas (Class 14.1 property) are often the most valuable QFFP after real property. Para. (d) includes a farm or fishing quota; and a fishing licence (VIEWS doc 2017-0717401E5). See also 70(9.8) re leased property.

In *Sevy*, 2004 CarswellNat 3281 (TCC), a farmer's continuing attempts to make his cattle ranch profitable by adding a feedlot were found to be sufficient "use" over 5 years (see (a)(vii)(B)) to entitle him to the exemption.

In *Healy Estate*, [2005] 5 C.T.C. 2053 (TCC), property did not qualify because there was insufficient evidence that farming had been carried on in a businesslike way; sales of timber did not constitute farming.

In *Otteson*, 2014 TCC 250 (taxpayers' appeals to FCA discontinued A-417-14), the portion of a farm owned by two spouses but used by a partnership of them for tree farming was held to qualify under (a)(v).

Due to 110.6(1)"child", the term "parent" can refer to a grandparent or great-grandparent, but not a great-great-grandparent: VIEWS doc 2012-0454701I7.

For CRA interpretation of this definition and 110.6(1.3), see VIEWS docs 2014-0536881E5 (woodlot owned since before 1987); 2015-0552551E5 (sale of right to exploit sand pit on farm property can qualify); 2015-0567231E5 (general comments; sharecropping income is rental income, not farming); 2015-0572791E5 (woodlot may qualify); 2017-0709161C6 [2017 APFF q.16] ("property" includes both land and home).

For some CRA interpretations of the previous "qualified farm property" definition, see VIEWS docs 2003-0054531R3 (children who inherited a property farmed by the parent need not have used it themselves in farming); 2004-0056741E5 (gross revenue test in (a)(vi)(A) can be met by another person); 2004-0057061E5 (election under 110.6(19) gives property a post-1987 acquisition date for (a)(vii)); 2004-0065501E5 (interpretation when attribution rules in 74.2 apply); 2004-0103051217 (break in continuous family ownership not fatal to 5-year test); 2004-0103341E5 (land farmed by taxpayer's parents in the past qualifies); 2005-0121232E5 (property did not qualify); 2005-0138381E5 (life interest in real property can qualify); 2005-0140771E5 (land farmed in the 1980s qualifies); 2005-0142411E5 (property may qualify); 2005-0144881E5 (property qualifies); 2005-0151071E5 (exemption applies to grandson selling land farmed by grandfather that meets the 2-year test); 2005-0154441R3 (property qualifies); 2005-0155861E5 (property farmed by deceased taxpayer qualifies); 2005-0161881E5 (property qualifies); 2006-0179431E5 (general comments); 2006-0181771E5 (property appears to qualify); 2006-0183341E5 (property qualifies under pre-1987 rules); 2006-0205321E5 (QFP can include undivided interest in farmland); 2007-0259521E5 (tending herds for third parties leasing the land does not qualify); 2008-0285271C6 (qualification after death of spouse); 2009-0316191E5 (general discussion); 2009-0312701E5 (granting of pipeline easement can qualify); 2009-0329231E5 (property appears to qualify); 2009-033287117 (property does not qualify where ownership by great-grandfather was interrupted by sale to third party); 2009-0344851E5 (property previously worked by taxpayer's father); 2010-0356961E5 (break in continuous ownership where property acquired by non-farming sibling); 2010-0363401E5 (general comments); 2010-0365181E5 (land owned by estate following owner's death); 2010-0381321E5 (general discussion); 2011-0396391E5 (property farmed 1964-71, rented 1971-2011, then sold); 2011-0400731E5 (milk quota qualifies); 2011-0401231E5 (property does not qualify); 2011-041334117 (property may qualify). See also Notes to 110.6(1.3).

For CRA interpretation of the previous "qualified fishing property" definition see 2007-026029117 (inclusion in 2006 of reserve from 2005 disposition does not qualify).

See also Heather Dawe, "Section 110.6 Capital Gains Deduction — Qualified Farm and Fishing Property", 9(9) *Tax Hyperion* (Carswell) 5-8 (Sept. 2012).

Para. (d) amended by 2016 budget bill #2, effective 2017, as part of changing the eligible capital property rules to CCA Class 14.1 (see Notes to 20(1)(b)). Before 2017, read:

> (d) an eligible capital property (which is deemed to include capital property to which paragraph 70(5.1)(b) or 73(3.1)(f) applies) used by a person or partnership referred to in any of subparagraphs (a)(i) to (v), or by a personal trust from which the individual acquired the property, in the course of carrying on a farming or fishing business in Canada;

Definition added by 2014 budget bill #2, effective for dispositions and transfers in the 2014 and later taxation years.

Interpretation Bulletins: See at end of 110.6.

"qualified farm property" — [Repealed]

Notes: 110.6(1)"qualified farm property" repealed by 2014 budget bill #2, for dispositions and transfers in the 2014 and later tax years. It was replaced by "qualified farm *or fishing* property". QFP was eligible for the lifetime capital gains exemption ($750,000 for 2007-13). For interpretation see Notes to the new definition.

Definition amended by 2002-2013 technical bill (for dispositions after May 1, 2006), 2006 budget bill #2, 2000 same-sex partners bill, 1991 technical bill.

"qualified fishing property" — [Repealed]

Notes: 110.6(1)"qualified fishing property" repealed by 2014 budget bill #2, for dispositions and transfers in the 2014 and later tax years. It was replaced by "qualified *farm or* fishing property". For interpretation see Notes to the new definition.

Definition amended by 2002-2013 technical bill, for dispositions after May 1, 2006. Added by 2006 budget bill #2.

"qualified small business corporation share" of an individual

(other than a trust that is not a personal trust) at any time (in this definition referred to as the "determination time") means a share of the capital stock of a corporation that,

(a) at the determination time, is a share of the capital stock of a small business corporation owned by the individual, the individual's spouse or common-law partner or a partnership related to the individual,

(b) throughout the 24 months immediately preceding the determination time, was not owned by anyone other than the individual or a person or partnership related to the individual, and

(c) throughout that part of the 24 months immediately preceding the determination time while it was owned by the individual or a person or partnership related to the individual, was a share of the capital stock of a Canadian-controlled private corporation more than 50% of the fair market value of the assets of which was attributable to

(i) assets used principally in an active business carried on primarily in Canada by the corporation or by a corporation related to it,

(ii) shares of the capital stock or indebtedness of one or more other corporations that were connected (within the meaning of subsection 186(4) on the assumption that each of the other corporations was a "payer corporation" within the meaning of that subsection) with the corporation where

(A) throughout that part of the 24 months immediately preceding the determination time that ends at the time the corporation acquired such a share or indebtedness, the share or indebtedness was not owned by anyone other than the corporation, a person or partnership related to the corporation or a person or partnership related to such a person or partnership, and

(B) throughout that part of the 24 months immediately preceding the determination time while such a share or indebtedness was owned by the corporation, a person or partnership related to the corporation or a person or partnership related to such a person or partnership, it was a share or indebtedness of a Canadian-controlled private corporation more than 50% of the fair market value of the assets of which was attributable to assets described in subparagraph (iii), or

(iii) assets described in either of subparagraph (i) or (ii)

except that

(d) where, for any particular period of time in the 24-month period ending at the determination time, all or substantially all of the fair market value of the assets of a particular corporation that is the corporation or another corporation that was connected with the corporation cannot be attributed to assets described in subparagraph (c)(i), shares or indebtedness of corporations described in clause (c)(ii)(B), or any combination thereof, the reference in clause (c)(ii)(B) to "more than 50%" shall, for the particular period of time, be read as a reference to "all or substantially all" in respect of each other corporation that was connected with the particular corporation and, for the purpose of this paragraph, a corporation is connected with another corporation only where

(i) the corporation is connected (within the meaning of subsection 186(4) on the assumption that the corporation was a "payer corporation" within the meaning of that subsection) with the other corporation, and

(ii) the other corporation owns shares of the capital stock of the corporation and, for the purpose of this subparagraph, the other corporation shall be deemed to own the shares of the capital stock of any corporation that are owned by a corporation any shares of the capital stock of which are owned or are deemed by this subparagraph to be owned by the other corporation,

(e) where, at any time in the 24-month period ending at the determination time, the share was substituted for another share, the share shall be considered to have met the requirements of this definition only where the other share

(i) was not owned by any person or partnership other than a person or partnership described in paragraph (b) throughout the period beginning 24 months before the determination time and ending at the time of substitution, and

(ii) was a share of the capital stock of a corporation described in paragraph (c) throughout that part of the period referred to in subparagraph (i) during which such share was owned by a person or partnership described in paragraph (b), and

(f) where, at any time in the 24-month period ending at the determination time, a share referred to in subparagraph (c)(ii) is substituted for another share, that share shall be considered to meet the requirements of subparagraph (c)(ii) only where the other share

(i) was not owned by any person or partnership other than a person or partnership described in clause (c)(ii)(A) throughout the period beginning 24 months before the determination time and ending at the time of substitution, and

(ii) was a share of the capital stock of a corporation described in paragraph (c) throughout that part of the period referred to in subparagraph (i) during which the share was owned by a person or partnership described in clause (c)(ii)(A);

Related Provisions: 80.03(8) — Deemed qualified small business corporation share where capital gain deemed on disposition following debt forgiveness; 108(1)"qualified small business corporation share" — Trusts; 110.6(1.1) — Fair market value of net income stabilization account; 110.6(14) — Various rules of interpretation; 110.6(15) — Value of assets of corporation; 110.6(16) — Personal trust; 120.4(1)"excluded amount"(d) — No income-splitting tax on most dispositions of QSBCS; 186(7) — Interpretation of "connected" for subparas. (c)(ii), (d)(i); 248(5) — Substituted property. See also at end of s. 110.6.

Notes: A QSBC share is eligible for the lifetime capital gains exemption ($750,000 for 2007-13, $800,000 for 2014, $813,600 for 2015, $824,176 for 2016, $835,716 for 2017, $848,252 for 2018, $866,912 for 2019, $883,384 for 2020, $892,218 for 2021) under 110.6(2.1). The basic concept is that: in para. (a), the corporation must be a Canadian-controlled private corporation using substantially all of its assets in carrying on an "active business" (see 248(1), and note the exclusion for a "specified investment business") in Canada (see 248(1)"small business corporation" and 125(7)"Canadian-controlled private corporation"); and in para. (c), throughout all of (2013-0495631C6) the 2-year period preceding the disposition, more than 50% of the corporation's assets were used "principally" [interpreted as more than 50%: VIEWS doc 2009-0307931E5] in carrying on an active business in Canada (but see also para. (d)). For both tests, shares or debt of other corporations that meet the test can qualify as such assets; also, the assets can be used actively by a related corporation, so if A owns Opco and A's spouse owns Realtyco which rents business premises to Opco, Realtyco can qualify. A lease (as lessee) of an asset does not qualify as an asset for this purpose: 2016-0652941C6 [2016 APFF q.11]. Future income tax assets are excluded, but a receivable tax refund relating to an active business qualifies: 2012-0473261E5, 2013-0499671C6, 2014-0537611C6 [Tremblay, "Is a Future Income Tax Asset an Asset Used in an Active Business?", 4(4) *Canadian Tax Focus* (ctf.ca) 1-2 (Nov. 2014)]. (Assets of a trust of which the corp is sole beneficiary do not qualify: 2006-0217301E5.) See also 2011-0410871E5, 2012-0459741E5, 2013-0483891E5, 2013-0504661E5 (general comments). When valuing a corporation's assets for this purpose, see 110.6(15) and Notes to 248(1)"small business corporation".

A corporation can be "purified" by fixing the asset mix to meet the "small business corporation" definition: see Moore, "Failure to Purify Can Be Costly", 7(4) *Tax for the Owner-Manager* (ctf.ca) 6-7 (Oct. 2007); Lewin, "Structuring the Sale of a Private Corporation in the Context of the New Dividend Rules", 2007 Cdn Tax Foundation conference report at 30:16-20. For rulings approving purification see VIEWS docs 912689, 9705823. In transferring shares to purify a corp, FIFO applies due to 110.6(14)(a): 2013-0481361E5 [Tollstam, "FIFO Derails QSBC Planning", 21(9) *Canadian Tax Highlights* (ctf.ca) 9-10 (Sept. 2013)]. Writing cheques that have not yet been cashed does not work in CRA's view (in Quebec): 2012-0435351I7; Drouin, "Purification Strategies in Quebec", 2(4) *Canadian Tax Focus* (ctf.ca) 7-8 (Nov. 2012). For purification attempts that do not work see 2011-0415161E5. A dividend paid to purify a corp could trigger 55(2): Cdn Tax Foundation 2017 conference roundtable q.3.

A website run from a server in Canada, "where any related manual activity takes place in Canada" is normally a business carried on in Canada: VIEWS doc 2011-0423951E5.

Under para. (b), shares must generally be held for 2 years to qualify for the exemption. (CRA considers that a holding of exactly 2 years does not qualify, so that one more day is needed: doc 2011-0411831C6.) See 110.6(14)(f), which deems new treasury shares to have been held by an unrelated person (and thus not to qualify) unless certain conditions are met. A trust that meets the 2-year test can flow out the exemption under 104(21.2) even to a person who has been a beneficiary for less than 2 years: 2012-0439271E5. In *Pellerin*, 2015 TCC 130, the Court said the "related" test applies only at time of sale; a child under 2 was in any event related to the trust (that held the shares) from the time he was conceived, so the 2-year test was satisfied!

In *Weaver*, 2008 FCA 238, shares did not qualify because the corporation earned only property income and was not a "small business corporation". See VIEWS doc 2005-0141021C6 to the same effect.

In *Chartier*, 2007 TCC 37, shares qualified because a right conferred by a stock option agreement did not cause the company to cease to be a CCPC, due to 110.6(14)(b).

An agreement to sell the shares to a public corporation or non-resident will not invalidate the shares' eligibility for the exemption. See 110.6(14)(b).

Where a corporation owns an interest in a limited partnership that carries on an active business in Canada, CRA considers that the corporate partner uses its proportionate share of each partnership asset for purposes of this definition. See Revenue Canada Round Table, 1993 Cdn Tax Foundation conference report, 58:34-35, Q. 58. See also VIEWS docs 9636835; 2012-0449651E5; 2012-0453991C6 (effect of recent Quebec case law); 2013-0500941E5 (any partnership, not just LP).

See also Notes to 248(1)"active business" and to 110.6(2.1).

CRA considers that "substantially all", used in the opening words of para. (d), means 90% or more.

See also Cepparo, "Cash: Active Business Asset?", 26(5) *Canadian Tax Highlights* (ctf.ca) 3-4 (May 2018); and Watson article in Notes to 110.6(15).

Quebec has additional conditions to qualify for the exemption for provincial tax purposes (except for the "primary" and manufacturing sectors: March 2016 QC budget), including that the vendor have played an active role in the business and not be involved in it after the sale.

Para. (a) amended by 2000 same-sex partners bill to refer to "common-law partner", effective as per Notes to 248(1)"common-law partner".

Definition "qualified small business corporation share" amended by 1991 technical bill, retroactive to dispositions of shares after June 17, 1987 (introduction of the definition).

Interpretation Bulletins: See list at end of s. 110.6.

Information Circulars: 88-2, para. 15: General anti-avoidance rule — section 245 of the *Income Tax Act*; 88-2 Supplement, paras. 3, 4: General anti-avoidance rule — section 245 of the *Income Tax Act*.

Advance Tax Rulings: ATR-53: Purification of a small business corporation; ATR-55: Amalgamation followed by sale of shares.

"share of the capital stock of a family farm corporation" — [Repealed]

Notes: Definition replaced with "share of the capital stock of a family farm *or fishing* corporation" by 2014 budget bill #2, for dispositions and transfers in the 2014 and later tax years. For interpretation see Notes to the new definition. Earlier amended by 2006 budget bill #2, 2000 same-sex partners bill, 1992 and 1991 technical bills.

"share of the capital stock of a family farm or fishing corporation", of an individual (other than a trust that is not a personal trust) at any time, means a share of the capital stock of a corporation owned by the individual at that time if

(a) throughout any 24-month period ending before that time, more than 50% of the fair market value of the property owned by the corporation was attributable to

(i) property that was used principally in the course of carrying on a farming or fishing business in Canada in which the individual, a beneficiary referred to in clause (C) or a spouse or common-law partner, child or parent of the individual or of a beneficiary referred to in clause (C), was actively engaged on a regular and continuous basis, by

(A) the corporation,

(B) the individual,

(C) if the individual is a personal trust, a beneficiary of the trust,

(D) a spouse, common-law partner, child or parent of the individual or of a beneficiary referred to in clause (C),

(E) another corporation that is related to the corporation and of which a share of the capital stock was a share of the capital stock of a family farm or fishing corporation of the individual, a beneficiary referred to in clause (C) or a spouse, common-law partner, child or parent of the individual or of a beneficiary referred to in clause (C), or

(F) a partnership, an interest in which was an interest in a family farm or fishing partnership of the individual, a beneficiary referred to in clause (C) or a spouse, common-law partner, child or parent of the individual or of such a beneficiary,

(ii) shares of the capital stock or indebtedness of one or more corporations of which all or substantially all of the fair market value of the property was attributable to property described in subparagraph (iv),

(iii) a partnership interest in or indebtedness of one or more partnerships of which all or substantially all of the fair market value of the property was attributable to properties described in subparagraph (iv), or

(iv) properties described in any of subparagraphs (i) to (iii), and

(b) at that time, all or substantially all of the fair market value of the property owned by the corporation was attributable to property described in subparagraph (a)(iv).

Related Provisions: 110.6(15) — Value of assets of corporation; 248(29) — Property used in a combination of farming and fishing. See also at end of s. 110.6.

Notes: This term has replaced "share of the capital stock of a family farm corporation" and "share of the capital stock of a family fishing corporation", and allows farming and fishing to be combined: see 248(29). It is used in 110.6(1)"qualified farm or fishing property" and (1.3), as well as 40(1.1), 70(9.2)-(9.8), 73(4)-(4.1).

CRA considers that "all or substantially all" means 90% or more.

AgriInvest and Agri-Québec accounts do not affect the calculation: see Notes to 110.6(1.1).

A residence used more than 50% for farm employees is accepted as used principally in the business: IT-268R4 para. 22, but only *qua* employees so this does not apply to the shareholders' home: VIEWS doc 2016-0652921C6 [2016 APFF q.9].

See also VIEWS doc 2013-0478961E5 (share owned by family farm partnership).

For interpretation of the pre-2014 "...family farm corp" definition see VIEWS docs 2001-0088115; 2004-0061271E5; 2008-029974117 (corporate partners are considered to use the farmland); 2010-0374861E5 ("used principally" is based on the entire period of ownership); 2011-0423061E5 (general comments); 2012-0457881E5 (use of property includes period before corporation acquired it).

Definition added by 2014 budget bill #2, for dispositions and transfers in the 2014 and later tax years.

Interpretation Bulletins: See at end of 110.6.

"share of the capital stock of a family fishing corporation" — [Repealed]

Notes: Definition replaced with "share of the capital stock of a family *farm or* fishing corporation" by 2014 budget bill #2, for dispositions and transfers in the 2014 and later tax years. See Notes to the new definition. Added by 2006 budget bill #2.

Related Provisions [subsec. 110.6(1)]: 110.6(1.1) — Fair market value of net income stabilization account; 110.6(15) — Value of assets of corporation; 257 — Formula cannot calculate to less than zero. See also at end of s. 110.6.

Income Tax Folios: S4-F8-C1: Business investment losses [replaces IT-484R2].

Advance Tax Rulings: ATR-56: Purification of a family farm corporation.

(1.1) Value of NISA — For the purposes of the definitions "qualified small business corporation share" and "share of the capital stock of a family farm or fishing corporation" in subsection (1), the fair market value of a net income stabilization account is deemed to be nil.

Notes: Due to this rule, funds in AgriInvest and Agri-Québec accounts do not taint eligibility for the exemption: VIEWS doc 2015-0583561E5. This does not apply to "excess deposits" in CRA's view: 2017-0688831E5.

110.6(1.1) amended by 2014 budget bill #2, for dispositions and transfers in the 2014 and later taxation years, to add "or fishing".

110.6(1.1) added by 1992 technical bill, effective 1991.

(1.2) [Repealed]

Notes: 110.6(1.2) repealed by 2014 budget bill #2, effective for dispositions and transfers in the 2014 and later taxation years. It has been incorporated into 110.6(1.3), combining farming and fishing.

110.6(1.2) added by 2006 budget bill #2, effective for dispositions of property after May 1, 2006.

(1.3) Farming or fishing property — conditions — For the purpose of applying the definition "qualified farm or fishing property", in subsection (1), of an individual, at any time, a property owned at that time by the individual, the spouse or common-law partner of the individual, or a partnership, an interest in which is an interest in a family farm or fishing partnership of the individual or of the individual's spouse or common-law partner, will not be con-

sidered to have been used in the course of carrying on a farming or fishing business in Canada, unless

(a) the following apply in respect of the property or property for which the property was substituted (in this paragraph referred to as "the property"),

(i) the property was owned throughout the period of at least 24 months immediately preceding that time by one or more of

(A) the individual, or a spouse, common-law partner, child or parent of the individual,

(B) a partnership, an interest in which is an interest in a family farm or fishing partnership of the individual or of the individual's spouse or common-law partner,

(C) if the individual is a personal trust, the individual from whom the trust acquired the property or a spouse, common-law partner, child or parent of that individual, or

(D) a personal trust from which the individual or a child or parent of the individual acquired the property, and

(ii) either

(A) in at least two years while the property was owned by one or more persons or partnerships referred to in subparagraph (i),

(I) the gross revenue of a person (in this subclause referred to as the "operator") referred to in subparagraph (i) from the farming or fishing business referred to in subclause (II) for the period during which the property was owned by a person or partnership described in subparagraph (i) exceeded the income of the operator from all other sources for that period, and

(II) the property was used principally in a farming or fishing business carried on in Canada in which an individual referred to in subparagraph (i), or where the individual is a personal trust, a beneficiary of the trust, was actively engaged on a regular and continuous basis, or

(B) throughout a period of at least 24 months while the property was owned by one or more persons or partnerships referred to in subparagraph (i), the property was used by a corporation referred to in subparagraph (a)(iv) of the definition "qualified farm or fishing property" in subsection (1) or by a partnership referred to in subparagraph (a)(v) of that definition in a farming or fishing business in which an individual referred to in any of subparagraphs (a)(i) to (iii) of that definition was actively engaged on a regular and continuous basis; or

(b) [Repealed]

(c) if the property or property for which the property was substituted was last acquired by the individual or partnership before June 18, 1987 or after June 17, 1987 under an agreement in writing entered into before that date,

(i) in the year the property was disposed of by the individual, the property was used principally in the course of carrying on the business of farming in Canada by

(A) the individual, or a spouse, common-law partner, child or parent of the individual,

(B) a beneficiary referred to in subparagraph (a)(ii) of the definition "qualified farm or fishing property" in subsection (1) or a spouse, common-law partner, child or parent of that beneficiary,

(C) a corporation referred to in subparagraph (a)(iv) of the definition "qualified farm or fishing property" in subsection (1),

(D) a partnership referred to in subparagraph (a)(v) of the definition "qualified farm or fishing property" in subsection (1), or

(E) a personal trust from which the individual acquired the property, or

(ii) in at least five years during which the property was owned by a person described in any of clauses (A) to (E), the property was used principally in the course of carrying on the business of farming in Canada by

(A) the individual, or a spouse, common-law partner, child or parent of the individual,

(B) a beneficiary referred to in subparagraph (a)(ii) of the definition "qualified farm or fishing property" in subsection (1) or a spouse, common-law partner, child or parent of that beneficiary,

(C) a corporation referred to in subparagraph (a)(iv) of the definition "qualified farm or fishing property" in subsection (1),

(D) a partnership referred to in subparagraph (a)(v) of the definition "qualified farm or fishing property" in subsection (1), or

(E) a personal trust from which the individual acquired the property.

Related Provisions: 248(5) — Substituted property; 248(29) — Property used in a combination of farming and fishing.

Notes: See Notes to 110.6(1)"qualified farm or fishing property".

CRA considers that the "used in farming" test applies separately to each legal parcel of land: VIEWS doc 2013-0474461E5. For more on 110.6(1.3) see 2007-0256811E5, 2007-0257221E5; 2008-0270251E5; 2008-0285271C6 (effect of death of spouse); 2009-0344851E5 (attribution rules and 69(11)); 2010-0356961E5 (siblings); 2010-0363401E5 (sharecropping); 2010-0367961E5 (creditor proofing); 2010-0372631E5; 2010-037580117; 2010-0380951E5 (who is the operator); 2010-0381361E5 (rental arrangements); 2010-0385871E5 (application of 24-month test); 2010-0386401E5; 2011-0392691E5 (what constitutes farming business); 2011-0394041E5 (whether income test includes capital gain); 2011-0394201M4; 2011-039964117 (subdivision and development); 2011-0421301E5; 2011-0421791E5; 2011-0423381E5 (interaction with principal residence exemption); 2011-0426061E5; 2011-0427821E5 (allocation among partners); 2012-0460791E5 (interaction with Canadian resource property rules); 2012-0463801E5 (application of 110.6(1.3)(a)(ii)(B)); 2012-0468321E5; 2014-0517601E5; 2014-0554381E5; 2016-0652931C6 [2016 APFF q.10] ("personal trust" in (a)(i) includes an estate); 2017-0688901E5 (para. (c) is satisfied).

On whether an "in-law" relationship continues after the connecting person's death (to meet the condition in (a)(i)(A), (c)(i)(A) or (c)(ii)(A)), see Notes to 252(2).

In *Otteson*, 2014 TCC 250 (FCA appeal discontinued A-417-14), the conditions in former (b)(ii) (see below) were met where two spouses owned property used by their partnership for tree farming.

110.6(1.3) amended by 2014 budget bill #2 (for dispositions/transfers in the 2014 and later tax years, to add "or fishing" references), 2002-2013 technical bill. Added by 2006 budget bill #2 (moved from 110.6(1)"qualified farm property"(a)(vi)-(vii)).

(2) Capital gains deduction — qualified farm or fishing property — In computing the taxable income for a taxation year of an individual (other than a trust) who was resident in Canada throughout the year and who disposed of qualified farm or fishing property in the year or a preceding taxation year (or who disposed of before 2014 property that was qualified farm property or qualified fishing property at the time of disposition), there may be deducted such amount as the individual may claim not exceeding the least of

(a) the amount determined by the formula

$$[\$400{,}000^9 - (A + B + C + D)] \times E$$

where

A is the total of all amounts each of which is an amount deducted under this section in computing the individual's taxable income for a preceding taxation year that ended

(i) before 1988, or

(ii) after October 17, 2000,

B is the total of all amounts each of which is

(i) ¾ of an amount deducted under this section in computing the individual's taxable income for a preceding taxa-

tion year that ended after 1987 and before 1990 (other than amounts deducted under this section for a taxation year in respect of an amount that was included in computing an individual's income for that year because of subparagraph 14(1)(a)(v) as that subparagraph applied for taxation years that ended before February 28, 2000), or

(ii) ¾ of an amount deducted under this section in computing the individual's taxable income for a preceding taxation year that began after February 27, 2000 and ended before October 18, 2000,

C is ⅔ of the total of all amounts each of which is an amount deducted under this section in computing the individual's taxable income

(i) for a preceding taxation year that ended after 1989 and before February 28, 2000, or

(ii) in respect of an amount that was included because of subparagraph 14(1)(a)(v) (as that subparagraph applied for taxation years that ended before February 28, 2000) in computing the individual's income for a taxation year that began after 1987 and ended before 1990,

D is the product obtained when the reciprocal of the fraction determined for E that applied to the taxpayer for a preceding taxation year that began before and included February 28, 2000 or October 17, 2000 is multiplied by the amount deducted under this subsection in computing the individual's taxable income for that preceding year, and

E is

(i) in the case of a taxation year that includes February 28, 2000 or October 17, 2000, the amount determined by the formula

$$2 \times (F + G)/H$$

where

F is the amount deemed by subsection 14(1.1) to be a taxable capital gain of the taxpayer for the taxation year;

G is the amount by which the amount determined in respect of the taxpayer for the year under paragraph 3(b) exceeds the amount determined for F; and

H is the total of

(A) the amount deemed by subsection 14(1.1) to be a taxable capital gain of the taxpayer for the taxation year multiplied by

(I) where that amount is determined by reference to paragraph 14(1.1)(a), the reciprocal of the fraction obtained by multiplying the fraction ¾ by the fraction in paragraph 14(1)(b) that applies to the taxpayer for the taxation year,

(II) where that amount is determined by reference to paragraph 14(1.1)(b), and the taxation year does not end after February 27, 2000 and before October 18, 2000, 2, and

(III) where that amount is determined by reference to paragraph 14(1.1)(b), and the taxation year ends after February 27, 2000 and before October 18, 2000, 3/2, and

(B) the amount determined for G multiplied by the reciprocal of the fraction in paragraph 38(a) that applies to the taxpayer for the taxation year; and

(ii) in any other case, 1,

(b) the individual's cumulative gains limit at the end of the year,

(c) the individual's annual gains limit for the year, and

(d) the amount that would be determined in respect of the individual for the year under paragraph 3(b) in respect of capital gains

---

[9] Indexed after 2014 by 117.1(1) — ed.

and capital losses if the only properties referred to in that paragraph were properties that, at the time they were disposed of, were qualified farm properties, qualified fishing properties or qualified farm or fishing properties.

Related Provisions: 40(1.1) — Extended capital gains reserve where farm property disposed of to child; 40(3.1) — Deemed disposition where negative ACB of partnership interest creates deemed gain; 73(3)–(4.1) — Intergenerational rollover of farm property; 110.6(2.2) — Increased deduction since April 21, 2015; 110.6(4) — Maximum deduction; 110.6(5) — Individual deemed resident in Canada throughout year; 110.6(6) — Failure to report gain; 110.6(7)–(11) — Restrictions; 110.6(13) — Meaning of "amount determined under para. 3(b)"; 110.6(17) — Order of deduction; 110.6(31) — Deduction limited to dollar limit applicable to year of disposition; 117.1(2)(c) — Amount of $400,000 indexed to inflation after 2014; 127.52(1)(h)(i) — Deduction allowed for minimum tax purposes; 257 — Formula cannot calculate to less than zero. See also at end of s. 110.6.

Notes: This deduction is topped up by 110.6(2.2) to $500,000 ($1 million exemption from capital gains), a fixed amount that is not indexed.

See generally Munro & Oelschlagel, *Taxation of Farmers and Fishermen* (Carswell, looseleaf or *Taxnet Pro* Reference Centre), chap. 7A; Notes to 110.6(1)"qualified farm or fishing property" and 110.6(1.3); Shew & Wong, "Multi-Level Farming Structures and the Capital Gains Exemption", 6(3) *Canadian Tax Focus* (ctf.ca) 10-11 (Aug. 2016); Bodie, Novotny & Ritchie, "Farming Taxation, With an Emphasis on Farm Succession", 2017 Prairie Provinces Tax Conference [PPTC] (ctf.ca); Friedley & Leenstra, "Opportunities, Pitfalls and Traps Accessing the Capital Gains Exemption on Qualified Farm Property", 2018 PPTC; Herbert & Stephan, "Taxation of Farming", 2019 PPTC; BDO, "Multiply capital gains exemption for farm property", March 21, 2021 (tinyurl.com/bdo-cge-farm and 2021(7) *Tax Times* 2-3 (April 16, 2021)).

The 1994 federal budget announced a review of the $500,000 exemptions for small business shares and farms to determine whether other measures would be more appropriate. The 1995 budget announced completion of this review and that no changes would be made. The 1998 Mintz Committee report recommended eliminating the exemptions. The 2006 budget extended them to fishing property, and the 2007 Budget increased them to $750,000. The 2013 budget increased the exemptions to $800,000, indexed after 2014. The 2015 budget increased the farm/fishing property exemption to $1m (not indexed): 110.6(2.2).

Note that 73(3)–(4.1) provide a rollover that may be an alternative to this exemption when transferring farm or fishing property to one's children or grandchildren.

The exemption can be combined with the principal-residence exemption for the home located on the property: VIEWS doc 2005-0132391E5. The exemption can apply to a grant of servitude in Quebec: doc 2006-0196071C6, and to the notional gain on change of use to inventory (no deemed disposition under 45(1)): 2007-0248391E5.

On sale of a farming business, amounts allocated to inventory are fully taxable (net of the inventory's cost) and not eligible for the exemption: *Marcon*, 2008 TCC 116.

A taxpayer claiming a large deduction under 110.6(2) may run into Alternative Minimum Tax under 127.5–127.55, since 30% of the gain is taxed for AMT purposes (see 127.52(1)(d)(i)).

In *Fournie v. Cromarty*, 2011 ONSC 6587, C died with 3 farms eligible for the exemption but total gains exceeding his exemption limit. C's will left one farm to F, provided F paid the capital gains tax on that farm. F was held entitled to share proportionally in the benefit of the exemption.

See also Notes to 110.6(2.1).

110.6(2) opening words and (d) amended by 2014 budget bill #2, for dispositions and transfers in the 2014 and later taxation years, to accommodate the new combined term "qualified farm or fishing property".

110.6(2)(a) formula amount changed from $375,000 to $400,000 by 2013 budget bill #2, for 2014 and later taxation years.

110.6(2)(a) formula amended by 2007 budget bill #2, for tax years that begin after March 19, 2007, to change $250,000 to $375,000.

110.6(2) earlier amended by 2006 budget bill #2 (last change effective for taxation years that end after May 1, 2006), 2000 and 1994 Budgets and 1992 technical bill.

Income Tax Folios: S1-F3-C2: Principal residence [replaces IT-120R6, IT-437R]; S4-F8-C1: Business investment losses [replaces IT-484R2].

Interpretation Bulletins: IT-426R: Shares sold subject to an earnout agreement. Also see list at end of s. 110.6.

Advance Tax Rulings: ATR-28: Redemption of capital stock of family farm corporation; ATR-56: Purification of a family farm corporation.

Forms: T1 Sched. 3: Capital gains (or losses); T3 Sched. 3: Eligible taxable capital gains; T657: Calculation of capital gains deduction; T936: Calculation of cumulative net investment loss; T1161: List of properties by an emigrant of Canada; T1237: Saskatchewan farm and small business capital gains tax credit.

(2.1) Capital gains deduction — qualified small business corporation shares — In computing the taxable income for a taxation year of an individual (other than a trust) who was resident in Canada throughout the year and who disposed of a share of a corporation in the year or a preceding taxation year and after June

17, 1987 that, at the time of disposition, was a qualified small business corporation share of the individual, there may be deducted such amount as the individual may claim not exceeding the least of

(a) the amount determined by the formula in paragraph (2)(a) in respect of the individual for the year,

(b) the amount, if any, by which the individual's cumulative gains limit at the end of the year exceeds the amount deducted under subsection (2) in computing the individual's taxable income for the year,

(c) the amount, if any, by which the individual's annual gains limit for the year exceeds the amount deducted under subsection (2) in computing the individual's taxable income for the year, and

(d) the amount that would be determined in respect of the individual for the year under paragraph 3(b) (to the extent that that amount is not included in computing the amount determined under paragraph (2)(d) in respect of the individual) in respect of capital gains and capital losses if the only properties referred to in paragraph 3(b) were qualified small business corporation shares of the individual.

Related Provisions: 40(1.1)(c) — extended capital gains reserve where small business corporation disposed of to child; 48.1 — Deemed disposition to trigger exemption before small business corp goes public; 69(11)(a)(i) — Exception to rule deeming proceeds at FMV where CG deduction claimed after incorporation or dissolution of partnership; 110.6(4) — Maximum deduction; 110.6(5) — Individual deemed resident in Canada throughout year; 110.6(6) — Failure to report gain; 110.6(7)–(11) — Restrictions; 110.6(13) — Meaning of "amount determined under para. 3(b)"; 110.6(31) — Deduction limited to dollar limit for year of disposition; 127.52(1)(h)(i) — Deduction allowed for minimum tax. See also at end of s. 110.6.

Notes: The $441,692 deduction (2020) or $446,109 deduction (2021; indexed annually) offsets an underlying $883,384 ($892,218 for 2021) of capital gains on qualified small business corporation shares, since $\frac{1}{2}$ of the gain is included in income (see 38(a)). This exemption is shared with the farming/fishing property exemption under 110.6(2), but the limit for that deduction is $500,000 ($1m of capital gain): 110.6(2.2).

See Notes to 110.6(1)"qualified small business corporation share" for the conditions shares must meet to qualify for the exemption. Note also other conditions: not having CNIL (see Notes to 110.6(1)"cumulative net investment loss"); not having past ABILs or certain capital loss claims (see Notes to 110.6(1)"cumulative gains limit"); being resident in Canada (but see 110.6(5)); reporting the gain and claiming the deduction (see 110.6(6)); not having higher capital gain due to not paying dividends on preferred shares (110.6(8)); and others.

Note that if the vendor provides a non-competition agreement when selling shares, payment for that "restrictive covenant" may be fully taxable. See Notes to 56.4(2).

In para. (d), note that "3(b)" (no initial parenthesis) refers to para. (b) of s. 3, while "(2)(d)" refers to 110.6(2)(d).

On a sale to a public corporation, the exemption was technically unavailable due to 256(9) and the *La Survivance* case (VIEWS docs 2006-0214781E5, 2008-0285221C6). This has been corrected by amendment to 256(9) in 2009, generally retroactive to 2006.

A sale to a family member can qualify: VIEWS doc 2010-0359871E5. On a sale to a related corporation, 84.1 might convert the capital gain to a dividend so that it is not eligible for the exemption.

A carried-back loss on QSBC shares from an estate via 164(6) must be netted (110.6(2.1)(d)) against the QSBC gain on the terminal return: doc 2004-0088061I7.

Crystallizing the exemption with a sale can be useful to lock in a cost base increase before incurring investment expenses that create CNIL (see 110.6(1)"cumulative net investment loss"), but note possible traps: (1) it reduces future ability to claim ABILs (see 39(9)); (2) if only part of the shares are later sold, the full dollar limit of free gain may not be available at that time; (3) alternative minimum tax (127.5-127.55); (4) tax on split income under 120.4(4); (5) US citizens may have US tax to pay on the sale. See also Patrick Uzan, "Crystallizations Can Be Beneficial Even in Asset Sales", 11(1) *Tax for the Owner-Manager [TfOM]* (ctf.ca) 8-9 (Jan. 2011); David Wilkenfeld, "Crystallization Planning", 16(2) *TfOM* 2-3 (April 2016).

In *Gervais*, 2018 FCA 3, half of a capital gain was transferred by the husband so the wife could claim the exemption: this violated GAAR (245(2)).

In *Laplante*, 2018 FCA 193 (leave to appeal denied 2019 CarswellNat 1522 (SCC)), sharing the exemption with six family members, with them paying the proceeds back to L and L paying their Alternative Minimum Tax, was held to be ineffective as a "simulation" under the Quebec *Civil Code*. (See Notes to 245(2) for discussion of "sham".)

See also VanderDuim & Williams, *Taxation of Private Corporations and their Shareholders* (ctf.ca, 5th ed., 2020), chap. 15; Hermann, "The Capital Gains Exemption", 2000 Cdn Tax Foundation conference report, 29:1-59; Kakkar & Yan, "Practical Considerations in Claiming an ABIL or the Capital Gains Exemption", 2012 Ontario Tax Conference (ctf.ca.), 5:1-28; Mammola & Youn, "The Capital Gains Exemption: Selected Planning Issues", 65(1) *Canadian Tax Journal* 191-213 (2017).

For a ruling see VIEWS doc 2005-0134731R3 (structure minimizing tax on transfer of CCPC from parent to child — but CRA said in 2015-0610711C6 [2015 CTF q.11] that in light of *Descarries* it would no longer approve this case), and *contra* (on a sale to a sibling) see 2008-0269441E5. The individual must be resident in Canada throughout the year, but need not be for the 24-month holding period in 110.6(1)"qualified small business corporation share": 2010-0359781E5. Where an error was made in the sale agreement so that the shares do not qualify, consider rectification, discussed in Notes to 169(1): 2010-0381961E5.

A taxpayer claiming a large deduction under 110.6(2.1) may run into Alternative Minimum Tax under 127.5–127.55, since 30% of the gain is taxed for AMT purposes (see 127.52(1)(d)(i)).

See Notes to 110.6(2) re the history of this exemption, consideration given to repealing it, and its gradual increase over the years.

120.4(4)-(5) (part of the Tax on Split Income rules) are targeted in part at the capital gains exemption.

110.6(2.1) amended by 2014 budget bill #2 (for dispositions/transfers in the 2014 and later tax years), 2006 budget bill #2, 2000 Budget, 1995-97 technical bill, 1994 Budget.

Interpretation Bulletins: IT-426R: Shares sold subject to an earnout agreement. Also see list at end of s. 110.6.

Information Circulars: 88-2, para. 15: General anti-avoidance rule — section 245 of the *Income Tax Act*; 88-2 Supplement, paras. 3, 4: General anti-avoidance rule — section 245 of the *Income Tax Act*.

Advance Tax Rulings: ATR-42: Transfer of shares; ATR-53: Purification of a small business corporation; ATR-55: Amalgamation followed by sale of shares.

Forms: T1 Sched. 3: Capital gains (or losses); T3 Sched. 3: Eligible taxable capital gains; T657: Calculation of capital gains deduction; T936: Calculation of cumulative net investment loss; T1161: List of properties by an emigrant of Canada; T1237: Saskatchewan farm and small business capital gains tax credit.

(2.2) Additional deduction — qualified farm or fishing property [total $500,000]

— In computing the taxable income for a taxation year of an individual (other than a trust) who was resident in Canada throughout the year and who disposed of qualified farm or fishing property in the year or a preceding taxation year and after April 20, 2015, there may be deducted an amount claimed by the individual that does not exceed the least of

(a) the amount, if any, by which $500,000[10] exceeds the total of

(i) $400,000[9] adjusted for each year after 2014 in the manner set out by section 117.1, and

(ii) the total of all amounts each of which is an amount deducted under this subsection in computing the individual's taxable income for a preceding taxation year that ended after 2014,

(b) the amount, if any, by which the individual's cumulative gains limit at the end of the year exceeds the total of all amounts each of which is an amount deducted by the individual under subsection (2) or (2.1) in computing the individual's taxable income for the year,

(c) the amount, if any, by which the individual's annual gains limit for the year exceeds the total of all amounts each of which is an amount deducted by the individual under subsection (2) or (2.1) in computing the individual's taxable income for the year, and

(d) the amount that would be determined in respect of the individual for the year under paragraph 3(b) in respect of capital gains and capital losses if the only properties referred to in that paragraph were qualified farm or fishing properties disposed of by the individual after April 20, 2015.

Related Provisions: 110.6(2.3) — Top-up under (2.2) applies after maximum claims under (2) and (2.1).

Notes: 110.6(2.2) tops up the farm/fishing property exemption to $1,000,000, from the 110.6(2) indexed amount ($892,218 for 2021) that is shared with the 110.6(2.1) exemption for small business shares. The top-up (needed only if the indexed maximum is being claimed: 110.6(2.3)) remains at $1m without indexing (so it approaches zero as the indexed amount approaches $1m). Added by 2015 Budget bill, for tax years ending after April 20, 2015.

Former 110.6(2.2), "Capital gains deduction — qualified fishing property", added by 2006 budget bill #2, and repealed by 2014 budget bill #2 for the 2014 and later tax

years. It was incorporated into 110.6(2) using the combined term "qualified farm or fishing property".

Forms: T1 Sched. 3: Capital gains (or losses); T3 Sched. 3: Eligible taxable capital gains; T657: Calculation of capital gains deduction; T936: Calculation of cumulative net investment loss; T1161: List of properties of an emigrant of Canada; T1237: Saskatchewan farm and small business capital gains tax credit.

(2.3) Additional deduction — ordering rule

— Subsection (2.2) does not apply in computing the taxable income for a taxation year of an individual unless the individual has claimed the maximum amount that could be claimed under subsections (2) and (2.1) for the taxation year.

Notes: 110.6(2.3) added by 2015 Budget bill, for tax years ending after April 20, 2015.

Former 110.6(2.3) (added by 2007 budget bill #2; repealed by 2014 budget bill #2 for dispositions and transfers in 2014 and later tax years) provided a transitional rule for 2007, due to the limit being increased from $250,000 to $375,000.

(3) [Repealed]

Notes: 110.6(3) repealed by 1994 Budget, effective 1996. It provided a general exemption against up to $100,000 of capital gains, expressed as a $75,000 deduction against taxable capital gains (¾ of a capital gain was then included in income under 38(a)). It was usable to Feb. 22, 1994 for regular gains, and for 1994-95 for deemed gains under 110.6(19), which could be made up to 2 years late under 110.6(26).

110.6(3) previously amended by 1992 technical bill, effective 1990.

(4) Maximum capital gains deduction

— Notwithstanding subsections (2) and (2.1), the total amount that may be deducted under this section in computing an individual's income for a taxation year shall not exceed the total of the amount determined by the formula in paragraph (2)(a) and the amount that may be deducted under subsection (2.2), in respect of the individual for the year.

Notes: 110.6(4) ensures that the lifetime total of all exemptions claimed — for farm and fishing property, small business shares, and the general $100,000 exemption until Feb. 22, 1994 — cannot exceed the dollar limit ($883,384 for 2020, $892,218 for 2021, indexed annually, and $1m for farm/fishing property under 110.6(2.2)).

110.6(4) amended by 2015 Budget bill (for tax years ending after April 20, 2015), 2014, 2007 and 2006 budget bills #2, 2000 and 1994 Budgets.

(5) Deemed resident in Canada

— For the purposes of subsections (2) to (2.2), an individual is deemed to have been resident in Canada throughout a particular taxation year if

(a) the individual was resident in Canada at any time in the particular taxation year; and

(b) the individual was resident in Canada throughout the immediately preceding taxation year or throughout the immediately following taxation year.

Related Provisions: 110.6(13) — No exemption while non-resident.

Notes: 110.6(5) gives the benefit of the capital gains deduction to someone who becomes resident in Canada, or ceases to be resident in Canada, during a year. (Note that 128.1(1) bumps up cost to fair market value (FMV) on immigration, while 128.1(4) deems most shares disposed of at FMV on emigration.) 110.6(13) effectively eliminates the exemption for a non-resident.

110.6(5) amended by 2015 Budget bill (for tax years that end after April 20, 2015); 2014, 2007 and 2006 budget bills #2; 1994 Budget.

(6) Failure to report capital gain

— Notwithstanding subsections (2) to (2.2), no amount may be deducted under this section in respect of a capital gain of an individual for a particular taxation year in computing the individual's taxable income for the particular taxation year or any subsequent year, if

(a) the individual knowingly or under circumstances amounting to gross negligence

(i) fails to file the individual's return of income for the particular taxation year within one year after the taxpayer's filing-due date for the particular taxation year, or

(ii) fails to report the capital gain in the individual's return of income for the particular taxation year; and

(b) the Minister establishes the facts justifying the denial of such an amount under this section.

---

[9] Indexed after 2014 by 117.1(1) — ed.

[10] Not indexed to inflation — ed.

Related Provisions: *Interpretation Act* 27(5) — Meaning of "within one year".

Notes: The "knowingly or gross negligence" test is the same wording as the 163(2) penalty, so there is extensive case law interpreting it. See Notes to 163(2).

For examples of 110.6(6) applying to disallow the exemption, see *Dymond*, [1990] 2 C.T.C. 2509 (TCC); *Malleck*, [1998] 1 C.T.C. 3015 (TCC); *Vitti*, [1999] 2 C.T.C. 2164 (TCC); *Greenwood*, [2000] 2 C.T.C. 2093 (TCC); *Roy*, [2001] 3 C.T.C. 226 (FCA); *Sidhu*, 2004 TCC 174.

For cases where the Tax Court found no gross negligence so the exemption was allowed, see *Ragobar*, [1995] 1 C.T.C. 2364; *Godin*, [1995] 1 C.T.C. 2825; *Adams*, [1996] 3 C.T.C. 2592; *Corday*, 1995 CarswellNat 2119; *Trépanier*, 1995 CarswellNat 2122; *Nicholas*, [1998] 1 C.T.C. 3015; *Carlson*, [1998] 2 C.T.C. 2476; *Colangelo Estate*, [1998] 2 C.T.C. 2823; *Mercille*, [2000] 2 C.T.C. 2434; *Findlay*, [2000] 3 C.T.C. 152 (FCA) (accountant's negligence not attributed to taxpayer who was not privy to accountant's actions); *Foisy*, [2001] 1 C.T.C. 2606; *Ounpuu*, 2009 TCC 121.

110.6(6) amended by 2015 Budget bill (for tax years that end after April 20, 2015), 2014 budget bill #2, 2002-2013 technical bill, 2007 and 2006 budget bills #2, 1994 Budget.

CRA Audit Manual: 28.4.15: Application of penalty in specific income tax situations — taxable capital gains.

(7) Deduction not permitted — Notwithstanding subsections (2) to (2.2), no amount may be deducted under this section in computing an individual's taxable income for a taxation year in respect of a capital gain of the individual for the taxation year if the capital gain is from a disposition of property which disposition is part of a series of transactions or events

 (a) that includes a dividend received by a corporation to which dividend subsection 55(2) does not apply but would apply if this Act were read without reference to paragraph 55(3)(b); or

 (b) in which any property is acquired by a corporation or partnership for consideration that is significantly less than the fair market value of the property at the time of acquisition (other than an acquisition as the result of an amalgamation or merger of corporations or the winding-up of a corporation or partnership or a distribution of property of a trust in satisfaction of all or part of a corporation's capital interest in the trust).

Related Provisions: 248(10) — Series of transactions or events. See also at end of s. 110.6.

Notes: For CRA views on whether 110.6(7)(b) applies see docs 2005-0152031E5 (no), 2012-0454181C6 (maybe), 2012-0456711I7 (yes), 2013-0503511E5 (maybe).

110.6(7) amended by 2015 Budget bill (for tax years that end after April 20, 2015); 2014, 2007 and 2006 budget bills #2; 1994 Budget.

Advance Tax Rulings: ATR-56: Purification of a family farm corporation.

(8) Deduction not permitted — Notwithstanding subsections (2) to (2.2), if an individual has a capital gain for a taxation year from the disposition of a property and it can reasonably be concluded, having regard to all the circumstances, that a significant part of the capital gain is attributable to the fact that dividends were not paid on a share (other than a prescribed share) or that dividends paid on such a share in the taxation year or in any preceding taxation year were less than 90% of the average annual rate of return on that share for that year, no amount in respect of that capital gain shall be deducted under this section in computing the individual's taxable income for the year.

Related Provisions: 110.6(9) — Average annual rate of return; 183.1(7) — Tax on corporate distributions — application of s. 110.6(8). See also at end of s. 110.6.

Notes: 110.6(8) is designed to prevent conversion of dividend income into exempt capital gains. Corporations could issue shares with attributes designed to yield capital gains — e.g., preferred shares paying low or no dividends but redeemable at a substantial premium. 110.6(8) denies the deduction, but does not apply to prescribed shares under Reg. 6205.

See Mark Brender, "The *De Minimis* Dividend Test under 110.6(8)", 41(4) *Canadian Tax Journal* 808-27 and 41(5) 1034-44 (1993); Manu Kakkar, "Capital Gains Exemption: Freeze Shares", 12(2) *Tax for the Owner-Manager* (ctf.ca) 9 (April 2012).

110.6(8) amended by 2015 Budget bill (for tax years that end after April 20, 2015); 2014, 2007 and 2006 budget bills #2; 1994 Budget.

Regulations: 6205 (prescribed share).

(9) Average annual rate of return — For the purpose of subsection (8), the average annual rate of return on a share (other than a prescribed share) of a corporation for a taxation year is the annual rate of return by way of dividends that a knowledgeable and prudent investor who purchased the share on the day it was issued would expect to receive in that year, other than the first year after the issue, in respect of the share if

 (a) there was no delay or postponement of the payment of dividends and no failure to pay dividends in respect of the share;

 (b) there was no variation from year to year in the amount of dividends payable in respect of the share (other than where the amount of dividends payable is expressed as an invariant percentage of or by reference to an invariant difference between the dividend expressed as a rate of interest and a generally quoted market interest rate); and

 (c) the proceeds to be received by the investor on the disposition of the share are the same amount the corporation received as consideration on the issue of the share.

Notes: For CRA interpretation see VIEWS doc 2013-0495641C6 [APFF 2013 q.4].

Regulations: 6205 (prescribed share).

(10) [Repealed under former Act]

Notes: 110.6(10) repealed by 1988 tax reform, effective 1988. It prevented the use of extensions or renewal of options to defer capital gains during the phase-in of the exemption from 1985 to 1988.

(11) Where deduction not permitted — Where it is reasonable to consider that one of the main reasons for an individual acquiring, holding or having an interest in a partnership or trust (other than an interest in a personal trust) or a share of an investment corporation, mortgage investment corporation or mutual fund corporation, or for the existence of any terms, conditions, rights or other attributes of the interest or share, is to enable the individual to receive or have allocated to the individual a percentage of any capital gain or taxable capital gain of the partnership, trust or corporation that is larger than the individual's percentage of the income of the partnership, trust or corporation, as the case may be, notwithstanding any other provision of this Act,

 (a) no amount may be deducted under this section by the individual in respect of any such gain allocated or distributed to the individual after November 21, 1985; and

 (b) where the individual is a trust, any such gain allocated or distributed to it after November 21, 1985 shall not be included in computing its eligible taxable capital gain (within the meaning assigned by subsection 108(1)).

Notes: For the meaning of "one of the main reasons" see Notes to 83(2.1).

(12) [Repealed]

Notes: 110.6(12), "Trust deduction — death of spouse or common-law partner", repealed by 2014 budget bill #2 for 2016 and later tax years, due to new 104(13.4) and amendments to 104(6). Earlier amended by 2014 budget bill #2, 2002-2013 technical bill, 2006 budget bill #2, 2001 technical bill, 2000 same-sex partners bill, 2000 and 1994 Budgets, 1992 technical bill.

Abandoned Proposed Addition — 110.6(12), (12.1)

Notes: Dept. of Finance consultation paper *Tax Planning Using Private Corporations*, July 18, 2017 (reproduced here in the 53rd ed.), proposed new 110.6(12) and (12.1) and related amendments (including 110.6(16), (17.1)-(18.1), (24)-(30.1) and other provisions), to limit use of the capital gains exemption in many cases, including for gains accrued while the person was under 18, and gains accrued before rollout from a personal trust. The government dropped these proposals, as announced in Finance news release and Backgrounder, Oct. 16, 2017 (also reproduced here in the 53rd ed.). Related changes announced in July 2017 to extend the tax on income splitting (120.4) proceeded with revisions; changes re the passive income of private corporations (under 123.3 in the 53rd ed.) were replaced by limitations on the small business deduction (125(5.1)(b)) and dividend refund (s. 129); changes to catch conversion of income to capital gains (84.1, 246.1) were dropped.

(13) Determination under para. 3(b) — For the purposes of this section, the amount determined under paragraph 3(b) in respect of an individual for a period throughout which the individual was not resident in Canada is nil.

Related Provisions: 110.6(5) — Year of immigration or emigration. See also at end of s. 110.6.

Notes: Deeming the 3(b) amount to be zero eliminates the exemption for a non-resident, via 110.6(2)(d), (2.1)(d) and (2.2)(d). However, see 110.6(5).

(14) Related persons, etc. [miscellaneous rules re shares] — For the purposes of the definition "qualified small business corporation share" in subsection (1),

(a) a taxpayer shall be deemed to have disposed of shares that are identical properties in the order in which the taxpayer acquired them;

(b) in determining whether a corporation is a small business corporation or a Canadian-controlled private corporation at any time, a right referred to in paragraph 251(5)(b) shall not include a right under a purchase and sale agreement relating to a share of the capital stock of a corporation;

(c) a personal trust shall be deemed

(i) to be related to a person or partnership for any period throughout which the person or partnership was a beneficiary of the trust, and

(ii) in respect of shares of the capital stock of a corporation, to be related to the person from whom it acquired those shares where, at the time the trust disposed of the shares, all of the beneficiaries (other than registered charities) of the trust were related to that person or would have been so related if that person were living at that time;

(d) a partnership shall be deemed to be related to a person for any period throughout which the person was a member of the partnership;

(d.1) a person who is a member of a partnership that is a member of another partnership is deemed to be a member of the other partnership;

(e) where a corporation acquires shares of a class of the capital stock of another corporation from any person, it shall be deemed in respect of those shares to be related to the person where all or substantially all the consideration received by that person from the corporation in respect of those shares was common shares of the capital stock of the corporation;

(f) shares issued after June 13, 1988 by a corporation to a particular person or partnership shall be deemed to have been owned immediately before their issue by a person who was not related to the particular person or partnership unless the shares were issued

(i) as consideration for other shares,

(ii) as part of a transaction or series of transactions in which the person or partnership disposed of property to the corporation that consisted of

(A) all or substantially all the assets used in an active business carried on by that person or the members of that partnership, or

(B) an interest in a partnership all or substantially all the assets of which were used in an active business carried on by the members of the partnership, or

(iii) as payment of a stock dividend; and

(g) where, immediately before the death of an individual, or, in the case of a deemed transfer under subsection 248(23), immediately before the time that is immediately before the death of an individual, a share would, but for paragraph (a) of the definition "qualified small business corporation share" in subsection (1), be a qualified small business corporation share of the individual, the share shall be deemed to be a qualified small business corporation share of the individual if it was a qualified small business corporation share of the individual at any time in the 12-month period immediately preceding the death of the individual.

Related Provisions: 54.2 — Sale of shares after incorporation of business; 110.6(16) — Personal trust for 110.6(14)(c); 248(1) — "business" does not include adventure or concern under 110.6(14)(f); 248(5)(b) — Effect of stock dividend; 248(10) — Series of transactions or events; 248(12) — Identical properties. See also at end of 110.6.

Notes: *110.6(14)(a)* imposes FIFO when purifying a corporation (see Notes to 110.6(1)"qualifying small business corporation share"): VIEWS doc 2013-0481361E5.

110.6(14)(b) applied in *Chartier*, 2007 TCC 37: a right under a stock option agreement was held to be a right under an agreement of purchase and sale. See also docs 2006-0190931E5, 2006-0196121C6, 2006-0214691E5, 2007-0243371C6 (distinguishing *Chartier*); 2011-0428371I7 (share put/call rights: distinguishing *Chartier*); Karen Yull, "Incorporation of Professionals: 24-Month Holding Period Test", 4(9) *Tax Hyperion* (Carswell, Sept. 2007).

110.6(14)(a) and (c): see Heather Dawe, "Capital Gains Exemption — Deeming Provisions", 12(8) *Tax Hyperion* 9-11 (Aug. 2015).

110.6(14)(d): for an example see VIEWS doc 2009-0310231E5.

110.6(14)(d.1) allows the exemption on disposition of shares by a lower-tier partnership. See Bryant Frydberg, "Top Technical Bill Issues for Owner-Managers", 2013 Prairie Provinces Tax Conference (ctf.ca), 11:1, §4.

110.6(14)(f): A two-year holding period is required for a new company, unless (f)(i), (ii) or (iii) is satisfied: VIEWS docs 2010-0367031E5, 2011-0421821E5, 2014-0519071E5. 110.6(14)(f)(i) can apply to an 85(1) transfer: 2005-0117791E5. In *Twomey*, 2012 TCC 310, inadvertent issuance of only 1 share when 100 shares were intended to be issued was corrected by directors' resolution and retroactively met the holding period.

In *Gillen*, 2019 FCA 62, the "assets used in active business" test in (f)(ii)(A) was not met, as assets were sold immediately upon their acquisition.

The conditions in (f)(ii)(A) are consistent with the rule in 54.2 that lets an individual incorporate a business, immediately sell the shares and claim the exemption under 110.6(2.1). They do not apply to a transfer of real property the corporation is acquiring to use in its business: VIEWS doc 2006-0208691E5. See also 1988 Cdn Tax Foundation roundtable p. 53:9, and 2011-0424331E5, where the business and building are not transferred together; 2011-0426481E5 ((f)(ii) applies). Note that if a "shelf" company with existing shares is used instead of newly incorporated, 110.6(1)"qualified small business corporation share"(b) may not be satisfied!

110.6(14)(f)(ii)(B) applies to a partial disposition of a partnership interest: 2004-0101761E5.

CRA considers that "substantially all", used in (e) and (f)(ii), means 90% or more.

110.6(14)(d.1) added by 2002-2013 technical bill, for dispositions after Dec. 20, 2002; and for dispositions made by a taxpayer after 1999, by election. 110.6(14) earlier amended by 1995-97 and 1991 technical bills.

Advance Tax Rulings: ATR-55: Amalgamation followed by sale of shares.

(15) Value of assets of corporations — For the purposes of the definitions "qualified small business corporation share" and "share of the capital stock of a family farm or fishing corporation" in subsection (1), the definition "share of the capital stock of a family farm or fishing corporation" in subsection 70(10) and the definition "small business corporation" in subsection 248(1),

(a) where a person (in this subsection referred to as the "insured"), whose life was insured under an insurance policy owned by a particular corporation, owned shares of the capital stock (in this subsection referred to as the "subject shares") of the particular corporation, any corporation connected with the particular corporation or with which the particular corporation is connected or any corporation connected with any such corporation or with which any such corporation is connected (within the meaning of subsection 186(4) on the assumption that the corporation referred to in this subsection was a payer corporation within the meaning of that subsection),

(i) the fair market value of the life insurance policy shall, at any time before the death of the insured, be deemed to be its cash surrender value (within the meaning assigned by subsection 148(9)) at that time, and

(ii) the total fair market value of assets — other than assets described in any of subparagraphs (c)(i) to (iii) of the definition "qualified small business corporation share" in subsection (1), any of subparagraphs (a)(i) to (iii) of the definition "share of the capital stock of a family farm or fishing corporation" in subsection (1) or any of paragraphs (a) to (c) of the definition "small business corporation" in subsection 248(1), as the case may be — of any of those corporations that are

(A) the proceeds, the right to receive the proceeds or attributable to the proceeds, of the life insurance policy of which the particular corporation was a beneficiary, and

(B) used, directly or indirectly, within the 24-month period beginning at the time of the death of the insured or, where written application therefor is made by the particular corporation within that period, within such longer period as the Minister considers reasonable in the circumstances, to redeem, acquire or cancel the subject shares owned by the insured immediately before the death of the insured,

not in excess of the fair market value of the assets immediately after the death of the insured, shall, until the later of

(C) the redemption, acquisition or cancellation, and

(D) the day that is 60 days after the payment of the proceeds under the policy,

be deemed not to exceed the cash surrender value (within the meaning assigned by subsection 148(9)) of the policy immediately before the death of the insured; and

(b) the fair market value of an asset of a particular corporation that is a share of the capital stock or indebtedness of another corporation with which the particular corporation is connected shall be deemed to be nil and, for the purpose of this paragraph, a particular corporation is connected with another corporation only where

(i) the particular corporation is connected (within the meaning assigned by paragraph (d) of the definition "qualified small business corporation share" in subsection (1)) with the other corporation, and

(ii) the other corporation is not connected (within the meaning of subsection 186(4) as determined without reference to subsection 186(2) and on the assumption that the other corporation is a payer corporation within the meaning of subsection 186(4)) with the particular corporation,

except that this paragraph applies only in determining whether a share of the capital stock of another corporation with which the particular corporation is connected is a qualified small business corporation share or a share of the capital stock of a family farm or fishing corporation and in determining whether the other corporation is a small business corporation.

Related Provisions: 186(7) — Interpretation of "connected" for para. (a).

Notes: For interpretation of para. (a) (life insurance policy valued at cash surrender value), see VIEWS docs 1999-0006485, 2013-0473981E5, 2016-0651801C6 [2016 APFF q.9]. See also 70(5.3) Notes; Watson, "Intercorporate Shareholdings and 110.6(15)(b)", 18(2) *Tax Hyperion* (Carswell) 1-5 (March-April 2021) (circularity issue).

For the meaning of "indirectly" in (a)(ii)(B), see Notes to 17.1(1).

110.6(15) amended by 2014 budget bill #2 (for dispositions and transfers in the 2014 and later tax years), 1993 and 1991 technical bills.

(16) Personal trust — For the purposes of the definition "qualified small business corporation share" in subsection (1) and of paragraph (14)(c), a personal trust shall be deemed to include a trust described in subsection 7(2).

Notes: 110.6(16) added by 1991 technical bill, for dispositions after June 17, 1987.

(17) Order of deduction — For the purpose of clause (2)(a)(iii)(A), amounts deducted under this section in computing an individual's taxable income for a taxation year that ended before 1990 shall be deemed to have first been deducted in respect of amounts that were included in computing the individual's income under this Part for the year because of subparagraph 14(1)(a)(v) before being deducted in respect of any other amounts that were included in computing the individual's income under this Part for the year.

Notes: 110.6(17) added by 1992 technical bill, effective 1990, and amended by 1994 Budget effective 1996. It is intended to ensure that individuals who have not claimed the maximum exemption do not have their exemption inappropriately reduced as a result of the change in the capital gains inclusion rate after 1988-89.

(18) [Repealed]

Notes: Former 110.6(18) added by 1992 Budget/technical bill, effective 1992 and repealed by 1994 Budget, effective 1996, due to the elimination of the general $100,000 exemption in 110.6(3). It provided rules of interpretation for "eligible real property gain" and "eligible real property loss".

(19)–(30) [No longer relevant.]

Notes: 110.6(19)-(30) (added by 1994 Budget; reproduced here up to the 42nd ed., or see PITA DVD version or *Taxnet Pro*) provided an election to crystallize accrued capital gains as of Feb, 22, 1994, to use the $100,000 capital gains deduction (CGD) under 110.6(3). The election applied to the 1994 return in most cases, and was generally due by April 30, 1995. It could be made up to 2 years late on paying a penalty: 110.6(26)-(30). See *Foisy*, [2001] 1 C.T.C. 2606 (TCC), para. 22; *Saab*, 2005 TCC 331; *Sicurella*, 2013 TCC 79 (election did not change CCA entitlement for building); VIEWS docs 2006-018596I17, 2008-0285331C6. The election could be used for "flow-through entities" until 2004: see 39.1. The election was not validly made by filing a T664 and T657A, without reporting the gain and offsetting CGD on the return: *McCullock-Finney*, 2017 TCC 103. The election is part of the taxpayer's "permanent" file, not destroyed until 10 years after death, available on request from CRA: 2020-0851641C6 [2020 APFF Financial q.8].

110.6(20) provided conditions for 110.6(19). 110.6(21) ensured that making the 110.6(19) election on non-qualifying real property (investment real estate) would not require tax to be paid on the portion of the gain that was ineligible for the exemption (under rules in effect from March 1992). Such tax was deferred until later disposition of the property.

110.6(22) grinds down the ACB of property where the amount designated under a 110.6(19) election exceeds 110% of the fair market value on Feb. 22, 1994, effectively imposing a penalty on guessing too high as to the value of the property. Bowman CJ stated in *Nanji*, [2002] 2 C.T.C. 2627 (TCC), para. 19: "Whether the Act says so or not, [110.6(22)] is a penalty and obviously intended to be such. This is confirmed by subsection 110.6(28)".

110.6(23) applied on a 110.6(19) election to dispose of a partnership interest. 110.6(24) provided the deadline for filing a 110.6(19) election. 110.6(25) permitted revocation of an election before 1998. 110.6(26) permitted an election to be filed up to 2 years late. 110.6(27) permitted a 110.6(26) election to be amended before 1998. No extension is available, since this election is not listed in Reg. 600: VIEWS doc 2005-0122191E5.

110.6(28) provided that a 110.6(19) election could not be revoked or amended if the designated amount exceeded 11/10 of FMV. 110.6(29) provided a penalty for a late or amended election. 110.6(30) provided for assessment of the 110.6(29) penalty.

Remission Orders: *Karen Smedley and George Smedley Remission Order*, P.C. 2004-264 (remission of tax where CRA failed to advise that election could be amended under 110.6(27)).

Income Tax Folios: S1-F3-C2; Principal residence [replaces IT-120R6, IT-437R]; S4-F8-C1; Business investment losses [replaces IT-484R2].

I.T. Technical News: 7 (principal residence and the capital gains election).

(31) Reserve limit [deduction limited to dollar limit for year of disposition] — If an amount is included in an individual's income for a particular taxation year because of subparagraph 40(1)(a)(ii) in respect of a disposition of property in a preceding taxation year that, at the time of the disposition, is qualified farm or fishing property, a qualified small business corporation share, qualified farm property or qualified fishing property, the total of all amounts deductible by the individual for the particular year under this section is reduced by the amount, if any, determined by the formula

$$A - B$$

where

A is the total of all amounts each of which is an amount deductible under this section by the individual for the particular year or a preceding taxation year, computed without reference to this subsection; and

B is the total of all amounts each of which is an amount that would be deductible under this section by the individual for the particular year or a preceding taxation year if the individual had not for any preceding taxation year claimed a reserve under subparagraph 40(1)(a)(iii) and had claimed, for each taxation year ending before the particular year, the amount that would have been deductible under this section.

Notes: 110.6(31) prevents increases in the exemption (due to amendment to 110.6(2)(a) or inflation indexing under 117.1(1)) from applying to a 40(1)(a) capital gains reserve included in income in a later year to the extent the gain would not have qualified for the exemption in the year of disposition. See also VIEWS doc 2018-075535117 (trust realized gain, claimed reserve, then flowed out reserve amount under 104(21), (21.1)).

110.6(31) amended by 2014 budget bill #2, for dispositions and transfers in the 2014 and later taxation years, to add reference to qualified farm or fishing property (see Notes to definition of that term in 110.6(1)). The old terms were retained because an earlier disposition may have been before 2014.

110.6(31) amended by 2013 budget bill #2, for taxation years that end after March 19, 2007. The earlier 110.6(31), which applied to taxation years that end after March 18,

2007 (i.e., only to the 2007 year, for individuals), prevented the increase from $250,000 to $375,000 (of taxable capital gains deduction) from applying to dispositions made before the increase was announced on March 19, 2007 (see also 110.6(2.3)).

(32) [Repealed]

Notes: 110.6(32) added by 2007 budget bill #2 for taxation years that end after March 18, 2007, and repealed by 2013 budget bill #2 for taxation years that begin after March 19, 2007, so for individuals it applied to 2007 only. It related to the former 110.6(31).

Related Provisions [s. 110.6]: 39(9) — Reduction of business investment loss; 39(11) — Bad debt recovery; 39(13) — Repayment of assistance; 40(3) — Deemed gain when ACB adjusted below nil; 42 — Deemed loss on warranty; 70(2) — Rollovers on death; 98(1)(c) — Disposition of partnership property; 111(8)"non-capital loss"A:E — Carryforward of exemption deduction as non-capital loss; 111(8)"pre-1986 capital loss balance"C, D, E — Balance reduced by exemption claims; 111.1 — Order of applying provisions; 131(1)(b) — Election re capital gains dividend.

Definitions [s. 110.6]: "active business" — 248(1); "adjusted cost base" — 54, 248(1); "allowable business investment loss" — 38(c), 248(1); "alter ego trust", "amount" — 248(1); "annual gains limit" — 110.6(1); "assessment" — 248(1); "average annual rate of return" — 110.6(9); "balance-due day" — 248(1); "beneficiary" — 248(25) Notes; "borrowed money", "business" — 248(1); "calendar year" — Interpretation Act 37(1)(a); "Canada" — 255; "Canadian-controlled private corporation" — 125(7), 248(1); "capital gain" — 39(1)(a), 248(1); "capital interest" — 108(1), 248(1); "capital loss" — 39(1)(b), 248(1); "capital property" — 54, 248(1); "carrying on business" — 253; "child" — 70(10), 110.6(1), 252(1); "class of shares" — 248(6); "common-law partner", "common share" — 248(1); "corporation" — 248(1), Interpretation Act 35(1); "credit union" — 137(6), 248(1); "cumulative gains limit", "cumulative net investment loss" — 110.6(1); "deferred profit sharing plan" — 147(1), 248(1); "depreciable property" — 13(21), 248(1); "disposition", "dividend" — 248(1); "election filing date" — 110.6(26); "elector" — 110.6(19); "eligible capital property" — 54, 248(1); "eligible real property loss" — 110.6(1); "employee" — 248(1); "fair market value" — see 69(1) Notes; "farming" — 248(1); "filing-due date" — 150(1), 248(1); "fiscal period" — 249(2)(b), 249.1; "fishing", "gross revenue" — 248(1); "identical" — 248(12); "immovable" — Quebec Civil Code art. 900–907; "income-averaging annuity contract" — 61(4), 248(1); "individual", "insurance policy" — 248(1); "interest in a family farm or fishing partnership" — 110.6(1); "investment corporation" — 130(3)(a), 248(1); "investment expense", "investment income" — 110.6(1); "joint spousal or common-law partner trust", "Minister" — 248(1); "month" — Interpretation Act 35(1); "mortgage investment corporation" — 130.1(6), 248(1); "mutual fund corporation" — 131(8), 248(1); "mutual fund trust" — 132(6)–(7), 132.2(3)(n), 248(1); "net capital loss" — 111(8), 248(1); "net income stabilization account" — 110.6(1.1), 248(1); "non-qualifying real property" — 110.6(1), 248(1); "parent" — 70(10)"child", 252(2)(a); "partnership" — see 96(1) Notes; "person" — 248(1); "personal trust" — 110.6(16), 248(1); "pooled registered pension plan" — 147.5(1), 248(1); "prescribed", "property" — 248(1); "qualified farm or fishing property", "qualified small business corporation share" — 110.6(1); "registered charity", "registered pension plan" — 248(1); "registered retirement savings plan" — 146(1), 248(1); "related" — 110.6(14)(c)–(e), 251(2); "related segregated fund trust" — 138.1(1)(a); "rental property" — Reg. 1100(14); "resident in Canada" — 110.6(5), 250; "series of transactions" — 248(10); "share" — 248(1); "share of the capital stock of a family farm or fishing corporation" — 110.6(1); "small business corporation" — 110.6(14)(b), 248(1); "specified member", "stock dividend" — 248(1); "substituted" — 248(5); "taxable capital gain" — 38(a), 248(1); "taxable income" — 2(2), 248(1); "taxation year" — 249; "taxpayer" — 248(1); "trust" — 104(1), 248(1), (3); "writing" — Interpretation Act 35(1).

Income Tax Folios [s. 110.6]: S4-F8-C1: Business investment losses [replaces IT-484R2].

Interpretation Bulletins [s. 110.6]: IT-123R6: Transactions involving eligible capital property; IT-236R4: Reserves — disposition of capital property (cancelled); IT-242R: Retired partners; IT-268R3: Inter vivos transfer of farm property to child; IT-268R4: Inter vivos transfer of farm property to child; IT-278R2: Death of a partner or of a retired partner; IT-281R2: Elections on single payments from a deferred profit-sharing plan (cancelled); IT-330R: Dispositions of capital property subject to warranty, covenant, etc. (cancelled); IT-369R: Attribution of trust income to settlor; IT-381R3; Trusts — capital gains and losses and the flow-through of taxable capital gains to beneficiaries; IT-442R: Bad debts and reserves for doubtful debts; IT-451R: Deemed disposition and acquisition on ceasing to be or becoming resident in Canada; IT-504R2: Visual artists and writers.

110.7 (1) Residing in prescribed zone [northern Canada deduction] — Where, throughout a period (in this section referred to as the "qualifying period") of not less than 6 consecutive months beginning or ending in a taxation year, a taxpayer who is an individual has resided in one or more particular areas each of which is a prescribed northern zone or prescribed intermediate zone for the

year and files for the year a claim in prescribed form, there may be deducted in computing the taxpayer's taxable income for the year

(a) the total of all amounts each of which is the product obtained by multiplying the specified percentage for a particular area for the year in which the taxpayer so resided by an amount received, or the value of a benefit received or enjoyed, in the year by the taxpayer in respect of the taxpayer's employment in the particular area by a person with whom the taxpayer was dealing at arm's length in respect of travel expenses incurred by the taxpayer or another individual who was a member of the taxpayer's household during the part of the year in which the taxpayer resided in the particular area, to the extent that

(i) the amount received or the value of the benefit, as the case may be,

(A) does not exceed a prescribed amount in respect of the taxpayer for the period in the year in which the taxpayer resided in the particular area,

(B) is included and is not otherwise deducted in computing the taxpayer's income for the year or any other taxation year, and

(C) is not included in determining an amount deducted under subsection 118.2(1) for the year or any other taxation year,

(ii) the travel expenses were incurred in respect of trips made in the year by the taxpayer or another individual who was a member of the taxpayer's household during the part of the year in which the taxpayer resided in the particular area, and

(iii) neither the taxpayer nor a member of the taxpayer's household is at any time entitled to a reimbursement or any form of assistance (other than a reimbursement or assistance included in computing the income of the taxpayer or the member) in respect of travel expenses to which subparagraph (ii) applies; and

(b) the lesser of

(i) 20% of the taxpayer's income for the year, and

(ii) the total of all amounts each of which is the product obtained by multiplying the specified percentage for a particular area for the year in which the taxpayer so resided by the total of

(A) $11.00* multiplied by the number of days in the year included in the qualifying period in which the taxpayer resided in the particular area, and

(B) $11.00* multiplied by the number of days in the year included in that portion of the qualifying period throughout which the taxpayer maintained and resided in a self-contained domestic establishment in the particular area (except any day included in computing a deduction claimed under this paragraph by another person who resided on that day in the establishment).

Proposed Amendment — Northern residents' deduction — "Lowest airfare" requirement

CRA news release, March 18, 2019: See under Reg. 7304(2)(c).

Proposed Amendment — Northern residents' deduction for travel

Federal Budget, Notice of Ways and Means Motion, April 19, 2021: *Northern Residents Deductions*

4 The Act [mostly the Regulations — ed.] is modified to give effect to the proposals relating to Northern Residents Deductions as described in the budget documents tabled by the Minister of Finance in the House of Commons on April 19, 2021.

Federal Budget, Supplementary Information, April 19, 2021: See under Reg. 7304(2).

Prime Minister's mandate letter to Minister of Northern Affairs, Dec. 2019: I will expect you to work with your colleagues and through established legislative, regu-

---

* Not indexed for inflation, but increased from $7.50 to $8.25 in 2008 and to $11 in 2016 — ed.

latory and Cabinet processes to deliver on your top priorities. In particular, you will:
...

- Work with the Minister of Finance to increase the Northern Residents Deduction for travel costs to at least $1,200 in the Northern Zone and at least $600 in the Intermediate Zone so that it benefits all Northerners who travel. You will work with the Minister of Innovation, Science and Industry who is the Minister responsible for the Competition Bureau to ensure that these savings are for the benefit of citizens in the North rather than transportation providers.

Liberal.ca election platform, Oct. 2019: *Travel for Northerners*

We will make life more affordable for people living in Canada's North.

Whether for school, medical appointments, or to visit with family, people who call Canada's North home need to travel — but the high cost of airfare can make it unaffordable for many. The current Northern Residents Deduction only allows people who already receive travel benefits through work to deduct travel costs, with no help for people whose work doesn't help cover those costs.

To make travel more affordable for everyone in the North, we will move forward with improvements to the Northern Resident Deduction, giving people living in the Northern Zone at least $1,200 in deductible travel costs, with $600 in deductible travel costs for people in the Intermediate Zone.

To make sure that these savings are not simply passed on to airlines and other transportation companies, we will direct the Competition Bureau to oversee the pricing of transportation in the North, and will review the communities covered by these zones to ensure that Northerners in all parts of the country get the help they need to make life affordable.

Related Provisions: 6(6) — Employment at special work site or remote area — non-taxable benefits; 110.7(4) — Limitation on 110.7(1)(b)(ii); 111.1 — Order of applying provisions; 127.52(1)(h)(i) — Deduction allowed for minimum tax purposes.

Notes: See Guide RC4650, instructions on Form T2222, and "Tax information for northern residents" (April 9, 2021), tinyurl.com/cra-north. See Notes to Reg. 7303.1 for discussion of the prescribed zones.

Per IC 73-21R9 and tinyurl.com/travel-cra, travel expenses for 110.7 can optionally be calculated without receipts: $23/meal or $69/day (since 2020; $17 and $51 for 2006-2019: tinyurl.com/travel-cra); and vehicle expenses per qualifying km driven (to cover both ownership and operating expenses), using the table in 62(3) Notes.

110.7(1) requires a full 6 months, not parts of calendar months, despite the definition of "month" in the *Interpretation Act*. Thus, June 18–December 9 was not "6 consecutive months": *McCombie*, [2000] 4 C.T.C. 2251 (TCC).

Temporary absences: In *Morecroft*, 1991 CarswellNat 587 (TCC), temporary absences did not cause loss of the 6-month "residence" requirement. However, in *Talbot*, 2018 TCC 94, T had so many absences from the region when off work, without leaving his belongings there, that he did not "reside" there. CRA VIEWS: miners who come to the northern zone for 4 or 14 days at a time, then return home for a few days, do not qualify: 2005-0141731E5. Where an employee lives permanently outside the region, it will be a question of fact whether temporary absences break the 6-month requirement: 2005-0147241E5, 2007-0235791E5, 2008-0274361E5, 2008-0287721E5, 2009-0306571E5, 2010-0360801E5, 2010-0363521E5, 2010-0364801E5, 2011-0396721I7, 2015-0582091E5.

For "member of the taxpayer's household" see VIEWS doc 2009-0349531E5.

For the (b)(ii)(B) extra deduction, see Notes to 248(1)"self-contained domestic establishment".

CRA accepts a reasonable travel reimbursement before or after a trip, but not recharacterization of existing salary as travel reimbursement: docs 2004-0089071E5, 2010-0373421E5, 2014-0528201E5; nor a combined payment that includes settlement and housing allowances (2006-0197431R3).

CRA reportedly audits and reassesses this claim excessively: "Federal minister to look at 'abnormal' number of tax reviews in Northern Canada", tinyurl.com/cbc-110-7 (April 2018).

110.7(1)(b)(ii)(A)-(B) amended by 2016 budget bill #1, for 2016 and later taxation years, to change $8.25 to $11. This had been proposed in the Oct. 2015 Liberal election platform, along with indexing the amount to inflation, which was not done.

Cls. (b)(ii)(A)-(B) amended by 2008 budget bill #1 to change $7.50 to $8.25, for 2008 and later taxation years. 110.7 earlier amended by 1992, 1991 technical bills.

Interpretation Bulletins: IT-91R4: Employment at special work sites or remote work locations.

Regulations: 100(3.1) (deduction reduces source withholdings); 7303.1 (prescribed northern zone, prescribed intermediate zone); 7304(4) (prescribed amount for 110.7(1)(a)(i)(A)).

Forms: RC4054: Ceiling amounts for housing benefits paid in prescribed zones [information sheet]; T2222: Northern residents deductions.

(2) Specified percentage — For the purpose of subsection (1), the specified percentage for a particular area for a taxation year is

(a) where the area is a prescribed northern zone for the year, 100%; and

(b) where the area is a prescribed intermediate zone for the year, 50%.

Regulations: 7303.1 (prescribed northern zone, prescribed intermediate zone).

Interpretation Bulletins: IT-91R4: Employment at special work sites or remote work locations.

(3) Restriction — The total determined under paragraph (1)(a) for a taxpayer in respect of travel expenses incurred in a taxation year in respect of an individual shall not be in respect of more than 2 trips made by the individual in the year, other than trips to obtain medical services that are not available in the locality in which the taxpayer resided.

Related Provisions [s. 110.7(3)]: 118.2(2)(g), (h) — Medical expense credit for travel expenses.

Notes: Two spouses can each claim 2 trips for each: VIEWS doc 2009-0318891E5.

(4) Board and lodging allowances, etc. — The amount determined under subparagraph (1)(b)(ii) for a particular area for a taxpayer for a taxation year shall not exceed the amount by which the amount otherwise determined under that subparagraph for the particular area for the year exceeds the value of, or an allowance in respect of expenses incurred by the taxpayer for, the taxpayer's board and lodging in the particular area (other than at a work site described in paragraph 67.1(2)(e)) that

(a) would, but for subparagraph 6(6)(a)(i), be included in computing the taxpayer's income for the year; and

(b) can reasonably be considered to be attributable to that portion of the qualifying period that is in the year and during which the taxpayer maintained a self-contained domestic establishment as the taxpayer's principal place of residence in an area other than a prescribed northern zone or a prescribed intermediate zone for the year.

Notes: 110.7(4) provides that non-taxable benefits received by employees at special work sites reduce the 110.7(1) deduction. Since 67.1(2)(e) allows full deductibility for meals at special work sites more than 30 km from an urban area of at least 40,000 people, 110.7(4) provides that only those non-taxable benefits received in respect of special work sites that are *within* 30 km of such an area will reduce the deduction.

For CRA interpretation see VIEWS docs 2013-0505481E5, 2014-055841117.

See also Notes to 248(1)"self-contained domestic establishment".

110.7(4) amended by 1998 Budget to add "(other than at a work site described in paragraph 67.1(2)(e))" in the opening words, effective for 1998 and later taxation years.

Regulations: 7303.1 (prescribed northern zone, prescribed intermediate zone).

Interpretation Bulletins: IT-91R4: Employment at special work sites or remote work locations.

Forms: RC4054: Ceiling amounts for housing benefits paid in prescribed zones [information sheet].

(5) Idem — Where on any day an individual resides in more than one particular area referred to in subsection (1), for the purpose of that subsection, the individual shall be deemed to reside in only one such area on that day.

Definitions [s. 110.7]: "amount" — 248(1); "arm's length" — 251(1); "employment", "individual", "person", "prescribed" — 248(1); "prescribed intermediate zone" — Reg. 7303.1(2); "prescribed northern zone" — Reg. 7303.1(1); "qualifying period" — 110.7(1); "self-contained domestic establishment" — 248(1); "specified percentage" — 110.7(2); "taxable income" — 2(2), 248(1); "taxation year" — 249.

111. (1) Losses deductible — For the purpose of computing the taxable income of a taxpayer for a taxation year, there may be deducted such portion as the taxpayer may claim of the taxpayer's

(a) **non-capital losses** — non-capital losses for the 20 taxation years immediately preceding and the 3 taxation years immediately following the year;

Related Provisions: 88(1.1) — Windup — non-capital losses of subsidiary; 88(1.3) — Windup — rules relating to computation of income and tax of parent; 111(7.2) — Non-capital loss of life insurer; 111(7.3)-(7.5), 144.1(13) — Special rules for non-capital losses of employee life and health trust; 115(1)(c), (d) — Application of losses to non-resident; 127.52(1)(i)(i) — Limitation on deduction for minimum tax purposes; 186(1)(d)(i) — Application of non-capital loss to Part IV tax. See also at end of subsec. 111(1) and s. 111.

Notes: The claim under 111(1)(a) for losses from the 20 taxation years *preceding* implements a 20-year carry*forward* of losses, since the legislation is written from the point of view of the year in which the loss is *claimed*. (Note however that non-capital losses that arose in taxation years ending before March 23, 2004 were carried forward only 7 years, and those in taxation years ending from March 23, 2004 through Dec. 31, 2005 were carried forward only 10 years.) Similarly, the reference to the 3 taxation years *following* implements a carry*back* of losses for 3 years. Losses cannot be carried back more than 3 years: VIEWS doc 2018-0789661M4.

The losses under 111(1)(a) are business losses (excluding farm, fishing and limited partnership losses: see 111(1)(c)-(e)), property losses, employment losses (see Notes to 5(2)), losses from deductible legal fees exceeding support received (VIEWS doc 2010-0386271E5: see 56(1)(b) Notes), and allowable business investment losses (only 10-year carryforward for ABILs), after which they revert to being net capital losses under 111(1)(b). See 111(8)"non-capital loss".

A formal loss determination is necessary to start the statute-barred clock ticking, if a loss is left over for a later year; but a loss need not be reported in one year to claim it in a later year. See Notes to 152(1.1).

The taxpayer has absolute discretion as to what year to apply carryovers from other years: *CCLI*, 2007 FCA 185. However, a loss can be used only based on the year it is incurred, not from when it is accepted by CRA or the Courts: VIEWS doc 2014-0533871E5. CRA audit policy on reassessing year X is to ask if the taxpayer wants to apply other years' loss carryovers to reduce year X tax; but in *Building Products*, 2020 FC 784, CRA failed to do this, BP failed to object in time, and by the time BP asked for the losses to be applied it was too late to reassess (and 152(4.2) does not apply to corporations). CRA's refusal to waive the resulting interest was held reasonable. See also 152(1.1) Notes.

For an individual, use Form T1A to carry back a loss; for a corporation, T2 Schedule 4; for a trust, Form T3A.

See 111(5) Notes re loss trading, moving losses within a corporate group, refreshing losses and other planning. See also CRA *Income Tax Audit Manual* chap. 29.

Total corporate non-capital loss carryovers were projected to cost the federal government $6.6 billion in each of 2019 and 2020, $6.8b in 2021 and $7.2b in 2022: *Report on Federal Tax Expenditures 2021*. All loss carryback claims over $200,000 are apparently referred for audit: *Posteraro*, 2014 BCPC 31, para. 15.

Where a loss carryback reverses a dividend refund, the refund can be recovered by the CRA under 160.1(1).

111(1)(a) amended from "10 years" to "20 years" by 2006 budget bill #1 (implementing a Nov. 14/05 proposal), effective for losses that arise in 2006 and later taxation years. Amended from "7 years" to "10 years" by 2004 Budget, effective for losses that arise in taxation years that end after March 22, 2004.

Remission Orders: *Kathryn Strigner Remission Order*, P.C. 2011-488 (remission of tax on condition taxpayer does not claim non-capital loss from repayment of disability income replacement benefits); *Pierre Dupuis Remission Order*, P.C. 2011-489 (remission of tax on condition taxpayer does not claim NCL from repayment of wage loss replacement benefits); *Blackberry Limited Remission Order*, P.C. 2013-1404 (Blackberry allowed to do a transaction that triggered an extra year-end without losing a carryback year); *Allan Pysher Remission Order*, P.C. 2015-54 (remission of tax on condition taxpayer does not claim NCL from repayment of disability benefits); *Céline Hamel Remission Order*, P.C. 2015-839 (same); *Marie-Rose Denis Income Tax Remission Order*, P.C. 2017-163 (same as *Dupuis*).

Income Tax Folios: S4-F8-C1: Business investment losses [replaces IT-484R2].

Interpretation Bulletins: IT-393R2: Election re tax on rents and timber royalties — non-residents. See also at end of s. 111.

Information Circulars: 88-2, para. 8: General anti-avoidance rule — section 245 of the *Income Tax Act*.

I.T. Technical News: 3 (loss utilization within a corporate group); 25 (refreshing losses).

CRA Audit Manual: 11.3.3: Application of losses; 11.3.6: Examples of loss allocation and the business investment tax credit; 29.1.0: Non-capital losses; 29.5.0: Loss carryovers.

Advance Tax Rulings: ATR-44: Utilization of deductions and credits within a related corporate group.

Forms: T1 General return, Line 25200 [former 252]; T1A: Request for loss carryback; T2 Sched. 4: Corporation loss continuity and application; T3A: Request for loss carryback by a trust.

(b) **net capital losses** — net capital losses for taxation years preceding and the three taxation years immediately following the year;

Related Provisions: 88(1.2) — Wind-up — net capital losses of subsidiary; 88(1.3) — Wind-up — computation of income of parent; 104(21)(a) — Trusts — portion of taxable capital gains deemed gain of beneficiary; 110.6(1) — "annual gains limit"; 111(1.1) — Adjustments to net capital losses; 111(2) — Net capital losses when taxpayer dies; 115(1)(c), (d) — Application of losses to non-resident; 127.52(1)(i)(i) — Limitation on deduction for minimum tax purposes; 180.01 — Election to reduce tax on stock-option shares that have dropped in value. See also at end of subsec. 111(1) and s. 111.

Notes: 111(1)(b) provides an indefinite carryforward, and 3-year carryback, of unused allowable capital losses. See 111(8)"net capital loss" and Notes to 111(1)(a). Except for the year of death, net capital losses of other years can be used only against taxable

capital gains (net of allowable capital losses); and $2,000 of pre-1986 capital losses per year can be used against other income. See 111(1.1).

A trust can carry back a net capital loss only to years where its taxable capital gains were included in its taxable income and not allocated out to beneficiaries: VIEWS doc 2006-021626117.

Income Tax Folios: S5-F2-C1: Foreign tax credit [replaces IT-270R3, IT-395R2, IT-520].

Income Tax Folios: S4-F8-C1: Business investment losses [replaces IT-484R2].

Interpretation Bulletins: IT-98R2: Investment corporations (cancelled); IT-243R4: Dividend refund to private corporations. See also at end of s. 111.

CRA Audit Manual: 11.3.3: Application of losses; 29.2.0: Capital losses; 29.5.0: Loss carryovers.

Forms: T1 General return, Line 25300 [former 253]; T3A: Request for loss carryback by a trust.

(c) **restricted farm losses** — restricted farm losses for the 20 taxation years immediately preceding and the 3 taxation years immediately following the year, but no amount is deductible for the year in respect of restricted farm losses except to the extent of the taxpayer's incomes for the year from all farming businesses carried on by the taxpayer;

Related Provisions: 31 — Loss from farming where chief source of income not from farming; 53(1)(i) — Addition to ACB of farmland; 88(1.3) — Winding-up — computation of income and tax payable by parent; 101 — Loss carryforward claimed on disposition of farmland by partnership; 115(1)(c), (d) — Application of losses to non-resident; 127.52(1)(i)(i) — Limitation on deduction for minimum tax purposes. See also at end of subsec. 111(1) and s. 111.

Notes: 111(1)(c) provides a 20-year carryforward, and 3-year carryback, of unused restricted farm losses (as defined in 31(1.1)). See Notes to 111(1)(a) and 31(1).

111(1)(c) amended from "10 years" to "20 years" by 2006 budget bill #1 (implementing a Nov. 14/05 proposal), for losses that arise in 2006 and later taxation years.

Interpretation Bulletins: See list at end of s. 111.

CRA Audit Manual: 11.3.3: Application of losses; 11.6.5 and Appendix A-11.2.23: Farm losses and restricted farm loss report; 29.5.0: Loss carryovers.

Forms: T3A: Request for loss carryback by a trust.

(d) **farm losses** — farm losses for the 20 taxation years immediately preceding and the 3 taxation years immediately following the year; and

Related Provisions: 53(1)(i) — Addition to ACB of farmland; 101 — Claim of loss after disposition of farmland by partnership; 127.52(1)(i)(i) — Limitation on deduction for minimum tax purposes.

Notes: 111(1)(d) provides a 20-year carryforward, and 3-year carryback, of unused farm and fishing losses. See 111(8)"farm loss" and Notes to 111(1)(a) and 31(1).

111(1)(d) amended from "10 years" to "20 years" by 2006 budget bill #1 (implementing a Nov. 14/05 proposal), for losses that arise in 2006 and later taxation years.

CRA Audit Manual: 11.3.3: Application of losses; 11.6.5 and Appendix A-11.2.23: Farm losses and restricted farm loss report; 29.5.0: Loss carryovers.

Forms: T3A: Request for loss carryback by a trust.

(e) **limited partnership losses** — limited partnership losses in respect of a partnership for taxation years preceding the year, but no amount is deductible for the year in respect of a limited partnership loss except to the extent of the amount by which

(i) the taxpayer's at-risk amount in respect of the partnership (within the meaning assigned by subsection 96(2.2)) at the end of the last fiscal period of the partnership ending in the taxation year

exceeds

(ii) the total of all amounts each of which is

(A) the amount required by subsection 127(8) in respect of the partnership to be added in computing the investment tax credit of the taxpayer for the taxation year,

(B) the taxpayer's share of any losses of the partnership for that fiscal period from a business or property, or

(C) the taxpayer's share of

(I) the foreign resource pool expenses, if any, incurred by the partnership in that fiscal period,

(II) the Canadian exploration expense, if any, incurred by the partnership in that fiscal period,

(III) the Canadian development expense, if any, incurred by the partnership in that fiscal period, and

(IV) the Canadian oil and gas property expense, if any, incurred by the partnership in that fiscal period.

Related Provisions [para. 111(1)(e)]: 53(2)(c)(i.1) — Reduction in ACB of partnership interest for LP loss except to the extent deducted; 88(1.1) — Wind-up — non-capital losses of subsidiary; 96(2.1) — Determination of limited partnership losses; 96(2.4) — Limited partner — extended definition; 127.52(1)(i)(i) — Limitation on deduction for minimum tax purposes. See also at end of subsec. 111(1) and s. 111.

Notes: 111(1)(e) provides an indefinite carryforward of limited partnership (LP) losses (as defined in 96(2.1)(e)) that cannot be deducted because of the "at-risk" rules. The losses can be claimed only against new capital contributions, plus future income earned by the LP; the at-risk amount (the cap in 111(1)(e)(i)) is increased by that income: 96(2.2)(b). See Notes to 96(2.1) and 111(1)(a).

111(1)(e)(ii)(C)(I) amended by 2000 Budget, for taxation years that begin after 2000.

CRA Audit Manual: 11.3.3: Application of losses; 29.5.0: Loss carryovers.

Related Provisions [subsec. 111(1)]: 111(3) — Limitations on deductibility; 111(4), (5) — Limitations where change of control of corporation or trust; 111(9) — Where taxpayer not resident in Canada; 132.2(3)(j) — No loss carryforward after mutual fund rollover; 152(6)(c) — CRA required to reassess earlier year to allow carryback; 164(5), (5.1) — Effect of carryback of loss; 164(6) — Carryback of losses of estate to deceased's year of death; 256(7) — Where control deemed not to have been acquired; 256(8) — Where share deemed to have been acquired; 261(7)(a), 261(15) — Functional currency reporting. See also at end of s. 111. For other carryovers, see under "carryforward" in Topical Index.

Interpretation Bulletins [subsec. 111(1)]: IT-232R3: Losses — their deductibility in the loss year or in other years; IT-262R2: Losses of non-residents and part-year residents; IT-302R3: Losses of a corporation — the effect that acquisitions of control, amalgamations, and windings-up have on their deductibility. See also at end of s. 111.

Forms [subsec. 111(1)]: T1A: Request for loss carryback; T2 Sched. 4: Corporation loss continuity and application; T3A: Request for loss carryback by a trust.

(1.1) [Adjustments to] Net capital losses — Notwithstanding paragraph (1)(b), the amount that may be deducted under that paragraph in computing a taxpayer's taxable income for a particular taxation year is the total of

(a) the lesser of

(i) the amount, if any, determined under paragraph 3(b) in respect of the taxpayer for the particular year, and

(ii) the total of all amounts each of which is an amount determined by the formula

$$A \times B / C$$

where

A   is the amount claimed under paragraph (1)(b) for the particular year by the taxpayer in respect of a net capital loss for a taxation year (in this paragraph referred to as the "loss year"),

B   is the fraction that would be used for the particular year under section 38 in respect of the taxpayer if the taxpayer had a capital loss for the particular year, and

C   is the fraction required to be used under section 38 in respect of the taxpayer for the loss year;

(b) where the taxpayer is an individual, the least of

(i) $2,000,

(ii) the taxpayer's pre-1986 capital loss balance for the particular year, and

(iii) the amount, if any, by which

(A) the amount claimed under paragraph (1)(b) in respect of the taxpayer's net capital losses for the particular year

exceeds

(B) the total of the amounts in respect of the taxpayer's net capital losses that, using the formula in subparagraph (a)(ii), would be required to be claimed under paragraph (1)(b) for the particular year to produce the amount determined under paragraph (a) for the particular year; and

(c) the amount, if any, that the Minister determines to be reasonable in the circumstances for the particular year and after considering the application to the taxpayer of subsections 104(21.6), 130.1(4), 131(1) and 138.1(3.2) as they read in their application to the taxpayer's last taxation year that began before November 2011.

Related Provisions: 111(2) — Year of death. See also at end of s. 111.

Notes: The basic rule for past- or future-year net capital losses is that they can only be applied against current-year taxable capital gains (net of current allowable capital losses) determined under 3(b): 111(1.1)(a)(i).

In addition, for an individual, any capital losses from before May 23, 1985 that are not yet used up can be claimed at the rate of $2,000 per year: 111(1.1)(b) and 111(8)"pre-1986 capital loss balance".

On death, 111(2)(b) amends 111(1.1)(b) for that year and the previous year so that *all* unused capital losses can be used, except to the extent the taxpayer claimed the capital gains exemption in earlier years. Thus, any net capital losses not previously used can offset business, employment or other income for those years.

111(1.1)(c) amended by 2002-2013 technical bill (Part 5 — technical) for tax years that begin after Oct. 2011; added by same bill, for 2000 and later tax years.

111(1.1) amended by 1991 technical bill, retroactive to 1985.

Interpretation Bulletins: IT-232R3: Losses — their deductibility in the loss year or in other years; IT-262R2: Losses of non-residents and part-year residents. See also at end of s. 111.

(2) Year of death — Where a taxpayer dies in a taxation year, for the purpose of computing the taxpayer's taxable income for that year and the immediately preceding taxation year, the following rules apply:

(a) paragraph (1)(b) shall be read as follows:

"(b) the taxpayer's net capital losses for all taxation years not claimed for the purpose of computing the taxpayer's taxable income for any other taxation year;"; and

(b) paragraph (1.1)(b) shall be read as follows:

"(b) the amount, if any, by which

(i) the amount claimed under paragraph (1)(b) in respect of the taxpayer's net capital losses for the particular year

exceeds the total of

(ii) all amounts in respect of the taxpayer's net capital losses that, using the formula in subparagraph (a)(ii), would be required to be claimed under paragraph (1)(b) for the particular year to produce the amount determined under paragraph (a) for the particular year, and

(iii) all amounts each of which is an amount deducted under section 110.6 in computing the taxpayer's taxable income for a taxation year, except to the extent that, where the particular year is the year in which the taxpayer died, the amount, if any, by which the amount determined under subparagraph (i) in respect of the taxpayer for the immediately preceding taxation year exceeds the amount so determined under subparagraph (ii)."

Notes: 111(2) allows deduction of unused capital loss carryovers against any income source for the year of death and the previous year. See IT-232R3 para. 30 and VIEWS doc 2017-0690651E5.

111(2) amended by 1991 technical bill, retroactive to 1985.

Interpretation Bulletins: IT-232R3: Losses — their deductibility in the loss year or in other years. See also at end of s. 111.

(3) Limitation on deductibility — For the purposes of subsection (1),

(a) an amount in respect of a non-capital loss, restricted farm loss, farm loss or limited partnership loss, as the case may be, for a taxation year is deductible, and an amount in respect of a net capital loss for a taxation year may be claimed, in computing the taxable income of a taxpayer for a particular taxation year only to the extent that it exceeds the total of

(i) amounts deducted under this section in respect of that non-capital loss, restricted farm loss, farm loss or limited partnership loss in computing taxable income for taxation years preceding the particular taxation year,

(i.1) the amount that was claimed under paragraph (1)(b) in respect of that net capital loss for taxation years preceding the particular taxation year, and

(ii) amounts claimed in respect of that loss under paragraph 186(1)(c) for the year in which the loss was incurred or under paragraph 186(1)(d) for the particular taxation year and taxation years preceding the particular taxation year, and

(b) no amount is deductible in respect of a non-capital loss, net capital loss, restricted farm loss, farm loss or limited partnership loss, as the case may be, for a taxation year until

(i) in the case of a non-capital loss, the deductible non-capital losses,

(ii) in the case of a net capital loss, the deductible net capital losses,

(iii) in the case of a restricted farm loss, the deductible restricted farm losses,

(iv) in the case of a farm loss, the deductible farm losses, and

(v) in the case of a limited partnership loss, the deductible limited partnership losses,

for preceding taxation years have been deducted.

Related Provisions: 87(2.1)(b) — Determining loss after amalgamation; 88(1.1) — Non-capital losses of subsidiary; 88(1.2) — Net capital losses of subsidiary; 88(1.3) — Winding-up — computation of income and tax payable by parent; 149(10)(c) — No loss carryover on corp becoming or ceasing to be exempt. See also at end of s. 111.

Notes: 111(3)(b) did not restrict a taxpayer from carrying forward a loss that could not be carried back to a statute-barred year: *CCLI (1994) Inc.*, 2007 FCA 185. However, CRA will not reassess to change a loss application to a nil-assessed year; VIEWS doc 2013-0504491I7 (see Notes to 152(1.1)).

Opening words of 111(3)(a) amended by 1991 technical bill, retroactive to 1985.

Interpretation Bulletins: IT-232R3: Losses — their deductibility in the loss year or in other years; IT-262R2: Losses of non-residents and part-year residents; IT-302R3: Losses of a corporation — the effect that acquisitions of control, amalgamations, and windings-up have on their deductibility. See also at end of s. 111.

(4) Loss restriction event [change in control] — capital losses — Notwithstanding subsection (1), and subject to subsection (5.5), if at any time (in this subsection referred to as "that time") a taxpayer is subject to a loss restriction event,

(a) no amount in respect of a net capital loss for a taxation year that ended before that time is deductible in computing the taxpayer's taxable income for a taxation year that ends after that time;

(b) no amount in respect of a net capital loss for a taxation year that ends after that time is deductible in computing the taxpayer's taxable income for a taxation year that ends before that time;

(c) in computing the adjusted cost base to the taxpayer at and after that time of each capital property, other than a depreciable property, of the taxpayer immediately before that time, there is to be deducted the amount, if any, by which the adjusted cost base to the taxpayer of the property immediately before that time exceeds its fair market value immediately before that time;

(d) each amount required by paragraph (c) to be deducted in computing the adjusted cost base to the taxpayer of a property is deemed to be a capital loss of the taxpayer for the taxation year that ended immediately before that time from the disposition of the property;

(e) if the taxpayer designates — in its return of income under this Part for the taxation year that ended immediately before that time or in a prescribed form filed with the Minister on or before the day that is 90 days after the day on which a notice of assessment of tax payable for the year or notification that no tax is payable for the year is sent to the taxpayer — a property that was a capital property of the taxpayer immediately before that time (other than a property in respect of which an amount would, but for this paragraph, be required by paragraph (c) to be deducted in computing its adjusted cost base to the taxpayer or a depreciable property of a prescribed class to which, but for this paragraph, subsection (5.1) would apply),

(i) the taxpayer is deemed to have disposed of the property at the time that is immediately before the time that is immedi-

ately before that time for proceeds of disposition equal to the lesser of

(A) the fair market value of the property immediately before that time, and

(B) the greater of the adjusted cost base to the taxpayer of the property immediately before the disposition and such amount as is designated by the taxpayer in respect of the property,

(ii) subject to subparagraph (iii), the taxpayer is deemed to have reacquired the property at that time at a cost equal to those proceeds of disposition, and

(iii) if the property is depreciable property of the taxpayer the capital cost of which to the taxpayer immediately before the disposition exceeds those proceeds of disposition, for the purposes of sections 13 and 20 and any regulations made for the purposes of paragraph 20(1)(a),

(A) the capital cost of the property to the taxpayer at that time is deemed to be the amount that was its capital cost immediately before the disposition, and

(B) the excess is deemed to have been allowed to the taxpayer in respect of the property under regulations made for the purposes of paragraph 20(1)(a) in computing the taxpayer's income for taxation years that ended before that time; and

(f) for the purposes of the definition "capital dividend account" in subsection 89(1), each amount that because of paragraph (d) or (e) is a capital loss or gain of the taxpayer from a disposition of a property for the taxation year that ended immediately before that time is deemed to be a capital loss or gain, as the case may be, of the taxpayer from the disposition of the property immediately before the time that a capital property of the taxpayer in respect of which paragraph (e) would be applicable would be deemed by that paragraph to have been disposed of by the taxpayer.

Related Provisions: 13(7)(f) — Rules applicable to depreciable property; 53(2)(b.2) — Reduction in ACB; 53(4) — Effect on ACB of share, partnership interest or trust interest; 87(2.1)(b) — Determining loss after amalgamation; 107(1.1)(b)(ii) — Deemed cost of income interest in trust; 110.1(1.2) — Parallel rule for charitable donation credits; 111(5) — Parallel rule for non-capital losses; 111(5.5) — Anti-avoidance rule; 111(12) — Gain or loss on foreign debt after change in control; 244(14), (14.1) — Date when notice sent; 249(3.1) — Deemed year end on becoming or ceasing to be CCPC; 249(4) — Deemed year end where change of control occurs; 251.2 — Loss restriction event; Reg. 5905(5.2), (5.3) — Rule where foreign affiliate is acquired. See also at end of s. 111 and under "Control of corporation: change of" in Topical Index.

Notes: See Notes to 111(5). The purpose of 111(4) is the same: capital losses cannot be carried either forward to after a change in control (now called a "loss restriction event"), nor back to before one. 111(4)(c)-(d) trigger accrued losses on capital property, so the cost base of the property is written down and thus the accrued loss also cannot be used after the change in control. However, 111(4)(e) provides an election to realize capital gains to offset the capital losses that will otherwise disappear on the change in control, to bump up the cost base of the gain properties. For this purpose, land and building can be treated as separate properties: VIEWS doc 2008-0304991E5; and goodwill qualifies since it is now Class 14.1 property: 2017-0709141C6 [2017 APFF q.15]; 2020-0841791I7 (internally generated goodwill; Class 12 intellectual property also). See also 2011-0421491I7 (interaction with 96(2.2), (2.3)); 2012-0452821R3 and 2012-0462141R3 (111(4)(d) applies); 2012-0454161C6 (no adjustment to capital dividend account to reflect net capital losses being lost on change in control); 2015-0581641C6 [2015 IFA q.10] (111(4)(e) designation and 212.3).

See Notes to 111(12) re the deadline for a designation under 111(4)(e) where an election is made to have 111(12) apply from 2006.

For a corporation filing Quebec returns, a designation under para. (e) must be copied to Revenu Québec: *Taxation Act* ss. 736, 21.4.6.

111(4) amended by 2013 budget bill #2 (effective March 21, 2013, to change references from control of a corp being acquired to "loss restriction event" (251.2(2)) so as to apply to trusts); 2010 budget bill #2; 1991 technical bill.

Interpretation Bulletins: IT-302R3: Losses of a corporation — the effect that acquisitions of control, amalgamations, and windings-up have on their deductibility. See also at end of s. 111.

I.T. Technical News: 7 (control by a group — 50/50 arrangement); 9 (loss consolidation within a corporate group); 30 (corporate loss utilization transactions).

Forms: T2 Sched. 6: Summary of dispositions of capital property.

(5) Loss restriction event [change in control] — non-capital losses and farm losses — If at any time a taxpayer is subject to a loss restriction event,

(a) no amount in respect of the taxpayer's non-capital loss or farm loss for a taxation year that ended before that time is deductible by the taxpayer for a taxation year that ends after that time, except that the portion of the taxpayer's non-capital loss or farm loss, as the case may be, for a taxation year that ended before that time as may reasonably be regarded as the taxpayer's loss from carrying on a business and, if a business was carried on by the taxpayer in that year, the portion of the non-capital loss as may reasonably be regarded as being in respect of an amount deductible under paragraph 110(1)(k) in computing the taxpayer's taxable income for that year is deductible by the taxpayer for a particular taxation year that ends after that time

  (i) only if that business was carried on by the taxpayer for profit or with a reasonable expectation of profit throughout the particular year, and

  (ii) only to the extent of the total of the taxpayer's income for the particular year from

   (A) that business, and

   (B) if properties were sold, leased, rented or developed or services rendered in the course of carrying on that business before that time, any other business substantially all the income of which was derived from the sale, leasing, rental or development, as the case may be, of similar properties or the rendering of similar services; and

(b) no amount in respect of the taxpayer's non-capital loss or farm loss for a taxation year that ends after that time is deductible by the taxpayer for a taxation year that ended before that time, except that the portion of the taxpayer's non-capital loss or farm loss, as the case may be, for a taxation year that ended after that time as may reasonably be regarded as the taxpayer's loss from carrying on a business and, if a business was carried on by the taxpayer in that year, the portion of the non-capital loss as may reasonably be regarded as being in respect of an amount deductible under paragraph 110(1)(k) in computing the taxpayer's taxable income for that year is deductible by the taxpayer for a particular taxation year that ends before that time

  (i) only if throughout the taxation year and in the particular year that business was carried on by the taxpayer for profit or with a reasonable expectation of profit, and

  (ii) only to the extent of the taxpayer's income for the particular year from

   (A) that business, and

   (B) if properties were sold, leased, rented or developed or services rendered in the course of carrying on that business before that time, any other business substantially all the income of which was derived from the sale, leasing, rental or development, as the case may be, of similar properties or the rendering of similar services.

Related Provisions: 10(11) — Adventure in the nature of trade deemed to be business carried on by corporation or trust; 69(11) — Restriction on loss consolidation outside corporate group; 87(2.1)(b) — Determining loss after amalgamation; 110.1(1.2) — Parallel rule for charitable donation credits; 111(4) — Parallel rule for capital losses; 111(12) — Gain or loss on foreign debt after change in control; 249(3.1) — Deemed year end on becoming or ceasing to be CCPC; 249(4) — Deemed year end when change of control occurs; 251.2 — Loss restriction event. See also at end of 111(1) and of s. 111.

Notes: 111(5) is designed to limit "trading" in loss corporations or trusts, where an entity is acquired for its loss carryforwards and the assets of a profitable business are rolled into it (e.g., under 85(1)), so that the losses soak up the profits from the business. 111(5) was extended to trusts in 2013 by changing "control of a corporation has been acquired" to "a taxpayer is subject to a loss restriction event": see Notes to 251.2(2). Note that acquisition by a related person generally does not trigger a change of control: 256(7)(a)(i)(B). See also 256(7)-(9) and 256.1 re acquisition of control.

For similar rules (e.g., 88(1.1) for windups, 111(4) for capital losses, 110.1(1.2) for charitable donation credits), see Topical Index under "Control of corporation: change of", and "Loss restriction event". Similar rules apply in the US under *Internal Revenue*

Code §382. Income trust unwindings in 2008-10 involved mergers with loss companies that avoided 111(5) (see Notes to 85.1(8)); this led to the 2010 amendments to 256(7).

(Other reasons to shift income and expenses include "tax rate arbitrage" by moving income to lower-tax provinces; using up undepreciated capital cost with CCA; and using non-refundable SR&ED tax credits. See also Notes to 247(2) re transfer pricing.)

If 111(5) applies, CRA will reassess to deny claimed losses in later years, but will not reassess the acquisition year to change the loss: VIEWS doc 2012-0437901I7 (and see Notes to 152(1.1)).

Provided the *same* business is still carried on with reasonable expectation of profit, 111(5) allows past losses against income from that or a "similar" business. This recognizes that reviving a failed business is a positive goal (despite the loss trading). Loss carryforwards were allowed in: *Gaz Métropolitain*, [1999] 2 C.T.C. 2116 (TCC) (company converting vehicles to run on natural gas was held to have sale of natural gas as its principal activity, for the same rule under 88(1)); *Crystal Beach*, 2006 TCC 183 (amusement park that became condominium and marina was the same business of "exploitation of a recreational site"); *S.T.B. Holdings*, 2011 TCC 144 (land speculation and land development were same business for 88(1.1)(e)). They were disallowed in: *Manac Inc.*, [1998] 4 C.T.C. 60 (FCA) (trailer panels and trailers were not same business); *NRT Technology*, 2013 FCA 221 (purchased company's business of Telepanel electronic shelf labels had ended, although buyer used the technology in other applications). See also VIEWS docs 2005-0113461R3, 2005-0140981C6, 2006-0172311R3; 2017-0695131C6 [2017 CPTS q.4] (oil & gas industry); Notes to Reg. 1101(1) re "same business"; Nijhawan, "When is Loss Trading Permissible?", 2015 Cdn Tax Foundation conference report, 9:1-26.

GAAR applied to schemes circumventing 111(5) in *Mathew (Kaulius)* and *OSFC Holdings* (the policy prohibiting transfer of losses outside a corporate group is clear), *Water's Edge*, *MacKay*, and *Birchcliff Energy*; and did not apply in *Husky Oil*, *Deans Knight* and *MMV Capital*. See Notes to 245(2) for these cases. In VIEWS doc 2011-0392171R3, 111(5) did not prevent pre-amalgamation losses from being claimed by the new corp, but CRA applied GAAR to debt capitalization transactions considered to misuse s. 80. Other anti-avoidance provisions can also apply to sales of tax losses: 69(11), 112(2.4), 256(7)(b), (c), 256(8).

In 2011-0392171R3, 111(5) did not prevent pre-amalgamation losses from being claimed by the new corp, but GAAR applied to pre-amalgamation debt capitalization transactions considered to be an abuse of s. 80.

Loss consolidations: CRA generally accepts plans that shift losses within a corporate group. See Information Circular 88-2 paras. 8, 9; *Income Tax Technical News* 3, 30 ("Corporate Loss Utilization Transactions"); Advance Tax Ruling ATR-44; 1994 Cdn Tax Foundation conference report p. 47:2; VIEWS doc 2014-0522251E5 (key criterion "is the existence of other assets in the parent company that can generate sufficient income to pay the dividends on the preferred shares held by the subsidiary"). For rulings approving such plans see 2004-0089181R3, 2004-0088541R3, 2004-0098071R3, 2004-0098561R3, 2004-0101341R3, 2005-0118951R3, 2005-0132891R3, 2005-0134461R3, 2005-0139621R3, 2005-0152431E5, 2005-0155451R3, 2005-0158931R3, 2005-0160471R3, 2006-0171291R3, 2006-0178651R3, 2006-0179471R3, 2006-0180321R3 (preferred share debt loop), 2006-0184571R3, 2006-0185221R3, 2006-0192521R3, 2006-0198421R3, 2006-0219051R3, 2007-0220051R3, 2007-0226151R3, 2007-0226931R3, 2007-0227931R3, 2007-0243471R3, 2007-0248301R3, 2007-0248441R3, 2007-0249251E5, 2007-0252501R3, 2008-0266221R3, 2008-0273471R3, 2008-0279991R3, 2008-0280391R3, 2008-0284621R3, 2008-0289761R3 ("standard loss consolidation ruling without significant provincial allocation issues"), 2008-0289771R3, 2008-0295751R3 (set-offs of notes at redemption are acceptable), 2008-0297571R3, 2008-0299591R3, 2008-0304741R3 (arrangement using a partnership), 2008-0304881R3 [Yull, "Utilizing Losses within an Affiliated Group", 6(10) *Tax Hyperion [TH]* (Carswell, Oct. 2009)], 2008-0312611R3, 2009-0308921R3, 2009-0317831R3, 2009-0324861R3 (standard shift of current-year losses to affiliate through interest expense on intercorporate debt), 2009-0344191R3, 2009-0347041R3, 2009-0332571R3 [Cyna, "Related but Unaffiliated Companies and Loss Consolidation", 8(1) *TH* (Jan. 2011)], 2010-0353911R3, 2010-0355031R3, 2010-0355671R3, 2010-0364221R3 (loss consolidation using LP), 2010-0367251R3, 2010-0370751R3, 2010-0371661R3, 2010-0375301R3, 2010-0379631R3, 2010-0389321R3, 2010-0390291R3, 2011-0408241R3, 2011-0409601R3, 2011-0411821R3, 2011-0416921R3, 2011-0425461R3, 2011-0422481R3, 2011-0426581R3, 2011-0427951R3, 2011-0431851R3 (and supp. 2012-0472151R3), 2012-0437881R3, 2012-0439191R3, 2012-0451431R3, 2012-0458671R3, 2012-0472291R3, 2013-0458091R3 (multiple Losscos and 3 Profitcos), 2013-0483051R3, 2013-0483491R3 (limited-recourse loan to comply with debt indenture), 2013-0483601R3, 2013-0496351R3, 2013-0498551R3, 2013-0504301R3, 2013-0505431R3, 2013-0511991R3, 2013-0512321R3, 2013-0515351R3, 2014-0518451R3; 2014-0525081R3, 2014-0525441R3 (arrangement unwound after less than a month), 2014-0536651R3, 2014-0543911R3, 2014-0547181R3, 2014-0554411R3, 2014-0556781R3, 2014-0563151R3, 2015-0564731R3 [revised 2015-0622091R3, 2018-0765041R3, 2018-0784941R3], 2015-0569861R3, 2015-0576421R3, 2015-0582101R3, 2015-0593341R3, 2015-0596971R3, 2015-0604071R3, 2015-0611061R3, 2015-0624601R3, 2016-0626531R3, 2016-0640371R3, 2016-0645351R3, 2016-0652041R3, 2016-0663831R3, 2016-0671701R3 [2018-0768161R3], 2016-0673141R3, 2016-0680261R3, 2017-0688351R3, 2017-0706211R3 [2018-0766701R3] (annual shifting of losses from Losscos in group), 2017-0711911R3, 2018-0741691R3, 2018-0742641R3, 2018-0771891R3, 2018-0772921R3 (moving capital losses), 2018-0777621R3, 2018-0781971R3, 2018-0782751R3, 2018-0788031R3, 2019-0794891R3, 2019-0818291R3 [2020-0869891R3]; 2019-0819871R3 (US corp with Canadian branch continuing into ULC); 2019-0819971R3; 2019-

0834901R3 (Profitco transfers depreciable property to Lossco at cost and gets it back at FMV); 2019-0835141R3, 2020-0865971R3. A ruling was refused where Lossco did not have the borrowing capacity required: 2007-0253031E5. Finance was considering legislation to permit loss consolidations within groups, but has dropped the idea: see below.

Budgets 2010 and 2012, under "Taxation of Corporate Groups", announced that Canada would consider a formal system of loss transfers or consolidated reporting. After consultation, Budget 2013 announced that no changes will be made. See also Finance news release 2010-112, "Minister of Finance Announces Public Consultations on the Taxation of Corporate Groups" (Nov. 23, 2010) with 37-page consultation paper; TEI letters to Finance, Oct. 6, 2010 and April 8, 2011; "Policy Forum", 59(2) *Canadian Tax Journal [CTJ]* 239-313 (2011); Ting, "The Unthinkable Policy Option?", 59(3) *CTJ* 421-62 (2011); Pantaleo & Johns, "Toward a New System for the Taxation of Corporate Groups", 2010 Cdn Tax Foundation conference report, 35:1-38; Ting, *The Taxation of Corporate Groups Under Consolidation: An International Comparison* (Cambridge University Press, 2013, 321 pp.), reviewed at 61(4) *CTJ* 1243-44 (2013).

CRA requires a "positive spread between the interest paid and the dividends earned" to provide a ruling; and will consider ruling requests where the corporations are related and/or affiliated: doc 2014-0546911C6 [2014 CTF q.2].

CRA ruling 2003-0031823 and supplementary rulings 2004-0056501 and 2004-0069151R3 were reportedly issued to allow MDS Inc. to use $300 million in losses of Hemosol Corp.

CRA rejected attempted loss consolidations in doc 2012-0454061C6.

Losses from property cannot be carried forward: doc 2011-0401721I7.

Provincial impact: CRA stated at the 2005 CTF conference (*Income Tax Technical News* 34) that ruling requests must now contain analysis of the provincial tax implications (shifting income to low-tax provinces); CRA will discuss the ruling with the province, except AB and QC since it does not have Tax Collection Agreements with them. At the 2008 conference (report p. 3:18; *Technical News* 41), CRA said that before issuing a ruling, Rulings will "recommend practitioners obtain comfort from provincial tax authorities to minimize the risk of double taxation". At the 2009 conference, q.22 (report, 3:19-20; *Technical News* 44), CRA said "incidental" shifting of provincial income on a typical loss consolidation is acceptable, but on deliberate shifting to a lower-rate province, "provincial concerns will have to be considered". The 2013 Budget, in announcing no loss consolidation regime will be introduced (above), stated: "the Government will continue to work with provinces and territories regarding their concerns about the uncertainty of the cost associated with the current approach to loss utilization". If a main reason for an arrangement is to shift income among provinces, CRA may challenge it under provincial GAAR: 2014 conference roundtable, q.2. Some of the rulings listed above now include provincial GAAR rulings.

Income Tax Folio S3-F6-C1 ¶1.71-1.75 and *Income Tax Technical News* 30 discuss loss consolidations.

The Auditor General's fall 2009 report (oag-bvg.gc.ca), Chap. 3, §3.46 raised concerns about "tech-wreck" restructurings, where losses are traded within the technology sector. CRA has asked Finance to address this issue. (256.1, introduced in 2013, is a partial solution.) See also *Income Tax Technical News* 34. In *Cormark Securities*, [2012] 3 C.T.C. 49 (FC), CRA was allowed to obtain information about such deals from a company that was involved in them.

Other ways to use up losses in a group can include: paying intercompany fees (see 67 Notes); intercompany loans paying interest; amalgamating corps (see 87(2.1) Notes); liquidating a subsidiary (see 88(1.1), 111(5.4)); transferring assets with accrued gains; transferring business assets that generate income. Moving equipment from Xco to Yco in the same group, with Xco still running the equipment under an agency agreement, worked in *J.D. Irving Ltd.*, 2020 QCCQ 2423 (it was not "leasing property" under the Quebec version of Reg. 1100(15)).

"Refreshing" losses that would otherwise expire, by cycling funds and interest expense within a corporate group to use up the losses and create new losses elsewhere, can be acceptable if 111(5) is not being circumvented and the loss is being deducted within the original carryforward period: *Income Tax Technical News* 25 [2002 CTF conference report pp. 15:12-13]. See 2007-0251081E5 on using options to refresh losses. Refreshing nearly-expired losses or resurrecting expired losses to extend the carryforward period by amending past CCA claims (using 111(5.1), IC84-1 paras. 9-10 or 152(4.2)) is disallowed as "retroactive tax planning" that undermines the time limits in 111(1): VIEWS docs 2001-0090213, 2013-047411I7; 2013 Cdn Tax Foundation conference Roundtable (Jeff Sadrian); *St. Benedict Trust*, 2020 TCC 109 (under appeal to FCA).

See Richardson et al., *Taxation of Private Corporations and their Shareholders* (ctf.ca, 5th ed., 2020), chap. 17; Stadtegger, "Corporate Loss Utilization", 2003 Cdn Tax Foundation conference report, 30:1-19; Finkelstein & Nixon, "Takeovers", 2004 conference report at 21:14-59; Rowe and Bond, "Loss Utilization And Acquisition Of Control" 19 *Canadian Petroleum Tax Journal [CPTJ]* (2006) §2; Forget, "Strategies and Issues Relating to the Transfer of Businesses or Assets Within a Corporate Group", 2007 conference report, 7:1-27; Finnigan & Blom, "Use of Corporate Losses", 2007 Prairie Provinces Tax Conference [PPTC] (ctf.ca), 11:1-26; Munoz, "Loss Utilization in Arm's-Length Business Combinations", 57(3) *Canadian Tax Journal* 660-98 (2009); Power et al., "Loss Utilization Strategies within a Related Group", 2009 Atlantic Provinces Tax Conf. 4A:1-28; Man & Tse, "Tax in Troubled Times", 2009 BC Tax Conf. [BCTC] 5:1-40; Truster, "Effective Loss Utilization within a Closely Held Group", 2009 Ontario Tax Conf. 4:1-16; Burghardt & Chiu, "Loss is Just a Four Letter Word", 2013 conference report, 14:1-43; Bodie & Novotny, "Acquisitions of Control", 2013

PPTC 6:1-27; Jamal, "Revisiting Affiliated Group Loss Consolidations: Effective Strategies & Techniques", 2013 BCTC 3:1-34; Wharram, "Loss Utilization", 2013 Ontario Tax Conf. 4:1-33; Baxter, "Loss Consolidation Transactions", 11(5) *Tax Hyperion* (Carswell) 1-3 (May 2014); Lindsay & Couture, "Update on Planning With Losses", 27(1) *CPTJ* (2014); Ross & Weaver, "Introduction to Losses", *YP Focus Virtual Conference* (ctf.ca, Sept. 2020), 1:1-48. See also 251.2(2) Notes.

The flip side of loss trading, gain trading, is caught by 69(11) in some cases. Gain trading was not subject to GAAR in *Loyens*, 2003 TCC 214.

De jure control: Duha Printers, [1998] 3 C.T.C. 303 (SCC), held that "control" under 111(5) means *de jure* (legal) control, so 111(5) was averted through a scheme that maintained technical control despite a shareholders' agreement that affected real control. (This would now be caught by 256.1(6).) The SCC stated that *de jure* control is normally found by determining who can elect a majority of the board from the articles, by-laws and share register, but one must also look at a unanimous shareholders' agreement (UShA), which is a constating document that supplants the long-standing principle of shareholder non-interference with the directors' powers to manage the corp. See Ewens, "Relevance of Shareholders' Agreements in Interpreting Acquisition of Control", IV(3) *Corporate Structures & Groups* (Federated Press) 220-24 (1997). In *Sedona Networks*, 2007 FCA 169, a voting agreement by all shareholders was held not to be a UShA because it did not restrict the directors' powers. In *Kruger Wayagamack*, 2015 TCC 90, paras. 44-70 (aff'd on other grounds 2016 FCA 192), a UShA that gave KW power to elect 3 of 5 directors did not give it *de jure* control, because the UShA required many decisions to have unanimous director or shareholder approval. CRA says it will apply GAAR to *Duha*-like schemes (1998 Cdn Tax Foundation conference report, p. 52:21). See also VIEWS docs 2009-031435117 (specific UShA did not remove control from majority shareholder), 2009-034333117 (agreement is not a UShA); CRA Round Table, 2010 conference report, q.34, p. 4:30; Lamarre, "Unanimous Shareholder Agreements and CCPC Status" (2010), on davidsherman.ca/files. Note that a bequest of shares on death in violation of a UShA is valid: *Frye v. Frye Estate*, 2008 ONCA 606 (leave to appeal denied 2009 CanLII 4209 (SCC)). See also Nitikman, "Who has *De Jure* Control of a Corporation When Its Shares Are Held by a Limited Partnership?", 59(4) *Canadian Tax Journal* 765-82 (2011); Goldberg, "Part 1 ... The Impact of Control", 2457 *Tax Topics* (CCH) 1-4 (April 11, 2019); Keey, *Checklist 1 — Acquisition of Control, Taxnet Pro* Corporate Tax Centre (2020, 34pp). CRA ruled in 2011-0402571R3 (also 2012 CTF conference report, p. 5:14) that "control in the long run", via the ability to do a consolidation squeeze-out, is *de jure* control. In *MMV Capital*, 2020 TCC 82 (under appeal by Crown to FCA), taking on a new business to use up losses, transferring all the equity but only 48% of the votes, did not trigger GAAR.

In *Silicon Graphics*, 2002 FCA 260, dispersed ownership by non-residents was not "control". Thus, a minor change in a corp's ownership should not constitute change in control. Similarly, in *Crystal Beach*, 2006 TCC 183, two shareholders were held not to have sufficient common connection to be a "group of persons". In *Alberta Printed Circuits*, 2011 TCC 232, para. 93, a Barbados corp was held to be controlled by the Canadian beneficiaries of an insurance policy that owned the corp's parent. In *Bresse Syndics (CO2 Solution)*, 2021 FCA 115, Xco controlled Yco because Yco was owned by a trust whose trustees had to be directors of Xco [Arrigo, "Troubling Interpretation", 10(2) *Canadian Tax Focus* (ctf.ca) 4-5 (May 2020)].

For the meaning of "derived" in 111(5)(a)(ii), see Notes to 18.1(12).

See also Couzin, "Some Reflections on Corporate Control", 53(2) *Canadian Tax Journal* 305-32 (2005); Brender, "Developments in the Concept of Corporate Control", 2007 Cdn Tax Foundation conference report, 31:1-52; McDougall & Lai, "Selected Aspects of Corporate Control", 2010 conference report, 11:1-38; Notes to 125(7)"Canadian-controlled private corporation"; Wen, "Control and Acquisition of Control", *YP Focus Virtual Conference* (ctf.ca, Sept. 2020), 3C:1-31.

See also VIEWS docs 2009-0308611R3 (no acquisition of control on transfer to executors of estate); 2012-0454111C6 [2012 APFF q.17] (trigger of power of attorney on incapacity ("homologation of the mandate", in Quebec) does not cause change in control); 2013-0494981E5 (whether beneficiary B having right to replace trustee gives B control of corp held by trust).

A change in trustees of a trust that owns shares may change control: *Consolidated Holding*, [1972] C.T.C. 18 (SCC). CRA says that replacing even one trustee changes control, as the trustees form a group due to fiduciary obligations: *Income Tax Technical News* 34, 38; VIEWS docs 2004-0087761E5, 2007-0240431C6, 2007-0255461C6, 2011-0401931C6 (except where 256(7)(a) applies). (IT-302R3 para. 10 may be withdrawn.) This issue has been raised with Finance. See also Brender, above at 31:8-15. See Notes to 250(1) re where a trust is resident.

For more on control and change in control see Notes to 251(2), 251.2(2) and 256(7).

CRA considers that "substantially all", used in 111(5)(a)(ii), (b)(ii), means 90% or more.

111(5) amended by 2013 budget bill #2, effective March 21, 2013, to refer to a "loss restriction event" so as to extend the rule to trusts (see Notes to 251.2(2)).

Interpretation Bulletins: IT-206R: Separate businesses; IT-302R3: Losses of a corporation — the effect that acquisitions of control, amalgamations, and windings-up have on their deductibility. See also at end of s. 111.

I.T. Technical News: 7 (control by a group — 50/50 arrangement); 9 (loss consolidation within a corporate group); 16 (*Duha Printers* case); 25 (refreshing losses); 30 (corporate loss utilization transactions); 34 (loss consolidation — unanimous shareholder agreements; sale of tax losses; change in trustees and control); 38 (control of corporation owned by income trust — impact of change in trustees); 41 (loss consolidation and provincial GAAR); 44 (loss consolidation).

Advance Tax Rulings: ATR-7: Amalgamation involving losses and control; ATR-44: Utilization of deductions and credits within a related corporate group.

(5.1) Loss restriction event — UCC computation — Subject

to subsection (5.5), if at any time a taxpayer is subject to a loss restriction event and, if this Act were read without reference to subsection 13(24), the undepreciated capital cost to the taxpayer of depreciable property of a prescribed class immediately before that time would have exceeded the total of

(a) the fair market value of all the property of that class immediately before that time, and

(b) the amount in respect of property of that class otherwise allowed under regulations made under paragraph 20(1)(a) or deductible under subsection 20(16) in computing the taxpayer's income for the taxation year that ended immediately before that time,

the excess is to be deducted in computing the taxpayer's income for the taxation year that ended immediately before that time and is deemed to have been allowed in respect of property of that class under regulations made under paragraph 20(1)(a).

Related Provisions: 87(2.1)(b) — Determining loss after amalgamation; 111(5.5) — Anti-avoidance rule; 251.2 — Loss restriction event. See also at end of s. 111.

Notes: For CRA interpretation of 111(5.1) see VIEWS doc 2006-0195951C6. See Notes to 111(5) re using 111(5.1) to resurrect expired losses.

111(5.1) amended by 2013 budget bill #2, effective March 21, 2013, to extend its application to trusts (by referring to a "loss restriction event" instead of control of a corporation being acquired: see Notes to 251.2(2)).

Interpretation Bulletins: IT-302R3: Losses of a corporation — the effect that acquisitions of control, amalgamations, and windings-up have on their deductibility. See also at end of s. 111.

I.T. Technical News: 7 (control by a group — 50/50 arrangement); 9 (loss consolidation within a corporate group); 30 (corporate loss utilization transactions).

(5.2) [Repealed]

Notes: 111(5.2) repealed by 2016 budget bill #2, effective 2017, as part of changing the eligible capital property rules to CCA Class 14.1 (see Notes to 20(1)(b)). From March 21, 2013 through 2016, read:

(5.2) Loss restriction event — CEC computation — Subject to subsection (5.5), if at any time a taxpayer is subject to a loss restriction event and immediately before that time the taxpayer's cumulative eligible capital in respect of a business exceeds the total of

(a) ¾ of the fair market value of the eligible capital property in respect of the business, and

(b) the amount otherwise deducted under paragraph 20(1)(b) in computing the taxpayer's income from the business for the taxation year that ended immediately before that time,

the excess is to be deducted under paragraph 20(1)(b) in computing the taxpayer's income for the taxation year that ended immediately before that time.

111(5.2) amended by 2013 budget bill #2, effective March 21, 2013, to extend its application to trusts (by referring to a "loss restriction event" instead of control of a corporation being acquired: see Notes to 251.2(2)).

(5.3) Loss restriction event — doubtful debts and bad debts — Subject to subsection (5.5), if at any time a taxpayer is subject to a loss restriction event,

(a) no amount may be deducted under paragraph 20(1)(l) in computing the taxpayer's income for the taxation year that ended immediately before that time; and

(b) in respect of each debt owing to the taxpayer immediately before that time

(i) the amount that is the greatest amount that would, but for this subsection and subsection 26(2) of this Act and subsection 33(1) of the *Income Tax Act*, chapter 148 of the Revised Statutes of Canada, 1952, have been deductible under paragraph 20(1)(l)

(A) is deemed to be a separate debt, and

(B) notwithstanding any other provision of this Act, is to be deducted as a bad debt under paragraph 20(1)(p) in computing the taxpayer's income for its taxation year that ended immediately before that time, and

(ii) the amount by which the debt exceeds that separate debt is deemed to be a separate debt incurred at the same time and under the same circumstances as the debt was incurred.

Related Provisions: 50(1)(a) — Deemed disposition where debt becomes bad debt; 87(2.1)(b) — Determining loss after amalgamation; 88(1.1) — Non-capital losses, etc., of subsidiary; 111(5.5) — Anti-avoidance rule; 251.2 — Loss restriction event. See also at end of s. 111.

Notes: 111(5.3) amended by 2013 budget bill #2, effective March 21, 2013, to extend its application to trusts (by referring to a "loss restriction event" instead of control of a corporation being acquired: see Notes to 251.2(2)).

I.T. Application Rules: 69 (meaning of "chapter 148 of ...").

Interpretation Bulletins: IT-302R3: Losses of a corporation — the effect that acquisitions of control, amalgamations, and windings-up have on their deductibility.

I.T. Technical News: 7 (control by a group — 50/50 arrangement); 9 (loss consolidation within a corporate group).

(5.4) Non-capital loss — Where, at any time, control of a corporation has been acquired by a person or persons, such portion of the corporation's non-capital loss for a taxation year ending before that time as

(a) was not deductible in computing the corporation's income for a taxation year ending before that time, and

(b) can reasonably be considered to be a non-capital loss of a subsidiary corporation (in this subsection referred to as the "former subsidiary corporation") from carrying on a particular business (in this subsection referred to as the "former subsidiary corporation's loss business") that was deemed by subsection 88(1.1) of the *Income Tax Act*, chapter 148 of the Revised Statutes of Canada, 1952, as read on November 12, 1981 to be the non-capital loss of the corporation for the taxation year of the corporation in which the former subsidiary corporation's loss year ended

shall be deemed to be a non-capital loss of the corporation from carrying on the former subsidiary corporation's loss business.

Related Provisions: 87(2.1)(b) — Determining loss after amalgamation; 256(6)–(9) — Whether control acquired; 256.1 — Deemed change in control if 75% FMV acquired. See also at end of s. 111.

I.T. Application Rules: 69 (meaning of "chapter 148 of ...").

Interpretation Bulletins: IT-302R3: Losses of a corporation — the effect that acquisitions of control, amalgamations, and windings-up have on their deductibility. See also at end of s. 111.

I.T. Technical News: 7 (control by a group — 50/50 arrangement); 9 (loss consolidation within a corporate group).

(5.5) Loss restriction event — special rules — If at any time a taxpayer is subject to a loss restriction event,

(a) paragraphs (4)(c) to (f) and subsections (5.1) to (5.3) do not apply to the taxpayer in respect of the loss restriction event if at that time the taxpayer becomes or ceases to be exempt from tax under this Part on its taxable income; and

(b) if it can reasonably be considered that the main reason that the taxpayer is subject to the loss restriction event is to cause paragraph (4)(d) or any of subsections (5.1) to (5.3) to apply with respect to the loss restriction event, the following do not apply with respect to the loss restriction event:

(i) that provision and paragraph (4)(e), and

(ii) if that provision is paragraph (4)(d), paragraph (4)(c).

Related Provisions: 87(2.1)(b) — Determining loss after amalgamation; 107.3(3)(a) — Trust that ceases to be qualifying environmental trust ceases being exempt from Part I tax; 251.2 — Loss restriction event.

Notes: 111(5.5) amended by 2013 budget bill #2, effective March 21, 2013, to extend its application to trusts (by referring to a "loss restriction event" instead of control of a corporation being acquired: see Notes to 251.2(2)).

Interpretation Bulletins: IT-302R3: Losses of a corporation — the effect that acquisitions of control, amalgamations, and windings-up have on their deductibility. See also at end of s. 111.

(6) Limitation — For the purposes of this section and paragraph 53(1)(i), any loss of a taxpayer for a taxation year from a farming business shall, after the taxpayer disposes of the land used in that farming business and to the extent that the amount of the loss is

required by paragraph 53(1)(i) to be added in computing the adjusted cost base to the taxpayer of the land immediately before the disposition, be deemed not to be a loss.

Notes: "Land" can include buildings; see 70(5.2) Notes.

(7) Idem — For the purposes of this section, any loss of a taxpayer for a taxation year from a farming business shall, to the extent that the loss is included in the amount of any deduction permitted by section 101 in computing the taxpayer's income for any subsequent taxation year, be deemed not to be a loss of the taxpayer for the purpose of computing the taxpayer's taxable income for that subsequent year or any taxation year subsequent thereto.

(7.1), (7.11), (7.2) [Repealed]

Notes: 111(7.1), (7.11) and (7.2) repealed by 2002-2013 technical bill (Part 5 — technical) for taxation years that begin after Oct. 2011. They provided relief for certain pre-1977 losses of life insurance companies, and applied only to years before 1978.

(7.3) Non-capital losses of employee life and health trusts — Paragraph (1)(a) does not apply in computing the taxable income of a trust for a taxation year if the trust is, in the year, an employee life and health trust.

Related Provisions: 111(7.4) — Carryback and carryforward for ELHT; 111(7.5) — No carryforward where ELHT loses status or deduction rights.

Notes: An ELHT cannot claim a regular 20-year loss carryforward, but can claim a 7-year carryforward under 111(7.4), as long as it remains an ELHT (see 111(7.5)).

111(7.3) added by 2010 budget bill #2, effective 2010.

(7.4) Non-capital losses of employee life and health trusts — For the purposes of computing the taxable income of an employee life and health trust for a taxation year, there may be deducted such portion as the trust may claim of the trust's non-capital losses for the seven taxation years immediately preceding and the three taxation years immediately following the year.

Related Provisions: 111(7.3) — Regular non-capital loss carryovers not allowed; 111(7.5) — No carryforward where ELHT loses status or deduction rights; 111(8)"non-capital loss"(a.1) — Amount deductible in calculating loss of ELHT; 144.1(10) — Non-capital losses to ELHT only as allowed by 111(7.3)–(7.5).

Notes: See 111(7.3) Notes. 111(7.4) amended by 2021 budget bill #1, effective Feb. 27, 2018, to change "three" to "seven". Added by 2010 budget bill #2, effective 2010.

(7.5) Non-capital losses of employee life and health trusts — Notwithstanding paragraph (1)(a) and subsection (7.4), no amount in respect of the trust's non-capital losses for a taxation year in which the trust was an employee life and health trust may be deducted in computing the trust's taxable income for another taxation year (referred to in this subsection as the "specified year") if

(a) the trust was not an employee life and health trust for the specified year; or

(b) the trust is an employee life and health trust that, because of the application of subsection 144.1(3), is not permitted to deduct any amount under subsection 104(6) for the specified year.

Notes: 111(7.5) added by 2010 budget bill #2, effective 2010. See Notes to 111(7.3).

(8) Definitions — In this section,

"exchange rate", at any time in respect of a currency of a country other than Canada, means the rate of exchange between that currency and Canadian currency quoted by the Bank of Canada on the day that includes that time or, if that day is not a business day, on the day that immediately precedes that day, or a rate of exchange acceptable to the Minister;

Related Provisions: 261(5)(d) — Application when using functional currency reporting; 261(5)(f)(i) — Interpretation when functional currency election in effect; *Interpretation Act* s. 29 — Time referred to is standard time.

Notes: bankofcanada.ca/rates has daily exchange rates since April 28, 2017, and earlier historical noon and closing rates back to 2007.

Definition amended by 2017 budget bill #2, to delete "at noon" after "Bank of Canada", effective March 2017 (since the BoC now publishes only one rate per day).

111(8)"exchange rate" added by 2008 budget bill #2, effective on the same basis as 111(12).

"farm loss" of a taxpayer for a taxation year means the amount determined by the formula

$$A - C$$

where

A is the lesser of

    (a) the amount, if any, by which

        (i) the total of all amounts each of which is the taxpayer's loss for the year from a farming or fishing business

    exceeds

        (ii) the total of all amounts each of which is the taxpayer's income for the year from a farming or fishing business, and

    (b) the amount that would be the taxpayer's non-capital loss for the year if the amount determined for D in the definition "non-capital loss" in this subsection were nil, and

B [Repealed]

C is the total of all amounts by which the farm loss of the taxpayer for the year is required to be reduced because of section 80;

Related Provisions: 31(1), (1.1) — Restricted farm loss; 53(1)(i) — Addition to ACB of farmland; 80(3)(b) — Reduction in farm loss on debt forgiveness; 87(2.1)(a) — Amalgamation — farm loss carried forward; 96(1) — Farm loss of partner; 111(9) — Farm loss where taxpayer not resident in Canada; 127.52(1)(i)(ii)(B) — Calculation of previous year's farm loss for minimum tax purposes; 161(7) — Effect of carryback of loss; 248(1)"farm loss" — Definition applies to entire Act; 257 — Formula cannot calculate to less than zero. See also at end of s. 111.

Notes: See Notes to 111(1)(d) and 31(1).

A(b) amended by 2013 budget bill #2, effective Dec. 12, 2013, to change "each of the amounts determined for C and D" to "the amount determined for D" (and "zero" to "nil"). (111(8)"non-capital loss"C was repealed in 2000.)

Definition amended by 1994 technical bill (for taxation years ending after Feb. 21, 1994) and 1999 Budget.

111(8)"farm loss" was 111(8)(b.1) before RSC 1985 (5th Supp) consolidation for tax years ending after Nov. 1991.

Interpretation Bulletins: IT-302R3: Losses of a corporation — the effect that acquisitions of control, amalgamations, and windings-up have on their deductibility. See also at end of s. 111.

CRA Audit Manual: 29.4.0: Farm losses and restricted farm losses.

"foreign currency debt" means a debt obligation denominated in a currency of a country other than Canada;

Related Provisions: 248(1)"foreign currency debt" — Definition applies to entire Act; 261(5)(f)(ii) — Interpretation when functional currency election in effect.

Notes: 111(8)"foreign currency debt" added by 2008 budget bill #2, effective on the same basis as 111(12).

"net capital loss" of a taxpayer for a taxation year means the amount determined by the formula

$$A - B + C - D$$

where

A is the amount, if any, determined under subparagraph 3(b)(ii) in respect of the taxpayer for the year,

B is the lesser of the total determined under subparagraph 3(b)(i) in respect of the taxpayer for the year and the amount determined for A in respect of the taxpayer for the year,

C is the least of

    (a) the amount of the allowable business investment losses of the taxpayer for the taxpayer's tenth preceding taxation year,

    (b) the amount, if any, by which the amount of the non-capital loss of the taxpayer for the taxpayer's tenth preceding taxation year exceeds the total of all amounts in respect of that non-capital loss deducted in computing the taxpayer's taxable income or claimed by the taxpayer under paragraph 186(1)(c) or (d) for the year or for any preceding taxation year, and

    (c) if the taxpayer was subject to a loss restriction event before the end of the year and after the end of the taxpayer's tenth preceding taxation year, nil, and

D is the total of all amounts by which the net capital loss of the taxpayer for the year is required to be reduced because of section 80;

Related Provisions: 80(4)(b) — Reduction in net capital loss on debt forgiveness; 87(2.1)(a) — Amalgamation — net capital loss carried forward; 96(1) — Net capital loss of partner; 96(8)(b) — Loss of partnership that previously had only non-resident partners; 96(8)(c) — Disposition of property by partnership that previously had only non-resident partners; 111(1)(b) — Application of net capital loss; 111(7.2) — Non-capital loss of life insurer; 111(9) — Net capital loss of non-resident; 127.52(1)(i)(ii) — Calculation of previous year's loss for minimum tax purposes; 142.7(12)(f) — Net capital loss on conversion of foreign bank affiliate to branch; 161(7) — Effect of carryback of loss; 180.01 — Election to reduce tax on stock-option shares that have dropped in value; 248(1)"net capital loss" — Definition applies to entire Act; 251.2 — Loss restriction event; 257 — Formula cannot calculate to less than zero. See also at end of s. 111.

Notes: See Notes to 111(1)(b).

C(c) amended by 2013 budget bill #2, effective March 21, 2013, to refer to a "loss restriction event" instead of acquisition of control, so as to extend the rule to trusts (see Notes to 251.2(2)).

C(a)-(c) amended by 2004 Budget to change "seventh" to "tenth", effective for losses that arise in taxation years that end after March 22, 2004; but for a taxpayer's taxation year before the 8th taxation year that ends after March 22, 2004, read "seventh" in C(c). Since 111(8) looks back to claim earlier losses, these changes generally took effect around 2012, but earlier for a corporation that has short taxation years (e.g., due to 249(4) on change of control).

111(8)"net capital loss" was 111(8)(a) before RSC 1985 (5th Supp) consolidation for tax years ending after Nov. 1991.

Income Tax Folios: S4-F8-C1: Business investment losses [replaces IT-484R2].

Interpretation Bulletins: IT-302R3: Losses of a corporation — the effect that acquisitions of control, amalgamations, and windings-up have on their deductibility. See also at end of s. 111.

"non-capital loss" of a taxpayer for a taxation year means, at any time, the amount determined by the formula

$$(A + B) - (D + D.1 + D.2)$$

where

A is the amount determined by the formula

$$E - F$$

where

E is the total of all amounts each of which is

(a) the taxpayer's loss for the year from an office, employment, business or property,

(a.1) an amount deductible under paragraph 104(6)(a.4) in computing the taxpayer's income for the year;[11]

(b) an amount deducted under paragraph (1)(b) or section 110.6, or deductible under any of paragraphs 110(1)(d) to (g) and (k), section 112 and subsections 113(1) and 138(6), in computing the taxpayer's taxable income for the year, or

(c) if that time is before the taxpayer's eleventh following taxation year, the taxpayer's allowable business investment loss for the year, and

F is the amount determined under paragraph 3(c) in respect of the taxpayer for the year,

B is the amount, if any, determined in respect of the taxpayer for the year under section 110.5 or subparagraph 115(1)(a)(vii),

C [Repealed]

D is the amount that would be the taxpayer's farm loss for the year if the amount determined for B in the definition "farm loss" in this subsection were zero,

D.1 is the total of all amounts deducted under subsection (10) in respect of the taxpayer for the year, and

D.2 is the total of all amounts by which the non-capital loss of the taxpayer for the year is required to be reduced because of section 80;

Related Provisions: 80(3)(a), 80(4)(a) — Reduction in non-capital loss on debt forgiveness; 87(2.1)(a) — Amalgamation — non-capital loss carried forward; 96(1) — Non-capital loss of partner; 96(8)(b), (c) — Loss of partnership that previously had only non-resident partners; 111(1)(a) — Application of non-capital loss; 111(5.4) — Non-capital loss after change of control; 111(9) — Non-capital loss where taxpayer not

resident in Canada; 127.52(1)(i)(ii)(B) — Calculation of previous year's non-capital loss for minimum tax purposes; 138.1(2.1) — Related segregated fund trust — pre-2018 non-capital losses; 142.7(12)(d) — Non-capital loss on converting foreign bank affiliate to branch; 161(7) — Effect of carryback of loss; 248(1)"non-capital loss" — Definition applies to entire Act; 257 — Formula amounts cannot calculate to less than zero. See also at end of s. 111.

Notes: See Notes to 111(1)(a).

Due to the reference in A to 111(1)(b), business losses of a taxation year that have been used to reduce a taxable capital gain for that year may be reinstated where net capital losses of other years are carried over to that year.

For application of D.2 see VIEWS doc 2011-0418071I7.

E(b) amended by 2021 budget bill #1, effective July 2021, to change "110(1)(d) to (d.3), (f), (g)" to "110(1)(d) to (g)", effectively adding 110(1)(e).

E(b) amended to delete reference to 110(1)(j) by 2017 budget bill #1, effective 2018.

E(a.1) added by 2010 budget bill #2, effective 2010.

111(8)"non-capital loss" opening words amended (to add "at any time") and E amended (effectively to introduce the 10-year cap on ABILs in E(c), due to 111(1)(a) going to 20 years) by 2006 budget bill #1, effective for losses that arise in 2006 and later taxation years. For earlier losses, read:

E is the total of all amounts each of which is the taxpayer's loss for the year from an office, employment, business or property, the taxpayer's allowable business investment loss for the year, an amount deducted under paragraph (1)(b) or section 110.6 in computing the taxpayer's taxable income for the year or an amount that may be deducted under any of paragraphs 110(1)(d) to (d.3), (f), (g), (j) and (k), section 112 and subsections 113(1) and 138(6) in computing the taxpayer's taxable income for the year, and

B amended by 2001 technical bill to refer to 115(1)(a)(vii), effective June 28, 1999.

E amended by 2001 Budget to add reference to 110(1)(g), for 1997 and later tax years and, notwithstanding 152(4)-(5), any assessment of tax, interest or penalty for any tax year shall be made that is necessary to give effect to the amendment.

Definition earlier amended by 2000 Budget, effective for 2000 and later taxation years (reference to 110(1)(d.01) added to E); 1999 Budget, effective 1998 and later taxation years (C deleted); 1994 technical bill (D.2 added); 1992 transportation support bill (D.1 added); 1992 technical bill (A amended).

111(8)"non-capital loss" was 111(8)(b) before RSC 1985 (5th Supp) consolidation.

Income Tax Folios: S4-F8-C1: Business investment losses [replaces IT-484R2].

Interpretation Bulletins: IT-302R3: Losses of a corporation — the effect that acquisitions of control, amalgamations, and windings-up have on their deductibility. See also at end of s. 111.

I.T. Technical News: 25 (refreshing losses).

CRA Audit Manual: 29.1.0: Non-capital losses.

Forms: T1A: Request for loss carryback.

"pre-1986 capital loss balance" of an individual for a particular taxation year means the amount determined by the formula

$$(A + B) - (C + D + E + E.1)$$

where

A is the total of all amounts each of which is an amount determined by the formula

$$F - G$$

where

F is the individual's net capital loss for a taxation year ending before 1985, and

G is the total of all amounts claimed under this section by the individual in respect of that loss in computing the individual's taxable income for taxation years preceding the particular taxation year, and

B is the amount determined by the formula

$$H - I$$

where

H is the lesser of

(a) the amount of the individual's net capital loss for the 1985 taxation year, and

(b) the amount, if any, by which the amount determined under subparagraph 3(e)(ii) of the *Income Tax Act*, chapter 148 of the Revised Statutes of Canada, 1952, in respect of

---

11 Should be a comma — ed.

the individual for the 1985 taxation year exceeds the amount deductible by reason of paragraph 3(e) of that Act in computing the individual's taxable income for the 1985 taxation year, and

I is the total of all amounts claimed under this section by the individual in respect of the individual's net capital loss for the 1985 taxation year in computing the individual's taxable income for taxation years preceding the particular taxation year,

C is the total of all amounts deducted under section 110.6 in computing the individual's taxable income for taxation years that ended before 1988 or begin after October 17, 2000,

D is ¾ of the total of all amounts each of which is an amount deducted under section 110.6 in computing the individual's taxable income for a taxation year, preceding the particular year, that

(a) ended after 1987 and before 1990, or

(b) began after February 27, 2000 and ended before October 18, 2000,

E is ⅔ of the total of all amounts deducted under section 110.6 in computing the individual's taxable income for taxation years, preceding the particular year, that ended after 1989 and before February 28, 2000, and

E.1 is amount determined by the formula

$$J \times (0.5/K)$$

where

J is the amount deducted by the individual under section 110.6 for a taxation year of the individual, preceding the particular year, that includes February 28, 2000 or October 17, 2000, and

K is the fraction in paragraph 38(a) that applies to the individual for the individual's taxation year referred to in the description of J.

Related Provisions: 161(7) — Effect of carryback of loss; 257 — Formula amounts cannot calculate to less than zero. See also at end of s. 111.

Notes: $2,000 per year of an individual's pre-1986 capital loss balance can be deducted against other sources of income each year. See 111(1.1)(b)(i).

Description of C amended by 2002-2013 technical bill (Part 5 — technical) to add "begin", for 2000 and later taxation years.

Description of C amended (to add "or after October 17, 2000"), D amended (to add para. (b)), E amended (to add "and before February 28, 2000"), and E.1 added, by 2000 Budget, effective for taxation years that end after February 27, 2000.

111(8)"pre-1986 capital loss balance" was 111(8)(b.2) before RSC 1985 (5th Supp) consolidation for tax years ending after Nov. 1991.

111(8)(b.2)(i)(B) and (ii)(C) (now 111(8)"pre-1986 capital loss balance"A and B) amended by 1991 technical bill, retroactive to 1985.

I.T. Application Rules: 69 (meaning of "chapter 148 of ...").

Interpretation Bulletins: IT-232R3: Losses — their deductibility in the loss year or in other years; IT-262R2: Losses of non-residents and part-year residents. See also at end of s. 111.

(9) Exception [non-residents] — In this section, a taxpayer's non-capital loss, net capital loss, restricted farm loss, farm loss and limited partnership loss for a taxation year during which the taxpayer was not resident in Canada shall be determined as if

(a) in the part of the year throughout which the taxpayer was non-resident, if section 114 applies to the taxpayer in respect of the year, and

(b) throughout the year, in any other case,

the taxpayer had no income other than income described in any of subparagraphs 115(1)(a)(i) to (vi), the taxpayer's only taxable capital gains, allowable capital losses and allowable business investment losses were from dispositions of taxable Canadian property (other than treaty-protected property) and the taxpayer's only other losses were losses from the duties of an office or employment performed by the taxpayer in Canada and businesses (other than treaty-protected businesses) carried on by the taxpayer in Canada.

Related Provisions: 80(1)"excluded property" — Properties to which debt forgiveness rules do not apply; 94(3)(a)(v) — Application to trust deemed resident in Canada;

115(1)(c) — Treaty-protected business losses not usable against Canadian business profits; 161(7) — Effect of carryback of loss. See also at end of s. 111.

Notes: Capital losses realized before becoming non-resident can be carried forward against taxable Canadian property gains and are not subject to 111(9): VIEWS doc 2017-0705801I7.

111(9) amended by 2001 technical bill (effective 1998 and later taxation years), 1998 Budget and 1992 technical bill. 111(9) was 111(8)(c) before RSC 1985 (5th Supp) consolidation for tax years ending after Nov. 1991.

Interpretation Bulletins: IT-262R2: Losses of non-residents and part-year residents; IT-393R2: Election re tax on rents and timber royalties — non-residents.

(10), (11) [No longer relevant.]

Notes: 111(10) and (11) reduce losses where a fuel tax rebate under *Excise Tax Act* s. 68.4 is claimed. This was a 1991-92 rebate for truckers and a 1996-99 rebate for airlines, available in exchange for giving up losses. See Notes to 12(1)(x.1).

111(10), (11) amended by 1997 budget bill #1. They were 111(9), (10) before RSC 1985 (5th Supp) consolidation for tax years ending after Nov. 1991. Added by 1992 transportation support bill.

(12) Foreign currency debt on loss restriction event — For the purposes of subsection (4), if at any time a taxpayer owes a foreign currency debt in respect of which the taxpayer would have had, if the foreign currency debt had been repaid at that time, a capital loss or gain, the taxpayer is deemed to own at the time (in this subsection referred to as the "measurement time") that is immediately before that time a property

(a) the adjusted cost base of which at the measurement time is the amount determined by the formula

$$A + B - C$$

where

A is the amount of principal owed by the taxpayer under the foreign currency debt at the measurement time, calculated, for greater certainty, using the exchange rate applicable at the measurement time,

B is the portion of any gain, previously recognized in respect of the foreign currency debt because of this section, that is reasonably attributable to the amount described in A, and

C is the portion of any capital loss previously recognized in respect of the foreign currency debt because of this section, that is reasonably attributable to the amount described in A; and

(b) the fair market value of which is the amount that would be the amount of the principal owed by the taxpayer under the foreign currency debt at the measurement time if that amount were calculated using the exchange rate applicable at the time of the original borrowing.

Related Provisions: 39(2) — Capital gain or loss on foreign currency; 40(10), (11) — Calculation of gain or loss on foreign currency debt; 251.2 — Loss restriction event; 257 — Formula cannot calculate to less than zero.

Notes: Under 111(4), on change in control a corporation must recognize all its accrued capital losses on property it owns. Those losses (and net capital losses carried forward), cannot be used, but the corporation can elect to realize any accrued capital gains on other property it owns, to apply the capital losses against them.

Before 111(12), capital gains and losses resulting from foreign currency fluctuations on a corporation's debt liabilities were not subject to these rules, even though in other respects the Act generally treats them like other capital gains and losses (see 39(2)).

111(12) extends the general treatment of accrued capital gains and losses on change in control to those resulting from foreign currency fluctuations on debt liabilities denominated in a foreign currency. (These rules apply only to foreign currency debts the repayment of which would have generated a *capital* loss/gain.) 111(12) provides that for purposes of 111(4), if at any time a corporation owes a foreign currency debt, the corporation is deemed to own, immediately before that time (the "measurement time"), a property with ACB and FMV determined by the formulas in 111(12)(a)-(b). Establishing ACB and an FMV for this notional property allows for the calculation of capital losses or gains on the foreign currency debt. (See also 40(11).)

See also VIEWS doc 2014-0544941E5 (interaction with 80.01(3)); Smit, "Foreign Currency Debts and Acquisitions of Control", 92 *International Tax* (CCH) 2-5 (Feb. 2017).

111(12) amended by 2013 budget bill #2, effective March 21, 2013, to extend the rule to trusts. Added by 2008 budget bill #2, for acquisitions of control after March 7, 2008 (after 2008 in some cases).

Related Provisions [s. 111]: 31(1) — Loss from farming where chief source of income not farming; 66.8(1) — Resource expenses of limited partner; 87(2.1) — Non-capital loss, net capital loss, restricted farm loss and farm loss of predecessor corporation; 87(2.11) — Losses, etc., on amalgamation with subsidiary wholly-owned corporation; 88.1 — Non-capital loss, net capital loss, restricted farm loss, and farm loss of subsidiary; 96(2.2) — At-risk amount; 104(21) — Portion of taxable capital gains deemed gain of beneficiary; 111.1 — Ordering of applying provisions; 127.52(1) — Adjusted taxable income determined; 128(1)(g), 128(2)(g) — Where corporation or individual is bankrupt; 152(1.1)–(1.3) — Determination of losses; 152(6) — Reassessment; 164(6) — Where disposition of property by legal representative of deceased taxpayer; 256(8) — Deemed acquisition of shares.

Definitions [s. 111]: "acquired" — 256(7)–(9); "active business" — 248(1); "adjusted cost base" — 54, 248(1); "allowable business investment loss" — 38(c), 248(1); "allowable capital loss" — 38(b), 248(1); "amount" — 248(1); "arm's length" — 251(1); "assessment" — 248(1); "at-risk amount" — 96(2.2); "business" — 248(1); "Canada" — 255; "Canadian development expense" — 66.2(5), 248(1); "Canadian exploration expense" — 66.1(6), 248(1); "Canadian oil and gas property expense" — 66.4(5), 248(1); "capital loss" — 39(1)(b), 248(1); "capital property" — 54, 248(1); "carrying on business" — 253; "control" — 256(6)–(9), 256.1(3); "corporation" — 248(1), *Interpretation Act* 35(1); "cumulative eligible capital" — 14(5), 248(1); "currency of a country other than Canada" — 261(5)(f)(ii); "depreciable property" — 13(21), 248(1); "disposition" — 248(1); "eligible capital property" — 54, 248(1); "employee life and health trust" — 144.1(2), 248(1); "employment" — 248(1); "exchange rate" — 111(8), 261(5)(d); "fair market value" — see 69(1) Notes; "farming" — 248(1); "farm loss" — 111(8), 248(1); "fiscal period" — 249(2)(b), 249.1; "fishing", "foreign currency" — 248(1); "foreign currency debt" — 111(8), 248(1); "foreign resource pool expense", "individual", "insurer" — 248(1); "investment tax credit" — 127(9), 248(1); "land" — see 70(5.2) Notes; "life insurer" — 248(1); "limited partner" — 96(2.4); "limited partnership loss" — 96(2.1)(e), 248(1); "loss restriction event" — 251.2; "measurement time" — 111(12); "Minister" — 248(1); "net capital loss" — 111(8), 248(1); "1975 branch accounting election deficiency" — 111(7.11), 138(12); "non-capital loss" — 111(8), 248(1); "non-resident", "office", "person", "prescribed", "property", "regulation" — 248(1); "resident in Canada" — 94(3)(a), 250; "restricted farm loss" — 31, 248(1); "sent" — 244(14), (14.1); "specified year" — 111(7.5); "tax payable" — 248(2); "taxable capital gain" — 38, 248(1); "taxable income" — 2(2), 248(1); "taxation year" — 249; "taxpayer", "treaty-protected business", "treaty-protected property" — 248(1); "undepreciated capital cost" — 13(21), 248(1).

Income Tax Folios [s. 111]: S4-F7-C1: Amalgamations of Canadian corporations [replaces IT-474R2].

Interpretation Bulletins [s. 111]: IT-171R2: Non-resident individuals — computation of taxable income earned in Canada and non-refundable tax credits (cancelled); IT-381R3: Trusts — capital gains and losses and the flow-through of taxable capital gains to beneficiaries.

111.1 Order of applying provisions — In computing an individual's taxable income for a taxation year, the provisions of this Division shall be applied in the following order: sections 110, 110.2, 111, 110.6 and 110.7.

Notes: 111.1 amended by 1999 Budget, effective for 1998 and later taxation years, to add reference to 110.2 and to delete reference to 110.4(2).

Definitions [s. 111.1]: "individual" — 248(1); "taxable income" — 2(2), 248(1); "taxation year" — 249.

Interpretation Bulletins: IT-232R3: Losses — their deductibility in the loss year or in other years; IT-523: Order of provisions applicable in computing an individual's taxable income and tax payable.

CRA Audit Manual: 29.5.8: Loss carryovers — order of certain deductions.

112. (1) Deduction of taxable dividends received by corporation resident in Canada — Where a corporation in a taxation year has received a taxable dividend from

(a) a taxable Canadian corporation, or

(b) a corporation resident in Canada (other than a non-resident-owned investment corporation or a corporation exempt from tax under this Part) and controlled by it,

an amount equal to the dividend may be deducted from the income of the receiving corporation for the year for the purpose of computing its taxable income.

Related Provisions: 52(3)(a)(ii) — Deduction from cost of share received as stock dividend; 53(1)(b)(ii) — Reduced addition to ACB of share after 84(1) applies; 55(2) — Capital gains stripping; 104(16) — Distributions tax on income trusts; 104(19) — Taxable dividends flowed through trust; 111(8)"non-capital loss"A:E — Amount included in non-capital loss; 112(2) — Dividends received from non-resident corporation; 112(2.1)–(2.6) — Where no deduction permitted; 112(3)–(3.32) — Denial of capital loss on share where intercorporate dividend previously paid; 112(4)–(4.3) — Loss on share held as inventory; 112(5.2)B(b)(i), (ii) — Adjustment for dividends received on mark-to-market property; 115(1)(d.1) — Deduction from income of non-resident; 137(5.2) — Credit union — allocations of taxable dividends and capital gains; 138(6) — Life insurer; 186(1) — Tax payable on certain taxable dividends; 186(3)"as-

sessable dividend" — Part IV tax; 219(1)(b) — Branch tax on non-resident corporations; 256(6), (6.1) — Meaning of "controlled". See also at end of s. 112.

Notes: 112(1) offsets 82(1)(a)(i) and (a.1)(i), and thus allows many intercorporate dividends to be received tax-free. Conceptually, the same income, after being taxed once in the corporation that earns it, can be paid up as dividends through an arbitrarily long chain of holding companies without triggering tax until it reaches an individual.

The two major exceptions to the treatment of intercorporate dividends are 112(2.1)–(2.9) (exclusion for dividends on certain preferred shares and other shares used as financing vehicles to obtain the intercorporate dividend deduction) and Part IV (refundable tax under 186 on "portfolio" dividends and on dividends from a corporation receiving a dividend refund). As well, dividends deducted under 112(1) may trigger the stop-loss rules in 112(3)-(5.6).

For the meaning of "dividend" see Notes to 248(1)"dividend".

If the dividend's purpose is to reduce the value of the shares or the capital gain realized on their sale (i.e., a capital gain strip), it may be deemed to be a capital gain. See Notes to 55(2) and (2.1).

In *Spruce Credit Union*, 2014 FCA 143, dividends received by credit unions from a deposit insurance corporation (as part of cycling funds to another DIC) were deductible under 112(1), even if they were taxable under 137.1 rather than 82(1).

For dividends from foreign corporations, see 113(1).

A corporate partner may claim the deduction under 112(1) on dividends allocated to it from a partnership: VIEWS doc 2003-0027745.

Income Tax Folios: S3-F2-C1: Capital Dividends [replaces IT-66R6]; S6-F2-C1: Disposition of an income interest in a trust [replaces IT-385R2].

Interpretation Bulletins: IT-88R2: Stock dividends; IT-98R2: Investment corporations (cancelled); IT-269R4: Part IV tax on dividends received by a private corporation or a subject corporation; IT-328R3: Losses on shares on which dividends have been received; IT-524: Trusts — flow-through of taxable dividends to a beneficiary — after 1987.

Information Circulars: 88-2, para. 13: General anti-avoidance rule — section 245 of the *Income Tax Act*.

Advance Tax Rulings: ATR-16: Inter-company dividends and interest expense; ATR-18: Term preferred shares; ATR-22R: Estate freeze using share exchange; ATR-27: Exchange and acquisition of interests in capital properties through rollovers and winding-up ("butterfly"); ATR-32: Rollover of fixed assets from Opco into Holdco; ATR-35: Partitioning of assets to get specific ownership — "butterfly"; ATR-46: Financial difficulty; ATR-57: Transfer of property for estate planning purposes; ATR-58: Divisive reorganization.

(2) Dividends received from non-resident corporation — Where a taxpayer that is a corporation has, in a taxation year, received a dividend from a corporation (other than a foreign affiliate of the taxpayer) that was taxable under subsection 2(3) for the year and that has, throughout the period from June 18, 1971 to the time when the dividend was received, carried on a business in Canada through a permanent establishment as defined by regulation, an amount equal to that proportion of the dividend that the paying corporation's taxable income earned in Canada for the immediately preceding year is of the whole of the amount that its taxable income for that year would have been if it had been resident in Canada throughout that year, may be deducted from the income of the receiving corporation for the taxation year for the purpose of computing its taxable income.

Related Provisions: 55(2) — Capital gains stripping; 112(2.1)–(2.6) — Where no deduction permitted; 112(5.2)B(b)(i), (ii) — Adjustment for dividends received on mark-to-market property; 113(1) — Deduction for dividend from foreign affiliate; 115(1)(d.1) — Deduction from income of non-resident; 137(5.2) — Credit union — allocations of taxable dividends and capital gains; 186(3)"assessable dividend" — Part IV tax; 247(1) — Dividend stripping. See also at end of s. 112.

Regulations: 400(2) (meaning of "permanent establishment" until April 26, 1989); 8201 (meaning of "permanent establishment" effective 10:00 p.m., April 26, 1989).

(2.1) No deduction permitted — No deduction may be made under subsection (1) or (2) in computing the taxable income of a specified financial institution in respect of a dividend received by it on a share that was, at the time the dividend was received, a term preferred share, other than a dividend on a share of the capital stock of a corporation that was not acquired in the ordinary course of the business carried on by the institution, and for the purposes of this subsection, if a restricted financial institution received the dividend on a share of the capital stock of a mutual fund corporation or an investment corporation at any time after the mutual fund or investment corporation has elected under subsection 131(10) not to be a restricted financial institution, the share is deemed to be a term preferred share acquired in the ordinary course of business.

Related Provisions: 84(4.2) — Deemed dividend where paid-up capital of term preferred share reduced; 191(4) — Subsection 112(2.1) deemed not to apply; 248(1) — "amount" of a stock dividend; 248(14) — Specified financial institution — corporations deemed related; 258(2) — Deemed dividend on term preferred share. See also at end of s. 112.

Notes: See Notes to 248(1)"term preferred share". For interpretation of "in the ordinary course of business" see VIEWS doc 2005-0133341I7. For examples of rulings that 112(2.1)–(2.4) do not apply see 2011-0416001R3 (split-up butterfly); 2019-0819971R3 (loss consolidation).

112(2.1) amended by 2002-2013 technical bill for dividends received after Nov. 4, 2010.

Interpretation Bulletins: IT-52R4: Income bonds and income debentures (cancelled); IT-88R2: Stock dividends.

Advance Tax Rulings: ATR-10: Issue of term preferred shares; ATR-16: Intercompany dividends and interest expense; ATR-18: Term preferred shares; ATR-46: Financial difficulty.

(2.2) Guaranteed shares — No deduction may be made under subsection (1), (2) or 138(6) in computing the taxable income of a particular corporation in respect of a dividend received on a share of the capital stock of a corporation that was issued after 8:00 p.m. Eastern Daylight Saving Time, June 18, 1987 where

(a) a person or partnership (in this subsection and subsection (2.21) referred to as the "guarantor") that is a specified financial institution or a specified person in relation to a specified financial institution, but that is not the issuer of the share or an individual other than a trust, is, at or immediately before the time the dividend was received, obligated, either absolutely or contingently and either immediately or in the future, to effect any undertaking (in this subsection and subsections (2.21) and (2.22) referred to as a "guarantee agreement"), including any guarantee, covenant or agreement to purchase or repurchase the share and including the lending of funds to or the placing of amounts on deposit with, or on behalf of, the particular corporation or any specified person in relation to the particular corporation given to ensure that

(i) any loss that the particular corporation or a specified person in relation to the particular corporation may sustain by reason of the ownership, holding or disposition of the share or any other property is limited in any respect, or

(ii) the particular corporation or a specified person in relation to the particular corporation will derive earnings by reason of the ownership, holding or disposition of the share or any other property; and

(b) the guarantee agreement was given as part of a transaction or event or a series of transactions or events that included the issuance of the share.

Related Provisions: 84(4.3) — Deemed dividend where paid-up capital of guaranteed share reduced; 87(4.2) — Amalgamations; 112(2.21) — Exceptions; 112(2.22) — Interpretation; 248(1) — "amount" of a stock dividend; 248(10) — Series of transactions; 248(14) — Specified financial institution — corporations deemed related; 258(3) — Deemed interest on preferred shares. See also at end of s. 112.

Notes: 112(2.2)(a) opening words amended by 2002-2013 technical bill (for dividends received after Nov. 4, 2010, to change "paid" to "received").

112(2.2) amended by 2001 technical bill, for dividends received after 1998. This appears to override earlier grandfathering for shares issued before certain dates. 112(2.2) amended by 1988 tax reform, for dividends on shares issued (or deemed issued by para. (f)) after 8pm EDT June 18, 1987. However, it does not apply to a 248(1)"grandfathered share". For dividends on shares issued from May 24, 1985 to 8pm EDST June 18, 1987 (unless issued per an agreement in writing entered into by May 23, 1985, or distributed to the public per a prospectus, preliminary prospectus or registration statement filed by that date and subject to other conditions), 112(2.2) reads differently (unless superseded by the 2001 amendment): see up to PITA 58th ed. For insurance corporations (other than life insurance corps), 112(2.2) applied only to dividends on shares acquired after Oct. 23, 1979, but again this may be overridden by the 2001 amendment.

Regulations: 6201(3) (prescribed share for 112(2.2)(g)); 6201(8) (prescribed share for 112(2.2)(d)).

Advance Tax Rulings: ATR-16: Inter-company dividends and interest expense; ATR-46: Financial difficulty.

(2.21) Exceptions — Subsection (2.2) does not apply to a dividend received by a particular corporation on

(a) a share that is at the time the dividend is received a share described in paragraph (e) of the definition "term preferred share" in subsection 248(1);

(b) a grandfathered share, a taxable preferred share issued before December 16, 1987 or a prescribed share;

(c) a taxable preferred share issued after December 15, 1987 and of a class of the capital stock of a corporation that is listed on a designated stock exchange where all guarantee agreements in respect of the share were given by one or more of the issuer of the share and persons that are related (otherwise than because of a right referred to in paragraph 251(5)(b)) to the issuer unless, at the time the dividend is paid to the particular corporation, dividends in respect of more than 10 per cent of the issued and outstanding shares to which the guarantee agreement applies are paid to the particular corporation or the particular corporation and specified persons in relation to the particular corporation; or

(d) a share

(i) that was not acquired by the particular corporation in the ordinary course of its business,

(ii) in respect of which the guarantee agreement was not given in the ordinary course of the guarantor's business, and

(iii) the issuer of which is, at the time the dividend is paid, related (otherwise than because of a right referred to in paragraph 251(5)(b)) to both the particular corporation and the guarantor.

Related Provisions: 112(2.22) — Interpretation. See also at end of s. 112.

Notes: 112(2.21)(c) amended by 2007 budget bill #2, effective Dec. 14, 2007, to change "prescribed stock exchange" to "designated stock exchange".

112(2.21) added by 2001 technical bill, effective for dividends received after 1998.

(2.22) Interpretation — For the purposes of subsections (2.2) and (2.21),

(a) where a guarantee agreement in respect of a share is given at any particular time after 8:00 p.m. Eastern Daylight Saving Time, June 18, 1987, otherwise than under a written arrangement to do so entered into before 8:00 p.m. Eastern Daylight Saving Time, June 18, 1987, the share is deemed to have been issued at the particular time and the guarantee agreement is deemed to have been given as part of a series of transactions that included the issuance of the share; and

(b) **"specified person"** has the meaning assigned by paragraph (h) of the definition "taxable preferred share" in subsection 248(1).

Related Provisions: 248(1)"grandfathered share" — Share deemed not to be grandfathered; 258(3) — Deemed interest on preferred share. See also at end of s. 112.

Notes: 112(2.22) added by 2001 technical bill, for dividends received after 1998.

(2.3) Where no deduction permitted [dividend rental arrangement or synthetic equity arrangement] — No deduction may be made under subsection (1) or (2) or 138(6) in computing the taxable income of a particular corporation in respect of a dividend received on a share of the capital stock of a corporation where there is, in respect of the share, a dividend rental arrangement of the particular corporation, a partnership of which the particular corporation is directly or indirectly a member or a trust under which the particular corporation is a beneficiary.

Related Provisions: 112(2.31) — Exception — certain synthetic equity arrangements; 126(4.2) — No foreign tax credit on short-term securities acquisitions; 248(1)"dividend rental arrangement"(b)(i) — DRA includes arrangement where 112(2.3) applies; 260(6.1) — Deductible amount under securities lending arrangement. See also at end of s. 112.

Notes: 112(2.3) denies a 112(1) intercorporate dividend deduction on dividends received as part of a "dividend rental arrangement" (DRA), defined in 248(1) to include not only dividend rentals but also a "synthetic equity arrangement" and other arrangements. See also 112(2.31)-(2.34).

The 2016 amendments (112(2.3)-(2.34)), announced in the 2015 Budget, target the following [Finance Technical Notes]: Certain taxpayers, typically financial institutions, would enter into particular arrangements (248(1)"synthetic equity arrangements"

(SEAs)) where the taxpayer retains legal ownership of an underlying Canadian share, but substantially all the risk of loss and opportunity for gain/profit on the share is transferred to a counterparty using an equity derivative. Some taxpayers took the position that the pre-2016 DRA rules did not catch these arrangements, and claimed a 112(1) deduction on the dividends received on the underlying share. A taxpayer that enters into a SEA in respect of a share is generally required to transfer the economic benefit of any dividends received through "dividend-equivalent payments" to the counterparty. On the premise that the DRA rules did not apply, the taxpayer realized a tax loss on the arrangement by taking advantage of the 112(1) deduction, resulting in tax-free dividend income, while also deducting the dividend-equivalent payments.

To protect the Canadian tax base, the amendments modify the DRA rules to deny the 112(1) deduction on dividends received on a Canadian share in respect of which there is a SEA: 112(2.3), 248(1)"dividend rental arrangement"(c). A SEA, in respect of a share owned by a taxpayer, is considered to exist where the taxpayer (or a person not at arm's length with the taxpayer) enters into one or more agreements that have the effect of providing to a counterparty substantially all the risk of loss and opportunity for gain/profit on the share. Where a person not at arm's length with the taxpayer enters into such an agreement, a SEA is considered to exist if it is reasonable to conclude that the non-arm's length person knew, or ought to have known, that the effect described above would result: 248(1)"synthetic equity arrangement"(a)(iii).

In general terms, an exception to the DRA rule is provided if a taxpayer can establish (112(2.31)(b)) that no tax-indifferent investor (TII) has substantially all the risk of loss and opportunity for gain/profit on the share by virtue of a SEA or another equity derivative that is entered into in connection with the SEA. A taxpayer will be presumed to qualify for this exception (112(2.32)) if it obtains accurate representations from its counterparty to the SEA arrangement that the counterparty is not a TII and either:

- does not reasonably expect to eliminate substantially all of its risk of loss and opportunity for gain/profit on the share; or

- has transferred all or substantially all its risk of loss and opportunity for gain/profit on the share to its own counterparty and has obtained the same representations from that counterparty.

If the representations are later found inaccurate, the arrangement will be treated as a DRA.

This measure does not apply to agreements traded on a recognized derivatives exchange unless it can reasonably be considered that the taxpayer knows, or ought to know, the identity of the counterparty to the agreement: 248(1)"synthetic equity arrangement"(b)(i).

112(2.3), 248(1)"dividend rental arrangement" and 248(1)"synthetic equity arrangement" apply on a dividend-per-dividend basis: for each dividend received on a share, the share must be tested to determine whether the definitions are met. Even if a share is part of a DRA for a given dividend, it may not be for a later dividend.

For criticism of these changes as affecting legitimate non-tax arrangements (e.g. hedging for notional share-based compensation plans), see TEI letter to Finance, Aug. 28, 2015. See also Pham, "The Proposed Synthetic Equity Arrangement Rules", XIII(3) *Corporate Structures & Groups* (Federated Press) 733-36 (2015); Fraser, "Proposed Synthetic Equity Arrangement Rules", XX(1) *Corporate Finance* (Federated Press) 2710-13 (2015); Juneja, "Taxation of Equity Derivatives", 2015 Cdn Tax Foundation conference report, 17:1-22.

112(2.3) amended by 2016 budget bill #1 to add "a partnership of which the particular corporation is directly or indirectly a member or a trust under which the particular corporation is a beneficiary", effective for

(a) dividends paid or that become payable after April 2017;

(b) dividends paid or that become payable from Nov. 2015 through April 2017 on a share if

(i) there is a synthetic equity arrangement (SEA), or one or more agreements or arrangements described by 248(1)"dividend rental arrangement"(d), in respect of the share at that time, and

(ii) (ii) after April 21, 2015, and before that time, all or any part of the above SEA, or agreements or arrangements — including an option, swap, futures contract, forward contract or other financial or commodity contract or instrument as well as a right or obligation under the terms of such a contract or instrument — that contributes or could contribute to the effect of providing all or substantially all of the risk of loss and opportunity for gain or profit, in respect of the share, to one or more persons or partnerships is

(A) entered into, acquired, extended or renewed after April 21, 2015, or

(B) in the case of a right to increase the notional amount under an agreement that is or is part of the SEA, is exercised or acquired after April 21, 2015.

112(2.3) added by 1989 Budget, effective for dividends on shares acquired after April 1989. For explanation, see Notes to 248(1)"dividend rental arrangement".

Former 112(2.3) repealed by 1988 tax reform, with the introduction of Part VI.1 tax in 191.1. It applied to short-term preferred shares (as then defined in 248(1)) issued before 8pm EDST, June 18, 1987.

Advance Tax Rulings: ATR-16: Inter-company dividends and interest expense.

(2.31) Dividend rental arrangements — exception — Subsection (2.3) does not apply to a dividend received on a share where

there is, in respect of the share, a dividend rental arrangement of a person or partnership (referred to in this subsection and subsection (2.32) as the "taxpayer") throughout a particular period during which the synthetic equity arrangement referred to in paragraph (c) of the definition "dividend rental arrangement" is in effect if

(a) the dividend rental arrangement is a dividend rental arrangement because of that paragraph; and

(b) the taxpayer establishes that, throughout the particular period, no tax-indifferent investor or group of tax-indifferent investors, each member of which is affiliated with every other member, has all or substantially all of the risk of loss and opportunity for gain or profit in respect of the share.

Related Provisions: 112(2.32) — How taxpayer can satisfy condition in (2.31)(b); 112(2.33) — Where counterparty expects to become tax-indifferent or eliminate risk; 248(42) — Synthetic equity arrangement relating to multiple identical shares.

Notes: See Notes to 112(2.3). 112(2.31) provides an exception to 112(2.3) if the DRA is one because of 248(1)"dividend rental arrangement"(c) (i.e., it involves a synthetic equity arrangement (SEA)), and the taxpayer establishes that, throughout the particular period, no tax-indifferent investor (or group of them, each member of which is affiliated with every other member), has substantially all the risk of loss and opportunity for gain or profit in respect of the share because of the SEA or a specified SEA. See 112(2.32) for ways to satisfy this condition.

There is no exception to 112(2.3) if the DRA is one because of 248(1)"dividend rental arrangement"(d).

112(2.31)(b) amended by 2018 budget bill #2, for dividends paid or that become payable after Feb. 26, 2018, to delete "because of the synthetic equity arrangement or a specified synthetic equity arrangement" (at the end). This and related amendments to 112(2.32)-(2.33) implement a 2018 Budget proposal under the heading "Artificial Losses Using Equity-Based Financial Arrangements".

112(2.31) added by 2016 budget bill #1, effective on the same basis as the amendment to 112(2.3).

(2.32) Representations [whether tax-indifferent investor has risk for (2.31)(b)] — A taxpayer is considered to have satisfied the condition described in paragraph (2.31)(b) in respect of a share if

(a) the taxpayer or the connected person referred to in paragraph (a) of the definition "synthetic equity arrangement" in subsection 248(1) (either of which is referred to in this subsection as the "synthetic equity arrangement party") obtains accurate representations in writing from its counterparty, or from each member of a group comprised of all its counterparties each of which is affiliated with each other (each member of this group of counterparties is referred to in this subsection as an "affiliated counterparty"), with respect to the synthetic equity arrangement, as appropriate, that

(i) it is not a tax-indifferent investor and it does not reasonably expect to become a tax-indifferent investor during the particular period referred to in subsection (2.31), and

(ii) all or substantially all of its risk of loss and opportunity for gain or profit in respect of the share during the particular period referred to in subsection (2.31) has not been eliminated and cannot reasonably be expected by it to be eliminated;

(b) the synthetic equity arrangement party obtains accurate representations in writing from its counterparty, or from each affiliated counterparty, with respect to the synthetic equity arrangement that the counterparty, or each affiliated counterparty, as appropriate

(i) is not a tax-indifferent investor and does not reasonably expect to become a tax-indifferent investor during the particular period referred to in subsection (2.31),

(ii) has entered into one or more specified synthetic equity arrangements that have the effect of eliminating all or substantially all of its risk of loss and opportunity for gain or profit, in respect of the share, in one of the following circumstances:

(A) in the case of a counterparty, that counterparty

(I) has entered into a specified synthetic equity arrangement with its own counterparty (a counterparty of a counterparty or of an affiliated counterparty is referred to in this subsection as a "specified counterparty"), or

(II) has entered into a specified synthetic equity arrangement with each member of a group of its own counterparties each member of which is affiliated with each other member (each member of this group of counterparties is referred to in this subsection as an "affiliated specified counterparty"), or

(B) in the case of an affiliated counterparty, each affiliated counterparty

(I) has entered into a specified synthetic equity arrangement with the same specified counterparty, or

(II) has entered into a specified synthetic equity arrangement with an affiliated specified counterparty that is part of the same group of affiliated specified counterparties, and

(iii) has obtained accurate representations in writing from each of its specified counterparties, or from each member of the group of affiliated specified counterparties referred to in subclause (A)(II) or (B)(II), as appropriate, that

(A) it is not a tax-indifferent investor and it does not reasonably expect to become a tax-indifferent investor during the particular period referred to in subsection (2.31), and

(B) all or substantially all of its risk of loss and opportunity for gain or profit in respect of the share during the particular period referred to in subsection (2.31) has not been eliminated and cannot reasonably be expected by it to be eliminated;

(c) the synthetic equity arrangement party obtains accurate representations in writing from its counterparty, or from each affiliated counterparty, with respect to the synthetic equity arrangement that the counterparty, or each affiliated counterparty, as appropriate

(i) is not a tax-indifferent investor and does not reasonably expect to become a tax-indifferent investor during the particular period referred to in subsection (2.31),

(ii) has entered into specified synthetic equity arrangements

(A) that have the effect of eliminating all or substantially all of its risk of loss and opportunity for gain or profit in respect of the share,

(B) where no single specified counterparty or group of affiliated specified counterparties has been provided with all or substantially all of the risk of loss and opportunity for gain or profit in respect of the share, and

(C) where each specified counterparty or affiliated specified counterparty deals at arm's length with each other (other than in the case of affiliated specified counterparties, within the same group, of affiliated specified counterparties), and

(iii) has obtained accurate representations in writing from each of its specified counterparties, or from each of its affiliated specified counterparties, that

(A) it is a person resident in Canada and it does not reasonably expect to cease to be resident in Canada during the particular period referred to in subsection (2.31), and

(B) all or substantially all of its risk of loss and opportunity for gain or profit in respect of the share during the particular period referred to in subsection (2.31) has not been eliminated and cannot reasonably be expected by it to be eliminated;

(d) where a person or partnership is a party to a synthetic equity arrangement chain in respect of the share, the person or partnership

(i) has obtained all or substantially all of the risk of loss and opportunity for gain or profit in respect of the share under the synthetic equity arrangement chain,

(ii) has entered into one or more specified synthetic equity arrangements that have the effect of eliminating all or substantially all of its risk of loss and opportunity for gain or profit in respect of the share, and

(iii) obtains accurate representations in writing of the type described in paragraph (a), (b) or (c), as if it were a synthetic equity arrangement party, from each of its counterparties where each such counterparty deals at arm's length with that person or partnership.

Related Provisions: 248(42) — Synthetic equity arrangement relating to multiple identical shares.

Notes: See Notes to 112(2.3). 112(2.32) sets out rules under which a taxpayer can satisfy the 112(2.31)(b) condition by obtaining specific representations from its synthetic equity arrangement (SEA) counterparty(ies). In its simplest form, these rules require the taxpayer to obtain two representations: (1) the counterparty is not a tax-indifferent investor (TII), and (2) the counterparty does not reasonably expect to eliminate all or substantially all its risk of loss and opportunity for gain/profit on the share. The second representation is used as a substitute for a back-to-back anti-avoidance rule, and is intended to prevent a taxpayer from avoiding the application of the SEA rules by interposing a counterparty between itself and a TII. It is intended that the representations provide taxpayers and CRA with additional certainty as to whether an intermediate counterparty has, in fact, entered into a specified SEA with a TII.

These representation rules apply only to shorter chains of derivatives as the veracity of representations in longer chains would not be practicably verifiable by CRA.

112(2.32) requires that the representations obtained by the taxpayer be accurate. If a taxpayer relies on specified representations to claim a 112(1) deduction but CRA later determines them to be inaccurate, then the 112(2.31) exception will not apply, and the arrangement will be a dividend rental arrangement throughout the period.

112(2.32) requires that the representations be in writing. They could be included in a confirmation under an ISDA Master Agreement between the parties, if one exists. (Finance Technical Notes)

112(2.32)(a)(ii), (b)(iii)(B) and (c)(iii)(B) amended by 2018 budget bill #2, for dividends paid or that become payable after Feb. 26, 2018 (see Notes to 112(2.31)). For earlier dividends, each one read:

it has not eliminated and it does not reasonably expect to eliminate all or substantially all of its risk of loss and opportunity for gain or profit in respect of the share during the particular period referred to in subsection (2.31);

112(2.32) added by 2016 budget bill #1, effective on the same basis as the amendment to 112(2.3).

(2.33) End of particular period [where counterparty expects to become tax-indifferent or eliminate risk] — If, at a time during a particular period referred to in subsection (2.31), a counterparty, specified counterparty, affiliated counterparty or affiliated specified counterparty reasonably expects to become a tax-indifferent investor or — if it has provided a representation described by subparagraph (2.32)(a)(ii) or clause (2.32)(b)(iii)(B) or (c)(iii)(B) in respect of a share — that all or substantially all of its risk of loss and opportunity for gain or profit in respect of the share will be eliminated, the particular period for which it has provided a representation in respect of the share is deemed to end at that time.

Notes: See Notes to 112(2.3). 112(2.33) is intended to ensure that the 112(2.31) exception is available only for the period during which the representations that have been provided remain accurate.

112(2.33) amended by 2018 budget bill #2, for dividends paid or that become payable after Feb. 26, 2018 (see Notes to 112(2.31)), to change "to eliminate all or substantially all of its risk of loss and opportunity for gain or profit in respect of the share" to "that all or substantially all of its risk of loss and opportunity for gain or profit in respect of the share will be eliminated".

112(2.33) added by 2016 budget bill #1, effective on the same basis as the amendment to 112(2.3).

(2.34) Interpretation [references to counterparties] — For greater certainty, each reference in subsection (2.32) to a "counterparty", a "specified counterparty", an "affiliated counterparty" or an "affiliated specified counterparty" is to be read as referring only to a person or partnership that obtains all or any

portion of the risk of loss or opportunity for gain or profit in respect of the share.

Related Provisions: 248(1)"synthetic equity arrangement"(a)(i) — meaning of "counterparty".

Notes: See Notes to 112(2.3). 112(2.34) clarifies that the representations in 112(2.32) do not have to be obtained from certain contractual parties that may be involved in an equity derivative transaction, such as third-party calculation agents, if they do not obtain any economic exposure in respect of the share.

112(2.34) added by 2016 budget bill #1, effective on the same basis as the amendment to 112(2.3).

(2.4) Where no deduction permitted — No deduction may be made under subsection (1) or (2) or subsection 138(6) in computing the taxable income of a particular corporation in respect of a dividend received on a share (in this subsection referred to as the "subject share"), other than an exempt share, of the capital stock of another corporation where

(a) any person or partnership was obligated, either absolutely or contingently, to effect an undertaking, including any guarantee, covenant or agreement to purchase or repurchase the subject share, under which an investor is entitled, either immediately or in the future, to receive or obtain any amount or benefit for the purpose of reducing the impact, in whole or in part, of any loss that an investor may sustain by virtue of the ownership, holding or disposition of the subject share, and any property is used, in whole or in part, either directly or indirectly in any manner whatever, to secure the undertaking; or

(b) the consideration for which the subject share was issued or any other property received, either directly or indirectly, by an issuer from an investor, or any property substituted therefor, is or includes

(i) an obligation of an investor to make payments that are required to be included, in whole or in part, in computing the income of the issuer, other than an obligation of a corporation that, immediately before the subject share was issued, would be related to the corporation that issued the subject share if this Act were read without reference to paragraph 251(5)(b), or

(ii) any right to receive payments that are required to be included, in whole or in part, in computing the income of the issuer where that right is held on condition that it or property substituted therefor may revert or pass to an investor or a person or partnership to be determined by an investor,

where that obligation or right was acquired by the issuer as part of a transaction or event or a series of transactions or events that included the issuance or acquisition of the subject share, or a share for which the subject share was substituted.

Related Provisions: 87(4.2) — Amalgamations; 112(2.5) — Application of subsec. (2.4); 112(2.6) — Definitions; 112(2.8) — Loss sustained by investor; 112(2.9) — Related corporations; 248(1) — "amount" of a stock dividend; 248(5) — Substituted property; 248(10) — Series of transactions. See also at end of s. 112.

Notes: The shares described in 112(2.4) are generally referred to as "collateralized preferred shares".

For the meaning of "indirectly", see Notes to 17.1(1).

Interpretation Bulletins: IT-88R2: Stock dividends.

(2.5) Application of subsec. (2.4) — Subsection (2.4) applies only in respect of a dividend on a share where, having regard to all the circumstances, it may reasonably be considered that the share was issued or acquired as part of a transaction or event or a series of transactions or events that enabled any corporation to earn investment income, or any income substituted therefor, and, as a result, the amount of its taxes payable under this Act for a taxation year is less than the amount that its taxes payable under this Act would be for the year if that investment income were the only income of the corporation for the year and all other taxation years and no amount were deductible under subsections 127(5) and 127.2(1) in computing its taxes payable under this Act.

Related Provisions: 248(10) — Series of transactions.

(2.6) Definitions — For the purposes of this subsection and subsection (2.4),

"exempt share" means

(a) a prescribed share,

(b) a share of the capital stock of a corporation issued before 5:00 p.m. Eastern Standard Time, November 27, 1986, other than a share held at that time

(i) by the issuer, or

(ii) by any person or partnership where the issuer may become entitled to receive any amount after that time by way of subscription proceeds or contribution of capital with respect to that share pursuant to an agreement made before that time, or

(c) a share that was, at the time the dividend referred to in subsection (2.4) was received, a share described in paragraph (e) of the definition "term preferred share" in subsection 248(1) during the applicable time period referred to in that paragraph;

Related Provisions: 112(2.7) — Change in agreement or condition; 248(13) — Interests in trusts and partnerships. See also at end of s. 112.

Notes: Para. (c) added by 1993 technical bill, effective Dec. 22, 1992.

"investor" means the particular corporation referred to in subsection (2.4) and a person with whom that corporation does not deal at arm's length and any partnership or trust of which that corporation, or a person with whom that corporation does not deal at arm's length, is a member or beneficiary, but does not include the other corporation referred to in that subsection;

"issuer" means the other corporation referred to in subsection (2.4) and a person with whom that corporation does not deal at arm's length and any partnership or trust of which that corporation, or a person with whom that corporation does not deal at arm's length, is a member or beneficiary, but does not include the particular corporation referred to in that subsection.

(2.7) Change in agreement or condition — For the purposes of the definition "exempt share" in subsection (2.6), where at any time after 5:00 p.m. Eastern Standard Time, November 27, 1986 the terms or conditions of a share of the capital stock of a corporation have been changed or any agreement in respect of the share has been changed or entered into by the corporation, the share shall be deemed to have been issued at that time.

(2.8) Loss sustained by investor — For the purposes of paragraph (2.4)(a), any loss that an investor may sustain by virtue of the ownership, holding or disposition of the subject share referred to in that paragraph shall be deemed to include any loss with respect to an obligation or share that was issued or acquired as part of a transaction or event or a series of transactions or events that included the issuance or acquisition of the subject share, or a share for which the subject share was substituted.

Related Provisions: 248(10) — Series of transactions.

(2.9) Related corporations — For the purposes of subparagraph (2.4)(b)(i), where it may reasonably be considered having regard to all the circumstances that a corporation has become related to any other corporation for the purpose of avoiding any limitation upon the deduction of a dividend under subsection (1), (2) or 138(6), the corporation shall be deemed not to be related to the other corporation.

Related Provisions: 87(2)(rr) — Amalgamations — tax on taxable preferred shares. See also at end of s. 112.

(3) Loss on share that is capital property — Subject to subsections (5.5) and (5.6), the amount of any loss of a taxpayer (other than a trust) from the disposition of a share that is capital property of the taxpayer (other than a share that is property of a partnership) is deemed to be the amount of the loss determined without reference to this subsection minus,

(a) where the taxpayer is an individual, the lesser of

(i) the total of all amounts each of which is a dividend received by the taxpayer on the share in respect of which an election was made under subsection 83(2) where subsection 83(2.1) does not deem the dividend to be a taxable dividend, and

(ii) the loss determined without reference to this subsection minus all taxable dividends received by the taxpayer on the share; and

(b) where the taxpayer is a corporation, the total of all amounts received by the taxpayer on the share each of which is

(i) a taxable dividend, to the extent of the amount of the dividend that was deductible under this section or subsection 115(1) or 138(6) in computing the taxpayer's taxable income or taxable income earned in Canada for any taxation year,

(ii) a dividend in respect of which an election was made under subsection 83(2) where subsection 83(2.1) does not deem the dividend to be a taxable dividend, or

(iii) a life insurance capital dividend.

Related Provisions: 40(2)(g) — Restriction on capital losses; 40(3.3), (3.4) — Limitation on loss where share acquired by affiliated person; 40(3.7) — Application to non-resident individual; 53(1)(f) — Addition to ACB; 87(2)(x) — Amalgamations — flow-through to new corporation; 93(2) — Parallel rule on disposition of shares of foreign affiliate; 107(1)(c), (d) — Parallel stop-loss rule on disposition of interest in trust that flowed dividends out to corporation; 107.4(3)(b)(ii) — Application of stop-loss rule to qualifying disposition; 112(3.01) — Exclusion for certain dividends; 112(3.1), (3.2) — Loss on share that is capital property of partnership or trust; 112(4)–(4.22) — Shares held as inventory; 112(5.2)C(b) — Adjustment for dividends received on mark-to-market property; 112(7) — Rules where shares exchanged; 112(10) — Synthetic equity arrangement — identical properties. See also at end of s. 112.

Notes: 112(3) is a "stop-loss" rule reducing a loss from disposition of a share that is capital property, where the taxpayer received capital dividends on the share. There is no offsetting addition to adjusted cost base; the denial of deduction is permanent. Analogous rules for shares held by partnerships and trusts, or held as inventory, appear in 112(3.1)-(4.22).

112(3) applies only where dividends were paid on the same shares, and not on shares of a different class, no matter how similar the share attributes: *Toronto Dominion Bank*, 2011 FCA 221, para. 59. For an example of 112(3) applying see VIEWS doc 2011-0416001R3 (split-up butterfly).

For discussion of 112(3)–(3.32), see Burpee, "The New Stop-Loss Rules", 46(3) *Canadian Tax Journal* 678-95 (1998); Suarez, "The Capital Property Dividend Stop-Loss Rules", 53(1) *CTJ* 269-91 (2005); Kakkar, "Section 112 Stop-Loss Rules Prevail", 5(3) *Tax for the Owner-Manager* (ctf.ca) 3-4 (July 2005).

112(3) amended by 1995-97 technical bill, for dispositions after April 26, 1995, other than:

(a) a disposition pursuant to an agreement in writing made before April 27, 1995;

(b) a disposition of a share of the capital stock of a corporation that is made to the corporation if

(i) on April 26, 1995 the share was owned by an individual (other than a trust) or by a particular trust under which an individual (other than a trust) was a beneficiary,

(ii) on April 26, 1995 a corporation, or a partnership of which a corporation is a member, was a beneficiary of a life insurance policy that insured the life of the individual or the individual's spouse,

(iii) it was reasonable to conclude on April 26, 1995 that a main purpose of the life insurance policy was to fund, directly or indirectly, in whole or in part, a redemption, acquisition or cancellation of the share by the corporation that issued the share, and

(iv) [per Part 6 of 2001 technical bill: for 2001 and later taxation years, and for 2000 taxation year if an election is made for the common-law partner rules to apply to 2000; see Notes to 248(1)"common-law partner")] the disposition is made by

(A) the individual or the individual's spouse or common-law partner,

(B) the estate of the individual or of the individual's spouse or common-law partner within the estate's first taxation year,

(C) the particular trust where it is a post-1971 spousal or common-law partner trust or a trust described in 104(4)(a.1), the individual's spouse or common-law partner, as the case may be, is the beneficiary referred to in subpara. (i) above and the disposition occurs before the end of the trust's third taxation year that begins after the death of the individual's spouse or common-law partner, as the case may be, or

(D) a trust described in 73(1.01)(c) created by the individual, or a trust described in 70(6)(b) created by the individual's will in respect of the individual's spouse or common-law partner, before the end of the trust's third taxation year that begins after the death of the individual or the individual's spouse or common-law partner, as the case may be;

(iv) [per Part 6 of 2001 technical bill and per 1995-97 technical bill: different conditions apply for 1995-97, 1998-99 and 2000 taxation years otherwise; no longer reproduced here]; or

(c)-(e): [grandfathering for various dispositions before 1997, no longer reproduced]

For purposes of the above, subsec. 131(12) of the 1995-97 technical bill provides:

(12) For the purposes of paragraph [(b) above] and this subsection, a share of the capital stock of a corporation acquired in exchange for another share in a transaction to which section 51, 85, 86 or 87 of the Act applies is deemed to be the same share as the other share.

(In other words, grandfathering continues despite any number of rollovers under the listed provisions.) Grandfathering is not affected by life insurance replacement or conversion: VIEWS doc 2005-0124311E5. See also 2005-0136041E5, 2005-0145111E5, 2005-0147401I7, 2005-0161291R3, 2007-0241981C6, 2010-0359431C6, 2011-0398401C6 and 2011-0399401C6, on whether amendments to an agreement (or change in policy ownership or beneficiary designation) cause loss of grandfathering; Stephens, "CRA Looks at the Grandfathering Rules", XII(2) *Insurance Planning [IP]* (Federated Press) 767-71 (2006); Wark, "Stop-Loss Grandfathering Revisited", XII(3) *IP* 783-84 (2006); Truster, "Corporate-Owned Life Insurance: Grandfathering", 10(3) *Tax for the Owner-Manager* (ctf.ca) 6-7 (July 2010).

Before the amendment, since Oct. 31, 1994, read:

(3) Loss on share that is capital property — Subject to subsections (5.5) and (5.6), where a corporation owns a share that is a capital property and receives a taxable dividend, a capital dividend or a life insurance capital dividend in respect of that share, the amount of any loss of the corporation arising from transactions with reference to the share on which the dividend was received shall, unless it is established by the corporation that

(a) the corporation owned the share 365 days or longer before the loss was sustained, and

(b) the corporation and persons with whom the corporation was not dealing at arm's length did not, at the time the dividend was received, own in the aggregate more than 5% of the issued shares of any class of the capital stock of the corporation from which the dividend was received,

be deemed to be the amount of that loss otherwise determined, minus the total of all amounts each of which is an amount received by the corporation in respect of

(c) a taxable dividend on the share to the extent that the amount of the dividend was deductible from the corporation's income for any taxation year by virtue of this section or subsection 138(6) and was not an amount on which the corporation was required to pay tax under Part VII of the *Income Tax Act*, chapter 148 of the Revised Statutes of Canada, 1952, as it read on March 31, 1977,

(d) a capital dividend on the share, or

(e) a life insurance capital dividend on the share.

Reference to 112(5.5) and (5.6) added to 112(3) by 1994 technical bill, effective for dispositions occurring after October 30, 1994.

I.T. Application Rules: 69 (meaning of "chapter 148 of ...").

Income Tax Folios: S3-F2-C1: Capital Dividends [replaces IT-66R6].

Interpretation Bulletins: IT-88R2: Stock dividends; IT-328R3: Losses on shares on which dividends have been received.

I.T. Technical News: 12 (stop-loss provisions — grandfathering).

CRA Audit Manual: 29.2.4: Specific exceptions to capital gain and loss rules.

(3.01) Loss on share that is capital property — excluded dividends — A qualified dividend shall not be included in the total determined under subparagraph (3)(a)(i) or paragraph (3)(b) if the taxpayer establishes that

(a) it was received when the taxpayer and persons with whom the taxpayer was not dealing at arm's length did not own in total more than 5% of the issued shares of any class of the capital stock of the corporation from which the dividend was received; and

(b) it was received on a share that the taxpayer owned throughout the 365-day period that ended immediately before the disposition.

Related Provisions: 87(2)(x) — Amalgamations — flow-through to new corporation; 112(5.6) — Stop-loss rules restricted; 112(6.1) — Qualified dividend; 112(8), (9) — Effect of synthetic disposition.

Notes: In CRA's view, the "issued shares" of the "class" in 112(3.01)(a) is the actual number of shares in the class, not the "separate class" created by an 84(3) deemed dividend: VIEWS doc 2005-0112921E5.

112(3.01) amended by 2011 budget bill #2, for dispositions after March 21, 2011, to change "dividend" to "qualified dividend" (see 112(6.1)). Added by 1995-97 technical bill, effective on the same basis as the amendments to 112(3).

(3.1) Loss on share held by partnership — Subject to subsections (5.5) and (5.6), where a taxpayer (other than a partnership or a mutual fund trust) is a member of a partnership, the taxpayer's share of any loss of the partnership from the disposition of a share that is held by a particular partnership as capital property is deemed to be that share of the loss determined without reference to this subsection minus,

(a) where the taxpayer is an individual, the lesser of

(i) the total of all amounts each of which is a dividend received by the taxpayer on the share in respect of which an election was made under subsection 83(2) where subsection 83(2.1) does not deem the dividend to be a taxable dividend, and

(ii) that share of the loss determined without reference to this subsection minus all taxable dividends received by the taxpayer on the share;

(b) where the taxpayer is a corporation, the total of all amounts received by the taxpayer on the share each of which is

(i) a taxable dividend, to the extent of the amount of the dividend that was deductible under this section or subsection 115(1) or 138(6) in computing the taxpayer's taxable income or taxable income earned in Canada for any taxation year,

(ii) a dividend in respect of which an election was made under subsection 83(2) where subsection 83(2.1) does not deem the dividend to be a taxable dividend, or

(iii) a life insurance capital dividend; and

(c) where the taxpayer is a trust, the total of all amounts each of which is

(i) a taxable dividend, or

(ii) a life insurance capital dividend

received on the share and designated under subsection 104(19) or (20) by the trust in respect of a beneficiary that was a corporation, partnership or trust.

Related Provisions: 40(3.3), (3.4) — Limitation on loss where share acquired by affiliated person; 40(3.7) — Application to non-resident individual; 53(1)(f) — Addition to ACB; 53(2)(c)(i)(C) — Rule ignored in determining reduction in ACB; 87(2)(x) — Amalgamations — flow-through to new corporation; 100(4) — Application of stop-loss rule to disposition of interest in partnership; 104(20) — Designation re non-taxable dividends; 107.4(3)(b)(ii) — Application of stop-loss rule to qualifying disposition; 112(3.11) — Exclusion for certain dividends; 112(3.12) — Amount designated by trust to beneficiary that is a partnership or trust; 112(5.2)C(c) — Adjustment for dividends received on mark-to-market property; 112(7) — Rules where shares exchanged; 112(10) — Synthetic equity arrangement — identical properties. See also at end of s. 112.

Notes: In *Bank of Montreal*, 2020 FCA 82, since pre-2013 39(2) deemed a loss on shares in a tower structure to be a loss on currency, 112(3.1) did not apply to deny the loss, and GAAR did not apply as there was no "tax benefit".

112(3.1) amended by 1995-97 technical bill, effective on the same basis as the amendments to 112(3) (i.e., generally April 27, 1995 but subject to extensive grandfathering).

Before the amendment, since Oct. 31, 1994, read:

(3.1) Loss on share that is capital property of partnership — Subject to subsections (5.5) and (5.6), where a corporation is a member of a partnership and the corporation receives a taxable dividend, a capital dividend or a life insurance capital dividend in respect of a share that is a capital property of the partnership, the corporation's share of any loss of the partnership arising with respect to the share on which the dividend was received shall, unless it is established by the corporation that

(a) the partnership held the share 365 days or longer before the loss was sustained, and

(b) the partnership, the corporation and persons with whom the corporation was not dealing at arm's length did not, at the time the dividend was received, hold in the aggregate more than 5% of the issued shares of any class of the capital stock of the corporation from which the dividend was received,

be deemed to be the amount of that loss otherwise determined, minus the total of all amounts each of which is an amount received by the corporation in respect of

(c) a taxable dividend on the share to the extent that the amount of the dividend was deductible from the corporation's income for any taxation year by

virtue of this section or subsection 138(6) and was not an amount on which the corporation was required to pay tax under Part VII of the *Income Tax Act*, chapter 148 of the Revised Statutes of Canada, 1952, as it read on March 31, 1977,

(d) a capital dividend on the share, or

(e) a life insurance capital dividend on the share.

Reference to 112(5.5) and (5.6) added to 112(3.1) by 1994 technical bill, for dispositions after Oct. 30, 1994.

I.T. Application Rules: 69 (meaning of "chapter 148 of ...").

Income Tax Folios: S3-F2-C1: Capital Dividends [replaces IT-66R6].

Interpretation Bulletins: IT-88R2: Stock dividends; IT-328R3: Losses on shares on which dividends have been received.

I.T. Technical News: 12 (stop-loss provisions — grandfathering).

(3.11) Loss on share held by partnership — excluded dividends — A qualified dividend shall not be included in the total determined under subparagraph (3.1)(a)(i) or paragraph (3.1)(b) or (c) if the taxpayer establishes that

(a) it was received when the particular partnership, the taxpayer and persons with whom the taxpayer was not dealing at arm's length did not hold in total more than 5% of the issued shares of any class of the capital stock of the corporation from which the dividend was received; and

(b) it was received on a share that the particular partnership held throughout the 365-day period that ended immediately before the disposition.

Related Provisions: 87(2)(x) — Amalgamations — flow-through to new corporation; 112(5.6) — Stop-loss rules restricted; 112(6.1) — Qualified dividend; 112(8), (9) — Effect of synthetic disposition.

Notes: 112(3.11) amended by 2011 budget bill #2, for dispositions after March 21, 2011, to change "dividend" to "qualified dividend" (see 112(6.1)). Added by 1995-97 technical bill, effective on the same basis as the amendments to 112(3).

(3.12) Loss on share held by partnership — excluded dividends — A taxable dividend received on a share and designated under subsection 104(19) by a particular trust in respect of a beneficiary that was a partnership or trust shall not be included in the total determined under paragraph (3.1)(c) where the particular trust establishes that the dividend was received by an individual (other than a trust).

Notes: 112(3.12) added by 1995-97 technical bill, effective on the same basis as the amendments to 112(3) (i.e., generally April 27, 1995 but subject to extensive grandfathering).

(3.2) Loss on share held by trust — Subject to subsections (5.5) and (5.6), the amount of any loss of a trust (other than a mutual fund trust) from the disposition of a share of the capital stock of a corporation that is capital property of the trust is deemed to be the amount of the loss determined without reference to this subsection minus the total of

(a) the amount, if any, by which the lesser of

(i) the total of all amounts each of which is a dividend received by the trust on the share in respect of which an election was made under subsection 83(2) where subsection 83(2.1) does not deem the dividend to be a taxable dividend, and

(ii) the loss determined without reference to this subsection minus the total of all amounts each of which is the amount of a taxable dividend

(A) received by the trust on the share,

(B) received on the share and designated under subsection 104(19) by the trust in respect of a beneficiary who is an individual (other than a trust), or

(C) that is a qualified dividend received on the share and designated under subsection 104(19) by the trust in respect of a beneficiary that was a corporation, partnership or another trust where the trust establishes that

(I) it owned the share throughout the 365-day period that ended immediately before the disposition, and

(II) the dividend was received while the trust, the beneficiary and persons not dealing at arm's length with the beneficiary owned in total less than 5% of the issued shares of any class of the capital stock of the corporation from which the dividend was received

exceeds

(iii) if the trust is an individual's graduated rate estate, the share was acquired as a consequence of the individual's death and the disposition occurs during the trust's first taxation year, ½ of the lesser of

(A) the loss determined without reference to this subsection, and

(B) the individual's capital gain from the disposition of the share immediately before the individual's death, and

(b) the total of all amounts each of which is

(i) a taxable dividend, or

(ii) a life insurance capital dividend

received on the share and designated under subsection 104(19) or (20) by the trust in respect of a beneficiary that was a corporation, partnership or trust.

Related Provisions: 40(3.7) — Application to non-resident individual; 53(1)(f) — Addition to ACB; 87(2)(x) — Amalgamations — flow-through to new corp; 104(20) — Designation re non-taxable dividends; 107.4(3)(b)(ii) — Application of stop-loss rule to qualifying disposition; 112(3.3), (3.31) — Exceptions; 112(5.2)C(b) — Adjustment for dividends received on mark-to-market property; 112(5.6) — Stop-loss rules restricted; 112(6.1) — Qualified dividend; 112(7) — Rules where shares exchanged; 112(8), (9) — Effect of synthetic disposition. See also at end of s. 112.

Notes: See Notes to 112(3). 112(3.2) will apply to an estate (as well as other trusts); the ½ allowance in 112(3.2)(a)(iii) allows a capital dividend, funded by corporate-owned life insurance, to reduce the tax payable on freeze shares (high value, low PUC) on death. See Joel Cuperfain, "Life Insurance and the Reduction of Tax Liability", VI(4) *Insurance Planning* (Federated Press) 398-401 (1999). Starting 2016, 112(3.2)(a)(iii) can be used only by a GRE: see Notes to 248(1)"graduated rate estate".

The stop-loss reduction in 112(3.2) is computed on a share-by-share basis: VIEWS doc 2007-0224371I7. Thus, on redemptions of shares on two consecutive days, each transaction is considered separately: doc 2009-0310601I7.

See also Stephens, "The 'Spousal Rollover and Redeem' Strategy", XI(2) *Insurance Planning* 694-96 (2005); docs 2009-0346261I7, 2018-0744151C6 [STEP 2018 q.15].

112(3.2)(a)(iii) opening words amended by 2014 budget bill #2, for 2016 and later taxation years, to change "estate" to "graduated rate estate".

112(3.2)(a)(ii)(C) opening words amended by 2011 budget bill #2, effective for dispositions occurring after March 21, 2011, to add "that is a qualified dividend" (see 112(6.1)).

112(3.2)(a)(iii) amended by 2000 Budget to change "¼" to "½", effective for dispositions that occur after October 17, 2000; for dispositions that occurred from February 27, 2000 through October 17, 2000, read as "⅓".

112(3.2) amended by 1995-97 technical bill, effective on the same basis as the amendments to 112(3) (i.e., generally April 27, 1995 but subject to extensive grandfathering). Before the amendment, since October 31, 1994, read:

> (3.2) Loss on share that is capital property of trust — Subject to subsections (5.5) and (5.6), where a corporation is a beneficiary of a trust (other than a prescribed trust) that owns a share that is capital property and the corporation receives a taxable dividend in respect of that share pursuant to a designation under subsection 104(19) or the trust has made a designation under subsection 104(20) in respect of the corporation for a capital dividend or a life insurance capital dividend on that share, the amount of any loss of the trust arising with respect to the share on which the dividend was subject to a designation shall, unless it is established by the corporation that
>
> (a) the trust owned the share 365 days or longer before the loss was sustained, and
>
> (b) the trust, the corporation and persons with whom the corporation was not dealing at arm's length did not, at the time the dividend was received, own in the aggregate more than 5% of the issued shares of any class of the capital stock of the corporation from which the dividend was received,
>
> be deemed to be the amount of that loss otherwise determined, minus the total of all amounts each of which is a taxable dividend, a capital dividend or a life insurance capital dividend in respect of that share that was designated under subsection 104(19) or (20) in respect of a beneficiary that was a corporation.

Reference to 112(5.5) and (5.6) added to 112(3.2) by 1994 technical bill, effective for dispositions occurring after October 30, 1994.

Income Tax Folios: S3-F2-C1: Capital Dividends [replaces IT-66R6].

Interpretation Bulletins: IT-88R2: Stock dividends; IT-328R3: Losses on shares on which dividends have been received.

I.T. Technical News: 12 (stop-loss provisions — grandfathering).

(3.3) Loss on share held by trust — special cases — Notwithstanding subsection (3.2), where a trust has at any time acquired a share of the capital stock of a corporation because of subsection 104(4), the amount of any loss of the trust from a disposition after that time is deemed to be the amount of the loss determined without reference to subsection (3.2) and this subsection minus the total of

(a) the amount, if any, by which the lesser of

(i) the total of all amounts each of which is a dividend received after that time by the trust on the share in respect of which an election was made under subsection 83(2) where subsection 83(2.1) does not deem the dividend to be a taxable dividend, and

(ii) the loss determined without reference to subsection (3.2) and this subsection minus the total of all amounts each of which is the amount of a taxable dividend

(A) received by the trust on the share after that time,

(B) received on the share after that time and designated under subsection 104(19) by the trust in respect of a beneficiary who is an individual (other than a trust), or

(C) that is a qualified dividend received on the share after that time and designated under subsection 104(19) by the trust in respect of a beneficiary that was a corporation, partnership or another trust where the trust establishes that

(I) it owned the share throughout the 365-day period that ended immediately before the disposition, and

(II) the dividend was received when the trust, the beneficiary and persons not dealing at arm's length with the beneficiary owned in total less than 5% of the issued shares of any class of the capital stock of the corporation from which the dividend was received

exceeds

(iii) ½ of the lesser of

(A) the loss from the disposition, determined without reference to subsection (3.2) and this subsection, and

(B) the trust's capital gain from the disposition immediately before that time of the share because of subsection 104(4), and

(b) the total of all amounts each of which is a taxable dividend received on the share after that time and designated under subsection 104(19) by the trust in respect of a beneficiary that was a corporation, partnership or trust.

Related Provisions: 40(3.7) — Application to non-resident individual; 87(2)(x) — Amalgamations — flow-through to new corporation; 107.4(3)(b)(ii) — Application of stop-loss rule to qualifying disposition; 112(3.31), (3.32) — Excluded dividends; 112(5.6) — Stop-loss rules restricted; 112(6.1) — Qualified dividend; 112(7) — Rules where shares exchanged; 112(8), (9) — Effect of synthetic disposition.

Notes: 112(3.3)(a)(ii)(C) opening words amended by 2011 budget bill #2, effective for dispositions occurring after March 21, 2011, to add "that is a qualified dividend" (see 112(6.1)).

112(3.3)(a)(iii) amended by 2000 Budget to change "¼" to "½", effective for dispositions that occur after Oct. 17, 2000; for dispositions that occurred from Feb. 27, 2000 through Oct. 17, 2000, read as "⅓".

112(3.3) added by 1995-97 technical bill, effective on the same basis as the amendments to 112(3) (i.e., generally April 27, 1995 but subject to extensive grandfathering).

Income Tax Folios: S3-F2-C1: Capital Dividends [replaces IT-66R6].

(3.31) Loss on share held by trust — excluded dividends — A qualified dividend received by a trust shall not be included under subparagraph (3.2)(a)(i) or (b)(ii) or (3.3)(a)(i) if the trust establishes that the dividend

(a) was received,

(i) in any case where the dividend was designated under subsection 104(19) or (20) by the trust, when the trust, the beneficiary and persons with whom the beneficiary was not dealing at arm's length did not own in total more than 5% of the issued shares of any class of the capital stock of the corporation from which the dividend was received, or

(ii) in any other case, when the trust and persons with whom the trust was not dealing at arm's length did not own in total more than 5% of the issued shares of any class of the capital stock of the corporation from which the dividend was received, and

(b) was received on a share that the trust owned throughout the 365-day period that ended immediately before the disposition.

Related Provisions: 87(2)(x) — Amalgamations — flow-through to new corporation; 104(20) — Designation re non-taxable dividends; 112(5.6) — Stop-loss rules restricted; 112(6.1) — Qualified dividend; 112(7) — Rules where shares exchanged; 112(8), (9) — Effect of synthetic disposition.

Notes: 112(3.31) opening words amended by 2011 budget bill #2, effective for dispositions occurring after March 21, 2011, to change "No dividend ... shall be" to "A qualified dividend ... shall not be". (See 112(6.1).)

112(3.31) added by 1995-97 technical bill, effective on the same basis as the amendments to 112(3) (i.e., generally April 27, 1995 but subject to extensive grandfathering).

(3.32) Loss on share held by trust — excluded dividends — A qualified dividend that is a taxable dividend received on the share and that is designated under subsection 104(19) by the trust in respect of a beneficiary that was a corporation, partnership or trust, shall not be included under paragraph (3.2)(b) or (3.3)(b) if the trust establishes that the dividend was received by an individual (other than a trust), or

(a) was received when the trust, the beneficiary and persons with whom the beneficiary was not dealing at arm's length did not own in total more than 5% of the issued shares of any class of the capital stock of the corporation from which the dividend was received; and

(b) was received on a share that the trust owned throughout the 365-day period that ended immediately before the disposition.

Related Provisions: 87(2)(x) — Amalgamations — flow-through to new corporation; 112(6.1) — Qualified dividend; 112(8), (9) — Effect of synthetic disposition.

Notes: 112(3.32) opening words amended by 2011 budget bill #2, effective for dispositions occurring after March 21, 2011, to change "No taxable dividend ... shall be" to "A qualified dividend that is a taxable dividend ... shall not be". (See 112(6.1).)

112(3.32) added by 1995-97 technical bill, effective on the same basis as the amendments to 112(3) (i.e., generally April 27, 1995 but subject to extensive grandfathering).

(4) Loss on share that is not capital property — Subject to subsections (5.5) and (5.6), the amount of any loss of a taxpayer (other than a trust) from the disposition of a share of the capital stock of a corporation that is property (other than capital property) of the taxpayer is deemed to be the amount of the loss determined without reference to this subsection minus,

(a) where the taxpayer is an individual and the corporation is resident in Canada, the total of all dividends received by the individual on the share;

(b) where the taxpayer is a partnership, the total of all dividends received by the partnership on the share; and

(c) where the taxpayer is a corporation, the total of all amounts received by the taxpayer on the share each of which is

(i) a taxable dividend, to the extent of the amount of the dividend that was deductible under this section, section 113 or subsection 115(1) or 138(6) in computing the taxpayer's taxable income or taxable income earned in Canada for any taxation year, or

(ii) a dividend (other than a taxable dividend).

Related Provisions: 53(2)(c)(i)(C) — Rule ignored in determining ACB reduction; 87(2)(x) — Amalgamation — flow-through to new corp; 93(2)–(2.3) — Loss limitation on disposition of share; 112(4.01) — Exclusion for certain dividends; 112(5.2)C(b) — Adjustment for dividend received on mark-to-market property; 112(10) — Synthetic equity arrangement — identical property. See also at end of s. 112.

Notes: See VIEWS doc 2008-0265311E5 (interaction with 186(1)).

112(4) amended by 1995-97 technical bill (effective for dispositions after April 26, 1995), 1994 technical bill and 1993 and 1991 technical bills.

Interpretation Bulletins: IT-88R2: Stock dividends; IT-328R3: Losses on shares on which dividends have been received.

(4.01) Loss on share that is not capital property — excluded dividends — A qualified dividend shall not be included in the total determined under paragraph (4)(a), (b) or (c) if the taxpayer establishes that

(a) it was received when the taxpayer and persons with whom the taxpayer was not dealing at arm's length did not own in total more than 5% of the issued shares of any class of the capital stock of the corporation from which the dividend was received; and

(b) it was received on a share that the taxpayer owned throughout the 365-day period that ended immediately before the disposition.

Related Provisions: 87(2)(x) — Amalgamations — flow-through to new corporation; 112(5.6) — Stop-loss rules restricted; 112(6.1) — Qualified dividend; 112(8), (9) — Effect of synthetic disposition.

Notes: 112(4.01) opening words amended by 2011 budget bill #2, effective for dispositions occurring after March 21, 2011, to change "dividend" to "qualified dividend" (see 112(6.1)).

112(4.01) added by 1995-97 technical bill, for dispositions after April 26, 1995.

(4.1) Fair market value of shares held as inventory — For the purpose of section 10, the fair market value at any time of a share of the capital stock of a corporation is deemed to be equal to the fair market value of the share at that time, plus

(a) where the shareholder is a corporation, the total of all amounts received by the shareholder on the share before that time each of which is

(i) a taxable dividend, to the extent of the amount of the dividend that was deductible under this section, section 113 or subsection 115(1) or 138(6) in computing the shareholder's taxable income or taxable income earned in Canada for any taxation year, or

(ii) a dividend (other than a taxable dividend);

(b) where the shareholder is a partnership, the total of all amounts each of which is a dividend received by the shareholder on the share before that time; and

(c) where the shareholder is an individual and the corporation is resident in Canada, the total of all amounts each of which is a dividend received by the shareholder on the share before that time (or, where the shareholder is a trust, that would have been so received if this Act were read without reference to subsection 104(19)).

Related Provisions: 87(2)(x) — Amalgamations — flow-through to new corporation; 112(4.11) — Exclusion for certain dividends; 112(10) — Synthetic equity arrangement — identical properties. See also at end of s. 112.

Notes: 112(4.1) amended by 1995-97 technical bill (effective for taxation years that end after April 26, 1995) and 1993 and 1991 technical bills.

Interpretation Bulletins: IT-88R2: Stock dividends; IT-328R3: Losses on shares on which dividends have been received.

(4.11) Fair market value of shares held as inventory — excluded dividends — A qualified dividend shall not be included in the total determined under paragraph (4.1)(a), (b) or (c) if the shareholder establishes that

(a) it was received while the shareholder and persons with whom the shareholder was not dealing at arm's length did not hold in total more than 5% of the issued shares of any class of the capital stock of the corporation from which the dividend was received; and

(b) it was received on a share that the shareholder held throughout the 365-day period that ended at the time referred to in subsection (4.1).

Related Provisions: 87(2)(x) — Amalgamations — flow-through to new corporation; 112(6.1) — Qualified dividend; 112(8), (9) — Effect of synthetic disposition.

Notes: 112(4.11) opening words amended by 2011 budget bill #2, effective for dispositions occurring after March 21, 2011, to change "dividend" to "qualified dividend" (see 112(6.1)).

112(4.11) added by 1995-97 technical bill, effective for taxation years that end after April 26, 1995.

(4.2) Loss on share held by trust — Subject to subsections (5.5) and (5.6), the amount of any loss of a trust from the disposition of a share that is property (other than capital property) of the trust is deemed to be the amount of the loss determined without reference to this subsection minus

(a) the total of all amounts each of which is a dividend received by the trust on the share, to the extent that the amount was not designated under subsection 104(20) in respect of a beneficiary of the trust; and

(b) the total of all amounts each of which is a dividend received on the share that was designated under subsection 104(19) or (20) by the trust in respect of a beneficiary of the trust.

Related Provisions: 87(2)(x) — Amalgamations — flow-through to new corporation; 104(20) — Designation re non-taxable dividends; 112(3.2) — Stop-loss rule; 112(4.21), (4.22) — Exclusions for certain dividends; 112(5.2)C(b) — Adjustment for dividends received on mark-to-market property. See also at end of s. 112.

Notes: 112(4.2) amended by 1995-97 technical bill (for dispositions after April 26, 1995). For earlier dispositions (still needed for 53(2)(c)(i)(C)), read:

(4.2) Where no deduction permitted — Subject to subsections (5.5) and (5.6), where a taxpayer is a member of a partnership and the taxpayer receives a dividend in respect of a share that is not a capital property of the partnership, the taxpayer's share of any loss of the partnership arising with respect to the share on which the dividend was received shall, unless it is established by the taxpayer that

(a) the partnership held the share 365 days or longer before the loss was sustained, and

(b) the partnership, the taxpayer and persons with whom the taxpayer was not dealing at arm's length did not, at the time the dividend was received, hold in the aggregate more than 5% of the issued shares of any class of the capital stock of the corporation from which the dividend was received, be deemed to be the amount of that loss otherwise determined, minus

(c) where the taxpayer is an individual and the corporation is a taxable Canadian corporation, the total of all amounts each of which is a dividend (other than a capital gains dividend within the meaning assigned by subsection 131(1)) on the share received by the taxpayer,

(d) where the taxpayer is a corporation, the total of all amounts each of which is

(i) a taxable dividend, to the extent of the amount thereof that was deductible under this section or subsection 115(1) or 138(6) in computing the taxpayer's taxable income or taxable income earned in Canada for any taxation year, or

(ii) a dividend (other than a taxable dividend or a dividend deemed by subsection 131(1) to be a capital gains dividend),

on the share received by the taxpayer, and

(e) in any other case, nil.

112(4.2) earlier amended by 1994 technical bill, 1993 and 1991 technical bills.

Interpretation Bulletins: IT-88R2: Stock dividends; IT-328R3: Losses on shares on which dividends have been received.

(4.21) Loss on share held by trust — excluded dividends — A qualified dividend shall not be included in the total determined under paragraph (4.2)(a) if the taxpayer establishes that

(a) it was received when the trust and persons with whom the trust was not dealing at arm's length did not own in total more than 5% of the issued shares of any class of the capital stock of the corporation from which the dividend was received; and

(b) it was received on a share that the trust owned throughout the 365-day period that ended immediately before the disposition.

Related Provisions: 87(2)(x) — Amalgamations — flow-through to new corporation; 112(5.6) — Stop-loss rules restricted; 112(6.1) — Qualified dividend; 112(8), (9) — Effect of synthetic disposition.

Notes: 112(4.21) opening words amended by 2011 budget bill #2, effective for dispositions occurring after March 21, 2011, to change "dividend" to "qualified dividend" (see 112(6.1)).

112(4.21) added by 1995-97 technical bill, for dispositions after April 26, 1995.

(4.22) Loss on share held by trust — excluded dividends — A qualified dividend shall not be included in the total determined under paragraph (4.2)(b) if the taxpayer establishes that

(a) it was received when the trust, the beneficiary and persons with whom the beneficiary was not dealing at arm's length did not own in total more than 5% of the issued shares of any class of the capital stock of the corporation from which the dividend was received; and

(b) it was received on a share that the trust owned throughout the 365-day period that ended immediately before the disposition.

Related Provisions: 87(2)(x) — Amalgamations — flow-through to new corporation; 112(5.6) — Stop-loss rules restricted; 112(6.1) — Qualified dividend; 112(8), (9) — Effect of synthetic disposition.

Notes: 112(4.22) opening words amended by 2011 budget bill #2, effective for dispositions occurring after March 21, 2011, to change "dividend" to "qualified dividend" (see 112(6.1)).

112(4.22) added by 1995-97 technical bill, for dispositions after April 26, 1995.

(4.3) [Repealed]

Notes: 112(4.3) repealed by 1995-97 technical bill, for dispositions after April 26, 1995. It dealt with a trust beneficiary receiving a dividend designated under 104(19) on a share that was not capital property. Earlier amended by 1994 technical bill.

(5) Disposition of share by financial institution — Subsection (5.2) applies to the disposition of a share by a taxpayer in a taxation year where

(a) the taxpayer is a financial institution in the year;

(b) the share is a mark-to-market property for the year; and

(c) the taxpayer received

(i) a dividend on the share at a time when the taxpayer and persons with whom the taxpayer was not dealing at arm's length held in total more than 5% of the issued shares of any class of the capital stock of the corporation from which the dividend was received, or

(ii) a dividend on the share under subsection 84(3).

Related Provisions: 87(2)(e.5) — Amalgamation — continuing corporation; 88(1)(h) — Windup — continuing corporation; 112(5.4) — Deemed dispositions and reacquisitions ignored; 138(11.5)(k.2) — Transfer of business by non-resident insurer.

Notes: 112(5)(c)(ii) added by 2011 budget bill #2, effective for dispositions occurring after March 21, 2011.

112(5) added by 1994 technical bill, effective for dispositions in taxation years that begin after October 1994.

(5.1) Share held for less than one year — Subsection (5.2) applies to the disposition of a share by a taxpayer in a taxation year where

(a) the disposition is an actual disposition;

(b) the taxpayer did not hold the share throughout the 365-day period that ended immediately before the disposition; and

(c) the share was a mark-to-market property of the taxpayer for a taxation year that begins after October 1994 and in which the taxpayer was a financial institution.

Related Provisions: 87(2)(e.5) — Amalgamation — continuing corporation; 88(1)(h) — Windup — continuing corporation; 112(5.4) — Deemed dispositions and reacquisitions to be ignored; 112(8), (9) — Effect of synthetic disposition; 138(11.5)(k.2) — Transfer of business by non-resident insurer.

Notes: 112(5.1)(b) amended by 1995-97 technical bill, effective for dispositions after April 26, 1995. 112(5.1) added by 1994 technical bill, for dispositions in taxation years that begin after October 1994.

(5.2) Adjustment re dividends — Subject to subsection (5.3), where subsection (5) or (5.1) provides that this subsection applies to the disposition of a share by a taxpayer at any time, the taxpayer's proceeds of disposition shall be deemed to be the amount determined by the formula

$$A + B - (C - D)$$

where

A is the taxpayer's proceeds determined without reference to this subsection,

B is

(a) if the taxpayer received a dividend under subsection 84(3) in respect of the share, the total determined under subparagraph (b)(ii), and

(b) in any other case, the lesser of

(i) the loss, if any, from the disposition of the share that would be determined before the application of this subsection if the cost of the share to any taxpayer were determined without reference to

(A) paragraphs 87(2)(e.2) and (e.4), 88(1)(c), 138(11.5)(e) and 142.5(2)(b),

(B) subsection 85(1), where the provisions of that subsection are required by paragraph 138(11.5)(e) to be applied, and

(C) paragraph 142.6(1)(d), and

(ii) the total of all amounts each of which is

(A) where the taxpayer is a corporation, a taxable dividend received by the taxpayer on the share, to the extent of the amount that was deductible under this section or subsection 115(1) or 138(6) in computing the taxpayer's taxable income or taxable income earned in Canada for any taxation year,

(B) where the taxpayer is a partnership, a taxable dividend received by the taxpayer on the share, to the extent of the amount that was deductible under this section or subsection 115(1) or 138(6) in computing the taxable income or taxable income earned in Canada for any taxation year of members of the partnership,

(C) where the taxpayer is a trust, an amount designated under subsection 104(19) in respect of a taxable dividend on the share, or

(D) a dividend (other than a taxable dividend) received by the taxpayer on the share,

C is the total of all amounts each of which is the amount by which

(a) the taxpayer's proceeds of disposition on a deemed disposition of the share before that time were increased because of this subsection,

(b) where the taxpayer is a corporation or trust, a loss of the taxpayer on a deemed disposition of the share before that time was reduced because of subsection (3), (3.2), (4) or (4.2), or

(c) where the taxpayer is a partnership, a loss of a member of the partnership on a deemed disposition of the share before that time was reduced because of subsection (3.1) or (4), and

D is the total of all amounts each of which is the amount by which the taxpayer's proceeds of disposition on a deemed disposition of the share before that time were decreased because of this subsection.

Related Provisions: 53(2)(c)(i)(C) — Rule ignored in determining reduction in ACB; 87(2)(e.5) — Amalgamation — continuing corp; 88(1)(h) — Windup — continuing corp; 112(5.21) — Exclusion for certain dividends; 112(5.3), (5.4) — Application; 112(5.5), (5.6) — Stop-loss rules not applicable; 112(10) — Synthetic equity arrangement — identical properties; 138(11.5)(k.2) — Transfer of business by non-resident insurer; 257 — Formula cannot calculate to less than zero. See also at end of 112(1).

Notes: For CRA interpretation see VIEWS doc 2009-0315901I7.

112(5.2)B and C(c) amended by 2018 budget bill #2, for dispositions after Feb. 26, 2018, effectively to add B(a) (former (a)-(b) are now (b)(i)-(ii)) and change "(3.1) or (4.2)" to "(3.1) or (4)" in C(c). For earlier dispositions, read B as:

B   is the lesser of

(a) the loss, if any, from the disposition of the share that would be determined before the application of this subsection if the cost of the share to any taxpayer were determined without reference to

(i) paragraphs 87(2)(e.2) and (e.4), 88(1)(c), 138(11.5)(e) and 142.5(2)(b),

(ii) subsection 85(1), where the provisions of that subsection are required by paragraph 138(11.5)(e) to be applied, and

(iii) paragraph 142.6(1)(d), and

(b) the total of all amounts each of which is

(i) where the taxpayer is a corporation, a taxable dividend received by the taxpayer on the share, to the extent of the amount that was deductible under this section or subsection 115(1) or 138(6) in computing the taxpayer's taxable income or taxable income earned in Canada for any taxation year,

(ii) where the taxpayer is a partnership, a taxable dividend received by the taxpayer on the share, to the extent of the amount that was deductible under this section or subsection 115(1) or 138(6) in computing the taxable income or taxable income earned in Canada for any taxation year of members of the partnership,

(iii) where the taxpayer is a trust, an amount designated under subsection 104(19) in respect of a taxable dividend on the share, or

(iv) a dividend (other than a taxable dividend) received by the taxpayer on the share,

In general terms, the amendment prevents X from realizing a loss on a share repurchase that exceeds any mark-to-market (M2M) income previously realized on the share and taxed in X's hands. To the extent the repurchased share was fully hedged (which is typically the case), any M2M income realized on the share due to its increase in value would be fully offset under the hedge and X would have paid no net tax. The amendment generally limits the loss on the share repurchase to the excess, if any, of its M2M cost (rather than the original cost) over its redemption price. (Finance Technical Notes)

For discussion of this amendment see Kelly & Dhawan, "Share Repurchase Program", 26(6) *Canadian Tax Highlights* (ctf.ca) 9-10 (June 2018).

112(5.2) amended by 1995-97 technical bill (for dispositions after April 26, 1995), 1994 technical bill.

(5.21) Subsec. (5.2) — excluded dividends — A dividend, other than a dividend received under subsection 84(3), shall not be included in the total determined under subparagraph (b)(ii) of the description of B in subsection (5.2) unless

(a) the dividend was received when the taxpayer and persons with whom the taxpayer did not deal at arm's length held in total more than 5% of the issued shares of any class of the capital stock of the corporation from which the dividend was received; or

(b) the share was not held by the taxpayer throughout the 365-day period that ended immediately before the disposition.

Related Provisions: 112(8), (9) — Effect of synthetic disposition.

Notes: 112(5.21) opening words amended by 2018 budget bill #2, for dispositions after Feb. 26, 2018, to change "paragraph (b)" to "subparagraph (b)(ii)".

112(5.21) amended by 2011 budget bill #2 (for dispositions after March 21, 2011), 1995-97 technical bill.

(5.3) Adjustment not applicable — For the purpose of determining the cost of a share to a taxpayer on a deemed reacquisition of the share after a deemed disposition of the share, the taxpayer's proceeds of disposition shall be determined without regard to subsection (5.2).

Notes: 112(5.3) added by 1994 technical bill, effective for dispositions in taxation years that begin after October 1994.

(5.4) Deemed dispositions — Where a taxpayer disposes of a share at any time,

(a) for the purpose of determining whether subsection (5.2) applies to the disposition, the conditions in subsections (5) and (5.1) shall be applied without regard to a deemed disposition and reacquisition of the share before that time; and

(b) total amounts under subsection (5.2) in respect of the disposition shall be determined from the time when the taxpayer actually acquired the share.

Related Provisions: 87(2)(e.5) — Amalgamation — continuing corporation; 88(1)(h) — Windup — continuing corporation; 138(11.5)(k.2) — Transfer of business by non-resident insurer.

Notes: 112(5.4) added by 1994 technical bill, effective for dispositions in taxation years that begin after October 1994.

(5.5) Stop-loss rules not applicable — Subsections (3) to (4) and (4.2) do not apply to the disposition of a share by a taxpayer in a taxation year that begins after October 1994 where

(a) the share is a mark-to-market property for the year and the taxpayer is a financial institution in the year; or

(b) subsection (5.2) applies to the disposition.

Related Provisions: 112(5.6) — Transitional rules.

Notes: Reference to 112(4.3) deleted from opening words of 112(5.5) by 1995-97 technical bill, effective for dispositions after April 26, 1995.

112(5.5) added by 1994 technical bill, effective for dispositions in taxation years that begin after October 1994.

(5.6) Stop-loss rules restricted — In determining whether any of subsections (3) to (4) and (4.2) apply to reduce a loss of a taxpayer from the disposition of a share, this Act shall be read without reference to paragraphs (3.01)(b) and (3.11)(b), subclauses (3.2)(a)(ii)(C)(I) and (3.3)(a)(ii)(C)(I) and paragraphs (3.31)(b), (3.32)(b), (4.01)(b), (4.21)(b) and (4.22)(b) where

(a) the disposition occurs

(i) because of subsection 142.5(2) in a taxation year that includes October 31, 1994, or

(ii) because of paragraph 142.6(1)(b) after October 30, 1994; or

(b) the share was a mark-to-market property of the taxpayer for a taxation year that begins after October 1994 in which the taxpayer was a financial institution.

Notes: Opening words of 112(5.6) amended by 1995-97 technical bill, for dispositions after April 26, 1995.

112(5.6) added by 1994 technical bill, for dispositions after Oct. 30, 1994.

(6) Meaning of certain expressions — For the purposes of this section,

(a) **["dividend", "taxable dividend"]** — "dividend" and "taxable dividend" do not include a capital gains dividend (within the meaning assigned by subsection 131(1)) or any dividend received by a taxpayer on which the taxpayer was required to pay tax under Part VII of the *Income Tax Act*, chapter 148 of the Revised Statutes of Canada, 1952, as it read on March 31, 1977;

Related Provisions: 248(1) — Definitions of "dividend" and "taxable dividend".

Notes: 112(6)(a) amended by 1995-97 technical bill, effective April 27, 1995.

(b) **["control"]** — one corporation is controlled by another corporation if more than 50% of its issued share capital (having full voting rights under all circumstances) belongs to the other corporation, to persons with whom the other corporation does not deal at arm's length, or to the other corporation and persons with whom the other corporation does not deal at arm's length; and

(c) **["financial institution", "mark-to-market property"]** — "financial institution" and "mark-to-market property" have the meanings assigned by subsection 142.2(1).

Related Provisions: See Related Provisions at end of s. 112.

Notes: 112(6)(c) added by 1994 technical bill, effective for taxation years that begin after October 1994.

(6.1) Interpretation — qualified dividend — For the purposes of this section, a dividend on a share is a qualified dividend to the extent that

(a) it is a dividend other than a dividend received under subsection 84(3); or

(b) it is received under subsection 84(3) and,

(i) if the share is held by an individual other than a trust, the dividend is received by the individual,

(ii) if the share is held by a corporation, the dividend is received by the corporation while it is a private corporation, and is paid by another private corporation,

(iii) if the share is held by a trust,

(A) the dividend is received by the trust,

(B) the dividend is designated under subsection 104(19) by the trust in respect of a beneficiary and

(I) the beneficiary is an individual other than a trust,

(II) the beneficiary is a private corporation when the dividend is received by it and the dividend is paid by another private corporation,

(III) the beneficiary is another trust that does not designate the dividend under subsection 104(19), or

(IV) the beneficiary is a partnership all of the members of which are, when the dividend is received, a person described by any of subclauses (I) to (III), or

(C) the dividend is designated by the trust under subsection 104(19) in respect of a beneficiary that is another trust or a partnership and the trust establishes that the dividend is received by a person described by any of subclauses (B)(I) to (III), and

(iv) if the share is held by a partnership,

(A) the dividend is included in the income of a member of a partnership and

(I) the member is an individual, or

(II) the member is a private corporation when the dividend is received by it and the dividend is paid by another private corporation, or

(B) the dividend is designated under subsection 104(19) by a member of a partnership that is a trust in respect of a beneficiary described by any of subclauses (iii)(B)(I) to (IV) or is described by clause (iii)(C).

Notes: 112(6.1) added by 2011 budget bill #2, for dispositions after March 21, 2011. The stop-loss rules in 112(3)–(5.2) contain exceptions that generally apply to shares held for at least a year where the shareholder and non-arm's-length persons own 5% or less of the class of shares on which the dividend is received. Some corps were avoiding the stop-loss rules by entering into arrangements that relied on these exceptions to, in effect, claim a double deduction on the redemption of shares. A deemed dividend arises on redemption of shares (excess of redemption price over PUC: see 84(3)), and the corp would claim the 112(1) deduction. Where PUC was below the redemption price, the deemed dividend would also result in a loss. The 2011 Budget therefore amended all the stop-loss rules so that the exception applies only to a "qualified dividend", defined here. In effect, the stop-loss rules are extended to any dividend deemed received on redemption of shares held by a corp (including held indirectly through a partnership or trust), other than dividends deemed received on redemption of shares of a private corp that are held by a private corp (other than a financial institution) whether directly or indirectly through a partnership or trust (other than a partnership or trust that is a FI).

(7) Rules where shares exchanged — Where a share (in this subsection referred to as the "new share") has been acquired in exchange for another share (in this subsection referred to as the "old share") in a transaction to which section 51, 85.1, 86 or 87 applies, for the purposes of the application of any of subsections (3) to (3.32) in respect of a disposition of the new share, the new share is deemed to be the same share as the old share, except that

(a) any dividend received on the old share is deemed for those purposes to have been received on the new share only to the extent of the proportion of the dividend that

(i) the shareholder's adjusted cost base of the new share immediately after the exchange

is of

(ii) the shareholder's adjusted cost base of all new shares immediately after the exchange acquired in exchange for the old share; and

(b) the amount, if any, by which a loss from the disposition of the new share is reduced because of the application of this subsection shall not exceed the proportion of the shareholder's adjusted cost base of the old share immediately before the exchange that

(i) the shareholder's adjusted cost base of the new share immediately after the exchange

is of

(ii) the shareholder's adjusted cost base of all new shares, immediately after the exchange, acquired in exchange for the old share.

Related Provisions: 40(3.7) — Application to non-resident individual.

Notes: Although 112(7) does not apply to s. 85, CRA may apply GAAR to avoidance of the stop-loss rules using 85(1): VIEWS doc 2011-0412171C6.

112(7) amended by 1995-97 technical bill (for dispositions after April 26, 1995) and 1993 technical bill. See also at end of 112(1).

Interpretation Bulletins [subsec. 112(7)]: IT-88R2: Stock dividends; IT-269R4: Part IV tax on dividends received by a private corporation or a subject corporation; IT-328R3: Losses on shares on which dividends have been received.

(8) Synthetic disposition — holding period

— If a synthetic disposition arrangement is entered into in respect of a property owned by a taxpayer and the synthetic disposition period of the arrangement is 30 days or more, for the purposes of paragraphs (3.01)(b) and (3.11)(b), subclauses (3.2)(a)(ii)(C)(I) and (3.3)(a)(ii)(C)(I) and paragraphs (3.31)(b), (3.32)(b), (4.01)(b), (4.11)(b), (4.21)(b), (4.22)(b), (5.1)(b) and (5.21)(b) and subsection (9), the taxpayer is deemed not to own the property during the synthetic disposition period.

Related Provisions: 112(9) — Exception where property owned for one year before SDP; 112(9.1) — Exception during synthetic disposition period.

Notes: See Notes to 248(1)"synthetic disposition arrangement". 112(8) ensures taxpayers cannot circumvent the stop-loss rules in 112(3)–(7) by entering into an SDA so as to meet the 365-day ownership requirement. See also Notes to the exception in 112(9).

112(8) added by 2013 budget bill #2, effective for an agreement or arrangement entered into after March 20, 2013; it also applies to an agreement or arrangement entered into before March 21, 2013, the term of which is extended after March 20, 2013, as if the agreement or arrangement were entered into at the time of the extension.

(9) Exception

— Subsection (8) does not apply in respect of a property owned by a taxpayer in respect of a synthetic disposition arrangement if the taxpayer owned the property throughout the 365-day period (determined without reference to this subsection) that ended immediately before the synthetic disposition period of the arrangement.

Notes: 112(9) provides an exception to 112(8) if the taxpayer owned the property throughout the 365 days ending immediately before the synthetic disposition period. In determining this, the taxpayer is not considered to own the property throughout that period if 112(8) previously applied to the property during that period (or would have applied if the determination in 112(8) were made without reference to 112(9)). This ensures that 112(8) applies only where a SDA is used to allow a taxpayer to meet a 365-day hold period test that the taxpayer otherwise would not have met.

112(9) added by 2013 budget bill #2, effective for an agreement or arrangement entered into after March 20, 2013, or up to that date where its term is extended after that date, as if it were entered into at the time of extension. In such case, if the agreement or arrangement was entered into by Sept. 12, 2013 and its term is not extended after that date, read 112(9) without "(determined without reference to this subsection)".

(9.1) Exception

— Subsection (8) does not apply for the purpose of paragraph (5.21)(b) in respect of a dividend received on a share, referred to in paragraph (a) of the description of B in subsection (5.2), during a synthetic disposition period of a synthetic disposition arrangement in respect of that share.

Notes: 112(9.1) added by 2018 budget bill #2, for dispositions after Feb. 26, 2018. It is intended to ensure that an actual dividend received on a share before its repurchase, which absent 112(8) would qualify as a 112(5.21) excluded dividend, will not increase the proceeds of disposition otherwise determined under 112(5.2) unless a synthetic disposition arrangement with respect to the share was entered into after the payment of the actual dividend in order to meet the 365-day ownership requirement under 112(5.21)(b). (Finance Technical Notes)

(10) Synthetic equity arrangements — ordering

— For the purposes of subsections (3), (3.1), (4), (4.1) and (5.2), if a synthetic equity arrangement is in respect of a number of shares that are identical properties (referred to in this subsection as "identical shares") that is less than the total number of such identical shares owned by a person or partnership at that time and in respect of which there is no other synthetic equity arrangement, the synthetic equity arrangement is deemed to be in respect of those identical shares in the order in which the person or partnership acquired them.

Related Provisions: 248(12) — Identical properties; 248(42) — Synthetic equity arrangement relating to multiple identical shares.

Notes: See Notes to 112(2.3)–(2.34).

112(10) added by 2016 budget bill #1, effective April 22, 2015.

(11) Interest in a partnership — cost reduction

— In computing the cost to a taxpayer, at any time, of an interest in a partnership that is property (other than capital property) of the taxpayer, there is to be deducted an amount equal to the total of all amounts each of which is the taxpayer's share of any loss of the partnership from the disposition by the partnership, or another partnership of which the partnership is directly or indirectly a member, of a share of the capital stock of a corporation (referred to in this subsection and subsection (12) as the "partnership loss") in a fiscal period of the partnership that includes that time or a prior fiscal period, computed without reference to subsections (3.1), (4) and (5.2), to the extent that the taxpayer's share of the partnership loss has not previously reduced the taxpayer's cost of the interest in the partnership because of the application of this subsection.

Related Provisions: 112(12) — Where taxpayer disposes of partnership interest; 112(13) — Where taxpayer acquires partnership interest.

Notes: 112(11)-(13) added by 2017 budget bill #2, effective Sept. 16, 2016. Together with an amendment to 53(2)(c)(i)(C), they are intended to ensure that taxpayers do not circumvent the dividend stop-loss rules in 112(3)-(7) by holding shares through a partnership instead of directly. These rules deny the inappropriate loss created in certain circumstances through fluctuation of the cost to the taxpayer of an interest in a partnership arising from the shares held or disposed of by the partnership.

(12) Application

— For the purposes of subsection (11), if a taxpayer disposes of an interest in a partnership at any particular time, the taxpayer's share of a partnership loss is to be computed as if

(a) the fiscal period of each partnership of which the taxpayer is directly or indirectly a member had ended immediately before the time that is immediately before the particular time;

(b) any share of the capital stock of a corporation that was property of a partnership referred to in paragraph (a) at the particular time had been disposed of by the relevant partnership immediately before the end of that fiscal period for proceeds equal to its fair market value at the particular time; and

(c) each member of a partnership referred to in paragraph (a) were allocated a share of any loss (computed without reference to subsections (3.1), (4) and (5.2)) in respect of dispositions described in paragraph (b) determined by reference to the member's specified proportion for the fiscal period referred to in paragraph (a).

Notes: See Notes to 112(11).

(13) Application

— For the purposes of subsection (11), if a taxpayer (referred to as the "transferee" in this subsection) acquires an interest in a partnership at any time from another taxpayer (referred to as the "transferor" in this subsection), in computing the cost of the partnership interest to the transferee there is to be added an amount equal to the total of all amounts each of which is an amount deducted from the transferor's cost of the partnership interest because of subsection (11), other than an amount to which subsection (3.1) would apply.

Notes: See Notes to 112(11).

Related Provisions [s. 112]: 66(1) — Exploration development expenses of principal-business corporations; 82(2) — Certain dividends deemed received by taxpayer; 104(19) — Taxable dividends flowed through trust; 138(6) — Insurance corporations — Deduction for dividends from taxable corporations; 187.2 — Tax on dividends on taxable preferred shares; 187.3 — Tax on dividends on taxable RFI shares.

Definitions [s. 112]: "adjusted cost base" — 54, 248(1); "affiliated" — 251.1; "affiliated counterparty" — 112(2.32)(a), 112(2.34); "affiliated specified counterparty" — 112(2.32)(b)(ii)(A)(II), 112(2.34); "amount" — 248(1); "arm's length" — 251(1); "beneficiary" — 248(25) [Notes]; "business" — 248(1); "Canada" — 255; "capital dividend" — 83(2), 248(1); "capital property" — 54, 248(1); "carried on a business in Canada" — 253; "class" — 248(6); "connected person" — 248(1)"synthetic equity arrangement"(a); "consequence of the individual's death" — 248(8); "controlled" — 112(6)(b), 256(6), (6.1); "corporation" — 248(1), *Interpretation Act* 35(1); "counterparty" — 112(2.34); "designated stock exchange" — 248(1), 262; "disposition" — 248(1); "dividend" — 112(6)(a), 248(1); "dividend rental arrangement" — 248(1); "exempt share" — 112(2.6), (2.7); "fair market value" — see 69(1) Notes; "financial institution" — 112(6)(c), 142.2(1); "fiscal period" — 249.1; "foreign affiliate" — 95(1), 248(1); "graduated rate estate", "grandfathered share" — 248(1); "guarantee agreement", "guarantor" — 112(2.2)(a); "identical properties" — 248(12); "identical shares" — 112(10); "individual", "insurance corporation" — 248(1); "investment corporation" — 130(3)(a), 248(1); "investor", "issuer" — 112(2.6); "life insurance capital dividend" — 248(1); "mark-to-market property" — 112(6)(c), 142.2(1); "mutual fund corporation" — 131(8), 248(1); "mutual fund trust" — 132(6)–(7), 132.2(3)(n), 248(1); "non-resident-owned investment corporation" — 133(8), 248(1); "partnership" — see 96(1) Notes; "partnership loss" — 112(11); "permanent establishment" — Reg. 8201; "person", "prescribed", "property" — 248(1); "qualified dividend" — 112(6.1); "received" — 248(7); "regulation" — 248(1); "related" — 112(2.9), 251; "resident in Canada" — 250; "restricted financial institution" — 248(1); "series of transactions" — 248(10); "share" — 112(7), 248(1); "short-term preferred share" — 248(1); "specified counterparty" — 112(2.32)(b)(ii)(A)(I), 112(2.34); "specified financial institution" — 248(1), 248(14); "specified person" — 112(2.22)(b); "specified proportion", "specified synthetic equity arrangement" — 248(1); "substituted" — 248(5); "synthetic disposition arrangement", "synthetic disposition period", "synthetic equity arrangement", "synthetic equity arrangement chain" — 248(1); "synthetic equity arrangement party" — 112(2.32)(a); "tax payable" — 248(2); "tax-indifferent investor" — 248(1); "taxable Canadian corporation" — 89(1), 248(1); "taxable dividend" — 89(1), 112(6)(a), 248(1); "taxable income" — 2(2), 248(1); "taxable income earned in Canada" — 115(1), 248(1); "taxable preferred share" — 248(1); "taxation year" — 249; "taxpayer" — 112(2.31), 248(1); "term preferred share" — 248(1); "trust" — 104(1), 248(1), (3); "writing", "written" — *Interpretation Act* 35(1)"writing".

113. (1) Deduction in respect of dividend received from foreign affiliate — Where in a taxation year a corporation resident in Canada has received a dividend on a share owned by it of the capital stock of a foreign affiliate of the corporation, there may be deducted from the income for the year of the corporation for the purpose of computing its taxable income for the year, an amount equal to the total of

(a) an amount equal to such portion of the dividend as is prescribed to have been paid out of the exempt surplus, as defined by regulation (in this Part referred to as **"exempt surplus"**) of the affiliate,

Announced Administrative Change — Residence of foreign affiliate for exempt surplus

CRA notice (tinyurl.com/cra-internat, April 27, 2021): See under 250(1)(a), section I.B "Income tax residency: Corporations", paragraph "This administrative approach...".

(a.1) an amount equal to the total of

(i) one-half of the portion of the dividend that is prescribed to have been paid out of the hybrid surplus, as defined by regulation (in this Part referred to as **"hybrid surplus"**), of the affiliate, and

(ii) the lesser of

(A) the total of

(I) the product obtained when the foreign tax prescribed to be applicable to the portion of the dividend referred to in subparagraph (i) is multiplied by the amount by which

1. the corporation's relevant tax factor for the year exceeds

2. one-half, and

(II) the product obtained when

1. the non-business-income tax paid by the corporation applicable to the portion of the dividend referred to in subparagraph (i)

is multiplied by

2. the corporation's relevant tax factor for the year, and

(B) the amount determined under subparagraph (i),

(b) an amount equal to the lesser of

(i) the product obtained when the foreign tax prescribed to be applicable to such portion of the dividend as is prescribed to have been paid out of the taxable surplus, as defined by regulation (in this Part referred to as **"taxable surplus"**) of the affiliate is multiplied by the amount by which

(A) the corporation's relevant tax factor for the year exceeds

(B) one, and

(ii) that portion of the dividend,

(c) an amount equal to the lesser of

(i) the product obtained when

(A) the non-business-income tax paid by the corporation applicable to such portion of the dividend as is prescribed to have been paid out of the taxable surplus of the affiliate

is multiplied by

(B) the corporation's relevant tax factor for the year, and

(ii) the amount by which such portion of the dividend as is prescribed to have been paid out of the taxable surplus of the affiliate exceeds the deduction in respect thereof referred to in paragraph (b); and

(d) an amount equal to such portion of the dividend as is prescribed to have been paid out of the pre-acquisition surplus of the affiliate,

and for the purposes of this subsection and Subdivision I of Division B, the corporation may make such elections as may be prescribed.

Related Provisions: 20(13) — Deduction for dividend; 90(9)(a) — Deduction against upstream loan inclusion from foreign affiliate where dividend would be deductible under 113(1)(a)–(b); 91(5) — Amounts deductible in respect of dividends received; 92(2) — ACB reduction where amount deductible under 113(1)(d); 92(4)–(6) — Where dividend from pre-acquisition surplus received by partnership; 93(1.2) — Disposition of share of foreign affiliate held by partnership; 93(2)–(2.31) — Stop-loss rules; 93(3) — Exempt dividends; 93.1(1) — Where shares are owned by partnership; 93.1(2) — Dividend on shares of foreign affiliate held by partnership; 111(8)"non-capital loss"A:E — Carryforward of dividend deduction as non-capital loss; 112(2) — Deduction for dividend received from corporation that is not a foreign affiliate; 113(4) — Dividend received before 1976; 186(1) — Part IV tax on certain taxable dividends; 186(3)"assessable dividend" — Part IV tax; Reg. 5907(2.02) — Anti-avoidance rule — surplus. See also at end of s. 113.

Notes: In very simplified terms, for a corporation resident in Canada, a dividend from active income in a treaty or TIEA country is tax-free (exempt surplus), and a dividend from passive income (taxed as FAPI: 91(1), with a deduction under 91(4) for foreign tax paid) is taxable except to the extent foreign tax was paid on it (taxable surplus).

A dividend from a foreign affiliate (FA) is included in income under 90(1). A dividend out of exempt surplus or pre-acquisition surplus can then be deducted under 113(1)(a) or (d), resulting in no corporate tax (but pre-acquisition surplus reduces ACB (92(2), 53(2)(b)) and thus can trigger a capital gain). The same is true for half of a dividend from hybrid surplus. A dividend from taxable surplus (and the other half of hybrid surplus) is included in income, but a deduction is allowed for underlying foreign tax paid by the FA and for foreign withholding tax paid on the dividend (113(1)((a.1), (b) and (c)) — if high foreign tax was paid, this can net out to tax-free. (For dividends from Canadian corporations, see 112(1).)

Dividends are normally deemed to come first from exempt surplus (net of any exempt deficit), then from hybrid surplus (net of any hybrid deficit), then from taxable surplus (net of any taxable deficit), then pre-acquisition surplus (Reg. 5901). Under Reg. 5901(1.1) the receiving corporation can elect for taxable surplus to come before hybrid surplus (as that may be more beneficial in certain cases). The FA may elect to pay out of taxable surplus first (Reg. 5902), e.g. to let the Canadian resident corporation use up loss carryovers.

Exempt surplus (Reg. 5907(1)) is, very generally, active business income earned by the FA in treaty or TIEA countries ("designated treaty country" in Reg. 5907(11); see list of Canada's tax treaties at end of book, and Notes to 95(1)"non-qualifying country"), and certain capital gains. Hybrid surplus is, generally, capital gains on the sale of partnership interests and shares in other FAs. Taxable surplus (Reg. 5907(1)) is generally income earned in other countries, as well as passive income (earned anywhere) and certain capital gains. Pre-acquisition surplus (Reg. 5900(1)(c), 5901(1)(c), 5902(1)(b)) is essentially a non-taxable return of capital that reduces adjusted cost base (92(2), 53(2)(b)). A corp claiming a 113(1) deduction needs complete surplus calculations: VIEWS doc 2019-0798761C6 [2019 IFA q.9], 2019-0821311C6 [2019 APFF q.8] (see also Notes to Reg. 5901(2.1)).

Dividends deductible under 113(1) (before deducting foreign withholding tax) are included in GRIP from which eligible dividends are paid: see 89(1)"general rate income pool"E(b).

See also Vidal, *Introduction to International Tax in Canada* (Carswell, 8th ed., 2020), chap. 16; Dolson, "Exempt Surplus and TIEAs: A Bad Deal", 6(3) *Canadian Tax Focus* (ctf.ca) 6 (Aug. 2016); Samuel, "Interaction of the Foreign Affiliate Surplus and Safe-Income Regimes", 66(2) *Canadian Tax Journal* 269-307 (2018).

See also VIEWS doc 2014-0523341C6 (treatment of life insurance proceeds received by foreign affiliate).

113(1) amended by 2002-2013 technical bill, last change effective for dividends received after Aug. 19, 2011.

Regulations: 5900–5902, 5906, 5907 (prescribed portion, prescribed foreign tax, prescribed elections, definitions); 5900(1)(c) (pre-acquisition surplus); 5907(1.01) (exempt surplus, taxable surplus).

Interpretation Bulletins: IT-269R4: Part IV tax on taxable dividends received by a private corporation or a subject corporation; IT-328R3: Losses on shares on which dividends have been received.

Information Circulars: 77-9R: Books, records and other requirements for taxpayers having foreign affiliates.

CRA Audit Manual: 15.11.4: Tax treaties — relief from double taxation; 15.12.2: Foreign accrual property income (FAPI) and foreign affiliates.

(2) Additional deduction — Where, at any particular time in a taxation year ending after 1975, a corporation resident in Canada has received a dividend on a share owned by it at the end of its 1975 taxation year of the capital stock of a foreign affiliate of the corporation, there may be deducted from the income for the year of the corporation for the purpose of computing its taxable income for the year, an amount in respect of the dividend equal to the lesser of

(a) the amount, if any, by which the amount of the dividend so received exceeds the total of

(i) the deduction in respect of the dividend permitted by subsection 91(5) in computing the corporation's income for the year, and

(ii) the deduction in respect of the dividend permitted by subsection (1) from the income for the year of the corporation for the purpose of computing its taxable income, and

(b) the amount, if any, by which

(i) the adjusted cost base to the corporation of the share at the end of its 1975 taxation year

exceeds the total of

(ii) [Repealed under former Act]

(iii) such amounts in respect of dividends received by the corporation on the share after the end of its 1975 taxation year and before the particular time as are deductible under paragraph (1)(d) in computing the taxable income of the corporation for taxation years ending after 1975,

(iii.1) the total of all amounts received by the corporation on the share after the end of its 1975 taxation year and before the particular time

(A) on a reduction, before August 20, 2011, of the paid-up capital of the foreign affiliate in respect of the share, or

(B) on a reduction, after August 19, 2011, of the paid-up capital of the foreign affiliate in respect of the share that is a qualifying return of capital (within the meaning assigned by subsection 90(3)) in respect of the share, and

(iv) the total of all amounts deducted under this subsection in respect of dividends received by the corporation on the share before the particular time.

Related Provisions: 92 — ACB of share in foreign affiliate; 113(1) — Deduction in respect of dividend received from foreign affiliate; 186(3)"assessable dividend" — Part IV tax. See also at end of s. 113.

Notes: 113(2)(b)(iii.1) amended, effectively to add cl. (B), by 2002-2013 technical bill (Part 3 — FA reorganizations), effective Aug. 20, 2011.

Cl. (iii.1)(B) was not in the Aug. 19/11 draft.

Interpretation Bulletins: IT-98R2: Investment corporations (cancelled); IT-269R4: Part IV tax on taxable dividends received by a private corporation or a subject corporation.

(3) Definitions — In this section,

"non-business-income tax" paid by a taxpayer has the meaning assigned by subsection 126(7);

"relevant tax factor" has the meaning assigned by subsection 95(1).

Notes: 113(3)"non-business-income tax" was 113(3)(b) and "relevant tax factor" was 113(3)(a) before RSC 1985 (5th Supp) consolidation for tax years ending after Nov. 1991.

(4) Portion of dividend deemed paid out of exempt surplus — Such portion of any dividend received at any time in a taxation year by a corporation resident in Canada on a share owned by it of the capital stock of a foreign affiliate of the corporation, that was received after the 1971 taxation year of the affiliate and before the affiliate's 1976 taxation year, as exceeds the amount deductible in respect of the dividend under paragraph (1)(d) in computing the corporation's taxable income for the year shall, for the purposes of paragraph (1)(a), be deemed to be the portion of the dividend prescribed to have been paid out of the exempt surplus of the affiliate.

Related Provisions: 113(1) — Deduction in respect of dividend received from foreign affiliate. See also at end of s. 113.

Related Provisions [s. 113]: 66(1) — Exploration and development expenses of principal-business corporations; 80.1(4) — Assets acquired from foreign affiliate of taxpayer as dividend in kind or as benefit to shareholder; 82(2) — Dividend deemed received by taxpayer; 126(4) — Portion of foreign tax not included; 187.2 — Tax on dividends on taxable preferred shares; 187.3 — Tax on dividends on taxable RFI shares; 258(3) — Certain dividends on preferred shares deemed to be interest; 258(5) — Deemed interest on certain shares.

Definitions [s. 113]: "adjusted cost base" — 54; "amount" — 248(1); "Canada" — 255; "corporation" — 248(1), Interpretation Act 35(1); "dividend" — 248(1); "exempt surplus" — 113(1)(a), Reg. 5907(1), (1.01); "foreign affiliate" — 93.1(1), 95(1), 248(1); "hybrid surplus" — 113(1)(a.1)(i), Reg. 5900(1)(a.1), 5901(1)(a.1), 5907(1), (1.01); "individual" — 248(1); "non-business-income tax" — 113(3), 126(7); "paid-up capital" — 89(1), 248(1); "portion of the dividend" — Reg. 5900(1); "pre-acquisition surplus" — Reg. 5900(1)(c), 5901(1)(c); "prescribed", "regulation" — 248(1); "qualifying return of capital" — 90(3); "relevant tax factor" — 95(1), 113(3); "resident in Canada" — 250; "share" — 248(1); "taxable income" — 2(2), 248(1); "taxable surplus" — 113(1)(b)(i), Reg. 5900(1)(b), 5901(1)(b), 5907(1), (1.01); "taxation year" — 249; "taxpayer" — 248(1).

114. Individual resident in Canada for only part of year — Notwithstanding subsection 2(2), the taxable income for a taxation year of an individual who is resident in Canada throughout part of the year and non-resident throughout another part of the year is the amount, if any, by which

(a) the amount that would be the individual's income for the year if the individual had no income or losses, for the part of the year throughout which the individual was non-resident, other than

(i) income or losses described in paragraphs 115(1)(a) to (c), and

(ii) income that would have been included in the individual's taxable income earned in Canada for the year under subparagraph 115(1)(a)(v) if the part of the year throughout which the individual was non-resident were the whole taxation year,

exceeds the total of

(b) the deductions permitted by subsection 111(1) and, to the extent that they relate to amounts included in computing the amount determined under paragraph (a), the deductions permitted by any of paragraphs 110(1)(d) to (d.2) and (f), and

(c) any other deduction permitted for the purpose of computing taxable income to the extent that

(i) it can reasonably be considered to be applicable to the part of the year throughout which the individual was resident in Canada, or

(ii) if all or substantially all of the individual's income for the part of the year throughout which the individual was non-resident is included in the amount determined under paragraph (a), it can reasonably be considered to be applicable to that part of the year.

Related Provisions: 66(4.3) — Foreign exploration and development expenses of part-year resident [PYR]; 110.6(5) — Capital gains exemption available for year of immigration or emigration; 111(9) — Losses where taxpayer not resident in Canada; 118.91 — Tax credits for PYR; 119 — Credit to former resident where stop-loss rule applies; 120(3)(a) — Effect of s. 114 where income earned in no province or in Quebec; 122.5(6.2) — GST/HST Credit for PYR; 122.61(3) — Canada Child Benefit for PYR; 122.8(6) — Child fitness credit (pre-2017) for PYR; 122.9(5) — Teacher school-supplies credit for PYR; 126(2.1) — Foreign tax credit where s. 114 applies; 128.1 — Change in residence.

Notes: An individual deemed resident under 250(1)(a), by "sojourning" in Canada for 183 days or more, is deemed resident *throughout* the year, and s. 114 does not apply. It applies only to someone who immigrates (becomes resident in Canada) or emigrates (ceases to be resident) during a year. See 128.1 for the effect of immigration or emigration. See Notes to 250(1) re the meaning of "resident", and tinyurl.com/cra-emigrants.

114 cannot apply to a trust, since on change of residence a new taxation year starts under 128.1(1)(a) or (4)(a): IT-262R2 para. 27.

114(c) applies only in computing *taxable* income (not net income), so it could not be used for accrued interest on a "departure trade" (see Notes to 128.1(4)): *Grant*, 2007 FCA 174 (leave to appeal denied 2007 CarswellNat 3852 (SCC)).

In *Zhu*, 2016 FCA 113, a loss on shares acquired while in Canada was non-deductible because the taxpayer sold the shares after emigration and at that point was no longer carrying on business in Canada.

A taxpayer resident in Alberta part of the year, who earns employment income in Quebec while non-resident, pays Alberta tax on that income: VIEWS doc 2011-0407601E5.

114 amended by 2001 technical bill (effective for 1998 and later taxation years), 1994 technical bill and 1993 and 1991 technical bills.

Definitions [s. 114]: "amount", "individual", "non-resident" — 248(1); "resident in Canada" — 94(3)(a), 250; "taxable income", "taxable income earned in Canada" — 248(1); "taxation year" — 249.

Income Tax Folios [s. 114]: S5-F1-C1: Determining an individual's residence status [replaces IT-221R3].

Interpretation Bulletins [s. 114]: IT-262R2: Losses of non-residents and part-year residents; IT-497R4: Overseas employment tax credit.

Forms: T1248 Sched. D: Information about your residency status; T4056: Emigrants and income tax [guide]; T4058: Non-residents and income tax [guide].

114.1 [Repealed]

Notes: 114.1 repealed by 2001 technical bill, for 1998 and later taxation years. With the restructuring of s. 114, this rule is no longer needed. It provided an interpretation of 115(2) for purposes of 114.

114.2 Deductions in separate returns

114.2 Deductions in separate returns — Where a separate return of income with respect to a taxpayer is filed under subsection 70(2), 104(23) or 150(4) for a particular period and another return of income under this Part with respect to the taxpayer is filed for a period ending in the calendar year in which the particular period ends, for the purpose of computing the taxable income under this Part of the taxpayer in those returns, the total of all deductions claimed in all those returns under section 110 shall not exceed the total that could be deducted under that section for the year with respect to the taxpayer if no separate returns were filed under subsections 70(2), 104(23) and 150(4).

Related Provisions: 118.93 — Credits in separate returns.

Definitions [s. 114.2]: "calendar year" — *Interpretation Act* 37(1)(a); "taxable income" — 2(2), 248(1); "taxpayer" — 248(1).

Interpretation Bulletins: IT-326R3: Returns of deceased persons as "another person".

DIVISION D — TAXABLE INCOME EARNED IN CANADA BY NON-RESIDENTS

115. (1) Non-resident's taxable income [earned] in Canada — For the purposes of this Act, the taxable income earned in Canada for a taxation year of a person who at no time in the year is resident in Canada is the amount, if any, by which the amount that would be the non-resident person's income for the year under section 3 if

(a) the non-resident person had no income other than

(i) incomes from the duties of offices and employments performed by the non-resident person in Canada and, if the person was resident in Canada at the time the person performed the duties, outside Canada,

(ii) incomes from businesses carried on by the non-resident person in Canada which, in the case of the Canadian banking business of an authorized foreign bank, is, subject to this Part, the profit from that business computed using the bank's branch financial statements (within the meaning assigned by subsection 20.2(1)),

Announced Administrative Change — 115(1)(a)(ii) — COVID-19

CRA notice (tinyurl.com/cra-internat, April 27, 2021): See under 250(1)(a), sections II "Carrying on business in Canada/Permanent establishment" and VII.B "Permanent establishment".

(iii) taxable capital gains from dispositions described in paragraph (b),

(iii.1) the amount by which the amount required by paragraph 59(3.2)(c) to be included in computing the non-resident person's income for the year exceeds any portion of that amount that was included in computing the non-resident per-

son's income from a business carried on by the non-resident person in Canada,

(iii.2) amounts required by section 13 to be included in computing the non-resident person's income for the year in respect of dispositions of properties to the extent that those amounts were not included in computing the non-resident person's income from a business carried on by the non-resident person in Canada,

(iii.21) the total of all amounts, each of which is an amount included under subparagraph 56(1)(r)(v) or section 56.3 in computing the non-resident person's income for the year,

(iii.22) the total of all amounts, each of which is an amount included under subparagraph 56(1)(r)(iv.1) in computing the non-resident person's income for the year,

(iii.3) in any case where, in the year, the non-resident person carried on a business in Canada described in any of paragraphs (a) to (g) of the definition "principal-business corporation" in subsection 66(15), all amounts in respect of a Canadian resource property that would be required to be included in computing the non-resident person's income for the year under this Part if the non-resident person were resident in Canada at any time in the year, to the extent that those amounts are not included in computing the non-resident person's income by virtue of subparagraph (ii) or (iii.1),

(iv) the amount, if any, by which any amount required by subsection 106(2) to be included in computing the non-resident person's income for the year as proceeds of the disposition of an income interest in a trust resident in Canada exceeds the amount in respect of that income interest that would, if the non-resident person had been resident in Canada throughout the year, be deductible under subsection 106(1) in computing the non-resident person's income for the year,

(iv.1) the amount, if any, by which any amount required by subsection 96(1.2) to be included in computing the non-resident person's income for the year as proceeds of the disposition of a right to a share of the income or loss under an agreement referred to in paragraph 96(1.1)(a) exceeds the amount in respect of that right that would, if the non-resident person had been resident in Canada throughout the year, be deductible under subsection 96(1.3) in computing the non-resident person's income for the year,

(v) in the case of a non-resident person described in subsection (2), the total determined under paragraph (2)(e) in respect of the non-resident person,

(vi) the amount that would have been required to be included in computing the non-resident person's income in respect of a life insurance policy in Canada by virtue of subsection 148(1) or (1.1) if the non-resident person had been resident in Canada throughout the year, and

(vii) in the case of an authorized foreign bank, the amount claimed by the bank to the extent that the inclusion of the amount in income

(A) increases any amount deductible by the bank under subsection 126(1) for the year, and

(B) does not increase an amount deductible by the bank under section 127 for the year,

(b) the only taxable capital gains and allowable capital losses referred to in paragraph 3(b) were taxable capital gains and allowable capital losses from dispositions, other than dispositions deemed under subsection 218.3(2), of taxable Canadian properties (other than treaty-protected properties), and

Proposed Amendment — Additional tax on vacant housing owned by non-residents

Federal Budget, Annex 7, April 19, 2021: *Tax on Unproductive Use of Canadian Housing by Foreign Non-resident Owners*

Budget 2021 proposes to introduce a new national 1% tax on the value of non-resident, non-Canadian owned residential real estate considered to be vacant or underused. This tax would be levied annually beginning in 2022.

Beginning in 2023, all owners of residential property in Canada, other than Canadian citizens or permanent residents of Canada, would be required to file an annual declaration for the prior calendar year with the Canada Revenue Agency in respect of each Canadian residential property they own. The requirement to file this declaration would apply irrespective of whether the owner is subject to tax in respect of the property for the year.

In a declaration in respect of a property, the owner would be required to report information such as the property address, the property value and the owner's interest in the property. The owner may also be eligible to claim in their declaration an exemption from the tax in respect of a property for the year. An exemption may be available, for instance, where a property is leased to one or more qualified tenants in relation to the owner for a minimum period in a calendar year. Where an exemption in respect of a property for the year is not available, the owner would be required to calculate the amount of tax owing and report and remit it to the Canada Revenue Agency by the filing due date.

The failure to file a declaration with respect to a property for a calendar year as and when required could result in the loss of any available exemptions in respect of the property for the calendar year. Penalties and interest would also be applicable and the assessment period would be unlimited.

In the coming months, the government will release a backgrounder to provide stakeholders with an opportunity to comment on further parameters of the proposed tax. These parameters would include, for example, the definition of residential property, the value on which the tax would apply, how the tax would apply where a property is owned by multiple individuals and/or non-individuals, potential exemptions and compliance and enforcement mechanisms. Additionally, the consultation will consider whether, how and when the proposed tax would apply in smaller, resort and tourism communities.

Notes: Budget Table 1 projects that this measure will generate revenue for the federal government of $200 million in 2022-23, $170m in 2023-24, and $165m in each of 2024-25 and 2025-26.

Federal Economic Statement, Chapter 4, Nov. 30, 2020: *§4.8.2.2 Taxing Unproductive Use of Canadian Housing by Foreign Non-resident Owners*

Too often, the price of homes is out of reach for Canadians, in particular for those looking to buy their first home. Speculative demand from foreign, non-resident investors contributes to unaffordable housing prices for many Canadians. To help make the housing market more secure and affordable for Canadians, the government is committed to ensuring that foreign, non-resident owners, who simply use Canada as a place to passively store their wealth in housing, pay their fair share.

The government will take steps over the coming year to implement a national, tax-based measure targeting the unproductive use of domestic housing that is owned by non-resident, non-Canadians, which removes these assets from the domestic housing supply.

(b.1) [Repealed]

(c) the only losses for the year referred to in paragraph 3(d) were losses from duties of an office or employment performed by the person in Canada and businesses (other than treaty-protected businesses) carried on by the person in Canada and allowable business investment losses in respect of property any gain from the disposition of which would, because of this subsection, be included in computing the person's taxable income earned in Canada,

exceeds the total of

(d) the deductions permitted by subsection 111(1) and, to the extent that they relate to amounts included in computing the amount determined under any of paragraphs (a) to (c), the deductions permitted by any of paragraphs 110(1)(d) to (d.2), (e) and (f) and subsection 110.1(1),

(e) the deductions permitted by any of subsections 112(1) and (2) and 138(6) in respect of a dividend received by the non-resident person, to the extent that the dividend is included in computing the non-resident person's taxable income earned in Canada for the year,

(e.1) the deduction permitted by subsection (4.1), and

(f) where all or substantially all of the non-resident person's income for the year is included in computing the non-resident person's taxable income earned in Canada for the year, such of the other deductions permitted for the purpose of computing taxable income as may reasonably be considered wholly applicable.

Federal Budget, Annex 7, April 19, 2021: *Digital Services Tax*

Context

Digital technology has resulted in the development of new business models and ways of creating value. In the digital economy, data is a key commodity and the collection, processing and monetization of data is a key commercial activity. New business models have developed involving online platforms that attract users through certain service offerings, collect data and content contributions from the users, and then monetize that data and content in order to earn a profit. Examples of such business models include:

- social media platforms and search engines that earn revenue from advertising that they target based on data they have gathered about their users' interests; and

- intermediation platforms that create online markets for sellers and buyers of goods or services (e.g., taxi rides, short-term accommodations), exchange information across the platform about those on the other side of the market and facilitate transactions between them.

In these business models, the users are not mere customers of the platform or passive recipients of its services. The active participation of users, in interacting with the platform and providing data and content contributions, is a key contributor to the product offering of the platform. This user participation is a key input in the platform business's production process in a way similar to labour and physical capital in a more traditional business. For example:

- a search engine cannot earn advertising revenue without users to view ads and provide information allowing those ads to be targeted; and

- an accommodation platform cannot facilitate transactions without information about available apartments to share with potential renters and information about renters seeking premises to share with apartment providers.

Current tax systems, however, were generally designed for a bricks-and-mortar economy and effectively assume that value is created only in places where physical resources, like employees, facilities and equipment, are located. Given their reliance on digital technology, businesses of this type do not require a local physical presence in order to engage with users and collect their data and content. These businesses nevertheless can reasonably be considered to be conducting this part of their value-creating activity, even if it is controlled remotely, in the location of the users. This activity, however, is not always subject to local tax under current rules.

Since user-intensive commercial activity of this kind is dominated by businesses that are multinational in scope, this issue would be best addressed multilaterally. To this end, the international community has been discussing possible approaches for a number of years. In the project on Base Erosion and Profit Shifting (BEPS) undertaken by the members of the Organisation for Economic Co-operation and Development (OECD) and the G20 from 2013 to 2015, digital economy challenges were designated as Action 1 of the 15 action items. No agreement, however, was reached under Action 1 on a common approach with respect to corporate-level tax. Intensive discussions on the challenges of digitalization re-started in 2017 through the OECD-led Inclusive Framework on BEPS (which now has 139 member jurisdictions). Due to the inability to reach consensus, however, in October 2020 the target date for agreement was deferred to mid-2021.

Canada has a strong preference for a multilateral approach and so continues to work actively toward this goal with our international partners. However, there have been delays in reaching agreement and there is uncertainty about when an eventual agreed approach will come into effect. **The government therefore proposes to implement an interim measure.**

Proposed Measure

As announced in the November 2020 Fall Economic Statement, Budget 2021 proposes to **implement a Digital Services Tax (DST)**. The proposed tax is intended to ensure that revenue earned by large businesses — foreign or domestic — from engagement with online users in Canada, including through the collection, processing and monetizing of data and content contributions from those users, is subject to Canadian tax. The DST is intended to be interim in nature — it would apply as of January 1, 2022 until an acceptable multilateral approach comes into effect with respect to the implicated businesses.

The proposed tax would have the following key features.

- *Rate and Base*: The DST would apply at a rate of **3% on revenue from certain digital services** reliant on the engagement, data and content contributions of Canadian users. For greater certainty, revenue would not include any applicable value-added tax or sales tax amounts collected on the revenue transaction.

- *In-Scope Revenue*: The DST would apply to revenue from online business models in which the participation of users, including by the provision of data and content contributions, is a key value driver. Specifically, it would apply to revenue from:

  — *Online marketplaces*: Services provided through an online marketplace that helps match sellers of goods and services with potential buyers, whether or not the platform facilitates completion of the sale. Included would be optional (e.g., "premium") services that enhance the basic intermediation function or affect its commercial terms. This category would not generally include:

    - revenue in respect of the storage or shipping of tangible goods sold through the marketplace, to the extent the revenue reflects a reasonable rate of compensation for those services;

- the sale of goods and services (including the sale, licensing or streaming of digital content such as audio, video, games, software, e-books, newspapers and magazines) by a seller on its own account; and

- trading in financial instruments and commodities.

— *Social media*: Services provided through an online interface to facilitate interaction between users or between users and user-generated content. This category would not generally include an interface of which the sole purpose is to provide communications services (such as telephone service through Voice over Internet Protocol).

— *Online advertising*: Services aimed at the placing of online advertisements that are targeted based on data gathered from users of an online interface. This would include online interfaces such as online marketplaces, social media platforms, internet search engines, digital content streaming services, and online communications services. Advertisements would include preferential search listings. The scope would encompass both revenue earned by an interface operator from the display of advertising on the interface as well as revenue earned from systems for facilitating online advertising placement by third parties (including demand-side platforms, supply-side platforms, ad exchanges and advertising performance monitoring services).

— *User data*: The sale or licensing of data gathered from users of an online interface, including anonymized and aggregated data.

• *Taxpayers*:

— *Thresholds*: The DST would apply to businesses organized under various forms including corporations, trusts and partnerships. The DST would apply in a particular calendar year to an entity that meets, or is a member of a business group that meets, both of the following thresholds:

- global revenue from all sources of €750 million or more (the threshold for country-by-country reporting under an OECD standard) in the previous calendar year; and

- in-scope revenue associated with Canadian users of more than $20 million in the particular calendar year.

For such entities or groups, the DST would apply only to in-scope revenue associated with Canadian users in excess of the $20 million threshold.

— *Group-level calculation*: Group-level calculation of thresholds is important because a firm's administrative capacity is linked to its overall size and the revenue-generating activities linked to Canadian users may be dispersed across multiple entities in a business group. It is anticipated that groups will generally be defined in the same manner as for country-by-country reporting.

— *Large firms*: Large firms are the focus of the proposed tax for several reasons.

- Successful leveraging of user participation, data and content as a key value creation method in an online platform involves significant economies of scale and important network effects. Users are attracted by the presence of other users with whom they can interact, so market share tends to gravitate toward platforms that attract large user groups. Larger platforms thus tend to have a greater ability to generate value from user engagement.

- Larger, more mature firms are more likely to be profitable and able to bear the burden of a tax on revenue, which is not sensitive to profitability. Exclusion from the tax of smaller firms, from all countries, will help ensure that smaller, less mature and growing firms, which are less likely to be profitable, are not prejudiced in their ability to compete against larger, more established firms.

- Large firms are better able to manage the burden of compliance associated with a new tax and can absorb the relevant costs over a larger amount of revenue. The relative costs of administration for government are also proportionately smaller relative to the tax revenue for larger firms. In particular, the costs of administering a tax applicable to large numbers of smaller firms, many of which have little or no local physical presence, would be inordinate.

• *Revenue Sourcing*: When revenue of an entity is contractually related to both activities within the scope of the DST and other activities, the in-scope revenue would need to be determined on a reasonable basis. In determining an entity's in-scope revenue associated with users in Canada (as opposed to users in another jurisdiction), two general methods would be used. Where it is possible to trace revenues to relevant users in Canada on the basis of transactional information, such tracing would be required. Where such tracing is not possible, a specified formulaic allocation would be required. Revenue sourcing principles would vary according to the nature of the revenue.

— Online marketplaces: Fee revenue of online marketplaces would generally be sourced to the locations of the users who interact through the interface.

- *Transactional*: Fee revenue associated with a particular transaction between users (e.g., a fee set as a percentage of the transaction price or as a fixed amount per transaction, or a fee otherwise set for a particular transaction) would generally be considered to be sourced 50:50 to the locations of the buyer and seller. This allocation recognizes that regardless of the legal arrangement for payment of the fee, the intermediation service of the marketplace is reliant on the engagement and data contributions of both

parties. However, where the transaction is an arrangement for the performance of a tangible service in a particular location (e.g., accommodations, food delivery, taxi ride), the revenue would be sourced to the location where the service is performed.

- *Non-transactional*: Fee revenue that is not associated with a particular transaction (e.g., interface subscription fees) and revenue from advertising goods or services listed for sale on the marketplace would be sourced to the locations of the interface users on a formulaic basis. The revenue associated with users in Canada would be considered to be equal to the total of the relevant revenue multiplied by the ratio of the number of marketplace transaction participants in Canada to the total number of transaction participants. For this purpose, the buyer and seller in a transaction would each be considered a 'transaction participant' and a participant would be counted each time it participates in a transaction. This allocation reflects the fact that non-transactional interface fees are generally paid for the ultimate purpose of concluding transactions with other interface users, even if those users cannot be identified at the time the fee is paid.

— *Social media*: Fee revenue of social media interfaces (e.g., interface subscription fees) would be sourced to the locations of the interface users on a formulaic basis. The revenue associated with users in Canada would be considered to be equal to the total of the relevant revenue multiplied by the ratio of the number of active users of the interface that are users in Canada to the total number of active users in all locations. This allocation reflects the fact that interface fees are generally paid for the purpose of facilitating interactions with other interface users, including those who do not pay fees.

— *Online advertising*: Online advertising revenue would generally be sourced based on the location of the user who views, listens to, clicks on, or otherwise consumes the advertisement. This user would often be the same user whose data has been used to target the advertisement. As an exception, revenue of an online marketplace from advertising goods or services listed for sale on the marketplace would be sourced using the formula applicable to non-transactional marketplace fee revenue (outlined above). Outside of this exception, advertising revenue would be sourced using tracing or a formulaic basis, according to the circumstances.

- Tracing: Advertising revenue would be required to be traced to viewers in Canada where possible. For example, this would include revenue from a series of advertisements that is shown all or substantially all (generally 90% or more) to viewers in Canada and revenue from individual advertisements that are shown to viewers in Canada (e.g., where advertising fees are contractually charged on the basis of a user viewing or clicking on the advertisement or taking some other action).

- Formula: Where under a contract advertising revenue associated with users in Canada and other jurisdictions is not separately identifiable, revenue associated with users in Canada would be considered to be equal to the total contract revenue multiplied by the ratio of the number of advertisement views by viewers in Canada to the total number of advertisement views by viewers in all locations.

— *User data*: Revenue from the sale of user data would be sourced where possible to the location of the user to whom the data relates. If particular revenue relates to data in respect of both users in Canada and users in other locations, the revenue associated with users in Canada would be considered to be equal to the total of the relevant revenue multiplied by the ratio of the number of users from which the data was collected that are users in Canada to the total number of users.

• *User Location*:

— *Ordinary location*: The determination of whether a user of an interface is located in Canada or some other country for purposes of revenue sourcing would generally be based on the ordinary (i.e., usual) location of an individual user and the ordinary place of business of a business user. The determination of the ordinary location, or ordinary place of business, of a user would be based on information generally available to the digital service provider. This would include such indicators as recurring data on device geolocation or internet protocol (IP) address, billing address, delivery address (where relevant), and telephone area code.

— *Real-time location*: By exception, in the cases of advertising targeted based on the real-time location of a user and the sale of data based on the real-time location of a user, the real-time location of a user would be based on device geolocation if available, or other information if not.

— *Consistency*: Firms would be expected to use a consistent approach in determining user location, though different approaches might be used for different services depending on differences in data availability.

• *Treatment for Income Tax Purposes*: As with other non-income taxes, the deductibility of the DST liability of an entity in computing taxable income for Canadian income tax purposes would be determined based on general principles [9(1) — ed.] — e.g., whether it is incurred for the purpose of earning the entity's income subject to Canadian income tax [18(1)(a) — ed.]. DST liability would not be eligible for a credit against Canadian income tax payable [see also 18(1)(t) — ed.].

- **Administration**: It is proposed that firms subject to DST be required to file an annual return following the end of the reporting period, which is proposed to be the calendar year. It is contemplated that:
  - one annual payment would be required after the end of the reporting period;
  - a group would be able to designate an entity to file the DST return and pay the DST liability on behalf of the group; and
  - to facilitate enforcement, each entity in a group would be jointly and severally liable for DST payable by any other group member.

Coming Into Force

The DST would apply as of January 1, 2022.

Consultation

The government plans to engage with the provinces and territories to discuss the implications of the DST.

The government welcomes feedback from stakeholders on the proposed approach to implementing the DST. Interested parties are invited to send written representations by June 18, 2021 to the Department of Finance Canada, Tax Policy Branch at: DST-TSN@canada.ca.

It is anticipated that draft legislation for a new statute implementing the DST would be released for public comment during summer 2021, taking into account the feedback received. The legislation would subsequently be included in a bill to be introduced in Parliament.

Nov. 30, 2020 Economic Statement, Chapter 4: *International Corporate Tax and Digitalization*

The government is committed to ensuring that everyone pays their fair share, so that Canada continues to have the resources needed to invest in people and keep our economy strong. When it comes to corporate level tax, this means ensuring that corporations in all sectors, including digital corporations, pay their fair share of taxes in respect of their activity in Canada. It is important that tax rules take account of new ways in which businesses carry out value-creating activities in a jurisdiction, including remote digital means such as the collection of user data and content contributions. It is also important that countries have tools to protect their tax bases against avoidance in the form of international profit shifting.

The government recognizes the mutual benefits of multilateral coordination in international taxation and therefore has a strong preference for a multilateral approach to address these issues. We need a modern tax system where all corporations pay their fair share. Canada has been working with our international partners in a process led by the Organisation for Economic Co-operation and Development with a view to developing a coordinated approach by mid-2021. The government remains committed to a multilateral solution, but is concerned about the delay in arriving at consensus. The government therefore proposes to implement a tax on corporations providing digital services, with effect from January 1, 2022, which would apply until such time as an acceptable common approach comes into effect. On a provisional basis, it is estimated that the new measure would increase federal revenues by $3.4 billion over 5 years, starting in 2021-22. Further details will be announced in Budget 2021.

Prime Minister's "mandate letter" to Minister of Finance, Dec. 2019: I will expect you to work with your colleagues and through established legislative, regulatory and Cabinet processes to deliver on your top priorities. In particular, you will: . . .

- Ensure that multinational tech giants pay appropriate corporate tax on the revenue that they generate within Canada.

Oct. 2019 Liberal election platform: "We will . . . make sure that multinational tech giants pay corporate tax on the revenue they generate in Canada."

Notes: One might think that, for companies resident in treaty countries, the treaty would prevent Canada from taxing income not arising from a permanent establishment (PE) in Canada. However, Finance advises that the DST will be a tax on gross revenue, not on income, and thus not protected by tax treaty. Given that Art. 7 of each treaty requires a PE for Canada to tax "business profits" (not revenues), this interpretation appears to be correct.

The Finance Minister stated on June 5, 2021 that this proposal will proceed until the new BEPS tax system is in place (see Proposed Amendments at end of s. 95, under "Action 1"): tinyurl.com/cbc-g7-beps.

Budget Table 1 projects that this measure will generate revenue for the federal government of $200 million in 2021-22, $700m in 2022-23 [implying digital revenues from Canada of $23.3 billion!], $800m in each of 2023-24 and 2024-25, and $900m in 2025-26 (minus relatively small annual administrative costs).

Related Provisions: 2(3) — Tax on non-resident's taxable income earned in Canada; 4(3) — Whether deductions applicable to a particular source; 40(9) — Prorating for gains not taxed before April 27, 1995; 52(8) — Cost to non-resident of share of corporation that becomes resident in Canada; 94(3)(a)(iv) — Application to beneficiary of trust deemed resident in Canada; 95(1)"taxable Canadian business"(a) — Business of foreign affiliate; 107.3(1)(b) — Income of non-resident beneficiary of qualifying environmental trust; 111(8)"non-capital loss"B — Carryforward of 115(1)(b)(vii) amount; 111(9) — Carryover of losses of non-resident taxpayer; 112(3)(b)(i) — Reduction in loss under 115(1)(d.1) on subsequent disposition of share; 112(5.2)B(b)(i), (ii) — Adjustment for dividends received on mark-to-market property; 114 — Individual resident in Canada for only part of year; 115(2.1) — Non-resident actors — income excluded; 115(3) — Non-resident employed as airline pilot; 115.1 — Competent

authority agreements under tax treaties; 115.2 — Non-resident investment or pension fund deemed not carrying on business in Canada; 116 — Certificate required where non-resident disposes of TCP; 118.94 — Limitation on credits available; 217 — Election re certain payments; 219(1) — Branch tax on non-resident corporations; 248(1)"taxable income earned in Canada" — Definition applies to entire Act but cannot be less than nil; 250.1(a) — Taxation year of non-resident person; Canada-U.S. Tax Treaty:Art. VII — Business profits of U.S. resident; Canada-U.S. Tax Treaty:Art. XIII — Taxation of capital gains.

Notes: See Reg. 102 and 105 re payors' withholding obligations. A non-resident individual who does not have a Social Insurance Number should apply for an Individual Tax Number (see Notes to 237(1)).

The tax imposed by 2(3) and 115(1) is relieved in certain cases by Canada's bilateral tax treaties. The Canada-U.S. and Canada-U.K. treaties are reproduced at the end of this book. For example, the tax on gains under 115(1)(b) is usually relieved by treaty for gains on personal property (but not real property). On a sale of real property, see s. 116 re withholding and certificate obligations.

Amendments effective April 26, 1995 increased the scope of taxation of capital gains of non-residents, to include shares of non-resident corps whose value is "primarily" (greater than 50%) attributable to real property in Canada, provided the specific share being acquired also meets this test (see 248(1)"taxable Canadian property"(d)). A transitional rule in 40(9) prorates this gain to reduce it by months before May 1995. In addition, Canada-US tax treaty Art. XVIII prevents this tax from applying to US residents in respect of non-resident corps.

See also Notes to 2(3).

115(1)(a)(i) applies to: payment of annual leave credits accumulated while working in Canada (VIEWS doc 2010-0377821E5); non-resident sending employee to Canada under Interchange Canada program (2017-0731441E5) [Begun, "No Need for Second Thoughts on Secondments", XXVI(1) *Taxation of Executive Compensation & Retirement* (Federated Press) 10-12 (2018)]. It does not apply to: a 6(6) non-taxable allowance (2008-0297661E5); non-resident systems analysts working physically outside Canada on servers in Canada (2012-0440411E5).

115(1)(a)(i) includes wage loss insurance benefits taxable to residents under 6(1)(f), even though they are not income from "duties performed": *Price*, 2012 FCA 332 (overruling *Blauer*, 2007 TCC 706, which had said 212(1)(h) should apply instead).

Athletes: In *Austin*, 2004 TCC 6, a Canadian Football League player played 3-4 of 18 games a season in the US, and was paid per game. The Court held that the allocation of his income to time worked outside Canada for 115(1)(a)(i) was 3-4 out of 18, not 6 or 8 days out of 180 as CRA claimed. In VIEWS doc 2017-0702061E5, a professional athlete's games were 60% in the US so 40% of his income was allocated to Canada; amounts paid to his RCA, exempted by 6(1)(a)(ii), could not be all allocated to Canada. See also Notes to Reg. 2602(1) re allocation of a non-resident's income to provinces; and note that signing bonuses for US-resident players in Canada are limited to 15% Canadian tax under Canada-US Tax Treaty Art. XVI:4.

Pilots: Both *Sutcliffe*, 2005 TCC 812 (later reasons 2006 TCC 581), and *Price*, 2011 TCC 449 (appeal dismissed on this issue 2012 FCA 332) determined the allocation to Canada of flight time by a non-resident Air Canada pilot based on flight time in Canadian airspace. The TCC in *Price* recommended that Parliament "set a firm percentage" to stop "endless maneuvering" through the Courts, and Finance responded on Dec. 21/12 with a simpler rule in 115(3), enacted by 2013 budget bill #1.

115(1)(a)(ii) does not tax business income earned by person X resident in a country with which Canada has a tax treaty, unless X has a "permanent establishment" in Canada: e.g., Canada-US treaty Art. VII:1. However, this worldwide approach may change: see OECD Proposed Amendments at end of s. 95, under "Action 1"; and see the proposed Digital Services Tax above.

Where a non-resident disposes of an interest in a life insurance policy that is not a "life insurance policy in Canada" so 115(1)(a)(vi) does not apply, see VIEWS doc 2006-0207001E6.

115(1)(a) does not catch property income (passive income) earned by a non-resident such as interest, dividends, rents and royalties (see Notes to 9(1) under "Business income vs property income"). See instead 212(1) and (2).

CRA considers that "substantially all" in 115(1)(f) means 90% or more.

115(1)(a)(iii.22) added by 2021 budget bill #1, effective 2020.

115(1)(d) amended to refer to 110(1)(e) by 2021 budget bill #1, effective July 2021.

115(1) amended by 2008 budget bill #2 (for 2008 and later tax years), 2004 Budget, 2001 technical bill (moving "taxable Canadian property" definition to 248(1)), 2000 and 1998 Budgets, 1995-97 technical bill, 1996 Budget, 1994, 1992 and 1991 technical bills.

Regulations: 105 (withholding on payments of fees, commissions, etc.).

I.T. Application Rules: 26(30) (taxable Canadian property under new rules effective April 26, 1995).

Interpretation Bulletins: IT-113R4: Benefits to employees — stock options; IT-150R2: Acquisition from a non-resident of certain property by death or mortgage foreclosure or by virtue of a deemed disposition (cancelled); IT-176R2: Taxable Canadian property — Interests in and options on real property and shares; IT-242R: Retired partners; IT-262R2: Losses of non-residents and part-year residents; IT-379R: Employees profit sharing plans — allocations to beneficiaries; IT-393R2: Election re tax on rents and timber royalties — non-residents; IT-421R2: Benefits to individuals, corporations and shareholders from loans or debt; IT-434R: Rental of real property by individual; IT-451R: Deemed disposition and acquisition on ceasing to be or becoming resident in Canada; IT-465R: Non-resident beneficiaries of trusts See also at end of s. 115.

Information Circulars: 72-17R6: Procedures concerning the disposition of taxable Canadian property by non-residents of Canada — section 116; 88-2 Supplement, para. 7: General anti-avoidance rule — section 245 of the *Income Tax Act*.

CRA Audit Manual: 15.2.0: Income of a non-resident.

Advance Tax Rulings: ATR-70: Distribution of taxable Canadian property by a trust to a non-resident.

Forms: R105: Regulation 105 waiver application; T2 Sched. 91: Information concerning claims for treaty-based exemptions; T1243: Deemed disposition of property by an emigrant of Canada; T1248 Sched. D: Information about your residency status; T1261: Application for a CRA individual tax number (ITN) for non-residents; T2061A: Election by an emigrant to report deemed dispositions of taxable Canadian property and capital gains and/or losses thereon; T4058: Non-residents and income tax [guide].

(2) Idem [persons deemed employed in Canada] — Where, in a taxation year, a non-resident person was

(a) a student in full-time attendance at an educational institution in Canada that is a university, college or other educational institution providing courses at a post-secondary school level in Canada,

(b) a student attending, or a teacher teaching at, an educational institution outside Canada that is a university, college or other educational institution providing courses at a post-secondary school level, who in any preceding taxation year ceased to be resident in Canada in the course of or subsequent to moving to attend or to teach at the institution,

(b.1) an individual who in any preceding taxation year ceased to be resident in Canada in the course of or subsequent to moving to carry on research or any similar work under a grant received by the individual to enable the individual to carry on the research or work,

(c) an individual

(i) who had, in any previous year, ceased to be resident in Canada,

(ii) who received, in the taxation year, salary or wages or other remuneration in respect of an office or employment that was paid to the individual directly or indirectly by a person resident in Canada, and

(iii) who was, under an agreement or a convention with one or more countries that has the force of law in Canada, entitled to an exemption from an income tax otherwise payable in any of those countries in respect of the salary or wages or other remuneration, or

(c.1) a person who received in the year an amount, under a contract, that was or will be deductible in computing the income of a taxpayer subject to tax under this Part and the amount can, irrespective of when the contract was entered into or the form or legal effect of the contract, reasonably be regarded as having been received, in whole or in part,

(i) as consideration or partial consideration for entering into a contract of service or an agreement to perform a service where any such service is to be performed in Canada, or for undertaking not to enter into such a contract or agreement with another party, or

(ii) as remuneration or partial remuneration from the duties of an office or employment or as compensation or partial compensation for services to be performed in Canada,

the following rules apply:

(d) for the purposes of subsection 2(3) the non-resident person shall be deemed to have been employed in Canada in the year,

(e) for the purposes of subparagraph (1)(a)(v), the total determined under this paragraph in respect of the non-resident person is the total of

(i) any remuneration in respect of an office or employment that was paid to the non-resident person directly or indirectly by a person resident in Canada and was received by the non-resident person in the year, except to the extent that such re-

muneration is attributable to the duties of an office or employment performed by the non-resident person anywhere outside Canada and

(A) is subject to an income or profits tax imposed by the government of a country other than Canada, or

(B) is paid in connection with the selling of property, the negotiating of contracts or the rendering of services for the non-resident person's employer, or a foreign affiliate of the employer, or any other person with whom the employer does not deal at arm's length, in the ordinary course of a business carried on by the employer, that foreign affiliate or that person,

(ii) amounts that would be required by paragraph 56(1)(n) or (o) to be included in computing the non-resident person's income for the year if the non-resident person were resident in Canada throughout the year and the reference in the applicable paragraph to "received by the taxpayer in the year" were read as a reference to "received by the taxpayer in the year from a source in Canada",

(iii) [Repealed]

(iv) amounts that would be required by paragraph 56(1)(q) to be included in computing the non-resident person's income for the year if the non-resident person were resident in Canada throughout the year, and

(v) amounts described in paragraph (c.1) received by the non-resident person in the year, except to the extent that they are otherwise required to be included in computing the non-resident person's taxable income earned in Canada for the year, and

(f) there may be deducted in computing the taxable income of the non-resident person for the year the amount that would be deductible in computing the non-resident person's income for the year by virtue of section 62 if

(i) the definition "eligible relocation" in subsection 248(1) were read without reference to subparagraph (a)(i) of that definition, and

(ii) the amounts described in subparagraph 62(1)(c)(ii) were the amounts described in subparagraph (e)(ii) of this subsection.

Related Provisions: 4(3) — Deductions applicable; 52(8) — Reduction in cost base of share of corporation that becomes resident in Canada; 146(1)"earned income"(d) — RRSPs — "earned income"; 153(1)(o) — Withholding of tax on amount described in 115(2)(c.1); 250(1) — Individuals deemed resident in Canada; Reg. 104(2) — Withholding required for payments taxed under 115(2)(e)(i).

Notes: For the meaning of "post-secondary", used in 115(2)(a) and (b), see Notes to 118.5(1)(a); and for "full-time attendance", see Notes to 118.5(1)(b).

A former Canadian resident employed at a Canadian consulate outside Canada falls under 115(2)(b): VIEWS doc 2011-0415151E5.

115(2)(c) effectively allows Canada to tax foreign employment income of an expatriate if the other country has agreed in a tax treaty with Canada to refrain from doing so. However, if the income is not paid directly or indirectly by a Canadian resident it will not be taxed. See VIEWS doc 2008-0295221E5.

See Notes to 17.1(1) re "indirectly" in (c)(ii) and (e)(i).

115(2)(c.1) is designed for signing bonuses; see 6(3) for this rule for Canadian residents. In *Nonis*, 2021 TCC 31, it did not apply to the Toronto Maple Leafs' general manager, who was fired in April 2015 and continued to receive salary to 2016. He was taxed only on the fraction of his income representing his days actually in Canada (37 in 2015, 0 in 2016), not on all the income, which would be "absurd" (para. 76).

A non-resident moving to Canada should be sure to receive any bonus for work done *outside* Canada *before* becoming resident here; otherwise it is taxable under 5(1). See *Garcia*, 2007 TCC 548.

Salary payments to a non-resident who was formerly resident in Canada, for work outside Canada, are taxable under 115(2)(e)(i) unless taxed in the foreign country or paid in the ordinary course of a business carried on by the employer (which can include a Canadian college's campus in a foreign country: VIEWS doc 2008-027672I7), and withholding is required by 153(1) and Reg. 104(2).

For the meaning of "income or profits tax" in (e)(i)(A), see Notes to 126(4).

An educational institution might or might not be carrying on "business" for purposes of 115(2)(e)(i)(B): VIEWS doc 2007-023796I7.

115(2) amended by 2001 technical bill (for 1998 and later tax years), 1998 Budget and 1992 Child Benefit bill.

Income Tax Folios: S1-F2-C3: Scholarships, research grants and other education assistance [replaces IT-340R]; S1-F3-C4: Moving expenses [replaces IT-178R3].

Interpretation Bulletins: IT-161R3: Non-residents — exemption from tax deductions at source on employment income (cancelled). See also at end of s. 115.

Forms: T1248 Sched. D: Information about your residency status; T1261: Application for a CRA individual tax number (ITN) for non-residents; T4058: Non-residents and income tax [guide].

(2.1) Non-resident actors — Notwithstanding subsection (1), where a non-resident person is liable to tax under subsection 212(5.1), or would if this Act were read without reference to subsection 212(5.2) be so liable, in respect of an amount paid, credited or provided in a particular taxation year, the amount shall not be included in computing the non-resident person's taxable income earned in Canada for any taxation year unless a valid election is made under subsection 216.1(1) in respect of the non-resident person for the particular year.

Related Provisions: 115(2.2) — Deferred payment by actor's corporation; 150(1)(a)(i)(B) — No requirement for actor to file Canadian tax return.

Notes: 115(2.1) added by 2001 technical bill, effective for amounts paid, credited or provided after 2000. (This measure, along with 212(5.1)–(5.3) and 216.1, was first announced on March 16, 2001.)

(2.2) Deferred payment by actor's corporation — Where a corporation is liable to tax under subsection 212(5.1) in respect of a corporation payment (within the meaning assigned by subsection 212(5.2)) made in a taxation year in respect of an actor and, in a subsequent year, the corporation makes an actor payment (within the meaning assigned by subsection 212(5.2)) to or for the benefit of the actor, the amount of the actor payment is not deductible in computing the income of the corporation for any taxation year and is not included in computing the taxable income earned in Canada of the actor for any taxation year.

Notes: 115(2.2) added by 2001 technical bill, effective for amounts paid, credited or provided after 2000. See Notes to 115(2.1).

Regulations: 202(1.1) (information return).

(2.3) Non-resident persons — 2010 Olympic and Paralympic Winter Games — [No longer relevant]

Notes: 115(2.3) (added by 2007 budget bill #2 effective Dec. 14, 2007) exempts Jan.-March 2010 income of various non-residents (athletes, officials, etc.) in connection with the Vancouver Winter Olympics and Paralympics held Feb. 12-28, 2010. (CRA considers Olympic medals taxable to Canadians: see Reg. 7700 Notes.)

(3) Non-resident employed as aircraft pilot — For the purpose of applying subparagraph (1)(a)(i) to a non-resident person employed as an aircraft pilot, income of the non-resident person that is attributable to a flight (including a leg of a flight) and paid directly or indirectly by a person resident in Canada is attributable to duties performed in Canada in the following proportions:

(a) all of the income attributable to the flight if the flight departs from a location in Canada and arrives at a location in Canada;

(b) one-half of the income attributable to the flight if the flight departs from a location in Canada and arrives at a location outside Canada;

(c) one-half of the income attributable to the flight if the flight departs from a location outside Canada and arrives at a location in Canada; and

(d) none of the income attributable to the flight if the flight departs from a location outside Canada and arrives at a location outside Canada.

Notes: See Notes to 115(1) re *Sutcliffe* and *Price*, which led to this much simpler rule. If a treaty provides a better result, the treaty applies, but CRA's view is that a pilot must use one rule or the other throughout a year: doc 2014-0559751E5. For the meaning of "aircraft" see 8(1)(j) Notes. For "indirectly" see 17.1(1) Notes.

115(3) added by 2013 budget bill #1, for 2013 and later tax years.

Former 115(3) repealed by 2001 technical bill, effective Oct. 2, 1996 (earlier amended by 1995-97, 1991 technical bills). See now 248(1)"taxable Canadian property"(l) for a similar rule, but see Notes there re VIEWS doc 2002-0151795.

(4) Non-resident's income from Canadian resource property — Where a non-resident person ceases at any particular time in a taxation year to carry on such of the businesses described in any of paragraphs (a) to (g) of the definition "principal business corporation" in subsection 66(15) as were carried on by the non-resident person immediately before that time at one or more fixed places of business in Canada and either does not commence after that time and during the year to carry on any business so described at a fixed place of business in Canada or disposes of Canadian resource property at any time in the year during which the non-resident person was not carrying on any business so described at a fixed place of business in Canada, the following rules apply:

(a) the taxation year of the non-resident person that would otherwise have included the particular time shall be deemed to have ended at such time and a new taxation year shall be deemed to have commenced immediately thereafter;

(b) the non-resident person or any partnership of which the non-resident person was a member immediately after the particular time shall be deemed, for the purpose only of computing the non-resident person's income earned in Canada for the taxation year that is deemed to have ended, to have disposed immediately before the particular time of each Canadian resource property that was owned by the non-resident person or by the partnership immediately after the particular time and to have received therefor immediately before the particular time proceeds of disposition equal to the fair market value thereof at the particular time; and

(c) the non-resident person or any partnership of which the non-resident person was a member immediately after the particular time shall be deemed, for the purpose only of computing the non-resident person's income earned in Canada for a taxation year commencing after the particular time, to have reacquired immediately after the particular time, at a cost equal to the amount deemed by paragraph (b) to have been received by the non-resident person or the partnership as the proceeds of disposition therefor, each property deemed by that paragraph to have been disposed of.

Related Provisions: 4(3) — Deductions applicable; 66.2(7) — Exception — Canadian development expense; 66.4(7) — Share of partner; 115(5) — Partnership excludes prescribed partnership; 115.1 — Competent authority agreements under tax treaties.

Interpretation Bulletins: IT-125R4: Dispositions of resource properties.

(4.1) Foreign resource pool expenses — Where a taxpayer ceases at any time after February 27, 2000 to be resident in Canada, a particular taxation year of the taxpayer ends after that time and the taxpayer was non-resident throughout the period (in this subsection referred to as the "non-resident period") that begins at that time and ends at the end of the particular year,

(a) in computing the taxpayer's taxable income earned in Canada for the particular year, there may be deducted each amount that would be permitted to be deducted in computing the taxpayer's income for the particular year under subsection 66(4) or 66.21(4) if

(i) subsection 66(4) were read without reference to the words "who is resident throughout a taxation year in Canada" and as if the amount determined under subparagraph 66(4)(b)(ii) were nil, and

(ii) subsection 66.21(4) were read without reference to the words "throughout which the taxpayer is resident in Canada" and as if the amounts determined under subparagraph 66.21(4)(a)(ii) and paragraph 66.21(4)(b) were nil; and

(b) an amount deducted under this subsection in computing the taxpayer's taxable income earned in Canada for the particular year is deemed, for the purpose of applying subsection 66(4) or 66.21(4), as the case may be, to a subsequent taxation year, to have been deducted in computing the taxpayer's income for the particular year.

Notifications

Notes: 115(4.1) added by 2000 Budget, for tax years that begin after Feb. 27, 2000.

(5) Interpretation of "partnership" — For the purposes of subsection (4), "partnership" does not include a prescribed partnership.

Regulations: No prescribed partnerships to date.

(6) Application of subsec. 138(12) — The definitions in subsection 138(12) apply to this section.

Notes: 115(6) added in the RSC 1985 (5th Supp) consolidation, effective for tax years ending after Nov. 1991. This rule was formerly in the opening words of 138(12). It is now superfluous, since "designated insurance policy" and "life insurance policy in Canada" are both defined in 248(1).

Definitions [s. 115]: "allowable business investment loss" — 38(c), 248(1); "allowable capital loss" — 38(b), 248(1); "amount" — 248(1); "associated" — 256; "authorized foreign bank", "business" — 248(1); "branch financial statements" — 20.2(1); "Canada" — 255, *Interpretation Act* 35(1); "Canadian banking business" — 248(1); "Canadian resource property" — 66(15), 248(1); "capital interest" — in a trust 108(1), 248(1); "capital property" — 54, 248(1); "carried on a business in Canada" — 253; "class of shares" — 248(6); "corporation" — 248(1), *Interpretation Act* 35(1); "corporation payment" — 212(5.2); "designated insurance property" — 138(12), 248(1); "dividend", "employed", "employee", "employment" — 248(1); "fair market value" — see 69(1) Notes; "foreign affiliate" — 95(1), 248(1); "foreign resource pool expense" — 248(1); "income interest" — 108(1), 248(1); "individual" — 248(1); "interest" — in real property 248(4); "international traffic" — 248(1); "life insurance policy in Canada" — 138(12), 248(1); "listed" — 87(10); "mutual fund corporation" — 131(8), 248(1); "mutual fund trust" — 132(6)–(7), 132.2(3)(n), 248(1); "non-resident", "office", "officer" — 248(1); "partnership" — 115(5) (and see 96(1) Notes); "person", "prescribed" — 248(1); "principal-business corporation" — 66(15); "property" — 248(1); "property used by it in the year in, or held by it in the year in the course of carrying on an insurance business" — 115(6), 138(12); "public corporation" — 89(1), 248(1); "resident in Canada" — 94(3)(a), 250; "salary or wages", "share" — 248(1); "taxable Canadian property" — 248(1); "taxable capital gain" — 38(a), 248(1); "taxable income" — 2(2), 248(1); "taxable income earned in Canada" — 115(1), 248(1); "taxation year" — 249, 250.1(a); "taxpayer" — 248(1); "timber resource property" — 13(21), 248(1); "treaty-protected business", "treaty-protected property" — 248(1); "trust" — 104(1), 248(1), (3); "unit trust" — 108(2), 248(1).

Income Tax Folios [s. 115]: S5-F1-C1: Determining an individual's residence status [replaces IT-221R3].

Interpretation Bulletins [s. 115]: IT-81R: Partnerships — income of non-resident partners; IT-168R3: Athletes and players employed by football, hockey and similar clubs; IT-171R2: Non-resident individuals — computation of taxable income earned in Canada and non-refundable tax credits (cancelled); IT-328R3: Losses on shares on which dividends have been received; IT-393R2: Election re tax on rents and timber royalties — non-residents; IT-420R3: Non-residents — income earned in Canada.

115.1 (1) Competent authority [tax treaty] agreements — Notwithstanding any other provision of this Act, where the Minister and another person have, under a provision contained in a tax convention or agreement with another country that has the force of law in Canada, entered into an agreement with respect to the taxation of the other person, all determinations made in accordance with the terms and conditions of the agreement shall be deemed to be in accordance with this Act.

(2) Transfer of rights and obligations — Where rights and obligations under an agreement described in subsection (1) have been transferred to another person with the concurrence of the Minister, that other person shall be deemed, for the purpose of subsection (1), to have entered into the agreement with the Minister.

Related Provisions [s. 115.1]: 115(1) — Non-resident's taxable income earned in Canada; 116(1) — Disposition by non-resident of certain property; Canada-U.S. Tax Treaty:Art. XXVI — Mutual agreement procedure; Canada-U.K. Tax Treaty:Art. 23 — Mutual agreement procedure.

Notes [s. 115.1]: To request competent authority assistance in resolving a double taxation problem, see Information Circular 71-17R6. One may need to file a waiver under 152(4) to ensure the Canadian return remains open for reassessment (see also 152(4)(b)(iii), which extends the deadline by 3 years for non-arm's length transactions with non-residents). The treaty may have a deadline for applying for competent authority assistance, e.g. 6 years from the end of the relevant taxation year (Canada-US treaty Art. XXVI:2), or 2 years "from the first notification of the action which gives rise to taxation not in accordance with the Convention" (Canada-France treaty Art. 25:1).

As of fall 2020, Canada's designated "competent authorities" for tax treaty disputes involving specific taxpayers are Bob Hamilton (CRA Commissioner and CEO) and Christine Donoghue (Deputy Commissioner, 613-957-3688, christine.donoghue@cra.gc.ca). The delegated competent authorities for issues not involving specific taxpayers including general interpretation, non-discrimination, treaty shopping and double-non-taxation issues are Bob Hamilton; Christine Donoghue; Geoff Trueman (Assistant Commissioner, Legislative Policy & Regulatory Affairs [LPRA]);

Randy Hewlett (Director General, Legislative Policy Directorate [LPD], LPRA, 613-670-9058, randy.hewlett@cra.gc.ca); Robert Demeter (Director, Intl Relations & Treaties, LPD); Nancy Tremblay and Eli Moore (Senior Treaty Negotiators, Competent Authority Policy Section, LPD).

The CA will not agree to defer Canadian recognition of income that is exempt under the other country's law, as its role is to address double tax: VIEWS doc 2012-0444161C6.

"Another country" in 115.1(1) includes Hong Kong and Taiwan: see Notes to 219.2.

In *Teletech Canada*, 2013 FC 572, CRA refused Competent Authority assistance on transfer pricing because the reporting that triggered the problem (increasing parent's US income and decreasing sub's Canadian income) was not initiated by the CRA or the IRS. The Court dismissed an application for judicial review as filed too late.

A case resolved at competent authority and agreed to by the taxpayer was binding as a "settlement" in *Sifto Canada*, 2017 TCC 37, so CRA could not reassess SC after further audit. See Robson, "Subsection 115.1(1): Unanswered Questions from Sifto", 25(8) *Canadian Tax Highlights* (ctf.ca) 3-4 (Aug. 2017). In *Kerry Canada*, 2019 FC 377, a request to hold objections in abeyance pending consideration by the competent authority was held to be an implied waiver, so CRA could reassess late in K's favour.

See also *CRA Mutual Agreement Procedure Program Report 2019* (14pp), which explains the MAP process and timelines, and includes program statistics and contact information; and Information Circular 71-17R6, "Competent Authority Assistance".

See tinyurl.com/comp-authority for tax treaty Notices including agreements between the competent authorities on various treaty issues.

See also Skretkowicz & Diebel, "Canadian Competent Authority Update", 2006 Cdn Tax Foundation conference report, 18:1-24; Akin et al., "The Role of the Competent Authority in Canada and the United States", 2009 conference report, 16:1-16; Murray & Oatway, "The Competent Authority Function", 2012 conference report, 23:1-5; Shafer & Boychuk, "Understanding the Competent Authority Process"; 2016 conference report at 7:15-21; Notes to Canada-U.S. tax treaty, Art. XXVI:3 and XXIX-A:1.

115.1 rewritten by 1992 technical bill, retroactive to 1985, to extend its application. It previously applied only to the disposition of property by a non-resident where the Minister agreed to defer taxation pursuant to a prescribed tax treaty provision; para. XIII(8) of the Canada-U.S. treaty and para. 13(6) of the Canada-Netherlands treaty were prescribed in Reg. 7400 for this purpose. The new 115.1 is much more general.

Definitions [s. 115.1]: "Minister", "person" — 248(1).

Income Tax Folios [s. 115.1]: S5-F2-C1: Foreign tax credit [replaces IT-270R3, IT-395R2, IT-520].

Interpretation Bulletins [s. 115.1]: IT-173R2: Capital gains derived in Canada by residents of the United States; IT-420R3: Non-residents — income earned in Canada.

Information Circulars [s. 115.1]: 71-17R6: Guidance on competent authority assistance under Canada's tax conventions.

I.T. Technical News: 34 (Canada-U.S. competent authority Memorandum of Understanding).

Transfer Pricing Memoranda: TPM-12: Accelerated Competent Authority Procedure (ACAP).

CRA Audit Manual: 15.12.4: Competent authority division.

Forms [s. 115.1]: T2029: Waiver in respect of the normal reassessment period or extended reassessment period.

115.2 Non-residents with Canadian investment service providers — (1) Definitions — The definitions in this subsection apply in this section.

"Canadian investor", at any time in respect of a non-resident person, means a person that the non-resident person knows, or ought to know after reasonable inquiry, is at that time resident in Canada.

Notes: Definition "Canadian investor" added by 2001 Budget, this version effective for 2002 and later taxation years.

"Canadian service provider" means a corporation resident in Canada, a trust resident in Canada or a Canadian partnership.

"designated investment services" provided to a person or partnership means any one or more of the services described in the following paragraphs:

(a) investment management and advice with respect to qualified investments, regardless of whether the manager has discretionary authority to buy or sell;

(b) purchasing and selling qualified investments, exercising rights incidental to the ownership of qualified investments such as voting, conversion and exchange, and entering into and executing agreements with respect to such purchasing and selling and the exercising of such rights;

(c) investment administration services, such as receiving, delivering and having custody of investments, calculating and reporting investment values, receiving subscription amounts from, and paying distributions and proceeds of disposition to, investors in and beneficiaries of the person or partnership, record keeping, accounting and reporting to the person or partnership and its investors and beneficiaries; and

(d) in the case of a corporation, trust or partnership the only undertaking of which is the investing of its funds in qualified investments, marketing investments in the corporation, trust or partnership to non-resident investors.

Notes: See Notes at end of 115.2.

Definition "designated investment services" amended by 2001 Budget, for 2002 and later taxation years.

"promoter" of a corporation, trust or partnership means a particular person or partnership that initiates or directs the founding, organization or substantial reorganization of the corporation, trust or partnership, and a person or partnership that is affiliated with the particular person or partnership.

Notes: Definition "promoter" amended by 2001 Budget, effective for 2002 and later taxation years, effectively to change references from "qualified non-resident" to "corporation, trust or partnership".

"qualified investment" of a person or partnership means

(a) a share of the capital stock of a corporation, or an interest in a partnership, trust, entity, fund or organization, other than a share or an interest

(i) that is either

(A) not listed on a designated stock exchange, or

(B) listed on a designated stock exchange, if the person or partnership, together with all persons with whom the person or partnership does not deal at arm's length, owns 25% or more of the issued shares of any class of the capital stock of the corporation or of the total value of interests in the partnership, entity, trust, fund or organization, as the case may be, and

(ii) of which more than 50% of the fair market value is derived from one or more of

(A) real or immovable property situated in Canada,

(B) Canadian resource property, and

(C) timber resource property;

(b) indebtedness;

(c) annuities;

(d) commodities or commodities futures purchased or sold, directly or indirectly in any manner whatever, on a commodities or commodities futures exchange;

(e) currency; and

(f) options, interests, rights and forward and futures agreements in respect of property described in any of paragraphs (a) to (e) or this paragraph, and agreements under which obligations are derived from interest rates, from the price of property described in any of those paragraphs, from payments made in respect of such a property by its issuer to holders of the property, or from an index reflecting a composite measure of such rates, prices or payments, whether or not the agreement creates any rights in or obligations regarding the referenced property itself.

Notes: When an investment ceases to be a QI, CRA allows the Canadian service provider 15 days to dispose of it before 115.2(2) applies: VIEWS doc 2007-0225911E5.

Para. (d): for the meaning of "indirectly" see Notes to 17.1(1). Exchanges selling electricity can be "commodities exchanges": VIEWS doc 2005-0118881E5.

Definition amended by 2002-2013 technical bill (effective June 26, 2013), 2007 budget bill #2, 2001 Budget.

"qualified non-resident" — [Repealed]

Notes: Definition "qualified non-resident" repealed by 2001 Budget, for 2002 and later tax years.

(2) Not carrying on business in Canada — For the purposes of subsections 115(1) and 150(1) and Part XIV, a non-resident person is not considered to be carrying on business in Canada at any particular time solely because of the provision to the person, or to a partnership of which the person is a member, at the particular time of designated investment services by a Canadian service provider if

(a) in the case of services provided to a non-resident individual other than a trust, the individual is not affiliated at the particular time with the Canadian service provider;

(b) in the case of services provided to a non-resident person that is a corporation or trust,

(i) the person has not, before the particular time, directly or through its agents,

(A) directed any promotion of investments in itself principally at Canadian investors, or

(B) sold an investment in itself that is outstanding at the particular time to a person who was a Canadian investor at the time of the sale and who is a Canadian investor at the particular time,

(ii) the person has not, before the particular time, directly or through its agents, filed any document with a public authority in Canada in accordance with the securities legislation of Canada or of any province in order to permit the distribution of interests in the person to persons resident in Canada, and

(iii) when the particular time is more than one year after the time at which the person was created, the total of the fair market value, at the particular time, of investments in the person that are beneficially owned by persons and partnerships (other than a designated entity in respect of the Canadian service provider) that are affiliated with the Canadian service provider does not exceed 25% of the fair market value, at the particular time, of all investments in the person; and

(c) in the case of services provided to a partnership of which the non-resident person is a member,

(i) the particular time is not more than one year after the partnership was formed,

(ii) where the non-resident person is, or is affiliated with, a person or partnership described in clause (A) or (B), the total of the fair market value of all investments in the partnership at the particular time is not less than four times the total of the fair market value of each investment in the partnership beneficially owned at the particular time by

(A) a person or partnership (other than a designated entity in respect of the Canadian service provider), more than 25% of the total of the fair market value, at the particular time, of investments in which are beneficially owned by persons and partnerships (other than a designated entity in respect of the Canadian service provider) that are affiliated with the Canadian service provider, or

(B) a person or partnership (other than a designated entity in respect of the Canadian service provider) that is affiliated with the Canadian service provider, or

(iii) at the particular time, the non-resident person is not affiliated with the Canadian service provider and is not affiliated with any person or partnership (other than the partnership to which the services are provided) described in clause (ii)(A) or (B).

Related Provisions: 115.2(3) — Interpretation.

Notes: See Notes at end of 115.2. 115.2(2) amended by 2002-2013 technical bill (for 2002 and later tax years, or after Oct. 2011 by election), 2001 Budget.

(3) Interpretation — For the purposes of this subsection and subparagraphs (2)(b)(iii) and (c)(ii),

(a) the fair market value of an investment in a corporation, trust or partnership shall be determined without regard to any voting rights attaching to that investment; and

(b) a person or partnership is, at a particular time, a designated entity in respect of a Canadian service provider if the total of the fair market value at the particular time, of investments in the entity that are beneficially owned by persons and partnerships (other than another designated entity in respect of the Canadian service provider) that are affiliated with the Canadian service provider does not exceed 25% of the fair market value, at the particular time, of all investments in the entity.

Notes: 115.2(3) opening words amended by 2002-2013 technical bill (Part 5 — technical) to add reference to 115.2(2)(c)(ii), for 2002 and later taxation years.

(4) Transfer pricing — For the purpose of section 247, where subsection (2) applies in respect of services provided to a person that is a corporation or trust or to a partnership, if the Canadian service provider referred to in that subsection does not deal at arm's length with the promoter of the person or of the partnership, the service provider is deemed not to deal at arm's length with the person or partnership.

Notes: 115.2(4) amended by 2001 Budget, for 2002 and later taxation years.

(5) [Repealed]

Notes: 115.2(5) added and repealed by 2002-2013 technical bill. In force from 2008 taxation year, it provided in effect that designated investment services did not cause a partnership interest to become taxable Canadian property before March 5, 2010.

Notes [s. 115.2]: 115.2 ensures that a non-resident investment or pension fund is not considered to be carrying on business in Canada (see 253) solely by engaging a Canadian firm to provide investment management and administration services, if certain conditions are met. See Yvette Morelli, "Section 115.2", 11(3) *Tax Law Update* (Ontario Bar Assn) 23-27 (May 2001); Judith Harris, "Section 115.2 — Safe Harbour for Off-Shore Funds", XI(1) *Business Vehicles* (Federated Press) 562-67 (2007). For CRA interpretation see VIEWS docs 2002-0157313, 2006-0172401R3, 2007-0224751R3, 2013-0513431E3, 2014-0550421C6 [2014 TEI q.E6], 2017-0699531R3.

115.2 added by 1999 Budget, for tax years ending after 1998.

Definitions [s. 115.2]: "affiliated" — 251.1; "amount", "annuity" — 248(1); "arm's length" — 251(1); "beneficially owned" — 248(3); "business" — 248(1); "Canada" — 255, *Interpretation Act* 35(1); "Canadian investor" — 115.2(1); "Canadian partnership" — 102(1), 248(1); "Canadian resource property" — 66(15), 248(1); "Canadian service provider" — 115.2(1); "corporation" — 248(1), *Interpretation Act* 35(1); "designated entity" — 115.2(3)(b); "designated investment services" — 115.2(1); "designated stock exchange" — 248(1), 262; "disposition" — 248(1); "fair market value" — 115.2(3)(a) and see 69(1) Notes; "immovable" — Quebec *Civil Code* art. 900–907; "individual", "non-resident" — 248(1); "partnership" — see 96(1) Notes; "person", "prescribed" — 248(1); "promoter" — 115.2(1); "property" — 248(1); "province" — *Interpretation Act* 35(1); "qualified investment", "qualified non-resident" — 115.2(1); "record" — 248(1); "resident in Canada" — 94(3)(a), 250; "share", "taxable Canadian property" — 248(1); "taxation year" — 249; "timber resource property" — 13(21), 248(1); "trust" — 104(1), 248(1), (3).

116. (1) Disposition by non-resident person of certain property — If a non-resident person proposes to dispose of any taxable Canadian property (other than property described in subsection (5.2) and excluded property) the non-resident person may, at any time before the disposition, send to the Minister a notice setting out

(a) the name and address of the person to whom he proposes to dispose of the property (in this section referred to as the "proposed purchaser");

(b) a description of the property sufficient to identify it;

(c) the estimated amount of the proceeds of disposition to be received by the non-resident person for the property; and

(d) the amount of the adjusted cost base to him [the non-resident person] of the property at the time of the sending of the notice.

Announced Administrative Change — COVID-19 — Email requests for section 116 certificates and comfort letters

CRA notice (tinyurl.com/cra-internat, April 27, 2021): See under 250(1)(a), sections "V. Disposition of taxable Canadian property by non-residents of Canada", and at end, "How to obtain international waivers and certificates of compliance during the COVID-19 crisis" and "CRA Fax Numbers for International Waivers or Non-Resident Disposition".

Proposed Amendment — Additional tax on vacant housing owned by non-residents

Federal Budget, Annex 7, April 19, 2021: See under 115(1)(b).

Related Provisions: 115.1 — Competent authority agreements under tax treaties; 116(2) — Certificate in respect of proposed disposition; 116(3) — Notice to Minister; 116(5) — Purchaser liable to withhold if no certificate obtained; 116(5.1) — Gift or non-arm's length transfer; 116(6) — Excluded property; 244.2(1) — Bank etc. required to report international electronic funds transfers of $10,000 or more.

Notes: 116 protects the Canadian government's ability to collect tax on capital gains on real estate in Canada, as it has no direct jurisdiction over the non-resident (**NR**) vendor (see Notes to 223(3) re collection of tax from NRs). Since 2010, 116 no longer applies to private corporation shares or to partnership or trust units unless (anytime within the past 60 months) most of their value is attributable to real property in Canada or certain other Canadian property: see 248(1)"taxable Canadian property". See also 116(6) for "excluded property".

To apply (Form T2062), the NR needs a tax number: Social Insurance Number (former Cdn resident), Temporary Tax Number, or Individual Tax Number (requested on Form T1261). Send the application to the CRA "Section 116 Centre of Expertise" based on the real property location, corporate head office (for shares) or trustee's location (for an interest in a trust or estate). Montreal TSO for Quebec; International TSO for Ontario; Edmonton TSO for prairie provinces; Vancouver TSO for BC. A bank acting on power of sale could not obtain a Court order to file the certificate on behalf of the NR: *Bank of Montreal v. Nielsen*, 2017 BCSC 891.

116(1) is optional in that a NR is not technically required to apply for a certificate in respect of a proposed disposition. However, if no certificate is obtained under 116(2) or (4), the purchaser is liable under 116(5) for 25% of the purchase price (50% for depreciable property and real property inventory: 116(5.3)), and should withhold that amount on closing. The amount must be remitted: there is no prescribed form; for what goes in the remittance letter see 2016 Alberta CPA (tinyurl.com/cra-abtax), q.14. If too much is withheld, the NR can claim a refund provided it files a return reporting the disposition within 3 years of year-end (164(1)): VIEWS doc 2015-0596851E5. See also CRA web page tinyurl.com/s116-cra.

There is no limitation period for 116(5) liability to be assessed: see 227(10.1). As well, 227(9.3) imposes interest and 227(9) imposes penalty on the unremitted amount.

S. 116 applies to a sale of a purchaser's right under an Agreement of Purchase and Sale (e.g. a right to buy a condominium under construction), since 248(1)"taxable Canadian property"(f) includes an interest in real property in Canada: VIEWS doc 2015-0608211E5. The right might be "treaty-protected property" requiring notice to CRA but no certificate (see 116(5.01), (5.02)), depending on whether the relevant tax treaty treats an NR's interest in real property as real property that Canada can tax. Under Canada-US treaty Art. XIII:3(b)(i) and VI:2, it appears to be real property, as an "option or similar right"; a CRA answer to the author's 2014 query on this point will be in doc 2014-0547171E5, which CRA confirmed in July 2020 is still(!) to be issued. 116 does not apply to a forfeited deposit on cancellation of a sale: 2013-0479861I7.

116(1) applies to a gift, and to a transfer to a related person for less than market value: see 116(5.1). "Cost" in 116(5)(c) means the price the taxpayer gave up to get the asset: *Coast Capital*, 2016 FCA 181, para. 31.

116(5) can apply on marriage breakdown, if (say) H becomes non-resident and then transfers his interest in the family home to W. It may not always be certain what W's "cost" is for 116(5)(c), but W likely must pay CRA 25% of the value transferred to her, even though H will benefit from the 40(2)(b) principal-residence exemption for the years H was in Canada, and can thus recover most of the tax from CRA. 116(5) closing words *might* allow W to "recover" the 25% from H since the tax is ultimately not payable, but this may be difficult if H is outside Canada. See Kakkar & Dubois, "Timing is Everything", 9(2) *Tax for the Owner-Manager* (ctf.ca) 6 (April 2009).

Following the disposition, the NR must notify CRA, or a penalty applies: 116(3), 162(7). VIEWS doc 2013-049812117 suggests the penalty can be waived if there was no gain on the property (and notes that a former foreign diplomat is not exempt from the penalty). In *Suissa*, 2013 FC 897, disposition of 4 properties by 6 related co-owners led to penalties under 162(7) of $60,000 ($2,500 each property per person), and the Court upheld CRA's refusal to waive the penalties.

A notice mechanism applies to treaty-protected property since 2009, per 116(5.01)–(5.02), but the 2010 amendments to 248(1)"taxable Canadian property" effectively prevent s. 116 from applying in most such cases. The NR must normally file a Canadian tax return to report the gain: VIEWS doc 2019-0798861C6 [2019 IFA q.6].

116(5)(a) provides a "due diligence" defence if the purchaser did not know the vendor was NR, but not if the purchaser did not know the property was TCP (e.g., whether the value of shares was "derived" from real property any time in the past 60 months). CRA says obtaining a statutory declaration (of not being NR) from an arm's length vendor "would generally qualify as reasonable inquiry", absent facts suggesting the purchaser should make more inquiry, such as a foreign mailing address: VIEWS doc 2017-0703351E5. CRA will not issue a certificate to confirm property is not TCP, but will issue a certificate on request as if the property were TCP: 2010-0387141C6 [2010 CTF conf report p.4:16, q.16]. In *McKean v. Wang*, 2020 ONSC 7901, paras. 76-80, a dispute over a failed closing, one issue was whether the seller could provide a statutory declaration signed by Power of Attorney (not personally), or the buyer could refuse to close; the Court declined to decide the issue. (One would think a buyer unsatisfied that the seller is resident should tender 75% of the purchase price and pay 25% to CRA. Since the 25% stands to the seller's credit with CRA, the seller loses nothing and must accept the 75%: see *RJM56 v. Kurnik* in 227(1) Notes, and 227(13).) In *Kau*, 2018 TCC 156 (FCA appeal discontinued A-290-18), it was not "reasonable inquiry" to accept a one-line unsworn affidavit ("declared" before a California notary public) from vendor V saying he was not NR, when the purchaser's lawyer knew V's address was in

California and V signed the closing documents there, as these were "red flags" requiring more inquiry.

In *Scotia Mortgage v. Gladu*, 2017 BCSC 1182, a mortgagee who sold on foreclosure sought a declaration that the purchaser bought from the mortgagee, not the (NR) owner, so that 116(1) would not apply. The BCSC declined to rule, since the Tax Court would have jurisdiction over the assessment to be issued.

In *Mao v. Liu*, 2017 BCSC 226, a notary who handled a purchase was liable to the purchaser for not having 25% withheld and sent to CRA. The sale was by Court order under power of sale but since the registered owner was NR, CRA assessed the purchaser for not withholding. (The notary's claim against the vendor's lawyers was ongoing: *Liu v. Borden Ladner*, 2020 BCCA 50.)

In *Cindric v. Mesic*, 2020 ONSC 7021, a litigation settlement involving buying a property from a non-resident was satisfied by withholding and remitting 25% to CRA; the buyer had no further tax liability and thus should have finalized the settlement.

CRA "pre-audits" s. 116 applications, looking at such issues as ACB, PUC of shares and s. 85 issues before issuing a certificate.

Part XIII tax: When a s. 116 certificate is requested, CRA practice is to ask for information about past rental of the property, and to request any unpaid withholding tax on rent (212(1)(d)). Legally, once tax on the gain is paid, CRA may be required by 116(2) or (4) to issue the certificate even if Part XIII tax is owing. However, in *Morris (RCI Trust)*, 2009 FCA 373 (leave to appeal denied 2010 CarswellNat 1311 (SCC)), the FC had ordered CRA to issue a certificate to a Barbados trust selling property, despite CRA concerns about Canadian tax avoidance on the transactions that put the property into the trust; but the FCA ruled the FC had no jurisdiction to address the issue, and the trust should file a Part I return and appeal the resulting assessment to the Tax Court.

Trust/estate distribution: 116 may apply where a Canadian resident trust or estate distributes property to beneficiary B in satisfaction of B's capital interest. (Note that 116(3)(a) defines "purchaser" as anyone to whom a NR disposes of taxable Canadian property.) See VIEWS docs 2001-0093155, 2002-0131015, 2003-0000695, 2004-0062121E5, 2005-0149961E5, 2006-0181711E5, 2006-0184741E5, 2006-0185641C6, 2012-0465081I7; 2015-0578541C6 [2015 STEP q.10] (estate distribution to trust); Frankovic, "Application of Section 116 to Distributions by Canadian Resident Trusts", 1779 *Tax Topics* (CCH) 1-3 (April 13, 2006). Even monthly distributions are caught, but only one Form T2062 is required each year if a payment schedule is provided with it: CRA May 2005 ICAA roundtable (tinyurl.com/cra-abtax), q. 12. However, note the "treaty-protected property" rules in 116(5.01)–(5.02), and amendments to 248(1)"taxable Canadian property" in 2010 so that it applies to a trust only if its value is primarily Canadian real property; and see Uzan, "Section 116 Loophole?", 10(4) *Tax for the Owner-Manager* (ctf.ca) 8-9 (Oct. 2010); Klyguine, Breaks & Odina, "No Need for Section 116 Clearance Certificate for Capital Distributions from an Estate to a US Beneficiary", tinyurl.com/BLG-s116. In *Lipson*, 2012 TCC 20, 116(3) was held not to apply to a distribution by an estate (a Quebec succession) because an estate is not the same as a trust, but that case was overruled by a 2013 amendment to 248(1)"trust". 116 can apply to a transfer of real property by an estate with US executors to Canadian beneficiaries: 2012-0448681E5. A NR trust with NR beneficiaries might also be subject to s. 116: 2017-0717981E5.

Bare trustee: On disposition by a NR with only legal title where a Canadian resident has beneficial interest (see Notes to 54"capital property"), 116 should not apply. The purchaser may insist on a certificate, but with no beneficial ownership the NR cannot obtain one! CRA may be willing to issue a letter confirming no certificate is needed.

In *1074022 B.C. v. Li*, 2020 BCSC 65, non-resident L did not pay his mortgage and 25% was withheld from a court-ordered sale. The Court ordered CRA to refund the balance (in excess of L's tax liability on the sale) to L's lawyer in trust, as per L's direction, so it could be paid to the mortgagees.

See also Tunney, "Section 116 Update", 10(4) *Canadian Tax Highlights [CTH]* (ctf.ca) 28 (April 2002) (s. 116 applying to s. 51 rollover and to options; comfort letter for CRA delay; amending certificate to reflect price adjustment; accounts receivable and prepaid expenses as TCP); Lang, "Section 116 Certificates", XIV(4) *Corporate Finance* (Federated Press) 1555-60 (2008); Arkin, "Section 116 Certificates", 2010 Atlantic Provinces Tax Conf. (ctf.ca), 1C:1-19; Falk & Morand, "Section 116 Clearance Certificates", 2010 BC Tax Conf. (ctf.ca), 12:1-41; Rudick, "No Section 116 Safe Harbour", 2044 *Tax Topics [TT]* (CCH) 1-3 (May 12, 2011); Suarez & Gosselin, "Canada's Section 116 System", 66(2) *Tax Notes International [TNI]* (taxnotes.com) 175-96 (April 9, 2012); Parks, "Canadian Real Estate and Taxable Canadian Property", XVIII(3) *International Tax Planning [ITP]* (Federated Press) 1250-53 (2013); Bernstein, "Update on Nonresident Investment in Canadian Real Estate", 81(6) *TNI* 529-32 (Feb. 8, 2016) (shorter version at "Non-Resident Invests in Canadian Realty", 23(8) *CTH* 9-10 (Aug. 2015)); Zittlau, "Corporate Reorganizations Involving Taxable Canadian Property", XX(3) *ITP* 6-9 (2016); Choudhury, "Section 116: Tips and Traps", 2350 *TT* 1-4 (March 23, 2017); Smith & Wen, "The Taxation of Taxable Canadian Properties", 2019 Ont. Tax Conf. 11 (55pp).

If a self-directed RRSP acquires TCP from an NR, the RRSP trustee (not the plan or annuitant) is liable for the s. 116 withholding: *Olympia Trust*, 2015 FCA 279. An appeal on this issue, *Coast Capital* (see 2016 FCA 181), was withdrawn Sept. 14/17: TCC file 2013-1860(IT)G.

A NR individual who does not have a Social Insurance Number can apply on Form T1261 for an Individual Tax Number (see Notes to 237(1)). However, CRA waives the T1261 requirement if the disposition is a distribution of personal-use property by a personal trust: VIEWS doc 2008-0275871C6.

Where an Ontario corporation acquires real property in Ontario, see Notes to 248(4).

Where a partnership disposes of TCP, each partner is required to notify CRA, but CRA accepts a notification filed on behalf of all partners: VIEWS docs 2012-0444081C6, 2020-0862451C6 [2020 CTF q.4] (purchaser liability only for portion of TCP attributed to non-resident partners).

Property in Quebec: A parallel certificate is required from Revenu Québec, failing which the purchaser can be liable for an additional 12.875% of the purchase price (30% for depreciable property or real property inventory): *Taxation Act* ss. 1101, 1102.2; RQ Interpretation Bulletin IMP. 1097-1/R1. The federal withholding is not reduced for Quebec property: VIEWS doc 2005-0141101C6.

Death: No s. 116 certificate is required for a transfer: Information Circular 72-17R6 paras. 67-68; but this applies only to the transfer from deceased to estate, not from the estate to beneficiaries: VIEWS docs 2002-0117975, 2006-0181711E5.

See also docs 2006-0201651I7 (interaction of 116(3) and (5) with 44(2) where NR's property is expropriated); 2007-0244291E5 (sale by estate of Canadian resident, where 1 of 2 executors is US resident); 2008-0301701E5 (corporation's liability on redemption of shares if no certificate obtained); 2010-0387151E5 (withholding under *both* 212(2) and 116(5) on redemption of shares); 2011-0391741I7 and 2011-0429021E5 (116 does not apply to disposition of shares under 87(4)); 2011-0399501E5 (distribution by NR trust to beneficiary); 2012-0457741E5 and Cdn Tax Foundation 2017 conference roundtable q.14 (amalgamation of foreign corps); 2012-0465221E5 (CRA will not rule on whether property is TCP when issuing certificate); 2012-0470331E5 (no s. 116 certificate required for land held in inventory if CRA provides a "qualified business exemption" under IC 72-17R6 para. 36); 2015-0602781E5 (gift of family farm to child under 73(4.1)); 2017-0724241C6 [2017 CTF q.14], 2017-0734841C6 [2017 TEI q.E3] (interaction with 87(8.4) election).

An NR who exercises warrants to acquire shares of a private Canadian corp has a disposition to which 116 applies, but the issuer of the warrant is apparently not a "purchaser" under 116(5) so there is no withholding obligation: VIEWS doc 2005-0111741E5.

Note that even the sale of shares in NR corporations and interests in NR trusts and partnerships may require a s. 116 certificate. See 248(1)"taxable Canadian property"(e), (g) and (k).

A US resident selling Canadian capital property owned since before 1981 may be able to prorate the capital gain using Canada-US tax treaty Art. XIII:9.

116(1) amended by 2001 technical bill (effective Oct. 2, 1996), 1995-97 technical bill.

Income Tax Folios: S4-F5-C1: Share for share exchange [replaces IT-450R].

Interpretation Bulletins: See Interpretation Bulletins and Information Circulars at end of s. 116.

I.T. Technical News: 38 (anti-discrimination provisions).

CRA Audit Manual: 12.13.0: Disposals of taxable Canadian property; 15.2.12: Disposition of taxable Canadian property by a non-resident; 15.10.10: Section 116 audit guide and reference manual; 16.2.2: Estate of a deceased person — non-residents.

Forms: T1261: Application for a Canada Revenue Agency individual tax number (ITN) for non-residents; T2062: Request by a non-resident of Canada for a certificate of compliance related to the disposition of taxable Canadian property; T2062A: Request by a non-resident of Canada for a certificate of compliance related to the disposition of Canadian resource or timber resource property, Canadian real property (other than capital property), or depreciable taxable Canadian property; T2062A Sched. 1: Disposition of Canadian resource property by non-residents.

(2) Certificate in respect of proposed disposition — Where a non-resident person who has sent to the Minister a notice under subsection (1) in respect of a proposed disposition of any property has

(a) paid to the Receiver General, as or on account of tax under this Part payable by the non-resident person for the year, 25% of the amount, if any, by which the estimated amount set out in the notice in accordance with paragraph (1)(c) exceeds the amount set out in the notice in accordance with paragraph (1)(d), or

(b) furnished the Minister with security acceptable to the Minister in respect of the proposed disposition of the property,

the Minister shall forthwith issue to the non-resident person and the proposed purchaser a certificate in prescribed form in respect of the proposed disposition, fixing therein an amount (in this section referred to as the "certificate limit") equal to the estimated amount set out in the notice in accordance with paragraph (1)(c).

Related Provisions: 116(5) — Non-residents — Liability of purchaser; 164(1.7) — Security not to be released while appeal pending.

Notes: See Notes to 116(1). 116(2) amended by 2000 Budget to change "33⅓%" to "25%", effective for taxation years that end after Oct. 17, 2000; for a taxation year that ended from Feb. 28, 2000 through Oct. 17, 2000, read as "30%".

Interpretation Bulletins: See Interpretation Bulletins and Information Circulars at end of s. 116.

(3) Notice to Minister — Every non-resident person who in a taxation year disposes of any taxable Canadian property of that person (other than property described in subsection (5.2) and excluded property) shall, not later than 10 days after the disposition, send to the Minister, by registered mail, a notice setting out

(a) the name and address of the person to whom the non-resident person disposed of the property (in this section referred to as the **"purchaser"**),

(b) a description of the property sufficient to identify it, and

(c) a statement of the proceeds of disposition of the property and the amount of its adjusted cost base to the non-resident person immediately before the disposition,

unless the non-resident person has, at any time before the disposition, sent to the Minister a notice under subsection (1) in respect of any proposed disposition of that property and

(d) the purchaser was the proposed purchaser referred to in that notice,

(e) the estimated amount set out in that notice in accordance with paragraph (1)(c) is equal to or greater than the proceeds of disposition of the property, and

(f) the amount set out in that notice in accordance with paragraph (1)(d) does not exceed the adjusted cost base to the non-resident person of the property immediately before the disposition.

Related Provisions: 116(5.1) — Gift or non-arm's length transfer; 116(6) — Excluded property; 162(7) — Penalty for failure to send notice; 238(1) — Offences; 248(7) — Mail deemed received on day mailed.

Notes: See Notes to 116(1).

Opening words of 116(3) amended by 1995-97 technical bill, effective April 27, 1995.

Interpretation Bulletins: See Interpretation Bulletins and Information Circulars at end of s. 116.

Forms: T1261: Application for a Canada Revenue Agency individual tax number (ITN) for non-residents; T2062: Request by a non-resident of Canada for a certificate of compliance related to the disposition of taxable Canadian property; T2062A: Request by a non-resident of Canada for a certificate of compliance related to the disposition of Canadian resource or timber resource property, Canadian real property (other than capital property), or depreciable taxable Canadian property; T2062A Sched. 1: Disposition of Canadian resource property by non-residents.

(4) Certificate in respect of property disposed of — Where a non-resident person who has sent to the Minister a notice under subsection (3) in respect of a disposition of any property has

(a) paid to the Receiver General, as or on account of tax under this Part payable by the non-resident person for the year, 25% of the amount, if any, by which the proceeds of disposition of the property exceed the adjusted cost base to the non-resident person of the property immediately before the disposition, or

(b) furnished the Minister with security acceptable to the Minister in respect of the disposition of the property,

the Minister shall forthwith issue to the non-resident person and the purchaser a certificate in prescribed form in respect of the disposition.

Related Provisions: 116(5) — Non-residents — liability of purchaser; 116(5.1) — Gift or non-arm's length transfer; 164(1.7) — Security not to be released while appeal pending.

Notes: See Notes to 116(1).

116(4) amended by 2000 Budget to change "33⅓%" to "25%", effective for taxation years that end after October 17, 2000; for a taxation year that ended from February 28, 2000 through October 17, 2000, read as "30%".

Interpretation Bulletins: See Interpretation Bulletins and Information Circulars at end of s. 116.

(5) Liability of purchaser — Where in a taxation year a purchaser has acquired from a non-resident person any taxable Canadian property (other than depreciable property or excluded property) of the non-resident person, the purchaser, unless

(a) after reasonable inquiry the purchaser had no reason to believe that the non-resident person was not resident in Canada,

(a.1) subsection (5.01) applies to the acquisition, or

(b) a certificate under subsection (4) has been issued to the purchaser by the Minister in respect of the property,

is liable to pay, and shall remit to the Receiver General within 30 days after the end of the month in which the purchaser acquired the property, as tax under this Part for the year on behalf of the non-resident person, 25% of the amount, if any, by which

(c) the cost to the purchaser of the property so acquired

exceeds

(d) the certificate limit fixed by the certificate, if any, issued under subsection (2) in respect of the disposition of the property by the non-resident person to the purchaser,

and is entitled to deduct or withhold from any amount paid or credited by the purchaser to the non-resident person or otherwise recover from the non-resident person any amount paid by the purchaser as such a tax.

> **Announced Administrative Change — 116(5) — COVID-19**
>
> **CRA notice (tinyurl.com/cra-internat, April 27, 2021)**: See under 250(1)(a), sections "V. Disposition of taxable Canadian property by non-residents of Canada", and at end, "How to obtain international waivers and certificates of compliance during the COVID-19 crisis" and "CRA Fax Numbers for International Waivers or Non-Resident Disposition".
>
> **CRA notice (tinyurl.com/cra-internat)**: See under 116(1).

Related Provisions: 116(2) — Certificate in respect of proposed disposition; 116(4) — Certificate in respect of property disposed of; 116(5.1) — Gift or non-arm's length transfer; 116(6) — Excluded property; 164(1.5)(c)(ii) — Late refund of amount overpaid due to assessment under 116(5); 227(9) — Failure to remit tax — penalty; 227(9.3) — Interest on tax not paid; 227(10.1) — Assessment; 248(7) — Mail deemed received on day mailed; *Interpretation Act* 27(5) — Meaning of "within 30 days".

Notes: See Notes to 116(1).

116(5) amended by 2008 budget bill #1 (for dispositions after 2008), 2000 and 1989 Budgets.

Interpretation Bulletins: See Interpretation Bulletins and Information Circulars at end of s. 116.

Registered Plans Compliance Bulletins: 4 (abusive schemes — RRSP stripping).

CRA Audit Manual: 12.13.0: Disposals of taxable Canadian property; 15.2.12: Disposition of taxable Canadian property by a non-resident; 15.10.10: Section 116 audit guide and reference manual.

(5.01) Treaty-protected property — This subsection applies to the acquisition of a property by a person (referred to in this subsection as the "purchaser") from a non-resident person if

(a) the purchaser concludes after reasonable inquiry that the non-resident person is, under a tax treaty that Canada has with a particular country, resident in the particular country;

(b) the property would be treaty-protected property of the non-resident person if the non-resident person were, under the tax treaty referred to in paragraph (a), resident in the particular country; and

(c) the purchaser provides notice under subsection (5.02) in respect of the acquisition.

Related Provisions: 116(5)(a.1), (5.3)(a), (6)(i) — No certificate required.

Notes: 116(5.01) provides relief (via 116(5)(a.1), (5.3)(a) and (6)(i)) from the certificate requirements (see Notes to 116(1)) for gains that are not taxed due to a treaty, such as on a non-resident's sale of private corporation shares, or receipt of capital distributions from a trust. For discussion see Newcombe & Lecocq, "Changes to Section 116 for Dispositions of Treaty-Protected Property", 5(8) *Tax Hyperion* (Carswell, Aug. 2008); Bernstein, "New Section 116 Certificates", 17(2) *Cdn Tax Highlights* (ctf.ca) 4-5 (Feb. 2009); Bernstein & Worndl, "Is It Necessary To Comply with Section 116 of the *Income Tax Act* if the Property is Treaty-Exempt Property?", 177 *The Estate Planner* (CCH) 2-4 (Oct. 2009); Bernstein & Choudhury, "Section 116 Notice", 19(3) *CTH* 2-3 (March 2011); Falk & Morand, "Section 116 Clearance Certificates: Relief for Treaty-Exempt and Treaty-Protected Property", *International Tax Newsletter* (Taxnet Pro Corporate Tax Centre), May 2011.

In *Landbouwbedrijf Backx*, 2018 TCC 142 (sent back for new decision on other grounds 2019 FCA 310; later decision 2021 TCC 2 (under appeal to FCA)), a farm was not treaty-protected property because the corp that owned it was held to be resident in Canada (under "central management and control").

For CRA interpretation see VIEWS docs 2008-0278801C6 q.7 (general discussion); 2008-0289051E5 (notice under 116(5.02) need not be filed for treaty-protected property); 2009-031737117 (sale by partnership: "non-resident person" means each partner individually, so purchaser can provide T2062C for treaty country partners only and must withhold for other partners; sale by LLC: "non-resident person" means the LLC); 2009-0347711C6 (116(5.02) notice can be filed using an estimate); 2011-0429961R3 (shares exempt under Canada-UK treaty).

"Country" in para. (a) includes Hong Kong and Taiwan: see Notes to 219.2.

Before 2009, CRA could not be forced to issue a certificate on the sale of treaty-protected property: *Morris (RCI Trust)*, 2009 FCA 373; leave to appeal denied 2010 CarswellNat 1311 (SCC).

116(5.01) added by 2008 budget bill #1, effective for dispositions of property that occur after 2008.

Forms: T2062C: Notification of an acquisition of treaty-protected property from a non-resident vendor.

(5.02) Notice by purchaser in respect of an acquisition of property — A person (referred to in this subsection as the "purchaser") who acquires property from a non-resident person provides notice under this subsection in respect of the acquisition if the purchaser sends to the Minister, on or before the day that is 30 days after the date of the acquisition, a notice setting out

(a) the date of the acquisition;

(b) the name and address of the non-resident person;

(c) a description of the property sufficient to identify it;

(d) the amount paid or payable, as the case may be, by the purchaser for the property; and

(e) the name of the country with which Canada has concluded a tax treaty under which the property is a treaty-protected property for the purposes of subsection (5.01) or (6.1), as the case may be.

Related Provisions: 116(6.1) — Property subject to notice is treaty-exempt property.

Notes: See Notes to 116(5.01). 116(5.02) added by 2008 budget bill #1, effective for dispositions of property that occur after 2008.

(5.1) Gifts, etc. — If a non-resident person has disposed of or proposes to dispose of a life insurance policy in Canada, a Canadian resource property or a taxable Canadian property other than

(a) excluded property, or

(b) property that has been transferred or distributed on or after the non-resident person's death and as a consequence thereof

to any person by way of gift *inter vivos* or to a person with whom the non-resident person was not dealing at arm's length for no proceeds of disposition or for proceeds of disposition less than the fair market value of the property at the time the non-resident person so disposed of it or proposes to dispose of it, as the case may be, the following rules apply:

(c) the reference in paragraph (1)(c) to "the proceeds of disposition to be received by the non-resident person for the property" shall be read as a reference to "the fair market value of the property at the time the non-resident person proposes to dispose of it",

(d) the references in subsections (3) and (4) to "the proceeds of disposition of the property" shall be read as references to "the fair market value of the property immediately before the disposition",

(e) the references in subsection (5) to "the cost to the purchaser of the property so acquired" shall be read as references to "the fair market value of the property at the time it was so acquired", and

(f) the reference in subsection (5.3) to "the amount payable by the taxpayer for the property so acquired" shall be read as a reference to "the fair market value of the property at the time it was so acquired".

Related Provisions: 116(6) — Excluded property.

Notes: It is uncertain whether "*inter vivos*" (literally, "between living persons") refers only to individuals: VIEWS doc 2013-0484321E5.

Opening words of 116(5.1) amended by 2001 technical bill to change "property that would, if the non-resident person disposed of it, be taxable Canadian property of the non-resident person" to simply "taxable Canadian property", effective October 2, 1996. (The definition of TCP no longer requires it to be disposed of.)

Interpretation Bulletins: IT-150R2: Taxable Canadian property — acquisition from a non-resident of certain property on death or mortgage foreclosure or by virtue of a deemed disposition (cancelled). See also Interpretation Bulletins and Information Circulars at end of s. 116.

Forms: T2062B: Notice of disposition of life insurance policy in Canada by a non-resident; T2062B Sched. 1: Certification and remittance notice.

(5.2) Certificates for dispositions — If a non-resident person has, in respect of a disposition, or a proposed disposition, in a taxation year to a taxpayer of property (other than excluded property) that is a life insurance policy in Canada, a Canadian resource property, a property (other than capital property) that is real property, or an immovable, situated in Canada, a timber resource property, depreciable property that is a taxable Canadian property or any interest in, or for civil law any right in, or any option in respect of, a property to which this subsection applies (whether or not that property exists),

(a) paid to the Receiver General, as or on account of tax under this Part payable by the non-resident person for the year, such amount as is acceptable to the Minister in respect of the disposition or proposed disposition of the property, or

(b) furnished the Minister with security acceptable to the Minister in respect of the disposition or proposed disposition of the property,

the Minister shall forthwith issue to the non-resident person and to the taxpayer a certificate in prescribed form in respect of the disposition or proposed disposition fixing therein an amount equal to the proceeds of disposition, proposed proceeds of disposition or such other amount as is reasonable in the circumstances.

Related Provisions: 116(5.1), (5.3) — Liability of purchaser; 164(1.7) — Security not to be released while appeal pending; 248(4) — Interest in real property.

Notes: The amount "acceptable to the Minister" in 116(5.2)(a) is the applicable tax rate on the recapture: Information Circular 72-17R6 para. 43(a)(ii).

116(5.2) opening words amended by 2016 budget bill #2, effective 2017, to delete "eligible capital property that is taxable Canadian property or" before "any interest" (as part of changing the ECP rules to CCA Class 14.1: see 20(1)(b) Notes). 116(5.2) earlier amended by 2002-2013 technical bill (effective Dec. 24, 1998), 2001 technical bill, 1995-97 technical bill, 1990 Budget.

Interpretation Bulletins: See Interpretation Bulletins and Information Circulars at end of s. 116.

(5.3) Liability of purchaser in certain cases — Where in a taxation year a taxpayer has acquired from a non-resident person property referred to in subsection (5.2),

(a) the taxpayer, unless subsection (5.01) applies to the acquisition or unless after reasonable inquiry the taxpayer had no reason to believe that the non-resident person was not resident in Canada, is liable to pay, as tax under this Part for the year on behalf of the non-resident person, 50% of the amount, if any, by which

(i) the amount payable by the taxpayer for the property so acquired

exceeds

(ii) the amount fixed in the certificate, if any, issued under subsection (5.2) in respect of the disposition of the property by the non-resident person to the taxpayer

and is entitled to deduct or withhold from any amount paid or credited by the taxpayer to the non-resident person or to otherwise recover from the non-resident person any amount paid by the taxpayer as such a tax; and

(b) the taxpayer shall, within 30 days after the end of the month in which the taxpayer acquired the property, remit to the Receiver General the tax for which the taxpayer is liable under paragraph (a).

Related Provisions: 116(5.1) — Gift or non-arm's length transfer; 164(1.5)(c)(ii) — Late refund of amount overpaid due to assessment under 116(5.3); 227(9) — Failure to remit tax — penalty; 227(9.3) — Interest on tax not paid; 227(10.1) — Assessment; 248(7) — Mail deemed received on day mailed; *Interpretation Act* 27(5) — Meaning of "within 30 days".

Notes: Withholding for a life insurance policy is based on FMV, not cash surrender value: VIEWS doc 2013-0481411C6.

Para. (a) amended by 2008 budget bill #1 to add "unless subsection (5.01) applies to the acquisition", effective for dispositions of property that occur after 2008.

Interpretation Bulletins: See Interpretation Bulletins and Information Circulars at end of s. 116.

(5.4) Presumption — Where there has been a disposition by a non-resident of a life insurance policy in Canada by virtue of subsection 148(2) or any of paragraphs (a) to (c) and (e) of the definition "disposition" in subsection 148(9), the insurer under the policy shall, for the purposes of subsections (5.2) and (5.3) be deemed to be the taxpayer who acquired the property for an amount equal to the proceeds of disposition as determined under section 148.

Interpretation Bulletins: See Interpretation Bulletins and Information Circulars at end of s. 116.

(6) Definition of "excluded property" — For the purposes of this section, "excluded property" of a non-resident person means

(a) a property that is a taxable Canadian property solely because a provision of this Act deems it to be a taxable Canadian property;

(a.1) a property (other than real or immovable property situated in Canada, a Canadian resource property or a timber resource property) that is described in an inventory of a business carried on in Canada by the person;

(b) a security that is

  (i) listed on a recognized stock exchange, and

  (ii) either

    (A) a share of the capital stock of a corporation, or

    (B) SIFT wind-up entity equity;

(c) a unit of a mutual fund trust;

(d) a bond, debenture, bill, note, mortgage, hypothecary claim or similar obligation;

(e) property of a non-resident insurer that

  (i) is licensed or otherwise authorized under the laws of Canada or a province to carry on an insurance business in Canada; and

  (ii) carries on an insurance business, within the meaning of subsection 138(1) of the Act, in Canada;

(f) property of an authorized foreign bank that carries on a Canadian banking business;

(g) an option in respect of property referred to in any of paragraphs (a) to (f) whether or not such property is in existence;

(h) an interest, or for civil law a right, in property referred to in any of paragraphs (a) to (g); and

(i) a property that is, at the time of its disposition, a treaty-exempt property of the person.

Related Provisions: 40(3)(d) — Deemed disposition (and gain) when ACB of property goes negative; 40(3.1)(b) — Deemed disposition of partnership interest when its ACB goes negative; 55(6) — Reorganization share deemed listed on designated stock exchange for purposes of 116(6); 87(10) — New share issued on amalgamation of public corp deemed listed; 132.2(3)(g)(ii) — Effect of mutual fund reorganization; 150(5) — Disposition of excluded property may be "excluded disposition" not requiring tax return.

Notes: See Notes to 116(5.01).

The term "bond, debenture, bill, note, ..." in para. (d) may not include bankers' acceptances: *Federated Co-operatives*, 2001 FCA 217; leave to appeal denied 2001 CarswellNat 1788 (SCC).

See VIEWS docs 2010-0366651R3 (spinoff butterfly: para. (b)); 2012-0431891R3 (mortgage pool: para. (d)).

116(6) amended by 2002-2013 technical bill (Part 4 — bijuralism), effective June 26, 2013, to add "or immovable" (para. (a.1)) and "or for civil law a right" (para. (h)).

116(6)(f) changed from "property of an authorized foreign bank that is used or held in the course of the bank's Canadian banking business" by 2002-2013 technical bill, effective June 28, 1999. 116(6) earlier amended by 2008 budget bills #1 and #2, 2007 budget bill #2, 2001 *Civil Code* harmonization bill, 2001 and 1995-97 technical bills.

Income Tax Folios: S4-F5-C1: Share for share exchange [replaces IT-450R].

(6.1) Treaty-exempt property — For the purpose of subsection (6), a property is a treaty-exempt property of a non-resident person, at the time of the non-resident person's disposition of the property to another person (referred to in this subsection as the "purchaser"), if

(a) it is, at that time, a treaty-protected property of the non-resident person; and

(b) where the purchaser and the non-resident person are related at that time, the purchaser provides notice under subsection (5.02) in respect of the disposition.

Related Provisions: 40(3)(d) — Deemed disposition (and gain) when ACB of property goes negative; 40(3.1)(b) — Deemed disposition of partnership interest when its ACB goes negative.

Notes: Note the distinction between treaty-protected property (defined in 248(1)) and treaty-exempt property (defined here), which requires notice under 116(5.02).

See Notes to 116(5.01). 116(6.1) added by 2008 budget bill #1, effective for dispositions of property that occur after 2008.

(7) Application of subsec. 138(12) — The definitions in subsection 138(12) apply to this section.

Notes: 116(7) added in the RSC 1985 (5th Supp) consolidation, for tax years ending after Nov. 1991. This rule was formerly in the opening words of 138(12).

Definitions [s. 116]: "adjusted cost base" — 54, 248(1); "amount" — 248(1); "arm's length" — 251(1); "authorized foreign bank", "bank", "business" — 248(1); "Canada" — 255, *Interpretation Act* 35(1); "Canadian banking business" — 248(1); "Canadian resource property" — 66(15), 248(1); "capital property" — 54, 248(1); "certificate limit" — 116(2); "class of shares" — 248(6); "consequence" — 248(8); "corporation" — 248(1), *Interpretation Act* 35(1); "depreciable property" — 13(21), 248(1); "disposition" — 248(1); "eligible capital property" — 54, 248(1); "excluded property" — 116(6); "fair market value" — see 69(1) Notes; "immovable" — Quebec *Civil Code* art. 900–907; "insurer" — 248(1); "interest" in real property — 248(4); "inventory" — 248(1); "life insurance policy in Canada" — 138(12), 248(1); "listed" — 87(10); "Minister" — 248(1); "month" — *Interpretation Act* 35(1); "mutual fund trust" — 132(6)–(7), 132.2(3)(n), 248(1); "non-resident", "person", "prescribed" — 248(1); "property" — 248(1); "proposed purchaser" — 116(1)(a); "province" — *Interpretation Act* 35(1); "public corporation" — 89(1), 248(1); "purchaser" — 116(3)(a); "recognized stock exchange" — 248(1); "related" — 251(2)–(6); "resident" — 250; "security" — *Interpretation Act* 35(1); "SIFT wind-up entity equity", "share", "tax treaty", "taxable Canadian property" — 248(1); "taxation year" — 249, 250.1(a); "taxpayer" — 248(1); "timber resource property" — 13(21), 248(1); "treaty-exempt property" — 116(6.1); "treaty-protected property" — 248(1). See also 116(7).

Income Tax Folios [s. 116]: S4-F7-C1: Amalgamations of Canadian corporations [replaces IT-474R2].

Interpretation Bulletins [s. 116]: IT-150R2: Acquisition from non-resident of certain property on death or mortgage foreclosure or by virtue of a deemed disposition (cancelled).

Information Circulars [s. 116]: 72-17R6: Procedures concerning the disposition of taxable Canadian property by non-residents of Canada — section 116.

DIVISION E — COMPUTATION OF TAX

Subdivision A — Rules Applicable to Individuals

117. (1) Tax payable under this Part — For the purposes of this Division, except section 120 (other than subparagraph (a)(ii) of the definition "tax otherwise payable under this Part" in subsection 120(4)), tax payable under this Part, tax otherwise payable under this Part and tax under this Part shall be computed as if this Part were read without reference to Division E.1.

Notes: Division E.1 is 127.5 to 127.55, the Alternative Minimum Tax.

"Tax otherwise payable under this Part" includes pre-2008 corporate surtax under 123.2: VIEWS doc 2008-0311211I7.

117(1) amended by 1999 Budget, last change effective for 2000 and later tax years.

(2) Rates for taxation years after 2015 — The tax payable under this Part by an individual on the individual's taxable income or taxable income earned in Canada, as the case may be (in this

Subdivision referred to as the "amount taxable") for a taxation year is

> (a) 15% of the amount taxable, if the amount taxable is equal to or less than the amount determined for the taxation year in respect of $45,282[12];

> (b) if the amount taxable is greater than $45,282[12] and is equal to or less than $90,563[12], the maximum amount determinable in respect of the taxation year under paragraph (a), plus 20.5% of the amount by which the amount taxable exceeds $45,282[12] for the year;

> (c) if the amount taxable is greater than $90,563[12], but is equal to or less than $140,388[12], the maximum amount determinable in respect of the taxation year under paragraph (b), plus 26% of the amount by which the amount taxable exceeds $90,563[12] for the year;

> (d) if the amount taxable is greater than $140,388[12], but is equal to or less than $200,000[12], the maximum amount determinable in respect of the taxation year under paragraph (c), plus 29% of the amount by which the amount taxable exceeds $140,388[12] for the year; and

> (e) if the amount taxable is greater than $200,000[12], the maximum amount determinable in respect of the taxation year under paragraph (d), plus 33% of the amount by which the amount taxable exceeds $200,000[12] for the year.

Related Provisions: 117(1) — Minimum tax to be ignored for purposes of 117(2); 117(3) — Minimum thresholds for 2004; 117.1(2)(d) — Indexing for inflation; 120(2) — Rate reduction for residents of Quebec; 122 — Top rate of tax payable by *inter vivos* trust; 127.5 — Minimum tax; 180.2 — "Clawback" tax on old age security.

Notes: The rates as now enacted are for 2016 and indexed by 117.1 after 2016. For 2021, the bracket thresholds are $49,020, $98,040, $151,978 and $216,511 (for earlier years see table at end of 117.1). These reflect the 2016 Budget "middle class tax cut" amendments, reducing the 22% bracket to 20.5% and increasing the rate over $200,000 taxable income (2016) from 29% to 33%. The charitable donation credit in 118.1(3) was adjusted at the same time to provide a 33% credit for donations from income taxed at 33%. See Parliamentary Budget Officer, "Revisiting the Middle Class Tax Cut" (April 18, 2019), tinyurl.com/pbo-taxcut, on the fiscal impact of these changes including behavioural responses. The new top rate did not produce anywhere near the expected revenue, due to changes in taxpayer behaviour: Laurin, "Unhappy Returns" (C.D. Howe Institute, 2018), tinyurl.com/unhappy-returns.

In addition to tax under 117, an individual is also subject to provincial or territorial income tax. Except for Quebec, which collects its own tax on separate returns, each province/territory imposes personal income tax that is collected for it by the CRA on a joint tax return (since 2001, all provinces and territories impose tax calculated on taxable income rather than on federal tax). See *Provincial TaxPartner* (CD-ROM) or *Taxnet Pro*. Income of an individual is taxed by the province in which the individual is resident on Dec. 31: Reg. 2601(1). For rates see introductory pages. For income not earned in a province, there is additional federal tax under 120(1).

The federal rates for residents of Quebec are actually 83.5% of the rates shown here. See 120(2) and Notes thereto.

The 15% lowest rate in 117(2)(a) is the 248(1)"appropriate percentage" for calculating personal credits (118-118.81) and minimum tax (127.51:A). The 33% rate in 117(2)(e) is the 248(1)"highest individual percentage", used as the tax rate for trusts (122(1)(a)), TOSI (120.4(2)) and charitable credit for high-income donors (118.1(3)C).

For corporate tax rates, see 123.4(2) Notes, or tables at beginning of book.

117(2) amended by 2016 tax-rate bill (for 2016 and later years), 2009 budget bill #1, 2007 Economic Statement, 2006 budget bills #1, #2. See table after 117.1.

Income Tax Folios: S1-F1-C1: Medical expense tax credit [replaces IT-519R2]; S1-F2-C1: Education and textbook tax credits [replaces IT-515R2]; S1-F2-C2: Tuition tax credit [replaces IT-516R2].

Interpretation Bulletins: IT-406R2: Tax payable by an *inter vivos* trust; IT-513R: Personal tax credits.

CRA Audit Manual: 15.2.15: Tax calculations.

(2.1) Tax payable — WITB [CWB] advance payment — The tax payable under this Part on the individual's taxable income for a taxation year, as computed under subsection (2), is deemed to be the total of the amount otherwise computed under that subsection and, except for the purposes of sections 118 to 118.9, 120.2, 121, 122.3 and Subdivision C, the total of all amounts received by the individual in respect of the taxation year under subsection 122.7(7).

Notes: 117(2.1) makes the Canada Workers Benefit advance payment repayable, if the taxpayer does not qualify for it.

117(2.1) added by 2007 budget bill #2, effective for 2008 and later taxation years.

(3) Minimum thresholds for 2004 — [No longer relevant]

Notes: 117(3) added by 2000 Budget, in force June 14, 2001.

(4)–(5.2) [Repealed under former Act]

Notes: Former 117(3)–(5.2), repealed by 1988 tax reform, set out the personal tax rates for years before 1988.

(6), (7) [Repealed]

Notes: 117(6) repealed by 1999 Budget for 1998 and later taxation years. It allowed tax tables to be used instead of calculations. See Notes to Reg. 2500.

117(7) repealed by 1992 Child Benefit Bill, effective 1993. It provided the "notch provision", allowing a reduction for a dependant's medical expenses. See now 118.2(1).

Definitions [s. 117]: "amount" — 248(1); "amount taxable" — 117(2); "Federal Court" — *Federal Courts Act* s. 4; "individual", "person", "prescribed" — 248(1); "tax payable" — 117(1), 248(2); "taxable income" — 2(2), 248(1); "taxable income earned in Canada" — 115(1), 248(1); "taxation year" — 249; "taxpayer" — 248(1); "writing" — *Interpretation Act* 35(1).

117.1 (1) Annual adjustment [inflation indexing] — Each specified amount in relation to tax payable under this Part or Part I.2 for a taxation year shall be adjusted so that the amount to be used for the year under the provision for which the amount is relevant is the total of

> (a) the amount that would, but for subsection (3), be the amount to be used under the relevant provision for the preceding taxation year, and

> (b) the product obtained by multiplying

>> (i) the amount referred to in paragraph (a)

> by

>> (ii) the amount, adjusted in such manner as may be prescribed and rounded to the nearest one-thousandth, or, where the result obtained is equidistant from two consecutive one-thousandths, to the higher thereof, that is determined by the formula

$$\frac{A}{B} - 1$$

where

A   is the Consumer Price Index for the 12 month period that ended on September 30 next before that year, and

B   is the Consumer Price Index for the 12 month period immediately preceding the period mentioned in the description of A.

Related Provisions: 117(1.1) — Indexing of specific amounts; 122.5(3.1) — Indexing of GST Credit amounts; 122.61(5) — Indexing of Child Tax Benefit before July 2016; 205(1)"ALDA dollar limit"(b) — Indexing of limit for advanced life deferred annuity; 207.01(1)"TFSA dollar limit"(d) — Indexing of tax-free savings account contribution limit; 257 — Formula cannot calculate to less than zero.

Notes: 117.1(1) provides relief from inflation, by indexing many credits, deductions and tax brackets to the Consumer Price Index. For the indexing factor for recent years, see first line of table at end of 117.1.

Indexing of each amount in 117.1(1) begins as per the in-force rule adding that amount; for example, the $400,000 in 110.6(2)(a) is indexed only after 2014. For the applicable year in each case, see the footnotes to the amounts as printed in the relevant provisions.

See Notes to 118(1)B(b.1) for the rule for indexing of the amount in that para.

Most provinces index provincial brackets and credits, but since they use provincial inflation rates, the annual adjustments differ slightly from the federal.

117.1(1) opening words and (a) amended by 2021 budget bill #1, for 2021 and later tax years. The list of indexed provisions was moved to 117.1(2).

117.1(1) opening words amended by 2019 budget bill #1 to add the $10,000 in 122.91(2)B (earned income to qualify for the Canada Training Credit), indexed for 2021 and later tax years.

117.1(1) amended by 2016 budget bill #2 (s. 67), intended to be effective for 2019 and later tax years, to change the references to the dollar amounts in 122.7; but this amendment repealed by 2018 budget bill #1 (s. 39) and replaced with a new amendment to 117.1(1), since the dollar amounts in 122.7 were increased further.

---

[12] Indexed by 117.1 after 2016 — ed.

117.1(1) opening words amended by 2013 budget bill #2, for 2015 and later taxation years, to add "the amount of $400,000 referred to in the formula in paragraph 110.6(2)(a)" [i.e., the lifetime capital gains exemption threshold].

117.1(1) earlier amended by 2010 budget bill #2 (for 2009 and later years), 2007 budget bill #2, S.C. 2007 c. 16, 2006 budget bills #1 and #2, 2004 Budget, 2000 budget first bill, 1999, 1998, 1997, 1996 and 1995 Budgets, 1990 GST.

The 2000 amendment changed "1.03" in the formula to "1", to restore full indexing. From 1988-99, "1.03" meant that brackets and credits were indexed only to the extent inflation to the previous September exceeded 3%. Since it was under 3% from 1992-98, the brackets and credits were unchanged 1992-99.

Interpretation Bulletins: IT-406R2: Tax payable by an *inter vivos* trust.

(1.1) [Repealed]

Notes: 117.1(1.1) repealed by 2017 budget bill #1, for 2017 and later taxation years. (It set a 2000 base for inflation indexing of amounts in subsec. 118(1)B(a)-(d), which were re-enacted with a 2017 base.) It read:

> (1.1) Adjustment of certain amounts — Notwithstanding any other provision of this section, for the purpose of making the adjustment provided under subsection (1) for the 2000 taxation year, the amounts used for the 1999 taxation year
>
> > (a) in respect of the amounts of $6,000, $5,000 and $500 referred to in paragraphs (a), (b) and (c) of the description of B in subsection 118(1) and the amount of $625 referred to in subparagraph 180.2(4)(a)(ii) are deemed to be $7,131, $6,055, $606 and $665, respectively; and
> >
> > (b) in respect of the amounts of $6,456 and $4,103 referred to in paragraph (d) of the description of B in subsection 118(1) are deemed to be $7,131 and $4,778, respectively.

117.1(1.1) added by 2000 budget bill #1, for 2000 and later taxation years.

(2) Annual adjustment — amounts

For the purposes of subsection (1), each of the following amounts is a **specified amount** in relation to tax payable under this Part or Part I.2 for a taxation year:

(a) the amount of $300 referred to in subparagraph 6(1)(b)(v.1);

(b) the amount of $1,000 referred to in the formula in paragraph 8(1)(s);

(c) the amount of $400,000 referred to in the formula in paragraph 110.6(2)(a);

(d) each of the amounts expressed in dollars in subsection 117(2);

(e) each of the amounts expressed in dollars in the description of B in subsection 118(1);

(f) the amount of $12,298 in the description of A in subsection 118(1.1);

(g) the amount of $15,000 in paragraph (d) of the description of F in subsection 118(1.1);

(h) each of the amounts expressed in dollars in subsection 118(2);

(i) the amount of $1,000 referred to in subsection 118(10);

(j) the amount of $15,000 referred to in subsection 118.01(2);

(k) each of the amounts expressed in dollars in subsection 118.2(1);

(l) each of the amounts expressed in dollars in subsection 118.3(1);

(m) each of the amounts expressed in dollars in subsection 122.5(3);

(n) the amount of $2,500 referred to in subsection 122.51(1);

(o) each of the amounts expressed in dollars in subsection 122.51(2);

(p) the amount of $14,000 referred to in subsection 122.7(1.3);

(q) the amounts of $1,395 and $2,403 in the description of A, and each of the amounts expressed in dollars in the description of B, in subsection 122.7(2);

(r) the amount of $720 in the description of C, and each of the amounts expressed in dollars in the description of D, in subsection 122.7(3);

(s) the amount of $10,000 in the description of B in subsection 122.91(2); and

(t) each of the amounts expressed in dollars in Part I.2.

Notes: Re-enacting the entire list of indexed provisions in 2021 (and moving it from 117.1(1) to new 117.1(2)) does not mean that each amount should be indexed only from 2021, since the indexing for each year is based on the previous year's indexed value, as already enacted before this amendment. Still, in the author's view, it would be clearer if 117.1(2) showed, for each indexed dollar amount, the base year from which that amount is indexed.

117.1(2) added by 2021 budget bill #1, for 2021 and later tax years, but 117.1(2)(g) does not apply to the 2021-2023 tax years, and 117.1(2)(p)-(r) do not apply to the 2021 tax year. The list of indexed provisions was moved from 117.1(1).

Former 117.1(2) repealed by 1999 Budget, for 1999 and later tax years.

(3) Rounding

Where an amount referred to in this section, when adjusted as provided in this section, is not a multiple of one dollar, it shall be rounded to the nearest multiple of one dollar or, where it is equidistant from two such consecutive multiples, to the higher thereof.

(4) Consumer Price Index

In this section, the Consumer Price Index for any 12 month period is the result arrived at by

> (a) aggregating the Consumer Price Index for Canada, as published by Statistics Canada under the authority of the *Statistics Act*, adjusted in such manner as is prescribed, for each month in that period;
>
> (b) dividing the aggregate obtained under paragraph (a) by twelve; and
>
> (c) rounding the result obtained under paragraph (b) to the nearest one-thousandth or, where the result obtained is equidistant from two consecutive one-thousandths, to the higher thereof.

Notes: 117.1(4)(a) amended by 2000 budget bill #1, for 2000 and later tax years.

(5)–(8) [Repealed under former Act]

Notes: 117.1(5), repealed in 1986, provided indexing for the notch provision in former 117(7). 117.1(6), repealed by 1988 tax reform, provided for rounding of amounts (now covered by 117(1)(d)). 117.1(7), repealed by 1988 tax reform, provided the definition now in 117.1(4). 117.1(7.1)-(8), repealed in 1985-86, provided indexing before 1986.

INDEXED PERSONAL TAX CREDITS (see introductory pages for more details)

	2014	2015	2016	2017	2018	2019	2020	2021
Indexing factor from previous year	1.009	1.017	1.013	1.014	1.015	1.022	1.019	1.010
110.6(2): capital gains exemption	$800,000	$813,600	$824,176	$835,716	$848,252	$866,912	$883,384	$892,218
118(1)B(c), 118(1.1): basic personal credit	1,671	1,699	1,721	1,745	1,771	1,810	1,845–1,984	1,863–2,071
118(1)B(a), (b), 118(1.1): spousal/partner and wholly dependent person	1,671	1,699	1,721	1,745	1,771	1,810	1,845–1,984	1,863–2,071
118(1)B(b.1): living with child under 18	338	0	0	0	0	0	0	0
118(1)B(d): 18 and over and infirm	680	691	700	710	721	737	751	759
— income limit for phaseout	6,607	6,720	6,807	6,902	7,006	7,160	7,296	7,369
118(1)B(a)(ii)C(A), (b)(iv)D(A), (b.1), (c.1)E(I), (d): Family Caregiver credit	309	314	318	323	327	335	341	344
118(2): age 65 or older (low-income only, since 1994)	1,037	1,055	1,069	1,084	1,100	1,124	1,146	1,157
— income limit for phaseout	34,873	35,466	35,927	36,430	36,976	37,790	38,508	38,893
118(3): maximum pension credit	300	300	300	300	300	300	300	300
118.3(1): disability credit	1,165	1,185	1,200	1,217	1,235	1,262	1,286	1,299
118(1)B(c.1): caregiver	680	691	700	—	—	—	—	—
118(10): Canada Employment Credit	169	172	174	177	179	183	187	189

INDEXED PERSONAL TAX CREDITS (see introductory pages for more details)

	2014	2015	2016	2017	2018	2019	2020	2021
118.01(2): maximum adoption expenses credit	2,250	2,288	2,318	2,350	2,386	2,438	2,484	2,509
118.2(1): medical expense credit — income threshold	2,171	2,208	2,237	2,268	2,302	2,352	2,397	2,421
122.51(2): refundable medical expense supplement	1,152	1,172	1,187	1,203	1,222	1,248	1,272	1,285
— family income limit for phaseout	25,506	25,939	26,277	26,644	27,044	27,639	28,164	28,446
122.7(2)A(a): Canada Workers Benefit — single	998	1,015	1,028	1,042	1,058	1,081	1,102	1,113
122.7(2)A(b): — family CWB	1,813	1,844	1,868	1,894	1,922	1,964	2,001	2,021
122.7(3)C: — maximum CWB supplement	499	507	514	521	529	541	551	557
180.2(1): OAS/family allowance clawback — income threshold	71,592	72,809	73,756	74,788	75,910	77,580	79,054	79,845
180.2(4): OAS monthly grind-down	895	910	922	935	949	970	988	998
207.01(1)"TFSA dollar limit" — maximum annual contribution	5,500	10,000	5,500	5,500	5,500	6,000	6,000	6,000

INDEXED FEDERAL TAX RATES FOR INDIVIDUALS
(plus provincial tax; surtaxes under 180.1 before 2001)

1992–1999 Income Tax Rate Schedule

Taxable Income	Tax on Lower Limit	Tax Rate on Excess
(inflation less than 3% per year)		
$0 – 29,590	$ —	17%
29,591 – 59,180	5,030	26%
59,181 and over	12,724	29%

2000 Income Tax Rate Schedule

Taxable Income	Tax on Lower Limit	Tax Rate on Excess
$0 – 30,004	$ —	17%
30,005 – 60,009	5,101	25%
60,010 and over	12,602	29%

2001 Income Tax Rate Schedule

Taxable Income	Tax on Lower Limit	Tax Rate on Excess
$0 – 30,754	$ —	16%
30,755 – 61,509	4,921	22%
61,510 – 100,000	11,687	26%
100,001 and over	21,694	29%

2002 Income Tax Rate Schedule

Taxable Income	Tax on Lower Limit	Tax Rate on Excess
$0 – 31,677	$ —	16%
31,678 – 63,354	5,068	22%
63,355 – 103,000	12,037	26%
103,001 and over	22,345	29%

2003 Income Tax Rate Schedule

Taxable Income	Tax on Lower Limit	Tax Rate on Excess
$0 – 32,183	$ —	16%
32,184 – 64,368	5,149	22%
64,369 – 104,648	12,229	26%
104,649 and over	22,702	29%

2004 Income Tax Rate Schedule

Taxable Income	Tax on Lower Limit	Tax Rate on Excess
$0 – 35,000	$ —	16%
35,001 – 70,000	5,600	22%
70,001 – 113,804	13,300	26%
113,805 and over	24,689	29%

2005 Income Tax Rate Schedule

Taxable Income	Tax on Lower Limit	Tax Rate on Excess
$0 – 35,595	$ —	15%
35,596 – 71,190	5,339	22%
71,191 – 115,739	13,170	26%
115,740 and over	24,753	29%

2006 Income Tax Rate Schedule

Taxable Income	Tax on Lower Limit	Tax Rate on Excess
$0 – 36,378	$ —	15.25%
36,379 – 72,756	5,548	22%
72,757 – 118,285	13,551	26%
118,286 and over	25,388	29%

2007 Income Tax Rate Schedule

Taxable Income	Tax on Lower Limit	Tax Rate on Excess
$0 – 37,178	$ —	15%
37,179 – 74,357	5,577	22%
74,358 – 120,887	13,756	26%
120,888 and over	25,854	29%

2008 Income Tax Rate Schedule

Taxable Income	Tax on Lower Limit	Tax Rate on Excess
$0 – 37,885	$ —	15%
37,886 – 75,769	5,683	22%
75,770 – 123,184	14,017	26%
123,185 and over	26,345	29%

2009 Income Tax Rate Schedule

Taxable Income	Tax on Lower Limit	Tax Rate on Excess
$0 – 40,726	$ —	15%
40,727 – 81,452	6,109	22%
81,453 – 126,264	15,068	26%
126,265 and over	26,719	29%

2010 Income Tax Rate Schedule

Taxable Income	Tax on Lower Limit	Tax Rate on Excess
$0 – 40,970	$ —	15%
40,971 – 81,941	6,146	22%
81,942 – 127,021	15,159	26%
127,022 and over	26,880	29%

2011 Income Tax Rate Schedule

Taxable Income	Tax on Lower Limit	Tax Rate on Excess
$0 – 41,544	$ —	15%
41,545 – 83,088	6,232	22%
83,089 – 128,800	15,371	26%
128,801 and over	27,256	29%

2012 Income Tax Rate Schedule

Taxable Income	Tax on Lower Limit	Tax Rate on Excess
$0 – 42,707	$ —	15%
42,708 – 85,414	6,406	22%
85,415 – 132,406	15,802	26%
132,407 and over	28,020	29%

2013 Income Tax Rate Schedule

Taxable Income	Tax on Lower Limit	Tax Rate on Excess
$0 – 43,561	$ —	15%
43,562 – 87,123	6,534	22%
87,124 – 135,054	16,118	26%
135,055 and over	28,579	29%

2014 Income Tax Rate Schedule

Taxable Income	Tax on Lower Limit	Tax Rate on Excess
$0 – 43,953	$ —	15%
43,954 – 87,907	6,593	22%
87,908 – 136,270	16,263	26%
136,271 and over	28,837	29%

2015 Income Tax Rate Schedule

Taxable Income	Tax on Lower Limit	Tax Rate on Excess
$0 – 44,701	$ —	15%
44,702 – 89,401	6,705	22%
89,402 – 138,586	16,539	26%
138,587 and over	29,327	29%

2016 Income Tax Rate Schedule

Taxable Income	Tax on Lower Limit	Tax Rate on Excess
$0 – 45,282	$ —	15%
45,283 – 90,563	6,792	20.5%
90,564 – 140,388	16,075	26%
140,389 – 200,000	29,029	29%
200,001 and over	46,316	33%

2017 Income Tax Rate Schedule

Taxable Income	Tax on Lower Limit	Tax Rate on Excess
$0 – 45,916	$ —	15%
45,917 – 91,831	6,888	20.5%
91,832 – 142,353	16,300	26%
142,354 – 202,800	29,435	29%
202,801 and over	46,965	33%

2018 Income Tax Rate Schedule

Taxable Income	Tax on Lower Limit	Tax Rate on Excess
$0 – 46,605	$ —	15%
46,606 – 93,208	6,991	20.5%
93,209 – 144,489	16,544	26%
144,490 – 205,842	29,877	29%
205,843 and over	47,669	33%

2019 Income Tax Rate Schedule

Taxable Income	Tax on Lower Limit	Tax Rate on Excess
$0 – 47,630	$ —	15%
47,631 – 95,259	7,145	20.5%
95,260 – 147,667	16,908	26%
147,668 – 210,371	30,534	29%
210,372 and over	48,718	33%

2020 Income Tax Rate Schedule

Taxable Income	Tax on Lower Limit	Tax Rate on Excess
$0 – 48,535	$ —	15%
48,536 – 97,069	7,280	20.5%
97,070 – 150,473	17,230	26%
150,474 – 214,368	31,114	29%
214,369 and over	49,644	33%

2021 Income Tax Rate Schedule

Taxable Income	Tax on Lower Limit	Tax Rate on Excess
$0 – 49,020	$ —	15%
49,021 – 98,040	7,353	20.5%
98,041 – 151,978	17,402	26%
151,979 – 216,511	31,426	29%
216,512 and over	50,140	33%

See detailed current tables in introductory pages of the book.

Definitions [s. 117.1]: "amount" — 248(1); "Consumer Price Index" — 117.1(4); "individual", "prescribed", "regulation" — 248(1); "specified amount" — 117.1(2); "taxation year" — 249.

118. (1) Personal credits — For the purpose of computing the tax payable under this Part by an individual for a taxation year, there may be deducted an amount determined by the formula

$$A \times B$$

where

A is the appropriate percentage for the year, and

B is the total of,

Notes: The "appropriate percentage" (248(1)) is 15%, the same as the lowest bracket rate under 117(2)(a). The effect of a credit at this rate is the same as a deduction from the "bottom" rather than the "top" of income. For a taxpayer with taxable income under $48,535 (2020) or $49,020 (2021), a credit is worth the same as a deduction.

All the credits under 118-118.7 are "non-refundable" credits, so if federal tax is zero they are worthless (though some can be transfered to another taxpayer: 118.8-118.9). They *can* create a refund on filing, for a taxpayer who had tax withheld at source or has paid instalments. Some other credits are "refundable" (by being deemed paid on account of tax) even for a taxpayer with no income, such as the GST/HST Credit (122.5), Canada Child Benefit (122.61(1)), medical expense supplement (122.51), Canada Workers Benefit (122.7), Climate Action Incentive (122.8), school supplies credit (122.9), Canada Training Credit (122.91), film production credits (125.4(3), 125.5(3)), and SR&ED refundable investment tax credit (127.1(1)).

On the 118(1) credit generally see Income Tax Folio S1-F4-C2.

(a) **married or common-law partnership status** — in the case of an individual who at any time in the year is a married person or a person who is in a common-law partnership who supports the individual's spouse or common-law partner and is not living separate and apart from the spouse or common-law partner by reason of a breakdown of their marriage or common-law partnership, an amount equal to the total of

(i) the basic personal amount of the individual for the year, and

(ii) the amount determined by the formula

$$C + C.01 - C.1$$

where

C is

(A) $2,150[13] if the spouse or common-law partner is dependent on the individual by reason of mental or physical infirmity, and

(B) in any other case, nil,

C.01 is the basic personal amount of the individual for the year, and

C.1 is the income of the individual's spouse or common-law partner for the year or, if the individual and the individual's spouse or common-law partner are living separate and apart at the end of the year because of a breakdown of their marriage or common-law partnership, the spouse's or common-law partner's income for the year while married to, or in a common-law partnership with, the individual and not so separated,

Related Provisions: 82(3) — Optional inclusion into income of dividends received by spouse; 117.1(2)(e) — Indexing for inflation; 118(1.1) — Basic personal amount; 118(4) — Limitations; 118(5) — No deduction where claim made for support;

---

[13] Indexed after 2017 by 117.1(1) — ed.

118.91 — Individual resident in Canada for part of the year; 118.95(b) — Application in year individual becomes bankrupt; 257 — Formula cannot calculate to less than zero.

Notes: The "appropriate percentage" (248(1)) is 15%. The credit for having a spouse or common-law partner (CLP) is equal to 118(1)B(b) + (c) (equivalent-to-spouse credit + basic personal credit). See the table before s. 118 and Table I-2 in the introductory pages. If the spouse/CLP is infirm, there is an additional amount of $2,295 (for 2021); see Notes to 118(1)B(b.1).

The spouse's "income" is s. 3 income ("net income" on the tax return). It includes the spouse's income security benefits, even if obtained by fraud and later repaid: *Langlois*, 2007 TCC 460; and the 1995-2005 reserve under former 34.2: *Murphy*, 2003 TCC 898.

See Notes to 118.8 for the meaning of "living separate and apart".

For the meaning of "support" see Income Tax Folio S1-F4-C2 ¶2.18-2.20. In *Brobbey*, 2010 TCC 536, the credit was denied because B did not in fact support his wife, who was in Ghana.

Amendments by 2021 budget bill #1, for 2020 and later tax years, to reflect the "basic personal amount" changing from a fixed amount to a range (see 118(1.1)): (a)(i) changed from "$10,527 and"; (a)(ii) formula changed from "$10,527 + C – C.1"; C.01 added.

118(1)B(a)(ii)C(A) amended by 2017 budget bill #1, for 2017 and later tax years, to change "$2,000" to "2,150", but 117.1(1) does not apply to this number for 2017. This amendment did nothing, as the $2,000 was already indexed to $2,150 for 2017.

118(1)B(a) earlier amended by 2011 budget bill #2 (for 2012 and later years), 2009 and 2007 budget bills #1, 2000 same-sex partners bill, 1999 and 1996 Budgets.

Interpretation Bulletins: IT-295R4: Taxable dividends received after 1987 by a spouse; IT-513R: Personal tax credits.

Forms: T1 General return, Lines 30300, 30425; T1 Sched. 6: Canada Workers Benefit.

(b) wholly dependent person ["equivalent to spouse" credit] — in the case of an individual who does not claim a deduction for the year because of paragraph (a) and who, at any time in the year,

    (i) is

        (A) a person who is unmarried and who does not live in a common-law partnership, or

        (B) a person who is married or in a common-law partnership, who neither supported nor lived with their spouse or common-law partner and who is not supported by that spouse or common-law partner, and

    (ii) whether alone or jointly with one or more other persons, maintains a self-contained domestic establishment (in which the individual lives) and actually supports in that establishment a person who, at that time, is

        (A) except in the case of a child of the individual, resident in Canada,

        (B) wholly dependent for support on the individual, or the individual and the other person or persons, as the case may be,

        (C) related to the individual, and

        (D) except in the case of a parent or grandparent of the individual, either under 18 years of age or so dependent by reason of mental or physical infirmity,

an amount equal to the total of

    (iii) the basic personal amount of the individual for the year, and

    (iv) the amount determined by the formula

$$D + D.01 – D.1$$

    where

    D is

        (A) $2,150[13] if

           (I) the dependent person is, at the end of the taxation year, 18 years of age or older and is, at any time in the year, dependent on the individual by reason of mental or physical infirmity, or

           (II) the dependent person is a person, other than a child of the individual in respect of whom paragraph (b.1) applies, who, at the end of the taxation year, is under the age of 18 years and who, by reason of mental or physical infirmity, is likely to be, for a long and continuous period of indefinite duration, dependent on others for significantly more assistance in attending to the dependent person's personal needs and care, when compared to persons of the same age, and is so dependent on the individual at any time in the year, and

        (B) in any other case, nil,

    D.01 is the basic personal amount of the individual for the year, and

    D.1 is the dependent person's income for the year,

Related Provisions: 117.1(2)(e) — Indexing for inflation; 118(1.1) — Basic personal amount; 118(4) — Limitations; 118(5) — No deduction where claim made for support; 118(5.1) — Restriction in 118(5) does not apply if neither parent can claim child; 118.3(2) — Dependant having impairment; 118.91 — Individual resident in Canada for part of the year; 118.95(b) — Application in year individual becomes bankrupt; 257 — Formula cannot calculate to less than zero.

Notes: See generally Income Tax Folio S1-F4-C2. The "equivalent to spouse" credit is for a person who has no cohabiting spouse or common-law partner (CLP) but supports a child or other relative. With the 2021 amendments, it works out to $1,845 to $1,984 for 2020 ($12,298 to $13,229 × 15%), and $1,863 to $2,071 for 2021 ($12,421 to $13,808 × 15%). (See 118(1.1) Notes for why each number is a range.) There is a parallel provincial credit also. See the table before s. 118 and Table I-2 in the introductory pages. If the dependant is infirm, there is an additional amount of $2,273 (2020) or $2,295 (2021); see Notes to 118(1)B(b.1). This credit and the one in (b.1) can be claimed only by the same parent, so shared-custody parents cannot split them: VIEWS doc 2017-0721711E5.

See Notes to 118.8 on being separated while living under the same roof. For "maintains" in (b)(ii), see Notes to 248(1)"self-contained domestic establishment".

"At any time in the year" can refer to intermittent periods during the year, and "wholly dependent" in (ii)(B) can relate to those intermittent periods: *Isaac*, [1995] 1 C.T.C. 2387D (TCC); *Geddes*, [2000] 2 C.T.C. 2577 (TCC). In *Bruno*, 2007 TCC 360, a father who continued to live in the family home, in a self-contained unit, was allowed to claim one child under pre-2015 para. (b.1), even though the child normally lived in the main part of the home.

"Wholly dependent": see Income Tax Folio S1-F4-C2 ¶2.47: "the person is financially dependent on the individual such that the individual provides almost entirely for the person's well-being... the parent must be responsible for the usual day-to-day activities of raising the child, such as ensuring the child attends school and providing necessities such as food, shelter and clothing." See also VIEWS docs 2011-0397251E5, 2018-0768651E5. Where grandparent X receives support payments from an agency to care for grandchild Y, Y is not "wholly dependent" on X: 2012-0433851M4.

Both parties must live in the same home, so a child who visits does not qualify: *Narsing*, 1998 CarswellNat 172 (FCA), para. 2; *Karim*, 2016 TCC 91, para. 37; *Kimber*, 2017 TCC 197. Where the parent is separated from the other parent, has custody of the child and is in a new relationship but makes no claim under para. (a), the credit is available if at any time in the year they are not yet living with a new CLP: VIEWS doc 2009-0344151I7. See also Notes to 118(4) and (5).

For the meaning of "support" see Folio S1-F4-C2 ¶2.18-2.20. It includes both financial and non-financial support: VIEWS doc 2010-038121117.

Where the taxpayer and his estranged spouse both supported their children and each claimed one child, neither child was "wholly dependent" on the taxpayer so the credit was disallowed: *Charlebois*, 2004 TCC 785. Similarly, where each spouse had the child for 6 months and received support from the other, neither could claim the credit: *de Moissac*, [2007] 1 C.T.C. 2001 (TCC); this has now been fixed by 118(5.1).

Limiting the credit to children under 18 does not infringe the *Charter of Rights*: *Mercier*, 1996 CarswellNat 3187 (FCTD); *Pilette*, 2009 FCA 367; VIEWS doc 2013-0476541E5.

A parent cannot claim a credit for a child who is in a group home or other facility and not living with the parent: doc 2006-0180021E5. A parent need not have legal custody to claim a child: 2006-01976701E5, 2016-0674861C6 [CPA QC 2017 q.1.6]. A child placed with a person by a youth centre can qualify: 2007-023962117. A child who has not yet immigrated to Canada does not qualify: 2009-0313021E5; but if the parent is deemed resident by 250(1) and claims a child outside Canada, see 2009-032816117. A child over 18 does not qualify unless dependent due to infirmity: (b)(ii)(D), 2009-0321781E5. On 5 scenarios involving former spouses see 2018-078570117.

A claim for a parent can be made only if the parent lives with the taxpayer: VIEWS doc 2010-0365391E5.

---

[13] Indexed after 2017 by 117.1(1) — ed.

Amendments by 2021 budget bill #1, for 2020 and later tax years, to reflect the "basic personal amount" changing from a fixed amount to a range (see 118(1.1)): (b)(iii) changed from "$10,527 and"; (b)(iv) formula changed from "$10,527 + D – D.1"; D.01 added.

Feb. 2020 correction (laws.justice.gc.ca/corrections): "common law partner" in (b)(i)(B) changed to "common-law partner".

118(1)B(b)(iv)D(A) amended by 2017 budget bill #1, for 2017 and later tax years, to change "$2,000" to "2,150", but 117.1(1) does not apply to this number for 2017. This amendment did nothing, as the $2,000 was already indexed to $2,150 for 2017.

118(1)B(b) amended by 2011 budget bill #2, for 2012 and later years, to add the infirm-dependant amount. Earlier amended by 2009 and 2007 budget bills #1, 2000 same-sex partners bill, 1999 and 1996 Budgets.

Income Tax Folios: S1-F1-C2: Disability tax credit [replaces IT-519R2].

Interpretation Bulletins: IT-513R: Personal tax credits.

Forms: T1 General return, Line 30300; T1 Sched. 5: Details of dependant.

(b.1) caregiver amount for infirm child — $2,150[13] for each child, who is under the age of 18 years at the end of the taxation year, of the individual and who, by reason of mental or physical infirmity, is likely to be, for a long and continuous period of indefinite duration, dependent on others for significantly more assistance in attending to the child's personal needs and care, when compared to children of the same age if

(i) the child ordinarily resides throughout the taxation year with the individual together with another parent of the child, or

(ii) except if subparagraph (i) applies, the individual

(A) may deduct an amount under paragraph (b) in respect of the child, or

(B) could deduct an amount under paragraph (b) in respect of the child if

(I) paragraph (4)(a) and the reference in paragraph (4)(b) to "or the same domestic establishment" did not apply to the individual for the taxation year, and

(II) the child had no income for the year,

Related Provisions: 117.1(2)(e) — Indexing for inflation; 118(4) — Limitations; 118(5) — No deduction where claim made for support; 118(5.1) — Restriction in 118(5) does not apply if neither parent can claim child; 118(9.1) — Where child is born, adopted or dies during year; 118.3(2) — Dependant having impairment; 118.8 — Transfer of unused credit to spouse or common-law partner; 118.91 — Individual resident in Canada for part of the year; 118.95(b) — Application in year individual becomes bankrupt.

Notes: See generally Income Tax Folio S1-F4-C2. Since 2015, 118(1)B(b.1) is only the "infirm child under 18" credit, equal to the additional infirm-dependant amounts in 118(1)B(a)(ii)C(A), (b)(iv)D(A), (c.1)E(I) and (before 2017) (d). The amount is $2,273 (credit of $341) for 2020, $2,295 ($344) for 2021. See also 118(1)B(d).

For interpretation of "ordinarily resides throughout the taxation year" see VIEWS docs 2008-0274401E5, 2013-0513701E5.

This credit and the one in 118(1)B(b) can be claimed only by the same parent: VIEWS doc 2017-0721711E5.

Death: Where the child dies in the year, the credit is allowed (118(9.1)) but not if the child would have turned 18 before year-end: VIEWS doc 2012-0440261E5. Where a child is born and dies in the same year, the credit is allowed: 2011-040389117. Where a parent dies during the year, the child can be claimed on the deceased's return: 2013-047830117. (These docs written for the pre-2015 credit would still seem to apply.)

Before 2015, (b.1) implemented a non-refundable Child Tax Credit. It was replaced by an enhanced Universal Child Care Benefit (56(6) Notes); the UCCB was replaced in 2016 with a higher 122.61 Child Tax Benefit (now Canada Child Benefit). (The pre-1993 Child Tax Credit was in 122.2. Before 1988, a dependent child *deduction* was available under 109. From 1988-2006 there was no deduction or credit for a dependent child other than an infirm adult child (118(1)B(d)) or equivalent-to-spouse credit (118(1)B(b)).)

118(1)B(b.1) amended by 2017 budget bill #1 (for 2017 and later tax years, to change $2,000 to $2,150, but the $2,000 was already indexed to $2,150 for 2017); 2015 budget bill #1, 2011 budget bill #2, 2007 budget bill #2. Added by 2007 budget bill #1. Earlier (b.1), added by 1998 Budget and repealed by 1999 Budget, implemented a supplementary personal credit for low-income taxpayers.

Income Tax Folios: S1-F1-C2: Disability tax credit [replaces IT-519R2].

Forms: T1 General return, Lines 30499, 30500.

(c) **single status** — except in the case of an individual entitled to a deduction because of paragraph (a) or (b), the basic personal amount of the individual for the year,

Related Provisions: 117.1(2)(e) — Indexing for inflation; 118.91 — Individual resident in Canada for part of the year; 118.95(b) — Application in year individual becomes bankrupt; 122(1.1) — No personal credits allowed to trust.

Notes: With the 2021 amendments, the basic personal credit works out to $1,845 to $1,984 for 2020 ($12,298 to $13,229 × 15%), and $1,863 to $2,071 for 2021 ($12,421 to $13,808 × 15%). (See 118(1.1) Notes for why each number is a range.) There is a parallel provincial credit also. See the table preceding s. 118.

118(1)B(c) amended by 2021 budget bill #1, for 2020 and later tax years, to change "$10,320" to "the basic personal amount of the individual for the year".

118(1)B(c) amended by 2009 Budget (for 2009 and later years), 1999 Budget.

Income Tax Folios: S1-F1-C2: Disability tax credit [replaces IT-519R2]; S1-F2-C2: Tuition tax credit [replaces IT-516R2]; S1-F3-C1: Child care expense deduction [replaces IT-495R3].

Interpretation Bulletins: IT-500R: RRSPs — death of an annuitant; IT-513R: Personal tax credits.

Forms: T1 General return, Line 30000.

(c.1) [Repealed]

Notes: 118(1)B(c.1) repealed by 2017 budget bill #1 for 2017 and later taxation years, as part of consolidating the "caregiver" credit in para. (d). It read:

(c.1) in-home care of relative [caregiver credit] — in the case of an individual who, at any time in the year alone or jointly with one or more persons, maintains a self-contained domestic establishment which is the ordinary place of residence of the individual and of a particular person

(i) who has attained the age of 18 years before that time,

(ii) who is

(A) the individual's child or grandchild, or

(B) resident in Canada and is the parent, grandparent, brother, sister, aunt, uncle, nephew or niece of the individual or of the individual's spouse or common-law partner, and

(iii) who is

(A) the individual's parent or grandparent and has attained the age of 65 years before that time, or

(B) dependent on the individual because of the particular person's mental or physical infirmity,

the amount determined by the formula

$$\$18,906 + E - E.1$$

where

E   is

(I) $2,000 if the particular person is dependent on the individual by reason of mental or physical infirmity, and

(II) in any other case, nil, and

E.1 is the greater of $14,624 and the particular person's income for the year,

118(1)B(c.1) provided before 2017 a "caregiver" federal credit of up to $700 (for 2016: $4,667 × 15%) (plus a parallel provincial credit) for individuals residing with and providing in-home care to a parent or grandparent (including in-laws) 65 or over or an infirm dependent relative. The federal credit was reduced by 15¢ for each dollar of the dependant's net income over $15,940 (2016). If the dependant was infirm, there was an additional amount of $2,121 (2016); see Notes to 118(1)B(b.1).

In *Vaynshteyn*, 2004 TCC 573, V moved into her parents' apartment for three 2-month periods to help care for them (though continuing to return to her home); she was allowed the credit. In *Solanki*, 2010 TCC 221, the credit was disallowed because S no longer lived in the condo in which he supported his elderly parents. In CRA's view, the cared-for individual cannot have two "ordinary places of residence", so a relative who moves back and forth between two homes does not qualify: VIEWS doc 2006-0179381E5.

See also VIEWS docs 2009-0344401M4 (general discussion); 2010-0384881E5 (credit for disabled adult daughter); 2011-0394591E5 (meaning of "maintained a dwelling" [see also Notes to 248(1)"self-contained domestic establishment"]; documentation needed; adjustment of previous years; claims for multiple relatives allowed); 2013-0479671E5 (taxpayer does not qualify for caregiver amount).

---

[13] Indexed after 2017 by 117.1(1) — ed.

118(1)B(c.1) amended by 2011 budget bill #2, for 2012 and later tax years, to add the infirm-dependant amount. Earlier amended by 2001 technical bill, 2000 Budget; added by 1998 Budget.

(d) Canada caregiver credit [infirm adult dependant] — for each person who, at any time in the year,

(i) is dependent on the individual because of mental or physical infirmity, and

(ii) either

(A) is a spouse or common-law partner of the individual, or

(B) has attained the age of 18 years and is a dependant of the individual,

the amount determined by the formula

$$\$6,883^{13} - E$$

where

E is the amount, if any, by which the dependant's income for the year exceeds $16,163^{13}, and

Related Provisions: 108(1)"preferred beneficiary"(a)(ii)(A) — Infirm dependant can be a preferred beneficiary of trust; 117.1(2)(e) — Indexing for inflation; 118(1)B(e) — Credit for infirm dependant who also qualifies for equivalent-to-spouse credit; 118(4) — Limitations; 118(6) — Definition of dependant; 118.3(2) — Dependant having impairment; 118.91 — Individual resident in Canada for part of the year; 118.92 — Ordering of credits; 118.95(b) — Application in year individual becomes bankrupt; 257 — Formula cannot calculate to less than zero; Canada-U.S. Tax Treaty:Art. XXV:3 — US-resident dependant qualifies.

Notes: 118(1)B(d) provides the "Canada Caregiver Credit", simplified by the 2017 Budget as $7,276 for 2020 ($7,348 for 2021) for infirm dependants who are parents/grandparents, siblings, aunts/uncles, nieces/nephews, adult children of the claimant or of the claimant's spouse or common law partner, and $2,273 for 2020 ($2,295 for 2021) for an infirm dependent spouse or common-law partner for whom the individual claims the spouse or common-law partner amount [118(1)B(a)(ii)(A)], or an infirm dependant for whom the individual claims an eligible dependant credit [118(1)B(b)(iv)(A)], or an infirm child who is under 18 at year-end [118(1)B(b.1)]. The credit is reduced dollar-for-dollar by the dependant's net income above $17,085 (2020) or $17,256 (2021) [118(1)B(d)E]. The dependant is not required to live with the caregiver for the credit. This credit is no longer available for non-infirm seniors who live with their adult children. Note that "infirm" is a lower standard than required for the 118.3 disability credit.

See generally Income Tax Folio S1-F4-C2 ¶2.60-2.67. This credit requires an infirm "dependant" (118(6): resident in Canada if not a child or grandchild). A US resident can qualify due to Canada-US tax treaty Art. XXV:2: VIEWS doc 2006-0182461I7. For other non-resident relatives, the medical expense credit can be allowed in some cases: 2019-0833721M4.

Where the dependant has net income up to $17,085 (2020) or $17,256 (2021), the calculation is $7,276 (2020) or $7,348 (2021), 15% of which = $1,091 or $1,102, plus a parallel provincial tax credit. See the table before s. 118 and Table I-2. (The 2012 $2,000 amount is now included in the $7,276 for 2020 [$2,273 plus the base $5,003] or $7,348 for 2021 [$2,295 plus $5,053].)

In *Borden*, 2003 TCC 297, the taxpayer supported his adult son, who had paranoid psychosis and was driving around the US. The Court held the son was dependent on his father due to mental infirmity, so the credit was allowed. In *Jordan*, 2010 TCC 46, the credit was denied due to insufficient evidence of the taxpayer's son's infirmity.

CRA suggests a married child can qualify for this credit, noting "If your child is in receipt of social assistance or any other type of support, you must be able to show that the other assistance is insufficient to fully meet your child's basic needs and that she had to rely on the support you provided": doc 2004-0092741E5. For an example of a claim ground down by the child having income, see 2010-0384881E5.

118(1)B(d) amended by 2017 budget bill #1, for 2017 and later taxation years, but 117.1(1) does not apply to the dollar amounts for 2017. For 2012-16, read:

(d) dependants — for each dependant of the individual for the year who

(i) attained the age of 18 years before the end of the year, and

(ii) was dependent on the individual because of mental or physical infirmity,

the amount determined by the formula

$$\$10,358 + \$2,000 - F$$

where

F is the greater of $6,076 and the dependant's income for the year, and

118(1)B(d) amended by 2011 budget bill #2 (for 2012 and later taxation years), 2000, 1999 and 1996 Budgets, 1992 Child Benefit Bill.

Income Tax Folios: S1-F1-C2: Disability tax credit [replaces IT-519R2].

Forms: T1 General return, Lines 30425, 30450.

(e) additional amount [re dependant] — in the case of an individual entitled to a deduction in respect of a person because of paragraph (a) or (b) and who would also be entitled, but for paragraph (4)(c), to a deduction because of paragraph (d) in respect of the person, the amount by which the amount that would be determined under paragraph (d) exceeds the amount determined under paragraph (a) or (b), as the case may be, in respect of the person.

Related Provisions: 118(6) — Definition of dependant; 118.91 — Individual resident in Canada for part of the year; 118.92 — Ordering of credits; 118.95(b) — Application in year individual becomes bankrupt.

Notes: Taxpayer X with an infirm dependant over 17 may qualify for both 118(1)B(b) and (d). If this happens, 118(4)(c) restricts X to claiming under 118(1)B(b). The credit under (d) can exceed that under (b), if the dependant's income becomes too high. To ensure X is not penalized by having to claim a lower credit under (b), para. (e) provides that the amount under (b) is increased up to the level of (d).

118(1)B(e) amended by 2017 budget bill #1 for 2017 and later taxation years. For 1998-2016, read:

(e) in the case of an individual entitled to a deduction in respect of a person because of paragraph (b) and who would also be entitled, but for paragraph (4)(c), to a deduction because of paragraph (c.1) or (d) in respect of the person, the amount by which the amount that would be determined under paragraph (c.1) or (d), as the case may be, exceeds the amount determined under paragraph (b) in respect of the person.

118(1)B(e) earlier amended by 1998 Budget; added by 1996 Budget.

Income Tax Folios: S1-F3-C1: Child care expense deduction [replaces IT-495R3].

Interpretation Bulletins: IT-394R2: Preferred beneficiary election; IT-513R: Personal tax credits.

Information Circulars: 07-1R1: Taxpayer relief provisions.

Forms: RC4064: Medical and disability-related information [guide].

(1.1) Definition of "basic personal amount" — For the purposes of subsection (1), **"basic personal amount"**, of an individual for a taxation year, means the amount determined by the formula

$$A + B$$

where

A is $12,298; and

B is the amount determined by the formula

$$C - D \times E$$

where

C is the amount determined by the formula

$$F - G$$

where

F is

(a) for the 2020 taxation year, $13,229,

(b) for the 2021 taxation year, $13,808,

(c) for the 2022 taxation year, $14,398, and

(d) for the 2023 and subsequent taxation years, $15,000, and

G is the amount determined for A,

D is the amount determined for C, and

E is

(a) if the individual's income for the year is less than or equal to the first dollar amount for the year referred to in paragraph 117(2)(d), nil, and

(b) in any other case, the lesser of 1 and the amount determined by the formula

$$(H - I)/J$$

where

H is the individual's income for the year,

---

13 Indexed after 2017 by 117.1(1) — ed.

I   is the first dollar amount for the year referred to in paragraph 117(2)(d), and

J   is the amount determined by the formula

$$K - L$$

where

K   is the first dollar amount for the year referred to in paragraph 117(2)(e), and

L   is the amount determined for I.

Related Provisions: 117.1(2)(f), (g) — Indexing for inflation; 257 — Formula cannot calculate to less than zero.

Notes: Under the calculation, for 2020 the minimum basic personal amount (BPA) is $12,298 (where net income exceeds $214,368), and the maximum is $13,229 (where net income is below $150,473). For 2021, the minimum is $12,421 and max is $13,808 (net income below $151,978).

The formula is A+B, where A is $12,298 for 2020, $12,421 for 2021 (the base amount, indexed from 2019 and previous years) and B is a maximum of F−A, meaning the excess of F over A. A is the minimum BPA for each year, and F is the maximum for each year (if net income is low enough).

If net income is above the threshold for the 33% bracket (117(2)(e): $214,368 for 2020, $216,411 for 2021), then D × E will equal D [because E is 1; see below], and C−(D × E) will be zero. Then B will be zero and the BPA will be $12,298 for 2020, $12,421 for 2021.

[The reason E is 1 above is because E is the lesser of 1 and (H−I)/(K−I), which for 2020 is (net income−$150,473)/($214,368−$150,473), so if net income exceeds $214,368, the fraction comes out to more than 1 and thus E is 1. The same happens each year as the amounts in 117(2)(d) and (e) continue to be indexed past 2020. Thus, for 2021, it is (net income−$151,978)/($216,511−$151,978), so if net income exceeds $216,511, the fraction comes out to more than 1 and E is 1.]

If net income is below the threshold for the 29% bracket (117(2)(d); $150,473 for 2020, $151,978 for 2021), then D × E will be zero because E is zero (see E(a)). Then C−(D × E) will be the same as C, and B will be the same as C, which again is F−G (the maximum additional amount to bring the total to the amount in F). Therefore, the BPA for 2020 is $13,229, for 2021 is $13,808, and so on (see F).

Between the 117(2)(d) and (e) amounts of net income ($150,473 to $214,368 for 2020, $151,978 to $216,511 for 2021), the BPA is phased down from $13,229 to $12,298 (for 2020), or from $13,808 to $12,421 (for 2021), through the calculation of E as (H−I)/(K−I), gradually approaching 1.

118(1.1) added by 2021 budget bill #1, for 2020 and later tax years (as proposed in Finance news release, Dec. 9, 2019).

(2) Age [senior citizen] credit

— For the purpose of computing the tax payable under this Part for a taxation year by an individual who, before the end of the year, has attained the age of 65 years, there may be deducted the amount determined by the formula

$$A \times (\$6,408^{14} - B)$$

where

A   is the appropriate percentage for the year; and

B   is 15% of the amount, if any, by which the individual's income for the year would exceed $25,921[15] if, in computing that income, no amount were included in respect of a gain from a disposition of property to which section 79 applies and no amount were deductible under paragraph 20(1)(ww).

Related Provisions: 117.1(2)(h) — Indexing for inflation; 118.8 — Transfer of unused credits to spouse; 118.91 — Individual resident in Canada for part of the year; 118.92 — Ordering of credits; 118.95(b) — Application in year individual becomes bankrupt; 180.2 — "Clawback" tax and withholding of old age security benefits.

Notes: The $6,408 figure is indexed by 117.1(1) after 2009. The credit for low-income seniors is $1,146 for 2020 ($7,637 × 15%) and $1,157 for 2021 ($7,713 × 15%), plus a parallel provincial credit. See table preceding s. 118 and Notes at beginning of 118(1).

"B" phases out the credit as net income increases. Once net income reaches $89,421 in 2020 ($7,637 / 0.15 + $38,508) or $90,313 in 2021 ($7,713 / 0.15 + $38,893), no credit remains.

For purposes of 118(2), income untaxed due to a tax treaty does not reduce the available credit: *Peter*, [1997] 2 C.T.C. 2504 (TCC). This contrasts with *Swantje*, which applies to the old age security clawback; see Notes to 180.2. In *Sveinson*, 2011 TCC 34, a

large workers' compensation payment (taxed under 56(1)(v) and deducted under 110(1)(f)) disentitled the taxpayer to the age credit.

Quebec also has a "career extension" credit for taxpayers over 65 who have "eligible work income" (such as employment or business income) over $5,000. Ontario also has the Ontario Senior Homeowners' Property Tax Grant. NL offers a Seniors Benefit and SK has a Senior Supplementary Amount.

118(2)B amended by 2018 budget bill #1 to add "and no amount were deductible under paragraph 20(1)(ww)", for 2018 and later tax years.

118(2) earlier amended by 2009 budget bill #1 (for 2009 and later tax years), 2007 budget bill #1, 1995-97 technical bill and 1994 Budget.

Interpretation Bulletins: IT-513R: Personal tax credits.

Information Circulars: 07-1R1: Taxpayer relief provisions.

Remission Orders: *Keith Kirby Remission Order*, P.C. 2005-1533; *Josephine Pastorious Remission Order*, P.C. 2005-1534.

Forms: T1 General return, Line 30100.

(3) Pension credit

— For the purpose of computing the tax payable under this Part by an individual for a taxation year, there may be deducted an amount determined by the formula

$$A \times B$$

where

A   is the appropriate percentage for the year; and

B   is the lesser of

   (a) $2,000[2], and

   (b) the total of

      (i) the eligible pension income of the individual for the taxation year,

      (ii) the total of all amounts received by the individual in the year on account of a retirement income security benefit under Part 2 of the *Veterans Well-being Act*, and

      (iii) the total of all amounts received by the individual in the year on account of an income replacement benefit payable to the individual under Part 2 of the *Veterans Well-being Act*, if the amount is determined under subsection 19.1(1), paragraph 23(1)(b) or subsection 26.1(1) of that Act (as modified, where applicable, under Part 5 of that Act).

Related Provisions: 60.03 — Pension income splitting with spouse; 104(27) — Deemed income of beneficiary; 118(7) — Definition of "eligible pension income"; 118.8 — Transfer of unused credits to spouse; 118.91 — Individual resident in Canada for part of the year; 118.92 — Ordering of credits; 118.93 — Separate returns; 118.95(a) — Application in year individual becomes bankrupt; 122(1.1) — Credits not permitted to trust.

Notes: See Notes to 118(7) "qualified pension income".

The maximum value of the pension credit since 2007 is $300 ($2,000 × 15%), plus a parallel provincial credit. The effect is to exempt $2,000 of pension income off the "bottom" of income (at the lowest bracket) rather than a deduction from the "top". See Notes at the beginning of 118(1). The credit can be doubled by splitting the pension income with the spouse under 60.03.

A person aged 65-71 with no pension can convert RRSP funds to a RRIF and draw $2,000 per year tax-free from the RRIF, using this credit. CRA refused to say whether doing this and then recontributing to an RRSP would trigger GAAR: doc 2009-0323701E5.

For information on obtaining Old Age Security and the Guaranteed Income Supplement, see tinyurl.com/oas-canada.

Para. B(b)(ii) amended and (iii) added by 2018 budget bill #1, effective April 2019. Before then, read:

   (ii) the total of all amounts received by the individual in the year on account of a retirement income security benefit payable to the individual under Part 2 of the *Veterans Well-being Act*.

Para. B(b)(ii) effectively amended by S.C. 2017, c. 20 (Bill C-44, Royal Assent June 22, 2017), subsec. 292(2), to change "*Canadian Forces Members and Veterans Re-establishment and Compensation Act*" (with all other such references in federal legislation) to "*Veterans Well-being Act*" effective April 2018.

---

[2] Not indexed for inflation — ed.

[14] Indexed after 2009 by 117.1.

[15] Indexed after 1995 by 117.1. See Notes to 117.1(1).

118(3)B changed from "is the lesser of $2,000 and the eligible pension income of the individual for the taxation year" (effectively adding (b)(ii)) by 2017 budget bill #2, for 2015 and later taxation years.

118(3) earlier amended by 2007 budget bill #1 (for 2007 and later taxation years), 2006 budget second bill, 1992 technical bill.

Interpretation Bulletins: IT-500R: RRSPs — death of an annuitant; IT-517R: Pension tax credit (cancelled).

Information Circulars: 07-1R1: Taxpayer relief provisions.

Forms: T1 General return, Line 31400.

(3.1)–(3.3) [Repealed]

Notes: 118(3.1)-(3.2) repealed by 2009 budget bill #1, for 2009 and later years. They provided the real numbers for 118(1)B(a)-(c) for 2005-08. They were amended by 2007 Economic Statement, 2006 Budget and 2005 budget bill #1 (which added 118(3.2)). 118(3.1) added by 2000 Budget, effective 2004. 118(3.3) repealed by 2007 budget bill #1, for 2007 and later taxation years.

An Oct. 7/05 Liberal government proposal to have 118(3.1)-(3.3) increase the personal credits to use up 1/3 of federal budget surpluses (Bill C-67, *Unanticipated Surpluses Act*) was not enacted. Instead, the (Conservative) 2007 budget bill #1 enacted the *Tax-back Guarantee Act*, which provides:

1. Short title — This Act may be cited as the *Tax-back Guarantee Act.*

2. Direction to provide personal tax relief — The Government of Canada shall apply any imputed interest savings resulting from reductions of federal debt to measures that provide tax relief for individuals.

3. Meaning of "federal debt" — In this Act, "federal debt" means the accumulated deficit as stated in the Public Accounts prepared in accordance with sections 63 and 64 of the *Financial Administration Act* in respect of a fiscal year.

4. Imputed interest savings — The imputed interest savings in respect of a fiscal year of the Government of Canada is the amount determined by the Minister of Finance to be the product of multiplying the total amount by which federal debt was reduced in the year by the effective interest rate for the year.

5. Effective interest rate — The effective interest rate for a fiscal year is the ratio of the amount of public debt charges related to unmatured debt (as stated in the Public Accounts for the year) to the average amount of unmatured debt for the year (determined by dividing by two the sum of the amount of unmatured debt at the beginning of the year and the amount of unmatured debt at the end of the year, as those amounts are stated in the Public Accounts for the year).

6. Public announcement — At least once every fiscal year, the Minister of Finance shall report, by way of a statement tabled in the House of Commons or other public announcement,

(a) the finalized determination of the imputed interest savings in respect of the previous fiscal year; and

(b) an accounting of the measures to which those savings have been applied in accordance with section 2.

With annual deficits, the *Tax-back Guarantee Act* has been irrelevant since 2009 (and, since COVID-19, will remain so for many years). However, it can be repealed, or simply ignored by later legislation: see *Progressive Conservative Party v. Manitoba*, 2014 MBQB 155, where a legislated requirement for a referendum before increasing the retail sales tax rate did not fetter the legislature's right to pass such an increase, even without repealing the requirement.

(4) Limitations re subsec. (1) — For the purposes of subsection (1), the following rules apply:

(a) no amount may be deducted under subsection (1) because of paragraphs (a) and (b) of the description of B in subsection (1) by an individual in a taxation year for more than one other person;

(a.1) no amount may be deducted under subsection (1) because of paragraph (b) of the description of B in subsection (1) by an individual for a taxation year for a person in respect of whom an amount is deducted because of paragraph (a) of that description by another individual for the year if, throughout the year, the person and that other individual are married to each other or in a common-law partnership with each other and are not living separate and apart because of a breakdown of their marriage or the common-law partnership, as the case may be;

(a.2) a reference to income for a year is to be read as a reference to that income determined as if, in computing that income, no amount were deductible under paragraph 20(1)(ww);

(b) not more than one individual is entitled to a deduction under subsection (1) because of paragraph (b) of the description of B in that subsection for a taxation year in respect of the same person or the same domestic establishment and where two or more individuals otherwise entitled to such a deduction fail to agree as to the individual by whom the deduction may be made, no such deduction for the year shall be allowed to either or any of them;

(b.1) not more than one individual is entitled to a deduction under subsection (1) because of paragraph (b.1) of the description of B in that subsection for a taxation year in respect of the same child and where two or more individuals otherwise entitled to such a deduction fail to agree as to the individual by whom the deduction may be made, no such deduction for the year shall be allowed to either or any of them;

(c) if an individual is entitled to a deduction under subsection (1) because of paragraph (a) or (b) of the description of B in subsection (1) for a taxation year in respect of any person, no amount may be deducted because of paragraph (d) of that description by any individual for the year in respect of the person; and

(d) if more than one individual is entitled to a deduction under subsection (1) because of paragraph (d) of the description of B in subsection (1) for a taxation year in respect of the same person,

(i) the total of all amounts so deductible for the year shall not exceed the maximum amount that would be so deductible for the year by any one of those individuals for that person if that individual were the only individual entitled to deduct an amount for the year because of that paragraph for that person, and

(ii) if the individuals cannot agree as to what portion of the amount each can so deduct, the Minister may fix the portions.

(e) [Repealed]

Related Provisions: 118(6) — Definition of "dependant".

Notes: See Income Tax Folio S1-F4-C2.

118(4)(a.1) denies an equivalent-to-spouse credit to X for person Y if X's spouse (or common-law partner) S has claimed a *spousal* credit for Y (which would be rare), but not if X and S are separated; and not if S had so little income that no amount was actually deducted from tax: *Ullah*, 2013 TCC 387, para. 13.

118(4)(b) applied to disallow a 118(1)B(b) credit in *Krashinsky*, 2010 TCC 78, because the separated spouses could not agree on who would get it (para. 16): "This is an issue that should routinely be addressed at the time of the separation agreement, where joint custody is an issue ... the zero sum approach of denying any credit without agreement can ... create a harsh and unfair result"; and the same in *Ruel*, 2017 TCC 93, para. 32. See also VIEWS docs 2009-034309117 and 2017-0721711E5 on the interaction of 118(4)(b) with 118(1)B(b) and (b.1). In *Nault*, 2011 TCC 428, the father was denied the credit because he did not satisfy the Court that the child did not reside with the mother for part of the year.

The words "entitled to a deduction" in 118(4)(c) are ambiguous. A person who makes a claim for one child under 118(1)B(b) is arguably no longer "entitled to a deduction" for a second child under that paragraph. (See *United Parcel Service*, 2009 SCC 20, where a rebate was not "payable" if no claim was made for it.)

See also Notes to 118(5).

118(4)(a.2) added by 2018 budget bill #1, for 2018 and later tax years.

118(4)(c)-(e) changed to (c)-(d) by 2017 budget bill #1, for 2017 and later taxation years, consequential on amendments to 118(1). For 2011-16, read:

(d) where an individual is entitled to a deduction under subsection (1) because of paragraph (c.1) of the description of B in subsection (1) for a taxation year in respect of any person, the person is deemed not to be a dependant of any individual for the year for the purpose of paragraph (d) of that description; and

118(4)(b) amended (so as to apply only to 118(1)B(b) and not (b.1)) and 118(4)(b.1) added, by 2011 budget bill #2, for 2011 and later taxation years. Before the amendment, only one person could claim the Child Tax Credit (118(1)B(b.1)) in respect of the same domestic establishment, so if two families shared a home (e.g. two adult sisters living together, each with one child), only one person could claim it (see *Cheung*, 2010 TCC 297). The limitation was moved to new 118(4)(b.1), which does not refer to a domestic establishment as 118(4)(b) does, "to ensure that sharing a home does not prevent otherwise-eligible parents from claiming the CTC in respect of their children".

Before the 2011 amendment, 118(4) "generally precludes two taxpayers from claiming either for the same dependent or in respect of the same domestic establishment", and 118(4)(a) refers to 118(1)B(a) and (b): *Lutz*, 2009 TCC 436.

118(4)(b) amended by 2007 budget bill #1, for 2007 and later taxation years, to refer to 118(1)B(b.1). 118(4) earlier amended by 2000 same-sex partners bill, 1998 Budget and 1992 Child Benefit bill.

Interpretation Bulletins: IT-513R: Personal tax credits.

(5) Support — No amount may be deducted under subsection (1) in computing an individual's tax payable under this Part for a taxation year in respect of a person where the individual is required to pay a support amount (within the meaning assigned by subsection 56.1(4)) to the individual's spouse or common-law partner or former spouse or common-law partner in respect of the person and the individual

(a) lives separate and apart from the spouse or common-law partner or former spouse or common-law partner throughout the year because of the breakdown of their marriage or common-law partnership; or

(b) claims a deduction for the year because of section 60 in respect of a support amount paid to the spouse or common-law partner or former spouse or common-law partner.

Related Provisions: 118(5.1) — Restriction does not apply when two people both pay child support.

Notes: The equivalent-to-spouse credit is lost if the parent is required to pay child support, and either claims a support deduction or lives apart from the other spouse *throughout* the year (meaning the entire year; *Chu*, 2005 TCC 169). See *Cornelius*, 2008 TCC 615; *Scott*, 2009 TCC 36; *St-Germain*, 2009 TCC 518, para. 18; *Pineau*, 2009 TCC 559 (FCA appeal discontinued A-477-09); *Persaud*, 2011 TCC 163; *Giroux*, 2012 TCC 284; *Curry*, 2015 TCC 152; *Luschtinetz*, 2015 TCC 320; VIEWS doc 2018-0768651E5. This is true even in cases such as: support is not paid, or is paid but not claimed for tax purposes (*Szuch*, 2006 FCA 383); the parent is the primary caregiver (*Chu*, 2007 TCC 262); the amount payable is arrears from an earlier year (*LeClair*, 2005 TCC 363, *Whitty*, 2009 TCC 333); the requirement is under an agreement rather than a court order (*Perrin*, 2010 TCC 331); the court order purports to allocate the credit to this parent (*Beaudoin*, 2010 TCC 600); the other spouse has waived the court-ordered support (*Roy*, 2011 TCC 511, 2014-0516711E5: such waiver is void); the child is now residing with the taxpayer so that the support obligation could be cancelled (*Foreman*, 2012 TCC 36; *Larivière*, 2016 TCC 287, para. 19); the taxpayer stopped paying child support because he was taking care of both children (*Duke*, 2012 TCC 41); the taxpayer claims that the order for him to pay child support violates the *Charter of Rights* (*D'Ambrosio*, 2014 TCC 70; FCA appeal discontinued A-187-14).

118(5) applies even if the amount paid is a "net" for shared custody under the Child Support Guidelines: *Verones*, 2013 FCA 69; *Ladell*, 2011 TCC 314; *Sauve*, 2014 TCC 99; *Commet*, 2016 TCC 48; *Harder*, 2016 TCC 197; *Groves*, 2017 TCC 66. Where the Court Order required H to pay W $1,200 and W to pay H $800 monthly in respect of different children, 118(5) still prevented H's deduction because the Order also said this required a "net payment" of $400. If the parents pay each other support during different months of shared custody, the credit was lost before 2007, but this is fixed by 118(5.1): docs 2010-0369571E5, 2012-0443301E5, 2013-0502091E5 (parents can claim in alternate years). Different drafting of the support order with the same net effect can result in both parents, one or neither getting the credit, which is unfair: *Ochitwa*, 2014 TCC 263, para. 8; *Letoria*, 2015 TCC 221. See also Notes to 118(5.1). Where each parent has custody of one child and they pay each other support, each can claim the credit: 2010-0380431E5. For claims in the year of separation see 2010-0373061E5. See also 2008-0298881E5, 2009-034173117, 2010-0374871E5, 2014-0532311M4. An obligation to pay only *spousal* support does not trigger 118(5): 2011-042643117.

Similarly, 118(5) applies to prevent claiming the disability credit (118.3(2)) for a child for whom the taxpayer is required to pay support: *Scott* (above); again, 118(5.1) provides relief in a shared custody situation so that the parents can alternate the claims each year: doc 2012-0443101E5.

Retroactive cancellation of earlier support can result in 118(5) not applying, since 118(5) does not state when the "requirement to pay a support amount" can be created or extinguished: *Barthels*, [2003] 3 C.T.C. 2756 (TCC); *Antalya*, 2005 TCC 31; *Giroux*, 2012 TCC 284; *Abiola*, 2013 TCC 115; *Cook*, 2017 TCC 188. *Contra*, retroactive cancellation did not stop 118(5) from having applied in *Lavoie*, 2001 CarswellNat 3858 (TCC); *Young*, 2003 CarswellNat 157 (TCC); *Dubis*, 2010 TCC 121. In VIEWS doc 2007-0230421I7, the CRA says a retroactive *agreement* would be ineffective.

See Notes to 118.8 for the meaning of "living separate and apart".

118(5) does not violate the *Charter of Rights*: *Donovan*, 2005 TCC 667; *Calogeracos*, 2008 CarswellNat 2076 (TCC); *Sears*, [2009] 4 C.T.C. 2119 (TCC); *Dubuc*, 2014 CarswellNat 1343 (TCC). The Canadian Human Rights Commission cannot be forced to investigate this issue: *Donovan*, 2008 CarswellNat 1159 (FC). 118(5) cannot be overridden by provincial Court order: *Calogeracos* (above). See Drache, "Fairness or Double Dipping", xxxi(4) *The Canadian Taxpayer* (Carswell) 31-32 (Feb. 17, 2009).

118(5) amended by 2001 technical bill (effective 2001), 2000 same-sex partners bill and 1996 Budget.

Income Tax Folios: S1-F3-C3: Support payments [replaces IT-530R].

Interpretation Bulletins: IT-513R: Personal tax credits.

Information Circulars: 07-1R1: Taxpayer relief provisions.

(5.1) Where subsec. 118(5) does not apply — Where, if this Act were read without reference to this subsection, solely because of the application of subsection (5), no individual is entitled to a deduction under paragraph (b) or (b.1) of the description of B in subsection (1) for a taxation year in respect of a child, subsection (5) shall not apply in respect of that child for that taxation year.

Notes: See Notes to 118(5). 118(5.1) corrects a problem that arose in *Slade*, 2005 TCC 641, *Leclerc*, 2005 TCC 689, and *de Moissac*, [2007] 1 C.T.C. 2001 (TCC), where both parents paid each other support during different months of shared custody, and both parents were denied the credit.

118(5.1) does not apply when child support is payable only in one direction, even if that support is calculated as a "net" of amounts the spouses owe each other due to sharing of custody: *Verones*, 2013 FCA 69; *Perrin*, 2010 TCC 331; *Cunningham*, 2012 TCC 279; *Haynes*, 2013 TCC 84; *Jantzi*, 2013 TCC 119; *Belway*, 2015 TCC 249; *Harder*, 2016 TCC 197; *Groves*, 2017 TCC 66 (even though CRA website was misleading); *Huneault*, 2017 TCC 70; *Stevenson*, 2008 TCC 176; *Bayrack*, 2019 TCC 53.

118(5.1) also does not provide relief where the other spouse could have claimed the credit but did not have enough income for it to be of use: *Beaudoin*, 2010 TCC 600; *Betts*, 2012 TCC 224.

However, 118(5.1) provided relief where each parent was *required* under an agreement to pay support for one or more children, even though the actual payment was a net: *Judickas*, 2016 TCC 225; *Ruel*, 2017 TCC 93 [but 118(4) disallowed the credits because the ex-spouses did not agree which one should get them]. 118(5.1) also applied in *Lawson*, 2017 TCC 131, where only the father was required to pay, but the agreement stated the monthly amount "represents the difference between the child support payments they would otherwise pay to each other", and the evidence showed it was so calculated.

For CRA interpretation see VIEWS docs 2010-0368381E5, 2011-0396611E5 (where "set-off" used so that one parent pays the other only the difference), 2012-0445401E5, 2015-0570791E5; 2019-081810117 (*Verones* applies to deny credit on set-off unless legal payment obligations exist in both directions).

118(5.1) added by 2007 budget bill #2, effective for 2007 and later taxation years.

(6) Definition of "dependant" — For the purposes of paragraph (d) of the description of B in subsection (1), "dependant", of an individual for a taxation year, means a person who at any time in the year is dependent on the individual for support and is

(a) the child or grandchild of the individual or of the individual's spouse or common-law partner; or

(b) the parent, grandparent, brother, sister, uncle, aunt, niece or nephew, if resident in Canada at any time in the year, of the individual or of the individual's spouse or common-law partner.

Related Provisions: 252(1), (2) — Extended meaning of "child", "parent", "brother", etc.

Notes: A parent of a taxpayer's deceased spouse is still considered a parent by CRA administrative practice; see Notes to 252(2). A brother who was a Canadian citizen but had resided outside Canada for several years was not a "dependant" for the medical expense credit: *Hagos*, [2009] 2 C.T.C. 2030 (TCC) (under appeal to FCA).

"Dependent for support" refers to basic necessities of life such as food, shelter and clothing: VIEWS doc 2012-0436431E5. If a person receives provincial disability support, "it would have to be shown that this income was insufficient to meet her basic needs and that she had to rely on the support provided by the taxpayer": 2009-032672117. However, in *Savoy*, 2011 CarswellNat 193 (TCC), S's quadriplegic brother B was held to be S's "dependant" (even though S was not providing B food and shelter) because S was renovating his garage into a living unit for B, who passed away before the unit was ready.

118(6) opening words amended by 2017 budget bill #1, for 2017 and later taxation years, to no longer apply to 118(1)B(e) and 118(4)(e).

118(6) amended by 2000 same-sex partners bill (last change effective 2001) and 1996 Budget.

Income Tax Folios: S1-F1-C1: Medical expense tax credit [replaces IT-519R2]; S1-F1-C2: Disability tax credit [replaces IT-519R2].

Interpretation Bulletins: IT-394R2: Preferred beneficiary election; IT-513R: Personal tax credits.

(7) Definitions — Subject to subsections (8) and (8.1), for the purposes of this subsection and subsection (3),

Notes: Opening words of 118(7) amended by 2007 budget bill #1, effective for 2007 and later taxation years, to add reference to 118(8.1) and to "this subsection".

"eligible pension income" of an individual for a taxation year means

(a) if the individual has attained the age of 65 years before the end of the taxation year, the pension income received by the individual in the taxation year, and

(b) if the individual has not attained the age of 65 years before the end of the taxation year, the qualified pension income received by the individual in the taxation year;

Related Provisions: 60.03(1)"eligible pension income" — Expanded definition for purposes of pension income splitting rules.

Notes: 118(7)"eligible pension income" added by 2007 budget bill #1, for 2007 and later taxation years. These rules were formerly in the pension credit in 118(3)B.

"pension income" received by an individual in a taxation year means the total of

(a) the total of all amounts each of which is an amount included in computing the individual's income for the year that is

(i) a payment in respect of a life annuity out of or under a superannuation or pension plan (other than a pooled registered pension plan) or a specified pension plan,

(ii) an annuity payment under a registered retirement savings plan, under an "amended plan" as referred to in subsection 146(12) or under an annuity in respect of which an amount is included in computing the individual's income by reason of paragraph 56(1)(d.2),

(iii) a payment out of or under a registered retirement income fund or under an "amended fund" as referred to in subsection 146.3(11),

(iii.1) a payment (other than a payment described in subparagraph (i)) payable on a periodic basis under a money purchase provision (within the meaning assigned by subsection 147.1(1)) of a registered pension plan,

(iii.2) an amount included under section 147.5,

(iii.3) an amount included under subsection 146.5(2),

(iv) an annuity payment under a deferred profit sharing plan or under a "revoked plan" as referred to in subsection 147(15),

(v) a payment described in subparagraph 147(2)(k)(v), or

(vi) the amount by which an annuity payment included in computing the individual's income for the year by reason of paragraph 56(1)(d) exceeds the capital element of that payment as determined or established under paragraph 60(a), and

(b) the total of all amounts each of which is an amount included in computing the individual's income for the year by reason of section 12.2 of this Act or paragraph 56(1)(d.1) of the *Income Tax Act*, chapter 148 of the Revised Statutes of Canada, 1952;

Related Provisions: 60.03(1)"pension income" — Expanded definition for purposes of pension income splitting rules; 104(27) — Flow-out of pension benefits by trust; 118(8) — Limitations; 118(8.1) — Bridging benefits included in "payment in respect of a life annuity under a superannuation or pension plan".

Notes: If one is 65 or older by year-end, all "pension income" qualifies for the 118(3) pension credit: 118(7)"eligible pension income"(a). Otherwise, only "qualified pension income" (below) is eligible.

Old Age Security and CPP benefits are not "pension income": 118(8).

Subpara. (a)(ii): A simple withdrawal of funds from an RRSP is not an "annuity": *Taylor*, 2014 TCC 102; *Way*, 2018 TCC 198.

(a)(iii): CRA says an amount deemed *received* by 146.3(6) does not qualify because it is not deemed to be a "payment": VIEWS doc 2019-0813281C6 [2019 APFF Financial q.9] (this is wrong in the author's view, as "deemed" is conclusive (see Notes to 244(15)) and the "out of or under a RRIF" wording tracks exactly between the two provisions).

(a)(iii.1), covering periodic payments under an RPP money purchase provision, is needed due to 2008 amendments to Reg. 8506 which allow money purchase RPPs to provide members with retirement benefits that are payable in the same manner as under a RRIF. These benefits are not considered to be lifetime annuity payments, but they qualify for the pension credit (118(3)) and pension income splitting (60.03).

Para. (b): The reference to 56(1)(d.1) is to a provision repealed in 1990 that still applies to annuity contracts acquired before 1990. See Notes to 56(1)(d.1).

Subpara. (a)(iii.3) added by 2021 budget bill #1, effective 2020.

Definition amended by 2002-2013 technical bill (for 2004 and later tax years), 2012 budget bill #2 (effective Dec. 14, 2012), 2011 budget bill #2.

Regulations: 7800 (Saskatchewan Pension Plan is specified pension plan, for subpara. (a)(i)).

I.T. Application Rules: 69 (meaning of "chapter 148 of ...").

"qualified pension income" received by an individual in a taxation year means the total of all amounts each of which is an amount included in computing the individual's income for the year and described in

(a) subparagraph (a)(i) of the definition "pension income" in this subsection, or

(b) any of subparagraphs (a)(ii) to (vi) or paragraph (b) of the definition "pension income" in this subsection received by the individual as a consequence of the death of a spouse or common-law partner of the individual.

Related Provisions: 104(27) — Flow-out of pension benefits by trust; 118(5) — Alimony and maintenance; 118(8) — Limitations; 118.7 — Credit for EI premium and CPP contribution; 248(8) — Meaning of "consequence" of death.

Notes: See Notes to "pension income" above.

For a taxpayer under 65, pension income must be "qualified pension income" (QPE) to qualify for 118(3) credit or 60.03 income splitting.

An RRSP or RRIF does not produce QPE: *Whalen*, [1995] 1 C.T.C. 2339 (TCC); VIEWS docs 2008-0273681E5, 2008-0281261M4, 2008-0282561E5. Payments from a RRIF are not payments out of a pension plan merely because the original source of funds was a pension plan: *Kennedy*, [2001] 4 C.T.C. 2192 (TCC); 2003-0011587, 2006-0201251M4. Payments from a locked-in retirement fund or life income fund are not QPE, since the fund is not a life annuity: *Cheberiak*, [2002] 2 C.T.C. 2348 (TCC); *Letarte*, 2005 TCC 420; 2014-0523311C6 [2014 CALU q.4]. Nor, in the CRA's view, is life annuity income attributed from an under-65 spouse to an over-65 spouse under 74.1(1): 2008-0284411C6; or RRIF income attributed under 146.3(5.4): 2007-0257001E5. For "as a consequence of the death", see 248(8) and 2008-0284401C6. See also the exclusions in 118(8); and 60.03 Notes for other cases where pension income splitting was denied.

Para. (b) amended by 2000 same-sex partners bill (effective 2001), 1992 technical bill.

Interpretation Bulletins: IT-500R: RRSPS — death of an annuitant; IT-517R: Pension tax credit (cancelled).

(8) Interpretation — For the purposes of subsection (7), "pension income" and "qualified pension income" received by an individual in a taxation year do not include any amount that is

(a) the amount of a pension or supplement under the *Old Age Security Act* or of any similar payment under a law of a province;

(b) the amount of a benefit under the *Canada Pension Plan* or under a provincial pension plan as defined in section 3 of that Act;

(c) a death benefit;

(d) the amount, if any, by which

(i) an amount required to be included in computing the individual's income for the year

exceeds

(ii) the amount, if any, by which the amount referred to in subparagraph (i) exceeds the total of all amounts deducted (other than under paragraph 60(c)) by the individual for the year in respect of that amount;

(e) a payment received out of or under a salary deferral arrangement, a retirement compensation arrangement, an employee benefit plan or an employee trust; or

(f) a payment (other than a payment under the *Judges Act* or the *Lieutenant Governors Superannuation Act*) received out of or under an unfunded supplemental plan or arrangement, being a plan or arrangement where

(i) the payment was in respect of services rendered to an employer by the individual or the individual's spouse or common-law partner or former spouse or common-law partner as an employee, and

(ii) the plan or arrangement would have been a retirement compensation arrangement or an employee benefit plan had the employer made a contribution in respect of the payment to a trust governed by the plan or arrangement.

Related Provisions: 118.91 — Individual resident in Canada for part of the year; 118.92 — Ordering of credits; 118.93 — Credits in separate returns; 118.94 — Credit restriction for non-resident individual.

Notes: In *Talbot*, 2013 TCC 2, a Hydro-Québec lump sum pension prepayment during phased retirement fell under 118(8)(e).

A pension paid from a provincial supplemental pension plan appears to fall under 118(8)(f): VIEWS doc 2008-0299941E5. See also 2011-0425871E5.

118(8)(e) amended by 2011 budget bill #2, effective 2010, to delete "or a prescribed provincial pension plan". 118(7)"pension income"(a)(i) now covers a "specified pension plan" (the Saskatchewan Pension Plan).

118(8) amended by 2007 budget bill #1, for 2007 and later tax years.

Interpretation Bulletins: IT-517R: Pension tax credit (cancelled).

(8.1) Bridging benefits — For the purposes of subsection (7), a payment in respect of a life annuity under a superannuation or pension plan is deemed to include a payment in respect of bridging benefits, being benefits payable under a registered pension plan on a periodic basis and not less frequently than annually to an individual where

(a) the individual or the individual's spouse or common-law partner or former spouse or common-law partner was a member (as defined in subsection 147.1(1)) of the registered pension plan;

(b) the benefits are payable for a period ending no later than the end of the month following the month in which the member attains 65 years of age or would have attained that age if the member had survived to that day; and

(c) the amount (expressed on an annualized basis) of the benefits payable to the individual for a calendar year does not exceed the total of the maximum amount of benefits payable for that year

under Part I of the *Old Age Security Act* and the maximum amount of benefits (other than disability, death or survivor benefits) payable for that year under either the *Canada Pension Plan* or a provincial pension plan as defined in section 3 of that Act.

Notes: 118(8.1) added by 2007 budget bill #1, for 2007 and later taxation years.

(9) [Repealed]

Notes: 118(9) repealed by 2009 budget bill #1, for 2009 and later taxation years. It provided for rounding of certain amounts in 118(3.1) and (3.2) to the nearest dollar. Added by 2006 Budget and amended by 2007 budget bill #1.

(9.1) Child tax credit — For greater certainty, in the case of a child who in a taxation year is born, adopted or dies, the reference to "throughout the taxation year" in subparagraph 118(1)(b.1)(i) is to be read as a reference to "throughout the portion of the taxation year that is after the child's birth or adoption or before the child's death".

Notes: This rule was applied in *Kimber*, 2017 TCC 197, para. 17. For CRA interpretation see VIEWS docs 2009-0308111I7, 2010-0382341E5, 2011-040389117, 2012-0440261E5 and Notes to 118(1)B(b.1).

118(9.1) added by 2007 budget bill #1, for 2007 and later tax years.

(10) Canada Employment Credit — For the purpose of computing the tax payable under this Part by an individual for a taxation year, there may be deducted the amount determined by the formula

$$A \times B$$

where

A is the appropriate percentage for the taxation year; and

B is the lesser of

(a) $1,000[16], and

(b) the total of all amounts, each of which is an amount included in computing the individual's income for the taxation year from an office or employment or an amount included in the taxpayer's income for the taxation year because of subparagraph 56(1)(r)(v).

Related Provisions: 8(1)(r)(ii)B(B)(I) — Apprentice mechanics' tools deduction based on amount of Canada Employment Credit; 117.1(2)(i) — Indexing of $1,000 to inflation after 2007; 118.8 — Application of credit on transfer of unused credits to spouse; 118.91 — Part-year resident; 118.95(b) — Application in year individual becomes bankrupt.

Notes: This credit is worth $187 for 2020 ($1,245 × 15%) and $189 for 2021 ($1,257 × 15%). It helps compensate for relatively few employment expenses being deductible (8(1), 8(2)); see Notes to 8(1)(a) re pre-1988 8(1)(a); VIEWS doc 2010-0365351E5. See also the Canada Workers Benefit in 122.7, for low-income workers.

118(10) (Canada Employment Credit) applies only to income from office/employment, and EI-like benefits under 56(1)(r)(iv) (including the Canada Emergency Response Benefit). CRA T1 Guide, Line 31260 says it applies to "the total of the employment income you reported on line 10100 and line 10400" [former lines 101, 104], but this still means only *employment* income, not research grants (56(1)(o)) and certain other amounts that go on Line 10400. Note that employment need not have been in Canada.

The credit is available for post-retirement income, if it is taxed as employment income: VIEWS doc 2010-0373051E5.

118(10)B(b) amended for 2008 and later tax years by 2008 budget bill #2, effectively to refer to 56(1)(r)(v). Deleting "if this Act were read without reference to section 8" means that deductions from employment income are allowed in the calculation.

118(10) added by 2006 budget bill #2, for 2006 and later taxation years, but for 2006, read "$1,000" as "$250".

Forms: T1 General return, Line 31260 [former 363].

Definitions [s. 118]: "amount", "annuity", "appropriate percentage" — 248(1); "aunt" — 252(2)(e); "basic personal amount" — 118(1.1); "brother" — 252(2); "calendar year" — *Interpretation Act* 37(1)(a); "Canada" — 255; "child" — 118(5), 252(1); "common-law partner", "common-law partnership" — 248(1); "consequence of the death" — 248(8); "death benefit" — 248(1); "deferred profit sharing plan" — 147(1), 248(1); "dependant" — 118(5), (6); "disposition" — 248(1); "eligible pension income" — 248(1); "employee", "employer", "employee benefit plan", "employee trust" — 248(1); "grandparent" — 252(2); "income" — 118(4)(a.2); "individual", "Minister" — 248(1); "money purchase provision" — 147.1(1); "month" — *Interpretation Act* 35(1); "nephew", "niece" — 252(2)(g); "parent" — 252(2)(a); "payment in respect of a life annuity" — 118(8.1); "pension income" — 118(7), (8); "person" — 248(1); "pooled registered pension plan" — 147.5(1), 248(1); "prescribed", "property" — 248(1); "province" — *Interpretation Act* 35(1); "provincial pension plan" —

---

[16] Indexed after 2007 by 117.1 — ed.

Canada Pension Plan s. 3; "qualified pension income" — 118(7), (8); "real servitude" — Quebec *Civil Code* art. 1177; "received" — 248(7); "registered pension plan" — 248(1); "registered retirement income fund" — 146.3(1), 248(1); "registered retirement savings plan" — 146(1), 248(1); "related" — 251(2); "resident in Canada" — 250; "retirement compensation arrangement", "salary deferral arrangement", "self-contained domestic establishment" — 248(1); "sister" — 252(2); "specified pension plan" — 248(1), Reg. 7800; "spouse" — 118(5); "surplus adjustment" — 122.52(1); "tax payable" — 248(2); "taxation year" — 249; "trust" — 104(1), 248(1), (3); "uncle" — 252(2)(e).

Interpretation Bulletins [s. 118]: IT-83R3: Non-profit organizations — Taxation of income from property; IT-171R2: Non-resident individuals — computation of taxable income earned in Canada and non-refundable tax credits (cancelled); IT-326R3: Returns of deceased persons as "another person"; IT-393R2: Election re tax on rents and timber royalties — non-residents.

Information Circulars [s. 118]: 07-1R1: Taxpayer relief provisions.

118.01 [Adoption expense credit] — (1) Definitions — The following definitions apply in this section.

"adoption period", in respect of an eligible child of an individual, means the period that

(a) begins at the earlier of the time that an application is made for registration with a provincial ministry responsible for adoption (or with an adoption agency licensed by a provincial government) and the time, if any, that an application related to the adoption is made to a Canadian court; and

(b) ends at the later of the time an adoption order is issued by, or recognized by, a government in Canada in respect of that child, and the time that the child first begins to reside permanently with the individual.

Notes: Para. (a) amended by 2013 budget bill #1 to change "the eligible child's adoption file is opened" to "an application is made for registration". The Budget papers stated that this is "to better recognize that there are costs that adoptive parents must incur prior to being matched with a child". The amendment was stated to apply "to the 2013 and subsequent taxation years". CRA interprets this to mean adoption credit claims made for 2013 and later years (rather than only if the extended adoption period begins in 2013 or later): VIEWS doc 2013-0515791E5, addressed to the author.

"eligible adoption expense", in respect of an eligible child of an individual, means an amount paid for expenses incurred during the adoption period in respect of the adoption of that child, including

(a) fees paid to an adoption agency licensed by a provincial government;

(b) court costs and legal and administrative expenses related to an adoption order in respect of that child;

(c) reasonable and necessary travel and living expenses of that child and the adoptive parents;

(d) document translation fees;

(e) mandatory fees paid to a foreign institution;

(f) mandatory expenses paid in respect of the immigration of that child; and

(g) any other reasonable expenses related to the adoption required by a provincial government or an adoption agency licensed by a provincial government.

Related Provisions: 67.1(1) — Food and entertainment 50% rule does not apply.

Notes: Where fees are paid to multiple agencies, para. (a) applies only to those that result in an adoption: VIEWS doc 2017-0692561E5.

CRA considers that para. (g) does not include moving expenses, because parents naturally bearing children incur such expenses: VIEWS doc 2010-0377851E5. Surrogacy costs do not qualify: 2014-0518931E5.

"eligible child", of an individual, means a child who has not attained the age of 18 years at the time that an adoption order is issued or recognized by a government in Canada in respect of the adoption of that child by that individual.

Notes: Adoption by a step-parent qualifies: VIEWS doc 2019-0797671E5.

(2) Adoption expense tax credit — For the purpose of computing the tax payable under this Part by an individual for the taxation

year that includes the end of the adoption period in respect of an eligible child of the individual, there may be deducted the amount determined by the formula

$$A \times B$$

where

A   is the appropriate percentage for the taxation year; and

B   is the lesser of

(a) \$15,000[17], and

(b) the amount determined by the formula

$$C - D$$

where

C   is the total of all eligible adoption expenses in respect of the eligible child, and

D   is the total of all amounts each of which is the amount of a reimbursement or any other form of assistance (other than an amount that is included in computing the individual's income and that is not deductible in computing the individual's taxable income) that any individual is or was entitled to receive in respect of an amount included in computing the value of C.

Related Provisions: 117.1(2)(j) — Indexing for inflation; 118.01(3) — Apportionment of credit between parents; 118.91 — Part-year resident; 118.92 — Ordering of credits; 118.93 — Credits in separate returns; 118.94 — Credit restriction for non-resident individual; 118.95(a) — Application in year individual becomes bankrupt; 257 — Formula cannot calculate to less than zero.

Notes: See at end of 118.01.

118.01(2)B(a) amended to change \$10,000 to \$15,000 by 2014 budget bill #1, for 2014 and later tax years; the \$15,000 is indexed after 2014.

Forms: T1 General return, Line 31300.

(3) Apportionment of credit — Where more than one individual is entitled to a deduction under this section for a taxation year in respect of the adoption of an eligible child, the total of all amounts so deductible shall not exceed the maximum amount that would be so deductible for the year by any one of those individuals for that child if that individual were the only individual entitled to deduct an amount for the year under this section, and if the individuals cannot agree as to what portion of the amount each can so deduct, the Minister may fix the portions.

Notes [s. 118.01]: 118.01 provides a federal credit of 15% of "eligible adoption expenses" (118.01(1)) on completed adoption of an "eligible child" (118.01(1)), up to maximum expenses of \$16,563 (2020) or \$16,729 (2021). The expenses must have been incurred during the "adoption period" (118.01(1)), and are claimed for the year in which the adoption period ends. The parent must submit proof of adoption in the form of a Canadian or foreign adoption order, or otherwise demonstrate that all legal requirements of the parent's jurisdiction have been met. Any expenses for which the adoptive parent has been or is entitled to be reimbursed are excluded: 118.01(2)D.

Expenses of attempting to adopt child A, if child B is adopted instead, do not qualify: VIEWS doc 2012-0444001E5.

Several provinces offer a parallel credit. Quebec's is in *Taxation Act* ss. 1029.8.63–1029.8.66.

118.01 added by 2006 budget bill #1 for 2005 and later tax years.

Definitions [s. 118.01]: "adoption period" — 118.01(1); "amount", "appropriate percentage" — 248(1); "Canada" — 255, *Interpretation Act* 35(1); "child" — 252(1); "eligible adoption expense", "eligible child" — 118.01(1); "individual", "Minister" — 248(1); "parent" — 252(2)(a); "provincial" — *Interpretation Act* 33(3), 35(1)"province"; "related" — 251(2)–(6); "taxable income" — 248(1); "taxation year" — 249.

Income Tax Folios [s. 118.01]: S1-F1-C2: Disability tax credit [replaces IT-519R2].

118.02 [Digital news subscription credit] — (1) Definitions — The following definitions apply in this section.

"digital news subscription", of an individual with a qualified Canadian journalism organization, means an agreement entered into

---

[17] Indexed by 117.1 after 2014 — ed.

between the individual and the qualified Canadian journalism organization, if

(a) the agreement entitles an individual to access content of the qualified Canadian journalism organization in digital form and that content is primarily original written news; and

(b) the qualified Canadian journalism organization does not hold a "licence" as defined in subsection 2(1) of the *Broadcasting Act*.

Notes: For the meaning of "primarily" see 73(3) Notes. For "broadcasting undertaking" in para. (b), see Notes to 125.6(1)"qualifying journalism organization".

Broadcasting Act s. 2(1) defines "licence" as "a licence to carry on a broadcasting undertaking issued by the Commission under this Act", and defines "Commission" as the Canadian Radio-television and Telecommunications Commission.

Paras. (a), (b) amended by 2021 budget bill #1, effective 2020. The previous version (now replaced retroactively, so never in force) read:

(a) the agreement entitles an individual to access content of the qualified Canadian journalism organization in digital form; and

(b) the qualified Canadian journalism organization is primarily engaged in the production of original written news content and is not engaged in a "broadcasting undertaking" as defined in subsection 2(1) of the *Broadcasting Act*.

"qualifying subscription expense", for a taxation year, means the amount paid in the year for a digital news subscription of an individual with a qualified Canadian journalism organization and, for this purpose, if the digital news subscription provides access to content in non-digital form or content other than content of qualified Canadian journalism organizations, the amount considered to be paid for the digital news subscription shall not exceed

(a) the cost of a comparable digital news subscription with the qualified Canadian journalism organization that solely provides access to content of qualified Canadian journalism organizations in digital form; and

(b) if there is no such comparable digital news subscription, 1/2 of the amount actually paid.

Related Provisions: 118.02(4), (5) — If expense ceases to qualify; 241(3.4) — CRA may publish list of qualifying subscriptions.

Notes: CRA is permitted to publish a list of qualifying subscriptions: 241(3.4).

This definition does not directly require CRA's agreement, but the organization must be a QCJO to qualify, and 248(1)"qualifying Canadian journalism organization"(b) requires designation by the Minister. An organization that CRA refuses to designate would have to apply to the Federal Court for judicial review (see 220(3.1) Notes re the *Vavilov* standard of "reasonable"), before subscribers can claim the 118.02 credit.

(2) Digital news subscription tax credit

— For the purpose of computing the tax payable under this Part by an individual for a taxation year that is before 2025, there may be deducted the amount determined by the formula

$$A \times B$$

where

A   is the appropriate percentage for the year; and

B   is the lesser of

(a) $500[2], and

(b) the total of all amounts each of which is a qualifying subscription expense of the individual for the year.

Related Provisions: 118.02(3) — Apportionment of credit; 118.92 — Ordering of credits; 241(3.4) — CRA may publish list of qualifying subscriptions.

Notes: The "appropriate percentage" in 248(1) is 15%, so this credit is for up to $75 ($500 of digital news subscriptions per year). See CRA Q&A, "Digital news subscription tax credit" (May 3, 2019), tinyurl.com/cra-dnstc; *Guidance on the income tax measures to support journalism* (tinyurl.com/cra-journalism, Dec. 2019), §4.

For the other 2019 Budget measures supporting journalism see Notes to 248(1)"qualified Canadian journalism organization". Budget Table 1 predicts this credit will cost the federal government $5 million in 2019-20, $26m in 2020-21, $31m in 2021-22, $36m in 2022-23 and $41m in 2023-24.

(3) Apportionment of credit

— If more than one individual is entitled to a deduction under this section for a taxation year in respect of a qualifying subscription expense, the total of all amounts

so deductible shall not exceed the maximum amount that would be so deductible for the year by any one of those individuals in respect of the qualifying subscription expense, if that individual were the only individual entitled to deduct an amount for the year under this section, and if the individuals cannot agree as to what portion of the amount each can so deduct, the Minister may fix the portions.

(4) Ceasing to qualify

— For the purposes of subsection (1), if amounts paid under an agreement cease to be qualifying subscription expenses at any particular time in a calendar year and, at the particular time, the Minister has communicated or otherwise made available pursuant to paragraph 241(3.4)(b) that these amounts qualify as qualifying subscription expenses, amounts paid under that agreement are deemed to be qualifying subscription expenses — to the same extent that the amounts paid were considered to be qualifying subscription expenses immediately before the particular time — until the end of the calendar year in which the Minister communicates or otherwise makes available pursuant to paragraph 241(3.4)(b) that amounts paid under the agreement no longer qualify as qualifying subscription expenses.

Related Provisions: 118.02(5) — Notice to subscribers if expenses cease to qualify.

Notes: If a subscription has been listed by CRA as qualifying, then once it ceases to qualify it continues to be eligible for the credit until the end of the year that CRA publishes a notice that it no longer qualifies. The organization must notify subscribers if subscriptions cease to qualify: 118.02(5).

118.02(4) added by 2021 budget bill #1, effective 2020.

(5) Notice to individuals

— If an organization enters into a digital news subscription agreement with an individual and amounts paid under the agreement cease to be qualifying subscription expenses, the organization shall inform the individual that amounts paid under the agreement are no longer qualifying subscription expenses.

Notes: 118.02(5) added by 2021 budget bill #1, effective 2020.

Notes [s. 118.02]: 118.02 added by 2019 budget bill #1, for 2020 and later tax years. See Notes to 118.02(2).

Former 118.02 repealed by 2017 Budget first bill, effective 2018. From July 2006 through July 2017 it provided the **Public Transit Pass Credit**, of 15% of the amount paid for a public transit pass that met certain conditions. It had been introduced by the Conservatives and was eliminated by the Liberal government.

The amendment to 118.02(2)C before repeal means that a taxpayer who stocked up on a year's worth of passes early in 2017, expecting the credit to be eliminated, does not get the credit for passes used after June 2017. A pass that crosses over July 1 can be claimed *pro rata*, e.g. 1/2 for a full-2017 pass: tinyurl.com/cra-transit.

2016 Budget Table 1 predicted that the repeal of 118.02 would save the federal government $150 million in 2017-18, $205m in 2018-19, $210m in 2019-20, $220m in 2020-21 and $225m in 2021-22. The Parliamentary Budget Officer (May 23, 2017) reported that 1.2 million Canadians will pay on average an extra $137 in (annual?) federal tax due to the credit's repeal; that 185,000 people benefiting from the credit (15.4% of all those benefiting) earn annual after-tax income below $22,600; and that "it is unlikely the elimination of this single tax incentive will materially affect ridership choices".

Ontario provides a 15% credit for those over 65, since July 2017: Didkovsky, "Ontario Seniors' Public Transit Credit", 7(4) *Canadian Tax Focus* (ctf.ca) 6-7 (Nov. 2017); VIEWS doc 2017-0733511E5.

118.02 provided:

118.02 [Pre-July 2017 public transit pass credit] — (1) Definitions — The following definitions apply in this section.

"eligible electronic payment card" means an electronic payment card that is

(a) used by an individual for at least 32 one-way trips, between the place of origin of the trip and its termination, during an uninterrupted period not exceeding 31 days, and

(b) issued by or on behalf of a qualified Canadian transit organization, which organization records and receipts the cost and usage of the electronic payment card and identifies the right, of the individual who is the holder or owner of such a card, to use public commuter transit services of that qualified Canadian transit organization.

Notes [Former 118.02(1)"eligible electronic payment card"]: A round trip counts as two one-way trips: VIEWS doc 2009-0316211E5. "Uninterrupted period" means that at least 32 trips must be taken during the 31-day period, but not that a trip must be taken on each day in the period: 2011-0393491E5. See also 2013-0510991I7.

---

[2] Not indexed for inflation — ed.

118.02(1)"eligible electronic payment card" added by 2007 Budget second bill, effective for 2007 and later taxation years.

"eligible public transit pass" means a document

    (a) issued by or on behalf of a qualified Canadian transit organization; and

    (b) identifying the right of an individual who is the holder or owner of the document to use public commuter transit services of that qualified Canadian transit organization

        (i) on an unlimited number of occasions and on any day on which the public commuter transit services are offered during an uninterrupted period of at least 28 days, or

        (ii) on an unlimited number of occasions during an uninterrupted period of at least 5 consecutive days, if the combination of that document and one or more other such documents gives the right to the individual to use those public commuter transit services on at least 20 days in a 28-day period.

Notes [Former 118.02(1)"eligible public transit pass"]: This test can be met by a combination of weekly passes that together entitle the rider to ride on at least 20 days in a 28-day period: VIEWS doc 2010-038249117.

118.02(1)"eligible public transit pass"(b)(ii) added by 2007 Budget second bill, effective for 2007 and later taxation years. See Notes to 118.02(2).

"public commuter transit services" means services offered to the general public, ordinarily for a period of at least five days per week, of transporting individuals, from a place in Canada to another place in Canada, by means of bus, ferry, subway, train or tram, and in respect of which it can reasonably be expected that those individuals would return daily to the place of their departure.

"qualified Canadian transit organization" means a person authorised, under a law of Canada or a province, to carry on in Canada a business that is the provision of public commuter transit services, which is carried on through a permanent establishment (as defined by regulation) in Canada.

Notes [Former 118.02(1)"qualified Canadian transit organization"]: Definition amended by 2002-2013 technical bill (Part 5 — technical) to change "permanent establishment (as defined by regulation)" from "permanent establishment", effective for 2009 and later taxation years. (See Reg. 8201.)

Regulations [Former 118.02(1)"qualified Canadian transit organization"]: 8201 (meaning of "permanent establishment").

"qualifying relation" of an individual for a taxation year means a person who is

    (a) the individual's spouse or common-law partner at any time in the taxation year; or

    (b) a child of the individual who has not, during the taxation year, attained the age of 19 years.

(2) Transit pass tax credit — For the purpose of computing the tax payable under this Part by an individual for a taxation year, there may be deducted the amount determined by the formula

$$A \times B$$

where

A   is the appropriate percentage for the taxation year; and

B   is the amount determined by the formula

$$C - D$$

where

C   is the total of all amounts each of which is the portion of the cost of an eligible public transit pass or of an eligible electronic payment card, attributable to the use of public commuter transit services in the taxation year and before July 2017 by the individual or by a person who is in the taxation year a qualifying relation of the individual, and

D   is the total of all amounts each of which is the amount of a reimbursement, allowance or any other form of assistance that any person is or was entitled to receive in respect of an amount included in computing the value of C (other than an amount that is included in computing the income for any taxation year of that person and that is not deductible in computing the taxable income of that person).

Related Provisions [Former 118.02(2)]: 118.02(3) — Apportionment of credit where more than one person eligible; 118.91 — Part-year resident; 118.92 — Ordering of credits; 118.93 — Credits in separate returns; 118.94 — Credit restriction for non-resident individual; 118.95(a) — Application in year individual becomes bankrupt; 257 — Formula cannot calculate to less than zero.

Notes [Former 118.02(2)]: The credit applied at the lowest marginal rate (15% since 2007); see 248(1)"appropriate percentage", 117(2), VIEWS doc 2006-0208541M4), and so was equivalent to a deduction from the "bottom" of income rather than the top. The credit applied before the tuition and education credits (118.92; 2006-0207361M4).

Ten-ride paper tickets do not qualify: *Taino*, 2012 TCC 272; *Stewart*, 2012 TCC 435.

A Presto card (bought from Toronto Transit Commission) qualified in *Mendoza*, 2016 TCC 112; the credit was not lost merely because the TTC refused to produce a usage report.

In *Komarynsky*, 2014 TCC 342, para. 7, the credit was disallowed because the taxpayer failed to establish that he purchased monthly transit passes.

A daily pass or cash fare is not eligible for the credit (but weekly passes can be eligible); see 118.02(1)"eligible public transit pass" (VIEWS docs 2006-0204311M4, 2006-0204321M4, 2006-006491M4, 2006-0216211M4, 2007-0240601M4, 2007-0243821M4). Nor is a GO Transit 10-ride pass: 2008-0298991E5. Swipe cards that provide a fixed number of rides did not qualify: 2007-0225892M4, but see now 118.02(1)"eligible electronic payment card". An 8-passenger commuter van does not qualify: see 118.02(1)"public commuter transit services" (2006-0187801E5, 2007-0225601M4, 2007-0232661M4). Ferry service qualifies, including car ferries, but only the fare charged for the individual (without car) qualifies for the credit: 2006-0208601E5. A privately-owned company can be a qualified Canadian transit organization: 2006-0209281M4, 2007-0244091M4; but not an employer that is reimbursing employee commuting costs: 2012-044071117. Transporting public school students on a school bus under a user-pay system is likely not "services offered to the general public" for 118.02(1)"public commuter transit services": 2009-0323321E5. A bike-sharing program does not qualify: 2010-0377101M4.

118.02(2)B:C amended by 2017 Budget first bill, for the 2017 taxation year, to add "and before July 2017".

118.02(2)C amended by 2007 Budget second bill, effective for 2007 and later taxation years, to add reference to "eligible electronic payment card".

(3) Apportionment of credit — If more than one individual is entitled to a deduction under this section for a taxation year in respect of an eligible public transit pass or of an eligible electronic payment card, the total of all amounts so deductible shall not exceed the maximum amount that would be so deductible for the year by any one of those individuals for that eligible public transit pass or eligible electronic payment card if that individual were the only individual entitled to deduct an amount for the year under this section, and if the individuals cannot agree as to what portion of the amount each can so deduct, the Minister may fix the portions.

Notes [Former 118.02(3)]: 118.02(3) amended by 2007 Budget second bill, effective for 2007 and later taxation years, to add references to "eligible electronic payment card".

Notes [Former 118.02]: 118.02 added by 2006 Budget second bill, for 2006 and later tax years, for use of public commuter transit services after June 2006.

Definitions [Former 118.02]: "amount", "appropriate percentage", "business" — 248(1); "Canada" — 255, *Interpretation Act* 35(1); "child" — 252(1); "common-law partner" — 248(1); "eligible electronic payment card", "eligible public transit pass" — 118.02(1); "individual", "Minister" — 248(1); "permanent establishment" — Reg. 8201; "person" — 248(1); "province" — *Interpretation Act* 35(1); "public commuter transit services", "qualified Canadian transit organization", "qualifying relation" — 118.02(1); "record", "regulation", "taxable income" — 248(1); "taxation year" — 249.

Definitions [s. 118.02]: "amount", "appropriate percentage" — 248(1); "calendar year" — *Interpretation Act* 37(1)(a); "digital news subscription" — 118.02(1); "individual", "Minister", "qualified Canadian journalism organization" — 248(1); "qualifying subscription expense" — 118.02(1); "taxation year" — 249; "written" — *Interpretation Act* 35(1)"writing".

118.03 [Repealed]

Notes: 118.03 provided the Children's Fitness Credit, 15% of up to $1,000 of qualifying expenses. Repealed by 2014 budget bill #2 for 2015 and later tax years, as it was moved to 122.8 as a refundable credit (eliminated after 2016). 118.03 added by 2006 budget bill #2, for 2007 and later tax years; amended by 2007 budget bill #2 retroactive to its introduction.

118.031 [Repealed]

Notes: 118.031 implemented the Children's Arts Tax Credit, giving parents a $75 non-refundable credit per child (15% of max $500, not indexed for inflation) for eligible expenses. It was available for enrolment of a child, under 16 at start of year, in an eligible program of artistic, cultural, recreational or developmental activities (Reg. 9401). For a child under 18 at start of year who was eligible for the disability credit, 15% could be claimed on an extra $500 once at least $100 was paid in eligible expenses.

118.031 added by 2011 (Conservative) budget bill #2, for 2011 and later tax years. The Liberals halved it for 2016 and repealed it for 2017 and later years. For 2016, read:

    118.031 [Children's arts tax credit] — (1) Definitions — The following definitions apply in this section.

    "eligible expense" in respect of a qualifying child of an individual for a taxation year means the amount of a fee paid to a qualifying entity (other than an amount paid to a person who is, at the time the amount is paid, the individual's spouse or common-law partner or another individual who is under 18 years of age) to the extent that the fee is attributable to the cost of registration or membership of the qualifying child in a prescribed program of artistic, cultural, recreational or developmental activity and, for the purposes of this section, that cost

(a) includes the cost to the qualifying entity of the program in respect of its administration, instruction, rental of required facilities, and uniforms and equipment that are not available to be acquired by a participant in the program for an amount less than their fair market value at the time, if any, they are so acquired; and

(b) does not include

(i) the cost of accommodation, travel, food or beverages,

(ii) any amount deductible in computing any person's income for any taxation year, or

(iii) any amount included in computing a deduction from any person's tax payable under any Part of this Act, for any taxation year.

Notes [former 118.031(1)"eligible expense"]: Costs of programs includes sales taxes: VIEWS doc 2012-0437491M4. For a list of what should appear on receipts see that doc or 2011-0422861M4 (also notes that the supplier can be an individual). Where an expense may also qualify for the Children's Fitness Credit and/or as a child-care expense, see Notes to 118.03(2).

The following can qualify: Beaver Scouts (VIEWS doc 2012-04387311M4); math tutoring (2011-0423081M4); music therapy (2011-0418751M4); optional 6-day school trip outside school's curriculum (2012-0441061M4); photography lessons (2012-0328041M4); piano and vocal lessons (2011-0418771M4); specialized arts program (2011-0421401M4). Martial arts programs do not qualify because they are eligible under 118.03: doc 2012-0437311M4 (Reg. 9401(1) opening words exclude a "physical activity"). Driving school does not qualify: 2012-0434191E5.

Regulations [former 118.031(1)"eligible expense"]: 9401 (prescribed program) "qualifying child" of an individual has the meaning assigned by subsection 122.8(1).

Notes [former 118.031(1)"qualifying child"]: Definition amended by 2014 budget bill #2, for 2015 and later taxation years, to change "118.03(1)" to "122.8(1)".

"qualifying entity" means a person or partnership that offers one or more programs of artistic, cultural, recreational or developmental activity prescribed for the purposes of the definition "eligible expense".

(2) **Children's arts tax credit** — For the purpose of computing the tax payable under this Part by an individual for a taxation year, there may be deducted the amount determined by the formula

$$A \times B$$

where

A   is the appropriate percentage for the taxation year; and

B   is the total of all amounts each of which is, in respect of a qualifying child of the individual for the taxation year, the lesser of $250 and the amount determined by the formula

$$C - D$$

where

C   is total of all amounts each of which is an amount paid in the taxation year by the individual, or by the individual's spouse or common-law partner, that is an eligible expense in respect of the qualifying child of the individual, and

D   is the total of all amounts that any person is or was entitled to receive, each of which relates to an amount included in computing the value determined for C in respect of the qualifying child that is the amount of a reimbursement, allowance or any other form of assistance (other than an amount that is included in computing the income for any taxation year of that person and that is not deductible in computing the taxable income of that person).

Related Provisions [former 118.031(2)]: 118.031(3) — Credit for child with disability; 118.031(4) — Apportionment of credit; 118.91 — Part-year resident; 118.92 — Ordering of credits; 118.93 — Credits in separate returns; 118.94 — Credit restriction for non-resident individual; 118.95(a) — Application in year individual becomes bankrupt.

Notes [former 118.031(2)]: The "appropriate percentage" (248(1)) is 15%, so this credit is 15% of up to $500 (maximum $75) for 2011-15, and 15% of up to $250 for 2016.

B amended by 2016 budget bill #1, effective for the 2016 taxation year, to change "$500" to "$250", en route to eliminating this credit as of 2017.

(3) **Children's arts tax credit — child with disability** — For the purpose of computing the tax payable under this Part by an individual for a taxation year there may be deducted in respect of a qualifying child of the individual an amount equal to $500 multiplied by the appropriate percentage for the taxation year if

(a) the amount referred to in the description of B in subsection (2) is $100 or more; and

(b) an amount is deductible in respect of the qualifying child under section 118.3 in computing any person's tax payable under this Part for the taxation year.

Notes [former 118.031(3)]: The credit under 118.031(3) is in addition to the credit under 118.031(2).

(4) **Apportionment of credit** — If more than one individual is entitled to a deduction under this section for a taxation year in respect of a qualifying child, the total of all amounts so deductible shall not exceed the maximum amount that would be so deductible for the year by any one of those individuals in respect of that qualifying child if that individual were the only individual entitled to deduct an amount for the year under this section in respect of that qualifying child, and if the individuals cannot agree as to what portion of the amount each can so deduct, the Minister may fix the portions.

Definitions [former 118.031]: "amount", "appropriate percentage" — 248(1); "child" — 252(1); "common-law partner" — 248(1); "eligible expense" — 118.031(1); "fair market value" — see Notes to 69(1); "individual", "Minister" — 248(1); "partnership" — see Notes to 96(1); "person", "prescribed" — 248(1); "prescribed program" — Reg. 9401; "qualifying child" — 118.031(1), 122.8(1); "qualifying entity" — 118.031(1); "taxable income" — 248(1); "taxation year" — 249.

Income Tax Folios [former 118.031]: S1-F3-C1: Child care expense deduction [replaces IT-495R3]

See also Notes to 118.031(1)"eligible expense". If the organization refuses to issue a receipt, it cannot be forced to, but the taxpayer may provide other proof of payment: 2012-0439611M4.

For discussion of this and the parallel provincial credits in SK, MB, ON, NS and YK see M. Lori Adams, "Children's Arts and Cultural Activities", 4 *Provincial Tax News* (CCH) 3-5 (Sept. 2011). BC introduced a parallel credit in its March 2012 Budget.

118.04 [Home renovation tax credit — 2009 only] — [No longer relevant.]

Notes [s. 118.04]: 118.04 provided a non-refundable Home Renovation Tax Credit for the 2009 tax year only, as announced in the 2009 federal Budget, of 15% of qualifying expenditures over $1,000 and up to $10,000 (maximum $1,350 credit), for renovation expenses incurred from Jan. 28/09 through Jan. 31/10. For detailed discussion including VIEWS docs approving specific renovations (possibly still relevant for 118.041(1)"qualifying expenditure" and "qualifying renovation"), see these Notes up to PITA 54th ed., or the Notes in the current electronic version on DVD or *Taxnet Pro*.

118.041 [Home accessibility tax credit] — (1) Definitions — The following definitions apply in this section.

"eligible dwelling" of an individual, at any time in a taxation year, means a housing unit (including the land subjacent to the housing unit and the immediately contiguous land, but not including the portion of that land that exceeds the greater of ½ hectare and the portion of that land that the individual establishes is necessary for the use and enjoyment of the housing unit as a residence) located in Canada if

(a) the individual (or a trust under which the individual is a beneficiary) owns — whether jointly with another person or otherwise — at that time, the housing unit or a share of the capital stock of a co-operative housing corporation acquired for the sole purpose of acquiring the right to inhabit the housing unit owned by the corporation; and

(b) the housing unit is ordinarily inhabited, or is reasonably expected to be ordinarily inhabited, at any time in the taxation year

(i) by the individual, if the individual is a qualifying individual, or

(ii) by the individual and a qualifying individual, if

(A) the individual is an eligible individual in respect of the qualifying individual, and

(B) the qualifying individual does not, throughout the taxation year, own — whether jointly with another person or otherwise — and ordinarily inhabit another housing unit in Canada.

Notes: This definition (largely copied from 118.04(1)) is drawn in part from 54"principal residence"; see Notes to that definition for interpretation.

"eligible individual", in respect of a qualifying individual for a taxation year, means

(a) an individual who is the qualifying individual's spouse or common-law partner in the year;

(b) except if paragraph (c) applies, an individual who is entitled to deduct an amount under subsection 118.3(2) for the year in respect of the qualifying individual or would be if no amount was claimed for the year by the qualifying individual under subsection 118.3(1) or by the qualifying individual's spouse or common-law partner under section 118.8; or

(c) in the case of a qualifying individual who has attained the age of 65 before the end of the year, an individual who

(i) claimed for the year a deduction under subsection 118(1) in respect of the qualifying individual because of

(A) paragraph (b) of the description of B in that subsection, or

(B) paragraph (d) of the description of B in that subsection where the qualifying individual is a parent, grandparent, child, grandchild, brother, sister, aunt, uncle, nephew or niece of the individual, or of the individual's spouse or common-law partner, or

(ii) could have claimed for the year a deduction referred to in subparagraph (i) in respect of the qualifying individual if

(A) the qualifying individual had no income for the year,

(B) in the case of a deduction referred to in clause (i)(A), the individual were not married and not in a common-law partnership, and

(C) in the case of a deduction under subsection 118(1) because of paragraph (d) of the description of B in that subsection in respect of a qualifying individual who is a dependant (within the meaning of subsection 118(6)) of the individual, the qualifying individual was dependent on the individual because of mental or physical infirmity.

Related Provisions: 118.041(7)(a) — If individual dies before turning 65.

Notes: Cl. (c)(i)(B) amended by 2017 budget bill #1, for 2017 and later taxation years, to delete "(c.1) or" before "(d)".

"individual" does not include a trust.

Notes: Other than excluding a trust, 248(1)"individual" applies: a person other than a corporation. Thus, it means only a human being.

"qualifying expenditure" of an individual means an outlay or expense that is made or incurred, during a taxation year, that is directly attributable to a qualifying renovation — of an eligible dwelling of a qualifying individual or an eligible individual in respect of a qualifying individual — and that is the cost of goods acquired or services received during the year and includes an outlay or expense for permits required for, or for the rental of equipment used in the course of, the qualifying renovation, but does not include an outlay or expense

(a) to acquire a property that can be used independently of the qualifying renovation;

(b) that is the cost of annual, recurring or routine repair or maintenance;

(c) to acquire a household appliance;

(d) to acquire an electronic home-entertainment device;

(e) that is the cost of housekeeping, security monitoring, gardening, outdoor maintenance or similar services;

(f) for financing costs in respect of the qualifying renovation;

(g) made or incurred primarily for the purpose of increasing or maintaining the value of the eligible dwelling;

(h) made or incurred for the purpose of gaining or producing income from a business or property;

(i) in respect of goods or services provided by a person not dealing at arm's length with the qualifying individual or the eligible individual, unless the person is registered for the purposes of Part IX of the *Excise Tax Act*; or

(j) to the extent that the outlay or expense can reasonably be considered to be have been reimbursed, otherwise than as assistance from the federal or a provincial government including a grant, subsidy, forgivable loan or a deduction from tax.

Notes: *Para. (g)*: in *Patrie*, 2019 TCC 276, "rickety" stairs to the back garden were replaced with a new deck, stairs and railing. This qualified, since the purpose was to allow Mrs. P access to the garden, not to increase the home's value.

Para. (i) permits a non-arm's length payment if the payee is GST-registered, even if the registration is for a business that has nothing to do with the renovation work — but this ensures that GST/HST is paid on the renovation.

Para. (j): see 12(1)(x) Notes for meaning of "assistance" and related words.

See Notes to 118.04 (the general home renovation credit for 2009) up to the 54th ed. (or the electronic version) for many VIEWS docs on "qualifying expenditure", though this definition is somewhat different.

"qualifying individual", in respect of a taxation year, means an individual

(a) who has attained the age of 65 years before the end of the taxation year; or

(b) in respect of whom an amount is deductible, or would be deductible if this Act were read without reference to paragraph 118.3(1)(c), under section 118.3 in computing a taxpayer's tax payable under this Part for the taxation year.

Related Provisions: 118.041(7) — Effect of bankruptcy or death.

"qualifying renovation" means a renovation or alteration of an eligible dwelling of a qualifying individual or an eligible individual in respect of a qualifying individual that

(a) is of an enduring nature and integral to the eligible dwelling; and

(b) is undertaken to

(i) enable the qualifying individual to gain access to, or to be mobile or functional within, the eligible dwelling, or

(ii) reduce the risk of harm to the qualifying individual within the eligible dwelling or in gaining access to the dwelling.

Notes: Para. (a) is copied from 118.04(1)"qualifying renovation".

For CRA interpretation see VIEWS doc 2015-0598591M4 (general comments).

In *Patrie*, 2019 TCC 276, outside stairs were replaced with a new deck, stairs and railing, to allow Mrs. P access to the garden. This qualified as increasing her access to the "eligible dwelling": paras. 14-16.

(2) Qualifying expenditure rules — For the purpose of this section,

(a) a qualifying expenditure in respect of an eligible dwelling of a particular individual — who is a qualifying individual or an eligible individual in respect of a qualifying individual — includes an outlay or expense made or incurred by a co-operative housing corporation, a condominium corporation (or, for civil law, a syndicate of co-owners) or a similar entity (in this paragraph referred to as the "corporation"), in respect of a property that is owned, administered or managed by that corporation and that includes the eligible dwelling, to the extent of the share of that outlay or expense that is reasonably attributable to the eligible dwelling, if

(i) the outlay or expense would be a qualifying expenditure of the corporation if the corporation were an individual and the property were an eligible dwelling of that individual, and

(ii) the corporation has notified, in writing, either the particular individual or, if the particular individual is an eligible individual in respect of a qualifying individual, the qualifying individual, of the share of the outlay or expense that is attributable to the eligible dwelling; and

(b) a qualifying expenditure in respect of an eligible dwelling of a particular individual — who is a qualifying individual or an eligible individual in respect of a qualifying individual — includes an outlay or expense made or incurred by a trust, in respect of a property owned by the trust that includes the eligible dwelling, to the extent of the share of that outlay or expense that is reasonably attributable to the eligible dwelling, having regard to the amount of the outlays or expenses made or incurred in respect of the eligible dwelling (including, for this purpose, common areas relevant to more than one eligible dwelling), if

    (i) the outlay or expense would be a qualifying expenditure of the trust if the trust were an individual and the property were an eligible dwelling of that individual, and

    (ii) the trust has notified, in writing, either the particular individual or, if the particular individual is an eligible individual in respect of a qualifying individual, the qualifying individual, of the share of the outlay or expense that is attributable to the eligible dwelling.

Related Provisions: 118.04(2) — Similar rules for 2009 home renovation credit.

(3) Home accessibility tax credit — For the purpose of computing the tax payable under this Part by a qualifying individual or an eligible individual, in respect of an eligible dwelling for a taxation year, there may be deducted the amount determined by the formula

$$A \times B$$

where

A is the appropriate percentage for the taxation year; and

B is the lesser of

    (a) $10,000, and

    (b) the total of all amounts, each of which is a qualifying expenditure of the individual in respect of the eligible dwelling for the taxation year.

Related Provisions: 118.041(4) — Double-dipping with medical expense credit; 118.041(5) — Apportionment where more than one person can claim credit; 118.041(6), (7) — Effect of bankruptcy or death; 118.2(2)(l.2) — Medical expense credit for home renovations; 118.91 — Part-year resident; 118.92 — Ordering of credits; 118.93 — Credits in separate returns; 118.94 — Restriction on credit for non-resident individual; 118.95(a) — Credit in year of bankruptcy.

Notes: 118.041 implements the Home Accessibility Tax Credit announced in the 2015 Budget, for accessibility renovations for a person who is over 65 *or* qualifies for the disability tax credit (118.041(1)"qualifying individual"): VIEWS doc 2019-0791601E5.

The credit is non-refundable (see Notes to 118(1)B opening words). It is 15% of up to $10,000 of "qualifying expenditures" (118.041(1)) on "qualifying renovations" (118.041(1)), per "qualifying individual" (118.041(1)), to a maximum of $10,000 per "eligible dwelling" (118.041(1)). Total expenses claimed for any one "qualifying individual" are limited to $10,000: 118.041(5)(a). Two people who qualify (e.g. a married couple both over 65) can claim only one $10,000 amount for the same house: 118.041(5)(b). The expense must be made or incurred by a "qualifying individual" or "eligible individual": VIEWS doc 2015-0606911E5.

See Notes to 118.04 (the general home renovation credit for 2009) up to the 54th ed. for many VIEWS docs on that credit, though 118.041 has some different wording.

The "appropriate percentage" (248(1)) is 15%, the same as the lowest bracket rate under 117(2)(a). The credit is thus 15% of up to $10,000 of qualifying expenditures (i.e., maximum $1,500).

This credit can be doubled up with the medical expense credit under 118.2(2)(l.2) for the same renovation: 118.041(4). For a home *purchase* (rather than renovation) for a person with a disability, see 118.05.

See also Edwin Harris, "Home Accessibility Tax Credit", 12(9) *Tax Hyperion* (Carswell) 1-2 (Sept. 2015); Keith McIntyre, "Introduction of the Home Accessibility Tax Credit", 2015(11) *Tax Times* (Carswell) 1-2 (June 12, 2015).

Some provinces offer a similar credit, e.g. Ontario Seniors' Home Safety Credit (2021), Sask. Home Renovation Tax Credit (Oct. 2020–2022).

Forms: T1 General return, Line 31285.

(4) Interaction with medical expense credit [double dipping allowed] — Despite paragraph 248(28)(b), an amount may be included in determining both an amount under subsection (3) and under section 118.2 if those amounts otherwise qualify to be included for the purposes of those provisions.

Related Provisions: 118.04(4) — Same rule for 2009 home renovation credit.

Notes: See Notes to 118.041(3).

(5) Limits [apportionment of credit] — For the purpose of this section,

    (a) a maximum of $10,000 of qualifying expenditures for a taxation year in respect of a qualifying individual can be claimed

under subsection (3) by the qualifying individual and all eligible individuals in respect of the qualifying individual;

    (b) if there is more than one qualifying individual in respect of an eligible dwelling, a maximum of $10,000 of qualifying expenditures for a taxation year in respect of the eligible dwelling can be claimed under subsection (3) by the qualifying individuals and all eligible individuals in respect of the qualifying individuals; and

    (c) if more than one individual is entitled to a deduction under subsection (3) for a taxation year in respect of the same qualifying individual or the same eligible dwelling and the individuals cannot agree as to what portion of the amount each can so deduct, the Minister may fix the portions.

Related Provisions: 118.03(6) — Effect of bankruptcy.

(6) Effect of bankruptcy — For the purpose of subsection (5), if an individual becomes bankrupt in a particular calendar year, despite subsection 128(2), any reference to the taxation year of the individual is deemed to be a reference to the particular calendar year.

(7) In the event of death and bankruptcy — For the purpose of this section,

    (a) if an individual dies during a calendar year and would have attained 65 years of age if the individual were alive at the end of the year, the individual is deemed to have attained 65 years of age at the beginning of the year;

    (b) if an individual becomes a qualifying individual during a calendar year and becomes bankrupt in that year, the individual is deemed to be a qualifying individual at the beginning of that year; and

    (c) if an individual becomes a qualifying individual during a calendar year and an eligible individual in respect of the qualifying individual becomes bankrupt in that year, the individual is deemed to be a qualifying individual at the beginning of the year.

Notes: 118.041 added by 2015 Budget bill, for 2016 and later tax years. See 118.041(3) Notes.

Definitions [s. 118.041]: "amount", "appropriate percentage" — 248(1); "arm's length" — 251(1); "aunt" — 252(2)(e); "bankrupt" — 248(1); "beneficiary" — 248(25) [Notes]; "brother" — 252(2)(b); "business" — 248(1); "calendar year" — *Interpretation Act* 37(1)(a); "Canada" — 255, *Interpretation Act* 35(1); "child" — 252(1); "common-law partner", "common-law partnership" — 248(1); "corporation" — 248(1), *Interpretation Act* 35(1); "eligible dwelling", "eligible individual" — 118.41(1); "grandparent" — 252(2)(d); "individual" — 118.41(1); "Minister" — 248(1); "nephew", "niece" — 252(2)(g); "parent" — 252(2)(a); "person", "property" — 248(1); "provincial" — *Interpretation Act* 33(3), 35(1)"province"; "qualifying expenditure", "qualifying individual" — 118.41(1); "share" — 248(1); "sister" — 252(2)(c); "taxation year" — 249; "taxpayer" — 248(1); "trust" — 104(1), 248(1), (3); "uncle" — 252(2)(e); "writing" — *Interpretation Act* 35(1).

118.05 [First-time home buyer's credit and disability home purchase credit] — (1) Definitions — The following definitions apply in this section.

"qualifying home" in respect of an individual, means a "qualifying home" as defined in subsection 146.01(1) that is acquired, whether jointly or otherwise, after January 27, 2009 if

    (a) the home is acquired by the individual, or by the individual's spouse or common-law partner, and

    (i) the individual intends to inhabit the home as a principal place of residence not later than one year after its acquisition,

    (ii) the individual did not own, whether jointly or otherwise, a home that was occupied by the individual in the period

        (A) that began at the beginning of the fourth preceding calendar year that ended before the acquisition, and

        (B) that ended on the day before the acquisition, and

(iii) the individual's spouse or common-law partner did not, in the period referred to in subparagraph (ii), own, whether jointly or otherwise, a home

(A) that was inhabited by the individual during the marriage to or common-law partnership with the individual, or

(B) that was a share of the capital stock of a cooperative housing corporation that relates to a housing unit inhabited by the individual during the marriage to or common-law partnership with the individual; or

(b) the home is acquired by the individual for the benefit of a specified person in respect of the individual, and

(i) the individual intends that the home be inhabited by the specified person as a principal place of residence not later than one year after its acquisition by the individual, and

(ii) the purpose of the acquisition of the home by the individual is to enable the specified person to live in

(A) a home that is more accessible by the specified person or in which the specified person is more mobile or functional, or

(B) an environment better suited to the specified person's personal needs and care.

Related Provisions: 118.05(2) — Transfer of land must be registered to qualify as "acquired".

Notes: A home built on land acquired before Jan. 27, 2009 qualifies: VIEWS doc 2009-0338571M4.

If a couple is buying their first home and the parents of one of them (who own their own home) are also on title, the home is still a "qualifying home" for the couple: doc 2010-0360131E5. A widowed person whose deceased spouse owned a home qualifies: 2019-0811881C6 [2019 APFF Financial q.2]. A home purchased by a partnership can be administratively accepted as a "qualifying home" of the partners: 2010-0368991E5. In a duplex or triplex, the "home" is the apartment, not the building: 2011-0394311E5.

"specified person" in respect of an individual, at any time, means a person who

(a) is the individual or is related at that time to the individual; and

(b) would be entitled to a deduction under subsection 118.3(1) in computing tax payable under this Part for the person's taxation year that includes that time if that subsection were read without reference to paragraph (c) of that subsection.

(2) Rules of application — For the purposes of this section, an individual is considered to have acquired a qualifying home only if the individual's interest (or for civil law, right) in it is registered in accordance with the land registration system or other similar system applicable where it is located.

Notes: A condominium does not qualify until the condominium is registered so that the purchaser has legal ownership: VIEWS doc 2010-0357201E5.

(3) First-time home buyers' tax credit [and disability home purchase credit] — In computing the tax payable under this Part by an individual for a taxation year in which a qualifying home in respect of the individual is acquired, there may be deducted the amount determined by multiplying $5,000 by the appropriate percentage for the taxation year.

Related Provisions: 118.05(4) — Apportionment of credit where more than one person eligible; 118.91 — Part-year resident; 118.92 — Ordering of credits; 118.93 — Credits in separate returns; 118.94 — Credit restriction for non-resident individual; 118.95(a) — Application in year individual becomes bankrupt.

Notes: See Notes at end of 118.05. The "appropriate percentage" (248(1)) is 15% (the lowest bracket rate under 117(2)(a)), so the credit is $750.

The credit can be claimed even if the taxpayer pays only $1 for the home (VIEWS doc 2013-047822E5) or only assumes a mortgage: 2009-0333141M4, 2009-0333181M4.

Forms: T1 General return, Line 31270.

(4) Apportionment of credit — If more than one individual is entitled to a deduction under this section for a taxation year in respect of a particular qualifying home, the total of all amounts so deductible shall not exceed the maximum amount that would be so deductible for the year by any one of those individuals in respect of the qualifying home, if that individual were the only individual entitled to deduct an amount for the year under this section, and if the individuals cannot agree as to what portion of the amount each can so deduct, the Minister may fix the portions.

Notes: The credit can be split between spouses, but the total credit cannot exceed $750: VIEWS doc 2011-0394311E5.

Notes [s. 118.05]: 118.05 implements the $750 First-Time Home Buyer's Credit (118.05(3)) and the $750 Disability Home Purchase Credit (118.05(1)"qualifying home"(b) and 118.05(1)"specified person"), as announced in the 2009 federal Budget. The credit is available even if the home is acquired by way of gift: VIEWS doc 2016-0674851C6 [CPA QC 2017 q.1.8].

Quebec introduced a parallel first-time homebuyer $750 credit in its March 2018 budget. Ontario has a similar "first-time buyer" credit against provincial land transfer tax, refunding up to $4,000 of LTT (on the first $368,000 of purchase price). BC has the "BC HOME Partnership", 5-year interest-free loan to first-time buyers.

For renovations to a home to make it more accessible, see the 118.041 credit and the medical expense credit under 118.2(2)(l.2).

The "CMHC First-Time Home Buyer Incentive", introduced by the March 2019 federal Budget, is a shared equity mortgage, allowing buyers to reduce borrowing costs by sharing the home cost with Canada Mortgage and Housing Corp. It provides funding of 5% or 10% of the home purchase price, repayable after 25 years or on sale of the home. See tinyurl.com/cmhc-hbi. The Nov. 30, 2020 Economic Statement (§3.3.1.11) proposes to enhance eligibility for this program in Toronto, Vancouver and Victoria.

118.05 added by 2009 budget bill #2, for 2009 and later taxation years.

Definitions [s. 118.05]: "acquired" — 118.05(2); "amount", "appropriate percentage" — 248(1); "calendar year" — *Interpretation Act* 37(1)(a); "common-law partner", "common-law partnership" — 248(1); "corporation" — 248(1), *Interpretation Act* 35(1); "individual", "Minister", "person", "property" — 248(1); "qualifying home" — 118.05(1); "related" — 251(2)–(6); "share" — 248(1); "specified person" — 118.05(1); "taxation year" — 249.

Income Tax Folios [s. 118.05]: S1-F1-C2: Disability tax credit [replaces IT-519R2].

118.06 (1) Definition of "eligible volunteer firefighting services" — In this section and section 118.07, "eligible volunteer firefighting services" means services provided by an individual in the individual's capacity as a volunteer firefighter to a fire department that consist primarily of responding to and being on call for firefighting and related emergency calls, attending meetings held by the fire department and participating in required training related to the prevention or suppression of fires, but does not include services provided to a particular fire department if the individual provides firefighting services to the department otherwise than as a volunteer.

Notes: See Notes at end of 118.06.

118.06(1) amended to add reference to 118.07 by 2014 budget bill #1, effective for 2014 and later taxation years.

(2) Volunteer firefighter tax credit — For the purpose of computing the tax payable under this Part for a taxation year by an individual who performs eligible volunteer firefighting services in the year, there may be deducted the amount determined by multiplying $3,000 by the appropriate percentage for the taxation year if the individual

(a) performs in the year not less than 200 hours of service each of which is an hour of

(i) eligible volunteer firefighting service for a fire department, or

(ii) eligible search and rescue volunteer service for an eligible search and rescue organization; and

(b) provides the certificates referred to in subsections (3) and 118.07(3) as and when requested by the Minister.

Related Provisions: 81(4) — Honorarium fully included in income if credit claimed; 118.06(3) — Certificate required if demanded by CRA; 118.91 — Part-year resident; 118.92 — Ordering of credits; 118.93 — Credits in separate returns; 118.94 — Credit restriction for non-resident individual; 118.95(a) — Application in year individual becomes bankrupt.

Notes: See Notes to 81(4) for the meaning of "volunteer". The "appropriate percentage" (248(1)) is 15%, so this credit is worth $450. (Nova Scotia offers a $500 refundable "Volunteer Firefighters and Ground Search & Rescue Tax Credit": gov.ns.ca.)

The certification requirement in 118.06(2)(b) is similar to that in 8(10) for many employment expenses, but applies only if CRA asks for it.

118.06(2) amended by 2014 budget bill #1, effective for 2014 and later taxation years, to add "who performs eligible volunteer firefighting services in the year" and subpara. (a)(ii), and add reference to 118.07(3) in para. (b). See Notes at end of 118.06.

Forms: T1 General return, Line 31220 [former 362].

(3) Certificate — If the Minister so demands, an individual making a claim under this section in respect of a taxation year shall provide to the Minister a written certificate from the fire chief or a delegated official of each fire department to which the individual provided eligible volunteer firefighting services for the year, attesting to the number of hours of eligible volunteer firefighting services performed in the year by the individual for the particular fire department.

Notes [s. 118.06]: 118.06 added by 2011 budget bill #2, for 2011 and later tax years. It implements the Volunteer Firefighter Credit. The person must perform at least 200 hours of volunteer firefighting services in a taxation year, for one or more fire departments, primarily of responding to and being on call for firefighting and related emergency calls, attending meetings held by the fire department and participating in required training related to the prevention or suppression of fires. Volunteer service hours are ineligible if the firefighter also provides paid firefighting services to the same fire department (or if the volunteer firefighter is employed by the company the firefighter is serving: VIEWS doc 2013-0495011E5). The taxpayer must obtain written certification from the chief (or a delegated official) of the fire department confirming the number of hours of eligible volunteer firefighting services performed. Since 2014, this credit is integrated with that in 118.07 so that the maximum combined credit is $450.

CRA accepts "secondary" services as being eligible, such as equipment maintenance, medical training, simulation drills and preventive visits, as long as "primary" service hours exceed secondary: doc 2014-0559501E5.

Being "on call" qualifies. CRA "expects that each fire department will examine its on call procedures to certify the number of hours of eligible services", as simply carrying a pager or cellphone does not establish the person was on call: VIEWS docs 2012-0436861M4, 2012-0439071M4, 2012-0433181E5, 2013-0481951E5. For other activities that can make up the 200 hours see 2011-0431921E5, 2013-0481951E5. "Related emergency calls" in 118.06(1) include medical emergencies and vehicle accidents: 2012-0436941M4.

Where there is no fire chief, the person who approves purchases of firefighting equipment can be considered the "delegated official" for 118.06(3): doc 2012-0434951E5.

A US fire department qualifies: doc 2012-0432221I7. CRA says that a fire department at an industrial facility (where the volunteer firefighter is employed at the facility) does not qualify because it is not a "fire department" under provincial legislation: 2012-0444191E5. (The Courts might disagree: see *Angels of Flight*, 2009 TCC 279.)

CRA interprets "volunteer firefighter" consistently between 81(4) and 118.06: VIEWS doc 2011-0421551E5. See Notes to 81(4).

See also the Saskatchewan credit for volunteer first responders, introduced in 2019.

The 2014 budget bill #1 amendments integrate this credit with the new search-and-rescue volunteer credit in 118.07, so that only one total credit is allowed for a volunteer who does both.

Definitions [s. 118.06]: "amount", "appropriate percentage" — 248(1); "eligible search and rescue volunteer service" — 118.07(1); "eligible volunteer firefighting services" — 118.06(1); "individual", "Minister" — 248(1); "taxation year" — 249; "written" — *Interpretation Act* 35(1).

118.07 [Search and rescue volunteer credit] — (1) Definitions — The following definitions apply in this section and section 118.06.

"eligible search and rescue organization" means a search and rescue organization

(a) that is a member of the Search and Rescue Volunteer Association of Canada, the Civil Air Search and Rescue Association or the Canadian Coast Guard Auxiliary; or

(b) whose status as a search and rescue organization is recognized by a provincial, municipal or public authority.

Notes: For who can attest to the hours of eligible service, what activities qualify, and who determines the organization qualifies, see VIEWS doc 2014-0527411E5.

"eligible search and rescue volunteer services" means services, other than eligible volunteer firefighting services, provided by an individual in the individual's capacity as a volunteer to an eligible search and rescue organization that consist primarily of responding to and being on call for search and rescue and related emergency calls, attending meetings held by the organization and participating in required training related to search and rescue services, but does not include services provided to an organization if the individual provides search and rescue services to the organization otherwise than as a volunteer.

Notes: See Notes to 81(4) for the meaning of "volunteer".

(2) Search and rescue volunteer tax credit — For the purpose of computing the tax payable under this Part for a taxation year by an individual who performs eligible search and rescue volunteer services in the year, there may be deducted the amount determined by multiplying $3,000 by the appropriate percentage for the taxation year if the individual

(a) performs in the year not less than 200 hours of service each of which is an hour of

(i) eligible search and rescue volunteer service for an eligible search and rescue organization, or

(ii) eligible volunteer firefighting services for a fire department;

(b) provides the certificates referred to in subsections (3) and 118.06(3) as and when requested by the Minister; and

(c) has not deducted an amount under section 118.06 for the year.

Related Provisions: 81(4) — Honorarium fully included in income if credit claimed; 118.07(3) — Certificate required if demanded by CRA; 118.91 — Part-year resident; 118.92 — Ordering of credits; 118.93 — Credits in separate returns; 118.94 — Credit restriction for non-resident individual; 118.95(a) — Application in year individual becomes bankrupt.

Notes: The "appropriate percentage" (248(1)) is 15%, so this credit is worth $450.

The certification requirement in 118.07(2)(b) is similar to that in 8(10) for many employment expenses, but applies only if the CRA asks for it.

Forms: T1 General return, Line 31240 [former 395].

(3) Certificate — If the Minister so demands, an individual making a claim under this section in respect of a taxation year shall provide to the Minister a written certificate from the team president, or other individual who fulfils a similar role, of each eligible search and rescue organization to which the individual provided eligible search and rescue volunteer services for the year, attesting to the number of hours of eligible search and rescue volunteer services performed in the year by the individual for the particular organization.

Notes: 118.07, added by 2014 budget bill #1 for 2014 and later taxation years, implements the search-and-rescue volunteers credit announced in the 2014 Budget. It is integrated with the volunteer firefighter credit; see Notes at end of 118.06.

Definitions [s. 118.07]: "amount", "appropriate percentage" — 248(1); "eligible search and rescue organization", "eligible search and rescue volunteer services" — 118.07(1); "eligible volunteer firefighting services" — 118.06(1); "individual", "Minister" — 248(1); "provincial" — *Interpretation Act* 33(3), 35(1)"province"; "taxation year" — 249; "written" — *Interpretation Act* 35(1)"writing".

118.1 (1) Definitions — In this section,

"first-time donor" — [Repealed]

Related Provisions: 118.1(3.1), (3.2) — Super credit for first-time donor.

Notes: See Notes to 118.1(3.1). "First-time donor" added by 2013 budget bill #1, for gifts made after March 20, 2013, then repealed (by the same bill) for 2018 and later taxation years.

"total charitable gifts", of an individual for a particular taxation year, means the total of all amounts each of which is the eligible amount — to the extent it is not otherwise included in determining an amount that is deducted under this section in computing any individual's tax payable under this Part for any taxation year — of a gift (other than a gift any part of the eligible amount of which is included in the total cultural gifts or the total ecological gifts of any individual for any taxation year) that is made

(a) to a qualified donee,

(b) in a taxation year that is not a year for which an amount is deducted under subsection 110(2) in computing the individual's taxable income, and

(c) if the individual is

  (i) not a trust,

    (A) by the individual, or the individual's spouse or common-law partner, in the particular year or any of the five preceding taxation years,

    (B) by the individual in the year in which the individual dies if the particular year is the taxation year that precedes the taxation year in which the individual dies, or

    (C) by the individual's estate if subsection (5.1) applies to the gift and the particular year is the taxation year in which the individual dies or the preceding taxation year, or

  (ii) a trust

    (A) by the trust in the particular year or any of the five preceding taxation years,

    (B) by the trust if

      (I) the trust is an individual's estate,

      (II) subsection (5.1) applies to the gift, and

      (III) the particular year is a taxation year

        1 in which the estate is the individual's graduated rate estate, and

        2 that precedes the taxation year in which the gift is made, or

    (C) by the trust if

      (I) the end of the particular year is determined by paragraph 104(13.4)(a) because of an individual's death,

      (II) the gift is made after the particular year and on or before the trust's filing-due date for the particular year, and

      (III) the subject of the gift is property that is held by the trust at the time of the individual's death or is property that was substituted for that property;

Related Provisions: 38(a.1) — No capital gain on donation of publicly-traded shares; 43.1(1) — Charitable gifts excluded from rules re life interests in real property; 46(1), (5) — Capital gain on certain donations; 69(1)(b)(ii) — Donor deemed to have disposed of property at market value; 110(1)(d.01) — Deduction on donating employee stock-option shares to charity; 110.1(1)(a) — Parallel deduction for corporations; 118.1(1)"total gifts"(a)(ii) — Charitable gifts limited to 75% of net income; 118.1(2.1) — Ordering of claims; 118.1(5.2) — Designation of charity as beneficiary of insurance policy, RRSP, RRIF or TFSA; 118.1(6) — Election for reduced proceeds on donation of property; 118.1(13) — Donation of non-qualifying securities; 118.1(16) — Loanback arrangements; 118.1(21)–(24) — Effect of individual granting option to charity; 118.1(25)–(28) — Donation denied where property returned to donor; 143(3.1) — Hutterite colonies — election re gifts; 149.1(1)"qualified donee" — Entities to which donations can be made; 149.1(6.4) — Donations to registered national arts service org; 149.1 — CRA registration and control over charities and other qualified donees; 188.2(3)(a) — Effect of suspension of charity's receipting privileges; 225.1(7) — Donation shelter assessment can be half-collected while under appeal; 237.1(1)"gifting arrangement", "tax shelter" — Tax shelter registration requirement; 248(30)–(33) — Determination of eligible amount; 248(35)–(39) — Value of gift limited to cost if acquired within 3 years or as tax shelter; 248(41) — Donation value deemed nil if taxpayer does not inform donee of circumstances requiring reduction; Canada-U.S. Tax Treaty:Art. XXI:7 — Donations to US charities qualify for taxpayer with US-source income; Canada-U.S. Tax Treaty:Art. XXIX-B:1 — Property left to US charity on death.

Notes: See Notes to 118.1(1)"total gifts" for calculation of the credit and carrying donations forward. To check a charity's status and other info: tinyurl.com/list-charities or charitydata.ca. Total projected federal donation credits were $3.1 billion in each of 2019 and 2020, $3.4b in each of 2021-22: *Report on Federal Tax Expenditures 2021*.

To qualify, a gift must be to a registered charity or another "qualified donee" as defined in 149.1(1). Denying credit for a gift to a foreign charity that is not a qualified donee does not violate the *Charter of Rights*: *Hall*, 2013 TCC 314.

Spouses: CRA has for decades permitted a claim for donations made in the name of one's spouse: *T1 General Income Tax Guide*, Line 34900 [former 349]. Thus, receipts in both spouses' (or common-law partners') names can be pooled and claimed on one return. This applies to donation carryforwards also: VIEWS doc 2010-0377811E5. Before 2016, this administrative practice was not legally enforceable: *Douziech*, 2000 CarswellNat 1000 (TCC); since 2016, it is allowed by (c)(i)(A), and also continues administratively so that a gift can be split between spouses: 2015-0590501E5. See also Drache, "Income Splitting with Charitable Tax Credits", xxxiv(7) *The Canadian Tax-*

payer (Carswell) 54-55 (April 6, 2012). See however Notes to 118.1(4.1) re splitting donations made by will or after death.

On the timing of when a gift of securities takes place, see discussion of 38(a.1) in Notes to s. 38.

Meaning of "gift": see Income Tax Folio S7-F1-C1 ¶1.1-1.3. A gift is "a voluntary transfer of property owned by a donor to a donee in return for which no benefit or consideration flows to the donor": *Friedberg*, [1992] 1 C.T.C. 1 (FCA), para. 4 (aff'd on other grounds [1993] 2 C.T.C. 306 (SCC)); *McBurney*, [1985] 2 C.T.C. 214 (FCA); *Berg*, 2014 FCA 25, para. 23; for discussion see also *McNamee*, 2011 ONCA 533; *Kossow*, 2013 FCA 283 (leave to appeal denied 2014 CarswellNat 1529 (SCC)); *Cassan*, 2017 TCC 174 (FCA appeal settled A-304-17), paras. 263-298; *Jensen*, 2018 TCC 60 and *Goheen*, 2019 FCA 104 (Global Prosperity scheme: taxpayers must have received benefit in the form of investment return; gross-negligence penalties imposed); *Markou*, 2019 FCA 299 (leave to appeal denied 2020 CarswellNat 1486) (McKellar/Trinity leveraged donations: interconnected transactions, no gift). At common law, gift requires "impoverishment" of the donor and no benefit or consideration in return (other than the tax credit): *Boisselle*, [1989] 1 C.T.C. 2385 (TCC); *Friedberg* (above); *Maréchaux*, 2010 FCA 287 (leave to appeal denied 2011 CarswellNat 1911); *Mariano*, 2015 TCC 244, paras. 19-24 (expectation of inflated receipt vitiates the gift); VIEWS doc 2012-0469971E5; but see the 248(30)-(33) "split-receipting" rules, allowing an "advantage" of up to 80% of the gift.

A gift must be voluntary, so the following do not qualify: donation ordered by a court as a penalty [e.g. *Bekkerus*, 2018 ABPC 201, para. 19] (*Registered Charities Newsletter* 18); gift required by contract (doc 2011-0409551E5, but it may be deductible as a business expense: 2010-0388751E5); donation required by a collective agreement (2013-0477981E5); gift with a kickback provided by a third party (*van der Steen*, 2020 FCA 168; *McPherson*, 2006 TCC 648 (FCA appeal discontinued A-14-07); *Norton*, 2008 TCC 91; gift required by trust terms with no discretion to trustees (2019-0798491C6 [2019 STEP q.2]).

There must be donative intent (*Mariano*, 2015 TCC 244, para. 17; *Tudora*, 2020 TCC 11, para. 29), and a lack of a connection to the charity or pattern of past donations can indicate no real donation was made: *Coombs (Rigutto)*, 2008 TCC 289 (aff'd due to delay 2009 FCA 74); *Jensen*, 2018 TCC 60, paras. 46-65; VIEWS doc 2009-0314031E5. However, there can be another motive while still having donative intent, and there need not be "disinterested generosity": *Cassan*, 2017 TCC 174 (FCA appeal settled A-304-17), paras. 288, 296. (Arguably a "split gift" (only part donation) no longer needs "donative intent" due to 248(30): *Markou*, 2018 TCC 66, para. 113; the FCA refused to comment on this point because there was no split gift: 2019 FCA 299 (leave to appeal denied 2020 CarswellNat 1486), para. 61, but required "donative intent" and "impoverishment" in the case: para. 60.)

A donation by forgiveness of loan is valid: Drache, "Loaned Funds Can Serve Many Purposes", 22(7) *Canadian Not-for-Profit News* (Carswell) 49-50 (July 2014). In *Benquesus*, 2006 TCC 193, a father donated to a foundation, specifying this was a loan from his 4 children; each of them later forgave part of the loan, thus making a valid donation.

A gift can include advice on how to spend the funds, provided there is no legal obligation on the charity to comply: *Curlett*, [1966] C.T.C. 243 (Ex. Ct); Drache, "Advising on Donor-Advised Funds", xxvi(11) *The Canadian Taxpayer* (Carswell) 86-87 (May 25, 2004); VIEWS docs 2005-0159771R3, 2011-0405881E5. As between donor and charity, a donor cannot retrieve a gift on the ground the funds were not used as requested: *Faas v. CAMH*, 2019 ONCA 192; *McKay Cross Foundation v. Innovative Community*, 2018 ONSC 6422. A gift restricted to a particular purpose (scholarships) could not be changed to another purpose (new school building) even by Court order and even with the donors' consent: *Musgrave School Foundation*, 2014 BCSC 1900; and in *Doukhobor Heritage v. Vancouver Foundation*, 2020 BCCA 80 (reversing the BCSC), a "permanent fund" set up by a charity at a foundation could not be reversed when the fund underperformed, as "a person who has made a gift cannot retract it" (para. 56). A demand loan that became a donation on death created a trust and was a valid gift, not an invalid testamentary disposition: *Norman Estate v. Watch Tower*, 2014 BCCA 277.

A donation of services is not a gift: Charities Policy CPC-017; *Slobodrian*, 2003 FCA 350 and 2005 FCA 336 (leave to appeal denied 2006 CarswellNat 164 (SCC)); *Oloya*, 2011 TCC 308; but expenses reimbursed to a volunteer by cheque can be signed back to the charity and qualify as a donation: *Beaulieu*, [1998] 2 C.T.C. 2431 (TCC), Charities Policies CPC-012, CPC-025, doc 2010-0391511E5; Drache, "Receipting Volunteer Expenses", 28(4) *Canadian Not-for-Profit News [CNfPN]* (Carswell) 27-28 (April 2020). (The practice of a charity paying a speaker an inflated speaking fee and then having the fee donated back, with the speaker benefiting from the donation credit being higher than the tax on the income, could be challenged by CRA as not being a genuine transaction or under GAAR, and might endanger the charity's status.) The US Tax Court has allowed a volunteer to deduct expenses: Drache, "Unreimbursed Volunteer Expenses American Style", 20(1) *CNfPN* 7-8 (Jan. 2012). Note also the credits for firefighting and search-and-rescue volunteers in 118.06 and 118.07.

Delivery: A gift is not complete until it is delivered, and a gift by cheque is not complete until the cheque is cashed or cleared: *Teixeira v. Markgraf*, 2017 ONCA 819, para. 46. (So despite 248(7)(a), mailing a cheque to a charity on December 31 does not appear to qualify for a credit that year.)

For gifts "in kind" (not money), see IT-297R2, VIEWS doc 2014-0526131E5; and see Notes to 69(1) re valuing the donation. A gift of free rent can be a gift of property if the rental income is reported: *Oloya*, 2011 TCC 308, para. 16; *Carson*, 2013 TCC 353 (in neither case did it qualify). A donation of Air Miles or similar points, or an air ticket acquired with points, qualifies if its value can be reasonably estimated: docs 9921267, 2003-0000175, 2006-0173251E5, 2006-0193261E5; Drache, "Airlines Points, Tickets and Charity", 14(9) *Canadian Not-for-Profit News [CNfPN]* (Carswell) 70-71 (Sept. 2006) (however, Air Canada's Aeroplan refuses to value its points: Drache, "Donation of Aeroplan Points Gives Valuation Problems", 16(2) *CNfPN* 12-13 (Feb. 2008)). A barter club's barter dollars qualify: 2008-0274411I7. Merchant rewards can qualify if the customer owns the reward before assigning it to a charity: 2018-0761161E5. Loyalty card rebates can qualify: 2017-0704951E5. A gift certificate or gift card can qualify, but see Charities Guidance CG-007 (earlier, see 2000-0030237). A right to use software the taxpayer developed can qualify: 2004-0108721I7. A donation of art with a lifetime loan back to the donor qualifies, minus the value of the 248(32) "advantage": 2006-0170391R3, 2007-0229281R3. Blood and organ donations qualify, but there may be practical difficulties getting a receipt: Yasny, "Tax Credit for Donations of Blood and Body Parts", 22(6) *CNfPN* 46-47 (June 2014) and xxxvii(24) *The Canadian Taxpayer* (Carswell) 191-92 (Dec. 18, 2015). Donations of goods of unproven value were disallowed in: *Le*, 2011 TCC 292; *Ehiozomwangie*, 2013 TCC 145; *Ashaolu*, 2013 TCC 138. In practice, CRA wants a professional appraisal for goods worth over $1,000: tinyurl.com/non-cash-gifts.

Donating shares: see 118.1(13), limiting the credit on certain donations of private company shares. If publicly traded securities are donated, the capital gain on them is deemed nil: 38(a.1), (a.3). A 2015 proposal to eliminate the capital gain on *private* company shares and real estate starting 2017, to the extent cash equal to the proceeds was donated, was dropped per the 2016 Budget (former proposed 38(a.4), 38.3, 38.4). Donating private company shares is tax-effective compared to redeeming them and donating after-tax proceeds, but there are many pitfalls: Fabbro, "Donations of Securities to Private Foundations", 2435 *Tax Topics* (CCH) 1-6 (Nov. 8, 2018); Janzen, "Donation of Private Company Shares", 67(3) *Canadian Tax Journal* 789-808 (2019); Balasingam, "Donating Private Company Shares", tinyurl.com/don-pcs. See also 118.1(6), election to reduce the capital gain (and donation value) on donating *any* capital property.

See also Adam Parachin, "Reforming the Meaning of 'Charitable Gift' ", 57(4) *Canadian Tax Journal* 787-838 (2009); Drache, "Gifts with Conditions Subsequent", 19(5) *CNfPN* 38-39 (May 2011); Terrance Carter, "Pitfalls in Drafting Gift Agreements", 2017 STEP Canada conference (contact memberservices@step.ca); and discussion of "leveraged donation" shelters below.

In Quebec, where the *Civil Code* applies (see *Interpretation Act* ss. 8.1, 8.2), a "gift" can include a sale for less than market value, and a gift can be revoked on account of ingratitude. 248(30) does not apply in Quebec: VIEWS doc 2007-0248451E5. In common-law provinces a gift cannot be for consideration (but see the "eligible amount" rules in 248(30)-(33)). See Drache, "Common Law, Civil Law or Both", XXIII(21) *The Canadian Taxpayer* (Carswell) 165-67 (Oct. 23, 2001). In *French*, 2016 FCA 64 (reversing the TCC), non-Quebec taxpayers were allowed to plead the *Civil Code* was relevant to their appeals, as it was arguable that Parliament intended the civil law rule to apply. In *Fonds de solidarité*, 2018 TCC 3 (aff'd on other grounds 2019 FCA 36), a $9m payment to the local town to invest in something to replace a failed paper plant was held not to be a donation under the *Civil Code*, because it relieved the donor of an obligation to invest the funds in another project.

A sale for less than fair market value is a gift of the excess, even before enactment of the "eligible amount" rules: see Notes to 248(31).

Tuition to private schools for religious studies (including Christian and Jewish day schools that also teach secular subjects) qualifies for charitable donation under a 1975 CRA policy that also allows a school to allocate its outside funding to secular education so as to increase the donation amount: Information Circular 75-23 and tinyurl.com/cra-ic75-23. This effectively overrides *Zandstra*, [1974] C.T.C. 503 (FCTD), on the theory that one cannot pay for religious education (but see *Smith*, 2019 TCC 274, para. 16). Taxpayers who donated to Swim Canada to pay for their children's swimming lessons cannot challenge this policy as discriminatory, as it is the policy that should be changed if it is wrong: *Fluevog*, 2011 FCA 338; the Court expressed "no opinion" on whether CRA was legally correct in allowing religious tuition as a donation. In *Coleman (Ballard)*, 2011 FCA 82 (leave to appeal denied 2011 CarswellNat 4679 (SCC)), donations to the National Foundation for Christian Leadership were disallowed, as they were used for scholarships that were largely for the donors' children (and were not for religious education per IC75-23). *Emms v. Christian Economic Assistance Foundation*, a class action claiming parents were promised donation credits that CRA denied, was settled for $1.5 million (1/3 of which went to legal fees): 2015 ONSC 7664. A similar action in BC, seeking refund of the donations, failed: *Neville v. National Foundation for Christian Leadership*, 2014 BCCA 38 (leave to appeal denied 2014 CarswellBC 1447).

For donations to US charities see Notes to 118.1(9).

Receipt required with full details: see Notes to 118.1(2) and Reg. 3501(1).

Fraud: CRA reassessed hundreds of donors to three charities that engaged in fraudulent schemes of giving cash back to the "donors": the Lebanese Antonine Maronite Order; and the Or Hamaarav Sephardic Congregation and Abarbanel S Learning Centre (for which the charities' director was convicted of fraud: *Edery*, 2001 CarswellOnt 2209 (Ont. CJ)). Most taxpayers who appealed lost in both the TCC and the FCA (2002-07): *Abinader* (FCA appeal discontinued), *Abouantoun*, *Atallah*, *Bassila*, *Chamoun*, *Cortbaoui*, *Daou*, *Dargham*, *Kiwan (Nassar)*, *Nasrallah*, *Nassif*, *Nawar*, *Tawil*, *Younes* (Maronites); *Benarroch*, *Boutarieh*, *Buzaglo*, *Halajian*, *Kadoch*, *Soberano* (Edery charities). Some of the Edery appeals won on the ground that their donation amount was reasonable for them and was not proven to have been part of the fraud, so CRA did not meet the onus to assess statute-barred years: *Benitah*, *Benmergui*, *Bentolila*, *Cohen*. CRA also conceded some cases at the objection stage on this basis.

A similar "cash-back" scheme involving Ambrose Danso-Dapaah and George Gudu, and charities Bible Teaching Ministries, PanAfrican Canadian Multicultural Centre, CanAfrica International Foundation and Heaven's Gate Healing Ministry, led to credits disallowed in *Tuar*, 2010 TCC 236; *Scott*, 2010 TCC 237; *Grossett*, 2012 TCC 179; *Adomphwe*, 2010 TCC 240; *Le*, 2011 TCC 292; *Clarke*, 2011 TCC 547 and 548; *Patel*, 2011 TCC 555; *Sarsonas*, 2011 TCC 559; *Johnson*, 2014 TCC 84; *Perry*, 2016 TCC 210. See also CRA news release Dec. 18/08, re conviction of Ambrose Dapaah and sentence of 51 months in prison, and news release April 8/10, re charges laid against other individuals. CRA news releases, June 29/10, Sept. 14/10 and Dec. 1/10 reported conviction and sentencing of tax preparers Leslie George Walker and Faiz Khan for filing clients' returns with false donation claims to the above charities and Ave Development Foundation, City Chapel Ministries International, Destiny Ministries International Christian Mission and Faith Full Gospel Tabernacle. In *Leo-Mensah*, [2010] 3 C.T.C. 299 (Ont CA) (leave to appeal to SCC denied 2010 CarswellOnt 9113), providing $11.7 million in false charitable receipts led to 2 years in prison beyond 11 months in pre-trial custody, plus $145,000 in fines.

Similarly, donations to Mehfuz Children's Welfare Trust (false receipts by accountants Fareed and Saheem Raza) were disallowed in *Bani*, 2014 TCC 340; *Vekkal*, 2014 TCC 341; *Komarynsky*, 2014 TCC 342; *Abootaleby-Pour*, 2014 TCC 343; *Izkendar*, 2014 TCC 344; *Nocon*, 2014 TCC 345; *Rasuli*, 2014 TCC 346; and cash donations to Revival Time Ministries [RTM] were disallowed in *Imoh*, 2014 TCC 258; *Arthur*, 2015 TCC 43; *Bope*, 2015 TCC 120; *Mapish*, 2015 TCC 122; *Okeke*, 2016 FCA 293; *Heno*, 2020 TCC 127 (also Redemption Power Intl Ministries).

Donations to various charities were similarly disallowed as implausible or unproven in *Afovia*, 2012 TCC 391; *Sklodowski*, 2013 TCC 37; *Ehiozomwangie*, 2013 TCC 145; *Clarke*, 2013 TCC 191 [return prepared by Festus Bayden]; *Sowa [Sowah]*, 2015 FCA 103; *Vo*, 2013 TCC 343 [scheme masterminded by Bayden, Eric Armah]; *Dhillon*, 2014 TCC 25, *Syla*, 2016 TCC 266, *Amaoko-Boatey*, 2016 TCC 282 and *Zubeiru*, 2017 TCC 199 [false receipts from William Ankomah: Holy Alpha and Omega Church, New Hope for Africa]; *Ofori-Darko*, 2014 TCC 54 [Redemption Faith Ministries]; *Holst*, 2014 TCC 104 and *Akinbo*, 2014 TCC 214 [Israelite Church of Christ, Liberty Parish Celestial Church of Christ]; *Hassan*, 2014 TCC 144 [Operation Save Canada's Teenagers (OSCT); costs awarded in Informal Procedure for lying in Court]; *McCalla*, 2014 TCC 199 and *Ampomah*, 2014 TCC 217 [Jesus Healing Center]; *Duggan*, 2015 TCC 175 [Mega Church, OSCT]; *Iqbal*, 2015 TCC 324 [Africanadian Mediation Community Services, OSCT]; *Omoruan*, 2016 TCC 138 [Redemption Power Intl Ministries, Celestial Church of Christ, Christ Apostolic Church Intl (CACI), Hope Economic Relief Org]; *Guobadia*, 2016 TCC 182 [OSCT, Nations for Christ Ministries, House of Evidence Christian Fellowship]; *Purba*, 2016 TCC 218 [CACI]; *Khan*, 2017 TCC 171 [CACI, Evidence Ministries, Christ Healing Church]; *Langboung*, 2017 TCC 186; *Isah*, 2018 TCC 28; *Ruremesha*, 2018 TCC 57 [RTM, OSCT]; *Tutu*, 2018 TCC 128 [Liberty Wellness]; *Seepersad*, 2018 TCC 226 [City Chapel Ministries [CCM], Faith Assemblies, World Council for African Development]; *Ampratwum-Duah*, 2020 TCC 18 (CCM: receipts for donations by church leader were signed by him with no other supporting evidence; church should have kept records per 230(6)); *Kyei*, 2021 TCC 10 (Raymond Frempong / Orbit Financial; statute-barred assessments upheld).

In *Castro*, 2015 FCA 225 (leave to appeal denied 2016 CarswellNat 1067 (SCC)) (reversing several TCC appeals reported as *David*, 2014 TCC 117), inflated CanAfrica tax receipts were held not to be benefits or advantages on the facts of the case, but since the amount of the receipt did not match the cash donated, no credit was allowed even for the cash. In *Mattacchione*, 2015 TCC 283, para. 97, inflated receipts and appraisals meant that a "buy low donate high" promoter had no donative intent. See Adam Aptowitzer, "New Tax Court Decision in Mattacchione: Intuitive but Unsettling", xxxviii(4) *The Canadian Taxpayer* (Carswell) 30-31 (Feb. 19, 2016).

In *Okoroafor*, 2010 ONSC 2477, CRA had seized documents in an investigation into false donations to Christ Embassy Christian Centre, and after a year was allowed to keep the seized items for another 9 months due to the investigation's complexity.

Convictions of tax preparers for claiming false donations (FD) for clients: Bernard Sarfo (LTS Direct, Liberty Tax Service): 14 months jail [CRA news release (NR), Feb. 21/11]; Eric Armah (E&F Tax Associates, Bankay Financial Services): 3 years for $34m of FD [NR June 8/11]; Isaac (Ike) Amoako (Orbit Financial Services): 2 years for $34m of FD on 5,800 returns [June 17/11]; Christopher Paterson: 18 months conditional and 200 hrs community service for $1m of FD over 5 years [NR March 21/12]; Saturday Oton: 6 months + 1 year probation for FD to Siva Vishnu Temple or Hindu Temple Society on 26 returns [2014 CarswellOnt 2175 (Ont CA); leave to appeal denied 2015 CarswellOnt 4017 (SCC)]; Samuel Yeboah Tanoh (Trans Xpress Cash Inc.): $6,789 fine for $13,579 of FD [NR Oct. 18/12]; Penelope Donick: 1 year and $200,000 fine for $4m of FD on 269 returns over 4 years [NR Oct. 19/12]; Rodrigo Layco: 2 years less a day conditional for $3.1m of FD to CanAfrica [NR Jan. 29/13]; Adegboyega Adenekanad Adebukunola: time served in custody + 6 months conditional for $858,897 of FD on 129 returns [NR March 5/13]; Dele Afolabi: 6 months conditional + $10,000 fine for $373,000 of FD on 59 returns [NR May 6/13]; Imad Kutum, CA: 2 years + $100,000 fine for $3.6m of FD on 487 returns [2013 ONCJ 241]; Doreen Tennina: 10 years for $58.5 million of FD on 4,200 returns [2013 ONSC 4694] [NR Sept. 8/15: extradited from Italy to serve sentence]; Lawrence Aimurie: 12 months conditional + $25,000 fine for $641,000 of FD, receipts from Faith Assemblies International [NR July 22/13]; David Ajise and Eto Ekpenyong Eto: 30 months in jail, and 2 years less a day conditional (respectively) for $5m of FD, receipts from Tractors for

Our Daily Bread Canada [NR Jan. 14/14; 2018 SCC 51]; Ekue Kuevioakoe: 12 months conditional + $70,000 fine for $235,000 of FD on 431 returns [2015 ONCJ 681; NR Dec. 3/15]; Fareed & Saheem Raza: $11.4m of FD on 1,700 returns, 51 months prison each [2015 BCSC 2512, 2016 BCSC 1030]; George Nnane: $1.9m federal tax evaded, 3 years prison [NR Feb. 7/20]; John Oladapo Oladehinde: 2 years less a day conditional + $412,000 fine for $13m of FD on 1,400 returns [NR July 8/20].

Convictions of charity administrators for issuing false receipts to each other: Taiba Djalal and Marcel Fragé (news release Dec. 8/15: charity SOCADE; conditional sentences of 12 and 18 months).

Acquittal: In *Bromley*, [2004] 3 C.T.C. 58 (BC Prov Ct), charities lawyer B was acquitted of making sham donations (pre-248(31)) to V foundation, where X had loaned $500,000 to V but could not use the credit, and B and his family donated $500,000 to V, which repaid the loan and X gave the funds back to B. There was no attempt to deceive CRA, and the Crown did not prove beyond reasonable doubt that the donations were invalid for tax purposes.

For revocations of charities involved in abusive schemes see Notes to 168(1).

Undoing a donation (returning a gift): see Notes to 118.1(26).

Where cash is donated to a charity and then loaned back to the donor with interest, the CRA considers that no donation has been made: VIEWS doc 2002-0152695. It is possible that under the new "eligible amount" split-receipt rules in 248(30)-(33), the Courts would consider this as a gift of the cash minus the "value" of the loan back (however that be calculated). See also 118.1(16) if the donor and charity are not at arm's length.

If a taxpayer fails to inform a charity before a receipt is issued of facts that will cause a reduction in value due to 248(31)-(39), the donation is deemed to be nil: 248(41). This should deny a credit even for "cash paid" in some donation shelter schemes (below).

Donation shelters: In a typical "art flip", art was purchased by a donor to give to a charity to sell by auction, and valued for donation receipt purposes at far more than the donor paid, on the theory that "fair market value" (FMV) was the highest possible retail price (see Notes to 69(1)); the entire valuation, donation and auction process was organized by a promoter. 46(5) and the 163.2 penalties target such shelters, and the 2003 budget added them to 237.1(1)"tax shelter", so the credit is disallowed unless the shelter is registered and a T5004 is filed with the return: 237.1(6). They were shut down by 248(35)-(39) (as of Dec. 5, 2003, though not enacted until June 26, 2013), which limits the donation amount to the cost of the property. Due to these amendments and CRA enforcement, there was "no reported participation in gifting tax shelters in 2015-16": *CRA Departmental Performance Report 2015-16*, p. 55.

In these shelters, the Courts generally rule that the gift is real but the value is what the donor paid for the art (and the Courts have upheld some 163(2) gross-negligence penalties): *Langlois*, 2000 CarswellNat 3241 (FCA); *Duguay*, [2002] 1 C.T.C. 8 (FCA); *Klotz*, 2005 FCA 158 (leave to appeal denied 2006 CarswellNat 930 (SCC)) (FMV of 250 prints was what K paid for them because the prints had to be valued as a group, not individually); *Malette*, 2004 FCA 187 ("block discount" applied to 981 paintings, so their value was what M paid); *Nash (Tolley, Quinn)*, 2005 FCA 386 (leave to appeal denied 2006 CarswellNat 932) (FMV of blocks of prints was what the taxpayers paid because that was the best price the taxpayers could have obtained had they sold them at the time); *Nguyen*, 2008 TCC 401; *Russell*, 2009 TCC 548 (Canadian Art Advisory Services program: the "market" for FMV is not the retail market because an individual cannot sell into that market as a gallery can; and what the donor buys is not art but an "investment" that includes the tax credit); *Nantel*, 2009 TCC 599; *Roher (Kaur)*, 2019 FCA 313 (leave to appeal denied 2020 CarswellNat 1394) (Artistic Ideas shelter — prints to be valued as a group).

The shelters spread from art to other products including software and drugs, but always failed in Court. See *Robichaud*, 2004 TCC 661 (Scott guide on stamp values is not reliable for determining FMV); *Morisset*, 2007 TCC 114 (Court rejected claimed value of donated polar bear skins); *Lockie*, 2010 TCC 142 (FCA appeal discontinued A-164-10) (donations to In Kind Canada of toothbrushes, gel pens and school packs, purchased at low cost from China, were valued at cost [see also *Groscki*, 2017 TCC 249, paras. 19-33]); *Eisbrenner (Morrison)*, 2020 FCA 93 (leave to appeal denied 2021 CarswellNat 72 (SCC)) (drugs — Canadian Gift Initiative, Canadian Humanitarian Trust [CRA allowed cash portion of donation: para. 7]); *Abreo*, 2019 TCC 122 (under appeal to FCA as *Chibani*; appeal as *Klepatch* discontinued A-262-19) (software — donations to National Children's Burn Society); *Eusebe*, 2018 TCC 254 (Universal Donation Program: appeals dismissed where no receipts).

"Leveraged donation" shelters (80% of the cash provided by lengthy interest-free loan) failed in *Maréchaux*, 2010 FCA 287 (leave to appeal denied 2011 CarswellNat 1911 (SCC)) and *Markou*, 2019 FCA 299 (leave to appeal denied 2020 CarswellNat 1486) [both Trinity Capital], and *Kossow*, 2013 FCA 283 [Berkshire Funding]: there was no "gift" because of the expectation of a benefit, so no credit was allowed even for the cash paid. In *Cassan*, 2017 TCC 174 (FCA appeal settled A-304-17), paras. 361-363, the EquiGenesis shelter donation credit was nil (even though the loan was not sufficiently related to the donation to be a benefit: para. 306) because the principal amount of the loan was a "limited-recourse amount" under 248(32)(b), and the interest rate payable on the loan was below market rate (248(32)(a)) [McIsaac, "Charitable Donation and Investment Program", 25(11) *Canadian Tax Highlights* (ctf.ca) 12-14 (Nov. 2017); Sorenson, "Donation, Deduction, Deferral", XX(4) *Corporate Finance* (Federated Press) 2-7 (2017)]. [The Equigenesis appeals were mostly settled and a class action against CRA abandoned: *Gordon*, 2019 ONSC 6499.] The cash portion of a donation shelter was also denied in: *Bandi*, 2013 TCC 230 [Charitable Technology Gifting Program — "alleged cash gift cannot be considered in isolation from the overall plan": para. 19]; *Glover*, 2015 TCC 199; *Mariano*, 2015 TCC 244 [Global Learning Gift Initiative (GLGI) — see also 2016 TCC 161, awarding $490,000 costs against the appellants and promoter]; *Abdalla*, 2019 FCA 5 (GLGI; leave to appeal denied 2019 CarswellNat 2472); *Miller*, 2019 TCC 204 (GLGI); *Tudora*, 2020 TCC 11 (GLGI). (See also 174(1) Notes re CRA's attempt to consolidate GLGI appeals.) In *Sweetman*, 2020 TCC 36, a non-resident GLGI appellant, with evidently little chance of success, was required to post $19,375 security to continue his appeal. In *Berg*, 2014 FCA 25, the cash paid on the purchase of timeshare units was disallowed (B had conceded the 90% that came from a promissory note), based on *Maréchaux* and because B intended to profit from the deal and thus had no donative intent to "impoverish" himself. The existence of a "gift" may change since the enactment of 248(30) in 2013; in *Edwards*, 2012 FCA 330 (Parklane shelter), the FCA put an appeal on hold until it was enacted.

Claims under the Strategic Gifting shelter were denied in *Lappan*, 2017 TCC 240; *Murji*, 2018 TCC 7 (donation of worthless foreign shares, similar to the Innovative Gifting shelter; no donative intent and scheme was unregistered tax shelter; the cash paid net of the promoter's fee had been allowed by CRA).

Shelter appeal procedural decisions include *Gould*, 2009 TCC 107 (FCA appeal discontinued A-66-09); *Sputek*, 2011 TCC 540; *van der Steen*, 2016 TCC 205 (Canadian Literary Enhancement Society shelter); *Amrite*, 2018 TCC 11 (Canadian Literacy Initiatives shelter: appeals filed too late); *Larson*, 2018 TCC 242 (Initiatives Canada shelter; extension of time to appeal denied); *Mudge*, 2020 TCC 77 (Canadian Humanitarian Trust); *Foroglou*, 2020 TCC 117 (GLGI; TCC denied F's request for $2.2 million interim costs); *Kloppers*, 2020 TCC 118 (GLGI: CRA processing objections very slowly was not "divide and conquer" abuse of process); *Sweetman*, 2021 TCC 32 (GLGI: TCC refused to hold appeal in abeyance until other GLGI reassessments confirmed).

Where shelter litigation of a test case takes years, interest relief might be available for appeals put on hold: see 220(3.1) and Drache, "Fairness Provisions May Help Art Flip Taxpayers", 30(8) *The Canadian Taxpayer* (Carswell) 61-63 (April 15-28, 2008).

CRA will not rule on donation shelters: VIEWS docs 2010-0372311E5, 2010-0389111C6 [2010 CTF conf report, q. 34, pp. 4:30-31]. CRA audits all donation shelters and denies almost all claims. As of a Jan. 10, 2014 news release, CRA had denied more than $5.9 billion in donation claims and reassessed over 182,000 taxpayers who participated in gifting shelters, and had assessed $137 million in third-party penalties against promoters and tax preparers. For revocations of charities involved in shelters see Notes to 168(1). CRA statistics show total claimed donations in abusive shelters down from $1.3 billion in 2006 to $100 million in 2013 (blumbergs.ca, May 3, 2014).

In *Diewold*, 2018 SKQB 149, D's use of the GLGI shelter, which she believed was valid, was reason for harsh treatment in bankruptcy (see Notes to 128(2)).

CRA policy since 2012 is to refuse to assess a return claiming a donation shelter, and (news release Nov. 27, 2014) that it will assess if the claim is deleted. If the purpose were to allow time to audit the shelter, this could be reasonable based on the cases on "all due dispatch" (see Notes to 152(1)). However, a stated purpose is to deter the use of such shelters, and this is improper: *Ficek*, 2013 FC 502 (re GLGI); *McNally*, 2015 FC 767 (Crown's appeal dismissed as moot 2015 FCA 248) (re Equigenesis: CRA ordered to assess within 30 days). In *Rae*, 2015 FC 707, a request to certify a class action against CRA for refusing to assess was denied, because the class was not properly defined and R was not an appropriate representative plaintiff.

Half the amount in dispute on a donation shelter must be paid while under appeal: see 225.1(7).

The shelters have led to lawsuits against law firms, promoters, charities, directors and advisors. The Banyan Tree shelter claim (*Robinson v. Rochester Financial*, 2010 ONSC 463 (leave to appeal denied 2010 ONSC 1899 (Div. Ct)) was settled for $11 million with no admission of liability by Fraser Milner Casgrain LLP: 2012 ONSC 911. A class action on the Athletic Trust (Caribbean timeshare) shelter could proceed since the 2-year lawsuit limitation period might not have started until a TCC test case had settled: *Lipson v. Cassels Brock*, 2013 ONCA 165 [costs award 2013 ONSC 6450; more procedural decisions 2014 ONSC 6106, 6163; 2019 ONSC 5524, 5483]. A class action on the Parklane/Trafalgar "Donations Canada" shelter was certified in *Cannon v. Funds for Canada*, 2012 ONSC 399 (leave to appeal denied 2012 ONSC 6101); it settled with the lawyers (Patterson Palmer, McInnis Cooper, Ed Harris) for $28.2 million (class counsel receiving $9.4m): 2013 ONSC 7686, and settled with the promoters for $17.5m at 2017 ONSC 2670 (class counsel receiving $5.8m). *Mossman v. Berkshire Funding* (ONSC, file 14-CV-512061) was a class action over the Berkshire program (*Kossow*, above); the defendants included Thorsteinssons and Gowlings (a similar claim *Schoep* (BCSC) was not certified). The claim was discontinued on Nov. 18, 2019: tinyurl.com/berk-class. A class action against GLGI, law and accounting firms was certified in Ont.: *Wintercorn v. Global Learning*, tinyurl.com/glgi-class, glgiclassaction.com (and see 2020 ONSC 1326); a parallel claim *Piett v. Global Learning*, 2018 SKQB 144, is not (yet) certified. A class action over a program where parents of students "donated" to Redeemer University, and it lent the funds to their children and then forgave the loans, was settled: classactionlaw.ca; "Redeemer settles $6-million lawsuit with families", *Hamilton Spectator*, Jan. 31, 2013. See also cba.org/classaction. In *Lemberg v. Perris*, 2010 ONSC 3690, a chartered accountant was liable to his clients for recommending an art-flip shelter from which he was receiving a secret commission, in breach of his fiduciary obligation to them. See also Hayhoe & Stacey, "Charities and Non-Profits", 2010 Cdn Tax Foundation conference report at 33:17-20; Thompson, "Dangerous Opinions", tinyurl.com/dangerous-opinions (Feb. 2011); Jakolev & Turner, "Tax Shelter Lawsuits", 19(12) *Canadian Tax Highlights* (ctf.ca) 6-7 (Dec. 2011); Baker & Schwartz, "Risk Management Issues", 2012 conference report at 7:13-16. For earlier discussion of tax opinions and law-firm liability see Smith, "Dealing with Tax Risk in an Opinion", 1994 conference report, 38:1-23. See also *Donor Beware: Investi-*

gation into the sufficiency of the CRA's warnings about questionable tax shelter schemes, Taxpayers' Ombudsman (oto-boc.gc.ca), Dec. 2013; and commentary by Aptowitzer, "Bolting the Barn Door After It's Burned to the Ground", xxxvi(11) *The Canadian Taxpayer* (Carswell) 86-88 (May 30, 2014). See 237.1(1)"tax shelter" Notes for lawsuits against promoters of other kinds of shelters.

For more on a **lawsuit limitation clock** not running until the tax appeal fails (*Lipson* case in last para.), see *King Lofts v. Emmons*, 2014 ONCA 215, para. 10; *Presidential MSH v. Marr*, 2017 ONCA 325, para. 53 (not "appropriate" to sue until CRA appeal process exhausted); *National Money Mart v. 24 Gold*, 2017 ONSC 6373 (GST/HST claim against purchaser arises when vendor pays CRA assessment); *Winmill v. Woodstock*, 2017 ONCA 962 (assault claim against police could wait until plaintiff's criminal charges resolved); *Nelson v. Lavoie*, 2019 ONCA 431 (not "appropriate" to sue financial planner for setting up invalid pension plan until CRA confirmed plan was invalid); and the SCC has granted leave to appeal in *Grant Thornton v. New Brunswick*, 2020 NBCA 18 (relying on audit report — non-tax case). *Contra*, see *Halsall v. Champion Consulting*, [2017] EWHC 1079 (England) (clock started running for lawyer-investors once they knew donation shelter was being investigated by revenue authority); *Coveley v. Thorsteinssons*, 2018 ONSC 4804 (claim that tax litigators did not initially tell taxpayers they had a weak case; clock started running once such advice was given); *Naples Pizza*, 2019 QCCS 710 (3-year clock for suing Revenu Québec for assessing GST started when auditor issued assessment, not when NP won TCC appeal); *Utah*, 2020 FCA 224 (time limit on lawsuit for failing to process refugee claim did not start when Access to Information request processed, but when injury caused by government delay was known). In *Charette v. Trinity Capital*, 2012 ONSC 2824 (leveraged-donation shelters: see *Maréchaux*), motions for summary judgment on the basis the claims were statute-barred were denied, because the law firm being sued (FMC) had represented the plaintiff in his dispute with CRA, likely stopping the limitation period from running (the action later settled for $37 million: 2019 ONSC 3153, para. 50).

Lawsuits against CRA, for not warning taxpayers that shelters would fail, or for not taking action to deregister charities, were struck out in *Scheuer*, 2016 FCA 7 (reversing the FC) (Global Learning shelters) and *Deluca*, 2016 ONSC 3865 (Liberty Wellness shelter; "Imposing tort liability in any way measured in relation to the disallowed tax benefit would simply confer the illicit benefit indirectly instead of directly": para. 63). See 171(1) Notes.

In *Whent*, [2000] 1 C.T.C. 329 (FCA) (leave to appeal denied 2000 CarswellNat 2397 (SCC)), an art-flip purchase for donation purposes was held not to be an adventure in the nature of trade, so the gain on the donation was a capital gain.

Art donations have led to prosecutions of promoters for evasion: Claude Simard (CRA news release [NR] July 14/10); Stéphane Saintonge (pled guilty and fined $840,000: NR June 21/12).

The one donation shelter that works and is accepted by CRA, though its value was reduced in 2011, is the purchase and donation of flow-through shares. See 40(12), 38(a.1) Notes and 66(12.6).

In *De Santis*, 2015 TCC 95, wine donated for auction was valued at $350 to $6,500 per bottle, based on international market values; the Court accepted the appellant's evidence as shifting the onus of proof to the Crown, which did not lead any better evidence. In *Balkwill*, 2018 TCC 99, donated wine was valued at auction prices excluding taxes, customs duties and Liquor Control Board markups.

For Quebec provincial tax purposes, a gift of art to a charity cannot be claimed until the charity sells the art, which must be within 5 years of the gift. The credit is limited by the sale price the charity obtains. This rule does not apply to donations to museums, galleries, recognized artistic organizations, governments or municipalities. (*Taxation Act*, ss. 752.0.10.11.1 and 11.2.)

In *Walsh*, 2008 TCC 282, the Crown was not allowed to argue that shares had been overvalued, after initially assessing on the basis there was no donation; but in *Lockie*, 2010 TCC 142 (FCA appeal discontinued A-164-10), the Crown was allowed under 152(9) to amend its Reply to allege "no donative intent" rather than just valuation.

An insurance policy is valued at cash surrender value minus policy loan outstanding: IT-244R3 para. 3; Information Circular 89-3 paras. 40-41; VIEWS docs 2006-0168591E5, 2007-0241901C6, 2007-0270391C6, 2009-0312021E5, 2011-0398461C6, 2012-0432601E5. See Blumenfeld & Manwaring, "Gifting New and In-force Insurance Policies to Charities", XVI(2) *Insurance Planning* (Federated Press) 1005-10 (2010); and Notes to 248(35). BC's Financial Services Authority had said that a charity accepting a gift of life insurance from a BC resident violates the province's *Insurance Act*, but after blowback now says "solicitation by *bona fide* charities of donations of life insurance policies or benefits" is OK: Bulletin INS-20-003 (tinyurl.com/ins-20-03), though it will investigate any practices that may involve vulnerable British Columbians [Manwaring & Fitzpatrick, "Charities and Gifts of Life Insurance: Clarification from BC's Financial Regulator", XXV(3) *Insurance Planning* (Federated Press) 17-20 (2020)]. See also Notes to 70(5.3) on valuing a policy.

See also Notes to 69(1) for more on "fair market value", and Patrick Boyle, "Gifts, Partial Gifts, Split Receipting, and Valuations", 20(3) *The Philanthropist* (thephilanthropist.ca) 205 at 225-41 (2006).

For gifts on death (bequests) see Notes to 118.1(4.1).

For a ruling allowing donations to a municipality to pay legal fees for a matter benefitting the community, see doc 2016-0634031R3.

For more discussion see Kerr & Chan, "Charities and Charitable Donations", *Practical Insights*, *Taxnet Pro* Tax Disputes Centre (Dec. 2020, 85pp); Drache et al., *Charities Taxation, Policy and Practice — Taxation*, chap. 17 (*Taxnet Pro* Reference Centre); Hoffstein & West, *Charitable Giving in Canada* (Carswell, 2013, 155pp); Campbell & Sprague, "Aligning Tax-Planning Strategies with Philanthropy", 66(1) *Canadian Tax Journal* 159-84 (2018). See also Notes to 248(31), (32), (35).

"Super" or "stretch" credits: Pre-2018 additional credit for first-time donors: 118.1(3.1). Pre-2018 credit for donating medicine for use abroad: 110.1(8), (9). Credit for Ontario farmers donating product to certain charities (*Taxation Act, 2007* s. 103.1.2): tinyurl.com/ont-farmdonate. Similar BC credit: tinyurl.com/bc-farm-food.

A person who has taken a vow of perpetual poverty (see Notes to 110(2)) will deduct all income under 110(2) and pay no tax, and cannot claim a 118.1 credit: para. (b).

The Standing Committee on Finance issued a report on tax incentives for charitable donations on Feb. 11, 2013: tinyurl.com/fin-charity. See Drache, "Flaccid Finance Committee Report on Charities", 21(3) *Canadian Not-for-Profit News* (Carswell) 17-19 (March 2013); Carole Fernando, "Finance Committee Reports on Tax Incentives for Charitable Giving", 10(4) *Tax Hyperion* (Carswell) 3-4 (April 2013). See also the very detailed "Evaluation of the Charitable Donation Tax Credit", in Dept. of Finance (fin.gc.ca), *Tax Expenditures and Evaluations 2014* (March 2015), pp. 30-70.

Bill C-458 (MP Peter Braid; Second Reading May 29, 2013) proposed to amend this definition, "total Crown gifts", "total cultural gifts" and "total ecological gifts" to allow donations up to 60 days after year-end. While the bill was originally expected to pass, it will not proceed. (Critics have suggested that moving the deadline to Feb. 28 might result in charitable giving losing out to RRSP contributions.)

Cls. (c)(i)(C) and (c)(ii)(B) amended and (c)(ii)(C) added by 2016 budget bill #2, for 2016 and later taxation years, to change "graduated rate estate" to "estate" in (c)(i)(C). This allows donations by an estate after 36 months (when it is no longer a GRE) up to 60 months after death: see 118.1(5.1).

Definition amended by 2014 budget bill #2, for 2016 and later taxation years.

Effective 2012, the provisions for donations to municipalities, Indian bands, foreign universities, governments, UN agencies and certain other entities (former paras. (b)-(g.1) of this definition) were changed (along with registered charities) to refer to "qualified donee", in conjunction with 2011 Budget changes giving CRA more control over donation receipts. See Notes to 149.1(1)"qualified donee".

Definition earlier amended by 2002-2013 technical bill, 2011 budget bill #2, 1997 and 1995 Budgets.

Regulations: 3503, Sch. VIII (prescribed universities outside Canada [since 2012, prescribed for 149.1(1)"qualified donee"(a)(iv)]).

Income Tax Folios: S7-F1-C1: Split-receipting and deemed fair market value [replaces IT-110R3].

Interpretation Bulletins: See lists at end of 118.1(1) and 118.1.

Information Circulars: 75-23: Tuition fees and charitable donations paid to privately supported secular and religious schools; 84-3R6: Gifts to certain charitable organizations outside Canada. See also at end of 118.1.

I.T. Technical News: 17 (loan of property as a gift).

Registered Charities Newsletters: 1 (donation of services); 2 (issuing official donation receipts where there are prizes); 3 (gifts of property other than cash); 4 (issuing receipts for gifts of art); 6 (can registered charities issue donation receipts for tuition fees?; the "art" of issuing official donation receipts); 7 (fundraising golf tournaments; fundraising auctions); 8 (further questions on golf tournaments; directed donations; issuing receipts for gifts of art; gifts of units in a hedge fund; membership fees; official donation receipts — Quebec donors); 9 (how do you establish the value of gifts-in-kind?); 11 (audit of tax preparer lands registered charities in hot water); 12 (valuing gifts of public securities); 14 (abusive donation scheme not allowed); 16 (donations of items of a speculative value); 18 (charitable donation tax shelter arrangements; what is a gift in kind? how should charitable gifts in kind be valued? donation of time-shares, including recreational property; can businesses receive receipts for donations made out of their inventory? can shares or stock options be gifts? can a charity issue a charitable receipt for a court-ordered payment made to it?); 22 (rent-free accommodations; donate-a-car programs); 23 (court news: volunteering services is not a gift); 24 (First Nations and qualified donee status); 25 (reimbursing funds to volunteers); 27 (receipts — who is the donor?); 29 (tax shelter gifting arrangements; valuing donations); 33 (improper receipting); *Charities Connection* 8 (golf tournaments; East Africa Drought Relief Fund).

Charities Policies: CPC-006: Gift-in-kind; CPC-008: Gift — payment to a registered charity instead of paying union dues; CPC-012: Out of pocket expenses; CPC-017: Official donation receipts — gifts of services; CPC-018: Official donation receipts — gifts out of inventory; CPC-019: Official donation receipts — payment for participation in a youth band or choir; CPC-025: Gift — expenses — volunteer; CPC-030: Organizations outside Canada to which Her Majesty has made a gift.

Charities Guidance: CG-007: Donation of gift certificates or gift cards; CG-010: Qualified donees; CG-015: Charitable organizations outside Canada that have received a gift from Her Majesty in Right of Canada; CG-016: Qualified donees — Consequences of returning donated property.

CRA Audit Manual: 12.16.0: Requesting appraisal or valuation.

Forms: RC4142: Tax advantages of donating to a charity [guide]; T1 General return, Line 34900; T1 General return, Sched. 9: Donations and gifts; T1236: Qualified donees worksheet/amounts provided to other organizations.

"total Crown gifts" — [Repealed]

Notes: "Total Crown gifts" repealed by 2014 budget bill #2, for 2016 and later taxation years. Even before repeal, the definition no longer applied except for a gift made under an agreement signed by Feb. 18, 1997. Gifts to the Crown, which pre-1997 could be for up to 100% of net income, were subject to the same 75% limit as charitable donations 1997-2015: 118.1(1)"total gifts"(a)(i), (b), 118.1(1)"total charitable gifts", 149.1(1)"qualified donee"(d). This responded to universities and hospitals setting up Crown foundations (created by the province but redirecting funds to the institution), which had an unfair advantage over other charities in competing for major gifts.

Definition amended by 2002-2013 technical bill (for gifts made after Dec. 20, 2002), 1997 and 1995 Budgets.

"total cultural gifts", of an individual for a particular taxation year, means the total of all amounts each of which is the eligible amount — to the extent it is not otherwise included in determining an amount that is deducted under this section in computing any individual's tax payable under this Part for any taxation year — of a gift

(a) of an object that the Canadian Cultural Property Export Review Board has determined meets the criterion set out in paragraph 29(3)(b) of the *Cultural Property Export and Import Act*,

(b) that is made to an institution or a public authority in Canada that is, at the time the gift is made, designated under subsection 32(2) of the *Cultural Property Export and Import Act* either generally or for a specified purpose related to that object, and

(c) that is made

(i) if the individual is not a trust,

(A) by the individual, or the individual's spouse or common-law partner, in the particular year or any of the five preceding taxation years,

(B) by the individual in the year in which the individual dies if the particular year is the taxation year that precedes the taxation year in which the individual dies, or

(C) by the individual's estate if subsection (5.1) applies to the gift and the particular year is the taxation year in which the individual dies or the preceding taxation year, or

(ii) if the individual is a trust,

(A) by the trust in the particular year or any of the five preceding taxation years,

(B) by the trust if

(I) the trust is an individual's estate,

(II) subsection (5.1) applies to the gift, and

(III) the particular year is a taxation year

1 in which the estate is the individual's graduated rate estate, and

2 that precedes the taxation year in which the gift is made, or

(C) by the trust if

(I) the end of the particular year is determined by paragraph 104(13.4)(a) because of an individual's death,

(II) the gift is made after the particular year and on or before the trust's filing-due date for the particular year, and

(III) the subject of the gift is property that is held by the trust at the time of the individual's death or is property that was substituted for that property;

(d) [Repealed]

Related Provisions: 39(1)(a)(i.1) — No capital gain on gift of cultural property to designated institution; 110.1(1)(c) — Parallel deduction for corporations; 118.1(1)"total gifts"(c) — Cultural gifts not limited to 75% of net income; 118.1(2.1) — Ordering of claims; 118.1(7.1) — Gifts of cultural property — deemed proceeds; 118.1(10), (10.1) — Fair market value; 118.1(21) — Granting of option is not cultural gift; 143(3.1) — Election in respect of gifts; 207.3 — Tax on institution that disposes of cultural property; 248(30)–(33) — Determination of eligible amount; 248(35)–(39) — Value of gift limited to cost if acquired within 3 years or as tax shelter.

Notes: Cultural gifts that qualify under this definition can be for up to 100% of net income, rather than the 75% limit that applies to charitable donations; see 118.1(1)"total gifts"(a)(i) and (c). Also, any capital gain on the donation is exempt: 39(1)(a)(i.1).

Due to *Heffel Gallery*, 2018 FC 605, cultural property would have needed a Canadian connection to qualify; but this was reversed both at 2019 FCA 82 and by the 2019 Budget amendment to this definition. See Notes to 118.1(10).

The Canadian Cultural Property Export Review Board has indicated that, where donated art has not been held for at least two years, the Board will normally not value the art at higher than the price at which the donor purchased it. (This no longer matters in light of 248(35).) See also 118.1(10.1).

A gift of an interest (including a residual interest) in an object is considered by CRA not to be a gift of an "object", and thus not to qualify: VIEWS doc 9524775.

Para. (a) amended by 2019 budget bill #1, effective March 19, 2019, to change "criteria set out in paragraphs 29(3)(b) and (c)" to "criterion set out in paragraph 29(3)(b)". See Notes to 39(1) re 39(1)(a)(i.1).

Cls. (c)(i)(C) and (c)(ii)(B) amended and (c)(ii)(C) added by 2016 budget bill #2, for 2016 and later taxation years, to change "graduated rate estate" to "estate" in (c)(i)(C). This allows donations by an estate after 36 months (when it is no longer a GRE) up to 60 months after death: see 118.1(5.1).

Definition (other than para. (a)) amended by 2014 budget bill #2, for 2016 and later taxation years.

Opening words of definition amended by 2002-2013 technical bill, for gifts made after Dec. 20, 2002, to change "fair market value" to "eligible amount" (see 248(31)).

Interpretation Bulletins: IT-407R4: Dispositions of cultural property to designated Canadian institutions. See also at end of 118.1.

I.T. Technical News: 17 (loan of property as a gift).

Registered Charities Newsletters: 24 (cultural property as gifts).

"total ecological gifts", of an individual for a particular taxation year, means the total of all amounts each of which is the eligible amount — to the extent it is not otherwise included in determining an amount that is deducted under this section in computing any individual's tax payable under this Part for any taxation year — of a gift (other than a gift any part of the eligible amount of which is included in the total cultural gifts of any individual for any taxation year)

(a) of land (including a covenant or an easement to which land is subject or, in the case of land in the Province of Quebec, a personal servitude (the rights to which the land is subject and which has a term of not less than 100 years) or a real servitude)

(i) the fair market value of which is certified by the Minister of the Environment, and

(ii) that is certified by that Minister, or by a person designated by that Minister, to be ecologically sensitive land, the conservation and protection of which is, in the opinion of that Minister or the designated person, important to the preservation of Canada's environmental heritage,

(b) that is made to a qualified donee that is

(i) Her Majesty in right of Canada or of a province,

(i.1) a municipality in Canada, or a municipal or public body performing a function of government in Canada, that is approved by that Minister or the designated person in respect of the gift, or

(ii) a registered charity (other than a private foundation) one of the main purposes of which is, in the opinion of that Minister, the conservation and protection of Canada's environmental heritage, and that is approved by that Minister or the designated person in respect of the gift, and

(c) that is made

(i) if the individual is not a trust,

(A) by the individual, or the individual's spouse or common-law partner, in the particular year or any of the 10 preceding taxation years,

(B) by the individual in the year in which the individual dies if the particular year is the taxation year that precedes the taxation year in which the individual dies, or

(C) by the individual's estate if subsection (5.1) applies to the gift and the particular year is the taxation year in which the individual dies or the preceding taxation year, or

(ii) if the individual is a trust,

(A) by the trust in the particular year or any of the 10 preceding taxation years,

(B) by the trust if

(I) the trust is an individual's estate,

(II) subsection (5.1) applies to the gift, and

(III) the particular year is a taxation year

1 in which the estate is the individual's graduated rate estate, and

2 that precedes the taxation year in which the gift is made, or

(C) by the trust if

(I) the end of the particular year is determined by paragraph 104(13.4)(a) because of an individual's death,

(II) the gift is made after the particular year and on or before the trust's filing-due date for the particular year, and

(III) the subject of the gift is property that is held by the trust at the time of the individual's death or is property that was substituted for that property;

Related Provisions: 38(a.2) — Reduced capital gain inclusion on ecological gift; 110.1(1)(d) — Parallel deduction for corporations; 118.1(1)"total gifts"(d) — Ecological gifts not limited to 20% of net income; 118.1(2.1) — Ordering of claims; 118.1(10.1)–(10.5) — Determination of fair market value by Minister of the Environment; 118.1(12) — Fair market value of ecological servitude, covenant or easement; 118.1(21) — Granting of option is not ecological gift; 207.31 — Tax if donee disposes of the property; 248(30)–(33) — Determination of eligible amount.

Notes: Ecological gifts that qualify under this definition can be for up to 100% of net income, rather than the 75% limit that applies to charitable donations; see 118.1(1)"total gifts"(a)(i) and (d). As well, the donation can be carried forward 10 years rather than the usual 5: para. (c). "Land" can include buildings: see 70(5.2) Notes.

If the donee ever disposes of the land without authorization from the Minister of the Environment, a special 50% tax applies under 207.31.

For the administrative definition of "ecologically sensitive land" and more detail on this credit, see Environment Canada, *The Ecological Gifts Program*, at ec.gc.ca/pde-egp or call 1-800-668-6767. For interpretation of the definition by the CRA, see VIEWS docs 2002-0163405, 2004-0063831E5, 2004-0106211E5, 2008-0275041E5, 2009-0338871R3.

In *Yellow Point*, 2020 FCA 195, the ecological gift was made when the property was transferred, not the next year when it was designated as ecological property.

On donation of a conservation easement, see 118.1(12) and VIEWS docs 2002-0174285, 2013-0513251E5. In *Coal Property* (2019), 153 T.C. No. 7 (US Tax Court), a $155m donation for a conservation easement was denied because the easement was not "protected in perpetuity".

See also Blom, "Ecologically Sensitive Land and Estate Planning", 4(7) *Tax Hyperion* (Carswell, July 2007); Zweibel & Cooper, "Charitable Gift of Conservation Easements", 58(1) *Canadian Tax Journal* 26-61 (2010).

Para. (a) opening words and (b)(i)-(ii) amended (adding (i.1)) by 2017 budget bill #2, for gifts made after March 21, 2017. For earlier gifts, read:

(a) of land (including a covenant or an easement to which land is subject or, in the case of land in the Province of Quebec, a real servitude) ...

(b) ...

(i) Her Majesty in right of Canada or of a province, a municipality in Canada or a municipal or public body performing a function of government in Canada, or

(ii) a registered charity one of the main purposes of which is, in the opinion of that Minister, the conservation and protection of Canada's environmental heritage, and that is approved by that Minister or the designated person in respect of the gift, and

Cls. (c)(i)(A), (c)(i)(C) and (c)(ii)(B) amended and (c)(ii)(C) added by 2016 budget bill #2, for 2016 and later taxation years, to change "five" to "10" in (c)(i)(A) and "graduated rate estate" to "estate" in (c)(i)(C) (this allows donations by an estate after 36 months, when it is no longer a GRE, up to 60 months after death: see 118.1(5.1)). (c)(ii)(B) previously read (this version now deemed never to have been in force):

(B) by the trust if the trust is a graduated rate estate, subsection (5.1) applies to the gift and the particular year is the taxation year in which the gift is made or a preceding taxation year of the estate;

Definition amended by 2014 budget bill #2, for 2016 and later taxation years. Before the amendment, read:

"total ecological gifts", of an individual for a taxation year, means the total of all amounts each of which is the eligible amount of a gift (other than a gift de-

scribed in the definition "total cultural gifts") of land (including a covenant or an easement to which land is subject or, in the case of land in the Province of Quebec, a real servitude) if

(a) the fair market value of the gift is certified by the Minister of the Environment,

(b) the land is certified by that Minister, or by a person designated by that Minister, to be ecologically sensitive land, the conservation and protection of which is, in the opinion of that Minister or the designated person, important to the preservation of Canada's environmental heritage, and

(c) the gift was made by the individual in the year or in any of the 10 preceding taxation years to a qualified donee that is

(i) Her Majesty in right of Canada or of a province,

(ii) a municipality in Canada,

(iii) a municipal or public body performing a function of government in Canada, or

(iv) a registered charity one of the main purposes of which is, in the opinion of that Minister, the conservation and protection of Canada's environmental heritage, and that is approved by that Minister or the designated person in respect of the gift,

to the extent that those amounts were not included in determining an amount that was deducted under this section in computing the individual's tax payable under this Part for a preceding taxation year;

Para. (c) opening words amended by 2014 budget bill #2, for gifts made after Feb. 10, 2014, to add "a qualified donee that is" (so the definition in 149.1(1) must be satisfied); and to change "five" to "10" (so an unclaimed donation can be carried forward up to 10 years).

Definition amended by 2002-2013 technical bill (Part 5 — technical) for gifts made after Dec. 20, 2002, to use the term "eligible amount" (see 248(31)) instead of "fair market value", make various minor wording changes and accommodate Quebec civil law terms.

Para. (a) (now subpara. (c)(iii)) amended by 2002-2013 technical bill (Part 5 — technical) for gifts made after May 8, 2000, to add "or a municipal or a public body performing a function of government in Canada". (See Notes to 118.1(1)"total charitable gifts" re former para. (d.1) of that definition.)

Opening words of 118.1(1)"total ecological gifts" amended by 2000 Budget to change "that is certified by the Minister of the Environment" to "the fair market value of which is certified by the Minister of the Environment and that is certified by that Minister", effective for gifts made, or proposed to be made, after February 27, 2000. Thus, it is not just the *existence* of the gift that must be certified by the MoE, but also its value (see 118.1(10.1)–(10.5) for administrative procedures).

Definition "total ecological gifts" added by 1995 Budget, effective for gifts made after February 27, 1995. Para. (a) amended by 1997 Budget, effective for gifts made after February 18, 1997, to add reference to Her Majesty in right of Canada or a province. Crown gifts are no longer given a special preference of up to 100% of net income (see Notes to "total Crown gifts"). Therefore ecological gifts to the Crown are now included in this definition so that they continue to benefit from the 100% rate.

Income Tax Folios: S7-F1-C1: Split-receipting and deemed fair market value [replaces IT-110R3].

I.T. Technical News: 17 (loan of property as a gift).

Registered Charities Newsletters: 22 (ecological gifts).

"total gifts" of an individual for a taxation year means the total of

(a) the least of

(i) the individual's total charitable gifts for the year,

(ii) the individual's income for the year where the individual dies in the year or in the following taxation year, and

(iii) in any other case, the lesser of the individual's income for the year and the amount determined by the formula

$$0.75A + 0.25(B + C + D - E)$$

where

A is the individual's income for the year,

B is the total of all amounts, each of which is that proportion of the individual's taxable capital gain for the taxation year in respect of a gift made by the individual in the taxation year (in respect of which gift an eligible amount is included in the individual's total charitable gifts for the taxation year) that the eligible amount of the gift is of the individual's proceeds of disposition in respect of the gift,

C is the total of all amounts each of which is a taxable capital gain of the individual for the year, because of subsection 40(1.01), from a disposition of a property in a preceding taxation year,

D is the total of all amounts each of which is determined in respect of the individual's depreciable property of a prescribed class and equal to the lesser of

(A) the amount included under subsection 13(1) in respect of the class in computing the individual's income for the year, and

(B) the total of all amounts each of which is determined in respect of a disposition that is the making of a gift of property of the class made by the individual in the year (in respect of which gift an eligible amount is included in the individual's total charitable gifts for the taxation year) equal to the lesser of

(I) that proportion, of the amount by which the proceeds of disposition of the property exceed any outlays and expenses, to the extent that they were made or incurred by the individual for the purpose of making the disposition, that the eligible amount of the gift is of the individual's proceeds of disposition in respect of the gift, and

(II) that proportion, of the capital cost to the individual of the property, that the eligible amount of the gift is of the individual's proceeds of disposition in respect of the gift, and

E is the total of all amounts each of which is the portion of an amount deducted under section 110.6 in computing the individual's taxable income for the year that can reasonably be considered to be in respect of a gift referred to in the description of B or C,

(b) [Repealed]

(c) the individual's total cultural gifts for the year, and

(d) the individual's total ecological gifts for the year.

Related Provisions: 248(35)–(39) — Value of gift limited to cost if acquired within 3 years or as tax shelter; 257 — Formula cannot calculate to less than zero.

Notes: Charitable donations (118.1(1)"total charitable gifts") are limited to 75% of net income (subpara. (a)(iii)), but 100% for "total cultural gifts" and "total ecological gifts" (see Notes to each of those definitions). Crown gifts (gifts to the government) are now treated as charitable donations: see Notes to 118.1(1)"total Crown gifts". The taxpayer can choose not to claim donations so as to use other credits (or for any other reason), and carry the donations forward: VIEWS doc 2011-0410641E5. Unclaimed amounts can be claimed in any of the next 5 years (see (c)(i)(A) of each definition; 10 years for ecological gifts). For an example of the carryforward see *Tufts*, 2008 TCC 68.

On the 0.25(B+C+D–E) calculation (note that B applies only to a gain "in respect of a gift", see Wen, "Charitable Gifts by Life Interest Trust After Beneficiary's Death", 10(3) *Canadian Tax Focus* (ctf.ca) 15-16 (Aug. 2020).

For provincial tax, Quebec eliminated the "75% of income" limit in its 2016 Budget.

For a good review of the rules see CRA pamphlet P113, *Gifts and Income Tax*. See also Notes to 118.1(1)"total charitable gifts" and 118.1(3).

For an *alter ego* or similar trust, element B for the year a beneficiary dies includes a gift of capital property made the next year: VIEWS doc 2019-0799641E5.

Definition amended by 2014 budget bill #2 (for 2016 and later tax years); 2002-2013 technical bill; 1997, 1996 and 1995 Budgets.

I.T. Technical News: 17 (loan of property as a gift).

Forms: T1 General return, Line 34900; T1 General return, Sched. 9: Donations and gifts.

Notes [subsec. 118.1(1)]: 118.1(1) amended by 1991 technical bill, effective December 11, 1988.

Interpretation Bulletins: See list at end of s. 118.1.

Information Circulars: See list at end of s. 118.1.

(2) Proof of gift — An eligible amount of a gift is not to be included in the total charitable gifts, total cultural gifts or total ecological gifts of an individual unless the making of the gift is evidenced by filing with the Minister

(a) a receipt for the gift that contains prescribed information;

(b) in the case of a gift described in the definition "total cultural gifts" in subsection (1), the certificate issued under subsection 33(1) of the *Cultural Property Export and Import Act*; and

(c) in the case of a gift described in the definition "total ecological gifts" in subsection (1), both certificates referred to in that definition.

Related Provisions: 110.1(2) — Parallel rule for corporations; 188.2 — Suspension of charity's receipting privileges; 230(2) — Books and records to be kept by charity; 248(30)–(33) — Determination of eligible amount; 248(41) — Donation value deemed nil if taxpayer does not inform donee of circumstances requiring reduction.

Notes: See Notes to 118.1(1)"total charitable gifts". See also Notes to 110.1(1) re taking a business deduction instead of a donation receipt. See Notes to Reg. 3501(1) re receipt requirements. A receipt that does not accurately reflect the money or value of goods donated is not a "receipt": *Guobadia*, 2016 TCC 182, para. 32.

A charity must verify the "true donor" before issuing a receipt: tinyurl.com/true-donor [Drache, "Issuing Receipts", 26(2) *Canadian Not-for-Profit News* (Carswell) 9-10 (Feb. 2018)]. Receipts for raffles and fundraising that give the donor an "advantage": see Notes to 248(32).

A charity is not legally required to issue a receipt: VIEWS doc 2012-0469971E5. See also Drache, "Receipt Issuing and Donor Goodwill", 25(2) *Canadian Not-for-Profit News* (Carswell) 10-11 (Feb. 2017).

118.1(2) opening words amended by 2014 budget bill #2, for 2016 and later taxation years, to delete "total Crown gifts" before "total cultural gifts".

118.1(2) opening words amended by 2002-2013 technical bill (Part 5 — technical) effective for gifts made after Dec. 20, 2002, to add "An eligible amount of" and change "proven" to "evidenced".

118.1(2) amended by 2000 Budget (last change effective for gifts made after Dec. 20, 2000) and 1995 Budget.

Regulations: 3501 (prescribed information).

Income Tax Folios: S7-F1-C1: Split-receipting and deemed fair market value [replaces IT-110R3].

Interpretation Bulletins: IT-407R4: Dispositions of cultural property to designated Canadian institutions. See also at end of s. 118.1.

Information Circulars: See list at end of s. 118.1.

Advance Tax Rulings: ATR-63: Donations to agents of the Crown.

Registered Charities Newsletters: See under 118.1(1)"total charitable gifts" and Reg. 3501(1).

(2.1) Ordering of gifts — For the purpose of determining an individual's total charitable gifts, total cultural gifts and total ecological gifts for a taxation year, no amount in respect of a gift described in any of the definitions of those expressions and made in a particular taxation year is to be considered to have been included in determining an amount that was deducted under this section in computing the individual's tax payable under this Part for a taxation year until amounts in respect of such gifts made in taxation years preceding the particular year that can be so considered are so considered.

Related Provisions: 110.1(1.1)(b) — Parallel ordering rule for corporations.

Notes: 118.1(2.1) opening words amended by 2014 budget bill #2, for 2016 and later taxation years, to delete "total Crown gifts" before "total cultural gifts".

118.1(2.1) added by 1997 Budget, for taxation years that begin after 1996.

(3) Deduction by individuals [credit] for gifts — For the purpose of computing the tax payable under this Part by an individual for a taxation year, there may be deducted such amount as the individual claims not exceeding the amount determined by the formula

$$A \times B + C \times D + E \times F$$

where

A is the appropriate percentage for the year;

B is the lesser of $200 and the individual's total gifts for the year;

C is the highest individual percentage for the year;

D is

(a) in the case of a trust (other than a graduated rate estate or a "qualified disability trust" as defined in subsection 122(3)), the amount, if any, by which its total gifts for the year exceeds $200, and

(b) in any other case, the lesser of

(i) the amount, if any, by which the individual's total gifts for the year exceeds $200, and

(ii) the amount, if any, by which the individual's amount taxable for the year for the purposes of subsection 117(2) exceeds the first dollar amount for the year referred to in paragraph 117(2)(e);

E is 29%; and

F is the amount, if any, by which the individual's total gifts for the year exceeds the total of $200 and the amount determined for D.

Related Provisions: 37(5) — Scientific research and experimental development expenditures; 110(2) — Deduction for member of religious order who has taken vow of perpetual poverty; 110.1 — Deduction for gifts by corporations; 117(1) — Tax payable under this Part; 118.1(3.1) — Additional credit for first-time donors; 118.1(4)–(5.3) [before 2016], 118.1(4.1)–(5.2) [after 2015] — Gift on death; 118.1(5.4), (6) — Gift of capital property — designation of value; 118.1(7) — Gift of art by artist; 118.1(13)–(20) — No credit for gift of non-qualifying securities; 118.91 — Individual resident in Canada for part of the year; 118.95(a), 128(2)(e)(iii)(B), 128(2)(f)(iv), 128(2)(g)(ii)(B) — Application to bankrupt individual; 152(6) — Reassessment; 164(5), (5.1) — Effect of carryback of loss; 225.1(7) — Donation shelter assessment can be half-collected while under appeal.

Notes: Ordinary donations qualify up to 75% of net income. See Notes to 118.1(1)"total gifts" and "total charitable gifts".

The formula works out to 15% (248(1)"appropriate percentage") on the first $200 and 29% on gifts over $200, but 33% (248(1)"highest individual percentage") on gifts over $200 to the extent the taxpayer's income is taxed at the 33% rate (over $214,368 taxable income for 2020 and $216,511 for 2021: see 117(2)). The credit is then enhanced to 20-30% (first $200) and 40-54% (over $200) by a parallel provincial tax credit. In some provinces (ON, QC, NB, Yukon), the combined credit is lower than the top marginal rate, so a high-income taxpayer who earns an extra $1,000 and donates it all to charity loses money. CRA provides a phone/web app for an individual to calculate the effect of the credit for themselves: tinyurl.com/cra-mobapps.

(For a trust that pays tax at the top marginal rate on all income (see 122(1)), the credit is 33% on all donations above $200 per year: D(a).)

Since either spouse can claim the credit (118.1(1)"total charitable gifts"(c)(i)(A)), it can be better for a lower-income spouse (with tax withheld at source) to claim it, and invest the resulting tax refund without 74.1(1) attribution to the other spouse.

A trust can claim the donation credit: VIEWS doc 2003-0015041E5.

118.1(3) amended by 2016 tax-rate bill and 2016 budget bill #1, for 2016 and later taxation years; and when calculating D, an individual's total gifts for the year are determined without reference to gifts made before the 2016 taxation year [this affects a trust with an off-calendar year-end].

118.1(3)B amended by 1994 Budget, effective 1994, to reduce the threshold at which the high credit cuts in from $250 to $200.

Income Tax Folios: S7-F1-C1: Split-receipting and deemed fair market value [replaces IT-110R3].

Interpretation Bulletins: IT-226R: Gift to a charity of a residual interest in real property or an equitable interest in a trust; IT-297R2: Gifts in kind to charity and others; IT-407R4: Dispositions of cultural property to designated Canadian institutions. See also at end of s. 118.1.

Information Circulars: 75-23: Tuition fees and charitable donations paid to privately supported secular and religious schools.

Registered Charities Newsletters: See under 118.1(1)"total charitable gifts".

Forms: T1 General return, Line 34900; T1 General return, Sched. 9: Donations and gifts.

(3.1) [First-time donor super credit — Repealed]

Related Provisions: 118.1(1)"first-time donor" — Definition; 118.1(3.2) — Allocation of super credit between spouses.

Notes: 118.1(3.1), added by 2013 budget bill #1 for donations made after March 20, 2013 but only through the end of 2017 and repealed by the same bill for 2018 and later taxation years, supplemented the regular credit under 118.1(3), which is 15% on the first $200 and 29% on additional donations (33% to the extent of income earned in the top bracket). For someone who (and whose spouse or common-law partner) did not claim a donation credit for any year after 2007 [118.1(1)"first-time donor"], the federal credit on the first $1,000 of donations in any of 2013-2017 was an extra 25% (i.e., 40% on the first $200 and 54% on the rest (58% for a person in the top bracket)). This is sometimes called a "stretch" credit or "super" credit. 118.1(3.1) read:

> (3.1) First-time donor [stretch] credit — For the purpose of computing the tax payable under this Part by a first-time donor for a taxation year that begins after 2012 and ends before 2018, the first-time donor may deduct an amount not exceeding the lesser of $250 and the amount that is 25% of the total of all amounts, each of which is an eligible amount of a gift of money in the year or in any of the four preceding taxation years and in respect of which the first-time donor — or a person who is, at the end of the year, the first-time donor's spouse (other than a person who was at that time separated from the first-time donor by reason of a breakdown of their marriage) or common- law partner — has deducted an amount for the year under subsection (3).

The extra credit could be claimed only once. New donors were thus advised to consider accumulating donations from March 21/13 until $1,000 and claiming them all at once, but no later than the 2017 return.

2013 Budget table A2.1 forecast that this would cost the federal government $25 million in each of 2013-14 through 2015-16, $30m in 2016-17 and $20m in 2017-18; but Finance's *Tax Expenditures and Evaluations 2017* reports costs of only $4-5m for each year 2013-17. CRA reported 98,010 people claimed the credit in 2013: Drache, "Charitable Donation Data", 23(4) *Canadian Not-for-Profit News* (Carswell) 31-32 (April 2015). For economic and policy discussion see Policy Forum articles, 61(4) *Canadian Tax Journal* 1087-1122 (2013).

(3.2) [Repealed]

Notes: See Notes to 118.1(3.1). 118.1(3.2) added by 2013 budget bill #1, for gifts made after March 20, 2013, then by the same bill repealed for 2018 and later taxation years.

(4) Gifts — deaths before 2016 — If an individual dies before 2016 and any of this subsection and subsections (5), (5.2), (5.3), (7) and (7.1) (as they read for the taxation year in which the death occurred) applied to deem the individual to have made a gift at a time before the death, then for the purposes of this section the gift is deemed not to have been made by any other taxpayer or at any other time.

Related Provisions: 70(5) — Deemed disposition of property immediately before death; 118.1(5) — Gift made by will deemed made in year of death.

Notes: This rule ensures that if the old rules apply to a pre-2016 death, none of the new rules in 118.1(4.1)-(5.2) will apply. See Notes to 118.1(4.1) for post-2015 deaths, and to 118.1(5) for pre-2016 deaths.

118.1(4) amended by 2014 budget bill #2, for 2016 and later taxation years.

Earlier amended by 2000 Budget (last change effective 2000) and 1997 Budget.

Interpretation Bulletins: IT-288R2: Gifts of capital properties to a charity and others; IT-407R4: Dispositions of cultural property to designated Canadian institutions. See also at end of s. 118.1.

(4.1) Gifts — deaths after 2015 [conditions for 118.1(5) to apply] — Subsection (5) applies to a gift if an estate arises on and as a consequence of the death after 2015 of an individual and the gift is

(a) made by the individual by the individual's will;

(b) deemed by subsection (5.2) to have been made in respect of the death; or

(c) made by the estate.

Notes: Amendments to 118.1(4.1)-(5.2) change the rules for donations on death, providing more flexibility for deaths after 2015.

Donations made by will, by the estate and "designation" donations [RRSP, RRIF, TFSA or life insurance policy: 118.1(5.2)] are now all deemed to have been made by the estate, at the time the property is transferred to the charity [118.1(4.1), (5)]. The estate can then allocate the donation among any of: the estate's taxation year in which the donation is made; any earlier year of the estate [118.1(1)"total charitable gifts" *["tcg"]* (c)(ii)(B)]; or the last 2 taxation years of the deceased [tcg(c)(i)(C), 118.1(5.1)]. (There are parallel rules in 118.1(1)"total cultural gifts" and "total ecological gifts".) The 118.1(1)"total gifts" limits apply to whichever one claims the donation.

The estate trustee may need a (full or partial) clearance certificate from the CRA before making a donation. See Notes to 159(3).

The 2016 budget bill #2 amendments to 118.1(5.1), first released Jan. 15, 2016 (and related amendments to 38(a.1), (a.2), 39(1), 118.1(1)), further relaxed the rules by allowing the estate to make the donation up to 60 months after death, rather than requiring it to be made by a "graduated rate estate" (up to 36 months after death).

Donated property (except for "designation" donations) must have been acquired by the estate on and as a consequence of the death, or have been substituted for such property [118.1(5.1), 248(5), (8)]. For other property, the estate can claim the credit in the year the donation is made or any of the 5 following years: tcg(c)(ii)(B).

Because of these changes, one no longer need track whether a donation was provided for in the deceased's will rather than made by the estate. Also, the gift is valued (for donation purposes) when paid to the charity in all cases, rather than at death if made by will. CRA is reviewing its practice of allowing a gift for the year of death as long as the estate advises the charity in writing of the gift and the charity states it will accept it: 2018-0745851C6 [2018 CALU q.4].

However, the rule permitting either spouse to claim a donation, which was long-time CRA administrative policy and is now in tcg(c)(i)(A), does not apply to tcg(c)(i)(C), so a spouse can no longer claim a donation made in the deceased's will (as VIEWS doc 2010-0377811E5 permitted before 2016). The CRA advised the author (2014-0555511E5) that it will no longer apply the 2010 policy, and reconfirmed this in 2016-0624851C6 [CPA QC 2016 q.8]. The author then raised this issue with Finance, but no further amendment will be made. (Note that the point of the spousal-sharing rule is to have spouses not worry about whose name appears on a receipt, since many spouses pool funds in one account, yet they may not know until after year-end who will claim donations. This account sharing does not continue after death.)

See also docs 2016-0652821C6 [2016 APFF q.6] (tcg(c)(i)(A) and (c)(ii)(A) apply to a graduated rate estate (GRE) up to 60 months); 2016-0651731C6 [2016 APFF q.7] (tcg(c)(ii)(B) applies to GRE up to 60 months); 2017-0698191E5 (estate donation of shares, carried back to deceased's return, eliminates capital gain via 38(a.1)); 2019-0799641E5 ((c)(ii)(C) applies to *alter ego* trust).

In CRA's view, a common-law gift "*donatio mortis causa*" (DMC) is subject to a condition precedent (that the donor die), and so cannot be claimed until the year of death: 2007-0228411E5. Gail Black (millerthomson.com Charities Newsletter Jan. 2008) argues that the CRA is wrong, as a DMC is a present gift subject to a condition subsequent, and once death occurs it is retrospective to when the gift was made.

In *Turcotte*, 2015 QCCA 396 (leave to appeal denied 2015 CarswellQue 7382 (SCC)), a donation by will triggered a credit and could not also be a 104(6) deduction to the estate as an amount paid to a beneficiary.

For charitable remainder trusts see Ho, "Will Planning", 2(1) *Canadian Tax Focus* (ctf.ca) 5 (Feb. 2012); Chenier, "CRTs are Alive and Well in Canada", 21(9) *Canadian Not-for-Profit News* (Carswell) 67-68 (Sept. 2013); Hoffstein, "CRA's views on charitable remainder trusts", Miller Thomson *Social Impact*, March 18, 2021 (tinyurl.com/hoffs-crt); docs 2011-0403611R3, 2016-0625841E5, 2017-0734261E5.

See generally tinyurl.com/estate-donations-cra.

See also Valentine & Smith, "Proposed Changes to Charitable Gifts by Will", 7(4) *Taxes & Wealth Management* (Carswell) 10-12 (Sept. 2014); Marino, "Charitable Gifts at Death", XX(3) *Insurance Planning* (Federated Press) 1289-92 (2014); Fabbro, "Dying to Donate", 2249 *Tax Topics* (CCH) 1-4 (April 16, 2015) and 244 *The Estate Planner* 1-4 (May 2015); Eisenbraun et al., "Graduated Rate Estates and Gifting on Death", 2015 Prairie Provinces Tax Conf. (ctf.ca), 9:1-18; Schusheim & Katz, "Charitable Gift Planning", 63(3) *Canadian Tax Journal* 803-24 (2015); Lee-Kennedy & Kleinman, "Philanthropy: Recent Developments", 2015 Cdn Tax Foundation conference report, 40:1-24; Corbin, "Donating Pre-Retirement Death Benefits" and "Letter to Finance", 33(11) *Money & Family Law* (Carswell) 81-82 (Nov. 2018).

118.1(4.1) added by 2014 budget bill #2, for 2016 and later taxation years.

(5) Gifts — deaths after 2015 — If this subsection applies to a gift, then for the purposes of the Act (other than subsections (4.1) and (5.2)) the gift is deemed to be made

    (a) by the estate referred to in subsection (4.1) and not by any other taxpayer; and

    (b) subject to subsection (13), at the time that the property that is the subject of the gift is transferred to the donee and not at any other time.

Related Provisions: 38(a.1)(ii) — Gift of publicly-traded securities made on death; 38(a.2) — Reduced capital gain inclusion on ecological gift; 39(1)(a)(i.1) — Gain on disposition not capital gain; 70(5) — Deemed disposition of property immediately before death; 104(7.02) — No deduction to estate for amount claimed as donation; 118.1(4) — Carryback of gift made in year of death; 118.1(4.1) — Conditions for 118.1(5) to apply; 118.1(5.1) [after 2015] — Where gift is made by graduated rate estate; 118.1(5.1), (5.2) [before 2016], 118.1(5.2)(a) [after 2015] — Gift of life insurance on death. See also at end of s. 118.1.

Notes: See Notes to 118.1(4.1) for post-2015 deaths.

118.1(5) amended by 2014 budget bill #2, for 2016 and later taxation years.

Pre-2016 deaths:

The CRA considers that a gift by will of a specific amount to a list of charities, giving the executor discretion as to how much to allocate to each charity, can qualify under former 118.1(5). Similarly, a gift to charity without naming one, allowing the executor discretion to choose the charity, qualifies: VIEWS doc 2001-0090205. Similarly, a gift to a private foundation to be created by the executors qualifies, even though the foundation did not exist at time of death: 2000-0055825. See also 9727787, 2004-0081021R3, 2005-0142121E5, 2010-0370491C6, 2012-0453131C6; 2012-0472161I7 (distinguishing between donation and settlement of capital interest in the estate); 2013-0490141I7, 2014-054062117. Similarly, a bequest allowing a spouse to select some pieces of art for herself, with the rest going to charity, qualifies: 2005-0139611E5. A gift of an equitable interest in a testamentary spousal trust qualified in 2006-0182881R3. The gift should be valued as of death date even if not received by the charity until much later: 2010-0363131C6, 2011-0430131E5; *Registered Charities Newsletter* #27, q.7. A gift does not qualify if the value of the donation cannot reasonably be determined when it is made, or if it is unclear who will receive the capital: 2007-0259841E5. Similarly, a gift of "$100,000 minus the amount my corporation will be able to donate" would not qualify: 2013-0492791C6 [2013 APFF q.1].

If a beneficiary disclaims a right to the capital of a trust in favour of a charity, there may be an immediate gift under the will for purposes of former 118.1(5): 2002-0117823.

Where a will provides for transfer of preferred shares to a charity followed by redemption of the shares for cash, see 2002-0174333. Where a will provides for a spousal trust with trustee encroachment power plus a charity bequest on the spouse's death, see 2011-0428021E5. On a gift by will of non-qualifying securities, see 2013-0486701E5.

Where the residue of an estate is donated to charity and the deceased's return is due before the amount under former 118.1(5) can be calculated, the CRA states that the "gift should occur within a reasonable time period" after death and a later adjustment

request can be filed after the return is assessed: 2000-0053185. Wolfe Goodman suggested estimating the gift, requesting assessment be delayed until the amount is known, and filing a protective objection if an assessment is issued: XI(2) *Goodman on Estate Planning* (Federated Press) 879 (2002).

Where an amount was bequeathed to a priest who had taken a vow of perpetual poverty (see 110(2)), but was paid by the estate to a charity the priest served, the donation did not qualify as made by the deceased: *MacDonald Estate*, 2004 TCC 333.

See also Notes to 118.1(4.1) re common-law gifts "*donatio mortis causa*", and re charitable remainder trusts.

For more on pre-2016 118.1(5) see Ball & Dietrich, "Charitable Bequests and Estate Planning", 59(1) *Canadian Tax Journal* 103-24 (2001); Newcombe, "Charitable Giving by Alter Ego and Joint Partner Trusts", 6(6) *Tax Hyperion* (Carswell, June 2009) and "Donations by Will", 8(1) (Jan. 2011); Corbin, "Charitable Gifts Made in Settlement of a Will Challenge", 25(1) *Money & Family Law* (Carswell) 1-3 (Jan. 2010) and "The Gift That Keeps on Giving", 26(2) 9-10 (Feb. 2011); Sharma, "Testamentary Gifts to U.S. Charities: Some Words of Caution", 4(4) *It's Personal* (Carswell) 1-3 (Nov. 2011); Bromley, "Devising Without Denial: Charitable Gift Planning In Revocationland", 2013 B.C. Tax Conf. (ctf.ca), 13:1-23.

118.1(5) earlier amended by 1997 Budget, for gifts made after July 1997.

Interpretation Bulletins: IT-226R: Gift to a charity of a residual interest in real property or an equitable interest in a trust; IT-407R4: Dispositions of cultural property to designated Canadian institutions. See also at end of s. 118.1.

Registered Charities Newsletters: 1 (donation of services); 2 (issuing official donation receipts where there are prizes); 3 (gifts of property other than cash); 4 (issuing receipts for gifts of art); 6 (can registered charities issue donation tax receipts for tuition fees?; the "art" of issuing official donation receipts); 7 (fundraising golf tournaments; fundraising auctions); 8 (further questions on golf tournaments; directed donations; issuing receipts for gifts of art; gifts of units in a hedge fund; Membership fees; official donation receipts — Quebec donors); 9 (how do you establish the value of gifts-in-kind?); 11 (audit of tax preparer lands registered charities in hot water); 12 (valuing gifts of public securities); 27 (gift of residue of an estate can qualify).

(5.1) Gifts by graduated rate estate — This subsection applies to a gift made by an individual's graduated rate estate (determined without reference to paragraph (a) of the definition "graduated rate estate" in subsection 248(1)) if the gift is made no more than 60 months after the individual's death, the death occurs after 2015 and either

    (a) the gift is deemed by subsection (5.2) to have been made in respect of the death, or

    (b) the subject of the gift is property that was acquired by the estate on and as a consequence of the death or is property that was substituted for that property.

Related Provisions: 118.1(1)"total charitable gifts"(c), "total cultural gifts"(c), "total ecological gifts"(c) — Donation credit to deceased or estate; 248(5) — Substituted property; 248(8) — Meaning of "consequence of death".

Notes: Once 118.1(5.1) applies, either the deceased or the estate can claim the donation credit. See Notes to 118.1(4.1). For pre-2016 deaths, see Notes to 118.1(5).

See VIEWS docs 2015-0578551C6 [2015 STEP q.11] (cash cannot be "substituted" property for shares, for 118.1(5.1)(b)); 2016-0625841E5 (will establishes testamentary trust and equitable interest in trust is gifted to charity: 118.1(5.1) does not apply); 2017-0734261E5 (charitable remainder trust created by GRE is not substituted for property received on death, so 118.1(5.1)(b) does not apply).

118.1(5.1) opening words amended by 2016 budget bill #2, for 2016 and later taxation years, to allow donations up to 60 months after death (in sync with 118.1(1)"total charitable gifts"(c)(i)(A)).

118.1(5.1) amended by 2014 budget bill #2, for 2016 and later taxation years.

118.1(5.1) added by 2000 Budget, for deaths after 1998.

Registered Charities Newsletters: 15 (gifts by direct designation).

(5.2) Deemed gifts — eligible transfers — For the purposes of this section, money or a negotiable instrument transferred to a qualified donee is deemed to be property that is the subject of a gift, in respect of an individual's death, made to the qualified donee, if the death occurs after 2015 and the transfer is

    (a) a transfer — other than a transfer the amount of which is not included in computing the income of the individual or the individual's estate for any taxation year but would have been included in computing the income of the individual or the estate for a taxation year if the transfer had been made to the individual's legal representative for the estate's benefit and this Act were read without reference to subsection 70(3) — made

        (i) as a consequence of the death,

(ii) solely because of the obligations under a life insurance policy under which, immediately before the death, the individual's life was insured, and the individual's consent would have been required to change the recipient of the transfer, and

(iii) from an insurer to a person that is the qualified donee and that was, immediately before the death, neither a policyholder under the policy nor an assignee of the individual's interest under the policy; or

(b) a transfer made

(i) as a consequence of the death,

(ii) solely because of the qualified donee's interest or, for civil law a right, as a beneficiary under an arrangement (other than an arrangement of which a licensed annuities provider is the issuer or carrier)

(A) that is a registered retirement savings plan or registered retirement income fund or that was, immediately before the death, a TFSA, and

(B) under which the individual was, immediately before the death, the annuitant or holder, and

(iii) from the arrangement to the qualified donee.

Related Provisions: 118.1(4.1)(b) — Subsec. (5) applies to gift.

Notes: See Notes to 118.1(4.1). 118.1(5.2)(a) extends the donation credit to eligible transfers under a life insurance policy made due to designations under the policy. As a result, the credit can be claimed on death as a consequence of transfers to charities under life insurance policies. Combined with the 100%-of-income donation limit in the year of death (118.1(1)"total gifts"(a)(ii)), a purchase of life insurance with a charity designated as the beneficiary can be used to shelter capital gains triggered under 70(5) on death. (Finance Technical Notes)

118.1(5.2) applies to designation of a charity as beneficiary of a segregated fund policy: VIEWS doc 2016-0632621C6 [2016 CALU q.3].

118.1(5.2)(b) provides for a credit on direct designation by an RRSP, RRIF or TFSA to a beneficiary charity. As discussed in Notes to 118.1(4.1), the credit can be claimed by either the estate or the deceased.

118.1(5.2) amended by 2014 budget bill #2, for 2016 and later taxation years.

Pre-2016 118.1(5.2):

Insurance proceeds received by a charity under an irrevocable beneficiary designation could qualify as a donation in the deceased's final year: VIEWS doc 2004-0065451C5. See also 2012-0434761E5; Corbin, "Charity As Beneficiary Of Life Insurance Proceeds", 25(1) *Money & Family Law* (Carswell) 3-5 (Jan. 2010); and 118.1(5) Notes.

118.1(5.2) added by 2000 Budget, effective in respect of deaths that occur after 1998, and amended by 2004 Budget retroactive to its introduction.

Registered Charities Newsletters: 15 (gifts by direct designation).

(5.3) [Repealed]

Related Provisions: 118.1(4) — Carryback of gift made in year of death.

Notes: See Notes to 118.1(4.1) for post-2015 deaths; to 118.1(5) re pre-2016 deaths.

118.1(5.3) repealed by 2014 budget bill #2, for 2016 and later taxation years. It addressed direct designation of a donation on death from an RRSP, RRIF or TFSA.

118.1(5.3) earlier amended by 2008 budget bills #1 and #2 (for 2009 and later tax years), 2004 Budget. Added by 2000 Budget.

Registered Charities Newsletters: 15 (gifts by direct designation).

(5.4) Where subsec. (6) applies — Subsection (6) applies in circumstances where

(a) an individual

(i) makes a gift at any time of capital property to a qualified donee, or

(ii) who is non-resident, makes a gift at any time of real or immovable property situated in Canada to a prescribed donee who provides an undertaking, in a form satisfactory to the Minister, to the effect that the property will be held for use in the public interest; and

(b) the fair market value of the property otherwise determined at that time exceeds

(i) in the case of depreciable property of a prescribed class, the lesser of the undepreciated capital cost of that class at the end of the taxation year of the individual that includes that time (determined without reference to proceeds of disposi-

tion designated in respect of the property under subsection (6)) and the adjusted cost base to the individual of the property immediately before that time, and

(ii) in any other case, the adjusted cost base to the individual of the property immediately before that time.

Related Provisions: 110.1(2.1) — Parallel rule for corporations; 248(35)–(39) — Value of gift limited to cost if acquired within 3 years or as tax shelter.

Notes: 118.1(5.4) amended by 2014 budget bill #2 (for 2016 and later tax years). Added by 2002-2013 technical bill.

Regulations: 3504 (prescribed donee for 118.1(5.4)(a)(ii)).

Income Tax Folios: S7-F1-C1: Split-receipting and deemed fair market value [replaces IT-110R3].

(6) Gifts of capital property — If this subsection applies in respect of a gift by an individual of property, and the individual or the individual's legal representative designates an amount in respect of the gift in the individual's return of income under section 150 for the year in which the gift is made, the amount so designated is deemed to be the individual's proceeds of disposition of the property and, for the purpose of subsection 248(31), the fair market value of the gift, but the amount so designated may not exceed the fair market value of the property otherwise determined and may not be less than the greater of

(a) in the case of a gift made after December 20, 2002, the amount of the advantage, if any, in respect of the gift, and

(b) the amount determined under subparagraph (5.4)(b)(i) or (ii), as the case may be, in respect of the property.

Related Provisions: 38(a.1) — Donation of listed securities; 110.1(3) — Parallel rule for corporations; 118.1(5.4) — Conditions for 118.1(6) to apply; 248(32) — Determination of amount of advantage; 248(35)–(39) — Value of gift limited to cost if acquired within 3 years or as tax shelter.

Notes: 118.1(5.4)-(6) [110.1(2.1)-(3) for corporations] allow a designation to have capital property that has been donated (or real property of a non-resident) deemed sold at an amount lower than value (not lower than cost), with the donation deemed at the same amount. This is useful where the donation cannot be used for credit (e.g. a non-resident with no Canadian-source income donating Canadian real property, or a taxpayer with donations over the annual limit), to eliminate recapture and capital gains in exchange for a reduced donation value. It may also be useful in Ontario and any other province where the value of a donation is less than the top marginal rate on income (see Notes to 118.1(3)), to reduce recapture (13(1)) which would cost more than the donation savings. Also, where valuation of the property is uncertain, designating a lower value avoids valuation problems with the CRA. Where no tax is payable due to the donation, no payment or security is needed for a non-resident to get a s. 116 certificate, but the person must still file a T1, report the gain and claim the donation credit: VIEWS doc 2013-0496461E5. Where a designation is made, the donation receipt should still show the actual value: 2015-0593921E5.

A designation by an individual resident in Quebec must be copied to Revenu Québec: *Taxation Act* ss. 752.0.10.12, 21.4.6.

118.1(6) amended by 2002-2013 technical bill (for gifts made after 1999), 2011 budget bill #2 (retroactively superseded by later amendment), 2001 technical bill, 1995 Budget, 1992 technical bill.

Income Tax Folios: S7-F1-C1: Split-receipting and deemed fair market value [replaces IT-110R3].

Interpretation Bulletins: IT-226R: Gift to a charity of a residual interest in real property or an equitable interest in a trust; IT-288R2: Gifts of capital properties to a charity and others; IT-504R2: Visual artists and writers.

Forms: T3 Sched. 1A, T1170: Capital gains on gifts of certain capital property.

(7) Gift of art [by artist] — Subsection (7.1) applies to a gift made by an individual if the gift is described in the definition "total charitable gifts" or "total cultural gifts" in subsection (1) and the property that is the subject of the gift is a work of art that

(a) was created by the individual and is in the individual's inventory;

(b) was acquired by the individual under circumstances where subsection 70(3) applies; or

(c) if the individual is an estate that arose on and as a consequence of the death of a particular individual who created the work of art, was in the particular individual's inventory immediately before the death.

Related Provisions: 10(6) — Artist's inventory.

Notes: See Notes to 118.1(7.1). 118.1(7) amended by 2014 budget bill #2, for 2016 and later taxation years.

118.1(7) earlier amended by 2002-2013 technical bill (for gifts made after Dec. 20, 2002), 2001 and 1991 technical bills.

Interpretation Bulletins: IT-288R2: Gifts of capital properties to a charity and others; IT-504R2: Visual artists and writers.

(7.1) Gift of art [by artist] — If this subsection applies to a gift made by an individual, the following rules apply:

(a) in the case of a gift described in the definition "total cultural gifts" in subsection (1),

(i) if at the time the gift is made the fair market value of the work of art that is the subject of the gift exceeds its cost amount to the individual, the individual is deemed to receive at that time proceeds of disposition in respect of the work of art equal to the greater of its cost amount to the individual at that time and the amount of the advantage, if any, in respect of the gift, and

(ii) if the individual is the graduated rate estate of a particular individual who created the work of art that is the subject of the gift and at the time immediately before the particular individual's death the fair market value of the work of art exceeds its cost amount to the particular individual, the particular individual is deemed to receive at that time proceeds of disposition in respect of the work of art equal to the cost amount to the particular individual at that time and the estate is deemed to have acquired the work of art at a cost equal to those proceeds; and

(b) in the case of a gift described in the definition "total charitable gifts" in subsection (1),

(i) if at the time the gift is made the fair market value of the work of art that is the subject of the gift exceeds its cost amount to the individual, then the amount designated in the individual's return of income under section 150 for the taxation year that includes that time is deemed to be

(A) the individual's proceeds of disposition in respect of the work of art, and

(B) the fair market value of the work of art for the purposes of subsection 248(31),

(ii) a designation under subparagraph (i) is of no effect to the extent that the amount designated

(A) exceeds the fair market value of the work of art otherwise determined, or

(B) is less than the greater of the amount of the advantage, if any, in respect of the gift, and the cost amount to the individual of the work of art,

(iii) if the individual is the graduated rate estate of a particular individual who created the work of art that is the subject of the gift and at the time immediately before the particular individual's death the fair market value of the work of art exceeds its cost amount to the particular individual,

(A) the amount designated in the particular individual's return of income under section 150 for the taxation year that includes that time is deemed to be the value of the work of art at the time of the death, and

(B) the estate is deemed to have acquired the work of art at a cost equal to that value, and

(iv) a designation under subparagraph (iii) is of no effect to the extent that the amount designated

(A) exceeds the fair market value of the work of art otherwise determined, or

(B) is less than the cost amount to the particular individual of the work of art.

Related Provisions: 118.1(7) — Conditions for 118.1(7.1) to apply.

Notes: 118.1(7) and (7.1) provide special relief where an artist (or the artist's estate) donates artwork created by the artist and held in the artist's inventory, and the value of the artwork exceeds its cost amount to the artist. See Income Tax Folio S4-F14-C1 ¶1.88-1.98.

If the inventory item is cultural property (39(1)(a)(i.1) — if it were capital property there would be no capital gain), then under (7.1)(a), the artist (or the estate, if a graduated rate estate) is deemed to have received proceeds of disposition equal to the cost amount to the artist of the work, but the fair market value (FMV) of the artwork is not affected. The artist or estate is thus entitled to a donation credit based on the FMV, but the artist recognizes neither business profit nor loss on disposing of the art.

For other property, under (7.1)(b) the artist can designate in their return a value no lower than cost and no higher than FMV, to be treated both as proceeds of disposition in calculating the artist's income and the amount of the gift for the donation credit. If the artist has died, the legal representative may, under (7.1)(b), designate such value to be the deemed proceeds in calculating the artist's income for the year of death. The artist's estate is deemed to have acquired the work at a cost equal to those proceeds.

As of 2016, 118.1(7) and (7.1) no longer treat a gift made as a consequence [248(8)] of the artist's death as being made immediately before death. Instead, 118.1(7) provides that 118.1(7.1) applies where the gift is made by an artist's "graduated rate estate" (GRE) [meaning within 36 months: definition in 248(1)] out of the artist's inventory.

Where 118.1(7.1) applies to a gift of art made by an artist's GRE, and immediately before death the FMV of the artwork exceeds its cost amount to the artist, then (7.1)(a)(ii), (b)(iii) and (iv) apply. If the artwork is a cultural gift, (a)(ii) deems the artist to receive, before death, proceeds equal to the art's cost amount to the artist, and the GRE is deemed to have acquired the art at the same amount. As a result, no income for the artwork's value is recognized under s. 70 by the artist for the year of death.

The rules in 118.1(5)–(5.2) apply to determine the tax treatment of the gift, in conjunction with 118.1(1)"total charitable gifts"(c) and "total cultural gifts"(c).

If the individual is resident in Quebec, any designation under 118.1(7.1)(b) must be copied to Revenu Québec: *Taxation Act* ss. 752.0.10.14, 21.4.6.

For discussion of the pre-2016 rules, see VIEWS doc 2008-0304871E5.

118.1(7.1) amended by 2014 budget bill #2, for 2016 and later taxation years.

118.1(7.1) earlier amended by 2002-2013 technical bill (for gifts made after Dec. 20, 2002), 2001 and 1991 technical bills.

Interpretation Bulletins: IT-407R4: Dispositions of cultural property to designated Canadian institutions; IT-504R2: Visual artists and writers. See also at end of s. 118.1.

(8) Gifts made by partnership — If at the end of a fiscal period of a partnership an individual is a member of the partnership, the individual's share of any amount that would, if the partnership were a person, be the eligible amount of a gift made by the partnership to any donee is, for the purpose of this section, deemed to be the eligible amount of a gift made to that donee by the individual in the individual's taxation year in which the fiscal period of the partnership ends.

Related Provisions: 53(2)(c)(iii) — Deduction from ACB of partnership interest; 110.1(4) — Parallel rule for corporations; 248(30)–(33) — Determination of eligible amount.

Notes: 118.1(8) amended by 2002-2013 technical bill for gifts made after Dec. 20, 2002.

(9) Commuter's charitable donations — Where throughout a taxation year an individual resided in Canada near the boundary between Canada and the United States, if

(a) the individual commuted to the individual's principal place of employment or business in the United States, and

(b) the individual's chief source of income for the year was that employment or business,

a gift made by the individual in the year to a religious, charitable, scientific, literary or educational organization created or organized in or under the laws of the United States that would be allowed as a deduction under the *United States Internal Revenue Code* shall, for the purpose of the definition "total charitable gifts" in subsection (1), be deemed to have been made to a registered charity.

Related Provisions: Canada-U.S. Tax Treaty:Art. XXI:6 — Cross-border donations.

Notes: Canada-U.S. tax treaty Art. XXI:7 allows donations to U.S. charities to be treated as donations to Canadian charities, up to a limit of 75% of U.S.-source income. The taxpayer need not be a commuter. Some U.S. charities also qualify under 149.1(1)"qualified donee"(a)(iv) (universities in Schedule VIII) and (v) (charities to which the Canadian government has recently donated).

See also Drache, "Donating to U.S. Charities", 9(1) *Canadian Not-for-Profit News* (Carswell) 5-6 (Jan. 2001); VIEWS doc 2009-0322801E5.

(10) Determination of fair market value — For the purposes of paragraph 110.1(1)(c) and the definition "total cultural gifts" in subsection (1), the fair market value of an object is deemed to be the fair market value determined by the Canadian Cultural Property Export Review Board.

Related Provisions: 118.1(10.1) — Determination by Board applies for 2 years; 118.1(11) — Assessment consequential on determination of value by Board; 241(4)(d)(xii) — Disclosure of information to Dept. of Canadian Heritage or Board.

Notes: See Notes to 39(1). Cultural property that is either donated or sold to a designated institution is exempt from capital gains tax: 39(1)(a)(i.1). See also Notes to 69(1) for principles for determining FMV; and to 118.1(1)"total cultural gifts".

118.1(11) requires CRA to assess late to allow a cultural gift if certification takes years. If certification is refused, the gift can still be claimed as a regular donation for the year it was made: VIEWS doc 2019-0826691E5.

Malette, 2004 FCA 187, was an appeal from a CCPERB valuation.

In *Heffel Gallery*, 2019 FCA 82 (reversing the FC), "national importance" for cultural property was held to apply to foreign works, so an important French impressionist painting needed CCPERB approval to be exported, and qualified under 118.1(1)"total cultural gifts" even without the 2019 Budget amendment to that definition.

Under *Cultural Property Export and Import Act* s. 33.1, a determination by the CCPERB can be appealed to the TCC. Such appeal must use the General Procedure: *Maréchal*, 2004 TCC 464, para. 26, aff'd 2005 FCA 124. See also Customs Memorandum D19-4-1, *Export and Import of Cultural Property*.

See also Steven Nemetz, "Gifting Cultural Property in Canada", 85(3) *Canadian Bar Review* 457-93 (2006).

118.1(10) amended by 1995 cultural property bill (Bill C-93), in force July 12, 1996 (per Order in Council SI/96-73, *Canada Gazette*, Part II, Vol 130, No. 15, p. 2573).

118.1(10) added by 1991 Budget, effective for gifts made after February 20, 1990.

Interpretation Bulletins: IT-407R4: Dispositions of cultural property to designated Canadian institutions; IT-504R2: Visual artists and writers.

(10.1) Determination of fair market value [cultural or ecological property] — For the purposes of this section, subparagraph 69(1)(b)(ii), subsection 70(5) and sections 110.1 and 207.31, if at any time the Canadian Cultural Property Export Review Board or the Minister of the Environment determines or redetermines an amount to be the fair market value of a property that is the subject of a gift described in paragraph 110.1(1)(a), or in the definition "total charitable gifts" in subsection (1), made by a taxpayer within the two-year period that begins at that time, an amount equal to the last amount so determined or redetermined within the period is deemed to be the fair market value of the gift at the time the gift was made and, subject to subsections (6), (7.1) and 110.1(3), to be the taxpayer's proceeds of disposition of the gift.

Related Provisions: 118.1(10.2)–(11) — Related administrative procedures.

Notes: If the fair market value of a property is determined by the CCPERB, that value will apply to the property for all income tax purposes related to charitable gifts for 2 years from the determination.

A determination by the CCPERB can be appealed to the TCC under *Cultural Property Export and Import Act* s. 33.1. Such appeal must use the General Procedure: *Maréchal*, 2004 TCC 464, para. 26, aff'd 2005 FCA 124.

For criticism of CCPERB practices as deferring too much to the CRA, see Drache, "Cultural Property Review Board Has Lost Its Way", 22(7) *Canadian Not-for-Profit News* (Carswell) 53 (July 2014).

118.1(10.1) amended by 2014 budget bill #2, for 2016 and later taxation years, to change "subject to subsections (6), (7), (7.1)" to "subject to subsections (6), (7.1)".

118.1(10.1) amended by 2000 Budget, for gifts made, or proposed to be made, after Feb. 27, 2000. Added by 1998 Budget, for determinations and redeterminations made after Feb. 23, 1998.

(10.2) Request for determination by the Minister of the Environment — Where a person disposes or proposes to dispose of a property that would, if the disposition were made and the certificates described in paragraph 110.1(1)(d) or in the definition "total ecological gifts" in subsection (1) were issued by the Minister of the Environment, be a gift described in those provisions, the person may request, by notice in writing to that Minister, a determination of the fair market value of the property.

Related Provisions: 118.1(10.3) — Duty of Minister on receipt of request.

Notes: 118.1(10.2) added by 2000 Budget, effective for gifts made, or proposed to be made, after February 27, 2000.

(10.3) Duty of Minister of the Environment — In response to a request made under subsection (10.2), the Minister of the Environment shall with all due dispatch make a determination in accordance with subsection (12) or 110.1(5), as the case may be, of the fair market value of the property referred to in that request and give notice of the determination in writing to the person who has disposed of, or who proposes to dispose of, the property, except that

no such determination shall be made if the request is received by that Minister after three years after the end of the person's taxation year in which the disposition occurred.

Related Provisions: 118.1(10.4) — Redetermination by Minister; 118.1(10.5) — Certificate of fair market value.

Notes: See Notes to 152(1) on the meaning of "all due dispatch".

118.1(10.3) added by 2000 Budget, effective for gifts made, or proposed to be made, after February 27, 2000.

(10.4) Ecological gifts — redetermination — Where the Minister of the Environment has, under subsection (10.3), notified a person of the amount determined by that Minister to be the fair market value of a property in respect of its disposition or proposed disposition,

(a) that Minister shall, on receipt of a written request made by the person on or before the day that is 90 days after the day that the person was so notified of the first such determination, with all due dispatch confirm or redetermine the fair market value;

(b) that Minister may, on that Minister's own initiative, at any time redetermine the fair market value;

(c) that Minister shall in either case notify the person in writing of that Minister's confirmation or redetermination; and

(d) any such redetermination is deemed to replace all preceding determinations and redeterminations of the fair market value of that property from the time at which the first such determination was made.

Related Provisions: 118.1(10.5) — Certificate of fair market value; 169(1.1) — Appeal of valuation to Tax Court of Canada.

Notes: 118.1(10.4) added by 2000 Budget, effective for gifts made, or proposed to be made, after February 27, 2000.

(10.5) Certificate of fair market value — Where the Minister of the Environment determines under subsection (10.3) the fair market value of a property, or redetermines that value under subsection (10.4), and the property has been disposed of to a qualified donee described in paragraph 110.1(1)(d) or in the definition "total ecological gifts" in subsection (1), that Minister shall issue to the person who made the disposition a certificate that states the fair market value of the property so determined or redetermined and, where more than one certificate has been so issued, the last certificate is deemed to replace all preceding certificates from the time at which the first certificate was issued.

Related Provisions: 118.1(12) — Reassessment beyond limitation period to give effect to certificate; 169(1.1) — Appeal of certificate value to Tax Court of Canada.

Notes: 118.1(10.5) added by 2000 Budget, effective for gifts made, or proposed to be made, after February 27, 2000.

(11) Assessments — Notwithstanding subsections 152(4) to (5), such assessments or reassessments of a taxpayer's tax, interest or penalties payable under this Act for any taxation year shall be made as are necessary to give effect

(a) to a certificate issued under subsection 33(1) of the *Cultural Property Export and Import Act* or to a decision of a court resulting from an appeal made pursuant to section 33.1 of that Act; or

(b) to a certificate issued under subsection (10.5) or to a decision of a court resulting from an appeal made pursuant to subsection 169(1.1).

Related Provisions: 165(1.2) — No objection allowed to assessment under 118.1(11).

Notes: See Notes to 118.1(10). 118.1(11) amended by 2000 Budget, for gifts made or proposed after Feb. 27, 2000. Added by 1995 cultural property bill.

(12) Ecological gifts [fair market value] — For the purposes of applying subparagraph 69(1)(b)(ii), subsection 70(5), this section and section 207.31 in respect of a gift described in the definition "total ecological gifts" in subsection (1) that is made by an individual, the amount that is the fair market value (or, for the purpose of subsection (6), the fair market value otherwise determined) of the gift at the time the gift was made and, subject to subsection (6), the individual's proceeds of disposition of the gift, is deemed to be the amount determined by the Minister of the Environment to be

(a) where the gift is land, the fair market value of the gift; or

(b) where the gift is a servitude, covenant or easement to which land is subject, the greater of

(i) the fair market value otherwise determined of the gift, and

(ii) the amount by which the fair market value of the land is reduced as a result of the making of the gift.

Related Provisions: 43(2) — Calculation for 118.1(12) also applies for determining capital gain or loss on disposition; 110.1(5) — Parallel rule for donation deduction for corporations; 118.1(10.1)–(10.5) — Determination of fair market value by Minister of the Environment.

Notes: See VIEWS docs 2002-0174285, 2013-0513251E5. "Land" can include buildings: see 70(5.2) Notes.

118.1(12) amended by 2000 Budget/2001 technical bill, this version effective for gifts made, or proposed to be made, after Feb. 27, 2000. Added by 1997 Budget, effective for gifts made after Feb. 27, 1995.

(13) Non-qualifying securities — For the purposes of this section (other than this subsection), if at any particular time an individual makes a gift (including a gift that, but for this subsection, would be deemed by subsection (5) to be made at the particular time) of a non-qualifying security of the individual and the gift is not an excepted gift,

(a) except for the purpose of applying subsection (6) to determine the individual's proceeds of disposition of the security, the gift is deemed not to have been made;

(b) if the security ceases to be a non-qualifying security of the individual at a subsequent time that is within 60 months after the particular time and the donee has not disposed of the security at or before the subsequent time, the individual is deemed to have made a gift to the donee of property at the subsequent time and the fair market value of that property is deemed to be the lesser of the fair market value of the security at the subsequent time and the fair market value of the security at the particular time that would, if this Act were read without reference to this subsection, have been included in calculating the individual's total charitable gifts for a taxation year;

(c) if the security is disposed of by the donee within 60 months after the particular time and paragraph (b) does not apply to the security, the individual is deemed to have made a gift to the donee of property at the time of the disposition and the fair market value of that property is deemed to be the lesser of the fair market value of any consideration (other than a non-qualifying security of any person) received by the donee for the disposition and the fair market value of the security at the particular time that would, if this Act were read without reference to this subsection, have been included in calculating the individual's total charitable gifts for a taxation year; and

(d) a designation under subsection (6) or 110.1(3) in respect of the gift made at the particular time may be made in the individual's return of income for the year that includes the subsequent time referred to in paragraph (b) or the time of the disposition referred to in paragraph (c).

Related Provisions: 40(1.01) — Capital gains reserve on disposition of non-qualifying security (NQS); 88(1)(e.61) — Winding-up of subsidiary — gift deemed made by parent corporation; 110.1(6), (7) — Application to corporation; 118.1(13.1)–(13.3) — Anti-avoidance rules; 118.1(14) — When security exchanged for another NQS; 118.1(14.1) — Exchange of beneficial interest in trust for other NQS; 118.1(15) — Death of donor; 118.1(18) — Definition of NQS; 118.1(19) — Excepted gift; *Interpretation Act* 27(5) — Meaning of "within 60 months".

Notes: A donation credit (or deduction under 110.1) generally should not be available to a donor until the use and benefits of the donor's property have been transferred to the charity. 118.1(13) (110.1(6) for corporations) applies to donations of non-qualifying securities (NQS), generally defined (118.1(18)) as a share, debt obligation or other security issued by the donor or non-arm's-length person. (Certain financial-institution obligations and publicly listed securities are excluded.) 118(13) defers the credit (or deduction) of the donation of a NQS until the charity has disposed of the NQS for consideration that is not anyone's NQS (and this must be within 5 years). See also 118.1(13.1)–(13.3), which provide further anti-avoidance rules.

118.1(13) does not apply to an "excepted gift", defined in 118.1(19) as a gift of a share to an arm's length donee that is not a private foundation, provided that if the donee is a charitable organization or a public foundation the donor deals at arm's length with all of the foundation's directors and officers.

The "denial of credit" in 118.1(13) replaces resolution (21) of the February 1997 Budget, which would have imposed a tax on the charity on the receipt of donations of non-qualifying securities.

In *Remai*, 2009 FCA 340, R's $10.5 million donation to his private foundation of promissory notes issued by his company was allowed once the foundation sold the notes to his nephew's company, which was held to deal at arm's length with R. (The plan did not violate GAAR.) See Drache, "FCA Rules on Case Involving Foundation Divestiture of Assets", 18(1) *Canadian Not-for-Profit News* 6-7 (Jan. 2010).

For CRA interpretation of 118.1(13) see VIEWS docs 2005-0148381R3, 2009-0326991C6, 2010-0369261E5, 2012-0486701E5, 2016-0628181R3.

118.1(13) amended by 2014 budget bill #2 (for 2016 and later tax years), 2002-2013 technical bill, 2011 budget bill #2. Added by 1997 Budget.

(13.1) Application of subsec. (13.2) — Subsection (13.2) applies if, as part of a series of transactions,

(a) an individual makes, at a particular time, a gift of a particular property to a qualified donee;

(b) a particular person holds a non-qualifying security of the individual; and

(c) the qualified donee acquires, directly or indirectly, a non-qualifying security of the individual or of the particular person.

Related Provisions: 118.1(13.3) — Where series of transactions leads to donee acquiring NQS.

Notes: 118.1(13.1) added by 2011 budget bill #2, effective March 22, 2011.

(13.2) Non-qualifying securities — third-party accommodation [indirect gift] — If this subsection applies,

(a) for the purposes of this section, the fair market value of the particular property is deemed to be reduced by an amount equal to the fair market value of the non-qualifying security acquired by the qualified donee; and

(b) for the purposes of subsection (13),

(i) if the non-qualifying security acquired by the qualified donee is a non-qualifying security of the particular person, it is deemed to be a non-qualifying security of the individual,

(ii) the individual is deemed to have made, at the particular time referred to in subsection (13.1), a gift of the non-qualifying security acquired by the qualified donee, the fair market value of which does not exceed the amount, if any, by which

(A) the fair market value of the particular property determined without reference to paragraph (a)

exceeds

(B) the fair market value of the particular property determined under paragraph (a), and

(iii) paragraph (13)(b) does not apply in respect of the gift.

Related Provisions: 118.1(13.1) — Conditions for 118.1(13.2) to apply; 118.1(13.3) — Where series of transactions leads to donee acquiring NQS; 248(35)–(39) — Value of donation limited to cost if acquired within 3 years or as tax shelter.

Notes: 118.1(13.2) added by 2011 budget bill #2, effective March 22, 2011.

Income Tax Folios: S7-F1-C1: Split-receipting and deemed fair market value [replaces IT-110R3].

(13.3) Non-qualifying securities — anti-avoidance — For the purposes of subsections (13.1) and (13.2), if, as part of a series of transactions, an individual makes a gift to a qualified donee and the qualified donee acquires a non-qualifying security of a person (other than the individual or particular person referred to in subsection (13.1)) and it may reasonably be considered, having regard to all the circumstances, that one of the purposes or results of the acquisition of the non-qualifying security by the qualified donee was to facilitate, directly or indirectly, the making of the gift by the individual, then the non-qualifying security acquired by the qualified donee is deemed to be a non-qualifying security of the individual.

Related Provisions: 248(10) — Series of transactions.

Notes: For the meaning of "indirectly" see Notes to 17.1(1).

118.1(13.3) added by 2011 budget bill #2, effective March 22, 2011.

(14) Exchanged security — Where a share (in this subsection referred to as the "new share") that is a non-qualifying security of an individual has been acquired by a donee referred to in subsection (13) in exchange for another share (in this subsection referred to as the "original share") that is a non-qualifying security of the individual by means of a transaction to which section 51, subparagraphs 85.1(1)(a)(i) and (ii) or section 86 or 87 applies, the new share is deemed for the purposes of this subsection and subsection (13) to be the same share as the original share.

Related Provisions: 110.1(6) — Application to corporation; 118.1(18) — Definition of non-qualifying security.

Notes: 118.1(14) added by 1997 Budget, effective for gifts made after July 1997.

(14.1) Exchange of beneficial interest in trust — Where a donee disposes of a beneficial interest in a trust that is a non-qualifying security of an individual in circumstances where paragraph (13)(c) would, but for this subsection, apply in respect of the disposition, and in respect of which the donee receives no consideration other than other non-qualifying securities of the individual, for the purpose of subsection (13) the gift referred to in that subsection is to be read as a reference to a gift of those other non-qualifying securities.

Notes: 118.1(14.1) provides that if, in the course of disposition of a beneficial interest in a trust that is a non-qualifying security (NQS) of an individual, the donee receives as consideration only other NQS of the individual, the gift referred to in 118.1(13) is considered a gift of those other NQS, rather than a gift of the interest in the trust. For example, if X donates an interest in a trust, that interest may be a NQS of the individual under 118.1(18) because the trust holds other NQS of X. If the trust is wound up and those other NQS are distributed from the trust to the donee, X will not be permitted a donation credit (originally denied when the gift was made of the interest in the trust) until those other NQS are disposed of by the donee.

See also 118.1(18)(b.1).

118.1(14.1) added by 2007 budget bill #2, effective in respect of gifts made after March 18, 2007.

(15) Death of donor — If, but for this subsection, an individual would be deemed by subsection (13) to have made a gift after the individual's death, for the purpose of this section the individual is deemed to have made the gift in the taxation year in which the individual died, except that the amount of interest payable under any provision of this Act is the amount that it would be if this subsection did not apply to the gift.

Related Provisions: 118.1(4) — Carryback of gift made in year of death; 152(4)(b)(vi) — Three-year extension to reassessment period; 161(1) — Imposition of interest on late payments of tax.

Notes: 118.1(15) added by 1997 Budget, effective for gifts made after July 1997.

(16) Loanbacks — For the purpose of this section, where

(a) at any particular time an individual makes a gift of property,

(b) if the property is a non-qualifying security of the individual, the gift is an excepted gift, and

(c) within 60 months after the particular time

(i) the donee holds a non-qualifying security of the individual that was acquired by the donee after the time that is 60 months before the particular time, or

(ii) the individual or any person or partnership with which the individual does not deal at arm's length uses property of the donee under an agreement that was made or modified after the time that is 60 months before the particular time, and the property was not used in the carrying on of the donee's charitable activities,

the fair market value of the gift is deemed to be that value otherwise determined minus the total of all amounts each of which is the fair market value of the consideration given by the donee to so acquire a non-qualifying security so held or the fair market value of such a property so used, as the case may be.

Federal Budget, Supplementary Information, April 21, 2015: The non-qualifying security rules and the loanback rules that apply to donations of shares will also apply to donations of interests in limited partnerships.

Notes: This proposal was not included in the draft Budget legislation of July 31, 2015 (later incorporated into 2016 budget bill #1), which includes the related proposal at 253.1(2). Finance has not yet determined for certain whether this proposal will be necessary. It is probably not, but Finance is open to be convinced otherwise (Nov 2016).

Related Provisions: 110.1(6) — Application to corporation; 118.1(17) — Ordering rule; 118.1(18) — Definition of non-qualifying security; 152(4)(b)(vi) — Three-year extension to reassessment period.

Notes: For CRA interpretation see Charities Summary Policy CSP-L07; Charities and Giving Notice "Loanbacks" (Nov. 24, 2010); VIEWS docs 2009-0307941E5, 2019-080187I17. See Notes to 118.1(1)"total charitable gifts" for discussion of cash donated to a charity and loaned back to the donor.

For meaning of "charitable activities" in (c)(ii) see Notes to 149.1(1)"charitable activities".

118.1(16)(c)(ii) amended by 2007 budget bill #2, effective in respect of gifts made after March 18, 2007, to delete from the opening words "where the individual and the donee do not deal at arm's length with each other" (and to fold former clauses (A) and (B) into the body of (ii)).

118.1(16) added by 1997 Budget, for acquisitions, or beginning use, after July 1997.

(17) Ordering rule — For the purpose of applying subsection (16) to determine the fair market value of a gift made at any time by a taxpayer, the fair market value of consideration given to acquire property described in subparagraph (16)(c)(i) or of property described in subparagraph (16)(c)(ii) is deemed to be that value otherwise determined minus any portion of it that has been applied under that subsection to reduce the fair market value of another gift made before that time by the taxpayer.

Related Provisions: 110.1(6) — Application to corporation.

Notes: 118.1(17) added by 1997 Budget, effective August 1997, and corrected by *Miscellaneous Statute Law Amendment Act, 1999*.

(18) Non-qualifying security defined — For the purposes of this section, "non-qualifying security" of an individual at any time means

(a) an obligation (other than an obligation of a financial institution to repay an amount deposited with the institution or an obligation listed on a designated stock exchange) of the individual or the individual's estate or of any person or partnership with which the individual or the estate does not deal at arm's length immediately after that time;

(b) a share (other than a share listed on a designated stock exchange) of the capital stock of a corporation with which the individual or the estate or, where the individual is a trust, a person affiliated with the trust, does not deal at arm's length immediately after that time;

(b.1) a beneficial interest of the individual or the estate in a trust that

(i) immediately after that time is affiliated with the individual or the estate, or

(ii) holds, immediately after that time, a non-qualifying security of the individual or estate, or held, at or before that time, a share described in paragraph (b) that is, after that time, held by the donee; or

(c) any other security (other than a security listed on a designated stock exchange) issued by the individual or the estate or by any person or partnership with which the individual or the estate does not deal at arm's length (or, in the case where the person is a trust, with which the individual or estate is affiliated) immediately after that time.

See under 118.1(16).

Related Provisions: 110.1(6) — Application to corporation; 118.1(20) — Meaning of "financial institution".

Notes: See Notes to 118.1(13). The "time" in para. (b) is the time that the gift is made: VIEWS doc 2004-008018117. For interpretation of 118.1(18)(b.1)(i) see 2009-0326991C6. For a ruling that an interest in a trust is not a NQS see 2011-0402611R3.

118.1(18)(a)–(c) amended by 2007 budget bill #2, effective Dec. 14, 2007, to change "prescribed stock exchange" to "designated stock exchange".

118.1(18)(b.1) added, and (b) and (c) amended to refer to a person affiliated with a trust, by 2007 budget bill #2, effective for gifts made after March 18, 2007.

118.1(18) added by 1997 Budget, effective August 1997.

(19) Excepted gift — For the purposes of this section, a gift made by a taxpayer is an excepted gift if

(a) the security is a share;

(b) the donee is not a private foundation;

(c) either,

(i) if the taxpayer is an individual's graduated rate estate,

(A) the individual dealt at arm's length with the donee immediately before the individual's death, and

(B) the graduated rate estate deals at arm's length with the donee (determined without reference to paragraph 251(1)(b)), or

(ii) if subparagraph (i) does not apply, the taxpayer deals at arm's length with the donee; and

(d) where the donee is a charitable organization or a public foundation, the taxpayer deals at arm's length with each director, trustee, officer and like official of the donee.

Related Provisions: 110.1(6) — Application to corporation; 251(1) — Meaning of arm's length.

Notes: A testamentary gift cannot be an excepted gift, due to 118.1(5)(a) and 251(1)(b): VIEWS doc 2015-0578561C6 [2015 STEP q.12].

118.1(19)(c) changed from "the taxpayer deals at arm's length with the donee" by 2016 budget bill #2, for 2016 and later taxation years.

118.1(19) added by 1997 Budget, effective for gifts made after July 1997.

(20) Financial institution defined — For the purpose of subsection (18), "financial institution" means a corporation that is

(a) a member of the Canadian Payments Association; or

(b) a credit union that is a shareholder or member of a body corporate or organization that is a central for the purposes of the *Canadian Payments Act*.

Related Provisions: 110.1(6) — Application to corporation.

Notes: 118.1(20) added by 1997 Budget, effective August 1997.

118.1(20)(b) amended by 2017 budget bill #2, effective Oct. 24, 2001, to change "*Canadian Payments Association Act*" to "*Canadian Payments Act*".

(21) Options [granted by individual to qualified donee] — Subject to subsections (23) and (24), if an individual has granted an option to a qualified donee in a taxation year, no amount in respect of the option is to be included in computing the total charitable gifts, total cultural gifts or total ecological gifts in respect of any taxpayer for any taxation year.

Related Provisions: 110.1(10) — Parallel rule for corporations.

Notes: 118.1(21)–(24) (110.1(10)–(13) for corporations) provide that no donation credit (deduction) is available for granting an option to a charity to acquire a property of the taxpayer until the charity acquires the property. The taxpayer will then be allowed a credit (deduction) based on the fair market value of the property at that time, minus any amount paid by the charity for the option and the property. Consistent with the split-receipting rules in 248(30)-(33), no credit (deduction) is allowed if the total paid by the charity for the property + option exceeds 80% of the value of the property at the time of acquisition.

118.1(21) amended by 2014 budget bill #2, for 2016 and later taxation years, to delete "total Crown gifts" after "total charitable gifts" and change "in respect of the individual" to "in respect of any taxpayer".

118.1(21) added by 2011 budget bill #2, for options granted after March 21, 2011.

(22) Application of subsec. (23) — Subsection (23) applies if

(a) an option to acquire a property of an individual is granted to a qualified donee;

(b) the option is exercised so that the property is disposed of by the individual and acquired by the qualified donee at a particular time; and

(c) either

(i) the amount that is 80% of the fair market value of the property at the particular time is greater than or equal to the total of

(A) the consideration received by the individual from the qualified donee for the property, and

(B) the consideration received by the individual from the qualified donee for the option, or

(ii) the individual establishes to the satisfaction of the Minister that the granting of the option or the disposition of the property was made by the individual with the intention to make a gift to the qualified donee.

Related Provisions: 49 — Treatment of options generally; 110.1(11) — Parallel rule for corporations.

Notes: 118.1(22) added by 2011 budget bill #2, effective for options granted after March 21, 2011.

(23) Granting of an option — If this subsection applies, notwithstanding subsection 49(3),

(a) the individual is deemed to have received proceeds of disposition of the property equal to the property's fair market value at the particular time; and

(b) there shall be included in the individual's total charitable gifts, for the taxation year that includes the particular time, the amount by which the property's fair market value exceeds the total described in subparagraph (22)(c)(i).

Related Provisions: 110.1(12) — Parallel rule for corporations; 118.1(22) — Conditions for 118.1(23) to apply.

Notes: See Notes to 118.1(21). 118.1(23) added by 2011 budget bill #2, effective for options granted after March 21, 2011.

(24) Disposition of an option — If an option to acquire a particular property of an individual is granted to a qualified donee and the option is disposed of by the qualified donee (otherwise than by the exercise of the option) at a particular time

(a) the individual is deemed to have disposed of a property at the particular time

(i) the adjusted cost base of which to the individual immediately before the particular time is equal to the consideration, if any, paid by the qualified donee for the option, and

(ii) the proceeds of disposition of which are equal to the lesser of the fair market value of the particular property at the particular time and the fair market value of any consideration (other than a non-qualifying security of any person) received by the qualified donee for the option; and

(b) there shall be included in the total charitable gifts of the individual for the individual's taxation year that includes the particular time the amount, if any, by which the proceeds of disposition as determined by paragraph (a) exceed the consideration, if any, paid by the donee for the option.

Related Provisions: 110.1(13) — Parallel rule for corporations.

Notes: 118.1(24) added by 2011 budget bill #2, effective for options granted after March 21, 2011.

(25) Returned property — Subsection (26) applies if a qualified donee has issued to an individual a receipt referred to in subsection (2) in respect of a transfer of a property (in this subsection and subsection (26) referred to as the "original property") and a particular property that is

(a) the original property is later transferred to the individual (unless that later transfer is reasonable consideration or remuneration for property acquired by or services rendered to a person); or

(b) any other property that may reasonably be considered compensation for or a substitute for, in whole or in part, the original property, is later transferred to the individual.

Related Provisions: 110.1(14) — Parallel rule for corporations.

Notes: See Notes to 118.1(26). 118.1(25) added by 2011 budget bill #2, for transfers of property after March 21, 2011.

Charities Guidance: CG-016: Qualified donees — Consequences of returning donated property.

(26) Returned property — If this subsection applies, then

(a) irrespective of whether the transfer of the original property by the individual to the qualified donee referred to in subsection (25) was a gift, the individual is deemed not to have disposed of the original property at the time of that transfer nor to have made a gift;

(b) if the particular property is identical to the original property, the particular property is deemed to be the original property; and

(c) if the particular property is not the original property, then

(i) the individual is deemed to have disposed of the original property at the time that the particular property is transferred to the individual for proceeds of disposition equal to the greater of the fair market value of the particular property at that time and the fair market value of the original property at the time that it was transferred by the individual to the donee, and

(ii) if the transfer of the original property by the individual would be a gift if this section were read without reference to paragraph (a), the individual is deemed to have, at the time of that transfer, transferred to the donee a property that is the subject of a gift having a fair market value equal to the amount, if any, by which the fair market value of the original property at the time of that transfer exceeds the fair market value of the particular property at the time that it is transferred to the individual.

Related Provisions: 110.1(15) — Parallel rule for corporations; 118.1(25) — Conditions for 118.1(26) to apply; 118.1(27) — Information return required; 118.1(28) — Reassessment to undo donation credit.

Notes: 118.1(25)–(28) (110.1(14)–(17) for corporations) apply where a charity receives property from a taxpayer, issues a tax receipt but later returns the property to the taxpayer. To ensure the credit (deduction) is not improperly retained, the CRA can reassess to disallow the donor's credit (deduction). The charity must issue a revised receipt, and must send a copy to the CRA if the receipt amount has changed by more than $50: 118.1(27), 110.1(16), Reg. 3501.1.

This rule "is not meant to encourage or sanction the return of property to a donor... registered charities that return donated property may be found to have made a gift to a non-qualified donee ... [and] provincial and federal legislation, as well as common law, may affect their ability to legally return property": Director General, Charities Directorate (Cathy Hawara), at National Charity Law Symposium, May 4, 2012.

See also Guidance CG-016; VIEWS doc 2016-0630351E5; Drache, "Returning a Gift", 17(6) *Canadian Not-for-Profit News* 46-48 (June 2009) and 25(8) 57-58 (Aug. 2017).

118.1(26) added by 2011 budget bill #2, for transfers of property after March 21, 2011.

Charities Guidance: CG-016: Qualified donees — Consequences of returning donated property.

(27) Information return — If subsection (26) applies in respect of a transfer of property to an individual and that property has a fair market value greater than $50, the transferor must file an information return containing prescribed information with the Minister not later than 90 days after the day on which the property was transferred and provide a copy of the return to the individual.

Related Provisions: 110.1(16) — Parallel rule for corporations.

Notes: See Notes to 118.1(26). 118.1(27) added by 2011 budget bill #2, effective for transfers of property made after March 21, 2011, and an information return filed by Nov. 15, 2011 is deemed filed on time.

Regulations: 3501.1 (contents of information return).

Charities Guidance: CG-016: Qualified donees — Consequences of returning donated property.

(28) Reassessment — If subsection (26) applies in respect of a transfer of property to an individual, the Minister may reassess a return of income of any person to the extent that the reassessment can reasonably be regarded as relating to the transfer.

Related Provisions: 110.1(17) — Parallel rule for corporations.

Notes: 118.1(28) added by 2011 budget bill #2, for transfers of property after March 21, 2011.

Definitions [s. 118.1]: "adjusted cost base" — 54, 248(1); "advantage" — 248(32); "affiliated" — 251.1; "amount" — 248(1); "amount taxable" — 117(2); "appropriate percentage" — 248(1); "annuitant" — 146(1), 146.3(1); "arm's length" — 251(1); "assessment" — 248(1); "beneficiary" — 248(25) [Notes]; "business" — 248(1); "Canada" — 255, *Interpretation Act* 35(1); "capital property" — 54, 248(1); "charitable organization" — 149.1(1) [technically does not apply to 118.1]; "common-law partner", "common-law partnership" — 248(1); "consequence" — 248(8); "corporation" — 248(1), *Interpretation Act* 35(1); "cost amount" — 248(1); "credit union" — 137(6), 248(1); "depreciable property" — 13(21), 248(1); "designated stock exchange" — 248(1), 262; "disposition", "employment" — 248(1); "eligible amount" — 248(31), (41); "estate" — 104(1), 248(1); "excepted gift" — 118.1(19); "fair market value" — 118.1(13), 248(35) and see 69(1) Notes; "filing-due date" — 150(1), 248(1); "financial institution" — 118.1(20); "first-time donor" — 118.1(1); "fiscal period" — 249(2)(b), 249.1; "graduated rate estate" — 248(1); "Her Majesty" — *Interpretation Act* 35(1); "highest individual percentage" — 248(1); "identical" — 248(12); "immovable" — Quebec *Civil Code* art. 900–907; "individual", "insurer", "inventory" — 248(1); "land" — see 70(5.2) Notes; "legal representative" — 248(1); "licensed annuities provider" — 147(1), 248(1); "life insurance policy" — 138(12), 248(1); "Minister" — 248(1); "month" — *Interpretation Act* 35(1); "non-qualifying security" — 118.1(18); "non-resident" — 248(1); "office", "officer" — 248(1); "original property" — 118.1(25); "partnership" — see 96(1) Notes; "person", "prescribed" — 248(1); "private foundation" — 149.1(1), 248(1); "property" — 248(1); "province" — *Interpretation Act* 35(1); "public foundation" — 149.1(1), 248(1); "qualified disability trust" — 122(3); "qualified donee" — 149.1(1), 188.2(3)(a), 248(1); "qualified pension income" — 118(7); "registered Canadian amateur athletic association", "registered charity" — 248(1); "registered retirement income fund" — 146.3(1), 248(1); "registered retirement savings plan" — 146(1), 248(1); "resident in Canada" — 250; "series of transactions" — 248(10); "share", "shareholder" — 248(1); "substituted" — 248(5); "TFSA" — 146.2(5), 248(1); "tax payable" — 248(2); "taxable capital gain" — 38(a), 248(1); "taxable income" — 2(2), 248(1); "taxation year" — 249; "taxpayer" — 248(1); "that Minister" — 118.1(10.2); "total charitable gifts", "total Crown gifts", "total cultural gifts", "total ecological gifts", "total gifts" — 118.1(1); "trust" — 104(1), 248(1), (3); "undepreciated capital cost" — 13(21), 248(1); "United States", "writing" — *Interpretation Act* 35(1); "written" — *Interpretation Act* 35(1)"writing".

Interpretation Bulletins [s. 118.1]: IT-86R: Vow of perpetual poverty; IT-171R2: Non-resident individuals — computation of taxable income earned in Canada and non-refundable tax credits (cancelled); IT-226R: Gift to a charity of a residual interest in real property or an equitable interest in a trust; IT-244R3: Gifts by individuals of life insurance policies as charitable donations; IT-288R2: Gifts of capital properties to a charity and others; IT-297R2: Gifts in kind to charity and others; IT-326R3: Returns of deceased persons as "another person"; IT-393R2: Election re tax on rents and timber royalties — non-residents; IT-407R4: Dispositions of cultural property to designated Canadian institutions; IT-504R2: Visual artists and writers.

Information Circulars [s. 118.1]: 75-23: Tuition fees and charitable donations paid to privately supported schools; 07-1R1: Taxpayer relief provisions.

118.2 (1) Medical expense credit — For the purpose of computing the tax payable under this Part by an individual for a taxation year, there may be deducted the amount determined by the formula

$$A \times [(B - C) + D]$$

where

A is the appropriate percentage for the taxation year;

B is the total of the individual's medical expenses in respect of the individual, the individual's spouse or common-law partner or a child of the individual who has not attained the age of 18 years before the end of the taxation year

(a) that are evidenced by receipts filed with the Minister,

(b) that were not included in determining an amount under this subsection, section 64 or subsection 122.51(2), for a preceding taxation year,

(c) that are not included in determining an amount under this subsection, section 64 or subsection 122.51(2), by any other taxpayer for any taxation year, and

(d) that were paid by the individual or the individual's legal representative within any period of 12 months that ends in the taxation year or, if those expenses were in respect of a person (including the individual) who died in the taxation year, within any period of 24 months that includes the day of the person's death;

C   is the lesser of $1,813[18] and 3% of the individual's income for the taxation year; and

D   is the total of all amounts each of which is, in respect of a dependant of the individual (within the meaning assigned by subsection 118(6), other than a child of the individual who has not attained the age of 18 years before the end of the taxation year), the amount determined by the formula

$$E - F$$

where

E   is the total of the individual's medical expenses in respect of the dependant

     (a) that are evidenced by receipts filed with the Minister,

     (b) that were not included in determining an amount under this subsection, or subsection 122.51(2), in respect of the individual for a preceding taxation year,

     (c) that are not included in determining an amount under this subsection, or subsection 122.51(2), by any other taxpayer for any taxation year, and

     (d) that were paid by the individual or the individual's legal representative within the period referred to in paragraph (d) of the description of B; and

F   is the lesser of $1,813[18] and 3% of the dependant's income for the taxation year.

Related Provisions: 110.7(1) — Residing in prescribed zone; 117(1) — Tax payable under this Part; 117.1(2)(k) — Indexing for inflation; 118.2(3)(a) — Taxable employment benefits deemed paid by employee as medical expense; 118.2(3)(b) — Reimbursed or reimbursable amounts excluded; 118.3 — Mental or physical impairment; 118.4(1) — Severe and prolonged impairment; 118.4(2) — Reference to medical practitioner; 118.91 — Individual resident in Canada for part of the year; 118.92 — Ordering of credits; 118.93 — Credits in separate returns; 118.94 — Credit restriction for non-resident individual; 118.95(a) — Application in year individual becomes bankrupt; 122(1.1) — Trust cannot claim credit; 122.51 — Refundable credit of up to $500; 257 — Formula cannot calculate to less than zero.

Notes: The effect of the credit is that medical expenses over $2,397 (for 2020) or $2,421 (for 2021) (or "3% of net income" if that is lower) entitle the taxpayer to a credit of 15%, which including a provincial credit is worth about 21% — equivalent to a deduction for a taxpayer in the lowest bracket. Quebec provides a 20% credit but has no dollar limit to the 3% threshold, so very high-income taxpayers are effectively precluded from claiming medical expenses for Quebec tax purposes.

Expenses are pooled for the taxpayer, spouse or common-law partner, and children under 18 (regardless of their income), after which the threshold amount is deducted. If a taxpayer has a spouse in a nursing home as well as a common-law partner, both might qualify, but CRA disagrees: VIEWS doc 2009-0330301C6. The amendment to 118.2(1)B enacted in 2013 supposedly ensures that both do not qualify, but it is unclear whether it actually does so. Expenses can be claimed for an Indian spouse whose income is exempt (see Notes to 81(1)(a)): VIEWS doc 2011-0397631E5.

Medical expenses can be grouped into a 12-month period to qualify (see B(d)). CRA confusingly says that for 118.2.2, expenses must be *incurred*, and can be paid at any time, but for 118.2(1) they must be *paid* during the 12-month period chosen: VIEWS doc 2015-0589041E5 (which also says 2005-0133261I7 is "confusing" and does not represent CRA policy. See also 2012-0456201E5. The 12-month period picked can be changed from year to year, as long as no expense is double-claimed: 2014-0529851E5.

Taxpayers must file receipts, but there is no obligation on suppliers to issue receipts: VIEWS docs 2007-0230921M4, 2011-0420021E5.

Taxpayers can claim medical expenses actually paid *by the taxpayer* for a dependent relative (beyond a spouse, common-law partner and children under 18) that exceed the relative's threshold; before 2011 this was limited to $10,000. In *Savoy*, 2011 TCC 73, S was allowed $10,000 of the cost of renovating his garage (pre-Feb. 22/05 under 118.2(2)(l.2)) into a living unit for his quadriplegic brother B, who passed away before the unit was ready. Even though S was not providing B food and shelter, doing the renovations meant that B was S's "dependant".

Medical services provided as taxable employee benefits are considered to be the employee's medical expenses: 118.2(3)(a). Expenses are excluded to the extent they are reimbursed by an insurance plan: 118.2(3)(b). The unreimbursed balance can be claimed.

An additional credit for low-income earners is available in 122.51. See also the Disability Supports Deduction in s. 64 as an alternative to claiming this credit.

Where medical expenses are paid for using (non-taxable) funds received under provincial programs for children with autism, they cannot be claimed under 118.2: VIEWS doc 2003-0054611E5.

118.2(1) amended by 2002-2013 technical bill (for tax years that end after Oct. 2011), 2011 budget bill #2 (to remove a pre-2011 $10,000 limitation on claims for family members other than spouse and minor children), 2006 budget bill #1, 2004 Budget (before 2004, medical expenses for dependent relatives were reduced by 4.25 × the excess of the relative's income over the basic personal amount), 2000 same-sex partners bill, 1999, 1998 and 1997 Budget bills, 1992 Child Benefit bill.

Income Tax Folios: S1-F1-C1: Medical expense tax credit [replaces IT-519R2]; S1-F1-C2: Disability tax credit [replaces IT-519R2]; S1-F1-C3: Disability supports deduction [replaces IT-519R2].

Interpretation Bulletins: IT-171R2: Non-resident individuals — computation of taxable income earned in Canada and non-refundable tax credits (cancelled); IT-393R2: Election re tax on rents and timber royalties — non-residents.

Information Circulars: 07-1R1: Taxpayer relief provisions.

Forms: RC4065: Medical Expenses 2016 [guide]; T1 General return, Lines 33099, 33200 [former 330].

(2) Medical expenses — For the purposes of subsection (1), a medical expense of an individual is an amount paid

     (a) **[medical and dental services]** — to a medical practitioner, dentist or nurse or a public or licensed private hospital in respect of medical or dental services provided to a person (in this subsection referred to as the "patient") who is the individual, the individual's spouse or common-law partner or a dependant of the individual (within the meaning assigned by subsection 118(6)) in the taxation year in which the expense was incurred;

     (b) **[attendant or nursing home care]** — as remuneration for one full-time attendant (other than a person who, at the time the remuneration is paid, is the individual's spouse or common-law partner or is under 18 years of age) on, or for the full-time care in a nursing home of, the patient in respect of whom an amount would, but for paragraph 118.3(1)(c), be deductible under section 118.3 in computing a taxpayer's tax payable under this Part for the taxation year in which the expense was incurred;

     (b.1) **[attendant]** — as remuneration for attendant care provided in Canada to the patient if

         (i) the patient is a person in respect of whom an amount may be deducted under section 118.3 in computing a taxpayer's tax payable under this Part for the taxation year in which the expense was incurred,

         (ii) no part of the remuneration is included in computing a deduction claimed in respect of the patient under section 63 or 64 or paragraph (b), (b.2), (c), (d) or (e) for any taxation year,

         (iii) at the time the remuneration is paid, the attendant is neither the individual's spouse or common-law partner nor under 18 years of age, and

         (iv) each receipt filed with the Minister to prove payment of the remuneration was issued by the payee and contains, where the payee is an individual, that individual's Social Insurance Number,

to the extent that the total of amounts so paid does not exceed $10,000[2] (or $20,000[2] if the individual dies in the year);

     (b.2) **[group home care]** — as remuneration for the patient's care or supervision provided in a group home in Canada maintained and operated exclusively for the benefit of individuals who have a severe and prolonged impairment if

         (i) because of the patient's impairment, the patient is a person in respect of whom an amount may be deducted under section 118.3 in computing a taxpayer's tax payable under this Part for the taxation year in which the expense is incurred,

---

[2] Not indexed for inflation — ed.

[18] Indexed by 117.1(1) after 2004 — ed.

(ii) no part of the remuneration is included in computing a deduction claimed in respect of the patient under section 63 or 64 or paragraph (b), (b.1), (c), (d) or (e) for any taxation year, and

(iii) each receipt filed with the Minister to prove payment of the remuneration was issued by the payee and contains, where the payee is an individual, that individual's Social Insurance Number;

(c) **[full-time attendant at home]** — as remuneration for one full-time attendant upon the patient in a self-contained domestic establishment in which the patient lives, if

(i) the patient is, and has been certified in writing by a medical practitioner to be, a person who, by reason of mental or physical infirmity, is and is likely to be for a long-continued period of indefinite duration dependent on others for the patient's personal needs and care and who, as a result, requires a full-time attendant,

(ii) at the time the remuneration is paid, the attendant is neither the individual's spouse or common-law partner nor under 18 years of age, and

(iii) each receipt filed with the Minister to prove payment of the remuneration was issued by the payee and contains, where the payee is an individual, that individual's Social Insurance Number;

(d) **[nursing home care]** — for the full-time care in a nursing home of the patient, who has been certified in writing by a medical practitioner to be a person who, by reason of lack of normal mental capacity, is and in the foreseeable future will continue to be dependent on others for the patient's personal needs and care;

(e) **[school, institution, etc.]** — for the care, or the care and training, at a school, an institution or another place of the patient, who has been certified in writing by an appropriately qualified person to be a person who, by reason of a physical or mental handicap, requires the equipment, facilities or personnel specially provided by that school, institution or other place for the care, or the care and training, of individuals suffering from the handicap suffered by the patient;

(f) **[ambulance fees]** — for transportation by ambulance to or from a public or licensed private hospital for the patient;

(g) **[transportation]** — to a person engaged in the business of providing transportation services, to the extent that the payment is made for the transportation of

(i) the patient, and

(ii) one individual who accompanied the patient, where the patient was, and has been certified in writing by a medical practitioner to be, incapable of travelling without the assistance of an attendant

from the locality where the patient dwells to a place, not less than 40 kilometres from that locality, where medical services are normally provided, or from that place to that locality, if

(iii) substantially equivalent medical services are not available in that locality,

(iv) the route travelled by the patient is, having regard to the circumstances, a reasonably direct route, and

(v) the patient travels to that place to obtain medical services for himself or herself and it is reasonable, having regard to the circumstances, for the patient to travel to that place to obtain those services;

(h) **[travel expenses]** — for reasonable travel expenses (other than expenses described in paragraph (g)) incurred in respect of the patient and, where the patient was, and has been certified in writing by a medical practitioner to be, incapable of travelling without the assistance of an attendant, in respect of one individual who accompanied the patient, to obtain medical services in a place that is not less than 80 km from the locality where the patient dwells if the circumstances described in subparagraphs (g)(iii) to (v) apply;

(i) **[devices]** — for, or in respect of, an artificial limb, an iron lung, a rocking bed for poliomyelitis victims, a wheel chair, crutches, a spinal brace, a brace for a limb, an ileostomy or colostomy pad, a truss for hernia, an artificial eye, a laryngeal speaking aid, an aid to hearing, an artificial kidney machine, phototherapy equipment for the treatment of psoriasis or other skin disorders, or an oxygen concentrator, for the patient;

(i.1) **[devices for incontinence]** — for or in respect of diapers, disposable briefs, catheters, catheter trays, tubing or other products required by the patient by reason of incontinence caused by illness, injury or affliction;

(j) **[eyeglasses]** — for eye glasses or other devices for the treatment or correction of a defect of vision of the patient as prescribed by a medical practitioner or optometrist;

(k) **[various]** — for an oxygen tent or other equipment necessary to administer oxygen or for insulin, oxygen, liver extract injectible for pernicious anaemia or vitamin B12 for pernicious anaemia, for use by the patient as prescribed by a medical practitioner;

(l) **[guide dogs, other service animals]** — on behalf of the patient who is blind or profoundly deaf or has severe autism, severe diabetes, severe epilepsy, severe mental impairment or a severe and prolonged impairment that markedly restricts the use of the patient's arms or legs,

(i) for an animal that is

(A) specially trained to

(I) in the case of severe mental impairment, perform specific tasks (excluding, for greater certainty, the provision of emotional support) that assist the patient in coping with the impairment, and

(II) in all other cases, assist the patient in coping with the impairment, and

(B) provided by a person or organization one of whose main purposes is such training of animals,

(ii) for the care and maintenance of such an animal, including food and veterinary care,

(iii) for reasonable travel expenses of the patient incurred for the purpose of attending a school, institution or other facility that trains, in the handling of such animals, individuals who are so impaired, and

(iv) for reasonable board and lodging expenses of the patient incurred for the purpose of the patient's full-time attendance at a school, institution or other facility referred to in subparagraph (iii);

(l.1) **[transplant costs]** — on behalf of the patient who requires a bone marrow or organ transplant,

(i) for reasonable expenses (other than expenses described in subparagraph (ii)), including legal fees and insurance premiums, to locate a compatible donor and to arrange for the transplant, and

(ii) for reasonable travel, board and lodging expenses (other than expenses described in paragraphs (g) and (h)) of the donor (and one other person who accompanies the donor) and the patient (and one other person who accompanies the patient) incurred in respect of the transplant;

(l.2) **[alterations to home]** — for reasonable expenses relating to renovations or alterations to a dwelling of the patient who lacks normal physical development or has a severe and prolonged mobility impairment, to enable the patient to gain access to, or to be mobile or functional within, the dwelling, provided that such expenses

(i) are not of a type that would typically be expected to increase the value of the dwelling, and

(ii) are of a type that would not normally be incurred by persons who have normal physical development or who do not have a severe and prolonged mobility impairment;

765

(l.21) **[home construction costs]** — for reasonable expenses relating to the construction of the principal place of residence of the patient who lacks normal physical development or has a severe and prolonged mobility impairment, that can reasonably be considered to be incremental costs incurred to enable the patient to gain access to, or to be mobile or functional within, the patient's principal place of residence, provided that such expenses

(i) are not of a type that would typically be expected to increase the value of the dwelling, and

(ii) are of a type that would not normally be incurred by persons who have normal physical development or who do not have a severe and prolonged mobility impairment;

(l.3) **[lip reading and sign language training]** — for reasonable expenses relating to rehabilitative therapy, including training in lip reading and sign language, incurred to adjust for the patient's hearing or speech loss;

(l.4) **[sign language services]** — on behalf of the patient who has a speech or hearing impairment, for sign language interpretation services or real-time captioning services, to the extent that the payment is made to a person in the business of providing such services;

(l.41) **[note-taking services]** — on behalf of the patient who has a mental or physical impairment, for note-taking services, if

(i) the patient has been certified in writing by a medical practitioner to be a person who, because of that impairment, requires such services, and

(ii) the payment is made to a person in the business of providing such services;

(l.42) **[voice recognition software]** — on behalf of the patient who has a physical impairment, for the cost of voice recognition software, if the patient has been certified in writing by a medical practitioner to be a person who, because of that impairment, requires that software;

(l.43) **[reading services]** — on behalf of the patient who is blind or has a severe learning disability, for reading services, if

(i) the patient has been certified in writing by a medical practitioner to be a person who, because of that impairment, requires such services, and

(ii) the payment is made to a person in the business of providing such services;

(l.44) **[deaf-blind intervening services]** — on behalf of the patient who is blind and profoundly deaf, for deaf-blind intervening services, if the payment is made to a person in the business of providing those services;

(l.5) **[moving expenses]** — for reasonable moving expenses (within the meaning of subsection 62(3), but not including any expense deducted under section 62 for any taxation year) of the patient, who lacks normal physical development or has a severe and prolonged mobility impairment, incurred for the purpose of the patient's move to a dwelling that is more accessible by the patient or in which the patient is more mobile or functional, if the total of the expenses claimed under this paragraph by all persons in respect of the move does not exceed $2,000;

(l.6) **[driveway alterations]** — for reasonable expenses relating to alterations to the driveway of the principal place of residence of the patient who has a severe and prolonged mobility impairment, to facilitate the patient's access to a bus;

(l.7) **[van for wheelchair]** — for a van that, at the time of its acquisition or within 6 months after that time, has been adapted for the transportation of the patient who requires the use of a wheelchair, to the extent of the lesser of $5,000 and 20% of the amount by which

(i) the amount paid for the acquisition of the van

exceeds

(ii) the portion, if any, of the amount referred to in subparagraph (i) that is included because of paragraph (m) in computing the individual's deduction under this section for any taxation year;

(l.8) **[caregiver training]** — for reasonable expenses (other than amounts paid to a person who was at the time of the payment the individual's spouse or common-law partner or a person under 18 years of age) to train the individual, or a person related to the individual, if the training relates to the mental or physical infirmity of a person who

(i) is related to the individual, and

(ii) is a member of the individual's household or is dependent on the individual for support;

(l.9) **[therapy]** — as remuneration for therapy provided to the patient because of the patient's severe and prolonged impairment, if

(i) because of the patient's impairment, an amount may be deducted under section 118.3 in computing a taxpayer's tax payable under this Part for the taxation year in which the remuneration is paid,

(ii) the therapy is prescribed by, and administered under the general supervision of,

(A) a medical doctor, a nurse practitioner or a psychologist, in the case of mental impairment, and

(B) a medical doctor, a nurse practitioner or an occupational therapist, in the case of a physical impairment,

(iii) at the time the remuneration is paid, the payee is neither the individual's spouse or common-law partner nor under 18 years of age, and

(iv) each receipt filed with the Minister to prove payment of the remuneration was issued by the payee and contains, where the payee is an individual, that individual's Social Insurance Number;

(l.91) **[tutoring services]** — as remuneration for tutoring services that are rendered to, and are supplementary to the primary education of, the patient who

(i) has a learning disability or a mental impairment, and

(ii) has been certified in writing by a medical practitioner to be a person who, because of that disability or impairment, requires those services,

if the payment is made to a person ordinarily engaged in the business of providing such services to individuals who are not related to the payee;

(l.92) **[design of therapy plan]** — as remuneration for the design of an individualized therapy plan for the patient because of the patient's severe and prolonged impairment, if

(i) because of the patient's impairment, an amount would be, if this Act were read without reference to paragraph 118.3(1)(c), deductible under section 118.3 in computing a taxpayer's tax payable under this Part for the taxation year in which the remuneration is paid,

(ii) the plan is required to access public funding for specialized therapy or is prescribed by

(A) a medical doctor, a nurse practitioner or a psychologist, in the case of mental impairment, or

(B) a medical doctor, a nurse practitioner or an occupational therapist, in the case of a physical impairment,

(iii) the therapy set out in the plan is prescribed by and, if undertaken, administered under the general supervision of

(A) a medical doctor, a nurse practitioner or a psychologist, in the case of mental impairment, or

(B) a medical doctor, a nurse practitioner or an occupational therapist, in the case of a physical impairment, and

(iv) the payment is made to a person ordinarily engaged in a business that includes the design of such plans for individuals who are not related to the payee;

(m) **[prescribed in regulations]** — for any device or equipment for use by the patient that

    (i) is of a prescribed kind,

    (ii) is prescribed by a medical practitioner,

    (iii) is not described in any other paragraph of this subsection, and

    (iv) meets such conditions as may be prescribed as to its use or the reason for its acquisition,

to the extent that the amount so paid does not exceed the amount, if any, prescribed in respect of the device or equipment;

(n) **[drugs]** — for

    (i) drugs, medicaments or other preparations or substances (other than those described in paragraph (k))

        (A) that are manufactured, sold or represented for use in the diagnosis, treatment or prevention of a disease, disorder or abnormal physical state, or its symptoms, or in restoring, correcting or modifying an organic function,

        (B) that can lawfully be acquired for use by the patient only if prescribed by a medical practitioner or dentist, and

        (C) the purchase of which is recorded by a pharmacist, or

    (ii) drugs, medicaments or other preparations or substances that are prescribed by regulation;

(o) **[lab tests]** — for laboratory, radiological or other diagnostic procedures or services together with necessary interpretations, for maintaining health, preventing disease or assisting in the diagnosis or treatment of any injury, illness or disability, for the patient as prescribed by a medical practitioner or dentist;

(p) **[dentures]** — to a person authorized under the laws of a province to carry on the business of a dental mechanic, for the making or repairing of an upper or lower denture, or for the taking of impressions, bite registrations and insertions in respect of the making, producing, constructing and furnishing of an upper or lower denture, for the patient;

(q) **[health plan premiums]** — as a premium, contribution or other consideration under a private health services plan in respect of one or more of the individual, the individual's spouse or common-law partner and any member of the individual's household with whom the individual is connected by blood relationship, marriage, common-law partnership or adoption, except to the extent that the premium, contribution or consideration is deducted under subsection 20.01(1) in computing an individual's income from a business for any taxation year;

(r) **[gluten-free food]** — on behalf of the patient who has celiac disease, the incremental cost of acquiring gluten-free food products as compared to the cost of comparable non-gluten-free food products, if the patient has been certified in writing by a medical practitioner to be a person who, because of that disease, requires a gluten-free diet;

(s) **[Special Access Programme drugs]** — for drugs obtained under Health Canada's Special Access Programme in accordance with sections C.08.010 and C.08.011 of the *Food and Drug Regulations* and purchased for use by the patient;

(t) **[Special Access Programme devices]** — for medical devices obtained under Health Canada's Special Access Programme in accordance with Part 2 of the *Medical Devices Regulations* and purchased for use by the patient; or

(u) **[medical marijuana]** — on behalf of the patient who is the holder of a "medical document" (as defined in subsection 264(1) of the *Cannabis Regulations*) to support their use of cannabis for medical purposes, for the cost of cannabis, cannabis oil, cannabis plant seeds or cannabis products purchased for medical purposes from a holder of a "licence for sale" (as defined in subsection 264(1) of the *Cannabis Regulations*).

(v) **[medical marijuana]** — [Repealed]

Possible Future Amendment — Fertility-Related Expenses

Federal Budget, March 19, 2019, Chapter 4, Part 1: See under 118.2(2.2).

Related Provisions: 20(1)(qq), (rr) — Business deduction for disability-related modifications to buildings and disability-related equipment; 20.01 — Deduction from business income for private health plan premiums; 63(3)"child care expense"(d) — Medical expenses are not child care expenses; 64 — Disability supports deduction for attendant care and other expenses; 67.1(1) — Food and entertainment 50% restriction does not apply; 110.7(3) — Northern Canada residents — trips to obtain medical services; 118.041(4) — Home accessibility credit and medical expense credit can both be claimed for same expense; 118.2(2.1) — Expenses for purely cosmetic procedures disallowed; 118.2(2.2) — Fertility expenses allowed; 118.2(3) — Taxable benefit counts as employee's expense; 118.2(4) — Use of own vehicle for transportation under (2)(g); 118.3(1)(c) — No disability credit if attendant or nursing home care claimed; 118.3(2) — Dependant having impairment; 144.1(10) — Employee contributions to employee life and health trust deemed to be contributions to private health services plan for 118.2(2)(q) if so identified; 251(6) — Meaning of "connected by blood relationship, marriage or adoption".

Notes: "Patient", defined in 118.2(2)(a) for all of 118.2(2), includes various relatives including in-laws. See 118(6) and 252. It does not include a surrogate mother, so ultrasound and prescription drug expenses of a surrogate were denied to the parents: *Warnock*, 2014 TCC 240.

Medical expenses include GST/HST paid on them: VIEWS doc 2018-0767261M4.

118.2(2) is to be interpreted "liberally and humanely", expansively and compassionately, as long as the legislation can be (slightly) stretched to accommodate the claim: *Olney*, 2014 TCC 262, paras. 13, 27.

118.2(2)(a): "Medical practitioner" (see 118.4(2)) under CRA policy includes a regulated health profession. Obviously it includes physicians and surgeons. Depending on the province, the list can include (Income Tax Folio S1-F1-C1 ¶1.23; list at tinyurl.com/cra-medprac): acupuncturist, audiologist, chiropodist, chiropractor, combined lab + X-ray technologist, counselling therapist, criminologist, dental assistant, dental hygienist, dental nurse, dental technician / technologist / therapist, dentist, denturist, dental mechanic, denturologist, dietician, emergency medical technician, hearing aid practitioner, homeopath, kinesiologist, licensed or registered practical nurse, marriage and family therapist, massage therapist [see below], medical laboratory technologist, medical radiation technologist, midwife [2017-0728281M4], naturopath [2012-0462011E5], nurse [2009-0332141E5], nurse practitioner, occupational therapist, ophthalmic medical assistant, optician, optometrist, pharmacist [2011-0395531E5, 2011-0407091E5], physiotherapist (physical therapist), podiatrist, professional technologist in orthoses/prostheses, psychoeducator, psychological associate, psychologist, registered nursing assistant, registered nutritionist, registered psychiatric nurse, registered psychotherapist, respiratory therapist, sexologist, social worker, speech language pathologist, traditional Chinese medicine practitioner, vocational guidance counsellor. The following did not qualify: Board Certified Behaviour Analyst in Ontario (2016-0633581E5); Christian Science practitioner (2005-0126931E5, 2006-0180991M4, 2008-0296611I7); clinical counsellor in BC (2007-0246011E5, 2007-0250511E5); doula in Alberta (2013-0490121E5, 2017-0728281M4); homeopath or naturopath in NB (2010-0407341E5); laser technician (2011-0427631E5); naturopath or osteopath in QC (*Parent*, 2007 TCC 608; *Chevalier*, 2008 TCC 11 [no *Charter* violation], 2015-0585011I7, 2016-0624871C6 [CPA QC 2016 q.3]); orthotherapist or osteopath in QC (2014-0533911E5); personal trainer recommended by physician (2009-0342711E5, 2010-0391051E5, 2011-0429001E5); pulse electromagnetic technician (2014-0551781M4); "podologue" in QC (2009-0337771E5); psychometrist (2011-0427011E5, but see 118.2(2)(o)); Reiki practitioner (*Tall*, 2008 TCC 677 (aff'd on other grounds 2009 FCA 342); this allegedly "Euro-centric" rule was not a *Charter* violation); Rolf therapist (2007-0235861E5); shiatsu therapist in BC (2015-0571341E5); speech therapy technician in QC (2012-0465171E5); thalassotherapy centre (*Roy*, 2004 TCC 753); unregistered nurse providing Christian and native healing processes (2007-0224311E5). Registered massage therapists qualify in ON and BC and apparently in SK (*Knechtel*, [2001] 4 C.T.C. 2444 (TCC)), but not in AB (*Pagnotta*, [2001] 4 C.T.C. 2613 (TCC); *Ross*, 2014 TCC 317, paras. 33-42), QC (*Rogers*, 2010 TCC 548, VIEWS doc 2011-0392401E5), NS (*Laurie*, 2003 TCC 105) or NB (*Noddin*, 2004 TCC 687 [no *Charter* violation]; *Davar*, 2005 TCC 715); but tinyurl.com/cra-medprac now says NB qualifies as well as BC, ON, NL. In *Pickwoad*, 2005 TCC 409, the Court ruled that despite CRA policy, "medical practitioner" means *only* a physician or surgeon, and a registered social worker did not qualify. In *Couture*, 2008 FCA 412, an acupuncturist (in ON, where they were not regulated) was held not to be a "medical practitioner", as "authorized to practise" in 118.4(2) means specifically authorized by legislation, not simply permitted; but in *Murphy*, 2010 TCC 434, an acupuncturist was a "medical practitioner" in 2007 because Ontario had passed the *Traditional Chinese Medicine Act*; but in *Power*, 2012 TCC 113, a different judge ruled an acupuncturist still did not qualify in 2009 because the *TCMA* had not yet been proclaimed in force! Since *Couture*, CRA looks for "specific legislation that enables, permits or empowers a person to perform medical services": 2009-0337771E5. Changes to CRA's list are initiated by the provinces: 2019-0803411I7. See also Thompson, "Referential Tax Legislation: The Role of Provincial Law in the Medical Expense Tax Credit", 91 *Canadian Bar Review* 211-40 (2012).

In appropriate cases, consider whether para. (e), (l.9) or (o) may apply to a service that does not fall under 118.2(2)(a).

118.2(2)(a) applies only to an *existing* medical condition in CRA's view, so storing umbilical cord blood or stem cells does not qualify: docs 2005-0137781E5, 2010-0386621E5, 2010-0390981E5, 2011-0422941E5 (see also under 118.2(2)(o) below); and *Shapiro*, 2014 CarswellNat 594 (TCC). Doc 2006-0218131E5 states: "it has generally been the Agency's position that services provided by a medical practitioner are medical services", so that payments for medico-legal reports (for litigation) qualify; but 2011-0436011E5 states the opposite, and that they do not qualify.

For 118.2(2)(a), counselling services are considered to qualify if (a) the counsellor is working in a recognized mental health clinic, community agency or hospital; (b) the counsellor is a member of an association governing their profession; and (c) the treatment is at the request of, or in association with, a physician: docs 2002-0171795, 2005-0153591E5, 2006-0213231E5.

118.2(2)(a) does not cover membership or access fees to a private health clinic in CRA's view (2006-0166961E5: this might not be correct). It does cover medical clinic block fees for uninsured services (2007-0255741I7, 2014-0540731E5 — provided they are "medical" services, but a doctor's note explaining absence from work qualifies, as does any "certificate or report": doc 9726515); and an "executive medical" health assessment by a physician: 2006-0175831E5. It does not cover payment to a physician for a missed appointment: *Zaffino*, 2007 TCC 388, paras. 11-13. It does not cover cosmetic procedures such as laser hair removal, due to 118.2(2.1): 2010-0361271E5 (overrides 2004-0078231I7).

Legal expenses of trying to get a provincial health care plan to pay for medical treatment, or to correct medical records, do not qualify in CRA's view: docs 2010-0358201E5, 2010-0389841E5; nor the cost of obtaining records from a medical records company: 2014-0553301E5. Similarly, interest on a bank loan taken to pay for dental treatments does not qualify: 2011-0416651I7.

The following can qualify under 118.2(2)(a): assisted suicide ["medical assistance in dying"] (2017-0703891C6 [2017 CTF q.16]); complex continuing care co-payment to Ontario hospital while awaiting nursing home placement, even if identified as for meals and accommodation (2015-0574831E5); dental implants done by a dentist (2006-0218021E5, 2011-0397151E5 — note that tooth whitening no longer qualifies due to 118.2(2.1)); fertility clinic fees (*Ismael*, 2014 TCC 157, para. 7, on consent, and see now 118.2(2.2)); hip replacement prosthesis (ceramic femoral head), but only because paid to hospital (2014-0533671E5); hyperbaric oxygen therapy (2014-0529101E5); *in vitro* fertility costs (see now 118.2(2.2)), including sperm freezing, egg freezing, embryo freezing, thawing and storage (2003-0035715, 2011-0396951E5, 2011-0415601E5, 2011-0416451E5, 2015-0589741E5, 2015-0612331I7, 2018-0763791I7, 2020-0842461E5) (but not amounts paid to cover the donor's costs: 2009-0311051E5, 2015-0572891E5, 2018-0751891I7); intrauterine insemination (2010-0381401E5); lap band surgery, where not purely cosmetic (2011-0395451E5); medical digital infrared thermal imaging (or possibly under 118.2(2)(o); 2009-0307921E5); nuchal translucency and nasal bone detection, if performed by a medical practitioner or nurse (2007-0246741E5); pain management, if fees paid to a physician or hospital for a pre-existing medical condition (2011-0397731E5); photodymamic therapy (2010-0383831I7); pulsed electromagnetic field therapy (PEMF) (2019-0807521E5); sex reassignment surgery and related treatments (2012-0463201E5); Special Authority status-request fee paid to a physician (for BC PharmaCare coverage for a particular drug) (2013-0499731E5); stem cell therapy provided by a medical practitioner or hospital (2008-0285981E5, 2009-0319341E5, 2012-0448971E5 [but not collection and storage of stem cells since this does not relate to an existing medical condition: 2010-0386621E5]); surgery in the United States, and travel to get it (2012-0437281E5); vasectomy reversal, since it relates to "existing medical condition" of infertility (2014-0529901E5); weight loss program provided by medical practitioner (2010-0358421E5, 2010-0361011E5, 2011-0402881E5, 2011-0429001E5). For ultrasound tests, see below re 118.2(2)(o). See also Notes to 118.2(2.1).

Payments to a corporation or clinic qualify under 118.2(2)(a) as long as they are for medical services performed by (or under supervision of) physicians: *Mudry*, 2008 TCC 160; docs 2003-0045561E5, 2006-0171931I7.

A claim under 118.2(2)(a) for payment to a hospital for long-term care could disentitle the patient to the disability credit; see Notes to 118.3(1) re 118.3(1)(c).

118.2(2)(b): For CRA's list of approved nursing homes throughout Canada (some only on a "case by case" basis), see "CRA List of Nursing Homes" on *TaxPartner* or *Taxnet Pro*. "Nursing home" does not include a retirement residence or seniors' residence even if it provides 24-hour nursing care (*Miles*, [2000] 2 C.T.C. 2165 (TCC); VIEWS docs 2011-0395531E5, 2016-0624871C6 [CPA QC 2016 q.3]); or the taxpayer's home even if fully adapted to the patient's needs (2007-0253621E5). For administrative definitions of nursing home, see Income Tax Folio S1-F1-C1 ¶1.33 and docs 2008-0285321C6, 2008-0291121E5, 2009-0346431E5, 2011-0399061E5, 2014-0529851E5; 2016 Alberta CPA (tinyurl.com/cra-abtax), q. 16(a) [home not on the list will not be disallowed until it is contacted to determine eligibility]. However, where a portion of retirement home costs is identified as paid for attendant care, it qualifies under 118.2(2)(b.1): 2003-0030965, 2005-0142361E5. See also 118.2(2)(e) below; the Disability Supports Deduction under s. 64; Champagne & Meville, "Credit Where It's Due: Tax Credit for Elder-Care Expenses and Other Tax Considerations", 66(4) *Canadian Tax Journal* 1013-40 (2018).

If a claim is made under 118.2(2)(b), no disability credit can be claimed: 118.3(1)(c), VIEWS docs 2011-0395031E5, 2011-0415541M4.

A therapist working intensively with a disabled child could qualify under 118.2(2)(b): VIEWS doc 2009-0343381E5.

Certification under 118.2(2)(b) requires a Form T2201, but for 118.2(2)(d), a doctor's letter is sufficient: VIEWS doc 2005-0149621E5.

(Note that payments received to allow the taxpayer to care for a disabled child or spouse may not be taxable: see Notes to s. 3 at bullet "attendant-care".)

118.2(2)(b.1): "Attendant care" includes salaries of retirement home employees for health care, meal preparation, housekeeping, laundry service, transportation driver and security in unsecured units: VIEWS doc 2004-0101081E5. It included payment to a service to clean the appellant's home, in *Zaffino*, 2007 TCC 388; and payment for clothes alterations, by a Thalidomide victim who could not do the work herself, in *Olney*, 2014 TCC 262, para. 27. CRA says it does not include provision of only maid or cleaning services (Income Tax Folio S1-F1-C1 ¶1.32); snow cleaning or lawn maintenance (2014-0552351E5); or recreational camp assistance (2018-0778121E5). CRA says nursing home care does not qualify unless the receipt shows a specific amount for attendant care: 2011-0418081E5. The $10,000 limit applies to each taxpayer claiming for the same patient: 2006-0172181I7.

The dollar limit in 118.2(2)(b.1) closing words is not indexed to inflation. It was $5,000 when introduced in 1991 and became $10,000 in 1997.

118.2(2)(b.1) and (c) refer to "remuneration" of an attendant (rather than "cost" as in 64(a)A(ii)(J)), which suggests that employer EI and CPP premiums are not included, but CRA allows them: Income Tax Folio S1-F1-C1 ¶1.43. 118.2(2)(d) uses "full-time care", which suggests all care costs but possibly not accommodation, although the French wording "séjour à plein temps" suggests that accommodation is included.

118.2(2)(c): Sequential part-time attendants can equal a full-time attendant: doc 2007-0253621E5.

118.2(2)(d): See under 118.2(2)(b) and (b.1) above.

118.2(2)(e): A retirement community qualified in *McKinley*, 2004 TCC 50, for a blind patient with severe dementia. However, in *Lister*, 2006 FCA 331 (leave to appeal denied 2007 CarswellNat 1229 (SCC)), assisted living in a retirement community did not qualify, as 118.2(2)(e) "contemplates institutional care" (para. 18), and in general "no tax relief is provided for the ordinary expenses of living" (para. 15). A retirement home again did not qualify in *Shultis*, 2006 TCC 499, though it might have if the patient required the "safe unit" for dementia patients under constant supervision. A personal care home or seniors' residence can qualify if it has specialized equipment or specially trained personnel: docs 2005-0113121E5, 2011-0395531E5. The taxpayer's home does not qualify in CRA's view: 2007-0253621E5.

Sending an autistic child to an integrated day care or private school does not qualify under 118.2(2)(e) in CRA's view, unless the school has specialized equipment, facilities or trained personnel to care for such a child: docs 2004-0065621E5, 2010-0403181E5. A residential treatment centre, addiction treatment centre or detoxification clinic can qualify: 2012-0436431E5, 2012-0444341E5. A summer camp does not: 2018-0778121E5 (it may be a s. 63 child-care expense).

Specific schools, whether fees allowed (Y/N): Calgary Academy: Y (*Karn*, 2013 TCC 78: school only for students with learning disabilities). Crestwood Preparatory: N (*Bauskin*, 2013 TCC 64: no evidence of special equipment, facilities or personnel in mainstream program). Foothills Academy: Y, in part (*Lang*, 2009 TCC 182, but under 118.2(2)(l.91), not (e)). Glenlyon Norfolk: N (*Piper*, 2010 TCC 492: it was not a special school for children with disabilities). Laureate Academy: N (*MacDuff*, 2009 TCC 179: insufficient evidence). Robert Land Academy: Y (*Marshall*, 2003 TCC 356) and N (*Kushnir*, [1986] 1 C.T.C. 2514 (TCC): insufficient evidence). Rothesay Collegiate: N (*Scott*, 2008 FCA 286: school's "focus was not on the provision of medical services"; and physician had not given formal certification). Rundle College: N (*Flower*, 2005 TCC 268: no care given in a "medical context"). St. George's School, Montreal: N (*Leibovich*, 2016 TCC 6: school did not specifically cater to students with learning disorders). TALC Academy: Y (*Lucarelli*, 2012 TCC 301). Unnamed school: N (*Vita-Finzi*, 2008 TCC 565: school not principally focused on children with learning disabilities).

A school for gifted children generally will not qualify: doc 2005-0115011E5 and cases it cites (*Collins*, *Burns*, *Robinson*, *Giroday*). A therapeutic equestrian centre does not qualify in CRA's view: 2007-0240721I7. Driving lessons for a disabled person do not qualify since a driving school does not provide "care": 2007-0244411E5. A school providing an allergy-free environment for a severely allergic student does not qualify: 2013-0507021E5.

"Certified" in 118.2(2)(e) was satisfied by a doctor's letter combined with a follow-up assessment by a resource centre: *Lucarelli*, 2012 TCC 301.

Where a school qualifies under 118.2(2)(e), travel to the school can qualify, but not rental of accommodation near the school: doc 2009-0349551E5 (but see new policy under 118.2(2)(g)-(h) below).

A nursing home can qualify under 118.2(2)(e) even though it is also under 118.2(2)(b). See Notes to 118.3(1) re 118.3(1)(c).

See also Golombek, Pearl-Weinberg & Francis, "Tuition Expense and Tutoring Fees as Medical Expenses", 63(2) *Canadian Tax Journal* 543-64 (2015); and consider 118.2(2)(l.91) as an alternative to (e).

118.2(2)(g) and (h) (travel): if commercial transport is unavailable, see 118.2(4). "Medical services" include a school under 118.2(2)(e), so travel to the school qualified: *Patton*, 2005 TCC 704. Travel costs can include a spouse's daily visits to the patient, not just when travelling to the hospital with the patient: *Bell*, 2009 TCC 523; *Jordan*, 2012 TCC 394. Travel does not qualify if it is not strictly for medical care (Ottawa patient's wife had to be cared for by their children in Alberta while he was in hospital):

Young, 2009 TCC 628. (However, under a "liberal and compassionate approach", since surgeons in Calgary would perform a procedure on the husband that those in Ottawa would not, "substantially equivalent medical services" were held not to be available in Ottawa: para. 11.) "Available" does not refer to cost, so where a taxpayer flew to Poland for dental work she could not afford in Canada, the travel did not qualify: *Tokarski*, 2012 TCC 115. Similarly, in *AB* [formerly *Ismael*], 2014 TCC 157, paras. 24-26, *in vitro* fertilization outside Canada was disallowed for a Toronto person who could have obtained it in Toronto, but wanted a particular type of donor and a cheaper procedure. Swimming therapy recommended by a physician might qualify, but did not where the 40km/80km conditions were not met: *Scully*, 2008 TCC 617 (parents' vacations to have a rest from caring for their disabled children also did not qualify). Travel to visit a child undergoing hospital treatment, where the parents also needed training at the hospital to care for the child, was allowed by consent judgment in *Desbiens* (*Law Times*, Nov. 16/09, p. 2; Court file 2008-2239(IT)I). In *Sienema*, 2010 TCC 468, travel expenses were allowed for the taxpayer to go to his parents' home for hot-tub treatment (but the taxpayer and attendant could not both claim travel when they went in the same vehicle).

In *Tallon*, 2015 FCA 156, winter travel to warm climates (needed for severe pain) was disallowed: "medical services" in (g) has the same meaning as in 118.2(2)(a) (para. 38). CRA says the same: docs 2008-0289291E5, 2012-0437331E5, 2012-0461911E5, 2015-0610741C6 [2015 CTF q.13]. In *Tallon*, 2017 TCC 244, the same taxpayer argued that travel to Thailand qualified because she had some medical services while there; it did not because her reason for the travel was still to get away from the cold.

Meals and accommodation for the accompanying person qualify if it is reasonable for the patient to remain at the facility: docs 2010-0353251M4, 2010-0377291M4, 2010-0384471M4, 2010-0385321M4, 2010-0391371M4, 2010-0391871M4, 2013-0507301C6 [2010 CTF conf p. 4:22-23, q.23], 2014-0530721E5. (This reverses 2008-0303871E5, 2009-0305671E5, 2009-0306221E5.) Parking also qualifies: 2011-0394771E5.

See also docs 2002-0121825 (whether "substantially equivalent" services available); 2004-0092971E5 (travel to allow patient in mental health facility to come home for monthly visits does not qualify); 2007-0253261E5 (newborn baby visits); 2007-0255831E5 (patient travelling 400 km for heart transplant could claim food and lodging near hospital for 3 months' post-op care, as travel was medically inadvisable); 2007-0255351I7; 2008-0285981E5 ("reasonable" test can be met even if medical services available nearer the locality); 2008-0285981E5, 2012-0437281E5, 2012-0435931E5, 2009-0337761E5 (meals and hotel while travelling >80km); 2011-0395911E5 (travel for high school student to move to school with sign language interpreter, but not rent); 2011-0396951E5 (travel for *in vitro* fertilization in Japan qualified due to long waiting periods in Canada); 2011-0423231E5 (only 1 accompanying person qualifies [this cannot be challenged using *Interpretation Act* s. 33(2), since the French is "un seul particulier"]); 2012-0448971E5 and 2012-0457461E5 ((g)(iii) test met if travel was reasonable even if medical services are available closer); 2012-0463351E5 (travel to US medical specialist); 2013-0478271E5 (travel needed due to shortage of family doctors in patient's locality); 2013-0483171E5 (40km rule prevents claim even where three 60km round trips needed daily); 2013-0510121E5 (travel to optometrist to prescribe contact lenses would likely not qualify); 2014-0520551E5 (travel to foreign country for surgery: various questions); 2015-0584181E5 (where baby is in hospital and one parent stays nearby, other parent's travel does not qualify); 2016-0624871C6 [CPA QC 2016 q.3] (orthodontist's travel paid by patient does not qualify [in the author's view, this is wrong as the patient is paying for the orthodontist's services, not for travel: cf. GST/HST "single supply" concept in Policy P-077R2]).

The measurement of 40 km and 80km for 118.2(2)(g) and (h) should use normal road distance. See Notes to 248(1)"eligible relocation".

In *Johnson*, 2010 TCC 321, payment with frequent-flyer points qualified as payment. See also Notes to 6(1)(a) under "Frequent-flyer points".

Per Income Tax Folio S1-F1-C1 ¶1.72 and tinyurl.com/travel-cra, 118.2(2)(h) travel expenses can optionally be calculated without receipts as $23/meal or $69/day (since 2020 [see under 62(3)]; $17 and $51 for 2006-2019); and vehicle expenses per qualifying km driven (covers both ownership and operating expenses), using the rates in the Notes to 62(3). This recognizes that the Courts allow much more than the older CRA policy of 5¢/km: see *Enns*, [1996] 2 C.T.C. 2630 (TCC), and *Watt*, [1997] 2 C.T.C. 2651 (TCC); docs 2014-0555801M4; 2018-0761301M4 (method used to establish Treasury Board rates, which CRA considers "fair and reasonable"). Where a taxpayer claimed the same travel expenses for herself and for her spouse to accompany her, the duplicate claim was denied: *Bartlett*, 2008 TCC 494 (and see *Sienema* case above).

118.2(2)(i): A "wheel chair" can include: rickshaw [bike trailer for disabled persons that can be converted to wheelchair by reattaching front detachable wheels] (VIEWS doc 2002-0161665); scooter purchased in place of wheelchair (2011-0378071E5); "standing wheelchair" (2015-0596311I7); stroller designed for disabled child (2003-0046145); tricycle wheelchair or rolling geriatric chair (2009-0351781E5). It does not include: battery-powered bicycle (2009-0323571E5); power-lift armchair (2014-0524211E5); Segway (2015-0596311I7) (but devices designed exclusively to enable a Segway to be used by a disabled person qualify; 2016 Alberta CPA (tinyurl.com/cra-abtax), q. 16(b)). A wheelchair cushion qualifies (as "in respect of" a wheelchair) but a bath cushion does not: 2010-0361221E5. A Joint Activation System Elbow rehabilitative splinting system likely qualifies as a "brace for a limb": 2011-0429871E5.

Because 118.2(2)(i) uses "in respect of", it covers operating and maintaining the listed equipment (e.g. wheelchair repairs and a computer unit to reconfigure the controls for a wheelchair: doc 2011-0395531E5), as well as purchase: Income Tax Folio S1-F1-C1 ¶1.73-1.86; 2007-0247031E5 (hearing aid extended warranty), 2009-0332141E5 (moulds and creams for hearing aid), 2009-0342421I7 (climate-controlled storage space for home dialysis supplies, and many other costs relating to home dialysis), 2011-0408941E5 (renting equipment and buying disposable bags for Topical Pressurized Oxygen Therapy). It does not cover a Torso Body Sock seamless T-shirt to be worn under a thoraco-lumbo-sacral orthosis in CRA's view, because such a T-shirt "is not a requirement": 2011-0429441E5.

118.2(2)(i.1) does not not cover baby wipes: VIEWS doc 2010-0356391E5 (note that a baby's incontinence is normal, not caused by "illness, injury or affliction"). "Other products" is considered to refer to products designed for use by incontinent persons, and so does not cover bed clothing, disposable gloves for caregivers or body ointments: 2010-0359861E5; or moist wipes: 2012-0437351E5.

118.2(2)(j) covers glasses prescribed to treat or correct a defect of vision (including contact lenses and prescription swimming goggles: Folio S1-F1-C1 ¶1.89, VIEWS doc 2017-0690361E5), but in CRA's view does not cover glasses prescribed by an optometrist to treat photosensitivity, which causes a person to suffer from headaches caused by the sun or bright light: 2003-0046081E5 (the Courts might disagree). In *Young*, 2009 TCC 628, para. 19, reading glasses were disallowed without evidence of a prescription. Lacrisert (ophthalmic insert to treat dry eye) can qualify "in special cases" if prescribed by a physician or optometrist "specifically for the treatment or correction of a specified defect of vision": 2010-0371881E5.

118.2(2)(k) does not cover a mobile app that monitors (but does not measure) a diabetic's blood sugar and advises what to do, in CRA's view: doc 2019-0804001E5.

118.2(2)(l) applies to guide dogs and other service animals. It applies to a trained diabetic alert dog: VIEWS doc 2014-0519971M4. It would not apply to a riding horse purchased for therapeutic riding; 2010-0378461E5, or a service dog for people with PTSD: 2016-0647181M4 (unless the 2018 change applies). Since 2018, it is expanded to service animals assisting a person with severe mental impairment in performing specific tasks: see tinyurl.com/cra-animals.

118.2(2)(l.1) covers legal and other expenses of transplant costs. For other deductible legal expenses, see Notes to 60(o). Travel expenses of parents of a transplant patient qualify, but only for 1 accompanying person under (l.1)(ii), unless para. (g) or (h) applies: VIEWS doc 2007-0237541I7.

In *Zieber*, 2008 TCC 328, expenses of a surrogate mother were allowed on the basis that an embryo is an "organ" being transplanted; but other judges declined to follow *Zieber* in *Warnock*, 2014 TCC 240, *Zanatta*, 2014 TCC 293 and *Pearen*, 2014 TCC 294, as the transplant recipient is the surrogate, not the "patient" defined in 118.2(2)(a); this was not *Charter* discrimination against gay couples (*Zanatta*, para. 22); and CRA will not follow *Zieber*: 2010-0391691E5. 118.2(2.2), introduced in 2017, does not help, since the surrogate is not a "patient": 2019-0828011M4. An unfertilized egg is not an "organ" so (l.1) does not apply: *Ismael*, 2014 TCC 157, para. 23.

118.2(2)(l.2)-(l.21) apply to renovations and construction of a home respectively, subject to subparas. (i)-(ii) discussed below. See generally VIEWS doc 2019-0791601E5. They can apply to: dock landing gate as wheelchair safety measure (2010-0379331E5); generator to ensure power for breathing equipment (2014-0535011E5); power flush toilets for person with Crohn's disease (2007-0251071E5); RV (recreational vehicle) used as a home (2005-0133691I7); stair lift for child with MS (2005-0163161E5); walk-in bathtub and high toilet, possibly (2012-0448781E5). Some provinces provide a Seniors' Home Renovation Tax Credit on the T1, a percentage of expenses on certain home modifications. These credits reduce the 118.2 expense: 118.2(3)(b), 2012-0470381E5. 118.2(2)(l.2) can be claimed along with the Home Accessibility Credit for the same expense: 118.041(4).

118.2(2)(l.2) was originally held to allow hardwood flooring to replace carpet for a patient with severe allergies (*Seely*, 2003 TCC 342) and a hot tub (*Gibson*, 2001 FCA 356 and many TCC cases). These cases were overturned as of 2005 by subparas. (l.2)(i)-(ii) and (l.21)(i)-(ii). Hardwood floors were thus denied in *Hendricks*, 2008 TCC 497, and hot tubs denied in *Johnston*, 2012 TCC 177 and *Anthony*, 2012 TCC 334. However, *Sotski*, 2013 TCC 286, allowed low-end laminate flooring for a patient with Parkinson's who would trip on carpet, as it replaced carpet that was fairly new and there was "no element of personal consumption" (para. 11); and in *Sienema*, 2010 TCC 468, S was allowed travel expenses to go to his parents' home for hot-tub treatments. Renovations to a pool do not qualify because they increase the value of the home: VIEWS doc 2006-0198081E5. See also 2008-0304581E5, 2009-0342291E5, 2009-0342581E5, 2009-0345491E5, 2011-0422991E5, 2017-0683371E5. In *Barnes*, 2009 TCC 429, a swimming pool required for B's daughter did not increase the value of the home because it took up the whole backyard, but did not qualify because it was a pool of the type able-bodied people would install.

In *Chobotar*, 2009 TCC 260, no credit was allowed for $35,000 spent to add a room and accessible bathroom for a person with multiple sclerosis, because it increased the home's value by $21,000 (although the addition, designed to accommodate a wheelchair, met the "not normally incurred" test). In *Young*, 2009 TCC 628, para. 15, a pedestal sink did not qualify because it could be purchased by someone with normal development. In *Henschel*, 2010 TCC 344, para. 10, a fireplace safety gate did not qualify because it "was designed also to protect normal children". In *Shallhorn*, 2019 QCCQ 449, an elevator for a paraplegic's home was allowed (for the parallel Quebec rule) even though it could be used by someone without a disability. See also under 118.2(2)(l.6) below re driveway alterations.

118.2(2)(l.21) applied to new home construction costs in *Totten*, 2003 TCC 457 (T had multiple sclerosis and was providing for future needs; "incremental" costs are the extra costs over the standard costs of the home). In *Meredith*, 2007 TCC 694 (later appeal denied 2008 TCC 172 due to issue estoppel), "incremental cost" was the $72,000 extra cost of an adapted condominium relative to a similar unadapted condo, not relative to M's previous condo.

118.2(2)(l.4) together with paras. (g)-(h) allows travel for a student to a school with a sign language interpreter: doc 2011-0395911E5.

118.2(2)(l.42): Voice recognition software for a person with a learning disability does not qualify unless the person requires the software because of a physical impairment: 2011-0431291E5. (Would a brain scan showing physical evidence of the learning disability suffice?) If the device is needed to read print, see Reg. 5700(L.1).

118.2(2)(l.5): Moving expenses include a person with severe and prolonged mobility impairment moving from a 2-storey home to a bungalow, or moving from a home with entrance stairs to one with a ramp: doc 2011-0403471E5.

118.2(2)(l.6): Driveway alterations can include resurfacing: doc 2011-0404911E5.

118.2(2)(l.7) applies to purchase of a van, but not maintenance or operating expenses: *Scully*, [2009] 2 C.T.C. 2225 (TCC), para. 26 (unlike para. (i), (l.7) uses "for", not "in respect of"). Reg. 5700(m)-(n) can be used to claim amounts over the $5,000 limit, by claiming the cost of a power-operated lift and hand-control modifications: 2011-0420021E5. See also 2007-0223571E5, 2007-024900117, 2014-0535011E5, 2015-0593261M4.

118.2(2)(l.8): See also 118(1)B(c.1) for a credit for caring for elderly relatives.

118.2(2)(l.9) does not cover homeopathic medicaments and herbal supplements: *Herzig*, 2004 TCC 344; or a "massageur par acupression thermique": VIEWS doc 2006-0204181E5. Talk therapy could qualify, but not where paid to the spouse due to subpara. (iii): 2011-0394341E5. Speech therapy technician not under a physician's supervision does not qualify: 2012-0465171E5. Monitoring of therapy by a physician does not meet the test of "administered under the general supervision": 2008-0291501E5, 2010-0355211E5 (skating coach, but skating might qualify for the fitness credit under 118.03). Side alteration vibration training does not qualify where not administered under the general supervision of a medical doctor or occupational therapist: 2010-0358821E5. 118.2(2)(l.9) did not cover supplies (e.g. weight vest, puzzles) that parents purchased for therapists to use with their autistic children: *Henschel*, 2010 TCC 344, para. 15. Aquatherapy was stated not to qualify in 2011-0397731E5, but that letter did not consider 118.2(2)(l.9). A personal trainer qualified in *Olney*, 2014 TCC 262, para. 25, for a Thalidomide victim who used her feet for many daily tasks and needed to maintain strength in her core and legs. Music therapy, play therapy, yoga and horseback riding therapy can all qualify if the conditions are met.

118.2(2)(l.91) (tutoring) applied in *Hoare*, 2007 TCC 292, to hiring a full-time teacher at H's home for his children with severe learning disabilities, as this was "supplementary" to the distance learning program the teacher used. In *Lang*, 2009 TCC 182, high school tuition at Foothills Academy for L's children was allowed in part (see also under 118.2(2)(e) above). See also doc 2011-042970117.

118.2(2)(m): see Notes to Reg. 5700.

118.2(2)(n) does not apply to over-the-counter products (including vitamins, dietary supplements, aspirin and organic products), due to "that can lawfully be acquired" in (n)(i)(B) (but Reg. 5701 allows drugs that require a medical practitioner's [including a pharmacist!: docs 2011-0395531E5, 2011-0407091E5] "intervention" to obtain, i.e., behind-the-counter drugs, if prescribed by a medical practitioner). Before Feb. 26/08, these might be allowed if prescribed by a doctor and recorded by a pharmacist (*Breger*, 2007 TCC 254; *Norton*, 2008 TCC 29), but not if those conditions were not both satisfied: *Ray*, 2004 FCA 1 and several TCC cases and VIEWS docs. Naturopathic medicines do not qualify: *Bentley*, 2009 TCC 316. *Charter of Rights* challenges by taxpayers needing non-prescription drugs were rejected in *Ali*, 2008 FCA 190 (leave to appeal denied 2008 CarswellNat 4095 (SCC)); *Tall*, 2009 FCA 342; *Ray*, 2010 FCA 17 (leave to appeal denied 2010 CarswellNat 1752; *Chevalier*, 2008 TCC 11; *Leeper*, 2015 TCC 82. See now docs 2008-0284881E5, 2010-0378121M4, 2010-0384271M4, 2011-0391961E5, 2011-0399851E5, 2011-0419231E5, 2011-0426031E5, 2012-0433101E5, 2012-0462011E5, 2012-0465121E5, 2013-0488841M4, 2014-0529511E5; *Berg*, 2011 TCC 528. Fertility medications can qualify: 2010-0381401E5, 2018-075189117. If an expense does not fall under 118.2(2)(n), consider whether it qualifies under para. (i.1) as a product required by reason of incontinence, or as a drug listed in para. (k).

118.2(2)(o) covers: embryo freezing costs (VIEWS doc 2018-0763791117); fertility clinic cycle monitoring (2011-0401711E5); *in-vitro* fertilization and related costs (Income Tax Folio S1-F1-C1 ¶1.130-1.131, docs 2011-0396951E5, 2011-0415601E5, 2011-0416451E5, 2018-075189117; and see now 118.2(2.2)); learning disability assessment, possibly (2011-0427011E5); MRI procedure (2011-0415671E5); medical digital infrared thermal imaging, probably (2009-0307921E5); pharmacogenomics test and consultation, possibly (2018-0760741E5); sleep evaluation study (2011-0397231E5); ultrasound tests (2009-0349731E5).

In CRA's view, 118.2(2)(o) does not cover: gym membership and weight loss clinic (2010-0361011E5 and 2011-0402881E5, but see above re 118.2(2)(a)); speech therapy technician whose services do not assist medical practitioner or speech therapist in reaching diagnosis or establishing treatment (2012-0465171E5); sperm banking by an individual who is to have an operation that could affect his ability to have children (2002-0148245; it may qualify under 118.2(2)(a)); umbilical cord blood (or stem cell) extraction and storage for possible future use in treating illness, because it does not treat an existing medical condition (*Shapiro*, 2014 TCC 74; 2003-0042615, 2010-0386621E5, 2010-0390981E5, 2011-0422941E5); genetic counsellor report, for the same reason (2010-0386651E5). In *Chen*, 2019 TCC 192, 118.2(2)(o) might have cov-

ered harvesting stem cells from a newborn's umbilical cord, but a doctor's letter saying "all patients are advised to do this" did not meet the "prescribed" test.

118.2(2)(q) does not cover the Ontario Health Premium, both because it is a tax not a premium, and because it is public not private health insurance: VIEWS doc 2004-0083531I7. Nor does it cover Alberta Health Care Insurance premiums: *Ross*, 2014 CarswellNat 4420 (TCC), para. 44. Nor does it cover membership or access fees to a private health clinic in CRA's view: 2006-0166961E5. It does cover premiums and prescription co-payments to the Nova Scotia Seniors' Pharmacare Program: 2006-0205931E5; premiums to the New Brunswick Drug Plan: 2014-052432117; and health plans for travel outside Canada: 2007-0229901E5. It may cover US Medicare: 2007-0254661E5. See also 2006-0197131C6 (long-term care policy) and Notes to 248(1)"private health services plan".

118.2(2)(r): For CRA guidelines on gluten-free products see tinyurl.com/gluten-cra. Minutes from CRA's informal Disabilities Advisory Committee, April 3/08 (*Access to Information Act* disclosure p. 000039) state: "CRA has no requirement for definitive diagnosis, only requires a letter from QP [qualified practitioner] saying person needs GF [gluten-free] foods ... In practice, one receipt per product is all that we have requested, but the person has to track how many they buy". Gluten-free foods do not qualify if required medically by an autistic child (doc 2010-0403181E5) or by a person with multiple food allergies but not celiac disease (2011-0427621E5).

118.2(2)(u): *Cannabis Regulations* s. 264(1) provides:

> "**medical document**" means a document provided by a health care practitioner to support the use of cannabis for medical purposes.

> "**health care practitioner**" means, except as otherwise provided, a medical practitioner or a nurse practitioner.

> "**medical practitioner**" means an individual who
>> (a) is entitled under the laws of a province to practise medicine in that province;
>> (b) is not restricted, under the laws of the province in which they practise, from authorizing the use of cannabis; and
>> (c) is not named in a notice issued under section 335 that has not been retracted.

> "**nurse practitioner**" means an individual who
>> (a) is entitled under the laws of a province to practise as a nurse practitioner or an equivalent designation and is practising as a nurse practitioner or an equivalent designation in that province;
>> (b) is not restricted, under the laws of the province in which they practise, from authorizing the use of cannabis; and
>> (c) is not named in a notice issued under section 335 that has not been retracted.

> "**licence for sale**" means a licence for sale for medical purposes.

Thus, only purchases from a holder of a licence for sale *for medical purposes* qualify, not from a regular cannabis retailer: VIEWS doc 2019-0800911E5.

For pre-2019 interpretation, see docs 2006-0209581E5, 2011-0405191E5, 2015-0588751E5, 2018-0777751E5. Monitoring, counselling and assistance with medical marijuana use, and a vaporizer, do not qualify: 2012-0432791E5, 2017-0700781E5.

The following do not qualify even if medically necessary (*Young*, 2009 TCC 628, para. 16; Guide RC4064) because they are not listed in 118.2(2) or Reg. 5700: apartment rental to reduce COVID-19 risk (2020-0866561E5); cell phone (*Olney*, 2014 TCC 262, para. 22); Chi machine (*Ross*, 2014 TCC 317, para. 26); Cryo-Cuff cold therapy device (2011-0395281E5); custom mattress or pillow (2017-0724441E5); electric breast pump (2007-0248701E5); exercise equipment for patient with high cholesterol (2010-0385911E5, 2011-0402881E5); fitness classes (*Ross*, para. 27, but see above re 118.2(2)(l.9)); G-tube (feeding tube) insertion and apparatus (except for the syringe, under Reg. 5700(b)) (2007-0220531E5); GPS tracking device (2012-0456201E5); health club membership (*Roberts*, 2012 TCC 319); hydrotherapy pool fees (2015-0567251E5); iPad for autistic child or person with speech impairment (2010-0383021E5, 2017-0719651E5); Lifeline emergency alarm (*Mattinson*, 2008 TCC 40); Liftware spoon (2017-0719651E5); light therapy device (2008-0305071E5); memory foam mattress (not for hospital bed), over-bed rolling table, oximeter and probes, second stairway hall hand railing, bite-activated nipples for sippy-cup dressings, tape liquid bandage and antiseptic (2009-0332141E5); organic food (2016-0646001M4); orthopedic chair for back pain (2010-0389391E5); orthopedic shoes not custom-made (2012-04562012E5); Polar Care Cube motorized cold therapy device (2011-0428191E5); power of attorney fees to manage finances for person with dementia (2010-0390001E5); power-lift armchair (2014-0524211E5); prenatal classes (2017-0696851E5); pulsed electromagnetic field therapy (PEMF) device (2019-0798981E5, 2019-0812161E5); recumbent exercise bike (2014-0528671E5); snowblower or snow-clearing service (2014-0552351E5); surrogacy fees to carry embryo and deliver baby (2010-0391691E5, and see above re 118.2(2)(l.1)); undergarments to hold breast prosthesis after mastectomy (2012-0436991E5); vaporization system for inhaling marijuana (2012-0432791E5); Water Well for warm water therapy for post-polio Syndrome (2011-0392871E5); window film to filter out UV rays (2010-0379331E5); wiring and bank fees and interest charges (*Ismael*, 2014 TCC 157); yoga fees (2011-0423231E5).

A device need not be new to qualify: doc 2011-0395281E5.

A deduction under 20.01 is often preferable to a credit under 118.2(2)(q), either because the taxpayer is not otherwise over the threshold in 118.2(1)C, or because the taxpayer is in a higher bracket than the 15% (federal) rate at which the credit applies (see 117(2)). Note that a 118.2 credit and a deduction (including as a business expense under 9(1)) cannot both be claimed for the same expense: 248(28), VIEWS doc 2014-0562151E5. (118.041(4) allows a double credit for certain home renovation expenses.)

For more CRA interpretation see Income Tax Folio S1-F1-C1; Guide RC4064. For a detailed (though dated) discussion of the eligible expenses, see David M. Sherman, *Taxes, Health & Disabilities* (Carswell, 1995). For a detailed (current) alphabetical list see "Medical Expense Credit Quick Reference Table", *Taxnet Pro* Tax & Estate Planning Centre (2020, 42pp). See also Choran & Farina, "Medical Expenses Abroad", 21(4) *Canadian Tax Highlights* (ctf.ca) 8-9 (April 2013).

See also Notes to Reg. 5700.

118.2(2)(u) amended by 2019 budget bill #1, effective Oct. 17, 2018, due to the new *Cannabis Act* and *Cannabis Regulations* (legalizing marijuana). Before that date, read:

> (u) on behalf of the patient who is authorized to possess marihuana, marihuana plants or seeds, cannabis or cannabis oil for their own medical use under the *Access to Cannabis for Medical Purposes Regulations* or section 56 of the *Controlled Drugs and Substances Act*, for the cost of marihuana, marihuana plants or seeds, cannabis or cannabis oil purchased in accordance with the *Access to Cannabis for Medical Purposes Regulations* or section 56 of the *Controlled Drugs and Substances Act*.

118.2(2)(l) amended by 2018 budget bill #1, for expenses incurred after 2017, to add "severe mental impairment" and (i)(A)(I). For earlier expenses, read everything before subpara. (i) as:

> (l) [guide dogs, etc.] — on behalf of the patient who is blind or profoundly deaf or has severe autism, severe diabetes, severe epilepsy or a severe and prolonged impairment that markedly restricts the use of the patient's arms or legs,
>
> > (i) for an animal specially trained to assist the patient in coping with the impairment and provided by a person or organization one of whose main purposes is such training of animals,

118.2(2)(l.9)(ii)(A), (B), (l.92)(ii)(A), (B) and (l.92)(iii)(A), (B) amended by 2017 budget bill #2, for expenses incurred after Sept. 7, 2017, to add "a nurse practitioner".

118.2(2)(v) added effective June 7, 2013, but then repealed and para. (u) amended effective Aug. 24, 2016, both by 2017 budget bill #2. Before Aug. 24, 2016, read (u) as:

> (u) [medical marijuana] — on behalf of the patient who is authorized to possess marihuana for medical purposes under the *Marihuana Medical Access Regulations* or section 56 of the *Controlled Drugs and Substances Act*, for
>
> > (i) the cost of medical marihuana or marihuana seeds purchased from Health Canada, or
> >
> > (ii) the cost of marihuana purchased from an individual who possesses, on behalf of that patient, a Designated-person Production license to produce marihuana under the *Marihuana Medical Access Regulations* or an Exemption for cultivation or production under section 56 of the *Controlled Drugs and Substances Act*; or

From June 7, 2013 through Aug. 23, 2016, read (v) as:

> (v) [medical marijuana] — on behalf of the patient who is authorized to possess marihuana for medical purposes under the *Marihuana for Medical Purposes Regulations* or section 56 of the *Controlled Drugs and Substances Act*, for the cost of marihuana purchased from
>
> > (i) a "licensed producer" (as defined in subsection 1(1) of the *Marihuana for Medical Purposes Regulations*), in accordance with a "medical document" (as defined in subsection 1(1) of the *Marihuana for Medical Purposes Regulations*),
> >
> > (ii) a "health care practitioner" (as defined in subsection 1(1) of the *Marihuana for Medical Purposes Regulations*) in the course of treatment for a medical condition,
> >
> > (iii) a hospital, under subsection 65(2.1) of the *Narcotics Control Regulations*, or
> >
> > (iv) an individual who possesses an exemption for cultivation or production under section 56 of the *Controlled Drugs and Substances Act*.

118.2(2)(l) opening words amended to add "severe diabetes", and 118.2(2)(l.92) added, by 2014 budget bill #1, both effective for expenses incurred after 2013.

118.2(2) earlier amended by 2002-2013 technical bill, last change effective Oct. 24, 2012 (paras. (c)-(e), (g)-(i), (l.9)); 2008 budget bill #1 (paras. (l), (n)); 2006 budget bill #1 ((i), (l.2)-(l.21), (l.43)-(l.44), (s)-(u)); 2003 Budget ((l.4)-(l.42), (r)); 2001 technical bill ((q)); 2000 same-sex partners bill ((b)-(c), (l.8), (q)); 2000 Budget ((l.21)); 1999 Budget ((b.1)-(b.2), (l.9)-(l.91)); 1998 Budget ((l.8), (q)); 1997 Budget ((b.1), (l.4)-(l.7), (m)); 1992 Child Benefit bill ((a)); 1992 Budget/technical bill ((l.3)); 1991 Budget/technical bill ((b)-(c), (h)-(i.1), (l), (l.2), (m)); 1989 Budget ((l.1)-(l.2)).

Regulations: 5700 (prescribed device or equipment for 118.2(2)(m)); 5701 (prescribed drugs or substances for 118.2(2)(n)).

Income Tax Folios: S1-F1-C1: Medical expense tax credit [replaces IT-519R2]; S1-F1-C2: Disability tax credit [replaces IT-519R2]; S1-F1-C3: Disability supports deduction [replaces IT-519R2]; S1-F3-C1: Child care expense deduction [replaces IT-495R3]; S2-F1-C1: Health and welfare trusts [replaces IT-85R2].

Interpretation Bulletins: IT-339R2: Meaning of "private health services plan"; IT-393R2: Election re tax on rents and timber royalties — non-residents.

Information Circulars: 82-2R2: SIN legislation that relates to the preparation of information slips (re 118.2(2)(b.1)(iv), (c)(iii)).

Forms: RC4064: Medical and disability-related information [guide].

(2.1) Cosmetic purposes — The medical expenses referred to in subsection (2) do not include amounts paid for medical or dental services, nor any related expenses, provided purely for cosmetic purposes, unless necessary for medical or reconstructive purposes.

Notes: 118.2(2.1) implements a March 2010 Budget proposal to deny the medical expense credit for cosmetic procedures unless they are necessary for medical or reconstructive purposes. Table A5.1 in the Budget papers projects that this measure will generate revenue for the federal government of $40 million in each of 2010-11 through 2014-15. See generally VIEWS doc 2012-0448691E5.

The following are considered ineligible unless medically required (tinyurl.com/cra-cosmetic; VIEWS docs 2010-0361271E5, 2010-0362981M4, 2010-0365801E5, 2012-0462471M4): augmentations (e.g. chin, cheek, lips); body modifications (e.g. tongue splits); body shaping, contouring or lifts (e.g. body, breasts, buttocks, face, and stomach); botulinum injections; chemical peels; implants (e.g. jewellery implanted into an eye or tooth, or microdermal, transdermal, or subdermal cosmetic implants); filler injections for removal of wrinkles; hair removal; hair replacement; laser treatments (skin resurfacing and removal of age spots); liposuction; reshaping such as rhinoplasty and otoplasty; rib removal; tattoo removal; teeth whitening; and tooth contouring and reshaping. See also Folio S1-F1-C1 ¶1.143-1.146.

The following still qualify (same sources as above): breast implant and related procedures for reconstructive purposes after a mastectomy; breast reduction to reduce back and shoulder pain; dental braces (if required to correct a misaligned bite); dental veneers to correct decayed or misaligned teeth; gastric bypass surgery or gastric stapling; laser eye surgery; removal of excess skin after rapid weight loss due to infection risk.

The following also qualify: cosmetic procedures to treat melasma or acne that is severe, persistent and disfiguring (VIEWS docs 2010-0378051E5, 2011-0412591E5); endovenous laser therapy for varicose veins (2011-0411181E5, 2013-0477051E5); gastric sleeve surgery (2012-0439481E5); hair removal required due to Polycystic Ovarian Syndrome (2011-0401221E5, 2011-0405091E5); lap band surgery for patient who is obese and has high blood pressure and sleep apnea (2011-0395451E5); photodynamic therapy for patient with severe Rosacea (2010-0383831I7); removing excess skin for medical reasons (2013-0480831E5); treatment for a rare skin condition and scalp itching (2010-0386581E5).

CRA often says the determination is one of fact depending on the circumstances: docs 2011-0414811E5 (mammoplasty of a second breast to match one done for medical reasons); 2011-0429431E5 (tightening skin).

Circumcision of an infant male for religious reasons, in the author's view, is not "purely for cosmetic purposes" but for religious purposes, and should still qualify for the credit if performed by a physician. "Cosmetic" is defined as "to enhance beauty", and a religious circumcision is not displayed to others and is unrelated to beauty or looks. As well, there is extensive evidence of health and medical benefit: circinfo.net. (VIEWS doc 2011-0411641E5 avoids answering the question, other than to say the taxpayer needs to substantiate that the procedure is not cosmetic.)

See also Macnaughton, "Cosmetic Medical Services and PSHPs", 18(5) *Canadian Tax Highlights* (ctf.ca) 10-11 (May 2010); Chu et al., "Curtailing Income Tax Relief for Cosmetic Medical Expenses?", 58(3) *Canadian Tax Journal* 529-75 (2010) (suggests *inter alia* that "psychological distress" might be accepted as a medical reason for allowing expenses).

To prove an expense qualifies (a statement on the physician's receipt that the service is not cosmetic is not sufficient), see VIEWS doc 2011-0392051E5.

Parallel amendments to the *Excise Tax Act* (Schedule V, Part II, s. 1.1 and Schedule VI, Part II, s 1.2; see David M. Sherman, *Practitioner's Goods and Services Tax Annotated*) exclude purely cosmetic procedures and related devices from the GST/HST exemption for health care services and from the zero-rating for medical devices.

118.2(2.1) added by 2010 budget bill #1, effective for expenses incurred after March 4, 2010 ("incurred" refers to a legal obligation: VIEWS doc 2012-0433661E5).

(2.2) Fertility expenses — An amount is deemed to be a medical expense of an individual for the purposes of this section if the amount

> (a) is paid for the purpose of a "patient" (within the meaning of subsection (2)) conceiving a child; and
>
> (b) would be a medical expense of the individual (within the meaning of subsection (2)) if the patient were incapable of conceiving a child because of a medical condition.

> **Possible Future Amendment — Fertility-Related Expenses**
>
> **Federal Budget, March 19, 2019, Chapter 4, Part 1:** *Expanding Health-Related Tax Relief*

The Government is also committed to ensuring that the Medical Expense Tax Credit reflects medically related developments. To this end, the Government will be reviewing the income tax treatment of fertility-related medical expenses under the Medical Expense Tax Credit for fairness and consistency, and in light of work being undertaken by Health Canada in relation to the *Assisted Human Reproduction Act* and supporting regulations.

Notes: 118.2(2.2) applies whether or not there is a medical need. Thus, it covers a woman with no male partner who chooses *in vitro* fertilization to have a child.

See VIEWS docs 2017-0699941E5 and 2018-0753891E5 (general discussion); 2018-0751891I7 (cost of eggs and sperm); 2018-076379117 (embryo freezing). See also Notes to 118.2(2), under 118.2(2)(a), (g)-(h), (l.1), (n) and (o).

118.2(2.2) cannot cover hiring a surrogate mother, as the surrogate is not a 118.2(2)(a) "patient". (See 118.2(2) Notes, under 118.2(2)(l.1), para. "In *Zieber*".)

118.2(2.2) added by 2017 budget bill #1, for 2017 and later tax years, as well as for an earlier year for which an individual requests a refund from the Minister within the time limit in 164(1.5)(a) (i.e., 10 years back).

(3) Deemed medical expense — For the purposes of subsection (1),

(a) any amount included in computing an individual's income for a taxation year from an office or employment in respect of a medical expense described in subsection (2) paid or provided by an employer at a particular time shall be deemed to be a medical expense paid by the individual at that time; and

(b) there shall not be included as a medical expense of an individual any expense to the extent that

(i) the individual,

(ii) the person referred to in subsection (2) as the patient,

(iii) any person related to a person referred to in subparagraph (i) or (ii), or

(iv) the legal representative of any person referred to in any of subparagraphs (i) to (iii)

is entitled to be reimbursed for the expense, except to the extent that the amount of the reimbursement is required to be included in computing income and is not deductible in computing taxable income.

Related Provisions: 251(2) — Related persons.

Notes: 118.2(3)(a) allows taxable health-care benefits (see Notes to 6(1)(a)) to count as paid by the employee, to put the employee in the same position as receiving cash and paying the expense directly.

118.2(3)(b) disallows a claim to the extent reimbursement of the cost is available. This includes funds provided under Alberta's Self-Managed Care Program: VIEWS doc 2009-0351971E5; and a private insurer: 2011-042883117; and the Hiring Credit for Small Business where it pays for an attendant: 2012-047265117.

The Ontario Healthy Homes Renovation Tax Credit [eliminated as of 2017] and BC Seniors' Home Renovation Tax Credit (on the T1 return) do not reduce the expense for 118.2, despite 118.2(3)(b): VIEWS doc 2013-049090117 (reversing 2012-0470381E5, addressed to the author). Nor do the Quebec CIALB (refundable credit to help seniors living independently) or CISUT (refundable credit for seniors staying in functional rehab transition units): 2014-0527291E5.

Where an employee or retiree receives a lump sum to replace ongoing health or dental coverage (e.g. if the employer is insolvent), CRA now says this is *not* a 118.2(3)(b) reimbursement, retroactive to 2012: doc 2020-0869481E5.

The reference to a person related to the patient in 118.2(3)(b)(iii) covers a reimbursement that is provided under a health care plan that covers family members. For example, a father might be claiming expenses for a child, while the mother is entitled to reimbursement through her employer-paid drug plan.

CRA states that insurance statements must be provided even where the insurer will deny the claim, because "one is to assume that the expenses need to be submitted to the insurance company before the amount can be considered by the CRA": May 2013 ICAA Roundtable q.18 (tinyurl.com/cra-abtax).

118.2(3)(b) amended by 1997 Budget, for 1997 and later tax years; and by 1992 technical bill, effective 1992.

Income Tax Folios: S1-F1-C1: Medical expense tax credit [replaces IT-519R2]; S1-F1-C2: Disability tax credit [replaces IT-519R2]; S1-F1-C3: Disability supports deduction [replaces IT-519R2].

Interpretation Bulletins: IT-339R2: Meaning of "private health services plan"; IT-393R2: Election re tax on rents and timber royalties — non-residents.

(4) Deemed payment of medical expenses — Where, in circumstances in which a person engaged in the business of providing transportation services is not readily available, an individual makes use of a vehicle for a purpose described in paragraph (2)(g), the individual or the individual's legal representative shall be deemed to have paid to a person engaged in the business of providing transportation services, in respect of the operation of the vehicle, such amount as is reasonable in the circumstances.

Definitions [s. 118.2]: "amount", "appropriate percentage" — 248(1); "blood relationship" — 251(6)(a); "business" — 248(1); "carrying on business" — 253; "child" — 252(1); "common-law partner", "common-law partnership" — 248(1); "connected" — 251(6); "dentist" — 118.4(2); "employment", "individual", "legal representative" — 248(1); "medical doctor" — 118.4(2); "medical expense" — 118.2(2), (2.1), (2.2), (3); "medical practitioner" — 118.4(2); "Minister" — 248(1); "month" — *Interpretation Act* 28, 35(1); "nurse", "nurse practitioner", "occupational therapist" — 118.4(2); "office" — 248(1); "optometrist" — 118.4(2); "patient" — 118.2(2)(a); "person" — 248(1); "pharmacist" — 118.4(2); "prescribed", "private health services plan" — 248(1); "province" — *Interpretation Act* 35(1); "psychologist" — 118.4(2); "regulation" — 248(1); "related" — 251(2); "resident in Canada" — 250; "self-contained domestic establishment" — 248(1); "tax payable" — 248(2); "taxation year" — 249; "taxpayer" — 248(1); "writing" — *Interpretation Act* 35(1).

Interpretation Bulletins: IT-326R3: Returns of deceased persons as "another person"; IT-518R: Food, beverages and entertainment expenses.

118.3 (1) Credit for mental or physical impairment — Where

(a) an individual has one or more severe and prolonged impairments in physical or mental functions,

(a.1) the effects of the impairment or impairments are such that the individual's ability to perform more than one basic activity of daily living is significantly restricted where the cumulative effect of those restrictions is equivalent to having a marked restriction in the ability to perform a basic activity of daily living or are such that the individual's ability to perform a basic activity of daily living is markedly restricted or would be markedly restricted but for therapy that

(i) is essential to sustain a vital function of the individual,

(ii) is required to be administered at least three times each week for a total duration averaging not less than 14 hours a week, and

(iii) cannot reasonably be expected to be of significant benefit to persons who are not so impaired,

(a.2) in the case of an impairment in physical or mental functions the effects of which are such that the individual's ability to perform a single basic activity of daily living is markedly restricted or would be so restricted but for therapy referred to in paragraph (a.1), a medical practitioner has certified in prescribed form that the impairment is a severe and prolonged impairment in physical or mental functions the effects of which are such that the individual's ability to perform a basic activity of daily living is markedly restricted or would be markedly restricted, but for therapy referred to in paragraph (a.1), where the medical practitioner is a medical doctor, a nurse practitioner or, in the case of

(i) a sight impairment, an optometrist,

(ii) a speech impairment, a speech-language pathologist,

(iii) a hearing impairment, an audiologist,

(iv) an impairment with respect to an individual's ability in feeding or dressing themself, an occupational therapist,

(v) an impairment with respect to an individual's ability in walking, an occupational therapist, or after February 22, 2005, a physiotherapist, and

(vi) an impairment with respect to an individual's ability in mental functions necessary for everyday life, a psychologist,

(a.3) in the case of one or more impairments in physical or mental functions the effects of which are such that the individual's ability to perform more than one basic activity of daily living is significantly restricted, a medical practitioner has certified in prescribed form that the impairment or impairments are severe and prolonged impairments in physical or mental functions the effects of which are such that the individual's ability to perform more than one basic activity of daily living is significantly restricted and that the cumulative effect of those restrictions is equivalent to having a marked restriction in the ability to perform a single basic activity of daily living, where the medical practitioner is, in the case of

(i) an impairment with respect to the individual's ability in feeding or dressing themself, or in walking, a medical doctor, a nurse practitioner or an occupational therapist, and

(ii) in the case of any other impairment, a medical doctor or nurse practitioner,

(b) the individual has filed for a taxation year with the Minister the certificate described in paragraph (a.2) or (a.3), and

(c) no amount in respect of remuneration for an attendant or care in a nursing home, in respect of the individual, is included in calculating a deduction under section 118.2 (otherwise than because of paragraph 118.2(2)(b.1)) for the year by the individual or by any other person,

there may be deducted in computing the individual's tax payable under this Part for the year the amount determined by the formula

$$A \times (B + C)$$

where

A is the appropriate percentage for the year,

B is $6,000, and

C is

(a) where the individual has not attained the age of 18 years before the end of the year, the amount, if any, by which

(i) $3,500

exceeds

(ii) the amount, if any, by which

(A) the total of all amounts each of which is an amount paid in the year for the care or supervision of the individual and included in computing a deduction under section 63, 64 or 118.2 for a taxation year

exceeds

(B) $2,050, and

(b) in any other case, zero.

Enacted Amendment — COVID-19 — Payments to persons eligible for disability credit

CRA notice, Aug. 11, 2020, updated to April 26, 2021 (tinyurl.com/covid-disab): *One-time payment to persons with disabilities*

This *non-taxable, non-reportable*, one-time payment provides *up to $600* in recognition of the extraordinary expenses faced by persons with disabilities during the COVID-19 pandemic.

This payment complements other emergency supports, such as the one-time special payment through the Goods and Services Tax Credit and the one-time payment to seniors.

Eligibility

To be eligible for this one time payment, you needed to ensure your personal information was up to date by the end of February 2021.

We will automatically issue this one-time payment if by *March 5, 2021*:

• you had an existing valid Disability Tax Credit (DTC) certificate from the Canada Revenue Agency (CRA)

• you were eligible and applied for the DTC by *December 31, 2020*

• you were a beneficiary as at July 1, 2020 of:

— Canada Pension Plan Disability (CPPD)

— Quebec Pension Plan Disability Pension (QPPD)

— Veterans Affairs Canada (VAC) disability supports provided to veterans (War Service and Canadian Armed Forces) and former Royal Canadian Mounted Police, including:

• Disability Pension

• Disability Award

• Pain and Suffering Compensation

• Critical Injury Benefit

• Rehabilitation Services and Vocational Assistance Program

• Income Replacement Benefit

• Canadian Forces Income Support

Note: The CRA generally takes 8 weeks to review a *complete* DTC application and inform you of their decision as to whether you are eligible for the DTC. Cases that are more complex can take longer.

This one-time payment is to provide financial support to the person with the disability. Caregivers, survivors, and dependents are not eligible for this payment.

Payment for seniors

If you received the one-time seniors payment you may also be eligible for the one-time payment to persons with disabilities.

You will receive a cumulative amount of up to $600, broken into 2 payments:

• if you received the $300 one-time seniors payment for the Old Age Security (OAS) pension, you will receive an additional $300

• if you received the $500 one-time seniors payment for both the OAS pension and the Guaranteed Income Supplement (GIS) or the Allowance, you will receive an additional $100

If your Canada Pension Plan Disability benefit converted to Old Age Security in 2020

The CPPD benefit automatically converts to OAS pension the month following your 65th birthday.

If you are still in receipt of CPPD for the month of July 2020 (converting in August 2020 to OAS), you should receive this one-time payment.

If you are no longer in receipt of CPPD, and not currently eligible for DTC, QPPD, or one of the disability supports provided by VAC, you are not eligible for this payment.

In this case, you needed to apply for the DTC before *December 31, 2020*. If the CRA determined that you are eligible for the DTC by March 5, 2021, you may receive a payment starting April 23, 2021.

Payment for children with disabilities

If you are the parents of children with disabilities, you should receive the one-time payment.

For cases of shared custody, the payment will be split among care providers, like the Child Disability Benefit payment and the Canada Child Benefit.

In cases where there has been a change in custody, the primary care giver of a child with a disability as of June 30, 2020 should receive the $600 payment on behalf of the child.

You can visit the CRA Canada Child Benefit [guide T4114 — ed.] for more information on eligibility for cases of shared custody or a change in custody.

Agencies and care providers of children in their care will receive the payment as per the *Children's Special Allowance Act*.

In rare cases where we were not able to identify the caregiver(s), the payment will be issued directly to the child.

Payment to the estate

For individuals who were eligible for the DTC in 2020, but passed away, the estate should receive the payment (regardless of the client's date of death in 2020).

For CPPD, QPPD, and VAC eligible clients who were alive as at July 1, 2020 but have since passed away, the estate will receive the payment.

How to apply

You do not have to apply for this one time payment. You will automatically receive this payment if you are eligible.

Date of payment

You may receive this one-time payment starting April 23, 2021 if:

• you were confirmed eligible by March 5, 2021; and

• your personal information was up to date by the end of February 2021; and

• you did not receive a payment in October 2020 or January 2021.

Payment amount

This is a separate one-time payment of up to $600.

Method of payment

To issue the payment, we use the direct deposit and mailing address you have on file at:

• Canada Pension Plan Disability (CPPD)

• Quebec Pension Plan Disability Pension (QPPD)

• Veterans Affairs Canada (VAC)

• Canada Revenue Agency (CRA)

To be eligible for this one time payment, you needed to:

• be *confirmed* eligible by CPPD, QPPD, VAC, or the CRA by *March 5, 2021*; and

• ensure that your personal information was up to date by end of *February 2021*

Returning a payment

If you received a payment and you wish to return it, you can send it by mail or return it to a Service Canada Centre.

Return your payment by mail

Cheque received by mail

If you receive your cheque by mail, send it with a covering note to the Receiver General of Canada to the following address:

Cheque Redemption and Control Directorate - Returned Cheques, PO Box 2000, Matane QC, G4W 4N5

Payment via direct deposit

If you receive your payment via direct deposit:

1. please ensure to clearly mark all the following information on your cheque:
   - your name
   - your SIN, and
   - the statement "One-time Payment to persons with Disabilities"
2. send it to the address below

ESDC – National Accounts Receivable, 100-1081 Main Street, Moncton, NB, E1C 1H1

Return your payment in a Service Canada Centre

You can return your cheque to any Service Canada Centre.

Note: If you received the payment via direct deposit, you have to make a cheque payable to the Receiver General of Canada.

Contact us

Questions about your eligibility.

Canada Pension Plan Disability
Telephone: 1-800-277-9914; TTY: 1-800-255-4786

Disability Tax Credit
Telephone: 1-800-959-8281; TTY: 1-800-665-0354

Quebec Pension Plan Disability Pension
Telephone: 1-800-463-5185

Veterans Affairs Canada
Telephone: 1-866-522-2122; TTY: 1-800-567-5803.

Questions about your payment

Before contacting us:

- review the eligibility criteria
- check the payment date
- allow at least *5 business days* from your estimated payment date

Canada Pensions Plan

Telephone: 1-800-277-9914; TTY: 1-800-255-4786

Benefit finder

You can visit the COVID-19 benefits finder [covid-benefits.alpha.canada.ca/en/start] for more information on the Disability one-time payment, or other benefits for which you may qualify.

Related Provisions: 241(4)(h.1) — Disclosure of information by CRA for purposes of payment.

Notes: Legal authority to pay this benefit is the *Public Health Events of National Concern Payments Act*, enacted by 2020 COVID bill #1. The announcements about it from Finance and CRA say it is non-taxable and need not be reported. (Technically, one might call it needs-based since the news releases announcing it focused on the needs of persons with disabilities, so 56(1)(u) could require it to be added to net income, with offsetting 110(1)(f) deduction in computing taxable income which could reduce the next year's GST/HST Credit and other credits. However, CRA does not administer it this way.)

241(4)(h.1) permits CRA to share information about the Disability Credit to enable this payment to be made, as well as any followup administrative action.

Proposed Amendments — Disability Tax Credit

Federal Budget, Notice of Ways and Means Motion, April 19, 2021: *Disability Tax Credit*

1 The Act is modified to give effect to the proposals relating to the Disability Tax Credit as described in the budget documents tabled by the Minister of Finance in the House of Commons on April 19, 2021.

Federal Budget, Supplementary Information, April 19, 2021: *Disability Tax Credit*

The Disability Tax Credit (DTC) is a non-refundable tax credit that is intended to recognize the impact of non-itemizable disability-related costs on the ability to pay tax. For 2021, the value of the credit is $1,299 [plus a provincial credit — ed.].

To be eligible for the DTC, an individual must have a certificate [118.3(1)(a.2), (a.3) — ed.] confirming that they have a severe and prolonged impairment in physical or mental functions. The effects of the impairment must be such that, even with appropriate devices, medication and therapy, the individual is blind or is:

- markedly restricted in their ability to perform a basic activity of daily living, or would be so restricted were it not for certain therapy (commonly referred to as "extensive life-sustaining therapy"); or

- significantly restricted in their ability to perform more than one basic activity of daily living where the cumulative effect of those restrictions is comparable to being markedly restricted in a basic activity of daily living.

For these purposes, the *Income Tax Act* recognizes the following basic activities of daily living [118.4(1)(c) — ed.]: walking; feeding or dressing oneself; mental functions necessary for everyday life; speaking; hearing; eliminating bodily waste; and, for the purposes of the "significantly restricted" test noted above, includes seeing.

A valid DTC certificate is also a requirement for accessing certain other tax-related measures, including Registered Disability Savings Plans, the Child Disability Benefit and the disability supplement to the Canada Workers Benefit.

Mental Functions Necessary for Everyday Life

Under current rules, mental functions necessary for everyday life include [118.4(1)(c.1) — ed.]:

- memory;
- problem-solving, goal-setting and judgement (taken together); and
- adaptive functioning.

To ensure that the eligibility criteria for the DTC better articulate the range of mental functions necessary for everyday life, Budget 2021 proposes that, for the purposes of the DTC, mental functions necessary for everyday life include:

- attention;
- concentration;
- memory;
- judgement;
- perception of reality;
- problem-solving;
- goal-setting;
- regulation of behaviour and emotions;
- verbal and non-verbal comprehension; and
- adaptive functioning.

Life-Sustaining Therapy

Under current rules, extensive life-sustaining therapy is therapy that [118.3(1)(a.1) — ed.]:

- is essential to sustain a vital function;
- is required to be administered at least three times each week for a total duration averaging not less than 14 hours a week; and
- cannot reasonably be expected to be of significant benefit to an individual who does not have a severe and prolonged impairment in physical or mental functions.

These requirements are intended to allow individuals to qualify for the DTC where they are undergoing therapies that have a significant impact on everyday living, comparable to the impact of being directly restricted in basic activities of daily living.

Under the current rules, time spent on the following activities may be included in determining time spent receiving therapy [118.3(1.1)(a)-(c) — ed.]:

- activities that require the individual to take time away from normal, everyday activities in order to receive the therapy;
- where the therapy requires a regular dosage of medication that needs to be adjusted on a daily basis, activities directly involved in determining the appropriate dosage; and
- in the case of a child who is unable to perform the activities related to the therapy as a result of their age, the time spent by the child's primary caregivers to perform and supervise these activities for the child.

Time spent on the following activities cannot be included in determining time spent receiving therapy [118.3(1.1)(d) — ed.]: activities related to dietary or exercise restrictions or regimes (even if those restrictions or regimes are a factor in determining the daily dosage of medication), travel time, medical appointments, shopping for medication and recuperation after therapy.

These rules can result in important components of therapy being excluded from the calculation of therapy time. For example, the determination of the appropriate dosage of medicine for treating diabetes in individuals who are insulin-dependent may require precise recording of dietary intake. In a similar fashion, therapy that involves the consumption of medical food or medical formula (such as for treating certain inherited metabolic conditions) may require, as part of the treatment, the precise recording of the dietary intake of particular compounds. [See the *Mullings* and *Hughes* cases discussed in 118.3(1.1) Notes — ed.]

To better recognize these aspects of therapy for the purposes of calculating time spent on therapy, while ensuring that everyday activities (such as normal management of a healthy diet) and discretionary activities are not taken into account for that purpose, Budget 2021 proposes to:

- allow reasonable time spent determining dietary intake and/or physical exertion to be considered part of the therapy, where this information is essential to, and is undertaken for the purpose of, determining the dosage of medication that must be adjusted on a daily basis;

- clarify that the exclusion of time for medical appointments does not apply to appointments to receive therapy or to determine the daily dosage of medication;

- provide that the exclusion of time for recuperation after therapy does not apply to medically required recuperation; and

- in the case of therapy that requires the daily consumption of a medical food or medical formula to limit intake of a particular compound to levels required for the proper development or functioning of the body, allow reasonable time spent on activities that are directly related to the determination of the amount of the compound that can be safely consumed to be considered part of the therapy.

Budget 2021 also proposes that, where an individual is incapable of performing their therapy on their own due to the impacts of their disability, the time reasonably required by another person to assist the individual in performing and supervising the therapy would be allowed to be counted.

Budget 2021 further proposes that the requirement that therapy be administered at least three times each week be reduced to two times each week. The requirement that therapy be of a duration averaging not less than 14 hours a week would remain unchanged.

These proposed changes would apply to the 2021 and subsequent taxation years, in respect of DTC certificates filed with the Minister of National Revenue on or after Royal Assent.

Federal Budget, Chapter 7, April 19, 2021: *Improving Access to the Disability Tax Credit*

In 2017, the Government of Canada reinstated the Canada Revenue Agency's Disability Advisory Committee to ensure tax measures for persons with disabilities are administered in a fair, transparent, and accessible way. Since the release of the committee's first annual report in 2019, the government has introduced many important changes, including improvements to its communications and outreach activities for the Disability Tax Credit and changes to Registered Disability Savings Plans to better protect beneficiaries. As the government considers new recommendations from the committee, released in a second report on April 9, 2021, the government is proposing to take further steps to act on the guidance of the committee by improving the eligibility criteria for mental functions and life-sustaining therapy. To help more families and people living with disabilities access the Disability Tax Credit, and other related support measures like the Registered Disability Savings Plan and the Child Disability Benefit:

Budget 2021 proposes to update the list of mental functions of everyday life that is used for assessment for the Disability Tax Credit. Using terms that are more clinically relevant would make it easier to be assessed, reduce delays, and improve access to benefits.

Budget 2021 also proposes to recognize more activities in determining time spent on life-sustaining therapy and to reduce the minimum required frequency of therapy to qualify for the Disability Tax Credit. To ensure these changes enable applicants to have a fair and proper assessment of their eligibility for the Disability Tax Credit, the government will undertake a review of these changes in 2023.

It is estimated that, as a result of these measures, an additional 45,000 people will qualify for the Disability Tax Credit, and related benefit programs linked to its eligibility, each year. This represents $376 million in additional support over five years, starting in 2021-22.

Notes: Budget Table 1 projects that these measures will cost the federal government $19 million in 2021-22, $84m in 2022-23, $90m in 2023-24, $91m in 2024-25 and $92m in 2025-26.

Proposed Addition (non-tax) — Canada Disability Benefit

Employment and Social Development Canada news release, June 22, 2021: *Government of Canada introduces legislation to create the new Canada Disability Benefit*

Canadians with disabilities are twice as likely to live in poverty than those without disabilities, a situation that has been made even worse by the impacts of the COVID-19 pandemic. By addressing the longstanding inequities that lead to financial insecurity, hardships and social exclusion faced by persons with disabilities, the Government of Canada is delivering on its commitment to building a disability-inclusive Canada.

As part of the Government of Canada's plan to ensure an inclusive recovery that "leaves no one behind", the Minister of Employment, Workforce Development and Disability Inclusion, Carla Qualtrough, introduced new legislation today that would establish the framework for a new Canada Disability Benefit.

This ground-breaking legislation would enable the Government of Canada to take a proactive approach in the creation and delivery of the new benefit, to support working-age Canadians with disabilities. The Canada Disability Benefit would supplement, not replace, existing federal and provincial-territorial supports with a goal of lifting hundreds of thousands of persons with disabilities out of poverty.

In the spirit of "Nothing Without Us", the Government of Canada will build on the legislation introduced today to engage with stakeholders and persons with disabilities to have their voices heard on the design of the benefit leading up to the development of regulations. This engagement has already started with the recent launch of the Disability Inclusion Action Plan, a public survey that asks Canadians how the Government of Canada can build a barrier-free country. Engagement activities will continue through the summer and fall.

The legislation also recognizes the leading role that provinces and territories play in providing supports and services to Canadians with disabilities and the importance of engaging with them in developing income and other supports. Federal, Provincial and Territorial (FPT) Ministers responsible for Social Services and Disability intend to meet this summer for an initial discussion on the proposed new benefit.

The Government of Canada committed in the 2020 Speech from the Throne to develop the first-ever Disability Inclusion Action Plan (DIAP). This plan will include:

- a new Canada Disability Benefit;

- a robust employment strategy for Canadians with disabilities;

- and a better process to determine eligibility for federal disability programs and benefits.

The new Canada Disability Benefit is the cornerstone of this plan.

Notes: Bill C-35, to enact this benefit, received First Reading on June 22, 2021. It leaves all the details (including eligibility criteria and amount of benefit) to be determined by regulation. It adds ITA 241(4)(d)(vii.51) to allow CRA to communicate information for purposes of administering the benefit, which will apparently be run by ESDC (one would not be surprised to see CRA take over payment).

Related Provisions: 6(16) — Non-taxable disability-related employment benefits; 64 — Disability supports deduction for attendant care and other expenses; 108(1)"preferred beneficiary" — PB election available only to beneficiary with severe and prolonged impairment; 117.1(2)(l) — Indexing for inflation; 118.05(1)"specified person" — Disability Home Purchase Credit; 118.2 — Credit for medical expenses; 118.3(1.1) — Determining time spent on therapy; 118.3(4) — Additional information requested by CRA; 118.4(1) — Meaning of severe and prolonged impairment; 118.4(2) — Reference to medical practitioner; 118.6(3) — Student eligible for disability credit; 118.8 — Transfer of unused credits to spouse; 118.91 — Individual resident in Canada for part of year; 118.92 — Ordering of credits; 118.93 — Credits in separate returns; 118.94 — Credit restriction for non-resident individual; 118.95(b) — Application in year individual becomes bankrupt; 120.4(3)A — Disability credit deductible against income-splitting tax; 122.7(3) — Canada Workers Benefit — disability supplement; 146.4(1)"DTC-eligible individual" — Registered disability savings plan for person eligible for 118.3 credit; 152(1.01), (1.2) — eligibility for credit can be appealed to Tax Court; 241(4)(h.1) — Disclosure of information by CRA for purposes of COVID-19 payment in 2020.

Notes: See canada.ca/disability-tax-credit. The federal disability tax credit (DTC) works out to $1,286 ($8,576 × 15%) for 2020 and $1,299 ($8,662 × 15%) for 2021. There is a parallel provincial credit as well. A disabled dependant can be claimed under 118.3(2). About 770,000 people claimed DTCs of $1.3 billion in 2016-17: CRA news release, Dec. 8, 2017.

DTC eligibility creates other entitlements: $600 COVID-19 payment in 2020 (see Enacted Amendment above); non-taxable disability-related employment benefits (6(16)); higher child-care deductions (63(3)"annual child care expense amount"(a)); disability supports deduction (indirectly: 64(a)A(ii)); trust preferred-beneficiary election (108(1)"preferred beneficiary", 104(14)); home accessibility credit (118.041(1)"qualifying individual"(b)); disability home purchase credit (118.05(1)"qualifying home", "specified person"); medical expense credit for nursing home care, attendant, group home care or therapy (118.2(2)(b), (b.1), (b.2), (l.9)); limited exclusion from income-splitting tax (120.4(1)"excluded amount"(a)(ii)(B)); qualified disability trust taxed at low marginal rates (122(1)); higher Canada Child Benefit (122.61(1)M:N(a)); higher Canada Workers Benefit (122.7(3)); enhanced Home Buyer's Plan (146.01(1)"specified disabled person"); enhanced RESP entitlements (146.1(1)"specified plan", 146.1(1.1)(a), (2.2)); RDSP eligibility (146.4(1)"DTC-eligible individual", 152(1.01)); Lifelong Learning Plan reduced withholdings (Reg. 104.1(1)(a)); and various provincial benefits and tax breaks. As well, a person with "an impairment of mobility to such a degree that using public transportation would be hazardous" can claim a refund of 1.5¢ per litre of gasoline purchased, under the Federal Excise Gasoline Tax Refund Program: CRA Form XE8. See also *Enabling access to disability tax measures*, tinyurl.com/disab-report1 (2019), Appendices 7-8; Granelli, "Providing for the Disabled Beneficiary", 2254 *Tax Topics* (CCH) 1-5 (May 21, 2015) and 2256:1-5 (June 4, 2015); Sprysak, "Income Tax Supports for Canadians With Disabilities", 66(3) *Canadian Tax Journal* 679-705 (2018); Golombek & Pearl-Weinberg, "Planning for Disabled Beneficiaries Using Life Insurance Trusts", XXIV(2) *Insurance Planning* (Federated Press) 2-6 (2019).

Note that DTC-eligible is not the same as being "infirm" in provisions that use that term (which is not defined).

When reading 118.3(1), **read the rules in 118.3(1.1) and 118.4(1) as well**. The FCA ruled in *Johnston*, [1998] 2 C.T.C. 262, para. 10, that 118.3 should be given a "humane and compassionate" interpretation. For detailed review of the case law to 1995, see David M. Sherman, *Taxes, Health & Disabilities* (Carswell, 1995).

118.3(1)(a): "Severe" means "sharp, grave, distressing, violent, extreme, rigorous, difficult to be endured... grievous": *Mantle*, 1995 CarswellNat 309 (TCC), paras. 9-10.

118.3(1)(a.1): Life-sustaining therapy for (a.1)(i) includes capping therapy to help breathe, or kidney dialysis to filter blood. CRA says it does not include implanted devices such as a pacemaker, or special programs of diet, exercise, hygiene or medication: Fact Sheet, July 2003 (doc 2003-07B on *TaxPartner* or *Taxnet Pro*). See also 118.3(1.1) re time involved.

AIDS: *Corbett*, 2008 TCC 499, rejected a claim by a man with AIDS that his medications were life-sustaining therapy that took a lot of time.

Diabetes can qualify if insulin therapy requires at least 14 hours/week (118.3(1.1)), but CRA was disallowing such claims (*Toronto Star*, Dec. 5, 2017, p. A6). The Minister of National Revenue issued a news release Dec. 4, 2017 (tinyurl.com/mnr-dtc) saying "no change has been made to the eligibility criteria", but CRA then backed down: a Dec. 8, 2017 news release said "CRA will return to using the pre-May 2017 clarification letter for applications related to Life-Sustaining Therapy. The CRA will also review the applications that have been denied since May 2017". This review was completed in 2018: of 2,267 denials, 1,326 were changed to "accepted". No followup letter was sent to those who were not (CRA letter to Diabetes Canada and Disability Tax Fairness Alliance, Jan. 28, 2019). Juvenile diabetes qualified in *Mantle*, 1995 CarswellNat 309 (TCC), and *Brazeau*, 2010 TCC 546. In both *Pelletier*, 2008 TCC 425 and *Hutchings*, 2009 TCC 375, the credit was disallowed because the patient spent insufficient time on their insulin dosage; but in *Brazeau*, 2010 TCC 546, a young diabetic qualified as requiring 15 hours a week.

PKU can qualify: see 118.3(1.1) Notes.

Sleep apnea requiring a CPAP machine to assist in breathing while asleep does not qualify: *Girard*, 2006 FCA 65; *Biron*, 2004 TCC 154; *Boisvert*, 2005 TCC 249; *Beauchamp*, 2008 TCC 189.

Other illnesses: see 118.4(1) Notes.

118.3(1)(a.2), (a.3): See 118.4(2) Notes re certification by a practitioner. In 2017-18, the laws.justice.gc.ca "official" version of the Act showed closing words to (a.3) that were not enacted by Parliament and did not "correct grammatical or typographical errors" (*Legislation Revision and Consolidation Act* s. 27(c)). The author brought this to Finance's attention (and see *Mullings*, 2017 TCC 133, footnote 5 to heading before para. 8), and the extra words were deleted.

118.3(1)(b): Form T2201 can be filed any time, not only with a return or T1 Adjustment: ICABC/CRA Pacific Region liaison meeting, Jan. 2013, q. 20. It can be filed online through My Account or (per E-File news release, May 14, 2020) Represent a Client. CRA approval is either temporary or indefinite; status can be checked online. A CRA assessment denying DTC entitlement does not bind the taxpayer to later years if not appealed: *Connolly*, 2019 TCC 160, para. 6.

The certificate requirement is mandatory, not merely directory: *Partanen*, [1999] 3 C.T.C. 79 (FCA); *MacIsaac*, [2000] 1 C.T.C. 307 (FCA); *Nancarrow*, 2013 TCC 258; but the judge can "determine, based on medical evidence, whether a negative certificate should be treated as a positive certificate": *Buchanan*, 2002 FCA 231, para. 25. CRA says the certification cannot first be provided after death: VIEWS doc 2002-0134625. Certification can be provided for a past year: 2010-0363321E5; but in *Arciresi*, 2013 TCC 331, a T2201 for 2010 could not be used for a 2009 claim. Even someone with a permanent disability may require periodic recertification, to confirm they are "permanently markedly restricted all or substantially all of the time" [see 118.4(1) and 118.3(4)]: ICABC 2013 (above), q.19.

118.3(1)(c) denies the DTC if nursing home or attendant care expenses are claimed as medical expenses under 118.2(2)(b) or (d). 118.2(2)(b.1), limited to $10,000, does not affect the DTC; but see 118.2(2) Notes re (b.1). CRA's view *was* that 118.2(2)(b.2) and (e) also do not prevent a DTC claim (even though they are not excluded in 118.3(1)(c), because care under (b.2) and (e) is not nursing-home care even if the institution happens to be a nursing home: docs 2001-0116207, 2005-0155731E5, 2008-0293121I7; but 2014-0529851E5 reverses this. If nursing home care is provided in a hospital, the 118.2(2)(a) and DTC claims can both be made: doc 9708237; in *Greenaway*, 2010 TCC 42 the TCC agreed and a nursing home was treated as being under 118.2(2)(e): "to the extent an expense can qualify under different paragraphs of subsection 118.2(2), taxpayers are free to choose the more favourable treatment" (para. 18); but in 2011-0395031E5, CRA stated that amounts for long-term care (and that are not for medical care) in a hospital can be claimed only as attendant care (and thus disentitle the patient to the DTC). CRA does not necessarily agree that one can choose the more favourable treatment, in light of *Lister*, 2006 FCA 331, suggesting that a particular provision in 118.2(2) contemplates a particular kind of care. Note also that 118.92 says the 118.3 credit is claimed before 118.2, which could mean that no 118.2 credit has been claimed at the time 118.3 is claimed. When a patient dies, medical expenses can be claimed for the year of death for a 24-month period (118.2(1)B(a)). As long as the 118.2(2)(b) and DTC are claimed for different years, the time periods to which the claims relate can overlap (i.e., the disability credit can be claimed for a year during which medical expenses were paid but were claimed for a later year).

Disability Advisory Committee (DAC): CRA announced a new DAC in 2017 (an earlier one was disbanded in 2006), advising CRA on disability issues. See its first report, *Enabling access to disability tax measures* (May 2019, 112pp), tinyurl.com/disab-report1. CRA news release May 24, 2019, "Government of Canada delivers on Disability Advisory Committee's recommendations", describes changes, including enhanced phone service and online T2201 submission. The DAC's second annual report (April 2021, 163pp) is at tinyurl.com/disab-report2; CRA's response to its recommendations (April 9, 2021) at tinyurl.com/cra-disab-resp. The Senate Standing Committee on Social Affairs issued a detailed report with recommendations: *Breaking Down Barriers* (June 2018, 35pp).

118.3(1)(a.2) opening words and (a.3)(i)-(ii) amended by 2017 budget bill #1, for certifications after March 21, 2017, to add references to "nurse practitioner". (Before, a NP could not certify a T2201: VIEWS doc 2014-0531061M4.) 118.3(1) earlier amended by 2006 budget bill #2, 2003, 2000, 1998 and 1997 Budgets.

Promoters: There are businesses that approach taxpayers to file DTC claims for them and charge a percentage of refunds obtained. The Manitoba Consumers' Bureau issued an alert March 11, 2010 that such persons require a "direct seller's licence" if operating in Manitoba, and noting that consumers can cancel direct-sales contracts within 10 days. CRA announced on April 9, 2013 that retired Dr. Clarita Vianzon and the three partners of J & J Canadian Grants Company (Jose Diogo, Jim Kussy, John Lopes) pled guilty to creating false DTC certificates to get individuals refunds. Each was fined $89,000 and given an 18-month conditional sentence (6 months for the doctor).

The *Disability Tax Credit Promoters Restrictions Act* (DTCPRA) was introduced as a private member's bill (C-462) and enacted as S.C. 2014, c. 7. It comes into force Nov. 15, 2021: P.C. 2021-212. It **limits the fee that can be charged for a DTC claim** and effectively prevents contingency fees, effectively destroying the business of DTC promoters. The maximum fee is set at $100 per taxation year: *Disability Tax Credit Promoters Restrictions Regulations*, P.C. 2021-213. It will be adjusted for inflation in 2025 and every 5 years thereafter. For CRA's DTCPRA consultations before the Regulations were passed, see tinyurl.com/dtc-consult. The DTCPRA provides:

1. Short title — This Act may be cited as the *Disability Tax Credit Promoters Restrictions Act*.

Interpretation

2. Definitions — The following definitions apply in this Act.

"claimant" means an individual who is the subject of a disability tax credit request or who has a dependant on behalf of whom a disability tax credit request is made.

"disability tax credit request" means a request, made in respect of a claimant,

(a) for determination of disability tax credit eligibility under subsection 152(1.01) of the *Income Tax Act*;

(b) in respect of a deduction under subsection 118.3(1) or (2) of the *Income Tax Act*; or

(c) in respect of any deduction or overpayment of tax under the *Income Tax Act* that is contingent upon the eligibility for a deduction under subsection 118.3(1) or (2) of that Act.

"fee" means the fair market value of any consideration accepted or charged by a person, directly or indirectly, to prepare a disability tax credit request.

"maximum fee" means the maximum fee set by regulations made under section 9.

"Minister" means the Minister of National Revenue.

"person" has the same meaning as in subsection 248(1) of the *Income Tax Act*.

"prescribed" means prescribed by regulation.

"promoter" means a person who, directly or indirectly, accepts or charges a fee in respect of a disability tax credit request.

Promoter's Fee

3. (1) Prohibition — It is prohibited for a promoter to accept or charge a fee that exceeds the maximum fee.

(2) Penalty for fee exceeding maximum fee — Every promoter who contravenes subsection (1) is liable to a penalty in respect of the fee equal to the total of $1,000 and the amount determined by the formula:

$$A - (B + C)$$

where

A   is the fee in respect of a disability tax credit request,

B   is the maximum fee, and

C   is the amount of the fee in respect of the disability tax credit request that is repaid to the claimant within 120 days after notification is given to the Minister in accordance with section 4 or any longer period that is acceptable to the Minister.

4. Reporting requirement — promoter — Every promoter, other than a prescribed exempt promoter, must notify the Minister, in a form and manner authorized by the Minister, of the fee accepted or charged by the promoter in respect of a disability tax credit request if it exceeds the maximum fee.

5. Deceptive information — It is prohibited for a promoter to make, participate in, assent to or acquiesce in the making of any false or deceptive entries in a notification required under section 4.

Offences

6. Offences — Every promoter who fails to notify the Minister under section 4 or who contravenes section 5 is guilty of an offence and, in addition to any penalty otherwise provided, is liable on summary conviction to a fine of not less than $1,000 and not more than $25,000.

7. Offences — Every promoter who contravenes section 3 is guilty of an offence and, in addition to any penalty otherwise provided, is liable on summary conviction to a fine of not less than 100% and not more than 200% of the total of all amounts by which the fee exceeds the maximum fee amount in respect of a disability tax credit request.

Disclosure of Information

8. **Information may be disclosed** — Section 241 of the *Income Tax Act* does not apply to information or documents that can reasonably be regarded as necessary for the administration or enforcement of this Act and an official or authorized person, as defined for the purposes of that section, may make that information or a copy of any such documents available to any person for a purpose related to the administration or enforcement of this Act.

Regulations

9. **Regulations** — The Governor in Council may make regulations for carrying out the purposes and provisions of this Act including, without restricting the generality of the foregoing, regulations

(a) setting the maximum fee;

(b) exempting certain promoters from the notifying requirements set out in section 4; and

(c) prescribing anything that by this Act is to be prescribed.

Application of the *Income Tax Act*

10. **Provisions applicable** — Sections 152, 158 and 159, subsections 161(1) and (11), sections 162 to 167 and 257, Division J of Part I and Part XV of the *Income Tax Act* are applicable with respect to the circumstances related to a disability tax credit request, with such modifications as the circumstances require.

Consequential Amendments — *Tax Court of Canada Act*

11. Subsection 12(1) of the *Tax Court of Canada Act* is replaced by the following:

12. (1) **Jurisdiction** — The Court has exclusive original jurisdiction to hear and determine references and appeals to the Court on matters arising under the *Air Travellers Security Charge Act*, the *Canada Pension Plan*, the *Cultural Property Export and Import Act*, Part V.1 of the *Customs Act*, the *Disability Tax Credit Promoters Restrictions Act*, the *Employment Insurance Act*, the *Excise Act, 2001*, Part IX of the *Excise Tax Act*, Part 1 of the *Greenhouse Gas Pollution Pricing Act* [added by 2018 budget bill #1 s. 198 — ed.], the *Income Tax Act*, the *Old Age Security Act*, the *Petroleum and Gas Revenue Tax Act* and the *Softwood Lumber Products Export Charge Act, 2006* when references or appeals to the Court are provided for in those Acts.

Coming into Force

12. **Order in council** — This Act comes into force on a day to be fixed by order of the Governor in Council.

The *Disability Tax Credit Promoters Restrictions Regulations* provide:

MAXIMUM FEE

1. (1) **Setting of maximum fee** — For the purposes of subsection 3(1) of the *Disability Tax Credit Promoters Restrictions Act*, the maximum fee for a disability tax credit request made by a promoter is set at

(a) $100, for a request for a determination of disability tax credit eligibility under subsection 152(1.01) of the *Income Tax Act*;

(b) $100 per taxation year, for a request made in respect of a deduction under subsection 118.3(1) or (2) of the *Income Tax Act*; or

(c) $100 per taxation year, for a request made in respect of any deduction or overpayment of tax under the *Income Tax Act* that is contingent upon the eligibility for a deduction under subsection 118.3(1) or (2) of that Act.

(2) **Total fee accepted or charged** — If more than one disability tax credit request is made in respect of a claimant for a taxation year under either paragraph (1)(b) or (c), or both, the total fee that a promoter accepts or charges must not exceed $100.

ADJUSTED MAXIMUM FEE

2. (1) **Inflationary adjusted year** — In this section, "inflationary adjusted year" means 2025 and every fifth year after that year.

(2) **Maximum fee adjusted on December 1** — Subject to subsections (3) and (4), the maximum fee set out in section 1 is to be adjusted on December 1 of a particular inflationary adjusted year so that the maximum fee is equal to the greater of

(a) the fee determined by the formula

$$A \times B$$

where

A   is the maximum fee on November 30 of the particular inflationary adjusted year, and

B   is the amount determined by the formula in subparagraph (i) or (ii), whichever is applicable, rounded to the nearest one-thousandth, or, if the

amount is equidistant from two consecutive one-thousandths, rounded to the higher one-thousandth,

(i) if the particular inflationary adjusted year is 2025,

$$C/D$$

where

C   is the Consumer Price Index for the 12-month period ending on September 30, 2025, and

D   is the Consumer Price Index for the 12-month period that ended on September 30, 2019,

(ii) for any other particular inflationary adjusted year,

$$E/F$$

where

E   is the Consumer Price Index for the 12-month period ending on September 30 of the particular inflationary adjusted year, and,

F   is the Consumer Price Index for the 12-month period ending on September 30 of the last inflationary adjusted year in which the maximum fee was adjusted; and

(b) the fee referred to in the description of A in paragraph (a).

(3) **Application of adjustment** — The adjustment referred to in subsection (2) is to be applied only if the amount determined under that subsection exceeds the amount of the maximum fee described in the description of A in paragraph (2)(a) by $5 or more.

(4) **Rounding** — If the adjustment referred to in subsection (2) is applied, the maximum fee determined under that subsection is to be rounded to the nearest dollar or, if the result is equidistant from two consecutive dollar amounts, to the higher dollar amount.

(5) **Consumer Price Index** — In this section, the Consumer Price Index for any 12-month period is the result arrived at by

(a) aggregating the Consumer Price Index for Canada, as published by Statistics Canada under the authority of the *Statistics Act*, for each month in that period;

(b) dividing the aggregate obtained under paragraph (a) by 12; and

(c) rounding the result obtained under paragraph (b) to the nearest one-thousandth or, if the result obtained is equidistant from two consecutive one-thousandths, to the higher one-thousandth.

COMING INTO FORCE

3. **S.C. 2014, c. 7** — These Regulations come into force on the day on which the *Disability Tax Credit Promoters Restrictions Act* comes into force, but if they are registered after that day, they come into force on the day on which they are registered.

Income Tax Folios: S1-F3-C1: Child care expense deduction [replaces IT-495R3].

Interpretation Bulletins: IT-394R2: Preferred beneficiary election.

Information Circulars: 07-1R1: Taxpayer relief provisions.

Forms: RC4064: Medical and disability-related information [guide]; T1 General return, Line 31600; T2201 and T2201-1: Disability tax credit certificate.

(1.1) Time spent on therapy — For the purpose of paragraph 118.3(1)(a.1), in determining whether therapy is required to be administered at least three times each week for a total duration averaging not less than an average of 14 hours a week, the time spent on administering therapy

(a) includes only time spent on activities that require the individual to take time away from normal everyday activities in order to receive the therapy;

(b) in the case of therapy that requires a regular dosage of medication that is required to be adjusted on a daily basis, includes (subject to paragraph (d)) time spent on activities that are directly related to the determination of the dosage of the medication;

(c) in the case of a child who is unable to perform the activities related to the administration of the therapy as a result of the child's age, includes the time, if any, spent by the child's primary caregivers performing or supervising those activities for the child; and

(d) does not include time spent on activities related to dietary or exercise restrictions or regimes (even if these restrictions or regimes are a factor in determining the daily dosage of medication), travel time, medical appointments, shopping for medication or recuperation after therapy.

Notes: *Diabetes*: see 118.3(1) Notes.

PKU: In both *Mullings*, 2017 TCC 133, and *Hughes*, 2018 TCC 42, a child with phenylketonuria qualified, as her mother spent at least 14 hours/week (rounded up from 13.5 in *Hughes*) to precisely regulate the phenylalanine (1 of the 20 amino acids in proteins) entering her body, to prevent brain damage. This was therapy administration, not "diet". For CRA interpretation since *Mullings* see VIEWS doc 2017-0724351I7. The April 2021 Budget changes (see under 118.3(1)) will legislatively approve these decisions.

Teachers and daycare providers are not "primary caregivers" for para. (c): doc 2018-0753261I7.

118.3(1.1) added by 2006 budget bill #1 (implementing a 2005 Budget proposal), for 2005 and later tax years.

(2) Dependant having impairment — Where

(a) an individual has, in respect of a person (other than a person in respect of whom the person's spouse or common-law partner deducts for a taxation year an amount under section 118 or 118.8) who is resident in Canada at any time in the year and who is entitled to deduct an amount under subsection (1) for the year,

    (i) claimed for the year a deduction under subsection 118(1) because of

        (A) paragraph (b) of the description of B in that subsection, or

        (B) paragraph (d) of that description where the person is a parent, grandparent, child, grandchild, brother, sister, aunt, uncle, nephew or niece of the individual, or of the individual's spouse or common-law partner, or

    (ii) could have claimed for the year a deduction referred to in subparagraph (i) in respect of the person if

        (A) the person had no income for the year and had attained the age of 18 years before the end of the year, and

        (B) in the case of a deduction referred to in clause (i)(A), the individual were not married or not in a common-law partnership, and

(b) no amount in respect of remuneration for an attendant, or care in a nursing home, because of that person's mental or physical impairment, is included in calculating a deduction under section 118.2 (otherwise than under paragraph 118.2(2)(b.1)) for the year by the individual or by any other person,

there may be deducted, for the purpose of computing the tax payable under this Part by the individual for the year, the amount, if any, by which

    (c) the amount deductible under subsection (1) in computing that person's tax payable under this Part for the year

exceeds

    (d) the amount of that person's tax payable under this Part for the year computed before any deductions under this Division (other than under sections 118 to 118.07 and 118.7).

Related Provisions: 63(1)(e)(ii)(A)(II), 63(2)(b)(i)(B), 63(3)"child care expense"(c)(i)(B) — Higher child care expenses deduction for disabled child over 7; 118.031(3) — Enhanced Children's Arts Tax Credit (pre-2017) for child with disability; 118.3(3) — Apportionment of credit between taxpayers; 118.3(4) — Additional information requested by CRA; 118.8 — Transfer of disability credit to spouse; 118.91 — Individual resident in Canada for part of the year; 118.92 — Ordering of credits; 118.93 — Credits in separate returns; 118.94 — Credit restriction for non-resident individual; 118.95(b) — Application in year individual becomes bankrupt; 120.4(3)A — Disability credit deductible against income-splitting tax; Canada-U.S. Tax Treaty:Art. XXV:3 — US-resident dependant qualifies.

Notes: See 118.8 for transfer of the disability credit from a spouse or common-law partner. 118.3(2) provides a different mechanism, usually used to claim a dependent child who qualifies for the credit. See also 118(1)B(d) for the Caregiver credit; and 122.61(1)M:N(a) for the Child Disability Benefit (an increase to the Canada Child Benefit).

When reading a VIEWS doc or article in French about 118.3(2), note that the para. numbering is totally different in French than English!

The *dependant* need not file a return to establish net income for this credit: VIEWS doc 2006-0198641I7. A US-resident dependant qualifies: Canada-US tax treaty Art. XXV:2; 2006-0182461I7.

Separated parents sharing custody: see VIEWS doc 2018-0768651E5. In *Scott*, 2009 TCC 36, no 118.3(2) credit could be claimed for a child for whom S paid support, due to 118(5); but see now 118(5.1).

In *O'Neill*, 2008 TCC 548, the credit was disallowed both because the dependant was O's cousin (despite being treated like a sister) and because she was in a nursing home.

118.3(2)(a)(i)(B) amended by 2017 budget bill #1, for 2017 and later tax years, to delete "(c.1) or" before "(d)". 118.3(2) earlier amended by 2011 and 2009 budget bills #2, 2001 technical bill, 2000 same-sex partners bill, 1998 Budget, 1993 and 1992 technical bills.

Interpretation Bulletins: See list at end of 118.3.

Information Circulars: 07-1R1: Taxpayer relief provisions.

Forms: RC4064: Medical and disability-related information [guide]; T1 General return, Line 31800.

(3) Partial dependency [appointment of credit] — Where

more than one individual is entitled to deduct an amount under subsection (2) for a taxation year in respect of the same person, the total of all amounts so deductible for the year shall not exceed the maximum amount that would be deductible under that subsection for the year by an individual in respect of that person if that individual were the only individual entitled to deduct an amount under that subsection in respect of that person, and where the individuals cannot agree as to what portion of the amount each can deduct, the Minister may fix the portions.

(4) Additional information — Where a claim under this section or under section 118.8 is made in respect of an individual's impairment

    (a) if the Minister requests in writing information with respect to the individual's impairment, its effects on the individual and, where applicable, the therapy referred to in paragraph (1)(a.1) that is required to be administered, from any person referred to in subsection (1) or (2) or section 118.8 in connection with such a claim, that person shall provide the information so requested to the Minister in writing; and

    (b) if the information referred to in paragraph (a) is provided by a person referred to in paragraph (1)(a.2) or (a.3), the information so provided is deemed to be included in a certificate in prescribed form.

Related Provisions: 162(7) — Penalty for failure to comply with request for information.

Notes: Additional information provided by the doctor under 118.3(4) "forms part of the doctor's certificate": *Pham*, 2010 TCC 588, para. 8; *Poehlke*, 2010 TCC 604, para. 4.

118.3(4)(b) amended by 2002-2013 technical bill (Part 5 — technical) to add reference to 118.3(1)(a.3), effective for 2005 and later taxation years.

118.3(4) amended by 2000 Budget, effective for 2000 and later taxation years.

Notes [s. 118.3]: "National Health and Welfare" changed to "Human Resources Development" by S.C. 1996, c. 11, effective July 12, 1996. 118.3 amended by 1991 Budget/technical bill, effective 1991.

Definitions [s. 118.3]: "amount" — 248(1); "appropriate percentage" — 248(1); "audiologist" — 118.4(2); "aunt" — 252(2)(e); "basic activity of daily living" — 118.4(1)(c), (d); "brother" — 252(2)(b); "Canada" — 255; "child" — 252(1); "common-law partner", "common-law partnership" — 248(1); "dressing" — 118.4(1)(f); "feeding" — 118.4(1)(e); "grandparent" — 252(2)(d); "individual" — 248(1); "markedly restricted" — 118.4(1)(b); "medical doctor", "medical practitioner" — 118.4(2); "Minister" — 248(1); "nephew", "niece" — 252(2)(g); "nurse practitioner", "occupational therapist", "optometrist" — 118.4(2); "parent" — 252(2)(a); "person" — 248(1); "physiotherapist" — 118.4(2); "prescribed" — 248(1); "prolonged" — 118.4(1)(a); "psychologist" — 118.4(2); "resident in Canada" — 250; "sister" — 252(2)(c); "speech-language pathologist" — 118.4(2); "taxation year" — 249; "uncle" — 252(2)(e); "writing" — *Interpretation Act* 35(1).

Income Tax Folios [s. 118.3]: S1-F1-C1: Medical expense tax credit [replaces IT-519R2]; S1-F1-C2: Disability tax credit [replaces IT-519R2]; S1-F1-C3: Disability supports deduction [replaces IT-519R2]; S1-F2-C2: Tuition tax credit [replaces IT-516R2]; S1-F3-C1: Child care expense deduction [replaces IT-495R3].

Interpretation Bulletins [s. 118.3]: IT-171R2: Non-resident individuals — computation of taxable income earned in Canada and non-refundable tax credits (cancelled); IT-326R3: Returns of deceased persons as "another person"; IT-393R2: Election re tax on rents and timber royalties — non-residents.

Forms [s. 118.3]: T929: Disability supports deduction; T2201 and T2201-1: Disability tax credit certificate.

118.4 (1) Nature of impairment — For the purposes of subsection 6(16), sections 118.2 and 118.3 and this subsection,

(a) an impairment is prolonged where it has lasted, or can reasonably be expected to last, for a continuous period of at least 12 months;

(b) an individual's ability to perform a basic activity of daily living is markedly restricted only where all or substantially all of the time, even with therapy and the use of appropriate devices and medication, the individual is blind or is unable (or requires an inordinate amount of time) to perform a basic activity of daily living;

(b.1) an individual is considered to have the equivalent of a marked restriction in a basic activity of daily living only where all or substantially all of the time, even with therapy and the use of appropriate devices and medication, the individual's ability to perform more than one basic activity of daily living (including for this purpose, the ability to see) is significantly restricted, and the cumulative effect of those restrictions is tantamount to the individual's ability to perform a basic activity of daily living being markedly restricted;

(c) a basic activity of daily living in relation to an individual means

(i) mental functions necessary for everyday life,

(ii) feeding oneself or dressing oneself,

(iii) speaking so as to be understood, in a quiet setting, by another person familiar with the individual,

(iv) hearing so as to understand, in a quiet setting, another person familiar with the individual,

(v) eliminating (bowel or bladder functions), or

(vi) walking;

(c.1) mental functions necessary for everyday life include

(i) memory,

(ii) problem solving, goal-setting and judgement (taken together), and

(iii) adaptive functioning;

(d) for greater certainty, no other activity, including working, housekeeping or a social or recreational activity, shall be considered as a basic activity of daily living;

(e) feeding oneself does not include

(i) any of the activities of identifying, finding, shopping for or otherwise procuring food, or

(ii) the activity of preparing food to the extent that the time associated with the activity would not have been necessary in the absence of a dietary restriction or regime; and

(f) dressing oneself does not include any of the activities of identifying, finding, shopping for or otherwise procuring clothing.

Proposed Amendment — 118.4(1)

Federal Budget, Supplementary Information, April 19, 2021: See under 118.3(1).

Notes: See Notes to 118.3(1).

CRA's "check-the box" format on Form T2201 is too restrictive in some cases, and "Taxpayers should not be denied relief simply because the questions in the prescribed form do not neatly fit the circumstances": *Gibson*, 2014 TCC 236, para. 25.

CRA interprets "blind" as meaning having visual acuity in the better eye of 20/200 or less, or the diameter in the field of vision in the better eye is no greater than 20° (Form T2201; VIEWS doc 2004-0066181E5). This interpretation has no legal status, and "blind" means "deprived of the use of sight": *Blondin*, [1996] 1 C.T.C. 2063 (TCC). Blindness in only one eye is insufficient: *Doré*, 1995 CarswellNat 1701 (TCC); *Hoben*, 2003 TCC 658; *Riley*, 2003 TCC 916; *Marrone*, 2004 TCC 507; *Islam*, 2013 TCC 175; and this does not violate the *Charter of Rights*: *Bleiler*, 2014 TCC 296. In *Lewis*, 2007 TCC 416, a child was totally blind in one eye and had 20/50 vision in the other eye, but

without knowing what this meant "in layman's terms", the Court dismissed the appeal for lack of evidence.

The following have qualified: ADHD, learning disabilities, impulse control and conduct disorder (combined), impairing child's ability to engage socially (*Jungen*, 2021 TCC 16); bipolar disorder (*Buchanan*, 2002 FCA 231: markedly restricted in perceiving, thinking and remembering even though B's psychiatrist indicated on the T2201 that B did not qualify); chronic fatigue (*Gibson*, 2014 TCC 236: (c.1)(ii) means one must "look at all three mental functions together and decide whether the combination results in a severe impairment" (para. 24)); cumulative effect of essential tremor disorder, bipolar disorder, depression, anxiety and panic attacks (*Benoit*, 2014 TCC 95); cumulative effect of fibromyalgia, rheumatoid arthritis and other conditions once they became severe enough (*Connolly*, 2019 TCC 160); learning disability (*McDermid*, 2014 TCC 264: one child qualified but not another); severe anxiety disorder (*Green*, 2019 TCC 74: (c.1)(iii) applied); social anxiety and panic attacks (*Cochrane*, 2018 TCC 212: C was unable to leave her house); Tourette Syndrome, comorbid ADHD and dyslexia (*Pekofsky*, 2014 TCC 183).

The following did not qualify: allergies and eczema (*Brassard*, 2014 TCC 82); Asperger's (*Ostlund*, 2011 TCC 197); attention deficit-hyperactivity disorder (ADHD) (*Walkowiak*, 2012 TCC 453; *Vrantsidis*, 2017 TCC 204); bipolar disorder plus irritable bowel syndrome (*Laing*, 2019 TCC 267); hearing loss (*Pham*, 2010 TCC 588); mental illness (*Cook*, 2008 TCC 458; *Pakarinen*, 2010 TCC 456); migraine or cluster headaches (*Fontaine*, 2009 TCC 162; *Wood*, 2011 TCC 168); mild intellectual disability (*Poehlke*, 2010 TCC 604). The April 2021 Budget changes (see under 118.3(1)) will legislatively accept some of these cases.

CRA considers that "substantially all", used in 118.4(1)(b), means 90% or more.

118.4(1)(c)(ii): the phrase "feeding and dressing oneself" was changed to "feeding oneself or dressing oneself", first by Tax Court interpretation (*Lawlor*, [1996] 2 C.T.C. 2005D; *Dippel*, [1996] 3 C.T.C. 2202; *Mercier*, [1998] 2 C.T.C. 2610; *Tanguay*, [1998] 2 C.T.C. 2963); and then by 2003 Budget bill.

118.4(1)(c.1)(ii): "taken together" means the three functions must be "considered in the aggregate"; one activity will not suffice: VIEWS doc 2016-0681201I7.

118.4(1)(e), *(f)*: the definitions of "feeding" and "dressing" were introduced by 2003 Budget to overturn *Hamilton*, 2002 FCA 118, where a person on a special diet due to celiac disease, who spent a lot of time selecting and preparing the foods he could eat, was allowed the credit. These proposals were originally more restrictive in Aug. 30, 2002 draft legislation, but were withdrawn after public protest. The new definition of "feeding" still excludes a person with celiac disease who must spend excessive time finding gluten-free foods. However, such foods now qualify for medical expense credit in 118.2(2)(r). The new definition of "feeding" does cover someone who takes a long time to prepare their food because of a disability (e.g. a person with only one hand). No credit is allowed for food preparation for a child with allergies: *Kash*, 2006 TCC 662; *Marceau*, 2007 FCA 352 (but see Notes to 118.3(1.1) re PKU).

In *Droin*, 2005 TCC 793, a taxpayer with an atrophied left arm was found to be markedly restricted in feeding and dressing himself, so he was eligible for the credit even though he was not otherwise restricted in activities of daily living. In *Wiley*, 2013 TCC 237, a taxpayer with fibromyalgia and nerve damage who took a long time to dress herself "at times" (according to her doctor) did not qualify. However, "dressing" should be considered to include bathing and grooming: *Johnston*, [1998] 2 C.T.C. 262 (FCA), para. 37; *Wiley*, paras. 15, 17.

118.4(1) amended by 2006 budget bill #1 (for 2005 and later tax years), 2003 and 1991 Budgets.

Income Tax Folios: S1-F1-C1: Medical expense tax credit [replaces IT-519R2]; S1-F1-C2: Disability tax credit [replaces IT-519R2].

Interpretation Bulletins: IT-326R3: Returns of deceased persons as "another person".

(2) Reference to medical practitioners, etc. — For the purposes of sections 63, 64, 118.2, 118.3 and 118.6, a reference to an audiologist, dentist, medical doctor, medical practitioner, nurse, nurse practitioner, occupational therapist, optometrist, pharmacist, physiotherapist, psychologist or speech-language pathologist is a reference to a person authorized to practise as such,

(a) where the reference is used in respect of a service rendered to a taxpayer, pursuant to the laws of the jurisdiction in which the service is rendered;

(b) where the reference is used in respect of a certificate issued by the person in respect of a taxpayer, pursuant to the laws of the jurisdiction in which the taxpayer resides or of a province; and

(c) where the reference is used in respect of a prescription issued by the person for property to be provided to or for the use of a taxpayer, pursuant to the laws of the jurisdiction in which the taxpayer resides, of a province or of the jurisdiction in which the property is provided.

Notes: See Notes to 118.2(2) (at *118.2(2)(a)*) re meaning of "medical practitioner" for purposes of the medical expense credit.

For certifying disability on Form T2201 (118.3(1)(a.2), (a.3)), a dentist does not qualify but a psychiatrist does (as a physician): VIEWS doc 2016-0632181E5. Changes to the list of qualifying professions come from Finance, not CRA: 2019-080341117.

Minutes from CRA's informal Disabilities Advisory Committee, April 3, 2008 (*Access to Information Act* disclosure p. 000039) state: "Question about whether a physiotherapist whose provincial organization doesn't issue a number is considered a QP [qualifying practitioner] and allows their clients to claim for treatments. The Act (118.4(2)) speaks to 'authorized to practice' — this is interpreted as 'licensed'. We do not record 'numbers' on the T2201 for the very reason that different jurisdictions may approach things differently. So as long as the physiotherapist is licensed, no problem." See also *Couture*, 2008 FCA 412, and *Murphy*, 2010 TCC 434, on the meaning of "authorized" ("some formality of formal recognition as a discipline that is legally countenanced under Ontario law").

118.4(2)(a) opening words amended by 2017 budget bill #1, effective March 22, 2017, to add "nurse practitioner".

118.4(2) opening words amended by 2006 budget bill #1 (implementing a 2005 Budget proposal) to add "physiotherapist" effective Feb, 23, 2005, and reference to s. 64 effective 2004 and later taxation years. 118.4(2) earlier amended by 2000 Budget (for certifications made after Oct. 17, 2000), 1998 and 1997 Budgets.

Definitions [s. 118.4]: "basic activity of daily living" — 118.4(1)(c), (d); "dressing" — 118.4(1)(f); "feeding" — 118.4(1)(e); "individual" — 248(1); "mental functions necessary for everyday life" — 118.4(1)(c.1); "Minister", "person", "property" — 248(1); "province" — *Interpretation Act* 35(1); "taxpayer" — 248(1).

Forms [s. 118.4]: T2201 and T2201-1: Disability tax credit certificate.

118.5 (1) Tuition credit — Subject to subsection (1.2), for the purpose of computing the tax payable under this Part by an individual for a taxation year, there may be deducted,

Notes: Opening words amended by 2019 budget bill #1, effective 2019, to add "Subject to subsection (1.2)".

(a) **[institution in Canada]** — subject to subsection (1.1), where the individual was during the year a student enrolled at an educational institution in Canada that is

(i) a university, college or other educational institution providing courses at a post-secondary school level, or

(ii) certified by the Minister of Employment and Social Development to be an educational institution providing courses, other than courses designed for university credit, that furnish a person with skills for, or improve a person's skills in, an occupation,

an amount equal to the product obtained when the appropriate percentage for the year is multiplied by the amount of any fees for the individual's tuition paid in respect of the year to the educational institution, except to the extent that those fees

(ii.1) are paid to an educational institution described in subparagraph (i) in respect of courses that are not at the post-secondary school level, if

(A) the individual had not attained the age of 16 years before the end of the year, or

(B) the purpose of the individual's enrolment at the institution cannot reasonably be regarded as being to provide the individual with skills, or to improve the individual's skills, in an occupation,

(ii.2) are paid to an educational institution described in subparagraph (ii) if

(A) the individual had not attained the age of 16 years before the end of the year, or

(B) the purpose of the individual's enrolment at the institution cannot reasonably be regarded as being to provide the individual with skills, or to improve the individual's skills, in an occupation,

(iii) are paid on behalf of, or reimbursed to, the individual by the individual's employer and the amount paid or reimbursed is not included in the individual's income,

(iii.1) are fees in respect of which the individual is or was entitled to receive a reimbursement or any form of assistance under a program of Her Majesty in right of Canada or a province designed to facilitate the entry or re-entry of workers into the labour force, where the amount of the reimbursement

or assistance is not included in computing the individual's income,

(iv) were included as part of an allowance received by the individual's parent on the individual's behalf from an employer and are not included in computing the income of the parent by reason of subparagraph 6(1)(b)(ix), or

(v) are paid on the individual's behalf, or are fees in respect of which the individual is or was entitled to receive a reimbursement, under a program of Her Majesty in right of Canada designed to assist athletes, where the payment or reimbursement is not included in computing the individual's income;

Related Provisions: 118.5(1.1) — Minimum $100 fees per institution; 118.5(1.2) — Reduction for Canada Training Credit claimed. See also Related Provisions at end of s. 118.5.

Notes: The federal credit is 15% since 2007. See 117(2)(a) and 248(1)"appropriate percentage". There may also be a provincial credit (Ontario eliminated its credit as of Sept. 5, 2017: *Taxation Act, 2007* s. 9(15)). CRA practice is not to require the Form T2202A to be filed with the return, but audit inquiries for the form are frequently made after the return has been assessed.

The calculation of fees paid "in respect of the year", not "in the year", so a university can issue a T2202A for a prior year when fees are not paid until the next year: VIEWS doc 2004-007067117. Where fees are prepaid, the credit is for courses taken in the year: 2004-0099741E5, 2010-0361981E5.

Where fees are paid by an employer as a taxable benefit, they qualify as if paid by the individual: 118.5(1)(a)(iii), VIEWS docs 2009-0338271E5, 2011-0412502E5. This puts the employee in the same position as receiving cash and paying the tuition directly. Fees paid by a student to an employer to reimburse it for tuition fees paid (where the student dropped out of the course, or where a physician did not practise in a particular area as promised) may qualify if the employer issues a receipt to the student: 2003-0009597, 2011-0412502E5; or may be deductible under 8(1)(n): 2010-0376491E5.

Where tuition fees are paid for or reduced by the school, this may be a scholarship taxable under 56(1)(n) (effectively exempt under 56(3)), or an employee benefit under 6(1))(a). See Notes to 56(1)(n). In either case, the tuition credit is available on the unreduced tuition, and the institution should issue a T2202A for the full tuition before the reduction: VIEWS doc 2009-0308201E5.

There is no legal obligation on the institution to issue Form T2202A. If the institution has a fee dispute with a student, it would be "inappropriate" to withhold the form: VIEWS doc 2005-0119471E5. Where a student pays tuition arrears to a collection agency acting for the institution, the institution should issue a revised T2202A for that year showing the amount paid: doc 2008-027216117. The student need not be registered on the university's computer system and the T2202A can be done manually: 2014-0526991E5.

118.5(1)(a)(i): For "other educational institution", see Income Tax Folio S1-F2-C2 ¶2.5 (can include organization governing a profession); VIEWS docs 2016-0681131E5; 2019-0803661E5 (truck driving mandatory entry-level training (MELT) qualifies).

In *Setchell*, 2006 TCC 37, a 4-week SAP computer course did not qualify because SAP Canada was not a college and did not require secondary school education. However, the cost was allowed as a business expense.

118.5(1)(a)(ii): In *East*, [2001] 1 C.T.C. 2033 (TCC), the Court held that only the institution, not its location, needs to be certified. A certification purporting to apply to only certain locations of SHL Computer Innovations was held to apply to all its locations. However, in *Kiprenko*, [2001] 1 C.T.C. 2226 (TCC), a different judge, unaware of *East*, concluded that SHL was not certified at all!

CRA must prove non-certification, since this information is in the Minister's hands, and must prove that its list of institutions certified by Human Resources Development Canada is accurate; the Tax Court therefore allowed the credit for the Toronto Truck Driving School in *Edwards*, [1998] 4 C.T.C. 2906, and for the Canadian Transportation Specialist School in *Ahmad*, 2007 TCC 382. (CRA allows a certified institution to provide the student with a letter of certification rather than Form T2202A: VIEWS doc 2007-0237521E5.)

The requirement that a student be 16 to qualify for a certified institution does not breach the *Charter of Rights*, because it is the parents who are denied the credit: *Troupe*, [2002] 2 C.T.C. 2449 (TCC), *Sulcs*, 2007 TCC 637.

For the meaning of "post-secondary" and "education" see *Hillman*, 2006 TCC 578 (bar review courses did not qualify); VIEWS docs 2010-0384101E5, 2016-0656111E5, 2016-0675551E5. A private career college registered under the Ontario *Private Career Colleges Act* qualifies: 2012-044539117. An aviation academy was not providing "post-secondary" level courses, even though N graduated from high school before enrolling: *Napier*, 2001 FCA 358. However, in *Dean*, 2005 TCC 138, helicopter pilot courses at Nelson Marlborough Institute of Technology in New Zealand qualified because they were creditable towards a Bachelor of Commerce and Nelson was held to be a "university". Flying school classes and certain amounts of flight time qualify: 2012-0472331E5. Piano classes past Grade 8 at the Mississauga School of Music were "post-secondary", since that level qualified for Grade 12 high school credit: *Tarkowski*, 2007 TCC 632; but Grade 10 piano taught by an individual 1 hour a week did not qualify in

Kam, 2013 TCC 266. Fees to a professional program at a university qualify even if they are not transferable to an academic program: 2012-0447351I7, 2013-0483291I7. A high school offering post-secondary courses qualifies: 2019-0815841E5. Courses with no admission requirement did not qualify in 2014-0540411E5.

In *Jacejko*, [1999] 4 C.T.C. 2032 (TCC), 40% of the cost of a theological college's non-credit instructional Holy Land tour qualified for a student enrolled at the college.

Lab fees, library fees, exam fees and diploma fees qualify as tuition: Income Tax Folio S1-F2-C2 ¶2.34. Student activities, board and lodging and "goods of enduring value" do not: ¶2.35. Dentistry students' fees for use of dental equipment, instruments and chairs are similar to a lab fee and qualify: doc 2003-0012557. Books do not unless included in a correspondence course charge: ¶2.35. See VIEWS doc 2005-0117321E5 for detailed discussion. Fees to "audit" a course qualify: 2006-0167441E5, but 2011-0403811E5 suggests they may not. Application fees qualify even for a course the student is not accepted to (2008-0301351E5), provided (in CRA's view) the student subsequently enrolls at the institution: Income Tax Folio S1-F2-C2 ¶2.34 (this restriction may not be correct in the author's view). Costs to fly instructors to an overseas site qualify: 2010-0354201E5. Fees required by the university to be paid directly to a coach who is the course instructor do not qualify: 2016-0659941E5.

English or French second-language training at an HRSDC-certified institution can qualify if required for employment: VIEWS doc 2009-031845I17. An "additional qualification" (AQ) course offered by a teachers' college qualifies: doc 2003-0042283. High-school "advance placement" (AP) course examination fees that give university credit can qualify: doc 2002-0137817. Training under a Canada Job Grant can qualify: 2014-0559561I7.

Examination fees can qualify under 118.5(1)(d) since 2011 (reversing *Arrioja*, 2005 TCC 95). Other fees not paid to an educational institution generally do not qualify: VIEWS doc 2019-0801361E5 (medical residency fees such as matching fees, registration fees, certification fees, translation costs and travel costs; but the 122.91 Canada Training Credit may be available).

A medical resident qualifies for the credit: VIEWS doc 2003-0011245 (see also Notes to 118.6(1)"qualifying educational program").

"Enrolled" includes part-time students and means "registered with the registrar of the institution such that the student would be liable for any tuition fees": Income Tax Folio S1-F2-C2 ¶2.22; doc 2014-0526991E5.

The requirement is "enrolled at an *educational institution in Canada*" ("situé au Canada", in French), not "enrolled in Canada at an educational institution", so a student taking courses in Canada from a US company to qualify for the New York State Bar could not claim the credit (quite aside from the fact the company was not an educational institution): *Hillman*, 2006 TCC 578. CRA refers to the Canadian Information Centre for International Credentials (CICIC) list, though it is not definitive, and the Canadian campus of a foreign university can qualify: VIEWS doc 2008-028986I17. The Univ. of Phoenix was held to qualify since it has campuses in Canada, for students taking online instruction in Canada from its Arizona campus: *Robinson*, 2006 TCC 664 (Beaubier J) and *Cammidge*, 2011 TCC 172 (Little J); but this argument was rejected in: *Faint*, 2011 TCC 260 (Margeson J), *Abdalla*, 2011 TCC 328 (Webb J, who allowed the credit under 118.5(1)(b)), and *Rose*, 2012 TCC 161 (FCA appeal discontinued A-159-12) (V. Miller J, who did not). A private piano teacher is not an educational institution: *Van Helden*, 2014 TCC 196.

For carryforward of the tuition credit, and interaction with the foreign tax credit, see Notes to 118.61(1).

118.5(1)(a)(ii.1)(A) and (B) conditions added by 2017 budget bill #1, for 2017 and later taxation years. The amendment makes this rule consistent with the rules for certified educational institutions, extended by the Budget to include occupational skills courses that are not at the post-secondary level (see 118.6(1)"qualifying educational program").

118.5(1)(a)(ii) amended by 2013 budget bill #2 (s. 238(1)(i)(i)), effective Dec. 12, 2013, to change "Minister of Human Resources and Skills Development" to "Minister of Employment and Social Development".

118.5(1)(a)(iii) amended by 2002-2013 technical bill, effective June 26, 2013.

118.5(1)(a) amended by 2011 budget bill #2, for 2011 and later taxation years, to add "subject to subsection (1.1)" in opening words and to delete "if the total of these fees exceeds $100" before subpara. (ii.1) [no substantive change, as the $100 threshold was moved to 118.5(1.1)].

118.5(1) earlier amended by 1995-97 technical bill, S.C. 1996 c. 11, S.C. 2005 c. 34, and 1992 and 1991 technical bills.

Regulations: 203 (university required to issue tuition certificate).

Income Tax Folios: S1-F2-C2: Tuition tax credit [replaces IT-516R2].

Interpretation Bulletins: IT-171R2: Non-resident individuals — computation of taxable income earned in Canada and non-refundable tax credits (cancelled); IT-393R2: Election re tax on rents and timber royalties — non-residents; IT-470R: Employees' fringe benefits.

Information Circulars: 75-23: Tuition fees and charitable donations paid to privately supported secular and religious schools; 07-1R1: Taxpayer relief provisions.

Forms: T1 General return, Line 32300; and Sched. 11: Federal tuition, education, and textbook amounts; T2202A: Tuition, education, and textbook amounts certificate; TL11B: Tuition, education, and textbook amounts certificate — Flying school or club.

(b) [university outside Canada] — where the individual was during the year a student in full-time attendance at a university outside Canada in a course leading to a degree, an amount equal to the product obtained when the appropriate percentage for the year is multiplied by the amount of any fees for the individual's tuition paid in respect of the year to the university, except any such fees

(i) paid in respect of a course of less than three consecutive weeks duration,

(ii) paid on the individual's behalf by the individual's employer to the extent that the amount of the fees is not included in computing the individual's income, or

(iii) paid on the individual's behalf by the employer of the individual's parent, to the extent that the amount of the fees is not included in computing the income of the parent by reason of subparagraph 6(1)(b)(ix);

Related Provisions: See Related Provisions at end of 118.5.

Notes: See Guides RC190, *Information for Educational Institutions Outside Canada*; RC192, *Information for Students — Educational Institutions Outside Canada*.

A "university outside Canada" must, according to CRA (Income Tax Folio S1-F2-C2 ¶2.12), be recognized by a nationally accepted accrediting body of its country as being an educational institution that confers at least bachelor or equivalent level degrees. It need not have "University" in its name: VIEWS doc 2008-0288251E5. It must have degree-granting powers: *Klassen*, 2007 FCA 339. Historically, all those in former Reg. Schedule VIII qualified: former IT-516R2 para. 5. That list is now at tinyurl.com/univs-cra for the donation credit; CRA uses a second list of institutions for 118.5 (tinyurl.com/cra-tuition-univs; 2011-0429531E5). An institution on *either* list is recognized as qualifying for the tuition credit: tinyurl.com/cra-educ-rec; S1-F2-C2 ¶2.13 (CRA will consider adding to the list "at the request of the institution").

The following have qualified for 118.5(1)(b): California Coast University (*Kitura*, 2003 TCC 892; it was approved by the State of California even though not listed by the American Council on Education or the Western Association of Schools and Colleges); Groupe École Supérieure de Commerce, France (*Laprairie*, 2007 TCC 135; it had authorization from the French education ministry to award degrees); Institut ÉCO-Conseil de Strasbourg, France (*Drouin*, [1999] 2 C.T.C. 2413 (TCC)); London School of Economics (*Shea*, 2008 TCC 184: it was part of Univ. of London and did not need to be in Sch. VIII to qualify); Musicians Institute College of Contemporary Music (*Zailo*, 2014 TCC 60, but not for a program leading to an associate's degree); Univ. of Phoenix (*Abdalla*, 2011 TCC 328; and see Notes to 118.5(1)(a) re it qualifying because it has a campus in Canada); Walden University, AZ (*Lowry*, 2011 TCC 329); unnamed university confirmed by IRPPD (VIEWS doc 2007-0260961E5).

The following have not qualified: Aeroservice Aviation Centre, Miami (*Rivington*, 2006 TCC 468; it was not a university and provided a certificate, not a degree); American Academy of Dramatic Arts (*Zaluski*, 2010 TCC 338: it did not grant degrees); Cottey College, Missouri (*Gillich*, 2006 TCC 49; it offered only a 2-year "associate degree", not a full bachelor's); Divers Institute of Technology, Seattle (*Humphreys*, 2010 TCC 88; it did not offer courses leading to a degree); London Academy of Music and Dramatic Art, England (*Andrews*, 2003 TCC 830 and *Goldberg*, 2006 TCC 676; it granted a diploma in professional acting, not a degree, which is a "recognition in writing of academic achievement which is called a degree, and includes the degrees of bachelor, master and doctor"); Minot State University–Bottineau Campus (*Klassen*, 2007 FCA 339; it was a school separate from Minot State University and not a degree-granting institution); New South Wales Technical and Further Education School, Australia (*Wise*, 2007 TCC 741; it conferred a diploma, not a degree); Sotheby's Institute of Art New York, pre-2010 (*Yacubowicz*, 2011 TCC 64; even though the taxpayer got credit at Univ. of Manchester for her year there, it did not yet have degree-granting powers). In *Alexander College*, 2016 FCA 269, a Canadian college that offered only "associate" degrees but whose credits were transferable to universities was a "university" for GST purposes (but the GST use is in an "entirely different statutory context" from the ITA: para. 22).

The degree need not be granted by the same institution that the taxpayer attends: *Laprairie*, 2007 TCC 135; but see VIEWS doc 2008-0301631I7, which based on *Klassen* (FCA, above) says that if the institution the student attends cannot itself grant a bachelor's degree, the fact another university grants one will not entitle the student to the credit. The course in question must be towards a bachelor's degree or higher; an associate's degree does not qualify: *Zailo*, 2014 TCC 60.

Whether enrolment is "full-time" is left to the institution to determine: *Ferre*, 2010 TCC 593, para. 26; *Archibald*, 2018 FCA 2 (A spending 25-30 hours a week on an online MBA did not make it full-time when the university called it part-time); VIEWS docs 2011-0398871E5, 2012-0437811E5, 2012-0442181E5; but see also guidelines in Income Tax Folio S1-F2-C2 ¶2.17-2.21. Travel time and study time do not count: *Nwar-Ahmad*, 2016 TCC 113. Part-time enrolments in two institutions can be combined and counted as full-time: 2005-0119011E5, 2010-0360511E5.

Before 2011, the 3-consecutive-week requirement in (b)(i) was 13 consecutive weeks; the cases below are still relevant in satisfying the 3-week requirement. A US university program of three 10-week semesters, each followed by one week of exams, did not qualify: VIEWS doc 2003-0011695. In *Fayle*, 2005 TCC 71, a 6-week University of Oslo course did not qualify even though it was identical to a 13-week course of fewer hours per week. In *Ali*, 2004 TCC 726, a US university full-time program did not qualify because the university was on a quarterly rather than a trimester system, with only 11-12 weeks in some terms (the Court suggested that relief be granted by remission order). In *Larsen*, 2012 TCC 74, a 6-week course at a university in Spain did not qualify. In *Zochowski*, 2012 TCC 277, 4 semesters of 10 weeks each, with a break of a few weeks between each semester, did not qualify. See also Notes to 118.6(1) "designated educational institution" for case law on the parallel requirement in para. (b) of that definition. The TCC considered the 13-week requirement to apply to each individual course, not the entire program: *Ferre*, 2010 TCC 593 (Paris J), *Faint*, 2011 TCC 260 (Margeson J), and *Rose*, 2012 TCC 161 (FCA appeal discontinued A-159-12) (V. Miller J); but in *Siddell*, 2011 TCC 250, Bowie J disagreed and held that "course" means "the entire curriculum pursued throughout the academic year" (see also doc 2011-0403991E5); and in *Abdalla*, 2011 TCC 328 Webb J ruled that due to *Interpretation Act* s. 33(2), 2 consecutive courses totalling more than 13 weeks qualified. In *Lowry*, 2011 TCC 329 (Webb J), where the student took two 12-week courses with one week off in between, the 13-week test was not met.

The 3-week requirement was met by 10 consecutive 1-2 week courses in a 1-year MBA program: *Fortnum*, 2018 TCC 126. CRA says in doc 2019-0791521I7 that *Fortnum* is not binding and CRA's interpretation has not changed, but also says it will apply *Fortnum* in "factually similar" cases; Folio S1-F2-C2 ¶2.31.1.

Remote learning: The case law was conflicted as to whether a student taking courses by correspondence or Internet "attends" a university. The credit was disallowed in *Hlopina*, [1998] 2 C.T.C. 2669 (TCC) and *Cleveland*, 2004 TCC 34 but allowed in *Krause*, 2004 TCC 594, *Valente*, 2006 TCC 145, *Kuwalek*, 2006 TCC 624, *McGrath*, 2007 TCC 295 and *Cammidge*, 2011 TCC 172. CRA's view was that Internet courses did not qualify (docs 2003-0036885, 2004-0091151E5, 2004-0108331M4, 2005-0116531M4), but CRA changed its position for taxation years after 2006, and accepts Internet attendance (but not correspondence courses): Income Tax Folio S1-F2-C2 ¶2.19-2.20; 2007-0233661I7, 2007-0260931E5, 2008-0292531I7. (See also Notes to 118.5(1)(c) re commuting.)

A Canadian agent can issue Form TL11A on behalf of the university: VIEWS doc 2007-0260931E5. A TL11A may show fees in foreign currency; the credit is based on the exchange rate when the fees are paid: 2019-0802711E5. The TL11A is not mandatory for claiming the credit: *Fortnum*, 2018 TCC 126, para. 8.

See also Caiella & Webel, "Post-Secondary Education Outside Canada", 20(1) *Canadian Tax Highlights* (ctf.ca) 6-7 (2012) and 20(4) 8-9 (April 2012); Lam, "Tax Credits for Cross-Border Students", 2013(16) *Tax Times* (Carswell) 1-3 (Aug. 30, 2013).

118.5(1)(b)(i) amended by 2011 budget bill #2, for tuition fees paid for 2011 and later tax years, to change "13" to "three".

Regulations: 203 (university required to issue tuition certificate).

Income Tax Folios: S1-F2-C2: Tuition tax credit [replaces IT-516R2].

Forms: TL11A: Tuition, education, and textbook amounts certificate — University outside Canada; T1 General return, Line 32300; T1 General return, Sched. 11: Federal tuition, education, and textbook amounts.

(c) [cross-border commuter] — where the individual resided throughout the year in Canada near the boundary between Canada and the United States if the individual

(i) was at any time in the year a student enrolled at an educational institution in the United States that is a university, college or other educational institution providing courses at a post-secondary school level, and

(ii) commuted to that educational institution in the United States,

an amount equal to the product obtained when the appropriate percentage for the year is multiplied by the amount of any fees for the individual's tuition paid in respect of the year to the educational institution if those fees exceed $100, except to the extent that those fees

(iii) are paid on the individual's behalf by the individual's employer and are not included in computing the individual's income, or

(iv) were included as part of an allowance received by the individual's parent on the individual's behalf from an employer and are not included in computing the income of the parent by reason of subparagraph 6(1)(b)(ix); and

Notes: The term "commuted" requires physical travel, and does not include telecommuting by taking a course over the Internet: *Wellington*, 2004 TCC 313. (See however Notes to 118.5(1)(b).)

In *Van de Water*, [1991] 1 C.T.C. 2200 (TCC), 80 km from a Montreal suburb to Plattsburg NY was held not to be "near", so the credit was disallowed. In *Yankson*, 2005 TCC 527, Calgary was held not to be "near" Seattle. However, in *Humphreys*, 2010 TCC 88, Brentwood Bay BC was considered "near" Seattle even though the commute (partly by ferry) took over 4 hours; the Court stated the *Van de Water* test does not apply "in the watery expanses of the Pacific coast".

For the meaning of "post-secondary", see Notes to 118.5(1)(a).

Forms: T1 General return, Line 32300; T1 General return, Sched. 11: Federal tuition, education, and textbook amounts.

(d) [licensing examination fees] — subject to subsection (1.1), if the individual has taken an examination (in this section referred to as an "occupational, trade or professional examination") in the year that is required to obtain a professional status recognized under a federal or provincial statute, or to be licensed or certified as a tradesperson, where that status, licence or certification allows the individual to practise the profession or trade in Canada, an amount equal to the product obtained when the appropriate percentage for the year is multiplied by the amount of any fees paid in respect of the occupational, trade or professional examination to an educational institution referred to in paragraph (a), a professional association, a provincial ministry or other similar institution, except to the extent that the occupational, trade or professional examination fees

(i) are paid on behalf of, or reimbursed to, the individual by the individual's employer and the amount paid or reimbursed is not included in the individual's income, or

(ii) are fees in respect of which the individual is or was entitled to receive a reimbursement or any form of assistance under a program of Her Majesty in right of Canada or a province designed to facilitate the entry or re-entry of workers into the labour force, where the amount of the reimbursement or assistance is not included in computing the individual's income.

Related Provisions: 118.5(1.1) — Minimum $100 fees per institution; 118.5(4) — Meaning of "fees paid in respect of. . .". See also Related Provisions at end of 118.5.

Notes: See Income Tax Folio S1-F2-C2, ¶2.40-2.42. Exam fees that qualify include: foreign-trained lawyer's fee to provincial law society for licensing exam (VIEWS doc 2012-0439811E5); Medical Council of Canada Qualifying Examination, and College of Family Physicians (2012-0444181M4); Society of Actuaries (2013-0480991E5); truck driving Class 1 licence (2019-0803661E5).

The following do not qualify: foreign-trained lawyer's fee to a university for the National Committee on Accreditation Challenge Examination Review Program, as this is not required for those writing the exam (VIEWS doc 2012-0439811E5); International Qualification Examination (IQEX) for a Canadian CA to become a US CPA (2013-0478801E5); Certified Human Resources Professional designation in Alberta (2013-0490671E5); other fees to qualify for a profession not recognized by a Canadian statute (2014-0530681E5, 2018-0786171E5). For a taxpayer carrying on business, exam fees are non-deductible capital expenses (18(1)(b)), but may be eligible for capital cost allowance as Class 14.1 property.

118.5(1)(d) added by 2011 budget bill #2, for 2011 and later tax years.

Forms: T1 General return, Line 32300; T1 General return, Sched. 11: Federal tuition, education, and textbook amounts.

Related Provisions [subsec. 118.5(1)]: See Related Provisions at end of 118.5.

Income Tax Folios: S1-F2-C2: Tuition tax credit [replaces IT-516R2]; S1-F2-C3: Scholarships, research grants and other education assistance [replaces IT-340R].

I.T. Technical News: 13 (employer-paid educational costs).

Forms: T2202A: Tuition, education, and textbook amounts certificate; TL11C: Tuition, education, and textbook amounts certificate — Commuter to United States.

(1.1) Minimum amount — No amount may be deducted for a taxation year by an individual under paragraph (1)(a) or (d) in respect of any fees paid to a particular institution unless the total of the fees described in those paragraphs and paid to the particular institution in the year by the individual exceeds $100[2].

Notes: 118.5(1.1) added by 2011 budget bill #2, for 2011 and later tax years. This $100 limit was formerly in 118.5(1)(a), and is still in 118.5(1)(c). No $100 limit applies

---

[2] Not indexed for inflation — ed.

to 118.5(1)(b), presumably because it is only for university tuition, which will always be higher.

(1.2) Canada training credit reduction

— The amount that may be deducted for a taxation year by an individual under subsection (1) is to be reduced by the amount determined by the formula

$$A \times B$$

where

A   is the appropriate percentage for the taxation year; and

B   is the amount, if any, deemed to have been paid by the individual under subsection 122.91(1) in respect of the taxation year.

Notes: 118.5(1.2) provides that the portion of tuition fees refunded via the Canada Training Credit (CTC, 122.91) is not eligible for the tuition credit. This is done by reducing the tuition credit by 15% of the CTC for the year.

118.5(1.2) added by 2019 budget bill #1, effective 2019.

(2) Application to deemed residents

— Where an individual is deemed by section 250 to be resident in Canada throughout all or part of a taxation year, in applying subsection (1) in respect of the individual for the period when the individual is so deemed to be resident in Canada, paragraph (1)(a) shall be read without reference to the words "in Canada".

Forms: TL11D: Tuition fees certificate — educational institutions outside Canada for a deemed resident of Canada.

(3) Inclusion of ancillary fees and charges

— For the purpose of this section, "fees for an individual's tuition" includes ancillary fees and charges that are paid

(a) to an educational institution referred to in subparagraph (1)(a)(i), and

(b) in respect of the individual's enrolment at the institution in a program at a post-secondary school level,

but does not include

(c) any fee or charge to the extent that it is levied in respect of

(i) a student association,

(ii) property to be acquired by students,

(iii) services not ordinarily provided at educational institutions in Canada that offer courses at a post-secondary school level,

(iv) the provision of financial assistance to students, except to the extent that, if this Act were read without reference to subsection 56(3), the amount of the assistance would be required to be included in computing the income, and not be deductible in computing the taxable income, of the students to whom the assistance is provided, or

(v) the construction, renovation or maintenance of any building or facility, except to the extent that the building or facility is owned by the institution and used to provide

(A) courses at the post-secondary school level, or

(B) services for which, if fees or charges in respect of the services were required to be paid by all students of the institution, the fees or charges would be included because of this subsection in the fees for an individual's tuition, and

(d) any fee or charge for a taxation year that, but for this paragraph, would be included because of this subsection in the fees for the individual's tuition and that is not required to be paid by

(i) all of the institution's full-time students, where the individual is a full-time student at the institution, and

(ii) all of the institution's part-time students, where the individual is a part-time student at the institution,

to the extent that the total for the year of all such fees and charges paid in respect of the individual's enrolment at the institution exceeds $250[2].

Notes: Since 118.5(3)(c)(ii) excludes "property" to be "acquired", a paramedic's first aid kit and a cooking student's utensils are excluded, but food can qualify since it is consumed: VIEWS doc 2010-0356101E5. A computer is excluded: 2011-0394391E5.

A fee charged only to students in certain programs is a "non-universal fee" limited to $250 per year by 118.5(3)(d): VIEWS doc 2004-0054761E5. The $250 limitation in 118.5(3)(d) also applies to fees to obtain course credit for work experience (which may actually be excluded by 118.5(3)(c)(iii) if they are for services not ordinarily offered by post-secondary institutions): doc 2006-085161E5. The $250 limit has not been increased since it was introduced in 1997.

Textbooks may be included in the cost of a correspondence course from a Canadian institution: Income Tax Folio S1-F2-C2 ¶2.35; VIEWS doc 2006-0215121E5. See also the pre-2017 textbook credit in 118.6(2.1).

For the meaning of "post-secondary", see Notes to 118.5(1)(a).

118.5(3)(c)(iv) amended by 2013 budget bill #2, for 2012 and later taxation years, to change "if the reference in paragraph 56(1)(n) to '$500' were read as a reference to 'nil'" to "if this Act were read without reference to subsection 56(3)". This will "clarify that fees related to the provision of financial assistance are excluded except to the extent that the amount of the assistance is required to be included in computing the income of the individual or would be required to be included but for the scholarship exemption in 56(3)" [Finance Technical Notes].

118.5(3) added by 1997 Budget, effective for 1997 and later taxation years.

(4) Ancillary fees and charges for examinations

— For the purpose of this section, "fees paid in respect of the occupational, trade or professional examination" of an individual includes ancillary fees and charges, other than fees and charges included in subsection (3), that are paid to an educational institution referred to in subparagraph (1)(a)(i), a professional association, a provincial ministry or other similar institution, in respect of an occupation, trade or professional examination taken by the individual, but does not include any fee or charge to the extent that it is levied in respect of

(a) property to be acquired by an individual;

(b) the provision of financial assistance to an individual, except to the extent that, if this Act were read without reference to subsection 56(3), the financial assistance would be required to be included in computing the income, and would not be deductible in computing the taxable income, of the individual;

(c) the construction, renovation or maintenance of any building or facility; or

(d) any fee or charge for a taxation year that, but for this paragraph, would be included because of this subsection in the fees for the individual's occupational, trade or professional examination and that is not required to be paid by all the individuals taking the occupational, trade or professional examination to the extent that the total for the year of all such fees and charges paid in respect of the individual's fees for the occupational, trade or professional examination exceeds $250.

Notes: Online seminar fees paid to a professor to prepare for an exam do not qualify under 118.5(4): VIEWS doc 2013-0480991E5.

118.5(4) added by 2011 budget bill #2, effective for 2011 and later taxation years. This was 118.5(3.1) in the June 6, 2011 Budget draft legislation.

Related Provisions [s. 118.5]: 64(a)A(ii)(I) — Deduction for talking textbooks for disabled students; 110(1)(g) — Deduction for tuition assistance that does not qualify under 118.5; 117(1) — Tax payable under this Part; 118.5(1.2) — Reduction for amount allowed as Canada Training Credit; 118.61(2) — Carryforward of unused credits; 118.8 — Transfer of unused credits to spouse; 118.9 — Transfers to supporting person; 118.91 — Individual resident in Canada for part of the year; 118.92 — Ordering of credits; 118.93 — Credits in separate returns; 118.94 — Credit restriction for non-resident individual; 118.95(a) — Application in year individual becomes bankrupt; Reg. 5700(w) — Medical expense credit for talking textbooks for disabled students.

Definitions [s. 118.5]: "amount", "appropriate percentage" — 248(1); "Canada" — 255, *Interpretation Act* 35(1); "employer" — 248(1); "fees for tuition" — 118.5(3); "fees paid in respect of" — 118.5(4); "Her Majesty" — *Interpretation Act* 35(1); "individual", "Minister" — 248(1); "occupational, trade or professional examination" — 118.5(1)(d); "parent" — 252(2)(a); "person", "property" — 248(1); "province" — *Interpretation Act* 35(1); "provincial" — *Interpretation Act* 33(3), 35(1)"province"; "resident in Canada" — 250; "tax payable" — 248(2); "taxable income" — 248(1); "taxation year" — 249; "United States" — *Interpretation Act* 35(1).

Income Tax Folios: S1-F2-C2: Tuition tax credit [replaces IT-516R2].

Interpretation Bulletins: IT-326R3: Returns of deceased persons as "another person".

---

[2] Not indexed for inflation — ed.

118.6 (1) [Pre-2017 education credit —] Definitions — For the purposes of sections 63 and 64 and this Subdivision,

Notes: 118.6(1) opening words amended by 2000 Budget (effective 2000), 1998 Budget, 1991 technical bill.

"designated educational institution" means

(a) an educational institution in Canada that is

(i) a university, college or other educational institution designated by the lieutenant governor in council of a province as a specified educational institution under the *Canada Student Loans Act*, designated by an appropriate authority under the *Canada Student Financial Assistance Act*, or designated, for the purposes of *An Act respecting financial assistance for education expenses*, R.S.Q., c. A-13.3, by the Minister of the Province of Quebec responsible for the administration of that Act, or

(ii) certified by the Minister of Employment and Social Development to be an educational institution providing courses, other than courses designed for university credit, that furnish a person with skills for, or improve a person's skills in, an occupation,

(b) a university outside Canada at which the individual referred to in the definition "qualifying student" in this subsection was enrolled in a course, of not less than three consecutive weeks duration, leading to a degree, or

(c) if the individual referred to in the definition "qualifying student" in this subsection resided, throughout the year referred to in that definition, in Canada near the boundary between Canada and the United States, an educational institution in the United States to which the individual commuted that is a university, college or other educational institution providing courses at a post-secondary school level;

Related Provisions: 122.7(1)"designated educational institution" — Definition applies to Canada Workers Benefit; 146.1(1)"post-secondary educational institution"(a) — DEI qualifies for RESP purposes; 146.02(1)"qualifying educational program" — DEI qualifies for Lifelong Learning Plan RRSP withdrawal; Reg. 203 — Institution under para. (a) required to file tuition certificates.

Notes: This definition applied before 2017 to determine the education credit under 118.6(2). That credit has been repealed and the definition was amended; it is still used by other provisions such as 56(3.1).

For the meaning of "post-secondary" in para. (c) see Notes to 118.5(1)(a). For "university outside Canada" and attendance by Internet, see Notes to 118.5(1)(b).

CRA does not maintain a list of designated institutions: VIEWS doc 2006-0179011E5. See also 2008-0279601E5 (rejecting an unnamed program); 2009-033393117; 2011-043079117 and 2013-047428117 (accepting HRSDC-certified institutions). For foreign institutions, see Notes to 118.5(1)(b).

Enrolment in a provincial CGA (Certified General Accountant) program does not qualify unless the student is at an institution under this definition: VIEWS doc 2005-016373117. Nor do Professional Development courses qualify an organization: 2019-0823261E5.

A Canadian agent can issue Form TL11A on behalf of a foreign university: VIEWS doc 2007-0260931E5.

The pre-2011 13-week requirement for a foreign university in para. (b) was not satisfied for a Ph.D. student whose courses lasted only 10 weeks while he also worked on his dissertation, so he was ineligible for the Lifelong Learning Plan RRSP withdrawal in 146.02: *Haringa*, 2010 TCC 589. See also Notes to 118.5(1)(b), which had the same 13-week requirement.

Paras. (b)-(c) amended by 2016 budget bill #1, for 2017 and later tax years, to change "referred to in subsection (2)" to "referred to in the definition "qualifying student" in this subsection" (in both), and "in that subsection" to "in that definition" (para. (c)).

Definition earlier amended by 2013 budget bill #2 (effective Dec. 12, 2013), 2002-2013 technical bill, 2011 budget bill #2 (changing "13" in para. (b) to "three"); S.C. 1996, c. 11; S.C. 1994, c. 28.

Forms: TL11A: Tuition, education, and textbook amounts certificate — University outside Canada.

"qualifying educational program" means a program of not less than three consecutive weeks duration that provides that each student taking the program spend not less than 10 hours per week on courses or work in the program and, in respect of a program at an institution described in the definition "designated educational institution" (other than an institution described in subparagraph (a)(ii) of that definition), that is a program that does not consist primarily of research (unless the program leads to a diploma from a college or a Collège d'enseignement général et professionnel, or a bachelor, masters, doctoral or equivalent degree) but, in relation to any particular student, does not include a program if the student receives, from a person with whom the student is dealing at arm's length, any allowance, benefit, grant or reimbursement for expenses in respect of the program other than

(a) an amount received by the student as or on account of a scholarship, fellowship or bursary, or a prize for achievement in a field of endeavour ordinarily carried on by the student,

(b) a benefit, if any, received by the student because of a loan made to the student in accordance with the requirements of the *Canada Student Loans Act*, the *Apprentice Loans Act* or *An Act respecting financial assistance for education expenses*, R.S.Q., c. A-13.3, or because of financial assistance given to the student in accordance with the requirements of the *Canada Student Financial Assistance Act*, or

(c) an amount that is received by the student in the year under a program referred to in subparagraph 56(1)(r)(ii) or (iii), a program established under the authority of the *Department of Employment and Social Development Act* or a prescribed program;

Related Provisions: 146.1(1)"qualifying educational program" — Only para. (b) of definition applies to RESPs; 146.02(1)"qualifying educational program" — Definition for purposes of LLP (borrowing from RRSP).

Notes: For the meaning of "post-secondary", see Notes to 118.5(1)(a). The 2011 amendment excludes research that does not lead to a degree, so postdoctoral fees did not qualify for the pre-2017 education credit and postdoctoral fellowships do not qualify for the scholarship exemption (see Notes to 56(3)).

"Three consecutive weeks" means 21 days, not parts of 3 calendar weeks running from a Friday to a Monday: VIEWS doc 2006-0185081E5. However, "program" refers to the program of study rather than each course, so a series of modules can be combined to meet the tests: 2011-0403991E5. (See also Notes to 118.5(1)(b).)

Medical residency programs qualified in *Kandasamy*, 2014 TCC 47, as the residents spent more than 10 hours a week on "courses or work in the program", even though they also received salary from the hospital for the work. CRA now accepts this for "similar or identical fact situations": VIEWS docs 2014-0551931E5, 2015-059205117 (reversing 2011-0396601E5). See also Notes to 118.5(1)(a).

A distance-learning program at a foreign university qualifies: VIEWS doc 2005-015783117. Flying hours at a flight school can qualify: 2011-0402091E5. A post-doctoral fellowship (see Notes to 56(3)) did not, even before the 2011 amendment, in CRA's view, because the student is not working towards a degree: 2007-0236551E5, 2008-0275961E5, 2008-0278331M4, 2008-0301601M4, 2009-0308561E5.

Any benefit or reimbursement disqualifies the entire program: VIEWS docs 2007-0227011E5, 2008-0290421E5; 2010-038491117 (employer reimbursement for 1 course out of 4 disqualifies all 4). It is unclear whether a salary received on an internship counts as such a "benefit": 2010-0368431E5 does not say. If the student repays the entire benefit, the credit is allowed: 2011-0412502E5.

Where free tuition is offered to all, there is no "benefit"; but if only some students get free tuition, CRA's view was that this is a "benefit" and the program is not a qualifying educational program for them: docs 2005-0127341E5, 2006-0174061E5 (post-graduate medical students). However, *Pan*, 2010 TCC 147, held there is no "benefit" to domestic students getting free medical residency when foreign residents are charged.

Pre-2005 para. (b) did not apply to a teacher taking courses that enhanced her profession but were not part of her employment duties: *Reiner*, 2005 TCC 115; *Cunningham*, 2005 TCC 455. There is no longer any restriction on programs that relate to one's employment: docs 2007-0227011E5, 2007-0227621E5.

Opening words amended by 2017 budget bill #1, for 2017 and later tax years, to delete "at a post-secondary school level" before "that does not consist primarily of research". The Budget thus expanded the definition to include occupational skills courses that *are not* at the post-secondary level.

Definition amended by 2016 budget bill #1 (effective Jan. 2, 2015); 2013 and 2011 budget bills #2; SC 2005 c. 34; 2004, 2001 Budgets; SC 1994 c. 28; 1991 technical bill.

Regulations: No prescribed programs yet for para. (c).

Income Tax Folios: S1-F3-C1: Child care expense deduction [replaces IT-495R3].

"qualifying student", for a month in a taxation year, means an individual who,

(a) in the month,

(i) is enrolled in a qualifying educational program as a full-time student at a designated educational institution, or

(ii) is not described in subparagraph (i) and is enrolled at a designated educational institution in a specified educational program that provides that each student in the program spend not less than 12 hours in the month on courses in the program,

(b) if requested by the Minister, proves the enrolment by filing with the Minister a certificate in prescribed form issued by the designated educational institution and containing prescribed information,

(c) in the case of an individual who is enrolled in a program (other than a program at the post-secondary school level) at a designated educational institution described in subparagraph (a)(i) of the definition "designated educational institution" or who is enrolled in a program at a designated educational institution described in subparagraph (a)(ii) of that definition,

(i) has attained the age of 16 years before the end of the year, and

(ii) is enrolled in the program to obtain skills for, or improve the individual's skills in, an occupation; and

(d) in the case of an individual who is enrolled at a designated educational institution described in paragraph (c) of the definition "designated educational institution", is enrolled in a program that is at the post-secondary level;

Related Provisions: Reg. 203 — Institution required to file tuition certificate.

Notes: Para. (c) opening words amended (to add everything from the first "who is" through "or"), and (d) added, by 2017 budget bill #1, for 2017 and later tax years.

Definition added by 2016 budget bill #1, for 2017 and later taxation years (due to repeal of the education credit in 118.6(2); other provisions that referred to entitlement to that credit (such as 56(3), (3.1)) now refer to a qualifying student).

Forms: See under 118.6(2).

"specified educational program" means a program that would be a qualifying educational program if the definition "qualifying educational program" were read without reference to the words "that provides that each student taking the program spend not less than 10 hours per week on courses or work in the program".

Notes: A "specified educational program" is a part-time "qualifying educational program". Professional Development courses do not qualify in CRA's view, even if a student takes 12 hours in a month (118.6(1)"qualifying student"(a)(ii)): doc 2019-0823261E5.

Definition added by 1998 Budget, for 1998 and later tax years.

(2) [Repealed]

Notes: 118.6(2) provided the Education Credit for post-secondary students. Repealed by 2016 budget bill #1, for 2017 and later tax years (it was replaced with more funding for students needing tuition assistance; the tuition credit in 118.5 is still provided). For 2001-2016, read:

(2) Education credit — There may be deducted in computing an individual's tax payable under this Part for a taxation year the amount determined by the formula

$$A \times B$$

where

A   is the appropriate percentage for the year; and

B   is the total of the products obtained when

(a) $400 is multiplied by the number of months in the year during which the individual is enrolled in a qualifying educational program as a full-time student at a designated educational institution, and

(b) $120 is multiplied by the number of months in the year (other than months described in paragraph (a)), each of which is a month during which the individual is enrolled at a designated educational institution in a specified educational program that provides that each student in the program spend not less than 12 hours in the month on courses in the program,

if the enrolment is proven by filing with the Minister a certificate in prescribed form issued by the designated educational institution and containing prescribed information and, in respect of a designated educational institution described in subparagraph (a)(ii) of the definition "designated educational institution" in subsection (1), the individual has attained the age of 16 years before the end of the year and is enrolled in the program to obtain skills for, or improve the individual's skills in, an occupation.

The credit was actually higher than shown, due to the textbook credit in 118.6(2.1). The dollar amounts remained the same from 2001, not indexed for inflation.

The "appropriate percentage" was 15% from 2007-16 (see 117(2)(a) and 248(1)). Note that the credit applied to months "during" which the student was enrolled; "month" is defined in *Interpretation Act* 35(1) to mean a calendar month. If a student was enrolled

from August 31 to December 2, that was 5 months. "Enrolment" could presumably be effective before classes start.

For discussion of the credit see Income Tax Folio S1-F2-C1, VIEWS doc 2007-0242651E5. Tuition reimbursement from the parent's employer (whether falling under 6(1)(a) or 56(1)(n)) does not affect the student's entitlement to the credit: 2009-0307721E5, 2013-0484631E5.

Whether enrolment is "full-time": see Notes to 118.5(1)(b). English or French second-language training can qualify if required for employment: VIEWS doc 2009-031845117. See also 2015-0568921E5 (a part-time course designed to be 12 months still counts as 12 for a student who finishes sooner).

CRA's view is that where the term was extended due to the 2012 Quebec student strike, the original calendar determines the number of months: 2013-0477151E5.

There is no legal obligation on the institution to issue a Form T2202A. If the institution has a dispute with a student over fees, it would be "inappropriate" to withhold the form: VIEWS doc 2005-0119471E5. Even if a student's tuition is all covered by funding sources, the student should get a T2202A: 2010-0382261E5. Not having the form is fatal to this credit as well as to the scholarship exemption in excess of $500 under 56(3): *Zhang*, 2010 TCC 592.

Some provinces still offer an education credit or other incentives, e.g. Saskatchewan Graduate Retention Program. See M. Lori Adams, "Tax Incentives for Post-Secondary Graduates", 5 *Provincial Tax News* (CCH) 2-3 (Oct. 2011).

118.6(2) earlier amended by 2000 Budget (for 2001 and later taxation years), 1998, 1997, 1996 and 1992 Budgets, 1991 technical bill.

(2.1) [Repealed]

Notes: 118.6(2.1) provided the Textbook Credit. Introduced in the 2006 Budget, it was allegedly for textbooks but did not require any proof of purchase. It could have been enacted by increasing the $400 and $120 amounts in 118.6(2) to $465 and $140, but the Conservatives wanted to keep it separate for political reasons, so that it looked like a different or "new" credit. Repealed by 2016 budget bill #1 for 2017 and later tax years (along with 118.6(2)). For 2006-2016, read:

(2.1) Post-secondary textbook credit — If an amount may be deducted under subsection (2) in computing the individual's tax payable for a taxation year, there may be deducted in computing the individual's tax payable under this Part for the year the amount determined by the formula

$$A \times B$$

where

A   is the appropriate percentage for the year; and

B   is the total of the products obtained when

(a) $65 is multiplied by the number of months referred to in paragraph (a) of the description of B in subsection (2), and

(b) $20 is multiplied by the number of months referred to in paragraph (b) of that description.

118.6(2.1) added by 2006 budget bill #2, for 2006 and later taxation years.

(3) Students eligible for the disability tax credit — For the purposes of subparagraph (a)(i) of the definition "qualifying student" in subsection (1), the reference to "full-time student" is to be read as "student" if

(a) an amount may be deducted under section 118.3 in respect of the individual for the year; or

(b) the individual has in the year a mental or physical impairment the effects of which on the individual have been certified in writing, to be such that the individual cannot reasonably be expected to be enrolled as a full-time student while so impaired, by a medical doctor, a nurse practitioner or, where the impairment is

(i) an impairment of sight, by a medical doctor, a nurse practitioner or an optometrist,

(i.1) a speech impairment, by a medical doctor, a nurse practitioner or a speech-language pathologist,

(ii) a hearing impairment, by a medical doctor, a nurse practitioner or an audiologist,

(iii) an impairment with respect to the individual's ability in feeding or dressing themself, by a medical doctor, a nurse practitioner or an occupational therapist,

(iii.1) an impairment with respect to the individual's ability in walking, by a medical doctor, a nurse practitioner, an occupational therapist or a physiotherapist, or

(iv) an impairment with respect to the individual's ability in mental functions necessary for everyday life (within the meaning assigned by paragraph 118.4(1)(c.1)), by a medical doctor, a nurse practitioner or a psychologist.

Related Provisions: 64(a)A(ii)(I) — Disability supports deduction for talking textbooks; 146.02(1)"full-time student" — Student eligible under 118.6(3) qualifies as full-time student for LLP (loan from RRSP to fund education); 146.1(2)(g.1)(i)(B) — Disabled student may receive RESP funds when enrolled part-time; Reg. 5700(w) — Medical expense credit for talking textbooks.

Notes: Before 2017, 118.6(3) allowed disabled students the full education and textbook credits (118.6(2), (2.1)) even if they were not enrolled on a full-time basis. Now it continues to treat disabled part-time students as though they were full-time, for purposes of other provisions.

118.6(3)(b) amended by 2017 budget bill #2 to add "a nurse practitioner" (7 places), for certifications made after Sept. 7, 2017.

Opening words amended by 2016 budget bill #1 for 2017 and later tax years. For earlier years, read:

> (3) In calculating the amount deductible under subsection (2) or (2.1), the reference in subsection (2) to "full-time student" is to be read as "student" if

118.6(3) earlier amended by 2006 budget bill #2 (for 2006 and later tax years), 2003 and 1998 Budgets, 1992 Budget/technical bill.

Definitions [s. 118.6]: "amount", "appropriate percentage" — 248(1); "arm's length" — 251(1); "audiologist" — 118.4(2); "Canada" — 255, *Interpretation Act* 35(1); "designated educational institution" — 118.6(1); "employment", "individual" — 248(1); "Lieutenant Governor in Council" — *Interpretation Act* 35(1); "medical doctor" — 118.4(2); "Minister" — 248(1); "month" — *Interpretation Act* 35(1); "nurse practitioner", "occupational therapist" — 118.4(2); "office" — 248(1); "optometrist" — 118.4(2); "person" — 248(1); "physiotherapist" — 118.4(2); "prescribed" — 248(1); "province" — *Interpretation Act* 35(1); "psychologist" — 118.4(2); "qualifying educational program", "qualifying student", "specified educational program" — 118.6(1); "speech-language pathologist" — 118.4(2); "tax payable" — 248(2); "taxation year" — 249; "United States" — *Interpretation Act* 35(1); "writing" — *Interpretation Act* 35(1).

Income Tax Folios [s. 118.6]: S1-F2-C1: Education and textbook tax credits [replaces IT-515R2]; S1-F2-C2: Tuition tax credit [replaces IT-516R2].

Interpretation Bulletins [s. 118.6]: IT-171R2: Non-resident individuals — computation of taxable income earned in Canada and non-refundable tax credits (cancelled); IT-326R3: Returns of deceased persons as "another person"; IT-393R2: Election re tax on rents and timber royalties — non-residents.

Information Circulars [s. 118.6]: 07-1R1: Taxpayer relief provisions.

118.61 (1) Unused tuition, textbook and education tax credits — In this section, an individual's unused tuition, textbook and education tax credits at the end of a taxation year is the amount determined by the formula

$$A + (B - C) - (D + E)$$

where

A is the amount determined under this subsection in respect of the individual at the end of the preceding taxation year;

B is the total of all amounts each of which may be deducted under section 118.5 in computing the individual's tax payable under this Part for the year;

C is the lesser of the value of B and the amount that would be the individual's tax payable under this Part for the year if no amount were deductible under this Division (other than an amount deductible under this section and any of sections 118 to 118.07, 118.3 and 118.7);

D is the amount that the individual may deduct under subsection (2) for the year; and

E is the tuition tax credit transferred for the year by the individual to the individual's spouse, common-law partner, parent or grandparent.

Related Provisions: 118.81 — Tuition, textbook and education credits transferred; 257 — Formula cannot calculate to less than zero; 128(2)(g)(ii) — Effect of bankruptcy on unused credits.

Notes: A student attending school outside Canada but remaining Canadian resident can obtain the credit and carry it forward indefinitely; CRA's T1 Schedule 11 may be incorrect, and the legislation governs: *Gallant*, 2012 TCC 119. A non-resident (NR) who becomes resident in Canada cannot use tuition paid while NR: *Marino*, 2020 TCC 50 (under appeal to FCA); *Cristofaro*, 2021 QCCA 1025 (parallel Quebec rule). A student who becomes non-resident with no income subject to Canadian tax is not entitled to the credit: VIEWS doc 2002-0150305; but previous carryforward can be used if they resume Canadian residency: 2018-0784491E5. The formula grinds down the car-

ryforward for any credit available even if the credit was not taken (e.g. the student claims foreign tax credits instead), so there is no point not claiming the credit if it can be claimed: 2004-0090261I7, 2011-0416691E5.

The formula works so that a student with significant dividend income that is absorbed by the dividend tax credit (s. 121) has no credit under 118.61. In *Zhang*, 2017 TCC 258, such dividend income wiped out the carryforward for later years, since "may deduct" in D means "is permitted to deduct", not "did deduct". (The same interpretation applied in another context in *David M. Sherman*, 1999 CarswellNat 2296 (TCC).)

The credit cannot be carried forward into a year of bankruptcy: 128(2)(f)(iv)(C), VIEWS doc 2010-0379861E5 (and see *Delisle*, 2005 CarswellNat 6457 (TCC)).

B amended to delete reference to 118.6, and E amended to change "tuition, textbook and education tax credits" to "tuition tax credit", by 2016 budget bill #1, for 2017 and later tax years. 118.61(1) earlier amended by 2011 budget bill #2 (for 2011 and later tax years), 2009 and 2006 budget bills #2, 2006 budget bill #1, 2001 technical bill, 2000 same-sex partners bill.

(2) Deduction of carryforward — For the purpose of computing an individual's tax payable under this Part for a taxation year, there may be deducted the lesser of

(a) the amount determined under subsection (1) in respect of the individual at the end of the preceding taxation year, and

(b) the amount that would be the individual's tax payable under this Part for the year if no amount were deductible under this Division (other than an amount deductible under this section and any of sections 118 to 118.07, 118.3 and 118.7).

Related Provisions: 118.61(4) — Where credit rate changes from year to year; 118.91 — Individual resident in Canada for part of the year; 118.92 — Ordering of credits; 128(2)(e), 128(2)(f)(iv) — On bankruptcy, only trustee can claim carryforward.

Notes: 118.61(2) amended by 2011 budget bill #2 (for 2011 and later tax years), 2009 budget bill #2, 2006 budget bills #1 and 2, 2001 technical bill.

Forms: T1 General return, Sched. 11: Federal tuition, education, and textbook amounts.

(3) [Repealed]

Notes: 118.61(3) repealed by 2006 budget bill #2, effective for 2006 and later taxation years. It was a transitional rule to account for the change in the "appropriate percentage" (bottom tax rate in 117(2)) from 17% to 16% as of 2001. It was added by 2000 Budget, effective for 2001 and later taxation years.

(4) Change of appropriate percentage — For the purpose of determining the amount that may be deducted under subsection (2) in computing an individual's tax payable for a taxation year, in circumstances where the appropriate percentage for the taxation year is different from the appropriate percentage for the preceding taxation year, the individual's unused tuition, textbook and education tax credits at the end of the preceding taxation year is deemed to be the amount determined by the formula

$$A/B \times C$$

where

A is the appropriate percentage for the current taxation year;

B is the appropriate percentage for the preceding taxation year; and

C is the amount that would be the individual's unused tuition, textbook and education tax credits at the end of the preceding taxation year if this section were read without reference to this subsection.

Notes: 118.61(4) accommodates changes in the lowest tax bracket rate (which is used for personal credits) from 16% (2001-04) to 15% (2005), 15.25% (2006) and 15% (2007-). See 117(2)(a) and 248(1)"appropriate percentage".

Opening words amended by 2016 budget bill #1, for 2017 and later taxation years, to delete "or 118.6(2.1)" (after "subsection (2)").

118.61(4) added by 2006 Budget and amended by 2006 budget bill #2, effective for 2005 and later taxation years.

Notes [s. 118.61]: 118.61 added by 1997 Budget, effective for 1997 and later taxation years.

Definitions [s. 118.61]: "amount", "appropriate percentage", "common-law partner" — 248(1); "grandparent" — 252(2)(d); "individual" — 248(1); "parent" — 252(2)(a); "taxation year" — 249; "tuition, textbook and education tax credits transferred" — 118.81; "unused tuition, textbook and education tax credits" — 118.61(1).

Income Tax Folios [s. 118.61]: S1-F2-C1: Education and textbook tax credits [replaces IT-515R2]; S1-F2-C2: Tuition tax credit [replaces IT-516R2].

118.62 Credit for interest on student loan — For the purpose of computing an individual's tax payable under this Part for a taxation year, there may be deducted the amount determined by the formula

$$A \times B$$

where

A is the appropriate percentage for the year; and

B is the total of all amounts (other than any amount paid on account of or in satisfaction of a judgement) each of which is an amount of interest paid in the year (or in any of the five preceding taxation years that are after 1997, to the extent that it was not included in computing a deduction under this section for any other taxation year) by the individual or a person related to the individual on a loan made to, or other amount owing by, the individual under the *Canada Student Loans Act*, the *Canada Student Financial Assistance Act*, the *Apprentice Loans Act* or a law of a province governing the granting of financial assistance to students at the post-secondary school level.

Enacted and Proposed Non-Tax Change — COVID-19 — Student loans — no interest March 30-Sept 2020 and April 2021-March 2022

Dept. of Finance Backgrounder, March 18, 2020: *Canada's COVID-19 Economic Response Plan: Support for Canadians and Businesses*

Income Support for Individuals Who Need It Most

To ensure that certain groups who may be vulnerable to the impacts of COVID-19 have the support they need, the Government is proposing targeted help by: . . .

- Placing a six-month interest-free moratorium on the repayment of Canada Student Loans for all individuals currently in the process of repaying these loans.

Dept. of Finance news release, Dec. 2, 2020: *Government introduces legislation to provide critical support to Canadians and businesses during the pandemic*

. . .

Bill C-14 includes measures that would: . . .

- ease the financial burden of student debt for up to 1.4 million Canadians by eliminating the interest on repayment of the federal portion of the Canada Student Loans and Canada Apprentice Loans for one year (2021-22);

Federal Budget, Chapter 3, April 19, 2021: *Waiving Interest on Student Loans for an Additional Year*

To ensure that the cost of post-secondary education in Canada remains predictable and affordable for everyone during the economic recovery: The government proposes to introduce legislation that would extend the waiver of interest accrual on Canada Student Loans and Canada Apprentice Loans until March 31, 2023. This change has an estimated cost of $392.7 million in 2022-23.

This action would mean savings for approximately 1.5 million Canadians repaying student loans, the majority of whom are women.

Notes: The relief announced in March 2020 (no interest March 30 to Sept. 30, 2020) was enacted by 2020 COVID bill #1 in *Canada Student Loans Act* s. 11.2, *Canada Student Financial Assistance Act* s. 9.3 and *Apprentice Loans Act* s. 8.1. Interest relief from April 1, 2021 to March 30, 2022 was enacted by 2021 COVID bill #1, in *CSLA* s. 11.3, *CSFAA* s. 9.4 and *ALA* s. 8.2.

Related Provisions: 20(1)(c) — Interest deductible when money borrowed to earn income; 118.91 — Individual resident in Canada for part of the year; 118.92 — Ordering of credits; 118.93 — Credits in separate returns; 118.94 — Credit restriction for non-resident individual; 118.95(a) — Application in year individual becomes bankrupt.

Notes: 118.62 provides a credit for interest paid on a student loan. The federal credit is 15% of the interest paid in the year or in any of the 5 prior years, to the extent it was not already counted. (Including a parallel provincial credit, the total credit is about 21%.) The interest must have been paid under one of the indicated federal or provincial student-loan programs, and not under a judgment (for default in payment); "judgment" means a court judgment, so payments to a collection agency on a loan in collection status still qualify: VIEWS doc 2010-0376461I7. Forgiven interest and interest accrued but not paid do not qualify. However, capitalization of unpaid interest may constitute "payment" if there is a novation of the loan, though as a new loan, later interest payments would not qualify: 2018-0757501E5 [Cheaib, "Novation", 11(2) *Canadian Tax Focus* (ctf.ca) 10 (May 2021)]. The fact a loan is used for student education is not enough, if it is not made under one of the specified programs: *Renz*, [2003] 1 C.T.C. 2307 (TCC); *Wilkins*, 2009 TCC 61; *Sandhu*, 2010 TCC 223; *Mueller*, 2013 TCC 3.

For the meaning of "post-secondary", see Notes to 118.5(1)(a).

A student loan that is refinanced to obtain a better interest rate does not qualify if the new loan is not under the *Canada Student Loans Act*: *Vilenski*, 2003 TCC 418. However, a loan qualified where it was made directly by the university to a student who had been rejected by the provincial student assistance plan: *Napier*, 2007 TCC 14.

Only the student to whom the student loan was made can claim the credit; the words "a person related to the individual" do not allow the related person (such as a spouse) to make the claim on their own return: *Lazarescu-King*, 2003 TCC 806.

Overpaid interest recovered by class action lawsuit is not taxable: VIEWS doc 2008-0285311C6.

A bank loan under the *Canada Student Loans Act* that is not repaid can be offset by the CRA against income tax refunds. See IC 13-2 and *Hérold*, 2013 FCA 19.

Reference to *Apprentice Loans Act* added by 2014 budget bill #2, effective Jan. 2, 2015 (in-force date of 2014 budget bill #1, Part 6, Div. 30, per P.C. 2014-1242).

118.62 added by 1998 Budget, effective for 1998 and later taxation years.

Definitions [s. 118.62]: "amount", "appropriate percentage" — 248(1); "individual", "person" — 248(1); "province" — *Interpretation Act* 35(1); "related" — 251(2)–(6); "taxation year" — 249.

Information Circulars: 13-2R1: Government programs collection policies.

118.7 Credit for EI and QPIP premiums and CPP contributions — For the purpose of computing the tax payable under this Part by an individual for a taxation year, there may be deducted the amount determined by the formula

$$A \times B$$

where

A is the appropriate percentage for the year; and

B is the total of

(a) the total of all amounts each of which is an amount payable by the individual as an employee's premium or a self-employment premium for the year under the *Employment Insurance Act*, not exceeding the maximum amount of such premiums payable by the individual for the year under that Act,

(a.1) the total of all amounts each of which is an amount payable by the individual as an employee's premium for the year under the *Act respecting parental insurance*, R.S.Q., c. A-29.011, not exceeding the maximum amount of such premiums payable by the individual for the year under that Act,

(a.2) the amount, if any, by which the total of all amounts each of which is an amount payable by the individual in respect of self-employed earnings for the year as a premium under the *Act respecting parental insurance*, R.S.Q., c. A-29.011, (not exceeding the maximum amount of such premiums payable by the individual for the year under that Act) exceeds the amount deductible under paragraph 60(g) in computing the individual's income for the year,

(b) the total of all amounts each of which is an amount payable by the individual for the year as an employee's contribution under subsection 8(1) of the *Canada Pension Plan* or as a like contribution under a "provincial pension plan", as defined in section 3 of that Act, not exceeding the maximum amount of such contributions payable by the individual for the year under the plan, and

(c) the amount by which

(i) the total of all amounts each of which is an amount payable by the individual in respect of self-employed earnings for the year as a contribution under the *Canada Pension Plan* or under a provincial pension plan within the meaning assigned by section 3 of that Act (not exceeding the maximum amount of such contributions payable by the individual for the year under the plan)

exceeds

(ii) the amount deductible under paragraph 60(e) in computing the individual's income for the year.

Related Provisions: 56(1)(a) — CPP, EI and QPIP benefits taxable; 60(e) — Deduction for other half of CPP contributions; 60(g) — Deduction for portion of QPIP contributions; 118.91 — Individual resident in Canada for part of the year; 118.92 — Ordering of credits; 118.93 — Credits in separate returns; 118.94 — Application to non-resident individual; 118.95(a) — Application in year individual becomes bankrupt.

Notes: For information about the *Canada Pension Plan*, see Notes to 56(1)(a).

The "appropriate percentage" (248(1)) is 15%, leading to a credit worth about 21% including a parallel provincial credit. See Notes to 118(1)B opening words.

For an *employed* person, this credit is for CPP contributions paid at the 2018 level plus inflation indexing; the extra amounts payable starting 2019 due to CPP enhancements are eligible for full 60(e.1) deduction instead. (Deduction is worth more than a credit for those in a higher bracket than 15%; see table at end of 117.1.)

For a *self-employed* person, this credit is for half of CPP contributions paid at the 2018 level plus inflation indexing. The other half, plus all extra amounts payable starting 2019, are eligible for full deduction instead: 60(e).

Self-employed CPP contributions are calculated and paid on the T1 General return (Schedule 8 and Line 42100 [former 421]). Taxpayers with sufficient pensionable income require both employer-paid and employee-paid contributions while age 60-65 even if they are receiving CPP benefits; from 65-70 they can elect to stop contributing (Form CPT30); from age 70 they do not contribute. See canada.ca/cpp.

Where CPP and EI are withheld from pay in error, and the payor later determines that the payment was not employment income (and amends the T4), CRA may reassess to deny the 118.7 credit for the CPP and EI. The CPP/EI withheld in error can be refunded by the payor filing a PD24, or the taxpayer can file a T1-Adj adjustment request within the time limits of 4 years (*CPP* s. 38) or 3 years (*EI Act* s. 96): VIEWS doc 2012-0462421E5.

Contributions to social security systems in other countries may qualify for credit due to Canada's tax treaties. See Form RC269 and *Guidance for Taxpayers Requesting Tax Treaty Relief for Cross-Border Pension Contributions* (tinyurl.com/cross-border-pens), re Chile, Colombia, Ecuador, Estonia, Finland, France, Germany [also VIEWS doc 2012-0439441E5], Greece, Ireland, Italy, Latvia, Lithuania, Netherlands, Slovenia, South Africa, Sweden, Switzerland, UK and Venezuela. For the US, see Canada-US tax treaty Art. XXIV:2(a)(ii) and Information Circular 84-6.

EI Act Part VII.1 allows self-employed persons to opt into the EI system for certain purposes such as maternity benefits (but once in, they cannot leave); see Drache, "Legislation Proposed to Grant Partial EI Coverage for Self-Employed", xxxi(23) *The Canadian Taxpayer [TCT]* (Carswell) 177-78 (Nov. 24, 2009). The reference to "a self-employment premium" in 118.7:B(a) allows a credit for such premiums. See also VIEWS doc 2010-0365421E5 (partner can show no income for purposes of EI self-employed benefits when on maternity leave). Part VII.1 is little used: Drache, "Intuition Should Lose to Facts in Policy Making", xxxvii(15) *TCT* 113-115 (July 31, 2015). In 2020, all self-employed persons are eligible for the Canada Emergency Response Benefit (for COVID-19); the benefit is taxable under 56(1)(a)(iv).

118.7:B(b) amended by 2016 budget bill #2, effective 2019, to add "subsection 8(1) of" and "as a like contribution", to cap the credit at 2018 levels plus indexing (the non-inflation increases in CPP contributions are deductible under 60(e) and (e.1)).

118.7 amended by 2002-2013 technical bill (for 2010 and later years), 2000 Budget.

Proposed **118.71** was in a 2010 Bloc Québécois private member's bill (C-288) that would have enacted a credit for new graduates settling in a "designated region". It passed the (minority-government) House of Commons but not the Senate, and will not likely be reintroduced.

Definitions [s. 118.7]: "amount", "appropriate percentage", "employee", "individual" — 248(1); "provincial pension plan" — *Canada Pension Plan* s. 3; "tax payable" — 248(2); "taxation year" — 249.

Income Tax Folios: S1-F1-C2: Disability tax credit [replaces IT-519R2]; S1-F2-C2: Tuition tax credit [replaces IT-516R2].

Interpretation Bulletins: IT-171R2: Non-resident individuals — computation of taxable income earned in Canada and non-refundable tax credits (cancelled); IT-326R3: Returns of deceased persons as "another person"; IT-393R2: Election re tax on rents and timber royalties — non-residents.

Information Circulars: 07-1R1: Taxpayer relief provisions.

Forms: RC269: Employee contributions to a foreign pension plan or social security arrangement for 2017 — non-United States plans or arrangements; T1 General return, Line 42100 [former 421]; T1 General, Sched. 8: Canada Pension Plan contributions and overpayment for 2019.

118.8 Transfer of unused credits to spouse [or common-law partner]

— For the purpose of computing the tax payable under this Part for a taxation year by an individual who, at any time in the year, is a married person or a person who is in a common-law partnership (other than an individual who, by reason of a breakdown of their marriage or common-law partnership, is living separate and apart from the individual's spouse or common-law partner at the end of the year and for a period of 90 days commencing in the year), there may be deducted an amount determined by the formula

$$A + B - C$$

where

A is the tuition tax credit transferred for the year by the spouse or common-law partner to the individual;

B is the total of all amounts each of which is deductible under subsection 118(1), because of paragraph (b.1) of the description of

B in that subsection, or subsection 118(2) or (3) or 118.3(1) in computing the spouse's or common-law partner's tax payable under this Part for the year; and

C is the amount, if any, by which

(a) the amount that would be the spouse's or common-law partner's tax payable under this Part for the year if no amount were deductible under this Division (other than an amount deductible under subsection 118(1) because of paragraph (c) of the description of B in that subsection, under subsection 118(10) or under any of sections 118.01 to 118.07, 118.3, 118.61 and 118.7)

exceeds

(b) the lesser of

(i) the total of all amounts that may be deducted under section 118.5 in computing the spouse's or common-law partner's tax payable under this Part for the year, and

(ii) the amount that would be the spouse's or common-law partner's tax payable under this Part for the year if no amount were deductible under this Division (other than an amount deductible under any of sections 118 to 118.07, 118.3, 118.61 and 118.7).

Related Provisions: 117(1) — Tax payable under this Part; 118.3(2) — Disability credit claim for disabled dependant; 118.3(4) — Additional information requested by CRA; 118.61(2) — Carryforward of unused credits; 118.91 — Individual resident in Canada for part of the year; 118.92 — Ordering of credits; 118.93 — Credits in separate returns; 118.94 — Credit restriction for non-resident individual; 118.95(b) — Application in year individual becomes bankrupt; 257 — Formula cannot calculate to less than zero.

Notes: *"Separate and apart" (S&A)*: A couple can live S&A under the same roof, if they live separate lives (social, communication, sexual, meals, not presenting themselves as a couple): *Longchamps*, [1986] 2 C.T.C. 2231 (TCC); *Kelner*, 1995 CarswellNat 1207 (TCC); *Rangwala*, [2000] 4 C.T.C. 2430 (TCC); *Sigouin*, 2001 CarswellNat 2683 (TCC); *Roby*, 2001 CarswellNat 2756 (TCC); *Uwasomba*, 2002 CarswellNat 3737 (TCC) (husband living in the basement was not "under the same roof"); *Benson*, 2003 CarswellNat 147 (TCC); *Bellavance*, 2004 TCC 5; *Chibuluzo*, 2005 TCC 195; *Bruno*, 2007 TCC 360; *Aukstinaitis*, 2008 TCC 104; *Perron*, 2010 TCC 547; *Scott*, 2015 TCC 9; *JB*, 2018 QCCQ 4200 (Quebec law); VIEWS docs 9902035, 9933028, 2010-0364841E5, 2010-0377532M4 (lists factors CRA considers), 2011-0406701E5 (see also Notes to 248(1)"common-law partner"). However, the relationship must have broken down: 2008-0278401E5; a husband who had his own home was not S&A from his disabled wife, whom he came to see and care for almost daily for most of the day: *Kara*, 2009 TCC 82. Similarly, in *Sookochoff*, 2020 TCC 131, a married couple could not live together as their respective children did not get along, but their relationship had not broken down. In *Grau*, 2009 TCC 60, false claims of being S&A, disbelieved by the Court, led to gross negligence penalties.

CRA says a non-resident is not a "taxpayer" eligible for the 118.3 disability credit, and so cannot transfer the credit to a resident spouse: doc 2019-0834041I7 (neither 118.3 nor 118.8 uses "taxpayer", but this is consistent with *Marino*, 2020 TCC 50 (under appeal to FCA): see 248(1)"taxpayer" Notes).

118.8:A amended by 2016 budget bill #1, for 2017 and later tax years, to change "tuition, textbook and education tax credits" to "tuition tax credit", and C(b)(i) amended to delete "or 118.6" (after 118.5).

C(a) and (b)(ii) both amended by 2014 budget bill #2, for 2014 and later taxation years, to change "to 118.06" to "to 118.07".

118.8 earlier amended by 2011 budget bill #2 (for 2011 and later years), 2009 Budget bill, 2007 budget bill #1, 2006 budget bill #2, 2000 same-sex partners bill, 1999, 1998, 1997 and 1996 Budgets and 1992 Budget/technical bill.

Definitions [s. 118.8]: "amount", "common-law partner", "common-law partnership", "individual" — 248(1); "tax payable" — 248(2); "taxation year" — 249; "tuition, textbook and education tax credits transferred" — 118.81.

Income Tax Folios: S1-F1-C1: Medical expense tax credit [replaces IT-519R2]; S1-F1-C2: Disability tax credit [replaces IT-519R2]; S1-F2-C1: Education and textbook tax credits [replaces IT-515R2]; S1-F2-C2: Tuition tax credit [replaces IT-516R2].

Interpretation Bulletins: IT-171R2: Non-resident individuals — computation of taxable income earned in Canada and non-refundable tax credits (cancelled); IT-326R3: Returns of deceased persons as "another person"; IT-393R2: Election re tax on rents and timber royalties — non-residents; IT-470R: Employees' fringe benefits; IT-513R: Personal tax credits; IT-517R: Pension tax credit (cancelled).

Forms: T1 Sched. 2: Federal amounts transferred from your spouse or common-law partner.

118.81 Tuition tax credit transferred — In this Subdivision, the tuition tax credit transferred for a taxation year by a person to an individual is the lesser of

(a) the amount determined by the formula

$$A - B$$

where

A is the lesser of

(i) the total of all amounts that may be deducted under section 118.5 in computing the person's tax payable under this Part for the year, and

(ii) the amount determined by the formula

$$C \times D$$

where

C is the appropriate percentage for the taxation year, and

D is $5,000.

B is the amount that would be the person's tax payable under this Part for the year if no amount were deductible under this Division (other than an amount deductible under any of sections 118 to 118.07, 118.3, 118.61 and 118.7), and

(b) the amount for the year that the person designates in writing for the purpose of section 118.8 or 118.9.

Related Provisions: 118.61(2) — Carryforward of unused credits; 257 — Formula cannot calculate to less than zero.

Notes: No transfer of tuition/education credits is possible if the student has substantial dividend income, because the dividend tax credit is not subtracted under B. See TI Schedule 11.

Unused credits carried forward from previous years cannot be transferred to a parent or grandparent: *Maou*, 2005 TCC 435. For an example of a claim for a sister's credits see VIEWS doc 2006-0193891I7.

118.81 opening words amended to change "tuition, textbook and education tax credits" to "tuition tax credit" and 118.81(a)A(i) amended to delete "or 118.6" (after 118.05) by 2016 budget bill #1, for 2017 and later taxation years.

118.81(a)B amended by 2011 budget bill #2, for 2011 and later taxation years, to change "118 to 118.05" to "118 to 118.06", and by 2014 budget bill #1, for 2014 and later years, to change to "118 to 118.07".

118.81(a)B amended to to change "118, 118.01, 118.02, 118.03" to "118 to 118.05" by 2009 budget bill #2, effective for 2009 and later taxation years.

118.1 earlier amended by 2006 Budget bills (last change effective 2006 and later taxation years), 2000 and 1997 Budgets.

Definitions [s. 118.81]: "amount", "appropriate percentage", "individual", "person" — 248(1); "tax payable" — 248(2); "taxation year" — 249; "writing" — *Interpretation Act* 35(1).

Income Tax Folios: S1-F2-C2: Tuition tax credit [replaces IT-516R2].

118.9 Transfer to parent or grandparent — If for a taxation year a parent or grandparent of an individual (other than an individual in respect of whom the individual's spouse or common-law partner deducts an amount under section 118 or 118.8 for the year) is the only person designated in writing by the individual for the year for the purpose of this section, there may be deducted in computing the tax payable under this Part for the year by the parent or grandparent, as the case may be, the tuition tax credit transferred for the year by the individual to the parent or grandparent, as the case may be.

Notes [s. 118.9]: A student is not required to be resident or deemed resident in Canada to transfer the tuition credit to the parent, but unless the student is a "taxpayer" with Canadian-source income, there is no credit available to be transferred: VIEWS docs 2002-0122195, 2003-0026827. In *Cristofaro*, 2021 QCCA 1025 (on the parallel Quebec rule), an Ontario taxpayer paying QC tax (on national partnership income allocated to him) was not allowed a credit for his non-resident daughter's tuition paid in Scotland. Similarly, see 118.61(1) Notes re *Marino*. For provincial tax credit, the province may require the tuition to have been paid while resident in the province (e.g., Ontario *Taxation Act, 2007* s. 9(14.1), for tuition paid before the Ont. tuition credit was eliminated).

Unused credits carried forward from previous years cannot be transferred to a parent or grandparent: *Maou*, 2005 TCC 435.

118.9 amended to change "tuition, textbook and education tax credits" to "tuition tax credit" by 2016 budget bill #1, for 2017 and later taxation years.

118.9 earlier amended by 2006 budget bill #2 (for 2006 and later taxation years), 2000 same-sex partners bill, 1997 and 1996 Budgets, 1992 Budget/technical bill.

Definitions [s. 118.9]: "amount", "common-law partner" — 248(1); "grandparent" — 252(2)(d); "individual", "Minister" — 248(1); "parent" — 252(2)(a); "prescribed" — 248(1); "tax payable" — 248(2); "taxation year" — 249; "tuition, textbook and education tax credits transferred" — 118.81; "writing" — *Interpretation Act* 35(1).

Income Tax Folios [s. 118.9]: S1-F2-C1: Education and textbook tax credits [replaces IT-515R2]; S1-F2-C2: Tuition tax credit [replaces IT-516R2].

Interpretation Bulletins [s. 118.9]: IT-171R2: Non-resident individuals — computation of taxable income earned in Canada and non-refundable tax credits (cancelled); IT-326R3: Returns of deceased persons as "another person"; IT-393R2: Election re tax on rents and timber royalties — non-residents; IT-470R: Employees' fringe benefits.

118.91 Part-year residents — Notwithstanding sections 118 to 118.9, where an individual is resident in Canada throughout part of a taxation year and throughout another part of the year is non-resident, for the purpose of computing the individual's tax payable under this Part for the year,

(a) the amount deductible for the year under each such provision in respect of the part of the year that is not included in the period or periods referred to in paragraph (b) shall be computed as though such part were the whole taxation year; and

(b) the individual shall be allowed only

(i) such of the deductions permitted under subsections 118(3) and (10) and sections 118.01 to 118.2, 118.5, 118.62 and 118.7 as can reasonably be considered wholly applicable to the period or periods in the year throughout which the individual is resident in Canada, computed as though that period or those periods were the whole taxation year, and

(ii) such part of the deductions permitted under sections 118 (other than subsections 118(3) and (10)), 118.3, 118.8 and 118.9 as can reasonably be considered applicable to the period or periods in the year throughout which the individual is resident in Canada, computed as though that period or those periods were the whole taxation year,

except that the amount deductible for the year by the individual under each such provision shall not exceed the amount that would have been deductible under that provision had the individual been resident in Canada throughout the year.

Related Provisions: 114 — Individual resident in Canada during only part of year; 117(1) — Tax payable under this Part; 217(c) — Election respecting certain payments.

Notes: 118.91(b)(i) amended by 2016 budget bill #1, for 2017 and later taxation years, to delete reference to 118.6(2.1) and 118.6.

118.91(b)(i) and (ii) amended by 2009 budget bill #2, effective for 2009 and later taxation years to add reference to 118.04-118.05 in subpara. (i) and to 118(10) in subpara. (ii), and to add "to the period ... whole taxation year" to both.

118.91 earlier amended by 2006 Budget bills (last change effective for 2006 and later taxation years), 1998 Budget, 1993 and 1991 technical bills.

Definitions [s. 118.91]: "amount" — 248(1); "Canada" — 255; "carrying on business" — 253; "employed", "individual", "non-resident" — 248(1); "resident in Canada" — 250; "tax payable" — 248(2); "taxation year" — 249; "taxpayer" — 248(1).

118.92 Ordering of credits — In computing an individual's tax payable under this Part, the following provisions shall be applied in the following order: subsections 118(1) and (2), section 118.7, subsections 118(3) and (10) and sections 118.01, 118.02, 118.04, 118.041, 118.05, 118.06, 118.07, 118.3, 118.61, 118.5, 118.9, 118.8, 118.2, 118.1, 118.62 and 121.

Related Provisions: 117(1) — Tax payable under this Part.

Notes: For examples of 118.92 applying, see VIEWS docs 2009-0309211E5, 2011-0410641E5.

118.92 means that the various personal credits must be used up before claiming the dividend tax credit: *Zhang*, 2017 TCC 258, para. 12.

118.92 amended by 2019 budget bill #1 to add reference to 118.02 (credit for digital news subscriptions), effective 2020; by 2017 budget bill #1 to delete reference to 118.02 (after 118.01), effective 2018; by 2016 budget bill #1, for 2017 and later taxation years, to delete reference to 118.031 (after 118.02) and 118.6 (after 118.5).

118.92 amended by 2016 budget bill #1 to delete reference to 119.1 for 2016 and later taxation years; by 2015 Budget bill to add 118.041 for 2016 and later years and delete 118.03 for 2015 and later years; by 2015 Budget bill to add 119.1 for 2014 and later years [and preserving deletion of 118.03 as only from 2015]; by 2014 budget bill #1 to add 118.07 for 2014 and later years. Earlier amended by 2011 and 2009 budget bills #2, 2006 Budget bill, 1998 and 1997 Budgets.

Definitions [s. 118.92]: "individual" — 248(1); "tax payable" — 248(2).

Interpretation Bulletins: IT-523: Order of provisions applicable in computing an individual's taxable income and tax payable.

118.93 Credits in separate returns

118.93 Credits in separate returns — If a separate return of income with respect to a taxpayer is filed under subsection 70(2), 104(23) or 150(4) for a particular period and another return of income under this Part with respect to the taxpayer is filed for a period ending in the calendar year in which the particular period ends, for the purpose of computing the tax payable under this Part by the taxpayer in those returns, the total of all deductions claimed in all those returns under any of subsections 118(3) and (10) and sections 118.01 to 118.7 and 118.9 shall not exceed the total that could be deducted under those provisions for the year with respect to the taxpayer if no separate returns were filed under any of subsections 70(2), 104(23) and 150(4).

Related Provisions: 114.2 — Deductions in separate returns; 117(1) — Tax payable under this Part.

Notes: The wording of 118.93 means that the personal and dependant credits in 118(1), and the age credit in 118(2), can be doubled up and claimed on both returns when filing one of the indicated "separate" returns.

118.93 amended by 2006 budget bill #1, for 2005 and later taxation years.

Definitions [s. 118.93]: "calendar year" — *Interpretation Act* 37(1)(a); "taxpayer" — 248(1).

Interpretation Bulletins: IT-326R3: Returns of deceased persons as "another person"; IT-513R: Personal tax credits; IT-517R: Pension tax credit (cancelled).

118.94 Tax payable by non-residents (credits restricted)

118.94 Tax payable by non-residents (credits restricted) — Sections 118 to 118.07 and 118.2, subsections 118.3(2) and (3) and sections 118.8 and 118.9 do not apply for the purpose of computing the tax payable under this Part for a taxation year by an individual who at no time in the year is resident in Canada unless all or substantially all the individual's income for the year is included in computing the individual's taxable income earned in Canada for the year.

Related Provisions: 117(1) — Tax payable under this Part; 217 — Election respecting certain payments.

Notes: CRA considers that "substantially all" means 90% or more.

118.94 applied in *Luscher*, 2012 TCC 151, where income (from all sources) was less than taxable income earned in Canada (TIEC). "Income for the year" meant worldwide income after netting capital gains with capital losses as required by s. 3, so US capital losses reduced Canadian capital gains. TIEC included taxable capital gains only on Canadian (not US) real property, due to 115(1)(a)(iii). No part of US-source income was included in TIEC.

118.94 applied in *Kenny*, 2018 TCC 2: an Irish resident worked in Canada for a few weeks, but 40% of his income was social assistance received in Ireland (not income there but would be income in Canada under 56(1)(u)), so his Canadian income was not "substantially all".

A non-taxable allowance is not included in "income for the year" in 118.94: VIEWS doc 2008-0297661E5.

118.94 amended to delete reference to 118.6 by 2016 budget bill #1, for 2017 and later taxation years.

118.94 amended by 2011 budget bill #2, for 2011 and later taxation years, to change "118 to 118.05" to "118 to 118.06", and by 2014 budget bill #1, for 2014 and later years, to change to "118 to 118.07".

118.94 amended to change "118, 118.01, 118.02, 118.03" to "118 to 118.05" by 2009 budget bill #2, effective for 2009 and later taxation years.

118.94 earlier amended by 2006 Budget bills (last change effective for 2006 and later taxation years) and 1991 technical bill.

Definitions [s. 118.94]: "individual", "non-resident" — 248(1); "resident in Canada" — 250; "taxable income earned in Canada" — 248(1); "taxation year" — 249.

Interpretation Bulletins: IT-171R2: Non-resident individuals — computation of taxable income earned in Canada and non-refundable tax credits (cancelled); IT-513R: Personal tax credits.

CRA Audit Manual: 15.2.15: Tax calculations.

118.95 Credits in year of bankruptcy

118.95 Credits in year of bankruptcy — Notwithstanding sections 118 to 118.9, for the purpose of computing an individual's tax payable under this Part for a taxation year that ends in a calendar year in which the individual becomes bankrupt, the individual shall be allowed only

(a) such of the deductions as the individual is entitled to under any of subsections 118(3) and (10) and sections 118.01 to 118.2, 118.5, 118.62 and 118.7, as can reasonably be considered wholly applicable to the taxation year, and

(b) such part of the deductions as the individual is entitled to under any of sections 118 (other than subsections 118(3) and (10)), 118.3, 118.8 and 118.9 as can reasonably be considered applicable to the taxation year,

except that the total of the amounts so deductible for all taxation years of the individual in the calendar year under any of those provisions shall not exceed the amount that would have been deductible under that provision in respect of the calendar year if the individual had not become bankrupt.

Related Provisions [s. 118.95]: 122.5(7) — Parallel rule for GST credit; 122.61(3.1) — Parallel rule for Canada Child Benefit; 128(2)(e)(iii) — Credits allowed on return by trustee.

Notes: Absent 118.95, an individual who went bankrupt could claim full credits on both pre- and post-bankruptcy returns for the same year (see Notes to 128(2)). The credits must be prorated (or allocated to one return or the other, for credits based on expenditures or the receipt of certain types of income).

118.95(a) amended to delete reference to 118.6 by 2016 budget bill #1, for 2017 and later tax years.

118.95 earlier amended by 2006 Budget bills (last change effective for 2006 and later tax years), 1998 Budget. Added by 1995-97 technical bill.

Definitions [s. 118.95]: "bankrupt" — 248(1); "calendar year" — *Interpretation Act* 37(1)(a); "individual" — 248(1); "taxation year" — 249.

Interpretation Bulletins [s. 118.95]: IT-513R: Personal tax credits.

119. Former resident — credit for tax paid

119. Former resident — credit for tax paid — If at any particular time an individual was deemed by subsection 128.1(4) to have disposed of a capital property that was a taxable Canadian property of the individual throughout the period that began at the particular time and that ends at the first time, after the particular time, at which the individual disposes of the property, there may be deducted in computing the individual's tax payable under this Part for the taxation year that includes the particular time the lesser of

(a) that proportion of the individual's tax for the year otherwise payable under this Part (within the meaning assigned by paragraph (a) of the definition "tax for the year otherwise payable under this Part" in subsection 126(7)) that

  (i) the individual's taxable capital gain from the disposition of the property at the particular time

is of

  (ii) the amount determined under paragraph 114(a) in respect of the individual for the year, and

(b) that proportion of the individual's tax payable under Part XIII in respect of dividends received during the period by the individual in respect of the property and amounts deemed under Part XIII to have been paid during the period to the individual as dividends from corporations resident in Canada, to the extent that the amounts can reasonably be considered to relate to the property, that

  (i) the amount by which the individual's loss from the disposition of the property at the end of the period is reduced by subsection 40(3.7)

is of

  (ii) the total amount of those dividends.

Related Provisions: 126(2.21) — Foreign tax credit for former resident; 128.1(6)(b)(iii) — Effect of election by returning former resident; 128.3 — Shares acquired on rollover deemed to be same shares for s. 119; 127.531(a) — Credit allowed for alternative minimum tax; 152(6.3) — Reassessment to allow s. 119 credit; 161(7)(a)(i), 164(5)(a.1) — Effect of carryback of loss.

Notes: 119 provides a credit in certain cases where the "stop-loss" rule in 40(3.7) applies to an individual who ceased to be resident in Canada. Under 128.1(4), emigrants are treated as having disposed of most properties for proceeds equal to their value. An individual may therefore be treated as having realized an accrued gain when leaving Canada, and will be taxed on the gain. If the individual later receives dividends on the property, a loss on a later disposition may be reduced by 40(3.7), and thus may not be available to offset the gain on the 128.1(4) deemed disposition. Part or all of the tax liability arising from the gain would thus remain payable. However, the individual may also have paid tax on those post-departure dividends under 212(2).

119 addresses this possible overlap between the tax on the 128.1(4) deemed disposition of a capital property and the Part XIII tax on dividends that reduce the taxpayer's loss on the property. In general terms, it allows a credit equal to the tax on those dividends, up to the amount of the tax on the gain that arose on emigration. 119 applies only to property that is "taxable Canadian property" (248(1)) but is also subject to the 128.1(4) deemed disposition, such as shares in a Canadian corp whose value is primarily real estate in Canada. 152(6.3) allows late reassessment of the credit. See VIEWS doc 2011-0430021E5.

The "tax payable under Part XIII" in 119(b) is the rate reduced by treaty, due to ITAR 10(6): VIEWS doc 2003-0033421E5.

It is unclear whether 119 applies to reduce Part XIII tax withheld on a deemed dividend on shares of a corp that wound up after emigrating to the US: doc 2012-0438521E5.

However, 119 does not work for shares that were TCP on emigration but no longer are due to the 2010 amendments to 248(1)"taxable Canadian property": VIEWS doc 2016-0652791C6 [2016 APFF q.18]. See also Henry Shew, "Section 119: Flawed Relief", 6(2) *Canadian Tax Focus* (ctf.ca) 9-10 (May 2016).

119 added by 2001 technical bill, effective for disposition after Dec. 23, 1998 by individuals who cease to be resident in Canada after Oct. 1, 1996.

Former 119 repealed by 2001 technical bill, for 1995 and later tax years. It implemented "block averaging" for farmers and fishermen, but was effectively eliminated by the 1988 tax reform. For taxpayers with fluctuating incomes, some income averaging may be possible with RRSPs. See 146(5) and (8) and Notes to 146(10). See also 15(2) Notes, and the averaging for lump-sum payments in 110.2 and 120.31.

Definitions [s. 119]: "amount" — 248(1); "capital property" — 54, 248(1); "corporation" — 248(1), *Interpretation Act* 35(1); "dividend", "individual", "property" — 248(1); "resident in Canada" — 250; "taxable Canadian property" — 248(1); "taxable capital gain" — 38(a), 248(1); "taxation year" — 249; "trust" — 104(1), 248(1), (3).

119.1 [Family Tax Cut — Repealed]

Notes: 119.1 repealed by 2016 budget bill #1, for 2016 and later tax years, as promised in the Oct. 2015 Liberal election platform. It implemented the Conservative "Family Tax Cut" income-splitting announced in the Oct. 30, 2014 "benefits for families" news release, which also included increased child care expense deductions (63(3)"annual child care expense amount") and expanded Universal Child Care Benefit (now replaced by a higher Canada Child Benefit — see Notes to 56(6)).

The economic effect of 119.1(2) was to permit income splitting with a lower-income spouse, but the mechanics were very different from the pension income splitting under 60.03. Under 119.1, the higher-income spouse received a credit of up to $2,000.

See Golombek, "Crunching the new Family Tax Cut Credit", 2015(6) *Tax Times* (Carswell) 1-2 (March 31, 2015) [2015-6]. For discussion of the cost to government and effect on taxpayers, see Parliamentary Budget Officer, *The Family Tax Cut* (March 17, 2015, paper and slides).

119.1 added by 2015 Budget bill (Part 2), for 2014 and later tax years.

120. (1) Income not earned in a province — There shall be added to the tax otherwise payable under this Part by an individual for a taxation year the amount that bears the same relation to 48% of the tax otherwise payable under this Part by the individual for the year that

(a) the individual's income for the year, other than the individual's income earned in the year in a province,

bears to

(b) the individual's income for the year.

Related Provisions: 117(1) — Tax payable under this Part; 120(3) — "Income for the year" defined; 120(4) — Income earned in the year in a province.

Notes: 120(1) replaces the provincial tax imposed on individuals' income earned in a province (see tables in introductory pages, and Notes to 117(2) and Reg. 2601(1)). See also Remission Orders annotation below, and Notes to 120(2) re the *Income Earned in Quebec Income Tax Remission Order*.

Although the tax rate at 48% of federal tax may be lower than some provincial rates, no provincial personal credits are available as they are for income earned in a province.

Income earned in the Newfoundland offshore area is not considered earned in a province, so it is subject to this surtax: VIEWS doc 2014-0539571I7.

See also VIEWS doc 2013-0513641I7 (120(1) applies to an estate deemed resident in Canada under 94(3)).

120(1) amended by 1989 Budget and by 2000 Budget. For 1990-99 taxation years, read "52%"; for 1989, "49.5%"; for 1982-88, "47%".

Interpretation Bulletins: IT-393R2: Election re tax on rents and timber royalties — non-residents; IT-434R: Rental of real property by individual.

Remission Orders: *Income Earned in Quebec Income Tax Remission Order*, P.C. 1989-1204 (reduction in withholdings for certain income related to Quebec); *Locally Engaged Employees of the Canadian Embassy and Consulates in the United States Remission Order*, P.C. 2018-345 (remission of 120(1) tax).

(2) Amount deemed paid in prescribed manner [Quebec abatement] — Each individual is deemed to have paid, in prescribed manner and on prescribed dates, on account of the individual's tax under this Part for a taxation year an amount that bears the same relation to 3% of the tax otherwise payable under this Part by the individual for the year that

(a) the individual's income earned in the year in a province that, on January 1, 1973, was a province providing schooling allowances within the meaning of the *Youth Allowances Act*, chapter Y-1 of the Revised Statutes of Canada, 1970,

bears to

(b) the individual's income for the year.

Related Provisions: 117(1) — Tax payable under this Part; 120(3) — "Income for the year" defined; 152(1)(b) — Determination of amount on assessment; 152(4.2)(b) — Redetermination of credit at taxpayer's request; 160.1 — Where excess refunded.

Notes: 120(2)(a) refers to Quebec; 120(2) effectively provides a 3% refundable credit against federal tax for residents of Quebec. A further 13.5% credit is allowed under s. 27 of the *Federal-Provincial Fiscal Arrangements Act*, R.S.C. 1985, c. F-8. The combined 16.5% credit is calculated on *tax*, not income. Thus, federal tax is multiplied by 0.835 to apply the credit. The 15%, 22%, 26% and 29% federal brackets are thus 12.525%, 18.37%, 21.71% and 24.215% respectively for Quebec residents. See also "Quebec Abatement" (fin.gc.ca/fedprov/altpay-eng.asp).

The *Income Earned in Quebec Income Tax Remission Order*, which prevents double tax on certain non-residents, will be extended to years after 1996: VIEWS doc 2009-0330381C6.

Regulations: 6401 (prescribed date is December 31 of each year).

Remission Orders: *Income Earned in Quebec Income Tax Remission Order*, P.C. 1989-1204 (reduction in withholdings for certain income related to Quebec).

Forms: T1 General return, Line 44000 [former 440; on Quebec-residents form only].

(2.1) [Repealed]

Notes: 120(2.1) repealed by 2001 technical bill, effective for 1996 and later taxation years. It related to block averaging under former 119.

(2.2) Amount deemed paid [First Nations tax] — An individual is deemed to have paid on the last day of a taxation year, on account of the individual's tax under this Part for the year, an amount equal to the individual's income tax payable for the year to an Aboriginal government pursuant to a law of that government made in accordance with a tax sharing agreement between that government and the Government of Canada.

Related Provisions: 81(1)(a) — Deduction for amounts exempted under *Indian Act*; 152(1)(b) — Determination of amount on assessment; 152(4.2)(b) — Redetermination of credit at taxpayer's request; 156.1(1)"net tax owing"(b)B, E, F, 156.1(1.3) — First Nations tax counted for instalment purposes; 239(5) — 120(2.2) to be ignored in determining whether offence committed.

Notes: 120(2.2) (added by 1999 Budget, for 1999 and later tax years) ensures that any income tax payable to a First Nations (aboriginal) government is fully credited against income tax payable for the year (whether or not it is paid), so it is not an income tax liability. However, this provision cannot be used as a defence against criminal charges of tax evasion: see 239(5). See also Notes to 81(1)(a).

(3) Definition of "the individual's income for the year" — For the purpose of this section, "the individual's income for the year" means

(a) if section 114 applies to the individual in respect of the year, the amount determined under paragraph 114(a) in respect of the individual for the year;

(b) if the individual was non-resident throughout the year, the individual's taxable income earned in Canada for the year determined without reference to paragraphs 115(1)(d) to (f);

(c) in the case of an individual who is a specified individual in relation to the year, the individual's income for the year computed without reference to paragraph 20(1)(ww); and

(d) in the case of a SIFT trust, the amount, if any, by which its income for the year determined without reference to this paragraph exceeds its taxable SIFT trust distributions (as defined in subsection 122(3)) for the year.

Notes: Despite "means" in the opening words (see Notes to 188.1(5)), if none of 120(3)(a)-(d) applies, "income" simply means net income as determined under s. 3.

120(3)(d) added by 2007 budget bill #1, effective Oct. 31, 2006. By deducting "taxable SIFT trust distributions", it ensures that a SIFT trust does not pay provincial tax or the substitute federal tax on distributions that have already been taxed at a federal rate that includes a factor for provincial tax (see 122(1)(b) and Notes to 104(16)).

120(3) earlier amended by 2001 technical bill and 1999 Budget, last change effective for 2000 and later taxation years.

(3.1) [Repealed under former Act]

Notes: 120(3.1), repealed by 1985 Budget, provided a federal tax reduction, which varied over the years from $50 to $200 per person.

(4) Definitions — In this section,

"income earned in the year in a province" means amounts determined under rules prescribed for the purpose by regulations made on the recommendation of the Minister of Finance;

Notes: A taxpayer cannot challenge the allocation of income among the provinces in a Tax Court appeal, as that requires an appeal under the provincial ITA: *Sutcliffe*, 2004 FCA 376. See "An appeal of only provincial tax" under "Jurisdiction" in 169(1) Notes.

120(4)"income earned in the year in a province" was para. 120(4)(a) before RSC 1985 (5th Supp) consolidation for tax years ending after Nov. 1991.

Regulations: 2600–2607 (rules determining income earned in the year in a province).

Income Tax Folios: S5-F1-C1: Determining an individual's residence status [replaces IT-221R3].

Interpretation Bulletins: IT-434R: Rental of real property by individual.

"province [para. 120(4)(b)]" — [Repealed under former Act]

Notes: Para. 120(4)(b), which defined "province", was repealed in 1980. See the definition of "province" in subsec. 35(1) of the *Interpretation Act*.

"tax otherwise payable under this Part" by an individual for a taxation year means the total of

(a) the greater of

(i) the individual's minimum amount for the year determined under section 127.51, and

(ii) the amount that, but for this section, would be the individual's tax payable under this Part for the year if this Part were read without reference to

(A) subsection 117(2.1), section 119, subsection 120.4(2) and sections 126, 127, 127.4 and 127.41, and

(B) where the individual is a specified individual in relation to the year, section 121 in its application to dividends included in computing the individual's split income for the year, and

(b) where the individual is a specified individual in relation to the year, the amount, if any, by which

(i) the highest individual percentage for the year multiplied by the individual's split income for the year

exceeds

(ii) the total of all amounts each of which is an amount that may be deducted under section 121 and that can reasonably be considered to be in respect of a dividend included in computing the individual's split income for the year.

Related Provisions: 117(1) — Tax payable under this Part.

Notes: Subpara. (b)(i) amended by 2016 tax-rate bill, for 2016 and later taxation years, to change "29% of" to "the highest individual percentage for the year multiplied by". The rate is now 33%; see 248(1)"highest individual percentage" and 117(2)(e).

Cl. (a)(ii)(A) amended by 2007 budget bill #2, for 2008 and later taxation years, to add reference to 117(2.1). Thus, a Canada Workers Benefit advance payment is not included in "tax otherwise payable" for purposes of the additional tax on income not earned in a province and the Quebec abatement.

Definition earlier amended by 2001 technical bill (for 2000 and later tax years), 1999 and 1998 Budgets. 120(4)"tax otherwise payable under this Part" was para. 120(4)(c) before RSC 1985 (5th Supp) consolidation for tax years ending after Nov. 1991.

Definitions [s. 120]: "amount" — 248(1); "Canada" — 255; "highest individual percentage" — 248(1); "income earned in the year in a province" — 120(4); "income for the year" — 120(3); "individual" — 248(1); "minimum amount" — 127.51; "Minister of Finance" — *Financial Administration Act* 14; "prescribed", "non-resident" —

248(1); "province" — *Interpretation Act* 35(1); "regulation" — 248(1); "resident in Canada" — 250; "SIFT trust" — 122.1(1), (2), 248(1); "specified individual", "split income" — 120.4(1), 248(1); "tax otherwise payable" — 120(4); "tax payable" — 248(2); "taxable income" — 2(2), 248(1); "taxable SIFT trust distributions" — 122(3); "taxation year" — 249; "taxpayer" — 248(1).

120.1 [Repealed]

Notes: 120.1 repealed by 1999 Budget, for 1998 and later taxation years. It provided a credit for amounts forward-averaged before 1988. See Notes to repealed 110.4.

120.2 (1) Minimum tax carry-over — There may be deducted from the amount that, but for this section, section 120 and subsection 120.4(2), would be an individual's tax payable under this Part for a particular taxation year such amount as the individual claims not exceeding the lesser of

(a) the portion of the total of the individual's additional taxes determined under subsection (3) for the 7 taxation years immediately preceding the particular year that was not deducted in computing the individual's tax payable under this Part for a taxation year preceding the particular year, and

(b) the amount, if any, by which

(i) the amount that, but for this section, section 120 and subsection 120.4(2), would be the individual's tax payable under this Part for the particular year if the individual were not entitled to any deduction under any of sections 126, 127 and 127.4

exceeds

(ii) the individual's minimum amount for the particular year determined under section 127.51.

Notes: See Notes to 127.5 for an overview of the Alternative Minimum Tax (AMT) in 127.5–127.55 and this carryover.

120.2(1) amended by 1999 Budget, for 2000 and later tax years.

Remission Orders: *Vera Henderson Income Tax Remission Order*, P.C. 2008-983 (remission "due to unintended results of the legislation", provided the taxpayer makes no claim under 120.2(1)).

Forms: T691: Alternative minimum tax.

(2) [Repealed under former Act]

Notes: 120.2(2), repealed by 1988 tax reform, provided a carryback of minimum tax credit from the year of death. Minimum tax no longer applies to that year: 127.55(c).

(3) Additional tax determined — For the purposes of subsection (1), additional tax of an individual for a taxation year is the amount, if any, by which

(a) the individual's minimum amount for the year determined under section 127.51

exceeds the total of

(b) the amount that, if this Act were read without reference to section 120, would be the individual's tax payable under this Part for the year if the individual were not entitled to any deduction under any of sections 126, 127 and 127.4, and

(c) that proportion of the amount, if any, by which

(i) the individual's special foreign tax credit for the year determined under section 127.54

exceeds

(ii) the total of all amounts deductible under section 126 from the individual's tax for the year

that

(iii) the amount of the individual's foreign taxes for the year within the meaning assigned by subsection 127.54(1)

is of

(iv) the amount that would be the individual's foreign taxes for the year within the meaning assigned by subsection 127.54(1) if the definition "foreign taxes" in that subsection were read without reference to "⅔ of".

Related Provisions: 117(1) — Tax payable under this Part; 180.01(2)(g) — Application to 2010-14 election re deferred employee stock option benefits.

Notes: 120.2(3)(b) amended by 2002-2013 technical bill, for 2000 and later tax years, to ensure the additional tax for the minimum tax does not include the 33% "tax on split income" under 120.4. Earlier amended by 1999 Budget.

(4) Where subsec. (1) does not apply — Subsection (1) does

not apply in respect of an individual's return of income filed under subsection 70(2), paragraph 104(23)(d) or 128(2)(f) or subsection 150(4).

Notes: 120.2(4) amended by 2000 Budget (for 1996 and later tax years), 1995-97 technical bill.

Definitions [s. 120.2]: "amount", "individual" — 248(1); "minimum amount" — 127.51; "tax payable" — 248(2); "taxation year" — 249.

120.3 CPP/QPP disability [or other] benefits for previous

years — There shall be added in computing an individual's tax payable under this Part for a particular taxation year the total of all amounts each of which is the amount, if any, by which

(a) the amount that would have been the tax payable under this Part by the individual for a preceding taxation year if that portion of any amount not included in computing the individual's income for the particular year because of subsection 56(8) and that relates to the preceding year had been included in computing the individual's income for the preceding year

exceeds

(b) the tax payable under this Part by the individual for the preceding year.

Related Provisions: 120.31 — Lump-sum payment averaging.

Notes: 120.3 added by 1991 Budget, effective 1990. See Notes to 56(8).

Definitions [s. 120.3]: "amount", "individual" — 248(1); "tax payable" — 248(2); "taxation year" — 249.

Remission Orders: *Rosa Amorim Remission Order*, P.C. 2009-1224 (remission of tax, interest and penalty incurred due to CRA's incorrect calculation under 120.3).

120.31 Lump-sum payments [averaging] — (1) Defini-

tions — The definitions in subsection 110.2(1) apply in this section.

Notes: See Notes at end of 120.31.

(2) Addition to tax payable — There shall be added in computing an individual's tax payable under this Part for a particular taxation year the total of all amounts each of which is the amount, if any, by which

(a) the individual's notional tax payable for an eligible taxation year to which a specified portion of a qualifying amount received by the individual relates and in respect of which an amount is deducted under section 110.2 in computing the individual's taxable income for the particular year

exceeds

(b) the individual's tax payable under this Part for the eligible taxation year.

Forms: T1198: Statement of qualifying retroactive lump-sum payment.

(3) Notional tax payable — For the purpose of subsection (2), an individual's notional tax payable for an eligible taxation year, calculated for the purpose of computing the individual's tax payable under this Part for a taxation year (in this subsection referred to as "the year of receipt") in which the individual received a qualifying amount, is the total of

(a) the amount, if any, by which

(i) the amount that would be the individual's tax payable under this Part for the eligible taxation year if the total of all amounts, each of which is the specified portion, in relation to the eligible taxation year, of a qualifying amount received by the individual before the end of the year of receipt, were added in computing the individual's taxable income for the eligible taxation year

exceeds

(ii) the total of all amounts each of which is an amount, in respect of a qualifying amount received by the individual

before the year of receipt, that was included because of this paragraph in computing the individual's notional tax payable under this Part for the eligible taxation year, and

(b) if the eligible taxation year ended before the taxation year preceding the year of receipt, an amount equal to the amount that would be calculated as interest payable on the amount, if any, by which the amount determined under paragraph (a) in respect of the eligible taxation year exceeds the taxpayer's tax payable under this Part for that year, if the amount that would be calculated as interest payable on that excess were calculated

(i) for the period that began on May 1 of the year following the eligible taxation year and that ended immediately before the year of receipt, and

(ii) at the prescribed rate that is applicable for the purpose of subsection 164(3) with respect to the period.

Regulations: 4301(b) (prescribed rate of interest).

Notes [s. 120.31]: 120.31, combined with 110.2, provides a somewhat ineffective retroactive averaging of certain kinds of lump-sum income payments. See Notes to 110.2. It was added by 1999 Budget, effective for 1995 and later taxation years, and notwithstanding 152(4)-(5), any assessment for any taxation year that ended before 1999 shall be made as necessary to take into account the application of 120.31.

The amount "calculated as interest" under 120.31(3)(b) is not interest and thus cannot be waived under 220(3.1) (Taxpayer Relief, formerly called Fairness): VIEWS doc 2004-0075531I7.

120.31(3)(b) opening words amended by 2002-2013 technical bill (Part 5 — technical), effective for 1995 and later taxation years.

Definitions [s. 120.31]: "amount" — 248(1); "eligible taxation year" — 110.2(1), 120.31(1); "individual" — 248(1); "notional tax payable" — 120.31(3); "prescribed" — 248(1); "qualifying amount", "specified portion" — 110.2(1), 120.31(1); "taxable income" — 248(1); "taxation year" — 249; "year of receipt" — 120.31(3).

120.4 Tax on split income [TOSI] — (1) Definitions — The

definitions in this subsection apply in this section.

"arm's length capital", of a specified individual, means property of the individual if the property, or property for which it is a substitute, was not

(a) acquired as income from, or a taxable capital gain or profit from the disposition of, another property that was derived directly or indirectly from a related business in respect of the specified individual;

(b) borrowed by the specified individual under a loan or other indebtedness; or

(c) transferred, directly or indirectly by any means whatever, to the specified individual from a person who was related to the specified individual (other than as a consequence of the death of a person).

Related Provisions: 120.4(1.1)(d) — Extended meaning of "derived directly or indirectly"; 248(8) — Meaning of "consequence" of death.

Notes: See Notes at end of 120.4. Due to 120.4(1)"excluded amount"(f)(ii), if X is age 17-23 at start of year, X is subject to TOSI only to the extent the amount exceeds a "reasonable return" on "arm's length capital" contributed by X. See 120.4(1)"reasonable return".

For the meaning of "derived directly or indirectly" in para. (a), see 120.4(1.1)(d). For "transferred directly or indirectly" in (c), see Notes to 17.1(1).

Definition added by 2018 budget bill #1, for 2018 and later tax years.

"excluded amount", in respect of an individual for a taxation year, means an amount that is the individual's income for the year from, or the individual's taxable capital gain or profit for the year from the disposition of, a property to the extent that the amount

(a) if the individual has not attained the age of 24 years before the year, is from a property that was acquired by, or for the benefit of, the individual as a consequence of the death of a person who is

(i) a parent of the individual, or

(ii) any person, if the individual is

(A) enrolled as a full-time student during the year at a "post-secondary educational institution" (as defined in subsection 146.1(1)), or

(B) an individual in respect of whom an amount may be deducted under section 118.3 in computing a taxpayer's tax payable under this Part for the year;

(b) is from a property acquired by the individual under a transfer described in subsection 160(4);

(c) is a taxable capital gain that arises because of subsection 70(5);

(d) is a taxable capital gain for the year from the disposition by the individual of property that is, at the time of the disposition, "qualified farm or fishing property" or "qualified small business corporation shares" (as those terms are defined in subsection 110.6(1)), unless the amount would be deemed to be a dividend under subsection 120.4(4) or (5) if this definition were read without reference to this paragraph;

(e) if the individual has attained the age of 17 years before the year, is

    (i) not derived directly or indirectly from a related business in respect of the individual for the year, or

    (ii) derived directly or indirectly from an excluded business of the individual for the year;

(f) if the individual has attained the age of 17 years but not the age of 24 years before the year, is

    (i) a safe harbour capital return of the individual, or

    (ii) a reasonable return in respect of the individual, having regard only to the contributions of arm's length capital by the individual; or

(g) if the individual has attained the age of 24 years before the year, is

    (i) income from, or a taxable capital gain from the disposition of, excluded shares of the individual, or

    (ii) a reasonable return in respect of the individual.

Related Provisions: 120.4(1.1)(c) — Deemed excluded amount from spouse or common-law partner; 120.4(1.1)(d) — Extended meaning of "derived directly or indirectly"; 248(8) — Meaning of "consequence" of death.

Notes: See Notes at end of 120.4. An "excluded amount" is excluded from the tax on split income (TOSI): see opening words of 120.4(1)"split income". It covers X's income or gains from various sources:

Para. (a) covers an amount from property inherited by X if X is under 24 at start of year in certain cases, as a "consequence" of death (see 248(8)). This exclusion does not extend to substituted or replacement property: VIEWS doc 2005-0126831E5.

Para. (b) excludes from TOSI an amount from property acquired on breakdown of marriage or common-law partnership, if the conditions of 160(4) are met.

Para. (c) excludes a gain arising on X's death (70(5)).

Para. (d) excludes gains from property eligible for the capital gains exemption (110.6), except for a deemed dividend under 120.4(4) or (5). For an example see VIEWS doc 2018-0768661C6 [2018 APFF q.13].

Para. (e) applies if X is 17 or over at start of year. Only income from a 120.4(1)"related business" [Canadian-resident person related to X is sufficiently connected to the business] is subject to TOSI, and even then, income from a 120.4(1)"excluded business" [where X has made sufficient labour contribution] is not. For interpretation see VIEWS docs 2018-0765811C6 [2018 APFF Financial q.4], 2018-0768661C6 [2018 APFF q.13], 2018-0779981C6 [2018 CTF q. 9], 2018-0780081C6 [2018 CTF q.10]; 2019-0824421C6 [2019 CTF q.9] (where business has been sold but "source individual" still works there on transitional basis, TOSI applies).

Where a child owns shares in Holdco which has both a related business and portfolio investments, if Holdco tracks its cash and pays dividends from the revenue from the investments, TOSI will not apply: VIEWS doc 2018-0768821C6 [2018 APFF q.11].

On the meaning of "derived directly or indirectly", see VIEWS docs 2018-0771861E5 (secondary income is not caught); 2019-0824421C6 [2019 CTF q.9] (phrase is broadly interpreted, but does not apply where business no longer carried on). See also Notes to 94(1)"resident portion" on "derived"; and Notes to 17.1(1) on "indirectly".

Para. (f) applies if X is 17-23 at start of year. A 120.4(1)"safe harbour capital return" is excluded from TOSI, based on the prescribed rate (currently 1%: Reg. 4301(c)). A 120.4(1)"reasonable return" is also allowed, but based only on 120.4(1)"arm's length capital" contributed, not X's labour (which may be covered under (e) above). For interpretation see VIEWS doc 2018-0768661C6 [2018 APFF q.13].

Para. (g) applies if X is 24 or over at start of year. Dividends or gain from 120.4(1)"excluded shares" [generally, shares of a corp carrying on a non-services business if X owns 10% or more of its shares] are excluded from TOSI by (g)(i). For an example see VIEWS doc 2018-0768661C6 [2018 APFF q.13]. Under (g)(ii), a 120.4(1)"reasonable

return" is also excluded: generally, a reasonable return taking into account the relative contributions made to the business (labour, capital, risks) by X and related persons related to the individual.

"Excluded amount" amended by 2018 budget bill #1, for 2018 and later tax years. For earlier years, read:

"excluded amount", in respect of an individual for a taxation year, means an amount that is the income from, or the taxable capital gain from the disposition of, a property acquired by or for the benefit of the individual as a consequence of the death of

    (a) a parent of the individual; or

    (b) any person, if the individual is

        (i) enrolled as a full-time student during the year at a post-secondary educational institution (as defined in subsection 146.1(1)), or

        (ii) an individual in respect of whom an amount may be deducted under section 118.3 in computing a taxpayer's tax payable under this Part for the year.

Opening words amended by 2011 budget bill #2, for dispositions after March 21, 2011, to add "or the taxable capital gain from the disposition of".

"excluded business", of a specified individual for a taxation year, means a business if the specified individual is actively engaged on a regular, continuous and substantial basis in the activities of the business in either

    (a) the taxation year, except in respect of an amount described in paragraph (e) of the definition "split income"; or

    (b) any five prior taxation years of the specified individual.

Notes: See Notes to 120.4(1)"excluded amount" and at end of 120.4. If X was at least 17 at start of year, and X is "actively engaged on a regular, continuous and substantial basis in the activities of the business", then X's income is excluded from TOSI: 120.4(1)"excluded amount"(e). *Gains* on shares of the business are excluded only if X has met the test in at least 5 prior years: para. (b) and 120.4(1)"split income"(e). The years need not be continuous, and could be long ago: VIEWS doc 2018-0783741E5. Pre-incorporation or -amalgamation years qualify for the 5 years, as it is the same "business": 2019-0814181E5.

"Actively engaged" is not defined, other than a deeming rule based on average 20 hrs/week of work: 120.4(1.1)(a). The meaning generally turns on the time, work and energy that X devotes to the business. The more X is involved in management and current activities, the more likely X will be considered to participate on a regular, continuous and substantial basis. The more X's contributions are integral to the success of the business, the more substantial they are. Also "if the business, by its nature, does not demand a higher number of hours worked and the individual's labour contributions are integral to the success of the business". Involvement in the business pre-incorporation counts. [Finance Technical Notes] See also VIEWS docs 2015-0595521C6 [2015 APFF q.2], 2018-0761601E5; 2019-0799901C6 [2019 STEP q.3] and 2020-0837631C6 [2020 STEP q.9] (5 hours/week by each spouse qualifies if that is enough to run the business); 2019-0812771C6 [2019 APFF q.18] (maternity or injury leave throughout year disqualifies X).

Where active business ceases and the corp uses the profits to carry on an investment business, it is not the same business and thus not an "excluded business": VIEWS docs 2019-0792001E5, 2019-0824411C6 [2019 CTF q.8], 2020-0837641C6 [2020 STEP q.10].

See also Georgina Tollstam, "CRA on Excluded Business Test", 26(11) *Canadian Tax Highlights* (ctf.ca) 11-12 (Nov. 2018).

Definition added by 2018 budget bill #1, for 2018 and later tax years.

"excluded shares", of a specified individual at any time, means shares of the capital stock of a corporation owned by the specified individual if

    (a) the following conditions are met:

        (i) less than 90% of the business income of the corporation for the last taxation year of the corporation that ends at or before that time (or, if no such taxation year exists, for the taxation year of the corporation that includes that time) was from the provision of services, and

        (ii) the corporation is not a professional corporation;

    (b) immediately before that time, the specified individual owns shares of the capital stock of the corporation that

        (i) give the holders thereof 10% or more of the votes that could be cast at an annual meeting of the shareholders of the corporation, and

        (ii) have a fair market value of 10% or more of the fair market value of all of the issued and outstanding shares of the capital stock of the corporation; and

(c) all or substantially all of the income of the corporation for the relevant taxation year in subparagraph (a)(i) is income that is not derived, directly or indirectly, from one or more related businesses in respect of the specified individual other than a business of the corporation.

Related Provisions: 120.4(1.1)(d) — Extended meaning of "derived directly or indirectly".

Notes: See Notes at end of 120.4. This definition applies at the point when a dividend is being paid or the shares are being sold. Dividends or gains from "excluded shares" are excluded from TOSI if the taxpayer is 24 or older by start of year: 120.4(1)"excluded amount"(g)(i).

Subpara. (a)(i): "income" for the 90% test (which is for the *previous* taxation year) could be net income, or could be gross revenue as per *Novopharm* and *Ludco*, discussed at beginning of Notes to 18(1)(a). CRA says it is gross revenue: VIEWS doc 2018-0743961C6 [STEP 2018 q.5]. CRA says a corp needs to have some business income for (a)(i) to apply: 2018-0744031C6 [STEP 2018 q.7]; this might not be correct, and note that it is unclear where to draw the line between "business income" and income from property (see Notes to 9(1) on this). See also 2018-0768801C6 [2018 APFF q.9]; tinyurl.com/excluded-shares (examples of the gross business income test).

120.4 does not apply to dividends unless they are derived from a "related business" (for a person 17 or older at start of year): 120.4(1)"excluded amount"(e)(i). Thus, if activity is sufficiently low that there is no "business", 120.4 does not apply and (a)(i) need not be considered. However, the level of activity required for 248(1)"business" is low, and uncertain: doc 2018-0771861E5 [Infanti, "CRA Clarifies TOSI's 'Derived'...", 19(1) *Tax for the Owner-Manager* (ctf.ca) 2-3 (Jan. 2019)]. See also Notes to 18.1(12) on "derived", but note that the wording here is "derived directly or indirectly" (see Notes to 17.1(1) re "indirectly").

To avoid providing 90% services under (a)(i), a business might charge for goods where possible. However, in VIEWS doc 2018-0743961C6 [STEP 2018 q.5], CRA seems to use a "single supply" test (but without referring to GST). There is extensive GST/HST case law holding that if components of a supply are inextricably intertwined, the supplier provides a "single supply" of the dominant element (services in this case). See, e.g., *Hurd Dentistry*, 2017 TCC 142: an orthodontist supplied only a service, not both a service and braces. See Cases annotation to 123(1)"supply" in David M. Sherman, *Practitioner's Goods and Services Tax, Annotated*, and CRA Policy P-077R2. See also Notes to 127(9)"qualified property" re *Will-Kare* and related cases. However, in tinyurl.com/excluded-shares Example 6, CRA accepts that a business of constructing decks can treat the materials supplied as sale of goods.

Having a business whose principal purpose is to derive income from property (see Notes to 9(1) under "Business income vs property income", and to 125(7)"specified investment business" [SIB — business income even though taxed as investment income]), so as to increase non-services income, risks triggering 120.4 by having business income in the first place. Note also that putting investment assets in a corp can endanger its status for 110.6(1)"qualified small business corporation share" (capital gains exemption), as well as for 125(5.1)(b) (excessive passive income grinds down small business deduction). See also De Palma & Schechter, "Tax on Split Income: Applicability for Investment and Holding Companies", 2436 *Tax Topics* (CCH) 1-2 (Nov. 15, 2018). See VIEWS docs 2018-0765791C6 [2018 APFF Financial q.2] (corp can carry on business of earning income from property); 2018-0779981C6 [2018 CTF q. 9], 2018-0780081C6 [2018 CTF q.10] (excluded shares and related business).

See also VIEWS docs 2018-0745871C6 [CALU 2018 q.6] (providing drivers for trucks is providing services); 2019-0819431E5, 2020-0839581E5 (GAAR may apply where restructuring done to fit definition); 2019-0833181E5 (right to download digital videos is intangible property, not services).

See also Kathryn Walker, "The Services Carve-Out from TOSI", 8(2) *Canadian Tax Focus* (ctf.ca) 12-13 (May 2018).

Shares owned by a trust cannot be excluded shares: see opening words. This makes family trusts less attractive as a mechanism to hold private company shares.

Subpara. (a)(ii): note that 248(1)"professional corporation" means only an incorporated accountant, chiropractor, dentist, lawyer, Quebec notary, physician or veterinarian.

Para. (b): Before the March 2018 redraft, the same shares would have had to meet both the "votes" and the "value" tests; the Joint Committee raised this with Finance as a concern. With the revised wording, separate shares with votes and value now qualify if owned by the same person: VIEWS doc 2018-0771811E5. Note also that for 2018, the test can be met at year-end as an alternative to the "point in time": 2018-0761601E5.

For more on para. (b) see VIEWS docs 2018-0768661C6 [2018 APFF q.13] ((b) applies); 2018-0777361E5 (on facts, (b) applies to common shares, not pref shares redeemed by estate after death).

Para. (c): See 120.4(1.1)(d) for extended meaning of "derived directly or indirectly". Interposing a Holdco above the active business corp will cause the Holdco shares not to qualify as "excluded shares", due to para. (c). See VIEWS docs 2018-0743971C6 [STEP 2018 q.6], 2018-0745871C6 [CALU 2018 q.6], 2018-0761601E5. The rule also catches a corp that earns rent from a related professional corp.

"Income" in para. (c) means gross revenue from all sources in CRA's view: doc 2018-0743961C6 [2018 STEP q.5]; and includes taxable capital gains without deducting al-

lowable capital losses: 2019-0802331E5. (This may be correct: as with (a)(i) above, see beginning of Notes to 18(1)(a).) It includes intercorporate dividends deducted under 112(1).

For more on para. (c) see VIEWS docs 2018-0768661C6 [2018 APFF q.13] ((c) applies); 2018-0768801C6 [2018 APFF q.9]; 2018-0777361E5 ((c) applies to corp whose only income for 30 years was from investment business); 2019-0792011E5 (whether funds held by Holdco are "derived" from related business); 2019-0813021E5 ("a business of the corporation" includes partnership business).

"Excluded shares" added by 2018 budget bill #1, for 2018 and later tax years, but for 2018, read opening words of (b) as "immediately before that time or the end of 2018, the shares".

"reasonable return", in respect of a specified individual for a taxation year, means a particular amount derived directly or indirectly from a related business in respect of the specified individual that

(a) would, if this subsection were read without reference to subparagraph (f)(ii) or (g)(ii) of the definition "excluded amount", be an amount described in the definition "split income" in respect of the specified individual for the year; and

(b) is reasonable having regard to the following factors relating to the relative contributions of the specified individual, and each source individual in respect of the specified individual, in respect of the related business:

(i) the work they performed in support of the related business,

(ii) the property they contributed, directly or indirectly, in support of the related business,

(iii) the risks they assumed in respect of the related business,

(iv) the total of all amounts that were paid or that became payable, directly or indirectly, by any person or partnership to, or for the benefit of, them in respect of the related business, and

(v) such other factors as may be relevant.

Related Provisions: 120.4(1.1)(d) — Extended meaning of "derived directly or indirectly".

Notes: See 120.4(1)"excluded amount"(f)(ii) and (g)(ii). If X is age 17-23 at start of year, X is subject to TOSI only to the extent the amount exceeds a "reasonable return" (RR) on "arm's length capital" contributed by X. If X is 24 or over, a RR is also excluded, but taking into account *all* of X's contributions to the business (labour, capital, risks). The RR exclusion is unavailable to a child under 17 at start of year.

CRA states in its *Guidance* (tinyurl.com/cra-splitinc): "In determining whether the payment is a Reasonable Return, the Agency does not intend to generally substitute its judgment of what would be considered a reasonable amount unless there has not been a good faith attempt to determine a reasonable amount based on the Reasonableness Criteria.". See also VIEWS docs 2018-0771851E5 (start-up risk when business began can be considered); 2018-0777361E5 (general discussion); 2019-0814161E5 (investment from spouses' joint account unlikely to count as passive spouse contributing property).

The words "in support of" (the business) are broader than "for" or "in". *Quaere* whether a spouse that takes care of the home and children, so that the other spouse has more time to work in the business, is doing work "in support of" the business.

For the meaning of "derived directly or indirectly" in opening words, see 120.4(1.1)(d). For "indirectly" in (b)(ii) and (iv), see Notes to 17.1(1).

Definition added by 2018 budget bill #1, for 2018 and later tax years.

"related business", in respect of a specified individual for a taxation year, means

(a) a business carried on by

(i) a source individual in respect of the specified individual at any time in the year, or

(ii) a partnership, corporation or trust if a source individual in respect of the specified individual at any time in the year is actively engaged on a regular basis in the activities of the partnership, corporation or trust related to earning income from the business;

(b) a business of a particular partnership, if a source individual in respect of the specified individual at any time in the year has an interest — including directly or indirectly — in the particular partnership; and

(c) a business of a corporation, if the following conditions are met at any time in the year:

(i) a source individual in respect of the specified individual owns

(A) shares of the capital stock of the corporation, or

(B) property that derives, directly or indirectly, all or part of its fair market value from shares of the capital stock of the corporation, and

(ii) it is the case that

$$0.1A \leq B + C$$

where

A   is the total fair market value of all of the issued and outstanding shares of the capital stock of the corporation,

B   is the total fair market value at that time of property described in clause (i)(A), and

C   is the portion of the total fair market value of property described in clause (i)(B) that is derived from shares of the capital stock of the corporation.

Related Provisions: 120.4(1)"split income"(b)(ii)(A), (c)(ii)(C) — Income derived from related business; 120.4(1.1)(d) — Extended meaning of "derived directly or indirectly".

Notes: "Related business" (**RB**) applies in determining the application of tax on split income (TOSI) to individuals who are at least 17 by the start of the year. Under 120.4(1)"excluded amount"(e)(i), TOSI applies to an amount only if it is derived directly or indirectly from a "related business".

See Notes to 9(1) and 248(1)"business" on the meaning of "business".

Since this definition applies only to 2018 and later tax years, it appears that if the business ceased before 2018 there is no RB.

RB is defined for a "specified individual" for a year and refers to a "source individual" (both as defined in 120.4(1)). Income sprinkling arrangements seek to reduce tax by decreasing income from the RB by a higher-income individual (the source individual) with a matching increase in the income derived from the RB by a lower-income individual (the specified individual).

For a business to be a RB for a specified individual, a "source individual" in respect of the specified individual must be sufficiently connected to the business. Para. (a) applies where the source individual is actively involved in the business. (For the meaning of "actively engaged....", see Notes to 120.4(1)"excluded business".) Paras. (b) and (c) apply where the source individual has a sufficient interest in the partnership or corporation carrying on the business.

The wording "means (a) ... and (b) ... and (c)" is satisfied by any of (a), (b) or (c), since grammatically it is the same as "means (a) ... and means (b) ... and means (c)".

For CRA interpretation see VIEWS docs 2018-0777361E5 (RB continues after death); 2018-0779981C6 [2018 CTF q.9] (various scenarios), 2018-0780081C6 [2018 CTF q.10] (general comments); 2019-0795291E5 (no RB after father's death as taxpayer no longer related to stepmother); 2019-0819431E5, 2020-0839581E5 (doctor stops professional corp carrying on business and sells shares to spouse, then starts new prof corp: portfolio investment management is likely a business, but RB may still exist, and GAAR may apply).

Examples of (c)(i)(B) can include shares, and trust or partnership interests; an interest in a discretionary trust is "property" for (c)(i)(B) in CRA's view: doc 2018-0768811C6 [2018 APFF q.10].

See also Lee, "TOSI and Valuing a Discretionary Interest in a Trust", 9(1) *Canadian Tax Focus [CTFo]* (ctf.ca) 2 (Feb. 2019) and "Property with Nominal Value: An Exception to TOSI?", 9(3) *CTFo* 7 (Aug. 2019) (re partnership interest where partnership liabilities exceed assets); Saxe & Carson, "TOSI: Reconciling Related Business", 27(10) *Canadian Tax Highlights* (ctf.ca) 11-12 (Oct. 2019).

"Related business" added by 2018 budget bill #1, for 2018 and later tax years.

"safe harbour capital return", of a specified individual for a taxation year, means an amount that does not exceed the amount determined by the formula

$$A \times B$$

where

A   is the rate equal to the highest rate of interest prescribed under paragraph 4301(c) of the *Income Tax Regulations* in effect for a quarter in the year; and

B   is the total of all amounts each of which is determined by the formula

$$C \times D/E$$

where

C   is the fair market value of property contributed by the specified individual in support of a related business at the time it was contributed,

D   is the number of days in the year that the property (or property substituted for it) is used in support of the related business and has not directly or indirectly, in any manner whatever, been returned to the specified individual, and

E   is the number of days in the year.

Notes: 120.4(1)"excluded amount"(f)(i) exempts from TOSI a return on a capital investment in support of a related business made by X aged 17-23 (at start of year) that is a "safe harbour capital return" (SHCR).

X's SHCR means a return up to a prescribed rate based on the value of property contributed by X in support of a related business (prorated to the number of days in the year that the property, or property substituted for it, is used in support of the related business). The prescribed rate used is in Reg. 4301(c). (The Dec. 13, 2017 draft was ambiguous as to what rate of interest applied, and could have been interpreted as that in Reg. 4301(a). This was clarified in the March 2018 draft which was enacted.)

For the meaning of "indirectly" in D, see Notes to 17.1(1).

Definition added by 2018 budget bill #1, for 2018 and later tax years.

"source individual", in respect of a specified individual for a taxation year, means an individual (other than a trust) who, at any time in the year, is

(a) resident in Canada; and

(b) related to the specified individual.

Notes: This refers to the person whose income is sought to be reduced by income splitting (but there is no requirement for intent). See Notes to 120.4(1)"related business". For an interpretation finding a "source individual" (after a death) see VIEWS doc 2018-0777361E5.

Definition added by 2018 budget bill #1, for 2018 and later tax years.

"specified individual", for a taxation year, means an individual (other than a trust) who

(a) is resident in Canada

(i) in the case where the individual dies in the year, immediately before the death, and

(ii) in any other case, at the end of the year; and

(b) if the individual has not attained the age of 17 years before the year, has a parent resident in Canada at any time in the year.

Related Provisions: 120.4(1.1) — Additional rules for specified individual; 248(1)"specified individual" — Definition applies to entire Act.

Notes: This refers to the person whose tax may be increased by the tax on income splitting (TOSI); the other person is the "source individual". See 120.4(1)"split income" opening words, and Notes to 120.4(1)"related business". For an interpretation finding a "specified individual" (after a death) see VIEWS doc 2018-0777361E5.

Definition amended by 2018 budget bill #1, for 2018 and later tax years. For 2000-2017, read:

"specified individual", in relation to a taxation year, means an individual who

(a) had not attained the age of 17 years before the year;

(b) at no time in the year was non-resident; and

(c) has a parent who is resident in Canada at any time in the year.

"split income", of a specified individual for a taxation year, means the total of all amounts (other than excluded amounts) each of which is

(a) an amount required to be included in computing the individual's income for the year

(i) in respect of taxable dividends received by the individual in respect of shares of the capital stock of a corporation (other than shares of a class listed on a designated stock exchange or shares of the capital stock of a mutual fund corporation), or

(ii) because of the application of section 15 in respect of the ownership by any person of shares of the capital stock of a corporation (other than shares of a class listed on a designated stock exchange),

(b) a portion of an amount included because of the application of paragraph 96(1)(f) in computing the individual's income for the year, to the extent that the portion

(i) is not included in an amount described in paragraph (a), and

(ii) can reasonably be considered to be income derived directly or indirectly from

(A) one or more related businesses in respect of the individual for the year, or

(B) the rental of property by a particular partnership or trust, if a person who is related to the individual at any time in the year

(I) is actively engaged on a regular basis in the activities of the particular partnership or trust related to the rental of property, or

(II) in the case of a particular partnership, has an interest in the particular partnership directly or indirectly through one or more other partnerships,

(c) a portion of an amount included because of the application of subsection 104(13) or 105(2) in respect of a trust (other than a mutual fund trust or a trust that is deemed to be in existence by subsection 143(1)) in computing the individual's income for the year, to the extent that the portion

(i) is not included in an amount described in paragraph (a), and

(ii) can reasonably be considered

(A) to be in respect of taxable dividends received in respect of shares of the capital stock of a corporation (other than shares of a class listed on a designated stock exchange or shares of the capital stock of a mutual fund corporation),

(B) to arise because of the application of section 15 in respect of the ownership by any person of shares of the capital stock of a corporation (other than shares of a class listed on a designated stock exchange),

(C) to be income derived directly or indirectly from one or more related businesses in respect of the individual for the year, or

(D) to be income derived from the rental of property by a particular partnership or trust, if a person who is related to the individual at any time in the year is actively engaged on a regular basis in the activities of the particular partnership or trust related to the rental of property,

(d) an amount included in computing the individual's income for the year to the extent that the amount is in respect of a debt obligation that

(i) is of a corporation (other than a mutual fund corporation or a corporation shares of a class of the capital stock of which are listed on a designated stock exchange), partnership or trust (other than a mutual fund trust), and

(ii) is not

(A) described in paragraph (a) of the definition "fully exempt interest" in subsection 212(3),

(B) listed or traded on a public market, or

(C) a deposit, standing to the credit of the individual,

(I) within the meaning assigned by the *Canada Deposit Insurance Corporation Act*, or

(II) with a credit union or a branch in Canada of a bank, and

(e) an amount in respect of a property, to the extent that

(i) the amount

(A) is a taxable capital gain, or a profit, of the individual for the year from the disposition after 2017 of the property, or

(B) is included under subsection 104(13) or 105(2) in computing the individual's income for the year and can reasonably be considered to be attributable to a taxable capital gain, or a profit, of any person or partnership for the year from the disposition after 2017 of the property, and

(ii) the property is

(A) a share of the capital stock of a corporation (other than a share of a class listed on a designated stock exchange or a share of the capital stock of a mutual fund corporation), or

(B) a property in respect of which the following conditions are met:

(I) the property is

1 an interest in a partnership,

2 an interest as a beneficiary under a trust (other than a mutual fund or a trust that is deemed to be in existence by subsection 143(1)), or

3 a debt obligation (other than a debt obligation described in any of clauses (d)(ii)(A) to (C)), and

(II) either

1 in respect of the property an amount is included in the individual's split income for the year or an earlier taxation year, or

2 all or any part of the fair market value of the property, immediately before the disposition referred to in clause (i)(A) or (B), as the case may be, is derived, directly or indirectly, from a share described in clause (A).

Related Provisions: 20(1)(ww) — Split income deducted from income for regular tax purposes; 56(5), 74.4(2)(g), 74.5(13) — Attribution rules do not apply to split income; 108(5) — Split income paid out by trust to beneficiary retains its characteristics; 120.4(1)"related business" — Definition; 120.4(1.1)(b) — Application to property acquired on a death; 120.4(1.1)(d) — Extended meaning of "derived directly or indirectly"; 120.4(2) — Tax on split income; 120.4(4) — Certain capital gains deemed to be dividends; 120.4(5) — Certain capital gains earned through trust deemed to be dividends; 248(1)"split income" — Definition applies to entire Act.

Notes: See Notes at end of 120.4. "Split income" describes the types of income subject to TOSI under 120.4(2). Note that it applies to dividends, gains and partnership and other income, but not salary (and not *co-ownership* rental income or capital gain, since that comes from direct ownership of the property: VIEWS doc 2020-0837611C6 [2020 STEP q.7]). (Partnership income can also be reallocated by CRA under 103(1).) Where it applies to a capital gain (para. (e)), offsetting capital losses cannot be used to first eliminate the capital gain, but half may be turned into a non-capital loss via 20(1)(ww). For the meaning of "derived directly or indirectly", see 120.4(1.1)(d).

Para. (a), on its face, catches all dividends or appropriations from private corporations. See Notes to 120.4(1)"excluded amount" (especially paras. (e)-(g)) for the exclusions.

A preferred-beneficiary amount under 104(14), if designated under 104(19), falls under (a)(i): see Notes to 104(14).

Subpara. (a)(i), clause (e)(ii)(A): The exclusion of dividends and gains from publicly listed shares means that a family partnership, with children receiving such amounts as partnership income, is not subject to TOSI, but other rules such as 74.1, 96(1.8), 103(1) and (1.1) can apply: VIEWS doc 2018-0768831C6 [2018 APFF q.12]. Stock market gains retain their non-TOSI status when flowed out through a trust: 2018-0765801C6 [2018 APFF Financial q.3].

Paras. (b), (c): For the meaning of "actively engaged" in (b)(ii)(B)(I) and (c)(ii)(D), see Notes to 120.4(1)"excluded business".

CRA considers that an interest-bearing loan made to a trust constitutes provision of "property" under *(b)(ii)*: VIEWS doc 2003-0181705.

For an example of (c)(ii)(D) see doc 2018-0765811C6 [2018 APFF Financial q.4].

Para. (d) extends the definition to apply to interest. Generally, *interest* received by a "specified individual" from a debtor corporation, partnership or trust will be split income if *dividends* received from that debtor would be split income. The exception for interest from publicly traded shares and mutual funds in (d)(i) (sometimes called "excluded debt") applies to such income allocated by a family trust to beneficiaries, since 108(5)(a) does not apply to 120.4: doc 2019-0812741C6 [2019 APFF q.15].

Para. (e) extends the definition to include taxable capital gains and income from disposition of property, not otherwise included in the definition, in situations where income from the property would be split income in the individual's hands.

A trust (if its terms permit) could stream "good" income to minors and "bad" income to adult beneficiaries, and the minors would not have split income: docs 2001-0112945,

2011-0422531E5; 2013-0495651C6; but these precede the 2014 and 2018 amendments.

(b)(ii) and (c)(ii)(C)-(D) amended and (d)-(e) added by 2018 budget bill #1, for 2018 and later tax years. For earlier years, read:

(b) ...

    (ii) can reasonably be considered to be income derived

        (A) from the provision of property or services by a partnership or trust to, or in support of, a business carried on by

            (I) a person who is related to the individual at any time in the year,

            (II) a corporation of which a person who is related to the individual is a specified shareholder at any time in the year, or

            (III) a professional corporation of which a person related to the individual is a shareholder at any time in the year, or

        (B) from a business of, or the rental of property by, a particular partnership or trust, if a person who is related to the individual at any time in the year

            (I) is actively engaged on a regular basis in the activities of the particular partnership or trust related to earning income from a business or the rental of property, or

            (II) in the case of a particular partnership, has an interest in the particular partnership directly or indirectly through one or more other partnerships, or

(c) ...

    (ii) can reasonably be considered ...

        (C) to be income derived from the provision of property or services by a partnership or trust to, or in support of, a business carried on by

            (I) a person who is related to the individual at any time in the year,

            (II) a corporation of which a person who is related to the individual is a specified shareholder at any time in the year, or

            (III) a professional corporation of which a person related to the individual is a shareholder at any time in the year, or

        (D) to be income derived from a business of, or the rental of property by, a particular partnership or trust, if a person who is related to the individual at any time in the year is actively engaged on a regular basis in the activities of the particular partnership or trust related to earning income from a business or the rental of property.

Definition amended by 2014 budget bill #2, for 2014 and later tax years: to add (b)(ii)(B); to add (c)(ii)(D); and to add reference to a 143(1) trust in (c) opening words. The first two changes implement a Budget proposal to apply TOSI where a child is allocated income from a partnership or trust that is derived from business or rental activities conducted by an adult with third parties.

Definition earlier amended by 2002-2013 technical bill (generally for taxation years that begin after Dec. 20, 2002), 2007 budget bill #2.

Forms: T1206: Tax on split income.

(1.1) Additional rules — specified individual — For the purpose of applying this section in respect of a specified individual in respect of a taxation year,

(a) an individual is deemed to be actively engaged on a regular, continuous and substantial basis in the activities of a business in a taxation year of the individual if the individual works in the business at least an average of 20 hours per week during the portion of the year in which the business operates;

(b) if an amount would — if this section were read without reference to this paragraph — be split income of a specified individual who has attained the age of 17 years before the year in respect of a property, and that property was acquired by, or for the benefit of, the specified individual as a consequence of the death of another person, then

    (i) for the purpose of applying paragraph (b) of the definition "reasonable return" in subsection (1), to the extent that the particular amount referred to in that paragraph is in respect of the property, then the factors referred to in that paragraph in respect of the other person are to be included for the purpose of determining a reasonable return in respect of the individual,

    (ii) for the purposes of this subparagraph and the definition "excluded business" in subsection (1), if the other person was actively engaged on a regular, substantial and continuous basis in the activities of a business throughout five previous taxation years, then the individual is deemed to have been actively engaged on a regular, substantial and continuous basis in the business throughout those five years, and

    (iii) for the purpose of applying paragraph (g) of the definition "excluded amount" in subsection (1) in respect of that property, the individual is deemed to have attained the age of 24 years before the year if the other person had attained the age of 24 years before the year;

(c) an amount that is a specified individual's income for a taxation year from, or the specified individual's taxable capital gain or profit for the year from the disposition of, a property is deemed to be an excluded amount in respect of the specified individual for the taxation year if

    (i) the following conditions are met:

        (A) the amount would be an excluded amount in respect of the specified individual's spouse or common-law partner for the year, if the amount were included in computing the spouse or common-law partner's income for the year, and

        (B) the spouse or common-law partner has attained the age of 64 years before the year, or

    (ii) the amount would have been an excluded amount in respect of an individual who was, immediately before their death, the specified individual's spouse or common-law partner, if the amount were included in computing the spouse or common-law partner's income for their last taxation year (determined as if this section applies in respect of that year);

(d) for greater certainty, an amount derived directly or indirectly from a business includes

    (i) an amount that

        (A) is derived from the provision of property or services to, or in support of, the business, or

        (B) arises in connection with the ownership or disposition of an interest in the person or partnership carrying on the business, and

    (ii) an amount derived from an amount described in this paragraph; and

(e) for the purposes of this section, an individual is deemed not to be related to their spouse or common-law partner at any time in a year if, at the end of the year, the individual is living separate and apart from their spouse or common-law partner because of a breakdown of their marriage or common-law partnership.

Related Provisions: 110.6(12)(d) — Effect of 120.4(1.1)(e) on capital gains exemption; 248(8) — Meaning of "consequence" of death.

Notes: *Para. (a)* provides a deeming rule for 120.4(1)"excluded business", "related business"(a)(ii), "split income"(b)(ii)(B)(I), (c)(ii)(D), and 120.4(1.1)(b)(ii), but a person who does not meet the 20 hrs/week test can factually still be "actively engaged on a regular, continuous and substantial basis"; see Notes to 120.4(1)"excluded business".

For the test, X does not need to work every week the business operates in a year. For example, the test is satisfied if X works 30 hrs/week for 20 weeks in a year for a business that operates only 25 weeks of the year ($30 \times 20 / 25 \geq 20$).

A person who works more than 20 hrs/week but cannot work for a period, such as after having a baby, may still qualify (under 120.4(1)"excluded business"): VIEWS doc 2018-0770911E5. See also 2018-0761601E5 (criteria CRA will consider); 2019-0792001E5 (paid leave cannot be included in the 20 hrs/week); 2019-0799911C6 [2019 STEP q.4] (spouse working 20 hrs/week as receptionist qualifies even without salary); 2020-0837631C6 [2020 STEP q.9] (working for multiple related companies cannot be combined to reach 20 hrs/week).

Para. (b) provides a continuity rule for inherited property. It applies to amounts that would, absent this rule, be split income of X if X is at least 17 at start of year, for property that was acquired by or for the benefit of X as a "consequence" (248(8)) of the death of another person. (b)(i) allows X to avoid TOSI to the extent that an amount, had it been received by the deceased, would have been a "reasonable return" for 120.4(1)"excluded amount"(g)(ii).

(b)(ii) provides that income on inherited property qualifies as an "excluded amount" to the extent the amount, had it been received by the deceased, would have been from an "excluded business" under 120.4(1)"excluded amount"(e)(ii) because the deceased was actively engaged on a regular, continuous and substantial basis in the activities of the related business throughout any 5 previous years (for the meaning of "actively engaged...", see Notes to 120.4(1)"excluded business"). See also VIEWS docs 2019-0799941C6 [2019 STEP q.6] (tracing on multiple deaths; (b)(ii) deems the individual's status with respect to *all* shares owned, once it applies); 2019-0824401C6 [2019 CTF q.7] (application where *inter vivos* trust requires distribution of property on death).

(b)(iii) provides that, for the "excluded shares" and "reasonable return" tests in 120.4(1)"excluded amount"(g) (which generally apply only if X is at least 24 at start of year), if the deceased had reached age 24 before the year of death, X is deemed to have reached age 24 before the year. This deeming rule applies only for determining whether TOSI applies to amounts derived from the inherited property acquired by or for the benefit of X. This allows an X who is 17-23 at start of year to potentially qualify for these exclusions from TOSI if the deceased qualified before death.

For interpretation of para. (b) see VIEWS doc 2018-0777361E5 (general discussion).

Para. (c) applies to amounts received by X in a year, if X's spouse or common law partner (S-CLP) turned 64 years by the start of the year, or died before the end of the year. An amount is an "excluded amount" (EA) in X's hands if it would have been an EA in the hands of the S-CLP, if it had been received by the S-CLP as income in the year (or in their last taxation year, if dead). (In determining whether an amount would have been an EA in the last taxation year of an individual for a taxation year before the 2018 amendments came into force, the new definition of EA applies.)

This exclusion of a S-CLP over 65 means that a corporation can be used to split retirement income, just as 60.03 allows pension income splitting.

For (c)(ii) see VIEWS docs 2018-0765801C6 [2018 APFF Financial q.3]; 2019-0799961C6 [2019 STEP q.5] (holding through trust after spouse's death).

Para. (d) clarifies that certain amounts are included in what is "derived, directly or indirectly, from a business". The first is an amount derived from provision of property or services to, or in support of, the business. This is based on 120.4(1)"split income"(b)(ii) and (c)(ii). Second is an equity return on an interest in a partnership, corporation or trust carrying on a business. Third, (d)(ii) is an iterative rule so that income derived from income derived from a business is caught; but despite (d)(ii), CRA says second-generation income (earned from investing income from a related business) is not caught: docs 2018-0771861E5, 2018-0778661C6 [2018 APFF q.13], 2018-0779981C6 [2018 CTF q.9]. See also 2019-0792001E5 (investment income from corp acquired with proceeds from sale of active Opco: not considered from "excluded business").

Para. (d) uses "includes" rather than "means", so the ordinary meaning of "derived directly or indirectly" also applies: see Notes to 188.1(5). For "derived" see Notes to 94(1)"resident portion". For "indirectly" see Notes to 17.1(1).

Para. (e) provides that spouses and common-law partners are deemed not related for 120.4 if they are living separate and apart due to breakdown of the marriage or c-l partnership. See Kyle Lamothe, "TOSI on a Marriage Breakdown", 26(7) *Canadian Tax Highlights* (ctf.ca) 7 (July 2018).

120.4(1.1) in the July 18, 2017 draft legislation included several more rules, including an extended definition of "related" that included aunt, uncle, niece and nephew (draft 120.4(1.1)(a)). These have been dropped.

120.4(1.1) added by 2018 budget bill #1, for 2018 and later tax years. (c)(i)(B) corrected from "common law partner" to "common-law partner", Feb. 2020: laws.justice.gc.ca/eng/corrections.

(2) Tax on split income — There shall be added to a specified individual's tax payable under this Part for a taxation year the highest individual percentage for the year multiplied by the individual's split income for the year.

Related Provisions: 20(1)(ww) — Split income deducted from income for regular tax purposes; 120.2(1), 120.2(1)(b)(i) — No AMT carryover allowed against split-income tax; 120.4(3) — Minimum amount of income-splitting tax; 127.5 — Alternative minimum tax cannot be less than split-income tax; 160(1.2) — Parent (or other person) jointly liable with child (or other specified individual) for tax.

Notes: The "highest individual percentage" (248(1)) is 33%, the top rate in 117(2). The effect is to tax a child's "split income" (or that of another "specified individual"), such as dividends from private corporations, at the rate that applies to high-income taxpayers. See Notes at end of 120.4. If the split income is most or all of the child's income, see also 120.4(3).

120.4(2) amended by 2016 tax-rate bill, for 2016 and later taxation years, to change "29% of" to "the highest individual percentage for the year multiplied by".

Forms: T1206: Tax on split income.

(3) Tax payable by a specified individual — Notwithstanding any other provision of this Act, if an individual is a specified individual for a taxation year, the individual's tax payable under this Part for the year shall not be less than the amount by which the amount added under subsection (2) to the individual's tax payable under this Part for the year exceeds the amount determined by the formula

$$A + B$$

where

A is the amount deducted under section 118.3 in computing the individual's tax payable under this Part for the year; and

B is the total of all amounts each of which is the amount that

(a) may be deducted under section 121 or 126 in computing the individual's tax payable under this Part for the year, and

(b) can reasonably be considered to be in respect of an amount included in computing the individual's split income for the year.

Notes: 120.4(3) provides that if X is a "specified individual", X's federal tax payable is not less than X's split income for the year times 33%, reduced only by the dividend tax credit and the foreign tax credit on that income. (No personal and other credits, such as the charitable donation credit: VIEWS doc 2020-0837621C6 [2020 STEP q.8].) However, the disability credit under 118.3 can still be claimed. This subsection catches cases where the split income is most or all of the child's taxable income.

120.4(3) amended by 2018 budget bill #1, for 2018 and later tax years, essentially to add formula element A. For 2000-2017, read:

(3) Notwithstanding any other provision of this Act, where an individual is a specified individual in relation to a taxation year, the individual's tax payable under this Part for the year shall not be less than the amount by which

(a) the amount added under subsection (2) to the individual's tax payable under this Part for the year

exceeds

(b) the total of all amounts each of which is an amount that

(i) may be deducted under section 121 or 126 in computing the individual's tax payable under this Part for the year, and

(ii) can reasonably be considered to be in respect of an amount included in computing the individual's split income for the year.

(4) Taxable capital gain — If a specified individual who has not attained the age of 17 years before a taxation year would have for the taxation year, if this Act were read without reference to this section, a taxable capital gain (other than an excluded amount) from a disposition of shares (other than shares of a class listed on a designated stock exchange or shares of a mutual fund corporation) that are transferred, either directly or indirectly, in any manner whatever, to a person with whom the specified individual does not deal at arm's length, then the amount of that taxable capital gain is deemed not to be a taxable capital gain and twice the amount is deemed to be received by the specified individual in the year as a taxable dividend that is not an eligible dividend.

Related Provisions: 48.1(1) — Deemed disposition when small business corporation goes public does not apply to 120.4(4); 104(21.2)(b) — Deemed taxable capital gain when trust designates gain to flow out to beneficiary.

Notes: 120.4(4) generally provides that if X is a "specified individual" under 18 at year-end, X's capital gain from disposition of certain shares transferred to a non-arm's length person is subject to TOSI. The amount that would have been X's capital gain is deemed to be a taxable dividend received by X and included in X's split income.

As announced in the 2011 Budget, 120.4(4)-(5) extended the kiddie tax to capital gains, and apply dividend tax rates instead of capital gains rates. This responded to income-splitting techniques that used capital gains to avoid TOSI, by having capital gains realized for the benefit of a minor on disposition of shares to a person not dealing at arm's length with the minor. Before 120.4(4)-(5), TOSI did not apply in: *McClarty Family Trust*, 2012 TCC 80 (stock dividends and circular payments converted dividend income to capital gains; GAAR did not apply as there was a genuine creditor-proofing purpose); *Gwartz*, 2013 TCC 86 (dividends on high-low shares to a family trust generated capital gains; this did not violate GAAR).

The deemed taxable dividend under 120.4(4) and (5) is deemed for all purposes of the Act, not just 120.4. Thus, the gross-up (82(1)) and dividend tax credit (s. 121) apply. A child's crystallization of the capital gains exemption would be deemed not to have happened: VIEWS doc 2012-0432241E5. However, no dividend refund is created because the corporation is not deemed to have *paid* a dividend: 2013-0480261C6.

For the meaning of "indirectly", see Notes to 17.1(1).

See Hudson, "Section 120.4: Finance Not Kidding About the Kiddie Tax", 11(4) *Tax for the Owner-Manager* (ctf.ca) 3 (Oct. 2011); Goldberg, "Update — Federal Budget Targets Planning Involving Minors", 201 *The Estate Planner* (CCH) 1-3 (Oct. 2011); Gasparro, "Current Issues", 2011 Ontario Tax Conference (ctf.ca), 1B:1-27.

120.4(4) amended by 2018 budget bill #1, for 2018 and later tax years, to add "who has not attained the age of 17 years before taxation year", to keep the rule applying only to those under 18 at year-end. Added by 2011 budget bill #2, for dispositions after March 21, 2011.

(5) Taxable capital gain of trust — If a specified individual who has not attained the age of 17 years before a taxation year would be, if this Act were read without reference to this section, required under subsection 104(13) or 105(2) to include an amount in computing the specified individual's income for the taxation

year, then to the extent that the amount can reasonably be considered to be attributable to a taxable capital gain (other than an excluded amount) of a trust from a disposition of shares (other than shares of a class listed on a designated stock exchange or shares of a mutual fund corporation) that are transferred, either directly or indirectly, in any manner whatever, to a person with whom the specified individual does not deal at arm's length, subsections 104(13) and 105(2) do not apply in respect of the amount and twice the amount is deemed to be received by the specified individual in the year as a taxable dividend that is not an eligible dividend.

Related Provisions: 48.1(1) — Deemed disposition when small business corporation goes public does not apply to 120.4(5).

Notes: See Notes to 120.4(4). 120.4(5) generally applies in a similar manner, where X would otherwise have income from a trust under 104(13)(a) or 105(2) that is attributable to capital gains of the trust.

120.4(5) amended by 2018 budget bill #1, for 2018 and later tax years, to add "who has not attained the age of 17 years before a taxation year" ("a the" corrected to "a": laws.justice.gc.ca/eng/corrections). This keeps the rule applying only to those under 18 at year-end. Added by 2011 budget bill #2, for dispositions after March 21, 2011.

Notes [s. 120.4]: 120.4 implements the "tax on split income" (TOSI), known as the "kiddie tax" before 2018, but now applicable to adults as well. It taxes "split income" (defined in 120.4(1)) at the top marginal rate of 33% federal tax, plus provincial tax, and prevents most credits from reducing this tax if the split income is the person's only income: 120.4(2), (3).

120.4 was extensively amended by 2018 budget bill #1, for 2018 and later tax years (see Notes to each definition and subsection). TOSI now catches income sprinkling to adult (close) family members, most commonly by dividend, but also shareholder appropriations and through trusts and partnerships. There are numerous exceptions: see 120.4(1)"excluded amount", "excluded business" and "excluded shares", and 120.4(1.1)(a) (working 20 hours/week or more in the business) and (c)(i) (sprinkling to a spouse of a business owner over age 65). See also Notes to 120.4(1)"excluded amount" and "related business". Comprehensive discussion is in the CRA *Guidance* (tinyurl.com/cra-splitinc).

To analyse a TOSI problem, start from 120.4(2) and determine if there is 120.4(1)"split income"(a)-(e), carving out a 120.4(1)"excluded amount", which requires stepping through that definition in detail and considering 120.4(1)"related business" [which depends on there being a "source individual"] (bad), "excluded business" (good), "excluded shares" (good), "reasonable return" (good) and "safe harbour capital return" (good). And consider the additional rules in 120.4(1.1). For a flowchart see tinyurl.com/moodys-tosi, or *Tax on Split Income (TOSI) Navigation Tool* (*Taxnet Pro* Tax & Estate Planning Centre, March 2021, 17pp). For software that does the analysis see *Tax on Split Income Navigator* at bluejlegal.com.

Note that 120.4 does not apply to salary, although s. 67 may apply; and arguably an unreasonable salary could be a shareholder benefit (15(1)) triggering 120.4(1)"split income"(a)(ii). See CRA *Guidance*, Example 5B; Klyguine, "Income Splitting ... Salaries Paid to Family Members", 8(1) *Canadian Tax Focus* (ctf.ca) 1-2 (Feb. 2018). 120.4 does not apply to income from an unincorporated business that is not earned via partnership or trust (see 120.4(1)"split income").

The parent or other "source individual" may be jointly liable for the tax if the person subject to TOSI is under 25 at year-end: 160(1.2).

The amendments were first proposed in a July 18, 2017 consultation paper (reproduced here in PITA 53rd ed.) that also proposed to: (1) limit use of the capital gains exemption (later abandoned: see under 110.6(12)); (2) prevent conversions of dividends to capital gains (later abandoned: see under 84.1(1) and 246.1); (3) tax passive income of CCPCs at a high rate (later changed to a grind-down of the small business deduction: see 125(5.1)(b) and under 123.3). This caused a storm of protest from the tax community, small business, doctors, farmers, the Conservative Party and others. News releases and Backgrounders of Oct. 3, 16, 18, 19 and 20 and Dec. 13, 2017 announced changes to and dropping of many of the proposals. The TOSI rules were substantially simplified in the Dec. 13 draft, which was enacted largely unchanged.

For more discussion see Sideris & Espiritu, *Taxation of Private Corporations and their Shareholders* (ctf.ca, 5th ed., 2020), chap. 8; Keey, "Revised TOSI Rules", *General Corporate Tax* newsletter, *Taxnet Pro* Corporate Tax Centre, Jan. 2018 (26pp); Keung, "The Income Sprinkling Trilogy", March 26, 2018 (tinyurl.com/moodys-v3tosi); Ratnam, "How the New TOSI Rules Impact your Family", XXIII(1) *Insurance Planning* (Federated Press) 14-17 (2018); Santia, "Revisiting Planning for Private Company Shareholders", 66(2) *Canadian Tax Journal* 421-45 (2018); Zuchetto & Brown, "Estate Freezing and the TOSI", VII(1) *Personal Tax & Estate Planning* (Federated Press) 8-15 (2018); Gervais & Sideris, "Do the New Income Sprinkling Rules Affect My Family?", 2017 Cdn Tax Foundation conference report, 14:1-24; Gallant, "TOSI Rules", 2018 Prairie Provinces Tax Conference [PPTC] (ctf.ca); Bolleter, "Tax on Split Income", 2018 Ontario Tax Conference (ctf.ca), 12:1-11; Ideias, "Tax on Split Income... What a Tax Planner Needs to Know" (*Taxnet Pro* Tax & Estate Planning Centre, 2021, 9pp); Abrams, "Income from Publicly-Traded Partnerships: Subject to TOSI?", 19(2) *Tax for the Owner-Manager [TfOM]* (ctf.ca) 6-7 (April 2019); Jotic, Robinet &

Bonanno, "Potential Uncertainty When Capital Gains are Subject to TOSI", 27(4) *Canadian Tax Highlights* (ctf.ca) 9-10 (April 2019); Lee, "Shareholder Loan: Does TOSI Prevent a Deduction on Repayment?", 9(2) *Canadian Tax Focus* (ctf.ca) 1-2 (May 2019); Malik & Kim, "Planning in the Brave New World of TOSI", 2019 PPTC (85pp); Ni & Fabbro, "An Overview of Tax on Split Income", *ibid.* (73pp); Katlai, "TOSI and Dividends from Rental Income" 19(3) *TfOM* 8-9 (July 2019); VanGilst, "Four TOSI Exceptions Available to Farmers", 2019(21) *Tax Times* (Carswell) 1-2 (Nov. 8, 2019); Woolley & Ong, "Planning for Distribution Under TOSI: A Dozen TOSI Tips", 2019 BC Tax Conf. 10:1-86; Baxter, "Prescribed-Rate Loan Planning and TOSI", 16(6) *Tax Hyperion* (Carswell) 4-6 (Nov-Dec 2019); Shadrin, Kakkar & Ghani, "FAPI and TOSI Overlap: 107% Tax Is Not Fair", 20(1) *TfOM* 5-6 (Jan. 2020); de Gannes, Jaggi & Jessa, "Tax on Split Income — A Practical Approach", 2019 Ont. Tax Conf. 8 (153pp); Conrad, "TOSI — Things You Need To Know", 2019 Atlantic Provinces Tax Conf. 4:1-39.

CRA interpretations: see Notes to the definitions and subsections above; "TOSI for Adults" PowerPoint, in VIEWS doc 2018-0773811C6; Keung, "A critical review of recent CRA views on TOSI and how to use them to your advantage", tinyurl.com/tosi-views (Jan. 31, 2019); "Tax on Split Income: CRA Views and Guidance Quick Reference Table", *Taxnet Pro* Tax & Estate Planning Centre (March 2021, 15pp); Mancell, "A Comprehensive Review of Every Interpretation of the Revised TOSI Rules", 2452 *Tax Topics* (CCH) 1-9 (March 7, 2019).

On application to partnerships and trusts see Potechin, "What Canada's new income-splitting rules mean for partnerships" (tinyurl.com/tosi-pships); Ross & Potechin, "Canada's new income splitting tax rules and family trusts" (tinyurl.com/tosi-trusts).

These changes will generate tax revenue of $435m-$1.07b: Parliamentary Budget Officer, *Income Sprinkling Using Private Corporations* (March 8, 2018, 22pp).

The Standing Senate Committee on National Finance issued a detailed report in Dec. 2017, *Fair, Simple and Competitive Taxation*, recommending the (revised) proposed changes be withdrawn and the government "undertake an independent, comprehensive review of Canada's tax system", or at least that the proposals be delayed until 2019. Despite lobbying to the Senate, the Budget bill containing these rules was enacted in June 2018.

Pre-2018 120.4 applied to income of a child under 18 attributable to dividends, capital gains or shareholder appropriations from private corporations, or to income earned through a trust or partnership derived from goods or services provided to (or in support of) a related person's business (former 120.4(1)"split income"). It thus effectively overrode *Ferrel*, [1999] 2 C.T.C. 101 (FCA), and caught income of a parent that was diverted, through a trust or otherwise, to a child. Since 2018 TOSI is much extended.

On the pre-2018 rules see VIEWS docs 2012-0465001E5 (general discussion); 2013-0480261C6 (120.4 can apply if one parent is resident in Canada, even if not the contributing parent; 120.4 can apply to a capital gains exemption crystallization); 2013-049397117 (120.4 may apply where parent splits income with LLP of which trust for children is a partner); and Notes to 120.4(4) and 120.4(1)"split income".

For discussion of pre-2018 120.4, see Donnelly et al., "Income Splitting and the New Kiddie Tax", 48(4) *Canadian Tax Journal* 979-1018 (2000); Sherloski & Faye, "The Kiddie Tax", 2000 Prairie Provinces Tax Conference (ctf.ca), 8:1-17.

Pre-2018, CRA wrote to many children reporting dividend income, asking them to prove the income was not "split income" and stating that without such proof, the return would be reassessed on the assumption it was. Perhaps this will now be expanded to include young adults.

The pre-2018 kiddie tax applied in *Jeannotte*, 2011 TCC 247 (arrangement set up in 1994 for granddaughters' education). For other case law see Notes to 120.4(4).

120.4 added by 1999 Budget for 2000 and later taxation years.

Definitions [s. 120.4]: "actively engaged" — 120.4(1.1)(a); "amount", "business" — 248(1); "arm's length" — 251(1); "arm's length capital" — 120.4(1); "bank" — 248(1); "beneficiary" — 248(25) [Notes]; "Canada" — 255, *Interpretation Act* 35(1); "capital gain" — 39(1)(a), 248(1); "common-law partner" — 248(1); "consequence of the death" — 248(8); "corporation" — 248(1), *Interpretation Act* 35(1); "credit union" — 137(6), 248(1); "derived directly or indirectly" — 120.4(1.1)(d); "designated stock exchange" — 248(1), 262; "disposition" — 248(1); "eligible dividend" — 89(1), 248(1); "excluded amount", "excluded business", "excluded shares" — 120.4(1); "fair market value" — see 69(1) Notes; "highest individual percentage", "individual" — 248(1); "mutual fund corporation" — 131(8), 248(1); "mutual fund trust" — 132(6)-(7), 132.2(3)(n), 248(1); "non-resident" — 248(1); "parent" — 252(2)(a); "partnership" — see 96(1) Notes; "person" — 248(1); "post-secondary educational institution" — 146.1(1); "prescribed", "professional corporation", "property" — 248(1); "public market" — 122.1(1), 248(1); "qualified farm or fishing property", "qualified small business corporation share" — 110.6(1) *[technically do not apply to 120.4]*; "reasonable return", "related business" — 120.4(1); "resident in Canada" — 250; "safe harbour capital return" — 120.4(1); "share", "shareholder", "small business corporation" — 248(1); "source individual" — 120.4(1); "specified individual" — 120.4(1), 248(1); "specified shareholder" — 248(1); "split income" — 120.4(1), 248(1); "substitute", "substituted" — 248(5); "taxable capital gain" — 38(a), 248(1); "taxable dividend" — 89(1), 120.4(4), (5), 248(1); "taxpayer" — 248(1); "trust" — 104(1), 248(1), (3).

121. Deduction for taxable dividends [dividend tax credit] — There may be deducted from the tax otherwise payable under this Part by an individual for a taxation year the total of

(a) **[non-eligible dividends]** — the product of the amount, if any, that is required by subparagraph 82(1)(b)(i) to be included in computing the individual's income for the year multiplied by

(i) for the 2018 taxation year, $^8/_{11}$, and

(ii) for taxation years after 2018, $^9/_{13}$, and

(b) **[eligible dividends]** — the product of the amount, if any, that is required by subparagraph 82(1)(b)(ii) to be included in computing the individual's income for the year multiplied by

(i) for the 2009 taxation year, $^{11}/_{18}$,

(ii) for the 2010 taxation year, $^{10}/_{17}$,

(iii) for the 2011 taxation year, $^{13}/_{23}$, and

(iv) for taxation years after 2011, $^6/_{11}$.

Related Provisions: 82(2) — Dividends deemed received by taxpayer; 117(1) — Tax payable under this Part; 118.92 — Ordering of credits; 120.4(3)B(a) — Dividend tax credit deductible against income-splitting tax.

Notes: See Notes to 82(1). The 82(1)(b)(i) "gross-up" increases the amount on which personal tax is paid to the theoretical pre-tax corporate income. For **non-eligible dividends (NED)**, the 15% gross-up (since 2019) presumes a federal-provincial corporate tax rate of 13.04% (15/115ths: 15% of $86.96 — which is what is left of $100 after paying 13.04% tax — is $13.04). The dividend tax credit (DTC) in s. 121 then refunds an amount equal to the tax paid, in theory, by the corp (i.e., the gross-up), to achieve "integration". The 9/13ths in 121(a)(ii) is for the underlying federal tax only. Each province provides a credit for the provincial corporate tax; since the credit varies by province, the effective DTC is not exactly the same as the gross-up. For **eligible dividends (ED)**, the same principle applies to the 38% gross-up under 82(1)(b)(ii), which presumes a 27.5% (38/138ths) federal+provincial tax for public companies; the 6/11 DTC similarly refunds only the presumed federal tax and leaves room for the province to refund provincial corporate tax. These amounts are adjusted periodically to reflect changes in corp tax rates. See also Tobias, *Taxation of Corporations, Partnerships and Trusts* (Carswell, 5th ed., 2017), chap. 9.

For 2019 and later years (15% gross-up for NED), the 9/13 fraction (of the gross-up) means the federal credit is 9.03% (9/13 × 15 / 1.15) of the grossed-up dividend [note this is essentially the same as the 9% small business federal corporate rate due to 125(1.1)], and 10.38% (9/13 × 15%) of the actual dividend. The top federal tax on NED is thus 33% on 115% of the dividend [0.33 × 1.15 = 37.95%], minus 10.38% dividend tax credit, or **27.57%**.

For 2018 (16% gross-up for NED), the 8/11 fraction (of the gross-up) means the federal credit was 10.03% (8/11 × 16 / 1.16) of the grossed-up dividend [note this is essentially the same as the 10% small business federal corp rate due to 125(1.1)], and 11.64% (8/11 × 16%) of the actual dividend. The top federal tax on NED was thus 33% on 116% of the dividend [0.33 × 1.16 = 38.28%], minus 11.64% dividend tax credit, or 26.64%.

For 2016-2017 (17% gross-up), the 121(a) fraction was 21/29ths. For 2014-2015 (18% gross-up) it was 13/18.

"There may be deducted" means the DTC claim is optional, but a partial claim is not allowed: VIEWS doc 2012-043904E5.

121 amended by 2018 budget bill #1 (to change the 121(a) fraction for 2018 and later tax years), 2016 budget bill #1 and 2015 Budget bill (both to change it for 2016 and later tax years), 2013 and 2008 budget bills #1, 2006 budget bill #2.

Definitions [s. 121]: "amount", "individual" — 248(1); "taxation year" — 249.

Interpretation Bulletins: IT-67R3: Taxable dividends from corporations resident in Canada; IT-295R4: Taxable dividends received after 1987 by spouse; IT-379R: Employees profit sharing plans — allocations to beneficiaries; IT-524: Trusts — flow-through of taxable dividends to a beneficiary after 1987.

Forms: T1 General return, Sched. 1, Line 40425 [former 425].

122. (1) Tax payable by trust — Notwithstanding section 117, the tax payable under this Part for a taxation year by a trust (other than a graduated rate estate or qualified disability trust) is the total of

(a) the highest individual percentage for the taxation year multiplied by the trust's amount taxable for the taxation year,

(b) if the trust is a SIFT trust for the taxation year, the positive or negative amount determined by the formula

$$A \times B$$

where

A is the positive or negative decimal fraction determined by the formula

$$C + D - E$$

where

C is the net corporate income tax rate in respect of the SIFT trust for the taxation year,

D is the provincial SIFT tax rate of the SIFT trust for the taxation year, and

E is the decimal fraction equivalent of the percentage rate of tax provided in paragraph (a) for the taxation year, and

B is the SIFT trust's taxable SIFT trust distributions for the taxation year, and

(c) if subsection (2) applies to the trust for the taxation year, the amount determined by the formula

$$A - (B - C)$$

where

A is the amount that would be determined for B for the year if

(i) the rate of tax payable under this Part by the trust for each taxation year referred to in the description of B were the highest individual percentage for the taxation year, and

(ii) the trust's taxable income for a particular taxation year referred to in the description of B were reduced by the total of

(A) the amount, if any, that was paid or distributed in satisfaction of all or part of an individual's interest as a beneficiary under the trust if

(I) the individual was an electing beneficiary of the trust for the particular year,

(II) the payment or distribution can reasonably be considered to be made out of that taxable income, and

(III) the payment or distribution was made in a taxation year referred to in the description of B,

(B) the amount that is the portion of the tax payable under this Part by the trust for the particular year that can reasonably be considered to relate to the amount determined under clause (A), and

(C) the amount that is the portion of the tax payable, under the law of the province in which the trust is resident for the particular year, that can reasonably be considered to relate to the amount determined under clause (A),

B is the total of all amounts each of which is the amount of tax payable under this Part by the trust for a taxation year that precedes the year if that preceding taxation year is

(i) the later of

(A) the first taxation year for which the trust was a qualified disability trust, and

(B) the last taxation year, if any, for which subsection (2) applied to the trust, or

(ii) a taxation year that ends after the taxation year described in subparagraph (i), and

C is the total of all amounts each of which is an amount determined for clause (ii)(B) of the description of A in determining the amount for A for the year.

Related Provisions: 117(2) — Amount taxable; 120(3)(d) — SIFT trust distribution not taxed provincially; 122(2) — Qualified disability trust — application of 122(1)(c); 157(2) — SIFT trust pays same instalments as a corporation; 197(2) — Taxation of SIFT partnership distributions; 257 — Formula cannot calculate to less than zero.

Notes: *122(1)(a)* provides that all trusts, other than a GRE (see Notes to 248(1)"graduated rate estate") or QDT (122(3)"qualified disability trust"), pay flat tax at the top marginal rate, which is 33% (federal tax) starting 2016. Before 2016, both estates and testamentary trusts (TTs) paid at the 15%-29% marginal rates that applied to individuals (122(1) applies only to *inter vivos* trusts). As of 2016, a TT does not qualify for low rates unless it is a QDT, and an estate qualifies for only 3 years, and only if it meets the GRE definition. These changes respond to the use of TTs for income splitting. See generally tinyurl.com/cra-gre.

Related pre-2016 benefits for TTs that were repealed or changed to apply only to GREs include: 80.04(6)(a)(ii)(B) (deadline for filing debt forgiveness transfer agreement); 104(23)(e) (exemption from income tax instalment rules); 127(7) (investment tax credit flow-out to beneficiaries); 127.51, 127.53 ($40,000 exemption from minimum tax); 152(4.2) (statute-barred reassessment to reduce tax); 164(1.5) (refund where return filed more than 3 years after year-end); 165(1)(a)(i) (extended objection deadline for recent year); 210(1)"designated beneficiary"(d), 210(2)(a) (preferential treatment under Part XII.2); 248(1)"personal trust"(a) (personal trust status); 249(1)(c) (exemption from requirement to use the calendar year).

These changes were first floated in the March 2013 Budget, then introduced as proposals for comment on June 3, 2013, then enacted by 2014 budget bill #2. For discussion see Glover, "Testamentary Trusts", 3(2) *Canadian Tax Focus* (ctf.ca) 2 (May 2013); CBA/CPA Canada Joint Committee on Taxation letter to Finance, Dec. 2, 2013 (recommended no change, or expanding the preferred beneficiary election to compensate); STEP Canada letter, Dec. 2, 2013 (criticized proposals as not based on empirical or tax policy analysis, and recommended relief for trusts for disadvantaged beneficiaries and for spouses, as well as grandfathering; APFF letter (apff.org), Dec. 2, 2013 (various criticisms and recommendations).

Even before these changes, if an estate took too long to wind up, intending to continue with the graduated rates, the beneficiary could be taxed on the income: *Grayson*, [1990] 1 C.T.C. 2303 (TCC).

122(1)(b) implements the distributions tax on income trusts (see Notes to 104(16)). The "net corporate income tax rate" (248(1)) was 21% for 2007, 19.5% for 2008, 19% for 2009, 18% for 2010, 16.5% for 2011 and 15% since 2012 — the same rate as under 123.4(2). The "provincial SIFT tax rate" (248(1)) is added. Thus, the combined tax under 122(1)(b) is equivalent to the federal and provincial corporate tax rates. (There is no additional provincial tax: see 120(3)(d).) This tax has applied since 2011, or earlier for new trusts or those that exceed "normal growth" guidelines: see 122.1(2).

122(1)(c) provides for "recovery" of tax from a trust that elected in an earlier year to be a qualified disability trust (QDT). The amount recovered is, in effect, the tax for the earlier year on the trust's income for that year that is not distributed to an individual who was an "electing beneficiary" of the trust for the earlier year. 122(2) sets out the conditions for 122(1)(c). When it applies, 122(1)(c) requires the trust to pay, in addition to the 29% tax under 122(1)(a), the formula amount A−B. In general terms, A is the total tax the trust would have paid under Part I for an earlier year if the trust had not been a QDT and it flowed out to an electing beneficiary the amount of its taxable income for that year that was later distributed to that beneficiary (i.e., as a capital distribution). B computes the actual tax paid by the trust on its taxable income for each such earlier year. The difference between these amounts is the tax recovered for the year in which 122(1)(c) applies. (The Finance Technical Notes contain more detail and examples.) See VIEWS doc 2016-0651751C6 [2016 APFF q.7] (application to undistributed income after beneficiary dies).

122(1)(c) formula changed from "A−B", and C added, by 2017 budget bill #2, for taxation years that end after Sept. 15, 2016. The effect of C is to ensure that, to the extent credit is given in computing A for federal income tax paid in respect of an electing beneficiary's share of the trust's taxable income for an earlier year, credit for that amount is not also provided for under B. (Finance Technical Notes)

122(1)(a) changed from "29% of its amount taxable for the taxation year" by 2016 tax-rate bill, for 2016 and later taxation years. The rate is now 33%; see 248(1)"highest individual percentage" and 117(2)(e).

122(1)(c)A(i) amended by 2016 budget bill #1, for 2016 and later taxation years, to change "29%" to "the highest individual percentage for the taxation year" (due to the top rate in 117(2) rising to 33%).

122(1) opening words amended and (c) added by 2014 budget bill #2, for 2016 and later taxation years.

122(1) earlier amended by 2008 budget bill #1 (for 2009 and later taxation years), 2007 budget bill #1.

Interpretation Bulletins: IT-83R3: Non-profit organizations — taxation of income from property.

Information Circulars: 78-5R3: Communal organizations.

Forms: T3QDT: Joint election for a trust to be a qualified disability trust; T3QDT-WS: Recovery tax worksheet.

(1.1) Credits available to trusts — No deduction may be made under this Subdivision (other than section 118.1, 120.2 or 121) in computing the tax payable by a trust for a taxation year.

Notes: 122(1.1) prevents a trust from claiming any credits under 117-122.51, other than donations (118.1), minimum tax carryover (120.2) and dividend tax credit (121).

122(1.1) amended by 2014 budget bill #2, for 2016 and later taxation years. For 1988-2015, read: "No deduction may be made under section 118 in computing the tax payable by a trust for a taxation year".

Interpretation Bulletins: IT-83R3: Non-profit organizations — taxation of income from property; IT-406R2: Tax payable by an *inter vivos* trust.

(2) Qualified disability trust — application of (1)(c) — This subsection applies to a trust for a particular taxation year if the trust was a qualified disability trust for a preceding taxation year and

(a) none of the beneficiaries under the trust at the end of the particular year was an electing beneficiary of the trust for a preceding year;

(b) the particular year ended immediately before the trust ceased to be resident in Canada; or

(c) an amount is paid or distributed in the particular year to a beneficiary under the trust in satisfaction of all or part of the beneficiary's interest in the trust unless

(i) the beneficiary is an electing beneficiary of the trust for the particular year or a preceding year,

(ii) the amount is deducted under paragraph 104(6)(b) in computing the trust's income for the particular year, or

(iii) the amount is paid or distributed in satisfaction of a right to enforce payment of an amount that was deducted under paragraph 104(6)(b) in computing the trust's income for a preceding year.

Notes: See Notes to 122(1) re 122(1)(c).

122(2) replaced by 2014 budget bill #2, for 2016 and later taxation years. For 2003-2015, a different 122(2) provided a grandfathering that no longer applies.

122(2) earlier amended by 2002-2013 technical bill (for taxation years beginning after 2002), 2001 technical bill.

(3) Definitions — The following definitions apply in this section.

"beneficiary", under a trust, includes a person beneficially interested in the trust.

Notes: This definition is not really necessary, since the FCA effectively extended the same definition in 108(1) to the entire Act in *Propep Inc.*, 2009 CarswellNat 2923 (leave to appeal denied 2010 CarswellNat 506 (SCC)), ruling that 248(25) applied to "beneficiary" in 256(1.2)(f)(ii).

See Notes to 188.1(5) re meaning of "includes".

Definition added by 2014 budget bill #2, for 2016 and later taxation years.

"electing beneficiary", for a taxation year of a qualified disability trust, means a beneficiary under the trust that for the year

(a) makes an election described in clause (a)(iii)(A) of the definition "qualified disability trust" in this subsection; and

(b) is described in paragraph (b) of that definition.

Notes: Definition added by 2014 budget bill #2, for 2016 and later taxation years.

"non-deductible distributions amount" for a taxation year has the meaning assigned by subsection 104(16).

"qualified disability trust", for a taxation year (in this definition referred to as the "trust year"), means a trust, if

(a) the trust

(i) is, at the end of the trust year, a testamentary trust that arose on and as a consequence of a particular individual's death,

(ii) is resident in Canada for the trust year, and

(iii) includes in its return of income under this Part for the trust year

(A) an election, made jointly with one or more beneficiaries under the trust in prescribed form, to be a qualified disability trust for the trust year, and

(B) the Social Insurance Number of each of those beneficiaries;

(b) each of those beneficiaries is an individual, named as a beneficiary by the particular individual in the instrument under which the trust was created,

(i) in respect of whom paragraphs 118.3(1)(a) to (b) apply for the individual's taxation year (in this definition referred to as the "beneficiary year") in which the trust year ends, and

(ii) who does not jointly elect with any other trust, for a taxation year of the other trust that ends in the beneficiary year, to be a qualified disability trust; and

(c) subsection (2) does not apply to the trust for the trust year.

Related Provisions: 54"principal residence"(c.1)(iii.1)(B) — Principal residence exemption; 94(4)(b) — Deeming non-resident trust to be resident in Canada does not apply.

Notes: A QDT pays low marginal rates of tax (122(1) opening words), but a clawback applies if anyone other than an electing disabled beneficiary benefits from the trust: 122(1)(c), 122(2).

Note that (a)(ii) requires the trust to be *factually* resident in Canada (see Notes to 250(1)), since 94(4)(b) excludes 94(3) from applying to it.

The (a)(iii)(A) election must be copied to Revenu Québec, for a trust or beneficiary filing a Quebec return: *Taxation Act* ss. 768.2, 21.4.6.

In para. (b), "named" cannot include an unborn person: VIEWS doc 2016-0651741C6 [2016 APFF q.6].

Subpara. (b)(ii) means that a disabled person can benefit from only one QDT, so two parents cannot each separately leave funds for a trust for the same child and have those trusts qualify for low marginal rates.

A QDT can make a preferred beneficiary election under 104(14): docs 2015-0605111E5, 2016-0645801C6 [2016 STEP q.4]. A graduated rate estate whose beneficiary becomes disabled likely cannot become a QDT: 2019-0805771C6 [2019 STEP q.11].

See also Lund, "...the New Qualified Disability Trust", V(3) *Personal Tax and Estate Planning* (Federated Press) 239-43 (2015); Blumenfeld, "The New Qualified Disability Trust", 9(1) *Taxes & Wealth Management* (Carswell) 12-14 (Feb. 2016). See also Notes to 60.011 re a Henson trust.

Definition added by 2014 budget bill #2, for 2016 and later taxation years.

Forms: T3QDT: Joint election for a trust to be a qualified disability trust.

"taxable SIFT trust distributions", of a SIFT trust for a taxation year, means the lesser of

(a) its amount taxable for the taxation year, and

(b) the amount determined by the formula

$$A/(1 - (B + C))$$

where

A   is its non-deductible distributions amount for the taxation year,

B   is the net corporate income tax rate in respect of the SIFT trust for the taxation year, and

C   is the provincial SIFT tax rate of the SIFT trust for the taxation year.

Notes: 122(3)"taxable SIFT trust distributions"C amended by 2008 budget bill #1, making the same change as to 122(1)(b)A:D.

Related Provisions: 117(2) — Amount taxable.

Notes [subsec. 122(3)]: 122(3) added by 2007 budget bill #1, effective Oct. 31, 2006. Former 122(3), repealed by 1985 technical bill, set out the tax rate for a mutual fund trust, now covered by 122(1).

Definitions [s. 122]: "allowable capital loss" — 38(b), 248(1); "amount" — 248(1); "amount taxable" — 117(2); "balance-due day" — 248(1); "business" — 248(1); "beneficial ownership" — 248(3); "beneficially interested" — 248(25); "beneficiary" — 122(3); "Canada" — 255; "contribution" — 94(1); "electing beneficiary" — 122(3); "graduated rate estate" — 248(1); "highest individual percentage", "individual" — 248(1); "inter vivos trust" — 108(1), 248(1); "months specified" — 122.5(4); "mutual fund trust" — 132(6)–(7), 132.2(3)(n), 248(1); "net corporate income tax rate" — 248(1); "non-deductible distributions amount" — 104(16), 122(3); "person", "prescribed", "property" — 248(1); "province" — *Interpretation Act* 35(1); "provincial SIFT tax rate" — 248(1); "qualified disability trust" — 122(3); "resident" — 250; "resident in Canada" — 94(3)(a), 250; "SIFT trust" — 122.1(1), (2), 248(1); "tax payable" — 248(2); "taxable capital gain" — 38(a), 248(1); "taxable income" — 2(2), 248(1); "taxable SIFT trust distributions" — 122(3); "taxation year" — 249; "testamentary trust" — 108(1), 248(1); "trust" — 104(1), 248(1), (3), "trust year" — 122(3)"qualified disability trust".

122.1 (1) Definitions — The following definitions apply in this section and in sections 104 and 122.

"eligible resale property", of an entity, means real or immovable property (other than capital property) of the entity

(a) that is contiguous to a particular real or immovable property that is capital property or eligible resale property, held by

(i) the entity, or

(ii) another entity affiliated with the entity; and

(b) the holding of which is ancillary to the holding of the particular property.

Related Provisions: 122.1(1)"qualified REIT property"(b)(ii) — Revenue from managing eligible resale properties; 122.1(1)"real estate investment trust"(b)(vi) — Gains from dispositions of eligible resale properties.

Notes: 122.1(1)"eligible resale property" added by 2002-2013 technical bill (Part 5 — technical), effective on same basis as 122.1(1.1).

"entity" means a corporation, trust or partnership.

Related Provisions: 12.6(1), 18.3(1)"entity" — Definition applies to stapled-security rules.

"equity", of an entity, means

(a) if the entity is a corporation, a share of the capital stock of the corporation;

(b) if the entity is a trust, an income or capital interest in the trust;

(c) if the entity is a partnership, an interest as a member of the partnership;

(d) a liability of the entity (and, for purposes of the definition "publicly-traded liability" in this section, a security of the entity that is a liability of another entity) if

(i) the liability is convertible into, or exchangeable for, equity of the entity or of another entity, or

(ii) any amount paid or payable in respect of the liability is contingent or dependent on the use of or production from property, or is computed by reference to revenue, profit, cash flow, commodity price or any other similar criterion or by reference to dividends paid or payable to shareholders of any class of shares of the capital stock of a corporation, or to income or capital paid or payable to any member of a partnership or beneficiary under a trust; and

(e) a right to, or to acquire, anything described in this paragraph and any of paragraphs (a) to (d).

Notes: Participating debt is treated as equity: subpara. (d)(ii).

122.1(1)"equity" added by 2008 budget bill #2, retroactive to Oct. 31, 2006.

"equity value", of an entity at any time, means the total fair market value at that time of

(a) if the entity is a corporation, all of the issued and outstanding shares of the capital stock of the corporation;

(b) if the entity is a trust, all of the income or capital interests in the trust; or

(c) if the entity is a partnership, all of the interests in the partnership.

Related Provisions: 12.6(1), 18.3(1)"equity value" — Definition applies to stapled-security rules.

Notes: For the meaning of "fair market value" see Notes to 69(1).

"excluded subsidiary entity", for a taxation year, means an entity none of the equity of which is at any time in the taxation year

(a) listed or traded on a stock exchange or other public market; nor

(b) held by any person or partnership other than

(i) a real estate investment trust,

(ii) a taxable Canadian corporation,

(iii) a SIFT trust (determined without reference to subsection (2)),

(iv) a SIFT partnership (determined without reference to subsection 197(8)),

(v) a person or partnership that does not have, in connection with the holding of a security of the entity, property the value of which is determined, all or in part, by reference to a security that is listed or traded on a stock exchange or other public market, or

(vi) an excluded subsidiary entity for the taxation year.

Related Provisions: 122.1(1)"SIFT trust" — Excluded subsidiary entity is not a SIFT trust.

Notes: For a ruling that a partnership is an excluded subsidiary entity following a reorganization, see VIEWS doc 2010-0358731R3.

Subpara. (b)(v) added (and former (b)(v) renumbered (vi)) by 2013 budget bill #2, effective Oct. 31, 2006, except that it does not apply for determining if an entity is an excluded subsidiary entity for taxation years of the entity that begin before July 21, 2011 if the entity so elects in writing filed with the Minister by Dec. 12, 2014.

122.1(1)"excluded subsidiary entity" added by 2008 budget bill #2, effective Oct. 31, 2006.

"gross REIT revenue", of an entity for a taxation year, means the amount, if any, by which the total of all amounts received or receivable in the year (depending on the method regularly followed by the entity in computing the entity's income) by the entity exceeds the total of all amounts each of which is the cost to the entity of a property disposed of in the year.

Related Provisions: 122.1(1.1), (1.2) — Character preservation rule.

Notes: Loans payable, equity contributions, GST/HST input tax credits, and rebates can generally be excluded from GRR: VIEWS doc 2018-0784661E5.

Definition added by 2002-2013 technical bill, effective on same basis as 122.1(1.1).

"investment", in a trust or partnership,

(a) means

(i) a property that is a security of the trust or partnership, or

(ii) a right which may reasonably be considered to replicate a return on, or the value of, a security of the trust or partnership; but

(b) does not include

(i) an unaffiliated publicly-traded liability of the trust or partnership, nor

(ii) regulated innovative capital.

Notes: The broad definitions of "investment" and "security" in 122.1(1) led the CBA/CICA Joint Committee to ask CRA how "SIFT trust" and "SIFT partnership" will apply to private partnerships and private trusts (letter, Feb. 3, 2009). For CRA's response re partnerships, see Notes to 197(1)"SIFT partnership". See also VIEWS doc 2010-0386841E5.

Para. (b) added by 2008 budget bill #2, retroactive to Oct. 31, 2006 (subparas. (a)(i), (ii) were formerly paras. (a), (b)).

"non-portfolio earnings", of a SIFT trust for a taxation year, means the total of

(a) the amount, if any, by which

(i) the total of all amounts each of which is the SIFT trust's income for the taxation year from a business carried on by it in Canada or from a non-portfolio property, other than income that is a taxable dividend received by the SIFT trust,

exceeds

(ii) the total of all amounts each of which is the SIFT trust's loss for the taxation year from a business carried on by it in Canada or from a non-portfolio property, and

(b) the amount, if any, by which

(i) the total of

(A) all taxable capital gains of the SIFT trust from dispositions of non-portfolio properties during the taxation year, and

(B) one-half of the total of all amounts each of which is deemed under subsection 131(1) to be a capital gain of the SIFT trust for the taxation year in respect of a non-portfolio property of the SIFT trust for the taxation year

exceeds

(ii) the total of the allowable capital losses of the SIFT trust for the taxation year from dispositions of non-portfolio properties during the taxation year.

Related Provisions: 197(1)"non-portfolio earnings" — Parallel definition for SIFT partnerships; 197(3) — Ignore 96(1.11) when applying definition to partnerships.

Notes: See VIEWS doc 2010-0377081E5 (interpretation of parallel definition for partnerships).

I.T. Technical News: 38 (definition of "non-portfolio earnings").

"non-portfolio property", of a particular entity for a taxation year, means a property, held by the particular entity at any time in the taxation year, that is

(a) a security of a subject entity (other than a portfolio investment entity), if at that time the particular entity holds

(i) securities of the subject entity that have a total fair market value that is greater than 10% of the equity value of the subject entity, or

(ii) securities of the subject entity that, together with all the securities that the particular entity holds of entities affiliated with the subject entity, have a total fair market value that is greater than 50% of the equity value of the particular entity;

(b) a Canadian real, immovable or resource property, if at any time in the taxation year the total fair market value of all properties held by the particular entity that are Canadian real, immovable or resource properties is greater than 50% of the equity value of the particular entity; or

(c) a property that the particular entity, or a person or partnership with whom the particular entity does not deal at arm's length, uses at that time in the course of carrying on a business in Canada.

Related Provisions: 122.1(1)"SIFT trust" — Real estate investment trust excluded from SIFT rules; 248(1)"non-portfolio property" — Definition applies to entire Act.

Notes: See Notes to 122.1(1)"SIFT trust".

Definition amended by 2013 budget bill #2, for tax years that end after July 20, 2011, so that it applies to a corporation.

122.1(1)"non-portfolio property"(a) amended by 2008 budget bill #2, retroactive to Oct. 31, 2006, to add "(other than a portfolio investment entity)".

"portfolio investment entity" at any time means an entity that does not at that time hold any non-portfolio property.

Notes: 122.1(1)"portfolio investment entity" added by 2008 budget bill #2, retroactive to Oct. 31, 2006.

"public market" includes any trading system or other organized facility on which securities that are qualified for public distribution are listed or traded, but does not include a facility that is operated solely to carry out the issuance of a security or its redemption, acquisition or cancellation by its issuer.

Related Provisions: 248(1)"public market" — Definition applies to entire Act.

Notes: See Notes to 188.1(5) re meaning of "includes".

"publicly-traded liability", of an entity, means a liability that is a security of the entity, that is not equity of the entity and that is listed or traded on a stock exchange or other public market.

Notes: 122.1(1)"publicly-traded liability" added by 2008 budget bill #2, retroactive to Oct. 31, 2006.

"qualified REIT property", of a trust at any time, means a property that, at that time, is held by the trust and is

(a) a real or immovable property that is capital property, an eligible resale property, an indebtedness of a Canadian corporation represented by a bankers' acceptance, a property described by paragraph (a) or (b) of the definition "qualified investment" in section 204 or a deposit with a credit union;

(b) a security of a subject entity all or substantially all of the gross REIT revenue of which, for its taxation year that ends in the trust's taxation year that includes that time, is from maintaining, improving, leasing or managing real or immovable properties that are capital properties of the trust or of an entity of which the trust holds a share or an interest, including real or immovable properties that the trust, or an entity of which the trust holds a share or an interest, holds together with one or more other persons or partnerships;

(c) a security of a subject entity, if the entity holds no property other than

(i) legal title to real or immovable property of the trust or of another subject entity all of the securities of which are held by the trust (including real or immovable property that the trust or the other subject entity holds together with one or more other persons or partnerships), and

(ii) property described in paragraph (d); or

(d) ancillary to the earning by the trust of amounts described in subparagraphs (b)(i) and (iii) of the definition "real estate investment trust", other than

(i) an equity of an entity, or

(ii) a mortgage, hypothecary claim, mezzanine loan or similar obligation.

Notes: Note that "real or immovable property" is defined below in 122.1(1). An oil or gas pipeline would appear to be included in "qualified REIT property".

For CRA interpretation see VIEWS doc 2007-0255861E5 (sewers and roads acquired to service an apartment building were "ancillary" for para. (d)).

Definition amended by 2002-2013 technical bill (Part 5 — technical), effective on same basis as 122.1(1.1).

122.1(1)"qualified REIT property"(a) and (c)(i) amended by 2008 budget bill #2, retroactive to Oct. 31, 2006. The former versions, now deemed never to have been in force, appear in PITA 32nd-36th ed.

"real estate investment trust", for a taxation year, means a trust that is resident in Canada throughout the taxation year, if

(a) at each time in the taxation year the total fair market value at that time of all non-portfolio properties that are qualified REIT properties held by the trust is at least 90% of the total fair market value at that time of all non-portfolio properties held by the trust;

(b) not less than 90% of the trust's gross REIT revenue for the taxation year is from one or more of the following:

(i) rent from real or immovable properties,

(ii) interest,

(iii) dispositions of real or immovable properties that are capital properties,

(iv) dividends,

(v) royalties, and

(vi) dispositions of eligible resale properties;

(c) not less than 75% of the trust's gross REIT revenue for the taxation year is from one or more of the following:

(i) rent from real or immovable properties,

(ii) interest from mortgages, or hypothecs, on real or immovable properties, and

(iii) dispositions of real or immovable properties that are capital properties;

(d) at each time in the taxation year an amount, that is equal to 75% or more of the equity value of the trust at that time, is the amount that is the total fair market value of all properties held by the trust each of which is a real or immovable property that is capital property, an eligible resale property, an indebtedness of a Canadian corporation represented by a bankers' acceptance, a property described by paragraph (a) or (b) of the definition "qualified investment" in section 204 or a deposit with a credit union; and

(e) investments in the trust are, at any time in the taxation year, listed or traded on a stock exchange or other public market.

Related Provisions: 12.6(1), 18.3(1)"real estate investment trust" — Definition applies to stapled-security rules; 18.3(3) — No deduction for rent or other amount payable to REIT on stapled security; 122.1(1)"SIFT trust" — REIT excluded from SIFT rules; 122.1(1.1), (1.2) — Character preservation rule; 122.1(1.3) — Character of revenue — hedging arrangements.

Notes: A REIT as defined is not subject to the SIFT rules (see 122.1(1)"SIFT trust" opening words), but non-resident investors are subject to withholding tax under 218.3.

For purposes of the revenue tests before the amendments enacted in 2013, trust income normally does not retain its underlying character when earned by a beneficiary, due to 108(5): *Income Tax Technical News* 38; 2007 Cdn Tax Foundation conference report p. 4:14. However, if a subtrust has designated taxable capital gains under 104(21), the character is preserved: 2010-0368211E5. Trust income earned through a partnership is measured based on the trust's share of that income: 2010-0369251E5. See also 2007-0244171E5 (trust investing only in mortgages would not likely be a REIT); 2007-0244691R3, 2008-0300451R3, 2009-0350481R3 and 2016-0660321R3 (REIT reorganizations); 2010-0376801R3 (solar panel revenues qualify); 2010-0385511E5 (subtrust income qualifies).

Note that the sometimes-subtle distinction between income from business and income from property can determine whether a trust is a REIT. See Notes to 9(1) under "Busines income vs property income".

Since the 2008 amendments but before the 2013 amendments announced in Dec. 2010, see Berry & Freeman, "Righting REITs", 2008 Cdn Tax Foundation conference report, 17:1-20 (purifying to avoid SIFT rules); Lorne Shillinger & John Ulmer, "Advanced Topics in Real Estate Tax Planning", 2009 conference report, 33:1-17; Smit & Pyra, "Recent Transactions of Interest", 2011 Cdn Tax Foundation conference report, 10:1-5 and 11:5-11 (discussing RioCan and Dundee International REITs); Chagnon & Provost, "Cross-Border Canadian REITs", 2011 conference report, 22:1-25.

Since the 2013 amendments, see Kraus *et al.*, "Update on Real Estate Investment Trusts", 2013 Cdn Tax Foundation conference report, 15:1-64; Leitner & Northup, "The US Inversion Rules and Their Impact on Cross-Border Offerings", *ibid.*, 21:1-35; Bernstein, "Canadian Syndication of US Real Estate", 21(1) *Canadian Tax Highlights* (ctf.ca) 9-10 (Jan. 2013); Armstrong & Glicklich, "Conversion of Killam Properties to a REIT"; 2016 conference report at 7:15-21; Freeman & Schiefer, "Issues and Traps with the REIT Rules", 2017 Cdn Tax Foundation annual conference (slides; no paper written); VIEWS doc 2014-0547491R3 (new LP without revenues qualifies as REIT).

A REIT income distribution to a non-resident is subject to withholding tax under 212(1)(c): VIEWS doc 2014-0522271E5.

Definition amended by 2002-2013 technical bill, effective on same basis as 122.1(1.1), except that, for tax years that end before 2013, read para. (d) without the words "that is capital property, an eligible resale property".

Definition amended by 2008 budget bill #2, retroactive to Oct. 31, 2006. The former version, now deemed never to have been in force, appears in the 32nd-36th ed.

Para. (d) amended by 2007 budget bill #2, effective 2008, to change reference from 212(1)(b)(ii)(C) to 212(3)"fully exempt interest"(a) (due to changes to 212(1)(b)).

I.T. Technical News: 38 (SIFT entities — definition of REIT).

CRA Audit Manual: 16.2.7: Real estate investment trusts.

"real or immovable property", of a taxpayer,

(a) includes

(i) a security held by the taxpayer, if the security is a security of a trust that satisfies (or of any other entity that would, if it were a trust, satisfy) the conditions set out in paragraphs (a) to (d) of the definition "real estate investment trust", or

(ii) an interest in real property or a real right in immovables (other than a right to a rental or royalty described in paragraph (d) or (e) of the definition "Canadian resource property" in subsection 66(15)); but

(b) does not include any depreciable property, other than

(i) a property included, otherwise than by an election permitted by regulation, in Class 1, 3 or 31 of Schedule II to the *Income Tax Regulations*,

(ii) a property ancillary to the ownership or utilization of a property described in subparagraph (i), or

(iii) a lease in, or a leasehold interest in respect of, land or property described in subparagraph (i).

Notes: See Notes to 122.1(1)"rent from real or immovable properties" below.

"regulated innovative capital" means equity of a trust, where

(a) since November 2006, the equity has been authorized, by the Superintendent of Financial Institutions or by a provincial regulatory authority having powers similar to those of the Superintendent, as Tier 1 or Tier 2 capital of a financial institution (as defined by subsection 181(1));

(b) the terms and conditions of the equity have not changed after August 1, 2008;

(c) the trust has not issued any equity after October 31, 2006; and

(d) the trust does not hold any non-portfolio property other than

(i) liabilities of the financial institution, and

(ii) shares of the capital stock of the financial institution that were acquired by the trust for the sole purpose of satisfying a right to require the trust to accept, as demanded by a holder of the equity, the surrender of the equity.

Notes: 122.1(1)"regulated innovative capital" added by 2008 budget bill #2, retroactive to Oct. 31, 2006. See Finance news release 2008-056, "Government of Canada Takes Further Steps to Strengthen Housing Market" (Aug. 1/08), at fin.gc.ca.

"rent from real or immovable properties"

(a) includes

(i) rent or similar payments for the use of, or right to use, real or immovable properties, and

(ii) payment for services ancillary to the rental of real or immovable properties and customarily supplied or rendered in connection with the rental of real or immovable properties, but

(iii) [Repealed]

(b) does not include

(i) payment for services supplied or rendered, other than those described in subparagraph (a)(ii), to the tenants of such properties,

(ii) fees for managing or operating such properties,

(iii) payment for the occupation of, use of, or right to use a room in a hotel or other similar lodging facility, or

(iv) rent based on profits.

Notes: For CRA interpretation see VIEWS docs 2007-0244171E5 (several questions); 2010-0376801R3 (solar panels are "real or immovable properties" [this conflicts with GST/HST Info Sheet GI-122]); 2010-0385511E5 (sub-trust income qualifies); 2018-0784701E5 (furnished apartment rent qualifies with no need to deduct furniture rental value).

See Notes to 188.1(5) re meaning of "includes" in para. (a).

The InnVest REIT split up hotel income by having the property owned by a REIT which was not a SIFT (because it merely leased property to the other trust), while the SIFT trust paid tax only on the hotel operations income: Cannon, Pashkowich & Thompson, "2010 Transactions of Interest", 2010 Cdn Tax Foundation conference report at 6:18-24. The 2002-2013 technical bill amendments to 122.1 have shut down this approach.

Subpara. (a)(iii) repealed by 2002-2013 technical bill (Part 5 — technical), effective on same basis as 122.1(1.1) (which along with 122.1(1.2) has replaced this rule).

Subpara. (a)(iii) added by 2008 budget bill #2, retroactive to Oct. 31, 2006.

"SIFT trust", being a specified investment flow-through trust, for

a taxation year means a trust (other than an excluded subsidiary entity, or a real estate investment trust, for the taxation year) that meets the following conditions at any time during the taxation year:

(a) the trust is resident in Canada;

(b) investments in the trust are listed or traded on a stock exchange or other public market; and

(c) the trust holds one or more non-portfolio properties.

Related Provisions: 18.3(3) — No deduction for certain amounts payable on stapled security; 85.1(8), 88.1(2), 107(3.1) — Mechanisms for conversion of SIFT trust to corporation; 104(6)(b)B(ii) — Amount distributed not deductible to SIFT trust; 104(16) — Trust distribution deemed received as dividend; 122.1(2) — Application of definition from 2006-2010; 157(2) — SIFT trust pays same instalments as a corporation; 197(1)"SIFT partnership" — Parallel definition for partnership; 248(1)"SIFT trust" — Definition applies to entire Act; Reg. 2608 — Determining province of residence of SIFT trust.

Notes: See CRA, "What is a SIFT trust", tinyurl.com/cra-sift. To calculate a SIFT trust's income and tax, see tinyurl.com/sift-calc.

For a trust to be "resident in Canada" (para. (a)), its central management and control must be in Canada. See Notes to 250(1).

SIFT status is determined on a year-by-year basis. The definition requires holding one or more "non-portfolio properties", whose definition in 122.1(1) is based on 122.1(1)"subject entity", which requires a Canadian entity or Canadian-source income. Cross-border income trusts are thus not SIFT trusts: see Notes to 104(16).

See Johnson et al., "Current Transactions", 2012 Cdn Tax Foundation conference report, 8:1-39; Bennett & Rowe, "Recent Transactions of Interest", 2014 conference report, 15:1-11, 15:38-49. On amendments to 122.1(1) enacted in 2008, see Finance news release 2007-106 (Dec. 20/07); Harris, "The 'SIFT' Tax", XI(4) *Business Vehicles*

(Federated Press) 602-06 (2008); Sherman & Freeman, "New SIFT Proposals", XIV(4) *Corporate Finance* (Federated Press) 1552-54 (2008).

For CRA interpretation see VIEWS doc 2007-0261591E5 (subsidiary entity of an income trust).

See also articles referenced in Notes to 104(16); and Notes to 122.1(1)"investment".

122.1(1)"SIFT trust" amended by 2008 budget bill #2, retroactive to Oct. 31, 2006, to add "an excluded subsidiary entity, or".

"security" of a particular entity means any right, whether absolute

or contingent, conferred by the particular entity or by an entity that is affiliated with the particular entity, to receive, either immediately or in the future, an amount that can reasonably be regarded as all or any part of the capital, of the revenue or of the income of the particular entity, or as interest paid or payable by the particular entity, and for greater certainty includes

(a) a liability of the particular entity;

(b) if the particular entity is a corporation,

(i) a share of the capital stock of the corporation, and

(ii) a right to control in any manner whatever the voting rights of a share of the capital stock of the corporation;

(c) if the particular entity is a trust, an income or a capital interest in the trust;

(d) if the particular entity is a partnership, an interest as a member of the partnership; and

(e) a right to, or to acquire, anything described in this paragraph and any of paragraphs (a) to (d).

Notes: See Notes to 122.1(1)"investment".

"subject entity" means a person or partnership that is

(a) a corporation resident in Canada;

(b) a trust resident in Canada;

(c) a Canadian resident partnership; or

(d) a non-resident person, or a partnership that is not described in paragraph (c), the principal source of income of which is one or any combination of sources in Canada.

Notes: See Notes to 122.1(1)"SIFT trust".

"unaffiliated publicly-traded liability", of an entity at any time

means a publicly-traded liability of the entity if, at that time the total fair market value of all publicly-traded liabilities of the entity that are held at that time by persons or partnerships that are not affiliated with the entity is at least 90% of the total fair market value of all publicly-traded liabilities of the entity.

Notes: 122.1(1)"unaffiliated publicly-traded liability" added by 2008 budget bill #2, retroactive to Oct. 31, 2006.

(1.1) Application of subsec. (1.2) — Subsection (1.2) applies to an entity for a taxation year in respect of an amount and another entity (referred to in this subsection and subsection (1.2) as the "parent entity", "specified amount" and "source entity", respectively), if

(a) at any time in the taxation year the parent entity

(i) is affiliated with the source entity, or

(ii) holds securities of the source entity that

(A) are described by any of paragraphs (a) to (c) of the definition "equity" in subsection (1), and

(B) have a total fair market value that is greater than 10% of the equity value of the source entity;

(b) the specified amount is included in computing the parent entity's gross REIT revenue for the taxation year in respect of a security of the source entity held by the parent entity; and

(c) in the case of a source entity that is a subject entity described in paragraph (b) of the definition "qualified REIT property" in subsection (1) in respect of the parent entity at each time during the taxation year at which the parent entity holds securities of the source entity, the specified amount cannot reasonably be considered to be derived from the source entity's gross REIT revenue from maintaining, improving, leasing or managing real or immovable properties that are capital properties of the parent entity or of an entity of which the parent entity holds a share or an interest, including real or immovable properties that the parent entity, or an entity of which the parent entity holds a share or an interest, holds together with one or more other persons or partnerships.

Notes: 122.1(1.1) added by 2002-2013 technical bill, for 2011 and later taxation years; and also, by election, for taxation years of a trust that end after 2006.

(1.2) Character preservation rule — If this subsection applies to a parent entity for a taxation year in respect of a specified amount and a source entity, then for the purposes of the definition "real estate investment trust" in subsection (1), to the extent that the specified amount can reasonably be considered to be derived from gross REIT revenue of the source entity having a particular character, the specified amount is deemed to be gross REIT revenue of the parent entity having the same character and not having any other character.

Related Provisions: 122.1(1.1) — Conditions for 122.1(1.2) to apply.

Notes: 122.1(1.2) added by 2002-2013 technical bill (Part 5 — technical), effective on same basis as 122.1(1.1).

(1.3) Character of revenue — hedging arrangements — For the purposes of the definition "real estate investment trust" in subsection (1),

(a) if an amount is included in gross REIT revenue of a trust for a taxation year and it results from an agreement that can reasonably be considered to have been made by the trust to reduce its risk from fluctuations in interest rates in respect of debt incurred by the trust to acquire or refinance real or immovable property, the amount is deemed to have the same character as gross REIT revenue in respect of the real or immovable property and not any other character; and

(b) if a real or immovable property is situated in a country other than Canada and an amount included in gross REIT revenue of a trust for a taxation year

(i) is a gain from fluctuations in the value of the currency of that country relative to Canadian currency recognized on

(A) revenue in respect of the real or immovable property, or

(B) debt incurred by the trust for the purpose of earning revenue in respect of the real or immovable property, or

(ii) results from an agreement that

(A) provides for the purchase, sale or exchange of currency, and

(B) can reasonably be considered to have been made by the trust to reduce its risk from currency fluctuations described in subparagraph (i),

the amount is deemed to have the same character as gross REIT revenue in respect of the real or immovable property and not any other character.

Notes: 122.1(1.3) added by 2002-2013 technical bill (Part 5 — technical), effective on same basis as 122.1(1.1).

(2) Application of definition "SIFT trust" — The definition "SIFT trust" applies to a trust for a taxation year of the trust that ends after 2006, except that if the trust would have been a SIFT trust on October 31, 2006 had that definition been in force and applied to the trust as of that date, that definition does not apply to the trust for a taxation year of the trust that ends before the earlier of

(a) 2011, and

(b) the first day after December 15, 2006 on which the trust exceeds normal growth as determined by reference to the normal growth guidelines issued by the Department of Finance on December 15, 2006, as amended from time to time, unless that excess arose as a result of a prescribed transaction.

Related Provisions: 197(8) — Parallel rules for partnerships.

Notes: The guidelines, in Finance news release 2006-082 (Dec. 15, 2006) and Finance Technical Notes of Dec. 4, 2008, are reproduced here up to PITA 48th ed. SIFTs that

exceeded the guidelines were subject to the new rules before 2011 even if their growth was "normal": *Income Tax Technical News* 38; 2007 Cdn Tax Foundation conference report, 4:12-13. See also VIEWS docs 2007-0244691R3, 2007-0245281R3, 2007-0255821E5, 2009-0351591E5.

I.T. Technical News: 38 (SIFT rules — transitional normal growth).

Notes [s. 122.1]: 122.1 added by 2007 budget bill #1, effective Oct. 31, 2006 (but for actual effective dates see 122.1(2) above). It implements the rules for SIFT trusts. See Notes to 122(1) and 104(16). For discussion of the 2002-2013 technical bill amendments see Notes to 122.1(1.1).

Former 122.1, repealed by 1985 technical bill, reduced tax for 1977 and 1978.

Definitions [s. 122.1]: "affiliated" — 251.1; "allowable capital loss" — 38(b), 248(1); "amount" — 248(1); "arm's length" — 251(1); "business" — 248(1); "Canada" — 255, *Interpretation Act* 35(1); "Canadian corporation" — 89(1), 248(1); "Canadian real, immovable or resource property", "Canadian resident partnership" — 248(1); "capital gain" — 39(1)(a), 248(1); "capital interest" — 108(1), 248(1); "capital property" — 54, 248(1); "class of shares" — 248(6); "corporation" — 248(1), *Interpretation Act* 35(1); "credit union" — 137(6), 248(1); "depreciable property" — 13(21), 248(1); "disposition", "dividend" — 248(1); "eligible resale property", "entity", "equity", "equity value", "excluded subsidiary entity" — 122.1(1); "fair market value" — see 69(1) Notes; "financial institution" — 181(1); "fully exempt interest" — 212(3); "gross REIT revenue" — 122.1(1); "immovable" — 122.1(1), Quebec *Civil Code* art. 900–907; "interest in real property" — 248(4); "investment" — 122.1(1); "land" — see 70(5.2) Notes; "non-portfolio property" — 122.1(1); "non-resident" — 248(1); "parent entity" — 122.1(1.1); "partnership" — see 96(1) Notes; "person" — 248(1); "portfolio investment entity" — 122.1(1); "prescribed", "property" — 248(1); "provincial" — *Interpretation Act* 33(3), 35(1)"province"; "public market", "publicly-traded liability", "qualified REIT property", "real estate investment trust", "real or immovable property" — 122.1(1); "real right" — 248(4.1); "regulated innovative capital" — 122.1(1); "regulation" — 248(1); "rent from real or immovable property" — 122.1(1); "resident in Canada" — 250; "SIFT partnership" — 197(1), (8), 248(1); "SIFT trust" — 122.1(1), (2), 248(1); "security" — 122.1(1); "share", "shareholder" — 248(1); "source entity", "specified amount" — 122.1(1.1); "specified investment flow-through trust" — 122.1(1)"SIFT trust"; "subject entity" — 122.1(1); "taxable Canadian corporation" — 89(1), 248(1); "taxable capital gain" — 38(a), 248(1); "taxable dividend" — 89(1), 248(1); "taxation year" — 249; "taxpayer" — 248(1); "trust" — 104(1), 248(1), (3); "unaffiliated publicly-traded liability" — 122.1(1).

122.2 [Child Tax Credit — Repealed]

Notes: 122.2 repealed by 1992 Child Benefit bill, effective 1993. The refundable Child Tax Credit was replaced with a monthly non-taxable Child Tax Benefit for lower-income families, renamed Canada Child Benefit (CCB) in 2016. See 122.6-122.63. (The dependent child deduction in s. 109, replaced by the Child Tax Credit in 122.2 in 1988, was restored in 2007 as a credit in 118(1)B(b.1), replaced in 2015 by an increased Universal Child Care Benefit (see 56(6) Notes, itself replaced in 2016 by an enhanced CCB.)

122.3 (1) Overseas employment tax credit [pre-2016] — If an individual is resident in Canada in a taxation year and, throughout any period of more than six consecutive months that began before the end of the year and included any part of the year (in this section referred to as the **"qualifying period"**)

(a) was employed by a person who was a specified employer, other than for the performance of services under a prescribed international development assistance program of the Government of Canada, and

(b) performed all or substantially all the duties of the individual's employment outside Canada

(i) in connection with a contract under which the specified employer carried on business outside Canada with respect to

(A) the exploration for or exploitation of petroleum, natural gas, minerals or other similar resources,

(B) any construction, installation, agricultural or engineering activity, or

(C) any prescribed activity, or

(ii) for the purpose of obtaining, on behalf of the specified employer, a contract to undertake any of the activities referred to in clause (i)(A), (B) or (C),

there may be deducted, from the amount that would, but for this section, be the individual's tax payable under this Part for the year, an amount equal to that proportion of the tax otherwise payable under this Part for the year by the individual that the lesser of

(c) an amount equal to that proportion of the specified amount for the year that the number of days

(i) in that portion of the qualifying period that is in the year, and

(ii) on which the individual was resident in Canada

is of 365, and

(d) the specified percentage for the year of the individual's income for the year from that employment that is reasonably attributable to duties performed on the days referred to in paragraph (c)

is of

(e) the amount, if any, by which

(i) if the individual is resident in Canada throughout the year, the individual's income for the year, and

(ii) if the individual is non-resident at any time in the year, the amount determined under paragraph 114(a) in respect of the taxpayer for the year

exceeds

(iii) the total of all amounts each of which is an amount deducted under section 110.6 or paragraph 111(1)(b), or deductible under paragraph 110(1)(d.2), (d.3), (f) or (g), in computing the individual's taxable income for the year.

Related Provisions: 117(1) — Tax payable under this Part; 122.3(1.01) — Specified amount; 122.3(1.02) — Specified percentage; 122.3(1.1) — No credit for incorporated employee; 126(1)(b)(i)(E)(II), 126(7)"non-business-income tax"(f) — Foreign tax credit disallowed.

Notes: The overseas employment tax credit (phased out completely as of 2016: 122.3(1.01), (1.02)) effectively allowed a qualifying individual to eliminate 80% of Canadian tax on income earned on an overseas project that lasted at least 6 months. ("Overseas" is a misnomer; it can include the US, and can apply to an employee who lives in Canada and commutes across the border: *Purves*, 2005 TCC 290.) For discussion see IT-497R4, VIEWS docs 2007-0219991E5, 2007-0229931E5, 2007-0248761E5, 2011-0401611E5, 2016-0655681E5.

For a thorough review see Sanjana Bhatia & Pooja Samtani, "Employees on Foreign Ground: the Overseas Employment Tax Credit", 17(8) *Taxation of Executive Compensation & Retirement* (Federated Press) 663-68 (April 2006).

Where some but not all overseas work is financed by CIDA (see Reg. 3400), 122.3(1)(a) disallows the credit: VIEWS docs 2005-0152871E5, 2005-0158871E5. (However, allowances paid to an employee working on a CIDA program may be tax-free due to 6(1)(b)(iii) and 250(1)(d): 2010-0361561E5.)

122.3(1)(b) reads "outside Canada" rather than "in a country other than Canada" so that the credit is available to a person working on a project in international waters. However, "Canada" is considered to extend 200 nautical miles offshore for natural resource exploration or exploitation, and 12 miles for other qualifying activities: VIEWS doc 2013-0493081E5.

The opening words of 122.3(1) require the conditions in (a) and (b) to be met for 6 consecutive months, but do not require physical absence from Canada for 6 consecutive months: *Rooke*, 2002 FCA 393; the "substantially all" test means that employment in Canada must be no more than 10% during the period: VIEWS doc 2007-0230991E5. The 6 months is measured as e.g., April 15 through October 14: 2007-0262351E5. In *Rooke*, an individual who returned to Canada for substantial periods of time between projects for the same employer qualified for the credit. If there is a break between employments, each must qualify separately for the 6 months: *Ward*, 2003 TCC 725, doc 2009-0312641E5; even if the employee remains overseas: 2008-0271011E5. A daily commute from Canada to the work site may qualify: 2002-0148385. Sick leave spent in Canada can qualify: 2005-0123991E5, 2009-0314421E5, 2009-0333601E5, 2013-0497011E5. Preparatory work not exceeding 10% can be done in Canada: 2010-0383871E5. For further discussion see 2008-0304311E5, 2010-0362181E5; 2011-039200117 (time at sea in a particular example); 2011-0393431E5 (how to count paid compensatory leave); 2011-0395721E5 (the "substantially all" test applies to each qualifying employment); 2011-0402901E5 (effect of vacation time); 2011-0415991E5 (employees evacuated to Canada due to civil unrest, and either teleworking or on call).

The employer must be resident in Canada, a foreign affiliate of a Canadian resident or certain partnerships: see 122.3(2)"specified employer".

On whether the employer "carried on business [cob] outside Canada" in 122.3(1)(b)(i), see VIEWS doc 2002-0137407, which reviews the case law, such as *Betteridge*, [1999] 1 C.T.C. 2569 (TCC) and *Fonta*, [2002] 3 C.T.C. 2177 (TCC). CRA claims that a Canadian placement agency placing employees outside Canada does not cob outside Canada merely because the employees work outside Canada; but the credit was allowed on the basis that the agency was subcontracting employees outside Canada, in *Purves*, 2005 TCC 290; *Adams*, 2005 TCC 237; *Dunbar*, 2005 TCC 769; *Mys*, 2007

TCC 736; *MacIsaac*, 2010 TCC 436. Similarly, in *Suprenant (Claveri)*, 2005 TCC 192, MCI Canada was held to cob in France when it sent employees (who remained its employees) to work at MCI France. A non-profit organization can cob for purposes of 122.3: *Timmins*, [1999] 2 C.T.C. 133 (FCA); doc 2002-0172925.

CRA will allow the credit to an employee of a subcontractor on a specific project where the main contractor qualifies: VIEWS doc 2007-02359671E5.

In *Smyth*, 2007 TCC 366 (FCA appeal dismissed for procedural reasons A-118-07), an Edmonton police officer serving in Kosovo did not qualify, since he continued to be employed by the Edmonton police force, which was not carrying on business for profit.

"Exploitation of petroleum" in 122.3(1)(b)(i)(A) includes shipping crude oil to a refinery, so an oil tanker captain qualified for the credit: *Dunbar*, 2005 TCC 769. Based on *Dunbar*, transportation of refined petroleum does not qualify: VIEWS doc 2007-0237261E5. The meaning of "exploitation" will depend on the particular resource being exploited: doc 2008-026947117.

"Construction" in 122.3(1)(b)(i): see Notes to 125.1(3)"manufacturing or processing".

"Engineering" in 122.3(1)(b)(i)(B) can include software engineering, and need not be performed by a professional engineer: *Gabie*, [1999] 1 C.T.C. 2352 (TCC); *Purves*, 2005 TCC 290; *Mys*, 2007 TCC 736; VIEWS doc 2005-0144921E5. CRA said an engineer supervising ship-building was not doing "engineering": 2008-0285901E5, 2011-0413641E5. Teaching engineering at a college's foreign campus did not qualify in *Humber*, 2010 TCC 253, but did in *Legge*, 2011 TCC 413 (late claims by other employees of the same college: *Adey*, 2019 FC 1001). See also 2011-0394351E5 (audit referral to determine if activity was engineering); Russell, "OETC/Qatar", 10(12) *Tax Hyperion* (Carswell) 8 (Dec. 2013).

The words "equal to" before para. (c) mean that the whole credit or no credit must be claimed, rather than a partial credit (where the taxpayer wants to increase a foreign tax credit: see 126(1)(b)(i)(E)(II) and 126(7)"non-business-income tax"(f)): VIEWS doc 2007-023083117.

Where employment income is partly stock options, CRA normally considers the services rendered *in the year the option was granted* to determine whether the income is eligible for the OETC: doc 2011-04299721E5.

For rulings approving the credit see VIEWS docs 2006-0186631R3, 2008-0282451R3.

CRA considers that "substantially all" in 122.3(1)(b) means 90% or more.

122.3(1)(e)(iii) amended by 2017 budget bill #1 to delete reference to 110(1)(j), effective 2018 (unnecessary since 122.3 is inoperative after 2016).

122.3(1) opening words amended non-substantively by 2002-2013 technical bill, for tax years that begin after June 26, 2013.

122.3(1) amended by 2012 budget bill #2, effective for 2013 and later taxation years, to change "of $80,000" to "the specified amount for the year" (para. (c)) and "80%" to "the specified percentage for the year" (para. (d)), so as to phase out the credit. (See 122.3(1.01) and (1.02).)

122.3(1) amended by 2001 technical bill (effective for 1998 and later taxation years), 2001 Budget, 1999 Budget, 1993 technical bill and 1991 technical bill.

Regulations: 3400 (prescribed international development assistance program for 122.3(1)(a)); 6000 (prescribed activity for 122.3(1)(b)(i)(C) is activity under contract with UN).

Income Tax Folios: S5-F2-C1: Foreign tax credit [replaces IT-270R3, IT-395R2, IT-520].

Interpretation Bulletins: IT-497R4: Overseas employment tax credit.

Information Circulars: 07-1R1: Taxpayer relief provisions.

Forms: T626: Overseas employment tax credit.

(1.01) Specified amount — For the purposes of paragraph (1)(c), the specified amount for a taxation year of an individual is

(a) for the 2013 to 2015 taxation years, the amount determined by the formula

$$[\$80,000 \times A/(A + B)] + [C \times B/(A + B)]$$

where

A is the individual's income described in paragraph (1)(d) for the taxation year that is earned in connection with a contract that was committed to in writing before March 29, 2012 by a specified employer of the individual,

B is the individual's income described in paragraph (1)(d) for the taxation year, other than income included in the description of A, and

C is

(i) for the 2013 taxation year, $60,000,

(ii) for the 2014 taxation year, $40,000, and

(iii) for the 2015 taxation year, $20,000; and

(b) for the 2016 and subsequent taxation years, nil.

Notes: 122.3(1.01) and (1.02) phase out the OETC over 2013-16. During the phase-out period, the pre-2013 80% factor (applied to an employee's qualifying foreign employment income in determining the OETC) is reduced to 60% for 2013, 40% for 2014 and 20% for 2015 [122.3(1.02)A(c)]. As well, the limit on qualifying income is reduced from $80,000 to $60,000 for 2013, $40,000 for 2014 and $20,000 for 2015 [122.3(1.01)A(c)]. The OETC is eliminated as of 2016.

These phase-out rules do not apply to qualifying foreign employment income earned on a project or activity to which the employer had committed in writing before March 29, 2012 [122.3(1.01)A(a)]. In such instances, the 80% factor and $80,000 limit continue to apply through 2015; the OETC is still eliminated in 2016.

A contract is "committed to in writing" when the employer has signed a written contract or tendered an irrevocable bid, and a renewal provided for in the contract is included: VIEWS doc 2013-0514311E5; but not if the original contract is materially changed, or extended after expiring: 2014-0521751E5.

In both 122.3(1.01) and (1.02), "$80,000 × A/(A+B)" or "80% × A/(A+B)" allows the grandfathered amount, and "C × B/(A+B)" allows the 60-40-20 reduced credit.

122.3(1.01), (1.02) added by 2012 budget bill #2, for 2013 and later tax years. See Notes to 122.3(1).

(1.02) Specified percentage — For the purposes of paragraph (1)(d), the specified percentage for a taxation year of an individual is

(a) for the 2013 to 2015 taxation years, the amount determined by the formula

$$[80\% \times A/(A + B)] + [C \times B/(A + B)]$$

where

A   is the value of A in subsection (1.01),

B   is the value of B in subsection (1.01), and

C   is

    (i) for the 2013 taxation year, 60%,

    (ii) for the 2014 taxation year, 40%, and

    (iii) for the 2015 taxation year, 20%; and

(b) for the 2016 and subsequent taxation years, 0%.

Notes: See Notes to 122.3(1.01).

(1.1) Excluded income — No amount may be included under paragraph (1)(d) in respect of an individual's income for a taxation year from the individual's employment by an employer

(a) if

    (i) the employer carries on a business of providing services and does not employ in the business throughout the year more than five full-time employees,

    (ii) the individual

        (A) does not deal at arm's length with the employer, or is a specified shareholder of the employer, or

        (B) where the employer is a partnership, does not deal at arm's length with a member of the partnership, or is a specified shareholder of a member of the partnership, and

    (iii) but for the existence of the employer, the individual would reasonably be regarded as being an employee of a person or partnership that is not a specified employer; or

(b) if at any time in that portion of the qualifying period that is in the taxation year

    (i) the employer provides the services of the individual to a corporation, partnership or trust with which the employer does not deal at arm's length, and

    (ii) the fair market value of all the issued shares of the capital stock of the corporation or of all interests in the partnership or trust, as the case may be, that are held, directly or indirectly, by persons who are resident in Canada is less than 10% of the fair market value of all those shares or interests.

Notes: The test for disallowance of the credit is essentially one of "incorporated employee", similar to that for a personal services business as defined in 125(7). See 18(1)(p). Subpara. (a)(iii) (former para. (c)) requires that the relationship with the non-resident entity that is paying would be an employment relationship were it not for the corporation (see Notes to 248(1)"employee"). An individual whose work can qualify as an independent contractor (i.e., carrying on business rather than employed) can still incorporate that business and claim the credit for salary paid to the individual by the

individual's own corporation, since the relationship between the individual and the non-resident was not an employment relationship in the first place. 122.3(1.1) was held to apply in *Gillespie*, 2009 TCC 26 (FCA appeal discontinued A-92-09), and was held not to apply in *Perrin*, 2007 TCC 138. See also VIEWS doc 2008-0292471E5.

For the meaning of "more than 5 full-time employees", see Notes to 125(7)"specified investment business".

122.3(1.1)(b) added by 2002-2013 technical bill, for tax years that begin after June 26, 2013.

122.3(1.1) added by 1996 Budget, effective 1997.

I.T. Technical News: 41 (the "more than five full-time employees" test).

(2) Definitions — In subsection (1),

"specified employer" means

(a) a person resident in Canada,

(b) a partnership in which interests that exceed in total value 10% of the fair market value of all interests in the partnership are owned by persons resident in Canada or corporations controlled by persons resident in Canada, or

(c) a corporation that is a foreign affiliate of a person resident in Canada;

Related Provisions: 256(6), (6.1) — Meaning of "controlled".

Notes: For a ruling that a company will be a specified employer after a restructuring, see VIEWS doc 2007-0219291R3. See also 2011-0409951E5 (general discussion).

"tax otherwise payable under this Part for the year" means the amount that, but for this section, sections 120 and 120.2, subsection 120.4(2) and sections 121, 126, 127 and 127.4, would be the tax payable under this Part for the year.

Notes: 122.3(2)"tax otherwise payable under this Part for the year" amended by 1999 Budget, effective for 2000 and later taxation years, to delete references to 120.1, 127.2 and 127.3 and add reference to 120.4(2).

122.3(2)"specified employer" was 122.3(2)(a) and "tax otherwise payable under this Part for the year" was 122.3(2)(b) before RSC 1985 (5th Supp) consolidation for tax years ending after Nov. 1991.

Definitions [s. 122.3]: "amount" — 248(1); "arm's length" — 251(1); "business" — 248(1); "controlled" — 256(6), (6.1); "corporation" — 248(1), *Interpretation Act* 35(1); "employed", "employee", "employer", "employment" — 248(1); "fair market value" — see 69(1) Notes; "foreign affiliate" — 95(1), 248(1); "individual" — 248(1); "month" — *Interpretation Act* 35(1); "non-resident" — 248(1); "partnership" — see 96(1) Notes; "person" — 248(1); "qualifying period" — 122.3(1); "resident in Canada" — 94(3)(a), 250; "share" — 248(1); "specified amount" — 122.3(1.01); "specified employer" — 122.3(2); "specified percentage" — 122.3(1.02); "specified shareholder" — 248(1); "tax otherwise payable" — 122.3(2); "tax payable" — 248(2); "taxable income" — 2(2), 248(1); "taxation year" — 249; "trust" — 104(1), 248(1), (3); "writing" — *Interpretation Act* 35(1).

122.4 [Repealed under former Act]

Notes: 122.4, repealed by 1990 GST effective 1991, enacted the federal sales tax credit, designed to offset the pre-1991 federal sales tax paid indirectly by low-income taxpayers. It was replaced by the GST (now GST/HST) Credit in 122.5.

122.5 [GST/HST credit] — **(1) Definitions** — The following definitions apply in this section.

"adjusted income", of an individual for a taxation year in relation to a month specified for the taxation year, means the total of the individual's income for the taxation year and the income for the taxation year of the individual's qualified relation, if any, in relation to the specified month, both calculated as if in computing that income no amount were

(a) included

    (i) under paragraph 56(1)(q.1) or subsection 56(6),

    (ii) in respect of any gain from a disposition of property to which section 79 applies, or

    (iii) in respect of a gain described in subsection 40(3.21); or

(b) deductible under paragraph 20(1)(ww) or 60(y) or (z).

Notes: See Notes to 122.6"adjusted income", which is essentially the same. See also Notes at end of 122.5.

Para. (b) amended by 2018 budget bill #1 to refer to 20(1)(ww), for 2018 and later tax years. Definition earlier amended by 2010 budget bill #2, 2007 RDSPs bill, 2006 budget bill #1, 2001 Budget, 1995-97 technical bill.

"cohabiting spouse or common-law partner" of an individual at any time has the meaning assigned by section 122.6.

Notes: Definition added by 2001 Budget, effective for amounts that are deemed to be paid during months specified for the 2001 and later taxation years (i.e., effective with the July 2002 payment).

Forms: RC65: Marital status change.

"eligible individual", in relation to a month specified for a taxation year, means an individual (other than a trust) who

(a) has, before the specified month, attained the age of 19 years; or

(b) was, at any time before the specified month,

(i) a parent who resided with their child, or

(ii) married or in a common-law partnership.

Related Provisions: 122.5(2) — Persons deemed not to be eligible individuals; 122.5(5) — Only one eligible individual.

Notes: See Notes to 122.6(2) re non-residents not qualifying.

The requirement to be 19 or older does not violate the *Charter of Rights*: *Lister*, [1994] 2 C.T.C. 365 (FCA).

Definition "eligible individual" amended by 2001 Budget, effective for amounts that are deemed to be paid during months specified for the 2001 and later taxation years (i.e., effective with the July 2002 payment). Earlier amended by 2000 same-sex partners bill and 1995-97 technical bill, effective April 27, 1995.

Forms: RC65: Marital status change.

"qualified dependant" of an individual, in relation to a month specified for a taxation year, means a person who at the beginning of the specified month

(a) is the individual's child or is dependent for support on the individual or on the individual's cohabiting spouse or common-law partner;

(b) resides with the individual;

(c) is under the age of 19 years;

(d) is not an eligible individual in relation to the specified month; and

(e) is not a qualified relation of any individual in relation to the specified month.

Related Provisions: 122.5(2) — Persons deemed not to be qualified dependants.

Notes: Definition "qualified dependant" amended by 2001 Budget, effective for amounts that are deemed to be paid during months specified for the 2001 and later taxation years (i.e., effective with the July 2002 payment).

Forms: RC4210: GST/HST credit [guide].

"qualified relation" of an individual, in relation to a month specified for a taxation year, means the person, if any, who, at the beginning of the specified month, is the individual's cohabiting spouse or common-law partner.

Related Provisions: 122.5(2) — Persons deemed not to be qualified relations; 163(2)(c.1) — False statements or omissions.

Notes: Definition "qualified relation" amended by 2001 Budget, effective for amounts that are deemed to be paid during months specified for the 2001 and later taxation years (i.e., effective with the July 2002 payment).

122.5(1)"qualified relation" amended by 2000 same-sex partners bill to refer to "common-law partner", effective as per Notes to 248(1)"common-law partner".

"Qualified relation" amended by 1992 technical bill, effective 1993.

See also Notes at end of 122.5.

"return of income", in respect of a person for a taxation year, means

(a) for a person who is resident in Canada at the end of the taxation year, the person's return of income (other than a return of income under subsection 70(2) or 104(23), paragraph 128(2)(e) or subsection 150(4)) that is required to be filed for the taxation year or that would be required to be filed if the person had tax payable under this Part for the taxation year; and

(b) in any other case, a prescribed form containing prescribed information that is filed for the taxation year with the Minister.

Notes: Definition "return of income" added by 2001 Budget, effective for amounts that are deemed to be paid during months specified for the 2001 and later taxation years (i.e., effective with the July 2002 payment).

(2) Persons not eligible individuals, qualified relations or qualified dependants — Notwithstanding subsection (1), a person is not an eligible individual, is not a qualified relation and is not a qualified dependant, in relation to a month specified for a taxation year, if the person

(a) died before the specified month;

(b) is confined to a prison or similar institution for a period of at least 90 days that includes the first day of the specified month;

(c) is at the beginning of the specified month a non-resident person, other than a non-resident person who

(i) is at that time the cohabiting spouse or common-law partner of a person who is deemed under subsection 250(1) to be resident in Canada throughout the taxation year that includes the first day of the specified month, and

(ii) was resident in Canada at any time before the specified month;

(d) is at the beginning of the specified month a person described in paragraph 149(1)(a) or (b); or

(e) is a person in respect of whom a special allowance under the *Children's Special Allowances Act* is payable for the specified month.

Notes: CRA states (VIEWS doc 9206605) that "a prison or similar institution" for para. (c) includes penitentiaries, detention centres, reformatories and mental hospitals designated to be used for detention of the criminally insane. The exclusion of prisoners does not violate the *Charter of Rights*: *Wells*, [1998] 1 C.T.C. 2118 (TCC); *Bradley*, 2009 TCC 15. (A prisoner can claim the Canada Child Benefit: see Notes to 122.6"eligible individual".)

Non-residents did not qualify for the credit in: *Goldstein*, 2014 FCA 27; *Manotas*, 2011 TCC 408; *Bower*, 2013 TCC 183; *Agrebi*, 2014 TCC 141; *Corkum*, 2015 TCC 38.

122.5(2) amended by 2001 Budget, for amounts deemed paid during months specified for 2001 and later tax years (i.e., as of the July 2002 payment).

(3) Deemed payment on account of tax — An eligible individual in relation to a month specified for a taxation year who files a return of income for the taxation year is deemed to have paid during the specified month on account of their tax payable under this Part for the taxation year an amount equal to $1/4$ of the amount, if any, determined by the formula

$$A - B$$

where

A is the total of

(a) $213[19],

(b) $213[19] for the qualified relation, if any, of the individual in relation to the specified month,

(c) if the individual has no qualified relation in relation to the specified month and is entitled to deduct an amount for the taxation year under subsection 118(1) because of paragraph (b) of the description of B in that subsection in respect of a qualified dependant of the individual in relation to the specified month, $213[19],

(d) $112[19] times the number of qualified dependants of the individual in relation to the specified month, other than a qualified dependant in respect of whom an amount is included under paragraph (c) in computing the total for the specified month,

(e) if the individual has no qualified relation and has one or more qualified dependants, in relation to the specified month, $112, and

---

[19] Indexed by 117.1 after 1990 — ed.

(f) if the individual has no qualified relation and no qualified dependant, in relation to the specified month, the lesser of $112[20] and 2% of the amount, if any, by which the individual's income for the taxation year exceeds $6,911[20]; and

B is 5% of the amount, if any, by which the individual's adjusted income for the taxation year in relation to the specified month exceeds $27,749[21].

Related Provisions: 117.1(2)(m) — Inflation indexing; 122.5(3.001) — Additional COVID-19 benefit for 2020; 122.5(3.1), (3.2) — Advance payment; 122.5(5) — Only 1 eligible individual per family; 152(1)(b) — Assessment; 152(1.2)(d) — Notice of determination denying credit at taxpayer's request; 152(4.2)(b) — Redetermination of credit at taxpayer's request; 160.1(1), (1.1) — Taxpayer and spouse both liable for overpaid credit; 163(2)(c.1) — False statement or omission — penalty; 164(1) — Refund of credit if no tax payable; 164(2.1) — Application of credit to other debt; 164(3) — No interest on late payment of credit; 239(1.1) — Offence of claiming false credits; 257 — Formula cannot calculate to less than zero.

Notes: See Notes at end of 122.5. The maximum credit per adult is $296 for 2020, $299 for 2021. The maximum per child is $155 (2020), $157 (2021). The "specified months" are Jan., April, July and Oct.: 122.5(4). For 2020, there was an extra $580 ($306 per child) for the COVID-19 emergency: 122.5(3.001).

Under B in the formula, the credit is gradually phased out once *net* income exceeds $38,507 (2020) or $38,892 (2021), even if taxable income is lower due to amounts included but not taxed (e.g., *Farah*, 2013 TCC 16 — workers' comp payments under 56(1)(v)).

Before the 2014 tax year, taxpayers had to check a box on the T1 return to apply for the credit. Now CRA considers it automatically.

122.5(3) amended by 2014 budget bill #1 (for 2014 and later tax years), 2001 Budget, 2000 and 1999 budget bills #1, 1993 technical bill, 1992 Child Benefit bill

Information Circulars: 07-1R1: Taxpayer relief provisions.

Remission Orders: *Debbie Johnston Remission Order*, P.C. 2013-38 (remission of overpaid GST Credit due to "financial setback with extenuating circumstances"); *Trena LaHaye Remission Order*, P.C. 2016-868 (remission due to incorrect action by CRA officials, as collection "is unjust").

Forms: RC65: Marital status change; RC151: GST/HST credit application for individuals who become residents of Canada; RC4210: GST/HST credit [guide].

(3.001) COVID-19 — additional deemed payment [COVID-19 GST Credit for 2020] — An eligible individual in relation to a month specified for a taxation year who files a return of income for the taxation year is deemed to have paid during the specified month on account of their tax payable under this Part for the taxation year an amount determined by the formula

$$0.5(A - B)$$

where

A is the total of

(a) $580,

(b) $580 for the qualified relation, if any, of the individual in relation to the specified month,

(c) if the individual has no qualified relation in relation to the specified month and is entitled to deduct an amount for the taxation year under subsection 118(1) because of paragraph (b) of the description of B in that subsection in respect of a qualified dependant of the individual in relation to the specified month, $580,

(d) $306 times the number of qualified dependants of the individual in relation to the specified month, other than a qualified dependant in respect of whom an amount is included under paragraph (c) in computing the total for the specified month,

(e) if the individual has no qualified relation and has one or more qualified dependants, in relation to the specified month, $306, and

(f) if the individual has no qualified relation and no qualified dependant, in relation to the specified month, the lesser of $306 and 2% of the amount, if any, by which the individual's income for the taxation year exceeds $9,412; and

B is 5% of the amount, if any, by which the individual's adjusted income for the taxation year in relation to the specified month exceeds $37,789.

Related Provisions: 122.5(3.02) — Calculation for shared-custody parents; 122.5(4.1) — Specified month for this payment; 122.5(5) — Only one eligible individual per family; 152(1)(b) — Assessment; 152(1.2)(d) — Notice of determination denying credit to be issued at taxpayer's request; 152(4.2)(b) — Redetermination of credit at taxpayer's request; 257 — Formula cannot calculate to less than zero.

Notes: 122.5(3.001) provides a one-time emergency payment for the COVID-19 coronavirus crisis (for May 2020: 122.5(4.1)). The dollar amounts shown are the actual amounts, not indexed (117.1(1) does not apply to this subsection). For the calculation for shared-custody parents, see 122.5(3.02). See CRA, "COVID-19 — Frequently asked questions: Increase to the GST/HST credit amount", tinyurl.com/covid-gstc.

122.5(3.001) added by 2020 COVID bill #1, effective March 25, 2020. Further COVID-19 support is provided by: 122.61(1.01) (increased Canada Child Benefit); 125.7 (Canada Emergency Wage Subsidy, Canada Emergency Rent Subsidy); 153(1.02)–(1.04) (10% payroll deduction subsidy to employers); delaying income tax payment and instalment deadlines to Sept. 30, 2020 (see Notes to 150(1) opening words); the *Canada Emergency Response Benefit Act* ($2,000 monthly to workers who do not qualify for EI); *Canada Emergency Student Benefit Act* ($1,250 monthly to students); *Public Health Events of National Concern Payments Act* (used for one-time $300 to seniors [see under 56(1)(a)(i)(A)] and $600 to persons with disabilities [see 118.3(1) Notes]); increased Canada Student Grants and suspending Canada Student Loan repayments and interest [see under 118.62]; Indigenous Community Support Fund grants; Canada Emergency Business Account interest-free loans for small businesses and not-for-profits; Canada Emergency Commercial Rent Assistance; expanded EI program; *Canada Recovery Benefits Act* with the Canada Recovery Benefit ($500 weekly for self-employed persons seeking work), Canada Recovery Sickness Benefit (persons who are sick or must self-isolate) and Canada Recovery Caregiving Benefit; and other measures. Many of these benefits are taxed under 56(1)(r) (for individuals) or 12(1)(x) (for businesses). See Ryan Keey, *COVID-19 Tax and Economic Relief Measures* (*Taxnet Pro*, 248pp as of June 30, 2021).

(3.01) Shared-custody parent — Notwithstanding subsection (3), if an eligible individual is a shared-custody parent (within the meaning assigned by section 122.6, but with the words "qualified dependant" in that section having the meaning assigned by subsection (1)) in respect of one or more qualified dependants at the beginning of a month, the amount deemed by subsection (3) to have been paid during a specified month is equal to the amount determined by the following formula

$$1/2 \times (A + B)$$

where

A is the amount determined by the formula in subsection (3), calculated without reference to this subsection, and

B is the amount determined by the formula in subsection (3), calculated without reference to this subsection and subparagraph (b)(ii) of the definition "eligible individual" in section 122.6.

Related Provisions: 122.5(3.02) — Additional one-time COVID-19 benefit for 2020 for shared-custody parent; 122.61(1.1) — Parallel rule for Canada Child Benefit.

Notes: 122.5(3.01) added by 2010 budget bill #2, effective for amounts deemed paid during months after June 2011. See Notes to 122.61(1.1).

(3.02) COVID-19 — shared-custody parent — Notwithstanding subsection (3.001), if an eligible individual is a "shared-custody parent" (within the meaning assigned by section 122.6, but with the words "qualified dependant" in that section having the meaning assigned by subsection (1)) in respect of one or more qualified dependants at the beginning of a month, the amount deemed by subsection (3.001) to have been paid during the specified month is equal to the amount determined by the following formula:

$$0.5(A + B)$$

where

A is the amount determined by the formula in subsection (3.001), calculated without reference to this subsection; and

B is the amount determined by the formula in subsection (3.001), calculated without reference to this subsection and subparagraph (b)(ii) of the definition "eligible individual" in section 122.6.

---

[20] Indexed by 117.1 after 1999 — ed.

[21] Indexed by 117.1 after 1992. See Notes to 117.1(1) — ed.

Notes: 122.5(3.02) added by 2020 COVID bill #1, effective March 25, 2020. It provides the GSTC calculation for shared-custody parents for the one-time COVID-19 payment for 2020. See 122.5(3.001) Notes.

(3.1) When advance payment applies — Subsection (3.2) applies in respect of an eligible individual in relation to a particular month specified for a taxation year, and each subsequent month specified for the taxation year, if

(a) the amount deemed by that subsection to have been paid by the eligible individual during the particular month specified for the taxation year is less than $50; and

(b) it is reasonable to conclude that the amount deemed by that subsection to have been paid by the eligible individual during each subsequent month specified for the taxation year will be less than $50.

Related Provisions: 122.61(2) — Parallel rule for Canada Child Benefit.

Notes: The GST/HST Credit can be paid out annually instead of quarterly when each quarterly entitlement is expected to be less than $50.

122.5(3.1)(a) and (b) amended by 2011 budget bill #2, for amounts deemed paid during months specified for 2010 and later taxation years, to change $25 to $50.

122.5(3.1) amended by 2001 Budget, effective as of the July 2002 payment. Added by 2000 budget bill #1.

Forms: RC4210: GST/HST credit [guide].

(3.2) Advance payment — If this subsection applies, the total of the amounts that would otherwise be deemed by subsection (3) to have been paid on account of the eligible individual's tax payable under this Part for the taxation year during the particular month specified for the taxation year, and during each subsequent month specified for the taxation year, is deemed to have been paid by the eligible individual on account of their tax payable under this Part for the taxation year during the particular specified month for the taxation year, and the amount deemed by subsection (3) to have been paid by the eligible individual during those subsequent months specified for the taxation year is deemed, except for the purpose of this subsection, not to have been paid to the extent that it is included in an amount deemed to have been paid by this subsection.

Related Provisions: 122.7(7) — Advance payment of Canada Workers Benefit; 160.1(1)(b), 160.1(3) — No interest payable on overpaid credit.

Notes: 122.5(3.2) added by 2001 Budget, effective for the July 2002 payment. It is part of what is developing into a "universal income" for all.

(4) Months specified — For the purposes of this section, the months specified for a taxation year are July and October of the immediately following taxation year and January and April of the second immediately following taxation year.

Notes: The April 1993 federal budget proposed to pay the GST credit twice a year, in April and October, rather than four times a year. This would have taken effect in 1994, and was designed by the Conservative government to give the appearance of reducing the federal deficit for the year ended March 31, 1994 (by not paying the credit in January). It was included in Bill C-136, tabled on June 14, 1993. With the election of a Liberal government in November 1993, it became politically desirable to maximize the 1993-94 deficit (attributable to the Tories). The proposed amendment was thus dropped, as announced in a Dec. 20, 1993 Finance news release.

Forms: RC4210: GST/HST credit [guide].

(4.1) COVID-19 — month specified — Notwithstanding subsection (4) and for the purposes of this section, the month specified in subsection (3.001) is May 2020 (or an earlier month designated by the Minister) and the taxation year is the 2018 taxation year.

Notes: 122.5(4.1) added by 2020 COVID bill #1, effective March 25, 2020. It determines the "specified month" for the one-time COVID-19 payment for 2020. See 122.5(3.001) Notes.

(5) Only one eligible individual — If an individual is a qualified relation of another individual in relation to a month specified for a taxation year and both those individuals would be, but for this subsection, eligible individuals in relation to the specified month, only the individual that the Minister designates is the eligible individual in relation to the specified month.

Notes: 122.5(5) amended by 2014 budget bill #1, for 2014 and later taxation years, due to the change in 122.5(3) of no application being required for the credit.

122.5(5) amended by 2001 Budget, effective for the July 2002 payment. Earlier amended by 1993 technical bill, 1992 technical bill and 1990 GST.

(5.1) [Repealed]

Notes: 122.5(5.1) (a temporary measure introduced pending a more general reform of the GST Credit) repealed by 2001 Budget, effective for the July 2002 payment.

(6) Exception re qualified dependant — If a person would, if this Act were read without reference to this subsection, be the qualified dependant of two or more individuals, in relation to a month specified for a taxation year,

(a) the person is deemed to be a qualified dependant, in relation to that month, of the one of those individuals on whom those individuals agree;

(b) in the absence of an agreement referred to in paragraph (a), the person is deemed to be, in relation to that month, a qualified dependant of the individuals, if any, who are, at the beginning of that month, eligible individuals (within the meaning assigned by section 122.6, but with the words "qualified dependant" in that section having the meaning assigned by subsection (1)) in respect of that person; and

(c) in any other case, the person is deemed to be, in relation to that month, a qualified dependant only of the individual that the Minister designates.

Notes: 122.5(6)(a) applied to allocate the credit in *Fraser*, 2010 TCC 23; and *Ross*, 2011 TCC 515 (the Court noted that the GST Credit is different from the Canada Child Benefit in this respect). The court was willing to split the credit as between the spouses in *Nixon*, 2014 SKQB 264, para. 38, but did not have sufficient information to do so. In *Laurin*, 2007 FCA 44, the FCA ruled a separation agreement could not specify which spouse got the credit, but overlooked 122.5(6). In *Perron*, 2017 TCC 220, paras. 23-27, an agreement referring to the Child Tax Benefit and Child Tax Credit did not cover the GST Credit; and in any event the shared-custody rule in 122.5(3.01) overrides 122.5(6)(a): paras. 31-32.

122.5(6)(b) amended by 2010 budget bill #2, for amounts deemed paid after June 2011. Earlier amended by 2001 Budget, 1993 and 1992 technical bills.

(6.1) Notification to Minister — An individual shall notify the Minister of the occurrence of any of the following events before the end of the month following the month in which the event occurs:

(a) the individual ceases to be an eligible individual;

(b) a person becomes or ceases to be the individual's qualified relation; and

(c) a person ceases to be a qualified dependant of the individual, otherwise than because of attaining the age of 19 years.

Related Provisions: 122.62(6) — Parallel rule for Canada Child Benefit.

Notes: 122.5(6.1) added by 2001 Budget, effective for the July 2002 payment.

Forms: RC65: Marital status change.

(6.2) Non-residents and part-year residents — For the purpose of this section, the income of a person who is non-resident at any time in a taxation year is deemed to be equal to the amount that would, if the person were resident in Canada throughout the year, be the person's income for the year.

Notes: 122.5(6.2) added by 2001 Budget, effective for the July 2002 payment.

Forms: RC151: GST/HST credit application for individuals who become residents of Canada.

(7) Effect of bankruptcy — For the purpose of this section, if in a taxation year an individual becomes bankrupt, the individual's income for the taxation year shall include the individual's income for the taxation year that begins on January 1 of the calendar year that includes the date of bankruptcy.

Related Provisions: 118.95 — Parallel rule for other credits; 122.61(3.1) — Parallel rule for Canada Child Benefit.

Notes: 122.5(7)(b) repealed by 2002-2013 technical bill, effective June 26, 2013 (and para. (a) folded into 122.5(7)). The GST credit for a single person with no dependents is now in 122.5(3)(f), without reference to s. 118.

122.5(7) added by 1995-97 technical bill, effective for bankruptcies that occur after April 26, 1995. It allows the GST credit to be based on income from both the pre- and post-bankruptcy period. See also 128(2), 118.95 and 122.61(3.1).

Notes [s. 122.5]: 122.5 enacts the GST Credit or GST/HST Credit (GSTC), designed to offset Goods and Services Tax and Harmonized Sales Tax paid by low-income taxpayers. This is a refundable credit, even for taxpayers with no income, because 122.5(3) deems it paid on account of tax (like instalments or source deductions). In practice the credit is prepaid by CRA 4 times a year, in the "months specified" in

122.5(4) (with a one-time additional payment in 2020 for COVID-19). CRA also administers several similar provincial credits: Guide RC4210.

Despite its name, this GSTC has nothing to do with the GST except in its economic objective. It is enacted in the ITA, and denial is appealed under s. 169. An appeal of denial of the credit under the *Excise Tax Act* (GST/HST legislation) was quashed in *Burchell*, 2013 TCC 102 (FCA appeal dismissed for delay A-148-13).

Until 2014, one applied for the credit by ticking a box on the T1 personal income tax return. Now CRA considers it automatically for taxpayers who file returns.

To calculate the GSTC based on family income, use tinyurl.com/benefits-calc. To find out whether a taxpayer is eligible for the credit and when payment will be made, use canada.ca/my-cra-account or /taxes-representatives.

Various inclusions in income that are offset by matching deductions, so that no tax is paid directly, result in the GSTC being reduced or eliminated due to higher "net income". See Notes to 56(1)(u) and (v). Foster care "kinship" payments were exempted under 81(1)(h.1), in 2019, to eliminate this problem.

Spouses can decide between them which one gets the GSTC: 122.5(6). A non-resident normally does not qualify: 122.5(2)(c). For explanation of the timing of the calculation when the taxpayer's circumstances change, see *Frenna*, 2011 TCC 411.

The credit is generally excluded from a bankrupt's estate available to creditors: *Bankruptcy & Insolvency Act* s. 67(1)(b.1); *Bankruptcy and Insolvency General Rules*, C.R.C. 1978, c. 30, s. 59; *Marcotte*, 2006 CanLII 40675 (Ont. SCJ); *MacIntyre*, 2018 ABQB 380; *Glasgow*, 2018 ONSC 4608.

From July 2017-June 2018, CRA paid total GSTC of $4.39 billion to 10.5 million persons. See tinyurl.com/stats-gstc.

For the additional credit for heating expenses, paid in 2000-01 to persons eligible for the GSTC, see Notes to 81(1)(g.4).

122.5 added by 1990 GST, effective 1989. It replaced the former federal sales tax credit in 122.4.

Definitions [s. 122.5]: "adjusted income" — 122.5(1); "amount", "bankrupt" — 248(1); "calendar year" — *Interpretation Act* 37(1)(a); "Canada" — 255; "child" — 252(1); "cohabiting spouse or common-law partner" — 122.5(1), 122.6; "common-law partner", "common-law partnership" — 248(1); "eligible individual" — 122.5(1); "individual" — 248(1); "Minister" — 248(1); "month" — *Interpretation Act* 35(1); "non-resident" — 248(1); "parent" — 252(2)(a); "person", "prescribed" — 248(1); "qualified dependant", "qualified relation" — 122.5(1); "registered disability savings plan" — 146.4(1), 248(1); "resident", "resident in Canada" — 250; "return of income" — 122.5(1); "specified month" — 122.5(4), (4.1); "taxation year" — 249; "writing" — *Interpretation Act* 35(1).

122.51 (1) [Refundable medical expense supplement —] Definitions — The definitions in this subsection apply in this section.

"adjusted income" of an individual for a taxation year has the meaning assigned by section 122.6.

Notes: See Notes to 122.6"adjusted income".

"eligible individual" for a taxation year means an individual (other than a trust)

(a) who is resident in Canada throughout the year (or, if the individual dies in the year, throughout the portion of the year before the individual's death);

(b) who, before the end of the year, has attained the age of 18 years; and

(c) the total of whose incomes for the year from the following sources is at least $2,500[22]:

(i) offices and employments (computed without reference to paragraph 6(1)(f)),

(ii) businesses each of which is a business carried on by the individual either alone or as a partner actively engaged in the business, and

(iii) the program established under the *Wage Earner Protection Program Act*.

Related Provisions: 117.1(2)(n) — Annual indexing for inflation.

Notes: See Notes at end of 122.51.

122.51(1)"eligible individual"(c) amended for 2008 and later tax years by 2008 budget bill #2.

(2) Deemed payment on account of tax — Where a return of income (other than a return of income filed under subsection 70(2),

paragraph 104(23)(d) or 128(2)(e) or subsection 150(4)) is filed in respect of an eligible individual for a particular taxation year that ends at the end of a calendar year, there is deemed to be paid at the end of the particular year on account of the individual's tax payable under this Part for the particular year the amount determined by the formula

$$A - B$$

where

A is the lesser of

(a) $1,000[22], and

(b) the total of

(i) the amount determined by the formula

$$(0.25/C) \times D$$

where

C is the appropriate percentage for the particular taxation year, and

D is the total of all amounts each of which is the amount determined by the formula in subsection 118.2(1) for the purpose of computing the individual's tax payable under this Part for a taxation year that ends in the calendar year, and

(ii) 25% of the total of all amounts each of which is the amount deductible under section 64 in computing the individual's income for a taxation year that ends in the calendar year; and

B is 5% of the amount, if any, by which

(a) the total of all amounts each of which is the individual's adjusted income for a taxation year that ends in the calendar year

exceeds

(b) $21,663[22].

Related Provisions: 117.1(2)(o) — Annual indexing for inflation; 152(1)(b) — Assessment; 152(4.2)(b) — Redetermination of credit at taxpayer's request; 163(2)(c.2) — False statements or omissions — penalty; 257 — Formula cannot calculate to less than zero.

Forms: T1 General return, Line 45200 [former 452].

Notes [s. 122.51]: 122.51 provides a refundable medical expense supplement of up to $1,272 (2020) or $1,285 (2021) for low-income workers with medical expenses. Because the amount is deemed paid on account of the individual's tax payable, it, like source deductions or instalments paid, creates a refund under 164(1) if the total exceeds tax owing for the year. The supplement is phased out after the couple's net income (122.51(1)"adjusted income") exceeds $28,164 (2020) or $28,446 (2021): 122.51(2)B(b). The dollar amounts are indexed to inflation: see 117.1(1).

For comment and an example see Arthur Drache, "Medical Expense Supplement Credit", xxiv(22) *The Canadian Taxpayer* (Carswell) 172-3 (Nov. 12, 2002), but note that the calculation changed as of 2005.

The calculation in 122.51(2) allows the credit to a person who has two businesses, one with income and one with a loss, netting to a loss: VIEWS doc 2008-0295731E5.

122.51(2)A(b)(i) formula corrected from "(25/C) × D" by 2017 budget bill #2, for 2005 and later taxation years.

122.51(2) amended by 2006 budget bills #1 and #2 (last change effective for 2006 and later taxation years), 2005 budget bill #1, 2004, 2000 and 1999 Budgets. 122.51 added by 1997 Budget.

Proposed **122.52** was a minority Liberal government proposal to apply ⅓ of federal budget surpluses to tax reductions (Bill C-67, *Unanticipated Surpluses Act*, First Reading Oct. 7, 2005). It will not be implemented; see Notes to repealed 118(3.1)-(3.3).

Definitions [s. 122.51]: "adjusted income" — 122.51(1); "amount", "business" — 248(1); "calendar year" — *Interpretation Act* 37(1)(a); "eligible individual" — 122.51(1); "employment", "individual", "office" — 248(1); "partner" — see 96(1) Notes; "resident in Canada" — 250; "tax payable" — 248(2); "taxation year" — 249.

Income Tax Folios [s. 122.51]: S1-F1-C2: Disability tax credit [replaces IT-519R2].

[22] Indexed by 117.1(1) — ed.

Subdivision A.1 — Canada Child Benefit

122.6 Definitions — In this Subdivision,

Notes: Subdivision title changed from "Canada Child Tax Benefit" by 2016 budget bill #1, effective July 2016.

"adjusted earned income" — [Repealed]

Notes: Definition "adjusted earned income" repealed by 1998 first budget bill, effective July 1998.

"adjusted income", of an individual for a taxation year, means the total of all amounts each of which would be the income for the year of the individual and or of the person who was the individual's cohabiting spouse or common-law partner at the end of the year if in computing that income no amount were

(a) included

(i) under paragraph 56(1)(q.1) or subsection 56(6),

(ii) in respect of any gain from a disposition of property to which section 79 applies, or

(iii) in respect of a gain described in subsection 40(3.21), or

(b) deductible under paragraph 20(1)(ww) or 60(y) or (z);

Related Provisions: 122.51(1)"adjusted income" — Definition applies for purposes of refundable medical expense supplement; 122.62(5) — Death of cohabiting spouse; 122.62(6) — Separation from cohabiting spouse.

Notes: This term is called "net family income" in CRA publications. This definition applies for the Canada Child Benefit (**CCB**), refundable medical expense credit (122.51(1)), Canada Education Savings Grant (see *CES Act* in 146.1 Notes) and Canada Disability Savings Grant (see *CDS Act* in 146.4 Notes). Essentially the same definition is in 122.5(1) for the GST/HST Credit.

Adjusted income includes workers' compensation, welfare and other payments that are included in income (56(1)(u), (v)) but not taxed due to 110(1)(f) deduction: *Nicholson*, 2006 TCC 398; *Farah*, 2013 TCC 16. It includes trust income (other than from an RDSP: 56(1)(q.1), VIEWS doc 2015-0600081I7). It excludes the pre-July 2016 Universal Child Care Benefit (56(6)), and an Indian's exempt income (see 81(1)(a)): 2016-0645991M4.

The income of a deceased spouse (or common-law partner) is counted: VIEWS doc 2014-0536771E5.

The requirement to pool spouses' incomes (eliminating the CCB if joint income is too high: e.g. *Kvito*, 2009 TCC 207) does not violate the *Charter of Rights* or *Canadian Human Rights Code* based on marital status: *McFadyen*, [2001] 1 C.T.C. 140 (FCA); *McFadyen*, 2006 FCA 11 (leave to appeal denied 2006 CarswellNat 1230 (SCC)); *Astley*, 2012 TCC 155 (married people are not a disadvantaged group). *Gouskos*, 2020 TCC 110, para. 10, rejected the wife's argument that she had no access to the husband's income, but allowed her to argue that his income was lower than assessed even though he had not appealed his assessment (see 160(1) Notes at "Challenging underlying liability").

Para. (b) amended by 2018 budget bill #1 to add reference to 20(1)(ww), for 2018 and later tax years. Definition earlier amended by 2010 budget bill #2, 2007 RDSPs bill, 2006 budget bill #1, 2000 same-sex partners bill, 1995-97 technical bill.

"base taxation year", in relation to a month, means

(a) where the month is any of the first 6 months of a calendar year, the taxation year that ended on December 31 of the second preceding calendar year, and

(b) where the month is any of the last 6 months of a calendar year, the taxation year that ended on December 31 of the preceding calendar year;

Notes: Adjusted income for BTY 2019 determines the CCB for July 2020-June 2021.

"cohabiting spouse or common-law partner" of an individual at any time means the person who at that time is the individual's spouse or common-law partner and who is not at that time living separate and apart from the individual and, for the purpose of this definition, a person shall not be considered to be living separate and apart from an individual at any time unless they were living separate and apart at that time, because of a breakdown of their marriage or common-law partnership, for a period of at least 90 days that includes that time;

Related Provisions: 122.5(1)"cohabiting spouse..." — Definition applies to GST Credit; 122.7(1)"cohabiting spouse..." — Definition applies to Canada Workers Benefit; 122.8(1)"cohabiting spouse..." — Definition applies to Climate Action Incentive.

Notes: See Notes to 118.8 for the meaning of "living separate and apart".

In *Sookochoff*, 2020 TCC 131, a couple married but could not live together as their respective children did not get along. The Court held they were committed to the marriage and so met this definition, and their income had to be pooled when calculating the CCB (see 122.61(1) Notes).

Timing of disentitlement to the CCB on marrying someone with high income: see *MacIntosh*, 2019 TCC 155, paras. 28-35 (FCA appeal discontinued A-346-19).

CRA announced on May 12, 2009 that following breakdown of a marriage or relationship, "benefit recipients who worry that the CRA will not receive their former spouse's information may immediately submit two letters from independent third parties to show that they live at a residential address different from their former spouse". However, there have been problems and unfairness in CRA's administration of this process. See Taxpayer's Ombudsman, *Proving Your Status* (Oct. 2016), tinyurl.com/ombud-proving. CRA, at "Supporting documents" (July 2019), tinyurl.com/cra-marital, is now slightly more flexible but still needs independent confirmation.

If a taxpayer has a spouse in a nursing home (no breakdown of marriage — see *Kara*, 2009 TCC 82) as well as a common-law partner, both might fall within this definition, but CRA does not take this view: VIEWS doc 2009-0330301C6.

Definition amended by 2000 same-sex partners bill, effective 2001 or earlier.

Income Tax Folios: S1-F1-C1: Medical expense credit [replaces IT-519R2].

"earned income" — [Repealed]

Notes: Definition "earned income" repealed by 1998 budget bill #1, effective July 1998. It referred to the definition in 63(3).

"eligible individual" in respect of a qualified dependant at any time means a person who at that time

(a) resides with the qualified dependant,

(b) is a parent of the qualified dependant who

(i) is the parent who primarily fulfils the responsibility for the care and upbringing of the qualified dependant and who is not a shared-custody parent in respect of the qualified dependant, or

(ii) is a shared-custody parent in respect of the qualified dependant,

(c) is resident in Canada or, where the person is the cohabiting spouse or common-law partner of a person who is deemed under subsection 250(1) to be resident in Canada throughout the taxation year that includes that time, was resident in Canada in any preceding taxation year,

(d) is not described in paragraph 149(1)(a) or (b), and

(e) is, or whose cohabiting spouse or common-law partner is, a Canadian citizen or a person who

(i) is a permanent resident within the meaning of subsection 2(1) of the *Immigration and Refugee Protection Act*,

(ii) is a temporary resident within the meaning of the *Immigration and Refugee Protection Act*, who was resident in Canada throughout the 18 month period preceding that time,

(iii) is a protected person within the meaning of the *Immigration and Refugee Protection Act*,

(iv) was determined before that time to be a member of a class defined in the *Humanitarian Designated Classes Regulations* made under the *Immigration Act*, or

(v) is an Indian within the meaning of the *Indian Act*,

and, for the purposes of this definition,

(f) where a qualified dependant resides with the dependant's female parent, the parent who primarily fulfils the responsibility for the care and upbringing of the qualified dependant is presumed to be the female parent,

(g) the presumption referred to in paragraph (f) does not apply in prescribed circumstances,

(h) prescribed factors shall be considered in determining what constitutes care and upbringing, and

(i) an individual shall not fail to qualify as a parent (within the meaning assigned by section 252) of another individual solely because of the receipt of a social assistance amount that is payable under a program of the Government of Canada or the government of a province for the benefit of the other individual;

Related Provisions: 122.62(1) — Eligible individuals.

Notes: Note that 252(1)(b) and 252(2)(a) extend the definition of "parent" to include other persons with "custody and control".

The parties cannot agree on who gets the CCB: see Notes to 122.61(1).

Para. (a): the child must actually reside with the parent, not just visit: *SR*, 2003 TCC 649; *Angba*, 2006 TCC 17; *Kervin*, 2006 TCC 697; *Fiogbe*, 2007 TCC 454; *Lessard*, 2008 TCC 174; *Arab*, 2008 TCC 193; *Constantin*, 2008 TCC 222; *Dubois*, 2008 TCC 460; *Moïse*, 2009 TCC 187; *Demerais*, 2010 TCC 628; *Waters*, 2010 TCC 631; *Demers*, 2011 TCC 54; *Dubuc*, 2011 TCC 55; *Dostie*, 2011 TCC 467; *Nadalin*, 2012 TCC 48; *Bertrand*, 2015 TCC 174; *Karim*, 2016 TCC 91; *Struck*, 2016 TCC 285; *Jiang*, 2019 TCC 188; but need not "primarily" reside with that parent: *Carnochan*, 2006 TCC 13. See also *Goodwin*, 2008 TCC 183. Once a child was living elsewhere in the custody of Children's Aid, the parent ceased to qualify: *Matthews*, 2009 TCC 270; *Weidenfeld*, 2010 FCA 333 (in *MS*, 2020 FC 982 (under appeal to FCA), the Federal Court did not have jurisdiction to hear a class action on this issue). In *Attia*, 2010 TCC 308, when the other spouse abducted the children, the taxpayer ceased to qualify. However, children not *physically* with a parent were held to *legally* reside with them in: *Bouchard*, 2009 TCC 38 (father in prison); *Charafeddine*, 2010 TCC 417 (father F abducted children and kept them in Lebanon for years; denying the credit to the mother "would be tantamount to condoning [F's] illegal acts"); *Jhanji*, 2014 TCC 126 (J's intention to bring son to Canada temporarily frustrated by his wife's death, so son in boarding school in India "constructively resided" with J in Canada); *Shevchyk*, 2016 TCC 64 (father was injured and unable to care for his children for a time). In *Couture*, 2010 TCC 233 and *Grenier*, 2010 TCC 234, the Court concluded that the child resided with the mother rather than another woman who had a relationship with the child's father.

Para. (c): see Notes to 250(1) for the meaning of "resident in Canada". Non-resident parents did not qualify in: *Goldstein*, 2014 FCA 27; *Manotas*, 2011 TCC 408; *Vegh*, 2012 TCC 95; *Hasin*, 2013 TCC 72; *Bower*, 2013 TCC 183; *Agrebi*, 2014 TCC 141; *Luo*, 2014 TCC 143 (FCA appeal dismissed for delay A-273-14); *Kaplan*, 2014 TCC 215; *Corkum*, 2015 TCC 38. The parent qualified in *Fatima*, 2012 TCC 49, and qualified for some years in *Snow*, 2012 TCC 78.

A non-custodial parent can be an "eligible individual" for months during which the child actually lives with that parent: *Matte*, 2003 FCA 19; *Sanderson*, 2008 TCC 609.

Para. (e) imposes conditions re citizenship and immigration status. (The exclusion of refugees and others with "precarious immigration status" is being taken to Federal Court: "Legal clinic challenges part of *Income Tax Act*", *Law Times*, Feb. 12, 2018, p. 3.) If neither parent qualifies, the fact the children are Canadian citizens does not help: *Ahansaz*, 2007 TCC 568; *Kwangwari*, 2013 TCC 302. A foreign student living with a Canadian family on an exchange program does not qualify: *Therrien*, 2007 TCC 717. Nor does a refugee or visitor who has received a work permit: *Bituala-Mayala*, 2008 TCC 125 (fixed by *Nelly Bituala-Mayala Remission Order*, P.C. 2009-968); *Davidson*, 2015 TCC 54; *Almadhoun*, 2018 FCA 112. CRA considers "resident in Canada" in (e)(ii) to mean *Immigration and Refugee Protection Act* residence, not income tax residence: doc 2010-0386951I7.

Subpara. (e)(v) allows persons who are not Canadian citizens or "permanent residents" under the *Immigration and Refugee Act*, but are Indians under the *Indian Act* and thus have the right to stay in Canada, to receive the CCB if they meet all other requirements. See VIEWS doc 2016-0675991E5. This rule is now retroactive to 2005, so one can use 152(4.2) to request that it apply to past years.

Para. (f): The presumption that the mother is the eligible individual can be overridden not only by Reg. 6301-2 (per paras. (g)-(h)), but also by other factors: *Cabot*, [1998] 4 C.T.C. 2893 (TCC); *Bénard*, [2004] 2 C.T.C. 2569 (TCC); *Theriault*, 2006 TCC 405 (stepmother, deemed parent under 252(1)(c), wanted nothing to do with the child). The presumption does not violate the *Charter of Rights*: *Campbell*, 2005 FCA 420. The presumption does not apply in certain cases such as conflicting CTB applications: Reg. 6301; *Walsh*, 2007 TCC 263; or where Reg. 6302 favours the other parent: VIEWS doc 2009-0308031E5. It applied in *Dexter*, 2012 TCC 176; *D'Elia*, 2012 TCC 180; *Burchell*, 2013 TCC 102 (appeal to FCA dismissed for delay A-147-13) (mother took precedence over grandmother).

In *Murray*, 2005 TCC 514, a truck driver lived with a woman who was not the mother of his children. She applied for and received CTB cheques, but was not their primary caregiver. The father was entitled to the payments. In *Mesamour*, 2010 TCC 131, a foster caregiver was denied the CTB because she was not entirely responsible for the children's care and education.

Para. (h): If both parents qualify, preference is given to the primary caregiver. See Notes to Reg. 6302.

Para. (i) ensures that federal or provincial social assistance for a child does not disqualify the child as being "wholly dependent" on the parent.

Before the 2011 "shared-custody parent" amendments (122.6"shared-custody parent", 122.61(1.1)), CRA policy already allowed parents to split the CTB 6 months each in shared-custody cases. The TCC had no jurisdiction to reject this policy: *Vigeant*, 2007 TCC 492, and approved it in *Pantelidis*, 2010 TCC 639. In several cases the TCC found each parent to be the "primary" caregiver for certain months, so as to split the CTB: *Connolly*, 2010 TCC 231; *Campbell*, 2010 TCC 67; *White*, 2010 TCC 394.

Where both spouses have claims, the Crown should use 174(1) to bind both to the result of an appeal; where it does not, the non-participating spouse, even if a witness in the other appeal, is not bound by it: *Pearson*, 2011 TCC 455.

Para. (i) added by 2018 budget bill #2, retroactive to 2008.

Subpara. (e)(v) added by 2016 budget bill #1, originally effective July 2016 but made retroactive to 2005 by 2018 budget bill #1 (s. 38).

Para. (b) amended by 2010 budget bill #2, for overpayments deemed to arise after June 2011, to refer to shared-custody parents.

Definition amended by S.C. 2001, c. 27 (*Immigration and Refugee Protection Act*), effective June 28, 2002 per P.C. 2002-996; 2001 technical bill, 2000 same-sex partners bill, 1998 Budget and 1995-97 technical bill.

Regulations: 6301 (for para. (g) — circumstances where the presumption in para. (f) does not apply); 6302 (for para. (h) — factors to be considered).

Forms: RC66 Sched.: Status in Canada/statement of income.

"qualified dependant" at any time means a person who at that time

(a) has not attained the age of 18 years,

(b) is not a person in respect of whom an amount was deducted under paragraph (a) of the description of B in subsection 118(1) in computing the tax payable under this Part by the person's spouse or common-law partner for the base taxation year in relation to the month that includes that time, and

(c) is not a person in respect of whom a special allowance under the *Children's Special Allowances Act* is payable for the month that includes that time;

Notes: For para. (c) see *Jahnke*, 2008 TCC 544; *Weidenfeld*, 2010 FCA 333 (child in temporary care of Jewish Family and Child Service was in para. (c)).

122.6"qualified dependant"(b) amended by 2000 same-sex partners bill to refer to "common-law partner", effective as per Notes to 248(1)"common-law partner".

"return of income" filed by an individual for a taxation year means

(a) where the individual was resident in Canada throughout the year, the individual's return of income (other than a return of income filed under subsection 70(2) or 104(23), paragraph 128(2)(e) or subsection 150(4)) that is filed or required to be filed under this Part for the year, and

(b) in any other case, a prescribed form containing prescribed information, that is filed with the Minister.

"shared-custody parent" in respect of a qualified dependant at a particular time means, where the presumption referred to in paragraph (f) of the definition "eligible individual" does not apply in respect of the qualified dependant, an individual who is one of the two parents of the qualified dependant who

(a) are not at that time cohabitating spouses or common-law partners of each other,

(b) reside with the qualified dependant either

(i) at least 40% of the time in the month in which the particular time occurs, or

(ii) on an approximately equal basis, and

(c) primarily fulfil the responsibility for the care and upbringing of the qualified dependant when residing with the qualified dependant, as determined in consideration of prescribed factors,

Related Provisions: 122.5(3.01) — Dividing GST/HST Credit; 122.6"eligible individual"(b)(ii) — Shared-custody parent is eligible individual; 122.61(1.1) — Dividing Canada Child Tax Benefit.

Notes: See Notes to 122.61(1.1). Para. (b) changed from "reside with the qualified dependant on an equal or near equal basis" by 2021 budget bill #1, retroactive to July 2011. This ensures that anything up to a 60-40 split, or otherwise "approximately equal", qualifies as shared custody. The Finance Technical Notes say "approximately equal" might apply if the intent is to be near-equal but due to illness or summer vacation the split is 62-38 in a given month.

The amendment overrules *Lavrinenko*, 2019 FCA 51, and *Morrissey*, 2019 FCA 56 (leave to appeal denied 2019 CarswellNat 4990 (SCC)), which had held that "near equal" meant only up to 55-45, and that the Federal Child Support Guidelines definition of "shared custody" was irrelevant (*Lavrinenko* para. 28).

Lavrinenko and *Morrissey* had overruled many earlier cases finding shared-custody parents, cited here up to PITA 59th ed. Later cases (*Sprong*, 2019 TCC 261; *Jersak (Best)*, 2020 TCC 136) are also overruled by the retroactive amendment.

122.6"shared-custody parent" added by 2010 budget bill #2.

Related Provisions: 164(2.3) — Form deemed to be a return of income.

Notes [s. 122.6]: 122.6 added by 1992 Child Benefit bill, effective for overpayments deemed to arise in 1993 or later.

Definitions [s. 122.6]: "amount" — 248(1); "base taxation year" — 122.6; "calendar year" — *Interpretation Act* 37(1)(a); "Canada" — 255; "cohabiting spouse or common-law partner" — 122.6; "common-law partner", "common-law partnership" — 248(1); "earned income" — 63(3), 122.6; "individual" — 248(1); "Minister" — 248(1); "parent" — 252(2)(a); "prescribed" — 248(1); "qualified dependant" — 122.6; "registered disability savings plan" — 146.4(1), 248(1); "resident" — 250; "shared-custody parent" — 122.6; "taxation year" — 249.

122.61 (1) Deemed overpayment [Canada Child Benefit] —

If a person and, if the Minister so demands, the person's cohabiting spouse or common-law partner at the end of a taxation year have filed a return of income for the year, an overpayment on account of the person's liability under this Part for the year is deemed to have arisen during a month in relation to which the year is the base taxation year, equal to the amount determined by the formula

$$(A + M)/12$$

where

A   is the amount determined by the formula

$$E - Q$$

where

E   is the total of

(a) the product obtained by multiplying $6,400[23] by the number of qualified dependants in respect of whom the person was an eligible individual at the beginning of the month who have not reached the age of six years at the beginning of the month, and

(b) the product obtained by multiplying $5,400[23] by the number of qualified dependants, other than those qualified dependants referred to in paragraph (a), in respect of whom the person was an eligible individual at the beginning of the month, and

Q   is

(a) if the person's adjusted income for the year is less than or equal to $30,000[23], nil,

(b) if the person's adjusted income for the year is greater than $30,000[23] but less than or equal to $65,000[23], and if the person is, at the beginning of the month, an eligible individual in respect of

(i) only one qualified dependant, 7% of the person's adjusted income for the year in excess of $30,000[23],

(ii) only two qualified dependants, 13.5% of the person's adjusted income for the year in excess of $30,000[23],

(iii) only three qualified dependants, 19% of the person's adjusted income for the year in excess of $30,000[23], or

(iv) more than three qualified dependants, 23% of the person's adjusted income for the year in excess of $30,000[23], and

(c) if the person's adjusted income for the year is greater than $65,000[23], and if the person is, at the beginning of the month, an eligible individual in respect of

(i) only one qualified dependant, the total of $2,450[23] and 3.2% of the person's adjusted income for the year in excess of $65,000[23],

(ii) only two qualified dependants, the total of $4,725[23] and 5.7% of the person's adjusted income for the year in excess of $65,000[23],

(iii) only three qualified dependants, the total of $6,650[23] and 8% of the person's adjusted income for the year in excess of $65,000[23], or

(iv) more than three qualified dependants, the total of $8,050[23] and 9.5% of the person's adjusted income for the year in excess of $65,000[23];

R   [Repealed]

C   [Repealed]

M   is the amount determined by the formula

$$N - O$$

where

N   is the product obtained by multiplying $2,730[23] by the number of qualified dependants in respect of whom both

(a) an amount may be deducted under section 118.3 for the taxation year that includes the month, and

(b) the person is an eligible individual at the beginning of the month, and

O   is

(a) if the person's adjusted income for the year is less than or equal to $65,000[23], nil, and

(b) if the person's adjusted income for the year is greater than $65,000[23],

(i) where the person is an eligible individual in respect of only one qualified dependant described in N, 3.2% of the person's adjusted income for the year in excess of $65,000[23], and

(ii) where the person is an eligible individual in respect of two or more qualified dependants described in N, 5.7% of the person's adjusted income for the year in excess of $65,000[23].

Possible Future Amendment — $1,000 increase in CCB for children under 1

Prime Minister's mandate letter to Minister of Families, Dec. 2019: I will expect you to work with your colleagues and through established legislative, regulatory and Cabinet processes to deliver on your top priorities. In particular, you will: . . .

- To help families when the costs of raising kids are highest, starting next summer, increase the Canada Child Benefit by 15% for children under the age of 1.

Liberal.ca election platform, Oct. 2019: Building on the successful Canada Child Benefit (CCB) — which gives more money every month to nine out of 10 families and helped lift 300,000 children out of poverty — we will move forward with the next steps in helping families make ends meet. We will:

- give up to $1,000 more to families to help when the costs of raising kids are highest, by boosting the CCB by 15% for children under the age of one; ...

Notes: The Parliamentary Budget Officer (Election Cost Estimates, Sept. 2019) reports that, under this measure, the base benefit for newborns would be $7,750 as of July 2020. See now 122.61(1.2), which provides up to $1,200, but for 2021 only.

Possible Future Amendment — 122.61(1)M:N — Increase in Child Disability Benefit

Prime Minister's mandate letter to Minister of Employment, Workforce Development and Disability Inclusion, Dec. 2019: I will expect you to work with your colleagues and through established legislative, regulatory and Cabinet processes to deliver on your top priorities. In particular, you will: . . .

- Double the Child Disability Benefit and work with families and experts to ensure the Benefit is effective in providing help as most needed;

Liberal.ca election platform, Oct. 2019: *Child Disability Benefit*

We will double support to parents who care for special needs kids.

Parents who care for their special needs children go the extra mile every day. They take care of their kids' physical, emotional, and education needs; they advocate to get the care and services their kids need to be healthy and happy; they often work multiple jobs to pay for expensive services; and they never stop worrying about what other challenges the future might bring. These hard-working parents deserve our respect — and need our help.

We will move forward with more help for these family caregivers by immediately doubling the Child Disability Benefit. This tax-free monthly benefit helps children whose impairment is severe, and prolonged by certain conditions such as learning and speech disabilities, psychological disorders, and autism spectrum disorder, among others. We also recognize that there is more to do to improve how children and families

---

[23] Indexed by 122.61(5) after 2016 — ed.

access this benefit. We will work closely with families and experts as the benefit is increased, to ensure children get the help they need.

This increased benefit would give families of a child with a disability more than $2,800 in extra help, right away, with up to $5,664 in total financial support available each year — giving more than 150,000 children and their families more money to help with the costs of care.

Related Provisions: 56(6) — Universal Child Care Benefit is taxable; 74.1(2) — No attribution of income from Canada Child Benefit (CCB); 75(3)(d) — Trust from CCB payments — exclusion from reversionary trust rules; 122.61(1.01) — Additional one-time COVID-19 benefit for May 2020; 122.61(3)(a) — Determining family income where spouse is non-resident; 122.61(5) — Indexing to inflation; 122.62(5)–(7) — Effect of changes in spousal status; 122.63 — Agreement with province to vary calculation; 152(1.2), (3.2), (3.3) — Request for determination of CCB; 152(4.2)(b) — Redetermination of deemed overpayment at taxpayer's request; 160.1(1), (2.1) — Taxpayer and spouse both liable for overpaid CCB; 164(1), (2.3) — Refund of CCB if no tax payable; 164(2.2) — CCB cannot normally be applied to other debts; 164(3) — No interest on late payment of CCB; 241(4)(j.1) — Information may be provided to designated person for adjusting social assistance payment; 257 — Formula amounts cannot calculate to less than zero; *Canada Emergency Student Benefit Act* s. 14(2) — Overpaid emergency student benefit cannot be offset against CCB.

Notes: Since July 2016, the Canada Child Benefit (CCB) replaces the former Canada Child Tax Benefit (which was in this section) as well as the former Universal Child Care Benefit (see Notes to 56(6)) and National Child Benefit Supplement (in this section). Payments are integrated and paid together with provincial child benefits in most provinces. Payment is generally made on the 20th of the month. See tinyurl.com/cra-child-benefit and Guide T4114. For May 2020 only, there is an extra $300 per child for the COVID-19 emergency: 122.61(1.01). For 2021, there is an additional $600-$1200 for children under 6, paid quarterly: 122.61(1.2).

122.61(1) creates an "overpayment", so the CCB, like instalments or source deductions withheld, is payable or refundable under 164 even if no tax is payable for the year (thus, it is a "refundable credit"). It cannot normally be offset by other debts: 164(2.2), though once deposited in a bank account that account can presumably be garnished.

The CCB, indexed by 122.61(5), is (from July 2020) $6,765 per child under 6 and $5,708 per child age 6-17 (from July 2021, **$6,833** and **$5,765**): 122.61(1)A:E. However, it is reduced (122.61(1)A:Q) if the parent's or couple's previous-year net income (122.6"adjusted income") exceeds $31,711 (July 2020) or $32,028 (July 2021). From there to $68,708 (July 2020) or $69,395 (July 2021), the reduction is 7% for a 1-child family, 13.5% for 2, 19% for 3 and 23% for larger families. Over $68,708 (July 2020) or $69,395 (2021), remaining benefits are phased out at 3.2% for a 1-child family, 5.7% for 2, 8% for 3 and 9.5% for larger families. The lower phase-out rates seem intended for political reasons to still give fairly high-income taxpayers some benefit. For example, as of July 2021 with 4 children age 6-17 the benefit disappears entirely only if 2020 family income exceeds $221,689 ({[$5,765 × 4] − [[$69,395 − 32,028] × .23]} / .095 + $69,395).

The phase-out is based on family net income, even if taxable income is lower due to amounts included in income but subject to an offsetting deduction (e.g., *Dakiri*, 2013 TCC 18 — workers' comp payments under 56(1)(v)).

For an overview of the rules see *Wachal*, 2020 TCC 78, paras. 5-6. To calculate the CCB and integrated provincial benefits: tinyurl.com/cra-ccbcalc. To check if a taxpayer is eligible for the benefit and when payment will be made, use canada.ca/my-cra-account or /taxes-representatives. One can apply for the benefit online: canada.ca/my-cra-account. One can also apply online when registering a newborn in all provinces and NWT, but not yet YK or NU: tinyurl.com/cra-aba; guides RC4476-BC, RC4476-NS, etc.

Formula element M provides the Child Disability Benefit supplement for each child eligible for the 118.3 disability credit. For July 2020-June 2021, it is $2,886 for families with net income up to $68,708 (tinyurl.com/cra-cdb21), after which it is reduced at the rates in formula element O.

CRA's target (tinyurl.com/cra-standards) is to process digital applications within 8 weeks and paper applications within 11 weeks, 95% of the time; in 2019-20, it did 96% (digital) and 98% (paper).

Evaluation: See Taxpayers' Ombudsman, *Benefits Unsheltered* (Dec. 2017), re how CRA communicates to people staying in shelters about benefits such as the CCB; CRA, "How to get your benefit payments while staying in a shelter", tinyurl.com/cra-ben-shelter; CRA study *Ethnography of Homeless and Housing-Insecure Canadians' Experiences Filing Taxes and Accessing Benefits* (March 2018, 35pp); news release "Updates on CRA Service Improvements" (Sept. 7, 2018); Auditor General 2021 Report 4, "Canada Child Benefit" recommendations (tinyurl.com/ccb-audit), and Minister's response of Feb. 25, 2021, tinyurl.com/cra-ccb-resp.

Who gets the CCB: Neither an agreement by the parties, nor a provincial superior court order, can determine which parent gets it, as only the Act governs: *Laurin*, 2007 FCA 44; *Ross*, 2011 TCC 515; *Desmarais*, 2013 TCC 83, para. 24; *Perron*, 2017 TCC 220, paras. 17-21; but see last para. of Notes to Reg. 6302 for cases that did consider the parties' agreement. (For the GST/HST Credit, 122.5(6) allows such agreement, subject to 122.5(3.01).) A dispute as to which parent gets the CCB must be resolved in Tax Court, not in litigation between the spouses: *Silverman v. Silverman*, 2015 BCSC 157.

Overpaid benefits: An overpaid CCB is recovered from the taxpayer under 160.1(1), or from the spouse under 160.1(2.1). This can be appealed to the TCC, as it is not strictly a collection matter: *Surikov*, 2008 TCC 161 (saying *Cheung* was wrong on this point).

In *Robertson*, 2008 TCC 154, R was found not to have been living common-law, so the other person's adjusted income was not included in the calculation. Conversely, in *Harrison*, 2008 TCC 314, H was held to be living common-law, so he had to repay the CCB. The CCB was recovered from taxpayers who had failed to report their spouse's income, once CRA identified that family income was too high, in *Dionne*, [2004] 2 C.T.C. 2828 (TCC), and *Findlay*, 2009 TCC 542. In *Atlantic Technologist*, [2009] 2 C.T.C. 20 (Nfld. Prov. Ct), a woman was convicted of claiming the CCB when she knew her husband had income he was not reporting.

See Notes to 122.62(4) for cases where CRA sought to recover a CCB overpaid to a spouse who had left the home.

Various inclusions in income that are offset by matching deductions, so that no tax is paid directly, result in the CCB being reduced due to higher "net income". See Notes to 56(1)(u) and (v). Foster care "kinship" payments were exempted under 81(1)(h.1), in 2019, to eliminate this problem.

See also Tollstam, "New Canada Child Benefit", 24(8) *Canadian Tax Highlights* (ctf.ca) 7-8 (Aug. 2016); Terekhova, "Post-Divorce Monthly: Canada Child Tax Benefit: Second Caveat", 33(4) *Money & Family Law* (Carswell) 32 (April 2018).

122.61(1) amended by 2016 budget bill #1, effective July 2018, to change the formulas from "(A+C+M)/12" and "E−Q−R" and repeal formula elements C and R, to eliminate references to the national child benefit supplement. The references had been left in place for two years, without affecting the CCB calculation, "to provide time for provinces and territories to make the necessary changes to their social assistance and child benefit programs following the elimination of the National Child Benefit supplement". Formula elements C and R read:

R is the amount determined for C;

C is the amount determined by the formula

$$F − (G × H)$$

where

F is, if the person is, at the beginning of the month, an eligible individual in respect of

(a) only one qualified dependant, $2,308, and

(b) two or more qualified dependants, the total of

(i) $2,308 for the first qualified dependant,

(ii) $2,042 for the second qualified dependant, and

(iii) $1,943 for each of the third and subsequent qualified dependants,

G is the amount determined by the formula

$$J − [K − (L/0.122)]$$

where

J is the person's adjusted income for the year,

K is $45,282, and

L is the amount referred to in paragraph (a) of the description of F, and

H is

(a) if the person is an eligible individual in respect of only one qualified dependant, 12.2%, and

(b) if the person is an eligible individual in respect of two or more qualified dependants, the fraction (expressed as a percentage rounded to the nearest one-tenth of one per cent) of which

(i) the numerator is the total that would be determined under the description of F in respect of the eligible individual if that description were applied without reference to the fourth and subsequent qualified dependants in respect of whom the person is an eligible individual, and

(ii) the denominator is the amount referred to in paragraph (a) of the description of F, divided by 0.122; and

122.61(1) amended by 2016 budget bill #1, effective July 2016.

122.61(1)A(c) repealed by 2006 budget bill #1 (Part 6 — Universal Child Care Benefit), effective for overpayments deemed to arise during months after June 2007. This amendment eliminates the supplement for children under 7, due to the introduction of the Universal Child Care Benefit (see Notes to 56(6)). As a transitional measure, the supplement continued to be paid for children who were 6 years old at the beginning of each month from July 2006 through June 2007.

122.61(1) amended by 2006 budget bill #1 (for overpayments deemed to arise after June 2006), 2005 budget bill #1, 2003 same-sex partners bill, and 2003, 2000, 1999, 1998 and 1997 Budgets.

See also Notes at end of 122.61.

Income Tax Folios: S1-F3-C1: Child care expense deduction [replaces IT-495R3].

Forms: CTB9: Canada child tax benefit statement; RC64: Children's special allowances; RC66: Canada child benefits application; RC66 Sched.: Status in Canada/statement of income; RC113: Direct deposit request for children's special allowances; RC4476-AB; RC4476-BC; RC4476-MB; RC4476-NB; RC4476-NL;

RC4476-NS; RC4476-ON; RC4476-PE; RC4476-QC; RC4476-SK: Birth registration and Canada Child Benefits [guide]; T4114: Canada child benefits [guide].

(1.01) COVID-19 — additional amount [for May 2020] — If the month referred to in subsection (1) is May 2020, each amount expressed in dollars referred to in paragraphs (a) and (b) of the description of E in subsection (1) is deemed, for that month, to be equal to that amount (as adjusted under subsection (5)) plus an additional amount of $3,600. For greater certainty, the adjustment in subsection (5) shall not take into account this additional amount.

Related Provisions: 122.5(3.001) — Increased GST Credit for COVID-19; 122.61(1.2) — Additional COVID-19 amount for 2021; *Canada Emergency Student Benefit Act* s. 14(2) — Overpaid emergency student benefit cannot be offset against CCB.

Notes: 122.61(1.01) provides a one-time emergency $300 additional Child Tax Benefit per child, for the COVID-19 coronavirus crisis. Adding $3,600 to E(a) and (b) means adding $300 per child for May 2020 only. (122.61(5) does not apply to this subsection, so these are the actual dollar amounts, not indexed.)

122.61(1.01) added by 2020 COVID bill #1, effective March 25, 2020. See CRA, "One-time increase to CCB payment in May 2020", tinyurl.com/covid-ccb. For other COVID-19 support measures, see 122.5(3.001) Notes.

(1.1) Shared-custody parent — Notwithstanding subsection (1), if an eligible individual is a shared-custody parent in respect of one or more qualified dependants at the beginning of a month, the overpayment deemed by subsection (1) to have arisen during the month is equal to the amount determined by the formula

$$1/2 \times (A + B)$$

where

A   is the amount determined by the formula in subsection (1), calculated without reference to this subsection, and

B   is the amount determined by the formula in subsection (1), calculated without reference to this subsection and subparagraph (b)(ii) of the definition "eligible individual" in section 122.6.

Related Provisions: 122.5(3.01) — Parallel rule for GST Credit; *Universal Child Care Benefit Act* s. 4(1)(a) [in Notes to ITA 56(6)] — Parallel rule for UCCB.

Notes: See Notes to 122.6 "shared-custody parent", and tinyurl.com/cra-child-benefit. The shared-custody credit can be claimed retroactively: VIEWS doc 2013-0500821E5. In *Jersak (Best)*, 2020 TCC 136, CRA recovered half the CCB from J; the fact it might be too late for her ex to claim half for most years did not help her (also, CRA could use 122.62(2) to extend time for him to apply).

See also Budd & Robinson, "The Canada Child Benefit and Child Custody", 6(3) *Canadian Tax Focus* (ctf.ca) 5-6 (Aug. 2016); Ranot, "Who Receives the Canada Child Benefits", 34(11) *Money & Family Law* (Carswell) 83-84 (Nov. 2019).

In *Nixon v. Nixon*, 2014 SKQB 264, the parties had agreed to share the CTB, but the father could not claim an offset for not having received half of it since it was up to CRA to determine whether they were shared-custody parents.

122.61(1.1) added by 2010 budget bill #2, effective for overpayments deemed to arise after June 2011.

(1.2) Deemed overpayment — COVID-19 [young child supplement] — If the Minister determines before 2024 that an overpayment (for greater certainty, in an amount greater than nil) on account of a person's liability under this Part for a taxation year is deemed to have arisen during a month under subsection (1), or would be so deemed if this section were read without reference to subsection (2), then an overpayment on account of the person's liability under this Part for the year is deemed to have arisen during the month, equal to the total of all amounts each of which is an amount in respect of a qualified dependant — in respect of whom the person was an eligible individual at the beginning of the month who has not reached the age of six years at the beginning of the month — determined by the formula

$$A \times B$$

where

A   is

(a) 0.5, if the person is a shared-custody parent in respect of the qualified dependant, and

(b) 1, in any other case; and

B   is

(a) if the month is January 2021 or April 2021,

  (i) $300, if the person's adjusted income for 2019 is less than or equal to $120,000, and

  (ii) $150 in any other case,

(b) if the month is July 2021 or October 2021,

  (i) $300, if the person's adjusted income for 2020 is less than or equal to $120,000, and

  (ii) $150 in any other case, and

(c) in any other case, nil.

Related Provisions: 122.61(1.01) — Additional COVID-19 amount for May 2020; 122.62(5)–(7) — Effect of changes in spousal status.

Notes: 122.61(1.2) provides COVID-19 relief in the form of 4 additional CCB payments of $300 per child under 6 to families entitled to the CCB with family net income (122.6 "adjusted income") up to $120,000, and $150 per child under 6 to families entitled to the CCB with higher net income. CRA calls this the "young child supplement" (CCBYCS): tinyurl.com/cra-ccbycs. Shared-custody parents split these payments: para. A(a).

Eligibility for these quarterly amounts requires the individual to be entitled to a CCB payment in the particular month. To qualify, an individual must be determined by the end of 2023 to be entitled to the CCB: 122.61(1.2) opening words.

Nov. 30, 2020 Economic Statement Table 1 forecasts that this will cost the government $580 million in 2020-21 and $1,775m in 2021-22.

122.61(1.2) added by 2021 COVID bill #1, effective May 6, 2021.

(2) Exceptions — Notwithstanding subsection (1), if a particular month is the first month during which an overpayment that is less than $20 (or such other amount as is prescribed) is deemed under that subsection to have arisen on account of a person's liability under this Part for the base taxation year in relation to the particular month, any such overpayment that would, but for this subsection, reasonably be expected at the end of the particular month to arise during another month in relation to which the year is the base taxation year is deemed to arise under that subsection during the particular month and not during the other month.

Related Provisions: 122.5(3.1) — Parallel rule for GST/HST Credit.

Notes: The Canada Child Benefit can be paid out annually instead of monthly when each monthly entitlement is expected to be less than $20.

122.61(2) amended by 2011 budget bill #2, effective with respect to overpayments deemed to arise during months that are after June 2011, to change $10 to $20.

Regulations: No alternate amount has been prescribed.

(3) Non-residents and part-year residents — For the purposes of this section, if a person was non-resident at any time in a taxation year, the person's income for the year is, for greater certainty, deemed to be the amount that would have been the person's income for the year had the person been resident in Canada throughout the year.

Notes: 122.61(3) counts a non-resident spouse's worldwide income for purposes of determining family income, which erodes the Canada Child Benefit over a given threshold. Strangely, this rule did not apply to a spouse who was deemed non-resident throughout the year due to the Canada-US tax treaty: *Thorpe*, 2007 TCC 410 (CRA is expected to ignore this Informal Procedure decision).

122.61(3) amended by 2013 budget bill #2, effective Dec. 12, 2013, effectively to delete former para. (b) (which applied to "earned income", repealed from 122.6 in 1998).

Forms: RC66 Sched.: Status in Canada/statement of income.

(3.1) Effect of bankruptcy — For the purposes of this Subdivision, where in a taxation year an individual becomes bankrupt,

(a) the individual's income for the year shall include the individual's income for the taxation year that begins on January 1 of the calendar year that includes the date of bankruptcy; and

(b) the total of all amounts deducted under section 63 in computing the individual's income for the year shall include the amount deducted under that section for the individual's taxation year that begins on January 1 of the calendar year that includes the date of bankruptcy.

(c) [Repealed]

Related Provisions: 118.95, 122.5(7) — Parallel rule for personal credits, GST credit.

Notes: See Notes to 122.5(7). 122.61(3.1) amended by 1998 budget bill #1, effective June 18, 1998. Added by 1995-97 technical bill, for bankruptcies after April 26, 1995.

(4) Amount not to be charged, etc. — A refund of an amount deemed by this section to be an overpayment on account of a person's liability under this Part for a taxation year

(a) shall not be subject to the operation of any law relating to bankruptcy or insolvency;

(b) cannot be assigned, charged, attached or given as security;

(c) does not qualify as a refund of tax for the purposes of the *Tax Rebate Discounting Act*;

(d) cannot be retained by way of deduction or set-off under the *Financial Administration Act*; and

(e) is not garnishable moneys for the purposes of the *Family Orders and Agreements Enforcement Assistance Act*.

Related Provisions: 164(2.2) — No set-off against other tax debts.

(5) Annual adjustment [indexing] — Each amount expressed in dollars in subsection (1) shall be adjusted so that, where the base taxation year in relation to a particular month is after 2016, the amount to be used under that subsection for the month is the total of

(a) the amount that would, but for subsection (7), be the relevant amount used under subsection (1) for the month that is one year before the particular month, and

(b) the product obtained by multiplying

(i) the amount referred to in paragraph (a)

by

(ii) the amount, adjusted in such manner as is prescribed and rounded to the nearest one-thousandth or, where the result obtained is equidistant from 2 such consecutive one-thousandths, to the higher thereof, that is determined by the formula

$$(A/B) - 1$$

where

A   is the "Consumer Price Index" (within the meaning assigned by subsection 117.1(4)) for the 12-month period that ended on September 30 of the base taxation year, and

B   is the Consumer Price Index for the 12 month period preceding the period referred to in the description of A.

Related Provisions: 117.1(1) — Indexing of other amounts; 122.61(7) — Rounding of adjusted amounts; 257 — Formula cannot calculate to less than zero.

Notes: 122.61(5) provides for indexing of the Canada Child Benefit (CCB) to inflation since July 2018 (due to the words "after 2016": see 122.6"base taxation year" and 122.61(1) opening words).

The CCB as announced in the March 2016 Budget was much higher than the previous Child Tax Benefit, and was not going to be indexed, so 122.61(5) was repealed. (Either the Liberal government wanted future political credit for announcing increases in the CCB, or it wanted the CCB's real cost eroded over time to reduce the federal deficit.) However, the Parliamentary Budget Officer, in *Fiscal Analysis of Federal Children's Benefits* (Sept. 1, 2016), reported that the new program would cost the government less than the old program by about 2025. Due to the resulting publicity, indexing was first restored by reintroducing 122.61(5) (2016 budget bill #2) applying "after 2018" to start indexing in July 2020. 2018 budget bill #1 then changed this to "after 2016", starting indexing in July 2018, as announced in Dept. of Finance Backgrounder, Oct. 24, 2017.

Before July 2016, 122.61(5) read as it does now, but "2016" read "1998".

(5.1) [Repealed]

Notes: 122.61(5.1) repealed by 1998 budget bill #1, effective for overpayments deemed to arise during months that are after June 1998. It provided an annual adjustment to an amount in 122.61(1), originally added by 1997 Budget (first bill).

(6) [Applies to 2005-07 only.]

(6.1) [Applies to 2001-02 only.]

(7) Rounding — If an amount referred to in subsection (1), when adjusted as provided in subsection (5), is not a multiple of one dollar, it shall be rounded to the nearest multiple of one dollar or, where it is equidistant from 2 such consecutive multiples, to the higher thereof.

Notes: 122.61(7) added by 2016 budget bill #2, effective Dec. 15, 2016, after being repealed by 2016 budget bill #1 effective July 2016. With indexing in 122.61(5) eliminated, rounding to the nearest dollar was no longer needed until indexing was restored. Before July 2016, 122.61(7) read as it does now.

Notes [s. 122.61]: 122.61 added by 1992 Child Benefit bill, effective for overpayments deemed to arise in 1993 or later, with transitional rules for 1992 and 1993.

Definitions [s. 122.61]: "adjusted earned income", "adjusted income" — 122.6; "amount", "bankrupt" — 248(1); "base taxation year" — 122.6; "calendar year" — *Interpretation Act* 37(1)(a); "Canada" — 255; "cohabiting spouse or common-law partner" — 122.6; "common-law partner" — 248(1); "earned income", "eligible individual" — 122.6; "Minister" — 248(1); "month" — *Interpretation Act* 35(1); "person" — 248(1); "qualified dependant" — 122.6; "resident" — 250; "return of income", "shared-custody parent" — 122.6; "taxable income" — 2(2), 248(1); "taxable income earned in Canada" — 115(1), 248(1); "taxation year" — 249.

122.62 (1) Eligible individuals — For the purposes of this Subdivision, a person may be considered to be an eligible individual in respect of a particular qualified dependant at the beginning of a month only if the person has, no later than 11 months after the end of the month, filed with the Minister a notice in prescribed form containing prescribed information.

Related Provisions: 122.62(5)–(8) — Change in status; 220(2.1) — Waiver of requirement under 122.62(1) to file notice; 241(4)(b) — Disclosure of taxpayer information for purposes of administering the Act; 241(4)(j.1) — Information may be provided to provincial officials for certain purposes.

Notes: It appears that not filing a change in marital status triggers this rule, but in *Guest*, 2010 TCC 336, the Canada Child Benefit was allowed because CRA had not considered that it could waive or extend the notice period under 122.62(2) or 220(2.1), and CRA's T4114 guide was confusing. See also Notes to 122.6"eligible individual". See now 122.62(4)-(8).

Calculation of the deadline for objecting to a disallowed CTB required determining how to apply 152(1.2), and in the circumstances, the taxpayer's objection deadline had not yet started: *Reynolds*, 2013 TCC 288 (FCA appeal discontinued A-354-13).

122.62(1) amended by 1995-97 technical bill, effective August 28, 1995. "National Health and Welfare" changed to "Human Resources Development" by S.C. 1996, c. 11, effective July 12, 1996. See also Notes at end of 122.62.

Forms: RC65: Marital status change [possibly: *Guest v. R.*, 2010 TCC 336, para. 14].

(2) Extension for notices — The Minister may, on or before the day that is 10 years after the beginning of the month referred to in subsection (1), extend the time for filing a notice under that subsection.

Notes: A CRA refusal to extend time can be challenged by judicial review application in Federal Court (see Notes to 220(3.1)). In *Nicholls*, 2010 FC 1235, CRA paid retroactive benefits only back as far as it could reassess N's estranged wife to recover the benefits it had paid her; the Court held this to be a reasonable exercise of discretion. The TCC cannot then bypass the Minister's discretion by determining eligibility for the benefit: *Nicholls*, 2012 FCA 243. See also VIEWS doc 2013-0500821E5.

122.62(2) amended by 2016 budget bill #1, effective July 2016, to add "on or before the day that is 10 years after the beginning of the month referred to in subsection (1)". The 10-year limitation period is consistent with 152(4.2) and 220(3.1). 122.62(2) allows 10 years for the CRA to extend the time to make a late claim: *Jersak (Best)*, 2020 TCC 136, para. 25.

122.62(2) amended by 1995-97 technical bill (effective Aug. 28, 1995) and S.C. 1996, c. 11 (effective July 12, 1996).

(3) [No longer relevant]

Notes: 122.62(3) provides a transitional rule for children who qualified before 1993.

(4) Person ceasing to be an eligible individual — Where during a particular month a person ceases to be an eligible individual in respect of a particular qualified dependant (otherwise than because of the qualified dependant attaining the age of 18 years), the person shall notify the Minister of that fact before the end of the first month following the particular month.

Related Provisions: 241(4)(j.2) — Information may be provided to provincial officials for certain purposes.

Notes: A notification under 122.62(4) or election under 122.62(5)–(7) is also deemed to be a notification or election under Ontario *Taxation Act, 2007* s. 104(2), for purposes of the Ontario child benefit.

In all of *Healey*, [2005] 3 C.T.C. 2218 (TCC), *Badia*, 2007 TCC 570, *Milliard*, 2009 TCC 41, *Sitter*, 2010 TCC 263 and *Gaucher*, 2012 TCC 43, wife **W** moved out and separated from husband **H**. Payments continued to be made to a joint account (in *Badia*, the account was changed to be in H's name only; in *Milliard*, W testified she had lost her bank card; in *Gaucher*, W returned the card to H and had no access to the account) and H used the funds. In all these cases, W was held to have received the payments and was required to repay them since she had not been entitled to them! Similarly, in *Cheung*, 2006 TCC 171, W's appeal was dismissed on the basis this was "strictly a collection matter" (*contra*, see Notes to 122.61(1) re *Surikov*). Similarly, in *Willis*, 2012 TCC 23, the CRA could recover amounts sent after W left but before she notified the CRA of her move, even though H had cashed the cheques, a "blatant wrong" on his part. However, in *Moore*, 2006 TCC 587, on similar facts, W was not required to repay the benefit because she had not received the funds. Where W told the CRA she was leaving the family home, but the CRA continued to send her the cheques, the CRA could not recover the funds from her because it had treated her "as the trustee for the proper recipient", so she had received the funds in trust for H: *Forbes*, 2006 TCC 377. See also *Luo*, 2014 TCC 143 (FCA appeal dismissed for delay A-273-14), where W was not entitled to the CCTB she had received because she was not resident in Canada, and argued unsuccessfully that H and not she should have to repay it.

CRA refusal to accept that W was separated because H had not provided a new address was not a human rights violation: *Maximova*, 2019 FCA 37.

See the Remission Orders annotation below for cases where recovery of an overpaid CCTB was waived by Cabinet order. Arguably, in cases of hardship CRA has discretion not to collect, based on *Surdivall v. Ontario*, 2014 ONCA 240.

122.62(4) amended by 1995-97 technical bill, effective August 28, 1995.

Remission Orders: *Nelly Bituala-Mayala Remission Order*, P.C. 2009-968 (remission of overpaid child tax benefit (CTB) due to extreme hardship and CRA error); *Xiu Que Hong Remission Order*, P.C. 2013-39 (remission of overpaid CTB due to 'extreme hardship and financial setback with an extenuating circumstance'); *Yolande Laurence Remission Order*, P.C. 2014-952 (remission of overpaid CTB due to "incorrect action on the part of federal government officials"); *Trena LaHaye Remission Order*, P.C. 2016-868 (same); *Milca Kwangwari Remission Order*, P.C. 2017-1507 (same); *Janet De La Torre Remission Order*, P.C. 2017-1506 (remission of overpaid CTB due to "extreme hardship"); *Tonele Benoit Remission Order*, P.C. 2019-1145 (incorrect CRA action and extreme hardship).

Forms: RC65: Marital status change.

(5) Death of cohabiting spouse [or common-law partner] — If the cohabiting spouse or common-law partner of an eligible individual in respect of a qualified dependant dies,

(a) the eligible individual shall notify the Minister in prescribed form of that event before the end of the first calendar month that begins after that event; and

(b) subject to subsection (8), for the purpose of determining the amount deemed under subsection 122.61(1) or (1.2) to be an overpayment arising in that first month and any subsequent month on account of the eligible individual's liability under this Part for the base taxation year in relation to that first month, the eligible individual's adjusted income for the year is deemed to be equal to the eligible individual's income for the year.

Related Provisions: 122.62(8) — Where two events happen in same month; 241(4)(j.2) — Information may be provided to provincial officials for certain purposes.

Notes: 122.62(5)–(8) now require an individual receiving the CCB to notify CRA of a marital (or common-law) status change (death, separation, marriage, etc.) by the end of the month after the change (consistent with 122.5(6.1) for the GST/HST Credit). If the change results in a change to CCB amounts, revised entitlements will be effective in the first month after the month of change in status: VIEWS doc 2013-0475271E5. See Taxpayers' Ombudsman, "Systemic Examination of Service Issues Arising from the Canada Revenue Agency's Interpretation and Application of the June 2011 Legislative Changes Affecting the Canada Child Tax Benefit" (March 9, 2016).

122.62(5)(b) amended by 2021 COVID bill #1, effective May 6, 2021, to add "or (1.2)".

122.62(5) amended by 2011 budget bill #2 (for events after June 2011), 2000 same-sex partners bill, 1995-97 technical bill (renumbered from (6)).

Forms: RC65: Marital status change.

(6) Separation from cohabiting spouse [or common-law partner] — If a person ceases to be an eligible individual's cohabiting spouse or common-law partner,

(a) the eligible individual shall notify the Minister in prescribed form of that event before the end of the first calendar month that begins after that event; and

(b) subject to subsection (8), for the purpose of determining the amount deemed under subsection 122.61(1) or (1.2) to be an overpayment arising in that first month and any subsequent month on account of the eligible individual's liability under this Part for the base taxation year in relation to that first month, the eligible individual's adjusted income for the year is deemed to be equal to the eligible individual's income for the year.

Related Provisions: 122.5(6.1) — Parallel rule for GST/HST Credit; 122.62(8) — Where two events happen in same month; 241(4)(j.2) — Information may be provided to provincial officials for certain purposes.

Notes: See 122.62(5) Notes. 122.62(6)(b) amended by 2021 COVID bill #1, effective May 6, 2021, to add "or (1.2)". 122.62(6) amended by 2011 budget bill #2 (for events after June 2011), 2000 same-sex partners bill, 1995-97 technical bill (renumbered from (7)).

Forms: RC65: Marital status change.

(7) Person becoming a cohabiting spouse [or common-law partner] — If a taxpayer becomes the cohabiting spouse or common-law partner of an eligible individual,

(a) the eligible individual shall notify the Minister in prescribed form of that event before the end of the first calendar month that begins after that event; and

(b) subject to subsection (8), for the purpose of determining the amount deemed under subsection 122.61(1) or (1.2) to be an overpayment arising in that first month and any subsequent month on account of the eligible individual's liability under this Part for the base taxation year in relation to that first month, the taxpayer is deemed to have been the eligible individual's cohabiting spouse or common-law partner at the end of the base taxation year in relation to that month.

Related Provisions: 122.62(8) — Where two events happen in same month; 241(4)(j.2) — Information may be provided to provincial officials for certain purposes.

Notes: See 122.62(5) Notes. 122.62(7)(b) amended by 2021 COVID bill #1, effective May 6, 2021, to add "or (1.2)". 122.62(7) amended by 2011 budget bill #2 (for events after June 2011), 2000 same-sex partners bill, 1995-97 technical bill (renumbered from (8)).

Forms: RC65: Marital status change.

(8) Ordering of events — If more than one event referred to in subsections (5) to (7) occur in a calendar month, only the subsection relating to the last of those events to have occurred applies.

Notes: 122.62(8) added by 2011 budget bill #2, for events after June 2011.

(9) [Repealed]

Notes: 122.62(9) repealed by 1995-97 technical bill, effective Aug. 28, 1995. It allowed Revenue Canada to obtain advice from Human Resources Development Canada on particular taxpayers.

Notes [s. 122.62]: 122.62 added by 1992 Child Benefit bill, effective for overpayments deemed to arise in 1993 or later.

Definitions [s. 122.62]: "adjusted earned income", "adjusted income" — 122.6; "amount" — 248(1); "cohabiting spouse or common-law partner" — 122.6; "common-law partner", "common-law partnership" — 248(1); "eligible individual" — 122.6; "individual" — 248(1); "Minister" — 248(1); "month" — *Interpretation Act* 35(1); "person", "prescribed" — 248(1); "qualified dependant" — 122.6; "taxation year" — 249; "taxpayer" — 248(1).

122.63 (1) Agreement — The Minister of Finance may enter into an agreement with the government of a province whereby the amounts determined under the description of E in subsection 122.61(1) with respect to persons resident in the province shall, for the purpose of calculating overpayments deemed to arise under that subsection, be replaced by amounts determined in accordance with the agreement.

(2) Agreement — The amounts determined under the description of E in subsection 122.61(1) for a base taxation year because of any agreement entered into with a province and referred to in subsection (1) shall be based on the age of qualified dependants of eligible individuals, or on the number of such qualified dependants, or both, and shall result in an amount in respect of a qualified dependant that is not less, in respect of that qualified dependant, than 85% of the amount that would otherwise be determined under that description in respect of that qualified dependant for that year.

(3) Agreement — Any agreement entered into with a province and referred to in subsection (1) shall provide that, where the operation of the agreement results in a total of all amounts, each of which is an amount deemed under subsection 122.61(1) to be an overpayment on account of the liability under this Part for a taxation year of a person subject to the agreement, that exceeds 101% of the total of such overpayments that would have otherwise been deemed to have arisen under subsection 122.61(1), the excess shall be reimbursed by the government of the province to the Government of Canada.

Notes [s. 122.63]: Provinces and territories can enter into an agreement with the federal government to restructure Canada Child Benefit base benefit amounts (within the same fiscal envelope), based on the age of the child and/or number of children in a family. This was not possible from July 2016 through June 2017, when the former Canada Child Tax Benefit was first revised and increased by the 2016 Budget.

122.63 repealed by 2016 budget bill #1 effective July 2016, and re-enacted by 2017 budget bill #1 effective July 2017. The pre-July 2016 version was substantively identical to the current one.

122.63 amended by 1995-97 technical bill; added by 1992 Child Benefit bill.

Definitions [s. 122.63]: "amount" — 248(1); "base taxation year", "eligible individual" — 122.6; "Minister of Finance" — *Financial Administration Act* 14; "person" — 248(1); "province" — *Interpretation Act* 35(1); "qualified dependant" — 122.6; "resident" — 250.

122.64 [Repealed]

Notes: 122.64 repealed by 2013 budget bill #2, effective Dec. 12, 2013. It was not needed as it is covered by 241(4)(e), (j.1) and (j.2) and 239(2.21). It provided for confidentiality of information relating to the Child Tax Benefit.

122.64 earlier amended by 1995-97 technical bill, S.C. 1996 c. 11 and S.C. 2005 c. 35. Added by 1992 Child Benefit bill.

Definitions [s. 122.64]: "authorized person", "official" — 241(10); "person", "prescribed" — 248(1); "province" — *Interpretation Act* 35(1); "taxpayer" — 248(1).

Subdivision A.2 — Canada Workers Benefit [former Working Income Tax Benefit — ed.]

Notes: Heading changed from "Working Income Tax Benefit" by 2018 budget bill #1, effective 2019.

122.7 (1) Definitions — The following definitions apply in this section.

"adjusted net income" of an individual for a taxation year means the amount that would be the individual's income for the taxation year if

(a) [Repealed]

(b) in computing that income, no amount were included under paragraph 56(1)(q.1) or subsection 56(6), in respect of any gain from a disposition of property to which section 79 applies or in respect of a gain described in subsection 40(3.21); and

(c) in computing that income, no amount were deductible under paragraph 20(1)(ww) or 60(y) or (z).

Related Provisions: 122.7(1.1) — Optional method of determining working income for taxpayer with exempt income.

Notes: Para. (a) repealed by 2018 budget bill #2, effective 2019. It read "[if] this Act were read without reference to paragraph 81(1)(a) and subsection 81(4)". Before 2019, a status Indian's exempt income, including social assistance, reduced WITB entitlement: VIEWS doc 2016-0665081E5.

Para. (c) amended by 2018 budget bill #1 to add reference to 20(1)(ww), for 2018 and later tax years.

Para. (b) amended by 2010 budget bill #2, for 2000 and later tax years.

"cohabiting spouse or common-law partner" of an individual at any time has the meaning assigned by section 122.6.

"designated educational institution" has the meaning assigned by subsection 118.6(1).

"eligible dependant" of an individual for a taxation year means a child of the individual who, at the end of the year,

(a) resided with the individual;

(b) was under the age of 19 years; and

(c) was not an eligible individual.

Related Provisions: 122.7(1.2) — Effect of social assistance under kinship care program; 122.7(10) — No eligible dependant if both parents claim.

"eligible individual" for a taxation year means an individual (other than an ineligible individual) who was resident in Canada throughout the taxation year and who was, at the end of the taxation year,

(a) 19 years of age or older;

(b) the cohabiting spouse or common-law partner of another individual; or

(c) the parent of a child with whom the individual resides.

Related Provisions: 122.7(1.2) — Effect of social assistance under kinship care program; 122.7(4) — Where eligible spouse deemed not to be eligible individual.

Notes: On the meaning of "with whom the individual resides", see Notes to 122.6"eligible individual".

"eligible spouse" of an eligible individual for a taxation year means an individual (other than an ineligible individual) who was resident in Canada throughout the taxation year and who was, at the end of the taxation year, the cohabiting spouse or common-law partner of the eligible individual.

Related Provisions: 122.7(4) — Where eligible spouse deemed not to be eligible individual.

"ineligible individual" for a taxation year means an individual

(a) who is described in paragraph 149(1)(a) or (b) at any time in the taxation year;

(b) who, except where the individual has an eligible dependant for the taxation year, was enrolled as a full-time student at a designated educational institution for a total of more than 13 weeks in the taxation year; or

(c) who was confined to a prison or similar institution for a period of at least 90 days during the taxation year.

Notes: If a student's university T2202A (see 118.6) shows 4 months of being a full-time student, but the program was only 13 weeks, the student still qualifies under para. (b) but the CRA may reject the 122.7 claim: Joseph Rosenthal letter, "We regret to inform you", Sept. 2009 *CAmagazine* (cica.ca) 4. See also Notes to 118.5(1)(b) re calculation of weeks.

"return of income" filed by an individual for a taxation year means a return of income (other than a return of income filed under subsection 70(2) or 104(23), paragraph 128(2)(e) or subsection 150(4)) that is required to be filed for the taxation year or that would be required to be filed if the individual had tax payable under this Part for the taxation year.

"working income", of an individual for a taxation year, means the total of

(a) the total of all amounts each of which would, if this Act were read without reference to section 8, be the individual's income for the taxation year from an office or employment,

(b) all amounts that are included because of paragraph 56(1)(n) or (o) or subparagraph 56(1)(r)(v) in computing the individual's income for a period in the taxation year, and

(c) the total of all amounts each of which is the individual's income for the taxation year from a business carried on by the individual otherwise than as a specified member of a partnership.

Related Provisions: 117(2.1) — Amount paid in advance is part of tax payable; 122.7(1.1) — Optional method of determining working income for taxpayer with exempt income; Reg. 203 — Mandatory tuition certificates to allow CRA to determine working income.

Notes: CRA considered an allocation from a 143(1) communal organization not to be working income: VIEWS doc 2013-050627117, but 143(2)(d) fixes this.

Paras (a)-(c) amended by 2018 budget bill #2, effective 2019, to delete references to 81(1)(a) and 81(4) (see now 122.7(1.1)). Before 2019, read:

> (a) the total of all amounts each of which would, if this Act were read without reference to section 8, paragraph 81(1)(a) and subsection 81(4), be the individual's income for the taxation year from an office or employment;
>
> (b) all amounts that are included, or that would, but for paragraph 81(1)(a), be included, because of paragraph 56(1)(n) or (o) or subparagraph 56(1)(r)(v) in computing the individual's income for a period in the taxation year; and
>
> (c) the total of all amounts each of which would, if this Act were read without reference to paragraph 81(1)(a), be the individual's income for the taxation year from a business carried on by the individual otherwise than as a specified member of a partnership.

Para. (b) amended by 2008 budget bill #2 to add reference to 56(1)(r)(v), for 2008 and later taxation years.

(1.1) Optional amounts — An individual may determine the total amount for the definition "working income" for both the individual and the individual's eligible spouse, if applicable, for a taxation year as if the Act were read without reference to paragraph 81(1)(a) and subsection 81(4) and if so, the individual shall determine the total amount for the definition "adjusted net income" for both the individual and the individual's eligible spouse, if applicable, for the taxation year as if the Act were read without reference to paragraph 81(1)(a) and subsection 81(4).

Notes: 122.7(1.1) allows X to opt to include amounts in 122.7(1)"working income" (WI) that would be excluded due to 81(1)(a) (exempt income due to another Act, including status Indian) or 81(4) (payments for volunteer emergency services). If X includes these amounts in WI, X must also include amounts that would be excluded by 81(1)(a) or 81(4) from X's spouse's WI. As well, X must also include amounts that would normally be excluded from X's (and spouse's) 122.7(1)"adjusted net income" due to 81(1)(a) or 81(4). This option can increase 122.7 credit entitlement if X has insufficient WI, but limits "cherry-picking" part of the income.

122.7(1.1) added by 2018 budget bill #2, effective 2019.

(1.2) Receipt of social assistance — For the purposes of applying the definitions "eligible dependant" and "eligible individual" in subsection (1) for a taxation year, an individual shall not fail to qualify as a parent (within the meaning assigned by section 252) of another individual solely because of the receipt of a social assistance amount that is payable under a program of the Government of Canada or the government of a province for the benefit of the other individual, unless the amount is a special allowance under the *Children's Special Allowances Act* in respect of the other individual in the taxation year.

Related Provisions: 81(1)(h), (h.1) — Foster care payments do not increase net income.

Notes: See Notes to 81(1)(h.1), which exempts "kinship care" payments. 122.7(1.2) ensures such payments do not disentitle the recipient from being a parent for purposes of the CWB. Added by 2019 budget bill #1, effective 2009.

(1.3) Secondary earner exemption — For the purposes of subsections (2) and (3),

(a) if an eligible individual had an eligible spouse for a taxation year and the working income for the year of the eligible individual was less than the working income for the year of the eligible spouse, the eligible individual's adjusted net income for the year is deemed to be the amount, if any, by which the eligible individual's adjusted net income for the year (determined without reference to this subsection) exceeds the lesser of

(i) the eligible individual's working income for the year, and

(ii) $14,000[24]; and

(b) if an eligible individual had an eligible spouse for a taxation year and the working income for the year of the eligible individual was greater than or equal to the working income for the year of the eligible spouse, the eligible spouse's adjusted net income for the year is deemed to be the amount, if any, by which the eligible spouse's adjusted net income for the year (determined without reference to this subsection) exceeds the lesser of

(i) the eligible spouse's working income for the year, and

(ii) $14,000[24].

Related Provisions: 117.1(2)(p) — Inflation indexing.

Notes: See 122.7(2) Notes. 122.7(1.3) added by 2021 budget bill #1, effective 2021.

(2) Deemed payment on account of tax — Subject to subsections (4) and (5), an eligible individual for a taxation year who files a return of income for the taxation year is deemed to have paid, at the end of the taxation year, on account of tax payable under this Part for the taxation year, an amount equal to the amount, if any, determined by the formula

$$A - B$$

where

A is

(a) if the individual had neither an eligible spouse nor an eligible dependant, for the taxation year, the lesser of $1,395[24]

and 27% of the amount, if any, by which the individual's working income for the taxation year exceeds $3,000, and

(b) if the individual had an eligible spouse or an eligible dependant, for the taxation year, the lesser of $2,403[24] and 27% of the amount, if any, by which the total of the working incomes of the individual and, if applicable, of the eligible spouse, for the taxation year, exceeds $3,000; and

B is

(a) if the individual had neither an eligible spouse nor an eligible dependant, for the taxation year, 15% of the amount, if any, by which the adjusted net income of the individual for the taxation year exceeds $22,944[24], and

(b) if the individual had an eligible spouse or an eligible dependant, for the taxation year, 15% of the amount, if any, by which the total of the adjusted net incomes of the individual and, if applicable, of the eligible spouse, for the taxation year, exceeds $26,177[24].

Related Provisions: 117.1(2)(q) — Inflation indexing; 122.7(3) — Disability supplement; 122.7(5) — If individual and spouse both claim, benefit is nil for both; 122.7(11), (12) — Special rules on bankruptcy or death; 122.71 — Provincial credit possible; 152(1)(b) — Assessment; 152(4.2)(b) — Redetermination of credit at taxpayer's request; 163(2)(c.3) — Penalty for false statement; 257 — Formula cannot calculate to less than zero; Reg. 203 — Mandatory tuition certificates to allow CRA to determine benefit without taxpayer applying.

Notes: 122.7 (tinyurl.com/cra-cwb) provides the Canada Workers Benefit (CWB), called Working Income Tax Benefit (WITB) before 2019. Introduced (as WITB) in 2007 and enhanced in 2009, 2019 and 2021, it is payable to low-income individuals who have employment or business income ("working income"). Its goal is to encourage low-income people to work or work more, by reducing marginal rates on new income, which can be 75% or higher due to clawbacks of other benefits.

The CWB is a "refundable" credit: the 122.7(2) and (3) amounts are *deemed paid* by the taxpayer so, like source deductions or instalments paid, they reduce tax liability and create a s. 164 refund if the total exceeds tax owing for the year (see Notes at beginning of 118(1)B). The credit is prepaid by CRA in advance, but is repayable if overpaid: 122.7(7), 117(2.1). Since 2019, the CWB need not be specifically claimed other than by filing a return.

The CWB has 2 parts: basic CWB (122.7(2)) and a supplement for individuals entitled to the 118.3 disability credit (122.7(3)). The basic CWB is a refund of 25% of all working income over $3,000 (not indexed), to a maximum $1,102 for 2020, $1,113 for 2021 credit for single individuals without dependants (Single CWB) and $2,001 for 2020, $2,021 for 2021 for couples and single parents (Family CWB). The CWB Supplement is a refund of 25% of all working income over $1,150 (not indexed) to a maximum $551 (2020) or $557 (2021). To target low-income individuals and families, both Basic CWB and CWB Supplement are reduced if income (combined with spouse or common-law partner) exceeds certain thresholds (formula elements B and D). These thresholds and reductions were changed in 2021, as per April 2021 Budget, to enhance the CWB: see tinyurl.com/cra-cwb-2021. As well, 122.7(1.3) provides a "secondary earner exemption", so a spouse's income up to $14,000 does not reduce CWB eligibility.

Some provinces provide parallel benefits.

See also the Canada Employment Credit in 118(10), available to *all* employees.

See CRA "Warning: Don't be fooled by the working income tax benefit tax scheme" (2018, tinyurl.com/cra-warn-witb), re schemes where tax preparers create false T4s and claim the CWB for people who are not employees.

The WITB was disallowed in *Ali*, 2015 TCC 196, para. 42, because family net income was too high.

Refraining from claiming the (pre-2017) 118.6 education credit did not help entitle a person to the WITB: VIEWS doc 2014-0563291E5.

122.7(2) amended by 2021 budget bill #1, effective 2021, to reduce the phase-out: A(a) changed $1,355 to $1,395 and 26% to 27%; A(b) changed $2,355 to $2,403 and 26% to 27%; B(a) changed $12,820 to $22,944 and 12% to 15%; B(b) changed $17,025 to $26,177 and 12% to 15%. (122.7(1.3) was added at the same time.)

122.7(2) opening words amended by 2018 budget bill #2, effective 2019, to delete "and who makes a claim under this subsection" before "is deemed to have" (so that filing a return is sufficient to claim the credit).

122.7(2)A, B amended by 2016 budget bill #2 (s. 69) to enhance the benefit, intended to be effective 2019; but overridden effective 2019 by 2018 budget bill #1: A(a) $925, 25% changed to $1,355, 26%; A(b) $1,680, 25% to $2,335, 26%; B(a) 15% $10,500 to 12%, $12,820; B(b) 15%, $14,500 to $17,025.

122.7(2) earlier amended by 2009 budget bill #2.

Forms: RC201: Canada workers benefit advance payments application; T1 Sched. 6: Canada Workers Benefit.

---

[24] Indexed by 117.1 after 2021 — ed.

(3) Deemed payment on account of tax — disability supplement — An eligible individual for a taxation year who files a return of income for the taxation year and who may deduct an amount under subsection 118.3(1) in computing tax payable under this Part for the taxation year is deemed to have paid, at the end of the taxation year, on account of tax payable under this Part for the taxation year, an amount equal to the amount, if any, determined by the formula

$$C - D$$

where

C is the lesser of $720[24] and 27% of the amount, if any, by which the individual's working income for the taxation year exceeds $1,150; and

D is

(a) if the individual had neither an eligible spouse nor an eligible dependant, for the taxation year, 15% of the amount, if any, by which the individual's adjusted net income for the taxation year exceeds $32,244[24],

(b) if the individual had an eligible spouse for the taxation year who was not entitled to deduct an amount under subsection 118.3(1) for the taxation year, or had an eligible dependant for the taxation year, 15% of the amount, if any, by which the total of the adjusted net incomes of the individual and, if applicable, of the eligible spouse, for the taxation year, exceeds $42,197[24], and

(c) if the individual had an eligible spouse for the taxation year who was entitled to deduct an amount under subsection 118.3(1) for the taxation year, 7.5% of the amount, if any, by which the total of the adjusted net incomes of the individual and of the eligible spouse, for the taxation year, exceeds $42,197[24].

Related Provisions: 117.1(2)(r) — Inflation indexing; 122.71 — Provincial credit possible; 152(1)(b) — Assessment; 152(4.2)(b) — Redetermination of credit at taxpayer's request; 163(2)(c.3) — Penalty for false statement; 257 — Formula cannot calculate to less than zero.

Notes: See Notes to 122.7(2).

122.7(3)C, D amended by 2021 budget bill #1, effective 2021, to reduce the phase-out: C changed $700 and 26% to $720 and 27%; D(a) changed 12% and $24,111 to 15% and $32,224; D(b) changed 12% and $36,483 to 15% and $42,197; D(c) changed 6% and $36,483 to 7.5% and $42,197.

122.7(3)C, D amended by 2016 budget bill #2 to enhance the benefit, intended to be effective 2019; but overridden effective 2019 by 2018 budget bill #1: $462.50 and 25% changed to $700 and 26%; 15% and $16,667 to 12% and $24,111; 15% and $25,700 to 12% and $36,483; and 7.5% and $25,700 to 6% and $36,483.

122.7(3) earlier amended by 2009 budget bill #2.

(4) Eligible spouse deemed not to be an eligible individual — An eligible spouse of an eligible individual for a taxation year is deemed, for the purpose of subsection (2), not to be an eligible individual for the taxation year if the eligible spouse made a joint application described in subsection (6) with the eligible individual and the eligible individual received an amount under subsection (7) in respect of the taxation year.

(5) Only one eligible individual — If an eligible individual has an eligible spouse for a taxation year and both those individuals would be, but for this subsection, eligible individuals for the purposes of subsection (2) in respect of the taxation year,

(a) if the individuals agree on which individual is the eligible individual for the taxation year, only that individual shall be an eligible individual for the purposes of subsection (2) in respect of the taxation year; and

(b) in any other case, only the individual that the Minister designates is the eligible individual for the purposes of subsection (2) in respect of the taxation year.

Notes: 122.7(5) amended by 2018 budget bill #2, effective 2019. Before 2019, only one spouse could apply (now, per 122.7(2), no application is made other than filing a return):

(5) Amount deemed to be nil — If an eligible individual had an eligible spouse for a taxation year and both the eligible individual and the eligible spouse make a claim for the taxation year under subsection (2), the amount deemed to have been paid under that subsection by each of them on account of tax payable under this Part for the taxation year, is nil.

(6) Application for advance payment — Subsection (7) applies to an individual for a taxation year if,

(a) at any time after January 1 and before September 1 of the taxation year, the individual makes an application (or in the case of an individual who has, at that time, a cohabiting spouse or common-law partner, the two of them make a joint application designating the individual for the purpose of subsection (7)), to the Minister in prescribed form, containing prescribed information; and

(b) where the individual and a cohabiting spouse or common-law partner have made a joint application referred to in paragraph (a)

(i) the individual's working income for the taxation year can reasonably be expected to be greater than the working income of the individual's cohabiting spouse or common-law partner for the taxation year, or

(ii) the individual can reasonably be expected to be deemed by subsection (3) to have paid an amount on account of tax payable under this Part for the taxation year.

Related Provisions: 122.7(9) — Notification required of change in circumstances.

(7) Advance payment — Subject to subsection (8), the Minister may pay to an individual before the end of January of the year following a taxation year, one or more amounts that, in total, do not exceed one-half of the total of the amounts that the Minister estimates will be deemed to be paid by the individual under subsection (2) or (3) at the end of the taxation year, and any amount paid by the Minister under this subsection is deemed to have been received by the individual in respect of the taxation year.

Related Provisions: 117(2.1) — Tax payable — Advance payment is repayable; 122.5(3.2) — Advance payment of GST/HST credit; 122.7(6), (8) — Conditions for advance payment.

(8) Limitation — advance payment — No payment shall be made under subsection (7) to an individual in respect of a taxation year

(a) if the total amount that the Minister may pay under that subsection is less than $100; or

(b) before the day on which the individual has filed a return of income for a preceding taxation year in respect of which the individual received a payment under that subsection.

(9) Notification to Minister — If, in a taxation year, an individual makes an application described in subsection (6), the individual shall notify the Minister of the occurrence of any of the following events before the end of the month following the month in which the event occurs

(a) the individual ceases to be resident in Canada in the taxation year;

(b) the individual ceases, before the end of the taxation year, to be a cohabiting spouse or common-law partner of another person with whom the individual made the application;

(c) the individual enrols as a full-time student at a designated educational institution in the taxation year; or

(d) the individual is confined to a prison or similar institution in the taxation year.

(10) Special rule for eligible dependant — For the purpose of applying subsections (2) and (3), if an individual (referred to in this subsection as the "child") would be, but for this subsection, an eli-

---

[24] Indexed by 117.1 after 2021 — ed.

gible dependant of more than one eligible individual for a taxation year, the child is deemed only to be an eligible dependant of

(a) if the individuals agree, the agreed upon individual; and

(b) in any other case, the individual designated by the Minister.

Notes: 122.7(10) amended by 2018 budget bill #2, effective 2019 (due to elimination of a requirement in 122.7(2) to "claim" the credit). Before 2019, read:

(10) For the purpose of applying subsections (2) and (3), an individual (referred to in this subsection as the "child") is deemed not to be an eligible dependant of an eligible individual for a taxation year if the child is an eligible dependant of another eligible individual for the taxation year and both eligible individuals identified the child as an eligible dependant for the purpose of claiming or computing an amount under this section for the taxation year.

(11) Effect of bankruptcy — For the purpose of this Subdivision, if an individual becomes bankrupt in a particular calendar year

(a) notwithstanding subsection 128(2), any reference to the taxation year of the individual (other than in this subsection) is deemed to be a reference to the particular calendar year; and

(b) the individual's working income and adjusted net income for the taxation year ending on December 31 of the particular calendar year is deemed to include the individual's working income and adjusted net income for the taxation year that begins on January 1 of the particular calendar year.

(12) Special rules in the event of death — For the purpose of this Subdivision, if an individual dies after June 30 of a calendar year

(a) the individual is deemed to be resident in Canada from the time of death until the end of the year and to reside at the same place in Canada as the place where the individual resided immediately before death;

(b) the individual is deemed to be the same age at the end of the year as the individual would have been if the individual were alive at the end of the year;

(c) the individual is deemed to be the cohabiting spouse or common-law partner of another individual (referred to in this paragraph as the "surviving spouse") at the end of the year if,

(i) immediately before death, the individual was the cohabiting spouse or common-law partner of the surviving spouse, and

(ii) the surviving spouse is not the cohabiting spouse or common-law partner of another individual at the end of the year; and

(d) any return of income filed by a legal representative of the individual is deemed to be a return of income filed by the individual.

Notes [s. 122.7]: See Notes to 122.7(2).

122.7 added by 2007 budget bill #2, effective 2007 (some parts 2008) and later tax years.

An earlier proposed 122.7 (Dec. 23, 1997 draft legislation) provided $50 to US social security recipients in lieu of interest due to Canada-US tax treaty changes. It was enacted instead as Part 2 of the 1998 Budget bill.

Definitions [s. 122.7]: "adjusted net income" — 122.7(1); "amount", "bankrupt", "business" — 248(1); "calendar year" — *Interpretation Act* 37(1)(a); "Canada" — 255, *Interpretation Act* 35(1); "child" — 252(1); "cohabiting spouse or common-law partner" — 122.7(1); "common-law partner" — 248(1); "designated educational institution" — 122.7(1); "disposition" — 248(1); "eligible dependant" — 122.7(1), (10); "eligible individual" — 122.7(1); "eligible spouse" — 122.7(1), (4); "employment", "individual" — 248(1); "ineligible individual" — 122.7(1); "legal representative", "Minister" — 248(1); "month" — *Interpretation Act* 35(1); "office" — 248(1); "parent" — 122.7(1.2), 252(2)(a); "partnership" — see 96(1) Notes; "person", "prescribed", "property" — 248(1); "province" — *Interpretation Act* 35(1); "registered disability savings plan" — 146.4(1), 248(1); "resident in Canada" — 122.7(12), 250; "return of income" — 122.7(1); "specified member" — 248(1); "taxation year" — 122.7(11), 249; "working income" — 122.7(1).

122.71 Modification for purposes of provincial program — The Minister of Finance may enter into an agreement with the government of a province whereby the amounts determined under subsections 122.7(2) and (3) with respect to an eligible individual resident in the province at the end of the taxation year shall, for the purpose of calculating amounts deemed to be paid on account of the tax payable of an individual under those subsections, be replaced by amounts determined in accordance with the agreement.

Notes [s. 122.71]: 122.71 allows the Minister of Finance to enter into an agreement with the government of a province (or territory) to modify the CWB (see 122.7) with respect to residents of that province. This is intended to allow the federal Government to implement province-specific changes to the CWB to better harmonize it with existing provincial income support programs.

122.71 added by 2007 budget bill #2, for 2007 and later taxation years.

Definitions [s. 122.71]: "amount" — 248(1); "eligible individual" — 122.7(1); "individual" — 248(1); "Minister of Finance" — *Financial Administration Act* 14; "province" — *Interpretation Act* 35(1); "resident" — 250; "taxation year" — 249.

Subdivision A.3 — Climate Action Incentive

122.8 (1) Definitions — The following definitions apply in this section.

Notes: See Notes to 122.8(4).

"cohabiting spouse or common-law partner", of an individual at any time, has the same meaning as in section 122.6.

"eligible individual", for a taxation year, means an individual (other than a trust) who is, at the end of the taxation year,

(a) 18 years of age or older;

(b) a parent who resides with their child; or

(c) married or in a common-law partnership.

Related Provisions: 122.8(2) — Certain persons excluded from "eligible individual"; 122.8(3) — Person deemed to reside only at principal place of residence; 122.8(7) — One only eligible individual.

"qualified dependant", of an individual for a taxation year, means a person who, at the end of the taxation year,

(a) is the individual's child or is dependent for support on the individual or on the individual's cohabiting spouse or common-law partner;

(b) resides with the individual;

(c) is under the age of 18 years;

(d) is not an eligible individual for the taxation year; and

(e) is not a qualified relation of any individual for the taxation year.

Related Provisions: 122.8(2) — Certain persons excluded from "qualified dependant"; 122.8(3) — Person deemed to reside only at principal place of residence; 122.8(8) — Where person would be QD of two individuals.

"qualified relation", of an individual for a taxation year, means the person, if any, who, at the end of the taxation year, is the individual's cohabiting spouse or common-law partner.

Related Provisions: 122.8(2) — Certain persons excluded from "qualified relation".

"return of income", in respect of a person for a taxation year, means the person's return of income (other than a return of income under subsection 70(2) or 104(23), paragraph 128(2)(e) or subsection 150(4)) that is required to be filed for the taxation year or that would be required to be filed if the person had tax payable under this Part for the taxation year.

(2) Persons not eligible individuals, qualified relations or qualified dependants — Notwithstanding subsection (1), a person is not an eligible individual, is not a qualified relation and is not a qualified dependant, for a taxation year, if the person

(a) died before April of the year following the taxation year;

(b) is confined to a prison or similar institution for a period of at least 90 days during the taxation year;

(c) is a non-resident person at any time in the taxation year;

(d) is a person described in paragraph 149(1)(a) or (b) at any time in the taxation year; or

(e) is a person in respect of whom a special allowance under the *Children's Special Allowances Act* is payable at any time in the taxation year.

Notes: For interpretation of 122.8(2)(e) see Notes to 122.6"qualified dependant".

(3) Residence — For the purposes of this section, an individual is considered to reside at any time only at their principal place of residence.

(4) Deemed overpayment [Carbon tax credit] — An eligible individual who files a return of income for a taxation year and who makes a claim under this subsection is deemed to have paid, at the end of the taxation year, on account of tax payable under this Part for the taxation year, an amount equal to the amount determined by the formula

$$(A + B + C \times D) \times E$$

where

A   is the amount specified by the Minister of Finance for an eligible individual for the taxation year for the province (in this subsection and subsection (6) referred to as the "relevant province") in which the eligible individual resides at the end of the taxation year;

B   is

(a) the amount specified by the Minister of Finance for a qualified relation for the taxation year for the relevant province, if

(i) the eligible individual has a qualified relation at the end of the taxation year, or

(ii) subparagraph (i) does not apply and the eligible individual has a qualified dependant at the end of the taxation year, and

(b) in any other case, nil;

C   is the amount specified by the Minister of Finance for a qualified dependant for the taxation year for the relevant province;

D   is the number of qualified dependants of the eligible individual at the end of the taxation year, other than a qualified dependant in respect of whom an amount is included because of subparagraph (a)(ii) of the description of B for the taxation year; and

E   is

(a) 1.1, if there is a census metropolitan area, as determined in the last census published by Statistics Canada before the taxation year, in the relevant province and the individual does not reside in a census metropolitan area at the end of the taxation year, and

(b) 1, in any other case.

Proposed Amendment — Climate action incentive to be paid quarterly

Federal Budget, Chapter 5, April 19, 2021: Budget 2021 proposes to change the delivery of Climate Action Incentive payments from a refundable credit claimed annually on personal income tax returns to quarterly payments made through the benefit system starting in 2022. This will deliver Canadians' Climate Action Incentive payments on a more regular basis. Further details will be announced later in 2021.

Notes: Quarterly payments, along with the quarterly GST/HST Credit (122.5) and monthly Canada Child Benefit (122.61), move Canada closer to a "universal income" system whereby every resident gets a regular income even if they are not working.

Related Provisions: 122.8(3) — Person deemed to reside only at principal place of residence; 152(1)(b) — Assessment; 152(4.2)(b) — Redetermination of credit at taxpayer's request; 163(2)(c.4) — False statement or omission — penalty.

Notes: The Climate Action Incentive (CAI) is a distribution to all individual taxpayers, in provinces and territories that have no carbon tax (SK, MB, ON, NB for 2019-March 31, 2020; AB, SK, MB, ON for 2020), of carbon tax charged to businesses under the *Greenhouse Gas Pollution Pricing Act*, to give the illusion of a tax reduction/refund while discouraging the use of oil & gas. (See Roberge, "Review of the Evolution of Canada's Carbon Taxation", 2496 *Tax Topics* (CCH) 1-3 (Jan. 9, 2020).) 122.8(4) creates an "overpayment", so the CAI, like instalments or source deductions withheld or the Canada Child Benefit, is payable or refundable under 164 even if no tax is payable for the year (thus, it is a "refundable credit"), provided a return is filed within 3 years of year-end. See also VIEWS doc 2020-0841911M4 (general info).

Per Finance news release "Government Announces Climate Action Incentive Payment Amounts for 2020" (Dec. 16, 2019), the payments in 2020 (refunded when assessing 2019 returns) are:

		Ontario	Manitoba	Sask.	Alberta
A	Single adult, or first adult in a couple	$224	$243	$405	$444
B	Second adult in a couple, or first child of a single parent	$112	$121	$202	$222
C	Each child under 18 (starting with the second child for single parents)	$56	$61	$101	$111

Note: Exceptionally, the 2020 Climate Action Incentive payment claimed by eligible Albertans will reflect fuel charge proceeds generated over a 15-month period. This consists of three months (January–March 2020) with a carbon price of $20, plus 12 months (April 2020–March 2021) with a carbon price of $30.

Per Finance Backgrounder "Climate Action Incentive Payment Amounts for 2021" (tinyurl.com/climate-pay21, Dec. 16, 2020), the payments in 2021 (refunded when assessing 2020 returns) are:

		Ontario	Manitoba	Sask.	Alberta
A	Single adult, or first adult in a couple[1]	$300	$360	$500	$490
B	Second adult in a couple, or first child of a single parent[2]	$150	$180	$250	$245
C	Each child under 18 (starting with the second child for single parents)[3]	$75	$90	$125	$123

[1] Referred to as a qualified individual in the legislation.

[2] Referred to as a qualified relation in the legislation.

[3] Referred to as a qualified dependant in the legislation.

A supplementary 10% is paid to taxpayers residing outside a census metropolitan area (CMA), as defined by Statistics Canada (at least 100,000 people, at least 50,000 in the core), "in recognition of their increased energy needs and reduced access to alternative transportation options". For the 35 CMAs see tinyurl.com/canada-cma.

Other provinces have their own carbon taxes and will handle payments to their residents.

Forms: T1 General return, Line 45110 [former 449]; T1 General return, Sched. 14: Climate Action Incentive.

(5) Authority to specify amounts — The Minister of Finance may specify amounts for a province for a taxation year for the purposes of this section. If the Minister of Finance does not specify a particular amount that is relevant for the purposes of this section, that particular amount is deemed to be nil for the purpose of applying this section.

(6) Deemed rebate in respect of fuel charges — The amount deemed by this section to have been paid on account of tax payable for a taxation year is deemed to have been paid in the year following the taxation year as a rebate in respect of charges levied under Part 1 of the *Greenhouse Gas Pollution Pricing Act* in respect of the relevant province.

(7) Only one eligible individual — If an individual is a qualified relation of another individual for a taxation year and both those individuals would be, but for this subsection, eligible individuals for the taxation year, only the individual that the Minister designates is the eligible individual for the taxation year.

(8) Exception — qualified dependant — If a person would, if this Act were read without reference to this subsection, be the qualified dependant of two or more individuals, for a taxation year,

(a) the person is deemed to be a qualified dependant, for the taxation year, of the one of those individuals on whom those individuals agree; and

(b) in any other case, the person is deemed to be, for the taxation year, a qualified dependant only of the individual that the Minister designates.

(9) Effect of bankruptcy — For the purposes of this section, if an individual becomes bankrupt in a particular calendar year, notwithstanding subsection 128(2), any reference to the taxation year of the individual (other than in this subsection) is deemed to be a reference to the particular calendar year.

Notes: 122.8 (Subdivision a.3) added by 2018 budget bill #2, for 2018 and later tax years. See Notes to 122.8(4).

Former 122.8 implemented the refundable **Child Fitness Credit** for 2015-16, replacing an identical but non-refundable credit in 118.03 (2007-14). This was a Conservative measure that was cut in half by the Liberals for 2016 and repealed by 2016 budget bill #1 for 2017 and later tax years. For the 2016 year, read:

122.8 (1) Definitions — The following definitions apply in this section.

"eligible fitness expense" in respect of a qualifying child of an individual for a taxation year means the amount of a fee paid to a qualifying entity (other than an amount paid to a person that is, at the time the amount is paid, the individual's spouse or common-law partner or another individual who is under 18 years of age) to the extent that the fee is attributable to the cost of registration or membership of the qualifying child in a prescribed program of physical activity and, for the purposes of this section, that cost

(a) includes the cost to the qualifying entity of the program in respect of its administration, instruction, rental of required facilities, and uniforms and equipment that are not available to be acquired by a participant in the program for an amount less than their fair market value at the time, if any, they are so acquired; and

(b) does not include

(i) the cost of accommodation, travel, food or beverages, or

(ii) any amount deductible under section 63 in computing any person's income for any taxation year.

Regulations [former 122.8(1)"eligible fitness expense"]: 9400 (prescribed program of physical activity).

"qualifying child" of an individual for a taxation year means a child of the individual who is, at the beginning of the year,

(a) under 16 years of age; or

(b) in the case where an amount is deductible under section 118.3 in computing any person's tax payable under this Part for the year in respect of that child, under 18 years of age.

Notes [former 122.8(1)"qualifying child"]: The child need not live with the parent claiming the credit: VIEWS doc 2011-0403581E5.

"qualifying entity" means a person or partnership that offers one or more prescribed programs of physical activity.

Notes [former 122.8(1)"qualifying entity"]: The qualifying entity need not be in Canada: VIEWS doc 2010-036027117.

"return of income" filed by an individual for a taxation year means a return of income (other than a return of income filed under subsection 70(2) or 104(23), paragraph 128(2)(e) or subsection 150(4)) that is required to be filed for the year or that would be required to be filed if the individual had tax payable under this Part for the year.

(2) Deemed overpayment — An individual who files a return of income for a taxation year and who makes a claim under this subsection is deemed to have paid, at the end of the year, on account of tax payable under this Part for the year, an amount equal to the amount determined by the formula

$$A \times B$$

where

A is the appropriate percentage for the year; and

B is the total of all amounts each of which is, in respect of a qualifying child of the individual for the year, the lesser of $500 and the amount determined by the formula

$$C - D$$

where

C is the total of all amounts each of which is an amount paid in the year by the individual, or by the individual's spouse or common law partner, that is an eligible fitness expense in respect of the qualifying child of the individual, and

D is the total of all amounts that any person is or was entitled to receive, each of which relates to an amount included in computing the value of C in respect of the qualifying child that is the amount of a reimbursement, allowance or any other form of assistance (other than an amount that is included in computing the income for any taxation year of that person

and that is not deductible in computing the taxable income of that person).

Related Provisions [former 122.8(2)]: 122.8(3) — Additional credit for child with disability; 122.8(4) — Apportionment of credit among multiple taxpayers; 122.8(5) — Effect of bankruptcy; 122.8(6) — Application to part-year resident; 122.8(7) — Application to non-resident; 152(1)(b) — Assessment; 152(4.2)(b) — Redetermination of credit at taxpayer's request; 163(2)(c.4) — False statement or omission — penalty; 257 — Formula cannot calculate to less than zero.

Notes [former 122.8(2)]: The "appropriate percentage" (248(1)) is 15%, so this credit is 15% of up to $1,000 (maximum $150) before 2016, and 15% of up to $500 for 2016.

Before 2015, this credit was in 118.03 and was only for taxpayers with tax payable for the year. By deeming the taxpayer to have paid an amount on account of tax, 122.8(2) creates a *refundable* credit, like instalments or source deductions withheld, refundable under 164(1) even if no tax is payable for the year.

See Reg. 9400 for prescribed programs of physical activity. There is no permit or authorization system (VIEWS doc 2007-0222451M4) and no list of qualifying activities, but "sports studies" do not qualify: 2007-0228351M4. Family memberships at civic centres, and travelling costs, do not qualify: 2007-0222131M4. Wakeboarding and waterskiing could be excluded if motorized vehicles are used: 2007-0237391M4 and Reg. 9400(1)"physical activity". Whether a given activity qualifies depends on the facts, and it is the organization that is usually in the best position to make the determination: 2007-0222141M4, 2007-0222151M4, 2007-0222161M4, 2007-0222171M4, 2007-0230441E5, 2007-0237401M4, 2007-0247081M4, 2007-0248651M4 (bowling likely qualifies), 2016-062625117 (each program must be reviewed separately). The following do or may qualify: equestrian therapy (2007-024072117); junior golf membership (2015-0607311E5); martial arts programs (2012-0437311M4); personal trainer (2009-0348201M4); skating (2007-0232041E5); ski courses, including ski lift tickets (2013-0480231E5); swimming for preschoolers, even if the focus is on getting the child used to the water (2008-028012117).

Children's camps qualify only if at least 5 consecutive days and more than 50% of program time is devoted to physical activity: Reg. 9400(2)(b), docs 2007-0235931M4, 2007-0241341E5, 2008-0267561M4. Swimming lessons can qualify under this 5-day test: 2009-0311931E5. A program of lessons (e.g., swimming) must be at least 8 weeks: Reg. 9400(2)(a), doc 2008-0266981M4; the 8 weeks need not be consecutive if interrupted by a statutory holiday: 2008-0301711E5, 2009-0310931E5. The requirement is 5 consecutive days or more but there is no minimum daily duration time, so swimming lessons of 2 weeks, 5 times a week, 45 minutes per lesson will qualify: 2009-0325901E5. A volleyball/basketball camp held 3 days a week for 4 consecutive weeks does not qualify: 2009-0319811M4. School sports programs generally do not qualify because they are part of the curriculum: 2009-0328401E5. For an organization that does not have more than 50% of children's activities with significant physical activity, membership still qualifies on a prorated basis: 2009-0318021M4. Fees paid in 2007 for a program that began in 2006 can qualify: 2008-0269091E5.

The physical activity need not take place in Canada: VIEWS doc 2010-036027117.

The cost of a uniform or jersey can be included in the amount paid: VIEWS docs 2007-0233601M4, 2007-0247341E5. A discounted fee for low-income families does not affect eligibility, but only the actual fee paid qualifies: 2007-0240891M4 (net of any reimbursement: 2008-0268151E5).

Receipts should include the name and address of the organization, name of the program or activity, total amount received, date, allowable amount for the credit, full name of payor, child's name and date of birth, and authorized signature: VIEWS docs 2007-0228551M4, 2007-0248341M4, 2008-0267001E5. A dance studio program eligible for both 122.8 (dance) and 118.031 (song — Children's Arts Tax Credit) or similar program should split up receipts to show each program separately: 2012-0438981M4, 2013-0485741M4. (A physical program cannot qualify for 118.031, as Reg. 9401(1) excludes a "physical activity".) The same expense may also qualify as a child care expense, and can be claimed under s. 63 to the extent possible, using the same receipt: 2011-0428341E5. If the organization refuses to issue a receipt, it cannot be forced to, but the taxpayer may provide other proof of payment: 2012-0439611M4.

Additional credit is available for children with serious disabilities: 122.8(3), VIEWS doc 2007-0239821M4.

A human rights challenge to 122.8 as discriminating against "split families" is proceeding: *Fannon*, 2017 FC 58.

On the extent to which pre-2015 118.03 was used see Fisher et al., "Awareness and Use of Canada's Children's Fitness Tax Credit", 61(3) *Canadian Tax Journal* 599-632 (2013).

Several provinces/territories also have a provincial fitness credit.

122.8(2)B opening words amended by 2016 budget bill #1, effective for the 2016 taxation year, to change $1,000 to $500, en route to eliminating this credit as of 2017.

(3) Child with disability — An individual who files a return of income for a taxation year and who makes a claim under this subsection is deemed to have

paid, in respect of a qualifying child of the individual, at the end of the year, on account of tax payable under this Part for the year, an amount equal to $500 multiplied by the appropriate percentage for the year, if

(a) the amount referred to in the description of B in subsection (2) is $100 or more; and

(b) an amount is deductible in respect of the qualifying child under section 118.3 in computing any person's tax payable under this Part for the year.

Related Provisions [former 122.8(3)]: See under 122.8(2).

(4) Apportionment of overpayment — If more than one individual is entitled to make a claim under this section for a taxation year in respect of a qualifying child, the total of all amounts deemed to have been paid shall not exceed the maximum amount that could be deemed to have been paid for the year by any one of those individuals in respect of that qualifying child if that individual were the only individual entitled to claim an amount for the year under this section in respect of that qualifying child. If the individuals cannot agree as to what portion of the maximum amount each can so claim, the Minister may fix the portions.

(5) Effect of bankruptcy — For the purposes of this subdivision, if an individual becomes bankrupt in a particular calendar year, notwithstanding subsection 128(2), any reference to the taxation year of the individual (other than in this subsection) is deemed to be a reference to the particular calendar year.

(6) Part-year residents — If an individual is resident in Canada throughout part of a taxation year and is non-resident throughout another part of the year, the total of the amounts that are deemed to be paid by the individual under subsection (2) and (3) for the year cannot exceed the lesser of

(a) the total of

(i) the amounts deemed to be paid under those subsections that can reasonably be considered as wholly applicable to the period or periods in the year throughout which the individual is not resident in Canada, computed as though that period or those periods were the whole taxation year, and

(ii) the amounts deemed to be paid under those subsections that can reasonably be considered as wholly applicable to the period or periods in the year throughout which the individual is resident in Canada, computed as though that period or those periods were the whole taxation year, and

(b) the total of the amounts that would have been deemed to have been paid under those subsections for the year had the individual been resident in Canada throughout the year.

(7) Non-residents — Subsections (2) and (3) do not apply in respect of a taxation year of an individual if the individual is, at no time in the year, resident in Canada, unless all or substantially all the individual's income for the year is included in computing the individual's taxable income earned in Canada for the year.

Definitions [former s. 122.8]: "amount", "appropriate percentage", "bankrupt" — 248(1); "calendar year" — *Interpretation Act* 37(1)(a); "child" — 252(1); "common-law partner" — 248(1); "eligible fitness expense" — 122.8(1); "fair market value" — see Notes to 69(1); "individual", "Minister" — 248(1); "partnership" — see Notes to 96(1); "person", "prescribed" — 248(1); "qualifying child", "qualifying entity" — 122.8(1); "resident in Canada" — 250; "return of income" — 122.8; "taxable income" — 2(2), 248(1); "taxable income earned in Canada" — 248(1); "taxation year" — 249.

122.8 added by 2014 budget bill #2, for 2015 and later taxation years.

Definitions [s. 122.8]: "amount", "bankrupt" — 248(1); "calendar year" — *Interpretation Act* 37(1)(a); "child" — 252(1); "cohabiting spouse or common-law partner" — 122.8(1); "common-law partner", "common-law partnership" — 248(1); "eligible individual" — 122.8(1), 122.8(2), (7); "individual", "Minister" — 248(1); "Minister of Finance" — *Financial Administration Act* s. 14; "non-resident" — 248(1); "parent" — 252(2)(a); "person" — 248(1); "province" — *Interpretation Act* 35(1); "qualified dependant" — 122.8(1), 122.8(2), (8); "qualified relation" — 122.8(1), 122.8(2); "relevant province" — 122.8(4)A; "reside" — 122.8(3); "return of income" — 122.8(1); "taxation year" — 122.8(9), 249; "trust" — 104(1), 248(1), (3).

Subdivision A.4 — School Supplies Tax Credit

122.9 (1) Definitions — The following definitions apply in this section.

"eligible educator", in respect of a taxation year, means an individual who, at any time during the taxation year,

(a) is employed in Canada as a teacher or an early childhood educator at

(i) an elementary or secondary school, or

(ii) a regulated child care facility; and

(b) holds a valid and recognized (in the province or territory in which the individual is employed)

(i) teaching certificate, licence, permit or diploma, or

(ii) certificate or diploma in early childhood education.

Notes: The words "or territory" in (b)(i) are unnecessary, due to *Interpretation Act* 35(1)"province". This has been pointed out to Finance.

"eligible supplies expense", of an eligible educator for a taxation year, means an amount (other than any amount deducted in computing any person's income for any taxation year or any amount otherwise included in computing a deduction from any person's tax payable under this Act for any taxation year) paid by the eligible educator in the taxation year for teaching supplies to the extent that

(a) the teaching supplies were

(i) purchased by the eligible educator for the purpose of teaching or facilitating students' learning, and

(ii) directly consumed or used in an elementary or secondary school or in a regulated child care facility in the performance of the duties of the eligible educator's employment; and

(b) the eligible educator is not entitled to receive a reimbursement, allowance or any other form of assistance (other than an amount that is included in computing the income for any taxation year of the eligible educator and that is not deductible in computing the taxable income of the eligible educator) in respect of the amount paid.

"return of income" filed by an eligible educator for a taxation year means a return of income (other than a return of income filed under subsection 70(2) or 104(23), paragraph 128(2)(e) or subsection 150(4)) that is required to be filed for the year or that would be required to be filed if the eligible educator had tax payable under this Part for the year.

"teaching supplies" means

(a) consumable supplies; and

(b) prescribed durable goods.

Regulations: 9600 (prescribed durable goods).

(2) Deemed overpayment — An eligible educator who files a return of income for a taxation year and who makes a claim under this subsection is deemed to have paid, at the end of the year, on account of tax payable under this Part for the year, an amount equal to the amount determined by the formula

$$A \times B$$

where

A is the appropriate percentage for the year; and

B is the least of

(a) $1,000[2],

(b) the total of all amounts each of which is an eligible supplies expense of the eligible educator for the year, and

(c) if the eligible educator fails to provide the certificate referred to in subsection (3) in respect of the year, as and when requested by the Minister, nil.

Related Provisions: 122.9(3) — Employer's certificate required on request by CRA; 122.9(4) — Effect of bankruptcy; 122.9(5) — Application to part-year resident; 122.9(6) — Application to non-resident; 152(1)(b) — Assessment; 152(4.2)(b) — Redetermination of credit at taxpayer's request; 163(2)(c.5) — False statement or omission — penalty.

Notes: See canada.ca/school-supply-credit. 122.9 provides a credit for teachers who use their own money to buy school supplies for students, as promised in the Oct. 2015 Liberal election platform. The "appropriate percentage" (248(1)) is 15%, so this credit is 15% of up to $1,000 (max $150), not indexed for inflation. (Better tax relief is available from 8(1)(i)(iii), if its conditions can be met.)

By deeming the taxpayer to have paid an amount on account of tax, 122.9(2) creates a *refundable* credit, like instalments or source deductions withheld, refundable under

---

[2] Not indexed for inflation — ed.

164(1) even if no tax is payable for the year. (This seems unnecessary, since teachers normally have taxable income.)

(3) Certificate — If the Minister so demands, an eligible educator making a claim under this section in respect of a taxation year shall provide to the Minister a written certificate from their employer, or a delegated official of the employer, attesting to the eligible supplies expenses of the eligible educator for the year.

Related Provisions: 122.9(2)B(c) — No credit allowed if certificate requested and not provided.

Notes: This certificate is needed only if the CRA requests it. See Notes to 8(10), the more general "employer certificate" provision, about such certificates.

(4) Effect of bankruptcy — For the purposes of this Subdivision, if an eligible educator becomes bankrupt in a particular calendar year, notwithstanding subsection 128(2), any reference to the taxation year of the eligible educator (other than in this subsection) is deemed to be a reference to the particular calendar year.

(5) Part-year residents — If an eligible educator is resident in Canada throughout part of a taxation year and is non-resident throughout another part of the year, the total of the amounts that are deemed to be paid by the eligible educator under subsection (2) for the year cannot exceed the lesser of

(a) the total of

(i) the amounts deemed to be paid under subsection (2) that can reasonably be considered as wholly applicable to the period or periods in the year throughout which the eligible educator is not resident in Canada, computed as though that period or those periods were the whole taxation year, and

(ii) the amounts deemed to be paid under subsection (2) that can reasonably be considered as wholly applicable to the period or periods in the year throughout which the eligible educator is resident in Canada, computed as though that period or those periods were the whole taxation year; and

(b) the total of the amounts that would have been deemed to have been paid under subsection (2) for the year had the eligible educator been resident in Canada throughout the year.

(6) Non-residents — Subsection (2) does not apply in respect of a taxation year of an eligible educator if the eligible educator is, at no time in the year, resident in Canada, unless all or substantially all the eligible educator's income for the year is included in computing the eligible educator's taxable income earned in Canada for the year.

Notes: 122.9 added by 2016 budget bill #1, effective for 2016 and later taxation years. See Notes to 122.9(2).

Definitions [s. 122.9]: "amount", "appropriate percentage", "bankrupt" — 248(1); "calendar year" — *Interpretation Act* 37(1)(a); "Canada" — 255, *Interpretation Act* 35(1); "child" — 252(1); "eligible educator", "eligible supplies expense" — 122.9(1); "employed", "employer", "employment", "individual", "Minister", "non-resident", "person", "prescribed" — 248(1); "province" — *Interpretation Act* 35(1); "resident", "resident in Canada" — 250; "return of income" — 122.9(1); "taxable income" — 2(2), 248(1); "taxable income earned in Canada" — 248(1); "taxation year" — 249; "teaching supplies" — 122.9(1); "territory" — *Interpretation Act* 35(1); "written" — *Interpretation Act* 35(1)"writing".

Subdivision A.5 — Canada Training Credit

122.91 (1) Claimed amount — An individual who is resident in Canada throughout a taxation year, files a return of income for the taxation year and makes a claim under this subsection is deemed to have paid, at the end of the taxation year, on account of tax payable under this Part for the taxation year, an amount claimed by the individual that does not exceed the lesser of

(a) the training amount limit of the individual for the taxation year, and

(b) 50% of the amount that would be deductible under paragraph 118.5(1)(a) or (d) in computing the individual's tax payable under this Part for the taxation year if

(i) this Act were read without reference to subsections 118.5(1.2) and (2), and

(ii) the appropriate percentage for the taxation year were 100%.

Related Provisions: 118.5(1.2) — Credit reduces tuition credit; 122.91(2) — Training amount limit; 122.91(3) — Effect of bankruptcy; 122.91(4) — Effect of death; 152(1)(b) — Assessment; 152(4.2)(b) — Redetermination of credit at taxpayer's request; 163(2)(c.6) — False statement or omission — penalty.

Notes: The $250 under 122.91(2) starts accumulating in 2019; the credit can first be claimed in 2020. By deeming the taxpayer to have paid an amount on account of tax, 122.91(1) creates a *refundable* credit, like instalments or source deductions withheld, refundable under 164(1) even if no tax is payable for the year. For detail see tiny-url.com/cra-training-credit.

(2) Training amount limit — For the purposes of this section, the training amount limit of an individual for a taxation year is

(a) if the taxation year is after 2019 and the individual has attained the age of 26 years, and has not attained the age of 66 years, before the end of the taxation year, the lesser of

(i) the amount determined by the formula

$$A + B - C$$

where

A   is the individual's training amount limit for the preceding taxation year,

B   is

(A) $250[2], if

(I) the individual has filed a return of income for the preceding taxation year,

(II) the individual was resident in Canada throughout the preceding taxation year,

(III) the total of the following amounts is greater than or equal to $10,000[25]:

1 the amount that would be the individual's "working income" (as defined in subsection 122.7(1)) for the preceding taxation year, if this Act were read without reference to paragraph 81(1)(a) and subsection 81(4),

2 the total of all amounts each of which is an amount payable to the individual under subsection 22(1), 23(1), 152.04(1) or 152.05(1) of the *Employment Insurance Act* in the preceding taxation year, and

3 the amount that would be included in the individual's income because of subparagraph 56(1)(a)(vii) in computing the individual's income for the preceding taxation year, if this Act were read without reference to paragraph 81(1)(a), and

(IV) the individual's income for the preceding taxation year under this Part does not exceed the higher dollar amount referred to in paragraph 117(2)(c), as adjusted under this Act for the preceding taxation year, and

(B) nil, in any other case, and

C   is the amount deemed to have been paid by the individual under subsection (1) in respect of the preceding taxation year, and

(ii) the amount determined by the formula

$$\$5,000^{2} - D$$

---

[2] Not indexed for inflation — ed.

[25] Indexed by 117.1(1) after 2020 — ed.

where

    D is the total of all amounts deemed to have been paid by the individual under subsection (1) in respect of a preceding taxation year; and

    (b) nil, in any other case.

Related Provisions: 117.1(2)(s) — Inflation indexing.

Notes: For (a)(i)B(A)(III), the $10,000 (2020) is indexed to $10,100 for 2021. For (a)(i)B(A)(IV), the net income limit is $147,667 for 2020 (the "preceding" year is 2019, the first year the $250 can accumulate), $150,473 for 2021, $151,978 for 2022.

(3) Effect of bankruptcy — For the purpose of this Subdivision, if an individual becomes bankrupt in a particular calendar year,

    (a) notwithstanding subsection 128(2), any reference to the taxation year of the individual (other than in this subsection) is deemed to be a reference to the particular calendar year; and

    (b) the individual's working income and income under this Part for the taxation year ending on December 31 of the particular calendar year is deemed to include the individual's working income and the income under this Part for the taxation year that begins on January 1 of the particular calendar year.

(4) Special rules in the event of death — For the purposes of this section, if an individual dies in a calendar year,

    (a) the individual is deemed to be resident in Canada from the time of death until the end of the year;

    (b) the individual is deemed to be the same age at the end of the year as the individual would have been if the individual were alive at the end of the year; and

    (c) any return of income filed by a legal representative of the individual is deemed to be a return of income filed by the individual.

Notes: See Notes to 122.91(1).

The Parliamentary Budget Officer (April 30, 2019) estimates that this credit (net of the reduction in the tuition credit) will cost the federal government $30 million in 2019-20, $155m in 2020-21, $178m in 2021-22, $296m in 2022-23 and $211m in 2023-24.

122.91 (Subdiv. a.5) added by 2019 budget bill #1, effective 2019.

Definitions [s. 122.91]: "amount", "appropriate percentage", "bankrupt" — 248(1); "calendar year" — *Interpretation Act* 37(1)(a); "individual", "legal representative" — 248(1); "resident in Canada" — 122.91(4)(a), 250; "taxation year" — 122.91(3)(a), 249; "training amount limit" — 122.91(2); "working income limit" — 122.7(1).

Subdivision B — Rules Applicable to Corporations

123. (1) Rate for corporations — The tax payable under this Part for a taxation year by a corporation on its taxable income or taxable income earned in Canada, as the case may be, (in this section referred to as its "amount taxable") for the year is, except where otherwise provided,

    (a) 38% of its amount taxable for the year.

    (b)–(d) [Repealed under former Act]

Related Provisions: 123.4(2) — General reduction in tax rate; 124 — Provincial tax abatement for corporations; 125 — Small business deduction; 125.1 — Manufacturing and processing credit; 137.1(9) — Tax rate for deposit insurance corporation; 157(1) — Monthly instalment requirements; 161(4.1) — Interest on unpaid taxes; 182 — Surtax on tobacco manufacturers; 219(1) — Additional tax on foreign corporations; 261(7)(h) — Functional currency reporting.

Notes: The 38% rate is reduced to 28% by 124(1), to allow room for the provinces to levy tax, and further reduced to 15% on most corporations' income (but not personal services business income) by 123.4(2), or to 10% (2018) or 9% (2019) by the small business deduction in 125(1). See Notes to 123.4(2) and 125(1.1). Income not earned in a province is not eligible for the abatement (but see 124(4)"province"). There is no corporate surtax since 2008: 123.2. For provincial corporate tax, see tinyurl.com/provcorp-cra, and Tables C-1 to C-9 at beginning of this book.

On how corporations are taxed, see Norman Tobias, *Taxation of Corporations, Partnerships and Trusts* (Carswell, 5th ed., 2017), chaps. 6-12; *Taxation of Private Corporations and their Shareholders* (ctf.ca, 5th ed., 2020).

Forms: T2 Sched. 7: Aggregate investment income and active business income.

(2) [Repealed under former Act]

Notes: 123(2) repealed by 1988 Canada-Nova Scotia Offshore Petroleum Resources Accord. For taxation years beginning before Dec. 23, 1989, it dealt with the Nova Scotia offshore area. See 124(4)"province" now.

Definitions [s. 123]: "amount taxable" — 123(1); "corporation" — 248(1), *Interpretation Act* 35(1); "taxable income" — 2(2), 248(1); "taxable income earned in Canada" — 115(1), 248(1).

123.1 [No longer relevant.]

Notes: 123.1 imposes the corporate surtax for 1985-86.

123.2 [Corporate surtax — repealed]

Notes: 123.2 repealed by 2006 budget bill #1, for taxation years that begin after 2007. It imposed a 4% corporate surtax (see 123.4(2) Notes).

123.2 earlier amended by 2005 budget bill #1, 2000, 1998 and 1995 Budgets, 1992 technical bill and 1989 Budget.

123.3 Refundable tax on CCPC's investment income —

There shall be added to the tax otherwise payable under this Part for each taxation year by a corporation that is throughout the year a Canadian-controlled private corporation an amount equal to $10\frac{2}{3}\%$ of the lesser of

    (a) the corporation's aggregate investment income for the year (within the meaning assigned by subsection 129(4)), and

    (b) the amount, if any, by which its taxable income for the year exceeds the least of the amounts determined in respect of it for the year under paragraphs 125(1)(a) to (c).

Abandoned Proposed Amendment — Additional tax on private corporation's passive income

Notes: Dept. of Finance consultation paper *Tax Planning Using Private Corporations*, July 18, 2017 (reproduced here in the 53rd ed.), proposed various ways to tax passive income of private corps at high rates, to compensate for the small business deduction having applied to the profits used to generate such passive income. The resulting uproar from small business and the media caused the government to back down and to propose that changes would apply only to passive income exceeding $50,000 per year (representing a 5% return on $1 million of investments): news release, Oct. 20, 2017. After more criticism, Finance proposed instead in the 2018 Budget to grind down the small business deduction when passive income exceeds $50,000 (125(5.1), (5.2)), and to limit the refundable tax on investment income (129(1)-(5)). See also 120.4 Notes.

Related Provisions: 125(1)(b)(i), 126(7)"tax for the year otherwise payable under this Part"(b), (c) — Refundable tax ignored for foreign tax credit purposes; 129(4)"non-eligible refundable dividend tax on hand"(a)(i)A — Refund of tax (plus 20 points of regular tax on the same income).

Notes [s. 123.3]: The 10.67% tax under 123.3 (6.67% before 2016) is refundable (see 129(4)"non-eligible refundable dividend tax on hand"(a)(i)A) once sufficient dividends are paid out; it combines with the 20% dividend refund for a total refund of 30.67% (26.67% before 2016) of investment income (integration). See Notes to 129(1). The purpose of 123.3 is to ensure that most corporations pay upfront about 51% total tax including provincial tax (about 47% before 2016) on investment income, rather than about 25% (see Notes to 123.4(2)); thus there is no incentive to earn interest income in a corporation rather than personally. However, once sufficient dividends are paid out, the dividend refund under 129(1) combined with the gross-up (82(1)(b)) and dividend tax credit (s. 121) ensures that the total tax on investment income earned through a corporation and paid out as dividends is about the same as on investment income earned directly by an individual (integration).

For a private company that earns only investment income and does not pay out dividends, it is better *not* to be a CCPC (125(7)) so as not to pay this refundable tax and to be eligible for the 13% reduction in 123.4 (see 123.4(1)"full-rate taxable income"(b)(iii)). One way to do this is to use a foreign (e.g. Cayman Islands) company that is managed from Canada and thus resident in Canada (see Notes to 250(3)), but is not a "Canadian corporation" (89(1)) and thus not a CCPC. (GAAR could apply, or conceivably the CRA could say the company is non-resident so FAPI applies.) Another (possibly subject to GAAR or still held to be a CCPC) is to put a foreign company or trust in the ownership chain, e.g. Canadian individual owns a BVI company that owns a Canadian company. Note that 249(3.1) will apply if a CCPC ceases to be a CCPC. (The election in 89(11) does not deem a company not to be a CCPC for purposes of 123.3.)

123.3 opening words amended to change "6 2/3%" to "10 2/3%" by 2016 tax-rate bill, for taxation years that end after 2015, but for such years that begin before 2016, read "10 2/3%" as "6 2/3% + 4%(A/B), where A is the number of days in the taxation year that are after 2015, and B is the total number of days in the taxation year". (In other words, the increase to 10 2/3% is prorated based on the number of days after 2015.) This increase is consequential on the top rate increase from 29% to 33% in 117(2).

123.3 added by 1995 Budget, effective for taxation years that end after June 1995.

Former 123.3, repealed by 1985 technical bill, set out the corporate surtaxes for 1981, 1982 and 1983.

Definitions [s. 123.3]: "Canadian-controlled private corporation" — 125(7), 248(1); "corporation" — 248(1), *Interpretation Act* 35(1); "taxable income" — 2(2), 248(1); "taxation year" — 249.

123.4 Corporation tax reductions — (1) Definitions — The definitions in this subsection apply in this section.

"CCPC rate reduction percentage" [Repealed]

Notes: Definition "CCPC rate reduction percentage" repealed by 2003 Budget, effective for 2005 and later taxation years. It is no longer needed with the repeal of 123.4(3).

"full rate taxable income" of a corporation for a taxation year is

(a) if the corporation is not a corporation described in paragraph (b) or (c) for the year, the amount by which that portion of the corporation's taxable income for the year (or, for greater certainty, if the corporation is non-resident, that portion of its taxable income earned in Canada for the year) that is subject to tax under subsection 123(1) exceeds the total of

(i) if an amount is deducted under subsection 125.1(1) from the corporation's tax otherwise payable under this Part for the year, the amount obtained by dividing the amount so deducted by the corporation's general rate reduction percentage for the taxation year,

(ii) if an amount is deducted under subsection 125.1(2) from the corporation's tax otherwise payable under this Part for the year, the amount determined, in respect of the deduction, by the formula in that subsection,

(iii) the corporation's income for the year from a personal services business; and

(iv) if the corporation is a credit union throughout the year and the corporation deducted an amount for the year under subsection 125(1) (because of the application of subsections 137(3) and (4)), the amount, if any, that is the product of the amount, if any, determined for B in subsection 137(3) multiplied by the amount determined for C in subsection 137(3) in respect of the corporation for the year;

(b) if the corporation is a Canadian-controlled private corporation throughout the year, the amount by which that portion of the corporation's taxable income for the year that is subject to tax under subsection 123(1) exceeds the total of

(i) the amounts that would, if paragraph (a) applied to the corporation, be determined under subparagraphs (a)(i) to (iv) in respect of the corporation for the year,

(ii) the least of the amounts, if any, determined under paragraphs 125(1)(a) to (c) in respect of the corporation for the year, and

(iii) except for a corporation that is, throughout the year, a cooperative corporation (within the meaning assigned by subsection 136(2)) or a credit union, the corporation's aggregate investment income for the year, within the meaning assigned by subsection 129(4), and

(iv) [Repealed]

(c) if the corporation is throughout the year an investment corporation, a mortgage investment corporation or a mutual fund corporation, nil.

Related Provisions: 123.5 — Additional 5% tax on personal services business income; 125.11 — Resource rate reduction 2003-06.

Notes: See Notes to 123.4(2).

Subpara. (a)(iii), announced on Oct. 31, 2011, increases tax on a PSB (see 125(7)"personal services business") by 13 percentage points. It is aimed at stopping PSBs from being used intentionally for planning purposes, now that general corporate tax rates have been substantially reduced. See also Brodlieb, "Should I be taking it personally?", 2071 *Tax Topics* (CCH) 1-4 (Nov. 17, 2011).

Definition amended by 2002-2013 technical bill (for tax years that begin after Oct. 2011), 2013 budget bills #1 and #2 (for tax years that end after March 20, 2013), 2006 budget bills #1 and #2, 2003 resource bill, 2003 and 2000 Budgets.

"general rate reduction percentage" of a corporation for a taxation year is the total of

(a) that proportion of 7% that the number of days in the taxation year that are before 2008 is of the number of days in the taxation year,

(b) that proportion of 8.5% that the number of days in the taxation year that are in 2008 is of the number of days in the taxation year,

(c) that proportion of 9% that the number of days in the taxation year that are in 2009 is of the number of days in the taxation year,

(d) that proportion of 10% that the number of days in the taxation year that are in 2010 is of the number of days in the taxation year,

(e) that proportion of 11.5% that the number of days in the taxation year that are in 2011 is of the number of days in the taxation year, and

(f) that proportion of 13% that the number of days in the taxation year that are after 2011 is of the number of days in the taxation year.

Related Provisions: 125.1(1), (2) — Application to M&P credit.

Notes: See Notes to 123.4(2).

Paras. (b)-(e) amended and (f) added by 2007 Economic Statement, to reduce the rate (from 28%: see 123(1) and 124(1)) gradually to 15% as of January 2012. Table A.1 in the Economic Statement estimates that this measure will cost the federal government $1.28 billion in 2008-09, $1.62b in 2009-10, $1.725b in 2010-11, $3.355b in 2011-12 and $6.12b in 2012-13.

Para (d) amended and (e) added by 2007 budget bill #1. The rate was to have been reduced by 7.5% for 2008, 8% for 2009, 9% for 2010 and 9.5% as of 2011.

123.4(1)"general rate reduction percentage" amended by 2006 budget bill #1 (implementing a 2005 Budget proposal temporarily suspended due to a Liberal minority government deal with the NDP), effective June 22, 2006. Under the previous version, the reduction was 1% for calendar 2001, 3% for 2002, 5% for 2003 and 7% for 2004-07.

(2) General deduction from tax — There may be deducted from a corporation's tax otherwise payable under this Part for a taxation year the product obtained by multiplying the corporation's general rate reduction percentage for the year by the corporation's full rate taxable income for the year.

Proposed Amendment — Corporate tax rate cut in half for clean tech businesses

Federal Budget, Supplementary Information, April 19, 2021: *Rate Reduction for Zero-Emission Technology Manufacturers*

Budget 2021 proposes a temporary measure to reduce corporate income tax rates for qualifying zero-emission technology manufacturers. Specifically, taxpayers would be able to apply reduced tax rates on eligible zero-emission technology manufacturing and processing income of:

- 7.5%, where that income would otherwise be taxed at the 15% general corporate tax rate; and
- 4.5%, where that income would otherwise be taxed at the 9% small business tax rate.

Eligible Zero-Emission Technology Manufacturing or Processing Activities

This measure would apply in respect of income from the following zero-emission technology manufacturing or processing activities:

- manufacturing of solar energy conversion equipment, such as solar thermal collectors, photovoltaic solar arrays and bespoke supporting structures or frames, but excluding passive solar heating equipment (e.g., a masonry wall installed to absorb solar energy);
- manufacturing of wind energy conversion equipment, such as wind turbine towers, nacelles and rotor blades;
- manufacturing of water energy conversion equipment, such as hydroelectric, water current, tidal and wave energy conversion equipment;
- manufacturing of geothermal energy equipment;
- manufacturing of equipment for a ground source heat pump system;
- manufacturing of electrical energy storage equipment used for storage of renewable energy or for providing grid-scale storage or other ancillary services (e.g., voltage regulation), including battery, compressed air and flywheel storage systems;
- manufacturing of zero-emission vehicles (i.e., plug-in hybrid vehicles with a battery capacity of at least seven kilowatt-hours, electric vehicles and hydrogen-powered vehicles) and the conversion of vehicles into zero-emission vehicles;

- manufacturing of batteries and fuel cells for zero-emission vehicles;

- manufacturing of electric vehicle charging systems and hydrogen refuelling stations for vehicles;

- manufacturing of equipment used for the production of hydrogen by electrolysis of water;

- production of hydrogen by electrolysis of water; and

- production of solid, liquid or gaseous fuel (e.g., wood pellets, renewable diesel and biogas) from either carbon dioxide or specified waste material (i.e., wood waste, municipal waste, sludge from an eligible sewage treatment facility, plant residue, spent pulping liquor, food and animal waste, manure, pulp and paper by-product and separated organics), but excluding the production of by-products which is a standard part of another industrial or manufacturing process (e.g., the production of wood chips, black liquor or hog fuel as part of another wood transformation process).

For each of the manufacturing activities described above, eligible activities would include the manufacturing of components or sub-assemblies only if such equipment is purpose-built or designed exclusively to form an integral part of the relevant system. For example, manufacturing of wind turbine rotor blades may be an eligible activity, but manufacturing of general use tires, fasteners, wiring, transformers, paint, piping or concrete would not.

Eligible activities would exclude all activities that do not qualify as manufacturing or processing for the purposes of the capital cost allowance rules.

Calculation of Eligible Income

It is proposed that a taxpayer's eligible income generally be equal to its "adjusted business income" multiplied by the proportion of its total labour and capital costs that are used in eligible activities. The definition of "adjusted business income" as well as the method used to determine labour and capital costs would be substantially based on those used in calculating manufacturing and processing profits under current tax rules.

All of a taxpayer's labour and capital costs would be deemed to be labour and capital costs that are used in eligible activities if all or substantially all of its labour and capital costs are related to eligible activities.

The government welcomes feedback from stakeholders on the proposed allocation method for these purposes. Interested parties are invited to send written representations by June 18, 2021 to the Department of Finance Canada, Tax Policy Branch at: ZETM-FTZE@canada.ca.

Minimum Proportion of Eligible Activities

A taxpayer would qualify for the reduced tax rates on its eligible income only if at least 10% of its gross revenue from all active businesses carried on in Canada is derived from eligible activities.

Reduced Rate for Small Businesses

Certain small businesses currently benefit from a reduced federal corporate income tax rate of 9% — a preference relative to the general corporate income tax rate of 15%. This rate reduction is provided through the "small business deduction" [125(1), (1.1) — ed.] and applies on up to $500,000 per year of qualifying active business income (i.e., up to the business limit [125(2) — ed.]) of a Canadian-controlled private corporation (CCPC).

For taxpayers with income subject to both the general and the small business corporate tax rates, taxpayers would be able to choose to have their eligible income taxed at either the reduced rate of 4.5% for small businesses or the general reduced rate of 7.5%. The amount of income taxed at the 4.5% rate plus the amount of income taxed at the small business rate of 9% would not be allowed to exceed the business limit.

Treatment of Dividends

The tax system has two dividend tax credit (DTC) rates and gross-up factors to recognize the two different corporate income tax rates that generally apply to corporations. The enhanced DTC [121(b) — ed.] and gross-up [82(1)(b)(ii) — ed.] are applied to dividends distributed to an individual from corporate income taxed at the general corporate tax rate ("eligible dividends"). The ordinary DTC [121(a) — ed.] and gross-up [82(1)(b)(i) — ed.] are applied to dividends distributed to an individual from corporate income not taxed at the general corporate tax rate ("non-eligible dividends"). At the federal level, the enhanced and ordinary dividend tax credit correspond to 15% and 9% of the grossed-up amount of the dividend, respectively.

Given the targeted application, temporary nature, and gradual phase-out of the proposed measure, no changes to the DTC rates or the allocation of corporate income for the purpose of dividend distributions are proposed. That is, income subject to the general reduced rate would continue to give rise to eligible dividends and the enhanced dividend tax credit, while income subject to the reduced rate for small businesses would continue to give rise to non-eligible dividends and the ordinary dividend tax credit.

Application and Phase-Out

The reduced tax rates would apply to taxation years that begin after 2021. The reduced rates would be gradually phased out starting in taxation years that begin in 2029 and fully phased out for taxation years that begin after 2031 (as shown in Table 8).

Table 8 — Schedule of Reduced Tax Rates

Taxation years that begin in:	2022 to 2028	2029	2030	2031	2032 or later
Reduced Tax Rate on Income Eligible for the Small Business Deduction	4.5%	5.625%	6.75%	7.875%	9%
Reduced Tax Rate on Other Eligible Income	7.5%	9.375%	11.25%	13.125%	15%

Strategic Environmental Assessment Statement

Overall, the measure is expected to have positive environmental impacts by lowering emissions of greenhouse gases and air particulates.

The measure could indirectly lower the price of zero-emission technology equipment, which could lead to a greater adoption of zero-emission technology in Canada, helping to reduce emissions of greenhouse gases and air particulates. This would contribute to achieving the Federal Sustainable Development Strategy targets relating to increasing the percentage of Canadians living in areas where air quality standards are achieved to 85% by 2030, and having 90% of electricity generated from renewable and non-emitting sources by 2030. In addition, the proposal would help advance the government's commitment to exceed Canada's target of reducing total greenhouse gas emissions by 30% relative to 2005 levels by 2030, and the government's commitment of net-zero greenhouse gas emissions by 2050.

However, increased manufacturing activities in Canada could directly increase emissions of greenhouse gases and air particulates, as well as increase production of industrial waste. This could partially offset some of the positive environmental impacts of the measure.

Consultation document, Dept of Finance April 19, 2021: *Tax Reduction for Zero-Emission Technology Manufacturing*

Current Status: Open until June 18, 2021

Join In

As more countries commit to achieving net-zero emissions by 2050, the demand for zero-emission technology will only grow. To create jobs and support the growth of clean technology manufacturing in Canada, Budget 2021 proposes to reduce — by half — the general corporate and small business income tax rates for businesses that manufacture zero-emission technologies. The proposed measure is described in detail in the Budget 2021 annex entitled Tax Measures: Supplementary Information.

This consultation seeks views and feedback on the proposed allocation method for determining income eligible for the reduced tax rates on zero-emission technology manufacturing. Specifically, Budget 2021 proposes to determine income eligible for the reduced tax rates on zero-emission technology manufacturing based on the share of a taxpayers' labour and capital costs used in eligible zero-emission technology manufacturing activities.

We also welcome any additional comments or feedback relevant to the scope of this consultation.

Who is the focus of this consultation?

Through this consultation, we want to hear from tax practitioners and members of the public. In submitting your comments, please include:

- Full name;

- Name of the organization;

- Telephone number, including area code; and

- Reply e-mail address.

Participate through email

Due to COVID-19 public health considerations, email submissions are preferred. Send us your comments at ZETM-FTZE@canada.ca with "Zero-Emission Technology Manufacturing Consultation" as the subject line.

Should you wish to provide comments by mail, please direct your submission to the attention of the Tax Policy Branch.

What's next?

Our conversation doesn't end here.

We'll be collecting your feedback and will consider your input alongside the analysis of departmental officials to help inform decisions on the proposed tax rate reductions for businesses that manufacture zero-emission technologies.

Information received through this comment process is subject to the *Access to Information Act* and the *Privacy Act*. Those providing comments are asked to indicate clearly the name of the individual or the organization that should be identified as having made the submission. In order to respect privacy and confidentiality, please advise when providing your comments whether you:

- consent to the disclosure of your comments in whole or in part;

- request that your identity and any personal identifiers be removed prior to release; or
- wish that any portions of your comments be kept confidential (if so, clearly identify the confidential portions).

Should you indicate that your comments, or any portions thereof, be considered confidential, the Department of Finance will make all reasonable efforts to protect this information.

Get in touch

ZETM-FTZE@canada.ca

Federal Budget, Chapter 5, April 19, 2021: *Growing Zero-emission Technology Manufacturing*

As more countries commit to achieving net-zero emissions by 2050, the demand for zero-emission technology will only grow. With a highly educated and motivated workforce, Canada is well positioned to take advantage of this opportunity. Strengthening our manufacturing sector and creating good, well-paying jobs is key to growing a resilient, competitive middle class.

To create jobs and support the growth of clean technology manufacturing in Canada:

Budget 2021 proposes to reduce — by 50% — the general corporate and small business income tax rates for businesses that manufacture zero-emission technologies. The reductions would go into effect on January 1, 2022, and would be gradually phased out starting January 1, 2029 and eliminated by January 1, 2032. The Department of Finance Canada will regularly review new technologies that might be eligible, in consultation with Environment and Climate Change Canada, Natural Resources Canada, Sustainable Development Technology Canada, and other key stakeholders across government and industry.

These proposed tax rate reductions will enhance Canada's competitiveness in attracting investment in zero-emission technology manufacturing, while also supporting existing businesses in the sector. This will advance Canada's economic recovery and help create well-paying jobs for Canadians. It is estimated that this measure will reduce federal revenues by $45 million over five years, starting in 2021-22.

In addition, the government will undertake an analysis to ensure that Canada keeps pace with the U.S. and other jurisdictions in providing the appropriate tax structures and incentives to encourage clean economy businesses to invest, grow, and deploy solutions here in Canada.

Examples of zero-emission technology manufacturing in Canada:

- Manufacturing of wind turbines, solar panels, and equipment used in hydroelectric facilities.
- Manufacturing of geothermal energy systems.
- Manufacturing of electric cars, busses, trucks, and other vehicles.
- Manufacturing of batteries and fuel cells for electric vehicles.
- Production of biofuels from waste materials.
- Production of green hydrogen.
- Manufacturing of electric vehicle charging systems.
- Manufacturing of certain energy storage equipment.

Speech from the Throne, Sept. 23, 2020: The Government will launch a new fund to attract investments in making zero-emissions products and **cut the corporate tax rate in half for these companies** to create jobs and make Canada a world leader in clean technology. The Government will ensure Canada is the most competitive jurisdiction in the world for clean technology companies.

Prime Minister's mandate letter to Minister of Finance, Dec. 2019: I will expect you to work with your colleagues and through established legislative, regulatory and Cabinet processes to deliver on your top priorities. In particular, you will:

- Cut tax rates by 50% for companies that develop and manufacture zero-emissions technology. Eligible sectors should include but not be limited to: manufacturing related to renewable energy, renewable fuels production, zero-emission vehicles, carbon sequestration and removal technology, batteries for use in zero-emission vehicles, and grid storage and electric vehicle charging systems.

Liberal.ca election platform, Oct. 2019: *Lower Taxes For Clean Tech Businesses*

We will cut corporate taxes in half for businesses that develop technologies or manufacture products that have zero emissions.

The market for clean technology — which uses renewable energy and emits less pollution — is expected to exceed $2.5 trillion by 2022. That's good news for our economy, and for our environment.

To take advantage of this opportunity to attract and grow businesses that will help us meet the ambitious goal of achieving net-zero emissions by 2050, we will cut in half the corporate tax paid by companies that develop and manufacture zero-emissions technology. These lower taxes will create a strong incentive for businesses to set up shop in Canada, and help make Canada a true world leader in zero-emissions clean tech.

Notes: See also Proposed Amendments under Reg. Schedule II, Class 43.1, increasing the CCA rate on purchase of various clean tech products.

Budget Table 1 projects that this measure will cost the federal government $1 million in 2021-22, $10m in each of 2022-23 to 2024-25 and $15m in 2025-26.

Related Provisions: 136(1) — Cooperative can be private corporation for purposes of 123.4; 137(7) — Credit union can be private corporation for purposes of 123.4.

Notes: The general federal corporate tax rate (for non-manufacturing, large businesses in a province) is 15%: 38% (123(1)), minus 10% (124(1)), minus 13% (123.4(2)). With provincial tax the total is about 25%, varying by province. See Tables C1-C6 at beginning of book; Di Maio & Hibbard, "Corporate Rate Update", 27(8) *Canadian Tax Highlights* (ctf.ca) 4-5 (Aug. 2019).

In the past, the federal rate was: 28% + surtax [123.2] = 29.12% (2000); 27% + surtax = 28.12% (2001); 25% + surtax = 26.12% (2002); 23% + surtax = 24.12% (2003); 21% + surtax = 22.12% (2004-07); 19.5%, surtax repealed (2008), 19% (2009), 18% (2010), 16.5% (2011), 15% (since 2012).

The reductions in corporate rates change the planning where profits over the small business deduction limit ($500,000) would be bonused out to owners. With a combined federal-provincial rate of about 25% on large corporation active business income, keeping profits in the corporation provides substantial tax deferral relative to personal income tax rates. However, for income from a PSB (125(7)"personal services business"), 123.4(1)"full rate taxable income"(a)(iii) increases the rate by 13 percentage points, and 123.5 adds a further 5% tax.

Due to the wording of 123.4(1)"full rate taxable income"(b)(ii), a corp entitled to claim the small business deduction does not get a higher 123.4(2) deduction by not claiming it: VIEWS doc 2016-0674221C6 [CPA QC 2017 q.1.1]

For the rate for small businesses on active business income, see Notes to 125(1).

Despite the drop in US corporate rates under 2017 tax reform, Canada's subsequent Budgets have made no changes to remain competitive.

In 123.4(2), "full-rate taxable income" corrected to "full rate taxable income" (no hyphen): laws.justice.gc.ca/eng/corrections.

Income Tax Folios: S4-F15-C1: Manufacturing and processing [replaces IT-147R3].

Interpretation Bulletins: IT-73R6: The small business deduction.

(3) [Repealed]

Notes: 123.4(3) repealed by 2003 Budget, for 2005 and later taxation years. As of 2004, 123.4(3) is no longer needed because the general rate reduction matches the CCPC rate reduction that it provided. See Notes to 123.4(2).

Notes [s. 123.4]: 123.4 added by 2000 Budget, for 2001 and later tax years.

Definitions [s. 123.4]: "aggregate investment income" — 129(4), 248(1); "amount", "business", "business limit" — 248(1); "CCPC rate reduction percentage" — 123.4(1); "Canadian-controlled private corporation" — 125(7), 248(1); "cooperative corporation" — 136(2); "corporation" — 248(1), *Interpretation Act* 35(1); "credit union" — 137(6), 248(1); "fiscal period" — 249.1; "full rate taxable income", "general rate reduction percentage" — 123.4(1); "investment corporation" — 130(3), 248(1); "mortgage investment corporation" — 130.1(6), 248(1); "mutual fund corporation" — 131(8), 248(1); "non-resident" — 248(1); "non-resident-owned investment corporation" — 133(8), 248(1); "personal services business" — 125(7), 248(1); "property" — 248(1); "taxable income" — 2(2), 248(1); "taxable income earned in Canada" — 248(1); "taxable resource income" — 125.11(1); "taxation year" — 249.

123.5 Tax on personal services business income — There shall be added to the tax otherwise payable under this Part for each taxation year by a corporation an amount equal to 5% of the corporation's taxable income for the year from a personal services business.

Related Provisions: 123.4(1)"full rate taxable income"(a)(iii) — Additional 13% tax above general corporate rate.

Notes: See Notes to 125(7)"personal services business". The federal tax on a corporation's PSB income is now 33%: it is 38% (123(1)), minus 10% (124(1)), minus 0% (123.4(2), due to 123.4(1)"full rate taxable income"(a)(iii) reducing FRTI to nil), plus 5% (123.5). 123.5 was introduced along with the top personal tax rate increasing from 29% to 33% in 2016 (see 117(2)(e)).

123.5 added by 2016 budget bill #1, for taxation years that end after 2015 except that, for such years that begin before 2016, read "5%" as "5% (A/B)" where A is the number of days in the year that are after 2015, and B is the total number of days in the taxation year. (In other words, the tax is prorated to the number of days in 2016.)

Former 123.4-123.5, repealed by 1985 technical bill, enacted the corporate surtax for 1982-1983.

Definitions [s. 123.5]: "amount" — 248(1); "corporation" — 248(1), *Interpretation Act* 35(1); "personal services business" — 125(7), 248(1); "taxable income" — 2(2), 248(1); "taxation year" — 249.

124. (1) Deduction from corporation tax — There may be deducted from the tax otherwise payable by a corporation under this Part for a taxation year an amount equal to 10% of the corporation's taxable income earned in the year in a province.

Related Provisions: 117(1) — Tax payable under this Part; 123.4(2) — Further rate reduction.

Notes: The 10% abatement in 124(1), from 38% to 28%, gives the provinces and territories "room" to levy provincial corporate taxes, which are imposed on income attributable to a permanent establishment in the province. See Tables C-1 and C-3 in the introductory pages and Notes at beginning of Reg. Part IV (before Reg. 400). To the extent corporate income is not allocated to a province (see 124(4)"taxable income ..." and Reg. 400–413), it remains taxable at the full 38% under s. 123.

A further reduction for most corporations is provided by 123.4(2). See Notes to 123(1).

124(1) does not apply to a non-resident that elects to report net rental income under 216(1), even though Quebec will tax the rent: VIEWS doc 2006-0196171C6.

Interpretation Bulletins: IT-177R2: Permanent establishment of a corporation in a province; IT-347R2: Crown corporations (cancelled); IT-393R2: Election re tax on rents and timber royalties — non-residents.

(2)–(2.2) [Repealed under former Act]

Notes: 124(2) to (2.2), repealed in 1974, provided for a deduction from corporate tax for production profits from mineral resources.

(3) Crown agents — Notwithstanding subsection (1), no deduction may be made under this section from the tax otherwise payable under this Part for a taxation year by a corporation in respect of any taxable income of the corporation for the year that is not, because of an Act of Parliament, subject to tax under this Part or by a prescribed federal Crown corporation that is an agent of Her Majesty.

Related Provisions: 27 — Prescribed federal Crown corporations are subject to Part I tax; 149(6) — Apportionment rule.

Notes: 124(3) ensures that the objective of s. 27 is met. 27(2) requires certain federal Crown corporations that operate in the commercial sector to pay tax, in order not to give them an unfair advantage over private-sector businesses. Since such corps are not subject to provincial corporate income tax for constitutional reasons (provinces cannot tax the federal Crown), 124(3) provides that they get no abatement under 124(1). The abatement is designed to allow room for the provinces to levy a tax of about 10%.

124(3) amended by 1992 technical bill, for 1992 and later taxation years, to ensure that a corporation that is exempt (under s. 149 or otherwise) cannot have the portion of its income that is taxable reduced by an abatement under 124(1) for the exempt income.

Regulations: 7100 (prescribed federal Crown corporation).

Interpretation Bulletins: IT-347R2: Crown corporations (cancelled).

(4) Definitions — In this section,

> ### Proposed Amendment — 124(4) opening words
>
> **(4) Definitions** — The following definitions apply in this section.
>
> **Application**: Bill C-74 (First Reading June 18, 2015; requires reintroduction in new Parliament), subsec. 252(1), will amend the opening words of subsec. 124(4) to read as above, in force on Royal Assent.

"province" includes the Newfoundland offshore area and the Nova Scotia offshore area;

> ### Proposed Amendment — 124(4)"province"
>
> **"province"** includes the joint management area, the Nova Scotia offshore area and the Newfoundland offshore area.
>
> **Application**: Bill C-74 (First Reading June 18, 2015; requires reintroduction in new Parliament), subsec. 252(2), will amend the definition "province" in subsec. 124(4) to read as above, applicable to taxation years that begin after the day on which an administration agreement in respect of tax imposed under s. 235 of the *Canada–Quebec Gulf of St. Lawrence Petroleum Resources Accord Implementation Act* comes into effect.

Related Provisions: Reg. 414(1)"province" — Same definition applies to SIFT trusts and partnerships.

Notes: Under *Interpretation Act* s. 35(1), "province" also includes Yukon, the Northwest Territories and Nunavut.

124(4)"province" was 124(4)(b) before RSC 1985 (5th Supp) consolidation for tax years ending after Nov. 1991.

Regulations: 400–413 (taxable income earned in the year in a province).

"taxable income earned in the year in a province" means the amount determined under rules prescribed for the purpose by regulations made on the recommendation of the Minister of Finance.

Notes: 124(4)"taxable income earned in the year in a province" was 124(4)(a) before RSC 1985 (5th Supp) consolidation for tax years ending after Nov. 1991.

Regulations: 400–413 (taxable income earned in the year in a province).

Definitions [s. 124]: "amount" — 248(1); "corporation" — 248(1), *Interpretation Act* 35(1); "Her Majesty" — *Interpretation Act* 35(1); "joint management area", "mineral resource" — 248(1); "Minister of Finance" — *Financial Administration Act* 14; "Newfoundland offshore area", "Nova Scotia offshore area" — 248(1); "Parliament" — *Interpretation Act* 35(1); "province" — 124(4), *Interpretation Act* 35(1);

"taxable income" — 2(2), 248(1); "taxable income earned in the year in a province" — 124(4); "taxation year" — 249.

124.1, 124.2 [Repealed under former Act]

Notes: 124.1 and 124.2, repealed in 1976, defined terms that are no longer used.

125. (1) Small business deduction — There may be deducted from the tax otherwise payable under this Part for a taxation year by a corporation that was, throughout the taxation year, a Canadian-controlled private corporation, an amount equal to the corporation's small business deduction rate for the taxation year multiplied by the least of

> (a) the amount, if any, by which the total of
>
>> (i) the total of all amounts each of which is the amount of income of the corporation for the year from an active business carried on in Canada, other than an amount that is
>>
>>> (A) described in paragraph (a) of the description of A in the definition "specified partnership income" in subsection (7) for the year,
>>>
>>> (B) described in subparagraph (a)(i) of the definition "specified corporate income" in subsection (7) for the year, or
>>>
>>> (C) paid or payable to the corporation by another corporation with which it is associated, that is deemed by subsection 129(6) to be income for the year from an active business carried on by the corporation in circumstances where the associated corporation is not a Canadian-controlled private corporation or is a Canadian-controlled private corporation that has made an election under subsection 256(2) in respect of its taxation year in which the amount was paid or payable,
>>
>> (ii) the specified partnership income of the corporation for the year, and
>>
>> (ii.1) the specified corporate income of the corporation for the year
>
> exceeds the total of
>
>> (iii) the total of all amounts each of which is a loss of the corporation for the year from an active business carried on in Canada (other than a loss of the corporation for the year from a business carried on by it as a member of a partnership), and
>>
>> (iv) the specified partnership loss of the corporation for the year,
>
> (b) the amount, if any, by which the corporation's taxable income for the year exceeds the total of
>
>> (i) 100/28 of the total of the amounts that would be deductible under subsection 126(1) from the tax for the year otherwise payable under this Part by it if those amounts were determined without reference to sections 123.3 and 123.4,
>>
>> (ii) the amount determined by multiplying the total of the amounts that would be deductible under subsection 126(2) from the tax for the year otherwise payable under this Part by it, if those amounts were determined without reference to section 123.4, by the relevant factor for the year, and
>>
>> (iii) the amount, if any, of the corporation's taxable income for the year that is not, because of an Act of Parliament, subject to tax under this Part, and
>
> (c) the corporation's business limit for the year.

> ### Proposed Amendment — Rate Reduction for zero-emission technology manufacturers
>
> **Federal Budget, Supplementary Information, April 19, 2021**: See under 123.4(2).

Related Provisions: 89(1)"general rate income pool", "low rate income pool" — Income subject to small business deduction ineligible for 45% dividend gross-up; 125(1.1) — Small business deduction rate; 125(2)–(5) — Restriction of deduction to $500,000 of active business income; 125(5.1) — Elimination of small business deduction for large corporations; 125(7)"Canadian-controlled private corporation"(d) — Election not to be CCPC for purposes of 125(1); 125(9) — Anti-avoidance rule;

125(10) — Computational rule — specified corporate income; 136(1) — Cooperative can be private corporation for purposes of s. 125; 137(3), (4) — Credit unions — small business deduction; 137(7) — Credit union can be private corporation for s. 125.

Notes: 125(1) provides the "small business deduction" (SBD), a deduction from *tax* — i.e., a credit against tax otherwise owing. It reduces from 28% to 10.5% [see Notes to 125(1.1)] the federal tax on the first $500,000 [125(2)] of a Canadian-controlled private corporation's active business income (ABI) in Canada. Associated corporations must share the $500,000 limit: 125(2)–(5). Large corporations lose part or all of the deduction: 125(5.1)(a). Having passive income over $50,000 can grind down the availability of the deduction starting 2019-20: 125(5.1)(b).

Advantages of incorporating a business include: income splitting by having dividends go to family members [see Notes to 56(2)]; low corporate tax rate as long as funds are kept in the corporation; choice of salary vs dividends; limited liability; perpetual existence of the corp; no instalments required for first year [157(1)]; off-calendar year-end [249(1)(a)]; accruing bonuses at year-end [see 78(4)]; the capital gains exemption on selling the shares [110.6(2.1)]; allowable business investment loss if the business fails [39(1)(c)]. Disadvantages include: business losses cannot be claimed by owners; investment income subject to high tax rates until paid out [see 123.3, 123.4, 129]; associated corporations [125(3), and 256(2.1) if the family has another corp]; extreme complexity in complying with the rules enacted in 2016 [see next para.]; payroll taxes on owner salaries (e.g., Ontario Employer Health Tax); loss of ITAR 23(3) reserve; the costs of incorporating and maintaining the corporation and filing its returns (with no current savings if all business profits are needed personally); and shareholder benefit traps [15(1), 15(2)]. See also Purse & Taylor, "The Decision to Incorporate", 8(4) *Taxes and Wealth Management* (Carswell) 4-8 (Nov. 2015).

2016 anti-avoidance changes: For taxation years beginning after March 21, 2016, the very complex 2016 amendments target structures used to multiply the SBD. Pre-existing 125(1)(a)(ii) and 125(7)"specified partnership income" already limited a corporate partner to its *pro rata* share of a notional $500,000 business limit determined at the partnership level, but this was widely circumvented, typically by having a CCPC provide a partner's services to the partnership. (The CRA approved this: see the many rulings cited in Notes to 125(7)"personal services business".) 125(7)"designated member" and "specified partnership income" now deem a CCPC to be a partner in many cases, and treat the CCPC's ABI from the partnership as being partnership ABI. Claiming the SBD on any income earned by a partner or a designated partner from the partnership (either via 96(1) or from providing service/property to the partnership) is allowed to the extent of a *pro rata* share of the "specified partnership business limit" [125(7)] of $500,000, which may be assigned by a partner to a non-arm's length designated partner [125(8)].

The amendments also apply if CCPC Xco earns ABI from providing services or property to private corp Yco (this can include a co-op, a credit union or a subsidiary of a foreign public corp) in which Xco or its shareholders have *any* interest. See 125(1)(a)(i)(B), 125(1)(a)(ii.1) and 125(7)"specified corporate income". 125(10) provides an exception for most transactions between associated corps. Under 125(3.1)-(3.2), Yco (if it is a CCPC) can assign all or part of its unused business limit to Xco (subject to CRA override: 125(7)"specified corporate income"(b)).

Relief from these rules for sales of farming/fishing products is in 125(7)"specified farming and fishing income", which is excluded from "specified corporate income".

For discussion of the new rules, see: tinyurl.com/sbd-moodys (includes flowcharts); CBA/CPA Canada Joint Committee letter to Finance, Aug. 25, 2016, suggesting numerous changes (largely ignored, other than the 125(10) exception); Keung, "New Small Business Deduction Rules", 2016 Cdn Tax Foundation conference report, 27:1-26, "New Rules Regarding the Small Business Deduction" 2017 STEP Canada conference (61 detailed slides, contact memberservices@step.ca), and "Anti-Intermediary Rules in Section 125", 25(2) *Canadian Tax Highlights* (ctf.ca) 9-10 (Feb. 2017); Joint Committee letter to Finance, June 2, 2017 enclosing Feb. 14/17 letter to CRA (numerous examples of problems with the rules, plus flowcharts showing how they operate); Harris, "Recent Amendments to the Small Business Deduction", 2017 Prairie Provinces Tax Conference (ctf.ca); Purse & Hansen, "A Review of the Specified Corporate Income and Specified Partnership Income Rules", 2018 Prairie Provinces Tax Conf.; Brown & Kind, "Family Trusts and the Small Business Deduction", IX(2) *Personal Tax & Estate Planning* (Federated Press) 2-9 (2020). For CRA interpretation see VIEWS doc 2016-0679721E5 (income is specified corporate income and reduces SBD).

Some commentators are of the view that the 2016 amendments made s. 125 so complex and unmanageable that the government should simply repeal the small business deduction entirely and reduce the general corporate tax rate. See Lauchlin MacEachern, "The Small Business Deduction: Is Its Complexity Justified?", 17(3) *Tax for the Owner-Manager* (ctf.ca) 2-3 (July 2017).

Professionals such as lawyers, accountants, physicians, dentists, engineers and architects are allowed by provincial licensing bodies to incorporate to access the SBD. Pre-2016 articles on this subject (see these Notes up to the 56th ed.) are obsolete, due to the 2016 amendments to s. 125 and the 2018 amendments to 120.4 (TOSI). See now Kietaibl & Arnold, *Taxation of Private Corporations and their Shareholders* (ctf.ca, 5th ed., 2020), chap. 5; Professional Corporation Checklist (*Taxnet Pro* Tax & Estate Planning Centre, 2020, 7pp); Ideias, "Professional Corporations: What a Tax Planner Needs to Know", *ibid.* (2021, 8pp).

Income ineligible for the SBD is subject to 15% federal tax plus provincial tax (see Notes to 123.4(2)), plus 10.67% under 123.3. Part of this tax is then refunded to the corporation on payment of sufficient dividends from NERDTOH (129(4)"non-eligible refundable dividend tax on hand"(a)(i)A): see Notes to 129(1).

Provincial tax: Each province has a parallel SBD to reduce provincial corporate tax to about 2-4% (even 0% in some cases). See Table C-6 at beginning of book.

US citizens should be cautious of using a private corporation. See Notes to 128.1(1); Bickley, "Pitfalls for US Citizens in Canadian Tax-Planning Structures", 2(4) *Canadian Tax Focus* (ctf.ca) 10 (Nov. 2012); Bandoblu, "US-Owned Professional Corps", 21(4) *CTH* 4 (April 2013); but *contra* see Brown, "US-Owned Professional Corps Revisited", 22(3) 7-8 (March 2014).

Corps with exempt income (e.g. under 81(1), *Indian Act* or a tax treaty) cannot have the portion of income that is taxable reduced by the exempt income's SBD: 125(1)(b)(iii).

Planning: Corporations formerly "bonused out" profits to owner-managers to get income down to the SBD threshold. CRA generally allows this: see Notes to 67 (including on the best salary-dividend mix). There is now less need for this due to the reduced general corporate tax rate (Notes to 123.4(2)); see LeBreux & Moody, "CCPC Bonus Down and Out?" 13(12) *CTH* 5-6 (Dec. 2005); Bernstein, "Owner-Manager Remuneration", 16(3) *CTH* 6 (March 2008); Louis & Goldberg, "Corporate Deferral Strategies", 172 *The Estate Planner* (CCH) 1-4 (May 2009); Carson & Lim, "Corporate Rate Update", 18(6) *CTH* 6-7 (June 2010); Amirault & Baxter, "Professional Groups + Small Business Deduction Opportunities", 2017 Atlantic Provinces Tax Conf. (ctf.ca).

A corporation can elect not to be a CCPC for purposes of 125(1), which can increase the dividend tax credit: see Notes to 89(11). Also, since 125(1) begins "There *may* be deducted", a CCPC can choose not to claim the deduction so as to maximize GRIP (89(1)"general rate income pool"): VIEWS doc 2016-0648481E5.

125(1)(a)(i) amended and (ii.1) added (and other amendments made to s. 125) by 2016 budget bill #2, effective for

(a) taxation years that begin after March 21, 2016; and

(b) person X's taxation year that begins before March 22, 2016 and ends after March 21, 2016 if

(i) X would be entitled to make an assignment to a corporation under 125(3.2) or (8) if amended s. 125 applied to that year,

(ii) the taxation year of the corporation referred to in (i) above begins after March 21, 2016,

(iii) X makes such an assignment for that year and the assignment is to the corporation for its taxation year that begins after March 21, 2016, and

(iv) X files with the Minister the prescribed form required by 125(3.2) in its return of income for that year, by the later of X's "filing-due date" (see 248(1)) and Feb. 13, 2017 (i.e., 60 days after Royal Assent).

Before the amendments, read 125(1)(a)(i) as:

(i) the total of all amounts each of which is the income of the corporation for the year from an active business carried on in Canada (other than the income of the corporation for the year from a business carried on by it as a member of a partnership), and

125(1)(b)(i) amended to change "10/3" to "100/28" by 2002-2013 technical bill (Part 5 — technical), for taxation years that end after Oct. 31, 2011, and prorated by the number of days in the taxation year up to and after that date.

125(1) earlier amended by 2002-2013 technical bill (Part 5 — technical) (for 2003 and later taxation years), 2006 budget bill #2 (for 2008 and later taxation years), 2000 Budget, 1995-97 technical bill, 1995 Budget and 1992 technical bill.

Interpretation Bulletins: IT-73R6: The small business deduction; IT-189R2: Corporations used by practising members of professions; IT-243R4: Dividend refund to private corporations; IT-362R: Patronage dividends; IT-458R2: Canadian-controlled private corporation.

Information Circulars: 88-2, para. 11: General anti-avoidance rule — section 245 of the *Income Tax Act*.

I.T. Technical News: 16 (Parthenon Investments case).

Forms: T2 Sched. 7: Aggregate investment income and active business income; T2 Sched. 341: Nova Scotia corporate tax reduction for new small businesses; T700: Saskatchewan new small business corporate tax reduction; T701: Nova Scotia corporate tax reduction for new small businesses; T708: Prince Edward Island small business deduction; T745: Newfoundland new small business deduction; T1001: Northwest Territories small business deduction; T1258: New Brunswick small business investor tax credit.

(1.1) Small business deduction rate — For the purpose of subsection (1), a corporation's small business deduction rate for a taxation year is the total of

(a) that proportion of 17.5% that the number of days in the taxation year that are before 2018 is of the number of days in the taxation year,

(b) that proportion of 18% that the number of days in the taxation year that are in 2018 is of the number of days in the taxation year, and

(c) that proportion of 19% that the number of days in the taxation year that are after 2018 is of the number of days in the taxation year.

(d), (e) [Repealed]

Related Provisions: 137(3) — Deduction rate applies to credit union; 137.1(9) — Application of rate to deposit insurance corporation.

Notes: The percentage reduction shown is deducted from 28% (38% under 123(1) minus 10% under 124(1)), so the small business federal corporate tax rate is 9% since 2019 (10% for calendar 2018; 10.5% for 2016-17; 11% 2008-2015; 12% for 2007).

The reduction for each year is prorated to the number of days in the calendar year that are in the corporation's tax year. For example, a corp with a June 30 year-end has a blended deduction (from 28%) for 2018-2019 of about 18.5% (not exactly since there are 184 days in July-December and 181 in January-June).

125(1.1) amended by 2018 budget bill #1, for 2018 and later tax years. Before the amendment, the 17.5% deduction (10.5% small business rate) applied to all days after 2015. The reduction in the rate from 10.5% to 10% (2018) and 9% (2019+) was announced Oct. 16, 2017, after complaints about the July 18, 2017 proposals (see Notes to 120.4). Note however that for dividends paid after 2017 on pre-2018 active business income, the increase in the gross-up and dividend tax credit (82(1)(b)(i), 121(a)) means the total tax rate paid by corp (before 2018) + individual (after 2017) is *higher* than if the small business rate had not been reduced.

125(1.1)(b)-(e) replaced with (b) by 2016 budget bill #1, for 2016 and later tax years, to maintain the small business deduction at 17.5% rather than increasing it to 19% over 2017-19 as had been planned. Before the amendment, the 17.5% rate would have applied to days in 2016, 18% to days in 2017, 18.5% in 2018 and 19% starting 2019.

125(1.1) amended by 2015 Budget bill, for 2016 and later tax years. Before the amendment, the rate was 17% for all days after 2007. Earlier amended by 2007 Economic Statement; added by 2006 budget bill #2.

Former 125(1.1), repealed in 1984, provided a reduced small business deduction for CCPCs carrying on a "non-qualifying business" (e.g., certain professionals). Such corps now get the regular deduction.

(2) Business limit — For the purpose of this section, a corporation's business limit for a taxation year is $500,000 unless the corporation is associated in the taxation year with one or more other Canadian-controlled private corporations, in which case, except as otherwise provided in this section, its business limit is nil.

Related Provisions: 125(3)-(5) — Business limit to be shared among associated corporations; 125(3.1), (3.2) — Reduction where business limit assigned to another corp; 125(5.1) — Elimination of small business deduction for large corps; 248(1)"business limit" — Definition applies to entire Act.

Notes: The business limit was $200,000 from 1982-2002, then gradually increased, and has been $500,000 since 2009.

Most provinces have a $500,000 threshold for provincial corporate tax; see Table C-7 or tinyurl.com/provcorp-cra. Sask. is $600,000.

125(2) amended by 2009 budget bill #1 (for 2009 and later taxation years), 2006 budget bill #2, 2004 and 2003 Budgets to change the limit as per the table above.

Interpretation Bulletins: IT-73R6: The small business deduction.

Information Circulars: 88-2, para. 18: General anti-avoidance rule — section 245 of the *Income Tax Act*.

(3) Associated corporations — Notwithstanding subsection (2), if all the Canadian-controlled private corporations that are associated with each other in a taxation year file with the Minister in prescribed form an agreement that assigns for the purpose of this section a percentage to one or more of them for the year, the business limit for the year of each of the corporations is

(a) if the total of the percentages assigned in the agreement does not exceed 100%, $500,000 multiplied by the percentage assigned to that corporation in the agreement; and

(b) in any other case, nil.

Related Provisions: 125(3.1), (3.2) — Reduction where business limit assigned to another corp; 125(4) — Failure to file agreement; 125(5) — Special rules for business limit; 256(1) — Associated corporations.

Notes: *Deneschuk Building Supplies*, [1996] 3 C.T.C. 2039 (TCC), ruled that the agreement under 125(3) can be filed at any time, where no notice was issued by the Minister under 125(4). CRA now accepts amended allocations: VIEWS doc 2009-0351721E5; Chiu & Dolson, "Business Limit Allocation Do-Overs", 11(3) *Tax for the Owner-Manager* (ctf.ca) 5-6 (July 2011).

The reference to "year" in 125(3) is to the taxation year: VIEWS doc 2004-0091711E5.

See table in Notes to 125(2); the dollar amount shown in 125(3) is prorated based on the calendar year.

See also Roy et al., *Taxation of Private Corporations and their Shareholders* (ctf.ca, 5th ed., 2020), chap. 5.

125(3)(a) amended by 2009 budget bill #1 (for 2009 and later taxation years), 2006 budget bill #2 and 2003 Budget.

Interpretation Bulletins: IT-73R6: The small business deduction.

Forms: T2 Sched. 23: Agreement among associated Canadian-controlled private corporations to allocate the business limit; T2 Sched. 49: Agreement among associated Canadian-controlled private corporations to allocate the expenditure limit.

(3.1) Reduction — business limit — The business limit for the year of a corporation under subsection (2), (3) or (4) is reduced by the total of all amounts each of which is the portion, if any, of the business limit that the corporation assigns to another corporation under subsection (3.2).

Notes: 125(3.1) added by 2016 budget bill #2, effective on the same basis as the amendments to 125(1) (years that begin or end after March 21, 2016).

(3.2) Assignment [of business limit] — For the purpose of this section, a Canadian-controlled private corporation (in this subsection referred to as the "first corporation") may assign all or any portion of its business limit under subsection (2), (3) or (4) for a taxation year of the first corporation to another Canadian-controlled private corporation (in this subsection referred to as the "second corporation") for a taxation year of the second corporation if

(a) the second corporation has an amount of income, for its taxation year, referred to in subparagraph (a)(i) of the definition "specified corporate income" in subsection (7) from the provision of services or property directly to the first corporation;

(b) the first corporation's taxation year ends in the second corporation's taxation year;

(c) the amount assigned does not exceed the amount determined by the formula

$$A - B$$

where

A is the amount of income referred to in paragraph (a), and

B is the portion of the amount described in A that is deductible by the first corporation in respect of the amount of income referred to in clause (1)(a)(i)(A) or (B) for the year; and

(d) a prescribed form is filed with the Minister by

(i) the first corporation in its return of income for its taxation year, and

(ii) the second corporation in its return of income for its taxation year.

Related Provisions: 125(3.1) — Reduction in business limit to extent assigned; 249(2)(a) — Reference to a year ending in another year; 257 — Formula cannot calculate to less than zero.

Notes: See Notes to 125(1), under "The amendments also apply". The reference in 125(3.2)(b) to "ends in the second corporation's taxation year" includes years that end at the same time: 249(2)(a).

The prescribed form for 125(3.2)(d) is T2 Schedule 7, Part 6. (For a corp filing a Quebec return, it must be copied to Revenu Québec: *Taxation Act* ss. 771.2.1.6.1, 21.4.6.) CRA generally accepts an amended assignment, provided there is no change to any statute-barred year: VIEWS doc 2017-072858117 (earlier, see 2017-0713051E5).

For more CRA interpretation see 2016-0651831E5 (125(3.2) applies, but problem identified there was later fixed with 125(10)); 2017-0709241E5 (business limit that can be assigned is after applying 125(5.1)).

See also Lorenzo Bonnano & Guy Buckley, "Business Limit Assignment", 26(10) *Canadian Tax Highlights* (ctf.ca) 10-12 (Oct. 2018).

125(3.2) added by 2016 budget bill #2, effective on the same basis as the amendments to 125(1) (years that begin or end after March 21, 2016).

(4) Failure to file agreement — If any of the Canadian-controlled private corporations that are associated with each other in a taxation year has failed to file with the Minister an agreement as contemplated by subsection (3) within 30 days after notice in writing by the Minister has been forwarded to any of them that such an agreement is required for the purpose of any assessment of tax under this Part, the Minister shall, for the purpose of this section, allocate an amount to one or more of them for the taxation year. The total amount so allocated must equal the least of the amounts that would, if none of the corporations were associated with any other corporation during the year and if this Act were read without reference to subsections (5) and (5.1), be the business limits of the corporations for the year.

Related Provisions: 256(1) — Associated corporations; *Interpretation Act* 27(5) — Meaning of "within 30 days".

Notes: 125(4) amended by 2003 Budget, for 2003 and later tax years, to reflect the increase in the business limit from $200,000 to $300,000.

Interpretation Bulletins: IT-73R6: The small business deduction.

(5) Special rules for business limit — Notwithstanding subsections (2), (3) and (4),

(a) where a Canadian-controlled private corporation (in this paragraph referred to as the "first corporation") has more than one taxation year ending in the same calendar year and it is associated in 2 or more of those taxation years with another Canadian-controlled private corporation that has a taxation year ending in that calendar year, the business limit of the first corporation for each taxation year ending in the calendar year in which it is associated with the other corporation that ends after the first such taxation year ending in that calendar year is, subject to the application of paragraph (b), an amount equal to the lesser of

(i) its business limit determined under subsection (3) or (4) for the first such taxation year ending in the calendar year, and

(ii) its business limit determined under subsection (3) or (4) for the particular taxation year ending in the calendar year; and

(b) where a Canadian-controlled private corporation has a taxation year that is less than 51 weeks, its business limit for the year is that proportion of its business limit for the year determined without reference to this paragraph that the number of days in the year is of 365.

Notes: 125(5)(a) applies when a corporation with two taxation years ending in the same calendar year (such as due to a 249(4) change in control) is associated with the same corporation in both of those years: VIEWS doc 2002-0157415. See also 2009-0306401E5.

125(5) opening words amended by 2016 budget bill #2, effective on the same basis as the amendments to 125(1) (years that begin or end after March 21, 2016), to change "subsections (2) to (4)" to "subsections (2), (3) and (4)" (so as not to override new 125(3.1)-(3.2)).

2009 budget bill #1 s. 39(3) provides in effect that, in applying 125(5) to a corporation for a year that crossed over Jan. 1/09, the prorated figure from 125(3) is used for 125(5)(a)(i). The 2006 Budget bill provided the same rule for a year that crossed over Jan. 1/07.

Opening words of 125(5) changed from "Notwithstanding any other provision of this section" to "Notwithstanding subsections (2) to (4)" by 1994 Budget, effective for taxation years that end after June 1994. 125(5) is now subject to 125(5.1).

125(5)(a) amended by 1992 technical bill, for tax years that end after Dec. 20, 1991, to prevent a group of corporations that has more than one tax year ending in a calendar year from allocating extra business limit to a corporation that becomes a new member of the group in a second tax year ending in the same calendar year.

Interpretation Bulletins: IT-73R6: The small business deduction.

(5.1) Business limit reduction — Notwithstanding subsections (2), (3), (4) and (5), a Canadian-controlled private corporation's business limit for a particular taxation year ending in a calendar year is the amount, if any, by which its business limit otherwise determined for the particular taxation year exceeds the greater of

(a) the amount determined by the formula

$$A \times B / \$11,250$$

where

A is the amount that would, but for this subsection, be the corporation's business limit for the particular taxation year, and

B is the amount determined by the formula

$$0.225\% \times (C - \$10 \text{ million})$$

where

C is

(i) if, in both the particular taxation year and the preceding taxation year, the corporation is not associated with any corporation, the taxable capital employed in

Canada (within the meaning assigned by subsection 181.2(1) or 181.3(1) or section 181.4, as the case may be) of the corporation for the preceding taxation year,

(ii) if, in the particular taxation year, the corporation is not associated with any corporation but was associated with one or more corporations in the preceding taxation year, the taxable capital employed in Canada (within the meaning assigned by subsection 181.2(1) or 181.3(1) or section 181.4, as the case may be) of the corporation for the particular taxation year, or

(iii) if, in the particular taxation year, the corporation is associated with one or more particular corporations, the total of all amounts each of which is the taxable capital employed in Canada (within the meaning assigned by subsection 181.2(1) or 181.3(1) or section 181.4, as the case may be) of the corporation or of any of the particular corporations for its last taxation year that ended in the preceding calendar year, and

(b) the amount determined by the formula

$$D/\$500,000 \times 5(E - \$50,000)$$

where

D is the amount determined for A in paragraph (a), and

E is the total of all amounts each of which is the adjusted aggregate investment income of the corporation, or of any corporation with which it is associated at any time in the particular taxation year, for each taxation year of the corporation, or associated corporation, as the case may be, that ended in the preceding calendar year.

Related Provisions: 87(2)(j.92) — Amalgamation — continuing corporation; 125(5.2) — Anti-avoidance — expanded meaning of "associated"; 127(10.2) — Reduction in SR&ED investment tax credits for large corporations; 181.1(1.2), 181.5(1.1), (4.1) — Application of calculation to large corporations; 257 — Formula amounts cannot calculate to less than zero.

Notes: *125(5.1)(a)* eliminates the small business deduction for large corporations, by reducing the deduction for corps with group "taxable capital

Pre-2016 planning: If corp A exceeded $15m TCEC and associated corp B thus had nil business limit, one could incorporate C, associated with A (e.g. through 256(1)(c)) but not B. Then B and C were associated only through A; and if A elected under 256(2) to be associated with neither, B got its business limit back since it was deemed not associated with A! The 2016 amendment to 256(2) prevents this: now B and C "are deemed not to be associated *with each other*", but each remains associated with A.

For CRA interpretations and calculations under the formula, see docs 2005-0153791E5, 2005-0161611I7, 2008-0285371C6; 2011-0401731E5 (application to partly-exempt farm mutual insurance corp); 2011-0424631E5; 2012-0468831E5 (associated corporation that is exempt NPO is counted in measuring TCEC).

125(5.1)(b) grinds down the business limit by $5 for every $1 of passive income the corp (and associated corps: see extended meaning of "associated" in 125(5.2)) has over $50,000. If the corp otherwise has a $500,000 limit, it disappears at $150,000 of passive income, so there is no 125(1) deduction and all business income is taxed at the general rate (see 123.4(2) Notes). This rule is targeted at companies that keep money that was taxed at only the small business rate. Note that (net) investment income in one corp is not reduced by an investment loss in an associated corp when calculating 125(7)"adjusted aggregate investment income", so the grind may apply. A 55(2) deemed gain is active income if the share meets 125(7)"active asset"(b): VIEWS doc 2020-0852251C6 [2020 APFF q.13].

This is a major change from the July and Oct. 2017 proposals to tax private corporations' passive income at high rates (see "Abandoned Proposed Amendment" under 123.3). See now Woo & Friedley, *Taxation of Private Corporations and their Shareholders* (ctf.ca, 5th ed., 2020), pp. 9:27-45; Baxter, "The New Passive Income Rules", 2017 Cdn Tax Foundation conference report at 13:15-34.

Shorter articles: Pisesky, "Incentive Effects of the New SBD Clawback", 8(2) *Canadian Tax Focus [CTFo]* (ctf.ca) 1-2 (May 2018); Fowlis & Hogan, "Planning for the New Passive Income Rules", XXIII(2) *Insurance Planning* (Federated Press) 14-19 (2018); Goldberg, "The Passive Investment Rules", 2426 *Tax Topics* (CCH) 1-3 (Sept. 6, 2018); Kakkar & Ghani, "The New Passive Income SBD Grind Rules", 19(1) *Tax for the Owner-Manager [TfOM]* (ctf.ca) 1-2 (2019) and 19(2) 4 (April 2019); Lee & Raveendran, "Possible Anomaly in the Passive Income SBD Grind?", 9(4) *CTFo* 1-2 (Nov. 2019) (windup of corp may avoid the grind); Shadrin, Ghani & Harnett, "Corporate Partnership May Avoid the Para. 125(5.1) Grind", 20(4) *TfOM* 4-5 (Oct. 2020); Rau & Dupuis, "Managing Adjusted Aggregate Investment Income", tinyurl.com/manage-aaii.

Ontario announced in its Nov. 2018 Economic Statement that it will *not* copy this measure for purposes of Ont. corporate income tax. NB made the same announcement in its

March 2019 Budget. This provides an incentive for certain corps to shift wages or a permanent establishment to those provinces. See Golombek & Goodis, "Lack of Integration a Win for Some Ontario and New Brunswick Taxpayers", 21(2) *Tax for the Owner-Manager* (ctf.ca) 2-3 (April 2021).

For CRA VIEWS on 125(5.1)(b) see docs 2018-0771871E5 and 2018-0780031C6 [2018 CTF q.16] (transitional application to 2018-21).

125(5.1)(b) added by 2018 budget bill #1, effective on the same basis as 87(2)(aa) amendment (taxation years that begin after 2018, but earlier if planning was used to try to trigger a year-end before 125(5.1)(b) applied).

125(5.1) opening words amended by 2016 budget bill #2, effective on the same basis as the amendments to 125(1) (years that begin or end after March 21, 2016), to change "subsections (2) to (5)" to "subsections (2), (3), (4) and (5)" (so as not to override new 125(3.1)-(3.2)).

125(5.1)B amended by 2002-2013 technical bill, for taxation years that begin after Dec. 20, 2002 (with a different reading for a corp described in 181.1(3) for its taxation years that began before June 26, 2013). 125(5.1) earlier amended by 1995 Budget; added by 1994 Budget.

Interpretation Bulletins: IT-73R6: The small business deduction.

(5.2) Anti-avoidance — A particular corporation and another corporation are deemed to be associated with each other at a particular time for the purposes of paragraph (5.1)(b) if

    (a) the particular corporation lends or transfers property at any time, either directly or indirectly, by means of a trust or by any other means whatever, to the other corporation;

    (b) the other corporation is, at the particular time, related to the particular corporation but is not associated with it; and

    (c) it may reasonably be considered that one of the reasons the loan or transfer was made was to reduce the amount determined for E in paragraph (5.1)(b) in respect of the particular corporation, or of any corporation with which it is associated, for a taxation year.

Notes: See Notes to 125(5.1); Comeau & Antel, "Subsection 125(5.2)", 19(2) *Tax for the Owner-Manager* (ctf.ca) 5-6 (April 2019); Blucher, "Dissociation of Corporations", 16(4) *Tax Hyperion* (Carswell) 1-3 (July-Aug. 2019).

For the meaning of "indirectly" in para. (a), see Notes to 17.1(1).

Note that "one of the reasons" in para. (c) is a broader test than "one of the main reasons" (e.g., 256(2.1)).

Paying annual dividends can trigger 125(5.2): VIEWS doc 2019-0798461C6 [2019 STEP q.16]. CRA declined to say whether transferring active business assets can trigger it: 2020-0839961C6 [2020 STEP q.14].

125(5.2) added by 2018 budget bill #1, effective on the same basis as 87(2)(aa) amendment (tax years that begin after 2018, but earlier if planning was used to try to trigger a year-end before 125(5.1)(b) applied).

(6) Corporate partnerships — Where in a taxation year a corporation is a member of a particular partnership and in the year the corporation or a corporation with which it is associated in the year is a member of one or more other partnerships and it may reasonably be considered that one of the main reasons for the separate existence of the partnerships is to increase the amount of a deduction of any corporation under subsection (1), the specified partnership income of the corporation for the year shall, for the purposes of this section, be computed in respect of those partnerships as if all amounts each of which is the income of one of the partnerships for a fiscal period ending in the year from an active business carried on in Canada were nil except for the greatest of those amounts.

Related Provisions: 125(6.1) — Corporation deemed member of partnership; 125(6.2) — Specified partnership income deemed nil.

Notes: For the meaning of "one of the main reasons" see Notes to 83(2.1).

(6.1) Corporation deemed member of partnership — For the purposes of this section, a corporation that is a member, or is deemed by this subsection to be a member, of a partnership that is a member of another partnership shall be deemed to be a member of the other partnership and the corporation's share of the income of the other partnership for a fiscal period shall be deemed to be equal to the amount of that income to which the corporation was directly or indirectly entitled.

(6.2) Specified partnership income deemed nil — Notwithstanding any other provision of this section, where a corporation is a member of a partnership that was controlled, directly or indirectly

in any manner whatever, by one or more non-resident persons, by one or more public corporations (other than a prescribed venture capital corporation) or by any combination thereof at any time in its fiscal period ending in a taxation year of the corporation, the income of the partnership for that fiscal period from an active business carried on in Canada shall, for the purposes of computing the specified partnership income of a corporation for the year, be deemed to be nil.

Related Provisions: 125(6.3) — Partnership deemed to be controlled; 256(5.1), (6.2) — Controlled directly or indirectly.

Regulations: 6700 (prescribed venture capital corporation).

(6.3) Partnership deemed to be controlled — For the purposes of subsection (6.2), a partnership shall be deemed to be controlled by one or more persons at any time if the total of the shares of that person or those persons of the income of the partnership from any source for the fiscal period of the partnership that includes that time exceeds $^{1}/_{2}$ of the income of the partnership from that source for that period.

(7) Definitions — In this section,

"active asset", of a particular corporation at any time, means property that is

    (a) used at that time principally in an active business carried on primarily in Canada by the particular corporation or by a Canadian-controlled private corporation that is related to the particular corporation,

    (b) a share of the capital stock of another corporation if, at that time,

        (i) the other corporation is connected with the particular corporation (within the meaning assigned by subsection 186(4) on the assumption that the other corporation is at that time a payer corporation within the meaning of that subsection), and

        (ii) the share would be a "qualified small business corporation share" (as defined in subsection 110.6(1)) if

            (A) the references in that definition to an "individual" were references to the particular corporation, and

            (B) that definition were read without reference to "the individual's spouse or common-law partner", or

    (c) an interest in a partnership, if

        (i) at that time, the fair market value of the particular corporation's interest in the partnership is equal to or greater than 10% of the total fair market value of all interests in the partnership,

        (ii) throughout the 24-month period ending before that time, more than 50% of the fair market value of the property of the partnership was attributable to property described in this paragraph or in paragraph (a) or (b), and

        (iii) at that time, all or substantially all of the fair market value of the property of the partnership was attributable to property described in this paragraph or in paragraph (a) or (b);

Notes: See 125(5.1) Notes. This term is used in 125(7)"adjusted aggregate investment income". The 10% investment threshold in (b)(i) and (c)(i) allows venture capital and "angel" investors to invest without penalty.

"Active asset" added by 2018 budget bill #1, effective on the same basis as 87(2)(aa) amendment (taxation years that begin after 2018, but earlier if planning was used to try to trigger a year-end before 125(5.1)(b) applied).

"active business carried on by a corporation" means any business carried on by the corporation other than a specified investment business or a personal services business and includes an adventure or concern in the nature of trade;

Related Provisions: 129(6) — Investment income from associated corporation deemed to be active business income; 248(1) — Definition of "active business" for purposes other than s. 125.

Notes: This rule was introduced to counter cases such as *Rockmore Investments*, [1976] C.T.C. 291 (FCA) and *Supreme Theatres*, [1981] C.T.C. 190 (FCTD).

The business carried on need not actually be "active": *Ollenberger*, 2013 FCA 74. (See Notes to 248(1)"eligible relocation", under "New work location".)

See also Notes to 248(1)"active business", 125(7)"income of the corporation..." and 125(7)"specified investment business".

125(7)"active business" was 125(7)(a) before RSC 1985 (5th Supp) consolidation for tax years ending after Nov. 1991.

Interpretation Bulletins: IT-73R6: The small business deduction; IT-243R4: Dividend refund to private corporations.

"adjusted aggregate investment income", of a corporation (other than a corporation that is deemed not to be a private corporation by subsection 136(1) or 137(7) or section 141.1) for a taxation year, means the amount that would be the "aggregate investment income" (as defined in subsection 129(4)) of the corporation for the year, if

(a) paragraph (a) of that definition read as follows:

(a) the amount, if any, by which

(i) the eligible portion of the corporation's taxable capital gains (other than taxable capital gains from the disposition of property that is, at the time of disposition, an active asset of the corporation) for the year

exceeds

(ii) the eligible portion of its allowable capital losses (other than allowable capital losses from the disposition of property that is, at the time of disposition, an active asset of the corporation) for the year, or

(b) subparagraph (b)(iii) of that definition read as follows:

(iii) a dividend from a corporation connected with it (within the meaning assigned by subsection 186(4) on the assumption that the corporation is at that time a payer corporation within the meaning of that subsection), and

(c) paragraph (a) of the definition "income" or "loss" in subsection 129(4) read as follows:

(a) includes

(i) the income or loss from a specified investment business carried on by it, and

(ii) amounts in respect of a life insurance policy that are included in computing the corporation's income for the year, to the extent that the amounts would not otherwise be included in the computation of the corporation's aggregate investment income, but

and

(d) no amount were deducted under subsection 91(4) by the corporation in computing its income for the year;

Notes: See 125(5.1) Notes. Definition added by 2018 budget bill #1, effective on the same basis as 87(2)(aa) amendment (tax years that begin after 2018, but earlier if planning aimed to trigger a year-end before 125(5.1)(b) applied).

"Canadian-controlled private corporation" means a private corporation that is a Canadian corporation other than

(a) a corporation controlled, directly or indirectly in any manner whatever, by one or more non-resident persons, by one or more public corporations (other than a prescribed venture capital corporation), by one or more corporations described in paragraph (c), or by any combination of them,

(b) a corporation that would, if each share of the capital stock of a corporation that is owned by a non-resident person, by a public corporation (other than a prescribed venture capital corporation), or by a corporation described in paragraph (c) were owned by a particular person, be controlled by the particular person,

(c) a corporation a class of the shares of the capital stock of which is listed on a designated stock exchange, or

(d) in applying subsection (1), paragraphs 87(2)(vv) and (ww) (including, for greater certainty, in applying those paragraphs as provided under paragraph 88(1)(e.2)), the definitions "excessive eligible dividend designation", "general rate income pool" and "low rate income pool" in subsection 89(1) and subsections 89(4) to (6), (8) to (10) and 249(3.1), a corporation that has

made an election under subsection 89(11) and that has not revoked the election under subsection 89(12);

Related Provisions: 89(4) — GRIP addition on becoming CCPC; 89(8) — LRIP addition on ceasing to be CCPC; 89(11) — Election not to be CCPC for purposes of para. (d); 123.3 — Refundable tax on CCPC's investment income; 125(1) — Small business deduction for CCPC; 136 — Co-operative corporation may be private corporation for purposes of s. 125; 137(7) — Credit union may be private corporation for purposes of s. 125; 248(1)"Canadian-controlled private corporation" — Definition applies to entire Act; 249(3.1) — Deemed year-end on becoming or ceasing to be CCPC; 251(5) — Control by related groups, options, etc.; 256(5.1), (6.2) — Controlled directly or indirectly.

Notes: Generally a corp wants to be a CCPC to benefit from the small business deduction (125(1)), higher and refundable SR&ED credits (127(10.1), 127.1(1)"qualifying corporation"), capital gains deduction on its shares (110.6(2.1)), deferral of stock option benefits (7(1.1)), small business share rollover (44.1(1)"eligible small business corporation"), ABIL on shares or debt (39(1)(c)(iv)), shorter reassessment period (152(3.1)(b)) and later payment (248(1)"balance-due day"(d)(i)(B)). A downside is that investment income is subject to higher tax until it is paid out as dividends (123.3 and see Table C-6 at beginning of book).

The definition of a CCPC does not require Canadian control, but the *lack* of control by non-residents and/or public companies. 50% private Canadian resident voting power is normally sufficient. However, "directly or indirectly in any manner whatever" in para. (a) applies the 256(5.1) *de facto* control test. (Either test can apply to deny CCPC status: *Lyrtech RD*, 2014 FCA 267, para. 38 (leave to appeal denied 2015 CarswellNat 2528 (SCC)).) See Notes to 256(5.1) for cases finding *de facto* control. In *Ekamant Canada*, 2009 TCC 408, 75% ownership by three US-resident members of the same family meant the company was not a CCPC even though the Canadian shareholder had a 251(5)(b) right to purchase their shares. CRA applied para. (a) in VIEWS docs 2008-0279441I7, 2010-0366611I7. 94(3)(a)'s deeming a non-resident trust to be resident in Canada for certain purposes does not apply for determining CCPC status: 2016-0644911C6 [2016 STEP q.7].

Para. (b) provides that ownership of more than 50% of the voting shares by non-residents is sufficient to prevent a corporation from being a CCPC. This overrides *Silicon Graphics*, 2002 FCA 260, where dispersed ownership by non-residents was held not to be "control". However, the *Silicon Graphics* principle still applies elsewhere in the Act; *Income Tax Technical News* No. 25 (but 95(1)"controlled foreign affiliate"(c) will override it for that definition). A share option is deemed to be ownership under 251(5)(b)(i) for purposes of para. (b): *Sedona Networks*, 2007 FCA 169, but CRA considers this comment to be *obiter* and non-binding: *Income Tax Technical News* 38; 2007 Cdn Tax Foundation conference report at 4:6-7. See also Brender, "Developments in the Concept of Corporate Control", 2007 conference report at 31:15-29, 39-49. Para. (b) does not say "directly or indirectly in any manner whatever", so 256(5.1) does not apply to it and there must be *de jure* control (see Notes to 111(5)). See also VIEWS docs 2007-0253591I7, 2008-0265901I7, 2008-0265902I7, 2010-0379351I7, 2010-0388101E5; 2011-0426411C6 [2011 CTF conf report q.7, p.4:5] (despite *Sedona*, CRA applies 251(5)(b) on a "holder by holder" basis).

In applying para. (b), a unanimous shareholders' agreement (UShA) ensuring Canadian residents can elect a majority of the directors took priority over the fact that non-residents plus public-corporations had more than 50% of the share votes: *Price Waterhouse [Bioartifical Gel, Bagtech]*, 2013 FCA 164; thus, the corp was a CCPC. This overrules former CRA policy [*Income Tax Technical News* 44; 2009 CTF Conf. p. 3:13-15, q.14], and CRA accepts this result: VIEWS doc 2014-0523301C6 [2014 CALU q.3]. (A sole shareholder's declaration can be equivalent to a UShA: e.g. *Canada Business Corporations Act* s. 146(2), Ontario *BCA* s. 108(3).) In *Ekamant* (above), documents signed by the US shareholders did not constitute a UShA taking away the directors' powers. See also Notes to 111(5) for CRA docs on UShAs.

See also Notes to 251(5).

Parthenon Investments, [1997] 3 C.T.C. 152 (FCA) held that "control" means only ultimate control, on the theory that "control cannot allow for two masters simultaneously". Thus, on a chain of corporations with Canadian control at the top and a US corp in the middle, the lowest tier was not "controlled" by a non-resident. 256(6.1) and (6.2) have reversed this rule since 1999, and provide that the top and middle levels have simultaneous control. In *Perfect Fry*, 2008 FCA 218, the *Parthenon* principle (pre-256(6.1)) applied to PF, which was controlled by a public company which in turn was controlled by a group of Canadian residents, so PF was a CCPC.

In *Kaleidescape v. Computershare*, 2014 ONSC 4983, a trust deed was rectified so that a company not be controlled by non-residents and remain a CCPC. (See Notes to 169(1) re rectification; due to *Fairmont Hotels* this would no longer be granted.)

See Notes to 89(11) re the election for para. (d).

Where a corporation wishes *not* to be a CCPC because it earns investment income, see Notes to 123.3.

See also Foreman, "Selected Tax Aspects Related to CCPCs", 2006 BC Tax Conference (ctf.ca), 19:1-31; Keey, "CCPC Status: An Update", *General Corporate Tax* newsletter (*Taxnet Pro* Corporate Tax Centre), Nov. 2010, pp. 1-21; Keey, *Checklist 11 — Corporate Status*, *Taxnet Pro* Corporate Tax Centre (2020, 17pp). For software that assists in the determination see *CCPC Status Navigator* at bluejlegal.com.

Para. (c) amended by 2007 budget bill #2, effective Dec. 14, 2007.

Para. (d) added by 2006 budget bill #2, for 2006 and later taxation years.

Definition earlier amended by 2000 Budget (for tax years that begin after 1999), 1995-97 technical bill. 125(7)"Canadian-controlled private corporation" was 125(7)(b) before RSC 1985 (5th Supp) consolidation for tax years ending after Nov. 1991.

Regulations: 6700 (prescribed venture capital corporation).

Income Tax Folios: S4-F8-C1: Business investment losses [replaces IT-484R2].

Interpretation Bulletins: IT-73R6: The small business deduction; IT-113R4: Benefits to employees — stock options; IT-243R4: Dividend refund to private corporations; IT-458R2: Canadian-controlled private corporation.

I.T. Technical News: 3 (Canadian-controlled private corporation); 16 (*Parthenon Investments* case); 25 (*Silicon Graphics* case and para. (b)); 38 (CCPC determination — impact of the *Sedona* decision); 44 (unanimous shareholder agreements and the CCPC definition).

"designated member", of a particular partnership in a taxation year, means a Canadian-controlled private corporation that provides (directly or indirectly, in any manner whatever) services or property to the particular partnership at any time in the corporation's taxation year where, at any time in the year,

(a) the corporation is not a member of the particular partnership, and

(b) either

(i) one of its shareholders holds a direct or indirect interest in the particular partnership, or

(ii) if subparagraph (i) does not apply,

(A) the corporation does not deal at arm's length with a person that holds a direct or indirect interest in the particular partnership, and

(B) it is not the case that all or substantially all of the corporation's income for the year from an active business is from providing services or property to

(I) persons with which the corporation deals at arm's length, or

(II) partnerships (other than the particular partnership) with which the corporation deals at arm's length, other than a partnership in which a person that does not deal at arm's length with the corporation holds a direct or indirect interest;

Notes: See Notes to 125(1); Michelle Chang, "Designated Member Draft Rule for SBD", 24(7) *Canadian Tax Highlights* (ctf.ca) 11-12 (July 2016).

For the meaning of "indirectly" in opening words, see Notes to 17.1(1). The CRA interprets "substantially all", used in (b)(ii)(B), as meaning 90% or more.

Definition added by 2016 budget bill #2, effective on the same basis as the amendments to 125(1) (years that begin or end after March 21, 2016).

"income of the corporation for the year from an active business" means the total of

(a) the corporation's income for the year from an active business carried on by it including any income for the year pertaining to or incident to that business, other than income for the year from a source in Canada that is a property (within the meaning assigned by subsection 129(4)), and

(b) the amount, if any, included under subsection 12(10.2) in computing the corporation's income for the year;

Related Provisions: 125(1)(a)(ii.1), 125(7)"specified corporate income" — Limitation where property or services provided to private corp with any cross-ownership; 129(6) — Investment income from associated corporation deemed to be active business income.

Notes: See Notes to 125(1) re limitations on active business income starting 2016.

Interest on overpaid income taxes relating to a business may be considered income from the business: see Notes to 12(1)(c). IT-73R6 para. 9 accepts certain items after cessation of business as qualifying, e.g. bad debt recoveries, sale of inventory, recapture and similar items; VIEWS doc 2011-0423071E5 accepts an SR&ED investment tax credit refund as well. See also Notes to 9(1) under "Business income vs property income", and Notes to 125(7)"active business carried on by a corporation". See also 2008-0280941E5; 2011-0407051E5 and 2014-0540041E5 (whether parking or other rental income is incidental to active business); 2011-0422971E5 (status of income under Ontario's Feed-in Tariff and microFIT programs).

125(7)"income of the corporation..." was 125(7)(c) before RSC 1985 (5th Supp) consolidation for tax years ending after Nov. 1991. Para. (b) (formerly 125(7)(c)(ii)) added by 1992 technical bill, for 1991 and later taxation years.

Interpretation Bulletins: IT-73R6: The small business deduction; IT-243R4: Dividend refund to private corporations.

"personal services business" carried on by a corporation in a taxation year means a business of providing services where

(a) an individual who performs services on behalf of the corporation (in this definition and paragraph 18(1)(p) referred to as an "incorporated employee"), or

(b) any person related to the incorporated employee

is a specified shareholder of the corporation and the incorporated employee would reasonably be regarded as an officer or employee of the person or partnership to whom or to which the services were provided but for the existence of the corporation, unless

(c) the corporation employs in the business throughout the year more than five full-time employees, or

(d) the amount paid or payable to the corporation in the year for the services is received or receivable by it from a corporation with which it was associated in the year;

Related Provisions: 18(1)(p) — Limitation on deductions from personal services business income; 123.4(1)"full rate taxable income"(a)(iii) — PSB income ineligible for 13% general corporate rate reduction; 123.5 — Additional 5% tax on PSB income; 207.6(3) — Retirement compensation arrangement for incorporated employee; 248(1)"personal services business" — Definition applies to entire Act.

Notes: See Notes to 18(1)(p) re the consequences of having a personal services business. See Notes to Reg. 1101(1) re what constitutes a separate "business".

A PSB exists where the relationship between individual A and corporation B's client C would be one of employment if corporation B did not exist (and A or A's family members own 10% or more of B's shares, or may have a right to such shares: 248(1)"specified shareholder"). Note that the question is whether A would be considered an employee of C. It is irrelevant whether A might be considered an employee of D if D is a client of C and A has been working at D (this often happens with computer consultants). This is because the phrase "but for the existence of the corporation" refers *only* to B. C cannot be "but-for"ed out of existence when applying the definition, unless A is a specified shareholder of C; and "the person or partnership to whom or to which the services were provided" refers back to the services in the opening words of the definition, which are the services provided by B, and so "the person" can only be C. (However, see both *758997 Alberta Ltd.*, 2004 TCC 755, and *Carreau*, 2006 TCC 20, where the TCC *did* look at the relationship between A and D. In *Carreau*, the Court stated at para. 12: "We can accordingly assert that it was [B] that provided services to [D] in its capacity as a subcontractor of [C]", but did not address the "but-for" issue.)

The leading PSB case is *Dynamic Industries*, 2005 FCA 211.

In *Criterion Capital*, [2001] 4 C.T.C. 2844 (TCC), a President/CEO of a company was held to be an independent contractor in respect of additional services he provided outside the scope of those positions, and thus his corporation was not carrying on a PSB. The same was the result in *Peter Cedar Products*, 2009 TCC 463, for 3 directors of a company who ceased being employees and whose corps went into business as its sales representatives. However, in *Ivan Cassell Ltd.*, 2016 TCC 53 (FCA appeal discontinued A-107-16), a company's President who provided his services through his corp was carrying on a PSB; his corp did not operate in a businesslike manner and its compensation was like that of an employee. See also discussion of owner-managers, and when they can be contractors to their own company, in Notes to 248(1)"employee".

However, "officer or employee" may be broader than "employee". In *9098-9005 Quebec*, 2012 TCC 324, an individual was held to be carrying on a PSB because, absent his corporation, he would have been an "officer" of a partnership of which he was a member, and of an estate he managed.

Real estate agents in Ontario can incorporate since 2020, but must be "employed" by the brokerage (O.Reg. 536/20, s. 3), so there will likely be a PSB.

Single client: Companies providing services to only one client were held not to be carrying on PSB in *Dynamic Industries* (above) (it *had* had other clients, and was responsible to correct its errors) and *C.J. McCarty Inc.*, 2015 TCC 201 (large project but client did not require exclusivity, and there was risk). *Contra*, there was a PSB in *G & J Muirhead Holdings*, 2014 TCC 49 (all of owner's working hours were spent on daily activity, controlled by payor, that was integral to payor's business).

For more cases finding a PSB, see *533702 Ontario*, [1991] 2 C.T.C. 2102 (TCC) (running plumbing business's showroom); *Tedco Apparel*, [1991] 2 C.T.C. 2669 (TCC) (sales director); *Placements Marcel Lapointe*, [1993] 1 C.T.C. 2506 (TCC) (where corporation's fees were a share of payor's profits, this was not partnership arrangement because losses were not also shared); *Morley Law Corp.*, [2002] 2 C.T.C. 2483 (TCC) (in-house counsel); *W.B. Pletch Co.*, 2005 TCC 400 (owner was former senior executive and continued to provide management services to same company); *1166787 Ontario*, 2008 TCC 93 (FCA appeal dismissed for delay A-101-08) (company's owner managed cruise vacation company); *609309 Alberta*, 2010 TCC 166 (ironworking supervisor); *Gomez Consulting*, 2013 TCC 135 (applications analyst programmer); *1165632 Ontario*, 2014 TCC 189 (general manager of building-supply business); *9016-9202 Québec*, 2014 TCC 281 (FCA appeal discontinued A-469-14) (garbage collectors, under arrangements set up by the payor); *Arora Trading*, 2019 TCC 98, paras. 30-31 (5 employees + independent contractor is not "more than five full time employees").

For more TCC cases finding no PSB, see *Huschi*, [1989] 1 C.T.C. 2057 (radio station manager); *David T. McDonald Co.*, [1992] 2 C.T.C. 2607 (shoe sales rep); *Société de Projets ETPA*, [1993] 1 C.T.C. 2392 (developing advertising pamphlets for customers); *Crestglen Investments*, [1993] 2 C.T.C. 3210 (managing shopping plazas); *Healy Financial*, [1994] 2 C.T.C. 2168 (computer consultant that had other customers); *Gitchee Gumee Consultants*, [1995] 2 C.T.C. 2764 (consulting services and flower decorating); *S & C Ross Enterprises*, [2002] 4 C.T.C. 2598 (corporate VP doing extra due-diligence work); *Galaxy Management*, 2005 TCC 674 (company owner not subject to any meaningful degree of control by third parties); *Robertson*, 2009 TCC 183 (owner had his own clients and provided engineering services as his own business); *Aniger Consulting*, 2011 FCA 349 (consulting services); *TAP Consultant*, 2011 QCCQ 6626 and *Pragma Services*, 2011 QCCQ 12977 [Jim Yager, "Quebec IT Consultants: No PSB", 20(4) *Canadian Tax Highlights* (ctf.ca) 9-10 (April 2012)]; *6305521 Canada*, 2017 QCCQ 14869 (aircraft maintenance with multiple clients); *Arora Trading*, 2019 TCC 98, para. 26 (for first year, AT had no employees, so could not have an incorporated employee).

See also the case law in Notes to 248(1)"employee" for many cases on whether a relationship was that of employment.

The intention of the parties to create an independent-contractor relationship is not relevant to determining a PSB (unlike 248(1)"employee"): *1166787 Ontario* (above) para. 31; *609309 Alberta* para. 23; *Muirhead Holdings* paras. 4-10; *C.J. McCarty*, para. 44.

Note that para. (d) excludes from PSB income amounts received from an associated corp (see s. 256), so the corporations continue to share the small business limit.

See also VIEWS docs 2005-0160891E5, 2007-0243411C6, 2008-027098117 (anti-avoidance), 2008-0285161C6 (para. (d)), 2009-0334501M4 (finding of PSB), 2012-0455101M4 (general discussion of PSBs); 2019-0805901M4 (incorporated truck drivers: see tinyurl.com/cra-truck-drivers).

Before the 2016 amendments (see 125(1) Notes), a professional corp could provide partners' services without being a PSB or creating specified partnership income: see these Notes up to PITA 59th ed. for rulings and published articles. These rulings no longer apply: VIEWS doc 2016-0646411E5.

For the meaning of "more than 5 full-time employees", see 125(7)"specified investment business" Notes.

See House of Commons Finance Committee, June 2010 report, "Servant or Master? Differing Interpretations of a Personal Services Business", which recommends amending the PSB rules to "reflect the realities of the modern labour market, particularly in terms of small information technology companies, in order to ensure tax fairness for those small business owners who are deemed to be 'incorporated employees'." See also Taxpayers' Ombudsman report, "Systemic Investigation into whether the Canada Revenue Agency Provides Sufficient Information Regarding Personal Services Businesses" [re corps formed to bid on federal government contracts] (Feb. 25, 2016).

See also Kietaibl & Arnold, *Taxation of Private Corporations and their Shareholders* (ctf.ca, 5th ed., 2020), pp. 5:37-48; Lindsay & James, "Personal Services Businesses in the Oil and Gas Sector", 26(2) *Canadian Petroleum Tax Journal* (2013); Virji, "Old News, New Trend: PSBs on the Rise", 2192 *Tax Topics* (CCH) 1-4 (March 13, 2014).

125(7)"personal services business" was 125(7)(d) before RSC 1985 (5th Supp) consolidation for tax years ending after Nov. 1991.

Interpretation Bulletins: IT-73R6: The small business deduction; IT-168R3: Athletes and players employed by football, hockey and similar clubs; IT-189R2: Corporations used by practising members of professions; IT-406R2: Tax payable by an *inter vivos* trust; IT-421R2: Benefits to individuals, corporations and shareholders from loans or debt.

I.T. Technical News: 41 (the "more than five full-time employees" test).

Forms: CPT-1: Request for a ruling as to the status of a worker under the *Canada Pension Plan* or *Employment Insurance Act*.

"specified cooperative income" — [Repealed]

Notes: "Specified cooperative income" (SCI) has been replaced retroactively by "specified farming or fishing income", which applies more broadly. It was added by 2017 budget bill #2, for tax years that begin after March 21, 2016, and repealed by 2019 budget bill #1 on the same basis. Any assessment of taxpayer X's tax, interest and penalties payable for any tax year that ends before March 19, 2019 that would, absent the repeal, be precluded by 152(4)-(5), if requested by X, is to be made to the extent necessary to take the repeal into account. Now deemed never to have been in force, the definition read:

"specified cooperative income", of a corporation (in this definition referred to as the "selling corporation") for a taxation year, means income of the selling corporation (other than an amount included in the selling corporation's income under subsection 135(7)) from the sale of the farming products or fishing catches of the selling corporation's farming or fishing business to a corporation (in this definition referred to as the "purchasing corporation") if

(a) the purchasing corporation deals at arm's length with the selling corporation, and

(b) either

(i) the purchasing corporation would be a "cooperative corporation", as defined in subsection 136(2), if the reference in paragraph (c) of that

subsection to "business of farming" were read as "business of farming or fishing", or

(ii) the following conditions are met:

(A) the selling corporation (or one of its shareholders) or a person who does not deal at arm's length with the selling corporation (or one of its shareholders) holds a direct or indirect interest in a corporation that

(I) would be a "cooperative corporation", as defined in subsection 136(2), if the reference in paragraph (c) of that subsection to "business of farming" were read as "business of farming or fishing", and

(II) holds a direct or indirect interest in the purchasing corporation, and

(B) the income from the sale of the farming products or fishing catches would not be an amount described in subparagraph (a)(i) of the definition "specified corporate income" if

(I) the condition in subclause (A)(I) were not met, and

(II) that subparagraph were read without reference to "(other than specified cooperative income)";

SCI enabled certain income arising in connection with sales to farming or fishing co-ops to be excluded from 125(7)"specified corporate income", so it remained eligible for the small business deduction. See now Notes to 125(7)"specified farming or fishing income".

"specified corporate income", of a corporation for a taxation year, means the lesser of

(a) the lesser of

(i) the total of all amounts each of which is income (other than specified farming or fishing income of the corporation for the year) from an active business of the corporation for the year from the provision of services or property to a private corporation (directly or indirectly, in any manner whatever) if

(A) at any time in the year, the corporation (or one of its shareholders) or a person who does not deal at arm's length with the corporation (or one of its shareholders) holds a direct or indirect interest in the private corporation, and

(B) it is not the case that all or substantially all of the corporation's income for the year from an active business is from the provision of services or property to

(I) persons (other than the private corporation) with which the corporation deals at arm's length, or

(II) partnerships with which the corporation deals at arm's length, other than a partnership in which a person that does not deal at arm's length with the corporation holds a direct or indirect interest, and

(ii) the total of all amounts each of which is the portion, if any, of the business limit of a private corporation described in subparagraph (i) for a taxation year that the private corporation assigns to the corporation under subsection (3.2), and

(b) an amount that the Minister determines to be reasonable in the circumstances;

Related Provisions: 125(1)(a)(i)(B) — Exclusion of amount in (a) from small business deduction; 125(9) — Anti-avoidance; 125(10) — Computational rule for SCI.

Notes: The SCI (a)(i) amount is normally denied the small business deduction: 125(1)(a)(i)(B), except to the extent another corp in the group assigns business limit under 125(3.2): 125(1)(a)(ii.1). See 125(1) Notes; Kakkar & Ghani, "The Scary New World of Specified Corporate Income". 16(3) *Tax for the Owner-Manager* (ctf.ca) 2 (July 2016); Budd & Robinson, "Specified Corporate Income When Year-Ends Differ", 8(1) *Canadian Tax Focus* (ctf.ca) 2 (Feb. 2018).

For the meaning of "indirectly" in (a)(i) opening words, see Notes to 17.1(1). CRA interprets "substantially all", used in (a)(i)(B), as meaning 90% or more.

Para. (b) allows CRA to determine SCI at a "reasonable" amount, effectively as an anti-avoidance rule. CRA cannot yet give specific examples: VIEWS doc 2017-0693461C6 [2017 STEP q.1], but disproportionately allocating expenses to SCI is likely not reasonable: 2017-0706401E5. A CRA determination can possibly be challenged only by judicial review in Federal Court (see Notes to 220(3.1)).

(a)(i) opening words amended by 2019 budget bill #1, to change "other than specified cooperative income" to "other than specified farming or fishing income of the corporation for the year", on the same basis as 125(7)"specified farming and fishing income" (tax years that begin after March 21, 2016, with a late-assessment rule).

(a)(i) opening words amended by 2017 budget bill #2, for tax years that begin after March 21, 2016, to exclude "specified cooperative income". See Notes to that term in 125(7).

Definition added by 2016 budget bill #2, effective on the same basis as the amendments to 125(1).

"specified farming or fishing income", of a particular corporation for a taxation year, means income of the particular corporation (other than an amount included in the particular corporation's income under subsection 135(7)), if

(a) the income is from the sale of the farming products or fishing catches of the particular corporation's farming or fishing business to another corporation, and

(b) the particular corporation deals at arm's length with the other corporation;

Notes: This definition was introduced by the 2019 Budget to retroactively replace "specified cooperative income", eliminating the need for farming/fishing sales to be to a co-op to be excluded from "specified corporate income", which is ineligible for the small business deduction (125(1)(a)(ii.1)).

For discussion of the former rule see Gislason, "Proposed Legislation to Insulate Cooperative Corporations", 2362 *Tax Topics* (CCH) 1-3 (June 15, 2017); Campbell, "Only One Lifeboat?", 14(4) *Tax Hyperion* (Carswell) 1-3 (July-Aug. 2017).

Amounts included in a corporation's income under 135(7) (patronage dividends paid by a co-op to its members out of profits) are not income from sale of the corp's farming products or fishing catches. "This is in keeping with the principle that a single business, including a cooperative business, is entitled to one business limit only": Finance Technical Notes to the former definition, Oct. 2017.

Definition added by 2019 budget bill #1, for tax years that begin after March 21, 2016. Any assessment of taxpayer X's tax, interest and penalties payable for any tax year that ends before March 19, 2019 that would, absent the addition, be precluded by 152(4)-(5), if requested by X, is to be made to the extent necessary to take the addition into account. Technically, this means CRA is *required* to assess to allow the change, but only if the assessment would otherwise be statute-barred. In other words, a corp should wait for the 3-year 152(4) period to run out and can then force CRA to reassess! (In practice, CRA will retroactively apply the new rule.)

"specified investment business", carried on by a corporation in a taxation year, means a business (other than a business carried on by a credit union or a business of leasing property other than real or immovable property) the principal purpose of which is to derive income (including interest, dividends, rents and royalties) from property but, except where the corporation was a prescribed labour-sponsored venture capital corporation at any time in the year, does not include a business carried on by the corporation in the year where

(a) the corporation employs in the business throughout the year more than 5 full-time employees, or

(b) any other corporation associated with the corporation provides, in the course of carrying on an active business, managerial, administrative, financial, maintenance or other similar services to the corporation in the year and the corporation could reasonably be expected to require more than 5 full-time employees if those services had not been provided;

Related Provisions: 95(1) — Analogous definition of "investment business" for FAPI purposes; 125(7)"active business" — No small business deduction for specified investment business; 129(4)"income" — Dividend refund available for income from specified investment business; 129(6) — Income from associated corporation deemed to be active business income; 248(1)"specified investment business" — Definition applies to entire Act.

Notes: See Notes to 9(1) under "Business income vs property income". Although it is a "business", the income of a specified investment business (SIB) is taxed as investment income, and ineligible for the 125(1) small business deduction, as it is excluded from 125(7)"active business". It is eligible for the dividend refund: see 129(4)"income" or "loss". (Investment income from an associated corp may be deemed by 129(6) to be active business income, and thus excluded from SIB income.) See generally VIEWS doc 2018-0754581E5.

The "principal purpose" (of deriving income from property, except leasing of personal property) is determined not by a corporation's stated objects but by "what the corporation in fact does and what its sources of income are": *Ben Barbary Co.*, [1989] 1 C.T.C. 2364 (TCC); *Prosperous Investments*, [1992] 1 C.T.C. 2218 (TCC), para. 13.

There was SIB in: *0742443 B.C. [R-Xtra]*, 2015 FCA 231 (self-storage lockers); *Weaver*, 2008 FCA 238 (corp winding down active land development business was earning mostly rental income); *Lee*, [1999] 3 C.T.C. 2200 (TCC) (mobile home park); *Skartaris Holdings*, 2016 TCC 278 (corp's principal purpose was renting out properties, not buying them for resale); *1717398 Ontario [Lost Forest Park]*, 2019 TCC 183

(FCA appeal discontinued A-362-19) (campground for RVs and mobile homes). There was no SIB in: *Langille*, 2009 TCC 139 (trading inventories of liquidated goods); *Rocco Gagliese Productions*, 2018 TCC 136 (music writer's corporation royalties from his ongoing work [CRA accepts this: doc 2019-0798321C6 (2019 STEP q.7)]).

Campgrounds and self-storage facilities: as announced in the 2015 Budget, Finance reviewed these, but announced in the 2016 Budget that no changes will be made. See also Oakey, "SIB or SBD? Which camp are you in?", 13(7) *Tax Hyperion* (Carswell) 3-4 (July 2016); and cases above. CRA news release "Eligibility Requirements for Campgrounds" (Aug. 23, 2016) says a campground is normally renting property, but one that provides "significant additional services integral to the success of its business operations", e.g. coin operated laundry, swimming pool/lifeguard, playground, refuse disposal, retailing food and supplies, may qualify as active business (see also VIEWS doc 2016-0647271E5).

CRA considered the following not to be SIB: property management and landscaping services (VIEWS doc 2010-0391671E5); taxi licensing income (2002-0168555: it was a business of leasing taxis, which are not real property); work camp whose services included meals, lodging, fresh linens, housekeeping, laundromat and fuel sales (2005-0150361E5: similar to a hotel); active securities trading (2019-0826051E5). Owning a gravel pit and being paid for sand and gravel removed from it is a SIB: 2011-0398011E5 [one might think it is not even a business].

Number of employees: the para. (a) exception applies if the corp employs more than 5 full-time employees (FTEs) "in the business"; see Notes to Reg. 1101(1) re what is a separate "business". The phrase "more than 5" FTEs can mean 5 plus a part-time employee (PTE): *489599 B.C.*, 2008 TCC 332; and CRA accepts this: VIEWS doc 2008-0300581C6, *Income Tax Technical News* 41, 2008 Cdn Tax Foundation conference report at 3:5-6 (superseding IT-73R6 para. 15). 5 FTEs plus an independent contractor do not qualify: *Arora Trading*, 2019 TCC 98, paras. 30-31. Multiple PTEs cannot be added up to get 5 FTEs: *Lerric Investments*, [1999] 2 C.T.C. 2718 (TCC), para. 14 (aff'd 2001 FCA 14 without discussing this point); *Baker (Town Properties)*, 2005 FCA 185, para. 14; *Mini Entrepôt Longueuil*, 2018 TCC 106 (total 12,000 hours, but only employees working at least 29-30 hrs/week were "full time". (95(1)"investment business"(c)(ii) offers an *equivalent of* more than 5" test that is not found here.) Fractions of employees cannot be allocated to co-owners: *Lerric* (FCA). 4 hours/day is not "full-time" even if that is standard in the industry: *Baker*. In *625041 Ontario*, 2004 TCC 693, evidence that 6 members of a family all worked full-time in the business was not believed, based on the salaries paid. See also 2004-0101771E5, 2005-0139641E5 (30 hrs/week is not "full time"), 2007-025801117 (employees of partnership cannot be counted as employees of corporate partner), 2008-0284681E5 and 2009-0335731E5 (corps forming partnership rather than co-ownership solves the problem), 2009-0329951C6 (whether shareholders can be considered FTEs). See also Cheng & Qubti, "Rental Income and ABI: Structuring Around the Five-Employee Test", 8(2) *Canadian Tax Focus* (ctf.ca) 7 (May 2018).

Para. (b): on calculating whether associated corps combined with the corp required more than 5 FTEs, see *Grist*, 2011 TCC 304 (insufficient evidence that test met); *Huntly Investments*, 2017 TCC 255 (test not met); VIEWS doc 2005-0120751E5.

VIEWS doc 2002-0179825 discusses combining 6 owners' apartment buildings, each with 1 employee, into a new corp with a separate class of shares "tracking" the interest in each building. The new corp would have 6 full-time employees. CRA's view is that, because of the tracking shares, each building is a separate business which is still a SIB.

If SIB income is converted to active business income by shifting it to a relateed management company that charges management fees, CRA will apply s. 67 or GAAR: doc 2005-0146001E5. (Since 2016, the "specified corporate income" rules will likely catch this also: see Notes to 125(1).)

See also Plant, "A Review of Specified Investment Business Rules", 2019 Atlantic Provinces Tax Conference (ctf.ca), 3B:1-26; Herman, "Single-Family Offices: A Tax Deferral Opportunity", 11(1) *Canadian Tax Focus* (ctf.ca) 10-11 (Feb. 2021).

Definition amended by 2002-2013 technical bill (Part 4 — bijuralism, effective June 26, 2013), 1995-97 technical bill. 125(7)"specified investment business" was 125(7)(e) before RSC 1985 (5th Supp) consolidation for tax years ending after Nov. 1991.

Regulations: 6701 (prescribed labour-sponsored venture capital corporation).

Interpretation Bulletins: IT-73R6: The small business deduction; IT-189R2: Corporations used by practising members of professions; IT-243R4: Dividend refund to private corporations; IT-406R2: Tax payable by an *inter vivos* trust.

I.T. Technical News: 41 (the "more than five full-time employees" test).

"specified partnership business limit", of a person for a taxation year, at any particular time, means the amount determined by the formula

$$(K/L) \times M - T$$

where

K is the total of all amounts each of which is the person's share of the income (determined in accordance with Subdivision J of Division B) of a partnership of which the person was a member for a fiscal period ending in the year from an active business carried on in Canada,

L is the total of all amounts each of which is the income of the partnership for a fiscal period referred to in paragraph (a) of the description of A in the definition "specified partnership income" in this subsection from an active business carried on in Canada,

M is the lesser of

(a) the amount of the business limit indicated in subsection (2) for a corporation that is not associated in a taxation year with one or more other Canadian-controlled private corporations, and

(b) the product obtained by the formula

$$(Q/R) \times S$$

where

Q is the amount referred to in paragraph (a),

R is 365, and

S is the total of all amounts each of which is the number of days in a fiscal period of the partnership that ends in the year, and

T is the total of all amounts each of which is an amount, if any, that the person assigns under subsection (8);

Related Provisions: 125(8) — Assignment of SPBL; 257 — Formula cannot calculate to less than zero.

Notes: Definition added by 2016 budget bill #2, effective on the same basis as the amendments to 125(1) (years that begin or end after March 21, 2016).

"specified partnership income" of a corporation for a taxation year means the amount determined by the formula

$$A + B$$

where

A is the total of all amounts each of which is an amount in respect of a partnership of which the corporation was a member, or a designated member, in the year equal to the least of

(a) the total of all amounts each of which is an amount in respect of an active business carried on in Canada by the corporation as a member, or a designated member, of the partnership determined by the formula

$$G - H$$

where

G is the total of all amounts each of which is

(i) the corporation's share of the income (determined in accordance with Subdivision J of Division B) of the partnership for a fiscal period of the business that ends in the year,

(ii) income of the corporation for the year from the provision (directly or indirectly, in any manner whatever) of services or property to the partnership, or

(iii) an amount included in the corporation's income for the year in respect of the business under any of subsections 34.2(2), (3) and (12), and

H is the total of all amounts deducted in computing the corporation's income for the year from the business (other than amounts that were deducted in computing the income of the partnership from the business or the income of the corporation described under subparagraph (ii) of the description of G) or in respect of the business under subsection 34.2(4) or (11),

(b) an amount equal to

(i) if the corporation was a member of the partnership, the corporation's specified partnership business limit for the year, and

(ii) if the corporation was a designated member of the partnership, the total of all amounts assigned to it under subsection (8) for the year and, where no such amounts have been assigned, nil, and

(c) nil, if

(i) the corporation is a member, or a designated member, of the partnership (including indirectly through one or more other partnerships) in the year, and

(ii) the partnership provides services or property to either

(A) a private corporation (directly or indirectly in any manner whatever) in the year, if

(I) the corporation (or one of its shareholders) or a person who does not deal at arm's length with the corporation (or one of its shareholders) holds a direct or indirect interest in the private corporation, and

(II) it is not the case that all or substantially all of the partnership's income for the year from an active business is from the provision of services or property to

1 persons (other than the private corporation) that deal at arm's length with the partnership and each person that holds a direct or indirect interest in the partnership, or

2 partnerships with which the partnership deals at arm's length, other than a partnership in which a person that does not deal at arm's length with the corporation holds a direct or indirect interest, or

(B) a particular partnership (directly or indirectly in any manner whatever) in the year, if

(I) the corporation (or one of its shareholders) does not deal at arm's length with the particular partnership or a person that holds a direct or indirect interest in the particular partnership, and

(II) it is not the case that all or substantially all of the partnership's income for the year from an active business is from the provision of services or property to

1 persons that deal at arm's length with the partnership and each person that holds a direct or indirect interest in the partnership, or

2 partnerships (other than the particular partnership) with which the partnership deals at arm's length, other than a partnership in which a person that does not deal at arm's length with the corporation holds a direct or indirect interest, and

B is the lesser of

(a) the total of the amounts determined in respect of the corporation for the year under subparagraphs (1)(a)(iii) and (iv), and

(b) the total of all amounts each of which is an amount in respect of a partnership of which the corporation was a member, or a designated member, in the year equal to the amount determined by the formula

$$N - O$$

where

N is the amount determined in respect of the partnership for the year under paragraph (a) of the description of A, and

O is the amount determined in respect of the partnership for the year

(i) if the corporation was a member of the partnership, under subparagraph (b)(i) of the description of A, and

(ii) if the corporation was a designated member of the partnership, under subparagraph (b)(ii) of the description of A;

Related Provisions: 125(1)(a)(i)(A), (a)(ii.1) — SPI limits small business deduction; 125(6) — Corporate partnerships; 125(6.2) — Specified partnership income deemed nil; 125(8) — Assignment of specified partnership business limit; 125(9) — Anti-avoidance rule; 257 — Formulas cannot calculate to less than zero. See also at end of s. 125.

Notes: See Notes to 125(1). For pre-2016 rulings that a professional corp could provide partners' services without creating SPI, see 125(7)"personal services business" Notes. See also VIEWS doc 2013-0498081E5 (impact of 34.2 and of multi-tier partnership).

CRA interprets "substantially all", used in A(c)(ii)(A)(II) and (B)(II), as meaning 90% or more. For "indirectly", see Notes to 17.1(1).

Definition amended by 2016 budget bill #2, effective on the same basis as the amendments to 125(1). Before the amendments, read:

"specified partnership income" of a corporation for a taxation year means the amount determined by the formula

$$A + B$$

where

A   is the total of all amounts each of which is an amount in respect of a partnership of which the corporation was a member in the year equal to the lesser of

(a) the total of all amounts each of which is an amount in respect of an active business carried on in Canada by the corporation as a member of the partnership determined by the formula

$$G - H$$

where

G   is the total of all amounts each of which is the corporation's share of the income (determined in accordance with subdivision j of Division B) of the partnership for a fiscal period of the business that ends in the year, or an amount included in the corporation's income for the year in respect of the business under any of subsections 34.2(2), (3) and (12), and

H   is the total of all amounts deducted in computing the corporation's income for the year from the business (other than amounts that were deducted in computing the income of the partnership from the business) or in respect of the business under subsection 34.2(4) or (11), and

(b) the amount determined by the formula

$$K/L \times M$$

where

K   is the total of all amounts each of which is the corporation's share of the income (determined in accordance with subdivision j of Division B) of the partnership for a fiscal period ending in the year from an active business carried on in Canada,

L   is the total of all amounts each of which is the income of the partnership for a fiscal period referred to in paragraph (a) from an active business carried on in Canada, and

M   is the lesser of

(i) $500,000, and

(ii) the product obtained when $1,370 is multiplied by the total of all amounts each of which is the number of days in a fiscal period of the partnership that ends in the year, and

B   is the lesser of

(a) the total of the amounts determined in respect of the corporation for the year under subparagraphs (1)(a)(iii) and (iv), and

(b) the total of all amounts each of which is an amount in respect of a partnership of which the corporation was a member in the year equal to the amount determined by the formula

$$N - O$$

where

N   is the amount determined in respect of the partnership for the year under paragraph (a) of the description of A, and

O   is the amount determined in respect of the partnership for the year under paragraph (b) of the description of A;

G and H amended by 2013 budget bill #2, for taxation years that end after March 22, 2013, to change "from the business because of subsection 34.2(5)" to "in respect of the business under any of subsections 34.2(2), (3) and (12)" in G and to add "or in respect of the business under subsection 34.2(4) or (11)" in H.

Definition earlier amended by 2009 budget bill #1 (for partnership fiscal periods that end after 2008), 2006 budget bill #2, 2003 and 1995 Budgets, 1991 technical bill. 125(7)"specified partnership income" was 125(7)(f) before RSC 1985 (5th Supp) consolidation for tax years ending after Nov. 1991.

Interpretation Bulletins: IT-73R6: The small business deduction.

Forms: T2 Sched. 7: Aggregate investment income and active business income.

"specified partnership loss" of a corporation for a taxation year means the total of all amounts each of which is an amount in respect of a partnership of which the corporation was a member in the year determined by the formula

$$A + B$$

where

A   is the total of all amounts each of which is the corporation's share of the loss (determined in accordance with Subdivision J of Division B) of the partnership for a fiscal period ending in the year from an active business carried on in Canada by the corporation as a member of the partnership, and

B   is the total of all amounts each of which is an amount determined by the formula

$$G - H$$

where

G   is the amount determined for H in the definition "specified partnership income" in this subsection for the year in respect of the corporation's income from an active business carried on in Canada by the corporation as a member of the partnership, and

H   is the amount determined for G in the definition "specified partnership income" in this subsection for the year in respect of the corporation's share of the income from the business.

Related Provisions: 125(1)(a)(iv) — SPL deducted from income eligible for small business deduction; 257 — Formula cannot calculate to less than zero.

Notes: Formula element B (formerly 125(7)(g)(ii)) added by 1991 technical bill, retroactive to 1986, to clarify that amounts deducted by a corporate partner are included in specified partnership loss if they were deducted in computing the corporation's income from the business carried on in Canada by the corporation as a member of the partnership.

125(7)"specified partnership loss" was 125(7)(g) before RSC 1985 (5th Supp) consolidation for tax years ending after Nov. 1991.

Interpretation Bulletins: IT-73R6: The small business deduction.

Related Provisions [subsec. 125(7)]: 48.1 — Election to trigger capital gains exemption on ceasing to be CCPC.

(8) Assignment — specified partnership business limit —

For the purpose of the definition "specified partnership income" in subsection (7), a person that is a member of a partnership in a taxation year may assign to a designated member of the partnership — for a taxation year of the designated member — all or any portion of the person's specified partnership business limit (determined without reference to this assignment) in respect of the person's taxation year if

(a) the person is described in paragraph (b) of the definition "designated member" in subsection (7) in respect of the designated member in the designated member's taxation year;

(b) the specified partnership business limit of the person is in respect of a fiscal period of the partnership that ends in the designated member's taxation year; and

(c) a prescribed form is filed with the Minister by

(i) the designated member in its return of income for the designated member's taxation year, and

(ii) the person in its return of income for the person's taxation year.

Related Provisions: 249(2)(b) — Reference to a fiscal period ending in a year.

Notes: See Notes to 125(1), under "2016 anti-avoidance changes". The reference in 125(8)(b) to "ends in the designated member's taxation year" includes a fiscal period that ends at the same time as that year: 249(2)(b).

The prescribed form for 125(8)(c) is T2 Schedule 7, Part 3. (For a corp filing a Quebec return, it must be copied to Revenu Québec: *Taxation Act* ss. 771.2.1.6.2, 21.4.6.) CRA generally accepts an amended assignment provided there is no change to any statute-barred year; and a person can make an assignment to more than one designated member [DM] (and a DM can receive one from more than one person): VIEWS doc 2017-072858I17. See also 2018-0768761C6 [2018 APFF q.5] (partner P cannot assign to corp of which P is not a shareholder); 2019 CPA Alberta (tinyurl.com/cra-abtax), income tax q.14 (where there is a non-corporate partner).

See also Lorenzo Bonnano & Guy Buckley, "Business Limit Assignment", 26(10) *Canadian Tax Highlights* (ctf.ca) 10-12 (Oct. 2018).

125(8) added by 2016 budget bill #2, effective on the same basis as the amendments to 125(1) (years that begin or end after March 21, 2016).

Forms: T2 Sched. 7, Part 3: Calculation of aggregate investment income and active business income.

(8.1)–(8.6) [Repealed under former Act]

(9) Anti-avoidance — If a corporation provides services or property to a person or partnership that holds a direct or indirect interest in a particular partnership or corporation and one of the reasons for the provision of the services or property to the person or partnership, instead of to the particular partnership or corporation, is to avoid the application of subparagraph (1)(a)(ii) or (ii.1) in respect of the income from the provision of the services or property, no amount in respect of the corporation's income from the provision of the services or property is to be included in the total amount determined under paragraph (1)(a).

Notes: 125(9) added by 2016 budget bill #2, effective on the same basis as the amendments to 125(1).

(9.1) [Repealed under former Act]

(10) Computational rule — specified corporate income — For the purpose of determining an amount for a taxation year in respect of a corporation under clause (1)(a)(i)(B) or subparagraph (1)(a)(ii.1), an amount of income is to be excluded if the amount is

(a) income from an active business of the corporation for the year from the provision of services or property to another corporation with which the corporation is associated (in this subsection referred to as the "associated corporation"); and

(b) not deductible by the associated corporation for its taxation year in respect of an amount included in the income of the associated corporation that is

(i) referred to in any of clauses (1)(a)(i)(A) to (C), or

(ii) reasonable to consider as being attributable to or derived from an amount referred to in clause (1)(a)(i)(C).

Notes: See Notes to 125(1). 125(10) added by 2016 budget bill #2, effective on the same basis as the amendments to 125(1) (years that begin or end after March 21, 2016). First released in Oct. 2016 (it was not in the July 29/16 draft legislation), it fixes a problem identified in VIEWS doc 2016-0651831E5. See 2016-0669731C6 [2016 CTF q.15].

Former 125(8)–(15) repealed in 1984, to simplify the small business deduction. (That was the last time simplification played a role in ITA design, until the eligible capital property system was replaced by Class 14.1 as of 2017.)

(11)–(15) [Repealed under former Act]

Definitions [s. 125]: "active asset", "active business" — 125(7) (see also "income from ..."), 248(1); "adjusted aggregate investment income" — 125(7); "aggregate investment income" — 129(4), 248(1); "amount" — 248(1); "arm's length" — 251(1); "assessment" — 248(1); "associated" — 125(5.2), 256; "business" — 248(1); "business limit" — 125(2)–(5); "calendar year" — *Interpretation Act* 37(1)(a); "Canada" — 255, *Interpretation Act* 35(1); "Canadian-controlled private corporation" — 125(7), 248(1); "carrying on business" — 253; "class" — 248(6); "connected" — 186(4); "controlled directly or indirectly" — 256(5.1)–(6); "cooperative corporation" — 136(2); "corporation" — 248(1), *Interpretation Act* 35(1); "credit union" — 137(6), 248(1); "designated member" — 125(7); "designated stock exchange" — 248(1), 262; "dividend", "employee" — 248(1); "fair market value" — see 69(1) Notes; "farming", "fishing" — 248(1); "fiscal period" — 249(2)(b), 249.1; "immovable" — Quebec *Civil Code* art. 900–907; "in Canada" — 255; "income from active business" — 125(7); "incorporated employee" — 125(7)"personal services business"(a); "Minister", "non-resident" — 248(1); "Parliament" — *Interpretation Act* 35(1); "partnership" — see 96(1) Notes; "payer corporation" — 186(4); "person" — 248(1); "personal services business" — 125(7), 248(1); "prescribed" — 248(1); "prescribed labour-sponsored venture capital corporation" — Reg. 6701; "prescribed venture capital corporation" — Reg. 6700; "private corporation" — 89(1), 136, 248(1); "property" — 248(1); "public corporation" — 89(1), 248(1); "qualified small business corporation share" — 110.6(1); "related" — 251(2)–(6); "relevant factor", "share", "shareholder", "small business corporation" — 248(1); "small business deduction rate" — 125(1.1); "specified corporate income", "specified farming or fishing income" — 125(7); "specified investment business" — 125(7), 248(1); "specified partnership business limit", "specified partnership income", "specified partnership loss" — 125(7); "specified shareholder" — 248(1); "taxable capital employed in Canada" — 181.2(1), 181.3(1), 181.4; "taxable dividend" — 89(1), 248(1); "taxable income" — 2(2), 248(1); "taxation year" — 249; "trust" — 104(1), 248(1), (3); "writing" — *Interpretation Act* 35(1).

125.1 (1) Manufacturing and processing profits deductions [M&P credit] — There may be deducted from the tax otherwise payable under this Part by a corporation for a taxation year an amount equal to the corporation's general rate reduction percentage for the taxation year (within the meaning assigned by subsection 123.4(1)) multiplied by the lesser of

(a) the amount, if any, by which the corporation's Canadian manufacturing and processing profits for the year exceed, where the corporation was a Canadian-controlled private corporation throughout the year, the least of the amounts determined under paragraphs 125(1)(a) to (c) in respect of the corporation for the year, and

(b) the amount, if any, by which the corporation's taxable income for the year exceeds the total of

(i) where the corporation was a Canadian-controlled private corporation throughout the year, the least of the amounts determined under paragraphs 125(1)(a) to (c) in respect of the corporation for the year,

(ii) the amount determined by multiplying the total of the amounts that would be deductible under subsection 126(2) from the tax for the year otherwise payable under this Part by it, if those amounts were determined without reference to section 123.4, by the relevant factor for the year, and

(iii) where the corporation was a Canadian-controlled private corporation throughout the year, its aggregate investment income for the year (within the meaning assigned by subsection 129(4)).

Proposed Amendment — Rate Reduction for zero-emission technology manufacturers

Federal Budget, Supplementary Information, April 19, 2021: See under 123.4(2).

Related Provisions: 125.1(2) — Credit for generating electrical energy; 136(1) — Cooperative can be private corporation for 125.1; 137(7) — Credit union can be private corporation for 125.1; 182 — Tobacco manufacturing surtax.

Notes: The manufacturing and processing (M&P) credit is now generally inoperative, as it reduces the general tax rate from 28% to the same level as per the general corporate rate reduction under 123.4 (see Notes to 123.4(2)). 125.1 is still relevant because some provinces have a reduced rate on M&P income (e.g., Manitoba: VIEWS doc 2014-0517371E5; and see Forms annotation below).

See Reg. Sch. II-Cl. 8(a), 29 and 43 for accelerated CCA on certain M&P machinery and equipment. A building used for M&P is eligible for extra CCA: Reg. 1100(1)(a.1).

See also Notes at end of 125.1; Fenton, "Manufacturing & Processing Income Credit", 2535 *Tax Topics* (CCH) 1-5 (Oct. 6, 2020), and "Calculation of Manufacturing and Processing Income", 2536 1-4 (Oct. 13, 2020).

125.1(1) amended by 2002-2013 technical bill (for 2003 and later tax years), 2006 budget bill #1 (effective 2008), 2000 and 1995 Budgets, 1992 technical bill.

Interpretation Bulletins: IT-145R: Canadian manufacturing and processing profits — reduced rate of corporate tax.

Forms: T2 Sched. 27: Calculation of Canadian manufacturing and processing profits deduction; T2 Sched. 300: Newfoundland and Labrador manufacturing and processing profits tax credit; T2 Sched. 321: PEI corporate investment tax credit; T2 Sched. 344: Nova Scotia manufacturing and processing investment tax credit; T2 Sched. 381: Manitoba manufacturing investment tax credit; T2 Sched. 402: Saskatchewan manufacturing and processing investment tax credit; T2 Sched. 404: Saskatchewan manufacturing and processing profits tax reduction; T2 Sched. 426: B.C. manufacturing and processing tax credit; T2 Sched. 440: Yukon manufacturing and processing profits tax credit; T2 Sched. 460: NWT investment tax credit; T2 Sched. 480: Nunavut Territory investment tax credit.

(2) Electrical energy and steam — A corporation that generates electrical energy for sale, or produces steam for sale, in a taxation year may deduct from its tax otherwise payable under this Part for the year an amount equal to the corporation's general rate reduction percentage for the taxation year (within the meaning assigned by subsection 123.4(1)) multiplied by the amount determined by the formula

$$A - B$$

where

A is the amount, if any, that would, if the definition "manufacturing or processing" in subsection (3), and in subsection 1104(9) of the *Income Tax Regulations*, were read without reference to paragraph (h) of those definitions (other than for the purpose of applying section 5201 of the *Income Tax Regulations*) and if subsection (5) applied for the purpose of subsection (1), be the lesser of

(a) the amount determined under paragraph (1)(a) in respect of the corporation for the year, and

(b) the amount determined under paragraph (1)(b) in respect of the corporation for the year; and

B is the amount, if any, that is the lesser of

(a) the amount determined under paragraph (1)(a) in respect of the corporation for the year, and

(b) the amount determined under paragraph (1)(b) in respect of the corporation for the year.

Related Provisions: 125.1(5) — Interpretation; 257 — Formula cannot calculate to less than zero.

Notes: 125.1(2) extends the M&P credit (see Notes to 125.1(1)) to corporations that generate electrical energy or produce steam for sale. Amended by 2006 budget bill #1 (effective June 22, 2006), 2000 and 1999 Budgets.

Former 125.1(2), repealed by 1988 tax reform, provided transitional rules for 1973-76.

(3) Definitions — In this section,

"Canadian manufacturing and processing profits" of a corporation for a taxation year means such portion of the total of all amounts each of which is the income of the corporation for the year from an active business carried on in Canada as is determined under rules prescribed for that purpose by regulation made on the recommendation of the Minister of Finance to be applicable to the manufacturing or processing in Canada of goods for sale or lease; and

Notes: In *Will-Kare Paving*, 2000 SCC 36, asphalt produced by WK for its paving business was not considered produced "for sale or lease", but was supplied in the course of contracts for work and materials. CRA accepts that a separate company can be set up in this situation to sell asphalt to the paving company and qualify for the M&P credit: VIEWS doc 2013-0504601E5.

In *C.R.I. Environnement*, 2007 TCC 206, a company that treated waste products and shipped them to disposal facilities (which it paid) was not manufacturing for "sale" (under Quebec law). Its argument that it "sold" the waste for a higher price than it acquired it (albeit a "negative price") was rejected.

See also Notes to 125.1(3)"manufacturing or processing" below.

125.1(3)"Canadian manufacturing and processing profits" was 125.1(3)(a) before RSC 1985 (5th Supp) consolidation for tax years ending after Nov. 1991.

Regulations: 5200–5204 (Canadian manufacturing and processing profits).

Interpretation Bulletins: IT-145R: Canadian manufacturing and processing profits — reduced rate of corporate tax.

"manufacturing or processing" does not include

(a) farming or fishing,

(b) logging,

(c) construction,

(d) operating an oil or gas well or extracting petroleum or natural gas from a natural accumulation of petroleum or natural gas,

(e) extracting minerals from a mineral resource,

(f) processing

(i) ore (other than iron ore or tar sands ore) from a mineral resource located in Canada to any stage that is not beyond the prime metal stage or its equivalent,

(ii) iron ore from a mineral resource located in Canada to any stage that is not beyond the pellet stage or its equivalent, or

(iii) tar sands ore from a mineral resource located in Canada to any stage that is not beyond the crude oil stage or its equivalent,

(g) producing industrial minerals,

(h) producing or processing electrical energy or steam, for sale,

(i) processing natural gas as part of the business of selling or distributing gas in the course of operating a public utility,

(j) processing heavy crude oil recovered from a natural reservoir in Canada to a stage that is not beyond the crude oil stage or its equivalent,

(k) Canadian field processing, or

(l) any manufacturing or processing of goods for sale or lease, if, for any taxation year of a corporation in respect of which the expression is being applied, less than 10% of its gross revenue from all active businesses carried on in Canada was from

(i) the selling or leasing of goods manufactured or processed in Canada by it, and

(ii) the manufacturing or processing in Canada of goods for sale or lease, other than goods for sale or lease by it.

Related Provisions: 127(11)(a) — Meaning of "manufacturing or processing" for investment tax credit purposes; Reg. 1104(9) — Definition of manufacturing or processing for Class 29 purposes.

Notes: For the meaning of "manufacturing or processing" see Income Tax Folio S4-F15-C1. In *Federal Farms*, 1967 CarswellNat 355 (SCC), selecting potatoes and carrots, washing, brushing, spraying, drying and sorting was held to be "processing". "Processing" implies application of a uniform process to each item (*Tenneco*, [1991] 1 C.T.C. 323 (FCA)) or subjecting the product to a method, system or technique of preparation, handling or other treatment (*Harvey C. Smith Drugs*, [1995] 1 C.T.C. 143 (FCA)). It does not require creating a new product: a change can be enough, so regasifying liquid natural gas qualified in *Repsol Canada*, 2017 FCA 193, paras. 52-57. In *TDS Group*, 2005 TCC 40, assembly and packing of auto and truck parts was "processing". In *Pacific National Processing*, 2013 BCSC 279, fish processing including evisceration that "transforms the dead fish into a marketable food product" was "processing" and not simply cleaning, grading and packaging, for BC retail sales tax. Allowing dirty oil to settle and separate was "processing", so trucks doing this qualified for the Quebec version of 127(9)"qualified property"(c)(i): *Environnement Sanivac*, 2016 QCCQ 9461. See also VIEWS doc 2015-0624191E5; Notes to 248(1)"farming".

In *Charles McCann Ltd. v. O'Culuchain*, [1986] I.R. 96 (Supreme Court of Ireland), artificially ripening bananas was held to be "manufacturing".

Para. (a): In *Ferme Lunick*, 2020 QCCQ 1703, potato farming and washing/bagging (in separate divisions) were a single business, so this exclusion applied.

Para. (c): For CRA interpretation of "construction" (C) see docs 2001-0108575 (prefabrication of log homes is not C); 2010-0360641E5 (road contractor placing material on road is C, but subcontracted processing of material in a pit qualifies); 2014-0537121E5 (dredging is C).

Para. (f): For the meaning of "prime metal stage or its equivalent" in (f)(i), see Notes to Reg. 1104(5).

Para. (g): "Industrial minerals" (IM) are considered by the CRA to be non-metallic minerals such as gravel, clay, stone, limestone, sand and feldspar: IT-145R para. 11; doc 2014-0520941E5. Sand and gravel products are IM, but "processing" them to produce specialized IM products is not "producing" IM: *Nova Scotia Sand*, 1980 CarswellNat 1354 (FCA), paras. 6, 13, 15. Excavating and extracting slate from a pit constitutes producing IM: 2007-0227421E5. "Producing IM is considered to include all activities connected with the mining, excavating and extracting the mineral material from the mine or pit area, including any primary crushing operation required to make it transportable from the mine or pit area as well as the transporting of the material from the mine or pit. Subsequent activities such as crushing, washing, screening and sorting of the mineral material in order to make the product of mine or pit marketable are considered to be processing": 2007-024239117.

For more CRA views see docs 2003-0020535 (R&D can qualify under Reg. 5202"qualified activities"(c)); 2008-0290971E5 (activity that does not change product's form or characteristics does not qualify); 2008-0293291E5 (blast-freezing is processing but maintaining frozen food is not); 2008-0299321E5 (managing forestry output for related company); 2008-0304611E5 (cutting and installing granite countertops does not qualify); 2010-0355981E5 (potash mining excluded by paras. (e) and (f), as potash is an "ore"); 2011-041557117 (corporation that does only SR&ED is not manufacturing); 2012-0465071E5 (taking, editing and printing photos — uncertain); 2012-0470501E5 (converting water to ice for sale — maybe); 2014-0530631E5 (SR&ED can be part of M&P); 2014-0548101E5 (applying alloy to steel rods — maybe); 2018-078151117 (photocopying — uncertain). See also Notes to 127(9)"qualified property", which uses the same phrase.

Definition amended by 1996 Budget (for tax years that begin after 1996), 1991 technical bill. 125.1(3)"manufacturing or processing" was 125.1(3)(b) before consolidation in RSC 1985 (5th Supp) for tax years ending after Nov. 1991.

Interpretation Bulletins: IT-92R2: Income of contractors; IT-145R: Canadian manufacturing and processing profits — reduced rate of corporate tax; IT-411R: Meaning of "construction".

I.T. Technical News: 8 (pre-delivery service of new vehicles); 19 (Canadian manufacturing and processing profits — change to Interpretation Bulletin IT-145R).

(4) Determination of gross revenue — For the purposes of paragraph (l) of the definition "manufacturing or processing" in subsection (3), where a corporation was a member of a partnership at any time in a taxation year,

(a) there shall be included in the gross revenue of the corporation for the year from all active businesses carried on in Canada, that proportion of the gross revenue from each such business carried on in Canada by means of the partnership, for the fiscal period of the partnership coinciding with or ending in that year, that the corporation's share of the income of the partnership from that business for that fiscal period is of the income of the partnership from that business for that fiscal period; and

(b) there shall be included in the gross revenue of the corporation for the year from all activities described in subparagraphs (l)(i) and (ii) of the definition "manufacturing or processing" in subsection (3), that proportion of the gross revenue from each such activity engaged in in the course of a business carried on by means of the partnership, for the fiscal period of the partnership coinciding with or ending in that year, that the corporation's share of the income of the partnership from that business for that fiscal period is of the income of the partnership from that business for that fiscal period.

(5) Interpretation — For the purpose of the description of A in subsection 125.1(2) and for the purpose of applying the *Income Tax Regulations* (other than section 5201 of the Regulations) to that subsection other than the description of B,

(a) electrical energy and steam are deemed to be goods; and

(b) the generation of electrical energy for sale, and the production of steam for sale, are deemed to be, subject to paragraph (l) of the definition "manufacturing or processing" in subsection (3), manufacturing or processing.

Notes [subsec. 125.1(5)]: 125.1(5)(a) and (b) amended by 2000 Budget, effective for taxation years that end after 1999, to add the references to steam.

125.1(5) added by 1999 Budget, effective for taxation years that end after 1998.

Notes [s. 125.1]: An opposition party can initiate consideration of a reduction or removal of the 125.1 credit. S.C. 1973-74, c. 29, subsecs. 1(3)-(4) provide:

(3) Procedure where motion filed with speaker — Where, at any time after March 31, 1974, a motion for the consideration of the House of Commons, signed by not less than sixty members of the House, is filed with the Speaker to the effect that section 125.1 of the *Income Tax Act*, as enacted by subsection (1), be amended, or to the effect that subsection (2) be amended, so as to

(a) discontinue the deduction that would otherwise be permitted by the said section 125.1,

(b) reduce the amount of the deduction that would otherwise be permitted by that section, or

(c) in any other manner, restrict the application of the provisions of that section,

for any period commencing after the motion is filed, the House of Commons shall, within the first fifteen days next after the motion is filed that the House is sitting, in accordance with the Rules of the House, take up and consider the motion, and if the motion, with or without amendments, is approved by the House, the Minister of Finance shall forthwith take such steps as are necessary in order that a measure in his name giving effect to the motion may be placed before the House without delay.

(4) Time for deciding questions — All questions in connection with any motion taken up and considered by the House of Commons pursuant to subsection (3) shall be debated without interruption and decided not later than the end of the third sitting day next after the day the motion is first so taken up and considered, and any measure required to be placed before the House pursuant to that subsection giving effect to any such motion shall be placed before the House not later than the end of the fifteenth sitting day next after the day the motion, with or without amendments, is approved by the House, and all questions in connection with any such measure shall be debated without interruption and decided not later than the end of the seventh sitting day next after the day the measure is first so placed before the House.

This rule was not in the reconsolidation of s. 125.1 in RSC 1985 (5th Supp) which took effect March 1, 1994. However, it should still be in force; see ITAR 75.

Definitions [s. 125.1]: "amount", "business" — 248(1); "Canadian-controlled private corporation" — 125(7), 248(1); "Canadian field processing" — 248(1); "Canadian manufacturing and processing profits" — 125.1(3); "corporation" — 248(1), *Interpretation Act* 35(1); "farming", "fishing" — 248(1); "general rate reduction percentage" — 123.4(1); "gross revenue" — 125.1(4), 248(1); "manufacturing or processing" — 125.1(3); "mineral resource" — 248(1); "Minister of Finance" — *Financial Administration Act* 14; "oil or gas well", "relevant factor", "tar sands" — 248(1); "taxable income" — 2(2), 248(1); "taxation year" — 249.

Income Tax Folios [s. 125.1]: S4-F15-C1: Manufacturing and processing [replaces IT-147R3].

125.11 [Repealed]

Notes [s. 125.11]: 125.11 added by 2003 resource bill for 2003 and later tax years and repealed by the same bill for tax years that begin after 2006. Effective 2007, the rate reduction under 123.4 applies and the corporate tax rate is the same for resource income and other income. The 2002-2013 technical bill amended 125.11(1)"taxable resource income" for taxation years that begin after Feb. 27, 2004 until its repeal.

125.2 [Repealed]

Notes: 125.2 and 125.3 provided credits for pre-1992 Part I.3 and Part VI tax.

See Notes to 181.1(6)"Canadian surtax payable" for the text of 125.3(4)"Canadian surtax payable", which is still relevant for that definition.

125.21 Part XIII tax — eligible bank affiliate — There may be deducted in computing the tax payable under this Part for a taxation year by a particular corporation that is throughout the year an eligible Canadian bank (as defined in subsection 95(2.43)) the total of all amounts, each of which is the amount, if any, by which

(a) an amount paid under paragraph 212(1)(b) in respect of interest paid or credited in the year by the particular corporation in respect of an upstream deposit (as defined in subsection 95(2.43)) owing to a non-resident corporation that is, throughout the year, an eligible bank affiliate (as defined in subsection 95(2.43)) of the particular corporation

exceeds

(b) the total of all amounts each of which is a portion of the amount described in paragraph (a) that is available to the non-resident corporation or any other person or partnership at any time as a credit or reduction of, or deduction from, any amount otherwise payable to the government of a country other than Canada, or a political subdivision of that country, having regard to all available provisions of the laws of that country, or political subdivision, as the case may be, any tax treaty with that country and any other agreements entered into by that country or political subdivision.

Related Provisions [s. 125.21]: 95(2.31), (3.01) — Relief from FAPI on certain securities transactions; 95(2.43)–(2.45) — Rules for eligible bank affiliate.

Notes: 125.21 added by 2014 budget bill #2, for tax years that begin after Oct. 2012. It generally allows a Canadian parent corp to bank a non-refundable credit, against its Part I tax payable, for certain amounts of non-resident withholding tax paid on interest on an upstream deposit made by a foreign affiliate of the bank.

Definitions [s. 125.21]: "amount", "bank" — 248(1); "Canada" — 255, *Interpretation Act* 35(1); "corporation" — 248(1), *Interpretation Act* 35(1); "eligible bank affiliate", "eligible Canadian bank" — 95(2.43); "mark-to-market property" — 142.2(1); "non-resident" — 248(1); "partnership" — see 96(1) Notes; "person", "tax treaty" — 248(1); "taxation year" — 249; "upstream deposit" — 95(2.43).

125.3 [Deduction of pre-1992 Part I.3 tax — No longer relevant.]

Notes: See under 125.2.

Canadian Film or Video Production Tax Credit

125.4 (1) Definitions — The definitions in this subsection apply in this section.

"assistance" means an amount, other than a prescribed amount or an amount deemed under subsection (3) to have been paid, that would be included under paragraph 12(1)(x) in computing a taxpayer's income for any taxation year if that paragraph were read without reference to

(a) subparagraphs 12(1)(x)(v) to (viii), if the amount were received

(i) from a person or partnership described in subparagraph 12(1)(x)(ii), or

(ii) in circumstances where clause 12(1)(x)(i)(C) applies; and

(b) subparagraphs 12(1)(x)(v) to (vii), in any other case.

Related Provisions: 87(2)(j.94) — Amalgamation — continuing corporation; 125.4(5) — Credit is deemed to be assistance for all purposes under the Act; 241(4)(d)(xv) — Disclosure of information to government agency providing assistance.

Notes: For interpretation of this definition see VIEWS docs 2005-0119061I7, 2008-0296351E5. See also Joseph Gill, "Financing Canadian Films Through Crowdfunding", 3(1) *Canadian Tax Focus* (ctf.ca) 4-5 (Feb. 2013).

Prescribed amounts (Reg. 1106(11)) include amounts received from the Canada Television and Cable Production Fund (CTCPF) under its Licence Fee Program.

Paras. (a) and (b) added in place of "subparagraphs (v) to (vii)" by 2014 budget bill #2, generally effective for production commencement time after Nov. 13, 2003, with some grandfathering (see these Notes up to the 53rd ed.).

125.4(1)"assistance" amended by 1998 Budget for amounts received after Feb. 23, 1998.

See also Notes at end of 125.4.

Regulations: 1106(11) (prescribed amount).

"Canadian film or video production" has the meaning assigned by regulation.

Notes: See Notes to 125.4(1)"Canadian film or video production certificate".

Regulations: 1101(5k.1) (separate class for Canadian film or video production); 1106(3) (treaty co-production); 1106(4) (definition of "Canadian film or video production"); Sch. II:Cl. 10(x) (CCA class for Canadian film or video production).

"Canadian film or video production certificate" means a certificate issued in respect of a production by the Minister of Canadian Heritage certifying that the production is a Canadian film or video production in respect of which that Minister is satisfied that, except where the production is a treaty co-production (as defined in subsection 1106(3) of the *Income Tax Regulations*), an acceptable share of revenues from the exploitation of the production in non-Canadian markets is, under the terms of any agreement, retained by

(a) a qualified corporation that owns or owned an interest in, or for civil law a right in, the production;

(b) a prescribed taxable Canadian corporation related to the qualified corporation; or

(c) any combination of corporations described in paragraph (a) or (b).

Related Provisions: 125.4(3) — Tax credit where certificate issued; 125.4(6) — Revocation of certificate; 125.4(7) — Guidelines from Minister of Canadian Heritage; 152(4.2)(b) — Redetermination of credit at taxpayer's request; 241(3.3) — Disclosure to public of information on certificate.

Notes: In *Tricon Television29*, 2011 FC 435, the "docu-soap" *Beautiful People* was found not to be "Canadian" under Reg. 1106(6), and the Dept. of Canadian Heritage's Canadian Audio-Visual Certification Office refused to issue a certificate. The Court denied judicial review.

Definition amended by 2014 budget bill #2, for film or video productions for which certificates are issued by the Minister of Canadian Heritage after Dec. 20, 2002 (with different reading for those for which certificates were issued before 2004).

This amendment was changed from that proposed in 2007 to refer to Reg. 1106(3) instead of "as defined by regulation", and to delete former proposed para. (b), which would have required that "public financial support of the production would not be contrary to public policy". The "public policy" requirement was one reason Bill C-10 (2007) was stalled in the Senate in 2007-08, after passing the Commons (the other reason was the non-resident trust and foreign investment entity (FIE) rules in then-proposed 94-94.4 — the FIE rules were later dropped). The proposal raised concerns about government censorship of the film industry: Drache, "Films, Tax Credits and Public Policy", 16(4) *Canadian Not-for-Profit News* (Carswell) 27-28 (April 2008). The Oct. 7, 2008 Conservative election platform proposed to remove the "public policy" requirement. The huge technical package was eventually enacted in the 2002-2013 technical bill without any of the amendments to 125.4 (or 241(3.3)). These amendments were finally enacted in 2014.

Regulations: 1106(2) (prescribed taxable Canadian corporation); 1106(3) (treaty co-production).

"investor" — [Repealed]

Notes: Definition repealed by 2014 budget bill #2, effective

(a) for tax years ending after Nov. 14, 2003 (earlier in some cases); and

(b) for a film or video production in respect of which a corporation has, in a return of income filed before Nov. 14, 2003, claimed an amount under 125.4(3) for a labour expenditure incurred after 1997.

"labour expenditure", of a corporation for a taxation year in respect of a Canadian film or video production, means, in the case of a corporation that is not a qualified corporation for the taxation year, nil, and in the case of a corporation that is a qualified corpora-

tion for the taxation year, subject to subsection (2), the total of the following amounts to the extent that they are reasonable in the circumstances and included in the cost to, or in the case of depreciable property the capital cost to, the corporation, or any other person or partnership, of the production:

(a) the salary or wages directly attributable to the production that are incurred after 1994 and in the taxation year, or the preceding taxation year, by the corporation for the stages of production of the property, from the production commencement time to the end of the post-production stage, and paid by it in the taxation year or within 60 days after the end of the taxation year (other than amounts incurred in that preceding taxation year that were paid within 60 days after the end of that preceding taxation year),

(b) that portion of the remuneration (other than salary or wages and other than remuneration that relates to services rendered in the preceding taxation year and that was paid within 60 days after the end of that preceding taxation year) that is directly attributable to the production of property, that relates to services rendered after 1994 and in the taxation year, or that preceding taxation year, to the corporation for the stages of production, from the production commencement time to the end of the post-production stage, and that is paid by it in the taxation year or within 60 days after the end of the taxation year to

(i) an individual who is not an employee of the corporation, to the extent that the amount paid

(A) is attributable to services personally rendered by the individual for the production of the property, or

(B) is attributable to and does not exceed the salary or wages of the individual's employees for personally rendering services for the production of the property,

(ii) another taxable Canadian corporation, to the extent that the amount paid is attributable to and does not exceed the salary or wages of the other corporation's employees for personally rendering services for the production of the property,

(iii) another taxable Canadian corporation all the issued and outstanding shares of the capital stock of which (except directors' qualifying shares) belong to an individual and the activities of which consist principally of the provision of the individual's services, to the extent that the amount paid is attributable to services rendered personally by the individual for the production of the property, or

(iv) a partnership that is carrying on business in Canada, to the extent that the amount paid

(A) is attributable to services personally rendered by an individual who is a member of the partnership for the production of the property, or

(B) is attributable to and does not exceed the salary or wages of the partnership's employees for personally rendering services for the production of the property, and

(c) where

(i) the corporation is a subsidiary wholly-owned corporation of another taxable Canadian corporation (in this section referred to as the "parent"), and

(ii) the corporation and the parent have agreed that this paragraph apply in respect of the production,

the reimbursement made by the corporation in the year, or within 60 days after the end of the year, of an expenditure that was incurred by the parent in a particular taxation year of the parent in respect of that production and that would be included in the labour expenditure of the corporation in respect of the property for the particular taxation year because of paragraph (a) or (b) if

(iii) the corporation had had such a particular taxation year, and

(iv) the expenditure were incurred by the corporation for the same purpose as it was by the parent and were paid at the same time and to the same person or partnership as it was by the parent.

Related Provisions: 13(7)–(7.4) — Capital cost of depreciable property; 125.4(1), 248(1) — Extended meaning of salary or wages; 125.4(2) — Rules governing labour expenditure; *Interpretation Act* 27(5) — Meaning of "within 60 days".

Notes: The word "from" in "from the production commencement time to the end of the post-production stage" is inclusive of both dates: *Rookie Blue Two*, 2015 ONSC 1618 (dealing with the parallel Ontario credit; this was overturned by retroactive amendment announced in the April 24/15 Ontario budget, p. 329).

For "directors' qualifying shares" in (b)(iii), see Notes to 85(1.3).

Everything before (b)(i) amended by 2014 budget bill #2, effective on the same basis as the amendment to 125.4(1)"assistance".

"production commencement time", in respect of a Canadian film or video production, means the earlier of

(a) the time at which principal photography of the production begins, and

(b) the latest of

(i) the time at which a qualified corporation that has an interest in, or for civil law a right in, the production, or the parent of the corporation, first makes an expenditure for salary or wages or other remuneration for activities, of scriptwriters, that are directly attributable to the development by the corporation of script material of the production,

(ii) the time at which the corporation or the parent of the corporation acquires a property, on which the production is based, that is a published literary work, screenplay, play, personal history or all or part of the script material of the production, and

(iii) two years before the date on which principal photography of the production begins.

Notes: Definition added by 2014 budget bill #2, effective on the same basis as the amendment to 125.4(1)"assistance". It is identical to that proposed in 2007; see Notes to 125.4(1)"Canadian film or video production certificate".

"qualified corporation" for a taxation year means a corporation that is throughout the year a prescribed taxable Canadian corporation the activities of which in the year are primarily the carrying on through a permanent establishment (as defined by regulation) in Canada of a business that is a Canadian film or video production business.

Notes: In *Global Video*, 2005 TCC 742, the credit was denied because production of Canadian films was not the taxpayer's primary business activity.

A single purpose corporation (incorporated for one production) can qualify, whether or not its parent is a qualified corporation: VIEWS doc 2005-0155621E5.

Regulations: 1106(2) (prescribed taxable Canadian corporation); 8201 (permanent establishment).

"qualified labour expenditure", of a corporation for a taxation year in respect of a Canadian film or video production, means the lesser of

(a) the amount, if any, by which

(i) the total of

(A) the labour expenditure of the corporation for the year in respect of the production, and

(B) the amount by which the total of all amounts each of which is the labour expenditure of the corporation for a preceding taxation year in respect of the production exceeds the total of all amounts each of which is a qualified labour expenditure of the corporation in respect of the production for a preceding taxation year before the end of which the principal filming or taping of the production began

exceeds

(ii) where the corporation is a parent, the total of all amounts each of which is an amount that is the subject of an agreement in respect of the production referred to in paragraph (c) of the definition "labour expenditure" between the corporation and its wholly-owned corporation, and

(b) the amount determined by the formula

$$A - B$$

where

A is 60% of the amount by which

(i) the total of all amounts each of which is an expenditure by the corporation in respect of the production that is included in the cost to, or in the case of depreciable property the capital cost to, the corporation or any other person or partnership of the production at the end of the taxation year,

exceeds

(ii) the total of all amounts each of which is an amount of assistance in respect of that cost that, at the time of the filing of its return of income for the year, the corporation or any other person or partnership has received, is entitled to receive or can reasonably be expected to receive, that has not been repaid before that time pursuant to a legal obligation to do so (and that does not otherwise reduce that cost), and

B is the total of all amounts each of which is the qualified labour expenditure of the corporation in respect of the production for a preceding taxation year before the end of which the principal filming or taping of the production began.

Related Provisions: 257 — Formula cannot calculate to less than zero.

Notes: If a conditional loan is repaid in a later year, the taxpayer cannot refile its earlier return to delete the "assistance", but effectively gets the claim in the later year: VIEWS doc 2005-0111129I7.

Fees received by a producer will be counted as either income or proceeds of disposition, and not double-counted for purposes of the credit: VIEWS doc 2006-0167941E5.

Definition amended by 2014 budget bill #2, effective on the same basis as the amendment to 125.4(1)"assistance". The amendment is identical to one proposed in 2007; see Notes to 125.4(1)"Canadian film or video production certificate".

"salary or wages" does not include an amount

(a) described in section 7;

(b) determined by reference to profits or revenues; or

(c) paid to a person in respect of services rendered by the person at a time when the person was non-resident, unless the person was at that time a Canadian citizen.

Related Provisions: 125.4(2)(a) — Meaning of "remuneration"; 248(1)"salary or wages" — Definition extended to include all income from employment.

Notes: "Salary or wages", as defined in 248(1), includes taxable employment benefits, but due to this definition does not include stock option benefits, profit-sharing or sales-based bonuses or commissions.

Para. (c) added by 2014 budget bill #2 [(a) and (b) were formerly in the body of the definition], effective on the same basis as the amendment to 125.4(1)"assistance". This amendment is identical to one proposed in 2007; see Notes to 125.4(1)"Canadian film or video production certificate".

"script material", in respect of a production, means written material describing the story on which the production is based and, for greater certainty, includes a draft script, an original story, a screen story, a narration, a television production concept, an outline or a scene-by-scene schematic, synopsis or treatment.

Notes: Definition added by 2014 budget bill #2, effective on the same basis as the amendment to 125.4(1)"assistance". It is identical to that proposed in 2007; see Notes to 125.4(1)"Canadian film or video production certificate".

(2) Rules governing labour expenditures of a corporation — For the purposes of the definitions "labour expenditure" and "qualified labour expenditure" in subsection (1),

(a) remuneration does not include remuneration

(i) determined by reference to profits or revenues, or

(ii) in respect of services rendered by a person at a time when the person was non-resident, unless the person was at that time a Canadian citizen;

(b) services referred to in paragraph (b) of that definition that relate to the post-production stage of the production include only the services that are rendered at that stage by a person who performs the duties of animation cameraman, assistant colourist, assistant mixer, assistant sound-effects technician, boom operator, colourist, computer graphics designer, cutter, developing technician, director of post production, dubbing technician, encoding technician, inspection technician — clean up, mixer, optical effects technician, picture editor, printing technician, projectionist, recording technician, senior editor, sound editor, sound-effects technician, special effects editor, subtitle technician, timer, video-film recorder operator, videotape operator or by a person who performs a prescribed duty;

(c) that definition does not apply to an amount to which section 37 applies; and

(d) an expenditure incurred in respect of a film or video production by a qualified corporation (in this paragraph referred to as the "co-producer") in respect of goods supplied or services rendered by another qualified corporation to the co-producer in respect of the production is not a labour expenditure to the co-producer or, for the purpose of applying this section to the co-producer, a cost or capital cost of the production.

Notes: 125.4(2)(a)(ii) and (d) added, and opening words amended to refer to a qualified labour expenditure, by 2014 budget bill #2, effective on the same basis as the amendment to 125.4(1)"assistance". These amendments are identical to those proposed in 2007; see Notes to 125.4(1)"Canadian film or video production certificate".

125.4(2)(c) added by 2001 technical bill, effective December 1999.

(3) Tax credit — Where

(a) a qualified corporation for a taxation year files with its return of income for the year

    (i) a Canadian film or video production certificate issued in respect of a Canadian film or video production of the corporation,

    (ii) a prescribed form containing prescribed information, and

    (iii) each other document prescribed in respect of the production, and

(b) the principal filming or taping of the production began before the end of the year,

the corporation is deemed to have paid on its balance-due day for the year an amount on account of its tax payable under this Part for the year equal to 25% of its qualified labour expenditure for the year in respect of the production.

Proposed Amendments — Canadian Film or Video Production Tax Credit — Extended timelines due to COVID-19

Federal Budget, Supplementary Information, April 19, 2021: See under Reg. 1106(1)"application for a certificate of completion".

Related Provisions: 87(2)(j.94) — Amalgamation — continuing corporation; 125.4(4) — No credit where investor can claim deduction; 125.4(5) — Credit constitutes assistance for purposes of the Act generally; 125.4(6) — Credit lost retroactively if certificate revoked; 125.5(4) — No film/video production services credit if Canadian film/video credit is available under 125.4; 152(1)(b) — Assessment of credit; 157(3)(e), 157(3.1)(c) — Reduction in instalments to reflect credit; 163(2)(f) — Penalty for false statement or omission; 164(1)(a)(ii) — Refund of credit before assessment; 220(6) — Assignment of refund permitted.

Notes: Because the credit is deemed paid on account of tax, it is refunded under 164(1) even if the corporation has no tax to pay for the year. Thus, it operates as a grant to a corporation that is not yet profitable.

In *AJE Productions*, 2003 TCC 517, CRA reduced AJE's claim by 20% because AJE granted the right to 20% of net revenues from a production to a TV network (WTN). The Court held that AJE had not given WTN a 20% ownership interest in the production, and allowed AJE the full credit.

Closing words of 125.4(3) amended by 1996 Budget, effective for 1996 and later taxation years (non-substantive change).

See also Notes at end of 125.4, and Notes to 125.5(3).

Regulations: 1101(5k.1)(a) (separate class for CCA purposes).

Forms: RC4164: Claiming a Canadian film or video production tax credit — guide to Form T1131; T2 Sched. 302: Additional certificate numbers for the Newfoundland and Labrador film and video industry tax credit; T2 Sched. 345: Additional certificate numbers for the Nova Scotia film industry tax credit; T2 Sched. 365: Additional certificate numbers for the New Brunswick film tax credit; T2 Sched. 382: Additional certificate numbers for the Manitoba film and video production tax credit; T2 Sched. 388: Manitoba film and video production tax credit; T2 Sched. 410: Additional certificate numbers for the Saskatchewan film employment tax credit; T1131: Claiming a Canadian

film or video production tax credit; T1196: B.C. film and television tax credit; T1197: B.C. production services tax credit; T2 Sched. 556: Ontario film and television tax credit.

(4) Exception — This section does not apply to a Canadian film or video production if the production — or an interest in a person or partnership that has, directly or indirectly, an interest in, or for civil law a right in, the production — is a tax shelter investment for the purpose of section 143.2.

Notes: In *Big Comfy Corp.*, [2002] 3 C.T.C. 2151 (TCC), 125.4(4) did not apply because the investors' financing arrangement did not give them ownership rights entitling them to claim a deduction for financing costs.

125.4(4) amended by 2014 budget bill #2, effective on the same basis as the amendment to 125.4(1)"investor". This amendment is identical to that proposed in 2007; see Notes to 125.4(1)"Canadian film or video production certificate".

See also Notes at end of 125.4.

(5) When assistance received — For the purposes of this Act other than this section, and for greater certainty, the amount that a corporation is deemed under subsection (3) to have paid for a taxation year is assistance received by the corporation from a government immediately before the end of the year.

Related Provisions: 12(1)(x) — Inclusion of assistance in income; 13(7.4) — Reduction in capital cost of depreciable property to reflect assistance; 53(2)(k) — Reduction in ACB of capital property to reflect assistance.

Notes: Because the amount of the credit is deemed to be government assistance received *before* the end of the year, it reduces the capital cost of production for purposes of claiming capital cost allowance.

See also Notes at end of 125.4. See Notes to 12(1)(x) re treatment of assistance.

(6) Revocation of certificate — If an omission or incorrect statement was made for the purpose of obtaining a Canadian film or video production certificate in respect of a production, or if the production is not a Canadian film or video production,

(a) the Minister of Canadian Heritage may

    (i) revoke the certificate, or

    (ii) if the certificate was issued in respect of productions included in an episodic television series, revoke the certificate in respect of one or more episodes in the series;

(b) for greater certainty, for the purposes of this section, the expenditures and cost of production in respect of productions included in an episodic television series that relate to an episode in the series in respect of which a certificate has been revoked are not attributable to a Canadian film or video production; and

(c) for the purpose of subparagraph (3)(a)(i), a certificate that has been revoked is deemed never to have been issued.

Related Provisions: 241(3.3) — Disclosure to public of information on revoked certificate.

Notes: In *Studios St-Antoine*, 2011 FC 1521, a certificate revocation was overturned as unreasonable, where the French co-producer had gone into receivership and the Canadian producer bought back its interest from the receiver (without clearing this first with Telefilm Canada), so that the film was no longer a treaty co-production under Reg. 1106(3). The Court sent the file back to the Minister of Canadian Heritage on the basis that Telefilm had enough information by the deadline to recommend the certificate be issued. However, in *Productions Espace Vert VIII*, 2011 FC 1522 (decided at the same time as *St-Antoine* by the same judge), a revocation on the same facts were upheld, as the process was not as far along and the film lost its coproduction status.

In *Productions Tooncan XIII*, 2011 FC 1520 (also same time, same judge), a Part A certificate for a co-production with Spain was revoked because the treaty with Spain was not expanded to include TV productions in time to meet the 48-month filing deadline (Reg. 1106(1)"application for a certificate of completion" and "certificate of completion"). The Minister of Canadian Heritage breached procedural fairness, but could not have reached any other decision (since there was no legal authority to grant the certificate), so the revocation was upheld.

125.4(6) amended by 2014 budget bill #2, effective Nov. 15, 2003, effectively to add (a)(ii) and (b). This amendment is identical to that proposed in 2007; see Notes to 125.4(1)"Canadian film or video production certificate".

(7) Guidelines — The Minister of Canadian Heritage shall issue guidelines respecting the circumstances under which the conditions in the definition "Canadian film or video production certificate" in subsection (1) are satisfied. For greater certainty, those guidelines are not statutory instruments as defined in the *Statutory Instruments Act*.

Notes: 125.4(7) added by 2014 budget bill #2, effective for film or video productions in respect of which certificates are issued by the Minister of Canadian Heritage after Dec. 20, 2002. It is almost identical to 125.4(7) proposed in 2007, which referred to "paragraphs (a) and (b) of the definition" of CFVPC; see Notes to 125.4(1)"Canadian film or video production certificate".

Notes [s. 125.4]: 125.4 provides the Canadian film or video production tax credit, which has replaced an exemption from the at-risk rules in 96(2.2)(d)(ii). Generally, this credit (125.4(3)) is 25% of qualified labour expenditures incurred by a qualified corporation for production of a Canadian film or video production, capped at 15% of the production cost (125.4(1)"qualified labour expenditure"(b)A: 25% × 60%). See guide RC4164 and canada.ca/taxes-film. (See also the film production *services* credit in 125.5.) Total projected 125.4 credits were $290 million in 2019, $220 in 2020, $265m in 2021 and $310m in 2022: *Report on Federal Tax Expenditures 2021*.

For case law, see Notes to the 125.4 subsections and Reg. 1106(1)"excluded production". For a dispute between investors and producers over rights to film credits, see *Grosvenor Park v. Arc Productions*, 2020 ONSC 5651 (220(6) permits a corporation to assign a tax refund).

For detailed discussion of 125.4 (before the 2014 amendments) and the film shelter rules that preceded it, see Bacal et al., "Raise the Curtain", 43(6) *Canadian Tax Journal* 1965-2007 (1995). See also Notes to 18.1(17) and 96(2.2); Zitzerman, "Structuring an International Treaty Co-Production", 3 *Privately Held Companies & Taxes* (Carswell) 5-11 (Oct. 2014); Duarte, *Canadian Film & Television Business and Legal Practice* (Carswell, looseleaf or ProView), chap. 17.

For an interpretation on transfer of a Canadian film or video production to a parent company, see VIEWS doc 2009-0348461I7. The production is Class 10(x) property, deemed a separate class by Reg. 1101(5k.1). On whether the production costs are current or capital, see 2010-0355761I7 (no specific rules). Where corporate producers are amalgamated or wound up, see 2012-0449101E5.

CRA has Film Services Units in several Tax Services Offices to provide specialized assistance with the credit. See canada.ca/taxes-film. The target (tinyurl.com/cra-standards) is to process film-credit claims within 120 days if audited, 90% of the time; in 2019-20, it did 93%. See also the Canadian Audio-Visual Certification Office (CAVCO) website.

The Film Industry Advisory Committee, which provided input to the CRA, was disbanded along with all other CRA advisory committees on Sept. 25, 2006, as part of a Conservative government cost-cutting measure.

Revenue Canada published a detailed "Questions and Answers About Film Tax Credit Programs" in 1999. It is reproduced on *TaxPartner* and *Taxnet Pro* under "Selected CRA Releases" (1999-05-28).

Most provinces also offer a film credit, e.g. Ontario Film and Television Tax Credit (omdc.on.ca), Film Incentive BC (bcfilm.bc.ca). See tinyurl.com/pwc-films (PWC, *The big table*) for a list with credit rates and links to each province's program.

125.4 added by 1995 Budget, for 1995 and later taxation years (and substantially amended by 2014 budget bill #2, as per Notes to subsections above).

Definitions [s. 125.4]: "amount" — 248(1); "assistance" — 125.4(1), (5); "balance-due day" — 248(1); "business" — 248(1); "Canada" — 255; "Canadian film or video production", "Canadian film or video production certificate" — 125.4(1); "capital cost" — of depreciable property 13(7)–(7.4), (10), 70(13), 128.1(1)(c), 128.1(4)(c); "carrying on business in Canada" — 253; "corporation" — 248(1), *Interpretation Act* 35(1); "depreciable property" — 13(21), 248(1); "employee", "individual" — 248(1); "labour expenditure" — 125.4(1), (2); "non-resident" — 248(1); "parent" — 125.4(1)"labour expenditure"(c)(i); "partnership" — see 96(1) Notes; "permanent establishment" — Reg. 8201; "person", "prescribed" — 248(1); "prescribed taxable Canadian corporation" — Reg. 1106(2); "production commencement time" — 125.4(1); "property" — 248(1); "qualified corporation", "qualified labour expenditure" — 125.4(1); "qualifying share" — 192(6), 248(1) *[not intended to apply to s. 125.4]*; "regulation" — 248(1); "related" — 251(2)–(6); "remuneration" — 125.4(2)(a); "salary or wages" — 125.4(1), 248(1); "script material" — 125.4(1); "share", "subsidiary wholly-owned corporation" — 248(1); "tax shelter investment" — 143.2(1); "taxable Canadian corporation" — 89(1), 248(1); "taxation year" — 249; "taxpayer" — 248(1); "treaty co-production" — Reg. 1106(3); "written" — *Interpretation Act* 35(1)"writing".

CRA Audit Manual [s. 125.4]: 10.11.12: Consultation regarding film tax credits; 15.12.1: Film services unit.

Film or Video Production Services Tax Credit

125.5 (1) Definitions — The definitions in this subsection apply in this section.

"accredited film or video production certificate", in respect of a film or video production, means a certificate issued by the Minister of Canadian Heritage certifying that the production is an accredited production.

Related Provisions: 125.5(3) — Tax credit if certificate issued; 125.5(6) — Revocation of certificate; 152(4.2)(b) — Redetermination of credit at taxpayer's request.

"accredited production" has the meaning assigned by regulation.

Regulations: 9300 (meaning of accredited production).

"assistance" means an amount, other than an amount deemed under subsection (3) to have been paid, that would be included under paragraph 12(1)(x) in computing the income of a taxpayer for any taxation year if that paragraph were read without reference to subparagraphs (v) to (vii).

Related Provisions: 241(4)(d)(xv) — Disclosure of information to government agency providing assistance.

"Canadian labour expenditure" of a corporation for a taxation year in respect of an accredited production means, in the case of a corporation that is not an eligible production corporation in respect of the production for the year, nil, and in any other case, subject to subsection (2), the total of the following amounts in respect of the production to the extent that they are reasonable in the circumstances:

(a) the salary or wages directly attributable to the production that are incurred by the corporation after October 1997, and in the year or the preceding taxation year, and that relate to services rendered in Canada for the stages of production of the production, from the final script stage to the end of the post-production stage, and paid by it in the year or within 60 days after the end of the year to employees of the corporation who were resident in Canada at the time the payments were made (other than amounts incurred in that preceding year that were paid within 60 days after the end of that preceding year),

(b) that portion of the remuneration (other than salary or wages and other than remuneration that relates to services rendered in the preceding taxation year and that was paid within 60 days after the end of that preceding year) that is directly attributable to the production, that relates to services rendered in Canada after October 1997 and in the year, or that preceding year, to the corporation for the stages of production of the production, from the final script stage to the end of the post-production stage, and that is paid by it in the year or within 60 days after the end of the year to a person or a partnership, that carries on a business in Canada through a permanent establishment (as defined by regulation), and that is

(i) an individual resident in Canada at the time the amount is paid and who is not an employee of the corporation, to the extent that the amount paid

(A) is attributable to services personally rendered by the individual in Canada in respect of the accredited production, or

(B) is attributable to and does not exceed the salary or wages paid by the individual to the individual's employees at a time when they were resident in Canada for personally rendering services in Canada in respect of the accredited production,

(ii) another corporation that is a taxable Canadian corporation, to the extent that the amount paid is attributable to and does not exceed the salary or wages paid to the other corporation's employees at a time when they were resident in Canada for personally rendering services in Canada in respect of the accredited production,

(iii) another corporation that is a taxable Canadian corporation, all the issued and outstanding shares of the capital stock of which (except directors' qualifying shares) belong to an individual who was resident in Canada and the activities of which consist principally of the provision of the individual's services, to the extent that the amount paid is attributable to services rendered personally in Canada by the individual in respect of the accredited production, or

(iv) a partnership, to the extent that the amount paid

(A) is attributable to services personally rendered in respect of the accredited production by an individual who is resident in Canada and who is a member of the partnership, or

(B) is attributable to and does not exceed the salary or wages paid by the partnership to its employees at a time when they were resident in Canada for personally rendering services in Canada in respect of the accredited production, and

(c) where

(i) the corporation is a subsidiary wholly-owned corporation of another corporation that is a taxable Canadian corporation (in this section referred to as the "parent"), and

(ii) the corporation and the parent have filed with the Minister an agreement that this paragraph apply in respect of the production,

the reimbursement made by the corporation in the year, or within 60 days after the end of the year, of an expenditure that was incurred by the parent in a particular taxation year of the parent in respect of the production and that would be included in the Canadian labour expenditure of the corporation in respect of the production for the particular taxation year because of paragraph (a) or (b) if

(iii) the corporation had had such a particular taxation year, and

(iv) the expenditure were incurred by the corporation for the same purpose as it was incurred by the parent and were paid at the same time and to the same person or partnership as it was paid by the parent.

Related Provisions: 13(7)–(7.4) — Capital cost of depreciable property; 87(2)(j.94) — Amalgamation — continuing corporation; 125.5(1), 248(1) — Extended meaning of salary or wages; 125.5(2) — Rules governing labour expenditure; *Interpretation Act* 27(5) — Meaning of "within 60 days".

Notes: The word "from" in "from the final script stage to the end of the post-production stage" is inclusive of both dates; see Notes to 125.4(1)"labour expenditure".

For "directors' qualifying shares" in (b)(iii), see Notes to 85(1.3).

Regulations: 8201 (permanent establishment).

"eligible production corporation", in respect of an accredited production for a taxation year, means a corporation, the activities of which in the year in Canada are primarily the carrying on through a permanent establishment (as defined by regulation) in Canada of a film or video production business or a film or video production services business and that

(a) owns the copyright in the accredited production throughout the period during which the production is produced in Canada, or

(b) has contracted directly with the owner of the copyright in the accredited production to provide production services in respect of the production, where the owner of the copyright is not an eligible production corporation in respect of the production,

except a corporation that is, at any time in the year,

(c) a person all or part of whose taxable income is exempt from tax under this Part,

(d) controlled directly or indirectly in any manner whatever by one or more persons all or part of whose taxable income is exempt from tax under this Part, or

(e) prescribed to be a labour-sponsored venture capital corporation for the purpose of section 127.4.

Related Provisions: 256(5.1), (6.2) — Controlled directly or indirectly.

Notes: In *Snow White Productions v. PMP*, 2004 BCSC 604, the Court rectified a production arrangement to meet the definition's conditions, where it was clear the parties intended to obtain the production credit. (See Notes to 169(1) re rectification; due to *Fairmont Hotels* this would no longer be granted.)

The words "and that" before para. (a) refer to the corporation, not the business, and introduce a distinct test: VIEWS doc 2014-0532801I7.

A corporation indirectly controlled by a province probably cannot be an eligible production corporation due to para. (d): VIEWS doc 2003-0014655.

Words between paras. (b) and (c) amended by 2001 technical bill to add "at any time in the year", effective December 1999.

Regulations: 6701 (prescribed labour-sponsored venture capital corporation); 8201 (permanent establishment).

"qualified Canadian labour expenditure" of an eligible production corporation for a taxation year in respect of an accredited production means the amount, if any, by which

(a) the total of all amounts each of which is the corporation's Canadian labour expenditure for the year or a preceding taxation year

exceeds the aggregate of

(b) the total of all amounts, each of which is an amount of assistance that can reasonably be considered to be in respect of amounts included in the total determined under paragraph (a) in respect of the corporation for the year that, at the time of filing its return of income for the year, the corporation or any other person or partnership has received, is entitled to receive or can reasonably be expected to receive, that has not been repaid before that time pursuant to a legal obligation to do so (and that does not otherwise reduce that expenditure),

(c) the total of all amounts, each of which is the qualified Canadian labour expenditure of the corporation in respect of the accredited production for a preceding taxation year before the end of which the principal filming or taping of the production began, and

(d) where the corporation is a parent, the total of all amounts each of which is included in the total determined under paragraph (a) in respect of the corporation for the year and is the subject of an agreement in respect of the accredited production referred to in paragraph (c) of the definition "Canadian labour expenditure" between the corporation and its subsidiary wholly-owned corporation.

Notes: See Notes at end of 125.5.

"salary or wages" does not include an amount described in section 7 or an amount determined by reference to profits or revenues.

Related Provisions: 125.5(2)(a) — Meaning of "remuneration"; 248(1)"salary or wages" — Definition extended to include all income from employment.

Notes: "Salary or wages", as defined in 248(1), includes taxable employment benefits, but due to this definition does not include stock option benefits, or profit-sharing or sales-based bonuses.

(2) Rules governing Canadian labour expenditure of a corporation — For the purpose of the definition "Canadian labour expenditure" in subsection (1),

(a) remuneration does not include remuneration determined by reference to profits or revenues;

(b) services referred to in paragraph (b) of that definition that relate to the post-production stage of the accredited production include only the services that are rendered at that stage by a person who performs the duties of animation cameraman, assistant colourist, assistant mixer, assistant sound-effects technician, boom operator, colourist, computer graphics designer, cutter, developing technician, director of post production, dubbing technician, encoding technician, inspection technician — clean up, mixer, optical effects technician, picture editor, printing technician, projectionist, recording technician, senior editor, sound editor, sound-effects technician, special effects editor, subtitle technician, timer, video-film recorder operator, videotape operator or by a person who performs a prescribed duty;

(c) that definition does not apply to an amount to which section 37 applies; and

(d) for greater certainty, that definition does not apply to an amount that is not a production cost including an amount in respect of advertising, marketing, promotion, market research or an amount related in any way to another film or video production.

(3) Tax credit — An eligible production corporation in respect of an accredited production for a taxation year is deemed to have paid on its balance-due day for the year an amount on account of its tax payable under this Part for the year equal to 16% of its qualified

Canadian labour expenditure for the year in respect of the production, if

>　(a) the corporation files with its return of income for the year
>
>>　(i) a prescribed form containing prescribed information in respect of the production,
>>
>>　(ii) an accredited film or video production certificate in respect of the production, and
>>
>>　(iii) each other document prescribed in respect of the production; and
>
>　(b) the principal filming or taping of the production began before the end of the year.

Proposed Amendments — Film or Video Production Services Tax Credit — Extended timelines due to COVID-19

Federal Budget, Supplementary Information, April 19, 2021: See under Reg. 1106(1)"application for a certificate of completion".

Related Provisions: 87(2)(j.94) — Amalgamation — continuing corporation; 125.5(4) — No credit if 125.4 credit allowed; 125.5(5) — Credit constitutes assistance for purposes of the Act; 125.5(6) — Credit lost retroactively if certificate revoked; 152(1)(b) — Assessment of credit; 157(3)(e), 157(3.1)(c) — Reduction in instalments to reflect credit; 163(2)(g) — Penalty for false statement or omission; 164(1)(a)(ii) — Refund of credit before assessment.

Notes: Because the credit is deemed paid on account of tax (like an instalment), it is refunded to the corporation even if the corp has no tax to pay for the year.

This credit is for *foreign* films and videos that are produced in Canada. The 125.4 credit, which takes precedence over this one (see 125.5(4)), is for *Canadian* productions.

125.5(3) amended by 2003 Budget, for Canadian labour expenditures incurred after Feb. 18, 2003, primarily to increase the credit from 11% to 16%.

See also Notes at end of 125.5 and at end of 125.4.

Forms: RC4385: Guide to Form T1177; T1177: Film or video production services tax credit.

(4) Canadian film or video production

— Subsection (3) does not apply in respect of a production in respect of which an amount is deemed to have been paid under subsection 125.4(3).

(5) When assistance received

— For the purposes of this Act other than this section, and for greater certainty, the amount that a corporation is deemed under subsection (3) to have paid for a taxation year is assistance received by the corporation from a government immediately before the end of the year.

Related Provisions: 12(1)(x) — Inclusion of assistance into income; 13(7.4) — Reduction in capital cost of depreciable property to reflect assistance; 53(2)(k) — Reduction in ACB of capital property to reflect assistance.

Notes: See Notes to 12(1)(x) re treatment of assistance, and Notes at end of 125.5 re enactment.

(6) Revocation of certificate

— An accredited film or video production certificate in respect of an accredited production may be revoked by the Minister of Canadian Heritage where

>　(a) an omission or incorrect statement was made for the purpose of obtaining the certificate, or
>
>　(b) the production is not an accredited production,

and, for the purpose of subparagraph (3)(a)(ii), a certificate that has been revoked is deemed never to have been issued.

Notes [125.5]: 125.5 (added by 1995-97 technical bill, for tax years ending after Oct. 1997) implements a refundable (see 125.5(3)) 16% credit for film production services, to stimulate the production of foreign films in Canada. See Guide RC4385 and canada.ca/taxes-film. For a parallel credit for Canadian film productions, see 125.4. Total projected 125.5 credits were $315 million in 2019, $235m in 2020, $285m in 2021 and $335m in 2022: *Report on Federal Tax Expenditures 2021*.

See Notes at end of 125.4 re CRA Film Services Units and service standards.

Most provinces offer a similar credit: see tinyurl.com/pwc-films. In *Confessions Productions*, 2014 BCSC 813, the CRA as administrator of the BC credit could not refuse that credit when it had allowed the federal one.

See also Tony Duarte, *Canadian Film & Television Business and Legal Practice* (Carswell, looseleaf or ProView), chap. 17.

Definitions [s. 125.5]: "accredited film or video production certificate", "accredited production" — 125.5(1); "amount" — 248(1); "assistance" — 125.5(1), (5); "balance-

due day", "business" — 248(1); "Canada" — 255; "Canadian labour expenditure" — 125.5(1); "carries on business in Canada", "carries on a business in Canada" — 253; "controlled directly or indirectly" — 256(5.1)–(6); "corporation" — 248(1), *Interpretation Act* 35(1); eligible production corporation" — 248(1); "employee", "individual" — 248(1); "labour-sponsored venture capital corporation" — Reg. 6701; "parent" — 125.5(1)"Canadian labour expenditure"(c)(i); "partnership" — see 96(1) Notes; "permanent establishment" — Reg. 8201; "person", "prescribed" — 248(1); "qualified Canadian labour expenditure" — 125.5(1); "qualifying share" — 192(6), 248(1) *[not intended to apply to s. 125.5]*; "regulation" — 248(1); "remuneration" — 125.5(2)(a); "resident in Canada" — 250; "salary or wages" — 125.5(1), 248(1); "share" — 248(1); "subsidiary wholly-owned corporation" — 248(1); "taxable Canadian corporation" — 89(1), 248(1); "taxation year" — 249.

CRA Audit Manual [s. 125.5]: 10.11.12: Consultation regarding film tax credits; 15.12.1: Film services unit.

[Labour Credit for Journalism Organizations]

125.6 (1) Definitions — The following definitions apply in this section.

"assistance" means an amount, other than an amount received from the Aid to Publishers component of the Canada Periodical Fund or an amount deemed under subsection (2) to have been paid, that would be included under paragraph 12(1)(x) in computing the income of a taxpayer for any taxation year if that paragraph were read without reference to

>　(a) subparagraphs 12(1)(x)(v) to (viii), if the amount were received
>
>>　(i) from a person or partnership described in subparagraph 12(1)(x)(ii), or
>>
>>　(ii) in circumstances where clause 12(1)(x)(i)(C) applies; and
>
>　(b) subparagraphs 12(1)(x)(v) to (vii), in any other case.

Related Provisions: 125.6(1)"qualifying labour expenditure"(b)B — Assistance reduces entitlement to credit.

Notes: Opening words amended by 2021 budget bill #1, retroactive to 2019, to add "other than an amount received from the Aid to Publishers *[A2P]* component of the Canada Periodical Fund or". Instead of being "assistance" that reduces the credit via 125.6(1)"qualifying labour expenditure"B, A2P funding reduces the credit directly via 125.6(2)B, (2.1)B.

"Assistance" describes amounts that reduce the cost of 125.6(1)"qualifying labour expenditures". The definition is based on amounts that would be included in income under 12(1)(x), and is the same as 125.4(1)"assistance", which applies for the Canadian film/video production credit. It excludes the 125.6 credit itself.

"eligible newsroom employee", in respect of a qualifying journalism organization in a taxation year, means an individual who

>　(a) is employed by the organization in the taxation year;
>
>　(b) works, on average, a minimum of 26 hours per week throughout the portion of the taxation year in which the individual is employed by the organization;
>
>　(c) at any time in the taxation year, has been, or is reasonably expected to be, employed by the organization for a minimum period of 40 consecutive weeks that includes that time;
>
>　(d) spends at least 75% of their time engaged in the production of original written news content, including by researching, collecting information, verifying facts, photographing, writing, editing, designing and otherwise preparing content; and
>
>　(e) meets any prescribed conditions.

Related Provisions: 125.6(1)"qualifying labour expenditure"(b)A — Salary of employee generates credit.

Notes: The employee must spend at least 75% of their time in the production of (original) news content. This is not limited to journalists; it can include editors, photographers and graphic designers. (Finance Technical Notes)

Para. (d) amended by 2021 budget bill #1, retroactive to 2019, to add "original written" (due to 125.6(1)"qualifying journalism organization"(a) being deleted).

"qualifying journalism organization", at any time, means a qualified Canadian journalism organization that meets the following conditions:

>　(a) it does not hold a "licence", as defined in subsection 2(1) of the *Broadcasting Act*; and

(b) if it is a corporation having share capital, it meets the conditions in subparagraph (e)(iii) of the definition "Canadian newspaper" in subsection 19(5).

(c) [Repealed]

(d) [Repealed]

Related Provisions: 87(2)(j.96) — Amalgamation — continuing corporation.

Notes: This definition is different from that of the same term in 149.1(1). It is also distinct from "qualified Canadian journalism organization" and "registered journalism organization", both defined in 248(1).

Paras. (a)-(d) changed to (a)-(b) by 2021 budget bill #1, retroactive to 2019. The previous version, now deemed never to have been in force, read:

> (a) it is primarily engaged in the production of original written news content;
>
> (b) it does not carry on a "broadcasting undertaking" as defined in subsection 2(1) of the *Broadcasting Act*;
>
> (c) it does not, in the taxation year in which the time occurs, receive an amount from the Aid to Publishers component of the Canada Periodical Fund; and
>
> (d) if it is a corporation having share capital, it meets the conditions in subparagraph (e)(iii) of the definition "Canadian newspaper" in subsection 19(5).

Former (a) was deleted to remove the "primarily" requirement; an "original news content" requirement continues in 248(1)"qualified Canadian journalism organization"(a)(v), and was added to 125.6(1)"eligible newsroom employee"(d). The change to (b) [new (a)] allows broadcasting of podcasts, as these do not require a "licence" (*Broadcasting Act* s. 2(1) defines "licence" as "a licence to carry on a broadcasting undertaking issued by the Commission under this Act", and defines "Commission" as the Canadian Radio-television and Telecommunications Commission). Deletion of (c) means that Aid to Publishers funding does not disqualify an organization; instead it reduces the credit via 125.6(2)B, (2.1)B. Para. (d) was renumbered (b).

"qualifying labour expenditure", of a taxpayer for a taxation year in respect of an eligible newsroom employee, means the lesser of

(a) the amount determined by the formula

$$\$55,000^2 \times A/365$$

where

A is the lesser of 365 and the number of days in the taxation year in which the taxpayer is a qualifying journalism organization, and

(b) the amount determined by the formula

$$A - B$$

where

A is the salary or wages payable by the taxpayer to the eligible newsroom employee in respect of the portion of the taxation year throughout which the taxpayer is a qualifying journalism organization, and

B is the total of all amounts each of which is an amount of assistance that

(i) the taxpayer has received, is entitled to receive or can reasonably be expected to receive, in respect of amounts described in A, and

(ii) has not been repaid before the end of the year pursuant to a legal obligation to do so.

Related Provisions: 125.6(2)A — Refundable credit of 25% of QLE; 257 — Formula cannot calculate to less than zero.

Notes: The 125.6(2) credit is 25% of a qualifying journalism organization's qualifying labour expenditures (QLE). QLE is defined in respect of an eligible newsroom employee and is generally the salary or wages payable by the organization to the employee. QLE is decreased by any "assistance" (defined in 125.6(1)) received in respect of the employee. QLE is subject to an annual cap of $55,000 per employee, prorated for short tax years. Due to "lesser of 365..." in A, in a leap year the maximum QLE is still $55,000.

"A" amended by 2021 budget bill #1, retroactive to 2019, to add "in which the taxpayer is a qualifying journalism organization".

(2) Tax credit — A taxpayer (other than a partnership) that is a qualifying journalism organization at any time in a taxation year and that files a prescribed form containing prescribed information with its return of income for the year is deemed to have, on its bal-ance-due day for the year, paid on account of its tax payable under this Part for the year an amount determined by the formula

$$0.25(A) - B$$

where

A is the total of all amounts each of which is a qualifying labour expenditure of the qualifying journalism organization for the year in respect of an eligible newsroom employee; and

B is the amount received by the taxpayer from the Aid to Publishers component of the Canada Periodical Fund in the year.

Related Provisions: 87(2)(j.96) — Amalgamation — continuing corporation; 125.6(2.1) — Active partner eligible for credit if partnership is QJO; 125.6(2.2) — "Taxpayer" includes partnership; 125.6(3) — Credit deemed received as assistance before year-end for other purposes; 152(1)(b) — Assessment of credit; 157(3)(e), 157(3.1)(c) — Reduction in instalments to reflect credit; 163(2)(h) — Penalty for false statement or omission; 164(1)(a)(ii) — Refund of credit before assessment; 257 — Formula cannot calculate to less than zero.

Notes: 125.6(2) provides the refundable labour tax credit for journalism organizations (corporations claim it on T2 Sched. 58), of 25% of "qualifying labour expenditures" for the year. (If the organization is a partnership, the credit is provided to the active partners under 125.6(2.1).) Because the taxpayer is "deemed to have paid" the amount, it, like instalments or source deductions, is treated as a credit to the account that is fully refundable even if no tax is payable for the year, and even if the organization is a non-profit or charity that never pays income tax.

See CRA Q&A, "Refundable labour tax credit" (May 3, 2019), tinyurl.com/cra-rltc; *Guidance on the income tax measures to support journalism* (tinyurl.com/cra-journalism, Dec. 2019), §3.

For other 2019 Budget measures supporting journalism see 248(1)"qualified Canadian journalism organization" Notes. Budget Table 1 predicts this credit will cost the federal government $75 million in 2020-21 and $95m in each of 2021-22 to 2023-24.

Formula element B added by 2021 budget bill #1, retroactive to 2019. See Notes to 125.6(1)"assistance".

Forms: T2 Sched. 58: Canadian journalism labour tax credit.

(2.1) Partnership — tax credit — If a taxpayer (other than a partnership) is a member of a partnership (other than a specified member of the partnership) at the end of a fiscal period of the partnership that ends in a taxation year of the taxpayer, the partnership is a qualifying journalism organization at any time in that fiscal period and the partnership files an information return in prescribed form containing prescribed information for that fiscal period, then the taxpayer is deemed to have, on the taxpayer's balance-due day for the taxation year, paid on account of the taxpayer's tax payable under this Part for the taxation year an amount determined by the formula

$$(0.25A - B)C/D$$

where

A is the total of all amounts each of which is a qualifying labour expenditure of the qualifying journalism organization for the fiscal period in respect of an eligible newsroom employee;

B is the amount received by the qualifying journalism organization from the Aid to Publishers component of the Canada Periodical Fund in the fiscal period;

C is the specified proportion of the taxpayer for the fiscal period; and

D is the total of all specified proportions of members of the partnership for the fiscal period, other than members that are partnerships or specified members of the partnership.

Notes: 125.6(2.1) added by 2021 budget bill #1, retroactive to 2019.

Forms: T5013 Sched. 58: Canadian journalism labour tax credit.

(2.2) Partnership — application rule — In this section a taxpayer includes a partnership.

Notes: 125.6(2.2) added by 2021 budget bill #1, retroactive to 2019.

(3) When assistance received — For the purposes of this Act other than this section, and for greater certainty, the amount that a taxpayer is deemed under subsection (2) or (2.1) to have paid for a

---

2 Not indexed for inflation — ed.

taxation year is assistance received by the taxpayer from a government immediately before the end of the year.

Notes: For purposes other than the credit itself, the credit is deemed to be "assistance". See Notes to 12(1)(x) for the treatment of assistance, under 12(1)(x)(iv) and other provisions.

125.6(3) amended by 2021 budget bill #1, retroactive to 2019, to add reference to 125.6(2.1), the labour credit for active partners of qualifying journalism organizations that are structured as partnerships.

Notes [s. 125.6]: See Notes to s. 125.6(2). 125.6 added by 2019 budget bill #1, effective 2019, except that for greater certainty, it does not apply in respect of salary or wages that are in respect of a period before 2019.

Definitions [s. 125.6]: "amount" — 248(1); "assistance" — 125.6(1); "balance-due day" — 248(1); "Canadian newspaper" — 19(5); "corporation" — 248(1), *Interpretation Act* 35(1); "eligible newsroom employee" — 125.6(1); "employed", "employee" — 248(1); "fiscal period" — 249.1; "individual" — 248(1); "partnership" — see 96(1) Notes; "person", "prescribed", "qualified Canadian journalism organization" — 248(1); "qualifying journalism organization", "qualifying labour expenditure" — 125.6(1); "salary or wages", "share", "specified member", "specified proportion" — 248(1); "taxation year" — 249; "taxpayer" — 125.6(2.2), 248(1); "writing", "written" — *Interpretation Act* 35(1)"writing".

[Canada Emergency Wage Subsidy, Canada Emergency Rent Subsidy]

125.7 (1) Definitions — The following definitions apply in this section and in subsection 163(2.901).

"base percentage", of an eligible entity for a qualifying period, means

(a) for the fifth qualifying period,

(i) if the entity's revenue reduction percentage is greater than or equal to 50%, 60%, and

(ii) in any other case, 1.2 multiplied by the revenue reduction percentage;

(b) for the sixth qualifying period,

(i) if the entity's revenue reduction percentage is greater than or equal to 50%, 60%, and

(ii) in any other case, 1.2 multiplied by the revenue reduction percentage;

(c) for the seventh qualifying period,

(i) if the entity's revenue reduction percentage is greater than or equal to 50%, 50%, and

(ii) in any other case, 1 multiplied by the revenue reduction percentage;

(d) for the eighth qualifying period,

(i) if the entity's revenue reduction percentage is greater than or equal to 50%, 40%, and

(ii) in any other case, 0.8 multiplied by the revenue reduction percentage;

(e) for the ninth qualifying period,

(i) if the entity's revenue reduction percentage is greater than or equal to 50%, 40%, and

(ii) in any other case, 0.8 multiplied by the revenue reduction percentage;

(f) for the tenth qualifying period,

(i) if the entity's revenue reduction percentage is greater than or equal to 50%, 40%, and

(ii) in any other case, 0.8 multiplied by the revenue reduction percentage;

(g) for the eleventh qualifying period to the seventeenth qualifying period,

(i) if the entity's revenue reduction percentage is greater than or equal to 50%, 40%, and

(ii) in any other case, the percentage determined by the formula

$$0.8 \times A$$

where

A is the revenue reduction percentage;

(h) for the eighteenth qualifying period,

(i) if the entity's revenue reduction percentage is greater than or equal to 50%, 35%, and

(ii) in any other case, the percentage determined by the formula

$$0.875 \times (A - 10\%)$$

where

A is the revenue reduction percentage;

(i) for the nineteenth qualifying period,

(i) if the entity's revenue reduction percentage is greater than or equal to 50%, 25%, and

(ii) in any other case, the percentage determined by the formula

$$0.625 \times (A - 10\%)$$

where

A is the revenue reduction percentage;

(j) for the twentieth qualifying period,

(i) if the entity's revenue reduction percentage is greater than or equal to 50%, 10%, and

(ii) in any other case, the percentage determined by the formula

$$0.25 \times (A - 10\%)$$

where

A is the revenue reduction percentage; and

(k) for a qualifying period after the twentieth qualifying period, a percentage determined by regulation in respect of the eligible entity or, if there is no percentage determined by regulation for the qualifying period, nil.

Related Provisions: 125.7(8)(a) — Amounts that can be prescribed.

Notes: Paras. (a)-(f) opening words and (g) amended, and (h)-(k) added, by 2021 budget bill #1, effective June 29, 2021, to add from Periods 11 on and refer to all periods by number. Before that date, read:

(a) for the qualifying period referred to in paragraph (c.2) of the definition "qualifying period",

[...]

(b) for the qualifying period referred to in paragraph (c.3) of the definition "qualifying period",

[...]

(c) for the qualifying period referred to in paragraph (c.4) of the definition "qualifying period",

[...]

(d) for the qualifying period referred to in paragraph (c.5) of the definition "qualifying period",

[...]

(e) for the qualifying period referred to in paragraph (c.6) of the definition "qualifying period",

[...]

(f) for the qualifying period referred to in paragraph (c.7) of the definition "qualifying period",

[...]

(g) for a qualifying period referred to in paragraph (d) of the definition "qualifying period", a percentage determined by regulation in respect of the eligible entity.

Before the above amendments, Reg. 8901.2(2) prescribed the percentage (for para. (g)), for Dec. 20/20-June 5/21 (Periods 11-16), as $0.8 \times$ the revenue reduction percentage, max 40%.

Definition amended by 2020 COVID bill #5 retroactive to its introduction (April 11, 2020): (e)(i)-(ii) changed 20% to 40% and 0.4 to 0.8; (f) renumbered as (g) [changed "the" to "a" qualifying period]; new (f) added.

"Base percentage" added by 2020 COVID bill #3, effective April 11, 2020. See 125.7(2) Notes re CEWS Stage 2.

Regulations: 8901.2(2) (prescribed percentages for Dec. 20/20-June 4/21, for para. (g); replaced by amendments to this definition).

"baseline remuneration", in respect of an eligible employee of an eligible entity, means the average weekly eligible remuneration, excluding any period of seven or more consecutive days for which the employee was not remunerated, paid to the eligible employee by the eligible entity during the period that

(a) begins on January 1, 2020 and ends on March 15, 2020; or

(b) if the eligible entity elects,

(i) begins on March 1, 2019 and ends on May 31, 2019, in respect of any of the first qualifying period to the third qualifying period,

(ii) begins on March 1, 2019 and ends on June 30, 2019, in respect of the fourth qualifying period, unless the eligible entity elects to use the period that begins on March 1, 2019 and ends on May 31, 2019 for that qualifying period,

(iii) begins on July 1, 2019 and ends on December 31, 2019, in respect of any of the fifth qualifying period to the thirteenth qualifying period,

(iii.1) begins on March 1, 2019 and ends on June 30, 2019, in respect of any of the fourteenth qualifying period to the seventeenth qualifying period, unless the eligible entity elects to use the period that begins on July 1, 2019 and ends on December 31, 2019 for that qualifying period,

(iii.2) begins on July 1, 2019 and ends on December 31, 2019, in respect of the eighteenth qualifying period and any subsequent qualifying period, or

(iv) if the eligible employee was on leave for any reason mentioned in subsection 12(3) of the *Employment Insurance Act* or section 2 of the *Act respecting parental insurance*, CQLR, c. A-29.011 throughout the period that begins on July 1, 2019 and ends on March 15, 2020, begins 90 days prior to the date on which the employee commenced that leave and ends on the day prior to the date on which they commenced their leave, in respect of the fifth qualifying period and any subsequent qualifying period.

Related Provisions: 125.7(2)A(b)(ii) — Baseline remuneration used as one determinant for CEWS; 125.7(10) — Amending or revoking election.

Notes: For (b)(iv), *EI Act* s. 12(3) refers to pregnancy, newborn child care, prescribed illness/injury and certain family caregiving. The Quebec Act s. 2 refers to maternity, newborn and adopted-child care.

See 125.7(2) Notes, and tinyurl.com/cews-cra-faq qq. 18 to 19.

Subpara. (b)(i)-(iv) amended by 2021 budget bill #1, effective June 29, 2021, to refer to the periods by number and extend to more periods. See 125.7(2) Notes. Before that date, read:

(b) if the eligible entity elects,

(i) begins on March 1, 2019 and ends on May 31, 2019, in respect of a qualifying period described in any of paragraphs (a) to (c) of the definition "qualifying period",

(ii) begins on March 1, 2019 and ends on June 30, 2019, in respect of a qualifying period described in paragraph (c.1) of the definition "qualifying period", unless the eligible entity elects to use the period that begins on March 1, 2019 and ends on May 31, 2019 for that qualifying period,

(iii) begins on July 1, 2019 and ends on December 31, 2019, in respect of a qualifying period described in any of paragraphs (c.2) to (d) of the definition "qualifying period", or

(iv) if the eligible employee was on leave for any reason mentioned in subsection 12(3) of the *Employment Insurance Act* or section 2 of the *Act respecting parental insurance*, CQLR, c. A-29.011 throughout the period that begins on July 1, 2019 and ends on March 15, 2020, begins 90 days prior to the date on which the employee commenced that leave and ends on the day prior to the date on which they commenced their leave, in respect of a qualifying period referred to in any of paragraphs (c.2) to (d) of the definition "qualifying period".

Subpara. (b)(iv) added by 2020 COVID bill #5, retroactive to definition's introduction (April 11, 2020).

Para. (b) added by 2020 COVID bill #3, retroactive to April 11, 2020.

Forms: RC661: CEWS attestation.

"current reference period", for a qualifying period, means

(a) for the first qualifying period, March 2020;

(b) for the second qualifying period, April 2020;

(c) for the third qualifying period, May 2020;

(c.1) for the fourth qualifying period, June 2020;

(c.2) for the fifth qualifying period, July 2020;

(c.3) for the sixth qualifying period, August 2020;

(c.4) for the seventh qualifying period, September 2020;

(c.5) for the eighth qualifying period, October 2020;

(c.6) for the ninth qualifying period, November 2020;

(c.7) for the tenth qualifying period, December 2020;

(c.8) for the eleventh qualifying period, December 2020;

(c.9) for the twelfth qualifying period, January 2021;

(c.91) for the thirteenth qualifying period, February 2021;

(c.92) for the fourteenth qualifying period, March 2021;

(c.93) for the fifteenth qualifying period, April 2021;

(c.94) for the sixteenth qualifying period, May 2021;

(c.95) for the seventeenth qualifying period, June 2021;

(c.96) for the eighteenth qualifying period, July 2021;

(c.97) for the nineteenth qualifying period, August 2021;

(c.98) for the twentieth qualifying period, September 2021;

(c.99) for the twenty-first qualifying period, October 2021;

(c.991) for the twenty-second qualifying period, November 2021; and

Related Provisions: 125.7(1)"qualifying entity"(c) — Current reference period revenues must be sufficiently below earlier revenues; 125.7(9) — Entity that meets conditions for a period qualifies for the next period.

Notes: See 125.7(1)"qualifying period" for the numbers of the qualifying periods.

Paras. (a)-(c.7) changed to (a)-(c.991) by 2021 budget bill #1, effective June 29, 2021, to refer to the periods by number and extend to more periods. See 125.7(2) Notes. Before that date, read:

(a) for the qualifying period referred to in paragraph (a) of the definition "qualifying period", March 2020;

(b) for the qualifying period referred to in paragraph (b) of the definition "qualifying period", April 2020;

(c) for the qualifying period referred to in paragraph (c) of the definition "qualifying period", May 2020;

(c.1) for the qualifying period referred to in paragraph (c.1) of the definition "qualifying period", June 2020;

(c.2) for the qualifying period referred to in paragraph (c.2) of the definition "qualifying period", July 2020;

(c.3) for the qualifying period referred to in paragraph (c.3) of the definition "qualifying period", August 2020;

(c.4) for the qualifying period referred to in paragraph (c.4) of the definition "qualifying period", September 2020;

(c.5) for the qualifying period referred to in paragraph (c.5) of the definition "qualifying period", October 2020;

(c.6) for the qualifying period referred to in paragraph (c.6) of the definition "qualifying period", November 2020;

(c.7) for the qualifying period referred to in paragraph (c.7) of the definition "qualifying period", December 2020; and

Before the above amendments, Reg. 8901.2(3) prescribed the reference periods for Periods 11-16. Now these appear in the definition.

Para. (c.7) added by 2020 COVID-19 bill #5 and (c.1)-(c.6) added by 2020 COVID bill #3, both retroactive to definition's introduction (April 11, 2020).

Regulations: 8901.2(3) (prescribed periods for Dec. 20/20-June 4/21, for para. (d); replaced by amendments to this definition). An earlier Reg. 8901.2(1), which prescribed the June 2020 period, was repealed and retroactively superseded by paras. (c.1)-(c.6).

"eligible employee", of an eligible entity in respect of a week in a qualifying period, means an individual employed by the eligible entity primarily in Canada throughout the qualifying period (or the portion of the qualifying period throughout which the individual was employed by the eligible entity), other than, if the qualifying period is any of the first qualifying period to the fourth qualifying period, an individual who is without remuneration by the eligible entity in respect of 14 or more consecutive days in the qualifying period.

Notes: For a non-arm's length employee such as a controlling shareholder, the subsidy is available but the calculation is restricted by 125.7(2)A(a)(i)(C), A(b)(ii)G(C) or A(b)(iv)(C)(I). See 125.7(2) Notes.

See tinyurl.com/cews-cra-faq qq. 13 to 16, 22 and 23. CRA says taxable benefits are *included* in determining "without remuneration", which is different from 125.7(1)"eligible remuneration": doc 2020-0847781E5. Independent contractors who are not employees [see 248(1)"employee" Notes] do not qualify; nor do outsourced staff employed by a staffing agency (but the staffing agency may itself qualify for CEWS): 2020-0856781E5.

Definition amended by 2021 budget bill #1, effective June 29, 2021, to refer to the periods by number (see 125.7(1)"qualifying period"). Before that date, read:

> "eligible employee", of an eligible entity in respect of a week in a qualifying period, means an individual employed by the eligible entity primarily in Canada throughout the qualifying period (or the portion of the qualifying period throughout which the individual was employed by the eligible entity), other than, if the qualifying period is described in any of paragraphs (a) to (c.1) of the definition "qualifying period", an individual who is without remuneration by the eligible entity in respect of 14 or more consecutive days in the qualifying period.

Definition amended by 2020 COVID bill #5, retroactive to its introduction (April 11, 2020), but for applications made before Nov. 19, 2020, read as originally enacted:

> "eligible employee", of an eligible entity in respect of a week in a qualifying period, means an individual employed in Canada by the eligible entity in the qualifying period, other than, if the qualifying period is described in any of paragraphs (a) to (c.1) of the definition "qualifying period", an individual who is without remuneration by the eligible entity in respect of 14 or more consecutive days in the qualifying period.

Definition amended by 2020 COVID bill #3, retroactive to April 11, 2020, to limit the exception to "qualifying period"(a)-(c.1).

"eligible entity" means

(a) a corporation or a trust, other than a corporation or a trust that is exempt from tax under this Part or is a public institution;

(b) an individual other than a trust;

(c) a registered charity, other than a public institution;

(d) a person that is exempt from tax under this Part because of paragraph 149(1)(e), (j), (k) or (l), other than a public institution;

(e) a partnership, all of the members of which are described in this paragraph or any of paragraphs (a) to (d); or

(f) a prescribed organization.

Related Provisions: 87(2)(g.6) — Amalgamation — continuing corporation; 125.7(1)"qualifying entity" — QE defined as eligible entity that meets conditions; 125.7(1)"qualifying renter" — QR defined as eligible entity that meets conditions.

Notes: A charity (para. (c)) or non-profit (para. (d)) can choose whether to count government assistance as revenue when applying the 15% or 30% drop-in-revenue test: 125.7(1)"qualifying revenue"(a)(ii), (b)(ii). See 125.7(2) Notes.

For CEWS for a non-resident corp and to a partnership, see tinyurl.com/cews-cra-faq qq. 3-02, 3-1.

Para. (a): "exempt from tax" means a 149(1) exemption, not an 81(1) (including tax-treaty) exemption of specific income: VIEWS doc 2020-0847791E5.

Definition amended by 2020 COVID bill #3, retroactive to its introduction (April 11, 2020), except that in respect of qualifying periods March 15–April 11 and April 12–May 9, 2020, read (a)-(b) as they were before the amendment:

> (a) a corporation, other than a corporation that is exempt from tax under this Part or is a public institution;
>
> (b) an individual;

Regulations: 8901.1 (prescribed organizations for para. (f)).

"eligible remuneration", of an eligible employee of an eligible entity, means amounts described in paragraph 153(1)(a) or (g), other than

(a) for greater certainty, a retiring allowance;

(b) amounts deemed to have been received by the eligible employee as a benefit under or because of any of paragraphs 7(1)(a) to (d.1);

(c) any amount received that can reasonably be expected to be paid or returned, directly or indirectly, in any manner whatever, to

(i) the eligible entity,

(ii) a person or partnership not dealing at arm's length with the eligible entity, or

(iii) another person or partnership at the direction of the eligible entity; and

(d) any amount that is paid in respect of a week in the qualifying period, if, as part of an arrangement involving the eligible employee and the eligible entity,

(i) the amount is in excess of the eligible employee's baseline remuneration,

(ii) after the qualifying period, the eligible employee is reasonably expected to be paid a lower weekly amount than their baseline remuneration, and

(iii) one of the main purposes for the arrangement is to increase the amount of the deemed overpayment under subsection (2).

Notes: "Eligible remuneration" is used in calculating the amount of subsidy in A(a)(i)(A), A(a)(ii)(A) and A(b)(ii)G(A), and in 125.7(1)"baseline remuneration" for CEWS Stage 2. CPP and EI costs are reimbursed to the employer under 125.7(2)D.

The definition covers salary, wages and taxable benefits (153(1)(a)), plus fees and commissions (153(1)(g)), but excludes: (a) retiring allowances, including severance pay (248(1)"retiring allowance"); (b) stock option benefits, except those deemed on death by 7(1)(e); (c) kickbacks to the employer or at the employer's direction; (d) artificial increases in pay.

The Finance Backgrounder of April 11, 2020 (see 125.7(2) Notes) says benefits from use of a corporate vehicle are excluded, but this is not in the legislation. Such benefits fall under 153(1)(a) and so are included, in the author's view. Finance has indicated that the word "paid" in 125.7(2)A(a)(i) and (b)(i) was intended to exclude automobile benefits, but if that interpretation were correct, 153(1)(a) would not apply to *any* taxable benefits (since 153(1) opening words uses "paying"), and it does, as CRA considers that "paying" in 153(1) requires withholding on benefits.

See also tinyurl.com/cews-cra-faq qq. 17 to 17-3.

See also VIEWS docs 2020-0848881E5 (para. (c) does not apply to employee costs billed to related company for services rendered); 2020-0865791I7 (para. (c) catches salary returned by shareholder as capital contribution or loan).

"executive compensation repayment amount", of an eligible entity, means

(a) nil, unless

(i) shares of the capital stock of the eligible entity are listed or traded on a stock exchange or other public market, or

(ii) the eligible entity is controlled by a corporation described in subparagraph (i); and

(b) if the conditions in subparagraph (a)(i) or (ii) are met, the amount determined by the formula

$$A \times B$$

where

A is

(i) a percentage assigned to the eligible entity under an agreement if

(A) the agreement is entered into by

(I) the eligible entity,

(II) an eligible entity, shares of the capital stock of which are listed or traded on a stock exchange or other public market, that controls the eligible entity (referred to in this definition as the "public parent corporation"), if the public parent corporation received a deemed overpayment under subsection (2) in respect of the seventeenth qualifying period or any subsequent qualifying period, and

(III) each other eligible entity that received a deemed overpayment under subsection (2) in respect of the seventeenth qualifying period or any subsequent qualifying period and was controlled in that period by the eligible entity or the public parent corporation, if any,

(B) the agreement is filed in prescribed form and manner with the Minister,

(C) the agreement assigns, for the purposes of this definition, a percentage in respect of each eligible entity referred to in clause (A) of this description,

(D) the total of all the percentages assigned under the agreement equals 100%, and

(E) the percentage allocated to any eligible entity under the agreement would not result in an amount allocated to the eligible entity in excess of the total of all amounts of deemed overpayments of the eligible entity under subsection (2) for the seventeenth qualifying period and any subsequent qualifying period, and

(ii) in any other case, 100%, and

B   is the lesser of

(i) the total of all amounts each of which is an amount of a deemed overpayment under subsection (2) for each of the entities described in clause (i)(A) of the description of A for the seventeenth qualifying period and each subsequent qualifying period, other than amounts in respect of employees on leave with pay, and

(ii) the amount determined by the formula

$$C - D$$

where

C   is the executive remuneration of the eligible entity, or of the public parent corporation that controls the eligible entity, if any, for the 2021 calendar year (prorated based upon the number of days of the eligible entity's, or the public parent corporation's, fiscal periods in the calendar year, if those fiscal periods are not the calendar year), and

D   is the executive remuneration of the eligible entity, or of the public parent corporation that controls the eligible entity, if any, for the 2019 calendar year (prorated based upon the number of days of the eligible entity's, or the public parent corporation's, fiscal periods in the calendar year, if those fiscal periods are not the calendar year).

Related Provisions: 125.7(14) — ECRA reduces wage subsidy.

Notes: See 125.7(14). Definition added by 2021 budget bill #1, effective June 29, 2021.

"executive remuneration", of an eligible entity, means

(a) the total amount of compensation that is reported in the eligible entity's Statement of Executive Compensation for Named Executive Officers pursuant to National Instrument 51-102 Continuous Disclosure Obligations, as amended from time to time, of the Canadian Securities Administrators in respect of Named Executive Officers of the eligible entity;

(b) if paragraph (a) does not apply and the eligible entity is required to make a similar disclosure to shareholders under the laws of another jurisdiction, the amount of total compensation reported in that disclosure (if the compensation of more than five individuals is required to be reported under that disclosure, using the five most highly compensated of those individuals); and

(c) if paragraphs (a) and (b) do not apply, the amount that would be required to be reported by the eligible entity using the methodology for preparing the Statement of Executive Compensation referred to in paragraph (a).

Related Provisions: 125.7(15) — Foreign currency rule.

Notes: See 125.7(14). Definition added by 2021 budget bill #1, effective June 29, 2021.

"prior reference period", for a qualifying period of an eligible entity, means

(a) subject to paragraph (b),

(i) for the first qualifying period, March 2019,

(ii) for the second qualifying period, April 2019,

(iii) for the third qualifying period, May 2019,

(iv) for the fourth qualifying period, June 2019,

(v) for the fifth qualifying period, July 2019,

(vi) for the sixth qualifying period, August 2019,

(vii) for the seventh qualifying period, September 2019,

(viii) for the eighth qualifying period, October 2019,

(ix) for the ninth qualifying period, November 2019,

(x) for the tenth qualifying period, December 2019,

(xi) for the eleventh qualifying period, December 2019,

(xii) for the twelfth qualifying period, January 2020,

(xiii) for the thirteenth qualifying period, February 2020,

(xiv) for the fourteenth qualifying period, March 2019,

(xv) for the fifteenth qualifying period, April 2019,

(xvi) for the sixteenth qualifying period, May 2019,

(xvii) for the seventeenth qualifying period, June 2019,

(xviii) for the eighteenth qualifying period, July 2019,

(xix) for the nineteenth qualifying period, August 2019,

(xx) for the twentieth qualifying period, September 2019,

(xxi) for the twenty-first qualifying period, October 2019, and

(xxii) for the twenty-second qualifying period, November 2019;

(b) January and February 2020, if

(i) on March 1, 2019, the eligible entity was not carrying on business or otherwise carrying on its ordinary activities and the qualifying period is referred to in any of paragraphs (a) to (c.1) of the definition "qualifying period", or

(ii) the qualifying period is referred to in any of

(A) paragraphs (a) to (c.1) of the definition "qualifying period" and the eligible entity elects for all of the periods set out in paragraphs (a) to (c) of that definition, or

(B) paragraphs (c.2) to (d) of the definition "qualifying period" and the eligible entity elects for all of the periods set out in those paragraphs; and

(c) for the qualifying period referred to in paragraph (d) of the definition "qualifying period", a prescribed period.

Related Provisions: 87(2)(g.6) — Amalgamation — continuing corporation; 125.7(1)"qualifying entity"(c) — Qualification for subsidy; 125.7(4.2)(e) — Asset sale — when business deemed commenced; 125.7(10) — Amending or revoking election.

Notes: See 125.7(1)"qualifying period" for the numbers of the qualifying periods.

The "prior reference period" is the baseline period used to determine that revenue has dropped, for CEWS entitlement. For any given month, it is the same calendar month of 2019 (but 2020 for Jan-Feb), but for an entity that elects under (b)(ii), it is Jan.-Feb. 2020. See 125.7(1)"qualifying entity"(c) and Notes to 125.7(2).

Subparas. (a)(i)-(x) changed to (i)-(xxii) by 2021 budget bill #1, effective June 29, 2021, to refer to the periods by number and extend to more periods. See 125.7(2) Notes. Before that date, read:

(a) subject to paragraph (b),

(i) for the qualifying period referred to in paragraph (a) of the definition "qualifying period", March 2019,

(ii) for the qualifying period referred to in paragraph (b) of the definition "qualifying period", April 2019,

(iii) for the qualifying period referred to in paragraph (c) of the definition "qualifying period", May 2019,

(iv) for the qualifying period referred to in paragraph (c.1) of the definition "qualifying period", June 2019,

(v) for the qualifying period referred to in paragraph (c.2) of the definition "qualifying period", July 2019,

(vi) for the qualifying period referred to in paragraph (c.3) of the definition "qualifying period", August 2019,

(vii) for the qualifying period referred to in paragraph (c.4) of the definition "qualifying period", September 2019,

(viii) for the qualifying period referred to in paragraph (c.5) of the definition "qualifying period", October 2019,

(ix) for the qualifying period referred to in paragraph (c.6) of the definition "qualifying period", November 2019, and

(x) for the qualifying period referred to in paragraph (c.7) of the definition "qualifying period", December 2019;

Before the above amendments, Reg. 8901.2(4) prescribed the prior reference periods for Periods 11-16. Now these appear in the definition.

Subpara. (a)(x) added by 2020 COVID bill #5, retroactive to definition's introduction (April 11, 2020). Subparas. (a)(iv)-(ix) added and (b)(i)-(ii) amended by 2020 COVID bill #3, retroactive to April 11, 2020.

Regulations: 8901.2(4) (prescribed periods for Dec. 20/20-June 4/21, for para. (c); replaced by amendments to this definition). An earlier Reg. 8901.2(2), which prescribed a period, was repealed and retroactively superseded by subparas. (a)(iv)-(ix).

Forms: RC661: CEWS attestation; RC665: CERS attestation.

"public health restriction", in respect of a qualifying property of an eligible entity for a qualifying period, means an order or decision in respect of which the following conditions are met:

(a) it is made under a law of Canada or a province, or the authority granted under such a law;

(b) it is made in response to the coronavirus disease 2019 (COVID-19) pandemic;

(c) it is limited in scope based on one or more factors, such as

(i) defined geographical boundaries,

(ii) type of business or other activity, or

(iii) risks associated with a particular location;

(d) non-compliance with the order or decision is a federal or provincial offence or can result in the imposition of an administrative monetary penalty or other sanction by the Government of Canada or a province;

(e) it does not result from a violation by the eligible entity — or a party with which the eligible entity does not deal at arm's length that rents, directly or indirectly, the qualifying property from the eligible entity (referred to in this definition as the "specified tenant") — of an order or decision that meets the conditions in paragraphs (a) to (d);

(f) as a result of the order or decision, some or all of the activities of the eligible entity — or the specified tenant — at, or in connection with, the qualifying property (that it is reasonable to expect the eligible entity — or the specified tenant — would, absent the order or decision, otherwise have engaged in) are required to cease (referred to in this definition as the "restricted activities") based, for greater certainty, on the type of activity rather than the extent to which an activity may be performed or limits placed on the time during which an activity may be performed;

(g) it is reasonable to conclude that at least approximately 25% of the qualifying revenues of the eligible entity — or the specified tenant — for the prior reference period that were earned from, or in connection with, the qualifying property were derived from the restricted activities; and

(h) the restricted activities are required to cease for a period of at least one week.

Related Provisions: 125.7(1)"rent top-up percentage" — Extra CERS while property is subject to PHR.

Notes: This is for the "lockdown support" in 125.7(2.1)B: see 125.7(1)"rent top-up percentage" and "qualifying rent expense". See VIEWS docs 2020-0873601I7 (application to a travel agency); 2021-0880401I7 (retail store or restaurant with curbside pickup).

The "specified tenant" references in paras. (e)-(g) implement a Feb. 21, 2021 Finance announcement, to address cases where the entity that operates the business rents the space from a related entity.

Paras. (e)-(g) amended by 2021 budget bill #1 to add "specified tenant" references, retroactive to Sept. 27, 2020. Before the amendment, they read (now deemed never in force):

(e) it does not result from a violation by the eligible entity of an order or decision that meets the conditions in paragraphs (a) to (d);

(f) as a result of the order or decision, some or all of the activities of the eligible entity at, or in connection with, the qualifying property (that it is reasonable to expect the eligible entity would, absent the order or decision, otherwise have engaged in) are required to cease (referred to in this definition as the "restricted

activities") based, for greater certainty, on the type of activity rather than the extent to which an activity may be performed or limits placed on the time during which an activity may be performed;

(g) it is reasonable to conclude that at least approximately 25% of the qualifying revenues of the eligible entity for the prior reference period that were earned from, or in connection with, the qualifying property were derived from the restricted activities; and

Definition added by 2020 COVID bill #5, effective Sept. 27, 2020.

"public institution" means

(a) an organization described in any of paragraphs 149(1)(a) to (d.6); or

(b) a school, school board, hospital, health authority, public university or college.

Related Provisions: 125.7(1)"eligible entity"(a), (c), (d) — Public institution does not qualify for subsidy.

Notes: Para. (a) purports to apply to 149(1)(a) and (b), perhaps to exclude foreign government employees and their family members from getting the subsidy for paying employees of any business they operate; but since such a person is an individual and not an "organization", para. (a) might not actually apply to them.

For CRA interpretation see VIEWS docs 2020-0846831E5, 2020-0846931E5, 2020-0848441E5, 2020-0848721E5, 2020-0849211E5, 2020-0849221E5, 2020-0849761E5 (general comments; CRA will not provide rulings as there have been too many enquiries).

"qualifying entity", for a qualifying period, means an eligible entity that meets the following conditions:

(a) it files an application with the Minister in respect of the qualifying period in prescribed form and manner on or before the later of

(i) January 31, 2021, and

(ii) 180 days after the end of the qualifying period;

(b) the individual who has principal responsibility for the financial activities of the eligible entity attests that the application is complete and accurate in all material respects;

(c) if the qualifying period is any of the first qualifying period to the fourth qualifying period, its qualifying revenues for the current reference period are equal to or less than the specified percentage, for the qualifying period, of

(i) if paragraph (a) or (c) of the definition "prior reference period" applies, its qualifying revenues for the prior reference period, and

(ii) if paragraph (b) of the definition "prior reference period" applies, the amount determined by the formula

$$0.5A(B/C)$$

where

A   is its qualifying revenues for the prior reference period,

B   is the number of days in the prior reference period, and

C   is the number of days in the prior reference period during which the eligible entity was carrying on business; and

(d) it meets either of the following conditions:

(i) it had, on March 15, 2020, a business number in respect of which it is registered with the Minister to make remittances required under section 153, or

(ii) it is the case that

(A) on March 15, 2020,

(I) it employed one or more individuals in Canada,

(II) the payroll for its employees was administered by another person or partnership (referred to in this subparagraph as the "payroll service provider"), and

(III) the payroll service provider had a business number in respect of which it is registered with the Minister to make remittances required under section 153,

(B) the payroll service provider used its business number to make the remittances referred to in subclause (A)(III) in respect of the employees of the eligible entity, and

(C) the Minister is satisfied that the conditions in clauses (A) and (B) are met.

Related Provisions: 87(2)(g.6) — Amalgamation — continuing corporation; 125.7(4.2)(d) — Application where business was sold to new entity; 125.7(4.2)(e) — Asset sale — when business deemed commenced; 125.7(5)(a) — CEWS limited to amount claimed; 125.7(9)(a) — Entity that meets conditions for any of first 3 periods qualifies for the next period; 163.2(4) — Individual attesting under para. (b) liable to penalty for misrepresentation (subject to 163.2(15)); 241(3.5) — CRA may publicize names of applicants.

Notes: See 125.7(2) Notes. The application under para. (a) is done online. The "attestation" under para. (b) is done as part of the online process, but if done by a representative such as an accountant, the person required to attest must complete and sign Form RC661, which the representative should keep.

For the application deadline for each period see VIEWS doc 2021-0879631C6 [TEI 2021], q.2.

Para. (c) opening words amended by 2021 budget bill #1, effective June 29, 2021, to refer to the periods by number (see 125.7(1)"qualifying period"). Before that date, read:

(c) if the qualifying period is described in any of paragraphs (a) to (c.1) of the definition "qualifying period", its qualifying revenues for the current reference period are equal to or less than the specified percentage, for the qualifying period, of

Para. (a) amended by 2020 COVID bill #5, retroactive to definition's introduction (April 11, 2020), effectively to add (a)(ii).

Definition amended by 2020 COVID bill #3, retroactive to its introduction (April 11, 2020): (a) changed Oct. 2020 to Feb. 2021; (c) opening words limited to "qualifying period"(a)-(c.1); (d)(ii) added.

Forms: RC661: CEWS attestation.

"qualifying period" means

(a) [Period 1 — ed.] the period that begins on March 15, 2020 and ends on April 11, 2020 (referred to in this section as the "first qualifying period");

(b) [Period 2 — ed.] the period that begins on April 12, 2020 and ends on May 9, 2020 (referred to in this section as the "second qualifying period");

(c) [Period 3 — ed.] the period that begins on May 10, 2020 and ends on June 6, 2020 (referred to in this section as the "third qualifying period");

(c.1) [Period 4 — ed.] the period that begins on June 7, 2020 and ends on July 4, 2020 (referred to in this section as the "fourth qualifying period");

(c.2) [Period 5 — ed.] the period that begins on July 5, 2020 and ends on August 1, 2020 (referred to in this section as the "fifth qualifying period");

(c.3) [Period 6 — ed.] the period that begins on August 2, 2020 and ends on August 29, 2020 (referred to in this section as the "sixth qualifying period");

(c.4) [Period 7 — ed.] the period that begins on August 30, 2020 and ends on September 26, 2020 (referred to in this section as the "seventh qualifying period");

(c.5) [Period 8 — ed.] the period that begins on September 27, 2020 and ends on October 24, 2020 (referred to in this section as the "eighth qualifying period");

(c.6) [Period 9 — ed.] the period that begins on October 25, 2020 and ends on November 21, 2020 (referred to in this section as the "ninth qualifying period");

(c.7) [Period 10 — ed.] the period that begins on November 22, 2020 and ends on December 19, 2020 (referred to in this section as the "tenth qualifying period");

(c.8) [Period 11 — ed.] the period that begins on December 20, 2020 and ends on January 16, 2021 (referred to in this section as the "eleventh qualifying period");

(c.9) [Period 12 — ed.] the period that begins on January 17, 2021 and ends on February 13, 2021 (referred to in this section as the "twelfth qualifying period");

(c.91) [Period 13 — ed.] the period that begins on February 14, 2021 and ends on March 13, 2021 (referred to in this section as the "thirteenth qualifying period");

(c.92) [Period 14 — ed.] the period that begins on March 14, 2021 and ends on April 10, 2021 (referred to in this section as the "fourteenth qualifying period");

(c.93) [Period 15 — ed.] the period that begins on April 11, 2021 and ends on May 8, 2021 (referred to in this section as the "fifteenth qualifying period");

(c.94) [Period 16 — ed.] the period that begins on May 9, 2021 and ends on June 5, 2021 (referred to in this section as the "sixteenth qualifying period");

(c.95) [Period 17 — ed.] the period that begins on June 6, 2021 and ends on July 3, 2021 (referred to in this section as the "seventeenth qualifying period");

(c.96) [Period 18 — ed.] the period that begins on July 4, 2021 and ends on July 31, 2021 (referred to in this section as the "eighteenth qualifying period");

(c.97) [Period 19 — ed.] the period that begins on August 1, 2021 and ends on August 28, 2021 (referred to in this section as the "nineteenth qualifying period");

(c.98) [Period 20 — ed.] the period that begins on August 29, 2021 and ends on September 25, 2021 (referred to in this section as the "twentieth qualifying period");

(c.99) [Period 21 — ed.] the period that begins on September 26, 2021 and ends on October 23, 2021 (referred to in this section as the "twenty-first qualifying period");

(c.991) [Period 22 — ed.] the period that begins on October 24, 2021 and ends on November 20, 2021 (referred to in this section as the "twenty-second qualifying period"); and

(d) a prescribed period that ends no later than November 30, 2021.

Related Provisions: 125.7(8) — Percentages and amounts can be prescribed for para. (d).

Notes: See 125.7(2) Notes. Paras. (a)-(c.7) and (d) changed to (a)-(c.991) and (d) by 2021 budget bill #1, effective June 29, 2021, to number the periods and extend to more of them. Before that date, read:

(a) [Period 1 — ed.] the period that begins on March 15, 2020 and ends on April 11, 2020;

(b) [Period 2 — ed.] the period that begins on April 12, 2020 and ends on May 9, 2020;

(c) [Period 3 — ed.] the period that begins on May 10, 2020 and ends on June 6, 2020;

(c.1) [Period 4 — ed.] the period that begins on June 7, 2020 and ends on July 4, 2020;

(c.2) [Period 5 — ed.] the period that begins on July 5, 2020 and ends on August 1, 2020;

(c.3) [Period 6 — ed.] the period that begins on August 2, 2020 and ends on August 29, 2020;

(c.4) [Period 7 — ed.] the period that begins on August 30, 2020 and ends on September 26, 2020;

(c.5) [Period 8 — ed.] the period that begins on September 27, 2020 and ends on October 24, 2020;

(c.6) [Period 9 — ed.] the period that begins on October 25, 2020 and ends on November 21, 2020;

(c.7) [Period 10 — ed.] the period that begins on November 22, 2020 and ends on December 19, 2020; or

(d) [Periods 11+ — ed.] a prescribed period that ends no later than June 30, 2021.

Before the above amendments, Reg. 8901.2(1) prescribed Periods 11-16.

Para. (c.7) added, and (d) changed Dec. 31/20 to June 30/21, by 2020 COVID bill #5, retroactive to April 11, 2020. Paras. (c.1)-(c.6) added, and (d) changed Sept. 30/20 to Dec. 31/20, by 2020 COVID bill #3, also retroactive to April 11, 2020.

Regulations: 8901.2(1) (prescribed periods Dec. 20/20 - June 4/21 for para. (d); replaced by amendments to this definition) (an earlier Reg. 8901.2(3), which applied to the previous version of para. (d), was repealed and retroactively superseded by paras. (c.1)-(c.6)).

"qualifying property", of an eligible entity for a qualifying period, means real or immovable property (other than property that is a self-contained domestic establishment used by the eligible entity or by a person not dealing at arm's length with the eligible entity, or part of such a self-contained domestic establishment, the land subjacent to the self-contained domestic establishment and such portion of any immediately contiguous land as can reasonably be regarded as contributing to the use and enjoyment of the self-contained domestic establishment as a residence) in Canada used by the eligible entity in the course of its ordinary activities.

Notes: Despite exclusion of a "self-contained domestic establishment", the part of a property that is not the home can still qualify: VIEWS doc 2020-0870041I7. A boat slip can be QP if it is real or immovable property: 2021-0875571I7.

Definition added by 2020 COVID bill #5, effective Sept. 27, 2020.

"qualifying recovery entity", for a qualifying period, means an eligible entity that meets the following conditions:

(a) it files an application with the Minister in respect of the qualifying period in prescribed form and manner no later than 180 days after the end of the qualifying period;

(b) it is a qualifying entity for the qualifying period;

(c) if it is a corporation (other than a corporation that is exempt from tax under this Part), it

(i) is a Canadian-controlled private corporation, or

(ii) would be a Canadian-controlled private corporation absent the application of subsection 136(1);

(d) if it is a partnership, throughout the qualifying period it is the case that

$$A \leq 0.5B$$

where

A is the total of all amounts, each of which is the fair market value of an interest in the partnership held — directly or indirectly, through one or more partnerships — by

(i) a person or partnership other than an eligible entity, or

(ii) a corporation, other than a corporation that

(A) is exempt from tax under this Part, or

(B) is described in subparagraph (c)(i) or (ii), and

B is the total fair market value of all interests in the partnership; and

(e) it has a revenue reduction percentage

(i) greater than 0%, if it is the seventeenth qualifying period, or

(ii) greater than 10%, if it is any of the eighteenth qualifying period to the twenty-second qualifying period.

Related Provisions: 125.7(2.2) — Recovery hiring subsidy for QRE.

Notes: See 125.7(2.2). Definition added by 2021 budget bill #1, effective June 29, 2021.

"qualifying rent expense", in respect of a qualifying property for an eligible entity for a qualifying period, means the amount determined by the formula

$$A - B$$

where

A is the lesser of $75,000 and the total of all amounts paid — under a written agreement entered into before October 9, 2020, or pursuant to the renewal (on substantially similar terms) or assignment of a written agreement entered into before October 9, 2020 — in respect of the qualifying period by the eligible entity to a party with which the eligible entity deals at arm's length, each of which is

(a) rent for the use of, or right to use, the qualifying property,

(i) including

(A) gross rent,

(B) rent based on a percentage of sales, profit or a similar criterion,

(C) amounts required to be paid under a net lease by the eligible entity either to the lessor or a third party, as

(I) base rent,

(II) regular instalments of operating expenses, such as insurance, utilities and common area maintenance expenses, customarily charged to the lessee under a net lease,

(III) property and similar taxes, including school and municipal taxes, and

(IV) regular instalments of other amounts payable to the lessor for services ancillary to the rental of real or immovable properties and customarily supplied or rendered in connection with the rental of real or immovable properties, and

(D) amounts received by the lessor under the Canada Emergency Commercial Rent Assistance program that were applied against rent payable in respect of the qualifying period, if those amounts would otherwise be required to be refunded to the eligible entity, and

(ii) excluding

(A) sales taxes,

(B) amounts paid as, on account of, in lieu of payment of or in satisfaction of, damages,

(C) amounts paid under a guarantee, security or similar indemnity or covenant,

(D) payments arising due to default under the agreement by the eligible entity,

(E) interest and penalties on unpaid amounts,

(F) fees payable for discrete items or special services, and

(G) reconciliation adjustment payments, and

(b) in the case of qualifying property owned by the eligible entity that is not used by the eligible entity primarily to earn rental income or, where the qualifying property is used primarily by the eligible entity to earn rental income directly or indirectly from a person or partnership not dealing at arm's length with the eligible entity, that is not used by that person or partnership primarily to earn rental income,

(i) if there is a debt obligation secured by a mortgage or hypothec on the qualifying property, interest on the debt obligation to the extent that the amount of the debt obligation does not exceed the lesser of

(A) the lowest total principal amount secured by one or more mortgages or hypothecs (provided the mortgage or hypothec has an amortization period) on the qualifying property at any time after it was acquired by the eligible entity (excluding any temporary period in the course of a refinancing transaction between the time when an existing mortgage is discharged and a new mortgage is registered), and

(B) the cost amount of the qualifying property,

(ii) amounts paid for insurance on the qualifying property, and

(iii) property and similar taxes on the qualifying property, including school and municipal taxes; and

B is the total of all amounts, each of which is received or receivable by the eligible entity in respect of the qualifying period, either directly or indirectly, from a party with which the entity deals at arm's length and is described in paragraph (a) of the description of A.

Related Provisions: 125.7(6)(a)(ii) — Anti-avoidance rule; 125.7(8)(c) — Amounts that can be prescribed; 125.7(12), (13) — Amount deemed paid when due, if renter pays within 60 days of getting refund; 257 — Formula cannot calculate to less than zero.

Notes: This amount is used in the CERS formula: see 125.7(2.1)B:G. Note that it is not only rent; for an owner, it covers mortgage interest, property taxes and insurance. For CRA interpretation see VIEWS docs 2020-0869981I7 (hair salon chair "rent" may qualify [i.e., "right to use" includes a non-exclusive licence to space]); 2020-0873491E5 and 2021-0879631C6 [TEI 2021], q.1 (whether tenant's payment of utilities is part of QRE).

Definition added by 2020 COVID bill #5, effective Sept. 27, 2020.

"qualifying renter", for a qualifying period, means an eligible entity that meets the following conditions:

(a) it files an application with the Minister in respect of the qualifying period in prescribed form and manner no later than 180 days after the end of the qualifying period;

(b) the individual who has principal responsibility for the financial activities of the eligible entity attests that the application is complete and accurate in all material respects; and

(c) it meets any of the following conditions:

(i) it meets the condition in paragraph (d) of the definition "qualifying entity",

(ii) it had a business number on September 27, 2020 and provides records and other information satisfactory to the Minister in support of its application, or

(iii) it meets prescribed conditions.

Related Provisions: 125.7(5)(a) — CERS limited to amount claimed.

Notes: Definition added by 2020 COVID bill #5, effective Sept. 27, 2020.

Forms: RC665: CERS attestation.

"qualifying revenue", of an eligible entity for a prior reference period or a current reference period, means the inflow of cash, receivables or other consideration arising in the course of the ordinary activities of the eligible entity — generally from the sale of goods, the rendering of services and the use by others of resources of the eligible entity — in Canada in the particular period, subject to the following:

(a) in the case of an eligible entity described in paragraph (c) of the definition "eligible entity",

(i) it includes revenue from a "related business" (as defined in subsection 149.1(1)), gifts and other amounts received in the course of its ordinary activities, and

(ii) notwithstanding subparagraph (i), the eligible entity may elect to exclude funding received from government sources in the determination of its qualifying revenue for all of its prior reference periods and current reference periods;

(b) in the case of an eligible entity described in paragraph (d) of the definition "eligible entity",

(i) it includes membership fees and other amounts received in the course of its ordinary activities, and

(ii) notwithstanding subparagraph (i), the eligible entity may elect to exclude funding received from government sources in the determination of its qualifying revenue for all of its prior reference periods and current reference periods;

(b.1) in the case of an eligible entity prescribed in paragraph (f) of the definition "eligible entity" that would be described in paragraph (c) or (d) of that definition if it were not a public institution, subparagraphs (a)(i) and (ii) apply to an eligible entity that would be described in paragraph (c) of that definition and subparagraphs (b)(i) and (ii) apply to an eligible entity that would be described in paragraph (d) of that definition;

(c) it excludes, for greater certainty, extraordinary items;

(d) it excludes amounts derived from persons or partnerships not dealing at arm's length with the eligible entity; and

(e) it excludes, for greater certainty, deemed overpayments under subsection (2) and deemed remittances under subsection 153(1.02).

Related Provisions: 125.7(4) — Computation of QR (accounting principles, etc.); 125.7(4.2) — Application where business was sold to new entity; 125.7(6)(a)(i) — Anti-avoidance rule; 125.7(10) — Amending or revoking election.

Notes: "Inflow" is calculated using normal accounting practices: 125.7(4); VIEWS doc 2020-0856791E5 (CRA will not issue rulings on this).

Revenue "in Canada" would appear to include revenue arising outside Canada but earned from operations in Canada. See discussion of "arising" in Notes to Canada-US Treaty Art. XXI:7.

CRA says QR includes revenue determined under the "percentage of completion" method, but not unrealized gains/losses from mark-to-market valuation: doc 2020-

0855831E5. CRA says QR must be calculated the same way for both CEWS and CERS: 2021-0879631C6 [TEI 2021], q.2.

CRA says a para. (c) "extraordinary item" is non-recurring, is not typical of the entity's normal activities and is primarily outside its control (and COVID-19 emergency funding qualifies): VIEWS docs 2020-0846711I7, 2020-0847141E5; tinyurl.com/cews-cra-faq q. 6-2; and normally does not include business interruption insurance: 2020-0852571I7. Donations to a charity from a special COVID-19 fundraising campaign do not qualify: 2020-0855601E5.

Bad debts cannot be used to reduce revenue: tinyurl.com/cews-cra-faq q. 6-3. See qq. 6-6 to 8 for more on qualifying revenue.

Para. (b.1) (added by 2020 COVID bill #3, retroactive to April 11, 2020) allows prescribed organizations (Reg. 8901.1) that are charities or NPOs to choose whether to include government-source revenue in "qualifying revenue".

Forms: RC661: CEWS attestation; RC665: CERS attestation.

"recovery wage subsidy rate", for a qualifying period, means

(a) for any of the seventeenth qualifying period to the nineteenth qualifying period, 50%;

(b) for the twentieth qualifying period, 40%;

(c) for the twenty-first qualifying period, 30%; and

(d) for the twenty-second qualifying period, 20%.

Related Provisions: 125.7(2.2) — Recovery hiring subsidy.

Notes: See 125.7(2.2). Definition added by 2021 budget bill #1, effective June 29, 2021.

"rent subsidy percentage", of an eligible entity for a qualifying period, means

(a) if the qualifying period is any of the eighth qualifying period to the seventeenth qualifying period,

(i) if the eligible entity's revenue reduction percentage is greater than or equal to 70%, 65%,

(ii) if the eligible entity's revenue reduction percentage is greater than or equal to 50%, but less than 70%, the percentage determined by the formula

$$40\% + (A - 50\%) \times 1.25$$

where

A is the eligible entity's revenue reduction percentage, and

(iii) if the eligible entity's revenue reduction percentage is less than 50%, the percentage determined by the formula

$$0.8 \times B$$

where

B is the eligible entity's revenue reduction percentage;

(a.1) if the qualifying period is any of the eighteenth qualifying period to the twentieth qualifying period, the percentage determined by the formula

$$A + B$$

where

A is the eligible entity's base percentage for the qualifying period, and

B is the eligible entity's top-up percentage for the qualifying period; and

(b) for a qualifying period after the twentieth qualifying period, a percentage determined by regulation in respect of the eligible entity or, if there is no percentage determined by regulation for the qualifying period, nil.

Related Provisions: 125.7(8)(b) — Amounts that can be prescribed.

Notes: (a) opening words and (b) amended and (a.1) added by 2021 budget bill #1, effective June 29, 2021, to refer to the periods by number and extend to more periods. See 125.7(1)"qualifying period". Before that date, read:

(a) if the qualifying period is described in any of paragraphs (c.5) to (c.7) of the definition "qualifying period",

. . . . .

(b) for a qualifying period referred to in paragraph (d) of the definition "qualifying period", a percentage determined by regulation in respect of the qualifying period.

Before the above amendments, Reg. 8901.2(5) prescribed the percentages for Periods 11-16.

Definition added by 2020 COVID bill #5, effective Sept. 27, 2020.

Regulations: 8901.2(5) (prescribed percentages for Dec. 20/20-June 4/21, for para. (b); replaced by amendments to this definition).

"rent top-up percentage", of an eligible entity in respect of a qualifying property for a qualifying period, means the percentage determined by the formula

$$A \times B \div C$$

where

A   is 25%, or a prescribed percentage, for any of the eighth qualifying period to the twentieth qualifying period and nil, or a prescribed percentage, for any subsequent qualifying period,

B   is the number of days in the qualifying period throughout which the qualifying property is subject to a public health restriction, and

C   is the number of days in the qualifying period.

Notes: Description of A changed from "is 25% or a prescribed percentage" by 2021 budget bill #1, effective June 29, 2021.

Definition added by 2020 COVID bill #5, effective Sept. 27, 2020.

"revenue reduction percentage", of an eligible entity for a qualifying period, means the result (expressed as a percentage) of the formula

$$1 - A/B$$

where

A   is the eligible entity's qualifying revenue for the current reference period for the qualifying period; and

B   is the eligible entity's qualifying revenue for the prior reference period for the qualifying period — or, if the prior reference period is January and February 2020, the amount determined by the formula in subparagraph (c)(ii) of the definition "qualifying entity" — or a period prescribed by regulation in respect of the eligible entity for the qualifying period.

Related Provisions: 257 — Formula cannot calculate to less than zero.

Notes: Definition added by 2020 COVID bill #3, effective April 11, 2020. See 125.7(2) Notes re CEWS Stage 2.

"specified percentage", for a qualifying period, means

(a) for the first qualifying period, 85%; and

(b) for any of the second qualifying period to the fourth qualifying period, 70%.

(c) [Repealed]

Related Provisions: 125.7(1)"qualifying entity"(c) — Reduction in revenues to no more than specified percentage of prior reference period, to qualify for subsidy.

Notes: Revenue must drop to the "specified percentage" or less of pre-pandemic "prior reference period" revenue, to qualify for subsidy: 125.7(1)"qualifying entity"(c).

Paras. (a)-(c) replaced with (a)-(b) by 2021 budget bill #1, effective June 29, 2021, to refer to the periods by number and cover more periods. Before that date, read:

> (a) for the qualifying period referred to in paragraph (a) of the definition "qualifying period", 85%;
>
> (b) for the qualifying period referred to in any of paragraphs (b) to (c.1) of the definition "qualifying period", 70%; and
>
> (c) for the qualifying period referred to in paragraph (d) of the definition "qualifying period", the prescribed percentage.

Para. (b) amended by 2020 COVID bill #5, retroactive to definition's introduction (April 11, 2020), to change "paragraph (b) or (c)" to "any of paragraphs (b) to (c.1)".

Regulations: None yet for para. (c) (an earlier Reg. 8901.2(4) was retroactively repealed and superseded by para. (b)).

"top-up percentage", of an eligible entity for a qualifying period, means the percentage determined by regulation for the qualifying period or, if there is no percentage determined by regulation for the qualifying period,

(a) for any of the fifth qualifying period to the tenth qualifying period, the lesser of 25% and the percentage determined by the formula

$$1.25 \times (A - 50\%)$$

where

A   is the entity's top-up revenue reduction percentage for the qualifying period;

(b) for any of the eleventh qualifying period to the seventeenth qualifying period, the lesser of 35% and the percentage determined by the formula

$$1.75 \times (A - 50\%)$$

where

A   is the entity's top-up revenue reduction percentage for the qualifying period;

(c) for the eighteenth qualifying period, the lesser of 25% and the percentage determined by the formula

$$1.25 \times (A - 50\%)$$

where

A   is the entity's top-up revenue reduction percentage for the qualifying period;

(d) for the nineteenth qualifying period, the lesser of 15% and the percentage determined by the formula

$$0.75 \times (A - 50\%)$$

where

A   is the entity's top-up revenue reduction percentage for the qualifying period;

(e) for the twentieth qualifying period, the lesser of 10% and the percentage determined by the formula

$$0.5 \times (A - 50\%)$$

where

A   is the entity's top-up revenue reduction percentage for the qualifying period; and

(f) for each qualifying period after the twentieth qualifying period, nil.

Related Provisions: 257 — Formula cannot calculate to less than zero.

Notes: See 125.7(2) Notes. The top-up percentage of up to 25% can increase the total CEWS support: 125.7(2)A(b)(ii).

Definition amended by 2021 budget bill #1, effective June 29, 2021. Before that date, read:

> "top-up percentage", of an eligible entity for a qualifying period, means the percentage determined by regulation for the qualifying period or, if there is no percentage determined by regulation for the qualifying period, the lesser of 25% and the percentage determined by the formula
>
> $$1.25 \times (A - 50\%)$$
>
> where
>
> A   is the entity's top-up revenue reduction percentage for the qualifying period.

Before the above amendment, Reg. 8901.2(6) prescribed the percentages for Dec. 20/20-March 13/21 (Periods 11-13).

Opening words amended by 2020 COVID bill #5, retroactive to definition's introduction (April 11, 2020), to refer to a percentage determined by regulation. "Top-up percentage" added by 2020 COVID bill #3, effective April 11, 2020.

Regulations: 8901.2(6) (prescribed percentage for Dec. 20/20-June 4/21; replaced by amendments to this definition).

"top-up revenue reduction percentage", of an eligible entity for a qualifying period, means

(a) for any of the fifth qualifying period to the seventh qualifying period, the result (expressed as a percentage) of the formula

$$1 - A/B$$

where

A   is the average monthly qualifying revenue of the eligible entity for the last three calendar months that ended prior to the current reference period for the qualifying period, and

B is the average monthly qualifying revenue of the eligible entity for

    (i) if the prior reference period for the qualifying period is January and February 2020, January and February 2020, and

    (ii) in any other case, the last three calendar months that ended prior to the prior reference period for the qualifying period;

(b) for any of the eighth qualifying period to the tenth qualifying period, the greater of

    (i) the result (expressed as a percentage) of the formula in paragraph (a), and

    (ii) the revenue reduction percentage of the eligible entity for the qualifying period; and

(c) for the eleventh qualifying period and each subsequent qualifying period, the eligible entity's revenue reduction percentage for the qualifying period.

Related Provisions: 257 — Formula cannot calculate to less than zero.

Notes: The TRRP is used in 125.7(1)"top-up percentage", for the "top-up" CEWS calculation (125.7(2)A(b)(i)(B) and A(b)(ii)). TRRP for a period is the percentage drop in revenue for the last 3 months relative to pre-pandemic ("prior reference period") revenue. See 125.7(2) Notes.

Opening words of (a)-(b), and para. (c), amended by 2021 budget bill #1, effective June 29, 2021, to refer to periods by number and cover more periods. Before that date, read:

(a) for a qualifying period referred to in any of paragraphs (c.2) to (c.4) of the definition "qualifying period", the result (expressed as a percentage) of the formula

[...]

(b) for a qualifying period referred to in any of paragraphs (c.5) to (c.7) of the definition "qualifying period", the greater of

[...]

(c) for a qualifying period referred to in paragraph (d) of the definition "qualifying period", the revenue reduction percentage of the eligible entity for the qualifying period.

Definition amended by 2020 COVID bill #5, retroactive to its introduction, to limit para. (a) to "qualifying period"(c.2)-(c.4) and add paras. (b), (c). Added by 2020 COVID bill #3, effective April 11, 2020.

"total base period remuneration", of an eligible entity, means the total of all amounts, each of which is for an eligible employee in respect of a week in the fourteenth qualifying period, equal to the least of

(a) $1,129,

(b) the eligible remuneration paid to the eligible employee in respect of the week,

(c) if the eligible employee does not deal at arm's length with the eligible entity in the qualifying period, the baseline remuneration in respect of the eligible employee determined for that week, and

(d) if the eligible employee is on leave with pay in the week, nil.

Related Provisions: 125.7(2.2) — Recovery hiring subsidy.

Notes: See 125.7(2.2). Definition added by 2021 budget bill #1, effective June 29, 2021.

"total current period remuneration", of an eligible entity for a qualifying period, means the total of all amounts, each of which is for an eligible employee in respect of a week in the qualifying period, equal to the least of

(a) $1,129,

(b) the eligible remuneration paid to the eligible employee in respect of the week,

(c) if the eligible employee does not deal at arm's length with the eligible entity in the qualifying period, the baseline remuneration in respect of the eligible employee determined for that week, and

(d) if the eligible employee is on leave with pay in the week, nil.

Related Provisions: 125.7(2.2) — Recovery hiring subsidy; 125.7(6.1) — Anti-avoidance rule.

Notes: See 125.7(2.2). Definition added by 2021 budget bill #1, effective June 29, 2021.

(2) COVID-19 — wage subsidy — For a qualifying entity for a qualifying period, an overpayment on account of the qualifying entity's liability under this Part for the taxation year in which the qualifying period ends is deemed to have arisen during the qualifying period in an amount determined by the formula

$$A - B - C + D$$

where

A is the total of all amounts, each of which is for an eligible employee in respect of a week in the qualifying period,

    (a) if the qualifying period is described in any of paragraphs (a) to (c.1) of the definition "qualifying period" in subsection (1), equal to the greater of

        (i) the least of

            (A) 75% of eligible remuneration paid to the eligible employee by the qualifying entity in respect of that week,

            (B) $847, and

            (C) if the eligible employee does not deal at arm's length with the qualifying entity in the qualifying period, nil, and

        (ii) the least of

            (A) the amount of eligible remuneration paid to the eligible employee by the qualifying entity in respect of that week,

            (B) 75% of baseline remuneration in respect of the eligible employee determined for that week, and

            (C) $847, and

    (b) if the qualifying period is described in any of paragraphs (c.2) to (d) of the definition "qualifying period" in subsection (1),

        (i) if the eligible employee is not on leave with pay for that week and the qualifying period is described in paragraph (c.2) or (c.3) of the definition "qualifying period" in subsection (1), the greater of

            (A) an amount equal to

                (I) nil, if the revenue reduction percentage of the qualifying entity for the qualifying period is less than 30%, and

                (II) in any other case, the greater of the amount determined under subparagraph (a)(i) and the amount determined under subparagraph (a)(ii), and

            (B) the amount determined by the formula in subparagraph (ii),

        (ii) if the eligible employee is not on leave with pay for that week and the qualifying period is described in any of paragraphs (c.4) to (d) of the definition "qualifying period" in subsection (1), the amount determined by the formula

$$(E + F) \times G$$

where

E is the qualifying entity's base percentage for the qualifying period,

F is the qualifying entity's top-up percentage for the qualifying period, and

G is the least of

    (A) the amount of eligible remuneration paid to the eligible employee by the qualifying entity in respect of that week,

    (B) $1,129, and

    (C) if the eligible employee does not deal at arm's length with the qualifying entity in the qualifying period, the baseline remuneration in respect of the eligible employee determined for that week,

(iii) if the eligible employee is on leave with pay for that week and the qualifying period is described in paragraph (c.2) or (c.3) of the definition "qualifying period" in subsection (1),

(A) nil, unless

(I) the revenue reduction percentage of the qualifying entity for the qualifying period is greater than 0%, or

(II) the top-up percentage of the qualifying entity for the qualifying period is greater than 0%, and

(B) in any other case, the greater of the amount determined under subparagraph (a)(i) and the amount determined under subparagraph (a)(ii), and

(iv) if the eligible employee is on leave with pay for that week and the qualifying period is described in any of paragraphs (c.4) to (d) of the definition "qualifying period" in subsection (1), the least of

(A) the amount of eligible remuneration paid to the eligible employee by the qualifying entity in respect of that week,

(B) an amount determined by regulation *[Reg. 8901.2(7) — ed.]* in respect of the qualifying entity for the qualifying period,

(C) nil, if

(I) the eligible employee does not deal at arm's length with the qualifying entity in the qualifying period, and

(II) the baseline remuneration of the eligible employee for that week is nil, and

(D) nil, unless

(I) the revenue reduction percentage of the qualifying entity for the qualifying period is greater than 0%, or

(II) the top-up percentage of the qualifying entity for the qualifying period is greater than 0%;

B is the total of all amounts each of which is an amount deemed to have been remitted under subsection 153(1.02) by the qualifying entity in the qualifying period;

C is the total of all amounts received by the eligible employee for each week in the qualifying period as a work-sharing benefit under the *Employment Insurance Act*; and

D is

(a) nil, if the qualifying period is described in any of paragraphs (c.2) to (d) of the definition "qualifying period" in subsection (1), unless

(i) the revenue reduction percentage of the qualifying entity for the qualifying period is greater than 0%, or

(ii) the top-up percentage of the qualifying entity for the qualifying period is greater than 0%, and

(b) in any other case, the total of all amounts, each of which is for an eligible employee in respect of a week in the qualifying period, if the eligible employee is on leave with pay for that week and the amount is

(i) an amount payable by the qualifying entity

(A) as an employer's premium under the *Employment Insurance Act*, or

(B) as an employer's contribution under the *Canada Pension Plan* or under a "provincial pension plan" as defined in section 3 of the *Canada Pension Plan*, or

(ii) an amount payable by the qualifying entity as an employer's premium under the *Act respecting parental insurance*, CQLR, c. A-29.011.

Related Provisions: 87(2)(g.6) — Amalgamation — continuing corporation; 125.7(2.2) — Canada Recovery Hiring Program; 125.7(3) — CEWS deemed to be government assistance; 125.7(5) — Limitations on CEWS; 125.7(6) — Anti-avoidance rule; 125.7(7) — Application to partnerships; 125.7(9)(a) — Entity that qualifies for any of first 3 periods qualifies for the next period; 125.7(9.2) — Entity can claim wage subsidy or recovery hiring subsidy, not both; 125.7(14) — Requirement to repay excessive executive compensation from June 6, 2021; 152(1)(b) — Assessment of deemed payment (CEWS); 152(3.4) — CEWS notice of determination; 163(2)(i), 163(2.901) — Gross negligence penalty; 164(1.6) — CRA can pay CEWS any time in the year; 164(3) — No interest on late payment of CEWS by CRA; 241(3.5) — CRA may publicize names of applicants for CEWS; 257 — Formula cannot calculate to less than zero.

Notes: 125.7 provides the Canada Emergency Wage Subsidy (CEWS), which covers up to 75% of employee salaries for employees that are kept on the payroll during the 2020 COVID-19 crisis, provided the employer has a sufficient drop in arm's-length revenues (see 125.7(1)"qualifying entity"). Although worded as a deemed overpayment (so that it is refundable), the subsidy can be paid by CRA immediately once a business has applied: 164(1.6). A CEWS determination can be objected to and appealed: 152(3.4), 152(1.2). Excessive executive compensation while receiving CEWS will cause a business to be required to repay some of the benefit: 125.7(14).

See 125.7(1)"qualifying period" for Periods 1-13 to which CEWS applies.

The application is done online, through My Business Account or Represent a Client. A claim can be amended via the "adjustment to a prior claim" option.

CEWS Stage 1 (March 15 to July 4, 2020) is explained in the April 11, 2020 Dept. of Finance news release and Backgrounder introducing the legislation (which are similar to the April 8 versions announcing changes from an April 1, 2020 detailed announcement) [legislative references shown editorially are to the legislation as later amended retroactively]:

Government Introduces COVID-19 Emergency Response Act, No. 2 to Help Businesses Keep Canadians in their Jobs

The Government of Canada is taking immediate, significant and decisive action to support Canadians and businesses facing hardship as a result of the global COVID-19 outbreak.

Today, Finance Minister Bill Morneau introduced in Parliament Bill C-14, the *COVID-19 Emergency Response Act, No. 2*, which, upon receiving Royal Assent [received on the same day, April 11, 2020 — ed.], would bring this measure into law. The legislation introduced today includes additional flexibilities that would provide effective support to those eligible employers that are hardest hit by the COVID-19 pandemic and would help protect the jobs Canadians depend on during these difficult times.

Taking action to protect a strong economy includes taking action to protect jobs. The proposed CEWS is a key measure in the Government of Canada's COVID-19 Economic Response Plan. It would provide a strong incentive for employers to pay employees who have been sent home for health and safety reasons or due to lack of work. It would enable employers to retain employees who are still on the payroll and to rehire workers previously laid off. With the CEWS program, families across Canada would be able to count on a steady income.

The proposed CEWS [125.7(2)A(a) — ed.] would apply at a rate of 75% of the first $58,700 earned by employees — representing a benefit of up to $847 per week, per employee [$58,700 is the Year's Maximum Pensionable Earnings for 2020 under the CPP — ed.]. The program would be in place for a 12-week period, from March 15 to June 6, 2020 [later extended to Aug. 29, 2020, then to November, then to December, then to June 2021 — ed.]. Employers of all sizes and across all sectors of the economy would be eligible, with certain exceptions including public sector entities [125.7(1)"eligible entity" — ed.]. Flexibility in the measurement of revenue for the purpose of applying the revenue decline test would also ensure more consistent access to the wage subsidy across impacted organizations, including newly created businesses and high-growth companies, as well as non-profit organizations and registered charities.

An eligible employer's entitlement to this wage subsidy would be based on the salary or wages actually paid to employees. All employers would be expected to at least make best efforts to bring employees' wages to their pre-crisis levels.

Bill C-14 introduced today includes proposed improvements to the Canada Emergency Wage Subsidy that were announced in detail on April 8, 2020 and subsequently refined as part of the legislative process. These improvements include the following:

- To measure their revenue loss, it is proposed that employers compare their revenue of March, April and May 2020 [and later months — ed.] to that of the same month of 2019 or, in order to provide added flexibility, to an average of their revenue earned in January and February 2020. [See 125.7(1)"prior reference period"(b) — ed.]

- For March, the government proposes to make the CEWS more accessible than originally announced by reducing this 30% benchmark to 15%, in recognition of the fact that many businesses did not begin to be affected by the crisis until partway through the month. [See 125.7(1)"specified percentage"(a) — ed.]

- To provide certainty for employers, the government is also proposing that once an employer is found eligible for a specific period, they would automatically qualify for the next period of the program. For example, an employer with a revenue drop of more than 15% in March would qualify for the first and second periods of the program, covering remuneration paid between March 15 and May 9. Similarly, an employer with a revenue drop of 30% in April would qualify for the second and third periods of the program, covering remuneration paid between May 10 to June 6. [See 125.7(9)(a) — ed.]

- To recognize the challenges in measuring revenues of non-profit organizations and registered charities, it is proposed that they be allowed to choose whether or not to include government assistance in revenues for the purpose of applying the revenue decline test. Once chosen, the same approach would have to be maintained by the organization throughout the program period. [See 125.7(1)"qualifying revenue"(a)(ii), (b)(ii) and (b.1) — ed.]

- It is also proposed that employers be allowed to measure revenues either on the basis of accrual accounting (as they are earned) or cash accounting (as they are received). Once chosen, the same accounting method would have to be used by the employer throughout the program period. [See 125.7(4)(e) — ed.]

- It is also proposed that the CEWS provide an additional amount to compensate employers for their contributions to the *Canada Pension Plan*, Employment Insurance, Quebec Pension Plan and Quebec Parental Insurance Plan paid in respect of eligible employees who are on leave with pay due to COVID-19. [See 125.7(2)D(b) — ed.]

In order to maintain the integrity of the program and to ensure that it helps Canadians keep their jobs, the employer would be required to repay amounts paid under the CEWS if they do not meet the eligibility requirements [152(1)(b) allows assessment of the amount deemed paid by 125.7(2), so all the consequences of assessment follow; and a CEWS determination under 152(3.4) is effectively treated as an assessment due to 152(1.2) — ed.]. The government is also proposing a penalty of 25% of the CEWS received by an employer if the employer has engaged in transactions that artificially reduce the employer's revenue in order to qualify for the subsidy [125.7(6), 163(2.901) — ed.]. As well, under existing provisions of the *Income Tax Act* [239(1) — ed.], persons making, or participating in making, a false or deceptive statement could be prosecuted with a summary or indictable offence [and/or assessed a gross-negligence penalty: 163(2)(i), 163.2(4) — ed.]. Anyone found guilty could be sentenced to prison for up to 5 years [239(2)(b) — ed.].

The government will continue to carefully monitor all developments relating to the COVID-19 outbreak and will continue to take further action to protect Canadians and the economy.

Backgrounder: Additional Details on the Canada Emergency Wage Subsidy

What It Means for Canadian Employers

To help employers keep and return workers to their payroll through the challenges posed by the COVID-19 pandemic, the Prime Minister, Justin Trudeau, announced the new Canada Emergency Wage Subsidy on March 27, 2020. This would provide a 75% wage subsidy to eligible employers for up to 12 weeks [later extended to many more weeks — ed.], retroactive to March 15, 2020.

This wage subsidy aims to prevent further job losses, encourage employers to rehire workers previously laid off as a result of COVID-19, and help better position Canadian companies and other employers to more easily resume normal operations following the crisis. While the Government has designed the proposed wage subsidy to provide generous and timely financial support to employers, it has done so with the expectation that employers will do their part by using the subsidy in a manner that supports the health and well-being of their employees.

Eligible Employers

Eligible employers [125.7(1)"eligible entity" — ed.] would include individuals, taxable corporations, partnerships consisting of eligible employers, non-profit organizations and registered charities [and later, entities prescribed in Reg. 8901.1 — ed.].

Public bodies would not be eligible for this subsidy [125.7(1)"eligible entity", exclusions of "public institution" — ed.]. Public bodies [125.7(1)"public institution" — ed.] would generally include municipalities and local governments, Crown corporations, wholly owned municipal corporations, public universities, colleges, schools and hospitals [and, perhaps unintentionally, foreign diplomats and their families — ed.].

This subsidy would be available to eligible employers that see [125.7(1)"qualifying entity"(c) — ed.] a drop of at least 15% of their revenue in March 2020 [125.7(1)"specified percentage"(a) — ed.] and 30% for the following months [125.7(1)"specified percentage"(b) — ed.] (see Eligible Periods). In applying for the subsidy, employers would be required to attest to the decline in revenue [125.7(1)"qualifying entity"(b), Form RC661 — ed.].

We encourage all eligible employers to rehire employees as quickly as possible and to apply for the Canada Emergency Wage Subsidy [125.7(1)"qualifying entity"(a) — ed.] if they are eligible. To ensure that the Canada Emergency Response Benefit (CERB) applies as intended, the Government will consider implementing an approach to limit duplication. This could include a process to allow individuals rehired by their employer during the same eligibility period to cancel their CERB claim and repay that amount.

Calculating Revenues

An employer's revenue for this purpose would be its revenue in Canada earned from arm's-length sources [125.7(1)"qualifying revenue"(d) — ed.]. Revenue would be calculated using the employer's normal accounting method [125.7(4) opening words — ed.], and would exclude revenues from extraordinary items [125.7(1)"qualifying revenue"(c) — ed.] and amounts on account of capital [according to Finance, this comes from the reference to "normal accounting practices" in 125.7(4) opening words — ed.].

On April 8, 2020, the government clarified that employers would be allowed to calculate their revenues under the accrual method or the cash method, but not a combination of both [125.7(4)(e) — ed.]. Employers would select an accounting method when first applying for the CEWS and would be required to use that method for the entire duration of the program.

For registered charities and non-profit organizations, the calculation will include most forms of revenue, excluding revenues from non-arm's length persons [125.7(1)"qualifying revenue"(d) — ed.]. These organizations would be allowed to choose whether or not to include revenue from government sources as part of the calculation [125.7(1)"qualifying revenue"(a)(ii), (b)(ii), (b.1) — ed.]. Once chosen, the same approach would have to apply throughout the program period.

Special rules for the computation of revenue would be provided to take into account certain non-arm's length transactions, such as where an employer sells all of its output to a related company that in turn earns arm's length revenue [125.7(4)(d) — ed.]. As well, affiliated groups would be able to compute revenue on a consolidated basis [125.7(4)(a), (b) — ed.].

Amount of Subsidy

The subsidy amount for a given employee on eligible remuneration paid for the period between March 15 and June 6, 2020 would be the greater of:

- 75% of the amount of remuneration paid, up to a maximum benefit of $847 per week [125.7(2)A(a)(i), only for arm's-length employees — ed.]; and

- the amount of remuneration paid, up to a maximum benefit of $847 per week or 75% of the employee's pre-crisis weekly remuneration, whichever is less [125.7(2)A(a)(ii) — ed.].

In effect, employers may be eligible for a subsidy of up to 100% of the first 75% of pre-crisis wages or salaries of existing employees. These employers would be expected where possible to maintain existing employees' pre-crisis employment earnings [but this is not required by the legislation — ed.].

The pre-crisis remuneration for a given employee [125.7(1)"baseline remuneration"(a) — ed.] would be based on the average weekly remuneration paid between January 1 and March 15 inclusively, excluding any seven-day periods in respect of which the employee did not receive remuneration.

Employers will also be eligible for a subsidy of up to 75% of salaries and wages paid to new employees [125.7(1)"eligible employee" — ed.].

Eligible remuneration [125.7(1)"eligible remuneration" — ed.] may include salary, wages, and other remuneration like taxable benefits. These are amounts for which employers would generally be required to withhold or deduct amounts to remit to the Receiver General on account of the employee's income tax obligation [153(1)(a), (g) — ed.]. However, it does not include severance pay [125.7(1)"eligible remuneration"(a) — ed.], or items such as stock option benefits [125.7(1)"eligible remuneration"(b), though stock option death benefits under 7(1)(e) may be included, if 153(1) catches them despite 153(1.01) not applying — ed.] or the personal use of a corporate vehicle.

A special rule will apply to employees that do not deal at arm's length with the employer [125.7(2)A(a)(i)(C) — ed.]. The subsidy amount for such employees will be limited to the eligible remuneration paid in any pay period between March 15 and June 6, 2020, up to a maximum benefit of the lesser of $847 per week and 75% of the employee's pre-crisis weekly remuneration [125.7(2)A(a)(ii)(B) — ed.]. The subsidy would only be available in respect of non-arm's length employees employed prior to March 15, 2020 [125.7(1)"baseline remuneration"(a) — ed.]

There would be no overall limit on the subsidy amount that an eligible employer may claim.

Employers are expected to make their best effort to top-up employees' salaries to bring them to pre-crisis levels [this is not mandatory — ed.].

Refund for Certain Payroll Contributions

On April 8, 2020, the Government proposed to expand the CEWS by introducing a new 100% refund for certain employer-paid contributions to Employment Insurance, the *Canada Pension Plan*, the Quebec Pension Plan, and the Quebec Parental Insurance Plan. This refund would cover 100% of employer-paid contributions for eligible employees for each week throughout which those employees are on leave with pay and for which the employer is eligible to claim for the CEWS for those employees [125.7(2)D — ed.].

In general, an employee will be considered to be on leave with pay throughout a week if that employee is remunerated by the employer for that week but does not perform any work for the employer in that week [125.7(2)D(b) opening words — ed.]. This refund would not be available for eligible employees that are on leave with pay for only a portion of a week.

This refund would not be subject to the weekly maximum benefit per employee of $847 that an eligible employer may claim in respect of the CEWS [but 2020

CPP contributions are limited to $58,700 per year per employee anyway — ed.]. There would be no overall limit on the refund amount that an eligible employer may claim.

For greater certainty, employers would be required to continue to collect and remit employer and employee contributions to each program [CPP, EI, etc. — ed.] as usual. Eligible employers would apply for a refund, as described above, at the same time that they apply for the CEWS.

Eligible Periods

Eligibility would generally be determined by the change in an eligible employer's monthly revenues, year-over-year, for the calendar month in which the period began [125.7(1)"qualifying entity"(c)(i) — ed.].

On April 8, 2020, the Government announced that all employers would be allowed to calculate their change in revenue using an alternative benchmark to determine their eligibility. This would provide more flexibility to employers for which the general approach may not be appropriate, including high-growth firms, sectors that faced difficulties in 2019, non-profits and charities, as well as employers established after February 2019. Under this alternative approach [125.7(1)"qualifying entity"(c)(ii) — ed.], employers would be allowed to compare their revenue using an average of their revenue earned in January and February 2020 [125.7(1)"prior reference period"(b) — ed.]. Employers would select the general year-over-year approach or this alternative approach when first applying for the CEWS and would be required to use the same approach for the entire duration of the program.

The Government is also announcing that, in order to provide certainty to employers, once an employer is found eligible for a specific period, the employer would automatically qualify for the next period [125.7(9)(a) — ed.].

- ABC Inc. is a start-up that started its operations last September. It reported revenues of $100,000 in January and $140,000 in February, for a monthly average of $120,000. In March, its revenues dropped to $90,000. Because revenues in March are 25% lower than $120,000, ABC Inc. would be eligible for the CEWS for the first and second claiming period. To be eligible for the third claiming period, ABC Inc. revenues would have to be $84,000 or less for the month of April or May (that is, 30% lower than $120,000).

The amount of wage subsidy (provided under the COVID-19 Economic Response Plan) received by the employer in a given month would be ignored for the purpose of measuring year-over-year changes in monthly revenues [125.7(3), reference to "other than this section" — ed.].

- For example, if revenues in March 2020 were down 20% compared to March 2019, the employer would be allowed to claim the CEWS (as calculated above) on remuneration paid between March 15 and April 11, 2020, as well as between April 12 to May 9.

- Alternatively, this employer could use its average revenue from the months of January and February 2020, instead of March 2019, to determine if it is eligible for the CEWS.

- Once an approach is chosen, the employer would have to apply it throughout the program period [125.7(1)"prior reference period"(b)(ii)(A) — ed.].

The table below outlines each claiming period, the required reduction in revenue and the reference period for eligibility.

Claiming period	Required reduction in revenue	Reference period for eligibility
Period 1 March 15 to April 11	15%	March 2020 over: • March 2019 or • Average of January and February 2020
Period 2 April 12 to May 9	30%	Eligible for Period 1 OR April 2020 over: • April 2019 or • Average of January and February 2020
Period 3 May 10 to June 6	30%	Eligible for Period 2 OR May 2020 over: • May 2019 or • Average of January and February 2020

Eligible employees

An eligible employee [defined in 125.7(1) — ed.] is an individual who is employed in Canada.

Eligibility for the CEWS of an employee's remuneration will be available to employees other than those who have been without remuneration for 14 or more consecutive days in the eligibility period, i.e., from March 15 to April 11, from April 12 to May 9, or from May 10 to June 6 [125.7(1)"eligible employee" and "qualifying period"(a)-(c) — ed.].

This rule replaces the previously announced restriction that an employer would not be eligible to claim the CEWS for remuneration paid to an employee in a week that falls within a 4-week period for which the employee is eligible for the Canadian [*Canada* — ed.] Emergency Response Benefit.

How to Apply

Eligible employers would be able to apply for the CEWS [125.7(1)"qualifying entity"(a) — ed.] through the Canada Revenue Agency's My Business Account portal as well as a web-based application. Employers would have to keep records demonstrating their reduction in arm's-length revenues and remuneration paid to employees [230(1) — ed.]. More details about the application process will be made available shortly.

Ensuring Compliance

In order to maintain the integrity of the program and to ensure that it helps Canadians keep their jobs, the employer would be required to repay amounts paid under the CEWS if they do not meet the eligibility requirements [when the 125.7(2) amount is assessed under 152(1)(b), the usual assessment and collection rules apply; and per 152(1.2), the usual rules apply to a CEWS determination under 152(3.4) — ed.]. Penalties may apply in cases of fraudulent claims [163(2)(i), or third-party penalty under 163.2(4) for an individual providing false information under 125.7(1)"qualifying entity"(b) — ed.]. The penalties may include fines or even imprisonment [239(1), (1.1), (2) — ed.]. In addition, anti abuse rules would be put in place to ensure that the subsidy is not inappropriately obtained [125.7(1)"eligible remuneration"(d), 125.7(6), 163(2.901) — ed.] and to help ensure that employees are paid the amounts they are owed [125.7(1)"eligible remuneration"(c) — ed.].

Employers that engage in artificial transactions to reduce revenue for the purpose of claiming the CEWS would be subject to a penalty equal to 25% of the value of the subsidy claimed [163(2)(i), 163(2.901) — ed.], in addition to the requirement to repay in full the subsidy that was improperly claimed [following assessment under 152(1)(b) or CEWS determination under 152(3.4) — ed.].

Interaction with 10% Wage Subsidy

On March 25, 2020, the *COVID-19 Emergency Response Act*, which included the implementation of a temporary 10% wage subsidy [153(1.02)-(1.04) — ed.], received Royal Assent. For employers that are eligible for both the CEWS and the 10% wage subsidy for a period, any benefit from the 10% wage subsidy for remuneration paid in a specific period would generally reduce the amount available to be claimed under the CEWS in that same period [125.7(2)B — ed.].

Interaction with the Work-Sharing Program

On March 18, 2020, the Prime Minister announced an extension of the maximum duration of the Work-Sharing program from 38 weeks to 76 weeks for employers affected by COVID-19. This measure will provide income support to employees eligible for Employment Insurance who agree to reduce their normal working hours because of developments beyond the control of their employers.

For employers and employees that are participating in a Work-Sharing program, EI benefits received by employees through the Work-Sharing program will reduce the benefit that their employer is entitled to receive under the CEWS [125.7(2)C — ed.].

Government Assistance

The usual treatment of tax credits and other benefits provided by the government would apply. As a consequence, the wage subsidy received by an employer would be considered government assistance and be included in the employer's taxable income [12(1)(x), 125.7(3) — ed.].

Assistance received under either wage subsidy would reduce the amount of remuneration expenses eligible for other federal tax credits calculated on the same remuneration [e.g., via 127(18)-(21) for the investment tax credit — ed.].

How employers will benefit from the CEWS

Maude and Stéphane own a corporation that operates an automobile repair shop in Saint Boniface, Manitoba. They are working full time, each drawing a salary of $1,300 per week, and have three part-time employees, each earning $800 per week, for a total weekly payroll of $5,000. Maude and Stéphane have reduced their opening hours due to decreased demand for their services. They had initially laid off their employees, but they have now decided to re-hire them following the announcement of the Canada Emergency Wage Subsidy. Their employees are not being asked to report to work during this challenging period.

Maude and Stéphane are now keeping their employees on the payroll, paying them 75% of their pre-crisis salary ($600 per week). Maude and Stéphane would be eligible for a weekly wage subsidy of $3,494 ($847 for each of themselves and $600 for each of their employees). Maude and Stéphane would also be eligible for a 100% refund of their employer-paid contributions to Employment Insurance and the *Canada Pension Plan* in respect of their employees, providing an additional benefit of up to $124 per week.

At the end of each claiming period, Maude and Stéphane would submit an application through the Canada Revenue Agency portal, attesting that their decline in revenues in each month is sufficient to qualify, when compared to the average of January and February. [However, once they qualify for a period, they do not need to attest for the one next period: 125.7(9) — ed.] They would also report the total remuneration paid to themselves and their furloughed employees during the month. As Maude and Stéphane have access to direct deposits with the Canada Revenue Agency, they would receive their subsidy shortly after each application.

CEWS Stage 2 (July 5 to Nov. 21, 2020) is explained in Finance Backgrounder "Adapting the Canada Emergency Wage Subsidy to Protect Jobs and Promote Growth", July 17, 2020 (introductory portion omitted):

Effective July 5, 2020 [starting from 125.7(1)"qualifying period"(c.2) — ed.], the CEWS would [now does — ed.] consist of two parts:

- a base subsidy available to all eligible employers that are experiencing a decline in revenues, with the subsidy amount varying depending on the scale of revenue decline [125.7(2)A(b)(i) — ed.]; and

- a top-up subsidy of up to an additional 25% for those employers that have been most adversely affected by the COVID-19 crisis [125.7(2)A(b)(i)(B), (ii) — ed.].

The two-part CEWS would apply with respect to the remuneration of active employees ["not on leave with pay" in 125.7(2)A(b)(i) and (ii) — ed.]. A separate CEWS rate structure would apply to furloughed employees (as described further below) ["on leave with pay" in 125.7(2)A(b)(iii), (iv) — ed.]. In addition, a safe harbour would be available [125.7(2)A(b)(iii)(B) — ed.] to ensure that, through August 29 (periods 5 and 6 [125.7(1)"qualifying period"(c.2), (c.3) — ed.]), employers would have access to a CEWS rate that is at least as generous as they would have had under the initial CEWS structure, as described further below (see *Safe harbour rule for Periods 5 and 6* below).

Base subsidy for all employers impacted by the crisis

Effective July 5, 2020 (i.e., Period 5 and subsequent periods), employers that have been affected by the COVID-19 crisis would be eligible for a base CEWS amount for active employees ["not on leave with pay" in 125.7(2)A(b)(ii) — ed.]. This base CEWS would be a specified rate, applied to the amount of remuneration paid to the employee for the eligibility period, on remuneration of up to $1,129 per week [125.7(2)A(b)(ii)G(B) — ed.]. The rate of the base CEWS would now vary depending on the level of revenue decline [125.7(1)"base percentage" — ed.], and its application would be extended to employers with a revenue decline of less than 30% (see Table 1) [125.7(1)"base percentage"(a)(ii), (b)(ii), etc. — ed.]. This expansion would mean that **all** eligible employers with a revenue decline would now qualify for CEWS support.

The specified rate would be determined [125.7(1)"base percentage" — ed.] based on the change in an eligible employer's monthly revenues, as described further below (see *Reference Periods for the Drop-in-Revenues Test* below).

The maximum base CEWS rate would be provided to employers with a revenue drop of 50% or more [125.7(1)"base percentage"(a)(i), (b)(i), etc. — ed.]. Employers with a revenue drop of less than 50% would be eligible for a lower base CEWS rate, as shown in Table 1 [125.7(1)"base percentage"(a)(ii), (b)(ii), etc. — ed.]. The decline in the base CEWS rate between a 50% revenue drop and zero provides a smooth phase-out so that businesses can grow and rehire without worrying about a sharp drop in support as economic activity returns.

The maximum base CEWS rate would be gradually reduced from 60% in Periods 5 and 6 (July 5 to August 29) [125.7(1)"base percentage"(a)(i) — ed.] to 20% in Period 9 (October 25 to November 21) [125.7(1)"base percentage"(e)(i) — ed.].

Table 1: Rate structure of the base CEWS

Timing	Period 5*: July 5–August 1	Period 6*: August 2–August 29	Period 7: August 30–September 26	Period 8: September 27–October 24	Period 9: October 25–November 21
Maximum weekly benefit per employee	Up to $677	Up to $677	Up to $565	Up to $452	Up to $226
Revenue drop					
Revenue drop 50% and over	60%	60%	50%	40%	20%
0% to 49%	1.2 × revenue drop (e.g., 1.2 × 20% revenue drop = 24% base CEWS rate)	1.2 × revenue drop (e.g., 1.2 × 20% revenue drop = 24% base CEWS rate)	1.0 × revenue drop (e.g., 1.0 × 20% revenue drop = 20% base CEWS rate)	0.8 × revenue drop (e.g., 0.8 × 20% revenue drop = 16% base CEWS rate)	0.4 × revenue drop (e.g., 0.4 × 20% revenue drop = 8% base CEWS rate)

* In Periods 5 and 6, employers who would have been better off in the CEWS design in Periods 1 to 4 would be eligible for a 75% wage subsidy if they have a revenue decline of 30% or more. As described further below (see *Safe harbour rule for Periods 5 and 6* below).

Top-up subsidy for the most adversely affected employers

A top-up CEWS of up to 25% [i.e., to maximum 85% support for July 5 to Aug. 29 — ed.] would be available to employers that were the most adversely impacted by the pandemic [125.7(2)A(b)(i)(B), (ii) — ed.]. Generally, an eligible employer's top-up CEWS would be determined based on the revenue drop experienced when comparing revenues in the preceding 3 months to the same months in the prior year [125.7(1)"top-up revenue reduction percentage"A — ed.]. Under the **alternative approach** to the calculation of baseline revenues, an eligible employer's top-up CEWS would be determined based on the revenue drop experienced when comparing average monthly revenue in the preceding 3 months to the average monthly revenue in January and February 2020 [125.7(1)"top-up revenue reduction percentage"B(a) — ed.].

- For example, if an employer had $600,000 in revenue between April 1 and June 30, 2019, and $210,000 in revenue between April 1 and June 30, 2020, the employer would have a 3-month revenue drop of 65%.

- Under the alternative approach, if an employer had $400,000 in revenue between January 1 and February 29, 2020 (average monthly revenue of $200,000), and $210,000 in revenue between April 1 and June 30, 2020 (average monthly revenue of $70,000), the employer would have a 3-month revenue drop of 65%.

Employers that have experienced a 3-month average revenue drop of more than 50% would receive a top-up CEWS rate equal to 1.25 times the average revenue drop that exceeds 50%, up to a maximum top-up CEWS rate of 25% [125.7(1)"top-up percentage" — ed.], which is attained at a 70% revenue decline. As with the base CEWS rate, the top-up CEWS rate would apply to remuneration of up to $1,129 per week [125.7(2)A(b)(ii)G(B) — ed.]. The top-up CEWS rate for selected average revenue drop levels is illustrated in Table 2 below.

Table 2: Top-up CEWS rates for selected levels of average revenue drop over the preceding three months

3-month average revenue drop	Top-up CEWS rate	Top-up calculation = 1.25 × (3 month revenue drop – 50%)
70% and over	25%	1.25 × (70%-50%) = 25%
65%	18.75%	1.25 × (65%-50%) = 18.75%
60%	12.5%	1.25 × (60%-50%) = 12.5%
55%	6.25%	1.25 × (55%-50%) = 6.25%
50% and under	0.0%	1.25 × (50%-50%) = 0.0%

The overall CEWS rate would be equal to the top-up CEWS rate plus the base CEWS rate. Table 3 shows the combined base and top-up CEWS rates for Periods 5 to 9 for the most adversely affected employers.

Table 3: Rate structure of the combined base CEWS and the top-up CEWS for the most affected employers (i.e., those that experienced an average revenue drop of 70% or more in the preceding 3 months)

Timing	Period 5*: July 5–August 1	Period 6*: August 2–August 29	Period 7: August 30–September 26	Period 8: September 27–October 24	Period 9: October 25–November 21
Maximum weekly benefit per employee	Up to $960	Up to $960	Up to $847	Up to $734	Up to $508
Revenue drop in the current 1-month reference period					
50% or more	85% (60% base CEWS + 25% top-up)	85% (60% base CEWS + 25% top-up)	75% (50% base CEWS + 25% top-up)	65% (40% base CEWS + 25% top-up)	45% (20% base CEWS + 25% top-up)
0% to 49%	1.2 × revenue drop + 25% (e.g., 1.2 × 20% revenue drop + 25% = 49% CEWS rate)	1.2 × revenue drop + 25% (e.g., 1.2 × 20% revenue drop + 25% = 49% CEWS rate)	1 × revenue drop + 25% (e.g., 1 × 20% revenue drop + 25% = 45% CEWS rate)	0.8 × revenue drop + 25% (e.g., 0.8 × 20% revenue drop + 25% = 41% CEWS rate)	0.4 × revenue drop + 25% (e.g., 0.4 × 20% revenue drop + 25% = 33% CEWS rate)

* In Periods 5 and 6, employers who would have been better off in the CEWS design in Periods 1 to 4 would be eligible for a 75% wage subsidy if they have a revenue decline of 30% or more. As described further below (see *Safe harbour rule for Periods 5 and 6* below).

Table 4 illustrates the interaction of the 3-month drop in revenue test for the top-up CEWS and the month-over-month revenue test for the base CEWS for Periods 5 and 6. For example, an employer that is recovering with a revenue drop of

20% in Period 5 and a preceding 3-month average revenue drop of 60% would benefit from a base CEWS rate of 24% and a top-up CEWS rate of 12.5%, which would provide a combined CEWS rate of 36.5%.

Table 4: Rate structure of the combined base CEWS and the top-up CEWS for Periods 5 and 6*

Average revenue drop in the preceding 3 months

Revenue drop in the current 1-month reference period	70% or more	50% to 69%	0% to 49%
50% or more	85% (60% base CEWS + 25% top-up)	60% + 1.25 × (3 month revenue drop-50%) (e.g., 60% base CEWS + 1.25 × (60% 3 month revenue drop – 50%) = 72.5% CEWS rate)	60% (60% base CEWS + 0% top-up)
0% to 49%	1.2 × revenue drop + 25% (e.g., 1.2 × 20% revenue drop + 25% = 49% CEWS rate)	1.2 × revenue drop + 1.25 × (3 month revenue drop-50%) (e.g., 1.2 × 20% revenue drop + 1.25 × (60% 3-month revenue drop-50%) = 36.5% CEWS rate)	1.2 × revenue drop (e.g., 1.2 × 20% revenue drop = 24% CEWS rate)
No revenue drop	25% (0% base CEWS + 25% top-up)	1.25 × (3 month revenue drop-50%) (e.g., 1.25 × (60% 3-month revenue drop-50%) = 12.5% CEWS rate)	nil

* In Periods 5 and 6, employers who would have been better off in the CEWS design in Periods 1 to 4 would be eligible for a 75% wage subsidy if they have a revenue decline of 30% or more. As described further below (see *Safe harbour rule for Periods 5 and 6* below).

Safe harbour rule for Periods 5 and 6

For Periods 5 and 6 [July 5 to Aug. 29: 125.7(1)"qualifying period"(c.2), (c.3) — ed.], an eligible employer would be entitled to a CEWS rate not lower than the rate that they would be entitled to if their entitlement were calculated under the CEWS rules that were in place for Periods 1 to 4 [125.7(2)A(b)(i)(A)(II) — ed.]. This means that in Periods 5 and 6, an eligible employer with a revenue decline of 30% or more in the relevant reference period would receive a CEWS rate of at least 75% or potentially an even higher CEWS rate using the new rules outlined above for the most adversely affected employers (up to 85%).

CEWS for Furloughed Employees

For Periods 5 and 6 [July 5 to Aug. 29: 125.7(1)"qualifying period"(c.2), (c.3) — ed.], the subsidy calculation for a furloughed employee would remain the same as for Periods 1 to 4 [125.7(2)A(b)(iii)(B) — ed.]. It would be the greater of:

- For arm's-length employees, 75% of the amount of remuneration paid, up to a maximum benefit of $847 per week; and

- 75% of the employee's pre-crisis weekly remuneration up to a maximum benefit of $847 per week or the amount of remuneration paid, whichever is less.

Beginning in Period 7 [from Aug. 30: 125.7(1)"qualifying period"(c.4) — ed.], CEWS support for furloughed employees would be adjusted [125.7(2)A(b)(iv), and see Reg. 8901.2(7) for (b)(iv)(B) for Periods 7-10 — ed.] to align with the benefits provided through the Canada Emergency Response Benefit (CERB) and/or Employment Insurance (EI). This would ensure equitable treatment of employees on furlough between both programs, provide greater clarity to workers as to their compensation as compared to a changing subsidy rate based on their employer's revenue in a given month and, when combined with draft legislative changes to the interaction with the CERB (i.e., the elimination of the 14-days rule, as discussed below), make it easier to transition employees on to CEWS so that they are reconnected with their employer.

For Period 5 and subsequent periods [from July 5 — ed.], the CEWS for furloughed employees would be available to eligible employers that qualify for either the base rate or the top-up for active employees in the relevant period [125.7(2)A(b)(i)(A), (iii)(A) — ed.].

The employer portion of contributions in respect of the *Canada Pension Plan*, Employment Insurance, the Quebec Pension Plan, and the Quebec Parental Insurance Plan in respect of furloughed employees would continue to be refunded to the employer.

Eligible Remuneration

No changes are proposed to the definition of eligible remuneration [125.7(1) — ed.]. Eligible remuneration may include salary, wages, and other remuneration like taxable benefits. These are amounts for which employers would generally be required to withhold or deduct amounts to remit to the Receiver General on account of the employee's income tax obligation. However, it does not include

severance pay, or items such as stock option benefits or the personal use of a corporate vehicle.

For active arm's-length employees, the amount of remuneration would be based solely on actual remuneration paid for the eligibility period, without reference to the pre-crisis remuneration concept used for earlier CEWS periods, which is explained in the Finance Canada backgrounder of April 11, 2020. A modified special rule would apply to active employees that do not deal at arm's length with the employer. For Period 5 and subsequent periods, the wage subsidy for such employees would be based on the employee's weekly eligible remuneration or pre-crisis remuneration, whichever is less, up to a maximum of $1,129 [125.7(2)A(b)(ii)G(B) — ed.]. The subsidy would only be available in respect of non-arm's-length employees that were employed prior to March 16, 2020 [125.7(2)A(b)(ii)G(C), 125.7(1)"baseline remuneration"(a) — ed.].

For Period 4, the pre-crisis remuneration of an employee would be based on the average weekly remuneration paid to the employee from January 1 to March 15, 2020; from March 1, 2019 to May 31, 2019; or from March 1, 2019 to June 30, 2019 [125.7(1)"baseline remuneration" — ed.]. For Period 5 and subsequent periods, the pre-crisis remuneration of an employee would be based on the average weekly remuneration paid to the employee from January 1 to March 15, 2020 or from July 1, 2019 to December 31, 2019 [125.7(1)"baseline remuneration"(a), (b)(iii) — ed.]. In all cases, the calculation of average weekly remuneration would exclude any period of 7 or more consecutive days without remuneration [125.7(1)"baseline remuneration" opening words — ed.]. Employers can choose which period to use on an employee-by-employee basis.

Eligible Employers and Employees

Eligible employers [125.7(1)"eligible entity" — ed.] include individuals, taxable corporations and trusts, partnerships consisting of eligible employers, non profit organizations and registered charities. Public institutions are generally not eligible for the subsidy [125.7(1)"eligible entity"(a), (c), (d), 125.7(1)"public institution" — ed.]. As announced on May 15, 2020, eligible employers also include the following groups [prescribed in Reg. 8901.1 — ed.]:

- Partnerships that are up to 50% owned by non-eligible members;

- Indigenous government-owned corporations that are carrying on a business, as well as partnerships where the partners are Indigenous governments and eligible employers;

- Registered Canadian Amateur Athletic Associations;

- Registered Journalism Organizations; and

- Non-public colleges and schools, including institutions that offer specialized services, such as arts schools, driving schools, language schools or flight schools.

An eligible employee is an individual who is employed in Canada. Effective July 5, 2020, the eligibility criteria would no longer exclude employees that are without remuneration in respect of 14 or more consecutive days in an eligibility period [125.7(1)"eligible employee" — ed.].

Calculating Revenues

An employer's revenue for the purposes of the CEWS is its revenue in Canada earned from arm's-length sources [125.7(1)"qualifying revenue" — ed.]. Revenues from extraordinary items and amounts on account of capital are excluded [para. (c) — ed.].

For registered charities and non-profit organizations, the calculation includes most forms of revenue, excluding revenues from non-arm's length persons. These organizations are allowed to choose whether to include revenue from government sources as part of the calculation [125.7(1)"qualifying revenue"(a)(ii), (b)(ii), (b.1) — ed.]. Once chosen, the same approach would have to apply throughout the program period.

Special rules for the computation of revenue are provided to take into account certain non-arm's-length transactions, such as where an employer sells all of its output to a related company that in turn earns arm's-length revenue [125.7(4)(d) — ed.]. As well, affiliated groups are able to elect to compute revenue on a consolidated basis [125.7(4)(b) — ed.].

Reference Periods for the Drop-in-Revenues Test

For the purpose of the base CEWS [125.7(2)A(b)(ii) — ed.], eligibility would generally be determined by the change in an eligible employer's monthly revenues, year-over-year, for the applicable calendar month [125.7(1)"revenue reduction percentage", "current reference period", "prior reference period" — ed.]. Table 5 below outlines each claiming period and the relevant period for determining an eligible employer's change in revenue. For Period 5 and all subsequent periods, an eligible employer would be able to use the greater of its percentage revenue decline in the current period and that in the previous period for the purpose of determining its qualification for the base CEWS and its base CEWS rate in the current period [125.7(9)(b) — ed.]. This would provide certainty and be a continuation of the rules for Periods 1 to 4 that allowed an employer that met the revenue test in one period to automatically qualify for the following period [125.7(9)(a) — ed.].

Employers that have elected to use the alternative approach for the first 4 periods [125.7(1)"prior reference period"(b) opening words — ed.] would be able to either maintain that election for Period 5 and onward or revert to the general approach. Similarly, employers that have used the general approach for the first 4 periods would be able to either continue with the general approach or elect to use the alternative approach for Period 5 and onward. Whichever approach they choose would apply for Period 5 and onward and would apply to the calculation of the base CEWS and the top-up CEWS. This would provide flexibility for employers to adjust their approach in light of new circumstances they may be experiencing as the CEWS is extended.

Table 5: Reference periods for the base CEWS

	Claim period	General approach	Alternative approach
Period 5	July 5 to August 1, 2020	July 2020 over July 2019 *or* June 2020 over June 2019	July 2020 *or* June 2020 over average of January and February 2020
Period 6	August 2 to August 29, 2020	August 2020 over August 2019 *or* July 2020 over July 2019	August 2020 *or* July 2020 over average of January and February 2020
Period 7	August 30 to September 26, 2020	September 2020 over September 2019 *or* August 2020 over August 2019	September 2020 *or* August 2020 over average of January and February 2020
Period 8	September 27 to October 24, 2020	October 2020 over October 2019 *or* September 2020 over September 2019	October 2020 *or* September 2020 over average of January and February 2020
Period 9	October 25 to November 21, 2020	November 2020 over November 2019 *or* October 2020 over October 2019	November 2020 *or* October 2020 over average of January and February 2020

For the purpose of the top-up CEWS, eligibility would generally be determined by the change in an eligible employer's revenues for a 3-month period. Table 6 below outlines each claiming period and the relevant period for determining an eligible employer's average change in revenue.

Table 6: Reference periods for the top-up CEWS

	Claim period	General approach	Alternative approach
Period 5	July 5 to August 1, 2020	April to June 2020 over April to June 2019	April to June 2020 average over January and February 2020 average*
Period 6	August 2 to August 29, 2020	May to July 2020 over May to July 2019	May to July 2020 average over January and February 2020 average*
Period 7	August 30 to September 26, 2020	June to August 2020 over June to August 2019	June to August 2020 average over January and February 2020 average*
Period 8	September 27 to October 24, 2020	July to September 2020 over July to September 2019	July to September 2020 average over January and February 2020 average*
Period 9	October 25 to November 21, 2020	August to October 2020 over August to October 2019	August to October 2020 average over January and February 2020 average*

* The calculation would equal the average monthly revenue over the 3 months of the reference period divided by the average revenue for the months of January and February 2020.

Legislative Amendments

The government has shared draft legislative proposals [news release, May 15, 2020 — ed.] to make the changes to the CEWS described in this backgrounder as well as changes in response to feedback received from stakeholders. These proposed changes, which would generally apply as of March 15, 2020, include:

- providing an appeal process based on the existing procedure for notices of determination that allows for an appeal to the Tax Court of Canada [152(3.4), 152(1.2) — ed.];

- providing continuity rules for the calculation of an employer's drop in revenues in certain circumstances where the employer purchased all or substantially all the assets used in carrying on business by the seller [125.7(4.1), (4.2) — ed.];

- allowing prescribed organizations [listed in Reg. 8901.1 — ed.] that are registered charities or non-profit organizations to choose whether to include government-source revenue for the purpose of computing their reductions in qualifying revenue [125.7(1)"qualifying revenue"(b.1) — ed.]; and

- allowing entities that use the cash method of accounting to elect to use accrual based accounting to compute their revenues for the purpose of the CEWS [125.7(4)(e)(ii) — ed.].

The government is also proposing to move forward with previously released legislative changes, including relieving changes for calculating pre-crisis "baseline" remuneration, for corporations that have amalgamated [87(2)(g.6) — ed.] and for eligible entities that use payroll service providers [125.7(1)"qualifying entity"(d)(ii) — ed.]. The government is also proposing to move forward with the

amendment that would align the treatment of trusts and corporations for the purposes of the CEWS [125.7(1)"eligible entity"(a), (b) — ed.]. Some of these proposed measures can be found in the May 15, 2020 backgrounder entitled "Extending eligibility for the Canada Emergency Wage Subsidy".

How Employers Would Benefit From the Redesigned CEWS

Example: Hard hit employer eligible for an 85% combined subsidy rate

Joanne and Hal run a sporting goods store in Fredericton, New Brunswick. They have 10 full time employees, each earning $800 per week for a total weekly payroll of $8,000. Joanne and Hal closed their store on March 15, and reopened for curbside pick-up May 1. With the help of the CEWS, they have kept half of their employees on the payroll, paying them their full regular wages. Over the first 16 weeks of the CEWS, they benefitted from the 75% wage subsidy and they received $48,000 in CEWS support. In July, with the economy reopening, they intend to rehire all of their employees and have them return to their pre-crisis schedule. As revenues were down over 50% year-over-year in June, they would qualify for the maximum base CEWS rate of 60% in Period 5. In addition, because their revenues from April to June 2020 were down over 70% when compared to April to June 2019, they would be eligible for the 25% CEWS top-up, increasing their combined subsidy rate to 85%. This would translate into $27,200 in CEWS support in Period 5, to help them pay their employees' salaries.

Example: Employer that becomes eligible for the CEWS as a result of the removal of the 30% revenue decline threshold

Shelf Life Foods is a mid-size frozen food manufacturer in Kingston, Ontario. It has 200 full time employees, each earning $1,000 per week for a total monthly payroll of $800,000. Most of its pre-crisis sales were to supermarkets and have kept steady since the crisis began but the drop in its sales to restaurants during the crisis have contributed to reducing its overall revenues by 15% each month. Because the revenue drop the company experienced was less than the 30% threshold over the first 16 weeks of the CEWS, the company did not qualify for the CEWS. Deciding that it could not operate at a loss much longer, the company was preparing to reduce staff hours by 15%, or $120,000 per month. With the new design of the CEWS, however, the company, with a 15% revenue drop, would qualify for the base CEWS in Period 5, starting on July 5, 2020, and Period 6, starting on August 2, 2020. In Periods 5 and 6, it would receive a subsidy of 18% of its wages, equivalent to $144,000 for each period. Because it would qualify for the CEWS, the company decides it would not have to reduce staff hours.

Example: Employer who becomes eligible for the CEWS as a result of extension to users of payroll services

Maude runs a non-profit organization in Vancouver, providing services to youth in her community. In addition to volunteers, she hires part-time students to help organize these services. Her revenues dropped significantly because of the overall economic decline but, because she makes use of a centralized payroll service available to such non-profit organizations in her province and did not obtain her own payroll program account with the CRA, she could not qualify for the CEWS. Now, with the change of rules regarding the use of payroll service providers [125.7(1)"qualifying entity"(d)(ii) — ed.], her organization would qualify for the CEWS and be able to claim benefits retroactive to March 15, 2020.

Example: Recovering employer that is assured of continued support from future CEWS benefits

Maya and her brother Petr run a linen cleaning services business north of Montreal. Their cleaning services for hotels and inns have been shut down temporarily, but they managed to keep most of their other commercial linen cleaning services active. Throughout the crisis, they have been able to maintain 10 full-time employees, each being paid $800 per week for a total weekly payroll of $8,000. Over the preceding three months, revenues were down 50% compared to the same period last year. During Periods 1 through 4, they qualified for the maximum subsidy rate of 75%. Customers are gradually returning and they are considering seeking new lines of business. In June, their revenues are down 35%. This means that, under the new CEWS rules, they would qualify for a base CEWS rate of 42% in Period 5 [125.7(1)"base percentage"(a)(ii) — ed.]. However, with the safe harbour rule [125.7(9)(b) — ed.], they would be eligible for a rate of 75% in Period 5 — the rate they would have qualified for under the original CEWS rules. This would provide Maya and Petr a total subsidy amount of $24,000 in Period 5. In July, they have secured a new client, and revenues in July and August would be down 25% from last year. With the elimination of the 30% revenue test, they would now be eligible for a CEWS rate of 30% in Period 6. The extension and expansion of the CEWS would provide them with additional financial support as they rebuild their business.

[See also discussion of CEWS Stage 1 above for administrative and other rules — ed.]

CRA detailed information: tinyurl.com/cews-cra-faq and tinyurl.com/cews-cra. Application Guide: tinyurl.com/cews-guide. Calculator: tinyurl.com/cews-calc.

Changes for Sept. 27 to Dec. 19, 2020 (Periods 8-10), enacted in Bill C-9 (2020 COVID bill #5), are explained in Finance Backgrounder "Details on the Canada Emergency Wage Subsidy Extension", Nov. 5, 2020 (introductory portion omitted):

The wage subsidy includes a base subsidy for all employers whose revenues have been impacted by the pandemic. The base subsidy rate for Period 8 (September 27 to October 24, 2020) would continue to apply for Periods 9 and 10

(October 25 to December 19, 2020). As such, the maximum base subsidy rate would be set at 40% for this period. Table 1, below, shows the new rate structure of the base subsidy.

Table 1: New Rate Structure of the Base Subsidy, Periods 8–10

Timing	Period 8: September 27–October 24	Period 9: October 25–November 21	Period 10: November 22–December 19
Maximum weekly benefit per employee	Up to $452	Up to $452	Up to $452
Revenue drop			
50% and over	40%	40%	40%
0% to 49%	0.8 × revenue drop (e.g., 0.8 × 20% revenue drop = 16% base subsidy rate)	0.8 × revenue drop (e.g., 0.8 × 20% revenue drop = 16% base subsidy rate)	0.8 × revenue drop (e.g., 0.8 × 20% revenue drop = 16% base subsidy rate)

The new rate structure for the base wage subsidy would replace the one previously announced on July 17, 2020 for Period 9.

Top-up Wage Subsidy More Responsive to Support the Most Affected Employers

A top-up wage subsidy of up to 25% [125.7(2)A(b)(ii), 125.7(1)"top-up percentage" — ed.] is available to employers most adversely impacted by the pandemic. Currently, an eligible employer's top-up wage subsidy is generally determined based on the revenue drop over the preceding three months compared to the same months in the prior year. Under the alternative approach to the calculation of baseline revenues, the top-up wage subsidy is determined based on the revenue drop experienced when comparing average monthly revenue in the preceding three months to the average monthly revenue in January and February 2020 [125.7(1)"prior reference period"(b) — ed.].

To make the top-up wage subsidy more responsive to sudden changes in revenue, the revenue-decline test for the base subsidy and the top-up wage subsidy would be harmonized from September 27, 2020 onward. Instead of using the current three-month revenue-decline test for the top-up wage subsidy, both the base and top-up wage subsidies would be determined by the change in an eligible employer's monthly revenues, year-over-year, for either the current or previous calendar month [125.7(1)"top-up revenue reduction percentage"(b), added by 2020 COVID bill #5 — ed.]. This means an employer with a 70% or greater revenue loss in a single period would be eligible for a 65% wage subsidy. For employers using the alternative method (announced on April 8, 2020), both the base subsidy and the top-up wage subsidy would be determined by comparing its current monthly revenues with the average of its January 2020 and February 2020 revenues.

Because the wage subsidy would now be based on the current month's revenue losses, instead of the preceding three months', an employer who had strong revenues over the summer, but is facing a revenue decline of over 50% in Period 8, would qualify for a more generous wage subsidy this fall.

Table 2, below, shows the new combined rate structure with the base subsidy and the top-up wage subsidy.

Table 2: Rate Structure of the Combined Base Subsidy and the Top-up Wage Subsidy, Periods 8–10

Timing	Period 8: September 27–October 24	Period 9: October 25–November 21	Period 10: November 22–December 19
Maximum weekly benefit per employee	Up to $734	Up to $734	Up to $734
Revenue drop			
70% and over	65%	65%	65%
50% to 69%	40% + 1.25 × (revenue drop - 50%) (e.g., 40% + 1.25 × (60% revenue drop - 50%) = 52.5% combined base and top-up wage subsidy rate)	40% + 1.25 × (revenue drop - 50%) (e.g., 40% + 1.25 × (60% revenue drop - 50%) = 52.5% combined base and top-up wage subsidy rate)	40% + 1.25 × (revenue drop - 50%) (e.g., 40% + 1.25 × (60% revenue drop - 50%) = 52.5% combined base and top-up wage subsidy rate)
0% to 49%	0.8 × revenue drop	0.8 × revenue drop	0.8 × revenue drop

Under the alternative approach, both the base subsidy and the top-up wage subsidy would be determined by the change in an eligible employer's monthly revenues relative to the average of its January 2020 and February 2020 revenues

[125.7(1)"revenue reduction percentage", "top-up percentage"(b) — ed.]. Table 3, below, outlines each qualifying period and the relevant period for determining an eligible employer's change in revenue.

Employers that had chosen to use the general approach to choosing a prior reference period for Period 5 (July 5 to August 1) and onward would continue to use that approach. Similarly, employers that had chosen to use the alternative approach for Period 5 and onward would continue to use the alternative approach.

An eligible employer would use the greater of its percentage revenue decline for the current qualifying period and that for the previous qualifying period for the purpose of determining its combined base subsidy and top-up wage subsidy rate for the current qualifying period.

Table 3: Reference Periods for the Base Subsidy and the Top-up Wage Subsidy

Timing	Period 8: September 27–October 24	Period 9: October 25–November 21	Period 10: November 22–December 19
General approach	October 2020 over October 2019 or September 2020 over September 2019	November 2020 over November 2019 or October 2020 over October 2019	December 2020 over December 2019 or November 2020 over November 2019
Alternative approach	October 2020 or September 2020 over average of January and February 2020	November 2020 or October 2020 over average of January and February 2020	December 2020 or November 2020 over average of January and February 2020

Safe Harbour Rule for the Top-up Wage Subsidy for Periods 8 through 10

For Periods 8 through 10, an eligible employer would be entitled to a top-up wage subsidy rate not lower than the rate that it would be entitled to if its entitlement were calculated under the three month revenue-decline test ["the greater of" in 125.7(1)"top-up revenue reduction percentage"(b) — ed.]. Under this safe harbour rule, an eligible employer's top-up wage subsidy would generally be determined based on the revenue drop experienced when comparing revenues in the preceding three months to the same months in the prior year. Under the alternative approach to the calculation of baseline revenues, an eligible employer's top-up wage subsidy would be determined based on the revenue drop experienced when comparing average monthly revenue in the preceding three months to the average monthly revenue in January and February 2020. Table 4, below, outlines the reference periods for the safe harbour rule.

Table 4: Reference Periods for the Top-up wage Subsidy Safe Harbour Rule

Timing	Period 8: September 27–October 24	Period 9: October 25–November 21	Period 10: November 22–December 19
General approach	July to September 2020 over July to September 2019	August to October 2020 over August to October 2019	September to November 2020 over September to November 2019
Alternative approach	July to September 2020 average over January and February 2020 average*	August to October 2020 average over January and February 2020 average*	September to November 2020 average over January and February 2020 average*

* The calculation would equal the average monthly revenue over the three months of the reference period divided by the average revenue for the months of January and February 2020.

Alignment of Benefits for Furloughed Employees

As announced on October 14, 2020, for Periods 9 (October 25 to November 21) and 10 (November 22 to December 19), the wage subsidy for furloughed employees would be adjusted to align with the benefits provided through Employment Insurance (EI) to ensure equitable treatment of employees on furlough between both programs [125.7(2)A(b)(iv), Reg. 8901.2(7)(b) — ed.].

Specifically, the wage subsidy calculation for a furloughed employee would be the lesser of:

- the amount of eligible remuneration paid in respect of the week; and
- the greater of:
  - $500, and
  - 55% of pre-crisis remuneration for the employee, up to a maximum subsidy amount of $573.

The employer portion of contributions in respect if the Canada Pension Plan, EI, the Quebec Pension Plan, and the Quebec Parental Insurance Plan in respect of furloughed employees would continue to be refunded.

Special Baseline Remuneration Period for Employees Returning from Leave

Under the general rules, an eligible employer's entitlement to the wage subsidy for a furloughed employee, as well as an active employee in certain circumstances, is determined through a calculation that takes into account both the employee's current and baseline (pre-crisis) remuneration.

Baseline remuneration [defined in 125.7(1) — ed.] means the average weekly eligible remuneration paid to an eligible employee by an eligible employer during the period beginning January 1, 2020, and ending March 15, 2020. Any period of seven or more consecutive days for which the employee was not remunerated is excluded from the calculation. However, the eligible employer may elect, for each qualifying period in respect of an employee, an alternative baseline period for calculating the average weekly eligible remuneration. For Periods 5 through 9 (July 5 to November 21, 2020), the alternative baseline remuneration period begins on July 1, 2019 and ends on December 31, 2019. An eligible employer may elect the alternative baseline remuneration period because, for example, an eligible employee was on leave through the duration of the regular baseline remuneration period.

Under proposed new rules [125.7(1)"baseline remuneration"(b)(iv) — ed.], employers would be given greater flexibility to claim the wage subsidy in respect of employees returning from maternity leave, parental leave, caregiver leave or long-term sick leave. An eligible employer would be able to elect for each qualifying period from Periods 5 to 10 (July 5 to December 19, 2020), a special baseline remuneration period in respect of an eligible employee returning from a continuous maternity, parental, caregiver, or long-term sick leave that began before July 1, 2019 and ended after March 15, 2020. The special remuneration period would be the 90-day period ending immediately before the beginning of the employee's leave period.

The proposed new baseline remuneration periods for Periods 5 to 10 (July 5 to December 19, 2020) are summarized in table 5 below:

Table 5: Baseline Remuneration Periods for Periods 5 to 10

Regular baseline remuneration period	Alternative baseline remuneration period	Special baseline remuneration period*
January 1 to March 15, 2020	July 1, 2019 to December 31, 2019	90-day period ending immediately before the beginning of the employee's leave period

* Available for eligible employees returning from a continuous maternity, parental, caregiver, or long-term sick leave that began before July 1, 2019 and ended after March 15, 2020.

Application Period

Currently, to qualify for the wage subsidy for a qualifying period, an eligible employer must make an application for the qualifying period, in a prescribed form and manner, no later than January 31, 2021.

With the extension of the wage subsidy, to ensure that employers have sufficient time to make their wage subsidy applications, the proposed new deadline to make an application for a qualifying period would be the later of January 31, 2021 or 180 days after the end of the qualifying period [125.7(1)"qualifying entity"(a) — ed.].

Asset Purchases

The wage subsidy has a relieving rule that applies when an entity purchases all or substantially all of business assets of a seller. If the purchaser and seller jointly elect, the purchaser can use the prior reference period revenues associated with those assets for the purpose of computing its revenue decline.

This rule would be expanded to allow it to be used when an entity purchases the assets of a business, or of a distinct part of a business, of an arm's length seller and the purchaser uses those assets to carry on a business [125.7(4.1)(b)(ii) — ed.]. As with the existing rule, the purchaser and seller would need to make a joint election.

Eligible Employees

Eligible employees are employees for whom the wage subsidy can be claimed. An amendment to the definition "eligible employee" [in 125.7(1) — ed.] would ensure that only employees of an eligible entity employed primarily in Canada throughout a qualifying period (or portion of a qualifying period during which the employee was employed by the eligible entity) would be considered eligible employees for the purpose of the wage subsidy.

CEWS from Dec. 20, 2020 to March 13, 2021 (Periods 11-13) was initially announced in Finance news release, Oct. 9, 2020:

Government announces new, targeted support to help businesses through pandemic

. . .

While some parts of our economy are recovering, others continue to struggle with reduced revenues, increased costs, and uncertainty because of the COVID-19 pandemic.

That is why today the Deputy Prime Minister and Finance Minister, the Honourable Chrystia Freeland, announced the government's intention to introduce new, targeted supports to help hard-hit businesses and other organizations experiencing a drop in revenue. The government plans to introduce legislation to provide support that would help these businesses safely get through the second

wave of the virus and the winter, cover costs so they can continue to serve their communities, and be positioned for a strong recovery, including: [see 125.7(2.1) for CERS and Lockdown Support — ed.] . . .

• The extension of the Canada Emergency Wage Subsidy until June 2021 [implemented initially by Reg. 8901.2(1) through March — ed.], which would continue to protect jobs by helping businesses keep employees on the payroll and encouraging employers to re-hire their workers. The subsidy would remain at the current subsidy rate of up to a maximum of 65% of eligible wages until December 19, 2020. This measure is part of the government's commitment to create over 1 million jobs and restore employment to the level it was before the pandemic.

The Federal Economic Statement, Supplementary Information, Nov. 30, 2020, stated:

Emergency Business Supports

The Government has introduced a number of support measures to help businesses and other organizations affected by the COVID-19 pandemic, including the Canada Emergency Wage Subsidy [125.7(2) — ed.], the Canada Emergency Rent Subsidy [125.7(2.1)A — ed.] and the Lockdown Support [125.7(2.1)B — ed.].

Program details in respect of these three measures have been legislated through December 19, 2020 and the application of these measures can be extended by regulation until June 2021. Proposed program details from December 20, 2020 to March 13, 2021 for the three measures [now enacted — ed.] are described below.

Canada Emergency Wage Subsidy Extension

The Government introduced the Canada Emergency Wage Subsidy to prevent further job losses and encourage employers to quickly rehire workers previously laid off as a result of COVID 19. The wage subsidy provides eligible employers that have experienced a decline in revenues with a wage subsidy for eligible remuneration paid to their employees.

Support for active employees

The wage subsidy for active employees includes a base subsidy for all employers that have experienced a decline in revenues, as well as a top-up wage subsidy available to employers most adversely impacted by the pandemic. The maximum combined base subsidy and top-up wage subsidy rate is set at 65% for the current qualifying period, which ends on December 19, 2020.

The Government proposes to increase the maximum wage subsidy to 75% for the 11th to 13th qualifying periods, which run from December 20, 2020 to January 16, 2021, from January 17, 2021 to February 13, 2021 and from February 14, 2021 to March 13, 2021, respectively [this has now been done, by regulatory amendments in P.C. 2020-1124 — ed.]. The maximum base subsidy would remain at 40% [Reg. 8901.2(2)(a), now 125.7(1)"base percentage" — ed.] and the maximum top-up wage subsidy rate would increase to 35% [Reg. 8901.2(6), now 125.7(1)"top-up percentage" — ed.], as set out in Table 2.

Table 2: Canada Emergency Wage Subsidy Rate Structure, Periods 11 to 13

(December 20, 2020 to March 13, 2021)

Revenue decline	Base subsidy	Top-up wage subsidy
70% and over	40%	35%
50–69%	40%	(Revenue decline – 50%) × 1.75
1–49%	Revenue decline × 0.8	0%

Support for furloughed employees

A separate wage subsidy rate structure applies for furloughed employees. The wage subsidy for furloughed employees is aligned with the benefits provided through Employment Insurance (EI) through December 19, 2020 to ensure equitable treatment of such employees between both programs.

To ensure that the wage subsidy for furloughed employees remains aligned with benefits available under EI, the Government proposes that the weekly wage subsidy for a furloughed employee from December 20, 2020 to March 13, 2021 be the lesser of [now done in Reg. 8901.2(7)(c) — ed.]:

• the amount of eligible remuneration paid in respect of the week; and

• the greater of:

— $500, and

— 55% of pre-crisis remuneration for the employee, up to a maximum subsidy amount of $595.

Employers will also continue to be entitled to claim under the wage subsidy their portion of contributions in respect of the Canada Pension Plan, EI, the Quebec Pension Plan and the Quebec Parental Insurance Plan in respect of furloughed employees.

Reference periods

For the purposes of the wage subsidy (and the rent subsidy, as discussed below [under 125.7(2.1) — ed.]), an employer's decline in revenues is generally determined by comparing the change in the employer's monthly revenues, year-over-year. An employer may also elect to use an alternative approach, which compares the change in the employer's monthly revenues relative to the average of its January 2020 and February 2020 revenues [125.7(1)"prior reference period"(b) — ed.]. A deeming rule provides that an employer's decline in revenues for any particular qualifying period is the greater of its decline in revenues for the particular qualifying period and the immediately preceding qualifying period [125.7(9)(b) — ed.].

Table 3 below outlines the proposed reference periods for determining an eligible employer's decline in revenues from December 20, 2020 to March 13, 2021 [done in Reg. 8901.2(3) — ed.].

Table 3: Canada Emergency Wage Subsidy Reference Periods, Periods 11 to 13

(December 20, 2020 to March 13, 2021)

Timing	Period 11 December 20, 2020–January 16, 2021	Period 12 January 17, 2021–February 13, 2021	Period 13 February 14, 2021–March 13, 2021
General approach	December 2020 over December 2019 *or* November 2020 over November 2019	January 2021 over January 2020 *or* December 2020 over December 2019	February 2021 over February 2020 *or* January 2021 over January 2020
Alternative approach	December 2020 *or* November 2020 over average of January and February 2020	January 2021 *or* December 2020 over average of January and February 2020	February 2021 *or* January 2021 over average of January and February 2020

Employers that had chosen to use the general approach for prior periods would continue to use that approach. Similarly, employers that had chosen to use the alternative approach would continue to use the alternative approach.

All the other parameters of the program would remain unchanged. Details for the wage subsidy for any periods beyond March 13, 2021 will be proposed at a later date.

A Finance news release of Dec. 18, 2020 provided further changes:

Government announces wage subsidy rate increase to 75%

Since March, the Canada Emergency Wage Subsidy has protected more than 4 million jobs, helping businesses and workers through the challenges of the pandemic.

Today, the Deputy Prime Minister and Minister of Finance, the Honourable Chrystia Freeland, announced that the government has concluded the necessary regulatory changes [amending Reg. 8901.2 — ed.] to raise the maximum wage subsidy rate to 75% for the period beginning Sunday, December 20, 2020, until March 13, 2021 [Reg. 8901.2(2)(a) 40% + Reg. 8901.2(6) 35%; these are now in 125.7(1)"base percentage" and "top-up percentage" instead — ed.]. This support will be there for workers and businesses through the tough months ahead as we face the second wave of the COVID-19 pandemic.

The wage subsidy is now more flexible and targeted, allowing employers to access the maximum subsidy rate based on a single month's revenue decline instead of having to demonstrate three months' decline, giving employers support that better reflects their current or evolving needs.

The wage subsidy will continue to support workers at businesses of every size, across Canada. The government will monitor health and economic conditions to determine details for subsequent periods.

Analysis in the Fall Economic Statement demonstrates that government support measures offset about half of the negative economic effects of the pandemic on the unemployment rate. This support has helped Canada to recover almost eight in ten of the lost jobs, compared to just over half in the United States.

CEWS from March 14 to June 5, 2021 (Periods 14-16) was initially announced in Finance news release, March 3, 2021:

Government Announces Wage and Rent Subsidy Amounts to Remain Unchanged Through to June

... Through the pandemic, applicants have demonstrated revenue declines by comparing revenue to the previous year. Given that we are approaching a full year of the COVID-19 pandemic, the government is today announcing that applicants would be able to continue to use a pre-pandemic 2019 reference month, effective for the upcoming periods from March 14 to June 5, 2021.

Backgrounder: Government Announces Wage and Rent Subsidy Amounts to Remain Unchanged Through to June

Businesses, non-profits, and charities that have experienced a decline in revenues while weathering the COVID-19 crisis are eligible for a variety of government support measures including direct subsidies to support workers and pay rent.

- The Canada Emergency Wage Subsidy [125.7(2) — ed.] helps employers retain and quickly rehire workers previously laid off.

- The Canada Emergency Rent Subsidy [125.7(2.1)A — ed.] provides direct and easy-to-access rent and mortgage interest support to tenants and property owners.

- Lockdown Support [125.7(2.1)B — ed.] provides additional rent relief to organizations that are subject to a lockdown and must shut their doors or significantly restrict their activities under a public health order issued under the laws of Canada, or a province or a territory.

The wage subsidy, the rent subsidy, and Lockdown Support are legislated to be available until June 2021. Proposed program details, from March 14 to June 5, 2021, for the three measures are described below.

Maintaining the Current Rate Structures Until June 5, 2021

The rate structures for the wage subsidy for active employees, the rent subsidy, and Lockdown Support that are currently in place until March 13, 2021, would be extended for March 14 to June 5, 2021. This means that:

- The maximum base wage subsidy rate for active employees would remain at 40% [Reg. 8901.2(2)(a), now 125.7(1)"base percentage" — ed.], and the maximum top-up wage subsidy rate for employers most adversely impacted by the pandemic would remain at 35%. [Reg. 8901.2(6), now 125.7(1)"top-up percentage" — ed.]. As such, the maximum combined wage subsidy rate would remain at 75%.

- The maximum rent subsidy rate would remain at 65% [125.7(1)"rent subsidy percentage"(a)(i), 125.7(2.1)A:C — ed.].

- Lockdown Support would remain at 25% [125.7(1)"rent top-up percentage"A — ed.] and continue to be provided in addition to the rent subsidy, providing eligible hard hit businesses with rent support of up to 90%.

Support for Furloughed Employees

A separate wage subsidy rate structure applies for furloughed employees. To ensure that the wage subsidy for furloughed employees remains aligned with benefits available under Employment Insurance (EI), and that workers are provided with equitable treatment between the two programs, the weekly wage subsidy for a furloughed employee, from March 14 to June 5, 2021, would remain the same and continue to be the lesser of [Reg. 8901.2(7)(c), now Reg. 8901.2(c) — ed.]:

- the amount of eligible remuneration paid in respect of the week; and

- the greater of:

  — $500; and

  — 55% of pre-crisis remuneration for the employee, up to a maximum subsidy amount of $595.

Employers would also continue to be entitled to claim under the wage subsidy their portion of contributions in respect of the *Canada Pension Plan*, EI, the Quebec Pension Plan and the Quebec Parental Insurance Plan for furloughed employees.

Revenue-decline Reference Periods Until June 2021

Since the wage subsidy and rent subsidy programs launched, an organization's decline in revenues has generally been determined by comparing the change in the organization's revenues in a current calendar month with its revenues in the same calendar month of the previous year. An organization may also elect to use an alternative approach, which compares the change in the organization's monthly revenues relative to the average of its January 2020 and February 2020 revenues. A deeming rule provides that an organization's decline in revenues for any particular qualifying period is the greater of its decline in revenues for the particular qualifying period and the immediately preceding qualifying period.

Given that we are approaching a full year of the COVID-19 pandemic, to ensure that the general approach continues to calculate an organization's decline in revenues relative to a pre-pandemic month, the prior reference periods would be based on calendar months from 2019, effective as of the qualifying period from March 14 to April 10, 2021 [125.7(1)"baseline remuneration"(b)(iii.1) — ed.]. The proposed reference periods are summarized in Table 1.

Table 1

Canada Emergency Wage Subsidy and Canada Emergency Rent Subsidy Reference Periods, Periods 14 to 16

(March 14 to June 5, 2021)

Timing	Period 14 March 14–April 10	Period 15 April 11–May 8	Period 16 May 9–June 5
General approach	March 2021 over March 2019 *or* February 2021 over February 2020	April 2021 over April 2019 *or* March 2021 over March 2019	May 2021 over May 2019 *or* April 2021 over April 2019
Alternative approach	March 2021 *or* February 2021 over average of January and February 2020	April 2021 *or* March 2021 over average of January and February 2020	May 2021 *or* April 2021 over average of January and February 2020

Employers that had chosen to use the general approach for prior periods would continue to use that approach. Similarly, employers that had chosen to use the alternative approach would continue to use the alternative approach.

More Flexible Baseline Remuneration Periods

An eligible employer's entitlement to the wage subsidy for a furloughed employee or an active non-arm's length employee is determined through a calculation that takes into account both the employee's current and baseline (pre-crisis) remuneration.

By default, baseline remuneration [125.7(1) — ed.] means the average weekly eligible remuneration paid to an eligible employee by an eligible employer during the period beginning January 1, 2020, and ending March 15, 2020. Any period of seven or more consecutive days for which the employee was not remunerated is excluded from the calculation. However, the eligible employer may elect an alternative baseline period for calculating the average weekly eligible remuneration.

An additional elective alternative baseline remuneration computation for March 14 to June 5, 2021 (Qualifying Periods 14 to 16), is proposed [125.7(1)"baseline remuneration"(b)(iii.1) — ed.] to ensure that the baseline remuneration comparator remains appropriate. In particular, an eligible employer would be allowed to elect, for qualifying periods from March 14 to June 5, 2021, to use the period of March 1, 2019 to June 30, 2019, or July 1 to December 31, 2019 (the current alternative period), to calculate baseline remuneration.

The Canada Revenue Agency will administer this measure on the basis of draft legislative proposals released with today's announcement.

The estimated cost for the wage subsidy from March 14 to June 5, 2021, is $13.9 billion in 2021-22 and the estimated cost for the rent subsidy and Lockdown Support from March 14 to June 5, 2021 is $2.1 billion in 2021-22. Costs may change depending on changing public health restrictions and economic activity.

CEWS from June 6 to Sept. 24, 2021 (Periods 17-24)) was announced in the Federal Budget Supplementary Information, April 19, 2021:

Emergency Business Supports

The government has introduced a number of support measures to help businesses and other organizations affected by the COVID-19 pandemic, including the Canada Emergency Wage Subsidy, the Canada Emergency Rent Subsidy and the Lockdown Support.

Program details in respect of these three measures have been announced through June 5, 2021 and the application of these measures cannot be extended by regulation beyond June 2021.

Budget 2021 proposes to extend the Canada Emergency Wage Subsidy, the Canada Emergency Rent Subsidy and the Lockdown Support until September 2021. The subsidy rates would gradually decline over the July-to-September period. The proposed details of these programs from June 6, 2021 to September 25, 2021 are described below.

Budget 2021 also proposes to provide the government with the legislative authority to add additional qualifying periods for the wage subsidy, the rent subsidy and the Lockdown Support until November 20, 2021, should the economic and public health situation warrant it.

Canada Emergency Wage Subsidy

The government introduced the Canada Emergency Wage Subsidy to prevent further job losses and encourage employers to quickly rehire workers previously laid off as a result of COVID-19. The measure provides eligible employers that have experienced a decline in revenues with a wage subsidy for eligible remuneration paid to their employees.

Support for Active Employees

The wage subsidy for active employees includes a base subsidy for employers that have experienced a decline in revenues as well as a top-up wage subsidy that is available to employers that have experienced a decline in revenues of at least 50%. The maximum combined base subsidy and top-up wage subsidy rate is set at 75% through the qualifying period ending on June 5, 2021 [Reg. 8901.2(2)(a) 40% + Reg. 8901.2(6) 35%, now 125.7(1)"base percentage"(g) 40% + 125.7(1)"top-up percentage"(b) 35% — ed.].

Budget 2021 proposes the wage subsidy rate structures set out in Table 2 for June 6, 2021 to September 25, 2021. As illustrated in the table, the subsidy rates would be gradually phased out starting on July 4, 2021. Furthermore, only employers with a decline in revenues of more than 10% would be eligible for the wage subsidy as of that date.

Table 2 — Canada Emergency Wage Subsidy Base and Top-up Rate Structure, Periods 17 to 20

(June 6, 2021 to September 25, 2021)

	Period 17 June 6–July 3	Period 18 July 4–July 31	Period 19 August 1–August 28	Period 20 August 29–September 25
*Maximum weekly benefit per employee**	$847	$677	$452	$226
Revenue decline:				

Table 2 — Canada Emergency Wage Subsidy Base and Top-up Rate Structure, Periods 17 to 20

(June 6, 2021 to September 25, 2021)

	Period 17 June 6–July 3	Period 18 July 4–July 31	Period 19 August 1–August 28	Period 20 August 29–September 25
70% and over	75% (i.e., Base: 40% + Top-up: 35%)	60% (i.e., Base: 35% + Top-up: 25%)	40% (i.e., Base: 25% + Top-up: 15%)	20% (i.e., Base: 10% + Top-up: 10%)
50–69%	Base: 40% + Top-up: (revenue decline - 50%) × 1.75 (e.g., 40% + (60% revenue decline - 50%) × 1.75 = 57.5% subsidy rate)	Base: 35% + Top-up: (revenue decline - 50%) × 1.25 (e.g., 35% + (60% revenue decline - 50%) × 1.25 = 47.5% subsidy rate)	Base: 25% + Top-up: (revenue decline - 50%) × 0.75 (e.g., 25% + (60% revenue decline - 50%) × 0.75 = 32.5% subsidy rate)	Base: 10% + Top-up: (revenue decline - 50%) × 0.5 (e.g., 10% + (60% revenue decline - 50%) × 0.5 = 15% subsidy rate)
>10–50%	Base: revenue decline × 0.8 (e.g., 30% revenue decline × 0.8 = 24% subsidy rate)	Base: (revenue decline - 10%) × 0.875 (e.g., (30% revenue decline - 10%) × 0.875 = 17.5% subsidy rate)	Base: (revenue decline - 10%) × 0.625 (e.g., (30% revenue decline - 10%) × 0.625 = 12.5% subsidy rate)	Base: (revenue decline - 10%) × 0.25 (e.g., (30% revenue decline - 10%) × 0.25 = 5% subsidy rate)
0–10%	Base: revenue decline × 0.8 (e.g., 5% revenue decline × 0.8 = 4% subsidy rate)	0%	0%	0%

Notes:

* The maximum weekly benefit per employee is equal to the maximum combined base subsidy and top-up wage subsidy for the qualifying period applied to the amount of eligible remuneration paid to the employee for the qualifying period, on remuneration of up to $1,129 per week.

Requirement to Repay Wage Subsidy

Budget 2021 proposes to require a publicly listed corporation to repay [125.7(14), 125.7(1)"executive compensation repayment amount" — ed.] wage subsidy amounts received for a qualifying period that begins after June 5, 2021 in the event that its aggregate compensation for specified executives during the 2021 calendar year [125.7(1)"executive remuneration" — ed.] exceeds its aggregate compensation for specified executives during the 2019 calendar year.

For the purpose of this proposed rule, a publicly listed corporation's specified executives will be its Named Executive Officers whose compensation is required to be disclosed under Canadian securities laws in its annual information circular provided to shareholders, or similar executives in the case of a corporation listed in another jurisdiction [125.7(1)"executive remuneration" — ed.]. This generally includes its chief executive officer, chief financial officer, and three other most highly compensated executives. A corporation's executive compensation for a calendar year will be calculated by prorating the aggregate compensation of its specified executives for each of its taxation years that overlap with the calendar year.

The amount of the wage subsidy required to be repaid [125.7(14) — ed.] would be equal to the lesser of:

• the total of all wage subsidy amounts received in respect of active employees for qualifying periods that begin after June 5, 2021; and

• the amount by which the corporation's aggregate specified executives' compensation for 2021 exceeds its aggregate specified executives' compensation for 2019.

This requirement to repay would be applied at the group level and would apply to wage subsidy amounts paid to any entity in the group.

[See also Possible Future Amendment under 125.7(14), re public companies that pay dividends while receiving CEWS — ed.]

Support for Furloughed Employees

A separate wage subsidy rate structure applies for furloughed employees. The wage subsidy for furloughed employees is aligned with the benefits provided through Employment Insurance (EI) through June 5, 2021 to ensure equitable treatment of such employees between the two programs.

To ensure that the wage subsidy for furloughed employees remains aligned with benefits available under EI, Budget 2021 proposes that the weekly wage subsidy for a furloughed employee from June 6, 2021 to August 28, 2021 be the lesser of [Reg. 8901.2(7)(c), now changed to Reg. 8901.2(c) — ed.]:

- the amount of eligible remuneration paid in respect of the week; and
- the greater of:
  - — $500; and
  - — 55% of pre-crisis remuneration for the employee, up to a maximum subsidy amount of $595.

The wage subsidy for furloughed employees would continue to be available to eligible employers that qualify for the wage subsidy for active employees for the relevant period until August 28, 2021. Employers will also continue to be entitled to claim under the wage subsidy their portion of contributions in respect of the *Canada Pension Plan*, EI, the Quebec Pension Plan and the Quebec Parental Insurance Plan in respect of furloughed employees.

Reference Periods

For the purposes of the wage subsidy, an employer's decline in revenues is generally determined by comparing the employer's revenues in a current calendar month with its revenues in the same calendar month, pre-pandemic [125.7(1)"prior reference period"(a) — ed.]. An employer may also elect to use an alternative approach, which compares the employer's monthly revenues relative to the average of its January 2020 and February 2020 revenues [125.7(1)"prior reference period"(b)(ii) — ed.]. A deeming rule provides that an employer's decline in revenues for any particular qualifying period is the greater of its decline in revenues for the particular qualifying period and the immediately preceding qualifying period.

Budget 2021 proposes the reference periods set out in Table 3 for determining an eligible employer's decline in revenues for the qualifying periods from June 6, 2021 to September 25, 2021.

Table 3 — Canada Emergency Wage Subsidy Reference Periods, Periods 17 to 20

(June 6, 2021 to September 25, 2021)

Timing	Period 17 June 6–July 3	Period 18 July 4–July 31	Period 19 August 1–August 28	Period 20 August 29–September 25
General approach	June 2021 over June 2019 *or* May 2021 over May 2019	July 2021 over July 2019 *or* June 2021 over June 2019	August 2021 over August 2019 *or* July 2021 over July 2019	September 2021 over September 2019 *or* August 2021 over August 2019
Alternative approach	June 2021 *or* May 2021 over average of January and February 2020	July 2021 *or* June 2021 over average of January and February 2020	August 2021 *or* July 2021 over average of January and February 2020	September 2021 *or* August 2021 over average of January and February 2020

Employers that had chosen to use the general approach for prior periods would continue to use that approach. Similarly, employers that had chosen to use the alternative approach would continue to use the alternative approach.

Baseline Remuneration

Under the general rules, an eligible employer's entitlement to the wage subsidy for a furloughed employee, as well as an active employee in certain circumstances, is determined through a calculation that takes into account both the employee's current and baseline (pre-crisis) remuneration.

Baseline remuneration [defined in 125.7(1) — ed.] means the average weekly eligible remuneration paid to an eligible employee by an eligible employer during the period beginning January 1, 2020 and ending March 15, 2020. Any period of seven or more consecutive days for which the employee was not remunerated is excluded from the calculation. However, the eligible employer may elect, for each qualifying period in respect of an employee, an alternative baseline period for calculating the average weekly eligible remuneration.

To ensure that the alternative baseline remuneration periods for a particular qualifying period continue to generally reflect the corresponding calendar months covered by the qualifying period, Budget 2021 proposes to allow an eligible employer to elect to use the following alternative baseline remuneration periods [125.7(1)"baseline remuneration"(b) — ed.]:

- March 1 to June 30, 2019 or July 1 to December 31, 2019, for the qualifying period between June 6, 2021 and July 3, 2021; and
- July 1 to December 31, 2019, for qualifying periods beginning after July 3, 2021.

An employer can apply for less than it is entitled to by excluding some employees: VIEWS doc 2020-0850231E5.

See also CRA, "Businesses: Watch out for Canada Emergency Wage Subsidy tax schemes" (tinyurl.com/cews-schemes, June 17, 2021), re "schemes that artificially inflate or falsify eligibility criteria".

For detailed analysis see also Keey, *COVID-19 — Canada Emergency Wage Subsidy* (*Taxnet Pro*, 253pp as of June 22, 2021) and "The Canada Emergency Wage Subsidy", xlii(8) *The Canadian Taxpayer* (Carswell) 57-70 (June 19, 2020), xlii(9) 73-88 (July 10, 2020), xlii(10) 89-95 (July 24, 2020); Katlai, "Technology Corporations' Access to COVID-19 Subsidies", 20(3) *Tax for the Owner-Manager* (ctf.ca) 8-9 (July 2020) (impact on SR&ED credits); Ghani et al., "How does CEWS Apply to Non-Resident Employers?", *COVID-19 and Canadian Tax* (ctf.ca) 4-5 (July 2020) (and other articles in that issue); Keung et al., "Moodys Tax Explains CEWS v. 2.0" (tinyurl.com/moodys-cews2); Humphries & Demner, "COVID-19 Tax Update", tinyurl.com/thor-cews or 2528 *Tax Topics* (CCH) 1-11 (Aug. 18, 2020). For a spreadsheet calculator see taxtemplates.ca. For a flowchart (Moodys) see tinyurl.com/cews-flow.

Audits: Keung & Moody, "Here Come the CEWS Audits" (Sept. 15, 2020), tinyurl.com/moody-cews-audit; Keung & Mah, "CRA Audit Issues Relating to CEWS", Cdn Tax Foundation Sept. 2020 Owner-Manager Taxation Conference, pp. 1-25.

See also the Auditor General's 2021 Report #7 on CEWS, generally concluding that CEWS development was done well in a very short time-frame, and making some recommendations that Finance and CRA have accepted.

For a list of other COVID-19 support measures, see Notes to 122.5(3.001).

125.7(2)A and D amended by 2020 COVID bill #3, retroactive to enactment of 125.7 on April 11, 2020, effectively to add A(b) and D(a) for post-July 4/20 periods.

Regulations: 8901.2(7) [to be all of s. 8901.2] (amount determined for 125.7(2)A(b)(iv)(B)).

Forms: RC661: CEWS attestation [note: application for CEWS is online].

(2.1) COVID-19 — rent subsidy [Canada Emergency Rent Subsidy] — For a qualifying renter for a qualifying period referred to in any of paragraphs (c.5) to (d) of the definition "qualifying period" in subsection (1), an overpayment on account of the qualifying renter's liability under this Part for the taxation year in which the qualifying period ends is deemed to have arisen during the qualifying period in an amount determined by the formula

$$A + B$$

where

A   is the amount determined by the formula

$$C \times D$$

where

C   is the qualifying renter's rent subsidy percentage for the qualifying period, and

D   is the lesser of

(a) the total of all amounts, each of which is the qualifying renter's qualifying rent expense for a qualifying property for the qualifying period, and

(b) the amount determined by the formula

$$\$300,000 \times E$$

where

E   is

(i) 100%, unless the qualifying renter is affiliated at any time in the qualifying period with one or more eligible entities that claims an amount under this subsection in respect of the qualifying period,

(ii) a percentage assigned to the qualifying renter under an agreement, if

(A) the agreement is entered into by the qualifying renter and each eligible entity that

(I) is affiliated with the qualifying renter in the qualifying period, and

(II) claims an amount under this subsection in respect of the qualifying period,

(B) the agreement is filed in prescribed form and manner with the Minister in respect of the qualifying period by the qualifying renter and each eligible entity referred to in clause (A) with their application for the qualifying period,

(C) the agreement assigns, for the purposes of this subsection, a percentage in respect of each eligible entity referred to in clause (B) for the qualifying period, and

(D) the total of all the percentages assigned under the agreement does not exceed 100%, and

(iii) in any other case, nil; and

B   is the total of all amounts, each of which is an amount in respect of a qualifying property for the qualifying period, determined by the formula

$$F \times G$$

where

F   is

(i) nil, unless the rent subsidy percentage of the qualifying renter for the qualifying period is greater than 0%, and

(ii) in any other case, the rent top-up percentage of the qualifying renter in respect of the qualifying property for the qualifying period, and

G   is the qualifying rent expense of the qualifying renter in respect of the qualifying property for the qualifying period.

Enacted Amendment — Extension of CERS to June 2021

Federal Economic Statement, Supplementary Information, Nov. 30, 2020: *Canada Emergency Rent Subsidy Extension*

The Government introduced the Canada Emergency Rent Subsidy to provide direct relief to organizations that continue to be economically impacted by the COVID 19 pandemic. Under the rent subsidy, qualifying organizations that have experienced a decline in revenues are eligible for a subsidy on qualifying expenses.

Rate structure

The Government proposes to extend, until March 13, 2021, the current rate structure for the base rent subsidy (which applies until December 19, 2020), as shown in Table 4.

Table 4: Canada Emergency Rent Subsidy Rate Structure, Periods 11* to 13 (December 20, 2020 to March 13, 2021)

Revenue decline	Base subsidy
70% and over	65%
50–69%	40% + (revenue decline − 50%) × 1.25
1–49%	Revenue decline × 0.8

Notes:

*   Period 11 of the Canada Emergency Wage Subsidy is the fourth period of the Canada Emergency Rent Subsidy. Period identifiers have been aligned for simplicity.

Revenue decline calculation

Both the rent subsidy and the wage subsidy use the same calculation to determine an organization's revenue decline. As a result, the same reference periods are used to calculate an organization's decline in revenues for the wage subsidy and the rent subsidy. Likewise, if an entity elects to use an alternative method for computing its revenue decline under the wage subsidy, it must use that alternate method for the rent subsidy.

The Government also confirms its intention to proceed with the proposed change to the rent subsidy, details of which were announced on November 19, 2020, that would **allow amounts to be considered to have been paid when they become due**, provided certain conditions are met [see 125.7(12), (13) — ed.].

Details for the rent subsidy for any period beyond March 13, 2021 will be proposed at a later date.

Lockdown Support Extension

For locations that must cease operations or significantly limit their activities under a public health order issued under the laws of Canada, a province or territory, the Government introduced the Lockdown Support through the Canada Emergency Rent Subsidy program to provide additional help. In order to qualify for the Lockdown Support, an applicant must qualify for the base rent subsidy.

The Government proposes to extend, until March 13, 2021, the current 25% rate for the Lockdown Support. Details for the Lockdown Support for any period beyond March 13, 2021 will be proposed at a later date.

Dept. of Finance news release, March 3, 2021: *Government Announces Wage and Rent Subsidy Amounts to Remain Unchanged Through to June*

[For the text of the news release, see under 125.7(1)"qualifying period" — ed.]

Notes: Table 1 in the Economic Statement forecasts that these extensions will cost the government $2.18 billion in 2020-21.

Related Provisions: 87(2)(g.6) — Amalgamation — continuing corporation; 125.7(3) — CERS deemed to be government assistance; 125.7(5)(a) — CERS limited to amount claimed; 125.7(6)(b)(iii) — Anti-avoidance rule; 125.7(7) — Application to partnerships; 125.7(11) — Extended meaning of "affiliated" for formula element E; 152(1)(b) — Assessment of deemed payment (CERS); 152(3.4) — CERS notice of determination; 163(2)(i), 163(2.901) — Gross negligence penalty; 164(1.6) — CRA can pay CERS any time in the year; 164(3) — No interest on late payment of CERS by CRA; 241(3.5) — CRA may publicize names of applicants for CERS; 241(4)(d)(vii.10) — Disclosure of information to provincial government for COVID-19 rent or interest assistance.

Notes: 125.7(2.1) implements the Canada Emergency Rent Subsidy (CERS) and "Lockdown Support", for property owners as well as renters, announced Nov. 2, 2020. (They replace Canada Emergency Commercial Rent Assistance (CECRA) payments to landlords.) For CRA detail see tinyurl.com/cra-cers, which includes sections "Who can apply", "Periods you can apply for", "Expenses you can claim", "Calculate your subsidy amount" (online calculator), "How to apply", "After you apply" and "Contact us about CERS" (CRA business inquiry line 1-800-959-5525). See also "Technical Guidance" (tinyurl.com/cra-cers-tech), with additional technical information.

CERS (125.7(1)"rent subsidy percentage", 125.7(2.1)A) provides direct rent and mortgage interest support to tenants and property owners until June 2021 for qualifying organizations affected by COVID-19. It supports businesses, charities, and non-profits that have suffered a revenue drop by covering up to 65% of eligible expenses until Dec. 19, 2020. Retroactive claims are allowed for the Sept. 27-Oct. 24 period.

Lockdown Support [125.7(1)"rent top-up percentage", 125.7(2.1)B — ed.] provides an extra 25% for qualifying organizations that are subject to a lockdown and must shut their doors or sharply limit their activities under a public health order. Combined with CERS, hard-hit businesses subject to a lockdown can receive rent support of up to 90%.

Rent not yet paid can qualify for subsidy, as long as it is paid within 60 days of the subsidy being received: 125.7(12), (13).

The Finance Backgrounder of Nov. 5, 2020 "Canada Emergency Wage Subsidy, Canada Emergency Rent Subsidy and Lockdown Support" provides the following overview table of the three programs:

Rate Structures Applicable in Periods 8, 9 and 10 (September 27 to December 19, 2020)

	Canada Emergency Wage Subsidy (CEWS)	Canada Emergency Rent Subsidy (CERS) and Lockdown Support		
Revenue Decline	Wage Subsidy	CERS Base Rent Subsidy	Lockdown Support Rent Subsidy	Total Rent Subsidy if Eligible for Lockdown Support
70% and over	65%	65%	25%	90%
50% to 69%	40% + (revenue drop - 50%) × 1.25	40% + (revenue drop - 50%) × 1.25	25%	65% + (revenue drop - 50%) × 1.25
1% to 49%	Revenue drop × 0.8	Revenue drop × 0.8	25%	25% + Revenue drop × 0.8

The Finance Backgrounder of Nov. 5, 2020 on **CERS** states:

With the introduction of the new rent subsidy, qualifying organizations that have suffered a revenue drop would be eligible for a subsidy on eligible expenses. As shown in Table 1 [reproduced below — ed.] and Figure 1 [not reproduced — ed.], the maximum base rate subsidy would be 65% [125.7(1)"rent subsidy percentage"(a)(i), 125.7(2.1)A:C — ed.], and available to organizations with a revenue drop of 70% or more [125.7(1)"rent subsidy percentage"(a)(i) — ed.]. The base rate would then decline to a rate of 40% for organizations with a revenue drop of 50% [125.7(1)"rent subsidy percentage"(a)(ii) — ed.], and then would gradually reduce to zero for those not experiencing a decline in revenues. This structure mirrors the Canada Emergency Wage Subsidy rate structure [125.7(2) — ed.].

Table 1

Revenue Decline	Base Subsidy Rate
70% and over	65%
50% to 69%	40% + (revenue drop - 50%) × 1.25
	(e.g., 40% + (60% revenue drop − 50%) × 1.25 = 52.5% subsidy rate)
1% to 49%	Revenue drop × 0.8
	(e.g., 25% revenue drop × 0.8 = 20% subsidy rate)

Eligible Expenses

Eligible expenses for a location for a qualifying period [125.7(1)"qualifying rent expense" — ed.] would include commercial rent [para. A(a) — ed.], property taxes (including school taxes and municipal taxes) [A(a)(C)(III) — ed.], property insurance [A(a)(C)(II) — ed.], and interest on commercial mortgages (subject to limits) [A(b)(i) — ed.] for a qualifying property, less any subleasing revenues [formula element B — ed.]. Any sales tax (e.g., GST/HST) component of these costs would not be an eligible expense [A(a)(ii)(A) — ed.].

Eligible expenses would be limited to those paid under agreements in writing entered into before October 9, 2020 (and continuations of those agreements) [125.7(1)"qualifying rent expense"A opening words — ed.] and would be limited to expenses related to real property located in Canada [125.7(1)"qualifying property" — ed.]. Expenses that relate to residential property used by the taxpayer (e.g., their house or cottage) would not be eligible [125.7(1)"qualifying property" — ed.]. Payments made between non-arm's-length entities would not be eligible expenses [125.7(1)"qualifying rent expense"A opening words — ed.]. Mortgage interest expenses in respect of a property primarily used to earn, directly or indirectly, rental income from arms-length entities would not be eligible [125.7(1)"qualifying rent expense"A(b) opening words — ed.].

Expenses for each qualifying period would be capped at $75,000 per location [125.7(1)"qualifying rent expense"A opening words — ed.] and be subject to an overall cap of $300,000 that would be shared among affiliated entities [125.7(2.1)A:D(b) — ed.].

Eligible Entities

Eligibility criteria for the new rent subsidy would generally align with the Canada Emergency Wage Subsidy program. Eligible entities [125.7(1)"eligible entity", Reg. 8901.1 — ed.] include individuals, taxable corporations and trusts, non-profit organizations and registered charities. Public institutions are generally not eligible for the subsidy [125.7(1)"eligible entity"(a), (c), (d) — ed.]. Eligible entities also include the following groups [Reg. 8901.1 — ed.]:

- Partnerships that are up to 50% owned by non-eligible members;

- Indigenous government-owned corporations that are carrying on a business, as well as partnerships where the partners are Indigenous governments and eligible entities;

- Registered Canadian Amateur Athletic Associations;

- Registered Journalism Organizations; and

- Non-public colleges and schools, including institutions that offer specialized services, such as arts schools, driving schools, language schools or flight schools.

In addition, an eligible entity must meet one of the following criteria [125.7(1)"qualifying renter"(c), 125.7(1)"qualifying entity"(d) — ed.]:

- have a payroll account as of March 15, 2020 or have been using a payroll service provider;

- have a business number as of September 27, 2020 (and satisfy the Canada Revenue Agency that it is a bona fide rent subsidy claim); or

- meet other conditions that may be prescribed in the future.

Calculating Revenues

Revenues will be calculated in the same manner as under the Canada Emergency Wage Subsidy program [125.7(1)"qualifying revenue" — ed.].

- An entity's revenue for the purposes of the rent subsidy is its revenue from its ordinary activities in Canada earned from arm's-length sources [125.7(1)"qualifying revenue"(d) — ed.], determined using its normal accounting practices [125.7(4) opening words — ed.]. Revenues from extraordinary items [125.7(1)"qualifying revenue"(c) — ed.] and amounts on account of capital are excluded [according to Finance, capital is excluded by the words "normal accounting practices" in 125.7(4) opening words — ed.].

- For registered charities and non-profit organizations, the calculation includes most forms of revenue, excluding revenues from non-arm's length persons [125.7(1)"qualifying revenue"(d) — ed.]. These organizations are allowed to choose whether to include revenue from government sources as part of the calculation [125.7(1)"qualifying revenue"(a)(ii), (b)(ii) — ed.]. Once chosen, the same approach would have to apply throughout the program period.

- Special rules for the computation of revenue are provided to take into account certain non-arm's-length transactions, such as where an entity sells all of its output to a related company that in turn earns arm's-length revenue [125.7(4)(d) — ed.].

- Affiliated groups that do not normally compute revenue on a consolidated basis may elect to do so [125.7(4)(b) — ed.].

Reference Periods for the Drop-in-Revenues Test

Eligibility would generally be determined by the change in an eligible entity's monthly revenues, year-over-year, for the applicable calendar month [125.7(1)"revenue reduction percentage", "prior reference period"(a), (c), Reg. 8901.2(4) — ed.].

Alternatively, an entity can choose to calculate its revenue decline by comparing its current reference month revenues with the average of its January and February 2020 revenues [125.7(1)"prior reference period"(b) — ed.].

Once an entity has chosen to use either the general or alternative approach, they must use that approach for each of the three periods [125.7(1)"prior reference

period"(b)(ii)(B), which covers all periods from July 5/20 — ed.]. The approach chosen would apply to both the base Canada Emergency Wage Subsidy and the Canada Emergency Rent Subsidy [125.7(1)"qualifying entity"(c) and "revenue reduction percentage" — ed.].

An eligible entity would use the greater of its percentage revenue decline for the current qualifying period and that for the previous qualifying period in order to determine its subsidy rate [125.7(9)(b) — ed.]. This would provide certainty to businesses regarding their expected minimum subsidy rate and aligns with the practice under the Canada Emergency Wage Subsidy [also 125.7(9)(b) — ed.].

Table 2, below, outlines each qualifying period and the relevant reference period for determining the change in revenue.

Table 2: Reference Periods

	Qualifying period	General approach	Alternative approach
Period 8	September 27 to October 24, 2020	October 2020 over October 2019 *or* September 2020 over September 2019	October 2020 *or* September 2020 over average of January and February 2020
Period 9	October 25 to November 21, 2020	November 2020 over November 2019 *or* October 2020 over October 2019	November 2020 *or* October 2020 over average of January and February 2020
Period 10	November 22 to December 19, 2020	December 2020 over December 2019 *or* November 2020 over November 2019	December 2020 *or* November 2020 over average of January and February 2020

Note: The period numbers align with those used for the Canada Emergency Wage Subsidy, for simplicity. Period 8 of the Canada Emergency Wage Subsidy program [beginning Sept. 27, 2020 — ed.] is the first period for which the rent subsidy will be in effect.

All applications must be made on or before 180 days after the end of the qualifying period [125.7(1)"qualifying renter"(a) — ed.].

The estimated cost for the first three periods of the rent subsidy program, including the new Lockdown Support for locations significantly affected by public health restrictions, is $2.2 billion in 2020-21.

[Examples follow — ed.]

The Finance Backgrounder of Nov. 5, 2020 on **Lockdown Support** states:

The new Lockdown Support would be available retroactive to September 27, 2020, until June 2021, during periods when businesses are facing eligible public health restrictions. The government is providing the proposed details for the first 12 weeks of the program, until December 19, 2020. The proposed program would align with many aspects of the Canada Emergency Wage Subsidy [125.7(2) — ed.] to provide a simple, easy-to-understand program directly to renters and property owners.

This backgrounder provides information for organizations that have been significantly affected by public health restrictions and may be eligible for additional support for certain rent or property expenses. If your organization is not subject to qualifying public health lockdown restrictions, but you are currently experiencing a decline in revenues, you may still be eligible for the Canada Emergency Rent Subsidy.

Base Rent Subsidy for Organizations Impacted by the Crisis

With the introduction of the new Canada Emergency Rent Subsidy, qualifying organizations that have suffered a revenue drop would be eligible for a subsidy on certain expenses [125.7(2.1)A — ed.]. As shown in Table 1 [reproduced below — ed.] and Figure 1 [not reproduced — ed.], the maximum base rate would be 65% [125.7(1)"rent subsidy percentage"(a)(i) — ed.], available to organizations with a revenue drop of 70% or more. The base rate would then gradually decline to a rate of 40% for organizations with a revenue drop of 50% [125.7(1)"rent subsidy percentage"(a)(ii) — ed.], and then would gradually reduce to zero for those not experiencing a decline in revenues. This structure mirrors the Canada Emergency Wage Subsidy rate structure for the relevant periods.

Lockdown Support for Locations Significantly Affected by Public Health Restrictions

The new Lockdown Support of 25% [125.7(2.1)B, 125.7(1)"rent top-up percentage"A — ed.] would be available to organizations with locations that are temporarily forced to close or temporarily have their business activities significantly restricted by a public health order issued under the laws of Canada or a province or territory [125.7(1)"rent top-up percentage"B, "public health restriction" — ed.]. This would include a shutdown of a location as a result COVID-19 outbreak (as declared by a provincial, territorial or regional health authority). This follows a commitment in the Speech from the Throne to provide direct financial support to businesses temporarily shut down as a result of a local public health decision.

Specifically, a public health restriction would be an order that meets the following conditions:

- it is made under the laws of Canada, a province or territory (including orders made by a municipality or regional health authority under one of those laws) in response to the COVID-19 pandemic [125.7(1)"public health restriction"(a), (b) — ed.];

- it is limited in scope based on factors such as defined geographical boundaries, type of business or other activity, or risks associated with a particular location [125.7(1)"public health restriction"(c) — ed.];

- non-compliance with the order is a federal, provincial or territorial offence or can result in the imposition of an administrative monetary penalty or other sanction imposed by the Government of Canada or a province or territory [125.7(1)"public health restriction"(d) — ed.];

- it cannot result from a violation of an order that meets the above conditions [125.7(1)"public health restriction"(e) — ed.]; and

- it must be in effect, for a period of at least a week [125.7(1)"public health restriction"(h) — ed.], so that some or all of the activities of the eligible entity at, or in connection with, the qualifying property are required to completely cease [125.7(1)"public health restriction"(f) — ed.]. In other words, limitations would be on the type of activity rather than the extent to which an activity may be performed or limits placed on the time during which an activity may be performed.

For an organization to qualify for the Lockdown Support for a qualifying property, the following conditions must apply:

- the organization qualifies for the base Canada Emergency Rent Subsidy [125.7(2.1)B:F(i) — ed.]; and

- the public health order requires that the organization

  — completely shut down the location [implied by 125.7(1)"public health restriction"(g) — ed.]; or,

  — cease some or all of the activities at the location and it is reasonable to conclude that the ceased activities, in the appropriate pre-pandemic prior reference period, were responsible for at least approximately 25% of the revenues of the entity at that location [125.7(1)"public health restriction"(g) — ed.].

If the organization is subject to a public health restriction and has to cease activities for only part of a qualifying period, the Lockdown Support would be prorated for the number of days in the period during which the relevant location was affected [125.7(1)"rent top-up percentage"B/C — ed.].

The following examples illustrate some common circumstances where an organization qualifying for the base subsidy may have qualifying property (i.e., a location) that would be eligible for the Lockdown Support.

- Restrictions on indoor dining: a restaurant that normally earns approximately 25% or more of its revenues in connection with indoor dining could qualify due to its dining room being shut down even if it shifts its activities to take-out orders to make up some of the lost revenues from indoor dining.

- Closure of bars: a bar that is ordered to close down due to a regional public health restriction, and, anticipating low demand for take-out, does not continue operating, could qualify.

- Closure of fitness centres: a fitness center providing group fitness classes that is ordered to close down could qualify, even if, for instance, it moves to online instruction.

- Closure of retail stores: a retail store that is ordered to close down its location in a shopping mall, but that continues to operate providing online sales and curbside pick-up, could qualify so long as its in-store sales normally accounted for at least approximately 25% of its revenues.

- Restrictions on types of personal services: an esthetics studio that earned most of its pre-pandemic revenues from services that cannot be performed while wearing a mask and can no longer be provided due to a public health restriction, could qualify.

- Other closures of certain indoor activities: a theater or an interactive museum that is ordered to close down would qualify.

- Closure in relation to a COVID-19 outbreak on the premises: a soup kitchen that is ordered to close down due to a specific public health restriction arising from a number of its employees contracting COVID-19 would qualify.

The following examples illustrate some common circumstances where an organization would generally not be eligible for the Lockdown Support:

- Reduction in business hours: a bar that is subject to a restriction requiring bars in a region to shut down by 10:00 pm each day would not qualify, as their activities would not be required to cease for a period of at least one week [125.7(1)"public health restriction"(h) — ed.].

- Requirements for physical distancing: a restaurant that earns most of its revenues in connection with indoor dining would not qualify due to a public health restriction limiting patrons to six persons per table, as it could continue to carry on its indoor dining activities.

- Restrictions on travel: a bed and breakfast that sees a decrease in the number of clients due to travel restrictions would not qualify as it can continue to operate, and there is no order to cease its activities.

- Reduction in the number of clients at any one time: a movie theater that is required to limit the number of clients would not qualify, as it would not be required to cease any of its activities.

- Violation of a public health order: a factory that is required to close down due to violating a public health restriction would not qualify because the shut-down resulted from a contravention of public health orders.

Table 1

Revenue Decline	Base subsidy rate	Lockdown Support
70% and over	65%	25%
50% to 69%	40% + (revenue drop - 50%) × 1.25 (e.g., 40% + (60% revenue drop – 50%) × 1.25 = 52.5% subsidy rate)	25%
1% to 49%	Revenue drop × 0.8 (e.g., 25% revenue drop × 0.8 = 20% subsidy rate)	25%

Eligible Expenses

[These rules are the same as for CERS, and are described in the Backgrounder above — ed.]

For the purpose of the new Lockdown Support for those affected by public health restrictions, eligible expenses would be capped at $75,000 per location [125.7(1)"qualifying rent expense"A opening words — ed.], but no overall cap would apply [125.7(2.1)B does not have the $300,000 cap that appears in 125.7(2.1)A:D(b) — ed.].

Eligible Entities

Calculating Revenues

Reference Periods for the Drop-in-Revenues Test

[The rules under the above 3 headings are the same as for CERS, and are described in the Backgrounder above — ed.]

All applications must be made on or before 180 days after the end of the qualifying period [125.7(1)"qualifying renter"(a) — ed.].

The estimated cost for the first three periods of the rent subsidy program, including the top-up for locations significantly affected by public health restrictions, is $2.2 billion in 2020-21.

[Examples follow — ed.]

For later periods, see the Proposed Amendment boxes above.

For discussion (in addition to CRA's at tinyurl.com/cra-cers), see Keey, *COVID-19 — Canada Emergency Wage Subsidy* (Taxnet Pro, June 22, 2021, 253pp, updated regularly), section "Canada Emergency Rent Subsidy"; Walsh et al, "Government introduces the new Canada emergency rent subsidy program", tinyurl.com/bdo-cers (Nov. 11, 2020); Mancell, "Canada Emergency Rent Subsidy", 2541 *Tax Topics* (CCH) 1-4 (Nov. 17, 2020); Minden Gross, "CECRA is Dead, Long Live CERS", tinyurl.com/mindengross-cers. For a flowchart see Keung, tinyurl.com/moodys-cers (Nov. 30, 2020). For a spreadsheet calculator see taxtemplates.ca.

125.7(2.1) added by 2020 COVID bill #5, effective Sept. 27, 2020.

Forms: RC665: CERS attestation.

(2.2) Canada Recovery Hiring Program [CRHP] — For a qualifying recovery entity for a qualifying period, an overpayment on account of the qualifying entity's liability under this Part for the taxation year in which the qualifying period ends is deemed to have arisen during the qualifying period in an amount determined by the formula

$$A \times (B - C)$$

where

A is the recovery wage subsidy rate for the qualifying period;

B is the qualifying recovery entity's total current period remuneration for the qualifying period; and

C is the qualifying recovery entity's total base period remuneration.

Related Provisions: 125.7(6.1) — Anti-avoidance rule; 125.7(9.2) — Entity can claim wage subsidy or recovery hiring subsidy, not both; 257 — Formula cannot calculate to less than zero.

Notes: The Canada Recovery Hiring Program (CRHP) runs to Nov. 20, 2021, while CEWS (125.7(2)) is currently scheduled to expire on Sept. 24, 2021. See tinyurl.com/cra-crhp.

The key difference between CRHP and CEWS is that CEWS is based on "eligible remuneration", while CRHP is based on *incremental* remuneration ("total current period remuneration" minus "total base period remuneration"). As well, the CRHP subsidy is a fixed percentage per claim period (125.7(1)"recovery wage subsidy rate") once there is sufficient revenue reduction to qualify, rather than varying based on "revenue reduction percentage".

An entity must choose which of CEWS and CRHP to claim (the higher one) and cannot claim both: 125.7(9.2).

The Federal Budget Supplementary Information, April 19, 2021, introduced CRHP as follows:

> Budget 2021 proposes to introduce the new Canada Recovery Hiring Program [125.7(2.2) — ed.] to provide eligible employers with a subsidy of up to 50% on the incremental remuneration paid to eligible employees between June 6, 2021 and November 20, 2021.

> An eligible employer would be permitted to claim either the hiring subsidy or the Canada Emergency Wage Subsidy for a particular qualifying period, but not both [125.7(9.2) — ed.].

> The proposed details of the hiring subsidy are described below.

Eligible Employers

Employers eligible for the Canada Emergency Wage Subsidy [125.7(1)"eligible entity" — ed.] would generally be eligible for the hiring subsidy. However, a for-profit corporation would be eligible for the hiring subsidy only if it is a Canadian-controlled private corporation (including a cooperative corporation that is eligible for the small business deduction) [125.7(1)"qualifying recovery entity"(c) — ed.]. Other eligible employers would include individuals, non-profit organizations, registered charities, and certain partnerships [125.7(1)"qualifying recovery entity"(d) — ed.].

Corporations and trusts that are ineligible for the Canada Emergency Wage Subsidy because they are public institutions [125.7(1)"eligible entity" — ed.] would not be eligible for the hiring subsidy [125.7(1)"qualifying recovery entity" opening words — ed]. Public institutions generally include municipalities and local governments, Crown corporations, wholly owned municipal corporations, public universities, colleges, schools and hospitals.

Eligible employers (or their payroll service provider) would be required to have had a payroll account open with the Canada Revenue Agency on March 15, 2020 [125.7(1)"qualifying recovery entity"(b), "qualifying entity"(d) — ed.].

Eligible Employees

An eligible employee [125.7(1) — ed.] must be employed primarily in Canada by an eligible employer throughout a qualifying period (or the portion of the qualifying period throughout which the individual was employed by the eligible employer).

The hiring subsidy would not be available for furloughed employees. A furloughed employee is an employee who is on leave with pay, meaning they are remunerated by the eligible employer but do not perform any work for the employer. An employee would not be considered to be on leave with pay for the purposes of the hiring subsidy if they are on a period of paid absence, such as vacation leave, sick leave, or a sabbatical.

Eligible Remuneration and Incremental Remuneration

The types of remuneration eligible for the Canada Emergency Wage Subsidy would also be eligible for the hiring subsidy. Eligible remuneration [defined in 125.7(1) — ed.] generally includes salary, wages, and other remuneration for which employers are required to withhold or deduct amounts on account of the employee's income tax obligations. However, it does not include severance pay, or items such as stock option benefits or the personal use of a corporate vehicle. The amount of remuneration for employees would be based solely on remuneration paid in respect of the qualifying period.

Incremental remuneration for a qualifying period means the difference between an employer's total eligible remuneration paid to eligible employees for the qualifying period and its total eligible remuneration paid to eligible employees for the baseline period. In both the qualifying period and the baseline period, eligible remuneration for each eligible employee would be subject to a maximum of $1,129 per week.

As is currently the case for the Canada Emergency Wage Subsidy, the eligible remuneration for a non-arm's length employee for a week could not exceed their baseline remuneration determined for that week. More information on baseline remuneration is available in the supplementary information on Emergency Business Supports.

The applicable dates for the calculation of the incremental remuneration [125.7(2.2) — ed.] are shown in Table 5.

Table 5 — Canada Recovery Hiring Program Dates Used to Calculate Incremental Remuneration, Periods 17* to 22

(June 6, 2021 to November 20, 2021)

Qualifying period	Period 17	Period 18	Period 19	Period 20	Period 21	Period 22
Qualifying period dates	June 6 to July 3, 2021	July 4 to July 31, 2021	August 1 to August 28, 2021	August 29 to September 25, 2021	September 26 to October 23, 2021	October 24 to November 20, 2021
Baseline period	March 14 to April 10, 2021					

Notes:

* Period 17 of the Canada Emergency Wage Subsidy would be the first period of the Canada Recovery Hiring Program. Period identifiers have been aligned for ease of reference.

Subsidy Amount

Provided that an eligible employer's decline in revenues exceeds the revenue-decline threshold for a qualifying period (see Revenue-Decline Threshold below), its subsidy in that qualifying period would be equal to its incremental remuneration multiplied by the applicable hiring subsidy rate for that qualifying period. These hiring subsidy rates are shown in Table 6.

Table 6 — Canada Recovery Hiring Program Rates, Periods 17* to 22

(June 6, 2021 to November 20, 2021)

	Period 17 June 6–July 3	Period 18 July 4–July 31	Period 19 August 1–Aug. 28	Period 20 August 29–Sept. 25	Period 21 September 26–October 23	Period 22 October 24–Nov. 20
Hiring subsidy rate	50%	50%	50%	40%	30%	20%

Notes:

* Period 17 of the Canada Emergency Wage Subsidy would be the first period of the Canada Recovery Hiring Program. Period identifiers have been aligned for ease of reference.

Revenue-Decline Threshold

To qualify for a hiring subsidy in a qualifying period, an eligible employer would have to have experienced a decline in revenues sufficient to qualify for the Canada Emergency Wage Subsidy in that qualifying period. For qualifying periods where the Canada Emergency Wage Subsidy is no longer in effect, an eligible employer would have to have experienced a decline in revenues of more than 10%. As such, an eligible employer's decline in revenues would have to be more than [125.7(1)"qualifying recovery entity"(e) — ed.]:

- 0%, for the qualifying period between June 6, 2021 and July 3, 2021; and

- 10%, for qualifying periods between July 4, 2021 and November 20, 2021.

An employer's decline in revenues would be determined in the same manner as under the Canada Emergency Wage Subsidy [125.7(1)"revenue reduction percentage" — ed.]. This method compares the employer's revenues in a current calendar month with its revenues in the same calendar month, pre-pandemic. An employer can also elect to use an alternative approach, which compares the employer's monthly revenues relative to the average of its January 2020 and February 2020 revenues. A deeming rule [125.7(9)(b) — ed.] provides that an employer's decline in revenues for any particular qualifying period is the greater of its decline in revenues for the particular qualifying period and the immediately preceding qualifying period.

Employers that had chosen to use the general approach for prior periods of the Canada Emergency Wage Subsidy would be required to continue to use that approach for the hiring subsidy. Similarly, employers that had chosen to use the alternative approach would be required to continue to use the alternative approach.

The reference periods set out in Table 7 would be used to determine an eligible employer's decline in revenues for the qualifying periods from June 6, 2021 to November 20, 2021.

Table 7 — Canada Recovery Hiring Program Reference Periods, Periods 17* to 22

(June 6, 2021 to November 20, 2021)

Timing	Period 17	Period 18	Period 19	Period 20	Period 21	Period 22
	June 6–July 3	July 4–July 31	August 1–Aug. 28	August 29–Sept. 25	September 26–October 23	October 24–Nov. 20
General approach	June 2021 over June 2019 *or* May 2021 over May 2019	July 2021 over July 2019 *or* June 2021 over June 2019	August 2021 over August 2019 *or* July 2021 over July 2019	September 2021 over September 2019 *or* August 2021 over August 2019	October 2021 over October 2019 *or* September 2021 over September 2019	November 2021 over November 2019 *or* October 2021 over October 2019
Alternative approach	June 2021 *or* May 2021 over average of January and February 2020	July 2021 *or* June 2021 over average of January and February 2020	August 2021 *or* July 2021 over average of January and February 2020	September 2021 *or* August 2021 over average of January and February 2020	October 2021 *or* September 2021 over average of January and February 2020	November 2021 *or* October 2021 over average of January and February 2020

Notes:

* Period 17 of the Canada Emergency Wage Subsidy would be the first period of the Canada Recovery Hiring Program. Period identifiers have been aligned for ease of reference.

An application for the hiring subsidy for a qualifying period would be required to be made no later than 180 days after the end of the qualifying period.

Chapter 4 of the Budget provided the following additional information:

For businesses that have been hit hardest by the pandemic, hiring the workers they need to grow is a cost they may worry about taking on. The government wants these businesses to be able to recover and grow by hiring more people so that workers are at the forefront of our recovery.

Budget 2021 proposes to introduce the new Canada Recovery Hiring Program for eligible employers that continue to experience qualifying declines in revenues relative to before the pandemic. The proposed subsidy would offset a portion of the extra costs employers take on as they reopen, either by increasing wages or hours worked, or hiring more staff. This support would only be available for active employees and will be available from June 6 to November 20, 2021. Eligible employers would claim the higher of the Canada Emergency Wage Subsidy or the new proposed subsidy. The aim is to make it as easy as possible for businesses to hire new workers as the economy reopens.

As the rates for both the wage subsidy and the hiring program will slowly ramp down over time, employers will have a strong incentive to begin hiring as soon as possible and maximize their benefit. Further details can be found in Annex 6. The Canada Recovery Hiring Program will help Canadian-controlled private corporations, individuals, charities, and non-profits hire the workers they need so that the economy can fully recover, more quickly and without leaving people behind. It is estimated that this program will cost $595 million in 2021-22.

Example

Dorothy and Stan run a bookstore whose storefront was shut down sporadically through the winter and spring due to public health restrictions. While their business survived, they had to lay off three of their 10 employees, whom they pay $600 per week. Their baseline payroll from March 14 to April 10 was $16,800 (i.e., 7 employees × $600 × 4 weeks).

As public health restrictions are lifted and the vaccination campaign continues, their business begins to recover. In May, their revenues are still down 50% from their level before the pandemic, but are only down 20% in June, and by July are close to their pre-pandemic level. As a result, they are able to hire back their three laid-off employees starting June 6, and are even able to add an additional employee starting July 4.

As a result of measures proposed in this Budget, Dorothy and Stan's business will benefit from either the extended Canada Emergency Wage Subsidy or the new Canada Recovery Hiring Program:

- For June 6 to July 3, their payroll is $24,000. Their business would be eligible for a wage subsidy rate of 40% (based on a 50% revenue decline), resulting in a wage subsidy of $9,600.

  Alternatively, the business would be eligible for a hiring subsidy rate of 50%, which would be applied to the difference between its current payroll and its baseline payroll, resulting in a hiring incentive of $3,600. They are better off claiming the wage subsidy of $9,600 for this period.

- For July 4 to July 31, their payroll is $26,400. Their business would be eligible for a wage subsidy rate of 8.75% (based on a 20% revenue decline), resulting in a wage subsidy of $2,310.

  Alternatively, the business would be eligible for a hiring subsidy rate of 50%, which would be applied to the difference between its current payroll and its baseline payroll, resulting in a hiring incentive of $4,800. In this instance, they are better off claiming the hiring incentive of $4,800 for this period.

In total, Dorothy and Stan will be eligible for at least $14,400 in support from these two measures to help their business rebuild as the economy recovers.

Finance news release, June 2, 2021, provided additional detail:

Government of Canada Announces Details of the New Canada Recovery Hiring Program and Extension of Business Support Programs

Today, Deputy Prime Minister and Minister of Finance, the Honourable Chrystia Freeland, and the Minister of Small Business, Export Promotion and International Trade, the Honourable Mary Ng, announced that the new Canada Recovery Hiring Program, would be available retroactively to June 6, 2021.

The proposed Canada Recovery Hiring Program [125.7(2.2) — ed.] would help hard hit businesses hire the workers they need to recover and grow as local economies reopen. The program would provide a subsidy of up to 50% of eligible salary or wages. It would be available to eligible employers who have experienced qualifying revenue declines so they can hire more workers, increase workers' hours, or increase wages. This support would afford businesses with certainty that they can take on the extra costs needed to rehire and be ready to return to growth. Like with the Canada Emergency Wage Subsidy and Canada Emergency Rent Subsidy, businesses would be able to access the program through the Canada Revenue Agency (CRA). Support would be available retroactively to this Sunday, June 6, 2021, and businesses would be able to hire workers as their local economy reopens, or as they are ready.

The Deputy Prime Minister and the Minister of Small Business also detailed the proposed extension of business support programs that have served as a lifeline to Canadian businesses through the pandemic. This includes the proposed extension of the Wage Subsidy [125.7(2) — ed.], Rent Subsidy [125.7(2.1)A — ed.], and Lockdown Support [125.7(2.1)B — ed.] until September 25, 2021. These programs are currently set to expire this month. Both the Hiring Program and proposed extensions are part of Bill C-30, the *Budget Implementation Act*, which is currently before Parliament.

The Hiring Program [125.7(2.2) — ed.] is designed to interact with the Wage Subsidy [125.7(2) — ed.]. The programs overlap so that, as Wage Subsidy rates gradually decline, eligible employers would still be able to receive the maximum support from the Hiring Program this summer if they hire more workers or increase workers' hours or wages. This will make it easy for businesses to quickly hire new workers and do so at a pace that works best for them, as different jurisdictions reopen their economies at different paces.

The Deputy Prime Minister and the Minister of Small Business also announced that the Business Credit Availability Program and Highly Affected Sectors Credit Availability Program are being extended to December 31, 2021. Both programs were set to expire on June 30, 2021. This will ensure, with economies reopening and a path to recovery ahead, businesses will have the liquidity support they need to invest in their recovery.

Through these programs, the government is ensuring that businesses can continue to get the support they need and enabling them to invest in their longer-term prosperity, including businesses in hard-hit sectors like tourism and hospitality, hotels, arts and entertainment.

Quick facts

- The proposed Canada Recovery Hiring Program would be available to support active employees from June 6, 2021 to November 20, 2021. This will allow eligible employers to use the program at a pace that works for them.

- As with the Wage Subsidy, eligible employers would receive support after each four week period of the program.

- Support would be available retroactively once Bill C-30 receives Royal Assent.

- Eligible employers would be able to access support through the CRA and the application portal would be available after Royal Assent.

- The program is estimated to cost $595 million in 2021-22.

- The Canada Emergency Wage Subsidy has protected more than 5.3 million jobs, to date. The program is currently set to expire in June 2021.

- To give workers and employers certainty and stability over the coming months, the recent federal budget proposed to extend the Wage Subsidy until September 25, 2021.

- This extension would see a gradual decrease of the Wage Subsidy rate, beginning July 4, 2021, in order to ensure an orderly phase-out of the program as the economy reopens.

- Employers would be able to shift to the Canada Recovery Hiring Program as they transition to recovery and hire new workers.

- The Canada Emergency Rent Subsidy and Lockdown Support have helped more than 187,000 organizations with rent, mortgage, and other property expenses. The program is currently set to expire in June 2021.

- To bridge Canadians through to recovery, the recent federal budget proposed to extend the Rent Subsidy and Lockdown Support until September 25, 2021.

- This extension would see a gradual decrease of the Rent Subsidy rate, beginning July 4, 2021, in order to ensure an orderly phase-out of this program as the economy reopens.

- The Business Credit Availability Program (BCAP) loan guarantee and co-lending programs provide credit of up to $6.25 million and $12.5 million respectively. BCAP also provides support for mid-sized businesses including loans of up to $60 million per company, and guarantees of up to $80 million.

- Through the Highly Affected Sectors Credit Availability Program (HAS-CAP), BDC partners with participating Canadian financial institutions to offer government-guaranteed, low-interest loans of $25,000 to $1 million to businesses across the country, with repayment periods of up to 10 years, in all sectors that have been hit hard by the pandemic. This includes restaurants, businesses in the tourism and hospitality sectors, and those that rely on in-person service.

- For additional information on BCAP or HASCAP or to apply, businesses should contact their primary financial institution with whom they have a pre-existing relationship.

- The Organisation for Economic Cooperation and Development's May 2021 Economic Outlook stated that "the Canadian economy will rebound strongly and grow by 6.1% in 2021 and 3.8% in 2022, thanks to reduced COVID-19 restrictions in the second half of this year and buoyant external demand. These developments will be echoed in a recovery in the labour market." It also assessed that "Reforms proposed in [Budget 2021] suggest positive advances in social and environmental policy and for the business environment."

Backgrounder: Helping hard-hit businesses hire more workers with the Canada Recovery Hiring Program

For businesses that have been hit hardest by the pandemic, hiring the workers they need to grow is a cost they may worry about taking on. The federal government wants these businesses to be able to recover and grow by hiring more people.

The recent federal budget proposed the new Canada Recovery Hiring Program [125.7(2.2) — ed.] to provide support to eligible employers that continue to experience qualifying declines in revenues relative to before the pandemic. The proposed Hiring Program is included in Bill C-30, *An Act to implement certain provisions of the budget tabled in Parliament on April 19, 2021 and other measures*, which is currently before Parliament. The program would offset a portion of the extra costs employers take on as they reopen, either by increasing wages or hours worked or hiring more staff. This support would only be available for active employees and will be available from June 6, 2021, to November 20, 2021. The aim is to make it as easy as possible for businesses to hire new workers as the economy reopens.

As the rates for both the Wage Subsidy and the Hiring Program will slowly ramp down over time, employers will have a strong incentive to begin hiring as soon as possible and maximize their benefit. The program is also designed so that employers can hire at their own pace, as different jurisdictions reopen at different paces.

The Hiring Program will help eligible employers hire the workers they need so that the economy can fully recover more quickly and without leaving people behind. The program will be available through the Canada Revenue Agency, just like the Wage Subsidy [125.7(2) — ed.] and Rent Subsidy [125.7(2.1) — ed.]. The application portal will open following Royal Assent of Bill C-30, the *Budget Implementation Act*.

It is estimated that this program will cost $595 million in 2021-22.

How the Canada Recovery Hiring Program Works

The proposed Canada Recovery Hiring Program [125.7(2.2) — ed.] would provide eligible employers with a subsidy of up to 50% of incremental remuneration paid to eligible active employees between June 6, 2021, and November 20, 2021.

Eligible Employers

Employers eligible for the Canada Emergency Wage Subsidy [125.7(1)"eligible entity" — ed.] would generally be eligible for the Canada Recovery Hiring Program. Eligible employers must be Canadian-controlled private corporations (including a cooperative corporation that is eligible for the small business deduction) [125.7(1)"qualifying recovery entity"(c) — ed.], and also include individuals, non-profit organizations, registered charities, and certain partnerships.

Corporations and trusts that are ineligible for the Canada Emergency Wage Subsidy because they are public institutions [125.7(1)"eligible entity" — ed.] would also not be eligible for the Hiring Program [125.7(1)"qualifying recovery entity" opening words — ed.]. Public institutions [defined in 125.7(1) — ed.] generally include municipalities and local governments, Crown corporations, wholly owned municipal corporations, public universities, colleges, schools, and hospitals.

Eligible employers, or their payroll service provider, would be required to have had a payroll account open with the Canada Revenue Agency on March 15, 2020 [125.7(1)"qualifying recovery entity"(b), "qualifying entity"(d) — ed.].

Eligible Employees

An eligible employee [defined in 125.7(1) — ed.] must be actively employed by an eligible employer throughout a qualifying period (or the portion of the qualifying period throughout which the individual was employed by the eligible employer) and are primarily employed in Canada.

The Hiring Program would not be available for furloughed employees, meaning those who are on leave with pay but do not perform any work for the employer. An employee would not be considered to be on leave with pay for the purposes of the Hiring Program if they are on a period of paid absence such as vacation leave, sick leave, or sabbatical.

Eligible Remuneration and Incremental Remuneration

The types of remuneration eligible for the Canada Emergency Wage Subsidy would also be eligible for the Hiring Program.

Eligible remuneration [defined in 125.7(1) — ed.] generally includes salary, wages, and other remuneration for which employers are required to withhold or deduct amounts on account of the employee's income tax obligations. However, severance pay, stock option benefits, or the personal use of a corporate vehicle are not eligible. The amount of remuneration for employees would be based solely on remuneration paid during the qualifying period.

Incremental remuneration for a qualifying period [125.7(2.2)B minus C — ed.] is the difference between total eligible remuneration paid to eligible employees during the qualifying period and total eligible remuneration paid to them during the baseline period. For calculation of total eligible remuneration paid for both the qualifying period and the baseline period, eligible remuneration for each eligible employee would be subject to a maximum of $1,129 per week [125.7(1)"total current period remuneration"(a), "total base period remuneration"(a) — ed.].

As with the Canada Emergency Wage Subsidy, the eligible remuneration for a non-arm's length employee for a week could not exceed their baseline remuneration determined for that week. More information on baseline remuneration is available in Annex 6 of Budget 2021.

Table 1, below, outlines the dates used for calculating incremental remuneration [125.7(2.2) — ed.].

Table 1

Canada Recovery Hiring Program Dates Used to Calculate Incremental Remuneration, Periods 17* to 22

(June 6, 2021 to November 20, 2021)

Qualifying period	Period 17	Period 18	Period 19	Period 20	Period 21	Period 22
Qualifying period dates	June 6 to July 3, 2021	July 4 to July 31, 2021	August 1 to August 28, 2021	August 29 to September 25, 2021	September 26 to October 23, 2021	October 24 to November 20, 2021
Baseline period	March 14 to April 10, 2021					

* Period 17 of the Canada Emergency Wage Subsidy would be the first period of the Canada Recovery Hiring Program. Period identifiers have been aligned for ease of reference.

Revenue-Decline Threshold

To be eligible for the Hiring Program an employer would have to demonstrate a decline in revenues sufficient to qualify for the Canada Emergency Wage Subsidy during a qualifying period. If an employer is applying during a period when the Canada Emergency Wage Subsidy is no longer in effect, they would have to demonstrate a revenue decline of more than 10%. As such, an eligible employer's decline in revenues would have to be [125.7(1)"qualifying recovery entity"(e) — ed.]:

- More than 0%, for the qualifying period between June 6, 2021 and July 3, 2021.

- More than 10%, for qualifying periods between July 4, 2021 and November 20, 2021.

An employer's decline in revenues would be determined in the same manner as under the Canada Emergency Wage Subsidy [125.7(1)"revenue reduction percentage" — ed.]. This method compares the employer's revenues in a current calendar month with its revenues in the same calendar month, pre-pandemic. An employer can also elect to use an alternative approach, which compares the employer's monthly revenues relative to the average of its January 2020 and February 2020 revenues. An employer's decline in revenues for any particular qualifying period is the greater of its decline in revenues for the particular qualifying period and the immediately preceding qualifying period.

Employers that had chosen to use the general approach for prior periods of the Canada Emergency Wage Subsidy would be required to continue to use that approach for the Hiring Program. Similarly, employers that had chosen to use the alternative approach would be required to continue to use the alternative approach.

Table 2 sets out the reference periods used to determine an eligible employer's revenue decline or the qualifying periods.

Table 2

Canada Recovery Hiring Program Reference Periods, Periods 17* to 22

(June 6, 2021 to November 20, 2021)

Timing	Period 17 June 6 - July 3	Period 18 July 4 - July 31	Period 19 August 1 - August 28	Period 20 August 29 - September 25	Period 21 September 26 - October 23	Period 22 October 24 - November 20
General approach	June 2021 over June 2019 *or* May 2021 over May 2019	July 2021 over July 2019 *or* June 2021 over June 2019	August 2021 over August 2019 *or* July 2021 over July 2019	September 2021 over September 2019 *or* August 2021 over August 2019	October 2021 over October 2019 *or* September 2021 over September 2019	November 2021 over November 2019 *or* October 2021 over October 2019
Alternative approach	June 2021 *or* May 2021 over average of January and February 2020	July 2021 *or* June 2021 over average of January and February 2020	August 2021 *or* July 2021 over average of January and February 2020	September 2021 *or* August 2021 over average of January and February 2020	October 2021 *or* September 2021 over average of January and February 2020	November 2021 *or* October 2021 over average of January and February 2020

* Period 17 of the Canada Emergency Wage Subsidy would be the first period of the Canada Recovery Hiring Program. Period identifiers have been aligned for ease of reference.

Employers seeking access support from the Hiring Program must apply no later than 180 days after the end of each qualifying period [125.7(1)"qualifying entity"(a) — ed.].

An eligible employer would be permitted to claim either the hiring subsidy or the Canada Emergency Wage Subsidy for a particular qualifying period, but not both [125.7(9.2) — ed.].

Subsidy Amount

If an eligible employer meets the revenue-decline threshold for a qualifying period, its subsidy amount would be equal to its eligible incremental remuneration multiplied by the Hiring subsidy rate (e.g. 50%, 40%, 30% or 20%) for the qualifying period. The rates for each period are shown below, in Table 3.

Table 3

Canada Recovery Hiring Program Rates, Periods 17* to 22

(June 6, 2021 to November 20, 2021)

	Period 17 June 6 - July 3	Period 18 July 4 - July 31	Period 19 August 1 - August 28	Period 20 August 29 - September 25	Period 21 September 26 - October 23	Period 22 October 24 - November 20
Hiring subsidy rate	50%	50%	50%	40%	30%	20%

* Period 17 of the Canada Emergency Wage Subsidy would be the first period of the Canada Recovery Hiring Program. Period identifiers have been aligned for ease of reference.

Example

Max and Chinmay run a bookstore whose storefront was shut down sporadically through the winter and spring due to public health restrictions. While their business survived, they had to lay off three of their 10 employees, each of whom they pay $600 per week. Their baseline payroll from March 14 to April 10 was $16,800 (i.e., seven employees × $600 × four weeks).

As public health restrictions are lifted and the vaccination campaign continues, their business begins to recover. In May, their revenues were still down 50% from their level before the pandemic, but are only down 20% in June, and by July are close to their pre-pandemic level. As a result, they are able to hire back their three laid-off employees starting June 6, and are even able to add an additional employee starting July 4.

As a result of proposed measures in the federal government's recovery plan, Max and Chinmay's business will benefit from either the extended Canada Emergency Wage Subsidy or the new Canada Recovery Hiring Program:

- For June 6 to July 3, their payroll is $24,000. Their business would be eligible for a wage subsidy rate of 40% (based on a 50% revenue decline), resulting in a wage subsidy of $9,600. Alternatively, the business would be eligible for a hiring subsidy rate of 50%, which would be applied to the difference between its current payroll and its baseline payroll, resulting in a hiring incentive of $3,600. They are better off claiming the wage subsidy of $9,600 for this period.

- For July 4 to July 31, their payroll is $26,400. Their business would be eligible for a wage subsidy rate of 8.75% (based on a 20% revenue decline), resulting in a wage subsidy of $2,310. Alternatively, the business would be eligible for a hiring subsidy rate of 50%, which would be applied to the difference between its current payroll and its baseline payroll, resulting in a hiring incentive of $4,800. In this instance, they are better off claiming the hiring incentive of $4,800 for this period.

In total, Max and Chinmay will be eligible for at least $14,400 in support from these two measures to help their business rebuild as the economy recovers.

125.7(2.2) added by 2021 budget bill #1, effective June 29, 2021.

(3) When assistance received — For the purposes of this Act other than this section, and for greater certainty, an amount that an eligible entity is deemed under any of subsections (2) to (2.2) to have overpaid is assistance received by it from a government immediately before the end of the qualifying period to which it relates.

Notes: CEWS and CERS are normally taxable to the business under 12(1)(x). See 125.7(2) Notes, Finance Backgrounder, at "Government Assistance".

125.7(3) amended by 2021 budget bill #1, effective June 29, 2021, to add reference to 125.7(2.2) (CRHP). Amended by 2020 COVID bill #5, effective Sept. 27, 2020, to add references to "qualifying renter" and 125.7(2.1) (CERS).

(4) Computation of revenue — For the purposes of the definition "qualifying revenue" in subsection (1), the qualifying revenue of an eligible entity is to be determined in accordance with its normal accounting practices, except that

(a) if a group of eligible entities normally prepares consolidated financial statements, each member of the group may determine its qualifying revenue separately, provided every member of the group determines its qualifying revenue on that basis;

(b) if an eligible entity and each member of an affiliated group of eligible entities of which the eligible entity is a member jointly elect, the qualifying revenue of the group determined on a consolidated basis in accordance with relevant accounting principles is to be used for each member of the group;

(c) if all of the interests in an eligible entity are owned by participants in a joint venture and all or substantially all of the qualifying revenue of the eligible entity for a qualifying period is in respect of the joint venture, then the eligible entity may use the qualifying revenues of the joint venture (determined as if the joint venture were an eligible entity) as its qualifying revenues for the qualifying period for the purposes of this section;

(d) if all or substantially all of an eligible entity's qualifying revenue — determined without reference to paragraph (d) of the definition "qualifying revenue" in subsection (1) — for a qualifying period is from one or more particular persons or partnerships with which it does not deal at arm's length and each particular person or partnership jointly elects with the eligible entity, for the purposes of this section

(i) the eligible entity's qualifying revenue for the prior reference period is deemed to be $100, and

(ii) the eligible entity's qualifying revenue for the current reference period is deemed to be the total of all amounts, each of which is determined by the formula

$$\$100(A/B)(C/D)$$

where

A   is the eligible entity's qualifying revenue (determined without reference to paragraph (d) of the definition "qualifying revenue" in subsection (1)) for the current reference period attributable to a particular person or partnership,

B   is the total of all amounts, each of which is the eligible entity's qualifying revenue (determined without reference to paragraph (d) of the definition "qualifying revenue" in subsection (1)) for the current reference period attributable to a particular person or partnership,

C   is the particular person or partnership's qualifying revenue (determined as if the definition "qualifying revenue" in subsection (1) were read without reference to "in Canada") for the current reference period, and

D   is the particular person or partnership's qualifying revenue (determined as if the definition "qualifying revenue" in subsection (1) were read without reference to "in Canada") for the prior reference period; and

(e) an eligible entity may make an election, which must apply for all qualifying periods, to determine its qualifying revenues based on

(i) the cash method, within the meaning assigned by subsection 28(1) with any modifications that the circumstances require, or

(ii) the accrual method, in accordance with generally accepted accounting principles.

Related Provisions: 125.7(10) — Amending or revoking election.

Notes: See under 125.7(2). On 125.7(4)(b) see Carolin & Kakkar, "The Canada Emergency Wage Subsidy: Affiliated Group Issues", *COVID-19 and Canadian Tax* (ctf.ca) 1-3 (July 2020); Lee & Raveendran, "Affiliation Election for CEWS: Private Corporation Applications", *ibid* 3-4. See also tinyurl.com/cews-cra-faq, especially qq. 8 to 12-1. On (e)(ii) see International Fiscal Assn CRA Q&A (Aug. 6, 2020), tinyurl.com/ifa-covid-qa, q. 15.

See also VIEWS docs 2020-0851731E5 (para. (d) election not allowed for a multi-tiered chain, such as Canco selling to one foreign sub that sells to another); 2021-0879631C6 [TEI 2021], q.2 (qualifying revenue should be calculated the same way for both CEWS and CERS).

125.7(4) amended by 2020 COVID bill #5, retroactive to introduction of 125.7 (April 11, 2020), to change in (c) "instead of its qualifying revenues for the purposes of paragraph (c) of the definition "qualifying entity" in subsection (1);" to "as its qualifying revenues for the qualifying period for the purposes of this section", and to change (d) from applying to 125.7(1)"qualifying entity"(c) to applying to all of 125.7.

125.7(4)(e) amended by 2020 COVID bill #3, retroactive to April 11, 2020, to change "revenues" to "qualifying revenues" and add (e)(ii).

Forms: RC661: CEWS attestation; RC665: CERS attestation.

(4.1) Asset sales — conditions — Subsection (4.2) applies to an eligible entity in respect of a qualifying period if

(a) the eligible entity acquired assets (referred to in this subsection and subsection (4.2) as the **"acquired assets"**) of a person or partnership (referred to in this subsection and subsection (4.2) as the **"seller"**) during the qualifying period or at any time before that period;

(b) immediately prior to the acquisition, the fair market value of the acquired assets constituted

(i) all or substantially all of the fair market value of the property of the seller used in the course of carrying on business, or

(ii) if the seller and the eligible entity deal with each other at arm's length, all or substantially all of the property of the seller that can reasonably be regarded as being necessary for the eligible entity to be capable of carrying on a business of the seller, or part of a business of the seller, as a business;

(c) the acquired assets were used by the seller in the course of a business carried on in Canada by the seller;

(d) it is reasonable to conclude that none of the main purposes of the acquisition was to increase the amount of a deemed overpayment under subsection (2); and

(e) the eligible entity elects in respect of the qualifying period and files the election in prescribed form and manner with the Minister or, if the seller is in existence during the qualifying period, the eligible entity and the seller jointly elect in respect of that period and so file with the Minister.

Related Provisions: 125.7(10) — Amending or revoking election.

Notes: (b)(ii) is similar to *Excise Tax Act* s. 167(1) for no GST/HST on transfer of a business; for CRA interpretation see GST/HST Menmorandum 14-4 paras. 7-9.

125.7(4.1)(b) amended by 2020 COVID bill #5, retroactive to introduction of 125.7 (April 11, 2020), effectively to add the arm's-length requirement and reference to "part of" a business in (b)(ii). Former (b), now deemed never to have been in force, read:

> (b) immediately prior to the acquisition, the fair market value of the acquired assets constituted all or substantially all of the fair market value of the property of the seller used in the course of carrying on business;

125.7(4.1) added by 2020 COVID bill #3, effective April 11, 2020.

Forms: RC665: CERS attestation.

(4.2) Asset sales — application — If this subsection applies to an eligible entity in respect of a qualifying period,

(a) the amount of the qualifying revenue of the seller for the prior reference period, or the current reference period, for the qualifying period that is reasonably attributable to the acquired assets (referred to in this subsection as the "assigned revenue") is to be included in determining the qualifying revenue of the eligible entity for its prior reference period or current reference period, as the case may be, for the qualifying period;

(b) the assigned revenue is to be subtracted from the qualifying revenue of the seller for its prior reference period or current reference period, as the case may be, for the qualifying period;

(c) if a portion of the assigned revenue is from a person or partnership that did not deal at arm's length with the seller and that person or partnership deals at arm's length with the eligible entity throughout the current reference period, then that portion of the assigned revenue is deemed to not be derived from persons or partnerships not dealing at arm's length for the purposes of paragraph (d) of the definition "qualifying revenue" in subsection (1);

(d) if the seller meets any of the following conditions, the eligible entity is deemed to meet that condition:

(i) either of the conditions in paragraph (d) of the definition "qualifying entity" in subsection (1), and

(ii) both of the conditions in subparagraph (c)(ii), or the condition in subparagraph (c)(iii), of the definition "qualifying renter" in subsection (1); and

(e) for the purposes of subparagraph (b)(i) of the definition "prior reference period" in subsection (1) and the description of C in subparagraph (c)(ii) of the definition "qualifying entity" in subsection (1), the eligible entity is deemed to have commenced carrying on the business in which the acquired assets are used at the earlier of

(i) the date on which the eligible entity commenced carrying on that business, and

(ii) the date on which the seller commenced carrying on the business in which the acquired assets were used.

Related Provisions: 125.7(4.1) — Conditions and election for 125.7(4.2) to apply.

Notes: For a loophole in this rule see Lee & Raveendran, "CEWS 2.0: Subsidizing Corporate Reorganizations?", 10(4) *Canadian Tax Focus* (ctf.ca) 1-2 (Nov. 2020). For CRA interpretation see VIEWS doc 2020-0870981E5 (where asset transfer happens in middle of qualifying period).

Subpara. (d)(ii) added by 2021 budget bill #1, effective Sept. 27, 2020. Before that date, read:

> (d) if the seller meets either of the conditions in paragraph (d) of the definition "qualifying entity" in subsection (1), the eligible entity is deemed to meet that condition; and

Para. (e) added by 2020 COVID bill #5, retroactive to introduction of 125.7 (April 11, 2020).

125.7(4.2) added by 2020 COVID bill #3, effective April 11, 2020.

(5) Deemed overpayment — For the purposes of this section,

(a) the amount of any deemed overpayment by an eligible entity under any of subsections (2) to (2.2) in respect of a qualifying period cannot exceed the amount claimed by the eligible entity in the application referred to in paragraph (a) of the definition "qualifying entity" in subsection (1) — or paragraph (a) of the definition "qualifying renter" in subsection (1) or paragraph (a) of the definition "qualifying recovery entity" in subsection (1) — in respect of that qualifying period; and

(b) if an eligible employee is employed in a week by two or more qualifying entities that do not deal with each other at arm's length, the total amount of the deemed overpayment under subsection (2) or (2.2) in respect of the eligible employee for that week shall not exceed the amount that would arise if the eligible employee's eligible remuneration for that week were paid by one qualifying entity.

Notes: Paras. (a), (b) amended by 2021 budget bill #1, effective June 29, 2021, to apply to CRHP (125.7(2.2)). From Sept. 27, 2020 until then, read:

(a) the amount of any deemed overpayment by an eligible entity under subsection (2) or (2.1) in respect of a qualifying period cannot exceed the amount claimed by the eligible entity — in the application referred to in paragraph (a) of the definition "qualifying entity" in subsection (1) or paragraph (a) of the definition "qualifying renter" in subsection (1) — in respect of that qualifying period; and

(b) if an eligible employee is employed in a week by two or more qualifying entities that do not deal with each other at arm's length, the total amount of the deemed overpayment under subsection (2) in respect of the eligible employee for that week shall not exceed the amount that would arise if the eligible employee's eligible remuneration for that week were paid by one qualifying entity.

Para. (a) amended by 2020 COVID bill #5, effective Sept. 27, 2020, to apply to CERS. Before that date, read:

(a) the amount of any deemed overpayment by an eligible entity under subsection (2) in respect of a qualifying period cannot exceed the amount claimed by the qualifying entity — in the application referred to in paragraph (a) of the definition "qualifying entity" in subsection (1) — in respect of that qualifying period; and

(6) Anti-avoidance — qualifying revenues — Notwithstanding any other provision in this section, the qualifying revenue of an eligible entity for a current reference period for a qualifying period is deemed to be equal to the qualifying revenue of the eligible entity for the relevant prior reference period, if

(a) the eligible entity, or a person or partnership not dealing at arm's length with the eligible entity, enters into a transaction or participates in an event (or a series of transactions or events) or takes an action (or fails to take an action) — other than, for greater certainty, a decision under subparagraph (a)(ii) or (b)(ii) of the definition "qualifying revenue" in subsection (1) or the decision to use one of the methods of computing qualifying revenues under subsection (4) — that has the effect of

(i) reducing the qualifying revenues (determined without reference to this subsection) of the eligible entity for the current reference period, or

(ii) increasing the qualifying rent expenses of the eligible entity for the qualifying period; and

(b) it is reasonable to conclude that one of the main purposes of the transaction, event, series or action in paragraph (a) is to

(i) cause an eligible entity to qualify for the deemed overpayment under subsection (2) in respect of that qualifying period,

(ii) in respect of the fifth qualifying period and subsequent qualifying periods, increase the amount of a deemed overpayment under subsection (2), or

(iii) increase the amount of a deemed overpayment under subsection (2.1).

Related Provisions: 163(2.901) — Penalty of 25% of overclaimed subsidy.

Notes: Subpara. (b)(ii) amended by 2021 budget bill #1, effective June 29, 2021, to refer to periods by number. Before that date, read:

(ii) in respect of qualifying periods described in any of paragraphs (c.2) to (d) of the definition "qualifying period" in subsection (1), increase the amount of a deemed overpayment under subsection (2), or

125.7(6) amended by 2020 COVID bill #5, effective Sept. 27, 2020, to add the opening "Notwithstanding" clause, and to add (a)(ii) and (b)(iii) (for CERS). Before that date, read:

(6) The qualifying revenue of an eligible entity for a current reference period for a qualifying period is deemed to be equal to the qualifying revenue of the eligible entity for the relevant prior reference period, if

(a) the eligible entity, or a person or partnership not dealing at arm's length with the eligible entity, enters into a transaction or participates in an event (or a series of transactions or events) or takes an action (or fails to take an action) — other than, for greater certainty, a decision under subparagraph (a)(ii) or (b)(ii) of the definition "qualifying revenue" in subsection (1) or the decision to use one of the methods of computing qualifying revenues under subsection (4) — that has the effect of reducing the qualifying revenues (determined without reference to this subsection) of the eligible entity for the current reference period; and

(b) it is reasonable to conclude that one of the main purposes of the transaction, event, series or action in paragraph (a) is to

(i) cause an eligible entity to qualify for the deemed overpayment under subsection (2) in respect of that qualifying period, or

(ii) in respect of qualifying periods described in any of paragraphs (c.2) to (d) of the definition "qualifying period" in subsection (1), increase the amount of a deemed overpayment under subsection (2).

125.7(6)(b)(ii) added by 2020 COVID bill #3, retroactive to introduction of 125.7 (April 11, 2020).

(6.1) Anti-avoidance — recovery wage subsidy — Notwithstanding any other provision in this section, the total current period remuneration of an eligible entity for a qualifying period is deemed to be equal to the total base period remuneration of the eligible entity, if

(a) the eligible entity, or a person or partnership not dealing at arm's length with the eligible entity, enters into a transaction or participates in an event (or a series of transactions or events) or takes an action (or fails to take an action) that has the effect of increasing the difference between the total current period remuneration and the total base period remuneration of the eligible entity for the qualifying period; and

(b) it is reasonable to conclude that one of the main purposes of the transaction, event, series or action in paragraph (a) is to increase the amount of a deemed overpayment under subsection (2.2).

Related Provisions: 163(2.902) — Penalty of 25% of overclaimed subsidy.

Notes: 125.7(6.1) added by 2021 budget bill #1, effective June 29, 2021.

(7) Partnerships — A partnership is deemed

(a) for the purposes of subsections (2) to (2.2) and subsections 152(3.4) and 160.1(1), to be a taxpayer; and

(b) for the purposes of subsections (2) to (2.2), to have a liability under this Part for a taxation year in which a qualifying period ends.

Notes: 125.7(7)(a), (b) amended by 2021 budget bill #1, effective June 29, 2021, to refer to 125.7(2.2) (CRHP); by 2020 COVID bill #5, effective Sept. 27, 2020, to refer to 125.7(2.1) (CERS).

125.7(7)(a) amended by 2020 COVID bill #3 to refer to 152(3.4), retroactive to introduction of 125.7 (April 11, 2020).

(8) Prescribed amounts — The following may be prescribed for the purposes of:

(a) the definition "base percentage" in subsection (1),

(i) the percentages in subparagraphs (a)(i), (b)(i), (c)(i), (d)(i), (e)(i), (f)(i), (g)(i), (h)(i), (i)(i) and (j)(i), and

(ii) the factors in subparagraphs (a)(ii), (b)(ii), (c)(ii), (d)(ii), (e)(ii), (f)(ii), (g)(ii), (h)(ii), (i)(ii) and (j)(ii); and

(b) the definition "rent subsidy percentage" in subsection (1), the factors and percentages in paragraphs (a) and (a.1) of that definition;

(b.1) the definition "recovery wage subsidy rate" in subsection (1), the percentages in that definition; and

(c) the definition "qualifying rent expense" in subsection (1), specific, or classes of, expenses that are included or excluded as qualifying rent expenses under paragraph (a) or (b) of that definition.

Notes: This rule seems to say that even where the indicated legislative provisions do not refer to "prescribed" amounts but provide fixed amounts or percentages, they can be overridden by amendments to the *Income Tax Regulations*. See Reg. 8901.1 and 8901.2.

Paras. (a), (b) amended, and (b.1) added, by 2021 budget bill #1, effective June 29, 2021. Before that date, read:

(a) the definition "base percentage" in subsection (1),

(i) the percentages in subparagraphs (a)(i), (b)(i), (c)(i), (d)(i), (e)(i) and (f)(i), and

(ii) the factors in subparagraphs (a)(ii), (b)(ii), (c)(ii), (d)(ii), (e)(ii) and (f)(ii);

(b) the definition "rent subsidy percentage" in subsection (1), the factors and percentages in paragraph (a) of that definition; and

125.7(8) amended by 2020 COVID bill #5, effective Sept. 27, 2020, to apply to CERS. Before that date, read:

(8) For the purposes of the definition "base percentage" in subsection (1), the following may be prescribed:

(a) the percentages in subparagraphs (a)(i), (b)(i), (c)(i), (d)(i) and (e)(i); and

(b) the factors in subparagraphs (a)(ii), (b)(ii), (c)(ii), (d)(ii) and (e)(ii).

125.7(8) amended by 2020 COVID bill #3, retroactive to introduction of 125.7 (April 11, 2020). The previous version, now superseded, read:

(8) For any period referred to in paragraph (d) of the definition "qualifying period" in subsection (1), the following may be prescribed:

(a) the percentages in subparagraphs (a)(i) and (b)(ii) of the description of A in subsection (2); and

(b) the amounts in subparagraphs (a)(ii) and (b)(iii) of the description of A in subsection (2).

(9) Deeming rules — revenue decline tests — If, absent the application of this subsection,

(a) an eligible entity meets the conditions in paragraph (c) of the definition "qualifying entity" in subsection (1) in respect of a particular qualifying period described in any of paragraphs (a) to (c) of the definition "qualifying period" in subsection (1), then the eligible entity is deemed to meet the conditions of that paragraph in respect of the immediately following qualifying period; or

(b) a lower revenue reduction percentage is determined in respect of an eligible entity for a particular qualifying period described in any of paragraphs (c.2) to (d) of the definition "qualifying period" in subsection (1) than for the immediately preceding qualifying period, then the revenue reduction percentage in respect of the eligible entity for the particular qualifying period is deemed to be equal to its revenue reduction percentage for the immediately preceding qualifying period.

Related Provisions: 125.7(9.1) — Special case for Dec. 20, 2020 to Jan. 16, 2021.

Notes: See 125.7(2) Notes. 125.7(9)(b) added, and (a) limited to "qualifying period"(a)-(c), by 2020 COVID bill #3, retroactive to introduction of 125.7 (April 11, 2020).

(9.1) Special case [for Dec. 20/20 to Jan. 16/21] — For the purposes of paragraph (9)(b), if the particular qualifying period is the eleventh qualifying period, then the immediately preceding qualifying period is deemed to be the ninth qualifying period.

Notes: 125.7(9.1) (added by 2021 budget bill #1, effective June 29, 2021) was announced in a Finance news release, Feb. 24, 2021 as giving applicants "more flexibility in determining the revenue decline for the wage and rent subsidies for the qualifying period from Dec. 20, 2020 to Jan. 16, 2021". The Backgrounder explains: "Qualifying applicants must demonstrate a decline in revenues between a current reference period and a prior reference period: either the same period in the previous year or their average revenue for the months of Jan. and Feb. 2020. To provide certainty for subsidy applicants at the start of a qualifying period, a deeming rule [125.7(9) — ed.] provides that an entity's percentage revenue decline for a qualifying period cannot be less than its percentage revenue decline for the immediately preceding qualifying period... it is proposed that ... an applicant's percentage revenue decline for the 11th qualifying period (Dec. 20, 2020 to Jan. 16, 2021) cannot be less than the applicant's percentage

revenue decline for the 9th qualifying period (Oct. 25, 2020 to Nov. 21, 2020). This provides greater flexibility for applicants, as the 11th and 10th qualifying periods both use the same reference months (Dec. 2020 over Dec. 2019 by default), which means the percentage revenue decline for those two periods would otherwise be the same."

(9.2) Greater of wage and recovery subsidies — For a qualifying period,

(a) if the amount of any deemed overpayment under subsection (2) is equal to or greater than the amount of any deemed overpayment under subsection (2.2), the amount of any deemed overpayment under subsection (2.2) is deemed to be nil; and

(b) if the amount of any deemed overpayment under subsection (2.2) is greater than the amount of any deemed overpayment under subsection (2), the amount of any deemed overpayment under subsection (2) is deemed to be nil.

Notes: This means an entity claims the higher of the Wage Subsidy (125.7(2)) or the Recovery Hiring Subsidy (125.7(2.2)), but cannot claim both, as the lower one is deemed to be nil (if they are equal, the 125.7(2.2) amount is deemed nil).

125.7(9.2) added by 2021 budget bill #1, effective June 29, 2021.

(10) Amending or revoking elections — An eligible entity may amend or revoke an election made under this section on or before the date that the application is due for the first qualifying period in respect of which the election is made.

Notes: 125.7(10) added by 2020 COVID bill #5, effective Sept. 27, 2020.

(11) Affiliated entities — For the purposes of the description of E in subsection (2.1), if two eligible entities are affiliated with the same eligible entity, they are deemed to be affiliated with each other.

Notes: 125.7(11) added by 2020 COVID bill #5, effective Sept. 27, 2020.

(12) Deeming rule — qualifying rent expense — For the purposes of the definition "qualifying rent expense" in subsection (1), an amount is deemed to have been paid by an eligible entity on the date it first became due under an agreement, and not at a later date, if the individual referred to in paragraph (b) of the definition "qualifying renter" in subsection (1) attests that the eligible entity intends to pay the amount due under the agreement no later than 60 days after the day on which the Minister makes the first refund under subsection 164(1.6) in respect of the amount deemed to have been paid (referred to in subsection (13) as the "payment deadline").

Related Provisions: 125.7(13) — Rule does not apply unless amount is actually paid by deadline.

Notes: 125.7(12) and (13) allow CERS (125.7(2.1)) to be paid even if the rent being subsidized has not yet been paid, as long as it is actually paid within 60 days of the CERS payment to the tenant. Added by 2021 COVID bill #1, effective Sept. 27, 2020.

(13) Deeming rule — qualifying rent expense — Subsection (12) is deemed not to have produced its effect if the amount due referred to in subsection (12) is not actually paid on or before the payment deadline.

Notes: See Notes to 125.7(12).

(14) Executive compensation — The amount of a refund made by the Minister to an eligible entity in respect of a deemed overpayment under subsection (2) on a particular date under subsection 164(1.6), in respect of any of the seventeenth qualifying period to the twenty-second qualifying period, is deemed to be an amount that has been refunded to the eligible entity on that particular date (for the taxation year in which the refund was made) in excess of the amount to which the eligible entity was entitled as a refund under this Act to the extent of the lesser of the amount of the refund and the amount determined by the formula

$$A - B$$

where

A is the executive compensation repayment amount of the eligible entity; and

B is the total of all amounts deemed to be an excess refund to the eligible entity under this subsection in respect of refunds made after the particular date.

884

Possible Future Amendment — CEWS while paying dividends or repurchasing shares

2021 budget bill #1 (Bill C-30) was amended by the Commons Finance Committee to add subsecs. 24(32.1) and (32.2):

(32.1) The Minister of Finance must prepare a report on proposed measures to

(a) prevent publicly traded companies and their subsidiaries from paying dividends or repurchasing their own shares while receiving the Canada Emergency Wage Subsidy, for the period that is after the tabling of the report under subsection (32.2); and

(b) recover wage subsidy amounts from publicly traded companies and their subsidiaries that paid dividends or repurchased their own shares while receiving the Canada Emergency Wage Subsidy, for the period that is before the tabling of the report under subsection (32.2).

(32.2) The Minister of Finance must cause the report to be tabled in each House of Parliament no later than 30 days after the day on which this Act receives royal assent or, if either House is not then sitting, on any of the first 15 days on which that House is sitting.

Related Provisions: 257 — Formula cannot calculate to less than zero.

Notes: This measure was described in the April 2021 federal Budget as follows:

Budget 2021 proposes to require a publicly listed corporation to repay wage subsidy amounts received for a qualifying period that begins after June 5, 2021 in the event that its aggregate compensation for specified executives during the 2021 calendar year exceeds its aggregate compensation for specified executives during the 2019 calendar year.

...

The amount of the wage subsidy required to be repaid would be equal to the lesser of:

- the total of all wage subsidy amounts received in respect of active employees for qualifying periods that begin after June 5, 2021; and

- the amount by which the corporation's aggregate specified executives' compensation for 2021 exceeds its aggregate specified executives' compensation for 2019.

This requirement to repay would be applied at the group level and would apply to wage subsidy amounts paid to any entity in the group.

A related measure may be introduced to recover CEWS from public companies that pay dividends while receiving CEWS, as per amendments made by the Commons Finance Committee before enactment of 2021 budget bill #1. See Possible Future Amendment above.

125.7(14) added by 2021 budget bill #1, effective June 29, 2021.

(15) Foreign currency — executive remuneration — For the purposes of paragraphs 261(2)(b) and (5)(c), amounts referred to in the definition "executive remuneration" in subsection (1) are deemed to arise on the last day of the eligible entity's fiscal period to which the amount relates and not at any other time.

Notes: 125.7(15) added by 2021 budget bill #1, effective June 29, 2021.

Notes [s. 125.7]: See 125.7(2) Notes. 125.7 added by 2020 COVID bill #2, effective April 11, 2020.

Definitions [s. 125.7]: "acquired assets" — 125.7(4.1)(a); "affiliated" — 125.7(11), 251.1; "amount" — 248(1); "arm's length" — 251(1); "associated" — 256; "base percentage" — 125.7(1), Reg. 8901.2(2); "baseline remuneration" — 125.7(1); "business", "business number" — 248(1); "calendar year" — *Interpretation Act* 37(1)(a); "Canada" — 255, *Interpretation Act* 35(1); "Canadian-controlled private corporation" — 125.7(7), 248(1); "cash method" — 28(1), 248(1); "corporation" — 248(1), *Interpretation Act* 35(1); "cost amount" — 248(1); "current reference period" — 125.7(1), Reg. 8901.2(3); "eighteenth qualifying period" — 125.7(1)"qualifying period"(c.96); "eighth qualifying period" — 125.7(1)"qualifying period"(c.5); "eleventh qualifying period" — 125.7(1)"qualifying period"(c.8); "eligible employee" — 125.7(1); "eligible entity" — 125.7(1), Reg. 8901.1; "eligible remuneration" — 125.7(1); "employed", "employee", "employer" — 248(1); "executive compensation repayment amount", "executive remuneration" — 125.7(1); "fair market value" — see 69(1) Notes; "fifteenth qualifying period" — 125.7(1)"qualifying period"(c.93); "fifth qualifying period" — 125.7(1)"qualifying period"(c.2); "first qualifying period" — 125.7(1)"qualifying period"(a); "fiscal period" — 249.1; "fourteenth qualifying period" — 125.7(1)"qualifying period"(c.92); "fourth qualifying period" — 125.7(1)"qualifying period"(c.1); "immovable" — Quebec *Civil Code* art. 900-907; "individual", "Minister" — 248(1); "month" — *Interpretation Act* 35(1); "nineteenth qualifying period" — 125.7(1)"qualifying period"(c.97); "ninth qualifying period" — 125.7(1)"qualifying period"(c.6); "partnership" — see 96(1) Notes; "payment deadline" — 125.7(12); "person", "prescribed", "principal amount" — 248(1); "prior reference period" — 125.7(1), Reg. 8901.2(4); "property" — 248(1); "province" — *Interpretation Act* 35(1); "provincial" — *Interpretation Act* 33(3), 35(1)"province"; "provincial pension plan" — *Canada Pension Plan* s. 3; "public health restriction",

"public institution" — 125.7(1); "public market" — 122.1(1), 248(1); "qualifying entity" — 125.7(1); "qualifying period" — 125.7(1), Reg. 8901.2(1); "qualifying property", "qualifying recovery entity", "qualifying rent expense", "qualifying renter" — 125.7(1); "qualifying revenue" — 125.7(1); "record" — 248(1); "recovery wage subsidy rate" — 125.7(1); "registered charity", "regulation" — 248(1); "related business" — 149.1(1); "rent subsidy percentage" — 125.7(1), Reg. 8901.2(5); "rent top-up percentage" — 125.7(1); "restricted activities" — 125.7(1)"public health restriction"(f); "retiring allowance" — 248(1); "revenue reduction percentage" — 125.7(1); "second qualifying period" — 125.7(1)"qualifying period"(b); "security" — *Interpretation Act* 35(1); "self-contained domestic establishment" — 248(1); "seller" — 125.7(4.1)(a); "series of transactions" — 248(10); "seventeenth qualifying period" — 125.7(1)"qualifying period"(c.95); "seventh qualifying period" — 125.7(1)"qualifying period"(c.4); "share", "shareholder" — 248(1); "sixteenth qualifying period" — 125.7(1)"qualifying period"(c.94); "sixth qualifying period" — 125.7(1)"qualifying period"(c.3); "specified percentage" — 125.7(1); "specified tenant" — 125.7(1)"public health restriction"(e); "taxation year" — 249; "taxpayer" — 248(1); "tenth qualifying period" — 125.7(1)"qualifying period"(c.7); "third qualifying period" — 125.7(1)"qualifying period"(c); "thirteenth qualifying period" — 125.7(1)"qualifying period"(c.91); "top-up percentage" — 125.7(1), Reg. 8901.2(6); "top-up revenue reduction percentage" — 125.7(1); "total base period remuneration" — 125.7(1); "total current period remuneration" — 125.7(1), (6.1); "trust" — 104(1), 248(1), (3); "twelfth qualifying period" — 125.7(1)"qualifying period"(c.9); "twentieth qualifying period" — 125.7(1)"qualifying period"(c.98); "twenty-first qualifying period" — 125.7(1)"qualifying period"(c.99); "twenty-second qualifying period" — 125.7(1)"qualifying period"(c.991); "written" — *Interpretation Act* 35(1)"writing".

Subdivision C — Rules Applicable to All Taxpayers

126. (1) Foreign tax deduction [foreign tax credit — non-business income] — A taxpayer who was resident in Canada at any time in a taxation year may deduct from the tax for the year otherwise payable under this Part by the taxpayer an amount equal to

(a) such part of any non-business-income tax paid by the taxpayer for the year to the government of a country other than Canada (except, where the taxpayer is a corporation, any such tax or part thereof that may reasonably be regarded as having been paid by the taxpayer in respect of income from a share of the capital stock of a foreign affiliate of the taxpayer) as the taxpayer may claim,

not exceeding, however,

(b) that proportion of the tax for the year otherwise payable under this Part by the taxpayer that

(i) the amount, if any, by which the total of the taxpayer's qualifying incomes exceeds the total of the taxpayer's qualifying losses

(A) for the year, if the taxpayer is resident in Canada throughout the year, and

(B) for the part of the year throughout which the taxpayer is resident in Canada, if the taxpayer is non-resident at any time in the year,

from sources in that country, on the assumption that

(C) no businesses were carried on by the taxpayer in that country,

(D) where the taxpayer is a corporation, it had no income from shares of the capital stock of a foreign affiliate of the taxpayer, and

(E) where the taxpayer is an individual,

(I) no amount was deducted under subsection 91(5) in computing the taxpayer's income for the year, and

(II) if the taxpayer deducted an amount under subsection 122.3(1) from the taxpayer's tax otherwise payable under this Part for the year, the taxpayer's income from employment in that country was not from a source in that country to the extent of the lesser of the amounts determined in respect thereof under paragraphs 122.3(1)(c) and (d) for the year,

is of

(ii) the total of

(A) the amount, if any, by which,

(I) if the taxpayer was resident in Canada throughout the year, the taxpayer's income for the year computed without reference to paragraph 20(1)(ww), and

(II) if the taxpayer was non-resident at any time in the year, the amount determined under paragraph 114(a) in respect of the taxpayer for the year

exceeds

(III) the total of all amounts each of which is an amount deducted under section 110.6 or paragraph 111(1)(b), or deductible under any of paragraphs 110(1)(d) to (g) and sections 112 and 113, in computing the taxpayer's taxable income for the year, and

(B) the amount, if any, added under section 110.5 in computing the taxpayer's taxable income for the year.

Related Provisions: 20(11), 20(12) — Deduction instead of credit for foreign taxes paid; 20(12) — Foreign non-business income tax; 94(3)(b) — Application to trust deemed resident in Canada; 104(22.1) — Foreign tax credit (FTC) allocated to beneficiary of trust; 110.5 — Optional addition to income to create FTC; 120.4(3)B(a) — FTC deductible against income-splitting tax; 126(1.1) — Application to authorized foreign bank; 126(6) — Separate deduction in respect of each country and source; 126(7)"tax for the year otherwise payable under this Part" — Tax otherwise payable; 138(8) — No deduction for tax paid on life insurance business income; 144(8.1) — Employees profit sharing plan — foreign tax deduction; 161(6.1) — Delay in interest on FTC adjustment; Canada-U.S. Tax Treaty:Art. XXIV:4 — Credit for U.S. citizen resident in Canada; Canada-U.S. Tax Treaty:Art. XXIX-B:6, 7 — Credit for U.S. estate taxes. See also at end of s. 126.

Notes: In general terms, the foreign tax credit (FTC) prevents double tax by allowing a credit to a Canadian resident for foreign income tax paid on foreign-source income, up to a limit of the Canadian tax on that income determined on a proportional basis. (For a non-resident, see 126(2.2)–(2.23).) The effect is that the taxpayer pays total tax equal to the higher of the two rates of tax (Canadian and foreign) on the foreign-source income. The actual implementation of the credit is complex. 126(1) covers non-business income such as dividends on which foreign tax was withheld; 126(2) covers income from carrying on business in a foreign country. See Notes to 126(7)"non-business-income tax" and "business-income tax".

The calculation is done on a country-by-country basis: 126(1)(b) (but CRA will stop asking for a breakdown of income from a mutual fund, as long as the information slips are consistent with the FTC claimed: VIEWS doc 2018-0761581C6 [2018 APFF Financial q.12]). An individual can claim only up to 15% foreign tax against tax on income from property: 126(7)"non-business-income tax"(b); any excess is allowed as deduction under 20(11). Unclaimed credits are also allowed under 20(12); and see 110.5 for a temporary addition to income to maximize the credit. See also Income Tax Folio S5-F2-C1 for detailed discussion and examples.

In 126(1)(b), "tax for the year otherwise payable…" is defined in 126(7). In the 126(1)(b) calculation, only certain deductions are allowed, so the denominator is not the same as taxable income.

If Canadian tax was payable on the income but was not paid and the year is statute-barred, Taxpayer Relief cannot be used to claim a FTC, as "tax for the year" under 126(7) is based on "tax payable", which under 248(2) is the tax "as fixed by assessment".

The attribution rules in 56(4.1), 74.1 and 75(2) attribute income but not foreign tax, resulting in a mismatch so that no FTC can be claimed: VIEWS doc 2007-0233701C6. However, deductions under 20(11) and (12) can be claimed, since the income attributed is *net* income from the source after such deductions.

No FTC is available to the owner for tax paid by a limited-liability corp, as the LLC is a separate person: 2010-0369311E5 (see also Canada-US tax treaty Art. IV:6). Where a trust allocates foreign income to a beneficiary under 104(22), the FTC is available under 104(22.1)–(22.4) but 20(11)–(12) cannot be used; see IT-201R2.

A part-year resident can claim an FTC for foreign tax paid for the entire year: VIEWS doc 2013-0480311C6 [2013 STEP q.5].

CRA considers a gain on a *deemed* disposition to be Canadian-source income ineligible for FTC: doc 2014-052523117.

See Vidal, *Introduction to International Tax in Canada* (Carswell, 8th ed., 2020), chap. 14; Li & Cockfield, *International Taxation in Canada*, 4th ed. (LexisNexis, 2018), chap. 11; Snider, "The Foreign Tax Credit Rules", 2001 Cdn Tax Foundation conference report, pp. 14:1-42; Welters, "Foreign Tax Credits and the Locality of the Source of Employment Income", 21(8) *Taxation of Executive Compensation & Retirement* (Federated Press) 1278-79 (April 2010); Vo, "Foreign Tax Credits: Problems with Timing", 2(2) *Canadian Tax Focus* (ctf.ca) 6 (Aug. 2012); Singh & Spiro, "The Canadian Income Tax Treatment of Foreign Taxes", 2014 conference report, 22:1-37; Bernstein, "Canadian Foreign Tax Credit: US Inversions", 24(7) *Canadian Tax Highlights* (ctf.ca) 9-10 (July 2016).

For the exchange rate to use in computing the credit, see 261(2) and VIEWS docs 2010-037596117, 2019-0824381C6 [2019 CTF q.2] (use date of payment of foreign tax).

The foreign-source income should be included before deducting foreign tax: *Yankulov*, 2008 TCC 657.

Where the foreign tax is reassessed so that the FTC is reduced, the taxpayer has 90 days to report and pay the additional Canadian tax with no interest: 161(6.1).

As an alternative (or in addition) to the FTC, relief may be available under Canada's bilateral tax treaties. See the Canada-U.S. and Canada-U.K. treaties reproduced at the end of this book. Many foreign countries, like Canada, also offer an FTC in respect of income not arising in those countries.

For the parallel provincial FTC see Snider & Platt, "The Ontario Foreign Tax Credit Regime After Harmonization", 16 *Provincial Tax News* (CCH) 1-4 (Sept. 2012); Lamothe, "The Missing Provincial Tax Credit for Foreign Business-Income Tax", 6(2) *Canadian Tax Focus [CTFo]* (ctf.ca) 10 (May 2016); McLeod & Pulla, "Misalignment of Federal and Provincial Tax Credits", 9(4) *CTFo* 8 (Nov. 2019). Canada-Brazil tax sparing does not apply to Ontario tax: VIEWS doc 2016-063271117. A provincial FTC cannot be appealed to the TCC: *Baluyot*, 2007 TCC 682 (FCA appeal discontinued A-566-07), and Notes to 169(1).

The FTC for a US citizen resident in Canada is determined under Canada-US treaty Art. XXIV:4. See *Glen Taylor*, [2000] 3 C.T.C. 456 (FCTD); VIEWS doc 2010-0355551E5.

In *Dagenais*, [2000] 2 C.T.C. 2022 (TCC), no FTC was allowed for US tax on lottery winnings because they are not income under the ITA. See Sider & Beaulne, "FTCs: Treaty Versus Act", 8(5) *Canadian Tax Highlights* (ctf.ca) 35 (May 2000).

See also VIEWS docs 2010-0359571E5 (income from a TV broadcast is royalty income eligible for FTC under 126(1)); 2012-046165117 (loss-consolidation structure using 110.5 to prevent wasting FTC was acceptable); 2013-047638117 (FTC for trust deemed resident under 94(3)); 2013-0480321C6 (US tax paid by Canadian resident owner of an LLC qualifies for credit against FAPI from the LLC); 2016-0676431E5 (FTC on employees profit sharing plan); 2019-083221117 (cross-border restricted share units granted to employees who work in both Canada and another country).

See Notes to 15(1) re forms of ownership of U.S. vacation property.

In determining net foreign business income, the formulary apportionment method used for US state taxes is not appropriate; see VIEWS doc 2006-018191117.

126(1)(b)(ii)(A)(III) amended by 2021 budget bill #1, effective July 2021, to change "110(1)(d) to (d.3), (f) and (g)" to "110(1)(d) to (g)" (effectively adding (e)).

126(1)(b)(ii)(A)(III) amended by 2017 budget bill #1 to delete reference to 110(1)(j), effective 2018.

126(1) amended by 2000 Budget (last change effective for 1998 and later taxation years), 2001, 1999 and 1998 Budgets, 1993 technical bill.

Income Tax Folios: S5-F2-C1: Foreign tax credit [replaces IT-270R3, IT-395R2, IT-520].

Interpretation Bulletins: IT-167R6: Registered pension plans — employee's contributions; IT-201R2: Foreign tax credit — trust and beneficiaries; IT-273R2: Government assistance — general comments; IT-243R4: Dividend refund to private corporations; IT-379R: Employees profit sharing plans — allocations to beneficiaries; IT-393R2: Election re tax on rents and timber royalties — non-residents; IT-506: Foreign income taxes as a deduction from income.

I.T. Technical News: 30 (tax avoidance); 31R2 (social security taxes and the foreign tax credit).

CRA Audit Manual: 15.11.4: Tax treaties — relief from double taxation.

Forms: T2 Sched. 5: Tax calculation supplementary — corporations; T2 Sched. 21: Federal and provincial or territorial foreign income tax credits and federal logging tax credit; T3FFT: T3 Federal foreign tax credits; T3PFT: T3 Provincial or territorial foreign tax credits; T2036: Provincial or territorial foreign tax credits; T2209: Federal foreign tax credits.

(1.1) Authorized foreign bank — In applying subsections 20(12) and (12.1) and this section in respect of an authorized foreign bank,

(a) the bank is deemed, for the purposes of subsections (1), (4) to (5), (6) and (7), to be resident in Canada in respect of its Canadian banking business;

(b) the references in subsection 20(12) and paragraph (1)(a) to "country other than Canada" shall be read as a reference to "country that is neither Canada nor a country in which the taxpayer is resident at any time in the taxation year";

(c) the reference in subparagraph (1)(b)(i) to "from sources in that country" shall be read as a reference to "in respect of its Canadian banking business from sources in that country";

(d) subparagraph (1)(b)(ii) shall be read as follows:

"(ii) the lesser of

(A) the taxpayer's taxable income earned in Canada for the year, and

(B) the total of the taxpayer's income for the year from its Canadian banking business and the amount determined in respect of the taxpayer under subparagraph 115(1)(a)(vii) for the year.";

(e) in computing the non-business income tax paid by the bank for a taxation year to the government of a country other than Canada, there shall be included only taxes that relate to amounts that are included in computing the bank's taxable income earned in Canada from its Canadian banking business; and

(f) the definition "tax-exempt income" in subsection (7) shall be read as follows:

"tax-exempt income" means income of a taxpayer from a source in a particular country in respect of which

(a) the taxpayer is, because of a comprehensive agreement or convention for the elimination of double taxation on income, which has the force of law in the particular country and to which a country in which the taxpayer is resident is a party, entitled to an exemption from all income or profits taxes, imposed in the particular country, to which the agreement or convention applies, and

(b) no income or profits tax to which the agreement or convention does not apply is imposed in the particular country;".

Notes: 126(1.1) added by 2001 technical bill, effective June 28, 1999. See Notes to 248(1)"authorized foreign bank".

(2) Idem [foreign tax credit — business income] — Where a taxpayer who was resident in Canada at any time in a taxation year carried on business in the year in a country other than Canada, the taxpayer may deduct from the tax for the year otherwise payable under this Part by the taxpayer an amount not exceeding the least of

(a) such part of the total of the business-income tax paid by the taxpayer for the year in respect of businesses carried on by the taxpayer in that country and the taxpayer's unused foreign tax credits in respect of that country for the 10 taxation years immediately preceding and the 3 taxation years immediately following the year as the taxpayer may claim,

(b) the amount determined under subsection (2.1) for the year in respect of businesses carried on by the taxpayer in that country, and

(c) the amount by which

(i) the tax for the year otherwise payable under this Part by the taxpayer

exceeds

(ii) the amount or the total of amounts, as the case may be, deducted under subsection (1) by the taxpayer from the tax for the year otherwise payable under this Part.

Related Provisions: 87(2)(z) — Amalgamation; 88(1)(e.7) — Winding-up; 94(3)(b) — Application to trust deemed resident in Canada; 104(22.1) — FTC allocated to beneficiary of trust; 110.5 — Optional addition to income to create FTC; 120.4(3)B(a) — FTC deductible against income-splitting tax; 126(2.1) — Amount determined for para. (2)(b); 126(2.3) — Rules relating to unused FTC; 126(6) — Separate deduction in respect of each country; 129(4)"non-eligible refundable dividend tax on hand"(a)(ii)(C) — Effect on dividend refund; 138(8) — No FTC for life insurance business; 152(6) — Reassessment; 152(6)(f.1) — Minister required to reassess past year to allow unused FTC; 161(6.1) — Delay in interest on FTC adjustment; 161(7)(a)(iv.1), 164(5)(e), 164(5.1) — Effect of loss carryback; 261(7)(a), 261(15) — Functional currency reporting. See also at end of s. 126.

Notes: See Notes to 126(1). For interpretation where a corporation has permanent establishments in several provinces and a foreign country, see VIEWS doc 2003-0051241E5. For the meaning of "paid by the taxpayer", see Notes to 126(7)"non-business-income tax".

126(2)(a) amended to change "7" to "10" by 2004 Budget, for unused foreign tax credits computed for tax years that end after March 22, 2004. (This parallels a change to 111(1)(a).)

Income Tax Folios: S5-F2-C1: Foreign tax credit [replaces IT-270R3, IT-395R2, IT-520].

Interpretation Bulletins: IT-243R4: Dividend refund to private corporations; IT-273R2: Government assistance — general comments.

I.T. Technical News: 8 (treatment of United States unitary state taxes).

CRA Audit Manual: 11.3.4: Tax credits; 15.11.4: Tax treaties — relief from double taxation.

Forms: T2 Sched. 5: Tax calculation supplementary — corporations; T2 Sched. 21: Federal and provincial or territorial foreign income tax credits and federal logging tax credit; T3FFT: T3 Federal foreign tax credits; T3PFT: T3 Provincial or territorial foreign tax credits; T2036: Provincial or territorial foreign tax credits; T2209: Federal foreign tax credits.

(2.1) Amount determined for purposes of para. (2)(b) — For the purposes of paragraph (2)(b), the amount determined under this subsection for a year in respect of businesses carried on by a taxpayer in a country other than Canada is the total of

(a) that proportion of the tax for the year otherwise payable under this Part by the taxpayer that

(i) the amount, if any, by which the total of the taxpayer's qualifying incomes exceeds the total of the taxpayer's qualifying losses

(A) for the year, if the taxpayer is resident in Canada throughout the year, and

(B) for the part of the year throughout which the taxpayer is resident in Canada, if the taxpayer is non-resident at any time in the year,

from businesses carried on by the taxpayer in that country

is of

(ii) the total of

(A) the amount, if any, by which

(I) if the taxpayer is resident in Canada throughout the year, the taxpayer's income for the year computed without reference to paragraph 20(1)(ww), and

(II) if the taxpayer is non-resident at any time in the year, the amount determined under paragraph 114(a) in respect of the taxpayer for the year

exceeds

(III) the total of all amounts each of which is an amount deducted under section 110.6 or paragraph 111(1)(b), or deductible under any of paragraphs 110(1)(d) to (g) and sections 112 and 113, in computing the taxpayer's taxable income for the year, and

(B) the amount, if any, added under section 110.5 in computing the taxpayer's taxable income for the year, and

(b) that proportion of the amount, if any, added under subsection 120(1) to the tax for the year otherwise payable under this Part by the taxpayer that

(i) the amount determined under subparagraph (a)(i) in respect of the country

is of

(ii) the amount, if any, by which,

(A) where section 114 does not apply to the taxpayer in respect of the year, the taxpayer's income for the year, and

(B) where section 114 applies to the taxpayer in respect of the year, the total of the taxpayer's income for the period or periods referred to in paragraph 114(a) and the amount that would be determined under paragraph 114(b) in respect of the taxpayer for the year if subsection 115(1) were read without reference to paragraphs 115(1)(d) to (f)

exceeds

(C) the taxpayer's income earned in the year in a province (within the meaning assigned by subsection 120(4)).

Related Provisions: 126(6)(c) — Incomes deemed from separate sources. See also at end of s. 126.

Notes: See Notes to 126(1).

126(2.1)(a)(ii)(A)(III) amended by 2021 budget bill #1, effective July 2021, to change "110(1)(d) to (d.3), (f) and (g)" to "110(1)(d) to (g)" (effectively adding (e)).

126(2.1)(a)(ii)(A)(III) amended by 2017 budget bill #1 to delete reference to 110(1)(j), effective 2018.

126(2.1) amended by 2000 Budget (last change effective for 2000 and later taxation years), 2001, 1999 and 1998 Budgets and 1993 and 1991 technical bills.

Income Tax Folios: S5-F2-C1: Foreign tax credit [replaces IT-270R3, IT-395R2, IT-520].

Forms: T3PFT: T3 Provincial or territorial foreign tax credits; T2036: Provincial or territorial foreign tax credits.

(2.2) Non-resident's foreign tax deduction — If at any time in a taxation year a taxpayer who is not at that time resident in Canada disposes of a property that was deemed by subsection 48(2), as it read in its application before 1993, or by paragraph 128.1(4)(e), as it read in its application before October 2, 1996, to be taxable Canadian property of the taxpayer, the taxpayer may deduct from the tax for the year otherwise payable under this Part by the taxpayer an amount equal to the lesser of

(a) the amount of any non-business-income tax paid by the taxpayer for the year to the government of a country other than Canada that can reasonably be regarded as having been paid by the taxpayer in respect of any gain or profit from the disposition of the property, and

(b) that proportion of the tax for the year otherwise payable under this Part by the taxpayer that

(i) the taxable capital gain from the disposition of that property

is of

(ii) if the taxpayer is non-resident throughout the year, the taxpayer's taxable income earned in Canada for the year determined without reference to paragraphs 115(1)(d) to (f), and

(iii) if the taxpayer is resident in Canada at any time in the year, the amount that would have been the taxpayer's taxable income earned in Canada for the year if the part of the year throughout which the taxpayer was non-resident were the whole taxation year.

Related Provisions: 114 — Residence in Canada for part of year; 126(2.21)–(2.23) — Credit for former resident; 115(1) — Non-resident's taxable income; 126(7) — "tax for the year otherwise payable under this Part". See also at end of s. 126.

Notes: 126(2.2) amended by 2001 technical bill (last change effective for 1998 and later taxation years) and 1993 technical bill.

Interpretation Bulletins: IT-273R2: Government assistance — general comments; IT-451R: Deemed disposition and acquisition on ceasing to be or becoming resident.

(2.21) Former resident — deduction — If at any particular time in a particular taxation year a non-resident individual disposes of a property that the individual last acquired because of the application, at any time (in this subsection referred to as the "acquisition time") after October 1, 1996, of paragraph 128.1(4)(c), there may be deducted from the individual's tax otherwise payable under this Part for the year (in this subsection referred to as the "emigration year") that includes the time immediately before the acquisition time an amount not exceeding the lesser of

(a) the total of all amounts each of which is the amount of any business-income tax or non-business-income tax paid by the individual for the particular year

(i) where the property is real or immovable property situated in a country other than Canada,

(A) to the government of that country, or

(B) to the government of a country with which Canada has a tax treaty at the particular time and in which the individual is resident at the particular time, or

(ii) where the property is not real or immovable property, to the government of a country with which Canada has a tax treaty at the particular time and in which the individual is resident at the particular time,

that can reasonably be regarded as having been paid in respect of that portion of any gain or profit from the disposition of the property that accrued while the individual was resident in Canada and before the time the individual last ceased to be resident in Canada, and

(b) the amount, if any, by which

(i) the amount of tax under this Part that was, after taking into account the application of this subsection in respect of dispositions that occurred before the particular time, otherwise payable by the individual for the emigration year

exceeds

(ii) the amount of such tax that would have been payable if the particular property had not been deemed by subsection 128.1(4) to have been disposed of in the emigration year.

Related Provisions: 119 — Former resident — credit for tax paid; 126(2.22) — Parallel credit to trust after distribution to non-resident beneficiary; 126(2.23) — Reduction where foreign tax credit available under foreign system; 128.3 — Shares acquired on rollover deemed to be same shares for 126(2.21); 152(6)(f.1) — Minister required to reassess past year to allow credit; 161(7)(a)(iv.1), 164(5)(e), 164(5.1) — Effect of carryback of loss; Canada-U.S. Tax Treaty:Art. XIII:1 — Gain on real property taxable by country in which property is situated.

Notes: 126(2.21) added by 2001 technical bill, for 1996 and later tax years. It addresses the case where former resident of Canada X is subject to tax in another country on a gain that accrued while X was resident in Canada, and that was subject to Canadian tax on emigration due to 128.1(4).

The best way to alleviate such results is to modify Canada's tax treaties to ensure appropriate recognition for the Canadian tax that arises on departure. (This has now been done in many recent treaties. See Notes to 128.1(4).) However, since treaty changes take years, 126(2.21) provides interim relief in the form of a limited credit against Canadian tax that arises in the year of departure from Canada, for post-departure foreign taxes. These foreign taxes can comprise both business-income and non-business-income taxes (defined in subsection 126(7)). 126(2.22) provides similar limited credits against a trust's Canadian tax that arose in the year of a distribution by the trust to a non-resident beneficiary, for the beneficiary's subsequent foreign taxes. It is intended that these interim foreign tax credits will be reviewed by the Government as appropriate treaty changes are put in place.

126(2.21) and (2.22) apply, in most cases, only for taxes paid to countries with which Canada has a tax treaty. Exceptions are provided for taxes imposed by a foreign country on gains on real property situated in that country. In keeping with the general international principle that the country in which real property is located has the first right to tax gains on that property, Canada will always provide credit for such taxes, regardless whether Canada has a tax treaty with the particular country.

126(2.21) cannot be used to reduce departure tax on a corporation's shares by Canadian withholding tax on a deemed dividend on windup of that corporation, as it applies only to foreign tax: VIEWS doc 2011-0427211E5.

A 126(2.21) reassessment is subject to the 152(4) deadline, and CRA says 152(4.2) does not allow extending the deadline for the emigration year (though it does not explain why), but that a waiver can be filed to keep the year open: docs 2016-0660421E5, 2016-0673171E5.

"Country" in para. (a) includes Hong Kong and Taiwan: see Notes to 219.2.

126(2.21)(a)(i) opening words and (a)(ii) amended by 2002-2013 technical bill (Part 4 — bijuralism), effective June 26, 2013, to add "or immovable".

Income Tax Folios: S5-F2-C1: Foreign tax credit [replaces IT-270R3, IT-395R2, IT-520].

(2.22) Former resident — trust beneficiary — If at any particular time in a particular taxation year a non-resident individual disposes of a property that the individual last acquired at any time (in this subsection referred to as the "acquisition time") on a distribution after October 1, 1996 to which paragraphs 107(2)(a) to (c) do not apply only because of subsection 107(5), the trust may deduct from its tax otherwise payable under this Part for the year (in this subsection referred to as the "distribution year") that includes the acquisition time an amount not exceeding the lesser of

(a) the total of all amounts each of which is the amount of any business-income tax or non-business-income tax paid by the individual for the particular year

(i) where the property is real or immovable property situated in a country other than Canada,

(A) to the government of that country, or

(B) to the government of a country with which Canada has a tax treaty at the particular time and in which the individual is resident at the particular time, or

(ii) where the property is not real or immovable property, to the government of a country with which Canada has a tax treaty at the particular time and in which the individual is resident at the particular time,

that can reasonably be regarded as having been paid in respect of that portion of any gain or profit from the disposition of the property that accrued before the distribution and after the latest of the times, before the distribution, at which

(iii) the trust became resident in Canada,

(iv) the individual became a beneficiary under the trust, or

(v) the trust acquired the property, and

(b) the amount, if any, by which

(i) the amount of tax under this Part that was, after taking into account the application of this subsection in respect of dispositions that occurred before the particular time, otherwise payable by the trust for the distribution year

exceeds

(ii) the amount of such tax that would have been payable by the trust for the distribution year if the particular property had not been distributed to the individual.

Related Provisions: 104(22.1) — FTC to beneficiary of trust; 126(2.23) — Reduction where FTC available under foreign system; 128.3 — Shares acquired on rollover deemed to be same shares for 126(2.22); 152(6)(f.1) — Minister required to reassess past year to allow credit; 161(7)(a)(iv.1), 164(5)(e), 164(5.1) — Effect of carryback of loss; 220(4.6)–(4.63) — Security for tax on distribution of taxable Canadian property by trust to non-resident beneficiary; Canada-U.S. Tax Treaty:Art. XIII:1 — Gain on real property taxable by country in which property is situated.

Notes: 126(2.22)(a)(i) opening words and (a)(ii) amended by 2002-2013 technical bill (Part 4 — bijuralism), effective June 26, 2013, to add "or immovable".

126(2.22) added by 2001 technical bill, effective for 1996 and later taxation years. See Notes to 126(2.21).

(2.23) Where foreign credit available — For the purposes of subsections (2.21) and (2.22), in computing, in respect of the disposition of a property by an individual in a taxation year, the total amount of taxes paid by the individual for the year to one or more governments of countries other than Canada, there shall be deducted any tax credit (or other reduction in the amount of a tax) to which the individual was entitled for the year, under the law of any of those countries or under a tax treaty between Canada and any of those countries, because of taxes paid or payable by the individual under this Act in respect of the disposition or a previous disposition of the property.

Related Provisions: 128.3 — Shares acquired on rollover deemed to be same shares for 126(2.23).

Notes: 126(2.23) added by 2001 technical bill, for 1996 and later taxation years.

(2.3) Rules relating to unused foreign tax credit — For the purposes of this section,

(a) the amount claimed under paragraph (2)(a) by a taxpayer for a taxation year in respect of a country shall be deemed to be in respect of the business-income tax paid by the taxpayer for the year in respect of businesses carried on by the taxpayer in that country to the extent of the amount of that tax, and the remainder, if any, of the amount so claimed shall be deemed to be in respect of the taxpayer's unused foreign tax credits in respect of that country that may be claimed for the taxation year;

(b) no amount may be claimed under paragraph (2)(a) in computing a taxpayer's tax payable under this Part for a particular taxation year in respect of the taxpayer's unused foreign tax credit in respect of a country for a taxation year until the taxpayer's unused foreign tax credits in respect of that country for taxation years preceding the taxation year that may be claimed for the particular taxation year have been claimed; and

(c) an amount in respect of a taxpayer's unused foreign tax credit in respect of a country for a taxation year may be claimed under paragraph (2)(a) in computing the taxpayer's tax payable under this Part for a particular taxation year only to the extent that it exceeds the aggregate of all amounts each of which is the amount that may reasonably be considered to have been claimed in respect of that unused foreign tax credit in computing the taxpayer's tax payable under this Part for a taxation year preceding the particular taxation year.

Related Provisions: 87(2)(z) — Amalgamations; 88(1)(e.7) — Winding-up.

Notes: 126(2.3)(b), (c) amended by 2000 Budget, for 2001 and later taxation years.

Income Tax Folios: S5-F2-C1: Foreign Tax Credit [replaces IT-270R3, IT-395R2, IT-520].

(3) Employees of international organizations — Where an individual is resident in Canada at any time in a taxation year, there may be deducted from the individual's tax for the year otherwise payable under this Part an amount equal to that proportion of the tax for the year otherwise payable under this Part by the individual that

(a) the individual's income

(i) for the year, if the individual is resident in Canada throughout the year, and

(ii) for the part of the year throughout which the individual was resident in Canada, if the individual is non-resident at any time in the year,

from employment with an international organization (other than a prescribed international organization), as defined for the purposes of section 2 of the *Foreign Missions and International Organizations Act*

is of

(b) the amount, if any, by which

(i) if the taxpayer is resident in Canada throughout the year, the taxpayer's income for the year computed without reference to paragraph 20(1)(ww), and

(ii) if the taxpayer is non-resident at any time in the year, the amount determined under paragraph 114(a) in respect of the taxpayer for the year

exceeds

(iii) the total of all amounts each of which is an amount deducted under section 110.6 or paragraph 111(1)(b), or deductible under any of paragraphs 110(1)(d) to (d.3), (f) and (g), in computing the taxpayer's taxable income for the year,

except that the amount deductible under this subsection in computing the individual's tax payable under this Part for the year may not exceed that proportion of the total of all amounts each of which is an amount paid by the individual to the organization as a levy (the proceeds of which are used to defray expenses of the organization), computed by reference to the remuneration received by the individual in the year from the organization in a manner similar to the manner in which income tax is computed, that

(c) the individual's income for the year from employment with the organization

is of

(d) the amount that would be the individual's income for the year from employment with the organization if this Act were read without reference to paragraph 81(1)(a).

Related Provisions: 110(1)(f)(iii), (iv) — Deductions for income from certain international organizations; 126(7)"tax for the year otherwise payable under this Part" — Tax for year otherwise payable defined. See also at end of s. 126.

Notes: OECD employees do not qualify for this credit: VIEWS doc 2006-0211341E5 (though the CRA was reconsidering its position then). Tax withheld by the EU does not qualify: 2013-0500491E5, 2016-0634231I7.

Income from certain "prescribed" international organizations (listed in Reg. 8900(1)) is excluded because there is a deduction from taxable income under 110(1)(f)(iii). See also 110(1)(f)(iv).

S. 2 of the *Foreign Missions and International Organizations Act*, S.C. 1991, c. 41, defines "international organization" as follows:

> "international organization" means an inter-governmental organization, whether or not established by treaty, of which two or more states are members, and includes an inter-governmental conference in which two or more states participate;

The Organization of American States and the Inter-American Institute for Cooperation on Agriculture are international organizations: VIEWS doc 2000-0054485.

126(3)(b)(iii) amended by 2017 budget bill #1 to delete reference to 110(1)(j), effective 2018.

126(3) amended by 2001 technical bill (effective for 1998 and later taxation years), 2001, 2000 and 1999 Budgets and 1993 and 1992 technical bills.

Regulations: 8900(1) (prescribed international organization for para. (a) closing words).

(4) Portion of foreign tax not included — For the purposes of this Act, an income or profits tax paid by a person resident in Canada to the government of a country other than Canada does not include a tax, or that portion of a tax, imposed by that government that would not be imposed if the person were not entitled under section 113 or this section to a deduction in respect of the tax or that portion of the tax.

Related Provisions: 126(5) — Foreign oil and gas levies deemed to be income or profits tax; 126(6)(a) — Interpretation of "government of a country...". See also at end of s. 126.

Notes: Note that the rule in 126(4) applies for purposes of the entire Act.

CRA considers that "income or profits tax" (IPT) includes a tax on gross revenue if it is under a statute that allows annual election to pay on gross or net, and the tax rate on net income is not unreasonably high: VIEWS doc 2013-0508171C6 [2013 CTF conf]. IPT includes Guatemala's tax on gross revenue and its withholding tax on dividends (2011-0431031E5), but not the former Mexican Assets Tax (2003-0022651E5), nor certain Costa Rica withholding tax (2009-0337531E5, 2010-0356621E5). Foreign oil and gas levies are deemed to be IPT: 126(5).

126(4) applies to deny a foreign tax credit (FTC) if the foreign country imposes tax only if a FTC is available. This applies to certain taxes of Kyrgyz Republic (VIEWS doc 2000-0062815) and Costa Rica (2009-0337531E5, 2010-0356621E5).

126(4) amended by 2001 technical bill, effective June 28, 1999, to use the term "government of a country other than Canada" (see 126(6)).

(4.1) No economic profit — If a taxpayer acquires a property, other than a capital property, at any time after February 23, 1998 and it is reasonable to expect at that time that the taxpayer will not realize an economic profit in respect of the property for the period that begins at that time and ends when the taxpayer next disposes of the property, the total amount of all income or profits taxes (referred to as the "foreign tax" for the purpose of subsection 20(12.1)) in respect of the property for the period, and in respect of related transactions, paid by the taxpayer for any year to the government of any country other than Canada, is not included in computing the taxpayer's business-income tax or non-business-income tax for any taxation year.

Related Provisions: 20(12.1) — Deduction from income for amount disallowed as credit by 126(4.1); 126(4.4) — Certain dispositions ignored for 126(4.1); 126(6)(a) — Interpretation of "government of a country...".

Notes: 126(4.1) amended by 2001 technical bill, effective June 28, 1999; added by 1998 Budget for 1998 and later taxation years. See 126(7)"economic profit". The foreign tax credit operates on a country-by-country pooling basis, so income from a source taxed in a foreign country at a higher rate than in Canada creates excess credits that may be used to reduce Canadian tax on income from other sources in the country that are taxed at rates lower than the Canadian rate. This cross-crediting can make an otherwise uneconomic transaction attractive, and can amount to a subsidy by the Canadian tax system for such transactions. To limit this effect, 126(4.1) denies the credit in situations where, without the credit, there is no expected economic profit.

(4.11) [Foreign tax credit generator —] Denial of foreign tax credit — If a taxpayer is a member of a partnership, any income or profits tax paid to the government of a particular country other than Canada — in respect of the income of the partnership for a period during which the taxpayer's direct or indirect share of the income of the partnership under the income tax laws (referred to in

subsection (4.12) as the "relevant foreign tax law") of any country other than Canada under the laws of which any income of the partnership is subject to income taxation, is less than the taxpayer's direct or indirect share of the income for the purposes of this Act — is not included in computing the taxpayer's business-income tax or non-business-income tax for any taxation year.

Related Provisions: 91(4.1), Reg. 5907(1.03) — Parallel rules; 126(4.12) — Exceptions; 126(4.13) — Look-through rule for tiered partnerships.

Notes: 126(4.11)–(4.13) are part of the "foreign tax credit generator" rules, along with 91(4.1)–(4.7) and Reg. 5907(1.03)–(1.09). These rules, first announced in the March 2010 federal budget, seek to prevent artificial schemes that generate foreign tax credits where the burden of the foreign tax is not actually being borne by the taxpayer.

Finance confirmed at the May 2010 IFA conference that these proposals "are intended to apply only to hybrid instruments that are a common feature of all the targeted schemes": see Barnicke & Huynh, "IFA 2010 on Foreign Affiliates", 18(6) *Canadian Tax Highlights* (ctf.ca) 9-10 (June 2010), with examples.

For discussion see Barnicke & Huynh, "Foreign Tax Credit Generators", 18(4) *Canadian Tax Highlights* [*CTH*] (ctf.ca) 6-7 (April 2010) and "Foreign Tax Credit Generators: Redraft", 18(10) *CTH* 7-8 (Oct. 2010); Juneja & Turner, "Foreign Tax Credit Generator Proposals — An Inadvertent Attack on Hybrids?", 2001 *Tax Topics* (CCH) 1-6 (July 15, 2010); Buttenham & Matteo, "The Foreign Tax Credit Generator Proposals", XVI(1) *International Tax Planning* [*ITP*] (Federated Press) 1092-96 (2010); CBA/CICA Joint Committee submission to Finance, May 3, 2010 (on *Taxnet Pro*), pp. 7-16 (following the submission that the rules were too broad, Finance changed the parallel amendments at 91(4.1)-(4.7) and Reg. 5907(1.03)-(1.09)); McDowell et al., "Upstream Loans", 2012 Cdn Tax Foundation conference report, 21:1-29; Bradley & Buttenham, "The New Foreign Tax Credit Generator Rules", XVIII(2) *ITP* 1228-32 (2012); Barnicke & Huynh, "Losing the FAT", 21(2) *CTH* 1-2 (Feb. 2013); O'Hagan, "Foreign Tax Credit Generator Rules Can Cause FAPI Heartache", 2(3) *The Newsletter* (Tax Executives Institute, Toronto Chapter) 8-10 (March 2013).

For a foreign tax credit generator plan that preceded these rules and succeeded at the TCC, see *4145356 Canada*, in Notes to 126(7)"non-business-income tax".

126(4.11) added by 2002-2013 technical bill (Part 5 — technical), effective for income or profits tax paid for taxation years of a taxpayer that end after March 4, 2010; but for taxation years of the taxpayer that end before Aug. 28, 2010, read both instances of "direct or indirect share" as "share".

(4.12) Exceptions — For the purposes of subsection (4.11), a taxpayer is not to be considered to have a lesser direct or indirect share of the income of a partnership under the relevant foreign tax law than for the purposes of this Act solely because of one or more of the following:

(a) a difference between the relevant foreign tax law and this Act in the manner of

(i) computing the income of the partnership, or

(ii) allocating the income of the partnership because of the admission to, or withdrawal from, the partnership of any of its members;

(b) the treatment of the partnership as a corporation under the relevant foreign tax law; or

(c) the fact that the taxpayer is not treated as a corporation under the relevant foreign tax law.

Related Provisions: 91(4.3), Reg. 5907(1.05) — Parallel rules; 126(4.13) — Look-through rule for tiered partnerships.

Notes: See Notes to 126(4.11). 126(4.12) added by 2002-2013 technical bill (Part 5 — technical), effective for income or profits tax paid for taxation years of a taxpayer that end after March 4, 2010; but for taxation years of the taxpayer that end before Aug. 28, 2010, read "direct or indirect share" as "share".

(4.13) Tiered partnerships — For the purposes of subsections (4.11) and (4.12), if a taxpayer is (or is deemed by this subsection to be) a member of a particular partnership that is a member of another partnership, the taxpayer is deemed to be a member of the other partnership.

Related Provisions: 91(4.4) — Parallel rules; 93.1(3) — Parallel rule for FAPI.

Notes: See Notes to 126(4.11). 126(4.13) added by 2002-2013 technical bill (Part 5 — technical), effective for income or profits tax paid for taxation years of a taxpayer that end after Aug 27, 2010.

(4.2) Short-term securities acquisitions — If at any particular time a taxpayer disposes of a property that is a share or debt obligation and the period that began at the time the taxpayer last acquired the property and ended at the particular time is one year or less, the amount included in business-income tax or non-business-income

tax paid by the taxpayer for a particular taxation year on account of all taxes (referred to in this subsection and subsections (4.3) and 161(6.1) as the "foreign tax") that are

(a) paid by the taxpayer in respect of dividends or interest in respect of the period that are included in computing the taxpayer's income from the property for any taxation year,

(b) otherwise included in business-income tax or non-business-income tax for any taxation year, and

(c) similar to the tax levied under Part XIII

shall, subject to subsection (4.3), not exceed the amount determined by the formula

$$A \times (B - C) \times D / E$$

where

A   is

(a) if the foreign tax would otherwise be included in business-income tax, the total of

(i) that proportion of 26.5% that the number of days in the taxation year that are in 2011 is of the number of days in the taxation year, and

(ii) that proportion of 25% that the number of days in the taxation year that are after 2011 is of the number of days in the taxation year, and

(b) if the foreign tax would otherwise be included in non-business-income tax, the total of

(i) if the taxpayer is a corporation that is a Canadian-controlled private corporation throughout the taxation year, that proportion of 28% that the number of days in the taxation year that are after 2010 is of the number of days in the taxation year, and

(ii) if the taxpayer is not a Canadian-controlled private corporation throughout the taxation year, the total of

(A) that proportion of 16.5% that the number of days in the taxation year that are in 2011 is of the number of days in the taxation year, and

(B) that proportion of 15% that the number of days in the taxation year that are after 2011 is of the number of days in the taxation year,

B   is the total of the taxpayer's proceeds from the disposition of the property at the particular time and the amount of all dividends or interest from the property in respect of the period included in computing the taxpayer's income for any taxation year,

C   is the total of the cost at which the taxpayer last acquired the property and any outlays or expenses made or incurred by the taxpayer for the purpose of disposing of the property at the particular time,

D   is the amount of foreign tax that would otherwise be included in computing the taxpayer's business-income tax or non-business-income tax for the particular year, and

E   is the total amount of foreign tax that would otherwise be included in computing the taxpayer's business-income tax or non-business-income tax for all taxation years.

Related Provisions: 112(2.3) — No domestic deduction on dividend rental arrangement; 126(4.3) — Exceptions; 126(4.4) — Certain dispositions ignored for 126(4.2); 161(6.1) — Delay in interest on foreign tax credit adjustment; 257 — Formula cannot calculate to less than zero. See also at end of s. 126.

Notes: 126(4.2) limits the foreign tax credit in respect of dividends or interest on a share or debt obligation that is held by the taxpayer for one year or less. The credit is limited to the Canadian tax that would be payable at a notional rate on the gross income from the security for the hold period. The effect is generally to prevent an excess credit that could be used to shelter other income from the foreign country in respect of which the tax was paid. See the limitations on this rule in 126(4.3) and (4.4).

The rule applies to foreign taxes on dividends or interest that are similar to the Part XIII withholding tax. It limits the foreign tax included in business-income tax or non-business-income tax to 40% or 30% respectively of gross profit from the share or debt. The difference in rates is because non-business foreign income of a corporation resident in Canada is typically taxable by a province, entitling the corporation to a 10%

abatement under 124(1). Foreign business income earned through a permanent establishment outside Canada is not taxable by a province.

Gross profit is not defined but is in effect measured by a formula as the total of proceeds from disposing of the property and interest or dividends received during the ownership period, less the cost of acquiring the property and expenses of disposition. No deduction is made for carrying charges.

If the ownership period falls into more than one taxation year, the allowable foreign tax is allocated between those years, through D and E in the formula, in the same proportion as it would be allocated without the limit. In this case, if tax payable for the first year increases due to 126(4.2) after disposition of the property in the second year, 161(6.1) provides some relief from payment of interest. The resulting reduction in foreign tax credit is also a "specified future tax consequence" as defined in 248(1).

126(4.2)A amended by 2002-2013 technical bill (Part 5 — technical), effective for taxation years that begin after Oct. 2011.

126(4.2) added by 1998 Budget, effective for 1998 and later taxation years.

(4.3) Exceptions — Subsection (4.2) does not apply to a property of a taxpayer

(a) that is a capital property;

(b) that is a debt obligation issued to the taxpayer that has a term of one year or less and that is held by no one other than the taxpayer at any time;

(c) that was last acquired by the taxpayer before February 24, 1998; or

(d) in respect of which any foreign tax is, because of subsection (4.1), not included in computing the taxpayer's business-income tax or non-business-income tax.

Notes: 126(4.3) added by 1998 Budget, effective for 1998 and later taxation years.

(4.4) Dispositions ignored — For the purposes of subsections (4.1) and (4.2) and the definition "economic profit" in subsection (7),

(a) a disposition or acquisition of property deemed to be made by subsection 10(12) or (13) or 45(1), section 70, 128.1 or 132.2, subsections 138(11.3), 138.2(4) or 142.5(2), paragraph 142.6(1)(b) or subsections 142.6(1.1) or (1.2) or 149(10) is not a disposition or acquisition, as the case may be; and

(b) a disposition

(i) to which section 51.1 applies, of a convertible obligation in exchange for a new obligation,

(ii) to which subsection 86(1) applies, of old shares in exchange for new shares, or

(iii) to which subsections 87(4) and (8) apply, of old shares in exchange for new shares,

is not a disposition, and the convertible obligation and the new obligation, or the old shares and the new shares, as the case may be, are deemed to be the same property.

Notes: 126(4.4)(a) amended by 2017 budget bill #2 to add reference to 138.2(4), for taxation years that begin after 2017.

126(4.4)(a) amended by 2016 budget bill #2, effective 2017, to delete reference to 14(14), (15) (as part of changing the eligible capital property rules to CCA Class 14.1: see Notes to 20(1)(b)).

126(4.4)(a) amended by 2002-2013 technical bill (Part 5 — technical) to change reference from 132.2(1)(f) to 132.2, effective for dispositions and acquisitions that occur after 1998 (earlier in-force rules from the 2001 technical bill were preserved).

126(4.4) amended by 2001 technical bill (effective June 28, 1999) and 1998 Budget.

(4.5) Synthetic disposition — holding period — If a synthetic disposition arrangement is entered into in respect of a property owned by a taxpayer and the synthetic disposition period of the arrangement is 30 days or more,

(a) for the purpose of determining whether the period referred to in subsection (4.2) is one year or less, the period is deemed to begin at the earlier of

(i) the time that is immediately before the particular time referred to in subsection (4.2), and

(ii) the end, if any, of the synthetic disposition period; and

(b) for the purposes of subsection (4.6), the taxpayer is deemed not to own the property during the synthetic disposition period.

Related Provisions: 126(4.6) — Exception where property owned for one year before SDP.

Notes: See Notes to 248(1)"synthetic disposition arrangement". 126(4.5) ensures taxpayers cannot circumvent 126(4.2) by entering into an SDA that allows the taxpayer to legally own a property for more than a year without having substantial risk of loss or opportunity for gain on the property. See also Notes to the exception in 126(4.6).

126(4.5) added by 2013 budget bill #2, effective for an agreement or arrangement entered into after March 20, 2013; it also applies to an agreement or arrangement entered into before March 21, 2013, the term of which is extended after March 20, 2013, as if the agreement or arrangement were entered into at the time of the extension.

(4.6) Exception — Subsection (4.5) does not apply in respect of a property owned by a taxpayer in respect of a synthetic disposition arrangement if the taxpayer owned the property throughout the one-year period (determined without reference to this subsection) that ended immediately before the synthetic disposition period of the arrangement.

Notes: 126(4.6) provides an exception to 126(4.5) if the taxpayer owned the property throughout the 365 days ending immediately before the synthetic disposition period. In determining this, the taxpayer is not considered to own the property throughout that period if 126(4.5) applied in respect of the property during that period (or would have applied if the determination in 126(4.5) were made without reference to 126(4.6)). This ensures that 126(4.5) applies only where an SDA is used to allow a taxpayer to meet a 365-day hold period test that the taxpayer otherwise would not have met.

126(4.6) added by 2013 budget bill #2, effective

(a) for an agreement or arrangement entered into after March 20, 2013, and

(b) for an agreement or arrangement entered into before March 21, 2013, the term of which is extended after March 20, 2013, as if the agreement or arrangement were entered into at the time of the extension.

For an agreement or arrangement in (a) or (b) above that was entered into by Sept. 12, 2013, and the term of which is not extended after that date, read 126(4.6) without the words "(determined without reference to this subsection)".

(5) Foreign oil and gas levies — A taxpayer who is resident in Canada throughout a taxation year and carries on a foreign oil and gas business in a taxing country in the year is deemed for the purposes of this section to have paid in the year as an income or profits tax to the government of the taxing country an amount equal to the lesser of

(a) the amount, if any, by which

(i) the amount obtained by multiplying the taxpayer's income from the business in the taxing country for the year by the total of

(A) that proportion of 26.5% that the number of days in the taxation year that are in 2011 is of the number of days in the taxation year, and

(B) that proportion of 25% that the number of days in the taxation year that are after 2011 is of the number of days in the taxation year

exceeds

(ii) the total of all amounts that would, but for this subsection, be income or profits taxes paid in the year in respect of the business to the government of the taxing country, and

(b) the taxpayer's production tax amount for the business in the taxing country for the year.

Related Provisions: 126(7)"production tax amount" — Definition; Reg. 5910 — Parallel rules for FAPI. See also Related Provisions at end of s. 126.

Notes: 126(5)(a)(i) changed from "40% of the taxpayer's income from the business in the taxing country for the year" by 2002-2013 technical bill (Part 5 — technical), effective for taxation years that begin after Oct. 2011.

126(5) replaced by 2000 Budget/2001 technical bill, effective for taxation years of a taxpayer that begin after Dec. 31, 1999 (or earlier by designation. See Notes in 20th to 34th editions). The former 126(5) was moved to 126(6)(a).

(5.1) Deductions for specified capital gains — Where in a taxation year an individual has claimed a deduction under section 110.6 in computing the individual's taxable income for the year, for the purposes of this section the individual shall be deemed to have claimed the deduction under section 110.6 in respect of such taxable capital gains or portion thereof as the individual may specify in the individual's return of income required to be filed pursuant to section 150 for the year or, where the individual has failed to so specify, in respect of such taxable capital gains as the Minister may specify in respect of the taxpayer for the year.

Related Provisions: See Related Provisions at end of s. 126.

(6) Rules of construction — For the purposes of this section,

(a) the government of a country other than Canada includes the government of a state, province or other political subdivision of that country;

(b) where a taxpayer's income for a taxation year is in whole or in part from sources in more than one country other than Canada, subsections (1) and (2) shall be read as providing for separate deductions in respect of each of the countries other than Canada;

(c) if any income from a source in a particular country would be tax-exempt income but for the fact that a portion of the income is subject to an income or profits tax imposed by the government of a country other than Canada, the portion is deemed to be income from a separate source in the particular country; and

(d) if, in computing a taxpayer's income for a taxation year from a business carried on by the taxpayer in Canada, an amount is included in respect of interest paid or payable to the taxpayer by a person resident in a country other than Canada, and the taxpayer has paid to the government of that other country a non-business income tax for the year with respect to the amount, the amount is, in applying the definition "qualifying incomes" in subsection (7) for the purpose of subsection (1), deemed to be income from a source in that other country.

Related Provisions: See Related Provisions at end of s. 126.

Notes: "Political subdivision" in 126(6)(a) includes a city or municipality. A US state franchise tax qualifies for credit due to 126(6)(a): VIEWS doc 2011-0428791E5. The European Union is not considered a "country": 2013-0500491E5, 2016-0634231I7. For an example of 126(6)(c) applying see 2012-0462151I7. See also Notes to Canada-UK treaty Art. 21:3.

126(6)(d) added by 2002-2013 technical bill (Part 5 — technical), effective for amounts received after Feb. 27, 2004.

126(6) amended by 2001 technical bill, effective June 28, 1999.

Income Tax Folios: S5-F2-C1: Foreign tax credit [replaces IT-270R3, IT-395R2, IT-520].

(7) Definitions — In this section,

"business-income tax" paid by a taxpayer for a taxation year in respect of businesses carried on by the taxpayer in a country other than Canada (referred to in this definition as the "business country") means, subject to subsections (4.1) to (4.2), the portion of any income or profits tax paid by the taxpayer for the year to the government of a country other than Canada that can reasonably be regarded as tax in respect of the income of the taxpayer from a business carried on by the taxpayer in the business country, but does not include a tax, or the portion of a tax, that can reasonably be regarded as relating to an amount that

(a) any other person or partnership has received or is entitled to receive from that government, or

(b) was deductible under subparagraph 110(1)(f)(i) in computing the taxpayer's taxable income for the year;

Related Provisions: 94(3)(b) — Application to trust deemed resident in Canada; 94(16)(d), (e) — Non-resident trust — electing contributor deemed to have paid BIT; 104(22.3) — Deduction in computing non-business-income tax of trust; 126(4) — Exclusion of certain amounts; 126(4.11) — Exclusion of artificially generated amounts; 126(5) — Foreign tax; 126(6)(a) — Interpretation of "government of a country..."; 126(8) — Foreign-source income from SIFT partnership reduced by Part IX.1 tax payable. See also at end of s. 126.

Notes: See Notes to 126(1) and 126(7)"non-business-income tax". As to whether a business is carried on in the foreign country, see VIEWS doc 2010-0388651I7 and Notes to 2(3). Foreign tax paid by a parent on behalf of its Canadian subsidiary qualifies as BIT, as the parent is considered to act as agent for the sub: 2013-0477461E5.

Opening words amended to change "(4.1) and (4.2)" to "(4.1) to (4.2)", thus adding reference to 126(4.11), (4.12) and (4.13), by 2002-2013 technical bill (Part 5 — technical), effective for income or profits tax paid for taxation years of a taxpayer that end after March 4, 2010. (See Notes to 126(4.11).)

Opening words of definition amended by 2001 technical bill (effective June 28, 1999), 1998 Budget and 1991 technical bill. 126(7)"business-income tax" was 126(7)(a) before RSC 1985 (5th Supp) consolidation for tax years ending after Nov. 1991.

Income Tax Folios: S5-F2-C1: Foreign tax credit [replaces IT-270R3, IT-395R2, IT-520].

Interpretation Bulletins: IT-201R2: Foreign tax credit — trust and beneficiaries; IT-273R2: Government assistance — general comments; IT-506: Foreign income taxes as a deduction from income.

I.T. Technical News: 8 (treatment of United States unitary state taxes).

"commercial obligation" in respect of a taxpayer's foreign oil and gas business in a country means an obligation of the taxpayer to a particular person, undertaken in the course of carrying on the business or in contemplation of the business, if the law of the country would have allowed the taxpayer to undertake an obligation, on substantially the same terms, to a person other than the particular person;

Notes: 126(7)"commercial obligation" added by 2000 Budget, effective on the same basis as 126(5).

"economic profit" of a taxpayer in respect of a property for a period means the part of the taxpayer's profit, from the business in which the property is used, that is attributable to the property in respect of the period or to related transactions, determined as if the only amounts deducted in computing that part of the profit were

(a) interest and financing expenses incurred by the taxpayer and attributable to the acquisition or holding of the property in respect of the period or to a related transaction,

(b) income or profits taxes payable by the taxpayer for any year to the government of a country other than Canada, in respect of the property for the period or in respect of a related transaction, or

(c) other outlays and expenses that are directly attributable to the acquisition, holding or disposition of the property in respect of the period or to a related transaction;

Related Provisions: 126(4.4) — Certain dispositions ignored for purposes of this definition; 126(6)(a) — Interpretation of "government of a country...".

Notes: See Notes to 126(4.1). 126(7)"economic profit"(b) amended by 2001 technical bill, effective June 28, 1999. Definition added by 1998 Budget, effective for 1998 and later taxation years.

"foreign oil and gas business" of a taxpayer means a business, carried on by the taxpayer in a taxing country, the principal activity of which is the extraction from natural accumulations, or from oil or gas wells, of petroleum, natural gas or related hydrocarbons;

Related Provisions: Reg. 5910(4) — Definition applies to FAPI rules.

Notes: 126(7)"foreign oil and gas business" added by 2000 Budget, effective on the same basis as 126(5).

"foreign-tax carryover [para. 126(7)(b)]" — [Repealed under former Act]

Notes: 126(7)(b), repealed in 1984, defined "foreign-tax carryover", a term no longer used. For the carryover of unused foreign tax credits, see 126(2)(a), 126(2.3) and 126(7)"unused foreign tax credit".

"non-business-income tax" paid by a taxpayer for a taxation year to the government of a country other than Canada means, subject to subsections (4.1) to (4.2), the portion of any income or profits tax paid by the taxpayer for the year to the government of that country that

(a) was not included in computing the taxpayer's business-income tax for the year in respect of any business carried on by the taxpayer in any country other than Canada,

(b) was not deductible by virtue of subsection 20(11) in computing the taxpayer's income for the year, and

(c) was not deducted by virtue of subsection 20(12) in computing the taxpayer's income for the year,

but does not include a tax, or the portion of a tax,

(c.1) that is in respect of an amount deducted because of subsection 104(22.3) in computing the taxpayer's business-income tax,

(d) that would not have been payable had the taxpayer not been a citizen of that country and that cannot reasonably be regarded as attributable to income from a source outside Canada,

(e) that may reasonably be regarded as relating to an amount that any other person or partnership has received or is entitled to receive from that government,

(f) that, where the taxpayer deducted an amount under subsection 122.3(1) from the taxpayer's tax otherwise payable under this Part for the year, may reasonably be regarded as attributable to the taxpayer's income from employment to the extent of the lesser of the amounts determined in respect thereof under paragraphs 122.3(1)(c) and (d) for the year,

(g) that can reasonably be attributed to a taxable capital gain or a portion thereof in respect of which the taxpayer or a spouse or common-law partner of the taxpayer has claimed a deduction under section 110.6, or

(h) [Repealed]

(i) that can reasonably be regarded as relating to an amount that was deductible under subparagraph 110(1)(f)(i) in computing the taxpayer's taxable income for the year;

Related Provisions: 4(1) — Income or loss from a source; 94(3)(b) — Application to deemed-resident trust; 94(16)(d), (e) — Non-resident trust — electing contributor deemed to have paid NBIT; 104(22.3) — Deduction in computing trust's NBIT; 126(4), 126(4.11) — Exclusion of uneconomic or artificially generated amounts; 126(6)(a) — Interpretation of "government of a country..."; 126(8) — Foreign-source income from SIFT partnership grossed up for Part IX.1 tax; Canada-U.S. Tax Treaty:Art. XXIX-B:6 — U.S. estate tax allowed for foreign tax credit purposes. See additional Related Provisions and Definitions at end of s. 126.

Notes: See Notes to 126(1). Non-business-income tax (**NBIT**) is foreign "income or profits tax" not included in 126(7)"business-income tax" (BIT), which depends on whether the source of income is a "business" under the ITA (see Notes to 9(1) under "Business income vs property income"). The reference is to foreign tax paid "for the year", including amounts paid after year-end. Each foreign country's tax must be considered separately: 126(6)(b). A part-year resident apportions Canadian tax under 126(1)(b) (which refers to s. 114), but need not apportion NBIT or BIT to amounts paid while resident in Canada.

CRA audits many FTCs and requires a copy of the foreign assessment, or proof of payment or refund (or Canadian information slips such as a T3): VIEWS doc 2016-0634941C6 [2016 STEP q.9]; 2016-0669851C6 [2016 CTF q.12]; 2016 Alberta CPA roundtable (tinyurl.com/cra-abtax), q.10 [Nataly Urena, "More Documentation Required for FTC Claims", 6(4) *Canadian Tax Focus* (ctf.ca) 12 (Nov. 2016)].

In calculating NBIT or BIT, note that Canada's tax treaty with the foreign country (e.g. Bangladesh, Brazil, India, Jamaica, Nigeria, Pakistan, Tunisia) may provide for "tax sparing", whereby foreign tax waived to encourage development is considered paid (and thus is NBIT or BIT) for purposes of the ITA: VIEWS doc 2014-0525961I7 (but this will not create a provincial FTC). See also Notes to Reg. 5907(10).

A US state's franchise tax qualifies as BIT, due to 126(6)(a): VIEWS doc 2011-0428791E5; Sunita Doobay, "Foreign Tax Credit for Franchise Tax", 21(6) *Canadian Tax Highlights* (ctf.ca) 11-12 (June 2013).

For the meaning of "income or profits tax", see Notes to 126(4). For the meaning of "country" see Notes to 126(6). NBIT includes the 10% additional US tax payable on early withdrawal from an Individual Retirement Account: doc 2011-0398741I7 (reversing earlier position in 9330140, 9304595 [Earle, "CRA Changes Position", 8(7) *Tax Hyperion* (Carswell, July 2011); Yager, "Canadian FTC: US Pension Early Withdrawal", 19(7) *Canadian Tax Highlights [CTH]* (ctf.ca) 4-5 (July 2011)]. NBIT also includes: US alternative minimum tax, in some cases (2003-0019751E5); US FICA payments (2008-0304081E5, Canada-US tax treaty Art. XXIV(2)(a)(ii)); US tax paid by a Cdn resident individual on US LLC income (2014-0548111E5); US 2018 transition tax, though FTC may not be available (2018-0748811C6 [STEP 2018 q.12]).

NBIT does not include: mandatory premiums to a US state public sector retirement plan (*Nadeau*, 2004 TCC 433); Medicare taxes (2007-0254661E5; Bilkey, "No FTC for Medicare Surtax", 21(3) *CTH* 6-7 (March 2013)); most non-US social security taxes (since the payments are voluntary and the taxpayer derives financial benefit from them: *Income Tax Technical News* 31R2, VIEWS doc 2005-0123101M4); US tax paid by an LLC, which is not considered paid by the LLC's shareholder (2015-0601781E5; see Notes to 248(1)"corporation"); South Africa's Secondary Tax on Companies (because it is not paid by the taxpayer: 2014-0546571E5); UK mandatory national insurance contributions (the payer receives a benefit so the payments are not for a "public purpose": *Yates*, [2001] 3 C.T.C. 2565 (TCC); *Zong*, 2019 TCC 270).

When a Canadian inherits a US IRA or pension plan subject to US estate tax, no FTC is available, but see Notes to Canada-US tax treaty Art. XVIII:1 for a deduction.

Where Canadian resident R is working in non-treaty country C that treats R as resident in C and subject to tax on world income, NBIT will be only the C tax on income sourced in C: VIEWS doc 2013-0495091E5.

Where a person pays more tax to country C than Canada's tax treaty with C requires, the excess is a voluntary payment, not "tax", and is not NBIT: *Meyer*, 2004 TCC 199; *Marchan*, 2008 TCC 158; Income Tax Folio S5-F2-C1 ¶1.34; VIEWS docs 2008-0264221E5 (US), 2010-0390061E5 (Pakistan), 2012-0451251C6 [2012 APFF q.10] (excess tax on ADRs), 2014-052523117 (Japan). However, in *Shindle*, 2009 TCC 133, small amounts of tax apparently overpaid to various US states and cities were allowed, due in part to the Crown not properly pleading its assumptions.

NBIT means the amount actually paid by the taxpayer, net of refunds such as US child tax credit (*Zhang*, 2008 FCA 198), US foreign tax credit (*Arsove*, 2016 TCC 283) and Economic Stimulus Package credits and advance payments (2009-030642117).

In a "foreign tax credit generator" case, the test of "paid by the taxpayer" was met for a partner when the *partnership* paid the tax, in *4145356 Canada*, 2011 TCC 220 (Crown's FCA appeal discontinued on settlement, A-193-11). See Mitchell Sherman, "Talkin' 'bout My Generation", XVII(2) *Corporate Finance* (Federated Press) 1981-87 (2011). See now 126(4.11)-(4.13), which are targeted at such cases.

Partner P is considered to have paid NBIT paid by the partnership, due to 96(1)(f), generally but not always P's *pro rata* share: VIEWS doc 2014-0558601E5 [Brown & Spiro, "Partners' Credit for Foreign Withholding Tax", 8(2) *Canadian Tax Focus* (ctf.ca) 4-5 (May 2018)].

Where a trust earns income from US real property but the beneficiary is required to pay US tax on the income, the beneficiary can normally claim the FTC: VIEWS doc 2003-0049081E5. See also 2015-0570291R3 (FTC allowed on income from a US trust), 2015-0572541R3 (FTC on transfer of US 401(k) to RRSP, even though 60(j) allows an offsetting deduction); 2017-0695141C6 [2017 STEP q.4] (contributor to US grantor trust can claim credit); 2018-0744161C6 [STEP 2018 q.13] (if *alter ego* trust pays foreign withholding tax on dividends attributed to the settlor by 75(2), the tax paid is not attributed).

Tax on pension income qualifies as NBIT, including tax paid by a person renouncing US citizenship (see Notes to 128.1(1)): VIEWS doc 2013-0477121E5. Where foreign pension income is split between spouses under 60.03, the foreign tax can also be split: May 2008 ICAA roundtable (tinyurl.com/cra-abtax), q. 22.

Australian company "fully-franked" dividends, paid under an imputation system, do not qualify because the Canadian shareholder is not directly paying the Australian tax: *White*, 2003 TCC 668; presumably this will apply to dividends from other (former British Empire) countries that use the same imputation system.

Para. (g) applied to the pre-1994 general capital gains exemption in 110.6(3) (e.g. on a Florida condo). It will rarely apply now, since 110.6 applies only to Canadian property, not normally subject to foreign tax.

Para. (i) denies the credit for income exempt from Canadian tax due to a treaty.

See also Notes to 126(1) and 20(12).

Opening words amended to change "(4.1) and (4.2)" to "(4.1) to (4.2)", thus adding reference to 126(4.11), (4.12) and (4.13), by 2002-2013 technical bill (Part 5 — technical), effective for income or profits tax paid for taxation years of a taxpayer that end after March 4, 2010. (See Notes to 126(4.11).)

Para. (h) repealed by 2013 budget bill #1, for taxation years that begin after March 20, 2013 (on elimination of international banking centres in 33.1).

Definition earlier amended by 2001 technical bill, 2000 same-sex partners bill, 1998 and 1994 Budgets, 1993 and 1991 technical bills. 126(7)"non-business-income tax" was 126(7)(c) before RSC 1985 (5th Supp) consolidation for tax years ending after Nov. 1991.

Income Tax Folios: S5-F2-C1: Foreign tax credit [replaces IT-270R3, IT-395R2, IT-520].

Interpretation Bulletins: IT-201R2: Foreign tax credit — trust and beneficiaries; IT-273R2: Government assistance — general comments; IT-497R4: Overseas employment tax credit; IT-506: Foreign income taxes as a deduction from income. See also at end of s. 126.

I.T. Technical News: 30 (tax avoidance).

"production tax amount" of a taxpayer for a foreign oil and gas business carried on by the taxpayer in a taxing country for a taxation year means the total of all amounts each of which

(a) became receivable in the year by the government of the country because of an obligation (other than a commercial obligation) of the taxpayer, in respect of the business, to the government or an agent or instrumentality of the government,

(b) is computed by reference to the amount by which

(i) the amount or value of petroleum, natural gas or related hydrocarbons produced or extracted by the taxpayer in the course of carrying on the business in the year

exceeds

(ii) an allowance or other deduction that

(A) is deductible, under the agreement or law that creates the obligation described in paragraph (a), in computing

the amount receivable by the government of the country, and

(B) is intended to take into account the taxpayer's operating and capital costs of that production or extraction, and can reasonably be considered to have that effect,

(c) would not, if this Act were read without reference to subsection (5), be an income or profits tax, and

(d) is not identified as a royalty under the agreement that creates the obligation or under any law of the country;

Related Provisions: 12(1)(o.1) — Production tax amount included in income; Reg. 5910(4) — Definition applies to FAPI rules.

Notes: 126(7)"production tax amount" added by 2000 Budget, effective on the same basis as 126(5).

Regulations: 5910 (production sharing rules apply to foreign affiliate system).

"qualifying incomes" of a taxpayer from sources in a country means incomes from sources in the country, determined in accordance with subsection (9);

Related Provisions: 126(6)(d) — Application to interest paid by non-resident-Canadian business.

Notes: 126(7)"qualifying incomes" amended by 2000 Budget, effective on the same basis as 126(5). Definition added by 1998 Budget, effective for taxation years that begin after February 24, 1998.

"qualifying losses" of a taxpayer from sources in a country means losses from sources in the country, determined in accordance with subsection (9);

Notes: 126(7)"qualifying losses" amended by 2000 Budget, effective on the same basis as 126(5). Definition added by 1998 Budget, effective for taxation years that begin after February 24, 1998.

"related transactions", in respect of a taxpayer's ownership of a property for a period, means transactions entered into by the taxpayer as part of the arrangement under which the property was owned;

Notes: Definition added by 1998 Budget, effective for 1998 and later taxation years.

"tax for the year otherwise payable under this Part" by a taxpayer means

(a) in paragraph (1)(b) and subsection (3), the amount determined by the formula

$$A - B$$

where

A is the amount that would be the tax payable under this Part for the year by the taxpayer if that tax were determined without reference to section 120.3 and before making any deduction under any of sections 121, 122.3, 125 to 127.41 and, if the taxpayer is a Canadian-controlled private corporation throughout the year, section 123.4, and

B is the amounts deemed by subsections 120(2) and (2.2) to have been paid on account of tax payable under this Part by the taxpayer,

(b) in subparagraph (2)(c)(i) and paragraph (2.2)(b), the amount that would be the tax payable under this Part for the year by the taxpayer if that tax were determined without reference to sections 120.3 and 123.3 and before making any deduction under any of sections 121 and 122.3, subsection 123.4(3), and sections 124 to 127.41, and

(c) in subsection (2.1), the amount that would be the tax payable under this Part for the year by the taxpayer if that tax were determined without reference to subsection 120(1) and sections 120.3 and 123.3 and before making any deduction under any of sections 121 and 122.3, subsection 123.4(3) and sections 124 to 127.41;

Related Provisions: 257 — Formula cannot calculate to less than zero. See also at end of s. 126.

Notes: Note that all personal credits are taken before the foreign tax credit (FTC), since 118-118.94 are not listed in A. There is no carryforward of an FTC; if a donation credit will wipe out the FTC, consider deferring the donation claim to a later year (up to 5 years: 118.1(1)"total charitable gifts").

Definition amended by 2000 Budget (for 2001 and later tax years), 1999, 1995 and 1994 Budgets, 1991 technical bill. 126(7)"tax for the year ..." was para. 126(7)(d) before RSC 1985 (5th Supp) consolidation for tax years ending after Nov. 1991.

I.T. Application Rules: 69 (meaning of "chapter 148 of ...").

Income Tax Folios: S5-F2-C1: Foreign tax credit [replaces IT-270R3, IT-395R2, IT-520].

"tax-exempt income" means income of a taxpayer from a source in a country in respect of which

(a) the taxpayer is, because of a tax treaty with that country, entitled to an exemption from all income or profits taxes, imposed in that country, to which the treaty applies, and

(b) no income or profits tax to which the treaty does not apply is imposed in any country other than Canada;

Related Provisions: 126(1.1)(f) — Application of definition to authorized foreign bank.

Notes: The exemption must be by treaty, not simply because the other country does not tax the income: VIEWS doc 2004-0081151I7.

Definition added by 1998 Budget, for tax years that begin after Feb. 24, 1998.

Income Tax Folios: S5-F2-C1: Foreign tax credit [replaces IT-270R3, IT-395R2, IT-520].

"taxing country" means a country (other than Canada) the government of which regularly imposes, in respect of income from businesses carried on in the country, a levy or charge of general application that would, if this Act were read without reference to subsection (5), be an income or profits tax.

Related Provisions: Reg. 5910(4) — Definition applies to FAPI rules.

Notes: 126(7)"taxing country" added by 2000 Budget, on the same basis as 126(5).

"unused foreign tax credit" of a taxpayer in respect of a country for a taxation year means the amount, if any, by which

(a) the business-income tax paid by the taxpayer for the year in respect of businesses carried on by the taxpayer in that country

exceeds

(b) the amount, if any, deductible under subsection (2) in respect of that country in computing the taxpayer's tax payable under this Part for the year.

Related Provisions: 152(6)(f.1) — Minister required to reassess past year to allow unused foreign tax credit; 257 — Formula cannot calculate to less than zero. See also at end of s. 126.

Notes: Definition amended by 2000 Budget, for 2001 and later tax years. 126(7)"unused foreign tax credit" was 126(7)(e) before RSC 1985 (5th Supp) consolidation for tax years ending after Nov. 1991. Formula elements A–C were subparas. (i)–(iii).

Income Tax Folios: S5-F2-C1: Foreign tax credit [replaces IT-270R3, IT-395R2, IT-520].

Interpretation Bulletins: IT-488R2: Winding-up of 90%-owned taxable Canadian corporations (cancelled).

CRA Audit Manual: 11.3.4: Tax credits.

(8) Deemed dividend — [SIFT] partnership — If an amount is deemed by subsection 96(1.11) to be a taxable dividend received by a person in a taxation year of the person in respect of a partnership, and it is reasonable to consider that all or part of the amount (in this subsection referred to as the "foreign-source portion") is attributable to income of the partnership from a source in a country other than Canada, the person is deemed for the purposes of this section to have an amount of income from that source for that taxation year equal to the amount determined by the formula

$$A \times B/C$$

where

A is the total amount included under subsection 82(1) in computing the income of the person in respect of the taxable dividend for that taxation year;

B is the foreign-source portion; and

C is the amount of the taxable dividend deemed to be received by the person.

Notes: 126(8) added by 2007 budget bill #1, effective Oct. 31, 2006. It is part of the SIFT rules (see Notes to 104(16)) for partnerships (see 96(1.11)). It ensures that, when calculating foreign tax credits, the full taxable dividend applicable to foreign-sourced

income that is non-portfolio earnings (NPE) ("grossed-up" by 82(1), if applicable) is included in the calculation. In addition, the dividend is deemed to be from a foreign source, despite 96(1.11)(b), to the extent the NPE are from a foreign source.

Former 126(8), "Deemed separate source", added by 1998 Budget for taxation years beginning after Feb. 24, 1998, and repealed by 2000 Budget effective June 28, 1999. This rule was moved to 126(6)(c).

(9) Computation of qualifying incomes and losses — The qualifying incomes and qualifying losses for a taxation year of a taxpayer from sources in a country shall be determined

(a) without reference to

(i) any portion of income that was deductible under subparagraph 110(1)(f)(i) in computing the taxpayer's taxable income,

(ii) for the purpose of subparagraph 126(1)(b)(i), any portion of income in respect of which an amount was deducted under section 110.6 in computing the taxpayer's income, or

(iii) any income or loss from a source in the country if any income of the taxpayer from the source would be tax-exempt income; and

(b) as if the total of all amounts each of which is that portion of an amount deducted under subsection 66(4), 66.21(4), 66.7(2) or 66.7(2.3) in computing those qualifying incomes and qualifying losses for the year that applies to those sources were the greater of

(i) the total of all amounts each of which is that portion of an amount deducted under subsection 66(4), 66.21(4), 66.7(2) or 66.7(2.3) in computing the taxpayer's income for the year that applies to those sources, and

(ii) the total of

(A) the portion of the maximum amount that would be deductible under subsection 66(4) in computing the taxpayer's income for the year that applies to those sources if the amount determined under subparagraph 66(4)(b)(ii) for the taxpayer in respect of the year were equal to the amount, if any, by which the total of

(I) the taxpayer's foreign resource income (within the meaning assigned by subsection 66.21(1)) for the year in respect of the country, determined as if the taxpayer had claimed the maximum amounts deductible for the year under subsections 66.7(2) and (2.3), and

(II) all amounts each of which would have been an amount included in computing the taxpayer's income for the year under subsection 59(1) in respect of a disposition of a foreign resource property in respect of the country, determined as if each amount determined under subparagraph 59(1)(b)(ii) were nil,

exceeds

(III) the total of all amounts each of which is a portion of an amount (other than a portion that results in a reduction of the amount otherwise determined under subclause (I)) that applies to those sources and that would be deducted under subsection 66.7(2) in computing the taxpayer's income for the year if the maximum amounts deductible for the year under that subsection were deducted,

(B) the maximum amount that would be deductible under subsection 66.21(4) in respect of those sources in computing the taxpayer's income for the year if

(I) the amount deducted under subsection 66(4) in respect of those sources in computing the taxpayer's income for the year were the amount determined under clause (A),

(II) the amounts deducted under subsections 66.7(2) and (2.3) in respect of those sources in computing the taxpayer's income for the year were the maximum amounts deductible under those subsections,

895

(III) for the purposes of the definition "cumulative foreign resource expense" in subsection 66.21(1), the total of the amounts designated under subparagraph 59(1)(b)(ii) for the year in respect of dispositions by the taxpayer of foreign resource properties in respect of the country in the year were the maximum total that could be so designated without any reduction in the maximum amount that would be determined under clause (A) in respect of the taxpayer for the year in respect of the country if no assumption had been made under subclause (A)(II) in respect of designations made under subparagraph 59(1)(b)(ii), and

(IV) the amount determined under paragraph 66.21(4)(b) were nil, and

(C) the total of all amounts each of which is the maximum amount, applicable to one of those sources, that is deductible under subsection 66.7(2) or (2.3) in computing the taxpayer's income for the year.

Related Provisions: 248(1)"foreign resource property" — Meaning of foreign resource property in respect of a country.

Notes: Under 126(9)(a), no foreign tax credit is available for amounts exempted by tax treaty: VIEWS doc 2007-0230391E5. Qualifying income (QI) refers to net income, not taxable income, so using a non-capital loss carryforward does not reduce QI: doc 2003-0025105. A gain on a foreign principal residence that is not taxed due to 40(2)(b) is not QI; if it is reported but offset with a loss carryforward, it is QI: 2004-0103431E5. QI does not include a gain on deemed disposition of mark-to-market securities, due to 126(6)(c): 2012-046215117. See also 2008-0280941E5 (general discussion).

126(9) added by 2000 Budget, effective on the same basis as 126(5). See Notes to 126(7)"qualifying incomes" and "qualifying losses".

Related Provisions [s. 126]: 4(3) — Whether deductions are applicable to a particular source; 60(o)(iii) — Deduction for legal expenses in appealing assessment of foreign tax; 80.1(2) — Election re interest for expropriation assets required; 87(2.11) — Vertical amalgamations; 104(22)–(22.4) — Trusts — allocation of foreign-source income to beneficiaries; 127.54(2) — foreign tax credit; 258(3) — Certain dividends on preferred shares deemed to be interest; 258(5) — Deemed interest on certain shares; Canada-U.S. Tax Treaty: Art. XXIV — Elimination of double taxation.

Definitions [s. 126]: "amount", "authorized foreign bank", "business" — 248(1); "business-income tax" — 126(7); "Canada" — 255, *Interpretation Act* 35(1); "Canadian banking business" — 248(1); "capital property" — 54, 248(1); "commercial obligation" — 126(7); "common-law partner" — 248(1); "corporation" — 248(1), *Interpretation Act* 35(1); "distribution year" — 126(2.22); "disposition", "dividend" — 248(1); "economic profit" — 126(7); "emigration year" — 126(2.21); "employment" — 248(1); "foreign affiliate" — 95(1), 248(1); "foreign oil and gas business" — 126(7); "foreign resource property" — 66(15), 248(1); "foreign resource property in respect of" — 248(1); "foreign tax" — 126(4.2); "government of a country" — 126(6)(a); "immovable" — Quebec *Civil Code* art. 900–907; "income or profits tax" — 126(4), (5); "individual" — 248(1); "non-business-income tax" — 126(7); "non-resident" — 126(1.1)(a), 248(1); "office", "oil or gas well" — 248(1); "partnership" — see 96(1) Notes; "person", "prescribed" — 248(1); "prescribed international organization" — Reg. 8900(1); "production tax amount" — 126(7); "property" — 248(1); "province" — *Interpretation Act* 35(1); "qualifying incomes", "qualifying losses" — 126(7), (9); "related transactions" — 126(7); "relevant foreign tax law" — 126(4.11); "resident", "resident in Canada" — 126(1.1)(a), 250; "share" — 248(1); "source" — 126(6)(c); "synthetic disposition arrangement", "synthetic disposition period" — 248(1); "tax for the year otherwise payable" — 126(7); "taxable dividend" — 89(1), 248(1); "tax-exempt income" — 126(7); "tax payable" — 248(2); "tax treaty", "taxable Canadian property" — 248(1); "taxable capital gain" — 38(a), 248(1); "taxable income" — 2(2), 248(1); "taxable income earned in Canada" — 248(1); "taxation year" — 249; "taxing country" — 126(7); "taxpayer" — 248(1); "time of disposition" — 128.1(4)(b); "trust" — 104(1), 248(1), (3); "unused foreign tax credit" — 126(7).

126.1 [Repealed]

Notes: 126.1 added by 1992 Economic Statement effective 1993; repealed by 2002-2013 technical bill for forms filed after March 20, 2003. It provided a credit, for 1993 only, to offset increases in Unemployment Insurance premiums payable by employers, to encourage employers to hire additional staff. An earlier 126.1, repealed in 1974, dealt with political contributions, now under 127(3).

127. [Investment tax credit, logging credit and political credit] — (1) Logging tax deduction [credit] — There may be

deducted from the tax otherwise payable by a taxpayer under this Part for a taxation year an amount equal to the lesser of

(a) ⅔ of any logging tax paid by the taxpayer to the government of a province in respect of income for the year from logging operations in the province, and

(b) 6⅔% of the taxpayer's income for the year from logging operations in the province referred to in paragraph (a),

except that in no case shall the total of amounts in respect of all provinces that would otherwise be deductible under this subsection from the tax otherwise payable under this Part for the year by the taxpayer exceed 6⅔% of the amount that would be the taxpayer's taxable income for the year or taxable income earned in Canada for the year, as the case may be, if this Part were read without reference to paragraphs 60(b), (c) to (c.2), (i) and (v) and sections 62, 63 and 64.

Related Provisions: 117(1) — "Tax otherwise payable".

Notes: This is actually a *credit* because it is a deduction from *tax*, not from income. See Notes to 127(2)"logging tax", and to Reg. 700(1) re *Weyerhaeuser* case.

"Tax otherwise payable under this Part" includes pre-2008 surtax under 123.2: VIEWS doc 2008-031121117.

127(1) amended by 1992 technical bill, for the 1991 and later tax years.

Interpretation Bulletins: IT-121R3: Election to capitalize cost of borrowed money (cancelled).

Forms: T2 Sched. 5: Tax calculation supplementary — corporations.

(2) Definitions — In subsection (1),

"income for the year from logging operations in the province" has the meaning assigned by regulation;

Notes: See Notes to Reg. 700(1). This definition was para. 127(2)(a) before RSC 1985 (5th Supp) consolidation for tax years ending after Nov. 1991.

Regulations: 700(1), (2) (meaning of "income for the year from logging operations in a province").

"logging tax" means a tax imposed by the legislature of a province that is declared by regulation to be a tax of general application on income from logging operations.

Notes: The relevant provinces are British Columbia and Quebec. Logging tax paid is ⅔ recoverable under 127(1) and ⅓ on the provincial income tax return, so in theory it is all recovered. This does not always work: Louis Tassé, "Not-so-neutral Logging Tax", III(2) *Resource Sector Taxation* (Federated Press) 209-11 (2005).

127(2)"logging tax" was para. 127(2)(b) before RSC 1985 (5th Supp) consolidation for tax years ending after Nov. 1991.

Regulations: 700(3) (provinces are B.C. and Quebec).

(3) [Political] Contributions to registered parties and candidates — There may be deducted from the tax otherwise payable by a taxpayer under this Part for a taxation year in respect of the total of all amounts each of which is the eligible amount of a monetary contribution that is referred to in the *Canada Elections Act* and that is made by the taxpayer in the year to a registered party, a registered association or a candidate, as those terms are defined in that Act,

(a) when that total does not exceed $400, 75% of that total,

(b) when that total exceeds $400 and does not exceed $750, $300 plus 50% of the amount by which that total exceeds $400, and

(c) when that total exceeds $750, the lesser of

(i) $650, and

(ii) $475 plus 33⅓% of the amount by which the total exceeds $750,

if payment of each monetary contribution that is included in that total is evidenced by filing with the Minister a receipt, signed by the agent authorized under that Act to accept that monetary contribution, that contains prescribed information.

Related Provisions: 18(1)(n) — No deduction from income for political contributions; 120(4) — "Tax otherwise payable under this Part"; 127(3.1) — Issue of receipts; 127(3.2) — Authorization required for receipts from registered associations; 127(3.3) — No receipts to be issued while judicial deregistration of party is pending; 127(4) — Interpretation; 127(4.2) — Allocation of amount contributed among partners; 230.1 — Books and records relating to political contributions; 248(30)–(33) — Eligible amount of monetary contribution; 248(41) — Donation value deemed nil if taxpayer does not inform donee of circumstances requiring reduction.

Notes: This is actually a *credit* because it is a deduction from *tax*, not from income. The maximum credit for federal political contributions (once they reach $1,275 for the year) is $650: 127(3)(c)(i), VIEWS docs 2013-0511591E5, 2014-0516961E5. See Reg. 2000-2002 for receipt requirements. This encourages small contributions. The *Canada Elections Act* imposes limits on contributions.

Corporations can no longer make federal political contributions, as *Canada Elections Act* s. 404.1(1) was repealed. Corporations can claim credits for provincial political contributions in most provinces. See CRA guide T4012 (2010). An individual who contributes to a provincial party but moves to another province before year-end generally cannot claim any credit: VIEWS doc 2010-0374351E5.

Political contributions are used to support party leadership candidates, although the credit was not intended to apply to this. See Arthur Drache, "Taxpayers Support All Leadership Candidates", XXIV(22) *The Canadian Taxpayer* (Carswell) 174-75 (Nov. 12-25, 2002). Someone seeking a nomination is not a "candidate" under the *Election Act*: tinyurl.com/cbc-lougheed.

In *Figueroa*, 2003 SCC 37, political parties were entitled to be recognized as parties and issue tax receipts even if they did not meet the *Canada Elections Act* (CEA) threshold of nominating 50 candidates for election. The government responded with amendments to the CEA (S.C. 2004, c. 24) replacing the 50-candidate requirement with new registration requirements, including that a party endorse and support at least one candidate, that it provide signed declarations of support from at least 250 members and that it have at least four officers. The amendments add a purpose-based definition of "political party" and require the party leader declare that one of its fundamental purposes meets the definition. The Commissioner of Canada Elections may apply for judicial deregistration under CEA 521.1 if these requirements are not met, and the party cannot issue tax receipts while the application is pending (see 127(3.3)). The amendments provide other anti-abuse measures as well.

The terms referred to in 127(3) are defined as follows in the *Canada Elections Act*:

2. (1) "*monetary contribution*" means an amount of money provided that is not repayable.

2. (1) "*registered party*" means a political party that is registered in the registry of political parties referred to in section 394 as a registered party.

2. (1) "*registered association*" means an electoral district association that is registered in the registry of electoral district associations referred to in section 455.

2. (1) "*candidate*" means a person whose nomination as a candidate at an election has been confirmed under subsection 71(1) and who, or whose official agent, has not yet complied with sections 477.59 to 477.72 and 477.8 to 477.84 in respect of that election. [Those sections deal with reporting of election funding and disposing of any surplus — ed.]

For the sections of the CEA referred to in the definitions above, see CanLii.org.

127(3) opening words amended by 2002-2013 technical bill (Part 5 — technical), effective for monetary contributions made after Dec. 20, 2002 to add "the eligible amount of" and to delete (after "registered party") "a provincial division of a registered party"; but for monetary contributions made before 2004, ignore the words "a registered association".

127(3) amended by 2003 election financing bill, effective for monetary contributions made in taxation years ending after 2003, with transitional rules for 2004.

127(3) amended by *Canada Elections Act* (CEA), S.C. 2000, c. 9, generally effective for 2000 and later taxation years. The effect of the amendment was to increase the 75% credit threshold so it applies on the first $200 rather than the first $100. The change from $300 to $325 in 127(3)(c) decreased the maximum contribution that generates a credit from $1,150 to $1,075. The maximum credit remains $500.

Regulations: 2000 (prescribed information).

Information Circulars: 75-2R9: Contributions to a registered party, a registered association or to a candidate at a federal election.

Forms: T1 General return, Sched. 1, Lines 409, 410; T2092: Contributions to a registered party or to a registered association — information return; T2093: Contributions to a candidate at an election — information return.

(3.1) Issue of receipts — A receipt referred to in subsection (3) must be issued only in respect of the monetary contribution that it provides evidence for and only to the contributor who made it.

Related Provisions: 238(1) — Offences.

Notes: 127(3.1) amended by 2003 election financing bill (for monetary contributions made in tax years ending after 2003), *Canada Elections Act* (effective Sept. 2000).

Information Circulars: 75-2R9: Contributions to a registered party, a registered association or to a candidate at a federal election.

(3.2) Authorization required for receipts from registered associations — No agent of a registered association of a registered party shall issue a receipt referred to in subsection (3) unless the leader of the registered party has, in writing, notified the financial agent, as referred to in the *Canada Elections Act*, of the regis-

tered association that its agents are authorized to issue those receipts.

Related Provisions: 238(1) — Offences.

Notes: 127(3.2) replaced by 2003 election financing bill, for monetary contributions made in tax years ending after 2003. Although it is completely different from the earlier version, violation is still subject to 238(1).

127(3.2) amended by *Canada Elections Act*, effective Sept. 2000.

Information Circulars: 75-2R9: Contributions to a registered party, a registered association or to a candidate at a federal election.

(3.3) Prohibition — issuance of receipts — If the Commissioner of Canada Elections makes an application under subsection 521.1(2) of the *Canada Elections Act* in respect of a registered party, no registered agent of the party — including, for greater certainty, a registered agent appointed by a provincial division of the party — and no electoral district agent of a registered association of the party shall issue a receipt referred to in subsection (3) unless the Commissioner withdraws the application or the court makes an order under subsection 521.1(6) of that Act or dismisses the application.

Notes: See Notes to 127(3) re the *Figueroa* case. CEA s. 521.1(2) allows the Commissioner to apply to a Court for deregistration of a political party where the "party does not have as one of its fundamental purposes participating in public affairs by endorsing one or more of its members as candidates and supporting their election". The onus of proof is on the party (521.1(4)). 521.1(6) permits the Court to exempt the party and its registered associations from ITA 127(3.3), subject to any conditions the Court considers appropriate, if "the public interest and the need to ensure fairness of the electoral process warrant it".

127(3.3) added by 2004, c. 24, s. 24, effective May 15, 2004, originally to be in force only until May 15, 2006 or, if Parliament was not then in session, until 90 days after the start of the next session. This "sunset provision" was amended by S.C. 2006, c. 1, and s. 26 of the 2004 bill now requires only a Senate committee report reviewing the amendments.

(4) [Repealed]

Notes: 127(4) repealed by 2003 election financing bill, for monetary contributions made in tax years ending after 2003. It defined various terms with reference to the *Canada Elections Act*, now done in 127(3). Amended in 2000.

(4.1) Monetary contributions — form and content — For the purpose of subsections (3) and (3.1), a monetary contribution made by a taxpayer may be in the form of cash or of a negotiable instrument issued by the taxpayer. However, it does not include

(a) a monetary contribution that a taxpayer who is an agent authorized under the *Canada Elections Act* to accept monetary contributions makes in that capacity; or

(b) a monetary contribution in respect of which a taxpayer has received or is entitled to receive a financial benefit of any kind (other than a prescribed financial benefit or a deduction under subsection (3)) from a government, municipality or other public authority, whether as a grant, subsidy, forgivable loan or deduction from tax or an allowance or otherwise.

Related Provisions: 237.1(1)"gifting arrangement", "tax shelter" — Tax shelter registration requirement.

Notes: "Monetary contribution" is "an amount of money provided that is not repayable": *Canada Elections Act* 2(1). For para. (b) interpretation see 12(1)(x) Notes.

127(4.1) amended by S.C. 2006, c. 9 (effective 2007 except for pre-2007 contributions); 2003 election financing bill; S.C. 2000, c. 9.

Information Circulars: 75-2R9: Contributions to a registered party, a registered association or to a candidate at a federal election.

(4.2) [Repealed]

Notes: 127(4.2) amended by 2002-2013 technical bill and repealed by *Federal Accountability Act* (S.C. 2006, c. 9), both effective 2007 (except in respect of monetary contributions made before 2007).

127(4.2) earlier amended by *Canada Elections Act*, effective Sept. 1, 2000.

(5) Investment tax credit — There may be deducted from the tax otherwise payable by a taxpayer under this Part for a taxation year an amount not exceeding the lesser of

(a) the total of

(i) the taxpayer's investment tax credit at the end of the year in respect of property acquired before the end of the year, of the taxpayer's apprenticeship expenditure for the year or a preceding taxation year, of the taxpayer's flow-through mining expenditure for the year or a preceding taxation year, of the taxpayer's pre-production mining expenditure for the year or a preceding taxation year or of the taxpayer's SR&ED qualified expenditure pool at the end of the year or at the end of a preceding taxation year, and

(ii) the lesser of

(A) the taxpayer's investment tax credit at the end of the year in respect of property acquired in a subsequent taxation year, of the taxpayer's apprenticeship expenditure for a subsequent taxation year, of the taxpayer's flow-through mining expenditure for a subsequent taxation year, of the taxpayer's pre-production mining expenditure for a subsequent taxation year or of the taxpayer's SR&ED qualified expenditure pool at the end of the subsequent taxation year to the extent that an investment tax credit was not deductible under this subsection for the subsequent taxation year, and

(B) the amount, if any, by which the taxpayer's tax otherwise payable under this Part for the year exceeds the amount, if any, determined under subparagraph (i), and

(b) where Division E.1 applies to the taxpayer for the year, the amount, if any, by which

(i) the taxpayer's tax otherwise payable under this Part for the year

exceeds

(ii) the taxpayer's minimum amount for the year determined under section 127.51.

Related Provisions: 12(1)(t) — Income inclusion for ITCs; 13(7.1) — Deemed capital cost; 13(21)"undepreciated capital cost"I — Reduction in UCC of property to reflect ITCs; 37(1)(e) — ITC reduces SR&ED deduction; 53(2)(k)(ii) — Reduction in ACB of property to reflect ITCs; 66.1(6)"cumulative Canadian exploration expense"L — Reduction in CCEE; 87(2.11) — Vertical amalgamations; 127(8) — ITC of partnership; 127(11.1) — Reduction for assistance, etc.; 127(11.2) — Time of expenditure and acquisition; 127(26) — Expenditure unpaid within 180 days of year-end; 127.1(3) — Refundable ITC deemed claimed under 127(5); 128(2)(e)(iii)(C) — No credit on return filed by trustee following individual's discharge from bankruptcy; 152(6)(d) — Reassessment; 164(5), (5.1) — Effect of carryback of loss; 220(6), (7) — Assignment of ITC refund by corporation; 261(7)(a), 261(15) — Functional currency reporting.

Notes: This is actually a *credit* because it is a deduction from *tax*, not from income. See 127(9)"specified percentage" and 127(9)"investment tax credit" for the calculation of the credit. The amount claimed is optional: for CRA policy on changes to amounts already claimed see Information Circular 84-1.

Ainsworth Lumber, [2001] 3 C.T.C. 2001 (TCC), para. 53, held that 127(5) does not provide an ordering rule that requires older ITCs to be claimed before current ITCs. See VIEWS doc 2005-014368I7; May 2011 ICAA roundtable (tinyurl.com/cra-abtax), q. 25.

Structures to transfer ITCs within an affiliated group of companies may be acceptable: VIEWS doc 2007-0222921R3.

127(5)(a)(i) and (a)(ii)(A) amended by 2017 budget bill #1, for expenditures incurred after March 21, 2017 (unless incurred before 2020 under a written agreement entered into by that date), to delete "of the taxpayer's child care space amount for the year or a preceding taxation year" before "of the taxpayer's flow-through mining expenditure" in (a)(i), and "of the taxpayer's child care space amount for a subsequent taxation year" before "of the taxpayer's flow-through mining expenditure" in (a)(ii)(A).

127(5)(a)(i) and (ii)(A) amended by 2007 budget bill #2, effective March 19, 2007, to add references to child care space amount (defined in 127(9)).

127(5)(a)(i) and (ii)(A) amended by 2006 budget bill #2, for tax years that end after May 1, 2006, to add references to apprenticeship expenditures (defined in 127(9)).

127(5) earlier amended by 2003 resource bill (for 2003 and later tax years) and by 2000, 1995 and 1993 Budgets.

Regulations: 4600–4609.

Income Tax Folios: S3-F8-C1: Principal-business corporations in the resource industries [replaces IT-400].

Interpretation Bulletins: IT-92R2: Income of contractors; IT-411R: Meaning of "construction".

Information Circulars: 78-4R3: Investment tax credit rates; 84-1: Revision of capital cost allowance claims and other permissive deductions.

Application Policies: SR&ED 96-03: Claimants' entitlements and responsibilities; SR&ED 96-05: Penalties under subsec. 163(2).

CRA Audit Manual: 11.3.4: Tax credits; 11.3.6: Examples of loss allocation and the business investment tax credit.

Advance Tax Rulings: ATR-44: Utilization of deductions and credits within a related corporate group.

Forms: RC4290: Refunds for small business R&D [guide]; T2 Sched. 31: Investment tax credit — corporations; T661: SR&ED expenditures claim; T1263: Third-party payments for SR&ED; T2038 (Ind.): Investment tax credit (individuals); T4088: Claiming scientific research and experimental development expenditures — guide to form T661.

(6) Investment tax credit of cooperative corporation —

Where at any particular time in a taxation year a taxpayer that is a cooperative corporation within the meaning assigned by subsection 136(2) has, as required by subsection 135(3), deducted or withheld an amount from a payment made by it to any person pursuant to an allocation in proportion to patronage, the taxpayer may deduct from the amount otherwise required by that subsection to be remitted to the Receiver General, an amount, not exceeding the amount, if any, by which

(a) its investment tax credit at the end of the immediately preceding taxation year in respect of property acquired and expenditures made before the end of that preceding taxation year

exceeds the total of

(b) the amount deducted under subsection (5) from its tax otherwise payable under this Part for the immediately preceding taxation year in respect of property acquired and expenditures made before the end of that preceding taxation year, and

(c) the total of all amounts each of which is the amount deducted by virtue of this subsection from any amount otherwise required to be remitted by subsection 135(3) in respect of payments made by it before the particular time and in the taxation year,

and the amount, if any, so deducted from the amount otherwise required to be remitted by subsection 135(3)

(d) shall be deducted in computing the taxpayer's investment tax credit at the end of the taxation year, and

(e) shall be deemed to have been remitted by the taxpayer to the Receiver General on account of tax under this Part of the person to whom that payment was made.

Related Provisions: 12(1)(t) — Inclusion in income of ITCs; 13(7.1) — Deemed capital cost; 13(21)"undepreciated capital cost"I — Reduction in UCC to reflect ITCs; 53(2)(k)(ii) — Reduction in ACB of property to reflect ITCs; 66.1(6)"cumulative Canadian exploration expense"L — Reduction in CCEE.

Interpretation Bulletins: IT-362R: Patronage dividends.

Forms: T2 Sched. 31: Investment tax credit — corporations.

(7) Investment tax credit of certain trusts —

If, in a particular taxation year of a taxpayer who is a beneficiary under a trust that is a graduated rate estate or that is deemed to be in existence by section 143, an amount is determined in respect of the trust under paragraph (a), (a.1), (a.4), (b) or (e.1) of the definition "investment tax credit" in subsection (9) for its taxation year that ends in that particular taxation year, the trust may, in its return of income for its taxation year that ends in that particular taxation year, designate the portion of that amount that can, having regard to all the circumstances including the terms and conditions of the trust, reasonably be considered to be attributable to the taxpayer and was not designated by the trust in respect of any other beneficiary of the trust, and that portion is to be added in computing the investment tax credit of the taxpayer at the end of that particular taxation year and is to be deducted in computing the investment tax credit of the trust at the end of its taxation year that ends in that particular taxation year.

Related Provisions: 53(2)(h)(ii) — Reduction in ACB of interest in trust; 127(11.1)(d) — Deemed receipt of assistance or contract payment; 127(11.2) — Time of expenditure and acquisition.

Notes: 127(7) amended to delete "(a.5)" (after "(a.4)") by 2017 budget bill #1, for expenditures incurred after March 21, 2017 (unless incurred before 2020 under a written agreement entered into by that date), due to repeal of the child-care spaces credit.

127(7) amended by 2014 budget bill #2, for 2016 and later taxation years, to change "a testamentary trust or under an *inter vivos* trust" to "a trust that is a graduated rate estate". (See Notes to 122(1).)

127(7) amended by 2007 budget bill #2, effective March 19, 2007, to add "(a.5)"; by 2006 budget bill #2, for tax years that end after May 1, 2006, to add "(a.4)"; and by 1995 Budget to add "(a.1)".

Application Policies: SR&ED 2000-01: Cost of materials.

Forms: T2038 (Ind.): Investment tax credit (individuals); T2 Sched. 31: Investment tax credit — corporations.

(8) Investment tax credit of partnership — Subject to subsection (28), where, in a particular taxation year of a taxpayer who is a member of a partnership, an amount would be determined in respect of the partnership, for its taxation year that ends in the particular taxation year, under paragraph (a), (a.1), (a.4), (b) or (e.1) of the definition "investment tax credit" in subsection (9), if

(a) except for the purpose of subsection (13), the partnership were a person and its fiscal period were its taxation year, and

(b) in the case of a taxpayer who is a specified member of the partnership in the taxation year of the partnership, that definition were read without reference to paragraph (a.1) thereof, and paragraph (e.1) of that definition were read without reference to subparagraphs (ii) to (iv) thereof,

the portion of that amount that can reasonably be considered to be the taxpayer's share thereof shall be added in computing the investment tax credit of the taxpayer at the end of the particular year.

Related Provisions: 53(2)(c)(vi) — Reduction in ACB of partnership interest; 96(2.1)–(2.4) — Limited partnerships; 127(8.1) — ITC of limited partner; 127(8.3) — ITC not allocated to limited partners; 127(8.4) — Election — renunciation of allocated credits; 127(11.1)(d) — Deemed receipt of assistance or contract payment; 127(11.2) — Time of expenditure and acquisition; 127(23) — Taxation year of partnership for rules governing allocation of assistance; 127(28) — Recapture of ITC where partnership property converted to commercial use.

Notes: For discussion of ITCs and partnerships, see Lee, "Flow-Through of Partnership R&D Tax Credits", III(4) *Business Vehicles* (Federated Press) 150-53 (1997).

127(8) does not cover 127(9)"investment tax credit"(e), so a partnership does not get the extra 20% ITC for SR&ED under 127(10.1): *Canadian Solifuels*, 2001 FCA 280.

A passive partner ("specified member") is ineligible for R&D investment tax credits: 127(8)(b); *Lauger*, 2007 TCC 650.

A joint venture that is not a partnership is not subject to 127(8): VIEWS doc 2008-0269721I7.

127(8) opening words amended by 2017 budget bill #1 to change "(28) and (28.1)" to "(28)" and "(a.4), (a.5)" to "(a.4)", for expenditures incurred after March 21, 2017 (unless incurred before 2020 under a written agreement entered into by that date), due to repeal of the child-care spaces credit.

127(8) earlier amended by 2007 budget bill #2 (effective March 19, 2007), 2006 budget bill #2, 1998 and 1995 Budgets.

Application Policies: SR&ED 2000-04R2: Recapture of investment tax credit; SR&ED 2004-02R5: Filing requirements for claiming SR&ED.

Forms: T2038 (Ind.): Investment tax credit (individuals); T2 Sched. 31: Investment tax credit — corporations.

(8.1) Investment tax credit of limited partner — Notwithstanding subsection (8), if a taxpayer is a limited partner of a partnership at the end of a fiscal period of the partnership, the amount, if any, determined under subsection (8) to be added in computing the taxpayer's investment tax credit at the end of the taxpayer's taxation year in which that fiscal period ends shall not exceed the lesser of

(a) the portion of the amount that would, if this section were read without reference to this subsection, be determined under subsection (8) to be the amount to be added in computing the taxpayer's investment tax credit at the end of the taxpayer's taxation year in which that fiscal period ends as is considered to have arisen because of the expenditure by the partnership of an amount equal to the taxpayer's expenditure base (as determined under subsection (8.2) in respect of the partnership) at the end of that fiscal period, and

(b) the taxpayer's at-risk amount in respect of the partnership at the end of that fiscal period.

Related Provisions: 96(2.2) — At-risk amount; 96(2.4) — Limited partner; 127(8.2) — Expenditure base; 127(8.3) — ITC not allocated to limited partners; 127(8.5) — "At-risk amount", "limited partner".

Notes: 127(8.1) restricts ITCs that can be allocated by a partnership to a limited partner, based on the limited partner's expenditure base (127(8.2)) and at-risk amount (96(2.2)) for the partnership.

127(8.1) amended by 2006 budget bill #2 (for tax years that end after May 1, 2006), 1995 Budget.

(8.2) Expenditure base — For the purposes of subsection (8.1), a taxpayer's expenditure base in respect of a partnership at the end of a taxation year of the partnership is the lesser of

(a) the amount, if any, by which the total of

(i) the taxpayer's at-risk amount in respect of the partnership at the time the taxpayer last became a limited partner of the partnership,

(ii) all amounts described in subparagraph 53(1)(e)(iv) contributed by the taxpayer after the time the taxpayer last became a limited partner of the partnership and before the end of the year that may reasonably be considered to have increased the taxpayer's at-risk amount in respect of the partnership at the end of the taxation year in which the contribution was made, and

(iii) the amount, if any, by which

(A) the total of all amounts each of which is the taxpayer's share of any income of the partnership as determined under paragraph 96(1)(f) for the year, or a preceding year ending after the time the taxpayer last became a limited partner of the partnership,

exceeds

(B) the total of all amounts each of which is the taxpayer's share of any loss of the partnership as determined under paragraph 96(1)(g) for one of those years

exceeds the total of

(iv) all amounts received by the taxpayer after the time the taxpayer last became a limited partner of the partnership and before the end of the year as, on account or in lieu of payment of, or in satisfaction of, a distribution of the taxpayer's share of partnership profits or partnership capital, and

(v) the total of all amounts each of which is the amount of an expenditure of the partnership referred to in paragraph (8.1)(a) in respect of the taxpayer for a preceding year, and

(b) that proportion of the lesser of

(i) the total of all amounts each of which is, if the partnership were a person and its fiscal period were its taxation year,

(A) an amount a specified percentage of which would be determined in respect of the partnership under paragraph (a), (b) or (e.1) of the definition "investment tax credit" in subsection (9) for the year,

(A.1) an amount that would be the apprenticeship expenditure of the partnership if the reference to "$2,000" in paragraph (a) of the definition "apprenticeship expenditure" in subsection (9) were read as a reference to "$20,000" and paragraph (b) of that definition were read without reference to "10% of", or

(A.2) [Repealed]

(B) the amount that would be the SR&ED qualified expenditure pool of the partnership at the end of the year, and

(ii) the total of all amounts each of which is the amount determined under paragraph (a) in respect of each of the limited partners of the partnership at the end of the year

that

(iii) the amount determined in respect of the taxpayer under paragraph (a) for the year

is of

(iv) the amount determined under subparagraph (ii).

Related Provisions: 96(2.2) — At-risk amount; 96(2.4) — Limited partner; 127(8.5) — "At-risk amount", "limited partner".

Notes: 127(8.2)(b)(i)(A.2) repealed by 2017 budget bill #1, for expenditures incurred after March 21, 2017 (other than incurred before 2020 under a written agreement entered into by that date), due to repeal of the child-care spaces credit. It read:

> (A.2) an amount that would be the child care space amount in respect of a property of the partnership if the reference to "$10,000" in paragraph (a) of the definition "child care space amount" in subsection (9) were read as a reference to "$40,000" and paragraph (b) of that definition were read without reference to "25% of", or

127(8.2) amended by 2007 budget bill #2 (effective March 19, 2007), 2006 budget bill #2, 1995 Budget.

(8.3) Investment tax credit — allocation of unallocated partnership ITCs

— For the purpose of subsection (8), and subject to subsection (8.4), if a taxpayer is a member of a partnership (other than a specified member) throughout a fiscal period of the partnership, there shall be added to the amount that can reasonably be considered to be that member's share of the amount determined under subsection (8) the amount, if any, that is such portion of the amount determined under subsection (8.31) in respect of that fiscal period as is reasonable in the circumstances (having regard to the investment in the partnership, including debt obligations of the partnership, of each of those members of the partnership who was a member of the partnership throughout the fiscal period of the partnership and who was not a specified member of the partnership during the fiscal period of the partnership).

Related Provisions: 96(2.2) — At-risk amount; 96(2.4) — Limited partner; 127(8) — Election — renunciation of allocated credits; 127(8.4) — Election; 127(8.5) — "At-risk amount", "limited partner".

Notes: 127(8.3) and (8.31) provide essentially that partnership ITCs that cannot be allocated to specified members may be added (for purposes of 127(8)) to the ITCs allocated to partners who were not specified members. This additional allocation is based on what is reasonable in the circumstances. See VIEWS doc 2010-0357461I7.

127(8.3) amended by 2006 budget bill #2 (last change effective for 2007 and later years), 1995 Budget.

(8.31) Amount of unallocated partnership ITC

— For the purpose of subsection (8.3), the amount determined under this subsection in respect of a fiscal period of a partnership is the amount, if any, by which

(a) the total of all amounts each of which is an amount that would, if the partnership were a person and its fiscal period were its taxation year, be determined in respect of the partnership under paragraph (a), (a.1), (a.4), (b) or (e.1) of the definition "investment tax credit" in subsection (9) for a taxation year that is the fiscal period,

exceeds

(b) the total of

(i) the total of all amounts each of which is the amount determined under subsection (8) in respect of the fiscal period to be the share of the total determined under paragraph (a) of a partner of the partnership (other than a member of the partnership who was at any time in the fiscal period of the partnership a specified member of the partnership), and

(ii) the total of all amounts each of which is the amount determined under subsection (8), with reference to subsection (8.1), in respect of the fiscal period to be the share of the total determined under paragraph (a) of a partner of the partnership who was at any time in the fiscal period of the partnership a specified member of the partnership.

(iii) [Repealed]

Notes: See 127(8.3) Notes. 127(8.31)(a) amended to delete "(a.5)" (after "(a.4)") by 2017 budget bill #1, for expenditures incurred after March 21, 2017 (other than incurred before 2020 under a written agreement entered into by that date), due to repeal of the child-care spaces credit.

127(8.31) earlier amended by 2007 budget bill #2. Added by 2006 budget bill #2.

(8.4) Idem

— Notwithstanding subsection (8), where, pursuant to subsections (8) and (8.3) an amount would, but for this subsection, be required to be added in computing the investment tax credit of a taxpayer for a taxation year, where the taxpayer so elects in prescribed form and manner in the taxpayer's return of income (other than a return of income filed under subsection 70(2) or 104(23), paragraph 128(2)(e) or subsection 150(4)) under this Part for the year, such portion of the amount as is elected by the taxpayer shall, for the purposes of this section, be deemed not to have been required by subsection (8) to have been added in computing the taxpayer's investment tax credit at the end of the year.

Related Provisions: 96(2.2) — At-risk amount; 96(2.4) — Limited partner; 127(8.5) — "At-risk amount", "limited partner".

Notes: An election "in the taxpayer's return" is valid even if the return is filed late. See Notes to 7(1.31).

Forms: T932: Election by a member of a partnership to renounce investment tax credits pursuant to subsection 127(8.4).

(8.5) Definitions

— In subsections (8.1) to (8.4), the words "at-risk amount" of a taxpayer and "limited partner" of a partnership have the meanings assigned to those words by subsections 96(2.2) and (2.4), respectively.

(9) Idem

— In this section,

Notes: 127(9) also applied to s. 127.1 before RSC 1985 (5th Supp) consolidation for tax years ending after Nov. 1991. That rule of application is now in 127.1(2.1).

"annual investment tax credit limit" — [Repealed]

Notes: Definition "annual investment tax credit limit" repealed by 1993 Budget, effective for taxation years that begin in 1994 or later. There is now no limit on the extent to which ITCs can soak up tax payable. See Notes to 127(5).

"apprenticeship expenditure" of a taxpayer for a taxation year in respect of an eligible apprentice is the lesser of

(a) $2,000, and

(b) 10% of the eligible salary and wages payable by the taxpayer in the taxation year to the eligible apprentice in respect of the eligible apprentice's employment, in the taxation year and on or after May 2, 2006, by the taxpayer in a business carried on in Canada by the taxpayer in the taxation year;

Related Provisions: 127(9)"investment tax credit"(a.4) — Credit for expenditure; 127(9)"investment tax credit"(c) — Carryforward or carryback; 127(11.1)(c.4) — Reduction for assistance received.

Notes: 127(9)"apprenticeship expenditure" added by 2006 budget bill #2, effective for taxation years that end after May 1, 2006. It provides the Apprenticeship Job Creation Tax Credit. See also Notes to 127(9)"eligible apprentice", 127(11.1) and Reg. 7310. For CRA information see tinyurl.com/appren-cra.

Taxpayers who filed returns before this measure was enacted can claim it by filing a T2SCH31 or T2038(IND) by the deadline in 127(9)"investment tax credit"(m): VIEWS doc 2007-0252621E5.

For interpretation see VIEWS docs 2007-0222751E5, 2007-0228491E5, 2007-0250141E5, 2007-0257041E5, 2008-0268881I7, 2008-0280681I7 (no prorating for short taxation year), 2008-0281111I7 (apprentice carpenter-joiner does not qualify for work on home renovation jobs), 2008-0285401C6 (apprenticeship credit and investment tax credit can both be claimed on same expenditure), 2009-0313821E5 (determining when the 24 months starts in Quebec or Saskatchewan), 2009-0332681M4 (general discussion), 2009-0333751I7 (Ontario apprenticeship credit is assistance that reduces the federal claim, but the federal credit does not reduce the Ontario claim); 2009-0349461E5 and 2010-0372651E5 (no cumulative claim limit, so amount of claim per apprentice can vary based on year-ends); 2013-0504411E5 (employer can qualify even though apprenticeship contract is between province and trade union).

The federal government also provides a $2,000 Apprenticeship Incentive Grant and a $2,000 Apprenticeship Completion Grant (both taxable: 56(1)(n.1)). See servicecanada.gc.ca/eng/goc/apprenticeship.

There are also provincial incentives, e.g. British Columbia Training Tax Credit (itabc.ca; CRA forms T2SCH428, T1014-1), Ontario Apprenticeship Training Tax Credit (form T2SCH552; Ontario Ministry of Revenue *Corporations Tax Information Bulletin* 4015, "Apprenticeship Training Tax Credit" (April 2010)), Quebec tax credit for on-the-job training periods (*Taxation Act* ss. 1029.8.33.2 to 1029.8.33.10; see VIEWS doc 2009-0330311C6).

Forms: T2 Sched. 31: Investment tax credit — corporations; T2038 (Ind.): Investment tax credit (individuals).

"approved project" means a project with a total capital cost of depreciable property, determined without reference to subsection 13(7.1) or (7.4), of not less than $25,000 that has, on application in writing before July, 1988, been approved by such member of the Queen's Privy Council for Canada as is designated by the Governor in Council for the purposes of this definition in relation to projects in the appropriate province or region of a province;

Notes: 127(9)"approved project" amended in 1990, effective February 23, 1990, to replace "the Minister of Regional Industrial Expansion" with "such member ... of a province".

"approved project property" — [Repealed]

Notes: Definition "approved project property" repealed by 1995 Budget, for taxation years that begin after 1995, as it is no longer relevant. It applied to certain buildings, machinery and equipment acquired before 1993 for approved projects in Cape Breton.

"Cape Breton" means Cape Breton Island and that portion of the Province of Nova Scotia within the following described boundary:

beginning at a point on the southwesterly shore of Chedabucto Bay near Red Head, said point being S 70 degrees E (Nova Scotia grid meridian) from Geodetic Station Sand, thence in a southwesterly direction to a point on the northwesterly boundary of highway 344, said point being southwesterly 240' from the intersection of King Brook with said highway boundary, thence northwesterly to Crown post 6678, thence continuing northwesterly to Crown post 6679, thence continuing northwesterly to Crown post 6680, thence continuing northwesterly to Crown post 6681, thence continuing northwesterly to Crown post 6632, thence continuing northwesterly to Crown post 6602, thence northerly to Crown post 8575; thence northerly to Crown post 6599, thence continuing northerly to Crown post 6600, thence northwesterly to the southwest angle of the Town of Mulgrave, thence along the westerly boundary of the Town of Mulgrave and a prolongation thereof northerly to the Antigonish-Guysborough county line, thence along said county line northeasterly to the southwesterly shore of the Strait of Canso, thence following the southwesterly shore of the Strait of Canso and the northwesterly shore of Chedabucto Bay southeasterly to the place of beginning;

"certified property" of a taxpayer means any property (other than an approved project property) described in paragraph (a) or (b) of the definition "qualified property" in this subsection

(a) that was acquired by the taxpayer

(i) after October 28, 1980 and

(A) before 1987, or

(B) before 1988 where the property is

(I) a building under construction before 1987, or

(II) machinery and equipment ordered in writing by the taxpayer before 1987,

(ii) after 1986 and before 1989, other than a property included in subparagraph (i),

(iii) after 1988 and before 1995,

(iv) after 1994 and before 1996 where

(A) the property is acquired by the taxpayer for use in a project that was substantially advanced by or on behalf of the taxpayer, as evidenced in writing, before February 22, 1994, and

(B) construction of the project by or on behalf of the taxpayer begins before 1995, or

(v) after 1994 where the property

(A) is acquired by the taxpayer under a written agreement of purchase and sale entered into by the taxpayer before February 22, 1994,

(B) was under construction by or on behalf of the taxpayer on February 22, 1994, or

(C) is machinery or equipment that will be a fixed and integral part of property under construction by or on behalf of the taxpayer on February 22, 1994,

and that has not been used, or acquired for use or lease, for any purpose whatever before it was acquired by the taxpayer, and

(b) that is part of a facility as defined for the purposes of the *Regional Development Incentives Act*, chapter R-3 of the Revised Statutes of Canada, 1970, and was acquired primarily for use by the taxpayer in a prescribed area;

Notes: In *Ainsworth Lumber*, [2001] 3 C.T.C. 2001 (TCC), a project was held to be "substantially advanced" by Feb. 22/94 and thus met the test in cl. (a)(iv)(A).

Subpara. (a)(iii) amended to add "and before 1995", and subparas. (a)(iv) and (v) added, by 1994 Budget, for property acquired and expenditures incurred after 1994.

Regulations: 4602 (prescribed area).

"child care space amount" — [Repealed]

Notes: This credit has been eliminated. Definition repealed by 2017 budget bill #1, for expenditures incurred after March 21, 2017 (unless incurred before 2020 under a written agreement entered into by that date). It read:

"child care space amount" of a taxpayer for a taxation year is, if the provision of child care spaces is ancillary to one or more businesses of the taxpayer that are carried on in Canada in the taxation year and that do not otherwise include the provision of child care spaces, the lesser of

(a) the amount obtained when $10,000 is multiplied by the number of new child care spaces created by the taxpayer during the taxation year in a licensed child care facility for the benefit of children of the taxpayer's employees, or of a combination of children of the taxpayer's employees and other children; and

(b) 25% of the taxpayer's eligible child care space expenditure for the taxation year;

The ITC for this amount arose under 127(9)"investment tax credit"(a.5).

For CRA interpretation see VIEWS doc 2009-0336831M4.

127(9)"child care space amount" added by 2007 budget bill #2, for expenditures incurred after March 18, 2007.

"contract payment" means

(a) an amount paid or payable to a taxpayer, by a taxable supplier in respect of the amount, for scientific research and experimental development to the extent that it is performed

(i) for or on behalf of a person or partnership entitled to a deduction in respect of the amount because of subparagraph 37(1)(a)(i.01) or (i.1), and

(ii) at a time when the taxpayer is dealing at arm's length with the person or partnership, or

(b) an amount in respect of an expenditure of a current nature (within the meaning assigned by paragraph 37(8)(d)) of a taxpayer, other than a prescribed amount, payable by a Canadian government or municipality or other Canadian public authority or by a person exempt, because of section 149, from tax under this Part on all or part of the person's taxable income for scientific research and experimental development to be performed for it or on its behalf;

Related Provisions: 127(18)–(22) — Reduction of qualified expenditures to reflect contract payment; 127(25) — Anti-avoidance — deemed contract payment.

Notes: 127(18)-(22) prevent double-claiming the SR&ED credit (see 127(9)"SR&ED qualified expenditure pool" Notes) by both the entity performing the work (receiving a "contract payment" **(CP)**) and the payer. The CP reduces the performer's SR&ED expenses. For the payer, only 80% qualifies for credit: 127(9)"qualified expenditure"(a)(ii).

In *Com Dev*, [1999] 2 C.T.C. 2566 (TCC), the federal government's contract with Spar Aerospace to design and manufacture the Radarsat satellite stated that the intellectual property (IP) Spar developed would belong to the Crown (para. 10). (The government payments to Spar were presumably CPs.) The Court held Spar's payments to Com Dev under a subcontract were not CPs, as Com Dev did not transfer its IP to Spar under the subcontract. In *MDA Systems*, 2020 QCCQ 4190 (under the parallel Quebec rule), government payments for computer work on Radarsat were CPs, as the IP was transferred to the government.

A reimbursement of costs by a non-resident that is included in business income (see 9(1) Notes at "Disbursements") is not a CP: VIEWS doc 2008-0276121E5.

See also Chung, "The Quagmire that is Contract Payments", 2004 BC Tax Conf (ctf.ca), 14:1-32.

Definition amended by 2012 budget bill #2 (changing "37(1)(a)(i)" to "37(1)(a)(i.01)" in (a)(i) for expenditures after 2012, and limiting (b) to *current* expenditures after 2013, due to repeal of 37(1)(b)); 1995 Budget; 1992 technical bill.

Regulations: 4606 (prescribed amount).

Application Policies: SR&ED 94-04: Definition of "contract payment" in subsec. 127(9); SR&ED 2002-03: Taxable supplier rules; SR&ED 2005-02: General rules concerning the treatment of government and non government assistance.

"designated region" — [Repealed under former Act]

Notes: See prescribed designated region in the definition of "specified percentage" in this subsection and in Reg. 4607.

"eligible apprentice" means an individual who is employed in Canada in a trade prescribed in respect of a province or in respect of Canada, during the first twenty-four months of the individual's apprenticeship contract registered with the province or Canada, as the case may be, under an apprenticeship program designed to certify or license individuals in the trade;

Notes: See Notes to 127(9)"apprenticeship expenditure", and to Reg. 7310 for list of prescribed (Red Seal) trades.

The apprentice need not sign a separate contract with the employer: VIEWS doc 2007-0228611E5. For interpretation of "during the first 24 months" see 2014-0532451E5.

127(9)"eligible apprentice" added by 2006 budget bill #2, effective for taxation years that end after May 1, 2006, and amended retroactive to its introduction by 2007 budget bill #2. The 2007 amendment specifies that prescribed trades are "in respect of a province" (the Red Seal trades differ by province), and changed "two years" to "24 months", but VIEWS doc 2007-0228611E5 had noted anyway that "two years" means two 12-month periods, based on *Interpretation Act* s. 37(1).

Regulations: 7310 (prescribed trades).

"eligible child care space expenditure" — [Repealed]

Notes: This credit has been eliminated. Definition repealed by 2017 budget bill #1, for expenditures incurred after March 21, 2017 (unless incurred before 2020 under a written agreement entered into by that date). It read:

> "eligible child care space expenditure" of a taxpayer for a taxation year is the total of all amounts each of which is an amount
>
> > (a) that is incurred by the taxpayer in the taxation year for the sole purpose of the creation of one or more new child care spaces in a licensed child care facility operated for the benefit of children of the taxpayer's employees, or of a combination of children of the taxpayer's employees and other children, and
> >
> > (b) that is
> >
> > > (i) incurred by the taxpayer to acquire depreciable property of a prescribed class (other than a specified property) for use in the child care facility, or
> > >
> > > (ii) incurred by the taxpayer to make a specified child care start-up expenditure in respect of the child care facility;

25% of this expenditure was included in 127(9)"child care space amount".

For CRA interpretation see VIEWS doc 2014-0526161E5.

127(9)"eligible child care space expenditure" added by 2007 budget bill #2, effective for expenditures incurred after March 18, 2007.

"eligible salary and wages" payable by a taxpayer to an eligible apprentice means the amount, if any, that is the salary and wages payable by the taxpayer to the eligible apprentice in respect of the first 24 months of the apprenticeship (other than a qualified expenditure incurred by the taxpayer in a taxation year, remuneration that is based on profits, bonuses, amounts described in section 6 or 7, and amounts deemed to be incurred by subsection 78(4));

Related Provisions: 127(11.1)(c.4) — Reduction for assistance; 127(11.4) — Special rule for eligible salary and wages.

Notes: See Notes to 127(9)"apprenticeship expenditure", and to 127(11.1) re application of 127(11.1)(c.4).

Definition amended by 2002-2013 technical bill, for tax years that end after Nov. 5, 2010, to exclude a qualified expenditure. 127(9)"eligible salary and wages" added by 2006 budget bill #2, for tax years that end after May 1, 2006.

"eligible taxpayer" — [No longer relevant.]

Notes: "Eligible taxpayer" added by 1992 Economic Statement, effective for property acquired after Dec. 2, 1992. It describes entities eligible to earn the 10% small business investment tax credit before 1994 (see 127(9)"qualified small-business property").

"first term shared-use-equipment", of a taxpayer, means depreciable property of the taxpayer (other than prescribed depreciable property of a taxpayer) acquired before 2014 that is used by the taxpayer, during its operating time in the period (in this subsection and subsection (11.1) referred to as the "first period") beginning at the time the property was acquired by the taxpayer and ending at the end of the taxpayer's first taxation year ending at least 12 months after that time, primarily for the prosecution of scientific research and experimental development in Canada, but does not include general purpose office equipment or furniture;

Related Provisions: 37(1.3) — SR&ED within 200 nautical miles offshore is deemed done in Canada; 88(1)(e.3) closing words — Winding-up — parent deemed continuation of subsidiary; 127(11.5)(b) — Adjustments to qualified expenditures.

Notes: For CRA interpretation see VIEWS doc 2009-0316561E5.

Words "acquired before 2014" added by 2012 budget bill #2, effective March 29, 2012.

Definition "first term shared-use-equipment" added by 1992 Economic Statement, effective for property acquired after December 2, 1992. See 127(11.1)(e).

Regulations: 2900(11) (prescribed depreciable property).

Application Policies: SR&ED 2005-01: Shared-use equipment.

"flow-through mining expenditure" of a taxpayer for a taxation year means an expense deemed by subsection 66(12.61) (or by subsection 66(18) as a consequence of the application of subsection 66(12.61) to the partnership, referred to in paragraph (c) of this definition, of which the taxpayer is a member) to be incurred by the taxpayer in the year

(a) that is a Canadian exploration expense incurred by a corporation after March 2019 and before 2025 (including, for greater certainty, an expense that is deemed by subsection 66(12.66) to be incurred before 2025) in conducting mining exploration activity from or above the surface of the earth for the purpose of determining the existence, location, extent or quality of a mineral resource described in paragraph (a) or (d) of the definition "mineral resource" in subsection 248(1),

(b) that

> (i) is an expense described in paragraph (f) of the definition "Canadian exploration expense" in subsection 66.1(6), and
>
> (ii) is not an expense in respect of
>
> > (A) trenching, if one of the purposes of the trenching is to carry out preliminary sampling (other than specified sampling),
> >
> > (B) digging test pits (other than digging test pits for the purpose of carrying out specified sampling), and
> >
> > (C) preliminary sampling (other than specified sampling),

(c) an amount in respect of which is renounced in accordance with subsection 66(12.6) by the corporation to the taxpayer (or a partnership of which the taxpayer is a member) under an agreement described in that subsection and made after March 2019 and before April 2024, and

(d) that is not an expense that was renounced under subsection 66(12.6) to the corporation (or a partnership of which the corporation is a member), unless that renunciation was under an agreement described in that subsection and made after March 2019 and before April 2024;

(e) [Repealed]

Related Provisions: 127(9)"investment tax credit"(a.2) — 15% credit for expenditure; 127(9)"investment tax credit"(c) — Carryforward or carryback; 127(11.1)(c.2) — Reduction for assistance.

Notes: Credit for flow-through mining expenditures is provided in 127(9)"investment tax credit"(a.2). The term generally means an expense deemed incurred by the taxpayer in the year as a result of a corporation's renunciation under a flow-through share agreement (66(12.6)-(12.61)) and that meets the conditions in paras. (a)-(e). See also 127(11.1)(c.2) and 127(9)"pre-production mining expenditure".

Several provinces offer parallel credits: e.g., BC Mining Flow-Through Share Tax Credit; Ontario Focused Flow-Through Share Tax Credit; Manitoba Mineral Exploration Tax Credit; Saskatchewan Mineral Exploration Tax Credit.

The federal Budget extended the credit, by one year, annually from 2003 through 2018. The Nov. 2018 Economic Statement and 2019 Budget finally extended it by 5 years.

Paras. (a), (c), (d) amended by 2019 budget bill #1, to change all instances of "2018" to "2019", "2019" to "2024" and "2020" to "2025", for expenses renounced under a flow-through share agreement entered into after March 2019.

Paras. (a), (c), (d) amended by 2018 budget bill #1 to change all instances of 2017 to 2018, 2018>2019 and 2019>2020, for expenses renounced under a flow-through share agreement entered into after March 2018.

Identical amendments to the above made each prior year to move all dates one year forward by 2017, 2016, 2015, 2014, 2013, 2012 budget bills #1; 2011 budget bill #2; 2010, 2009, 2008 budget bills #1. Earlier extensions by 2007 budget bill #2, 2006 budget bill #1, 2004 and 2003 Budgets. Definition added by 2000 Budget.

Income Tax Folios: S3-F8-C1: Principal-business corporations in the resource industries [replaces IT-400].

"Gaspé Peninsula" means that portion of the Gaspé region of the Province of Quebec that extends to the western border of Kamouraska County and includes the Magdalen Islands;

Notes: "Kamouraska County" means the regional municipality, not the electoral district of Kamouraska: VIEWS doc 2004-0101461E5.

"government assistance" means assistance from a government, municipality or other public authority whether as a grant, subsidy, forgivable loan, deduction from tax, investment allowance or as any other form of assistance other than as a deduction under subsection (5) or (6);

Related Provisions: 12(1)(x) — Income inclusion for assistance; 248(16), (18) — GST input tax credit and rebate deemed to be government assistance; 248(16.1), (18.1) — QST input tax credit and rebate deemed to be government assistance.

Notes: See 12(1)(x) Notes re meaning of "assistance" and related words.

Application Policies: SR&ED 2005-02: General rules concerning the treatment of government and non government assistance.

Transfer Pricing Memoranda: TPM-17: The impact of government assistance on transfer pricing.

"investment tax credit" of a taxpayer at the end of a taxation year means the amount, if any, by which the total of

(a) the total of all amounts each of which is the specified percentage of the capital cost to the taxpayer of qualified property or qualified resource property acquired by the taxpayer in the year,

(a.1) 15% of the amount by which the taxpayer's SR&ED qualified expenditure pool at the end of the year exceeds the total of all amounts each of which is the super-allowance benefit amount for the year in respect of the taxpayer in respect of a province,

(a.2) where the taxpayer is an individual (other than a trust), 15% of the taxpayer's flow-through mining expenditures for the year,

(a.3) if the taxpayer is a taxable Canadian corporation, the total of

(i) the specified percentage of the portion of the taxpayer's pre-production mining expenditure described in subparagraph (a)(i) of the definition "pre-production mining expenditure", and

(ii) the specified percentage of the portion of the taxpayer's pre-production mining expenditure described in subparagraph (a)(ii) of the definition "pre-production mining expenditure",

(a.4) the total of all amounts each of which is an apprenticeship expenditure of the taxpayer for the taxation year in respect of an eligible apprentice,

(a.5) [Repealed]

(b) the total of amounts required by subsection (7) or (8) to be added in computing the taxpayer's investment tax credit at the end of the year,

(c) the total of all amounts each of which is an amount determined under any of paragraphs (a) to (b) in respect of the taxpayer for any of the 10 taxation years immediately preceding or the 3 taxation years immediately following the year,

(d) [Repealed]

(e) the total of all amounts each of which is an amount required by subsection (10.1) to be added in computing the taxpayer's investment tax credit at the end of the year or at the end of any of the 10 taxation years immediately preceding or the 3 taxation years immediately following the year,

(e.1) the total of all amounts each of which is the specified percentage of that part of a repayment made by the taxpayer in the year or in any of the 10 taxation years immediately preceding or the 3 taxation years immediately following the year that can reasonably be considered to be a repayment of government assistance, non-government assistance or a contract payment that reduced

(i) the capital cost to the taxpayer of a property under paragraph (11.1)(b),

(ii) the amount of a qualified expenditure incurred by the taxpayer under paragraph (11.1)(c) for taxation years that began before 1996,

(iii) the prescribed proxy amount of the taxpayer under paragraph (11.1)(f) for taxation years that began before 1996,

(iv) a qualified expenditure incurred by the taxpayer under any of subsections (18) to (20),

(v) the amount of a pre-production mining expenditure of the taxpayer under paragraph (11.1)(c.3), or

(vi) the amount of eligible salary and wages payable by the taxpayer to an eligible apprentice under paragraph (11.1)(c.4), to the extent that that reduction had the effect of reducing the amount of an apprenticeship expenditure of the taxpayer, and

(vii) [Repealed]

(e.2) the total of all amounts each of which is the specified percentage of ¼ of that part of a repayment made by the taxpayer in the year or in any of the 10 taxation years immediately preceding or the 3 taxation years immediately following the year that can reasonably be considered to be a repayment of government assistance, non-government assistance or a contract payment that reduced

(i) the amount of a qualified expenditure incurred by the taxpayer under paragraph (11.1)(e) for taxation years that began before 1996, or

(ii) a qualified expenditure incurred by the taxpayer under any of subsections (18) to (20),

in respect of first term shared-use-equipment or second term shared-use-equipment, and, for that purpose, a repayment made by the taxpayer in any taxation year preceding the first taxation year that ends coincidentally with the first period or the second period in respect of first term shared-use-equipment or second term shared-use-equipment, respectively, is deemed to have been incurred by the taxpayer in that first taxation year,

exceeds the total of

(f) the total of all amounts each of which is an amount deducted under subsection (5) from the tax otherwise payable under this Part by the taxpayer for a preceding taxation year in respect of property acquired, or an expenditure incurred, in the year or in any of the 10 taxation years immediately preceding or the 2 taxation years immediately following the year, or in respect of the taxpayer's SR&ED qualified expenditure pool at the end of such a year,

(g) the total of all amounts each of which is an amount required by subsection (6) to be deducted in computing the taxpayer's investment tax credit

(i) at the end of the year, or

(ii) [Repealed]

(iii) at the end of any of the 9 taxation years immediately preceding or the 3 taxation years immediately following the year,

(h) the total of all amounts each of which is an amount required by subsection (7) to be deducted in computing the taxpayer's investment tax credit

(i) at the end of the year, or

(ii) [Repealed]

(iii) at the end of any of the 10 taxation years immediately preceding or the 3 taxation years immediately following the year,

(i) the total of all amounts each of which is an amount claimed under subparagraph 192(2)(a)(ii) by the taxpayer for the year or a preceding taxation year in respect of property acquired, or an expenditure made, in the year or the 10 taxation years immediately preceding the year,

(j) if the taxpayer is subject to a loss restriction event at any time before the end of the year, the amount determined under subsection (9.1) in respect of the taxpayer, and

(k) if the taxpayer is subject to a loss restriction event at any time after the end of the year, the amount determined under subsection (9.2) in respect of the taxpayer,

except that no amount shall be included in the total determined under any of paragraphs (a) to (e.2) in respect of an outlay, expense or expenditure that would, if this Act were read without reference to subsections (26) and 78(4), be made or incurred by the taxpayer in the course of earning income in a particular taxation year, and no amount shall be added under paragraph (b) in computing the taxpayer's investment tax credit at the end of a particular taxation year in respect of an outlay, expense or expenditure made or incurred by a trust or a partnership in the course of earning income, if

(l) any of the income is exempt income or is exempt from tax under this Part,

(m) the taxpayer does not file with the Minister a prescribed form containing prescribed information in respect of the amount on or before the day that is one year after the taxpayer's filing-due date for the particular year;

Proposed Amendment — ITC for carbon-capture technology

Federal Budget, Chapter 5, April 19, 2021: *Tax Incentive for Carbon Capture, Utilization, and Storage*

Canadian innovators and engineers have developed some of the leading global technologies for CCUS technologies that are in demand as more countries take action to fight climate change. The government intends to take significant action to support and accelerate the adoption of these technologies. By providing incentives to adopt CCUS technologies, the proposed measure will be an important element in Canada's plan to achieve net-zero emissions by 2050. This important new element of Canada's tax system is also intended to accelerate the growth of new businesses and jobs related to carbon capture.

Budget 2021 proposes to introduce an investment tax credit for capital invested in CCUS projects with the goal of reducing emissions by at least 15 megatonnes of CO2 annually. This measure will come into effect in 2022.

The government will move quickly with a 90-day consultation period with stakeholders on the design of the investment tax credit, after which it will announce more details — including the rate of the incentive. It is not intended that the investment tax credit be available for Enhanced Oil Recovery projects. The government intends to make the credit available for direct air capture projects. The government will be seeking input from all industrial subsectors (e.g. oil sands, refining, cement, fertilizer, power generation, direct air capture, etc.), recognizing that various subsectors face different challenges in adopting CCUS. The tax credit will also support hydrogen production. During the consultation, the government will consider how equivalent tax support could be provided to producers of green hydrogen. The consultation will include key provincial governments, encouraging them to create complementary measures for CCUS projects in their jurisdictions.

Following consultations, the government intends to introduce legislation at the earliest opportunity to implement the investment tax credit. The government will also analyze how the tax system can be used to further support the commercialization and deployment of breakthrough technologies that may be critical to creating our net-zero future.

Dept. of Finance news release, June 7, 2021: *Department of Finance launches consultations on investment tax credit for carbon capture, utilization, and storage*

Today, the Department of Finance is launching consultations with stakeholders on the recent federal budget's proposal to introduce a new investment tax credit for capital invested in carbon capture, utilization, and storage (CCUS) projects. Canadian innovators and engineers have developed some of the leading global technologies for CCUS, which are in demand as more countries take action to fight climate change. Investing in these technologies today is a significant step towards achieving Canada's climate targets — and a greener, more resilient future for all Canadians.

CCUS is an important tool for reducing emissions in high-emitting sectors. It uses advanced technologies to capture carbon dioxide emissions from fuel combustion, industrial processes, or directly from the air. The captured carbon can then be used to create new and innovative products or stored deep underground.

The federal government intends for the new investment tax credit to be available for a broad range of CCUS applications across different industrial subsectors (e.g. concrete, plastics, fuels), including blue hydrogen projects and direct air capture projects, but not enhanced oil recovery projects. The government is seeking input from all industrial

subsectors, recognizing that various subsectors face different challenges in adopting CCUS. The consultation will include key provincial governments, as part of efforts to encourage complementary measures for CCUS projects in their respective jurisdictions.

The CCUS investment tax credit will be available starting in 2022. On the same timeline, the government will also determine how comparable tax support could be provided to producers of green hydrogen.

Stakeholders are invited to provide comments on the government's proposed approach by September 7, 2021. Details regarding how to participate are found in the related link below.

Quick facts

- The proposed new investment tax credit will support and accelerate the adoption of CCUS technologies, with the goal of reducing emissions by at least 15 megatonnes of CO2 annually. Investment is needed to support research and development that will help to advance the technology, lower its costs, and make sure Canada stays ahead of the curve in the global market for CCUS.

- In addition to the proposed investment tax credit for CCUS, the recent federal budget also proposed to provide $319 million to Natural Resources Canada over seven years, starting in 2021-22, with $1.5 million in remaining amortization, to support research, development, and demonstrations that would improve the commercial viability of CCUS technologies.

Contacts

Media may contact: Media Relations, Department of Finance Canada, mediare@fin.gc.ca, 613-369-4000. General enquiries: 1-833-712-2292, email financepublic-financepublique@fin.gc.ca

Consultation — Investment Tax Credit for Carbon Capture, Utilization, and Storage

Join in: Open until September 7, 2021

In Budget 2021, the government proposed the introduction of an investment tax credit for capital invested in carbon capture, utilization, and storage (CCUS) projects with the goal of reducing emissions by at least 15 megatonnes of CO2 annually. Investment is needed to support research and development that will help to advance the technology, lower its costs, and make sure Canada stays ahead of the curve in the global market for CCUS.

The federal government intends for the new investment tax credit be available for a broad range of CCUS applications across different industrial subsectors (e.g. concrete, plastics, fuels), including blue hydrogen projects and direct air capture projects, to the extent that captured CO2 is not used in enhanced oil recovery projects. The government is seeking input from all industrial subsectors, recognizing that various subsectors face different challenges in adopting CCUS. The consultation will include key provincial governments, as part of efforts to encourage complementary measures for CCUS projects in their respective jurisdictions.

The CCUS investment tax credit will be available starting in 2022. On the same timeline, the government will also determine how comparable tax support could be provided to producers of green hydrogen.

Key questions for consideration

This consultation seeks input from stakeholders on the design of the investment tax credit for CCUS, including the rate of the incentive, to achieve the government's goal. Questions for discussion are outlined below. Additional comments or feedback relevant to the scope of this consultation are also welcome.

The government is also requesting information about potential CCUS project proposals from varying industrial subsectors that could contribute to the government's goal of reducing emissions by at least 15 megatonnes of CO2 annually.

General considerations

- What are the risks associated with investing in CCUS? How is this risk incorporated into the evaluation of prospective projects?

- What types of projects should be eligible for the investment tax credit?

- What are the main factors that contribute to the costs of adopting CCUS? Are there important variations in cost that can be identified by industrial subsector? Are there important differences in the efficiency of different CCUS technologies that impact cost of adoption? Do costs vary significantly by project, by technology type or by subsector of application?

- Given the environmental measures announced by the government, what level of tax support could achieve at least a 15 megatonne annual emission reduction? What barriers to CCUS deployment may remain?

- What are the limits to how rapidly CCUS can be deployed? With the right supports in place, how quickly could your company or sector contribute to the 15 megatonne emission reduction objective?

- In the case of industrial use projects (other than Enhanced Oil Recovery), how does the use of CO2 affect project economics? Are there additional revenue streams that can be generated? What types of usage projects are being considered and how would the permanent sequestration of CO2 be ensured?

- What environmental benefits, if any, can be produced through industrial use projects that may not lead to permanent sequestration?

Technical Tax Credit Design Considerations

- What CCUS capital investments should be eligible to receive tax support and why (e.g., CO2 capture and compression equipment, pipeline infrastructure, sequestration infrastructure, other)?

- Should greenfield and retrofit CCUS projects receive the same support on the same range of equipment?

- What financial risks are associated with pipelines to transport CO2? How do they differ from those of capture or sequestration projects?

- How would an investment tax credit help defray costs or share risks between a proponent and the government?

- What is the typical ownership and financing structure of a CCUS project in your industry and what type of players or partners are typically involved?

- Could the design of the tax credit encourage or ensure a certain performance standard? For example, the amount of sequestration per dollar invested?

- What key elements of the design of the tax credit would be most important to advancing a project in your industry?

- If CO2 is not permanently sequestered, or escapes back into the atmosphere, what circumstances could permit a recovery of tax support? Similarly, if a project changes to an ineligible project (e.g., to use Enhanced Oil Recovery) what consequences should be associated with such a change in use?

- Though projects may be required to capture and transport CO2 in accordance with the laws of Canada or a province or territory that regulates that capture in order to be eligible, what additional assurances could be provided that CO2 is permanently sequestered?

What ongoing monitoring and validating actions could be undertaken?

CCUS Project Proposals

- Please identify potential CCUS projects that could help the Government of Canada meet its emission reduction goal of reducing GHG emissions by at least 15 million tonnes. Projects will be used to identify the potential for CCUS deployment in Canada.

- To submit a project proposal, please complete the project proposal template. Instructions are included in the booklet and completion of all relevant fields is requested. Completed templates or questions regarding submissions can be emailed to CCUS-CUSC@fin.gc.ca with "CCUS Project" in the title.

CCUS Project Proposal Template [XLS - 32 KB]

Who is the focus of this consultation?

Through this consultation, we want to hear from all stakeholders, including environmental groups, advocacy groups, and industry (including all industrial subsectors, such as direct air capture, power generation, fertilizer, cement, refining, and oil sands). Interested tax practitioners and members of the public are also welcome to provide input.

In submitting your comments, please include:

- Full name of the official;
- Name of the organization;
- Telephone number, including area code; and
- Reply e-mail address.

The government will also be consulting with key provincial governments where there is the greatest potential for CCUS, encouraging them to create complementary measures for CCUS projects in their jurisdictions.

Participate through email

Due to COVID-19 public health considerations, email submissions are preferred. Send us your comments at CCUS-CUSC@fin.gc.ca with "CCUS Consultation" as the subject line. Should you wish to provide comments by mail, please direct your submission to the attention of the Tax Policy Branch.

Treatment of confidential information

- Input received as part of this consultation is subject to the *Access to Information Act* and the *Privacy Act*. We will protect the confidentiality of your information in accordance with these Acts.

- Confidential information contained in project proposals, including financial, commercial, scientific or technical information, that is treated consistently in a confidential manner by the third party, is exempt from disclosure under section 20 of the *Access to Information Act*.

- Reasonable efforts will be made to maintain the confidentiality of any confidential information provided to the Department. Please advise when providing your comments and project proposals whether you:

  — consent to the disclosure of your comments and proposal information in whole or in part;

  — request that your identity and any personal identifiers be removed prior to publication; or

  — wish that any portions of your comments and proposal information be kept confidential (if so, clearly identify the confidential portions).

What's next?

We'll be collecting feedback and will consider the input alongside the analysis of departmental officials to help inform decisions on the design and rate of the investment tax credit for CCUS projects.

Get in touch

CCUS-CUSC@fin.gc.ca

Related Provisions: 37(11) — Filing deadline for R&D claims; 66(10.1)(b) — Joint exploration corporation; 87(2)(qq) — Amalgamation — continuation of corporation; 87(2.11) — Vertical amalgamations; 88(1)(e.3) — Flow-through of ITC to parent on wind-up of corporation; 127(7) — ITC of testamentary trust; 127(8) — ITC of partnership; 127(9.01), (9.02) — Transitional rules for 20-year carryforward; 127(9.1) — Where control acquired before end of year; 127(9.2) — Where control acquired after beginning of year; 127(10.1) — Addition to ITC for SR&ED done by CCPC; 127(10.8) — Regeneration of ITCs where entitlement to assistance expires; 127(11.1), (11.2) — ITC calculation rules; 127(26) — Expenditure unpaid within 180 days of end of year; 127(27), (29) — Reduction of ITC where property converted to commercial use; 127(28) — Recapture of negative ITC; 127.1(2), (2.01) — Refundable ITC; 220(2.2) — No extension allowed for deadline in para. (m); 248(1)"investment tax credit" — Definition applies to entire Act; 251.2 — Loss restriction event.

Notes: See Notes to 127(9)"specified percentage" and "SR&ED qualified expenditure pool". Ignoring the special cases, the ITC is (a) the specified percentage of the cost of qualified property (see Reg. 4600), plus (a.1) 15% [20% before 2014] of R&D expenditures (but see also 127(10.1) as well as 127(9)"qualified expenditure"(a)(ii)), plus (a.2) 15% of flow-through mining expenditures, plus (a.3) the specified percentage of pre-production mining expenditures, plus (a.4) all apprenticeship expenditures (defined as 10% of certain wages paid to apprentices), plus (c) ITCs of other years (20 before, 3 after; see 127(9.01), (9.02)), minus (f) ITCs claimed in those other years.

The 10-year carryforward in paras. (c), (e), (e.1), (e.2), (f), (g), (h) and (i) is actually 20 years starting from 1998: see 127(9.01), (9.02).

When an ITC has been allowed on assessment and the year is statute-barred, the CRA can use the carryforward period to deny the ITCs in a later year: *Papier Cascades Cabano*, 2006 FCA 419.

Property is "acquired" for ITC purposes when title passes or when the purchaser has all incidents of title such as possession, use and risk: *Terexcavation Antoine Grant*, 2002 CarswellNat 5183 (TCC).

The "capital cost" for ITC purposes did not reflect a 44(1) rollover on expropriation of property, but was the actual cost of the new property, in *Gaston Cellard Inc.*, 2002 CarswellNat 5139 (TCC).

Para. (l) ensures that an ITC is available only where the income from the business to which the expenditure or property relates is subject to tax. It applies to both s. 81 exempt *income* and s. 149 exempt *taxpayers*.

Para. (m): for the mechanics of making the claim and the need to meet the deadline, see 37(11) Notes. During 2020, extension for COVID-19 was provided by TLOPA (see Enacted Amendment under 169(1)): deadlines from March 13-Dec. 30, 2020 were extended by 6 months but no later than Dec. 31, 2020. See tinyurl.com/sred-file-ext.

History:

Para. (a) amended by 2012 budget bill #2, for tax years ending after March 29, 2012, to change "certified property" to "qualified resource property".

Para. (a.1) amended by 2012 budget bill #2 to change "20%" to "15%", for tax years that end after 2013, but for years that include Jan. 1, 2014, the change applies proportionally effective that day, based on the number of days in 2013 and 2014.

Para. (a.3) amended by 2012 budget bill #2, for tax years ending after March 29, 2012. For earlier years read "where the taxpayer is a taxable Canadian corporation, the specified percentage of the taxpayer's pre-production mining expenditure for the year". Para. (a.3), reference to cover it in para. (c), and subpara. (e.1)(v) added by 2003 resource bill, for 2003 and later tax years.

Para (a.4) added by 2006 budget bill #2, for tax years that end after May 1, 2006. See Notes to 127(9)"apprenticeship expenditure".

Para. (a.5) added by 2007 budget bill #2, for expenditures incurred after March 18, 2007, and repealed by 2017 budget bill #1 for expenditures incurred after March 21, 2017 (unless incurred before 2020 under a written agreement entered into by that date). The credit for child-care spaces has been eliminated. It read:

> (a.5) the child care space amount of the taxpayer for the taxation year,

Para. (d) repealed by 2006 budget bill #1, for 2006 and later tax years. It dealt with ITCs under former 119, which implemented "block averaging" for farmers and fishermen and was eliminated by 1988 tax reform.

Subparas. (e.1)(vi) and (vii) added by 2007 budget bill #2, (vi) for tax years that end after May 1, 2006 and (vii) for tax years that end after March 18, 2007; and (vii) repealed on same basis as para. (a.5). It read:

> (vii) the amount of an eligible child care space expenditure of the taxpayer under paragraph (11.1)(c.5), to the extent that that reduction had the effect of reducing the amount of a child care space amount of the taxpayer, and

Paras. (j) and (k) amended by 2013 budget bill #2, effective March 21, 2013, to change references to control of a corporation being acquired to "loss restriction event", so as to extend the rule to trusts (see Notes to 251.2(2)).

Definition earlier amended by 2000, 1997 and 1995 Budgets, 1991 technical bill.

Remission Orders: *Blackberry Limited Remission Order*, P.C. 2013-1404 (Blackberry allowed to do a transaction that triggered an extra year-end without losing a carryback year).

Interpretation Bulletins: IT-121R3: Election to capitalize cost of borrowed money (cancelled); IT-273R: Government assistance — general comments.

Information Circulars: 78-4R3: Investment tax credit rates.

Application Policies: SR&ED 2004-02R5: Filing requirements for claiming SR&ED; SR&ED 2005-02: General rules concerning the treatment of government and non government assistance.

Forms: RC4290: Refunds for small business R&D [guide]; T2 Sched. 31: Investment tax credit (ITC) — corporations; T661: SR&ED expenditures claim; T1263: Third-party payments for SR&ED; T2038 (Ind.): Investment tax credit (individuals); T4088: Claiming scientific research and experimental development expenditures — guide to form T661.

"non-government assistance" means an amount that would be included in income under paragraph 12(1)(x) if that paragraph were read without reference to subparagraphs 12(1)(x)(v) to (vii);

Notes: Definition amended by 2013 budget bill #2, effective Dec. 21, 2012, to change "by virtue of" to "under" and to change "12(1)(x)(vi) and (vii)" to "12(1)(x)(v) to (vii)".

Application Policies: SR&ED 2005-02: General rules concerning the treatment of government and non government assistance.

"non-qualifying corporation" — [No longer relevant.]

Notes: Definition "non-qualifying corporation" added by 1992 Economic Statement, effective for property acquired after Dec. 2, 1992. It describes a corporation ineligible for the temporary 10% small business investment tax credit for "qualified small-business property". See 127(9)"eligible taxpayer"(a).

"phase", of a project, means a discrete expansion in the extraction, processing or production capacity of the project of a taxpayer beyond a capacity level that was attained before March 29, 2012 and which expansion in capacity was the taxpayer's demonstrated intention immediately before that date;

Notes: Definition added by 2012 budget bill #2, effective March 29, 2012. This term was "project phase" in the March 29, 2012 Budget proposals.

"pre-production mining expenditure", of a taxable Canadian corporation for a taxation year, means the total of all amounts each of which is an expenditure incurred after 2002 by the taxable Canadian corporation in the taxation year that

(a) is a Canadian exploration expense and would be

(i) described in paragraph (f) of the definition "Canadian exploration expense" in subsection 66.1(6) if the expression "mineral resource" in that paragraph were defined to mean a mineral deposit from which the principal mineral to be extracted is diamond, a base or precious metal deposit, or a mineral deposit from which the principal mineral to be extracted is an industrial mineral that, when refined, results in a base or precious metal, or

(ii) described in paragraph (g), (g.3) or (g.4) and not in paragraph (f), of the definition "Canadian exploration expense" in subsection 66.1(6) if the expression "mineral resource" in paragraph (g) of that definition were defined to mean a mineral deposit from which the principal mineral to be extracted is diamond, a base or precious metal deposit, or a mineral deposit from which the principal mineral to be extracted is an industrial mineral that, when refined, results in a base or precious metal, and

(b) is not an expense that

(i) was renounced under subsection 66(12.6) to the taxable Canadian corporation except if the corporation is, on the effective date of the renunciation,

(A) a corporation that would be a "principal business corporation", as defined in subsection 66(15), if that definition were read without reference to its paragraphs (a), (a.1), (f), (h) and (i), and

(B) the sole shareholder of the corporation that renounced the expenditure, or

(ii) is a member's share of an expense incurred by a partnership unless the expense was deemed by subsection 66(18) to

have been made or incurred at the end of the fiscal period of the partnership by the member and throughout the fiscal period of the partnership in which the expense was incurred

(A) each member of the partnership would (otherwise than because of being a member of the partnership) be a "principal-business corporation" as defined in subsection 66(15) of the Act, if that definition were read without reference to its paragraphs (a), (a.1), (f), (h) and (i), and

(B) the corporation is a member of the partnership at the time the expenditure is incurred and would not be a specified member of the partnership if the definition "specified member" in subsection 248(1) were read without reference to its subparagraph (b)(ii),

Related Provisions: 66(18) — Expenses of partnerships; 127(9)"investment tax credit"(a.3) — 5%, 7% or 10% credit for expenditure; 127(9)"investment tax credit"(c) — Carryforward or carryback; 127(11.1)(c.3) — Reduction for assistance.

Notes: The requirement in (b)(ii)(A) that every partner be a principal-business corp has been criticized as too restrictive: René Albert & Liam Fitzgerald, "2011 Mining Update", 2011 Cdn Tax Foundation annual conference, slides 28-33 (not in published conference report).

Subpara. (a)(ii) amended by 2013 budget bill #2, effective March 21, 2013, to add reference to paras. (g.3) and (g.4) and "of that definition"; and retroactively corrected by 2017 budget bill #2 to restore "or" at the end of (a)(i).

Para. (b) changed from "is not an expense that was renounced under subsection 66(12.6) to the taxable Canadian corporation" by 2002-2013 technical bill (Part 5 — technical), for 2003 and later taxation years.

Para. (a) amended and subpara. (a)(ii) added by 2012 budget bill #2, for expenditures incurred after March 28, 2012 (splitting into (i), (ii) allows different treatment under 127(9)"specified percentage"(j), (k)).

Definition "pre-production mining expenditure" added by 2003 resource bill, for 2003 and later taxation years. See Notes to 20(1)(v.1) for related changes.

A definition **"project phase"** in the March 29, 2012 Budget was enacted as "phase".

Income Tax Folios: S3-F8-C1: Principal-business corporations in the resource industries [replaces IT-400].

"qualified Canadian exploration expenditure", **"qualified construction equipment"** — [Repealed]

Notes: Definitions "qualified Canadian exploration expenditure" and "qualified construction equipment" repealed by 1995 Budget, for taxation years that begin after 1995, as they are no longer relevant. They applied to expenditures before 1991.

"qualified expenditure" incurred by a taxpayer in a taxation year means

(a) an amount that is an expenditure incurred in the year by the taxpayer in respect of scientific research and experimental development and is

(i) an expenditure described in subparagraph 37(1)(a)(i), or

(ii) 80% of an expenditure described in any of subparagraphs 37(1)(a)(i.01) to (iii),

(iii), (iv) [Repealed]

(b) a prescribed proxy amount of the taxpayer for the year,

but does not include

(c) a prescribed expenditure incurred in the year by the taxpayer,

(d) where the taxpayer is a corporation, an expenditure specified by the taxpayer for the year for the purpose of clause 194(2)(a)(ii)(A),

(e) [Repealed]

(f) an expenditure (other than an expenditure that is salary or wages of an employee of the taxpayer) incurred by the taxpayer in respect of scientific research and experimental development to the extent that it is performed by another person or partnership at a time when the taxpayer and the person or partnership to which the expenditure is paid or payable do not deal with each other at arm's length,

(g) an expenditure described in paragraph 37(1)(a) that is paid or payable by the taxpayer to or for the benefit of a person or partnership that is not a taxable supplier in respect of the expenditure, other than an expenditure in respect of scientific research and experimental development directly undertaken by the taxpayer, and

(h) an amount that would otherwise be a qualified expenditure incurred by the taxpayer in the year to the extent of any reduction in respect of the amount that is required under any of subsections (18) to (20) to be applied;

Related Provisions: 18(9)(e) — Prepaid expenses deemed incurred in later taxation year; 37(1.3) — SR&ED within 200 nautical miles offshore is deemed done in Canada; 127(11.5) — Adjustments to qualified expenditures; 127(13)–(16) — Agreement to transfer expenditures to non-arm's length person who performs research; 127(18)–(21) — Reduction to reflect government assistance; 127(24) — Anti-avoidance rule — exclusion from qualified expenditure; 127(26) — Amounts not paid within 180 days of end of year; 162(5.1)–(5.3) — Penalty for not providing details regarding SR&ED claim preparer fees.

Notes: A qualified expenditure (QE) on SR&ED (see Notes to 248(1)"scientific research ...") is deductible under 37(1), and also entitles the taxpayer to a 15% or 35% credit. See 127(9)"SR&ED qualified expenditure pool"A, 127(9)"investment tax credit"(a.1) and 127(5) for the first 15%; and 127(10.1) for the extra 20%. (The "specified percentage" of a QE, in 127(9)"specified percentage"(e)(v), is no longer included in 127(9)"investment tax credit".)

Para. (a) includes 100% of R&D undertaken *by* the taxpayer, 80% of R&D undertaken *on behalf of* the taxpayer and certain other amounts paid to third parties (but see (f) and (g) below). Capital expenses (former 37(1)(b)) are not allowed since 2014. "Expenditure" excludes issuing shares: see Notes to 143.3.

Para. (b) allows an amount for the "proxy method": a 55% gross-up of labour costs to cover overhead. See Notes to Reg. 2900(4).

Para. (c) excludes a prescribed expenditure (Reg. 2902), e.g. admin costs, legal fees, interest, advertising, convention expenses, memberships, penalties, upkeep costs, some property acquisition costs, R&D rights costs, donations, and reimbursable amounts (with some exceptions).

Para. (d) relates to the old scientific research tax credit from the 1980s.

Para. (f) excludes an amount paid for R&D performed by another person not at arm's length, so a payment to a contractor must be at arm's length to be eligible for credit (a 127(13) election may allow the expenditure to be transferred). If para. (f) applies, the payee may be able to claim it, since it will not be a "contract payment" (denied by 127(18)) due to 127(9)"contract payment"(a)(ii).

Para. (g) excludes an amount paid to a third party "that is not a taxable supplier", unless it is in respect of SR&ED "directly undertaken by the taxpayer". See 127(9)"taxable supplier". Third party payments do not qualify unless the payee is resident in Canada or using a permanent establishment in Canada. Where amounts are paid to a placement agency under a contract to carry out SR&ED, see Notes to 37(8).

Para. (h) excludes QE reductions under 127(18)-(22). See Notes to 127(18).

See also Notes to 127(9)"SR&ED qualified expenditure pool" and 37(1).

Subpara. (a)(iii), "an expenditure for first term shared-use-equipment or second term shared-use-equipment", repealed by 2012 budget bill #2, effective Feb. 2017.

Subpara. (a)(iv), "an expenditure described in subparagraph 37(1)(b)(i)" repealed by 2012 budget bill #2, for expenditures incurred after 2013 (due to repeal of 37(1)(b), which allowed deduction for capital expenditures made before 2014).

Paras. (a) and (b) amended by 2012 budget bill #2, for expenditures incurred after 2012. For earlier expenditures since 1996-97, read:

(a) an amount that is an expenditure incurred in the year by the taxpayer in respect of scientific research and experimental development that is an expenditure

(i) for first term shared-use-equipment or second term shared-use-equipment,

(ii) described in paragraph 37(1)(a), or

(iii) described in subparagraph 37(1)(b)(i), or

(b) a prescribed proxy amount of the taxpayer for the year (which, for the purpose of paragraph (e), is deemed to be an amount incurred in the year),

Definition amended by 1997 Budget (effective for taxation years that begin after 1995), 1995 Budget, 1993 technical bill and 1992 Economic Statement.

Regulations: 2900(4)–(9) (prescribed proxy amount); 2902 (prescribed expenditure).

Information Circulars: 97-1: SR&ED — Administrative guidelines for software development.

Application Policies: SR&ED 2002-03: Taxable supplier rules; SR&ED 2004-01: Retiring allowance; SR&ED 2005-02: General rules concerning the treatment of government and non government assistance.

Forms: T2 Sched. 301: Newfoundland and Labrador research and development tax credit; T2 Sched. 340: Nova Scotia research and development tax credit; T2 Sched. 360: New Brunswick research and development tax credit; T2 Sched. 380: Manitoba research and development tax credit; T2 Sched. 403: Saskatchewan research and development tax credit; T661: SR&ED expenditures claim; T1129: Newfoundland and Labrador research and development tax credit (individuals); T1232: Yukon research and development tax credit (individuals); T1263: Third-party payments for SR&ED;

T4088: Claiming scientific research and experimental development expenditures — guide to form T661.

"qualified property", of a taxpayer, means property (other than a qualified resource property) that is

(a) a prescribed building to the extent that it is acquired by the taxpayer after June 23, 1975,

(b) prescribed machinery and equipment acquired by the taxpayer after June 23, 1975, or

(b.1) prescribed energy generation and conservation property acquired by the taxpayer after March 28, 2012,

that has not been used, or acquired for use or lease, for any purpose whatever before it was acquired by the taxpayer and that is

(c) to be used by the taxpayer in Canada primarily for the purpose of

(i) manufacturing or processing goods for sale or lease,

(ii) farming or fishing,

(iii) logging,

(iv) storing grain, or

(v) harvesting peat,

(c.1) property (other than property described in paragraph (b.1)) to be used by the taxpayer in Canada primarily for the purpose of producing or processing electrical energy or steam in a prescribed area, if

(i) all or substantially all of the energy or steam

(A) is used by the taxpayer for the purpose of gaining or producing income from a business (other than the business of selling the product of the particular property), or

(B) is sold directly (or indirectly by way of sale to a provincially regulated power utility operating in the prescribed area) to a person related to the taxpayer, and

(ii) the energy or steam is used by the taxpayer or the person related to the taxpayer primarily for the purpose of manufacturing or processing goods in the prescribed area for sale or lease, or

(d) to be leased by the taxpayer to a lessee (other than a person exempt from tax under this Part because of section 149) who can reasonably be expected to use the property in Canada primarily for any of the purposes referred to in paragraph (c), but this paragraph does not apply to property that is prescribed for the purposes of paragraph (b) or (b.1) unless

(i) the property is leased in the ordinary course of carrying on a business in Canada by a corporation whose principal business is leasing property, lending money, purchasing conditional sales contracts, accounts receivable, bills of sale, chattel mortgages or hypothecary claims on movables, bills of exchange or other obligations representing all or part of the sale price of merchandise or services, or any combination thereof,

(ii) the property is manufactured and leased in the ordinary course of carrying on business in Canada by a corporation whose principal business is manufacturing property that it sells or leases,

(iii) the property is leased in the ordinary course of carrying on business in Canada by a corporation whose principal business is selling or servicing property of that type, or

(iv) the property is a fishing vessel, including the furniture, fittings and equipment attached to it, leased by an individual (other than a trust) to a corporation, controlled by the individual, that carries on a fishing business in connection with one or more commercial fishing licences issued by the Government of Canada to the individual,

and, for the purpose of this definition, "Canada" includes the offshore region prescribed for the purpose of the definition "specified percentage";

Related Provisions: 127(9)"investment tax credit"(a) — ITC for specified percentage of QP; 127(9)"specified percentage"(a)(iii)(D) — QP for use in Atlantic provinces; 127(11) — Interpretation.

Notes: *Paras. (a)-(b.1)*: see Notes to Reg. 4600(1), (2) and (3).

Words between (b.1) and (c): qualified property must be new and unused. Former IT-331R para. 24 permitted used equipment to be treated as new after "major renovations", but in *Pêcheries Yvon Savage*, 2011 TCC 477, fishing boat renovations were insufficient to create a new boat. In light of that case "and the inherent difficulties in consistently applying this administrative position", it no longer applies: VIEWS doc 2013-0490091I7, and each case depends on its facts: 2015-0599901E5. A tractor that had been used for 2 years but was guaranteed as new did not qualify: *Auray-Blais*, [2003] 3 C.T.C. 2473 (TCC).

On whether a manufacturer or dealer (of farm equipment) can claim the credit, see docs 2002-0122357, 2002-0149987, 2008-0278791E5. A lessee in a 16.1(1) election cannot claim it: 2012-0440531E5 (revoking 2011-0417811E5).

Para. (c): "to be used by the taxpayer in Canada primarily for the purpose of" is an intention-based test, but "primarily" refers to the purpose, and does not refer to "in Canada": *Bois Daaquam Inc.*, [2002] 1 C.T.C. 2650 (TCC). It is the purchaser's intention at time of acquisition that counts: *Stark International*, 2019 TCC 248, para. 78 (citing *Setrakov Construction, Dragon Construction, Produits L.B.*). In *Capilano International*, 1995 CarswellNat 919 (TCC), seismic recording equipment with expected 10-year life, acquired for a 2-year overseas project, qualified as intended to be used in Canada. Similarly, in *Stark* (above), equipment whose *initial* 10 months' use was processing a customer's oil was held to be intended to process oil for sale. "Primarily" requires the qualifying use in Canada to be more than 50% of the property's total use: doc 2015-0624191E5. See also the exclusions in 127(11).

For (c)(i), in *Will-Kare Paving*, 2000 SCC 36, an asphalt plant was not qualified property because the asphalt produced by the taxpayer for its paving business was not "for sale or lease", but was supplied in the course of contracts for work and materials. Similarly, in *Albert*, 2009 TCC 16, a dentist's imaging machine used to produce crowns did not qualify because the dentist was providing services to his patients. However, in *Ateliers Ferroviaires*, 2011 TCC 352, equipment qualified where it was used to manufacture steel parts for a related company to use in repairing railway structures, as the parts were "sold" under the Quebec *Civil Code*. In *Coop Belle-de-Jour*, 2019 QCCQ 6609, making floral arrangements for sale qualified (under Quebec law that excluded farming). See also VIEWS docs 2007-0228901I7; 2014-0528231I7 (machine used in SR&ED to create a prototype can qualify); and Notes to 125.1(3)"manufacturing or processing" for more interpretation.

Cl. (c.1)(i)(B): For the meaning of "indirectly", see Notes to 17.1(1).

Para. (d): for the meaning of "principal business", see Notes to 20(1)(bb).

Closing words: a new fishing vessel used primarily in the prescribed offshore region (Reg. 4609) qualifies: VIEWS doc 2015-0576511E5.

Definition amended by 2012 budget bill #2 (for property acquired after March 28, 2012), 2001 *Civil Code* harmonization bill, 1996 Budget, 1993 and 1991 technical bills.

Regulations: 4600(1) (prescribed building); 4600(2) (prescribed machinery and equipment); 4600(3) (prescribed energy generation and conservation property); 4609 (prescribed offshore region, for closing words); 4610 (prescribed area for para. (c.1)).

Income Tax Folios: S4-F15-C1: Manufacturing and processing [replaces IT-147R3].

Interpretation Bulletins: IT-145R: Canadian manufacturing and processing profits — reduced rate of corporate tax.

Forms: T2 Sched. 321: PEI corporate investment tax credit; T2 Sched. 304: Newfoundland and Labrador resort property investment tax credit.

"qualified resource property", of a taxpayer, means property that is a prescribed building or prescribed machinery and equipment, that is acquired by the taxpayer after March 28, 2012, that has not been used, or acquired for use or lease, for any purpose whatever before it was acquired by the taxpayer and that is

(a) to be used by the taxpayer in Canada primarily for the purpose of

  (i) operating an oil or gas well or extracting petroleum or natural gas from a natural accumulation of petroleum or natural gas,

  (ii) extracting minerals from a mineral resource,

  (iii) processing

    (A) ore (other than iron ore or tar sands ore) from a mineral resource to any stage that is not beyond the prime metal stage or its equivalent,

    (B) iron ore from a mineral resource to any stage that is not beyond the pellet stage or its equivalent, or

    (C) tar sands ore from a mineral resource to any stage that is not beyond the crude oil stage or its equivalent,

  (iv) producing industrial minerals,

  (v) processing heavy crude oil recovered from a natural reservoir in Canada to a stage that is not beyond the crude oil stage or its equivalent,

  (vi) Canadian field processing,

  (vii) exploring or drilling for petroleum or natural gas, or

  (viii) prospecting or exploring for or developing a mineral resource, or

(b) to be leased by the taxpayer to a lessee (other than a person exempt from tax under this Part because of section 149) who can reasonably be expected to use the property in Canada primarily for any of the purposes referred to in paragraph (a), but this paragraph does not apply to prescribed machinery and equipment unless

  (i) the property is leased in the ordinary course of carrying on a business in Canada by a corporation whose principal business is any of, or a combination of, leasing property, lending money, purchasing conditional sales contracts, accounts receivable, bills of sale, chattel mortgages or hypothecary claims on movables, bills of exchange or other obligations representing all or part of the sale price of merchandise or services,

  (ii) the property is manufactured and leased in the ordinary course of carrying on business in Canada by a corporation whose principal business is manufacturing property that it sells or leases, or

  (iii) the property is leased in the ordinary course of carrying on business in Canada by a corporation the principal business of which is selling or servicing property of that type,

and, for the purpose of this definition, "Canada" includes the offshore region prescribed for the purpose of the definition "specified percentage";

Related Provisions: 127(9)"investment tax credit"(a) — ITC of specified percentage of QRP; 127(9)"qualified property" — Qualified property excludes QRP; 127(11) — Interpretation.

Notes: QRP relates to the phase-out of the 10% Atlantic ITC for assets used in oil & gas and mining in the Atlantic provinces, Gaspé and their offshore regions. Subject to grandfathering, the ITC is 5% for 2014-15 and 0% after 2015 (127(9)"specified percentage"(a.1)). Assets acquired before 2017 as part of a grandfathered phase of a project remain eligible for 10% ITC. Essentially, QRP is property that would have been qualified property had it been acquired before March 29, 2012 for use in oil & gas or mining. (The activities in (a)(i)-(viii) were formerly listed in 127(9)"qualified property"(c)(iv)-(xi).)

QRP acquired after March 28/12 cannot be qualified property (opening words of 127(9)"qualified property"), so no other ITC rate than the QRP rate can apply. No other transitional relief is available for QRP acquired after March 28/12 (under other relieving provisions that might have previously applied to such property).

For the meaning of "prime metal stage or its equivalent" in (a)(iii)(A) see Notes to Reg. 1104(5). For "producing industrial minerals" in (a)(iv) see Notes to 125.1(3)"manufacturing or processing".

Definition added by 2012 budget bill #2, effective March 29, 2012.

Regulations: 4600(1) (prescribed building); 4600(2) (prescribed machinery and equipment).

"qualified small-business property" — [Repealed]

Notes: Definition "qualified small-business property" repealed by 1995 Budget, effective for taxation years that begin after 1995. It described property that qualified for the 10% small business investment tax credit from Dec. 3, 1992 through the end of 1993. It was added by 1992 Economic Statement.

"qualified transportation equipment" — [Repealed]

Notes: Definition "qualified transportation equipment" repealed by 1995 Budget, for tax years that begin after 1995, as it is no longer relevant. It applied to property acquired before 1989.

"SR&ED qualified expenditure pool" of a taxpayer at the end of a taxation year means the amount determined by the formula

$$A + B - C$$

where

A is the total of all amounts each of which is a qualified expenditure incurred by the taxpayer in the year,

B   is the total of all amounts each of which is an amount determined under paragraph (13)(e) for the year in respect of the taxpayer, and in respect of which the taxpayer files with the Minister a prescribed form containing prescribed information by the day that is 12 months after the taxpayer's filing-due date for the year, and

C   is the total of all amounts each of which is an amount determined under paragraph (13)(d) for the year in respect of the taxpayer;

Related Provisions: 37(1.3) — SR&ED within 200 nautical miles offshore is deemed done in Canada; 127(5)(a)(i), 127(5)(a)(ii)(A) — Investment tax credit; 127(9)"investment tax credit"(a.1) — 20% of pool claimable; 127(9)"qualified expenditure"(a) — Capital property excluded after 2013; 127(10.1)(b) — Additional ITC for CCPC; 127(13) — Transfer of pool to other taxpayer; 127(14) — Identification of amounts transferred as current or capital; 143.3 — Stock option benefits, whether SR&ED expenditures; 162(5.1)–(5.3) — Penalty for not providing details regarding SR&ED claim preparer fees; 220(2.2) — No extension allowed for filing deadline; 257 — Formula cannot calculate to less than zero.

Notes: SR&ED costs are deductible under 37(1) (current expenditures only, due to repeal of 37(1)(b)). They also create a 15% ITC under 127(9)"investment tax credit"(a.1) (but for amounts paid to third parties rather than the taxpayer's own R&D, generally 15% of 80%: 127(9)"qualified expenditure"(a)(ii)), and, for some CCPCs, a top-up from 15% to 35% under 127(10.1) (the 35% may be refundable: 127.1). See Notes to 127(9)"qualified expenditure" and "investment tax credit". The amount claimed is optional: 127(5).

Meaning of SR&ED: Notes to 248(1)"scientific research and experimental development".

COVID-19: CEWS reduces the expenditure pool. See "Guidance: How the Canada Emergency Wage Subsidy Affects SR&ED Claims", tinyurl.com/cews-sred.

Contract payments: see Notes to 127(9)"contract payment".

Government assistance: See Notes to 127(9)"government assistance" and 127(18).

HST recapture: The SR&ED claim is effectively used to determine eligible GST/HST input tax credits for the Ontario and PEI portion of the HST on certain purchases by large businesses, until June 2018 (ON) and March 2021 (PEI). See *Excise Tax Act* s. 236.01 and *New Harmonized Value-added Tax System Regulations, No. 2*, s. 31(1)"specified research energy", in David M. Sherman, *Practitioner's Goods and Services Tax Annotated* (Carswell).

Payments or accruals to owner as SR&ED: see Notes to 37(8). *Andre Lamy Medicine*, 2020 TCC 61, held that a surgeon's corporation was entitled to ITCs because it, not he, did the R&D.

Proxy method (55% gross-up of labour costs for overhead): see Notes to Reg. 2900(4).

Restrictive covenant rules (56.4) could apply to some SR&ED contracts. See Balaji Katlai, "Restrictive covenants and potential uncertainties with recapture rules for SR&ED", *Taxnet Pro* Tax Disputes Centre (Jan. 2020, 3pp).

In *Amirix Systems*, 2011 TCC 60, reducing tax by using later years' ITCs instead of current year's SR&ED pool resulted in interest liability.

SR&ED can also qualify for the manufacturing & processing credit under 125.1 (and thus provincial M&P credits): see Reg. 5202"qualified activities"(c) and VIEWS doc 2003-0020535.

Export Development Canada will guarantee exporters' bank loans based on 75% of expected SR&ED refunds: tinyurl.com/edc-sred.

Farm producers are eligible for SR&ED credits for their financial contributions towards R&D through agricultural organizations. These investments may be called check-offs, assessments, or levies to finance R&D. See *Third Party Payment Policy*, §8.

Making the claim: See Notes to 37(11) for the mechanics of making the claim and compliance with 127(9)"investment tax credit"(m); a *complete* claim *must* be filed no later than 1 year after the tax return deadline.

Processing and audits: All SR&ED claims are audited. For administration see: canada.ca/taxes-sred; the Policies listed below; *Financial Claim Review Manual* (revised June 2015); *SR&ED Technical Review: A Guide for Claimants* (April 2015).

See also 20 CRA policies released Dec. 19, 2012 and revised Dec. 18, 2014: Assistance and Contract Payments Policy; Contract Expenditures for SR&ED Performed on Behalf of a Claimant Policy; Eligibility of Work for SR&ED ITCs Policy; Materials for SR&ED Policy; Pool of Deductible SR&ED Expenditures Policy; Prescribed Proxy Amount Policy; Recapture of SR&ED Investment Tax Credit Policy; SR&ED Capital Expenditures Policy; SR&ED Claims for Partnerships Policy; SR&ED During Production Runs Policy (revised July 2016); SR&ED Filing Requirements Policy; SR&ED Investment Tax Credit Policy; SR&ED Lease Expenditures Policy; SR&ED Overhead & Other Expenditures Policy; SR&ED Salary or Wages Policy; SR&ED Shared-Use-Equipment Policy; SR&ED While Developing an Asset Policy (revised July 2016); Third-Party Payments Policy; Total Qualified SR&ED Expenditures for ITC Purposes Policy; Traditional & Proxy Methods Policy.

CRA's processing target for SR&ED claims selected for review or audit (tinyurl.com/cra-standards) is 180 days, 90% of the time; in 2019-20, it did 85%, but anticipated 90% for 2020-21.

Total SR&ED credits granted were projected as $2.6 billion in 2019, $2.4b in 2020, $2.5b in 2021, and $2.6b in 2022, including $1.5b-1.7b annually in s. 127.1 refundable credits: Dept. of Finance, *Report on Federal Tax Expenditures 2021*.

Once an initial assessment is issued, CRA may have no legal obligation to reassess to allow an SR&ED claim: see Notes to 152(1) under "Amending a return".

The Taxpayers' Ombudsman (oto-boc.gc.ca) began a "systemic review" of the SR&ED program in Sept. 2009, and issued an observation paper in Feb. 2012, noting that many claimants and representatives did not understand CRA's administrative SR&ED policies, and that there was a perception that claims are not being administered fairly.

In response, CRA announced on Jan. 24, 2013 a pilot project for a "formal pre-approval process" and an enhanced "online self-assessment eligibility tool". On Feb. 6, 2014, CRA announced the Self-Assessment Learning Tool, to help businesses determine if they qualify, and the First-Time Claimant Advisory Service: CRA staff will meet with first-time claimants at their place of business, to help them understand the program and what they need to do to qualify. On June 29, 2016 CRA launched "Pre-Claim Consultation", allowing CRA review before the work is done (tinyurl.com/cra-preclaim), and cancelled the Account Executive Service and the Preclaim Project Review Service. See also 2016 Alberta CPA (tinyurl.com/cra-abtax), q.12.

For a ruling on an SR&ED financing structure see VIEWS doc 2009-0313261R3.

Consultants: Finance conducted a study in 2012 on the impact of contingency fees charged by consultants (news release 2012-086). Finance (Brian Ernewein) said at the Cdn Tax Foundation annual conference, Nov. 27/12, that they received 125 written submissions and met with 90 stakeholders, and noted the problem might be the complexity of the SR&ED rules rather than contingency fees. The introduction in 2013 of 162(5.1)-(5.3), requiring disclosure of "claim preparer information", appears intended to allow CRA to scrutinize contingency claims more carefully, perhaps because advisors working on contingency might make more aggressive or unreasonable claims.

Objections: To dispute a CRA decision on a claim, see Notes to 165(1), Application Policy SR&ED 2000-02R3 (revised April 2019) and canada.ca/taxes-sred. Detailed procedures for reviewing an SR&ED objection are in *CRA Appeals Manual* §8.1. CRA announced on Dec. 7, 2012 improved objection processes, including additional staff with science and engineering expertise, more in-depth review and expanded contact with claimants. See also Anderson, "The Appeals Process in the Scientific Research and Development Context", XVII(3) *Tax Litigation* (Federated Press) 1058-62 (2010).

Policy: Major changes were expected in the March 2012 federal Budget, possibly including a move away from tax credits and towards grants as recommended by the Oct. 2011 Jenkins report (rd-review.ca), but the changes announced and enacted were relatively minor (reduction of the non-CCPC credit in 127(9)"investment tax credit"(a.1) from 20% to 15%, elimination of capital expenditures by repealing 37(1)(b), and reducing qualified expenditures on contract payments and the prescribed proxy amount). See De Luca et al., "The New SR&ED Regime", 2012 Cdn Tax Foundation conference report, 16:1-25. On recent changes making foreign investment impractical and hurting Canadian R&D, see Robin MacKnight, "Whither the SR & ED Program?", 17(3) *Tax for the Owner-Manager* (ctf.ca) 6-7 (July 2017).

Prosecution: Conviction for false SR&ED claims: *Global Enviro*, 2011 ABQB 32 (work done in earlier period than claimed; corp and director each fined $250,000); *Elhami*, 2018 CarswellQue 2349 (Que. SC) (backdated receipts submitted; accused each fined $1 million). In *Gordon*, 2019 FC 853 (FCA appeal dismissed on procedural grounds A-394-19), SR&ED advisors who backdated documents to inflate ITCs were charged with fraud; the Crown stayed the charges; their lawsuit for malicious prosecution was resoundingly dismissed, as CRA had ample grounds to prosecute ($675,000 costs award to Crown 2019 FC 1348).

Provinces: Most provinces also provide R&D credits. See Table C-9 at beginning of book; "Summary of provincial and territorial R&D tax credits" at canada.ca/taxes-sred; scitax.com/provinces; Viner, *Guide to the Taxation of R&D Expenses* (Carswell, looseleaf or *Taxnet Pro* Reference Centre), chap. 10; Hearn & Cadesky, "Astounding Differences in Provincial R&D Tax Credits", 5(1) *Provincial & Territorial Tax News* (Carswell) 1-5 (Jan. 2016); Smith & Ferland, "Provincial and Territorial R & D Tax Credit Update", 26(12) *Canadian Tax Highlights* (ctf.ca) 1-3 (Dec. 2018). On interaction of the federal + Alberta credits see May 2010 ICAA roundtable (tinyurl.com/cra-abtax), q.7; of federal + Ontario credits, VIEWS doc 2013-0478331I7. Quebec also provides a special deduction for commercialization of innovations, a "patent box" scheme reducing the effective provincial corporate tax rate to 2% on certain IP income.

More information: Viner (above); Scitax Bulletins at scitax.com/bulletins.html; Spicer, *Taxation of Private Corporations and their Shareholders* (ctf.ca, 5th ed., 2020), chap. 20; Hearn, "Are Tax Adviser Fees an Eligible SR & ED Expenditure", 8(2) *Tax for the Owner-Manager* (ctf.ca) 8-9 (April 2008); Reain & Farrow, "Canada's Scientific Research and Experimental Development Program", 2008 Prairie Provinces Tax Conference (ctf.ca) 8:1-25; Hausch & Shum, "Scientific Research and Experimental Development", 2010 BC Tax Conf 10:1-23.

Worldwide incentives: Alvarez & Marsal, *Global Guide to R&D Tax Incentives* (42 countries), at taxand.com; Deloitte, *Global Survey of R&D Tax Incentives* (27 countries), on *Taxnet Pro*.

Definition added by 1995 Budget, for taxation years that begin after 1995.

Information Circulars: 84-1: Revision of capital cost allowance claims and other permissive deductions.

Application Policies: SR&ED 94-01: Retroactive claims for scientific research (TPRs); SR&ED 95-04R: Conflict of interest with regard to outside consultants;

SR&ED 96-05: Penalties under subsec. 163(2); SR&ED 96-07: Prototypes, custom products/commercial assets, pilot plants and experimental production; SR&ED 2000-02R3: Guidelines for resolving claimants' SR&ED concerns; SR&ED 2004-02R5: Filing requirements for claiming SR&ED. See also under 248(1)"scientific research and experimental development".

Forms: RC532: Request for administrative review; RC4290: Refunds for small business R&D [guide]; T2 Sched. 380: Manitoba research and development tax credit; T661: SR&ED expenditures claim; T1263: Third-party payments for SR&ED; T4052: An introduction to the SR&ED program [guide]; T4088: Claiming scientific research and experimental development expenditures — guide to form T661.

"second term shared-use-equipment" of a taxpayer means property of the taxpayer that was first term shared-use-equipment of the taxpayer and that is used by the taxpayer, during its operating time in the period (in this subsection and subsection (11.1) referred to as the "second period") beginning at the time the property was acquired by the taxpayer and ending at the end of the taxpayer's first taxation year ending at least 24 months after that time, primarily for the prosecution of scientific research and experimental development in Canada;

Related Provisions: 37(1.3) — SR&ED within 200 nautical miles offshore is deemed done in Canada; 88(1)(e.3) closing words — Winding-up — parent deemed continuation of subsidiary; 127(11.5)(b) — Adjustments to qualified expenditures.

Notes: Definition "second term shared-use-equipment" added by 1992 Economic Statement, effective for property acquired after December 2, 1992. See 127(11.1)(e).

Application Policies: SR&ED 2005-01: Shared-use equipment.

"specified child care start-up expenditure" — [Repealed]

Notes: This term was used in 127(9)"eligible child care space expenditure".

This credit has been eliminated. Definition repealed by 2017 budget bill #1, for expenditures incurred after March 21, 2017 (unless incurred before 2020 under a written agreement entered into by that date). It read:

> "specified child care start-up expenditure" of a taxpayer in respect of a child care facility is an expenditure incurred by the taxpayer (other than to acquire a depreciable property) that is
>
> > (a) a landscaping cost incurred to create, at the child care facility, an outdoor play area for children,
> >
> > (b) an architectural fee for designing the child care facility or a fee for advice on planning, designing and establishing the child care facility,
> >
> > (c) a cost of construction permits in respect of the child care facility,
> >
> > (d) an initial licensing or regulatory fee in respect of the child care facility, including fees for mandatory inspections,
> >
> > (e) a cost of educational materials for children, or
> >
> > (f) a similar amount incurred for the sole purpose of the initial establishment of the child care facility;

127(9)"specified child care start-up expenditure" added by 2007 budget bill #2, effective for expenditures incurred after March 18, 2007.

"specified percentage" means

(a) in respect of a qualified property

(i) acquired before April, 1977, 5%,

(ii) acquired after March 31, 1977 and before November 17, 1978 primarily for use in

(A) the Province of Nova Scotia, New Brunswick, Prince Edward Island or Newfoundland or the Gaspé Peninsula, 10%,

(B) a prescribed designated region, 7½%, and

(C) any other area in Canada, 5%,

(iii) acquired primarily for use in the Province of Nova Scotia, New Brunswick, Prince Edward Island or Newfoundland or the Gaspé Peninsula,

(A) after November 16, 1978 and before 1989, 20%,

(B) after 1988 and before 1995, 15%,

(C) after 1994, 15% where the property

(I) is acquired by the taxpayer under a written agreement of purchase and sale entered into by the taxpayer before February 22, 1994,

(II) was under construction by or on behalf of the taxpayer on February 22, 1994, or

(III) is machinery or equipment that will be a fixed and integral part of property under construction by or on behalf of the taxpayer on February 22, 1994, and

(D) after 1994, 10% where the property is not property to which clause (C) applies,

(iv) acquired after November 16, 1978 and before February 26, 1986 primarily for use in a prescribed offshore region, 7%,

(v) acquired primarily for use in a prescribed offshore region and

(A) after February 25, 1986 and before 1989, 20%,

(B) after 1988 and before 1995, 15%,

(C) after 1994, 15% where the property

(I) is acquired by the taxpayer under a written agreement of purchase and sale entered into by the taxpayer before February 22, 1994,

(II) was under construction by or on behalf of the taxpayer on February 22, 1994, or

(III) is machinery or equipment that will be a fixed and integral part of property under construction by or on behalf of the taxpayer on February 22, 1994, and

(D) after 1994, 10% where the property is not property to which clause (C) applies,

(vi) acquired primarily for use in a prescribed designated region and

(A) after November 16, 1978 and before 1987, 10%,

(B) in 1987, 7%,

(C) in 1988, 3%, and

(D) after 1988, 0%, and

(vii) acquired primarily for use in Canada (other than a property described in subparagraph (iii), (iv), (v) or (vi)), and

(A) after November 16, 1978 and before 1987, 7%,

(B) in 1987, 5%,

(C) in 1988, 3%, and

(D) after 1988, 0%,

(a.1) in respect of a qualified resource property acquired by a taxpayer primarily for use in Nova Scotia, New Brunswick, Prince Edward Island, Newfoundland and Labrador, the Gaspé Peninsula or the prescribed offshore region, and that is acquired

(i) after March 28, 2012 and before 2014, 10%,

(ii) after 2013 and before 2017, 10% if the property

(A) is acquired by the taxpayer under a written agreement of purchase and sale entered into by the taxpayer before March 29, 2012, or

(B) is acquired as part of a phase of a project and

(I) the construction of the phase was started by, or on behalf of, the taxpayer before March 29, 2012 (and for this purpose construction does not include obtaining permits or regulatory approvals, conducting environmental assessments, community consultations or impact benefit studies, and similar activities), or

(II) the engineering and design work for the construction of the phase, as evidenced in writing, was started by, or on behalf of, the taxpayer before March 29, 2012 (and for this purpose engineering and design work does not include obtaining permits or regulatory approvals, conducting environmental assessments, community consultations or impact benefit studies, and similar activities), and

(iii) in any other case,

(A) in 2014 and 2015, 5%, and

(B) after 2015, 0%,

(b) in respect of qualified transportation equipment acquired

(i) before 1987, 7%

(ii) in 1987, 5%, and

(iii) in 1988, 3%,

(c) in respect of qualified construction equipment acquired

(i) before 1987, 7%,

(ii) in 1987, 5%, and

(iii) in 1988, 3%,

(d) in respect of certified property

(i) included in subparagraph (a)(i) of the definition "certified property" in this subsection, 50%,

(ii) included in subparagraph (a)(ii) of that definition, 40%, and

(iii) in any other case, 30%,

(e) in respect of a qualified expenditure

(i) made after March 31, 1977 and before November 17, 1978 in respect of scientific research and experimental development to be carried out in

(A) the Province of Nova Scotia, New Brunswick, Prince Edward Island or Newfoundland or the Gaspé Peninsula, 10%,

(B) a prescribed designated region, 7½%, and

(C) any other area in Canada, 5%,

(ii) made by a taxpayer after November 16, 1978 and before the taxpayer's taxation year that includes November 1, 1983 or made by the taxpayer in the taxpayer's taxation year that includes November 1, 1983 or a subsequent taxation year if the taxpayer deducted an amount under section 37.1 in computing the taxpayer's income for the year,

(A) where the expenditure was made by a Canadian-controlled private corporation in a taxation year of the corporation in which it is or would, if it had sufficient taxable income for the year, be entitled to a deduction under section 125 in computing its tax payable under this Part for the year, 25%, and

(B) where clause (A) is not applicable and the qualified expenditure was in respect of scientific research and experimental development to be carried out in

(I) the Province of Nova Scotia, New Brunswick, Prince Edward Island or Newfoundland or the Gaspé Peninsula, 20%, and

(II) any other area in Canada, 10%,

(iii) made by a taxpayer in the taxpayer's taxation year that ends after October 31, 1983 and before January 1, 1985, other than a qualified expenditure in respect of which subparagraph (ii) is applicable,

(A) where the expenditure was made by a Canadian-controlled private corporation in a taxation year of the corporation in which it is or would, if it had sufficient taxable income for the year, be entitled to a deduction under section 125 in computing its tax payable under this Part for the year, 35%, and

(B) where clause (A) is not applicable and the qualified expenditure was in respect of scientific research and experimental development to be carried out in

(I) the Province of Nova Scotia, New Brunswick, Prince Edward Island or Newfoundland or the Gaspé Peninsula, 30%, and

(II) any other area in Canada, 20%,

(iv) made by a taxpayer

(A) after the taxpayer's 1984 taxation year and before 1995, or

(B) after 1994 under a written agreement entered into by the taxpayer before February 22, 1994,

(other than a qualified expenditure in respect of which subparagraph (ii) applies) in respect of scientific research and experimental development to be carried out in

(C) the Province of Newfoundland, Prince Edward Island, Nova Scotia or New Brunswick or the Gaspé Peninsula, 30%, and

(D) in any other area in Canada, 20%, and

(v) made by a taxpayer after 1994, 20% where the amount is not an amount to which clause (iv)(B) applies,

(f) in respect of the repayment of government assistance, non-government assistance or a contract payment that reduced

(i) the capital cost to the taxpayer of a property under paragraph (11.1)(b),

(ii) the amount of a qualified expenditure incurred by the taxpayer under paragraph (11.1)(c) or (e) for taxation years that began before 1996, or

(iii) the prescribed proxy amount of the taxpayer under paragraph (11.1)(f) for taxation years that began before 1996,

the specified percentage that applied in respect of the property, the expenditure or the prescribed proxy amount, as the case may be,

(f.1) in respect of the repayment of government assistance, non-government assistance or a contract payment that reduced

(i) a qualified expenditure of a taxpayer under any of subsections (18) to (20), for the qualified expenditure incurred

(A) before 2015, 20%, and

(B) after 2014, 15%,

(ii) the amount of eligible salary and wages payable (by the taxpayer) to an eligible apprentice under paragraph (11.1)(c.4), 10%,

(iii) [Repealed]

(g) in respect of an approved project property acquired

(i) before 1989, 60%, and

(ii) after 1988, 45%,

(h) in respect of the qualified Canadian exploration expenditure of a taxpayer for a taxation year, 25%,

(i) in respect of qualified small-business property, 10%,

(j) in respect of a pre-production mining expenditure of the taxpayer that is described in subparagraph (a)(i) of the definition "pre-production mining expenditure" and that is incurred

(i) before 2013, 10%,

(ii) in 2013, 5%, and

(iii) after 2013, 0%, and

(k) in respect of a pre-production mining expenditure of the taxpayer that is described in subparagraph (a)(ii) of the definition "pre-production mining expenditure" and that is incurred

(i) before 2014, 10%,

(ii) after 2013 and before 2016, 10% if the expenditure is incurred

(A) under a written agreement entered into by the taxpayer before March 29, 2012, or

(B) as part of the development of a new mine and

(I) the construction of the mine was started by, or on behalf of, the taxpayer before March 29, 2012 (and for this purpose construction does not include obtaining permits or regulatory approvals, conducting environmental assessments, community consultations or impact benefit studies, and similar activities), or

(II) the engineering and design work for the construction of the mine, as evidenced in writing, was started by, or on behalf of, the taxpayer before March 29,

2012 (and for this purpose engineering and design work does not include obtaining permits or regulatory approvals, conducting environmental assessments, community consultations or impact benefit studies, and similar activities), and

(iii) in any other case,

(A) in 2014, 7%,

(B) in 2015, 5% if the expense is described in paragraph (a)(ii) of the definition "pre-production mining expenditure" because of paragraph (g.4) of the definition "Canadian exploration expense" in subsection 66.1(6), and 4% otherwise, and

(C) after 2015, 0%;

Related Provisions: 13(27)(f) — Interpretation — available for use; 127(10.1) — Additional amount for R&D; 127(10.8) — Regeneration of ITCs where entitlement to assistance expires.

Notes: For the current operative percentages for the credit, see (a)(iii)(D), (a)(v)(D), (f), (f.1), "investment tax credit"(a), (a.1), (a.2), (a.3), "apprenticeship expenditure"(b) and 127(10.1). The rest of the definition deals with expenditures incurred in the past. The 15% R&D credit is in "investment tax credit"(a.1); another 20% is provided by 127(10.1) to certain CCPCs. See Notes to 127(9)"investment tax credit" and "SR&ED qualified expenditure pool".

Subpara. (a)(iii) is the Atlantic Investment Tax Credit: see Income Tax Folio S3-F8-C2 ¶2.54-2.56; tinyurl.com/cra-aitc; VIEWS doc 2020-0839061E5 (general outline). "Primarily" in Atlantic provinces or the Gaspé means more than 50%: 2014-0517331E5; but may also mean "first in importance": see 73(3) Notes.

The Montérégie Rive-Sud area of Quebec does not fall under (a)(iii): VIEWS doc 2011-0425581E5.

(f.1)(i) changed from "a qualified expenditure incurred by the taxpayer under any of subsections (18) to (20), 20%, or" by 2017 budget bill #2, for repayments after Sept. 21, 2016. This puts it in sync with the rate in 127(9)"investment tax credit"(a.1).

(f.1)(iii) repealed by 2017 budget bill #1, for expenditures incurred after March 21, 2017 (unless incurred before 2020 under a written agreement entered into by that date), due to repeal of the child-care spaces credit. It read:

(iii) the amount of the taxpayer's eligible child care space expenditure under paragraph (11.1)(c.5), 25%;

(k)(iii)(B) changed from "in 2015, 4%" by 2013 budget bill #2, effective March 21, 2013.

(a.1) added by 2012 budget bill #2, for property acquired after March 28, 2012.

(j) amended and (k) added by 2012 budget bill #2, for expenditures incurred after March 28, 2012. For earlier expenditures since 2005, the rate was 10%; 2004, 7%, 2003, 5%.

(f.1)(ii) and (iii) added by 2007 budget bill #2, (ii) for tax years that end after May 1, 2006 and (iii) for tax years that end after March 18, 2007.

Definition earlier amended by 2003 resource bill (for 2003 and later tax years), 1995-97 technical bill, 1994 Budget, 1992 Economic Statement.

Regulations: 4607 (prescribed designated region); 4609 (prescribed offshore region).

Information Circulars: 78-4R3: Investment tax credit rates; 87-5: Capital cost of property where trade-in is involved.

"specified property" — [Repealed]

Notes: Definition repealed by 2017 budget bill #1, for expenditures incurred after March 21, 2017 (unless incurred before 2020 under a written agreement entered into by that date), as part of repeal of the child-care spaces credit. It read:

"specified property" in respect of a taxpayer means any property that is

(a) a motor vehicle or any other motorized vehicle, or

(b) a property that is, or is located in, or attached to, a residence

(i) of the taxpayer,

(ii) [of] an employee of the taxpayer,

(iii) [of] a person who holds an interest in the taxpayer, or

(iv) [of] a person related to a person referred to in any of subparagraphs (i) to (iii);

This term was used in 127(9)"eligible child care space expenditure".

127(9)"specified property" added by 2007 budget bill #2, effective for expenditures incurred after March 18, 2007.

"specified sampling" means the collecting and testing of samples in respect of a mineral resource except that specified sampling does not include

(a) the collecting or testing of a sample that, at the time the sample is collected, weighs more than 15 tonnes, and

(b) the collecting or testing of a sample collected at any time in a calendar year in respect of any one mineral resource if the total weight of all such samples collected (by any person or partnership or any combination of persons and partnerships) in the period in the calendar year that is before that time (other than samples each of which weighs less than one tonne) exceeds 1,000 tonnes.

Notes: 127(9)"specified sampling" added by 2000 Budget, effective October 18, 2000. The term is used only in 127(9)"flow-through mining expenditure"(b)(ii).

"super-allowance benefit amount" for a particular taxation year in respect of a corporation in respect of a province means the amount determined by the formula

$$(A - B) \times C$$

where

A   is the total of all amounts each of which is an amount that is or may become deductible by the corporation, in computing income or taxable income relevant in calculating an income tax payable by the corporation under a law of the province for any taxation year, in respect of an expenditure on scientific research and experimental development incurred in the particular year,

B   is the amount by which the amount of the expenditure exceeds the total of all amounts that would be required by subsections (18) to (20) to reduce the corporation's qualified expenditures otherwise determined under this section if the definitions "government assistance" and "non-government assistance" did not apply to assistance provided under that law, and

C   is,

(a) where the corporation's expenditure limit for the particular year is nil, the maximum rate of the province's income tax that applies for that year to active business income earned in the province by a corporation, and

(b) in any other case, the rate of the province's income tax for that year that would apply to the corporation if

(i) it were not associated with any other corporation in the year,

(ii) its taxable income for the year were less than $200,000, and

(iii) its taxable income for the year were earned in the province in respect of an active business carried on in the province.

Related Provisions: 37(1)(d.1) — Amount reduces R&D deduction pool; 127(9)"investment tax credit"(a.1) — No direct ITC for amount; 127(10.1)(b) — Addition to ITC for amount; 257 — Formula cannot calculate to less than zero.

Notes: The super-allowance benefit amount reduces the R&D deduction pool (see 37(1)(d.1)) and the ITC (see 127(9)"investment tax credit"(a.1) and 127(10.1)(b)). It refers to provincial R&D incentive deductions that exceed 100% of the expenditure.

In the formula, (A–B) is the amount by which a provincial income tax deduction exceeds the R&D expenditure (ignoring provincial income tax credits). C is the provincial tax rate applied to convert the excess deduction into a tax-credit equivalent. For corporations with an expenditure limit for the year for R&D purposes (see 127(10.2)) that is greater than nil, the tax rate for C is the rate that the province applies to small business income earned in the year. Where the taxpayer's expenditure limit is nil, the applicable rate is the general corporate income tax rate for the year in the province for active business income.

127(9)"super-allowance benefit amount" added by 2000 Budget, last change effective for taxation years that begin after 2000.

"taxable supplier" in respect of an amount means

(a) a person resident in Canada or a Canadian partnership, or

(b) a non-resident person, or a partnership that is not a Canadian partnership,

(i) by which the amount was payable, or

(ii) by or for whom the amount was receivable

in the course of carrying on a business through a permanent establishment (as defined by regulation) in Canada.

Notes: Despite the word "taxable", a university or hospital that is exempt from income tax as a registered charity (149(1)(f)) is a "taxable supplier" if resident in Canada. See Notes to 248(1)"eligible relocation", para. "New work location".

Definition "taxable supplier" added by 1995 Budget, effective for taxation years that begin after 1995, and amended retroactive to its introduction by 1997 Budget bill to correct a formatting error by moving the closing words out of subpara. (b)(ii).

Regulations: 8201 (permanent establishment).

Application Policies: SR&ED 2002-03: Taxable supplier rules.

(9.01) Transitional application of investment tax credit definition — For the purpose of applying each of paragraphs (c) to (f), (h) and (i) of the definition "investment tax credit" in subsection (9) in respect of a taxpayer, the reference to "10" in that paragraph is to be read as a reference to the number that is the lesser of

(a) 20, and

(b) the number that is the total of 10 and the number of taxation years by which the number of taxation years of the taxpayer that have ended after 1997 exceeds 11.

Notes: As of 2018, the carryforward is 20 years. For 2009-2017 the carryforward was from 1998; e.g. for 2016, (b) is 10 + (2016-1997-11) = 10 + 8, so it is 18 years back from 2016. See Notes to 111(1)(a) and Ironside, "Ontario Harmonization and the Doubling of the ITC Carryforward Period", 5(3) *Tax Hyperion* (Carswell, March 2008).

127(9.01) amended by 2008 budget bill #2, for 2008 and later tax years. Added by 2006 budget bill #1.

(9.02) Transitional application of investment tax credit definition — For the purpose of applying paragraph (g) of the definition "investment tax credit" in subsection (9) in respect of a taxpayer, the reference to "9" in that paragraph is to be read as a reference to the number that is the lesser of

(a) 19, and

(b) the number that is the total of 9 and the number of taxation years by which the number of taxation years of the taxpayer that have ended after 1997 exceeds 11.

Notes: See Notes to 127(9.01). 127(9.02) amended by 2008 budget bill #2, for 2008 and later tax years. Added by 2006 budget bill #1.

(9.1) Loss restriction event [change in control] before end of year — If a taxpayer is subject to a loss restriction event at any time (in this subsection referred to as "that time") before the end of a taxation year of the taxpayer, the amount determined for the purposes of paragraph (j) of the definition "investment tax credit" in subsection (9) with respect to the taxpayer is the amount, if any, by which

(a) the amount, if any, by which

(i) the total of all amounts added in computing its investment tax credit at the end of the year in respect of a property acquired, or an expenditure made, before that time

exceeds

(ii) the total of all amounts each of which is an amount

(A) deducted in computing its investment tax credit at the end of the year under paragraph (f) or (g) of the definition "investment tax credit" in subsection (9), or

(B) deducted in computing its investment tax credit at the end of the taxation year immediately preceding the year under paragraph (i) of that definition,

to the extent that the amount may reasonably be considered to have been so deducted in respect of a property or expenditure in respect of which an amount is included in subparagraph (i)

exceeds the total of

(b) [Repealed under former Act]

(c) the amount, if any, by which its refundable Part VII tax on hand at the end of the year exceeds the total of all amounts each of which is an amount designated under subsection 192(4) in respect of a share issued by it

(i) in the period commencing one month before that time and ending at that time, or

(ii) after that time,

and before the end of the year, and

(d) that proportion of the amount that, but for subsections (3) and (5) and sections 126, 127.2 and 127.3, would be its tax payable under this Part for the year that,

(i) if throughout the year the taxpayer carried on a particular business in the course of which a property was acquired, or an expenditure was made, before that time in respect of which an amount is included in computing its investment tax credit at the end of the year, the amount, if any, by which the total of all amounts each of which is

(A) its income for the year from the particular business, or

(B) its income for the year from any other business substantially all the income of which was derived from the sale, leasing, rental or development of properties or the rendering of services similar to the properties sold, leased, rented or developed, or the services rendered, as the case may be, by the taxpayer in carrying on the particular business before that time

exceeds

(C) the total of all amounts each of which is an amount deducted under paragraph 111(1)(a) or (d) for the year by the taxpayer in respect of a non-capital loss or a farm loss, as the case may be, for a taxation year in respect of the particular business or the other business,

is of the greater of

(ii) the amount determined under subparagraph (i), and

(iii) its taxable income for the year.

Related Provisions: 249(4) — Deemed year-end on change of control; 251.2 — Loss restriction event.

Notes: See Notes to 111(5), which has the same purpose. CRA considers that "substantially all", used in 127(9.1)(d)(i)(B), means 90% or more.

127(9.1) amended by 2013 budget bill #2, effective March 21, 2013, to extend the rule to trusts (see Notes to 251.2(2)).

I.T. Technical News: 7 (control by a group — 50/50 arrangement).

Forms: T2 Sched. 31: Investment tax credit — corporations.

(9.2) Loss restriction event [change in control] after end of year — If a taxpayer is subject to a loss restriction event at any time (in this subsection referred to as "that time") after the end of a taxation year of the taxpayer, the amount determined for the purposes of paragraph (k) of the definition "investment tax credit" in subsection (9) is the amount, if any, by which

(a) the total of all amounts each of which is an amount included in computing its investment tax credit at the end of the year in respect of a property acquired, or an expenditure made, after that time

exceeds the total of

(b) [Repealed under former Act]

(c) its refundable Part VII tax on hand at the end of the year, and

(d) that proportion of the amount that, but for subsections (3) and (5) and sections 126, 127.2 and 127.3, would be its tax payable under this Part for the year that,

(i) if the taxpayer acquired a property or made an expenditure, in the course of carrying on a particular business throughout the portion of a taxation year that is after that time, in respect of which an amount is included in computing its investment tax credit at the end of the year, the amount, if any, by which the total of all amounts each of which is

(A) its income for the year from the particular business, or

(B) if the taxpayer carried on a particular business in the year, its income for the year from any other business substantially all the income of which was derived from the sale, leasing, rental or development of properties or the rendering of services similar to the properties sold, leased, rented or developed, or the services rendered, as the case may be, by the taxpayer in carrying on the particular business before that time

exceeds

(C) the total of all amounts each of which is an amount deducted under paragraph 111(1)(a) or (d) for the year by the taxpayer in respect of a non-capital loss or a farm loss, as the case may be, for a taxation year in respect of the particular business or the other business

is of the greater of

(ii) the amount determined under subparagraph (i), and

(iii) its taxable income for the year.

Related Provisions: 249(4) — Deemed year-end on change of control; 251.2 — Loss restriction event.

Notes: See Notes to 111(5), which has the same purpose. CRA considers that "substantially all", used in 127(9.2)(d)(i)(B), means 90% or more.

127(9.2) amended by 2013 budget bill #2, effective March 21, 2013, to extend the rule to trusts (see Notes to 251.2(2)).

I.T. Technical News: 7 (control by a group — 50/50 arrangement).

Forms: T2 Sched. 31: Investment tax credit — corporations.

(10) Ascertainment of certain property — The Minister may

(a) obtain the advice of the appropriate minister for the purposes of the *Regional Development Incentives Act*, chapter R-3 of the Revised Statutes of Canada, 1970, as to whether any property is property as described in paragraph (b) of the definition "certified property" in subsection (9);

(b) obtain a certificate from the appropriate minister for the purposes of the *Regional Development Incentives Act* certifying that any property specified therein is property as described in paragraph (b) of that definition; or

(c) provide advice to the member of the Queen's Privy Council for Canada appointed to be the Minister for the purposes of the *Atlantic Canada Opportunities Agency Act* as to whether any property qualifies for certification under the definition "approved project property" in subsection (9).

Notes: 127(10) amended in 1990, effective February 23, 1990, to refer to various Ministers in place of the Minister of Regional Industrial Expansion.

(10.1) Additions to investment tax credit — For the purposes of paragraph (e) of the definition "investment tax credit" in subsection (9), if a corporation was throughout a taxation year a Canadian-controlled private corporation, there shall be added in computing the corporation's investment tax credit at the end of the year the amount that is 20% of the least of

(a) such amount as the corporation claims;

(b) the amount by which the corporation's SR&ED qualified expenditure pool at the end of the year exceeds the total of all amounts each of which is the super-allowance benefit amount for the year in respect of the corporation in respect of a province; and

(c) the corporation's expenditure limit for the year.

Related Provisions: 127(10.2)–(10.4) — Expenditure limit and associated corporations; 127(10.7) — Further additions to ITCs; 127.1(2)"refundable investment tax credit"(f)(i), 127.1(2.01) — Addition to refundable ITC; 136(1) — Cooperative can be private corp for purposes of 127(10.1); 137(7) — Credit union can be private corp for 127(10.1).

Notes: See Notes to 127(9)"SR&ED qualified expenditure pool". 127(10.1) provides an additional ITC (i.e., 35% instead of 15%) for qualifying R&D expenditures incurred by CCPCs. Group taxable capital employed in Canada over $10 million reduces or eliminates this ITC: see 127(10.2).

The 127(10.1) amount is not available to partnerships, since 127(8) does not refer to 127(9)"investment tax credit"(e): *Canadian Solifuels*, 2001 FCA 180.

127(10.1) opening words amended by 2012 budget bill #2 to change "15%" to "20%", for taxation years that end after 2013, except that for such years that include Jan. 1, 2014, read "20%" as the total of

(i) 15% multiplied by the proportion that the number of days that are in the taxation year and before 2014 is of the number of days in the taxation year, and

(ii) 20% multiplied by the proportion that the number of days that are in the taxation year and after 2013 is of the number of days in the taxation year.

(In other words, the change from 15% to 20% applies proportionally effective Jan. 1, 2014, based on the number of days in the taxation year on each side of that date. This matches the reduction in 127(9)"investment tax credit"(a.1) from 20% to 15%, so that the total for qualifying CCPCs remains 35%.)

127(10.1)(b) amended by 2000 Budget (last change effective for taxation years that end after 2000), 1995 and 1993 Budgets.

Forms: T2 Sched. 31: Investment tax credit — corporations. See also under 127(9)"SR&ED qualified expenditure pool".

(10.2) Expenditure limit — For the purpose of subsection (10.1), a particular corporation's expenditure limit for a particular taxation year is the amount determined by the formula

$$\$3 \text{ million} \times (\$40 \text{ million} - A)/\$40 \text{ million}$$

where

A is

(a) nil, if the following amount is less than or equal to $10 million:

(i) if the particular corporation is not associated with any other corporation in the particular taxation year, the amount that is its taxable capital employed in Canada (within the meaning assigned by section 181.2 or 181.3) for its immediately preceding taxation year, and

(ii) if the particular corporation is associated with one or more other corporations in the particular taxation year, the amount that is the total of all amounts, each of which is the taxable capital employed in Canada (within the meaning assigned by section 181.2 or 181.3) of the particular corporation for its, or of one of the other corporations for its, last taxation year that ended in the last calendar year that ended before the end of the particular taxation year, and

(b) in any other case, the lesser of $40 million and the amount by which the amount determined under subparagraph (a)(i) or (ii), as the case may be, exceeds $10 million.

Related Provisions: 87(2)(oo) — Effect of amalgamation; 88(1)(e.8) — Winding-up; 125(5.1) — Elimination of business limit (and therefore the expenditure limit) for large corporations; 127(10.21)–(10.6) — Expenditure limit to be shared among associated corporations; 127(10.22), (10.23) — Venture capital investors — exclusion from associated-corporation rules; 127(10.6)(c) — Short taxation year; 257 — Formula cannot calculate to less than zero.

Notes: 127(10.2) sets the "expenditure limit" (**EL**) for SR&ED claims. 127(10.1) increases the ITC on SR&ED expenditures from 15% to 35%, but the additional 20% is limited by 127(10.1)(c) to the EL (now based only on capital, not income).

If the group's taxable capital employed in Canada (TCEC) does not exceed $10 million, the EL is $3 million: 127(10.2)A(a). Thus, the maximum fully refundable ITC available for qualifying CCPCs (under 127.1) is $1.05 million (35%).

The additional 20% is phased out as TCEC increases from $10m to $50m. This is done via the calculation "× [($40m – A)/$40m]". If TCEC does not exceed $10m, A is zero (see s. 257), so this is "× 1". Once TCEC reaches $50m, then B (the excess of TCEC over $10m) is $40m, and this calculation is "× 0", so the EL is zero.

For tax years ending before March 19, 2019, the expenditure limit (and thus the extra 15% (20%) ITC) was phased out as taxable income increased from $500,000 to $800,000. This was done via the calculation (in the previous version) "$8m – 10A"; once A reaches $800,000, that is zero. High income in the group (including income of non-resident corps) would reduce the limit: VIEWS docs 2007-0227061E5, 2011-0423671E5. Where a CCPC acquired control of a non-CCPC, see 2011-0417971E5. Element A included the taxable incomes of all associated corps even if a 256(2) election had been filed, since that election applies only to s. 125: 2002-0145445.

The two parts of the calculation worked together; the first is a dollar limit (max $3m) and the second applied a fraction that would reduce that dollar limit proportionately.

127(10.2) amended by 2019 budget bill #1, for tax years that end after March 18, 2019, to change formula from "($8 million – 10A) × [($40 million – B) / $40 million]", to delete former element A and renumber element B to A. For earlier years, read A as:

A is the greater of

(a) $500,000, and

(b) the amount that is

(i) if the particular corporation is not associated with any other corporation in the particular taxation year, the particular corporation's taxable income for its immediately preceding taxation year (determined before taking into consideration the specified future tax consequences for that preceding year), or

(ii) if the particular corporation is associated with one or more other corporations in the particular taxation year, the total of all amounts each of which is the taxable income of the particular corporation for its, or of one of the other corporations for its, last taxation year that ended in the last calendar year that ended before the end of the particular taxation year (determined before taking into consideration the specified future tax consequences for that last taxation year), and

127(10.2) earlier amended by 2009 budget bill #1 (effective 2009-10), 2008 budget bills #1 and #2, 2006 budget bill #2, 2003, 1996, 1994 and 1993 Budgets.

(10.21) Expenditure limits — associated CCPCs — Notwithstanding subsection (10.2), the expenditure limit for a taxation year of a corporation that is associated in the taxation year with one or more other Canadian-controlled private corporations is, except as otherwise provided in this section, nil.

Related Provisions: 127(10.3) — Allocation of expenditure limit among associated corporations.

Notes: 127(10.21) added by 2003 Budget, for taxation years that end after 2002.

(10.22) Deemed non-association of corporations — If a particular Canadian-controlled private corporation is associated with another corporation in circumstances where those corporations would not be associated if the Act were read without reference to paragraph 256(1.2)(a), the particular corporation has issued shares to one or more persons who have been issued shares by the other corporation and there is at least one shareholder of the particular corporation who is not a shareholder of the other corporation or one shareholder of the other corporation who is not a shareholder of the particular corporation, the particular corporation is deemed not to be associated with the other corporation for the purpose of determining the particular corporation's expenditure limit under subsection (10.2).

Related Provisions: 127(10.23) — Limitation on application of 127(10.22); 127.1(2.2) — Parallel rule for refundability of credit.

Notes: For CRA interpretation see VIEWS doc 2009-0343841E5.

127(10.22) opening words amended by 2008 budget bill #2, effective for taxation years that end after March 8, 2009, effectively to repeal para. (b).

127(10.22) added by 2004 Budget, for tax years that end after March 22, 2004. It allows otherwise-associated corps to be considered not associated for purposes of SR&ED credits, if they are associated through a third corp and CRA is satisfied that the 127(10.23) tests are met. This facilitates venture capital investments that could otherwise result in corps being associated because they are controlled by the same investors. It does not give the corps access to more small business deduction under s. 125. For interpretation see VIEWS doc 2005-012689117; CRA May 2005 ICAA roundtable (tinyurl.com/cra-abtax), q. 23.

(10.23) Application of subsec. (10.22) — Subsection (10.22) applies to the particular corporation and the other corporation referred to in that subsection only if the Minister is satisfied that

(a) the particular corporation and the other corporation are not otherwise associated under this Act; and

(b) the existence of one or more shareholders of the particular corporation who is not a shareholder of the other corporation, or the existence of one or more shareholders of the other corporation who is not a shareholder of the particular corporation, is not for the purpose of satisfying the requirements of subsection (10.22) or 127.1(2.2).

Related Provisions: 127.1(2.3) — Parallel rule for refundability of credit.

Notes: For CRA interpretation see VIEWS doc 2009-0343841E5.

127(10.23) added by 2004 Budget, for tax years that end after March 22, 2004.

(10.3) Associated corporations — If all of the Canadian-controlled private corporations that are associated with each other in a taxation year file with the Minister in prescribed form an agreement whereby, for the purpose of subsection (10.1), they allocate an amount to one or more of them for the year and the amount so allocated or the total of the amounts so allocated, as the case may be, does not exceed the amount determined for the year by the formula in subsection (10.2), the expenditure limit for the year of each of the corporations is the amount so allocated to it.

Related Provisions: 127(10.4) — Failure to file agreement.

Notes: 127(10.3) amended by 1993 Budget, effective for taxation years that begin in 1994 or later.

Forms: T2 Sched. 23: Agreement among associated Canadian-controlled private corporations to allocate the business limit; T2 Sched. 49: Agreement among associated Canadian-controlled private corporations to allocate the expenditure limit.

(10.4) Failure to file agreement — If any of the Canadian-controlled private corporations that are associated with each other in a taxation year fails to file with the Minister an agreement as contemplated by subsection (10.3) within 30 days after notice in writing by the Minister is forwarded to any of them that such an agreement is required for the purposes of this Part, the Minister shall, for the purpose of subsection (10.1), allocate an amount to one or more of them for the year, which amount or the total of which amounts, as the case may be, shall equal the amount determined for the year by the formula in subsection (10.2), and in any such case the expenditure limit for the year of each of the corporations is the amount so allocated to it.

Related Provisions: *Interpretation Act* 27(5) — Meaning of "within 30 days".

Notes: 127(10.4) amended by 1993 Budget, for tax years that begin after 1993.

(10.5) [Repealed under former Act]

Notes: 127(10.5) repealed in 1985, retroactive to its introduction.

(10.6) Expenditure limit determination in certain cases — Notwithstanding any other provision of this section,

(a) where a Canadian-controlled private corporation (in this paragraph referred to as the "first corporation") has more than one taxation year ending in the same calendar year and it is associated in two or more of those taxation years with another Canadian-controlled private corporation that has a taxation year ending in that calendar year, the expenditure limit of the first corporation for each taxation year in which it is associated with the other corporation ending in that calendar year is, subject to the application of paragraph (b), an amount equal to its expenditure limit for the first such taxation year determined without reference to paragraph (b); and

(b) where a Canadian-controlled private corporation has a taxation year that is less than 51 weeks, its expenditure limit for the year is that proportion of its expenditure limit for the year determined without reference to this paragraph that the number of days in the year is of 365.

(c) [Repealed]

Notes: Where a CCPC acquires control of a non-CCPC, 127(10.6) does not apply: VIEWS doc 2011-0417971E5.

127(10.6)(c) repealed by 2019 budget bill #1, for tax years that end after March 18, 2019, due to the amendment to 127(10.2). It read:

(c) for the purpose of subsection (10.2), where a Canadian-controlled private corporation has a taxation year that is less than 51 weeks, the taxable income of the corporation for the year shall be determined by multiplying that amount by the ratio that 365 is of the number of days in that year.

127(10.6)(c) amended by 2008 budget bill #2, for tax years that end after March 8, 2009, so that it no longer applies to determine the business limit of the corporation.

127(10.6)(c) added by 1994 Budget, effective for taxation years that begin after 1995.

(10.7) Further additions to investment tax credit [repaid assistance] — Where a taxpayer has in a particular taxation year repaid an amount of government assistance, non-government assistance or a contract payment that was applied to reduce

(a) the amount of a qualified expenditure incurred by the taxpayer under paragraph (11.1)(c) for a preceding taxation year that began before 1996,

(b) the prescribed proxy amount of the taxpayer under paragraph (11.1)(f) for a preceding taxation year that began before 1996, or

(c) a qualified expenditure incurred by the taxpayer under any of subsections (18) to (20) for a preceding taxation year,

there shall be added to the amount otherwise determined under subsection (10.1) in respect of the taxpayer for the particular year the amount, if any, by which

(d) the amount that would have been determined under subsection (10.1) in respect of the taxpayer for that preceding year if subsections (11.1) and (18) to (20) had not applied in respect of the government assistance, non-government assistance or con-

915

tract payment, as the case may be, to the extent of the amount so repaid,

exceeds

(e) the amount determined under subsection (10.1) in respect of the taxpayer for that preceding year.

Related Provisions: 127(10.8) — Further additions to investment tax credits.

Notes: 127(10.7) amended by 1995 Budget, effective for taxation years that begin after 1995. Added by 1991 technical bill.

Application Policies: SR&ED 2005-02: General rules concerning the treatment of government and non government assistance.

(10.8) Further additions to investment tax credit [expired assistance] — For the purposes of paragraph (e.1) of the definition "investment tax credit" in subsection (9), subsection (10.7) and paragraph 37(1)(c), an amount of government assistance, non-government assistance or a contract payment that

(a) was applied to reduce

(i) the capital cost to a taxpayer of a property under paragraph (11.1)(b),

(ii) the amount of a qualified expenditure incurred by a taxpayer under paragraph (11.1)(c) for taxation years that began before 1996,

(iii) the prescribed proxy amount of a taxpayer under paragraph (11.1)(f) for taxation years that began before 1996, or

(iv) a qualified expenditure incurred by a taxpayer under any of subsections (18) to (20),

(b) was not received by the taxpayer, and

(c) ceased in a taxation year to be an amount that the taxpayer can reasonably be expected to receive,

is deemed to be the amount of a repayment by the taxpayer in the year of the government assistance, non-government assistance or contract payment, as the case may be.

Related Provisions: 127(9)"investment tax credit"(e.1), (e.2) — Repayment of assistance; 127(9)"specified percentage"(f) — Repayment of assistance.

Notes: 127(10.8) allows a taxpayer to regenerate an ITC where entitlement to assistance expires without the assistance being received.

127(10.8) amended by 1995 Budget, for tax years that begin after 1995. Added by 1992 technical bill.

Application Policies: SR&ED 2005-02: General rules concerning the treatment of government and non government assistance.

(11) Interpretation — For the purposes of the definitions "qualified property" and "qualified resource property" in subsection (9),

(a) "manufacturing or processing" does not include any of the activities

(i) referred to in any of paragraphs (a) to (e) and (g) to (i) of the definition "manufacturing or processing" in subsection 125.1(3),

(ii) that would be referred to in paragraph (f) of that definition if that paragraph were read without reference to the expression "located in Canada",

(iii) that would be referred to in paragraph (j) of that definition if that paragraph were read without reference to the expression "in Canada", or

(iv) that would be referred to in paragraph (k) of that definition if the definition "Canadian field processing" in subsection 248(1) were read without reference to the expression "in Canada"; and

(b) for greater certainty, the purposes referred to in paragraph (c) of the definition "qualified property" and paragraph (a) of the definition "qualified resource property" in subsection (9) do not include

(i) storing (other than the storing of grain), shipping, selling or leasing finished goods,

(ii) purchasing raw materials,

(iii) administration, including clerical and personnel activities,

(iv) purchase and resale operations,

(v) data processing, or

(vi) providing facilities for employees, including cafeterias, clinics and recreational facilities.

Notes: In *H.B. Barton Trucking*, 2009 TCC 376, tractors and chip trailers used to transport wood chips were still part of logging, and were not "shipping finished goods" under 127(11)(b)(i).

Bunk houses for seasonal farm workers are not qualified property due to 127(11)(b)(vi): VIEWS doc 2013-0482701E5.

See also 125.1(3)"manufacturing or processing" Notes.

127(11) amended by 2012 budget bill #2 (effective March 29, 2012), 1996 Budget, 1991 technical bill.

Income Tax Folios: S4-F15-C1: Manufacturing and processing [replaces IT-147R3].

Interpretation Bulletins: IT-411R: Meaning of "construction".

(11.1) Investment tax credit [reduction for assistance, etc.] — For the purposes of the definition "investment tax credit" in subsection (9),

(a) the capital cost to a taxpayer of a property shall be computed as if no amount were added thereto by virtue of section 21;

(b) the capital cost to a taxpayer of a property shall be deemed to be the capital cost to the taxpayer of the property, determined without reference to subsections 13(7.1) and (7.4), less the amount of any government assistance or non-government assistance that can reasonably be considered to be in respect of, or for the acquisition of, the property and that, at the time of the filing of the taxpayer's return of income under this Part for the taxation year in which the property was acquired, the taxpayer has received, is entitled to receive or can reasonably be expected to receive;

(c) [Repealed]

(c.1) the amount of a taxpayer's qualified Canadian exploration expenditure for a taxation year shall be deemed to be the amount of the taxpayer's qualified Canadian exploration expenditure for the year as otherwise determined less the amount of any government assistance, non-government assistance or contract payment (other than assistance under the *Petroleum Incentives Program Act* or the *Petroleum Incentives Program Act*, Chapter P-4.1 of the Statutes of Alberta, 1981) in respect of expenditures included in determining the taxpayer's qualified Canadian exploration expenditure for the year that, at the time of the filing of the taxpayer's return of income for the year, the taxpayer has received, is entitled to receive or can reasonably be expected to receive;

(c.2) the amount of a taxpayer's flow-through mining expenditure for a taxation year is deemed to be the amount of the taxpayer's flow-through mining expenditure for the year as otherwise determined less the amount of any government assistance or non-government assistance in respect of expenses included in determining the taxpayer's flow-through mining expenditure for the year that, at the time of the filing of the taxpayer's return of income for the year, the taxpayer has received, is entitled to receive or can reasonably be expected to receive;

(c.3) the amount of a taxpayer's pre-production mining expenditure for a taxation year is deemed to be the amount of the taxpayer's pre-production mining expenditure for the year as otherwise determined less the amount of any government assistance or non-government assistance in respect of expenses included in determining the taxpayer's pre-production mining expenditure for the year that, at the time of the filing of the taxpayer's return of income for the year, the taxpayer has received, is entitled to receive or can reasonably be expected to receive;

(c.4) the amount of a taxpayer's eligible salary and wages for a taxation year is deemed to be the amount of the taxpayer's eligible salary and wages for the year otherwise determined less the amount of any government assistance or non-government assistance in respect of the eligible salary and wages for the year that, at the time of the filing of the taxpayer's return of income for the year, the taxpayer has received, is entitled to receive or can reasonably be expected to receive; and

(c.5) [Repealed]

(d) where at a particular time a taxpayer who is a beneficiary of a trust or a member of a partnership has received, is entitled to receive or can reasonably be expected to receive government assistance, non-government assistance or a contract payment, the amount thereof that may reasonably be considered to be in respect of, or for the acquisition of, depreciable property of the trust or partnership or in respect of an expenditure by the trust or partnership shall be deemed to have been received at that time by the trust or partnership, as the case may be, as government assistance, non-government assistance or as a contract payment in respect of the property or the expenditure, as the case may be.

(e), (f) [Repealed]

Related Provisions: 12(1)(x) — Payments as inducement or reimbursement etc.; 127(9)"investment tax credit"(e.1), (e.2) — Inclusion in ITC; 127(10.7), (10.8) — Further additions to ITCs; 248(16), (16.1) — GST or QST input tax credit/refund and rebate; 248(18), (18.1) — GST or QST — repayment of input tax credit or refund.

Notes: See Notes to 127(9)"government assistance".

127(11.1)(a) prevents a taxpayer that capitalizes interest under s. 21 from claiming ITCs on such amount. The taxpayer cannot capitalize interest outside s. 21 to obtain the ITC: *Saskatchewan Wheat Pool and Alberta Wheat Pool*, [1999] 2 C.T.C. 369 (FCA).

127(11.1)(c.1) should be repealed, since "qualified Canadian exploration expenditure" in 127(9) was repealed effective 1996. (Finance is aware of this.)

127(11.1)(c.4) applies to the Quebec tax credit for on-the-job training, to reduce the "eligible salary and wages" (which reduces 127(9)"apprenticeship expenditure"): VIEWS doc 2009-0330311C6. It also applies to the Ontario Apprenticeship Training Tax Credit: 2013-0490321M6.

127(11.1)(c.5) repealed by 2017 budget bill #1, for expenditures incurred after March 21, 2017 (unless incurred before 2020 under a written agreement entered into by that date), as part of repeal of the child-care spaces credit. It read:

> (c.5) the amount of a taxpayer's eligible child care space expenditure for a taxation year is deemed to be the amount of the taxpayer's eligible child care space expenditure for the taxation year otherwise determined less the amount of any government assistance or non-government assistance in respect of the eligible child care space expenditure for the taxation year that, at the time of the filing of the taxpayer's return of income for the taxation year, the taxpayer has received, is entitled to receive or can reasonably be expected to receive; and

127(11.1) amended by 2007 budget bill #2 (for taxation years that end after March 18, 2007), 2006 budget bill #2, 2003 resources bill, 2000 and 1995 Budgets, 1992 Economic Statement.

(11.2) Time of acquisition — In applying subsections (5), (7) and (8), paragraphs (a) and (a.1) of the definition "investment tax credit" in subsection (9) and section 127.1, qualified property and qualified resource property are deemed not to have been acquired by a taxpayer before the property is considered to have become available for use by the taxpayer, determined without reference to paragraphs 13(27)(c) and (28)(d).

Related Provisions: 13(26) — No CCA until property available for use; 37(1.2) — No R&D deduction for capital expenditure until property available for use; 248(19) — When property available for use.

Notes: 127(11.2) amended by 2017 budget bill #1, for expenditures incurred after March 21, 2017 (unless incurred before 2020 under a written agreement entered into by that date), as part of repeal of the child-care spaces credit. For earlier expenditures, read:

> (11.2) Time of expenditure and acquisition — In applying subsections (5), (7) and (8), paragraphs (a), (a.1) and (a.5) of the definition "investment tax credit" in subsection (9) and section 127.1,
>
> > (a) qualified property and qualified resource property are deemed not to have been acquired, and
> >
> > (b) expenditures included in an eligible child care space expenditure are deemed not to have been incurred
>
> by a taxpayer before the property is considered to have become available for use by the taxpayer, determined without reference to paragraphs 13(27)(c) and 13(28)(d), and subparagraph (27.12)(b)(i).

127(11.2)(a) amended by 2012 budget bill #2, effective Feb. 2017, to delete "and first term shared-use-equipment" before "are deemed".

127(11.2)(b) amended by 2012 budget bill #2, effective in respect of expenditures made after 2013, due to the repeal of 37(1)(b) (which allowed capital expenditures).

127(11.2)(a) amended by 2012 budget bill #2, effective March 29, 2012, to change "certified property" to "qualified resource property".

127(11.2) amended by 2007 budget bill #2, effective March 19, 2007, to add references to "(a.5)", "eligible child care expenditure" and "(27.12)(b)(i)".

127(11.2) earlier amended by 1995 Budget (effective for taxation years that begin after 1995), 1994 Budget and 1991 technical bill.

Advance Tax Rulings: ATR-44: Utilization of deductions and credits within a related corporate group.

Application Policies: SR&ED 2005-01: Shared-use equipment.

(11.3) Decertification of approved project property — For the purposes of the definition "approved project property" in subsection (9), a property that has been certified by the Minister of Regional Industrial Expansion, the Minister of Industry, Science and Technology or the member of the Queen's Privy Council for Canada appointed to be the Minister for the purposes of the *Atlantic Canada Opportunities Agency Act* may have its certification revoked by the latter Minister where

(a) an incorrect statement was made in the furnishing of information for the purpose of obtaining the certificate, or

(b) the taxpayer does not conform to the plan described in that definition,

and a certificate that has been so revoked shall be void from the time of its issue.

Related Provisions: 241(4) — Communication of information — exception.

(11.4) Special rule for eligible salary and wages — apprentices — For the purpose of the definition "eligible salary and wages" in subsection (9), the eligible salary and wages payable by a taxpayer in a taxation year to an eligible apprentice in respect of the eligible apprentice's employment in the taxation year is, if the eligible apprentice is employed by any other taxpayer who is related to the taxpayer (including a partnership that has a member that is related to the taxpayer) in the calendar year that includes the end of the taxpayer's taxation year, deemed to be nil unless the taxpayer is designated in prescribed form by all of those related taxpayers to be the only employer of the eligible apprentice for the purpose of the taxpayer applying that definition to the salary and wages payable by the taxpayer to the eligible apprentice in that taxation year, in which case

(a) the eligible salary and wages payable by the taxpayer in the taxation year to the eligible apprentice in respect of the eligible apprentice's employment in the taxation year shall be the amount determined without reference to this subsection; and

(b) the eligible salary and wages payable to the eligible apprentice by each of the other related taxpayers in their respective taxation years that end in the calendar year is deemed to be nil.

Notes: 127(11.4) added by 2006 budget bill #2, effective for taxation years that end after May 1, 2006. See Notes to 127(9)"apprenticeship expenditure".

Former 127(11.4) repealed by 1997 Budget, effective for 1997 and later taxation years. See now 37(12). Earlier amended by 1995 Budget and 1993 technical bill.

(11.5) Adjustments to qualified expenditures — For the purposes of the definition "qualified expenditure" in subsection (9), the amount of an expenditure (other than a prescribed proxy amount) incurred by a taxpayer in a taxation year is deemed to be the amount of the expenditure determined under subsection (11.6).

Related Provisions: 12(1)(x)(vi) — Income inclusion from reimbursement or assistance; 127(11.6) — Non-arm's length costs; 127(18) — Reduction of qualified expenditures.

Notes: 127(11.5) is similar to pre-1996 127(11.1)(c) and (e), and reduces the qualified expenditures incurred by a taxpayer in a taxation year. For interpretation rules, see 127(11.6)–(11.8). See also 127(18).

127(11.5) amended by 2012 budget bill #2, effective Feb. 2017, effectively to delete para. (b). Before that date, read:

> (11.5) For the purpose of the definition "qualified expenditure" in subsection (9),
>
> > (a) the amount of an expenditure (other than a prescribed proxy amount or an amount described in paragraph (b)) incurred by a taxpayer in a taxation year is deemed to be the amount of the expenditure determined under subsection (11.6); and
> >
> > (b) the amount of an expenditure incurred by a taxpayer in the taxation year that ends coincidentally with the end of the first period (within the meaning assigned in the definition "first term shared-use-equipment" in subsection (9)) or the second period (within the meaning assigned in the definition "sec-

ond term shared-use-equipment" in subsection (9)) in respect of first term shared-use-equipment or second term shared-use-equipment, respectively, of the taxpayer is deemed to be ¼ of the capital cost of the equipment determined after the application of subsection (11.6) in accordance with the following rules:

> (i) the capital cost to the taxpayer shall be computed as if no amount were added thereto because of section 21, and

> (ii) the capital cost to the taxpayer is determined without reference to subsections 13(7.1) and (7.4).

127(11.5)(a) amended by 2012 budget bill #2, effective in respect of expenditures made after 2013, to change "determined without reference to subsection 13(7.1) and (7.4) and after the application of subsection 127(11.6)" to "determined under subsection 127(11.6)" (due to the repeal of 37(1)(b), which allowed capital expenditures).

127(11.5) added by 1995 Budget, effective for taxation years that begin after 1995.

Application Policies: SR&ED 2005-01: Shared-use equipment.

(11.6) Non-arm's length costs — For the purpose of subsection (11.5), where

(a) a taxpayer would, if this Act were read without reference to subsection (26), incur at any time an expenditure as consideration for a person or partnership (referred to in this subsection as the "supplier") rendering a service (other than a service rendered by a person as an employee of the taxpayer) or providing a property to the taxpayer, and

(b) at that time the taxpayer does not deal at arm's length with the supplier,

the amount of the expenditure incurred by the taxpayer for the service or property and the cost to the taxpayer of the property are deemed to be

(c) in the case of a service rendered to the taxpayer, the lesser of

> (i) the amount of the expenditure otherwise incurred by the taxpayer for the service, and

> (ii) the adjusted service cost to the supplier of rendering the service, and

(d) in the case of a property sold to the taxpayer, the lesser of

> (i) the cost to the taxpayer of the property otherwise determined, and

> (ii) the adjusted selling cost to the supplier of the property.

Related Provisions: 12(1)(x)(vi) — Income inclusion from reimbursement or assistance; 127(11.7) — Meaning of adjusted selling cost and adjusted service cost; 127(11.8) — Interpretation; 127(24) — Exclusion from qualified expenditure.

Notes: 127(11.6) provides rules for determining the expenditures in respect of purchases of goods and services from non-arm's length parties.

127(11.6) between (b) and (c), and (d)(i), both amended by 2012 budget bill #2 to change "capital cost" to "cost", effective Feb. 2017.

127(11.6) added by 1995 Budget, for taxation years that begin after 1995.

Application Policies: SR&ED 2005-01: Shared-use equipment.

(11.7) Definitions — The definitions in this subsection apply in this subsection and subsection (11.6).

"**adjusted selling cost**" to a person or partnership (referred to in this definition as the "supplier") of a property is the amount determined by the formula

$$A - B$$

where

A is

> (a) where the property is purchased from another person or partnership with which the supplier does not deal at arm's length, the lesser of

>> (i) the cost to the supplier of the property, and

>> (ii) the adjusted selling cost to the other person or partnership of the property, and

> (b) in any other case, the cost to the supplier of the property,

> and for the purpose of paragraph (b),

> (c) where part of the cost to a supplier of a particular property is attributable to another property acquired by the supplier from a person or partnership with which the supplier

does not deal at arm's length, that part of the cost is deemed to be the lesser of

> (i) the amount of that part of the cost otherwise determined, and

> (ii) the adjusted selling cost to the person or the partnership of the other property,

(d) where part of the cost to a supplier of a property is attributable to a service (other than a service rendered by a person as an employee of the supplier) rendered to the supplier by a person or partnership with which the supplier does not deal at arm's length, that part of the cost is deemed to be the lesser of

> (i) the amount of that part of the cost otherwise determined, and

> (ii) the adjusted service cost to the person or partnership of rendering the service, and

(e) no part of the cost to a supplier of a property that is attributable to remuneration based on profits or a bonus paid or payable to an employee of the supplier shall be included, and

B is the total of all amounts each of which is the amount of government assistance or non-government assistance that can reasonably be considered to be in respect of the property and that the supplier has received, is entitled to receive or can reasonably be expected to receive.

Related Provisions: 127(11.8) — Interpretation; 257 — Formula cannot calculate to less than zero.

Notes: Definition "adjusted selling cost" added by 1995 Budget, for tax years that begin after 1995. It traces the costs incurred by non-arm's length parties in providing a service or a property, for purposes of 127(11.6).

"**adjusted service cost**" to a person or partnership (referred to in this definition as the "supplier") of rendering a particular service is the amount determined by the formula:

$$A - B - C - D - E$$

where

A is the cost to the supplier of rendering the particular service,

B is the total of all amounts each of which is the amount, if any, by which

> (a) the cost to the supplier for a service (other than a service rendered by a person as an employee of the supplier) rendered by a person or partnership that does not deal at arm's length with the supplier to the extent that the cost is incurred for the purpose of rendering the particular service

> exceeds

> (b) the adjusted service cost to the person or partnership referred to in paragraph (a) of rendering the service referred to in that paragraph to the supplier,

C is the total of all amounts each of which is the amount, if any, by which

> (a) the cost to the supplier of a property acquired by the supplier from a person or partnership that does not deal at arm's length with the supplier

> exceeds

> (b) the adjusted selling cost to the person or partnership referred to in paragraph (a) of the property,

> to the extent that the excess relates to the cost of rendering the particular service,

D is the total of all amounts each of which is remuneration based on profits or a bonus paid or payable to an employee of the supplier to the extent that it is included in the cost to the supplier of rendering the particular service, and

E is the total of all amounts each of which is government assistance or non-government assistance that can reasonably be considered to be in respect of rendering the particular service and that the supplier has received, is entitled to receive or can reasonably be expected to receive;

Related Provisions: 257 — Formula cannot calculate to less than zero.

Notes: Definition "adjusted service cost" added by 1995 Budget, for tax years that begin after 1995. It traces the costs incurred by non-arm's length parties in providing a service or a property, for purposes of 127(11.6).

(11.8) Interpretation for non-arm's length costs — For the purposes of this subsection and subsections (11.6) and (11.7),

(a) the cost to a person or partnership (referred to in this paragraph as the "supplier") of rendering a service or providing a property to another person or partnership (referred to in this paragraph as the "recipient") with which the supplier does not deal at arm's length does not include,

(i) where the cost to the recipient of the service rendered or property provided by the supplier would, but for this paragraph, be a cost to the recipient incurred in rendering a particular service or providing a particular property to a person or partnership with which the recipient does not deal at arm's length, any expenditure of the supplier to the extent that it would, if it were incurred by the recipient in rendering the particular service or providing the particular property, be excluded from a cost to the recipient because of this paragraph, and

(ii) in any other case, any expenditure of the supplier to the extent that it would, if it were incurred by the recipient, not be a qualified expenditure of the recipient; and

(b) paragraph 69(1)(c) does not apply in determining the cost of a property;

(c) [Repealed]

Notes: 127(11.8) provides additional rules relating to non-arm's length purchases of goods and services. The intent of 127(11.8)(a) is to reduce to nil to cost of used equipment to a non-arm's length supplier, so that the SR&ED claimant is deemed to have nil qualified expenditure on leasing the equipment: VIEWS doc 2006-0206761I7.

127(11.8)(c), "the leasing of a property is deemed to be the rendering of a service", repealed by 2012 budget bill #2, for expenditures made after 2013 (due to repeal of 37(1)(b), which allowed capital expenditures).

127(11.8) added by 1995 Budget, effective for taxation years that begin after 1995.

(12) Interpretation — For the purposes of subsection 13(7.1), where, pursuant to a designation or an allocation from a trust or partnership, an amount is required by subsection (7) or (8) to be added in computing the investment tax credit of a taxpayer at the end of the taxpayer's taxation year, the portion thereof that can reasonably be considered to relate to depreciable property shall be deemed to have been received by the partnership or trust, as the case may be, at the end of its fiscal period in respect of which the designation or allocation was made as assistance from a government for the acquisition of depreciable property.

(12.1) Idem — For the purposes of section 37, where, pursuant to a designation or an allocation from a trust or partnership, an amount is required by subsection (7) or (8) to be added in computing the investment tax credit of a taxpayer at the end of the taxpayer's taxation year, the portion thereof that may reasonably be regarded as relating to expenditures of a current nature in respect of scientific research and experimental development that are qualified expenditures shall, at the end of the fiscal period of the trust or partnership, as the case may be, in respect of which the designation or allocation was made, reduce the total of such expenditures of a current nature as may be claimed by the trust or partnership in respect of scientific research and experimental development.

(12.2) Idem — For the purposes of paragraphs 53(2)(c), (h) and (k), where in a taxation year a taxpayer has deducted under subsection (5) an amount that may reasonably be regarded as attributable to amounts included in computing the investment tax credit of the taxpayer at the end of the year in respect of property acquired, or an expenditure made, in a subsequent taxation year, the taxpayer shall be deemed to have made the deduction under that subsection in that subsequent taxation year.

(12.3) Idem — For the purposes of the determination of J in the definition "cumulative Canadian exploration expense" in subsection 66.1(6), where, pursuant to a designation by a trust, an amount is required by subsection (7) to be added in computing the investment tax credit of a taxpayer at the end of the taxpayer's taxation year, the portion thereof that can reasonably be considered to relate to a qualified Canadian exploration expenditure of the trust for a taxation year shall be deemed to have been received by the trust at the end of its taxation year in respect of which the designation was made as assistance from a government in respect of that expenditure.

Related Provisions: 248(16), (16.1) — GST or QST input tax credit/refund and rebate; 248(18), (18.1) — GST or QST — repayment of input tax credit or refund.

(13) Agreement to transfer qualified expenditures — Where a taxpayer (referred to in this subsection and subsections (15) and (16) as the "transferor") and another taxpayer (referred to in this subsection and subsection (15) as the "transferee") file with the Minister an agreement or an amended agreement in respect of a particular taxation year of the transferor, the least of

(a) the amount specified in the agreement for the purpose of this subsection,

(b) the amount that but for the agreement would be the transferor's SR&ED qualified expenditure pool at the end of the particular year, and

(c) the total of all amounts each of which is an amount that, if the transferor were dealing at arm's length with the transferee, would be a contract payment

(i) for the performance of scientific research and experimental development for, or on behalf of, the transferee,

(ii) that is paid by the transferee to the transferor on or before the day that is 180 days after the end of the particular year, and

(iii) that would be in respect of

(A) a qualified expenditure that

(I) would be incurred by the transferor in the particular year (if this Act were read without reference to subsections (26) and 78(4)) in respect of that portion of the scientific research and experimental development that was performed at a time when the transferor did not deal at arm's length with the transferee, and

(II) is paid by the transferor on or before the day that is 180 days after the end of the particular year, or

(B) an amount added because of this subsection to the transferor's SR&ED qualified expenditure pool at the end of the particular year where the amount is attributable to an expenditure in respect of the scientific research and experimental development

is deemed to be

(d) an amount determined in respect of the transferor for the particular year for the purpose of determining the value of C in the definition "SR&ED qualified expenditure pool" in subsection (9), and

(e) an amount determined in respect of the transferee for the transferee's first taxation year that ends at or after the end of the particular year for the purpose of determining the value of B in the definition "SR&ED qualified expenditure pool" in subsection (9),

and where the total of all amounts each of which is an amount specified in an agreement filed with the Minister under this subsection in respect of a particular taxation year of a transferor exceeds the amount that would be the transferor's SR&ED qualified expenditure pool at the end of the particular year if no agreement were filed with the Minister in respect of the particular year, the least of the amounts determined under paragraphs (a) to (c) in respect of each such agreement is deemed to be nil.

Related Provisions: 37(1)(e)(iii) — Reduced SR&ED deduction; 127(8)(a) — Partnership not a person for purposes of this subsection; 127(14) — Identification of amounts transferred as current or capital; 127(15) — Filing requirements; 127(16) — Anti-avoidance; 127(17) — Assessment of other years to take agreement into account; 127(29) — Recapture of ITC of allocating taxpayer.

Notes: 127(13) added by 1995 Budget, for tax years that begin after 1995. It provides for the transfer of qualified expenditures between non-arm's length taxpayers. Otherwise, the payer's expenditures in respect of the contract would not be qualified expenditures for ITC purposes: 127(9)"qualified expenditure"(f). In addition, the amount received or receivable by the performer would not be considered to be a contract payment. Qualified expenditures of the performer may be transferred to the payer up to a maximum of the contract amount.

Former 127(13)–(16), repealed by 1988 tax reform effective 1989, enacted the employment tax credit, which no longer exists.

Application Policies: SR&ED 2000-04R2: Recapture of investment tax credit.

Forms: T1146: Agreement to transfer qualified expenditures incurred re SR&ED contracts between persons not dealing at arm's length.

(14) Identification of amounts transferred — Where

(a) a transferor and a transferee have filed an agreement under subsection (13) in respect of a taxation year of the transferor,

(b) the agreement includes a statement identifying the amount specified in the agreement for the purpose of subsection (13), or a part of that amount, as being related to

(i) a particular qualified expenditure included in the value of A in the formula in the definition "SR&ED qualified expenditure pool" in subsection (9) for the purpose of determining the transferor's SR&ED qualified expenditure pool at the end of the year, or

(ii) a particular amount included in the value of B in the formula in that definition for the purpose of determining the transferor's SR&ED qualified expenditure pool at the end of the year that is deemed by paragraph (d) to be a qualified expenditure, and

(c) the total of all amounts so identified in agreements filed by the transferor under subsection (13) as being related to the particular expenditure or the particular amount does not exceed the particular expenditure or the particular amount, as the case may be,

for the purposes of this section (other than the description of A in the definition "SR&ED qualified expenditure pool" in subsection (9)) and section 127.1,

(d) the amount so identified that is included in the value of B in the formula in that definition for the purpose of determining the transferee's SR&ED qualified expenditure pool at the end of the taxation year of the transferee is deemed to be a qualified expenditure either of a current nature or of a capital nature, incurred by the transferee in that year, where the particular expenditure or the particular amount was an expenditure of a current nature or of a capital nature, as the case may be, and

(e) except for the purpose of paragraph (b), the amount of the transferor's qualified expenditures of a current nature incurred in the taxation year of the transferor in respect of which the agreement is made is deemed not to exceed the amount by which the amount of such expenditures otherwise determined exceeds the total of all amounts identified under paragraph (b) by the transferor in agreements filed under subsection (13) in respect of the year as being related to expenditures of a current nature.

Notes: 127(14) added by 1995 Budget, for taxation years that begin after 1995.

(15) Invalid agreements — An agreement or amended agreement referred to in subsection (13) between a transferor and a transferee is deemed not to have been filed with the Minister for the purpose of that subsection where

(a) it is not in prescribed form;

(b) it is not filed

(i) on or before the transferor's filing-due date for the particular taxation year to which the agreement relates,

(ii) in the period within which the transferor may serve a notice of objection to an assessment of tax payable under this Part for the particular year, or

(iii) in the period within which the transferee may serve a notice of objection to an assessment of tax payable under this Part for its first taxation year that ends at or after the end of the transferor's particular year;

(c) it is not accompanied by,

(i) where the transferor is a corporation and its directors are legally entitled to administer its affairs, a certified copy of their resolution authorizing the agreement to be made,

(ii) where the transferor is a corporation and its directors are not legally entitled to administer its affairs, a certified copy of the document by which the person legally entitled to administer its affairs authorized the agreement to be made,

(iii) where the transferee is a corporation and its directors are legally entitled to administer its affairs, a certified copy of their resolution authorizing the agreement to be made, and

(iv) where the transferee is a corporation and its directors are not legally entitled to administer its affairs, a certified copy of the document by which the person legally entitled to administer its affairs authorized the agreement to be made; or

(d) an agreement amending the agreement has been filed in accordance with subsection (13) and this subsection, except where subsection (16) applies to the original agreement.

Notes: 127(15) added by 1995 Budget, for taxation years that begin after 1995.

(16) Non-arm's length parties — Where a taxpayer does not deal at arm's length with another taxpayer as a result of a transaction, event or arrangement, or a series of transactions or events, the principal purpose of which can reasonably be considered to have been to enable the taxpayers to enter into an agreement referred to in subsection (13), for the purpose of paragraph (13)(e) the least of the amounts determined under paragraphs (13)(a) to (c) in respect of the agreement is deemed to be nil.

Related Provisions: 248(10) — Series of transactions.

Notes: 127(16) added by 1995 Budget, for taxation years that begin after 1995.

(17) Assessment — Notwithstanding subsections 152(4) and (5), such assessment of the tax, interest and penalties payable by any taxpayer in respect of any taxation year that began before the day an agreement or amended agreement is filed under subsection (13) or (20) shall be made as is necessary to take into account the agreement or the amended agreement.

Notes: 127(17) added by 1995 Budget, for taxation years that begin after 1995.

(18) Reduction of qualified expenditures — Where on or before the filing-due date for a taxation year of a person or partnership (referred to in this subsection as the "taxpayer") the taxpayer has received, is entitled to receive or can reasonably be expected to receive a particular amount that is government assistance, non-government assistance or a contract payment that can reasonably be considered to be in respect of scientific research and experimental development, the amount by which the particular amount exceeds all amounts applied for preceding taxation years under this subsection or subsection (19) or (20) in respect of the particular amount shall be applied to reduce the taxpayer's qualified expenditures otherwise incurred in the year that can reasonably be considered to be in respect of the scientific research and experimental development.

Related Provisions: 127(9)"investment tax credit"(e.1)(iv), 127(9)"investment tax credit"(e.2)(ii) — Inclusion in ITC; 127(9)"qualified expenditure"(h) — Exclusion from qualified expenditure; 127(10.7)(c), (d) — Further addition to ITC; 127(11.5) — Adjustments to qualified expenditures; 127(21) — Failure to allocate; 127(23) — Partnership's taxation year and filing-due date.

Notes: Under 127(18), government or non-government assistance or a "contract payment" (see 127(9)"contract payment" Notes) reduces SR&ED credit eligibility.

Amounts under the Saskatchewan Petroleum Research Incentive and Alberta's Innovative Technologies Royalty Program constitute "government assistance" for 127(18): VIEWS doc 2004-0095621I7.

Grants that will almost certainly have to be repaid must still be included in the 127(18) calculation in the year received: doc 2005-0141131C6. A reimbursement of costs by a non-resident that is included in income under 9(1) will not be considered non-government assistance or a contract payment for purposes of 127(18): 2008-0276121E5.

For CRA interpretation of "can reasonably be considered to be in respect of" SR&ED, see docs 2007-0226411E5, 2008-0300591C6 (wording of 127(18) is broader than 12(1)(x)).

127(18) added by 1995 Budget, for taxation years that begin after 1995.

Application Policies: SR&ED 2005-01: Shared-use equipment; SR&ED 2005-02: General rules concerning the treatment of government and non government assistance.

(19) Reduction of qualified expenditures — Where on or before the filing-due date for a taxation year of a person or partnership (referred to in this subsection as the "recipient") the recipient has received, is entitled to receive or can reasonably be expected to receive a particular amount that is government assistance, non-government assistance or a contract payment that can reasonably be considered to be in respect of scientific research and experimental development and the particular amount exceeds the total of

(a) all amounts applied for preceding taxation years under this subsection or subsection (18) or (20) in respect of the particular amount,

(b) the total of all amounts each of which would be a qualified expenditure that is incurred in the year by the recipient and that can reasonably be considered to be in respect of the scientific research and experimental development if subsection (18) did not apply to the particular amount, and

(c) the total of all amounts each of which would, but for the application of this subsection to the particular amount, be a qualified expenditure

(i) that was incurred by a person or partnership in a taxation year of the person or partnership that ended in the recipient's taxation year, and

(ii) that can reasonably be considered to be in respect of the scientific research and experimental development to the extent that it was performed by the person or partnership at a time when the person or partnership was not dealing at arm's length with the recipient,

the particular amount shall be applied to reduce each qualified expenditure otherwise determined that is referred to in paragraph (c).

Related Provisions: 127(9)"investment tax credit"(e.1)(iv), 127(9)"investment tax credit"(e.2)(ii) — Inclusion in ITC; 127(9)"qualified expenditure"(h) — Exclusion from qualified expenditure; 127(21) — Failure to allocate; 127(23) — Partnership's taxation year and filing-due date.

Notes: 127(19) applied to 4 of 16 research projects in *PSC Elstow*, 2008 TCC 694, and thus 12(1)(x) did not tax the assistance.

127(19) added by 1995 Budget, effective for taxation years that begin after 1995.

(20) Agreement to allocate — Where

(a) on or before the filing-due date for a taxation year of a person or partnership (referred to in this subsection and subsection (22) as the "taxpayer") the taxpayer has received, is entitled to receive or can reasonably be expected to receive a particular amount that is government assistance, non-government assistance or a contract payment that can reasonably be considered to be in respect of scientific research and experimental development,

(b) subsection (19) does not apply to the particular amount in respect of the year, and

(c) the taxpayer and a person or partnership (referred to in this subsection and subsection (22) as the "transferee") with which the taxpayer does not deal at arm's length file an agreement or amended agreement with the Minister,

the lesser of

(d) the amount specified in the agreement, and

(e) the total of all amounts each of which would, but for the agreement, be a qualified expenditure

(i) that was incurred by the transferee in a particular taxation year of the transferee that ended in the taxpayer's taxation year, and

(ii) that can reasonably be considered to be in respect of the scientific research and experimental development to the extent that it was performed by the transferee at a time when the transferee was not dealing at arm's length with the taxpayer

shall be applied to reduce the qualified expenditures otherwise determined that are described in paragraph (e).

Related Provisions: 127(9)"investment tax credit"(e.1)(iv), (e.2)(ii) — Inclusion in ITC; 127(9)"qualified expenditure"(h) — Exclusion from qualified expenditure; 127(17) — Assessment of other years to take agreement into account; 127(21) — Failure to allocate; 127(22) — Filing requirements; 127(23) — Partnership's taxation year and filing-due date.

Notes: 127(20) added by 1995 Budget, for taxation years that begin after 1995.

Application Policies: SR&ED 2005-02: General rules concerning the treatment of government and non government assistance.

Forms: T1145: Agreement to allocate assistance for SR&ED between persons not dealing at arm's length.

(21) Failure to allocate — Where on or before the filing-due date for a taxation year of a person or partnership (referred to in this subsection as the "recipient") the recipient has received, is entitled to receive or can reasonably be expected to receive a particular amount that is government assistance, non-government assistance or a contract payment that can reasonably be considered to be in respect of scientific research and experimental development and subsection (19) does not apply to the particular amount in respect of the year, the lesser of

(a) the total of all amounts each of which is a qualified expenditure

(i) that was incurred by a particular person or partnership in a taxation year of the particular person or partnership that ended in the recipient's taxation year, and

(ii) that can reasonably be considered to be in respect of the scientific research and experimental development to the extent that it was performed by the particular person or partnership at a time when the particular person or partnership was not dealing at arm's length with the recipient, and

(b) the amount, if any, by which the particular amount exceeds the total of amounts applied for the year and preceding taxation years under subsection (18), (19) or (20) in respect of the particular amount

is deemed for the purposes of this section to be an amount of government assistance received at the end of the particular year by the particular person or partnership in respect of the scientific research and experimental development.

Related Provisions: 127(23) — Partnership's taxation year and filing-due date.

Notes: 127(21) added by 1995 Budget, for taxation years that begin after 1995.

(22) Invalid agreements — An agreement or amended agreement referred to in subsection (20) between a taxpayer and a transferee is deemed not to have been filed with the Minister where

(a) it is not in prescribed form;

(b) it is not filed

(i) on or before the taxpayer's filing-due date for the particular taxation year to which the agreement relates,

(ii) in the period within which the taxpayer may serve a notice of objection to an assessment of tax payable under this Part for the particular year, or

(iii) in the period within which the transferee may serve a notice of objection to an assessment of tax payable under this Part for its first taxation year that ends at or after the end of the taxpayer's particular year;

(c) it is not accompanied by,

(i) where the taxpayer is a corporation and its directors are legally entitled to administer its affairs, a certified copy of their resolution authorizing the agreement to be made,

(ii) where the taxpayer is a corporation and its directors are not legally entitled to administer its affairs, a certified copy of the document by which the person legally entitled to administer its affairs authorized the agreement to be made,

(iii) where the transferee is a corporation and its directors are legally entitled to administer its affairs, a certified copy of their resolution authorizing the agreement to be made, and

921

(iv) where the transferee is a corporation and its directors are not legally entitled to administer its affairs, a certified copy of the document by which the person legally entitled to administer its affairs authorized the agreement to be made; or

(d) an agreement amending the agreement has been filed in accordance with subsection (20) and this subsection.

Related Provisions: 127(23) — Partnership's taxation year and filing-due date.

Notes: 127(22) added by 1995 Budget, for taxation years that begin after 1995.

(23) Partnership's taxation year — For the purposes of subsections (18) to (22), the taxation year of a partnership is deemed to be its fiscal period and its filing-due date for a taxation year is deemed to be the day that would be its filing-due date for the year if it were a corporation.

Notes: 127(23) added by 1995 Budget, for taxation years that begin after 1995.

(24) Exclusion from qualified expenditure — Where

(a) a person or partnership (referred to in this subsection as the "first person") does not deal at arm's length with another person or partnership (referred to in this subsection as the "second person"),

(b) there is an arrangement under which an amount is paid or payable by the first person to a person or partnership with which the first person deals at arm's length and an amount is received or receivable by the second person from a person or partnership with which the second person deals at arm's length, and

(c) one of the main purposes of the arrangement can reasonably be considered to be to cause the amount paid or payable by the first person to be a qualified expenditure,

the amount paid or payable by the first person is deemed not to be a qualified expenditure.

Related Provisions: 127(11.6) — Non-arm's length costs.

Notes: For meaning of "one of the main purposes" in para. (c), see Notes to 83(2.1).

127(24) added by 1995 Budget, for taxation years that begin after 1995.

(25) Deemed contract payment — Where

(a) a person or partnership (referred to in this subsection as the "first person") deals at arm's length with another person or partnership (referred to in this subsection as the "second person"),

(b) there is an arrangement under which an amount is paid or payable by the first person to a person or partnership (other than the second person) and a particular amount is received or receivable in respect of scientific research and experimental development by the second person from a person or partnership that is not a taxable supplier in respect of the particular amount, and

(c) one of the main purposes of the arrangement can reasonably be considered to be to cause the amount received or receivable by the second person not to be a contract payment,

the amount received or receivable by the second person is deemed to be a contract payment in respect of scientific research and experimental development.

Notes: For meaning of "one of the main purposes" in para. (c), see Notes to 83(2.1).

127(25) added by 1995 Budget, for taxation years that begin after 1995.

Application Policies: SR&ED 2002-03: Taxable supplier rules.

(26) Unpaid amounts — For the purposes of subsections (5) to (25) and section 127.1, a taxpayer's expenditure described in paragraph 37(1)(a) that is unpaid on the day that is 180 days after the end of the taxation year in which the expenditure is otherwise incurred is deemed

(a) not to have been incurred in the year; and

(b) to be incurred at the time it is paid.

Related Provisions: 127(11.6) — Non-arm's length costs; 127(27) — ITC recapture.

Notes: 127(26) added by 1995 Budget, for amounts incurred at any time, except that it does not apply to amounts paid before Sept. 19, 1996.

(27) Recapture of investment tax credit — Where

(a) a taxpayer acquired a particular property from a person or partnership in a taxation year of the taxpayer or in any of the 10 preceding taxation years,

(b) the cost, or a portion of the cost, of the particular property was a qualified expenditure, or would if this Act were read without reference to subsection (26) be a qualified expenditure, to the taxpayer,

(c) the cost, or the portion of the cost, of the particular property is included, or would if this Act were read without reference to subsection (26) be included, in an amount, a percentage of which can reasonably be considered to be included in computing the taxpayer's investment tax credit at the end of the taxation year, and

(d) in the year and after February 23, 1998, the taxpayer converts to commercial use, or disposes of without having previously converted to commercial use, the particular property or another property that incorporates the particular property,

there shall be added to the taxpayer's tax otherwise payable under this Part for the year the lesser of

(e) the amount that can reasonably be considered to be included in the taxpayer's investment tax credit at the end of any taxation year, or that would be so included if this Act were read without reference to subsection (26), in respect of the particular property, and

(f) the amount that is the percentage — that is the sum of each percentage described in paragraph (c) that has been applied to compute the taxpayer's investment tax credit in respect of the particular property — of

(i) in the case where the particular property or the other property is disposed of to a person who deals at arm's length with the taxpayer,

(A) the proceeds of disposition of the property, if the property

(I) is the particular property and is neither first term shared-use equipment nor second term shared-use equipment, or

(II) is the other property,

(B) 25% of the proceeds of disposition of the property, if the property is the particular property, is first term shared-use equipment and is not second term shared-use equipment, and

(C) 50% of the proceeds of disposition of the property, if the property is the particular property and is second term shared-use equipment, and

(ii) in the case where the particular property or the other property is converted to commercial use or is disposed of to a person who does not deal at arm's length with the taxpayer,

(A) the fair market value of the property, if the property

(I) is the particular property and is neither first term shared-use equipment nor second term shared-use equipment, or

(II) is the other property,

(B) 25% of the fair market value of the property at the time of its conversion or disposition, if the particular property is first term shared-use equipment and is not second term shared-use equipment, and

(C) 50% of the fair market value of the property at the time of its conversion or disposition, if the particular property is second term shared-use equipment.

Related Provisions: 37(1)(c.2) — Deduction allowed in subsequent year; 127(28) — Recapture of ITC of partnership; 127(29) — Recapture of ITC of allocating taxpayer; 127(32) — Meaning of "cost of the particular property"; 127(33) — No application to certain non-arm's length transfers; 127(36) — Transitional application of 20-year recapture carryforward.

Notes: 127(27) provides for recapture (repayment) of ITCs claimed on the cost of property that is converted to commercial use or sold within 10 years. It thus overrules *Consoltex Inc.*, [1997] 2 C.T.C. 2846 (TCC).

Amounts added to tax payable under 127(27) will increase the SR&ED pool for the following year: 37(1)(c.2).

127(27) amended by 2002-2013 technical bill, for dispositions and conversions after Dec. 20, 2002.

127(27) added by 1998 Budget, for dispositions and conversions of property after Feb. 23, 1998.

Application Policies: SR&ED 2000-04R2: Recapture of investment tax credit; SR&ED 2002-02R2: Experimental production and commercial production with experimental development work — allowable SR&ED expenditures; SR&ED 2005-01: Shared-use equipment.

(27.1)–(27.12) [Repealed]

Notes: 127(27.1)-(27.12) repealed by 2017 budget bill #1, for expenditures incurred after March 21, 2017 (unless incurred before 2020 under a written agreement entered into by that date), as part of repeal of the child-care spaces credit. They read:

(27.1) Recapture of investment tax credit — child care space amount — There shall be added to a taxpayer's tax otherwise payable under this Part for a particular taxation year, the total of all amounts each of which is an amount determined under subsection (27.12) in respect of a disposition by the taxpayer in the particular taxation year of a property a percentage of the cost of which can reasonably be considered to have been included in the child care space amount of the taxpayer for a taxation year, if the property was acquired in respect of a child care space that was created at a time that is less than 60 months before the disposition.

(27.11) Disposition — For the purpose of subsection (27.1),

(a) if a particular child care space, in respect of which any amount is included in the child care space amount of a taxpayer or a partnership for a taxation year or a fiscal period, ceases at any particular time to be available, the child care space is, except where the child care space has been disposed of by the taxpayer or the partnership before the particular time, deemed to be a property

(i) disposed of by the taxpayer or the partnership, as the case may be, at the particular time,

(ii) a percentage of the cost of which can reasonably be considered to be included in the child care space amount of the taxpayer or the partnership, as the case maybe, for a taxation year or a fiscal period, and

(iii) acquired in respect of a child care space that was created at the time the child care space was created,

(b) child care spaces that cease to be available are deemed to so cease in reverse chronological order to their creation, and

(c) a property acquired by a taxpayer or a partnership in respect of a child care space is deemed to be disposed of by the taxpayer or the partnership, as the case may be, in a disposition described in clause (27.12)(b)(ii)(B) if the property is leased by the taxpayer or the partnership to a lessee for any purpose or is converted to a use by the taxpayer or the partnership other than to a use for the child care space.

(27.12) Amount of recapture — For the purposes of subsection (27.1) and (27.11), the amount determined under this subsection in respect of a disposition of a property by a taxpayer or a partnership is,

(a) where the property disposed of is a child care space, the amount that can reasonably be considered to have been included under paragraph (a.5) of the definition "investment tax credit" in subsection (9) in respect of the taxpayer or partnership in respect of the child care space, and

(b) in any other case, the lesser of,

(i) the amount that can reasonably be considered to have been included under paragraph (a.5) of the definition "investment tax credit" in subsection (9) in respect of the taxpayer or partnership in respect of the cost of the property, and

(ii) 25% of

(A) if the property, or a part of the property, is disposed of to a person who deals at arm's length with the taxpayer or the partnership, the proceeds of disposition of the property, or of the part of the property, and

(B) in any other case, the fair market value of the property or of the part of the property, at the time of the disposition.

127(27.1) applied if a taxpayer had claimed a child-care space ITC, and then "disposed" of the property (e.g., because the child care space was no longer available: see 127(27.11)) within 60 months. The ITC had to be repaid, as calculated under 127(27.12). A deduction from income was then allowed the next year under 20(1)(nn.1), since the ITC was included in income under 12(1)(t).

Because the repeal is based on "expenditures incurred on or after Budget Day", the recapture under 127(27.1)-(27.12) will apparently continue to apply for many years,

based on the original expenditure having been made before March 22, 2017, or else having been incurred through 2019 under a written agreement entered into before that date.

127(27.1)-(27.12) added by 2007 budget bill #2, effective March 19, 2007.

(28) Recapture of investment tax credit of partnership —

For the purpose of computing the amount determined under subsection (8) in respect of a partnership at the end of a particular fiscal period, where

(a) a particular property, the cost of which is a qualified expenditure, is acquired by the partnership from a person or partnership in the particular fiscal period or in any of the 10 preceding fiscal periods of the partnership,

(b) the cost of the particular property is included in an amount, a percentage of which can reasonably be considered to have been included in computing the amount determined under subsection (8) in respect of the partnership at the end of a fiscal period, and

(c) in the particular fiscal period and after February 23, 1998, the partnership converts to commercial use, or disposes of without having previously converted to commercial use, the particular property or another property that incorporates the particular property,

there shall be deducted in computing the amount determined under subsection (8) in respect of the partnership at the end of the particular fiscal period the lesser of

(d) the amount that can reasonably be considered to have been included in respect of the particular property in computing the amount determined under subsection (8) in respect of the partnership, and

(e) the percentage (described in paragraph (b)) of

(i) where the particular property or the other property is disposed of to a person who deals at arm's length with the partnership, the proceeds of disposition of that property, and

(ii) in any other case, the fair market value of the particular property or the other property at the time of the conversion or disposition.

Related Provisions: 127(30) — Addition to tax where ITC goes negative; 127(32) — Meaning of "cost of the particular property"; 127(33) — No application to certain non-arm's length transfers; 127(36) — Transitional application of 20-year recapture carryforward.

Notes: 127(28) added by 1998 Budget, effective for dispositions and conversions of property that occur after February 23, 1998. It implements the same rule as 127(27), but for a partnership.

Application Policies: SR&ED 2000-04R2: Recapture of investment tax credit; SR&ED 2002-02R2: Experimental production and commercial production with experimental development work — allowable SR&ED expenditures.

(28.1) [Repealed]

Notes: 127(28.1) repealed by 2017 budget bill #1, for expenditures incurred after March 21, 2017 (unless incurred before 2020 under a written agreement entered into by that date), as part of repeal of the child-care spaces credit. It read:

(28.1) Recapture of partnership's investment tax credits — child care property — For the purpose of computing the amount determined under subsection (8) in respect of a partnership at the end of a particular fiscal period of the partnership, there shall be deducted the total of all amounts, each of which is an amount determined under subsection (27.12) in respect of a disposition by the partnership in the particular fiscal period of a property a percentage of the cost of which can reasonably be considered to have been included in the child care space amount of the partnership for a fiscal period, if the property was acquired in respect of a child care space that was created at a time that is less than 60 months before the disposition.

127(28.1) added by 2007 budget bill #2, effective March 19, 2007. It provides the same rule as 127(27.1), for partnerships.

(29) Recapture of investment tax credit of allocating taxpayer — Where

(a) a taxpayer acquired a particular property from a person or partnership in a taxation year or in any of the 10 preceding taxation years,

(b) the cost of the particular property was a qualified expenditure to the taxpayer,

(c) all or part of the qualified expenditure can reasonably be considered to have been the subject of an agreement made under subsection (13) by the taxpayer and another taxpayer (in this subsection referred to as the "transferee"), and

(d) in the year and after February 23, 1998, the taxpayer converts to commercial use, or disposes of without having previously converted to commercial use, the particular property or another property that incorporates the particular property,

there shall be added to the taxpayer's tax otherwise payable under this Part for the year the lesser of

(e) the amount that can reasonably be considered to have been included in computing the transferee's investment tax credit in respect of the qualified expenditure that was the subject of the agreement, and

(f) the amount determined by the formula

$$A \times B - C$$

where

A   is the percentage applied by the transferee in determining its investment tax credit in respect of the qualified expenditure that was the subject of the agreement,

B   is

(i) where the particular property or the other property is disposed of to a person who deals at arm's length with the taxpayer, the proceeds of disposition of that property, and

(ii) in any other case, the fair market value of the particular property or the other property at the time of the conversion or disposition, and

C   is the amount, if any, added to the taxpayer's tax payable under subsection (27) in respect of the particular property.

Related Provisions: 37(1)(c.2) — Deduction allowed in subsequent year; 127(32) — Meaning of "cost of the particular property"; 127(33) — No application to certain non-arm's length transfers; 127(36) — Transitional application of 20-year recapture carryforward; 257 — Formula cannot calculate to less than zero.

Notes: 127(29) added by 1998 Budget, effective for dispositions and conversions of property that occur after February 23, 1998. It implements the same rule as 127(27), but where the original ITC was transferred by agreement under 127(13).

Application Policies: SR&ED 2000-04R2: Recapture of investment tax credit; SR&ED 2002-02R2: Experimental production and commercial production with experimental development work — allowable SR&ED expenditures.

(30) Addition to tax — Where a taxpayer is a member of a partnership at the end of a fiscal period of the partnership, there shall be added to the taxpayer's tax otherwise payable under this Part for the taxpayer's taxation year in which that fiscal period ends the amount that can reasonably be considered to be the taxpayer's share of the amount, if any, by which

(a) the total of

(i) the total of all amounts each of which is the lesser of the amounts described in paragraphs (28)(d) and (e) in respect of the partnership in respect of the fiscal period, and

(ii) the total of all amounts each of which is the lesser of the amounts described in paragraphs (35)(c) and (d) in respect of the partnership in respect of the fiscal period,

(iii) [Repealed]

exceeds

(b) the amount that would be determined in respect of the partnership under subsection (8) if that subsection were read without reference to subsections (28) and (35).

Related Provisions: 37(1)(c.3) — Deduction allowed in subsequent year; 53(1)(e)(xiii) — Addition to adjusted cost base of partnership interest; 127(31) — Tiered partnership.

Notes: 127(30) applies where, at the end of a taxation year, a taxpayer is a member of a partnership that does not have enough ITC otherwise available for allocation under 127(8) to offset the ITC recapture required by 127(28), (28.1) or (35). In such a case, the amounts added in calculating the partnership ITC for 127(8) would be less than the amounts that reduce the partnership ITC. The excess "negative" partnership ITC that can reasonably be considered to be the taxpayer's share is added to tax payable. Amounts payable under 127(30) by partners will increase the partnership's SR&ED

pool for the next year: 37(1)(c.3). As well, the ACB of the partnership interest will be increased: 53(1)(e)(xiii).

127(30)(a)(iii) repealed and (b) amended to delete reference to 127(28.1) by 2017 budget bill #1, for expenditures incurred after March 21, 2017 (unless incurred before 2020 under a written agreement entered into by that date), as part of repeal of the childcare spaces credit. (a)(iii) read:

(iii) the total of all amounts each of which is an amount required by subsection (28.1) to be deducted in computing the amount determined in respect of the partnership in respect of the fiscal period under subsection (8),

127(30) amended by 2007 budget bill #2, effective March 19, 2007, effectively to add references to 127(28.1).

127(30) added by 1998 Budget, effective for dispositions and conversions of property that occur after February 23, 1998.

Application Policies: SR&ED 2000-04R2: Recapture of investment tax credit.

(31) Tiered partnership — Where a taxpayer is a member of a particular partnership that is a member of another partnership and an amount would be added to the particular partnership's tax payable under this Part for the year pursuant to subsection (30) if the particular partnership were a person and its fiscal period were its taxation year, that amount is deemed to be an amount that is the lesser of the amounts described in paragraphs (28)(d) and (e), in respect of a property of the particular partnership, that is required by subsection (28) to be deducted in computing the amount under subsection (8) in respect of the particular partnership at the end of the fiscal period.

Notes: 127(31) added by 1998 Budget, effective for dispositions and conversions of property that occur after February 23, 1998. It is a "look-through" rule to deal with tiers of partnerships. It directs partnerships and their members to continue allocating these amounts down through their members until a level is reached at which the members are not partnerships. This is done by deeming the amount that would be the member partnership's addition to tax under 127(30) if the member were a taxpayer, to be the amount of an ITC recapture under 127(28) in respect of the member partnership. 127(28) will then apply to reduce the ITC available for allocation by the lower-tier partnership under 127(8). If the amount is, in turn, "negative", 127(30) will cause the lower-tier partnership to allocate the addition to tax to its members. If necessary, 127(31) will apply again to allocate the addition to tax down a further level, if the members of the partnership at the next level are partnerships as well.

Application Policies: SR&ED 2000-04R2: Recapture of investment tax credit.

(32) Meaning of cost — For the purposes of subsections (27), (28) and (29), "cost of the particular property" to a taxpayer shall not exceed the amount paid by the taxpayer to acquire the particular property from a transferor of the particular property and, for greater certainty, does not include amounts paid by the taxpayer to maintain, modify or transform the particular property.

Notes: 127(32) added by 1998 Budget, effective for dispositions and conversions of property that occur after February 23, 1998. It defines "cost" for purposes of the recapture rules in 127(27)-(29) as the laid-out cost for initial acquisition of the property, not including inputs (such as overhead) which might otherwise be imputed to the cost.

Application Policies: SR&ED 2000-04R2: Recapture of investment tax credit.

(33) Certain non-arm's length transfers — Subsections (27) to (29), (34) and (35) do not apply to a taxpayer or partnership (in this subsection referred to as the "transferor") that disposes of a property to a person or partnership (in this subsection and subsections (34) and (35) referred to as the "purchaser"), that does not deal at arm's length with the transferor, if the purchaser acquired the property in circumstances where the cost of the property to the purchaser would have been an expenditure of the purchaser described in subclause 37(8)(a)(ii)(A)(III) or (B)(III) (as those subclauses read on March 29, 2012) but for subparagraph 2902(b)(iii) of the *Income Tax Regulations*.

Related Provisions: 127(34), (35) — Recapture on disposition or conversion to commercial use.

Notes: 127(33) provides that the ITC recapture provisions (see Notes to 127(27)) do not apply if X disposes of SR&ED property to non-arm's length purchaser P if P continues to use the property substantially all for SR&ED (i.e., property can be moved around within a corporate group). However, on a later disposition or conversion to commercial use, recapture applies under 127(34) or (35).

127(33) amended by 2012 budget bill #2, effective March 29, 2012, to add "(as those subclauses read on March 29, 2012)".

127(33) added by 1998 Budget, effective for dispositions and conversions of property that occur after February 23, 1998.

Application Policies: SR&ED 2000-04R2: Recapture of investment tax credit.

(34) Recapture of investment tax credit — Where, at any particular time in a taxation year and after February 23, 1998, a purchaser (other than a partnership) converts to commercial use, or disposes of without having previously converted to commercial use, a property

(a) that was acquired by the purchaser in circumstances described in subsection (33) or that is another property that incorporates a property acquired in such circumstances; and

(b) that was first acquired, or that incorporates a property that was first acquired, by a person or partnership (in this subsection referred to as the "original user") with which the purchaser did not deal at arm's length at the time at which the purchaser acquired the property, in the original user's taxation year or fiscal period that includes the particular time (on the assumption that the original user had such a taxation year or fiscal period) or in any of the original user's 10 preceding taxation years or fiscal periods,

there shall be added to the purchaser's tax otherwise payable under this Part for the year the lesser of

(c) the amount

(i) included, in respect of the property, in the investment tax credit of the original user, or

(ii) where the original user is a partnership, that can reasonably be considered to have been included in respect of the property in computing the amount determined under subsection (8) in respect of the original user, and

(d) the amount determined by applying the percentage that was applied by the original user in determining the amount referred to in paragraph (c) to

(i) if the property or the other property is disposed of to a person who deals at arm's length with the purchaser, the proceeds of disposition of that property, and

(ii) in any other case, the fair market value of the property or the other property at the time of the conversion or disposition.

Related Provisions: 37(1)(c.2) — Deduction allowed in subsequent year; 127(33) — No application to certain non-arm's length transfers; 127(36) — Transitional application of 20-year recapture carryforward.

Notes: 127(34) added by 1998 Budget, for dispositions and conversions of property after Feb. 23, 1998. See Notes to 127(33).

Application Policies: SR&ED 2000-04R2: Recapture of investment tax credit.

(35) Recapture of investment tax credit — Where, at any particular time in a fiscal period and after February 23, 1998, a purchaser is a partnership that converts to commercial use, or disposes of without having previously converted to commercial use, a property

(a) that was acquired by the purchaser in circumstances described in subsection (33) or that is another property that incorporates a property acquired in such circumstances, and

(b) that was first acquired, or that incorporates a property that was first acquired, by a person or partnership (in this subsection referred to as the "original user") with which the purchaser did not deal at arm's length at the time at which the purchaser acquired the property, in the original user's taxation year or fiscal period that includes the particular time (on the assumption that the original user had such a taxation year or fiscal period) or in any of the original user's 10 preceding taxation years or fiscal periods,

there shall be deducted in computing the amount determined under subsection (8) in respect of the purchaser at the end of the fiscal period the lesser of

(c) the amount

(i) included, in respect of the property, in the investment tax credit of the original user, or

(ii) where the original user is a partnership, that can reasonably be considered to have been included in respect of the pro-

perty in computing the amount determined under subsection (8) in respect of the original user, and

(d) the amount determined by applying the percentage that was applied by the original user in determining the amount referred to in paragraph (c) to

(i) if the property or the other property is disposed of to a person who deals at arm's length with the purchaser, the proceeds of disposition of that property, and

(ii) in any other case, the fair market value of the property or the other property at the time of the conversion or disposition.

Related Provisions: 127(30) — Addition to tax where ITC goes negative; 127(33) — No application to certain non-arm's length transfers; 127(36) — Transitional application of 20-year recapture carryforward.

Notes: 127(35) added by 1998 Budget, for dispositions and conversions of property after Feb. 23, 1998. See Notes to 127(33).

(36) Transitional application of investment tax credit recapture — For the purpose of applying each of subsection (27) or (29) in respect of a taxpayer, subsection (28) in respect of a partnership or subsection (34) or (35) in respect of a purchaser and an original user, as the case may be, (which taxpayer, partnership or original user is, in this subsection, referred to as the "taxpayer"), the reference to "10" in that subsection is to be read as a reference to the number that is the lesser of

(a) 20, and

(b) the number that is the total of 10 and the number of taxation years or fiscal periods, as the case may be, by which the number of taxation years or fiscal periods of the taxpayer that have ended after 1997 exceeds 11.

Notes: 127(36)(b) amended by 2008 budget bill #2, effective in respect of the 2008 and later taxation years, to change "2005" to "1997". See Notes to 127(9.01).

127(36) added by 2006 budget bill #1 (implementing a Nov. 14/05 proposal to extend carryforwards from 10 to 20 years), for 2006 and later tax years. See Notes to 111(1)(a).

Definitions [s. 127]: "active business" — 248(1); "adjusted selling cost", "adjusted service cost" — 127(11.7); "advantage" — 248(32); "allowable capital loss" — 38(b), 248(1); "amount" — 127(11.6), 248(1); "annual investment tax credit limit", "apprenticeship expenditure", "approved project", "approved project property" — 127(9); "arm's length" — 251(1); "assessment" — 248(1); "assistance" — 79(4), 125.4(5), 248(16), (16.1), (18), (18.1); "associated" — 127(10.22), (10.23), 256; "at-risk amount" — 96(2.2), 127(8.5); "available for use" — 13(27)–(32), 248(19); "bank" — 248(1); "beneficially interested" — 248(25); "business" — 248(1); "calendar year" — *Interpretation Act* 37(1)(a); "Canada" — 37(1.3), 127(9)"qualified property"(d), 255, *Interpretation Act* 35(1); "Canadian-controlled private corporation" — 125(7), 136(1), 248(1); "Canadian field processing" — 248(1); "Canadian exploration expense" — 66.1(6), 248(1); "Canadian partnership" — 102(1), 248(1); "Cape Breton" — 127(9); "capital cost" — 13(7.1)–(7.4), 127(11.1)(a), (b); "capital gain" — 39(1)(a), 248(1); "capital property" — 54, 248(1); "carrying on a business in Canada", "carrying on business in Canada" — 253; "certified property" — 127(9); "contract payment" — 127(9), (25); "control", "controlled" — 256(6)–(9), 256.1(3); "corporation" — 248(1), *Interpretation Act* 35(1); "cost" — 127(11.8)(a); "cost of the particular property" — 127(32); "credit union" — 137(6), 248(1); "current nature" — 37(8)(d); "depreciable property" — 13(21), 248(1); "disposition" — 127(27.11), 248(1); "eligible amount" — 248(31), (41); "eligible apprentice" — 127(9); "eligible salary and wages" — 127(9), (11.4); "employed", "employee", "employer", "employment", "exempt income" — 248(1); "expenditure" — 127(11.6), (26); "expenditure limit" — 127(10.2), (10.21); "fair market value" — see 69(1) Notes; "farm loss" — 111(8), 248(1); "farming" — 248(1); "filing-due date" — 127(23), 248(1); "first period" — 127(9)"first-term shared-use-equipment"; "first-term shared-use-equipment" — 127(9); "fiscal period" — 249(2)(b), 249.1; "fishing" — 248(1); "flow-through mining expenditure" — 127(9), (11.1)(c.2); "Gaspé Peninsula", "government assistance" — 127(9); "graduated rate estate" — 248(1); "incurred" — 127(26); "individual" — 248(1); "*inter vivos* trust" — 108(1), 248(1); "investment tax credit" — 127(9), 248(1); "legislature" — *Interpretation Act* 35(1); "legislative assembly"; "limited partner" — 96(2.4), 127(8.5); "loss restriction event" — 251.2; "manufacturing or processing" — 127(11)(a); "mineral", "mineral resource" — 248(1); "minimum amount" — 127.51; "Minister" — 248(1); "monetary contribution" — 127(4.1), *Canada Elections Act* s. 2(1); "month" — *Interpretation Act* 35(1); "nominee" — *Senate Appointments Confirmation Act* s. 2(1); "non-capital loss" — 111(8), 248(1); "non-government assistance" — 127(9); "non-resident" — 248(1); "oil or gas well" — 248(1); "partnership" — see 96(1) Notes; "permanent establishment" — Reg. 8201; "person" — 248(1); "phase", "pre-production mining expenditure" — 127(9); "prescribed"; "prescribed proxy amount" — Reg. 2900(4)–(10); "principal-business corporation" — 66(15); "property" — 248(1); "province" — *Interpretation Act* 35(1); "provincial" — *Interpretation Act* 33(3), 35(1)"province"; "purchaser" — 127(33); "purposes" — 127(11)(b);

"qualified Canadian exploration expenditure" — 127(9), (11.1)(c.1); "qualified construction equipment" — 127(9); "qualified expenditure" — 127(9), (14), (24); "qualified property", "qualified resource property", "qualified small-business property", "qualified transportation equipment" — 127(9); "record" — 248(1); "refundable Part VII tax on hand" — 192(3), 248(1); "regulation" — 248(1); "related" — 251(2)–(6); "resident in Canada" — 250; "SR&ED qualified expenditure pool" — 127(9); "salary or wages" — 248(1); "scientific research and experimental development" — 37(13), 248(1); "second-term shared-use-equipment" — 127(9); "series of transactions" — 248(10); "service" — 127(11.8)(c); "share", "shareholder", "specified future tax consequence", "specified member" — 248(1); "specified percentage", "specified sampling", "super-allowance benefit amount" — 127(9); "tar sands" — 248(1); "tax otherwise payable" — 117(1), 120(4); "tax payable" — 248(2); "taxable Canadian corporation" — 89(1), 248(1); "taxable capital gain" — 38(a), 248(1); "taxable income" — 2(2), 248(1); "taxable income earned in Canada" — 115(1), 248(1); "taxable supplier" — 127(9); "taxation year" — 127(23), 249; "taxpayer" — 248(1); "transferee" — 127(13), (20), (29); "transferor" — 127(13), (33); "trust" — 104(1), 248(1), (3); "undepreciated capital cost" — 13(21), 248(1); "writing", "written" — *Interpretation Act* 35(1)"writing".

127.1 (1) Refundable investment tax credit — Where a taxpayer (other than a person exempt from tax under section 149) files

(a) with the taxpayer's return of income (other than a return of income filed under subsection 70(2) or 104(23), paragraph 128(2)(f) or subsection 150(4)) for a taxation year, or

(b) with a prescribed form amending a return referred to in paragraph (a)

a prescribed form containing prescribed information, the taxpayer is deemed to have paid on the taxpayer's balance-due day for the year an amount on account of the taxpayer's tax payable under this Part for the year equal to the lesser of

(c) the taxpayer's refundable investment tax credit for the year, and

(d) the amount designated by the taxpayer in the prescribed form.

Related Provisions: 13(24) — Acquisition of control — limitation re calculation of refundable investment tax credit; 127(14) — Identification of amounts transferred as current or capital; 127.1(3) — Refundable ITC deemed claimed under 127(5); 152(1) — Assessment; 152(4.2)(b) — Redetermination of credit at taxpayer's request; 157(3)(e), 157(3.1)(c) — Reduction in instalments to reflect credit; 160.1 — Where excess refunded; 164(1)(a) — Refunds; 220(6) — Assignment of refund by corporation permitted; 256(2.1) — Anti-avoidance.

Notes: Because the taxpayer is "deemed to have paid" the amount in question, it, like instalments or source deductions, is treated as a credit to the account that is fully refundable even if no tax is payable for the year.

The refundable ITC is available only to certain CCPCs: see 127.1(2)"qualifying corporation". It was allowed because the corp was a CCPC in *Price Waterhouse Coopers [Bioartifical Gel, Bagtech]*, 2013 FCA 164. It was denied because the corp was not a CCPC in: *Lyrtech RD*, 2014 FCA 267 (leave to appeal denied 2015 CarswellNat 2528 (SCC)); *Solutions MindReady*, 2015 TCC 17 (TCC, appeal to FCA discontinued A-62-15); *Kruger Wayagamack*, 2016 FCA 192; *Aeronautic Development*, 2018 FCA 67 (leave to appeal denied 2019 CarswellNat 595 (SCC)). A lawsuit for alleged negligent advice on how to qualify as a CCPC to get the refundable ITC, *Sigma Capital v. KPMG*, 2014 ONSC 3997, settled on a confidential basis in 2019.

The deadline for claiming a refundable ITC is based on CRA's "determination" after the form is filed, not on the assessment date: *Perfect Fry*, 2007 TCC 133, paras. 42-45 (aff'd on other grounds 2008 FCA 218). In *Signalgene R&D*, 2012 FC 1375 and *Theratechnologies*, 2012 FC 1376, the FC granted judicial review of CRA's refusal to issue a Notice of Determination of the amount of refundable ITCs. On how CRA addresses a retroactive change to CCPC status to reflect the case law, see doc 2015-0567981I7.

127.1(1) amended by 1995-97 technical bill (for tax years that begin after April 26, 1995), 1996 Budget.

Application Policies: SR&ED 96-03: Claimants' entitlements and responsibilities; SR&ED 96-05: Penalties under subsec. 163(2).

CRA Audit Manual: 11.3.4: Tax credits.

Forms: RC4290: Refunds for small business R&D [guide]; T1 General return, Line 45400 [former 454] (for individuals); T4052: An introduction to the SR&ED program [guide].

(2) Definitions — In this section,

"excluded corporation" for a taxation year means a corporation that is, at any time in the year,

(a) controlled directly or indirectly, in any manner whatever, by

(i) one or more persons exempt from tax under this Part by virtue of section 149,

(ii) Her Majesty in right of a province, a Canadian municipality or any other public authority, or

(iii) any combination of persons each of whom is a person referred to in subparagraph (i) or (ii), or

(b) related to any person referred to in paragraph (a);

Related Provisions: 256(5.1), (6.2) — Controlled directly or indirectly.

"qualifying corporation", for a particular taxation year that ends in a calendar year, means a particular corporation that is a Canadian-controlled private corporation in the particular taxation year the taxable income of which for its immediately preceding taxation year — together with, if the particular corporation is associated in the particular taxation year with one or more other corporations (in this subsection referred to as "associated corporations"), the taxable income of each associated corporation for its last taxation year that ended in the preceding calendar year (determined before taking into consideration the specified future tax consequences for that last year) — does not exceed the qualifying income limit, if any, of the particular corporation for the particular taxation year;

Related Provisions: 87(2)(oo), (oo.1) — Effect of amalgamation; 88(1)(e.9) — Winding-up; 88(1)(e.9)(i)(C), (ii)(C), (iii) — Qualifying income limit on windup of subsidiary; 127.1(2.01) — Additional refundable amount for corporation that is not a qualifying corporation; 127.1(2.2), (2.3) — Venture capital investors — exclusion from associated-corporation rules; 127.1(4) — Where CCPC has taxation year less than 51 weeks; 136(1) — Cooperative can be private corporation for 127.1; 137(7) — Credit union can be private corporation for 127.1.

Notes: See Notes to 127.1(1) and 248(1)"specified future tax consequences".

Definition amended by 2013 budget bill #2 to add "if any" [near the end], effective for taxation years that begin after Dec. 21, 2012.

127.1(2)"qualifying corporation" amended by 2008 budget bill #2, effective for taxation years that end after Feb. 25, 2008. Definition earlier amended by 1996 Budget (for taxation years that begin after 1995) and 1994 Budget.

"qualifying income limit" of a corporation for a particular taxation year is the amount determined by the formula

$$\$500{,}000 \times [(\$40 \text{ million} - A)/\$40 \text{ million}]$$

where

A is

(a) nil, if $10 million is greater than or equal to the amount (in paragraph (b) referred to as the "taxable capital amount") that is the total of the corporation's taxable capital employed in Canada (within the meaning assigned by section 181.2 or 181.3) for its immediately preceding taxation year and the taxable capital employed in Canada (within the meaning assigned by section 181.2 or 181.3) of each associated corporation for the associated corporation's last taxation year that ended in the last calendar year that ended before the end of the particular taxation year, or

(b) in any other case, the lesser of $40 million and the amount by which the taxable capital amount exceeds $10 million;

Related Provisions: 88(1)(e.9)(i)(C), (ii)(C), (iii) — Qualifying income limit on windup of subsidiary.

Notes: See Notes to 127(10.2). 127.1(2)"qualifying income limit" added by 2008 budget bill #2/2009 budget bill #1, effective for taxation years that end after Feb. 25, 2008, with a transitional calculation for years that included Feb. 26, 2008.

"refundable investment tax credit" of a taxpayer for a taxation year means, in the case of a taxpayer who is

(a) a qualifying corporation for the year,

(b) an individual other than a trust, or

(c) a trust each beneficiary of which is a person referred to in paragraph (a) or (b),

an amount equal to 40% of the amount, if any, by which

(d) the total of all amounts included in computing the taxpayer's investment tax credit at the end of the year

(i) in respect of property (other than qualified small-business property) acquired, or a qualified expenditure (other than an expenditure in respect of which an amount is included under paragraph (f) in computing the taxpayer's refundable investment tax credit for the year) incurred, by the taxpayer in the year, or

(ii) because of paragraph (b) of the definition "investment tax credit" in subsection 127(9) in respect of a property (other than qualified small-business property) acquired or a qualified expenditure (other than an expenditure in respect of which an amount is included under paragraph (f) in computing the taxpayer's refundable investment tax credit for the year) incurred

exceeds

(e) the total of

(i) the portion of the total of all amounts deducted under subsection 127(5) for the year or a preceding taxation year (other than an amount deemed by subsection (3) to be so deducted for the year) that can reasonably be considered to be in respect of the total determined under paragraph (d), and

(ii) the portion of the total of all amounts required by subsection 127(6) or (7) to be deducted in computing the taxpayer's investment tax credit at the end of the year that can reasonably be considered to be in respect of the total determined under paragraph (d),

plus, where the taxpayer is a qualifying corporation (other than an excluded corporation) for the year, the amount, if any, by which

(f) the total of

(i) the portion of the amount required by subsection 127(10.1) to be added in computing the taxpayer's investment tax credit at the end of the year that is in respect of qualified expenditures incurred by the taxpayer in the year, and

(ii) all amounts determined under paragraph (a.1) of the definition "investment tax credit" in subsection 127(9) in respect of expenditures for which an amount is included in subparagraph (i)

exceeds

(g) the total of

(i) the portion of the total of all amounts deducted by the taxpayer under subsection 127(5) for the year or a preceding taxation year (other than an amount deemed by subsection (3) to be so deducted for the year) that can reasonably be considered to be in respect of the total determined under paragraph (f), and

(ii) the portion of the total of all amounts required by subsection 127(6) to be deducted in computing the taxpayer's investment tax credit at the end of the year that can reasonably be considered to be in respect of the total determined under paragraph (f).

Related Provisions: 88(1)(e.8) — Winding-up; 127(14) — Identification of amounts transferred as current or capital; 127.1(2.01) — Addition to refundable investment tax credit; 127(10.22), (10.23) — Venture capital investors — exclusion from associated-corporation rules; 256(2.1) — Anti-avoidance; 256(5.1), (6.2) — Controlled directly or indirectly.

Notes: Subpara. (f)(i) amended by 2012 budget bill #2, effective Feb. 2017, to delete "(other than expenditures of a capital nature)" after "qualified expenditures".

Para (f) amended by 1995 Budget, for taxation years that begin after 1995.

Definition "refundable investment tax credit" amended by 1992 Economic Statement, effective for taxation years that end after December 2, 1992.

(2.01) Addition to refundable investment tax credit — In the case of a taxpayer that is a Canadian-controlled private corporation other than a qualifying corporation or an excluded corporation, the refundable investment tax credit of the taxpayer for a taxation year is the amount, if any, by which

(a) the total of

(i) the portion of the amount required by subsection 127(10.1) to be added in computing the taxpayer's investment tax credit at the end of the year that is in respect of

qualified expenditures incurred by the taxpayer in the year, and

(ii) all amounts determined under paragraph (a.1) of the definition "investment tax credit" in subsection 127(9) in respect of expenditures for which an amount is included in subparagraph (i)

exceeds

(b) the total of

(i) the portion of the total of all amounts deducted by the taxpayer under subsection 127(5) for the year or a preceding taxation year (other than an amount deemed by subsection (3) to have been so deducted for the year) that can reasonably be considered to be in respect of the total determined under paragraph (a), and

(ii) the portion of the total of all amounts required by subsection 127(6) to be deducted in computing the taxpayer's investment tax credit at the end of the year that can reasonably be considered to be in respect of the total determined under paragraph (a).

Notes: 127.1(2.01) permits a corporation with taxable income over $500,000 (i.e., not a "qualifying corporation" under 127.1(2)) to obtain partial refundability of the 35% ITC for R&D expenditures, phased out as taxable income increases.

127.1(2.01) amended by 2012 budget bill #2, effective Feb. 1, 2017, effectively to repeal former (a)-(b). Before that date, read:

(2.01) In the case of a taxpayer that is a Canadian-controlled private corporation other than a qualifying corporation or an excluded corporation, the refundable investment tax credit of the taxpayer for a taxation year is 40% of the amount, if any, by which

(a) the total of

(i) the portion of the amount required by subsection 127(10.1) to be added in computing the taxpayer's investment tax credit at the end of the year that is in respect of qualified expenditures (other than expenditures of a current nature) incurred by the taxpayer in the year, and

(ii) all amounts determined under paragraph (a.1) of the definition "investment tax credit" in subsection 127(9) in respect of expenditures for which an amount is included in subparagraph (i)

exceeds

(b) the total of

(i) the portion of the total of all amounts deducted by the taxpayer under subsection 127(5) for the year or a preceding taxation year (other than an amount deemed by subsection (3) to have been so deducted for the year) that can reasonably be considered to be in respect of the total determined under paragraph (a), and

(ii) the portion of the total of all amounts required by subsection 127(6) to be deducted in computing the taxpayer's investment tax credit at the end of the year that can reasonably be considered to be in respect of the total determined under paragraph (a)

plus the amount, if any, by which

(c) the total of

(i) the portion of the amount required by subsection 127(10.1) to be added in computing the taxpayer's investment tax credit at the end of the year that is in respect of qualified expenditures (other than expenditures of a capital nature) incurred by the taxpayer in the year, and

(ii) all amounts determined under paragraph (a.1) of the definition "investment tax credit" in subsection 127(9) in respect of expenditures for which an amount is included in subparagraph (i)

exceeds

(d) the total of

(i) the portion of the total of all amounts deducted by the taxpayer under subsection 127(5) for the year or a preceding taxation year (other than an amount deemed by subsection (3) to have been so deducted for the year) that can reasonably be considered to be in respect of the total determined under paragraph (c), and

(ii) the portion of the total of all amounts required by subsection 127(6) to be deducted in computing the taxpayer's investment tax credit at the end of the year that can reasonably be considered to be in respect of the total determined under paragraph (c).

127(2.01) amended by 1995 Budget, effective for taxation years that begin after 1995. Added by 1993 Budget, effective for taxation years that begin in 1994 or later. (It was originally proposed as 127.1(2.1).)

(2.1) Application of subsec. 127(9) — The definitions in subsection 127(9) apply to this section.

Notes: 127.1(2.1) added in the RSC 1985 (5th Supp) consolidation for tax years ending after Nov. 1991. This rule was formerly in the opening words of 127(9).

(2.2) Refundable investment tax credit — associated CCPCs — If a particular Canadian-controlled private corporation is associated with another corporation in circumstances where those corporations would not be associated if the Act were read without reference to paragraph 256(1.2)(a), the particular corporation has issued shares to one or more persons who have been issued shares by the other corporation and there is at least one shareholder of the particular corporation who is not a shareholder of the other corporation or one shareholder of the other corporation who is not a shareholder of the particular corporation, the particular corporation is not associated with the other corporation for the purpose of calculating that portion of the particular corporation's refundable investment tax credit that is in respect of qualified expenditures.

Related Provisions: 127(10.22) — Parallel rule for determining expenditure limit.

Notes: 127.1(2.2) added by 2004 Budget, effective for taxation years that end after March 22, 2004. Together with 127.1(2.3) it fulfills the same function as 127(10.22) and (10.23), with respect to the refundable ITC.

(2.3) Application of subsec. (2.2) — Subsection (2.2) applies to the particular corporation and the other corporation referred to in that subsection only if the Minister is satisfied that

(a) the particular corporation and the other corporation are not otherwise associated under this Act; and

(b) the existence of one or more shareholders of the particular corporation who is not a shareholder of the other corporation, or the existence of one or more shareholders of the other corporation who is not a shareholder of the particular corporation, is not for the purpose of satisfying the requirements of subsection (2.2) or 127(10.22).

Related Provisions: 127(10.23) — Parallel rule for determining expenditure limit.

Notes: 127.1(2.3) added by 2004 Budget, effective for taxation years that end after March 22, 2004. See Notes to 127.1(2.2).

(3) Deemed deduction — For the purposes of this Act, the amount deemed under subsection (1) to have been paid by a taxpayer for a taxation year shall be deemed to have been deducted by the taxpayer under subsection 127(5) for the year.

Notes: In CRA's view, a taxpayer cannot manipulate refundable ITCs to claim more in ITCs than the maximum under 127(5): VIEWS doc 2005-0143681I7.

(4) Qualifying income limit determined in certain cases — For the purpose of the definition of "qualifying corporation" in subsection (2), where a Canadian-controlled private corporation has a taxation year that is less than 51 weeks, the taxable income of the corporation for the year shall be determined by multiplying that amount by the ratio that 365 is of the number of days in that year.

Notes: 127.1(4) added by 2009 budget bill #1, effective in respect of the 2008 and later taxation years. It was not in the draft legislation of Nov. 28, 2008.

Definitions [s. 127.1]: "amount" — 248(1); "associated" — 256; "balance-due day" — 248(1); "calendar year" — *Interpretation Act* 37(1)(a); "Canada" — 255, *Interpretation Act* 35(1); "Canadian-controlled private corporation" — 125(7), 248(1); "controlled directly or indirectly" — 256(5.1)–(6); "corporation" — 248(1), *Interpretation Act* 35(1); "employed" — 248(1); "excluded corporation" — 127.1(2); "Her Majesty" — *Interpretation Act* 35(1); "individual" — 248(1); "investment tax credit" — 127(9), 248(1); "Minister", "person", "prescribed", "property" — 248(1); "province" — *Interpretation Act* 35(1); "qualifying corporation", "qualifying income limit", "refundable investment tax credit" — 127.1(2); "related" — 251(2)–(6); "share", "shareholder", "specified future tax consequence" — 248(1); "taxable income" — 127.1(4), 248(1); "taxation year" — 249; "taxpayer" — 248(1); "trust" — 104(1), 248(1), (3).

127.2 [Share-purchase tax credit — No longer relevant.]

Notes: Share-purchase tax credits under 127.2 have not formally been repealed, but they are no longer available. Under 192(4), no designation of an SPTC can be made after 1986. Section 127.2 is therefore generally irrelevant, except for 127.2(8), which determines the cost of a share designated for purposes of the credit as being the cost minus the amount designated under 192(4). See also Notes to 192, 193.

127.3 [Scientific research tax credit — No longer relevant.]

Notes: See Notes to 194, 195. Scientific research tax credits (SRTCs) have not formally been repealed, but under 194(4.2), no SRTC designation can be made after 1985. 127.3 is therefore generally irrelevant, except for 127.3(6), which determines the cost of a share, debt obligation or right designated for purposes of the SRTC (reproduced here up to the 51st ed.). For the current investment tax credit for scientific research, see Notes to 127(9)"SR&ED qualified expenditure pool".

127.4 (1) [Labour-sponsored funds tax credit] Definitions — In this section,

"approved share" means a share of the capital stock of a prescribed labour-sponsored venture capital corporation, but does not include

(a) a share issued by a registered labour-sponsored venture capital corporation the venture capital business of which was discontinued before the time of the issue, and

(b) a share issued by a prescribed labour-sponsored venture capital corporation that is not a registered labour-sponsored venture capital corporation if, at the time of the issue, no province under the laws (described in section 6701 of the *Income Tax Regulations*) of which the corporation is registered or established provides assistance in respect of the acquisition of the share;

Related Provisions: 131(8) — Prescribed LSVCC is a mutual fund corporation; 204.8(2) — Determining when an RLSVCC discontinues its business; 211.7(1)"approved share" — Definition applies to Part XII.5.

Notes: Para. (b) amended by 2002-2013 technical bill (Part 5 — technical), effective for acquisitions of shares that occur after 2003.

127.4(1)"approved share" amended by 1999 Budget (effective for 1999 and later taxation years), 1996 Budget and 1991 technical bill.

Regulations: 100(5) (reduction in withholding where share purchased from payroll); 6701 (prescribed labour-sponsored venture capital corporation).

"labour-sponsored funds tax credit" — [Repealed]

Notes: "Labour-sponsored funds tax credit" repealed by 1996 Budget, effective for 1996 and later taxation years. (See now 127.4(5) and (6).)

"net cost" to an individual of an approved share means the amount, if any, by which

(a) the amount of consideration paid by the individual to acquire or subscribe for the share

exceeds

(b) the amount of any assistance (other than an amount included in computing a tax credit of the individual in respect of that share) provided or to be provided by a government, municipality or any public authority in respect of, or for the acquisition of, the share;

Related Provisions: 211.7(1)"net cost" — Definition applies to Part XII.5.

Notes: "Net cost" amended by 1991 technical bill, effective 1989.

"original acquisition" of a share means the first acquisition of the share, except that

(a) where the share is irrevocably subscribed and paid for before its first acquisition, subject to paragraphs (b) and (c), the original acquisition of the share is the first transaction whereby the share is irrevocably subscribed and paid for,

(b) a share is deemed never to have been acquired and never to have been irrevocably subscribed and paid for unless the first registered holder of the share is, subject to paragraph (c), the first person to either acquire or irrevocably subscribe and pay for the share, and

(c) for the purpose of this definition, a broker or dealer in securities acting in that capacity is deemed never to acquire or subscribe and pay for the share and never to be the registered holder of the share;

Related Provisions: 127.4(5.1) — Direction for original acquisition to be deemed to occur at beginning of year; 204.8(1)"original acquisition" — Definition applies to Part X.3; 211.7(1)"original acquisition" — Definition applies to Part XII.5.

Notes: "Original acquisition" added by 1996 Budget, effective 1996.

"qualifying trust" for an individual in respect of a share means

(a) a trust governed by a registered retirement savings plan, under which the individual is the annuitant, that is not a spousal or common-law partner plan (in this definition having the meaning assigned by subsection 146(1)) in relation to another individual,

(b) a trust governed by a registered retirement savings plan, under which the individual or the individual's spouse or common-law partner is the annuitant, that is a spousal or common-law partner plan in relation to the individual or the individual's spouse or common-law partner, if the individual and no other person claims a deduction under subsection (2) in respect of the share, or

(c) a trust governed by a TFSA of which the individual is the holder;

Related Provisions: 127.4(6)(a) — Credit to individual for investment by qualifying trust; 211.7(1)"qualifying trust" — Definition applies to Part XII.5.

Notes: 127.4(1)"qualifying trust"(a) and (b) amended by 2008 budget bill #2 to change "spousal plan" to "spousal or common-law partner plan", effective on the same basis as 248(1)"common-law partner" (generally 2001). This amendment had been in drafts of what became the 2002-2013 technical bill, but was instead included in the 2008 Budget bill since para. (c) was being added.

Para. (c) added by 2008 budget bill #2, effective for 2009 and later taxation years.

127.4(1)"qualifying trust"(b) amended by 2000 same-sex partners bill to refer to "common-law partner", effective as per Notes to 248(1)"common-law partner".

Definition amended by 1998 Budget, for 1998 and later tax years. The amendment allows the acquisition by an RRSP trust to always be taken into account in claiming the LSVCC credit for the RRSP annuitant (or, for a spousal RRSP, for the contributor spouse or the annuitant spouse who claims the LSVCC credit). This amendment is linked to the repeal of the "3-year cooling-off period" in 127.4(3) and (4); the previous definition prevented reinvestment in shares issued by LSVCCs in some cases.

Definition "qualifying trust" added by 1992 Economic Statement, effective for 1992 and later taxation years. See 127.4(6)(a).

"tax otherwise payable" by an individual means the amount that, but for this section, would be the individual's tax payable under this Part.

Notes: 127.4(1)"tax otherwise payable" amended by 1999 Budget, effective for 1998 and later taxation years, to change "but for this section and section 120.1" to "but for this section".

(1.1) Amalgamations or mergers — Subsections 204.8(2) and 204.85(3) apply for the purpose of this section.

Notes: 127.4(1.1) added by 1999 Budget, effective February 17, 1999.

(2) Deduction of labour-sponsored funds tax credit — There may be deducted from the tax otherwise payable by an individual (other than a trust) for a taxation year such amount as the individual claims not exceeding the individual's labour-sponsored funds tax credit limit for the year.

Related Provisions: 127.4(5) — Determination of labour-sponsored funds tax credit limit; 211.8 — Repayment of credit on early disposition of share.

Notes: 127.4(2) repealed effective 2017 by 2013 budget bill #2, but that repeal was cancelled by 2016 budget bill #1, s. 61(1), which reinstated the credit, but only for investment in provincial labour-sponsored venture capital corps. See 127.4(5) Notes.

127.4(2) earlier amended by 1998 and 1996 Budgets, 1992 technical bill.

Regulations: 100(5) (reduction in withholding where share purchased from payroll).

(3) [Repealed]

Notes: 127.4(3) repealed by 1998 Budget, for 1998 and later tax years. It was amended by 1996 Budget, for 1996 and later tax years, to contain the "3-year cooling-off period" rule, which prevented someone from redeeming an LSVCC share and buying new shares shortly thereafter for an additional credit. That rule no longer applies.

Former 127.4(3) amended by 1992 Economic Statement, for 1992 and later tax years, to add references to a qualifying trust. The amendment allowed an individual's RRSP to subscribe for LSVCC shares directly with new money provided for that purpose, with the credit going to the individual. See 127.4(1)"qualifying trust", and see now 127.4(6)(a). Previously the individual had to purchase the shares on personal account and then transfer them to the RRSP.

Former 127.4(3) amended by 1991 technical bill, effective 1989.

(4) [Repealed]

Notes: 127.4(4) repealed by 1998 Budget, effective for 1998 and later taxation years. It provided exceptions to the cooling-off period in 127.4(3).

127.4(4) replaced by 1996 Budget, for 1996 and later tax years. Previously amended by 1992 Economic Statement.

(5) Labour-sponsored funds tax credit limit — For the purpose of subsection (2), an individual's labour-sponsored funds tax credit limit for a taxation year is the lesser of

(a) $750, and

(b) the amount, if any, by which

(i) the total of all amounts each of which is the individual's labour-sponsored funds tax credit in respect of an original acquisition in the year or in the first 60 days of the following taxation year of an approved share

exceeds

(ii) the portion of the total described in subparagraph (i) that was deducted under subsection (2) in computing the individual's tax payable under this Part for the preceding taxation year.

Related Provisions: 127.4(5.1) — Extension of investment deadline by CRA so that acquisition deemed made at beginning of year; 127.4(6) — Determination of labour-sponsored funds tax credit.

Notes: The maximum LSVCC credit is $750 (15% of an investment up to $5,000): 127.4(5)(a).

Several provinces provide a credit for investment of up to $5,000 in a labour-sponsored venture capital corporation, to parallel this 15% federal credit. See Reg. 6701 for the list of provincial statutes, some of which (e.g., Ontario) are now expired (i.e., no new provincial credit is offered). For rules allowing a provincial LSVCC to revoke its registration after the province discontinues its credit, see 204.81(8.3), (8.4).

The $750 federal credit was phased out by the 2013 (Conservative) budget bill #2 to $500 for 2015, $250 for 2016 and $0 as of 2017. However, the 2016 (Liberal) budget bill #1 restored it to $750 as of 2016 [the bill's s. 61(1) undid the repeal of 127.4(2), (5) and (6), and s. 36 amended 127.4(5) and (6)].

The 2016 Budget papers state that newly registered LSVCCs under existing provincial legislation will be eligible if the provincial legislation is currently prescribed for purposes of the federal LSVCC tax credit. New provincial regimes will be eligible provided the enabling provincial legislation is patterned on currently prescribed provincial legislation. To be eligible, any new provincial regime would need to: provide a provincial tax credit of at least 15% of an individual's net cost of shares purchased in an LSVCC; require that the LSVCC be sponsored by an eligible labour body; and mandate that the LSVCC invest and maintain a minimum of 60% of its shareholder equity in eligible investments, generally investments in small and medium-sized enterprises.

"While significant funding to small and medium-sized businesses has been provided in a number of provinces through provincial LSVCC programs, the national LSVCC program has not had a similar impact." As a result, the federal LSVCC tax credit remained at 5% for 2016 (127.4(6)(a.1)) and is eliminated as of 2017 (127.4(6)(a.2)). The prohibition on new federal LSVCC registrations (204.81(1) opening words) and the transition rules for federally registered LSVCCs have been maintained.

Where a taxpayer acquires LSVCC shares and contributes them to a spousal RRSP, only the taxpayer can claim the credit; if the taxpayer contributes cash and the RRSP acquires the shares, either one can claim the credit (but they cannot split it): VIEWS docs 2005-0154871E5, 2006-0178491E5.

See also Smith, "Labour-Sponsored Venture Capital Corporations", IV(1) *Business Vehicles* (Federated Press) 162-78 (1997); Osborne & Sandler, "A Tax Expenditure Analysis of Labour-Sponsored Venture Capital Corporations", 46(3) *Canadian Tax Journal* 499-574 (1998).

127.4(5)(a) amended by 2016 budget bill #1, for 2017 and later tax years. For the 2016 tax year, read:

(a) the amount determined by the formula

$$0.15 \times A + 0.05 \times B$$

where

A . is the lesser of

(i) $5,000, and

(ii) the total of all amounts each of which is the net cost of the original acquisition of shares of a prescribed labour-sponsored venture capital corporation (other than a corporation that is a prescribed labour-sponsored venture capital corporation solely because it is a registered labour-sponsored venture capital corporation), and

B   is the lesser of

(i) the amount if any by which $5,000 exceeds the amount determined for subparagraph (ii) in the description of A, and

(ii) the total of all amounts each of which is the net cost of the original acquisition of shares of a corporation that is a prescribed labour-sponsored venture capital corporation solely because it is a registered labour-sponsored venture capital corporation, and

127.4(5) un-repealed by 2016 budget bill #1 s. 61 and amended by same bill s. 36, effective for 2016 and later taxation years, to change $250 back to $750.

127.4(5) earlier amended by 1998 Budget; added by 1996 Budget.

(5.1) Deemed original acquisition — If the Minister so directs, an original acquisition of an approved share that occurs in an individual's taxation year (other than in the first 60 days of the year) is deemed for the purpose of this section to have occurred at the beginning of the year and not at the time it actually occurred.

Notes: 127.4(5.1) added by 1998 Budget, effective for acquisitions made after 1997. It provides a general authorization, in 127.4(5.1) (and 146(22) for RRSPs), allowing CRA to direct that a late contribution was made at the start of the year — and thus within the first 60 days, qualifying it for a credit for the previous year.

(6) Labour-sponsored funds tax credit — For the purpose of subsection (5), an individual's labour-sponsored funds tax credit in respect of an original acquisition of an approved share is equal to the least of

(a) 15% of the net cost to the individual (or to a qualifying trust for the individual in respect of the share) for the original acquisition of the share by the individual or by the trust, if the share is a share of a prescribed labour-sponsored venture capital corporation (other than a corporation that is a prescribed labour-sponsored venture capital corporation solely because it is a registered labour-sponsored venture capital corporation),

(a.1) 5% of the net cost to the individual (or to a qualifying trust for the individual in respect of the share) for the original acquisition of the share by the individual or by the trust, if

(i) the taxation year for which a claim is made under subsection (2) in respect of the original acquisition is 2016, and

(ii) the share is a share of a corporation that is a prescribed labour-sponsored venture capital corporation solely because it is a registered labour-sponsored venture capital corporation,

(a.2) nil, if

(i) the taxation year for which a claim is made under subsection (2) in respect of the original acquisition is after 2016, and

(ii) the share is a share of a corporation that is a prescribed labour-sponsored venture capital corporation solely because it is a registered labour-sponsored venture capital corporation,

(b) nil, where the share was issued by a registered labour-sponsored venture capital corporation unless the information return described in paragraph 204.81(6)(c) is filed with the individual's return of income for the taxation year for which a claim is made under subsection (2) in respect of the original acquisition of the share (other than a return of income filed under subsection 70(2), paragraph 104(23)(d) or 128(2)(e) or subsection 150(4)),

(c) nil, where the individual dies after December 5, 1996 and before the original acquisition of the share,

(d) nil, where a payment in respect of the disposition of the share has been made under section 211.9, and

(e) nil, if the share is issued in exchange for another share of the corporation.

Related Provisions: 211.7(1)"labour-sponsored funds tax credit" — Determination of credit for purposes of Part XII.5 where share redeemed early.

Notes: 127.4(6)(a) provides a 15% federal credit for investment in provincially-registered LSVCCs; (a.1) and (a.2) provide 5% and zero, for 2016 and after 2016, for investment in federally-registered LSVCCs.

127.4(6) was repealed effective 2017 by 2013 budget bill #2, but that repeal was cancelled by 2016 budget bill #1, which reinstated the credit, though only for investment in provincial LSVCCs. See Notes to 127.4(5). Before the amendment, (a)-(a.2) read:

(a) 10% of the net cost to the individual (or to a qualifying trust for the individual in respect of the share) for the original acquisition of the share by the individual or by the trust, if the taxation year for which a claim is made under subsection (2) in respect of the original acquisition is 2015,

(a.1) 5% of the net cost to the individual (or to a qualifying trust for the individual in respect of the share) for the original acquisition of the share by the individual or by the trust, if the taxation year for which a claim is made under subsection (2) in respect of the original acquisition is 2016,

127.4(6)(a) changed from 15% to 10% for 2015 acquisitions, and (a.1) added with 5% rate for 2016 acquisitions, by 2013 budget bill #2.

127.4(6)(e) added by 2002-2013 technical bill (Part 5 — technical), for 2004 and later taxation years.

127.4(6) earlier amended by 1998 Budget; added by 1996 Budget.

Forms: T1 General return, Sched. 1, Lines 413, 414.

Definitions [s. 127.4]: "amount" — 248(1); "annuitant" — 146(1); "approved share" — 127.4(1); "business", "common-law partner" — 248(1); "corporation" — 248(1), *Interpretation Act* 35(1); "discontinued" — 204.8(2); "individual" — 248(1); "labour-sponsored funds tax credit" — 127.4(1), (6); "labour-sponsored funds tax credit limit" — 127.4(5); "Minister" — 248(1); "net cost" — 127.4(1); "original acquisition", "person", "prescribed" — 248(1); "prescribed labour-sponsored venture capital corporation" — Reg. 6701; "province" — *Interpretation Act* 35(1); "qualifying trust" — 127.4(1); "registered labour-sponsored venture capital corporation" — 248(1); "registered retirement savings plan" — 146(1), 248(1); "regulation", "share" — 248(1); "spousal or common-law partner plan" — 146(1); "TFSA" — 146.2(5), 248(1); "tax otherwise payable" — 127.4(1); "tax payable" — 248(2); "taxation year" — 249; "trust" — 104(1), 248(1), (3).

Forms [s. 127.4]: T5006: Statement of registered LSVCC class A shares.

127.41 (1) Part XII.4 tax credit [qualifying environmental trust beneficiary] — In this section, the Part XII.4 tax credit of a taxpayer for a particular taxation year means the total of

(a) all amounts each of which is an amount determined by the formula

$$A \times \frac{B}{C}$$

where

A is the tax payable under Part XII.4 by a qualifying environmental trust for a taxation year (in this paragraph referred to as the "trust's year") that ends in the particular year,

B is the amount, if any, by which the total of all amounts in respect of the trust that were included (otherwise than because of being a member of a partnership) because of the application of subsection 107.3(1) in computing the taxpayer's income for the particular year exceeds the total of all amounts in respect of the trust that were deducted (otherwise than because of being a member of a partnership) because of the application of subsection 107.3(1) in computing that income, and

C is the trust's income for the trust's year, computed without reference to subsections 104(4) to (31) and sections 105 to 107, and

(b) in respect of each partnership of which the taxpayer was a member, the total of all amounts each of which is the amount that can reasonably be considered to be the taxpayer's share of the relevant credit in respect of the partnership and, for this purpose, the relevant credit in respect of a partnership is the amount that would, if a partnership were a person and its fiscal period were its taxation year, be the Part XII.4 tax credit of the partnership for its taxation year that ends in the particular year.

Related Provisions: 87(2)(j.93) — Amalgamation — continuing corporation; 126(7)"tax for the year otherwise payable under this Part" — Credit under 127.41 ignored for foreign tax credit purposes.

Notes: Description of A amended by 1997 Budget, for tax years that end after Feb. 18, 1997, to change "mining reclamation trust" to "qualifying environmental trust". (The same change was made throughout the Act.)

Description of B amended by 1995-97 technical bill, retroactive to its introduction (see Notes at end of 127.41).

(2) Reduction of Part I tax — There may be deducted from a taxpayer's tax otherwise payable under this Part for a taxation year such amount as the taxpayer claims not exceeding the taxpayer's Part XII.4 tax credit for the year.

Notes: See Notes at end of 127.41.

(3) Deemed payment of Part I tax — There is deemed to have been paid on account of the tax payable under this Part by a taxpayer (other than a taxpayer exempt from such tax) for a taxation year on the taxpayer's balance-due day for the year, such amount as the taxpayer claims not exceeding the amount, if any, by which

(a) the taxpayer's Part XII.4 tax credit for the year

exceeds

(b) the amount deducted under subsection (2) in computing the taxpayer's tax payable under this Part for the year.

Related Provisions: 152(1)(b) — Assessment of amount deemed paid; 152(4.2)(b) — Redetermination of credit at taxpayer's request; 157(3)(e), 157(3.1)(c) — Reduction in instalments to reflect credit; 163(2)(e) — Penalty for false statement or omission.

Notes: Since an amount elected under 127.41(3) is deemed paid on account of tax, the amount, like an instalment or an amount withheld at source, will create a refund under 164(1) even if the taxpayer pays no tax for the year, but will not reduce provincial tax. The credit is thus a "refundable credit".

127.41(3) amended by 1996 Budget, effective for 1996 and later taxation years, to use the expression "the taxpayer's balance-due day for the year" (see 248(1)"balance-due day"). The change is non-substantive.

Notes [s. 127.41]: 127.41 added by 1994 Budget, effective for taxation years that end after February 22, 1994. It provides a refundable tax credit to beneficiaries of a qualifying environmental trust (formerly a mining reclamation trust), since income subject to the special tax at the trust level under 211.6 is also included in computing a beneficiary's income under 107.3(1). The refundable credit avoids the double taxation of the same income in the hands of a QET and its beneficiaries. It is not taxable under 12(1)(x) as government assistance: VIEWS doc 2010-0364761E5.

Definitions [s. 127.41]: "amount", "balance-due day" — 248(1); "fiscal period" — 249(2)(b), 249.1; "Part XII.4 tax credit" — 127.41(1); "partnership" — see 96(1) Notes; "qualifying environmental trust" — 211.6(1), 248(1); "taxation year" — 11(2), 249; "taxpayer" — 248(1); "trust's year" — 107.3(1).

DIVISION E.1 — MINIMUM TAX

127.5 Obligation to pay minimum tax — Notwithstanding any other provision of this Act but subject to subsection 120.4(3) and section 127.55, where the amount that, but for section 120, would be determined under Division E to be an individual's tax payable for a taxation year is less than the amount determined under paragraph (a) in respect of the individual for the year, the individual's tax payable under this Part for the year is the total of

(a) the amount, if any, by which

(i) the individual's minimum amount for the year determined under section 127.51

exceeds

(ii) the individual's special foreign tax credit determined under section 127.54 for the year, and

(b) the amount, if any, required by section 120 to be added to the individual's tax otherwise payable under this Part for the year.

Related Provisions: 117(1) — "Tax payable" to be calculated without reference to minimum tax; 120.2 — Minimum tax carryover; 127.54(2) — Foreign tax credit; 127.55 — Where minimum tax not applicable.

Notes: Alternative Minimum Tax (AMT) is calculated under 127.5–127.55. The taxpayer must pay the higher of AMT and regular federal tax. Any excess (i.e., AMT minus regular basic federal tax) is available for carryforward under 120.2(1) for 7 years, and can be claimed to the extent regular federal tax exceeds AMT in those years, to reduce regular federal tax. The provinces have a parallel provincial AMT.

Calculate AMT as follows: Start with taxable income. Add back various preferences such as tax shelter deductions (127.52) to reach "adjusted taxable income". For an individual or a graduated rate estate, deduct $40,000 (127.51:C). Apply tax at 15% (127.51:A, 248(1)"appropriate percentage"). Deduct certain credits (127.531).

The AMT can catch taxpayers who claim the capital gains exemption, because 30% of the capital gain is considered a preference for AMT purposes. See 127.52(1)(d)(i). However, no AMT applied to the non-taxable portion of pre-2017 eligible capital property: VIEWS doc 2005-0111281I7.

127.5 amended by 1999 Budget, this version effective for 2000 and later taxation years.

Opening words of 127.5 amended by 1995-97 technical bill, effective 1992, to remove exclusions for related segregated fund trusts and mutual fund trusts from being subject to the section. These are now exempted in 127.55(f) instead.

Definitions [s. 127.5]: "amount", "individual" — 248(1); "minimum amount" — 127.51; "mutual fund trust" — 132(6)–(7), 132.2(3)(n), 248(1); "taxation year" — 249.

---

[2] Not indexed for inflation — ed.

Income Tax Folios: S5-F2-C1: Foreign tax credit [replaces IT-270R3, IT-395R2, IT-520].

Forms: T3 Sched. 12: Minimum tax; T3 Sched. 12A Chart 2: Ontario minimum tax carryover; T691: Alternative minimum tax; T1033-WS: Worksheet for calculating instalment payments; T1219: Provincial alternative minimum tax; T1219-ON: Ontario minimum tax carryover.

127.51 Minimum amount determined — An individual's minimum amount for a taxation year is the amount determined by the formula

$$A (B - C) - D$$

where

A is the appropriate percentage for the year;

B is the individual's adjusted taxable income for the year determined under section 127.52;

C is

(a) $40,000[2], in the case of an individual (other than a trust) or a graduated rate estate; and

(b) nil, in any other case; and

D is the individual's basic minimum tax credit for the year determined under section 127.531.

Related Provisions: 127(5) — Investment tax credit; 257 — Formula cannot calculate to less than zero.

Notes: See Notes to 127.5. C changed from "C is the individual's basic exemption for the year determined under section 127.53" by 2014 budget bill #2, for 2016 and later taxation years. The $40,000 figure was formerly in 127.53; the only substantive change is that the $40,000 is no longer available for testamentary trusts, only GREs.

Definitions [s. 127.51]: "appropriate percentage", "graduated rate estate", "individual" — 248(1); "taxable income" — 2(2), 248(1); "taxation year" — 249.

Income Tax Folios: S2-F1-C1: Health and welfare trusts [replaces IT-85R2].

Forms: T3 Sched. 12: Minimum tax; T3 Sched. 12A Chart 2: Ontario minimum tax carryover; T691: Alternative minimum tax; T1033-WS: Worksheet for calculating instalment payments; T1219: Provincial alternative minimum tax; T1219-ON: Ontario minimum tax carryover.

127.52 (1) Adjusted taxable income determined — Subject to subsection (2), an individual's adjusted taxable income for a taxation year is the amount that would be the individual's taxable income for the year or the individual's taxable income earned in Canada for the year, as the case may be, if it were computed on the assumption that

(a) [Repealed]

(b) the total of all amounts each of which is an amount deductible under paragraph 20(1)(a) or any of paragraphs 20(1)(c) to (f) in computing the individual's income for the year in respect of a rental or leasing property (other than an amount included in the individual's share of a loss referred to in paragraph (c.1)) were the lesser of the total of all amounts otherwise so deductible and the amount, if any, by which the total of

(i) the total of all amounts each of which is the individual's income for the year from the renting or leasing of a rental or leasing property owned by the individual or by a partnership, computed without reference to paragraphs 20(1)(a) and (c) to (f), and

(ii) the amount, if any, by which

(A) the total of all amounts each of which is the individual's taxable capital gain for the year from the disposition of a rental or leasing property owned by the individual or by a partnership

exceeds

(B) the total of all amounts each of which is the individual's allowable capital loss for the year from the disposition of a rental or leasing property owned by the individual or by a partnership exceeds the total of all amounts each of which is the individual's loss for the year from the renting or leasing of a rental or leasing property owned by the individual or by a partnership (other than an amount included in the individual's share of a loss referred to in paragraph (c.1)), computed without reference to paragraphs 20(1)(a) and (c) to (f);

(c) the total of all amounts each of which is an amount deductible under paragraph 20(1)(a) or any of paragraphs 20(1)(c) to (f) in computing the individual's income for the year in respect of a film property referred to in paragraph (w) of Class 10 of Schedule II to the *Income Tax Regulations* (other than an amount included in the individual's share of a loss referred to in paragraph (c.1)) were the lesser of the total of all amounts otherwise so deductible by the individual for the year and the amount, if any, by which the total of

(i) the total of all amounts each of which is the individual's income for the year from the renting or leasing of a film property owned by the individual or by a partnership, computed without reference to paragraphs 20(1)(a) and (c) to (f), and

(ii) the amount, if any, by which

(A) the total of all amounts each of which is the individual's taxable capital gain for the year from the disposition of such a film property owned by the individual or by a partnership

exceeds

(B) the total of all amounts each of which is the individual's allowable capital loss for the year from the disposition of such a film property owned by the individual or by a partnership

exceeds the total of all amounts each of which is the individual's loss for the year from such a film property owned by the individual or by a partnership (other than amounts included in the individual's share of a loss referred to in paragraph (c.1)), computed without reference to paragraphs 20(1)(a) and (c) to (f);

(c.1) if, during a partnership's fiscal period that ends in the year (other than a fiscal period that ends because of subsection 99(1)), the individual's interest in the partnership is an interest for which an identification number is required to be, or has been, obtained under section 237.1,

(i) the individual's share of allowable capital losses of the partnership for the fiscal period were the lesser of

(A) the total of all amounts each of which is the individual's

(I) share of a taxable capital gain for the fiscal period from the disposition of property (other than property acquired by the partnership in a transaction to which subsection 97(2) applied), or

(II) taxable capital gain for the year from the disposition of the individual's interest in the partnership if the individual, or a person who does not deal at arm's length with the individual, does not have an interest in the partnership (otherwise than because of the application of paragraph 98(1)(a) or 98.1(1)(a)) throughout the following taxation year, and

(B) the individual's share of allowable capital losses of the partnership for the fiscal period,

(ii) the individual's share of each loss from a business of the partnership for the fiscal period were the lesser of

(A) the individual's share of the loss, and

(B) the amount, if any, by which

(I) the total of all amounts each of which is the individual's

1. share of a taxable capital gain for the fiscal period from the disposition of property used by the partnership in the business (other than property ac-

quired by the partnership in a transaction to which subsection 97(2) applied), or

2. taxable capital gain for the year from the disposition of the individual's interest in the partnership if the individual, or a person who does not deal at arm's length with the individual, does not have an interest in the partnership (otherwise than because of the application of paragraph 98(1)(a) or 98.1(1)(a)) throughout the following taxation year

exceeds

(II) the total of all amounts each of which is the individual's share of an allowable capital loss for the fiscal period, and

(iii) the individual's share of losses from property of the partnership for the fiscal period were the lesser of

(A) the total of

(I) the individual's share of incomes for the fiscal period from properties of the partnership, and

(II) the amount, if any, by which the total of all amounts each of which is the individual's

1. share of a taxable capital gain for the fiscal period from the disposition of property held by the partnership for the purpose of earning income from property (other than property acquired by the partnership in a transaction to which subsection 97(2) applied), or

2. taxable capital gain for the year from the disposition of the individual's interest in the partnership if the individual, or a person who does not deal at arm's length with the individual, does not have an interest in the partnership (otherwise than because of the application of paragraph 98(1)(a) or 98.1(1)(a)) throughout the following taxation year,

exceeds the total of all amounts each of which is the individual's share of an allowable capital loss for the fiscal period, and

(B) the individual's share of losses from property of the partnership for the fiscal period;

(c.2) where, during a fiscal period of a partnership that ends in the year (other than a fiscal period that ends because of the application of subsection 99(1)),

(i) the individual is a limited partner of the partnership, or is a member of the partnership who was a specified member of the partnership at all times since becoming a member of the partnership, or

(ii) the partnership owns a rental or leasing property or a film property and the individual is a member of the partnership,

the total of all amounts each of which is an amount deductible under any of paragraphs 20(1)(c) to (f) in computing the individual's income for the year in respect of the individual's acquisition of the partnership interest were the lesser of

(iii) the total of all amounts otherwise so deductible, and

(iv) the total of all amounts each of which is the individual's share of any income of the partnership for the fiscal period, determined in accordance with subsection 96(1);

(c.3) the total of all amounts each of which is an amount deductible in computing the individual's income for the year in respect of a property for which an identification number is required to be, or has been, obtained under section 237.1 (other than an amount to which any of paragraphs (b) to (c.2) applies) were nil;

(d) except in respect of dispositions of property occurring before 1986 or to which section 79 applies,

(i) the references to the fraction applicable to the individual for the year in each of paragraphs 38(a), (b) and (c) and section 41 were read as a reference to "4/5", other than in the case of a capital gain from a disposition that is the making of a gift of property to a qualified donee, and

(ii) each amount that is designated by a trust for a particular year of the trust in respect of the individual and deemed by subsection 104(21) to be a taxable capital gain for the year of the individual were equal to the amount obtained by the formula

$$4/5 \ (A \times 1/B)$$

where

A is the amount so deemed to be a taxable capital gain for the year of the individual, and

B is the fraction in paragraph 38(a) applicable to the trust for the particular year of the trust for which the designation is made;

(iii) [Repealed]

(e) the total of all amounts deductible under section 65, 66, 66.1, 66.2, 66.21 or 66.4 or under subsection 29(10) or (12) of the *Income Tax Application Rules* in computing the individual's income for the year were the lesser of the amounts otherwise so deductible by the individual for the year and the total of

(i) the individual's income for the year from royalties in respect of, and such part of the individual's income, other than royalties, for the year as may reasonably be considered as attributable to, the production of petroleum, natural gas and minerals, determined before deducting those amounts,

(i.1) the individual's income for the year from property, or from the business of selling the product of property, described in Class 43.1 or 43.2 in Schedule II to the *Income Tax Regulations*, determined before deducting those amounts, and

(ii) all amounts included in computing the individual's income for the year under section 59;

(e.1) the total of all amounts each of which is an amount deductible under any of paragraphs 20(1)(c) to (f) in computing the individual's income for the year in respect of a property that is a flow-through share (if the individual is the person to whom the share was issued under an agreement referred to in the definition "flow-through share" in subsection 66(15)), a Canadian resource property or a foreign resource property were the lesser of the total of the amounts otherwise so determined for the year and the amount, if any, by which

(i) the total of all amounts each of which is an amount described in subparagraph (e)(i) or (ii), determined without reference to paragraphs 20(1)(c) to (f),

exceeds

(ii) the total of all amounts each of which is an amount deductible under section 65, 66, 66.1, 66.2, 66.21 or 66.4 or under subsection 29(10) or (12) of the *Income Tax Application Rules* in computing the individual's income for the year;

(f) subsection 82(1) were read without reference to paragraph 82(1)(b);

(g) the total of all amounts deductible under section 104 in computing the income of a trust for the year were equal to the total of

(i) the total of all amounts otherwise deductible under that section, and

(ii) the total of all amounts each of which is ³/₅ of

(A) amounts designated by the trust under subsection 104(21) for the year, or

(B) that portion of a net taxable capital gain of the trust that may reasonably be considered to

(I) be part of an amount included, by virtue of subsection 104(13) or section 105, in computing the income for the year of a non-resident beneficiary of the trust, or

(II) have been paid in the year by a trust governed by an employee benefit plan to a beneficiary thereunder;

(h) the only amounts deductible under sections 110 to 110.7 in computing the individual's taxable income for the year or taxable income earned in Canada for the year, as the case may be, were

(i) the amounts deducted under any of subsections 110(2), 110.6(2) and (2.1) and 110.7(1),

(ii) the amount deducted under paragraph 110(1)(d), not exceeding the total of

(A) the amount deducted under paragraph 110(1)(d.01), and

(B) ²/₅ of the amount, if any, by which

(I) the amount deducted under paragraph 110(1)(d)

exceeds

(II) the amount determined under clause (A),

(iii) the amount deducted under paragraph 110(1)(d.01),

(iv) ²/₅ of the amounts deducted under any of paragraphs 110(1)(d.1) to (d.3),

(v) the amount that would be deductible under paragraph 110(1)(f) if paragraph (d) were applicable in computing the individual's income for the year; and

(vi) the amount deducted under paragraph 110(1)(g);

(h.1) [applicable to the 1994 and 1995 taxation years only]

(i) in computing the individual's taxable income for the year or the individual's taxable income earned in Canada for the year, as the case may be, the only amounts deductible under

(i) paragraphs 111(1)(a), (c), (d) and (e) were the lesser of

(A) the amount deducted under those paragraphs for the year, and

(B) the total of all amounts that would be deductible under those paragraphs for the year if

(I) paragraphs (b), (c) and (e) of this subsection, as they read in respect of taxation years that began after 1985 and before 1995, applied in computing the individual's non-capital loss, restricted farm loss, farm loss and limited partnership loss for any of those years,

(II) paragraphs (b) to (c.3), (e) and (e.1) of this subsection, as they read in respect of taxation years that began after 1994 and ended before 2012, applied in computing the individual's non-capital loss, restricted farm loss, farm loss and limited partnership loss for any of those years, and

(III) paragraphs (b) to (c.3), (e) and (e.1) of this subsection applied in computing the individual's non-capital loss, restricted farm loss, farm loss and limited partnership loss for any taxation year that ends after 2011, and

(ii) paragraph 111(1)(b) were the lesser of

(A) the total of all amounts each of which is an amount that can reasonably be considered to be the amount that the individual would have deducted under paragraph 111(1)(b) had paragraph (d) of this subsection been applicable in computing the amount deductible under paragraph 111(1)(b), and

(B) the total of all amounts that would be deductible under that paragraph for the year if

(I) paragraph (d) of this subsection applied in computing the individual's net capital loss for any taxation year that began before 1995,

(II) paragraphs (c.1) and (d) of this subsection, as they read in respect of taxation years that began after 1994 and ended before 2012, applied in computing the individual's net capital loss for any of those years, and

(III) paragraphs (c.1) and (d) of this subsection applied in computing the individual's net capital loss for any taxation year that ends after 2011; and

(j) the *Income Tax Application Rules* were read without reference to section 40 of that Act.

Related Provisions: 127.52(2) — Certain CCA claims by partnership deemed claimed by partner; 127.52(2.1) — Specified member of partnership — anti-avoidance rule; 127.52(3) — Rental or leasing property; 180.01(2)(f) — Application to 2010-14 election re deferred employee stock option benefits; 248(8) — Meaning of "consequence" of death.

Notes: See Notes to 127.5.

RRSP contributions (under 146(5), (5.1)) and retiring-allowance rollovers (60(j.1)) are no longer added back for AMT purposes, since the repeal of para. (a) in 1998.

Under para. (d), capital gains are 80% taxable for AMT purposes, meaning that an extra 30% is added to taxable income beyond the 50% included by 38(a). Where the capital gains exemption in 110.6 is claimed, the 50% is exempt (see 127.52(1)(h)(i)) but the extra 30% is still taxed for AMT purposes.

Canadian Renewable and Conservation Expenses (CRCE) are not deductible under para. (e) beyond the royalty income reasonably attributable to resource production. No distinction is made between an active participant in a CRCE project and a flow-through share or limited partnership investor: VIEWS doc 2002-0166845.

127.52(1)(e)(i.1) implements a Sept. 28, 2010 Finance comfort letter.

A health and welfare trust can deduct expenses exceeding gross trust income for 127.52(1), despite IT-85R2 para. 12 (now Income Tax Folio S2-F1-C1 ¶1.52): doc 2013-0484061I7.

Rental property interest expense for AMT purposes is limited by 127.52(1)(b) to the income from the property, and thus reduced by a loss, even if the interest was not the cause of the loss: *Gélinas*, 2013 TCC 250.

127.52(1) amended by 2014 budget bill #2 (for 2015 and later tax years), 2013 budget bill #2, 2002-2013 technical bill, 2006 budget bills #1 and #2; 2001, 2000, 1998 and 1997 Budgets; 1995-97, 1992 and 1991 technical bills, 1990 pension bill.

Income Tax Folios: S2-F1-C1: Health and welfare trusts [replaces IT-85R2].

Advance Tax Rulings: ATR-28: Redemption of capital stock of family farm corporation.

(2) Partnerships — For the purposes of subsection (1) and this subsection, any amount deductible under a provision of this Act in computing the income or loss of a partnership for a fiscal period is, to the extent of a member's share of the partnership's income or loss, deemed to be deductible by the member under that provision in computing the member's income for the taxation year in which the fiscal period ends.

Notes: 127.52(2) amended by 1995-97 technical bill, for tax years of an individual that begin after 1994. It had been a special rule applying to CCA claims by a member of a partnership that owned a residential building or certified Canadian film production. It now applies to any amount deductible in computing partnership income or loss.

(2.1) Specified member of a partnership — Where it can reasonably be considered that one of the main reasons that a member of a partnership was not a specified member of the partnership at all times since becoming a member of the partnership is to avoid the application of this section to the member's interest in the partnership, the member is deemed for the purpose of this section to have been a specified member of the partnership at all times since becoming a member of the partnership.

Related Provisions: 40(3.131) — Parallel rule for negative adjusted cost base of partnership interest.

Notes: For the meaning of "one of the main reasons" see Notes to 83(2.1).

127.52(2.1) added by 1995-97 technical bill, effective April 27, 1995.

(3) Definitions — For the purposes of this section,

"film property" means a property described in paragraph (n) of Class 12, or paragraph (w) of Class 10, of Schedule II to the *Income Tax Regulations*;

"limited partner" has the meaning that would be assigned by subsection 96(2.4) if that subsection were read without reference to "if the member's partnership interest is not an exempt interest (within the meaning assigned by subsection (2.5)) at that time and";

Notes: Definition "limited partner" added by 1995-97 technical bill, effective for taxation years of an individual that begin after 1994.

"rental or leasing property" means a property that is a rental property or a leasing property for the purpose of section 1100 of the *Income Tax Regulations*.

Related Provisions: 127.52(1)(b), (c.2)(ii) — Application of minimum tax.

Notes: Definition "rental or leasing property" added by 1995-97 technical bill, effective for taxation years of an individual that begin after 1994.

Regulations: 1100(14)–(14.2) (definition of rental property); 1100(17)–(20) (definition of leasing property).

"residential property" — [Repealed]

Notes: Definition "residential property" repealed by 1995-97 technical bill, effective for taxation years of an individual that begin after 1994.

Definitions [s. 127.52]: "allowable capital loss" — 38(a), 248(1); "amount" — 248(1); "arm's length" — 251(1); "business" — 248(1); "Canada" — 255; "capital gain" — 54, 248(1); "deferred profit sharing plan" — 147(1), 248(1); "disposition", "employment" — 248(1); "farm loss" — 111(8), 248(1); "film property" — 127.52(3); "fiscal period" — 248(1), 249(2)(b), 249.1; "flow-through share" — 66(15), 248(1); "foreign retirement arrangement" — 248(1); "identical" — 40(3.5), 248(12); "individual" — 248(1); "limited partner" — 127.52(3); "limited partnership loss" — 96(2.1)(e), 248(1); "mineral" — 248(1); "non-capital loss" — 111(8), 248(1); "non-resident" — 248(1); "partnership" — see 96(1) Notes; "person", "property", "regulation" — 248(1); "qualified donee" — 149.1(1), 248(1); "rental or leasing property" — 127.52(3); "rental property" — Reg. 1100(14); "restricted farm loss" — 31, 248(1); "specified member" — 127.52(2.1), 248(1); "taxable capital gain" — 38(a), 248(1); "taxable income" — 2(2), 248(1); "taxable income earned in Canada" — 115(1), 248(1); "taxation year" — 249; "trust" — 104(1), 248(1), (3).

Forms [s. 127.52]: T3 Sched. 12: Minimum tax; T3 Sched. 12A Chart 2: Ontario minimum tax carryover; T691: Alternative minimum tax; T1033-WS: Worksheet for calculating instalment payments; T1219: Provincial alternative minimum tax; T1219-ON: Ontario minimum tax carryover.

127.53 [Repealed]

Notes: 127.53 repealed by 2014 budget bill #2, for 2016 and later tax years. The $40,000 exemption is now in 127.51:C(a). Since the exemption no longer applies to trusts other than a GRE (and a deceased can have only one: 248(1)"graduated rate estate"(e)), the rules in 127.53(2)-(3) are no longer needed.

On a short taxation year, the basic exemption had to be shared among the trusts: VIEWS doc 2005-0164621E5.

Forms [s. 127.53]: T3 Sched. 12: Minimum tax; T3 Sched. 12A Chart 2: Ontario minimum tax carryover; T691: Alternative minimum tax; T1219: Provincial alternative minimum tax; T1219-ON: Ontario minimum tax carryover.

127.531 Basic minimum tax credit determined — An individual's basic minimum tax credit for a taxation year is the total of all amounts each of which is

(a) an amount deducted under any of subsections 118(1), (2) and (10), sections 118.01 to 118.07, subsection 118.3(1), sections 118.5 to 118.7 and 119 and subsection 127(1) in computing the individual's tax payable for the year under this Part; or

(b) the amount that was claimed under section 118.1 or 118.2 in computing the individual's tax payable for the year under this Part, determined without reference to this Division, to the extent that the amount claimed does not exceed the maximum amount deductible under that section in computing the individual's tax payable for the year under this Part, determined without reference to this Division.

Notes: 127.531 amended by 2014 budget bill #1, effective for 2014 and later taxation years, to change "118.01 to 118.06" to "118.01 to 118.07".

127.531(a) amended by 2011 budget bill #2, this version effective for 2011 and later taxation years. For 2009 and 2010, read "118 to 118.06" as "118 to 118.05".

The 2011 budget bill #2 amendments supersede (and copy) those made by 2009 and 2006 budget bills #2 and 2006 budget bill #1. The added reference to 118.1 and 118.2 overrules *David M. Sherman*, 1999 CarswellNat 2296 (TCC), where the Court ruled that charitable donations and medical expenses that were available to the author for credit under 118.1 and 118.2, but were not claimed for regular tax purposes, could be claimed for AMT purposes. Now the same claims must be made for both. The reason for the special wording of para. (b) is because charitable and medical claims may have been carried forward from past years. CRA's Form T691 remained unchanged since the *Sherman* decision, and has continued throughout to refer to the amounts claimed on the T1 return as the basis for calculating the basic minimum tax credit.

The references to 119 and 127(1) were proposed in the Nov. 5, 2010 draft technical bill. The reference to 119 was originally proposed in Finance comfort letters dated Sept. 9, 2004 and Dec. 7, 2004 (the latter stated that it would apply to dispositions after Dec. 23, 1998 for individuals who ceased to be resident in Canada after Oct. 1, 1996).

Definitions [s. 127.531]: "amount", "individual" — 248(1); "tax payable" — 248(2); "taxation year" — 249.

127.54 (1) Definitions — In this section,

"foreign income" of an individual for a taxation year means the total of

(a) the individual's incomes for the year from businesses carried on by the individual in countries other than Canada, and

(b) the individual's incomes for the year from sources in countries other than Canada in respect of which the individual has paid non-business-income taxes, within the meaning assigned by subsection 126(7), to governments of countries other than Canada;

"foreign taxes" of an individual for a taxation year means the total of the business-income taxes, within the meaning assigned by subsection 126(7), paid by the individual for the year in respect of businesses carried on by the individual in countries other than Canada and ⅔ of the non-business-income taxes, within the meaning assigned by that subsection, paid by the individual for the year to the governments of countries other than Canada.

(2) Foreign tax credit — For the purposes of section 127.5, an individual's special foreign tax credit for a taxation year is the greater of

(a) the total of all amounts deductible under section 126 from the individual's tax for the year, and

(b) the lesser of

(i) the individual's foreign taxes for the year, and

(ii) the amount determined by the formula

$$A \times B$$

where

A   is the appropriate percentage for the taxation year, and

B   is the individual's foreign income for the year.

Notes: 127.54(2)(b)(ii) amended by 2006 budget bill #1, effective for 2005 and later taxation years, to use a calculation of the lowest tax bracket rate (see 248(1)"appropriate percentage" and 127.51:A).

Definitions [s. 127.54]: "amount", "appropriate percentage", "business" — 248(1); "Canada" — 255; "foreign income", "foreign taxes" — 127.54(1); "individual" — 248(1); "taxation year" — 249.

Income Tax Folios [s. 127.54]: S5-F2-C1: Foreign tax credit [replaces IT-270R3, IT-395R2, IT-520].

127.55 Application of section 127.5 — Section 127.5 does not apply in respect of

(a) a return of income of an individual filed under subsection 70(2), paragraph 104(23)(d) or 128(2)(e) or subsection 150(4);

(b) [Repealed]

(c) an individual for the taxation year in which the individual dies;

(d) an individual for the 1986 taxation year if the individual dies in 1987;

(e) a trust described in paragraph 104(4)(a) or (a.1) for its taxation year that includes the day determined in respect of the trust under that paragraph; and

(f) a taxation year of a trust throughout which the trust is

(i) a related segregated fund trust (within the meaning assigned by paragraph 138.1(1)(a)),

(ii) a mutual fund trust,

(iii) a trust prescribed to be a master trust, or

(iv) an employee life and health trust.

Notes: 127.55(f)(iv) added by 2010 budget bill #2, effective 2010. 127.55 earlier amended by 2001 technical bill, 1995-97 and 1991 technical bills.

Definitions [s. 127.55]: "employee life and health trust" — 144.1(2), 248(1); "individual" — 248(1); "mutual fund trust" — 132(6); "prescribed" — 248(1); "related seg-

regated fund trust" — 138.1(1)(a); "taxation year" — 249; "trust" — 104(1), 248(1), (3).

Regulations: 4802(1.1) (prescribed master trust for 127.55(f)(iii)).

Interpretation Bulletins [s. 127.55]: IT-326R3: Returns of deceased persons as "another person".

DIVISION F — SPECIAL RULES APPLICABLE IN CERTAIN CIRCUMSTANCES

Bankruptcies

128. (1) Where corporation bankrupt — Where a corporation has become a bankrupt, the following rules are applicable:

(a) the trustee in bankruptcy shall be deemed to be the agent of the bankrupt for all purposes of this Act;

(b) the estate of the bankrupt shall be deemed not to be a trust or an estate for the purposes of this Act;

(c) the income and the taxable income of the corporation for any taxation year of the corporation during which it was a bankrupt and for any subsequent year shall be calculated as if

(i) the property of the bankrupt did not pass to and vest in the trustee in bankruptcy on the bankruptcy order being made or the assignment filed but remained vested in the bankrupt, and

(ii) any dealing in the estate of the bankrupt or any act performed in the carrying on of the business of the bankrupt estate by the trustee was done as agent on behalf of the bankrupt and any income of the trustee from such dealing or carrying on is income of the bankrupt and not of the trustee;

(d) a taxation year of the corporation shall be deemed to have commenced on the day the corporation became a bankrupt and a taxation year of the corporation that would otherwise have ended after the corporation became a bankrupt shall be deemed to have ended on the day immediately before the day on which the corporation became a bankrupt;

(e) if, in the case of any taxation year of the corporation ending during the period the corporation is a bankrupt, the corporation fails to pay any tax payable by it under this Act for any such year, the corporation and the trustee in bankruptcy are jointly and severally, or solidarily, liable to pay the tax, except that

(i) the trustee is only liable to the extent of the property of the bankrupt in the trustee's possession, and

(ii) payment by either of them discharges the liability to the extent of the amount paid;

(f) in the case of any taxation year of the corporation ending during the period the corporation is a bankrupt, the corporation shall be deemed not to be associated with any other corporation in the year; and

(g) where an absolute order of discharge is granted in respect of the corporation, for the purposes of section 111 any loss of the corporation for any taxation year preceding the year in which the order of discharge was granted is not deductible by the corporation in computing its taxable income for the taxation year of the corporation in which the order was granted or any subsequent year.

Related Provisions: 34.2(7) — No inclusion of partnership stub-period income in year corporation becomes bankrupt; 39(1)(c)(iv)(B) — Business investment loss on debt of bankrupt corporation; 50(1) — Capital loss on debts and shares of bankrupt corporation; 56.3 — No debt forgiveness reserve inclusion while corporation bankrupt; 80(1)"forgiven amount"B(i) — Debt forgiveness rules do not apply; 129(1.1) — No dividend refund on dividend paid to bankrupt controlling corporation; 227(5) — Amount in trust not part of estate.

Notes: See Notes to 128(2).

128(1) amended by 2002-2013 technical bill (effective June 26, 2013), 2004 *Civil Code* harmonization bill.

Regulations: 206(2) (information return).

Interpretation Bulletins: IT-179R: Change of fiscal period (to be revised re bankrupt corporations — see I.T. Technical News No. 8); IT-206R: Separate businesses.

Information Circulars: 12-1: GST/HST compliance refund holds.

I.T. Technical News: 8 (bankrupt corporation — change of fiscal period).

CRA Audit Manual: 8.4.10: Analyzing risk and the potential for collection of assessment/reassessment [whether to audit a bankrupt company]; 29.5.8: Loss carryovers — loss carryover bankruptcy.

Forms: RC342: Request by an insolvency practitioner for a waiver of the requirement to file a T2 corporation income tax return.

(2) Where individual bankrupt — Where an individual has become a bankrupt, the following rules are applicable:

(a) the trustee in bankruptcy shall be deemed to be the agent of the bankrupt for all purposes of this Act;

(b) the estate of the bankrupt shall be deemed not to be a trust or an estate for the purposes of this Act;

(c) the income and the taxable income of the individual for any taxation year during which the individual was a bankrupt and for any subsequent year shall be calculated as if

(i) the property of the bankrupt did not pass to and vest in the trustee in bankruptcy on the bankruptcy order being made or the assignment filed but remained vested in the bankrupt, and

(ii) any dealing in the estate of the bankrupt or any act performed in the carrying on of the business of the bankrupt estate by the trustee was done as agent on behalf of the bankrupt and any income of the trustee from such dealing or carrying on is income of the bankrupt and not of the trustee;

(d) except for the purposes of subsections 146(1), 146.01(4) and 146.02(4) and Part X.1,

(i) a taxation year of the individual is deemed to have begun at the beginning of the day on which the individual became a bankrupt, and

(ii) the individual's last taxation year that began before that day is deemed to have ended immediately before that day;

(d.1) where, by reason of paragraph (d), a taxation year of the individual is not a calendar year,

(i) paragraph 146(5)(b) shall, for the purpose of the application of subsection 146(5) to the taxation year, be read as follows:

"(b) the amount, if any, by which

(i) the amount, if any, by which the taxpayer's RRSP deduction limit for the particular calendar year in which the taxation year ends exceeds the total of all contributions made by an employer in the particular calendar year to a pooled registered pension plan in respect of the taxpayer

exceeds

(ii) the total of the amounts deducted under this subsection and subsection (5.1) in computing the taxpayer's income for any preceding taxation year that ends in the particular calendar year.",

and

(ii) paragraph 146(5.1)(b) shall, for the purpose of the application of subsection 146(5.1) to the taxation year, be read as follows:

"(b) the amount, if any, by which

(i) the amount, if any, by which the taxpayer's RRSP deduction limit for the particular calendar year in which the taxation year ends exceeds the total of all contributions made by an employer in the particular calendar year to a pooled registered pension plan in respect of the taxpayer

exceeds

(ii) the total of the amount deducted under subsection (5) in computing the taxpayer's income for the year and the amounts deducted under this subsection and subsection (5) in computing the taxpayer's income for any preceding taxation year that ends in the particular calendar year.";

(d.2) where, by reason of paragraph (d), the individual has two taxation years ending in a calendar year, each amount deducted in computing the individual's income for either of the taxation years shall be deemed, for the purposes of the definition "unused RRSP deduction room" in subsection 146(1) and Part X.1, to have been deducted in computing the individual's income for the calendar year;

(e) where the individual was a bankrupt at any time in a calendar year the trustee shall, within 90 days from the end of the year, file a return with the Minister, in prescribed form, on behalf of the individual of the individual's income for any taxation year occurring in the calendar year computed as if

(i) the only income of the individual for that taxation year was the income for the year, if any, arising from dealings in the estate of the bankrupt or acts performed in the carrying on of the business of the bankrupt by the trustee,

(ii) in computing the individual's taxable income for that taxation year, no deduction were permitted by Division C, other than

(A) an amount under any of paragraphs 110(1)(d) to (d.3) and section 110.6 to the extent that the amount is in respect of an amount included in income under subparagraph (i) for that taxation year, and

(B) an amount under section 111 to the extent that the amount was in respect of a loss of the individual for any taxation year that ended before the individual was discharged absolutely from bankruptcy, and

(iii) in computing the individual's tax payable under this Part for that taxation year, no deduction were allowed

(A) under any of sections 118 to 118.07, 118.2, 118.3, 118.5, 118.8 and 118.9,

(B) under section 118.1 with respect to a gift made by the individual on or after the day the individual became bankrupt,

(B.1) under section 118.62 with respect to interest paid on or after the day on which the individual became bankrupt, and

(C) under subsection 127(5) with respect to an expenditure incurred or property acquired by the individual in any taxation year that ends after the individual was discharged absolutely from bankruptcy,

and the trustee is liable to pay any tax so determined for that taxation year;

(f) notwithstanding paragraph (e), the individual shall file a separate return of the individual's income for any taxation year during which the individual was a bankrupt, computed as if

(i) the income required to be reported in respect of the year by the trustee under paragraph (e) was not the income of the individual,

(ii) in computing income, the individual was not entitled to deduct any loss sustained by the trustee in the year in dealing with the estate of the bankrupt or in carrying on the business of the bankrupt,

(iii) in computing the individual's taxable income for the year, no amount were deductible under any of paragraphs 110(1)(d) to (d.3) and section 110.6 in respect of an amount included in income under subparagraph (e)(i), and no amount were deductible under section 111, and

(iv) in computing the individual's tax payable under this Part for the year, no amount were deductible under

(A) section 118.1 in respect of a gift made before the day on which the individual became bankrupt,

(B) section 118.62 in respect of interest paid before the day on which the individual became bankrupt, or

(C) section 118.61 or 120.2 or subsection 127(5),

and the individual is liable to pay any tax so determined for that taxation year;

(g) notwithstanding subparagraphs (e)(ii) and (iii) and (f)(iii) and (iv), where at any time an individual was discharged absolutely from bankruptcy,

(i) in computing the individual's taxable income for any taxation year that ends after that time, no amount shall be deducted under section 111 in respect of losses for taxation years that ended before that time,

(ii) in computing the individual's tax payable under this Part for any taxation year that ends after that time,

(A) no amount shall be deducted under section 118.61 or 120.2 in respect of an amount for any taxation year that ended before that time,

(B) no amount shall be deducted under section 118.1 in respect of a gift made before the individual became bankrupt,

(B.1) no amount shall be deducted under section 118.62 in respect of interest paid before the day on which the individual became bankrupt, and

(C) no amount shall be deducted under subsection 127(5) in respect of an expenditure incurred or a property acquired by the individual in any taxation year that ended before that time, and

(iii) the individual's unused tuition, textbook and education tax credits (as determined under subsection 118.61(1)) at the end of the last taxation year that ended before that time is deemed to be nil;

(h) where, in a taxation year commencing after an order of discharge has been granted in respect of the individual, the trustee deals in the estate of the individual who was a bankrupt or performs any act in the carrying on of the business of the individual, paragraphs (e), (f) and (g) shall apply as if the individual were a bankrupt in the year; and

(i) the portion of the individual's non-capital loss for a particular taxation year in which paragraph (e) applied in respect of the individual and any preceding taxation year that does not exceed the lesser of

(i) the amount of the individual's allowable business investment losses for the particular taxation year, and

(ii) any portion of the individual's non-capital loss for that particular year that was not deducted in computing the individual's taxable income for any taxation year in which paragraph (e) applied in respect of the individual or any preceding taxation year,

shall, for the purpose of determining the individual's cumulative gains limit under section 110.6 for taxation years following the taxation year in which paragraph (e) was last applicable in respect of the individual, be deemed not to have been an allowable business investment loss.

Related Provisions: 34.1(8) — No inclusion of partnership stub-period income in year individual becomes bankrupt; 56.2, 56.3 — No debt forgiveness reserve inclusion while individual bankrupt; 80(1)"forgiven amount"B(i) — Debt forgiveness rules do not apply; 118.95 — Credits allowed on return filed by bankrupt individual; 120.2(4)(a) — No minimum tax carryover on individual's return under 128(2)(f); 122.5(7) — GST/HST Credit for year of bankruptcy; 122.61(3.1) — Canada Child Benefit for year of bankruptcy; 122.7(11) — Effect of bankruptcy on Canada Workers Benefit; 122.8(9) — Effect of bankruptcy on Climate Action Incentive payment; 122.9(4) — Teacher school-supplies credit for year of bankruptcy; 127.1(1)(a) — No refundable investment tax credit on individual's return under 128(2)(f); 127.55 — Minimum tax not applicable; 150(3) — Trustee in bankruptcy required to file return; 227(5) — Amount in trust not part of estate; Reg. 2701(2) — Calculation of group term life insurance benefit where individual bankrupt; *Interpretation Act* 27(5) — Meaning of "within 90 days".

Notes: Under the *Bankruptcy & Insolvency Act* (**BIA**), bankruptcy is retroactive to the date of the bankruptcy petition. A proposal in bankruptcy is a payment offer made by an insolvent person to creditors, to stop collection action and also avoid being petitioned into bankruptcy. A consumer proposal is similar, but is subject to a fast-track procedure. It may be made where total debts (other than a mortgage on the principal residence) do not exceed $250,000. On whether a proposal is valid when the person has

non-liquid assets exceeding liabilities, see *Kormos v. Fast*, 2018 ONSC 6044, para. 34. In *Marshall & Associates*, 2019 NBQB 318, an Oct. 2018 consumer proposal was not allowed to count tax liability only to Dec. 2017; the taxpayer had to file a provisional return or at least calculate it up to the proposal date. Not declaring all assets can constitute tax evasion, e.g. CRA news release "Robert Kalfayan fined nearly half a million dollars for tax evasion" (July 8, 2020).

Per BIA 60(1.1), a proposal must provide for payment of garnishment super-priority debts related to source withholdings (ITA 224(1.2) and related CPP/EI and provincial rules), unless CRA agrees otherwise. Due to COVID-19, CRA will defer such payments to Sept. 1, 2020 without the proposal being in default: tinyurl.com/cra-bia60 (April 23, 2020).

While the proposal is only a proposal, 128(2) does not apply: VIEWS doc 2010-035880I7. If the proposal is accepted, the debt settlement rules in s. 80 may apply: 2015-0568411E5. If it is rejected, the person is bankrupt (BIA s. 57), and the Federal Court has no jurisdiction to stay the bankruptcy: *Edell*, 2010 FCA 26. If the proposal is annulled under BIA s. 61(1), see 2009-035103117, IT-293R para. 16, and CRA Round Table, 2010 Cdn Tax Foundation conference report, q.1, p. 4:1-3.

A bankrupt person's assets are turned over to the trustee in bankruptcy to distribute to the creditors: *Nielsen*, 2018 BCSC 1161. However, there are various exemptions under both federal and provincial law, such as food and some home equity: see tinyurl.com/bankr-exemptions or tinyurl.com/exempt-bankr. For the GST/HST Credit, see Notes at end of 122.5. For exemptions for RRSPs and other registered plans, see Notes to 146(4). Secured creditors get first priority, then possibly CRA under "Crown prerogative" (see Notes to 159(3)), then all unsecured creditors. The trustee does not get a clearance certificate under 159(2) and is not liable under 159(3), and there is no mechanism for the CRA to advise that the trustee has no liability for the bankrupt's tax: VIEWS doc 2012-0455801E5. A home co-owned with a spouse was exempt from seizure by creditors but was subject to CRA deemed security under 223(11.1) which survived the bankruptcy: *Barr*, 2009 BCSC 1433.

If the assessment is under objection or appeal, the trustee may reject the tax debt as contingent and unquantifiable so that CRA cannot vote at a creditors' meeting or participate in asset distribution; if no appeal rights are left, the trustee must accept the debt assessed: *Port Chevrolet*, 2004 BCCA 37; *CCI Industries*, 2005 ABQB 675; *Baran*, 2013 ONSC 7501; *Schnier*, 2016 ONCA 5; *Sorochan*, 2021 NSSC 200, paras. 32-39.

Bankruptcy does not prevent a spouse or relative who received money or property from the bankrupt from being assessed for the bankrupt's tax debt. See Notes to 160(1).

Discharge: the bankrupt can apply for discharge and a fresh slate free of debt (with exceptions in BIA s. 178, such as criminal fines [and some regulatory penalties: *Hennig*, 2020 ABQB 48], child support and many student loans). CRA often opposes automatic discharge and requests some payment over time and a Court order to make current tax filings and payments. The application is heard by a Registrar or Master of the provincial superior court, who ranks below a judge. BIA s. 172.1 provides that a "tax debtor" ($200,000 or more of personal income tax debt [excluding assessments under appeal: *Schnier*, 2015 ONCA 5], which is 75% or more of their total unsecured debt) is not entitled to early or automatic discharge, and the court must consider the circumstances of the tax debt in setting discharge conditions; see *Zhao (BDO Canada)*, 2020 SKQB 187; *Sorochan*, 2021 NSSC 200. In a 172.1 case, a CRA assessment is not evidence that the taxpayer acted fraudulently or with gross negligence, absent a Tax Court determination: *Fretz*, 2011 NSSC 467 (but *contra* see *Sorochan*, paras. 35-37).

The Court may refuse discharge to those who abuse the system with multiple bankruptcies: *Kusch*, 2007 BCSC 618; *Berenbaum*, 2011 ONSC 72; *Crischuk*, 2013 BCSC 1413; *Tronchin*, 2013 ABQB 38; *Rotenberg*, 2017 ONSC 3585 (tax lawyer); *Montgomery*, 2018 SKQB 274; *Ongo*, 2018 NSSC 326; *Donaldson*, 2019 NSSC 33; *Yeo*, 2020 NSSC 135. It cannot revoke discharge for later non-compliance: *Briant*, 2016 BCSC 1575. It can lift the restriction on creditors enforcing collection during bankruptcy: *Crischuk* (above); *Drosdevech*, 2014 BCSC 1757 (if payments are missed); *Blain*, 2015 BCSC 1153 (same). Or it may suspend discharge for a long time, e.g. *Bice*, 2007 ABQB 708 (7 years); *Diewold*, 2018 SKQB 149 (7 years due to using donation shelter); *Binning*, 2017 SKQB 207 (4 years); or may require payment equal to many years of suspension (*Fuiten*, 2018 SKQB 299: 7 years' worth). Or it may refuse to consider discharge until the bankrupt provides current financial information: *Werkman*, 2016 ABQB 6. Discharge was allowed on a 4th bankruptcy in: *Burns*, 2019 NSSC 155; *Flight*, 2019 ONSC 5048; *Sorochan*, 2021 NSSC 200.

The Court may order a large payment before discharge, e.g. *Haibeck*, 2016 BCSC 2166 ($273,000 — 27% of the debt); *Malo*, 2015 QCCA 1948 ($245,000 — 58%: long-uncooperative 2nd-time bankrupt); *Tran*, 2016 YKSC 70 ($235,000 — 20%); *Hagerman*, 2014 SKQB 185 ($213,000 — value of equity in home, exempt from seizure, that H and wife bought in year before bankruptcy); *McRudden*, 2014 BCSC 217 ($200,000 — 25%: M lived opulent lifestyle while bankrupt); *Saran*, 2018 ONSC 6045 ($200,000: S was a Paradigm "detaxer" [see Notes to 248(1)"person"]); *Rivers*, 2014 BCSC 1800 ($200,000 — 9%: R ran company that stripped taxpayers' RRSPs); *Dinh*, 2017 YKSC 24 ($196,000 — 20%); *Van Eeuwen*, 2013 BCSC 1113 ($180,000 — 20%); *Perrier*, 2018 BCSC 463 ($150,000 — 16%); *Hover*, 2019 ONSC 6348 ($150,000 — 22%: H transferred assets to sister to avoid debt); *Gelpke*, 2012 BCSC 1770 ($150,000 — 19%: various factors including G's high standard of living with husband's assistance); *Robb*, 2015 ABQB 34 ($142,600 — 50%: 3rd-time bankrupt); *Macdonald*, 2015 NSSC 262 ($138,000 — 66%); *Foerster*, 2014 BCSC 1565 ($136,000 — 15%); *Drosdevech*, 2014 BCSC 1757 ($120,000 — 16%: tax protester); *Monaghan*, 2018 SKQB 210 ($100,000 — using donation shelter for 6 years after CRA warnings and reassessments); *Smith*, 2021 NSSC 205 (the greater of $100,000 [5%] or 15% of next 5 years' income); *English (Charlie)*, 2016 YKSC 38 ($93,000 and $90,000 — 50.1% and 52% of the tax debts).

However, Courts often discharge tax bankrupts for 10% or less of the pre-interest tax (despite harshly critical reasons for judgment), e.g. *Tjelta*, 2012 BCSC 984; *Hardtke*, 2012 ONSC 4662; *Kinnaird*, 2012 ONSC 4506; *Besner*, 2013 BCSC 347; *McKinney*, 2013 BCSC 1311; *Fraser*, 2013 SKQB 418; *Schira*, 2014 SKQB 4; *Newson*, 2014 SKQB 106; *Olson*, 2014 BCSC 2340; *Meikle*, 2015 BCSC 1768; *Kreger*, 2016 SKQB 247; *Reid*, 2020 ONSC 1726; *Sorochan*, 2021 NSSC 200. Sometimes the payment requirement applies after discharge rather than before, e.g. *Janzen*, 2014 BCSC 1095; *Berg*, 2014 BCSC 1005.

In *Ballantyne*, 2015 BCSC 1292, B had $69,000 debt but failed to report jointly owning $500,000 cash with his wife, later used to buy a home in her name. The Court inexplicably granted him discharge for $4,000 rather than voiding the bankruptcy.

Some bankrupts applying for discharge get the Court's sympathy, e.g. *Farr*, 2014 SKQB 214 ($0: tax debt of $575,000, but principal was only $109,000, F had paid $139,000, and he was now 70, unable to work, and living "frugally" in a trailer on a small pension); *Stanzel*, 2014 SKQB 187 ($0: $550,000 of debt from investment losses, lawsuits and a tax shelter that S thought was legitimate); *Armstrong*, 2016 SKQB 14 ($0 of $276,000 debt: A had made significant payments); *Paton*, 2017 SKQB 216 ($0 of $764,000 debt: P was co-operative, ill, 73 and living on OAS and CPP, and had paid a lot towards his tax debts which were from the 1980s); *Baran*, 2013 ONSC 7501 ($8,000 — 1%: CRA refused to explain $850,000 assessment and B testified she did not know why her expenses were disallowed); *Desai*, 2014 ONSC 136 ($7,900 — 2%: CRA Collections ruined D's insurance agency business by wrongfully seizing funds held in trust for insurer, and tax debt resulted from art flip shelter that was "thought by hundreds of Canadians to have been acceptable to CRA"); *Usher*, 2014 ONSC 925 ($16,159 — 1.3%: honest taxpayer invested in bad shelters); *Ebenal*, 2019 SKQB 67 ($0 of $1 million: couple were honest and did not know they had tax debt when they paid other debts; pension was embezzled; accountant was unresponsive); *Morrison*, 2019 MBQB 101 ($26,000 of $5 million: M was "not indifferent to his obligations", not living lavishly, and would never be able to pay CRA's requested $1.3m).

Conditional discharge orders usually require the bankrupt to file all unfiled income tax and GST/HST returns, but this requirement may be eliminated if it is not feasible for old years: *Hendsbee*, 2014 NSSC 148. A deceased person can possibly not be discharged: *Re Simoes*, 2011 BCSC 63 and *Coleman Estate*, 2011 MBQB 300. A discharge order can be varied after a year if there is "no reasonable probability" of the bankrupt being able to comply, but the Courts often reject such requests, e.g. *Besner*, 2015 BCSC 27; *Frey*, 2016 BCSC 525; *Kielb*, 2016 BCSC 1760.

For an overview of tax issues on bankruptcy see Tessis & Gaertner, *Canadian Guide to Troubled Businesses and Bankruptcies* (Carswell, looseleaf), Chapter 10; Stocco et al., "Insolvency 101", 2009 BC Tax Conference (ctf.ca), 8:1-35. For CRA procedures see *National Collections Manual* (2015, on *TaxPartner* or *Taxnet Pro*), under "Bankruptcy — Tax programs"; VIEWS doc 2010-0360191I7. A corporation can obtain protection to continue in business, without going into bankruptcy, under the *Companies' Creditors Arrangement Act* (CCAA); see 224(1.2) Notes. On bankruptcy generally see Houlden & Morawetz, *Bankruptcy and Insolvency Law of Canada* (Carswell, 4th ed., looseleaf); *Bennett on Bankruptcy* (LexisNexis, 23rd ed., 2021, 2218pp); *Honsberger's Bankruptcy in Canada* (Canada Law Book, 5th ed., 2017).

Objections and appeals: While B is bankrupt, only the trustee can object to or appeal an assessment; B, directors and accountants have no standing to do so: *475830 Alberta*, [1998] G.S.T.C. 103 (TCC); *Biron*, [2001] 2 C.T.C. 258 (FCA, leave to appeal denied 2001 CarswellNat 1620 (SCC)); *4028490 Canada*, 2005 TCC 50; *Garage A.D.*, 2008 TCC 246; *Lawrence*, 2012 TCC 331 (discharged B could not object for years during which he was bankrupt); but if the Quebec Superior Court orders that another person may represent the company, the TCC may respect that: *Bâtiment Fafard*, 1999 CarswellNat 1897 (TCC); *Lacroix*, 2010 TCC 160, para. 1. However, *Zhao (BDO Canada)*, 2020 SKQB 187, at paras. 92, 95-98, 101, 108-109 and 121, says that only B, not the trustee, can pursue the objection or appeal! The trustee can approve B's appeal after it is filed: *Schnier*, 2015 TCC 160. B can bring Court actions for "personal" claims such as pain and suffering, mental distress or reputational damage: *Meisels v. LPIC*, 2015 ONCA 406, para. 13. B can request a 152(4.2) adjustment: VIEWS doc 2015-0614421I7 (reversing 2007-0246481A11 and *Ullah*, 2013 TCC 387, para. 8). In *International Hi-Tech*, 2014 TCC 198, B's receivers and secured creditors, deemed by *Excise Tax Act* s. 266 to be its agents and having entitlement to its GST net tax refunds, were allowed to bring its TCC appeal.

The trustee is required a keep a bankrupt corporation's records for 6 years: 2009-0352341I7. CRA may disclose information about the bankrupt to the trustee: 2009-0351631I7, 2012-0451131I7. CRA may provide a discharged bankrupt an account statement for the period of bankruptcy: 2010-0385281I7. The trustee is required to file the bankrupt's unfiled returns (for all years: 2012-0451131I7), and both income tax and GST/HST refunds will be withheld until this is done unless a waiver is obtained: see 164(2.01) and Notes to 150(3). In *Sylvain Girard*, 2014 CarswellQue 9825 (Que. CA) (leave to appeal denied 2015 CarswellQue 3236 (SCC)), the Court ruled that a CRA reassessment of a bankrupt for pre-bankruptcy tax has no legal effect during the bankruptcy stay period.

New tax debts created during bankruptcy are not protected from CRA collection action: *Mutter (Meyers Norris)*, 2014 ABCA 176; *Armstrong*, 2015 BCSC 1167.

The trustee cannot challenge the correctness of CRA's claim if the taxpayer has exhausted the TCC appeal route: *Jones*, 2012 CarswellBC 2339 (BCSC).

Where the trustee is discharged but the bankrupt is not, a new limitation period for claims starts, but it does not apply to CRA due to s. 222: *Dyrland*, 2008 ABQB 356.

The 128(1)(d) or 128(2)(d) deemed year-end (DYE) requires CRA's systems to be able to process 2 tax years in the same calendar year: VIEWS doc 2008-0300301I7. The DYE applies only on bankruptcy, not on a proposal: *Marchessault*, 2007 FCA 345 (overriding other cases including *Gollner*, 2003 CarswellOnt 3188 (Ont. SCJ)); doc 2007-0243601E5. CRA administrative practice formerly allowed a DYE on a proposal; in *Wilcox*, 2014 NSSC 291, this was done but the Court ruled that CRA could not allocate increases in estimated pre-proposal tax to the post-proposal debt so as to be able to collect it. See also *Harris*, 2014 NSSC 417, discussing the CAIRP industry standard for allocating pre- and post-proposal income.

In *Jones*, [2004] 1 C.T.C. 65 (Ont CA), the taxpayer's proposal was accepted by the creditors, and the CRA as an unsecured creditor was to receive only about 60¢ on the dollar. The taxpayer then made instalment payments in the year to meet his current tax obligations. The Court held that the CRA could not apply these payments to the pre-proposal obligations as this would give it more than it was entitled to under the proposal. The instalments were applied only to the post-proposal tax obligation.

Tax refunds paid during bankruptcy (before discharge) normally belong to the trustee: BIA 67(1)(c), VIEWS docs 2008-0304901I7, 2011-0410301I7 (lists exceptions), 2012-0435561I7 (refund on return for post-bankruptcy period); *Gabrielle*, 2014 MBQB 77. If inadvertently paid to the bankrupt, it should be reissued to the trustee, and if the bankrupt refuses to return it, this can be enforced only through the Federal Court: 2009-0349501I7. CRA may be able to recover an excess refund paid during bankruptcy from the bankrupt after discharge: 2011-0404211I7. See also 2010-0389171I7 re holding back a bankrupt's refund. Pre-bankruptcy caregiver and disability credits (often applied for after discharge) were held payable to the trustee in: *Henderson*, 2003 ABQB 877; *Phillips*, 2010 BCSC 437; *Nixon*, 2001 SKQB 221; but to the taxpayer in: *Ford*, 2009 NSSC 124; *Potter*, 2010 MBQB 83; *Chomistek*, 2018 ABQB 434; *Rafter*, 2018 NSSC 331; *Deveau*, 2019 NSSC 256 (mostly). In *Krasilowez*, 2008 TCC 666 (FCA appeal dismissed for delay A-2-09), CRA retained a pre-bankruptcy refund by way of set-off, and a post-bankruptcy refund was not ordered paid to K (so would presumably be paid to the trustee); see also 2009-0331691I7. In *Funk*, 2009 MBQB 136, a secured creditor was taxed under 12(1)(x) on government assistance payments the creditor seized. An amount payable to a bankrupt by the trustee due to a provincial exemption can be seized by CRA garnishment: *Mutter (Meyers Norris Penney)*, 2014 ABCA 176.

The bankrupt is not liable to pay tax on income earned on property that is vested in and managed by the trustee for the creditors' benefit: *Turner*, 2004 TCC 556. When B collapsed his RRSP and directed the funds to his trustee under a proposal, the RRSP withdrawal was taxable: *Bertrand*, 2006 TCC 515. Similarly, when CRA registered a (Quebec) hypothec against M's RRSP before M's bankruptcy proposal, and seized the funds, they were included in M's income: *Martin*, 2015 TCC 118. During bankruptcy, income earned by a bankrupt should be reported by the trustee on a 128(2)(e) return: VIEWS doc 2007-0260511A11, based on *Meltzer*, [1996] 1 C.T.C. 2493 (TCC). The bankrupt can claim most 118–118.9 credits: 128(2)(f), 2010-0364121E5.

CRA may claim a right to deemed-trust amounts including the bankrupt's surplus income even though the BIA is supposed to be a "complete code"; e.g. CRA's claim in *Zuke*, 2014 BCSC 794.

Bankruptcy eliminates some ongoing tax carryforwards per 128(2)(f)(iii) and (g), including loss carryforwards even while bankrupt: *Abtan*, 2005 TCC 482; VIEWS docs 2009-0316341I7, 2009-0354701I7; but losses of the year of discharge can be carried forward: 2010-0357321I7. New losses can be generated only after absolute (not conditional) discharge: *Painter*, 2003 TCC 917. (A corporation can continue to deduct loss carryforwards until discharge: 128(1)(g), 2009-0340241I7; and a corp can carry back a loss to before bankruptcy: 2010-0385131I7.) Due to 128(2)(g)(iii), tuition paid during bankruptcy cannot be carried forward and claimed after discharge even if the courses are taken after discharge: *Delisle*, 2005 TCC 140; 2010-0379861E5. Bankruptcy does not eliminate: cumulative net investment loss for 110.6 (2004-0081811I7); moving expense carryforward (2008-0279271E5); obligation to repay Home Buyer's Plan amounts withdrawn from RRSP under 146.01, and presumably Lifelong Learning Plan amounts under 146.02 (2009-0318591E5); undeducted RRSP contributions (2013-0474741E5). See also 2007-0235211I7 for various effects of bankruptcy.

In *Lorrain*, [2004] 3 C.T.C. 2313 (TCC), an income averaging calculation under 110.2 and 120.31, spreading a pay equity settlement over several years, did not relieve L, who had been bankrupt, from payment for the earlier years, as the averaging provisions merely provide a calculation method without making the tax retroactive to those years.

For more CRA interpretation see VIEWS docs 2004-0092961E5 (provincial credits should be pro-rated); 2009-0314641I7 and 2009-0344491I7 (various questions where company filed Chapter 11 US bankruptcy and then had it recognized as a "foreign proceeding" under CCAA s. 18.6); 2009-0334351I7 (effect of bankrupt obtaining and cashing a duplicate cheque from CRA after discharge); 2009-0336001E5 (whether bankrupt corporation has a permanent establishment in a province); 2009-0345831I7 (treatment of tax refunds from two bankruptcies of same taxpayer); 2009-0351631I7 (disclosure of taxpayer information to the trustee); 2010-0356611I7 (undischarged bankrupt can be assessed for pre-bankruptcy year); 2015-0589051E5 (pension income splitting allowed by or with bankrupt spouse).

128(2)(e)(iii)(A) amended to delete reference to 118.6 by 2016 budget bill #1, for 2017 and later taxation years.

128(2) amended by 2016 budget bill #1 (for 2016 and later years, to delete reference to 119.1), 2015 budget bill #1 (to add that reference from 2014), 2002-2013 technical bill; 2012, 2011, 2009 and 2006 budget bills #2; 2006 budget bill #1, 2004 *Civil Code* harmonization bill; 2000, 1998 Budgets; 1995-97, 1992 technical bills; 1992 Economic Statement, 1990 pension bill.

Regulations: 206(2) (information return).

Remission Orders: *Investors in the Norbourg and Evolution Funds Remission Order*, P.C. 2012-816 (remission of bankruptcy dividend in respect of tax payable by bankrupt Vincent Lacroix).

Interpretation Bulletins: IT-124R6: Contributions to registered retirement savings plans; IT-179R: Change of fiscal period; IT-206R: Separate businesses; IT-415R2: Deregistration of registered retirement savings plans (cancelled); IT-513R: Personal tax credits.

CRA Audit Manual: 29.5.8: Loss carryovers — loss carryover bankruptcy.

Forms: RC342: Request by an insolvency practitioner for a waiver of the requirement to file a T2 corporation income tax return.

(3) [Repealed]

Notes: 128(3) repealed by 1995-97 technical bill, for bankruptcies after April 26, 1995. It defined "bankrupt" and "estate of the bankrupt", both now in 248(1).

Definitions [s. 128]: "allowable business investment loss" — 38(c), 248(1); "amount" — 248(1); "associated" — 128(1)(f), 256; "bankrupt", "business" — 248(1); "calendar year" — *Interpretation Act* 37(1)(a); "capital gain", "capital loss" — 39(1), 248(1); "corporation" — 248(1), *Interpretation Act* 35(1); "employer", "estate of the bankrupt", "individual", "Minister" — 248(1); "non-capital loss" — 111(8), 248(1); "pooled registered pension plan" — 147.5(1), 248(1); "prescribed", "property" — 248(1); "RRSP deduction limit" — 146(1), 248(1); "tax payable" — 248(2); "taxable income" — 2(2), 248(1); "taxation year" — 128(2)(d), 249; "taxpayer" — 248(1); "trust" — 104(1), 248(1), (3); "unused RRSP deduction room" — 146(1); "unused tuition, textbook and education tax credits" — 118.61(1).

Changes in Residence

128.1 (1) Immigration — For the purposes of this Act, where at a particular time a taxpayer becomes resident in Canada,

(a) **year-end, fiscal period** — where the taxpayer is a corporation or a trust,

(i) the taxpayer's taxation year that would otherwise include the particular time shall be deemed to have ended immediately before the particular time and a new taxation year of the taxpayer shall be deemed to have begun at the particular time, and

(ii) for the purpose of determining the taxpayer's fiscal period after the particular time, the taxpayer shall be deemed not to have established a fiscal period before the particular time;

(b) **deemed disposition** — the taxpayer is deemed to have disposed, at the time (in this subsection referred to as the "time of disposition") that is immediately before the time that is immediately before the particular time, of each property owned by the taxpayer, other than, if the taxpayer is an individual,

(i) property that is a taxable Canadian property,

(ii) property that is described in the inventory of a business carried on by the taxpayer in Canada at the time of disposition,

(iii) property included in Class 14.1 of Schedule II to the *Income Tax Regulations*, in respect of a business carried on by the taxpayer in Canada at the time of disposition, and

(iv) an excluded right or interest of the taxpayer, other than an interest described in paragraph (k) of the definition "excluded right or interest" in subsection (10),

(v) [Repealed]

for proceeds equal to its fair market value at the time of disposition;

(c) **deemed acquisition** — the taxpayer shall be deemed to have acquired at the particular time each property deemed by paragraph (b) to have been disposed of by the taxpayer, at a cost equal to the proceeds of disposition of the property;

(c.1) **deemed dividend to immigrating corporation** — if the taxpayer is a particular corporation that immediately before the time of disposition owned a share of the capital stock of another corporation resident in Canada, a dividend is deemed to

have been paid by the other corporation, and received by the particular corporation, immediately before the time of disposition, equal to the amount, if any, by which the fair market value of the share immediately before the time of disposition exceeds the total of

(i) the paid-up capital in respect of the share immediately before the time of disposition, and

(ii) if the share immediately before the time of disposition was taxable Canadian property that is not treaty-protected property, the amount by which, at the time of disposition, the fair market value of the share exceeds its cost amount;

(c.2) **deemed dividend to shareholder of immigrating corporation** — if the taxpayer is a corporation and an amount has been added to the paid-up capital in respect of a class of shares of the corporation's capital stock because of paragraph (2)(b),

(i) the corporation is deemed to have paid, immediately before the time of disposition, a dividend on the issued shares of the class equal to the amount of the paid-up capital adjustment in respect of the class, and

(ii) a dividend is deemed to have been received, immediately before the time of disposition, by each person (other than a person in respect of whom the corporation is a foreign affiliate) who held any of the issued shares of the class equal to that proportion of the dividend so deemed to have been paid that the number of shares of the class held by the person immediately before the time of disposition is of the number of issued shares of the class outstanding immediately before the time of disposition;

(c.3) **foreign affiliate dumping — immigrating corporation [chain of non-residents]** — if the taxpayer is a corporation that was, immediately before the particular time, controlled by one non-resident person or, if no single non-resident person controlled the CRIC, a group of non-resident persons not dealing with each other at arm's length (in this section, that one non-resident person, or each member of the group of non-resident persons, as the case may be, is referred to as a "**parent**", and the group of non-resident persons, if any, is referred to as the "**group of parents**") and the taxpayer owned, immediately before the particular time, one or more shares of one or more non-resident corporations (each of which is in this paragraph referred to as a "subject affiliate") that, immediately after the particular time, were — or that became, as part of a transaction or event or series of transactions or events that includes the taxpayer having become resident in Canada — foreign affiliates of the taxpayer, then

(i) in computing the paid-up capital, at any time after the time that is immediately after the particular time, of any particular class of shares of the capital stock of the taxpayer there is to be deducted the amount determined by the formula

$$A \times B/C$$

where

A is the lesser of

(A) the paid-up capital in respect of all of the shares of the capital stock of the taxpayer at the time that is immediately after the particular time, and

(B) the total of all amounts each of which is the fair market value at the particular time of

(I) a share of the capital stock of a subject affiliate owned by the taxpayer at the particular time, or

(II) an amount owing by the subject affiliate to the taxpayer at the particular time,

B is the paid-up capital in respect of the particular class of shares of the capital stock of the taxpayer at the time that is immediately after the particular time, and

C　is the paid-up capital in respect of all the shares of the capital stock of the taxpayer at the time that is immediately after the particular time, and

(ii)　for the purposes of Part XIII, the taxpayer is deemed, immediately after the particular time, to have paid to each parent, and each parent is deemed, immediately after the particular time, to have received from the taxpayer, a dividend in an amount determined by the formula

$$(A - B) \times C/D$$

where

A　is the amount determined under clause (B) of the description of A in subparagraph (i),

B　is the amount determined under clause (A) of the description of A in subparagraph (i),

C　is the fair market value, immediately after the particular time, of the shares of the capital stock of the taxpayer that are held, directly or indirectly, by the parent, and

D　is the total of all amounts each of which is the fair market value, immediately after the particular time, of the shares of the capital stock of the taxpayer that are held, directly or indirectly, by a parent.

(d)　**foreign affiliate** — where the taxpayer was, immediately before the particular time, a foreign affiliate of another taxpayer that is resident in Canada,

(i)　the affiliate is deemed to have been a controlled foreign affiliate of the other taxpayer immediately before the particular time, and

(ii)　the prescribed amount is to be included in the foreign accrual property income of the affiliate for its taxation year that ends immediately before the particular time.

Related Provisions: 52(8) — Cost of corporation's shares on it becoming resident; 53(1)(b.1) — Addition to ACB for deemed dividend under 128.1(1)(c.2); 53(4) — Effect on ACB of share, partnership interest or trust interest; 54"superficial loss"(c) — Superficial loss rule does not apply; 66(4.3) — Foreign exploration and development expenses on becoming resident; 66.21(1)"cumulative foreign resource expense"A.1, 66.21(5) — Foreign resource expenses on becoming resident; 70(5.3) — Value of shares of corp holding life insurance policy; 84(7) — When deemed dividend payable; 93.1(1) — Where shares are owned by partnership — effect on foreign affiliate definition; 94(3)(c), 94(4)(d), 128.1(1.1) — Deemed residence of non-resident trust does not apply for purposes of determining whether trust ceases to be resident; 96(8) — Cost of properties of partnership when partner becomes resident; 106(1.1)(b) — Deemed cost of income interest in trust; 107(1.1)(b)(ii) — Deemed cost of capital interest in trust; 114 — Individual resident during only part of year; 128.1(1.2) — Trust and partnership look-through rule for para. (c.1); 139.1(5) — Value of ownership rights in insurer during demutualization; 212.3(15) — Foreign affiliate dumping — rule for para. (c.3); 212.3(25) — Application of para. (c.3) to partnerships; 212.3(26) — Determining "related" and "control" for a trust for certain purposes; 215(1.1) — Limitation on requirement to withhold tax on deemed dividend under para. (c.1); 248(10) — Series of transactions; 250 — Determining residence in Canada; 257 — Formula cannot calculate to less than zero; Reg. 808(1.1) — Investment allowance for branch tax deemed nil before immigration.

Notes: An immigrant seeking Canadian citizenship must show evidence of having filed any required tax returns in 3 of the past 5 years under *Citizenship Act* s. 5(1)(c)(iii).

An immigrant who is due to receive a large payment that is taxable once resident in Canada should ensure they get it *before* becoming resident: e.g., *Davis*, 2018 TCC 110.

128.1(1)(b) and (c) bump up the tax cost of most property on immigration to its fair market value (FMV: see 69(1) Notes) [but not for a trust becoming a deemed resident: 128.1(1.1)]. Canada seeks a similar "step-up" from other countries via tax treaty; see 128.1(4) Notes. Personal-use property cannot trigger a later capital loss: 40(2)(g)(iii) [including a home vacated in the former country: VIEWS doc 2012-0455621E5]. In *Landbouwbedrijf Backx*, 2018 TCC 142, rev'd 2019 FCA 310, the TCC held that LB was already resident in Canada (under "central management and control": see 250(4) Notes), so 128.1(1)(c) did not apply in 2009 as LB claimed. The FCA sent the matter back because the TCC had based its decision on LB not having "ceased to be resident in the Netherlands", which is not necessary for 128.1(1) to apply. The TCC then reaffirmed (2021 TCC 2, para. 30, under appeal to FCA) that LB had been resident in Canada since 1998 (CRA having assessed LB as non-resident did not create an estoppel: paras. 51-56), so 128.1(1) did not apply in 2009; and ruled that Canada-Netherlands treaty Art. 4 did not assist LB.

Immigrants to Canada (including relocating employees) may have to file a T1135 reporting foreign property (see 233.3(3)), not only due to investments left in the home country but also because a home left there and rented out has its cost bumped up to current value by 128.1(1)(c).

See also CRA pamphlet T4055, *Newcomers to Canada*; VIEWS docs 2009-0323151E5 (application of bump-up to a 7(1) stock option); 2008-0280781E5 (power of appointment is not "property" for 128.1(1)(b), but may create a trust interest that is); 2013-0506731E5 (where dividend payable on share before immigration); 2019-0798631C6 (estate becoming resident due to trustee change can be a graduated rate estate).

See also David M. Sherman, *The Lawyer's Guide to Income Tax and GST/HST*, 2017 ed. (Carswell), ch. 3, "Immigration Law"; Garry Duncan, *Migration to Canada 2018* (Carswell, 328pp.); Jack Bernstein, "Tax Planning for Immigration to Canada", 248 *The Estate Planner* (CCH) 1-8 (Sept. 2015) and 78(10) *Tax Notes International* (taxnotes.com) 951-56 (June 8, 2015); Choudhury & Gurmukh, "Tax Issues on Immigration to Canada", 2323 *Tax Topics* (CCH) 1-5 (Sept. 15, 2016).

US citizens moving to Canada remain liable for US tax under the *Internal Revenue Code* (IRC) even when US non-resident. Their bank and brokerage accounts may be reported by CRA to the IRS under FATCA: see Notes to 269. A US citizen with over $54,000 in tax debt (2021; indexed annually) or no valid Social Security Number may have their passport revoked: IRC §7345; FAST Act (*Fixing America's Surface Transportation Act*) §32101(f); Bandoblu, "IRS Begins Passport Revocation", tinyurl.com/passp-revoke (IRS site); as of mid-2019, the IRS had sent out 389,000 certification notices: Castillo, Kirkpatrick & Galek, "US Tax Update: US Passport Revocation" (Jan. 8, 2021), tinyurl.com/passp-moodys. (It is a US federal offence for a citizen to enter or leave the US without a valid US passport, even if the person has a Canadian passport and can enter Canada! See 8 USC §1185(b).) Revocation does not apply to failing to declare a foreign bank account under FBAR [233.3(3) Notes]: 2384 *Tax Topics* (CCH) 7 (Nov. 16, 2017).

US citizens are subject to the 3.8% "Obamacare" net investment income tax (NIIT) even if they owe no US income tax. Canada gives no foreign tax credit (FTC) on Canadian-source income, and US regulations (§1.1411-1(e)) say the NIIT does not qualify for US FTC. The IRS's position is that Canada-US Treaty Art. XXIV:1 does not apply because the NIIT is not a tax on income. See Turkovich, "IRS: No FTC for 3.8% NIIT", 22(1) *Canadian Tax Highlights [CTH]* (ctf.ca) 9-10 (Jan. 2014); Nightingale, "The New Investment Income Tax", 2188 *Tax Topics* (CCH) 1-7 (Feb. 13, 2014); Lobo & Ruchelman, "The US NIIT", 23(6) *CTH* 5-7 (June 2015); Doobay, "RRSPs, RRIFs and the US NIIT", 23(9) *CTH* 10-11 (Sept. 2015).

An American who renounces US citizenship (or a person who gives up a green card held for at least 8 of the past 15 years) may have a deemed disposition of property for US tax: Brody & Binder, "New Expatriation Rules", 56(2) *Canadian Tax Journal* 559-70 (2008); Nightingale & Turche, "Expatriation", 61(1) *CTJ* 1-40 (2013); Berg, "FATCA in Canada: The 'Cure' for a US Place of Birth", 2014 Cdn Tax Foundation conference report, 33:1-38; Joyce & Turkovich, "US Citizenship Renunciation Procedures in Canada", 24(9) *Canadian Tax Highlights [CTH]* (ctf.ca) 3-4 (Sept. 2016); Reed, "Divorcing Uncle Sam", 2322 *Tax Topics* (CCH) 1-5 (Sept. 8, 2016); Bernstein, "Relinquishing US Citizenship", 261 *The Estate Planner* (CCH) 1-2 (Oct. 2016); Kellogg, "Important Exception to US Expatriation Provisions", 27(9) *CTH* 2-3 (Sept. 2019). This tax also applies to the present value of Canadian pension and RRSP balances (but the taxpayer may elect to irrevocably waive treaty reduction from 30% US withholding on future pension payments, and if so, the s. 126 foreign tax credit can be used against that withholding tax: VIEWS doc 2013-0477121E5). There are also estate and gift tax effects: Bandoblu & Turkovich, "Covered Expatriates", 23(10) *CTH* 5-6 (Oct. 2015); "US Citizenship renunciation could mean a steep inheritance tax", tinyurl.com/renunc-effect. In 2014, the US increased the renunciation fee from $450 to $2,350. A person renouncing for tax purposes may be barred from ever re-entering the US. Increasing numbers are renouncing: 5,132 in 2017. IRS publishes a quarterly list of renouncers, e.g., tinyurl.com/irs-renounced. Possible relief for dual citizens was announced in the 2015 Obama budget: Berg, "US Relief for Renunciation", 23(3) *CTH* 7-8 (March 2015); and see Velarde, "Transition Tax Relief May Buy Time for Residency-Based Tax Bill", *Tax Notes* (taxnotes.com), June 14, 2018, and Bandoblu, "IRS Relief Procedures for Certain Former Citizens", 27(10) *CTH* 5-6 (Oct. 2019).

2017 US tax reform (including IRC §965 transition tax on shareholder of non-US corp with undistributed earnings): Reed & Ko, "The Mandatory Repatriation Tax", 2399 *Tax Topics [TT]* (CCH) 1-5 (March 1, 2018); Reed, "Pleading Not GILTI", 2400 *TT* 1-6 (March 8, 2018) (re "global intangible low-taxed income") and "Subpart F Income Earned by Canadian Corporations After US Tax Reform", 2406 *TT* 1-4 (April 19, 2018); Carman, "The Impact of US Tax Reform on Canadian-US Corporate Groups", XXI(2) *Corporate Finance* (Federated Press) 18-24 (2018); Wu & Clements, "US Professionals Living in Canada", 8(3) *Canadian Tax Focus [CTFo]* (ctf.ca) 13-14 (Aug. 2018); Oppenheimer, "A Section 962 Election?", 26(11) *Canadian Tax Highlights [CTH]* (ctf.ca) 12-13 (Nov. 2018); Boidman, "Proposed US Reg: GILTI Reduced on Canadian Operations", 27(4) *CTH* 3-4 (April 2019); Pereira et al., "Introduction to GILTI and its Application to US Shareholders of Canadian Corporations", 67(2) *Canadian Tax Journal* 411-35 (2019); Thériault, "The Impact of GILTI on Canadian Corporations", 10(1) *CTFo* 10-11 (Feb. 2020); Nightingale & Fayolle, "Maybe You're Not Really GILTI", 2526 *TT* 1-5 (Aug. 4, 2020); Meadow, "Recently Released GILTI Regulations May Create Tax Nightmares for Many US Shareholders Residing in Canada", tinyurl.com/moodys-gilti-oct20.

See also Notes to: 40(2)(b) re US citizen owning a principal residence; 70(5) re US estate tax; 125(1) re owning a Canadian professional corp; 131(8) and 132(1) re investing in a Canadian mutual fund; 146.1 and 146.2 re RESPs and TFSAs; 233.3(3) re FBAR and other filing obligations and penalties; 269 re FATCA; Canada-US treaty

Art. XVIII:7 re RRSPs and RRIFs; Art. XXIV:3-6 for relief from double tax on US-source passive income.

For detailed discussion of US citizens in Canada see Vidal, *Introduction to International Tax in Canada* (Carswell, 8th ed., 2020), chaps. 26 and 29; Wruk, *The American in Canada* (2nd ed., ecwpress.com, 351pp., 2015); Pound & Reed, *A Tax Guide for American Citizens in Canada* (Carswell, 2013, 421pp); Marino & Sloan, "Typical Issues When a US Person is Part of the Mix", 2015 Prairie Provinces Tax Conf. (ctf.ca) 3:1-33; Lee & Shinh, "Taxation of US Citizens or Residents Working for a Canadian Employer", 65(2) *Canadian Tax Journal [CTJ]* 479-502 (2017); Lobo et al., "US Citizens as Shareholders of Canadian Companies", 2016 Cdn Tax Foundation conference report, 21:1-39; Nightingale, "American Professionals in Canada", 65(4) *CTJ* 893-937 (2017); Nightingale & Smith, "Advanced Topics for American Shareholders of Private Canadian Companies", 2017 Ontario Tax Conf.

Shorter articles: Reed, "Solving Subpart F — Deferring Investment Income Earned by a CFC in Canada", 2239 *Tax Topics [TT]* (CCH) 1-4 (Feb. 5, 2015); Bernstein, "US Immigrant Tax Planning", 23(3) *Canadian Tax Highlights [CTH]* (ctf.ca) 4-6 (March 2015); Carol Fitzsimmons, "US Tax Return Filings", 23(6) *CTH* 2-3 (June 2015); Bernstein, "Canadian Resident Owns US S Corp", 23(7) *CTH* 5-6 (July 2015); Kellogg, "Housing and Foreign Earned Income", 23(9) *CTH* 4-5 (Sept. 2015); Abraham, "PFIC Exposure for US Citizens", 16(2) *Tax for the Owner-Manager* (ctf.ca) 5-6 (April 2016); Waiss, "Updated FAQs for Streamlined Procedures", 24(3) *CTH* 4 (March 2016); Reed, "The Application of the US PFIC Regime to Canadian Start-ups", 2352 *Tax Topics* (CCH) 1-2 (April 6, 2017); Hsu, "Revoking the US Revocable Trust", 10(2) *BorderCrossings* (Carswell) 1-6 (Aug. 2017); Berg & Manasuev, "US Citizen Living in Canada: Foreign-Currency Gain?" 25(8) *CTH* 12-13 (Aug. 2017). US citizens owning mutual fund trust units: see 132(1) Notes; DeBlis, "The Curious Case of Accidental Americans", 2432 *TT* 1-4 (Oct. 18, 2018); Turchen & Nightingale, "Passive Foreign Investment Companies and US Citizens in Canada", 2545 *TT* 1-2 (Dec. 15, 2020); Kirkpatrick, "Tax Planning with Life Insurance for US Persons in Canada", XXVI(2) *Insurance Planning* (Federated Press) 6-11 (2021).

128.1(1)(c.1) provides that if an immigrating corp (Forco) at time of immigration holds a share of a corp resident in Canada (Canco) [including looking through a trust or partnership: 128.1(1.2)], Canco is deemed to have paid a dividend to Forco immediately before Forco is deemed to dispose of its Canco shares. Generally, the deemed dividend is equal to the FMV of the share minus its paid-up capital. However, if the Canco share is taxable Canadian property and Canada's right to tax any gain on the share realized by Forco is not removed by a tax treaty, the deemed dividend is in effect reduced by any capital gain realized by Forco on the deemed disposition of the Canco share.

Effectively, 128.1(1)(c.1) treats Canco as if it had distributed to Forco the portion of Canco's surplus allocable to the shares held by Forco, except to the extent that surplus has been realized as a capital gain taxable in Canada. Since the dividend is deemed paid to Forco before immigration, it is subject to 212(2) withholding tax. If Canco and Forco deal at arm's length, 215(1.1) relieves Canco of the requirement to withhold tax.

Where a corporation immigrates to Canada, unremitted profits of a Canadian branch are treated similarly to undistributed surplus of a Canadian corp in which it holds shares. Reg. 808(1.1) provides that the corp's allowance in respect of its investment in property in Canada will be nil for the year deemed to end before immigration. Since the corp will have no investment allowance, it will pay s. 219 branch tax on any unremitted profits of a Cdn branch arising in the year or deferred from earlier years.

128.1(1)(c.2) provides that if a corporation becomes resident in Canada and elects to increase PUC under 128.1(2)(b), it is deemed to have paid a dividend (equal to the increase in PUC) on the shares of that class before immigrating. (PUC generally can be returned to shareholders tax-free.) The dividend primarily affects shareholders resident in Canada, for whom a dividend from a foreign corporation is generally taxable. No dividend is deemed received, however, by a shareholder for whom the immigrating corporation is a foreign affiliate (FA). Taxation of the accrued surplus of a FA that becomes resident in Canada is dealt with under 128.1(1)(d).

Where a resident shareholder is deemed to receive a dividend from an immigrating corporation by 128.1(1)(c.2), the amount of the deemed dividend is added to the ACB of the share under 53(1)(b.1).

128.1(1)(c.3) was added to deter certain corporate immigrations that could otherwise be used as substitutes for transactions addressed by the foreign affiliate (FA) dumping rules in 212.3. It can create a deemed dividend and/or PUC reduction where a non-resident (NR) corp immigrates to Canada, is controlled by another NR and the immigrating corp owns shares of a non-resident corp (which could include the foreign parent) that becomes a FA of the immigrating corp either immediately after the immigration or as part of a series of transactions or events that includes the immigration. In these circumstances, the immigration could otherwise lead to a result similar to what the FA dumping rules in 212.3 are aimed at preventing.

For purposes of 128.1(1)(c.3), the look-through rules in 93.1(1) and 212.3(25) apply where any partnerships are in the ownership structure. As well, the "multiple control" rule in 212.3(15)(a) applies so that, generally, only one NR corp is considered to control the immigrating corp.

Interest accrued on a Canadian investment before immigration might have to be included in income after immigration: see Notes to 12(4).

Where a Canadian resident becomes non-resident and then resident in Canada again, see VIEWS doc 2009-0311951E5.

128.1(1)(c.3) opening words and (ii) amended by 2021 budget bill #1, for transactions or events after March 18, 2019, due to 212.3 being expanded to include control by non-resident individuals. Before the amendment, read:

> (c.3) if the taxpayer is a corporation that was, immediately before the particular time, controlled by a particular non-resident corporation and the taxpayer owned, immediately before the particular time, one or more shares of one or more non-resident corporations (each of which is in this paragraph referred to as a "subject affiliate") that, immediately after the particular time, were — or that became, as part of a transaction or event or series of transactions or events that includes the taxpayer having become resident in Canada — foreign affiliates of the taxpayer, then ...
>
> > (ii) for the purposes of Part XIII, the taxpayer is deemed, immediately after the particular time, to have paid to the particular non-resident corporation, and the particular non-resident corporation is deemed, immediately after the particular time, to have received from the taxpayer, a dividend equal to the amount, if any, by which the amount determined under clause (B) of the description of A in subparagraph (i) exceeds the amount determined under clause (A) of the description of A in subparagraph (i); and

128.1(1)(b)(iii) amended by 2016 budget bill #2, effective 2017, to change "eligible capital property" to "property included in Class 14.1 of Schedule II to the *Income Tax Regulations*" (as part of replacing the ECP rules: see Notes to 20(1)(b)).

128.1(1)(b)(iv) amended by 2014 budget bill #2, for 2016 and later taxation years. For 1997-2015, read:

> (iv) an excluded right or interest of the taxpayer (other than an interest in a non-resident testamentary trust that was never acquired for consideration),

128.1(1)(d)(i), (ii) amended (non-substantively) by 2002-2013 technical bill (Part 3 — FA reorganizations), effective for taxation years that begin after 2006; before the amendment, "controlled foreign affiliate" and "foreign accrual property income" (now in 248(1)) were cross-referenced to the definitions of those terms in 95(1).

128.1(1)(c.3) added by 2012 budget bill #2, effective for corporations that become resident in Canada after March 28, 2012.

128.1(1) amended by 2001 technical bill (effective for changes in residence after Oct. 1, 1996) and 1998 Budget (effective for corporations that become resident in Canada after Feb. 23, 1998). See also Notes at end of 128.1.

Regulations: 5907(13)–(15) (prescribed amount to be included in FAPI).

I.T. Application Rules: 26(10) (ITAR 26 does not apply to property owned since before 1972).

Income Tax Folios: S5-F1-C1: Determining an individual's residence status [replaces IT-221R3].

Interpretation Bulletins: IT-259R4: Exchanges of property; IT-262R2: Losses of non-residents and part-year residents.

CRA Audit Manual: 15.4.4: Immigration — becoming resident in Canada.

Forms: NR74: Determination of residency status (entering Canada); T4055: Newcomers to Canada [pamphlet].

(1.1) Trusts subject to subsec. 94(3) — Paragraph (1)(b) does not apply, at a time in a trust's particular taxation year, to the trust if the trust is resident in Canada for the particular taxation year for the purpose of computing its income.

Related Provisions: 94(4)(e) — Deemed residence of non-resident trust does not apply for purposes of determining whether trust ceases to be resident.

Notes: 94(3)(a) deems a non-resident trust to be resident only for specific purposes which do not include 128.1. The interaction of 94 and 128.1(1) works as follows: First, 94(4)(d) prevents 128.1(1) from applying when a trust first becomes resident (for specific purposes) solely because of the deeming rule in 94(3)(a). However, 94(3)(c) bumps up the cost base of the trust's assets to fair market value in the same way that 128.1(1) would have. If a deemed-resident trust then becomes *actually* resident in Canada (e.g. changes to having majority Canadian-resident trustees), then 128.1 applies, so there is a deemed year-end under 128.1(1)(a); but 128.1(1.1) prevents 128.1(1)(b) and (c) from applying, because at the instant before becoming resident, when 128.1(1)(b) would otherwise trigger a deemed disposition of property, the trust is already "resident in Canada for the purpose of computing its income" (see 94(3)(a)(ii)). 128.1(1)(c) then cannot apply because it applies only to property to which 128.1(1)(b) applies. See also 94(5)–(5.2) on deemed cessation of residence.

128.1(1.1) added by 2002-2013 technical bill (Part 1 — NRTs), effective for trust taxation years that end after 2006, and also for each earlier taxation year of a trust to which amended 94(1) applies (see Notes at end of s. 94).

(1.2) Trusts and partnerships look-through rule — For the purposes of this subsection and paragraph (1)(c.1), if at any time shares of the capital stock of a corporation resident in Canada are owned by a trust or a partnership (each referred to in this subsection as a "conduit"), each person or partnership with an interest as a beneficiary under the conduit or that is a member of the conduit (each referred to in this subsection as a "holder"), as the case may be, is deemed to own the shares of each class of the capital stock of the

corporation that are owned by the conduit the number of which is determined by the formula

$$A \times B/C$$

where

A is the total number of shares of the class of the capital stock of the corporation that is owned by the conduit at that time;

B is the fair market value, at that time, of the holder's interest in the conduit; and

C is the total fair market value, at that time, of all interests in the conduit.

Notes: 128.1(1.2) is similar to 212.1(6), providing a look-through for the deemed-dividend rule in 128.1(1)(c.1) (see Notes to 128.1(1)). Added by 2018 budget bill #2, for transactions or events after Feb. 26, 2018.

(2) Paid-up capital adjustment — If a corporation becomes resident in Canada at a particular time,

(a) for the purposes of subsection (1) and this subsection, the "paid-up capital adjustment" in respect of a particular class of shares of the corporation's capital stock in respect of that acquisition of residence is the positive or negative amount determined by the formula

$$(A \times B/C) - D$$

where

A is the amount, if any, by which

(i) the total of all amounts each of which is an amount deemed by paragraph (1)(c) to be the cost to the corporation of property deemed under that paragraph to have been acquired by the corporation at the particular time

exceeds

(ii) the total of all amounts each of which is the amount of a debt owing by the corporation, or any other obligation of the corporation to pay an amount, that is outstanding at the particular time,

B is the fair market value at the particular time of all of the shares of the particular class,

C is the total of all amounts each of which is the fair market value at the particular time of all of the shares of a class of shares of the corporation's capital stock, and

D is the paid-up capital at the particular time, determined without reference to this subsection, in respect of the particular class; and

(b) for the purposes of this Act, in computing the paid-up capital in respect of a class of shares of the corporation's capital stock at any time after the particular time and before the time, if any, at which the corporation next becomes resident in Canada, there shall be

(i) added the amount of the paid-up capital adjustment in respect of the particular class, if that amount is positive and the corporation so elects for all such classes in respect of that acquisition of residence by notifying the Minister in writing within 90 days after the particular time, and

(ii) deducted, if the amount of the paid-up capital adjustment in respect of the particular class is negative, the absolute value of that amount.

Related Provisions: 128.1(1)(c.2) — Deemed dividend to shareholder of immigrating corporation; 257 — Formula cannot calculate to less than zero; *Interpretation Act* 27(5) — Meaning of "within 90 days".

Notes: The general anti-avoidance rule in s. 245 probably does not apply to schemes that extract paid-up capital, if 128.1(2) does not apply. See *Evans*, 2005 TCC 684, superseding *McNichol* and *RMM Canadian Enterprises*.

For a ruling on 128.1(2) see VIEWS doc 2015-0584151R3 (share premium from share issuances under foreign corporate law is contributed surplus, can be added to PUC).

128.1(2) amended by 1998 Budget (for corporations that become resident in Canada after Feb. 23, 1998), 1995-97 technical bill.

See also Notes at end of 128.1.

(3) Paid-up capital adjustment — In computing the paid-up capital at any time in respect of a class of shares of the capital stock of a corporation

(a) there is to be deducted an amount equal to the lesser of A and B, and added an amount equal to the lesser of A and C, where

A is the absolute value of the difference between

(i) the total of all amounts deemed by subsection 84(3), (4) or (4.1) to be a dividend on shares of the class paid before that time by the corporation, and

(ii) the total that would be determined under subparagraph (i) if this Act were read without reference to subsection (2),

B is the total of all amounts required by subsection (2) to be added in computing the paid-up capital in respect of the class before that time, and

C is the total of all amounts required by subsection (2) to be deducted in computing the paid-up capital in respect of the class before that time; and

(b) there is to be added an amount equal to the lesser of

(i) the amount, if any, by which

(A) the total of all amounts deemed by subsection 84(3), (4) or (4.1) to be a dividend on shares of the class paid after March 28, 2012 and before that time by the corporation

exceeds

(B) the total that would be determined under clause (A) if this Act were read without reference to subparagraph (c.3)(i), and

(ii) the total of all amounts required by subparagraph (c.3)(i) to be deducted in computing the paid-up capital in respect of the class before that time.

Related Provisions: 66(4.3) — Foreign exploration and development expenses on ceasing to be resident; 66.21(5) — Foreign resource expenses on ceasing to be resident.

Notes: 128.1(3) amended by 2012 budget bill #2, effective March 29, 2012. The substantive changes were "of the corporation" to "of a corporation" in the opening words, and adding para. (b).

128.1(3) amended by 1998 Budget, effective for corporations that become resident in Canada after Feb. 23, 1998.

(4) Emigration — For the purposes of this Act, where at any particular time a taxpayer ceases to be resident in Canada,

(a) **year-end, fiscal period** — where the taxpayer is a corporation or a trust,

(i) the taxpayer's taxation year that would otherwise include the particular time shall be deemed to have ended immediately before the particular time and a new taxation year of the taxpayer shall be deemed to have begun at the particular time, and

(ii) for the purpose of determining the taxpayer's fiscal period after the particular time, the taxpayer shall be deemed not to have established a fiscal period before the particular time;

(a.1) **fiscal period** — if the taxpayer is an individual (other than a trust) and carries on a business at the particular time, otherwise than through a permanent establishment (as defined by regulation) in Canada,

(i) the fiscal period of the business is deemed to have ended immediately before the particular time and a new fiscal period of the business is deemed to have begun at the particular time, and

(ii) for the purpose of determining the fiscal period of the business after the particular time, the taxpayer is deemed not to have established a fiscal period of the business before the particular time;

(b) **deemed disposition** — the taxpayer is deemed to have disposed, at the time (in this paragraph and paragraph (d) referred to as the "time of disposition") that is immediately before the time that is immediately before the particular time, of each property owned by the taxpayer other than, if the taxpayer is an individual,

(i) real or immovable property situated in Canada, a Canadian resource property or a timber resource property,

(ii) capital property used in, property included in Class 14.1 of Schedule II to the *Income Tax Regulations* in respect of or property described in the inventory of, a business carried on by the taxpayer through a "permanent establishment" (as defined by regulation) in Canada at the particular time,

(iii) an excluded right or interest of the taxpayer,

(iv) if the taxpayer is not a trust and was not, during the 120-month period that ends at the particular time, resident in Canada for more than 60 months, property that was owned by the taxpayer at the time the taxpayer last became resident in Canada or that was acquired by the taxpayer by inheritance or bequest after the taxpayer last became resident in Canada, and

(v) any property in respect of which the taxpayer elects under paragraph (6)(a) for the taxation year that includes the first time, after the particular time, at which the taxpayer becomes resident in Canada,

for proceeds equal to its fair market value at the time of disposition, which proceeds are deemed to have become receivable and to have been received by the taxpayer at the time of disposition;

(b.1) **employee life and health trust** — notwithstanding paragraph (b), if the taxpayer is or was at any time an employee life and health trust,

(i) the taxpayer is deemed

(A) to have disposed, at the time (in this paragraph referred to as the "time of disposition") that is immediately before the time that is immediately before the particular time, of each property owned by the taxpayer for proceeds equal to its fair market value at the time of disposition, which proceeds are deemed to have become receivable and to have been received by the taxpayer at the time of disposition, and

(B) to have carried on a business at the time of disposition, and

(ii) each property of the taxpayer is deemed

(A) to have been described in the inventory of the business referred to in clause (i)(B), and

(B) to have a cost of nil at the time of disposition;

(c) **reacquisition** — the taxpayer is deemed to have reacquired, at the particular time, each property deemed by paragraph (b) or (b.1) to have been disposed of by the taxpayer, at a cost equal to the proceeds of disposition of the property;

(d) **individual — elective disposition** — notwithstanding paragraphs (b) to (c), if the taxpayer is an individual (other than a trust) and so elects in prescribed form and manner in respect of a property described in subparagraph (b)(i) or (ii),

(i) the taxpayer is deemed to have disposed of the property at the time of disposition for proceeds equal to its fair market value at that time and to have reacquired the property at the particular time at a cost equal to those proceeds,

(ii) the taxpayer's income for the taxation year that includes the particular time is deemed to be the greater of

(A) that income determined without reference to this subparagraph, and

(B) the lesser of

(I) that income determined without reference to this subsection, and

(II) that income determined without reference to subparagraph (i), and

(iii) each of the taxpayer's non-capital loss, net capital loss, restricted farm loss, farm loss and limited partnership loss for the taxation year that includes the particular time is deemed to be the lesser of

(A) that amount determined without reference to this subparagraph, and

(B) the greater of

(I) that amount determined without reference to this subsection, and

(II) that amount determined without reference to subparagraph (i); and

(d.1) **employee CCPC stock option shares** — if the taxpayer is deemed by paragraph (b) to have disposed of a share that was acquired before February 28, 2000 under circumstances to which subsection 7(1.1) applied, there shall be deducted from the taxpayer's proceeds of disposition the amount that would, if section 7 were read without reference to subsection 7(1.6), be added under paragraph 53(1)(j) in computing the adjusted cost base to the taxpayer of the share as a consequence of the deemed disposition.

(e), (f) [Repealed]

Related Provisions: 7(1.6) — Deemed disposition does not apply to stock option rules; 10(12) — Non-resident ceasing to use inventory — deemed disposition; 28(4), (4.1) — Farmer or fisherman emigrating; 44(2) — Date of disposition for property stolen, destroyed or expropriated; 53(4) — Effect on ACB of share, partnership interest or trust interest; 54"superficial loss"(c) — Superficial loss rule does not apply; 66(4)(b) — Foreign exploration and development expenses — deduction after emigration; 70(5.3) — Value of shares of corp that owns life insurance policy; 74.2(3)–(4) — Application of spousal attribution rule to disposition on emigration; 94(4)(e), 94(5)–(5.1) — When trust deemed to cease being resident; 104(4)(a.3) — Deemed disposition of property by trust on emigration of transferor; 106(1.1)(b) — Deemed cost of income interest in trust; 107(1.1)(b)(ii) — Deemed cost of income interest in trust; 114 — Individual resident during only part of year; 119 — Credit where stop-loss rule in 40(3.7) applies; 126(2.2) — Foreign tax credit on property deemed to be taxable Canadian property; 126(2.21), (2.22) — Foreign tax credit after emigration; 128.1(1)(b) — Deemed disposition on immigration; 128.1(5) — Deemed disposition does not increase instalment requirements; 128.1(6) — Returning former resident; 128.1(8) — Post-emigration loss; 128.1(9) — Information reporting; 128.3 — Shares acquired on rollover deemed to be same shares for 128.1(4)(b)(iv); 146.01(5) — Repayment of Home Buyer's Plan amount on emigration; 146.02(5) — Repayment of Lifelong Learning Plan amount on emigration; 219.1(1) — Tax on corporate emigration; 219.1(2) — Foreign affiliate dumping — corporate emigration; 220(3.2), Reg. 600 — Late filing of 128.1(4)(d) elections; 220(4.5)–(4.54) — Deferral of payment of departure tax; 226 — Demand for payment of taxes owing when taxpayer leaving Canada, and seizure of goods; 250 — Determining residence in Canada; Canada-U.S. Tax Treaty:Art. XIII:5(b)(ii), 6, 7 — Effect of emigration to U.S. on future capital gains; Canada-U.K. Tax Treaty:Art. 13:9 — Effect of emigration to U.K. on future capital gains.

Notes: See 250(1) Notes on whether a person is resident in Canada.

128.1(4)(b) creates what is informally called "departure tax" or "emigration tax". See Forms T1161 and T1243. It triggers a deemed disposition of most property at its fair market value (FMV — see Notes to 69(1)) when a person becomes non-resident (see s. 250). For the exceptions see (b)(i)–(v) and Notes to 128.1(10)"excluded right or interest". Any resulting capital gain is then taxed under the normal rules for capital gains (see 38-40). Payment can be delayed by posting security: 220(4.5)-(4.54). A later loss on the property can offset the gain: 128.1(8). Taxpayers who become resident in Canada for 5 years or less are exempted from this rule for property they owned on the date they became resident, provided it is the same property (e.g., shares exchanged on a corporate reorganization do not qualify): 128.1(4)(b)(iv), VIEWS doc 2013-0485661E5; and also on property inherited while resident in Canada.

For a life insurance policy, or shares whose value is in part based on a life insurance policy, see 70(5.3) for a special rule.

If the taxpayer has no assets in Canada, the CRA can ask the tax authorities in certain other countries to collect the Canadian tax. See Notes to Canada-US tax treaty Art. XXVI-A:1.

For an RRSP (excluded by 128.1(10)"excluded right or interest"(a)(i)), see Notes to ITCIA 5"periodic pension payment" (reproduced before the MLI and Canada-US Tax Treaty) for a planning tip.

In its tax treaty negotiations, Canada has since 1997 sought to have other countries allow a step-up in the cost base of property to FMV on immigration (as we have under 128.1(1)(c)), to prevent double taxation when the property is later sold. This has now been agreed in most of Canada's treaties or Protocols, including the U.S. (Art. XIII:6, 7) and the U.K. (Art. 13:10). See also the foreign tax credit for former residents in 126(2.21), and s. 119.

In *Holzhey*, 2007 TCC 247, a right to receive accrued interest on a loan held at time of emigration was held to be fully taxable under 12(1)(c) rather than a capital gain.

On ceasing to be resident in Canada, the CRA says an individual should complete Form NR73. This is not a statutory requirement (unless requested under 231.2); some advisers recommend filing a change of address and ticking off "ceased to be resident in Canada" on the T1, but not completing the NR73 due to its questions' intrusive nature. However, the CRA will require it if the taxpayer needs confirmation of non-residence, e.g. for pension purposes. Some of the questions cannot properly be answered until after the move to the new country.

After ceasing to be resident, the taxpayer will be subject to withholding tax on certain income from Canada. See 212(1) and (2).

In a "departure trade", X borrows a huge sum of money before departure, buys an investment that will pay interest after departure, and claims interest paid before departure as a deduction against the tax arising on departure due to 128.1(4). The matching interest income is then earned when X is non-resident and not subject to Canadian tax. In *Grant*, 2007 FCA 174 (leave to appeal denied 2007 CarswellNat 3852 (SCC)), a departure trade failed because the interest was not actually paid until the day after the taxpayers became non-resident. (CRA also argued that it failed because of GAAR and 20(1)(c); the Court did not deal with those arguments.) *Walsh v. BDO Dunwoody*, 2013 BCSC 392, 2013 BCSC 1463, was a lawsuit over a failed departure trade; it settled after these preliminary decisions.

See also VIEWS doc 2013-0494251E5 (income stream from sale of client list is subject to 128.1(4) [Cepparo, "Departure Tax on Right to Payments for Client List", 24(4) *Canadian Tax Highlights* (ctf.ca) 7 (April 2016)]).

128.1(4)(d) allows an election (Form T2061A) for deemed disposition of real property or business property, otherwise exempted by 128.1(4)(b)(i) or (ii). One can do this to use otherwise-unusable losses; (d)(i) steps up the property's cost for a later sale to which 115(1)(b) and 116 will apply. The filing deadline is in Reg. 1302, which applies to former 48(1)(a) and will be amended to apply here. If the individual was resident in Quebec, the election must be copied to Revenu Québec: *Taxation Act* ss. 785.2, 21.4.6.

See also Wruk & Ritchie, *The Canadian in America* (3rd ed., ecwpress.com, 349pp., 2015); Vidal, *Introduction to International Tax in Canada* (Carswell, 8th ed., 2020), chap. 26; Duncan, *Canadians Resident Abroad* (Carswell, 22nd ed., 2020, 467pp); Bratz, "Canadians Moving to the United States", 46(6) *Canadian Tax Journal* 1322-48 (1998); Rajan, "Are You Sure You Want to Leave Canada?", 47(5) *CTJ* 1342-66 (1999); Rautenberg, "The New Emigration Rules", 1999 Prairie Provinces Tax Conference (ctf.ca), 2:1-22; Wilson, "Taxpayer Migration Rules", 1999 Ontario Tax Conf. 12:1-45; Smith, "Mobile Beneficiaries of Canadian Estate Plans", 55(2) *CTJ* 382-406 (2007); Tollstam, "Planning for High Net Worth Individuals Leaving Canada", 2007 Cdn Tax Foundation conference report, 38:1-16; Nelson, "IRS Emigrants' Guidance", 18(5) *Canadian Tax Highlights* (ctf.ca) 1-2 (May 2010); Papinko, "U.S. Tax Planning for Canadians with Investment Structures Moving to the United States", 2(1) *The Newsletter* (Tax Executives Institute, Toronto Chapter) 7-12 (Sept. 2012); Kerzner, "Finding More Financial Wellness on the Road to Immigrating to America", 5(5) *It's Personal* (Carswell) 2-6 (Nov. 2012); Adamski & Bast, "Preparing Clients (and Structures) for Emigration", 2018 Atlantic Provinces Tax Conference (ctf.ca), 7:1-19; *Emigrating from Canada Checklist* (*Taxnet Pro* Tax & Estate Planning Centre, 2020, 12pp).

Where an employee is transferred temporarily to a related employer, the Canadian employer can often apply to the CRA under the Social Security Agreement between Canada and the other country for a certificate of coverage, and pay CPP premiums rather than have the employee subject to local social security taxes (e.g., FICA and Medicare in the U.S.).

An appointee under a trust's power of appointment is not a beneficiary and has no deemed disposition of an interest in the trust on emigration: VIEWS doc 2007-0235231C6.

See Notes to 152(3.1) for a rule of application in the 2001 technical bill regarding the reassessment deadline for individuals who emigrated from October 2, 1996 through June 13, 1999.

A corporation incorporated in Canada can cease to be resident in Canada only by being continued in another jurisdiction, due to 250(4). If it is, see 219.1 and Notes to 250(5.1).

128.1(4)(b)(ii) amended by 2016 budget bill #2, effective 2017, to change "eligible capital property" to "property included in Class 14.1 of Schedule II to the *Income Tax Regulations*" (as part of replacing the ECP rules: see Notes to 20(1)(b)).

128.1(4)(b)(i) amended by 2002-2013 technical bill (Part 4 — bijuralism), effective June 26, 2013, to add "or immovable".

128.1(4)(b.1) added, and (c) amended to refer to it, by 2010 budget bill #2, effective 2010. See Notes to 144.1.

128.1(4) amended by 2001 technical bill (effective for changes in residence that occur after October 1, 1996) and 1997 Budget. See also Notes at end of 128.1.

Regulations: 600(c), (c.1) (late filing of elections under (4)(b)(iv) and (4)(d)); 1300 (election under 128.1(4)(b)(iv)); 1302 (election under 128.1(4)(d)); 8201 (permanent establishment for (4)(b)(ii)).

Income Tax Folios: S5-F2-C1: Foreign tax credit [replaces IT-270R3, IT-395R2, IT-520].

Interpretation Bulletins: IT-113R4: Benefits to employees — stock options; IT-137R3: Additional tax on certain corporations carrying on business in Canada; IT-259R4: Exchanges of property; IT-262R2: Losses of non-residents and part-year residents; IT-451R: Deemed disposition and acquisition on ceasing to be or becoming resident in Canada.

Information Circulars: 07-1R1: Taxpayer relief provisions.

CRA Audit Manual: 15.4.4: Emigration — ceasing to be resident in Canada.

Advance Tax Rulings: ATR-70: Distribution of taxable Canadian property by a trust to a non-resident. [This was the 1991 ruling criticized by the Auditor General in 1996 that led to the October 2, 1996 proposals — ed.].

Forms: NR73: Determination of residency status (leaving Canada); T1161: List of properties by an emigrant of Canada; T1243: Deemed disposition of property by an emigrant of Canada; T2061A: Election by an emigrant to report deemed dispositions of taxable Canadian property and capital gains and/or losses thereon; T4056: Emigrants and income tax [guide].

(5) Instalment interest — If an individual is deemed by subsection (4) to have disposed of a property in a taxation year, in applying sections 155 and 156 and subsections 156.1(1) to (3) and 161(2), (4) and (4.01) and any regulations made for the purposes of those provisions, the individual's total tax payable under this Part for the year is deemed to be the lesser of

(a) the individual's total tax payable under this Part for the year, determined before taking into consideration the specified future tax consequences for the year, and

(b) the amount that would be determined under paragraph (a) if subsection (4) did not apply to the individual for the year.

Notes: 128.1(5) prevents the departure tax under 128.1(4) from requiring increased instalments for the year.

128.1(5) opening words and para. (a) amended by 2002-2013 technical bill (Part 5 — technical), effective for taxation years that begin after Oct. 2011, to change "total taxes payable under this Part and Part I.1" to "total tax payable under this Part".

128.1(5) added by 2001 technical bill, for changes in residence after Oct. 1, 1996.

(6) Returning former resident — If an individual (other than a trust) becomes resident in Canada at a particular time in a taxation year and the last time (in this subsection referred to as the "emigration time"), before the particular time, at which the individual ceased to be resident in Canada was after October 1, 1996,

(a) subject to paragraph (b), if the individual so elects in writing and files the election with the Minister on or before the individual's filing-due date for the year, paragraphs (4)(b) and (c) do not apply to the individual's cessation of residence at the emigration time in respect of all properties that were taxable Canadian properties of the individual throughout the period that began at the emigration time and that ends at the particular time;

(b) where, if a property in respect of which an election under paragraph (a) is made had been acquired by the individual at the emigration time at a cost equal to its fair market value at the emigration time and had been disposed of by the individual immediately before the particular time for proceeds of disposition equal to its fair market value immediately before the particular time, the application of subsection 40(3.7) would reduce the amount that would, but for that subsection and this subsection, be the individual's loss from the disposition,

(i) the individual is deemed to have disposed of the property at the time of disposition (within the meaning assigned by paragraph (4)(b)) in respect of the emigration time for proceeds of disposition equal to the total of

(A) the adjusted cost base to the individual of the property immediately before the time of disposition, and

(B) the amount, if any, by which that reduction exceeds the lesser of

(I) the adjusted cost base to the individual of the property immediately before the time of disposition, and

(II) the amount, if any, that the individual specifies for the purposes of this paragraph in the election under paragraph (a) in respect of the property,

(ii) the individual is deemed to have reacquired the property at the emigration time at a cost equal to the amount, if any, by which the amount determined under clause (i)(A) exceeds the lesser of that reduction and the amount specified by the individual under subclause (i)(B)(II), and

(iii) for the purpose of section 119, the individual is deemed to have disposed of the property immediately before the particular time;

(c) if the individual so elects in writing and files the election with the Minister on or before the individual's filing-due date for the year, in respect of each property that the individual owned throughout the period that began at the emigration time and that ends at the particular time and that is deemed by paragraph (1)(b) to have been disposed of because the individual became resident in Canada, notwithstanding paragraphs (1)(c) and (4)(b) the individual's proceeds of disposition at the time of disposition (within the meaning assigned by paragraph (4)(b)), and the individual's cost of acquiring the property at the particular time, are deemed to be those proceeds and that cost, determined without reference to this paragraph, minus the least of

(i) the amount that would, but for this paragraph, have been the individual's gain from the disposition of the property deemed by paragraph (4)(b) to have occurred,

(ii) the fair market value of the property at the particular time, and

(iii) the amount that the individual specifies for the purposes of this paragraph in the election; and

(d) notwithstanding subsections 152(4) to (5), any assessment of tax that is payable under this Act by the individual for any taxation year that is before the year that includes the particular time and that is not before the year that includes the emigration time shall be made that is necessary to take an election under this subsection into account, except that no such assessment shall affect the computation of

(i) interest payable under this Act to or by a taxpayer in respect of any period that is before the day on which the taxpayer's return of income for the taxation year that includes the particular time is filed, or

(ii) any penalty payable under this Act.

Related Provisions: 40(3.7) — Stop-loss rule applicable while non-resident; 128.1(7) — Returning trust beneficiary; 128.3 — Shares acquired on rollover deemed to be same shares for 128.1(6); 161(7)(a)(xi), 164(5)(h.02), 164(5.1) — Effect of carryback of loss; 220(3.2), Reg. 600(c) — Late filing of elections under (6)(a) and (c); 220(4.5)–(4.54) — Deferral of payment of tax on emigration.

Notes: In broad terms, 128.1(6) provides that an emigrant who returns to Canada at any time after emigration is no longer treated as having realized accrued gains on departure. Because there is no certain way of knowing which emigrants will return to Canada, this rule does not directly affect the obligations on emigration under 128.1(4). Rather, it allows the returning individual to retrospectively modify the obligations. As a practical matter, emigrants who plan to return can use the security provisions of 220(4.5) to defer payment of departure tax. In that case, the main effect of 128.1(6) will be to allow the security to be given back intact to the returning emigrant.

128.1(6) does not affect interest or penalties owing, including interest and penalties levied on taxes in respect of the individual's emigration (see 128.1(6)(d)(i), (ii)).

128.1(6)(b) is designed to prevent surplus-stripping. Without it, a resident of Canada could use a temporary period of non-residence to extract, as dividends subject only to low-rate withholding tax, value that represents accrued gains.

128.1(6) requires separate elections in respect of taxable Canadian property (para. (a)) and other property (para. (c)). The effects of the elections differ: the para. (a) election removes TCP from the deemed disposition and reacquisition on emigration, subject to special rules in para. (b); while the para. (c) election adjusts the emigration proceeds of disposition and the returning ACB of the other properties. Each election covers all property of the given sort, but the returning individual may choose to make only one election.

The property need not be TCP on re-immigration for 128.1(6) to apply: VIEWS doc 2013-0494871E5. See also Notes to 248(1)"taxable Canadian property" re the 2010 amendments to that definition.

If the individual is resident in Quebec, a 128.1(6) election must be copied to Revenu Québec: *Taxation Act* ss. 785.2.2, 21.4.6.

128.1(6) added by 2001 technical bill, for changes in residence after Oct. 1, 1996.

Regulations: 600(c) (late filing of elections under (6)(a) and (c)).

(6.1) Deemed taxable Canadian property — For the purposes of paragraph (6)(a), a property is deemed to be taxable Canadian property of the individual throughout the period that began at the emigration time and that ends at the particular time if

(a) the emigration time is before March 5, 2010; and

(b) the property was taxable Canadian property of the individual on March 4, 2010.

Notes: 128.1(6.1) added by 2010 budget bill #1, for determining TCP after March 4, 2010. This amendment was made in sync with narrowing 248(1)"taxable Canadian property". It provides grandfathering relief for individuals who emigrated before March 5, 2010 where the property was TCP before the amendments.

(7) Returning trust beneficiary — If an individual (other than a trust)

(a) becomes resident in Canada at a particular time in a taxation year,

(b) owns at the particular time a property that the individual last acquired on a trust distribution to which subsection 107(2) would, but for subsection 107(5), have applied and at a time (in this subsection referred to as the "distribution time") that was after October 1, 1996 and before the particular time, and

(c) was a beneficiary of the trust at the last time, before the particular time, at which the individual ceased to be resident in Canada,

the following rules apply:

(d) subject to paragraphs (e) and (f), if the individual and the trust jointly so elect in writing and file the election with the Minister on or before the earlier of their filing-due dates for their taxation years that include the particular time, subsection 107(2.1) does not apply to the distribution in respect of all properties acquired by the individual on the distribution that were taxable Canadian properties of the individual throughout the period that began at the distribution time and that ends at the particular time,

(e) paragraph (f) applies in respect of the individual, the trust and a property in respect of which an election under paragraph (d) is made where, if the individual

(i) had been resident in Canada at the distribution time,

(ii) had acquired the property at the distribution time at a cost equal to its fair market value at that time,

(iii) had ceased to be resident in Canada immediately after the distribution time, and

(iv) had, immediately before the particular time, disposed of the property for proceeds of disposition equal to its fair market value immediately before the particular time,

the application of subsection 40(3.7) would reduce the amount that would, but for that subsection and this subsection, have been the individual's loss from the disposition,

(f) where this paragraph applies in respect of an individual, a trust and a property,

(i) notwithstanding paragraph 107(2.1)(a), the trust is deemed to have disposed of the property at the distribution time for proceeds of disposition equal to the total of

(A) the cost amount to the trust of the property immediately before the distribution time, and

(B) the amount, if any, by which the reduction under subsection 40(3.7) described in paragraph (e) exceeds the lesser of

(I) the cost amount to the trust of the property immediately before the distribution time, and

(II) the amount, if any, which the individual and the trust jointly specify for the purposes of this paragraph in the election under paragraph (d) in respect of the property, and

(ii) notwithstanding paragraph 107(2.1)(b), the individual is deemed to have acquired the property at the distribution time at a cost equal to the amount, if any, by which the amount otherwise determined under paragraph 107(2)(b) exceeds the lesser of the reduction under subsection 40(3.7) described in paragraph (e) and the amount specified under subclause (i)(B)(II),

(g) if the individual and the trust jointly so elect in writing and file the election with the Minister on or before the later of their filing-due dates for their taxation years that include the particular time, in respect of each property that the individual owned throughout the period that began at the distribution time and that ends at the particular time and that is deemed by paragraph (1)(b) to have been disposed of because the individual became resident in Canada, notwithstanding paragraphs 107(2.1)(a) and (b), the trust's proceeds of disposition under paragraph 107(2.1)(a) at the distribution time, and the individual's cost of acquiring the property at the particular time, are deemed to be those proceeds and that cost determined without reference to this paragraph, minus the least of

(i) the amount that would, but for this paragraph, have been the trust's gain from the disposition of the property deemed by paragraph 107(2.1)(a) to have occurred,

(ii) the fair market value of the property at the particular time, and

(iii) the amount that the individual and the trust jointly specify for the purposes of this paragraph in the election,

(h) if the trust ceases to exist before the individual's filing-due date for the individual's taxation year that includes the particular time,

(i) an election or specification described in this subsection may be made by the individual alone in writing if the election is filed with the Minister on or before that filing-due date, and

(ii) if the individual alone makes such an election or specification, the individual and the trust are jointly and severally, or solidarily, liable for any amount payable under this Act by the trust as a result of the election or specification, and

(i) notwithstanding subsections 152(4) to (5), such assessment of tax payable under the Act by the trust or the individual for any year that is before the year that includes the particular time and that is not before the year that includes the distribution time shall be made as is necessary to take an election under this subsection into account, except that no such assessment shall affect the computation of

(i) interest payable under this Act to or by the trust or the individual in respect of any period that is before the individual's filing-due date for the taxation year that includes the particular time, or

(ii) any penalty payable under this Act.

Related Provisions: 40(3.7) — Stop-loss rule applicable while non-resident; 128.1(6) — Returning former resident; 128.3 — Shares acquired on rollover deemed to be same shares for 128.1(7); 161(7)(a)(xi), 164(5)(h.02), 164(5.1) — Effect of carryback of loss; 220(3.2), Reg. 600(c) — Late filing of elections under (7)(d) and (g); 220(4.5)–(4.54) — Deferral of payment of tax on emigration.

Notes: This subsection is modelled on 128.1(6); see Notes thereto.

If the individual or the trust is resident in Quebec, a 128.1(7)(d) or (g) election must be copied to Revenu Québec: *Taxation Act* ss. 785.2.3, 21.4.6.

128.1(7)(h)(ii) amended by 2002-2013 technical bill (Part 4 — bijuralism), effective June 26, 2013, to add "or solidarily".

128.1(7) added by 2001 technical bill, effective for changes in residence that occur after October 1, 1996 (an election under para. (d) or (g) could be made by the individual's filing-due date for the taxation year that included June 14, 2001).

Regulations: 600(c) (late filed elections under (7)(d), (g)).

(8) Post-emigration loss — If an individual (other than a trust)

(a) was deemed by paragraph (4)(b) to have disposed of a capital property at any particular time after October 1, 1996,

(b) has disposed of the property at a later time at which the property was a taxable Canadian property of the individual, and

(c) so elects in writing in the individual's return of income for the taxation year that includes the later time,

there shall, except for the purpose of paragraph (4)(c), be deducted from the individual's proceeds of disposition of the property at the particular time, and added to the individual's proceeds of disposition of the property at the later time, an amount equal to the least of

(d) the amount specified in respect of the property in the election,

(e) the amount that would, but for the election, be the individual's gain from the disposition of the property at the particular time, and

(f) the amount that would be the individual's loss from the disposition of the property at the later time, if the loss were determined having reference to every other provision of this Act including, for greater certainty, subsection 40(3.7) and section 112, but without reference to the election.

Related Provisions: 128.3 — Shares acquired on rollover deemed to be same shares for 128.1(7); 152(6)(f.2) — Minister required to reassess past year to allow unused foreign tax credit; 161(7)(a)(xi), 164(5)(h.02), 164(5.1) — Effect of carryback of loss; 220(3.2), Reg. 600(c) — Late filing of election under (8)(c).

Notes: 128.1(8) provides relief where X disposes of TCP, after emigrating from Canada, for proceeds less than the 128.1(4)(b) deemed proceeds on emigration. X may elect to reduce the deemed gain to reflect the later loss. The elected amount is added to X's proceeds on the actual disposition.

Due to the 2010 amendments to 248(1)"taxable Canadian property", 128.1(8) cannot be used for shares in private corps that drop in value after emigration.

In CRA's view, the right to force a 128.1(8) reassessment is limited to 3 years after the statute-barred deadline, due to 152(4)(b)(i) and 152(6)(f.2): doc 2010-0353711E5; and 128.1(8) does not apply to property that was TCP on emigration but is no longer TCP on disposition: 2013-0486321E5.

If the individual is resident in Quebec, a 128.1(8) election must be copied to Revenu Québec: *Taxation Act* ss. 785.2.4, 21.4.6.

128.1(8) (128.1(7) in the Dec. 17, 1999 draft legislation) added by 2001 technical bill, for residence changes after Oct. 1, 1996.

Regulations: 600(c) (late filed elections under (8)(c)).

(9) Information reporting — An individual who ceases at a particular time in a taxation year to be resident in Canada, and who owns immediately after the particular time one or more reportable properties the total fair market value of which at the particular time is greater than $25,000, shall file with the Minister in prescribed form, on or before the individual's filing-due date for the year, a list of all the reportable properties that the individual owned immediately after the particular time.

Related Provisions: 128.1(10)"reportable property" — Exclusions.

Notes: A life insurance policyholder should report the fair market value of the policy (Information Circular 89-3 paras. 40-41) rather than its cash surrender value: VIEWS doc 2008-0270401C6.

128.1(9) added by 2001 technical bill, for changes in residence that occur after 1995.

Forms: T1161: List of properties by an emigrant of Canada.

(10) Definitions — The definitions in this subsection apply in this section.

"excluded right or interest" of a taxpayer who is an individual means

(a) a right of the individual under, or an interest of the individual in a trust governed by,

(i) a registered retirement savings plan or a plan referred to in subsection 146(12) as an "amended plan",

(ii) a registered retirement income fund,

(iii) a registered education savings plan,

(iii.1) a registered disability savings plan,

(iii.2) a TFSA,

(iv) a deferred profit sharing plan or a plan referred to in subsection 147(15) as a "revoked plan",

(v) an employees profit sharing plan,

(vi) an employee benefit plan (other than a plan described in subparagraph (b)(i) or (ii)), (vi.1) an employee life and health trust,

(vii) a plan or arrangement (other than an employee benefit plan) under which the individual has a right to receive in a year remuneration in respect of services rendered by the individual in the year or a prior year,

(viii) a superannuation or pension fund or plan (other than an employee benefit plan),

(ix) a retirement compensation arrangement,

(x) a foreign retirement arrangement, or

(xi) a registered supplementary unemployment benefit plan;

(b) a right of the individual to a benefit under an employee benefit plan that is

(i) a plan or arrangement described in paragraph (j) of the definition "salary deferral arrangement" in subsection 248(1) that would, but for paragraphs (j) and (k) of that definition, be a salary deferral arrangement, or

(ii) a plan or arrangement that would, but for paragraph 6801(c) of the *Income Tax Regulations*, be a salary deferral arrangement,

to the extent that the benefit can reasonably be considered to be attributable to services rendered by the individual in Canada;

(c) a right of the individual under an agreement referred to in subsection 7(1);

(d) a right of the individual to a retiring allowance;

(e) a right of the individual under, or an interest of the individual in, a trust that is

(i) an employee trust,

(ii) an amateur athlete trust,

(iii) a cemetery care trust, or

(iv) a trust governed by an eligible funeral arrangement;

(f) a right of the individual to receive a payment under

(i) an annuity contract, or

(ii) an income-averaging annuity contract;

(g) a right of the individual to a benefit under

(i) the *Canada Pension Plan* or a provincial plan described in section 3 of that Act,

(ii) the *Old Age Security Act*, or

(iii) [Repealed]

(iv) a plan or arrangement instituted by the social security legislation of a country other than Canada or of a state, province or other political subdivision of such a country;

(h) a right of the individual to a benefit described in any of subparagraphs 56(1)(a)(iii) to (vi);

(i) a right of the individual to a payment out of a NISA Fund No. 2;

(j) an interest of the individual in a personal trust resident in Canada if the interest was never acquired for consideration and did not arise as a consequence of a qualifying disposition by the individual (within the meaning that would be assigned by subsection 107.4(1) if that subsection were read without reference to paragraphs 107.4(1)(h) and (i));

(k) an interest of the individual in a non-resident testamentary trust that is an estate that arose on and as a consequence of a death if

(i) the interest was never acquired for consideration, and

(ii) the estate has been in existence for no more than 36 months; or

(l) an interest of the individual in a life insurance policy in Canada, except for that part of the policy in respect of which the individual is deemed by paragraph 138.1(1)(e) to have an interest in a related segregated fund trust.

Related Provisions: 108(6) — Where terms of trust are varied; 108(7) — Meaning of "acquired for consideration"; 128.1(1)(b)(iv) — No deemed disposition on immigra-

tion; 128.1(4)(b)(iii) — No deemed disposition on emigration; 128.1(4)(d.1) — Where share acquired under stock option before emigration; 128.1(10)"reportable property" — No requirement to report most excluded personal property; 135.2(4)(e)(ii) — Cdn Wheat Board Farmers' Trust unit deemed not to fall within definition; 146(21.2) — Sask. Pension Plan account deemed to be RRSP for purposes of (a)(i); 147.5(12) — Pooled registered pension plan deemed to be RRSP for purposes of (a)(i).

Notes: Subpara. (a)(i) also applies to a PRPP (147.5(12)) and a Sask. Pension Plan account: 146(21.2).

For interpretation of (a)(vii) see VIEWS doc 2008-0280301I7; for (c), see 2013-0487961E5; for (j) and (k), see 2003-0019531E5, 2007-0235231C6. A disability insurance policy does not fall within this definition (and does not necessarily have zero value): 2010-0359411C6.

In (g)(i), "provincial plan" should be "provincial pension plan". This has been pointed out to Finance.

Para. (k) amended by 2014 budget bill #2, for 2016 and later taxation years, to be consistent with new 248(1)"graduated rate estate". For 1997-2015, read:

(k) an interest of the individual in a non-resident testamentary trust if the interest was never acquired for consideration; or

Subpara. (g)(iii), "a provincial pension plan prescribed for the purpose of paragraph 60(v)" (i.e. the Saskatchewan Pension Plan), repealed by 2011 budget bill #2, effective for taxation years that begin after 2009. 146(21.2) now provides the same rule.

Subpara. (a)(vi.1) added by 2010 budget bill #2, effective 2010.

Subpara. (a)(iii.2) added by 2008 budget bill #1, effective for 2009 and later taxation years. Subpara. (a)(iii.1) added by 2007 RDSPs bill, for 2008 and later taxation years. 128.1(10)"excluded right or interest" added by 2001 technical bill, effective for changes in residence that occur after Oct. 1, 1996.

"reportable property" of an individual at a particular time means any property other than

(a) money that is legal tender in Canada and deposits of such money;

(b) property that would be an excluded right or interest of the individual if the definition "excluded right or interest" in this subsection were read without reference to paragraphs (c), (j) and (l) of that definition;

(c) if the individual is not a trust and was not, during the 120-month period that ends at the particular time, resident in Canada for more than 60 months, property described in subparagraph (4)(b)(iv) that is not taxable Canadian property; and

(d) any item of personal-use property the fair market value of which, at the particular time, is less than $10,000.

Notes: 128.1(10)"reportable property" added by 2001 technical bill, effective for changes in residence that occur after 1995. This definition was in 128.1(9) in the draft legislation of Dec. 17, 1999.

Notes [s. 128.1]: 128.1 added by 1993 technical bill, effective January 1, 1993 (or earlier by election, for a corporation). It replaced s. 48.

Definitions [s. 128.1]: "acquired for consideration" — 108(7); "adjusted cost base" — 54, 248(1); "amateur athlete trust" — 143.1(1.2)(a), 248(1); "amount", "annuity" — 248(1); "arm's length" — 251(1); "assessment", "balance-due day" — 248(1); "beneficiary" — 248(25) [Notes]; "business" — 248(1); "Canada" — 255, *Interpretation Act* 35(1); "Canadian exploration and development expenses", "Canadian resource property" — 66(15), 248(1); "capital property" — 54, 248(1); "cemetery care trust" — 148.1(1), 248(1); "class of shares" — 248(6); "consideration" — 108(7); "controlled" — 212.3(15), (26), 256(6)–(9); "controlled foreign affiliate" — 95(1), 248(1); "corporation" — 248(1), *Interpretation Act* 35(1); "cost amount" — 248(1); "deferred profit sharing plan" — 147(1), 248(1); "disposition" — 248(1); "distribution time" — 128.1(7)(b); "dividend" — 248(1); "eligible capital property" — 54, 248(1); "eligible funeral arrangement" — 148.1(1), 248(1); "emigration time" — 128.1(6); "employee benefit plan" — 248(1); "employee life and health trust" — 144.1(2), 248(1); "employee trust" — 248(1); "employees profit sharing plan" — 144(1), 248(1); "excluded right or interest" — 128.1(10); "fair market value" — see 69(1) Notes; "farm loss" — 111(8), 248(1); "filing-due date" — 248(1); "fiscal period" — 249.1; "foreign accrual property income" — 95(1), (2), 248(1); "foreign affiliate" — 93.1(1), 95(1), 248(1); "foreign retirement arrangement" — 248(1), Reg 6803; "group of parents" — 128.1(1)(c.3); "immovable" — Quebec *Civil Code* art. 900–907; "income-averaging annuity contract", "individual", "inventory" — 248(1); "life insurance policy in Canada" — 138(12), 248(1); "limited partnership loss" — 96(2.1), 248(1); "Minister" — 248(1); "month" — *Interpretation Act* 35(1); "NISA Fund No. 2" — 248(1); "net capital loss", "non-capital loss" — 111(8), 248(1); "non-resident" — 248(1); "paid-up capital" — 89(1), 248(1); "paid-up capital adjustment" — 128.1(2)(a); "parent" — 128.1(1)(c.3); "partnership" — see 96(1) Notes; "permanent establishment" — Reg. 8201; "person", "personal trust" — 248(1); "personal-use property" — 54, 248(1); "prescribed" — 248(1); "proceeds of disposition" — 54; "property" — 248(1); "province" — *Interpretation Act* 35(1); "provincial plan" — *Canada Pension Plan* s. 3(1)"provincial pension plan"; "registered disability savings plan" — 146.4(1), 248(1); "registered education savings plan" — 146.1(1), 248(1); "registered retirement income fund" — 146.3(1), 248(1); "registered retirement savings plan" — 146(1), 248(1); "registered supplementary unemployment benefit plan" — 145(1), 248(1); "regulation" — 248(1); "related segregated fund trust" — 138.1(1)(a); "reportable property" — 248(1); "resident in Canada" — 94(3)(a), 250; "restricted farm loss" — 31(1.1), 248(1); "retirement compensation arrangement", "retiring allowance", "salary deferral arrangement" — 248(1); "series of transactions" — 248(10); "share", "shareholder", "specified future tax consequence" — 248(1); "TFSA" — 146.2(5), 248(1); "taxable Canadian property" — 248(1); "taxation year" — 249, 250.1(a); "taxpayer" — 248(1); "timber resource property" — 13(21), 248(1); "time of disposition" — 128.1(1)(b), 128.1(4)(b); "treaty-protected property" — 248(1); "trust" — 104(1), 248(1), (3); "writing" — *Interpretation Act* 35(1).

128.2 (1) Cross-border mergers

128.2 (1) Cross-border mergers — Where a corporation formed at a particular time by the amalgamation or merger of, or by a plan of arrangement or other corporate reorganization in respect of, 2 or more corporations (each of which is referred to in this section as a "predecessor") is at the particular time resident in Canada, a predecessor that was not immediately before the particular time resident in Canada shall be deemed to have become resident in Canada immediately before the particular time.

(2) Idem — Where a corporation formed at a particular time by the amalgamation or merger of, or by a plan of arrangement or other corporate reorganization in respect of, 2 or more corporations is at the particular time not resident in Canada, a predecessor that was immediately before the particular time resident in Canada shall be deemed to have ceased to be resident in Canada immediately before the particular time.

(3) Windings-up excluded — For greater certainty, subsections (1) and (2) do not apply to reorganizations occurring solely because of the acquisition of property of one corporation by another corporation, pursuant to the purchase of the property by the other corporation or because of the distribution of the property to the other corporation on the winding-up of the corporation.

Notes [s. 128.2]: 128.2 added by 1993 technical bill, effective January 1, 1993 (or earlier by election).

Definitions [s. 128.2]: "corporation" — 248(1), *Interpretation Act* 35(1); "predecessor" — 128.2(1); "property" — 248(1); "resident in Canada" — 250.

128.3 Former resident — replaced shares

128.3 Former resident — replaced shares — If, in a transaction to which section 51, subparagraphs 85.1(1)(a)(i) and (ii), subsection 85.1(8) or section 86 or 87 applies, a person acquires a share (in this section referred to as the "new share") in exchange for another share or equity in a SIFT wind-up entity (in this section referred to as the "old share"), for the purposes of section 119, subsections 126(2.21) to (2.23), subparagraph 128.1(4)(b)(iv) and subsections 128.1(6) to (8), 180.1(1.4) and 220(4.5) and (4.6), the person is deemed not to have disposed of the old share, and the new share is deemed to be the same share as the old share.

Notes: 128.3 applies to new shares received in exchange for old shares on a tax-deferred basis under one of the listed rollover provisions. For the purposes of those provisions, the individual is deemed not to have disposed of the old shares, and the new shares are deemed to be the old shares. This ensures that the relief available under these provisions is not lost as a result of such a share-for-share exchange. Note that s. 85 is not included in the list of provisions that qualify; submissions have been made to Finance to add it.

128.3 amended by 2002-2013 technical bill (Part 5 — technical), for taxation years that begin after 2001, to add reference to 128.1(4)(b)(iv) (and preserving earlier amendments effective Dec. 20, 2007). This implements a June 2, 2003 Finance comfort letter.

128.3 amended by 2008 budget bill #2, effective Dec. 20, 2007, to add reference to 85.1(8) and "or equity in a SIFT wind-up entity". See Notes to 85.1(8).

128.3 added by 2001 technical bill, effective October 2, 1996.

Definitions [s. 128.3]: "new share", "old share" — 128.3; "person", "SIFT wind-up entity", "share" — 248(1).

Private Corporations

129. (1) Dividend refund to private corporation

129. (1) Dividend refund to private corporation — Where a return of a corporation's income under this Part for a taxation year is made within 3 years after the end of the year, the Minister

(a) may, on sending the notice of assessment for the year, refund without application an amount (in this Act referred to as its "div-idend refund" for the year) in respect of taxable dividends paid by the corporation on shares of its capital stock in the year, and at a time when it was a private corporation, equal to the total of

(i) in respect of eligible dividends, an amount equal to the lesser of

(A) $38\frac{1}{3}\%$ of the total of all eligible dividends paid by it in the year, and

(B) its eligible refundable dividend tax on hand at the end of the year, and

(ii) in respect of taxable dividends (other than eligible dividends), an amount equal to the total of

(A) the lesser of

(I) $38\frac{1}{3}\%$ of the total of all taxable dividends (other than eligible dividends) paid by it in the year, and

(II) its non-eligible refundable dividend tax on hand at the end of the year, and

(B) either

(I) if the amount determined under subclause (A)(I) exceeds the amount determined under subclause (A)(II), the lesser of

1 the amount of the excess, and

2 the amount by which the corporation's eligible refundable dividend tax on hand at the end of the year exceeds the amount, if any, determined under subparagraph (i) for the year, and

(II) in any other case, nil; and

(b) shall, with all due dispatch, make the dividend refund after sending the notice of assessment if an application for it has been made in writing by the corporation within the period within which the Minister would be allowed under subsection 152(4) to assess tax payable under this Part by the corporation for the year if that subsection were read without reference to paragraph 152(4)(a).

Related Provisions: 129(1.2) — Anti-avoidance; 129(2) — Application to other liability; 129(4)"non-eligible refundable dividend tax on hand"(a)(i)B(A), (a)(ii)(B) — Effect on dividend refund; 131(5) — Mutual fund corporation deemed to be a private corporation; 141.1 — Insurance corporation deemed not to be private corporation; 152(1)(a) — Determination of refund by Minister; 157(3) — Reduction in instalment obligations to reflect dividend refund; 160.1 — Where excess refunded; 186(5) — Deemed private corp — non-private corp controlled by individual or related group; 244(14), (14.1) — Date when notice sent; 260(7) — Securities lending arrangement — amount deemed paid as a taxable dividend; 260(11)(c) — Amounts deemed paid where partnership of corps enters into securities lending arrangement; 261(7)(a) — Functional currency reporting; *Interpretation Act* 27(5) — Meaning of "within 3 years".

Notes: The dividend refund is a refund of the temporary high corporate tax on income from property, including interest and rental income: see 129(4)"aggregate investment income", "eligible refundable dividend tax on hand" and "non-eligible refundable dividend tax on hand", and Notes to 123.3 and 186(1). Since 2016, the refund rate is 38 1/3% of the dividend paid out, so that, of $100 of corporate income, the dividend refund of $30.67 (see 129(4)"non-eligible refundable dividend tax on hand"(a)(i)A) will be refunded once $80 in dividends is paid ($30.67 / .38333). The $80 is what remains after 20% corporate tax, reflecting the expected refund. The up-front corporate tax is $40 (presumed federal/provincial rate of 40%, though the actual rate is now much lower) plus $10.67 under s. 123.3, or $50.67. That leaves the corporation with $49.33 which, added to the $30.67 dividend refund, gives the corporation $80 to pay out as a dividend. Once the corporation receives the dividend refund of $30.67, its total tax is reduced to $20 — the rate at which the dividend gross-up under 82(1) and the dividend tax credit under 121 lead to full integration (for 89(1)"low rate income pool"). Before 2016, the refund rate was 33.33%, and the 123.3 tax rate was 6.67% instead of 10.67%, reflecting the pre-2016 top federal rate of 29% in 117(2).

The 2018 Budget split RDTOH into "eligible" and "non-eligible" refundable dividend tax on hand (both defined in 129(4)), depending on whether the dividend giving rise to the RDTOH was an eligible dividend (89(1)), taxed at a high corporate rate and thus eligible for higher dividend tax credit under 121. This change was done in sync with introducing 125(5.1)(b) to grind down the small business deduction for corps with passive income over $50,000/year. These changes replace the July 18, 2017 proposals to tax private corps' passive income at a high rate (see under 123.3). See also Baxter, "The New Passive Income Rules", 2017 Cdn Tax Foundation conference report at 13:8-17; Infanti et al., "Getting a Grip on New Passive Investment Rules", 67(4) *Canadian Tax Journal* 1267-85 (2019); Maheux, "Dividend Payment Trap: ERDTOH Converted to NERDTOH", 11(1) *Canadian Tax Focus* (ctf.ca) 3 (Feb. 2021) (if corp pays eligible dividends to one corp and non-eligible to another in same tax year).

A private corp that is a 135.1 co-op or 136(2) co-op can qualify, but another co-op cannot: VIEWS doc 2013-0510751E5.

See Notes to 248(1)"dividend" re paying a dividend by promissory note.

See Notes to 152(1) on the meaning of "all due dispatch".

An overpaid dividend refund can be recovered by CRA under 160.1(1).

On calculating the dividend refund on cross-redemptions of shares between connected corporations, see VIEWS doc 2013-050841117.

A corp can in theory choose not to claim the dividend refund and carry pre-dividend RDTOH forward, which can create planning opportunities, but CRA policy is to pay it automatically: VIEWS doc 2016-0649841E5; Cherniawsky, "Are Dividend Refund Claims by Dividend-Paying Corporations Elective?", 17(4) *Tax for the Owner-Manager* (ctf.ca) 9-10 (Oct. 2017).

CRA's view is that a denied dividend refund can be disputed on a nil assessment: doc 2011-0420751E5 (March 2012, overruling a Nov. 2011 letter with the same document number — the author of the March 2012 letter has confirmed this). This is because, for purposes of 152(1.2), the denial is a "determination" under 152(1)(a) that the dividend refund is nil (see also Notes to 152(1.1)).

If the 3-year deadline is missed: 129(1) is inoperative and no refund can be paid: *1057513 Ontario Inc.*, 2015 FCA 207; *Tawa Developments*, 2011 TCC 440, para. 25; *Ottawa Ritz Hotel*, 2012 TCC 166; *Nacom Inc.*, 2013 TCC 90, para. 5; *Duplessis*, 2016 FCA 264. CRA cannot transfer the refund to another year under 221.2, because a dividend refund is not "an amount that was appropriated to a debt". However, *Bonnybrook Industrial*, 2018 FCA 136 (reversing *Binder Capital*, 2017 FC 642), held that CRA has discretion to extend the deadline under 220(3) (and left open whether CRA can also use 220(2.1)), overruling VIEWS docs 2011-040570117, 2011-042129117, 2011-0426331E5, 2013-049942117.

If the deadline is missed, no rectification appears possible, since rectification (see Notes to 169(1)) applies only to matters under provincial law. "We cannot envision a situation in which an action, whether a rectification order or other action, would enable a taxpayer to obtain a dividend refund beyond the period described": CRA, May 2011 ICAA roundtable (tinyurl.com/cra-abtax), q. 2.

See also Wilson, "The Problem with Dividend Refunds", 11(3) *Tax for the Owner-Manager [TfOM]* (ctf.ca) 1-2 (July 2011) and 12(1) 4-5 (Jan. 2012); Stedman, "Intercorporate Dividend Planning", 20(1) *TfOM* 7-8 (Jan. 2020). (See also Notes to 164(1), which has the same 3-year deadline.)

If no dividend refund is paid because the deadline expired, the RDTOH is not reduced: *1057513 Ontario* (FCA, above), para. 6, confirming the TCC's view in *Tawa* (above); *Ottawa Ritz* (above); *Presidential MSH*, 2015 TCC 61; *Nanica Holdings*, 2015 TCC 85. The CRA now accepts this (overriding docs 2002-0132427, 2004-0098611E5, 2012-0436181E5), and also says the dividend recipient is not subject to Part IV tax if the payer gets no dividend refund because the deadline expired: 2015-0595591C6 [2015 APFF q.8]; 2015-0610691C6 [2015 CTF q.1].

See also Notes to 186(1).

129(1)(a) amended by 2018 budget bill #1 as described above, effective on the same basis as 87(2)(aa) amendment (taxation years that begin after 2018, but earlier if planning was used to try to trigger a year-end before 125(5.1)(b) applied). Before the amendment, read:

(a) may, on sending the notice of assessment for the year, refund without application an amount (in this Act referred to as its "dividend refund" for the year) equal to the lesser of

(i) 38⅓% of all taxable dividends paid by the corporation on shares of its capital stock in the year and at a time when it was a private corporation, and

(ii) its refundable dividend tax on hand at the end of the year; and

129(1)(a)(i) amended to change "1/3" to "38 1/3%" by 2016 tax-rate bill, for taxation years that end after 2015, except that for such years that begin before 2016, read "38 1/3%" as "33 1/3% + 5%(A/B), where A is the number of days in the taxation year that are after 2015, and B is the total number of days in the taxation year". (In other words, the increase from 33 1/3% to 38 1/3% is prorated based on the number of days after 2015.) This increase is consequential on the top marginal rate increase from 29% to 33% in 117(2).

129(1) amended by 2010 budget bill #2 (effective Dec. 15, 2010), 1995 Budget, 1992 technical bill and 1989 Budget.

Interpretation Bulletins: IT-243R4: Dividend refund to private corporations; IT-432R2: Benefits conferred on shareholders.

(1.1) Dividends paid to bankrupt controlling corporation
— In determining the dividend refund for a taxation year ending after 1977 of a particular corporation, no amount may be included under clause (1)(a)(i)(A), subclause (1)(a)(ii)(A)(I) or subsubclause (1)(a)(ii)(B)(I)1 in respect of a taxable dividend paid to a shareholder that

(a) was a corporation that controlled (within the meaning assigned by subsection 186(2)) the particular corporation at the time the dividend was paid; and

(b) was a bankrupt at any time during that taxation year of the particular corporation.

Notes: 129(1.1) opening words amended by 2018 budget bill #1 in consequence of the amendments to 129(1), effective on the same basis as those amendments (taxation years that begin after 2018, but earlier if planning was used to try to trigger a year-end before 125(5.1)(b) applied). Before the amendment, read "no amount may be included by virtue of subparagraph (1)(a)(i)".

129(1.1)(b) amended by 2017 budget bill #2 to delete "(within the meaning assigned by subsection 128(3))" after "bankrupt", for bankruptcies after April 26, 1995. ("Bankrupt" is now defined in 248(1).)

Interpretation Bulletins: IT-243R4: Dividend refund to private corporations.

(1.2) Dividends deemed not to be taxable dividends
— Where a dividend is paid on a share of the capital stock of a corporation and the share (or another share for which the share was substituted) was acquired by its holder in a transaction or as part of a series of transactions one of the main purposes of which was to enable the corporation to obtain a dividend refund, the dividend shall, for the purpose of subsection (1), be deemed not to be a taxable dividend.

Related Provisions: 87(2)(aa), (ii) — Amalgamations; 129(7) — Capital gains dividend excluded; 248(10) — Series of transactions. See additional Related Provisions at end of s. 129.

Notes: 129(1.2) was held not to apply in *Canwest Capital*, [1996] 1 C.T.C. 2974 (TCC), as the corporate structure was set up for business reasons (and Bell J. criticized 129(1.2) as not "capable of ready comprehension"). See also Notes to 83(2.1) on "one of the main purposes".

See also Anthony Strawson, "When Does Subsection 129(1.2) Apply to Deny a Dividend Refund?", 17(3) *Tax for the Owner-Manager* (ctf.ca) 7-8 (July 2017).

For CRA interpretation on 129(1.2) see docs 2004-0088551R3 (does not apply to reorg that did not shift shareholdings so as to put dividends in the hands of a tax-exempt person); 2008-0296371E5 (applies); 2011-0416001R3 (does not apply on split-up butterfly); 2005 STEP Conference Roundtable q.3 (www.step.ca); 2013-0480361C6 [2013 STEP conf. q. 12] (application of purpose test in 129(1.2) depends on specific facts; if test is met, 129(1.2) can deny dividend refund to payer corp even if tax was paid by shareholder on dividend); 2016-0628181R3 and 2020-0851991C6 [2020 APFF Financial q.3] [Wen, "Dividend Refund Denied Upon Redemption of Donated Private Company Shares", 8(2) *Canadian Tax Focus* (ctf.ca) 11-12 (May 2018)].

Interpretation Bulletins: IT-243R4: Dividend refund to private corporations.

(2) Application to other liability
— Instead of making a refund that might otherwise be made under subsection (1), the Minister may, where the corporation is liable or about to become liable to make any payment under this Act, apply the amount that would otherwise be refundable to that other liability and notify the corporation of that action.

Related Provisions: 222(1)"action" — Ten-year limitation period applies to 129(2).

Interpretation Bulletins: IT-243R4: Dividend refund to private corporations.

(2.1) Interest on dividend refund
— Where a dividend refund for a taxation year is paid to, or applied to a liability of, a corporation, the Minister shall pay or apply interest on the refund at the prescribed rate for the period beginning on the day that is the later of

(a) the day that is 120 days after the end of the year, and

(b) the day that is 30 days after the day on which the corporation's return of income under this Part for the year was filed under section 150, unless the return was filed on or before the day on or before which it was required to be filed,

and ending on the day on which the refund is paid or applied.

Related Provisions: 161.1 — Offset of refund interest against arrears interest.

Notes: 129(2.1)(b) appears to have a drafting error: Madden, "Dividend Refund: A Matter of Interest", 7(3) *Tax for the Owner-Manager* (ctf.ca) 5-6 (July 2007).

129(2.1)(b) amended by 2003 Budget, for tax years that end after June 2003, to add "the day that is 30 days after".

129(2.1) added by 1992 technical bill, effective for dividend refunds paid or applied in respect of taxation years that begin after 1991.

Regulations: 4301(b) (prescribed rate of interest).

(2.2) Excess interest on dividend refund
— Where, at any particular time, interest has been paid to, or applied to a liability of, a corporation under subsection (2.1) in respect of a dividend refund and it is determined at a subsequent time that the dividend refund

was less than that in respect of which interest was so paid or applied,

(a) the amount by which the interest that was so paid or applied exceeds the interest, if any, computed in respect of the amount that is determined at the subsequent time to be the dividend refund shall be deemed to be an amount (in this subsection referred to as the "amount payable") that became payable under this Part by the corporation at the particular time;

(b) the corporation shall pay to the Receiver General interest at the prescribed rate on the amount payable, computed from the particular time to the day of payment; and

(c) the Minister may at any time assess the corporation in respect of the amount payable and, where the Minister makes such an assessment, the provisions of Divisions I and J apply, with such modifications as the circumstances require, in respect of the assessment as though it had been made under section 152.

Related Provisions: 20(1)(ll) — Deduction on repayment of interest; 161.1 — Offset of refund interest against arrears interest; 221.1 — Application of interest where legislation retroactive; 248(11) — Interest compounded daily.

Notes: 129(2.2) added by 1992 technical bill, effective for dividend refunds paid or applied in respect of taxation years that begin after 1991.

Regulations: 4301(a) (prescribed rate of interest).

(3) [Repealed — definition of "refundable dividend tax on hand"]

Related Provisions: 129(3.1) — Grandfathering for property disposed of before November 13, 1981; 141.1 — Insurance corporation deemed not to be private corporation; 257 — Formula cannot calculate to less than zero; 260(11)(c) — Amounts deemed paid where partnership of corporations enters into securities lending arrangement.

Notes: 129(3) repealed by 2018 budget bill #1, as RDTOH was split into "eligible" and "non-eligible" RDTOH (see Notes to 129(1)). The repeal is effective on the same basis as 87(2)(aa) amendment (taxation years that begin after 2018, but earlier if planning was used to try to trigger a year-end before 125(5.1)(b) applied). 129(3) read:

(3) Definition of "refundable dividend tax on hand" — In this section, "refundable dividend tax on hand" of a corporation at the end of a taxation year means the amount, if any, by which the total of

(a) where the corporation was a Canadian-controlled private corporation throughout the year, the least of

(i) the amount determined by the formula

$$A - B$$

where

A   is 30⅔% of the corporation's aggregate investment income for the year, and

B   is the amount, if any, by which

(I) the amount deducted under subsection 126(1) from the tax for the year otherwise payable by it under this Part

exceeds

(II) 8% of its foreign investment income for the year,

(ii) 30⅔% of the amount, if any, by which the corporation's taxable income for the year exceeds the total of

(A) the least of the amounts determined under paragraphs 125(1)(a) to (c) in respect of the corporation for the year,

(B) 100/(38⅔) of the total of amounts deducted under subsection 126(1) from its tax for the year otherwise payable under this Part, and

(C) the amount determined by multiplying the total of amounts deducted under subsection 126(2) from its tax for the year otherwise payable under this Part, by the relevant factor for the year, and

(iii) the corporation's tax for the year payable under this Part,

(b) the total of the taxes under Part IV payable by the corporation for the year, and

(c) where the corporation was a private corporation at the end of its preceding taxation year, the corporation's refundable dividend tax on hand at the end of that preceding year

exceeds

(d) the corporation's dividend refund for its preceding taxation year.

RDTOH before 2019-2020: See Notes to 129(1) for the calculation of the dividend refund, and what happens if the return is filed late so no dividend refund is paid. The calculation of B factors in the effect of the foreign tax credit.

See Hoegner, "Refundable Dividend Tax on Hand and the Dividend Refund: Planning to Maximize the Tax Benefits", 52(4) *Canadian Tax Journal* 1217-36 (2004).

VIEWS doc 2007-0243231C6 states that RDTOH should not be counted in valuing a corp's shares for purposes of an estate freeze. However, RDTOH is relevant when valuing a company in a shareholder dispute: *Kruco inc. c. 3356175 Canada inc.*, 2008 QCCA 1158 [Landy, "Kruco Inc. — Round 3", xxx(18) *The Canadian Taxpayer* (Carswell) 137-39 (Sept. 9, 2008)].

On allocating RDTOH to a departing shareholder, see VIEWS doc 2007-0237361R3; Kandev & Shragie, "RDTOH on Butterfly", 16(11) *Canadian Tax Highlights* (ctf.ca) 2-3 (Nov. 2008).

129(3)(a)(i)A and (a)(ii) opening words amended to change "26⅔%" to "30⅔%" by 2016 tax-rate bill, for taxation years that end after 2015, except that for such years that begin before 2016, read "30⅔%" as "26⅔% + 4%(A/B)", where A is the number of days in the taxation year that are after 2015, and B is the total number of days in the taxation year". In other words, the rate is pro-rated between 26⅔% and 30⅔% based on the number of days in the year before and during 2016.

129(3)(a)(i)B(II) amended to change "9⅓%" to "8%" by 2016 tax-rate bill, for taxation years that end after 2015 except that for such years that begin before 2016, read "8%" as "9⅓% – 1⅓% (A/B)", where A is the number of days in the taxation year that are after 2015, and B is the total number of days in the taxation year". In other words, the rate is pro-rated between 9⅓% and 8% based on the number of days in the year before and during 2016.

129(3)(a)(ii)(B) amended to change "100/35" to "100/(38⅔)" by 2016 tax-rate bill, for taxation years that end after 2015 except that for such years that begin before 2016, read "100/(38⅔)" as "100/(35 + 3⅔(A/B))", where A is the number of days in the taxation year that are after 2015, and B is the total number of days in the taxation year". In other words, the fraction is pro-rated between 100/35 and 100/38.667 based on the number of days in the year before and during 2016.

129(3)(a)(ii)(B) amended by 2002-2013 technical bill, for taxation years that begin after Oct. 2011, to change "25/9" to "100/35".

129(3) also amended by 2002-2013 technical bill (last change effective for taxation years that begin after 2007), 1995 Budget.

Interpretation Bulletins: IT-243R4: Dividend refund to private corporations; IT-269R4: Part IV tax on taxable dividends received by a private corporation or a subject corporation.

Forms: T713: Addition at December 31, 1986 of RDTOH.

(3.1) Application [for taxation years that end before 2003] — [No longer relevant]

Notes: 129(3.1) is a transitional rule allowing a private non-CCPC to include in RDTOH for taxation years beginning after Nov. 12, 1981 certain income in respect of property disposed of by it before Nov. 13, 1981.

(3.2)–(3.5) [Repealed]

Notes: 129(3.2)–(3.5) repealed by 1995 Budget, effective for taxation years that end after June 1995. They provided rules for calculating RDTOH.

(4) Definitions — The definitions in this subsection apply in this section.

"aggregate investment income" of a corporation for a taxation year means the amount, if any, by which the total of all amounts, each of which is

(a) the amount, if any, by which

(i) the eligible portion of the corporation's taxable capital gains for the year

exceeds the total of

(ii) the eligible portion of its allowable capital losses for the year, and

(iii) the amount, if any, deducted under paragraph 111(1)(b) in computing its taxable income for the year, or

(b) the corporation's income for the year from a source that is a property, other than

(i) exempt income,

(ii) an amount included under subsection 12(10.2) in computing the corporation's income for the year,

(iii) the portion of any dividend that was deductible in computing the corporation's taxable income for the year, and

(iv) income that, but for paragraph 108(5)(a), would not be income from a property,

exceeds the total of all amounts, each of which is the corporation's loss for the year from a source that is a property;

Related Provisions: 123.3 — Refundable tax on CCPC's investment income; 129(4)"income" or "loss" — Specified investment business income and income relating to an active business; 129(4)"non-eligible refundable dividend tax on hand"(a)(i)A — Refund of 30⅔% of aggregate investment income; 131(11)(b) — Application of definition to labour-sponsored venture capital corporation; 248(1)"aggregate investment income" — Definition applies to entire Act.

Notes: The following are income from property and thus included in "aggregate investment income" (AII): income under 17(1) and 94.1(1) (VIEWS doc 2011-0397961I7); income under s. 148 from disposition of a life insurance policy (2006-0174111C6). Interest portion of a softwood lumber duty refund, taxed under 12(1)(z.6), is business income and not AII: 2007-0252431E5. See also Notes to 9(1) under "Business income vs property income"; and 2015-0598261C6 [2015 APFF q.24] on how to complete T2 Schedule 7.

The exclusion under (b)(iv) means that active business income earned by an income trust and payable to corporate unitholders is not AII: docs 2002-0143935, 2005-0153561E5.

Definition "aggregate investment income" added by 1995 Budget, effective for taxation years that end after June 1995. (For earlier years, see "Canadian investment income".)

Income Tax Folios: S4-F8-C1: Business investment losses [replaces IT-484R2].

Forms: T2 Sched. 7: Aggregate investment income and active business income.

"Canadian investment income" — [Repealed]

Notes: Definition "Canadian investment income" repealed by 1995 Budget, effective for taxation years that end after June 1995. See now "aggregate investment income".

Previously amended by 1992 technical bill, effective for 1991 and later taxation years. 129(4)"Canadian investment income" was 129(4)(a) before RSC 1985 (5th Supp) consolidation for tax years ending after Nov. 1991.

"eligible portion" of a corporation's taxable capital gains or allowable capital losses for a taxation year is the total of all amounts each of which is the portion of a taxable capital gain or an allowable capital loss, as the case may be, of the corporation for the year from a disposition of a property that, except where the property was a designated property (within the meaning assigned by subsection 89(1)), cannot reasonably be regarded as having accrued while the property, or a property for which it was substituted, was property of a corporation other than a Canadian-controlled private corporation, an investment corporation, a mortgage investment corporation or a mutual fund corporation;

Related Provisions: 248(5) — Substituted property.

Notes: Definition "eligible portion" added by 1995 Budget, effective for taxation years that end after June 1995.

"eligible refundable dividend tax on hand", of a particular corporation at the end of a taxation year, means the amount, if any, by which the total of

(a) the total of the taxes payable under Part IV by the particular corporation for the year in respect of

(i) eligible dividends received by the particular corporation in the year from corporations other than corporations with which the particular corporation is connected (in this paragraph, within the meaning assigned by subsection 186(4) on the assumption that the other corporation is at that time a payer corporation within the meaning of that subsection), and

(ii) taxable dividends received by the particular corporation in the year from corporations that are connected with the particular corporation to the extent that such dividends caused a dividend refund to those corporations from their eligible refundable dividend tax on hand, and

(b) where the particular corporation was a private corporation at the end of its preceding taxation year, the particular corporation's eligible refundable dividend tax on hand at the end of that preceding year

exceeds

(c) the total of all amounts each of which is the portion, if any, of the particular corporation's dividend refund from its eligible refundable dividend tax on hand determined, for its preceding taxation year, under

(i) subparagraph (1)(a)(i), and

(ii) clause (1)(a)(ii)(B).

Related Provisions: 129(5) — 2019 transitional RDTOH; 141.1 — Insurance corp deemed not to be private corp; 260(11)(c) — Amounts deemed paid where partnership of corporations enters into securities lending arrangement.

Notes: ERDTOH and NERDTOH (eligible / non-eligible refundable dividend tax on hand) are needed for determining the dividend refund: 129(1). They replace pre-2019 RDTOH (129(3)). See Notes to 129(1).

ERDTOH tracks a corporation's tax paid under Part IV on eligible dividends received from non-connected corps ("connected" under s. 186(4)); and taxable dividends received from connected corps to the extent such dividends cause the payer corp to receive a dividend refund from its ERDTOH. ERDTOH is reduced by dividend refunds from ERDTOH for a preceding year: 129(1)(a)(i). For 2019 transition from RDTOH see 129(5).

An 84.1(1) deemed dividend can create RDTOH: see Notes to 84.1(1).

Definitions of ERDTOH and NERDTOH added by 2018 budget bill #1, effective on the same basis as 87(2)(aa) amendment (taxation years that begin after 2018, but earlier if planning was used to try to trigger a year-end before 125(5.1)(b) applied).

"foreign investment income" of a corporation for a taxation year is the amount that would be its aggregate investment income for the year if

(a) every amount of its income, loss, capital gain or capital loss for the year that can reasonably be regarded as being from a source in Canada were nil,

(b) no amount were deducted under paragraph 111(1)(b) in computing its taxable income for the year, and

(c) this Act were read without reference to paragraph (a) of the definition "income" or "loss" in this subsection;

Notes: Definition "foreign investment income" amended by 1995 Budget, effective for taxation years that end after June 1995.

129(4)"foreign investment income" was 129(4)(b) before RSC 1985 (5th Supp) consolidation for tax years ending after Nov. 1991.

"income" or "loss" of a corporation for a taxation year from a source that is a property

(a) includes the income or loss from a specified investment business carried on by it in Canada other than income or loss from a source outside Canada, but

(b) does not include the income or loss from any property

(i) that is incident to or pertains to an active business carried on by it, or

(ii) that is used or held principally for the purpose of gaining or producing income from an active business carried on by it.

Related Provisions: 129(4)"foreign investment income"(c) — Para. (a) ignored for purposes of determining foreign investment income.

Notes: In *Alamar Farms*, 1992 CarswellNat 515 (TCC), oil well royalty income on a farm property, where all the land surface was used for farming, fell into both 129(4.1) and (4.2) [now (b)(i) and (ii)] and was active business income.

See VIEWS doc 2008-0302821E5. Investment income of a qualifying environmental trust, attributed to a corporation under 107.3(1)(a), may fall within subpara. (b)(i): doc 2007-0243271C6.

Definition "income or loss" (formerly 129(4.1) and (4.2)) added by 1995 Budget, effective for taxation years ending after June 1995.

Interpretation Bulletins: IT-73R6: The small business deduction.

"non-eligible refundable dividend tax on hand", of a corporation at the end of a taxation year, means the amount, if any, by which the total of

(a) if the corporation was a Canadian-controlled private corporation throughout the year, the least of

(i) the amount determined by the formula

$$A - B$$

where

A is 30 ⅔% of the corporation's aggregate investment income for the year, and

B is the amount, if any, by which

(A) the amount deducted under subsection 126(1) from the tax for the year otherwise payable by it under this Part

exceeds

(B) 8% of its foreign investment income for the year,

(ii) 30 ⅔% of the amount, if any, by which the corporation's taxable income for the year exceeds the total of

(A) the least of the amounts determined under paragraphs 125(1)(a) to (c) in respect of the corporation for the year,

(B) 100/(38 ⅔) of the total of amounts deducted under subsection 126(1) from its tax for the year otherwise payable under this Part, and

(C) the amount determined by multiplying the total of amounts deducted under subsection 126(2) from its tax for the year otherwise payable under this Part, by the relevant factor for the year, and

(iii) the corporation's tax for the year payable under this Part,

(b) the total of the taxes payable under Part IV by the corporation for the year less the amount determined under paragraph (a) of the definition "eligible refundable dividend tax on hand" in respect of the corporation for the year, and

(c) if the corporation was a private corporation at the end of its preceding taxation year, the corporation's non-eligible refundable dividend tax on hand at the end of that preceding year

exceeds

(d) the portion, if any, of the corporation's dividend refund from its non-eligible refundable dividend tax on hand determined, for its preceding taxation year, under clause (1)(a)(ii)(A).

Related Provisions: 87(2)(aa) — Application after amalgamation; 129(5) — 2019 transitional RDTOH; 131(5)(a) — NERDTOH of mutual fund corp; 131(11) — NERDTOH of prescribed labour-sponsored venture capital corp; 141.1 — Insurance corp deemed not to be private corp; 186(5) — NERDTOH of non-private corp that is controlled by individual or related group; 257 — Formula cannot calculate to less than zero; 260(11)(c) — Amounts deemed paid where partnership of corps enters into securities lending arrangement.

Notes: See Notes to 129(4)"eligible refundable dividend tax on hand". NERDTOH tracks: the refundable Part I tax on a CCPC's investment income; and Part IV tax a corp pays on dividends other than those described under ERDTOH. Subparas. (a)(i)-(iii) correspond directly to pre-2019 129(3)(a)(i)-(iii). NERDTOH is reduced by dividend refunds from NERDTOH for a preceding taxation year, on payment of non-eligible dividends.

(4.1) Conditions for subsec. (4.2) — Subsection (4.2) applies in respect of a particular taxation year of a particular corporation if the following conditions are met:

(a) the particular corporation has an amount of tax payable for the year under Part IV;

(b) the particular corporation has claimed amounts under paragraph 186(1)(c) or (d) in respect of the year; and

(c) the particular corporation would, in the absence of paragraphs 186(1)(c) and (d), have an amount determined, at the end of the year, under both paragraph (a) of the definition "eligible refundable dividend tax on hand" and paragraph (b) of the definition "non-eligible refundable dividend tax on hand" in subsection (4).

Notes: 129(4.1) added by 2018 budget bill #2, for taxation years that begin after 2018. See Notes to 129(4.2).

Former 129(4.1) repealed by 1995 Budget, for taxation years ending after June 1995.

(4.2) Part IV tax — allocation of losses — If this subsection applies in respect of a particular taxation year of a corporation, for the purpose of determining the amount under paragraph (a) of the definition "eligible refundable dividend tax on hand" in subsection (4), in respect of the corporation at the end of the year, the amount determined under subsection 186(1) in respect of the corporation for the year is deemed to be the amount determined by the formula

$$A + B - C$$

where

A   is the amount determined under paragraph 186(1)(a) in respect of the corporation for the year in respect of eligible dividends;

B   is the amount determined under paragraph 186(1)(b) in respect of the corporation for the year in respect of dividends that resulted in dividend refunds from the eligible refundable dividend tax on hand of other corporations; and

C   is the amount determined by the formula

$$38\ 1/3\% \ (D + E) - (F + G)$$

where

D   is the amount claimed by the corporation under paragraph 186(1)(c) for the year,

E   is the amount claimed by the corporation under paragraph 186(1)(d) for the year,

F   is the amount determined under paragraph 186(1)(a) in respect of the corporation for the year in respect of taxable dividends (other than eligible dividends), and

G   is the amount determined under paragraph 186(1)(b) in respect of the corporation for the year in respect of dividends that resulted in dividend refunds from the non-eligible refundable dividend tax on hand of other corporations.

Related Provisions: 129(4.1) — Conditions for 129(4.2) to apply; 257 — Formula cannot calculate to less than zero.

Notes: 129(4.2), when it applies (see 129(4.1)), provides ordering rules to allocate a corporation's non-capital loss and farm loss claims, in respect of Part IV taxes otherwise payable, first to the amount otherwise added to its non-eligible RDTOH account. The excess is allocated to its eligible RDTOH.

129(4.2) added by 2018 budget bill #2, for taxation years that begin after 2018.

Former 129(4.2) repealed by 1995 Budget, for taxation years ending after June 1995.

(4.3) [Repealed]

Notes: Former 129(4.3), (5) repealed by 1995 Budget, for tax years ending after June 1995.

(5) 2019 transitional RDTOH — The following rules apply to a corporation's first taxation year in respect of which the definition "eligible refundable dividend tax on hand" in subsection (4) applies:

(a) if the corporation is a Canadian-controlled private corporation throughout the taxation year and its preceding taxation year and is not a corporation in respect of which an election under subsection 89(11) applies to the taxation year or the preceding taxation year,

(i) for the purpose of applying paragraph (b) of the definition "eligible refundable dividend tax on hand" in respect of the corporation at the end of the taxation year, the corporation's eligible refundable dividend tax on hand at the end of its preceding taxation year is deemed to be the amount, if any, that is the lesser of

(A) the amount determined by the formula

$$A - B$$

where

A   is the corporation's refundable dividend tax on hand at the end of its preceding taxation year, and

B   is the corporation's dividend refund for its preceding taxation year, and

(B) the amount determined by the formula

$$(C - D) \times E$$

where

C   is the corporation's general rate income pool at the end of its preceding taxation year,

D   is the amount, if any, by which

(I) the total of all amounts each of which is an eligible dividend paid by the corporation in its preceding taxation year

exceeds

(II) the total of all amounts each of which is an excessive eligible dividend designation made by the corporation in its preceding taxation year, and

E   is 38 ⅓%, and

(ii) for the purpose of applying paragraph (c) of the definition "non-eligible refundable dividend tax on hand" in respect of the corporation at the end of the taxation year, the corporation's non-eligible refundable dividend tax on hand at the end of its preceding taxation year is deemed to be the amount determined by the formula

$$A - B$$

where

A is the amount determined under clause (a)(i)(A) in respect of the corporation at the end of the preceding taxation year, and

B is the amount determined under clause (a)(i)(B) in respect of the corporation at the end of the preceding taxation year; and

(b) in any other case, for the purpose of applying paragraph (b) of the definition "eligible refundable dividend tax on hand" in respect of the corporation at the end of the taxation year, the corporation's eligible refundable dividend tax on hand at the end of its preceding taxation year is deemed to be the amount that would be determined for clause (a)(i)(A) if paragraph (a) applied to the corporation in respect of the taxation year.

Related Provisions: 129(5.1) — Transitional RDTOH — Amalgamation; 257 — Formula amounts cannot calculate to less than zero.

Notes: 129(5) provides rules to transition from RDTOH to the ERDTOH / NERDTOH regime. See Notes to 129(4)"eligible refundable dividend tax on hand".

If a corp is a CCPC in its first tax year under the new regime and its preceding year, and it does not have an 89(11) election in effect for either year, its net RDTOH balance for its preceding year (RDTOH net of dividend refund for that year) is allocated to its first year's ERDTOH to the extent of 38 1/3% of its net GRIP balance for the preceding year (i.e GRIP net of eligible dividends paid in that year), and the rest is allocated to NERDTOH. For any other corp, the net RDTOH balance is allocated entirely to ERDTOH. If there has been an amalgamation, see 129(5.1).

Where Part IV tax is payable by a corp that is under the new regime, on dividends from a connected corp that is not, see VIEWS docs 2020-0855571E5, 2020-085652117.

129(5) added by 2018 budget bill #1, effective on the same basis as 87(2)(aa) amendment (taxation years that begin after 2018, but earlier if planning was used to try to trigger a year-end before 125(5.1)(b) applied).

Former 129(5) repealed by 1995 Budget, for taxation years ending after June 1995.

(5.1) 2019 transitional RDTOH — amalgamations — Subsection (5) applies with such modifications as are necessary for the purpose of applying paragraph 87(2)(aa) in respect of a corporation if

(a) the corporation is a predecessor corporation (within the meaning assigned by subsection 87(1)) in respect of an amalgamation (within the meaning assigned by subsection 87(1));

(b) the corporation has an amount of refundable dividend tax on hand at the end of its taxation year that ends because of paragraph 87(2)(a); and

(c) the first taxation year of the new corporation (within the meaning assigned by subsection 87(1)) in respect of the amalgamation is one to which the definition "eligible refundable dividend tax on hand" in subsection (4) applies.

Notes: 129(5.1) integrates 129(5) and 87(2)(aa) on amalgamations where a predecessor has an RDTOH balance and the new corp is subject to the new ERDTOH and NERDTOH regime. Thus, the 129(5) transitional rule applies to each predecessor before the ERDTOH and NERDTOH balances are combined under 87(2)(aa) for the new corp.

129(5.1) added by 2018 budget bill #1, effective on the same basis as 87(2)(aa) amendment (taxation years that begin after 2018, but earlier if planning was used to try to trigger a year-end before 125(5.1)(b) applied).

(6) Investment income from associated corporation deemed to be active business income — Where any particular amount paid or payable to a corporation (in this subsection referred to as the "recipient corporation") by another corporation (in this subsection referred to as the "associated corporation") with which the recipient corporation was associated in any particular taxation year commencing after 1972, would otherwise be included in computing the income of the recipient corporation for the particular year from a source in Canada that is a property, the following rules apply:

(a) for the purposes of subsection (4), in computing the recipient corporation's income for the year from a source in Canada that is a property,

(i) there shall not be included any portion (in this subsection referred to as the "deductible portion") of the particular amount that was or may be deductible in computing the income of the associated corporation for any taxation year from an active business carried on by it in Canada, and

(ii) no deduction shall be made in respect of any outlay or expense, to the extent that that outlay or expense may reasonably be regarded as having been made or incurred by the recipient corporation for the purpose of gaining or producing the deductible portion; and

(b) for the purposes of this subsection and section 125,

(i) the deductible portion shall be deemed to be income of the recipient corporation for the particular year from an active business carried on by it in Canada, and

(ii) any outlay or expense, to the extent described in subparagraph (a)(ii), shall be deemed to have been made or incurred by the recipient corporation for the purpose of gaining or producing that income.

Related Provisions: 125(1)(a)(i)(C) — Exclusion of 129(6) amount from small business deduction in certain cases; 125(3) — Allocation of active business income among associated corporations; 256(1) — Associated corporations.

Notes: 129(6) preserves the character of active business income when paid as income from property (e.g. interest or rent) to an associated corporation. Thus, it remains eligible for the small business deduction (s. 125, but subject to the exception in 125(1)(a)(i)(C)), and will not be investment income that creates RDTOH under 129(4)"eligible refundable dividend tax on hand" or "non-eligible refundable dividend tax on hand". This rule applies only to 129(4) and s. 125, and not to 248(1)"small business corporation": VIEWS doc 2012-0435101E5. For a similar rule for FAPI, preserving a foreign affiliate's active business income when paid as property income to another foreign affiliate, see 95(2)(a)(ii)(B)(I).

The words "any particular taxation year" refer to the payer's year in CRA's view: doc 2019-0795751E5.

In *Norco Development*, [1985] 1 C.T.C. 130 (FCTD), 129(6) applied to a payment by a partnership of corporations associated with the payee corporation. CRA applies this rule: VIEWS docs 2012-0442791E5, 2012-0449651E5.

In *Marché d'alimentation Géo Pilon*, 2012 QCCA 472 (leave to appeal denied 2012 CarswellQue 9025 (SCC)), the parallel rule in the Quebec *Taxation Act* was held not to apply to rental income paid through a franchisor, as there were two separate payments.

For examples of 129(6) applying see VIEWS docs 2004-0065941E5, 2008-0302821E5, 2011-0424151E5. An election by two corps under 256(2), not to be associated through a third corp, does not affect the application of 129(6): 2003-0030905, 2003-0037075, 2010-0387591E5; Hickey, "Election Not to Be Associated", 19(3) *Canadian Tax Highlights* (ctf.ca) 8-9 (March 2011). CRA says 129(6) does not apply to insurance proceeds that replace rent from an associated corp after fire damaged a building: 2012-043638117. See also 9(1) Notes under "Business income vs property income".

Interpretation Bulletins: IT-73R6: The small business deduction; IT-243R4: Dividend refund to private corporations.

(7) Meaning of "taxable dividend" — For the purposes of this section, "taxable dividend" does not include a capital gains dividend within the meaning assigned by subsection 131(1).

Related Provisions: 129(1.2) — Dividends deemed not to be taxable dividends.

(8) Application of section 125 — Expressions used in this section and not otherwise defined for the purposes of this section have the same meanings as in section 125.

Definitions [s. 129]: "active business" — 125(7), 129(8), 248(1); "aggregate investment income" — 129(4), 248(1); "allowable capital loss" — 38(b), 248(1); "amalgamation" — 87(1); "amount", "assessment" — 248(1); "associated corporation" — 256(1); "bankrupt", "business" — 248(1); "Canada" — 255; "Canadian-controlled private corporation" — 125(7), 248(1); "carrying on business" — 253; "connected" — 186(4); "corporation" — 248(1), *Interpretation Act* 35(1); "designated property" — 89(1); "dividend" — 248(1); "dividend refund" — 129(1)(a); "eligible dividend" — 89(1), 248(1); "eligible portion", "eligible refundable dividend tax on hand" — 129(4); "excessive eligible dividend designation" — 89(1), 248(1); "exempt income" — 248(1); "general rate income pool" — 89(1), 248(1); "income" — from property 129(4.1), (4.2); "income of the corporation for the year from an active business" — 125(7), 129(6), 129(8); "investment corporation" — 130(3), 248(1); "investment tax credit" — 127(9), 248(1); "loss" — from property 129(4.1), (4.2); "Minister" —

248(1); "non-eligible refundable dividend tax on hand" — 129(4); "predecessor corporation" — 87(1); "prescribed rate" — Reg. 4301; "private corporation" — 89(1), 131(5), 186(5), 248(1); "property" — 129(4.1), (4.2), 248(1); "relevant factor" — 248(1); "series of transactions" — 248(10); "share" — 248(1); "specified investment business" — 125(7), 248(1); "substituted" — 248(5); "tax payable" — 248(2); "taxable capital gain" — 38(a), 248(1); "taxable dividend" — 89(1), 129(1.2), 129(7), 248(1); "taxable income" — 2(2), 248(1); "taxation year" — 249; "writing" — *Interpretation Act* 35(1).

Investment Corporations

130. (1) Deduction from tax — A corporation that was, throughout a taxation year, an investment corporation may deduct from the tax otherwise payable by it under this Part for the year an amount equal to 20% of the amount, if any, by which its taxable income for the year exceeds its taxed capital gains for the year.

Related Provisions: 131(10) — Investment corporation can elect not to be restricted financial institution; 142.2(1)"financial institution"(c)(i) — Investment corporation not subject to mark-to-market rules.

Interpretation Bulletins: IT-98R2: Investment corporations (cancelled).

(2) Application of subsecs. 131(1) to (3.2), (4.1) and (6) — Where a corporation was an investment corporation throughout a taxation year (other than a corporation that was a mutual fund corporation throughout the year), subsections 131(1) to (3.2), (4.1) and (6) apply in respect of the corporation for the year

    (a) as if the corporation had been a mutual fund corporation throughout that and all previous taxation years ending after 1971 throughout which it was an investment corporation; and

    (b) as if its capital gains redemptions for that and all previous taxation years ending after 1971, throughout which it would, but for the assumption made by paragraph (a), not have been a mutual fund corporation, were nil.

Notes: 130(2) opening words amended by 2016 budget bill #2, effective 2017, to add reference to 131(4.1) [the "switch fund" rule]. Earlier amended by 1995-57 and 1992 technical bills.

Interpretation Bulletins: IT-98R2: Investment corporations (cancelled).

Forms: RC257: Request for an information return program account (RZ); T2 Sched. 18: Federal and provincial or territorial capital gains refund; T5: Statement of investment income; T5 Summ: Return of investment income.

(3) Meaning of expressions "investment corporation" and "taxed capital gains" — For the purposes of this section,

    (a) a corporation is an "investment corporation" throughout any taxation year in respect of which the expression is being applied if it complied with the following conditions:

        (i) it was throughout the year a Canadian corporation that was a public corporation,

        (ii) at least 80% of its property throughout the year consisted of shares, bonds, marketable securities or cash,

        (iii) not less than 95% of its income (determined without reference to subsection 49(2)) for the year was derived from, or from dispositions of, investments described in subparagraph (ii),

        (iv) not less than 85% of its gross revenue for the year was from sources in Canada,

        (v) not more than 25% of its gross revenue for the year was from interest,

        (vi) at no time in the year did more than 10% of its property consist of shares, bonds or securities of any one corporation or debtor other than Her Majesty in right of Canada or of a province or a Canadian municipality,

        (vii) no person would have been a specified shareholder of the corporation in the year if

            (A) the portion of the definition "specified shareholder" in subsection 248(1) before paragraph (a) were read as follows:

            " "specified shareholder" of a corporation in a taxation year means a taxpayer who owns, directly or indirectly, at any time in the year, more than 25% of

the issued shares of any class of the capital stock of the corporation and, for the purposes of this definition,"

            (B) paragraph (a) of that definition were read as follows:

            "(a) a taxpayer is deemed to own each share of the capital stock of a corporation owned at that time by a person related to the taxpayer,"

            (B.1) [Repealed]

            (C) that definition were read without reference to paragraph (d) of that definition,

            (C.1) [Repealed]

and

            (D) paragraph 251(2)(a) were read as follows:

            "(a) an individual and

                (i) the individual's child (as defined in subsection 70(10)) who is under 19 years of age, or

                (ii) the individual's spouse or common-law partner;"

        (viii) an amount not less than 85% of the total of

            (A) $2/3$ of the amount, if any, by which its taxable income for the year exceeds its taxed capital gains for the year, and

            (B) the amount, if any, by which all taxable dividends received by it in the year to the extent of the amount thereof deductible under section 112 or 113 from its income for the year exceeds the amount that the corporation's non-capital loss for the year would be if the amount determined in respect of the corporation for the year under paragraph 3(b) was nil,

(less any dividends or interest received by it in the form of shares, bonds or other securities that had not been sold before the end of the year) was distributed, otherwise than by way of capital gains dividends, to its shareholders before the end of the year; and

    (b) the amount of the "taxed capital gains" of a taxpayer for a taxation year is the amount, if any, by which

        (i) its taxable capital gains for the year from dispositions of property

exceeds

        (ii) the total of its allowable capital losses for the year from dispositions of property and the amount, if any, deducted under paragraph 111(1)(b) for the purpose of computing its taxable income for the year.

Related Provisions: 4(1) — Income or loss from a source; 112 — Deduction of dividends received; 113 — Deduction for dividends from foreign affiliate; 130(2) — Application of mutual fund corporation rules; 130(4) — Wholly owned subsidiaries; 132(5) — Taxed capital gains definition applies to mutual fund trusts; 184(2) — Tax on excess dividend paid by corporation; 248(1)"investment corporation" — Definition applies to entire Act.

Notes: *130(3)(a)(iii)* amended by 1991 technical bill, effective 1990, to add the parenthetical instruction to ignore 49(2).

130(3)(a)(vii)(B.1) and (C.1) added by 2002-2013 technical bill (s. 371) effective June 18, 1998, and repealed by the same bill for taxation years that begin after Oct. 2011. They were not added directly to the Act but by amending subsec. 155(2) of the 1995-97 technical bill (see below), presumably so that the grandfathering rules in 155(4)-(11) of that bill (below) would apply to them. They read:

(B.1) paragraph (b) of that definition were read as follows:

"(b) each beneficiary of a trust (except a beneficiary of a trust governed by a registered education savings plan who has not attained 19 years of age) is deemed to own that proportion of all such shares owned by the trust at that time that the fair market value at that time of the beneficial interest of the beneficiary in the trust is of the fair market value at that time of all beneficial interests in the trust,"

...

(C.1) paragraph (e) of that definition were read as follows:

"(e) notwithstanding paragraph (b), where a beneficiary's share of the income or capital of the trust depends on the exercise by any person of, or the failure by any person to exercise, any discretionary power, the beneficiary (except a beneficiary of a trust governed by a registered education savings plan who has not attained 19 years of age) is deemed to own each share of the capital stock of a corporation owned at that time by the trust;"

130(3)(a)(vii)(D) amended by 2000 same-sex partners bill to refer to "common-law partner", effective as per Notes to 248(1)"common-law partner".

130(3)(a)(vii) amended by 1995-97 technical bill (subsec. 155(2) of the bill), as itself amended by 1998 Budget bill (s. 92) and by 2002-2013 technical bill (s. 371 — see above), effective for corporations' taxation years that begin after June 20, 1996. However, subsecs. 155(4)-(11) (originally 155(4)-(9)) of the 1995-97 technical bill, as amended by 1998 Budget bill (s. 92), provide the following extensive grandfathering for existing shareholders who would otherwise violate the new 25% test:

(4) [The amendment to 130(3)(a)(vii)] applies to corporations for taxation years that begin after June 20, 1996 except that, where

(a) a corporation was an investment corporation on June 20, 1996,

(b) a particular person is a specified shareholder of the corporation in the year, and

(c) the particular person

(i) was a specified shareholder of the corporation on June 20, 1996, or

(ii) both

(A) was a specified shareholder of the corporation at any time after June 20, 1996 and before August 14, 1998, and

(B) would have been a specified shareholder of the corporation on June 20, 1996 if subparagraph 130(3)(a)(vii), [as amended,] were read without reference to clauses (B) and (D),

subparagraph 130(3)(a)(vii), [as amended,] does not apply to the corporation, with respect to the particular person and persons related to the particular person, except as provided in subsections 155(5) to (11).

(5) [The amendment to 130(3)(a)(vii)] applies to a corporation that was an investment corporation on June 20, 1996 for a taxation year that begins after that day if, at any time after that day and before the end of the year, a particular person described in paragraph [155(4)(b) of the 1995-97 technical bill (above)] in respect of the corporation for the year contributes capital to the corporation or acquires a share of the capital stock of the corporation other than by a permitted acquisition.

(6) [The amendment to 130(3)(a)(vii)] applies to a corporation that was an investment corporation on June 20, 1996 for a taxation year that begins after that day where, at any time after that day and before the end of the year, a newly related person in respect of the corporation

(a) contributed capital to the corporation; or

(b) held at any particular time property (in this paragraph referred to as an "ineligible investment") that is

(i) a share of the capital stock of the corporation, or

(ii) a share of the capital stock of a corporation, or an interest in a partnership or trust, that held an ineligible investment at the particular time.

(7) For the purpose of subsection (6), a newly related person in respect of a corporation at any time means a person who, at any other time that is before that time and after June 20, 1996, became related to a particular person described in paragraph [155(4)(b) of the 1995-97 technical bill (above)] in respect of the corporation, but does not include a person who would, if the taxation year of the corporation that includes that other time had ended immediately before that other time, have been a particular person described in paragraph [155(4)(b) of the 1995-97 technical bill (above)] in respect of the corporation for the year.

(8) [Repealed by 1998 Budget bill]

(9) For the purposes of subsections (5) to (8),

(a) where at a particular time

(i) a trust that existed on June 20, 1996 distributes a share of the capital stock of a corporation to a person who was a beneficiary under the trust throughout the period from June 20, 1996 to the particular time in satisfaction of all or any part of the beneficiary's capital interest in the trust, or

(ii) a partnership that existed on June 20, 1996 distributes, on ceasing to exist, a share of the capital stock of a corporation or an interest in a share to a person who was a member of the partnership throughout the period from June 20, 1996 to the particular time,

the share is deemed to have been owned by the beneficiary or member from the later of June 20, 1996 and the time the share was acquired by the trust or partnership until the particular time; and

(b) where a person who is a beneficiary of a trust or a member of a partnership is deemed by paragraph (b), (c) or (e) of the definition "specified shareholder" in subsection 248(1) of the Act to own a share owned by the partnership or trust, the person is deemed to have acquired the share at the later of the time the share was acquired by the trust or partnership and the time the person last became a beneficiary of the trust or a member of the partnership.

(10) At any time on or after the day of the death of a person described in paragraph [155(4)(c) of the 1995-97 technical bill (above)] in respect of a corporation and before the third anniversary of that day,

(a) the estate of the deceased person is deemed to be a person described in paragraphs (4)(b) and (c) [of the said 1995-97 technical bill (above)] who is related to each person who, throughout the period that begins at the end of June 20, 1996 and ends at the time of death, was related to the deceased person;

(b) notwithstanding subsection (7), the estate is deemed not to be a newly related person in respect of the corporation;

(c) notwithstanding subsection (11), the acquisition of shares of the corporation's capital stock by the estate from the deceased person is deemed to be a permitted acquisition; and

(d) the estate is deemed not to be a trust for the purposes of subparagraph (9)(a)(i) of this Act and paragraphs (b) and (e) of the definition "specified shareholder" in subsection 248(1) of the *Income Tax Act*.

(11) The definitions in this subsection apply in subsections (4) to (10) [of the said 1995-97 technical bill (above)] and this subsection.

"permitted acquisition" means an acquisition by a particular person of a share of a class of the capital stock of a corporation that was

(a) held, at each particular time after June 20, 1996 and before the time at which the particular person acquired it, or

(b) issued after June 20, 1996 by the corporation as a stock dividend and held, at each particular time after the time the share was issued and before the time at which the particular person acquired it,

by the particular person or by a person who was related to the particular person throughout the period that begins at the end of June 20, 1996 and ends at the particular time if, immediately after the time at which the particular person acquires the share, the total percentage of the issued shares of that class held by the particular person and persons related to the particular person (or in the case of acquisitions before August 14, 1998, by the particular person and persons with whom the particular person did not deal at arm's length immediately after the acquisition) does not exceed the permitted percentage for the particular person in respect of that class of shares.

"permitted percentage" for a particular person in respect of any class of shares of the capital stock of a corporation means

(a) in respect of acquisitions of shares before August 14, 1998, the greatest percentage that is the total percentage of the issued shares of a class of the capital stock of the corporation held at the end of June 20, 1996 by the particular person and persons with whom the particular person did not at that time deal at arm's length; and

(b) in any other case, the greater of

(i) the greatest percentage that is the total percentage of the issued shares of a class of the capital stock of the corporation held at the end of June 20, 1996 by the particular person and persons related to the particular person, and

(ii) the greatest percentage that is the total percentage of the issued shares of a class of the capital stock of the corporation held at the beginning of August 14, 1998 by the particular person and persons related to the particular person.

"related persons" and persons related to each other have, for purposes other than applying the definitions "permitted acquisition" and "permitted percentage" in respect of acquisitions of shares before August 14, 1998, the meaning that would be assigned by section 251 of the Act if paragraph 251(2)(a) of the Act were read as follows:

(a) an individual and

(i) the individual's child (as defined in subsection 70(10)) who is under 19 years of age, or

(ii) the individual's spouse;

"specified shareholder" has the meaning assigned by subparagraph 130(3)(a)(vii) of the Act, as enacted by subsection (2).

These changes were first announced in a Finance news release, Aug. 14, 1998. Before the amendment by 1995-97 technical bill (as itself amended by 1998 Budget bill and by 2002-2013 technical bill s. 371), read:

(vii) none of its shareholders at any time in the year held more than 25% of the issued shares of the capital stock of the corporation, and

Interpretation Bulletins: IT-98R2: Investment corporations (cancelled).

(4) Wholly owned subsidiaries — Where a corporation so elects in its return of income under this Part for a taxation year, each of the corporation's properties that is a share or indebtedness of another Canadian corporation that is at any time in the year a subsidiary wholly owned corporation of the corporation shall, for the purposes of subparagraphs (3)(a)(ii) and (vi), be deemed not to be owned by the corporation at any such time in the year, and each

property owned by the other corporation at that time shall, for the purposes of those subparagraphs, be deemed to be owned by the corporation at that time.

Notes: 130(4) added by 1991 technical bill, effective 1987 (a late election could be filed until March 16/92).

Interpretation Bulletins: IT-98R2: Investment corporations (cancelled).

Definitions [s. 130]: "allowable capital loss" — 38(b), 248(1); "amount" — 248(1); "Canada" — 255; "Canadian corporation" — 89(1), 248(1); "capital gain" — 39(1)(a), 248(1); "common-law partner" — 248(1); "corporation" — 248(1), *Interpretation Act* 35(1); "dividend", "gross revenue" — 248(1); "Her Majesty" — *Interpretation Act* 35(1); "investment corporation" — 130(3)(a), 248(1); "mutual fund corporation" — 131(8), 248(1); "property" — 248(1); "public corporation" — 89(1), 248(1); "share", "shareholder", "specified shareholder", "subsidiary wholly owned corporation" — 248(1); "taxable capital gain" — 38(a), 248(1); "taxable dividend" — 89(1), 248(1); "taxable income" — 2(2), 248(1); "taxation year" — 249; "taxed capital gains" — 130(3)(b).

Information Circulars [s. 130]: 78-14R4: Guidelines for trust companies and other persons responsible for filing T3GR, T3D, T3P, T3S, T3RI, and T3F returns.

Mortgage Investment Corporations

130.1 (1) Deduction from tax — In computing the income for a taxation year of a corporation that was, throughout the year, a mortgage investment corporation,

(a) there may be deducted the total of

(i) all taxable dividends, other than capital gains dividends, paid by the corporation during the year or within 90 days after the end of the year to the extent that those dividends were not deductible by the corporation in computing its income for the preceding year, and

(ii) ½ of all capital gains dividends paid by the corporation during the period commencing 91 days after the commencement of the year and ending 90 days after the end of the year; and

(b) no deduction may be made under section 112 in respect of taxable dividends received by it from other corporations.

Related Provisions: 142.2(1)"financial institution"(c)(ii) — Mortgage investment corporation not subject to mark-to-market rules; *Interpretation Act* 27(5) — Meaning of "within 90 days".

Notes: A MIC (see definition in 130.1(6)) is normally taxed only at the shareholder level: it can deduct dividends under 130.1(1), and dividends are treated as interest in the shareholders' hands: 130.1(2).

See Chen & Ross, "Mortgage Investment Corporations Affected by IFRS Uncertainty", 9(4) *Canadian Tax Focus* (ctf.ca) 3-4 (Nov. 2019) (impact on 20(1)(l) deduction).

See also 207.01(1)"advantage" Notes re "TFSA maximizer schemes" using MICs.

130.1(1) amended by 2000 Budget, for tax years that end after Feb. 27, 2000.

(2) Dividend equated to bond interest — For the purposes of this Act, any amount received from a mortgage investment corporation by a shareholder of the corporation as or on account of a taxable dividend, other than a capital gains dividend, shall be deemed to have been received by the shareholder as interest payable on a bond issued by the corporation after 1971.

Related Provisions: 130.1(3) — Application; 214(3)(e) — Non-resident withholding tax.

Notes: Due to this rule, a MIC's payments to non-resident shareholders are subject to Part XIII withholding tax if they fall within 212(3)"participating debt interest": VIEWS doc 2013-0475701R3.

(3) Application of subsec. (2) — Subsection (2) applies where the taxable dividend (other than a capital gains dividend) described in that subsection was paid during a taxation year throughout which the paying corporation was a mortgage investment corporation or within 90 days thereafter.

(4) Election re capital gains dividend — Where at any particular time during the period that begins 91 days after the beginning of a taxation year of a corporation that was, throughout the year, a mortgage investment corporation and ends 90 days after the end of the year, a dividend is paid by the corporation to shareholders of the corporation, if the corporation so elects in respect of the full amount

of the dividend in prescribed manner and at or before the earlier of the particular time and the first day on which any part of the dividend was paid,

(a) the dividend shall be deemed to be a capital gains dividend to the extent that it does not exceed the amount, if any, by which

(i) twice the taxed capital gains of the corporation for the year

exceeds

(ii) the total of all dividends, and parts of dividends, paid by the corporation during the period and before the particular time that are deemed by this paragraph to be capital gains dividends; and

(b) notwithstanding any other provision of this Act, if an amount is received by a taxpayer in a taxation year as, on account of, in lieu of payment of or in satisfaction of, the dividend, the amount

(i) shall not be included in computing the taxpayer's income for the year as income from a share of the capital stock of the corporation, and

(ii) is deemed to be a capital gain of the taxpayer from the disposition of capital property in the year.

Related Provisions: 130.1(4.2) — Reporting to shareholder of capital gains tax rate; 184(2) — Tax on excessive elections; 184(3) — Election to treat excess as separate dividend; 185(4) — Joint and several liability from excessive elections.

Notes: 130.1(4) amended by 2002-2013 technical bill (for tax years that begin after Oct. 2011, with grandfathering for dividends declared on capital gains from dispositions before Oct. 18, 2000), 2000 and 1994 Budgets, 1992 technical bill.

Regulations: 2104.1 (prescribed manner, prescribed form).

Forms: RC257: Request for an information return program account (RZ); T5: Statement of investment income; T5 Summ: Return of investment income; T2012: Election in respect of a capital gains dividend under subsec. 130.1(4).

(4.1) Application of subsecs. 131(1.1) to (1.4) — Where at any particular time a mortgage investment corporation paid a dividend to its shareholders and subsection (4) would have applied to the dividend except that the corporation did not make an election under subsection (4) on or before the day on or before which it was required by that subsection to be made, subsections 131(1.1) to (1.4) apply with such modifications as the circumstances require.

(4.2)–(4.5) [Repealed]

Notes: 130.1(4.2)-(4.5) repealed by 2002-2013 technical bill (Part 5 — technical), for taxation years that begin after Oct. 2011. Added by 2000 Budget, they provided rules for reporting and allocating dividends paid in 2000, taking into account the reduction in capital gains inclusion rate from ¾ to ⅔ to ½ during 2000.

(5) Public corporation — Notwithstanding any other provision of this Act, a mortgage investment corporation shall be deemed to be a public corporation.

(6) Meaning of "mortgage investment corporation" — For the purposes of this section, a corporation is a "mortgage investment corporation" throughout a taxation year if, throughout the year,

(a) it was a Canadian corporation;

(b) its only undertaking was the investing of funds of the corporation and it did not manage or develop any real or immovable property;

(c) none of the property of the corporation consisted of

(i) debts owing to the corporation that were secured on real or immovable property situated outside Canada,

(ii) debts owing to the corporation by non-resident persons, except any such debts that were secured on real or immovable property situated in Canada,

(iii) shares of the capital stock of corporations not resident in Canada, or

(iv) real or immovable property situated outside Canada, or any leasehold interest in such property;

(d) there were 20 or more shareholders of the corporation and no person would have been a specified shareholder of the corporation at any time in the year if

(i) the portion of the definition "specified shareholder" in subsection 248(1) before paragraph (a) were read as follows:

""specified shareholder" of a corporation at any time means a taxpayer who owns, directly or indirectly, at that time, more than 25% of the issued shares of any class of the capital stock of the corporation and, for the purposes of this definition,"

(ii) paragraph (a) of that definition were read as follows:

"(a) a taxpayer is deemed to own each share of the capital stock of a corporation owned at that time by a person related to the taxpayer,"

(iii) that definition were read without reference to paragraph (d) of that definition, and

(iv) paragraph 251(2)(a) were read as follows:

"(a) an individual and

(i) the individual's child (as defined in subsection 70(10)) who is under 18 years of age, or

(ii) the individual's spouse or common-law partner;"

(e) any holders of preferred shares of the corporation had a right, after payment to them of their preferred dividends, and payment of dividends in a like amount per share to the holders of the common shares of the corporation, to participate *pari passu* with the holders of the common shares in any further payment of dividends;

(f) the cost amount to the corporation of such of its property as consisted of

(i) debts owing to the corporation that were secured, whether by mortgages, hypothecs or in any other manner, on houses (as defined in section 2 of the *National Housing Act*) or on property included within a housing project (as defined in that section as it read on June 16, 1999), and

(ii) amounts of any deposits standing to the corporation's credit in the records of

(A) a bank or other corporation any of whose deposits are insured by the Canada Deposit Insurance Corporation or the Régie de l'assurance-dépôts du Québec, or

(B) a credit union,

plus the amount of any money of the corporation was at least 50% of the cost amount to it of all of its property;

(g) the cost amount to the corporation of all real or immovable property of the corporation, including leasehold interests in such property (except real or immovable property acquired by the corporation by foreclosure or otherwise after default made on a mortgage, hypothec or agreement of sale of real or immovable property) did not exceed 25% of the cost amount to it of all of its property;

(h) its liabilities did not exceed 3 times the amount by which the cost amount to it of all of its property exceeded its liabilities, where at any time in the year the cost amount to it of such of its property as consisted of property described in subparagraphs (f)(i) and (ii) plus the amount of any money of the corporation was less than ⅔ of the cost amount to it of all of its property; and

(i) its liabilities did not exceed 5 times the amount by which the cost amount to it of all its property exceeded its liabilities, where paragraph (h) is not applicable.

Related Provisions: 130.1(7) — How shareholders counted; 130.1(8) — First taxation year; 142.2(1)"financial institution"(c)(ii) — Mortgage investment corporation not subject to mark-to-market rules; 248(1)"mortgage investment corporation" — Definition applies to entire Act; 253.1(1) — Limited partner not considered to carry on partnership business.

Notes: See Notes to 130.1(1).

For 130.1(6)(b) and (c), a MIC can generally invest in a mutual fund trust (but it will be considered to own units of the trust, and not an interest in its mortgages); it can hold unimproved real property acquired (for resale) by either purchase or foreclosure, but cannot develop the property pending sale; and it may (depending on the facts) be able to invest in a limited partnership that owns real property (see 253.1(1)): VIEWS docs 2002-0165325, 2004-0108821R3, 2007-0249571E5, 2011-0415641E5, 2013-0487911R3. It can own shares of a Canadian corp: 2012-0450291E5. If a MIC forecloses on a rental property and then manages it (e.g. repairs, maintenance, negotiating new leases), that will violate 130.1(6)(b) and it will no longer qualify: 2010-0387521E5. See also Notes to 130.1(2) re non-resident shareholders.

For 130.1(6)(d), X, X's RRSP and X's TFSA are all different "persons" (but note the prohibited-investment and advantage rules in 207.01–207.05): doc 2011-0403161E5. Spouses owning a share as joint tenants may be considered one shareholder: 2019-0833841E5. A MIC shareholder's sibling is not a specified shareholder for (d), since (d)(iv) redefines "related": 2014-0528311E5. The "20 or more shareholders" must be direct, so a wholly-owned sub of a public company does not qualify: 2015-0599021E5. See also 130.1(7) where an RPP or DPSP is a shareholder. For other provisions "counting" persons, see 94(1)"closely held corporation"(b), Reg. 4801, 4900(1)(h)(i).

For 130.1(6)(e), multiple classes of common shares with different dividend entitlements do not disqualify a MIC: doc 2010-0377991E5.

For 130.1(6)(f), see VIEWS doc 2016-0669431E5 (commercial facilities in a housing project should not exceed 20% of gross floor area).

For 130.1(6)(f), *National Housing Act* s. 2 defines "house" as:

"**house**" means a building or movable structure, or any part thereof, that is intended for human habitation and contains not more than two family housing units, together with any interest in land appurtenant to the building, movable structure or part thereof;

For 130.1(6)(f), *National Housing Act* s. 2 defined "housing project", *as of June 16, 1999*, as:

"**housing project**" means a project consisting of one or more houses, one or more multiple-family dwellings, housing accommodation of the hostel or dormitory type, one or more condominium units or any combination thereof, together with any public space, recreational facilities, commercial space and other buildings appropriate to the project, but does not include a hotel.

For the version of 130.1(6)(f) that applies to property acquired before Nov. 2011, before the 2002-2013 technical bill amendment (see below), *National Housing Act* s. 2 has defined "housing project" since June 28, 1999 as:

"**housing project**" means

(a) any building or movable structure, or any part thereof, that is intended for human habitation,

(b) any property that is intended to be improved, converted or developed to provide housing accommodation or services in support of housing accommodation, or

(c) any property that is associated with housing accommodation, including, without limiting the generality of the foregoing, land, buildings and movable structures, and public, recreational, commercial, institutional and parking facilities;

130.1(6)(f)(i) amended to add "as it read on June 16, 1999" by 2002-2013 technical bill, for property acquired by a corporation after Oct. 2011, with grandfathering for certain debt that replaced debt already in place (see up to PITA 58th ed.).

130.1(6) also amended by 2002-2013 technical bill (effective June 26, 2013, to add each "or immovable"), 2001 *Civil Code* harmonization bill, 2000 same-sex partners bill, 1998 Budget bill, 1995-97 technical bill.

(7) How shareholders counted — In paragraph (6)(d), a trust governed by a registered pension plan or deferred profit sharing plan by which shares of the capital stock of a corporation are held shall be counted as four shareholders of the corporation for the purpose of determining the number of shareholders of the corporation, but as one shareholder for the purpose of determining whether any person is a specified shareholder (as defined for the purpose of that paragraph).

Notes: 130.1(7) amended by 1998 Budget, effective on the same basis as the amendment to 130.1(6)(d).

(8) First taxation year — For the purposes of subsection (6), a corporation that was incorporated after 1971 shall be deemed to have complied with paragraph (6)(d) throughout the first taxation year of the corporation in which it carried on business if it complied with that paragraph on the last day of that taxation year.

(9) Definitions — In this section,

"**liabilities**" of a corporation at any particular time means the total of all debts owing by the corporation, and all other obligations of the corporation to pay an amount, that were outstanding at that time;

Notes: 130.1(9)"liabilities" was 130.1(9)(a) before RSC 1985 (5th Supp) consolidation for tax years ending after Nov. 1991.

"non-qualifying real property", "non-qualifying taxed capital gains", "qualifying taxed capital gains" — [Repealed]

Notes: Definitions "non-qualifying real property", "non-qualifying taxed capital gains" and "qualifying taxed capital gains" repealed by 1994 Budget, effective Feb. 23, 1994, due to repeal of the general capital gains exemption in 110.6(3). They were added by 1992 technical bill.

"taxed capital gains" has the meaning assigned by paragraph 130(3)(b).

Notes: Definition "taxed capital gains" added by 1994 Budget, effective February 23, 1994. (The same definition was in force before 1992.) It replaces the definitions "non-qualifying taxed capital gains" and "qualifying taxed capital gains". As a result of the repeal of the general capital gains exemption in 110.6(3), no distinction between such gains is needed any more. See Notes to 130.1(4).

Former 130.1(9)"taxed capital gains" repealed by 1992 technical bill.

Definitions [s. 130.1]: "allowable capital loss" — 38(b), 248(1); "amount" — 248(1); "bank" — 248(1); "capital gain" — 39(1)(a), 248(1); "capital gains dividend" — 130.1(4); "capital loss" — 39(1)(b), 248(1); "capital property" — 54, 248(1); "class of shares" — 248(6); "common share", "common-law partner" — 248(1); "corporation" — 248(1), *Interpretation Act* 35(1); "credit union" — 137(6), 248(1); "deferred profit sharing plan" — 147(1), 248(1); "disposition", "dividend" — 248(1); "immovable" — Quebec *Civil Code* art. 900–907; "liabilities" — 130.1(9); "mortgage investment corporation" — 130.1(6), 248(1); "non-qualifying taxed capital gains" — 130.1(9); "non-resident", "preferred share", "prescribed", "property" — 248(1); "province" — *Interpretation Act* 35(1); "public corporation" — 89(1), 130.1(5), 248(1); "qualifying taxed capital gains" — 130.1(9); "received" — 248(7); "record", "registered pension plan" — 248(1); "resident in Canada" — 250; "share", "shareholder", "specified shareholder" — 248(1); "taxable capital gain" — 38(a), 248(1); "taxation year" — 249; "taxed capital gains" — 130(3)(b), 130.1(9); "taxpayer" — 248(1); "trust" — 104(1), 248(1), (3).

Mutual Fund Corporations

131. (1) Election re capital gains dividend — Where at any particular time a dividend became payable by a corporation, that was throughout the taxation year in which the dividend became payable a mutual fund corporation, to shareholders of any class of its capital stock, if the corporation so elects in respect of the full amount of the dividend in prescribed manner and at or before the earlier of the particular time and the first day on which any part of the dividend was paid,

(a) the dividend shall be deemed to be a capital gains dividend payable out of the corporation's capital gains dividend account to the extent that it does not exceed the corporation's capital gains dividend account at the particular time; and

(b) notwithstanding any other provision of this Act (other than paragraph (5.1)(b)), if an amount is received by a taxpayer in a taxation year as, on account of, in lieu of payment of or in satisfaction of, the dividend, the amount

(i) shall not be included in computing the taxpayer's income for the year as income from a share of the capital stock of the corporation, and

(ii) is deemed to be a capital gain of the taxpayer from the disposition of capital property in the year.

Related Provisions: 84(7) — When deemed dividend deemed payable; 112(4)(d), 112(4.1)(d), 112(4.2)(d) — Capital gains dividend excluded from stop-loss and share inventory valuation rules; 112(6) — No deduction for capital gains dividend; 122.1(1)"non-portfolio earnings"(b)(i)(B) — Application of deemed capital gain to income trusts distributions tax; 129(7) — No dividend refund for capital gains dividend; 130(2) — Application to investment corporation; 130(3) — Meaning of investment corporation and taxed capital gains; 131(1.1) — Deemed date of election; 131(1.5) — Reporting to shareholder of capital gains tax rate; 131(4) — Application of s. 84; 131(5.1), (5.2) — TCP gains distribution to non-resident subject to withholding tax; 132.2(3)(l)(iii) — Effect of qualifying exchange; 132.2 — Mutual fund reorganizations; 152(1) — Assessment; 142.2(1)"financial institution"(c)(iii) — Mutual fund corporation not subject to mark-to-market rules; 184(2) — Tax on excessive elections; 184(3) — Election to treat excess as separate dividend; 212(2) — No withholding tax on capital gains dividend; 244(14), (14.1) — Date when notice sent.

Notes: See Notes to 131(8). Since a MFC must be a Canadian corporation, there is no flow-through of capital gains from a US mutual fund corp, and they are fully taxed as dividends under 90(1): VIEWS doc 2011-0405261C6.

131(1) amended by 2002-2013 technical bill (for tax years that begin after Oct. 2011, with grandfathering for dividends declared on capital gains from dispositions before Oct. 18, 2000), 2004, 2000 and 1994 Budgets, 1992 technical bill.

Regulations: 2104 (prescribed manner of making election).

Interpretation Bulletins: IT-98R2: Investment corporations (cancelled); IT-243R4: Dividend refund to private corporations; IT-328R3: Losses on shares on which dividends have been received.

Forms: RC257: Request for an information return program account (RZ); T5: Statement of investment income; T5 Summ: Return of investment income; T2055: Election in respect of a capital gains dividend under subsection 131(1); RC4169: Tax treatment of mutual funds for individuals [guide].

(1.1) Deemed date of election — Where at any particular time a dividend has become payable by a mutual fund corporation to shareholders of any class of shares of its capital stock and subsection (1) would have applied to the dividend except that the election referred to in that subsection was not made on or before the day on or before which the election was required by that subsection to be made, the election shall be deemed to have been made at the particular time or on the first day on which any part of the dividend was paid, whichever is the earlier, if

(a) the election is thereafter made in prescribed manner and prescribed form;

(b) an estimate of the penalty in respect of the election is paid by the corporation when the election is made; and

(c) the directors or other person or persons legally entitled to administer the affairs of the corporation have, before the time the election is made, authorized the election to be made.

Related Provisions: 130(2) — Application to investment corporation; 131(1.2) — Request to make election; 131(1.3), (1.4) — Penalty; 152(1) — Assessment.

Regulations: 2104(f) (prescribed manner).

(1.2) Request to make election — The Minister may at any time, by written request served personally or by registered mail, request that an election referred to in paragraph (1.1)(a) be made by a mutual fund corporation and where the mutual fund corporation on which such a request is served does not comply therewith within 90 days after service of the request, subsection (1.1) does not apply to such an election made thereafter by it.

Related Provisions: 248(7)(a) — Mail deemed received on day mailed; *Interpretation Act* 27(5) — Meaning of "within 90 days".

(1.3) Penalty — For the purposes of this section, the penalty in respect of an election referred to in paragraph (1.1)(b) is an amount equal to the lesser of

(a) 1% per annum of the amount of the dividend referred to in the election for each month or part of a month during the period commencing with the time that the dividend became payable, or the first day on which any part of the dividend was paid if that day is earlier, and ending with the day on which the election was made, and

(b) the product obtained when $500 is multiplied by the proportion that the number of months or parts of months during the period referred to in paragraph (a) bears to 12.

(1.4) Assessment and payment of penalty — The Minister shall, with all due dispatch, examine each election referred to in paragraph (1.1)(a), assess the penalty payable and send a notice of assessment to the mutual fund corporation and the corporation shall pay forthwith to the Receiver General, the amount, if any, by which the penalty so assessed exceeds the total of all amounts previously paid on account of that penalty.

Related Provisions: 152(1) — Assessment.

(1.5)–(1.9) [Repealed]

Notes: 131(1.5)-(1.9) repealed by 2002-2013 technical bill (Part 5 — technical), for taxation years that begin after Oct. 2011. Added by 2000 Budget, they provided rules for reporting and allocating dividends paid in 2000, taking into account the reduction in capital gains inclusion rate from ¾ to ⅔ to ½ during 2000.

(2) Capital gains refund to mutual fund corporation — Where a corporation was, throughout a taxation year, a mutual fund corporation and a return of its income for the year has been made within 3 years from the end of the year, the Minister

(a) may, on sending the notice of assessment for the year, refund an amount (in this subsection referred to as its "capital gains refund" for the year) equal to the lesser of

(i) the total of

(A) 14% of the total of

(I) all capital gains dividends paid by the corporation in the period commencing 60 days after the beginning of the year and ending 60 days after the end of the year, and

(II) its capital gains redemptions for the year, and

(B) the amount, if any, that the Minister determines to be reasonable in the circumstances, after giving consideration to the percentages applicable in determining the corporation's capital gains refund for the year and preceding taxation years and the percentages applicable in determining the corporation's refundable capital gains tax on hand at the end of the year, and

(ii) the corporation's refundable capital gains tax on hand at the end of the year; and

(b) shall, with all due dispatch, make that capital gains refund after sending the notice of assessment if an application for it has been made in writing by the corporation within the period within which the Minister would be allowed under subsection 152(4) to assess tax payable under this Part by the corporation for the year if that subsection were read without reference to paragraph 152(4)(a).

Related Provisions: 130(2) — Application; 131(3) — Application to other liability; 131(3.1), (3.2) — Interest; 131(5.1), (5.2) — TCP gains distribution to non-resident subject to withholding tax; 152(1) — Assessment; 157(3)(c) — Reduction in instalments to reflect capital gains refund; 160.1 — Where excess refunded; 244(14), (14.1) — Date when notice sent; *Interpretation Act* 27(5) — Meaning of "within 3 years".

Notes: 131(2)(b) amended by 2010 budget bill #2, effective Dec. 15, 2010, to change "mailing" to "sending" (to accommodate electronic notices under 244(14.1)).

131(2)(a) amended by 2000 Budget (last change effective for taxation years that end after October 17, 2000), 1995-97 technical bill and 1989 Budget.

Interpretation Bulletins: IT-98R2: Investment corporations (cancelled).

Forms: T2 Sched. 18: Federal and provincial or territorial capital gains refund.

(3) Application to other liability — Instead of making a refund that might otherwise be made under subsection (2), the Minister may, where the corporation is liable or about to become liable to make any payment under this Act, apply the amount that would otherwise be refunded to that other liability and notify the corporation of that action.

Related Provisions: 130(2) — Application to investment corporation; 152(1) — Assessment; 222(1)"action" — Ten-year limitation period applies to 131(3).

(3.1) Interest on capital gains refund — Where a capital gains refund for a taxation year is paid to, or applied to a liability of, a corporation, the Minister shall pay or apply interest on the refund at the prescribed rate for the period beginning on the day that is the later of

(a) the day that is 120 days after the end of the year, and

(b) the day that is 30 days after the day on which the corporation's return of income under this Part for the year was filed under section 150, unless the return was filed on or before the day on or before which it was required to be filed,

and ending on the day the refund is paid or applied.

Related Provisions: 130(2) — Application to investment corporation; 131(3.2) — Excess interest on capital gains refund; 161.1 — Offset of refund interest against arrears interest; 221.1 — Application of interest where legislation retroactive; 248(11) — Interest compounded daily.

Notes: 131(3.1)(b) amended by 2003 Budget, effective for taxation years that end after June 2003, to add "the day that is 30 days after".

131(3.1) added by 1992 technical bill, effective for capital gains refunds paid or applied in respect of taxation years that begin after 1991.

Regulations: 4301(b) (prescribed rate of interest).

(3.2) Excess interest on capital gains refund — Where at any particular time interest has been paid to, or applied to a liability of, a corporation under subsection (3.1) in respect of a capital gains refund and it is determined at a subsequent time that the capital gains refund was less than that in respect of which interest was so paid or applied,

(a) the amount by which the interest that was so paid or applied exceeds the interest, if any, computed in respect of the amount that is determined at the subsequent time to be the capital gains refund shall be deemed to be an amount (in this subsection referred to as the "amount payable") that became payable under this Part by the corporation at the particular time;

(b) the corporation shall pay to the Receiver General interest at the prescribed rate on the amount payable, computed from the particular time to the day of payment; and

(c) the Minister may at any time assess the corporation in respect of the amount payable and, where the Minister makes such an assessment, the provisions of Divisions I and J apply, with such modifications as the circumstances require, in respect of the assessment as though it had been made under section 152.

Related Provisions: 20(1)(ll) — Deduction on repayment of interest; 130(2) — Application to investment corporation; 161.1 — Offset of refund interest against arrears interest; 221.1 — Application of interest where legislation retroactive; 248(11) — Interest compounded daily.

Notes: 131(3.2) added by 1992 technical bill, for capital gains refunds paid or applied in respect of taxation years that begin after 1991.

Regulations: 4301(a) (prescribed rate of interest).

(4) Application of section 84 — Section 84 does not apply to deem a dividend to have been paid by a corporation to any of its shareholders, or to deem any of the shareholders of a corporation to have received a dividend on any shares of the capital stock of the corporation, if at the time the dividend would, but for this subsection, be deemed by that section to have been so paid or received, as the case may be, the corporation was a mutual fund corporation.

Related Provisions: 131(11)(c) — Rules re prescribed labour-sponsored venture capital corporations; 132.2(3)(l)(i) — Mutual fund reorganization.

(4.1) Sections [switch-fund rollovers] not applicable — Sections 51, 85, 85.1, 86 and 87 do not apply to a taxpayer that holds a share (in this subsection referred to as the "old share") of a class of shares, that is recognized under securities legislation as or as part of an investment fund, of a mutual fund corporation if the taxpayer exchanges or otherwise disposes of the old share for another share (in this subsection referred to as the "new share") of a mutual fund corporation, unless

(a) if the exchange or disposition occurs in the course of a transaction, event or series of transactions or events described in subsections 86(1) or 87(1),

(i) all shares of the class (determined without reference to subsection 248(6)) that includes the old share at the time of the exchange or disposition are exchanged for shares of the class that includes the new share,

(ii) the old share and the new share derive their value in the same proportion from the same property or group of properties, and

(iii) the transaction, event or series was undertaken solely for *bona fide* purposes and not to cause this paragraph to apply; or

(b) if the old share and the new share are shares of the same class (determined without reference to subsection 248(6)) of shares of the same mutual fund corporation,

(i) the old share and the new share derive their value in the same proportion from the same property or group of properties held by the corporation that is allocated to that class, and

(ii) that class is recognized under securities legislation as or as part of a single investment fund.

Proposed Amendment — 131(4.1) not to apply if underlying investments are unchanged (for Desjardins co-op)

Letter from Dept. of Finance, Oct. 25, 2018: Capital régional et coopératif Desjardins, Montréal, QC

Madame,

La présente est en réponse à vos lettres du 22 juin et du 11 juillet 2018 adressées aux fonctionnaires de la Division de la législation de l'impôt et pour donner suite aux discussions subséquentes avec eux concernant votre demande de lettre d'intention relativement au paragraphe 131(4.1) de la *Loi de l'impôt sur le revenu* (la Loi) dans le cadre de l'échange d'actions de Capital régional et coopératif Desjardins (la Société) par des actionnaires admissibles.

Vous avez présenté le scénario suivant. Le gouvernement du Québec, dans son budget déposé le 27 mars 2018, propose de modifier la loi régissant la Société de manière à créer une nouvelle catégorie d'actions de la Société. Cette nouvelle catégorie d'actions présentera le même risque économique et le même rendement que la catégorie d'actions existante de la Société. Seuls les actionnaires admissibles de la Société auront le droit de souscrire à la nouvelle catégorie d'actions par l'échange d'un nombre équivalent d'actions de la catégorie d'actions existante (l'« échange d'actions proposé »). L'échange d'actions proposé a effectivement pour objet de modifier les modalités des actions existantes qui sont immédiatement rachetables en actions qui ne sont rachetables qu'au terme d'une longue période.

De façon générale, le paragraphe 131(4.1) veille à la reconnaissance appropriée des gains en capital sur les actions des sociétés de placement à capital variable organisées comme des fonds de placement à plusieurs catégories (souvent appelés « fonds de substitution »). Les fonds de substitution offrent habituellement différents types d'expositions aux actifs dans des fonds de placement différents, mais en règle générale, chaque fonds de placement est organisé comme une catégorie d'actions distincte au sein de la même société de placement à capital variable. Malgré les dispositions particulières (comme l'article 51 de la Loi) qui permettent d'effectuer, avec report de l'impôt, un échange d'actions d'une société, le contribuable qui échange une action d'une société de placement à capital variable contre une autre action de la même société est considéré comme ayant disposé de l'action pour un produit de disposition égal à la juste valeur marchande de l'action.

À votre avis, il serait inapproprié d'appliquer le paragraphe 131(4.1) relativement à l'échange d'actions proposé lorsque la société de placement à capital variable est organisée comme un fonds de placement unique aux fins du droit des valeurs mobilières et que l'action reçue et l'action échangée, même si elles n'appartiennent pas à la même catégorie d'actions, tirent leurs valeurs du même groupe de biens.

Nos observations

Nous sommes d'accord qu'en matière de politique, le paragraphe 131(4.1) ne devrait pas s'appliquer à la situation que vous avez décrite. Nous sommes donc disposés à recommander au ministre des Finances de modifier le paragraphe 131(4.1) de manière à ce qu'il ne s'applique pas dans le contexte précis de l'échange d'actions proposé. En particulier, nous proposons d'exclure de l'application du paragraphe 131(4.1) l'échange d'actions d'une société visée si l'action échangée et l'action reçue en échange tirent leur valeur dans la même proportion du même bien ou groupe de biens et si, en vertu du droit canadien des valeurs mobilières, l'action échangée et l'action reçue font partie du même fonds de placement. La Société serait une société visée à cette fin.

Bien qu'il nous soit impossible de garantir que le ministre des Finances ou le Parlement accepteront notre recommandation à cet égard, nous espérons que le présent énoncé de nos intentions vous sera utile.

Veuillez agréer, Madame, l'expression de mes meilleurs sentiments.

Brian Ernewein, Sous-ministre adjoint – Législation fiscale, Direction de la politique de l'impôt

Related Provisions: 131(6)"capital gains redemptions"A(b)(i) — Application to capital gains redemptions.

Notes: 131(4.1) implements a 2016 Budget proposal to prevent the corporate rollover rules from being used to allow investors to switch tax-free between a mutual fund corp's "switch funds" (different classes of shares), something not possible with mutual fund trusts and considered inappropriate as tax policy. Limited exceptions are provided. The Budget predicted this will earn the government $75 million in each of 2016-17 and 2017-18, but this does not take into account changes in behaviour: many taxpayers will now refrain from switching funds and triggering capital gains, due to the tax cost.

With switch funds in a mutual fund corporation less attractive, the 2017 Budget introduced amendments to 132.2(1)"qualifying exchange" to permit one to be converted to multiple mutual fund trusts.

See Hugh Chasmar, "Corporate Class Funds", 25(8) *Canadian Tax Highlights* (ctf.ca) 6-8 (Aug. 2017); Mitchell Thaw, *Taxation of Mutual Fund Trusts and Corporations* (Carswell, looseleaf or *Taxnet Pro* Reference Centre), chap. 10.

131(4.1) added by 2016 budget bill #2, for transactions and events after 2016.

(5) Dividend refund to mutual fund corporation — A corporation that was a mutual fund corporation throughout a taxation year

(a) is deemed for the purposes of paragraph 87(2)(aa) and section 129 to have been a private corporation throughout the year, except that its "non-eligible refundable dividend tax on hand" (as defined in subsection 129(4)) at the end of the year shall be determined without reference to paragraph (a) of that definition; and

(b) where it was not an investment corporation throughout the year, is deemed for the purposes of Part IV to have been a private corporation throughout the year except that, in applying subsection 186(1) to the corporation in respect of the year, that subsection shall be read without reference to paragraph 186(1)(b).

Related Provisions: 112 — Deduction of dividends received by resident corporation; 113 — Deduction of dividend from foreign affiliate; 131(1) — Election re capital gains dividend; 131(2) — Capital gains refund; 131(4) — Application of s. 84; 131(11)(c) — Rules re prescribed labour-sponsored venture capital corps; 152(1) — Assessment; 157(3)(c) — Reduction in instalments to reflect dividend refund.

Notes: 131(5)(a) amended by 2018 budget bill #1 to change RDTOH reference from 129(3) (repealed) to 129(4)"non-eligible" RDTOH, effective on the same basis as 87(2)(aa) amendment (taxation years that begin after 2018, but earlier if planning was used to try to trigger a year-end before 125(5.1)(b) applied).

131(5) amended by 1995-97 technical bill, for 1993 and later tax years. This retroactively overrides amendments made by 1995 Budget bill.

(5.1) TCP gains distribution — If a mutual fund corporation elects under subsection (1) to treat a dividend as a capital gains dividend, for the purposes of this Part and Part XIII,

(a) each shareholder to whom the dividend is paid is deemed to receive from the corporation, at the time the dividend is paid, a TCP gains distribution equal to the lesser of the amount of the dividend and the shareholder's pro rata portion at that time of the mutual fund corporation's TCP gains balance; and

(b) where the dividend is paid to a shareholder who is a non-resident person or a partnership that is not a Canadian partnership,

(i) subparagraph (1)(b)(ii) does not apply in respect of the dividend, to the extent of the TCP gains distribution, and

(ii) the TCP gains distribution is a taxable dividend that, except for the purpose of the definition of "capital gains dividend account" in subsection (6), is not a capital gains dividend.

Related Provisions: 131(5.2) — Limitation on application of 131(5.1); 131(6) — Definitions of "pro rata portion" and "TCP gains distribution"; 131(6)"TCP gains balance"(a)(ii) — Dividend included in TCP gains balance of shareholder that is mutual fund corporation; 132(4)"TCP gains balance"(a)(ii) — Dividend included in TCP gains balance of shareholder that is mutual fund trust; 132(5.1) — Parallel rule for mutual fund trust; 132(5.3) — Allocation to redeemers; 212(2) — Withholding tax on taxable dividend deemed payable to non-resident; 218.3(2)(c) — Withholding tax on mutual fund distributions to non-residents.

Notes: 131(5.1) (subject to 131(5.2)) treats a distribution out of gains on taxable Canadian property as a taxable dividend (not a capital gains dividend), triggering non-resident withholding tax under 212(2).

131(5.1)(b)(i) amended by 2002-2013 technical bill, for taxation years that begin after Oct. 2011. 131(5.1) added by 2004 Budget, effective March 23, 2004.

(5.2) Application of subsec. (5.1) — Subsection (5.1) applies to a dividend paid by a mutual fund corporation in a taxation year only if more than 5% of the dividend is received by or on behalf of shareholders each of whom is a non-resident person or is a partnership that is not a Canadian partnership.

Related Provisions: 132(5.2) — Parallel rule for mutual fund corporation.

Notes: 131(5.2) added by 2004 Budget, effective March 23, 2004.

(6) Definitions — In this section,

"capital gains dividend account" of a mutual fund corporation at any time means the amount, if any, by which

(a) the total of

(i) its capital gains, for all taxation years that began more than 60 days before that time, from dispositions of property after 1971 and before that time while it was a mutual fund corporation, and

(ii) all amounts each of which is an amount in respect of a distribution made by a trust to the corporation, at a time that is after its 2004 taxation year and at which it is a mutual fund corporation, in respect of capital gains of the trust equal to twice the amount determined by the following formula:

$$A - B$$

where

A is the amount of the distribution, and

B is the amount designated under subsection 104(21) by the trust in respect of the net taxable capital gains of the trust attributable to those capital gains

exceeds

(b) the total of

(i) its capital losses, for all taxation years that began more than 60 days before that time, from dispositions of property after 1971 and before that time while it was a mutual fund corporation,

(ii) all capital gains dividends that became payable by the corporation before that time and more than 60 days after the end of the last taxation year that ended more than 60 days before that time, and

(iii) an amount equal to 100/14 of its capital gains refund for any taxation year throughout which it was a mutual fund corporation where the year ended more than 60 days before that time;

Related Provisions: 88(2)(a)(i.1) — Winding-up; 87(2)(bb) — Amalgamation — addition to amounts determined under paras. (a) and (b); 257 — Formula cannot calculate to less than zero.

Notes: Subpara. (b)(iii) amended by 2002-2013 technical bill, for tax years that begin after Oct. 31, 2011, with a transitional rule for 2011-12.

Subpara. (a)(ii) added by 2002-2013 technical bill, for 2005 and later taxation years. It implements a Nov. 9, 2005 Finance comfort letter.

131(6)"capital gains dividend account" amended by 2000 Budget (effective for taxation years that end after Oct. 17, 2000), 1994 Budget, 1992 Budget/technical bill.

131(6)"capital gains dividend account" was 131(6)(b) before RSC 1985 (5th Supp) consolidation for tax years ending after Nov. 1991.

"capital gains redemptions" of a mutual fund corporation for a taxation year means the amount determined by the formula

$$\frac{A}{B} \times (C + D)$$

where

A is the sum of

(a) the total of all amounts paid by the corporation in the year on the redemption of shares of its capital stock, and

(b) the total of all amounts each of which is an amount equal to the fair market value of the shares of the corporation's capital stock that were exchanged in the year for other shares of the corporation's capital stock if

(i) paragraph (4.1) applies to the exchange, and

(ii) the amount is not included in the amount determined for paragraph (a),

B is the total of the fair market value at the end of the year of all the issued shares of its capital stock and the amount determined for A in respect of the corporation for the year,

C is 100/14 of the corporation's refundable capital gains tax on hand at the end of the year, and

D is the amount determined by the formula

$$(K + L) - (M + N)$$

where

K is the amount of the fair market value at the end of the year of all the issued shares of the corporation's capital stock,

L is the total of all amounts each of which is the amount of any debt owing by the corporation, or of any other obligation of the corporation to pay an amount, that was outstanding at that time,

M is the total of the cost amounts to the corporation at that time of all its properties, and

N is the amount of any money of the corporation on hand at that time;

Related Provisions: 130(2) — Application to investment corporation; 132.2(3)(m) — Mutual fund reorganizations; 257 — Formula amount cannot calculate to less than zero.

Notes: Description of A changed from "is the total of all amounts paid by the corporation in the year on the redemption of shares of its capital stock" by 2016 budget bill #2, effective 2017 (consequential on introduction of 131(4.1)).

C amended by 2000 Budget, for tax years that end after Oct. 17, 2000. 131(6)"capital gains redemptions" was 131(6)(a) before RSC 1985 (5th Supp) consolidation for tax years ending after Nov. 1991.

"dividend refund [para. 131(6)(c)]" — [Repealed under former Act]

Notes: 131(6)(c), defining "dividend refund", repealed in 1985. It referred to the definition in 129(1).

"non-qualifying real property", "non-qualifying real property capital gains dividend account" — [Repealed]

Notes: Definitions "non-qualifying real property" and "non-qualifying real property capital gains dividend account" repealed by 1994 Budget, effective Feb. 23, 1994, due to repeal of the general capital gains exemption in 110.6(3). They were added by 1992 Budget/technical bill; amended by 1993 technical bill. Before redrafting to fit the RSC 1985 (5th Supp), they were 131(6)(c.1) and (c).

"pro rata portion", of a shareholder at any time, of a mutual fund corporation's TCP gains balance, in respect of a dividend paid by the mutual fund corporation on a class of shares of its capital stock, means the amount determined by the formula

$$A \times B/C$$

where

A is the mutual fund corporation's TCP gains balance immediately before that time,

B is the amount received in respect of the dividend by the shareholder, and

C is the total amount of the dividend;

Notes: Definition "pro rata portion" added by 2004 Budget, effective March 23, 2004. This term is used in 131(5.1).

"refundable capital gains tax on hand" of a mutual fund corporation at the end of a taxation year means the amount determined by the formula

$$A - B$$

where

A is the total of all amounts each of which is an amount in respect of that or any previous taxation year throughout which the corporation was a mutual fund corporation, equal to the least of

(a) 28% of its taxable income for the year,

(b) 28% of its taxed capital gains for the year, and

(c) the tax payable by it under this Part for the year determined without reference to section 123.2, and

B is the total of all amounts each of which is an amount in respect of any previous taxation year throughout which the corporation was a mutual fund corporation, equal to its capital gains refund for the year.

Related Provisions: 87(2)(bb) — Amalgamation — addition to amounts determined under 131(6)"refundable capital gains tax on hand"A, B; 130(2) — Application to investment corporation; 131(7) — Taxed capital gains defined; 132.2(3)(i) — Addition to RCGTOH of transferee on qualifying exchange of property between mutual funds; 257 — Formula cannot calculate to less than zero.

Notes: 131(6)"refundable capital gains tax on hand" was 131(6)(d) before RSC 1985 (5th Supp) consolidation for tax years ending after Nov. 1991.

"TCP gains balance", of a mutual fund corporation at any time, means the amount, if any, by which

(a) the total of

(i) the mutual fund corporation's capital gains from dispositions, after March 22, 2004 and at or before that time, of taxable Canadian properties, and

(ii) the TCP gains distributions (including those defined in section 132) received by the mutual fund corporation at or before that time

exceeds

(b) the total of

(i) the mutual fund corporation's capital losses from dispositions, after March 22, 2004 and at or before that time, of taxable Canadian properties, and

(ii) the total of all amounts deemed, in respect of dividends paid by the mutual fund corporation before that time, to be TCP gains distributions received by shareholders from the mutual fund corporation;

Notes: Definition "TCP gains balance" added by 2004 Budget, effective March 23, 2004. This term is used in 131(5.1).

"TCP gains distribution" means a TCP gains distribution described in subsection (5.1).

Related Provisions: 132(4)"TCP gains distribution" — Definition applies to mutual fund trust.

Notes: Definition "TCP gains distribution" added by 2004 Budget, effective March 23, 2004.

(7) Definition of "taxed capital gains" — In subsection (6), "taxed capital gains" of a taxpayer for a taxation year has the meaning assigned by subsection 130(3).

(8) Meaning of "mutual fund corporation" — Subject to subsection (8.1), a corporation is, for the purposes of this section, a mutual fund corporation at any time in a taxation year if, at that time, it was a prescribed labour-sponsored venture capital corporation or

(a) it was a Canadian corporation that was a public corporation;

(b) its only undertaking was

(i) the investing of its funds in property (other than real property or an interest in real property or an immovable or a real right in an immovable),

(ii) the acquiring, holding, maintaining, improving, leasing or managing of any real property (or interest in real property) or of any immovable (or real right in immovables) that is capital property of the corporation, or

(iii) any combination of the activities described in subparagraphs (i) and (ii), and

(c) the issued shares of the capital stock of the corporation included shares

(i) having conditions attached thereto that included conditions requiring the corporation to accept, at the demand of the holder thereof and at prices determined and payable in accordance with the conditions, the surrender of the shares, or fractions or parts thereof, that are fully paid, or

(ii) qualified in accordance with prescribed conditions relating to the redemption of the shares,

and the fair market value of such of the issued shares of its capital stock as had conditions attached thereto that included such conditions or as were so qualified, as the case may be, was not less than 95% of the fair market value of all of the issued shares of the capital stock of the corporation (such fair market values being determined without regard to any voting rights attaching to shares of the capital stock of the corporation).

Related Provisions: 39(5) — MFC can make election for Canadian securities; 131(8.01) — Transitional election to be a MFC (2016); 131(8.1) — Loss of MFC status; 132.2(3)(n) — Corporation deemed not to be MFC after rollover of property to MFT; 142.2(1)"financial institution"(c)(iii) — MFC not subject to mark-to-market rules; 157(3)(c) — Instalments required from MFC; 248(1)"mutual fund corpora-

tion" — Definition applies to entire Act; 248(4.1) — Meaning of "real right in an immovable"; 253.1(1) — Limited partner not considered to carry on partnership business.

Notes: Most mutual funds are trusts (s. 132), not corps (s. 131). Although 131(4.1) now prevents "switch funds" (tax-free switch between classes), corporate class MFCs still offer tax advantages: Tehranchian, "Reduce Your Taxes by Investing in Corporate Class", 13(1) *Taxes & Wealth Management* (Carswell) 8-9 (March 2020). For MFCs see CRA guide RC4169; Thaw, *Taxation of Mutual Fund Trusts and Corporations* (Carswell, looseleaf or Taxnet Pro Reference Centre); Young, "Mutual Fund and Segregated Fund Flowthrough Tax Rules", 52(3) *Canadian Tax Journal* 884-924 (2004); Ondercin, "Guaranteed Minimum Withdrawal Benefit Products", XIV(2) *Insurance Planning* (Federated Press) 886-88 (2008); Reed, "Canadian Mutual Fund: US PFIC?", 22(9) *Canadian Tax Highlights* (ctf.ca) 5-6 (Sept. 2014) (US citizens). See also 132.2.

A mutual fund corp can make a 39(4) election for sales of Canadian securities to be treated on capital account, even if it is a "trader or dealer". See 39(5).

A reasonable delay before shares can be redeemed, to allow assets to be sold, will not put a corporation offside of the requirement in 131(8)(c)(i) that its shares be redeemable on "demand": VIEWS doc 2003-0007243.

131(8) amended by 2002-2013 technical bill (Part 4 — bijuralism, effective June 26, 2013), 1995-97, 1994 and 1991 technical bills.

Regulations: 6701 (prescribed labour-sponsored venture capital corporation).

I.T. Technical News: 6 (mutual funds trading — meaning of "investing its funds in property" in 131(8)(b)(i)); 14 (reporting of derivative income by mutual funds).

Advance Tax Rulings: ATR-62: Mutual fund distribution limited partnership — amortization of selling commissions.

Forms: RC4169: Tax treatment of mutual funds for individuals [guide].

(8.01) Election to be a mutual fund corporation — A corporation is deemed to be a mutual fund corporation, from the date it was incorporated until the earlier of the date the corporation meets the conditions to qualify as a mutual fund corporation under subsection (8) and December 31, 2017, if the corporation

(a) was incorporated after 2014 and before March 22, 2016;

(b) would have been a mutual fund corporation on March 22, 2016 if it could have elected on or before that date to be a "public corporation" under paragraph (b) of the definition "public corporation" in subsection 89(1), had the conditions prescribed in paragraph 4800(1)(b) of the *Income Tax Regulations* been satisfied;

(c) on March 22, 2016, had at least one class of shares that was recognized under securities legislation as an investment fund; and

(d) elects to have this subsection apply in the corporation's return of income for the corporation's first taxation year that ends after March 21, 2016.

Notes: 131(8.01) is intended to provide relief where a newly formed corporation has difficulty qualifying as a MFC due to the introduction of 131(4.1). Added by 2016 budget bill #2, effective 2017.

(8.1) Idem — Where, at any time, it can reasonably be considered that a corporation, having regard to all the circumstances, including the terms and conditions of the shares of its capital stock, was established or is maintained primarily for the benefit of non-resident persons, the corporation shall be deemed not to be a mutual fund corporation after that time unless

(a) throughout the period that begins on the later of February 21, 1990 and the day of its incorporation and ends at that time, all or substantially all of its property consisted of property other than property that would be taxable Canadian property if the definition "taxable Canadian property" in subsection 248(1) were read without reference to paragraph (b) of that definition; or

(b) it has not issued a share (other than a share issued as a stock dividend) of its capital stock after February 20, 1990 and before that time to a person who, after reasonable inquiry, it had reason to believe was non-resident, except where the share was issued to that person under an agreement in writing entered into before February 21, 1990.

Related Provisions: 248(4) — Interest in real property.

Notes: See Notes to 132(7).

CRA considers that "substantially all", in 131(8.1)(a), means 90% or more.

131(8.1) added by 1991 Budget effective Feb. 21, 1990, and amended by 2001 technical bill effective October 2, 1996.

(9) Reduction of refundable capital gains tax on hand — Notwithstanding any other provision of this section, the amount determined for A in the definition "refundable capital gains tax on hand" in subsection (6) in respect of the 1972 or 1973 taxation year of a corporation is,

(a) in respect of its 1972 taxation year, 91.25% of the amount so determined; and

(b) in respect of its 1973 taxation year, the total of

(i) 91.25% of that proportion of the amount so determined that the number of days in that portion of the year that is before 1973 is of the number of days in the whole year, and

(ii) 100% of that proportion of the amount so determined that the number of days in that portion of the year that is after 1972 is of the number of days in the whole year.

Related Provisions: 131(1) — Election re capital gains dividend; 131(6) — Definitions.

(10) Restricted financial institution — Notwithstanding any other provision of this Act, a mutual fund corporation or an investment corporation that at any time would, but for this subsection, be a restricted financial institution shall, if it has so elected in prescribed manner and prescribed form before that time, be deemed not to be a restricted financial institution at that time.

Related Provisions: 112(2.1) — Where no deduction of dividend permitted.

Forms: T2143: Election not to be a restricted financial institution.

(11) Rules respecting prescribed labour-sponsored venture capital corporations — Notwithstanding any other provision of this Act, in applying this Act to a corporation that was at any time a prescribed labour-sponsored venture capital corporation,

(a) for the purposes of subparagraphs (a)(i) and (ii) of the definition "non-eligible refundable dividend tax on hand" in subsection 129(4), the amount deducted under paragraph 111(1)(b) from the corporation's income for each taxation year ending after that time shall be deemed to be nil;

(b) the definition "aggregate investment income" in subsection 129(4) shall be read without reference to paragraph (a) of that definition in its application to taxation years that end after that time;

(c) notwithstanding subsection (4), if it so elects in its return of income under this Part for a taxation year ending after that time, subsection 84(1) applies for that year and all subsequent taxation years;

(d) subsection (5) does not apply for taxation years ending after that time; and

(e) the amount of the corporation's capital dividend account at any time after that time shall be deemed to be nil.

Related Provisions: 157(3)(c) — Reduction in instalments to reflect dividend refund; 186.1 — Exempt corporations.

Notes: See Notes to 248(1)"registered labour-sponsored venture capital corporation".

131(11) amended by 2018 budget bill #1 to change RDTOH reference from 129(3) (repealed) to 129(4)"non-eligible" RDTOH, effective on the same basis as 87(2)(aa) amendment (taxation years that begin after 2018, but earlier if planning was used to try to trigger a year-end before 125(5.1)(b) applied).

131(11)(b) amended by 1995 Budget, for tax years that end after June 1995. 131(11) added by 1991 technical bill, effective 1990.

Definitions [s. 131]: "active business" — 248(1); "amount", "assessment", "business" — 248(1); "Canada" — 255; "Canadian corporation" — 89(1), 248(1); "Canadian partnership" — 102(1), 248(1); "capital gains dividend" — 131(1), (5.1)(b)(ii); "capital dividend account" — 89(1) [technically not applicable to s. 131]; "capital gain" — 39(1)(a), 248(1); "capital gains dividend account", "capital gains redemptions" — 131(6); "capital gains refund" — 131(2); "capital loss" — 39(1)(b), 248(1); "capital property" — 54, 248(1); "class of shares" — 248(6); "corporation" — 248(1), *Interpretation Act* 35(1); "cost amount" — 248(1); "credit union" — 137(6), 248(1); "disposition", "dividend" — 248(1); "fair market value" — see 69(1) Notes; "immovable" — Quebec *Civil Code* art. 900–907; "interest in real property" — 248(4); "investment corporation" — 130(3), 248(1); "Minister" — 248(1); "mutual fund corporation" — 131(8), (8.1), 132.2(3)(l)(i), 132.2(1)(n), 248(1); "non-eligible refundable dividend tax on hand" — 129(4); "non-resident" — 248(1); "partnership" — see 96(1) Notes; "payable" — 84(7); "person", "prescribed" — 248(1); "prescribed labour-spon-

sored venture capital corporation" — Reg. 6701; "prescribed rate" — Reg. 4301; "private corporation" — 89(1), 248(1); "pro rata portion" — 131(6); "property" — 248(1); "public corporation" — 89(1), 248(1); "real right" — 248(4.1); "received" — 248(7); "refundable capital gains tax on hand" — 131(6); "resident in Canada" — 250; "restricted financial institution" — 248(1); "series of transactions" — 248(10); "share", "shareholder", "stock dividend" — 248(1); "TCP gains balance" — 131(6); "TCP gains distribution" — 131(5.1), (6); "tax payable" — 248(2); "taxable Canadian property" — 248(1); "taxable capital gain" — 38(a), 248(1); "taxable dividend" — 89(1), 248(1); "taxable income" — 2(2), 248(1); "taxation year" — 249; "taxed capital gains" — 130(3)(b), 131(7); "taxpayer" — 248(1); "trust" — 104(1), 248(1), (3); "writing" — *Interpretation Act* 35(1).

Regulations [s. 131]: 6701 (prescribed labour-sponsored venture capital corporation).

Mutual Fund Trusts

132. (1) Capital gains refund to mutual fund trust — Where a trust was, throughout a taxation year, a mutual fund trust and a return of its income for the year has been made within 3 years from the end of the year, the Minister

(a) may, on sending the notice of assessment for the year, refund an amount (in this subsection referred to as its "capital gains refund" for the year) equal to the lesser of

(i) the total of

(A) 16.5% of the total of the trust's capital gains redemptions for the year, and

(B) the positive or negative amount, if any, that the Minister determines to be reasonable in the circumstances, after giving consideration to the percentages applicable in determining the trust's capital gains refunds for the year or any previous taxation year and the percentages applicable in determining the trust's refundable capital gains tax on hand at the end of the year, and

(ii) the trust's refundable capital gains tax on hand at the end of the year; and

(b) shall, with all due dispatch, make that capital gains refund after sending the notice of assessment if an application for it has been made in writing by the trust within the period within which the Minister would be allowed under subsection 152(4) to assess tax payable under this Part by the trust for the year if that subsection were read without reference to paragraph 152(4)(a).

Related Provisions: 104(21) — Allocation of capital gains and losses to beneficiaries; 127.55(f)(ii) — No minimum tax on mutual fund trust; 132(2) — Application to other liability; 132(2.1), (2.2) — Interest; 132(5.1), (5.2) — TCP gains distribution to non-resident subject to withholding tax; 132.1 — Deduction for certain amounts designated by mutual fund trust; 132.2 — Mutual fund reorganizations; 142.2(1)"financial institution"(d) — Mutual fund trust not subject to mark-to-market rules; 152(1) — Assessment; 160.1 — Where excess refunded; 244(14), (14.1) — Date when notice sent; *Interpretation Act* 27(5) — Meaning of "within 3 years".

Notes: For discussion of MFTs see Thaw, *Taxation of Mutual Fund Trusts and Corporations* (Carswell, looseleaf or *Taxnet Pro* Reference Centre); Roth et al., *Canadian Taxation of Trusts* (ctf.ca, 2016), pp. 1091-1130; Botz, "Mutual Fund Trusts and Unit Trusts: Selected Tax and Legal Issues", 42(4) *Canadian Tax Journal* 1037-58 (1994); McMullen, "Canadian Real Estate Investment Trusts", III(2) *Business Vehicles* (Federated Press) 125-27 (1997); Young, "Mutual Fund and Segregated Fund Flowthrough Tax Rules", 52(3) *CTJ* 884-924 (2004). See also Notes to 132(6), 122.1, and CRA guide RC4169, *Tax Treatment of Mutual Funds for Individuals*. For US citizens investing in a MFT see Reed, "Canadian Mutual Fund: US PFIC?", 22(9) *Canadian Tax Highlights* (ctf.ca) 5-6 (Sept. 2014); Albers & Reed, "Strategies for Avoiding the Application of the PFIC Regime to Canadian Mutual Fund Trusts", 2271 *Tax Topics* (CCH) 1-4 (Sept. 17, 2015); Reed & Chalhoub, "The US Tax Classification of Canadian Mutual Fund Trusts", 63(4) *CTJ* 947-89 (2015).

An MFT can elect under 39(4) for sales of Canadian securities to be treated on capital account, even if it is a "trader or dealer": 39(5).

132(1)(a)(i)(A) and (B) amended by 2016 budget bill #1, effective 2016, to change (in (A)) "14.5%" to "16.5%" [due to the change in the top personal rate in 117(2) from 29% to 33%] and (in (B)) "the amount" to "the positive or negative amount" and "capital gains refunds for the year and preceding taxation years" to "capital gains refunds for the year or any previous taxation year".

132(1) earlier amended by 2010 budget bill #2 (effective Dec. 15, 2010), 2000 Budget, 1995-97 technical bill and 1989 Budget.

Forms: RC4169: Tax treatment of mutual funds for individuals [guide]; T2 Sched. 18: Federal and provincial or territorial capital gains refund; T184: Capital gains refund to a mutual fund trust.

(2) Application to other liability — Instead of making a refund that might otherwise be made under subsection (1) the Minister may, where the trust is liable or about to become liable to make any payment under this Act, apply the amount that would otherwise be refunded to that other liability and notify the trust of that action.

Related Provisions: 132(4) — Definitions; 132(6) — Meaning of mutual fund corporation; 152(1) — Assessment; 222(1)"action" — Ten-year limitation period applies to 132(2).

(2.1) Interest on capital gains refund — If a capital gains refund for a taxation year is paid to, or applied to a liability of, a mutual fund trust, the Minister shall pay or apply interest on the refund at the prescribed rate for the period beginning on the day that is 30 days after the later of

(a) the day that is 90 days after the end of the year, and

(b) the day on which the trust's return of income under this Part for the year was filed under section 150

and ending on the day on which the refund is paid or applied.

Related Provisions: 132(2.2) — Excess interest on capital gains refund; 161.1 — Offset of refund interest against arrears interest; 221.1 — Application of interest where legislation retroactive; 248(11) — Interest compounded daily; 251.2(7)(a) — Interest start date extended to regular year's deadline, for short year deemed ended due to change in majority beneficiaries.

Notes: 132(2.1) amended by 2003 Budget, for tax years that end after June 2003, to change "45 days" to "30 days". Added by 1992 technical bill.

Regulations: 4301(b) (prescribed rate of interest).

(2.2) Excess interest on capital gains refund — Where at any particular time interest has been paid to, or applied to a liability of, a trust under subsection (2.1) in respect of a capital gains refund and it is determined at a subsequent time that the capital gains refund was less than that in respect of which interest was so paid or applied,

(a) the amount by which the interest that was so paid or applied exceeds the interest, if any, computed in respect of the amount that is determined at the subsequent time to be the capital gains refund shall be deemed to be an amount (in this subsection referred to as the "amount payable") that became payable under this Part by the trust at the particular time;

(b) the trust shall pay to the Receiver General interest at the prescribed rate on the amount payable, computed from the particular time to the day of payment; and

(c) the Minister may at any time assess the trust in respect of the amount payable and, where the Minister makes such an assessment, the provisions of Divisions I and J apply, with such modifications as the circumstances require, in respect of the assessment as though it had been made under section 152.

Related Provisions: 20(1)(ll) — Deduction on repayment of interest; 161.1 — Offset of refund interest against arrears interest; 221.1 — Application of interest where legislation retroactive; 248(11) — Interest compounded daily.

Notes: 132(2.2) added by 1992 technical bill, effective for capital gains refunds paid or applied with respect to taxation years that begin after 1991.

Regulations: 4301(a) (prescribed rate of interest).

(3) Application of subsec. 104(20) — In its application in respect of a mutual fund trust, subsection 104(20) shall be read as if the reference therein to "a dividend (other than a taxable dividend)" were read as a reference to "a capital dividend".

(4) Definitions — In this section,

"capital gains redemptions" of a mutual fund trust for a taxation year means the amount determined by the formula

$$\left(\frac{A}{B} \times (C + D)\right) - E$$

where

A is the total of all amounts each of which is the portion of an amount paid by the trust in the year on the redemption of a unit in the trust that is included in the proceeds of disposition in respect of that redemption,

B is the total of the fair market value at the end of the year of all the issued units of the trust and the amount determined for A in respect of the trust for the year,

C is 100/16.5 of the trust's refundable capital gains tax on hand at the end of the year,

D is the amount determined by the formula

$$(K + L) - (M + N)$$

where

K is the amount of the fair market value at the end of the year of all the issued units of the trust,

L is the total of all amounts each of which is the amount of any debt owing by the trust, or of any other obligation of the trust to pay an amount, that was outstanding at that time,

M is the total of the cost amounts to the trust at that time of all its properties, and

N is the amount of any money of the trust on hand at that time, and

E is twice the total of all amounts each of which is an amount designated under subsection 104(21) for the year by the trust in respect of a unit of the trust redeemed by the trust at any time in the year and after December 21, 2000;

Related Provisions: 132.2(3)(m) — Mutual fund reorganizations; 257 — Formula cannot calculate to less than zero.

Notes: C amended by 2016 budget bill #1, effective 2016, to change "100/14.5" to "100/16.5" (see parallel change in 132(1)(a)(i)).

Definition earlier amended by 2000 Budget (for taxation years ending after Oct. 17, 2000). 132(4)"capital gains redemptions" was 132(4)(a) before RSC 1985 (5th Supp) consolidation for tax years ending after Nov. 1991.

"pro rata portion", of a beneficiary, of a mutual fund trust's TCP gains balance for a taxation year, in respect of an amount designated under subsection 104(21) by the mutual fund trust for the taxation year, means the amount determined by the formula

$$A \times B/C$$

where

A is the mutual fund trust's TCP gains balance for the taxation year,

B is the amount the mutual fund trust has designated under that subsection in respect of the beneficiary for the taxation year, and

C is the total of all amounts designated under that subsection by the mutual fund trust for the taxation year;

Notes: Definition "pro rata portion" added by 2004 Budget, effective March 23, 2004. This term is used in 132(5.1).

"refundable capital gains tax on hand" of a mutual fund trust at the end of a taxation year means the amount determined by the formula

$$A - B$$

where

A is the total of all amounts each of which is an amount in respect of that or any previous taxation year throughout which the trust was a mutual fund trust, equal to the least of

(a) the highest individual percentage for the year multiplied by its taxable income for the year,

(b) the highest individual percentage for the year multiplied by its taxed capital gains for the year, and

(c) where the taxation year ended after May 6, 1974, the tax payable under this Part by it for the year, and

B is the total of all amounts each of which is an amount in respect of any previous taxation year throughout which the trust was a mutual fund trust, equal to its capital gains refund for the year.

Related Provisions: 132(5) — Taxed capital gains defined; 132.2(3)(i) — Addition to RCGTOH on qualifying exchange of property between mutual funds; 257 — Formula cannot calculate to less than zero.

Notes: A(a)-(b) amended by 2016 budget bill #1, effective 2016, to change "29%" to "the highest individual percentage..." (due to increase in the top rate under 117(2)).

132(4)"refundable capital gains tax on hand" was 132(4)(b) before RSC 1985 (5th Supp) consolidation for tax years ending after Nov. 1991.

Proposed 132(4)"specified property" [2004] has been withdrawn: see Notes to 132(7).

"TCP gains balance", of a mutual fund trust for a particular taxation year, means the amount, if any, by which

(a) the total of

(i) the mutual fund trust's capital gains from dispositions, after March 22, 2004 and at or before the end of the particular taxation year, of taxable Canadian properties, and

(ii) the TCP gains distributions (including those defined in section 131) received by the mutual fund trust at or before the end of the particular taxation year

exceeds

(b) the total of

(i) the mutual fund trust's capital losses from dispositions, after March 22, 2004 and at or before the end of the particular taxation year, of taxable Canadian properties, and

(ii) the total of all amounts deemed, in respect of amounts designated by the mutual fund trust under subsection 104(21) for taxation years that preceded the particular taxation year, to be TCP gains distributions received by beneficiaries under the mutual fund trust;

Notes: Definition "TCP gains balance" added by 2004 Budget, effective March 23, 2004. This term is used in 132(5.1).

"TCP gains distribution" means a TCP gains distribution described in subsection (5.1).

Notes: Definition "TCP gains distribution" added by 2004 Budget, effective March 23, 2004.

(5) Definition of "taxed capital gains" — In subsection (4), "taxed capital gains" of a taxpayer for a taxation year has the meaning assigned by subsection 130(3).

(5.1) TCP gains distribution — If a mutual fund trust designates an amount under subsection 104(21) for a taxation year of the trust in respect of a beneficiary under the trust, for the purposes of this Part and Part XIII,

(a) the beneficiary is deemed to have received from the mutual fund trust a TCP gains distribution equal to the lesser of

(i) twice the amount designated, and

(ii) the beneficiary's pro rata portion of the mutual fund trust's TCP gains balance for the taxation year; and

(b) where the beneficiary is a non-resident person or a partnership that is not a Canadian partnership,

(i) the amount designated is deemed by subsection 104(21) to be a taxable capital gain of the beneficiary only to the extent that it exceeds one half of the TCP gains distribution, and

(ii) one half of the TCP gains distribution is to be added to the amount otherwise included under subsection 104(13) in computing the income of the beneficiary, and is deemed to be an amount to which paragraph 212(1)(c) applies.

Related Provisions: 131(5.1) — Parallel rule for mutual fund corp; 131(6)"TCP gains balance"(a)(ii) — Dividend included in TCP gains balance of mutual fund corp; 132(4) — Definitions of "pro rata portion" and "TCP gains distribution"; 132(4)"TCP gains balance"(a)(ii) — Dividend included in TCP gains balance of mutual fund trust; 132(5.2) — Limitation on application of 132(5.1); 132(5.3) — Allocation to redeemers; 212(1)(c) — Withholding tax on taxable dividend deemed paid under (a)(ii); 218.3(2)(c) — Withholding tax on mutual fund distributions to non-residents.

Notes: 132(5.1) added by 2004 Budget, effective March 23, 2004. Subject to 132(5.2), it treats a distribution out of its gains on taxable Canadian property as Canadian-source trust income, triggering non-resident withholding tax under 212(1)(c). For discussion see Peter Jovicic, "Draft Income Tax Legislation Affecting Mutual Funds", X(1) *Business Vehicles* (Federated Press) 482-6 (2004). It was one response to the growing use of income trusts (others included Part XIII.2 tax, 89(1)"eligible dividend", and eventually the SIFT rules in 104(16) and 122.1).

(5.2) Application of subsection (5.1) — Subsection (5.1) applies to an amount designated under subsection 104(21) by a mutual fund trust for a taxation year only if more than 5% of the total of all amounts each of which is an amount designated under that subsection by the mutual fund trust for the taxation year was designated in respect of beneficiaries under the mutual fund trust each of whom is a non-resident person or is a partnership that is not a Canadian partnership.

Related Provisions: 131(5.2) — Parallel rule for mutual fund corporation.

Notes: 132(5.2) added by 2004 Budget, effective March 23, 2004.

(5.3) Allocation to redeemers — If a trust that is a mutual fund trust throughout a taxation year paid or made payable, at any time in the taxation year, to a beneficiary an amount on a redemption by that beneficiary of a unit of the trust (in this subsection referred to as the "allocated amount"), and the beneficiary's proceeds from the disposition of that unit do not include the allocated amount, in computing its income for the taxation year no deduction may be made by the trust in respect of

(a) the portion of the allocated amount that would be, without reference to subsection 104(6), an amount paid out of the income (other than taxable capital gains) of the trust; and

(b) the portion of the allocated amount determined by the formula

$$A - 1/2\,(B + C - D)$$

where

A is the portion of the allocated amount that would be, without reference to subsection 104(6), an amount paid out of the taxable capital gains of the trust,

B is the beneficiary's proceeds from the disposition of the unit on the redemption,

C is the allocated amount, and

D is the amount determined by the trustee to be the beneficiary's cost amount of that unit, using reasonable efforts to obtain the information required to determine the cost amount.

Related Provisions: 257 — Formula cannot calculate to less than zero.

Notes: 132(5.3) was introduced by the 2019 Budget, to counter mutual fund trusts using the "allocation to redeemers" method to allocate capital gains to redeeming unitholders in excess of the capital gains that would otherwise have been realized by these unitholders on the redemption of their units. See tinyurl.com/budg2019 at "Mutual Funds: Allocation to Redeemers", and the Finance Technical Notes.

2019 Budget Table 1 predicted this change would earn the federal government $25 million in 2019-20, $105m in 2020-21, $90m in 2021-22, $75m in 2022-23 and $55m in 2023-24.

For discussion of the July 30, 2019 revisions see Pereira & Kabouchi, "Mutual Fund Trusts — Revised Proposals", tinyurl.com/BLG-redeemers (Aug. 2019).

132(5.3) added by 2021 budget bill #1, for tax years that begin after March 18, 2019; however, para. (b) does not apply to a mutual fund trust's tax year that begins before March 20, 2020, if, in that tax year, units of the trust are:

(a) listed on a designated stock exchange in Canada; and

(b) in continuous distribution.

(6) Meaning of "mutual fund trust" — Subject to subsection (7), for the purposes of this section, a trust is a mutual fund trust at any time if at that time

(a) it was a unit trust resident in Canada,

(b) its only undertaking was

(i) the investing of its funds in property (other than real property or an interest in real property or an immovable or a real right in an immovable),

(ii) the acquiring, holding, maintaining, improving, leasing or managing of any real property (or interest in real property) or of any immovable (or real right in immovables) that is capital property of the trust, or

(iii) any combination of the activities described in subparagraphs (i) and (ii), and

(c) it complied with prescribed conditions.

Related Provisions: 39(5) — MFT can make election for Canadian securities; 94(1)"exempt foreign trust"(h) — Non-resident MFT exempt from NRT rules; 94(4)(b) — Deeming non-resident trust to be resident in Canada does not apply to 132(6)(a); 104(21) — Allocation of capital gains and losses to beneficiaries;

132(6.1) — Election to be MFT from beginning of first year; 132(6.2) — Retention of MFT status to end of year; 132(7) — Loss of MFT status; 132.11 — Optional Dec. 15 year-end; 132.1(1)(q) — Trust deemed not to be MFT after rollover of property to another trust; 142.2(1)"financial institution"(d) — MFT not subject to mark-to-market rules; 156(2) — Payment of tax by MFT; 210(2)(b) — MFT not subject to Part XII.2 tax; 212(9)(c) — Interest received by MFT and paid to non-residents — withholding tax exemption; 248(1)"mutual fund trust" — Definition applies to entire Act; 248(4.1) — Meaning of "real right in an immovable"; 251.2(1)"investment fund", 251.2(3)(f) — Most MFTs not subject to "loss restriction event" rules; 253.1(1) — Limited partner not considered to carry on partnership business.

Notes: See Notes to 132(1). For 132(6)(a), see 108(2) for the meaning of "unit trust", and Notes to 250(1) for determining when a trust is "resident in Canada".

CRA stated at the 2005 Cdn Tax Foundation annual conference (discussion re income trusts) (*Income Tax Technical News* No. 34) that holding a limited partnership interest is not carrying on business due to 253.1(1), and that since holding shares is generally accepted as "investing of funds", holding shares in the general partner is acceptable for an MFT (although in rulings issued to date, trustees of the MFT were never a majority of the board of the general partner). For the MFT to guarantee debts of a corporation or partnership might put the MFT offside, but see VIEWS docs 2002-0167675, 2004-0068221E5, 2004-0097111R3, 2007-0226891R3, 2008-0271251R3, 2008-0273501R3, 2010-0386081R3 (guarantees are not a separate undertaking causing loss of MFT status). Day trading qualifies as "investing of funds in property": 2012-0470991E5.

Mutual fund trusts that are SIFTs (most income trusts other than REITs) are subject to a distributions tax under 122(1)(b) and 104(16). Most MFTs are not subject to the "loss restriction event" (change in majority beneficiaries) rules: see 251.2(3).

If the number of unitholders drops below 150 (Reg. 4801(b)), see Florence, "Tax Consequences of the Loss of Mutual Fund Status", VIII(2) *Business Vehicles* (Federated Press) 390-95 (2002), updated 13(3) *Taxation Law* (Ontario Bar Assn, oba.org) 22-25 (March 2003); and VIEWS doc 2013-049796117 (effect on RCGTOH).

In *Grenon*, 2021 TCC 30 (under appeal to FCA), G created a trust with 171 small investors, so his RRSP could invest $150 million through it into LPs operating his businesses. The TCC held that Reg. 4801(a)(i)(A) was not met, so the trust was not a MFT.

For more rulings see VIEWS docs 2004-0088711R3 (acquisition of rights assigned under credit agreement met terms of 132(6)(b)(i)); 2006-0217441R3 (trust is MFT); 2017-0723421E5 (new MFT).

132(6) amended by 2002-2013 technical bill (last change effective June 26, 2013), 1995-97 and 1991 technical bills.

Regulations: 204, 204.1, 221 (information return requirements for mutual fund trust); 4801 (prescribed conditions).

I.T. Technical News: 6 (mutual funds trading — meaning of "investing its funds in property" in 132(6)(b)(i)); 14 (reporting of derivative income by mutual funds); 34 (income trusts and subparagraph 132(6)(b)(i)).

CRA Audit Manual: 16.2.6: Mutual fund trusts.

Advance Tax Rulings: ATR-62: Mutual fund distribution limited partnership — amortization of selling commissions.

Forms: RC4169: Tax treatment of mutual funds for individuals [guide].

(6.1) Election to be mutual fund [from beginning of first year] — Where a trust becomes a mutual fund trust at any particular time before the 91st day after the end of its first taxation year, and the trust so elects in its return of income for that year, the trust is deemed to have been a mutual fund trust from the beginning of that year until the particular time.

Related Provisions: 251.2(7)(b) — "91st day" extended to regular year's balance-due day, for short year deemed ended due to change in majority beneficiaries.

Notes: Since 132(6.1) makes the trust a MFT from the beginning of its first taxation year, it retroactively makes any investment in the trust by an RRSP a "qualified investment" under Reg. 4900(1)(d): VIEWS doc 2002-0159245.

If the trust is resident in Quebec, the election must be copied to Revenu Québec: *Taxation Act* ss. 1120.0.1, 21.4.6.

132(6.1) amended by 1998 Budget to change "the calendar year in which its first taxation year began" to "its first taxation year", effective for 1998 and later taxation years. The amendment is consequential on the introduction of 132.11, which allows qualifying trusts to elect to have a December 15 year-end. A related amendment was also made to 142.6(1).

132(6.1) added by 1995-97 technical bill, effective for 1994 and later taxation years. It replaces a rule formerly in the closing words of 132(6).

(6.2) Retention of status as mutual fund trust — A trust is deemed to be a mutual fund trust throughout a calendar year where

(a) at any time in the year, the trust would, if this section were read without reference to this subsection, have ceased to be a mutual fund trust

(i) because the condition described in paragraph 108(2)(a) ceased to be satisfied,

(ii) because of the application of paragraph (6)(c), or

(iii) because the trust ceased to exist;

(b) the trust was a mutual fund trust at the beginning of the year; and

(c) the trust would, throughout the portion of the year throughout which it was in existence, have been a mutual fund trust if

(i) in the case where the condition described in paragraph 108(2)(a) was satisfied at any time in the year, that condition were satisfied throughout the year,

(ii) subsection (6) were read without reference to paragraph (c) of that subsection, and

(iii) this section were read without reference to this subsection.

Related Provisions: 250(6.1) — Similar rule for trust's residence in Canada.

Notes: 132(6.2) added by 2001 technical bill, effective 1990 and later taxation years (as promised in Finance comfort letters in 1999-2000). It applies where a mutual fund trust ceases to exist. The trust's taxation year (249(1)(b)) is not affected by termination, unless 132.2(1)(b) applies, so the last taxation year of a MFT is normally the calendar year of termination. This led to unintended consequences for provisions that require that a trust be a MFT *throughout* a taxation year (e.g., 132(1) capital gains refund, 127.55(f)(ii) AMT exemption, 210(2) Part XII.2 tax exemption). For rulings applying 132(6.2) see VIEWS docs 2005-0152491R3, 2007-0237011R3.

(7) Idem [trust primarily for non-residents] — Where, at any time, it can reasonably be considered that a trust, having regard to all the circumstances, including the terms and conditions of the units of the trust, was established or is maintained primarily for the benefit of non-resident persons, the trust shall be deemed not to be a mutual fund trust after that time unless

(a) at that time, all or substantially all of its property consisted of property other than property that would be taxable Canadian property if the definition "taxable Canadian property" in subsection 248(1) were read without reference to paragraph (b) of that definition; or

(b) it has not issued any unit (other than a unit issued to a person as a payment, or in satisfaction of the person's right to enforce payment, of an amount out of the trust's income determined before the application of subsection 104(6), or out of the trust's capital gains) of the trust after February 20, 1990 and before that time to a person who, after reasonable inquiry, it had reason to believe was non-resident, except where the unit was issued to that person under an agreement in writing entered into before February 21, 1990.

Related Provisions: 248(4) — Interest in real property.

Notes: For discussion of 132(7) see Ross, "Non-resident Unitholders", I(4) *Resource Sector Taxation* (Federated Press) 76-79 (2003); Bies & Nobrega, "Recent Transactions of Interest", 2008 Cdn Tax Foundation conference report at 6:1-8; VIEWS doc 2003-0048881E5.

Proposed amendments of Sept. 16, 2004 (131(8.1), 132(4)"specified property", 132(7)), under which mutual fund status would be lost if non-resident ownership exceeded 50% of value, were withdrawn.

If MFT status is lost under 132(7), it is lost forever. CRA stated at the 2005 CTF annual conference (*Income Tax Technical News* 34) that trustees should monitor levels of non-resident ownership (including making reasonable inquiry on issuing any new unit), and have mechanisms to reduce or dilute such ownership to avoid 132(7).

For a ruling on transactions allowing a trust to fall within the 132(7)(a) exception, see VIEWS doc 2006-0174351R3.

CRA considers that "substantially all", in 132(7)(a), means 90% or more.

132(7)(a) amended by 2007 budget bill #1, effective 2004, to give effect to a Nov. 26/04 Finance comfort letter, so that a trust can maintain MFT status by applying the test only at the time the trust fund is non-resident owned (rather than at all times in the period since the trust was created or Feb. 21, 1990). Thus, 132(7)(a) applies to a trust that, at a time after 2003, becomes non-resident owned if, at that time, it meets the "taxable Canadian property" test.

132(7)(a) and (b) amended by 2001 technical bill, para. (a) effective October 2, 1996 and para. (b) retroactive to February 21, 1990. 132(7) added by 1991 technical bill, effective February 21, 1990.

I.T. Technical News: 34 (income trusts and non-resident ownership).

Definitions [s. 132]: "amount", "assessment" — 248(1); "beneficiary" — 248(25) [Notes]; "calendar year" — *Interpretation Act* 37(1)(a); "Canada" — 255; "Canadian partnership" — 102(1), 248(1); "Canadian resource property" — 66(15), 248(1); "capital dividend" — 83(2), 248(1); "capital gain" — 39(1)(a), 248(1); "capital gains redemptions" — 132(4); "capital gains refund" — 132(1); "capital loss" — 39(1)(b), 248(1); "capital property" — 54, 248(1); "cost amount", "disposition", "dividend" — 248(1); "fair market value" — see 69(1) Notes; "highest individual percentage" — 248(1); "immovable" — Quebec *Civil Code* art. 900–907; "interest in real property" — 248(4); "Minister" — 248(1); "mutual fund trust" — 132(6)–(7), 132.2(3)(n), 248(1); "non-resident" — 248(1); "partnership" — see 96(1) Notes; "person" — 248(1); "prescribed rate" — Reg. 4301; "pro rata portion" — 132(4); "property" — 248(1); "real right" — 248(4.1); "refundable capital gains tax on hand" — 132(4); "resident in Canada" — 94(3)(a), 250; "taxable Canadian property" — 248(1); "taxable capital gain" — 38(a), 248(1); "taxable dividend" — 89(1), 248(1); "taxable income" — 2(2), 248(1); "taxation year" — 249; "taxed capital gains" — 130(3), 132(5); "TCP gains balance" — 132(4); "TCP gains distribution" — 132(4), (5.1); "timber resource property" — 13(21), 248(1); "trust" — 104(1), 248(1), (3); "unit trust" — 108(2), 248(1); "writing" — *Interpretation Act* 35(1).

Information Circulars [s. 132]: 78-14R4: Guidelines for trust companies and other persons responsible for filing T3GR, T3D, T3P, T3S, T3RI, and T3F returns.

132.1 (1) Amounts designated by mutual fund trust [for inclusion in taxpayer's income] — Where a trust in its return of income under this Part for a taxation year throughout which it was a mutual fund trust designates an amount in respect of a particular unit of the trust owned by a taxpayer at any time in the year equal to the total of

(a) such amount as the trust may determine in respect of the particular unit for the year not exceeding the amount, if any, by which

(i) the total of all amounts that were determined by the trust under subsection 104(16) of the *Income Tax Act*, chapter 148 of the Revised Statutes of Canada, 1952, for taxation years of the trust commencing before 1988

exceeds

(ii) the total of all amounts determined by the trust under this paragraph for the year or a preceding taxation year in respect of all units of the trust, other than amounts determined in respect of the particular unit for the year under this paragraph, and

(b) such amount as the trust may determine in respect of the particular unit for the year not exceeding the amount, if any, by which

(i) the total of all amounts described in subparagraph 53(2)(h)(i.1) that became payable by the trust after 1987 and before the year

exceeds

(ii) the total of all amounts determined by the trust under this paragraph for the year or a preceding taxation year in respect of all units of the trust, other than amounts determined in respect of the particular unit for the year under this paragraph,

the amount so designated shall

(c) subject to subsection (3), be deductible in computing the income of the trust for the year, and

(d) be included in computing the income of the taxpayer for the taxpayer's taxation year in which the year of the trust ends, except that where the particular unit was owned by two or more taxpayers during the year, such part of the amount so designated as the trust may determine shall be included in computing the income of each such taxpayer for the taxpayer's taxation year in which the year of the trust ends if the total of the parts so determined is equal to the amount so designated.

Related Provisions: 12(1)(m) — Income inclusion — benefits from trust; 132.2(3)(k) — Mutual fund reorganization — continuation of trust; 214(3)(f.1) — Non-resident withholding tax.

Notes: See Notes to 12(1)(m).

I.T. Application Rules: 69 (meaning of "chapter 148 of ...").

Forms: RC4169: Tax treatment of mutual funds for individuals [guide].

(2) Adjusted cost base of unit where designation made — In computing, at any time in a taxation year of a taxpayer, the adjusted cost base to the taxpayer of a unit in a mutual fund trust, there shall be added that part of the amount included under subsection (1) in computing the taxpayer's income that is reasonably attributable to the amount determined under paragraph (1)(b) by the trust for its taxation year ending in the year in respect of the unit owned by the taxpayer.

Related Provisions: 12(1)(m) — Amounts to be included from business or property — benefits from trusts; 53(1)(d.2) — Addition to adjusted cost base of share.

(3) Limitation on current year deduction — The total of amounts deductible by reason of paragraph (1)(c) in computing the income of a trust for a taxation year shall not exceed the amount that would be the income of the trust for the year if no deductions were made under this section and subsection 104(6).

Related Provisions: 132.2(3)(k) — Mutual fund reorganization — continuation of trust.

(4) Carryover of excess — The amount, if any, by which the total of all amounts each of which is an amount designated for the year under subsection (1) exceeds the amount deductible under this section in computing the income of the trust for the year, shall, for the purposes of paragraph (1)(c) and subsection (3), be deemed designated under subsection (1) by the trust for its immediately following taxation year.

Related Provisions: 132.2(3)(k) — Mutual fund reorganization — continuation of trust.

(5) Where designation has no effect — Where it is reasonable to conclude that an amount determined by a mutual fund trust

(a) under paragraph (1)(a) or (b) for a taxation year of the trust in respect of a unit owned at any time in the year by a taxpayer who was a person exempt from tax under this Part by reason of subsection 149(1), or

(b) under paragraph (1)(d) for the year in respect of the amount designated under subsection (1) for the year in respect of the unit

differs from the amount that would have been so determined for the year in respect of the taxpayer had the taxpayer not been a person exempt from tax under this Part by reason of subsection 149(1), the amount designated for the year in respect of the unit under subsection (1) shall have no effect for the purposes of paragraph (1)(c).

Related Provisions: 132.2(3)(k) — Mutual fund reorganization.

Definitions [s. 132.1]: "adjusted cost base" — 54, 248(1); "amount" — 248(1); "Canadian property" — 133(8); "mutual fund trust" — 132(6)–(7), 132.2(3)(n), 248(1); "person" — 248(1); "taxation year" — 249; "taxpayer" — 248(1); "trust" — 104(1), 248(1), (3).

132.11 (1) Taxation year of mutual fund trust — Notwithstanding any other provision of this Act, where a trust (other than a prescribed trust) that was a mutual fund trust on the 74th day after the end of a particular calendar year so elects in writing filed with the Minister with the trust's return of income for the trust's taxation year that includes December 15 of the particular year,

(a) the trust's taxation year that began before December 16 of the particular year and, but for this paragraph, would end at the end of the particular year (or, where the first taxation year of the trust began after December 15 of the preceding calendar year and no return of income was filed for a taxation year of the trust that ended at the end of the preceding calendar year, at the end of the preceding calendar year) is deemed to end at the end of December 15 of the particular year;

(b) if the trust's taxation year ends on December 15 because of paragraph (a), subject to subsection (1.1), each subsequent taxation year of the trust is deemed to be the period that begins at the beginning of December 16 of a calendar year and that ends at the end of December 15 of the following calendar year or at any earlier time that is determined under paragraph 128.1(4)(a), 132.2(3)(b), 142.6(1)(a) or 249(4)(a); and

(c) each fiscal period of the trust that begins in a taxation year of the trust that ends on December 15 because of paragraph (a) or that ends in a subsequent taxation year of the trust shall end no later than the end of the year or the subsequent year, as the case may be.

Related Provisions: 132.11(1.1) — Revocation of election; 132.11(2) — Where trust is member of partnership; 132.11(3) — Where trust is beneficiary of another trust; 132.11(6) — Additional income.

Notes: If the trust is resident in Quebec, the election must be copied to Revenu Québec: *Taxation Act* ss. 1121.7, 21.4.6.

A mutual fund that has elected under 132.11(1) and is a registered investment can also file its T3-RI return under 204.7(1) with a December 15 year-end: VIEWS doc 2004-0064661I7.

See Notes at end of 132.11. 132.11(1) amended by 2016 budget bill #2 (effective March 21, 2013), 2002-2013 and 2001 technical bills.

Regulations: 4801.01 (prescribed trust).

(1.1) Revocation of election — Where a particular taxation year of a trust ends on December 15 of a calendar year because of an election made under paragraph (1)(a), the trust applies to the Minister in writing before December 15 of that calendar year (or before a later time that is acceptable to the Minister) to have this subsection apply to the trust, with the concurrence of the Minister

(a) the trust's taxation year following the particular taxation year is deemed to begin immediately after the end of the particular taxation year and end at the end of that calendar year; and

(b) each subsequent taxation year of the trust is deemed to be determined as if that election had not been made.

Notes: If the trust is resident in Quebec, the application must be copied to Revenu Québec: *Taxation Act* ss. 1121.7.1, 21.4.6.

132.11(1.1) added by 2001 technical bill, for 2000 and later tax years, implementing an Aug. 16, 2000 comfort letter.

(2) Electing trust's share of partnership income and losses — Where a trust is a member of a partnership a fiscal period of which ends in a calendar year after December 15 of the year and a particular taxation year of the trust ends on December 15 of the year because of subsection (1), each amount otherwise determined under paragraph 96(1)(f) or (g) to be the trust's income or loss for a subsequent taxation year of the trust is deemed to be the trust's income or loss determined under paragraph 96(1)(f) or (g) for the particular year and not for the subsequent year.

(3) Electing trust's income from other trusts — Where a particular trust is a beneficiary under another trust a taxation year of which (in this subsection referred to as the "other year") ends in a calendar year after December 15 of the year and a particular taxation year of the trust ends on December 15 of the year because of subsection (1), each amount determined or designated under subsection 104(13), (19), (21), (22) or (29) for the other year that would otherwise be included, or taken into account, in computing the income of the particular trust for a subsequent taxation year of the trust shall

(a) be included, or taken into account, in computing the particular trust's income for the particular year; and

(b) not be included, or taken into account, in computing the particular trust's income for the subsequent year.

Notes: See Notes at end of 132.11.

(4) Amounts paid or payable to beneficiaries — Notwithstanding subsection 104(24), for the purposes of subsections (5) and (6) and 104(6) and (13) and paragraph (i) of the definition "disposition" in subsection 248(1) each amount that is paid, or that becomes payable, by a trust to a beneficiary after the end of a particular taxation year of the trust that ends on December 15 of a calendar year because of subsection (1) and before the end of that calendar year, is deemed to have been paid or to have become payable, as the case may be, to the beneficiary at the end of the particular year and not at any other time.

Notes: 132.11(4) amended by 2002-2013 technical bill (for amounts paid or payable after 1999), 2001 technical bill.

(5) Special rules where change in status of beneficiary — Where an amount is deemed by subsection (4) to have been paid or to have become payable at the end of December 15 of a calendar year by a trust to a beneficiary who was not a beneficiary under the trust at that time,

(a) notwithstanding any other provision of this Act, where the beneficiary did not exist at that time, except for the purpose of this paragraph, the first taxation year of the beneficiary is deemed to include the period that begins at that time and ends immediately before the beginning of the first taxation year of the beneficiary;

(b) the beneficiary is deemed to exist throughout the period described in paragraph (a); and

(c) where the beneficiary was not a beneficiary under the trust at that time, the beneficiary is deemed to have been a beneficiary under the trust at that time.

Related Provisions: 132.11(4) — Amounts paid to beneficiary from Dec. 16-31.

(6) Additional income of electing trust — Where a particular amount is designated under this subsection by a trust in its return of income for a particular taxation year that ends on December 15 because of subsection (1) or throughout which the trust was a mutual fund trust and the trust does not designate an amount under subsection 104(13.1) or (13.2) for the particular year,

(a) the particular amount shall be added in computing its income for the particular year; and

(b) for the purposes of subsections 104(6) and (13), each portion of the particular amount that is allocated under this paragraph to a beneficiary under the trust in the trust's return of income for the particular year in respect of an amount paid or payable to the beneficiary in the particular year shall be considered to be additional income of the trust for the particular year (determined without reference to subsection 104(6)) that was paid or payable, as the case may be, to the beneficiary at the end of the particular year.

(c) [Repealed]

Related Provisions: 132.11(4) — Amounts paid to beneficiary from Dec. 16-31; 220(3.21)(b) — Late filing, amendment or revocation of designation or allocation.

Notes: 132.11(6)(c) repealed by 2001 technical bill, effective for 2000 and later taxation years, as a result of the repeal of 52(6).

(7) Deduction — Subject to subsection (8), the lesser of the amount designated under subsection (6) by a trust for a taxation year and the total of all amounts each of which is allocated by the trust under paragraph (6)(b) in respect of the year shall be deducted in computing the trust's income for the following taxation year.

Related Provisions: 132.11(8) — Anti-avoidance rule.

(8) Anti-avoidance — Subsection (7) does not apply in computing the income of a trust for a taxation year where it is reasonable to consider that the designation under subsection (6) for the preceding taxation year was part of a series of transactions or events that includes a change in the composition of beneficiaries under the trust.

Related Provisions: 248(10) — Series of transactions or events.

Notes [s. 132.11]: 132.11 added by 1998 Budget, for 1998 and later tax years. It generally allows mutual fund trusts (MFTs) to elect to have taxation years that end on Dec. 15 rather than Dec. 31. The purpose is to allow MFTs to calculate income and distributions for a taxation year on a more administratively workable basis, to allow for more accurate and timely reporting, and to minimize the risk of errors which can have adverse financial consequences for MFTs and their unitholders.

Where the election is made, the trust's income must be adjusted to take into account investments in partnership interests and units of other trusts. Special provision is also made to allow for the allocation to unitholders of income paid or payable during Dec. 16-31. In addition, "overdistributions" by the trust to unitholders may be treated as income for those unitholders. The trust is generally allowed to deduct the amount of those overdistributions for the next taxation year. The mechanism for overdistributions ensures that MFTs can maximize their capital gain refunds and provides for more straightforward tax consequences for unitholders.

See also VIEWS doc 2014-0546831E5 (various effects of election).

The optional Dec. 15 year-end in 132.11 is a change from the original proposal in the 1998 budget, which would have allowed distributions within a month after year-end. See Judith Harris, "Recent Legislative Proposals: Taxation Year End Election", V(1) *Business Vehicles* (Federated Press) 222–24 (1999).

Definitions [s. 132.11]: "amount" — 248(1); "calendar year" — *Interpretation Act* 37(1)(a); "fiscal period" — 249.1; "Minister" — 248(1); "mutual fund trust" — 132(6)–(7), 132.2(3)(n), 248(1); "partnership" — see 96(1) Notes; "prescribed" — 248(1); "series of transactions" — 248(10); "share" — 248(1); "taxation year" — 249; "trust" — 104(1), 248(1), (3); "writing" — *Interpretation Act* 35(1).

132.2 (1) Definitions re qualifying exchange [rollover] of mutual funds — The following definitions apply in this section.

"first post-exchange year", of a fund in respect of a qualifying exchange, means the taxation year of the fund that begins immediately after the acquisition time.

"qualifying exchange" means a transfer at any time (in this section referred to as the **"transfer time"**) if

(a) the transfer is a transfer of all or substantially all of the property (including an exchange of a unit of a mutual fund trust for another unit of that trust) of

(i) a mutual fund corporation (other than a SIFT wind-up corporation) to one or more mutual fund trusts, or

(ii) a mutual fund trust to a mutual fund trust;

(b) all or substantially all of the shares issued by the mutual fund corporation referred to in subparagraph (a)(i) or the first mutual fund trust referred to in subparagraph (a)(ii) (in this section referred to as the **"transferor"**) and outstanding immediately before the transfer time are within 60 days after the transfer time disposed of to the transferor;

(c) no person disposing of shares of the transferor to the transferor within that 60-day period (otherwise than pursuant to the exercise of a statutory right of dissent) receives any consideration for the shares other than units of one or more mutual fund trusts referred to in subparagraph (a)(i) or the second mutual fund trust referred to in subparagraph (a)(ii) (in this section referred to as a **"transferee"** and, together with the transferor, as the **"funds"**);

(d) if property of the transferor has been transferred to more than one transferee,

(i) all shares of each class of shares, that is recognized under securities legislation as or as part of an investment fund, of the transferor are disposed of to the transferor within 60 days after the transfer time, and

(ii) the units received in consideration for a particular share of a class of shares, that is recognized under securities legislation as or as part of an investment fund, of the transferor are units of the transferee to which all or substantially all of the assets that were allocated to that investment fund immediately before the transfer time were transferred; and

(e) the funds jointly so elect, by filing a prescribed form with the Minister on or before the election's due date.

Related Provisions: 7(1.4) — Exchange of options giving mutual fund trust employee right to acquire units; 54"superficial loss"(c) — No superficial loss on deemed disposition and reacquisition; 132.2(6) — Due date for election in para. (c); 132.2(7) — Amendment or revocation of election.

Notes: CRA considers that "substantially all" means 90% or more.

See Notes to 132.2(3) for discussion of qualifying exchanges.

See Notes at end of 132.2 for in-force rules; note in particular s. 280(6) of the 2002-2013 technical bill, providing that an election under the former 132.2(2)"qualifying exchange" continues to apply.

Definition amended by 2017 budget bill #2, for transfers after March 21, 2017. This extends the mutual fund merger rules to mergers of "switch funds", which funds are now unattractive since rollovers of mutual fund corp units were stopped (see Notes to 131(4.1)). For earlier transfers, read:

"qualifying exchange" means a transfer at any time (in this section referred to as the "transfer time") of all or substantially all of the property of a mutual fund corporation (other than a SIFT wind-up corporation) or a mutual fund trust to a

mutual fund trust (in this section referred to as the "transferor" and "transferee", respectively, and as the "funds") if

(a) all or substantially all of the shares issued by the transferor and outstanding immediately before the transfer time are within 60 days after the transfer time disposed of to the transferor;

(b) no person disposing of shares of the transferor to the transferor within that 60-day period (otherwise than pursuant to the exercise of a statutory right of dissent) receives any consideration for the shares other than units of the transferee; and

(c) the funds jointly so elect, by filing a prescribed form with the Minister on or before the election's due date.

Forms: T1169: Election on disposition of property by a mutual fund corporation (or a mutual fund trust) to a mutual fund trust.

"share" means a share of the capital stock of a mutual fund corporation and a unit of a mutual fund trust.

Regulations: 1105 (prescribed classes of depreciable property).

I.T. Technical News: 34 (income trust reorganizations).

(2) Timing — In respect of a qualifying exchange, a time referred to in the following list immediately follows the time that precedes it in the list

(a) the transfer time;

(b) the first intervening time;

(c) the acquisition time;

(d) the beginning of the funds' first post-exchange years;

(e) the depreciables disposition time;

(f) the second intervening time; and

(g) the depreciables acquisition time.

Notes: Paras. (a)-(g) define the terms listed. Each one is deemed to exist an instant after the previous one.

(3) General — In respect of a qualifying exchange,

(a) each property of a fund, other than property disposed of by the transferor to a transferee at the transfer time and depreciable property, is deemed to have been disposed of, and to have been reacquired by the fund, at the first intervening time, for an amount equal to the lesser of

(i) the fair market value of the property at the transfer time, and

(ii) the greater of

(A) its cost amount, and

(B) the amount that the fund designates in respect of the property in a notification to the Minister accompanying the election in respect of the qualifying exchange;

(a.1) in respect of each property transferred by the transferor to a transferee, including an exchange of a unit of a transferee for another unit of that transferee, the transferor is deemed to have disposed of the property to the transferee, and to have received units of the transferee as consideration for the disposition of the property, at the transfer time;

(b) subject to paragraph (l), the last taxation years of the funds that began before the transfer time are deemed to have ended at the acquisition time, and their first post-exchange years are deemed to have begun immediately after those last taxation years ended;

(c) each depreciable property of a fund (other than property to which subsection (5) applies and property to which paragraph (d) would, if this Act were read without reference to this paragraph, apply) is deemed to have been disposed of, and to have been reacquired, by the fund at the second intervening time for an amount equal to the lesser of

(i) the fair market value of the property at the depreciables disposition time, and

(ii) the greater of

(A) the lesser of its capital cost and its cost amount to the disposing fund at the depreciables disposition time, and

(B) the amount that the fund designates in respect of the property in a notification to the Minister accompanying the election in respect of the qualifying exchange;

(d) if at the second intervening time the undepreciated capital cost to a fund of depreciable property of a prescribed class exceeds the fair market value of all the property of that class, the excess is to be deducted in computing the fund's income for the taxation year that includes the transfer time and is deemed to have been allowed in respect of property of that class under regulations made for the purpose of paragraph 20(1)(a);

(e) except as provided in paragraph (m), the transferor's cost of any particular property received by the transferor from a transferee as consideration for the disposition of the property is deemed to be

(i) nil, if the particular property is a unit of the transferee, and

(ii) the particular property's fair market value at the transfer time, in any other case;

(f) the transferor's proceeds of disposition of any units of a transferee that were disposed of by the transferor at any particular time that is within 60 days after the transfer time in exchange for shares of the transferor, are deemed to be equal to the cost amount of the units to the transferor immediately before the particular time;

(g) if, at any particular time that is within 60 days after the transfer time, a taxpayer disposes of shares of the transferor to the transferor in exchange for units of a transferee

(i) the taxpayer's proceeds of disposition of the shares and the cost to the taxpayer of the units are deemed to be equal to the cost amount to the taxpayer of the shares immediately before the particular time,

(ii) for the purposes of applying section 116 in respect of the disposition, the shares are deemed to be excluded property of the taxpayer,

(iii) where the qualifying exchange occurs after 2004, for the purposes of applying section 218.3 in respect of that exchange, the payment or crediting of the units to the taxpayer by the transferor is deemed not to be an assessable distribution,

(iv) where all of the taxpayer's shares of the transferor have been so disposed of, for the purpose of applying section 39.1 in respect of the taxpayer after that disposition, the transferee is deemed to be the same entity as the transferor,

(v) for the purpose of the definition "designated beneficiary" in section 210, the units are deemed not to have been held at any time by the transferor, and

(vi) if the taxpayer is at the particular time affiliated with the transferor or the transferee,

(A) those units are deemed not to be identical to any other units of the transferee,

(B) if the taxpayer is the transferee, and the units cease to exist when the taxpayer acquires them (or, for greater certainty, when the taxpayer would but for that cessation have acquired them), the taxpayer is deemed

(I) to have acquired those units at the particular time, and

(II) to have disposed of those units immediately after the particular time for proceeds of disposition equal to the cost amount to the taxpayer of those units at the particular time, and

(C) in any other case, for the purpose of computing any gain or loss of the taxpayer from the taxpayer's first disposition, after the particular time, of each of those units,

(I) if that disposition is a renunciation or surrender of the unit by the taxpayer for no consideration, and is not in favour of any person other than the transferee, the taxpayer's proceeds of disposition of that unit are

deemed to be equal to that unit's cost amount to the taxpayer immediately before that disposition, and

(II) if subclause (I) does not apply, the taxpayer's proceeds of disposition of that unit are deemed to be equal to the greater of that unit's fair market value and its cost amount to the taxpayer immediately before that disposition;

(h) where a share to which paragraph (g) applies would, if this Act were read without reference to this paragraph, cease to be a "qualified investment" (within the meaning assigned by subsection 146(1), 146.1(1), 146.3(1) or 146.4(1), section 204 or subsection 207.01(1)) as a consequence of the qualifying exchange, the share is deemed to be a qualified investment until the earlier of the day that is 60 days after the day that includes the transfer time and the time at which it is disposed of in accordance with paragraph (g);

(i) there shall be added to the amount determined under the description of A in the definition "refundable capital gains tax on hand" in subsection 132(4) in respect of a transferee for its taxation years that begin after the transfer time the amount determined by the formula

$$(A - B) \times C/D$$

where

A is the transferor's "refundable capital gains tax on hand" (within the meaning assigned by subsection 131(6) or 132(4), as the case may be) at the end of its taxation year that includes the transfer time,

B is the transferor's "capital gains refund" (within the meaning assigned by paragraph 131(2)(a) or 132(1)(a), as the case may be) for that year,

C is the total fair market value of property of the transferor disposed of to, net of liabilities assumed by, the transferee on the qualifying exchange, and

D is the total fair market value of property of the transferor disposed of to, net of liabilities assumed by, all transferees on the qualifying exchange;

(j) no amount in respect of a non-capital loss, net capital loss, restricted farm loss, farm loss or limited partnership loss of a fund for a taxation year that began before the transfer time is deductible in computing the taxable income of any of the funds for a taxation year that begins after the transfer time;

(k) if the transferor is a mutual fund trust, for the purposes of subsections 132.1(1) and (3) to (5), the transferee is deemed after the transfer time to be the same mutual fund trust as, and a continuation of, the transferor;

(l) if the transferor is a mutual fund corporation

(i) for the purpose of subsection 131(4) but, for greater certainty, without having any effect on the computation of any amount determined under this Part, the transferor is deemed in respect of any share disposed of in accordance with paragraph (g) to be a mutual fund corporation at the time of the disposition,

(ii) for the purpose of Part I.3 but, for greater certainty, without having any effect on the computation of any amount determined under this Part, the transferor's taxation year that, if this Act were read without reference to this paragraph, would have included the transfer time is deemed to have ended immediately before the transfer time, and

(iii) for the purpose of subsection 131(1), a dividend that is made payable at a particular time after the acquisition time but within the 60-day period commencing immediately after the transfer time, and paid before the end of that period, by the transferor to taxpayers that held shares of a class of shares of the transferor, that was recognized under securities legislation as or as part of an investment fund, immediately before the transfer time is deemed to have become payable at the first intervening time if the transferor so elects in respect of the full amount of the dividend in prescribed manner on or before the day on which any part of the dividend was paid;

(m) for the purpose of determining the funds' capital gains redemptions (as defined in subsection 131(6) or 132(4), as the case may be), for their taxation years that include the transfer time,

(i) the total of the cost amounts to the transferor of all its properties at the end of the year is deemed to be the total of all amounts each of which is

(A) the transferor's proceeds of disposition of a property that was transferred to a transferee on the qualifying exchange, or

(B) the cost amount to the transferor at the end of the year of a property that was not transferred on the qualifying exchange;

(ii) a transferee is deemed not to have acquired any property that was transferred to it on the qualifying exchange; and

(iii) the amounts determined under the descriptions of A and B in the definition "capital gains redemptions" shall be determined as if the year ended immediately before the transfer time; and

(n) except as provided in subparagraph (l)(i), the transferor is, notwithstanding subsections 131(8) and (8.01) and 132(6), deemed to be neither a mutual fund corporation nor a mutual fund trust for taxation years that begin after the transfer time.

Related Provisions: 54"superficial loss"(c) — Superficial loss rule does not apply to disposition under 132.2(3)(a) or (c); 132.2(4) — Transfer of non-depreciable property; 132.2(5) — Transfer of depreciable property; 257 — Formula cannot calculate to less than zero.

Notes: For discussion of 132.2 see Chasmar & Chua, "Reorganizations of Investment Funds", 49(2) *Canadian Tax Journal* 482-500 (2001); Ruby & Shragie, "Hidden Tax Traps in Section 132.2 Mergers", 54(2) *CTJ* 450-56 (2006). For mergers of REITs see Neal Armstrong, "Real Estate Investment Trust Mergers Rely on Section 132.2", X(2) *Corporate Finance* (Federated Press) 942-46 (2002); Xiao & Juneja, "Recent Transactions of Interest", 2017 Cdn Tax Foundation conference report at 5:17-25 (OneREIT-SmartREIT merger).

Note that loss carryforwards disappear on the merger (132.2(3)(j)), so 132.2 is not advisable for trusts carrying losses.

For rulings on the new 132.2 (enacted in 2013 effective 1999), see VIEWS docs 2005-0117591R3, 2005-0117901R3, 2005-0119891R3, 2005-0123381R3, 2005-0160541R3, 2006-0172931R3, 2006-0173211R3, 2006-0178401R3, 2006-0182221R3, 2006-0182271R3, 2006-0190311R3, 2006-0190371R3, 2006-0191631R3 (REIT reorganization), 2006-0192561R3, 2006-0195411R3, 2006-0196401R3, 2006-0196451R3, 2006-0199751R3, 2006-0212021R3, 2006-0212481R3, 2006-0214421R3, 2006-0218911R3 (reorg with internal butterfly), 2007-0244691R3 (REIT reorg to eliminate subtrust), 2008-0267631R3 (income trust, stapled units and elimination of corporation), 2008-03000451R3 (REIT reorg to eliminate Holdco), 2009-0350481R3 (REIT reorg); 2011-0395091R3, 2013-0488351R3 and 2013-0507291R3 (MFC to MFT conversion); 2013-0492731R3 and 2014-0518511R3 (MFT reorg to eliminate subtrust); 2016-0660321R3 (REIT reorg), 2018-0778961R3 [2019-0792771R3] (split-up of MFTs).

CRA stated at the 2005 Cdn Tax Foundation annual conference (*Income Tax Technical News* 34) that income trust reorgs, including converting a MFC to a MFT, can be acceptable (see VIEWS doc 2003-0053981R3), but converting a regular corporation to a MFT via 132.2 without realizing gains would be challenged under GAAR.

See VIEWS doc 2009-0327881E5 on the T3 filing deadline after a qualifying exchange.

CRA wrote to the Investment Funds Institute of Canada on May 5, 2004, stating there would be no blanket extension of time for tax filings (T3 return, T3 Supp. and Summ., NR4, T5008) after mutual fund mergers. "However, we are prepared to review all requests for an extension of time for tax filings on a merging of mutual funds on a case-by-case basis. This will ensure that CRA has all requisite information on hand to make an informed decision." The letter lists the information to be provided with a request for extension of time, and the conditions under which the CRA may grant extension. (The letter also describes what to do when combining information from several funds onto one T3 slip; that information is now in Guide T4013.) For the text of the letter, see up to PITA 43rd ed. (under 132.2).

132.2(3)(m)(iii) added by 2017 budget bill #2, for qualifying exchanges where an election in respect of the qualifying exchange is filed or amended after Sept. 7, 2017.

132.2(3)(h) amended by 2017 budget bill #2 to change 205(1) to 146.4(1), effective March 23, 2017.

132.2(3) amended by 2017 budget bill #2, for transfers that occur after March 21, 2017, to change "*the* transferee" to "*a* transferee" in (a), (e)-(g) opening words and (m)(ii); "one or both of the funds" to "transferor or the transferee" in (g)(vi) opening words;

para. (i); "either of the funds" to "any of the funds" in (j); to add reference to 131(8.01) in (n); and to add (a.1) and (l)(iii). These changes recognize that 132.2(1)"qualifying exchange"(a)(ii) and (d) now permit transfer to multiple trusts. For earlier transfers, read para. (i) as:

(i) there shall be added to the amount determined under the description of A in the definition "refundable capital gains tax on hand" in subsection 132(4) in respect of the transferee for its taxation years that begin after the transfer time the amount, if any, by which

(i) the transferor's refundable capital gains tax on hand (within the meaning assigned by subsection 131(6) or 132(4), as the case may be) at the end of its taxation year that includes the transfer time

exceeds

(ii) the transferor's capital gains refund (within the meaning assigned by paragraph 131(2)(a) or 132(1)(a), as the case may be) for that year;

See Notes at end of 132.2 for in-force rules. 132.2(3)(g)(iv)-(vi) were (ii)-(iv) in the July 16/10 draft. Subparas. (ii)-(iii) were released on Oct. 31/11 as 132.2(3)(o), (p).

Regulations: 1105 (prescribed classes of depreciable property).

(4) Qualifying exchange — non-depreciable property — If a transferor transfers a property, other than a depreciable property, to a transferee in a qualifying exchange,

(a) the transferee is deemed to have acquired the property at the acquisition time and not to have acquired the property at the transfer time;

(b) the transferor's proceeds of disposition of the property and the transferee's cost of the property are deemed to be the lesser of

(i) the fair market value of the property at the transfer time, and

(ii) the greatest of

(A) the cost amount to the transferor of the property at the transfer time,

(B) the amount that the transferor and the transferee agree on in respect of the property in their election, and

(C) the fair market value at the transfer time of the consideration (other than units of the transferee) received by the transferor for the disposition of the property; and

(c) if the property is a unit of the transferee and the unit ceases to exist when the transferee acquires it (or, for greater certainty, when the transferee would but for that cessation have acquired it), paragraphs (a) and (b) do not apply to the transferee.

Notes: 132.2(4)(b)(ii)(B) amended to change "funds" to "transferor and the transferee", and para. (c) added, by 2017 budget bill #2, for transfers after March 21, 2017.

(5) Depreciable property — If a transferor transfers a depreciable property to a transferee in a qualifying exchange,

(a) the transferor is deemed to have disposed of the property at the depreciables disposition time, and not to have disposed of the property at the transfer time;

(b) the transferee is deemed to have acquired the property at the depreciables acquisition time, and not to have acquired the property at the transfer time;

(c) the transferor's proceeds of disposition of the property and the transferee's cost of the property are deemed to be the lesser of

(i) the fair market value of the property at the transfer time, and

(ii) the greatest of

(A) the lesser of its capital cost and its cost amount to the transferor immediately before the depreciables disposition time,

(B) the amount that the transferor and the transferee agree on in respect of the property in their election, and

(C) the fair market value at the transfer time of the consideration (other than units of the transferee) received by the transferor for the disposition of the property;

(d) where the capital cost of the property to the transferor exceeds the transferor's proceeds of disposition of the property under paragraph (c), for the purposes of sections 13 and 20 and any regulations made for the purpose of paragraph 20(1)(a),

(i) the property's capital cost to the transferee is deemed to be the amount that was its capital cost to the transferor, and

(ii) the excess is deemed to have been allowed to the transferee in respect of the property under regulations made for the purpose of paragraph 20(1)(a) in computing income for taxation years ending before the transfer time; and

(e) where two or more depreciable properties of a prescribed class are disposed of by the transferor to the transferee in the same qualifying exchange, paragraph (c) applies as if each property so disposed of had been separately disposed of in the order designated by the transferor at the time of making the election in respect of the qualifying exchange or, if the transferor does not so designate any such order, in the order designated by the Minister.

Notes: 132.2(5)(c)(ii)(B) amended by 2017 budget bill #2, for transfers that occur after March 21, 2017, to change "funds" to "transferor and the transferee".

(6) Due date — The due date of an election referred to in paragraph (c) of the definition "qualifying exchange" in subsection (1) is

(a) the day that is six months after the day that includes the transfer time; and

(b) on joint application by the funds, any later day that the Minister accepts.

Forms: T1169: Election on disposition of property by a mutual fund corporation (or a mutual fund trust) to a mutual fund trust.

(7) Amendment or revocation of election — The Minister may, on joint application by the funds on or before the due date of an election referred to in paragraph (e) of the definition "qualifying exchange" in subsection (1), grant permission to amend or revoke the election.

Notes: 132.2(7) amended by 2017 budget bill #2, for transfers that occur after March 21, 2017, to change "paragraph (c)" to "paragraph (e)".

Notes [s. 132.2]: See Notes to 132.2(3) for discussion of the operation of 132.2. Where a mutual fund merger is not a "qualifying exchange", CRA may allow the continuing fund to combine the funds' reporting for the past year, and may extend filing deadlines. See May 5, 2004 letter to Investment Funds Institute of Canada, reproduced in "Proposed Administrative Policy" box here up to the 52nd ed.

132.2 replaced by 2002-2013 technical bill, generally effective for qualifying exchanges that occur after 1998, with transitional rules for a qualifying exchange before July 18, 2005 and some text reading differently before the 2009 taxation year (see up to PITA 48th ed. for details). An election made under former 132.2(2)"qualifying exchange"(c) continues to have the effect of having new 132.2 (as modified from time to time) apply. [2002-2013 technical bill, subsec. 280(6)] If an election was filed by Sep. 30, 1998 under 1995-97 technical bill subsec. 159(4) to ignore former 132.2(1)(p) in respect of a transfer, then ignore new 132.2(3)(i) in respect of that transfer. [2002-2013 technical bill, subsec. 280(7)]

For former 132.2, in force from July 1994 through end of 1998 [as amended by subsecs. 280(3) and (4) of the 2002-2013 technical bill], see the 44th or 45th ed.

Definitions [s. 132.2]: "acquisition time" — 132.2(2)(c); "affiliated" — 251.1; "amount" — 248(1); "capital gain" — 39(1)(a), 248(1); "class of shares" — 248(6); "cost amount" — 248(1); "depreciable property" — 13(21), 248(1); "depreciables acquisition time" — 132.2(2)(g); "depreciables disposition time" — 132.2(2)(e); "disposition" — 248(1); "due date" — 132.2(6); "fair market value" — see 69(1) Notes; "farm loss" — 111(8), 248(1); "first intervening time" — 132.2(2)(b); "first post-exchange year" — 132.2(1); "funds" — 132.2(1)"qualifying exchange"; "limited partnership loss" — 96(2.1), 248(1); "Minister" — 248(1); "month" — *Interpretation Act* 35(1); "mutual fund corporation" — 131(8), 248(1); "mutual fund trust" — 132(6)–(7), 132.2(3)(n), 248(1); "net capital loss" — 111(8), 248(1); "non-capital loss" — 111(8), 248(1); "person" — 248(1); "prescribed", "property" — 248(1); "qualifying exchange" — 132.2(1); "regulation" — 248(1); "restricted farm loss" — 31(1.1), 248(1); "SIFT wind-up corporation" — 248(1); "second intervening time" — 132.2(2)(f); "share" — 132.2(1); "taxable income" — 248(1); "taxation year" — 249; "taxpayer" — 248(1); "transfer time", "transferee", "transferor" — 132.2(1)"qualifying exchange"; "undepreciated capital cost" — 13(21), 248(1).

Non-Resident-Owned Investment Corporations

133. [No longer relevant.]

Notes: 133 sets out rules for non-resident-owned investment corporations (NROs), which were eliminated by the 2000 budget. No new NROs can be created after Feb. 27, 2000, and existing NROs lost their status at end of 2003 at the latest. 133(8) provides:

"non-resident-owned investment corporation" means a corporation incorporated in Canada that, throughout the whole of the period commencing on the later of June 18, 1971 and the day on which it was incorporated and ending on the last day of the taxation year in respect of which the expression is being applied, complied with the following conditions:

[(a)-(f) conditions — ed.];

except that ...

(i) subject to section 134.1, a corporation is not a non-resident-owned investment corporation in any taxation year that ends after the earlier of,

(i) the first time, if any, after February 27, 2000 at which the corporation effects an increase in capital, and

(ii) the corporation's last taxation year that begins before 2003;

See Woo, "NROs No More!", X(2) *International Tax Planning* (Federated Press) 706-08 (2001); Morgan, "The Demise of the NRO", X(2) *Corporate Finance* (Federated Press) 938-41 (2002).

For an alternative that could for a time achieve the same effect, see Vowinckel, "Replacing NRO Structures with Reverse Hybrids", 2001 Cdn Tax Foundation conference report, 10:1-25; VIEWS docs 2000-0054593, 2001-0101813 and 2003-0005273; Barnicke & Roy, "NRO Replacement", 11(6) *Canadian Tax Highlights* (ctf.ca) 3-4 (June 2003); but this has been curtailed by amendments to the Canada-US tax treaty: see Notes to Art. IV:7.

In *Banner Pharmacaps*, 2003 FCA 367, para. 9, a corporation was not an NRO because its principal business was not making loans.

134. Non-resident-owned corporation not a Canadian corporation, etc. — [No longer relevant]

Notes: 134 applies only to NROs, which do not exist since 2003. See Notes to 133.

134.1, 134.2 [No longer relevant.]

Notes: 134.1 provides an election to continue to be an NRO (see Notes to 133) for certain purposes for one year only (thus not past 2003-04). It was added by 2000 Budget and amended retroactively by 2002-2013 technical bill to implement a Nov. 1, 2001 Finance comfort letter. It applied following an amalgamation in *CGU Holdings*, 2009 FCA 20, but due to the amalgamation, allowable refundable tax was nil: "the deemed NRO status provided by 134.1(2) does not extend to 87(2)(cc)(i)".

134.2, added by 2000 Budget, allows revocation of an election to be an NRO.

Patronage Dividends

135. (1) Deduction in computing income — Notwithstanding anything in this Part, other than subsections (1.1) to (2.1) and 135.1(3), there may be deducted, in computing the income of a taxpayer for a taxation year, the total of the payments made, pursuant to allocations in proportion to patronage, by the taxpayer

(a) within the year or within 12 months thereafter to the taxpayer's customers of the year; and

(b) within the year or within 12 months thereafter to the taxpayer's customers of a previous year, the deduction of which from income of a previous taxation year was not permitted.

Related Provisions: 20(1)(u) — Deduction from income for amount allowed under 135(1); 87(2)(g.5) — Amalgamation — continuing corp; 135(1.1) — No deduction for payment not at arm's length unless cooperative or credit union; 135(2) — Limitation — non-member customers; 135(4) — Definitions; 135(7) — Patronage dividend included in member's income; 135.1(3) — Limit on deductibility for tax deferred cooperative shares; 136 — Cooperative deemed not to be private corp; 212(1)(g) — Non-resident withholding tax; *Interpretation Act* 27(5) — Meaning of "within 12 months".

Notes: A patronage dividend is an amount paid by a cooperative society (co-op) to its members, usually at year-end, as a rebate or discount for their purchases from the co-op. Some co-ops are effectively retailers dealing with consumers buying groceries or other goods. Others include farm co-ops whose members are commercial farmers making taxable supplies.

For interpretation see VIEWS docs 2005-0140601E5, 2005-0146061E5, 2005-0161981E5, 2011-0414201E5, 2012-0436981E5, 2012-0467231E5, 2017-0702731E5. A distribution to non-active members based on member loan balances might not fall within 135(1): 2005-0130401R3.

135(1) amended by 2006 budget bill #1 (effective 2006), 2004 Budget.

Regulations: 218 (information return).

Interpretation Bulletins: See list at end of s. 135.

Forms: T2 Sched. 16: Patronage dividend deduction.

(1.1) Limitation where non-arm's length customer — Subsection (1) applies to a payment made by a taxpayer to a customer with whom the taxpayer does not deal at arm's length only if

(a) the taxpayer is a cooperative corporation described in subsection 136(2) or a credit union; or

(b) the payment is prescribed.

Notes: 135(1.1) added by 2004 Budget, effective for payments made by a taxpayer after March 22, 2004 with grandfathering for certain "qualifying payments" made in the taxation year that began before March 23, 2004 (see PITA 27th-36th ed.).

Regulations: 3200 (temporary) (prescribed payments from March 23/04 to Oct. 28/08).

(2) Limitation where non-member customer — If a taxpayer has not made allocations in proportion to patronage in respect of all of the taxpayer's customers of the year, at the same rate, with appropriate differences for different types, classes, grades or qualities of goods, products or services, the amount that may be deducted by the taxpayer under subsection (1) is an amount equal to the lesser of

(a) the total of the payments mentioned in that subsection, and

(b) the total of

(i) the part of the income of the taxpayer for the year attributable to business done with members, and

(ii) the allocations in proportion to patronage made to non-member customers of the year.

Related Provisions: 87(2)(g.5) — Amalgamation — continuing corporation; 135(2.1) — Carryforward.

Notes: For interpretation see VIEWS doc 2003-0020241R3, but note that 135(1) now prohibits non-arm's length patronage dividends except for co-ops and credit unions.

135(2) opening words amended by 2004 Budget, effective for payments made by a taxpayer after March 22, 2004. The changes were non-substantive.

Interpretation Bulletins: See list at end of s. 135.

(2.1) Deduction carried over — Where, in a taxation year ending after 1985, all or a portion of a payment made by a taxpayer pursuant to an allocation in proportion to patronage to the taxpayer's customers who are members is not deductible in computing the taxpayer's income for the year because of the application of subsection (2) (in this subsection referred to as the "undeducted amount"), there may be deducted in computing the taxpayer's income for a subsequent taxation year, an amount equal to the lesser of

(a) the undeducted amount, except to the extent that that amount was deducted in computing the taxpayer's income for any preceding taxation year, and

(b) the amount, if any, by which

(i) the taxpayer's income for the subsequent taxation year (computed without reference to this subsection) attributable to business done with the taxpayer's customers of that year who are members

exceeds

(ii) the amount deducted in computing the taxpayer's income for the subsequent taxation year by virtue of subsection (1) in respect of payments made by the taxpayer pursuant to allocations in proportion to patronage to the taxpayer's customers of that year who are members.

Related Provisions: 87(2)(g.5) — Amalgamation — continuing corporation.

Interpretation Bulletins: See list at end of s. 135.

(3) Amount to be deducted or withheld from payment to customer — Subject to subsection 135.1(6), a taxpayer who makes at any particular time in a calendar year a payment pursuant to an allocation in proportion to patronage to a person who is resident in Canada and is not exempt from tax under section 149 shall, notwithstanding any agreement or any law to the contrary, deduct or withhold from the payment an amount equal to 15% of the lesser of the amount of the payment and the amount, if any, by which

(a) the total of the amount of the payment and the amounts of all other payments pursuant to allocations in proportion to pa-

tronage made by the taxpayer to that person in the calendar year and before the particular time

exceeds

(b) $100,

and forthwith remit that amount to the Receiver General on behalf of that person on account of that person's tax under this Part.

Related Provisions: 87(2)(g.5) — Amalgamation — continuing corporation; 127(6) — Investment tax credit of cooperative corporation; 135(2) — Limitation — non-member customers; 135(6) — Amount of payment to customers; 135.1(6) — 135.1(6) — Exclusion from withholding — tax deferred cooperative shares; 227(1), (4), (5), (8.3), (8.4), (9), (9.2), (9.4), (11), (12), (13) — Witholding taxes — administration and enforcement; 227.1 — Liability of directors.

Notes: Under s. 227, withholdings under 135(3) are generally subject to the same stringent rules as employee source deduction (payroll) withholdings (s. 153) and non-resident withholding taxes (s. 212).

135(3) opening words amended by 2006 budget bill #1 (implementing a 2005 Budget proposal), effective 2006, effectively to add reference to 135.1(6).

Interpretation Bulletins: See list at end of s. 135.

Forms: T2 Sched. 16: Patronage dividend deduction; T4A: Statement of pension, retirement, annuity, and other income; RC4157: Deducting income tax on pension and other income, and filing the T4A slip and summary.

(4) Definitions — For the purposes of this section and section 135.1,

Notes: 135(4) opening words amended by 2006 budget bill #1 (implementing a 2005 Budget proposal), effective 2006, to add reference to 135.1.

"allocation in proportion to patronage" for a taxation year means an amount credited by a taxpayer to a customer of that year on terms that the customer is entitled to or will receive payment thereof, computed at a rate in relation to the quantity, quality or value of the goods or products acquired, marketed, handled, dealt in or sold, or services rendered by the taxpayer from, on behalf of or to the customer, whether as principal or as agent of the customer or otherwise, with appropriate differences in the rate for different classes, grades or qualities thereof, if

(a) the amount was credited

(i) within the year or within 12 months thereafter, and

(ii) at the same rate in relation to quantity, quality or value aforesaid as the rate at which amounts were similarly credited to all other customers of that year who were members or to all other customers of that year, as the case may be, with appropriate differences aforesaid for different classes, grades or qualities, and

(b) the prospect that amounts would be so credited was held out by the taxpayer to the taxpayer's customers of that year who were members or non-member customers of that year, as the case may be;

Related Provisions: 135(1) — Deduction for allocations; 212(1)(g) — Withholding tax on allocations to non-residents.

Notes: For CRA interpretation see VIEWS doc 2010-0364001E5.

135(4)"allocation in proportion to patronage" was 135(4)(a) before RSC 1985 (5th Supp) consolidation for tax years ending after Nov. 1991.

Regulations: 218 (information return).

"consumer goods or services" means goods or services the cost of which was not deductible by the taxpayer in computing the income from a business or property;

Notes: 135(4)"consumer goods or services" was 135(4)(b) before RSC 1985 (5th Supp) consolidation for tax years ending after Nov. 1991.

"customer" means a customer of a taxpayer and includes a person who sells or delivers goods or products to the taxpayer, or for whom the taxpayer renders services;

Notes: 135(4)"customer" was 135(4)(c) before RSC 1985 (5th Supp) consolidation for tax years ending after Nov. 1991.

"income of the taxpayer attributable to business done with members" of any taxation year means that proportion of the income of the taxpayer for the year (before making any deduction under this section) that the value of the goods or products acquired, marketed, handled, dealt in or sold or services rendered by the taxpayer from, on behalf of, or for members, is of the total value of goods or products acquired, marketed, handled, dealt in or sold or services rendered by the taxpayer from, on behalf of, or for all customers during the year;

Notes: The definition includes income earned through a partnership: VIEWS doc 2015-0613961E5.

135(4)"income of the taxpayer attributable ... members" was 135(4)(d) before RSC 1985 (5th Supp) consolidation for tax years ending after Nov. 1991.

"member" means a person who is entitled as a member or shareholder to full voting rights in the conduct of the affairs of the taxpayer (being a corporation) or of a corporation of which the taxpayer is a subsidiary wholly-owned corporation;

Notes: 135(4)"member" was 135(4)(e) before RSC 1985 (5th Supp) consolidation for tax years ending after Nov. 1991.

"non-member customer" means a customer who is not a member;

Notes: 135(4)"non-member customer" was 135(4)(f) before RSC 1985 (5th Supp) consolidation for tax years ending after Nov. 1991.

"payment" includes

(a) the issue of a certificate of indebtedness or shares of the taxpayer or of a corporation of which the taxpayer is a subsidiary wholly-owned corporation if the taxpayer or that corporation has in the year or within 12 months thereafter disbursed an amount of money equal to the total face value of all certificates or shares so issued in the course of redeeming or purchasing certificates of indebtedness or shares of the taxpayer or that corporation previously issued,

(b) the application by the taxpayer of an amount to a member's liability to the taxpayer (including, without restricting the generality of the foregoing, an amount applied in fulfilment of an obligation of the member to make a loan to the taxpayer and an amount applied on account of payment for shares issued to a member) pursuant to a by-law of the taxpayer, pursuant to statutory authority or at the request of the member, or

(c) the amount of a payment or transfer by the taxpayer that, under subsection 56(2), is required to be included in computing the income of a member.

Notes: See Notes to 188.1(5) re meaning of "includes" in the opening words.

For CRA interpretation see VIEWS docs 2009-0345461E5, 2011-0396771I7.

135(4)"payment" was 135(4)(g) before RSC 1985 (5th Supp) consolidation for tax years ending after Nov. 1991.

Interpretation Bulletins: See list at end of s. 135.

(5) Holding out prospect of allocations — For the purpose of this section a taxpayer shall be deemed to have held out the prospect that amounts would be credited to a customer of a taxation year by way of allocation in proportion to patronage, if

(a) throughout the year the statute under which the taxpayer was incorporated or registered, its charter, articles of association or by-laws or its contract with the customer held out the prospect that amounts would be so credited to customers who are members or non-member customers, as the case may be; or

(b) prior to the commencement of the year or prior to such other day as may be prescribed for the class of business in which the taxpayer is engaged, the taxpayer has published an advertisement in prescribed form in a newspaper or newspapers of general circulation throughout the greater part of the area in which the taxpayer carried on business holding out that prospect to customers who are members or non-member customers, as the case may be, and has filed copies of the newspapers with the Minister before the end of the 30th day of the taxation year or within 30 days from the prescribed day, as the case may be.

Related Provisions: 20(1)(u) — Patronage dividends; *Interpretation Act* 27(5) — Meaning of "within 30 days".

Interpretation Bulletins: See list at end of s. 135.

(6) Amount of payment to customer — For greater certainty, the amount of any payment pursuant to an allocation in proportion to patronage is the amount thereof determined before deducting any amount required by subsection (3) to be deducted or withheld from that payment.

Related Provisions: 20(1)(u) — Deduction — patronage dividends; 87(2)(g.5) — Amalgamation — continuing corporation; 135(3) — Amount to be deducted or withheld from payment to customer.

Interpretation Bulletins: See list at end of s. 135.

(7) Payment to customer to be included in income — Where a payment pursuant to an allocation in proportion to patronage (other than an allocation in respect of consumer goods or services) has been received by a taxpayer, the amount of the payment shall, subject to subsection 135.1(2), be included in computing the recipient's income for the taxation year in which the payment was received and, without restricting the generality of the foregoing, where a certificate of indebtedness or a share was issued to a person pursuant to an allocation in proportion to patronage, the amount of the payment by virtue of that issuance shall be included in computing the recipient's income for the taxation year in which the certificate or share was received and not in computing the recipient's income for the year in which the indebtedness was subsequently discharged or the share was redeemed.

Related Provisions: 20(1)(u) — Patronage dividend deduction; 87(2)(g.5) — Amalgamation — continuing corporation; 135.1(2) — Limitation on income inclusion — tax deferred cooperative shares; 212(1)(g) — Non-resident withholding tax.

Notes: For CRA interpretation see VIEWS doc 2010-0364001E5.

135(7) amended by 2006 budget bill #1, effective 2006.

Interpretation Bulletins: See list at end of s. 135.

Forms: RC4157: Deducting income tax on pension and other income, and filing the T4A slip and summary; T2 Sched. 16: Patronage dividend deduction; T4A: Statement of pension, retirement, annuity, and other income.

(8) Patronage dividends — For the purposes of this section, where

(a) a person has sold or delivered a quantity of goods or products to a marketing board established by or pursuant to a law of Canada or a province,

(b) the marketing board has sold or delivered the same quantity of goods or products of the same class, grade or quality to a taxpayer of which the person is a member, and

(c) the taxpayer has credited that person with an amount based on the quantity of goods or products of that class, grade or quality sold or delivered to it by the marketing board,

the quantity of goods or products referred to in paragraph (c) shall be deemed to have been sold or delivered by that person to the taxpayer and to have been acquired by the taxpayer from that person.

Definitions [s. 135]: "allocation in proportion to patronage" — 135(4); "amount" — 248(1); "arm's length" — 251(1); "business" — 248(1); "calendar year" — *Interpretation Act* 37(1)(a); "Canada" — 255; "consumer goods or services" — 135(4); "corporation" — 248(1), *Interpretation Act* 35(1); "credit union" — 137(6), 248(1); "customer", "income of the taxpayer attributable", "member" — 135(4); "Minister" — 248(1); "non-member customer", "payment" — 135(4); "person", "prescribed", "property" — 248(1); "province" — *Interpretation Act* 35(1); "resident in Canada" — 94(3)(a), 250; "share", "subsidiary wholly-owned corporation" — 248(1); "taxation year" — 249; "taxpayer" — 248(1).

Interpretation Bulletins [s. 135]: IT-362R: Patronage dividends; IT-493: Agency cooperative corporations (cancelled).

Agricultural Cooperatives — Tax-deferred Patronage Dividends

135.1 (1) Definitions — The following definitions apply in this section and section 135.

"agricultural business" means a business, carried on in Canada, that consists of one or any combination of

(a) farming (including, if the person carrying on the business is a corporation described in paragraph (a) of the definition "agricultural cooperative corporation", the production, processing, storing and wholesale marketing of the products of its members' farming activities); or

(b) the provision of goods or services (other than financial services) that are required for farming.

Notes: See Notes at end of 135.1.

"agricultural cooperative corporation" at any time means a corporation

(a) that was incorporated or continued by or under the provisions of a law, of Canada or of a province, that provide for the establishment of the corporation as a cooperative corporation or that provide for the establishment of cooperative corporations; and

(b) that has at that time

(i) as its principal business an agricultural business, or

(ii) members, making up at least 75% of all members of the corporation, each of whom

(A) is an agricultural cooperative corporation, or

(B) has as their principal business a farming business.

Related Provisions: 87(2)(s) — Amalgamation — continuing corporation.

Notes: See VIEWS docs 2010-0375361E5 (liquidation of agricultural cooperative); 2013-0510751E5 (agricultural cooperative under 135.1 might not be co-op under 136(2)). For the meaning of "principal business" see Notes to 20(1)(bb).

"allowable disposition" means a disposition by a taxpayer of a tax deferred cooperative share less than five years after the day on which the share was issued if

(a) before the disposition,

(i) the agricultural cooperative corporation is notified in writing that the taxpayer has after the share was issued become disabled and permanently unfit for work, or terminally ill, or

(ii) the taxpayer ceases to be a member of the agricultural cooperative corporation; or

(b) the agricultural cooperative corporation is notified in writing that the share is held by a person on whom the share has devolved as a consequence of the death of the taxpayer.

"eligible member" of an agricultural cooperative corporation means a member who carries on an agricultural business and who is

(a) an individual resident in Canada;

(b) an agricultural cooperative corporation;

(c) a corporation resident in Canada that carries on the business of farming in Canada; or

(d) a partnership that carries on the business of farming in Canada, all of the members of which are described in any of paragraphs (a) to (c) or this paragraph.

"tax deferred cooperative share" at any time means a share

(a) issued, after 2005 and before 2026, by an agricultural cooperative corporation to a person or partnership that is at the time the share is issued an eligible member of the agricultural cooperative corporation, pursuant to an allocation in proportion to patronage;

(b) the holder of which is not entitled to receive on the redemption, cancellation or acquisition of the share by the agricultural cooperative corporation or by any person with whom the agricultural cooperative corporation does not deal at arm's length an amount that is greater than the amount that would, if this Act were read without reference to this section, be included under subsection 135(7) in computing the eligible member's income for their taxation year in which the share was issued;

(c) that has not before that time been deemed by subsection (4) to have been disposed of; and

(d) that is of a class

(i) the terms of which provide that the agricultural cooperative corporation shall not, otherwise than pursuant to an allowable disposition, redeem, acquire or cancel a share of the class before the day that is five years after the day on which the share was issued, and

(ii) that is identified by the agricultural cooperative corporation in prescribed form and manner as a class of tax deferred cooperative shares.

Related Provisions: 87(2)(s) — Amalgamation.

Notes: For interpretation see VIEWS docs 2006-0198831R3, 2006-0217851E5.

Para. (a) amended by 2021 budget bill #1 to change 2021 to 2026, effective June 29, 2021, extending the tax deferral as proposed in the April 2021 federal Budget; and by 2015 Budget bill to change 2016 to 2021, effective June 23, 2015, extending the deferral as proposed in the April 2015 Budget.

"tax paid balance" of a taxpayer at the end of a particular taxation year of the taxpayer means the amount, if any, by which

(a) the total of

(i) the taxpayer's tax paid balance at the end of the immediately preceding taxation year, and

(ii) the amount, if any, that is included in computing the taxpayer's income under this Part for the particular taxation year because of an election described in subparagraph (2)(a)(ii),

exceeds

(b) the total of all amounts each of which is the taxpayer's proceeds of disposition of a tax deferred cooperative share that the taxpayer disposed of in the particular taxation year.

(2) Income inclusion — In computing the income of a taxpayer for a particular taxation year, there shall be included under subsection 135(7), in respect of the taxpayer's receipt, as an eligible member, of tax deferred cooperative shares of an agricultural cooperative corporation in the particular taxation year, only the total of

(a) the lesser of

(i) the total of all amounts, in respect of the taxpayer's receipt in the particular taxation year of tax deferred cooperative shares, that would, if this Act were read without reference to this section, be included under subsection 135(7) in computing the taxpayer's income for the particular taxation year, and

(ii) the greater of nil and the amount, if any, specified by the taxpayer in an election in prescribed form that is filed with the taxpayer's return of income for the particular taxation year, and

(b) the amount, if any, by which

(i) the total of all amounts each of which is the taxpayer's proceeds of disposition of a tax deferred cooperative share disposed of by the taxpayer in the particular taxation year

exceeds

(ii) the total of

(A) the taxpayer's tax paid balance at the end of the immediately preceding taxation year, and

(B) the amount, if any, that is included in computing the taxpayer's income for the particular taxation year because of an election described in subparagraph (a)(ii).

Related Provisions: 87(2)(s) — Amalgamation — continuing corporation.

Notes: See Notes at end of 135.1.

(3) Deductibility limit — The amount that may be deducted under subsection 135(1) for a particular taxation year by an agricultural cooperative corporation in respect of payments, in the form of tax deferred cooperative shares, made pursuant to allocations in proportion to patronage shall not exceed 85% of the agricultural cooperative corporation's income of the taxation year attributable to business done with members.

Notes: Amounts non-deductible due to 135.1(3) cannot be claimed in a later year: VIEWS doc 2013-0503941E5.

(4) Deemed disposition — A taxpayer who holds a tax deferred cooperative share is deemed to have disposed of the share, for proceeds of disposition equal to the amount that would, if this Act were read without reference to this section, have been included under subsection 135(7), in respect of the share, in computing the taxpayer's income for the taxation year in which the share was issued, at the earliest time at which

(a) the paid-up capital of the share is reduced otherwise than by way of a redemption of the share; or

(b) the taxpayer pledges, or for civil law hypothecates, assigns or in any way alienates the share as security for indebtedness of any kind.

Related Provisions: 135.1(5) — Reacquisition.

Notes: 135.1(4)(b) does not apply to indebtedness entered into before 2006; see Notes at end of 135.1.

(5) Reacquisition — A taxpayer who is deemed by subsection (4) to have disposed at any time of a tax deferred cooperative share is deemed to have reacquired the share, immediately after that time, at a cost equal to the taxpayer's proceeds of disposition from that disposition.

(6) Exclusion from withholding obligation — Subsection 135(3) does not apply to a payment pursuant to an allocation in proportion to patronage that is paid by an agricultural cooperative corporation through the issuance of a tax deferred cooperative share.

(7) Withholding on redemption — A person or partnership (in this subsection referred to as the "redeeming entity") that redeems, acquires or cancels a shareholder's share shall withhold and forthwith remit to the Receiver General, on account of the shareholder's tax liability, 15% from the amount otherwise payable on the redemption, acquisition or cancellation, if

(a) the share was, at the time it was issued, a tax deferred cooperative share;

(b) the redeeming entity is the corporation that issued the share, or a person or partnership with whom the corporation does not deal at arm's length; and

(c) the shareholder is not a trust whose taxable income is exempt from tax under this Part because of paragraph 149(1)(r) or (x).

Related Provisions: 87(2)(s) — Amalgamation — continuing corporation; 227(1), (4), (5), (8.3), (8.4), (9), (9.2), (9.4), (11), (12), (13) — Withholding taxes — administration and enforcement; 227.1 — Liability of directors for failing to withhold.

Notes: 135.1(7) amended by 2002-2013 technical bill (Part 5 — technical), effective for redemptions, acquisitions and cancellations that occur after 2007. The amendment implemented a March 4, 2008 Finance comfort letter.

(8) Application of subsecs. 84(2) and (3) — Subsections 84(2) and (3) do not apply to a tax deferred cooperative share.

(9) Application of subsec. (10) — Subsection (10) applies in respect of the disposition, after September 28, 2009, by a taxpayer of a tax deferred cooperative share (in this subsection and subsection (10) referred to as the "old share") of an agricultural cooperative corporation if

(a) the disposition results from the acquisition, cancellation or redemption of the old share in the course of a reorganization of the capital of the corporation;

(b) in exchange for the old share the corporation issues to the taxpayer a share (in this subsection and subsection (10) referred to as the "new share") that is described in all of paragraphs (b) to (d) of the definition "tax deferred cooperative share" in subsection (1); and

(c) the amount of paid-up capital, and the amount, if any, that the taxpayer is entitled to receive on a redemption, acquisition or cancellation, of the new share are equal to those amounts, respectively, in respect of the old share.

Notes: See Notes to 135.1(10).

(10) Shares issued on corporate reorganizations — If this subsection applies in respect of an exchange of a taxpayer's old share for a new share, for the purposes of this section (other than subsection (9)),

(a) the new share issued in exchange for the old share is deemed to have been issued, pursuant to an allocation in proportion to patronage, at the time the old share was issued; and

(b) provided that no person or partnership receives at any time any consideration (other than the new share) in exchange for the old share, for the purposes of subsections (2) and (7) the taxpayer is deemed to have disposed of the old share for nil proceeds.

Related Provisions: 87(2)(s)(ii) — Meaning of "new share" and "old share"; 135.1(9) — Conditions for 135.1(10) to apply.

Proposed Amendment — Triangular amalgamation of cooperative corps

Letter from Dept. of Finance, June 17, 2019: See under 87(9).

Notes: 135.1(9) and (10) implement a Sept 28, 2009 Finance comfort letter. They were added by 2002-2013 technical bill (Part 5 — technical), effective Sept. 29, 2009, but in their application to an exchange of shares described by 87(2)(s)(ii) (as amended by the 2002-2013 technical bill) that occurs before Oct. 31, 2011:

(a) with respect to a new share received on the exchange that has been disposed of before Oct. 31, 2011, read 135.1(10)(a) as:

(a) the new share issued in exchange for the old share is deemed to have been issued at the time the old share was issued; and

(b) read 135.1(10)(b) as:

(b) for the purposes of subsections (2) and (7) the taxpayer is deemed to have disposed of the old share for nil proceeds.

Notes [s. 135.1]: Due to the withholding requirements in 135, when patronage dividends were paid in shares, agricultural co-ops had to issue part of the dividend in cash to cover the tax liability. To relieve this, 135.1 provides that an "eligible member" (135.1(1)) of an "agricultural cooperative corporation" (ACC) (135.1(1)) may defer income inclusion of all or part of a payment made by an ACC in the form of a "tax deferred cooperative share" (135.1(1)) issued from 2006-2015, pursuant to an allocation in proportion to patronage. The deferral lasts until disposition (135.1(2)) or deemed disposition (135.1(4)) of the share. The 2005 Budget, introducing 135.1, stated: "The Government will monitor the effectiveness of this measure and ... will continue to assess the capitalization challenges of the agricultural cooperative sector."

On a triangular amalgamation of agricultural co-ops see VIEWS doc 2019-0793911E5; this will be fixed as per the June 17, 2019 comfort letter reproduced at 87(9).

135.1 added by 2006 budget bill #1 (implementing a 2005 Budget proposal), effective 2006 (but 135.1(4)(b) does not apply to indebtedness entered into before 2006).

Definitions [s. 135.1]: "agricultural business", "agricultural cooperative corporation" — 135.1(1); "allocation in proportion to patronage" — 135(4); "allowable disposition" — 135.1(1); "amount" — 248(1); "arm's length" — 251(1); "attributable" — 135(4)"income of the taxpayer attributable to business done with members"; "business" — 248(1); "Canada" — 255, *Interpretation Act* 35(1); "consequence" — 248(8); "corporation" — 248(1), *Interpretation Act* 35(1); "disposition" — 248(1); "eligible member" — 135.1(1); "farming" — 248(1); "individual" — 248(1); "member" — 135(4); "new share" — 87(2)(s)(ii), 135.1(9)(b); "old share" — 87(2)(s)(ii), 135.1(9); "paid-up capital" — 89(1), 248(1); "partnership" — see 96(1) Notes; "payment" — 135(4); "person", "prescribed" — 248(1); "province" — *Interpretation Act* 35(1); "redeeming entity" — 135.1(7); "resident in Canada" — 250; "security" — *Interpretation Act* 35(1); "share", "shareholder" — 248(1); "tax deferred cooperative share", "tax paid balance" — 135.1(1); "taxable income" — 2(2), 248(1); "taxation year" — 249; "taxpayer" — 248(1); "trust" — 104(1), 248(1), (3); "writing" — *Interpretation Act* 35(1).

Continuance of the Canadian Wheat Board

135.2 (1) Definitions — The following definitions apply in this section.

"application for continuance" means the application for continuance referred to in paragraph (a) of the definition "Canadian Wheat Board continuance".

"Canadian Wheat Board" means the corporation referred to in subsection 4(1) of the *Canadian Wheat Board (Interim Operations) Act*, as it read before its repeal, that is continued under the *Canada Business Corporations Act* pursuant to the application for continuance.

Notes: See Notes at end of 135.2. *Canadian Wheat Board (Interim Operations) Act* s. 4(1) provides: "The Canadian Wheat Board continued by subsection 3(1) of the *Canadian Wheat Board Act* is continued as a corporation."

"Canadian Wheat Board continuance" means the series of transactions or events that includes

(a) the application for continuance under the *Canada Business Corporations Act* that is

(i) made by the corporation referred to in subsection 4(1) of the *Canadian Wheat Board (Interim Operations) Act*, as it read before its repeal, and

(ii) approved by the Minister of Agriculture and Agri-Food under Part III of the *Marketing Freedom for Grain Farmers Act*;

(b) the issuance of a promissory note or other evidence of indebtedness by the Canadian Wheat Board to the eligible trust; and

(c) the disposition of the eligible debt by the eligible trust, in the same taxation year of the trust in which the eligible debt is issued to it, in exchange for consideration that includes the issuance of shares by the Canadian Wheat Board that have a total fair market value at the time of their issuance that is equal to the amount by which the principal amount of the eligible debt exceeds $10 million.

"eligible debt" means the promissory note or other evidence of indebtedness referred to in paragraph (b) of the definition "Canadian Wheat Board continuance".

Related Provisions: 135.2(4)(c) — Cost to trust of eligible debt deemed nil.

"eligible share" means a common share of the capital stock of the Canadian Wheat Board that is issued in exchange for the eligible debt, as referred to in paragraph (c) of the definition "Canadian Wheat Board continuance".

Related Provisions: 135.2(3) — Effect of trust exchanging CWB debt for eligible shares; 135.2(4)(c) — Cost to trust of eligible share deemed nil; 135.2(12) — Stock dividend on CWB shares.

"eligible trust", at any time, means a trust that meets the following conditions:

(a) it was established in connection with the application for continuance;

(b) it is resident in Canada at that time;

(c) immediately before it acquired the eligible debt, it held only property of nominal value;

(d) it is not exempt because of subsection 149(1) from tax on its taxable income for any period in its taxation year that includes that time;

(e) all of the interests of beneficiaries under it at that time are described by reference to units that are eligible units in it;

(f) the only persons who have acquired an interest as a beneficiary under the trust from it before that time are persons who were participating farmers at the time they acquired the interest;

(g) all or substantially all of the fair market value of its property at that time is based on the value of property that is

(i) eligible debt,

(ii) shares of the capital stock of the Canadian Wheat Board, or

(iii) property described in paragraph (a) or (b) of the definition "qualified investment" if in section 204 or a deposit with a credit union;

(h) the property that it has paid or distributed at or before that time to a beneficiary under the trust in satisfaction of the beneficiary's eligible unit in the trust is

(i) money denominated in Canadian dollars, or

(ii) shares distributed as an eligible wind-up distribution of the trust; and

(i) at no time in its taxation year that includes that time is any other trust an eligible trust.

Related Provisions: 94(4)(b) — Deeming non-resident trust to be resident in Canada does not apply for purposes of this definition; 135.2(3), (4) — Rules for eligible trust; 135.2(6)(b) — Effect of trust issuing unit to estate after farmer's death; 135.2(10) — Windup of trust; 135.2(11) — Where trust ceases to be eligible trust; 135.2(15) — Trust must file annual form.

Notes: This trust is called the Farmers Equity Trust. See g3.ca and farmersequity-trust.ca. CRA interprets "substantially all", used in para. (g), as meaning 90% or more.

"eligible unit", in a trust at any time, means a unit that describes all or part of an interest as a beneficiary under the trust, if

(a) the total of all amounts each of which is the value of a unit at the time it was issued by the trust to a participating farmer does not exceed the amount by which the principal amount of the eligible debt exceeds $10 million; and

(b) all of the interests as a beneficiary under the trust are "fixed interests" if (as defined in subsection 251.2(1)) in the trust.

Related Provisions: 135.2(5) — Effect of participating farmer acquiring eligible unit; 135.2(6) — Effect of trust issuing unit to estate after farmer's death; 135.2(7), (9) — Disposition of eligible unit.

Notes: This means units of the G3 Farmers Equity Trust (see 135.2(1)"eligible trust").

"eligible wind-up distribution", of a trust, means a distribution of property by the trust to a person if

(a) the distribution includes a share of the capital stock of the Canadian Wheat Board that is listed on a designated stock exchange;

(b) the only property (other than a share described in paragraph (a)) distributed by the trust on the distribution is money denominated in Canadian dollars;

(c) the distribution results in the disposition of all of the person's interest as a beneficiary under the trust; and

(d) the trust ceases to exist immediately after the distribution or immediately after the last of a series of eligible wind-up distributions (determined without reference to this paragraph) of the trust that includes the distribution.

Related Provisions: 135.2(10) — Effect of distribution.

"participating farmer", in respect of a trust at any time, means a person

(a) who is eligible to receive units of the trust pursuant to the plan under which the trust directs its trustees to grant units to persons who have delivered grain under a contract with the Canadian Wheat Board on or after August 1, 2013; and

(b) engaged in the production of grain or any person entitled, as landlord, vendor or mortgagee or hypothecary creditor, to grain produced by a person engaged in the production of grain or to any share of that grain.

Related Provisions: 135.2(5) — PF acquires an eligible unit of trust; 135.2(6), (8) — Death of PF; 135.2(9) — Where PF disposes of eligible unit.

"person" includes a partnership.

(2) Trust acquires an eligible debt — If, at any time, an eligible trust acquires eligible debt, the principal amount of the eligible debt is deemed not to be included in computing the income of the eligible trust for the taxation year of the eligible trust that includes that time.

Notes: Absent this rule, the concern was that 15(1) might require income inclusion, because the debt is being transferred to the trust by a corporation (CWB) of which the trust is a shareholder.

(3) Disposition of eligible debt — If, at any time, an eligible trust disposes of eligible debt in exchange for consideration that includes the issuance of eligible shares

(a) for the purpose of computing the income of the eligible trust for its taxation year that includes that time

(i) an amount, in respect of the disposition of the eligible debt, equal to the fair market value of all property (other than eligible shares) received on the exchange by the trust is included,

(ii) no amount in respect of the disposition of the eligible debt is included (other than the amount described in subparagraph (i)), and

(iii) no amount in respect of the receipt of the eligible shares is included;

(b) the cost to the eligible trust of each eligible share is deemed to be nil;

(c) in computing the paid-up capital in respect of the class of the capital stock of the Canadian Wheat Board that includes the eligible shares, at any time after the shares are issued, there shall be deducted an amount equal to the amount of the paid-up capital in respect of that class at the time the shares are issued;

(d) subsection 75(2) does not apply to property

(i) that is held by the trust in a taxation year that ends at or after that time, and

(ii) that is

(A) received by the trust on the exchange, or

(B) a substitute for property described in subparagraph (i); and

(e) subsections 84(2) and (3) and section 85 do not apply at any time to eligible shares.

Notes: See Notes at end of 135.2. Subsec. (3) applies to the transaction that will take place when the privatization deal closes: debt issued by CWB will be converted to shares held by the Farmers' Trust. Para. (e) refers generally to all "eligible shares" of CWB, for all taxpayers.

(4) Eligible trust — The following rules apply in respect of a trust that is an eligible trust at any time in a taxation year of the trust:

(a) in computing the trust's income for the year

(i) no deduction may be made by the trust under subsection 104(6), except to the extent of the income of the trust (determined without reference to subsection 104(6)) for the year that is paid in the year, and

(ii) no deduction may be made by the trust under subsection 104(6), if the trust ceased to be an eligible trust at the beginning of the following taxation year;

(b) for the purposes of applying Part XII.2 in respect of the year

(i) the trust's designated income for the year is deemed to be the trust's income for the year determined without reference to subsections 104(6) and (30), and

(ii) the designated beneficiaries under the trust at any time in the year are deemed to include any beneficiary under the trust that is at that time

(A) non-resident,

(B) a partnership (other than a partnership that is, throughout its fiscal period that includes that time, a Canadian partnership), or

(C) exempt because of subsection 149(1) from tax under this Part on the person's taxable income;

(c) each property held by the trust that is the eligible debt or an eligible share is deemed to have a cost amount to the trust of nil;

(d) if the trust disposes of a property,

(i) subject to subsection (14), the disposition is deemed to occur for proceeds equal to the fair market value of the property immediately before the disposition,

(ii) the gain, if any, of the trust from the disposition is

(A) deemed not to be a capital gain, and

(B) to be included in computing the trust's income for the trust's taxation year that includes the time of disposition, and

(iii) the loss, if any, of the trust from the disposition is

(A) deemed not to be a capital loss, and

(B) to be deducted in computing the trust's income for the trust's taxation year that includes the time of disposition;

(e) the trust is deemed not to be a

(i) personal trust,

(ii) unit trust,

(iii) trust prescribed for the purpose of subsection 107(2), or

(iv) trust any interest in which is an excluded right or interest in applying section 128.1;

(f) any "security" (in this paragraph and paragraph (g), as defined in subsection 122.1(1)) of the trust that is held by a trust governed by a deferred profit sharing plan, RDSP, RESP, RRIF, RRSP or TFSA (referred to in this paragraph and paragraph (g) as the "registered plan trust") is deemed not to be a qualified investment for the registered plan trust;

(g) if a registered plan trust governed by a TFSA acquires at any time a security of the trust, Part XI.01 applies in respect of the security as though the acquisition is an advantage

(i) in relation to the TFSA that is extended at that time to the controlling individual of the TFSA, and

(ii) that is a benefit the fair market value of which is the fair market value of the security at that time; and

(h) paragraph (h) of the definition "disposition" in subsection 248(1) does not apply in respect of eligible units of the trust.

Notes: See Notes at end of 135.2 and to 135.2(1) "eligible trust". 135.2(4)(b)(ii)(B) corrected by Commons Finance Committee, before Third Reading of 2016 budget bill #1, to add "a Canadian partnership".

(5) Participating farmer — acquisition of eligible unit — If, at any time, a participating farmer acquires an eligible unit in an eligible trust from the trust,

(a) no amount in respect of the acquisition of the eligible unit is included in computing the income of the participating farmer; and

(b) the cost amount to the participating farmer of the eligible unit is deemed to be nil.

(6) Eligible unit issued to estate — If a participating farmer has, immediately before the participating farmer's death, not received an eligible unit of an eligible trust for which the participating farmer was eligible — pursuant to the plan under which the eligible trust directs its trustees to grant units to persons who have delivered grain under a contract with the Canadian Wheat Board on or after August 1, 2013 — and the eligible trust issues the unit to the estate that arose on and as a consequence of the death,

(a) the participating farmer is deemed to have acquired the unit at the time that is immediately before the time that is immediately before the death, as a participating farmer from the eligible trust, and to own the unit at the time that is immediately before the death;

(b) for the purpose of paragraph (f) of the definition "eligible trust" in subsection (1), the estate is deemed not to have acquired the unit from the trust; and

(c) for the purposes of paragraphs (8)(b) and (c), the estate is deemed to have acquired the eligible unit on and as a consequence of the death.

(7) Eligible unit — gain (loss) — If a person disposes of an eligible unit in a trust that is an eligible trust at the time of the disposition

(a) the gain, if any, of the person from the disposition is

(i) deemed not to be a capital gain, and

(ii) to be included in computing the person's income for the person's taxation year that includes that time; and

(b) the loss, if any, of the person from the disposition is

(i) deemed not to be a capital loss, and

(ii) to be deducted in computing the person's income for the person's taxation year that includes that time.

Notes: The June 2015 draft of 135.2(7) did not say whether a gain (loss) is deemed to be an income gain (loss) or a "tax nothing". Finance advised that this would be changed to clarify that it is an income gain (loss); see also 135.2(9)(c) where the farmer is a CCPC, which makes this clear.

(8) Death of a participating farmer — If, immediately before an individual's death, the individual owns an eligible unit that the individual acquired as a participating farmer from an eligible trust

(a) the individual is deemed to dispose (referred to in this subsection as the "particular disposition") of the eligible unit immediately before death;

(b) if paragraph (d) does not apply,

(i) the individual's proceeds from the particular disposition are deemed to be equal to the unit's fair market value immediately before the particular disposition,

(ii) the gain from the particular disposition is deemed to be included, under subsection 70(1) and not under any other provision, in the individual's income for the individual's taxation year in which the individual dies,

(iii) subsection 159(5) applies in respect of the individual who has died (determined as though a reference in that subsection to subsection 70(5.2) includes a reference to subsection 70(1) in the application of subsection 159(5) to the gain from the particular disposition) in respect of the particular disposition, and

(iv) the person who acquires the eligible unit as a consequence of the individual's death is deemed to have acquired the eligible unit at the time of the death at a cost equal to the individual's proceeds, described in subparagraph (i), from the particular disposition;

(c) paragraph (d) applies if

(i) the individual is resident in Canada immediately before the individual's death,

(ii) the individual's graduated rate estate acquires the eligible unit on and as a consequence of the death,

(iii) the individual's legal representative elects in prescribed form in the course of administering the individual's graduated rate estate that paragraph (b) not apply to the individual in respect of the particular disposition,

(iv) the election is filed with the individual's return of income under this Part for the individual's taxation year in which the death occurred,

(v) the estate distributes the eligible unit to the individual's spouse or common-law partner at a time at which it is the individual's graduated rate estate,

(vi) the individual's spouse or common-law partner is resident in Canada at the time of the distribution, and

(vii) the estate does not dispose of the unit before the distribution; and

(d) if this paragraph applies,

(i) the individual's gain from the disposition is deemed to be nil,

(ii) the cost amount to the estate of the eligible unit is deemed to be nil,

(iii) any amount that is included in the estate's income (determined without reference to this subparagraph and subsections 104(6) and (12)) for a taxation year from a source that is the eligible unit is, notwithstanding subsection 104(24), deemed

(A) to have become payable in that taxation year by the estate to the spouse or common-law partner, and

(B) not be have become payable to any other beneficiary,

(iv) the distribution is deemed to be a disposition by the estate of the eligible unit for proceeds equal to the cost amount to the estate of the unit,

(v) the part of the spouse or common-law partner's interest as a beneficiary under the estate that is disposed of as a result of the distribution is deemed to be disposed of for proceeds of disposition equal to the cost amount to the spouse or com-

mon-law partner of that part immediately before the disposition,

(vi) the cost amount to the spouse or common-law partner of the eligible unit is deemed to be nil, and

(vii) the spouse or common-law partner is, except for the purposes of paragraph (c), deemed to have acquired the eligible unit as a participating farmer from an eligible trust.

(9) Participating farmer — disposition of eligible unit — If, at any time, an eligible unit of an eligible trust that was acquired by a participating farmer from the eligible trust is disposed of by the participating farmer (other than a disposition described in paragraph (8)(a), (10)(d) or (11)(b)),

(a) the participating farmer's proceeds from the disposition are deemed to be equal to the fair market value of the unit immediately before its disposition;

(b) if the disposition results from a distribution of money denominated in Canadian dollars by the trust to the participating farmer in a taxation year of the trust, the money is proceeds from the disposition in that taxation year by the trust of other property and, at the time of the disposition, the participating farmer is not a person described in any of clauses (4)(b)(ii)(A) to (C), the trust's gain, if any, from the disposition of the other property is reduced to the extent that the proceeds so distributed would, in the absence of this paragraph, be included under subsection 104(13) in the participating farmer's income for the taxation year of the participating farmer in which the taxation year of the trust ends; and

(c) if the participating farmer is a Canadian-controlled private corporation, for the purposes of section 125, the gain from the disposition is deemed to be income from an active business carried on by the corporation.

(10) Eligible wind-up distribution — If, at any time, an eligible trust distributes property as an eligible wind-up distribution of the trust to a person

(a) subsection 107(2.1) does not apply in respect of the distribution;

(b) the trust is deemed to have disposed of the property for proceeds equal to its fair market value at that time;

(c) the trust's gain from the disposition of the property is, notwithstanding subsection 104(24), deemed

(i) to have become payable at that time by the trust to the person, and

(ii) not to have become payable to any other beneficiary;

(d) the person is deemed to acquire the property at a cost equal to the trust's proceeds from the disposition;

(e) the person's proceeds from the disposition of the eligible unit, or part of it, that results from the distribution are deemed to be equal to the cost amount of the unit to the person immediately before that time; and

(f) for greater certainty, no part of the trust's gain from the disposition is to be included in the cost to the person of the property, other than as determined by paragraph (d).

(11) Ceasing to be an eligible trust — If a trust ceases to be an eligible trust at a particular time

(a) subsection 149(10) applies to the trust as if

(i) it ceased at that particular time to be exempt from tax under this Part on its taxable income, and

(ii) the list of provisions in paragraph 149(10)(c) included a reference to this section; and

(b) each person who holds at the particular time an eligible unit in the trust is deemed to have

(i) disposed of, at the time that is immediately before the time that is immediately before the particular time, each of the eligible units for proceeds equal to the cost amount of the unit to the person, and

(ii) reacquired the eligible unit at the time that is immediately before the particular time at a cost equal to the fair market value of the unit at the time that is immediately before the particular time.

(12) Stock dividends — Canadian Wheat Board shares — If, at any time, the eligible trust holds an eligible share (or another share of the Canadian Wheat Board acquired before that time as a stock dividend) and the Canadian Wheat Board issues, as a stock dividend paid in respect of such a share, a share of a class of its capital stock, the amount by which the paid-up capital is increased — in respect of the issuance of all shares paid by the Canadian Wheat Board to the eligible trust as the stock dividend or any other stock dividend paid to other shareholders in connection with that stock dividend — for all classes of shares of the Canadian Wheat Board is, for the purposes of this Act, deemed to be no more than $1.

(13) Reorganization of capital — Canadian Wheat Board — Subsection (14) applies in respect of the disposition by an eligible trust of all of the shares (in this subsection and subsection (14) referred to collectively as the "old shares" and individually as an "old share") of a class of the capital stock of the Canadian Wheat Board owned by the eligible trust if

(a) the disposition of the old shares results from the acquisition, cancellation or redemption in the course of a reorganization of the capital of the Canadian Wheat Board;

(b) the Canadian Wheat Board issues to the eligible trust, in exchange for the old shares, shares (in this subsection and subsection (14) referred to collectively as the "new shares" and individually as a "new share") of a class of the capital stock of the Canadian Wheat Board the terms and conditions of which — including the entitlement to receive an amount on a redemption, acquisition or cancellation — are in all material respects the same as those of the old shares;

(c) the amount that is the total fair market value of all of the new shares acquired by the eligible trust on the exchange equals the total fair market value of all of the old shares disposed of by the eligible trust; and

(d) the amount that is the total paid-up capital in respect of all of the new shares acquired by the eligible trust on the exchange is equal to the amount that is the total paid-up capital in respect of all of the old shares disposed of on the exchange.

(14) Rollover of shares on reorganization — If this subsection applies in respect of an exchange of an eligible trust's old share for a new share,

(a) the old share is deemed to be disposed of by the eligible trust for proceeds equal to its cost amount to the eligible trust;

(b) the new share acquired for the old share referred to in paragraph (a) is deemed to be acquired for a cost equal to the amount referred to in paragraph (a);

(c) if the old share was an eligible share, the new share is deemed to be an eligible share; and

(d) if new shares are deemed to be eligible shares because of paragraph (c) and those shares are included in a class of shares that also includes other shares that are not eligible shares, those eligible shares are deemed to have been issued in a separate series of the class and the other shares are deemed to have been issued in a separate series of the class.

(15) Information filing requirement — A trust shall file with the Minister a prescribed form in prescribed manner in respect of each taxation year of the trust in which it is an eligible trust on or before the trust's filing-due date for the year.

Related Provisions: 135.2(16) — Penalty and consequence of not filing.

Notes: This "prescribed form" could be an information return, or simply a letter containing the information the CRA will require each year. The trust is also required to file a T3 income tax return by 150(1)(c).

(16) Failure to file prescribed form — If a trust fails to file the form required by subsection (15) on or before the day that is the trust's filing-due date for a taxation year,

(a) in addition to any other penalty for which the trust may be liable under this Act in respect of the failure, the trust is liable to a penalty equal to the product obtained when $1,000 is multiplied by the number of days during which the failure continues; and

(b) if, within 30 days after the trust is served personally or by registered mail with a demand in writing from the Minister for the form to be filed, the trust has not filed the form with the Minister, the trust is deemed to cease to be an eligible trust at the end of the day on which the demand was served.

Notes: Unlike the per-day penalties in s. 162 which are capped at 100 days, this penalty is unlimited.

Notes [s. 135.2]: The Canadian Wheat Board was established in 1935 as the sole marketing board for wheat and barley in Western Canada. It was governed by the *Canadian Wheat Board Act* as a mandatory producer-marketing system for wheat and barley in Alberta, Sask., Manitoba and a small part of BC. It was illegal for a farmer in areas under the Board's jurisdiction to sell wheat or barley through any other channel.

The Board's "single desk" marketing power ended on Aug. 1, 2012 due to the *Marketing Freedom for Grain Farmers Act*. (Consequential ITA amendments were made to 76(5) and repealing 161(5).) The Board changed its name to CWB, which continues to operate as a grain company. That *Act* also set a timeline for CWB's privatization.

On April 15, 2015, it was announced that a 50.1% stake in CWB would be sold for $250 million to Global Grain Group (G3), a joint venture of Bunge Limited and SALIC Canada (subsidiary of Saudi Agricultural and Livestock Investment Company). The other 49.9% is kept in trust for farmers who deliver grain to the board, receiving equity of $5 per tonne. The sale was completed in July 2015. In 2022, G3 has the option to buy back the shares from the trust at market value. See g3.ca.

CWB says the sale will result in a new coast-to-coast grain processing and shipping network in Canada, and will increase Canada's ability to export grain, create jobs and spawn economic growth in the Prairies.

S. 135.2 implements the tax consequences for the Farmers Equity Trust (135.2(1) "eligible trust") and participating farmers. There is no tax on initial conversion of CWB debt to shares: 135.2(3). Thus, there is no tax until the trust sells shares of CWB or a farmer sells a unit of the trust. 135.2(3)(c)-(d) provide that when the trust sells any CWB shares, it will have a full income inclusion since its cost is nil and the gain is deemed not to be capital gain. Similarly, when a farmer sells a unit of the trust, 135.2(5)(b) deems the cost to be nil and 135.2(7) and (9) provide that the gain is business income (which makes sense since it originated from business sales of grain). If a farmer dies, see 135.2(6), (8). If the trust winds up, see 135.2(10).

135.2 added by 2016 budget bill #1, effective July 2015, but before Dec. 31, 2015 read every reference to "graduated rate estate" as "estate".

Definitions [s. 135.2]: "active business" — 248(1); "advantage" — 207.01(1); "amount" — 248(1); "application for continuance" — 135.2(1); "beneficiary" — 248(25) [Notes]; "Canadian partnership" — 102(1), 248(1); "Canadian Wheat Board", "Canadian Wheat Board continuance" — 135.2(1); "Canadian-controlled private corporation" — 125(7), 248(1); "capital gain" — 39(1)(a), 248(1); "capital loss" — 39(1)(b), 248(1); "class of shares" — 248(6); "common share", "common-law partner" — 248(1); "consequence" — 248(8); "corporation" — 248(1), *Interpretation Act* 35(1); "cost amount" — 248(1); "credit union" — 137(6), 248(1); "deferred profit sharing plan" — 147(1), 248(1); "designated stock exchange" — 248(1), 262; "disposition", "dividend" — 248(1); "eligible debt", "eligible share", "eligible trust", "eligible unit", "eligible wind-up distribution" — 135.2(1); "estate" — 104(1), 248(1); "fair market value" — see 69(1) Notes; "filing-due date" — 150(1), 248(1); "fixed interest" — 251.2(1); "fiscal period" — 249.1; "graduated rate estate", "individual", "legal representative", "Minister" — 248(1); "new share" — 135.2(13)(b); "non-resident" — 248(1); "old share" — 135.2(13); "paid-up capital" — 89(1), 248(1); "participating farmer" — 135.2(1); "partnership" — see 96(1) Notes; "person" — 135.2(1); "personal trust", "prescribed", "principal amount", "property" — 248(1); "RDSP" — 248(1) "registered disability savings plan"; "resident in Canada" — 94(3)(a), 250; "RESP" — 248(1) "registered education savings plan"; "RRIF" — 248(1) "registered retirement income fund"; "RRSP" — 248(1) "registered retirement savings plan"; "registered plan trust" — 135.2(4)(f); "security" — 122.1(1), 135.2(4)(f); "series of transactions" — 248(10); "share", "shareholder", "stock dividend" — 248(1); "taxable income" — 2(2), 248(1); "taxation year" — 249; "TFSA" — 146.2(5), 248(1); "trust" — 104(1), 248(1), (3); "unit trust" — 108(2), 248(1); "writing" — *Interpretation Act* 35(1).

Cooperative Corporations

136. (1) Cooperative not private corporation — Notwithstanding any other provision of this Act, a cooperative corporation that would, but for this section, be a private corporation is deemed not to be a private corporation except for the purposes of section 15.1, paragraphs 87(2)(vv) and (ww) (including, for greater certainty, in applying those paragraphs as provided under paragraph 88(1)(e.2)), the definitions "excessive eligible dividend designation", "general rate income pool" and "low rate income pool" in subsection 89(1), subsections 89(4) to (6) and (8) to (10), sections 123.4, 125, 125.1, 127 and 127.1, the definition "mark-to-market property" in subsection 142.2(1), sections 152 and 157, subsection 185.2(3), the definition "small business corporation" in subsection 248(1) (as it applies for the purposes of paragraph 39(1)(c)) and subsection 249(3.1).

Related Provisions: 89(1)"paid-up capital"(b) — Paid-up capital of cooperative corporation; 125 — Small business deduction; 127(6) — Investment tax credit of cooperative corporation; 135 — Patronage dividend; 137 — Deductions in computing income; 248(1) — "share" includes a share of a cooperative corporation.

Notes: For discussion of the tax rates applicable to a cooperative see VIEWS doc 2007-0243201C6. A co-op's gain on redeeming its shares is not taxable: 2015-0583221E5.

136(1) amended by 2013 budget bill #2, for tax years that begin after Dec. 21, 2012.

136(1) amended by 2002-2013 technical bill, for 2001 and later taxation years, to add reference to 123.4 (and change "but for this section" to "if this Act were read without reference to this section"). This change, as proposed in a March 20, 2001 Finance comfort letter, ensures that a co-op gets the rate reductions provided for CCPCs.

136(1) amended by 1995-97 technical bill (for tax years ending Feb. 22, 1994), 1991 technical bill, 1989 Budget.

Interpretation Bulletins: IT-493: Agency cooperative corporations (cancelled).

(2) Definition of "cooperative corporation" — In this section, "cooperative corporation" means a corporation that was incorporated or continued by or under the provisions of a law, of Canada or of a province, that provide for the establishment of the corporation as a cooperative corporation or that provide for the establishment of cooperative corporations, for the purpose of marketing (including processing incident to or connected to the marketing) natural products belonging to or acquired from its members or customers, of purchasing supplies, equipment or household necessaries for or to be sold to its members or customers or of performing services for its members or customers, if

(a) the statute by or under which it was incorporated, its charter, articles of association or by-laws or its contracts with its members or its members and customers held out the prospect that payments would be made to them in proportion to patronage;

(b) none of its members (except other cooperative corporations) have more than one vote in the conduct of the affairs of the corporation;

(c) at least 90% of its members are individuals, other cooperative corporations, or corporations or partnerships that carry on the business of farming; and

(d) at least 90% of its shares, if any, are held by members described in paragraph (c) or by trusts governed by registered retirement savings plans, registered retirement income funds, TFSAs or registered education savings plans, the annuitants, holders or subscribers under which are members described in that paragraph.

Notes: For interpretation of "member" (based on the governing cooperative corporation statute), see VIEWS doc 2015-0611691E5.

136(2) amended by 2002-2013 technical bill (for 1998 and later tax years, implementing a June 11, 1999 Finance comfort letter), 2006 budget bill #1 (effective July 2005).

Definitions [s. 136]: "business" — 248(1); "Canada" — 255, *Interpretation Act* 35(1); "corporation" — 248(1), *Interpretation Act* 35(1); "farming", "individual" — 248(1); "partnership" — see 96(1) Notes; "person" — 248(1); "private corporation" — 89(1), 248(1); "province" — *Interpretation Act* 35(1); "registered education savings plan" — 146.1(1), 248(1); "registered retirement income fund" — 146.3(1), 248(1); "registered retirement savings plan" — 146(1), 248(1); "share", "small business corporation" — 248(1); "TFSA" — 146.2(5), 248(1); "trust" — 104(1), 248(1), (3).

Credit Unions, Savings and Credit Unions, and Deposit Insurance Corporations

137. (1) [Repealed under former Act]

Notes: 137(1), repealed by 1988 tax reform, dealt with a credit union's reserve for doubtful debts. See now 20(1)(l) instead.

(2) Payments pursuant to allocations in proportion to borrowing [credit union] — Notwithstanding anything in this Part, there may be deducted, in computing the income for a taxation year of a credit union, the total of bonus interest payments and payments pursuant to allocations in proportion to borrowing made by the credit union within the year or within 12 months thereafter to members of the credit union, to the extent that those payments were not deductible under this subsection in computing the income of the credit union for the immediately preceding taxation year.

Related Provisions: 110.1(1)(a) — 137(2) ignored for purposes of charitable donations limit; 135 — Patronage dividends; 137(6) — Maximum cumulative reserve; *Interpretation Act* 27(5) — Meaning of "within 12 months".

Notes: CRA says that the 137(2) deduction requires payments to be credited to all taxpayers who were members of the class in the year: doc 2019-0824091E5.

Interpretation Bulletins: IT-483: Credit unions (cancelled).

Forms: T2 Sched. 17: Credit union deductions.

(3) Additional deduction [credit union, before 2017] — There may be deducted from the tax otherwise payable under this Part for a taxation year by a corporation that was, throughout the year, a credit union, an amount equal to the amount determined by the formula

$$A \times B \times C$$

where

A   is the rate that would, if subsection 125(1.1) applied to the corporation for the year, be its small business deduction rate for the year within the meaning assigned by that subsection,

B   is the amount, if any, determined by the formula

$$D - E$$

where

D   is the lesser of

(a) the corporation's taxable income for the year, and

(b) the amount, if any, by which $4/3$ of the corporation's maximum cumulative reserve at the end of the year exceeds the corporation's preferred-rate amount at the end of the immediately preceding taxation year, and

E   is the least of the amounts determined under paragraphs 125(1)(a) to (c) in respect of the corporation for the year, and

C   is the percentage that is the total of

(a) the proportion of 100% that the number of days in the year that are before March 21, 2013 is of the number of days in the year,

(b) the proportion of 80% that the number of days in the year that are after March 20, 2013 and before 2014 is of the number of days in the year,

(c) the proportion of 60% that the number of days in the year that are in 2014 is of the number of days in the year,

(d) the proportion of 40% that the number of days in the year in 2015 is of the number of days in the year,

(e) the proportion of 20% that the number of days in the year in 2016 is of the number of days in the year, and

(f) if one or more days in the year are after 2016, 0%.

Related Provisions: 137(4.3) — Preferred-rate amount.

Notes: The 2013 Budget amendments phased out (from 2013-17) a deduction that gave credit unions (CUs) the 125(1) small business rate for income over the $500,000 limit. The amount of taxable income eligible for the additional deduction was subject to a limit based on the CU's cumulative taxable income that was taxed at the preferential rate (including as a result of the additional deduction) and the amount of their deposits and member shares. (A CU is deemed by 137(7) not to be a private corporation, but that rule does not apply to s. 125 or certain other provisions.)

137(3) amended by 2013 budget bill #1, for tax years that end after March 20, 2013. Earlier amended by 2006 budget bill #2, for 2008 and later tax years.

Interpretation Bulletins: IT-483: Credit unions (cancelled).

Forms: T2 Sched. 17: Credit union deductions.

(4) Amount deemed deductible under section 125 — For the purposes of this Act, any amount deductible or any deduction under subsection (3) from the tax otherwise payable by a credit union under this Part for a taxation year shall be deemed to be an amount deductible or a deduction, as the case may be, under section 125 from that tax.

Related Provisions: 125 — Small business deduction; 137(6) — Maximum cumulative reserve.

Interpretation Bulletins: IT-483: Credit unions (cancelled).

(4.1) Payments in respect of shares — Notwithstanding any other provision of this Act, an amount paid or payable by a credit union to a person is deemed to be paid or payable, as the case may be, by the credit union as interest and to be received or receivable, as the case may be, by the person as interest, if

(a) the amount is in respect of a share held by the person of the capital stock of the credit union, other than an amount paid or payable as or on account of a reduction of the paid-up capital, redemption, acquisition or cancellation of the share by the credit union to the extent of the paid-up capital of the share;

(b) the share is not listed on a stock exchange; and

(c) the person is

(i) a member of the credit union, or

(ii) a member of another credit union if the share is issued by the credit union after March 28, 2012 and the other credit union is a member of the credit union.

Related Provisions: 12(1)(c) — Interest included in income; 84(3), (4) — Deemed dividend on reduction of paid-up capital; 137(4.2) — Deemed interest not a dividend.

Notes: Even though the dividends are deemed to be interest and not dividends (137(4.2)), the shares are still "shares" for purposes of the Act: VIEWS docs 2004-0098711R3, 2004-0109031R3, 2005-0158951R3, 2005-0161981E5. For rulings that no Part VI.1 tax applies because a stock dividend is deemed by 137(4.1) to be interest, see 2007-0241561R3, 2008-0283681R3. For a ruling that 137(4.1) does not apply see 2014-0530371R3 (combination of credit unions).

For "stock exchange" see Notes to 248(1)"recognized stock exchange".

137(4.1) amended by 2013 budget bill #2 (for 2012 and later tax years), 2007 budget bill #2.

Interpretation Bulletins: IT-483: Credit unions (cancelled).

(4.2) Deemed interest not a dividend — Notwithstanding any other provision of this Act, an amount that is deemed by subsection (4.1) to be interest shall be deemed not to be a dividend.

Related Provisions: 84(2) — Deemed dividend on winding-up; 84(3) — Deemed dividend on redemption of shares; 84(4) — Deemed dividend — reduction of paid-up capital.

Notes: 137(4.2) amended by 1993 technical bill, for transactions after Dec. 21, 1992.

Interpretation Bulletins: IT-483: Credit unions (cancelled).

(4.3) Determination of preferred-rate amount of a corporation — For the purposes of subsection (3),

(a) the preferred-rate amount of a corporation at the end of a taxation year is determined by the formula

$$A + B/C$$

where

A　is its preferred-rate amount at the end of its immediately preceding taxation year,

B　is the amount deductible under section 125 from the tax for the taxation year otherwise payable by it under this Part, and

C　is its small business deduction rate for the taxation year within the meaning of subsection 125(1.1);

(b) where at any time a new corporation has been formed as a result of an amalgamation of two or more predecessor corporations, within the meaning of subsection 87(1), it shall be deemed to have had a taxation year ending immediately before that time and to have had, at the end of that year, a preferred-rate amount equal to the total of the preferred-rate amounts of each of the predecessor corporations at the end of their last taxation years; and

(c) where there has been a winding-up as described in subsection 88(1), the preferred-rate amount of the parent (referred to in that subsection) at the end of its taxation year immediately preceding

its taxation year in which it received the assets of the subsidiary (referred to in that subsection) on the winding-up shall be deemed to be the total of the amount that would otherwise be its preferred-rate amount at the end of that year and the preferred-rate amount of the subsidiary at the end of its taxation year in which its assets were distributed to the parent on the winding-up.

Notes: The preferred-rate amount determination cannot be appealed separately where there is no tax to appeal for the year: *Interior Savings Credit Union*, 2007 FCA 151.

Para. (a) amended by 2015 Budget bill, for 2016 and later taxation years, consequential on changes to the small business deduction rate in 125(1.1).

137(4.3)(a) amended to change "25/4" to "100/17" by 2002-2013 technical bill, for 2008 and later tax years, and prorated by the number of days in the year.

Interpretation Bulletins: IT-483: Credit unions (cancelled).

(5) Member's income — Where a payment has been received by a taxpayer from a credit union in a taxation year in respect of an allocation in proportion to borrowing, the amount thereof shall, if the money so borrowed was used by the taxpayer for the purpose of earning income from a business or property (otherwise than to acquire property the income from which would be exempt or to acquire a life insurance policy), be included in computing the taxpayer's income for the year.

(5.1) Allocations of taxable dividends and capital gains — A credit union (referred to in this subsection and in subsection (5.2) as the "payer") may, at any time within 120 days after the end of its taxation year, elect in prescribed form to allocate in respect of the year to a member that is a credit union such portion of each of the following amounts as may reasonably be regarded as attributable to the member:

(a) the total of all amounts each of which is the amount of a taxable dividend received by the payer from a taxable Canadian corporation in the year;

(b) the amount if any, by which

(i) the total of all amounts each of which is the amount by which the payer's capital gain from the disposition of a property in the year exceeds the payer's taxable capital gain from the disposition

exceeds

(ii) the total of all amounts each of which is the amount by which the payer's capital loss from the disposition of a property in the year exceeds the payer's allowable capital loss from the disposition; and

(c) each amount deductible under paragraph (5.2)(c) in computing the payer's taxable income for the year.

Related Provisions: 137(5.2) — Allocations of taxable dividends and capital gains; *Interpretation Act* 27(5) — Meaning of "within 120 days".

Notes: For a credit union filing Quebec returns, the election must be copied to Revenu Québec: *Taxation Act* ss. 803.1, 21.4.6.

137(5.1)(b) amended to correct a technical deficiency and 137(5.1)(c) added by 1991 technical bill, effective 1988.

Interpretation Bulletins: IT-483: Credit unions (cancelled).

Forms: T2004: Election by a credit union to allocate taxable dividends and taxable capital gains to member credit unions.

(5.2) Idem — Notwithstanding any other provision of this Act,

(a) there shall be deducted from the amount that would, but for this subsection, be deductible under section 112 in computing a payer's taxable income for a taxation year such portion of the total referred to in paragraph (5.1)(a) as the payer allocated to its members under subsection (5.1) in respect of the year;

(b) there shall be included in computing the income of a payer for a taxation year an amount equal to that portion of the amount referred to in paragraphs (5.1)(b) and (c) that the payer allocated under subsection (5.1) in respect of the year to its members; and

(c) each amount allocated under subsection (5.1) to a member may be deducted by that member in computing the member's taxable income for its taxation year that includes the last day of the payer's taxation year in respect of which the amount was so allocated.

Notes: 137(5.2)(b) amended by 1991 technical bill, effective 1988.

137(5.2)(c) amended by 1992 technical bill, effective for 1991 and later taxation years.

Interpretation Bulletins: IT-483: Credit unions (cancelled).

(6) Definitions — In this section,

"allocation in proportion to borrowing" for a taxation year means an amount credited by a credit union to a person who was a member of the credit union in the year on terms that the member is entitled to or will receive payment thereof, computed at a rate in relation to

(a) the amount of interest payable by the member on money borrowed from the credit union, or

(b) the amount of money borrowed by the member from the credit union,

if the amount was credited at the same rate in relation to the amount of interest or money, as the case may be, as the rate at which amounts were similarly credited for the year to all other members of the credit union of the same class;

Notes: 137(6)"allocation in proportion to borrowing" was 137(6)(a) before RSC 1985 (5th Supp) consolidation for tax years ending after Nov. 1991.

"bonus interest payment" for a taxation year means an amount credited by a credit union to a person who was a member of the credit union in the year on terms that the member is entitled to or will receive payment thereof, computed at a rate in relation to

(a) the amount of interest payable in respect of the year by the credit union to the member on money standing to the member's credit from time to time in the records or books of account of the credit union, or

(b) the amount of money standing to the member's credit from time to time in the year in the records or books of account of the credit union,

if the amount was credited at the same rate in relation to the amount of interest or money, as the case may be, as the rate at which amounts were similarly credited in the year to all other members of the credit union of the same class;

Notes: 137(6)"bonus interest payment" was 137(6)(a.1) before RSC 1985 (5th Supp) consolidation for tax years ending after Nov. 1991.

"credit union" means a corporation, association or federation incorporated or organized as a credit union or cooperative credit society if

(a) it derived all or substantially all of its revenues from

(i) loans made to, or cashing cheques for, members,

(ii) debt obligations or securities of, or guaranteed by, the Government of Canada or a province, a Canadian municipality, or an agency thereof, or debt obligations or securities of a municipal or public body performing a function of government in Canada or an agency thereof,

(iii) debt obligations of or deposits with, or guaranteed by, a corporation, commission or association not less than 90% of the shares or capital of which was owned by the Government of Canada or a province or by a municipality in Canada,

(iv) debt obligations of or deposits with, or guaranteed by, a bank, or debt obligations of or deposits with a corporation licensed or otherwise authorized under a law of Canada or a province to carry on in Canada the business of offering to the public its services as trustee,

(v) charges, fees and dues levied against members or members of members,

(vi) loans made to or deposits with a credit union or cooperative credit society of which it is a member, or

(vii) a prescribed revenue source,

(b) all or substantially all the members thereof having full voting rights therein were corporations, associations or federations

(i) incorporated as credit unions or cooperative credit societies, all of which derived all or substantially all of their revenues from the sources described in paragraph (a), or all or substantially all of the members of which were credit unions, cooperatives or a combination thereof,

(ii) incorporated, organized or registered under, or governed by a law of Canada or a province with respect to cooperatives, or

(iii) incorporated or organized for charitable purposes,

or were corporations, associations or federations no part of the income of which was payable to, or otherwise available for the personal benefit of, any shareholder or member thereof, or

(c) the corporation, association or federation would be a credit union by virtue of paragraph (b) if all the members (other than individuals) having full voting rights in each member thereof that is a credit union were members having full voting rights in the corporation, association or federation;

Related Provisions: 89(1)"paid-up capital"(b) — PUC of credit union; 137.1(7) — Deposit insurance corporation deemed not credit union; 248(1)"credit union" — Definition applies to entire Act; 248(1)"share" — Share of a credit union is a share; Reg. 9002(3) — Mark-to-market rules — property held by credit union.

Notes: For an overview of the industry, see Department of Finance, *Canada's Credit Unions and Caisses Populaires* (Jan. 2002), on fin.gc.ca.

An association qualifying as a cooperative credit society under the *Cooperative Credit Associations Act*, or that is approved by the Minister of Finance to become a retail association under the *Retail Associations Regulations* made under s. 375.1 of that Act, is a cooperative credit society for this definition: VIEWS doc 2003-0033371E5.

For the meaning of "municipal or public body..." in (a)(ii), see Notes to 149(1)(c).

"No part of the income of which" in (b) closing words refers to net income, and "personal benefit" could result from one person being able to sign cheques. See Notes to 149(1)(l).

CRA considers that "substantially all" means 90% or more.

See also 248(1)"federal credit union", introduced in 2010.

137(6)"credit union" was 137(6)(b) before RSC 1985 (5th Supp) consolidation for tax years ending after Nov. 1991.

Interpretation Bulletins: IT-483: Credit unions (cancelled).

"maximum cumulative reserve" of a credit union at the end of any particular taxation year means an amount determined by the formula

$$0.05 \times (A + B)$$

where

A is the total of all amounts each of which is the amount of any debt owing by the credit union to a member thereof or of any other obligation of the credit union to pay an amount to a member thereof, that was outstanding at the end of the year, including, for greater certainty, the amount of any deposit standing to the credit of a member of the credit union in the records of the credit union, but excluding, for greater certainty, any share in the credit union of any member thereof, and

B is the total of all amounts each of which is the amount, as of the end of the year, of any share in the credit union of any member thereof;

Notes: 137(6)"maximum cumulative reserve" was 137(6)(c) before RSC 1985 (5th Supp) consolidation for tax years ending after Nov. 1991.

I.T. Application Rules: 58(3.2) (reduction in maximum cumulative reserve to reflect level at end of 1971).

"member", of a credit union, means

(a) a person who is recorded as a member on the records of the credit union and is entitled to participate in and use the services of the credit union, and

(b) a registered retirement savings plan, a registered retirement income fund, a TFSA or a registered education savings plan, the annuitant, holder or subscriber under which is a person described in paragraph (a).

Related Provisions: Reg. 1404(2)"acquisition costs"(a)(iii.1) — Insurer established to provide insurance to credit union members — policy reserves.

Notes: See 136(2)(d) re para. (b). Para. (b) added by 2002-2013 technical bill, for 1996 and later tax years, with the references to a TFSA and a "holder" applying only from the 2009 year.

137(6)"member" was 137(6)(d) before RSC 1985 (5th Supp) consolidation for tax years ending after Nov. 1991.

(7) Credit union not private corporation — Notwithstanding any other provision of this Act, a credit union that would, if this Act were read without reference to this section, be a private corporation is deemed not to be a private corporation except for the purposes of sections 123.1, 123.4, 125, 127, 127.1, 152 and 157 and the definition "small business corporation" in subsection 248(1) as it applies for the purpose of paragraph 39(1)(c).

Notes: Since s. 89 is not listed as an exception, a credit union is not a private corporation for s. 89 and is not required to file a T2 Schedule 53 GRIP calculation for 89(1)"general rate income pool" (though it might need to file a Sch. 54 LRIP calculation): VIEWS doc 2013-0487491I7.

137(7) amended by 2002-2013 technical bill, for 2001 and later tax years, to add 123.4. This change, as proposed in two Dec. 20, 2001 Finance comfort letters, ensures that a credit union gets the rate reduction provided for CCPCs in 123.4(2).

In 137(7), reference to 152 added by 1989 Budget, effective April 28, 1989.

Definitions [s. 137]: "allocation in proportion to borrowing" — 137(6); "allowable capital loss" — 38(b), 248(1); "amount" — 248(1); "bank" — 248(1); "bonus interest payment" — 137(6); "business" — 248(1); "class" — of shares 248(6); "corporation" — 248(1), *Interpretation Act* 35(1); "credit union" — 137(6), 248(1); "disposition" — 248(1); "dividend" — 137(4.1), (4.2), 248(1); "interest" — 137(4.1), (4.2); "life insurance policy" — 138(12), 248(1); "maximum cumulative reserve", "member" — 137(6); "paid-up capital" — 89(1), 248(1); "payer" — 137(5.1); "person" — 248(1); "preferred-rate amount" — 137(4.3); "prescribed" — 248(1); "private corporation" — 89(1), 137(7), 248(1); "property" — 248(1); "province" — *Interpretation Act* 35(1); "record", "share", "shareholder", "small business corporation" — 248(1); "small business deduction rate" — 125(1.1); "taxable Canadian corporation" — 89(1), 248(1); "taxable capital gain" — 38(a), 248(1); "taxable income" — 2(2), 248(1); "taxation year" — 249; "taxpayer" — 248(1).

I.T. Application Rules [s. 137]: 58 (property of credit union acquired before 1972).

Interpretation Bulletins [s. 137]: IT-483: Credit unions (cancelled).

137.1 (1) Amounts included in income of deposit insurance corporation — For the purpose of computing the income for a taxation year of a taxpayer that is a deposit insurance corporation, the following rules apply:

(a) the corporation's income shall, except as otherwise provided in this section, be computed in accordance with the rules applicable in computing income for the purposes of this Part; and

(b) there shall be included in computing the corporation's income such of the following amounts as are applicable:

(i) the total of profits or gains made in the year by the corporation in respect of bonds, debentures, mortgages, hypothecary claims, notes or other similar obligations owned by it that were disposed of by it in the year, and

(ii) the total of each such portion of each amount, if any, by which the principal amount, at the time it was acquired by the corporation, of a bond, debenture, mortgage, hypothecary claim, note or other similar obligation owned by the corporation at the end of the year exceeds the cost to the corporation of acquiring it as was included by the corporation in computing its profit for the year.

Related Provisions: 89(1)"general rate income pool"E(b) — No high-gross-up dividends; 137.1(3) — Deductions from income of deposit insurance corporation; 137.1(5) — Deposit insurance corporation defined; 137.1(10) — Amounts paid by a deposit insurance corporation; 137.2 — Valuation of property owned since before 1975; 142.2(1)"financial institution"(c)(iv) — Deposit insurance corporation not subject to mark-to-market rules.

Notes: The term "bond, debenture, mortgage, hypothecary claim, note or other similar obligation" may not include bankers' acceptances: *Federated Co-operatives*, 2001 FCA 217; leave to appeal denied 2001 CarswellNat 1788 (SCC).

References to "hypothecary claims" added by 2001 *Civil Code* harmonization bill, effective June 14, 2001. The change is non-substantive; see *Interpretation Act* s. 8.2.

Interpretation Bulletins: IT-483: Credit unions (cancelled).

(2) Amounts not included in income — The following amounts shall not be included in computing the income of a deposit insurance corporation for a taxation year:

(a) any premium or assessment received, or receivable, by the corporation in the year from a member institution; and

(b) any amount received by the corporation in the year from another deposit insurance corporation to the extent that that amount can reasonably be considered to have been paid out of amounts referred to in paragraph (a) received by that other deposit insurance corporation in any taxation year.

Related Provisions: 137.1(4) — Limitation on deduction; 137.1(11) — Deductions for payments by member institution.

Notes: The meaning of "assessment" was discussed in *Civil Service Co-op*, [2001] 4 C.T.C. 2350 (TCC).

137.1(2)(b) added by 2002-2013 technical bill, for 1998 and later tax years.

(3) Amounts deductible in computing income of deposit insurance corporation — There may be deducted in computing the income for a taxation year of a taxpayer that is a deposit insurance corporation such of the following amounts as are applicable:

(a) the total of losses sustained in the year by the corporation in respect of bonds, debentures, mortgages, hypothecary claims, notes or other similar obligations owned by it and issued by a person other than a member institution that were disposed of by it in the year;

(b) the total of each such portion of each amount, if any, by which the cost to the corporation of acquiring a bond, debenture, mortgage, hypothecary claim, note or other similar obligation owned by the corporation at the end of the year exceeds the principal amount of the bond, debenture, mortgage, hypothecary claim, note or other similar obligation, as the case may be, at the time it was so acquired as was deducted by the corporation in computing its profit for the year;

(c) [Repealed under former Act]

(d) the total of all expenses incurred by the taxpayer in collecting premiums or assessments from member institutions;

(e) the total of all expenses incurred by the taxpayer

(i) in the performance of its duties as curator of a bank, or as liquidator or receiver of a member institution when duly appointed as such a curator, liquidator or receiver,

(ii) in the course of making or causing to be made such inspections as may reasonably be considered to be appropriate for the purposes of assessing the solvency or financial stability of a member institution, and

(iii) in supervising or administering a member institution in financial difficulty; and

(f) the total of all amounts each of which is an amount that is not otherwise deductible by the taxpayer for the year or any other taxation year and that is

(i) an amount paid by the taxpayer in the year pursuant to a legal obligation to pay interest on borrowed money used

(A) to lend money to, or otherwise provide assistance to, a member institution in financial difficulty,

(B) to assist in the payment of any losses suffered by members or depositors of a member institution in financial difficulty,

(C) to lend money to a subsidiary wholly-owned corporation of the taxpayer where the subsidiary is deemed by subsection (5.1) to be a deposit insurance corporation,

(D) to acquire property from a member institution in financial difficulty, or

(E) to acquire shares of the capital stock of a member institution in financial difficulty, or

(ii) an amount paid by the taxpayer in the year pursuant to a legal obligation to pay interest on an amount that would be deductible under subparagraph (i) if it were paid in the year.

Related Provisions: 137.2 — Valuation of property owned since before 1975.

Notes: References to "hypothecary claims" added to 137.1(3)(a) and (b) by 2001 *Civil Code* harmonization bill, effective June 14, 2001. The change is non-substantive; see *Interpretation Act* s. 8.2. See also Notes to 137.1(1).

Interpretation Bulletins: IT-483: Credit unions (cancelled).

(4) Limitation on deduction — No deduction shall be made in computing the income for a taxation year of a taxpayer that is a deposit insurance corporation in respect of

(a) any grant, subsidy or other assistance to member institutions provided by it;

(b) an amount equal to the amount, if any, by which the amount paid or payable by it to acquire property exceeds the fair market value of the property at the time it was so acquired;

(c) any amounts paid to its member institutions as allocations in proportion to any amounts described in subsection (2);

(d) any amount paid by it to another deposit insurance corporation that is, because of paragraph (2)(b), not included in computing the income of that other deposit insurance corporation; or

(e) any amount that may otherwise be deductible under paragraph 20(1)(p) in respect of debts owing to it by any of its member institutions that has not been included in computing its income for the year or a preceding taxation year.

Related Provisions: 20(1)(p) — Bad debts; 137.1(2) — Amounts not included in income.

Notes: For the meaning of "in proportion to" in para. (c) see *Spruce Credit Union*, 2012 TCC 357, para. 49; aff'd 2014 FCA 143, paras. 49-50.

137.1(4)(d) added by 2002-2013 technical bill, for 1998 and later tax years.

(5) Definitions — In this section,

"amortized cost [para. 137.1(5)(d)]" — [Repealed under former Act]

Notes: 137.1(5)(d), repealed by 1988 tax reform, defined "amortized cost", a term now defined in 248(1) and no longer used in this section.

"deposit insurance corporation" means

(a) a corporation that was incorporated by or under a law of Canada or a province respecting the establishment of a stabilization fund or board if

(i) it was incorporated primarily

(A) to provide or administer a stabilization, liquidity or mutual aid fund for credit unions, and

(B) to assist in the payment of any losses suffered by members of credit unions in liquidation, and

(ii) throughout any taxation year in respect of which the expression is being applied,

(A) it was a Canadian corporation, and

(B) the cost amount to the corporation of its investment property was at least 50% of the cost amount to it of all its property (other than a debt obligation of, or a share of the capital stock of, a member institution issued by the member institution at a time when it was in financial difficulty), or

(b) a corporation incorporated by the *Canada Deposit Insurance Corporation Act*;

Related Provisions: 137.1(5.1) — Deeming provision; 137.1(8) — Deemed compliance with Act.

Notes: 137.1(5)"deposit insurance corporation" was 137.1(5)(a) before RSC 1985 (5th Supp) consolidation for tax years ending after Nov. 1991.

"investment property" means

(a) bonds, debentures, mortgages, hypothecary claims, notes or other similar obligations

(i) of or guaranteed by the Government of Canada,

(ii) of the government of a province or an agent thereof,

(iii) of a municipality in Canada or a municipal or public body performing a function of government in Canada,

(iv) of a corporation, commission or association not less than 90% of the shares or capital of which is owned by Her Majesty in right of a province or by a Canadian municipality, or of a subsidiary wholly-owned corporation that is subsidiary to such a corporation, commission or association, or

(v) of an educational institution or a hospital if repayment of the principal amount thereof and payment of the interest thereon is to be made, or is guaranteed, assured or otherwise specifically provided for or secured by the government of a province,

(b) any deposits, deposit certificates or guaranteed investment certificates with

(i) a bank,

(ii) a corporation licensed or otherwise authorized under the laws of Canada or a province to carry on in Canada the business of offering to the public its services as trustee, or

(iii) a credit union or central that is a member of the Canadian Payments Association or a credit union that is a shareholder or member of a central that is a member of the Canadian Payments Association,

(c) any money of the corporation, and

(d) in relation to a particular deposit insurance corporation, debt obligations of, and shares of the capital stock of, a subsidiary wholly-owned corporation of the particular corporation where the subsidiary is deemed by subsection (5.1) to be a deposit insurance corporation;

Notes: Reference to "hypothecary claims" added to opening words of para. (a) by 2001 *Civil Code* harmonization bill, effective June 14, 2001. The change is non-substantive; see *Interpretation Act* s. 8.2. 137.1(5)"investment property" was 137.1(5)(c) before RSC 1985 (5th Supp) consolidation for tax years ending after Nov. 1991.

"member institution", in relation to a particular deposit insurance corporation, means

(a) a corporation whose liabilities in respect of deposits are insured by, or

(b) a credit union that is qualified for assistance from

that deposit insurance corporation.

Related Provisions: 142.2(1)"financial institution"(c)(iv) — Deposit insurance corporation not subject to mark-to-market rules.

Notes: 137.1(5)"member institution" was 137.1(5)(b) before RSC 1985 (5th Supp) consolidation for tax years ending after Nov. 1991.

(5.1) Deeming provision — For the purposes of this section, other than subsection (2), paragraph (3)(d), subparagraph (3)(e)(i), subsection (9) and paragraph (11)(a), a subsidiary wholly-owned corporation of a particular corporation described in the definition "deposit insurance corporation" in subsection (5) shall be deemed to be a deposit insurance corporation, and any member institution of the particular corporation shall be deemed to be a member institution of the subsidiary, where all or substantially all of the property of the subsidiary has at all times since the subsidiary was incorporated consisted of

(a) investment property;

(b) shares of the capital stock of a member institution of the particular corporation obtained by the subsidiary at a time when the member institution was in financial difficulty;

(c) debt obligations issued by a member institution of the particular corporation at a time when the member institution was in financial difficulty;

(d) property acquired from a member institution of the particular corporation at a time when the member institution was in financial difficulty; or

(e) any combination of property described in paragraphs (a) to (d).

Notes: CRA considers that "substantially all", used in the opening words of 137.1(5.1), means 90% or more.

137.1(5.1) amended by 1993 technical bill, for 1992 and later tax years.

(6) Deemed not to be a private corporation — Notwithstanding any other provision of this Act, a deposit insurance corporation that would, but for this subsection, be a private corporation shall be deemed not to be a private corporation.

(7) Deposit insurance corporation deemed not a credit union — Notwithstanding any other provision of this Act, a deposit insurance corporation that would, but for this subsection, be a credit union shall be deemed not to be a credit union.

Related Provisions: 137 — Credit unions.

(8) Deemed compliance — For the purposes of subsection (5), a corporation shall be deemed to have complied with clause (a)(ii)(B) of the definition "deposit insurance corporation" in subsection (5) throughout the 1975 taxation year if it complied with that clause on the last day of that taxation year.

(9) Special tax rate — The tax payable under this Part by a corporation for a taxation year throughout which it was a deposit insurance corporation (other than a corporation incorporated under the *Canada Deposit Insurance Corporation Act*) is the amount determined by the formula:

$$(38\% - A) \times B$$

where

A is the rate that would, if subsection 125(1.1) applied to the corporation for the taxation year, be the corporation's small business deduction rate for the taxation year within the meaning assigned by that subsection; and

B is the corporation's taxable income for the taxation year.

Related Provisions: 220(4.3), (4.4) — Security furnished by member institution of a deposit insurance corporation.

Notes: 137.1(9) amended by 2006 budget bill #2, effective for 2008 and later taxation years, to change "22% of its taxable income for the year" to the formula.

(10) Amounts paid by a deposit insurance corporation — Where in a taxation year a taxpayer is a member institution, there shall be included in computing its income for the year the total of all amounts each of which is

(a) an amount received by the taxpayer in the year from a deposit insurance corporation that is an amount described in any of paragraphs (4)(a) to (c), to the extent that the taxpayer has not repaid the amount to the deposit insurance corporation in the year,

(b) an amount received from a deposit insurance corporation in the year by a depositor or member of the taxpayer as, on account of, in lieu of payment of, or in satisfaction of, deposits with, or share capital of, the taxpayer, to the extent that the taxpayer has not repaid the amount to the deposit insurance corporation in the year, or

(c) the amount by which

(i) the principal amount of any obligation of the taxpayer to pay an amount to a deposit insurance corporation that is settled or extinguished in the year without any payment by the taxpayer or by the payment by the taxpayer of an amount less than the principal amount

exceeds

(ii) the amount, if any, paid by the taxpayer on the settlement or extinguishment of the obligation

to the extent that the excess is not otherwise required to be included in computing the taxpayer's income for the year or a preceding taxation year.

Related Provisions: 80(1)"forgiven amount" — Debt forgiveness; 137.1(10.1) — Principal amount of an obligation to pay interest; 137.1(12) — Repayment excluded; 220(4.3), (4.4) — Security furnished by a member institution of a deposit insurance corporation.

Notes: Certain amounts paid by a deposit insurance corp were taxable under 137.1(10), rather than capital gain, in *Civil Service Co-op*, [2001] 4 C.T.C. 2350 (TCC), which discussed 137.1 in some detail.

In *Spruce Credit Union*, 2014 FCA 143, dividends received by credit unions from a DIC, as part of cycling funds to another DIC, were deductible under 112(1) (even if they were taxable under 137.1 rather than 82(1)).

(10.1) Principal amount of an obligation to pay interest — For the purposes of paragraph (10)(c), an amount of interest payable by a member institution to a deposit insurance corporation on an obligation shall be deemed to have a principal amount equal to that amount.

Related Provisions: 137.1(11) — Deduction for payments by member institution.

(11) Deduction by member institutions — There may be deducted in computing the income for a taxation year of a taxpayer that is a member institution such of the following amounts as are applicable:

(a) any amount paid or payable by the taxpayer in the year that is described in subsection (2) to the extent that it was not deducted in computing the taxpayer's income for a preceding taxation year; and

(b) any amount repaid by the taxpayer in the year to a deposit insurance corporation on account of an amount described in paragraph (10)(a) or (b) that was received in a preceding taxation year to the extent that it was not, by reason of subsection (12), excluded from the taxpayer's income for the preceding year.

(12) Repayment excluded — Where

(a) a member institution has in a taxation year repaid an amount to a deposit insurance corporation on account of an amount that was included by virtue of paragraph (10)(a) or (b) in computing its income for a preceding taxation year,

(b) the member institution has filed its return of income required by section 150 for the preceding year, and

(c) on or before the day on or before which the member institution is required by section 150 to file a return of income for the taxation year, it has filed an amended return for the preceding year excluding from its income for that year the amount repaid,

the amount repaid shall be excluded from the amount otherwise included by virtue of paragraph (10)(a) or (b) in computing the member institution's income for the preceding year and the Minister shall make such reassessment of the tax, interest and penalties payable by the member institution for preceding taxation years as is necessary to give effect to the exclusion.

Definitions [s. 137.1]: "amount" — 248(1); "Canadian corporation" — 89(1), 248(1); "corporation" — 248(1), *Interpretation Act* 35(1); "credit union" — 137(6), 137.1(7), 248(1); "deposit insurance corporation" — 137.1(5), (5.1); "fair market value" — see 69(1) Notes; "Her Majesty" — *Interpretation Act* 35(1); "insurance corporation" — 248(1); "investment property" — 137.1(5); "member institution" — 137.1(5); "Minister" — 248(1); "private corporation" — 89(1), 248(1); "property" — 248(1); "province" — *Interpretation Act* 35(1); "share", "shareholder" — 248(1); "small business deduction rate" — 125(1.1); "subsidiary wholly-owned corporation" — 248(1); "tax payable" — 248(2); "taxable income" — 2(2), 248(1); "taxation year" — 249; "taxpayer" — 248(1).

137.2 [Deposit insurance corporation —] Computation of income for 1975 and subsequent years — For the purpose of computing the income of a deposit insurance corporation for the 1975 and subsequent taxation years,

(a) property of the corporation that is a bond, debenture, mortgage, hypothecary claim, note or other similar obligation owned by it at the commencement of the corporation's 1975 taxation year shall be valued at its cost to the corporation less the total of all amounts that, before that time, the corporation was entitled to receive as, on account or in lieu of payment of, or in satisfaction of, the principal amount of the bond, debenture, mortgage, hypothecary claim, note or other similar obligation,

(i) plus a reasonable amount in respect of the amortization of the amount by which the principal amount of the property at the time it was acquired by the corporation exceeded its actual cost to the corporation, or

(ii) minus a reasonable amount in respect of the amortization of the amount by which its actual cost to the corporation exceeded the principal amount of the property at the time it was acquired by the corporation;

(b) property of the corporation that is a debt owing to the corporation (other than property described in paragraph (a) or a debt that became a bad debt before its 1975 taxation year) acquired by it before the commencement of its 1975 taxation year shall be valued at any time at the amount thereof outstanding at that time;

(c) property of the corporation (other than property in respect of which any amount for the year has been included under paragraph (a)) that was acquired, by foreclosure or otherwise, after default made under a mortgage or hypothec shall be valued at its cost amount to the corporation; and

(d) any other property shall be valued at its cost amount to the corporation.

Notes: References to "hypothecary claim" and "hypothec" added by 2001 *Civil Code* harmonization bill, effective June 14, 2001. The changes are non-substantive; *Interpretation Act* s. 8.2.

137.2 added in the RSC 1985 (5th Supp) consolidation for tax years ending after Nov. 1991. This was formerly in 1974-75-76, c. 26, s. 94.

Definitions [s. 137.2]: "amount", "cost amount" — 248(1); "deposit insurance corporation" — 137.1(5), (5.1) [does not explicitly apply to 137.2]; "income" — 3; "principal amount" — 248(1), (26); "property" — 248(1); "taxation year" — 249.

Insurance Corporations

138. (1) Insurance corporations — It is hereby declared that a corporation, whether or not it is a mutual corporation, that has, in a taxation year, been a party to insurance contracts or other arrangements or relationships of a particular class whereby it can reasonably be regarded as undertaking

(a) to insure other persons against loss, damage or expense of any kind, or

(b) to pay insurance moneys to other persons

(i) on the death of any person,

(ii) on the happening of an event or contingency dependent on human life,

(iii) for a term dependent on human life, or

(iv) at a fixed or determinable future time,

whether or not such persons are members or shareholders of the corporation, shall, regardless of the form or legal effect of those contracts, arrangements or relationships, be deemed, for the purposes of this Act, to have been carrying on an insurance business of that class in the year for profit, and in any such case, for the purpose of computing the income of the corporation, the following rules apply:

(c) every amount received by the corporation under, in consideration of, in respect of or on account of such a contract, arrangement or relationship shall be deemed to have been received by it in the course of that business,

(d) the income shall, except as otherwise provided in this section, be computed in accordance with the rules applicable in computing income for the purposes of this Part,

(e) all income from property vested in the corporation shall be deemed to be income of the corporation, and

(f) all taxable capital gains and allowable capital losses from dispositions of property vested in the corporation shall be deemed to be taxable capital gains or allowable capital losses, as the case may be, of the corporation.

Related Provisions: 87(2.2) — Amalgamation of insurance corporations; 138(6) — Deductions for dividends from taxable corporations; 138(9) — Computation of income; 139, 139.1 — Mutualization and demutualization of insurer; 142 — Taxable capital gains where insurer carries on business in Canada and outside Canada; 148(1) — Amount included in life insurance policyholder's income; 149(1)(m), (t) — Exemptions — insurers; 190.1 — Financial institutions capital tax; 211.1 — Tax on life insurer's investment income.

Notes: 138(1) deems a company to be carrying on an insurance business, but does not speak to where the business is carried on: *Standard Life*, 2015 TCC 97, para. 75 (aff'd as *SCDA (2015) Inc.*, 2017 FCA 177).

See also Notes at end of s. 138. (For life insurance policyholders, see s. 148.)

A foreign insurance company (not licensed to carry on an insurance business in Canada) that trades properties in Canada may be deemed to be carrying on *business* in Canada by s. 253, but would not be carrying on an *insurance* business in Canada: VIEWS doc 2005-0126031C6.

For a ruling that a corp transferring all its warranty contracts to a subsidiary ceases to be an insurance corp (so 84(1)(c.3) can apply), see VIEWS doc 2006-0173771R3.

(2) Insurer's income or loss — Notwithstanding any other provision of this Act,

(a) if a life insurer resident in Canada carries on an insurance business in Canada and in a country other than Canada in a taxation year, its income or loss for the year from carrying on an insurance business is the amount of its income or loss for the taxation year from carrying on the insurance business in Canada;

(b) if a life insurer resident in Canada carries on an insurance business in Canada and in a country other than Canada in a taxation year, for greater certainty,

(i) in computing the insurer's income or loss for the taxation year from the insurance business carried on by it in Canada, no amount is to be included in respect of the insurer's gross investment revenue for the taxation year derived from property used or held by it in the course of carrying on an insurance business that is not designated insurance property for the taxation year of the insurer, and

(ii) in computing the insurer's taxable capital gains or allowable capital losses for the taxation year from dispositions of capital property (referred to in this subparagraph as "insurance business property") that, at the time of the disposition, was used or held by the insurer in the course of carrying on an insurance business,

(A) there is to be included each taxable capital gain or allowable capital loss of the insurer for the taxation year from a disposition in the taxation year of an insurance business property that was a designated insurance property for the taxation year of the insurer, and

(B) there is not to be included any taxable capital gain or allowable capital loss of the insurer for the taxation year from a disposition in the taxation year of an insurance business property that was not a designated insurance property for the taxation year of the insurer;

(c) if a non-resident insurer carries on an insurance business in Canada in a taxation year, its income or loss for the taxation year from carrying on an insurance business is the amount of its income or loss for the taxation year from carrying on the insurance business in Canada; and

(d) if a non-resident insurer carries on an insurance business in Canada in a taxation year,

(i) in computing the non-resident insurer's income or loss for the taxation year from the insurance business carried on by it in Canada, no amount is to be included in respect of the non-resident insurer's gross investment revenue for the taxation year derived from property used or held by it in the course of carrying on an insurance business that is not designated insurance property for the taxation year of the non-resident insurer, and

(ii) in computing the non-resident insurer's taxable capital gains or allowable capital losses for the taxation year from dispositions of capital property (referred to in this subparagraph as "insurance business property") that, at the time of the disposition, was used or held by the non-resident insurer in the course of carrying on an insurance business,

(A) there is to be included each taxable capital gain or allowable capital loss of the non-resident insurer for the taxation year from a disposition in the taxation year of an insurance business property that was a designated insurance property for the taxation year of the non-resident insurer, and

(B) there is not to be included any taxable capital gain or allowable capital loss of the non-resident insurer for the taxation year from a disposition in the taxation year of an insurance business property that was not a designated insurance property for the taxation year of the non-resident insurer.

Possible Future Amendments — Insurance corporations (Consultation)

Dept. of Finance news release, May 28, 2021: *Department of Finance launches consultations on tax implications of international accounting rules for insurance contracts (IFRS 17)*

On January 1, 2023, new international accounting rules for insurance contracts — known as International Financial Reporting Standards (IFRS) 17 — will come into effect.

IFRS 17 aims to improve the financial reporting of insurance contracts by mandating a consistent framework across countries, industries, and types of insurance contracts. It also aims to provide more transparent and useful information about the value of insurance obligations and the profitability of insurance contracts.

To address these changes, today the government is launching consultations with industry stakeholders on its intention to maintain the current alignment between the taxation of profits and the timing of income earning activities.

In particular, the government is seeking input on how best to enact IFRS 17 in a way that facilitates implementation by insurance companies and is auditable by the Canada Revenue Agency. The government is also seeking views on other potential taxation issues that could arise from the implementation of, or transition to, the new standard. This consultation will assist the government in developing potential modifications to the *Income Tax Act* and other administrative tools.

Stakeholders are invited to provide comments on the government's proposed approach by July 30, 2021. Comments can be sent by email to ifrs17consultation-consultationifrs17@canada.ca.

Contacts: Media may contact: Media Relations, Department of Finance Canada, fin.media-media.fin@canada.ca, 613-369-4000. General enquiries: 1-833-712-2292, TTY 613-369-3230; email fin.financepublic-financepublique.fin@canada.ca

Backgrounder: Consultations on tax implications of international accounting rules for insurance contracts

Accounting standards specify how transactions are recognized, measured, presented and disclosed in financial statements. While these standards are set by national accounting bodies, many countries, including Canada, follow the standards set by an independent international body, the International Accounting Standards Board (IASB). The movement towards global accounting standards reflects businesses' increasing participation in the global marketplace. Investors also benefit from the consistency and reliability of international standards. Since 2011, Canadian publicly-traded enterprises have followed IASB's International Financial Reporting Standards (IFRS), the same standards used in more than 100 other countries.

Insurers in Canada adopted IFRS reporting standards, including the standards pertaining to the reporting of insurance contracts (IFRS 4), in 2011. IFRS 4 was intended to be an interim standard for insurance contracts, pending the completion of a more comprehensive and uniform standard — IFRS 17.

Changes to the Accounting Standards for Insurance Contracts

On January 1, 2023, under IFRS 17, accounting standards for insurance contracts will substantially change financial reporting, primarily for two broad categories of insurance companies: life insurers — which includes annuity, accident and health insurance providers; and property and casualty (P&C) insurers — which includes auto, personal property, commercial property and liability insurance providers.

Income, as measured using generally accepted accounting principles, typically serves as the basis for computing a corporation's taxable income. The current measurement of taxable income for insurers closely matches that of accounting income under IFRS 4.

IFRS 17 will significantly alter the measurement of corporate income from insurance contracts, particularly by changing deferred recognition into profits of a portion of insurance revenues, which is currently included in income when insurance contracts are sold. Deferring raises key tax policy questions about how profits from an insurance business should be measured for tax purposes.

The unique nature of insurance contracts, where premiums are pooled then invested in order to pay claims often years after contracts are sold, has led to specific rules regarding the computation of income. Special rules permit insurers to set aside tax-deductible reserves in recognition of the future claims to be paid from premiums received.

Reserves under IFRS 17 will continue to be determined actuarially when the insurance contracts are sold. IFRS 17 will introduce a new reserve, the Contractual Service Margins (CSM), that will contain a portion of the profits earned on underwritten insurance contracts to be deferred and gradually released into income over the estimated life of the insurance contracts. If adopted for tax purposes, the introduction of the CSM mechanism would lead to a deferred recognition of profits into taxable income. IFRS 17 will

also introduce an asymmetrical treatment of profit and losses, as only profits will be deferred through the CSM. If, at the moment of underwriting, a group of contracts is expected to generate a loss over its lifetime then the insurer will be required to immediately deduct the loss against income.

Government of Canada's Position

The government intends to implement changes that will generally support the use of IFRS 17 accounting for income tax purposes. However, adjustments would be made to recognize profits as taxable income so that it remains aligned with economic activities, as under current rules. More specifically, the CSM would not be considered a deductible reserve for tax purposes. This approach would largely preserve the existing tax rules.

In the absence of such adjustments, profits from insurance policies — both new policies and policies existing at the time of transition — would no longer be aligned with the timing of economic activity. IFRS 17's CSM would allow insurers to defer the recognition of profits until years following the taxation year in which the economic (income-earning) activities occurred. Deferring the recognition of profits for insurance contracts would result in deferred tax payments, which would raise equity concerns vis-à-vis other sectors of the economy. The proposed asymmetrical treatment between the profits and losses under IFRS 17, would exacerbate this concern.

Consultation Process and Next Steps

The government is seeking input on how best to achieve the desired tax policy outcome in a way that facilitates implementation by insurance companies, and is auditable by the Canada Revenue Agency. The government is also seeking views on other potential taxation issues that could arise from the implementation of and transition to the new standard This consultation will assist the government in developing potential modifications to the *Income Tax Act* and other administrative tools.

Stakeholders are invited to provide comments by July 30, 2021. Comments can be sent to ifrs17consultation-consultationifrs17@canada.ca.

Contacts

Media may contact: Media Relations, Department of Finance Canada, fin.media-media.fin@canada.ca, 613-369-4000. General enquiries: 1-833-712-2292, fax 613-369-4065, TTY 613-369-3230, email fin.financepublic-financepublique.fin@canada.ca

Consultations on tax implications of international accounting rules for insurance contracts (IFRS 17), May 28, 2021:

Join In: Open until July 30, 2021

On January 1, 2023, new international accounting rules for insurance contracts — known as International Financial Reporting Standards (IFRS) 17 — will come into effect.

IFRS 17 aims to improve the financial reporting of insurance contracts by mandating a consistent framework across countries, industries and types of insurance contracts. It also aims to provide more transparent and useful information about the value of insurance obligations and the profitability of insurance contracts.

To address these changes, the government is seeking input on its intention to maintain the current alignment between the taxation of profits and the timing of income earning activities. In particular, the government is requesting feedback on how to best enact IFRS 17 in a way that facilitates implementation by insurance companies and is auditable by the Canada Revenue Agency. The government also welcomes views on other potential taxation issues that could arise from the implementation of, or transition to the new standard.

Who is the focus of this consultation?

We want to hear from insurance industry stakeholders. Interested tax practitioners and members of the public are also welcome to provide input.

In submitting your comments, please include:

- Full name of the official;
- name of the organization;
- full mailing address, including postal code;
- telephone number, including area code; and
- Reply e-mail address.

Participate through email

Due to COVID-19 public health considerations, email submissions are preferred. Send us your comments at ifrs17consultation-consultationifrs17@canada.ca with "IFRS 17" as the subject line.

Should you wish to provide comments by mail, please direct your submission to the attention of the Tax Policy Branch.

What's next?

This consultation with stakeholders will assist the government in developing potential modifications to the *Income Tax Act* and other administrative tools.

Information received through this comment process is subject to the *Access to Information Act* and the *Privacy Act*. Those providing comments are asked to indicate clearly the name of the individual or the organization that should be identified as having made the submission. In order to respect privacy and confidentiality, please advise when providing your comments whether you:

- consent to the disclosure of your comments in whole or in part;

Related Provisions: 20(7)(c) — No deduction for certain reserves; 20(26) — Deduction for unpaid claims reserve adjustment; 138(1) — Insurance corporations; 138(2.1)–(2.6) — Anti-avoidance — foreign branch used to insure Canadian risks; 138(6) — Deduction for dividends; 138(9) — Computation of income; 140(1), (2) — Deductions and inclusions in income of insurer; 211.1 — Tax on investment income of life insurer.

Notes: 138(2) implements a "Canada only" rule taxing a life insurer on its Canadian insurance business, not one carried on in foreign branches: *Standard Life*, 2015 TCC 97, paras. 35-47 (aff'd as *SCDA (2015) Inc.*, 2017 FCA 177).

See also Notes at end of s. 138.

138(2) amended by 2002-2013 technical bill (for taxation years ending after 1999), 1996 Budget, 1991 technical bill.

(2.1) Income — designated foreign insurance business —
If a life insurer resident in Canada has a designated foreign insurance business in a taxation year,

(a) for the purposes of computing the life insurer's income or loss from carrying on an insurance business in Canada for that taxation year, the life insurer's insurance business carried on in Canada is deemed to include the insurance of the specified Canadian risks that are insured as part of the designated foreign insurance business;

(b) if, in the immediately preceding taxation year, the designated foreign insurance business was not a designated foreign insurance business, for the purposes of paragraph (4)(a), subsection (9), the definition "designated insurance property" in subsection (12) and paragraphs 12(1)(d) to (e), the life insurer is deemed to have carried on the business in Canada in that immediately preceding year and to have claimed the maximum amounts to which it would have been entitled under paragraphs (3)(a) (other than under subparagraph (3)(a)(ii.1), (iii) or (v)), 20(1)(l) and (l.1) and 20(7)(c) in respect of those specified Canadian risks if that designated foreign insurance business had been a designated foreign insurance business in that immediately preceding year; and

(c) for the purposes of subparagraph (3)(a)(ii.1) and subsection 20(22),

(i) the life insurer is deemed to have carried on the business in Canada in that immediately preceding year, and

(ii) the amounts, if any, that would have been prescribed in respect of the insurer for the purposes of paragraphs (4)(b) and 12(1)(e.1) for that immediately preceding year in respect of the insurance policies in respect of those specified Canadian risks are deemed to have been included in computing its income for that year.

Related Provisions: 95(2)(a.2) — Parallel FAPI rule.

Notes: 138(2.1)–(2.6) extend the "base erosion" rules to foreign branches of life insurers (LIs). A LI resident in Canada is not taxed on income from carrying on business in a foreign jurisdiction (through a branch): 138(2). Foreign branches are thus taxed similarly to foreign affiliates (FAs) of Canadian-resident corps, whose foreign business income generally is not taxable in Canada and, in most cases, is exempt from Canadian tax on repatriation (see Notes to 113(1)).

Before 138(2.1)–(2.6), the income tax regimes for LIs and FAs differed in the treatment of income from insuring Canadian risks (e.g., risks in respect of persons resident in Canada). 95(2)(a.2)–(a.23) treat income from insuring Canadian risks of a controlled FA of a Canadian taxpayer as FAPI and thus taxable to the Canadian taxpayer on an accrual basis. This is intended to prevent Canadian taxpayers from avoiding Canadian tax by shifting income from the insurance of Canadian risks into a controlled FA resident in a low- or no-tax jurisdiction. 138(2.1)–(2.6) provide a parallel rule to prevent shifting income from insuring Canadian risks to a foreign branch of a Canadian LI.

This rule applies where 10% or more of gross premium income (net of reinsurance ceded) earned by a foreign branch of a Canadian LI is premium income in respect of Canadian risks: 138(12)"designated foreign insurance business". Where the rule ap-

plies, it deems the insurance of Canadian risks by a Canadian LI's foreign branch to be part of a business carried on by the LI in Canada: 138(2.1)(a).

Further, anti-avoidance rules in the FAPI regime (95(2)(a.21)-(a.23)) are extended to foreign branches of LIs: 138(2.2)-(2.5). These rules are intended to ensure that the rule cannot be avoided through either "insurance swaps" or ceding of Canadian risks.

As well, if a LI has insured foreign risks through its foreign branch and it can reasonably be concluded that the foreign risks were insured by the LI as part of a transaction or series of transactions one of the purposes of which was to avoid 138(2.1)-(2.5), then the LI is treated as if it had insured Canadian risks: 138(2.6). A similar rule in 95(2)(a.24) applies for FAPI. (Finance Technical Notes)

138(2.1)-(2.6) added by 2017 budget bill #2, for a taxpayer's taxation years that begin after March 21, 2017.

(2.2) Insurance swaps — For the purposes of this section, one or more risks insured by a life insurer resident in Canada, as part of an insurance business carried on in a country other than Canada, that would not be specified Canadian risks if this Act were read without reference to this subsection, are deemed to be specified Canadian risks if those risks would be deemed to be specified Canadian risks because of paragraph 95(2)(a.21) if the life insurer were a foreign affiliate of a taxpayer.

Related Provisions: 95(2)(a.21) — Parallel FAPI rule.

Notes: See Notes to 138(2.1).

(2.3) Insurance swaps — Subsection (2.4) applies in respect of one or more agreements or arrangements if

(a) subsection (2.2) applies to deem one or more risks insured by a particular life insurer resident in Canada to be specified Canadian risks; and

(b) those agreements or arrangements are in respect of risks described in paragraph (a) and have been entered into by any of the following (in subsection (2.4), referred to as an "agreeing party"):

(i) the particular life insurer,

(ii) another life insurer resident in Canada that does not deal at arm's length with the particular life insurer,

(iii) a partnership of which a life insurer described in subparagraph (i) or (ii) is a member,

(iv) a foreign affiliate of either the particular life insurer or a person that does not deal at arm's length with the particular life insurer, and

(v) a partnership of which a foreign affiliate described in subparagraph (iv) is a member.

Related Provisions: 95(2)(a.21) — Parallel FAPI rule.

Notes: See Notes to 138(2.1).

(2.4) Insurance swaps — If this subsection applies in respect of one or more agreements or arrangements,

(a) to the extent that activities performed in connection with those agreements or arrangements can reasonably be considered to be performed for the purpose of obtaining the result described in subparagraph 95(2)(a.21)(ii) (with any modifications that the circumstances require), those activities are deemed to be,

(i) if the agreeing party is a life insurer resident in Canada, or a partnership of which such a life insurer is a member, part of the life insurer's insurance business carried on in Canada, and

(ii) if the agreeing party is a foreign affiliate of a taxpayer, or a partnership of which such an affiliate is a member, a separate business, other than an active business, carried on by the affiliate; and

(b) any income from those activities (including income that pertains to or is incident to those activities) is deemed to be,

(i) if the agreeing party is a life insurer resident in Canada, income from the life insurer's insurance business carried on in Canada, and

(ii) if the agreeing party is a foreign affiliate of a taxpayer, income from the business, other than an active business.

Related Provisions: 95(2)(a.22) — Parallel FAPI rule.

Notes: See Notes to 138(2.1).

(2.5) Ceding of Canadian risks — Any income of a life insurer resident in Canada for a taxation year, from its insurance business carried on in a country other than Canada, in respect of the ceding of specified Canadian risks that would, if the life insurer were a foreign affiliate of a taxpayer, be included in computing the life insurer's income from a business, other than an active business, for the taxation year because of subparagraph 95(2)(a.2)(iii), is to be included in computing the life insurer's income or loss for that taxation year from its insurance business carried on in Canada, except to the extent it is already included because of subsection (2.1), (2.2) or (2.4).

Notes: See Notes to 138(2.1).

(2.6) Anti-avoidance — For the purposes of this section,

(a) a risk is deemed to be a specified Canadian risk that is insured as part of an insurance business carried on in Canada by a particular life insurer resident in Canada if

(i) the particular life insurer insured the risk as part of a transaction or series of transactions,

(ii) the risk would not be a specified Canadian risk if this Act were read without reference to this subsection, and

(iii) it can reasonably be concluded that one of the purposes of the transaction or series of transactions was to avoid

(A) having a designated foreign insurance business, or

(B) the application of any of subsections (2.1) to (2.5) to the risk; and

(b) if one or more agreements or arrangements in respect of the risk have been entered into by any of the persons or partnerships described in subparagraphs (2.3)(b)(i) to (v) (in this paragraph, referred to as an "agreeing party"),

(i) any activities performed in connection with those agreements or arrangements are deemed to be

(A) if the agreeing party is a life insurer resident in Canada, or a partnership of which such a life insurer is a member, part of the life insurer's insurance business carried on in Canada, and

(B) if the agreeing party is a foreign affiliate of a taxpayer, or a partnership of which such an affiliate is a member, a separate business, other than an active business, carried on by the affiliate, and

(ii) any income from those activities (including income that pertains to or is incident to those activities) is deemed to be,

(A) if the agreeing party is a life insurer resident in Canada, income from the life insurer's insurance business carried on in Canada, and

(B) if the agreeing party is a foreign affiliate of a taxpayer, income from the business, other than an active business.

Related Provisions: 95(2)(a.24) — Parallel FAPI rule.

Notes: See Notes to 138(2.1).

(3) Deductions allowed in computing income [of life insurer] — In computing a life insurer's income for a taxation year from carrying on its life insurance business in Canada, there may be deducted

(a) such of the following amounts as are applicable:

(i) any amount that the insurer claims as a policy reserve for the year in respect of its life insurance policies, not exceeding the total of amounts that the insurer is allowed by regulation to deduct in respect of the policies,

(ii) any amount that the insurer claims as a reserve in respect of claims that were received by the insurer before the end of the year under its life insurance policies and that are unpaid at the end of the year, not exceeding the total of amounts that the insurer is allowed by regulation to deduct in respect of the policies,

(ii.1) the amount included under paragraph (4)(b) in computing the insurer's income for the taxation year preceding the year,

(iii) the amount determined by the following formula:

$$A - B$$

where

A is the total of policy dividends (except the portion paid out of segregated funds) that became payable by the insurer after its 1968 taxation year and before the end of the year under its participating life insurance policies, and

B is the total of amounts deductible under this subparagraph (including as determined under subsection (3.1) as it read in its application to the insurer's last taxation year that began before November 2011) in computing its incomes for taxation years before the year, and

(iv) [Repealed]

(v) each amount (other than an amount credited under a participating life insurance policy) that would be deductible under section 140 in computing the insurer's income for the year if the reference in that section to "an insurance business other than a life insurance business" were read as a reference to "a life insurance business in Canada";

(b) the total of amounts each of which is a policy loan made by the insurer in the year and after 1977; and

(c) the amount of tax under Part XII.3 payable by the insurer in respect of its taxable Canadian life investment income for the year.

(d)–(g) [Repealed]

Related Provisions: 18(1)(e.1) — No deduction for unpaid claims; 20(1)(l) — Deductions — reserve for doubtful debts; 20(7)(c) — Policy reserves for non-life insurance business; 20(26) — Deduction for unpaid claims reserve adjustment; 138(3.1) — Excess policy dividend deduction deemed deductible; 138(4) — Amounts included in computing income; 138(4.01) — Life insurance policy includes group life benefit or annuity contract; 138(9) — Computation of income; 138(11.91)(d.1) — Computation of income for non-resident insurer; 138(12) — "Maximum tax actuarial reserve"; 138(16)–(25) — Transitional rules for accounting changes; 140 — Adjustments to income of insurance corporation; 257 — Formula cannot calculate to less than zero.

Notes: In *National Life*, 2008 FCA 14, an insurance reserve under 138(3)(a)(i) was adjusted under Reg. 1406(b) to remove a negative reserve amount; this has been overruled by amendments to Reg. 1406(b) enacted in 2013. The TCC decision (2006 TCC 551) contains a lengthy discussion of the relevant tax policy.

138(3) amended by 2002-2013 technical bill (for tax years that begin after Oct. 2011), 1996 Budget. Former 138(3)(c), repealed by 1988 tax reform, provided a deduction for an investment reserve. A reserve can now be claimed under 20(1)(l)(ii).

Regulations: 1102(1)(j) (no CCA on property used in life insurance business outside Canada); 1404 (policy reserves); 1405 (unpaid claims reserves).

(3.1) [Repealed]

Notes: 138(3.1), "Excess policy dividend deduction deemed deductible", repealed by 2002-2013 technical bill (Part 5 — technical), for taxation years that begin after Oct. 2011.

(4) Amounts included in computing income — In computing a life insurer's income for a taxation year from carrying on its life insurance business in Canada, there shall be included

(a) each amount deducted under paragraph (3)(a), other than under subparagraph (3)(a)(ii.1), (iii) or (v), in computing the insurer's income for the preceding taxation year;

(b) the amount prescribed in respect of the insurer for the year in respect of its life insurance policies; and

(c) the total of all amounts received by the insurer in the year in respect of the repayment of policy loans or in respect of interest on policy loans.

Related Provisions: 138(1) — Insurance corporations; 138(3) — Deductions allowed in computing income; 138(4.01) — Life insurance policy includes group life benefit or annuity contract; 138(4.1)–(4.4) — Amounts included in computing income; 138(9) — Computation of income; 138(11.5)(j.1) — Transfer of business by non-resident insurer; 138(11.91)(d) — Computation of income of non-resident insurer.

Notes: 138(4)(a) amended by 2002-2013 technical bill (for taxation years beginning after Oct. 2011), 1996 Budget, 1994 technical bill.

Regulations: 1404(2) (amount prescribed for 138(4)(b)).

(4.01) Life insurance policy — For the purposes of subsections (3) and (4), a life insurance policy includes a benefit under a group life insurance policy or a group annuity contract.

Related Provisions: Reg. 1408(1)"life insurance policy in Canada" — Same definition for purposes of policy reserve regulations.

Notes: 138(4.01) added by 1996 Budget, effective for 1996 and later taxation years.

(4.1), (4.2), (4.3) [Repealed]

Notes: 138(4.1)-(4.3) repealed by 2002-2013 technical bill (Part 5 — technical), for taxation years that begin after Oct. 2011. They provided deemed deductions for 1976, 1977 and 1985 for 138(4)(a).

(4.4) Income inclusion — If, for a period of time in a taxation year, a life insurer

(a) owned land (other than land referred to in paragraph (c) or (d)) or an interest, or for civil law a right, therein that was not held primarily for the purpose of gaining or producing income from the land for the period,

(b) had an interest, or for civil law a right, in a building that was being constructed, renovated or altered,

(c) owned land subjacent to the building referred to in paragraph (b) or an interest, or for civil law a right, therein, or

(d) owned land immediately contiguous to the land referred to in paragraph (c) or an interest, or for civil law a right, therein that was used or was intended to be used for a parking area, driveway, yard, garden or other use necessary for the use or intended use of the building referred to in paragraph (b),

there shall be included in computing the insurer's income for the year, where the land, building, or interest or right, was designated insurance property of the insurer for the year, or property used or held by it in the year in the course of carrying on an insurance business in Canada, the total of all amounts each of which is the amount prescribed in respect of the insurer's cost or capital cost, as the case may be, of the land, building, or interest or right, for the period, and the amount prescribed shall, at the end of the period, be included in computing

(e) where the land, or interest or right there-in, is property described in paragraph (a), the cost to the insurer of the land, or of the interest or right therein, and

(f) where the land, building, or interest or right therein, is property described in paragraphs (b) to (d), the capital cost to the insurer of the interest or right in the building described in paragraph (b).

Related Provisions: 138(4.5) — Anti-avoidance rule; 138(4.6) — Meaning of "completed"; 248(4) — Interest in real property.

Notes: 138(4.4) amended by 2002-2013 technical bill (Part 4 — bijuralism, effective June 26, 2013), 1996 Budget.

Regulations: 2410 (prescribed amount).

(4.5) Application [of subsec. (4.4)] — Where a life insurer transfers or lends property, directly or indirectly in any manner whatever, to a person or partnership (in this subsection referred to as the "transferee") that is affiliated with the insurer or a person or partnership that does not deal at arm's length with the insurer and

(a) that property,

(b) property substituted for that property, or

(c) property the acquisition of which was assisted by the transfer or loan of that property

was property described in paragraph (4.4)(a), (b), (c) or (d) of the transferee for a period of time in a taxation year of the insurer, the following rules apply:

(d) subsection (4.4) shall apply to include an amount in the insurer's income for the year on the assumption that the property was owned by the insurer for the period, was property described in paragraph (4.4)(a), (b), (c) or (d) of the insurer and was used or held by it in the year in the course of carrying on an insurance business in Canada, and

(e) an amount included in the insurer's income for the year under subsection (4.4) by reason of the application of this subsection shall

(i) where subparagraph (ii) does not apply, be added by the insurer in computing the cost to it of shares of the capital stock of or an interest in the transferee at the end of the year, or

(ii) where the insurer and the transferee have jointly elected in prescribed form on or before the day that is the earliest of the days on or before which any taxpayer making the election is required to file a return pursuant to section 150 for the taxation year that includes the period, be added in computing

(A) where the property is land or an interest, or for civil law a right, therein of the transferee described in paragraph (4.4)(a), the cost to the transferee of the land, or of the interest or right therein, and

(B) where the property is land or a building, or an interest therein or for civil law a right therein, described in paragraphs (4.4)(b) to (d), the capital cost to the transferee of the interest or of the right in the building described in paragraph (4.4)(b).

Related Provisions: 248(4) — Interest in real property; 248(5) — Substituted property; 251.1 — Affiliated persons.

Notes: For meaning of "indirectly" in opening words, see Notes to 17.1(1).

For a taxpayer filing Quebec returns, the election under (e)(ii) must be copied to Revenu Québec: *Taxation Act* ss. 844.4, 21.4.6.

138(4.5)(e)(ii)(A)-(B) amended by 2002-2013 technical bill (Part 4 — bijuralism), effective June 26, 2013. 138(4.5) earlier amended by 1996 Budget.

(4.6) Completion [of building] — For the purposes of subsection (4.4), the construction, renovation or alteration of a building is completed at the earlier of the day on which the construction, renovation or alteration is actually completed and the day on which all or substantially all of the building is used for the purpose for which it was constructed, renovated or altered.

Notes: CRA considers that "substantially all" means 90% or more.

(5) Deductions not allowed — Notwithstanding any other provision of this Act,

(a) in the case of an insurer, no deduction may be made under paragraph 20(1)(l) in computing its income for a taxation year from an insurance business in Canada in respect of a premium or other consideration for a life insurance policy in Canada or an interest therein; and

(b) in the case of a non-resident insurer or a life insurer resident in Canada that carries on any of its insurance business in a country other than Canada, no deduction may be made under paragraph 20(1)(c) or (d) in computing its income for a taxation year from carrying on an insurance business in Canada, except in respect of

(i) interest on borrowed money used to acquire designated insurance property for the year, or to acquire property for which designated insurance property for the year was substituted, for the period in the year during which the designated insurance property was held by the insurer in respect of the business,

(ii) interest on amounts payable for designated insurance property for the year in respect of the business, or

(iii) interest on deposits received or other amounts held by the insurer that arose in connection with life insurance policies in Canada or with policies insuring Canadian risks.

(iv) [Repealed]

Related Provisions: 248(4) — Interest in real property; 248(5) — Substituted property.

Notes: For the application of 138(5)(b) in several scenarios, see VIEWS docs 2005-0126051C6, 2006-0167351I7.

138(5)(b) amended by 1996 Budget and 2001 technical bill, both effective for 1997 and later taxation years.

(5.1) No deduction — No deduction shall be made under subsection 20(12) in computing the income of a life insurer resident in Canada in respect of foreign taxes attributable to its insurance business.

Interpretation Bulletins: IT-506: Foreign income taxes as a deduction from income.

(5.2) [Repealed]

Notes: 138(5.2) repealed by 1994 technical bill, effective for dispositions occurring after Oct. 30, 1994, with certain grandfathering for a disposition of a debt obligation before July 1995.

(6) Deduction for dividends from taxable corporations — In computing the taxable income of a life insurer for a taxation year, no deduction from the income of the insurer for the year may be made under section 112 but, except as otherwise provided by that section, there may be deducted from that income the total of taxable dividends (other than dividends on term preferred shares that are acquired in the ordinary course of the business carried on by the life insurer) included in computing the insurer's income for the year and received by the insurer in the year from taxable Canadian corporations.

Related Provisions: 18(1)(c) — Limitation re exempt income; 55(2) — Deemed proceeds or capital gain; 87(2)(x) — Amalgamations; 111(7.2) — "Non-capital loss" of life insurer; 111(8)"non-capital loss"A:E — Amount included in non-capital loss; 112(2.2), (2.4) — Where no deduction permitted; 112(3)(b)(i) — Reduction in loss on subsequent disposition of share; 112(4)(d) — Loss on share held as inventory; 112(5.2)B(b)(i), (ii) — Adjustment for dividends received on mark-to-market property; 115(1)(d.1) — Deduction from income of non-resident; 141(2) — Life insurance corporation deemed to be public corporation; 148(4) — Income from disposition; 187.2 — Tax on dividends on taxable preferred shares; 187.3 — Tax on dividends on taxable RFI shares; 191(4) — Subsec. 138(6) deemed not to apply; 248(14) — Corporations deemed related; 258 — Deemed dividend on term preferred share.

Notes: In *Industrielle Alliance*, 2008 TCC 15, deduction under 138(6) was allowed despite an offsetting transaction that created deductible interest.

Income Tax Folios: S6-F2-C1: Disposition of an income interest in a trust [replaces IT-385R2].

Interpretation Bulletins: IT-52R4: Income bonds and income debentures (cancelled); IT-328R3: Losses on shares on which dividends have been received.

(7) [Repealed]

Notes: 138(7) repealed by 1996 Budget, for 1996 and later tax years. It was designed to tax profits accumulated before 1969, and certain foreign branch profits, when distributed to shareholders.

(8) No deduction for foreign tax — No deduction shall be made under section 126 from the tax payable under this Part for a taxation year by a life insurer resident in Canada in respect of such part of an income or profits tax as can reasonably be attributable to income from its insurance business.

Notes: For the meaning of "income or profits tax", see Notes to 126(4).

(9) Computation of income — Where in a taxation year an insurer (other than an insurer resident in Canada that does not carry on a life insurance business) carries on an insurance business in Canada and in a country other than Canada, there shall be included in computing its income for the year from carrying on its insurance businesses in Canada the total of

(a) its gross investment revenue for the year from its designated insurance property for the year, and

(b) the amount prescribed in respect of the insurer for the year.

Related Provisions: 88(1)(g) — Winding up — gross investment revenue; 111(7.1) — Effect of election by insurer under ss. 138(9) re 1975 taxation year; 138(2) — Insurer's income or loss; 138(3) — Deductions allowed in computing income; 138(7) — Amounts paid to shareholders included in taxable income; 138(11.5)(i) — Transfer of insurance business by non-resident insurer; 138(11.91)(d) — Computation of income for non-resident insurer; 138(11.92)(c) — Computation of income where insurance business transferred; 142 — Taxable capital gains, etc.; 148(1) — Amounts included in computing policyholder's income; 219(4) — Non-resident insurers.

Notes: See Notes to 138(12)"designated insurance property".

138(9) amended by 1996 Budget, effective for 1997 and later taxation years. The substance of the amendment was to use the new term "designated insurance property"; the other changes are cosmetic.

Regulations: 2411 (prescribed amount).

Forms: T2 Sched. 150: Net income (loss) for income tax purposes for life insurance companies; T2016: Part XIII tax return — tax on income from Canada of approved non-resident insurers.

(9.1) [Repealed under former Act]

Notes: 138(9.1) provided rules where an insurer had elected under the pre-1978 version of 138(9).

(10) Application of financial institution rules — Notwithstanding sections 142.3, 142.4, 142.5 and 142.51, where in a taxation year an insurer (other than an insurer resident in Canada that does not carry on a life insurance business) carries on an insurance business in Canada and in a country other than Canada, in computing its income for the year from carrying on an insurance business in Canada,

(a) sections 142.3, 142.5 and 142.51 apply only in respect of property that is designated insurance property for the year in respect of the business; and

(b) section 142.4 applies only in respect of the disposition of property that, for the taxation year in which the insurer disposed of it, was designated insurance property in respect of the business.

Notes: 138(10) amended by 2008 budget bill #2 (for taxation years beginning after Sept. 2006), 1996 Budget. Added by 1994 technical bill.

(11) [Repealed]

Notes: 138(11) repealed by 1994 technical bill, effective for taxation years that begin after Feb. 22, 1994. It defined the profit or loss on a "Canada security".

(11.1) Identical properties — For the purpose of section 47, any property of a life insurance corporation that would, but for this subsection, be identical to any other property of the corporation is deemed not to be identical to the other property unless both properties are

(a) designated insurance property of the insurer in respect of a life insurance business carried on in Canada; or

(b) designated insurance property of the insurer in respect of an insurance business in Canada other than a life insurance business.

Related Provisions: 248(12) — Identical properties.

Notes: 138(11.1) amended by 1996 Budget, for 1997 and later taxation years.

I.T. Application Rules: 26(8.1) (property owned since before 1972).

Interpretation Bulletins: IT-387R2: Meaning of "identical properties".

(11.2) Computation of capital gain on pre-1969 depreciable property — For the purposes of computing the amount of a capital gain from the disposition of any depreciable property acquired by a life insurer before 1969, the capital cost of the property to the insurer shall be its capital cost determined without reference to paragraph 32(1)(a) of *An Act to amend the Income Tax Act*, chapter 44 of the Statutes of Canada 1968-69, as it read in its application to the 1971 taxation year.

(11.3) Deemed disposition — Subject to subsection (11.31), where a property of a life insurer resident in Canada that carries on an insurance business in Canada and in a country other than Canada or of a non-resident insurer is

(a) designated insurance property of the insurer for a taxation year, was owned by the insurer at the end of the preceding taxation year and was not designated insurance property of the insurer for that preceding year, or

(b) not designated insurance property for a taxation year, was owned by the insurer at the end of the preceding taxation year and was designated insurance property of the insurer for that preceding year,

the following rules apply:

(c) the insurer is deemed to have disposed of the property at the beginning of the year for proceeds of disposition equal to its fair market value at that time and to have reacquired the property immediately after that time at a cost equal to that fair market value,

(d) where paragraph (a) applies, any gain or loss arising from the disposition is deemed not to be a gain or loss from designated insurance property of the insurer in the year, and

(e) where paragraph (b) applies, any gain or loss arising from the disposition is deemed to be a gain or loss from designated insurance property of the insurer in the year.

Related Provisions: 54"superficial loss"(c) — Superficial loss rule does not apply; 138(11.31) — Exception where mark-to-market deemed disposition has applied; 138(11.4) — Loss deductible only in year property disposed of.

Notes: Except for certain limited purposes, 138(11.3) provides for a deemed disposition and reacquisition of property owned by a resident multinational life insurer or a non-resident insurer where there is a change in use of the property.

In *Standard Life*, 2015 TCC 97, aff'd as *SCDA*, 2017 FCA 177, SL tried to use 138(11.3) to bump up the cost base of assets by purporting to carry on a Bermuda insurance business in 2006 (in advance of the mark-to-market rules applying from 2007). The TCC ruled that 138(11.3) applies only when the insurer is already a multinational insurer and had property it could have previously "not designated" (paras. 25, 61): "the property must get on the list while the insurer in already a multinational life insurer" (para. 58). The FCA confirmed that 138(11.3) begins to apply only in the second year the insurer is carrying on business in another country.

138(11.3)(d) and (e) added by 2001 technical bill, for 1997 and later taxation years.

138(11.3) amended by 1996 Budget, for 1997 and later tax years, to use the term "designated insurance property" (DIP), and provide that any deemed disposition or reacquisition is considered to have occurred at the start of the year. This reflects the fact that property either is, or is not, DIP for the *entire* year.

138(11.3) earlier amended by 1994 technical bill, 1991 technical bill.

I.T. Application Rules: 26(17.1) (ITAR 26 does not apply to property owned since before 1972 where 138(11.3) applies).

(11.31) Exclusion from deemed disposition — Subsection (11.3) does not apply

(a) to deem a disposition in a taxation year of a property of an insurer where subsection 142.5(2) deemed the insurer to have disposed of the property in its preceding taxation year; nor

(b) for the purposes of paragraph 20(1)(l), the description of A and paragraph (b) of the description of F in the definition "undepreciated capital cost" in subsection 13(21) and the definition "designated insurance property" in subsection (12).

Notes: 138(11.31) amended by 1996 Budget for 1997 and later taxation years. Added by 1994 technical bill.

(11.4) Deduction of loss — Notwithstanding any other provision of this Act, where an insurer has a loss for a taxation year from the disposition, because of subsection (11.3), of a property other than a specified debt obligation (as defined in subsection 142.2(1)), and the loss would, but for this subsection, have been deductible in the year, the loss shall be deductible only in the taxation year in which the taxpayer disposes of the property otherwise than because of subsection (11.3).

Notes: 138(11.4) amended by 1994 technical bill, effective for property deemed by 138(11.3) to be disposed of after 1994.

(11.41) [Repealed]

Notes: 138(11.41) repealed by 1994 technical bill for changes in use of property occurring after Feb. 22, 1994. It dealt with inclusion of gains on change in use under 138(11.3)(c) and (d).

(11.5) Transfer of insurance business by non-resident insurer — Where

(a) a non-resident insurer (in this subsection referred to as the "transferor") has, at any time in a taxation year, ceased to carry on all or substantially all of an insurance business carried on by it in Canada in that year,

(b) the transferor has, at that time or within 60 days after that time, transferred all or substantially all of the property (in this subsection referred to as the "transferred property") that is owned by it at that time and that was designated insurance property in respect of the business for the taxation year that, because of paragraph (h), ended immediately before that time

(i) to a corporation (in this subsection referred to as the "transferee") that is a qualified related corporation (within the meaning assigned by subsection 219(8)) of the transferor

that began immediately after that time to carry on that insurance business in Canada, and

(ii) for consideration that includes shares of the capital stock of the transferee,

(c) the transferee has, at that time or within 60 days thereafter, assumed or reinsured all or substantially all of the obligations of the transferor that arose in the course of carrying on that insurance business in Canada, and

(d) the transferor and the transferee have jointly elected in prescribed form and in accordance with subsection (11.6),

the following rules apply:

(e) subject to paragraph (k.1), where the fair market value, at that time, of the consideration (other than shares of the capital stock of the transferee or a right to receive any such shares) received or receivable by the transferor for the transferred property does not exceed the total of the cost amounts to the transferor, at that time, of the transferred property, the proceeds of disposition of the transferor and the cost to the transferee of the transferred property shall be deemed to be the cost amount, at that time, to the transferor of the transferred property, and in any other case, the provisions of subsection 85(1) shall be applied in respect of the transfer,

(f) where the provisions of subsection 85(1) are not required to be applied in respect of the transfer, the cost to the transferor of any particular property (other than shares of the capital stock of the transferee or a right to receive any such shares) received or receivable by it as consideration for the transferred property shall be deemed to be the fair market value, at that time, of the particular property,

(g) where the provisions of subsection 85(1) are not required to be applied in respect of the transfer, the cost to the transferor of any shares of the capital stock of the transferee received or receivable by the transferor as consideration for the transferred property shall be deemed to be

(i) where the shares are preferred shares of any class of the capital stock of the transferee, the lesser of

(A) the fair market value of those shares immediately after the transfer of the transferred property, and

(B) the amount determined by the formula

$$A \times B / C$$

where

A is the amount, if any, by which the proceeds of disposition of the transferor of the transferred property determined under paragraph (e) exceed the fair market value, at that time, of the consideration (other than shares of the capital stock of the transferee or a right to receive any such shares) received or receivable by the transferor for the transferred property,

B is the fair market value, immediately after the transfer of the transferred property, of those preferred shares of that class, and

C is the fair market value, immediately after the transfer of the transferred property, of all preferred shares of the capital stock of the transferee receivable by the transferor as consideration for the transferred property, and

(ii) where the shares are common shares of any class of the capital stock of the transferee, the amount determined by the formula

$$A \times B / C$$

where

A is the amount, if any, by which the proceeds of disposition of the transferor of the transferred property determined under paragraph (e) exceed the total of the fair market value, at that time, of the consideration (other than shares of the capital stock of the transferee or a right to receive any such shares) received or receivable by the transferor for the transferred property and the cost to the transferor of all preferred shares of the capital stock of the transferee receivable by the transferor as consideration for the transferred property,

B is the fair market value, immediately after the transfer of the transferred property, of those shares of that class, and

C is the fair market value, immediately after the transfer of the transferred property, of all common shares of the capital stock of the transferee receivable by the transferor as consideration for the transferred property,

(h) for the purposes of this Act, the transferor and the transferee shall be deemed to have had taxation years ending immediately before that time and, for the purposes of determining the fiscal periods of the transferor and transferee after that time, they shall be deemed not to have established fiscal periods before that time,

(i) for the purpose of determining the amount of gross investment revenue required by subsection (9) to be included in computing the transferor's income for the particular taxation year referred to in paragraph (h) and its gains and losses from its designated insurance property for its subsequent taxation years, the transferor is deemed to have transferred the business referred to in paragraph (a), the property referred to in paragraph (b) and the obligations referred to in paragraph (c) to the transferee on the last day of the particular year,

(j) for the purpose of determining the income of the transferor and the transferee for their taxation years following their taxation years referred to in paragraph (h), amounts deducted by the transferor as reserves under paragraph (3)(a) (other than under subparagraph (3)(a)(ii.1), (iii) or (v)), paragraphs 20(1)(l) and (l.1) and 20(7)(c) of this Act and section 33 and paragraph 138(3)(c) of the *Income Tax Act*, chapter 148 of the Revised Statutes of Canada, 1952, in its taxation year referred to in paragraph (h) in respect of the transferred property referred to in paragraph (b) or the obligations referred to in paragraph (c) are deemed to have been deducted by the transferee, and not the transferor, for its taxation year referred to in paragraph (h),

(j.1) for the purpose of determining the income of the transferor and the transferee for their taxation years following their taxation years referred to in paragraph (h), amounts included under paragraphs (4)(b) and 12(1)(e.1) in computing the transferor's income for its taxation year referred to in paragraph (h) in respect of the insurance policies of the business referred to in paragraph (a) are deemed to have been included in computing the income of the transferee, and not of the transferor, for their taxation years referred to in paragraph (h),

(k) for the purposes of this section, sections 12, 12.4, 20, 138.1, 140 and 142, paragraphs 142.4(4)(c) and (d), section 148 and Part XII.3, the transferee is, in its taxation years following its taxation year referred to in paragraph (h), deemed to be the same person as, and a continuation of, the transferor in respect of the business referred to in paragraph (a), the transferred property referred to in paragraph (b) and the obligations referred to in paragraph (c),

(k.1) except for the purpose of this subsection, where the provisions of subsection 85(1) are not required to be applied in respect of the transfer,

(i) the transferor shall be deemed not to have disposed of a transferred property that is a specified debt obligation (other than a mark-to-market property), and

(ii) the transferee shall be deemed, in respect of a transferred property that is a specified debt obligation (other than a mark-to-market property), to be the same person as, and a continuation of, the transferor,

and for the purpose of this paragraph, "mark-to-market property" and "specified debt obligation" have the meanings assigned by subsection 142.2(1),

(k.2) for the purposes of subsections 112(5) to (5.2) and (5.4) and the definition "mark-to-market property" in subsection 142.2(1), the transferee shall be deemed, in respect of the transferred property, to be the same person as, and a continuation of, the transferor,

(l) for the purposes of this subsection and subsections (11.7) and (11.9), the fair market value of consideration received by the transferor from the transferee in respect of the assumption or reinsurance of a particular obligation referred to in paragraph (c) is deemed to be the total of the amounts deducted by the transferor as a reserve under paragraph (3)(a) (other than under subparagraph (3)(a)(ii.1), (iii) or (v)) and paragraph 20(7)(c) in its taxation year referred to in paragraph (h) in respect of the particular obligation, and

(m) for the purpose of computing the income of the transferor or the transferee for their taxation years following their taxation years referred to in paragraph (h),

(i) an amount in respect of a reinsurance premium paid or payable by the transferor to the transferee in respect of the obligations referred to in paragraph (c), or

(ii) an amount in respect of a reinsurance commission paid or payable by the transferee to the transferor in respect of the amount referred to in subparagraph (i)

under a reinsurance arrangement undertaken to effect the transfer of the insurance business to which this subsection applied shall be included or deducted, as the case may be, only to the extent that may be reasonably regarded as necessary to determine the appropriate amount of income of both the transferor and the transferee.

Related Provisions: 116(6)(e) — No s. 116 certificate required on disposition of Canadian insurance business assets; 138(11.6) — Time of election; 138(11.7) — Computation of paid-up capital; 138(11.94) — Transfer of business by resident insurer; 142.6(5), (6) — Acquisition of specified debt obligation by financial institution in rollover transaction; 190.13(c)(i)(A)(III) — Effect on capital tax; 219(5.2) — Branch tax — election by non-resident insurer who has transferred business; Reg. 9204(3) — Residual portion of specified debt obligation; *Interpretation Act* 27(5) — Meaning of "within 60 days".

Notes: 138(11.5) allows "domestication" of a non-resident insurer's branch insurance operation by transferring it to a Canadian resident corp. 138(11.94) provides a similar rollover for a Canadian insurer. See Welch, "Rare Rollovers", 46(4) *Canadian Tax Journal* 908-18 (1998); Ali-Dabydeen & Leighl, "An Overview of Domestication Transactions", 51(5) *CTJ* 2026-50 (2003).

Para. (j.1) provides that negative policy reserves included in the transferor's income under 12(1)(e.1) and 138(4)(b) for the tax year deemed to have ended before the transfer are deemed to have been included in the transferee's income for that year. This lets the transferee claim a deduction in the following year under 20(22) or 138(3)(a)(ii.1).

For interpretation of para. (m) see VIEWS doc 2015-0597921E5.

CRA considers that "substantially all" means 90% or more.

138(11.5) amended by 2002-2013 technical bill (for taxation years that begin after Oct. 2011), 2001 technical bill, 1996 Budget, 1994 technical bill, 1991 technical bill.

I.T. Application Rules: 69 (meaning of "chapter 148 of ...").

Forms: T2100: Joint election in respect of an insurance business transferred by a non-resident insurer.

(11.6) Time of election — Any election under subsection (11.5) shall be made on or before the day that is the earliest of the days on or before which any taxpayer making the election is required to file a return of income pursuant to section 150 for the taxation year in which the transactions to which the election relates occurred.

(11.7) Computation of paid-up capital — Where, after December 15, 1987, subsection (11.5) is applicable in respect of a transfer of property by a non-resident insurer to a qualified related corporation of the insurer and the provisions of subsection 85(1) were not required to be applied in respect of the transfer, the following rules apply:

(a) in computing the paid-up capital, at any time after the transfer, in respect of any particular class of shares of the capital stock of the qualified related corporation, there shall be deducted an amount determined by the formula

$$(A - B) \times C / A$$

where

A is the increase, if any, determined without reference to this subsection as it applies to the transfer, in the paid-up capital in respect of all the shares of the capital stock of the corporation as a result of the transfer,

B is the amount, if any, by which the cost of the transferred property to the corporation, immediately after the transfer, exceeds the fair market value, immediately after the transfer, of any consideration (other than shares of the capital stock of the corporation) received or receivable by the insurer from the corporation for the property, and

C is the increase, if any, determined without reference to this subsection as it applies to the transfer, in the paid-up capital in respect of the particular class of shares as a result of the acquisition by the corporation of the transferred property; and

(b) in computing the paid-up capital, at any time after December 15, 1987, in respect of any particular class of shares of the capital stock of the qualified related corporation, there shall be added an amount equal to the lesser of

(i) the amount, if any, by which

(A) the total of all amounts each of which is an amount deemed by subsection 84(3), (4) or (4.1) to be a dividend on shares of that class paid after December 15, 1987 and before that time by the corporation

exceeds

(B) the total of such dividends that would have been determined under clause (A) if this Act were read without reference to paragraph (a), and

(ii) the total of all amounts each of which is an amount required by paragraph (a) to be deducted in computing the paid-up capital in respect of that class of shares after December 15, 1987 and before that time.

Related Provisions: 138(11.5)(l) — Transfer of insurance business by non-resident insurer; 257 — Formula cannot calculate to less than zero.

(11.8) Rules on transfers of depreciable property — Where

(a) subsection (11.5) is applicable in respect of a transfer of depreciable property by a non-resident insurer to a qualified related corporation,

(b) the provisions of subsection 85(1) were not required to be applied in respect of the transfer, and

(c) the capital cost to the insurer of the depreciable property exceeds its proceeds of disposition therefor,

for the purposes of sections 13 and 20 and any regulations made under paragraph 20(1)(a), the following rules apply:

(d) the capital cost of the depreciable property to the corporation shall be deemed to be the amount that was the capital cost thereof to the insurer, and

(e) the excess shall be deemed to have been allowed to the corporation in respect of the property under regulations made under paragraph 20(1)(a) in computing its income for taxation years ending before the transfer.

(11.9) Computation of contributed surplus — Where, after December 15, 1987, subsection (11.5) or 85(1) is applicable in respect of a transfer of property by a person or partnership to an insurance corporation resident in Canada and

(a) the total of

(i) the fair market value, immediately after the transfer, of any consideration (other than shares of the capital stock of the corporation) received or receivable by the person or partnership from the corporation for the transferred property,

(ii) the increase, if any, in the paid-up capital of all the shares of the capital stock of the corporation (determined without reference to subsection (11.7) or 85(2.1) as it applies in respect of the transfer) arising on the transfer, and

(iii) the increase, if any, in the contributed surplus of the corporation (determined without reference to this subsection as it applies in respect of the transfer) arising on the transfer

exceeds

(b) the total of

(i) the total of all amounts each of which is an amount required to be deducted in computing the paid-up capital of a class of shares of the capital stock of the corporation under subsection (11.7) or 85(2.1), as the case may be, as it applies in respect of the transfer, and

(ii) the cost to the corporation of the transferred property,

for the purposes of paragraph 84(1)(c.1) and subsections 219(5.2) and (5.3), the contributed surplus of the corporation arising on the transfer shall be deemed to be the amount, if any, by which the amount of the contributed surplus otherwise determined exceeds the amount, if any, by which the total determined under paragraph (a) exceeds the total determined under paragraph (b).

Related Provisions: 138(11.5)(l) — Transfer of insurance business by non-resident insurer.

(11.91) Computation of income of non-resident insurer — Where, at any time in a particular taxation year,

(a) a non-resident insurer carries on an insurance business in Canada, and

(b) immediately before that time, the insurer was not carrying on an insurance business in Canada or ceased to be exempt from tax under this Part on any income from such business by reason of any Act of Parliament or anything approved, made or declared to have the force of law thereunder,

for the purpose of computing the income of the insurer for the particular taxation year,

(c) the insurer shall be deemed to have had a taxation year ending immediately before the commencement of the particular taxation year,

(d) for the purposes of paragraph (4)(a), subsection (9), the definition "designated insurance property" in subsection (12) and paragraphs 12(1)(d), (d.1) and (e), the insurer is deemed to have carried on the business in Canada in that preceding year and to have claimed the maximum amounts to which it would have been entitled under paragraphs (3)(a) (other than under subparagraph (3)(a)(ii.1), (iii) or (v)), 20(1)(l) and (1.1) and 20(7)(c) for that year,

(d.1) for the purposes of subsection 20(22) and subparagraph (3)(a)(ii.1),

(i) the insurer is deemed to have carried on the business referred to in paragraph (a) in Canada in the preceding taxation year referred to in paragraph (c), and

(ii) the amounts, if any, that would have been prescribed in respect of the insurer for the purposes of paragraphs (4)(b) and 12(1)(e.1) for that preceding year in respect of the insurance policies of that business are deemed to have been included in computing its income for that year, and

(e) the insurer is deemed to have disposed, immediately before the beginning of the particular taxation year, of each property owned by it at that time that is designated insurance property in respect of the business referred to in paragraph (a) for the particular taxation year, for proceeds of disposition equal to the fair market value at that time and to have reacquired, at the beginning of the particular taxation year, the property at a cost equal to that fair market value,

(f) [Repealed]

Related Provisions: 95(2)(k.1) — Application to foreign affiliate.

Notes: 138(11.91)(d.1) deems the non-resident insurer to have carried on business in Canada in the prior year and to have included in income the negative policy reserves that would have been prescribed under 12(1)(e.1) and 138(4)(b). This enables the non-resident insurer to deduct these amounts under 20(22) or 138(3)(a)(ii.1).

138(11.91)(e) can create eligible capital expenditure (see Notes to 20(1)(b)): VIEWS doc 2014-0536581I7.

138(11.91)(d) amended by 2017 budget bill #2, for a taxpayer's taxation years that begin after March 21, 2017, to add reference to 12(1)(d.1).

138(11.91) amended by 2002-2013 technical bill (for tax years beginning after Oct. 2011), 2001 technical bill, 1996 Budget.

I.T. Application Rules: 69 (meaning of "chapter 148 of ...").

(11.92) Computation of income where insurance business is transferred

— Where, at any time in a taxation year, an insurer (in this subsection referred to as the "vendor") has disposed of

(a) all or substantially all of an insurance business carried on by it in Canada, or

(b) all or substantially all of a line of business of an insurance business carried on by it in Canada

to a person (in this subsection referred to as the "purchaser") and obligations in respect of the business or line of business, as the case may be, in respect of which a reserve may be claimed under subparagraph (3)(a)(i) or (ii) or paragraph 20(7)(c) (in this subsection referred to as the "obligations") were assumed by the purchaser, the following rules apply:

(c) for the purpose of determining the amount of the gross investment revenue required to be included in computing the income of the vendor and the purchaser under subsection (9) and the amount of the gains and losses of the vendor and the purchaser from designated insurance property for the year

(i) the vendor and the purchaser shall, in addition to their normal taxation years, be deemed to have had a taxation year ending immediately before that time, and

(ii) for the taxation years of the vendor and the purchaser following that time, the business or line of business, as the case may be, disposed of to, and the obligations assumed by, the purchaser shall be deemed to have been disposed of or assumed, as the case may be, on the last day of the taxation year referred to in subparagraph (i),

(d) for the purpose of computing the income of the vendor and the purchaser for taxation years ending after that time,

(i) an amount paid or payable by the vendor to the purchaser in respect of the obligations, or

(ii) an amount in respect of a commission paid or payable by the purchaser to the vendor in respect of the amount referred to in subparagraph (i)

shall be deemed to have been paid or payable or received or receivable, as the case may be, by the vendor or the purchaser, as the case may be, in the course of carrying on the business or line of business, as the case may be, and

(e) where the vendor has disposed of all or substantially all of an insurance business referred to in paragraph (a), the vendor shall, for the purposes of section 219, be deemed to have ceased to carry on that business at that time.

Related Provisions: 190.13(c)(i)(A)(III) — Effect on capital tax; Reg. 1403(8)–(10) — Revision of policy lapse rates — reserve deficiency.

Notes: Opening words of 138(11.92)(c) amended by 1996 Budget to reflect the new term "designated insurance property", effective for disposition by an insurer of an insurance business or a line of business in its 1997 or a later tax year.

CRA considers that "substantially all" means 90% or more.

(11.93) Property acquired on default in payment

— Where, at any time in a taxation year of an insurer, the beneficial ownership of property is acquired or reacquired by the insurer in consequence of the failure to pay all or any part of an amount (in this subsection referred to as the "insurer's claim") owing to the insurer at that time in respect of a bond, debenture, mortgage, hypothecary claim, agreement of sale or any other form of indebtedness owned by the insurer, the following rules apply to the insurer:

(a) section 79.1 does not apply in respect of the acquisition or reacquisition;

(b) the insurer shall be deemed to have acquired or reacquired, as the case may be, the property at an amount equal to the fair market value of the property, immediately before that time;

(c) the insurer shall be deemed to have disposed at that time of the portion of the indebtedness represented by the insurer's claim for proceeds of disposition equal to that fair market value and, immediately after that time, to have reacquired that portion of the indebtedness at a cost of nil;

(d) the acquisition or reacquisition shall be deemed to have no effect on the form of the indebtedness; and

(e) in computing the insurer's income for the year or a subsequent taxation year, no amount is deductible under paragraph 20(1)(l) in respect of the insurer's claim.

Notes: Reference to "hypothecary claim" added to 138(11.93) opening words by 2001 *Civil Code* harmonization bill, effective June 14, 2001. The change is non-substantive; see *Interpretation Act* s. 8.2.

138(11.93) amended by 1994 technical bill, for property acquired or reacquired after Feb. 21, 1994, other than pursuant to a court order made by that date.

(11.94) Transfer of insurance business by resident insurer

— Where

(a) an insurer resident in Canada (in this subsection referred to as the "transferor") has, at any time in a taxation year, ceased to carry on all or substantially all of an insurance business carried on by it in Canada in that year,

(b) the transferor has, at that time or within 60 days after that time,

(i) in the case of a transferor that is a life insurer and that carries on an insurance business in Canada and in a country other than Canada in the year, transferred all or substantially all of the property (in subsection (11.5) referred to as the "transferred property") that is owned by it at that time and that was designated insurance property in respect of the business for the taxation year that, because of paragraph (11.5)(h), ended immediately before that time, or

(ii) in any other case, transferred all or substantially all of the property owned by it at that time and used by it in the year in, or held by it in the year in the course of, carrying on that insurance business in Canada in that year (in subsection (11.5) referred to as the "transferred property")

to a corporation resident in Canada (in this subsection referred to as the "transferee") that is a qualified related corporation (within the meaning assigned by subsection 219(8)) of the transferor that, immediately after that time, began to carry on that insurance business in Canada for consideration that includes shares of the capital stock of the transferee,

(c) the transferee has, at that time or within 60 days thereafter, assumed or reinsured all or substantially all of the obligations of the transferor that arose in the course of carrying on that insurance business in Canada, and

(d) the transferor and the transferee have jointly elected in prescribed form and in accordance with subsection (11.6),

paragraphs (11.5)(e) to (m) and subsections (11.7) to (11.9) apply in respect of the transfer.

Related Provisions: 142.6(5), (6) — Acquisition of specified debt obligation by financial institution in rollover transaction; Reg. 9204(3) — Residual portion of specified debt obligation; *Interpretation Act* 27(5) — Meaning of "within 60 days".

Notes: See Notes to 138(11.5).

138(11.94) amended by 2002-2013 technical bill (for transfers made after Oct. 2004), 2001 technical bill and 1996 Budget.

(12) Definitions

— In this section,

Related Provisions [subsec. 138(12)]: 211(1) — Definitions.

Notes: Opening words of 138(12) redrafted in RSC 1985 (5th Supp) consolidation, for tax years ending after Nov. 1991; formerly applied explicitly for purposes of several other provisions. These rules of application are now in 12.2(12), 13(23.1), 20(27.1), 70(11), 89(1.01), 111(7.11), 115(6), 116(7) and 142.1. See also 211(1).

"accumulated 1968 deficit" — [Repealed]

Notes: Definition "accumulated 1968 deficit" repealed by 1996 Budget, for 1997 and later taxation years. It was moved to 219(7), as it is no longer used in 138 but is still used for the branch tax in Part XIV. 138(12)"accumulated 1968 deficit" was 138(12)(a) before RSC 1985 (5th Supp) consolidation for tax years ending after Nov. 1991.

"amortized cost [para. 138(12)(b)]" — [Repealed under former Act]

Notes: 138(12)(b), repealed by 1988 tax reform, defined "amortized cost", a term that now appears in 248(1).

"amount payable", in respect of a policy loan at a particular time, means the amount of the policy loan and the interest thereon that is outstanding at that time;

Related Provisions: 148(9) — "amount payable".

Notes: 138(12)"amount payable" was 138(12)(b.1) before RSC 1985 (5th Supp) consolidation for tax years ending after Nov. 1991.

"base year" of a life insurer means the life insurer's taxation year that immediately precedes its transition year;

Notes: 138(12)"base year" added by 2008 budget bill #2, effective for taxation years that begin after September 2006. See Notes to 138(16).

"Canada security" — [Repealed]

Notes: Definition "Canada security" repealed by 1994 technical bill for taxation years beginning after Feb. 22, 1994. It was 138(12)(c) before RSC 1985 (5th Supp) consolidation for tax years ending after Nov. 1991.

"cost" — [Repealed]

Notes: Definition "cost" repealed by 1994 technical bill for taxation years beginning after Feb. 22, 1994. It was 138(12)(d) before RSC 1985 (5th Supp) consolidation for tax years ending after Nov. 1991.

"deposit accounting insurance policy" in respect of a life insurer's taxation year means an insurance policy of the life insurer that, according to generally accepted accounting principles, is not an insurance contract for that taxation year;

Related Provisions: Reg. 1408(1)"deposit accounting insurance policy" — Definition applies to Reg. Part XIV.

Notes: 138(12)"deposit accounting insurance policy" added by 2010 budget bill #2, effective for taxation years that begin after 2010.

"designated foreign insurance business", of a life insurer resident in Canada in a taxation year, means an insurance business that is carried on by the life insurer in a country other than Canada in the year unless more than 90% of the gross premium revenue from the business for the year from the insurance of risks (net of reinsurance ceded) is in respect of the insurance of risks (other than specified Canadian risks) of persons with whom the life insurer deals at arm's length.

Related Provisions: 138(2.1) — Income of DFIB is subject to tax.

Notes: Definition added by 2017 budget bill #2, for a taxpayer's taxation years that begin after March 21, 2017. See Notes to 138(2.1).

"designated insurance property" for a taxation year of an insurer (other than an insurer resident in Canada that at no time in the year carried on a life insurance business) that, at any time in the year, carried on an insurance business in Canada and in a country other than Canada, means property determined in accordance with prescribed rules except that, in its application to any taxation year, "designated insurance property" for the 1998 or a preceding taxation year means property that was, under this subsection as it read in its application to taxation years that ended in 1996, property used by it in the year in, or held by it in the year in the course of, carrying on an insurance business in Canada;

Related Provisions: 138(11.31)(b) — Change in use rule for insurance properties does not apply for purposes of this definition; 248(1)"designated insurance property" — Definition applies to entire Act.

Notes: Interest on overpaid income taxes may be considered income from property used by the insurer in the course of its business: *Munich Reinsurance*, 2001 FCA 365.

See the amendment to 138(2) enacted in 2013. See also 9(1) Notes at "Business income vs property income".

Definition added by 1996 Budget and amended by 2001 technical bill, for 1997 and later taxation years. It replaces "property used by it in the year in, or held by it in the year in the course of".

Regulations: 2401 (prescribed rules).

"excluded policy" in respect of a life insurer's base year means an insurance policy of the life insurer that would be a deposit accounting insurance policy for the life insurer's base year if the International Financial Reporting Standards adopted by the Accounting Standards Board and effective as of January 1, 2011 applied for that base year;

Notes: 138(12)"excluded policy" added by 2010 budget bill #2, for taxation years that begin after 2010.

"gross investment revenue" of an insurer for a taxation year means the amount determined by the formula

$$A + B + C + D + E + F - G$$

where

A   is the total of the following amounts included in its gross revenue for the year:

    (a) taxable dividends, and

    (b) amounts received or receivable as, on account of, in lieu of or in satisfaction of, interest, rentals or royalties, other than amounts in respect of debt obligations to which subsection 142.3(1) applies for the year,

B   is its income for the year from each trust of which it is a beneficiary,

C   is its income for the year from each partnership of which it is a member,

D   is the total of all amounts required by subsection 16(1) to be included in computing its income for the year,

E   is the total of

    (a) all amounts required by paragraph 142.3(1)(a) to be included in computing its income for the year, and

    (b) all amounts required by subsection 12(3) or 20(14) to be included in computing its income for the year except to the extent that those amounts are included in the computation of A,

F   is the amount determined by the formula

$$V - W$$

    where

    V   is the total of all amounts included under paragraph 56(1)(d) in computing its income for the year, and

    W   is the total of all amounts deducted under paragraph 60(a) in computing its income for the year, and

G   is the total of all amounts each of which is

    (a) an amount deemed by subparagraph 16(6)(a)(ii) to be paid by it in respect of the year as interest, or

    (b) an amount deductible under paragraph 142.3(1)(b) in computing its income for the year;

Related Provisions: 148(9) — "interest"; 257 — Formula cannot calculate to less than zero.

Notes: Definition amended by 1994 technical bill (for taxation years ending after Feb. 22, 1994), 1991 technical bill. 138(12)"gross investment revenue" was 138(12)(e) before RSC 1985 (5th Supp) consolidation for tax years ending after Nov. 1991.

"group term insurance policy [para. 138(12)(p)]" — [Repealed under former Act]

Notes: This definition was moved from 138(12)(p) to 138(15) in the RSC 1985 (5th Supp) consolidation for tax years ending after Nov. 1991. See Notes to 138(15).

"insurance", of a risk, includes the reinsurance of the risk.

Notes: Definition added by 2017 budget bill #2, for a taxpayer's taxation years that begin after March 21, 2017. See Notes to 138(2.1).

"interest", in relation to a policy loan, means the amount in respect of the policy loan that is required to be paid under the terms and conditions of the policy in order to maintain the policyholder's interest in the policy;

Notes: 138(12)"interest" was 138(12)(e.1) before RSC 1985 (5th Supp) consolidation for tax years ending after Nov. 1991.

"life insurance policy" includes an annuity contract and a contract all or any part of the insurer's reserves for which vary in amount depending on the fair market value of a specified group of assets;

Related Provisions: 12.2(10) — Riders; 211(1) — "Life insurance policy" for Part XII.3 tax; 248(1)"life insurance policy" — Definition applies to entire Act.

Notes: See Notes to 188.1(5) re meaning of "includes".

Under 138(4.01), "life insurance policy" includes group life benefit or annuity contract for certain purposes.

A UK endowment policy is likely a life insurance policy: VIEWS doc 2004-0096291E5.

138(12)"life insurance policy" was 138(12)(f) before RSC 1985 (5th Supp) consolidation for tax years ending after Nov. 1991.

Income Tax Folios: S3-F6-C1: Interest deductibility [replaces IT-533].

Interpretation Bulletins: IT-87R2: Policyholders' income from life insurance policies; IT-291R3: Transfer of property to a corporation under subsection 85(1); IT-355R2: Interest on loans to buy life insurance policies and annuity contracts, and interest on policy loans (cancelled).

"life insurance policy in Canada" means a life insurance policy issued or effected by an insurer on the life of a person resident in Canada at the time the policy was issued or effected;

Related Provisions: 128.1(10)"excluded right or interest"(l) — Life insurance policy in Canada excluded from deemed disposition on emigration; 248(1)"life insurance policy in Canada" — Definition applies to entire Act.

Notes: 138(12)"life insurance policy in Canada" was 138(12)(g) before RSC 1985 (5th Supp) consolidation for tax years ending after Nov. 1991.

Income Tax Folios: S3-F6-C1: Interest deductibility [replaces IT-533].

Interpretation Bulletins: IT-355R2: Interest on loans to buy life insurance policies and annuity contracts, and interest on policy loans (cancelled).

"maximum tax actuarial reserve" for a particular class of life insurance policy for a taxation year of a life insurer means, except as otherwise expressly prescribed, the maximum amount allowable under subparagraph (3)(a)(i) as a policy reserve for the year in respect of policies of that class;

Notes: 138(12)"maximum tax actuarial reserve" was 138(12)(h) before RSC 1985 (5th Supp) consolidation for tax years ending after Nov. 1991.

"net Canadian life investment income [para. 138(12)(i)]" — [Repealed under former Act]

Notes: 138(12)(i), repealed in 1978, defined "net Canadian life investment income", a term no longer used.

"non-segregated property" of an insurer means its property other than property included in a segregated fund;

Notes: 138(12)"non-segregated property" was 138(12)(j) before RSC 1985 (5th Supp) consolidation for tax years ending after Nov. 1991.

"participating life insurance policy" means a life insurance policy under which the policyholder is entitled to share (other than by way of an experience rating refund) in the profits of the insurer other than profits in respect of property in a segregated fund;

Notes: 138(12)"participating life insurance policy" was 138(12)(k) before RSC 1985 (5th Supp) consolidation for tax years ending after Nov. 1991.

"policy loan" means an amount advanced at a particular time by an insurer to a policyholder in accordance with the terms and conditions of a life insurance policy in Canada;

Related Provisions: 148(9)"policy loan" — Similar definition for s. 148; 211(1)"policy loan" — Definition applies to 211–211.6.

Notes: 138(12)"policy loan" was 138(12)(k.1) before RSC 1985 (5th Supp) consolidation for tax years ending after Nov. 1991.

Income Tax Folios: S3-F6-C1: Interest deductibility [replaces IT-533].

Interpretation Bulletins: IT-355R2: Interest on loans to buy life insurance policies and annuity contracts, and interest on policy loans (cancelled).

"property used by it in the year in, or held by it in the year in the course of" — [Repealed]

Notes: Definition "property used by it in the year in, or held by it in the year in the course of" repealed by 1996 Budget, effective for 1997 and later taxation years. It has been replaced by "designated insurance property", above.

138(12)"property used by it ..." was 138(12)(l) before RSC 1985 (5th Supp) consolidation for tax years ending after Nov. 1991.

"qualified related corporation" of a non-resident insurer has the meaning assigned by subsection 219(8);

Notes: 138(12)"qualified related corporation" was 138(12)(l.1) before RSC 1985 (5th Supp) consolidation for tax years ending after Nov. 1991.

"relevant authority" — [Repealed]

Notes: Definition "relevant authority" repealed by 1996 Budget, effective for 1997 and later taxation years. The term is no longer used. It referred to the Superintendent of Financial Institutions or the superintendent of insurance.

138(12)"relevant authority" was 138(12)(m) before RSC 1985 (5th Supp) consolidation for tax years ending after Nov. 1991.

"reserve transition amount" — [No longer relevant]

Notes: 138(12)"reserve transition amount" added by 2008 budget bill #2, effective for taxation years that begin after September 2006. See Notes to 138(16)-(26).

"segregated fund" has the meaning given that expression in subsection 138.1(1);

Notes: 138(12)"segregated fund" was 138(12)(n) before RSC 1985 (5th Supp) consolidation for tax years ending after Nov. 1991.

"specified Canadian risk" has the same meaning as in paragraph 95(2)(a.23).

Notes: Definition added by 2017 budget bill #2, for a taxpayer's taxation years that begin after March 21, 2017. See Notes to 138(2.1).

"surplus funds derived from operations" of an insurer as of the end of a particular taxation year means the amount determined by the formula

$$(A + B + C) - (D + E + F + G)$$

where

A   is the total of the insurer's income for each taxation year in the period beginning with its 1969 taxation year and ending with the particular year from all insurance businesses carried on by it,

B   is the total of all amounts each of which is a portion of a non-capital loss that was deemed by subsection 111(7.1) as it read in its application to the 1976 taxation year to have been deductible in computing the insurer's income for a taxation year that ended before 1977,

C   is the total of all profits or gains made by the insurer in the period in respect of non-segregated property of the insurer disposed of by it that was used by it in, or held by it in the course of, carrying on an insurance business in Canada, except to the extent that those profits or gains have been or are included in computing the insurer's income or loss, if any, for any taxation year in the period from carrying on an insurance business,

D   is the total of its loss, if any, for each taxation year in the period from all insurance businesses carried on by it,

E   is the total of all losses sustained by the insurer in the period in respect of non-segregated property disposed of by it that was used by it in, or held by it in the course of, carrying on an insurance business in Canada, except to the extent that those losses have been or are included in computing the insurer's income or loss, if any, for any taxation year in the period from carrying on an insurance business,

F   is the total of

    (a) all taxes payable under this Part by the insurer, and all income taxes payable by it under the laws of each province, for each taxation year in the period, except such portion thereof as would not have been payable by it if subsection (7) had not been enacted, and

    (b) all taxes payable under Parts I.3 and VI by the insurer for each taxation year in the period,

and

G is the total of all gifts made in the period by the insurer to a qualified donee.

H [Repealed]

Related Provisions: 257 — Formula cannot calculate to less than zero.

Notes: Definition amended by 2002-2013 technical bill (for taxation years beginning after Oct. 2011), 2011 budget bill #2, 1993 technical bill. It was 138(12)(o) before RSC 1985 (5th Supp) consolidation for tax years ending after Nov. 1991.

I.T. Application Rules: 60.1 (reference to "this Part" in description of F includes Part IA of pre-1972 Act).

"transition year" — [No longer relevant]

Notes: See Notes to 138(16)-(26). Definition "transition year" amended by 2002-2013 technical bill (for 2012 and later tax years), 2010 budget bill #2. Added by 2008 budget bill #2.

"1975 branch accounting election deficiency", "1975–76 excess additional group term reserve", "1975–76 excess capital cost allowance", "1975–76 excess investment reserve", "1975–76 excess policy dividend deduction", "1975–76 excess policy dividend reserve", "1975–76 excess policy reserves" — [Repealed]

Notes: All these definitions repealed by 2002-2013 technical bill (Part 5 — technical), for taxation years that begin after Oct. 2011. These were 138(12)(q), (w), (u), (t), (r), (s) and (v) before consolidation in R.S.C. 1985, c. 1 (5th Supp.) for tax years ending after Nov. 1991. They defined various balances and amounts as of 1975-76.

(13) Variation in "tax basis" and "amortized cost" — Where

(a) in a taxation year that ended after 1968 and before 1978 an insurer carried on a life insurance business in Canada and an insurance business in a country other than Canada,

(b) the insurer did not make an election in respect of the year under subsection 138(9) of the *Income Tax Act*, chapter 148 of the Revised Statutes of Canada, 1952, as it applied to that year, and

(c) the ratio of the value for the year of the insurer's specified Canadian assets to its Canadian investment fund for the year exceeded one,

each of the amounts included or deducted as follows in respect of the year shall be multiplied by the ratio referred to in paragraph (c):

(d) under paragraph (c), (d), (k) or (l) of the definition "tax basis" in subsection 142.4(1) in determining the tax basis of a debt obligation to the insurer, or

(e) under paragraph (c), (d), (f) or (h) of the definition "amortized cost" in subsection 248(1) in determining the amortized cost of a debt obligation to the insurer.

Related Provisions: 138(14) — Meaning of certain expressions; 142.4(1)"tax basis"(c), (d), (k), (l) — Disposition of specified debt obligation by financial institution.

Notes: 138(13) amended by 1994 technical bill, effective for taxation years that end after February 22, 1994.

I.T. Application Rules: 69 (meaning of "chapter 148 of ...").

(14) Meaning of certain expressions — For the purposes of subsection (13), the expressions "Canadian investment fund for a taxation year", "specified Canadian assets" and "value for the taxation year" have the meanings prescribed therefor.

(15) Definition not to apply — In this section, in construing the meaning of the expression "group term insurance policy", the definition "group term life insurance policy" in subsection 248(1) does not apply.

Notes: 138(15) appears to be meaningless. The term "group term insurance policy" is not used in the Act or the Regulations. The term "group term life insurance policy" is defined in 248(1), but is not used anywhere in the Act other than s. 6. It is also used in Reg. 304, 1401 and 1900. See Reg. 1408(2).

138(15) was 138(12)(p) before RSC 1985 (5th Supp) consolidation for tax years ending after Nov. 1991.

(16)–(26) [Accounting transition 2006-2011] — [No longer relevant]

Notes: The rules in 138(16)-(26) are parallel to those in 12.5, 20.4 and 142.51 — transitional rules to phase in changes in accounting for financial instruments required by *CICA Handbook* §3855. See Notes to 12.5.

138(16)-(25), along with 138(12)"base year", "reserve transition amount" and "transition year", added by 2008 budget bill #2, for tax years that begin after Sept. 2006. 138(26) added by 2002-2013 technical bill, for 2012 and later tax years.

Notes [s. 138]: For additional taxes on life insurance corporations, see Part VI (financial institutions tax) and Part XII.3 (tax on investment income). See s. 148 for the treatment of life insurance policyholders. See also Sanderson, "Hidden (And Not So Hidden) Taxes on Insurance Products", XXII(3) *Insurance Planning* (Federated Press) 2-7 (2017).

For an overview of s. 138 and its history, see Strain, "Taxation of Life Insurance", 45(5) *Canadian Tax Journal* 1506–1546 (1995). See also Borgmann, Swales & Welch, *Canadian Insurance Taxation* (Butterworths, 3rd ed., 2009, 384pp).

For more on the industry see clhia.ca (Cdn Life and Health Insurance Association); Brown & Menezes, *Insurance Law in Canada* (Carswell, 2 vols. looseleaf); Billingsley, *General Principles of Insurance Law* (LexisNexis, 3rd ed., 2020, 450pp).

Accounting standards changes (IFRS 17, "Insurance Contracts") may require amendments to s. 138: Vienneau, "New Profit Accounting for Insurers", 25(10) *Canadian Tax Highlights* (ctf.ca) 10-11 (Oct. 2017).

Life insurers must file T2 Schedule 150: VIEWS doc 2013-0479101C6.

Definitions [s. 138]: "accumulated 1968 deficit" — 138(12); "active business" — 248(1); "affiliated" — 251.1; "agreeing party" — 138(2.3)(b), 138(2.6)(b); "allowable capital loss" — 38(b), 248(1); "amortized cost" — 138(13), 248(1); "amount" — 248(1); "amount payable" — (in respect of a policy loan) 138(12); "annuity" — 248(1); "arm's length" — 251(1); "base year" — 138(12); "beneficial ownership" — 248(3); "borrowed money", "business" — 248(1); "Canada" — 255, *Interpretation Act* 35(1); "Canada security" — 138(12); "Canadian investment fund" — 138(14), Reg. 2400(4)(a); "capital gain" — 39(1)(a), 248(1); "capital property" — 54, 248(1); "carrying on business" — 253; "class of shares" — 248(6); "common share" — 248(1); "completed" — 138(4.6); "corporation" — 248(1), *Interpretation Act* 35(1); "cost" — (to an insurer of acquiring a mortgage or hypothec) 138(12); "cost amount" — 248(1); "deposit accounting insurance policy" — 138(12); "depreciable property" — 13(21), 248(1); "designated foreign insurance business" — 138(12); "designated insurance property" — 138(12), 248(1); "disposition", "dividend" — 248(1); "excluded policy" — 138(12); "fair market value" — see 69(1) Notes; "fiscal period" — 249(2)(b), 249.1; "foreign affiliate" — 95(1), 248(1); "gross investment revenue" — 138(12); "gross revenue" — 248(1); "identical" — 138(11.1), 248(12); "income or profits tax" — 126(4); "insurance" — 138(12); "insurance policy", "insurer" — 248(1); "interest in real property" — 248(4); "interest" — in relation to a policy loan 138(12); "life insurance business" — 248(1); "life insurance policy" — 138(4.01), (12), 248(1); "life insurance policy in Canada" — 138(12), 248(1); "life insurer" — 248(1); "mark-to-market property" — 142.2(1); "maximum tax actuarial reserve" — 138(12); "Minister" — 248(1); "net Canadian life investment income" — 209(2); "non-capital loss" — 111(8), 248(1); "non-resident" — 248(1); "non-segregated property" — 138(12); "paid-up capital" — 89(1), 138(11.7), 248(1); "parent" — 138(20); "Parliament" — *Interpretation Act* 35(1); "participating life insurance policy" — 138(12); "partnership" — see 96(1) Notes; "person" — 248(1); "policy dividend" — 139.1(8)(a); "policy loan" — 138(12); "preferred share", "prescribed", "principal amount", "property" — 248(1); "property used by it in the year in, or held by it in the year in the course of" — carrying on an insurance business 138(12); "province" — *Interpretation Act* 35(1); "qualified donee" — 149.1(1), 188.2(3)(a), 248(1); "qualified related corporation" — 138(12), 219(8); "received" — 248(7); "registered pension plan" — 248(1); "registered retirement savings plan" — 146(1), 248(1); "regulation" — 248(1); "related" — 251(2)–(6); "relevant authority", "reserve transition amount" — 138(12); "resident in Canada" — 94(3)(a), 250; "segregated fund" — 138(12); "series of transactions" — 248(10); "share", "shareholder" — 248(1); "specified Canadian assets" — 138(14), Reg. 2400(4)(a); "specified Canadian risk" — 95(2)(a.23), (a.24), 138(2.6), (12); "specified debt obligation" — 142.2(1); "subsidiary wholly-owned corporation" — 248(1); "substituted" — 248(5); "surplus funds derived from operations" — 138(12); "taxable Canadian corporation" — 89(1), 248(1); "taxable capital gain" — 38(a), 248(1); "taxable dividend" — 89(1), 248(1); "taxable income" — 2(2), 248(1); "taxation year" — 249; "taxpayer", "term preferred share" — 248(1); "transferred business" — 138(22); "transferred property" — 138(11.94)(b)(i); "transition year" — 138(12); "used" — 138(12)"property used by it in the year in, or held by it in the year in the course of"; "value for the taxation year" — 138(14), Reg. 2400(4)(a).

138.1 (1) Rules relating to segregated funds — In respect of life insurance policies for which all or any portion of an insurer's reserves vary in amount depending on the fair market value of a specified group of properties (in this section referred to as a "segre-

gated fund"), for the purposes of this Part, the following rules apply:

(a) a trust (in this section and section 138.2 referred to as the **"related segregated fund trust"**) is deemed to be created at the time that is the later of

(i) the day that the segregated fund is created, and

(ii) the day on which the insurer's 1978 taxation year commences,

and to continue in existence throughout the period during which the fund determines any portion of the benefits under those policies that vary in amount depending on the fair market value of the property in the segregated fund (in this section referred to as **"segregated fund policies"**);

(b) property that has been allocated to and that remains a part of the segregated fund, and any income that has accrued on that property is deemed to be the property and income of the related segregated fund trust and not to be the property and income of the insurer;

(c) the insurer is deemed to be

(i) the trustee who has ownership or control of the related segregated fund trust property,

(ii) a resident of Canada in respect of the related segregated fund trust property used or held by it in the course of carrying on the insurer's life insurance business in Canada, and

(iii) a non-resident of Canada in respect of the related segregated fund trust property not used or held by it in the course of carrying on the insurer's life insurance business in Canada;

(d) where at a particular time there is property in the segregated fund that was not funded with premiums paid under a segregated fund policy,

(i) the insurer is deemed to have an interest in the related segregated fund trust that is not in respect of any particular property or source of income, and

(ii) the cost at any time of that interest to the insurer is deemed to be the total of

(A) for property of the trust at that time allocated by the insurer to the segregated fund prior to 1978, the amount that would be its adjusted cost base to the insurer if the interest had been a capital property at all relevant times prior to 1978 and if the rules in this section had been applicable for the taxation years after 1971 and before 1978, and

(B) for property of the trust at that time allocated by the insurer to the segregated fund after 1977, the fair market value of the property at the time it was last allocated to the segregated fund by the insurer;

(e) where at any particular time there is property in the segregated fund that was funded with a portion of the premiums paid before that time under a segregated fund policy,

(i) the respective segregated fund policyholder is deemed to have an interest in the related segregated fund trust that is not in respect of any particular property or source of income,

(ii) the cost of that interest is deemed to be the amount that is the total of

(A) the amount that would be its adjusted cost base to the insurer at December 31, 1977 if the interest had been a capital property at all relevant times prior to 1978 and if the rules in this section (if subsection (3) were read without reference to the expressions "or capital loss" and "or loss") had been applicable for taxation years after 1971 and before 1978, and

(B) the total of amounts each of which is that portion of a premium paid before that time and after the day referred to in subparagraph (a)(ii) under a segregated fund policy that was or is to be used by the insurer to fund property

allocated to the segregated fund (other than the portion of the premium that is an acquisition fee), and

(iii) the portion of a premium included in a segregated fund is deemed not to be an amount paid in respect of a premium under the policy;

(f) the taxable income of the related segregated fund trust is deemed for the purposes of subsections 104(6), (13) and (24) to be an amount that has become payable in the year to the beneficiaries under the segregated fund trust and the amount therefor in respect of any particular beneficiary is equal to the amount determined by reference to the terms and conditions of the segregated fund policy;

(g) where at a particular time the fair market value of property transferred by the insurer to the segregated fund results in an increase at that time in the portion of the insurer's reserves for a segregated fund policy held by a policyholder that vary with the fair market value of the segregated fund and a decrease in the portion of its reserves for the policy that do not so vary, the amount of that increase shall,

(i) for the purpose of the determination of H in the definition "adjusted cost basis" in subsection 148(9), be deemed to be proceeds of disposition that the policyholder became entitled to receive at that time,

(ii) for the purpose of computing the adjusted cost base to the policyholder of the policyholder's interest in the related segregated fund trust, be added at that time to the cost to the policyholder of that interest, and

(iii) for the purpose of computing the insurer's income, be deemed to be a payment under the terms and conditions of the policy at that time;

(h) where at a particular time the fair market value of property transferred by the insurer from the segregated fund results in an increase at that time in the portion of the insurer's reserves for a segregated fund policy that do not vary with the fair market value of the segregated fund and a decrease in the portion of its reserves for the policy that so vary, the amount of that increase shall, for the purpose of calculating the insurer's income, be deemed to be a premium received by the insurer at that time;

(i) where at a particular time the policyholder of a segregated fund policy disposes of all or a portion of the policyholder's interest in the related segregated fund trust, that proportion of the amount, if any, by which the acquisition fee with respect to the particular policy exceeds the total of amounts each of which is an amount determined under this paragraph with respect to the particular policy before that time, that

(i) the fair market value of the interest disposed of at that time

is of

(ii) the fair market value of the policyholder's interest in the particular segregated fund trust immediately before that time,

is deemed to be a capital loss of the related segregated fund trust that reduces the policyholder's benefits under the particular policy by that amount for the purposes of subsection (3);

(j) the obligations of an insurer in respect of a benefit that is payable under a segregated fund policy, the amount of which benefit varies with the fair market value of the segregated fund at the time the benefit becomes payable, are deemed to be obligations of the trustee under the related segregated fund trust and not of the insurer and any amount received by the policyholder or that the policyholder became entitled to receive at any particular time in a year in respect of those obligations is deemed to be proceeds from the disposition of an interest in the related segregated fund trust;

(k) a reference to "the terms and conditions of the trust arrangement" in section 104 or subsection 127.2(3) is deemed to include a reference to the terms and conditions of the related segregated fund policy and the trustee is deemed to have designated the amounts referred to in that section in accordance with those terms and conditions; and

(l) where at any time an insurer acquires a share as a first registered holder thereof and allocates the share to a related segregated fund trust, the trust shall be deemed to have acquired the share at that time as the first registered holder thereof for the purpose of computing its share-purchase tax credit and the insurer shall be deemed not to have acquired the share for the purpose of computing its share-purchase tax credit.

Related Provisions: 39(1)(a)(iii) — Meaning of capital gain; 53(1)(l), 53(2)(q) — Adjustments to cost base; 87(2.2) — Amalgamation of insurance corporations; 88(1)(g) — Winding-up of subsidiary insurance corporations; 107.4(3)(g) — Application of 138.1(1)(i) on qualifying disposition to trust; 127.55(f)(i) — No minimum tax on related segregated fund trust; 138(11.5)(k) — Transfer of business by non-resident insurer; 138.1(2.1) — Transition — pre-2018 capital losses; 138.1(7) — Where subsections (1) to (6) not to apply; 218.1 — Application to non-resident withholding tax; 248(1)"disposition"(f)(vi) — Rollover from one trust to another; Reg. 9000 — Certain segregated funds excluded from definition of "financial institution".

Notes: For general info about segregated funds, see tinyurl.com/segr-funds; Young, "Mutual Fund and Segregated Fund Flowthrough Tax Rules", 52(3) *Canadian Tax Journal* 884-924 (2004); Marino & Natale, *Canadian Taxation of Life Insurance* (Carswell, 10th ed., 2020), chap 19. The main differences between a seg fund and a mutual fund are that a seg fund guarantees the return of a minimum to the investor at maturity or on death (death benefit payable to designated beneficiary, like life insurance); and the seg fund may have creditor protection by being life insurance (see Notes to 146(4)). See also Lyle, "Segregated Funds in Estate Planning — Should they be Designated as Insurance or Registered Plans?", 10(3) *Tax Hyperion* (Carswell) 6-7 (March 2013).

The Act does not dictate the methodology to be used by issuers of segregated fund policies in computing allocations to the holders: VIEWS doc 2005-0156951E5. See also 2006-0174091E5.

Index-linked variable life insurance policies may be segregated funds under 138.1(1) even though they are not regarded as such by the Office of the Superintendent of Financial Institutions: VIEWS doc 2002-0147535. The particular policy must be reviewed to determine whether the insurer's reserves vary depending on the performance of a specified group of properties.

See also docs 9905255 and 2007-0241971C6 (resetting of seg fund guarantees); 2007-0229731C6 (questions re 107.4, non-capital losses, and 138.1(1)(j)).

138.1(1) amended by 2017 budget bill #2, for tax years that begin after 2017: reference to 138.2 added to para. (a) opening words, and "income" changed to "taxable income" in para. (f).

138.1(1)(a) opening words amended by 2014 budget bill #2, for 2016 and later tax years, to change "an *inter vivos* trust" to "a trust" (in sync with generally replacing "testamentary trust" with "graduated rate estate").

Opening words of 138.1(1) redrafted in RSC 1985 (5th Supp) consolidation for tax years ending after Nov. 1991, to change "this Part and Part XIII" to "this Part". The application to Part XIII is now in 218.1.

(2) Rules relating to property in segregated funds at end of 1977 taxation year — [No longer relevant]

(2.1) Transition — pre-2018 non-capital losses — For the purpose of determining the taxable income of a related segregated fund trust for a taxation year that begins after 2017, the non-capital losses of the related segregated fund trust that arise in a taxation year that begins before 2018 are deemed to be nil.

Notes: 138.1(2.1) added by 2017 budget bill #2, effective Dec. 14, 2017.

(3) Capital gains and capital losses of related segregated fund trusts — A capital gain or capital loss of a related segregated fund trust from the disposition of any property shall, to the extent that a policyholder's benefits under a policy or the interest in the trust of any other beneficiary is affected by that gain or loss, be deemed to be a capital gain or capital loss, as the case may be, of the policyholder or other beneficiary and not that of the trust.

Related Provisions: 53(1)(l)(iv), 53(2)(q)(ii) — Adjustments to cost base; 138.1(7) — Where subsections (1) to (6) not to apply; 138.2(5) — Loss limitation on qualifying transfer (merger).

(3.1), (3.2) [Repealed]

(4) Election and allocation — Where at any particular time after 1977, a policyholder withdraws all or part of the policyholder's interest in a segregated fund policy, the trustee of a related segregated fund trust may elect in prescribed manner and prescribed form to treat any capital property of the trust as having been disposed of,

whereupon the property shall be deemed to have been disposed of on any day designated by the trustee for proceeds of disposition equal to

(a) the fair market value of the property on that day,

(b) the adjusted cost base to the trust of the property on that day, or

(c) an amount that is neither greater than the greater of nor less than the lesser of the amounts determined under paragraphs (a) and (b),

whichever is designated by the trustee, and to have been reacquired by the trust immediately thereafter at a cost equal to those proceeds, and where the trustee of a related segregated fund trust has made such an election, the following rules apply:

(d) the amount of any capital gain or capital loss resulting from the deemed disposition shall be allocated by the trustee to any policyholder withdrawing all or part of the policyholder's interest in the policyholder's policy at that time to the extent that the amount of the policyholder's benefits under the policy at that time is affected by the capital gain or capital loss in respect of property held by the related segregated fund trust at that time,

(e) the allocation referred to in paragraph (d) is deemed to have been made immediately before the withdrawal,

(f) any capital gain not so allocated is deemed to be allocated in accordance with the terms and conditions of the policy, and

(g) any capital loss not so allocated is deemed to be a superficial loss of each policyholder to the extent that the policyholder's benefits under the policy would be affected by the loss.

Related Provisions: 53(1)(l)(iii), 53(2)(q)(i) — Adjustments to cost base; 138.1(7) — Where subsections (1) to (6) not to apply; 138.2(2)(e) — No application on qualifying transfer (merger).

Notes: The donation to a charity of an interest in a seg fund is not a withdrawal of an interest but a change of ownership, so no 138.1(4) election is available: VIEWS doc 2008-0270551C6.

For a trust filing Quebec returns, a designation under 138.1(4) must be copied to Revenu Québec: *Taxation Act* ss. 851.20, 21.4.6.

Regulations: 6100 (prescribed manner and time).

Forms: T3018: Election under subsection 138.1(4) of the deemed disposition of capital property of a life insurance segregated fund.

(5) Adjusted cost base of property in related segregated fund trust — At any particular time, the adjusted cost base of each capital property of a related segregated fund trust shall be deemed to be the amount, if any, by which

(a) the adjusted cost base of the property to the trust immediately before that time

exceeds

(b) the total of amounts each of which is an amount in respect of the disposition by a policyholder of all or part of the policyholder's interest in the related segregated fund trust at that time equal to that proportion of the amount, if any, by which

(i) the adjusted cost base to the policyholder of that interest at that time

exceeds

(ii) the policyholder's proceeds of the disposition of that interest in the trust

that

(iii) the fair market value of the capital property at that time

is of

(iv) the total of amounts each of which is the fair market value of a capital property of the related segregated fund trust at that time.

Related Provisions: 53(1)(l), 53(2)(q) — ACB of interest in related segregated fund trust; 138(11.5)(k) — Transfer of business by non-resident insurer; 138.1(7) — Where subsections (1) to (6) not to apply; 138.2(2)(e) — No application on qualifying transfer (merger).

(6) Definition of "acquisition fee" — In this section, "acquisition fee" means the amount, if any, by which the total of amounts each of which is

(a) that portion of a premium charged by the insurer under a segregated fund policy that is not included in the related segregated fund or cannot reasonably be regarded as an amount required to fund a mortality or maturity benefit,

(b) a transfer from the segregated fund that cannot reasonably be regarded as an amount required to fund a mortality or maturity benefit other than an annual administration fee or charge, or,

(c) any amount by which the proceeds payable to the policyholder under a particular segregated fund policy is reduced on the surrender or partial surrender of the policy that may reasonably be regarded as a surrender fee,

exceeds

(d) the total of amounts each of which is that portion of an amount described in paragraph (a), (b) or (c) that may reasonably be considered to be in respect of an interest in the segregated fund that was disposed of before 1978.

(7) Non-application of subsecs. (1) to (6) — Subsections (1) to (6) do not apply to the holder of a segregated fund policy with respect to such a policy that is issued or effected as or under a pooled registered pension plan, registered pension plan, registered retirement income fund, registered retirement savings plan or TFSA.

Related Provisions: 148(1) — Amounts included in computing policyholder's income.

Notes: 138.1(7) amended by 2012 budget bill #2 (effective Dec. 14, 2012), 2008 budget bill #1, 1992 technical bill.

Notes [s. 138.1]: See under 138.1(1).

Definitions [s. 138.1]: "acquisition fee" — 138.1(6); "adjusted cost base" — 54, 248(1); "amount" — 248(1); "arm's length" — 251(1); "capital gain", "capital loss" — 39(1), 248(1); "capital property" — 54, 248(1); "corporation" — 248(1), *Interpretation Act* 35(1); "disposition" — 248(1); "fair market value" — see 69(1) Notes; "insurer" — 248(1); "*inter vivos* trust" — 108(1), 248(1); "life insurance business" — 248(1); "pooled registered pension plan" — 147.5(1), 248(1); "prescribed", "property", "registered pension plan" — 248(1); "registered retirement income fund" — 146.3(1), 248(1); "registered retirement savings plan" — 146(1), 248(1); "related" — 251(2)–(6); "related segregated fund trust" — 138.1(1)(a); "segregated fund" — 138.1(1); "segregated fund policies" — 138.1(1)(a); "TFSA" — 146.2(5), 248(1); "taxation year" — 249; "taxpayer" — 248(1); "trust" — 104(1), 248(1), (3).

138.2 [Segregated fund mergers] — (1) Qualifying transfer of funds — For the purposes of this section, a qualifying transfer occurs at a particular time (in this section referred to as the **"transfer time"**) if

(a) all of the property that, immediately before the transfer time, was property of a related segregated fund trust has become, at the transfer time, the property of another related segregated fund trust (in this section referred to as the **"transferor"** and **"transferee"**, respectively, and collectively as the **"funds"**);

(b) every person that had an interest in the transferor immediately before the transfer time (in this section referred to as a **"beneficiary"**) has ceased to be a beneficiary of the transferor at the transfer time and has received no consideration for the interest other than an interest in the transferee;

(c) the trustee of the funds is a resident of Canada; and

(d) the trustee of the funds so elects, by filing a prescribed form with the Minister on or before the election's due date.

Related Provisions: 138.2(2)–(4) — Effects of qualifying transfer; 138.2(6) — Due date for election under (1)(d).

Notes: See Notes at end of 138.2.

Forms: T2185: Election on disposition of property by a segregated fund trust to a related segregated fund trust.

(2) General — If there has been a qualifying transfer,

(a) the last taxation years of the funds that began before the transfer time are deemed to have ended at the transfer time and

the next taxation year of the transferee is deemed to have begun immediately after the transfer time;

(b) no amount in respect of a non-capital loss, net capital loss, restricted farm loss, farm loss or limited partnership loss of a fund for a taxation year that began before the transfer time is deductible in computing the taxable income of the funds for a taxation year that begins after the transfer time;

(c) each beneficiary's interest in the transferor is deemed to have been disposed of at the transfer time for proceeds of disposition, and each beneficiary's interest in the transferee received in the qualifying transfer is deemed to have been acquired at a cost, equal to the cost amount to the beneficiary of the interest in the transferor immediately before the transfer time;

(d) any amount determined under subsection 138.1(6) in respect of a policyholder's interest in the transferor is deemed

(i) to have been charged, transferred or paid in respect of the policyholder's interest in the transferee that is acquired on the qualifying transfer, and

(ii) to not have been charged, transferred or paid in respect of the policyholder's interest in the transferor; and

(e) subsections 138.1(4) and (5) do not apply in respect of any disposition of an interest in the transferor arising on the qualifying transfer.

(3) Transferor — capital gains and losses — In respect of a qualifying transfer, each property of the transferor held immediately before the transfer time is deemed to have been disposed of by the transferor immediately before the transfer time for proceeds of disposition, and to have been acquired by the transferee at the transfer time for a cost, equal to the lesser of

(a) the fair market value of the property immediately before the transfer time, and

(b) the greater of

(i) the cost amount of the property to the transferor immediately before the transfer time, and

(ii) the amount that is designated in respect of the property in the election in respect of the qualifying transfer.

(4) Transferee — capital gains and losses — In respect of a qualifying transfer, each property of the transferee held immediately before the transfer time is deemed to have been disposed of by the transferee immediately before the transfer time for proceeds of disposition, and to have been reacquired by the transferee at the transfer time for a cost, equal to the lesser of

(a) the fair market value of the property immediately before the transfer time, and

(b) the greater of

(i) the cost amount of the property to the transferee immediately before the transfer time, and

(ii) the amount that is designated in respect of the property in the election in respect of the qualifying transfer.

(5) Loss limitation — Subsection 138.1(3) does not apply to capital losses of a fund from the disposition of property on a qualifying transfer under subsection (3) or (4) to the extent that the amount of such capital losses exceeds the amount of capital gains of the fund from the disposition of property on the qualifying transfer under subsection (3) or (4), as the case may be.

(6) Due date — The due date of an election referred to in paragraph (1)(d) is the later of

(a) the day that is six months after the day that includes the transfer time, and

(b) a day that the Minister may specify.

Forms: T2185: Election on disposition of property by a segregated fund trust to a related segregated fund trust.

Notes: 138.2 added by 2017 budget bill #2, effective 2018. It permits mergers of segregated funds.

Definitions [s. 138.2]: "amount" — 248(1); "beneficiary" — 138.2(1)(b); "capital gain" — 39(1)(a), 248(1); "capital loss" — 39(1)(b), 248(1); "cost amount", "disposition" — 248(1); "fair market value" — see 69(1) Notes; "farm loss" — 111(8), 248(1); "funds" — 138.2(1)(a); "limited partnership loss" — 96(2.1), 248(1); "Minister" — 248(1); "month" — *Interpretation Act* 35(1); "net capital loss", "non-capital loss" — 111(8), 248(1); "person", "prescribed", "property" — 248(1); "qualifying transfer" — 138.2(1); "related segregated fund trust" — 138.1(1)(a); "resident" — 250; "restricted farm loss" — 31(1.1), 248(1); "taxable income" — 2(2), 248(1); "taxation year" — 249; "transfer time" — 138.2(1); "transferee", "transferor" — 138.2(1)(a); "trust" — 104(1), 248(1), (3).

139. Conversion of insurance corporations into mutual corporations

139. Conversion of insurance corporations into mutual corporations — Where an insurance corporation that is a Canadian corporation applies an amount in payment for shares of the corporation purchased or otherwise acquired by it under a mutualization proposal under Division III of Part VI of the *Insurance Companies Act* or under a law of the province under the laws of which the corporation is incorporated that provides for the conversion of the corporation into a mutual corporation by the purchase of its shares in accordance with that law,

(a) section 15 does not apply to require the inclusion, in computing the income of a shareholder of the corporation, of any part of that amount; and

(b) no part of that amount shall be deemed, for the purpose of subsection 138(7), to have been paid to shareholders or, for the purpose of section 84, to have been received as a dividend.

Related Provisions: 139.1 — Demutualization.

Notes: Opening words of 139 referring to a mutualization proposal under the *Insurance Companies Act* added by 1991 financial institutions bill (S.C. 1994, c. 7, Sch. I (1991, c. 47), s. 734), effective June 1, 1992.

Definitions [s. 139]: "amount" — 248(1); "Canadian corporation" — 89(1), 248(1); "dividend", "insurance corporation" — 248(1); "province" — *Interpretation Act* 35(1); "share", "shareholder" — 248(1).

Demutualization of Insurance Corporations

139.1 (1) Definitions — The definitions in this subsection apply in this section and sections 139.2 and 147.4.

"conversion benefit" means a benefit received in connection with the demutualization of an insurance corporation because of an interest, before the demutualization, of any person in an insurance policy to which the insurance corporation has been a party.

Related Provisions: 139.1(2), (3) — Determining when benefit received; 139.1(11) — Conversion benefit is not a shareholder benefit. See also Related Provisions under "taxable conversion benefit".

Notes: See Notes at end of 139.1.

"deadline" for a payment in respect of a demutualization of an insurance corporation means the latest of

(a) the end of the day that is 13 months after the time of the demutualization,

(b) where the entire amount of the payment depends on the outcome of an initial public offering of shares of the corporation or a holding corporation in respect of the insurance corporation, the end of the day that is 60 days after the day on which the offering is completed,

(c) where the payment is made after the initial deadline for the payment and it is reasonable to conclude that the payment was postponed beyond that initial deadline because there was not sufficient information available 60 days before that initial deadline with regard to the location of a person, the end of the day that is six months after such information becomes available, and

(d) the end of any other day that is acceptable to the Minister.

Related Provisions: 139.1(1)"initial deadline" — Definition.

"demutualization" means the conversion of an insurance corporation from a mutual company into a corporation that is not a mutual company.

Related Provisions: 139.1(4) — Effect of demutualization; 237(4) — Authority to communicate SIN to agent of shareholder.

Notes: See Notes at end of 139.1 for demutualizations undertaken to date.

"holding corporation" means a corporation that

(a) in connection with the demutualization of an insurance corporation, has issued shares of its capital stock to stakeholders; and

(b) owns shares of the capital stock of the insurance corporation acquired in connection with the demutualization that entitle it to 90% or more of the votes that could be cast in respect of shares under all circumstances at an annual meeting of

(i) shareholders of the insurance corporation, or

(ii) shareholders of the insurance corporation and holders of insurance policies to which the insurance corporation is a party.

Related Provisions: 139.1(4)(e) — Cost to holding corporation of shares acquired on demutualization; 141(3) — Holding corporation deemed to be public corporation.

"initial deadline" for a payment is the time that would, if the definition "deadline" were read without reference to paragraph (c) of that definition, be the deadline for the payment.

"mutual holding corporation" in respect of an insurance corporation, means a mutual company established to hold shares of the capital stock of the insurance corporation, where the only persons entitled to vote at an annual meeting of the mutual company are policyholders of the insurance corporation.

Related Provisions: 139.1(4)(d) — Receipt of ownership rights in MHC on demutualization; 139.2 — Deemed dividend on distribution of property by MHC.

Notes: The word "hold" means the mutual company must directly own shares of the insurance corp: VIEWS doc 2012-0451411E5.

"ownership rights" means

(a) in a particular mutual holding corporation, the following rights and interests held by a person in respect of the particular corporation because of an interest or former interest of any person in an insurance policy to which an insurance corporation, in respect of which the particular corporation is the mutual holding corporation, has been a party:

(i) rights that are similar to rights attached to shares of the capital stock of a corporation, and

(ii) all other rights with respect to, and interests in, the particular corporation as a mutual company; and

(b) in a mutual insurance corporation, the following rights and interests held by a person in respect of the mutual insurance corporation because of an interest or former interest of any person in an insurance policy to which that corporation has been a party:

(i) rights that are similar to rights attached to shares of the capital stock of a corporation,

(ii) all other rights with respect to, and interests in, the mutual insurance corporation as a mutual company, and

(iii) any contingent or absolute right to receive a benefit in connection with the demutualization of the mutual insurance corporation.

Related Provisions: 139.1(4)(a), (d) — Rollover where shares acquired in exchange for ownership rights.

"person" includes a partnership.

"share" of the capital stock of a corporation includes a right granted by the corporation to acquire a share of its capital stock.

"specified insurance benefit" means a taxable conversion benefit that is

(a) an enhancement of benefits under an insurance policy;

(b) an issuance of an insurance policy;

(c) an undertaking by an insurance corporation of an obligation to pay a policy dividend; or

(d) a reduction in the amount of premiums that would otherwise be payable under an insurance policy.

Related Provisions: 139.1(8) — Effect of stakeholder receiving specified insurance benefit.

"stakeholder" means a person who is entitled to receive or who has received a conversion benefit but, in respect of the demutualization of an insurance corporation, does not include a holding corporation in connection with the demutualization or a mutual holding corporation in respect of the insurance corporation.

Related Provisions: 139.1(4) — Effect of demutualization on stakeholder.

"taxable conversion benefit" means a conversion benefit received by a stakeholder in connection with the demutualization of an insurance corporation, other than a conversion benefit that is

(a) a share of a class of the capital stock of the corporation;

(b) a share of a class of the capital stock of a corporation that is or becomes a holding corporation in connection with the demutualization; or

(c) an ownership right in a mutual holding corporation in respect of the insurance corporation.

Related Provisions: 139.1(2), (3) — Determining when benefit received; 139.1(4)(f) — TCB deemed to be a dividend; 139.1(8)(a) — Policy dividend that is TCB deemed not to be policy dividend; 139.1(10) — Cost of TCB.

(2) Rules of general application — For the purposes of this section,

(a) subject to paragraphs (b) to (g), if in providing a benefit in respect of a demutualization, a corporation becomes obligated, either absolutely or contingently, to make or arrange a payment, the person to whom the undertaking to make or arrange the payment was given is considered to have received a benefit

(i) as a consequence of the undertaking of the obligation, and

(ii) not as a consequence of the making of the payment;

(b) where, in providing a benefit in respect of a demutualization, a corporation makes a payment (other than a payment, made pursuant to the terms of an insurance policy, that is not a policy dividend) at any time on or before the deadline for the payment,

(i) subject to paragraphs (f) and (g), the recipient of the payment is considered to have received a benefit as a consequence of the making of the payment, and

(ii) no benefit is considered to have been received as a consequence of the undertaking of an obligation, that is either contingent or absolute, to make or arrange the payment;

(c) no benefit is considered to have been received as a consequence of the undertaking of an absolute or contingent obligation of a corporation to make or arrange a payment (other than a payment, made pursuant to the terms of an insurance policy, that is not a policy dividend) unless it is reasonable to conclude that there is sufficient information with regard to the location of a person to make or arrange the payment;

(d) where a corporation's obligation to make or arrange a payment in connection with a demutualization ceases on or before the initial deadline for the payment and without the payment being made in whole or in part, no benefit is considered to have been received as a consequence of the undertaking of the obligation unless the payment was to be a payment (other than a policy dividend) pursuant to the terms of an insurance policy;

(e) no benefit is considered to have been received as a consequence of the undertaking of an absolute or contingent obligation of a corporation to make or arrange a payment where

(i) paragraph (a) would, but for this paragraph, apply with respect to the obligation,

(ii) paragraph (d) would, if that paragraph were read without reference to the words "on or before the initial deadline for the payment", apply in respect of the obligation,

(iii) it is reasonable to conclude that there was not, before the initial deadline for the payment, sufficient information with regard to the location of a person to make or arrange the payment, and

(iv) such information becomes available on a particular day after the initial deadline and the obligation ceases not more than six months after the particular day;

(f) no benefit is considered to have been received as a consequence of

(i) an undertaking of an absolute or contingent obligation of a corporation to make or arrange an annuity payment through the issuance of an annuity contract, or

(ii) a receipt of an annuity payment under the contract so issued

where it is reasonable to conclude that the purpose of the undertaking or the making of the annuity payment is to supplement benefits provided under either an annuity contract to which subsection 147.4(1) or paragraph 254(a) applied or a group annuity contract that had been issued under, or pursuant to, a registered pension plan that has wound up;

(g) no benefit is considered to have been received as a consequence of

(i) an amendment to which subsection 147.4(2) would, but for subparagraph 147.4(2)(a)(ii), apply, or

(ii) a substitution to which paragraph 147.4(3)(a) applies;

(h) the time at which a stakeholder is considered to receive a benefit in connection with the demutualization of an insurance corporation is,

(i) where the benefit is a payment made at or before the time of demutualization or is a payment to which paragraph (b) applies, the time at which the payment is made, and

(ii) in any other case, the latest of

(A) the time of the demutualization,

(B) where the extent of the benefit or the stakeholder's entitlement to it depends on the outcome of an initial public offering of shares of the corporation or a holding corporation in respect of the insurance corporation and the offering is completed before the day that is 13 months after the time of the demutualization, the time at which the offering is completed,

(C) where the entire amount of the benefit depends on the outcome of an initial public offering of shares of the corporation or a holding corporation in respect of the insurance corporation, the time at which the offering is completed,

(D) where it is reasonable to conclude that the person conferring the benefit does not have sufficient information with regard to the location of the stakeholder before the later of the times determined under clauses (A) to (C), to advise the stakeholder of the benefit, the time at which sufficient information with regard to the location of the stakeholder to so advise the stakeholder was received by that person, and

(E) the end of any other day that is acceptable to the Minister;

(i) the time at which an insurance corporation is considered to demutualize is the time at which it first issues a share of its capital stock (other than shares of its capital stock issued by it when it was a mutual company if the corporation did not cease to be a mutual company because of the issuance of those shares); and

(j) subject to paragraph (3)(b), the value of a benefit received by a stakeholder is the fair market value of the benefit at the time the stakeholder receives the benefit.

Related Provisions: 49.1 — Acquisition in satisfaction of obligation deemed not to be a disposition.

Notes: See Notes at end of 139.1.

(3) Special cases — For the purposes of this section,

(a) where benefits under an insurance policy are enhanced (otherwise than by way of an amendment to which subsection 147.4(2) would, but for subparagraph 147.4(2)(a)(ii), apply) in connection with a demutualization, the value of the enhancement is deemed to be a benefit received by the policyholder and not by any other person;

(b) where premiums payable under an insurance policy to an insurance corporation are reduced in connection with a demutualization, the policyholder is deemed, as a consequence of the undertaking to reduce the premiums, to have received a benefit equal to the present value at the time of the demutualization of the additional premiums that would have been payable if the premiums had not been reduced in connection with the demutualization;

(c) the payment of a policy dividend by an insurance corporation or an undertaking of an obligation by the corporation to pay a policy dividend is considered to be in connection with the demutualization of the corporation only to the extent that

(i) the policy dividend is referred to in the demutualization proposal sent by the corporation to stakeholders,

(ii) the obligation to make the payment is contingent on stakeholder approval for the demutualization, and

(iii) the payment or undertaking cannot reasonably be considered to have been made or given, as the case may be, to ensure that policy dividends are not adversely affected by the demutualization;

(d) except for the purposes of paragraphs (c), (e) and (f), where part of a policy dividend is a conversion benefit in respect of the demutualization of an insurance corporation and part of it is not, each part of the dividend is deemed to be a policy dividend that is separate from the other part;

(e) a policy dividend includes an amount that is in lieu of payment of, or in satisfaction of, a policy dividend;

(f) the payment of a policy dividend includes the application of the policy dividend to pay a premium under an insurance policy or to repay a policy loan;

(g) where the demutualization of an insurance corporation is effected by the merger of the corporation with one or more other corporations to form one corporate entity, that entity is deemed to be the same corporation as, and a continuation of, the insurance corporation;

(h) an insurance corporation shall be considered to have become a party to an insurance policy at the time that the insurance corporation becomes liable in respect of obligations of an insurer under the policy; and

(i) notwithstanding paragraph 248(7)(a), where a cheque or other means of payment sent to an address is returned to the sender without being received by the addressee, it is deemed not to have been sent.

Related Provisions: 139.1(2)(i) — Determining time of demutualization; 87(2.2) — Amalgamation of insurers.

(4) Consequences of demutualization — Where a particular insurance corporation demutualizes,

(a) each of the income, loss, capital gain and capital loss of a taxpayer, from the disposition, alteration or dilution of the taxpayer's ownership rights in the particular corporation as a result of the demutualization, is deemed to be nil;

(b) no amount paid or payable to a stakeholder in connection with the disposition, alteration or dilution of the stakeholder's ownership rights in the particular corporation may be included in Class 14.1 of Schedule II to the *Income Tax Regulations*;

(c) no election may be made under subsection 85(1) or (2) in respect of ownership rights in the particular corporation;

(d) where the consideration given by a person for a share of the capital stock of the particular corporation or a holding corporation in connection with the demutualization (or for particular ownership rights in a mutual holding corporation in respect of the particular corporation) includes the transfer, surrender, alteration or dilution of ownership rights in the particular corpora-

tion, the cost of the share (or the particular ownership rights) to the person is deemed to be nil;

(e) where a holding corporation in connection with the demutualization acquires, in connection with the demutualization, a share of the capital stock of the particular corporation from the particular corporation and issues a share of its own capital stock to a stakeholder as consideration for the share of the capital stock of the particular corporation, the cost to the holding corporation of the share of the capital stock of the particular corporation is deemed to be nil;

(f) where at any time a stakeholder receives a taxable conversion benefit and subsection (14) does not apply to the benefit,

(i) the corporation that conferred the benefit is deemed to have paid a dividend at that time on shares of its capital stock equal to the value of the benefit, and

(ii) subject to subsection (16), the benefit received by the stakeholder is deemed to be a dividend received by the stakeholder at that time;

(g) for the purposes of this Part, where a dividend is deemed by paragraph (f) or by paragraph (16)(i) to have been paid by a non-resident corporation, that corporation is deemed in respect of the payment of the dividend to be a corporation resident in Canada that is a taxable Canadian corporation unless any amount is claimed under section 126 in respect of tax on the dividend;

(h) for the purposes of section 70, subsection 104(4) and section 128.1, the fair market value of rights to benefits that are to be received in connection with the demutualization is, before the time of the receipt, deemed to be nil; and

(i) where a person acquires an annuity contract in respect of which, because of the application of paragraph (2)(f), no benefit is considered to have been received for the purpose of this section,

(i) the cost of the annuity contract to the person is deemed to be nil, and

(ii) section 12.2 does not apply to the annuity contract.

Related Provisions: 12(1)(j), 82(1), 90 — Inclusion in income of deemed dividend; 87(2)(j.6) — Amalgamation — continuing corporation; 139 — Mutualization proposal; 139.1(2)(j) — Value of benefit; 212(2) — Non-resident withholding tax on deemed dividend.

Notes: In *Fraser*, 2006 TCC 134, 139.1(4)(d) applied so that proceeds of sale of insurance company shares were all capital gain.

139.1(4)(b) amended by 2016 budget bill #2, effective 2017, to change "is an eligible capital expenditure" to "may be included in Class 14.1 of Schedule II to the *Income Tax Regulations*" (eligible capital property changed to Class 14.1: see 20(1)(b) Notes).

(5) Fair market value of ownership rights — For the purposes of section 70, subsection 104(4) and section 128.1, where an insurance corporation makes, at any time, a public announcement that it intends to seek approval for its demutualization, the fair market value of ownership rights in the corporation is deemed to be nil throughout the period that

(a) begins at that time; and

(b) ends either at the time of the demutualization or, in the event that the corporation makes at any subsequent time a public announcement that it no longer intends to demutualize, at the subsequent time.

Related Provisions: 87(2)(j.6) — Amalgamation — continuing corporation.

(6) Paid-up capital — insurance corporation — Where an insurance corporation resident in Canada has demutualized, in computing the paid-up capital at any particular time in respect of a class of shares of the capital stock of the corporation,

(a) there shall be deducted the total of all amounts each of which would, but for this subsection, have been deemed by subsection 84(1) to have been paid at or before the particular time by the corporation as a dividend on a share of that class because of an increase in paid-up capital (determined without reference to this subsection) in connection with the demutualization; and

(b) there shall be added the amount, if any, by which

    (i) the total of all amounts each of which is deemed by subsection 84(3), (4) or (4.1) to be a dividend on shares of that class paid by the corporation before the particular time

exceeds

    (ii) the total of all amounts each of which would be deemed by subsection 84(3), (4) or (4.1) to be a dividend on shares of that class paid by the corporation before the particular time, if this Act were read without reference to this subsection.

Related Provisions: 87(2)(j.6) — Amalgamation — continuing corporation.

(7) Paid-up capital — holding corporation — Where a particular corporation resident in Canada was at any time a holding corporation in connection with the demutualization of an insurance corporation, in computing the paid-up capital at any particular time in respect of a class of shares of the capital stock of the particular corporation,

(a) there shall be deducted the total of all amounts each of which is an amount by which the paid-up capital would, but for this subsection, have increased at or before the particular time as a result of the acquisition of shares of a class of the capital stock of the insurance corporation from the corporation on its demutualization; and

(b) there shall be added the amount, if any, by which

    (i) the total of all amounts each of which is deemed by subsection 84(3), (4) or (4.1) to be a dividend on shares of that class paid by the particular corporation before the particular time

exceeds

    (ii) the total of all amounts each of which would be deemed by subsection 84(3), (4) or (4.1) to be a dividend on shares of that class paid by the particular corporation before the particular time, if this Act were read without reference to this subsection.

Related Provisions: 87(2)(j.6) — Amalgamation — continuing corporation.

(8) Policy dividends — Where the payment of a policy dividend by an insurance corporation is a taxable conversion benefit,

(a) for the purposes of this Act other than this section, the policy dividend is deemed not to be a policy dividend; and

(b) no amount in respect of the policy dividend may be included, either explicitly or implicitly, in the calculation of an amount deductible by the insurer for any taxation year under paragraph 20(7)(c) or subsection 138(3).

Related Provisions: 87(2)(j.6) — Amalgamation — continuing corporation.

(9) Payment and receipt of premium — Where, in connection with the demutualization of an insurance corporation, a person would, if subsection (2) were read without reference to paragraphs (f) and (g) and paragraph (3)(a) were read without reference to the application of subsection 147.4(2), receive a particular benefit that is a specified insurance benefit,

(a) the insurance corporation that is obligated to pay benefits under the policy to which the particular benefit relates is deemed to have received a premium at the time of the demutualization in respect of that policy equal to the value of the particular benefit;

(b) for the purpose of paragraph (a), to the extent that the obligations of a particular insurance corporation under the policy were assumed by another insurance corporation before the time of the demutualization, the particular corporation is deemed not to be obligated to pay benefits under the policy; and

(c) subject to paragraph (15)(e), where the person receives the particular benefit, the person is deemed to have paid, at the time of demutualization, a premium in respect of the policy to which the benefit relates equal to the value of the particular benefit.

Related Provisions: 139.1(2)(i) — Determining time of demutualization; 139.1(2)(j) — Value of benefit.

(10) Cost of taxable conversion benefit — Where, in connection with the demutualization of an insurance corporation, a stakeholder receives a taxable conversion benefit (other than a specified insurance benefit), the stakeholder is deemed to have acquired the benefit at a cost equal to the value of the benefit.

Related Provisions: 139.1(2)(j) — Value of benefit.

(11) No shareholder benefit — Subsection 15(1) does not apply to a conversion benefit.

(12) Exclusion of benefit from RRSP and other rules — Subject to subsection (14), for the purposes of the provisions of this Act (other than paragraph (9)(c)) that relate to registered retirement savings plans, registered retirement income funds, retirement compensation arrangements, deferred profit sharing plans and superannuation or pension funds or plans, the receipt of a conversion benefit shall be considered to be neither a contribution to, nor a distribution from, such a plan, fund or arrangement.

(13) RRSP registration rules, etc. — For the purposes of this Act, paragraphs 146(2)(c.4) and 146.3(2)(g) and subsection 198(6) shall be applied without reference to any conversion benefit.

(14) Retirement benefit — A conversion benefit received because of an interest in a life insurance policy held by a trust governed by a registered retirement savings plan, registered retirement income fund, deferred profit sharing plan or superannuation or pension fund or plan is deemed to be received under the plan or fund, as the case may be, if it is received by any person (other than the trust).

Related Provisions: 139.1(4)(j) — Deemed dividend where 139.1(12) does not apply.

(15) Employee-paid insurance — Where

(a) a stakeholder receives a conversion benefit because of the stakeholder's interest in a group insurance policy under which individuals have been insured in the course of or because of their employment,

(b) at all times before the payment of a premium described in paragraph (c), the full cost of a particular insurance coverage under the policy was borne by the individuals who were insured under the particular coverage,

(c) the stakeholder pays a premium under the policy in respect of the particular coverage or under another group insurance policy in respect of coverage that has replaced the particular coverage, and

(d) either

    (i) the premium is deemed by paragraph (9)(c) to have been paid, or

    (ii) it is reasonable to conclude that the purpose of the premium is to apply, for the benefit of the individuals who are insured under the particular coverage or the replacement coverage, all or part of the value of the portion of the conversion benefit that can reasonably be considered to be in respect of the particular coverage,

the following rules apply:

(e) for the purposes of paragraph 6(1)(f) and regulations made for the purposes of subsection 6(4), the premium is deemed to be an amount paid by the individuals who are insured under the particular coverage or the replacement coverage, as the case may be, and not to be an amount paid by the stakeholder, and

(f) no amount may be deducted in respect of the premium in computing the stakeholder's income.

Related Provisions: 87(2)(j.6) — Amalgamation — continuing corporation.

(16) Flow-through of conversion benefits to employees and others — Where

(a) a stakeholder receives a conversion benefit (in this subsection referred to as the "relevant conversion benefit") because of the interest of any person in an insurance policy,

(b) the stakeholder makes a payment of an amount (otherwise than by way of a transfer of a share that was received by the stakeholder as all or part of the relevant conversion benefit and that was not so received as a taxable conversion benefit) to a particular individual

(i) who has received benefits under the policy,

(ii) who has, or had at any time, an absolute or contingent right to receive benefits under the policy,

(iii) for whose benefit insurance coverage was provided under the policy, or

(iv) who received the amount because an individual satisfied the condition in subparagraph (i), (ii) or (iii),

(c) it is reasonable to conclude that the purpose of the payment is to distribute an amount in respect of the relevant conversion benefit to the particular individual,

(d) either

(i) the main purpose of the policy was to provide retirement benefits or insurance coverage to individuals in respect of their employment with an employer, or

(ii) all or part of the cost of insurance coverage under the policy had been borne by individuals (other than the stakeholder),

(e) subsection (14) does not apply to the relevant conversion benefit, and

(f) one of the following applies, namely,

(i) the particular individual is resident in Canada at the time of the payment, the stakeholder is a person the taxable income of which is exempt from tax under this Part and the payment would, if this section were read without reference to this subsection, be included in computing the income of the particular individual,

(ii) the payment is received before December 7, 1999 and the stakeholder elects in writing filed with the Minister, on a day that is not more than six months after the end of the taxation year in which the stakeholder receives the relevant conversion benefit (or a later day acceptable to the Minister), that this subsection applies in respect of the payment,

(iii) the payment is received after December 6, 1999, the payment would, if this section were read without reference to this subsection, be included in computing the income of the particular individual and the stakeholder elects in writing filed with the Minister, on a day that is not more than six months after the end of the taxation year in which the stakeholder receives the relevant conversion benefit (or a later day acceptable to the Minister), that this subsection applies in respect of the payment, or

(iv) the payment is received after December 6, 1999 and the payment would, if this section were read without reference to this subsection, not be included in computing the income of the particular individual,

the following rules apply:

(g) subject to paragraph (l), no amount is, because of the making of the payment, deductible in computing the stakeholder's income,

(h) except for the purpose of this subsection and without affecting the consequences to the particular individual of any transaction or event that occurs after the time that the payment was made, the payment is deemed not to have been received by, or made payable to, the particular individual,

(i) the corporation that conferred the relevant conversion benefit is deemed to have paid to the particular individual at the time the payment was made, and the particular individual is deemed to have received at that time, a dividend on shares of the capital stock of the corporation equal to the amount of the payment,

(j) all obligations that would, but for this subsection, be imposed by this Act or the Regulations on the corporation because of the payment of the dividend apply to the stakeholder as if the stakeholder were the corporation, and do not apply to the corporation,

(k) where the relevant conversion benefit is a taxable conversion benefit, except for the purpose of this subsection and the purposes of determining the obligations imposed by this Act or the Regulations on the corporation because of the conferral of the relevant conversion benefit, the stakeholder is deemed, to the extent of the fair market value of the payment, not to have received the relevant conversion benefit, and

(l) where the relevant conversion benefit was a share received by the stakeholder (otherwise than as a taxable conversion benefit),

(i) where the share is, at the time of the payment, capital property held by the stakeholder, the amount of the payment shall, after that time, be added in computing the adjusted cost base to the stakeholder of the share,

(ii) where subparagraph (i) does not apply and the share was capital property disposed of by the stakeholder before that time, the amount of the payment is deemed to be a capital loss of the stakeholder from the disposition of a property for the taxation year of the stakeholder in which the payment is made, and

(iii) in any other case, paragraph (g) shall not apply to the payment.

Related Provisions: 53(1)(d.01) — Addition to ACB for amount under 139.1(16)(l); 87(2)(j.6) — Amalgamation — continuing corporation; 96(3) — Election by members of partnership; 139.1(17) — Flow-through of share benefits.

(17) **Flow-through of share benefits to employees and others** — Where

(a) because of the interest of any person in an insurance policy, a stakeholder receives a conversion benefit (other than a taxable conversion benefit) that consists of shares of the capital stock of a corporation,

(b) the stakeholder transfers some or all of the shares at any time to a particular individual

(i) who has received benefits under the policy,

(ii) who has, or had at any time, an absolute or contingent right to receive benefits under the policy,

(iii) for whose benefit insurance coverage was provided under the policy, or

(iv) who received the shares because an individual satisfied the condition in subparagraph (i), (ii) or (iii),

(c) it is reasonable to conclude that the purpose of the transfer is to distribute all or any portion of the conversion benefit to the particular individual,

(d) either

(i) the main purpose of the policy was to provide retirement benefits or insurance coverage to individuals in respect of their employment with an employer, or

(ii) all or part of the cost of insurance coverage under the policy had been borne by individuals (other than the stakeholder),

(e) subsection (14) does not apply to the conversion benefit, and

(f) one of the following applies, namely,

(i) the particular individual is resident in Canada at the time of the transfer, the stakeholder is a person the taxable income of which is exempt from tax under this Part and the amount of the transfer would, if this section were read without reference to this subsection, be included in computing the income of the particular individual,

(ii) the transfer is made before December 7, 1999 and the stakeholder elects in writing filed with the Minister, on a day that is not more than six months after the end of the taxation year in which the stakeholder receives the conversion benefit (or a later day acceptable to the Minister), that this subsection applies in respect of the transfer,

(iii) the transfer is made after December 6, 1999, the amount of the transfer would, if this section were read without reference to this subsection, be included in computing the income of the particular individual and the stakeholder elects in writing filed with the Minister, on a day that is not more than six months after the end of the taxation year in which the stakeholder receives the conversion benefit (or a later day acceptable to the Minister), that this subsection applies in respect of the transfer, or

(iv) the transfer is made after December 6, 1999 and the amount of the transfer would, if this section were read without reference to this subsection, not be included in computing the income of the particular individual,

the following rules apply:

(g) no amount is, because of the transfer, deductible in computing the stakeholder's income,

(h) except for the purpose of this subsection and without affecting the consequences to the particular individual of any transaction or event that occurs after the time that the transfer was made, the transfer is deemed not to have been made to the particular individual nor to represent an amount payable to the particular individual, and

(i) the cost of the shares to the particular individual is deemed to be nil.

Related Provisions: 87(2)(j.6) — Amalgamation — continuing corporation; 139.1(16) — Flow-through of conversion benefits.

(18) Acquisition of control — For the purposes of subsections 10(10), 13(21.2) and (24) and 18(15), sections 18.1 and 37, subsection 40(3.4), the definition "superficial loss" in section 54, section 55, subsections 66(11), (11.4) and (11.5), 66.5(3) and 66.7(10) and (11), section 80, paragraph 80.04(4)(h), subsections 85(1.2) and 88(1.1) and (1.2), sections 111 and 127 and subsections 249(4) and 256(7), control of an insurance corporation (and each corporation controlled by it) is deemed not to be acquired solely because of the acquisition of shares of the capital stock of the insurance corporation, in connection with the demutualization of the insurance corporation, by a particular corporation that at a particular time becomes a holding corporation in connection with the demutualization where, immediately after the particular time,

(a) the particular corporation is not controlled by any person or group of persons; and

(b) 95% of the fair market value of all the assets of the particular corporation is less than the total of all amounts each of which is

(i) the amount of the particular corporation's money,

(ii) the amount of a deposit, with a financial institution, of such money standing to the credit of the particular corporation,

(iii) the fair market value of a bond, debenture, note or similar obligation that is owned by the particular corporation that had, at the time of its acquisition, a maturity date of not more than 24 months after that time, or

(iv) the fair market value of a share of the capital stock of the insurance corporation held by the particular corporation.

Related Provisions: 87(2)(j.6) — Amalgamation — continuing corporation; 256(6), (6.1) — Meaning of "controlled".

Notes: 139.1(18) opening words amended by 2016 budget bill #2, effective 2017, to delete reference to 14(12), as part of changing the eligible capital property rules to CCA Class 14.1 (see Notes to 20(1)(b)).

Notes [s. 139.1]: 139.1 provides rules for "demutualization" of insurance companies, whereby Canada's large life insurers, formerly owned by their policyholders as mutual insurance companies, converted themselves to share corporations and issued tradeable shares to their policyholders (canada.coop/en/demutualization). This was done by Canada Life, Industrial-Alliance Life, Manufacturer's Life, Mutual Life and Sun Life. The thrust of 139.1 is to provide that there is no tax consequence to the policyholder on receiving the shares (139.1(4)(a)), but that the shares have a zero cost base (139.1(4)(d)) so that all cash received on the sale of the shares will be taxed as capital gain. Some life insurers have remained as mutual insurers, e.g. Equitable Life, Assumption Life, UL Mutual.

See Nickerson & Wentzell, "Insurance Company Demutualization", 11(6) *Taxation of Executive Compensation & Retirement* (Federated Press) 235-39 (Feb. 2000).

The June 2011 and Feb. 2014 (chap. 3.2) budgets said demutualization rules would be developed for property/casualty insurers. This may not require changes to 139.1. Economical Insurance is the first to apply: tinyurl.com/demut-econ1, tinyurl.com/demut-econ2.

139.1 added by 1999 Budget bill, for transactions after Dec. 15, 1998.

Definitions [s. 139.1]: "adjusted cost base" — 54, 248(1); "amount", "annuity" — 248(1); "capital gain" — 39(1), 248(1); "capital loss" — 39(1)(b), 248(1); "capital property" — 54, 248(1); "class of shares" — 248(6); "controlled" — 256(6), (6.1). "conversion benefit" — 139.1(1); "corporation" — 248(1), *Interpretation Act* 35(1); "deadline" — 139.1(1); "deferred profit sharing plan" — 147(1), 248(1); "demutualization" — 139.1(1); "disposition", "dividend" — 248(1); "eligible capital expenditure" — 14(5), 248(1); "employee", "employer", "employment" — 248(1); "fair market value" — see 69(1) Notes; "holding corporation" — 139.1(1); "individual" — 248(1); "initial deadline" — 139.1(1); "insurance corporation", "insurance policy", "insurer" — 248(1); "life insurance policy" — 138(12), 248(1); "Minister" — 248(1); "month" — *Interpretation Act* 35(1); "mutual holding corporation" — 139.1(1); "non-resident" — 248(1); "ownership rights" — 139.1(1); "paid-up capital" — 89(1), 248(1); "partnership" — see 96(1) Notes; "person" — 139.1(1), 248(1); "property", "registered pension plan" — 248(1); "registered retirement income fund" — 146.3(1), 248(1); "registered retirement savings plan" — 146(1), 248(1); "relevant conversion benefit" — 139.1(16)(a); "resident in Canada" — 250; "retirement compensation arrangement" — 248(1); "share" — 139.1(1), 248(1); "shareholder" — 248(1); "specified insurance benefit", "stakeholder" — 139.1(1); "taxable Canadian corporation" — 89(1), 248(1); "taxable conversion benefit" — 139.1(1); "taxable income" — 248(1); "taxation year" — 249; "taxpayer" — 248(1); "trust" — 104(1), 248(1), (3); "writing" — *Interpretation Act* 35(1).

139.2 Mutual holding corporations — Where at any time a mutual holding corporation (as defined in subsection 139.1(1)) in respect of an insurance corporation distributes property to a policyholder of the insurance corporation, the mutual holding corporation is deemed to have paid, and the policyholder is deemed to have received from the mutual holding corporation, at that time a dividend on shares of the capital stock of the mutual holding corporation, equal to the fair market value of the property.

Related Provisions: 139.1 — Demutualization.

Notes: 139.2 added by 1999 Budget, effective for transactions that occur after December 15, 1998. Its most common application is with respect to the distribution by a mutual holding corporation of dividends received on shares of the insurance corporation.

Definitions [s. 139.2]: "corporation" — 248(1), *Interpretation Act* 35(1); "dividend" — 248(1); "fair market value" — see 69(1) Notes; "insurance corporation" — 248(1); "mutual holding corporation" — 139.1(1); "property", "share" — 248(1).

140. (1) [Insurance corporation] Deductions in computing income — In computing the income for a taxation year of an insurance corporation, whether a mutual corporation or a joint stock company, from carrying on an insurance business other than a life insurance business, there may be deducted every amount credited in respect of that business for the year or a preceding taxation year to a policyholder of the corporation by way of a policy dividend, refund of premiums or refund of premium deposits if the amount was, during the year or within 12 months thereafter,

(a) paid or unconditionally credited to the policyholder; or

(b) applied in discharge, in whole or in part, of a liability of the policyholder to pay premiums to the corporation.

Related Provisions: 87(2.2) — Amalgamation of insurance corps; 88(1)(g) — Winding-up of subsidiary insurance corps; 138(11.5)(k) — Transfer of business by non-resident insurer; *Interpretation Act* 27(5) — Meaning of "within 12 months".

Notes: 140(1) amended by 1999 Budget, effective December 16, 1998.

(2) Inclusion in computing income — There shall be included in computing the income of an insurance corporation, whether a mutual corporation or a joint stock company, from carrying on an insurance business for its first taxation year that commences after June 17, 1987 and ends after 1987 (in this subsection referred to as its "1988 taxation year") the amount, if any, by which

(a) the total of all amounts each of which is an amount deducted by the corporation in computing its income for a taxation year ending before its 1988 taxation year pursuant to paragraph 140(c) of the *Income Tax Act*, chapter 148 of the Revised Statutes of Canada, 1952, or pursuant to that paragraph by reason of subparagraph 138(3)(a)(v) of that Act as it read in respect of those taxation years in respect of amounts credited to the account of the policyholder on terms that the policyholder is entitled to payment thereof on or before the expiration or termination of the policy

exceeds

(b) the total of all amounts each of which is an amount paid or unconditionally credited to a policyholder or applied in discharge, in whole or in part, of a liability of the policyholder to pay premiums to the corporation before the corporation's 1988 taxation year in respect of the amounts credited to the account of the policyholder referred to in paragraph (a).

Related Provisions [subsec. 140(2)]: 87(2.2) — Amalgamation of insurance corporations; 88(1)(g) — Winding-up of insurance corporations; 138(3) — Deductions allowed in computing income; 138(11.5)(k) — Transfer of business by non-resident insurer.

I.T. Application Rules: 69 (meaning of "chapter 148 of ...").

Definitions [s. 140]: "amount", "business" — 248(1); "carrying on business" — 253; "corporation" — 248(1), *Interpretation Act* 35(1); "dividend", "insurance corporation", "life insurance business" — 248(1); "policy dividend" — 139.1(8)(a), 248(1); "taxation year" — 249.

141. (1) Definitions — In this section, "demutualization" and "holding corporation" have the same meaning as in subsection 139.1(1).

Notes: See Notes at end of s. 141.

(2) Life insurance corporation deemed to be public corporation — Notwithstanding any other provision of this Act, a life insurance corporation that is resident in Canada is deemed to be a public corporation.

(3) Holding corporation deemed to be public corporation — A corporation resident in Canada that is a holding corporation because of its acquisition of shares in connection with the demutualization of a life insurance corporation resident in Canada is deemed to be a public corporation at each time in the specified period of the holding corporation at which the holding corporation would have satisfied conditions prescribed under subparagraph (b)(i) of the definition "public corporation" in subsection 89(1) if the words "shareholders, the dispersal of ownership of its shares and the public trading of its shares" in that subparagraph were read as "shareholders and the dispersal of ownership of its shares".

Related Provisions: 141(4) — Meaning of "specified period"; 141(5) — Shares of holding corporation deemed not to be taxable Canadian property.

(4) Specified period — For the purpose of subsection (3), the specified period of a corporation

(a) begins at the time the corporation becomes a holding corporation; and

(b) ends at the first time the corporation is a public corporation because of any provision of this Act other than subsection (3).

(5) Exclusion from taxable Canadian property — For the purpose of paragraph (d) of the definition "taxable Canadian property" in subsection 248(1), a share of the capital stock of a corporation is deemed to be listed at any time on a designated stock exchange if

(a) the corporation is

(i) a life insurance corporation resident in Canada that has demutualized and that, at that time, would have satisfied conditions prescribed under subparagraph (b)(i) of the definition "public corporation" in subsection 89(1) if the words "shareholders, the dispersal of ownership of its shares and the public trading of its shares" in that subparagraph were read as "shareholders and the dispersal of ownership of its shares", or

(ii) a holding corporation that is deemed by subsection (3) to be a public corporation at that time;

(b) no share of the capital stock of the corporation is listed on any stock exchange at that time; and

(c) that time is not later than six months after the time of demutualization of

(i) the corporation, where the corporation is a life insurance corporation, and

(ii) in any other case, the life insurance corporation in respect of which the corporation is a holding corporation.

Notes: 141(5) opening words amended by 2007 budget bill #2, effective Dec. 14, 2007, to change "stock exchange prescribed for the purpose of that definition" to "designated stock exchange".

141(5) earlier amended by 2001 technical bill, effective Dec. 16, 1998.

Related Provisions: 138(1) — Insurance corporations; 141.1 — Insurance corporation deemed not to be private corporation; 142 — Taxable capital gains of life insurer.

Notes [s. 141]: 141 renumbered as 141(2) and the rest of 141 added by 1999 Budget, effective December 16, 1998.

Definitions [s. 141]: "Canada" — 255; "corporation" — 248(1), *Interpretation Act* 35(1); "demutualization" — 139.1(1), 141(1); "designated stock exchange" — 248(1), 262; "dividend" — 248(1); "holding corporation" — 139.1(1), 141(1); "insurance corporation", "life insurance corporation" — 248(1); "month" — *Interpretation Act* 35(1); "prescribed" — 248(1); "public corporation" — 89(1), 248(1); "resident in Canada" — 250; "share" — 248(1); "specified period" — 141(4); "taxable Canadian property" — 248(1).

141.1 [Insurance corporation] deemed not to be a private corporation — Notwithstanding any other provision of this Act, an insurance corporation (other than a life insurance corporation) that would, but for this section, be a private corporation is deemed not to be a private corporation for the purposes of subsection 55(5), the definition "capital dividend account" in subsection 89(1) and sections 123.3 and 129.

Related Provisions: 141(2) — Life insurance corporation deemed to be public corporation.

Notes: The deeming in 141.1 applies for all purposes for which the indicated provisions apply, so it applied to s. 129 as referenced within another provision: *Groupe Commerce*, [1999] 4 C.T.C. 54 (FCA).

141.1 amended by 1995-97 technical bill, for taxation years that end after June 1995.

Definitions [s. 141.1]: "insurance corporation", "life insurance corporation" — 248(1); "private corporation" — 89(1), 248(1).

I.T. Application Rules: 69 (meaning of "chapter 148 of ...").

142, 142.1 [Repealed]

Notes: 142 and 142.1 repealed by 1996 Budget, for 1997 and later taxation years. 142 has been incorporated into 138(2)(b). It excluded from income certain taxable capital gains on insurance property not used in a Canadian insurance business.

142.1 provided that the definitions in 138(12) applied to section 142. It was added in the RSC 1985 (5th Supp) consolidation for tax years ending after Nov. 1991.

Financial Institutions

Interpretation

142.2 (1) Definitions — In this section and sections 142.3 to 142.7,

Notes: Opening words of 142.2(1) amended by 2001 technical bill to extend application to 142.7, effective June 28, 1999.

"excluded property" of a taxpayer for a taxation year means property, held at any time in the taxation year by the taxpayer, that is

(a) a share of the capital stock of a corporation if, at any time in the taxation year, the taxpayer has a significant interest in the corporation,

(b) a property that is, at all times in the taxation year at which the taxpayer held the property, a prescribed payment card corporation share of the taxpayer,

(c) if the taxpayer is an investment dealer, a property that is, at all times in the taxation year at which the taxpayer held the property, a prescribed securities exchange investment of the taxpayer,

(d) a share of the capital stock of a corporation if

(i) control of the corporation is, at any time (referred to in this paragraph as the "acquisition of control time") that is in the 24-month period that begins immediately after the end of the year, acquired by

    (A) the taxpayer,

    (B) one or more persons related to the taxpayer (otherwise than by reason of a right referred to in paragraph 251(5)(b)), or

    (C) the taxpayer and one or more persons described in clause (B), and

  (ii) the taxpayer elects in writing to have subparagraph (i) apply and files the election with the Minister on or before the taxpayer's filing-due date for the taxpayer's taxation year that includes the acquisition of control time, or

  (e) a prescribed property;

Related Provisions: 142.2(2), (3) — Significant interest; 152(6.2) — Extended reassessment period where para. (d) applies.

Notes: 142.2(1)"excluded property" added by 2008 budget bill #2, for tax years that begin after Sept. 2006.

Regulations: 9001(2), 9002 (prescribed property for para. (e)); 9002.1 (prescribed payment card corporation share for para. (b)); 9002.2 [repealed] (prescribed securities exchange investment for para. (c), for taxation years that began before 2008).

"fair value property" of a taxpayer for a taxation year means property, held at any time in the taxation year by the taxpayer, that is — or it is reasonable to expect would, if the taxpayer held the property at the end of the taxation year, be — valued (otherwise than solely because its fair value was less than its cost to the taxpayer or, if the property is a specified debt obligation, because of a default of the debtor) in accordance with generally accepted accounting principles, at its fair value (determined in accordance with those principles) in the taxpayer's balance sheet as at the end of the taxation year;

Notes: Note that "fair value" is not necessarily identical to the tax term "fair market value" (discussed in Notes to 69(1)). See Marcovitz & Van Loan, "Amendments to the Rules Governing Securities Held by Financial Institutions", 2009 Cdn Tax Foundation conference report, 10:27-28.

Definition added by 2008 budget bill #2, for tax years that begin after Sept. 2006.

"financial institution" at any time means

  (a) a corporation that is, at that time,

    (i) a corporation referred to in any of paragraphs (a) to (e.1) of the definition "restricted financial institution" in subsection 248(1),

    (ii) an investment dealer, or

    (iii) a corporation controlled by one or more persons or partnerships each of which is a financial institution at that time, other than a corporation the control of which was acquired by reason of the default of a debtor where it is reasonable to consider that control is being retained solely for the purpose of minimizing any losses in respect of the debtor's default, and

  (b) a trust or partnership more than 50% of the fair market value of all interests in which are held at that time by one or more financial institutions,

but does not include

  (c) a corporation that is, at that time,

    (i) an investment corporation,

    (ii) a mortgage investment corporation,

    (iii) a mutual fund corporation, or

    (iv) a deposit insurance corporation (as defined in subsection 137.1(5)),

  (d) a trust that is a mutual fund trust at that time, nor

  (e) a prescribed person or partnership;

Related Provisions: 20(1)(l)(ii) — Reserve for doubtful debts; 20(1)(p)(ii) — Deduction for bad debts; 85(1.4), 87(1.5) — Definition applies to other provisions; 87(2)(e.3), (e.4) — Amalgamation — continuing corporation; 112(6)(c) — Definition applies to other provisions; 142.5 — Mark-to-market rules applicable to financial institution; 142.6(1) — Becoming or ceasing to be a financial institution; 248(1)"cost amount" — Definition applies to other provisions; 256(6)–(9) — Whether control ac-

quired; Reg. 9204(2) — Residual portion of specified debt obligation on ceasing to be a financial institution.

Notes: See Reg. 9000. 142.2(1)"financial institution"(a)(i) amended by 1998 Budget to change "(e)" to "(e.1)", effective for taxation years that begin after 1998.

Acquisition of units of an investment trust by a segregated fund does not cause the trust to become an FI if the seg fund is not an FI: VIEWS doc 2006-0187361R3.

See also Notes at end of 142.2.

Regulations: 9000 (prescribed persons for para. (e)).

I.T. Technical News: 14 (reporting of derivative income by mutual funds); 25 (*Silicon Graphics* case — dispersed control is not control).

"investment dealer" at any time means a corporation that is, at that time, a registered securities dealer;

Related Provisions: 142.2(1)"financial institution" — Investment dealer is a financial institution; 142.2(1)"mark-to-market property"(c) — debt held by investment dealer subject to mark-to-market rules.

"mark-to-market property" of a taxpayer for a taxation year means property (other than an excluded property) held at any time in the taxation year by the taxpayer that is

  (a) a share,

  (b) if the taxpayer is not an investment dealer, a specified debt obligation that is a fair value property of the taxpayer for the taxation year,

  (c) if the taxpayer is an investment dealer, a specified debt obligation, or

  (d) a tracking property of the taxpayer that is a fair value property of the taxpayer for the taxation year;

Related Provisions: 10.1(3)(a) — Derivatives deemed to be M2M property on election; 80.6(2)(b) — M2M property excluded from synthetic disposition arrangement rule; 85(1.4), 87(1.5) — Definition applies to other provisions; 87(2)(e.4), (e.5) — Amalgamation — continuing corporation; 88(1)(h) — Windup — continuing corporation; 112(6)(c) — Definition applies to other provisions; 136(1) — Cooperative not private corporation — exception; 138(11.5)(k.2) — Transfer of business by non-resident insurer; 142.2(2), (3) — Significant interest; 142.3(3) — M2M property not subject to rules re income from specified debt obligations; 142.5 — Mark-to-market rules; 248(1)"cost amount"(c.1) — Cost amount of M2M property; Reg. 6209(b)(i) — Prescribed securities for lending assets.

Notes: Most businesses must use accrual accounting: see Notes to 9(1) under "Cash-basis accounting". Financial institutions (FIs) must "mark" M2M property "to market", reporting all accrued gains and losses on income account whether or not the property is disposed of: 142.5(1), (2). See Friedlander, *Taxation of Corporate Finance* (Carswell, looseleaf or *Taxnet Pro* Reference Centre), chap. 6; Marcovitz & Van Loan, "Amendments to the Rules Governing Securities Held by Financial Institutions", 2009 Cdn Tax Foundation conference report, 10:1-40; VIEWS doc 2013-0505111I7.

Kruger Inc., 2016 FCA 186 ruled that a *non*-FI's foreign exchange option contracts were not "inventory", but the M2M method could be used for them. As of 2017, a non-FI requires a 10.1 election to use M2M.

142.2(1)"mark-to-market property" amended by 2008 budget bill #2, this version effective for tax years that begin after Nov. 6, 2007. For discussion of the 2008 amendments, which responded to changes in financial reporting in *CICA Handbook* §3855, see Backgrounder to Finance news release 2006-091 (Dec. 28/06) at fin.gc.ca; 2007-0240211C6; and Notes to 12.5. See also 2008-0289021E5 (adjustments due to revaluing under §3855 do not affect income). Before the 2008 amendments, see 2003-0003005 (units of a mutual fund trust are not M2M property); 2005-0126041C6 (non-resident insurer not carrying on business in Canada is subject to s. 116 on deemed disposition of a M2M property that is taxable Canadian property); 2005-0158791C5 (new standards in *CICA Handbook* §§1530 and 3955 will result in some specified debt obligations becoming M2M property for fiscal years that begin after Sept. 2006).

Regulations: See under 142.2(1)"excluded property"; those provisions applied to "mark-to-market property" for taxation years that began before Oct. 2006.

Interpretation Bulletins: IT-291R3: Transfer of property to a corporation under subsection 85(1).

"specified debt obligation" of a taxpayer means the interest held by the taxpayer in

  (a) a loan, bond, debenture, mortgage, hypothecary claim, note, agreement of sale or any other similar indebtedness, or

  (b) a debt obligation, where the taxpayer purchased the interest,

other than an interest in

  (c) an income bond, an income debenture, a small business development bond, a small business bond or a prescribed property, or

(d) an instrument issued by or made with a person to whom the taxpayer is related or with whom the taxpayer does not otherwise deal at arm's length, or in which the taxpayer has a significant interest.

Related Provisions: 85(1.4), 87(1.5) — Definition applies to other provisions; 87(2)(e.3) — Amalgamation of holder of obligation; 138(11.5)(k.1) — Definition applies to other provisions; 142.2(1)"mark-to-market property"(b), (c) — Mark-to-market rules for financial institutions; 142.2(2), (3) — Significant interest; 142.3(1) — Income from specified debt obligations; 142.4 — Disposition of specified debt obligation; 142.5 — Mark-to-market rules for financial institutions; 248(1)"cost amount" — Definition applies to other provisions; 248(1)"cost amount"(d.2) — Cost amount of specified debt obligation; 248(1) — Definition of "lending asset"; Reg. 6209(b)(ii) — Prescribed securities for lending assets.

Notes: For an SDO that is M2M property, see Notes to 142.2(1)"mark-to-market property". Otherwise, financial institutions compute income under 142.3 and Reg. 9100-9104. For details see Richard Marcovitz & Chris Van Loan, "Update on Financial Institutions Taxation", 2009 Cdn Tax Foundation conference report, 10:23-33.

A unit of a mutual fund trust is not an SDO: VIEWS doc 2003-0003005.

"Hypothecary claim" added to para. (a) by 2001 *Civil Code* harmonization bill, effective June 14, 2001. The change is non-substantive; see *Interpretation Act* s. 8.2.

Regulations: 9004 (prescribed property for para. (c)).

Interpretation Bulletins: IT-291R3: Transfer of property to a corporation under subsection 85(1).

"tracking property" of a taxpayer means property of the taxpayer the fair market value of which is determined primarily by reference to one or more criteria in respect of property (referred to in this definition as "tracked property") that, if owned by the taxpayer, would be mark-to-market property of the taxpayer, which criteria are

(a) the fair market value of the tracked property,

(b) the profits or gains from the disposition of the tracked property,

(c) the revenue, income or cash flow from the tracked property, or

(d) any other similar criteria in respect of the tracked property;

Notes: Tracking property includes mutual fund trusts, unit trusts, equity derivatives, American Depository Receipts and similar instruments: VIEWS docs 2009-0316681C6, 2009-0330051C6. It can also include partnership interests, insurance policies, segregated funds, interests in various trusts, options, total return swaps, equity forward contracts, other derivatives and interests held by a seller under securitizations: Richard Marcovitz & Chris Van Loan, "Update on Financial Institutions Taxation", 2009 Cdn Tax Foundation conference report, 10:3-23. Note that a partnership or trust controlled by an FI is an FI: 142.2(1)"financial institution"(b). See also 2009-0328781E5 (various issues on application of the tracking property rules).

"Primarily" is taken by the CRA to mean "more than 50%", but can mean "first in importance": see 73(3) Notes.

142.2(1)"tracking property" added by 2008 budget bill #2, effective for taxation years that begin after September 2006.

(2) Significant interest — For the purposes of the definitions "excluded property" and "specified debt obligation" in subsection (1) and subsection 142.6(1.6), a taxpayer has a significant interest in a corporation at any time if

(a) the taxpayer is related (otherwise than because of a right referred to in paragraph 251(5)(b)) to the corporation at that time; or

(b) the taxpayer holds, at that time,

(i) shares of the corporation that give the taxpayer 10% or more of the votes that could be cast under all circumstances at an annual meeting of shareholders of the corporation, and

(ii) shares of the corporation having a fair market value of 10% or more of the fair market value of all the issued shares of the corporation.

Related Provisions: 142.2(3) — Rules for determining significant interest; 142.2(4) — Extended meaning of "related".

Notes: See VIEWS doc 2009-0328781E5 (various issues on application of the tracking property rules).

142.2(2) opening words amended by 2013 budget bill #2, effective Dec. 12, 2013, to delete application to 142.2(1)"mark-to-market property" [which no longer refers directly to "significant interest"] and 142.2(5) [repealed in 2009].

142.2(2) opening words amended by 2008 budget bill #2, effective for taxation years that begin after September 2006, to add references to "excluded property", "specified debt obligation" and 142.6(1.6).

(3) Rules re significant interest — For the purpose of determining under subsection (2) whether a taxpayer has a significant interest in a corporation at any time,

(a) the taxpayer shall be deemed to hold each share that is held at that time by a person or partnership to whom the taxpayer is related (otherwise than because of a right referred to in paragraph 251(5)(b));

(b) a share of the corporation acquired by the taxpayer by reason of the default of a debtor shall be disregarded where it is reasonable to consider that the share is being retained for the purpose of minimizing any losses in respect of the debtor's default; and

(c) a share of the corporation that is prescribed in respect of the taxpayer shall be disregarded.

Related Provisions: 142.2(4) — Extended meaning of "related".

Regulations: 9003 (prescribed share for 142.2(3)(c)).

(4) Extension of meaning of "related" — For the purposes of this subsection and subsections (2) and (3), in determining if, at a particular time, a person or partnership is related to another person or partnership, the rules in section 251 are to be applied as if,

(a) a partnership (other than a partnership in respect of which any amount of the income or capital of the partnership that any entity may receive directly from the partnership at any time as a member of the partnership depends on the exercise by any entity of, or the failure by any entity to exercise, a discretionary power) were a corporation having capital stock of a single class divided into 100 issued shares and each member of the partnership owned, at the particular time, that proportion of the issued shares of that class that

(i) the fair market value of the member's interest in the partnership at the particular time

is of

(ii) the fair market value of all interests in the partnership at the particular time; and

(b) a trust (other than a trust in respect of which any amount of the income or capital of the trust that any entity may receive directly from the trust at any time as a beneficiary under the trust depends on the exercise by any entity of, or the failure by any entity to exercise, a discretionary power) were a corporation having capital stock of a single class divided into 100 issued shares and each beneficiary under the trust owned, at the particular time, that proportion of the issued shares of that class that

(i) the fair market value of the beneficiary's beneficial interest in the trust at the particular time

is of

(ii) the fair market value at that time of all beneficial interests in the trust.

Notes: 142.2(4) amended by 2008 budget bill #2, for taxation years that begin after Sept. 2006.

(5) [Repealed]

Notes: 142.2(5) repealed by 2008 budget bill #2, for tax years that begin after Sept. 2006.

Notes [s. 142.2]: 142.2 added by 1994 technical bill, for tax years that end after Feb. 22, 1994.

Definitions [s. 142.2]: "acquired" — 256(7)–(9); "acquisition of control time" — 142.2(1)"excluded property"(d)(i); "amount" — 248(1); "control" — 256(6)–(9); "controlled" — 256(6), (6.1); "corporation" — 248(1), *Interpretation Act* 35(1); "deposit insurance corporation" — 137.1(5); "disposition" — 248(1); "excluded property" — 142.2(1); "fair market value" — see 69(1) Notes; "fair value property" — 142.2(1); "filing-due date" — 248(1); "financial institution" — 142.2(1); "fiscal period" — 249(2)(b), 249.1; "income bond", "income debenture", "indexed debt obligation", "investment corporation" — 130(3)(a), 248(1); "investment dealer", "mark-to-market property" — 142.2(1); "Minister" — 248(1); "month" — *Interpretation Act* 35(1); "mortgage investment corporation" — 130.1(6), 248(1); "mutual fund corporation" — 131(8), 248(1); "mutual fund trust" — 132(6)–(7), 132.2(3)(n), 248(1); "partnership" — see 96(1) Notes; "person", "prescribed", "property", "registered securities dealer" — 248(1); "related" — 142.2(4), 251(2); "share", "shareholder" — 248(1); "significant interest" — 142.2(2), (3); "small business bond" — 15.2(3), 248(1); "small business development bond" — 15.1(3), 248(1); "specified debt obligation" — 142.2(1); "taxation year" — 249; "taxpayer" — 248(1); "tracking property" — 142.2(1); "trust" — 104(1), 248(1), (3); "writing" — *Interpretation Act* 35(1).

Income from Specified Debt Obligations

142.3 (1) Amounts to be included and deducted — Subject to subsections (3) and (4), where a taxpayer that is, in a taxation year, a financial institution holds a specified debt obligation at any time in the year,

(a) there shall be included in computing the income of the taxpayer for the year the amount, if any, prescribed in respect of the obligation;

(b) there shall be deducted in computing the income of the taxpayer for the year the amount, if any, prescribed in respect of the obligation; and

(c) except as provided by this section, paragraphs 12(1)(d) and (i) and 20(1)(l) and (p) and section 142.4, no amount shall be included or deducted in respect of payments under the obligation (other than fees and similar amounts) in computing the income of the taxpayer for the year.

Related Provisions: 87(2)(e.3) — Amalgamation — continuing corporation; 138(10)(a) — Application to insurance corporation; 138(12)"gross investment revenue"E(a), 138(12)"gross investment revenue"G(b) — Gross investment revenue of insurer; 142.3(3) — Exception for certain obligations; 142.3(4) — Impaired specified debt obligations; 142.4(1)"tax basis"(b), (i) — Disposition of specified debt obligation by financial institution; 142.4(9) — Disposition of part of obligation.

Notes: See Notes to 142.2(1)"specified debt obligation".

CRA considers a partnership to be a "taxpayer" for purposes of 142.3: VIEWS doc 2003-0182555.

Opening words of 142.3(1) amended by 1995-97 technical bill, last change effective on the same basis as the addition of 142.3(4).

For initial enactment of 142.3(1) see Notes at end of 142.3.

Regulations: 9101 (prescribed amounts).

(2) Failure to report accrued amounts — Subject to subsection (3), where

(a) a taxpayer holds a specified debt obligation at any time in a particular taxation year in which the taxpayer is a financial institution, and

(b) all or part of an amount required by paragraph (1)(a) or subsection 12(3) to be included in respect of the obligation in computing the taxpayer's income for a preceding taxation year was not so included,

that part of the amount shall be included in computing the taxpayer's income for the particular year, to the extent that it was not included in computing the taxpayer's income for a preceding taxation year.

Related Provisions: 142.3(3) — Exception for certain obligations; 142.4(1)"tax basis"(b) — Disposition of specified debt obligation by financial institution.

Notes: 142.3(2) added by 1995-97 technical bill, retroactive to the introduction of 142.3 (see Notes at end of 142.3). Former 142.3(2) was moved to 142.3(3).

(3) Exception for certain obligations — Subsections (1) and (2) do not apply for a taxation year in respect of a taxpayer's specified debt obligation that is

(a) a mark-to-market property for the year; or

(b) an indexed debt obligation, other than a prescribed obligation.

Notes: 142.3(3) renumbered from 142.3(2) and amended to refer to new (2) by 1995-97 technical bill, retroactive to the introduction of 142.3 (see Notes at end of 142.3).

(4) Impaired specified debt obligations — Subsection (1) does not apply to a taxpayer in respect of a specified debt obligation for the part of a taxation year throughout which the obligation is impaired where an amount in respect of the obligation is deductible because of subparagraph 20(1)(l)(ii) in computing the taxpayer's income for the year.

Notes: 142.3(4) added by 1995-97 technical bill, for tax years that end after Sept. 1997, or earlier by election (see Notes to 20(1)(l)).

Notes [s. 142.3]: 142.3 added by 1994 technical bill, effective for taxation years that end after February 22, 1994, except that it does not apply to debt obligations disposed of before February 23, 1994.

Definitions [s. 142.3]: "amount" — 248(1); "financial institution" — 142.2(1); "indexed debt obligation" — 248(1); "investment dealer", "mark-to-market property" — 142.2(1); "prescribed" — 248(1); "specified debt obligation" — 142.2(1); "taxation year" — 249; "taxpayer" — 248(1).

Disposition of Specified Debt Obligations

142.4 (1) Definitions — In this section,

"tax basis" of a specified debt obligation at any time to a taxpayer means the amount, if any, by which the total of all amounts each of which is

(a) the cost of the obligation to the taxpayer,

(b) an amount included under subsection 12(3) or 16(2) or (3), paragraph 142.3(1)(a) or subsection 142.3(2) in respect of the obligation in computing the taxpayer's income for a taxation year that began before that time,

(c) subject to subsection 138(13), where the taxpayer acquired the obligation in a taxation year ending before February 23, 1994, the part of the amount, if any, by which

(i) the principal amount of the obligation at the time it was acquired

exceeds

(ii) the cost to the taxpayer of the obligation

that was included in computing the taxpayer's income for a taxation year ending before February 23, 1994,

(d) subject to subsection 138(13), where the taxpayer is a life insurer, an amount in respect of the obligation that was deemed by paragraph 142(3)(a) of the *Income Tax Act*, chapter 148 of the Revised Statutes of Canada, 1952, as it read in its application to the 1977 taxation year, to be a gain for a taxation year ending before 1978,

(e) where the obligation is an indexed debt obligation, an amount determined under subparagraph 16(6)(a)(i) in respect of the obligation and included in computing the income of the taxpayer for a taxation year beginning before that time,

(f) an amount in respect of the obligation that was included in computing the taxpayer's income for a taxation year ending at or before that time in respect of changes in the value of the obligation attributable to the fluctuation in the value of a currency of a country other than Canada relative to Canadian currency, other than an amount included under paragraph 142.3(1)(a),

(g) an amount in respect of the obligation that was included under paragraph 12(1)(i) in computing the taxpayer's income for a taxation year beginning before that time, or

(h) where the obligation was a capital property of the taxpayer on February 22, 1994, an amount required by paragraph 53(1)(f) or (f.1) to be added in computing the adjusted cost base of the obligation to the taxpayer on that day

exceeds the total of all amounts each of which is

(i) an amount deducted under paragraph 142.3(1)(b) in respect of the obligation in computing the taxpayer's income for a taxation year beginning before that time,

(j) the amount of a payment received by the taxpayer under the obligation at or before that time, other than

(i) a fee or similar payment, and

(ii) proceeds of disposition of the obligation,

(k) subject to subsection 138(13), where the taxpayer acquired the obligation in a taxation year ending before February 23, 1994, the part of the amount, if any, by which

(i) the cost to the taxpayer of the obligation

exceeds

(ii) the principal amount of the obligation at the time it was acquired

that was deducted in computing the taxpayer's income for a taxation year ending before February 23, 1994,

(l) subject to subsection 138(13), where the taxpayer is a life insurer, an amount in respect of the obligation that was deemed by paragraph 142(3)(b) of the *Income Tax Act*, chapter 148 of the Revised Statutes of Canada, 1952, as it read in its application to the 1977 taxation year, to be a loss for a taxation year ending before 1978,

(m) an amount that was deducted under subsection 20(14) in respect of the obligation in computing the taxpayer's income for a taxation year beginning before that time,

(n) where the obligation is an indexed debt obligation, an amount determined under subparagraph 16(6)(a)(ii) in respect of the obligation and deducted in computing the income of the taxpayer for a taxation year beginning before that time,

(o) an amount in respect of the obligation that was deducted in computing the taxpayer's income for a taxation year ending at or before that time in respect of changes in the value of the obligation attributable to the fluctuation in the value of a currency of a country other than Canada relative to Canadian currency, other than an amount deducted under paragraph 142.3(1)(b),

(p) an amount in respect of the obligation that was deducted under paragraph 20(1)(p) in computing the taxpayer's income for a taxation year ending at or before that time, or

(q) where the obligation was a capital property of the taxpayer on February 22, 1994, an amount required by paragraph 53(2)(b.2) or (g) to be deducted in computing the adjusted cost base of the obligation to the taxpayer on that day;

Related Provisions: 138(13) — Variation in tax basis of certain insurers; 248(1)"cost amount"(d.2) — Cost amount of specified debt obligation is tax basis; 261(5)(f) — Interpretation when functional currency reporting in effect.

Notes: Definition amended retroactive to its introduction by 1995-97 technical bill.

"transition amount" of a taxpayer in respect of the disposition of a specified debt obligation has the meaning assigned by regulation.

Related Provisions: 142.4(7)A — Current amount based on transition amount.

Regulations: 9201 (transition amount).

(2) Scope of section — This section applies to the disposition of a specified debt obligation by a taxpayer that is a financial institution, except that this section does not apply to the disposition of a specified debt obligation that is a mark-to-market property for the taxation year in which the disposition occurs.

Related Provisions: 87(2)(e.3) — Amalgamation — continuing corporation; 138(10)(b) — Application to insurance corporation; 142.3(1)(c) — Amount deductible in respect of specified debt obligation; 142.4(9) — Disposition of part of obligation.

Notes: See at end of 142.4.

(3) Rules applicable to disposition — Where a taxpayer has disposed of a specified debt obligation after February 22, 1994,

(a) except as provided by paragraph 79.1(7)(d) or this section, no amount shall be included or deducted in respect of the disposition in computing the taxpayer's income; and

(b) except where the obligation is an indexed debt obligation (other than a prescribed obligation), paragraph 20(14)(a) shall not apply in respect of the disposition.

Related Provisions: 142.4(2) — Scope of section.

Notes: 142.4(3) amended retroactive to its introduction by 1995-97 technical bill.

(4) Inclusions and deductions re disposition — Subject to subsection (5), where after 1994 a taxpayer disposes of a specified debt obligation in a taxation year,

(a) where the transition amount in respect of the disposition of the obligation is positive, it shall be included in computing the income of the taxpayer for the year;

(b) where the transition amount in respect of the disposition of the obligation is negative, the absolute value of the transition amount shall be deducted in computing the income of the taxpayer for the year;

(c) where the taxpayer has a gain from the disposition of the obligation,

(i) the current amount of the gain shall be included in computing the income of the taxpayer for the year, and

(ii) there shall be included in computing the taxpayer's income for taxation years that end on or after the day of disposition the amount allocated, in accordance with prescribed rules, to the year in respect of the residual portion of the gain; and

(d) where the taxpayer has a loss from the disposition of the obligation,

(i) the current amount of the loss shall be deducted in computing the taxpayer's income for the year, and

(ii) there shall be deducted in computing the taxpayer's income for taxation years that end on or after the day of disposition the amount allocated, in accordance with prescribed rules, to the year in respect of the residual portion of the loss.

Related Provisions: 39(1)(a)(ii.2) — No capital gain on disposition; 87(2)(g.2) — Amalgamation — continuing corp; 142.4(2) — Scope of section; 142.4(5) — Where subsec. (4) does not apply; 142.4(7) — Current amount; 142.4(8) — Residual portion; 142.4(9) — Disposition of part of obligation; 142.4(11) — Payments received on or after disposition; 142.7(13) — Application on transfer of foreign bank business from Canadian affiliate to branch; Reg. 2405(3)"gross Canadian life investment income"(d.1), (i.1) — Inclusion in/deduction from life insurer's income; Reg. 2411(4.1) — Inclusion in insurer's net investment revenue.

Notes: CRA considers a partnership to be a "taxpayer" for 142.4: doc 2003-0182555.

142.4(4) amended retroactive to its introduction by 1995-97 technical bill.

Regulations: 9203, 9204 (prescribed rules — residual portion).

(5) Gain or loss not amortized — Where after February 22, 1994 a taxpayer disposes of a specified debt obligation in a taxation year, and

(a) the obligation is

(i) an indexed debt obligation (other than a prescribed obligation), or

(ii) a debt obligation prescribed in respect of the taxpayer,

(b) the disposition occurred

(i) before 1995,

(ii) after 1994 in connection with the transfer of all or part of a business of the taxpayer to a person or partnership, or

(iii) because of paragraph 142.6(1)(c), or

(c) in the case of a taxpayer other than a life insurance corporation,

(i) the disposition occurred before 1996, and

(ii) the taxpayer elects in writing, filed with the Minister before July 1997, to have this paragraph apply,

the following rules apply:

(d) subsection (4) does not apply to the disposition,

(e) there shall be included in computing the taxpayer's income for the year the amount, if any, by which the taxpayer's proceeds of disposition exceed the tax basis of the obligation to the taxpayer immediately before the disposition, and

(f) there shall be deducted in computing the taxpayer's income for the year the amount, if any, by which the tax basis of the obligation to the taxpayer immediately before the disposition exceeds the taxpayer's proceeds of disposition.

Related Provisions: 39(1)(a)(ii.2) — No capital gain on disposition; 142.4(2) — Scope of section; Reg. 2411(4)A(c.1), 2411(4)B(a.1) — Inclusion in insurer's net investment revenue.

Notes: 142.4(5) amended retroactive to its introduction by 1995-97 technical bill.

Regulations: 9202(2), (4), (5) (debt obligations prescribed for 142.2(5)(a)(ii)).

(6) Gain or loss from disposition of obligation — For the purposes of this section,

(a) where the amount determined under paragraph (c) in respect of the disposition of a specified debt obligation by a taxpayer is positive, that amount is the taxpayer's gain from the disposition of the obligation;

(b) where the amount determined under paragraph (c) in respect of the disposition of a specified debt obligation by a taxpayer is negative, the absolute value of that amount is the taxpayer's loss from the disposition of the obligation; and

(c) the amount determined under this paragraph in respect of the disposition of a specified debt obligation by a taxpayer is the positive or negative amount determined by the formula

$$A - (B + C)$$

where

A   is the taxpayer's proceeds of disposition,

B   is the tax basis of the obligation to the taxpayer immediately before the time of disposition, and

C   is the taxpayer's transition amount in respect of the disposition.

Related Provisions: 257 — Formula cannot calculate to less than zero.

Notes: 142.4(6) amended retroactive to its introduction by 1995-97 technical bill.

(7) Current amount — For the purposes of subsections (4) and (8), the current amount of a taxpayer's gain or loss from the disposition of a specified debt obligation is

(a) where the taxpayer has a gain from the disposition of the obligation, the part, if any, of the gain that is reasonably attributable to a material increase in the probability, or perceived probability, that the debtor will make all payments as required by the obligation; and

(b) where the taxpayer has a loss from the disposition of the obligation, the amount that the taxpayer claims not exceeding the part, if any, of the loss that is reasonably attributable to a default by the debtor or a material decrease in the probability, or perceived probability, that the debtor will make all payments as required by the obligation.

Notes: 142.4(7) amended retroactive to its introduction by 1995-97 technical bill.

(8) Residual portion of gain or loss — For the purpose of subsection (4), the residual portion of a taxpayer's gain or loss from the disposition of a specified debt obligation is the amount, if any, by which the gain or loss exceeds the current amount of the gain or loss.

Related Provisions: 142.4(7) — Current amount.

Notes: 142.4(8) amended retroactive to its introduction by 1995-97 technical bill.

(9) Disposition of part of obligation — Where a taxpayer disposes of part of a specified debt obligation, section 142.3 and this section apply as if the part disposed of and the part retained were separate specified debt obligations.

Related Provisions: 248(27) — Partial forgiveness of debt obligation — effect on debtor.

Notes: 142.4(9) amended retroactive to its introduction by 1995-97 technical bill.

(10) Penalties and bonuses — Notwithstanding subsection 18(9.1), where a taxpayer that holds a specified debt obligation receives a penalty or bonus because of the repayment before maturity of all or part of the principal amount of the debt obligation, the payment is deemed to be received by the taxpayer as proceeds of disposition of the specified debt obligation.

Notes: 142.4(10) added by 1995-97 technical bill, effective for taxation years that end after Feb. 22, 1994.

Income Tax Folios: S4-F2-C1: Deductibility of fines and penalties [replaces IT-104R3].

(11) Payments received on or after disposition — For the purposes of this section, where at any time a taxpayer receives a payment (other than proceeds of disposition) under a specified debt

obligation on or after the disposition of the obligation, the payment is deemed not to have been so received at that time but to have been so received immediately before the disposition.

Notes [subsec. 142.4(11)]: 142.4(11) added by 1995-97 technical bill, effective for taxation years that end after Feb. 22, 1994 (i.e., retroactive to introduction of 142.4).

Notes [s. 142.4]: 142.4 added by 1994 technical bill, effective for taxation years that end after February 22, 1994.

Definitions [s. 142.4]: "adjusted cost base" — 54, 248(1); "amount" — 248(1); "Canadian currency" — 261(5)(f)(i); "capital property" — 54, 248(1); "currency of a country other than Canada" — 261(5)(f)(ii); "current amount" — 142.4(7); "financial institution" — 142.2(1); "indexed debt obligation" — 248(1); "investment dealer" — 142.2(1); "life insurance corporation", "life insurer" — 248(1); "mark-to-market property" — 142.2(1); "Minister" — 248(1); "partnership" — see 96(1) Notes; "person", "prescribed" — 248(1); "principal amount" — 248(1), (26); "regulation" — 248(1); "residual portion" — 142.4(8); "specified debt obligation" — 142.2(1); "tax basis" — 142.4(1); "taxation year" — 249; "taxpayer" — 248(1); "transition amount" — 142.4(1); "writing" — *Interpretation Act* 35(1).

Mark-to-Market Properties

142.5 (1) Income treatment for profits and losses — Where, in a taxation year that begins after October 1994, a taxpayer that is a financial institution in the year disposes of a property that is a mark-to-market property for the year,

(a) there shall be included in computing the taxpayer's income for the year the profit, if any, from the disposition; and

(b) there shall be deducted in computing the taxpayer's income for the year the loss, if any, from the disposition.

Related Provisions: 39(1)(a)(ii.2) — No capital gain on disposition; 138(10)(a) — Application to insurance corporation; 142.5(2) — Deemed disposition at year-end.

Notes: See Notes to 142.2(1)"mark-to-market property".

(2) Mark-to-market requirement — Where a taxpayer that is a financial institution in a taxation year holds, at the end of the year, a mark-to-market property for the year, the taxpayer shall be deemed

(a) to have disposed of the property immediately before the end of the year for proceeds equal to its fair market value at the time of disposition, and

(b) to have reacquired the property at the end of the year at a cost equal to those proceeds.

Related Provisions: 10.1(3)(a) — Election for M2M treatment of derivatives; 54"superficial loss"(c) — Superficial loss rule does not apply; 88(1)(i) — Windup of sub into parent; 112(5.6)(a)(i) — Stop-loss rules inapplicable; 138(10)(a) — Application to insurer; 138(11.31)(a) — Change in use rules for insurer do not apply; 142.5(1) — Disposition is on income account; 142.5(8)–(9) — Transitional rules; 142.6(2) — Acquisition date under 142.5(2) to be ignored.

Notes: See Notes to 142.2(1)"mark-to-market property".

For the impact on the foreign tax credit of the mark-to-market deemed disposition, see VIEWS doc 2012-0462151I7.

I.T. Technical News: 14 (reporting of derivative income by mutual funds).

(3) Mark-to-market debt obligation — Where a taxpayer is a financial institution in a particular taxation year that begins after October 1994, the following rules apply with respect to a specified debt obligation that is a mark-to-market property of the taxpayer for the particular year:

(a) paragraph 12(1)(c) and subsections 12(3) and 20(14) and (21) do not apply to the obligation in computing the taxpayer's income for the particular year;

(b) there shall be included in computing the taxpayer's income for the particular year an amount received by the taxpayer in the particular year as, on account of, in lieu of payment of, or in satisfaction of, interest on the obligation, to the extent that the interest was not included in computing the taxpayer's income for a preceding taxation year; and

(c) for the purpose of paragraph (b), where the taxpayer was deemed by subsection (2) or paragraph 142.6(1)(b) to have disposed of the obligation in a preceding taxation year, no part of an amount included in computing the income of the taxpayer for that preceding year because of the disposition shall be considered to be in respect of interest on the obligation.

Related Provisions: 138(10)(a) — Application to insurance corporation.

(4) Proceeds — mark-to-market property — For greater certainty, if a taxpayer is a financial institution in a taxation year and disposes of a share that is mark-to-market property of the taxpayer for the year, the taxpayer's proceeds from the disposition do not include any amount that would otherwise be proceeds from the disposition to the extent that the amount is deemed by subsection 84(2) or (3) to be a dividend received except to the extent the dividend is deemed by subparagraph 88(2)(b)(ii) not to be a dividend.

Related Provisions: 112(5.2)B, 112(5.21) — Parallel rules re intercorporate dividend deduction.

Notes: 142.5(4) added by 2018 budget bill #2, for dispositions after Feb. 26, 2018.

Former 142.5(4): see Notes to repealed 142.5(5)-(7).

(5)–(7) [Repealed]

Notes: Former 142.5(4)-(7) repealed by 2002-2013 technical bill (Part 5 — technical), for tax years that begin after Oct. 2011. 142.5(4) and (6) applied only to tax years that included Oct. 31, 1994, and 142.5(5) and (7) to tax years that began before 1999. Added by 1994 technical bill and amended by 1995-97 technical bill.

(8) First deemed disposition of debt obligation — Where

(a) in a particular taxation year that ends after October 30, 1994, a taxpayer disposed of a specified debt obligation that is a mark-to-market property of the taxpayer for the following taxation year, and

(b) either

(i) the disposition occurred because of subsection (2) and the particular year includes October 31, 1994, or

(ii) the disposition occurred because of paragraph 142.6(1)(b),

the following rules apply:

(c) subsection 20(21) does not apply to the disposition, and

(d) where

(i) an amount has been deducted under paragraph 20(1)(p) in respect of the obligation in computing the taxpayer's income for the particular year or a preceding taxation year, and

(ii) section 12.4 does not apply to the disposition,

there shall be included in computing the taxpayer's income for the particular year the amount, if any, by which

(iii) the total of all amounts referred to in subparagraph (i)

exceeds

(iv) the total of all amounts included under paragraph 12(1)(i) in respect of the obligation in computing the taxpayer's income for the particular year or a preceding taxation year.

(8.1) Application of subsec. (8.2) — Subsection (8.2) applies to a taxpayer for its transition year if

(a) subsection (2) deems the taxpayer to have disposed of a particular specified debt obligation immediately before the end of its transition year (in subsection (8.2) referred to as "the particular disposition"); and

(b) the particular specified debt obligation was owned by the taxpayer at the end of its base year and was not a mark-to-market property of the taxpayer for its base year.

Related Provisions: 142.51(1) — Definitions apply to 142.5(8.1).

Notes: 142.5(8.1) added by 2008 budget bill #2, effective for taxation years that begin after September 2006.

(8.2) Rules applicable to first deemed disposition of debt obligation — If this subsection applies to a taxpayer for its transition year, the following rules apply to the taxpayer in respect of the particular disposition:

(a) subsection 20(21) does not apply to the taxpayer in respect of the particular disposition; and

(b) if section 12.4 does not apply to the taxpayer in respect of the particular disposition, there shall be included in computing

the taxpayer's income for its transition year the amount, if any, by which

(i) the total of all amounts each of which is

(A) an amount deducted under paragraph 20(1)(l) in respect of the particular specified debt obligation of the taxpayer in computing the taxpayer's income for its base year, or

(B) an amount deducted under paragraph 20(1)(p) in respect of the particular specified debt obligation of the taxpayer in computing the taxpayer's income for a taxation year that preceded its transition year,

exceeds

(ii) the total of all amounts each of which is

(A) an amount included under paragraph 12(1)(d) in respect of the particular specified debt obligation of the taxpayer in computing the taxpayer's income for its transition year, or

(B) an amount included under paragraph 12(1)(i) in respect of the particular specified debt obligation of the taxpayer in computing the taxpayer's income for its transition year or a preceding taxation year.

Related Provisions: 142.51(1) — Definitions apply to 142.5(8.2); 142.5(8.1) — Conditions for subsec. (8.2) to apply.

Notes: 142.5(8.2) added by 2008 budget bill #2, effective for taxation years that begin after September 2006.

(9) Transition — property acquired on rollover — Where

(a) a taxpayer acquired a property before October 31, 1994 at a cost less than the fair market value of the property at the time of acquisition,

(b) the property was transferred, directly or indirectly, to the taxpayer by a person that would never have been a financial institution before the transfer if the definition "financial institution" in subsection 142.2(1) had always applied,

(c) the cost is less than the fair market value because subsection 85(1) applied in respect of the disposition of the property by the person, and

(d) subsection (2) deemed the taxpayer to have disposed of the property in its particular taxation year that includes October 31, 1994,

the following rules apply:

(e) where the taxpayer would, but for this paragraph, have a taxable capital gain for the particular year from the disposition of the property, the part of the taxable capital gain that can reasonably be considered to have arisen while the property was held by a person described in paragraph (b) shall be deemed to be a taxable capital gain of the taxpayer from the disposition of the property for the taxation year in which the taxpayer disposes of the property otherwise than because of subsection (2), and not to be a taxable capital gain for the particular year, and

(f) where the taxpayer has a profit (other than a capital gain) from the disposition of the property, the part of the profit that can reasonably be considered to have arisen while the property was held by a person described in paragraph (b) shall be included in computing the taxpayer's income for the taxation year in which the taxpayer disposes of the property otherwise than because of subsection (2), and shall not be included in computing the taxpayer's income for the particular year.

Notes: For the meaning of "indirectly" in para. (b), see Notes to 17.1(1).

Notes [s. 142.5]: CRA considers a partnership to be a "taxpayer" for purposes of 142.5: VIEWS doc 2003-0182555.

142.5 added by 1994 technical bill, for taxation years that end after Oct. 30, 1994.

Definitions [s. 142.5]: "allowable capital loss" — 38(b), 248(1); "amount" — 248(1); "base year" — 142.51(1); "capital gain" — 39(1)(a), 248(1); "capital property" — 54, 248(1); "disposition", "dividend" — 248(1); "fair market value" — see 69(1) Notes; "financial institution", "mark-to-market property" — 142.2(1); "non-resident" — 248(1); "particular disposition" — 142.5(8.1)(a); "prescribed", "property", "share" — 248(1); "specified debt obligation" — 142.2(1); "taxable Canadian property" — 248(1); "taxable capital gain" — 38(a), 248(1); "taxation year" — 249; "taxpayer" — 248(1); "transition year" — 142.51(1).

142.51 [Financial institutions accounting rule changes — 2006-2011 transition] — [No longer relevant]

Notes: 142.51 is parallel to 12.5, 20.4 and 138(16)-(25) — transitional rules to phase in changes in accounting for financial instruments required by *CICA Handbook* §3855. See Notes to 12.5.

142.51 added by 2008 budget bill #2, for taxation years that begin after Sept. 2006.

Additional Rules

142.6 (1) Becoming or ceasing to be a financial institution — Where, at a particular time after February 22, 1994, a taxpayer becomes or ceases to be a financial institution,

(a) where a taxation year of the taxpayer would not, but for this paragraph, end immediately before the particular time,

(i) except for the purpose of subsection 132(6.1), the taxpayer's taxation year that would otherwise have included the particular time is deemed to have ended immediately before that time and a new taxation year of the taxpayer is deemed to have begun at that time, and

(ii) for the purpose of determining the taxpayer's fiscal period after the particular time, the taxpayer shall be deemed not to have established a fiscal period before that time;

(b) if the taxpayer becomes a financial institution, the taxpayer is deemed to have disposed, immediately before the end of its particular taxation year that ends immediately before the particular time, of each of the following properties held by the taxpayer for proceeds equal to the property's fair market value at the time of that disposition:

(i) a specified debt obligation, or

(ii) a mark-to-market property of the taxpayer for the particular taxation year or for the taxpayer's taxation year that includes the particular time;

(c) where the taxpayer ceases to be a financial institution, the taxpayer shall be deemed to have disposed, immediately before the end of its taxation year that ends immediately before the particular time, of each property held by the taxpayer that is a specified debt obligation (other than a mark-to-market property of the taxpayer for the year), for proceeds equal to its fair market value at the time of disposition; and

(d) the taxpayer is deemed to have reacquired, at the end of its taxation year that ends immediately before the particular time, each property deemed by paragraph (b) or (c) to have been disposed of by the taxpayer, at a cost equal to the proceeds of disposition of the property.

Related Provisions: 54"superficial loss"(c) — Superficial loss rule does not apply to disposition under 142.6(1)(b); 87(2)(g.2) — Application of rule to predecessor corporation on amalgamation; 112(5.6)(a)(ii) — Stop-loss rules inapplicable; 142.4(5)(b)(iii) — Gain or loss not amortized; 142.5(8)(b)(ii) — First deemed disposition of debt obligation; 142.6(2) — Acquisition date under 142.6(1) to be ignored.

Notes: CRA considers a partnership to be a "taxpayer" for purposes of 142.6: VIEWS doc 2003-0182555.

142.6(1)(b) and (d) amended by 2002-2013 technical bill (Part 5 — technical), for taxation years that end after 1998.

142.6(1) amended by 1998 Budget (effective 1998) and 1994 technical bill.

(1.1) Ceasing to use property in Canadian business — If at a particular time in a taxation year a taxpayer that is a non-resident financial institution (other than a life insurance corporation) ceases to use, in connection with a business or part of a business carried on by the taxpayer in Canada immediately before the particular time, a property that is a mark-to-market property of the taxpayer for the year or a specified debt obligation, but that is not a property that was disposed of by the taxpayer at the particular time,

(a) the taxpayer is deemed

(i) to have disposed of the property immediately before the time that was immediately before the particular time for pro-

ceeds equal to its fair market value at the time of disposition and to have received those proceeds at the time of disposition in the course of carrying on the business or the part of the business, as the case may be, and

(ii) to have reacquired the property at the particular time at a cost equal to those proceeds; and

(b) in determining the consequences of the disposition in subparagraph (a)(i), subsection 142.4(11) does not apply to any payment received by the taxpayer after the particular time.

Related Provisions: 10(12) — Parallel rule for inventory; 142.6(1.3) — Specified debt obligation market to market; 142.6(2) — No effect on determination of when share acquired.

Notes: 142.6(1.1) added by 2001 technical bill, effective June 28, 1999 in respect of an authorized foreign bank, and Aug. 9, 2000 in any other case.

(1.2) Beginning to use property in a Canadian business — If at a particular time a taxpayer that is a non-resident financial institution (other than a life insurance corporation) begins to use, in connection with a business or part of a business carried on by the taxpayer in Canada, a property that is a mark-to-market property of the taxpayer for the year that includes the particular time or a specified debt obligation, but that is not a property that was acquired by the taxpayer at the particular time, the taxpayer is deemed

(a) to have disposed of the property immediately before the time that was immediately before the particular time for proceeds equal to its fair market value at the time of disposition; and

(b) to have reacquired the property at the particular time at a cost equal to those proceeds.

Related Provisions: 10(14) — Parallel rule for inventory; 142.6(2) — No effect on determination of when share acquired.

Notes: 142.6(1.2) added by 2001 technical bill, effective June 28, 1999 in respect of an authorized foreign bank, and Aug. 9, 2000 in any other case.

(1.3) Specified debt obligation marked to market — In applying subsection (1.1) to a taxpayer in respect of a property in a taxation year,

(a) the definition "mark-to-market property" in subsection 142.2(1) shall be applied as if the year ended immediately before the particular time referred to in subsection (1.1); and

(b) if the taxpayer does not have financial statements for the period ending immediately before the particular time referred to in subsection (1.1), references in the definition to financial statements for the year shall be read as references to the financial statements that it is reasonable to expect would have been prepared if the year had ended immediately before the particular time.

Notes: 142.6(1.3) added by 2001 technical bill, effective June 28, 1999 in respect of an authorized foreign bank, and Aug. 9, 2000 in any other case.

(1.4) Change in status — prescribed payment card corporation share — If, at any particular time in a taxation year of a taxpayer that is a financial institution for the taxation year, a property becomes a mark-to-market property of the taxpayer for the taxation year because it ceased, at the particular time, to be a prescribed payment card corporation share of the taxpayer,

(a) the taxpayer is deemed

(i) to have disposed of the property immediately before the particular time for proceeds of disposition equal to its fair market value immediately before the particular time, and

(ii) to have acquired the property, at the particular time, at a cost equal to those proceeds; and

(b) subsection 142.5(1) does not apply to the disposition under subparagraph (a)(i).

Related Provisions: 142.6(2) — Rule does not affect determination of when taxpayer acquired share.

Notes: 142.6(1.4) added by 2008 budget bill #2, effective for taxation years that end after Feb. 22, 1994.

Regulations: 9002.1 (prescribed payment card corporation share).

(1.5) Change in status — prescribed securities exchange investment — If, at any particular time in a taxation year of a taxpayer that is a financial institution for the taxation year, a property becomes a mark-to-market property of the taxpayer for the taxation year because it ceased, at the particular time, to be a prescribed securities exchange investment of the taxpayer,

(a) the taxpayer is deemed

(i) to have disposed of the property immediately before the particular time for proceeds of disposition equal to its fair market value immediately before the particular time, and

(ii) to have acquired the property, at the particular time, at a cost equal to those proceeds; and

(b) subsection 142.5(1) does not apply to the disposition under subparagraph (a)(i).

Related Provisions: 142.6(2) — Rule does not affect determination of when taxpayer acquired share.

Notes: 142.6(1.5) added by 2008 budget bill #2, effective for taxation years that begin after 1998.

Regulations: 9002.2 [repealed] (prescribed securities exchange investment).

(1.6) Change in status — significant interest — If, at the end of a particular taxation year of a taxpayer that is a financial institution for the taxation year, the taxpayer holds a share of the capital stock of a corporation, the taxpayer has a significant interest in that corporation at any time in the particular taxation year and the share is mark-to-market property of the taxpayer for the immediately following taxation year, the taxpayer is deemed to have,

(a) disposed of the share immediately before the end of the particular taxation year for proceeds of disposition equal to the fair market value, at that time, of the share; and

(b) acquired the share at the end of the particular taxation year at a cost equal to those proceeds.

Related Provisions: 142.2(2), (3) — Significant interest; 142.6(2) — Rule does not affect determination of when taxpayer acquired share; 152(6.2) — Extended reassessment period.

Notes: 142.6(1.6) added by 2008 budget bill #2, effective for taxation years that begin after September 2006.

(2) Deemed disposition not applicable — For the purposes of this Act, the determination of when a taxpayer acquired a share shall be made without regard to a disposition or acquisition that occurred because of subsection 142.5(2) or subsection (1), (1.1), (1.2), (1.4), (1.5) or (1.6).

Notes: 142.6(2) amended by 2008 budget bill #2 to refer to (1.4)-(1.6), effective for taxation years that begin after September 2006.

142.6(2) amended by 2001 technical bill, last change effective Aug. 9, 2000.

142.6(2) added by 1994 technical bill, for tax years that end after Feb. 22, 1994.

(3) Property not inventory — Where a taxpayer is a financial institution in a taxation year, inventory of the taxpayer in the year does not include property that is

(a) a specified debt obligation (other than a mark-to-market property for the year); or

(b) where the year begins after October 1994, a mark-to-market property for the year.

Related Provisions: 66.3(1)(a)(ii) — Rule in 142.6(3) overrides rule for certain exploration and development shares; 142.6(4) — Property that was inventory before introduction of new rules.

Notes: 142.6(3) added by 1994 technical bill, effective for taxation years that end after February 22, 1994.

(4) [Applies to 1994 only]

Notes: 142.6(4) added by 1994 technical bill, effective for taxation years that end after February 22, 1994.

(5) Debt obligations acquired in rollover transactions — Where,

(a) on February 23, 1994, a financial institution that is a corporation held a specified debt obligation (other than a mark-to-market property for the taxation year that includes that day) that was

at any particular time before that day held by another corporation, and

(b) between the particular time and February 23, 1994, the only transactions affecting the ownership of the property were rollover transactions,

the financial institution shall be deemed, in respect of that obligation, to be the same corporation as, and a continuation of, the other corporation.

Related Provisions: 87(2)(e), (e.2) — Rule overrides normal rules on amalgamation; 87(2)(e.3) — Continuity of corporation on amalgamation; 138(11.5)(k.1) — Continuity of corporation on rollover of insurance business by non-resident; 142.6(6) — Rollover transaction.

Notes: 142.6(5) added by 1994 technical bill, effective for taxation years that end after February 22, 1994.

(6) Definition of "rollover transaction" — For the purpose of subsection (5), "rollover transaction" means a transaction to which subsection 87(2), 88(1) or 138(11.5) or (11.94) applies, other than a transaction to which paragraph 138(11.5)(e) requires the provisions of subsection 85(1) to be applied.

Notes: 142.6(6) added by 1994 technical bill, for tax years that end after Feb. 22, 1994.

(7) Superficial loss rule not applicable — Subsection 18(13) does not apply to the disposition of a property by a taxpayer after October 30, 1994 where

(a) the taxpayer is a financial institution when the disposition occurs and the property is a specified debt obligation or a mark-to-market property for the taxation year in which the disposition occurs; or

(b) the disposition occurs because of paragraph (1)(b).

Notes: 142.6(7) added by 1994 technical bill, effective for dispositions occurring after Oct. 30, 1994, with limited grandfathering for a disposition of a debt obligation before July 1995. (The same application applies to the repeal of 138(5.2).)

(8)–(10) [No longer relevant]

Notes: 142.6(8) (added by 1995-97 technical bill for 1993 and later taxation years) provided an election for a financial institution to trigger accrued capital gains and losses at the end of its last taxation year that ended before Feb. 23, 1994, with a deemed reacquisition of the property at FMV or another value; and (9)-(10) deemed the election not to have been made in certain cases. They are reproduced up to the 42nd ed.

Definitions [s. 142.6]: "adjusted cost base" — 54, 248(1); "allowable capital loss" — 38(b), 248(1); "amount", "assessment", "authorized foreign bank" — 248(1); "bank" — 248(1); "business" — 248(1); "Canada" — 255, Interpretation Act 35(1); "capital property" — 54, 248(1); "corporation" — 248(1), Interpretation Act 35(1); "depreciable property" — 13(21), 248(1); "disposition" — 248(1); "fair market value" — see 69(1) Notes; "filing-due date" — 248(1); "financial institution" — 142.2(1); "fiscal period" — 249.1; "inventory", "life insurance corporation" — 248(1); "mark-to-market property" — 142.2(1); "Minister" — 248(1); "net capital loss" — 111(8), 248(1); "non-resident", "prescribed", "property" — 248(1); "rollover transaction" — 142.6(6); "share" — 248(1); "significant interest" — 142.2(2), (3); "specified debt obligation" — 142.2(1); "taxable capital gain" — 38(a), 248(1); "taxation year" — 249; "taxpayer" — 248(1); "writing" — Interpretation Act 35(1).

Conversion of Foreign Bank Affiliate to Branch

142.7 (1) Definitions — The definitions in this subsection apply in this section.

"Canadian affiliate" of an entrant bank at any particular time means a Canadian corporation that was, immediately before the particular time, affiliated with the entrant bank and that was, at all times during the period that began on February 11, 1999 and ended immediately before the particular time,

(a) affiliated with either

(i) the entrant bank, or

(ii) a foreign bank (within the meaning assigned by section 2 of the Bank Act) that is affiliated with the entrant bank at the particular time; and

(b) either

(i) a bank,

(ii) a corporation authorized under the *Trust and Loan Companies Act* to carry on the business of offering to the public its services as trustee, or

(iii) a corporation of which the principal activity in Canada consists of any of the activities referred to in subparagraphs 518(3)(a)(i) to (v) of the *Bank Act* and in which the entrant bank or a non-resident person affiliated with the entrant bank holds shares under the authority, directly or indirectly, of an order issued by the Minister of Finance or the Governor in Council under subsection 521(1) of that Act.

Related Provisions: 142.7(2)(a) — Effect of qualifying foreign merger.

Notes: See Notes at end of 142.7.

"eligible property" of a Canadian affiliate at any time means a property described in any of paragraphs 85(1.1)(a) to (g.1) that is, immediately before that time, used or held by it in carrying on its business in Canada.

"entrant bank" means a non-resident corporation that is, or has applied to the Superintendent of Financial Institutions to become, an authorized foreign bank.

"qualifying foreign merger" means a merger or combination of two or more corporations that would be a "foreign merger" within the meaning assigned by subsection 87(8.1) if that subsection were read without reference to the words "and otherwise than as a result of the distribution of property to one corporation on the winding-up of another corporation.

(2) Qualifying foreign merger — Where an entrant bank was formed as the result of a qualifying foreign merger, after February 11, 1999, of two or more corporations (referred to in this subsection as "predecessors"), and at the time immediately before the merger, there were one or more Canadian corporations (referred to in this subsection as "predecessor affiliates"), each of which at that time would have been a Canadian affiliate of a predecessor if the predecessor were an entrant bank at that time,

(a) for the purpose of the definition "Canadian affiliate" in subsection (1),

(i) each predecessor affiliate is deemed to have been affiliated with the entrant bank throughout the period that began on February 11, 1999 and ended at the time of the merger,

(ii) the expression "entrant bank" in subparagraph (b)(iii) of the definition is deemed to include a predecessor, and

(iii) if two or more of the predecessor affiliates are amalgamated or merged at any time after February 11, 1999 to form a new corporation, the new corporation is deemed to have been affiliated with the entrant bank throughout the period that began on February 11, 1999 and ended at the time of the amalgamation or merger of the predecessor affiliates; and

(b) if at least one of the predecessors complied with the terms of subsection[26] (11)(a), the entrant bank is deemed to have complied with those terms.

Notes: See Notes at end of 142.7.

(3) Branch-establishment rollover — If a Canadian affiliate of an entrant bank transfers an eligible property to the entrant bank, the entrant bank begins immediately after the transfer to use or hold the transferred property in its Canadian banking business and the Canadian affiliate and the entrant bank jointly elect, in accordance with subsection (11), to have this subsection apply in respect of the transfer, subsections 85(1) (other than paragraph (e.2)), (1.1), (1.4) and (5) apply, with any modifications that the circumstances require, in respect of the transfer, except that the portion of subsection 85(1) before paragraph (a) shall be read as follows:

"85. (1) Where a taxpayer that is a Canadian affiliate of an entrant bank (within the meanings assigned by subsection 142.7(1)) has, in a taxation year, disposed of any of the tax-

payer's property to the entrant bank (referred to in this subsection as the "corporation"), if the taxpayer and the corporation have jointly elected under subsection 142.7(3), the following rules apply:".

Related Provisions: 142.7(4) — Deemed fair market value; 142.7(5) — Transfers of specified debt obligations; 142.7(11) — Requirements for election; 142.7(13) — Stop-loss rule on windup of affiliate; Reg. 5301(8) — Effect of transfer on instalment base of transferee.

Notes: The CRA will not accept a late-filed election under 142.7(3): VIEWS doc 2002-0169187. However, see Notes to 220(3.2).

(4) Deemed fair market value — If a Canadian affiliate of an entrant bank and the entrant bank make an election under subsection (3) in respect of a transfer of property by the Canadian affiliate to the entrant bank, for the purposes of subsections 15(1), 52(2), 69(1), (4) and (5), 246(1) and 247(2) in respect of the transfer, the fair market value of the property is deemed to be the amount agreed by the Canadian affiliate and the entrant bank in their election.

(5) Specified debt obligations — If a Canadian affiliate of an entrant bank transfers a specified debt obligation to the entrant bank in a transaction in respect of which an election is made under subsection (3), the Canadian affiliate is a financial institution in its taxation year in which the transfer is made, and the amount that the Canadian affiliate and the entrant bank agree on in their election in respect of the obligation is equal to the tax basis of the obligation within the meaning assigned by subsection 142.4(1), the entrant bank is deemed, in respect of the obligation, for the purposes of sections 142.2 to 142.4 and 142.6, to be the same corporation as, and a continuation of, the Canadian affiliate.

(6) Mark-to-market property — If a Canadian affiliate of an entrant bank described in paragraph (11)(a) transfers at any time within the period described in paragraph (11)(c) to the entrant bank a property that is, for the Canadian affiliate's taxation year in which the property is transferred, a mark-to-market property of the Canadian affiliate,

(a) for the purposes of subsections 112(5) to (5.21) and (5.4), the definition "mark-to-market property" in subsection 142.2(1) and subsection 142.5(9), the entrant bank is deemed, in respect of the property, to be the same corporation as and a continuation of, the Canadian affiliate; and

(b) for the purpose of applying subsection 142.5(2) in respect of the property, the Canadian affiliate's taxation year in which the property is transferred is deemed to have ended immediately before the time the property was transferred.

Related Provisions: 87(2)(e.5) — Parallel rule on amalgamations.

(7) Reserves — If

(a) at a particular time,

(i) a Canadian affiliate of an entrant bank transfers to the entrant bank property that is a loan or lending asset, or a right to receive an unpaid amount in respect of a disposition before the particular time of property by the affiliate, or

(ii) the entrant bank assumes an obligation of the Canadian affiliate that is an instrument or commitment described in paragraph 20(1)(l.1) or an obligation in respect of goods, services, land, or chattels or movable property, described in subparagraph 20(1)(m)(i), (ii) or (iii),

(b) the property is transferred or the obligation is assumed for an amount equal to its fair market value at the particular time,

(c) the entrant bank begins immediately after the particular time to use or hold the property or owe the obligation in its Canadian banking business, and

(d) the Canadian affiliate and the entrant bank jointly elect in accordance with subsection (11) to have this subsection apply in respect of the transfer or assumption,

---

[26] *Sic*. Should be "paragraph" — ed.

then

(e) in applying paragraphs 20(1)(l), (l.1), (m), (n) and (p) in respect of the obligation or property, the taxation year of the affiliate that would, but for this paragraph, include the particular time is deemed to end immediately before the particular time, and

(f) in computing the income of the Canadian affiliate and the entrant bank for taxation years that end on or after the particular time,

(i) any amount deducted under paragraph 20(1)(l), (l.1), (m) or (n) by the Canadian affiliate in respect of the property or obligation in computing its income for its taxation year that ended immediately before the particular time, or under paragraph 20(1)(p) in computing its income for that year or for a preceding taxation year (to the extent that the amount has not been included in the affiliate's income under paragraph 12(1)(i)), is deemed to have been so deducted by the entrant bank in computing its income for its last taxation year that ended before the particular time and not to have been deducted by the Canadian affiliate,

(ii) in applying paragraph 20(1)(m), an amount in respect of the goods, services, land, chattels or movable property, that was included under paragraph 12(1)(a) in computing the Canadian affiliate's income from a business is deemed to have been so included in computing the entrant bank's income from its Canadian banking business for a preceding taxation year,

(iii) in applying paragraph 20(1)(n) in respect of a property described in subparagraph (a)(i) and paragraphs (b), (c) and (d) sold by the Canadian affiliate in the course of a business, the property is deemed to have been disposed of by the entrant bank (and not by the Canadian affiliate) at the time it was disposed of by the Canadian affiliate, and the amount in respect of the sale that was included in computing the Canadian affiliate's income from a business is deemed to have been included in computing the entrant bank's income from its Canadian banking business for its taxation year that includes the time at which the property was so disposed of, and

(iv) in applying paragraph 40(1)(a) or 44(1)(e) in respect of a property described in subparagraph (a)(i) and paragraphs (b), (c) and (d) disposed of by the Canadian affiliate, the property is deemed to have been disposed of by the entrant bank (and not by the Canadian affiliate) at the time it was disposed of by the Canadian affiliate, the amount determined under subparagraph 40(1)(a)(i) or 44(1)(e)(i) in respect of the Canadian affiliate is deemed to be the amount determined under that subparagraph in respect of the entrant bank, and any amount claimed by the Canadian affiliate under subparagraph 40(1)(a)(iii) or 44(1)(e)(iii) in computing its gain from the disposition of the property for its last taxation year that ended before the particular time is deemed to have been so claimed by the entrant bank for its last taxation year that ended before the particular time.

Related Provisions: 142.7(11) — Requirements for election.

Notes: See Notes at end of 142.7.

142.7(7)(a)(ii), (f)(ii) amended by 2002-2013 technical bill (Part 4 — bijuralism), effective June 26, 2013, to add "movable property".

(8) Assumption of debt obligation — If a Canadian affiliate of an entrant bank described in paragraph (11)(a) transfers at any time within the period described in paragraph (11)(c) property to the entrant bank, and any part of the consideration for the transfer is the assumption by the entrant bank in respect of its Canadian banking business of a debt obligation of the Canadian affiliate,

(a) where the Canadian affiliate and the entrant bank jointly elect in accordance with subsection (11) to have this paragraph apply,

(i) both

(A) the value of that part of the consideration for the transfer of the property, and

(B) for the purpose of determining the consequences of the assumption of the obligation and any subsequent settlement or extinguishment of it, the value of the consideration given to the entrant bank for the assumption of the obligation,

are deemed to be an amount (in this paragraph referred to as the "assumption amount") equal to the amount outstanding on account of the principal amount of the obligation at that time, and

(ii) the assumption amount shall not be considered a term of the transaction that differs from that which would have been made between persons dealing at arm's length solely because it is not equal to the fair market value of the obligation at that time;

(a.1) [Repealed]

(b) where the obligation is denominated in a foreign currency, and the Canadian affiliate and the entrant bank jointly elect in accordance with subsection (11) to have this paragraph apply,

(i) the amount of any income, loss, capital gain or capital loss in respect of the obligation due to the fluctuation in the value of the foreign currency relative to Canadian currency realized by

(A) the Canadian affiliate on the assumption of the obligation is deemed to be nil, and

(B) the entrant bank on the settlement or extinguishment of the obligation shall be determined based on the amount of the obligation in Canadian currency at the time it became an obligation of the Canadian affiliate, and

(ii) for the purpose of an election made in respect of the obligation under paragraph (a), the amount outstanding on account of the principal amount of the obligation at that time is the total of all amounts each of which is an amount that was advanced to the Canadian affiliate on account of principal, that remains outstanding at that time, and that is determined using the exchange rate that applied between the foreign currency and Canadian currency at the time of the advance; and

(c) for the purpose of applying paragraphs 20(1)(e) and (f) in respect of the debt obligation, the obligation is deemed not to have been settled or extinguished by virtue of its assumption by the entrant bank and the entrant bank is deemed to be the same corporation as, and a continuation of, the Canadian affiliate.

Related Provisions: 142.7(11) — Requirements for election; 261(2)(b) — 142.7(8)(b) overrides general currency conversion rules; 261(5)(c) — Functional currency reporting; 261(5)(f)(i) — Functional currency reporting — meaning of "Canadian currency".

Notes: 142.7(8)(a.1) added and repealed by 2002-2013 technical bill (Part 5 — technical), in force from June 28, 1999 through 2007. It implemented a Dec. 18, 2011 Finance comfort letter.

(9) Branch-establishment dividend — Notwithstanding any other provision of this Act, the rules in subsection (10) apply if

(a) a dividend is paid by a Canadian affiliate of an entrant bank to the entrant bank or to a person that is affiliated with the Canadian affiliate and that is resident in the country in which the entrant bank is resident, or

(b) a dividend is deemed to be paid for the purposes of this Part or Part XIII (other than by paragraph 214(3)(a)) as a result of a transfer of property from the Canadian affiliate to such a person,

and the Canadian affiliate and the entrant bank jointly elect in accordance with subsection (11) to have subsection (10) apply in respect of the dividend.

(10) Treatment of dividend — If the conditions in subsection (9) are met,

(a) the dividend is deemed (except for the purposes of subsections 112(3) to (7)) not to be a taxable dividend; and

(b) there is added to the amount otherwise determined under paragraph 219(1)(g) in respect of the entrant bank for its first taxation year that ends after the time at which the dividend is paid,

1019

the amount of the dividend less, where the dividend is paid by means of, or arises as a result of, a transfer of eligible property in respect of which the Canadian affiliate and the entrant bank have jointly elected under subsection (3), the amount by which the fair market value of the property transferred exceeds the amount the Canadian affiliate and the entrant bank have agreed on in their election.

Related Provisions: 142.7(11) — Requirements for election.

(11) Elections — An election under subsection (3) or (7), paragraph (8)(a) or (b) or subsection (10), (12) or (14) is valid only if

(a) the entrant bank by which the election is made has, on or before the day that is 6 months after the day on which the *Income Tax Amendments Act, 2000* [2001, c. 17] receives royal assent [June 14, 2001], complied with paragraphs 1.1(b) and (c) of the "Guide to Foreign Bank Branching" in respect of the establishment and commencement of business of a foreign bank branch in Canada issued by the Office of the Superintendent of Financial Institutions, as it read on December 31, 2000;

(b) the election is made in prescribed form on or before the earlier of the filing-due date of the Canadian affiliate and the filing-due date of the entrant bank, for the taxation year that includes the time at which

(i) in the case of an election under subsection (3) or (7), paragraph (8)(a) or (b) or subsection (10), the dividend, transfer or assumption to which the election relates is paid, made or effected, or

(ii) in the case of an election under subsection (12), the dissolution order was granted or the winding up commenced; and

(c) in the case of an election under subsection (3) or (7), paragraph (8)(a) or (b) or subsection (10), the dividend, transfer or assumption to which the election relates is paid, made or effected within the period that

(i) begins on the day on which the Superintendent makes an order in respect of the entrant bank under subsection 534(1) of the *Bank Act*, and

(ii) ends on the later of

(A) the earlier of

(I) the day that is one year after the day referred to in subparagraph (i), and

(II) the day that is three years after the day on which the *Income Tax Amendments Act, 2000* [2001, c. 17] receives royal assent [June 14, 2001], and

(B) the day that is one year after the day on which the *Income Tax Amendments Act, 2000* [2001, c. 17] receives royal assent [June 14, 2001].

Related Provisions: 142.7(2)(b) — Entrant bank deemed to have complied with para. (11)(a) if predecessor did; 142.7(6) — Transfer of mark-to-market property; 142.7(8) — Assumption of debt obligation.

Notes: See Notes at end of 142.7.

(12) Winding-up of Canadian affiliate: losses — If

(a) within the period described in paragraph (11)(c) in respect of the entrant bank,

(i) the Minister of Finance has issued letters patent under section 342 of the *Bank Act* or section 347 of the *Trust and Loan Companies Act* dissolving the Canadian affiliate or an order under section 345 of the *Bank Act* or section 350 of the *Trust and Loan Companies Act* approving the Canadian affiliate's application for dissolution (such letters patent or order being referred to in this subsection as the "dissolution order"), or

(ii) the affiliate has been wound up under the terms of the corporate law that governs it,

(b) the entrant bank carries on all or part of the business in Canada that was formerly carried on by the Canadian affiliate, and

(c) the Canadian affiliate and the entrant bank jointly elect in accordance with subsection (11) to have this section apply

then in applying section 111 for the purpose of computing the taxable income earned in Canada of the entrant bank for any taxation year that begins after the date of the dissolution order or the commencement of the winding up, as the case may be,

(d) subject to paragraphs (e) and (h), the portion of a non-capital loss of the Canadian affiliate for a taxation year (in this paragraph referred to as the "Canadian affiliate's loss year") that can reasonably be regarded as being its loss from carrying on a business in Canada (in this paragraph referred to as the "loss business") or being in respect of a claim made under section 110.5, to the extent that it

(i) was not deducted in computing the taxable income of the Canadian affiliate or any other entrant bank for any taxation year, and

(ii) would have been deductible in computing the taxable income of the Canadian affiliate for any taxation year that begins after the date of the dissolution order or the commencement of the winding up, as the case may be, on the assumption that it had such a taxation year and that it had sufficient income for that year,

is deemed, for the taxation year of the entrant bank in which the Canadian affiliate's loss year ended, to be a non-capital loss of the entrant bank from carrying on the loss business (or, in respect of a claim made under section 110.5, to be a non-capital loss of the entrant bank in respect of a claim under subparagraph 115(1)(a)(vii)) that was not deductible by the entrant bank in computing its taxable income earned in Canada for any taxation year that began before the date of the dissolution order or the commencement of the winding up, as the case may be,

(e) if at any time control of the Canadian affiliate or entrant bank has been acquired by a person or group of persons, no amount in respect of the Canadian affiliate's non-capital loss for a taxation year that ends before that time is deductible in computing the taxable income earned in Canada of the entrant bank for a particular taxation year that ends after that time, except that the portion of the loss that can reasonably be regarded as the Canadian affiliate's loss from carrying on a business in Canada and, where a business was carried on by the Canadian affiliate in Canada in the earlier year, the portion of the loss that can reasonably be regarded as being in respect of an amount deductible under paragraph 110(1)(k) in computing its taxable income for the year are deductible only

(i) if that business is carried on by the Canadian affiliate or the entrant bank for profit or with a reasonable expectation of profit throughout the particular year, and

(ii) to the extent of the total of the entrant bank's income for the particular year from that business, and where properties were sold, leased, rented or developed or services rendered in the course of carrying on that business before that time, from any other business substantially all of the income of which was derived from the sale, leasing, rental or development, as the case may be, of similar properties or the rendering of similar services,

and, for the purpose of this paragraph, where subsection 88(1.1) applied to the dissolution of another corporation in respect of which the Canadian affiliate was the parent and paragraph 88(1.1)(e) applied in respect of losses of that other corporation, the Canadian affiliate is deemed to be the same corporation as, and a continuation of, that other corporation with respect to those losses,

(f) subject to paragraphs (g) and (h), a net capital loss of the Canadian affiliate for a taxation year (in this paragraph referred to as the "Canadian affiliate's loss year") is deemed to be a net capital loss of the entrant bank for its taxation year in which the Canadian affiliate's loss year ended to the extent that the loss

(i) was not deducted in computing the taxable income of the Canadian affiliate or any other entrant bank for any taxation year, and

(ii) would have been deductible in computing the taxable income of the Canadian affiliate for any taxation year beginning after the date of the dissolution order or the commencement of the winding-up, as the case may be, on the assumption that the Canadian affiliate had such a taxation year and that it had sufficient income and taxable capital gains for that year,

(g) if at any time control of the Canadian affiliate or the entrant bank has been acquired by a person or group of persons, no amount in respect of the Canadian affiliate's net capital loss for a taxation year that ends before that time is deductible in computing the entrant bank's taxable income earned in Canada for a taxation year that ends after that time, and

(h) any loss of the Canadian affiliate that would otherwise be deemed by paragraph (d) or (f) to be a loss of the entrant bank for a particular taxation year that begins after the date of the dissolution order or the commencement of the winding-up, as the case may be, is deemed, for the purpose of computing the entrant bank's taxable income earned in Canada for taxation years that begin after that date, to be such a loss of the entrant bank for its immediately preceding taxation year and not for the particular year, if the entrant bank so elects in its return of income for the particular year.

Related Provisions: 142.7(11) — Requirements for election; 142.7(13) — Stop-loss rule on windup of affiliate; 142.7(14) — Specified debt obligations.

(13) Winding-up of Canadian affiliate: stop loss — If a Canadian affiliate and its entrant bank have at any time made a joint election under either of subsection (3) or (12),

(a) in respect of any transfer of property, directly or indirectly, by the Canadian affiliate to the entrant bank or a person with whom the entrant bank does not deal at arm's length,

(i) subparagraph 13(21.2)(e)(iii) shall be read without reference to clause (E) of that subparagraph,

(ii) [Repealed]

(iii) paragraph 18(15)(b) shall be read without reference to subparagraph (iv) of that paragraph, and

(iv) paragraph 40(3.4)(b) shall be read without reference to subparagraph (v) of that paragraph;

(b) in respect of any property of the Canadian affiliate appropriated to or for the benefit of the entrant bank or any person with whom the entrant bank does not deal at arm's length, section 69(5) shall be read without reference to paragraph (d); and

(c) for the purposes of applying subsection 13(21.2), 18(15) and 40(3.4) to any property that was disposed of by the affiliate, after the dissolution or winding-up of the affiliate, the entrant bank is deemed to be the same corporation as, and a continuation of, the affiliate.

Notes: For the meaning of "indirectly" in para. (a), see Notes to 17.1(1).

142.7(13)(a)(ii), "subsection 14(12) shall be read without reference to paragraph (g) of that subsection", repealed and para. (c) amended to delete reference to 14(12), by 2016 budget bill #2, effective 2017 (as part of changing the eligible capital property rules to CCA Class 14.1: see Notes to 20(1)(b)).

Regulations: 9204(2.1) (winding-up into authorized foreign bank).

(14) Winding-up of Canadian affiliate: SDOs — If a Canadian affiliate of an entrant bank and the entrant bank meet the conditions set out in paragraphs (12)(a) and (b) and jointly elect in accordance with subsection (11) to have this subsection apply, and the Canadian affiliate has not made an election under this subsection with any other entrant bank, the entrant bank is deemed to be the same corporation as, and a continuation of, the Canadian affiliate for the purposes of paragraphs 142.4(4)(c) and (d) in respect of any specified debt obligation disposed of by the Canadian affiliate.

Related Provisions: 142.7(11) — Requirements for election.

Notes [142.7]: 142.7, added by 2001 technical bill effective June 28, 1999, provides special, time-limited rules to facilitate foreign banks' conversion of Canadian operations, previously carried out through subsidiaries, into Canadian branches of the foreign banks themselves (see 248(1)"authorized foreign bank").

See Christopher Van Loan, "Update on the Tax Implications of Foreign Bank Branch Conversion", 11(3) *Tax Law Update* (Ontario Bar Assn, oba.org) 5-8 (May 2001).

A GST/HST rollover of assets from the subsidiary to the branch is also available. See s. 167.11 of the *Excise Tax Act*.

Definitions [s. 142.7]: "affiliated" — 251.1; "amount" — 248(1); "arm's length" — 251(1); "authorized foreign bank", "bank", "business" — 248(1); "Canada" — 255, *Interpretation Act* 35(1); "Canadian affiliate" — 142.7(1); "Canadian banking business" — 248(1); "Canadian corporation" — 89(1), 248(1); "Canadian currency" — 261(5)(f)(i); "capital gain" — 39(1)(a), 248(1); "capital loss" — 39(1)(b), 248(1); "carrying on a business in Canada" — 253; "commencement" — *Interpretation Act* 35(1); "corporation" — 248(1), *Interpretation Act* 35(1); "dividend" — 248(1); "eligible property", "entrant bank" — 142.7(1); "fair market value" — see 69(1) Notes; "filing-due date" — 248(1); "financial institution" — 142.2(1); "foreign currency" — 248(1); "foreign merger" — 87(8.1); "Governor" — *Interpretation Act* 35(1); "land" — see 70(5.2) Notes; "lending asset" — 248(1); "mark-to-market property" — 142.2(1); "Minister" — 248(1); "Minister of Finance" — *Financial Administration Act* 14; "month" — *Interpretation Act* 35(1); "movable" — Quebec *Civil Code* art. 900–907; "net capital loss", "non-capital loss" — 111(8), 248(1); "non-resident" — 248(1); "parent" — 88(1.1); "person", "prescribed", "principal amount", "property" — 248(1); "qualifying foreign merger" — 142.7(1); "resident" — 250; "share", "shareholder" — 248(1); "specified debt obligation" — 142.2(1); "taxable capital gain" — 38(a), 248(1); "taxable dividend" — 89(1), 248(1); "taxable income", "taxable income earned in Canada" — 248(1); "taxation year" — 249; "taxpayer" — 248(1).

Communal Organizations

143. (1) Communal [religious] organizations — Where a congregation, or one or more business agencies of the congregation, carries on one or more businesses for purposes that include supporting or sustaining the congregation's members or the members of any other congregation, the following rules apply:

(a) a trust is deemed to be created on the day that is the later of

(i) December 31, 1976, and

(ii) the day the congregation came into existence;

(b) the trust is deemed to have been continuously in existence from the day determined under paragraph (a);

(c) the property of the congregation is deemed to be the property of the trust;

(d) the property of each business agency of the congregation in a calendar year is deemed to be property of the trust throughout the portion of the year throughout which the trust exists;

(e) where the congregation is a corporation, the corporation is deemed to be the trustee having control of the trust property;

(f) where the congregation is not a corporation, its council, committee of leaders, executive committee, administrative committee, officers or other group charged with its management are deemed to be the trustees having control of the trust property;

(g) the congregation is deemed to act and to have always acted as agent for the trust in all matters relating to its businesses and other activities;

(h) each business agency of the congregation in a calendar year is deemed to have acted as agent for the trust in all matters in the year relating to its businesses and other activities;

(i) the members of the congregation are deemed to be the beneficiaries under the trust;

(j) tax under this Part is payable by the trust on its taxable income for each taxation year;

(k) in computing the income of the trust for any taxation year,

(i) subject to paragraph (l), no deduction may be made in respect of salaries, wages or benefits of any kind provided to the members of the congregation, and

(ii) no deduction may be made under subsection 104(6), except to the extent that any portion of the trust's income (determined without reference to that subsection) is allocated to the members of the congregation in accordance with subsection (2);

(l) for the purpose of applying section 20.01 to the trust,

(i) each member of the congregation is deemed to be a member of the trust's household, and

(ii) section 20.01 shall be read without reference to paragraphs 20.01(2)(b) and (c) and subsection 20.01(3); and

(m) where the congregation or one of the business agencies is a corporation, section 15.1 shall, except for the purposes of paragraphs 15.1(2)(a) and (c) (other than subparagraphs 15.1(2)(c)(i) and (ii)), apply as if this subsection were read without reference to paragraphs (c), (d), (g) and (h).

Related Provisions: 108(1)"trust"(c) — S. 143 trust deemed not a trust for certain purposes; 120.4(1)"split income"(c) — Income-splitting tax does not apply; 127(7) — Investment tax credit of trust; 143(2) — Election re income.

Notes: S. 143 was enacted to deal with Hutterite colonies (Hutterian Brethren, religious farming communities in Alberta), and to overrule *Wipf*, [1975] C.T.C. 79 (FCA); aff'd [1976] C.T.C. 57 (SCC). Hutterites live communally and do not personally own property. 143(1) deems a trust to operate the community's business, and the community members to be its beneficiaries. The trust can deduct income it distributes to the members only if a 143(2) election is in place. Under the election, the trust's income is allocated to members using the formula in 143(2)(a); due to 143(2)(d) added in 2019, members report business income and can thus benefit from the Canada Workers' Benefit in 122.7. Since the members do not own property, in practice the community pays their tax. For CRA discussion see docs 2009-0314331E5, 2013-0490251M4. See also Notes to 143(4)"congregation" re *Blackmore* case.

See also *Excise Tax Act* s. 191(6.1) (in the *Practitioner's Goods and Services Tax Annotated*), which exempts such organizations from the GST/HST self-supply rules for residential property.

143(1)(a) opening words amended by 2014 budget bill #2, for 2016 and later taxation years, to change "an *inter vivos* trust" to "a trust" (in sync with generally replacing "testamentary trust" with "graduated rate estate").

143(1) earlier amended by 1999 Budget, 1993 technical bill.

Information Circulars: 78-5R3: Communal organizations.

(2) Election in respect of income — If the trust referred to in subsection (1) in respect of a congregation so elects in respect of a taxation year in writing filed with the Minister on or before the trust's filing-due date for the year and all the congregation's participating members are specified in the election in accordance with subsection (5), the following rules apply:

(a) for the purposes of subsections 104(6) and (13), the amount payable in the year to a particular participating member of the congregation out of the income of the trust (determined without reference to subsection 104(6)) is the amount determined by the formula

$$0.8\,(A \times B/C) + D + (0.2A - E)/F$$

where

A is the taxable income of the trust for the year (determined without reference to subsection 104(6) and specified future tax consequences for the year),

B is

(i) where the particular member is identified in the election as a person to whom this subparagraph applies (in this subsection referred to as a "designated member"), 1, and

(ii) in any other case, 0.5,

C is the total of

(i) the number of designated members of the congregation, and

(ii) ½ of the number of other participating members of the congregation in respect of the year,

D is the amount, if any, that is specified in the election as an additional allocation under this subsection to the particular member,

E is the total of all amounts each of which is an amount specified in the election as an additional allocation under this subsection to a participating member of the congregation in respect of the year, and

F is the number of participating members of the congregation in respect of the year;

(b) the designated member of each family at the end of the year is deemed to have supported the other members of the family during the year and the other members of the family are deemed to have been wholly dependent on the designated member for support during the year;

(c) the taxable income for the year of each member of the congregation shall be computed without reference to subsection 110(2); and

(d) if the trust earns income from a business in the year, then the portion of the amount payable in the year to a particular participating member of the congregation out of the income of the trust under paragraph (a) that can reasonably be considered to relate to that income from a business is deemed to be income from a business carried on by the particular member.

Related Provisions: 143(3) — Election not binding unless taxes paid; 143(5) — Specification of family members; 220(3.2), Reg. 600(b) — Late filing or revocation of election; 257 — Formula cannot calculate to less than zero.

Notes: See Notes to 143(1).

If the trust is resident in Quebec, the election must be copied to Revenu Québec: *Taxation Act* ss. 851.28, 21.4.6.

143(2)(d) added by 2019 budget bill #1, for 2014 and later tax years. The effect of business income retaining its character is that community members have business income for purposes of the Canada Workers Benefit (pre-2019 Working Income Tax Benefit) in 122.7. For background see tinyurl.com/hutterite-tax-mnp. This proposal was buried in tiny print as a one-line costing item under "Policy Actions Taken Since Budget 2018" in Annex 1 of the Nov. 2018 Economic Statement, and did not come to the author's attention until it was referenced in the March 2019 Budget. Perhaps it was hidden because of the political danger of "giving" $120 million to a religious community? The Economic Statement projected that it would cost the federal government $45 million in 2018-19 (it is retroactive to 2014) and $15m in each of 2019-20 to 2023-24.

143(2) opening words amended by 2014 budget bill #2, for 2016 and later tax years, to change "Where the *inter vivos* trust" to "If the trust".

143(2) amended by 1999 Budget, effective for 1998 and later taxation years.

Information Circulars: 78-5R3: Communal organizations.

(3) Refusal to accept election — An election under subsection (2) in respect of a congregation for a particular taxation year is not binding on the Minister unless all taxes, interest and penalties payable under this Part, as a consequence of the application of subsection (2) to the congregation for preceding taxation years, are paid at or before the end of the particular year.

Notes: 143(3) amended by 1999 Budget, effective for 1998 and later taxation years.

Information Circulars: 78-5R3: Communal organizations.

(3.1) Election in respect of gifts — For the purposes of section 118.1, if the eligible amount of a gift made in a taxation year by a trust referred to in subsection (1) in respect of a congregation would, but for this subsection, be included in the total charitable gifts, total cultural gifts or total ecological gifts of the trust for the year and the trust so elects in its return of income under this Part for the year,

(a) the trust is deemed not to have made the gift; and

(b) each participating member of the congregation is deemed to have made, in the year, such a gift the eligible amount of which is the amount determined by the formula

$$A \times B/C$$

where

A is the eligible amount of the gift made by the trust,

B is the amount determined for the year in respect of the member under paragraph (2)(a) as a consequence of an election under subsection (2) by the trust, and

C is the total of all amounts each of which is an amount determined for the year in respect of a participating member of the congregation under paragraph (2)(a) as a consequence of an election under subsection (2) by the trust.

Related Provisions: 248(30)–(33) — Determination of eligible amount.

Notes: If the trust is resident in Quebec, the election must be copied to Revenu Québec: *Taxation Act* ss. 851.33, 21.4.6.

143(3.1) amended by 2014 budget bill #2 (for 2016 and later tax years), 2002-2013 technical bill, 1999 Budget, 1993 technical bill.

Information Circulars: 78-5R3: Communal organizations.

(4) Definitions — For the purposes of this section,

"adult" means an individual who, before the time at which the term is applied, has attained the age of eighteen years or is married or in a common-law partnership;

Notes: 143(4)"adult" amended by 2000 same-sex partners bill to refer to "common-law partnership", effective as per Notes to 248(1)"common-law partner".

"business agency", of a congregation at any time in a particular calendar year, means a corporation, trust or other person, where the congregation owned all the shares of the capital stock of the corporation (except directors' qualifying shares) or every interest in the trust or other person, as the case may be, throughout the portion of the particular calendar year throughout which both the congregation and the corporation, trust or other person, as the case may be, were in existence;

Notes: A corporation can be a BA of an incorporated congregation, but a wholly-owned subsidiary of a BA likely cannot be: VIEWS doc 2009-0314331E5.

For "directors' qualifying shares", see Notes to 85(1.3).

143(4)"business agency" added by 1999 Budget, this version effective for 2001 and later taxation years.

"congregation" means a community, society or body of individuals, whether or not incorporated,

(a) the members of which live and work together,

(b) that adheres to the practices and beliefs of, and operates according to the principles of, the religious organization of which it is a constituent part,

(c) that does not permit any of its members to own any property in their own right, and

(d) that requires its members to devote their working lives to the activities of the congregation;

Notes: In *Blackmore*, 2014 FCA 210, the polygamous fundamentalist Mormon community of Bountiful, BC was held not to be a "congregation", as (a) the members did not all "live together" (in the same place) or "work together" (in the same place, on a consistent basis); (b) they were a group of independent Mormon fundamentalists (not part of the mainstream LDS church) rather than members of a "religious organization"; (c) Bountiful did not prohibit members from owning property; (d) there was no "explicit and ongoing" requirement that members devote their working lives to the community. Thus, none of the 4 mandatory conditions was met.

143(4)"congregation" amended by 1999 Budget, for 1998 and later taxation years.

"family" means,

(a) in the case of an adult who is unmarried and who is not in a common-law partnership, that person and the person's children who are not adults, not married and not in a common-law partnership, and

(b) in the case of an adult who is married or in a common-law partnership, that person and the person's spouse or common-law partner and the children of either or both of them who are not adults, not married and not in a common-law partnership

but does not include an individual who is included in any other family or who is not a member of the congregation in which the family is included;

Notes: 143(4)"family" amended by 2000 same-sex partners bill, effective 2001 or earlier, to refer to common-law partners (the irony of making this amendment to s. 143 seems to have escaped Parliament).

"member of a congregation" means

(a) an adult, living with the members of the congregation, who conforms to the practices of the religious organization of which the congregation is a constituent part whether or not that person has been formally accepted into the organization, and

(b) a child who is unmarried and not in common-law partnership, other than an adult, of an adult referred to in paragraph (a), if the child lives with the members of the congregation;

Notes: Para. (b) amended by 2000 same-sex partners bill and 2001 technical bill effective 2001 or earlier.

"participating member", of a congregation in respect of a taxation year, means an individual who, at the end of the year, is an adult who is a member of the congregation;

Notes: 143(4)"participating member" added by 1999 Budget, for 1998 and later taxation years.

"religious organization" means an organization, other than a registered charity, of which a congregation is a constituent part, that adheres to beliefs, evidenced by the religious and philosophical tenets of the organization, that include a belief in the existence of a supreme being;

"total charitable gifts" has the meaning assigned by subsection 118.1(1);

"total Crown gifts" — [Repealed]

Notes: Definition repealed by 2014 budget bill #2, for 2016 and later taxation years. It cross-referenced to the definition under 118.1(1), which was also repealed.

"total cultural gifts" has the meaning assigned by subsection 118.1(1).

"total ecological gifts" has the same meaning as in subsection 118.1(1).

Notes: Definition added by 1999 Budget, for gifts made after Feb. 27, 1995.

Notes [subsec. 143(4)]: 143(4)"adult" was 143(4)(a); "congregation", (b); "family", (c); "member of a congregation", (d); "religious organization", (e); "total charitable gifts", "total Crown gifts" and "total cultural gifts", 143(4)(f) before RSC 1985 (5th Supp) consolidation for tax years ending after Nov. 1991.

(5) Specification of family members — For the purpose of applying subsection (2) to a particular election by the trust referred to in subsection (1) in respect of a congregation for a particular taxation year,

(a) subject to paragraph (b), a participating member of the congregation is considered to have been specified in the particular election in accordance with this subsection only if the member is identified in the particular election and

(i) where the member's family includes only one adult at the end of the particular year, the member is identified in the particular election as a person to whom subparagraph (i) of the description of B in subsection (2) (in this subsection referred to as the "relevant subparagraph") applies, and

(ii) in any other case, only one of the adults in the member's family is identified in the particular election as a person to whom the relevant subparagraph applies; and

(b) an individual is considered not to have been specified in the particular election in accordance with this subsection if

(i) the individual is one of two individuals who were married to each other, or in a common-law partnership, at the end of a preceding taxation year of the trust and at the end of the particular year,

(ii) one of those individuals was

(A) where the preceding year ended before 1998, specified in an election under subsection (2) by the trust for the preceding year, and

(B) in any other case, identified in an election under subsection (2) by the trust for the preceding year as a person to whom the relevant subparagraph applied, and

(iii) the other individual is identified in the particular election as a person to whom the relevant subparagraph applies.

Notes: 143(5) opening words amended by 2014 budget bill #2, for 2016 and later taxation years, to change the *inter vivos* trust to "the trust".

143(5) amended by 2001 technical bill (last change effective for the 2001 and later taxation years) and 1999 Budget.

Definitions [s. 143]: "adult" — 143(4); "amount", "business" — 248(1); "business agency" — 143(4); "calendar year" — *Interpretation Act* 37(1)(a); "child" — 252(1); "congregation" — 143(4); "corporation" — 248(1), *Interpretation Act* 35(1); "eligible amount" — 248(31), (41); "fair market value" — see 69(1) Notes; "family" — 143(4); "filing-due date" — "individual" — 248(1); "member of a congregation" — 143(4); "Minister", "officer" — 248(1); "participating member" — 143(4); "person", "property" — 248(1); "qualifying share" — 192(6), 248(1); "registered charity" — 248(1); "religious organization" — 143(4); "share", "specified future tax consequence" — 248(1); "taxable income" — 248(1); "taxation year" — 249; "total charitable gifts", "total Crown gifts", "total cultural gifts", "total ecological gifts" — 143(4); "trust" — 143(1)(a); "writing" — *Interpretation Act* 35(1).

143.1 [Amateur athlete trusts] — (1) Definitions — The definitions in this subsection apply in this section.

"amateur athlete" at any time means an individual (other than a trust) who is, at that time,

(a) a member of a registered Canadian amateur athletic association;

(b) eligible to compete, in an international sporting event sanctioned by an international sports federation, as a Canadian national team member; and

(c) not a professional athlete.

"professional athlete" means an individual who receives income that is compensation for, or is otherwise attributable to, the individual's activities as a player or athlete in a professional sport.

"qualifying performance income" of an individual means income that

(a) is received by the individual in a taxation year in which

(i) the individual was, at any time, an amateur athlete, and

(ii) the individual was not, at any time, a professional athlete;

(b) may reasonably be considered to be in connection with the individual's participation as an amateur athlete in one or more international sporting events referred to in the definition "amateur athlete"; and

(c) is endorsement income, prize money, or income from public appearances or speeches.

Related Provisions: 146(1)"earned income"(b.2) — Earned income for RRSP purposes.

"third party" in respect of an arrangement described in paragraph (1.1)(b) means a person who deals at arm's length with the amateur athlete in respect of the arrangement.

Notes: 143.1(1) amended by 2008 budget bill #2, effective for 2008 and later taxation years. (The substantive rule was moved to 143.1(1.2).)

(1.1) Where subsec. (1.2) applies — Subsection (1.2) applies where, at any time,

(a) a national sport organization that is a registered Canadian amateur athletic association receives an amount for the benefit of an individual under an arrangement made under rules of an international sport federation that require amounts to be held, controlled and administered by the organization in order to preserve the eligibility of the individual to compete in a sporting event sanctioned by the federation; or

(b) an individual enters into an arrangement that

(i) is an account with an issuer described in paragraph (b) of the definition "qualifying arrangement" in subsection 146.2(1), or that would be so described if that definition applied at that time,

(ii) provides that no amount may be deposited, credited or added to the account, other than an amount that is qualifying performance income of the individual or that is interest or other income in respect of the property deposited, credited or added to the account,

(iii) provides that a third party is a mandatory signatory on any payment from the account, and

(iv) is not a registered retirement savings plan or a TFSA.

Notes: 143.1(1.1) added by 2008 budget bill #2, effective for 2008 and later taxation years.

(1.2) Amateur athletes' reserve funds — If this subsection applies in respect of an arrangement referred to in subsection (1.1),

(a) a trust (in this section referred to as the **"amateur athlete trust"**) is deemed

(i) to be created on the day on which the first amount referred to in paragraph (1.1)(a) or (b) is received by the sport organization or by the issuer, as the case may be, in respect of the arrangement, and

(ii) to exist until subsection (3) or (4) applies in respect of the trust;

(b) all property held under the arrangement is deemed to be the property of the amateur athlete trust and not property of any other person;

(c) if, at any time, the sport organization or the issuer, as the case may be, receives an amount under the arrangement and the amount would, in the absence of this subsection, be included in computing the income of the individual in respect of the arrangement for the taxation year that includes that time, the amount is deemed to be income of the amateur athlete trust for that taxation year and not to be income of the individual;

(d) if, at any time, the sport organization or the issuer, as the case may be, pays or transfers an amount under the arrangement to or for the benefit of the individual, the amount is deemed to be an amount distributed at that time to the individual by the amateur athlete trust;

(e) the individual is deemed to be the beneficiary under the amateur athlete trust;

(f) the sport organization or the third party, as the case may be, in respect of the arrangement is deemed to be the trustee of the amateur athlete trust; and

(g) no tax is payable under this Part by the amateur athlete trust on its taxable income for any taxation year.

Related Provisions: 128.1(10)"excluded right or interest"(e)(ii) — No deemed disposition on emigration of athlete; 143.1(1.1) — Conditions for 143.1(1.2) to apply; 146(1)"earned income"(b.2) — Earned income for RRSP purposes; 149(1)(v) — Exemptions — amateur athlete trust; 210.2(2) — Part XII.2 tax payable by amateur athlete trust; 248(1)"amateur athlete trust" — Definition applies to entire Act; 248(1)"disposition"(f)(vi) — Rollover from one trust to another.

Notes: For CRA VIEWs on 143.1 and the "eligibility rule" (now in 143.1(1.1)(a)), see docs 2004-0070381E5, 2012-0442581E5, 2012-0451611M4; 2014-0558991E5 (*bona fide* loan to athlete is not included in income). See also Drache, "Amateur Athletic Trusts", xxvi(17) *The Canadian Taxpayer* (Carswell) 131-32 (Aug. 24, 2004).

Tax planning on windup of some amateur athlete trusts has been problematic. See Toronto Star report re Donovan Bailey, tinyurl.com/star-aat; and *Lindsay v. Aird & Berlis*, 2018 ONSC 7424 (and resulting insurers' dispute *Continental Casualty v. LawPRO*, 2020 ONSC 7131).

143.1(1.2)(a) opening words amended by 2014 budget bill #2, for 2016 and later taxation years, to change "an *inter vivos* trust" to "a trust" (in sync with generally replacing "testamentary trust" with "graduated rate estate").

143.1(1.2) added by 2008 budget bill #2 (for 2008 and later taxation years, with an elective transitional rule for 2008-09). For explanation of the amendments see Finance news release 2008-113 (Dec. 29/08). The substantive rule before 2008 was in 143.1(1).

Forms: T3ATH-IND: Amateur athlete trust income tax return; T1061: Canadian amateur athletic trust group information return.

(2) Amounts included in beneficiary's income — In computing the income for a taxation year of the beneficiary under an amateur athlete trust, there shall be included the total of all amounts distributed in the year to the beneficiary by the trust.

Related Provisions: 12(1)(z) — Inclusion in income of amateur athlete trust payments; 210.2(2) — Part XII.2 tax payable by amateur athlete trust; 212(1)(u) — Non-resident withholding tax — amateur athlete trust payments; 214(3)(k) — Non-resident withholding tax.

Notes: See Notes to 143.1(1.2).

(3) Termination of amateur athlete trust — Where an amateur athlete trust holds property on behalf of a beneficiary who has not competed in an international sporting event as a Canadian national team member for a period of 8 years that ends in a particular taxation year and begins in the year that is the later of

> **Proposed Amendment — 143.1(3) opening words**

(3) Termination of amateur athlete trust — Subject to subsection (3.1), if an amateur athlete trust holds property on behalf of a beneficiary who has not competed in an international sporting event as a Canadian national team member for a period of 8 years that ends in a particular taxation year and that begins in the year that is the later of

Application: The Dec. 20, 2019 draft legislation, subsec. 1(1), will amend the opening words of subsec. 143.1(3) to read as above, deemed to have come into force on Jan. 1, 2019.

Technical Notes: Section 143.1 provides for the tax treatment of certain amounts received by or on behalf of individuals who are amateur athletes. Under the eligibility standards of certain international sport federations, in order to preserve the eligibility status of an athlete for international competition, certain types of income earned by the athlete must be deposited with, and controlled and administered by, the applicable national sport organization.

Subsection 143.1(3) is intended to ensure that amounts held by amateur athlete trusts are included in an individual's income within a reasonable period of time. This subsection provides that if an individual has not competed in an international sporting event as a Canadian national team member for eight years, the amounts held by the amateur athlete trust at the end of the year are deemed to be distributed to the individual athlete at that time. The eight-year period commences with the later of the last year in which the athlete so competed and the year in which the trust was created.

Consequential on the introduction of new subsection 143.1(3.1), subsection (3) is amended to provide that it is subject to the application of the new special rule in subsection (3.1). For more information, see the commentary on new subsection (3.1).

Dept. of Finance news release, Dec. 20, 2019: See under 143.1(3.1).

(a) where the beneficiary has competed in such an event, the year in which the beneficiary last so competed, and

(b) the year in which the trust was created,

the trust shall be deemed to have distributed, at the end of the particular taxation year to the beneficiary, an amount equal to

(c) if the trust is liable to pay tax under Part XII.2 in respect of the particular year, 60% of the fair market value of all property held by it at that time, and

(d) in any other case, the fair market value of all property held by it at that time.

Related Provisions: 143.1(3.1) — Extension of no-competition period to 9 years for 2019-20 only; 210.2(2) — Part XII.2 tax payable by amateur athlete trust.

Notes: 143.1(3)(c) amended by 2016 budget bill #1, effective 2016, to change "64%" to "60%" (due to increase in the Part XII.2 tax rate).

Proposed Addition — 143.1(3.1)

(3.1) Special rule — 2019 — If the particular taxation year referred to in subsection (3) in respect of an amateur athlete trust would, if this section were read without reference to this subsection, be the 2019 taxation year, the reference to "8 years" in subsection (3) is to be read as a reference to "9 years".

Application: The Dec. 20, 2019 draft legislation, subsec. 1(2), will add subsec. 143.1(3.1), deemed to have come into force on Jan. 1, 2019.

Technical Notes: New subsection 143.1(3.1) applies if the eight-year period referred to in subsection 143.1(3), determined without reference to subsection (3.1), would end in 2019. Where new subjection (3.1) applies, it extends that period to nine years. As a result, the period referred to in subsection (3) will instead end in 2020 and the deemed distribution under subsection (3) by a trust will occur at the end of the 2020 taxation year rather than the 2019 taxation year.

Dept. of Finance news release, Dec. 20, 2019: *Government Supporting Canadian Athletes With Greater Flexibility for Amateur Athlete Trusts*

Canadian athletes train hard and dedicate themselves to their sports, all with the goal of representing our country well in international competitions. The Government of Canada appreciates these efforts and sacrifices, and wants to make sure these athletes can excel for years to come.

At present, amateur athletes can benefit from a deferral of tax on income, through the use of an arrangement known as an amateur athlete trust. An amateur athlete is an individual who is a member of a registered Canadian amateur athletic association, eligible to compete in international sporting events as a Canadian national team member, and not a professional athlete. Income that can be contributed to an amateur athlete trust includes endorsements, prize money, or income from public appearances or speeches in connection with the athlete's participation in international sporting events.

To provide additional flexibility to amateur athletes whose trusts are maturing in 2019, Finance Minister Bill Morneau today announced the Government's intention to introduce in Parliament the legislative proposals accompanying this news release, which would extend the maturation period of these trusts by one year, from eight years to nine years. These trusts would now mature in 2020.

Additionally, the Government plans to review the tax treatment of amateur athlete trusts to ensure they continue to provide Canadian athletes with adequate financial flexibility.

Quote

"The amount of heart and hard work Canadian athletes pour into their sports is an example for others, and their success makes all Canadians proud. To help amateur ath-

letes focus on the game and continue to succeed for years to come, our Government is proposing to provide additional flexibility in the management of their finances. These athletes — and the families who support their training — have earned the rewards that come from their hard work."

— Bill Morneau, Minister of Finance

Quick Facts

- Contributions to an amateur athlete trust are exempt from income for tax purposes and investment income is not taxed as it is earned in the trust.
- Amateur athlete trust amounts (contributions plus investment income) are included in income for tax purposes upon distribution to the athlete or, at the latest, eight years after the later of the last year in which the athlete competed as a Canadian national team member and the year in which the trust was created. If any property remains in the trust at the end of the eight-year period, it is deemed to have been distributed to the amateur athlete.
- The Government is the single largest investor in Canada's amateur sport system, providing over $200 million per year to support sport development, sport excellence, and hosting for the Canada Games and international sport events.

Media may contact: Pierre-Olivier Herbert, Director of Media Relations, Office of the Minister of Finance, pierre-olivier.herbert@canada.ca, 613-369-5696; Media Relations, Department of Finance Canada, fin.media-media.fin@canada.ca, 613-369-4000.

General Enquiries: 613-369-371, fax 613-369-4065, E-mail fin.financepublic-financepublique.fin@canada.ca

Federal Budget, Supplementary Information, April 19, 2021: *Previously Announced Measures*

Budget 2021 confirms the government's intention to proceed with the following previously announced tax and related measures, as modified to take into account consultations and deliberations since their release: . . .

- The income tax measure announced on December 20, 2019 to extend the maturation period of amateur athletes trusts maturing in 2019 by one year, from eight years to nine years.

Notes: Quebec made the same change: Finances Quebec Information Bulletin 2020-2.

(4) Death of beneficiary — Where an amateur athlete trust holds property on behalf of a beneficiary who dies in a year, the trust shall be deemed to have distributed, immediately before the death, to the beneficiary, an amount equal to

(a) if the trust is liable to pay tax under Part XII.2 in respect of the year, 60% of the fair market value of all property held by it at that time; and

(b) in any other case, the fair market value of all property held by it at that time.

Notes: 143.1(4)(a) amended by 2016 budget bill #1, effective 2016, to change "64%" to "60%" (due to increase in the Part XII.2 tax rate).

Notes [s. 143.1]: 143.1 added by 1992 technical bill, effective for 1992 and later taxation years (and also for 1988–91 by election). See Notes to 143.1(1.2).

Definitions [s. 143.1]: "amateur athlete" — 143.1(1); "amateur athlete trust" — 143.1(1.2)(a), 248(1); "amount" — 248(1); "arm's length" — 251(1); "beneficiary" — 108(1); "fair market value" — see 69(2) Notes; "individual" — 248(1); "inter vivos trust" — 108(1), 248(1); "person" — 248(1); "professional athlete" — 143.1(1); "property" — 248(1); "qualifying performance income" — 143.1(1); "registered Canadian amateur athletic association" — 248(1); "registered retirement savings plan" — 146(1), 248(1); "TFSA" — 146.2(5), 248(1); "taxable income" — 248(1); "taxation year" — 11(2), 249; "third party" — 143.1(1); "trust" — 104(1), 248(1), (3).

Cost of Tax Shelter Investments and Limited-recourse Debt in Respect of Gifting Arrangements

Notes: Heading changed from "Cost of Tax Shelter Investments" by 2002-2013 technical bill (Part 5 — technical), effective Feb. 19, 2003.

143.2 (1) Definitions — The definitions in this subsection apply in this section.

"expenditure" means an outlay or expense or the cost or capital cost of a property.

Related Provisions: 143.2(2) — At-risk adjustment in respect of expenditures; 143.2(6) — Expenditures reduced by at-risk adjustment.

Notes: See Notes at end of 143.2.

"limited partner" has the meaning that would be assigned by subsection 96(2.4) if that subsection were read without reference to "if the member's partnership interest is not an exempt interest (within the meaning assigned by subsection (2.5)) at that time and".

"limited-recourse amount" means the unpaid principal amount of any indebtedness for which recourse is limited, either immediately or in the future and either absolutely or contingently.

Related Provisions: 143.2(7), (8), (13) — Whether unpaid principal deemed to be limited-recourse amount; 143.4(2)(b)(ii)(B) — Limited-recourse amount reduces expenditure for contingent amount; 237.1(1)"gifting arrangement"(b) — Limited-recourse amount creates tax shelter; 248(1) — Definition of "principal amount"; 248(1)"limited-recourse amount" — Definition applies to entire Act; Reg. 3100(1)(a)(iii) — Limited-recourse amount may be prescribed benefit for purposes of definition of tax shelter.

Notes: Appeals on this definition have been settled: *Kopstein*, 2010 TCC 448 [discontinued, 2008-2468(IT)G], and *Barker*, 2012 TCC 64 [discontinued, 2006-2167(IT)G]. See also Notes to 143.2(6) and (7).

Income Tax Folios: S7-F1-C1: Split-receipting and deemed fair market value.

"taxpayer" includes a partnership.

Notes: The effect of this definition is that the restrictions on tax shelter investments in 143.2 are calculated at the partnership level.

See also Notes at end of 143.2.

"tax shelter investment" means

(a) a property that is a tax shelter for the purpose of subsection 237.1(1); or

(b) a taxpayer's interest in a partnership where

(i) an interest in the taxpayer

(A) is a tax shelter investment, and

(B) the taxpayer's partnership interest would be a tax shelter investment if

(I) this Act were read without reference to this paragraph and to the words "having regard to statements or representations made or proposed to be made in connection with the property" in the definition "tax shelter" in subsection 237.1(1),

(II) the references in that definition to "represented" were read as references to "that can reasonably be expected", and

(III) the reference in that definition to "is represented" were read as a reference to "can reasonably be expected",

(ii) another interest in the partnership is a tax shelter investment, or

(iii) the taxpayer's interest in the partnership entitles the taxpayer, directly or indirectly, to a share of the income or loss of a particular partnership where

(A) another taxpayer holding a partnership interest is entitled, directly or indirectly, to a share of the income or loss of the particular partnership, and

(B) that other taxpayer's partnership interest is a tax shelter investment.

Related Provisions: 18.1(13) — Matchable expenditure deemed to be a tax shelter investment; 53(2)(c)(i.3) — Tax shelter investment excluded from certain ACB reductions; 125.4(4) — No Canadian film credit for a tax shelter investment; 143.2(6) — Limitation on cost of tax shelter investment; 150(1)(d)(ii)(A) — Tax shelter investment does not entitle individual to June 15 filing deadline; 249.1(5) — Election for non-calendar year-end not permitted for tax shelters; Reg. 1100(20.1), (20.2) — Limitation on CCA claim for computer tax shelter property.

Notes: See Notes to 237.1(1)"tax shelter" and to Reg. Sch. II:Cl. 12. For the meaning of "indirectly" in (b)(iii), see Notes to 17.1(1).

See Notes at end of 143.2 re in-force application.

I.T. Technical News: 22 (tax shelter news release — rulings position).

(2) At-risk adjustment — For the purpose of this section, an at-risk adjustment in respect of an expenditure of a particular taxpayer, other than the cost of a partnership interest to which subsection 96(2.2) applies, means any amount or benefit that the particular taxpayer, or another taxpayer not dealing at arm's length with the particular taxpayer, is entitled, either immediately or in the future and either absolutely or contingently, to receive or to obtain, whether by way of reimbursement, compensation, revenue guarantee, proceeds of disposition, loan or any other form of indebtedness, or in any other form or manner whatever, granted or to be granted for the purpose of reducing the impact, in whole or in part, of any loss that the particular taxpayer may sustain in respect of the expenditure or, where the expenditure is the cost or capital cost of a property, any loss from the holding or disposition of the property.

Related Provisions: 96(2.2) — At-risk amount for limited partnership; 143.2(3) — Exclusions from at-risk adjustment; 143.2(4) — Determination of amount or benefit; 143.2(6) — Expenditures reduced by at-risk adjustment; 143.2(9) — Timing.

Notes: To fall within 143.2(2), "a particular amount or benefit need not be received; entitlement thereto is sufficient": *Madell*, [2009] 5 C.T.C. 31 (FCA), para. 5.

See also Notes at end of 143.2.

(3) Amount or benefit not included — For the purpose of subsection (2), an at-risk adjustment in respect of a taxpayer's expenditure does not include an amount or benefit

(a) to the extent that it is included in determining the value of J in the definition "cumulative Canadian exploration expense" in subsection 66.1(6), of M in the definition "cumulative Canadian development expense" in subsection 66.2(5) or of I in the definition "cumulative Canadian oil and gas property expense" in subsection 66.4(5) in respect of the taxpayer; or

(b) the entitlement to which arises

(i) because of a contract of insurance with an insurance corporation dealing at arm's length with the taxpayer (and, where the expenditure is the cost of an interest in a partnership, with each member of the partnership) under which the taxpayer is insured against any claim arising as a result of a liability incurred in the ordinary course of carrying on the business of the taxpayer or the partnership,

(ii) as a consequence of the death of the taxpayer,

(iii) in respect of an amount not included in the expenditure, determined without reference to subparagraph (6)(b)(ii), or

(iv) because of an excluded obligation (as defined in subsection 6202.1(5) of the *Income Tax Regulations*) in relation to a share issued to the taxpayer or, where the expenditure is the cost of an interest in a partnership, to the partnership.

(4) Amount or benefit — For the purposes of subsections (2) and (3), where the amount or benefit to which a taxpayer is entitled at any time is provided by way of an agreement or other arrangement under which the taxpayer has a right, either immediately or in the future and either absolutely or contingently (otherwise than as a consequence of the death of the taxpayer), to acquire property, for greater certainty the amount or benefit to which the taxpayer is entitled under the agreement or arrangement is considered to be not less than the fair market value of the property at that time.

(5) Amount or benefit — For the purposes of subsections (2) and (3), where the amount or benefit to which a taxpayer is entitled at any time is provided by way of a guarantee, security or similar indemnity or covenant in respect of any loan or other obligation of the taxpayer, for greater certainty the amount or benefit to which the taxpayer is entitled under the guarantee or indemnity at any particular time is considered to be not less than the total of the unpaid amount of the loan or obligation at that time and all other amounts outstanding in respect of the loan or obligation at that time.

(6) Amount of expenditure — Notwithstanding any other provision of this Act, the amount of any expenditure that is, or is the cost or capital cost of, a taxpayer's tax shelter investment, and the amount of any expenditure of a taxpayer an interest in which is a tax shelter investment, shall be reduced to the amount, if any, by which

(a) the amount of the taxpayer's expenditure otherwise determined

exceeds

(b) the total of

(i) the limited-recourse amounts of

(A) the taxpayer, and

(B) all other taxpayers not dealing at arm's length with the taxpayer

that can reasonably be considered to relate to the expenditure,

(ii) the taxpayer's at-risk adjustment in respect of the expenditure, and

(iii) each limited-recourse amount and at-risk adjustment, determined under this section when this section is applied to each other taxpayer who deals at arm's length with and holds, directly or indirectly, an interest in the taxpayer, that can reasonably be considered to relate to the expenditure.

Related Provisions: 18.1(13) — Subpara. (6)(b)(ii) inapplicable for matchable expenditures; 143.4(2)(b)(ii)(B) — Limited-recourse amount reduces expenditure for contingent amount; 237.1(6) — No tax shelter deductions unless shelter registered with CRA; Reg. 1100(20.1), (20.2) — Limitation on CCA claim for computer tax shelter property.

Notes: In *Tolhoek*, 2008 FCA 128, a deduction for software purchased with a promissory note was limited to cash paid, as the unpaid balance was a limited-recourse amount due to 143.2(7). The same applied in *Lee*, 2020 QCCQ 780, paras. 406, 431, 451 (Prospector Networks shelter; parallel Quebec rule). See also 237.1(1)"tax shelter" Notes.

The unpaid balance of advance royalties was disallowed in *Madell*, 2009 FCA 193 (also *Caputo*, 2008 TCC 263, *Falkenberg*, 2008 TCC 265, and *Storwick*, 2008 TCC 268 — FCA appeals discontinued), as there were no *bona fide* repayment arrangements and no interest was paid.

(6.1) Limited-recourse debt in respect of a gift or monetary contribution — The limited-recourse debt in respect of a gift or monetary contribution of a taxpayer, at the time the gift or monetary contribution is made, is the total of

(a) each limited-recourse amount at that time, of the taxpayer and of all other taxpayers not dealing at arm's length with the taxpayer, that can reasonably be considered to relate to the gift or monetary contribution,

(b) each limited-recourse amount at that time, determined under this section when this section is applied to each other taxpayer who deals at arm's length with and holds, directly or indirectly, an interest in the taxpayer, that can reasonably be considered to relate to the gift or monetary contribution, and

(c) each amount that is the unpaid amount at that time of any other indebtedness, of any taxpayer referred to in paragraph (a) or (b), that can reasonably be considered to relate to the gift or monetary contribution if there is a guarantee, security or similar indemnity or covenant in respect of that or any other indebtedness.

Related Provisions: 237.1(1)"gifting arrangement"(b) — Incurring limited-recourse debt may require tax shelter registration; 248(32)(b) — Limited-recourse debt reduces value of donation; 248(34) — Repayment of limited-recourse debt.

Notes: See Notes to 143.2(7).

The term "monetary contribution" is used in this subsection without explicitly referring to the definition in 127(4.1). Finance has indicated that the term might be moved to 248(1) in the future, but that 143.2(6.1) works even without it: If anything, the ordinary meaning is broader than the meaning under 127(3), so more limited recourse debt would be included under 143.2(6.1). But 143.2(6.1) applies for 248(32), which applies for 248(31), which applies for 127(3). Thus the broad interpretation of 143.2(6.1), in the end, would only apply in the narrow circumstance in 127(3).

143.2(6.1) added by 2002-2013 technical bill, for expenditures, gifts and monetary contributions made after Feb. 18, 2003.

Income Tax Folios: S7-F1-C1: Split-receipting and deemed fair market value.

(7) Repayment of indebtedness — For the purpose of this section, the unpaid principal of an indebtedness is deemed to be a limited-recourse amount unless

(a) *bona fide* arrangements, evidenced in writing, were made, at the time the indebtedness arose, for repayment by the debtor of the indebtedness and all interest on the indebtedness within a reasonable period not exceeding 10 years; and

(b) interest is payable at least annually, at a rate equal to or greater than the lesser of

(i) the prescribed rate of interest in effect at the time the indebtedness arose, and

(ii) the prescribed rate of interest applicable from time to time during the term of the indebtedness,

and is paid in respect of the indebtedness by the debtor no later than 60 days after the end of each taxation year of the debtor that ends in the period.

Related Provisions: 143.2(12) — Series of loans or repayments; Reg. 4301(c) (prescribed rate of interest).

Notes: In *Tolhoek*, 2008 FCA 128, due to a revenue guarantee and other circumstances of a software purchase, the repayment arrangements were not *bona fide*, so the unpaid balance was not deductible (143.2(6)). The requirement of a *bona fide* arrangement in 143.2(7)(a) extends to both principal and interest: para. 50. In *O'Dea*, 2009 TCC 295, 143.2(7) applied because interest was not paid within 60 days of year-end. In *Cassan*, 2017 TCC 174 (FCA appeal settled A-304-17), paras. 339-368, loans to taxpayers as part of the EquiGenesis shelter did not have *bona fide* repayment arrangements (and were also part of a 19-year loan plan) and so fell under 143.2(6.1). The parallel Quebec rule applied in *Lee*, 2020 QCCQ 780, paras. 372-395 (Prospector Networks shelter).

In VIEWS doc 2006-0196251C6, CRA expresses the view that a particular structure creates a limited-recourse amount. See also doc 2008-0302981E5.

(8) Limited-recourse amount — For the purpose of this section, the unpaid principal of an indebtedness is deemed to be a limited-recourse amount of a taxpayer where the taxpayer is a partnership and recourse against any member of the partnership in respect of the indebtedness is limited, either immediately or in the future and either absolutely or contingently.

(9) Timing — Where at any time a taxpayer has paid an amount (in this subsection referred to as the "repaid amount") on account of the principal amount of an indebtedness that was, before that time, the unpaid principal amount of a loan or any other form of indebtedness to which subsection (2) applies (in this subsection referred to as the "former amount or benefit") relating to an expenditure of the taxpayer,

(a) the former amount or benefit is considered to have been an amount or benefit under subsection (2) in respect of the taxpayer at all times before that time; and

(b) the expenditure is, subject to subsection (6), deemed to have been made or incurred at that time to the extent of, and by the payment of, the repaid amount.

Notes: This was 143.2(5.1) in the draft legislation of December 14, 1995.

(10) Timing — Where at any time a taxpayer has paid an amount (in this subsection referred to as the "repaid amount") on account of the principal amount of an indebtedness which was, before that time, an unpaid principal amount that was a limited-recourse amount (in this subsection referred to as the "former limited-recourse indebtedness") relating to an expenditure of the taxpayer,

(a) the former limited-recourse indebtedness is considered to have been a limited-recourse amount at all times before that time; and

(b) the expenditure is, subject to subsection (6), deemed to have been made or incurred at that time to the extent of, and by the amount of, the repaid amount.

Related Provisions: 231.6 — Foreign-based information.

(11) Short-term debt — Where a taxpayer pays all of the principal of an indebtedness no later than 60 days after that indebtedness arose and the indebtedness would otherwise be considered to be a limited-recourse amount solely because of the application of subsection (7) or (8), that subsection does not apply to the indebtedness unless

(a) any portion of the repayment is made with a limited-recourse amount; or

(b) the repayment can reasonably be considered to be part of a series of loans or other indebtedness and repayments that ends more than 60 days after the indebtedness arose.

Related Provisions: 231.6 — Foreign-based information; 251(1) — Arm's length.

(12) Series of loans or repayments — For the purpose of paragraph (7)(a), a debtor is considered not to have made arrangements to repay an indebtedness within 10 years where the debtor's ar-

rangement to repay can reasonably be considered to be part of a series of loans or other indebtedness and repayments that ends more than 10 years after it begins.

Related Provisions: 248(10) — Series of transactions or events.

Notes: 143.2(12) applied in *Cassan*, 2017 TCC 174 (FCA appeal settled A-304-17), para. 366, where 10-year loans could "reasonably be considered" to be expected to be refinanced.

(13) Information located outside Canada — For the purpose of this section, if it can reasonably be considered that information relating to indebtedness that relates to a taxpayer's expenditure, gift or monetary contribution is available outside Canada and the Minister is not satisfied that the unpaid principal of the indebtedness is not a limited-recourse amount, the unpaid principal of the indebtedness relating to the taxpayer's expenditure, gift or monetary contribution is deemed to be a limited-recourse amount relating to the expenditure, gift or monetary contribution unless

(a) the information is provided to the Minister; or

(b) the information is located in a country with which the Government of Canada has entered into a tax convention or agreement that has the force of law in Canada and includes a provision under which the Minister can obtain the information.

Notes: In *Tolhoek*, 2008 FCA 128, software shelter records in Bermuda were subject to this rule even though the CRA auditor did not reference 143.2(13) when asking for them. 143.2(13) applies even if the taxpayer has no access to the records and the persons offshore do not cooperate (FCA, para. 62). As a result, the unpaid balance of the purchase price was a limited-recourse amount and only the cash paid out was deductible (143.2(6)).

143.2(13) amended by 2002-2013 technical bill (Part 5 — technical), effective for expenditures, gifts and monetary contributions made after Feb. 18, 2003, to add "gift or monetary contribution" thrice.

(14) Information located outside Canada — For the purpose of this section, where it can reasonably be considered that information relating to whether a taxpayer is not dealing at arm's length with another taxpayer is available outside Canada and the Minister is not satisfied that the taxpayer is dealing at arm's length with the other taxpayer, the taxpayer and the other taxpayer are deemed not to be dealing with each other at arm's length unless

(a) the information is provided to the Minister; or

(b) the information is located in a country with which the Government of Canada has entered into a tax convention or agreement that has the force of law in Canada and includes a provision under which the Minister can obtain the information.

(15) Assessments — Notwithstanding subsections 152(4) to (5), such assessments, determinations and redeterminations may be made as are necessary to give effect to this section.

Related Provisions: 237.1(6.2) — Late assessment to deny deduction when penalty unpaid.

Notes: Late reassessments were allowed under 143.2(15) in *Tolhoek*, 2008 FCA 128 (the words "as are necessary" did not restrict the rule); *O'Dea*, 2009 TCC 295 (143.2(7) applied).

Notes [s. 143.2]: See Notes to 237.1(1)"tax shelter".

143.2 added by 1995-97 technical bill, for property acquired and outlays and expenses made or incurred by a taxpayer after Nov. 1994, with certain grandfathering for 1994 and 1995.

Definitions [s. 143.2]: "amount" — 143.2(4), (5.1), (6), 248(1); "arm's length" — 143.2(11), 251(1); "at-risk adjustment" — 143.2(2), (3); "benefit" — 143.2(4), (5.1); "business" — 248(1); "Canada" — 255; "consequence of the death" — 248(8); "excluded obligation" — Reg. 6202.1(5); "expenditure" — 143.2(1), (6); "fair market value" — see 69(1) Notes; "former limited-recourse indebtedness" — 143.2(9); "insurance corporation" — 248(1); "limited partner" — 143.2(1); "limited-recourse amount" — 143.2(1), (7), (8); "Minister" — 248(1); "monetary contribution" — 127(4.1); "partnership" — see 96(1) Notes; "prescribed" — 248(1); "prescribed rate" — Reg. 4301; "principal amount" — 248(1), (26); "property" — 248(1); "repaid amount" — 143.2(9); "regulation" — 248(1); "security" — *Interpretation Act* 35(1); "series" — 248(10); "specified member" — 248(1); "tax shelter investment" — 143.2(1); "taxpayer" — 143.2(1), 248(1); "taxation year" — 249.

Expenditure — Limitations

143.3 [Issuing shares or options is not an expenditure] — **(1) Definitions** — The following definitions apply in this section.

"expenditure" of a taxpayer means an expense, expenditure or outlay made or incurred by the taxpayer, or a cost or capital cost of property acquired by the taxpayer.

"option" means

(a) a security that is issued or sold by a taxpayer under an agreement referred to in subsection 7(1); or

(b) an option, warrant or similar right, issued or granted by a taxpayer, giving the holder the right to acquire an interest in the taxpayer or in another taxpayer with whom the taxpayer does not, at the time the option, warrant or similar right is issued or granted, deal at arm's length.

Notes: Para. (a) was added in the Oct. 24/12 draft, and does not apply to securities issued or sold before that date (see Notes at end of 143.3).

"taxpayer" includes a partnership.

(2) Options — limitation — In computing a taxpayer's income, taxable income or tax payable or an amount considered to have been paid on account of the taxpayer's tax payable, an expenditure of the taxpayer is deemed not to include any portion of the expenditure that would — if this Act were read without reference to this subsection — be included in determining the expenditure because of the taxpayer having granted or issued an option on or after November 17, 2005.

Related Provisions: 7(3)(b) — No reduction in employer's income from issuing stock options; 49(2), (2.1) — Non-arm's length exclusion to rules on expiry of option; 110(1)(e), 143.3(5) — Deduction allowed for stock options in excess of $200,000/year where 110(1)(d) deduction disallowed; 143.3(5) — Exceptions.

Notes: See Notes at end of 143.3.

(3) Corporate shares — limitation — In computing a corporation's income, taxable income or tax payable or an amount considered to have been paid on account of the corporation's tax payable, an expenditure of the corporation that would — if this Act were read without reference to this subsection — include an amount because of the corporation having issued a share of its capital stock at any particular time on or after November 17, 2005 is reduced by

(a) if the issuance of the share is not a consequence of the exercise of an option, the amount, if any, by which the fair market value of the share at the particular time exceeds

(i) if the transaction under which the share is issued is a transaction to which section 85, 85.1 or 138 applies, the amount determined under that section to be the cost to the issuing corporation of the property acquired in consideration for issuing the share, or

(ii) in any other case, the amount of the consideration that is the fair market value of the property transferred or issued to, or the services provided to, the issuing corporation for issuing the share; and

(b) if the issuance of the share is a consequence of the exercise of an option, the amount, if any, by which the fair market value of the share at the particular time exceeds the amount paid, pursuant to the terms of the option, by the holder to the issuing taxpayer for issuing the share.

Related Provisions: 52(3)(a) — Cost of share received as stock dividend excludes amount deductible under 112(1); 110(1)(e), 143.3(5) — Deduction allowed for stock options in excess of $200,000/year where 110(1)(d) deduction disallowed; 143.3(5) — Exceptions.

Notes: For CRA interpretation see VIEWS docs 2006-0176321R3 (conversion of co-op to ordinary corp); 2006-0205771R3 (143.3(3) affects 88(1)(d) bump); 2008-0300101R3 (143.3(3) does not apply); 2008-0300102R3 (same); 2011-0425441R3 (cross-border butterfly); 2016-0670201C6 [2016 CTF q.3] (143.3(3) could apply to *Agnico-Eagle* [see Notes to 39(2)]).

See Notes to 143.3(5) re the words "or issued" in (3)(a)(ii); and Notes at end of 143.3.

(4) Non-corporate interests — limitation — In computing a taxpayer's (other than a corporation's) income, taxable income or tax payable or an amount considered to have been paid on account of the taxpayer's tax payable, an expenditure of the taxpayer that would — if this Act were read without reference to this subsection — include an amount because of the taxpayer having issued an interest, or because of an interest being created, in itself at any particular time on or after November 17, 2005 is reduced by

(a) if the issuance or creation of the interest is not a consequence of the exercise of an option, the amount, if any, by which the fair market value of the interest at the particular time exceeds

(i) if the transaction under which the interest is issued is a transaction to which paragraph 70(6)(b) or 73(1.01)(c), subsection 97(2) or section 107.4 or 132.2 applies, the amount determined under that provision to be the cost to the taxpayer of the property acquired for the interest, or

(ii) in any other case, the amount of the consideration that is the fair market value of the property transferred or issued to, or the services provided to, the taxpayer for the interest; and

(b) if the issuance or creation of the interest is a consequence of the exercise of an option, the amount, if any, by which the fair market value of the interest at the particular time exceeds the amount paid, pursuant to the terms of the option, by the holder to the taxpayer for the interest.

Related Provisions: 143.3(5) — Exceptions.

(5) Clarification — For greater certainty,

(a) subsection (2) does not apply to reduce an expenditure that is a commission, fee or other amount for services rendered by a person as a salesperson, agent or dealer in securities in the course of the issuance of an option;

(b) subsections (3) and (4) do not apply to reduce an expenditure of a taxpayer to the extent that the expenditure does not include an amount determined to be an excess under those subsections;

(c) this section does not apply to determine the cost or capital cost of property determined under subsection 70(6), section 73, 85 or 85.1, subsection 97(2) or section 107.4, 132.2 or 138;

(d) this section does not apply to determine the amount of a taxpayer's expenditure if the amount of the expenditure as determined under section 69 is less than the amount that would, if this subsection were read without reference to this paragraph, be the amount of the expenditure as determined under this section; and

(e) this section does not apply to prohibit the deduction of an amount under paragraph 110(1)(e).

Notes: 143.3(5)(e) added by 2021 budget bill #1, effective July 2021. (A former draft (e) (July 16/10), implementing Dec. 10, 2009 Finance comfort letters, was withdrawn, and "or issued" added to 143.3(3)(a)(ii) instead.)

Notes [s. 143.3]: 143.3 overrides *Alcatel*, 2005 TCC 149, where a company was allowed SR&ED credits for stock options it issued. Note that 7(3)(b) already prohibits an *income* deduction to the employer: VIEWS doc 2008-0301171I7, but see the *TransAlta* case in 7(3) Notes.

For discussion of 143.3 see Brad Warden, "The *Alcatel* Legacy", 17(3) *Taxation Law* (Ontario Bar Assn, oba.org) 9-13 (April 2007); Marc Ton-That & Sam Tyler, "Recent Developments Affecting the Taxation of Convertible Debentures", X(3) *Corporate Structures & Groups* (Federated Press) 556-65 (2007); Mark Brender, "Finance Strikes Back at Alcatel", X(3) *CS&G* 567-70; Marc Ton-That, "Unintended Section 143.3 Application", 17(5) *Canadian Tax Highlights* (ctf.ca) 4 (May 2009); Chris Falk, Stefanie Morand & Brian O'Neill, "Is There Always Certainty Regarding Tax Basis?", 2014 Cdn Tax Foundation conference report, 14:1-36.

143.3 added by 2002-2013 technical bill effective Nov. 17, 2005, but for securities issued or sold before Oct. 24, 2012, ignore 143.3(1)"option"(a).

Definitions [s. 143.3]: "amount" — 248(1); "arm's length" — 251(1); "corporation" — 248(1), *Interpretation Act* 35(1); "expenditure" — 143.3(1); "fair market value" — see 69(1) Notes; "option" — 143.3(1); "partnership" — see 96(1) Notes; "person", "property", "share", "taxable income" — 248(1); "taxpayer" — 143.3(1), 248(1).

Expenditure — Limit for Contingent Amount

143.4 (1) Definitions — The following definitions apply in this section.

"**contingent amount**", of a taxpayer at any time (other than a time at which the taxpayer is a bankrupt), includes an amount to the extent that the taxpayer, or another taxpayer that does not deal at arm's length with the taxpayer, has a right to reduce the amount at that time.

Related Provisions: 87(2)(l.5) — Amalgamation — continuing corporation.

Notes: Since the definition uses "includes" rather than "means" (see 188.1(5) Notes), the ordinary meaning of "contingent" should apply as well: see 18(1)(e) Notes. See also the definition of "right to reduce", below.

Due to *Century Services [Leroy Trucking]*, 2010 SCC 60, the exclusion during bankruptcy might also apply during *Companies' Creditors Arrangement Act* protection.

"**expenditure**", of a taxpayer, means an expense, expenditure or outlay made or incurred by the taxpayer, or a cost or capital cost of property acquired by the taxpayer.

Related Provisions: 87(2)(l.5) — Amalgamation — continuing corporation.

"**right to reduce**" means a right to reduce or eliminate an amount in respect of an expenditure at any time, including, for greater certainty, a right to reduce that is contingent upon the occurrence of an event, or in any other way contingent, if it is reasonable to conclude, having regard to all the circumstances, that the right will become exercisable.

Notes: For the meaning of "contingent" see Notes to 18(1)(e).

"**taxpayer**" includes a partnership.

(2) Limitation of amount of expenditure — For the purposes of this Act, if in a taxation year of a taxpayer an expenditure of the taxpayer occurs, the amount of the expenditure at any time is the lesser of

(a) the amount of the expenditure at the time calculated under this Act without reference to this section, and

(b) the least amount of the expenditure calculated by reducing the amount of the expenditure determined under paragraph (a) by the amount that is the amount, if any, by which

(i) the total of all amounts each of which is a contingent amount of the taxpayer in the year in respect of the expenditure

exceeds

(ii) the total of all amounts each of which is

(A) an amount paid by the taxpayer to obtain a right to reduce an amount in respect of the expenditure, or

(B) a limited-recourse amount for the purposes of paragraph 143.2(6)(b) that reduces the expenditure under subsection 143.2(6) to the extent that the amount is also a contingent amount described in subparagraph (i) in respect of the expenditure.

Related Provisions: 18(1)(e) — No deduction from business or property for contingent amount; 87(2)(l.5) — Amalgamation — continuing corporation; 143.4(3) — Where amount is later paid; 143.4(4) — Later year's right-to-reduce included in income; 143.4(6) — Anti-avoidance; 143.4(7) — Late reassessment permitted.

Notes: 143.4(2) overlaps with 18(1)(e), but is broader as it applies to any expenditure (e.g. for investment tax credit) rather than only deductions from business or property income, and applies to a "right to reduce" (overruling *Collins*, 2010 FCA 12). See also Notes to 143.4(1)"contingent amount" and "right to reduce".

For discussion see Frankovic, "Draft Legislation on Contingent Amounts", 2037 *Tax Topics* (CCH) 1-3 (March 24, 2011). For criticism see CBA/CICA Joint Committee letter to Finance, Nov. 7, 2011; Falk et al., "Is There Always Certainty Regarding Tax Basis?", 2014 Cdn Tax Foundation conference report, 14:1-36.

On interaction with s. 80 see VIEWS docs 2016-062874I7; 2016-0661071R3 (s. 80 applies instead of 143.4 if interest on commercial debt is forgiven and CCAA arrangement entered into in same year [Carrie Smit & Mitchell Sherman, "Wrong to Reduce", XIV *Corporate Structures & Groups* (Federated Press) 2-7 (2017)]).

Cl. (b)(ii)(B) was added in the Oct. 24, 2012 draft.

(3) Payment of contingent amount — For the purposes of this Act, if in a particular taxation year, a taxpayer pays all or a portion of a contingent amount referred to in paragraph (2)(b) that reduces the amount of the taxpayer's expenditure referred to in paragraph (2)(a), the portion of the contingent amount paid by the taxpayer in the particular year for the purpose of earning income, and to that extent only, is deemed

(a) to have been incurred by the taxpayer in the particular year;

(b) to have been incurred for the same purpose and to have the same character as the expenditure so reduced; and

(c) to have become payable by the taxpayer in respect of the particular year.

Related Provisions: 87(2)(l.5) — Amalgamation — continuing corporation.

(4) Subsequent years — Subject to subsection (6), if at any time in a taxation year that is after a taxation year in which an expenditure of the taxpayer occurred, the taxpayer, or another taxpayer not dealing at arm's length with the taxpayer, has a right to reduce an amount in respect of the expenditure (in this subsection and subsection (5) referred to as the "prior expenditure") that would, if the taxpayer or the other taxpayer had had the right to reduce in a particular taxation year that ended before the time, have resulted in subsection (2) applying in the particular taxation year to reduce or eliminate the amount of the prior expenditure, the taxpayer's subsequent contingent amount in respect of the prior expenditure, as determined under subsection (5), is deemed, to the extent subsection (2) and this subsection have not previously applied in respect of the expenditure,

(a) to be an amount received by the taxpayer at the time in the course of earning income from a business or property from a person described in subparagraph 12(1)(x)(i); and

(b) to be an amount referred to in subparagraph 12(1)(x)(iv).

Related Provisions: 143.4(5) — Meaning of "subsequent contingent amount".

(5) Subsequent contingent amount — For the purposes of subsection (4), a taxpayer's subsequent contingent amount in respect of a prior expenditure of the taxpayer is the amount, if any, by which

(a) the maximum amount by which the amount (in this subsection referred to as the "particular amount") in respect of the prior expenditure may be reduced pursuant to a right to reduce the particular amount

exceeds

(b) the amount, if any, paid to obtain the right to reduce the particular amount.

(6) Anti-avoidance — If a taxpayer, or another taxpayer that does not deal at arm's length with the taxpayer, has a right to reduce an amount in respect of an expenditure of the taxpayer in a taxation year that is after the taxation year in which the expenditure otherwise occurred, determined without reference to subsection (3), the taxpayer is deemed to have the right to reduce in the taxation year in which that expenditure otherwise occurred if it is reasonable to conclude having regard to all the circumstances that one of the purposes for having the right to reduce after the end of the year in which the expenditure otherwise occurred was to avoid the application of subsection (2) to the amount of the expenditure.

(7) Assessments [no limitation period] — Notwithstanding subsections 152(4) to (5), such assessments, determinations and redeterminations may be made as are necessary to give effect to this section.

Related Provisions: 87(2)(l.5) — Amalgamation — continuing corporation.

Notes [s. 143.4]: See Notes to 143.4(2). 143.4 added by 2002-2013 technical bill (Part 5 — technical), for taxation years that end after March 15, 2011.

Definitions [s. 143.4]: "amount" — 248(1); "arm's length" — 251(1); "assessment", "bankrupt", "business" — 248(1); "contingent amount", "expenditure" — 143.3(1); "limited-recourse amount" — 143.2(1); "partnership" — see 96(1) Notes; "person" — 248(1); "prior expenditure" — 143.4(4); "property" — 248(1); "right to reduce" — 143.4(1); "subsequent contingent amount" — 143.4(5); "taxation year" — 249; "taxpayer" — 143.4(1), 248(1).

Income Tax Folios: S3-F6-C1: Interest deductibility [replaces IT-533].

DIVISION G — DEFERRED AND OTHER SPECIAL INCOME ARRANGEMENTS

Employees Profit Sharing Plans

144. (1) Definitions — The definitions in this subsection apply in this section.

"employees profit sharing plan" at a particular time means an arrangement

(a) under which payments computed by reference to

(i) an employer's profits from the employer's business,

(ii) the profits from the business of a corporation with which the employer does not deal at arm's length, or

(iii) any combination of the amounts described in subparagraphs (i) and (ii)

are required to be made by the employer to a trustee under the arrangement for the benefit of employees of the employer or of a corporation with which the employer does not deal at arm's length; and

(b) in respect of which the trustee has, since the later of the beginning of the arrangement and the end of 1949, allocated, either contingently or absolutely, to those employees

(i) in each year that ended at or before the particular time, all amounts received in the year by the trustee from the employer or from a corporation with which the employer does not deal at arm's length,

(ii) in each year that ended at or before the particular time, all profits for the year from the property of the trust (determined without regard to any capital gain made by the trust or capital loss sustained by it at any time after 1955),

(iii) in each year that ended after 1971 and at or before the particular time, all capital gains and capital losses of the trust for the year,

(iv) in each year that ended after 1971, before 1993 and at or before the particular time, 100/15 of the total of all amounts each of which is deemed by subsection (9) to be paid on account of tax under this Part in respect of an employee because the employee ceased to be a beneficiary under the plan in the year, and

(v) in each year that ended after 1991 and at or before the particular time, the total of all amounts each of which is an amount that may be deducted under subsection (9) in computing the employee's income because the employee ceased to be a beneficiary under the plan in the year.

Possible Future Amendment — Employee ownership trusts

Federal Budget, Chapter 3, April 19, 2021: See under 7(1).

Related Provisions: 75(3)(a) — Reversionary trust rules do not apply to EPSP; 94(1)"exempt foreign trust"(e) — Non-resident EPSP excluded from non-resident trust rules; 108(1)"trust"(a) — "Trust" does not include an EPSP for certain purposes; 128.1(10)"excluded right or interest"(a)(v) — No deemed disposition on emigration; 144(9) — Refunds; 144(10) — Payments out of profits; 144(11) — Year-end on becoming DPSP; 147(6) — DPSP deemed not to be EPSP; 207.8 — Tax on excess EPSP amount; 233.2(1)"exempt trust"(b)(iv)(B) — foreign EPSP exempt from foreign trust reporting rules; 248(1)"disposition"(f)(vi) — Rollover from one trust to another; 248(1)"employees profit sharing plan" — Definition applies to entire Act; 251(1) — Arm's length.

Notes: An EPSP is a trust to which an employer pays an amount based on its profits for Year 1, to be allocated to employees. The employee pays tax based on the allocation (144(3)) and not when the funds are received (144(6), (7)). The employer can deduct the amount paid for Year 1 but can make payment up to 120 days into Year 2 (144(5)). No withholding tax applies to the payments (153(1)) does not apply), so in some cases the employee's tax payment can be deferred until April 30 of Year 3. Making an EPSP contribution every second year avoids having to include the EPSP allocation in the employee's instalment base under 156(1).

See Fowlis, "Planning Considerations With Respect to Employees Profit Sharing Plans", 16(6) *Taxation of Executive Compensation & Retirement* (Federated Press) 503-06 (Feb. 2005); Sweatman & Hodge, "Employee Benefit Plans and Employee

Profit Sharing Plans", 16(9) *TECR* 539-47 (May 2005); Léger, "The EPSP as a Tax-Planning Tool", 10(4) *Tax for the Owner-Manager* (ctf.ca) 2-3 (Oct. 2010); Blucher, "EPSP Update", 8(5) *Tax Hyperion* (Carswell, May 2011).

Employer CPP contributions need not be made when an EPSP is used to channel income to an employee: *Greber Professional Corp.*, 2007 TCC 78; CRA May 2007 ICAA roundtable (tinyurl.com/cra-abtax), Q10; Charles Rotenberg, "Planning with EPSPs", xxix(19) *The Canadian Taxpayer* (Carswell) 145-46 (Sept. 25, 2007).

For general CRA information on EPSPs, see IT-280R, IT-379R; VIEWS doc 2011-0412181E5. For a detailed example see ruling 2001-0112123. A plan allowing the employee to choose annually whether to direct the employer contribution to an RRSP or an EPSP is likely not a valid EPSP: 2006-0180081E5. There must be a "realistic formula in which profits are the principal variable... It is not enough that profits are used only as a means of calculating the employer's contribution": 2009-0328661E5. An EPSP cannot be amended to remove the employer's contribution obligation: 2018-0738561E5. Using a fully-leveraged EPSP to defer compensation was rejected: 2018-0762101I7 [Pitch, "The Meaning behind the Ruling", XXVI(3) *Taxation of Executive Compensation & Retirement* (Federated Press) 9-11 (2019)]. For more on CRA assessing procedures see May 2006 ICAA roundtable (tinyurl.com/cra-abtax), q. 19. No contribution can be made after an employee dies, since the person is no longer an employee: 2013-0503771E5.

In *Fischer*, 2003 TCC 272, a Nesbitt Burns "Employee Share Ownership Plan" was held to be an EPSP given the broad definition of EPSP and the lack of evidence as to the plan. In *Lade*, [1965] C.T.C. 525 (SCC), an employees share ownership plan was held not to be an EPSP because the matching contributions made by the employer were not "computed by reference to the employer's profits" in the year. In *Jackson Professional Corp.*, 2013 FCA 142, an attempted EPSP failed because payments were discretionary and no 144(10) election had been made.

In *Dimane Enterprises*, 2014 TCC 334, an EPSP was held to be a sham because distributions were not really paid to the company owner's children (the purported employees), as the owner retained control of the funds, and the children's "employment" was household chores. In *J.R. Saint & Associates*, 2010 TCC 168, salary paid through an EPSP was held in part to be genuine.

On collapsing an EPSP, see VIEWS doc 2007-0250341E5. A transfer from one employer's EPSP to another's, for the same employee, is not a "disposition" of property: 2010-0385471E5.

Definition amended by 1993 technical bill, for 1992 and later taxation years.

Regulations: 204(3)(b) (no requirement to file regular trust return); 212 (information return).

Interpretation Bulletins: IT-280R: Employees profit sharing plans — payments computed by reference to profits; IT-379R: Employees profit sharing plans — allocations to beneficiaries.

"unused portion of a beneficiary's exempt capital gains balance" in respect of a trust governed by an employees profit sharing plan, at any particular time in a taxation year of the beneficiary, means

(a) where the year ends before 2005, the amount, if any, by which the beneficiary's exempt capital gains balance (in this paragraph having the same meaning as in subsection 39.1(1)) in respect of the trust for the year exceeds the total of all amounts each of which is an amount by which a capital gain is reduced under section 39.1 in the year because of the beneficiary's exempt capital gains balance in respect of the trust; or

(b) where the year ends after 2004, the amount, if any, by which

(i) the amount, if any, that would, if the definition "exempt capital gains balance" in subsection 39.1(1) were read without reference to "that ends before 2005", be the beneficiary's exempt capital gains balance in respect of the trust for the year

exceeds

(ii) where there has been a disposition of an interest or a part of an interest of the beneficiary in the trust after the beneficiary's 2004 taxation year (other than a disposition that is a part of a transaction described in paragraph (7.1)(c) in which property is received in satisfaction of all or a portion of the beneficiary's interests in the trust), the total of all amounts each of which is an amount by which the adjusted cost base of an interest or a part of an interest disposed of by the beneficiary (other than an interest or a part of an interest that is all or a portion of the beneficiary's interests referred to in paragraph (7.1)(c)) was increased because of paragraph 53(1)(p), and

(iii) in any other case, nil.

Notes: Definition added by 1995-97 technical bill, for 1994 and later tax years.

(2) No tax while trust governed by a plan — No tax is payable under this Part by a trust on the taxable income of the trust for a taxation year throughout which the trust is governed by an employees profit sharing plan.

Related Provisions: 149(1)(p) — Exemption from tax.

Notes: 144(2) amended by 1993 technical bill, effective for 1993 and later taxation years, to require that the EPSP be in place "throughout" the year.

(3) Allocation contingent or absolute taxable — There shall be included in computing the income for a taxation year of an employee who is a beneficiary under an employees profit sharing plan each amount that is allocated to the employee contingently or absolutely by the trustee under the plan at any time in the year otherwise than in respect of

(a) a payment made by the employee to the trustee;

(b) a capital gain made by the trust before 1972;

(c) a capital gain of the trust for a taxation year ending after 1971;

(d) a gain made by the trust after 1971 from the disposition of a capital property except to the extent that the gain is a capital gain described in paragraph (c); or

(e) a dividend received by the trust from a taxable Canadian corporation.

(f) [Repealed]

Related Provisions: 6(1)(d) — Inclusion in income from employment; 144(8) — Allocation of credit for dividends; 147(11) — Portion of receipts deductible where EPSP later becomes a DPSP.

Notes: In *Fischer*, 2003 TCC 272, an employer's EPSP contribution was taxable even though the allocation to the employee may not have been absolute. Foreign tax credit on the allocation: VIEWS doc 2016-0676431E5.

144(3)(f) repealed by 1993 technical bill, effective for 1992 and later taxation years (or 1993 by election).

Regulations: 212 (information return).

Interpretation Bulletins: IT-379R: Employees' profit sharing plans — allocations to beneficiaries.

Forms: T4PS: Statement of employee profit sharing plan allocations and payments; T4PS Summary: Employee profit-sharing plan payments and allocations; T4PS Segment.

(4) Allocated capital gains and losses — Each capital gain and capital loss of a trust governed by an employees profit sharing plan from the disposition of any property shall, to the extent that it is allocated by the trust to an employee who is a beneficiary under the plan, be deemed to be a capital gain or capital loss, as the case may be, of the employee from the disposition of that property for the taxation year of the employee in which the allocation was made and, for the purposes of section 110.6, the property shall be deemed to have been disposed of by the employee on the day on which it was disposed of by the trust.

Related Provisions: 6(1)(d) — Allocations etc. under profit sharing plan.

Notes: Where an EPSP member forfeits a previously allocated capital gain and the EPSP re-allocates the gain, the amount is taxable to the member to whom it is allocated: VIEWS doc 2005-0161671E5.

144(4) amended by 1994 Budget, effective 1994.

Interpretation Bulletins: IT-379R: Employees profit sharing plans — allocations to beneficiaries.

(4.1) Idem — Notwithstanding subsection 26(6) of the *Income Tax Application Rules*, where at any time before 1976 the trustee of a trust governed by an employees profit sharing plan so elects in prescribed manner, the trust shall be deemed

(a) to have, on December 31, 1971, disposed of each property owned by the trust on that day for proceeds of disposition equal to the fair market value of the property on that day, and

(b) to have, on January 1, 1972, reacquired each property described in paragraph (a) for the amount referred to in that paragraph,

if the trustee under the plan has, before 1976, allocated the total of all capital gains and capital losses resulting from the deemed dispositions among the employees or other beneficiaries under the plan to the extent that the trustee under the plan has not previously so allocated them.

Related Provisions: 54"superficial loss"(c) — Superficial loss rule does not apply.

Regulations: 1500(1) (prescribed manner).

Interpretation Bulletins: IT-379R: Employees profit sharing plans — allocations to beneficiaries.

(4.2) Idem — Where a trust governed by an employees profit sharing plan

(a) was governed by an employees profit sharing plan on December 31, 1971, and the trustee of the trust has made an election under subsection (4.1), or

(b) was not governed by an employees profit sharing plan on December 31, 1971,

the trustee of the trust may, in any taxation year after 1973, elect in prescribed manner and prescribed form to treat any capital property of the trust as having been disposed of, in which event the property shall be deemed to have been disposed of on any day designated by the trustee for proceeds of disposition equal to

(c) the fair market value of the property on that day,

(d) the adjusted cost base to the trust of the property on that day, or

(e) an amount that is neither greater than the greater of the amounts determined under paragraphs (c) and (d) nor less than the lesser of the amounts determined under those paragraphs

whichever is designated by the trustee and to have been reacquired by the trust immediately thereafter at a cost equal to those proceeds.

Related Provisions: 54"superficial loss"(c) — Superficial loss rule does not apply.

Regulations: 1500(2) (prescribed manner).

Interpretation Bulletins: IT-379R: Employees profit sharing plans — allocations to beneficiaries.

Forms: T3009: Election for deemed disposition and reacquisition of any capital property of an employees profit sharing plan under subsection 144(4.2).

(5) Employer's contribution to trust deductible — An amount paid by an employer to a trustee under an employees profit sharing plan during a taxation year or within 120 days thereafter may be deducted in computing the employer's income for the taxation year to the extent that it was not deductible in computing income for a previous taxation year.

Related Provisions: 18(1)(k) — Limitation re employer's contribution under profit sharing plan; 20(1)(w) — Employer's contribution deductible; 207.8 — Tax on excess EPSP amount; *Interpretation Act* 27(5) — Meaning of "within 120 days".

Notes: A contribution in the first 120 days can be deducted in either the previous year or the current year: May 2010 ICAA roundtable (tinyurl.com/cra-abtax), q.2.

No deduction is allowed for a contribution after an employee dies: see Notes to 144(1)"employees profit sharing plan".

(6) Beneficiary's receipts deductible [not taxable] — An amount received in a taxation year by a beneficiary from a trustee under an employees profit sharing plan shall not be included in computing the beneficiary's income for the year.

Related Provisions: 144(7) — Exceptions.

(7) Beneficiary's receipts that are not deductible — Notwithstanding subsection (6), such portion of an amount received in a taxation year by a beneficiary from the trustee under an employees profit sharing plan as cannot be established to be attributable to

(a) payments made by the employee to the trustee,

(b) amounts required to be included in computing the income of the employee for that or a previous taxation year,

(c) a capital gain made by the trust before 1972,

(d) a capital gain made by the trust for a taxation year ending after 1971, to the extent allocated by the trust to the beneficiary,

(e) a gain made by the trust after 1971 from the disposition of a capital property, except to the extent that the gain is a capital gain made by the trust for a taxation year ending after 1971,

(f) the portion, if any, of the increase in the value of property transferred to the beneficiary by the trustee that would have been considered to be a capital gain made by the trust in 1971 if the trustee had sold the property on December 31, 1971 for its fair market value at that time, or

(g) a dividend received by the trust from a taxable Canadian corporation other than a dividend described in subsection 83(1), to the extent allocated by the trust to the beneficiary,

shall be included in computing the beneficiary's income for the year in which the amount was received, except that in determining the amount of any payments or other things described in any paragraph of this subsection, the amount thereof otherwise determined shall be reduced by such portion of the total of all capital losses of the trust for taxation years ending after 1971 as has been allocated by the trust to the beneficiary and has not been applied to reduce the amount of any payments or other things described in any other paragraph of this subsection.

Related Provisions: 6(1)(d) — Allocations etc. under profit sharing plan; 212 — Tax on Canadian income of non-resident persons.

Interpretation Bulletins: IT-379R: Employees profit sharing plan — allocations to beneficiaries.

Forms: T4PS: Statement of employee profit sharing plan allocations and payments; T4PS Summary: Employee profit-sharing plan payments and allocations; T4PS Segment.

(7.1) Where property other than money received by beneficiary — Where, at any particular time in a taxation year of a trust governed by an employees profit sharing plan, an amount was received by a beneficiary from the trustee under the plan and the amount so received was property other than money, the following rules apply in respect of each such property so received by the beneficiary at the particular time:

(a) the amount that was the cost amount to the trust of the property immediately before the particular time shall be deemed to be the trust's proceeds of disposition of the property; and

(b) that proportion of

(i) such portion of the amount received by the beneficiary as can be established to be attributable to the payments or other things described in paragraphs (7)(a) to (g) (on the assumption that the amount of any payments or other things described in any such paragraph is the amount thereof determined as provided in subsection (7))

that

(ii) the cost amount to the trust of the property immediately before the particular time

is of

(iii) the cost amounts to the trust of all properties, other than money, so received by the beneficiary at the particular time,

is, subject to paragraph (c), deemed to be

(iv) the cost to the beneficiary of the property, and

(v) for the purposes of subsection (7) but not for the purposes of this subsection, the amount so received by the beneficiary by virtue of the receipt by the beneficiary of the property.

(c) where a particular property received is all or a portion of property received in satisfaction of all or a portion of the beneficiary's interests in the trust and the beneficiary files with the Minister on or before the beneficiary's filing-due date for the taxation year that includes the particular time an election in respect of the particular property in prescribed form, there shall be included in the cost to the beneficiary of the particular property determined under paragraph (b) the least of

(i) the amount, if any, by which the unused portion of the beneficiary's exempt capital gains balance in respect of the trust at the particular time exceeds the total of all amounts each of which is an amount included because of this paragraph in the cost to the beneficiary of another property received by the beneficiary at or before the particular time in the year,

(ii) the amount, if any, by which the fair market value of the particular property at the particular time exceeds the amount deemed by subparagraph (b)(iv) to be the cost to the beneficiary of the particular property, and

(iii) the amount designated in the election in respect of the particular property.

Notes: 144(7.1)(c) (and reference to it in (b)) added by 1995-97 technical bill, effective for 1994 and later taxation years; and a prescribed form filed under 144(7.1)(c) by the end of 1998 is deemed filed on time.

Interpretation Bulletins: IT-379R: Employees profit sharing plan — allocations to beneficiaries.

Forms: T4PS: Statement of employee profit sharing plan allocations and payments; T4PS Summary: Employee profit-sharing plan payments and allocations; T4PS Segment.

(8) Allocation of credit for dividends — Where there has been included in computing the income of a trust for a taxation year during which the trust was governed by an employees profit sharing plan taxable dividends from taxable Canadian corporations and there has been allocated by the trustee under the plan for the purposes of this subsection an amount for the year to one or more of the employees who are beneficiaries under the plan, which amount or the total of which amounts does not exceed the amount of the taxable dividends so included, each of the employees who are beneficiaries under the plan shall be deemed to have received a taxable dividend from a taxable Canadian corporation equal to the lesser of

(a) the amount, if any, that would be included in computing the employee's income for the year by virtue of this section, if this section were read without reference to paragraph (3)(e), and

(b) the amount, if any, so allocated for the purposes of this subsection to the employee.

Interpretation Bulletins: IT-379R: Employees profit sharing plans — allocations to beneficiaries.

(8.1) Foreign tax deduction [foreign tax credit] — For the purpose of subsection 126(1), the following rules apply:

(a) such portion of the income for a taxation year of a trust governed by an employees profit sharing plan from sources (other than businesses carried on by it) in a foreign country as

(i) may reasonably be considered (having regard to all the circumstances including the terms and conditions of the plan) to be part of

(A) the income that, by virtue of subsection (3), was included in computing the income for a taxation year of a particular employee who was a beneficiary under the plan, or

(B) the amount, if any, by which

(I) the total of amounts each of which is a capital gain of the trust that, by virtue of subsection (4), was deemed to be a capital gain of the particular employee for a taxation year

exceeds

(II) the total of amounts each of which is a capital loss of the trust that, by virtue of subsection (4), was deemed to be a capital loss of the particular employee for the taxation year, and

(ii) was not designated by the trust in respect of any other employee who was a beneficiary under the plan,

shall, if so designated by the trust in respect of the particular employee in its return of income for the year under this Part, be deemed to be income of the particular employee for the taxation year from sources in that country; and

(b) an employee who is a beneficiary under an employees profit sharing plan shall be deemed to have paid as non-business-income tax for a taxation year, on the income that the employee is deemed by paragraph (a) to have for the year from sources in a foreign country, to the government of that country an amount equal to that proportion of the non-business-income tax paid by the trust governed by the plan for the year to the government of

that country, or to the government of a state, province or other political subdivision of that country (except such portion of that tax as was deductible under subsection 20(11) in computing its income for the year) that

(i) the income that the employee is deemed by paragraph (a) to have for the year from sources in that country

is of

(ii) the income of the trust for the year from sources (other than businesses carried on by it) in that country.

Notes: For an employer filing Quebec returns, the election must be copied to Revenu Québec: *Taxation Act* ss. 865, 21.4.6.

(8.2) [Repealed]

Notes: 144(8.2) repealed by 1993 technical bill, for 1992 and later tax years.

(9) Deduction for forfeited amounts — Where a person ceases at any time in a taxation year to be a beneficiary under an employees profit sharing plan and does not become a beneficiary under the plan after that time and in the year, there may be deducted in computing the person's income for the year the amount determined by the formula

$$A - B - \frac{C}{4} - D$$

where

A is the total of all amounts each of which is an amount included in computing the person's income for the year or a preceding taxation year (other than an amount received before that time under the plan or an amount under the plan that the person is entitled at that time to receive) because of an allocation (other than an allocation to which subsection (4) applies) to the person made contingently under the plan before that time;

B is the portion, if any, of the value of A that is included in the value of A because of paragraph 82(1)(b);

C is the total of all taxable dividends deemed to be received by the person because of allocations under subsection (8) in respect of the plan; and

D is the total of all amounts deductible under this subsection in computing the person's income for a preceding taxation year because the person ceased to be a beneficiary under the plan in a preceding taxation year.

Related Provisions: 8(1)(o.1) — Deduction from employment income; 144(3) — Allocation contingent or absolute taxable; 144(10) — Payments out of profits; 152(1) — Assessment; 160.1 — Where excess refunded; 257 — Formula cannot calculate to less than zero.

Notes: Where an EPSP member forfeits a previously allocated capital gain, CRA will not allow an adjustment to account for the amount taxed which will never actually be received: VIEWS doc 2005-0161671E5.

144(9) amended by 1993 technical bill, effective for 1992 and later taxation years (with an election that it apply for 1992).

(10) Payments out of profits — Where the terms of an arrangement under which an employer makes payments to a trustee specifically provide that the payments shall be made "out of profits", the arrangement shall, if the employer so elects in prescribed manner, be deemed, for the purpose of subsection (1), to be an arrangement under which payments computed by reference to the employer's profits are required.

Related Provisions: 87(2)(r) — Amalgamation — election by predecessor deemed made by new corporation.

Notes: "It is our view that an 'out of profit' formula must provide for an acceptable yearly minimum contribution per employee member. Any provision[s] in the arrangement that suspend employer's contributions or reduce them below an acceptable minimum would not be permitted": VIEWS doc 2009-0328661E5. See also Notes to 144(1)"employees profit sharing plan".

For a trust filing Quebec returns (and otherwise, possibly for employees resident in Quebec), a designation under para. (a) must be copied to Revenu Québec: *Taxation Act* ss. 853, 21.4.6.

144(10) amended by 1993 technical bill, effective for 1992 and later taxation years, to have the wording match 144(9).

Regulations: 1500(3) (prescribed manner).

Interpretation Bulletins: IT-280R; Employees' profit sharing plans — payments computed by reference to profits.

(11) Taxation year of trust — Where an employees profit sharing plan is accepted for registration by the Minister as a deferred profit sharing plan, the taxation year of the trust governed by the employees profit sharing plan shall be deemed to have ended immediately before the plan is deemed to have become registered as a deferred profit sharing plan pursuant to subsection 147(5).

Notes [s. 144]: See Notes to 144(1)"employees profit sharing plan".

Definitions [s. 144]: "adjusted cost base" — 54, 248(1); "amount", "business" — 248(1); "Canadian corporation" — 89(1), 248(1); "capital gain", "capital loss" — 39(1), 248(1); "capital property" — 54, 248(1); "corporation" — 248(1), *Interpretation Act* 35(1); "dividend", "employee" — 248(1); "employees profit sharing plan" — 144(1), 248(1); "employer" — 248(1); "fair market value" — see 69(1) Notes; "Minister", "officer", "prescribed", "property" — 248(1); "province" — *Interpretation Act* 35(1); "taxable Canadian corporation" — 89(1), 248(1); "taxable capital gain" — 38(a), 248(1); "taxable dividend" — 89(1), 248(1); "taxable income" — 2(2), 248(1); "taxation year" — 144(11), 249; "trust" — 104(1), 248(1); "unused portion of a beneficiary's exempt capital gains balance" — 144(1).

Information Circulars [s. 144]: 77-1R4: Deferred profit sharing plans.

Employee Life and Health Trust

144.1 (1) Definitions — The following definitions apply in this section.

"actuary" means a Fellow of the Canadian Institute of Actuaries.

Related Provisions: 144.1(5) — Actuarial determination of contributions required; 147.1(1)"actuary" — Same definition for RPP rules.

"class of beneficiaries" of a trust means a group of beneficiaries who have identical rights or interests under the trust.

"designated employee benefit" means a benefit that is

(a) from a group sickness or accident insurance plan;

(b) from a group term life insurance policy;

(c) from a private health services plan;

(d) in respect of a counselling service described in subparagraph 6(1)(a)(iv); or

(e) not a death benefit, but that would be a death benefit if the amounts determined for paragraphs (a) and (b) of the definition "death benefit" in subsection 248(1) were nil.

Related Provisions: 6(1)(a)(i) — Benefits non-taxable; 6(1)(g)(iv) — DEB excluded from employee benefit plan benefits; 18(9)(a)(iv) — Limitation on prepaid expenses; 144.1(2)(a) — Paying DEB must be only object of ELHT.

Notes: Paras. (d)-(e) added by 2021 budget bill #1, effective Feb. 27, 2018 (and applicable to trusts regardless of when established). Before the amendment, the definition was all one paragraph:

"designated employee benefit" means a benefit from a group sickness or accident insurance plan, a group term life insurance policy or a private health services plan.

"employee" means a current or former employee of an employer and includes an individual in respect of whom the employer has assumed responsibility for the provision of designated employee benefits as a result of the acquisition by the employer of a business in which the individual was employed.

Related Provisions: 128.1(4)(b.1) — ELHT ceasing to be resident in Canada.

"key employee", of an employer in respect of a taxation year, means an employee who

(a) was at any time in the taxation year or in a preceding taxation year, a specified employee of the employer; or

(b) was an employee whose employment income from the employer in any two of the five taxation years preceding the year exceeded five times the Year's Maximum Pensionable Earnings (as determined under section 18 of the *Canada Pension Plan*) for the calendar year in which the employment income was earned.

Related Provisions: 144.1(2)(e), (f) — ELHT must not give more rights to key employees than others; 144.1(3)(b) — No deduction if ELHT is operated primarily for benefit of key employees.

Notes: The YMPE for 2020 and 2021 is $58,700 and $61,600, so this threshold is $293,500 and $308,000. See Table I-8 for other years.

(2) Employee life and health trust — A trust that is established for employees of one or more employers (each referred to in this subsection as a "participating employer") is an employee life and health trust for a taxation year if, throughout the taxation year, under the terms that govern the trust,

(a) the only purpose of the trust is to provide benefits to, or for the benefit of, persons described in subparagraph (d)(i) or (ii) and all or substantially all of the total cost of the benefits is applicable to designated employee benefits;

(b) on wind-up or reorganization, the property of the trust may only be distributed to

(i) each remaining beneficiary of the trust who is described in subparagraph (d)(i) or (ii) (other than a key employee or an individual who is related to a key employee) on a *pro rata* basis,

(ii) another employee life and health trust, or

(iii) after the death of the last beneficiary described in subparagraph (d)(i) or (ii), Her Majesty in right of Canada or a province;

(c) the trust meets one of the following conditions:

(i) the trust is required to be resident in Canada, determined without reference to section 94, or

(ii) if the condition in subparagraph (i) is not met, it is the case that

(A) employee benefits are provided to employees who are resident in Canada and to employees who are not resident in Canada,

(B) one or more participating employers are employers that are resident in a country other than Canada, and

(C) the trust is required to be resident in a country in which a participating employer resides;

(d) the trust may not have any beneficiaries other than persons each of whom is

(i) an employee of a participating employer or former participating employer,

(ii) an individual who, in respect of an employee of a participating employer or former participating employer, is (or, if the employee is deceased, was, at the time of the employee's death)

(A) the spouse or common-law partner of the employee, or

(B) related to the employee and either a member of the employee's household or dependent on the employee for support,

(iii) another employee life and health trust, or

(iv) Her Majesty in right of Canada or a province;

(e) the trust meets one of the following conditions:

(i) it contains at least one class of beneficiaries where

(A) the members of the class represent at least 25% of all of the beneficiaries of the trust who are employees of the participating employers under the trust, and

(B) either of the following conditions is met:

(I) at least 75% of the members of the class are not key employees of any of the participating employers under the trust, or

(II) the contributions to the trust in respect of key employees who deal at arm's length with their employer are determined in connection with a collective bargaining agreement, or

(ii) in respect of the private health services plan under the trust, the total cost of benefits provided to each key employee (and to persons described in subparagraph (2)(d)(ii) in respect of the key employee) in relation to the year does not exceed the amount determined by the formula

$$\$2,500 \times A(B/C)$$

where

A   is the total number of persons each of whom

(A) is a person to whom designated employee benefits are provided under the plan, and

(B) is the key employee or a person described in subparagraph (2)(d)(ii) in respect of the key employee,

B   is the number of days in the year that the key employee was employed on a full-time basis by an employer that participates in the plan, and

C   is the number of days in the year;

(f) the rights under the trust of each key employee of a participating employer are not more advantageous than the rights of a class of beneficiaries described in paragraph (e);

(g) no participating employer, nor any person who does not deal at arm's length with a participating employer, has any rights under the trust as a beneficiary or otherwise, except rights to

(i) designated employee benefits,

(ii) to enforce covenants, warranties or similar provisions regarding

(A) the maintenance of the trust as an employee life and health trust, or

(B) the operation of the trust in a manner that prevents subsection (3) from applying to prohibit the deduction of an amount by the trust under subsection 104(6), or

(iii) prescribed payments; and

(h) [Repealed]

(i) trustees who do not deal at arm's length with one or more participating employers must not constitute the majority of the trustees of the trust.

Related Provisions: 6(1)(a)(i) — Employer contributions to ELHT are not a taxable benefit; 6(1)(f)(iii.1) — Benefits under insurance plan administered by ELHT may be taxable; 75(3)(b) — Reversionary trust rules do not apply to ELHT; 104(6)(a.4) — Deduction to trust for designated employee benefits payable; 107.1(a) — Distribution of property by ELHT deemed at FMV; 108(1)"trust"(a) — "Trust" does not include an ELHT for certain purposes; 127.55(f)(iv) — No minimum tax on ELHT; 128.1(4)(b.1) — ELHT ceasing to be resident in Canada; 144.1(3) — No deduction if terms violated or trust is operated primarily for benefit of key employee; 144.1(12) — Deemed separate trusts where more than one employer; 144.1(18) — Trust must notify CRA when it becomes ELHT; 207.9 — Tax on prohibited investment; 248(1)"employee benefit plan"(a) — ELHT deemed not to be EBP; 248(1)"retirement compensation arrangement"(f.1) — ELHT deemed not to be RCA; 248(1)"salary deferral arrangement"(e.1) — ELHT deemed not to be SDA; 248(1)"employee life and health trust" — Definition applies to entire Act.

Notes: See Notes at end of 144.1. A condition in 144.1(2)(d) in the Feb. 26/10 draft, that the trust not be maintained primarily for key employees, was moved to 144.1(3)(b).

Note the special definition of "employee" for this section in 144.1(1).

Para. (a): CRA considers that "substantially all" means 90% or more.

Para. (e): Finance has indicated that "class" of beneficiaries is intended to refer to classes established under the trust document.

A long-term disability plan could be held in an ELHT: VIEWS doc 2010-0374891E5. An ELHT solely for key employees does not qualify: 2011-0392641E5. For a ruling that an ELHT qualifies (and that s. 80 does not apply to the trust's assumption of the employer's obligation to provide post-retirement benefits) see 2010-0389651R3. The employer's bankruptcy does not cause an ELHT to lose its status: 2011-0419811E5.

144.1(2) amended by 2021 budget bill #1 effective Feb. 27, 2018 (and applicable to trusts regardless of when established): "all or substantially all" test added to (a); (c)(ii) added; references to "former participating employer" added to (d); (e)(i)(B)(II), (e)(ii) added; (h) repealed [replaced by a "prohibited investment" rule in 207.9] and (i) amended. Paras. (h), (i) read:

(h) the trust may not make a loan to, or an investment in, a participating employer or a person or partnership with whom the participating employer does not deal at arm's length;

(i) representatives of one or more participating employers do not constitute the majority of the trustees of the trust or otherwise control the trust.

Regulations: 9500 (prescribed payments for 144.1(2)(g)(iii) — to GM and Chrysler Canada).

Income Tax Folios: S2-F1-C1: Health and welfare trusts [replaces IT-85R2].

(3) Breach of terms, etc. — No amount may be deducted in a taxation year by an employee life and health trust pursuant to subsection 104(6) if in the taxation year the trust

(a) is not operated in accordance with the terms required by subsection (2) to govern the trust, unless it is reasonable to conclude that its trustees neither knew nor ought to have known that designated employee benefits have been provided to, or contributions have been made in respect of, beneficiaries other than those described in subparagraph (2)(d)(i) or (ii); or

(b) provides any benefit for which, if the benefit had been paid directly to the employee and not out of the trust, the contributions or premiums would not be deductible in computing the income of an employer in respect of any taxation year.

Related Provisions: 111(7.5) — No carryforward of losses when 144.1(3) applies.

Notes: 144.1(3)(a), (b) amended by 2021 budget bill #1 effective Feb. 27, 2018 (and applicable to trusts regardless of when established). Before that date, read:

(a) is not operated in accordance with the terms required by subsection (2) to govern the trust, or

(b) is operated or maintained primarily for the benefit of one or more key employees or their family members described in subparagraph (2)(d)(ii).

(4) Deductibility of employer contributions — In computing the income of an employer,

(a) the employer may deduct for a taxation year the portion of its contributions to an employee life and health trust made in the year that may reasonably be regarded as having been contributed to enable the trust to

(i) pay premiums to an insurance corporation that is licensed to provide insurance under the laws of Canada or a province for insurance coverage for the year or a prior year in respect of designated employee benefits for beneficiaries described in subparagraph (2)(d)(i) or (ii), or

(ii) otherwise provide

(A) group term life insurance as described in clause 18(9)(a)(iii)(B), or

(B) any designated employee benefits payable in the year or a prior year to, or for the benefit of, beneficiaries described in subparagraph (2)(d)(i) or (ii); and

(b) the portion of any contribution made to an employee life and health trust that exceeds the amount deductible under paragraph (a) and that may reasonably be regarded as enabling the trust to provide or pay benefits described in subparagraphs (a)(i) or (ii) in a subsequent taxation year is deductible for that year.

Related Provisions: 6(1)(a)(i) — Employer contributions to ELHT are not a taxable benefit; 6(1)(f)(iii.1) — Benefits under insurance plan administered by ELHT may be taxable; 18(1)(o.3) — No deduction to ELHT except as permitted by 144.1(4)–(7); 20(1)(s) — Deduction under 144.1(4)-(7) allowed as deduction from employer's business income; 87(2)(j.3) — Amalgamation — continuing corporation; 144.1(5) — Actuarial determination of contributions required; 144.1(7) — Maximum deductible; 144.1(8), (9) — Issuance of indebtedness is not contribution until paid.

(5) Actuarial determination — For the purposes of subsection (4), if, in respect of an employer's obligations to fund an employee life and health trust, a report has been prepared by an independent actuary, using accepted actuarial principles and practices, before the time of a contribution by the employer, the portion of the contribution that the report specifies to be the amount that the employee life and health trust is reasonably expected to pay or incur in a taxation year in order to provide designated employee benefits to beneficiaries described in subparagraph (2)(d)(i) or (ii) for a taxation year is, in the absence of evidence to the contrary, presumed to have been contributed to enable the trust to provide those benefits for the year.

Related Provisions: 87(2)(j.3) — Amalgamation — continuing corporation.

(6) Deductibility — collectively bargained or similar agreement — Despite subsection (4) and paragraph 18(9)(a), an employer may deduct in computing its income for a taxation year the amount that it is required to contribute for the year to an employee life and health trust if the following conditions are met at the time that the contribution is made:

(a) the employer contributes to the trust in accordance with a contribution formula that does not provide for any variation in contributions determined by reference to the financial experience of the trust and either of the following conditions is met:

(i) if there is a collective bargaining agreement, the trust provides benefits

(A) negotiated under the collective bargaining agreement, or

(B) under a participation agreement that are substantially the same as under the collective bargaining agreement, or

(ii) in any other case, the trust provides benefits in accordance with an arrangement that meets the following conditions:

(A) there is a legal requirement for each employer to participate in accordance with the terms and conditions that govern the trust,

(B) there are a minimum of 50 beneficiaries under the trust who are employees of the participating employers in respect of the trust, and

(C) each employee who is a beneficiary under the trust deals at arm's length with each participating employer in respect of the trust; and

(b) contributions that are to be made by each employer are determined, in whole or in part, by reference to the number of hours worked by individual employees of the employer or some other measure that is specific to each employee with respect to whom contributions are made to the trust.

Related Provisions: 6(1)(a)(i) — Employer contributions to ELHT are not a taxable benefit; 6(1)(f)(iii.1) — Benefits under insurance plan administered by ELHT may be taxable; 18(1)(o.3) — No deduction to ELHT except as permitted by 144.1(4)-(7); 20(1)(s) — Deduction under 144.1(4)-(7) allowed as deduction from employer's business income; 87(2)(j.3) — Amalgamation — continuing corporation; 144.1(5) — Actuarial determination of contributions required; 144.1(7) — Maximum deductible; 144.1(8) — Issuance of indebtedness is not contribution until paid.

Notes: 144.1(6) amended by 2021 budget bill #1 effective Feb. 27, 2018 (and applicable to trusts regardless of when established). Before that date, read:

(6) **Multi-employer plans** — Notwithstanding subsection (4) and paragraph 18(9)(a), an employer may deduct in computing its income for a taxation year the amount that it is required to contribute for the year to an employee life and health trust if the following conditions are met at the time that the contribution is made:

(a) it is reasonable to expect that

(i) at no time in the year will more than 95% of the employees who are beneficiaries of the trust be employed by a single employer or by a related group of employers, and

(ii) at least 15 employers will contribute to the trust in respect of the year or at least 10% of the employees who are beneficiaries of the trust will be employed in the year by more than one participating employer and, for the purpose of this condition, all employers who are related to each other are deemed to be a single employer;

(b) employers contribute to the trust under a collective bargaining agreement and in accordance with a negotiated contribution formula that does not provide for any variation in contributions determined by reference to the financial experience of the trust; and

(c) contributions that are to be made by each employer are determined, in whole or in part, by reference to the number of hours worked by individual employees of the employer or some other measure that is specific to each employee with respect to whom contributions are made to the trust.

(7) **Maximum deductible** — The amount deducted in a taxation year by an employer in computing its income in respect of contributions made to an employee life and health trust shall not exceed the amount determined by the formula

$$A - B$$

where

A is the total of all amounts contributed by the employer to the trust in the year or in a preceding taxation year; and

B is the total of all amounts deducted by the employer in a preceding taxation year in respect of amounts contributed by the employer to the trust.

Related Provisions: 6(1)(a)(i) — Employer contributions to ELHT are not a taxable benefit; 18(1)(o.3) — No deduction to ELHT except as permitted by 144.1(6)–(7); 20(1)(s) — Deduction under 144.1(4)-(7) allowed as deduction from employer's business income; 87(2)(j.3) — Amalgamation — continuing corporation; 257 — Formula cannot calculate to less than zero.

(8) **Employer promissory note** — If an employer issues a promissory note or provides other evidence of its indebtedness to an employee life and health trust in respect of its obligation to the trust,

(a) the issuance of the note or the provision of the evidence of indebtedness to the trust is not a contribution to the trust; and

(b) a payment by the employer to the trust in full or partial satisfaction of its liability under the note or the evidence of indebtedness, whether stated to be of principal or interest or any other amount, is deemed to be an employer contribution to the trust that is subject to this section and not a payment of principal or interest on the note or indebtedness.

Related Provisions: 144.1(9) — Trust status at later time when payment made on note.

(9) **Trust status — subsequent times** — For the purposes of determining whether an amount is deductible by an employer under subsection (4), if a trust was an employee life and health trust at the time that a promissory note or other evidence of indebtedness referred to in subsection (8) was issued or provided, the trust is deemed to be an employee life and health trust at each time that an employer contribution is deemed to have been made under paragraph (8)(b) in respect of the note or other indebtedness.

(10) **Employee contributions** — For the purposes of paragraph 6(1)(f), subsection 6(4) and paragraph 118.2(2)(q), employee contributions to an employee life and health trust, to the extent that they are, and are identified by the trust at the time of contribution as, contributions in respect of a particular designated employee benefit, are deemed to be payments by the employee in respect of the particular designated employee benefit.

(11) **Income inclusion** — If a trust that is, or was, at any time, an employee life and health trust pays an amount as a distribution from the trust to any person in a taxation year, the amount of the distribution shall be included in computing the person's income for the year, except to the extent that the amount is

(a) a payment of a designated employee benefit that is not included in the person's income because of section 6; or

(b) a distribution to another employee life and health trust that is a beneficiary of the employee life and health trust.

Related Provisions: 6(1)(a)(i) — Benefits non-taxable; 6(1)(f)(iii.1) — Benefits under insurance plan administered by ELHT may be taxable; 56(1)(z.2) — Amount under 144.1(11) included in income unless taxed under 70(2); 75(3)(b) — Reversionary trust rules do not apply to ELHT; 107.1(a) — Distribution of property by ELHT deemed at FMV; 111(7.3)–(7.5), 144.1(13) — Non-capital losses of ELHT; 128.1(10)"excluded right or interest"(a)(vi.1) — No deemed disposition of rights on emigration or immigration of beneficiary; 153(1)(s) — Withholding of tax at source; 212(1)(w) — Withholding tax on payment to non-resident.

(12) **Deemed separate trusts** — Where contributions have been received by an employee life and health trust from more than one employer, the trust is deemed to be a separate trust established in respect of the property held for the benefit of beneficiaries described in subparagraph (2)(d)(i) or (ii) in respect of a particular employer, if

(a) the trustee designates the property to be held in a separate trust for the benefit of those beneficiaries in an election made on or before the filing-due date of the first taxation year of the separate trust described in this subsection; and

(b) under the terms of the trust, contributions from the employer and the income derived from those contributions accrues solely for the benefit of those beneficiaries.

Notes: For a trust filing a Quebec return, a para. (a) election must be copied to Revenu Québec: *Taxation Act* ss. 869.12, 21.4.6.

(13) Non-capital losses — No non-capital loss is deductible by an employee life and health trust in computing its taxable income for a taxation year, except as provided by subsections 111(7.3) to (7.5).

(14) Conditions — deemed employee life and health trust — Subsection (15) applies in respect of a trust if

(a) the trust was established before February 28, 2018;

(b) the contributions to the trust are determined in connection with a collective bargaining agreement;

(c) all or substantially all of the employee benefits provided by the trust are designated employee benefits; and

(d) the trust elects in prescribed form and manner that subsection (15) applies as of a particular date after 2018.

Notes: See 144.1(15) Notes. Feb. 28, 2018 is the date of the 2018 Budget announcing that health and welfare trusts would need to convert to ELHTs and that new HWTs could not be created.

CRA considers that "substantially all", used in para. (c), means 90% or more.

144.1(14) added by 2021 budget bill #1 effective Feb. 27, 2018 (and applicable to trusts regardless of when established).

(15) Deemed employee life and health trust — If this subsection applies in respect of a trust,

(a) the trust is deemed for the purposes of the Act to be an employee life and health trust from the particular date referred to in paragraph (14)(d) until the earliest of

(i) the end of 2022,

(ii) the day that the trust satisfies the conditions in subsection (2), and

(iii) any day on which the condition in paragraph (14)(c) is not satisfied; and

(b) at any time that the trust is an employee life and health trust because of paragraph (a),

(i) subsection 111(7.5) applies to the trust as if the reference in paragraph (b) of that subsection to "subsection 144.1(3)" were read as a reference to "paragraph 144.1(3)(b)", and

(ii) subsection (3) applies to the trust without reference to its paragraph (a).

Related Provisions: 144.1(14) — Conditions for subsec. (15) to apply; 144.1(18) — Trust must notify CRA when it becomes ELHT.

Notes: 144.1(14)-(18), along with other amendments to 144.1 enacted in 2021, implement changes first announced in the Feb. 2018 Budget. See Notes at end of 144.1.

144.1(15) added by 2021 budget bill #1 effective Feb. 27, 2018 (and applicable to trusts regardless of when established).

(16) Trust-to-trust transfer — If a property is transferred from a trust that provides employee benefits substantially all of which are designated employee benefits (referred to in this subsection as the "transferor trust") to an employee life and health trust (referred to in this subsection as the "receiving trust"), and if the Minister has been so notified in prescribed form, then

(a) the transferred property is deemed to have been disposed of by the transferor trust, and to have been acquired by the receiving trust, for an amount equal to the cost amount of the property to the transferor trust immediately before the disposition; and

(b) section 107.1 does not apply to the transfer.

Related Provisions: 144.1(17) — Deductibility of transferred property.

Notes: 144.1(16) added by 2021 budget bill #1 effective Feb. 27, 2018 (and applicable to trusts regardless of when established).

(17) Deductibility of transferred property — If subsection (16) applies to a transfer of property to an employee life and health trust, the transfer shall not be considered to be a contribution to the

employee life and health trust for the purposes of subsections (4) and (6).

Notes: 144.1(17) added by 2021 budget bill #1 effective Feb. 27, 2018 (and applicable to trusts regardless of when established).

(18) Requirement to file — A trust shall, on or before its first filing-due date after 2021, notify the Minister in prescribed form that it is an employee life and health trust if

(a) prior to February 27, 2018, it provided employee benefits substantially all of which are designated employee benefits;

(b) after February 26, 2018, it becomes an employee life and health trust because it satisfies the conditions in subsection (2); and

(c) subsections (15) and (16) do not apply to the trust.

Notes: 144.1(18) added by 2021 budget bill #1 effective Feb. 27, 2018 (and applicable to trusts regardless of when established).

Notes [s. 144.1]: ELHTs were introduced in 2010, not to replace IT-85R2 (now Income Tax Folio S2-F1-C1) for Health and Welfare Trusts (HWTs), but to enable the 2008 auto industry bailout, allowing GM and Chrysler to offload payment of retirees' health care benefits to a trust: see Reg. 9500. The original ELHT legislation changed nothing for an employer that did not set up an ELHT: no rule prevented deduction of employer contributions, or caused employee benefits to be taxable, for HWTs. However, per CRA policy announced in the Feb. 2018 Budget and updated in a Nov. 27, 2020 Finance news release, HWTs must convert to ELHTs by the end of 2021 to continue to be tax-free; and those created after Feb. 27, 2018 do not qualify. 144.1(14)-(15) govern conversion of a HWT to an ELHT. See also VIEWS docs 2010-0363102C6, 2011-0398371C6, 2011-0424761C6 [2010 CTF q.22].

An ELHT is a taxable trust that meets the conditions in 144.1(2), including that its objects are limited to paying "designated employee benefits" (DEB), and it does not prefer a "key employee". The employer can deduct contributions, provided they are for DEB (144.1(7)-(8)). An employee can also make contributions, and they qualify for the medical expense credit (144.1(10), 118.2(2)(q)) and reduce taxable benefits (6(1)(f)(v)). The trust can deduct amounts paid to employees or retirees for benefits (104(6), 144.1(3)), and can carry losses back 3 years or forward 7 years (111(7.4)). The payment is tax-free to the employee if it would have been tax-free if received from the employer (144.1(11), 6(1)(a)(i)). Payments of DEB to non-residents are free of withholding tax: 212(1)(w). See also 144.1(2) Notes.

See *Canadian Health Insurance Tax Guide: Employee Life and Health Trusts*, tinyurl.com/sunlife-taxguides; Théroux, "Employee Life and Health Trust", 18(4) *Canadian Tax Highlights* 1-2 (April 2010); Cyna, "Employee Life and Health Trusts", 7(4) *Tax Hyperion* (Carswell, April 2010); Winfield & Firman, "Implementing an Employee Life and Health Trust", 22(3) *Taxation of Executive Compensation & Retirement* (Federated Press) 1331-36 (Oct. 2010) and 22(7) 1379-85 (March 2011); Boyd & McLeod, "Employee Life and Health Trusts", 2010 Ontario Tax Conference (ctf.ca), 10:1-18.

A "lump sum pre-retirement leave payment" paid into an ELHT is subject to source deductions, as there is no rollover: VIEWS doc 2012-0467221E5.

144.1 added by 2010 budget bill #2, for trusts established after 2009.

Definitions [s. 144.1]: "actuary" — 144.1(1); "amount" — 248(1); "arm's length" — 251(1); "beneficiary" — 248(25) Notes; "business" — 248(1); "calendar year" — *Interpretation Act* 37(1)(a); "Canada" — 255, *Interpretation Act* 35(1); "class of beneficiaries" — 144.1(1); "cost amount" — 248(1); "designated employee benefit" — 144.1(1); "disposition", "employed" — 248(1); "employee" — 144.1(1); "employee life and health trust" — 144.1(2), 248(1); "employer", "employment", "filing-due date", "group term life insurance policy" — 248(1); "Her Majesty" — *Interpretation Act* 35(1); "identical" — 248(12); "individual", "insurance corporation" — 248(1); "key employee" — 144.1(1); "Minister" — 248(1); "non-capital loss" — 111(8), 248(1); "partnership" — see 96(1) Notes; "person", "prescribed", "private health services plan", "property" — 248(1); "province" — *Interpretation Act* 35(1); "related" — 251(2)–(6); "related group" — 251(4); "resident in Canada" — 250; "specified employee", "taxable income" — 248(1); "taxation year" — 249; "trust" — 104(1), 248(1), (3).

Registered Supplementary Unemployment Benefit Plans

145. (1) Definitions — In this section,

"registered supplementary unemployment benefit plan" means a supplementary unemployment benefit plan accepted by the Minister for registration for the purposes of this Act in respect of its constitution and operations for the taxation year under consideration;

Related Provisions: 75(3)(a) — Reversionary trust rules do not apply to RSUBP; 108(1)"trust"(a) — "Trust" does not include a RSUBP for certain purposes; 128.1(10)"excluded right or interest"(a)(xi) — No deemed disposition on emigration;

248(1)"disposition"(f)(vi) — Rollover from one trust to another; 248(1)"registered supplementary unemployment benefit plan" — Definition applies to entire Act.

Notes: CRA advises that there were 92 RSUBPs registered at end of 2016 (93 at end of 2012, 126 at end of 2009, 149 in 2005, 148 in 2000 and 142 in 1995).

For detail on RSUBPs see Information Circular 72-5R2 and tinyurl.com/rsubps.

145(1)"registered supplementary unemployment benefit plan" was 145(1)(a) before RSC 1985 (5th Supp) consolidation for tax years ending after Nov. 1991.

Information Circulars: 72-5R2: Registered supplementary unemployment benefit plans.

Forms: T3S: Supplementary unemployment benefit plan — income tax return.

"supplementary unemployment benefit plan" means an arrangement, other than an arrangement in the nature of a superannuation or pension fund or plan or an employees profit sharing plan, under which payments are made by an employer to a trustee in trust exclusively for the payment of periodic amounts to employees or former employees of the employer who are or may be laid off for any temporary or indefinite period.

Notes: 145(1)"supplementary unemployment benefit plan" was 145(1)(b) before RSC 1985 (5th Supp) consolidation for tax years ending after Nov. 1991.

Information Circulars: 72-5R2: Registered supplementary unemployment benefit plans; 78-14R4: Guidelines for trust companies and other persons responsible for filing T3GR, T3D, T3P, T3S, T3RI, and T3F returns.

(2) No tax while trust governed by plan — No tax is payable under this Part by a trust on the taxable income of the trust for a period during which the trust was governed by a registered supplementary unemployment benefit plan.

Related Provisions: 149(1)(q) — Trust exempt from tax.

Information Circulars: 72-5R2: Registered supplementary unemployment benefit plans.

Forms: T3S: Supplementary unemployment benefit plan — income tax return.

(3) Amounts received taxable — There shall be included in computing the income of a taxpayer for a taxation year each amount received by the taxpayer under a supplementary unemployment benefit plan from the trustee under the plan at any time in the year.

Related Provisions: 56(1)(g) — Income inclusion; 153(1)(e) — Withholding; 212(1)(k) — Withholding tax on payment to non-resident.

(4) Amounts received on amendment or winding-up of plan — There shall be included in computing the income for a taxation year of a taxpayer who, as an employer, has made any payment to a trustee under a supplementary unemployment benefit plan, any amount received by the taxpayer in the year as a result of an amendment to or modification of the plan or as a result of the termination or winding-up of the plan.

Related Provisions: 56(1)(g) — Income inclusion; 153(1)(e) — Withholding; 212(1)(k) — Withholding tax on payment to non-resident.

(5) Payments by employer deductible — An amount paid by an employer to a trustee under a registered supplementary unemployment benefit plan during a taxation year or within 30 days thereafter may be deducted in computing the employer's income for the taxation year to the extent that it was not deductible in computing income for a previous taxation year.

Related Provisions: 6(1)(a)(i) — Employer's contribution is not a taxable benefit; 18(1)(i) — Limitation re employer's contribution under supplementary unemployment benefit plan; 20(1)(x) — Deduction for employer's contribution; *Interpretation Act* 27(5) — Meaning of "within 30 days".

Definitions [s. 145]: "amount", "employee" — 248(1); "employees profit sharing plan" — 144(1), 248(1); "employer", "Minister" — 248(1); "taxable income" — 2(2), 248(1); "taxation year" — 249; "taxpayer" — 248(1); "trust" — 104(1), 248(1).

Registered Plans Compliance Bulletins [s. 145]: 1, 2, 3 (how to contact us).

Forms [s. 145]: T2 Sched. 15: Deferred income plans.

Registered Retirement Savings Plans

146. (1) Definitions — In this section,

"annuitant" means

(a) until such time after maturity of the plan as an individual's spouse or common-law partner becomes entitled, as a conse-

quence of the individual's death, to receive benefits to be paid out of or under the plan, the individual referred to in paragraph (a) or (b) of the definition "retirement savings plan" in this subsection for whom, under a retirement savings plan, a retirement income is to be provided, and

(b) thereafter, the spouse or common-law partner referred to in paragraph (a);

Related Provisions: 60(l) — Transfer of RRSP premium refunds; 128.1(10)"excluded right or interest"(a)(i) — No deemed disposition on emigration of annuitant; 160.2(1) — Joint and several liability in respect of amounts received out of or under RRSP; 207.04 — Tax on annuitant if RRSP acquires prohibited or non-qualified investment; 248(8) — Meaning of "consequence" of death.

Notes: 146(1)"annuitant" amended by 2000 same-sex partners bill to refer to "common-law partner", effective 2001 or earlier.

146(1)"annuitant" was 146(1)(a) before RSC 1985 (5th Supp) consolidation for tax years ending after Nov. 1991. (It was also amended by 1995-97 technical bill, retroactive to the 5th Supp. change.)

Information Circulars: 72-22R9: Registered retirement savings plans.

Forms: RC4177: Death of an RRSP annuitant [guide].

"benefit" includes any amount received out of or under a retirement savings plan other than

(a) the portion thereof received by a person other than the annuitant that can reasonably be regarded as part of the amount included in computing the income of an annuitant by virtue of subsections (8.8) and (8.9),

(b) an amount received by the person with whom the annuitant has the contract or arrangement described in the definition "retirement savings plan" in this subsection as a premium under the plan,

(b.1) an amount in respect of which the annuitant pays a tax under Part XI.01, unless the tax is waived, cancelled or refunded,

(c) an amount, or part thereof, received in respect of the income of the trust under the plan for a taxation year for which the trust was not exempt from tax by virtue of paragraph (4)(c), and

(c.1) a tax-paid amount described in paragraph (b) of the definition "tax-paid amount" in this subsection that relates to interest or another amount included in computing income otherwise than because of this section

and without restricting the generality of the foregoing includes any amount paid to an annuitant under the plan

(d) in accordance with the terms of the plan,

(e) resulting from an amendment to or modification of the plan, or

(f) resulting from the termination of the plan;

Related Provisions: 146.3(5)(d) — Parallel rule for RRIFs; 160.2(1) — Joint and several liability in respect of amounts received out of or under RRSP; 207.01(1)"advantage", 207.05 — Tax on advantage received from RRSP.

Notes: See Notes to 188.1(5) re meaning of "includes" in the opening words.

Para. (b.1) added by 2011 budget bill #2, for transactions occurring, income earned, capital gains accruing and investments acquired after March 22, 2011. It excludes an amount taxed under 207.01–207.07.

Para. (c.1) added by 1995-97 technical bill, effective for deaths after 1992.

146(1)"benefit" was 146(1)(b) before RSC 1985 (5th Supp) consolidation for tax years ending after Nov. 1991.

Advance Tax Rulings: ATR-37: Refund of premiums transferred to spouse.

"earned income" of a taxpayer for a taxation year means the amount, if any, by which the total of all amounts each of which is

(a) the taxpayer's income (other than an amount described in paragraph 12(1)(z)) for a period in the year throughout which the taxpayer was resident in Canada from

(i) an office or employment, determined without reference to paragraphs 8(1)(c), (m) and (m.2),

(ii) a business carried on by the taxpayer either alone or as a partner actively engaged in the business, or

(iii) property, where the income is derived from the rental of real or immovable property or from royalties in respect of a work or invention of which the taxpayer was the author or inventor,

(b) an amount included under paragraph 56(1)(b), (c.2), (g) or (o) or subparagraph 56(1)(r)(v) in computing the taxpayer's income for a period in the year throughout which the taxpayer was resident in Canada,

---

Proposed Addition — 146(1)"earned income"(b.01)

(b.01) an amount included under paragraph 56(1)(n) in computing the taxpayer's income for a period in the year throughout which the taxpayer was resident in Canada in connection with a program that consists primarily of research and does not lead to a diploma from a college or a Collège d'enseignement général et professionnel, or a bachelor, masters, doctoral or equivalent degree,

Application: The April 19, 2021 Budget Notice of Ways and Means Motion, s. 5, will add para. (b.01) to the definition "earned income" in subsec. 146(1), applicable in respect of the definition for taxation years after 2020; however, it also applies in respect of the definition for the 2011 to 2020 taxation years, for the purpose of determining the taxpayer's "RRSP deduction limit" under subsec. 146(1) in respect of a taxation year after 2020 during which the taxpayer makes a request in writing with the Minister of National Revenue for an adjustment to their "earned income" for any of those prior years.

Federal Budget, Supplementary Information, April 19, 2021: *Postdoctoral Fellowship Income*

For income tax purposes, postdoctoral fellows are generally not considered to be students. Thus, postdoctoral fellowship income generally does not qualify for the scholarship exemption from income tax. Although fully included in taxable income, and similar in nature to employment income, postdoctoral fellowship income does not currently qualify as "earned income" for the purpose of determining an individual's contribution limit for a registered retirement savings plan (RRSP).

Budget 2021 proposes to include postdoctoral fellowship income in "earned income" for RRSP purposes. This would provide postdoctoral fellows with additional RRSP room in order to make deductible RRSP contributions.

This measure would apply in respect of postdoctoral fellowship income received in the 2021 and subsequent taxation years. This measure would also apply in respect of postdoctoral fellowship income received in the 2011 to 2020 taxation years, where the taxpayer submits a request in writing to the Canada Revenue Agency for an adjustment to their RRSP room for the relevant years.

Notes: See 56(3) Notes re how post-doctoral fellowship income is taxed.

Budget Table 1 projects that this measure will cost the federal government $1 million in each of 2024-25 and 2025-26 (nothing measurable in other years).

(b.1) an amount received by the taxpayer in the year and at a time when the taxpayer is resident in Canada as, on account of, in lieu of payment of or in satisfaction of, a disability pension under the *Canada Pension Plan* or a provincial pension plan as defined in section 3 of that Act,

(b.2) the taxpayer's qualifying performance income (as defined in subsection 143.1(1)) that is deemed by paragraph 143.1(1.2)(c) to be income of an amateur athlete trust for the year,

(c) the taxpayer's income (other than an amount described in paragraph 12(1)(z)) for a period in the year throughout which the taxpayer was not resident in Canada from

(i) the duties of an office or employment performed by the taxpayer in Canada, determined without reference to paragraphs 8(1)(c), (m) and (m.2), or

(ii) a business carried on by the taxpayer in Canada, either alone or as a partner actively engaged in the business

except to the extent that the income is exempt from income tax in Canada by reason of a provision contained in a tax convention or agreement with another country that has the force of law in Canada, or

(d) in the case of a taxpayer described in subsection 115(2), the total that would be determined under paragraph 115(2)(e) in respect of the taxpayer for the year if

(i) that paragraph were read without reference to subparagraphs 115(2)(e)(iv), and

(ii) subparagraph 115(2)(e)(ii) were read without any reference therein to paragraph 56(1)(n),

except any part thereof included in the total determined under this definition by reason of paragraph (c) or exempt from income tax in Canada by reason of a provision contained in a tax convention or agreement with another country that has the force of law in Canada,

exceeds the total of all amounts each of which is

(e) the taxpayer's loss for a period in the year throughout which the taxpayer was resident in Canada from

(i) a business carried on by the taxpayer, either alone or as a partner actively engaged in the business, or

(ii) property, where the loss is sustained from the rental of real or immovable property,

(f) an amount deductible under paragraph 60(b), or deducted under paragraph 60(c.2), in computing the taxpayer's income for the year, or

(g) the taxpayer's loss for a period in the year throughout which the taxpayer was not resident in Canada from a business carried on by the taxpayer in Canada, either alone or as a partner actively engaged in the business,

(h) [Repealed]

and, for the purposes of this definition, the income or loss of a taxpayer for any period in a taxation year is the taxpayer's income or loss computed as though that period were the whole taxation year;

Notes: "Earned income" is used as the basis for determining RRSP contribution eligibility. 18% of earned income in year 1, subject to a maximum dollar limit and minus the pension adjustment, is the contribution limit for year 2 (contribution made up to March 1 or Feb. 29, year 3). See Notes to 146(1)"RRSP deduction limit", 146(5).

Note that income from "office or employment" under (a)(i) includes all taxable benefits and stock option benefits under ss. 6 and 7 (e.g., earning-loss benefits under 6(1)(f) or (f.1): VIEWS doc 2013-0478851I7), as well as salary or wages taxable under s. 5. Business income and real property rental income in (a)(ii) and (iii) are *net* income from the business or property (i.e., after deductible expenses), as determined for 9(1).

Earned income includes rental income attributed from a 75(2) trust: VIEWS doc 2014-0538241C6 [2014 APFF q.5].

Earned income does not include capital gains, so Part X.1 overcontributions tax applied in *Larose*, 2002 FCA 151; leave to appeal denied 2002 CarswellNat 3772 (SCC).

Earned income does not include income exempt under 81(1)(a) (e.g., a NATO employee): VIEWS doc 2007-025504117, and see Notes to 81(1)(a) under "RRSPs" re Indians. (It does under 63(3).)

Para. (h) repealed by 2016 budget bill #2, effective 2017, as part of changing the eligible capital property rules to CCA Class 14.1 (see Notes to 20(1)(b)). It read:

(h) the portion of an amount included under subparagraph (a)(ii) or (c)(ii) in determining the taxpayer's earned income for the year because of paragraph 14(1)(b)

Para. (b.2) added (to include contributions to an amateur athlete trust in earned income), and (a) and (c) amended to exclude 12(1)(z) amounts, by 2014 budget bill #2, effective for an individual's 2014 and later taxation years, except that if an individual elects in writing under s. 50(4) of the bill in respect of the individual's 2011, 2012 or 2013 taxation year and the election is filed with the Minister by March 2, 2015, the amendments are effective for the taxation year in respect of which the election is filed and later taxation years.

Subparas. (a)(iii), (e)(ii) amended by 2002-2013 technical bill (Part 4 — bijuralism), effective June 26, 2013, to add "or immovable".

Definition earlier amended by 2002-2013 technical bill (last change effective 2000), 2008 budget bill #2 (for 2008 and later years); 1995-97 technical bill, 1997 Budget, 1992 technical bill, 1990 pension bill. 146(1)"earned income" was 146(1)(c) before RSC 1985 (5th Supp) consolidation for tax years ending after Nov. 1991.

Interpretation Bulletins: IT-377R: Director's, executor's or juror's fees (cancelled); IT-434R: Rental of real property by individual.

I.T. Technical News: 11 (reporting of amounts paid out of an employee benefit plan).

"issuer" means the person referred to in the definition "retirement savings plan" in this subsection with whom an annuitant has a contract or arrangement that is a retirement savings plan;

Notes: 146(1)"issuer" was 146(1)(c.1) before RSC 1985 (5th Supp) consolidation for tax years ending after Nov. 1991.

Registered Plans Frequently Asked Questions: RPFAQ-1 (RRSPs/RRIFs), q. 3 (change of issuer).

"maturity" means the date fixed under a retirement savings plan for the commencement of any retirement income the payment of which is provided for by the plan;

Notes: 146(1)"maturity" was 146(1)(d) before RSC 1985 (5th Supp) consolidation for tax years ending after Nov. 1991.

"net past service pension adjustment" of a taxpayer for a taxation year means the positive or negative amount determined by the formula

$$P + Q - G$$

where

P   is the total of all amounts each of which is the taxpayer's past service pension adjustment for the year in respect of an employer,

Q   is the total of all amounts each of which is a prescribed amount in respect of the taxpayer for the year, and

G   is the amount of the taxpayer's PSPA withdrawals for the year, determined as of the end of the year in accordance with prescribed rules;

Related Provisions: 204.2(1.3) — Net past service pension adjustment for purposes of Part X.1 tax; 257 — Formula cannot calculate to less than zero.

Notes: Q added by 1993 technical bill, effective for 1993 and later taxation years.

146(1)"net past service pension adjustment" was 146(1)(d.1) before RSC 1985 (5th Supp) consolidation for tax years ending after Nov. 1991. 146(1)(d.1) added by 1990 pension bill and amended by 1992 technical bill, effective 1989.

Regulations: 8307(5) (prescribed rules); 8308.4(2) (prescribed amount for formula element Q).

"non-qualified investment" has the same meaning as in subsection 207.01(1);

Notes: See Notes to 146(10.1) and 146(1)"qualified investment", and to 146(10) re "RRSP strips" where attempts are made to extract RRSP funds tax-free by investing them in private companies.

Definition amended by 2011 budget bill #2, effective in respect of investments acquired after March 22, 2011. For those acquired earlier, read:

"non-qualified investment", in relation to a trust governed by a registered retirement savings plan, means property acquired by the trust after 1971 that is not a qualified investment for the trust;

146(1)"non-qualified investment" was 146(1)(e) before RSC 1985 (5th Supp) consolidation for tax years ending after Nov. 1991.

Registered Plans Compliance Bulletins: 2 (general warning: use of RRSP funds to purchase property that is worthless, non-existent, or not a qualified investment); 3 (fraudulent RRSP arrangements); 4 (abusive schemes — RRSP stripping).

"premium" means any periodic or other amount paid or payable under a retirement savings plan

(a) as consideration for any contract referred to in paragraph (a) of the definition "retirement savings plan" to pay a retirement income, or

(b) as a contribution or deposit referred to in paragraph (b) of that definition for the purpose stated in that paragraph

but except for the purposes of paragraph (b) of the definition "benefit" in this subsection, paragraph (2)(b.3), subsection (22) and the definition "excluded premium" in subsection 146.02(1), does not include a repayment to which paragraph (b) or (d) of the definition "excluded withdrawal" in subsection 146.01(1), or paragraph (b) of the definition "excluded withdrawal" in subsection 146.02(1), applies or an amount that is designated under subsection 146.01(3) or 146.02(3);

Related Provisions: 60(j) — Transfer of superannuation benefits; 60(l) — Transfer of RRSP premium refunds; 146(21.1) — Contribution to Sask. Pension Plan deemed to be RRSP premium; 147.5(11) — Contribution to pooled registered pension plan deemed to be RRSP premium.

Notes: A retiring allowance contributed to an RRSP is a "premium": *Misir*, 2008 TCC 168, para. 15.

Closing words amended by 2019 budget bill #1, for repayments after 2019, to add reference to 146.01(1)"excluded withdrawal"(d) [technically, changing "paragraph (b) of the definition "excluded withdrawal" in either subsection 146.01(1) or 146.02(1)" to "paragraph (b) or (d) of the definition "excluded withdrawal" in subsection 146.01(1), or paragraph (b) of the definition "excluded withdrawal" in subsection 146.02(1)"].

Definition amended by 1998 Budget (effective for 1997 and later taxation years), 1994 Budget and 1992 technical bill. 146(1)"premium" was 146(1)(f) before RSC 1985 (5th Supp) consolidation for tax years ending after Nov. 1991.

Regulations: 100(3)(c) (no source withholding where premium is paid by employer directly to RRSP); 214.1 (information return).

Interpretation Bulletins: IT-528: Transfers of funds between registered plans.

"qualified investment" for a trust governed by a registered retirement savings plan means

(a) an investment that would be described by any of paragraphs (a) to (d), (f) and (g) of the definition "qualified investment" in section 204 if the reference in that definition to "a trust governed by a deferred profit sharing plan or revoked plan" were read as a reference to "a trust governed by a registered retirement savings plan" and if that definition were read without reference to the words "with the exception of excluded property in relation to the trust",

(b) [Repealed]

(c) an annuity described in the definition "retirement income" in respect of the annuitant under the plan, if purchased from a licensed annuities provider,

(c.1) a contract for an annuity issued by a licensed annuities provider where

(i) the trust is the only person who, disregarding any subsequent transfer of the contract by the trust, is or may become entitled to any annuity payments under the contract, and

(ii) the holder of the contract has a right to surrender the contract at any time for an amount that would, if reasonable sales and administration charges were ignored, approximate the value of funds that could otherwise be applied to fund future periodic payments under the contract,

(c.2) a contract for an annuity issued by a licensed annuities provider where

(i) annual or more frequent periodic payments are or may be made under the contract to the holder of the contract,

(ii) the trust is the only person who, disregarding any subsequent transfer of the contract by the trust, is or may become entitled to any annuity payments under the contract,

(iii) neither the time nor the amount of any payment under the contract may vary because of the length of any life, other than the life of the annuitant under the plan (in this definition referred to as the "RRSP annuitant"),

(iv) the day on which the periodic payments began or are to begin (in this paragraph referred to as the "start date") is not later than the end of the year in which the RRSP annuitant attains 72 years of age,

(v) either

(A) the periodic payments are payable for the life of the RRSP annuitant and either there is no guaranteed period under the contract or there is a guaranteed period that begins at the start date and does not exceed a term equal to 90 years minus the lesser of

(I) the age in whole years at the start date of the RRSP annuitant (determined on the assumption that the RRSP annuitant is alive at the start date), and

(II) the age in whole years at the start date of a spouse or common-law partner of the RRSP annuitant (determined on the assumption that a spouse or common-law partner of the RRSP annuitant at the time the contract was acquired is a spouse or common-law partner of the RRSP annuitant at the start date), or

(B) the periodic payments are payable for a term equal to

(I) 90 years minus the age described in subclause (A)(I), or

(II) 90 years minus the age described in subclause (A)(II), and

(vi) the periodic payments

(A) are equal, or

(B) are not equal solely because of one or more adjustments that would, if the contract were an annuity under a retirement savings plan, be in accordance with subparagraphs (3)(b)(iii) to (v) or that arise because of a uniform reduction in the entitlement to the periodic payments as a consequence of a partial surrender of rights to the periodic payments, and

(d) such other investments as may be prescribed by regulations of the Governor in Council made on the recommendation of the Minister of Finance;

Related Provisions: 87(10) — New share issued on amalgamation of public corporation deemed listed; 132.2(3)(h) — Where share ceases to be QI due to mutual fund reorganization; 146(10.1) — Tax payable on income from non-QI; 146(21.1) — Contribution to Sask. Pension Plan deemed to be RRSP premium; 207.01(6) — Deemed disposition by RRSP on property becoming or ceasing to be QI; 207.04 — Tax payable by annuitant if RRSP acquires non-QI.

Notes: See 204"qualified investment", which lists many qualified investments (per 146(1)"qualified investment"(a)), and that also qualify for RRIF, RESP, RDSP and TFSA purposes. See also Reg. 4900(1), which prescribes many more investments that qualify. For CRA interpretation see Income Tax Folio S3-F10-C1. If a non-qualified investment is acquired, see Notes to 146(9), (10) and (10.1).

An RRSP can write a covered call option, since that results only in cash being received in the plan: VIEWS doc 2004-0056251E5.

Para. (c.3), "an advanced life deferred annuity", was proposed in the July 30, 2019 draft legislation, but was not in 2021 budget bill #1, which enacted the ALDA rules (Finance decided not to permit RRSPs and RRIFs to hold an ALDA contract, but 146(16)(a.1) permits transfer of RRSP funds to an ALDA).

Definition amended by 2007 budget bill #1 (effective March 19, 2007), 2001 technical bill, 2000 same-sex partners bill, 1995-97 technical bill. 146(1)"qualified investment" was 146(1)(g) before RSC 1985 (5th Supp) consolidation for tax years ending after Nov. 1991.

Regulations: 221 (information return where mutual fund etc. claims its shares are QI); 4900 (prescribed investments).

Remission Orders: *Lionaird Capital Corporation Notes Remission Order*, P.C. 1999-737 (tax under 146(10) waived because taxpayers thought they were qualified investments).

Income Tax Folios: S3-F10-C1: Qualified investments — RRSPs, RESPs, RRIFs, RDSPs and TFSAs [replaces IT-320R3].

Registered Plans Compliance Bulletins: 2 (general warning: use of RRSP funds to purchase property that is worthless, non-existent, or not a qualified investment); 3 (fraudulent RRSP arrangements); 4 (abusive schemes — RRSP stripping); 6 (RRSP strips).

Forms: T3F: Investments prescribed to be qualified information return.

"RRSP deduction limit" of a taxpayer for a taxation year means the amount determined by the formula

$$A + B + R - C$$

where

A   is the taxpayer's unused RRSP deduction room at the end of the preceding taxation year,

B   is the amount, if any, by which

(a) the lesser of the RRSP dollar limit for the year and 18% of the taxpayer's earned income for the preceding taxation year

exceeds the total of all amounts each of which is

(b) the taxpayer's pension adjustment for the preceding taxation year in respect of an employer, or

(c) a prescribed amount in respect of the taxpayer for the year,

C   is the taxpayer's net past service pension adjustment for the year, and

R   is the taxpayer's total pension adjustment reversal for the year;

Related Provisions: 128(2)(d) — Where individual bankrupt; 146(5) — Amount of RRSP premiums deductible; 146(5.1) — Amount of spousal RRSP premiums deductible; 146(5.21) — Anti-avoidance; 204.1(2.1) — Tax payable by individuals — contributions after 1990; 248(1)"RRSP deduction limit" — Definition applies to entire Act; 257 — Formula cannot calculate to less than zero; Reg. 8307(2) — Prescribed condi-

tion for registered pension plan; Canada-U.S. Tax Treaty:Art. XVIII:11 — Limit to deductions to U.S. plan.

Notes: RRSP contributions (combined with PRPP contributions: 147.5(11)) accumulated since 1991 can be deducted under 146(5) up to the RRSP deduction limit, with carryforward per 146(1)"unused RRSP deduction room".

The RRSP deduction limit is the lesser of $X and 18% of the taxpayer's previous year's earned income, minus the previous year's pension adjustment (see 248(1)"pension adjustment" and Reg. 8301(1)). $X is $13,500 for 1996-2002, $14,500 for 2003, $15,500 for 2004, $16,500 for 2005, $18,000 for 2006, $19,000 for 2007, $20,000 for 2008, $21,000 for 2009, $22,000 for 2010, and indexed after 2010: $22,450 for 2011, $22,970 for 2012, $23,820 for 2013, $24,270 for 2014, $24,930 for 2015, $25,370 for 2016, $26,010 for 2017, $26,230 for 2018, $26,500 for 2019, $27,230 for 2020, $27,830 for 2021, $29,210 for 2022. The figures come from 146(1)"RRSP dollar limit" and 147.1(1)"money purchase limit".

The pension adjustment was held not to reduce the deduction limit where earlier contributions had been withdrawn and the taxpayers were no longer employed, in *Emmerson*, [1998] 1 C.T.C. 2182 (TCC) and *Bussière*, [2001] 2 C.T.C. 2005 (TCC). However, in *Graham*, 2013 TCC 294, the TCC rejected this argument for a taxpayer who had changed employers (calling his argument "vacuous and devoid of merit" and awarding costs against him in the Informal Procedure!).

Most taxpayers receive a statement on their annual Notice of Assessment (T451) showing their RRSP contribution limit. The limit can also be obtained from TIPS (Tax Information Phone Service), 1-800-267-6999 (see tinyurl.com/cra-tips) or canada.ca/my-cra-account. Where a taxpayer relies on incorrect information from CRA to make an RRSP withdrawal, relief may be provided: see *Donald Potter Income Tax Remission Order* for an example. In *Cheng*, 2020 TCC 95, C's deducting $20,000 of contributions she had not made was carelessness allowing 152(4)(a)(i) late reassessment; CRA telling her she had unused contributions was due to her original misreporting.

See also Willis Towers Watson, *Canadian Pensions and Retirement Income Planning*, 6th ed. (LexisNexis, 2017), chaps. 3-4; Manu Kakkar, "Foreign Pension Plan Contributions May Reduce RRSP Room", 9(1) *Tax for the Owner-Manager* (ctf.ca) 6-7 (Jan. 2009); VIEWS doc 2009-0306731E5.

Pension adjustment reversal: See Notes to Reg. 8403.1. Formula element R added by 1997 Budget, effective 1998.

146(1)"RRSP deduction limit" was 146(1)(g.1) (added by 1990 pension bill) before RSC 1985 (5th Supp) consolidation for tax years ending after Nov. 1991.

Regulations: 8304.1 (pension adjustment reversal); 8308(2), 8308.2, 8308.4(2), 8309 (prescribed amount).

Forms: RC268: Employee contributions to a United States retirement plan for 2017 — cross-border commuters; T1 General Sched. 7: RRSP unused contributions, transfers, and HBP or LLP activities.

"RRSP dollar limit" for a calendar year means

(a) for years other than 1996 and 2003, the money purchase limit for the preceding year,

(b) for 1996, $13,500, and

(c) for 2003, $14,500;

Related Provisions: 204.2(1.1) — Cumulative excess amount in respect of RRSPs; 248(1)"RRSP dollar limit" — Definition applies to entire Act.

Notes: See Notes to 146(1)"RRSP deduction limit" for the dollar limits.

Definition "RRSP dollar limit" amended by 2003 Budget, effective 2003, to add the special case for 2003. Amended by 1995 Budget to add the special case for 1996.

146(1)"RRSP dollar limit" was 146(1)(g.2) before RSC 1985 (5th Supp) consolidation for tax years ending after Nov. 1991. Added by 1990 pension bill, effective 1989.

"refund of premiums" means any amount paid out of or under a registered retirement savings plan (other than a tax-paid amount in respect of the plan) as a consequence of the death of the annuitant under the plan,

(a) to an individual who was, immediately before the death, a spouse or common-law partner of the annuitant, where the annuitant died before the maturity of the plan, or

(b) to a child or grandchild of the annuitant who was, immediately before the death, financially dependent on the annuitant for support;

Related Provisions: 60(l)(ii)(A), 60.011 — Rollover of premiums to Henson trust; 60(l)(v) — Rollover of refund of premiums to RRSP; 60.02(1)"eligible proceeds"(a) — Rollover of refund of premiums to RDSP on death; 146(1.1) — Where child presumed not financially dependent; 146(8.1) — Deemed receipt of refund of premiums; 146(8.9) — Effect of death where person other than spouse becomes entitled; 146.3(1)"designated benefit" — Application of definition to RRIFs; 248(8) — Meaning of "consequence" of death.

Notes: See Notes to 146(8.8).

For CRA interpretation of this definition see VIEWS docs 2003-0030815, 2004-0065471C6, 2009-0312421E5; 2014-0525241I7 (ward of the Crown cannot be financially dependent on parent). See also 60.011 and 60.02.

The parallel RRIF term is 146.3(1)"designated benefit".

Amounts paid to a spouse from an insured, unmatured RRSP of a deceased annuitant qualify as a refund of premiums: VIEWS doc 2006-0207371E5.

Definition amended by 2003 Budget (for deaths after 2002), 2000 same-sex partners bill, 1999 and 1998 Budgets, 1995-97 technical bill, 1992 Child Benefit bill, 1990 pension bill. 146(1)"refund of premiums" was 146(1)(h) before RSC 1985 (5th Supp) consolidation for tax years ending after Nov. 1991. In opening words, "as consequence" corrected to "as a consequence": laws.justice.gc.ca/eng/corrections.

Interpretation Bulletins: IT-500R: RRSPs — death of an annuitant.

Advance Tax Rulings: ATR-37: Refund of premiums transferred to spouse.

Forms: RC4177: Death of an RRSP annuitant [guide].

"registered retirement savings plan" means a retirement savings plan accepted by the Minister for registration for the purposes of this Act as complying with the requirements of this section;

Related Provisions: 75(3)(a) — Reversionary trust rules do not apply to RRSP; 108(1)"trust"(a) — "Trust" does not include RRSP for certain purposes; 128.1(10)"excluded right or interest"(a)(i) — No deemed disposition of RRSP on emigration; 146(21.1)–(21.3) — Sask. Pension Plan deemed to be RRSP for certain purposes; 207.01(1)"advantage", 207.05 — Tax on advantage received from RRSP; 207.04 — Tax on annuitant if RRSP acquires non-qualified or prohibited investment; 248(1)"foreign retirement arrangement" — U.S. Individual Retirement Account; 248(1)"registered retirement savings plan" — Definition applies to entire Act; Reg. 9006(a) — RRSP not reported to CRA for disclosure to foreign tax authorities; Canada-U.S. Tax Treaty:Art. XVIII:7 — Election to defer US tax on income accruing in RRSP.

Notes: See Notes to 146(2) for general discussion of RRSPs.

In *Natarajan*, 2010 TCC 582, CRA agreed that employment income paid by the employer to a US Deferred Income Plan was not taxable because it had not been "received" — effectively turning the US plan into an RRSP!

146(1)"registered retirement savings plan" was 146(1)(i) before RSC 1985 (5th Supp) consolidation for tax years ending after Nov. 1991.

Interpretation Bulletins: IT-415R2: Deregistration of RRSPs (cancelled); IT-528: Transfers of funds between registered plans.

"retirement income" means

(a) an annuity commencing at maturity, and with or without a guaranteed term commencing at maturity, not exceeding the term referred to in paragraph (b), or, in the case of a plan entered into before March 14, 1957, not exceeding 20 years, payable to

(i) the annuitant for the annuitant's life, or

(ii) the annuitant for the lives, jointly, of the annuitant and the annuitant's spouse or common-law partner and to the survivor of them for the survivor's life, or

(b) an annuity commencing at maturity, payable to the annuitant, or to the annuitant for the annuitant's life and to the spouse or common-law partner after the annuitant's death, for a term of years equal to 90 minus either

(i) the age in whole years of the annuitant at the maturity of the plan, or

(ii) where the annuitant's spouse or common-law partner is younger than the annuitant and the annuitant so elects, the age in whole years of the spouse or common-law partner at the maturity of the plan,

issued by a person described in the definition "retirement savings plan" in this subsection with whom an individual may have a contract or arrangement that is a retirement savings plan,

or any combination thereof;

Related Provisions: 146(1)"qualified investment"(c.3), 146.5 — Advanced life deferred annuity (ALDA) permitted.

Notes: The July 30, 2019 draft legislation proposed to amend both (a) and (b) opening words to exclude an advanced life deferred annuity, but those amendments were not in 2021 budget bill #1, which enacted the ALDA rules (Finance decided not to permit RRSPs and RRIFs to hold ALDA contracts, but 146(16)(a.1) permits transfer of RRSP funds to an ALDA).

Para. (b) amended by 2000 same-sex partners bill, effective 2001 or earlier. 146(1)"retirement income" was 146(1)(i.1) before RSC 1985 (5th Supp) consolidation for tax years ending after Nov. 1991.

Income Tax Folios: S3-F10-C1: Qualified investments — RRSPs, RESPs, RRIFs, RDSPs and TFSAs [replaces IT-320R3].

Information Circulars: 72-22R9: Registered retirement savings plans; 74-1R5: Form T2037, Notice of purchase of annuity with "plan" funds.

Forms: T2037: Notice of purchase of annuity with "plan" funds.

"retirement savings plan" means

(a) a contract between an individual and a person licensed or otherwise authorized under the laws of Canada or a province to carry on in Canada an annuities business, under which, in consideration of payment by the individual or the individual's spouse or common-law partner of any periodic or other amount as consideration under the contract, a retirement income commencing at maturity is to be provided for the individual, or

(b) an arrangement under which payment is made by an individual or the individual's spouse or common-law partner

(i) in trust to a corporation licensed or otherwise authorized under the laws of Canada or a province to carry on in Canada the business of offering to the public its services as trustee, of any periodic or other amount as a contribution under the trust,

(ii) to a corporation approved by the Governor in Council for the purposes of this section that is licensed or otherwise authorized under the laws of Canada or a province to issue investment contracts providing for the payment to or to the credit of the holder thereof of a fixed or determinable amount at maturity, of any periodic or other amount as a contribution under such a contract between the individual and that corporation, or

(iii) as a deposit with a branch or office, in Canada, of

(A) a person who is, or is eligible to become, a member of the Canadian Payments Association, or

(B) a credit union that is a shareholder or member of a body corporate referred to as a "central" for the purposes of the *Canadian Payments Act*,

(in this section referred to as a **"depositary"**)

to be used, invested or otherwise applied by that corporation or that depositary, as the case may be, for the purpose of providing for the individual, commencing at maturity, a retirement income;

Related Provisions: 146(1)"registered retirement savings plan" — RRSP; 146(4) — No tax on income earned in trust RRSP; 146(20) — No tax on income earned in depositary RRSP; 146.2(12) — TFSA deemed not to be RSP; 248(1)"foreign retirement arrangement" — U.S. Individual Retirement Account; 248(1)"retirement savings plan" — Definition applies to entire Act.

Notes: Re whether an RRSP is a contract, a trust or something else, see *Bank of Nova Scotia v. Thibault*, 2004 SCC 29 and Notes to 248(3).

A "depositary" RRSP is, per (b)(iii), a "deposit" with a bank or similar financial institution, traditionally kept in a cash account or in term deposits and GICs. A self-directed or "trusteed" RRSP, by contrast, is usually at a brokerage (with a trust company as trustee) and can invest in many securities (see 146(1)"qualified investment", Reg. 4900). CRA Guide T4079 (ch. 6) says: "Since most trust companies are also members of the Canadian Payments Association, they may offer RRSPs that satisfy the meaning of a depositary RRSP. The terms and conditions of the legal document establishing the plan will determine whether it is a depositary or a trusteed RRSP." In *Okanagan Court Bailiffs v. TD Waterhouse*, 2015 BCSC 1312, para. 63, a TD Waterhouse RRSP was (surprisingly) considered "depositary", even though it was invested in securities that had lost 80% of their value.

Cl. (b)(iii)(B) amended by 2017 budget bill #2, effective Oct. 24, 2001, to change "*Canadian Payments Association Act*" to "*Canadian Payments Act*".

Definition amended by 2000 same-sex partners bill, effective as per Notes to 248(1)"common-law partner". 146(1)"retirement savings plan" was 146(1)(j) before RSC 1985 (5th Supp) consolidation for tax years ending after Nov. 1991.

Information Circulars: 72-22R9: Registered retirement savings plans; 74-1R5: Form T2037: Notice of purchase of annuity with "plan" funds; 78-14R4: Guidelines for trust companies and other persons responsible for filing T3GR, T3D, T3P, T3S, T3RI, and T3F returns.

Forms: T3GR: Group income tax and information return for RRSP, RRIF, RESP, or RDSP trusts (and worksheets); T4RSP: Statement of RRSP income; T4RSP Summary; T4079: T4RSP and T4RIF guide.

"spousal or common-law partner plan", in relation to a taxpayer, means

(a) a registered retirement savings plan

(i) to which the taxpayer has, at a time when the taxpayer's spouse or common-law partner was the annuitant under the plan, paid a premium, or

(ii) that has received a payment out of or a transfer from a registered retirement savings plan or a registered retirement income fund that was a spousal or common-law partner plan in relation to the taxpayer, or

(b) a registered retirement income fund that has received a payment out of or a transfer from a spousal or common-law partner plan in relation to the taxpayer;

Related Provisions: 74.5(12) — Application; 146(5.1) — Deduction for contribution to spousal RRSP; 146(8.3) — Attribution on withdrawal from spousal RRSP; 146.3(5.1) — RRIF — amount included in income; 147.5(11) — Contribution to pooled registered pension plan deemed to be RRSP premium.

Notes: See 146(5.1) and Notes to 146(8.3).

On a transfer from a spousal RRSP to a RRIF, the RRIF automatically becomes a "spousal or common-law plan": VIEWS doc 2009-0340061E6.

Definition "spousal plan" replaced with this definition by 2001 technical bill, for 2001 and later tax years, or earlier by election.

146(1)"spousal plan" was 146(1)(k) before RSC 1985 (5th Supp) consolidation for tax years ending after Nov. 1991. Added by 1990 pension bill, effective 1989.

Registered Plans Frequently Asked Questions: RPFAQ-1 (RRSPs/RRIFs), q. 1 (spousal or common-law partner designation); q. 4 (common-law partner).

"tax-paid amount" paid to a person in respect of a registered retirement saving[s] plan means

(a) an amount paid to the person in respect of the amount that would, if this Act were read without reference to subsection 104(6), be income of a trust governed by the plan for a taxation year for which the trust was subject to tax because of paragraph (4)(c), or

(b) where

(i) the plan is a deposit with a depositary referred to in clause (b)(iii)(B) of the definition "retirement savings plan" in this subsection, and

(ii) an amount is received at any time out of or under the plan by the person,

the portion of the amount that can reasonably be considered to relate to interest or another amount in respect of the deposit that was required to be included in computing the income of any person (other than the annuitant) otherwise than because of this section;

Related Provisions: 146(1)"benefit"(c.1) — Whether tax-paid amount is a "benefit"; 146(1)"refund of premiums" — Exclusion of tax-paid amount; 146(8.9) — RRSP income inclusion on death; 146(8.92), (8.93) — Deduction to deceased for post-death RRSP losses; 146.3(5)(c) — Tax-paid amount from RRIF excluded from income; 146.3(6.2) — RRIF income inclusion on death.

Notes: See Notes to 146(8.8).

"Tax-paid amount" added by 1995-97 technical bill, effective for deaths after 1992. The first "tax-paid amounts" could be received beginning in 1995 in respect of post-1994 income, since 104(6)(c) applies for deaths in 1993 or later and allows one further calendar year of exemption. See also 146(1)"refund of premiums", which excludes a tax-paid amount; and 146(8.9) and 146.3(6.2), under which the RRSP and RRIF income inclusions on death are determined.

"unused RRSP deduction room" of a taxpayer at the end of a taxation year means,

(a) for taxation years ending before 1991, nil, and

(b) for taxation years that end after 1990, the amount, which can be positive or negative, determined by the formula

$$A + B + R - (C + D)$$

where

A is the taxpayer's unused RRSP deduction room at the end of the preceding taxation year,

B is the amount, if any, by which

(i) the lesser of the RRSP dollar limit for the year and 18% of the taxpayer's earned income for the preceding taxation year

exceeds the total of all amounts each of which is

(ii) the taxpayer's pension adjustment for the preceding taxation year in respect of an employer, or

(iii) a prescribed amount in respect of the taxpayer for the year,

C is the taxpayer's net past service pension adjustment for the year,

D is the total of all amounts each of which is

(i) an amount deducted by the taxpayer under any of subsections (5) to (5.2), in computing the taxpayer's income for the year,

(ii) an amount deducted by the taxpayer under paragraph 10 of Article XVIII of the *Canada-United States Tax Convention* signed at Washington on September 26, 1980 or a similar provision in another tax treaty, in computing the taxpayer's taxable income for the year,

(iii) a contribution made by an employer in the year to a pooled registered pension plan in respect of the taxpayer, or

(iv) the amount, if any, by which the taxpayer's exempt-income contribution amount (as defined in subsection 147.5(1)) for the year exceeds the taxpayer's unused non-deductible PRPP room (as defined in subsection 147.5(1)) at the end of the preceding taxation year, and

R is the taxpayer's total pension adjustment reversal for the year.

Related Provisions: 128(2)(d), (d.2) — Where individual bankrupt; 146(1) — RRSP deduction limit; 146(5.21) — Anti-avoidance; 204.2(1.1) — Cumulative excess amount re RRSPs; 248(1)"unused RRSP deduction room" — Definition applies to entire Act; 257 — Formula cannot calculate to less than zero.

Notes: All unused contribution room accumulated since 1991 can be contributed and deducted at any time: 146(5).

D(i) amended (to change "(5) or (5.1)" to "(5) to (5.2)" and delete reference to 60(v)), and D(iii)-(iv) added, by 2012 budget bill #2, effective Dec. 14, 2012.

D(ii) added by 2008 budget bill #2, for taxation years that begin after 2008.

Formula element R added by 1997 Budget, effective 1998 (technically added retroactive to 1989 along with some corrective restructuring of the language of the definition, but deemed to be nil for taxation years before 1998). For discussion of the pension adjustment reversal (PAR), see Notes to 146(1)"RRSP deduction limit".

Para. (b) amended by 1996 Budget, effective April 25, 1997. Taxpayers can now carry forward unused RRSP room indefinitely.

146(1)"unused RRSP deduction room" was 146(1)(l) before RSC 1985 (5th Supp) consolidation for tax years ending after Nov. 1991. 146(1)(l) added by 1990 pension bill, effective 1989.

Regulations: 8304.1 (pension adjustment reversal); 8308(2), 8308.2, 8308.4(2) (prescribed amount).

Forms: T1 General Sched. 7: RRSP unused contributions, transfers, and HBP or LLP activities.

Interpretation Bulletins [subsec. 146(1)]: IT-124R6: Contributions to registered retirement savings plans; IT-307R4: Spousal or common-law registered retirement savings plans; IT-415R2: Deregistration of RRSPs (cancelled).

(1.1) Restriction — financially dependent — For the purposes of paragraph (b) of the definition "refund of premiums" in subsection (1), clause 60(l)(v)(B.01), the definition "eligible individual" in subsection 60.02(1), subparagraph 104(27)(e)(i) and section 147.5, it is assumed, unless the contrary is established, that an individual's child or grandchild was not financially dependent on the individual for support immediately before the individual's death if the income of the child or grandchild for the taxation year preceding the taxation year in which the individual died exceeded the amount determined by the formula

$$A + B$$

where

1043

A is the amount determined for F in subsection 118(1.1) for that preceding taxation year; and

B is nil, unless the financial dependency was because of mental or physical infirmity, in which case it is $6,180 adjusted for each such preceding taxation year that is after 2002 in the manner set out in section 117.1.

Notes: "A" amended by 2021 budget bill #1, for 2021 and later tax years, to reflect the "basic personal amount" moving from 118(1)B(c) to 118(1.1)F.

146(1.1) amended to apply to 147.5 by 2012 budget bill #2, effective Dec. 14, 2012. Earlier amended by 2011 budget bill #2, 2003 Budget. (Former 146(1.1), added by 1990 pension bill and repealed by 1992 technical bill, defined "spouse" to include a common-law spouse for certain purposes. Since 2001, all ITA references to "spouse" now say "or common-law partner".)

(2) Acceptance of plan for registration [— conditions] — The Minister shall not accept for registration for the purposes of this Act any retirement savings plan unless, in the Minister's opinion, it complies with the following conditions:

(a) the plan does not provide for the payment of any benefit before maturity except

(i) a refund of premiums, and

(ii) a payment to the annuitant;

(b) the plan does not provide for the payment of any benefit after maturity except

(i) by way of retirement income to the annuitant,

(ii) to the annuitant in full or partial commutation of retirement income under the plan, and

(iii) in respect of a commutation referred to in paragraph (c.2);

(b.1) the plan does not provide for a payment to the annuitant of a retirement income except by way of equal annual or more frequent periodic payments until such time as there is a payment in full or partial commutation of the retirement income and, where that commutation is partial, equal annual or more frequent periodic payments thereafter;

(b.2) the plan does not provide for periodic payments in a year under an annuity after the death of the first annuitant, the total of which exceeds the total of the payments under the annuity in a year before that death;

(b.3) the plan does not provide for the payment of any premium after maturity;

(b.4) the plan does not provide for maturity after the end of the year in which the annuitant attains 71 years of age;

(c) the plan provides that retirement income under the plan may not be assigned in whole or in part;

(c.1) notwithstanding paragraph (a), the plan permits the payment of an amount to a taxpayer where the amount is paid to reduce the amount of tax otherwise payable under Part X.1 by the taxpayer;

(c.2) the plan requires the commutation of each annuity payable thereunder that would otherwise become payable to a person other than an annuitant under the plan;

(c.3) the plan, where it involves a depositary, includes provisions stipulating that

(i) the depositary has no right of offset as regards the property held under the plan in connection with any debt or obligation owing to the depositary, and

(ii) the property held under the plan cannot be pledged, assigned or in any way alienated as security for a loan or for any purpose other than that of providing for the annuitant, commencing at maturity, a retirement income; and

(c.4) [Repealed]

(d) the plan in all other respects complies with regulations of the Governor in Council made on the recommendation of the Minister of Finance.

Related Provisions: 139.1(13) — Para. 146(2)(c.4) inapplicable to conversion benefit on demutualization of insurer; 146(3) — Minister may accept plan despite certain

other conditions; 146(12) — Change in plan after registration; 204.2(1.2) — Undeducted RRSP premiums; 207.01(1)"advantage", 207.05 — Tax on advantage received from RRSP; 207.04 — Tax on annuitant if RRSP acquires non-qualified or prohibited investment; 248(3)(c) — RRSP set up in Quebec deemed to be trust; Reg. 9006(a) — RRSP not reported to CRA for disclosure to foreign tax authorities.

Notes: Contributions to an RRSP by 60 days after year-end (March 1, but Feb. 29 in a leap year) are deductible under 146(5) (or for a spousal plan 146(5.1)), up to limits based on previous year's earned income: 146(1)"RRSP deduction limit", "RRSP dollar limit". Funds grow tax-free in the RRSP: 146(4). They are taxed when withdrawn: 146(8). The RRSP must mature by the year the taxpayer turns 71: see below re 146(2)(b.4). A person age 65-71 who transfers part (or all) of their RRSP to a RRIF can take out $2,000 per year from the RRIF and claim the 118(3) pension credit (or more and split such income with the spouse under 60.03).

For discussion of RRSPs see *Miller Thomson on Estate Planning* (Carswell, looseleaf), chap. 6. See Notes to 146(4) re whether creditors can seize an RRSP, and to Canada-US treaty Art. XVIII:7 re US citizens owning RRSPs.

RRSP issuers and advisers: see tinyurl.com/rrsps.

The trustee (not the RRSP or the annuitant) is liable for s. 116 withholding on purchase of shares from a non-resident. See Notes to 116(1).

CRA's processing target (tinyurl.com/cra-standards) for responding to RRSP applications (to register, amend or terminate) is 90% within 60 days; in 2019-20, it did 100%.

See Notes to 146(4) re whether an RRSP can be seized by creditors, and requirements for U.S. filers to report RRSPs as foreign trusts. See Notes to 146(10) re taxpayers defrauded by "RRSP strip" schemes to access their locked-in RRSP funds.

There is no statutory requirement for the annuitant to have a Social Insurance Number, but CRA requires it before registering the RRSP: VIEWS doc 2007-0240191C6.

In addition to the conditions in 146(2), a group RRSP set up by an employer may have conditions restricting pre-retirement withdrawal of funds. See Jeffrey Smith, "Employer puts a stop to retirement plan withdrawals", 20(12) *Canadian Payroll Reporter* (Carswell) 1, 8 (Dec. 2008), discussing *Court Galvanizing Ltd. v. USW Local 8614*, 2008 CarswellOnt 8032 (Ont. Arb. Bd.).

146(2)(b.4) requires an RRSP to mature the year the taxpayer turns 71. By the end of the year the RRSP must be converted to a RRIF (146.3) or an annuity (146(2)(b), (b.1), 146(1)"retirement income"), or else it is all included in income under 146(8). Most plans provide that they automatically convert to a RRIF if the taxpayer does nothing.

146(2)(b.4) amended to change "69" to "71" by 2007 budget bill #1, effective 2007, to increase the RRSP age limit from 69 to 71. Amended by 1996 Budget to change "71 years" to "69 years", effective 1996 or 1997 depending on the circumstances.

146(2)(c.1) amended by 1990 pension bill, effective 1991.

A settlement annuity purchased for a beneficiary on the annuitant's death may not comply with *146(2)(c.2)*: VIEWS doc 2005-0120161E5.

146(2)(c.3) applies only to depositary plans (see Notes to 146(1)"retirement savings plan"). If assets in a self-directed plan are pledged, see 146(10); if this condition is violated, see 146(12). If a depositary RRSP is pledged in violation of the condition required by 146(2)(c.3), the pledge is valid and can be enforced: *Re Whaling*, [1999] 4 C.T.C. 221 (Ont CA); *Trainer*, 2001 BCSC 916. Where a bank seizes an RRSP to satisfy another debt, in breach of the requirement in 146(2)(c.3)(i), the bank will be liable for damages: *Belliveau v. Royal Bank* (2000), 14 C.B.R. (4th) 17 (NBCA).

146(2)(c.4) repealed by 2011 budget bill #2, effective March 23, 2011. With its repeal, the RRSP contract is no longer required to prohibit the taxpayer receiving an "advantage", and an "advantage" is taxed under 207.05 (instead of 146(13.1)).

146(2)(c.4) amended by 1989 Budget, for advantages extended after 1988.

Regulations: 214, 214.1 (issuer must file information returns).

Interpretation Bulletins: IT-124R6: Contributions to registered retirement savings plans; IT-307R4: Spousal or common-law registered retirement savings plans; IT-415R2: Deregistration of RRSPs (cancelled).

Information Circulars: 72-22R9: Registered retirement savings plans.

Registered Plans Compliance Bulletins: 1, 2, 3 (how to contact us).

Registered Plans Frequently Asked Questions: RPFAQ-1 (RRSPs/RRIFs), q. 1 (spousal or common-law partner designation); q. 3 (change of issuer); q. 4 (common-law partner); q. 5 (incentives for RRSPs); q. 6 (foreign content rule for RRSPs).

Forms: T550: Application for registration of RSPs, ESPs or RIFs under s. 146, 146.1 and 146.3 of the ITA.

(3) Idem — The Minister may accept for registration for the purposes of this Act any retirement savings plan notwithstanding that the plan

(a) provides for the payment of a benefit after maturity by way of dividend;

(b) provides for any annual or more frequent periodic amount payable

(i) to the annuitant referred to in subparagraph (a)(ii) of the definition "retirement income" in subsection (1) by way of an annuity described in paragraph (a) of that definition to be reduced, in the event of the death of the annuitant's spouse or common-law partner during the lifetime of the annuitant, in such manner as to provide for the payment of equal annual or more frequent periodic amounts throughout the lifetime of the annuitant thereafter,

(ii) to any person by way of an annuity, to be reduced if a pension becomes payable to that person under the *Old Age Security Act*, by an annual or other periodic amount not exceeding the amount payable to that person in that period under that Act,

(iii) to any person by way of an annuity, to be increased or reduced depending on the increase or reduction in the value of a specified group of assets constituting the assets of a separate and distinct account or fund maintained in respect of a variable annuities business by a person licensed or otherwise authorized under the laws of Canada or a province to carry on in Canada that business,

(iii.1) to any person by way of an annuity under a contract that provides for the increase or reduction of the annuity in accordance only with a change in the interest rate on which the annuity is based, if the interest rate, as increased or reduced, equals or approximates a generally available Canadian market interest rate,

(iv) that may be adjusted annually to reflect

(A) in whole or in part increases in the Consumer Price Index, as published by Statistics Canada under the authority of the *Statistics Act*, or

(B) increases at a rate specified in the annuity contract, not exceeding 4% per annum, or

(v) to the annuitant by way of an annuity to be increased annually to the extent the amount or rate of return that would have been earned on a pool of investment assets (available for purchase by the public and specified in the annuity contract) exceeds an amount or rate specified in the plan and provides that no other increase may be made in the amount payable;

(c) [Repealed under former Act]

(d) provides for the payment of any amount after the death of an annuitant thereunder;

(e) is adjoined to a contract or other arrangement that is not a retirement savings plan; or

(f) contains such other terms and provisions, not inconsistent with this section, as are authorized or permitted by regulations of the Governor in Council made on the recommendation of the Minister of Finance.

Related Provisions: 60(l)(ii) — Transfer of RRSP premium refunds; 172(3) — Appeal from refusal to register.

Notes: See VIEWS doc 2015-0567071E5.

146(3)(b)(i) amended by 2000 same-sex partners bill to refer to "common-law partner", effective as per Notes to 248(1)"common-law partner".

Interpretation Bulletins: IT-124R6: Contributions to registered retirement savings plans; IT-307R4: Spousal or common-law registered retirement savings plans; IT-415R2: Deregistration of RRSPs (cancelled).

Information Circulars: 72-22R9: Registered retirement savings plans.

(4) No tax while trust governed by plan — Except as provided in subsection (10.1), no tax is payable under this Part by a trust on the taxable income of the trust for a taxation year if, throughout the period in the year during which the trust was in existence, the trust was governed by a registered retirement savings plan, except that

(a) if the trust has borrowed money (other than money used in carrying on a business) in the year or has, after June 18, 1971, borrowed money (other than money used in carrying on a business) that it has not repaid before the commencement of the year, tax is payable under this Part by the trust on its taxable income for the year;

(b) in any case not described in paragraph (a), if the trust has carried on any business or businesses in the year, tax is payable under this Part by the trust on the amount, if any, by which

(i) the amount that its taxable income for the year would be if it had no incomes or losses from sources other than from that business or those businesses, as the case may be,

exceeds

(ii) such portion of the amount determined under subparagraph (i) in respect of the trust for the year as can reasonably be considered to be income from, or from the disposition of, qualified investments for the trust; and

(c) if the last annuitant under the plan has died, tax is payable under this Part by the trust on its taxable income for each year after the year following the year in which the last annuitant died.

Related Provisions: 104(6)(a.2) — Deduction for amounts paid out to beneficiaries; 138.1(7) — Segregated fund rules do not apply to RRSP; 146(8.9)A(b), (c) — No income inclusion for tax-paid amounts on death; 146(10.1) — Tax on income from non-qualified investment; 146(20) — Exemption for income earned in depositary RRSP; 149(1)(r) — No tax on RRSP; 204.6 — Tax in respect of registered investments; 207.01(1)"advantage", 207.05 — Tax on advantage received from RRSP; 207.04 — Tax on annuitant if RRSP acquires non-qualified or prohibited investment; Canada-U.S. Tax Treaty:Art. XVIII:7 — Election to defer U.S. tax on income accruing in RRSP; Canada-U.S. Tax Treaty:Art. XXI:2(a) — RRSP exempt from U.S. tax.

Notes: See Notes to 146(2) for general discussion of RRSPs.

146(4) exempts income earned in a "trusteed" RRSP. The exemption for income in a "depositary" RRSP (see Notes to 146(1)"retirement savings plan") is in 146(20).

Since the RRSP is exempt, a transaction changing the book value of shares has no effect: VIEWS doc 2014-0545181E5.

An RRSP that carries on business is taxed on the business income: 146(4)(b). This could include active stock trading (see 248(1)"business" and Notes to 54"capital property"), but CRA does not normally assess on this basis: VIEWS doc 2014-0538221C6 [2014 APFF q.2] (though it does for TFSAs, perhaps because those profits will otherwise never be taxed: see Notes to 146.2(6)). See also Notes to 146.3(3).

An RRSP or RRIF is exempt from US withholding tax on dividends and interest: Canada-U.S. tax treaty Art. XXI:2. If a plan holds US stocks, the trustee should advise the U.S. payor not to withhold tax on dividends.

US citizens or residents: see Notes to Canada-US tax treaty Art. XVIII:7.

Seizure by creditors: An RRSP, RRIF or DPSP cannot be seized on bankruptcy (except contributions made in the 12 months before bankruptcy — though provincial legislation can override this exception). *Bankruptcy and Insolvency Act* s. 67(1)(b.3) provides:

> 67. (1) The property of a bankrupt divisible among his creditors shall not comprise [...]
>
> (b) any property that as against the bankrupt is exempt from execution or seizure under any laws applicable in the province within which the property is situated and within which the bankrupt resides; [...]
>
> (b.3) without restricting the generality of paragraph (b), property in a registered retirement savings plan or a registered retirement income fund, as those expressions are defined in the *Income Tax Act*, or in any prescribed plan, other than property contributed to any such plan or fund in the 12 months before the date of bankruptcy,

(A DPSP is a "prescribed plan" for (b.3): *Bankruptcy and Insolvency General Rules*, C.R.C., c. 368, s. 59.2, added by P.C. 2008-1318.) See Notes to 128(2) for more on bankruptcy.

Outside of bankruptcy, an RRSP or RRIF cannot be seized by creditors in 6 provinces due to specific legislation, subject to various exceptions. BC: *Court Order Enforcement Act* s. 71.3 (and *Wills, Estates and Succession Act* s. 88(2)(a) if an irrevocable beneficiary designation is made). Alberta: *Civil Enforcement Act* ss. 81.1, 92.1. Sask.: *Registered Plan (Retirement Income) Exemption Act*. Manitoba: *Registered Retirement Savings Protection Act*. PEI: *Designation of Beneficiary under Benefit Plan Act* s. 10 [only if a beneficiary is designated]. Nfld & Labrador: *Judgment Enforcement Act* s. 131.1. However, CRA (and the federal government generally) is not subject to provincial exemption from garnishment: *Quebec v. Canada*, 2011 SCC 60 and Notes to 224(1).

Without such a provincial rule, an RRSP or RRIF can be seized, though 146(2)(c.3)(ii) and 146.3(2)(c)(ii) say they cannot be used as security: *Bodnarchuk*, [1995] 2 C.T.C. 269 (FCTD); *Whaling*, [1999] 4 C.T.C. 221 (Ont CA); *Blouin*, 2003 SCC 31 (re Quebec where the RRSP was given as security); *Bank of Nova Scotia v. Thibault*, 2004 SCC 29 (Quebec: exemption from seizure cannot result from mere intention of the parties); *Keith G. Collins Ltd.*, 2008 MBCA 92 (CRA was creditor). The seizure can be done by the Sheriff delivering an order to the financial institution: *Guterres*, [1994] 2 C.T.C. 308 (FCTD, in BC); *Cameron*, 2007 FC 319 (in Ontario). Seizure and garnishment are different; garnishment may not be possible in common-law provinces (unless the annuitant collapses the RRSP), as the RRSP trustee is likely not a debtor; in Quebec, a trust company was liable for failing to honour a garnishment notice in *Marrazza*, 2004 FC 139. Cdn Bar Association annual meeting resolution 11-01-A (Aug. 2011) urges the "federal, provincial and territorial governments to adopt a harmonized legislative framework to protect RRSPs and RRIFs from creditors with appropriate limits and exemptions" (and see CBA letter to Minister of Finance, March 21, 2012).

A general security pledge of "all accounts" was interpreted as not including an RRSP unless specifically listed, as otherwise the pledge would trigger 146(10) or (12) and include the RRSP in income, causing "havoc": *Okanagan Court Bailiffs v. TD Waterhouse*, 2015 BCSC 1312.

In *National Trust*, [1998] 4 C.T.C. 26 (FCA), the annuitant had asked the RRSP trustee to cancel the plan and pay him the proceeds, so the trustee was "liable to pay" him for purposes of 224(1) garnishment.

See also Uukkivi, "RRSPs: Limiting the Risk of Exposure", 8(1) *Tax for the Owner-Manager* (ctf.ca) 5-6 (Jan. 2008); Ballantyne, "Clarification of RRSP Creditor Protection", XII(2) *Insurance Planning* (Federated Press) 772 (2006) and "Protecting All Retirement Products", XIV(1) 870-72 (2007); Klotz, "Protective Planning Against Business Failure", 24(6) *Money & Family Law* (Carswell) 41 at 45-46. In **Quebec**, see Frajman, "Beneficiary Designations in Quebec", xxvii(8) *The Canadian Taxpayer* (Carswell) 62-64 (Apr. 13, 2005), "RRSP Unseizability", xxviii(3) 20-21 (Jan. 31, 2006) and "Protecting Self-Directed RRSPs From Creditors", xxix(18) 141-43 (Sept. 11, 2007).

For discussion of locked-in RRSPs see Notes to 147.3(1).

An RRSP or RRIF placed with an insurer may be exempt from seizure under provincial insurance legislation: *Maritime Life*, [2000] 4 C.T.C. 98 (FCA). Putting it into life insurance may not defeat creditors if done shortly before the taxpayer goes bankrupt: *Ramgotra v. North American Life*, [1996] 1 C.T.C. 356 (SCC). In *Moss*, [2009] 4 C.T.C. 118 (FCA) (leave to appeal to SCC discontinued May 25/09), CRA was not liable for proceeding with collection action that prevented the taxpayer from converting insurance policies into annuities exempt from seizure.

Where an RRSP has a designated beneficiary, proceeds paid to the beneficiary on death are not part of the estate (though the estate must pay any tax owing due to the death: 146(8.8)) and cannot be seized by the estate's creditors, under Ontario case law: *Amherst Crane v. Perring*, [2004] 5 C.T.C. 5 (Ont CA), leave to appeal denied 2005 CarswellOnt 354 (SCC), and in PEI due to the *Designation of Beneficiaries under Benefit Plans Act*, s. 9. Similarly, in Sask., an estate solicitor could not count the RRSP in the estate's value when calculating his fees: *Gheyssen v. TTH Law*, 2014 SKQB 158. For exceptions in Ontario, see Corbin, "Creditor Protection for RRSPs on Death", 20(3) *Money & Family Law [MFL]* (Carswell) 17-18 (March 2005). See also Goodman, "The Protection of RRSPs/RRIFs from Estate Creditors", XI(3) *Insurance Planning* (Federated Press) 710-12 (2005); Doobay, "Designated Beneficiary and Creditors", 22(6) *Canadian Tax Highlights* (ctf.ca) 6-8 (June 2014) (re *Kiperchuk* and *Higgins* cases); Corbin, "Estate Administration Tax and 'Plans' With a Designated Beneficiary", 29(8) *MFL* 57-58 (Aug. 2014). In *Love v. Love*, 2011 SKQB 176, a beneficiary change requested by email was invalid as it was not specific enough. In *Morrison Estate*, 2015 ABQB 769, a RRIF beneficiary designation to 1 of 4 children was held valid (not subject to *Pecore*, discussed in Notes to 69(1)), but the beneficiary had to reimburse the estate for the tax the estate had to pay on the RRIF. In *McConomy Estate*, 2009 CanLII 6164 (Ont. SCJ), para. 58, a RRIF designation to child X was found valid, but X held the RRIF proceeds in trust for all three children, as the deceased intended an equal split of her assets; similarly in *Calmusky*, 2020 ONSC 1506, a resulting trust applied to a RRIF designation [Corbin, "Twins' Pique", 35(7) *MFL* (Carswell) 49-50 (July 2020); Byun, "Calmusky", XXV(4) *Insurance Planning* (Federated Press) 13-16 (2020); Main & DeFilippis, "Presumption of Resulting Trust Applied to Beneficiary Designation of RRIF", 14(1) *Taxes & Wealth Management* (Carswell) 3-4 (March 2021). STEP Canada (Feb. 22, 2021), Adovicis, CALU and the Ontario Bar Assn (Nov. 2020) have all proposed to Ontario that *Calmusky* be overruled by legislation.]. In *Ashton Estate*, 2008 CanLII 21421 (Ont. SCJ), a will's "I revoke all testamentary dispositions" clause was held to cancel previous RRSP designations; and a clause bequeathing RRSPs was held to apply to RRIFs to which the RRSPs had been converted. In *Boulos v. Duca Financial*, 2020 ONSC 1946, a designation in an RRSP was held to apply to the RRIF to which the RRSP had been automatically converted [Corbin, "The Case of the (Non-)Disappearing Beneficiary Designation", 35(6) *MFL* 41-42 (June 2020)]. See also Johnson, "Will Revocation Clauses and RRSP/RRIF Beneficiary Designations", 15(6) *Tax Hyperion* (Carswell) 4-8 (Nov-Dec 2018).

Seizure of other plans: A RESP whose subscriber is bankrupt can be seized (even if its funds came from child tax benefits that were exempt from seizure): *Mackinnon*, 2007 SKQB 39. (A RESP can be garnished for the subscriber's tax debt: VIEWS doc 2012-045928I7.) CRA says an RDSP whose beneficiary is bankrupt can be cashed by the trustee: 2013-050447117; but the Court refused this in *Alary*, 2016 BCSC 2108. The March 2019 federal Budget, Chapter 4, Part 1, announced that RDSPs will be exempt from seizure in bankruptcy, except for contributions made in the 12 months before the bankruptcy filing. A retirement compensation account (RCA) was not protected from seizure in *Virc v. Blair*, 2017 ONCA 849, as it was not a pension plan.

To apply 146(4)(c) where the carrier is not aware of the annuitant's death until years later, see VIEWS doc 9820687.

A worthless security can be removed from an RRSP via withdrawal by the annuitant or sale to a third party: VIEWS doc 2009-0347081E5.

Where an RRSP carries on business (by actively trading stocks), see VIEWS doc 2009-0340431E5.

146(4)(b) and (c) amended by 1993 technical bill, effective for 1993 and later taxation years. Tax is now payable by the trust only from the second year following death. (The same applies to RRIFs, under 146.3(3,1).)

Income Tax Folios: S3-F10-C1: Qualified investments — RRSPs, RESPs, RRIFs, RDSPs and TFSAs [replaces IT-320R3].

Interpretation Bulletins: IT-415R2: Deregistration of RRSPs (cancelled).

Information Circulars: 72-22R9: Registered retirement savings plans.

I.T. Technical News: 39 (settlement of a shareholder class action suit).

Advance Tax Rulings: ATR-37: Refund of premiums transferred to spouse.

(5) Amount of RRSP premiums deductible — There may be deducted in computing a taxpayer's income for a taxation year such amount as the taxpayer claims not exceeding the lesser of

(a) the amount, if any, by which the total of all amounts each of which is a premium paid by the taxpayer after 1990 and on or before the day that is 60 days after the end of the year under a registered retirement savings plan under which the taxpayer was the annuitant at the time the premium was paid, other than the portion, if any, of the premium

(i) that was deducted in computing the taxpayer's income for a preceding taxation year,

(ii) that was designated for any taxation year for the purposes of paragraph 60(j), (j.1) or (l),

(iii) in respect of which the taxpayer received a payment that was deducted under subsection (8.2) in computing the taxpayer's income for a preceding taxation year,

(iii.1) that was an exempt-income contribution amount (as defined in subsection 147.5(1)) for any taxation year,

(iv) that was deductible under subsection (6.1) in computing the taxpayer's income for any taxation year, or

(iv.1) that would be considered to be withdrawn by the taxpayer as an eligible amount (as defined in subsection 146.01(1) or 146.02(1)) less than 90 days after it was paid, if earnings in respect of a registered retirement savings plan were considered to be withdrawn before premiums paid under that plan and premiums were considered to be withdrawn in the order in which they were paid

exceeds

(v) the amount, if any, by which

(A) the total of all amounts deducted under subsection 147.3(13.1) in computing the taxpayer's income for the year or a preceding taxation year

exceeds

(B) the total of all amounts, in respect of transfers occurring before 1991 from registered pension plans, deemed by paragraph 147.3(10)(b) or (c) to be a premium paid by the taxpayer to a registered retirement savings plan, and

(b) the amount, if any, by which the taxpayer's RRSP deduction limit for the year exceeds the total of all contributions made by an employer in the year to a pooled registered pension plan in respect of the taxpayer.

Related Provisions: 18(1)(u) — Investment counselling and administration fees for RRSP are non-deductible; 18(11)(b) — No deduction for interest on money borrowed to contribute to RRSP; 60(i) — Deduction for RRSP premium paid; 60(j), (j.1), (l) — Transfer of superannuation benefits, retiring allowances and RRSP premium refunds; 146(1)"unused RRSP deduction room"(b)D(i) — Deduction reduces unused deduction room; 146(5.1) — Deduction for contribution to spousal RRSP; 146(5.21) — Anti-avoidance; 146(8.2) — Deduction where non-deducted overcontribution withdrawn from plan; 146(8.21) — Premium deemed not paid; 146(16) — Deduction on transfer of funds; 146(21.1) — Contribution to Sask. Pension Plan deemed to be RRSP premium; 146(22) — Deadline extension for ice storm and for 1998 PAR; 147.3(13.1) — Withdrawal of excessive transfers to RRSPs and RRIFs; 147.5(11) — Pooled registered pension plan contribution deemed to be RRSP premium; 204.1(2.1) — Overcontribution tax; 204.2(1.2)I(a)(vi) — Amount non-deductible due to 146(5)(a)(iv.1) not counted for overcontribution tax; 204.94(2) — Tax on RESP accumulated income payment not contributed to RRSP; Canada-U.S. Tax Treaty:Art. XVIII:7 — Election to defer U.S. tax on income accruing in RRSP; Canada-U.S. Tax Treaty:Art. XXI:2(a) — RRSP exempt from U.S. tax.

Notes: See Notes to 146(1)"RRSP deduction limit" for the maximum contribution deductible under 146(5), cumulative since 1991. Contributions are not subject to minimum tax, since the 1998 repeal of 127.52(1)(a). Overcontributions exceeding cumulative $2,000 are subject to 1% monthly Part X.1 tax: 204.1(2.1).

The contribution deadline is 60 days after year-end, normally Mar. 1 but Feb. 29 in a leap year. It can be extended by 146(22) at CRA discretion, as was done for the Jan. 1998 ice storm and for taxpayers with 1998 pension adjustment reversals. VIEWS doc 2010-0363431E5 says a contribution mailed to the bank on March 1 does not meet the deadline, but this is wrong due to 248(7)(a), which deems anything (other than payment to CRA) to be received the day it is mailed. CRA was "revisiting the issue" in light of the author's Dec. 31/10 email on this, but never issued a correction.

A third-party contribution can be deducted by the annuitant, provided it is not a "gift to the RRSP" (how this is determined is unstated): VIEWS doc 2019-0799111C6 [2019 CLHIA q.3]. For spousal contributions (deductible by the contributing spouse) see 146(5.1). Pre-bankruptcy contributions can be deducted after bankruptcy: 2013-0474741E5.

For interpretation of 146(5)(a)(iv.1) see Notes at end of 146.01. In *Duxbury*, 2006 TCC 688, payments on a mortgage on D's home held by D's RRSP were not deductible.

See 146(4) Notes re whether a creditor can seize an RRSP, and US filers; and 7(1) Notes re valuing a stock option contributed to an RRSP.

146(5) amended by 2012 budget bill #2 (effective Dec. 14, 2012), 1998 and 1994 Budgets, 1993 and 1992 technical bills, 1990 pension bill. For 1989-90, the limit was 20% of current year's earned income, capped at $3,500 minus deductible RPP contributions for RPP members, $7,500 otherwise.

Regulations: 100(3)(c) (no source withholding where premium is paid by employer directly to RRSP); 214.1 (information return).

Remission Orders: *Certain Taxpayers Remission Order, 1998-2*, P.C. 1998-2092, s. 2 (judges in Quebec who made contributions in 1989 or 1990); *Certain Taxpayers Remission Order, 1999-2*, P.C. 1999-1855, s. 2 (remission to Quebec judges for excess contributions in 1989-90); *Donald Potter Remission Order*, P.C. 2004-264 (remission of tax on a withdrawal based on incorrect information from the CRA).

Interpretation Bulletins: IT-124R6: Contributions to registered retirement savings plans; IT-307R4: Spousal or common-law registered retirement savings plans; IT-500R: RRSPs — death of an annuitant.

Advance Tax Rulings: ATR-2: Contribution to pension plan for past service; ATR-17: Employee benefit plan — purchase of company shares; ATR-37: Refund of premiums transferred to spouse.

Forms: T1 Sched. 7: RRSP unused contributions, transfers, and HBP or LLP activities; T4040: RRSPs and other registered plans for retirement [guide].

(5.1) Amount of spousal RRSP premiums deductible — There may be deducted in computing a taxpayer's income for a taxation year such amount as the taxpayer claims not exceeding the lesser of

(a) the total of all amounts each of which is a premium paid by the taxpayer after 1990 and on or before the day that is 60 days after the end of the year under a registered retirement savings plan under which the taxpayer's spouse or common-law partner (or, where the taxpayer died in the year or within 60 days after the end of the year, an individual who was the taxpayer's spouse or common-law partner immediately before the death) was the annuitant at the time the premium was paid, other than the portion, if any, of the premium

(i) that was deducted in computing the taxpayer's income for a preceding taxation year,

(ii) that was designated for any taxation year for the purposes of paragraph 60(j.2),

(iii) in respect of which the taxpayer or the taxpayer's spouse or common-law partner has received a payment that has been deducted under subsection (8.2) in computing the taxpayer's income for a preceding taxation year, or

(iv) that would be considered to be withdrawn by the taxpayer's spouse or common-law partner as an eligible amount (as defined in subsection 146.01(1) or 146.02(1)) less than 90 days after it was paid, if earnings in respect of a registered retirement savings plan were considered to be withdrawn before premiums paid under that plan and premiums were considered to be withdrawn in the order in which they were paid, and

(b) the amount, if any, by which the taxpayer's RRSP deduction limit for the year exceeds the total of all amounts each of which is

(i) the amount deducted under subsection (5) in computing the taxpayer's income for the year, or

(ii) a contribution made by an employer in the year to a pooled registered pension plan in respect of the taxpayer.

Related Provisions: 60(i) — Deduction for RRSP premiums paid; 60(l) — Transfer of RRSP premium refunds; 74.5(12)(a) — Attribution rules do not apply to spousal contribution; 146(1)"unused RRSP deduction room"(b)D(i) — Deduction reduces unused deduction room; 146(5) — Deduction for contribution to own plan; 146(8.21) — Premium deemed not paid; 146(8.3) — Attribution of income when amount withdrawn from RRSP; 146(16) — Deduction on transfer of funds; 146(21.1) — Contribution to Sask. Pension Plan deemed to be RRSP premium; 146(22) — Deadline extension for ice storm; 146.3(5.1) — Attribution on withdrawal from RRIF; 146.3(5.4) — RRIF — Spouse's income; 147.5(11) — Pooled registered pension plan contribution deemed to be RRSP premium; 204.1(2.1) — Tax payable by individuals — contributions after 1990; 204.2(1.2)I(a)(vi) — Amount non-deductible due to 146(5.1)(a)(iv) not included for Part X.1 penalty tax purposes; 204.94(2) — Tax on RESP accumulated income payment not contributed to RRSP; 252(3) — Extended meaning of "spouse"; *Interpretation Act* 27(5) — Meaning of "within 60 days".

Notes: 146(5.1) allows X to contribute to X's spouse's (or common-law partner's) RRSP, within X's own contribution limit. Even though pension income can now be split (60.03), it can still be useful for splitting income further, withdrawing funds before X turns 71: Eatock, "Do Spousal RRSPs Still Have a Use?", 20(2) *Taxation of Executive Compensation & Retirement* (Federated Press) 1042-43 (Sept. 2008).

See Notes to 146(8.3) re attribution on withdrawals.

146(5.1)(b)(ii) added by 2012 budget bill #2, effective Dec. 14, 2012.

146(5.1) amended by 2000 same-sex partners bill (last change effective 2001), 1998 and 1994 Budgets, 1993 technical bill and 1990 pension bill.

Regulations: 100(3)(c) (no source withholding where premium is paid by employer directly to RRSP); 214.1 (information return).

Interpretation Bulletins: IT-124R6: Contributions to registered retirement savings plans; IT-307R4: Spousal or common-law registered retirement savings plans; IT-500R: RRSPs — death of an annuitant.

Information Circulars: 72-22R9: Registered retirement savings plans.

Forms: T4040: RRSPs and other registered plans for retirement [guide].

(5.2) RRSP premium [transfer of RPP benefits in 2009-2010 where employer insolvent] — [No longer relevant]

Notes: 146(5.2), added by 2011 budget bill #2, allowed a deduction for a transfer of certain RPP benefits before 2011. Former 146(5.2), repealed by 1990 pension bill, defined "pension fund or plan".

(5.201) [No longer relevant]

Notes: 146(5.201) added by 2011 budget bill #2, effective in respect of transfers made after February 2009. See Notes to 146(5.2).

(5.21) Anti-avoidance [applies to 1990 only] — [No longer relevant]

Notes: 146(5.21) added by 1990 pension bill, effective for 1990 only.

(5.3)–(5.5) [Repealed under former Act]

Notes: 146(5.3)–(5.5), repealed by 1985 Budget, dealt with a special rollover of farm property into an RRSP. It was abolished due to the introduction of the capital gains exemption in 110.6. See 110.6(2).

(6) [Repealed]

Notes: 146(6) repealed by 2011 budget bill #2, for investments acquired after March 22, 2011. (See now 207.04.) It read:

(6) Disposition of non-qualified investment — Where in a taxation year a trust governed by a registered retirement savings plan disposes of a property that, when acquired, was a non-qualified investment, there may be deducted, in computing the income for the taxation year of the taxpayer who is the annuitant under the plan, an amount equal to the lesser of

(a) the amount that, by virtue of subsection (10), was included in computing the income of that taxpayer in respect of the acquisition of that property, and

(b) the proceeds of disposition of the property.

See Notes to 146(10.1).

(6.1) Recontribution of certain withdrawals — There may be deducted in computing a taxpayer's income for a particular taxation year the total of all amounts each of which is such portion of a prescribed premium for the particular year as was not designated for any taxation year for the purposes of paragraph 60(j), (j.1) or (l).

Related Provisions: 60(i) — Deduction for RRSP premiums paid; 146(5) — Amount of RRSP premiums deductible; 146.01(1)"excluded premium"(c) — Premium deducted under 146(6.1) not eligible for Home Buyers' Plan; 146.02(1)"excluded premium"(d) — Premium deducted under 146(6.1) not eligible for LLP; 152(6)(b.1) — Reassessment where deductible claimed.

Notes: 146(6.1) provides a special deduction in respect of prescribed premiums (see Reg. 8307(7)) paid to an RRSP (except to the extent they are designated for the purposes of 60(j), (j.1) or (l)). In general terms, 146(6.1) is intended to allow a taxpayer to recontribute amounts withdrawn by the taxpayer from an RRSP in order to create enough room for past service benefits under an RPP. Recontribution is permitted where the amount withdrawn was larger than necessary due to reasonable error or because registration of a new plan was ultimately refused. The deduction in respect of recontribution is available for the year in which the corresponding withdrawal was made, thus offsetting the inclusion of the amount withdrawn. 152(6)(b.1) gives a taxpayer the right to amend a previously filed return in order to claim the deduction.

Regulations: 8307(7) (prescribed premium).

Interpretation Bulletins: IT-124R6: Contributions to registered retirement savings plans.

(7) Recovery of property used as security

— Where in a taxation year a loan, for which a trust governed by a registered retirement savings plan has used or permitted to be used trust property as security, ceases to be extant, and the fair market value of the property so used was included by virtue of subsection (10) in computing the income of the taxpayer who is the annuitant under the plan, there may be deducted, in computing the income of the taxpayer for the taxation year, an amount equal to the amount, if any, remaining when

(a) the net loss (exclusive of payments by the trust as or on account of interest) sustained by the trust in consequence of its using the property, or permitting it to be used, as security for the loan and not as a result of a change in the fair market value of the property

is deducted from

(b) the amount so included in computing the income of the taxpayer in consequence of the trust's using the property, or permitting it to be used, as security for the loan.

Related Provisions: 60(i) — Deduction in computing income; 146(10) — Inclusion in income of property used as security.

Notes: See Notes to 146(10).

Regulations: 214(2) (information return).

Forms: T3GR: Group income tax and information return for RRSP, RRIF, RESP, or RDSP trusts (and worksheets).

(8) Benefits [and withdrawals] taxable

— There shall be included in computing a taxpayer's income for a taxation year the total of all amounts received by the taxpayer in the year as benefits out of or under registered retirement savings plans, other than excluded withdrawals (as defined in subsection 146.01(1) or 146.02(1)) of the taxpayer and amounts that are included under paragraph (12)(b) in computing the taxpayer's income.

Related Provisions: 56(1)(h) — Income from RRSP; 56(12) — Income inclusion on conversion of foreign retirement arrangement; 60(l) — Rollover of refund of premium; 139.1(12) — Conversion benefit on demutualization of insurance corp not taxable; 146(8.01) — Benefits from RRSP re Home Buyers' Plan (HBP); 146(8.3) — Attribution from spousal RRSP; 146(8.8) — Deemed benefit received by annuitant on death; 146(8.92), (8.93) — Deduction to deceased for post-death RRSP losses; 146(12) — Change in plan after registration; 146(16) — Deduction on transfer of funds; 146(20) — Amount credited to deposit RRSP deemed not received by annuitant; 146.01(4)–(6) — HBP — income inclusions; 146.02(4)–(6) — Lifelong Learning Plan — income inclusions; 147.3(13.1) — Withdrawal of excessive transfer to RRSP; 153(1)(j) — Withholding of tax at source; 160.2(1) — Joint and several liability in respect of amounts received from RRSP; 204.2(1.2)J(a) — Reduction of excess contributions; 207.01(1)"advantage", 207.05 — Tax on advantage received from RRSP; 212(1)(l) — Withholding tax on payment to non-resident.

Notes: 146(8) includes RRSP withdrawals in income: *Andaluz*, 2015 TCC 165 (appeal to FCA dismissed for delay A-331-15). For Canadian residents, withholding under Reg. 103(4) and parallel provincial withholding is approximate prepayment of the extra tax that will be owing when the year's return is filed. For a non-resident, 212(1)(l) withholding tax is the actual tax. Home Buyer's Plan (146.01) and Lifelong Learning Plan (146.02) "excluded withdrawals" are exempt; Reg. 104(3) and 104.1 allow them to be paid with no withholding.

A fraudulent withdrawal made by an estranged spouse is not taxable to the annuitant: *Field*, [2001] 2 C.T.C. 2462 (TCC), VIEWS doc 2004-0070041I7. A withdrawal at an advisor's request, transferring the funds to the advisor who then stole them, was taxable: *Mignault*, 2011 TCC 500. Cash received from a promoter after having the RRSP buy a particular investment was taxable under 146(8): *Filiatrault*, 2016 TCC 58.

On taxpayers defrauded by schemes to access RRSP funds without having them taxed, see Notes to 146(9) and 146(10).

A Court Order confiscating T's RRSP due to criminal convictions left T liable to pay tax on the RRSP value due to 146(8): *Toth*, 2006 TCC 116. Similarly, where an insolvent taxpayer collapsed his RRSP and directed the funds paid to a trustee under a bankruptcy proposal, the withdrawal was taxable: *Bertrand*, 2006 TCC 515; and where CRA registered a (Quebec) hypothec against M's RRSP before M's bankruptcy proposal, and seized the funds, this "withdrawal" was included in M's income: *Martin*, 2015 TCC 118.

A reimbursement of losses caused by an investment manager can be paid to the RRSP and not be a benefit to the annuitant; if paid to the annuitant it is taxable unless he/she transfers the funds to the RRSP within 6 months: *Income Tax Technical News* 39; VIEWS docs 2003-0038105, 2005-0118591R3; *Lavoie*, 2010 CarswellNat 3777 (FCA). Similarly, funds recovered in legal action on an RRSP investment (such as foreclosure) should be deposited to the RRSP, and legal fees should be paid out of the RRSP: 2009-0341801E5.

In *Lankarani*, 2011 TCC 176, withdrawal of RRSP funds in 2008 disentitled the taxpayer to the Guaranteed Income Supplement for July 2009-June 2010. In *Springer*, 2013 TCC 332, the withdrawal bumped the taxpayer into a higher tax bracket.

In *Pelletier*, 2006 TCC 237, an excess contribution withdrawn in a later year was taxable when withdrawn. (See 146(8.2).)

An RRSP must be converted to an annuity or RRIF (see 146.3) by the end of the year the taxpayer turns 71: see 146(2)(b.4). Otherwise it matures and is fully included in income under 146(8). See Mawani & Paquette, "Pre-Retirement RRSP Withdrawals", 59(2) *Canadian Tax Journal* 183-219 (2011) (re the extent this is done).

Management fees and investment counsel fees paid from inside the plan are not a benefit conferred on the annuitant: see 18(1)(u) Notes. Nor is a settlement paid to the plan for an actionable loss: VIEWS doc 2020-0865641I7.

146(8) amended by 1998 Budget (for 1999 and later tax years), 1992 Budget.

Regulations: 100(1)"remuneration"(i) (payment from RRSP subject to source withholding); 103(4), (6) (withholding requirements on withdrawal from RRSP); 104(3) (no withholding on Home Buyers' Plan withdrawal); 104.1 (no withholding on Lifelong Learning Plan withdrawal); 214(1), (2) (information return).

I.T. Application Rules: 61(2) (where annuitant died before 1972).

Interpretation Bulletins: IT-307R4: Spousal or common-law registered retirement savings plans; IT-500R: RRSPs — death of an annuitant.

Information Circulars: 72-22R9: Registered retirement savings plans.

I.T. Technical News: 39 (settlement of a shareholder class action suit).

Advance Tax Rulings: ATR-37: Refund of premiums transferred to spouse.

Registered Plans Frequently Asked Questions: RPFAQ-1 (RRSPs/RRIFs), q. 2 (locked-in designation).

Forms: T1 General return, Line 12900 [former 129]; T4RSP: Statement of RRSP income; T4RSP Summary; T4040: RRSPs and other registered plans for retirement [guide]; T4079: T4RSP and T4RIF guide.

(8.01) Subsequent re-calculation [on HBP or LLP withdrawal]

— If a designated withdrawal (as defined in subsection 146.01(1)) or an amount referred to in paragraph (a) of the definition "eligible amount" in subsection 146.02(1) is received by a taxpayer in a taxation year and, at any time after that year, it is determined that the amount is not an excluded withdrawal (as defined in subsection 146.01(1) or 146.02(1)), notwithstanding subsections 152(4) to (5), such assessments of tax, interest and penalties shall be made as are necessary to give effect to the determination.

Notes: 146(8.01) provides that if an amount is withdrawn under the Home Buyers' Plan (146.01) or Lifelong Learning Plan (146.02) and it is later determined that it should have been taxable, the correcting assessment can be made outside the normal (3-year) time limit.

146(8.01) amended by 1998 Budget, for 1999 and later taxation years.

146(8.01) added by 1992 technical bill, effective 1992.

Interpretation Bulletins: IT-415R2: Deregistration of RRSPs (cancelled).

(8.1) Deemed receipt of refund of premiums

— If a payment out of or under a registered retirement savings plan of a deceased annuitant to the annuitant's legal representative would have been a refund of premiums if it had been paid under the plan to an individual who is a beneficiary (as defined in subsection 108(1)) under the deceased's estate, the payment is, to the extent it is so designated jointly by the legal representative and the individual in prescribed form filed with the Minister, deemed to be received by the individual (and not by the legal representative) at the time it was so paid as a benefit that is a refund of premiums.

Related Provisions: 60(l) — Transfer of RRSP premium refunds; 60(l)(v)(B.1) — Rollover of designated benefits to child or grandchild on death; 146(8.9) — Effect of death where person other than spouse becomes entitled; 146.3(6.1) — Parallel rule for

RRIFs; 160.2(1) — Joint and several liability in respect of amounts received out of or under RRSP; 214(3)(c) — Non-resident withholding tax.

Notes: The portion taxed in the deceased's hands cannot be transferred tax-free to beneficiary B's RRSP, since it is not B's income under 60(l)(v) to qualify for rollover. Of course, B can contribute it to B's RRSP using B's contribution room.

For CRA interpretation of 146(8.1) see docs 2004-0065471C6, 2004-0098241R3, 2005-0161941E5, 2005-0162591E5, 2006-0201261E5, 2012-0458231E5; 2019-0815181C6 [2019 APFF Financial q.12] (designated amount is deemed received by the individual, so is not reported in the estate's T3 return); 2020-0851621C6 [2020 APFF Financial q.4] (Form T2019 is required where the will makes specific bequest to surviving spouse and RRSP proceeds are paid directly to spouse). See also Corbin, "RRSP Rollover on Death", 32(12) *Money & Family Law* (Carswell) 89-90 (Dec. 2017).

146(8.1) amended by 2002-2013 technical bill, this version effective 1999, to implement an April 20, 2005 Finance comfort letter re extending the meaning of "beneficiary" to include persons beneficially interested (see 248(25)), while preserving the 1999 amendment below.

146(8.1) amended by 1999 Budget, for 1999 and later tax years, to clarify that the refund of premiums is deemed received by the beneficiary (and not by the legal representative) at the same time as the corresponding RRSP amount was paid to the legal representative. This matches a similar rule for RRIFs in 146.3(6.1).

Advance Tax Rulings: ATR-37: Refund of premiums transferred to spouse.

Forms: T2019: Death of an RRSP annuitant — refund of premiums or joint designation on the death of a PRPP member.

(8.2) Amount deductible [overcontribution withdrawn] — Where

(a) all or any portion of the premiums paid in a taxation year by a taxpayer to one or more registered retirement savings plans under which the taxpayer or the taxpayer's spouse or common-law partner was the annuitant was not deducted in computing the taxpayer's income for any taxation year,

(b) the taxpayer or the taxpayer's spouse or common-law partner can reasonably be regarded as having received a payment from a registered retirement savings plan or a registered retirement income fund in respect of such portion of the undeducted premiums as

(i) was not paid by way of a transfer of an amount from a registered pension plan to a registered retirement savings plan,

(ii) was not paid by way of a transfer of an amount from a deferred profit sharing plan to a registered retirement savings plan in accordance with subsection 147(19), and

(iii) was not paid by way of a transfer of an amount to a registered retirement savings plan from

(A) a pooled registered pension plan in circumstances to which subsection 147.5(21) applied, or

(B) a specified pension plan in circumstances to which subsection (21) applied,

(c) the payment is received by the taxpayer or the taxpayer's spouse or common-law partner in a particular taxation year that is

(i) the year in which the premiums were paid by the taxpayer,

(ii) the year in which a notice of assessment for the taxation year referred to in subparagraph (i) was sent to the taxpayer, or

(iii) the year immediately following the year referred to in subparagraph (i) or (ii), and

(d) the payment is included in computing the taxpayer's income for the particular year,

the payment (except to the extent that it is a prescribed withdrawal) may be deducted in computing the taxpayer's income for the particular year unless it is reasonable to consider that

(e) the taxpayer did not reasonably expect that the full amount of the premiums would be deductible in the taxation year in which the premiums were paid or in the immediately preceding taxation year, and

(f) the taxpayer paid all or any portion of the premiums with the intent of receiving a payment that, but for this paragraph and paragraph (e), would be deductible under this subsection.

Related Provisions: 60(i) — Deduction for RRSP premiums paid; 146(5) — Deduction for contribution to own RRSP; 146(5.1) — Deduction for contribution to spousal RRSP; 146(8.21) — Excess premium deemed not paid; 146(16) — Deduction on transfer of funds; 146(21.2) — Sask. Pension Plan account deemed to be RRSP for purposes of 146(8.2); 147.3(13.1) — Withdrawal of excessive transfers to RRSPs and RRIFs; 147.5(11), (12) — Pooled registered pension plan deemed to be RRSP for certain purposes; Reg. 8307(4) — Eligibility of withdrawn amount for designation.

Notes: 146(8.2) allows non-deducted RRSP [or PRPP; 147.5(12)] premiums (typically overcontributions, but also amounts contributed for a year when the Home Buyers' Plan or Lifelong Learning Plan was used) to be withdrawn tax-free within a specified timeframe. There is no requirement that there be an "excess amount" for 204.2(1.1): VIEWS doc 2017-0707781C6 [2017 APFF q.4]. Technically the withdrawal is not tax-free, but 146(8.2) provides a deduction to offset the income inclusion. (The 1% per month tax under 204.2(1.1) may still apply during the period when the overcontribution existed.) If property is contributed and then withdrawn, the deduction is based on the value of the property when withdrawn: 2003-0008155. For the consequences of overcontribution and withdrawal see 2009-0321001E5.

The withdrawal may be from a different RRSP than the one to which the overcontribution was made: *Vale*, 2004 TCC 107.

CRA interprets "notice of assessment for the taxation year" in 146(8.2)(c)(ii) as meaning only a Part I assessment: VIEWS doc 2009-0344121E5.

For the procedures for using 146(8.2) and obtaining approval on Form T3012A, see CRA May 2006 ICAA roundtable (tinyurl.com/cra-abtax), q. 8.

146(8.2) can be used for a deceased: VIEWS docs 2017-0685001E5, 2017-0710681C6 [2017 APFF q.2].

In *Misir*, 2008 TCC 168, a taxpayer who had overcontributed was allowed to use "first-in, first-out" to make her withdrawal deductible under 146(8.2).

In *Pelletier*, 2006 TCC 237 and *McNamee*, 2009 TCC 630, an excess contribution withdrawn in a later year did not fall within 146(8.2). In *Connolly* (TCC, as reported in 2017 FC 1006, para. 21), one year's contribution withdrawal was allowed a deduction but not the other as C had missed the deadline.

146(8.2)(b)(iii)(A) added by 2012 budget bill #2, effective Dec. 14, 2012.

146(8.2)(b)(iii) amended by 2011 budget bill #2, for taxation years that begin after 2009, to change "provincial pension plan prescribed for the purpose of paragraph 60(v)" to "specified pension plan" (still the Saskatchewan Pension Plan; see Notes to 248(1)"specified pension plan").

146(8.2) earlier amended by 2000 same-sex partners bill (last change effective 2001), 1993 and 1992 technical bills and 1990 pension bill.

Regulations: 7800 (Saskatchewan Pension Plan is specified pension plan for (b)(iii)(b)).

Interpretation Bulletins: IT-307R4: Spousal or common-law registered retirement savings plans; IT-124R6: Contributions to registered retirement savings plans.

Forms: T746: Calculating your deduction for refund of unused RRSP, PRPP, and SPP contributions; T3012A: Tax deduction waiver on the refund of your unused RRSP, PRPP, or SPP contributions.

(8.21) Premium deemed not paid — Where a taxpayer or the taxpayer's spouse or common-law partner has, at any time in a taxation year, received a payment from a registered retirement savings plan or a registered retirement income fund in respect of all or any portion of a premium paid by the taxpayer to a registered retirement savings plan and the payment has been deducted under subsection (8.2) in computing the taxpayer's income for the year, the premium or portion thereof, as the case may be, shall,

(a) for the purposes of determining, after that time, the amount that may be deducted under subsection (5) or (5.1) in computing the taxpayer's income for the year or a preceding taxation year, and

(b) for the purposes of subsections (8.3) and 146.3(5.1) after that time, in the case of a payment received by the taxpayer,

be deemed not to have been a premium paid by the taxpayer to a registered retirement savings plan.

Related Provisions: 146(8.6) — Spouse's income; 146(21.2) — Sask. Pension Plan account deemed to be RRSP for purposes of 146(8.21); 147.5(11), (12) — Pooled registered pension plan deemed to be RRSP for certain purposes.

Notes: 146(8.21) amended by 2000 same-sex partners bill to refer to "common-law partner", effective as per Notes to 248(1)"common-law partner".

146(8.21) added by 1990 pension bill, effective for premiums paid after 1990.

Interpretation Bulletins: IT-124R6: Contributions to registered retirement savings plans.

(8.3) Spousal or common-law partner payments [attribution rule] — Where at any time in a taxation year a particular amount in respect of a registered retirement savings plan that is

a spousal or common-law partner plan in relation to a taxpayer is required by reason of subsection (8) or paragraph (12)(b) to be included in computing the income of the taxpayer's spouse or common-law partner before the plan matures or as a payment in full or partial commutation of a retirement income under the plan and the taxpayer is not living separate and apart from the taxpayer's spouse or common-law partner at that time by reason of the breakdown of their marriage or common-law partnership, there shall be included at that time in computing the taxpayer's income for the year an amount equal to the lesser of

(a) the total of all amounts each of which is a premium paid by the taxpayer in the year or in one of the two immediately preceding taxation years to a registered retirement savings plan under which the taxpayer's spouse or common-law partner was the annuitant at the time the premium was paid, and

(b) the particular amount.

Related Provisions: 56(1)(h) — Income from RRSP; 74.5(12) — Regular attribution rule does not apply; 146(8.21) — Premium deemed not paid; 146(8.5) — Ordering; 146(8.6) — Spouse's income; 146(8.7) — Where subsec. (8.3) does not apply; 146(21.3) — Payment from Sask. Pension Plan deemed to be from RRSP for purposes of 146(8.3)–(8.7), starting 2011; 146.3(5.1) — Parallel rule for RRIFs; 146(5.4) — Spouse's income; 147.3(13.1) — Withdrawal of excessive transfer to RRSP; 153(1)(j) — Withholding of tax at source.

Notes: Premiums to one's spouse's plan can be deducted (within total RRSP contribution room allowed) under 146(5.1). If contributions to any spousal plan are withdrawn in the calendar year during which a contribution was made or in the next 2 calendar years, they are attributed back to the contributor (unless 146(8.7) applies), but only to the extent of those contributions (*Werby*, 2004 TCC 672; VIEWS doc 2006-0214161E5). It does not matter whether the withdrawal is from the same plan as was most recently contributed to. The same rule applies to a RRIF under 146.3(5.1), except that the minimum amount that must be withdrawn annually anyway is excluded from attribution: 146.3(5.1)(c)(ii).

Attribution to a spouse under 146(8.3) does not change the requirement under 153(1)(j) for withholding from the payment, so the wrong taxpayer will be credited with the tax withheld: VIEWS doc 2011-0408251C6.

If A and B are spouses, a gift or loan from A to B that enables B to contribute to B's plan could result in attribution back to A under 74.1 when the RRSP proceeds are taxed many years later. This can be avoided by A giving funds to B that B contributes to A's plan while A makes a spousal contribution to B's plan and waits for the period under 146(8.3) to expire! (There is no attribution on a spousal contribution except under 146(8.3); see 74.5(12).)

146(8.3) does not apply to a Home Buyers' Plan (146.01) income inclusion where the funds came from a spousal RRSP: VIEWS docs 2008-026991117, 2012-0462061E5.

If the spouses are separated, 146(8.3) does not apply. The RRSP is a spousal RRSP, but the plan need not be identified as such on the T4RSP: VIEWS doc 2009-0317201E5.

The Saskatchewan Pension Plan is treated as an RRSP for purposes of 146(8.3) beginning 2011: see 146(21.3).

146(8.3) amended by 2000 same-sex partners bill (last change effective 2001), 1990 pension bill.

Interpretation Bulletins: IT-124R6: Contributions to registered retirement savings plans; IT-307R4: Spousal or common-law registered retirement savings plans; IT-415R2: Deregistration of RRSPs (cancelled).

Forms: T1234 Sched. B: Allowable amounts of non-refundable tax credits; T2205: Amounts from a spousal or common-law partner RRSP, RRIF or SPP to include in income.

(8.4) [Repealed under former Act]

Notes: 146(8.4) repealed by 1990 pension bill, effective 1991.

(8.5) Ordering

— Where a taxpayer has paid more than one premium described in subsection (8.3), such a premium or part thereof paid by the taxpayer at any time shall be deemed to have been included in computing the taxpayer's income by virtue of that subsection before premiums or parts thereof paid by the taxpayer after that time.

Related Provisions: 146(21.3) — Payment from Sask. Pension Plan deemed to be from RRSP for purposes of 146(8.3)–(8.7).

Interpretation Bulletins: IT-307R4: Spousal or common-law registered retirement savings plans.

(8.6) Spouse's [or common-law partner's] income

— Where, in respect of an amount required at any time in a taxation year to be included in computing the income of a taxpayer's spouse or common-law partner, all or part of a premium has by reason of subsection (8.3) been included in computing the taxpayer's income for the year, the following rules apply:

(a) the premium or part thereof, as the case may be, shall, for the purposes of subsections (8.3) and 146.3(5.1) after that time, be deemed not to have been a premium paid to a registered retirement savings plan under which the taxpayer's spouse or common-law partner was the annuitant; and

(b) an amount equal to the premium or part thereof, as the case may be, may be deducted in computing the income of the spouse or common-law partner for the year.

Related Provisions: 146(8.21) — Premium deemed not paid; 146(21.3) — Payment from Sask. Pension Plan deemed to be from RRSP for purposes of 146(8.3)–(8.7); 146.3(5.4) — Spouse's income.

Notes: 146(8.6) amended by 2000 same-sex partners bill to refer to "common-law partner", effective as per Notes to 248(1)"common-law partner".

146(8.6) amended by 1990 pension bill, this version effective 1991.

Interpretation Bulletins: IT-307R4: Spousal or common-law registered retirement savings plans; IT-415R2: Deregistration of RRSPs (cancelled).

(8.7) Where subsec. (8.3) does not apply

— Subsection (8.3) does not apply

(a) in respect of a taxpayer at any time during the year in which the taxpayer died;

(b) in respect of a taxpayer where either the taxpayer or the taxpayer's spouse or common-law partner is a non-resident at the particular time referred to in that subsection;

(c) in respect of amounts paid out of or under a plan referred to in subsection (12) as an "amended plan" to which paragraph (12)(a) applied before May 26, 1976;

(d) to any payment that is received in full or partial commutation of a registered retirement income fund or a registered retirement savings plan and in respect of which a deduction was made under paragraph 60(l) if, where the deduction was in respect of the acquisition of an annuity, the terms of the annuity provide that it cannot be commuted, and it is not commuted, in whole or in part within 3 years after the acquisition; or

(e) in respect of an amount that is deemed by subsection (8.8) to have been received by an annuitant under a registered retirement savings plan immediately before the annuitant's death.

Related Provisions: 146(21.3) — Payment from Sask. Pension Plan deemed to be from RRSP for purposes of 146(8.3)–(8.7).

Notes: 146(8.7)(b) amended by 2000 same-sex partners bill to refer to "common-law partner", effective as per Notes to 248(1)"common-law partner".

146(8.7)(e) added by 1990 pension bill, effective 1988.

Interpretation Bulletins: IT-307R4: Spousal or common-law registered retirement savings plans; IT-415R2: Deregistration of RRSPs (cancelled).

(8.8) Effect of death where person other than spouse [actually, including spouse] becomes entitled

— Where the annuitant under a registered retirement savings plan (other than a plan that had matured before June 30, 1978) dies after June 29, 1978, the annuitant shall be deemed to have received, immediately before the annuitant's death, an amount as a benefit out of or under a registered retirement savings plan equal to the amount, if any, by which

(a) the fair market value of all the property of the plan at the time of death

exceeds

(b) where the annuitant died after the maturity of the plan, the fair market value at the time of the death of the portion of the property described in paragraph (a) that, as a consequence of the death, becomes receivable by a person who was the annuitant's spouse or common-law partner immediately before the death, or would become so receivable should that person survive throughout all guaranteed terms contained in the plan.

Related Provisions: 60(l)(v)(B.1) — Transfer of RRSP premium refunds; 60.02 — Rollover to RDSP; 118.1(5.3) [before 2016], 118.1(5.2)(b) [after 2015] — Designation of charity as beneficiary of RRSP; 146(8.7) — Where subsec. (8.3) does not apply; 146(8.9) — Offsetting deduction; 146(8.92), (8.93) — Deduction to deceased for post-death RRSP losses; 146.3(6) — Parallel rule for RRIFs; 160.2(1) — Joint and several liability in respect of amounts received out of or under RRSP; 214(3)(c), 214(3.1) — Non-resident withholding tax.

Notes: The income inclusion in (8.8) is reduced by (8.9), so they must be read together. Where a spouse is entitled to the RRSP (either through the will or by direct designation), (8.9) reduces the (8.8) inclusion, and the spouse is taxed under 146(8) on the "benefit" received (146(1)). This benefit is normally a "refund of premiums" (146(1)) and can be rolled into the spouse's RRSP via 60(l) deduction. See Reg. 214(4) Notes re the T4RSP reporting requirement.

If the RRSP is not fully distributed by the end of the calendar year following the year of death, "B" in (8.9) is zero and the (8.9) deduction results in no (8.8) inclusion to the deceased; but 146(4)(c) applies so the RRSP pays tax on its taxable income in later years. Such income is a "tax-paid amount" (146(1)) and is excluded from the "refund of premiums" (146(1)) that the spouse pays tax on, to prevent double tax. The (8.9) deduction is discretionary; it is unavailable if the RRSP has matured: VIEWS doc 2016-0668991E5.

See IT-500R (written before the "tax-paid amount" rules) and guides RC4177, T4079 for CRA interpretation; and Notes to 60(l).

Payments made on death are not subject to withholding, which applies only to payments made "during the lifetime of the annuitant": Reg. 100(1)"remuneration"(i) [(j.1), for a RRIF].

Where the deceased leaves the RRSP to a financially dependent child or grandchild, the estate has no income inclusion: see 146(1)"refund of premiums" and 146(1.1). The child or grandchild can then roll the amounts into their own RRSP to avoid tax: see 60(l)(v)(B.1). Where the deceased leaves the RRSP to a spouse, see also 146(8.91).

See Notes to 146(4) re the effect of an RRSP having a "designated beneficiary".

In *Murphy Estate*, 2015 TCC 8, the deceased's RRSP had been left to his children, who were in dispute with his widow W over the estate. In a settlement, they agreed to "release, convey and transfer" their interest in the RRSP to W. Because they did not *disclaim* their interest, the transfer did not go to W directly from the RRSP and was not a 146(1)"refund of premiums" that she could roll into her RRSP under 60(l), and was taxable to the estate under 146(8.8). (The Court did not discuss 248(8), (9) or (23.1).)

For discussion of 146(8.8) and (8.9), see Crawford, "Tax-Free Transfers and Rollovers of RRSPs and RRIFs After Death", IV(2) *RRSP Planning* (Federated Press) 244-48 (1997); Corbin, "Post-Mortem Possibilities with RRSPs", 32(9) *Money & Family Law* (Carswell) 65-66 (Sept. 2017); Tehranchian, "The RRSP and RRIF Beneficiary Designation Solution for Converting Your Estate Taxes to Charitable Donations", 12(2) *Taxes & Wealth Management* (Carswell) 15-16 (June 2019); VIEWS doc 2010-0380071E5. See also 2002-0124467 re an estate claiming a deduction under 146(8.9) on the deceased's final return for RRSP amounts still unclaimed by the beneficiary.

Where the deceased or spouse is non-resident, withholding tax applies under 212(1)(l): VIEWS docs 2002-0141355, 2013-0495281C6 [2013 APFF q. 9].

If the RRSP increases in value after death, the excess is taxable to the beneficiary under 146(8); if it drops in value after death, see 146(8.92).

A trust can be designated as the beneficiary of an RRSP, and could be a testamentary trust: VIEWS doc 2005-0116491E5.

Where the carrier is not aware of the annuitant's death and funds are received by the estate many years later, see VIEWS doc 9820687.

The income inclusion before death makes the estate liable, and if the estate does not pay the tax, a beneficiary who receives the RRSP funds is jointly liable for the tax: 160.2(1), VIEWS docs 2010-0352911E5, 2011-0402391I7 (the CRA may have no recourse if the beneficiaries are outside Canada: see also Notes to 223(3)).

Where a deceased's RRSP was paid to the provincial commission holding "unclaimed property", but later claimed by beneficiary B, it was taxable to B when received, under the *surrogatum* principle (see 9(1) Notes at "Damages"): VIEWS doc 2019-0802891E5.

146(8.8)(b) amended by 2000 same-sex partners bill (last change effective 2001) and 1993 technical bill.

Regulations: 214(4) (information return).

Interpretation Bulletins: IT-307R4: Spousal or common-law registered retirement savings plans; IT-500R: RRSPs — death of an annuitant.

Advance Tax Rulings: ATR-37: Refund of premiums transferred to spouse.

Forms: RC4177: Death of an RRSP annuitant [guide].

(8.9) Idem — There may be deducted from the amount deemed by subsection (8.8) to have been received by an annuitant as a benefit out of or under a registered retirement savings plan an amount not exceeding the amount determined by the formula

$$A \times [\, 1 - (B + C - D)\,/\,(B + C)\,]$$

where

A   is the total of

(a) all refunds of premiums in respect of the plan,

(b) all tax-paid amounts in respect of the plan paid to individuals who, otherwise than because of subsection (8.1), received refunds of premiums in respect of the plan, and

(c) all amounts each of which is a tax-paid amount in respect of the plan paid to the legal representative of the annuitant under the plan, to the extent that the legal representative would have been entitled to designate that tax-paid amount under subsection (8.1) if tax-paid amounts were not excluded in determining refunds of premiums;

B   is the fair market value of the property of the plan at the particular time that is the later of

(a) the end of the first calendar year that begins after the death of the annuitant, and

(b) the time immediately after the last time that any refund of premiums in respect of the plan is paid out of or under the plan;

C   is the total of all amounts paid out of or under the plan after the death of the annuitant and before the particular time; and

D   is the lesser of

(a) the fair market value of the property of the plan at the time of the annuitant's death, and

(b) the sum of the values of B and C in respect of the plan.

Related Provisions: 60(l) — Transfer of RRSP premium refunds; 146.3(6.2) — Parallel rule for RRIFs; 152(6)(f.3) — Reassessment to allow carryback of loss; 160.2(1) — Joint and several liability in respect of amounts received out of or under RRSP; 257 — Formula cannot calculate to less than zero.

Notes: See Notes to 146(8.8).

146(8.9) amended by 1993 and 1995-97 technical bills, for deaths after 1992.

Interpretation Bulletins: IT-500R: RRSPs — death of an annuitant.

Advance Tax Rulings: ATR-37: Refund of premiums transferred to spouse.

Forms: RC4177: Death of an RRSP annuitant [guide].

(8.91) Amounts deemed receivable by spouse [or common-law partner] — Where, as a consequence of the death of an annuitant after the maturity of the annuitant's registered retirement savings plan, the annuitant's legal representative has become entitled to receive amounts out of or under the plan for the benefit of the spouse or common-law partner of the deceased and the legal representative and the spouse or common-law partner file with the Minister a joint election in prescribed form,

(a) the spouse or common-law partner shall be deemed to have become the annuitant under the plan as a consequence of the annuitant's death; and

(b) such amounts shall be deemed to be receivable by the spouse or common-law partner and, when paid, to be received by the spouse or common-law partner as a benefit under the plan, and not to be received by any other person.

Related Provisions: 60(l) — Transfer of RRSP premium refunds; 160.2(1) — Joint and several liability in respect of amounts received out of or under RRSP; 214(3)(c) — Non-resident withholding tax; 248(8) — Meaning of "consequence" of death.

Notes: 146(8.91) amended by 2000 same-sex partners bill, effective 2001 or earlier.

Interpretation Bulletins: IT-307R4: Spousal or common-law registered retirement savings plans; IT-500R: RRSPs — death of an annuitant.

Forms: RC4177: Death of an RRSP annuitant [guide].

(8.92) Deduction for post-death reduction in value — If the annuitant under a registered retirement savings plan dies before the maturity of the plan, there may be deducted in computing the annuitant's income for the taxation year in which the annuitant dies an amount not exceeding the amount determined, after all amounts payable out of or under the plan have been paid, by the formula

$$A - B$$

where

A   is the total of all amounts each of which is

(a) the amount deemed by subsection (8.8) to have been received by the annuitant as a benefit out of or under the plan,

(b) an amount (other than an amount described in paragraph (c)) received, after the death of the annuitant, by a taxpayer as a benefit out of or under the plan and included, because of subsection (8), in computing the taxpayer's income, or

(c) a tax-paid amount in respect of the plan; and

B is the total of all amounts paid out of or under the plan after the death of the annuitant.

Related Provisions: 60(i) — Deduction in computing net income; 146(8.93) — Exceptions; 146.3(6.3) — Parallel rule for RRIF; 147.5(19) — Parallel rule for PRPP; 152(6)(f.3) — Reassessment to allow carryback of loss; 257 — Formula cannot calculate to less than zero; Reg. 214(6) — Information return required.

Notes: 146(8.92) and 146.3(6.3) implement a Jan. 27/09 Budget proposal to allow carryback of losses in a RRSP or RRIF to the deceased's final return, provided the RRSP or RRIF is wound up by Dec. 31 of the year following death (see 146(8.93)(b), 146.3(6.4)(b)). This responds to the 2008 market downturn, where a deceased could be taxed on large gains in the plan at death (146(8.8)), yet by the time the assets were sold and funds received by the estate, the gains had evaporated. 146(8.92) allows a deduction for any difference between the amounts included in the deceased's income and the amounts actually received on winding up the plan. Even without losses, this effectively allows a deduction for commissions on sale of securities, since it is the market value of the securities that is included in income by 146(8.8).

Absent this rule, no-one could claim the loss, so unless the funds remained sheltered due to a 60(l) transfer they were lost: VIEWS docs 1999-0013725, 2000-0006115, 2002-0168275; "A Double Whammy — RRSPs that Decrease in Value After Death", 159 *The Estate Planner* (CCH) 1-3 (April 2008).

CRA must reassess up to 6 years back to allow this claim: 152(6)(f.3), VIEWS doc 2015-0592681E5.

146(8.92) added by 2009 budget bill #1, effective in respect of an RRSP in respect of which the last payment out of the plan is made after 2008. Limited administrative relief is available for RRSPs wound up before 2009: VIEWS doc 2009-0329761C6.

Regulations: 214(6) (information return).

Forms: RC249: Post-death decline in the value of RRIF, an unmatured RRSP and Post-Death Increase or Decline in the Value of a PRPP.

(8.93) Subsec. (8.92) not applicable — Except where the Minister has waived in writing the application of this subsection with respect to all or any portion of the amount determined in subsection (8.92) in respect of a registered retirement savings plan, that subsection does not apply if

(a) at any time after the death of the annuitant, a trust governed by the plan held a non-qualified investment; or

(b) the last payment out of or under the plan was made after the end of the year following the year in which the annuitant died.

Related Provisions: 146.3(6.4) — Parallel rule for RRIF.

Notes: 146(8.93) added by 2009 budget bill #1, effective in respect of an RRSP in respect of which the last payment out of the plan is made after 2008.

(9) Where disposition of property by trust — Where in a taxation year a trust governed by a registered retirement savings plan

(a) disposes of property for a consideration less than the fair market value of the property at the time of the disposition, or for no consideration, or

(b) acquires property for a consideration greater than the fair market value of the property at the time of the acquisition,

the difference between the fair market value and the consideration, if any, shall be included in computing the income for the taxation year of the annuitant under the plan.

Related Provisions: 146(11) — Life insurance policies; 146(12) — Change in plan after registration; 146.3(4) — Parallel rule for RRIF; 214(3)(c) — Non-resident withholding tax.

Notes: See CRA news release, "Warning: Watch out for self-directed RRSP tax schemes" (Aug. 26, 2019), and canada.ca/tax-schemes.

In *St. Arnaud*, 2013 FCA 88, 146(9) (and 146.3(4) for RRIFs) did not apply to an intended RRSP/RRIF investment to improve returns which, induced by fraud, was in worthless stocks. The FCA ruled that the RRSP and RRIF did not acquire the shares, as the supposed vendors were the corporations that issued the shares and a corporation cannot own shares in itself, and because the corporations never received the funds.

In *St. Arnaud*, Sharlow J.A. also held that 146(9) and 146.3(4) apply only if there was a tax avoidance intention, not to an innocent overpayment by the RRSP or RRIF. The other two FCA judges refused to address this question (para. 7), so it is not yet resolved.

In *Barkwill*, 2013 FCA 34, 146(9) applied to shares transferred to RRSPs for more than their purchase price (though para. 2 says the shares were contributed and deductions

claimed under 146(5); it is hard to see how issuing a contribution receipt constitutes paying consideration).

In *Baker*, 2014 TCC 204 (FCA appeal dismissed for delay A-351-15), 146(9) applied to an RRSP purchase of private company shares under an "Institute of Global Prosperity" scheme.

In *Gorman*, 2016 TCC 153, 146(9) and pre-2011 146(10) both applied to an RRSP strip where funds were moved offshore and lost.

In *Stewart*, 2019 TCC 22, 146(9) and pre-2011 (10) did not apply where 119 defrauded taxpayers' RRSPs bought worthless mortgages, as the amount paid was market value.

See also Notes to 146(10).

Regulations: 214(2) (information return).

Registered Plans Compliance Bulletins: 4 (abusive schemes — RRSP stripping).

Forms: T3GR: Group income tax and information return for RRSP, RRIF, RESP, or RDSP trusts (and worksheets).

(10) Property used as security for loan — If at any time in a taxation year a trust governed by a registered retirement savings plan uses or permits to be used any property of the trust as security for a loan, the fair market value of the property at the time it commenced to be so used shall be included in computing the income for the year of the taxpayer who is the annuitant under the plan at that time.

Related Provisions: 146(6) — Disposition of non-qualified investment; 146(7) — Recovery of property used as security; 146(10.1) — Tax payable by trust; 146(11) — Life insurance policies; 146.3(4) — Parallel rule for RRIF; 207.01(1)"advantage", 207.05 — Tax on advantage received from RRSP; 207.04 — Tax on annuitant if RRSP acquires non-qualified or prohibited investment; 214(3)(c) — Non-resident withholding tax; 259(1) — Election for proportional holdings in trust property.

Notes: The rules for an RRSP that acquires a non-qualified investment were moved to 207.01 and 207.04 in 2011, and 146(10) was left addressing only an RRSP being used as security for a loan. Most of the discussion below relates to pre-2011 146(10). See also Notes to 146(9) and 146(10.1).

RRSP strips before 2011: In *Nunn*, 2006 FCA 403, N was defrauded into transferring locked-in RRSP funds to a company, and lost the money, but was still taxed under 146(10). (This overrides *St-Hilaire*, 2005 TCC 747 and *Lalancette*, 2007 TCC 748, where taxpayers defrauded by a promoter, who invested locked-in RRSPs in a sham non-qualifying company, had no 146(10) inclusion but only under 146(8) for amounts actually received.) *Nunn* was followed in *Deschamps*, 2007 TCC 194; *Boily*, 2008 FCA 393 (leave to appeal denied 2009 CarswellNat 1760 (SCC)); *Beaulieu*, 2012 FCA 186. See also *Beaulieu*, 2009 FC 1236; *Gougeon*, 2010 TCC 359; *Bonavia*, 2010 FCA 129; *Astorino*, 2010 TCC 144; *Noiseux Estate*, 2016 TCC 51; *Filiatrault*, 2016 TCC 58; *Bédard*, 2016 TCC 179 ("investment clubs" through Claude Lavigne — income taxed under 146(8)). 146(10) also applied in *Chamczuk*, 2007 TCC 446, and *Barkwill*, 2013 FCA 34. In *Demers*, 2010 TCC 402, the defrauded taxpayer was denied an allowable business investment loss; in *Demers*, 2014 TCC 368, para. 12, the amount extracted from the RRSP was taxed under 146(8) even though the contract with the fraudsters was nullified by the QC Superior Court; in *Gorman*, 2016 TCC 153, both 146(9) and 146(10) applied. In *Burke*, 2009 TCC 680, a taxpayer with this issue had enough merit to his case to have a default judgment set aside. In *Brewster*, 2012 TCC 187, the Crown pleaded only that B had acquired non-qualified investments; because the Reply did not plead specific facts, the appeal was allowed. CRA reassessed over 5,000 taxpayers for $250 million of taxable income in such schemes (March 17/09 Tax Alert, "Investing in schemes that promise you tax free withdrawals from RRSPs and RRIFs could result in the loss of your retirement savings"). An "RRSP strip" appeal that settled is *Schiesser*, 2009 TCC 513 (appeal discontinued, 2005-4451(IT)G). See also VIEWS doc 2008-0278801C6 [2008 STEP conf] q.13. See 239(1) Notes for convictions of RRSP strip promoters. Since 2011, see 207.01(1)"registered plan strip" and 207.05(2)(c) for RRSP strips.

Other pre-2011 cases: 146(10) applied in *Chiasson*, 2017 FCA 239, to an investment in a company (Landmark) whose assets were primarily a Barbados company.

An RRSP that goes into overdraft may be borrowing money and thus may trigger 146(10): VIEWS doc 2003-0182255. A non-qualified investment can be "acquired" and trigger 146(10) even if it has not yet been paid for: 2009-0335681E5.

146(10) does not apply when an existing investment becomes non-qualified, but the tax under 207.1(1) [later replaced by 207.04] does: VIEWS doc 2010-0354681E5.

146(10) can be used, together with 146(7), as a bizarre form of advance income averaging by pledging self-directed RRSP assets as security or acquiring a non-qualified investment. (A "depositary" RRSP (see Notes to 146(1)"retirement savings plan") also cannot be pledged; see 146(2)(c.3)(ii), but see also 146(12) Notes.) This can bring income into a low-tax (or loss) year and allow a deduction in a later high-tax year under 146(6) or (7), for a person who has funds in an RRSP and anticipates increases in income in future years. Spousal attribution will not apply because 146(8.3) does not refer to 146(10). (See also 15(2) Notes for another method.) GAAR (s. 245) might apply to this scheme, however, and tax would be payable under 146(10.1) and 207.04 on non-qualified investments. See *Foreman (Chambers)*, [1996] 1 C.T.C. 265 (FCTD), where a similar scheme that involved repaying the RRSP before year-end was found not to artificially reduce income. Also note that 146(10) arguably applies only if the trustee takes the action of using or permitting use of the property as security; a pledge by the annuitant to which the trustee does not consent might not trigger 146(10).

See also Notes to 146(4) re whether an RRSP can be seized by creditors, and requirements for U.S. filers to report RRSPs as foreign trusts.

146(10) amended by 2011 budget bill #2, effective in respect of investments acquired after March 22, 2011.

Regulations: 214(2) (information return).

Remission Orders: *Lionaird Capital Corporation Notes Remission Order*, P.C. 1999-737 (tax under 146(10) waived because taxpayers thought they were qualified investments).

Interpretation Bulletins: IT-415R2: Deregistration of RRSPs (cancelled).

Registered Plans Compliance Bulletins: See under 146(1)"qualified investment".

Forms: T3GR: Group income tax and information return for RRSP, RRIF, RESP, or RDSP trusts (and worksheets).

(10.1) Where tax payable [income from non-qualified investment] — Where in a taxation year a trust governed by a registered retirement savings plan holds a property that is a non-qualified investment,

(a) tax is payable under this Part by the trust on the amount that its taxable income for the year would be if it had no incomes or losses from sources other than non-qualified investments and no capital gains or losses other than from dispositions of non-qualified investments; and

(b) for the purposes of paragraph (a),

(i) "income" includes dividends described in section 83, and

(ii) paragraphs 38(a) and (b) are to be read as if the fraction set out in each of those paragraphs were replaced by the word "all".

Related Provisions: 146(4) — Tax not otherwise payable by trust; 146.3(9) — Parallel rule for RRIF; 207.04(3) — Where investment is both prohibited and non-qualified; 207.04 — Tax on annuitant if RRSP acquires non-qualified or prohibited investment; 259(1) — Election for proportional holdings in trust property.

Notes: 146(10.1) imposes tax on any *income or gain* from non-qualified investments: VIEWS doc 2014-0529681E5. 207.04(1) imposes a penalty tax on the *acquisition* of a non-qualified investment (refundable under 207.04(4) if it was inadvertent and the investment is disposed of quickly). 207.1(1), which imposed a monthly tax on *holding* a non-qualified investment, has been repealed. Note that if the investment is also a "prohibited investment" (207.01(1)), any income or gain from it falls under 207.01(1)"advantage"(c)(i) and is confiscated (taxed at 100%) by 207.05.

Where shares are delisted and so become a non-qualifying investment, 207.01(6) deems the RRSP to dispose of and reacquire the shares at current value; so there is no recognition for the drop in value to that point, but any later gain is taxed under 146(10.1): VIEWS doc 2012-0447191E5.

146(10.1)(b)(ii) amended by 2002-2013 technical bill, effective June 26, 2013.

Income Tax Folios: S3-F10-C1: Qualified investments — RRSPs, RESPs, RRIFs, RDSPs and TFSAs [replaces IT-320R3]; S3-F10-C2: Prohibited investments — RRSPs, RRIFs and TFSAs.

Registered Plans Compliance Bulletins: See under 146(1)"qualified investment".

(11), (11.1) [Repealed]

Notes: 146(11) and (11.1) repealed by 2011 budget bill #2, effective in respect of investments acquired after March 22, 2011. (See now 207.04 if an RRSP acquires a non-qualified investment.)

146(11.1) added by 1995-97 technical bill, effective 1998. In place of 146(11), 146(1)"qualified investment"(c)-(c.2) expressly provide the types of annuity contracts that are qualified investments for trusteed RRSPs.

(12) Change in plan after registration — Where, on any day after a retirement savings plan has been accepted by the Minister for registration for the purposes of this Act, the plan is revised or amended or a new plan is substituted for it, and the plan as revised or amended or the new plan, as the case may be (in this subsection referred to as the "amended plan"), does not comply with the requirements of this section for its acceptance by the Minister for registration for the purposes of this Act, subject to subsection (13.1), the following rules apply:

(a) the amended plan shall be deemed, for the purposes of this Act, not to be a registered retirement savings plan; and

(b) the taxpayer who was the annuitant under the plan before it became an amended plan shall, in computing the taxpayer's in-

come for the taxation year that includes that day, include as income received at that time an amount equal to the fair market value of all the property of the plan immediately before that time.

Related Provisions: 146(2) — Requirements for registration; 146(8.3) — Spousal RRSP payments; 146(8.7) — Where ss. (8.3) does not apply; 146(13) — Change in plan after registration; 147.3(13.1) — Withdrawal of excessive transfer to RRSP; 204.1 — Tax in respect of over-contribution to deferred income plans; 204.2(1.4) — Deemed receipt where RRSP or RRIF amended; 214(3)(c) — Non-resident withholding tax.

Notes: Where the prohibition against a "depositary" RRSP (see Notes to 146(1)"retirement savings plan") being pledged as security is violated, the RRSP is revocable, but the pledge is not void and the bank to which the RRSP is pledged can use it to set off a loan: *Whaling*, [1999] 4 C.T.C. 221 (Ont CA). Similarly, CRA deemed security under 223(11.1) for a tax debt could apply to an RRSP: *Keith G. Collins Ltd.*, 2008 MBCA 92. See also *Okanagan Court Bailiffs v. TD Waterhouse*, 2015 BCSC 1312. For a trusteed RRSP, see 146(10) instead. See also Notes to 146(2).

A creditor can acquire a hypothec (security) on an RRSP, under Quebec *Civil Code* s. 2730, without triggering 146(12), because this does not change the terms of the RRSP: VIEWS doc 2008-0284451C6; and even if the debtor is part of the process, such as a taxpayer giving CRA security for unpaid tax: 2007-0258051I7.

146(12) reworded and made subject to 146(13.1) by 1989 Budget, effective 1989.

Regulations: 214(3) (information return).

Interpretation Bulletins: IT-307R4: Spousal or common-law registered retirement savings plans; IT-415R2: Deregistration of RRSPs (cancelled).

Forms: T3GR: Group income tax and information return for RRSP, RRIF, RESP, or RDSP trusts (and worksheets); T4RSP: Statement of RRSP income; T4RSP Summary; T1234 Sched. B: Allowable amounts of non-refundable tax credits; T2205: Amounts from a spousal or common-law partner RRSP, RRIF or SPP to include in income; T4079: T4RSP and T4RIF guide.

(13) Idem — For the purposes of subsection (12), an arrangement under which a right or obligation under a retirement savings plan is released or extinguished either wholly or in part and either in exchange or substitution for any right or obligation, or otherwise (other than an arrangement the sole object and legal effect of which is to revise or amend the plan) or under which payment of any amount by way of loan or otherwise is made on the security of a right under a retirement savings plan, shall be deemed to be a new plan substituted for that retirement savings plan.

Related Provisions: 146(2), (3) — Acceptance of plan registration; 146(16) — Deduction on transfer of funds.

Interpretation Bulletins: IT-415R2: Deregistration of RRSPs (cancelled).

(13.1) [Repealed]

Notes: 146(13.1) repealed by 2011 budget bill #2, for transactions occurring, income earned, capital gains accruing and investments acquired after March 22, 2011. (The tax on an issuer extending an "advantage" was moved to 207.05(3).)

Where a broker provides a commission rebate to a client's non-RRSP account based on total RRSP and non-RRSP holdings, the CRA considered that an "advantage" was provided and 146(13.1) applied: VIEWS doc 2004-0056431E5.

Paying a higher rate of interest in the RRSP due to high combined RRSP non-RRSP investment is not conferring an advantage: Registered Plans Division, 2003 RRSP/RRIF Consultation Session, App. B, q. 12.

See Notes to 239(1) re the penalty.

(13.2), (13.3) [Repealed]

Notes: 146(13.2) repealed by 2007 budget bill #1, effective 2007, but the repeal does not apply to RSPs whose annuitant reached age 69 before 2007. It was enacted in 1997 when the RRSP age limit was increased from 69 to 71, and provided that existing plans would effectively terminate at the end of the year the annuitant turned 69. With the increase in age limit back to 71 in 2007, it is no longer needed.

146(13.2) added by 1996 Budget, effective 1997, but subject to grandfathering rules. Effectively, anyone born in 1926, 1927 or 1928 (age 69-71 at end of 1997) had his/her RRSP terminate at the end of 1997, and had to convert it to a life annuity or a RRIF (see 146.3) to avoid full income inclusion under 146(12)(b) of the amount in the RRSP.

146(13.3) repealed by 2007 budget bill #1, on the same basis as the repeal of 146(13.2). It provided for the issuer to give the annuitant notice of the upcoming maturity of the plan. Added by 1996 Budget, effective on the same basis as 146(13.2).

(14) Premiums paid in taxation year — Where any amount has been paid in a taxation year as a premium under a retirement savings plan that was, at the end of that taxation year, a registered retirement savings plan, the amount so paid shall be deemed, for the purposes of this Act, to have been paid in that year as a premium under a registered retirement savings plan.

Related Provisions: 146(1) — "Retirement savings plan".

(15) Plan not registered at end of year entered into — Notwithstanding anything in this section, where an amount is received in a taxation year as a benefit under a registered retirement savings plan that was not, at the end of the year in which the plan was entered into, a registered retirement savings plan, such part, if any, of the amount so received as may be prescribed shall be deemed, for the purposes of this Act, to have been received in the taxation year otherwise than as a benefit or other payment under a registered retirement savings plan.

Regulations: Part I.

(16) Transfer of funds [to RPP, RRSP, RRIF or ALDA] — Notwithstanding any other provision in this section, a registered retirement savings plan may at any time be revised or amended to provide for the payment or transfer before the maturity of the plan, on behalf of the annuitant under the plan (in this subsection referred to as the "transferor"), of any property thereunder by the issuer thereof

(a) to a registered pension plan for the benefit of the transferor or to a registered retirement savings plan or registered retirement income fund under which the transferor is the annuitant,

(a.1) to a licensed annuities provider to acquire an advanced life deferred annuity for the benefit of the transferor, or

(b) to a registered retirement savings plan or registered retirement income fund under which the spouse or common-law partner or former spouse or common-law partner of the transferor is the annuitant, where the transferor and the transferor's spouse or common-law partner or former spouse or common-law partner are living separate and apart and the payment or transfer is made under a decree, order or judgment of a competent tribunal, or under a written separation agreement, relating to a division of property between the transferor and the transferor's spouse or common-law partner or former spouse or common-law partner in settlement of rights arising out of, or on the breakdown of, their marriage or common-law partnership,

and, where there has been such a payment or transfer of such property on behalf of the transferor before the maturity of the plan,

(c) the amount of the payment or transfer shall not, solely because of the payment or transfer, be included in computing the income of the transferor or the transferor's spouse or common-law partner or former spouse or common-law partner,

(d) no deduction may be made under subsection (5), (5.1) or (8.2) or section 8 or 60 in respect of the payment or transfer in computing the income of any taxpayer, and

(e) where the payment or transfer was made to a registered retirement savings plan, for the purposes of subsection (8.2), the amount of the payment or transfer shall be deemed not to be a premium paid to that plan by the taxpayer.

Related Provisions: 60(l) — Transfer of RRSP premium refunds; 146(21.2) — Sask. Pension Plan account deemed to be RRSP for purposes of 146(16)(a)–(b); 146.3(14)(a) — Transfer of RRIF on marriage breakdown; 147.5(11), (12) — Pooled registered pension plan deemed to be RRSP for purposes of paras. (a), (b); 160.2(1) — Joint and several liability in respect of amounts received out of or under RRSP; 204.2(1) — Excess amount for a year for RRSP; 204.2(1.2)I(a)(iii) — Transfer under 146(16) excluded from cumulative excess RRSP amount; 204.2(2) — Where terminated plan deemed to continue to exist; 205(1)"excess ALDA transfer" — Excessive transfer to advanced life deferred annuity; 248(23.1)(a) — Where property transferred to spouse after death; 252(3) — Extended meaning of "spouse" and "former spouse"; Reg. 8300(1)"excluded contribution" — Amount transferred is excluded contribution; Reg. 8502(b)(iv) — RPP may accept transfer under 146(16).

Notes: On a marriage-breakdown transfer to an RRSP, RRIF or PRPP [147.5(12)], Form T2220 is used but is not filed with CRA (the transferring institution reports the amount on a T4RSP or T4RIF as per Form T2220 instructions; the transferee institution does not issue a receipt as the amount is not a deductible contribution). If both spouses' signatures are not provided, the institutions should keep the court order or separation agreement in their files: CRA 2002 RRSP/RRIF Consultation Session, q.2.

If either spouse dies before the 146(16) transfer is completed, CRA considers that 146(16) does not apply: docs 2004-0073441E5, 2012-0418821E5, 2016-0651721C6 [2016 APFF q.5]. (However, see *Kuchta*, 2015 TCC 289 (appeal to FCA discontinued

A-551-15 but the decision may be a nullity due to *Birchcliff Energy* — see Notes to 169(1) under "Replacement by the Chief Justice").)

For a CRA ruling that a transfer meets the requirements of 146(16), see VIEWS doc 2002-0161163. Where the savings portion of an insurance policy is in an RRSP, it cannot be transferred to a RRIF because a whole life policy cannot be held in a RRIF: doc 2006-181721E5. Re amending a separation agreement so that 146(16) applies, see 2008-0274371E5. An investment in a private corp can be transferred from one RRSP to another under 146(16), but must qualify under Reg. 4900(6) or (12) for the transferee RRSP: 2009-0321921E5. If a spousal RRSP is transferred to a RRIF with the same annuitant, it becomes a spousal RRIF: 2009-0348161E5. 146(16) cannot be used after the transferor's death: 2014-0539151E5; nor on transfer to an ex-spouse to satisfy a child-support claim: 2015-0564351E5 [Ranot, "Change to RRSP Rollover Policy?", 31(5) *Money & Family Law* (Carswell) 34-35 (May 2016)].

The phrase "settlement of rights arising out of" in 146(16)(b) was stated to include support rights as well as property rights: VIEWS doc 2002-0144225. However, docs 2006-0199271E5 and 2008-0304451E5 state that 146(16) cannot be used to pay arrears of spousal or child support, as the transfer must be in satisfaction of property rights. See Notes to 118.8 for the meaning of "living separate and apart".

See also Mitchell Ornstein, "TFSA & RRSP Planning on Separation", 28(3) *Money & Family Law* (Carswell) 19 (March 2013).

A Sask. Pension Plan account is treated as an RRSP for 146(16)(a)-(b): 146(21.2).

146(16)(a.1) added by 2021 budget bill #1, effective 2020 (see 146.5).

146(16) amended by 2000 same-sex partners bill (effective 2001), 1992 technical bill and 1990 pension bill. The 1992 amendment clarified that, if T has made overcontributions to a transferor RRSP, T will not be prevented from withdrawing the overcontributions on a tax-free basis under 146(8.2) from another RRSP to which amounts have been transferred from the transferor RRSP under 146(16).

Regulations: 214(5), (6) (information return); 216(2) (information return on transfer to ALDA).

Remission Orders: *Certain Taxpayers Remission Order, 1999-2*, P.C. 1999-1855, s. 2 (remission to Quebec judges for excess contributions transferred under 146(16)).

Interpretation Bulletins: IT-307R4: Spousal or common-law registered retirement savings plans; IT-415R2: Deregistration of RRSPs (cancelled); IT-528: Transfers of funds between registered plans.

Information Circulars: 72-22R9: Registered retirement savings plans; 74-1R5: Form T2037, Notice of purchase of annuity with "plan" funds.

Advance Tax Rulings: ATR-31: Funding of divorce settlement amount from DPSP.

Registered Plans Directorate Newsletters: 91-4R (registration rules for money purchase provisions); 16-1 (qualifying transfers to IPPs).

Registered Plans Frequently Asked Questions: RPFAQ-1 (RRSPs/RRIFs), q. 3 (change of issuer/carrier).

Forms: T2033: Direct transfer under subsec. 146.3(14.1), 147.5(21) or 146(21), or para. 146(16)(a) or 146.3(2)(e); T2220: Transfer from an RRSP, RRIF, PRPP or SPP to another RRSP, RRIF or SPP on breakdown of marriage or common-law partnership.

(17)–(19) [Repealed under former Act]

Notes: 146(17) repealed by 1991 pension bill, effective for premiums paid after 1990. It applied where a payment was made under the pre-1991 version of 146(2)(c.1). 146(18) and (19), repealed in 1986, provided rules that no longer apply.

(20) Credited or added amount deemed not received [depositary RRSP] — Where

(a) an amount is credited or added to a deposit with a depositary referred to in subparagraph (b)(iii) of the definition "retirement savings plan" in subsection (1) as interest or income in respect of the deposit,

(b) the deposit is a registered retirement savings plan at the time the amount is credited or added to the deposit, and

(c) during the calendar year in which the amount is credited or added or during the preceding calendar year, the annuitant under the plan was alive,

the amount shall be deemed not to be received by the annuitant or any other person solely because of the crediting or adding.

Related Provisions: 81(1)(r) — No income inclusion where amount credited or added to foreign retirement arrangement; 146(1)"tax-paid amount"(b), (8.8), (8.9) — Income inclusion on death; 146(4) — Exemption for income earned in trust RRSP; 146(8) — Tax on withdrawals from plan.

Notes: See Notes to 146(1)"retirement savings plan". 146(20) amended by 1993 technical bill, effective for deaths in 1993 or later.

Interpretation Bulletins: IT-415R2: Deregistration of RRSPs (cancelled).

Information Circulars: 72-22R9: Registered retirement savings plans.

(21) Specified pension plan — Where

(a) an amount (other than an amount that is part of a series of periodic payments) is transferred directly from an individual's account under a specified pension plan

(i) to a registered retirement savings plan or registered retirement income fund under which the individual, or a spouse or common-law partner or former spouse or common-law partner of the individual, is the annuitant,

(ii) to acquire from a licensed annuities provider an annuity that would be described in subparagraph 60(l)(ii) if the individual, or a spouse or common-law partner or former spouse or common-law partner of the individual, were the taxpayer referred to in that subparagraph and if that subparagraph were read without reference to clause 60(l)(ii)(B), or

(iii) to an account under the plan of a spouse or common-law partner or former spouse or common-law partner of the individual, and

(b) if the transfer is in respect of a spouse or common-law partner or former spouse or common-law partner of the individual,

(i) the individual and the spouse or common-law partner or former spouse or common-law partner are living separate and apart and the transfer is made under a decree, order or judgment of a competent tribunal, or under a written separation agreement, relating to a division of property in settlement of rights arising out of, or on the breakdown of, their marriage or common-law partnership, or

(ii) the amount is transferred as a consequence of the individual's death,

the following rules apply:

(c) the amount shall not, solely because of the transfer, be included because of subparagraph 56(1)(a)(i) in computing the income of a taxpayer, and

(d) no deduction may be made under any provision of this Act in respect of the transfer in computing the income of a taxpayer.

Related Provisions: 56(1)(d.2) — Income inclusion; 70(3.1) — "Rights or things" treatment on death; 146(21.1)–(21.3) — Sask. Pension Plan treated as RRSP for certain purposes; 146.3(2)(f)(vii) — Conditions for RRIF — transfer of funds under 146(21); 147.5(12) — Pooled registered pension plan deemed to be RRSP for purposes of (a)(i); 148(1)(e) — Amounts included in computing policyholder's income; 204.2(1.2)I(a)(iii) — Transfer under 146(21) excluded from cumulative excess RRSP amount; 212(1)(h)(iii.1)(A), 212(1)(h)(iv.1) — Transfers under 146(21) excluded from withholding tax on pension benefits.

Notes: 146(21) allows transfer of a lump sum from the Sask. Pension Plan to an RRSP, RRIF or PRPP [see 147.5(12)].

146(21) amended by 2011 budget bill #2 (for tax years that begin after 2009), 2000 same-sex partners bill, 1998 Budget. Added by 1993 technical bill.

Regulations: 7800 (Saskatchewan Pension Plan is specified pension plan).

Interpretation Bulletins: IT-528: Transfers of funds between registered plans.

(21.1) Specified pension plan — contribution — For the purposes of this section, paragraphs 18(11)(b), 60(j), (j.1) and (l), 74.5(12)(a), 146.01(3)(a) and 146.02(3)(a) and Parts X.1 and X.5, and for the purposes of section 214.1 of the *Income Tax Regulations*, a contribution made by an individual to an account of the individual, or of the individual's spouse or common-law partner, under a specified pension plan is deemed to be a premium paid by the individual to a registered retirement savings plan under which the individual, or the individual's spouse or common-law partner, as the case may be, is the annuitant.

Related Provisions: 146(21.2) — Sask. Pension Plan account treated as RRSP for certain purposes; 146(21.3) — SPP payment treated as RRSP payment for certain purposes.

Notes: 146(21.1)–(21.3) deem a specified pension plan (the Sask. Pension Plan) to be an RRSP for various purposes. See Notes to 248(1)"specified pension plan".

146(21.1) added by 2011 budget bill #2, effective for taxation years that begin after 2009, but for taxation years that begin before 2011, ignore "and for purposes of section 214.1 of the *Income Tax Regulations*".

(21.2) Specified pension plan — account — For the purposes of paragraph (8.2)(b), subsection (8.21), paragraphs (16)(a) and (b)

and 18(1)(u), subparagraph (a)(i) of the definition "excluded right or interest" in subsection 128.1(10), paragraph (b) of the definition "excluded premium" in subsection 146.01(1), paragraph (c) of the definition "excluded premium" in subsection 146.02(1), subsections 146.3(14) and 147(19), section 147.3 and paragraphs 147.5(21)(c) and 212(1)(j.1) and (m) and for the purposes of any regulations made under subsection 147.1(18), an individual's account under a specified pension plan is deemed to be a registered retirement savings plan under which the individual is the annuitant.

Related Provisions: 146(21.1) — Sask. Pension Plan contribution treated as RRSP premium for certain purposes; 146(21.3) — SPP payment treated as RRSP payment for certain purposes.

Notes: See Notes to 146(21.1).

146(21.2) amended by 2017 budget bill #2 to add reference to 212(1)(j.1) and (m), effective 2010.

146(21.2) amended by 2012 budget bill #2, effective Dec. 14, 2012, to refer to 147.5(21)(c).

146(21.2) added by 2011 budget bill #2, for taxation years that begin after 2009.

(21.3) Specified pension plan — payment — For the purposes of subsections (8.3) to (8.7), a payment received by an individual from a specified pension plan is deemed to be a payment received by the individual from a registered retirement savings plan.

Related Provisions: 146(21.1) — Sask. Pension Plan contribution treated as RRSP premium for certain purposes; 146(21.2) — SPP account treated as RRSP for certain purposes.

Notes: See Notes to 146(21.1). 146(21.3) added by 2011 budget bill #2, effective for taxation years that begin after 2010.

(22) Deemed payment of RRSP premiums [extension of contribution deadline] — If the Minister so directs,

(a) except for the purposes of subparagraphs (5)(a)(iv.1) and (5.1)(a)(iv), an amount paid by an individual in a taxation year (other than an amount paid in the first 60 days of the year) as a premium is deemed to have been paid at the beginning of the year and not at the time it was actually paid;

(b) all or part of the amount may be designated in writing by the individual for the purpose of paragraph 60(j), (j.1) or (l) or subsection 146.01(3) or 146.02(3); and

(c) the designation is deemed to have been made in the individual's return of income for the preceding taxation year or in a prescribed form filed with that return, as the case may be.

Related Provisions: 146(21.1) — Contribution to Sask. Pension Plan (after 2009) deemed to be RRSP premium.

Notes: 146(22) added by 1998 Budget, effective for amounts paid after 1997. It allows CRA to treat RRSP contributions made after March 1 as made on January 1, and thus deductible for the previous year. It was introduced to implement the contribution deadline extension announced by Revenue Canada on February 5 and 16, 1998 for taxpayers affected by the January 1998 ice storm.

The extension is implemented in the legislation as a general authorization, in 146(22) (and 127.4(5.1) for LSVCCs), allowing CRA to direct that a late contribution was made at the beginning of the year — and thus within the first 60 days, qualifying it for a deduction for the previous year.

This provision was also used as authority for extending the 1998 contribution deadline to April 30, 1999 for individuals with a 1998 pension adjustment reversal (Dept. of Finance news release, Oct. 2, 1998).

CRA allows late remittances of group RRSP contributions if (a) they are for a group RRSP that the issuer administers; and (b) all RRSP contributions were withheld before the contribution deadline; and (c) the deadline was missed by a few days to a month; and (d) the late remittance was due to an administrative or system error by the employer or RRSP issuer that was beyond the individual members' control. (Registered Plans Division, 2003 RRSP/RRIF Consultation Session, q. 9.)

146(22)(a) amended by 2011 budget bill #2, for tax years that begin after 2009, to delete "as a contribution to an account under a prescribed provincial pension plan or" (before "as a premium"). This rule (for the Sask. Pension Plan) is now in 146(21.1).

Definitions [s. 146]: "advanced life deferred annuity" — 146.5(1), 248(1); "amount" — 248(1); "annuitant" — 146(1); "annuity" — 248(1); "arm's length" — 251(1); "assessment", "authorized foreign bank" — 248(1); "beneficiary" — 108(1); "benefit" — 146(1); "business" — 248(1); "calendar year" — *Interpretation Act* 37(1)(a); "Canada" — 255; "carrying on business" — 253; "child" — 252(1); "common-law partner", "common-law partnership" — 248(1); "consequence of the death", "consequence of the annuitant's death", "consequence of the individual's death" — 248(8); "corporation" — 248(1), *Interpretation Act* 35(1); "credit union" — 137(6), 248(1); "death benefit" — 248(1); "deferred profit sharing plan" — 147(1), 248(1);

"depositary" — 146(1)"retirement savings plan"(b)(iii); "designated withdrawal" — 146.01(1); "earned income" — 146(1); "eligible individual" — 60.02(1); "employer", "employment" — 248(1); "estate" — 104(1), 248(1); "excluded withdrawal" — 146.01(1), 146.02(1); "exempt-income contribution amount" — 147.5(1); "fair market value" — see 69(1) Notes; "farm loss" — 111(8), 248(1); "farming" — 248(1); "financially dependent" — 146(1.1); "former spouse" — 252(3); "immovable" — Quebec *Civil Code* art. 900–907; "individual" — 248(1); "issuer" — 146(1); "legal representative" — 248(1); "licensed annuities provider" — 147(1), 248(1); "life insurance policy" — 138(12), 248(1); "listed" — 87(10); "listed personal property" — 54, 248(1); "maturity" — 146(1); "Minister" — 248(1); "Minister of Finance" — *Financial Administration Act* 14; "money purchase limit" — 147.1(1), 248(1); "net past service pension adjustment", "non-qualified investment" — 146(1); "non-resident", "office" — 248(1); "PSPA withdrawals" — Reg. 8307(5); "parent" — 252(2)(a); "past service pension adjustment" — 248(1), Reg. 8303; "pension adjustment" — 248(1), Reg. 8301(1); "person" — 248(1); "pooled registered pension plan" — 147.5(1), 248(1); "premium" — 146(1), 147.5(11); "prescribed" — 248(1); "prescribed premium" — Reg. 8307(7); "prescribed withdrawal" — Reg. 8306(6); "property" — 248(1); "province" — *Interpretation Act* 35(1); "provincial pension plan" — *Canada Pension Plan* s. 3; "qualified investment" — 146(1); "qualifying performance income" — 143.1(1); "RRSP deduction limit", "RRSP dollar limit" — 146(1), 248(1); "received" — 146(20); "refund of premiums", "refunds of premiums" — 146(1); "registered pension plan" — 248(1); "registered retirement income fund" — 146.3(1), 248(1); "registered retirement savings plan" — 146(1), (21.2), 147.5(12), 248(1); "regulation" — 248(1); "resident" — 250; "retirement income" — 146(1); "retirement savings plan" — 146(1), 248(1); "retiring allowance", "salary or wages" — 248(1); "security" — *Interpretation Act* 35(1); "separation agreement", "share" — 248(1); "specified pension plan" — 248(1), Reg. 7800; "spousal or common-law partner plan" — 146(1); "spouse" — 252(3); "superannuation or pension benefit" — 248(1); "tax-paid amount" — 146(1); "tax payable" — 248(2); "tax treaty" — 248(1); "taxable capital gain" — 38, 248(1); "taxable income" — 2(2), 248(1); "taxation year" — 249; "taxpayer" — 248(1); "total pension adjustment reversal" — 248(1); "trust" — 104(1), 248(1), (3); "unused non-deductible PRPP room" — 147.5(1); "unused RRSP deduction room" — 146(1), 248(1); "writing" — *Interpretation Act* 35(1).

Home Buyers' Plan

146.01 (1) Definitions — In this section,

"annuitant" has the meaning assigned by subsection 146(1);

"benefit" has the meaning assigned by subsection 146(1);

"completion date", in respect of an amount received by an individual, is

(a) where the amount was received before March 2, 1993, October 1, 1993,

(b) where the amount was received after March 1, 1993 and before March 2, 1994, October 1, 1994, and

(c) in any other case, October 1 of the calendar year following the calendar year in which the amount was received;

Notes: The completion date is generally the date before which a qualifying home must be acquired in order for an RRSP withdrawal to be an eligible amount under the Home Buyers' Plan. See 146.01(1)"regular eligible amount"(c) and "supplemental eligible amount"(d)(i).

Definition added by 1992 Economic Statement, retroactive to 1992 (see Notes at end of 146.01). Para. (b) amended (formerly read "in any other case, October 1, 1994") and para. (c) added by 1994 Budget, effective 1994.

"designated withdrawal" of an individual is an amount received by the individual, as a benefit out of or under a registered retirement savings plan, pursuant to the individual's written request in the prescribed form referred to in paragraph (a) of the definition "eligible amount" (as that definition read in its application to amounts received before 1999), paragraph (a) of the definition "regular eligible amount" or paragraph (a) of the definition "supplemental eligible amount";

Notes: Definition added by 1998 Budget, effective 1999.

"eligible amount" of an individual is a regular eligible amount or supplemental eligible amount of the individual;

Related Provisions: 146(5)(a)(iv.1), 146(5.1)(a)(iv) — Amount withdrawn within 90 days under Home Buyers' Plan ineligible for RRSP contribution; 146(8), 146.01(1)"excluded withdrawal" — Eligible amount can be withdrawn from RRSP without paying tax; 146.01(2) — Interpretation; 146.01(3), (4) — Repayment of eligible amounts to RRSP.

Notes: CRA considers that the amount paid out to the individual is whatever is left over after costs incurred by the RRSP in cashing in its investments (such as mutual fund redemption fees): VIEWS doc 2000-0018235.

Definition amended by 1998 Budget, effective for amounts received after 1998. Earlier amended by 1994 Budget and 1992 Economic Statement. For initial enactment of the definition and explanation of the HBP, see Notes at end of 146.01.

Regulations: 214(1) (information return).

Forms: RC471: Home buyers' plan — cancellation; T1036: Home buyers' plan — request to withdraw funds from an RRSP; RC4135: Home buyers' plan [guide].

"excluded premium" in respect of an individual means a premium under a registered retirement savings plan where the premium

(a) was designated by the individual for the purposes of paragraph 60(j), (j.1), (j.2) or (l),

(b) was an amount transferred directly from a registered retirement savings plan, registered pension plan, registered retirement income fund or deferred profit sharing plan,

(c) was deductible under subsection 146(6.1) in computing the individual's income for any taxation year, or

(d) was deducted in computing the individual's income for the 1991 taxation year;

Related Provisions: 146(21.2) — Sask. Pension Plan account deemed to be RRSP for purposes of para. (b); 147.5(12) — Pooled registered pension plan deemed to be RRSP for purposes of para. (b).

Notes: Para. (b) amended by 2011 budget bill #2, for tax years that begin after 2009, to delete "or a provincial pension plan prescribed for the purpose of paragraph 60(v)" at the end. This rule (for the Sask. Pension Plan) is now in 146(21.2).

Para. (b) of "excluded premium" amended by 1993 technical bill, effective for 1992 and later taxation years. See also Notes at end of 146.01.

"excluded withdrawal" of an individual means

(a) an eligible amount received by the individual,

(b) a particular amount (other than an eligible amount) received while the individual was resident in Canada and in a calendar year if

(i) the particular amount would be an eligible amount of the individual if the definition "regular eligible amount" were read without reference to paragraphs (c) and (g) of that definition and the definition "supplemental eligible amount" were read without reference to paragraphs (d) and (f) of that definition,

(ii) a payment (other than an excluded premium) equal to the particular amount is made by the individual under a retirement saving plan that is, at the end of the taxation year of the payment, a registered retirement savings plan under which the individual is the annuitant,

(iii) the payment is made before the particular time that is

(A) if the individual was not resident in Canada at the time the individual filed a return of income for the taxation year in which the particular amount was received, the earlier of

(I) the end of the following calendar year, and

(II) the time at which the individual filed the return,

(B) where clause (A) does not apply and the particular amount would, but for subclause (2)(c)(ii)(A)(II), be an eligible amount, the end of the second following calendar year, and

(C) in any other case, the end of the following calendar year, and

(iv) either

(A) if the particular time is before 2000, the payment is made, as a repayment of the particular amount, to the issuer of the registered retirement savings plan from which the particular amount was received, no other payment is made as a repayment of the particular amount and that issuer is notified of the payment in prescribed form submitted to the issuer at the time the payment is made, or

(B) the payment is made after 1999 and before the particular time and the payment (and no other payment) is designated under this clause as a repayment of the particular amount in prescribed form filed with the Minister on or before the particular time (or before such later time as is acceptable to the Minister),

(c) an amount (other than an eligible amount) that is received in a calendar year before 1999 and that would be an eligible amount of the individual if the definition "eligible amount", as it applied to amounts received before 1999, were read without reference to paragraphs (c) and (e) of that definition, where the individual

(i) died before the end of the following calendar year, and

(ii) was resident in Canada throughout the period that began immediately after the amount was received and ended at the time of the death, or

(d) a particular amount (other than an eligible amount) received while the individual was resident in Canada and in a calendar year if

(i) the particular amount would be a regular eligible amount if subsection (2.1) were read without reference to its subparagraph (a)(iii),

(ii) a payment (other than an excluded premium) equal to the particular amount is made by the individual under a retirement saving plan that is, at the end of the taxation year of the payment, a registered retirement savings plan under which the individual is the annuitant, and

(iii) the payment is made before the end of the second calendar year after the calendar year that includes the particular time referred to in subsection (2.1);

Related Provisions: 146(1)"premium" — Definition excludes repayment described in para. (b); 146(8) — Home Buyers' Plan withdrawal not to be included in income; 146.01(2)(c) — Special rules.

Notes: An "excluded withdrawal" is an amount received by an individual from their RRSP as a Home Buyer's Plan (HBP) withdrawal. Under 146(8), it is excluded from income. See also Notes to 146.01(1)"regular eligible amount" and at end of 146.01.

Under para. (d) (added by 2019 budget bill #1), for amounts received after 2019, if X makes a HBP withdrawal following breakdown of marriage or common-law partnership, and it fails to qualify as a "regular eligible amount" (e.g., X does not acquire a qualifying home within the specified period), the withdrawal is still an "excluded withdrawal" (not included in income) if X repays it to an RRSP before the end of the second year after the year of withdrawal. See also Notes to 146.01(2.1).

Definition earlier amended by 1998 Budget (last change effective for amounts received after 1998), 1992 Economic Statement. For enactment see Notes at end of 146.01.

Regulations: 104(3) — No tax withheld at source on excluded withdrawal.

"HBP balance" of an individual at any time means the amount, if any, by which the total of all eligible amounts received by the individual at or before that time exceeds the total of

(a) all amounts designated under subsection (3) by the individual for taxation years that ended before that time, and

(b) all amounts each of which is included under subsection (4) or (5) in computing the individual's income for a taxation year that ended before that time;

Related Provisions: 150(1.1)(b)(iv) — Individual with HBP balance must file tax return.

Notes: Definition added by 1998 Budget, effective 1999.

"issuer" has the meaning assigned by subsection 146(1);

"participation period" of an individual means each period

(a) that begins at the beginning of a calendar year in which the individual receives an eligible amount, and

(b) that ends immediately before the beginning of the first subsequent calendar year at the beginning of which the individual's HBP balance is nil;

Notes: Definition added by 1998 Budget, effective 1999.

"premium" has the meaning assigned by subsection 146(1);

"qualifying home" means

(a) a housing unit located in Canada, or

(b) a share of the capital stock of a cooperative housing corporation, the holder of which is entitled to possession of a housing unit located in Canada,

except that, where the context so requires, a reference to a qualifying home that is a share described in paragraph (b) means the housing unit to which the share described in that paragraph relates;

Related Provisions: 118.05(1)"qualifying home" — Application of definition for purposes of First-Time Home Buyer's Credit.

Notes: A mobile home on leased land is a QH: VIEWS doc 2009-0335901E5. A motor home is not: 2011-0423971E5, 2013-048229117.

"quarter" — [Repealed]

Notes: "Quarter" repealed by 2002-2013 technical bill (Part 5 — technical), for 2002 and later taxation years. It was used only in 146.01(8), also repealed, and referred to the calendar quarters.

"regular eligible amount" of an individual means an amount received at a particular time by the individual as a benefit out of or under a registered retirement savings plan if

(a) the amount is received pursuant to the individual's written request in a prescribed form in which the individual sets out the location of a qualifying home that the individual has begun, or intends not later than one year after its acquisition by the individual to begin, using as a principal place of residence,

(b) the individual entered into an agreement in writing before the particular time for the acquisition of it or with respect to its construction,

(c) the individual

(i) acquires the qualifying home (or a replacement property for the qualifying home) before the completion date in respect of the amount, or

(ii) dies before the end of the calendar year that includes the completion date in respect of the amount,

(d) neither the individual nor the individual's spouse or common-law partner acquired the qualifying home more than 30 days before the particular time,

(e) the individual did not have an owner-occupied home in the period

(i) that began at the beginning of the fourth preceding calendar year that ended before the particular time, and

(ii) that ended on the 31st day before the particular time,

(f) the individual's spouse or common-law partner did not, in the period referred to in paragraph (e), have an owner-occupied home

(i) that was inhabited by the individual during the spouse's or common-law partner's marriage or common-law partnership to the individual, or

(ii) that was a share of the capital stock of a cooperative housing corporation that relates to a housing unit inhabited by the individual during the spouse's or common-law partner's marriage or common-law partnership to the individual,

(g) the individual

(i) acquired the qualifying home before the particular time and is resident in Canada at the particular time, or

(ii) is resident in Canada throughout the period that begins at the particular time and ends at the earlier of the time of the individual's death and the earliest time at which the individual acquires the qualifying home or a replacement property for it,

(h) the total of the amount and all other eligible amounts received by the individual in the calendar year that includes the particular time does not exceed $35,000[2], and

(i) the individual's HBP balance at the beginning of the calendar year that includes the particular time is nil;

---

[2] Not indexed for inflation — ed.

Related Provisions: 146.01(1)"eligible amount" — Regular eligible amount included in "eligible amount"; 146.01(2)(a.1) — Meaning of "owner-occupied home"; 146.01(2.1) — Separation or breakup.

Notes: In *Lipczak*, 2009 TCC 507, withdrawals were held to meet all conditions of this definition, so the amounts withdrawn were not included in L's income under 146(8).

Para. (a): if the intention test is met but the taxpayer does not actually live in the house, the withdrawal still qualifies: VIEWS doc 2010-0387991E5. In *Osei-Yaw*, 2009 CarswellNat 4244 (TCC), 146.01 did not apply because the Court did not believe the taxpayer intended to use the (rental) property as his principal residence.

Para. (b): a home acquired by way of gift under an agreement can qualify: VIEWS docs 2010-0370831E5, 2014-0550871E5.

Para. (d): a condo is "acquired" when the purchaser is entitled to immediate vacant possession: VIEWS doc 2015-0610201E5.

Paras. (e), (f): See 146.01(2)(a.1) for the definition of "owner-occupied home". A divorced person who jointly owned a home with her former spouse within the past 4 years does not qualify: VIEWS doc 2009-0347091E5. A separated spouse living in a home owned by her spouse qualifies: 2014-0539581E5. A widowed person whose deceased spouse owned a home qualifies: 2019-0811881C6 [2019 APFF Financial q.2]. A person who rents a home from their wholly-owned corporation qualifies: 2009-0347991E5, but not one who rents from their own partnership, since they have an ownership interest in the partnership property: 2010-0364021E5. If a purchase of a home is nullified under Quebec *Civil Code* art. 1422, it was not owned: 2010-0356901E5; but 2012-0443711E5 says subsequent events do not affect HBP entitlement. A home outside Canada can be an owner-occupied home: 2013-0477881E5, 2013-0502611E5. See also *Income Tax Technical News* 31R2, 2010-0355931E5 and 2013-048229117 on meaning of "principal place of residence".

Adding a family member on title to help secure financing does not disqualify eligibility: 2010-0356641E5, 2013-0504681E5.

Subpara. (f)(i): for interpretation see VIEWS doc 2013-049401117.

Para. (i): In *Ho*, 2010 TCC 571, the taxpayer withdrew $6,000 in 2006 under the HBP (for a deposit on a condo being built), then another $13,000 in 2008. Since her HBP balance was not nil at the start of the year, the $13,000 was included in her 2008 income.

Para. (h) amended by 2019 budget bill #1, to change "$25,000" to "$35,000", for 2019 and later tax years in respect of amounts received after March 19, 2019. Budget Table 1 predicts that the cost of the increase to the federal government will be $20 million each year from 2019-20 through 2023-24. This figure would seem to presume that the same taxpayers would otherwise all take the same money out of their RRSPs anyway, which seems unlikely.

Para. (h) amended by 2009 budget bill #1, to change "$20,000" to "$25,000", for 2009 and later taxation years in respect of withdrawals made after Jan. 27, 2009.

Definition earlier amended by 2000 same-sex partners bill; added by 1998 Budget. (Before 1998, see "eligible amount".)

Regulations: 214(1) (information return).

I.T. Technical News: 31R2 (meaning of "principal place of residence").

"replacement property" for a particular qualifying home in respect of an individual, or of a specified disabled person in respect of the individual, means another qualifying home that

(a) the individual or the specified disabled person agrees to acquire, or begins the construction of, at a particular time that is after the latest time that the individual made a request described in the definition "designated withdrawal" in respect of the particular qualifying home,

(b) at the particular time, the individual intends to be used by the individual or the specified disabled person as a principal place of residence not later than one year after its acquisition, and

(c) none of the individual, the individual's spouse or common-law partner, the specified disabled person or that person's spouse or common-law partner had acquired before the particular time;

Notes: 146.01(1)"replacement property"(c) amended by 2000 same-sex partners bill, effective 2001 or earlier.

Definition amended by 1998 Budget, effective 1999.

"specified disabled person", in respect of an individual at any time, means a person who

(a) is the individual or is related at that time to the individual, and

(b) would be entitled to a deduction under subsection 118.3(1) in computing tax payable under this Part for the person's taxation year that includes that time if that subsection were read without reference to paragraph (c) of that subsection;

Related Provisions: 146.01(1)"replacement property", 146.01(2)(c) — Special rules for specified disabled person; 146.01(1)"supplemental eligible amount" — Withdrawal to acquire accessible home for specified disabled person.

Notes: Definition added by 1998 Budget, effective 1999.

"spouse" — [Repealed]

Notes: Definition of "spouse" added by 1992 technical bill for 1992 only (for 1993–2000 the extension of the term "spouse" to include a common-law spouse applied for all purposes under 252(4)). For 1992, it applied the meaning under 146(1.1).

"supplemental eligible amount" of an individual means an amount received at a particular time by the individual as a benefit out of or under a registered retirement savings plan if

(a) the amount is received pursuant to the individual's written request in a prescribed form identifying a specified disabled person in respect of the individual and setting out the location of a qualifying home

(i) that has begun to be used by that person as a principal place of residence, or

(ii) that the individual intends to be used by that person as a principal place of residence not later than one year after its first acquisition after the particular time,

(b) the purpose of receiving the amount is to enable the specified disabled person to live

(i) in a dwelling that is more accessible by that person or in which that person is more mobile or functional, or

(ii) in an environment better suited to the personal needs and care of that person,

(c) the individual or the specified disabled person entered into an agreement in writing before the particular time for the acquisition of the qualifying home or with respect to its construction,

(d) either

(i) the individual or the specified disabled person acquires the qualifying home (or a replacement property for it) after 1998 and before the completion date in respect of the amount, or

(ii) the individual dies before the end of the calendar year that includes the completion date in respect of the amount,

(e) none of the individual, the spouse or common-law partner of the individual, the specified disabled person or the spouse or common-law partner of that person acquired the qualifying home more than 30 days before the particular time,

(f) either

(i) the individual or the specified disabled person acquired the qualifying home before the particular time and the individual is resident in Canada at the particular time, or

(ii) the individual is resident in Canada throughout the period that begins at the particular time and ends at the earlier of the time of the individual's death and the earliest time at which

(A) the individual acquires the qualifying home or a replacement property for it, or

(B) the specified disabled person acquires the qualifying home or a replacement property for it,

(g) the total of the amount and all other eligible amounts received by the individual in the calendar year that includes the particular time does not exceed $35,000[2], and

(h) the individual's HBP balance at the beginning of the calendar year that includes the particular time is nil.

Related Provisions: 118.2(2)(l.2), (l.21) — Medical expense credit for disability-related renovations and construction costs; 146.01(1)"eligible amount" — Supplemental eligible amount included in "eligible amount".

---

[2] Not indexed for inflation — ed.

Notes: This definition allows greater access to the Home Buyers' Plan for persons with disabilities; e.g., VIEWS doc 2019-0819671E5. Either the taxpayer or the disabled person must contract for and buy the home (e.g., 2019-0832201E5), so a grandparent cannot use it for a disabled grandchild whose parent will own the home: 2013-0496481E5.

Para. (g) amended by 2019 budget bill #1, to change "$25,000" to "$35,000", for 2019 and later tax years for amounts received after March 19, 2019. Definition earlier amended by 2009 budget bill #1 (changed from $20,000), 2000 same-sex partners bill; added by 1998 budget.

Regulations: 214(1) (information return).

(2) Special rules — For the purposes of this section,

(a) an individual shall be considered to have acquired a qualifying home if the individual acquired it jointly with one or more other persons;

(a.1) an individual shall be considered to have an owner-occupied home at any time where, at that time, the individual owns, whether jointly with another person or otherwise, a housing unit or a share of the capital stock of a cooperative housing corporation and

   (i) the housing unit is inhabited by the individual as the individual's principal place of residence at that time, or

   (ii) the share was acquired for the purpose of acquiring a right to possess a housing unit owned by the corporation and that unit is inhabited by the individual as the individual's principal place of residence at that time;

(b) where an individual agrees to acquire a condominium unit, the individual shall be deemed to have acquired it on the day the individual is entitled to immediate vacant possession of it;

(c) except for the purposes of subparagraph (g)(ii) of the definition "regular eligible amount" and subparagraph (f)(ii) of the definition "supplemental eligible amount", an individual or a specified disabled person in respect of the individual is deemed to have acquired, before the completion date in respect of a designated withdrawal received by the individual, the qualifying home in respect of which the designated withdrawal was received if

   (i) neither the qualifying home nor a replacement property for it was acquired by the individual or the specified disabled person before that completion date, and

   (ii) either

      (A) the individual or the specified disabled person

         (I) is obliged under the terms of a written agreement in effect on that completion date to acquire the qualifying home (or a replacement property for it) on or after that date, and

         (II) acquires the qualifying home or a replacement property for it before the day that is one year after that completion date, or

      (B) the individual or the specified disabled person made payments, the total of which equalled or exceeded the total of all designated withdrawals that were received by the individual in respect of the qualifying home,

         (I) to persons with whom the individual was dealing at arm's length,

         (II) in respect of the construction of the qualifying home or a replacement property for it, and

         (III) in the period that begins at the time the individual first received a designated withdrawal in respect of the qualifying home and that ends before that completion date; and

(d) an amount received by an individual in a particular calendar year is deemed to have been received by the individual at the end of the preceding calendar year and not at any other time if

   (i) the amount is received in January of the particular year (or at such later time as is acceptable to the Minister),

   (ii) the amount would not be an eligible amount if this section were read without reference to this paragraph, and

   (iii) the amount would be an eligible amount if the definition "regular eligible amount" in subsection (1) were read without reference to paragraph (i) of that definition and the definition "supplemental eligible amount" were read without reference to paragraph (h) of that definition.

Related Provisions: 146(5)(a)(iv.1), 146(5.1)(a)(iv) — Amount withdrawn within 90 days under Home Buyers' Plan ineligible for RRSP contribution.

Notes: *Para. (a):* a percentage interest in a home qualifies: VIEWS doc 2017-0730991E5.

Para. (a.1): for "owner-occupied home" see Notes to 146.01(1)"regular eligible amount".

Para. (b) deems a condo to be acquired, and starts the 30-day clock in 146.01(1)"regular eligible amount"(d), when interim possession is obtained before closing: *Chitalia*, 2017 TCC 227 (the CRA Guide was misleading so the Court awarded costs to C and recommended a remission order).

Para. (c): The extension does not apply only to unforeseen delays. "As long as the amounts withdrawn from the RRSP were used for the construction of the qualifying home before the completion date, it does not matter after that when the housing unit was ready to be occupied. The only requirement ... is that the individual intends to take possession of the unit for the purpose of occupying it as a principal residence not later than one year after it is available for vacant possession. The time limit ... is complied with as long as payments equalling at least the total of the withdrawals are made to the contractors or the suppliers ... prior to that completion date": *Lipczak*, 2009 TCC 507, para. 27.

Para. (d): In *Loh*, 2007 TCC 740, the taxpayer made HBP withdrawals in Oct. 2003 and April 2004. As the Minister had not determined whether April was "such later time [than Jan. 2004] as is acceptable", the Court allowed the appeal since there was no evidence the assessment was correct!

Subpara. (d)(i): For CRA criteria on accepting a "later time" see VIEWS doc 2018-0761541C6 [2018 APFF Financial q.8].

146.01(2) amended by 1998 Budget (for amounts received after 1998), 1994 Budget, 1992 Economic Statement.

I.T. Technical News: 31R2 (meaning of "principal place of residence").

Forms: RC471: Home buyers' plan — cancellation; RC4135: Home buyers' plan [guide].

(2.1) Marriage or common-law partnership [separation or breakup] — Notwithstanding paragraph (2)(a.1), for the purposes of the definition "regular eligible amount",

(a) an individual, and a spouse or common-law partner of the individual, are deemed not to have an owner-occupied home in a period ending before a particular time referred to in that definition if

   (i) at the particular time, the individual

      (A) is living separate and apart from the individual's spouse or common-law partner because of a breakdown of their marriage or common-law partnership,

      (B) has been living separate and apart from the individual's spouse or common-law partner for a period of at least 90 days, and

      (C) began living separate and apart from the individual's spouse or common-law partner in the calendar year that includes the particular time or any time in the four preceding calendar years,

   (ii) in the absence of this subsection, the individual would not be precluded from having a regular eligible amount because of the application of paragraph (f) of that definition in respect of a spouse or common-law partner (other than the spouse or common-law partner referred to in clauses (i)(A) to (C)), and

   (iii) where the individual has an owner-occupied home at the particular time,

      (A) the home is not the qualifying home referred to in that definition and the individual disposes of the home no later than the end of the second calendar year after the calendar year that includes the particular time, or

(B) the individual acquires the interest, or for civil law the right, of the spouse or common-law partner in the home; and

(b) if an individual to whom paragraph (a) applies has an owner-occupied home at the particular time referred to in that paragraph and the individual acquires the interest, or for civil law the right, of a spouse or common-law partner in the home, the individual is deemed for the purposes of paragraphs (c) and (d) of that definition to have acquired a qualifying home on the date that the individual acquired the interest or the right.

Notes: 146.01(2.1) (added by 2019 budget bill #1, for amounts received after 2019) allows X access to the Home Buyers' Plan (HBP) after breakdown of a marriage or common-law partnership (MCLP), provided certain conditions are met, even if X might not otherwise qualify as a first-time homebuyer.

Subpara. (a)(i) requires that at the time X makes an HBP withdrawal from a RRSP, X be living separate and apart from their spouse or CLP (SCLP) for a continuous period of at least 90 days because of a breakdown of the MCLP. As well, X must have begun to live separate and apart in the year the withdrawal was made or in one of the 4 preceding years. (a)(ii) prohibits X from accessing the HBP if, after the breakdown, X begins to reside in a home owned by a new SCLP. Thus, 146.01(1)"regular eligible amount"(f) continues to apply to X in respect of the new SCLP. (a)(iii) requires X to either dispose of their previous home by the end of the 2nd year after the year in which the HBP withdrawal was made, or buy their SCLP's interest.

Para. (b) provides that for the purposes of 146.01(1)"regular eligible amount"(c) and (d) (the conditions relating to acquiring a qualifying home), if after the breakdown of a MCLP X buys the interest or right of their SCLP in a jointly-owned home, X is deemed to have acquired a qualifying home at that point. This ensures that X can satisfy the requirements under 146.01(2)(d) and (e).

For more detail see tinyurl.com/cra-hbp2019 (CRA Q&A, May 3, 2019).

Table 1 predicts that the cost to the federal government of this measure will be $5 million in 2019-20 and $10 million each year from 2020-21 through 2023-24.

(3) Repayment of eligible amount — An individual may designate a single amount for a taxation year in a prescribed form filed with the individual's return of income for the year if the amount does not exceed the lesser of

(a) the total of all amounts (other than excluded premiums, repayments to which paragraph (b) or (d) of the definition "excluded withdrawal" in subsection (1) applies and amounts paid by the individual in the first 60 days of the year that can reasonably be considered to have been deducted in computing the individual's income, or designated under this subsection, for the preceding taxation year) paid by the individual in the year or within 60 days after the end of the year under a retirement savings plan that is at the end of the year or the following taxation year a registered retirement savings plan under which the individual is the annuitant, and

(b) the amount, if any, by which

(i) the total of all eligible amounts received by the individual before the end of the year

exceeds the total of

(ii) all amounts designated by the individual under this subsection for preceding taxation years, and

(iii) all amounts each of which is an amount included in computing the income of the individual under subsection (4) or (5) for a preceding taxation year.

Related Provisions: 146(21.1) — Contribution to Sask. Pension Plan deemed to be RRSP premium for purposes of 146.01(3)(a); 146.02(1)"excluded premium"(a) — Amount claimed under Home Buyers' Plan ineligible for LLP; 147.5(11) — Pooled registered pension plan contribution deemed to be RRSP premium for 146.01(3)(a); *Interpretation Act* 27(5) — Meaning of "within 60 days".

Notes: Since the 146.01(3) calculation is for the year, a "repayment" can take place before the HBP withdrawal, if the taxpayer discovers an inadvertent RRSP contribution made earlier in the year and wishes to avoid the penalty tax under 204.1(2.1) by designating the contribution as a repayment. This is confirmed in VIEWS doc 2002-0138235.

See also Notes at end of 146.01.

Para. (a) amended by 2019 budget bill #1 to add reference to 146.01(1)"excluded withdrawal"(d), for repayments after 2019.

146.01(3) amended by 1998 Budget (for 1999 and later tax years), 1995 and 1994 Budgets.

Forms: RC471: Home buyers' plan — cancellation; RC4135: Home buyers' plan [guide]; T1 General Sched. 7: RRSP unused contributions, transfers, and HBP or LLP activities.

(4) Portion of eligible amount not repaid — There shall be included in computing an individual's income for a particular taxation year included in a particular participation period of the individual the amount determined by the formula

$$\frac{(A - B - C)}{(15 - D)} - E$$

where

A is

(a) where

(i) the individual died or ceased to be resident in Canada in the particular year, or

(ii) the completion date in respect of an eligible amount received by the individual was in the particular year

nil, and

(b) in any other case, the total of all eligible amounts received by the individual in preceding taxation years included in the particular period,

B is

(a) nil, if the completion date in respect of an eligible amount received by the individual was in the preceding taxation year, and

(b) in any other case, the total of all amounts each of which is designated under subsection (3) by the individual for a preceding taxation year included in the particular period;

C is the total of all amounts each of which is included under this subsection or subsection (5) in computing the individual's income for a preceding taxation year included in the particular period;

D is the lesser of 14 and the number of taxation years of the individual ending in the period beginning

(a) where the completion date in respect of an eligible amount received by the individual was before 1995, January 1, 1995, and

(b) in any other case, January 1 of the first calendar year beginning after the completion date in respect of an eligible amount received by the individual

and ending at the beginning of the particular year, and

E is

(a) if the completion date in respect of an eligible amount received by the individual was in the preceding taxation year, the total of all amounts each of which is designated under subsection (3) by the individual for the particular year or any preceding taxation year included in the particular period, and

(b) in any other case, the amount designated under subsection (3) by the individual for the particular year.

Related Provisions: 257 — Formula cannot calculate to less than zero.

Notes: See Notes at end of 146.01. In *Javor*, 2005 TCC 102 and 2012 FCA 134, 146.01(4) applied even though J had lost the home due to marriage breakdown. In *Gramaglia*, 2007 TCC 218, the amount not repaid to the RRSP was included in income and resulted in a reduced Guaranteed Income Supplement.

146.01(4) amended by 1998 Budget, effective for 1999 and later taxation years. Previously amended by 1994 Budget and 1992 Economic Statement.

Forms: RC471: Home buyers' plan — cancellation; RC4135: Home buyers' plan [guide].

(5) Where individual becomes a non-resident — Where at any time in a taxation year an individual ceases to be resident in Canada, there shall be included in computing the income of the individual for the period in the year during which the individual was resident in Canada the amount, if any, by which

(a) the total of all amounts each of which is an eligible amount received by the individual in the year or a preceding taxation year

exceeds the total of

(b) all amounts designated under subsection (3) by the individual in respect of amounts paid not later than 60 days after that time and before the individual files a return of income for the year, and

(c) all amounts included under subsection (4) or this subsection in computing the individual's income for preceding taxation years.

Related Provisions: 56(1)(h.1) — Home buyers' plan — income inclusion.

Notes: The entire HBP balance is included in income for the year in which the taxpayer ceases to be resident in Canada. See VIEWS doc 2011-0426861I7.

146.01(5) amended by 1998 Budget (for 1999 and later tax years), 1994 Budget.

(6) Death of individual — If an individual dies at any time in a taxation year, there shall be included in computing the individual's income for the year the amount, if any, by which

(a) the individual's HBP balance immediately before that time exceeds

(b) the amount designated under subsection (3) by the individual for the year.

Related Provisions: 56(1)(h.1) — Home buyers' plan — income inclusion; 146.01(7) — Optional transfer of repayment obligation to spouse.

Notes: 146.01(6) amended by 1998 Budget, last change effective for 2000 and later years.

(7) Exception — If a spouse or common-law partner of an individual was resident in Canada immediately before the individual's death at a particular time in a taxation year and the spouse or common-law partner and the individual's legal representatives jointly so elect in writing in the individual's return of income for the year,

(a) subsection (6) does not apply to the individual;

(b) the spouse or common-law partner is deemed to have received a particular eligible amount at the particular time equal to the amount that, but for this subsection, would be determined under subsection (6) in respect of the individual;

(c) for the purposes of subsection (4) and paragraph (d), the completion date in respect of the particular amount is deemed to be

(i) if the spouse or common-law partner received an eligible amount before the death (other than an eligible amount received in a participation period of the spouse or common-law partner that ended before the beginning of the year), the completion date in respect of that amount, and

(ii) in any other case, the completion date in respect of the last eligible amount received by the individual; and

(d) for the purpose of subsection (4), the completion date in respect of each eligible amount received by the spouse or common-law partner, after the death and before the end of the spouse or common-law partner's participation period that includes the time of the death, is deemed to be the completion date in respect of the particular amount.

Related Provisions: 220(3.2), Reg. 600(b) — Late filing or revocation of election.

Notes: 146.01(7) amended by 2000 same-sex partners bill to refer to "common-law partner", effective as per Notes to 248(1)"common-law partner".

146.01(7) amended by 1998 Budget, this version effective for deaths after 1999, by 1994 Budget effective 1994, and by 1992 Economic Statement, retroactive to 1992.

(8) [Repealed]

Notes: 146.01(8) repealed by 2002-2013 technical bill (Part 5 — technical), for 2002 and later taxation years. It provided a deadline for filing a prescribed form. Reg. 214(1) now provides for an annual information return.

Forms: T1 Sched. 7: RRSP unused contributions, transfers, and HBP or LLP activities; T1036: Home buyers' plan — request to withdraw funds from an RRSP.

(9)–(13) [Repealed]

Notes: 146.01(9)–(13) repealed by 1994 Budget, effective 1994. They provided income inclusions for 1992 and 1993 where recent RRSP contributions were withdrawn

under the HBP. The rules in 146(5)(a)(iv.1) and 146(5.1)(a)(iv) now prevent certain RRSP contributions from being deducted, if those contributions are withdrawn under the Home Buyers' Plan within 90 days of being contributed.

Notes [s. 146.01]: 146.01 provides the Home Buyers' Plan, which (simplified) allows up to $35,000 per person ($25,000 before March 19, 2019) to be withdrawn from RRSPs for purchasing or building a qualifying home, provided the person and spouse have not owned a home within the past 5 years (on marriage or relationship breakdown, see s. 146.01(1)"excluded withdrawal"(d) and 146.01(2.1)). See 146.01(1)"regular eligible amount"(e), (f), (h) and 146(8). The home must be acquired before Oct. 1 of the next year: 146.01(1)"completion date", "regular eligible amount"(c). No withholding applies to the withdrawal: see Reg. 104(3), but an information return is required: see Reg. 214(1). The amount withdrawn should be repaid to the RRSP over a 15-year period beginning the second year after the withdrawal: 146.01(4). To the extent the repayments are not made, the amounts will be included in income under 146.01(4). If the taxpayer becomes non-resident, the entire unpaid amount is included in income for the last year of residence in Canada: 146.01(5). A husband and wife can each use $35,000: 2009-0348001E5. The home must be in Canada: 146.01(1)"qualifying home", 2015-0574271E5.

See also CRA Guide RC4135; tinyurl.com/what-hbp; VIEWS doc 2004-0090031E5.

RRSP contributions in the 89-day period before an HBP withdrawal are deductible only if the taxpayer had at least as much in the RRSP at the start of that period as the HBP withdrawal: 146(5)(a)(iv.1), VIEWS doc 2010-0371701E5.

Quebec proposed in its Nov. 4/08 Economic Update to allow a 1-year deferral in the repayment requirement for provincial tax purposes, for the 2009 year, if the federal government would do the same. This offer was not taken up.

For 2015, 91,000 taxpayers withdrew $1.27 billion from RRSPs under the HBP, and $867 million was repaid to RRSPs. (*Access to Information Act* disclosure in 2019)

For investment in the home mortgage by the RRSP as an alternative to the Home Buyers' Plan, see Reg. 4900(1)(j).

146.01 added by 1992 Budget/technical bill, effective for 1992 and later taxation years.

Definitions [s. 146.01]: "amount" — 248(1); "annuitant" — 146(1), 146.01(1); "arm's length" — 251(1); "benefit" — 146(1), 146.01(1); "calendar year" — *Interpretation Act* 37(1)(a); "Canada" — 255; "common-law partner", "common-law partnership" — 248(1); "completion date" — 146.01(1); "corporation" — 248(1), *Interpretation Act* 35(1); "deferred profit sharing plan" — 147(1), 248(1); "designated withdrawal" — 146.01(1); "eligible amount", "excluded premium", "excluded withdrawal" — 146.01(1); "filing-due date" — 150(1), 248(1); "HBP balance" — 146.01(1); "have an owner-occupied home" — 146.01(2)(a.1); "individual" — 248(1); "issuer" — 146(1), 146.01(1); "legal representative", "Minister" — 248(1); "net premium balance" — 146.01(11), (12); "owner-occupied home" — 146.01(2)(a.1); "participation period" — 146.01(1); "person" — 248(1); "premium" — 146(1), 146.01(1); "prescribed", "property" — 248(1); "qualifying home" — 146.01(1); "registered pension plan" — 248(1); "registered retirement income fund" — 146.3(1), 248(1); "registered retirement savings plan" — 146(1), 248(1); "regular eligible amount" — 146.01(1); "related" — 251(2)–(6); "resident", "resident in Canada" — 250; "retirement savings plan" — 146(1), 248(1); "share" — 248(1); "specified disabled person" — 146.01(1); "spouse" — 252(3); "supplemental eligible amount" — 146.01(1); "taxation year" — 128(2)(d), 249; "writing" — *Interpretation Act* 35(1); "written" — *Interpretation Act* 35(1)"writing".

Lifelong Learning Plan

146.02 (1) Definitions — The definitions in this subsection apply in this section.

"annuitant" has the meaning assigned by subsection 146(1).

"benefit" has the meaning assigned by subsection 146(1).

"eligible amount" of an individual means a particular amount received at a particular time in a calendar year by the individual as a benefit out of or under a registered retirement savings plan if

(a) the particular amount is received after 1998 pursuant to the individual's written request in a prescribed form;

(b) in respect of the particular amount, the individual designates in the form a person (in this definition referred to as the "designated person") who is the individual or the individual's spouse or common-law partner;

(c) the total of the particular amount and all other eligible amounts received by the individual at or before the particular time and in the year does not exceed $10,000[2];

(d) the total of the particular amount and all other eligible amounts received by the individual at or before the particular

---

[2] Not indexed for inflation — ed.

time (other than amounts received in participation periods of the individual that ended before the year) does not exceed $20,000[2];

(e) the individual did not receive an eligible amount at or before the particular time in respect of which someone other than the designated person was designated (other than an amount received in a participation period of the individual that ended before the year);

(f) the designated person

(i) is enrolled at the particular time as a full-time student in a qualifying educational program, or

(ii) has received written notification before the particular time that the designated person is absolutely or contingently entitled to enrol before March of the following year as a full-time student in a qualifying educational program;

(g) the individual is resident in Canada throughout the period that begins at the particular time and ends immediately before the earlier of

(i) the beginning of the following year, and

(ii) the time of the individual's death;

(h) except where the individual dies after the particular time and before April of the following year, the designated person is enrolled as a full-time student in a qualifying educational program after the particular time and before March of the following year and

(i) the designated person completes the program before April of the following year,

(ii) the designated person does not withdraw from the program before April of the following year, or

(iii) less than 75% of the tuition paid, after the beginning of the year and before April of the following year, in respect of the designated person and the program is refundable; and

(i) if an eligible amount was received by the individual before the year, the particular time is neither

(i) in the individual's repayment period for the individual's participation period that includes the particular time, nor

(ii) after January (or a later month where the Minister so permits) of the fifth calendar year of that participation period.

Related Provisions: 146(5)(a)(iv.1), 146(5.1)(a)(iv) — Amount withdrawn within 90 days under LLP ineligible for RRSP contribution; 146.01(2) — Interpretation; 146.02(3), (4) — Repayment of eligible amounts to RRSP; Reg. 203 — Educational institutions required to report enrolment information.

Notes: CRA considers that the amount paid out to the individual for purposes of the LLP is whatever is left over after costs incurred by the RRSP in cashing in its investments (such as mutual fund redemption fees): VIEWS doc 2000-0018235.

In *Kitura*, 2003 TCC 892, the taxpayer did not qualify for the LLP because he was enrolled in a correspondence course, and so was not a full-time student for para. (f). A medical resident may be a full-time student: see Notes to 118.6(1)"qualifying educational program". A master's program requiring >10 hours of class per week still does not qualify if the institution considers the student to be a part-time student: 2009-0323581E5. See also Notes to 118.5(1)(b) on the meaning of "full-time".

146.02(1)"eligible amount"(b) amended by 2000 same-sex partners bill to refer to "common-law partner", effective as per Notes to 248(1)"common-law partner".

Regulations: 214(1) (information return).

Forms: RC96: LLP — request to withdraw funds from an RRSP; RC4112: Lifelong learning plan [guide].

"excluded premium" of an individual means a premium that

(a) was designated by the individual for the purpose of paragraph 60(j), (j.1) or (l) or subsection 146.01(3);

(b) was a repayment to which paragraph (b) or (d) of the definition "excluded withdrawal" in subsection 146.01(1) applies;

(c) was an amount transferred directly from a registered retirement savings plan, registered pension plan, registered retirement income fund or deferred profit sharing plan; or

(d) was deductible under subsection 146(6.1) in computing the individual's income for any taxation year.

Related Provisions: 146(21.2) — Sask. Pension Plan account deemed to be RRSP for purposes of para. (c); 147.5(12) — Pooled registered pension plan deemed to be RRSP for purposes of para. (c).

Notes: Para. (b) amended by 2019 budget bill #1 to add "or (d)", for repayments after 2019.

Para. (c) amended by 2011 budget bill #2, for tax years that begin after 2009, to delete "or a provincial pension plan prescribed for the purpose of paragraph 60(v)" at the end. This rule (covering the Sask. Pension Plan) is now provided by 146(21.2).

"excluded withdrawal" of an individual means

(a) an eligible amount received by the individual; or

(b) a particular amount (other than an eligible amount) received while the individual was resident in Canada and in a calendar year if

(i) the particular amount would be an eligible amount of the individual if the definition "eligible amount" were read without reference to paragraphs (g) and (h) of that definition,

(ii) a payment (other than an excluded premium) equal to the particular amount is paid by the individual under a retirement savings plan that is, at the end of the taxation year of payment, a registered retirement savings plan under which the individual is the annuitant,

(iii) the payment is made before the particular time that is,

(A) if the individual was not resident in Canada at the time the individual filed a return of income for the taxation year in which the particular amount was received, the earlier of

(I) the end of the following calendar year, and

(II) the time at which the individual filed the return, and

(B) in any other case, the end of the following calendar year, and

(iv) the payment (and no other payment) is designated under this subparagraph as a repayment of the particular amount in prescribed form filed with the Minister on or before the particular time (or before such later time as is acceptable to the Minister).

Related Provisions: 146(1)"premium" — Definition excludes repayment described in para. (b); 146(8) — LLP withdrawal not to be included in income.

Notes: In *Wood*, 2008 FCA 302 (leave to appeal denied 2009 CarswellNat 1082 (SCC)), the TCC allowed a withdrawal because the Crown did not prove that its (changed) assumptions were correct, but the FCA ordered a new trial because the TCC refused to allow the Crown to call the taxpayer as a witness.

"full-time student" in a taxation year includes an individual to whom subsection 118.6(3) applies for the purpose of computing tax payable under this Part for the year or the following taxation year.

"LLP balance" of an individual at any time means the amount, if any, by which the total of all eligible amounts received by the individual at or before that time exceeds the total of

(a) all amounts designated under subsection (3) by the individual for taxation years that ended before that time, and

(b) all amounts each of which is included under subsection (4) or (5) in computing the individual's income for a taxation year that ended before that time.

Related Provisions: 150(1.1)(b)(iv) — Individual with LLP balance must file tax return.

"participation period" of an individual means each period

(a) that begins at the beginning of a calendar year

(i) in which the individual receives an eligible amount, and

(ii) at the beginning of which the individual's LLP balance is nil; and

---

[2] Not indexed for inflation — ed.

(b) that ends immediately before the beginning of the first subsequent calendar year at the beginning of which the individual's LLP balance is nil.

"premium" has the meaning assigned by subsection 146(1).

"qualifying educational program" means a program at a designated educational institution, as defined in subsection 118.6(1), of not less than three consecutive months duration that requires that each student taking the program spend not less than ten hours per week on courses or work in the program and that is

(a) of a technical or vocational nature designed to furnish a person with skills for, or improve a person's skills in, an occupation, if the program is at an institution described in subparagraph (a)(ii) of that definition; and

(b) at a post-secondary school level, in any other case.

Notes: See Notes to 118.6(1)"designated educational institution" re the *Haringa* case.

Definition amended by 2004 Budget, effective 2004, consequential on amendments to 118.6(1)"qualifying educational program".

"repayment period" of an individual for a participation period of the individual in respect of a person designated under paragraph (b) of the definition "eligible amount" means the period, if any, within the participation period

(a) that begins

(i) at the beginning of the third calendar year within the participation period if, in each of the second and third calendar years within the participation period,

(A) for calendar years before 2017, the person would not be entitled to claim an amount under subsection 118.6(2) (as it read in the year) in respect of at least three months in the year, if that subsection were read without reference to paragraph (b) of the description of B in that subsection, and

(B) for calendar years after 2016, the person would not be a "qualifying student" (as defined in subsection 118.6(1)) in respect of at least three months in the year, if that definition were read without reference to its subparagraph (a)(ii),

(ii) at the beginning of the fourth calendar year within the participation period if, in each of the third and fourth calendar years within the participation period,

(A) for calendar years before 2017, the person would not be entitled to claim an amount under subsection 118.6(2) (as it read in the year) in respect of at least three months in the year, if that subsection were read without reference to paragraph (b) of the description of B in that subsection, and

(B) for calendar years after 2016, the person would not be a "qualifying student" (as defined in subsection 118.6(1)) in respect of at least three months in the year, if that definition were read without reference to its subparagraph (a)(ii),

(iii) at the beginning of the fifth calendar year within the participation period if, in each of the fourth and fifth calendar years within the participation period,

(A) for calendar years before 2017, the person would not be entitled to claim an amount under subsection 118.6(2) (as it read in the year) in respect of at least three months in the year, if that subsection were read without reference to paragraph (b) of the description of B in that subsection, and

(B) for calendar years after 2016, the person would not be a "qualifying student" (as defined in subsection 118.6(1)) in respect of at least three months in the year, if that definition were read without reference to its subparagraph (a)(ii), and

(iv) in any other case, at the beginning of the sixth calendar year within the participation period; and

(b) that ends at the end of the participation period.

Notes: See Notes at end of 146.02.

Subpara. (a)(i)-(iii) amended by 2016 budget bill #1, as of June 22, 2016, effectively adding (i)(B), (ii)(B), (iii)(B) as of 2017. This does not change the rules; it is consequential on elimination of the education and textbook credits in 118.6. 118.6(1)"qualifying student" now determines student status. Before the amendment, read:

(i) at the beginning of the third calendar year within the participation period, if the person would not be entitled to claim an amount under subsection 118.6(2) in respect of at least three months in each of the second and third calendar years within the participation period, if that subsection were read without reference to paragraph (b) of the description of B in that subsection,

(ii) at the beginning of the fourth calendar year within the participation period, if subparagraph (i) does not apply and the person would not be entitled to claim an amount under subsection 118.6(2) in respect of at least three months in each of the third and fourth calendar years within the participation period, if that subsection were read without reference to paragraph (b) of the description of B in that subsection,

(iii) at the beginning of the fifth calendar year within the participation period, if subparagraphs (i) and (ii) do not apply and the person would not be entitled to claim an amount under subsection 118.6(2) in respect of at least three months in each of the fourth and fifth calendar years within that period, if that subsection were read without reference to paragraph (b) of the description of B in that subsection, and

Forms: RC96: LLP — request to withdraw funds from an RRSP; RC4112: Lifelong learning plan [guide].

(2) Rule of application — For the purpose of the definition "eligible amount" in subsection (1), a particular person is deemed to be the only person in respect of whom a particular amount was designated under paragraph (b) of that definition if

(a) an individual received the particular amount;

(b) the individual files a prescribed form with the Minister in which the particular person is specified in connection with the receipt of the particular amount;

(c) the particular amount would be an eligible amount of the individual if

(i) that definition were read without reference to paragraphs (b) and (e) of that definition, and

(ii) each reference in the portion of that definition after paragraph (d) to "designated person" were read as "individual" or "individual's spouse or common-law partner"; and

(d) the Minister so permits.

Related Provisions: 146(5)(a)(iv.1), 146(5.1)(a)(iv) — Amount withdrawn within 90 days under LLP ineligible for RRSP contribution.

Notes: 146.02(2)(c)(ii) amended by 2000 same-sex partners bill to refer to "common-law partner", effective as per Notes to 248(1)"common-law partner".

Forms: RC96: LLP — request to withdraw funds from an RRSP.

(3) Repayment of eligible amount — An individual may designate a single amount for a taxation year in prescribed form filed with the individual's return of income for the year if the amount does not exceed the lesser of

(a) the total of all amounts (other than excluded premiums, repayments to which paragraph (b) of the definition "excluded withdrawal" in subsection (1) applies and amounts paid by the individual in the first 60 days of the year that can reasonably be considered to have been deducted in computing the individual's income, or designated under this subsection, for the preceding taxation year) paid by the individual in the year or within 60 days after the end of the year under a retirement savings plan that is at the end of the year or the following taxation year a registered retirement savings plan under which the individual is the annuitant, and

(b) the individual's LLP balance at the end of the year.

Related Provisions: 146(21.1) — Contribution to Sask. Pension Plan deemed to be RRSP premium for purposes of 146.02(3)(a); 147.5(11) — Pooled registered pension plan contribution deemed to be RRSP premium for 146.02(3)(a); *Interpretation Act* 27(5) — Meaning of "within 60 days".

Notes: See Notes at end of 146.02.

Forms: RC96: LLP — request to withdraw funds from an RRSP.

(4) If portion of eligible amount not repaid — There shall be included in computing an individual's income for a particular taxation year that begins after 2000 the amount determined by the formula

$$[(A - B - C)/(10 - D)] - E$$

where

A is

    (a) nil, if

        (i) the individual died or ceased to be resident in Canada in the particular year, or

        (ii) the beginning of the particular year is not included in a repayment period of the individual, and

    (b) in any other case, the total of all eligible amounts received by the individual in preceding taxation years (other than taxation years in participation periods of the individual that ended before the particular year);

B is

    (a) nil, if the particular year is the first taxation year in a repayment period of the individual, and

    (b) in any other case, the total of all amounts designated under subsection (3) by the individual for preceding taxation years (other than taxation years in participation periods of the individual that ended before the particular year);

C is the total of all amounts each of which is included under this subsection or subsection (5) in computing the individual's income for a preceding taxation year (other than a taxation year included in a participation period of the individual that ended before the particular year);

D is the lesser of nine and the number of taxation years of the individual that end in the period that

    (a) begins at the beginning of the individual's last repayment period that began at or before the beginning of the particular year, and

    (b) ends at the beginning of the particular year; and

E is

    (a) if the particular year is the first taxation year within a repayment period of the individual, the total of the amount designated under subsection (3) by the individual for the particular year and all amounts so designated for preceding taxation years (other than taxation years in participation periods of the individual that ended before the particular year), and

    (b) in any other case, the amount designated under subsection (3) by the individual for the particular year.

Related Provisions: 56(1)(h.1) — Inclusion in income; 257 — Formula cannot calculate to less than zero.

Notes: See Notes at end of 146.02.

Forms: RC4112: Lifelong learning plan [guide].

(5) Ceasing residence in Canada — If at any time in a taxation year an individual ceases to be resident in Canada, there shall be included in computing the individual's income for the period in the year during which the individual was resident in Canada the amount, if any, by which

    (a) the total of all amounts each of which is an eligible amount received by the individual in the year or a preceding taxation year

exceeds the total of

    (b) all amounts designated under subsection (3) by the individual in respect of amounts paid not later than 60 days after that time and before the individual files a return of income for the year, and

    (c) all amounts included under subsection (4) or this subsection in computing the individual's income for preceding taxation years.

Related Provisions: 56(1)(h.2) — LLP — income inclusion; 128.1(4) — Ceasing residence in Canada.

Notes: See Notes at end of 146.02. The entire LLP balance is included in income for the year in which the taxpayer ceases to be resident in Canada; see VIEWS doc 2011-0426861I7.

(6) Death of individual — If an individual dies at any time in a taxation year, there shall be included in computing the individual's income for the year the amount, if any, by which

    (a) the individual's LLP balance immediately before that time

exceeds

    (b) the amount designated under subsection (3) by the individual for the year.

Related Provisions: 56(1)(h.2) — LLP — income inclusion; 70(5) — Effect of death; 146.01(7) — Optional transfer of repayment obligation to spouse.

(7) Exception — If a spouse or common-law partner of an individual was resident in Canada immediately before the individual's death at a particular time in a taxation year and the spouse or common-law partner and the individual's legal representatives jointly so elect in writing in the individual's return of income for the year,

    (a) subsection (6) does not apply to the individual;

    (b) the spouse or common-law partner is deemed to have received a particular eligible amount at the particular time equal to the amount that, but for this subsection, would be determined under subsection (6) in respect of the individual;

    (c) subject to paragraph (d), for the purpose of applying this section after the particular time, the spouse or common-law partner is deemed to be the person designated under paragraph (b) of the definition "eligible amount" in subsection (1) in respect of the particular amount; and

    (d) where the spouse or common-law partner received an eligible amount before the particular time in the spouse's or common-law partner's participation period that included the particular time and the particular individual designated under paragraph (b) of the definition "eligible amount" in subsection (1) in respect of that eligible amount was not the spouse or common-law partner, for the purpose of applying this section after the particular time the particular individual is deemed to be the person designated under that paragraph in respect of the particular amount.

Notes [subsec. 146.02(7)]: 146.02(7) amended by 2000 same-sex partners bill to refer to "common-law partner", effective as per Notes to 248(1)"common-law partner".

Notes [s. 146.02]: 146.02 added by 1998 Budget, effective 1999. The Lifelong Learning Plan (LLP) allows withdrawal of funds from an RRSP to fund education. As with the Home Buyers' Plan (HBP) in 146.01, the amounts borrowed must be repaid over a period of time, failing which they are included into income under 146.02(4). See Guide RC4112.

A taxpayer can repay an amount under the LLP and then withdraw the same amount under the HBP without waiting 90 days: VIEWS doc 2004-0075021E5.

In *Boily*, 2005 TCC 473, a taxpayer who failed to repay 1/10 of his LLP withdrawals in the first year repayment was due was taxed on the income inclusion.

For 2012, 15,000 taxpayers withdrew $97 million from RRSPs under the LLP, and total LLP repayable balances were $630 million. (*Access to Information Act* disclosure)

Definitions [s. 146.02]: "amount" — 248(1); "annuitant", "benefit" — 146(1), 146.01(1); "calendar year" — *Interpretation Act* 37(1)(a); "Canada" — 255, *Interpretation Act* 35(1); "common-law partner" — 248(1); "deferred profit sharing plan" — 147(1), 248(1); "eligible amount", "excluded premium", "excluded withdrawal", "full-time student" — 146.02(1); "individual", "legal representative" — 248(1); "LLP balance" — 146.02(1); "Minister" — 248(1); "month" — *Interpretation Act* 35(1); "participation period" — 146.02(1); "person" — 248(1); "premium" — 146(1), 146.02(1); "prescribed", "registered pension plan" — 248(1); "qualifying educational program" — 146.02(1); "registered retirement income fund" — 146.3(1), 248(1); "registered retirement savings plan" — 146(1), 248(1); "repayment period" — 146.02(1); "resident in Canada" — 250; "retirement savings plan" — 146(1), 248(1); "revocable" — 146.1(2.1); "taxation year" — 249; "written" — *Interpretation Act* 35(1)"writing".

Forms: RC96: LLP — request to withdraw funds from an RRSP; RC4112: Lifelong learning plan [guide].

Registered Education Savings Plans

146.1 (1) Definitions — In this section,

Related Provisions: 204.9(1.1) — Application of subsec. 146.1(1).

Notes: The opening words of 146.1(1) redrafted in RSC 1985 (5th Supp) consolidation for tax years ending after Nov. 1991. The former version made reference to Part X.4. That rule is now in 204.9(1.1).

"accumulated income payment" under an education savings plan means any amount paid out of the plan, other than a payment described in any of paragraphs (a) and (c) to (e) of the definition "trust", to the extent that the amount so paid exceeds the fair market value of any consideration given to the plan for the payment of the amount;

Related Provisions: 146.1(1.1), (1.2) — Rollover of AIP to RDSP for disabled person; 146.1(2)(d.1) — Limitations on AIPs; 146.1(7.1) — AIP included in recipient's income; 153(1)(t) — Withholding of tax at source from payments; 204.94 — Tax on AIPs not transferred to RRSP.

Notes: "Accumulated income payment" added by 1997 Budget, effective 1998. These payments are included in the recipient's income under 146.1(7.1) and are relevant for the special 20% tax in 204.94. The circumstances in which they can be made are limited by 146.1(2)(d.1).

Definition amended by 1998 Budget to change "(c), (d) and (e)" to "(c) to (e)" (i.e., effectively adding reference to (c.1)), effective 1998.

Regulations: 103(4), 103(6)(g), 103(8) (withholding at source); 200(2)(j) (information return).

"beneficiary", in respect of an education savings plan, means a person, designated by a subscriber, to whom or on whose behalf an educational assistance payment under the plan is agreed to be paid if the person qualifies under the plan;

Related Provisions: 146.1(2)(j) — Restrictions on who can be beneficiaries.

Notes: 146.1(1)"beneficiary" was 146.1(1)(a) before RSC 1985 (5th Supp) consolidation for tax years ending after Nov. 1991.

"contribution" to an education savings plan does not include an amount paid into the plan under or because of

    (a) the *Canada Education Savings Act* or a designated provincial program, or

    (b) any other program that has a similar purpose to a designated provincial program and that is funded, directly or indirectly, by a province (other than an amount paid into the plan by a public primary caregiver in its capacity as subscriber under the plan);

Related Provisions: 146.1(14)(a) — Reference to *Canada Education Savings Act* includes reference to earlier *DHRD Act*.

Notes: For the *Canada Education Savings Act*, see Notes at end of 146.1. For the meaning of "indirectly" in para. (b), see Notes to 17.1(1).

Definition amended by 2010 budget bill #1 (for 2009 and later tax years), 2007 budget bill #2, 2004 RESPs bill. Added by 1998 budget bill #1.

RESP Bulletins: 1R1 (designated provincial program).

"designated provincial program" means

    (a) a program administered pursuant to an agreement entered into under section 12 of the *Canada Education Savings Act*, or

    (b) a program established under the laws of a province to encourage the financing of children's post-secondary education through savings in registered education savings plans.

Notes: Para. (b) changed from "a prescribed program" by 2010 budget bill #1, effective for 2007 and later taxation years.

146.1(1)"designated provincial program" added by 2007 budget bill #2, effective for 2007 and later taxation years. It implements a March 2007 Budget proposal to accommodate Quebec education savings grants.

Regulations: No prescribed programs as yet. The Dept. of Finance Technical Notes of Oct. 2, 2007 state: "It is intended that the education savings incentive program proposed by the Government of Quebec in its 2007 budget be prescribed for this purpose".

"education savings plan" means an arrangement entered into between

    (a) any of the following, namely,

        (i) an individual (other than a trust),

        (ii) an individual (other than a trust) and the spouse or common-law partner of the individual, and

        (iii) a public primary caregiver of a beneficiary, and

    (b) a person (in this definition referred to as the "promoter")

under which the promoter agrees to pay or to cause to be paid educational assistance payments to or for one or more beneficiaries;

Related Provisions: 146.2(12) — TFSA deemed not to be ESP.

Notes: Para. (b) changed from "a person or organization (in this section referred to as a "promoter")", by 2017 budget bill #2, effective March 23, 2017.

Opening words and para. (a) of definition amended by 2004 RESPs bill, effective December 15, 2004. The change from "contract" to "arrangement" allows a trust to be a RESP, as announced by Finance news release July 20, 1999.

146.1(1)"education savings plan" amended by 2000 same-sex partners bill to refer to "common-law partner", effective as per Notes to 248(1)"common-law partner".

"Education savings plan" amended by 1997 Budget, effective for contracts made in 1998 or later. For contracts made from 1972-97, read:

    "education savings plan" means a contract entered into at any time between an individual (in this section referred to as a "subscriber") and a person or organization (in this section referred to as a "promoter") under which, in consideration of payment by the subscriber of any periodic or other amount as consideration under the contract, the promoter agrees to pay or to cause to be paid to or for a beneficiary educational assistance payments;

146.1(1)"education savings plan" was 146.1(1)(c) before RSC 1985 (5th Supp) consolidation for tax years ending after Nov. 1991.

"educational assistance payment" means any amount, other than a refund of payments, paid out of an education savings plan to or for an individual to assist the individual to further the individual's education at a post-secondary school level;

Related Provisions: 56(1)(q), 146.1(7) — EAPs included in income; 146.1(2)(g.1), 204.9(1) — Limitations on EAPs; 146.1(2.21), (2.22) — EAP can be made up to 6 months after ceasing to be student; 212(1)(r) — Non-resident withholding tax on EAPs.

Notes: See Notes at end of 146.1.

The tests of being enrolled in a qualifying educational program (146.1(2)(g.1)) and the EAP being paid to further the person's education must be met each time an EAP is paid: VIEWS doc 2004-0092341E5. However, CRA accepts up to $24,432 (2020), $24,676 (2021, adjusted annually) of expenses as legitimate without needing to assess reasonableness: RESP Bulletin 1R1. The $5,000 limit for the first 13 consecutive weeks on enrolment in the previous 12-month period remains (146.1(2)(g.1)).

For the meaning of "post-secondary", see Notes to 118.5(1)(a).

An EAP may be paid in a foreign currency: VIEWS doc 2004-0098421M4. A payment in respect of past educational expenses would not qualify: 2007-0262171E5, but see now 146.1(2.21)–(2.22).

Definition amended by 1997 Budget, effective 1998. 146.1(1)"educational assistance payment" was 146.1(1)(b) before RSC 1985 (5th Supp) consolidation for tax years ending after Nov. 1991.

Regulations: 200(2)(j) (information return).

RESP Bulletins: 1R1 (amount of EAP accepted administratively as legitimate).

"post-secondary educational institution" means

    (a) an educational institution in Canada that is described in paragraph (a) of the definition "designated educational institution" in subsection 118.6(1), or

    (b) an educational institution outside Canada that provides courses at a post-secondary school level and that is

        (i) a university, college or other educational institution at which a beneficiary was enrolled in a course of not less than 13 consecutive weeks, or

        (ii) a university at which a beneficiary was enrolled on a full-time basis in a course of not less than three consecutive weeks;

Notes: For the meaning of "post-secondary", see Notes to 118.5(1)(a). An institution need not be listed in the current edition of the American Council on Education's *Accredited Institutions of Postsecondary Education* to qualify: VIEWS docs 2005-0135321C6, 2005-0135911E5.

Para. (b) amended by 2011 budget bill #2, effective for educational assistance payments made after 2010, effectively to add subpara. (ii).

146.1(1)"post-secondary education institution" (formerly para. 146.1(1)(c.1) before RSC 1985 (5th Supp) consolidation) added to subsec. 146.1(1) by 1990 Budget, effective February 21, 1990.

"post-secondary school level" includes a program of courses, at an institution described in subparagraph (a)(ii) of the definition "designated educational institution" in subsection 118.6(1), of a technical or vocational nature designed to furnish a person with skills for, or improve a person's skills in, an occupation;

Notes: This definition does not apply to other sections where the term is used, such as 94, 115, 118.5, 118.6, 118.62 and 146.02.

Definition "post-secondary school level" added by 2004 Budget, effective 2004.

"pre-1972 income" — [Repealed]

Notes: "Pre-1972 income" repealed by 1997 Budget, effective 1998, in conjunction with the repeal of 146.1(8)–(10).

"promoter", of an arrangement, means the person described as the promoter in the definition "education savings plan";

Notes: "Promoter" added by 2017 budget bill #2, effective March 23, 2017. This term was previously defined in 146.1(1)"education savings plan"(b) for all of 146.1.

"public primary caregiver", of a beneficiary under an education savings plan in respect of whom a special allowance is payable under the *Children's Special Allowances Act*, means the department, agency or institution that maintains the beneficiary or the public trustee or public curator of the province in which the beneficiary resides;

Related Provisions: 204.94(2) — Whether public primary caregiver exempt from Part X.5 tax.

Notes: "Public primary caregiver" added by 2004 RESPs bill, effective Dec. 15, 2004.

"qualified investment" for a trust governed by a registered education savings plan means

(a) an investment that would be described by any of paragraphs (a) to (d), (f) and (g) of the definition "qualified investment" in section 204 if the reference in that definition to "a trust governed by a deferred profit sharing plan or revoked plan" were read as a reference to "a trust governed by a registered education savings plan" and if that definition were read without reference to the words "with the exception of excluded property in relation to the trust",

(b) [Repealed]

(c) a contract for an annuity issued by a licensed annuities provider where

(i) the trust is the only person who, disregarding any subsequent transfer of the contract by the trust, is or may become entitled to any annuity payments under the contract, and

(ii) the holder of the contract has a right to surrender the contract at any time for an amount that would, if reasonable sales and administration charges were ignored, approximate the value of funds that could otherwise be applied to fund future periodic payments under the contract,

(d) an investment that was acquired by the trust before October 28, 1998, and

(e) a prescribed investment;

Related Provisions: 87(10) — New share issued on amalgamation of public corporation deemed listed; 132.2(3)(h) — Where share ceases to be QI due to mutual fund reorganization; 146.1(2.1)(a) — Acquisition of non-QI makes plan revocable; 207.01(6) — Deemed disposition by RESP on property becoming or ceasing to be QI; 207.04 — Tax payable by annuitant if RESP acquires non-QI; 207.1(3) — Tax payable by RESP on holding non-QI [until 2017].

Notes: See Notes to 146(1)"qualified investment".

Paras. (a) and (b) replaced with (a) by 2007 budget bill #1, effective in determining whether a property is, at any time after March 18, 2007, a qualified investment (QI). Along with amendments to 204"qualified investment", the effect is to broaden and simplify the categories of QI.

Regulations: 221 (information return where mutual fund etc. claims its shares are QI); 222 (information return where RESP acquires or disposes of non-QI, or QI status changes); 4900 (prescribed investments).

Income Tax Folios: S3-F10-C1: Qualified investments — RRSPs, RESPs, RRIFs, RDSPs and TFSAs [replaces IT-320R3].

"qualifying educational program" means a program at a post-secondary school level of not less than three consecutive weeks duration that requires that each student taking the program spend not less than ten hours per week on courses or work in the program;

Notes: A flight training program may now qualify: VIEWS doc 2007-0252741E5.

Definition amended by 2004 Budget, effective 2004, effectively to remove the application of former para. (b) of 118.6(1)"qualifying educational program", so that education related to the individual's current employment is not excluded for RESP purposes.

Definition amended by 1996 Budget, for 1996 and later taxation years, to add exclusion of para. (a) of the definition in 118.6(1). Thus, the condition that a student not receive certain benefits, allowances, grants or reimbursements does not apply. As a result, payments may be made out of a RESP to a student who is in receipt of other benefits.

146.1(1)"qualifying educational program" (formerly 146.1(1)(d.1) before RSC 1985 (5th Supp) consolidation) added by 1990 Budget, effective February 21, 1990.

["RESP"] — [See "registered education savings plan" below.]

"RESP annual limit" — [Repealed]

Related Provisions: 146.1(2)(k) — Contributions not to exceed RESP annual limit; 204.9"excess amount"(a) — Penalty tax on exceeding RESP annual limit.

Notes: "RESP annual limit" added by 1997 Budget effective 1990, and repealed by 2007 budget bill #1 effective for contributions made after 2006. It limited the maximum annual contributions to a RESP per beneficiary (146.1(2)(k), 204.9(1)"excess amount"(a)). There is now only a $50,000 lifetime limit and no annual limit.

"refund of payments" at any time under a particular registered education savings plan means

(a) a refund at that time of a contribution that had been made at a previous time, if the contribution was made

(i) otherwise than by way of a transfer from another registered education savings plan, and

(ii) into the particular plan by or on behalf of a subscriber under the particular plan, or

(b) a refund at that time of an amount that was paid at a previous time into the particular plan by way of a transfer from another registered education savings plan, where the amount would have been a refund of payments under the other plan if it had been paid at the previous time directly to a subscriber under the other plan;

Notes: "Refund of payments" amended by 1997 Budget, for 1997 and later tax years.

146.1(1)"refund of payments" was 146.1(1)(e) before RSC 1985 (5th Supp) consolidation for tax years ending after Nov. 1991.

"registered education savings plan" or "RESP" means

(a) an education savings plan registered for the purposes of this Act, or

(b) a registered education savings plan as it is amended from time to time

but, except for the purposes of subsections (7) and (7.1) and Part X.4, a plan ceases to be a registered education savings plan immediately after the day as of which its registration is revoked under subsection (13);

Related Provisions: 75(3)(a) — Reversionary trust rules do not apply to RESP; 108(1)"trust"(a) — "Trust" does not include a RESP for certain purposes; 128.1(10)"excluded right or interest"(a)(iii) — No deemed disposition of RESP on emigration; 207.04 — Tax on subscriber if RESP acquires non-qualified or prohibited investment; 207.05 — Tax on advantage received from RESP; 248(1)"disposition"(f)(vi) — Rollover from one trust to another; 248(1)"registered education savings plan" — Definition applies to entire Act; Reg. 9006(f) — RESP not reported to CRA for disclosure to foreign tax authorities.

Notes: See Notes at end of 146.1.

"RESP" acronym added by 2012 budget bill #2, effective Dec. 14, 2012.

Definition amended by 1997 Budget, effective 1998. 146.1(1)"registered education savings plan" was 146.1(1)(f) before RSC 1985 (5th Supp) consolidation for tax years ending after Nov. 1991.

Information Circulars: 93-3R1: Registered education savings plans.

"specified educational program" means a program at a post-secondary school level of not less than three consecutive weeks duration that requires each student taking the program to spend not less than 12 hours per month on courses in the program;

Notes: Definition "specified educational program" added by 2007 budget bill #1, effective for 2007 and later taxation years. See 146.1(2)(g.1)(i)(B).

"specified plan" means an education savings plan

(a) that does not allow more than one beneficiary under the plan at any one time,

(b) under which the beneficiary is an individual in respect of whom paragraphs 118.3(1)(a) to (b) apply for the beneficiary's taxation year that ends in the 31st year following the year in which the plan was entered into, and

(c) that provides that, at all times after the end of the 35th year following the year in which the plan was entered into, no other individual may be designated as a beneficiary under the plan;

Notes: This refers to a RESP for a disabled person. It is used in 146.1(2)(h)(i), (2)(i)(i) and (6.1)(b).

Paras. (b) and (c) amended by 2008 budget bill #1 to change "21st" to "31st" and "25th" to "35th", effective for 2008 and later taxation years. "Specified plan" added by 2005 budget bill #1, effective for 2005 and later taxation years.

"subscriber" under an education savings plan at any time means

(a) each individual or the public primary caregiver with whom the promoter of the plan enters into the plan,

(a.1) another individual or another public primary caregiver who has before that time, under a written agreement, acquired a public primary caregiver's rights as a subscriber under the plan,

(b) an individual who has before that time acquired a subscriber's rights under the plan pursuant to a decree, order or judgment of a competent tribunal, or under a written agreement, relating to a division of property between the individual and a subscriber under the plan in settlement of rights arising out of, or on the breakdown of, their marriage or common-law partnership, or

(c) after the death of an individual described in any of paragraphs (a) to (b), any other person (including the estate of the deceased individual) who acquires the individual's rights as a subscriber under the plan or who makes contributions into the plan in respect of a beneficiary

but does not include an individual or a public primary caregiver whose rights as a subscriber under the plan had, before that time, been acquired by an individual or public primary caregiver in the circumstances described in paragraph (a.1) or (b);

Related Provisions: 207.04 — Tax on subscriber if RESP acquires prohibited or non-qualified investment.

Notes: The subscriber cannot be an incorporated charity (unless it is a 146.1(1)"public primary caregiver"): VIEWS doc 2019-0832221E5.

On the subscriber's death, a testamentary trust can become the "subscriber": VIEWS doc 2005-0118891E5; and see Cole Southall, "Continuing RESPs Beyond the Death of the Subscriber", 8(1) *Canadian Tax Focus* (ctf.ca) 13-14 (Feb. 2018). There can be more than one subscriber: 2006-0169821E5.

One can effectively change subscribers by transferring the assets to a new RESP; see Notes to 146.1(2).

Definition "subscriber" amended by 2004 RESPs bill (effective Dec. 15, 2004), 2000 same-sex partners bill. Added by 1997 Budget, for contracts made in 1998 or later.

"tax-paid-income" — [Repealed]

Notes: "Tax-paid income" repealed by 1997 Budget, effective 1998, in conjunction with the repeal of 146.1(8)–(10). This was 146.1(1)(g) before RSC 1985 (5th Supp) consolidation for tax years ending after Nov. 1991.

"trust", except in this definition and the definition "education savings plan", means any person who irrevocably holds property under an education savings plan for any of, or any combination of, the following purposes:

(a) the payment of educational assistance payments,

(b) the payment after 1997 of accumulated income payments,

(c) the refund of payments,

(c.1) the repayment of amounts (and the payment of amounts related to that repayment) under the *Canada Education Savings Act* or under a designated provincial program,

(d) the payment to, or to a trust in favour of, designated educational institutions in Canada referred to in subparagraph (a)(i) of the definition of that expression in subsection 118.6(1), or

(e) the payment to a trust that irrevocably holds property pursuant to a registered education savings plan for any of the purposes set out in paragraphs (a) to (d).

Related Provisions: 104(1) — Reference to trust or estate; 108(1)"trust"(a) — "Trust" does not include a RESP for certain purposes; 146.1(14)(a) — Reference to *Canada Education Savings Act* includes reference to earlier *DHRD Act*.

Notes: For interpretation of this definition see VIEWS doc 2006-0216851E5.

Definition amended by 2007 budget bill #2 (for 2007 and later tax years), 2004 RESPs bill, 1998 and 1997 Budgets, 1991 technical bill. 146.1(1)"trust" was 146.1(1)(h) before RSC 1985 (5th Supp) consolidation for tax years ending after Nov. 1991.

RESP Bulletins: 1R1 (designated provincial program).

(1.1) Election — A subscriber under an RESP that allows accumulated income payments and a holder of an RDSP may jointly elect in prescribed form to have subsection (1.2) apply in respect of a beneficiary under the RESP if, at the time the election is made, the beneficiary is also the beneficiary under the RDSP and

(a) the beneficiary has a severe and prolonged mental impairment that prevents, or can reasonably be expected to prevent, the beneficiary from enrolling in a qualifying educational program at a post-secondary educational institution; or

(b) the RESP meets the conditions described in clause (2)(d.1)(iii)(A) or (B) to make an accumulated income payment.

Notes: See 146.1(1.2) Notes. 146.1(1.1) added by 2012 budget bill #2, effective 2014.

Forms: RC435: Rollover from a RESP to a RDSP.

(1.2) Effect of election — If an election is made under subsection (1.1) and is filed by the promoter of the RESP with the Minister without delay, then notwithstanding paragraph (2)(d.1) and any terms of the RESP required by that paragraph, an accumulated income payment under the RESP may be made to the RDSP.

Related Provisions: 146.1(7.1)(a) — AIP under (1.2) not included in recipient's income.

Notes: Although 146.1(1.2) says the form should be "filed with the Minister without delay", the instructions on Form RC435 say the form should be kept on file and not sent to CRA. Such waiver of filing is allowed by 220(2.1). However, for a person filing a Quebec return, *Taxation Act* ss. 894.1 and 21.4.6 say the form must be sent to Revenu Québec.

146.1(1.2) allows a rollover of RESP investment income to an RDSP. Added by 2012 budget bill #2, effective 2014.

(2) Conditions for registration — The Minister shall not accept for registration for the purposes of this Act any education savings plan of a promoter unless, in the Minister's opinion, the following conditions are complied with:

(a) the plan provides that the property of any trust governed by the plan (after the payment of trustee and administration charges) is irrevocably held for any of the purposes described in the definition "trust" in subsection (1) by a corporation licensed or otherwise authorized under the laws of Canada or a province to carry on in Canada the business of offering to the public its services as a trustee;

(b) at the time of the application by the promoter for registration of the plan, there are not fewer than 150 plans entered into with the promoter each of which complied, at the time it was entered into, with all the other conditions set out in this subsection, as it read at that time;

(b.1) application for registration of the plan is made by the promoter in prescribed form containing prescribed information;

(c) the promoter and all trusts governed by the plan are resident in Canada;

(d) the plan does not allow for any payment before 1998 to a subscriber, other than a refund of payments, unless the subscriber is also the beneficiary under the plan;

(d.1) subject to subsection (2.2), if the plan allows accumulated income payments, the plan provides that an accumulated income payment is permitted to be made only if

(i) the payment is made to, or on behalf of, a subscriber under the plan who is resident in Canada when the payment is made,

(ii) the payment is not made jointly to, or on behalf of, more than one subscriber, and

(iii) any of

(A) the payment is made after the 9th year that follows the year in which the plan was entered into and each individual (other than a deceased individual) who is or was a beneficiary under the plan has attained 21 years of age before the payment is made and is not, when the payment is made, eligible under the plan to receive an educational assistance payment,

(B) the payment is made in the year in which the plan is required to be terminated in accordance with paragraph (i), or

(C) each individual who was a beneficiary under the plan is deceased when the payment is made;

(e) the plan is substantially similar to the type of plan described in or annexed to a prospectus filed by the promoter with a securities commission in Canada or a body performing a similar function in a province;

(f) in the event that a trust governed by the plan is terminated, the property held by the trust is required to be used for any of the purposes described in the definition "trust" in subsection (1);

(g) the plan does not allow for the payment of educational assistance payments before 1997 to an individual unless the individual is, at the time the payment is made, a student in full-time attendance at a post-secondary educational institution and enrolled in a qualifying educational program at the institution;

(g.1) the plan does not allow for the payment of an educational assistance payment to or for an individual at any time after 1996 unless

(i) either

(A) the individual is, at that time, enrolled as a student in a qualifying educational program at a post-secondary educational institution, or

(B) the individual has, before that time, attained the age of 16 years and is, at that time, enrolled as a student in a specified educational program at a post-secondary educational institution, and

(ii) either

(A) the individual satisfies, at that time, the condition set out in clause (i)(A), and

(I) has satisfied that condition throughout at least 13 consecutive weeks in the 12-month period that ends at that time, or

(II) the total of the payment and all other educational assistance payments made under a registered education savings plan of the promoter to or for the individual in the 12-month period that ends at that time does not exceed $5,000 or any greater amount that the Minister designated for the purpose of the *Canada Education Savings Act* approves in writing with respect to the individual, or

(B) the individual satisfies, at that time, the condition set out in clause (i)(B) and the total of the payment and all other educational assistance payments made under a registered education savings plan of the promoter to or for the individual in the 13-week period that ends at that time does not exceed $2,500 or any greater amount that the Minister designated for the purpose of the *Canada Education Savings Act* approves in writing with respect to the individual;

(g.2) the plan does not allow for any contribution into the plan, other than a contribution made by or on behalf of a subscriber under the plan in respect of a beneficiary under the plan or a contribution made by way of transfer from another registered education savings plan;

(g.3) the plan provides that an individual is permitted to be designated as a beneficiary under the plan, and that a contribution to the plan in respect of an individual who is a beneficiary under the plan is permitted to be made, only if

(i) in the case of a designation, the individual's Social Insurance Number is provided to the promoter before the designation is made and either

(A) the individual is resident in Canada when the designation is made, or

(B) the designation is made in conjunction with a transfer of property into the plan from another registered education savings plan under which the individual was a beneficiary immediately before the transfer, and

(ii) in the case of a contribution, either

(A) the individual's Social Insurance Number is provided to the promoter before the contribution is made and the individual is resident in Canada when the contribution is made, or

(B) the contribution is made by way of transfer from another registered education savings plan under which the individual was a beneficiary immediately before the transfer;

(h) the plan provides that no contribution (other than a contribution made by way of a transfer from another registered education savings plan) may be made into the plan after

(i) in the case of a specified plan, the 35th year following the year in which the plan was entered into, and

(ii) in any other case, the 31st year following the year in which the plan was entered into;

(i) the plan provides that it must be terminated on or before the last day of

(i) in the case of a specified plan, the 40th year following the year in which the plan was entered into, and

(ii) in any other case, the 35th year following the year in which the plan was entered into;

(i.1) if the plan allows accumulated income payments, the plan provides that it must be terminated before March of the year following the year in which the first such payment is made out of the plan;

(i.2) the plan does not allow for the receipt of property by way of direct transfer from another registered education savings plan after the other plan has made any accumulated income payment;

(j) if the plan allows more than one beneficiary under the plan at any one time, the plan provides

(i) that each of the beneficiaries under the plan is required to be connected to each living subscriber under the plan, or to have been connected to a deceased original subscriber under the plan, by blood relationship or adoption,

(ii) that a contribution into the plan in respect of a beneficiary is permitted to be made only if

(A) the beneficiary had not attained 31 years of age before the time of the contribution, or

(B) the contribution is made by way of transfer from another registered education savings plan that allows more than one beneficiary at any one time, and

(iii) that an individual is permitted to become a beneficiary under the plan at any particular time only if

(A) the individual had not attained 21 years of age before the particular time, or

(B) the individual was, immediately before the particular time, a beneficiary under another registered education savings plan that allows more than one beneficiary at any one time;

(k) [Repealed]

(l) the plan provides that the promoter shall, within 90 days after an individual becomes a beneficiary under the plan, notify the individual (or, where the individual is under 19 years of age at that time and either ordinarily resides with a parent of the individual or is maintained by a public primary caregiver of the individual, that parent or public primary caregiver) in writing of the existence of the plan and the name and address of the subscriber in respect of the plan;

(m) the Minister has no reasonable basis to believe that the promoter will not take all reasonable measures to ensure that the plan will continue to comply with the conditions set out in paragraphs (a), (c) to (d.1) and (f) to (l) for its registration for the purposes of this Act; and

(n) the Minister has no reasonable basis to believe that the plan will become revocable.

Related Provisions: 146.1(1.1), (1.2) — Rollover of accumulated income payment to RDSP; 146.1(2.1) — RESP becoming revocable; 146.1(2.2) — Waiver of conditions for disabled beneficiary; 146.1(2.21), (2.22) — EAP can be made up to 6 months after ceasing to be student; 146.1(2.3) — Circumstances where Social Insurance Number not required; 146.1(3) — Deemed registration; 146.1(4) — Registration of plan without prospectus; 146.1(4.1) — Amendments must be filed with CRA; 146.1(13) — Revocation where plan ceases to comply with requirements; 146.1(14) — References to *Canada Education Savings Act* includes references to earlier *DHRD Act*; 172(3) — Appeal from refusal to register; 204.9(1)"excess amount" — Limit on RESP contributions; 204.9(5)(c) — RESP asset sharing among siblings; 204.91 — Tax payable by subscribers; 207.04 — Tax on subscriber if RESP acquires non-qualified or prohibited investment; 207.05 — Tax on advantage received from RESP; 248(3)(c) — RESP set up in Quebec deemed to be trust; Reg. 9006(f) — RESP not reported to CRA for disclosure to foreign tax authorities; *Interpretation Act* 27(5) — Meaning of "within 90 days".

Notes: See Notes at end of 146.1 and to 146.1(1)"educational assistance payment" and (5). If a promoter does not comply with 146.1(2)(b), see VIEWS doc 2007-0257611E5.

CRA's processing target (tinyurl.com/cra-standards) for responding to RESP applications (to register, amend or terminate) is 90% within 60 days; in 2019-20, it did 100%.

Ontario birth registration now includes information for parents about opening a RESP.

A transfer from one plan to another with the same beneficiary is permitted, as a way of changing subscribers (146.1(6.1) will apply): VIEWS doc 2019-0812841C6 [2019 APFF Financial q.10].

146.1(2)(g.3): See 146.1(2.3) for cases where the SIN is not required.

146.1(2) amended by 2002-2013 technical bill (effective 2004), 2012 budget bill #2 (last change effective 2014), 2008, 2007 and 2005 budget bills #1, 2004 RESPs bill, 1998 Budget (for plans entered into after 1998 or after Feb. 20, 1990), 1997 Budget (for applications made after 1997 or plans entered into after Feb. 20, 1990), 1990 Budget/1991 technical bill.

Proposed **146.1(2.01)**, in private member's Bill C-253 (2008), proposed a deduction for RESP contributions. See 60(i) Notes.

Regulations: No prescribed conditions for 146.1(2)(m).

I.T. Application Rules: 69 (meaning of "chapter 148 of ...").

Information Circulars: 93-3R1: Registered education savings plans.

Registered Plans Compliance Bulletins: 1 (educational assistance payments (EAP) and RESP contributions); 8 (prescribed information to register an education savings plan).

RESP Bulletins: 1R1 (amount of EAP accepted administratively as legitimate).

Forms: T3GR: Group income tax and information return for RRSP, RRIF, RESP, or RDSP trusts (and worksheets); T550: Application for registration of RSPs, ESPs or RIFs under s. 146, 146.1 and 146.3 of the ITA; T1171: Tax withholding waiver on accumulated income payments from RESPs; T1172: Additional tax on accumulated income payments from RESPs.

(2.1) RESP is revocable — For the purposes of paragraphs (2)(n) and (12.1)(d), a registered education savings plan is revocable at any time after October 27, 1998 at which

(a) [Repealed]

(b) [Repealed]

(c) a trust governed by the plan begins carrying on a business; or

(d) a trustee that holds property in connection with the plan borrows money for the purposes of the plan, except where

(i) the money is borrowed for a term not exceeding 90 days,

(ii) the money is not borrowed as part of a series of loans or other transactions and repayments, and

(iii) none of the property of the trust is used as security for the borrowed money.

Related Provisions: 146.1(12.1) — Notice of intent to revoke registration; 146.1(12.2), (13) — Revocation of registration; 248(10) — Series of transactions;

253.1(1) — Limited partner not considered to carry on partnership business; 259(1) — Election for proportional holdings in trust property.

Notes: 146.1(2.1)(a) and (b) repealed by 2017 budget bill #2, effective for any investment acquired after March 22, 2017 and any investment acquired earlier that ceases to be a 146.1(2)"qualified investment" after that date. (The rules in 207.01-207.07 now apply to RESPs.) It read:

> (a) a trust governed by the plan acquires property that is not a qualified investment for the trust;
>
> (b) property held by a trust governed by the plan ceases to be a qualified investment for the trust and the property is not disposed of by the trust within 60 days after that time;

146.1(2.1) added by 1998 Budget, effective 1998.

Income Tax Folios: S3-F10-C1: Qualified investments — RRSPs, RESPs, RRIFs, RDSPs and TFSAs [replaces IT-320R3].

(2.2) Waiver of conditions for accumulated income payments — The Minister may, on written application of the promoter of a registered education savings plan, waive the application of the conditions in clause (2)(d.1)(iii)(A) in respect of the plan where a beneficiary under the plan suffers from a severe and prolonged mental impairment that prevents, or can reasonably be expected to prevent, the beneficiary from enrolling in a qualifying educational program at a post-secondary educational institution.

Notes: 146.1(2.2) added by 1998 Budget, effective 1998.

(2.21) Extension for making educational assistance payments — Notwithstanding paragraph (2)(g.1), an education savings plan may allow for the payment of an educational assistance payment to or for an individual at any time in the six-month period immediately following the particular time at which the individual ceases to be enrolled as a student in a qualifying educational program or a specified educational program, as the case may be, if the payment would have complied with the requirements of paragraph (2)(g.1) had the payment been made immediately before the particular time.

Related Provisions: 146.1(2.22) — Timing of payment.

Notes: 146.1(2.21) cannot apply after the taxpayer's death: VIEWS doc 2014-0527981I7.

146.1(2.21) added by 2008 budget bill #1, effective for 2008 and later taxation years, except in respect of cessations of enrolment that occur before 2008. It allows a six-month grace period for receiving EAPs.

(2.22) Timing of payment — An educational assistance payment that is made at any time in accordance with subsection (2.21) but not in accordance with paragraph (2)(g.1) is deemed, for the purposes of applying that paragraph at and after that time, to have been made immediately before the particular time referred to in subsection (2.21).

Notes: 146.1(2.22) added by 2008 budget bill #1, effective on the same basis as new 146.1(2.21).

(2.3) Social Insurance Number not required — Notwithstanding paragraph (2)(g.3), an education savings plan may provide that an individual's Social Insurance Number need not be provided in respect of

(a) a contribution to the plan, if the plan was entered into before 1999; and

(b) a designation of a non-resident individual as a beneficiary under the plan, if the individual was not assigned a Social Insurance Number before the designation is made.

Notes: 146.1(2.3) added by 2002-2013 technical bill (Part 5 — technical), effective 2004.

(3) Deemed registration — Where in any year an education savings plan cannot be accepted for registration solely because the condition set out in paragraph (2)(b) has not been complied with, if the plan is subsequently registered, it shall be deemed to have been registered on the first day of January of

(a) the year in which all of the conditions set out in subsection (2) (except in paragraph (2)(b)) were complied with, or

(b) the year preceding the year in which the plan was subsequently registered, whichever is the later.

Related Provisions: 146.1(12) — Deemed date of registration; 212(1)(r) — Non-residents — registered education savings plan.

Information Circulars: 93-3R1: Registered education savings plans.

(4) Registration of plans without prospectus — Notwithstanding paragraph (2)(e), where a promoter has not filed a prospectus in respect of an education savings plan referred to in that paragraph, the Minister may register the plan if the promoter is not otherwise required by the laws of Canada or a province to file such a prospectus with a securities commission in Canada or a body performing a similar function in a province and the plan complies with the other conditions set out in subsection (2).

Notes: 146.1(4) amended by 1990 Budget, for plans registered after Feb. 20, 1990.

(4.1) Obligation to file amendment — When a registered education savings plan is amended, the promoter shall file the text of the amendment with the Minister not later than 60 days after the day on which the plan is amended.

Related Provisions: 162(7) — Penalty for failure to comply.

Notes: 146.1(4.1) added by 1997 Budget, effective June 18, 1998.

(5) Trust not taxable — No tax is payable under this Part by a trust that is governed by a RESP on its taxable income for a taxation year, except that, if at any time in the taxation year, it holds one or more properties that are not qualified investments for the trust, tax is payable under this Part by the trust on the amount that would be its taxable income for the taxation year if it had no income or losses from sources other than those properties, and no capital gains or capital losses other than from dispositions of those properties, and for that purpose,

  (a) income includes dividends described in section 83;

  (b) the trust's taxable capital gain or allowable capital loss from the disposition of a property is equal to its capital gain or capital loss, as the case may be, from the disposition; and

  (c) the trust's income shall be computed without reference to subsection 104(6).

Related Provisions: 146.1(1.1), (1.2) — Rollover of accumulated income payment to RDSP; 18(11)(h) — No deduction for interest paid on money borrowed to make RESP contribution; 149(1)(u) — Exemption from tax; 207.04 — Tax on subscriber if RESP acquires non-qualified or prohibited investment; 207.05 — Tax on advantage received from RESP.

Notes: A RESP can be seized by the subscriber's creditors, even if the funds in it came from Child Tax Benefit payments: *Mackinnon*, 2007 SKQB 39. In *Payne*, 2001 ABQB 894, RESPs were held not to be property held by a bankrupt in trust for another person; the RESP funds were part of the bankrupt's estate, available to all creditors. However, in *Vienneau*, 2007 NBQB 332, RESPs were ordered returned to the bankrupts because the trustee had disclaimed any interest in them. See also Notes to 146(4).

146.1(5) amended by 2017 budget bill #2, effective on the same basis as the repeal of 146.1(2.1)(a), (b). Previously read:

> (5) No tax is payable under this Part by a trust on the taxable income of the trust for a taxation year if, throughout the period in the year during which the trust was in existence, the trust was governed by a registered education savings plan.

(6) Subscriber not taxable — No tax is payable by a subscriber on the income of a trust for a taxation year after 1971 throughout which the trust was governed by a registered education savings plan.

Related Provisions: 146.1(5) — Trust not taxable; 204.91 — Tax payable by subscribers; 212(1)(r) — Non-residents — registered education savings plan.

(6.1) Transfers between plans — Where property irrevocably held by a trust governed by a registered education savings plan (in this subsection referred to as the "transferor plan") is transferred to a trust governed by another registered education savings plan (in this subsection referred to as the "transferee plan"),

  (a) [Repealed]

  (b) for the purposes of this paragraph, the definition "specified plan" in subsection (1) and paragraphs (2)(d.1), (h) and (i), the transferee plan is deemed to have been entered into on the day that is the earlier of

    (i) the day on which the transferee plan was entered into, and

    (ii) the day on which the transferor plan was entered into; and

  (c) notwithstanding subsections (7) and (7.1), no amount shall be included in computing the income of any person because of the transfer.

Related Provisions: 146.1(2)(g.2), (i.2) — Restrictions on transfers between RESPs; 204.9(5) — Transfers between RESPs.

Notes: 146.1(6.1) amended by 2005 budget bill #1 (for 2005 and later tax years), 2004 RESPs bill, 1997 Budget. Added by 1990 Budget/1991 technical bill.

Information Circulars: 93-3R1: Registered education savings plans.

(7) Educational assistance payments — There shall be included in computing an individual's income for a taxation year the total of all educational assistance payments paid out of registered education savings plans to or for the individual in the year that exceeds the total of all excluded amounts in respect of those plans and the individual for the year.

Related Provisions: 56(1)(q) — Income inclusion from RESP; 60(x) — Deduction for repayment of Canada Education Savings Grant; 146.1(2.21), (2.22) — EAP can be made up to 6 months after ceasing to be student; 153(1)(t) — Withholding of tax at source; 212(1)(r) — Withholding tax on RESP payments to non-residents.

Notes: 146.1(7) amended by 2017 budget bill #2, effective March 23, 2017, to add "that exceeds the total of all excluded amounts ... for the year". (See 146.1(7.2).)

146.1(7) amended by 1997 Budget, effective for 1998 and later taxation years.

Regulations: 200(2)(j) (information return).

Information Circulars: 93-3R1: Registered education savings plans.

RESP Bulletins: 1R1 (amount of EAP accepted administratively as legitimate).

Forms: T1 General return, Line 13000 [former 130]: Other income.

(7.1) Other income inclusions — There shall be included in computing a taxpayer's income for a taxation year

  (a) each accumulated income payment (other than an accumulated income payment made under subsection (1.2)) received in the year by the taxpayer under a registered education savings plan that exceeds the total of all excluded amounts in respect of those plans and the individual for the year; and

  (b) each amount received in the year by the taxpayer in full or partial satisfaction of a subscriber's interest under a registered education savings plan (other than any excluded amount in respect of the plan).

Related Provisions: 146.1(7.2) — Excluded amount; 153(1)(t) — Withholding of tax at source.

Notes: 146.1(7.1) requires accumulated income payments received from an RESP to be included in income for the year. In order to discourage trading of RESP interests, it also requires inclusion of any amounts received from the disposition of a subscriber's interest under an RESP, other than amounts excluded by 146.1(7.2).

A plan to donate a leftover RESP to a public foundation rather than taking an AIP will not work: VIEWS doc 2007-0241941C6.

146.1(7.1)(a) amended by 2017 budget bill #2 (effective March 23, 2017, to add "that exceeds the total ... for the year"), 2012 budget bill #2 (effective 2014, to add (1.2) exclusion). Added by 1997 Budget. For former proposed 146.1(7.1)(c), in a 2008 bill proposing deduction for RESP contributions, see 60(i) Notes.

Regulations: 103(4), 103(6)(g), 103(8) (withholding of 20% at source); 200(2)(j) (information return).

(7.2) Excluded amount — An excluded amount in respect of a registered education savings plan is,

  (a) for the purposes of subsection (7) and paragraph (7.1)(a), an amount in respect of which a subscriber pays a tax under section 207.05 in respect of the plan, or another plan for which the plan was substituted by the subscriber, that

    (i) has not been waived, cancelled or refunded, and

    (ii) has not reduced any other amount that would otherwise be included under subsections (7) or (7.1) in computing an individual's income for the year or a preceding year; and

  (b) for the purposes of paragraph (7.1)(b),

    (i) any amount received under the plan,

    (ii) any amount received in satisfaction of a right to a refund of payments under the plan, or

(iii) any amount received by a taxpayer under a decree, order or judgment of a competent tribunal, or under a written agreement, relating to a division of property between the taxpayer and the taxpayer's spouse or common-law partner or former spouse or common-law partner in settlement of rights arising out of, or on the breakdown of, their marriage or common-law partnership.

Notes: 146.1(7.2) amended by 2017 budget bill #2, effective March 23, 2017. Before that date, read:

(7.2) For the purpose of paragraph (7.1)(b), an excluded amount in respect of a registered education savings plan is

(a) any amount received under the plan;

(b) any amount received in satisfaction of a right to a refund of payments under the plan; or

(c) any amount received by a taxpayer under a decree, order or judgment of a competent tribunal, or under a written agreement, relating to a division of property between the taxpayer and the taxpayer's spouse or common-law partner or former spouse or common-law partner in settlement of rights arising out of, or on the breakdown of, their marriage or common-law partnership.

146.1(7.2) amended by 2000 same-sex partners bill, effective 2001 or earlier. Added by 1997 Budget. For proposed repeal of 146.1(7.2), in a 2008 bill proposing a deduction for RESP contributions, see 60(i) Notes.

(8)–(10) [Repealed]

Notes: 146.1(8), (9) and (10) repealed by 1997 Budget, for 1998 and later tax years. They contained income exclusion rules for distribution of property relating to pre-1972 income of a RESP. To the extent trust income earned before 1972 had been included in the subscriber's income, the rules provided a deduction for the portion of "tax-paid-income" included in payments to a beneficiary.

(11) [Repealed]

Notes: 146.1(11) repealed by 2014 budget bill #2, for 2016 and later taxation years (in sync with generally replacing "testamentary trust" with "graduated rate estate").

Income Tax Folios: S3-F10-C1: Qualified investments — RRSPs, RESPs, RRIFs, RDSPs and TFSAs [replaces IT-320R3].

(12) Deemed date of registration — Subject to subsection (3), an education savings plan that is registered

(a) before 1976 shall be deemed to have been registered since the later of

(i) January 1, 1972, and

(ii) the first day of January of the year in which the plan was created; and

(b) after 1975 shall be deemed to have been registered on the first day of January in the year of registration.

(12.1) Notice of intent to revoke registration — When a particular day is

(a) a day on which a registered education savings plan ceases to comply with the conditions of subsection (2) for the plan's registration,

(b) a day on which a registered education savings plan ceases to comply with any provision of the plan,

(c) the last day of a month in respect of which tax is payable under Part X.4 by an individual because of contributions made, or deemed for the purpose of Part X.4 to have been made, by or on behalf of the individual into a registered education savings plan,

(d) a day on which a registered education savings plan is revocable, or

(e) a day on which a person fails to comply with a condition or an obligation, imposed under the *Canada Education Savings Act* or under a program administered pursuant to an agreement entered into under section 12 of that Act, that applies with respect to a registered education savings plan,

the Minister may send written notice (referred to in this subsection and subsection (12.2) as a "notice of intent") to the promoter of the plan that the Minister proposes to revoke the registration of the plan as of the day specified in the notice of intent, which day shall not be earlier than the particular day.

Related Provisions: 146.1(2.1) — RESP becoming revocable; 146.1(12.2) — Notice of revocation; 146.1(14)(a) — Reference to *Canada Education Savings Act* includes reference to earlier *DHRD Act*; 172(3)(e.1) — Appeal to Federal Court of Appeal from giving of notice of intent; 180(1)(c.1) — Deadline for filing appeal to Federal Court of Appeal; 248(7) — Notice deemed received on day mailed.

Notes: 146.1(12.1) amended by 2004 RESPs bill (effective Dec. 15, 2004), 1998 Budget. Added by 1997 Budget.

Income Tax Folios: S3-F10-C1: Qualified investments — RRSPs, RESPs, RRIFs, RDSPs and TFSAs [replaces IT-320R3].

(12.2) Notice of revocation — When the Minister sends a notice of intent to revoke the registration of a registered education savings plan to the promoter of the plan, the Minister may, after 30 days after the receipt by the promoter of the notice, send written notice (referred to in this subsection and subsection (13) as a "notice of revocation") to the promoter that the registration of the plan is revoked as of the day specified in the notice of revocation, which day shall not be earlier than the day specified in the notice of intent.

Related Provisions: 146.1(13) — Revocation; 248(7) — Notice deemed received on day mailed.

Notes: 146.1(12.2) added by 1997 Budget, effective 1998.

Income Tax Folios: S3-F10-C1: Qualified investments — RRSPs, RESPs, RRIFs, RDSPs and TFSAs [replaces IT-320R3].

(13) Revocation of registration — When the Minister sends a notice of revocation of the registration of a registered education savings plan under subsection (12.2) to the promoter of the plan, the registration of the plan is revoked as of the day specified in the notice of revocation, unless the Federal Court of Appeal or a judge thereof, on application made at any time before the determination of an appeal under subsection 172(3), orders otherwise.

Related Provisions: 146.1(2) — Requirements for registration; 146.1(5) — Trust becomes taxable after revocation; 244(5) — Proof of service by mail; 248(7)(a) — Mail deemed received on day mailed.

Notes: 146.1(13) amended by 1997 Budget, effective 1998 (in conjunction with the introduction of (12.1) and (12.2)).

Income Tax Folios: S3-F10-C1: Qualified investments — RRSPs, RESPs, RRIFs, RDSPs and TFSAs [replaces IT-320R3].

(13.1) RESP information — Every trustee under a registered education savings plan shall, in prescribed form and manner, file with the Minister information returns in respect of the plan.

Related Provisions: 146.1(15) — Information returns by promoters.

Notes: 146.1(13.1) added by 1998 budget bill #1, effective June 18, 1998.

(14) Former Act — A reference

(a) in this section, in paragraph 60(x) or in subparagraph 241(4)(d)(vii.1) to the *Canada Education Savings Act*, to an amount paid, to the payment of an amount or to the repayment of an amount, or to a condition or an obligation imposed, under that Act includes a reference to Part III.1 of the *Department of Human Resources Development Act*, or to an amount paid, to the payment of an amount or to the repayment of an amount, or to a condition or an obligation imposed, as the case may be, under that Part as it read at the time the reference is relevant; and

(b) in clause (2)(g.1)(ii)(B) to an amount that the Minister designated for the purpose of the *Canada Education Savings Act* approves in writing with respect to an individual includes a reference to an amount that the Minister of Human Resources Development or the Minister of State to be styled Minister of Human Resources and Skills Development has approved in writing, before the day on which a Minister is designated for the purposes of that Act, with respect to the individual.

Notes: 2013 budget bill #2 s. 238(2) provides: "Unless the context requires otherwise, every reference to the Minister of Human Resources and Skills Development in any provision of an Act of Parliament ... is, with any grammatical adaptations, to be read as a reference to the Minister of Employment and Social Development." However, the reference in 146.1(14)(b) is to actions "before the day on which a Minister is designated for the purposes of that Act", so presumably the context otherwise requires and this rule does not apply.

146.1(14) added by 2004 RESPs bill, effective December 15, 2004. See Notes at end of 146.1 for the text of the *CES Act*.

Former 146.1(14) repealed by 1997 Budget, effective 1998. It is no longer necessary in light of other consequences of revocation of a RESP: inclusion in income under 146.1(7) and (7.1), and penalty tax under 204.94.

(15) Regulations — The Governor in Council may make regulations requiring promoters of education savings plans to file information returns in respect of the plans.

Related Provisions: 146.1(13.1) — Information returns by trustees.

Notes: 146.1(15) added by 1997 Budget, effective June 18, 1998.

Notes [s. 146.1]: A RESP is set up by a "subscriber" (146.1(1)) for one or more "beneficiaries" (146.1(1)). Contributions to a RESP (limited by 204.9 and by 146.1(2)(h) and (k) to $50,000 lifetime (formerly $4,000 per child per year and $42,000 lifetime)) are not deductible, but income earned in the plan grows tax-free (146.1(5), (6)). Contributions for children who are under 17 at end of the previous year can earn Canada Education Savings Grants of 20% (maximum $500 (formerly $400) per child per year). (See also the *Overpayments of Canada Education Savings Grants Remission Order* (reproduced under "Remission Orders" after the Regulations), where grants were paid to beneficiaries from 1998 to June 2005 and the minimum contributions had not been made.) Quebec provides a similar Quebec Education Savings Incentive of 10% (max $250 per child per year).

Withdrawals from a RESP can be chosen from: (i) return of contributions to subscriber or directed to anyone else (146.1(1)"refund of payments") — normally no tax consequences; (ii) "educational assistance payment" (146.1(1)) (EAP) from income earned (plus CES Grants, Canada Learning Bonds, Alberta Centennial Education Savings grants and income accumulated on these), paid to and taxable to the student (146.1(7) and 56(1)(q); the scholarship exemption under 56(3) does not apply); (iii) "accumulated income payment" (146.1(1)), specially taxed (see Notes to 204.94) to prevent funds being accumulated in a RESP not for education. See VIEWS doc 2015-0583031I7. For a student with no other income, the financial institution should normally be instructed to provide an EAP, to use up the personal credit (118(1)B(c): income of $11,809 in 2018, $12,069 in 2019) and low-income brackets.

Educational assistance payments can be paid only once the student is "enrolled": 146(2)(g.1), VIEWS doc 2007-0227411M4. They can be paid up to 6 months after the student finishes the course: 146(2.21).

US citizens (see Notes to 128.1(1)) who contribute to or receive funds from a RESP may need to file a Form 3520 (see Notes to 233.3(3)) with the IRS: Dawn Haley, "The Drawbacks of TFSAs and RESPs to US Citizens", 3(1) *Canadian Tax Focus* (ctf.ca) 2-3 (Feb. 2013). However, Reed & Albers, "The US Tax Classification of the Canadian RESP", 2304 *Tax Topics* (CCH) 1-7 (May 5, 2016) argue that a RESP is likely not a trust and can be disclosed by letter attached to the tax return. CPA Canada (Feb. 25, 2016), the AICPA (March 4, 2016) and the American Chamber of Commerce in Canada have written to the Dept. of Finance and US Dept. of the Treasury to seek relief for RESPs, RDSPs and TFSAs.

A RESP can be seized to pay the subscriber's tax debt. See Notes to 146(4). It arguably should be included in net family property for family-law purposes: Shawyer & Dart, "Faulty Reasoning", 34(11) *Money & Family Law* (Carswell) 85-86 (Nov. 2019).

For discussion of RESPs see Information Circular 93-3R2; guide RC4092; Frequently Asked Questions (tinyurl.com/faqs-cra) > "Registered Education Savings Plans"; Donnelly et al., "Registered Education Savings Plans", 47(1) *CTJ* 81-109 (1999); Provenzano & Lim, "RESPs Enhanced", 15(11) *Canadian Tax Highlights* (ctf.ca) 7-8 (Nov. 2007); Provenzano & Ross, "RESPs Re-Enhanced", 17(2) *CTH* 8-9 (Feb. 2009) and "RESP Withdrawals Part 1", 17(4) *CTH* 8-9 (2009); "...Part 2", 17(5) *CTH* 5-6 (May 2009); Weigl & West, "Estate Planning and RESPs", II(5) *Personal Tax and Estate Planning* (Federated Press) 90-97 (2009); Magee, "Tax Planning for Post-Secondary Education", 58(2) *Canadian Tax Journal* 393-416 (2010); Basi, "Treatment of Registered Assets on Death — RESPs and TFSAs", 2015 STEP Canada conference (contact memberservices@step.ca); Informetrica Ltd., *Review of Registered Education Savings Plan Industry Practices* (Aug. 2008), on *TaxPartner* or *Taxnet Pro* (discusses both individual/family plans and group scholarship providers, which are very different). See also VIEWS doc 2009-0348901E5 (pitfalls of swapping securities between RESP and other account).

See *Heritage Education Funds*, 2010 TCC 161, re calculation of a RESP promoter's income from enrolment fees.

The *Canada Education Savings Act* (2004 RESPs bill, S.C. 2004), as amended, provides:

1. **Short title** — This Act may be cited as the *Canada Education Savings Act*.

2. (1) **Definitions** — The definitions in this subsection apply in this Act.

"Canada child benefit" means a deemed overpayment under Subdivision A.1 of Division E of Part I of the *Income Tax Act*.

"Canada Learning Bond" means the bond payable or paid under section 6.

"CES grant" means a Canada Education Savings grant payable or paid under section 5 or under Part III.1 of the *Department of Human Resources Development Act*, as it read immediately before the coming into force of section 19 of this Act.

"child tax benefit" — [Repealed]

"first threshold" for a particular year means the dollar amount referred to in paragraph 117(2)(a) of the *Income Tax Act*, as adjusted under that Act for the particular year;

"national child benefit supplement" — [Repealed]

"prescribed" means prescribed by regulations.

"primary caregiver" means

(a) in the case of a beneficiary who is a qualified dependant, the eligible individual in respect of the beneficiary; and

(b) in the case of a beneficiary in respect of whom a special allowance is payable under the *Children's Special Allowances Act*, the department, agency or institution that maintains the beneficiary.

"second threshold" for a particular year means the higher dollar amount referred to in paragraph 117(2)(b) of the *Income Tax Act*, as adjusted under that Act for the particular year.

(2) *Income Tax Act* expressions — Unless a contrary intention appears, in this Act

(a) the expressions "adjusted income", "eligible individual" and "qualified dependant" have the meanings assigned by section 122.6 of the *Income Tax Act*;

(b) the expressions "beneficiary", "contribution", "designated provincial program", "promoter", "registered education savings plan", "subscriber" and "trust" have the meanings assigned by section 146.1 of the *Income Tax Act*; and

(c) any other expression has the meaning assigned by the *Income Tax Act*.

3. **Purpose** — The purpose of this Act is to encourage the financing of children's post-secondary education through savings, from early childhood, in registered education savings plans.

3.1 **Informational and promotional activities** — The Minister shall take measures necessary to carry out the purpose set out in section 3, including making known to Canadians, through informational and promotional activities, the existence of CES grants and Canada Learning Bonds and any terms and conditions.

4. **Power of Governor in Council** — The Governor in Council may designate a member of the Queen's Privy Council for Canada to be the Minister for the purposes of this Act.

5. (1) **CES grants** — Subject to this Act and the regulations, on application to the Minister in a form and manner approved by the Minister, the Minister may, in respect of any contribution made in 1998 or a subsequent year to a registered education savings plan by or on behalf of a subscriber under the plan in respect of a beneficiary under the plan who is less than 17 years of age at the end of the year preceding the contribution, pay to a trustee of a trust governed by the plan a CES grant for the benefit of the trust. The payment is to be made on any terms and conditions that the Minister may specify by agreement between the Minister and the trustee.

(2) **Amount of grant** — The amount of a CES grant that may be paid for a particular year at any time is equal to the lesser of

(a) 20% of the contribution, and

(b) the amount, if any, by which the lesser of

(i) $1,000, unless the particular year is any of 1998 to 2006, in which case, $800, and

(ii) the beneficiary's unused CES grant room for the particular year at that time

exceeds

(iii) the total of all CES grants paid before that time — other than those amounts paid under subsection (4) — in respect of contributions made in the particular year in respect of the beneficiary.

(3) **Unused CES grant room** — The unused CES grant room for a beneficiary for a particular year at any time is

(a) if the beneficiary was 17 years of age or older at the end of the preceding year, nil; or

(b) in any other case, determined by the formula

$$\$400A + \$500B - C$$

where

A   is the number of years after 1997 and before 2007 in which the beneficiary was alive, other than a year throughout which the beneficiary was

(i) an ineligible beneficiary in accordance with the regulations, or

(ii) not resident in Canada,

B   is the number of years after 2006 in which the beneficiary was alive, up to and including the particular year, other than a year throughout which the beneficiary was

(i) an ineligible beneficiary in accordance with the regulations, or

(ii) not resident in Canada, and

C   is the total of all CES grants paid before that time — other than those amounts paid under subsection (4) — in respect of contributions made in a preceding year in respect of the beneficiary.

D   [Repealed]

(4) Additional amount of grant — The amount of a CES grant that may be paid for a particular year at any time is increased by the lesser of

(a) the amount that is

(i) 20% of the contribution, if the beneficiary

(A) is a qualified dependant of an eligible individual whose adjusted income used to determine the amount of a Canada child benefit in respect of January in the particular year is the first threshold for the particular year or less, or

(B) is a person in respect of whom a special allowance under the *Children's Special Allowances Act* is payable for at least one month in the particular year, and

(ii) 10% of the contribution, if the beneficiary is a qualified dependant of an eligible individual whose adjusted income used to determine the amount of a Canada child benefit in respect of January in the particular year is more than the first threshold for the particular year but not more than the second threshold for the particular year, and

(b) the amount by which

(i) $100, in the case of a beneficiary referred to in subparagraph (a)(i), or

(ii) $50, in the case of a beneficiary referred to in subparagraph (a)(ii)

exceeds

(iii) the total of all amounts paid under this subsection before that time in respect of contributions made in the particular year in respect of the beneficiary.

(5) Eligible individual — first month — If there has been no determination of eligibility for a Canada child benefit in respect of January in a particular year, the adjusted income to be used for the purposes of subsection (4) is the adjusted income used to determine the amount of a Canada child benefit for the first month in the particular year in respect of which eligibility has been established.

(6) Beneficiary born in December — In applying subsection (5) in respect of a beneficiary born in December, the reference to "the first month in the particular year in respect of which eligibility has been established" in that subsection is to be read as a reference to "January of the next year".

(6.1) Change in care — If, in a month following January in a particular year, an individual who was not the primary caregiver of a beneficiary in January of that year becomes the beneficiary's primary caregiver, then the adjusted income to be used for the purposes of subsection (4) in respect of contributions made to the trustee of the trust designated by that individual is the adjusted income used to determine the amount of a Canada child benefit for the first month in the particular year in respect of which the individual's eligibility for the Canada child benefit has been established.

(6.2) Change in care in December — In applying subsection (6.1) in respect of a beneficiary for whom the individual becomes the beneficiary's primary caregiver in December, the reference to "the first month in the particular year in respect of which the individual's eligibility for the Canada child benefit has been established" in that subsection is to be read as a reference to "January of the next year".

(7) Designation — The amount referred to in subsection (4) is to be paid to the trustee of a trust designated, in the form and manner approved by the Minister, by the primary caregiver of the beneficiary at the time the contribution is made.

(7.1) More than one primary caregiver — If there is more than one primary caregiver of the beneficiary at the time a contribution is made, the amount referred to in subsection (4) is to be paid to the trustee of the trust designated under subsection (7) to which a contribution is first made.

(7.2) Additional grant less than maximum amount — For greater certainty, if there is more than one primary caregiver of the beneficiary and the total of all amounts paid under subsection (4) to the trustee of the trust to which a contribution is first made is less than the maximum amount that may be paid under that subsection, then amounts may be paid under that subsection to the trustee of a trust designated by any primary caregiver of the beneficiary.

(8) [Repealed]

(9) Restriction — Subsection (4) applies only to contributions made in 2005 or a subsequent year.

(10) Lifetime cap — Not more than $7,200 in CES grants may be paid in respect of a beneficiary during their lifetime.

6. (1) Canada Learning Bonds — Subject to this Act and the regulations, on application to the Minister, in the form and manner approved by the Minister, the Minister may, in respect of a beneficiary under a registered education savings plan who was born after 2003 and is less than 21 years of age at the time of the application, pay to a trustee of a trust governed by the plan a Canada Learning

Bond for the benefit of the trust. The bond is to be paid on any terms and conditions that the Minister may specify by agreement between the Minister and the trustee.

(2) Amount of bond — The amount of a Canada Learning Bond is equal to the sum of the following amounts:

(a) $500 in respect of the first benefit year in which the beneficiary is a person less than 15 years of age at the beginning of the month immediately before the benefit year, or is born during the benefit year or during the month immediately before it, and, for at least one month in that year,

(i) is a qualified dependant of an eligible individual whose adjusted income used to determine the amount of a Canada child benefit was,

(A) if the eligible individual has not more than three qualified dependants, less than or equal to the first threshold for the particular year in which the benefit year begins, or

(B) if the eligible individual has more than three qualified dependants, less than the amount determined in accordance with subsection (2.1), or

(ii) is a person in respect of whom a special allowance under the *Children's Special Allowances Act* is payable, and

(b) $100 in respect of any subsequent benefit year in which the beneficiary is a person less than 15 years of age at the beginning of the month immediately before the benefit year and, for at least one month in that year, is a person to whom subparagraph (a)(i) or (ii) applies.

(2.1) Formula — For the purposes of clause (2)(a)(i)(B), the amount is determined by the formula

$$A + [(B + C + (D \times E))/Y]$$

where

A   is the amount determined by the formula

$$F - (B/0.122)$$

where

F   is the first threshold for the particular year in which the benefit year begins, and

B   is $2,308.27,

B   is $2,308.27,

C   is $2,041.94,

D   is $1,942.55,

E   is the number of qualified dependants in excess of two, and

Y   is 0.333.

(2.2) Annual adjustment — The amounts expressed in dollars in subsection (2.1) are to be adjusted, as set out in section 117.1 of the *Income Tax Act*, for each particular year after 2016.

(2.3) Adjustment for a benefit year — The amounts adjusted under subsection (2.2) that are to be used in respect of a benefit year are those amounts so adjusted for the particular year in which that benefit year begins.

(2.4) Restriction — A Canada Learning Bond is, other than for the purposes of section 14 of the *Canada Education Savings Regulations*, not to be paid in respect of any beneficiary

(a) more than once in the beneficiary's lifetime under paragraph 6(2)(a); and

(b) more than once in respect of a benefit year under paragraph 6(2)(b).

(3) Meaning of "benefit year" — In this section, "benefit year" means the period that starts on July 1 in one year and ends on June 30 of the next year.

(4) Designation — The amount of a bond in respect of a benefit year is to be paid to the trustee of a trust designated, in the form and manner approved by the Minister, by the primary caregiver of the beneficiary or, if the beneficiary is 18 years of age or more, by the beneficiary.

(5) Additional payment — When the Minister pays the amount under paragraph (2)(a), the Minister may, in prescribed circumstances, pay into the trust an additional amount determined in accordance with the regulations in recognition of the cost of administering registered education savings plans.

7. Conditions — Neither a CES grant nor a Canada Learning Bond may be paid in respect of a beneficiary under a registered education savings plan unless

(a) the Minister is provided with the Social Insurance Number of the beneficiary;

(b) the Minister is provided with the Social Insurance Number of the individual, or the business number of the department, agency or institution, that made a designation under subsection 5(7) or 6(4); and

(c) the beneficiary is resident in Canada, in the case of a CES grant, at the time the contribution to the plan is made and, in the case of a Canada Learning Bond, immediately before the payment is made.

8. Interest — The Minister may, in prescribed circumstances, pay interest, determined in accordance with prescribed rules, in respect of CES grants or Canada Learning Bonds.

9. Payments out of CRF — All amounts payable by the Minister under this Act, the regulations or an agreement entered into under section 12 shall be paid out of the Consolidated Revenue Fund.

9.1 (1) Waiver — On application made by the primary caregiver of the beneficiary or, if the beneficiary is 18 years of age or more, by the beneficiary, the Minister may, to avoid undue hardship, waive any of the requirements of this Act or the regulations that relate to the payment of CES grants or Canada Learning Bonds and that are specified in regulations made under paragraph 13(g). The application must be in the form and manner approved by the Minister.

(2) Restriction — Despite subsection (1), the Minister may not waive any requirement related to the determination of eligibility for a Canada child benefit or for a special allowance under the *Children's Special Allowances Act*.

10. Recovery of payments and interest — An amount required to be repaid to the Minister under this Act, the regulations or under an agreement entered into under this Act, other than an agreement referred to in section 12, and any interest due in respect of the amount constitute a debt due to Her Majesty in right of Canada and is recoverable as such in the Federal Court or any other court of competent jurisdiction.

11. [Repealed 2005, c. 34, s. 83(2).]

12. (1) Authority to enter into agreements with provinces — The Minister may, with the approval of the Minister of Finance, enter into agreements with the government of any province to administer provincial programs consistent with the purpose of this Act.

(2) Fees and charges — An agreement entered into under subsection (1) may include provisions respecting the fees or charges to be paid for a service provided by or on behalf of the Minister under the agreement.

(3) Amounts charged — The amounts of the fees or charges referred to in subsection (2) may not exceed the cost of providing the service.

(4) Amounts received — Subject to conditions imposed by the Treasury Board, any amounts received by the Minister for services may be used by the Minister for administering the provincial programs referred to in subsection (1).

12.1 Collection of information — If the Minister considers it advisable, the Minister may, subject to conditions agreed on by the Minister and the Minister of National Revenue, collect the Social Insurance Number of any registered education savings plan subscriber as well as any prescribed information, for the administration of section 146.1 and Parts X.4 and X.5 of the *Income Tax Act*.

13. Regulations — The Governor in Council may make regulations for carrying out the purpose and provisions of this Act and, without limiting the generality of the foregoing, may make regulations

(a) respecting any matter or thing that by this Act is to be or may be prescribed or otherwise determined under the regulations;

(b) establishing conditions that must be met by a registered education savings plan and by persons in respect of the plan before a CES grant or a Canada Learning Bond may be paid in respect of the plan;

(c) establishing the manner of determining the amount of a CES grant that may be paid in respect of contributions to registered education savings plans or the amount of a Canada Learning Bond that may be paid into those plans;

(d) specifying terms and conditions to be included in agreements entered into between a trustee under a registered education savings plan and the Minister relating to the terms and conditions applicable to the payment of a CES grant or a Canada Learning Bond and specifying, for inclusion in the agreements, in addition to any other conditions that the Minister considers appropriate, the obligations of a trustee under an agreement;

(e) prescribing the circumstances in which an additional amount may be paid under subsection 6(5) and establishing the manner of determining the amount of the payment;

(f) specifying terms and conditions to be included in agreements entered into between promoters of registered education savings plans and the Minister;

(g) specifying the requirements of this Act or the regulations relating to the payment of CES grants or Canada Learning Bonds that may be waived by the Minister to avoid undue hardship;

(h) governing or prohibiting the sharing of CES grants or Canada Learning Bonds, and the earnings generated on them;

(i) specifying circumstances under which all or part of any amount paid under this Act is to be repaid to the Minister;

(j) specifying circumstances under which the earnings generated on Canada Learning Bonds repaid under regulations made under paragraph (i) are to be repaid to the Minister and establishing the manner of determining the amount of those earnings;

(k) establishing, for the purpose of determining an amount required to be repaid under this Act in respect of CES grants or Canada Learning Bonds, the manner of determining the portion, if any, of an educational assistance payment made under a registered education savings plan that is attributable to CES grants or Canada Learning Bonds, as the case may be; and

(l) specifying information that the Minister may collect under section 12.1.

14. Agreements — Every agreement entered into under Part III.1 of the *Department of Human Resources Development Act* that is in force immediately before the coming into force of section 5 of this Act is deemed to be an agreement entered into under that section and continues in force until it terminates.

14.1 (1) Applications for benefit years before July 1, 2016 — The provisions of this Act, of the *Income Tax Act* and of any regulations made under those Acts, as they read immediately before July 1, 2016, apply to an application for a Canada Learning Bond made in respect of any "benefit year", within the meaning of subsection 6(3) of this Act, before that date.

(2) Applications for benefit year 2016-2017 — The provisions of this Act, of the *Income Tax Act* and of any applicable regulations made under those Acts, as they read immediately before July 1, 2017, apply to an application for a Canada Learning Bond made in respect of the "benefit year", within the meaning of subsection 6(3) of this Act, starting on July 1, 2016.

The *Canada Education Savings Regulations* (P.C. 2005-933, amended by 2007 and 2010 budget bills #1, 2011 budget bill #2, P.C. 2018-1540) contain detailed rules for payment of CES grants and Canada Learning Bonds, and determining the portion of an educational assistance payment that is attributable to a CLB. They can be found on *Taxnet Pro* or canLii.org.

Remission Orders: *Overpayments of Canada Education Savings Grants Remission Order*, P.C. 2008-1053 (remission for 1998-June 2005 to beneficiaries aged 16-17 where grants paid but minimum contributions to the RESP had not been made).

Definitions [s. 146.1]: "accumulated income payment" — 146.1(1); "adoption" — 251(6)(c); "allowable capital loss" — 38(b), 248(1); "amount", "annuity", "authorized foreign bank" — 248(1); "beneficiary" — 146.1(1); "blood relationship" — 251(6)(a); "borrowed money", "business" — 248(1); "Canada" — 255, *Interpretation Act* 35(1); "capital gain" — 39(1)(a), 248(1); "capital loss" — 39(1)(b), 248(1); "common-law partner", "common-law partnership" — 248(1); "connected" — 251(6); "contribution" — 146.1(1); "corporation" — 248(1), *Interpretation Act* 35(1); "designated educational institution" — 118.6(1); "designated provincial program" — 146.1(1); "disposition", "dividend" — 248(1); "education savings plan", "educational assistance payment" — 146.1(1); "estate" — 104(1), 248(1); "excluded amount" — 146.1(7.2); "fair market value" — see 69(1) Notes; "Federal Court of Appeal" — *Federal Courts Act* s. 3; "Governor in Council" — *Interpretation Act* 35(1); "individual" — 248(1); "licensed annuities provider" — 147(1), 248(1); "listed" — 87(10); "Minister" — 248(1); "month" — *Interpretation Act* 35(1); "nephew", "niece" — 252(2)(g); "non-resident" — 248(1); "notice of intent" — 146.1(12.1); "notice of revocation" — 146.1(12.2); "parent" — 252(2)(a); "person" — 248(1); "portion" — 146.1(8); "post-secondary educational institution" — 146.1(1); "post-secondary school level" — 146.1(1); "prescribed" — 248(1); "promoter" — 146.1(1); "property" — 248(1); "province" — *Interpretation Act* 35(1); "public primary caregiver" — 146.1(1); "qualified investment", "qualifying educational program" — 146.1(1); "RESP" — 146.1(1)"registered education savings plan", 248(1)"registered education savings plan"; "RESP annual limit", "refund of payments" — 146.1(1); "registered education savings plan" — 146.1(1), 248(1); "regulation" — 248(1); "resident in Canada" — 250; "security" — *Interpretation Act* 35(1); "series of loans" — 248(10); "share" — 248(1); "specified educational program" — 146.1(1); "specified maximum amount" — 146.4(1); "specified plan" — 146.1(1); "subscriber" — 146.1(1); "substituted property" — 248(5); "taxable capital gain" — 38(a), 248(1); "taxable income" — 2(2), 248(1); "taxation year" — 249; "tax-paid income" — 146.1(1); "taxpayer" — 248(1); "trust" — 146.1(1); "writing" — *Interpretation Act* 35(1); "written" — *Interpretation Act* 35(1)"writing".

Tax-free Savings Accounts

146.2 (1) Definitions — The following definitions apply in this section and in Part XI.01.

"distribution" under an arrangement of which an individual is the holder means a payment out of or under the arrangement in satisfaction of all or part of the holder's interest in the arrangement.

Notes: A withdrawal fee charged to a TFSA is excluded from the "distribution", so if $1 is charged on a $500 withdrawal, the "distribution" is $499: VIEWS docs 2009-0330971E5, 2009-0348381E5.

A payment from a TFSA to a creditor of holder H (or seizure of TFSA funds by the creditor) is a "distribution" that increases H's contribution room next Jan. 1: VIEWS doc 2018-0774901E5 (see 207.01(1)"excess TFSA amount"C).

See also Notes at end of 146.2.

"holder" of an arrangement means

(a) until the death of the individual who entered into the arrangement with the issuer, the individual;

(b) at and after the death of the individual, the individual's survivor, if the survivor acquires

(i) all of the individual's rights as the holder of the arrangement, and

(ii) to the extent it is not included in the rights described in subparagraph (i), the unconditional right to revoke any beneficiary designation made, or similar direction imposed, by the individual under the arrangement or relating to property held in connection with the arrangement; and

(c) at and after the death of a holder described in paragraph (b) or in this paragraph, the holder's survivor, if the survivor acquires

(i) all of the holder's rights as the holder of the arrangement, and

(ii) to the extent it is not included in the rights described in subparagraph (i), the unconditional right to revoke any beneficiary designation made, or similar direction imposed, by the holder under the arrangement or relating to property held in connection with the arrangement.

Related Provisions: 207.04 — Tax on holder if TFSA acquires prohibited or nonqualified investment.

Notes: On death, see Notes to 146.2(1)"survivor".

Para. (c), which implements a May 1, 2009 Finance comfort letter, added by 2002-2013 technical bill (Part 5 — technical), for 2009 and later taxation years.

"issuer" of an arrangement means the person described as the issuer in the definition "qualifying arrangement".

"qualifying arrangement", at a particular time, means an arrangement

(a) that is entered into after 2008 between a person (in this definition referred to as the "issuer") and an individual (other than a trust) who is at least 18 years of age;

(b) that is

(i) an arrangement in trust with an issuer that is a corporation licensed or otherwise authorized under the laws of Canada or a province to carry on in Canada the business of offering to the public its services as trustee,

(ii) an annuity contract with an issuer that is a licensed annuities provider, or

(iii) a deposit with an issuer that is

(A) a person who is, or is eligible to become, a member of the Canadian Payments Association, or

(B) a credit union that is a shareholder or member of a body corporate referred to as a "central" for the purposes of the *Canadian Payments Act*;

(c) that provides for contributions to be made under the arrangement to the issuer in consideration of, or to be used, invested or otherwise applied for the purpose of, the issuer making distributions under the arrangement to the holder;

(d) under which the issuer and the individual agree, at the time the arrangement is entered into, that the issuer will file with the Minister an election to register the arrangement as a TFSA; and

(e) that, at all times throughout the period that begins at the time the arrangement is entered into and that ends at the particular time, complies with the conditions in subsection (2).

Related Provisions: 146.2(5) — Qualifying arrangement is a TFSA; 207.01–207.07 — Tax on excess contributions and inappropriate investments.

Notes: A CRA announcement of July 11, 2011, "Guaranteed payments under a Segregated Fund Annuity or similar arrangement" (available on *Taxnet Pro*) states that in order to meet the condition in 146.2(2)(e), "the arrangement should permit the holder to transfer all or any part of the property held in connection with the arrangement (or an amount equal to its value), including the value of their right to receive guaranteed payments to another TFSA of the holder", and otherwise will not qualify due to para. (e) of this definition. Due to 248(1)"amount" and "property", "the right to receive guaranteed

payments constitutes property under the arrangement. The issuer is responsible for calculating the value of such property, which may be determined on an actuarial basis."

Subpara. (b)(ii) amended by 2008 budget bill #2, for 2009 and later tax years.

Forms: RC4466: TFSA information sheet; RC4477: Tax-free savings account (TFSA) guide for issuers.

"survivor" of an individual means another individual who is, immediately before the individual's death, a spouse or common-law partner of the individual.

Related Provisions: 252(3) — Extended meaning of "spouse".

Notes: The provisions for a TFSA to pass on death [146.2(1)"holder", "survivor", 146.2(9)] work only if provincial legislation permits designation of a beneficiary on death: Alexander, "Tax-Free Savings Accounts and Beneficiary Designations", 1(2) *Personal Tax and Estate Planning* (Federated Press) 25-30 (2008); Allard & Fera, "Issues Relating to Beneficiary Designations", 20(1) *Taxation of Executive Compensation & Retirement* (Federated Press) 1026-27 (July/Aug. 2008); Yull, "TFSAs, Successor Holder and Beneficiary Designations", 6(9) *Tax Hyperion* (Carswell, Sept. 2009); Sklar, "Death of a TFSA Holder", 190 *Will Power* (CCH) 1-5 (Oct. 2010). Guide RC4466 states: "in provinces or territories that permit the TFSA beneficiary designation, a successor holder is a spouse or common-law partner of the holder at the time of death, named by the deceased as the successor holder of the TFSA, who acquires all of the rights of the holder under the arrangement including the right to revoke any beneficiary designation. This spouse or common-law partner becomes the new account holder." See also VIEWS docs 2010-0371961C6; 2012-0453171C6 (where there is more than one survivor).

All common-law provinces and territories have enacted such legislation. BC: *Wills, Estates and Succession Act*, ss. 1(1)"benefit plan"(e) and 85(1). AB: regulation under *Trustee Act* s. 27. SK: *Queen's Bench Act, 1998*, s. 72.1. MB: *Beneficiary Designation Act (Retirement, Savings and Other Plans)* s. 1"plan"(c). Ont. s. 2 of O.Reg. 54/95 under *Succession Law Reform Act* (Corbin, "Enabling TFSA Beneficiary Designations", 24(4) *Money & Family Law* [MFL] (Carswell) 30-31 (April 2009) and "TFSA Beneficiary Designations: The Last Word?", 26(7) *MFL* 49 (July 2011), and Ontario news release "McGuinty Government Streamlines Paperwork and Reduces Costs for Ontarians", June 16/09). NS: *Beneficiaries Designation Act* s. 9(1)(b). NB: *Retirement Plan Beneficiaries Act* s. 6.1(2) and Reg. 92-95 para. (c). PEI: *Designation of Beneficiaries Under Benefit Plans Act*, s. 1(d). Nfld: *Income Tax Plan Savings Act* s. 2(d)(iii). Yukon: *Retirement Plan Beneficiaries Act* s. 1"plan"(c). NWT: *Tax-Free Savings Account Regulations*. Nunavut: *Retirement Plan Beneficiaries Act* s. 1"plan"(c.1). However, under the Quebec *Civil Code* a TFSA is transferred only through the estate: Frajman & Persico, "Death of a TFSA Holder", at both 1968 *Tax Topics* 1-2 (Nov. 26, 2009) and 179 *The Estate Planner* 3-4 (Dec. 2009) (CCH).

See also Katy Basi, "Treatment of Registered Assets on Death — RESPs and TFSAs", 2015 STEP Canada conference (contact memberservices@step.ca).

See also 146.2(1)"holder"(c).

Forms: RC240: Designation of an exempt contribution, Tax-free savings account.

(2) Qualifying arrangement conditions — The conditions referred to in paragraph (e) of the definition "qualifying arrangement" in subsection (1) are as follows:

(a) the arrangement requires that it be maintained for the exclusive benefit of the holder (determined without regard to any right of a person to receive a payment out of or under the arrangement only on or after the death of the holder);

(b) the arrangement prohibits, while there is a holder of the arrangement, anyone that is neither the holder nor the issuer of the arrangement from having rights under the arrangement relating to the amount and timing of distributions and the investing of funds;

(c) the arrangement prohibits anyone other than the holder from making contributions under the arrangement;

(d) the arrangement permits distributions to be made to reduce the amount of tax otherwise payable by the holder under section 207.02 or 207.03;

(e) the arrangement provides that, at the direction of the holder, the issuer shall transfer all or any part of the property held in connection with the arrangement (or an amount equal to its value) to another TFSA of the holder;

(f) if the arrangement is an arrangement in trust, it prohibits the trust from borrowing money or other property for the purposes of the arrangement; and

(g) the arrangement complies with prescribed conditions.

Related Provisions: 146.2(3), (4) — Where TFSA can be used as security; 146.2(5)(c) — Arrangement ceases to be TFSA if conditions not complied with. See also Related Provisions under 146.2(5).

Notes: See Notes at end of 146.2 and VIEWS doc 2017-0708951E5 for general discussion. Violating a 146.2(2) condition triggers 146.2(5)(c), so the TFSA is deregistered.

146.2(2)(a) and (b) are violated by a bank having a setoff right to use the TFSA for the taxpayer's debt to the bank or its affiliates: VIEWS doc 2017-072742117 (but see 146.2(4) on using a TFSA as security).

146.2(2)(c) requires that only holder H be allowed to contribute, but contributions can be made on behalf of H by another person under an agency arrangement: 2008-029623117; or with H's concurrence or at H's direction: 2017-0731541E5, 2018-0739761E5. Parent P can write a cheque to adult child C which C deposits to their TFSA, if it is a genuine gift: 2010-0369721E5 (if it is not a gift and P still has rights to the funds, the TFSA ceases to be a TFSA). Similarly for spouses: 2015-0569601E5.

146.2(2)(e) means TFSA investments must be transferable in CRA's view, so a non-commutable life annuity is not allowed: doc 2019-0799121C6 [2019 CLHIA q.7].

Regulations: No prescribed conditions for 142.2(2)(g).

Income Tax Folios: S3-F10-C1: Qualified investments — RRSPs, RESPs, RRIFs, RDSPs and TFSAs [replaces IT-320R3].

Forms: RC4477: Tax-free savings account (TFSA) guide for issuers.

(3) Paras. (2)(a), (b) and (e) not applicable — The conditions in paragraphs (2)(a), (b) and (e) do not apply to the extent that they are inconsistent with subsection (4).

Notes: See also Notes at end of 146.2.

146.2(3) added by 2008 budget bill #2, effective for 2009 and later taxation years (i.e., retroactive to the introduction of 146.2). Former 146.2(3) was renumbered 146.2(5) and amended.

(4) Using TFSA interest as security for a loan — A holder of a TFSA may use the holder's interest or, for civil law, right in the TFSA as security for a loan or other indebtedness if

(a) the terms and conditions of the indebtedness are terms and conditions that persons dealing at arm's length with each other would have entered into; and

(b) it can reasonably be concluded that none of the main purposes for that use is to enable a person (other than the holder) or a partnership to benefit from the exemption from tax under this Part of any amount in respect of the TFSA.

Notes: The TFSA holder can use the TFSA but not its underlying assets as security: VIEWS doc 2013-0514261E5 (using the assets would seem possible only for a deposit-type TFSA, since the holder does not own the assets if it is a trust). If a creditor realizes on security by taking TFSA funds, see 146.2(1)"distribution".

146.2(4) added by 2008 budget bill #2, for 2009 and later tax years (i.e., retroactive to introduction of 146.2). Former 146.2(4) was renumbered 146.2(6).

Forms: RC4466: TFSA information sheet.

(5) TFSA [tax-free savings account] — If the issuer of an arrangement that is, at the time it is entered into, a qualifying arrangement files with the Minister, before March of the calendar year following the calendar year in which the arrangement was entered into, an election in prescribed form and manner to register the arrangement as a TFSA under the Social Insurance Number of the individual with whom the arrangement was entered into, the arrangement becomes a TFSA at the time the arrangement was entered into and ceases to be a TFSA at the earliest of the following times:

(a) the time at which the last holder of the arrangement dies;

(b) the time at which the arrangement ceases to be a qualifying arrangement; or

(c) the earliest time at which the arrangement is not administered in accordance with the conditions in subsection (2).

Related Provisions: 18(1)(u) — Investment counselling and administration fees for TFSA are non-deductible; 18(11) — No deduction for interest on money borrowed to contribute to TFSA; 56(1)(d)(iii) — Annuity from TFSA not taxable; 74.5(12)(c) — Attribution rules do not apply to contributions; 75(3)(a) — Reversionary trust rules do not apply to TFSA; 108(1)"trust"(a) — "Trust" does not include TFSA for certain purposes; 118.1(5.3) [before 2016], 118.1(5.2)(b) [after 2015] — Designation of charity as beneficiary of TFSA; 128.1(10)"excluded right or interest"(a)(iii.2) — No deemed disposition on emigration of holder; 138.1(7) — Segregated fund rules do not apply to TFSA; 146.2(8), (10), (11) — Effect of arrangement ceasing to be TFSA; 148(1)(b.2) — No income inclusion on disposition of life insurance policy; 207.02 — Tax on excess contributions; 207.03 — Tax on non-resident contributions; 207.04 — Tax on holder if TFSA acquires inappropriate investment; 211(1)"registered life insurance policy"(a) — TFSA exempt from tax on life insurers; 248(1)"disposition"(f)(vi) — Transfer from TFSA to TFSA is not a disposition; 248(1)"TFSA" —

Definition applies to entire Act; 248(3)(c) — TFSA set up in Quebec deemed to be trust; Reg. 9006(k) — TFSA not reported to CRA for disclosure to foreign tax authorities.

Notes: See Notes at end of 146.2. If a TFSA ceases to qualify, 75(2) will apply: see Notes to 75(3).

146.2(3) renumbered as 146.2(5) and amended by 2008 budget bill #2, for 2009 and later tax years (i.e., retroactive to the introduction of 146.2). (Former 146.2(5) was renumbered 146.2(7).)

Income Tax Folios: S3-F10-C1: Qualified investments — RRSPs, RESPs, RRIFs, RDSPs and TFSAs [replaces IT-320R3].

Forms: RC236: Application for a TFSA identification number; RC4466: TFSA information sheet.

(6) Trust not taxable — No tax is payable under this Part by a trust that is governed by a TFSA on its taxable income for a taxation year, except that, if at any time in the taxation year, it carries on one or more businesses or holds one or more properties that are non-qualified investments (as defined in subsection 207.01(1)) for the trust, tax is payable under this Part by the trust on the amount that would be its taxable income for the taxation year if it had no incomes or losses from sources other than those businesses and properties, and no capital gains or capital losses other than from dispositions of those properties, and for that purpose,

(a) "income" includes dividends described in section 83;

(b) the trust's taxable capital gain or allowable capital loss from the disposition of a property is equal to its capital gain or capital loss, as the case may be, from the disposition; and

(c) the trust's income shall be computed without reference to subsection 104(6).

Related Provisions: 12(11)"investment contract"(d.1) — Exemption from annual interest accrual rules; 146.2(6.1) — Tax on business income — liability of holder and trustee; 149(1)(u.2) — TFSA exempt to extent provided in 146.2; 207.01(1)"specified non-qualified investment income" — Income attributable to amount on which Part I tax was payable by TFSA; 207.04(3) — Where investment both prohibited and non-qualified; 207.04(4) — Refund of tax on disposition of investment; 207.061 — Certain amounts included in TFSA holder's income; 253.1(1) — Limited partner not considered to carry on partnership business; 259(1) — Election for proportional holdings in trust property.

Notes: Certain activities may be taxable as business income, including option writing, foreign currency trading or "too much" stock trading: Income Tax Folio S3-F10-C1 ¶1.40-1.46; IT-479R; VIEWS docs 2010-0381031E5, 2014-0538221C6 [2014 APFF q.2]. CRA audits many TFSAs and by mid-2017 had reassessed TFSAs $75 million: 2017-0693341C6 [2017 STEP q.13]. See also Notes to 9(1) at "Business income vs property income", to 54"capital property", and to 146(4) and 146.3(3) re RRSPs and RRIFs "carrying on business"; Woolley, "Income from a Business or Property", 2014 Cdn Tax Foundation conference report at 6:7-15; Drache, "TFSAs as a Business", xxx-vii(1) *The Canadian Taxpayer* (Carswell) 5-6 (Jan. 2, 2015); MacEachern & Clarke, "Taxing TFSAs That Carry On a Securities Trading Business", 5(1) *Canadian Tax Focus* (ctf.ca) 1 (Feb. 2015); Campbell et al., "CRA TFSA Audit Project", 8(2) *Taxes & Wealth Management* (Carswell) 1-3 (May 2015); Davies & Demner, "Taxing TFSAs on Business Income", 23(7) *Canadian Tax Highlights* (ctf.ca) 8-9 (July 2015).

An ongoing appeal on this issue is *Canadian Western Trust [Ahamed TFSA]*, 2020 FCA 213 (dispute over discovery).

CRA thinks a TFSA is always resident in Canada and so can be taxed on business income, even if the owner manages it from outside Canada: VIEWS doc 2018-073820117. Similarly, CRA says the province of the trustee office location (not the holder's residence) taxes the income (but if investment decisions are delegated, it is the investment firm's office): 2019-0800551E5.

146.2(6)(c) added by 2010 budget bill #2, for 2010 and later taxation years. 146.2(4) renumbered as 146.2(6) by 2008 budget bill #2, for 2009 and later taxation years (former 146.2(6) was renumbered 146.2(8)).

Regulations: 223(1) (information return).

Income Tax Folios: S3-F10-C1: Qualified investments — RRSPs, RESPs, RRIFs, RDSPs and TFSAs [replaces IT-320R3]; S3-F10-C2: Prohibited investments — RRSPs, RRIFs and TFSAs.

Forms: RC4466: TFSA information sheet.

(6.1) Carrying on a business — If tax is payable under this Part for a taxation year because of subsection (6) by a trust that is governed by a TFSA that carries on one or more businesses at any time in the taxation year,

(a) the holder of the TFSA is jointly and severally, or solidarily, liable with the trust to pay each amount payable under this Act by the trust that is attributable to that business or those businesses; and

(b) the issuer's liability at any time for amounts payable under this Act in respect of that business or those businesses shall not exceed the total of

(i) the amount of property of the trust that the issuer is in possession or control of at that time in its capacity as legal representative of the trust, and

(ii) the total amount of all distributions of property from the trust on or after the date that the notice of assessment was sent in respect of the taxation year and before that time.

Notes: Before 146.2(6.1), the TFSA trustee (financial institution) was jointly liable with the TFSA for any tax the TFSA owed on its 146.2(6) business income: 104(1), 159(1), 159(3) and *Olympia Trust*, 2015 FCA 279, paras. 63-64. (The TFSA holder was liable only for Part XI.01 tax on the TFSA's acquisition of a non-qualified or prohibited investment.) If the TFSA did not have assets to pay the tax (e.g., the holder withdrew the assets), the trustee would be stuck with the bill. Now the *holder* is liable, and the trustee's liability at any given time is limited to the property held in the TFSA at that time, plus all distributions from the TFSA from the date the notice of assessment is sent. (The words "and before that time" at the end of (b)(ii) link to "at any time" in para. (b) opening words; thus the issuer is not liable today for tomorrow's distribution.)

146.2(6.1) added by 2019 budget bill #1, effective in respect of business activities in a TFSA for 2019 and later tax years.

(7) Amount credited to a deposit — An amount that is credited or added to a deposit that is a TFSA as interest or other income in respect of the TFSA is deemed not to be received by the holder of the TFSA solely because of that crediting or adding.

Related Provisions: 56(1)(d)(iii) — Annuity from TFSA not taxable; 207.061 — Certain amounts included in TFSA holder's income.

Notes: 146.2(5) renumbered as 146.2(7) by 2008 budget bill #2, effective for 2009 and later taxation years (i.e., retroactive to the introduction of 146.2). (Former 146.2(7) was renumbered 146.2(10).)

(8) Trust ceasing to be a TFSA — If an arrangement that governs a trust ceases, at a particular time, to be a TFSA,

(a) the trust is deemed

(i) to have disposed, immediately before the particular time, of each property held by the trust for proceeds equal to the property's fair market value immediately before the particular time, and

(ii) to have acquired, at the particular time, each such property at a cost equal to that fair market value;

(b) the trust's last taxation year that began before the particular time is deemed to have ended immediately before the particular time; and

(c) a taxation year of the trust is deemed to begin at the particular time.

Related Provisions: 146.2(10), (11) — Parallel rules for annuity contract and deposit.

Notes: 146.2(6) renumbered as 146.2(8) by 2008 budget bill #2, for 2009 and later tax years (retroactive to introduction of 146.2). (Former 146.2(8) was renumbered 146.2(11).)

(9) Trust ceasing to be a TFSA on death of holder — If an arrangement that governs a trust ceases to be a TFSA because of the death of the holder of the TFSA,

(a) the arrangement is deemed, for the purposes of subsections (6) and (8), any regulations made under subsection (13), the definition "trust" in subsection 108(1), paragraph 149(1)(u.2) and the definitions "qualified investment" and "non-qualified investment" in subsection 207.01(1), to continue to be a TFSA until, and to cease to be a TFSA immediately after, the exemption-end time, being in this subsection the earlier of

(i) the time at which the trust ceases to exist, and

(ii) the end of the first calendar year that begins after the holder dies;

(b) there shall be included in computing a taxpayer's income for a taxation year the total of all amounts each of which is an amount determined by the formula

$$A - B$$

where

A is the amount of a payment made out of or under the trust, in satisfaction of all or part of the taxpayer's beneficial interest in the trust, in the taxation year, after the holder's death and at or before the exemption-end time, and

B is an amount designated by the trust not exceeding the lesser of

(i) the amount of the payment, and

(ii) the amount by which the fair market value of all of the property held by the trust immediately before the holder's death exceeds the total of all amounts each of which is the value of B in respect of any other payment made out of or under the trust; and

(c) there shall be included in computing the trust's income for its first taxation year, if any, that begins after the exemption-end time the amount determined by the formula

$$A - B$$

where

A is the fair market value of all of the property held by the trust at the exemption-end time, and

B is the amount by which the fair market value of all of the property held by the trust immediately before the holder's death exceeds the total of all amounts each of which is the value of B in paragraph (b) in respect of a payment made out of or under the trust.

Related Provisions: 12(1)(z.5) — Inclusion in income from property; 212(1)(p) — Non-resident withholding tax; 257 — Formula cannot calculate to less than zero.

Notes: See Notes to 146.2(1)"survivor". 146.2(9) added by 2008 budget bill #2, for 2009 and later tax years (i.e., retroactive to the introduction of 146.2). (Former 146.2(9) was renumbered 146.2(12).)

Regulations: 223(2) (information return).

(10) Annuity contract ceasing to be a TFSA — If an annuity contract ceases, at a particular time, to be a TFSA,

(a) the holder of the TFSA is deemed to have disposed of the contract immediately before the particular time for proceeds equal to its fair market value immediately before the particular time;

(b) the contract is deemed to be a separate annuity contract issued and effected at the particular time otherwise than pursuant to or as a TFSA; and

(c) each person who has an interest or, for civil law, a right in the separate annuity contract at the particular time is deemed to acquire the interest at the particular time at a cost equal to its fair market value at the particular time.

Notes: 146.2(7) renumbered as 146.2(10) by 2008 budget bill #2, effective for 2009 and later taxation years (i.e., retroactive to the introduction of 146.2).

(11) Deposit ceasing to be a TFSA — If a deposit ceases, at a particular time, to be a TFSA,

(a) the holder of the TFSA is deemed to have disposed of the deposit immediately before the particular time for proceeds equal to its fair market value immediately before the particular time; and

(b) each person who has an interest or, for civil law, a right in the deposit at the particular time is deemed to acquire the interest at the particular time at a cost equal to its fair market value at the particular time.

Notes: 146.2(8) renumbered as 146.2(11) by 2008 budget bill #2, effective for 2009 and later taxation years (i.e., retroactive to the introduction of 146.2).

(12) Arrangement is TFSA only — An arrangement that is a qualifying arrangement at the time it is entered into is deemed not to be a retirement savings plan, an education savings plan, a retirement income fund or a disability savings plan.

Notes: 146.2(9) renumbered as 146.2(12) by 2008 budget bill #2, effective for 2009 and later taxation years (i.e., retroactive to the introduction of 146.2).

(13) Regulations — The Governor in Council may make regulations requiring issuers of TFSAs to file information returns in respect of TFSAs.

Notes: 146.2(13) added by 2008 budget bill #2, for 2009 and later taxation years.

Notes [s. 146.2]: See canada.ca/tfsa. The Tax-Free Savings Account began in 2009. Every Canadian resident 18 and older can contribute to a TFSA, cumulatively up to $5,000 per year for 2009-2012, $5,500 for 2013-2014 and 2016-18, $10,000 for 2015, $6,000 for 2019-2021 (indexed, rounded to the nearest $500, since 2018). See 207.01(1)"TFSA dollar limit" Notes for cumulative limits. Where the age of majority is 19 (BC, NB, NS, NL, and all territories), a TFSA cannot actually be opened in practice until age 19, though contribution room accumulates from 18.

A TFSA is registered, like an RRSP: s. 146.2(2). TFSAs are widely available at financial institutions.

TFSA contributions are not deductible, but all interest, dividends, capital gains and other income earned in a TFSA are non-taxable: 146.2(6), 149(1)(u.2). As well, the income and capital can be withdrawn tax-free at any time, in any amount.

Any year the taxpayer does not contribute the maximum builds up contribution room to use in any future year, with no carryforward limit: 207.01(1)"unused TFSA contribution room". Withdrawals also recreate contribution room (element B of that definition), but only starting the next year, so taxpayers who recontribute too soon will exceed the limit and be subject to penalty tax of 1% per month: 207.02.

A taxpayer who becomes or ceases to be resident in Canada during a year (see 250(1) Notes) can contribute the full $5,500, $6,000, etc. for the year: 207.01(1)"excess TFSA amount"D(a), but only while resident in Canada, as 207.03 imposes a penalty on contributions made while non-resident. See also Uppal, "TFSAs and Change in Residence Status", 2(2) *Canadian Tax Focus* (ctf.ca) 5 (May 2012); VIEWS doc 2012-0468941E5.

A TFSA can invest in the same kinds of investments as an RRSP: 207.01(1)"qualified investment". See Notes to Reg. 4900(1). The holder must pay a 1% monthly penalty tax if the TFSA holds non-qualified investments: 207.04, and a 100% tax on an "advantage" (very broadly defined) received from a TFSA: 207.05(2). On the valuation of warrants contributed to a TFSA see VIEWS docs 2008-0303791E5, 2009-0305431E5. See also the very strict "advantage" and other rules in 207.01–207.07, limiting swaps between TFSA and other accounts and prohibiting certain kinds of investment. A TFSA can invest in foreign currency, but certain foreign exchange contracts are not qualified investments, and active currency trading could be a "business" whose income is taxed: 2009-0318671E5, 2010-0356811E5. A TFSA that invests in US stocks is subject to US withholding tax on dividends; Canada-US Treaty Art. XXI:2 exempts dividends to RRSPs and RRIFs but not TFSAs. A TFSA's purchase of an investment using existing property is not a contribution: 2017-0685071E5.

For the advantages of contributing stock options to a TFSA see Notes to 7(1).

The attribution rules do not apply to income earned in a TFSA: 74.5(12)(c) (but it is not a TFSA if the spouse contributes directly to it: 142.2(2)(c), VIEWS doc 2009-0309861E5). Interest on money borrowed to invest in a TFSA is non-deductible (18(11)(j)). A non-resident should not contribute to a TFSA: 207.03.

A TFSA can be used as security for a loan, subject to certain conditions: 146.2(4).

Deregistration: A TFSA that borrows money (146.2(2)(f)) ceases to be one (146.2(5)(c)) and is deregistered. (An accidental overdraft, quickly fixed, will not normally cause this: VIEWS doc 2013-0486491I7.) On ceasing to be a TFSA, see 146.2(8)-(11) for effects; thereafter 75(2) applies to the trust, which is no longer exempt under 149(1)(u.2): 2017-0718021I7. On death of a TFSA holder, see 146.2(9) and Notes to 146.2(1)"survivor".

A TFSA can be part of an employee's flexible benefit plan: see Notes to 6(1)(a) under "Flex credits".

On designation of a survivor to a TFSA, see Notes to 146.2(1)"survivor".

TFSA issuers and advisers: see tinyurl.com/tfsa-cra and Form RC236.

For TFSA penalties see Notes to 207.02 (overcontribution), 207.04(1) (prohibited investment) and 207.05(1) (advantage). As well as imposing penalties, CRA taxes TFSAs under 146.2(6) for carrying on business such as by actively trading stocks (see 54"capital property" Notes). For TFSA audits see 146.2(6) Notes. See also 207.01(1)"advantage" Notes re "TFSA maximizer schemes".

US citizens should be very cautious about opening TFSAs. The income may be taxable each year on their US return. The TFSA must be reported electronically as part of FBAR by each June 30 (see Notes to 233.3(3)), and possibly on IRS Forms 3520 and 3520-A as a foreign trust. US citizens with TFSAs should consider withdrawing the funds (there is no tax cost), and if relief (via treaty or IRS administrative concession) is provided in the future, their contribution room will have been reinstated. See also Dawn Haley, "The Drawbacks of TFSAs and RESPs to US Citizens", 3(1) *Canadian Tax Focus* (ctf.ca) 2-3 (Feb. 2013); Max Reed, "TFSA: US Tax Classification", 22(7) *Canadian Tax Highlights* (ctf.ca) 5-6 (July 2014). *Contra*, for a view that a TFSA is treaty-protected, see Nightingale & Turchen, "The US Tax Implications of a TFSA", 2146 *Tax Topics* (CCH) 1-4 (April 25, 2013). For a view that it is *not* a foreign trust see Reed, "Classification of the Canadian TFSA for US Tax Purposes", 2215 *Tax Topics* 1-4 (Aug. 21, 2014). See also Notes to 146.1 re submissions made to Finance and the US in 2016.

CRA's target (tinyurl.com/cra-standards) for responding to TFSA applications (to register, amend or terminate) is 90% within 60 days; in 2019-20, it did 100%. As of 2017,

there were 19.5 million TFSAs held by 14.1m taxpayers; total TFSA contributions $61.4 billion; total TFSA value $276.8b (tinyurl.com/stats-cra, as of Dec. 2020).

On the merits of TFSAs see Policy Forum, 60(2) *Canadian Tax Journal* 355-99 (2012); Parliamentary Budget Officer, *The Tax-Free Savings Account* (Feb. 24, 2015, and update April 27, 2015).

For more on TFSAs see CRA Guide RC4466 and Information Circular 18-1; Gascho, "Tax-Free Savings Accounts", 19(2) *Taxation of Executive Compensation & Retirement* (Federated Press) 875-78 (Sept. 2007); Nilson, "Tax-Free Savings Accounts", 1914 *Tax Topics* (CCH) 1-5 (Nov. 13, 2008) [discusses investment strategies and when TFSAs are useful]; Ballantyne, "The Tax-Free Savings Account", XV(1) *Insurance Planning* (Federated Press) 940-46 (2008); Evans & Domercq, "Policy Forum", 56(3) *Canadian Tax Journal* 708-18 (2008); Keey, "TFSAs — Are They Right for Your Client?", 2(1) *It's Personal* (Carswell) 3-5 (Feb. 2009); Louis, "Tax-Free Savings Accounts", 170 *The Estate Planner* (CCH) 1-5 (March 2009) and 1935 *Tax Topics* 1-6 (April 9, 2009); Roth, "TFSAs — Are they Always Tax-Free?", 6(9) *Tax Hyperion* (Carswell, Sept. 2009) [points out problems for US citizens, Canadian emigrants, and withholding tax on foreign securities]; Forgie, Sommers & Vandebeek, "Tax-Free Savings Accounts", 2008 Cdn Tax Foundation conference report, 31:1-12; C.D. Howe Institute, "Saver's Choice: Comparing the Marginal Effective Tax Burdens on RRSPs and TFSAs", tinyurl.com/cdhowe-tfsa; de Rose & Balsara, "TFSA Always Tax-Free?", 19(2) *Canadian Tax Highlights* (ctf.ca) 8-9 (Feb. 2011); Dept. of Finance (fin.gc.ca), *Tax Expenditures and Evaluations* 2012, pp. 31-45 (TFSA holder statistics); Ornstein, "TFSA & RRSP Planning on Separation", 28(3) *Money & Family Law* (Carswell) 19 (March 2013); Du & Grant, "Tax-Free Savings Accounts: Beware of the Pitfalls", 12(1) *Taxes & Wealth Management* (Carswell) 6-9 (March 2019).

146.2 added by 2008 budget bill #1, for 2009 and later tax years.

Former 146.2 dealt with registered home ownership savings plans (RHOSPs). 146.2(1)-(21) repealed by 1985 Budget. 146.2(22)-(23), applying only to 1985, repealed on enactment of new 146.2. Although RHOSP funds could be withdrawn for any purpose without federal tax, Quebec required that they be used for a home or certain furniture or appliances to avoid provincial tax on withdrawal. Some Quebec residents thus kept RHOSPs, but these were revoked at the end of 1999 and the beneficiary deemed to receive the value of the property (Quebec *Taxation Act* s. 946.1). All property in a RHOSP was deemed acquired at FMV on Jan. 1/86: 50(3).

Definitions [s. 146.2]: "allowable capital loss" — 38(b), 146.2(4)(b), 248(1); "amount", "annuity" — 248(1); "arm's length" — 251(1); "assessment" — 248(1); "beneficiary" — 248(25) [Notes]; "business" — 248(1); "calendar year" — *Interpretation Act* 37(1)(a); "Canada" — 255, *Interpretation Act* 35(1); "capital gain" — 39(1)(a), 248(1); "capital loss" — 39(1)(b), 248(1); "common-law partner" — 248(1); "corporation" — 248(1), *Interpretation Act* 35(1); "credit union" — 137(6), 248(1); "disposition" — 248(1); "distribution" — 146.2(1); "dividend" — 248(1); "exemption-end time" — 146.2(9)(a); "fair market value" — see 69(1) Notes; "Governor in Council" — *Interpretation Act* 35(1); "holder" — 146.2(1); "individual" — 248(1); "issuer" — 146.2(1); "legal representative" — 248(1); "licensed annuities provider" — 147(1), 248(1); "Minister" — 248(1); "partnership" — see 96(1) Notes; "person", "prescribed", "property" — 248(1); "province" — *Interpretation Act* 35(1); "qualifying arrangement" — 146.2(1); "regulation" — 248(1); "retirement income fund" — 146.3(1), 248(1); "retirement savings plan" — 146(1), 248(1); "security" — *Interpretation Act* 35(1); "shareholder" — 248(1); "spouse" — 252(3); "survivor" — 146.2(1); "TFSA" — 146.2(5), 248(1); "taxable capital gain" — 38(a), 146.2(4)(b), 248(1); "taxable income" — 248(1); "taxation year" — 249; "taxpayer" — 248(1); "trust" — 104(1), 248(1), (3).

Registered Plans Compliance Bulletins [s. 146.2]: 6 (TFSA compliance issues).

Forms [s. 146.2]: RC343: Worksheet — TFSA contribution room; RC4477: Tax-free savings account (TFSA) guide for issuers.

Registered Retirement Income Funds

146.3 (1) Definitions — In this section,

"annuitant" under a retirement income fund at any time means

(a) the first individual to whom the carrier has undertaken to make payments described in the definition "retirement income fund" out of or under the fund, where the first individual is alive at that time,

(b) after the death of the first individual, a spouse or common-law partner (in this definition referred to as the "survivor") of the first individual to whom the carrier has undertaken to make payments described in the definition "retirement income fund" out of or under the fund after the death of the first individual, if the survivor is alive at that time and the undertaking was made

(i) pursuant to an election that is described in that definition and that was made by the first individual, or

(ii) with the consent of the legal representative of the first individual, and

(c) after the death of the survivor, another spouse or common-law partner of the survivor to whom the carrier has undertaken, with the consent of the legal representative of the survivor, to make payments described in the definition "retirement income fund" out of or under the fund after the death of the survivor, where that other spouse or common-law partner is alive at that time;

Related Provisions: 207.04 — Tax on annuitant if RRIF acquires prohibited or non-qualified investment.

Notes: After an annuitant's death, if the election in para. (b) has been made, payments can be made to the deceased's spouse or common-law partner (CLP) as "successor annuitant". If this is not done, the RRIF is taxable on death, but 146(8.2) allows payments (a "designated benefit") to be taxed to a beneficiary. In some cases (spouse or CLP, or child or grandchild dependent on the deceased due to infirmity), the designated benefit can be rolled into an RRSP, RRIF or annuity under 60(l). See VIEWS doc 2003-0050485.

A spouse designated under (b)(i) as the successor, who dies before receiving any payments, is still an "annuitant", but a (b)(ii) spouse is not: VIEWS doc 2015-0592681E5.

Para. (b) amended by 2002-2013 technical bill (Part 5 — technical), effective on the same basis as 248(1)"common-law partner" (2001 or earlier), to split up the text into subparas. (i) and (ii) and add a missing "or" between them.

146.3(1)"annuitant"(b) and (c) amended by 2000 same-sex partners bill, effective as per Notes to 248(1)"common-law partner".

146.3(1)"annuitant" was 146.3(1)(a) before RSC 1985 (5th Supp) consolidation for tax years ending after Nov. 1991. Amended by 1992 technical bill, for deaths after 1990.

Forms: RC4178: Death of a RRIF annuitant [guide].

"carrier" of a retirement income fund means

(a) a person licensed or otherwise authorized under the laws of Canada or a province to carry on in Canada an annuities business,

(b) a corporation licensed or otherwise authorized under the laws of Canada or a province to carry on in Canada the business of offering to the public its services as trustee,

(c) a corporation approved by the Governor in Council for the purposes of section 146 that is licensed or otherwise authorized under the laws of Canada or a province to issue investment contracts, or

(d) a person referred to as a depositary in section 146,

that has agreed to make payments under a retirement income fund to the individual who is the annuitant under the fund;

Notes: 146.3(1)"carrier" was para. 146.3(1)(b) before RSC 1985 (5th Supp) consolidation for tax years ending after Nov. 1991.

Registered Plans Frequently Asked Questions: RPFAQ-1 (RRSPs/RRIFs), q. 3 (change of carrier).

Forms: T3GR: Group income tax and information return for RRSP, RRIF, RESP, or RDSP trusts (and worksheets).

"designated benefit" of an individual in respect of a registered retirement income fund means the total of

(a) such amounts paid out of or under the fund after the death of the last annuitant thereunder to the legal representative of that annuitant

(i) as would, had they been paid under the fund to the individual, have been refunds of premiums (in this paragraph having the meaning assigned by subsection 146(1)) if the fund were a registered retirement savings plan that had not matured before the death, and

(ii) as are designated jointly by the legal representative and the individual in prescribed form filed with the Minister, and

(b) amounts paid out of or under the fund after the death of the last annuitant thereunder to the individual that would be refunds of premiums had the fund been a registered retirement savings plan that had not matured before the death;

Related Provisions: 146.3(6.1) — Designated benefit deemed received; 146.3(6.11) — Transfer of designated benefit.

Notes: A designated benefit (DB) of beneficiary B is treated as a RRIF distribution made directly to B and taxed to B under 146.3(5) rather than a "refund of premiums" included in the deceased's estate's income. For CRA interpretation see docs 2003-0039621E5, 2005-0126621R3, 2006-0201371E5, 2017-0707791C6 [2017 APFF q.6];

2019-0815181C6 [2019 APFF Financial q.12] (designated amount is not reported in estate's T3 return); 2020-0867001E5 (no DB if spouse dies before RRIF distribution).

Definition "designated benefit" added by 1993 technical bill, effective for deaths after 1992. See 146.3(6.1) and (6.11).

Forms: T1090: Death of a RRIF annuitant — designated benefit.

"minimum amount" under a retirement income fund for a year means, for the year in which the fund was entered into, a nil amount, and, for any other year, the amount determined by the formula

$$(A \times B) + C$$

where

A is the total fair market value of all properties held in connection with the fund at the beginning of the year (other than annuity contracts held by a trust governed by the fund that, at the beginning of the year, are not described in paragraph (b.1) of the definition "qualified investment");

B is

(a) where the first annuitant under the fund elected in respect of the fund under paragraph (b) of the definition "minimum amount" in this subsection, as it read before 1992, or under subparagraph 146.3(1)(f)(i) of the *Income Tax Act*, chapter 148 of the Revised Statutes of Canada, 1952, to use the age of another individual, the prescribed factor for the year in respect of the other individual,

(b) where paragraph (a) does not apply and the first annuitant under the fund so elects before any payment has been made under the fund by the carrier, the prescribed factor for the year in respect of an individual who was the spouse or common-law partner of the first annuitant at the time of the election, and

(c) in any other case, the prescribed factor for the year in respect of the first annuitant under the fund, and

C is, where the fund governs a trust, the total of all amounts each of which is

(a) a periodic payment under an annuity contract held by the trust at the beginning of the year (other than an annuity contract described at the beginning of the year in paragraph (b.1) of the definition "qualified investment") that is paid to the trust in the year, or

(b) if the periodic payment under such an annuity contract is not made to the trust because the trust disposed of the right to that payment in the year, a reasonable estimate of that payment on the assumption that the annuity contract had been held throughout the year and no rights under the contract were disposed of in the year;

Related Provisions: 146.3(1)"retirement income fund" — Requirement to withdraw minimum amount annually; 146.3(1.3) — Minimum amount for 2015; 146.3(1.4), (1.5) — Minimum amount for 2020; 146.3(2)(e.1), (e.2) — Requirement for carrier to retain enough property to pay out minimum amount; 146.3(5.1) — Amount included in income; Reg. 100(1)"remuneration"(j.1), 103(6)(d.1) — Withholding tax on payments; *Income Tax Conventions Interpretation Act* 5"periodic pension payment"(c) — Withdrawal of more than twice the minimum amount per year is not "periodic".

Notes: See Reg. 7308(4) for the prescribed "minimum amount" (MA) that must be withdrawn from a RRIF each year (Reg. 7308(3) for a RRIF set up before 1993) (for 2020, it is reduced by 1/4 due to COVID-19: 146.3(1.4)). The MA must be withdrawn annually from *each* plan, starting in the calendar year following the year in which the plan is set up, even if the annuitant has two RRIFs with the same carrier. See 146.3(1)"retirement income fund" and VIEWS docs 2002-0133905, 2007-023031E5, 2016-0669361E5. See also 146.3(1.3) for 2015. For the year of death, the MA is the same as it would have been (and see 146.3(6.11) Notes): 2019-0811901C6 [2019 APFF Financial q.8]. For the parallel rules for registered pension plans, see Reg. 8506(5).

A "transitional prohibited investment benefit" extracted under 207.05(4) counts towards the minimum amount: VIEWS doc 2012-0453161C6.

The minimum amount need not be withdrawn in cash, so there is no need to sell assets to satisfy the withdrawal requirement. The Minister of Finance wrote to financial institutions on Nov. 20/08 (Finance news release 2008-093), asking them to ensure that in-kind withdrawals can be done at no cost "and that RRIF clients will be made aware of this option". (Of course, cash will be needed to pay tax on the withdrawal.)

If the value of the RRIF is nil the minimum amount is nil, but an annuity contract with guaranteed benefits does not have nil value: VIEWS doc 2009-0342961E5.

The minimum amount rates in Reg. 7308(3)-(4) needed to be reduced due to lower interest rates in recent years, and this was done in the 2015 Budget bill. Robson & Laurin, "Drawing Down Our Savings" (tinyurl.com/cdh-rrif, July 2015) recommends they be reduced further, due to low yields and increased longevity.

The required withdrawals can cause the taxpayer to lose the Guaranteed Income Supplement: *Ward*, 2008 TCC 25; *Gaisford*, 2011 FCA 28; *Katz*, 2012 TCC 232 (FCA appeal discontinued A-412-12) (unclear whether reduced income due to higher withdrawal in earlier year was a "loss of pension income").

Opening words of definition amended by 2007 budget bill #1, last change effective 2009.

146.3(1)"minimum amount"B(b) amended by 2000 same-sex partners bill to refer to "common-law partner", effective as per Notes to 248(1)"common-law partner".

146.3(1)"minimum amount" amended by 1995-97 technical bill, effective:

(a) for 1998 and later taxation years, with respect to

(i) RIFs entered into after February 1986, and

(ii) RIFs entered into before March 1986 and revised or amended after February 1986 and before 1998;

(b) for the year in which a RIF is first revised or amended after 1997, and for later years, if the RIF was entered into before March 1986 and was not revised or amended after February 1986 and before 1998; and

(c) with respect to a RIF that governs a trust that, after July 1997, holds a contract for an annuity, for all years that begin after the first day

(i) that is after July 1997, and

(ii) on which the trust holds such a contract.

Before the amendment, the definition read:

"minimum amount" under a retirement income fund for the year in which the fund is entered into is nil and for each subsequent year is the product obtained when the fair market value of the property held in connection with the fund at the beginning of that subsequent year is multiplied by

(a) where the first annuitant under the fund elected in respect of the fund under paragraph (b), as it read before 1992, or under subparagraph 146.3(1)(f)(i) of the *Income Tax Act*, chapter 148 of the Revised Statutes of Canada, 1952, as it read before 1986, to use the age of another individual, the prescribed amount for that subsequent year in respect of the other individual,

(b) where paragraph (a) does not apply and the first annuitant under the fund so elects before any payment has been made under the fund by the carrier, the prescribed amount for that subsequent year in respect of an individual who was the spouse of the first annuitant at the time of the election, or

(c) in any other case, the prescribed amount for that subsequent year in respect of the first annuitant under the fund;

(The amendments are largely consequential on new 146.3(1)"qualified investment"(b.1) and (b.2), which permit a trusteed RRIF to hold certain types of annuity contracts. These amendments avoid the difficulty of determining the value of a locked-in annuity each year, and make it practical for a minimum amount to be calculated and distributed where a locked-in annuity is held by an RRIF. If an RRIF holds only locked-in annuities at the beginning of a year, the minimum amount for the year will never exceed the annuity payments received by the trust in that year.)

146.3(1)"minimum amount" was 146.3(1)(b.1) before RSC 1985 (5th Supp) consolidation for tax years ending after Nov. 1991.

146.3(1)"minimum amount" (formerly 146.3(1)(b.1)) amended by 1992 Budget/technical bill, applicable

(a) to the 1992 and later taxation years with respect to

(i) retirement income funds entered into after February 1986, and

(ii) retirement income funds entered into before March 1986 and revised or amended after February 1986 and before 1992; and

(b) to the taxation year in which a retirement income fund is first revised or amended after February 1986 and to later taxation years, where the fund was entered into before March 1986 and was not revised or amended after February 1986 and before 1992.

However, for the purposes of determining withholding taxes (regulations made under 153(1)), for the application of the spousal attribution rule for RRIFs in 146.3(5.1), and for section 5 of the *Income Tax Conventions Interpretation Act*, the new definition is effective only for payments made in 1993 or later.

Regulations: 7308 (prescribed factor).

I.T. Application Rules: 69 (meaning of "chapter 148 of ...").

Interpretation Bulletins: IT-528: Transfers of funds between registered plans.

Information Circulars: 78-18R6: Registered retirement income funds.

"property held" in connection with a retirement income fund means property held by the carrier of the fund, whether held by the carrier as trustee or beneficial owner thereof, the value of which, or the income or loss from which, is relevant in determining the amount for a year payable to the annuitant under the fund;

Notes: 146.3(1)"property held" was 146.3(1)(c) before RSC 1985 (5th Supp) consolidation for tax years ending after Nov. 1991.

146.3(1)(c) (now 146.3(1)"property held") amended in 1986, effective for RRIFs entered into after February 1986. Where an earlier RRIF is revised or amended after February 1986, effective as of the taxation year in which it is revised or amended. For earlier RRIFs that are not revised or amended, read:

(c) "property held in connection with the arrangement" means property held by a carrier of a retirement income fund, whether held by the carrier as trustee or beneficial owner thereof,

(i) the value of which, or

(ii) the income or loss from which

is relevant in determining the amount payable in a year to the annuitant under the fund;

"qualified investment" for a trust governed by a registered retirement income fund means

(a) an investment that would be described by any of paragraphs (a) to (d), (f) and (g) of the definition "qualified investment" in section 204 if the reference in that definition to "a trust governed by a deferred profit sharing plan or revoked plan" were read as a reference to "a trust governed by a registered retirement income fund" and if that definition were read without reference to the words "with the exception of excluded property in relation to the trust",

(b) [Repealed]

(b.1) a contract for an annuity issued by a licensed annuities provider where

(i) the trust is the only person who, disregarding any subsequent transfer of the contract by the trust, is or may become entitled to any annuity payments under the contract, and

(ii) the holder of the contract has a right to surrender the contract at any time for an amount that would, if reasonable sales and administration charges were ignored, approximate the value of funds that could otherwise be applied to fund future periodic payments under the contract,

(b.2) a contract for an annuity issued by a licensed annuities provider where

(i) annual or more frequent periodic payments are or may be made under the contract to the holder of the contract,

(ii) the trust is the only person who, disregarding any subsequent transfer of the contract by the trust, is or may become entitled to any annuity payments under the contract,

(iii) neither the time nor the amount of any payment under the contract may vary because of the length of any life, other than

(A) if the annuitant under the fund (in this paragraph referred to as the "RRIF annuitant") has made the election referred to in the definition "retirement income fund" in respect of the fund and a spouse or common-law partner, the life of the RRIF annuitant or the life of the spouse or common-law partner, and

(B) in any other case, the life of the RRIF annuitant,

(iv) the day on which the periodic payments began or are to begin (in this paragraph referred to as the "start date") is not later than the end of the year following the year in which the contract was acquired by the trust,

(v) either

(A) the periodic payments are payable for the life of the RRIF annuitant or the joint lives of the RRIF annuitant and the RRIF annuitant's spouse or common-law partner and either there is no guaranteed period under the contract or there is a guaranteed period that begins at the start date and does not exceed a term equal to 90 years minus the lesser of

(I) the age in whole years at the start date of the RRIF annuitant (determined on the assumption that the RRIF annuitant is alive at the start date), and

(II) the age in whole years at the start date of a spouse or common-law partner of the RRIF annuitant (determined on the assumption that a spouse or common-law partner of the RRIF annuitant at the time the contract was acquired is a spouse or common-law partner of the RRIF annuitant at the start date), or

(B) the periodic payments are payable for a term equal to

(I) 90 years minus the age described in subclause (A)(I), or

(II) 90 years minus the age described in subclause (A)(II), and

(vi) the periodic payments

(A) are equal, or

(B) are not equal solely because of one or more adjustments that would, if the contract were an annuity under a retirement savings plan, be in accordance with subparagraphs 146(3)(b)(iii) to (v) or that arise because of a uniform reduction in the entitlement to the periodic payments as a consequence of a partial surrender of rights to the periodic payments, and

(c) such other investments as may be prescribed by regulations of the Governor in Council made on the recommendation of the Minister of Finance;

Related Provisions: 87(10) — New share issued on amalgamation of public corporation deemed listed; 132.2(3)(h) — Where share ceases to be QI due to mutual fund reorganization; 146.3(7) — Tax on acquisition of non-QI; 146.3(9) — Tax on income from non-QI; 207.01(6) — Deemed disposition by RRIF on property becoming or ceasing to be QI; 207.04 — Tax payable by annuitant if RRIF acquires non-QI.

Notes: See Notes to 146(1)"qualified investment"; many qualified investments are listed in 204"qualified investment" and Reg. 4900(1). See 146.3(9) Notes re acquisition of non-qualified investments.

Para. (b.2) annuities are called "locked-in annuities". 146(1)"qualified investment"(c.1)-(c.2) provide parallel rules for RRSPs.

Para. (b.3), "an advanced life deferred annuity", was proposed in the July 30, 2019 draft legislation, but was not in 2021 budget bill #1, which enacted the ALDA rules (Finance decided not to permit RRSPs and RRIFs to hold an ALDA contract, but 146.3(14.1)(c) permits transfer of RRIF funds to an ALDA).

Definition amended by 2007 budget bill #1 (effective March 19, 2007), 2001 technical bill, 2000 same-sex partners bill 1995-97 technical bill, effective 1997. 146.3(1)"qualified investment" was 146.3(1)(d) before RSC 1985 (5th Supp) consolidation for tax years ending after Nov. 1991.

Regulations: 221 (information return where mutual fund etc. claims its shares are QI); 4900 (prescribed investments).

Remission Orders: *Lionaird Capital Corporation Notes Remission Order*, P.C. 1999-737 (tax under 146.3(7) waived because taxpayers thought they were qualified investments).

Income Tax Folios: S3-F10-C1: Qualified investments — RRSPs, RESPs, RRIFs, RDSPs and TFSAs [replaces IT-320R3].

Information Circulars: 78-18R6: Registered retirement income funds.

Registered Plans Compliance Bulletins: 4 (abusive schemes — RRSP stripping).

Forms: T3F: Investments prescribed to be qualified information return.

"registered retirement income fund" means a retirement income fund accepted by the Minister for registration for the purposes of this Act and registered under the Social Insurance Number of the first annuitant under the fund;

Related Provisions: 18(1)(u) — Investment counselling fees for RRIF are non-deductible; 75(3)(a) — Reversionary trust rules do not apply to RRIF; 108(1)"trust"(a) — "Trust" does not include a RRIF for certain purposes; 128.1(10)"excluded right or interest"(a)(ii) — No deemed disposition of RRIF on emigration; 207.01(1)"advantage", 207.05 — Tax on advantage received from RRIF; 207.04 — Tax on annuitant if RRIF acquires non-qualified or prohibited investment; 248(1)"registered retirement income fund" — Definition applies to entire Act; Reg. 9006(b) — RRIF not reported to CRA for disclosure to foreign tax authorities.

Notes: RRIF issuers and advisers: see tinyurl.com/rrifs.

146.3(1)"registered retirement income fund" was 146.3(1)(e) before RSC 1985 (5th Supp) consolidation for tax years ending after Nov. 1991.

See also Notes at end of 146.3.

Interpretation Bulletins: IT-415R2: Deregistration of RRSPs (cancelled); IT-528: Transfers of funds between registered plans.

Forms: T2033: Direct transfer under subsec. 146.3(14.1), 147.5(21) or 146(21), or para. 146(16)(a) or 146.3(2)(e).

"retirement income fund" means an arrangement between a carrier and an annuitant under which, in consideration for the transfer to the carrier of property, the carrier undertakes to pay amounts to the annuitant (and, where the annuitant so elects, to the annuitant's spouse or common-law partner after the annuitant's death), the total of which is, in each year in which the minimum amount under the arrangement for the year is greater than nil, not less than the minimum amount under the arrangement for that year, but the amount of any such payment does not exceed the value of the property held in connection with the arrangement immediately before the time of the payment.

Related Provisions: 146.2(12) — TFSA deemed not to be RIF; 146.3(1)"minimum amount" — determination of minimum amount to be paid out; 248(1)"retirement income fund" — Definition applies to entire Act.

Notes: Definition amended by 2007 budget bill #1, effective 2007.

146.3(1)"retirement income fund" amended by 2000 same-sex partners bill to refer to "common-law partner", effective as per Notes to 248(1)"common-law partner".

Definition "retirement income fund" amended by 1993 technical bill, effective as follows:

- For a RIF entered into before March 1986 and not revised or amended, the new definition does not apply.

- For a RIF entered into before March 1986 and revised or amended from March 1986 through the end of 1991, the new definition is effective for 1992 and later tax years.

- For a RIF entered into before March 1986 and first revised or amended in 1992 or later, the new definition is effective for the tax year in which the RIF is first revised or amended and for all later tax years.

- For a RIF entered into after February 1986, the new definition is effective for 1992 and later tax years.

The amendment removes the requirement that the full value of the RIF be paid out at the end of the year in which the last payment is made. Under 146.3(1)"minimum amount", payments from a RRIF can now continue through the annuitant's lifetime. The old definition (now deemed never to have been in force since the amendment was retroactive to the in-force date of the previous amendments) is reproduced here up to PITA 46th ed.

146.3(1)"retirement income fund" was 146.3(1)(f) before RSC 1985 (5th Supp) consolidation for tax years ending after Nov. 1991.

146.3(1)(f) (now 146.3(1)"retirement income fund") amended in 1986, effective for RRIFs entered into after February 1986. Where an earlier RRIF is revised or amended after February 1986, the new version is effective as of the taxation year in which it is revised or amended. For earlier RRIFs that are not revised or amended, read:

(f) "retirement income fund" means an arrangement between a carrier and an individual under which, in consideration for the transfer to the carrier of property (including money), the carrier undertakes to pay to the individual and, where the individual so elects, to his spouse after his death should he die before the arrangement ceases,

(i) in each year, commencing with the first complete calendar year after the arrangement is entered into, one or more amounts, the aggregate of which is equal to the amount that would be payable in the year under a single premium annuity contract purchased at a cost equal to the fair market value of the property held in connection with the arrangement at the beginning of the year if

(A) the annuity provided for equal annual payments throughout its term,

(B) the interest rate, if any, used in computing the annuity payment were such rate as the annuitant designates in respect of the year, not exceeding 6% per annum, and

(C) the term of the annuity in years were equal to the number that is

(I) the difference between 90 and the number that is, or would be, the age in whole years of the individual at the beginning of the year, or

(II) if the individual's spouse is younger than the individual and he so elects before the beginning of the first complete calendar year after the arrangement is entered into, the difference between 90 and the number that is, or would be, the age in whole years of his spouse at the beginning of the year, but the amount of any such payment shall not exceed the value of the property held in connection with the arrangement immediately before the time of the payment, and

> (ii) at the end of the year in which the last payment under the arrangement is, in accordance with the terms and conditions of the arrangement, required to be made, an amount equal to the value of the property, if any, held in connection with the arrangement at that time.

See also Notes at end of 146.3.

Interpretation Bulletins: IT-415R2: Deregistration of RRSPs (cancelled).

Information Circulars: 78-18R6: Registered retirement income funds.

(1.1) Adjusted minimum amount for 2008 — The minimum amount under a retirement income fund for 2008 is 75 per cent of the amount that would, in the absence of this subsection, be the minimum amount under the fund for the year.

Related Provisions: 60.021 — Recontribution of overwithdrawn amount for 2008; 146.3(1.2) — Exceptions; 146.3(1.4) — Parallel rule for 2020; Reg. 8506(7)(b) — Parallel rule for registered pension plan.

Notes: 146.3(1.1)-(1.2) reduce mandatory RRIF withdrawals for 2008, to reduce the need to liquidate assets during the market crash. Added by 2008 budget bill #2, in force March 12, 2009.

Former 146.3(1.1) added by 1990 pension bill, effective 1988, and repealed by 1992 technical bill, effective 1993. It defined "spouse" to include a common-law spouse for purposes of certain provisions. A similar rule in 252(4) applied from 1993 to 2000 for all purposes of the Act.

(1.2) Exceptions — Subsection (1.1) does not apply to a retirement income fund

(a) for the purposes of subsections (5.1) and 153(1) and the definition "periodic pension payment" in section 5 of the *Income Tax Conventions Interpretation Act*; nor

(b) if the individual who was the annuitant under the fund on January 1, 2008 attained 70 years of age in 2007.

Notes: See Notes to 146.3(1.1).

(1.3) Exceptions [minimum amount for 2015 for certain purposes] — For the purposes of subsections (5.1) and 153(1) and the definition "periodic pension payment" in section 5 of the *Income Tax Conventions Interpretation Act*, the minimum amount under a retirement income fund for 2015 is the amount that would be the minimum amount under the fund for the year if it were determined using the prescribed factors under subsection 7308(3) or (4), as the case may be, of the *Income Tax Regulations* as they read on December 31, 2014.

Related Provisions: 146.3(1.4) — Minimum amount for 2020.

Notes: The "minimum amount" (MA) numbers in Reg. 7308(3) and (4) were reduced by the 2015 Budget to better reflect recent lower interest rates and longer lifespans. 146.3(1.3) provides that for certain specific purposes, the MA for 2015 remains what it would have been without the amendment. This rule is for 2015 only.

146.3(1.3) added by 2015 Budget bill, effective June 23, 2015.

(1.4) Adjusted minimum amount for 2020 [COVID-19] — The minimum amount under a retirement income fund for 2020 is 75% of the amount that would, in the absence of this subsection, be the minimum amount under the fund for the year.

Related Provisions: 146.3(1.5) — Exceptions; Reg. 8506(7.1) — Parallel rule for registered pension plan.

Notes: 146.3(1.4)–(1.5), added by 2020 COVID bill #1 effective March 25, 2020, reduce mandatory RRIF withdrawals for 2020, to reduce the need to liquidate assets during the initial COVID-19 market crash. A parallel change for variable benefits under a defined-contribution registered pension plan was made by adding Reg. 8506(7.1). These changes were announced in Dept. of Finance Backgrounder "Canada's COVID-19 Economic Response Plan: Support for Canadians and Businesses" (March 18, 2020). This measure does not include a recontribution option for annuitants, so no provision similar to 60.021 was added, as was done for 146.3(1.1) in 2008 (the 2020 announcement was made early in the year).

146.3(1.4)–(1.5) were modelled on 146.3(1.1)–(1.2), which applied for 2008.

(1.5) Exceptions — Subsection (1.4) does not apply to a retirement income fund for the purposes of subsections (5.1) and 153(1) and the definition "periodic pension payment" in section 5 of the *Income Tax Conventions Interpretation Act*.

Notes: See Notes to 146.3(1.4).

(2) Acceptance of fund for registration — The Minister shall not accept for registration for the purposes of this Act any retirement income fund of an individual unless, in the Minister's opinion, the following conditions are complied with:

(a) the fund provides that the carrier shall make only those payments described in any of paragraphs (d) and (e), the definition "retirement income fund" in subsection (1), and subsections (14) and (14.1);

(b) the fund provides that payments thereunder may not be assigned in whole or in part;

(c) if the carrier is a person referred to as a depositary in section 146, the fund provides that

> (i) the carrier has no right of offset as regards the property held in connection with the fund in respect of any debt or obligation owing to the carrier, and

> (ii) the property held in connection with the fund cannot be pledged, assigned or in any way alienated as security for a loan or for any purpose other than that of the making by the carrier to the annuitant those payments described in paragraph (a);

(d) the fund provides that, except where the annuitant's spouse or common-law partner becomes the annuitant under the fund, the carrier shall, as a consequence of the death of the annuitant, distribute the property held in connection with the fund at the time of the annuitant's death or an amount equal to the value of such property at that time;

(e) the fund provides that, at the direction of the annuitant, the carrier shall transfer all or part of the property held in connection with the fund, or an amount equal to its value at the time of the direction (other than property required to be retained in accordance with the provision described in paragraph (e.1) or (e.2)), together with all information necessary for the continuance of the fund, to a person who has agreed to be a carrier of another registered retirement income fund of the annuitant;

(e.1) where the fund does not govern a trust or the fund governs a trust created before 1998 that does not hold an annuity contract as a qualified investment for the trust, the fund provides that if an annuitant, at any time, directs that the carrier transfer all or part of the property held in connection with the fund, or an amount equal to its value at that time, to a person who has agreed to be a carrier of another registered retirement income fund of the annuitant or to a registered pension plan in accordance with subsection (14.1), the transferor shall retain an amount equal to the lesser of

> (i) the fair market value of such portion of the property as would, if the fair market value thereof does not decline after the transfer, be sufficient to ensure that the minimum amount under the fund for the year in which the transfer is made may be paid to the annuitant in the year, and

> (ii) the fair market value of all the property;

(e.2) where paragraph (e.1) does not apply, the fund provides that if an annuitant, at any time, directs that the carrier transfer all or part of the property held in connection with the fund, or an amount equal to its value at that time, to a person who has agreed to be a carrier of another registered retirement income fund of the annuitant or to a registered pension plan in accordance with subsection (14.1), the transferor shall retain property in the fund sufficient to ensure that the total of

> (i) all amounts each of which is the fair market value, immediately after the transfer, of a property held in connection with the fund that is

>> (A) property other than an annuity contract, or

>> (B) an annuity contract described, immediately after the transfer, in paragraph (b.1) of the definition "qualified investment" in subsection (1), and

(ii) all amounts each of which is a reasonable estimate, as of the time of the transfer, of the amount of an annual or more frequent periodic payment under an annuity contract (other than an annuity contract described in clause (i)(B)) that the trust may receive after the transfer and in the year of the transfer

is not less than the amount, if any, by which the minimum amount under the fund for that year exceeds the total of all amounts received out of or under the fund before the transfer that are included in computing the income of the annuitant under the fund for that year;

(f) the fund provides that the carrier shall not accept property as consideration thereunder other than property transferred from

(i) a registered retirement savings plan under which the individual is the annuitant,

(ii) another registered retirement income fund under which the individual is the annuitant,

(iii) the individual to the extent only that the amount of the consideration was an amount described in subparagraph 60(l)(v),

(iv) a registered retirement income fund or registered retirement savings plan of the individual's spouse or common-law partner or former spouse or common-law partner under a decree, order or judgment of a competent tribunal, or under a written separation agreement, relating to a division of property between the individual and the individual's spouse or common-law partner or former spouse or common-law partner in settlement of rights arising out of, or on the breakdown of, their marriage or common-law partnership,

(iv.1) a deferred profit sharing plan in accordance with subsection 147(19);

(v) a registered pension plan of which the individual is a member (within the meaning assigned by subsection 147.1(1)),

(vi) a registered pension plan in accordance with subsection 147.3(5) or (7),

(vii) a specified pension plan in circumstances to which subsection 146(21) applies;

(viii) a pooled registered pension plan in accordance with subsection 147.5(21); or

(ix) an advanced life deferred annuity under which the individual is the annuitant, if the transfer is a refund described under paragraph (g) of the definition "advanced life deferred annuity" in subsection 146.5(1);

(g) [Repealed]

(h) the fund in all other respects complies with regulations of the Governor in Council made on the recommendation of the Minister of Finance.

Related Provisions: 139.1(13) — Para. 146(2)(c.4) inapplicable to conversion benefit on demutualization of insurer; 146.3(11) — Change in fund after registration; 146.3(14)–(14.2) — Transfers; 172(3) — Appeal from refusal to register; 207.01(1)"advantage", 207.05 — Tax on advantage received from RRIF; 207.04 — Tax on annuitant if RRIF acquires non-qualified or prohibited investment; 248(3)(c) — RRIF set up in Quebec deemed to be trust; 248(8) — Meaning of "consequence" of death; 252(3) — Extended meaning of "spouse" and "former spouse"; Reg. 9006(b) — RRIF not reported to CRA for disclosure to foreign tax authorities.

Notes: See Notes at end of 146.3. RRIF issuers and advisers: see tinyurl.com/rrifs.

CRA's processing target (tinyurl.com/cra-standards) for responding to RRIF applications (to register, amend or terminate) is 90% within 60 days; in 2019-20, it did 100%.

See Notes to 146(4) re whether creditors can seize a RRIF, the effect of having a "designated beneficiary", and US filers.

146.3(2)(e.1)-(e.2) do not apply on marriage breakdown: VIEWS doc 2003-0182965.

146.3(2)(f)(ix) added by 2021 budget bill #1, effective 2020 (see 146.5).

146.3(2) amended by 1995-97 and 1991 technical bills, for RIFs entered into after July 13, 1990 (see these Notes up to PITA 59th ed. for details). Other amendments made by 2002-2013 technical bill (effective 2002); 2012 budget bill #2 (effective Dec. 14, 2012); 2011 budget bill #2; 2003 Budget; 2000 same-sex partners bill; 1995-97, 1993 and 1992 technical bills; 1990 pension bill.

Interpretation Bulletins: IT-307R4: Spousal or common-law registered retirement savings plans.

Information Circulars: 78-18R6: Registered retirement income funds.

Registered Plans Compliance Bulletins: 1, 2, 3 (how to contact us).

Registered Plans Frequently Asked Questions: RPFAQ-1 (RRSPs/RRIFs), q. 3 (change of carrier); q. 4 (common-law partner); q. 6 (foreign content rule for RRSPs).

Forms: T550: Application for registration of RSPs, ESPs or RIFs under s. 146, 146.1 and 146.3 of the ITA; T2033: Direct transfer under subsec. 146.3(14.1), 147.5(21) or 146(21), or para. 146(16)(a) or 146.3(2)(e).

(3) No tax while trust governed by fund — Except as provided in subsection (9), no tax is payable under this Part by a trust on the taxable income of the trust for a taxation year if, throughout the period in the year during which the trust was in existence, the trust was governed by a registered retirement income fund of an individual, except that if the trust has

(a) borrowed money in the year or has borrowed money that it has not repaid before the commencement of the year,

(b) received a gift of property (other than a transfer from a registered retirement savings plan under which the individual is the annuitant (within the meaning of subsection 146(1)) or a transfer from a registered retirement income fund under which the individual is the annuitant)

(i) in the year, or

(ii) in a preceding year and has not divested itself of the property or any property substituted therefor before the commencement of the year, or

(c) carried on any business or businesses in the year,

tax is payable under this Part by the trust,

(d) where paragraph (a) or (b) applies, on its taxable income for the year, and

(e) where neither paragraph (a) nor (b) applies and where paragraph (c) applies, on the amount, if any, by which

(i) the amount that its taxable income for the year would be if it had no incomes or losses from sources other than from the business or businesses, as the case may be,

exceeds

(ii) such portion of the amount determined under subparagraph (i) in respect of the trust for the year as can reasonably be considered to be income from, or from the disposition of, qualified investments for the trust.

Related Provisions: 138.1(7) — Segregated fund rules do not apply to RRIF; 146.3(3.1) — Exception; 146.3(9) — Tax on income from non-qualified investments; 146.3(15) — Amount earned on RRIF deposit account not taxable to annuitant; 149(1)(x) — RRIF exempt from tax; 207.01(1)"advantage", 207.05 — Tax on advantage received from RRIF; 207.04 — Tax on annuitant if RRIF acquires non-qualified or prohibited investment; 248(5) — Substituted property; Canada-U.S. Tax Treaty:Art. XVIII:5 — Deferral of income accruing in retirement plan.

Notes: A RRIF engaged in a securities lending practice for profit would likely be carrying on a business and so become taxable: VIEWS doc 2006-0213111E5.

See Notes to 146(4) re this rule for RRSPs, and re exemption from U.S. withholding taxes and from seizure by creditors.

146.3(3)(e)(ii) added by 1993 technical bill, for 1993 and later tax years. The amendment recognizes that business income may be allocated to units in limited partnerships that are held by RRIFs, and that the disposition of qualified investments can, in some cases, result in business income (rather than capital gains).

Income Tax Folios: S3-F10-C1: Qualified investments — RRSPs, RESPs, RRIFs, RDSPs and TFSAs [replaces IT-320R3].

Information Circulars: 78-18R6: Registered retirement income funds.

(3.1) Exception — Notwithstanding subsection (3), if the last annuitant under a registered retirement income fund has died, tax is payable under this Part by the trust governed by the fund on its taxable income for each year after the year following the year in which the last annuitant under the fund died.

Related Provisions: 104(6)(a.2) — Deduction for amounts paid out to beneficiaries.

Notes: 146(3.1) amended by 1993 technical bill, effective for 1993 and later taxation years.

(4) Disposition or acquisition of property by trust — Where at any time in a taxation year a trust governed by a registered retirement income fund

(a) disposes of property for a consideration less than the fair market value of the property at the time of the disposition, or for no consideration, or

(b) acquires property for a consideration greater than the fair market value of the property at the time of the acquisition,

2 times the difference between that fair market value and the consideration, if any, shall be included in computing the income for the taxation year of the taxpayer who is the annuitant under the fund at that time.

Related Provisions: 146(9) — Parallel rule for RRSP; 212(1)(q), 214(3)(i) — Non-resident withholding tax.

Notes: See Notes to 146(9).

Regulations: 215(3) (information return).

Information Circulars: 78-18R6: Registered retirement income funds.

Registered Plans Compliance Bulletins: 4 (abusive schemes — RRSP stripping).

(5) Benefits taxable — There shall be included in computing the income of a taxpayer for a taxation year all amounts received by the taxpayer in the year out of or under a registered retirement income fund other than the portion thereof that can reasonably be regarded as

(a) part of the amount included in computing the income of another taxpayer by virtue of subsections (6) and (6.2);

(b) an amount received in respect of the income of the trust under the fund for a taxation year for which the trust was not exempt from tax by virtue of subsection (3.1);

(c) an amount that relates to interest, or to another amount included in computing income otherwise than because of this section, and that would, if the fund were a registered retirement savings plan, be a tax-paid amount (within the meaning assigned by paragraph (b) of the definition "tax-paid amount" in subsection 146(1)); or

(d) an amount in respect of which the annuitant pays a tax under Part XI.01, unless the tax is waived, cancelled or refunded.

Related Provisions: 56(1)(t) — Income from RRIF; 60(l) — Transfer of refund of premium under RRSP; 139.1(12) — Conversion benefit on demutualization of insurance corporation not taxable; 146(1)"benefit" — Parallel rule for RRSPs; 146.3(1)"retirement income fund" — Requirement to withdraw minimum amount annually; 146.3(6.3), (6.4) — Deduction to deceased for post-death RRIF losses; 146.3(15) — Amount earned in RRIF deposit account not taxable; 147.3(13.1) — Withdrawal of excessive transfer to RRIF; 153(1)(l) — Withholding of tax on RRIF payments; 160.2(2) — Joint and several liability where non-annuitant receives amount from RRIF; 212(1)(q) — Withholding tax on RRIF payment to non-resident; Canada-U.S. Tax Treaty:Art. XXI:2(a) — RRSP exempt from U.S. tax.

Notes: Where a taxpayer tried to obtain a loan on the security of his RRIF payments, and signed a form that was fraudulently used to steal his RRIF funds, he was liable for tax on the withdrawal: *Bonavia*, 2010 FCA 129. (See also Notes to 146(10) re RRSP and RRIF frauds.) In *Visser*, 2009 TCC 306, there was no income inclusion where a T4RIF had been issued on dissolution of a corp held in the RRIF, but the taxpayer had received nothing. See also Notes to 146(10).

146.3(5)(d) added by 2011 budget bill #2, effective for transactions occurring, income earned, capital gains accruing and investments acquired after March 22, 2011. It excludes an amount taxed under 207.01–207.07.

146.3(5)(c) added by 1995-97 technical bill, effective for deaths after 1992.

See also Notes at end of 146.3.

Regulations: 215(2) (information return).

Information Circulars: 78-18R6: Registered retirement income funds.

I.T. Technical News: 39 (settlement of a shareholder class action suit).

Forms: T4RIF: Statement of income from a registered retirement income fund; T4RIF Summ: Return of income out of a registered retirement income fund; T4040: RRSPs and other registered plans for retirement [guide].

(5.1) Amount included in income [spousal attribution] — If at any time in a taxation year a particular amount in respect of a registered retirement income fund that is a spousal or common-law partner plan (within the meaning assigned by subsection 146(1)) in relation to a taxpayer is required to be included in the income of the taxpayer's spouse or common-law partner and the taxpayer is not living separate and apart from the taxpayer's spouse or common-law partner at that time by reason of the breakdown of their marriage or common-law partnership, there shall be included at that time in computing the taxpayer's income for the year an amount equal to the least of

(a) the total of all amounts each of which is a premium (within the meaning assigned by subsection 146(1)) paid by the taxpayer in the year or in one of the two immediately preceding taxation years to a registered retirement savings plan under which the taxpayer's spouse or common-law partner was the annuitant (within the meaning assigned by subsection 146(1)) at the time the premium was paid,

(b) the particular amount, and

(c) the amount, if any, by which

(i) the total of all amounts each of which is an amount in respect of the fund that is required, in the year and at or before that time, to be included in the income of the taxpayer's spouse or common-law partner

exceeds

(ii) the minimum amount under the fund for the year.

Related Provisions: 60(l) — Transfer of refund of premiums under RRSP; 146(8.21) — Premium deemed not paid; 146(8.3) — Parallel RRSP rule; 146(8.6) — RRSP — Spouse's income; 146.3(1.3) — Minimum amount for 2015; 146.3(5.4) — Spouse's income; 146.3(5.5) — Application of subsec. (5.1); 147.3(13.1) — Withdrawal of excessive transfer to RRIF.

Notes: See Notes to the parallel rule in 146(8.3).

146.3(5.1) opening words amended by 2002-2013 technical bill, effective 2001 or earlier, to change "spousal plan" to "spousal or common-law partner plan".

146.3(5.1) amended by 2000 same-sex partners bill (last change effective 2001), 1992 technical bill and 1990 pension bill.

Interpretation Bulletins: IT-307R4: Spousal or common-law registered retirement savings plans; IT-124R6: Contributions to registered retirement savings plans.

Forms: T4RIF: Statement of income from a registered retirement income fund; T4RIF Summ: Return of income out of a registered retirement income fund; T1234 Sched. B: Allowable amounts of non-refundable tax credits; T2205: Amounts from a spousal or common-law partner RRSP, RRIF or SPP to include in income.

(5.2) [Repealed under former Act]

Notes: 146.3(5.2) repealed by 1990 pension bill, effective 1991. It provided a rule of interpretation that is now superfluous.

(5.3) Ordering — Where a taxpayer has paid more than one premium described in subsection (5.1), such a premium or part thereof paid by the taxpayer at any time shall be deemed to have been included in computing the taxpayer's income by virtue of that subsection before premiums or parts thereof paid by the taxpayer after that time.

(5.4) Spouse's income — Where, in respect of an amount required at any time in a taxation year to be included in computing the income of a taxpayer's spouse or common-law partner, all or part of a premium has, by reason of subsection (5.1), been included in computing the taxpayer's income for the year, the following rules apply:

(a) the premium or part thereof, as the case may be, shall, for the purposes of subsections (5.1) and 146(8.3) after that time, be deemed not to have been a premium paid to a registered retirement savings plan under which the taxpayer's spouse or common-law partner was the annuitant (within the meaning assigned by subsection 146(1)); and

(b) an amount equal to the premium or part thereof, as the case may be, deducted in computing the income of the spouse or common-law partner for the year.

Related Provisions: 146(8.6) — Spouse's income.

Notes: 146.3(5.4) amended by 2000 same-sex partners bill to refer to "common-law partner", effective 2001 or earlier.

146.3(5.4) amended by 1990 pension bill, effective 1991.

(5.5) Where subsec. (5.1) does not apply — Subsection (5.1) does not apply

(a) in respect of a taxpayer at any time during the year in which the taxpayer dies;

(b) in respect of a taxpayer where either the taxpayer or the annuitant is a non-resident at the particular time referred to in that subsection;

(c) to any payment that is received in full or partial commutation of a registered retirement savings plan or a registered retirement income fund and in respect of which a deduction was made under paragraph 60(l) if, where the deduction was in respect of the acquisition of an annuity, the terms of the annuity provide that it cannot be commuted, and it is not commuted, in whole or in part within 3 years after the acquisition; or

(d) in respect of an amount that is deemed by subsection (6) to have been received by an annuitant under a registered retirement income fund immediately before the annuitant's death.

Notes: 146.3(5.5)(d) added by 1990 pension bill, effective 1988.

(6) Where last annuitant dies — Where the last annuitant under a registered retirement income fund dies, that annuitant shall be deemed to have received, immediately before death, an amount out of or under a registered retirement income fund equal to the fair market value of the property of the fund at the time of the death.

Related Provisions: 56(1)(t) — Income from RRIF; 60.02 — Rollover to RDSP; 146(8.8) — Parallel rule for RRSPs; 146.3(5.5) — Application of subsec. (5.1); 146.3(6.2) — Amount deductible; 146.3(6.3), (6.4) — Deduction to deceased for post-death RRIF losses; 160.2(2) — Joint and several liability for tax owing on payment from RRIF; 212(1)(q), 214(3)(i) — Non-resident withholding tax; 257 — Formula cannot calculate to less than zero.

Notes: See CRA guide RC4178; Notes to 146.3(1)"annuitant", 146(8.8). The beneficiary does not pay tax on RRIF amounts that are included in the deceased's income: VIEWS doc 2009-0318581E5. Where the deceased or spouse is non-resident, withholding tax applies under 212(1)(q): 2002-0141355, 2013-0495281C6 [2013 APFF q. 9]. If a designated-beneficiary spouse dies before the RRIF distribution, see 2020-0867001E5.

146.3(6) amended by 1993 technical bill, effective for deaths in 1993 or later.

Regulations: 215(4) (information return).

Forms: RC4178: Death of a RRIF annuitant [guide].

(6.1) Designated benefit deemed received — A designated benefit of an individual in respect of a registered retirement income fund that is received by the legal representative of the last annuitant under the fund shall be deemed

(a) to be received by the individual out of or under the fund at the time it is received by the legal representative; and

(b) except for the purpose of the definition "designated benefit" in subsection (1), not to be received out of or under the fund by any other person.

Related Provisions: 60(l)(v)(B.1) — Rollover of designated benefits to child or grandchild on death; 146(8.1) — Parallel rule for RRSPs; 212(1)(q), 214(3)(i) — Non-resident withholding tax.

Notes: See Notes to 146.3(1)"designated benefit".

146.3(6.1) amended by 1993 technical bill, effective for deaths in 1993 or later.

Forms: RC4178: Death of a RRIF annuitant [guide]; T1090: Death of a RRIF annuitant — designated benefit.

(6.11) Transfer of designated benefit — For the purpose of subparagraph 60(l)(v), the eligible amount of a particular individual for a taxation year in respect of a registered retirement income fund is nil unless the particular individual was

(a) a spouse or common-law partner of the last annuitant under the fund, or

(b) a child or grandchild of that annuitant who was dependent because of physical or mental infirmity on that annuitant,

in which case the eligible amount shall be determined by the formula

$$A \times \left[1 - \frac{(B - C)}{D}\right]$$

where

A is the portion of the designated benefit of the particular individual in respect of the fund that is included because of subsection (5) in computing the particular individual's income for the year,

B is the minimum amount under the fund for the year,

C is the lesser of

(a) the total amounts included because of subsection (5) in computing the income of an annuitant under the fund for the year in respect of amounts received by the annuitant out of or under the fund, and

(b) the minimum amount under the fund for the year, and

D is the total of all amounts each of which is the portion of a designated benefit of an individual in respect of the fund that is included because of subsection (5) in computing the individual's income for the year.

Related Provisions: 60(l)(ii)(a), 60.011 — Transfer to trust for infirm dependent child; 60.02(1)"eligible proceeds"(b) — Rollover of eligible amount to RDSP on death; 257 — Formula cannot calculate to less than zero.

Notes: For the calculation in 146.3(6.11), see Guide T4079, Appendix C; VIEWS doc 2019-0811901C6 [2019 APFF Financial q.8] (effect of death).

146.3(6.11)(a) amended by 2000 same-sex partners bill, effective 2001 or earlier.

146.3(6.11) added by 1993 technical bill, effective for deaths in 1993 or later.

Forms: RC4178: Death of a RRIF annuitant [guide]; T4079: T4RSP and T4RIF guide.

(6.2) Amount deductible — There may be deducted from the amount deemed by subsection (6) to be received by an annuitant out of or under a registered retirement income fund an amount not exceeding the amount determined by the formula

$$A \times \left[1 - \frac{(B + C - D)}{(B + C)}\right]$$

where

A is the total of

(a) all designated benefits of individuals in respect of the fund,

(b) all amounts that would, if the fund were a registered retirement savings plan, be tax-paid amounts (in this subsection having the meaning assigned by subsection 146(1)) in respect of the fund received by individuals who received, otherwise than because of subsection (6.1), designated benefits in respect of the fund, and

(c) all amounts each of which is an amount that would, if the fund were a registered retirement savings plan, be a tax-paid amount in respect of the fund received by the legal representative of the last annuitant under the fund, to the extent that the legal representative would have been entitled to designate that tax-paid amount under paragraph (a) of the definition "designated benefit" in subsection (1) if tax-paid amounts were not excluded in determining refunds of premiums (as defined in subsection 146(1));

B is the fair market value of the property of the fund at the particular time that is the later of

(a) the end of the first calendar year that begins after the death of the annuitant, and

(b) the time immediately after the last time that any designated benefit in respect of the fund is received by an individual;

C is the total of all amounts paid out of or under the fund after the death of the last annuitant thereunder and before the particular time; and

D is the lesser of

(a) the fair market value of the property of the fund at the time of the death of the last annuitant thereunder, and

(b) the sum of the values of B and C in respect of the fund.

Related Provisions: 118.1(5.2)(b) — Designation of charity as beneficiary of RRIF; 146(8.9) — Parallel rule for RRSPs; 152(6)(f.3) — Reassessment to allow loss carryback.

Notes: See Notes to 146.3(1)"annuitant".

146.3(6.2) amended by 1993 technical bill and by 1995-97 technical bill (to add paras. A(b) and (c)), both effective for deaths in 1993 or later.

Forms: RC4178: Death of a RRIF annuitant [guide].

(6.3) Deduction for post-death reduction in value — If the last annuitant under a registered retirement income fund dies, there may be deducted in computing the annuitant's income for the taxation year in which the annuitant dies an amount not exceeding the amount determined, after all amounts payable out of or under the fund have been paid, by the formula

$$A - B$$

where

A is the total of all amounts each of which is

(a) the amount deemed by subsection (6) to have been received by the annuitant out of or under the fund,

(b) an amount (other than an amount described in paragraph (c)) received, after the death of the annuitant, by a taxpayer out of or under the fund and included, because of subsection (5), in computing the taxpayer's income, or

(c) an amount that would, if the fund were a registered retirement savings plan, be a tax-paid amount (within the meaning assigned by subsection 146(1)) in respect of the fund; and

B is the total of all amounts paid out of or under the fund after the death of the annuitant.

Related Provisions: 60(i) — Deduction in computing net income; 146(8.92) — Parallel rule for RRSP; 146.3(6.4) — Exceptions; 147.5(19) — Parallel rule for PRPP; 152(6)(f.3) — Reassessment to allow carryback of loss; 257 — Formula cannot calculate to less than zero; Reg. 215(6) — Information return required.

Notes: See Notes to the parallel rule for RRSPs in 146(8.92).

146.3(6.3) added by 2009 budget bill #1, for a RRIF from which the last payment is made after 2008. Limited administrative relief was available for RRIFs wound up before 2009: VIEWS doc 2009-0329761C6.

Regulations: 215(6) (information return).

Forms: RC249: Post-death decline in the value of RRIF, an unmatured RRSP and Post-Death Increase or Decline in the Value of a PRPP.

(6.4) Subsec. (6.3) not applicable — Except where the Minister has waived in writing the application of this subsection with respect to all or any portion of the amount determined in subsection (6.3) in respect of a registered retirement income fund, that subsection does not apply if

(a) at any time after the death of the annuitant, a trust governed by the fund held an investment that is not a qualified investment; or

(b) the last payment out of or under the fund was made after the end of the year following the year in which the annuitant died.

Related Provisions: 146(8.93) — Parallel rule for RRSP.

Notes: 146.3(6.4) added by 2009 budget bill #1, effective in respect of a RRIF in respect of which the last payment out of the fund is made after 2008.

(7) Property used as security for loan — If at any time in a taxation year a trust governed by a registered retirement income fund uses or permits to be used any property of the trust as security for a loan, the fair market value of the property at the time it commenced to be so used shall be included in computing the income for the year of the taxpayer who is the annuitant under the fund at that time.

Related Provisions: 146.3(9) — Tax payable where non-qualified investment acquired; 146.3(10) — Recovery of property used as security; 212(1)(q), 214(3)(i) — Non-resident withholding tax; 259(1) — Election for proportional holdings in trust property.

Notes: 146.3(7) amended by 2011 budget bill #2, effective for investments acquired after March 22, 2011. Before amendment, it also required income inclusion on acquiring a non-qualified investment. (See now 207.04 instead.) See Notes to 146.3(9) and 146(10).

Regulations: 215(3) (information return).

Remission Orders: *Lionaird Capital Corporation Notes Remission Order*, P.C. 1999-737 (tax under 146.3(7) waived because taxpayers thought they were qualified investments).

Registered Plans Compliance Bulletins: 4 (abusive schemes — RRSP stripping).

(8) [Repealed]

Notes: 146.3(8) repealed by 2011 budget bill #2, effective in respect of investments acquired after March 22, 2011. It allowed a deduction on disposition of a non-qualified investment of the amount included under 146.3(7) as it then read. See now 207.04.

(9) Tax payable on income from non-qualified investment — If a trust that is governed by a registered retirement income fund holds, at any time in a taxation year, a property that is not a qualified investment,

(a) tax is payable under this Part by the trust on the amount that its taxable income for the year would be if it had no incomes or losses from sources other than the property that is not a qualified investment or no capital gains or capital losses other than from the disposition of that property, as the case may be; and

(b) for the purposes of paragraph (a),

(i) "income" includes dividends described in section 83, and

(ii) paragraphs 38(a) and (b) are to be read as if the fraction set out in each of those paragraphs were replaced by the word "all".

Related Provisions: 146(10.1) — Parallel rule for RRSP; 146.3(3) — No tax while trust governed by fund; 146.3(7) — Acquisition of non-qualified investment by trust; 149(1)(x) — RRIF exemption; 207.04 — Tax on annuitant if RRIF acquires non-qualified or prohibited investment; 259(1) — Election for proportional holdings in trust property.

Notes: 146.3(9) imposes tax on any *income or gain* from non-qualified investments. 207.04(1) imposes a penalty tax on the *acquisition* of a non-qualified investment (refundable under 207.04(4) if it was inadvertent and the investment is disposed of quickly). 207.1(4), which imposed a monthly tax on *holding* a non-qualified investment, has been repealed. See also Notes to the parallel rule in 146(10.1).

146.3(9) amended by 2002-2013 technical bill, last change effective June 26, 2013.

Income Tax Folios: S3-F10-C1: Qualified investments — RRSPs, RESPs, RRIFs, RDSPs and TFSAs [replaces IT-320R3]; S3-F10-C2: Prohibited investments — RRSPs, RRIFs and TFSAs.

Information Circulars: 78-18R6: Registered retirement income funds.

(10) Recovery of property used as security — Where at any time in a taxation year a loan for which a trust governed by a registered retirement income fund has used or permitted to be used trust property as security ceases to be extant, and the fair market value of the property so used was included by virtue of subsection (7) in computing the income of a taxpayer who was the annuitant under the fund, there may be deducted in computing the income for a taxation year of the taxpayer who is at that time the annuitant, an amount equal to the amount, if any, remaining when

(a) the net loss (exclusive of payments by the trust as or on account of interest) sustained by the trust in consequence of its using or permitting to be used the property as security for the loan and not as a result of a change in the fair market value of the property

is deducted from

(b) the amount so included in computing the income of a taxpayer in consequence of the trust's using or permitting to be used the property as security for the loan.

Regulations: 215(3) (information return).

(11) Change in fund after registration — Where, on any day after a retirement income fund has been accepted by the Minister for registration for the purposes of this Act, the fund is revised or amended or a new fund is substituted therefor, and the fund as revised or amended or the new fund substituted therefor, as the case may be, (in this subsection referred to as the "amended fund") does not comply with the requirements of this section for its acceptance by the Minister for registration for the purposes of this Act, the following rules apply:

(a) the amended fund shall be deemed, for the purposes of this Act, not to be a registered retirement income fund; and

(b) the taxpayer who was the annuitant under the fund before it became an amended fund shall, in computing the taxpayer's income for the taxation year that includes that day, include as income received out of the fund at that time an amount equal to the fair market value of all the property held in connection with the fund immediately before that time.

Related Provisions: 146.3(2) — Requirements for acceptance for registration; 146.3(12) — Where arrangement deemed to be new fund substituted for RRIF; 146.3(13) — Where fund deemed revised or amended; 147.3(13.1) — Withdrawal of excessive transfer to RRSP; 153(1)(l) — Withholdings; 204.2(1.4) — Deemed receipt where RRSP or RRIF amended; 212(1)(q), 214(3)(i) — Non-resident withholding tax.

Information Circulars: 78-18R6: Registered retirement income funds.

Forms: T1234 Sched. B: Allowable amounts of non-refundable tax credits; T2205: Amounts from a spousal or common-law partner RRSP, RRIF or SPP to include in income.

(12) Idem — For the purposes of subsection (11), an arrangement under which a right or obligation under a retirement income fund is released or extinguished either wholly or in part and either in exchange or substitution for any right or obligation, or otherwise (other than an arrangement the sole object and legal effect of which is to revise or amend the fund) or under which payment of any amount by way of loan or otherwise is made on the security of a right under a retirement income fund, shall be deemed to be a new fund substituted for the retirement income fund.

Regulations: 215(4) (information return).

(13) [Repealed]

Notes: 146.3(13) repealed by 2011 budget bill #2, effective for transactions occurring, income earned, capital gains accruing and investments acquired after March 22, 2011. It caused an RRSP to become deregistrable on extending a prohibited benefit or loan. A RRIF advantage is now taxed under 207.05.

(14) Transfer on breakdown of marriage or common-law partnership — An amount is transferred from a registered retirement income fund of an annuitant in accordance with this subsection if the amount

(a) is transferred on behalf of an individual who is a spouse or common-law partner or former spouse or common-law partner of the annuitant and who is entitled to the amount under a decree, an order or a judgment of a competent tribunal, or under a written agreement, that relates to a division of property between the annuitant and the individual in settlement of rights that arise out of, or on a breakdown of, their marriage or common-law partnership; and

(b) is transferred directly to

(i) a registered retirement income fund under which the individual is the annuitant, or

(ii) a registered retirement savings plan under which the individual is the annuitant (within the meaning assigned by subsection 146(1)).

Related Provisions: 146(16)(b) — Transfer of RRSP on marriage breakdown; 146(21.2) — Sask. Pension Plan account deemed to be RRSP for purposes of 146.3(14); 146.3(2)(e)–(e.2) — Conditions applying on transfer; 146.3(14.2) — Effect of transfer; 147.5(12) — Pooled registered pension plan deemed to be RRSP for purposes of 146.3(14); 252(3) — Extended meaning of "spouse" and "former spouse".

Notes: On transfer of a RRIF on marriage breakdown, the first RRIF carrier need not hold back assets to pay out the minimum amount for the year, as 146.3(2)(e.1) and (e.2) do not apply: VIEWS doc 2003-0182965.

Where spouses separate but one dies before 146.3(14) can apply, see VIEWS doc 2017-0707801C6 for a solution [2017 APFF q.5].

146.3(14) amended by 2003 Budget (effective 2004; partly moved to 146(14.2)), 2000 same-sex partners bill, 1992 technical bill and 1990 pension bill.

Regulations: 215(5) (information return).

Interpretation Bulletins: IT-307R4: Spousal or common-law registered retirement savings plans; IT-528: Transfers of funds between registered plans.

Remission Orders: *Certain Taxpayers Remission Order, 1999-2*, P.C. 1999-1855, s. 2 (remission to Quebec judges for excess contributions in 1989-90 transferred under 146.3(14)).

Information Circulars: 78-18R6: Registered retirement income funds.

Forms: T2033: Direct transfer under subsec. 146.3(14.1), 147.5(21) or 146(21), or para. 146(16)(a) or 146.3(2)(e); T2220: Transfer from an RRSP, RRIF, PRPP or SPP to another RRSP, RRIF or SPP on breakdown of marriage or common-law partnership.

(14.1) Transfer to PRPP or RPP [or ALDA] — An amount is transferred from a registered retirement income fund of an annuitant in accordance with this subsection if the amount

(a) is transferred at the direction of the annuitant directly to an account of the annuitant under a pooled registered pension plan;

(b) is transferred at the direction of the annuitant directly to a registered pension plan of which, at any time before the transfer, the annuitant was a member (within the meaning assigned by subsection 147.1(1)) or to a prescribed registered pension plan and is allocated to the annuitant under a money purchase provision (within the meaning assigned by subsection 147.1(1)) of the plan; or

(c) is transferred at the direction of the annuitant directly to a licensed annuities provider to acquire an advanced life deferred annuity for the benefit of the annuitant.

Related Provisions: 146.3(14.2) — Effect of transfer; 205(1)"excess ALDA transfer" — Excessive transfer to advanced life deferred annuity; Reg. 8300(1)"excluded contribution" — Amount transferred is excluded contribution; Reg. 8502(b)(iv) — RPP may accept transfer under 146.3(14.1).

Notes: 146.3(14.1)(b) (added as (14.1) by 2003 Budget effective 2004), permits direct transfer of an amount from a RRIF to a money purchase provision of an RPP for the same annuitant, provided the annuitant was previously a member of the RPP. It accommodates transfers of funds back to a money purchase RPP by former members who had previously transferred their money purchase account to an RRSP or RRIF and who now wish to benefit from the new RRIF-type payout option for money purchase RPPs announced in the 2003 Budget (see under Reg. 8506(1)(a)).

146.3(14.1)(c) added by 2021 budget bill #1, effective 2020 (see 146.5); (a) added by 2012 budget bill #2, effective Dec. 14, 2012.

Regulations: 216(2) (information return on transfer to ALDA).

(14.2) Taxation of amount transferred — An amount transferred on behalf of an individual in accordance with paragraph (2)(e) or subsection (14) or (14.1)

(a) is not, solely because of that transfer, to be included in computing the income of any taxpayer; and

(b) is not to be deducted in computing the income of any taxpayer.

Notes: 146.3(14.2) added by 2003 Budget, effective 2004. (Before 2004, see 146(14).)

(15) Credited or added amount deemed not received — Where

(a) an amount is credited or added to a deposit with a depositary referred to in paragraph (d) of the definition "carrier" in subsection (1) as interest or income in respect of the deposit,

(b) the deposit is a registered retirement income fund at the time the amount is credited or added to the deposit, and

(c) during the calendar year in which the amount is credited or added or during the preceding calendar year, the annuitant under the fund was alive,

the amount shall be deemed not to be received by the annuitant or any other person solely because of the crediting or adding.

Notes: 146.3(15) amended by 1993 technical bill, effective for deaths in 1993 or later. (The same change with respect to RRSPs was made in 146(20).)

Notes [s. 146.3]: For RRIFs generally see tinyurl.com/rrif-cra; Mark Kaplan, "Registered Retirement Income Funds: An Update", 47(1) *Canadian Tax Journal* 134-47 (1999); *Miller Thomson on Estate Planning* (Carswell, looseleaf), chap. 6.

A RRIF cannot be seized on bankruptcy: see Notes to 146(4).

Definitions [s. 146.3]: "advanced life deferred annuity" — 146.5(1), 248(1); "amount" — 248(1); "annuitant" — 146.3(1); "annuity" — 248(1); "arm's length" — 251(1); "authorized foreign bank" — 248(1); "beneficial owner" — 248(3); "calendar year" — *Interpretation Act* 37(1)(a); "capital gain", "capital loss" — 39(1), 248(1); "carrier" — 146.3(1); "common-law partner", "common-law partnership" — 248(1); "consequence of the death" — 248(8); "corporation" — 248(1), *Interpretation Act*; "deferred profit sharing plan" — 147(1), 248(1); "depositary" — 146(1)"retirement savings plan"(b)(iii), 146.3(1)"carrier"(d); "designated benefit" — 146.3(1); "eligible amount" — 146.3(6.11); "fair market value" — see 69(1) Notes; "former spouse" — 252(3); "held" — 146.3(1); "individual", "legal representative" — 248(1); "licensed annuities provider" — 147(1), 248(1); "listed" — 87(10); "minimum amount" — 146.3(1), (1.3); "Minister" — 248(1); "Minister of Finance" — *Financial Administration Act* 14; "non-resident", "person" — 248(1); "pooled registered pension plan" — 147.5(1), 248(1); "prescribed" — 248(1); "property" — 248(1); "property held" — 146.3(1); "province" — *Interpretation Act* 35(1); "qualified investment" — 146.3(1);

"received" — 146.3(15); "refunds of premiums" — 146(1)"refund of premiums"; "registered pension plan" — 248(1); "registered retirement income fund" — 146.3(1), 248(1); "registered retirement savings plan" — 146(1), 248(1); "retirement income fund" — 146.3(1), 248(1); "separation agreement" — 248(1); "specified pension plan" — 248(1), Reg. 7800; "spousal or common-law partner plan" — 146(1); "spouse" — 252(3); "substituted" — 248(5); "surviving spouse" — 146.3(1)"annuitant"(b); "tax-paid amount" — 146(1); "taxable income" — 2(2), 248(1); "taxation year" — 249; "taxpayer" — 248(1); "trust" — 104(1), 248(1), (3); "written" — *Interpretation Act* 35(1)"writing".

Registered Disability Savings Plan

146.4 (1) Definitions — The following definitions apply in this section.

"assistance holdback amount", in relation to a disability savings plan, has the meaning assigned under the *Canada Disability Savings Act*.

Notes: See Notes at end of 146.4 for the text of the CDSA. In general terms, the assistance holdback amount (AHA) is the amount that the plan would be required, under the CDSA, to repay to the government if a disability assistance payment (DAP) were made from the plan.

A DAP cannot be paid if the value of the plan's assets would fall below the AHA: 146.4(4)(j). This ensures that the plan has enough assets to satisfy its potential repayment obligations under the CDSA.

The AHA is used in calculating the non-taxable portion of a DAP (146.4(7)), and in the rules triggering de-registration if a plan becomes non-compliant (146.4(10)).

"contribution" to a disability savings plan does not include (other than for the purpose of paragraph (b) of the definition "disability savings plan")

(a) an amount paid into the plan under or because of the *Canada Disability Savings Act* or a designated provincial program;

(b) an amount paid into the plan under or because of any other program that has a similar purpose to a designated provincial program and that is funded, directly or indirectly, by a province (other than an amount paid into the plan by an entity described in subparagraph (a)(iii) of the definition "qualifying person" in its capacity as holder of the plan);

(c) an amount transferred to the plan in accordance with subsection (8); or

(d) other than for the purposes of paragraphs (4)(f) to (h) and (n),

    (i) a specified RDSP payment as defined in subsection 60.02(1), or

    (ii) an accumulated income payment made to the plan under subsection 146.1(1.2).

Notes: This definition excludes amounts paid into the plan under the CDSA (reproduced in Notes at end of 146.4) so CDSA grants and bonds paid to an RDSP are not counted towards the $200,000 lifetime contribution limit in 146.4(4)(g)(iii), and are taxable when paid out of the plan. The definition also excludes prescribed payments, anticipating that some provinces may contribute to RDSPs for their residents.

For the meaning of "indirectly" in para. (b), see Notes to 17.1(1).

Para. (d) opening words amended by 2017 budget bill #2, effective March 23, 2017, to delete reference to 205(1)"advantage"(b). (205-207 were repealed; 207.01-207.07 now apply to RDSPs.)

Definition earlier amended by 2012 budget bill #2 (effective 2014), 2010 budget bills #1 and #2.

Regulations: No "prescribed payment" has been proposed for purposes of this definition.

RDSP Bulletins: 4 (Bill C-45).

"DTC-eligible individual", in respect of a taxation year, means an individual in respect of whom an amount is deductible, or would if this Act were read without reference to paragraph 118.3(1)(c) be deductible, under section 118.3 in computing a taxpayer's tax payable under this Part for the taxation year.

Related Provisions: 152(1.01), (1.2) — DTC-eligible status can be appealed.

"designated provincial program" means a program that is established under the laws of a province and that supports savings in registered disability savings plans.

Notes: 146.4(1)"designated provincial program" added by 2010 budget bill #1, effective for 2009 and later taxation years.

"disability assistance payment", in relation to a disability savings plan of a beneficiary, means any payment made from the plan to the beneficiary or to the beneficiary's estate.

Related Provisions: 146.4(7) — Non-taxable portion of payment; 146.4(10)(b), (c) — Deemed disability assistance payment from non-compliant plan; 153(1)(i), Reg. 100(1)"remuneration"(o), 103.1 — Source withholding for taxable amount.

Notes: See Notes at end of 146.4 for the *Canada Disability Savings Act*. Under 146.4(4)(i), a "disability assistance payment" (DAP) is one of three types of payment an RDSP can make. (The others are transfers under 146.4(8) and repayments to the government required by the CDSA.) Under 146.4(6), the amount by which a DAP exceeds the "non-taxable portion" (146.4(7)) is included in the beneficiary's income.

146.4 does not restrict the timing or amount of a DAP, or the use to which the payment is put, apart from: prohibiting a DAP that would leave the plan unable to satisfy a repayment requirement under the (146.4(4)(j)); requiring that "lifetime DAPs" (146.4(1)) begin no later than the year the beneficiary turns 60 (146.4(4)(k)); placing an annual limit on lifetime DAPs (146.4(4)(l)); requiring that an RDSP specify whether non-lifetime DAPs are permitted (146.4(4)(m)); and, in some cases, imposing the limit that would otherwise apply only to lifetime DAPs on all DAPs and requiring, after the beneficiary turns 59, that this amount be paid out each year (146.4(4)(n)). Under the CDSA, a DAP made when there is an "assistance holdback amount" (146.4(1)) will trigger a requirement for the plan to repay that amount to the government.

"disability savings plan" of a beneficiary means an arrangement

(a) between

    (i) a corporation (in this definition referred to as the "issuer")

        (A) that is licensed or otherwise authorized under the laws of Canada or a province to carry on in Canada the business of offering to the public its services as trustee, and

        (B) with which the specified Minister has entered into an agreement that applies to the arrangement for the purposes of the *Canada Disability Savings Act*, and

    (ii) one or more of the following:

        (A) the beneficiary,

        (B) an entity that, at the time the arrangement is entered into, is a qualifying person described in paragraph (a) or (b) of the definition "qualifying person" in relation to the beneficiary,

        (B.1) if the arrangement is entered into before 2024, a qualifying family member in relation to the beneficiary who, at the time the arrangement is entered into, is a qualifying person in relation to the beneficiary,

        (B.2) a qualifying family member in relation to the beneficiary who, at the time the arrangement is entered into, is not a qualifying person in relation to the beneficiary but is a holder of another arrangement that is a registered disability savings plan of the beneficiary, and

        (C) a legal parent of the beneficiary who, at the time the arrangement is entered into, is not a qualifying person in relation to the beneficiary but is a holder of another arrangement that is a registered disability savings plan of the beneficiary;

(b) under which one or more contributions are to be made in trust to the issuer to be invested, used or otherwise applied by the issuer for the purpose of making payments from the arrangement to the beneficiary; and

(c) that is entered into in a taxation year in respect of which

    (i) the beneficiary is a DTC-eligible individual, or

    (ii) the beneficiary is not a DTC-eligible individual and an amount is to be transferred from a registered disability savings plan of the beneficiary to the arrangement in accordance with subsection (8).

Related Provisions: 146.2(12) — TFSA deemed not to be DSP. See also under 146.4(1)"registered disability savings plan".

Notes: Subpara. (c)(ii) added by 2021 budget bill #1, effective 2021.

Cl. (a)(ii)(B.1) amended by 2018 budget bill #1 to change "2019" to "2024", effective June 21, 2018. See 146.4(1)"qualifying family member" Notes.

Para. (a)(i) opening words amended by 2017 budget bill #2, effective March 23, 2017, to change "section" to "definition" ("issuer" is now defined in 146.4(1) for the whole section).

Earlier amendments by 2015 Budget bill (effective June 23, 2015); 2012 budget bill #1 (amendments do not apply to DSPs entered into before June 29, 2012: VIEWS doc 2012-0468571E5). The deadline for establishing an RDSP for 2008 (and applying for the Canada Disability Savings Grant and Bond) was extended from Dec. 31, 2008 to March 2, 2009 by 2008 budget bill #2 s. 81.

"holder" of a disability savings plan at any time means each of the following:

(a) an entity that has, at that time, rights as an entity with whom the issuer entered into the plan;

(b) an entity that has, at that time, rights as a successor or assignee of an entity described in paragraph (a) or in this paragraph; and

(c) the beneficiary if, at that time, the beneficiary is not an entity described in paragraph (a) or (b) and has rights under the plan to make decisions (either alone or with other holders of the plan) concerning the plan, except where the only such right is a right to direct that disability assistance payments be made as provided for in subparagraph (4)(n)(ii).

Related Provisions: 146.4(13)(a) — Notification required of change in holders; 160.21 — Liability of holder for non-compliance by RDSP; 207.04 — Tax on holder if RDSP acquires prohibited or non-qualified investment.

Notes: Para. (c) amended by 2012 budget bill #2, effective 2014, to change "(4)(n)(iii)" to "(4)(n)(ii)".

"issuer", of an arrangement, means the person described as the "issuer" in the definition "disability savings plan".

Notes: Definition added by 2017 budget bill #2, effective March 23, 2017. This term had been defined in 146.4(1)"disability savings plan"(a)(i) for all of 146.4.

"lifetime disability assistance payments" under a disability savings plan of a beneficiary means disability assistance payments that are identified under the terms of the plan as lifetime disability assistance payments and that, after they begin to be paid, are payable at least annually until the earlier of the day on which the beneficiary dies and the day on which the plan is terminated.

"plan trust", in relation to a disability savings plan, means the trust governed by the plan.

"qualified investment", for a trust governed by a RDSP, means

(a) an investment that would be described by any of paragraphs (a) to (d), (f) and (g) of the definition "qualified investment" in section 204 if the reference in that definition to "a trust governed by a deferred profit sharing plan or revoked plan" were read as a reference to "a trust governed by a RDSP" and if that definition were read without reference to the words "with the exception of excluded property in relation to the trust";

(b) a contract for an annuity issued by a licensed annuities provider where

(i) the trust is the only person who, disregarding any subsequent transfer of the contract by the trust, is or may become entitled to any annuity payments under the contract, and

(ii) the holder of the contract has a right to surrender the contract at any time for an amount that would, if reasonable sales and administration charges were ignored, approximate the value of funds that could otherwise be applied to fund future periodic payments under the contract;

(c) a contract for an annuity issued by a licensed annuities provider where

(i) annual or more frequent periodic payments are or may be made under the contract to the holder of the contract,

(ii) the trust is the only person who, disregarding any subsequent transfer of the contract by the trust, is or may become entitled to any annuity payments under the contract,

(iii) neither the time nor the amount of any payment under the contract may vary because of the length of any life, other than the life of the beneficiary under the plan,

(iv) the day on which the periodic payments began or are to begin is not later than the end of the later of

(A) the year in which the beneficiary under the plan attains the age of 60 years, and

(B) the year following the year in which the contract was acquired by the trust,

(v) the periodic payments are payable for the life of the beneficiary under the plan and either there is no guaranteed period under the contract or there is a guaranteed period that does not exceed 15 years,

(vi) the periodic payments

(A) are equal, or

(B) are not equal solely because of one or more adjustments that would, if the contract were an annuity under a retirement savings plan, be in accordance with subparagraphs 146(3)(b)(iii) to (v) or that arise because of a uniform reduction in the entitlement to the periodic payments as a consequence of a partial surrender of rights to the periodic payments, and

(vii) the contract requires that, in the event the plan must be terminated in accordance with paragraph (4)(p), any amounts that would otherwise be payable after the termination be commuted into a single payment; and

(d) a prescribed investment.

Notes: 207.01-207.07 now apply to RDSPs.

Definition added by 2017 budget bill #2, effective March 23, 2017.

Regulations: 221 (information return where mutual fund etc. claims its shares are QI); 222 (information return where RDSP acquires or disposes of non-QI, or QI status changes); 4900 (prescribed investment).

"qualifying family member", in relation to a beneficiary of a disability savings plan, at any time, means an individual who, at that time, is

(a) a legal parent of the beneficiary; or

(b) a spouse or common-law partner of the beneficiary who is not living separate and apart from the beneficiary by reason of a breakdown of their marriage or common-law partnership.

Related Provisions: 146.4(1)"disability savings plan"(a)(ii)(B.1), (B.2) — QFM can become holder of RDSP; 146.4(1)"qualifying person"(c) — QFM can become qualifying person; 146.4(1.5) — Beneficiary replacing holder; 146.4(1.6) — Legal representative replacing holder; 146.4(1.7) — Dispute over accepting qualifying family member as holder; 146.4(13) — Issuer must notify beneficiary if QFM becomes holder; 146.4(14) — Issuer liability limited re allowing QFM to become holder.

Notes: Normally, the plan holder of an RDSP for adult beneficiary B must be either B or, if B lacks capacity to enter into a contract, B's guardian or other legal representative (146.4(1)"qualifying person"(b)). However, some adults had difficulty establishing a plan because their capacity to contract was in doubt. In many provinces, the only way an RDSP could be opened for them was to declare them legally incompetent and have someone named as their legal guardian (which has other negative consequences). While the provinces develop better solutions for RDSPs, the 2012 Budget changes temporarily allow a family member to become the plan holder. This was to be only for RDSPs set up before 2017 (146.4(1)"disability savings plan"(a)(ii)(B.1)), but was extended by the 2015 Budget to RDSPs set up before 2019, and by the 2018 Budget to RDSPs set up before 2024, since not all provinces and territories had as yet "instituted streamlined processes that allow for the appointment of a trusted person to manage resources on behalf of an adult who lacks contractual capacity". See 146.4(1)"qualifying person"(c), 146(1.5)–(1.7), (4)(c), (13)(e) and (14).

The Feb. 11, 2014 federal Budget, chapter 3.4, summarized the issue and noted that ON, QC, NS, NB, PEI and NU had not yet solved it.

An individual "legally authorized to act" for B ("qualifying person"(a)(ii)) includes a person appointed by B where B is not contractually competent to enter into an RDSP but can appoint someone under the provincial legislation: VIEWS doc 2018-0787301E5.

"Qualifying family member" added by 2012 budget bill #1, effective June 29, 2012.

RDSP Bulletins: 3R1 (qualifying family member).

"qualifying person", in relation to a beneficiary of a disability savings plan, at any time, means

(a) if the beneficiary has not, at or before that time, attained the age of majority, an entity that is, at that time,

(i) a legal parent of the beneficiary,

(ii) a guardian, tutor, curator or other individual who is legally authorized to act on behalf of the beneficiary, or

(iii) a public department, agency or institution that is legally authorized to act on behalf of the beneficiary,

(b) if the beneficiary has, at or before that time, attained the age of majority and is not, at that time, contractually competent to enter into a disability savings plan, an entity that is, at that time, an entity described in subparagraph (a)(ii) or (iii), and

(c) other than for the purposes of subparagraph (4)(b)(iv), an individual who is a qualifying family member in relation to the beneficiary if

(i) at or before that time, the beneficiary has attained the age of majority and is not a beneficiary under a disability savings plan,

(ii) at that time, no entity described in subparagraph (a)(ii) or (iii) is legally authorized to act on behalf of the beneficiary, and

(iii) in the issuer's opinion after reasonable inquiry, the beneficiary's contractual competence to enter into a disability savings plan at that time is in doubt.

Related Provisions: 146.4(1)"disability savings plan"(a)(ii)(B.1), (B.2) — Qualifying family member who is QP can become holder of RDSP; 146.4(1.5) — Beneficiary replacing holder; 146.4(1.6) — Legal representative replacing holder; 146.4(1.7) — Dispute over accepting qualifying family member as holder; 146.4(13) — Issuer must notify beneficiary if para. (c) applies; 146.4(14) — Issuer not liable for applying para. (c) in good faith.

Notes: See Notes to 146.4(1)"qualifying family member". Para. (c) added by 2012 budget bill #1, effective June 29, 2012.

RDSP Bulletins: 3R1 (qualifying family member).

["RDSP"] — [See "registered disability savings plan" below.]

"registered disability savings plan" or **"RDSP"** means a disability savings plan that satisfies the conditions in subsection (2), but does not include a plan to which subsection (3) or (10) applies.

Related Provisions: 18(11)(i) — No deduction for interest paid on money borrowed to make contribution; 40(2)(g) — No capital loss on disposition of RDSP; 60.02 — Rollover of RRSP, RRIF or RPP to RDSP on death; 74.5(12)(a.2) — Attribution rules do not apply to RDSP; 75(3)(a) — Reversionary trust rules do not apply to RDSP; 108(1)"trust"(a) — "Trust" does not include a RDSP for certain purposes; 128.1(10)"excluded right or interest"(iii.1) — No capital gains tax on emigration from Canada; 146.4(2)–(4) — Conditions for plan to be and remain registered; 146.4(5) — Whether RSDP pays tax; 146.4(10)(a) — Non-compliant plan ceases to be RDSP; 206.2 — Tax on advantage extended other than by making disability assistance payment; 207.04 — Tax on holder if RDSP acquires non-qualified or prohibited investment; 207.05 — Tax on advantage received from RDSP; 248(1)"registered disability savings plan" — Definition applies to entire Act; Reg. 9006(e) — RDSP not reported to CRA for disclosure to foreign tax authorities.

Notes: "RDSP" acronym added by 2012 budget bill #2, effective Dec. 14, 2012.

Forms: RC4460: Registered disability savings plan [guide].

"specified maximum amount", for a calendar year in respect of a disability savings plan, means the amount that is the greater of

(a) the amount determined by the formula set out in paragraph (4)(l) in respect of the plan for the calendar year, and

(b) the amount determined by the formula

$$A + B$$

where

A   is 10% of the fair market value of the property held by the plan trust at the beginning of the calendar year (other than annuity contracts held by the plan trust that, at the beginning of the calendar year, are not described in paragraph (b) of the definition "qualified investment"), and

B   is the total of all amounts each of which is

(i) a periodic payment under an annuity contract held by the plan trust at the beginning of the calendar year (other than an annuity contract described at the beginning of the calendar year in paragraph (b) of the definition "qualified investment") that is paid to the plan trust in the calendar year, or

(ii) if the periodic payment under such an annuity contract is not made to the plan trust because the plan trust disposed of the right to that payment in the calendar year, a reasonable estimate of that payment on the assumption that the annuity contract had been held throughout the calendar year and no rights under the contract were disposed of in the calendar year.

Notes: Both A and B(i) amended by 2017 budget bill #2, effective March 23, 2017, to change "qualified investment in subsection 205(1)" to "qualified investment". (205-207 were repealed, and QI is now defined in 146.4(1).)

Definition added by 2012 budget bill #2, effective 2014.

RDSP Bulletins: 4 (Bill C-45).

"specified Minister" means the minister designated under section 4 of the *Canada Disability Savings Act*.

Notes: This is the Minister for Human Resources and Social Development. See s. 5 of the CDSA, reproduced in the Notes at end of 146.4.

"specified year", for a disability savings plan of a beneficiary means the particular calendar year in which a medical doctor or a nurse practitioner licensed to practise under the laws of a province (or of the place where the beneficiary resides) certifies in writing that the beneficiary's state of health is such that, in the professional opinion of the medical doctor or the nurse practitioner, the beneficiary is not likely to survive more than five years and

(a) if the plan is a specified disability savings plan, each subsequent calendar year, but does not include any calendar year prior to the calendar year in which the certification is provided to the issuer of the plan; or

(b) in any other case, each of the five calendar years following the particular calendar year, but does not include any calendar year prior to the calendar year in which the certification is provided to the issuer of the plan.

Related Provisions: 146.4(1.1)–(1.4) — Shortened life expectancy — plan becomes specified disability savings plan; 146.4(4)(n)(i) — Limitation on withdrawal if year is not specified year.

Notes: Opening words amended by 2017 budget bill #2 to add 2 references to a nurse practitioner, for certifications made after Sept. 7, 2017.

Definition amended by 2011 budget bill #1, effective for 2011 and later taxation years, effectively to add para. (a) (in conjunction with new 146.4(1.1)–(1.4)).

RDSP Bulletins: 2R2 (Bill C-3).

(1.1) **[Shortened life expectancy — plan becomes] Specified disability savings plan** — If, in respect of a beneficiary under a registered disability savings plan, a medical doctor or a nurse practitioner licensed to practise under the laws of a province (or of the place where the beneficiary resides) certifies in writing that the beneficiary's state of health is such that, in the professional opinion of the medical doctor or the nurse practitioner, the beneficiary is not likely to survive more than five years, the holder of the plan elects in prescribed form and provides the election and the medical certification in respect of the beneficiary to the issuer of the plan, and the issuer notifies the specified Minister of the election in a manner and format acceptable to the specified Minister, then the plan becomes a specified disability savings plan at the time the notification is received by the specified Minister.

Related Provisions: 146.4(1)"specified year"(a), 146.4(4)(n)(i) — Limitations on withdrawals do not apply to specified disability savings plan.

Notes: 146.4(1.1)-(1.4), along with 146.4(1)"specified year"(a), implement a 2011 Budget proposal to allow RDSP beneficiaries with shortened life expectancy greater access to the RDSP funds. Withdrawals made at any time following a 146.4(1.1) election will not trigger the repayment of CDSGs and CDSBs provided that the total of the taxable portions of the withdrawals does not exceed $10,000 annually. Total annual withdrawals may exceed $10,000 due to non-taxable portions.

146.4(1.1) amended by 2017 budget bill #2 to add 2 references to a nurse practitioner, for certifications made after Sept. 7, 2017.

146.4(1.1) added by 2011 budget bill #1, for 2011 and later taxation years, but no 146.1(1.1) election may be made before June 26, 2011.

RDSP Bulletins: 2R2 (specified disability savings plan).

(1.2) Ceasing to be a specified disability savings plan — A plan ceases to be a specified disability savings plan at the earliest of the following times:

(a) the time that the specified Minister receives a notification, in a manner and format acceptable to the specified Minister, from the issuer of the plan that the holder elects that the plan is to cease to be a specified disability savings plan;

(b) the time that is immediately before the earliest time in a calendar year when the total disability assistance payments, other than non-taxable portions, made from the plan in the year and while it was a specified disability savings plan exceeds $10,000 (or such greater amount as is required to satisfy the condition in subparagraph (d)(i));

(c) the time that is immediately before the time that

(i) a contribution is made to the plan,

(ii) an amount described in any of paragraphs (a) and (b) and subparagraph (d)(ii) of the definition "contribution" in subsection (1) is paid into the plan,

(iii) the plan is terminated,

(iv) the plan ceases to be a registered disability savings plan as a result of the application of paragraph (10)(a), or

(v) is the beginning of the first calendar year throughout which the beneficiary under the plan has no severe and prolonged impairments with the effects described in paragraph 118.3(1)(a.1); and

(d) the time immediately following the end of a calendar year if

(i) in the year the total amount of disability assistance payments made from the plan to the beneficiary is less than the amount determined by the formula set out in paragraph (4)(l) in respect of the plan for the year (or such lesser amount as is supported by the property of the plan), and

(ii) the year is not the calendar year in which the plan became a specified disability savings plan.

(e), (f) [Repealed]

Related Provisions: 146.4(1.3) — No election for 24 months after plan ceases to be SDSP; 146.4(1.4) — Minister may waive application of 146.4(1.2).

Notes: 146.4(1.2)(b)-(f) replaced with (b)-(d) by 2012 budget bill #2, effective 2014.

146.4(1.2) added by 2011 budget bill #1, effective for 2011 and later taxation years, but for a specified disability savings plan in respect of which the required medical certification is obtained before 2012, read "$10,000" as "$20,000" and read "from the plan in the year" as "from the plan".

RDSP Bulletins: 2R2 (Bill C-3); 4 (Bill C-45).

(1.3) Waiting period — If at any time, a plan has ceased to be a specified disability savings plan because of subsection (1.2), then the holder of the plan may not make an election under subsection (1.1) until 24 months after that time.

Related Provisions: 146.4(1.4) — Minister may waive application of 146.4(1.3).

Notes: 146.4(1.3) added by 2011 budget bill #1, for 2011 and later taxation years.

(1.4) Waiver — The Minister may waive the application of subsections (1.2) or (1.3) if it is just and equitable to do so.

Notes: For the meaning of "just and equitable", see Notes to 85(7.1).

146.4(1.4) added by 2011 budget bill #1, for 2011 and later taxation years.

(1.5) Beneficiary replacing holder — Any holder of a disability savings plan who was a qualifying person in relation to the beneficiary under the plan at the time the plan (or another registered disability savings plan of the beneficiary) was entered into solely because of paragraph (c) of the definition "qualifying person" in subsection (1) ceases to be a holder of the plan and the beneficiary becomes the holder of the plan if

(a) the beneficiary is determined to be contractually competent by a competent tribunal or other authority under the laws of a province or, in the issuer's opinion after reasonable inquiry, the beneficiary's contractual competence to enter into a disability savings plan is no longer in doubt; and

(b) the beneficiary notifies the issuer that the beneficiary chooses to become the holder of the plan.

Notes: See Notes to 146.4(1)"qualifying family member".

146.4(1.5) opening words amended by 2013 budget bill #1, effective June 29, 2012, to change "is" to "was" and add "at the time the plan (or another registered disability savings plan of the beneficiary) was entered into". (This amendment and those to 146.4(1.6), (1.7), (4)(c), (13)(e) and (14) were not in the March 21, 2013 Budget.)

146.4(1.5) added by 2012 budget bill #1, effective June 29, 2012.

(1.6) Entity replacing holder — If an entity described in subparagraph (a)(ii) or (iii) of the definition "qualifying person" in subsection (1) is appointed in respect of a beneficiary of a disability savings plan and a holder of the plan was a qualifying person in relation to the beneficiary at the time the plan (or another registered disability savings plan of the beneficiary) was entered into solely because of paragraph (c) of that definition,

(a) the entity shall notify the issuer without delay of the entity's appointment;

(b) the holder of the plan ceases to be a holder of the plan; and

(c) the entity becomes the holder of the plan.

Notes: See Notes to 146.4(1)"qualifying family member".

146.4(1.6) opening words amended by 2013 budget bill #1, effective June 29, 2012, to change "is" to "was" and add "in relation to the beneficiary at the time the plan (or another registered disability savings plan of the beneficiary) was entered into".

146.4(1.6) added by 2012 budget bill #1, effective June 29, 2012.

(1.7) Rules applicable in case of dispute — If a dispute arises as a result of an issuer's acceptance of a qualifying family member who was a qualifying person in relation to the beneficiary at the time the plan (or another registered disability savings plan of the beneficiary) was entered into solely because of paragraph (c) of the definition "qualifying person" in subsection (1) as a holder of a disability savings plan, from the time the dispute arises until the time that the dispute is resolved or an entity becomes the holder of the plan under subsection (1.5) or (1.6), the holder of the plan shall use their best efforts to avoid any reduction in the fair market value of the property held by the plan trust, having regard to the reasonable needs of the beneficiary under the plan.

Notes: See Notes to 146.4(1)"qualifying family member".

146.4(1.7) amended by 2013 budget bill #1, effective June 29, 2012, to change "is" to "was" and add "in relation to the beneficiary at the time the plan (or another registered disability savings plan of the beneficiary) was entered into".

146.4(1.7) added by 2012 budget bill #1, effective June 29, 2012.

(2) Registered status — The conditions that must be satisfied for a disability savings plan of a beneficiary to be a registered disability savings plan are as follows:

(a) before the plan is entered into, the issuer of the plan has received written notification from the Minister that, in the Minister's opinion, a plan whose terms are identical to the plan would, if entered into by entities eligible to enter into a disability savings plan, comply with the conditions in subsection (4);

(b) at or before the time the plan is entered into, the issuer of the plan has been provided with the Social Insurance Number of the beneficiary and the Social Insurance Number or business number, as the case may be, of each entity with which the issuer has entered into the plan; and

(c) at the time the plan is entered into, the beneficiary is resident in Canada, except that this condition does not apply if, at that time, the beneficiary is the beneficiary under another registered disability savings plan.

Related Provisions: Reg. 9006(e) — RDSP not reported to CRA for disclosure to foreign tax authorities.

Regulations: 204(3)(g) (no information return required unless RDSP is taxable).

Information Circulars: 99-1R2: Registered disability savings plans.

Registered Plans Compliance Bulletins: 7 (filing of RDSP applications).

(3) Registered status nullified — A disability savings plan is deemed never to have been a registered disability savings plan unless

(a) the issuer of the plan provides without delay notification of the plan's establishment in prescribed form containing prescribed information to the specified Minister; and

(b) if the beneficiary is the beneficiary under another registered disability savings plan at the time the plan is established, that other plan is terminated without delay.

Notes: 146.4(3) amended by 2012 budget bill #2, effective Dec. 14, 2012.

Information Circulars: 99-1R2: Registered disability savings plans.

RDSP Bulletins: 4 (Bill C-45); 7 (filing of RDSP applications).

(4) Plan conditions — The conditions referred to in paragraph (2)(a) are as follows:

(a) the plan stipulates

(i) that it is to be operated exclusively for the benefit of the beneficiary under the plan,

(ii) that the designation of the beneficiary under the plan is irrevocable, and

(iii) that no right of the beneficiary to receive payments from the plan is capable, either in whole or in part, of surrender or assignment;

(b) the plan allows an entity to acquire rights as a successor or assignee of a holder of the plan only if the entity is

(i) the beneficiary,

(ii) the beneficiary's estate,

(iii) a holder of the plan at the time the rights are acquired,

(iv) a qualifying person in relation to the beneficiary at the time the rights are acquired, or

(v) an individual who is a legal parent of the beneficiary and was previously a holder of the plan;

(c) the plan provides that, where an entity (other than a qualifying family member in relation to the beneficiary) that is a holder of the plan ceases to be a qualifying person in relation to the beneficiary at any time, the entity ceases at that time to be a holder of the plan;

(d) the plan provides for there to be at least one holder of the plan at all times that the plan is in existence and may provide for the beneficiary (or the beneficiary's estate, as the case may be) to automatically acquire rights as a successor or assignee of a holder in order to ensure compliance with this requirement;

(e) the plan provides that, where an entity becomes a holder of the plan after the plan is entered into, the entity is prohibited (except to the extent otherwise permitted by the Minister or the specified Minister) from exercising their rights as a holder of the plan until the issuer has been advised of the entity having become a holder of the plan and been provided with the entity's Social Insurance Number or business number, as the case may be;

(f) the plan prohibits contributions from being made to the plan at any time if

(i) the beneficiary is not a DTC-eligible individual in respect of the taxation year that includes that time, unless the contribution is a specified RDSP payment in respect of the beneficiary, or

(ii) the beneficiary died before that time;

(g) the plan prohibits a contribution from being made to the plan at any time if

(i) the beneficiary attained the age of 59 years before the calendar year that includes that time,

(ii) the beneficiary is not resident in Canada at that time, or

(iii) the total of the contribution and all other contributions made at or before that time to the plan or to any other regis-

tered disability savings plan of the beneficiary would exceed $200,000;

(h) the plan prohibits contributions to the plan by any entity that is not a holder of the plan, except with written consent of a holder of the plan;

(i) the plan provides that no payments may be made from the plan other than

(i) disability assistance payments,

(ii) a transfer in accordance with subsection (8), and

(iii) repayments under the *Canada Disability Savings Act* or a designated provincial program;

(j) the plan prohibits a disability assistance payment from being made if it would result in the fair market value of the property held by the plan trust immediately after the payment being less than the assistance holdback amount in relation to the plan;

(k) the plan provides for lifetime disability assistance payments to begin to be paid no later than the end of the particular calendar year in which the beneficiary attains the age of 60 years or, if the plan is established in or after the particular year, in the calendar year following the calendar year in which the plan is established;

(l) the plan provides that the total amount of lifetime disability assistance payments made in any particular calendar year (other than a specified year for the plan) shall not exceed the amount determined by the formula

$$A/(B + 3 - C) + D$$

where

A is the fair market value of the property held by the plan trust at the beginning of the calendar year (other than annuity contracts held by the plan trust that, at the beginning of the calendar year, are not described in paragraph (b) of the definition "qualified investment" in subsection (1)),

B is the greater of 80 and the age in whole years of the beneficiary at the beginning of the calendar year,

C is the age in whole years of the beneficiary at the beginning of the calendar year, and

D is the total of all amounts each of which is

(i) a periodic payment under an annuity contract held by the plan trust at the beginning of the calendar year (other than an annuity contract described at the beginning of the calendar year in paragraph (b) of the definition "qualified investment" in subsection (1)) that is paid to the plan trust in the calendar year, or

(ii) if the periodic payment under such an annuity contract is not made to the plan trust because the plan trust disposed of the right to that payment in the calendar year, a reasonable estimate of that payment on the assumption that the annuity contract had been held throughout the calendar year and no rights under the contract were disposed of in the calendar year;

(m) the plan stipulates whether or not disability assistance payments that are not lifetime disability assistance payments are to be permitted under the plan;

(n) the plan provides that when the total of all amounts paid under the *Canada Disability Savings Act* before the beginning of a calendar year to any registered disability savings plan of the beneficiary exceeds the total of all contributions made before the beginning of the calendar year to any registered disability savings plan of the beneficiary,

(i) if the calendar year is not a specified year for the plan and the conditions in clauses (p)(ii)(A) and (B) are not met in the calendar year, the total amount of disability assistance payments made from the plan to the beneficiary in the calendar year shall not exceed the specified maximum amount for the calendar year, except that, in calculating that total amount, any payment made following a transfer in the calendar year from another plan in accordance with subsection (8) is to be disregarded if it is made

> (A) to satisfy an undertaking described in paragraph (8)(d), or

> (B) in lieu of a payment that would otherwise have been permitted to be made from the other plan in the calendar year had the transfer not occurred, and

(ii) if the beneficiary attained the age of 27 years, but not the age of 59 years, before the calendar year, the beneficiary has the right to direct that, within the constraints imposed by subparagraph (i) and paragraph (j), one or more disability assistance payments be made from the plan to the beneficiary in the calendar year;

(n.1) the plan provides that, if the beneficiary attained the age of 59 years before a calendar year, the total amount of disability assistance payments made from the plan to the beneficiary in the calendar year shall not be less than the amount determined by the formula set out in paragraph (l) in respect of the plan for the calendar year (or such lesser amount as is supported by the property of the plan trust);

(o) the plan provides that, at the direction of the holders of the plan, the issuer shall transfer all of the property held by the plan trust (or an amount equal to its value) to another registered disability savings plan of the beneficiary, together with all information in its possession (other than information provided to the issuer of the other plan by the specified Minister) that may reasonably be considered necessary for compliance, in respect of the other plan, with the requirements of this Act and with any conditions and obligations imposed under the *Canada Disability Savings Act*; and

(p) the plan provides for any amounts remaining in the plan (after taking into consideration any repayments under the *Canada Disability Savings Act* or a designated provincial program) to be paid to the beneficiary or the beneficiary's estate, as the case may be, and for the plan to be terminated, by the end of the calendar year following the earlier of

(i) the calendar year in which the beneficiary dies, and

(ii) the first calendar year in which the following conditions are met:

> (A) the holder of the plan has requested that the issuer terminate the plan, and

> (B) throughout the year, the beneficiary has no severe and prolonged impairments with the effects described in paragraph 118.3(1)(a.1).

Related Provisions: 60.02 — Rollover of RRSP, RRIF or RPP to RDSP on death; 146.4(4.01) — Transitional rule for 2019-2020 if beneficiary ceased to qualify for disability credit; 146.4(4.1)-(4.2) — Election on ceasing to be DTC-eligible; 146.4(10)(c) — Effect of non-compliance with para. (4)(h); 146.4(11) — Non-compliance with subsec. (4); 146.4(13)(b) — No amendment to plan unless Minister rules amendments comply; 207.04 — Tax on holder if RDSP acquires non-qualified or prohibited investment; 207.05 — Tax on advantage received from RDSP; 248(3)(c) — RDSP set up in Quebec deemed to be trust.

Notes: See Notes to 146.4(1)"assistance holdback amount", "disability assistance payment" and at end of 146.4.

See VIEWS doc 2009-032276I7 re compliance with 146.4(4)(h) in one situation.

On the beneficiary's bankruptcy, the trustee can cash out the RDSP: VIEWS doc 2013-050447I7.

146.4(4) amended by 2021 budget bill #1, effective 2021, to implement changes allowing an RDSP to continue when the beneficiary no longer qualifies for the disability credit: deleted requirement in para. (f) that "at that time there was a valid election referred to in subsection (4.1) in respect of the beneficiary"; (n)(i) amended to add "and the conditions in clauses (p)(ii)(A) and (B) are not met in the calendar year"; (p)(ii) changed from:

(ii) the first calendar year

> (A) if an election is made under subsection (4.1), that includes the time that the election ceases because of paragraph (4.2)(b) to be valid, and

> (B) in any other case, throughout which the beneficiary has no severe and prolonged impairments with the effects described in paragraph 118.3(1)(a.1).

146.4(4)(f)(i) amended by 2017 budget bill #2, for 2014 and later taxation years to add everything from "unless".

146.4(4)(l)A and (l)D(i) amended by 2017 budget bill #2, effective March 23, 2017, to change "qualified investment in subsection 205(1)" to "qualified investment in subsection (1)". (205-207 were repealed, and QI is now defined in 146.4(1).)

146.4(4) earlier amended by 2012 budget bill #2 (effective 2014); 2013 budget bill #1 (effective June 29, 2012); 2010 and 2008 budget bills #1.

Information Circulars: 99-1R2: Registered disability savings plans.

RDSP Bulletins: 3R1 (Bill C-38); 4 (Bill C-45).

Forms: RC4460: Registered disability savings plan [guide].

(4.01) Transitional rule — If, after March 18, 2019 and before 2021, a registered disability savings plan would otherwise be required to be terminated because of subparagraph (4)(p)(ii) or any terms of the plan provided because of that subparagraph, then notwithstanding that subparagraph or those terms, the plan is not required to be terminated before 2021 in either of the following circumstances:

(a) the beneficiary of the plan has no severe and prolonged impairments with the effects described in paragraph 118.3(1)(a.1), or

(b) an election was made under subsection (4.1), as it read immediately before 2021, and the election ceases to be valid after March 18, 2019 and before 2021 because of paragraph (4.2)(b), as it read immediately before 2021.

Notes: This was 146.4(4.4) in the July 30/19 and Nov. 30/20 draft legislation. 146.4(4.01) added by 2021 budget bill #1, effective 2021.

(4.1)–(4.3) [Repealed]

Notes: 146.4(4.1)-(4.3) repealed by 2021 budget bill #1, effective 2021. They read:

(4.1) Election on cessation of DTC-eligibility — A holder of a registered disability savings plan may elect in respect of a beneficiary under the plan who is not a DTC-eligible individual for a particular taxation year if

> (a) a medical doctor or a nurse practitioner licensed to practise under the laws of a province certifies in writing that the nature of the beneficiary's condition is such that, in the professional opinion of the medical doctor or the nurse practitioner, the beneficiary is likely to become a DTC-eligible individual for a future taxation year;

> (b) the beneficiary was a DTC-eligible individual for the year that immediately precedes the particular taxation year;

> (c) the holder makes the election in a manner and format acceptable to the specified Minister before the end of the year immediately following the particular taxation year and provides the election and the medical certification in respect of the beneficiary to the issuer of the plan; and

> (d) the issuer notifies the specified Minister of the election in a manner and format acceptable to the specified Minister.

(4.2) Election — An election under subsection (4.1) ceases to be valid at the time that is the earlier of

> (a) the beginning of the first taxation year for which the beneficiary is again a DTC-eligible individual; and

> (b) the end of the fourth taxation year following the particular taxation year referred to in subsection (4.1).

(4.3) Transitional rule — Unless an election is made under subsection (4.1), if 2011 or 2012 is the first calendar year throughout which the beneficiary of a registered disability savings plan has no severe and prolonged impairments with the effects described in paragraph 118.3(1)(a.1) and the plan has not been terminated, then notwithstanding subparagraph (4)(p)(ii) as it read on March 28, 2012 and any terms of the plan required by that subparagraph, the plan must be terminated no later than December 31, 2014.

146.4(4.1)(a) amended by 2017 budget bill #2 to add 2 references to a nurse practitioner, for certifications made after Sept. 7, 2017.

146.4(4.1)-(4.3) added by 2012 budget bill #2, effective 2014.

(5) Trust not taxable — No tax is payable under this Part by a trust on the taxable income of the trust for a taxation year if, throughout the period in the year during which the trust was in existence, the trust was governed by a registered disability savings plan, except that

(a) tax is payable under this Part by the trust on its taxable income for the year if the trust has borrowed money

(i) in the year, or

(ii) in a preceding taxation year and has not repaid it before the beginning of the year; and

(b) if the trust is not otherwise taxable under paragraph (a) on its taxable income for the year and, at any time in the year, it carries on one or more businesses or holds one or more properties that are not qualified investments for the trust, tax is payable under this Part by the trust on the amount that its taxable income for the year would be if it had no incomes or losses from sources other than those businesses and properties, and no capital gains or losses other than from dispositions of those properties, and for this purpose,

(i) "income" includes dividends described in section 83, and

(ii) paragraphs 38(a) and (b) are to be read as if the fraction set out in each of those paragraphs were replaced by the word "all".

Related Provisions: 149(1)(u.1) — RDSP exempt to extent provided by 146.4; 205–207 (until 2017) — Other taxes on RDSPs; 207.04 — Tax on holder if RDSP acquires non-qualified or prohibited investment; 207.05 — Tax on advantage received from RDSP; 253.1(1) — Investing in limited partnership is not carrying on business for 146.4(5)(b).

Notes: See Notes to 146.2(6) re RDSP carrying on business, e.g. active stock trading.

146.4(5)(b) opening words amended by 2017 budget bill #2, to delete "(as defined in subsection 205(1))" after "qualified investment", effective March 23, 2017. (QI is now defined in 146.4(1).)

Regulations: 204(3)(g) (information return required if 146.4(5)(a) or (b) applies).

Income Tax Folios: S3-F10-C1: Qualified investments — RRSPs, RESPs, RRIFs, RDSPs and TFSAs [replaces IT-320R3].

(6) Taxation of disability assistance payments — Where a disability assistance payment is made from a registered disability savings plan of a beneficiary, the amount, if any, by which the amount of the payment exceeds the non-taxable portion of the payment shall be included,

(a) if the beneficiary is alive at the time the payment is made, in computing the beneficiary's income for the beneficiary's taxation year in which the payment is made; and

(b) in any other case, in computing the income of the beneficiary's estate for the estate's taxation year in which the payment is made.

Related Provisions: 56(1)(q.1) — Income inclusion; 60(z) — Repayment deductible; 74.5(12)(a.2) — Attribution rules do not apply to RDSP; 122.5(1)"adjusted income" — Income not counted for purposes of GST/HST Credit; 122.6"adjusted income" — Income not counted for purposes of Canada Child Benefit; 146.4(7) — Non-taxable portion of payment; 146.4(10)(b), (c) — Deemed payment from non-compliant plan; 153(1)(i), Reg. 100(1)"remuneration"(o), 103.1 — Source withholding; 180.2(1)"adjusted income" — Income not counted for purposes of Old Age Security clawback; 206.2 — Tax on advantage extended other than by making disability assistance payment.

Forms: T1 General return, Line 12500 [former 125].

(7) Non-taxable portion of disability assistance payment — The non-taxable portion of a disability assistance payment made at a particular time from a registered disability savings plan of a beneficiary is the lesser of the amount of the disability assistance payment and the amount determined by the formula

$$A \times B/C + D$$

where

A   is the amount of the disability assistance payment;

B   is the amount, if any, by which

(a) the total of all amounts each of which is the amount of a contribution made before the particular time to any registered disability savings plan of the beneficiary

exceeds

(b) the total of all amounts each of which is the amount that would be the non-taxable portion of a disability assistance payment made before the particular time from any registered disability savings plan of the beneficiary, if the formula in this subsection were read without reference to the description of D;

C   is the amount by which the fair market value of the property held by the plan trust immediately before the payment exceeds the assistance holdback amount in relation to the plan; and

D   is the amount in respect of which a holder of the plan pays a tax under section 207.05 in respect of the plan, or another plan for which the plan was substituted by the holder, that

(a) has not been waived, cancelled or refunded; and

(b) has not otherwise been used in the year or a preceding year in computing the non-taxable portion of a disability assistance payment made from the plan or another plan for which the plan was substituted.

Related Provisions: 146.4(6) — Remainder of payment is taxable.

Notes: 146.4(7) amended by 2017 budget bill #2, effective Dec. 14, 2017, to add formula element D, and to add both "the amount that would be" and "if the formula in this subsection were read without reference to description of D" to B(b).

146.4(7) amended by 2010 budget bill #1, for 2009 and later taxation years.

(8) Transfer of funds — An amount is transferred from a registered disability savings plan (in this subsection referred to as the "prior plan") of a beneficiary in accordance with this subsection if

(a) the amount is transferred directly to another registered disability savings plan (in this subsection referred to as the "new plan") of the beneficiary;

(b) the prior plan is terminated immediately after the transfer;

(c) the issuer of the prior plan provides the issuer of the new plan with all information in its possession concerning the prior plan (other than information provided to the issuer of the new plan by the specified Minister) as may reasonably be considered necessary for compliance, in respect of the new plan, with the requirements of this Act and with any conditions and obligations imposed under the *Canada Disability Savings Act*; and

(d) where the beneficiary attained the age of 59 years before the calendar year in which the transfer occurs, the issuer of the new plan undertakes to make (in addition to any other disability assistance payments that would otherwise have been made from the new plan in the year) one or more disability assistance payments from the plan in the year, the total of which is equal to the amount, if any, by which

(i) the total amount of disability assistance payments that would have been required to be made from the prior plan in the year if the transfer had not occurred

exceeds

(ii) the total amount of disability assistance payments made from the prior plan in the year.

Related Provisions: 146.4(9) — No tax on transfer; 248(1)"disposition"(f)(vi) — Transfer from RDSP to RDSP is not disposition.

Notes: 146.4(8)(c) amended by 2012 budget bill #2, effective Dec. 14, 2012, to add "(other than information provided to the issuer of the new plan by the specified Minister)".

RDSP Bulletins: 4 (Bill C-45).

(9) No income inclusion on transfer — An amount transferred in accordance with subsection (8) is not, solely because of that transfer, to be included in computing the income of any taxpayer.

(10) Non-compliance — cessation of registered status — Where, at any particular time, a registered disability savings plan is non-compliant as described in subsection (11),

(a) the plan ceases, as of the particular time, to be a registered disability savings plan (other than for the purposes of applying, as of the particular time, this subsection and subsection (11));

(b) a disability assistance payment is deemed to have been made from the plan at the time (in this subsection referred to as the "relevant time") immediately before the particular time to the beneficiary under the plan (or, if the beneficiary is deceased at the relevant time, to the beneficiary's estate), the amount of which payment is equal to the amount, if any, by which

(i) the fair market value of the property held by the plan trust at the relevant time

exceeds

(ii) the assistance holdback amount in relation to the plan; and

(c) if the plan is non-compliant because of a payment that is not in accordance with paragraph (4)(j), a disability assistance payment is deemed to have been made from the plan at the relevant time (in addition to the payment deemed by paragraph (b) to have been made) to the beneficiary under the plan (or, if the beneficiary is deceased at the relevant time, to the beneficiary's estate)

(i) the amount of which payment is equal to the amount by which the lesser of

(A) the assistance holdback amount in relation to the plan, and

(B) the fair market value of the property held by the plan trust at the relevant time

exceeds

(C) the fair market value of the property held by the plan trust immediately after the particular time, and

(ii) the non-taxable portion of which is deemed to be nil.

Related Provisions: 160.21 — Joint and several liability for tax.

Information Circulars: 99-1R2: Registered disability savings plans.

(11) Non-compliance — A registered disability savings plan is non-compliant

(a) at any time that the plan fails to comply with a condition in subsection (4);

(b) at any time that there is a failure to administer the plan in accordance with its terms (other than those terms which the plan is required by subparagraph (4)(a)(i) to stipulate); and

(c) at any time that a person fails to comply with a condition or an obligation imposed, with respect to the plan, under the *Canada Disability Savings Act*, and the specified Minister has notified the Minister that, in the specified Minister's opinion, it is appropriate that the plan be considered to be non-compliant because of the failure.

Related Provisions: 146.4(10) — Effect of non-compliance; 146.4(12) — Exceptions to subsec. (11); 146.4(13)(c) — Notification of non-compliance required.

(12) Non-application of subsec. (11) — Where a registered disability savings plan would otherwise be non-compliant at a particular time because of a failure described in paragraph (11)(a) or (b),

(a) the Minister may waive the application of the relevant paragraph with respect to the failure, if it is just and equitable to do so;

(b) the Minister may deem the failure to have occurred at a later time;

(c) if the failure consists of the making of a contribution that is prohibited under any of paragraphs (4)(f) to (h), an amount equal to the amount of the contribution has been withdrawn from the plan within such period as is specified by the Minister and the Minister has approved the application of this paragraph with respect to the failure,

(i) the contribution is deemed never to have been made, and

(ii) the withdrawal is deemed not to be a disability assistance payment and not to be in contravention of the condition in paragraph (4)(i); or

(d) if the failure consists of the plan not being terminated by the time set out in paragraph (4)(p) and the failure was due to the issuer being unaware of, or there being some uncertainty as to, the existence of circumstances requiring that the plan be terminated,

(i) the Minister may specify a later time by which the plan is to be terminated (but no later than is reasonably necessary for the plan to be terminated in an orderly manner), and

(ii) paragraph (4)(p) and the plan terms are, for the purposes of paragraphs (11)(a) and (b), to be read as though they required the plan to be terminated by the time so specified.

Notes: For the meaning of "just and equitable" in para. (a), see Notes to 85(7.1).

146.4(12)(d) amended by 2008 budget bill #1, retroactive to its introduction (2008 and later taxation years).

(13) Obligations of issuer — The issuer of a registered disability savings plan shall,

(a) where an entity becomes a holder of the plan after the plan is entered into, so notify the specified Minister in prescribed form containing prescribed information on or before the day that is 60 days after the later of

(i) the day on which the issuer is advised of the entity having become a holder of the plan, and

(ii) the day on which the issuer is provided with the new holder's Social Insurance Number or business number, as the case may be;

(b) not amend the plan before having received notification from the Minister that, in the Minister's opinion, a plan whose terms are identical to the amended plan would, if entered into by entities eligible to enter into a disability savings plan, comply with the conditions in subsection (4);

(c) where the issuer becomes aware that the plan is, or is likely to become, non-compliant (determined without reference to paragraph (11)(c) and subsection (12)), notify the Minister and the specified Minister of this fact on or before the day that is 30 days after the day on which the issuer becomes so aware; and

(d) [Repealed]

(e) if the issuer enters into the plan with a qualifying family member who was a qualifying person in relation to the beneficiary at the time the plan (or another registered disability savings plan of the beneficiary) was entered into solely because of paragraph (c) of the definition "qualifying person" in subsection (1),

(i) so notify the beneficiary under the plan without delay in writing and include in the notification information setting out the circumstances in which the holder of the plan may be replaced under subsection (1.5) or (1.6), and

(ii) collect and use any information provided by the holder of the plan that is relevant to the administration and operation of the plan.

Notes: The test in para (d) is the "due diligence" test; see Notes to 227.1(3).

146.4(13)(d) repealed by 2017 budget bill #2, effective March 23, 2017. With the extension of 207.01-207.07 to cover RDSPs, 207.01(5) now provides this rule. Before that date, read:

(d) exercise the care, diligence and skill of a reasonably prudent person to minimize the possibility that a holder of the plan may become liable to pay tax under Part XI in connection with the plan, and

146.4(13)(e) opening words amended by 2013 budget bill #1, effective June 29, 2012, to change "is" to "was" and add "in relation to the beneficiary at the time the plan (or another registered disability savings plan of the beneficiary) was entered into".

Para. (e) added by 2012 budget bill #1, effective June 29, 2012. See Notes to 146.4(1)"qualifying family member".

Income Tax Folios: S3-F10-C1: Qualified investments — RRSPs, RESPs, RRIFs, RDSPs and TFSAs [replaces IT-320R3].

(14) Issuer's liability — If, after reasonable inquiry, an issuer of a disability savings plan is of the opinion that an individual's contractual competence to enter into a disability savings plan is in doubt, no action lies against the issuer for entering into a plan, under which the individual is the beneficiary, with a qualifying family member who was a qualifying person in relation to the beneficiary at the time the plan (or another registered disability savings plan of the beneficiary) was entered into solely because of paragraph (c) of the definition "qualifying person" in subsection (1).

Notes: See Notes to 146.4(1)"qualifying family member".

146.4(14) amended by 2013 budget bill #1, effective June 29, 2012, to change "is" to "was" and add "at the time the plan (or another registered disability savings plan of the beneficiary) was entered into".

146.4(14) added by 2012 budget bill #1, effective June 29, 2012.

Notes [s. 146.4]: A registered disability savings plan (RDSP) is a trust arrangement for beneficiary B who qualifies for the disability tax credit (DTC: 118.3, 146.4(4)(f)(i)). Contributions (until age 59: 146.4(4)(g)(i)) can be made (by anyone, with the plan holder's written permission: 146.4(4)(h)) to improve B's long-term financial security. See Information Circular 99-1R2 and conditions in 146.4(2)-(4), including a $200,000 lifetime contribution limit excluding government contributions ((4)(g)(iii)). A proposed amendment to 146.4(4)(p)(ii) allows an RDSP to stay open even if B ceases to qualify for the DTC.

Contributions for a beneficiary under 50 qualify for Canada Disability Savings Grants based on family net income (annual maximum $3,500, lifetime max $70,000), plus Canada Disability Savings Bonds (annual max $1,000, lifetime max $20,000). See the *Canada Disability Savings Act* and *Regulations* (below).

RDSPs are similar to RESPs, in that contributions are not deductible and investment income accrues tax-free (146.4(5)). However, the treatment of payments from RDSPs is different: each payment is deemed to include an amount of grants, bonds and investment income (146.4(7)), and that amount is included in the beneficiary's income (146.4(6)). Withdrawals must begin by the end of the year the beneficiary turns 60 (146.4(4)(k)).

RDSP issuers and advisers: see tinyurl.com/rdsp-cra.

CRA's target (tinyurl.com/cra-standards) for responding to RDSP applications (to register, amend or terminate) is 90% within 60 days; in 2019-20, it did 100%. As of Sept. 2016 there were 142,816 RDSPs with total $3.1 billion in assets. For interesting statistics see *Registered Disability Savings Plan Dashboard*, obtained under the *Access to Information Act* and available on *TaxPartner* and *Taxnet Pro*. In BC, there were 31,000 RDSPs as of Oct. 1, 2019 ("Minister's statement on registered Disability Savings Plan Awareness Month").

US citizens who either contribute to an RDSP or receive funds from an RDSP must file a Form 3520 with the IRS. See Notes to 233.3(3).

For detailed discussion and examples see Golombek, "Planning with Registered Disability Savings Plans", 57(2) *Canadian Tax Journal* 338-360 (2009). See also *Miller Thomson on Estate Planning* (Carswell, looseleaf), chap. 5; Roth, "The New Registered Disability Savings Plan", 4(11) *Tax Hyperion [TH]* (Carswell, Nov. 2007); Friedlan & Wark, "New Savings Plan for the Disabled", XIV(2) *Insurance Planning* (Federated Press) 889-94 (2008); Savoy & Lim, "Registered Disability Savings Plans", 17(8) *Canadian Tax Highlights [CTH]* (ctf.ca) 4-5 (Aug. 2009); Sklar, "Registered Disability Savings Plans Revisited", 204 *The Estate Planner* (CCH) 1-4 (Jan. 2012); Ibrahim & Lim, "RDSPs More Effective", 20(9) *CTH* 8-9 (Sept. 2012) and 20(12) 6-7 (Dec. 2012) (re 2012 Budget changes); Watson, "RDSP or Henson Trust — Which is Right for Your Client?", 9(12) *TH* 4-6 (Dec. 2012); Adlington, "RDSP Planning", 10(6) *TH* 4-6 (June 2013); Kinnear, "Treatment of registered assets on death", 2015 STEP Canada conference (contact memberservices@step.ca); Nichols & Horning, "Supporting a Disabled Child", 3566 *Tax Topics* (CCH) 1-3 (May 11, 2021) or 317 *The Estate Planner* 1-3 (June 2021). See also tinyurl.com/rdsp-faq for a detailed Q&A; Information Circular 99-1R1; Guide RC4460; VIEWS doc 2009-0311851E5.

The Senate Standing Committee on Social Affairs issued a detailed report with recommendations on the RDSP: *Breaking Down Barriers* (June 2018, 35pp). See also CRA Disability Advisory Committee 2019 report, *Enabling access to disability tax measures*, tinyurl.com/disab-report1, Appendix 11.

146.4 added by 2007 RDSPs bill, for 2008 and later tax years.

The *Canada Disability Savings Act*, also enacted by 2007 RDSPs bill and proclaimed in force Dec. 1, 2008 (P.C. 2008-1004), and amended by 2010 and 2011 budget bills #1 and 2016 budget bill #2, provides:

SHORT TITLE

1. Short title — This Act may be cited as the *Canada Disability Savings Act*.

INTERPRETATION

2. (1) Definitions — The following definitions apply in this Act.

"Canada child benefit" means a deemed overpayment under Subdivision A.1 of Division E of Part I of the *Income Tax Act*.

"Canada Disability Savings Bond" means the bond payable or paid under section 7.

"Canada Disability Savings Grant" means the grant payable or paid under section 6.

"child tax benefit" — [Repealed]

"contribution" — [Repealed]

"family income" means the income determined by the Minister in accordance with the definition "adjusted income" in section 122.6 of the *Income Tax Act* by using the information provided by the Minister of National Revenue for that purpose.

"first threshold" for a particular year means the dollar amount referred to in paragraph 117(2)(a) of the *Income Tax Act*, as adjusted under that Act for the particular year.

"phase-out income" for a particular year means

(a) if the particular year is before 2017, the amount determined by the formula

$$A - \left(\frac{B}{0.122}\right)$$

where

A is the first threshold for the particular year, and

B is the amount referred to in paragraph (a) of the description of F in subsection 122.61(1) of the *Income Tax Act*, as that subsection read on January 1, 2016, as adjusted under that Act for the particular year; or

(b) if the particular year is 2017 or any subsequent year, the dollar amount referred to in paragraph (a) of the description of Q in subsection 122.61(1) of the *Income Tax Act*, as adjusted under that Act for the particular year.

"second threshold" for a particular year means the higher dollar amount referred to in paragraph 117(2)(b) of the *Income Tax Act*, as adjusted under the Act for the particular year.

(2) *Income Tax Act* expressions — Unless a contrary intention appears, in this Act

(a) the expressions "adjusted income", "eligible individual" and "qualified dependant" have the same meanings as in section 122.6 of the *Income Tax Act*;

(b) the expressions "contribution", "designated provincial program", "DTC-eligible individual", "holder", "issuer", "registered disability savings plan", "specified year" and "specified disability savings plan" have the same meanings as in section 146.4 of that Act; and

(c) any other expression has the same meaning as in that Act.

PURPOSE

3. Purpose — The purpose of this Act is to encourage long term savings through registered disability savings plans to provide for the financial security of persons with severe and prolonged impairments in physical or mental functions.

MINISTER

4. Designation of Minister — The Governor in Council may, by order, designate a minister of the Crown to be "the Minister" for the purposes of this Act.

5. Informing Canadians — The Minister may take any measures that the Minister considers appropriate to make known to Canadians the existence of Canada Disability Savings Grants and Canada Disability Savings Bonds.

PAYMENTS

6. (1) Canada Disability Savings Grants — Subject to this Act and the regulations, on application, the Minister may, in respect of any contribution made to a registered disability savings plan of a beneficiary, pay a Canada Disability Savings Grant into the plan. The grant is to be paid on any terms and conditions that the Minister may specify by agreement between the Minister and the issuer of the plan.

(2) Amount of grant — The amount of a Canada Disability Savings Grant that may be paid for a particular year is equal to

(a) 300% of the part of the total contributions made in the particular year that is less than or equal to $500, and 200% of the part of those contributions that is more than $500 but less than or equal to $1,500, if the beneficiary is

(i) an individual who is at least 18 years of age on December 31 of the year preceding the particular year and whose family income for the particular year is less than or equal to the second threshold for the particular year,

(ii) a qualified dependant of an eligible individual whose adjusted income used to determine the amount of a Canada child benefit in respect of January in the particular year is less than or equal to the second threshold for the particular year, or

(iii) a person in respect of whom a special allowance under the *Children's Special Allowances Act* is payable for at least one month in the particular year; or

(b) 100% of the total contributions made in the particular year, up to a maximum of $1,000, in any other case.

(2.1) Deemed year of contribution — For the purposes of subsection (2), a contribution allocated to a year under subsection (2.2) is deemed to have been made in that year.

(2.2) Allocation of contribution — The Minister may allocate a contribution made to the beneficiary's registered disability savings plan in a year after 2010, in parts — to the year in which it is actually made and to each of the previous 10 years that is after 2007 and in which the plan was not a specified disability savings plan (other than a year in which the plan became a specified disability savings plan) — in the following order:

(a) up to $500 to each year in which the beneficiary is one referred to in paragraph (2)(a), beginning with the earliest year, less any contributions allocated to the year in question;

(b) up to $1500 to each year in which the beneficiary is one referred to in paragraph (2)(a), beginning with the earliest year, less any contributions allocated to the year in question including those so allocated under paragraph (a); and

(c) up to $1000 to each year in which the beneficiary is not one referred to in paragraph (2)(a), beginning with the earliest year, less any contributions allocated to the year in question.

(2.3) Residency and DTC-eligibility — No contribution made to the plan in a year may be allocated to a previous year unless, during that previous year, the beneficiary was resident in Canada and a DTC-eligible individual.

(2.4) Limit — The Minister may allocate only the portion of contributions made to the plan in a year in respect of which, in accordance with subsection (2), a Canada Disability Savings Grant of up to $10,500 may be paid into the plan in that year.

(2.5) Contributions made before 2011 — For the purposes of determining the contributions allocated to the year in question under any of paragraphs (2.2)(a) to (c), contributions made to the plan in 2008, 2009 or 2010 are considered to have been allocated to the year in which they were actually made.

(3) Family income — For the purposes of subparagraph (2)(a)(i), the family income for a particular year is that income determined for the year that ended on December 31 of the second preceding year.

(4) No determination for January — If there has been no determination of eligibility for a child tax benefit in respect of January in a particular year, the adjusted income to be used for the purposes of subparagraph (2)(a)(ii) is the adjusted income used to determine the amount of a Canada child benefit for the first month in the particular year in respect of which eligibility has been established.

(5) Beneficiary born in December — In applying subsection (4) in respect of a beneficiary born in December, the reference to "the first month in the particular year in respect of which eligibility has been established" in that subsection is to be read as a reference to "January of the next year".

(6) Indexing — [Repealed]

(7) Lifetime cap — Not more than $70,000 in Canada Disability Savings Grants may be paid in respect of a beneficiary during their lifetime.

(8) Annual cap — Not more than $10,500 in Canada Disability Savings Grants may be paid in respect of a beneficiary in a year.

(9) Annual statement to plan holders — Once a year, the Minister shall cause each holder of a registered disability savings plan to be provided with a statement that sets out the amount of Canada Disability Savings Grants that may be paid for particular years on the basis of future contributions.

7. (1) Canada Disability Savings Bonds — Subject to this Act and the regulations, on application, the Minister may pay a Canada Disability Savings Bond into a registered disability savings plan of a beneficiary

(a) for each year after the year in which the plan is entered into; and

(b) for the year in which the plan is entered into and for each of the previous 10 years

(i) that is after 2007,

(ii) during which the beneficiary was resident in Canada, and

(iii) for which a Canada Disability Savings Bond has not previously been paid.

(1.1) Terms and conditions — A Canada Disability Savings Bond is to be paid on any terms and conditions that the Minister may specify by agreement between the Minister and the issuer of the plan.

(2) Amount of bond — The amount of a Canada Disability Savings Bond that may be paid for a particular year is

(a) $1,000, if the beneficiary is

(i) an individual who is at least 18 years of age on December 31 of the year preceding the particular year and whose family income for the particular year is less than or equal to the phase-out income for the particular year,

(ii) a qualified dependant of an eligible individual whose adjusted income used to determine the amount of a Canada child benefit in respect of January in the particular year is less than or equal to the phase-out income for the particular year, or

(iii) a person in respect of whom a special allowance under the Children's Special Allowances Act is payable for at least one month in the particular year; or

(b) the amount determined by the formula set out in subsection (4), if the beneficiary is

(i) an individual who is at least 18 years of age on December 31 of the year preceding the particular year and whose family income for the particular year is more than the phase-out income for the particular year but less than the first threshold for the particular year, or

(ii) a qualified dependant of an eligible individual whose adjusted income used to determine the amount of a Canada child benefit in respect of January in the particular year is more than the phase-out income for the particular year but less than the first threshold for the particular year.

(3) Family income — For the purposes of subparagraphs (2)(a)(i) and (b)(i), the family income for a particular year is that income determined for the year that ended on December 31 of the second preceding year.

(4) Formula — For the purposes of paragraph (2)(b), the formula is as follows:

$$\$1,000 - [\$1,000 \times \frac{(A-B)}{(C-B)}]$$

where

A is, as the case may be, the family income referred to in subparagraph (2)(b)(i) or the adjusted income referred to in subparagraph (2)(b)(ii);

B is the phase-out income for the particular year; and

C is the first threshold for the particular year.

(5) Rounding of amounts — If an amount calculated under subsection (4) contains a fraction of a cent, the amount is to be rounded to the nearest whole cent or, if the amount is equidistant from two whole cents, to the higher of them.

(6) No determination for January — If there has been no determination of eligibility for a Canada child benefit in respect of January in a particular year, the adjusted income to be used for the purposes of subparagraphs (2)(a)(ii) and (b)(ii) is the adjusted income used to determine the amount of a Canada child benefit for the first month in the particular year in respect of which eligibility has been established.

(7) Beneficiary born in December — In applying subsection (6) in respect of a beneficiary born in December, the reference to "the first month in the particular year in respect of which eligibility has been established" in that subsection is to be read as a reference to "January of the next year".

(8) Indexing — [Repealed]

(9) Lifetime cap — Not more than $20,000 in Canada Disability Savings Bonds may be paid in respect of a beneficiary during their lifetime.

8. Payment — Neither a Canada Disability Savings Grant nor a Canada Disability Savings Bond may be paid unless

(a) the Minister is provided with, as the case may be,

(i) the Social Insurance Number of the beneficiary,

(ii) the Social Insurance Number of the eligible individual referred to in subparagraph 6(2)(a)(ii) or 7(2)(a)(ii) or (b)(ii), and

(iii) the business number of the department, agency or institution that maintains the beneficiary in respect of whom a special allowance is payable under the Children's Special Allowances Act for a month in the particular year;

(b) the beneficiary is resident in Canada, in the case of a Canada Disability Savings Grant, at the time the contribution to the plan is made and, in the case of a Canada Disability Savings Bond, immediately before the payment is made; and

(c) the plan is not a specified disability savings plan, in the case of a Canada Disability Savings Grant, at the time the contribution to the plan is made and, in the case of a Canada Disability Savings Bond, immediately before the payment is made.

9. Interest — The Minister may, in prescribed circumstances, pay interest, calculated as prescribed, in respect of Canada Disability Savings Grants or Canada Disability Savings Bonds.

10. Payments out of CRF — All amounts payable by the Minister under this Act shall be paid out of the Consolidated Revenue Fund.

11. Waiver — On application made by the holder or the beneficiary, to avoid undue hardship, the Minister may, in prescribed circumstances, waive any of the prescribed requirements of this Act or the regulations that relate to the payment of any amount or the repayment of any amount or earnings generated by that amount. The application must be in the form and manner approved by the Minister.

GENERAL

12. (1) Debt due to Her Majesty — An amount required to be repaid under this Act, the regulations or an agreement entered into under this Act constitutes a debt due to Her Majesty in right of Canada as of the date on which the Minister issues a written notice to the person responsible for the debt indicating the amount that is due.

(2) Recovery of payments and interest — Debts due to Her Majesty in right of Canada under this Act are recoverable, including in the Federal Court or any other court of competent jurisdiction, by the Minister of National Revenue.

(3) Deduction and set-off — Despite subsection 14(1), debts due to Her Majesty in right of Canada under this Act may be recovered at any time by way of

deduction from, set-off against or, in Quebec, compensation against, any sum of money that may be due or payable by Her Majesty in right of Canada to the person responsible for the debt, other than an amount payable under section 122.61 of the *Income Tax Act*.

13. **Deduction and set-off by the Minister** — Despite subsections 12(2) and 14(1), an amount required to be repaid by a person under this Act, the regulations or an agreement entered into under this Act may be recovered by the Minister at any time by way of deduction from, set-off against or, in Quebec, compensation against, any sum of money that may be due or payable under this Act to the person.

14. (1) **Limitation or prescription period** — Subject to this section, no action or proceedings shall be taken to recover debts due to Her Majesty in right of Canada under this Act after the expiry of the six-year limitation or prescription period that begins on the day on which the Minister issues the notice referred to in subsection 12(1).

(2) **Acknowledgement of liability** — If a person's liability for debts due to Her Majesty in right of Canada under this Act is acknowledged in accordance with subsection (4), the time during which the limitation or prescription period has run before the acknowledgement does not count in the calculation of that period.

(3) **Acknowledgement after expiry of limitation or prescription period** — If a person's liability for debts due to Her Majesty in right of Canada under this Act is acknowledged in accordance with subsection (4) after the expiry of the limitation or prescription period, an action or proceedings to recover the money may, subject to subsections (2) and (5), be brought within six years after the date of the acknowledgement.

(4) **Types of acknowledgements** — An acknowledgement of liability means

(a) a written promise to pay the money owing, signed by the person or his or her agent or other representative;

(b) a written acknowledgement of the money owing, signed by the person or his or her agent or other representative, whether or not a promise to pay can be implied from it and whether or not it contains a refusal to pay;

(c) a part payment by the person or his or her agent or other representative of any money owing; or

(d) any acknowledgement of the money owing made by the person, his or her agent or other representative or the trustee or director in the course of proceedings under the *Bankruptcy and Insolvency Act* or any other legislation dealing with the payment of debts.

(5) **Limitation or prescription period suspended** — The running of a limitation or prescription period is suspended during

(a) the period beginning on the day on which the Minister receives an application under section 11 and ending on the day on which the Minister issues a decision;

(b) the period beginning on the day on which the Minister of National Revenue receives an application concerning subsection 146.4(12) of the *Income Tax Act* and ending on the day on which that Minister makes a decision;

(c) the period beginning on the day on which an application for judicial review, with respect to a decision of the Minister to issue a notice under subsection 12(1), is filed and ending on the day on which the final decision is rendered; and

(d) any period in which it is prohibited to commence or continue an action or other proceedings against the person to recover debts due to Her Majesty in right of Canada under this Act.

(6) **Enforcement proceedings** — This section does not apply in respect of an action or proceedings relating to the execution, renewal or enforcement of a judgment.

15. **Collection of information** — If the Minister considers it advisable, the Minister may, subject to conditions agreed on by the Minister and the Minister of National Revenue, collect any prescribed information for the administration of section 146.4 and Part XI of the *Income Tax Act*.

16. **Notification by Minister of National Revenue** — When the Minister of National Revenue considers that a registered disability savings plan is no longer registered by virtue of the application of paragraph 146.4(10)(a) of the *Income Tax Act*, the Minister of National Revenue shall as soon as possible notify the Minister in writing.

17. **Regulations** — The Governor in Council may make regulations for carrying out the purpose and provisions of this Act and, without limiting the generality of the foregoing, may make regulations

(a) establishing requirements that must be met by a registered disability savings plan and by persons in respect of the plan before a Canada Disability Savings Grant or a Canada Disability Savings Bond may be paid in respect of the plan;

(b) establishing the manner of determining the amount of a Canada Disability Savings Grant that may be paid in respect of contributions made to regis-

tered disability savings plans or the amount of a Canada Disability Savings Bond that may be paid into those plans;

(c) specifying terms and conditions to be included in agreements entered into between an issuer of a registered disability savings plan and the Minister;

(d) governing the repayment of any amount paid under this Act or earnings generated by those amounts including providing for the circumstances under which an amount or earnings must be repaid and the manner of calculating such an amount or earnings;

(e) specifying the circumstances in which the Minister may pay interest on Canada Disability Savings Grants or Canada Disability Savings Bonds as well as the manner of calculating interest;

(f) specifying the requirements of this Act or the regulations relating to the payment of any amount or the repayment of any amount or earnings generated by that amount that may be waived by the Minister to avoid undue hardship;

(g) specifying the circumstances in which the Minister may waive the requirements provided under paragraph (f);

(h) specifying information that the Minister may collect under section 15; and

(i) requiring issuers to keep any record, book or other document containing any information relevant to the administration or enforcement of this Act or the regulations, and respecting where, how and how long it is to be kept.

The *Canada Disability Savings Regulations* (P.C. 2008-1005; amended by 2010 and 2011 budget bills #1, 2012 budget bill #2, P.C. 2013-797, 2014-620 and 2021 budget bill #1) provide:

1. **Interpretation** — The following definitions apply in these Regulations.

"Act" means the *Canada Disability Savings Act*.

"assistance holdback amount" means, at a particular time,

(a) in the case of an RDSP that is, at the particular time, a specified disability savings plan, nil; and

(b) in any other case, the total amount of bonds and grants paid into an RDSP within the 10-year period before the particular time, less any amount of bond or grant paid in that 10-year period that has been repaid to the Minister.

"bond" means a Canada Disability Savings Bond.

"grant" means a Canada Disability Savings Grant.

"issuer agreement" means an agreement entered into by the Minister and an issuer of an RDSP that relates to the payment of a grant or bond.

"RDSP" means a registered disability savings plan under section 146.4 of the *Income Tax Act*.

2. **Requirements for Payment of Grant** — The Minister may pay a grant into an RDSP in respect of a contribution made to and not withdrawn from the RDSP if

(a) the issuer enters into an issuer agreement with the Minister that applies to the RDSP and includes the terms and conditions set out in section 4;

(b) the issuer submits, at the request of the holder of the RDSP, an application for the grant to the Minister;

(c) the beneficiary is less than 49 years of age at the end of the year preceding the year in which the contribution is made;

(d) the total of the contribution and all other contributions made to an RDSP of the beneficiary does not exceed $200,000;

(e) the beneficiary is a DTC-eligible individual in respect of the year in which the contribution is made, and in respect of the year or years to which the contribution is allocated; and

(f) the issuer complies with the requirements of these Regulations and the terms and conditions of the issuer agreement that applies to the RDSP.

3. **Requirements for Payment of Bond** — The Minister may pay a bond into an RDSP if

(a) the issuer enters into an issuer agreement with the Minister that applies to the RDSP and includes the terms and conditions set out in section 4;

(b) the holder requests, no later than December 31 of the year in which the beneficiary attains 49 years of age, that the issuer submit an application for the bond;

(c) the issuer submits an application for the bond to the Minister;

(d) the beneficiary is less than 49 years of age at the end of the year preceding the year for which the bond is payable;

(e) the beneficiary is a DTC-eligible individual in respect of the year for which the bond is payable; and

(f) the issuer complies with the requirements of these Regulations and the terms and conditions of the issuer agreement that applies to the RDSP.

4. Terms and Conditions of Issuer Agreements — Every issuer agreement shall include the following terms and conditions:

(a) the issuer shall provide the Minister with any information that the Minister requires for the purposes of the Act and these Regulations;

(b) the issuer shall maintain records and books of account that relate to the amounts paid under the Act in the form and containing any information that the Minister requires to ensure compliance with the Act and these Regulations;

(c) the issuer shall allow the Minister access to all documents and other information that the Minister requires for auditing amounts paid or repaid under the Act and these Regulations;

(d) the issuer shall report to the Minister annually or within any other period set out in the issuer agreement with respect to

(i) all contributions, payments and transfers to, and all payments and transfers from, an RDSP,

(ii) the assistance holdback amount, and

(iii) any other information related to the RDSP that is specified in the issuer agreement;

(e) the issuer shall submit all information to the Minister in a format and manner that is acceptable to the Minister;

(f) the issuer shall not charge fees related to the RDSP against the assistance holdback amount of the RDSP;

(g) the issuer shall, when transferring the property of the RDSP, provide to the issuer of the new plan all information that it is required to provide in accordance with paragraph 146.4(8)(c) of the *Income Tax Act*; and

(h) the issuer shall repay any amount required to be repaid to the Minister under these Regulations and shall do so within the period specified in the agreement.

5. Repayments — (1) Subject to section 5.1, an issuer of an RDSP shall repay to the Minister, within the period set out in the issuer agreement, the amount referred to in subsection (2) if

(a) the RDSP is terminated;

(b) the plan ceases to be an RDSP as a result of the application of paragraph 146.4(10)(a) of the *Income Tax Act*; or

(c) [Repealed]

(d) the beneficiary dies.

(2) The amount that must be repaid as a result of the occurrence of an event described in subsection (1) is the lesser of

(a) the fair market value, immediately before the occurrence, of the property held by the RDSP, and

(b) the assistance holdback amount of the RDSP immediately before the occurrence.

(3) Despite subsections (1) and (2), if the beneficiary of an RDSP that is a specified disability savings plan dies, the issuer of the RDSP shall repay to the Minister, within the period set out in the issuer agreement, any portion of an amount paid into the RDSP as a grant or bond within the 10-year period preceding the time of the death that remains in the RDSP at that time.

(4) This section does not apply if the event described in subsection (1) or (3) occurs after the calendar year in which the beneficiary attains 59 years of age.

5.1 If an event described in paragraph 5(1)(a), (b) or (d) occurs while the beneficiary of an RDSP is no longer a DTC-eligible individual, the issuer of the RDSP shall repay to the Minister, within the period set out in the issuer agreement, the lesser of

(a) the fair market value, immediately before the occurrence of the event, of the property held by the RDSP, and

(b) the amount determined by the formula

$$A + B - C$$

where

A is

(i) if the event occurs before the calendar year in which the beneficiary attains 51 years of age, the total amount of grants and bonds paid into the RDSP within the 10-year period before the day on which the beneficiary ceased to be a DTC-eligible individual, less any portion of that amount that was repaid to the Minister within that period,

(ii) if the event occurs after the calendar year in which the beneficiary attains 50 years of age but before the calendar year in which they attain 60 years of age and the beneficiary ceased to be a DTC-eligible individual before the calendar year in which they attained 50 years of age, the total amount of grants and bonds paid into the RDSP within the period (expressed in number of years) determined by the following formula that ended before the day on which the

beneficiary ceased to be a DTC-eligible individual, less any portion of that amount that was repaid to the Minister within that period:

$$60 - n$$

where

n is the beneficiary's age on — or the age that they would have attained by — December 31 of the calendar year in which the event occurs,

(iii) if the event occurs after the calendar year in which the beneficiary attains 50 years of age but before the calendar year in which they attain 60 years of age and the beneficiary ceased to be a DTC-eligible individual after the calendar year in which they attained 49 years of age, the total amount of grants and bonds paid into the RDSP during the period beginning on January 1 of the year that is 10 years before the year in which the event occurs and ending on the day preceding the day on which the beneficiary ceased to be a DTC-eligible individual, less any portion of that amount that was repaid to the Minister within that period, or

(iv) if the event occurs after the calendar year in which the beneficiary attains 59 years of age, nil,

B is the amount of any grant or bond that is paid into the RDSP during the period beginning on the day on which the beneficiary ceased to be a DTC-eligible individual and ending on the day on which the event occurs, and

C is the amount of any grant or bond that has been repaid since the day on which the beneficiary ceased to be a DTC-eligible individual.

5.2 [Repealed]

5.3 (1) Subject to section 5.4, if a disability assistance payment is made, the issuer of the RDSP shall repay to the Minister, within the period set out in the issuer agreement, the least of the following amounts:

(a) $3 for every $1 of disability assistance payment made,

(b) the fair market value, immediately before the making of the disability assistance payment, of the property held by the RDSP, and

(c) the assistance holdback amount of the RDSP immediately before the making of the disability assistance payment.

(2) An issuer that repays the amount referred to in paragraph (1)(a) is to do so from the grants and bonds that were paid into the RDSP within the 10-year period preceding the making of the disability assistance payment, in the order in which they were paid into it.

(3) Subsection (1) does not apply in respect of any disability assistance payment made after the calendar year in which the beneficiary attains 59 years of age.

5.4 (1) If a disability assistance payment is made to a beneficiary who is no longer a DTC-eligible individual, the issuer of the RDSP shall repay to the Minister, within the period set out in the issuer agreement, the least of the following amounts:

(a) $3 for every $1 of disability assistance payment made,

(b) the fair market value, immediately before the making of the disability assistance payment, of the property held by the RDSP, and

(c) the amount determined by the formula

$$A + B - C$$

where

A is

(i) if the disability assistance payment is made before the calendar year in which the beneficiary attains 51 years of age, the total amount of grants and bonds paid into the RDSP within the 10-year period before the day on which the beneficiary ceased to be a DTC-eligible individual, less any portion of that amount that was repaid to the Minister within that period,

(ii) if the disability assistance payment is made after the calendar year in which the beneficiary attains 50 years of age but before the calendar year in which they attain 60 years of age and the beneficiary ceased to be a DTC-eligible individual before the calendar year in which they attained 50 years of age, the total amount of grants and bonds paid into the RDSP within the period (expressed in number of years) determined by the following formula that ended before the day on which the beneficiary ceased to be a DTC-eligible individual, less any portion of that amount that was repaid to the Minister within that period:

$$60 - n$$

where

n is the beneficiary's age on December 31 of the calendar year in which the disability assistance payment is made,

(iii) if the disability assistance payment is made after the calendar year in which the beneficiary attains 50 years of age but before the calendar year in which they attain 60 years of age and the beneficiary ceased to be a DTC-eligible individual after the calendar year in which they attained 49 years of age, the total amount of grants and bonds paid into the RDSP during the period beginning on January 1 of the year that is 10 years before the year in which the disability assistance payment is made and ending on the day preceding the day on which the beneficiary ceased to be a DTC-eligible individual, less any portion of that amount that was repaid to the Minister within that period, or

(iv) if the disability assistance payment is made after the calendar year in which the beneficiary attains 59 years of age, nil,

B   is the amount of any grant or bond that is paid into the RDSP during the period beginning on the day on which the beneficiary ceased to be a DTC-eligible individual and ending on the day on which the disability assistance payment is made, and

C   is the amount of any grant or bond that has been repaid since the day on which the beneficiary ceased to be a DTC-eligible individual.

(2) An issuer that repays the amount referred to in paragraph (1)(a) is to do so from the grants and bonds that were paid into the RDSP within the applicable period referred to in the description of A in paragraph (1)(c) and within the period referred to in the description of B in paragraph (1)(c), in the order in which they were paid into it.

(3) Subsection (1) does not apply in respect of any disability assistance payment made in the calendar year in which the beneficiary of the RDSP attains 60 years of age, or in any subsequent calendar year, if the total amount of disability assistance payments made to the beneficiary in that calendar year is less than or equal to the amount determined in accordance with paragraph 146.4(4)(l) of the *Income Tax Act* for that calendar year.

6. (1) An issuer of an RDSP shall repay to the Minister, within the period set out in the issuer agreement, any portion of an amount paid into the RDSP as a grant or bond to which there was no entitlement under the Act or these Regulations.

(2) A beneficiary of an RDSP shall repay to the Minister any portion of a disability assistance payment attributable to a grant payment or bond payment to which the beneficiary was not entitled under the Act or these Regulations.

7. For the purposes of calculating an amount to be repaid under these Regulations with respect to amounts that are transferred from a prior RDSP to a new RDSP in accordance with subsection 146.4(8) of the *Income Tax Act*, all amounts of bonds, grants and contributions transferred are considered to have been paid into or made to the new RDSP as of the day on which the amounts were paid into or made to the prior RDSP.

8. Waiver — Undue Hardship — For the purposes of section 11 of the Act, the Minister may waive the requirement in subparagraph 6(2)(a)(i) or 7(2)(a)(i) or (b)(i) of the Act that the individual be at least 18 years of age on December 31 of the year preceding the particular year if the beneficiary is not a qualified dependant of an eligible individual.

9. Authorized Collection of Information — For the purposes of section 15 of the Act, the following are prescribed information:

(a) the beneficiary's name, address, date of birth, social insurance number and, if applicable, date of death;

(b) if the holder is an individual, the holder's name, address and social insurance number;

(c) if the holder is a department, agency or institution that maintains the beneficiary, its business name, business number and address;

(d) the name and address of the issuer;

(e) in relation to any specific RDSP, the number assigned to the corresponding plan in respect of which written notification was given by the Minister of National Revenue in accordance with paragraph 146.4(2)(a) of the *Income Tax Act*;

(f) the number assigned to the disability savings plan entered into between the issuer and the holder;

(g) the day on which the disability savings plan between the issuer and the holder was entered into;

(h) the day on which the disability savings plan entered into between the issuer and the holder ends;

(i) the date and amount of contributions paid into the RDSP;

(j) the total amount of contributions paid into the RDSP;

(k) the amount of total earnings in the RDSP;

(l) if there is a transfer of amounts from a prior RDSP to a new RDSP,

(i) the amounts transferred as well as the book value and fair market value of those amounts,

(ii) the transfer date,

(iii) the name and address of the new issuer,

(iv) with respect to both the prior RDSP and new RDSP, the number assigned to the corresponding plan in respect of which written notification was given by the Minister of National Revenue in accordance with paragraph 146.4(2)(a) of the *Income Tax Act*, and

(v) with respect to both the prior RDSP and new RDSP, the number assigned to the disability savings plan entered into between the issuer and the holder;

(m) if there is a new holder of an RDSP after the RDSP is entered into, the new holder's name, address and social insurance number or business number, as the case may be, and the day on which they became the new holder of the RDSP;

(n) the disability assistance payments made, indicating the taxable and non-taxable portions of the payments and the date of each payment made;

(o) the fair market value of the RDSP;

(p) if a contribution is withdrawn subsequent to a waiver granted by the Minister of National Revenue in accordance with paragraph 146.4(12)(c) of the *Income Tax Act*, the amount and date of the contribution withdrawn; and

(q) whether or not a beneficiary is a DTC-eligible individual.

10. Coming Into Force — These Regulations come into force on the day on which section 136 of the *Budget and Economic Statement Implementation Act, 2007*, chapter 35 of the Statutes of Canada 2007, comes into force.

Disclosure of information for purposes of CDSA enforcement is allowed by 241(4)(d)(vii.5).

RDSPs were announced in the March 19, 2007 federal budget, as recommended by an expert advisory panel (Finance news release 2006-079, Dec. 12, 2006).

Definitions [s. 146.4]: "amount", "annuity" — 248(1); "assistance holdback amount" — 146.4(1); "beneficiary" — 146.4(1)"disability savings plan"; "borrowed money", "business", "business number" — 248(1); "calendar year" — *Interpretation Act* 37(1)(a); "Canada" — 255, *Interpretation Act* 35(1); "capital gain" — 39(1)(a), 248(1); "common-law partner", "common-law partnership" — 248(1); "corporation" — 248(1), *Interpretation Act* 35(1); "DTC-eligible individual" — 146.4(1); "deferred profit sharing plan" — 147(1), 248(1); "designated provincial program", "disability assistance payment", "disability savings plan" — 146.4(1); "disposition", "dividend" — 248(1); "estate" — 104(1), 248(1); "fair market value" — see 69(1) Notes; "holder" — 146.4(1); "identical" — 248(12); "individual" — 248(1); "issuer" — 146.4(1); "licensed annuities provider" — 147(1), 248(1); "lifetime disability assistance payments" — 146.4(1); "Minister" — 248(1); "month" — *Interpretation Act* 35(1); "non-compliant" — 146.4(11), (12); "non-taxable portion" — 146.4(7); "parent" — 252(2)(a); "person" — 248(1); "plan trust" — 146.4(1); "prescribed", "property" — 248(1); "province" — *Interpretation Act* 35(1); "qualified investment", "qualifying family member", "qualifying person" — 146.4(1); "RDSP" — 146.1(1)"registered disability savings plan", 248(1)"registered disability savings plan"; "registered disability savings plan" — 146.4(1), 248(1); "relevant time" — 146.4(10)(b); "resident in Canada" — 250; "retirement savings plan" — 146(1), 248(1); "specified disability savings plan" — 146.4(1.1)–(1.4); "specified maximum amount" — 146.4(1); "specified Minister" — 146.4(1); "specified RDSP payment" — 60.02(1); "specified year" — 146.4(1); "taxable income" — 248(1); "taxation year" — 249; "taxpayer" — 248(1); "trust" — 104(1), 248(1), (3); "writing", "written" — *Interpretation Act* 35(1)"writing".

Advanced Life Deferred Annuity

146.5 (1) Definitions — The following definitions apply in this section.

"advanced life deferred annuity" means a contract for an annuity that meets the following conditions:

(a) it is issued by a licensed annuities provider;

(b) it specifies that it is intended to qualify as an advanced life deferred annuity under this Act;

(c) periodic annuity payments under the contract

(i) commence to be paid no later than the end of the calendar year in which the annuitant attains 85 years of age, and

(ii) are payable for the life of the annuitant or for the lives, jointly, of the annuitant and the annuitant's spouse or common-law partner;

(d) periodic annuity payments under the contract are payable

(i) in equal amounts, or

(ii) in amounts that are not equal only because the payments

(A) are adjusted in whole or in part to reflect

(I) increases in the Consumer Price Index, as published by Statistics Canada under the authority of the *Statistics Act*, or

(II) increases at a rate specified in the contract, not exceeding 2% per annum, or

(B) are reduced on the death of the annuitant or the annuitant's spouse or common-law partner;

(e) if an annuity is payable for the lives, jointly, of the annuitant and the annuitant's spouse or common-law partner and the annuitant dies before payments commence to be paid, then the payments to the annuitant's spouse or common-law partner shall

(i) commence no later than the date that they would have commenced if the annuitant were alive, and

(ii) be adjusted in accordance with generally accepted actuarial principles if the payments commence before the date they would have commenced if the annuitant were alive;

(f) the amount to be paid, if any, to one or more beneficiaries under the contract after the death of the annuitant — or, in the case of a joint-lives annuity, after the last death of the annuitant and the annuitant's spouse or common-law partner — shall

(i) be paid as soon as practicable after the death of the annuitant or the last death of the annuitant and the annuitant's spouse or common-law partner, as the case may be, and

(ii) not exceed the amount, if any, by which the total amount transferred to acquire the annuity exceeds the total amount of annuity payments made under the contract;

(g) it provides that all or part of the amount transferred to acquire the annuity may be refunded, if

(i) the refund is paid to reduce the amount of tax that would otherwise be payable by the annuitant under Part XI, and

(ii) the refund is

(A) paid to the annuitant, or

(B) transferred directly to

(I) the issuer of a registered retirement savings plan of the annuitant,

(II) the carrier of a registered retirement income fund of the annuitant,

(III) the administrator of a pooled registered pension plan under which the annuitant is a member, or

(IV) the administrator of a money purchase provision of a registered pension plan under which the annuitant is a member;

(h) if it provides that the spouse or common-law partner may request a payment in a single amount in full or partial satisfaction of the spouse's or common-law partner's entitlement to payments described in subparagraph (c)(ii) as a consequence of the death of the annuitant, then the single amount cannot exceed the present value (at the time the single amount is paid) of the other payments that, as a consequence of the payment of the single amount, cease to be provided;

(i) no right under the contract is capable of being assigned, charged, anticipated, given as security or surrendered; and

(j) it does not provide for any payment under the contract except as specified in this definition.

Related Provisions: 146.5(2) — Payments other than under (f) or (g) included in income; 146.5(3) — Death benefits under para. (f) included in income; 146.5(4) — Refunds under para. (g) included in income; 146.5(5) — Effect of (g)(ii)(B) applying; 146.5(6) — Where para. (f) applies and beneficiary is described in 146.5(3)(a); 146.5(7) — Where amendment to contract results in definition no longer applying; 205(1)"cumulative excess amount", "excess ALDA transfer" — Over-transfer to ALDA; 252(3) — Extended meaning of spouse.

Notes: See Notes at end of 146.5.

Regulations: 216(2) (information return on transfer to ALDA); 216(3) (information return on payment or refund from ALDA).

"annuitant" means an individual who has acquired a contract for an annuity from a licensed annuities provider.

"beneficiary", under a contract for an annuity, means an individual who has a right under the contract to receive a payment after the death of the annuitant or the annuitant's spouse or common-law partner.

(2) Taxable amount — annuity payments — Amounts (excluding amounts described in paragraph (f) or (g) of the definition "advanced life deferred annuity" in subsection (1) and including amounts deemed to have been received under paragraph (7)(a)) received by a taxpayer in a taxation year under an advanced life deferred annuity shall be included in computing the income of the taxpayer for the taxation year.

Related Provisions: 56(1)(d)(iv) — Amount not taxed by 146.5 not included in taxable annuity income; 56(1)(z.5) — Inclusion in total income; 118(7)"pension income"(a)(iii.3) — ALDA annuity payment qualifies as "pension income"; 153(1)(u) — Withholding on payment to Canadian resident; 212(1)(l.1) — Withholding tax on payment to non-resident.

Notes: See Notes at end of 146.5.

Regulations: 216(3) (information return on payment from ALDA).

(3) Taxable amount — death benefits — Amounts described in paragraph (f) of the definition "advanced life deferred annuity" in subsection (1) received by a taxpayer in a taxation year under an advanced life deferred annuity as a result of the death of an individual shall be included in computing the income of

(a) the taxpayer for the taxation year, if the taxpayer is

(i) the spouse or common-law partner of the individual, or

(ii) a child or grandchild of the individual who was, immediately before the death of the individual, financially dependent on the individual for support; and

(b) the individual for the taxation year in which the individual died, in any other case.

Related Provisions: 56(1)(z.5) — Inclusion in total income; 60(l)(v)(A.2) — Rollover of death benefit to RRSP etc. for spouse, child or grandchild; 146.5(6) — Where 146.5(1)"advanced life deferred annuity"(f) applies and beneficiary is described in (3)(a); 153(1)(u) — Withholding on payment to Canadian resident; 212(1)(l.1) — Withholding tax on payment to non-resident; 252(3) — Extended meaning of spouse.

Regulations: 216(3) (information return on payment from ALDA).

(4) Taxation of refunds — The amount of a refund described in clause (g)(ii)(A) of the definition "advanced life deferred annuity" in subsection (1) that is paid to an annuitant shall be included in the income of the annuitant.

Related Provisions: 56(1)(z.5) — Inclusion in total income; 153(1)(u) — Withholding on payment to Canadian resident; 212(1)(l.1) — Withholding tax on payment to non-resident.

Regulations: 216(3) (information return on payment from ALDA).

(5) Treatment of amount transferred — If an amount is paid in circumstances described in clause (g)(ii)(B) of the definition "advanced life deferred annuity" in subsection (1),

(a) the amount shall not, by reason only of that payment, be included by reason of paragraph 56(1)(z.5) in computing the income of any taxpayer;

(b) no deduction may be made under any provision of this Act in respect of the amount in computing the income of any taxpayer;

(c) in the case of an amount paid to a registered pension plan, the amount is deemed not to be a contribution for the purpose of applying Parts LXXXIII and LXXXV of the *Income Tax Regulations*; and

(d) in the case of an amount paid to a registered retirement savings plan or a pooled registered pension plan, the amount shall not be included in determining the amount of the individual's undeducted RRSP premiums under subsection 204.2(1.2).

(6) Deemed payment to beneficiary — An amount is deemed to have been received at a particular time by a "beneficiary" (as defined in subsection 108(1)) of a deceased annuitant's estate, and not by the legal representative of the deceased annuitant, if

(a) the amount is described in paragraph (f) of the definition "advanced life deferred annuity" in subsection (1);

(b) the amount was paid to the legal representative;

(c) the beneficiary is described in paragraph (3)(a);

(d) the beneficiary is entitled to the amount in full or partial satisfaction of their rights as a beneficiary under the deceased annuitant's estate; and

(e) the amount is designated jointly by the legal representative and the beneficiary in prescribed form filed with the Minister.

(7) Amended contract — If an amendment made at any time to a contract results in it no longer meeting the conditions in the definition "advanced life deferred annuity" in subsection (1), the following rules apply:

(a) the annuitant under the contract immediately before that time is deemed to have received under the contract at that time an amount equal to the fair market value of their interest in the contract at that time; and

(b) the annuitant is deemed to have acquired their interest in the contract at that time at a cost equal to the fair market value of the interest at that time.

Notes: The advanced life deferred annuity (ALDA) was introduced by the March 2019 Budget. (For variable payment life annuities, introduced at the same time, see Reg. 8506(1)(e.2).)

An ALDA is a life annuity whose payout may be deferred until the end of the year the annuitant turn 85 (146.5(1)"advanced life deferred annuity"(c)(i)). There is a lifetime ALDA dollar limit of $150,000 from all qualifying plans, indexed annually but rounded to the nearest $10,000 (205(1)"ALDA dollar limit", "cumulative excess amount", 205(2)).

An ALDA qualifies as an annuity purchase for an RRSP (146(16)(a.1)), RRIF (146.3(14.1)(c)), DPSP (147(19)(d)(v)), PRPP (147.5(21)(c)) and defined contribution RPP (146.3(1)(c)(iv)).

146.5 added by 2021 budget bill #1, effective 2020.

Definitions [s. 146.5]: "advanced life deferred annuity" — 146.5(1), 248(1); "amount", "annuity" — 248(1); "beneficiary" — 108(1); "calendar year" — *Interpretation Act* 37(1)(a); "child" — 252(1); "common-law partner" — 248(1); "consequence" — 248(8); "death benefit" — 248(1); "estate" — 104(1), 248(1); "fair market value" — see 69(1) Notes; "individual", "legal representative" — 248(1); "licensed annuities provider" — 147(1), 248(1); "Minister" — 248(1); "pooled registered pension plan" — 147.5(1), 248(1); "prescribed" — 248(1); "registered pension plan" — 248(1); "registered retirement income fund" — 146.3(1), 248(1); "registered retirement savings plan" — 146(1), 248(1); "RRSP" — 248(1)"registered retirement savings plan"; "security" — *Interpretation Act* 35(1); "spouse" — 252(3); "taxation year" — 249; "taxpayer" — 248(1); "undeducted RRSP premiums" — 204.2(1.2).

Deferred Profit Sharing Plans

147. (1) Definitions — In this section,

"deferred profit sharing plan" means a profit sharing plan accepted by the Minister for registration for the purposes of this Act, on application therefor in prescribed manner by a trustee under the plan and an employer of employees who are beneficiaries under the plan, as complying with the requirements of this section;

Possible Future Amendment — Employee ownership trusts

Federal Budget, Chapter 3, April 19, 2021: See under 7(1).

Related Provisions: 75(3)(a) — Reversionary trust rules do not apply to DPSP; 108(1)"trust"(a) — "Trust" does not include a DPSP for certain purposes; 128.1(10)"excluded right or interest"(a)(iv) — No deemed disposition of DPSP on emigration; Reg. 9006(g) — DPSP not reported to CRA for disclosure to foreign tax authorities.

Notes: A DPSP allows an employer to deduct payments made for the benefit of employees and former employees (147(8)), who are taxed on amounts paid out of the plan (147(10)). No tax applies to income as it is earned inside the plan: 147(7). Contributions can be cheaper than pay because they are not subject to EI, CPP and other payroll taxes. For annual contribution limits see 147(5.1). An owner-manager or family member cannot be a beneficiary (147(2)(k.2), and see 147(2) Notes), and in *Goldstein*, [1974] C.T.C. 2021 (TRB), a DPSP designed to benefit the controlling shareholders

(by having conditions such that the company's other employees could not qualify) was deemed not to exist. A non-profit employer such as a union cannot sponsor a DPSP (VIEWS doc 9603366). The profits being measured can be those of a related company such as a U.S. parent: 147(1)"profit sharing plan" and VIEWS doc 2004-0093441I7.

A DPSP must invest in only "qualified investments" (s. 204, Reg. 4900), but these may include shares of the employer under certain conditions (204"qualified investment"(e), VIEWS doc 9821195). Debt of the employer will not qualify: VIEWS doc 9606285.

A DPSP is not required to have a locking-in provision preventing withdrawals, but one such provision was upheld in *Forbes v. Canadian Tire*, 2013 ONSC 132 (Ont. SCJ). See Mark Firman, "The Key to DPSP Locking-in", 24(2) *Taxation of Executive Compensation & Retirement* (Federated Press) 1571-73 (Sept. 2012).

A DPSP normally cannot be seized on bankruptcy: see Notes to 146(4).

DPSP issuers and advisers: see tinyurl.com/dpsp-cra.

See also Dominic Belley, "Owner-Manager Compensation 2: Deferred Profit-Sharing Plans", 1(4) *Tax for the Owner-Manager* (ctf.ca) 23-24 (Oct. 2001).

Interpretation Bulletins: IT-528: Transfers of funds between registered plans.

Forms: T2214: Application for registration as a deferred profit sharing plan.

"forfeited amount", under a deferred profit sharing plan or a plan the registration of which has been revoked pursuant to subsection (14) or (14.1), means an amount to which a beneficiary under the plan has ceased to have any rights, other than the portion thereof, if any, that is payable as a consequence of the death of the beneficiary to a person who is entitled thereto by virtue of the participation of the beneficiary in the plan;

"licensed annuities provider" means a person licensed or otherwise authorized under the laws of Canada or a province to carry on in Canada an annuities business;

Related Provisions: 248(1)"licensed annuities provider" — Definition applies to entire Act.

Notes: Definition "licensed annuities provider" added by 1996 Budget, effective 1992.

"profit sharing plan" means an arrangement under which payments computed by reference to an employer's profits from the employer's business, or by reference to those profits and the profits, if any, from the business of a corporation with which the employer does not deal at arm's length, are or have been made by the employer to a trustee in trust for the benefit of employees or former employees of that employer.

Related Provisions: 147(16) — Payments out of profits; 248(1)"deferred profit sharing plan", "profit sharing plan" — Definitions apply to entire Act; 248(8) — Meaning of "consequence" of death.

Notes: See Notes to 147(1)"deferred profit sharing plan".

147(1) amended by 1990 pension bill, effective 1991. For 1972–90, 147(1)(a) defined "deferred profit sharing plan" and 147(1)(b), "profit sharing plan".

Regulations: 1501 (prescribed manner).

Interpretation Bulletins: IT-280R: Employees profit sharing plans — payments computed by reference to profits.

Information Circulars: 77-1R4: Deferred profit sharing plans. See also at end of s. 147.

Forms: T3D: Income tax return for DPSP or revoked DPSP.

(1.1) Participating employer — An employer is considered to participate in a profit sharing plan where the employer makes or has made payments under the plan to a trustee in trust for the benefit of employees or former employees of the employer.

Notes: 147(1.1) added by 1996 Budget, retroactive to 1989. The Department of Finance indicates that it was "added for clarity and does not represent a change in policy."

(2) Acceptance of plan for registration — The Minister shall not accept for registration for the purposes of this Act any profit sharing plan unless, in the Minister's opinion, it complies with the following conditions:

(a) the plan provides that each payment made under the plan to a trustee in trust for the benefit of beneficiaries thereunder is the total of amounts each of which is required to be allocated by the trustee in the year in which it is received by the trustee, to the individual beneficiary in respect of whom the amount was so paid;

(a.1) the plan includes a stipulation that no contribution may be made to the plan other than

(i) a contribution made in accordance with the terms of the plan by an employer for the benefit of the employer's employees who are beneficiaries under the plan, or

(ii) an amount transferred to the plan in accordance with subsection (19);

(b) the plan does not provide for the payment of any amount to an employee or other beneficiary thereunder by way of loan;

(c) the plan provides that no part of the funds of the trust governed by the plan may be invested in notes, bonds, debentures, bankers' acceptances or similar obligations of

(i) an employer by whom payments are made in trust to a trustee under the plan for the benefit of beneficiaries thereunder, or

(ii) a corporation with whom that employer does not deal at arm's length;

(d) the plan provides that no part of the funds of the trust governed by the plan may be invested in shares of a corporation at least 50% of the property of which consists of notes, bonds, debentures, bankers' acceptances or similar obligations of an employer or a corporation described in paragraph (c);

(e) the plan includes a provision stipulating that no right of a person under the plan is capable of any surrender or assignment other than

(i) an assignment under a decree, an order or a judgment of a competent tribunal, or under a written agreement, that relates to a division of property between an individual and the individual's spouse or common-law partner, or former spouse or common-law partner, in settlement of rights that arise out of, or on a breakdown of, their marriage or common-law partnership,

(ii) an assignment by a deceased individual's legal representative on the distribution of the individual's estate, and

(iii) a surrender of benefits to avoid revocation of the plan's registration;

(f) the plan includes a provision stipulating that each of the trustees under the plan shall be resident in Canada;

(g) the plan provides that, if a corporation licensed or otherwise authorized under the laws of Canada or a province to carry on in Canada the business of offering to the public its services as trustee is not a trustee under the plan, there shall be at least 3 trustees under the plan who shall be individuals;

(h) the plan provides that all income received, capital gains made and capital losses sustained by the trust governed by the plan must be allocated to beneficiaries under the plan on or before a day 90 days after the end of the year in which they were received, made or sustained, as the case may be, to the extent that they have not been allocated in years preceding that year;

(i) the plan provides that each amount allocated or reallocated by a trustee under the plan to a beneficiary under the plan vest irrevocably in that beneficiary,

(i) in the case of an amount allocated or reallocated before 1991, at a time that is not later than 5 years after the end of the year in which it was allocated or reallocated, unless the beneficiary becomes, before that time, an individual who is not an employee of any employer who participates in the plan, and

(ii) in the case of any other amount, not later than the later of the time of allocation or reallocation and the day on which the beneficiary completes a period of 24 consecutive months as a beneficiary under the plan or under any other deferred profit sharing plan for which the plan can reasonably be considered to have been substituted;

(i.1) the plan requires that each forfeited amount under the plan and all earnings of the plan reasonably attributable thereto be paid to employers who participate in the plan, or be reallocated to beneficiaries under the plan, on or before the later of December 31, 1991 and December 31 of the year immediately following the calendar year in which the amount is forfeited, or such later time as is permitted in writing by the Minister under subsection (2.2);

(j) the plan provides that a trustee under the plan inform, in writing, all new beneficiaries under the plan of their rights under the plan;

(k) the plan provides that, in respect of each beneficiary under the plan who has been employed by an employer who participates in the plan, all amounts vested under the plan in the beneficiary become payable

(i) to the beneficiary, or

(ii) in the event of the beneficiary's death, to another person designated by the beneficiary or to the beneficiary's estate,

not later than the earlier of

(iii) the end of the year in which the beneficiary attains 71 years of age, and

(iv) 90 days after the earliest of

(A) the death of the beneficiary,

(B) the day on which the beneficiary ceases to be employed by an employer who participates in the plan where, at the time of ceasing to be so employed, the beneficiary is not employed by another employer who participates in the plan, and

(C) the termination or winding-up of the plan,

except that the plan may provide that, on election by the beneficiary, all or any part of the amounts payable to the beneficiary may be paid

(v) in equal instalments payable not less frequently than annually over a period not exceeding 10 years from the day on which the amount became payable, or

(vi) by a trustee under the plan to a licensed annuities provider to purchase for the beneficiary an annuity (other than an advanced life deferred annuity), if

(A) payment of the annuity is to begin not later than the end of the year in which the beneficiary attains 71 years of age, and

(B) the guaranteed term, if any, of the annuity does not exceed 15 years;

(k.1) the plan requires that no benefit or loan, other than

(i) a benefit the amount of which is required to be included in computing the beneficiary's income,

(ii) an amount referred to in paragraph (10)(b),

(ii.1) an amount paid pursuant to or under the plan by a trustee under the plan to a licensed annuities provider to purchase for a beneficiary under the plan an annuity to which subparagraph (k)(vi) or (19)(d)(v) applies,

(iii) a benefit derived from an allocation or reallocation referred to in subsection (2), or

(iv) the benefit derived from the provision of administrative or investment services in respect of the plan,

that is conditional in any way on the existence of the plan may be extended to a beneficiary thereunder or to a person with whom the beneficiary was not dealing at arm's length;

(k.2) the plan provides that no individual who is

(i) a person related to the employer,

(ii) a person who is, or is related to, a specified shareholder of the employer or of a corporation related to the employer,

(iii) where the employer is a partnership, a person related to a member of the partnership, or

(iv) where the employer is a trust, a person who is, or is related to, a beneficiary under the trust may become a beneficiary under the plan; and

(l) the plan, in all other respects, complies with regulations of the Governor in Council made on the recommendation of the Minister of Finance.

Related Provisions: 56(1)(d.2)(iii) — Income from annuity purchased with plan funds is taxable; 146(5.21)(b) — Anti-avoidance re pension adjustment; 147(1.1) — Meaning of "participates" in a profit sharing plan; 147(2.1) — Terms limiting contributions; 147(2.2) — Reallocation of forfeitures; 147(10)(a) — Amount used to purchase annuity under 147(2)(k)(vi) is not taxable; 147(10.3) — Amount contributed to or forfeited under a plan; 147(10.6) — Where pre-1997 annuity has not begun by age 69; 147(14) — Revocation of registration where plan ceases to comply with requirements; 147(17) — Meaning of "other beneficiary"; 147(19) — Transfer to spouse's/partner's RPP, RRSP or RRIF on breakdown of relationship; 147(21) — Restrictions re transfers from DPSPs; 172(3) — Appeal from refusal to register, revocation of registration, etc.; 198–204 — Taxes on DPSPs and revoked plans; 204.1(3) — Tax payable by DPSP on excess contributions; 204.2(4) — Definition of "excess amount" for a DPSP; Reg. 8502(f) — RPP rules parallel to 147(2)(e); Reg. 9006(g) — DPSP not reported to CRA for disclosure to foreign tax authorities.

Notes: See tinyurl.com/dpsp-cra; Willis Towers Watson, *Canadian Pensions and Retirement Income Planning*, 6th ed. (LexisNexis, 2017), chap. 19. CRA's target (tinyurl.com/cra-standards) for processing DPSP and pension applications is 85% within 180 days; in 2019-20, it did 94%.

Employee withdrawals of DPSP funds can be permitted during employment; they are taxed under 147(10) unless transferred under 147(19): VIEWS doc 2008-0304761E5.

Where an employer promises to pay amounts after an employee's retirement but does not segregate assets to back that promise, CRA does not consider the promise to give rise to "vested" contributions under 147(2)(i) or (k): VIEWS doc 2000-0041245. See also Notes to 147(1)"deferred profit sharing plan".

An amount forfeited and paid to an employer under 147(2)(i.1) is subject to source withholding under 153(1)(h) and reporting under Reg. 200(1): VIEWS doc 2013-0500511E5.

See VIEWS doc 2004-0074771I7 for a CRA interpretation that executives of a company would be prohibited by 147(2)(k.2) from becoming members of its DPSP due to holding shares in other corporations in the group.

147(2)(k)(vi) opening words and (k.1)(ii.1) amended by 2021 budget bill #1, effective 2020, to accommodate ALDAs (see 146.5). Before 2020, read:

> (k)(vi) by a trustee under the plan to a licensed annuities provider to purchase for the beneficiary an annuity where
>
> . . . . .
>
> (k.1)(ii.1) an amount paid pursuant to or under the plan by a trustee under the plan to a licensed annuities provider to purchase for a beneficiary under the plan an annuity to which subparagraph (k)(vi) applies,

147(2) amended by 2002-2013 technical bill (effective March 21, 2003), 2007 budget bill #1, 1996 Budget, 1993 technical bill, 1990 pension bill.

Regulations: 4900(2) (obligations described in 147(2)(c) are not qualified investments).

Interpretation Bulletins: IT-280R: Employees profit sharing plans — payments computed by reference to profits; IT-281R2: Elections on single payments from a deferred profit-sharing plan (cancelled); IT-363R2: Deferred profit sharing plans — deductibility of employer contributions and taxation of amounts received by a beneficiary (cancelled); IT-517R: Pension tax credit (cancelled).

Information Circulars: 74-1R5: Form T2037 — Notice of purchase of annuity with "plan" funds; 78-14R4: Guidelines for trust companies and other persons responsible for filing T3GR, T3D, T3P, T3S, T3RI, and T3F returns.

Registered Plans Directorate Newsletters: 91-4R (registration rules for money purchase provisions).

Registered Plans Compliance Bulletins: 1, 2, 3 (how to contact us).

Forms: T2037: Notice of purchase of annuity with "plan" funds; T2214: Application for registration as a deferred profit sharing plan.

(2.1) Terms limiting contributions — The Minister shall not accept for registration for the purposes of this Act a profit sharing plan unless it includes terms that are adequate to ensure that the requirements of subsection (5.1) in respect of the plan will be satisfied for each calendar year.

Notes: 147(2.1) added by 1990 pension bill, effective 1991.

(2.2) Reallocation of forfeitures — The Minister may, on written application, extend the time for satisfying the requirements of paragraph (2)(i.1) where

(a) the total of the forfeited amounts arising in a calendar year is greater than normal because of unusual circumstances; and

(b) the forfeited amounts are to be reallocated on a reasonable basis to a majority of beneficiaries under the plan.

Notes: 147(2.2) added by 1990 pension bill, effective 1991.

(3) Acceptance of employees profit sharing plan for registration — The Minister shall not accept for registration for the purposes of this Act any employees profit sharing plan unless all the capital gains of or made by the trust governed by the plan before the date of application for registration of the plan and all the capital losses of or sustained by the trust before that date have been allocated by the trustee under the plan to employees and other beneficiaries thereunder.

(4) Capital gains determined — For the purposes of subsections (3) and (11), such amount as may be determined by the Minister, on request in prescribed manner by the trustee of a trust governed by an employees profit sharing plan, shall be deemed to be the amount of

(a) the capital gains of or made by the trust governed by the plan before the date of application for registration of the plan, or

(b) the capital losses of or sustained by the trust before that date,

as the case may be.

(5) Registration date — Where a profit sharing plan is accepted by the Minister for registration as a deferred profit sharing plan, the plan shall be deemed to have become registered as a deferred profit sharing plan

(a) on the date the application for registration of the plan was made; or

(b) where in the application for registration a later date is specified as the date on which the plan is to commence as a deferred profit sharing plan, on that date.

Related Provisions: 144(11) — Taxation year of trust accepted as DPSP.

(5.1) Contribution limits — For the purposes of subsections (2.1) and (9) and paragraph (14)(c.4), the requirements of this subsection in respect of a deferred profit sharing plan are satisfied for a calendar year if, in the case of each beneficiary under the plan and each employer in respect of whom the beneficiary's pension credit (as prescribed by regulation) for the year under the plan is greater than nil,

(a) the total of all amounts each of which is the beneficiary's pension credit (as prescribed by regulation) for the year in respect of the employer under a deferred profit sharing plan does not exceed the lesser of

(i) ½ of the money purchase limit for the year, and

(ii) 18% of the amount that would be the beneficiary's compensation (within the meaning assigned by subsection 147.1(1)) from the employer for the year if the definition "compensation" in subsection 147.1(1) were read without reference to paragraph (b) of that definition;

(b) the total of all amounts each of which is the beneficiary's pension credit (as prescribed by regulation) for the year under a deferred profit sharing plan in respect of

(i) the employer, or

(ii) any other employer who, at any time in the year, does not deal at arm's length with the employer

does not exceed ½ of the money purchase limit for the year; and

(c) the total of

(i) the beneficiary's pension adjustment for the year in respect of the employer, and

(ii) the total of all amounts each of which is the beneficiary's pension adjustment for the year in respect of any other employer who, at any time in the year, does not deal at arm's length with the employer

does not exceed the lesser of

(iii) the money purchase limit for the year, and

(iv) 18% of the total of all amounts each of which is the beneficiary's compensation (within the meaning assigned by subsection 147.1(1)) for the year from the employer or any other employer referred to in subparagraph (ii).

Related Provisions: 147(2.1) — Terms limiting contributions; 147(8) — Employer contributions deductible; 147(9) — Limitation on deduction; 147(14) — Revocation of registration; 147(22) — Excess transfer; 147.1(8) — Pension adjustment limits; Reg. 8301(11) — Timing of contributions.

Notes: 147(5.1) added by 1990 pension bill, effective 1991. The deduction limit is ½ the 147.1(1)"money purchase limit" for the year, and is: 1991-92: $6,250; 1993: $6,750; 1994: $7,250; 1995: $7,750; 1996-2002: $6,750; 2003: $7,750; 2004: $8,250; 2005: $9,000; 2006: $9,500; 2007: $10,000; 2008: $10,500; 2009: $11,000; 2010: $11,225; 2011: $11,485; 2012: $11,910; 2013: $12,135; 2014: $12,465; 2015: $12,685; 2016: $13,005; 2017: $13,115; 2018: $13,250; 2019: $13,615; 2020: $13,915; 2021: $14,605; 2022+: indexed to 147.1(1)"money purchase limit".

"Compensation" in 147(5.1)(a)(ii) includes all amounts taxable under ss. 5 and 6, so a member receiving disability benefits taxable under 6(1)(f) can still be included in group DPSP contributions: VIEWS doc 2006-021428117.

Regulations: 8301(2)–(3) (pension credit under DPSP).

Interpretation Bulletins: IT-528: Transfers of funds between registered plans.

Information Circulars: See list at end of s. 147.

Registered Plans Directorate Newsletters: 96-1 (changes to retirement savings limits).

(5.11) [Repealed]

Notes: 147(5.11) repealed by 2002-2013 technical bill, for cessations of employment after 2002. Added by 1990 pension bill, effective 1991.

(6) Deferred plan not employees profit sharing plan — For a period during which a plan is a deferred profit sharing plan, the plan shall be deemed, for the purposes of this Act, not to be an employees profit sharing plan.

Related Provisions: 144(11) — Year-end of EPSP on becoming DPSP.

(7) No tax while trust governed by plan — No tax is payable under this Part by a trust on the taxable income of the trust for a period during which the trust was governed by a deferred profit sharing plan.

Related Provisions: 149(1)(s) — Exemption for DPSP; 198 — Tax on acquisition of non-qualified investments and use of assets as security; 207.1(2) — Tax payable by DPSP on holding non-qualified investments.

(8) Amount of employer's contribution deductible — Subject to subsection (9), there may be deducted in computing the income of an employer for a taxation year the total of all amounts each of which is an amount paid by the employer in the year or within 120 days after the end of the year to a trustee under a deferred profit sharing plan for the benefit of the employer's employees who are beneficiaries under the plan, to the extent that the amount was paid in accordance with the terms of the plan and was not deducted in computing the employer's income for a preceding taxation year.

Related Provisions: 6(1)(a)(i) — Employer's contribution to DPSP not a taxable benefit; 20(1)(y) — Employer's contribution to DPSP deductible; 147(5.1) — Contribution limits; 147(9), (9.1) — Limitations on deduction; 147(20) — Taxation of amount transferred; 204.1(3) — Tax payable by DPSP on excess amount; *Interpretation Act* 27(5) — Meaning of "within 120 days".

Notes: 147(8) amended by 1990 pension bill, effective 1991 for amounts paid to DPSPs after 1990. Before 1991, the deduction was based on 20% of current year's earned income, and capped at $3,500 minus any deductible employee RPP contributions for the year.

Interpretation Bulletins: IT-280R: Employees profit sharing plans — payments computed by reference to profits; IT-363R2: Deferred profit sharing plans — deductibility of employer contributions and taxation of amounts received by a beneficiary (cancelled).

Forms: T2 Sched. 15: Deferred income plans.

(9) Limitation on deduction — Where the requirements of subsection (5.1) in respect of a deferred profit sharing plan are not satisfied for a calendar year by reason that the pension credits of a beneficiary under the plan in respect of a particular employer do not comply with paragraph (5.1)(a) or the beneficiary's pension credits or pension adjustments in respect of a particular employer and other employers who do not deal at arm's length with the particular employer do not comply with paragraph (5.1)(b) or (c), the particular employer is not entitled to a deduction under subsection (8) in computing the particular employer's income for any taxation year in re-

spect of an amount paid to a trustee under the plan in the calendar year except to the extent expressly permitted in writing by the Minister, and, for the purposes of this subsection, an amount paid to a trustee of a deferred profit sharing plan in the first two months of a calendar year shall be deemed to have been paid in the immediately preceding year and not to have been paid in the year to the extent that the amount can reasonably be considered to be in respect of the immediately preceding year.

Notes: 147(9) amended by 1990 pension bill, effective 1990 for amounts paid to DPSPs after 1990. Before 1991, it related to the pre-1991 version of 147(8).

Forms: T2 Sched. 15: Deferred income plans.

(9.1) No deduction — Notwithstanding subsection (8), no deduction shall be made in computing the income of an employer for a taxation year in respect of an amount paid by the employer for the year to a trustee under a deferred profit sharing plan in respect of a beneficiary who is described in paragraph (2)(k.2) in respect of the plan.

Interpretation Bulletins: IT-280R: Employees profit sharing plans — payments computed by reference to profits; IT-363R2: Deferred profit sharing plans — deductibility of employer contributions and taxation of amounts received by a beneficiary (cancelled).

(10) Amounts received taxable — There shall be included in computing the income of a beneficiary under a deferred profit sharing plan for a taxation year the amount, if any, by which

(a) the total of all amounts received by the beneficiary in the year from a trustee under the plan (other than as a result of acquiring an annuity described in subparagraph (2)(k)(vi) under which the beneficiary is the annuitant)

exceeds

(b) the total of all amounts each of which is an amount determined for the year under subsection (10.1), (11) or (12) in relation to the plan and in respect of the beneficiary.

Related Provisions: 56(1)(d.2)(iii) — Income from annuity purchased with plan funds is taxable; 56(1)(i) — Deferred profit sharing plan; 60(j) — Transfer of superannuation benefits; 104(27.1) — DPSP benefits; 128.1(10)"excluded right or interest"(a)(iv) — No deemed disposition of DPSP on emigration; 139.1(12) — Conversion benefit on demutualization of insurance corporation not taxable; 147(10.1) — Single payment on retirement etc.; 147(10.4) — Income on disposal of shares; 147(11) — Portion of receipts deductible; 147(18) — Inadequate consideration on purchase from or sale to trust; 147(20) — Taxation of amount transferred; 153(1)(h) — Withholdings; 212(1)(m), 214(3)(d) — Withholding tax on payments to non-residents.

Notes: 147(10)(b) added by 1996 Budget, retroactive to 1992, so that an amount paid to purchase an annuity does not reduce the amount included in beneficiary B's income under 147(10). Since the amount is not received by B, the purchase of the annuity is disregarded for the purpose of computing B's income.

Interpretation Bulletins: IT-280R: Employees profit sharing plans — payments computed by reference to profits; IT-281R2: Elections on single payments from a deferred profit-sharing plan (cancelled); IT-363R2: Deferred profit sharing plans — deductibility of employer contributions and taxation of amounts received by a beneficiary (cancelled); IT-528: Transfers of funds between registered plans.

Information Circulars: See list at end of s. 147.

Advance Tax Rulings: ATR-31: Funding of divorce settlement amount from DPSP.

(10.1) Single payment on retirement, etc. — For the purposes of subsections (10) and (10.2), where a beneficiary under a deferred profit sharing plan has received, in a taxation year and when the beneficiary was resident in Canada, from a trustee under the plan a single payment that included shares of the capital stock of a corporation that was an employer who contributed to the plan or of a corporation with which the employer did not deal at arm's length on the beneficiary's withdrawal from the plan or retirement from employment or on the death of an employee or former employee and has made an election in respect thereof in prescribed manner and prescribed form, the amount determined for the year under this subsection in relation to the plan and in respect of the beneficiary is the amount, if any, by which the fair market value of those shares, immediately before the single payment was made, exceeds the cost amount to the plan of those shares at that time.

Related Provisions: 47(3)(a) — No averaging of cost on disposition of securities; 147(10) — Amounts received taxable; 147(10.2) — Single payment on retirement etc.; 147(11) — Portion of receipts deductible.

Notes: 147(10.1) amended by 1985 Budget, effective for terminations of interests in DPSPs after May 23, 1985.

Regulations: 1503 (prescribed manner, prescribed form).

Interpretation Bulletins: IT-281R2: Election on single payments from a deferred profit-sharing plan (cancelled); IT-528: Transfers of funds between registered plans.

Forms: T2078: Election under subsection 147(10.1) for a single payment received from a deferred profit sharing plan.

(10.2) Idem — Where a trustee under a deferred profit sharing plan has at any time in a taxation year made under the plan a single payment that included shares referred to in subsection (10.1) to a beneficiary who was resident in Canada at the time and the beneficiary has made an election under that subsection in respect of that payment,

(a) the trustee shall be deemed to have disposed of those shares for proceeds of disposition equal to the cost amount to the trust of those shares immediately before the single payment was made;

(b) the cost to the beneficiary of those shares shall be deemed to be their cost amount to the trust immediately before the single payment was made;

(c) the cost to the beneficiary of each of those shares shall be deemed to be the amount determined by the formula

$$A \times B / C$$

where

A is the amount determined under paragraph (a) in respect of all of those shares,

B is the fair market value of that share at the time the single payment was made, and

C is the fair market value of all those shares at the time the single payment was made; and

(d) for the purposes of paragraph 60(j), the cost to the beneficiary of those shares is an eligible amount in respect of the beneficiary for the year.

Notes: 147(10.2)(d) added by 1990 pension bill, effective 1989.

147(10.2) amended by 1985 Budget, effective for terminations of interests in DPSPs after May 23, 1985.

Interpretation Bulletins: IT-281R2: Elections on single payments from a deferred profit-sharing plan (cancelled); IT-528: Transfers of funds between registered plans.

(10.3) Amount contributed to or forfeited under a plan — There shall be included in computing the income for a taxation year of a beneficiary described in paragraph (2)(k.2) the total of amounts allocated or reallocated to the beneficiary in the year in respect of

(a) any amount contributed after December 1, 1982 by an employer to, or

(b) any forfeited amount under

a deferred profit sharing plan or a plan the registration of which has been revoked pursuant to subsection (14) or (14.1).

Notes: Except where 147(10.3) applies, employer contributions to a DPSP are not a taxable benefit: 6(1)(a)(i), VIEWS doc 2011-0405431E5.

147(10.3) amended by 1990 pension bill, effective 1991.

Interpretation Bulletins: IT-363R2: Deferred profit sharing plans — deductibility of employer contributions and taxation of amounts received by a beneficiary (cancelled).

(10.4) Income on disposal of shares — Where a taxpayer has a share in respect of which the taxpayer has made an election under subsection (10.1), there shall be included in computing the taxpayer's income for the taxation year in which the taxpayer disposed of or exchanged the share or ceased to be a resident of Canada, whichever is the earlier, the amount, if any, by which the fair market value of the share at the time the taxpayer acquired it exceeds the cost to the taxpayer, determined under paragraph (10.2)(c), of the share at the time the taxpayer acquired it.

Related Provisions: 7(1.3) — Order of disposition of securities acquired under stock option agreement; 110(1)(d.3) — Employer's shares — deduction from taxable income.

Interpretation Bulletins: IT-281R2: Elections on single payments from a deferred profit-sharing plan (cancelled).

(10.5) Amended contract — Where an amendment is made to an annuity contract to which subparagraph (2)(k)(vi) applies, the sole effect of which is to defer annuity commencement to no later than the end of the calendar year in which the individual in respect of whom the contract was purchased attains 71 years of age, the annuity contract is deemed not to have been disposed of by the individual.

Notes: 147(10.5) added by 2007 budget bill #1, effective 2007, to permit amendments to a DPSP to extend the age from 69 to 71 (see 147(2)(k)(iii) and (vi)(A)).

Former 147(10.5), an ordering rule for 147(10.4), repealed by 2000 Budget, effective for shares acquired, but not disposed of, before February 28, 2000 and to shares acquired after February 27, 2000. See now 7(1.3).

(10.6) [Repealed]

Notes: 147(10.6) repealed by 2007 budget bill #1, effective 2007 (since the DPSP age limit was changed back to 71), but the repeal does not apply to annuities under which the annuitant reached age 69 before 2007. It contained rules relating to annuities purchased for a DPSP beneficiary before 1997, if annuity payments did not begin by the end of the year the beneficiary turned 69.

147(10.6) added by 1996 Budget, effective 1997, subject to certain transitional rules.

(11) Portion of receipts deductible — For the purposes of subsections (10), (10.1) and (12), where an amount was received in a taxation year from a trustee under a deferred profit sharing plan by an employee or other beneficiary thereunder, and the employee was a beneficiary under the plan at a time when the plan was an employees profit sharing plan, the amount determined for the year under this subsection in relation to the plan and in respect of the beneficiary is such portion of the total of the amounts so received in the year as does not exceed

(a) the total of

(i) each amount included in respect of the plan in computing the income of the employee for the year or for a previous taxation year by virtue of section 144,

(ii) each amount paid by the employee to a trustee under the plan at a time when it was an employees profit sharing plan, and

(iii) each amount that was allocated to the employee or other beneficiary by a trustee under the plan, at a time when it was an employees profit sharing plan, in respect of a capital gain made by the trust before 1972,

minus

(b) the total of

(i) each amount received by the employee or other beneficiary in a previous taxation year from a trustee under the plan at a time when it was an employees profit sharing plan,

(ii) each amount received by the employee or other beneficiary in a previous taxation year from a trustee under the plan at a time when it was a deferred profit sharing plan, and

(iii) each amount allocated to the employee or other beneficiary by a trustee under the plan, at a time when it was an employees profit sharing plan, in respect of a capital loss sustained by the trust before 1972.

Related Provisions: 147(10) — Amounts received taxable; 147(17) — Meaning of "other beneficiary".

Interpretation Bulletins: IT-281R2: Elections on single payments from a deferred profit-sharing plan (cancelled); IT-363R2: Deferred profit sharing plans — deductibility of employer contributions and taxation of amounts received by a beneficiary (cancelled).

(12) Idem — For the purposes of subsections (10) and (10.1), where an amount was received in a taxation year from a trustee under a deferred profit sharing plan by an employee or other beneficiary thereunder, and the employee has made a payment in the year or a previous year to a trustee under the plan at a time when the plan was a deferred profit sharing plan, the amount determined for the year under this subsection in relation to the plan and in respect of the beneficiary is such portion of the total of the amounts so received in the year (minus any amount determined for the year under subsection (11) in relation to the plan and in respect of the beneficiary) as does not exceed

(a) the total of all amounts each of which was so paid by the employee in the year or a previous year to the extent that the payment was not deductible in computing the employee's income,

minus

(b) the total of all amounts each of which was received by the employee or other beneficiary from a trustee under the plan, at a time when it was a deferred profit sharing plan, to the extent that it was included in the computation of an amount determined for a previous year under this subsection in relation to the plan and in respect of the employee or other beneficiary.

Related Provisions: 60(j) — Transfer of superannuation benefits; 147(10) — Amounts received taxable; 147(11) — Portion of receipts deductible; 147(17) — Meaning of "other beneficiary".

Interpretation Bulletins: IT-281R2: Elections on single payments from a deferred profit-sharing plan (cancelled); IT-363R2: Deferred profit sharing plans — deductibility of employer contributions and taxation of amounts received by a beneficiary (cancelled).

(13) Appropriation of trust property by employer — Where funds or property of a trust governed by a deferred profit sharing plan have been appropriated in any manner whatever to or for the benefit of a taxpayer who is

(a) an employer by whom payments are made in trust to a trustee under the plan, or

(b) a corporation with which that employer does not deal at arm's length,

otherwise than in payment of or on account of shares of the capital stock of the taxpayer purchased by the trust, the amount or value of the funds or property so appropriated shall be included in computing the income of the taxpayer for the taxation year of the taxpayer in which the funds or property were so appropriated, unless the funds or property or an amount in lieu thereof equal to the amount or value of the funds or property was repaid to the trust within one year from the end of the taxation year, and it is established by subsequent events or otherwise that the repayment was not made as part of a series of appropriations and repayments.

Related Provisions: 201 — Tax on forfeitures; 214(3)(d) — Non-resident withholding tax; 248(10) — Series of transactions; *Interpretation Act* 27(5) — Meaning of "within one year".

(14) Revocation of registration — Where, at any time after a profit sharing plan has been accepted by the Minister for registration for the purposes of this Act,

(a) the plan has been revised or amended or a new plan has been substituted therefor, and the plan as revised or amended or the new plan substituted therefor, as the case may be, ceased to comply with the requirements of this section for its acceptance by the Minister for registration for the purposes of this Act,

(b) any provision of the plan has not been complied with,

(c) the plan is a plan that did not, as of January 1, 1968,

(i) comply with the requirements of paragraphs (2)(a), (b) to (h), (j) and (k), and paragraph 147(2)(i) of the *Income Tax Act*, chapter 148 of the Revised Statutes of Canada, 1952, as it read on January 1, 1972, and

(ii) provide that the amounts held by the trust for the benefit of beneficiaries thereunder that remain unallocated on December 31, 1967 must be allocated or reallocated, as the case may be, before 1969,

(c.1) the plan becomes a revocable plan pursuant to subsection (21),

(c.2) the plan does not comply with the requirements of paragraphs (2)(a) to (k) and (l),

(c.3) in the case of a plan that became registered after March, 1983, the plan does not comply with the requirements of paragraphs (2)(k.1) and (k.2),

(c.4) the requirements of subsection (5.1) in respect of the plan are not satisfied for a calendar year, or

(c.5) an employer who participates in the plan fails to file an information return reporting a pension adjustment of a beneficiary under the plan as and when required by regulation,

the Minister may revoke the registration of the plan,

(d) where paragraph (a) applies, as of the date that the plan ceased so to comply, or any subsequent date,

(e) where paragraph (b) applies, as of the date that any provision of the plan was not so complied with, or any subsequent date,

(f) where paragraph (c) applies, as of any date following January 1, 1968,

(g) where paragraph (c.1) applies, as of the date on which the plan became a revocable plan, or any subsequent date,

(h) where paragraph (c.2) or (c.3) applies, as of the date on which the plan did not so comply, or any subsequent date, but not before January 1, 1991,

(i) where paragraph (c.4) applies, as of the end of the year for which the requirements of subsection (5.1) in respect of the plan are not satisfied, or any subsequent date, and

(j) where paragraph (c.5) applies, as of any date after the date by which the information return was required to be filed,

and the Minister shall thereafter give notice of the revocation by registered mail to a trustee under the plan and to an employer of employees who are beneficiaries under the plan.

Related Provisions: 147(2) — Requirements for registration; 147(10.3) — Amount contributed to or forfeited under a plan; 147(15) — Rules applicable to revoked plan; 172(3)(c) — Appeal from refusal to register, revocation of registration, etc.; 198 — Tax on non-qualified investments and use of assets as security; 204 — "Revoked plan"; 244(5) — Proof of service by mail; 248(7)(a) — Mail deemed received on day mailed.

Notes: 147(14) amended by 1990 pension bill, effective 1991 or earlier.

I.T. Application Rules: 69 (meaning of "chapter 148 of ...").

(14.1) Idem — Where on any day after June 30, 1982 a benefit or loan is extended or continues to be extended as a consequence of the existence of a deferred profit sharing plan and that benefit or loan would be prohibited if the plan met the requirement for registration contained in paragraph (2)(k.1), the Minister may revoke the registration of the plan as of that or any subsequent day that is specified by the Minister in a notice given by registered mail to a trustee under the plan and to an employer of employees who are beneficiaries under the plan.

Related Provisions: 147(15) — Rules applicable to revoked plan; 198 — Tax on non-qualified investments and use of assets as security; 204 — "Revoked plan"; 244(5) — Proof of service by mail; 248(7)(a) — Mail deemed received on day mailed.

(15) Rules applicable to revoked plan — Where the Minister revokes the registration of a deferred profit sharing plan, the plan (in this section referred to as the "revoked plan") shall be deemed, for the purposes of this Act, not to be a deferred profit sharing plan, and notwithstanding any other provision of this Act, the following rules shall apply:

(a) the revoked plan shall not be accepted for registration for the purposes of this Act or be deemed to have become registered as a deferred profit sharing plan at any time within a period of one year commencing on the date the plan became a revoked plan;

(b) subsection (7) does not apply to exempt the trust governed by the plan from tax under this Part on the taxable income of the trust for a taxation year in which, at any time therein, the trust was governed by the revoked plan;

(c) no deduction shall be made by an employer in computing the employer's income for a taxation year in respect of an amount paid by the employer to a trustee under the plan at a time when it was a revoked plan;

(d) there shall be included in computing the income of a taxpayer for a taxation year

(i) all amounts received by the taxpayer in the year from a trustee under the revoked plan that, by virtue of subsection

(10), would have been so included if the revoked plan had been a deferred profit sharing plan at the time the taxpayer received those amounts, and

(ii) the amount or value of any funds or property appropriated to or for the benefit of the taxpayer in the year that, by virtue of subsection (13), would have been so included if the revoked plan had been a deferred profit sharing plan at the time of the appropriation of the funds or property; and

(e) the revoked plan shall be deemed, for the purposes of this Act, not to be an employees profit sharing plan or a retirement compensation arrangement.

Related Provisions: 128.1(10)"excluded right or interest"(a)(iv) — Emigration — no deemed disposition of interest in revoked plan; 147(14), (14.1) — Revocation of DPSP; 147(18) — Inadequate consideration on purchase from or sale to trust; 214(3)(d) — Non-resident withholding tax.

Notes: 147(15)(e) amended by 1990 pension bill, effective Oct. 9, 1986.

(16) Payments out of profits — Where the terms of an arrangement under which an employer makes payments to a trustee specifically provide that the payments shall be made "out of profits", the arrangement shall be deemed, for the purpose of subsection (1), to be an arrangement for payments "computed by reference to an employer's profits from the employer's business".

Interpretation Bulletins: IT-280R: Employees profit sharing plans — payments computed by reference to profits.

(17) Interpretation of "other beneficiary" — Where the expression "employee or other beneficiary" under a profit sharing plan occurs in this section, the words "other beneficiary" shall be construed as meaning any person, other than the employee, to whom any amount is or may become payable by a trustee under the plan as a result of payments made to the trustee under the plan in trust for the benefit of employees, including the employee.

Related Provisions: 202(1) — Returns and payment of estimated tax.

(18) Inadequate consideration on purchase from or sale to trust — Where a trust governed by a deferred profit sharing plan or revoked plan

(a) disposes of property to a taxpayer for a consideration less than the fair market value of the property at the time of the transaction, or for no consideration, or

(b) acquires property from a taxpayer for a consideration greater than the fair market value of the property at the time of the transaction,

the difference between that fair market value and the consideration, if any

(c) shall, for the purposes of subsections (10) and (15), be deemed to be an amount received by the taxpayer at the time of the disposal or acquisition, as the case may be, from a trustee under the plan as if the taxpayer were a beneficiary under the plan, and

(d) is an amount taxable under section 201 for the calendar year in which the trust disposes of or acquires the property, as the case may be.

Related Provisions: 201 — 50% tax payable on amount taxable.

Notes: 147(18) amended by 1990 pension bill, effective 1991.

Information Circulars: 77-1R4 — Deferred profit sharing plans.

(19) Transfer to RPP, RRSP or DPSP — An amount is transferred from a deferred profit sharing plan in accordance with this subsection if the amount

(a) is not part of a series of periodic payments;

(b) is transferred on behalf of an individual

(i) who is an employee or former employee of an employer who participated in the plan on the employee's behalf, or

(ii) who is a spouse or common-law partner, or former spouse or common-law partner, of an employee or former

employee referred to in subparagraph (i) and who is entitled to the amount

(A) as a consequence of the death of the employee or former employee, or

(B) under a decree, an order or a judgment of a competent tribunal, or under a written agreement, that relates to a division of property between the employee or former employee and the individual in settlement of rights that arise out of, or on a breakdown of, their marriage or common-law partnership;

in full or partial satisfaction of the individual's entitlement to benefits under the plan;

(c) would, if it were paid directly to the individual, be included under subsection (10) in computing the individual's income for a taxation year; and

(d) is transferred for the benefit of the individual directly to

(i) a registered pension plan,

(ii) a registered retirement savings plan under which the individual is the annuitant (within the meaning assigned by subsection 146(1)),

(iii) a deferred profit sharing plan that can reasonably be expected to have at least 5 beneficiaries at all times throughout the calendar year in which the transfer is made,

(iv) a registered retirement income fund under which the individual is the annuitant (within the meaning assigned by subsection 146.3(1)), or

(v) a licensed annuities provider to acquire an advanced life deferred annuity, if the individual is an employee or former employee of an employer who participated in the plan on the employee's behalf.

Related Provisions: 60(j) — Transfer of superannuation benefits; 104(27.1) — DPSP benefits; 146(8.2) — Amount deductible where withdrawn after mistaken contribution; 146(21.2) — Sask. Pension Plan account deemed to be RRSP for purposes of 147(19); 146.3(2)(f)(iv.1) — Conditions for RRIF; 147(2)(a.1) — Acceptance of plan for registration; 147(2)(e)(i) — Transfer of DPSP rights to spouse or partner permitted; 147(10.2) — Single payment on retirement etc.; 147(20) — Taxation of amount transferred; 147(22) — Excess transfer; 147.5(12) — Pooled registered pension plan deemed to be RRSP for purposes of 147(19); 204.2(1.2)I(a)(iii) — Transfer under 147(19) excluded from cumulative excess RRSP amount; 204.2(1.2)I(a)(iii) — Transfer under 147(19) excluded from cumulative excess RRSP amount; 205(1)"excess ALDA transfer" — Excessive transfer to advanced life deferred annuity; 248(8) — Meaning of "consequence" of death; 248(10) — Series of transactions; 252(3) — Extended meaning of "spouse" and "former spouse"; Reg. 8300(1)"excluded contribution" — Amount transferred is excluded contribution; Reg. 8502(b)(iv) — RPP may accept transfer under 147(19).

Notes: 147(19)(d)(v) added by 2021 budget bill #1, effective 2020, to accommodate ALDAs (see 146.5).

147(19) earlier amended by 2002-2013 technical bill (for transfers after March 20, 2003), 2000 same-sex partners bill, 1995-97 technical bill, 1990 pension bill.

Regulations: 216(2) (information return on transfer to ALDA).

Interpretation Bulletins: IT-528: Transfers of funds between registered plans.

Information Circulars: See list at end of s. 147.

Registered Plans Directorate Newsletters: 91-4R (registration rules for money purchase provisions); 16-1 (qualifying transfers to IPPs).

Forms: T2151: Direct transfer of a single amount under subsec. 147(19) or s. 147.3.

(20) Taxation of amount transferred — Where an amount is transferred on behalf of an individual in accordance with subsection (19),

(a) the amount shall not, by reason only of that transfer, be included by virtue of this section in computing the income of any taxpayer; and

(b) no deduction may be made under any provision of this Act in respect of the amount in computing the income of any taxpayer.

Related Provisions: 56(1)(i) — Amount received taxable; 147.5(12) — Pooled registered pension plan deemed to be RRSP for purposes of 147(20); 212(1)(m)(i) — Transferred amount not subject to non-resident withholding tax.

Notes: 147(20) added by 1990 pension bill, for amounts transferred in 1989 or later.

Interpretation Bulletins: IT-528: Transfers of funds between registered plans.

(21) Restriction re transfers — A deferred profit sharing plan becomes a revocable plan at any time that an amount is transferred from the plan to a registered pension plan, a registered retirement savings plan or another deferred profit sharing plan unless

(a) the transfer is in accordance with subsection (19); or

(b) the amount is deductible under paragraph 60(j) or (j.2) of this Act or paragraph 60(k) of the *Income Tax Act*, chapter 148 of the Revised Statutes of Canada, 1952, by the individual on whose behalf the transfer is made.

Related Provisions: 147(14)(c.1) — Revocation of registration; 147.5(12) — Pooled registered pension plan deemed to be RRSP for purposes of 147(21).

Notes: 147(21) added by 1990 pension bill, for amounts transferred in 1989 or later.

I.T. Application Rules: 69 (meaning of "chapter 148 of ...").

Interpretation Bulletins: IT-528: Transfers of funds between registered plans.

(22) Excess transfer — Where

(a) the transfer of an amount from a deferred profit sharing plan in a calendar year on behalf of a beneficiary under the plan would, but for this subsection, be in accordance with subsection (19), and

(b) the requirements of subsection (5.1) in respect of the plan are not satisfied for the year by reason that the beneficiary's pension credits or pension adjustments do not comply with any of paragraphs (5.1)(a) to (c),

such portion of the amount transferred as may reasonably be considered to derive from amounts allocated or reallocated to the beneficiary in the year or from earnings reasonably attributable to those amounts shall, except to the extent otherwise expressly provided in writing by the Minister, be deemed to be an amount that was not transferred in accordance with subsection (19).

Notes: 147(22) added by 1990 pension bill, for amounts transferred in 1989 or later.

Interpretation Bulletins: IT-528: Transfers of funds between registered plans.

Definitions [s. 147]: "advanced life deferred annuity" — 146.5(1), 248(1); "amount" — 248(1); "annuitant" — 146.3(1); "annuity", "business" — 248(1); "calendar year" — *Interpretation Act* 37(1)(a); "Canada" — 255; "capital gain", "capital loss" — 39(1), 248(1); "common-law partner", "common-law partnership" — 248(1); "compensation" — 147.1(1); "consequence of the death" — 248(8); "corporation" — 248(1), *Interpretation Act* 35(1); "deferred profit sharing plan" — 147(1), 248(1); "employed", "employee" — 248(1); "employees profit sharing plan" — 144(1), 248(1); "employer", "employment" — 248(1); "estate" — 104(1), 248(1); "fair market value" — see 69(1) Notes; "forfeited amount" — 147(1); "identical" — 248(12); "individual", "legal representative" — 248(1); "licensed annuities provider" — 147(1); "Minister" — 248(1); "Minister of Finance" — *Financial Administration Act* 14; "money purchase limit" — 147.1(1), 248(1); "other beneficiary" — 147(17); "participate" — 147(1.1); "pension adjustment" — 248(1), Reg. 8301(1); "person", "prescribed" — 248(1); "profit sharing plan" — 147(1), 248(1); "property" — 248(1); "province" — *Interpretation Act* 35(1); "registered pension plan" — 248(1); "registered retirement income fund" — 146.3(1), 248(1); "registered retirement savings plan" — 146(1), 248(1); "regulation" — 248(1); "related" — 251(2); "resident in Canada", "resident of Canada" — 250; "retirement compensation arrangement" — 248(1); "revocable plan" — 147(21), Reg. 8408(2); "revoked plan" — 147(15); "series of appropriations", "series of transactions" — 248(10); "share", "specified shareholder" — 248(1); "spouse" — 252(3); "taxable income" — 2(2), 248(1); "taxation year" — 249; "taxpayer" — 248(1); "trust" — 104(1), 248(1), (3); "writing" — *Interpretation Act* 35(1); "written" — *Interpretation Act* 35(1)"writing".

Information Circulars [s. 147]: 74-1R5: Form T2037 — Notice of purchase of annuity with "plan" funds; 77-1R4: Deferred profit sharing plans.

Registered Pension Plans

Notes: See generally tinyurl.com/rpd-cra (Registered Plans Division).

147.1 (1) Definitions — In this section and sections 147.2 and 147.3,

"actuary" means a Fellow of the Canadian Institute of Actuaries;

Related Provisions: 144.1(1)"actuary" — Same definition for ELHT rules.

"administrator" of a pension plan means the person or body of persons that has ultimate responsibility for the administration of the plan;

Related Provisions: 147.1(6) — Administrator; 147.1(7) — Obligations of administrator; Reg. 213 — Administrator must file information return.

Registered Pension Plans Technical Manual: §1.4 (administrator).

"average wage" for a calendar year means the amount that is obtained by dividing by 12 the total of all amounts each of which is the wage measure for a month in the 12 month period ending on June 30 of the immediately preceding calendar year;

Notes: See Notes to 147.1(1)"wage measure".

Registered Pension Plans Technical Manual: §1.6 (average wage).

"compensation" of an individual from an employer for a calendar year means the total of all amounts each of which is

(a) an amount in respect of

(i) the individual's employment with the employer, or

(ii) an office in respect of which the individual is remunerated by the employer

that is required (or that would be required but for paragraph 81(1)(a) as it applies with respect to the *Indian Act* or the *Foreign Missions and International Organizations Act*) by section 5 or 6 to be included in computing the individual's income for the year, except such portion of the amount as

(iii) may reasonably be considered to relate to a period throughout which the individual was not resident in Canada, and

(iv) is not attributable to the performance of the duties of the office or employment in Canada or is exempt from income tax in Canada by reason of a provision contained in a tax convention or agreement with another country that has the force of law in Canada,

(b) a prescribed amount, or

(c) an amount acceptable to the Minister in respect of remuneration received by the individual from any employer for a period in the year throughout which the individual was not resident in Canada, to the extent that the amount is not otherwise included in the total;

Related Provisions: 87(2)(q) — Amalgamation — continuing corporation; 147(5.1) — DPSP contribution limits; 147.1(8), (9) — Pension adjustment limits.

Notes: "Compensation" includes any amount taxable under ss. 5 or 6, including amounts allocated under an EPSP: VIEWS doc 2004-0093431I7; but not a severance payment, which is taxed under s. 56 as a "retiring allowance": 2004-0097241I7. It includes a stock option benefit: CCRA RPP 2002 Consultation Session, q. 2. It can include an "excess EPSP amount" under 207.8(1): 2013-0480911E5.

Para. (a) amended to add "or the *Foreign Missions and International Organizations Act*" by 2002-2013 technical bill (Part 5 — technical), effective 1991.

Regulations: 8507 (prescribed amount).

Information Circulars: 98-2: Prescribed compensation for registered pension plans.

Registered Plans Compliance Bulletins: 2 (compensation for RPP purposes).

Registered Pension Plans Technical Manual: §1.12 (compensation).

"defined benefit provision" of a pension plan means terms of the plan under which benefits in respect of each member are determined in any way other than that described in the definition "money purchase provision" in this subsection;

Interpretation Bulletins: IT-167R6: Registered pension plans — employee's contributions; IT-528: Transfers of funds between registered plans.

Registered Pension Plans Technical Manual: §1.18 (defined benefit provision).

"former limit" for each calendar year after 2005 and before 2010 means the greater of

(a) the product (rounded to the nearest multiple of $10, or, if that product is equidistant from two such consecutive multiples, to the higher multiple) of

(i) $18,000, and

(ii) the quotient obtained when the average wage for the year is divided by the average wage for 2005, and

(b) for 2006, $18,000, and for any other of those calendar years, the former limit for the preceding calendar year;

Notes: "Former limit" added by 2005 budget bill #1, effective 2005. It is used in 147.1(1)"money purchase limit"(k)-(n).

"member" of a pension plan means an individual who has a right, either immediate or in the future and either absolute or contingent, to receive benefits under the plan, other than an individual who has such a right only by reason of the participation of another individual in the plan;

Related Provisions: 128.1(10)"excluded right or interest"(a)(viii) — No deemed disposition on emigration of member; Reg. 8300(1)"member" — Similar definition for the Regulations.

Notes: A person can be a member of two RPPs at once, but 147.1(8) will limit total contributions or benefits: VIEWS doc 2007-0225551E5.

Registered Pension Plans Technical Manual: §1.29 (member).

"money purchase limit" for a calendar year means

(a) for years before 1990, nil,

(b) for 1990, $11,500,

(c) for 1991 and 1992, $12,500,

(d) for 1993, $13,500,

(e) for 1994, $14,500,

(f) for 1995, $15,500, and

(g) for years after 1995 and before 2003, $13,500,

(h) for 2003, $15,500,

(i) for 2004, $16,500,

(j) for 2005, $18,000,

(k) for 2006, the greater of $19,000 and the former limit for the year,

(l) for 2007, the greater of $20,000 and the former limit for the year,

(m) for 2008, the greater of $21,000 and the former limit for the year,

(n) for 2009, the greater of $22,000 and the former limit for the year, and

(o) for each year after 2009, the greater of

    (i) the product (rounded to the nearest multiple of $10, or, if that product is equidistant from two such consecutive multiples, to the higher multiple) of

        (A) the money purchase limit for 2009, and

        (B) the quotient obtained when the average wage for the year is divided by the average wage for 2009, and

    (ii) the money purchase limit for the preceding year;

Related Provisions: 146(1) — RRSP dollar limit; 147.1(8) — Pension adjustment limits; 147.1(9) — Pension adjustment limits — multi-employer plans; 248(1)"money purchase limit" — Definition applies to entire Act.

Notes: The dollar amounts shown limit RRSP contributions for the next taxation year (except for 1996 and 2003). The indexed figures after 2009 are: 2010: $22,450; 2011: $22,970; 2012: $23,820; 2013: $24,270; 2014: $24,930; 2015: $25,370; 2016: $26,010; 2017: $26,230; 2018: $26,500; 2019: $27,230; 2020: $27,830; 2021: $29,210.

See Notes to 146(1)"RRSP deduction limit". For the effect on DPSP limits, see Notes to 147(5.1).

For the purpose of determining a pension credit of an individual for the 2002 calendar year under Reg. 8308.1 or 8308.3 or an amount prescribed in respect of an individual under Reg. 8308.2 or 8309 for the 2003 calendar year, the money purchase limit for 2002 is deemed to be $14,500 (2003 Budget bill, subsec. 84(2)).

Definition amended (to delay scheduled increases) by 2005 budget bill #1, 2003, 1996, 1995 and 1992 Budgets.

Registered Plans Directorate Newsletters: 96-1 (changes to retirement savings limits).

Registered Pension Plans Technical Manual: §1.30 (money purchase limit).

"money purchase provision" of a pension plan means terms of the plan

(a) which provide for a separate account to be maintained in respect of each member, to which are credited contributions made to the plan by, or in respect of, the member and any other amounts allocated to the member, and to which are charged payments made in respect of the member, and

(b) under which the only benefits in respect of a member are benefits determined solely with reference to, and provided by, the amount in the member's account;

Related Provisions: 60.021(4)(a) — Definition applies to 2008 RRIF minimum amount reduction; 60.022(5)(a) — Definition applies to 60.022.

Notes: A "money purchase" RPP, also known as a "defined contribution" RPP, is one where an amount is invested on behalf of an individual member, and the benefits will be based on whatever those funds have earned over time (like an RRSP/RRIF). The more traditional pension is a "defined benefit" RPP, where the benefits on retirement are predetermined.

Regulations: 8506 (rules for money purchase provisions).

Interpretation Bulletins: IT-167R6: Registered pension plans — employee's contributions; IT-528: Transfers of funds between registered plans.

Registered Plans Directorate Newsletters: 91-4R (registration rules for money purchase provisions).

Registered Pension Plans Technical Manual: §1.31 (money purchase provision).

"multi-employer plan" in a calendar year has the meaning assigned by regulation;

Related Provisions: 147.1(9) — Pension adjustment limits — multi-employer plans; 252.1 — All union locals deemed to be one employer.

Regulations: 8500(1), 8510(1) (meaning of "multi-employer plan").

Registered Pension Plans Technical Manual: §1.32 (multi-employer plan).

Registered Plans Frequently Asked Questions: RPFAQ-2 (RPPs), q. 13 (what is a MEP?).

"participating employer", in relation to a pension plan, means an employer who has made, or is required to make, contributions to the plan in respect of the employer's employees or former employees, or payments under the plan to the employer's employees or former employees, and includes a prescribed employer;

Related Provisions: 87(2)(q) — Amalgamation — continuing corporation.

Notes: An employer does not stop being a participating employer (PE) by ceasing involvement with the plan (even by ceasing to exist): VIEWS doc 2019-0791761I7. A PSB (see 125(7)"personal services business") can be a PE: 2005-0122731I7.

Regulations: 8308(7)(c) (prescribed employer).

Interpretation Bulletins: IT-363R2: Deferred profit sharing plans — deductibility of employer contributions and taxation of amounts received by a beneficiary (cancelled).

Registered Pension Plans Technical Manual: §1.33 (participating employer).

"past service event" has the meaning assigned by regulation;

Related Provisions: 147.1(10) — Past service benefits.

Regulations: 8300(1), (2) (past service event).

Registered Pension Plans Technical Manual: §1.34 (past service event).

"single amount" means an amount that is not part of a series of periodic payments;

Interpretation Bulletins: IT-528: Transfers of funds between registered plans.

Registered Pension Plans Technical Manual: §1.41 (single amount).

"specified multi-employer plan" in a calendar year has the meaning assigned by regulation;

Related Provisions: 252.1 — All union locals deemed to be one employer.

Regulations: 8510(2), (3) (meaning of "specified multi-employer plan").

Registered Pension Plans Technical Manual: §1.42 (specified multi-employer plan).

Registered Plans Frequently Asked Questions: RPFAQ-2 (RPPs), q. 13 (what is a SMEP?).

"spouse" — [Repealed]

Notes: Definition "spouse" repealed by 1992 technical bill, effective 1993. A similar rule, extending the meaning of "spouse" to include common-law spouses, applied from 1993 to 2000 for all purposes of the Act, in 252(4). For periods before 1993, "spouse" was defined here to have the meaning it had under 146(1.1). See now Reg. 8500(5).

"wage measure" for a month means the average weekly wages and salaries of

(a) the Industrial Aggregate in Canada for the month as published by Statistics Canada under the *Statistics Act*, or

(b) in the event that the Industrial Aggregate ceases to be published, such other measure for the month as is prescribed by regulation under the *Canada Pension Plan* for the purposes of paragraph 18(5)(b) of that Act.

Notes: For the StatsCan Industrial Aggregate average weekly earnings, see tinyurl.com/ind-aggr.

Interpretation Bulletins: IT-124R6: Contributions to registered retirement savings plans.

Registered Pension Plans Technical Manual: §1.46 (wage measure).

(2) Registration of plan — The following rules apply with respect to the registration of pension plans:

(a) the Minister shall not register a pension plan unless

(i) application for registration is made in prescribed manner by the plan administrator,

(ii) the plan complies with prescribed conditions for registration, and

(iii) where the plan is required to be registered under the *Pension Benefits Standards Act, 1985* or a similar law of a province, application for such registration has been made;

(b) where a pension plan that was submitted for registration before 1992 is registered by the Minister, the registration is effective from the day specified in writing by the Minister; and

(c) where a pension plan that is submitted for registration after 1991 is registered by the Minister, the registration is effective from the later of

(i) January 1 of the calendar year in which application for registration is made in prescribed manner by the plan administrator, and

(ii) the day the plan began.

Related Provisions: 147.5 — Pooled registered pension plans; 149(1)(o) — Exemption — pension trust; 172(5) — Deemed refusal to register; 241(4)(j) — Communication of information — exception; Reg. 9006(d) — RPP not reported to CRA for disclosure to foreign tax authorities.

Notes: For pension plan registration and administration see tinyurl.com/rpd-cra; Willis Towers Watson, *Canadian Pensions and Retirement Income Planning*, 6th ed. (LexisNexis, 2017), chaps. 16-18, 20-22; *Morneau Shepell Handbook of Canadian Pension and Benefit Plans* (LexisNexis, 17th ed., 2020, 742pp).

In addition to registration under the ITA, an RPP must be registered under the provincial *Pension Benefits Act* or similar legislation, or, for industries under federal jurisdiction (FJ), the *Pension Benefits Standards Act* (see 147.1(2)(a)(iii)). The investments a FJ pension plan may make are specified in the *Pension Benefits Standards Regulations* (see canLii.org). Most provinces have adopted these rules for investments by plans under their jurisdiction: Stephen Heller & Andrew Harrison, "Pension Fund Investment in Real Estate", 2002 Cdn Tax Foundation conference report, 31:1-40.

RPP issuers and advisors: see tinyurl.com/rpp-cra, including "Frequently Asked Questions" and "Consultations Sessions", with answers to questions posed by the industry.

CRA's target (tinyurl.com/cra-standards) for processing RPP applications is 85% within 180 days; in 2019-20, it did 94%.

CRA announced on July 4, 2005 that it now accepts photocopies (rather than only originals) of signed documents submitted at the registration or amendment stage, including actuarial valuation reports.

CRA allows retroactive registration only in limited circumstances where there is no break in pension coverage from an existing plan: RPP 2002 Consultation Session, q. 7.

See also Théroux, "Registered Pension Plans: What a Tax Planner Needs to Know", Tax Planner Guide 5 (*Taxnet Pro*, Sept. 2016, 11pp.); Kutsenko, "Pension Plan Taxation in Canada", 38(4) *Estates, Trusts and Pensions Journal* 349-415 (2019).

Alternatives to traditional RPPs are being developed. For pooled registered pension plans, see 147.5. For discussion of target benefit plans see Terra Klinck & Susie Taing, "How Target Benefit Plans Fit Info the Current *Income Tax Act* RPP Regime", 24(3) *Taxation of Executive Compensation & Retirement* (Federated Press) 1594-96 (Oct. 2012); and Finance news release, "Harper Government Completes Public Target Benefit Plan Consultations" (June 25, 2014).

147.1(2)(b) and (c) amended by 1992 technical bill to provide a one-year delay.

Regulations: 8500-8520; 8501(1) (prescribed conditions); 8512(1), (2) (prescribed conditions, prescribed manner).

Information Circulars: 72-13R8: Employees' pension plans [partly superseded by new Regulations].

Registered Plans Directorate Newsletters: 91-4R (registration rules for money purchase provisions); 95-1 (new approach to plan registration); 95-2R1 (registered plan division services); 95-6R1 (specimen pension plans — speeding up the process); 95-7 (Quebec simplified pension plans); 98-1 (simplified pension plans); 04-2R (RPP applications — processing an incomplete application); 15-1 (comprehensive risk-based cyclical review of registered pension plans).

Registered Pension Plans Technical Manual: §2.1 (registration of the plan).

Registered Plans Compliance Bulletins: 2 (general warning: establishing RPPs when there exists no valid employee-employer relationship); 1, 2, 3 (how to contact

us); 5 (reminder of primary purpose requirement for RPPs); 9 (what to expect during an RPP audit).

Registered Plans Frequently Asked Questions: RPFAQ-2 (RPPs), q. 22 (what is a complete application for registering a pension plan?).

Forms: T3P: Employees' pension plan income tax return; T10: Pension adjustment reversal; T10 Summ: Summary of PARs; T10 Segment; T510: Application to register a pension plan; T2014: Request for a priority review of a RPP; T4099: Registered pension plans.

(3) Deemed registration — Where application is made to the Minister for registration of a pension plan for the purposes of this Act and, where the manner for making the application has been prescribed, the application is made in that manner by the administrator,

(a) subject to paragraph (b), the plan is, for the purposes of this Act other than paragraphs 60(j) and (j.2) and sections 147.3 and 147.4, deemed to be a registered pension plan throughout the period that begins on the latest of

(i) January 1 of the calendar year in which the application is made,

(ii) the day of commencement of the plan, and

(iii) January 1, 1989

and ending on the day on which a final determination is made with respect to the application; and

(b) where the final determination made with respect to the application is a refusal to register the plan, this Act shall, after the day of the final determination, apply as if the plan had never been deemed, under paragraph (a), to be a registered pension plan, except that

(i) any information return otherwise required to be filed under subsection 207.7(3) before the particular day that is 90 days after the day of the final determination is not required to be filed until the particular day, and

(ii) subsections 227(8) and (8.2) are not applicable with respect to contributions made to the plan on or before the day of the final determination.

Related Provisions: 87(2)(q) — Amalgamation — continuing corporation; 172(3) — Appeal from refusal to register, revocation of registration, etc.; 172(5) — Deemed refusal to register.

Notes: See Notes to 147.1(2). Reference to 147.4 added to opening words of 147.1(3)(a) by 1995-97 technical bill, effective 1997.

Registered Plans Directorate Newsletters: 95-1 (new approach to plan registration); 95-2R1 (registered plan division services); 95-6R1 (specimen pension plans — speeding up the process); 95-7 (Quebec simplified pension plans); 98-1 (simplified pension plans).

Registered Pension Plans Technical Manual: §2.2 (deemed registration).

Registered Plans Frequently Asked Questions: RPFAQ-2 (RPPs), q. 22 (what is a complete application for registering a pension plan?).

Forms: T510: Application to register a pension plan.

(4) Acceptance of amendments — The Minister shall not accept an amendment to a registered pension plan unless

(a) application for the acceptance is made in prescribed manner by the plan administrator;

(b) the plan as amended complies with prescribed conditions for registration; and

(c) the amendment complies with prescribed conditions.

Related Provisions: 147.1(15) — Plan as registered.

Notes: See Notes to 147.1(2).

Regulations: 8501(1), 8511 (prescribed conditions); 8512 (prescribed manner).

Registered Plans Directorate Newsletters: 95-6R1 (specimen pension plans — speeding up the process); 95-7 (Quebec simplified pension plans); 98-1 (simplified pension plans); 16-3 (transfers from underfunded IPPs).

Registered Pension Plans Technical Manual: §2.3 (acceptance of amendments).

Registered Plans Frequently Asked Questions: RPFAQ-2 (RPPs), q. 23 (what is a complete application for amending an RPP?).

Forms: T920: Application to amend to an RPP; T2011: RPP change of information form; T2014: Request for a priority review of a RPP.

(5) Additional conditions — The Minister may, at any time, impose reasonable conditions applicable with respect to registered pension plans, a class of such plans or a particular registered pension plan.

Notes: See Notes to Reg. 8515(1) re individual pension plans.

Registered Plans Directorate Newsletters: 96-3 (flexible pension plans); 98-1 (simplified pension plans); 04-1 (transfer from a defined benefit provision).

Registered Pension Plans Technical Manual: §2.4 (additional conditions).

(6) Administrator — There shall, for each registered pension plan, be a person or a body of persons that has ultimate responsibility for the administration of the plan and, except as otherwise permitted in writing by the Minister, the person or a majority of the persons who constitute the body shall be a person or persons resident in Canada.

Related Provisions: 87(2)(q) — Amalgamation — continuing corporation; 147.1(7) — Obligations of administrator; 147.1(11) — Revocation of registration — notice of intention; 250 — Residents.

Notes: CRA interpretation of 147.1(6) was in RPP Consultation Sessions, tinyurl.com/rpd-consults, "Questions from the Industry" 2002 q.1 and 2003 q.1, but both have been removed.

Registered Pension Plans Technical Manual: §2.5 (administrator); §2.5.1 (nonresident administrator).

(7) Obligations of administrator — The administrator of a registered pension plan shall

(a) administer the plan in accordance with the terms of the plan as registered except that, where the plan fails to comply with the prescribed conditions for registration or any other requirement of this Act or the regulations, the administrator may administer the plan as if it were amended to so comply;

(b) before July, 1990, in the case of a person or body that is the administrator on January 1, 1989 or becomes the administrator before June, 1990, and, in any other case, within 30 days after becoming the administrator, inform the Minister in writing

(i) of the name and address of the person who is the administrator, or

(ii) of the names and addresses of the persons who constitute the body that is the administrator; and

(c) where there is any change in the information provided to the Minister in accordance with this paragraph or paragraph (b), inform the Minister in writing, within 60 days after the change, of the new information.

Related Provisions: 87(2)(q) — Amalgamation — continuing corporation; 147.1(11) — Revocation of registration; 147.1(15) — Reference to "plan as registered"; 147.1(18) — Regulations; 147.1(19) — Pension plan refund due to contribution made in error; 238(1) — Offences; 248(7)(a) — Mail deemed received on day mailed; *Interpretation Act* 27(5) — Meaning of "within 30 days" and "within 60 days".

Notes: If the administrator cannot locate a member even through the National Search Unit of Social Development Canada, the member's entitlement can be placed in an account in trust for the member, or paid into provincial court: RPP Consultation Sessions, tinyurl.com/rpd-consults, "Questions from the Industry" 2004 q.1.

Regulations: Part LXXXV (prescribed conditions).

Registered Pension Plans Technical Manual: §2.6 (obligations of the administrator).

Forms: T3P: Employees' pension plan income tax return.

(8) Pension adjustment limits — Except as otherwise provided by regulation, a registered pension plan (other than a multi-employer plan) becomes, at the end of a calendar year after 1990, a revocable plan where

(a) the pension adjustment for the year of a member of the plan in respect of a participating employer exceeds the lesser of

(i) the money purchase limit for the year, and

(ii) 18% of the member's compensation from the employer for the year; or

(b) the total of

(i) the pension adjustment for the year of a member of the plan in respect of a participating employer, and

(ii) the total of all amounts each of which is the member's pension adjustment for the year in respect of an employer

who, at any time in the year, does not deal at arm's length with the employer referred to in subparagraph (i)

exceeds the money purchase limit for the year.

Related Provisions: 87(2)(q) — Amalgamation — continuing corporation; 147(5.1)(c) — Contribution limits; 147.1(11) — Revocation of registration — notice of intention; 147.1(9), 147.3(12), Reg. 8301(14)(a), 8305(2)(a), 8408(2), 8501(2), 8503(11), (15), 8506(4), 8511(2), 8515(9) — Other ways plan becomes revocable plan; 147.3(13) — Excess transfer; 252.1 — All union locals deemed to be one employer.

Regulations: 8509(12) (limitation on application of 147.1(8)).

Interpretation Bulletins: IT-528: Transfers of funds between registered plans.

Information Circulars: 98-2: Prescribed compensation for registered pension plans.

Registered Plans Directorate Newsletters: 91-4R (registration rules for money purchase provisions); 96-1 (changes to retirement savings limits).

Registered Pension Plans Technical Manual: §2.7 (PA limits).

Forms: T10: Pension adjustment reversal.

(9) Idem — multi-employer plans — Except as otherwise provided by regulation, a registered pension plan that is a multi-employer plan (other than a specified multi-employer plan) in a calendar year after 1990 becomes, at the end of the year, a revocable plan where

(a) for a member and an employer, the total of all amounts each of which is the member's pension credit (as prescribed by regulation) for the year in respect of the employer under a defined benefit or money purchase provision of the plan exceeds the lesser of

(i) the money purchase limit for the year, and

(ii) 18% of the member's compensation from the employer for the year; or

(b) for a member, the total of all amounts each of which is the member's pension credit (as prescribed by regulation) for the year in respect of an employer under a defined benefit or money purchase provision of the plan exceeds the money purchase limit for the year.

Related Provisions: 87(2)(q) — Amalgamation — continuing corporation; 147.1(8), 147.3(12), Reg. 8301(14)(a), 8305(2)(a), 8408(2), 8501(2), 8503(11), (15), 8506(4), 8511(2), 8515(9) — Other ways plan becomes revocable plan; 147.1(11) — Revocation of registration — notice of intention; 147.1(14) — Anti-avoidance — multi-employer plans; 147.3(13) — Excess transfer; Reg. 8301 — Pension adjustment.

Regulations: 8301(4)–(6), (8) (pension credit); 8509(12) (limitation on application of 147.1(9)).

Interpretation Bulletins: IT-528: Transfers of funds between registered plans.

Information Circulars: 98-2: Prescribed compensation for registered pension plans.

Registered Plans Directorate Newsletters: 91-4R (registration rules for money purchase provisions); 95-7 (Quebec simplified pension plans); 96-1 (changes to retirement savings limits); 98-1 (simplified pension plans).

Registered Plans Compliance Bulletins: 7 (making contributions and calculating and reporting pension adjustment for SMEPs).

Registered Pension Plans Technical Manual: §2.8 (PA limits — multi-employer plans).

(10) Past service benefits — With respect to each past service event that is relevant to the determination of benefits in respect of a member under a defined benefit provision of a registered pension plan, such benefits as are in respect of periods after 1989 and before the calendar year in which the event occurred shall be determined, for the purpose of a payment to be made from the plan or a contribution to be made to the plan at a particular time, with regard to the event only if

(a) where the member is alive at the particular time and except as otherwise provided by regulation, the Minister has certified in writing, before the particular time, that prescribed conditions are satisfied,

(b) where the member died before the particular time and the event occurred before the death of the member,

(i) this subsection did not require that the event be disregarded in determining benefits that were payable to the member immediately before the member's death (or that would have been so payable had the member been entitled to receive benefits under the provision immediately before the member's death), or

(ii) the event, as it affects the benefits provided to each individual who is entitled to benefits as a consequence of the death of the member, is acceptable to the Minister,

(c) where the member died before the particular time and the event occurred after the death of the member, the event, as it affects the benefits provided to each individual who is entitled to benefits as a consequence of the death of the member, is acceptable to the Minister, and

(d) no past service event that occurred before the event is required by reason of the application of this subsection to be disregarded at the particular time in determining benefits in respect of the member,

and, for the purposes of this subsection as it applies with respect to contributions that may be made to a registered pension plan, where application has been made for a certification referred to in paragraph (a) and the Minister has not refused to issue the certification, the Minister shall be deemed to have issued the certification.

Related Provisions: 87(2)(q) — Amalgamation — continuing corporation; 147.1(11) — Revocation of registration — notice of intention; 147.1(18) — Regulations; 147.2(1) — Pension contributions deductible — employer contributions; 241(4)(c) — Communication of information — exception; 248(8) — Meaning of "consequence" of death.

Regulations: 8300(6) (prescribed rules); 8306 (certification not required); 8307(2) (prescribed conditions); 8308(1) (benefits provided before registration); 8519 (prescribed manner).

Interpretation Bulletins: IT-167R6: Registered pension plans — employee's contributions.

Registered Pension Plans Technical Manual: §2.9 (past service benefits).

Forms: T1004: Applying for the certification of a provisional PSPA.

(11) Revocation of registration — notice of intention —

Where, at any time after a pension plan has been registered by the Minister,

(a) the plan does not comply with the prescribed conditions for registration,

(b) the plan is not administered in accordance with the terms of the plan as registered,

(c) the plan becomes a revocable plan,

(d) a condition imposed by the Minister in writing and applicable with respect to the plan (including a condition applicable generally to registered pension plans or a class of such plans and a condition first imposed before 1989) is not complied with,

(e) a requirement under subsection (6) or (7) is not complied with,

(f) a benefit is paid by the plan, or a contribution is made to the plan, contrary to subsection (10),

(g) the administrator of the plan fails to file an information return or actuarial report relating to the plan or to a member of the plan as and when required by regulation,

(h) a participating employer fails to file an information return relating to the plan or to a member of the plan as and when required by regulation, or

(i) registration of the plan under the *Pension Benefits Standards Act, 1985* or a similar law of a province is refused or revoked,

the Minister may give notice (in this subsection and subsection (12) referred to as a "notice of intent") by registered mail to the plan administrator that the Minister proposes to revoke the registration of the plan as of a date specified in the notice of intent, which date shall not be earlier than the date as of which,

(j) where paragraph (a) applies, the plan failed to so comply,

(k) where paragraph (b) applies, the plan was not administered in accordance with its terms as registered,

(l) where paragraph (c) applies, the plan became a revocable plan,

(m) where paragraph (d) or (e) applies, the condition or requirement was not complied with,

(n) where paragraph (f) applies, the benefit was paid or the contribution was made,

(o) where paragraph (g) or (h) applies, the information return or actuarial report was required to be filed, and

(p) where paragraph (i) applies, the registration referred to in that paragraph was refused or revoked.

Related Provisions: 87(2)(q) — Amalgamation — continuing corporation; 147.1(8) — Pension adjustment limits; 147.1(9) — Pension adjustment limits — multi-employer plans; 147.1(12) — Notice of revocation; 147.1(13) — Revocation of registration; 147.1(15) — Meaning of "plan" as registered; 147.1(18)(b) — Regulations; 147.3(12) — Restriction re transfers; 147.4(1)(d) — RPP annuity contract; 172(3) — Appeal from refusal to register, revocation of registration, etc.; 244(5) — Proof of service by mail; 248(7)(a) — Mail deemed received on day mailed.

Notes: CRA will reject (or revoke) plans aimed at stripping funds out of an existing RPP rather than providing retirement benefits (see Registered Plans Frequently Asked Questions annotation below).

In *Boudreau*, 2005 FCA 304, a past member of an RPP applied for judicial review of CRA's Notice of Intention to revoke the plan (she did not have standing to appeal under 172(3)). The Court ruled that she had no remedy until 147.1(13) was triggered, but could intervene in the employer's 172(3) appeal. See Notes to 147.1(13) for subsequent decision.

Pension plans that received transfers from public sector plans were revoked in *Boudreau* (above); *Loba Ltd.*, 2004 FCA 342 (leave to appeal denied 2005 CarswellNat 848 (SCC); new registration application rejected 2008 FCA 403; leave to appeal denied 2009 CarswellNat 1028); *1346687 Ontario*, 2007 FCA 262 (leave to appeal denied 2008 CarswellNat 116); *Jordan Financial*, 2007 FCA 263 (leave to appeal denied 2008 CarswellNat 118); *1344746 Ontario Inc.*, 2008 FCA 314 (appeal not filed on time); *1398874 Ontario*, 2010 FCA 14. The primary purpose of the plan must be to provide lifetime retirement benefits to employees (Reg. 8502(a)), and the onus is on the appellant to show CRA erred in concluding this primary purpose was not met. In effect, CRA's determination can be challenged only if it is unreasonable.

Retroactive revocation of the plan results in income inclusion from the RRIF or RRSP from which the funds were transferred: *Bonavia*, 2010 FCA 129; *Astorino*, 2010 TCC 144. The same would have applied in *Ross*, 2013 TCC 333, para. 78, but the assessments were statute-barred [taxpayers from *Jordan* and *1346687* above].

See Théroux, "Purpose, Motive, and Pension Plans", 15(10) *Canadian Tax Highlights* (ctf.ca) 7-8 (Oct. 2007); Drache, "Pension Plans Determined Not to Be Valid", xxix(22) *The Canadian Taxpayer* (Carswell) 173-74 (Nov. 6/07); New Brunswick Securities Commission, "Investor Alert: Pension unlocking schemes" (Aug. 26, 2011).

Regulations: 8501(2) (failure to comply with various conditions); 8503(15) (past service employer contributions); 8506(4) (non-payment of minimum amount).

Registered Pension Plans Technical Manual: §2.10 (revocation of registration — notice of intention); §2.11 (notice of revocation).

Registered Plans Compliance Bulletins: 5 (reminder of primary purpose requirement for RPPs); 8 (over-contributions to an RPP).

Registered Plans Directorate Newsletters: 15-1 (comprehensive risk-based cyclical review of registered pension plans).

Registered Plans Frequently Asked Questions: RPFAQ-2 (RPPs), q. 11 (IPPs established primarily to transfer funds from an existing RPP).

(12) Notice of revocation — Where the Minister gives a notice

of intent to the administrator of a registered pension plan, or the plan administrator applies to the Minister in writing for the revocation of the plan's registration, the Minister may,

(a) where the plan administrator has applied to the Minister in writing for the revocation of the plan's registration, at any time after receiving the administrator's application, and

(b) in any other case, after 30 days after the day of mailing of the notice of intent,

give notice (in this subsection and in subsection (13) referred to as a "notice of revocation") by registered mail to the plan administrator that the registration of the plan is revoked as of the date specified in the notice of revocation, which date may not be earlier than the date specified in the notice of intent or the administrator's application, as the case may be.

Notes: In *Hodge*, 2009 FCA 210, the Court rejected H's argument that once the plan administrator has applied for revocation and specified a date, the Minister cannot revoke the plan retroactively.

In *Mammone*, 2019 FCA 45, CRA issued a revocation notice in 2013, purporting to revoke M's plan effective 2009, but failed to wait the full 30 days from the notice of intent. CRA then assessed M for 2009 (in 2013). In 2017, CRA validly revoked the plan effective 2009. The FCA overturned the 2013 assessment, as the facts justifying it did not exist in 2013.

Registered Pension Plans Technical Manual: §2.11 (notice of revocation).

(13) Revocation of registration — Where the Minister gives a notice of revocation to the administrator of a registered pension plan, the registration of the plan is revoked as of the date specified in the notice of revocation, unless the Federal Court of Appeal or a judge thereof, on application made at any time before the determination of an appeal pursuant to subsection 172(3), orders otherwise.

Related Provisions: 147.1(12) — Notice of revocation; 244(5) — Proof of service by mail; 248(7)(a) — Mail deemed received on day mailed.

Notes: In *Cryptic Web*, A-561-05, the FCA dismissed a revocation appeal because the appellant did not file its documents. Cryptic Web's plan was revoked because it was not a real pension plan but a scheme to allow federal public servants to obtain a premium by leaving public service and transferring their pensions. The FCA dismissed applications to change the revocation dates of such plans in: *Boudreau*, 2007 FCA 32 (leave to appeal denied 2007 CarswellNat 1203 (SCC)); *Anglehart*, 2008 FCA 282; *Hodge*, 2009 FCA 210. See also Notes to 147.1(11).

Registered Pension Plans Technical Manual: §2.12 (revocation of registration).

(14) Anti-avoidance — multi-employer plans — Where at any time the Minister gives written notice to the administrators of two or more registered pension plans, each of which is a multi-employer plan, that this subsection is applicable in relation to those plans with respect to a calendar year,

(a) each of those plans that is a specified multi-employer plan in the year shall, for the purposes of subsection (9) (other than for the purpose of determining the pension credits referred to in paragraphs (9)(a) and (b)), be deemed to be a multi-employer plan that is not a specified multi-employer plan; and

(b) the totals determined for the year under paragraphs (9)(a) and (b) shall be the amounts that would be determined if all the plans were a single plan.

Related Provisions: 87(2)(q) — Amalgamation — continuing corporation.

Registered Plans Directorate Newsletters: 95-7 (Quebec simplified pension plans); 98-1 (simplified pension plans).

Registered Pension Plans Technical Manual: §2.13 (anti-avoidance — multi-employer plans).

(15) Plan as registered — Any reference in this Act and the regulations to a pension plan as registered means the terms of the plan on the basis of which the Minister has registered the plan for the purposes of this Act and as amended by

(a) each amendment that has been accepted by the Minister, and

(b) each amendment that has been submitted to the Minister for acceptance and that the Minister has neither accepted nor refused to accept, if it is reasonable to expect the Minister to accept the amendment,

and includes all terms that are not contained in the documents constituting the plan but that are terms of the plan by reason of the *Pension Benefits Standards Act, 1985* or a similar law of a province.

Related Provisions: 87(2)(q) — Amalgamation — continuing corporation.

Registered Pension Plans Technical Manual: §2.14 (plan as registered).

(16) Separate liability for obligations — Every person who is a member of a body that is the administrator of a registered pension plan is subject to all obligations imposed on administrators by this Act or a regulation as if the person were the administrator of the plan.

Related Provisions: 238(1) — Offences.

Registered Pension Plans Technical Manual: §2.15 (separate liability for obligations).

(17) Superintendent of Financial Institutions — The Minister may, for the purposes of this Act, obtain the advice of the Superintendent of Financial Institutions with respect to any matter relating to pension plans.

Registered Pension Plans Technical Manual: §2.16 (Superintendent of Financial Institutions).

(18) Regulations — The Governor in Council may make regulations

(a) prescribing conditions for the registration of pension plans and enabling the Minister to impose additional conditions or waive any conditions that are prescribed;

(b) prescribing circumstances under which a registered pension plan becomes a revocable plan;

(c) specifying the manner of determining, or enabling the Minister to determine, the portion of a member's benefits under a registered pension plan that is in respect of any period;

(d) requiring administrators of registered pension plans to make determinations in connection with the computation of pension adjustments, past service pension adjustments, total pension adjustment reversals or any other related amounts (all such amounts referred to in this subsection as "specified amounts");

(e) requiring that the method used to determine a specified amount be acceptable to the Minister, where more than one method would otherwise comply with the regulations;

(f) enabling the Minister to permit or require a specified amount to be determined in a manner different from that set out in the regulations;

(g) requiring that any person who has information required by another person in order to determine a specified amount provide the other person with that information;

(h) enabling the Minister to require any person to provide the Minister with information relating to the method used to determine a specified amount;

(i) enabling the Minister to require any person to provide the Minister with information relevant to a claim that paragraph (10)(a) is not applicable by reason of an exemption provided by regulation;

(j) respecting applications for certifications for the purposes of subsection (10);

(k) enabling the Minister to waive the requirement for a certification for the purposes of subsection (10);

(l) prescribing rules for the purposes of subsection (10), so that that subsection applies or does not apply with respect to benefits provided as a consequence of particular transactions, events or circumstances;

(m) requiring any person to provide the Minister or the administrator of a registered pension plan with information in connection with an application for certification for the purposes of subsection (10);

(n) requiring any person who obtains a certification for the purposes of subsection (10) to provide the individual in respect of whom the certification was obtained with an information return;

(o) requiring administrators of registered pension plans to file information with respect to amendments to such plans and to the arrangements for funding benefits thereunder;

(p) requiring administrators of registered pension plans to file information returns respecting such plans;

(q) enabling the Minister to require any person to provide the Minister with information for the purpose of determining whether the registration of a pension plan may be revoked;

(r) requiring administrators of registered pension plans to submit reports to the Minister, prescribing the class of persons by whom the reports shall be prepared and prescribing information to be contained in those reports;

(s) enabling the Minister to impose any requirement that may be imposed by regulation made under paragraph (r);

(t) defining, for the purposes of this Act, the expressions "multi-employer plan", "past service event", "past service pension adjustment", "pension adjustment", "specified multi-employer plan" and "total pension adjustment reversal"; and

(u) generally to carry out the purposes and provisions of this Act relating to registered pension plans and the determination and reporting of specified amounts.

Related Provisions: 87(2)(q) — Amalgamation — continuing corporation; 221 — Regulations generally; 238(1) — Offences.

Notes: 147.1(18)(d) and (t) amended by 1997 Budget, effective 1997, to add reference to total pension adjustment reversals.

Regulations: 8300–8520.

Registered Pension Plans Technical Manual: §2.17 (regulations).

(19) Reasonable error [— return of contribution] — The administrator of a registered pension plan may make a payment (other than a payment made to avoid the revocation of the registration of the plan) that is a return of all or a portion of a contribution made by a member of the plan, or an employer who participates in the plan, if

(a) the contribution was made to the plan as a consequence of a reasonable error;

(b) the payment is made to the member or employer, as the case may be, who made the contribution; and

(c) the payment is made no later than December 31 of the year following the year in which the contribution was made.

Related Provisions: 56(1)(a)(i)(G) — Income inclusion.

Notes: 56(1)(a)(i)(G) exempts the return of the contribution, but provincial standards legislation in some provinces sets out conditions under which refunds of errant contributions must be approved by the provincial regulator [Finance Technical Notes].

147.1(19) added by 2013 budget bill #2, for contributions made after 2013.

Registered Pension Plans Technical Manual: §2.18 (reasonable error).

Notes [s. 147.1]: 147.1 added by 1990 pension bill, effective 1989 or earlier.

Definitions [s. 147.1]: "actuary", "administrator" — 147.1(1); "amount" — 248(1); "as registered" — 147.1(15); "average wage" — 147.1(1); "calendar year" — *Interpretation Act* 37(1)(a); "Canada" — 255; "compensation" — 147.1(1); "consequence of the death" — 248(8); "defined benefit provision" — 147.1(1); "employer", "employment" — 248(1); "Federal Court of Appeal" — *Federal Courts Act* s. 3; "former limit" — 147.1(1); "Governor in Council" — *Interpretation Act* 35(1); "individual" — 248(1); "member" — 147.1(1); "Minister" — 248(1); "money purchase limit" — 147.1(1), 248(1); "money purchase provision" — 147.1(1); "multi-employer plan" — 147.1(1), Reg. 8500(1), 8510(1); "notice of intent" — 147.1(11); "office" — 248(1); "participating employer" — 147.1(1); "past service event" — 147.1(1), Reg. 8300(1), (2); "past service pension adjustment" — 248(1), Reg. 8303; "pension adjustment" — 248(1), Reg. 8301(1); "pension credit" — Reg. 8301(2)–(8), (10), (16); "person" — 248(1); "plan as registered" — 147.1(15); "prescribed" — 248(1); "province" — *Interpretation Act* 35(1); "registered pension plan", "regulation" — 248(1); "resident in Canada" — 250; "revocable plan" — 147.1(8), (9), 147.3(12), Reg. 8301(14)(a), 8305(2), 8408(2), 8501(2), 8503(11), (15), 8506(4), 8511(2), 8515(9); "single amount" — 147.1(1); "specified amount" — 147.1(18)(d); "specified multi-employer plan" — 147.1(1), Reg. 8510(2), (3); "spouse" — 146(1.1), 147.1(1); "total pension adjustment reversal" — 248(1); "wage measure" — 147.1(1); "writing" — *Interpretation Act* 35(1).

147.2 (1) Pension contributions deductible — employer contributions — For a taxation year ending after 1990, there may be deducted in computing the income of a taxpayer who is an employer the total of all amounts each of which is a contribution made by the employer after 1990 and either in the taxation year or within 120 days after the end of the taxation year to a registered pension plan in respect of the employer's employees or former employees, to the extent that

(a) in the case of a contribution in respect of a money purchase provision of a plan, the contribution was made in accordance with the plan as registered and in respect of periods before the end of the taxation year;

(b) in the case of a contribution in respect of the defined benefit provisions of a plan (other than a specified multi-employer plan), the contribution

(i) is an eligible contribution,

(ii) was made to fund benefits provided to employees and former employees of the employer in respect of periods before the end of the taxation year, and

(iii) complies with subsection 147.1(10);

(c) in the case of a contribution made to a plan that is a specified multi-employer plan, the contribution was made in accordance with the plan as registered and in respect of periods before the end of the taxation year; and

(d) the contribution was not deducted in computing the income of the employer for a preceding taxation year.

Proposed Amendment — Fixing contribution errors in defined-contribution plans

Federal Budget, Notice of Ways and Means Motion, April 19, 2021: *Fixing Contribution Errors in Defined Contribution Pension Plans*

9 The Act is modified to give effect to the proposals relating to Fixing Contribution Errors in Defined Contribution Pension Plans as described in the budget documents tabled by the Minister of Finance in the House of Commons on April 19, 2021.

Federal Budget, Supplementary Information, April 19, 2021: *Fixing Contribution Errors in Defined Contribution Pension Plans*

The rules in the *Income Tax Act* do not currently permit pension plan administrators to accept retroactive contributions to employee accounts under a defined contribution pension plan in order to correct under-contribution errors in respect of prior years. Although in some circumstances over-contribution errors may be corrected by refunding the excess to the contributor, these rules have been found to be cumbersome.

Budget 2021 proposes to provide more flexibility to plan administrators of defined contribution pension plans to correct for both under-contributions and over-contributions. The proposals would permit certain types of errors to be corrected via additional contributions to an employee's account under a defined contribution pension plan to compensate for an under-contribution error made in any of the preceding five years, subject to a dollar limit. The proposals would also permit plan administrators to correct for pension over-contribution errors in respect of an employee for any of the five years prior to the year in which the excess amount is refunded to the employee or employer, as the case may be, who made the contribution.

To simplify reporting requirements, the proposed rules would require the plan administrator to file a prescribed form in respect of each affected employee, rather than to amend T4 slips for prior years. Additional contributions to correct for under-contributions would reduce the employee's registered retirement savings plan (RRSP) contribution room for the taxation year following the year in which the retroactive contribution is made. To the extent this results in negative RRSP room, it would only impact the employee's contributions in future years. Refunds of over-contributions would generally restore the employee's RRSP contribution room for the taxation year in which the refund is made.

This measure would apply in respect of additional contributions made, and amounts of over-contributions refunded, in the 2021 and subsequent taxation years.

Notes: Budget Table 1 projects that this measure will cost the federal government $1 million in 2021-22 and nothing measurable in any other year.

Related Provisions: 6(1)(a)(i) — Employer's contribution not a taxable benefit; 20(1)(q) — Employer's contributions deductible; 87(2)(q) — Amalgamation — continuing corporation; 147.1(8), (9) — Pension adjustment limits; 147.2(2) — Employer contributions — defined benefit provisions; 147.2(8) — Former employee of predecessor employer; *Interpretation Act* 27(5) — Meaning of "within 120 days".

Notes: An employer can establish an RPP with a Jan. 1 effective date, make an eligible contribution before April 30 for past service and deduct the contribution for the previous year: VIEWS doc 2005-016140117.

For CRA's restrictive interpretation of 147.2(1)(b)(ii) when the contribution period and corporation year do not match, see VIEWS doc 2008-0284471C6; but see also 2012-0460531E5. For a ruling that a remedial payment is not a "contribution" for 147.2(1)(a), see 2013-0506291R3.

Registered Plans Directorate Newsletters: 91-4R (registration rules for money purchase provisions).

Registered Plans Compliance Bulletins: 2 (compensation for RPP purposes); 3 (employer over-contributions to a registered pension plan: double taxation); 8 (over-contributions to an RPP).

Registered Pension Plans Technical Manual: §3.1 (deductible employer contributions).

Registered Plans Frequently Asked Questions: RPFAQ-2 (RPPs), q. 21 (successor pension plan where business assets purchased).

(2) Employer contributions — defined benefit provisions — For the purposes of subsection (1), a contribution made by an employer to a registered pension plan in respect of the defined benefit provisions of the plan is an eligible contribution if it is a prescribed contribution or if it complies with prescribed conditions and is made pursuant to a recommendation by an actuary in whose opinion the contribution is required to be made so that the plan will have sufficient assets to pay benefits under the defined

benefit provisions of the plan, as registered, in respect of the employees and former employees of the employer, where

(a) the recommendation is based on an actuarial valuation that complies with the following conditions, except the conditions in subparagraphs (iii) and (iv) to the extent that they are inconsistent with any other conditions that apply for the purpose of determining whether the contribution is an eligible contribution:

(i) the effective date of the valuation is not more than 4 years before the day on which the contribution is made,

(ii) actuarial liabilities and current service costs are determined in accordance with an actuarial funding method that produces a reasonable matching of contributions with accruing benefits,

(iii) all assumptions made for the purposes of the valuation are reasonable at the time the valuation is prepared and at the time the contribution is made,

(iv) the valuation is prepared in accordance with generally accepted actuarial principles,

(v) the valuation complies with prescribed conditions, which conditions may include conditions regarding the benefits that may be taken into account for the purposes of the valuation, and

(vi) where more than one employer participates in the plan, assets and actuarial liabilities are apportioned in a reasonable manner among participating employers in respect of their employees and former employees, and

(b) the recommendation is approved by the Minister in writing,

and, for the purposes of this subsection and except as otherwise provided by regulation,

(c) the benefits taken into account for the purposes of a recommendation may include anticipated cost-of-living and similar adjustments where the terms of a pension plan do not require that those adjustments be made but it is reasonable to expect that they will be made, and

(d) a recommendation with respect to the contributions required to be made by an employer in respect of the defined benefit provisions of a pension plan may be prepared without regard to such portion of the assets of the plan apportioned to the employer in respect of the employer's employees and former employees as does not exceed the lesser of

(i) the amount of actuarial surplus in respect of the employer, and

(ii) 25% of the amount of actuarial liabilities apportioned to the employer in respect of the employer's employees and former employees.

Related Provisions: 147.2(3) — Filing of actuarial report; 147.2(7) — Amount paid by letter-of-credit issuer deemed to be eligible contribution; 147.2(8) — Former employee of predecessor employer.

Notes: 147.2(2)(d) amended by 2010 budget bill #1, effective for contributions made after 2009 to fund benefits provided in respect of periods of pensionable service after 2009, to change "20%" to "25%" in (d)(ii) and to delete (d)(iii). This amendment (along with the repeal of Reg. 8516(4)) implements a proposal in Finance news release 2009-103, Oct. 27, 2009 (fin.gc.ca), to increase the pension surplus threshold from 10% to 25% in conjunction with amendments to the *Pension Benefits Standards Act* affecting federally-regulated pensions.

147.2(2)(b) amended by 1995-97 technical bill, effective April 1996.

Regulations: 8515(5) (prescribed conditions); 8516(1) (prescribed contribution).

Information Circulars: 72-13R8: Employees' pension plans.

Registered Plans Directorate Newsletters: 95-3 (actuarial report content); 96-1 (changes to retirement savings limits).

Registered Pension Plans Technical Manual: §3.2 (employer contributions — defined benefit provisions).

Registered Plans Compliance Bulletins: 2 (funding designated RPPs); 7 (making contributions and calculating and reporting pension adjustment for SMEPs).

Registered Plans Frequently Asked Questions: RPFAQ-2 (RPPs), q. 21 (successor pension plan where business assets purchased).

Registered Plans Directorate Actuarial Bulletins: 2 (eligible employer contributions to a designated plan); 4 (draft) (apportioning assets and actuarial liabilities for 147.2(2)(a)(vi)).

(3) Filing of actuarial report — Where, for the purposes of subsection (2), a person seeks the Minister's approval of a recommendation made by an actuary in connection with the contributions to be made by an employer to a registered pension plan in respect of the defined benefit provisions of the plan, the person shall file with the Minister a report prepared by the actuary that contains the recommendation and any other information required by the Minister.

Related Provisions: Reg. 8410 — Actuarial report required on demand.

Registered Plans Directorate Newsletters: 95-3 (actuarial report content).

Registered Pension Plans Technical Manual: §3.3 (filing of actuarial report).

Forms: T1200: Instructions for completing the actuarial information summary.

(4) Amount of employee's pension contributions deductible — There may be deducted in computing the income of an individual for a taxation year ending after 1990 an amount equal to the total of

(a) **service after 1989** — the total of all amounts each of which is a contribution (other than a prescribed contribution) made by the individual in the year to a registered pension plan that is in respect of a period after 1989 or that is a prescribed eligible contribution, to the extent that the contribution was made in accordance with the plan as registered,

(b) **service before 1990 while not a contributor** — the least of

(i) the amount, if any, by which

(A) the total of all amounts each of which is a contribution (other than an additional voluntary contribution or a prescribed contribution) made by the individual in the year or a preceding taxation year and after 1945 to a registered pension plan in respect of a particular year before 1990, if all or any part of the particular year is included in the individual's eligible service under the plan and if

(I) in the case of a contribution that the individual made before March 28, 1988 or was obliged to make under the terms of an agreement in writing entered into before March 28, 1988, the individual was not a contributor to the plan in the particular year, or

(II) in any other case, the individual was not a contributor to any registered pension plan in the particular year

exceeds

(B) the total of all amounts each of which is an amount deducted, in computing the individual's income for a preceding taxation year, in respect of contributions included in the total determined in respect of the individual for the year under clause (A),

(ii) $3,500, and

(iii) the amount determined by the formula

$$(\$3,500 \times Y) - Z$$

where

Y is the number of calendar years before 1990 each of which is a year

(A) all or any part of which is included in the individual's eligible service under a registered pension plan to which the individual has made a contribution that is included in the total determined under clause (i)(A) and in which the individual was not a contributor to any registered pension plan, or

(B) all or any part of which is included in the individual's eligible service under a registered pension plan to which the individual has made a contribution

(I) that is included in the total determined under clause (i)(A), and

(II) that the individual made before March 28, 1988 or was obliged to make under the terms of an agreement in writing entered into before March 28, 1988, and in which the individual was not a contributor to the plan, and

Z is the total of all amounts each of which is an amount deducted, in computing the individual's income for a preceding taxation year,

(A) in respect of contributions included in the total determined in respect of the individual for the year under clause (i)(A), or

(B) where the preceding year was before 1987, under subparagraph 8(1)(m)(ii) (as it read in its application to that preceding year) in respect of additional voluntary contributions made in respect of a year that satisfies the conditions in the description of Y, and

(c) **service before 1990 while a contributor** — the lesser of

(i) the amount, if any, by which

(A) the total of all amounts each of which is a contribution (other than an additional voluntary contribution, a prescribed contribution or a contribution included in the total determined in respect of the individual for the year under clause (b)(i)(A)) made by the individual in the year or a preceding taxation year and after 1962 to a registered pension plan in respect of a particular year before 1990 that is included, in whole or in part, in the individual's eligible service under the plan

exceeds

(B) the total of all amounts each of which is an amount deducted, in computing the individual's income for a preceding taxation year, in respect of contributions included in the total determined in respect of the individual for the year under clause (A), and

(ii) the amount, if any, by which $3,500 exceeds the total of the amounts deducted by reason of paragraphs (a) and (b) in computing the individual's income for the year.

Related Provisions: 8(1)(m) — Contributions deductible from employment income; 20(1)(q), 147.2(2) — Employer's contribution; 56(1)(a)(i) — Pension benefits taxable when received; 60(j), (j.04) — Transfer or repayment of pension benefits; 60(n.1) — Deduction for repayment of pension benefits received in error; 87(2)(q) — Amalgamation — continuing corporation; 146(1)"earned income"(a)(i), (c)(i) — RRSP earned income counted before 8(1)(m) deduction; 147.2(6), 152(6)(g) — Additional deduction for year of death; 257 — Formula cannot calculate to less than zero; Reg. 100(3)(a) — Deduction reduces source withholdings; Canada-U.S. Tax Treaty:Art. XVIII:8 — Contributions to US pension plan; Canada-U.K. Tax Treaty:Art. 27:7 — Contributions to UK pension plan.

Notes: Contributions to pensions in other countries may qualify for credit due to Canada's tax treaties. See Forms RC267, RC268; CRA *Guidance for Taxpayers Requesting Tax Treaty Relief for Cross-Border Pension Contributions* (Nov. 2013), re Chile, Colombia, Ecuador, Estonia, Finland, France, Germany [also VIEWS doc 2012-0439441E5], Greece, Ireland, Italy, Latvia, Lithuania, Netherlands, Slovenia, South Africa, Sweden, Switzerland, UK [also 2010-0380961E5, 2013-0498601E5], Venezuela. For the US, see Canada-US tax treaty Art. XXIV:2(a)(ii), Information Circular 84-6.

In *Corbett*, [1999] 4 C.T.C. 231 (FCA), contributions to purchase years of service (i.e., contributions for non-existent service) were held deductible when made in accordance with the terms of the plan.

In *Hatt*, 2015 TCC 207, pension contributions (from a retiring allowance received while H was non-resident) created a loss from employment that could be used in a later year under 111(1)(a), even though 147.2(4) does not allow carryforward.

See also VIEWS doc 2020-0868601E5 (past service pension contributions paid in instalments are deductible, including interest portion).

147.2(4)(a) amended by 2001 technical bill to add "or that is a prescribed eligible contribution", effective for contributions made after 1990.

147.2(4)(b)(iii)Z(B) amended by 1995-97 technical bill, retroactive to 1991, to refer to past service AVCs that were deducted in computing income for years before 1987, and to refer to 8(1)(m)(ii) as it read in the year in which the deductions were claimed rather than as it read for 1990. This amendment was made because 8(1)(m)(ii) did not permit the deduction of past service AVCs after 1986.

Regulations: 100(3)(a) (deduction of pension contribution from payroll reduces source withholding); 8501(6.2) (prescribed eligible contribution); 8502(b)(i), 8503(4)(a), (b) (RPP contributions permitted by employee).

Interpretation Bulletins: IT-167R6: Registered pension plans — employee's contributions.

Registered Plans Compliance Bulletins: 2 (compensation for RPP purposes).

Registered Pension Plans Technical Manual: §3.4 (deductible employee contributions).

Remission Orders: *Certain Taxpayers Remission Order, 2000-3*, P.C. 2001-429 (Newfoundland public employees — payments for non-existent service under a pre-1991 agreement); *Certain Taxpayers Remission Order, 2003-1*, P.C. 2003-912 (Memorial University pension plan members — payments for non-existent service under a pre-1990 agreement).

Forms: RC267: Employee contributions to a United States retirement plan for 2017 — temporary assignments; RC268: Employee contributions to a United States retirement plan for 2017 — cross-border commuters; T1 General return, Line 20700 [former 207]; T4040: RRSPs and other registered plans for retirement [guide].

(5) [No longer relevant.]

Notes: 147.2(5) allowed pension deductions for public sector teachers from 1991-94.

Registered Pension Plans Technical Manual: §3.5 (teachers).

(6) Deductible contributions when taxpayer dies — Where a taxpayer dies in a taxation year, for the purpose of computing the taxpayer's income for the year and the preceding taxation year,

(a) paragraph (4)(b) shall be read without reference to subparagraph (ii) and as if the reference to "the least of" were a reference to "the lesser of"; and

(b) paragraph (4)(c) shall be read without reference to subparagraph (ii) and the words "the lesser of".

Related Provisions: 152(6)(g) — Minister required to reassess past year to allow additional deduction; 163(4)(b.1) — Additional deduction ignored when calculating penalties; 164(5)(h.01), (5.1)(h.01) — No back interest on refund where past year reassessed.

Notes: 147.2(6) added by 1995-97 technical bill, for deaths after 1992. It provides that for the year of death and the preceding year, the $3,500 annual limits in 147.2(4)(b) and (c) do not apply.

Registered Pension Plans Technical Manual: §3.6 (deductible contributions when a taxpayer dies).

(7) Letter of credit — For the purposes of this section and any regulations made under subsection 147.1(18) in respect of eligible contributions, an amount paid to a registered pension plan by the issuer of a letter of credit issued in connection with an employer's funding obligations under a defined benefit provision of the plan is deemed to be an eligible contribution made to the plan in respect of the provision by the employer with respect to the employer's employees or former employees, if

(a) the amount is paid under the letter of credit;

(b) the use of the letter of credit is permitted under the *Pension Benefits Standards Act, 1985* or a similar law of a province; and

(c) the amount would have been an eligible contribution under subsection (2) if

(i) it had been paid to the plan by the employer, and

(ii) this section were read without reference to this subsection.

Related Provisions: 147.2(8) — Former employee of predecessor employer.

Notes: 147.2(7) added by 2006 budget bill #2, effective 2006. It accommodates a budget measure (that amended regulations under the *Pension Benefits Standards Act, 1985*) to provide funding relief for federally-regulated defined benefit RPPs — an extension of the 5-year solvency funding payment period to 10 years on condition that the difference in payment levels is secured by a letter of credit. 147.2(7) ensures that such use of letters of credit does not cause adverse tax consequences.

147.2(7) opening words amended by 2002-2013 technical bill (Part 5 — technical), effective Nov. 6, 2010, to change "and any regulations made under subsection (2) or under subsection 147.1(18)" to "and any regulations made under subsection 147.1(18) in respect of eligible contributions".

Registered Pension Plans Technical Manual: §3.7 (letter of credit).

(8) Former employee of predecessor employer — For the purposes of this section and any regulations made under subsection 147.1(18) in respect of eligible contributions, a former employee of a predecessor employer (as defined by regulation) of a participating employer in relation to a pension plan is deemed to be a former employee of the participating employer in relation to the plan if

(a) the former employee would not otherwise be an employee or former employee of the participating employer; and

(b) benefits are provided to the former employee under a defined benefit provision of the plan in respect of periods of employment with the predecessor employer.

Notes: 147.2(8) added by 2002-2013 technical bill (Part 5 — technical), effective for contributions made after 1990.

Regulations: 8500(1)"predecessor employer", (1.2) (meaning of "predecessor employer").

Registered Pension Plans Technical Manual: §3.8 (former employees of predecessor employer).

Notes [147.2]: 147.2 added by 1990 pension bill, effective 1989. For employee RPP deductions before 1991, see 8(1)(m), (m.1) and 8(6)–8(8).

Definitions [s. 147.2]: "actuary" — 147.1(1); "additional voluntary contribution", "amount" — 248(1); "as registered" — 147.1(15); "defined benefit provision" — 147.1(1); "eligible contribution" — 147.2(2), (7); "employee", "employer", "employment" — 248(1); "former employee" — 147.2(8); "Her Majesty" — *Interpretation Act* 35(1); "individual", "Minister" — 248(1); "money purchase provision", "participating employer" — 147.1(1); "person" — 248(1); "plan as registered" — 147.1(15); "predecessor employer" — 8500(1)"predecessor employer", (1.2); "prescribed" — 248(1); "province" — *Interpretation Act* 35(1); "registered pension plan", "regulation" — 248(1); "specified multi-employer plan" — 147.1(1), Reg. 8510(2), (3); "taxation year" — 249; "taxpayer" — 248(1); "writing" — *Interpretation Act* 35(1).

147.3 (1) Transfer — money purchase to money purchase, RRSP or RRIF [or ALDA] — An amount is transferred from a registered pension plan in accordance with this subsection if the amount

(a) is a single amount;

(b) is transferred on behalf of a member in full or partial satisfaction of the member's entitlement to benefits under a money purchase provision of the plan as registered; and

(c) is transferred directly to

(i) another registered pension plan to provide benefits in respect of the member under a money purchase provision of that plan,

(ii) a registered retirement savings plan under which the member is the annuitant (within the meaning assigned by subsection 146(1)),

(iii) a registered retirement income fund under which the member is the annuitant (within the meaning assigned by subsection 146.3(1)), or

(iv) a licensed annuities provider to acquire an advanced life deferred annuity for the benefit of the member.

Related Provisions: 146(8.2) — Amount deductible where withdrawn after mistaken contribution; 146(21.2) — Sask. Pension Plan account deemed to be RRSP for 147.3; 147.3(9) — Taxation of amount transferred; 147.3(13) — Excess transfer; 147.5(12) — PRPP deemed to be RRSP for 147.3; 204.2(1.2)I(a)(iii) — Transfer under 147.3(1) excluded from cumulative excess RRSP amount; 205(1)"excess ALDA transfer" — Excessive transfer to advanced life deferred annuity; Reg. 8300(1)"excluded contribution" — Amount transferred is excluded contribution; Reg. 8502(b)(iv) — RPP may accept transfer. See also at end of 147.3.

Notes: Although 147.3(1) and 147.3(4) permit transfers from an RPP to an RRSP or RRIF, provincial pensions legislation will generally require that any such transfers be to a locked-in RRSP or a life income fund (LIF, essentially a locked-in RRIF). Since 1996, LIFs can also be used for former federal employees, as well as those in federally-regulated industries such as banking and telecommunications.

See also Finance news release 2008-037 (May 8, 2008), "Regulatory Changes Related to Federally Regulated Life Income Funds" (including Q&A), implementing announcements in the Feb. 26/08 budget; Drache, "Unlocking Some 'Locked-In' Funds", xxx(11) *The Canadian Taxpayer* (Carswell) 85-86 (May 27/08); Sara Kinnear, "Treatment of registered assets on death", 2015 STEP Canada conference (contact memberservices@step.ca).

Damages for miscalculating pension entitlements on a transfer of plans were considered non-taxable in VIEWS doc 2010-0361101R3.

147.3(1(c)(iv) added by 2021 budget bill #1, effective 2020, to permit a transfer to an ALDA (see 146.5).

147.3(1)(c)(iii) added by 1992 technical bill, effective August 30, 1990.

Regulations: 216(2) (information return on transfer to ALDA).

Interpretation Bulletins: IT-528: Transfers of funds between registered plans.

Registered Plans Directorate Newsletters: 91-4R (registration rules for money purchase provisions).

Registered Pension Plans Technical Manual: §4 (transfers); §4.1 (money purchase to money purchase, RRSP or RRIF).

Forms: T2151: Direct transfer of a single amount under subsec. 147(19) or s. 147.3; T4040: RRSPs and other registered plans for retirement [guide].

(2) Transfer — money purchase to defined benefit — An amount is transferred from a registered pension plan in accordance with this subsection if the amount

(a) is a single amount;

(b) is transferred on behalf of a member in full or partial satisfaction of the member's entitlement to benefits under a money purchase provision of the plan as registered; and

(c) is transferred directly to another registered pension plan to fund benefits provided in respect of the member under a defined benefit provision of that plan.

Related Provisions: 147.1(10) — Past service benefits; 147.3(9) — Taxation of amount transferred; 147.3(13) — Excess transfer; Reg. 8300(1)"excluded contribution" — Amount transferred is excluded contribution; Reg. 8502(b)(iv) — RPP may accept transfer. See also at end of s. 147.3.

Notes: On conversion from a money purchase to defined benefit provision, if the amount in the MP provision exceeds the amount required to fund the DB benefits, see RPP Consultation Sessions, tinyurl.com/rpd-consults, "Questions from the Industry" 2003 q.2.

Interpretation Bulletins: IT-528: Transfers of funds between registered plans.

Registered Plans Directorate Newsletters: 91-4R (registration rules for money purchase provisions); 16-1 (qualifying transfers to IPPs).

Registered Pension Plans Technical Manual: §4 (transfers); §4.2 (money purchase to defined benefit); §6.1 (qualifying transfers).

Forms: T2151: Direct transfer of a single amount under subsec. 147(19) or s. 147.3; T4040: RRSPs and other registered plans for retirement [guide].

(3) Transfer — defined benefit to defined benefit — An amount is transferred from a registered pension plan (in this subsection referred to as the "transferor plan") in accordance with this subsection if the amount

(a) is a single amount;

(b) consists of all or any part of the property held in connection with a defined benefit provision of the transferor plan;

(c) is transferred directly to another registered pension plan to be held in connection with a defined benefit provision of the other plan, unless the transfer is to an "individual pension plan" (as defined in subsection 8300(1) of the *Income Tax Regulations*) and is in respect of benefits that are attributable to employment with a former employer that is not a participating employer (or its predecessor employer); and

(d) is transferred as a consequence of benefits becoming provided under the defined benefit provision of the other plan to one or more individuals who were members of the transferor plan.

Related Provisions: 147.3(9) — Taxation of amount transferred; Reg. 8300(1)"excluded contribution" — Amount transferred is excluded contribution; Reg. 8502(b)(iv) — RPP may accept transfer. See also at end of s. 147.3.

Notes: 147.3(3)(c) amended by 2021 budget bill #1, effective March 19, 2019, to add everything from "unless". As proposed in the March 2019 Budget, this prohibits an IPP from providing retirement benefits in respect of past years of employment that were pensionable service under a defined benefit plan of an employer other than the IPP's participating employer (or its predecessor). This is an anti-avoidance measure, aimed at plans that establish an IPP sponsored by a newly incorporated private corp controlled by an individual who has terminated employment with their former employer: "The individual then transfers the commuted value of their pension entitlement from the former employer's defined benefit plan to the new IPP. This planning seeks to obtain a 100% transfer of assets to the new IPP instead of the restricted transfer of assets to the individual's RRSP."

Regulations: 8300(1) (individual pension plan); 8517 (prescribed amount).

Interpretation Bulletins: IT-528: Transfers of funds between registered plans.

Registered Plans Directorate Newsletters: 04-1 (transfer from a defined benefit provision).

Registered Pension Plans Technical Manual: §4 (transfers); §4.3 (defined benefit to defined benefit).

Notes: 147.3(4.1) added by 1992 technical bill, effective 1991.

Interpretation Bulletins: IT-528: Transfers of funds between registered plans.

Registered Plans Directorate Newsletters: 91-4R (registration rules for money purchase provisions); 95-5 (conversion of a defined benefit provision to a money purchase provision).

Registered Pension Plans Technical Manual: §4 (transfers); §4.5 (transfer of surplus — defined benefit to money purchase).

Forms: T2151: Direct transfer of a single amount under subsec. 147(19) or s. 147.3.

Forms: T2151: Direct transfer of a single amount under subsec. 147(19) or s. 147.3;
T4040: RRSPs and other registered plans for retirement [guide].

(4) Transfer — defined benefit to money purchase, RRSP or RRIF — An amount is transferred from a registered pension plan in accordance with this subsection if the amount

(a) is a single amount no portion of which relates to an actuarial surplus;

(b) is transferred on behalf of a member in full or partial satisfaction of benefits to which the member is entitled, either absolutely or contingently, under a defined benefit provision of the plan as registered;

(c) does not exceed a prescribed amount; and

(d) is transferred directly to

(i) another registered pension plan and allocated to the member under a money purchase provision of that plan,

(ii) a registered retirement savings plan under which the member is the annuitant (within the meaning assigned by subsection 146(1)), or

(iii) a registered retirement income fund under which the member is the annuitant (within the meaning assigned by subsection 146.3(1)).

Related Provisions: 146(5.2), (5.201), Reg. 8517(3)–(3.02) — Commutation of benefits from insolvent employer — rollover to RRSP or RPP; 146(8.2) — Amount deductible where withdrawn after mistaken contribution; 146(21.2) — Sask. Pension Plan account deemed to be RRSP for purposes of 147.3; 147.3(9) — Taxation of amount transferred; 147.5(12) — Pooled registered pension plan deemed to be RRSP for purposes of 147.3; 204.2(1.2)I(a)(iii) — Transfer under 147.3(4) excluded from cumulative excess RRSP amount; Reg. 8300(1)"excluded contribution" — Amount transferred is excluded contribution; Reg. 8502(b)(iv) — RPP may accept transfer. See also at end of s. 147.3.

Notes: See Notes to 147.3(1).

In *Yudelson*, 2010 FCA 44, a transfer of an RPP's indexing benefits to an RRSP, after the purchase of a non-indexed annuity, resulted in an income inclusion under 147.3(10). The Court reviewed the interaction of 147.1 and 147.3 with Reg. 8517.

In *Mangal*, 2018 TCC 8, a pension surplus transferred to M's RRSP was an "actuarial surplus" and so was excluded by 147.3(4)(a) and taxable due to 147.3(10).

Form T2151 may be used but is not mandatory for a 147.3(4) transfer, and any excess over the prescribed amount under Reg. 8517 is taxed under 56(1)(a) and subject to withholding tax: VIEWS doc 2006-0198921E5.

A terminating member can transfer the commuted value to an RRSP, subject to the Reg. 8517 limits, then purchase an annuity. CRA was asked (tinyurl.com/rpd-consults, "Questions from the Industry" 2003 q.9) whether 147.3(4) could be amended to permit direct purchase of an annuity with the commuted value, as this would not contradict 147.4's objective and would permit administrators to comply with provincial pension standards legislation. Response: "Although the annuity purchase option is available under s. 147.4, the Dept. of Finance is not currently pursuing an amendment to the Act to provide for the purchase of an annuity where the rights under the annuity contract are materially different from those under the pension plan." However, this question has been removed.

147.3(4)(d)(iii) added by 1992 technical bill, effective Aug. 30, 1990, to permit transfers to RRIFs. (Other amendments were retroactive to 1989.)

Regulations: 8517 (prescribed amount).

Interpretation Bulletins: IT-528: Transfers of funds between registered plans.

Registered Plans Directorate Newsletters: 91-4R (registration rules for money purchase provisions); 04-1 (transfer from a defined benefit provision).

Registered Plans Compliance Bulletins: 8 (transfers from an RPP when the plan is underfunded at termination).

Registered Pension Plans Technical Manual: §4 (transfers); §4.4 (defined benefit to money purchase, RRSP or RRIF).

Forms: T2151: Direct transfer of a single amount under subsec. 147(19) or s. 147.3; T4040: RRSPs and other registered plans for retirement [guide].

(4.1) Transfer of surplus — defined benefit to money purchase — An amount is transferred from a registered pension plan in accordance with this subsection if the amount

(a) is transferred in respect of the actuarial surplus under a defined benefit provision of the plan; and

(b) is transferred directly to another registered pension plan and allocated under a money purchase provision of that plan to one or more members of that plan.

(5) Transfer to RPP, RRSP or RRIF for spouse [or common-law partner] on marriage [or partnership] breakdown — An amount is transferred from a registered pension plan in accordance with this subsection if the amount

(a) is a single amount no portion of which relates to an actuarial surplus;

(b) is transferred on behalf of an individual who is a spouse or common-law partner or former spouse or common-law partner of a member of the plan and who is entitled to the amount under a decree, order or judgment of a competent tribunal, or under a written agreement, relating to a division of property between the member and the individual in settlement of rights arising out of, or on a breakdown of, their marriage or common-law partnership; and

(c) is transferred directly to

(i) another registered pension plan for the benefit of the individual,

(ii) a registered retirement savings plan under which the individual is the annuitant (within the meaning assigned by subsection 146(1)), or

(iii) a registered retirement income fund under which the individual is the annuitant (within the meaning assigned by subsection 146.3(1)).

Related Provisions: 146.3(2)(f)(vi) — Conditions for RRIF; 146(21.2) — Sask. Pension Plan account deemed to be RRSP for purposes of 147.3; 147(2)(e)(i) — Transfer of DPSP rights permitted on breakdown of marriage or common-law partnership; 147.3(9) — Taxation of amount transferred; 147.5(12) — Pooled registered pension plan deemed to be RRSP for purposes of 147.3; 204.2(1.2)I(a)(iii) — Transfer under 147.3(5) excluded from cumulative excess RRSP amount; 252(3) — Extended meaning of "spouse" and "former spouse"; Reg. 8300(1)"excluded contribution" — Amount transferred is excluded contribution; Reg. 8502(b)(iv) — RPP may accept transfer. See also at end of s. 147.3.

Notes: 147.3 amended by 2000 same-sex partners bill (last change effective 2001), 2001 and 1992 technical bills.

Interpretation Bulletins: IT-440R2: Transfer of rights to income; IT-528: Transfers of funds between registered plans.

Registered Plans Directorate Newsletters: 91-4R (registration rules for money purchase provisions); 04-1 (transfer from a defined benefit provision); 16-1 (qualifying transfers to IPPs).

Registered Pension Plans Technical Manual: §4 (transfers); §4.6 (to an RPP, RRSP or RRIF for spouse...).

Forms: T2151: Direct transfer of a single amount under subsec. 147(19) or s. 147.3; T4040: RRSPs and other registered plans for retirement [guide].

(6) Transfer — pre-1991 contributions — An amount is transferred from a registered pension plan in accordance with this subsection if the amount

(a) is a single amount;

(b) is transferred on behalf of a member who is entitled to the amount as a return of contributions made (or deemed by regulation to have been made) by the member under a defined benefit provision of the plan before 1991, or as interest (computed at a rate not exceeding a reasonable rate) in respect of those contributions; and

(c) is transferred directly to

(i) another registered pension plan for the benefit of the member,

(ii) a registered retirement savings plan under which the member is the annuitant (within the meaning assigned by subsection 146(1)), or

(iii) a registered retirement income fund under which the member is the annuitant (within the meaning assigned by subsection 146.3(1)).

Related Provisions: 146(21.2) — Sask. Pension Plan account deemed to be RRSP for purposes of 147.3; 147.3(9) — Taxation of amount transferred; 204.2(1.2)I(a)(iii) — Transfer under 147.3(6) excluded from cumulative excess RRSP amount; Reg. 8300(1)"excluded contribution" — Amount transferred is excluded contribution; Reg. 8502(b)(iv) — RPP may accept transfer. See also at end of s. 147.3.

Notes: 147.3(6)(b) amended by 2002-2013 technical bill (Part 5 — technical), for transfers after 1999, to add "(or deemed by regulation to be made)" (see Reg. 8500(9)).

147.3(6)(c)(iii) added by 1992 technical bill, effective August 30, 1990, to permit transfers to RRIFs.

Regulations: 8500(9) (transfer of significant number of members to new plan).

Interpretation Bulletins: IT-528: Transfers of funds between registered plans.

Registered Plans Directorate Newsletters: 91-4R (registration rules for money purchase provisions); 98-2 (treating excess member contributions under a registered pension plan); 04-1 (transfer from a defined benefit provision).

Registered Pension Plans Technical Manual: §4 (transfers); §4.7 (pre-1991 contributions).

Forms: T2151: Direct transfer of a single amount under subsec. 147(19) or s. 147.3.

(7) Transfer — lump sum benefits on death — An amount is transferred from a registered pension plan in accordance with this subsection if the amount

(a) is a single amount no portion of which relates to an actuarial surplus;

(b) is transferred on behalf of an individual who is entitled to the amount as a consequence of the death of a member of the plan and who was a spouse or common-law partner or former spouse or common-law partner of the member at the date of the member's death; and

(c) is transferred directly to

(i) another registered pension plan for the benefit of the individual,

(ii) a registered retirement savings plan under which the individual is the annuitant (within the meaning assigned by subsection 146(1)), or

(iii) a registered retirement income fund under which the individual is the annuitant (within the meaning assigned by subsection 146.3(1)).

Related Provisions: 104(27) — Pension benefits; 146(21.2) — Sask. Pension Plan account deemed to be RRSP for purposes of 147.3; 146.3(2)(f)(vi) — Conditions for RRIF; 147.3(9) — Taxation of amount transferred; 204.2(1.2)I(a)(iii) — Transfer under 147.3(7) excluded from cumulative excess RRSP amount; 248(8) — Meaning of "consequence" of death; 252(3) — Extended definition of "spouse" and "former spouse"; Reg. 8300(1)"excluded contribution" — Amount transferred is excluded contribution; Reg. 8502(b)(iv) — RPP may accept transfer. See also at end of s. 147.3.

Notes: 147.3(7)(b) amended by 2000 same-sex partners bill to refer to "common-law partner", effective as per Notes to 248(1)"common-law partner".

147.3(7)(c)(iii) added by 1992 technical bill, effective Aug. 30, 1990, to permit transfers to RRIFs.

Interpretation Bulletins: IT-528: Transfers of funds between registered plans.

Registered Plans Directorate Newsletters: 91-4R (registration rules for money purchase provisions); 16-1 (qualifying transfers to IPPs).

Registered Pension Plans Technical Manual: §4 (transfers); §4.8 (lump-sum benefits on death).

Forms: T2151: Direct transfer of a single amount under subsec. 147(19) or s. 147.3.

(7.1) Transfer where money purchase plan replaces money purchase plan — An amount is transferred from a registered pension plan (in this subsection referred to as the "transferor plan") in accordance with this subsection if

(a) the amount is a single amount;

(b) the amount is transferred in respect of the surplus (as defined by regulation) under a money purchase provision (in this subsection referred to as the "former provision") of the transferor plan;

(c) the amount is transferred directly to another registered pension plan to be held in connection with a money purchase provision (in this subsection referred to as the "current provision") of the other plan;

(d) the amount is transferred in conjunction with the transfer of amounts from the former provision to the current provision on behalf of all or a significant number of members of the transferor plan whose benefits under the former provision are replaced by benefits under the current provision; and

(e) the transfer is acceptable to the Minister and the Minister has so notified the administrator of the transferor plan in writing.

Related Provisions: Reg. 8300(8)(a)(iv) — Certain allocations deemed to be employer contributions; Reg. 8301(4)(b)(ii.2) — Pension credit to include transferred surplus; Reg. 8500(7)(d) — Certain allocations deemed to be individual's contributions.

Notes: 147.3(7.1) added by 2001 technical bill, for transfers that occur after 1998.

Regulations: 8500(1)"surplus", 8500(1.1) (meaning of "surplus").

Registered Pension Plans Technical Manual: §4 (transfers); §4.9 (money purchase plan replaces money purchase plan).

(8) Transfer where money purchase plan replaces defined benefit plan — An amount is transferred from a registered pension plan (in this subsection referred to as the "transferor plan") in accordance with this subsection if

(a) the amount is a single amount;

(b) the amount is transferred in respect of the actuarial surplus under a defined benefit provision of the transferor plan;

(c) the amount is transferred directly to another registered pension plan to be held in connection with a money purchase provision of the other plan;

(d) the amount is transferred in conjunction with the transfer of amounts from the defined benefit provision to the money purchase provision on behalf of all or a significant number of members of the transferor plan whose benefits under the defined benefit provision are replaced by benefits under the money purchase provision; and

(e) the transfer is acceptable to the Minister and the Minister has so notified the administrator of the transferor plan in writing.

Related Provisions: 147.3(9) — Taxation of amount transferred; 147.3(10) — Division of transferred amount; Reg. 8502(b)(iv) — RPP may accept transfer. See also at end of s. 147.3.

Notes: 147.3(8)(b) and (c) amended by 2001 technical bill, effective for transfers that occur after 1990, to eliminate a condition that the surplus be used to satisfy employer contribution obligations.

Interpretation Bulletins: IT-528: Transfers of funds between registered plans.

Registered Plans Directorate Newsletters: 91-4R (registration rules for money purchase provisions); 95-5 (conversion of a defined benefit provision to a money purchase provision); 98-1 (simplified pension plans).

Registered Pension Plans Technical Manual: §4 (transfers); §4.10 (money purchase plan replaces defined benefit plan).

Forms: T2151: Direct transfer of a single amount under subsec. 147(19) or s. 147.3.

(9) Taxation of amount transferred — Where an amount is transferred in accordance with any of subsections (1) to (8),

(a) the amount shall not, by reason only of that transfer, be included by reason of subparagraph 56(1)(a)(i) in computing the income of any taxpayer; and

(b) no deduction may be made under any provision of this Act in respect of the amount in computing the income of any taxpayer.

Related Provisions: 147.3(11) — Division of transferred amount; 147.3(14.1) — Transfer of property between benefit provisions of the same plan; 212(1)(h)(iii.1)(A) — Amount transferred under 147.3 excluded from withholding tax on pension benefits. See additional Related provisions at end of s. 147.3.

Interpretation Bulletins: IT-528: Transfers of funds between registered plans.

Registered Pension Plans Technical Manual: §4.11 (taxation of amount transferred).

(10) Idem — Where, on behalf of an individual, an amount is transferred from a registered pension plan (in this subsection referred to as the "transferor plan") to another plan or fund (in this subsection referred to as the "transferee plan") that is a registered pension plan, a registered retirement savings plan or a registered retirement income fund and the transfer is not in accordance with any of subsections (1) to (7),

(a) the amount is deemed to have been paid from the transferor plan to the individual;

(b) subject to paragraph (c), the individual shall be deemed to have paid the amount as a contribution or premium to the transferee plan; and

(c) where the transferee plan is a registered retirement income fund, for the purposes of subsection 146(5) and Part X.1, the individual shall be deemed to have paid the amount at the time of the transfer as a premium under a registered retirement savings plan under which the individual was the annuitant (within the meaning assigned by subsection 146(1)).

Related Provisions: 146(5)(a)(v)(B) — Amount of RRSP premiums deductible; 147.3(11) — Division of transferred amount; 147.3(12) — Restriction re transfers; 147.3(13.1) — Withdrawal of excessive transfers to RRSPs and RRIFs; 147.3(14.1) — Transfer of property between benefit provisions of the same plan. See also at end of s. 147.3.

Notes: 147.3(10) applied in *Yudelson*, 2010 FCA 44, and *Mangal*, 2018 TCC 8. See Notes to 147.3(4).

147.3(10)(a) amended to delete the initial words "Notwithstanding section 254" by 1995-97 technical bill, effective for transfers after July 30, 1997. (See now 147.4.)

147.3(10)(c) and the reference to RRIFs in the opening words of 147.3(10) added by 1992 technical bill, effective Aug. 30, 1990. See Notes to 147.3(1), (4), (5), (6) and (7).

Interpretation Bulletins: IT-528: Transfers of funds between registered plans.

Registered Plans Directorate Newsletters: 04-1 (transfer from a defined benefit provision).

Registered Pension Plans Technical Manual: §4.11 (taxation of amount transferred).

(11) Division of transferred amount — Where an amount is transferred from a registered pension plan to another registered pension plan, to a registered retirement savings plan or to a registered retirement income fund and a portion, but not all, of the amount is transferred in accordance with any of subsections (1) to (8),

(a) subsection (9) applies with respect to the portion of the amount that is transferred in accordance with any of subsections (1) to (8); and

(b) subsection (10) applies with respect to the remainder of the amount.

Related Provisions: 146(21.2) — Sask. Pension Plan account deemed to be RRSP for purposes of 147.3; 147.3(14.1) — Transfer of property between benefit provisions of the same plan.

Notes: 147.3(11) amended by 1992 technical bill, effective Aug. 30, 1990.

Registered Pension Plans Technical Manual: §4.12 (division of transferred amount).

(12) Restriction re transfers — A registered pension plan becomes a revocable plan at any time that an amount is transferred from the plan to another registered pension plan, to a registered retirement savings plan or to a registered retirement income fund unless

(a) the amount is transferred in accordance with any of subsections (1) to (8); or

(b) where the amount is transferred on behalf of an individual,

(i) the amount is deductible by the individual under paragraph 60(j) or (j.2), or

(ii) the *Pension Benefits Standards Act, 1985* or a similar law of a province prohibits the payment of the amount to the individual.

Related Provisions: 146(21.2) — Sask. Pension Plan account deemed to be RRSP for purposes of 147.3; 147.1(11) — Revocation of registration — notice of intention; 147.1(8), (9), Reg. 8301(14)(a), 8305(2)(a), 8408(2), 8501(2), 8503(11), (15), 8506(4), 8511(2), 8515(9) — Other ways plan becomes revocable plan. See also at end of s. 147.3.

Notes: 147.3(12) amended by 1992 technical bill, effective Aug. 30, 1990.

Interpretation Bulletins: IT-528: Transfers of funds between registered plans.

Registered Plans Directorate Newsletters: 91-4R (registration rules for money purchase provisions); 04-1 (transfer from a defined benefit provision).

Registered Pension Plans Technical Manual: §4.13 (restrictions re transfers).

(13) Excess transfer — Where

(a) the transfer in a calendar year of an amount from a registered pension plan on behalf of a member of the plan would, but for this subsection, be in accordance with subsection (1) or (2), and

(b) the plan becomes, at the end of the year, a revocable plan as a consequence of an excess determined under any of paragraphs 147.1(8)(a) and (b) and (9)(a) and (b) with respect to the member (whether or not such an excess is also determined with respect to any other member),

such portion of the amount transferred as may reasonably be considered to derive from amounts allocated or reallocated to the member in the year or from earnings reasonably attributable to those amounts shall, except to the extent otherwise expressly provided in writing by the Minister, be deemed to be an amount that was not transferred in accordance with subsection (1) or (2), as the case may be.

Interpretation Bulletins: IT-528: Transfers of funds between registered plans.

Registered Pension Plans Technical Manual: §4.14 (excess transfer).

(13.1) Withdrawal of excessive transfers to RRSPs and RRIFs — There may be deducted in computing the income of an individual for a taxation year the lesser of

(a) the amount, if any, by which

(i) the total of all amounts each of which is an amount included under clause 56(1)(a)(i)(C), paragraph 56(1)(z.3), subsections 146(8), (8.3) or (12) or 146.3(5), (5.1) or (11) in computing the individual's income for the year, to the extent that the amount is not a prescribed withdrawal,

exceeds

(ii) the total of all amounts each of which is an amount deductible under paragraph 60(l) or subsection 146(8.2) in computing the income of the individual for the year, and

(b) the amount, if any, by which

(i) the total of all amounts each of which is an amount that was

(A) transferred to a registered retirement savings plan or registered retirement income fund under which the individual was the annuitant (within the meaning assigned by subsection 146(1) or 146.3(1), as the case may be),

(B) included in computing the income of the individual for the year or a preceding taxation year, and

(C) deemed by paragraph (10)(b) or (c) to have been paid by the individual as a premium to a registered retirement savings plan,

exceeds

(ii) the total of all amounts each of which is an amount

(A) deductible under this subsection in computing the individual's income for a preceding taxation year, or

(B) deducted under subsection 146(5) in computing the individual's income for a preceding taxation year, to the extent that the amount can reasonably be considered to be in respect of an amount referred to in subparagraph (i).

Related Provisions: 60(i) — Premium or payment under RRSP or RRIF; 146(5) — Amount of RRSP premiums deductible; 146(8.2) — Amount deductible where withdrawn after mistaken contribution; 146(21.2) — Sask. Pension Plan account deemed to be RRSP for purposes of 147.3; Reg. 8307(4) — Eligibility of withdrawn amount for designation.

Notes: 147.3(13.1)(a)(i) amended by 2017 budget bill #2, to add reference to 56(1)(a)(i)(C) effective 2010 and 56(1)(z.3) effective Dec. 14, 2012.

147.3(13.1) added by 1992 technical bill, this version effective 1993.

Regulations: 8307(6) (prescribed withdrawal).

Interpretation Bulletins: IT-124R6: Contributions to registered retirement savings plans; IT-528: Transfers of funds between registered plans.

Registered Pension Plans Technical Manual: §4.15 (withdrawal of excess transfers to RRSPs or RRIFs).

Forms: T1043: Deduction for excess RPP transfers you withdrew from an RRSP or RRIF.

(14) Deemed transfer — For the purposes of this section and the regulations, where property held in connection with a particular pension plan is made available to pay benefits under another pension plan, the property shall be deemed to have been transferred from the particular plan to the other plan.

Registered Pension Plans Technical Manual: §4.16 (deemed transfer).

(14.1) Transfer of property between provisions — Where property held in connection with a benefit provision of a registered pension plan is made available to pay benefits under another benefit provision of the plan, subsections (9) to (11) apply in respect of the transaction by which the property is made so available in the same manner as they would apply if the other benefit provision were in another registered pension plan.

Notes: 147.3(14.1) added by 1997 Budget, effective for transfers after July 30, 1997.

Registered Plans Directorate Newsletters: 04-1 (transfer from a defined benefit provision).

Registered Pension Plans Technical Manual: §4.17 (transfer of property between provisions).

(15) [Repealed]

Notes: 147.3(15), "Annuity contract commencing after age 69", added by 1996 Budget and repealed by 1995-97 technical bill, retroactive to its introduction (which was generally effective 1997). It was re-enacted as 147.4(4).

Related Provisions [s. 147.3]: 60(j) — Transfer of superannuation benefits; 60(j.1) — Transfer of retiring allowances; 60(l) — Transfer of refund of RRSP premium; 147(19)–(22) — Transfer to RPP, RRSP or DPSP; 147.1(3)(a) — Deemed registration; Reg. 8502(k).

Notes [s. 147.3]: 147.3 added by 1990 pension bill, this version effective for amounts transferred in 1989 or later. For amounts transferred in 1988, 147.3 read differently.

Definitions [s. 147.3]: "administrator" — 147.1(1); "advanced life deferred annuity" — 146.5(1), 248(1); "amount" — 248(1); "as registered" — 147.1(15); "calendar year" — *Interpretation Act* 37(1)(a); "common-law partner", "common-law partnership" — 248(1); "consequence of the death" — 248(8); "defined benefit provision" — 147.1(1); "employer", "employment" — 248(1); "former spouse" — 252(3); "individual" — 248(1); "individual pension plan" — Reg. 8300(1); "member" — 147.1(1); "Minister" — 248(1); "money purchase provision" — 147.1(1); "plan as registered" — 147.1(15); "prescribed withdrawal" — Reg. 8306(6); "property" — 248(1); "province" — *Interpretation Act* 35(1); "registered pension plan" — 248(1); "registered retirement savings plan" — 146(1), (21.2), 147.5(12), 248(1); "regulation" — 248(1); "revocable plan" — 147.1(8), (9), 147.3(12), Reg. 8301(14)(a), 8305(2), 8408(2), 8501(2), 8503(11), (15), 8506(4), 8511(2), 8515(9); "single amount" — 147.1(1); "spouse" — 252(3); "surplus" — Reg. 8500(1), (1.1); "taxpayer" — 248(1); "transfer", "transferred" — 147.3(14); "writing" — *Interpretation Act* 35(1).

147.4 (1) RPP annuity contract [buy-out annuity] — Where

(a) at any time an individual acquires, in full or partial satisfaction of the individual's entitlement to benefits under a registered pension plan, an interest in an annuity contract (other than an advanced life deferred annuity) purchased from a licensed annuities provider,

(b) the rights provided for under the contract are not materially different from those provided for under the plan as registered,

(c) the contract does not permit premiums to be paid at or after that time, other than a premium paid at that time out of or under the plan to purchase the contract,

(d) either the plan is not a plan in respect of which the Minister may, under subsection 147.1(11), give a notice of intent to revoke the registration of the plan or the Minister waives the application of this paragraph with respect to the contract and so notifies the administrator of the plan in writing, and

(e) the individual does not acquire the interest as a consequence of a transfer of property from the plan to a registered retirement savings plan or a registered retirement income fund,

the following rules apply for the purposes of this Act:

(f) the individual is deemed not to have received an amount out of or under the registered pension plan as a consequence of acquiring the interest, and

(g) other than for the purposes of sections 147.1 and 147.3, any amount received at or after that time by any individual under the contract is deemed to have been received under the registered pension plan.

Related Provisions: 147.4(2) — Amendment to RPP annuity contract.

Notes: For CRA interpretation of 147.4(1) see Registered Plans Directorate Newsletter 20-1 (July 8, 2020) [Dollar, "CRA Releases Guidance on Defined Benefit Pension Plan to Annuity Transfers", XXV(4) *Insurance Planning* (Federated Press) 17-22 (2020)]; VIEWS docs 2005-0153071I7 (147.4(1)(c)); 2012-0435781C6 (if commuted value of defined-benefit RPP is insufficient to buy annuity with same payout as plan); 2012-0458781E5 (if 147.4(1) not used, entire cost of annuity is taxed under 56(1)(a)).

"While 147.4(1)(g) deems amounts paid under an annuity not to have been paid under an RPP for the purpose of preventing double rollovers, it does not imply that benefits were not received": *Yudelson*, 2010 FCA 44 (see Notes to 147.3(4)).

147.4(1)(a) amended by 2021 budget bill #1, effective 2020, to add ALDA exclusion.

147.4(1) added by 1995-97 technical bill, for annuity contract acquisitions, amendments and substitutions that occur after July 30, 1997.

Registered Plans Directorate Newsletters: 20-1 (RPP annuity contracts).

Registered Plans Compliance Bulletins: 3 (purchase of annuity under subsec. 147.4(1)).

Registered Pension Plans Technical Manual: §5.1 (RPP annuity contract).

Registered Plans Frequently Asked Questions: RPFAQ-2 (RPPs), q. 20 (where administrator purchases single life annuity and member is later found to have a partner).

(2) Amended contract — Where

(a) an amendment is made at any time to an annuity contract to which subsection (1) or paragraph 254(a) applies, other than an amendment the sole effect of which is to

(i) defer annuity commencement to no later than the end of the calendar year in which the individual in respect of whom the contract was purchased attains 71 years of age, or

(ii) enhance benefits under the annuity contract in connection with the demutualization (as defined by subsection 139.1(1)) of an insurance corporation that is considered for the purpose of section 139.1 to have been a party to the annuity contract, and

(b) the rights provided for under the contract are materially altered as a consequence of the amendment,

the following rules apply for the purposes of this Act:

(c) each individual who has an interest in the contract immediately before that time is deemed to have received at that time the payment of an amount under a pension plan equal to the fair market value of the interest immediately before that time,

(d) the contract as amended is deemed to be a separate annuity contract issued at that time otherwise than pursuant to or under a superannuation or pension fund or plan, and

(e) each individual who has an interest in the separate annuity contract immediately after that time is deemed to have acquired the interest at that time at a cost equal to the fair market value of the interest immediately after that time.

Related Provisions: 139.1(2)(g) — No demutualization benefit.

Notes: 147.4(2)(a)(i) amended by 2007 budget bill #1, effective 2007, due to the repeal of 147.4(4) as part of raising RRSP and RPP age limits from 69 to 71. Before 2007, read:

(i) provide for an earlier annuity commencement that avoids the application of paragraph (4)(b), or

147.4(2)(a)(ii) added by 1999 Budget, effective for amendments and substitutions that occur after December 15, 1998.

147.4(2) added by 1995-97 technical bill, effective for annuity contract acquisitions, amendments and substitutions that occur after July 30, 1997.

Registered Pension Plans Technical Manual: §5.2 (amended contract).

(3) New contract — For the purposes of this Act, where an annuity contract (in this subsection referred to as the "original contract") to which subsection (1) or paragraph 254(a) applies is, at any time, substituted by another contract,

(a) if the rights provided for under the other contract

(i) are not materially different from those provided for under the original contract, or

(ii) are materially different from those provided for under the original contract only because of an enhancement of benefits that can reasonably be considered to have been provided solely in connection with the demutualization (as defined by subsection 139.1(1)) of an insurance corporation that is considered for the purposes of section 139.1 to have been a party to the original contract,

the other contract is deemed to be the same contract as, and a continuation of, the original contract; and

(b) in any other case, each individual who has an interest in the original contract immediately before that time is deemed to have received at that time the payment of an amount under a pension plan equal to the fair market value of the interest immediately before that time.

Related Provisions: 139.1(2)(g) — No demutualization benefit due to substitution under 147.4(3)(a).

Notes: For the meaning of "not materially different" in (a)(i), see Notes to 147.4(1).

147.4(3)(a)(ii) added by 1999 Budget, effective for amendments and substitutions that occur after December 15, 1998.

147.4(3) added by 1995-97 technical bill, effective for annuity contract acquisitions, amendments and substitutions that occur after July 30, 1997.

Registered Pension Plans Technical Manual: §5.3 (new contract).

(4) [Repealed]

Notes: 147.4(4) repealed by 2007 budget bill #1, effective 2007, except that the repeal does not apply to annuities under which the annuitant reached age 69 before 2007. It applied where 254(a) applied, an individual acquired an annuity before 1997 in satisfaction of their interest in an RPP, and payment had not begun by the end of the year the individual turned 69.

147.4(4) added by 1995-97 technical bill, effective 1997, subject to transitional rules.

Definitions [147.4]: "advanced life deferred annuity" — 146.5(1), 248(1); "annuity" — 248(1); "calendar year" — *Interpretation Act* 37(1)(a); "demutualization" — 139.1(1); "fair market value" — see 69(1) Notes; "individual", "licensed annuities provider", "Minister" — 248(1); "plan as registered" — 147.1(15); "registered pension plan" — 248(1); "registered retirement income fund" — 146.3(1), 248(1); "registered retirement savings plan" — 146(1), 248(1); "writing" — *Interpretation Act* 35(1).

Pooled Registered Pension Plans

147.5 (1) Definitions — The following definitions apply in this section.

"administrator", of a pooled pension plan, means

(a) a corporation resident in Canada that is responsible for the administration of the plan and that is authorized under the *Pooled Registered Pension Plans Act* or a similar law of a province to act as an administrator for one or more pooled pension plans; or

(b) an entity designated in respect of the plan under section 21 of the *Pooled Registered Pension Plans Act* or any provision of a law of a province that is similar to that section.

Related Provisions: Reg. 213 — Administrator must file information return.

Notes: See Notes at end of 147.5. Finance news release "Federally Registered Pooled Registered Pension Plans Now Available" (Oct. 7, 2014) states: "the five insurance companies that have federal PRPP licences (Sun Life, Great West Life, Manulife, Standard Life and Industrial-Alliance) have been registered with the Office of the Superintendent of Financial Institutions and the CRA. This was the final step necessary for the plan administrators to make federal PRPPs available to Canadians."

"designated pooled pension plan", for a calendar year, means a pooled pension plan that, at any time in the year (other than the year in which the plan became registered as a PRPP), meets any of the following conditions:

(a) the plan has fewer than 10 participating employers;

(b) the fair market value of the property held in connection with the accounts of all members of the plan employed by a particular participating employer exceeds 50% of the fair market value of the property held in connection with the plan;

(c) more than 50% of the members of the plan are employed by a particular participating employer; or

(d) it is reasonable to conclude that the participation in the plan of one or more participating employers occurs primarily to avoid the application of any of paragraphs (a) to (c).

Related Provisions: 147.5(29) — Related employers (and union locals) deemed to be single employer.

"exempt earned income", of a taxpayer for a taxation year, means the total of all amounts each of which is an amount that is

(a) not included in the taxpayer's earned income (as defined in subsection 146(1)) for the year and that would be so included but for paragraph 81(1)(a) as it applies with respect to the *Indian Act*; and

Forms: RC383: Tax-exempt earned income and contributions for a PRPP.

(b) reported by the taxpayer in prescribed form filed with the Minister by the taxpayer's filing-due date for the year, or such later date as is acceptable to the Minister, provided that the later date is within three calendar years following the end of the year.

Related Provisions: 147.5(1)"exempt-income contribution amount"; 147.5(31)–(34) — Exempt earned income eligible for PRPP contribution.

"exempt-income contribution amount", of a taxpayer for a taxation year, means the total of

(a) all amounts each of which is a contribution to a PRPP made by the taxpayer for the year that is not deductible in computing the income of the taxpayer because of subsection (32), and

(b) the amount, if any, designated under subsection (34) by the taxpayer for the year in prescribed form filed with the Minister by the taxpayer's filing-due date for the year, or such later date as is acceptable to the Minister, provided that the later date is within three calendar years following the end of the year.

Related Provisions: 146(1)"unused RRSP deduction room"(b)D(iv) — EICA reduces unused RRSP deduction room; 146(5)(a)(iii.1) — EICA not available for RRSP deduction.

"member", of a pooled pension plan, means an individual (other than a trust) who holds an account under the plan.

"participating employer", in relation to a pooled pension plan for a calendar year, means an employer that, in the year,

(a) makes contributions to the plan in respect of all or a class of its employees or former employees; or

(b) remits to the administrator of the plan contributions made by members of the plan under a contract with the administrator in respect of all or a class of its employees.

"pooled pension plan" means a plan that is registered under the *Pooled Registered Pensions Plans Act* or a similar law of a province.

Related Provisions: 248(1)"pooled pension plan" — Definition applies to entire Act.

Notes: *"Plan Act"* corrected to *"Plans Act"*: laws.justice.gc.ca/eng/corrections.

"pooled registered pension plan" or **"PRPP"** means a pooled pension plan that has been accepted for registration by the Minister for the purposes of this Act, which registration has not been revoked.

Related Provisions: 6(1)(a)(i) — Employer contribution not a taxable benefit; 18(11)(c) — Whether interest deductible on money borrowed to contribute to PRPP; 56(1)(z.3), 147.5(13)(a) — Benefits taxable; 60(l)(v)(A.1), (B.01), (B.1)(II)1 — Rollover of PRPP on death to survivor's RRSP; 75(3)(a) — Reversionary trust rules do not apply to PRPP; 108(1)"trust"(a) — "Trust" does not include a PRPP for certain purposes; 118(7)"pension income"(a)(iii.2) — PRPP income qualifies for pension credit; 146(1)"unused RRSP deduction room"D(iii), 146(5)(b), 146(5.1)(b)(ii) — Employer contribution reduces RRSP contribution room; 147.5(8) — PRPP not taxed; 147.5(10) — Employer contributions deductible; 147.5(11) — Member contributions deemed to be RRSP premiums; 148(1)(b.3) — No income inclusion on disposition of life insurance policy; 248(1)"pooled registered pension plan" — Definition applies to entire Act; 248(1)"retirement compensation arrangement"(a.1) — PRPP deemed not to be RCA; 248(1)"salary deferral arrangement"(a.1) — PRPP deemed not to be SDA; Reg. 9006(c) — PRPP not reported to CRA for disclosure to foreign tax authorities.

Notes: See at end of 147.5.

Information Circulars: 13-1R1: Pooled registered pension plans.

Forms: RC364-CA: Application to register a pooled pension plan; RC365: PRPP amendment information; RC365-CA: PRPP amendment information; RC368-CA: Pooled registered pension plan annual information return.

"qualifying annuity", for an individual, means an annuity (other than an advanced life deferred annuity) that

(a) is payable to

(i) the individual for the individual's life, or

(ii) the individual for the lives, jointly, of the individual and the individual's spouse or common-law partner and to the survivor of them for the survivor's life;

(b) is payable beginning no later than the later of

(i) the end of the calendar year in which the individual attains 71 years of age, and

(ii) the end of the calendar year in which the annuity is acquired;

(c) unless the annuity is subsequently commuted into a single payment, is payable

(i) at least annually, and

(ii) in equal amounts or is not so payable solely because of an adjustment that would, if the annuity were an annuity under a retirement savings plan, in accordance with any of subparagraphs 146(3)(b)(iii) to (v);

(d) if the annuity includes a guaranteed period, requires that

(i) the period not exceed 15 years, and

(ii) in the event of the later of the death of the individual and that of the individual's spouse or common-law partner during the period, any remaining amounts otherwise payable be commuted into a single payment as soon as practicable after the later death; and

(e) does not permit any premiums to be paid, other than the premium paid from the PRPP to acquire the annuity.

Related Provisions: 147.5(23) — Where amount transferred from PRPP to acquire qualifying annuity; 252(3) — Extended meaning of "spouse".

Notes: Opening words of definition amended to add ALDA exclusion (see 146.5) by 2021 budget bill #1, effective 2020.

"qualifying survivor", in relation to a member of a PRPP, means an individual who, immediately before the death of the member

(a) was a spouse or common-law partner of the member; or

(b) was a child or grandchild of the member who was financially dependent on the member for support.

Related Provisions: 146(1.1) — Where child presumed not financially dependent; 147.5(17) — Deemed distribution to qualifying survivor; 252(3) — Extended meaning of "spouse".

"restricted investment", for a pooled pension plan, means

(a) a debt of a member of the plan;

(b) a share of, an interest in, or a debt of

(i) a corporation, partnership or trust in which a member of the plan has a significant interest, or

(ii) a person or partnership that does not deal at arm's length with the member of the plan or with a person or partnership described in subparagraph (i);

(c) an interest (or, for civil law, a right) in, or a right to acquire, a share, interest or debt described in paragraph (a) or (b); or

(d) prescribed property.

Related Provisions: 147.5(30) — Meaning of "significant interest".

Regulations: No prescribed property has been proposed for para. (d).

"single amount" means an amount that is not part of a series of periodic payments.

"successor member" means an individual who was the spouse or common-law partner of a member of a PRPP immediately before the death of the member and who acquires, as a consequence of the death, all of the member's rights in respect of the member's account under the PRPP.

Related Provisions: 248(8) — Meaning of "consequence" of death; 252(3) — Extended meaning of "spouse".

"unused non-deductible PRPP room", of a taxpayer at the end of a taxation year, means the amount determined by the formula

$$A - B$$

where

A is the amount of the taxpayer's unused RRSP deduction room at the end of the year, determined in accordance with subsection (33); and

B is the taxpayer's unused RRSP deduction room at the end of the year.

Related Provisions: 146(1)"unused RRSP deduction room"(b)D(iv) — UNDPR affects unused RRSP deduction room; 147.5(34)(a) — Amount up to UNDPR may be designated for non-deductible contribution.

(2) Registration conditions — The Minister may accept for registration a pooled pension plan for the purposes of this Act, but shall not accept for registration any plan unless application for registration is made in prescribed manner by the plan administrator and, in the Minister's opinion, the plan complies with the following conditions:

(a) the primary purpose of the plan is to accept and invest contributions in order to provide retirement income to plan members, subject to the limits and other requirements under this Act;

(b) a single and separate account is maintained for each member under the member's Social Insurance Number

(i) to which are credited all contributions made to the plan in respect of the member, and any earnings of the plan allocated to the member, and

(ii) to which are charged all payments and distributions made in respect of the member;

(c) the only benefits provided under the plan in respect of each member are benefits determined solely with reference to, and provided by, the amount in the member's account;

(d) all earnings of the plan are allocated to plan members on a reasonable basis and no less frequently than annually;

(e) the arrangement under which property is held in connection with the plan is acceptable to the Minister;

(f) no right of a person under the plan is capable of being assigned, charged, anticipated, given as security or surrendered, other than

(i) an assignment pursuant to a decree, order or judgment of a competent tribunal, or under a written agreement, relating to a division of property between the member and the member's spouse or common-law partner or former spouse or common-law partner, in settlement of rights arising out of, or on a breakdown of, their marriage or common-law partnership, or

(ii) an assignment by the legal representative of a deceased individual on the distribution of the individual's estate;

(g) the plan requires that all amounts contributed or allocated to a member's account vest immediately and indefeasibly for the benefit of the member;

(h) the plan permits the payment of an amount to a member if the amount is paid to reduce the amount of tax that would otherwise be payable under Part X.1 by the member;

(i) any amount payable from an account of a member after the death of the member is paid as soon as practicable after the death;

(j) there is no reason to expect that the plan may become a revocable plan; and

(k) any prescribed conditions.

Related Provisions: 147.5(3), (4) — Revocable plan; 147.5(7) — Amendments to plan; 147.5(24)–(27) — Revocation of plan for non-compliance with conditions; 172(3)(h) — Appeal of Minister's refusal to accept plan for registration; 204.2(5) — Withdrawal from PRPP allowed to reduce Part X.1 overcontribution tax; 252(3) — Extended meaning of "spouse" and "former spouse". See also Related Provisions to 147.5(1)"pooled registered pension plan".

Notes: See Notes at end of 147.5. In (f)(i), "or a under" corrected to "or under": laws.justice.gc.ca/eng/corrections.

Regulations: 213 (administrator must file information return). No prescribed conditions proposed for para. (k).

Information Circulars: 13-1R1: Pooled registered pension plans.

Forms: RC364: Application to register a plan as a pooled registered pension plan; RC364-CA: Application to register a pooled pension plan; RC365: PRPP amendment information; RC365-CA: PRPP amendment information; RC368-CA: Pooled registered pension plan annual information return.

(3) Conditions applicable to PRPPs — A pooled registered pension plan becomes a revocable plan at any time that

(a) a contribution is made to the plan other than an amount

(i) paid by a member of the plan,

(ii) paid by an employer or former employer of a member of the plan in respect of the member, or

(iii) transferred to the plan in accordance with any of subsections (21), 146(16) and (21), 146.3(14) and (14.1), 147(19) and 147.3(1), (4) and (5) to (7);

(b) a contribution is made to the plan in respect of a member after the calendar year in which the member attains 71 years of age, other than an amount

(i) described in subparagraph (a)(iii), or

(ii) if subsection 60.022(1) applies, described in any of subclauses 60(l)(v)(B.2)(II) to (IV) as read in that subsection;

(c) a participating employer makes contributions to the plan in a calendar year in respect of a member of the plan in excess of the RRSP dollar limit for the year, except in accordance with a direction by the member;

(d) a distribution is made from the plan other than

(i) a payment of benefits in accordance with subsection (5), or

(ii) a return of contributions

(A) if a contribution to the plan has been made as a result of a reasonable error by a member of the plan or a participating employer in relation to the plan and the return of contributions is made to the person who made the contribution no later than December 31 of the year following the calendar year in which the contribution was made,

(B) to avoid the revocation of the registration of the plan,

(C) to reduce the amount of tax that would otherwise be payable under Part X.1 by a member, or

(D) to comply with any requirement under this Act;

(e) property is held in connection with the plan that

(i) the administrator knew or ought to have known was a restricted investment for the plan, or

(ii) in the case of a designated pooled pension plan, is a share or debt of, or an interest in, a participating employer of the plan or any person or partnership that does not deal at arm's length with a participating employer, or an interest (or, for civil law, a right) in, or a right to acquire, such a share, debt or interest;

(f) the value of a member's right under the plan depends on the value of, or income or capital gains in respect of, property that would be described in paragraph (e) if it were held in connection with the plan;

(g) the administrator borrows money or other property for the purposes of the plan; or

(h) the plan or the administrator does not comply with a prescribed condition.

Related Provisions: 56(1)(z.3)(i) — No tax on return of contributions under 147.5(3)(d)(ii)(A) or (B); 147.5(13)(b) — Return of employer contributions under (d)(ii)(A) is taxable; 147.5(24)–(27) — Revocation where plan becomes revocable plan; 147.5(32.1) — Returned contribution deemed not made.

Notes: 147.5(3)(b)(ii) added by 2015 Budget bill, effective June 23, 2015, as an exclusion from a plan becoming revocable. See Notes to 60.022(1).

Regulations: No prescribed conditions proposed for para. (h).

Information Circulars: 13-1R1: Pooled registered pension plans.

Forms: RC383: Tax-exempt earned income and contributions for a PRPP.

(4) Non-payment of minimum amount — A PRPP becomes a revocable plan at the beginning of a calendar year if the total amount distributed from a member's account under the PRPP in the calendar year is less than the amount that would be the minimum amount for the calendar year under subsection 8506(5) of the *Income Tax Regulations* if the member's account were an account under a money purchase provision of a registered pension plan.

Related Provisions: 147.5(24)–(27) — Revocation where plan becomes revocable plan.

(5) Permissible benefits — The following benefits may be provided under a pooled pension plan:

(a) the payment of benefits to a member that would be in accordance with paragraph 8506(1)(e.1) or (e.2) of the *Income Tax Regulations* if the benefits were provided under a money purchase provision of a registered pension plan; and

(b) the payment of a single amount from the member's account.

Notes: 147.5(5)(a) amended by 2021 budget bill #1, effective 2020, to add "or (e.2)".

Information Circulars: 13-1R1: Pooled registered pension plans.

(6) Additional conditions — The Minister may, at any time, impose reasonable conditions, in writing, applicable with respect to PRPPs, a class of PRPPs or a particular PRPP.

Related Provisions: 147.5(24)–(27) — Revocation of plan for non-compliance.

(7) Acceptance of amendments — The Minister shall not accept an amendment to a PRPP unless

(a) application for the acceptance is made in prescribed manner by the administrator of the PRPP; and

(b) the amendment and the PRPP as amended comply with the registration conditions specified in subsection (2).

Related Provisions: 172(3)(i) — Appeal of Minister's refusal to accept amendment.

Forms: RC365: PRPP amendment information; RC365-CA: PRPP amendment information.

(8) Trust not taxable — No tax is payable under this Part by a trust governed by a PRPP on its taxable income for a taxation year, except that, if at any time in the year, it carries on a business, tax is payable under this Part by the trust on the amount that would be its taxable income for the year if it had no income or losses from sources other than the business, and for this purpose,

(a) all capital gains and capital losses from the disposition of property held in connection with the business are deemed to be income or losses, as the case may be, from the business; and

(b) the trust's income is to be computed without reference to subsections 104(6), (19) and (21).

Related Provisions: 149(1)(u.3) — No tax on PRPP; 253.1(1) — Limited partner not considered to carry on partnership business.

Notes: See Notes to 146(4) regarding a PRPP carrying on business.

(9) Obligations of administrator — The administrator of a PRPP shall exercise the care, diligence and skill of a reasonably prudent trustee to minimize the possibility that the registration of the PRPP may be revoked other than at the request of the administrator.

Notes: This is the same test as for the due-diligence defence for directors under 227.1(3) in respect of a corporation's unremitted source deductions. The Finance Technical Notes state that an administrator failing this test is liable to a $25/day penalty (minimum $100, maximum $2,500) under 162(7).

(10) Employer contributions deductible — There may be deducted in computing a taxpayer's income for a taxation year, the total of all amounts each of which is a contribution made by the taxpayer in the year or within 120 days after the end of the year to a PRPP in respect of the taxpayer's employees or former employees to the extent that the contribution

(a) was made in accordance with the PRPP as registered and in respect of periods before the end of the year; and

(b) was not deducted in computing the taxpayer's income for a preceding taxation year.

Related Provisions: 56(1)(a)(i) — Employer contribution not a taxable benefit; 20(1)(q) — Employer contribution deductible; 146(5)(b), 146(5.1)(b)(ii) — Employer contributions reduce employee's RRSP deduction limit; 147.5(13)(b) — Return of employer contributions under 147.5(3)(d)(ii)(A) is taxable; 147.5(32.1) — Returned contribution deemed not made; 204.2(1.2)I(c) — Employer contribution included in cumulative excess RRSP amount; *Interpretation Act* 27(5) — Meaning of "within 120 days".

Forms: T1 General return, Line 20810 [former 205].

(11) Member contributions — For the purposes of paragraphs 60(j), (j.1) and (l), section 146 (other than subsections (8.3) to (8.7)), paragraphs 146.01(3)(a) and 146.02(3)(a) and Parts X.1 and X.5, a contribution made to a PRPP by a member of a PRPP is deemed to be a premium paid by the member to an RRSP under which the member is the annuitant.

Related Provisions: 147.5(32) — No deduction for contribution from Indian's exempt income; 147.5(32.1) — Returned contribution deemed not made; 147.5(33) — Part X.1 tax applies to PRPP overcontributions out of an Indian's exempt income; Reg. 100(3)(a) — Source withholdings to be reduced to reflect member's contribution.

Information Circulars: 13-1R1: Pooled registered pension plans.

(12) Member's account — For the purposes of paragraph 18(1)(u), subparagraph (a)(i) of the definition "excluded right or interest" in subsection 128.1(10), paragraph 146(8.2)(b), subsection 146(8.21), paragraphs 146(16)(a) and (b), subparagraph 146(21)(a)(i), paragraph (b) of the definition "excluded premium" in subsection 146.01(1), paragraph (c) of the definition "excluded premium" in subsection 146.02(1), subsections 146.3(14) and 147(19) to (21), section 147.3 and paragraphs 212(1)(j.1) and (m), and of regulations made under subsection 147.1(18), a member's account under a PRPP is deemed to be a registered retirement savings plan under which the member is the annuitant.

Notes: 147.5(12) amended by 2017 budget bill #2, effective Dec. 14, 2012, to add "subsection" before "147.1(18)".

(13) Taxable amounts — There shall be included in computing the income of a taxpayer for a taxation year

(a) if the taxpayer is a member of a PRPP, the total of all amounts each of which is a distribution made in the year from the member's account under the PRPP, other than an amount that is

(i) included in computing the income of another taxpayer for the year under paragraph (b),

(ii) described in subsection (22), or

(iii) distributed after the death of the member;

(b) if the taxpayer is a participating employer in relation to a PRPP, the total of all amounts each of which is a return of contributions that is described in clause (3)(d)(ii)(A) and that is made to the taxpayer in the year.

Related Provisions: 56(1)(z.3) — Inclusion in income; 204.2(1.2)J(a) — Benefits reduce cumulative excess RRSP amount; 204.2(5) — Withdrawal from PRPP allowed to reduce Part X.1 overcontribution tax; Reg. 100(1)"remuneration"(b)(i) — No source withholdings on untaxed PRPP distribution.

(14) Treatment on death — no successor member — If a member of a PRPP dies and there is no successor member in respect of the deceased member's account under the PRPP, an amount, equal to the amount by which the fair market value of all property held in connection with the account immediately before the death exceeds the total of all amounts distributed from the account that are described in subsection (16), is deemed to have been distributed from the account immediately before the death.

Related Provisions: 152(6)(f.3) — Reassessment to allow loss carryback; Reg. 100(1)"remuneration"(b)(ii) — No source withholdings on PRPP distribution deemed made by 147.5(14).

(15) Treatment on death — successor member — If a member of a PRPP dies and there is a successor member in respect of the deceased member's account under the PRPP,

(a) the account ceases to be an account of the deceased member at the time of the death;

(b) the successor member is, after the time of the death, deemed to hold the account as a member of the PRPP; and

(c) the successor member is deemed to be a separate member in respect of any other account under the PRPP that the successor member holds.

(16) Qualifying survivor — If, as a consequence of the death of a member of a PRPP, an amount is distributed in a taxation year from the member's account under the PRPP to, or on behalf of, a qualifying survivor of the member, the amount shall be included in computing the survivor's income for the year, except to the extent that it is an amount described in subsection (22).

Related Provisions: 56(1)(z.3) — Inclusion in income from other sources; 60(l)(v)(A.1), (B.01), (B.1)(II)1 — Rollover to survivor's RRSP; 147.5(17) — Deemed distribution to qualifying survivor; 147.5(18) — Post-death increase in value; 147.5(19) — Post-death decrease in value; 248(8) — Meaning of "consequence" of death.

(17) Deemed distribution to qualifying survivor — If an amount is distributed at any time from a deceased member's account under a PRPP to the member's legal representative and a qualifying survivor of the member is entitled to all or a portion of the amount in full or partial satisfaction of the survivor's rights as a beneficiary (as defined in subsection 108(1)) under the deceased's estate, then, for the purposes of subsection (16), the amount or portion of the amount, as the case may be, is deemed to have been distributed at that time from the member's account to the qualifying survivor (and not to the legal representative) to the extent that it is so designated jointly by the legal representative and the qualifying survivor in prescribed form filed with the Minister.

Forms: T2019: Death of an RRSP annuitant — refund of premiums or joint designation on the death of a PRPP member.

(18) Post-death increase in value — There shall be included in computing the income for a taxation year of a taxpayer who is not a qualifying survivor in relation to a member of a PRPP, the total of all amounts each of which is an amount determined by the formula

$$A - B$$

where

A is the amount of a distribution made in the year from the member's account under the PRPP as a consequence of the member's death to, or on behalf of, the taxpayer, and

B is an amount designated by the administrator of the PRPP not exceeding the lesser of

(a) the amount of the distribution, and

(b) the amount by which the fair market value of all property held in connection with the account immediately before the death exceeds the total of all amounts each of which is

(i) the value of B in respect of any prior distribution made from the account, or

(ii) an amount included under subsection (16) in computing the income of a qualifying survivor in relation to the member.

Related Provisions: 56(1)(z.3) — Inclusion in income from other sources; 147.5(19) — Post-death decrease in value; 212(1)(h)(ii) — Amount designated is exempt from non-resident withholding tax; 248(8) — Meaning of "consequence" of death; 257 — Formula cannot calculate to less than zero.

(19) Post-death decrease in value — There may be deducted in computing the income of a member of a PRPP for the taxation year in which the member dies, an amount not exceeding the amount determined, after all amounts payable from the member's account under the PRPP have been distributed, by the formula

$$A - B$$

where

A is the total of all amounts each of which is an amount in respect of the account

(a) included in the member's income under subsection (13) because of the application of subsection (14),

(b) included in the income of another taxpayer under subsection (16) or (18), or

(c) transferred in accordance with subsection (21) in circumstances described in subparagraph (21)(b)(iii); and

B is the total of all distributions made from the account after the member's death.

Related Provisions: 146(8.92) — Parallel rule for RRSP; 146.3(6.3) — Parallel rule for RRIF; 147.5(20) — Exception; 152(6)(f.3) — Reassessment to allow loss carryback; 257 — Formula cannot calculate to less than zero.

(20) Subsec. (19) not applicable — Except where the Minister has waived in writing the application of this subsection with respect to all or any portion of the amount determined in subsection (19) in respect of a member's account under a PRPP, that subsection does not apply if the last distribution from the account was made after the end of the calendar year following the year in which the member died.

(21) Transfer of amounts — An amount is transferred from a member's account under a PRPP in accordance with this subsection if the amount

(a) is a single amount;

(b) is transferred on behalf of an individual who

(i) is the member,

(ii) is a spouse or common-law partner or former spouse or common-law partner of the member and who is entitled to the amount under a decree, order or judgment of a competent tribunal, or under a written agreement, relating to a division of property between the member and the individual, in settlement of rights arising out of, or on a breakdown of, their marriage or common-law partnership, or

(iii) is entitled to the amount as a consequence of the death of the member and was a spouse or common-law partner of the member immediately before the death; and

(c) is transferred directly to

(i) the individual's account under the PRPP,

(ii) another PRPP in respect of the individual,

(iii) a registered pension plan for the benefit of the individual,

(iv) a registered retirement savings plan or registered retirement income fund under which the individual is the annuitant,

(v) a licensed annuities provider to acquire a qualifying annuity for the individual, or

(vi) a licensed annuities provider to acquire an advanced life deferred annuity for the benefit of the individual.

Related Provisions: 146(8.2)(b)(iii)(A) — Amount not eligible for RRSP overcontribution withdrawal; 146(21.2) — Sask. Pension Plan deemed RRSP for purposes of 147.5(21)(c); 147.5(22) — Effect of 147.5(21) applying; 147.5(23) — Where amount transferred to acquire qualifying annuity; 204.2(1.2)I(a)(iii) — Transfer under 147.5(21) excluded from cumulative excess RRSP amount; 205(1)"excess ALDA transfer" — Excessive transfer to advanced life deferred annuity; 248(8) — Meaning of "consequence" of death; 252(3) — Extended meaning of "spouse" and "former spouse"; Reg. 8502(b)(iv) — RPP may accept transfer.

Notes: 147.5(21)(c)(vi) added by 2021 budget bill #1, effective 2020. See 146.5.

Regulations: 216(2) (information return on transfer to ALDA).

Information Circulars: 13-1R1: Pooled registered pension plans.

(22) Taxation of transfers — If subsection (21) applies to an amount transferred from a member's account under a PRPP on behalf of an individual,

(a) the amount shall not, by reason only of that transfer, be included in computing the income of the individual; and

(b) no deduction may be made in respect of the amount in computing the income of any taxpayer.

Related Provisions: 212(1)(h)(iii.1) — Transfer under 147.5(21) exempt from non-resident withholding tax.

(23) Taxation of qualifying annuity — If an amount is transferred in accordance with subsection (21) to acquire a qualifying annuity, there shall be included — under this section and not under any other provision of this Act — in computing an individual's income for a taxation year any amount received by the individual during the year out of or under the annuity or as proceeds from a disposition in respect of the annuity.

(24) Notice of intent — The Minister may give notice (in subsections (25) and (26) referred to as a "notice of intent") to an administrator of a PRPP in writing that the Minister intends to revoke the registration of the plan as a PRPP if

(a) the plan does not comply with the conditions for registration in subsection (2);

(b) the plan is not administered in accordance with the terms of the plan as registered;

(c) the plan becomes a revocable plan;

(d) a condition imposed under subsection (6) that applies with respect to the plan is not complied with; or

(e) registration of the plan under the *Pooled Registered Pension Plans Act* or a similar law of a province is refused or revoked.

Related Provisions: 147.5(25) — Notice to specify date of revocation; 147.5(26), (27) — Revocation; 172(3)(h) — Appeal from notice.

(25) Date of revocation — The notice of intent shall specify the date on which revocation of a PRPP is to be effective, which date shall not be earlier than the earliest date on which one of the events described in subsection (24) occurs.

(26) Notice of revocation — At any time after 30 days after the day on which the notice of intent is mailed to an administrator of a PRPP, the Minister may give notice (in this subsection and in subsection (27) referred to as a "notice of revocation") in writing to the administrator that the registration of the PRPP is revoked as of the date specified in the notice of revocation and that date may not be earlier than the date specified in the notice of intent.

(27) Revocation of registration — If the Minister gives a notice of revocation to the administrator of a PRPP, the registration of the PRPP is revoked as of the date specified in the notice of revocation, unless the Federal Court of Appeal or a judge of that Court, on application made at any time before the determination of an appeal pursuant to subsection 172(3), orders otherwise.

(28) Voluntary revocation — If the administrator of a PRPP so requests in writing, the Minister may give notice in writing to the administrator that the registration of the PRPP is revoked as of a specified date and that date may not be earlier than the date specified in the administrator's request.

(29) Single employer — For the purposes of the definition "designated pooled pension plan" in subsection (1), all employers that are related to each other are deemed to be a single employer and all the structural units of a trade union, including each local, branch, national and international unit, are deemed to be a single employer.

Related Provisions: 252.1 — Union locals deemed to be single employer for other purposes.

(30) Significant interest — For the purposes of the definition "restricted investment" in subsection (1), a member of a pooled pension plan has a significant interest in a corporation, trust or partnership at any time if, at that time,

(a) in the case of a corporation, the member is a specified shareholder of the corporation; and

(b) in the case of a partnership or trust,

(i) the member is a specified unitholder of the partnership or the trust, as the case may be, or

(ii) the total fair market value of the member's interests in the partnership or the trust, as the case may be, together with all interests in the partnership or the trust held by persons or partnerships with whom the member does not deal at arm's length or is affiliated, is 10% or more of the fair market value of all interests in the partnership or the trust.

Information Circulars: 13-1R1: Pooled registered pension plans.

(31) Contributions from exempt income — Contributions may be made to a PRPP in respect of a member of the PRPP as if the member's earned income (as defined in subsection 146(1)) for a taxation year included the member's exempt earned income for the year.

Related Provisions: 147.5(32) — Contribution from exempt income is non-deductible.

Notes: See Notes to 147.5(32).

Forms: RC383: Tax-exempt earned income and contributions for a PRPP.

(32) Non-deductible contributions — A contribution made by a member of a PRPP to the member's account under the PRPP out of or from the member's exempt earned income may not be deducted in computing the income of the member for any taxation year.

Related Provisions: 147.5(1)"exempt-income contribution amount"(a) — Amount non-deductible due to subsec. (32).

Notes: Contributions from a status Indian's (untaxed) exempt income are non-deductible, and based on the "connecting factors" (see Notes to 81(1)(a)), the PRPP income when received as a pension will remain exempt. (The investment grows tax-free in the PRPP: 147.5(8).)

(32.1) [Returned] Contribution deemed not paid — Where a member of a PRPP or a participating employer in relation to the PRPP has, at any time in a taxation year, received a distribution from the member's account under the PRPP that is a return of a contribution described in clause 147.5(3)(d)(ii)(A) or (B), the contribution is deemed not to have been a contribution made by the member or the participating employer, as the case may be, to the PRPP to the extent that the contribution is not deducted in computing the taxpayer's income for the year or a preceding taxation year.

Notes: 147.5(32.1), added by 2017 budget bill #2 effective Dec. 14, 2012, provides that a refund of a contribution made to a PRPP by taxpayer T as a result of a reasonable error or a refund to avoid the revocation of the PRPP, which amount is not deducted as a PRPP contribution for the year in which the refund is made or any preceding taxation year, is deemed not to have been a contribution made by T to the PRPP. As a result, such amount is not a contribution for purposes of the deeming rule in 147.5(11) and provisions listed therein. This is relevant in particular for 146(5) and (5.1) and Part X.1, as these provisions apply because of 147.5(11) to PRPP contributions (i.e., generally deductible contributions and the tax on over-contributions). (Finance Technical Notes)

(33) Exempt contributions not over-contributions — For the purposes of Part X.1 as it applies because of subsection (11) in respect of contributions made to a PRPP,

(a) an individual's earned income (as defined in subsection 146(1)) for any taxation year after 2012 includes the individual's exempt earned income for that year;

(b) an individual's exempt-income contribution amount for any taxation year is deemed to have been deducted by the individual under subsection 146(5) in computing the individual's income for that year; and

(c) the description of D in paragraph (b) of the definition "unused RRSP deduction room" in subsection 146(1) is to be read without reference to subparagraph (iv).

(34) Designation of exempt-income contribution amount — A taxpayer may designate an amount as the taxpayer's exempt-income contribution amount for a taxation year if the amount designated does not exceed the lesser of

(a) the taxpayer's unused non-deductible PRPP room at the end of the preceding taxation year, and

(b) the total of the taxpayer's contributions as a member to a PRPP for the year (other than contributions to which subsection (32) applies).

Related Provisions: 147.5(1)"exempt-income contribution amount"(b) — Amount designated under subsec. (34).

(35) Regulations — other — The Governor in Council may make regulations

(a) prescribing conditions applicable to administrators;

(b) requiring administrators to file information returns respecting pooled pension plans;

(c) enabling the Minister to require any person to provide the Minister with information for the purposes and provisions of this Act relating to PRPPs; and

(d) generally to carry out the purposes and provisions of this Act relating to PRPPs.

Notes [s. 147.5]: A PRPP is a deferred income plan for employees and self-employed individuals who do not have a workplace pension. Because assets are pooled, it should offer RPP investment quality at lower administration costs. A PRPP is a defined-*contribution* plan administered by a licensed administrator (147.5(1)"administrator"), not managed by the employer. PRPPs are unlikely to become popular; RRSPs are simpler.

Once a member has a PRPP account, member and employer contributions are credited to it: 147.5(2)(b); funds are pooled with the other funds in the plan. They accumulate tax-free (147.5(8)) and must be used to provide retirement income: 147.5(5). Amounts paid out are included in income: 147.5(13).

An employer can enrol an employee, or if the employer chooses not to participate, an employee can open a PRPP directly with an administrator.

Employer contributions to an employee's PRPP account in a year or within 120 days after year-end are deductible: 147.5(10). Contributions can be made only up to the employee's RRSP dollar limit for the year, unless the employee provides written direction to contribute more: 147.5(3)(c). Employer contributions count against the employee's RRSP contribution limit for the year: 146(5)(b).

Employee (or self-employed member) contributions are deductible as RRSP contributions: 147.5(11), subject to the RRSP contribution limit for the year (see Notes to 146(1)"RRSP deduction limit") when combined with employer contributions.

See tinyurl.com/prpp-cra and Information Circular 13-1R1. For the list of PRPPs see tinyurl.com/prpp-list.

Until the provinces enact PRPP legislation, the only taxpayers who can join a PRPP are those employed under federal jurisdiction, such as banking or interprovincial transportation, and those employed or self-employed in Yukon, NWT and Nunavut. The provinces are at various stages in introducing and enacting PRPP legislation.

Finance announced on July 15, 2015 a proposal to streamline PRPP oversight by having the provinces agree to let the federal OSFI supervise them, and released a draft Multilateral Agreement Respecting Pooled Registered Pension Plans. Such an agreement was entered into by Canada, BC, Nova Scotia, Quebec and Saskatchewan: *Canada Gazette [CG]* Part I, June 25, 2016, pp. 2190-2202. *CG* Part I, June 18, 2016, p. 1994, states that the effective date for the agreement is June 15, 2016. Ontario joined in 2017: *CG* Part I, Jan. 14, 2017, p. 164.

See Finance news releases explaining PRPPs on fin.gc.ca: 2010-128 (Dec. 20/10); 2011-057 (July 18/11); 2011-100 (Oct. 14/11); 2011-111 (Nov. 4/11); 2011-119 (Nov. 17/11); 2011-134 (Dec. 14/11); 2012-008 (Jan. 27/12); 2012-019 (Feb. 24/12); 2012-067 (June 12/12); 2012-074 (June 28/12); 2012-080 (July 16/12); 2012-093 (Aug. 21/12); 2012-095 (Aug. 23/12); 2013-026 (Feb. 20/13). *Pooled Registered Pension Plans Act*, S.C. 2012, c. 16 (the non-tax provisions) received Royal Assent on June 28, 2012 and was proclaimed in force Dec. 14, 2012 by P.C. 2012-1743.

See also Cross & Nasrallah, "Pooled Registered Pension Plans", 22(10) *Taxation of Executive Compensation & Retirement* (Federated Press) 1420-24 (June 2011); Winfield, "Pooled Registered Pension Plans", 23(3) *TECR* 1451-53 (Oct. 2011); Griffin & Hnatiw, "Pooled Registered Pension Plans", 20(2) *Canadian Tax Highlights* (ctf.ca) 7-8 (Feb. 2012) and 20(3) 11-12 (March 2012); Ranger-Musiol, "Pooled Registered Pension Plans Are Coming", 23(6) *TECR* 1495-99 (Feb. 2012); Ideias, "Pooled Registered Pension Plans" (*Taxnet Pro* Tax & Estate Planning Centre, 2021, 8pp). For criticism see Pierlot & Laurin, *Pooled Registered Pension Plans: Pension Saviour — or a New Tax on the Poor?*, Commentary No. 359 (C.D. Howe Institute, Aug. 2012, 16pp); Allard, "Is Anyone Interested in PRPPs?", tinyurl.com/mccarthy-prpp.

CPP enhancements: Related to the PRPP, Canada and the provinces consulted on a possible voluntary supplement to the CPP. On June 20, 2016, Finance and 8 provinces announced increases in CPP coverage and contributions starting 2019, and consequential changes to allow a full deduction for the extra CPP contributions (60(e)(ii), 60(e.1)) and an increased Working Income Tax Benefit (122.7, now the Canada Workers Benefit). These changes reduce the need for provinces to introduce mandatory plans. All 9 CPP-participating provinces (Quebec has its own Quebec Pension Plan) agreed to the changes: "Prime Minister of Canada announces agreement on strengthened Canada Pension Plan" (Oct. 4, 2016); Drache, "Agreement in Principle on CPP Enhancement", xxxviii(14) *The Canadian Taxpayer* (Carswell) 105-107 (July 29, 2016).

Provincial plans: Ontario introduced the Ontario Retirement Pension Plan, a mandatory provincial pension plan for employees without a comparable workforce plan, but abandoned it in July 2016 due to the CPP enhancements.

Quebec has the so-called "voluntary retirement savings plan" (VRSP), really an "automatic unless you opt out" plan. Employers with 5 or more Quebec-based employees with at least 1 year of uninterrupted service (and no group RRSP or employer TFSA) are required to offer a VRSP (administered by a financial institution). Employer contributions are voluntary; employee contributions are automatic but the employee can opt out or withdraw the contributions. See Sheila Brawn, "Quebec's VRSP law stands out from other PRPPs", *Canadian Payroll Reporter* (Carswell), July 2014, pp. 1-3.

147.5 added by 2012 budget bill #2, effective Dec. 14, 2012 (proclamation of *Pooled Registered Pension Plans Act*: P.C. 2012-1743).

Definitions [s. 147.5]: "administrator" — 147.5(1); "advanced life deferred annuity" — 146.5(1), 248(1); "affiliated" — 251.1; "amount", "annuity" — 248(1); "arm's length" — 251(1); "beneficiary" — 248(25) [Notes]; "business" — 248(1); "calendar year" — *Interpretation Act* 37(1)(a); "capital gain" — 39(1)(a), 248(1); "capital loss" — 39(1)(b), 248(1); "child" — 252(1); "common-law partner", "common-law partnership" — 248(1); "consequence" — 248(8); "corporation" — 248(1), *Interpretation Act* 35(1); "designated pooled pension plan" — 147.5(1); "disposition", "employed", "employee", "employer" — 248(1); "estate" — 104(1), 248(1); "exempt earned income" — 147.5(1); "exempt income" — 248(1); "exempt-income contribution amount" — 147.5(1); "fair market value" — see 69(1) Notes; "Federal Court" — *Federal Courts Act* s. 4; "filing-due date" — 150(1), 248(1); "former spouse" — 252(3); "Governor in Council" — *Interpretation Act* 35(1); "individual", "legal representative" — 248(1); "licensed annuities provider" — 147(1), 248(1); "member" — 147.5(1); "minimum amount" — Reg. 8506(5); "Minister" — 248(1); "notice of intent" — 147.5(24); "PRPP" — 147.5(1)"pooled registered pension plan"; "participating employer" — 147.5(1); "partnership" — see 96(1) Notes; "person" — 248(1); "plan as registered" — 147.1(15); "pooled pension plan", "pooled registered pension plan" — 147.5(1); "prescribed", "property" — 248(1); "province" — *Interpretation Act* 35(1); "PRPP" — 147.5(1)"pooled registered pension plan"; "qualifying annuity", "qualifying survivor" — 147.5(1); "registered pension plan" — 248(1); "registered retirement income fund" — 146.3(1), 248(1); "registered retirement savings plan" — 146(1), 248(1); "regulation" — 248(1); "related" — 251(2)–(6); "resident in Canada" — 94(3)(a), 250; "restricted investment" — 147.5(1); "retirement savings plan" — 146(1), 248(1); "RRSP" — 248(1)"registered retirement savings plan"; "RRSP dollar limit" — 146(1), 248(1); "security" — *Interpretation Act* 35(1); "share" — 248(1); "significant interest" — 147.5(30); "single amount" — 147.5(1); "specified shareholder", "specified unitholder" — 248(1); "spouse" — 252(3); "successor member" — 147.5(1); "taxable income" — 2(2), 248(1); "taxation year" — 249; "taxpayer" — 248(1); "trust" — 104(1), 248(1), (3); "unused non-deductible PRPP room" — 147.5(1); "unused RRSP deduction room" — 146(1), 248(1); "written" — *Interpretation Act* 35(1)"writing".

Life Insurance Policies

148. (1) Amounts included in computing policyholder's income — There shall be included in computing the income for a taxation year of a policyholder in respect of the disposition of an interest in a life insurance policy, other than a policy that is or is issued pursuant to

    (a) a registered pension plan,

    (b) a registered retirement savings plan,

    (b.1) a registered retirement income fund,

    (b.2) a TFSA,

    (b.3) a pooled registered pension plan,

    (c) an income-averaging annuity contract,

    (d) a deferred profit sharing plan, or

    (e) an annuity contract if

        (i) the payment for the annuity contract was deductible under paragraph 60(l) in computing the policyholder's income,

        (i.1) the annuity contract is a qualifying trust annuity with respect to a taxpayer and the amount paid to acquire it was deductible under paragraph 60(l) in computing the taxpayer's income, or

        (ii) the policyholder acquired the annuity contract in circumstances to which subsection 146(21) applied,

the amount, if any, by which the proceeds of the disposition of the policyholder's interest in the policy that the policyholder, beneficiary or assignee, as the case may be, became entitled to receive in the year exceeds the adjusted cost basis to the policyholder of that interest immediately before the disposition.

Related Provisions: 20(1)(e.2) — Deduction for premiums on life insurance used as collateral; 56(1)(j) — Income inclusion — life insurance policy proceeds; 60(s) — Deduction of policy loan repayment; 138.1(7) — Where segregated fund policyholder deemed to be trust, etc.; 148(2) — Deemed proceeds of disposition; 148(7) — Disposition not at arm's length and similar cases; 148(9)"adjusted cost basis"C — Disposition amount included in AC basis; Reg. 304(1)(b) — Contract in 148(1)(c) or (e) is a prescribed annuity contract. See additional Related Provisions at end of s. 148.

Notes: If a life insurance policyholder surrenders a policy and receives the cash surrender value, that is a "disposition" under 148(9). If the "proceeds of the disposition" (148(9)) exceed the "adjusted cost basis" (148(9)), the excess is taxed under 148(1) and 56(1)(j), and cannot be treated as the underlying income such as dividend income: *Naidoo*, 2003 TCC 394; *Jarvis*, 2009 TCC 224; *Greenstreet*, 2019 TCC 237. Taking a

policy loan also triggers income inclusion: 148(9)"disposition"(b), "proceeds of disposition"(b); *Neszt*, 2019 TCC 139. See also Notes to 148(9)"value" and to Reg. 306(1). In *Andersen*, 2020 TCC 51, 148(1) did not apply because CRA's Reply did not plead an assumption about the amount of adjusted cost basis.

See VIEWS docs 2005-0145331E5, 2006-0181641E5, 2007-0230321E5, 2007-0257601E5, 2008-0269941M4, 2008-0301371E5, 2008-0303971E5, 2009-0312021E5, 2011-0404941E5, 2012-0438751E5, 2012-0443171E5, 2012-0446491E5, 2012-0464781E5, 2012-0460091E5, 2012-0473561E5, 2013-0477251M4, 2013-0481421C6, 2013-0483071M4, 2013-0515011E5; 2014-0524031E5 (grandfathered policy), 2014-0538281C6 [2014 APFF q.7]; 2014-0541941E5; 2016-0658641E5 (capitalized policy loan interest); 2018-0780421M4; and Notes to 148(9)"disposition". See also 148(8) where a policy is transferred to the policyholder's child. For an example of the calculation applying to a so-called "Return of Premium" benefit see *White*, 2008 TCC 414.

For planning see Marino & Natale, *Canadian Taxation of Life Insurance* (Carswell, 10th ed., 2020, 796pp.); *Miller Thomson on Estate Planning* (Carswell, looseleaf), chap. 15; all issues of *Insurance Planning* (Federated Press); Stephens, *Estate Planning with Life Insurance* (7th ed., CCH, 2019); Thomas, "Tax Consequences of Certain Transfers of Ownership of a Life Insurance Policy", XI(4) *Goodman on Estate Planning* (Federated Press) 904-07 (2003); Everett & Ireland, "Tax Planning Regarding the Ownership of Life Insurance", 52(3) *Canadian Tax Journal [CTJ]* 968-91 (2004); Cuperfain, "Leveraged Life Insurance", 2004 Cdn Tax Foundation conference report, 10:1-31; Corbin, "Pitfalls with Separate Insurance Trusts", 1(2) *It's Personal* (Carswell) 1-2 (April 2008); Goodman & Cuperfain, "Life Insurance Planning", 2008 conference report, 39:1-32; Giacomin, "Tax Planning with Life Insurance", 2009 Atlantic Provinces Tax Conf. 3A:1-17; Wark, "Life Insurance Planning Update", 2010 Ontario Tax Conf. 5:1-24; Thibault, "Life Insurance Taxation: An Update", 2010 Prairie Provinces Tax Conf. 9:1-16; Giacomin, "Tax Planning with Life Insurance", 2012 Atlantic Provinces Tax Conf. 7A:1-7; Goodman & Cuperfain, "Life Insurance Update", 60(4) *CTJ* 971-91 (2012); Everett, "Life Insurance Planning after the 2013 Budget", 2013 conference report, 32:1-23; Tehranchian, "Why Should a Corporation Own Life Insurance?", 8(2) *Taxes & Wealth Management* (Carswell) 3-4 (May 2015); McLeod, "Life Insurance: Why Would Your Owner-Manager Client Want It?", 16(3) *Tax for the Owner-Manager [TfOM]* (ctf.ca) 8-9 (July 2016); McLeod, "Transferring a Life Insurance Policy from a Corporation", 19(4) *TfOM* 9-10 (Oct. 2019).

For promoted schemes and CRA audit concerns see VIEWS docs 2018-0752971C6 [2018 CALU q.7], 2020-0842131C6 [2020 CALU q.1]; and Notes to 248(1)"LIA policy" (leveraged insurance annuities) and "10/8 policy".

A life insurer is required to pay a policy's surrender value to its owner, so this amount can be garnished under 224(1) if the owner owes tax (at least in Quebec, but likely common-law provinces too): *London Life*, 2014 FCA 106 (leave to appeal denied 2015 CarswellNat 95 (SCC)).

148(1)(e)(ii) permits a transfer of an amount from the Saskatchewan Pension Plan to acquire an annuity.

A "universal life" policy does not limit the amount an insured may invest in the "side account" without insurance: *Mosten Investment (Atwater, Ituna) v. Manufacturers Life*, 2021 SKCA 36 (see paras. 11-16 for explanation of ULPs).

See also Notes at end of s. 138.

148(1) amended by 2002-2013 technical bill (effective Sept. 1992), 2012 budget bill #2 (effective Dec. 14, 2012), 2008 budget bill #1, 1993 and 1992 technical bills.

Regulations: 217(2) (information return).

Interpretation Bulletins: IT-87R2: Policyholders' income from life insurance policies; IT-244R3: Gifts by individuals of life insurance policies as charitable donations; IT-379R: Employees profit sharing plans — allocations to beneficiaries.

(1.1) Amount included in computing taxpayer's income — There shall be included in computing the income for a taxation year of a taxpayer in respect of a disposition of an interest in a life insurance policy described in paragraph (e) of the definition "disposition" in subsection (9) the amount, if any, by which the amount of a payment described in paragraph (e) of that definition that the taxpayer became entitled to receive in the year exceeds the amount that would be the taxpayer's adjusted cost basis of the taxpayer's interest in the policy immediately before the disposition if, for the purposes of the definition "adjusted cost basis" in subsection (9), the taxpayer were, in respect of that interest in the policy, the policyholder.

Related Provisions: 56(1)(j) — Life insurance policy proceeds included in income. See also at end of s. 148.

Regulations: 217(2) (information return).

(2) Deemed proceeds of disposition — For the purposes of subsections (1) and 20(20) and the definition "adjusted cost basis" in subsection (9),

    (a) where at any time a policyholder becomes entitled to receive under a life insurance policy a particular amount as, on account of, in lieu of payment of or in satisfaction of, a policy dividend, the policyholder shall be deemed

(i) to have disposed of an interest in the policy at that time, and

(ii) to have become entitled to receive proceeds of the disposition equal to the amount, if any, by which

(A) the particular amount

exceeds

(B) the part of the particular amount applied immediately after that time to pay a premium under the policy or to repay a policy loan under the policy, as provided for under the terms and conditions of the policy;

(b) where in a taxation year a holder of an interest in, or a person whose life is insured or who is the annuitant under, a life insurance policy (other than an annuity contract or an exempt policy) last acquired after December 1, 1982 or an annuity contract (other than a life annuity contract, as defined by regulation, entered into before November 13, 1981 or a prescribed annuity contract) dies, the policyholder shall be deemed to have disposed of the policyholder's interest in the policy or the contract, as the case may be, immediately before the death;

(c) where, as a consequence of a death, a disposition of an interest in a life insurance policy is deemed to have occurred under paragraph (b), the policyholder immediately after the death shall be deemed to have acquired the interest at a cost equal to the accumulating fund in respect thereof, as determined in prescribed manner, immediately after the death;

(d) where at any time a life insurance policy last acquired after December 1, 1982, or a life insurance policy to which subsection 12.2(9) of the *Income Tax Act*, chapter 148 of the Revised Statutes of Canada, 1952, applies by virtue of paragraph 12.2(9)(b) of that Act, ceases to be an exempt policy (otherwise than as a consequence of the death of an individual whose life is insured under the policy or at a time when that individual is totally and permanently disabled), the policyholder shall be deemed to have disposed of the policyholder's interest in the policy at that time for proceeds of disposition equal to the accumulating fund with respect to the interest, as determined in prescribed manner, at that time and to have reacquired the interest immediately after that time at a cost equal to those proceeds; and

(e) a policyholder with an interest in a life insurance policy, issued after 2016, that gives rise to an entitlement (of the policyholder, beneficiary or assignee, as the case may be) to receive all or a portion of an excess described in subparagraph (iv) is deemed, at a particular time, to dispose of a part of the interest and to be entitled to receive proceeds of the disposition equal to that excess or portion, as the case may be, if

(i) the policy is an exempt policy,

(ii) a "benefit on death" (as defined in subsection 1401(3) of the *Income Tax Regulations*) under a "coverage" (as defined in section 310 of the *Income Tax Regulations* for the purposes of section 306 of the *Income Tax Regulations*) under the policy is paid at the particular time,

(iii) the payment results in the termination of the coverage but not the policy, and

(iv) the amount of the "fund value benefit" (as defined in subsection 1401(3) of the *Income Tax Regulations*) paid at the particular time in respect of the coverage exceeds the amount

(A) in the case where there is no "policy anniversary" (as defined in section 310 of the *Income Tax Regulations*) before the date of death of the individual whose life is insured under the coverage, that would be determined — on the policy anniversary that is on or that first follows that date of death and as though the coverage were not terminated — in respect of the coverage under subclause

(A)(I) of the description of B in subparagraph 306(4)(a)(iii) of the *Income Tax Regulations*, and

(B) in any other case, that is determined — on the last policy anniversary before the date of the death of the individual whose life is insured under the coverage — in respect of the coverage under subclause (A)(I) of the description of B in subparagraph 306(4)(a)(iii) of the *Income Tax Regulations* as it applies for the purpose of subparagraph 306(1)(b)(ii) of the *Income Tax Regulations*.

Related Provisions: 148(11) — Loss of pre-2016 grandfathering. See Related Provisions at end of s. 148.

Notes: For the application of 148(2)(b) and (c) to annuity contracts, see VIEWS doc 2004-0100241I7.

148(2)(e) amended by 2017 budget bill #2, effective Dec. 14, 2017. Before that date, read:

(e) if, in respect of a life insurance policy issued after 2016 that is an exempt policy, a benefit on death (as defined in subsection 1401(3) of the *Income Tax Regulations*) under a coverage (as defined in subsection 1401(3) of the *Income Tax Regulations*) under the policy is paid at any time, the payment results in the termination of the coverage but not the policy and the amount of the fund value benefit (as defined in subsection 1401(3) of the *Income Tax Regulations*) paid in respect of the coverage at that time exceeds the amount determined in respect of the coverage under subclause (A)(I) of the description of B in subparagraph 306(4)(a)(iii) of the *Income Tax Regulations* on the policy anniversary (as defined in section 310 of the *Income Tax Regulations*) that is on, or that first follows, the date of the death of an individual whose life is insured under the coverage, then a policyholder with an interest in the policy that gives rise to an entitlement (of the policyholder, beneficiary or assignee, as the case may be) to receive all or a portion of that excess, is deemed, at that time, to dispose of a part of the interest and to be entitled to receive proceeds of the disposition equal to that excess or portion, as the case may be.

148(2)(e) added by 2014 budget bill #2, effective Dec. 16, 2014.

148(2)(a)(ii) amended by 1992 technical bill, effective for policy dividends received or receivable in taxation years that begin after Dec. 20, 1991, to deal with the case where part of the policy dividend is automatically applied to pay a premium or repay a policy loan, as provided under the terms of the policy.

Regulations: 301 (life annuity contract); 304 (prescribed annuity contract); 307 (accumulating fund).

I.T. Application Rules: 69 (meaning of "chapter 148 of ...").

Interpretation Bulletins: IT-87R2: Policyholders' income from life insurance policies; IT-210R2: Income of deceased persons — periodic payments and investment tax credit; IT-430R3: Life insurance proceeds received by a private corporation or a partnership as a consequence of death.

(3) Special rules for certain policies — For the purposes of this section, where all or any part of an insurer's reserves for a life insurance policy vary in amount depending on the fair market value of a specified group of properties (in this subsection referred to as a "segregated fund"),

(a) in computing the adjusted cost basis of the policy,

(i) an amount paid by the policyholder or on the policyholder's behalf as or on account of premiums under the policy or to acquire an interest in the policy shall, to the extent that the amount was used by the insurer to acquire property for the purposes of the segregated fund, be deemed not to have been so paid, and

(ii) any transfer of property by the insurer from the segregated fund that resulted in an increase in the portion of its reserves for the policy that do not vary with the fair market value of the segregated fund shall be deemed to have been a premium paid under the policy by the policyholder; and

(b) the proceeds of the disposition of an interest in the policy shall be deemed not to include the portion thereof, if any, payable out of the segregated fund.

Notes: For CRA interpretation of 148(3) see VIEWS doc 2008-0301371E5.

(4) Partial surrender — ACB prorated — If a taxpayer disposes (other than because of paragraph (2)(a) or as described in paragraph (b) of the definition "disposition" in subsection (9)) of a part of the taxpayer's interest in a life insurance policy (other than an annuity contract) last acquired after December 1, 1982 or an annuity contract, the adjusted cost basis to the taxpayer, immediately before the disposition, of the part is the amount determined by the formula

$$A \times B/C$$

where

A is the adjusted cost basis to the taxpayer of the taxpayer's interest immediately before the disposition,

B is the proceeds of the disposition, and

C is

(a) if the policy is a policy (other than an annuity contract) issued after 2016, the amount determined by the formula

$$D - E$$

where

D is the interest's cash surrender value immediately before the disposition, and

E is the total of all amounts each of which is an amount payable, immediately before the disposition, by the taxpayer in respect of a policy loan in respect of the policy, and

(b) in any other case, the accumulating fund with respect to the taxpayer's interest, as determined in prescribed manner, immediately before the disposition.

Related Provisions: 257 — Formula cannot calculate to less than zero. See also Related Provisions at end of s. 148.

Notes: Where a policy acquired after Dec. 1, 1982 is partially surrendered, the ACB of the policy is normally prorated under 148(4); any gain resulting from the partial disposition is included in income under 148(1) and 56(1)(j): VIEWS doc 2006-0181641E5.

148(4) amended by 2014 budget bill #2, effective Dec. 16, 2014.

Regulations: 307 (accumulating fund).

Interpretation Bulletins: IT-87R2: Policyholders' income from life insurance policies.

(4.01) Repayment of policy loan on partial surrender — For the purposes of the definition "adjusted cost basis" in subsection (9) and paragraph 60(s), a particular amount is deemed to be a repayment made immediately before a particular time by a taxpayer in respect of a policy loan in respect of a life insurance policy if

(a) the policy is issued after 2016;

(b) the taxpayer disposes of a part of the taxpayer's interest in the policy at the particular time;

(c) paragraph (a) of the definition "proceeds of the disposition" in subsection (9) applies to determine the proceeds of the disposition of the interest;

(d) the particular amount is not

(i) otherwise a repayment by the taxpayer in respect of the policy loan, and

(ii) described in subparagraph (i) of the description of C in paragraph (a) of the definition "proceeds of the disposition" in subsection (9); and

(e) the amount payable by the taxpayer in respect of the policy loan is reduced by the particular amount as a consequence of the disposition.

Notes: 148(4.01) amended by 2017 budget bill #2, effective Dec. 14, 2017, to change "at" to "immediately before" in opening words, "immediately after" to "at" in para. (b), and to correct reference to 148(9)"adjusted cost basis"C(i) in (d)(ii) to 148(9)"proceeds of the disposition"(a)C(i).

148(4.01) added by 2014 budget bill #2, effective Dec. 16, 2014.

(4.1) [Repealed under former Act]

Notes: 148(4.1) repealed as of 1978.

(5) 10/8 policy surrender — If a policyholder has after March 20, 2013 and before April 2014 disposed of an interest in a 10/8 policy because of a partial or complete surrender of the policy, the policyholder may deduct in computing their income for the taxation

year in which the disposition occurs an amount that does not exceed the least of

(a) the portion of an amount, included under subsection (1) in computing their income for the year in respect of the disposition, that is attributable to an investment account described in paragraph (b) of the definition "10/8 policy" in subsection 248(1) in respect of the policy,

(b) the total of all amounts each of which is an amount, to the extent that the amount has not otherwise been included in determining an amount under this paragraph, of a payment made after March 20, 2013 and before April 2014 that reduces the amount outstanding of a borrowing or policy loan, as the case may be, described in paragraph (a) of the definition "10/8 policy" in subsection 248(1) in respect of the policy, and

(c) the total of all amounts each of which is an amount, to the extent that the amount has not otherwise been included in determining an amount under this paragraph, that the policyholder is entitled to receive as a result of the disposition and that is paid after March 20, 2013 and before April 2014 out of an investment account described in paragraph (b) of the definition "10/8 policy" in subsection 248(1) in respect of the policy.

Notes: See Notes to 248(1)"10/8 policy". 148(5) added by 2013 budget bill #2, for taxation years that end after March 20, 2013.

(6) Proceeds receivable as annuity — Where, under the terms of a life insurance policy (other than an annuity contract) last acquired before December 2, 1982, a policyholder became entitled to receive from the insurer at any time before the death of the person whose life was insured thereunder, all the proceeds (other than policy dividends) payable at that time under the policy in the form of an annuity contract or annuity payments,

(a) the payments shall be regarded as annuity payments made under an annuity contract;

(b) the purchase price of the annuity contract shall be deemed to be the adjusted cost basis of the policy to the policyholder immediately before the first payment under that contract became payable; and

(c) the annuity contract or annuity payments shall be deemed not to be proceeds of the disposition of an interest in the policy.

Related Provisions: 148(10)(b) — References to "person whose life was insured". See also at end of s. 148.

(7) Disposition at non-arm's length and similar cases — If an interest of a policyholder in a life insurance policy is, at any time (referred to in this subsection as the "disposition time"), disposed of (other than a disposition under paragraph (2)(b)) by way of a gift, by distribution from a corporation or by operation of law only to any person, or in any manner whatever to any person with whom the policyholder was not dealing at arm's length,

(a) the policyholder is deemed to become entitled to receive, at the disposition time, proceeds of the disposition equal to the greatest of

(i) the value of the interest at the disposition time,

(ii) an amount equal to

(A) if the disposition time is before March 22, 2016, nil, and

(B) if the disposition time is after March 21, 2016, the fair market value at the disposition time of the consideration, if any, given for the interest, and

(iii) an amount equal to

(A) if the disposition time is before March 22, 2016, nil, and

(B) if the disposition time is after March 21, 2016, the adjusted cost basis to the policyholder of the interest immediately before the disposition time;

(b) the person that acquires the interest because of the disposition is deemed to acquire it, at the disposition time, at a cost equal to the amount determined under paragraph (a) in respect of the disposition;

(c) in computing the paid-up capital in respect of each class of shares of the capital stock of a corporation at any time at or after the disposition time there shall be deducted the amount determined by the formula

$$(A - B \times C/D) \times E/A$$

where

A is the increase, if any, as a result of the disposition, in the paid-up capital in respect of all the shares of the capital stock of the corporation,

B is the amount determined under paragraph (a) in respect of the disposition,

C is

(i) if consideration is given for the interest, the fair market value at the disposition time of consideration that is shares of the capital stock of the corporation given for the interest, and

(ii) if no consideration is given for the interest, 1,

D is

(i) if consideration is given for the interest, the fair market value at the disposition time of the consideration given for the interest, and

(ii) if no consideration is given for the interest, 1, and

E is the increase, if any, as a result of the disposition, in the paid-up capital in respect of the class of shares, computed without reference to this paragraph as it applies to the disposition;

(d) any contribution of capital to a corporation or partnership in connection with the disposition is deemed, to the extent that it exceeds the amount determined under subparagraph (a)(i) in respect of the disposition, not to result in a contribution of capital for the purpose of applying paragraphs 53(1)(c) and (e) at or after the disposition time;

(e) any contributed surplus of a corporation that arose in connection with the disposition is deemed, to the extent that it exceeds the amount determined under subparagraph (a)(i) in respect of the disposition, not to be contributed surplus for the purpose of applying subsection 84(1) at or after the disposition time; and

(f) if the disposition time is before March 22, 2016,

(i) subparagraphs (ii) and (iii) and paragraphs (c) to (e) apply in respect of the disposition only if the disposition is after 1999 and at least one person whose life was insured under the policy before March 22, 2016 is alive on March 22, 2016,

(ii) in applying paragraphs (c) to (e) in respect of the disposition, a reference in those paragraphs to "the disposition time" is to be read as "the beginning of March 22, 2016",

(iii) if at any time (referred to in this subparagraph as the "conversion time") before March 22, 2016 the paid-up capital of a class of shares of the capital stock of a corporation was increased, the increase occurred as a result of any action by which the corporation converted any of its contributed surplus into paid-up capital in respect of the class of shares, the contributed surplus arose in connection with the disposition, and subsection 84(1) did not apply to deem the corporation to pay a dividend at the conversion time in respect of the increase, in computing the paid-up capital in respect of that class of shares after March 21, 2016, there shall be deducted the amount determined by the formula

$$(A - B \times A/D) \times C/A$$

where

A is the increase, if any, as a result of the conversion, in the paid-up capital in respect of all the shares of the capital stock of the corporation, computed without reference to this paragraph as it applies to the disposition,

B is the amount determined under subparagraph (a)(i) in respect of the disposition,

C is the increase, if any, as a result of the conversion, in the paid-up capital in respect of the class of shares, computed without reference to this paragraph as it applies to the disposition, and

D is the total amount of the corporation's contributed surplus that arose in connection with the disposition, and

(iv) if any consideration given for the interest includes a share of the capital stock of a corporation, the share (or a share substituted for the share) is disposed of (referred to in this subparagraph as the "share disposition") after March 21, 2016 by a taxpayer and subsection 84.1(1) applies in respect of the share disposition, then for the purposes of applying section 84.1, the adjusted cost base to the taxpayer of the share immediately before the share disposition is to be reduced by the amount determined by the formula

$$(A - B \times A/C)/D$$

where

A is the total of all amounts each of which is the fair market value at the disposition time of a share of that capital stock given as consideration for the interest,

B is the greater of the amount determined under subparagraph 148(7)(a)(i) in respect of the disposition and the adjusted cost basis to the policyholder of the interest immediately before the disposition,

C is the fair market value at the disposition time of the consideration, if any, given for the interest, and

D is the total number of shares of that capital stock given as consideration for the interest.

Related Provisions: 89(1)"capital dividend account"(d)(v) — Effect on CDA; 257 — Formula cannot calculate to less than zero. See also Related Provisions at end of s. 148.

Notes: See Notes to 148(1). Where a corporation transfers a policy on the life of an arm's length shareholder or employee to the insured, for proceeds equal to the fair market value of the policy, 148(7) will not apply, as the sale is not a "distribution": VIEWS doc 2003-0004285. For examples of 148(7) applying see 2006-0197211C6, 2008-0268631E5. Where the policy is donated to a charity see 2010-0363091C6, 2017-0705231C6 [2017 APFF q.9]. Transfer by way of dividend in kind: 2016-0671731E5, 2017-0690331C6 [2017 CLHIA q.2]; as payment of preferred share redemption proceeds, see 2018-0761521C6 [2018 APFF Financial q.1] (giving up share is "consideration" for 148(7)(b)(ii); also notes the inconsistent treatment is questionable and has been referred to Finance). Transfer from a corp can also trigger 6(1)(a), 15(1), 246(1) or GAAR: 2019-0799051C6 [2019 CLHIA q.2].

On a corporation windup to which 88(1) applies, 148(7) does not apply: VIEWS doc 2005-0116631C6; on an 88(2) windup, see 2016-0651761C6 [2016 APFF q.3]. On a criss-cross buy-sell life insurance arrangement, see 2009-0316671C6.

See Stephens, "Planning Issues Concerning the Transfer of Corporate-owned Life Insurance Policies", XXII(1) *Insurance Planning [IP]* (Federated Press) 2-7 (2017); Campagna, "Transferring Policies from One Corporation to Another", XXIII(3) *IP* 2-11 (2018); Stephens, "The Impact of an Amalgamation or Wind-up on Corporate-Owned Life Insurance", XXIV(2) *IP* 7-11 (2019); Stephens, "Transferring Personally-Owned Life Insurance Policies", XXIV(4) *IP* 2-7 (2019).

"Person" in 148(7) includes a partnership in CRA's view: doc 2007-0237291I7.

148(7) amended by 2016 budget bill #2, effective Dec. 15, 2016. Before that date, read:

(7) Where, otherwise than by virtue of a deemed disposition under paragraph (2)(b), an interest of a policyholder in a life insurance policy is disposed of by way of a gift (whether during the policyholder's lifetime or by the policyholder's will), by distribution from a corporation or by operation of law only to any person, or in any manner whatever to any person with whom the policyholder was not dealing at arm's length, the policyholder shall be deemed thereupon to become entitled to receive proceeds of the disposition equal to the value of the interest at the time of the disposition, and the person who acquires the interest by virtue of the disposition shall be deemed to acquire it at a cost equal to that value.

The amendment implements a change announced in the 2016 Budget, "to ensure that amounts are not inappropriately received tax-free by a policyholder as a result of a disposition of an interest in a life insurance policy". In applying the policy transfer rule in 148(7), the fair market value of any consideration given for an interest in a life insurance policy is now included in the policyholder's proceeds of the disposition and the acquiring person's cost. As well, where the disposition arises on a contribution of capital to a corporation or partnership, any resulting increase in the corporation's paid-up capital and the adjusted cost base of the shares (or of an interest in the partnership) is limited to the proceeds of the disposition. (Finance Technical Notes)

(8) Idem — Notwithstanding any other provision in this section, where

(a) an interest of a policyholder in a life insurance policy (other than an annuity contract) has been transferred to the policyholder's child for no consideration, and

(b) a child of the policyholder or a child of the transferee is the person whose life is insured under the policy,

the interest shall be deemed to have been disposed of by the policyholder for proceeds of the disposition equal to the adjusted cost basis to the policyholder of the interest immediately before the transfer, and to have been acquired by the person who acquired the interest at a cost equal to those proceeds.

Related Provisions: 148(8.1) — *Inter vivos* transfer to spouse; 148(8.2) — Transfer to spouse at death. See also at end of s. 148.

Notes: 148(8) does not apply to the transfer of a life insurance policy under which the life of more than one child is insured, despite *Interpretation Act* s. 33(2): VIEWS doc 2004-0065441C6. The child must be the only life insured under the policy at the time of the transfer: 2005-0125391E5. 148(8) applies to a transfer to the policyholder's child as subrogated policyholder under Quebec *Civil Code* art. 2446: 2005-0136701C6. 148(8) applies to a joint-last-to-die policy where the first life has died; and the "child" in para. (b) need not be the same child as in para. (a): 2005-0137151E5. 148(8) applies when the transfer is to a minor: 2008-0270431C6. 148(8) applies on transfer to a grandchild, due to 148(9)"child": 2008-0268631E5. 148(8) applies on parents' transfer of their joint interests in a policy on their son to that son: 2013-0481381E5. It applies on transfer of insurance on Child A to Child B (CRA is bringing this to Finance's attention as it may go against policy): 2018-0745831C6 [2018 CALU q.3].

148(8) extended by 1991 technical bill, effective for transfers and distributions in 1990 or later, to a spouse and former spouse.

Regulations: 6500(1) (prescribed provisions and prescribed class of persons, for former 148(8)(a)(iii)).

Interpretation Bulletins: IT-87R2: Policyholders' income from life insurance policies.

(8.1) *Inter vivos* transfer to spouse [or common-law partner] — Notwithstanding any other provision of this section, where

(a) an interest of a policyholder in a life insurance policy (other than a policy that is, or is issued under, a plan or contract referred to in any of paragraphs (1)(a) to (e)) is transferred to

(i) the policyholder's spouse or common-law partner, or

(ii) a former spouse or common-law partner of the policyholder in settlement of rights arising out of their marriage or common-law partnership, and

(iii) [Repealed]

(b) both the policyholder and the transferee are resident in Canada at the time of the transfer,

unless an election is made in the policyholder's return of income under this Part for the taxation year in which the interest was transferred to have this subsection not apply, the interest shall be deemed to have been disposed of by the policyholder for proceeds of the disposition equal to the adjusted cost basis to the policyholder of the interest immediately before the transfer and to have been acquired by the transferee at a cost equal to those proceeds.

Related Provisions: 73(1) — *Inter vivos* transfer of property of spouse, etc., or trust; 148(8.2) — Transfer to spouse at death; 252(3) — Extended meaning of "spouse" and "former spouse". See additional Related Provisions and Definitions at end of s. 148.

Notes: CRA stated in VIEWS doc 2001-0073505 that 148(8.1) does not apply where a life insurance contract owned by one spouse is split into two due to marriage breakdown, because a "transfer" of an interest in a life insurance policy cannot be said to have occurred when the result of the transactions is to create a new policy. See also 2012-0460091E5 (transfer of UK mortgage endowment policy under divorce settlement).

148(8.1) amended by 2000 same-sex partners bill (last change effective 2001) and 1992 technical bill. Added by 1991 technical bill.

Interpretation Bulletins: IT-87R2: Policyholders' income from life insurance policies.

(8.2) Transfer to spouse [or common-law partner] at death — Notwithstanding any other provision of this section, where, as a consequence of the death of a policyholder who was

resident in Canada immediately before the policyholder's death, an interest of the policyholder in a life insurance policy (other than a policy that is or is issued under a plan or contract referred to in any of paragraphs (1)(a) to (e)) is transferred or distributed to the policyholder's spouse or common-law partner who was resident in Canada immediately before the death, unless an election is made in the policyholder's return of income under this Part for the taxation year in which the policyholder died to have this subsection not apply, the interest shall be deemed to have been disposed of by the policyholder immediately before the death for proceeds of the disposition equal to the adjusted cost basis to the policyholder of the interest immediately before the transfer and to have been acquired by the spouse or common-law partner at a cost equal to those proceeds.

Related Provisions: 70(6) — Where transfer or distribution to spouse or trust; 148(9)"adjusted cost basis"G.1 — "adjusted cost basis"; 248(8) — Meaning of "consequence" of death; 252(3) — Extended meaning of "spouse". See also at end of s. 148.

Notes: 148(8.2) amended by 2000 same-sex partners bill (last change effective 2001). Added by 1991 technical bill.

Interpretation Bulletins: IT-87R2: Policyholders' income from life insurance policies.

(9) Definitions — In this section and paragraph 56(1)(d.1) of the *Income Tax Act*, chapter 148 of the Revised Statutes of Canada, 1952,

Related Provisions: 12.2(12) — Application of subsecs. 138(12) and 148(9). See also at end of s. 148.

Notes: The opening words of 148(9) redrafted in the RSC 1985 (5th Supp) consolidation for tax years ending after Nov. 1991. The former version made reference to section 12.2; that rule of application is now in 12.2(12).

I.T. Application Rules: 69 (meaning of "chapter 148 of ...").

Interpretation Bulletins: IT-379R: Employees profit sharing plans — allocations to beneficiaries.

"adjusted cost basis", at any time to a policyholder of the policyholder's interest in a life insurance policy, means the amount determined by the formula

$$(A + B + C + D + E + F + G + G.1) -$$
$$(H + I + J + K + L + M + N + O)$$

where

A is the total of all amounts each of which is the cost of an interest in the policy acquired by the policyholder before that time but not including an amount referred to in the description of B or E,

B is the total of all amounts each of which is an amount paid before that time by or on behalf of the policyholder in respect of a premium under the policy, other than amounts referred to in clause (2)(a)(ii)(B), in subparagraph (iii) of the description of C in paragraph (a) of the definition "proceeds of the disposition" or in subparagraph (b)(i) of that definition,

C is the total of all amounts each of which is an amount in respect of the disposition of an interest in the policy before that time that was required to be included in computing the policyholder's income or taxable income earned in Canada for a taxation year,

D is the total of all amounts each of which is an amount in respect of the policyholder's interest in the policy that was included by virtue of subsection 12(3) or section 12.2 or of paragraph 56(1)(d.1) of the *Income Tax Act*, chapter 148 of the Revised Statutes of Canada, 1952, in computing the policyholder's income for any taxation year ending before that time or the portion of an amount paid to the policyholder in respect of the policyholder's interest in the policy on which tax was imposed by virtue of paragraph 212(1)(o) before that time,

E is the total of all amounts each of which is an amount that is in respect of the repayment, before that time and after March 31, 1978, of a policy loan and that does not exceed the amount determined by the formula,

$$E.1 - E.2$$

where

E.1 is the total of

(a) the proceeds of the disposition, if any, in respect of the loan,

(b) if the policy is issued after 2016 (and, in the case where the particular time at which the policy is issued is determined under subsection (11), the repayment is at or after the particular time), the portion of the loan applied, immediately after the loan, to pay a premium under the policy as provided for under the terms and conditions of the policy (except to the extent that the portion is described in subparagraph (i) of the description of C in paragraph (a) of the definition "proceeds of the disposition" in this subsection), and

(c) the amount, if any, described in the description of J in this definition (but not including any payment of interest) in respect of the loan, and

E.2 is the total all amounts each of which is an amount in respect of a repayment, of the loan, referred to in clause (2)(a)(ii)(B) or deductible under paragraph 60(s) of this Act or paragraph 20(1)(hh) of the *Income Tax Act*, chapter 148 of the *Revised Statutes of Canada*, 1952 (as it applied in taxation years before 1985),

F is the amount, if any, by which the cash surrender value of the policy as at its first anniversary date after March 31, 1977 exceeds the adjusted cost basis (determined under the *Income Tax Act*, chapter 148 of the Revised Statutes of Canada, 1952, as it would have read on that date if subsection 148(8) of that Act, as it read in its application to the period ending immediately before April 1, 1978, had not been applicable) of the policyholder's interest in the policy on that date,

G is, in the case of an interest in a life annuity contract, as defined by regulation, to which subsection 12.2(1) applies for the taxation year that includes that time (or would apply if the contract had an anniversary day in the year at a time when the taxpayer held the interest), the total of all amounts each of which is a mortality gain, as defined by regulation and determined by the issuer of the contract in accordance with the regulations, in respect of the interest immediately before the end of the calendar year ending in a taxation year commencing before that time,

G.1 is, in the case of an interest in a life insurance policy (other than an annuity contract) to which subsection (8.2) applied before that time, the total of all amounts each of which is a mortality gain, as defined by regulation and determined by the issuer of the policy in accordance with the regulations, in respect of the interest immediately before the end of the calendar year that ended in a taxation year that began before that time,

H is the total of all amounts each of which is the proceeds of the disposition of the policyholder's interest in the policy that the policyholder became entitled to receive before that time,

I is the total of all amounts each of which is an amount in respect of the policyholder's interest in the policy that was deducted by virtue of subsection 20(19) in computing the policyholder's income for any taxation year commencing before that time,

J is the amount payable on March 31, 1978 in respect of a policy loan in respect of the policy,

K is the total of all amounts each of which is an amount received before that time in respect of the policy that the policyholder was entitled to deduct under paragraph 60(a) in computing the policyholder's income for a taxation year,

L is

(a) in the case of an interest in a life insurance policy (other than an annuity contract) that was last acquired after December 1, 1982 by the policyholder, the total of all amounts each of which is the net cost of pure insurance, as defined by regulation and determined by the issuer of the policy in accordance with the regulations, in respect of the interest immediately before the end of the calendar year ending in a taxation year commencing after May 31, 1985 and before that time,

(b) in the case of an interest in an annuity contract to which subsection 12.2(1) applies for the taxation year that includes that time (or would apply if the contract had an anniversary day in the year and while the taxpayer held the interest), the total of all annuity payments paid in respect of the interest before that time and while the policyholder held the interest, or

(c) in the case of an interest in a contract referred to in the description of G, the total of all amounts each of which is a mortality loss, as defined by regulation and determined by the issuer of the contract in accordance with the regulations, in respect of the interest before that time;

M is, in the case of a policy that is issued after 2016 and is not an annuity contract, the total of all amounts each of which is a premium paid by or on behalf of the policyholder, or a cost of insurance charge incurred by the policyholder, before that time (and, in the case where the particular time at which the policy is issued is determined under subsection (11), at or after the particular time), to the extent that the premium or charge is in respect of a benefit under the policy other than a benefit on death (as defined in subsection 1401(3) of the *Income Tax Regulations*),

N is, in the case of a policy that is issued after 2016 and is not an annuity contract, the total of all amounts each of which is the policyholder's interest in an amount paid — to the extent that the cash surrender value of the policy, if any, or the fund value of the policy (as defined in subsection 1401(3) of the *Income Tax Regulations*), if any, is reduced by the amount paid — before that time (and, in the case where the particular time at which the policy is issued is determined under subsection (11), at or after the particular time) that

(a) is a benefit on death (as defined in subsection 1401(3) of the *Income Tax Regulations*), or a disability benefit, under the policy, and

(b) does not result in the termination of a coverage (as defined in subsection 1401(3) of the *Income Tax Regulations*) under the policy,

O is, in the case of a policy that is issued after 2016 and is not an annuity contract, the total of all amounts each of which is — if a "benefit on death" (as defined in subsection 1401(3) of the *Income Tax Regulations*) under a "coverage" (as defined in section 310 of the *Income Tax Regulations* for the purposes of section 306 of the *Income Tax Regulations*) under the policy is paid before that time as a consequence of the death of an individual whose life is insured under the coverage (and, in the case where the particular time at which the policy is issued is determined under subsection (11), at or after the particular time) and the payment results in the termination of the coverage — the amount, if any, determined with respect to the coverage by the formula

$$[P \times (Q + R + S)/T] - U$$

where

P is the adjusted cost basis of the policyholder's interest immediately before the termination,

Q is the amount of the "fund value benefit" (as defined in subsection 1401(3) of the *Income Tax Regulations*) under the policy paid in respect of the "coverage" (as defined in section 310 of the *Income Tax Regulations* for the purposes of section 306 of the *Income Tax Regulations*) on the termination,

R is the total of all amounts — each of which is in respect of a "coverage" (as defined in subsection 1401(3) of the *Income Tax Regulations*) in respect of a specific life or two or more specific lives jointly insured under the coverage referred to in the description of O — that would be the present value, determined for the purposes of section 307 of the *Income Tax Regulations*, on the last "policy anniversary" (as defined in section 310 of the *Income Tax Regulations*) on or before the termination, of the "fund value of the coverage" (as defined in subsection 1401(3) of the *Income Tax Regulations*) if the fund value of the coverage on that policy anniversary were equal to the fund value of the coverage on the termination,

S is the total of all amounts — each of which is in respect of a "coverage" (as defined in subsection 1401(3) of the *Income Tax Regulations* and referred to in this description as a "particular coverage") in respect of a specific life or two or more specific lives jointly insured under the coverage referred to in the description of O — that would be determined, on that policy anniversary, for paragraph (a) of the description of C in the definition "net premium reserve" in subsection 1401(3) of the *Income Tax Regulations* in respect of the particular coverage, if the benefit on death under the particular coverage, and the "fund value of the coverage" (as defined in subsection 1401(3) of the *Income Tax Regulations*), on that policy anniversary were equal to the benefit on death under the particular coverage and the fund value of the coverage, as the case may be, on the termination,

T is the amount that would be, on that policy anniversary, the "net premium reserve" (as defined in subsection 1401(3) of the *Income Tax Regulations*) in respect of the policy for the purposes of section 307 of the *Income Tax Regulations*, if the "fund value benefit" (as defined in subsection 1401(3) of the *Income Tax Regulations*) under the policy, the benefit on death under each "coverage" (as defined in subsection 1401(3) of the *Income Tax Regulations*) and the fund value of each coverage (as defined in subsection 1401(3) of the *Income Tax Regulations*) on that policy anniversary were equal to the fund value benefit, the benefit on death under each coverage and the fund value of each coverage, as the case may be, under the policy on the termination, and

U is the amount, if any, determined under subsection (4) in respect of a disposition before that time of the interest because of paragraph (2)(e) in respect of the payment in respect of the fund value benefit under the policy paid in respect of the "coverage" (as defined in section 310 of the *Income Tax Regulations* for the purposes of section 306 of the *Income Tax Regulations*) on the termination;

Related Provisions: 12.2(5) — Amounts included in income — taxpayer's interest in an annuity contract; 148(2) — Deemed proceeds of disposition; 148(4) — ACB prorated on partial surrender; 148(4.01) — Repayment of policy loan on partial surrender; 148(11) — Loss of pre-2016 grandfathering; 257 — Formula cannot calculate to less than zero. See also at end of s. 148.

Notes: See Notes to 148(1). The adjusted cost basis (not to be confused with "adjusted cost base" of capital property under s. 54) is, in simplest terms, any amount paid to acquire the policy (A), plus premiums paid (B), plus various amounts included in income in respect of the policy (C, D). It is reduced by the proceeds of disposition of an interest in the policy (H) and various other amounts. For examples see *White*, 2008 TCC 414; *Kratochwil*, 2012 TCC 45.

See Everett, "Adjusted Cost Basis", XI(1) *Insurance Planning* (Federated Press) 674-77 (2004); Marino, "Life Insurance and Return of Premium Benefits", XV(3) *IP* 962-65 (2009) [re *White* and *Brousseau* cases]. Where an insurance advisor pays a rebate to the policyholder, nothing permits reduction of the adjusted cost basis: VIEWS doc 2010-0359401C6. See also 9423417, 2006-0175121C6, 2006-02109431E5, 2008-0264301E5; and *Brousseau*, 2006 TCC 646, where the net cost of pure insurance (Reg. 308(1)) was deducted from the adjusted cost basis as per formula element L. A disposition of an exempt policy was taxable despite para. (j) because the death was of the insured's spouse, who was not insured: doc 2008-0274111E5 (the TCC case referred to therein appears to be unreported).

Definition amended by 2017 budget bill #2, effective Dec. 14, 2017, to add "paragraph (a) of" in para. E.1(b), and to amend O opening words and Q-U. Before that date, read:

O is, in the case of a policy that is issued after 2016 and is not an annuity contract, the total of all amounts each of which is — if a benefit on death (as defined in subsection 1401(3) of the *Income Tax Regulations*) under a coverage (as defined in subsection 1401(3) of the *Income Tax Regulations*) under the policy is paid before that time (and, in the case where the particular time at which the policy is issued is determined under subsection (11), at or after the particular time) and the payment results in the termination of the coverage — the amount, if any, determined with respect to the coverage by the formula

. . . . .

Q is the amount of the fund value benefit (as defined in subsection 1401(3) of the *Income Tax Regulations*) under the policy paid in respect of the coverage on the termination,

R is the amount that would be the present value, determined for the purposes of section 307 of the *Income Tax Regulations*, on the last policy anniversary (as defined in section 310 of the *Income Tax Regulations*) on or before the termination, of the fund value of the coverage (as defined in subsection 1401(3) of the *Income Tax Regulations*) if the fund value of the coverage on that policy anniversary were equal to the fund value of the coverage on the termination,

S is the amount that would be determined, on that policy anniversary, for paragraph (a) of the description of C in the definition "net premium reserve" in subsection 1401(3) of the *Income Tax Regulations* in respect of the coverage, if the benefit on death under the coverage, and the fund value of coverage, on that policy anniversary were equal to the benefit on death under the coverage and the fund value of the coverage, as the case may be, on the termination,

T is the amount that would be, on that policy anniversary, the net premium reserve (as defined in subsection 1401(3) of the *Income Tax Regulations*) in respect of the policy for the purposes of section 307 of the *Income Tax Regulations*, if the fund value benefit under the policy, the benefit on death under each coverage and the fund value of each coverage on that policy anniversary were equal to the fund value benefit, the benefit on death under each coverage and the fund value of each coverage, as the case may be, under the policy on the termination, and

U is the amount, if any, determined under subsection (4) in respect of a disposition before that time of the interest because of paragraph (2)(e) in respect of the payment in respect of the fund value benefit under the policy paid in respect of the coverage on the termination;

Definition amended by 2014 budget bill #2, effective Dec. 16, 2014: in opening words, changed "to a policyholder as at a particular time" to "at any time to a policyholder"; in formula, added "M+N+O"; amended E; added E.1, E.2, M, N, O, P, Q, R, S, T and U. The amendment clarifies the definition's application to certain policy transactions involving the repayment of a policy loan, premiums or cost of insurance charges for ancillary benefits (benefits other than the benefit on death), capital disability or death benefits (savings paid as death or disability benefits that do not result in termination of a coverage) and benefits on death resulting in the termination of a coverage under the policy (but not of the policy itself). (Finance Technical Notes)

Description of G, and para. L(b) (formerly 148(9)(a)(v.1) and (x)), amended by 1989 Budget and 1991 technical bill, for policies last acquired in 1990 or later. For earlier policies read:

G is, in the case of an interest in a life annuity contract, as defined by regulation, to which subsection 12.2(1) or (3) applies for the taxation year that includes that time, the total of all amounts each of which is a mortality gain, as defined by regulation and determined by the issuer of the contract in accordance with the regulations, in respect of the interest immediately before the end of the calendar year ending in a taxation year commencing before that time.

. . . . .

(b) in the case of an interest in an annuity contract to which subsection 12.2(1) or (3) applies, the total of all amounts each of which is an annuity payment paid in respect of the interest before that time and while the policyholder held the interest, or

148(9)"adjusted cost basis" was 148(9)(a) before RSC 1985 (5th Supp) consolidation for tax years ending after Nov. 1991. B and E amended, and G.1 added, by 1992 technical bill.

Regulations: 301 (life annuity contract — for 148(9)"adjusted cost basis"G); 308 (net cost of pure insurance — for 148(9)"adjusted cost basis"L(a)).

I.T. Application Rules: 69 (meaning of "chapter 148 of ...").

Interpretation Bulletins: IT-87R2: Policyholders' income from life insurance policies; IT-149R4: Winding-up dividend; IT-355R2: Interest on loans to buy life insurance policies and annuity contracts, and interest on policy loans (cancelled); IT-430R3: Life insurance proceeds received by a private corporation or a partnership as a consequence of death. See additional Related Provisions and Definitions at end of s. 148.

"amount payable", in respect of a policy loan, has the meaning assigned by subsection 138(12);

Notes: 148(9)"amount payable" was 148(9)(a.1) before RSC 1985 (5th Supp) consolidation for tax years ending after Nov. 1991.

"cash surrender value" at a particular time of a life insurance policy means its cash surrender value at that time computed without regard to any policy loans made under the policy, any policy dividends (other than paid-up additions) payable under the policy or any interest payable on those dividends;

Related Provisions: Reg. 1408(1)"cash surrender value" — Definition applies for policy reserve calculation.

Notes: 148(9)"cash surrender value" was 148(9)(b) before RSC 1985 (5th Supp) consolidation for tax years ending after Nov. 1991.

"child" of a policyholder includes a child as defined in subsection 70(10);

Related Provisions: 252(1) — Extended meaning of "child".

Notes: 148(9)"child" was 148(9)(b.1) before RSC 1985 (5th Supp) consolidation for tax years ending after Nov. 1991.

"disposition", in relation to an interest in a life insurance policy, includes

(a) a surrender thereof,

(b) a policy loan made after March 31, 1978,

(c) the dissolution of that interest by virtue of the maturity of the policy,

(d) a disposition of that interest by operation of law only, and

(e) the payment by an insurer of an amount (other than an annuity payment, a policy loan or a policy dividend) in respect of a policy (other than a policy described in paragraph (1)(a), (b), (c), (d) or (e)) that is a life annuity contract, as defined by regulation, entered into after November 16, 1978, and before November 13, 1981,

but does not include

(f) an assignment of all or any part of an interest in the policy for the purpose of securing a debt or a loan other than a policy loan,

(g) a lapse of the policy in consequence of the premiums under the policy remaining unpaid, if the policy was reinstated not later than 60 days after the end of the calendar year in which the lapse occurred,

(h) a payment under a policy as a disability benefit or as an accidental death benefit,

(i) an annuity payment,

(j) a payment under a life insurance policy (other than an annuity contract) that

(i) was last acquired before December 2, 1982, or

(ii) is an exempt policy

in consequence of the death of any person whose life was insured under the policy, or

(k) any transaction or event by which an individual becomes entitled to receive, under the terms of an exempt policy, all of the proceeds (including or excluding policy dividends) payable under the policy in the form of an annuity contract or annuity payments, if, at the time of the transaction or event, the individual whose life is insured under the policy was totally and permanently disabled;

Related Provisions: 60(s) — Deduction of policy loan repayment; 148(4) — ACB prorated on partial surrender; 148(10)(b) — References to "person whose life was insured"; 248(1)"disposition"(b.1) — Definition applies to entire Act; 248(8) — Meaning of "consequence" of death.

Notes: See Notes to 148(1). For "includes" in the opening words, see 188.1(5) Notes.

On a joint last-to-die policy, CRA agrees that payment of the cash surrender value on the first death is not a "disposition" (**DSP**) and so is tax-free: doc 2000-0033885 (reversing 2000-0014250). On whether there is a DSP on various amendments to a last-to-die policy, see 2003-0042861E5.

Capitalization of interest on a policy loan by issuing a new policy loan triggers para. (b): 2009-0319451E5. For para. (d), see 2007-0257251E5; para. (h), 2007-0257591E5; para. (j), 2012-0446491E5, 2020-0842141C6 [2020 CALU q.2]; para. (k), 2009-0308411E5.

A life insurer may lend from its general funds to a terminally ill policyholder, secured by assignment of the policy (as approved by the Ontario Financial Services Commission). Provided there is no amendment to the policy, and the loan is not provided under the policy's terms (which would make it a "policy loan"), CRA's view is that such loan does not cause a DSP: VIEWS doc 2002-0138895.

Where a terminally ill person "sells" their policy for cash by designating another person as beneficiary, CRA considers this a DSP, so 148(1) includes the proceeds in income. This is an exception to the administrative rule that a change of beneficiary is not a disposition. See VIEWS doc 9828187F; Chu, "Viatical Settlements", 1858 *Tax Topics* (CCH) 1-4 (Oct. 18, 2007).

If, as an alternative to cashing in the policy, the insured effectively donates it to a charity by designating the charity as beneficiary, see 118.1(5.2)(a).

148(9)"disposition" was 148(9)(c) before RSC 1985 (5th Supp) consolidation for tax years ending after Nov. 1991.

Regulations: 301 (life annuity contract — for 148(9)"disposition"(e)).

Interpretation Bulletins: IT-87R2: Policyholders' income from life insurance policies.

"interest", in relation to a policy loan, has the meaning assigned by subsection 138(12);

Notes: 148(9)"interest" was 148(9)(c.1) before RSC 1985 (5th Supp) consolidation for tax years ending after Nov. 1991.

"life insurance policy" — [Repealed under former Act]

Notes: 148(9)(d), repealed in 1985, defined "life insurance policy" and "relevant authority". These definitions are now found in 248(1) and 148(9)"relevant authority" respectively.

"policy loan" means an amount advanced by an insurer to a policyholder in accordance with the terms and conditions of the life insurance policy;

Related Provisions: 138(12)"policy loan" — Similar definition for s. 138.

Notes: 148(9)"policy loan" was 148(9)(e) before RSC 1985 (5th Supp) consolidation for tax years ending after Nov. 1991.

"premium" under a policy includes

(a) interest paid after 1977 to a life insurer in respect of a policy loan, other than interest deductible in the 1978 or any subsequent taxation year pursuant to paragraph 20(1)(c) or (d), and

(b) a prepaid premium under the policy to the extent that it cannot be refunded otherwise than on termination or cancellation of the policy,

but does not include

(c) the portion of any amount paid under the policy with respect to an accidental death benefit, a disability benefit, an additional risk as a result of insuring a substandard life, an additional risk in respect of the conversion of a term policy into another policy after the end of the year, an additional risk under a settlement option, or an additional risk under a guaranteed insurability benefit, if

(i) in the case of an annuity contract, a policy issued before 2017 or in respect of which the particular time at which the policy is issued is determined under subsection (11), where the interest in the policy was last acquired after December 1, 1982, the payment is made after May 31, 1985 and, if the particular time at which the policy is issued is determined under subsection (11), before the particular time, or

(ii) in the case where the taxpayer's interest in the policy was last acquired before December 2, 1982,

(A) subsection 12.2(9) of the *Income Tax Act*, chapter 148 of the *Revised Statutes of Canada*, 1952, applies to the interest,

(B) the particular time at which the policy is issued is determined under subsection (11), and

(C) the payment is made in the period that starts at the later of May 31, 1985 and the first time at which that subsection 12.2(9) applies in respect of the interest and that ends at the particular time;

Related Provisions: 60(s) — Repayment of policy loan. See additional Related Provisions at end of s. 148.

Notes: On premiums paid under a universal life insurance policy where the life insured is a substandard risk, see VIEWS doc 2006-0175121C6.

For the meaning of "issued before 2017" in (c)(i), see Notes to 148(11).

Para. (c) amended by 2014 budget bill #2, effective Dec. 16, 2014. 148(9)"premium" was 148(9)(e.1) before RSC 1985 (5th Supp) consolidation for tax years ending after Nov. 1991.

"proceeds of the disposition" of an interest in a life insurance policy means the amount of the proceeds that the policyholder, beneficiary or assignee, as the case may be, is entitled to receive on a disposition of an interest in the policy and for greater certainty,

(a) in respect of a surrender or maturity thereof, means the amount determined by the formula

$$(A - B) - C$$

where

A is the cash surrender value of that interest in the policy at the time of surrender or maturity,

B is that portion of the cash surrender value represented by A that is applicable to the policyholder's interest in the related segregated fund trust as referred to in paragraph 138.1(1)(e), and

C is the total of amounts each of which is

(i) an amount by which the amount payable in respect of a policy loan in respect of the policy is reduced as a consequence of the disposition, except that if the policy is issued after 2016 and the disposition is of a part of the interest (and, in the case where the particular time at which the policy is issued is determined under subsection (11), the disposition occurs at or after the particular time), only to the extent that the amount represents the portion of the loan applied, immediately after the loan, to pay a premium under the policy, as provided for under the terms and conditions of the policy,

(ii) a premium under the policy that is due but unpaid at that time, or

(iii) an amount applied, immediately after the time of the surrender, to pay a premium under the policy, as provided for under the terms and conditions of the policy,

(b) in respect of a policy loan made after March 31, 1978 means the lesser of

(i) the amount of the loan, other than the part thereof applied, immediately after the loan, to pay a premium under the policy, as provided for under the terms and conditions of the policy, and

(ii) the amount, if any, by which the cash surrender value of the policy immediately before the loan was made exceeds the total of the balances outstanding at that time of any policy loans in respect of the policy,

(c) in respect of a payment described in paragraph (e) of the definition "disposition" in this subsection, means the amount of that payment, and

(d) in respect of a disposition deemed to have occurred under paragraph (2)(b), means the accumulating fund in respect of the interest, as determined in prescribed manner,

(i) immediately before the time of death in respect of a life insurance policy (other than an annuity contract) last acquired after December 1, 1982, or

(ii) immediately after the time of death in respect of an annuity contract;

Related Provisions: 148(4) — ACB prorated on partial surrender; 257 — Formula cannot calculate to less than zero. See also at end of s. 148.

Notes: Definition amended by 2014 budget bill #2 (effective Dec. 16, 2014); 1992 technical bill (for policy loans made in tax years beginning after Dec. 20, 1991). 148(9)"proceeds of the disposition" was 148(9)(e.2) before RSC 1985 (5th Supp) consolidation for tax years ending after Nov. 1991.

"relevant authority" — [Repealed]

Notes: Definition "relevant authority" repealed by 1996 Budget, effective April 25, 1997 (Royal Assent). It was defined with reference to the definition in 138(12), now also repealed. The only place it was used was in 148(5), a rule for computing a foreign tax credit in respect of allocations from a segregated fund, which was repealed long ago. The term is also defined in Reg. 1408(1).

148(9)"relevant authority" was 148(9)(e.3) before RSC 1985 (5th Supp) consolidation for tax years ending after Nov. 1991.

"tax anniversary date", in relation to a life insurance policy, means the second anniversary date of the policy to occur after October 22, 1968;

Notes: 148(9)"tax anniversary date" was 148(9)(f) before RSC 1985 (5th Supp) consolidation for tax years ending after Nov. 1991.

"value" at a particular time of an interest in a life insurance policy means

(a) where the interest includes an interest in the cash surrender value of the policy, the amount in respect thereof that the holder of the interest would be entitled to receive if the policy were surrendered at that time, and

(b) in any other case, nil.

Notes: It is unclear whether surrender charges can be deducted in computing "value" for purposes of a 148(7) disposition: VIEWS doc 2008-0270411C6. Fees for valuing the policy on transfer are not deducted: 2011-0408351C6. For the "value" on a criss-cross buy-sell insurance arrangement, see 2009-0316671C6. For the value for purposes of 233.3(3), see 2011-0399441C6. For the fair market value of a life insurance policy, see Notes to 69(1).

148(9)"value" was 148(9)(g) before RSC 1985 (5th Supp) consolidation for tax years ending after Nov. 1991.

(9.1) Application of subsec. 12.2(11) — The definitions in subsection 12.2(11) apply to this section.

Notes: 148(9.1) added in the RSC 1985 (5th Supp) consolidation for tax years ending after Nov. 1991. It was formerly in the opening words of 12.2(11).

(10) Life annuity contracts — For the purposes of this section,

(a) a reference to "insurer" or "life insurer" shall be deemed to include a reference to a person who is licensed or otherwise authorized under a law of Canada or a province to issue contracts that are annuity contracts;

(b) a reference to a "person whose life was insured" shall be deemed to include a reference to an annuitant under a life annuity contract, as defined by regulation, entered into before November 17, 1978;

(c) where a policyholder is a person who has held an interest in a life insurance policy continuously since its issue date, the interest shall be deemed to have been acquired on the later of the date on which

(i) the policy came into force, and

(ii) the application in respect of the policy signed by the policyholder was filed with the insurer;

(d) except as otherwise provided, a policyholder shall be deemed not to have disposed of or acquired an interest in a life insurance policy (other than an annuity contract) as a result only of the exercise of any provision (other than a conversion into an annuity contract) of the policy; and

(e) where an interest in a life insurance policy (other than an annuity contract) last acquired before December 2, 1982 to which subsection 12.2(9) of the *Income Tax Act*, chapter 148 of the Revised Statutes of Canada, 1952, does not apply has been acquired by a taxpayer from a person with whom the taxpayer was not dealing at arm's length, the interest shall be deemed to have been last acquired by the taxpayer before December 2, 1982.

Related Provisions: 12.2(13) — Application of subsec. 148(10); 56(1)(j) — Life insurance policy proceeds. See also below.

Notes: For interpretations of 148(10)(d) see VIEWS docs 2005-0160761E5, 2005-0164711C6, 2007-0229771C6; 2015-0608261E5 (148(10)(d) cannot be used to split a multiple life policy into several policies).

The opening words of 148(10) redrafted in the RSC 1985 (5th Supp) consolidation for tax years ending after Nov. 1991, to delete reference to 12.2. This rule of application is now in 12.2(13).

Regulations: 301 (meaning of "life annuity contract").

I.T. Application Rules: 69 (meaning of "chapter 148 of ...").

(11) Loss of [pre-2017] grandfathering — For the purposes of determining at and after a particular time whether a life insurance policy (other than an annuity contract) issued before 2017 is treated as issued after 2016 under this section (other than this subsection) and sections 306 (other than subsections (9) and (10)), 307, 308, 310, 1401 and 1403 of the *Income Tax Regulations* (except as they apply for the purposes of subsection 211.1(3)), the policy is deemed to be a policy issued at the particular time if the particular time is the first time after 2016 at which life insurance — in respect of a life, or two or more lives jointly insured, and in respect of which a particular schedule of premium or cost of insurance rates applies — is

(a) if the insurance is term insurance, converted to permanent life insurance within the policy; or

(b) if the insurance (other than insurance paid for with policy dividends or that is reinstated) is medically underwritten after 2016 (other than to obtain a reduction in the premium or cost of insurance rates under the policy), added to the policy.

Related Provisions: Reg. 306(3) — Exemption test where 148(11) applies; Reg. 306(10) — Effect on rules in Reg. 306.

Notes: See Reg. 306(10). For the meaning of "issued before 2017" in the opening words, see VIEWS doc 2016-0651181E5 [Tollstam, "Grandfathering for Pre-2017 Life Insurance Policies", 24(12) *Canadian Tax Highlights* (ctf.ca) 9-10 (Dec. 2016)].

148(11) amended by 2017 budget bill #2, effective Dec. 14, 2017, to add exclusion for Reg. 306(10) in opening words; and to change para. (a) from "converted (other than only because of a change in premium or cost of insurance rates) into another type of life insurance; or".

148(11) added by 2014 budget bill #2, effective Dec. 16, 2014.

Related Provisions [s. 148]: 12.2 — Accrual of income on certain life insurance policies including annuity contracts; 20(1)(c), 20(2.2) — Deductibility of interest and compound interest on money borrowed to acquire a life insurance policy; 20(2.1) — Deductibility of interest paid or incurred in respect of a policy loan; 20(19) — Deduction from payment under an annuity contract for amounts previously included in income; 20(20) — Deduction re disposition of policy for accrued income previously included in income; 56(1)(d), (d.1) — Inclusion in income of annuity payments in respect of annuities not subject to accrual rules under subsec. 12.2; 60(a) — Deduction of capital element of annuity payments; 70(3.1) — "Rights or things" not to include interest in a life insurance policy; 70(5.3) — Valuation of shares of a corporation where it is beneficiary of policy on deceased; 87(2.2) — Amalgamation of insurers; 88(1)(g) — Winding-up of subsidiary insurance corporations; 89(1)"capital dividend account"(d) — When gains on life insurance policy issued on or before June 28, 1982 included in capital dividend account; 89(2)(a) — When gain on life insurance policy issued before June 29, 1982, excluded from capital dividend account; 115(1)(a)(vi), 116(5.1), (5.2) — Proceeds of disposition by non-resident of life insurance policy in Canada; 138 — Insurance corporations; 138.1 — Rules relating to segregated funds.

Notes [s. 148]: See Notes to 148(1).

Definitions [s. 148]: "accumulating fund" — Reg. 307; "adjusted cost basis" — 148(9); "amount" — 248(1); "amount payable" — (in respect of a policy loan) 148(9); "anniversary day" — 12.2(11), 148(9.1); "annuity" — 248(1); "arm's length" — 251(1); "beneficiary" — 248(25) [Notes]; "benefit on death" — Reg. 1401(3); "calendar year" — *Interpretation Act* 37(1)(a); "Canada" — 255; "cash surrender value" — 148(9); "child" — 70(10), 148(9), 252(1); "class of shares" — 248(6); "common-law partner", "common-law partnership" — 248(1); "consequence of a death", "consequence of the death" — 248(8); "corporation" — 248(1), *Interpretation Act* 35(1); "coverage" — Reg. 310"coverage"(a), 1401(3); "death benefit" — 248(1) *[not intended to apply here]*; "disposition" — (in relation to an interest in a life insurance policy) 148(9); "dividend" — 248(1); "exempt policy" — 12.2(11), 148(9.1), Reg. 306; "fair market value" — see 69(1) Notes; "former spouse" — 252(3); "fund value benefit" — Reg. 1401(3); "fund value of the coverage" — Reg. 1401(3); "gross revenue", "income-averaging annuity contract", "individual" — 248(1); "insurer" — 148(10)(a), 248(1); "interest" — (in relation to a policy loan) 148(9); "issued after 2015", "issued before 2016" — 148(11); "life annuity contract" — Reg. 301; "life insurance policy" — 138(12), 248(1); "life insurer" — 148(10)(a), 248(1); "net cost of pure insurance" — Reg. 308; "net premium reserve" — Reg. 1401(3); "non-resident" — 248(1); "paid-up addition" — 12.2(10); "paid-up capital" — 89(1), 248(1); "partnership" — see 96(1) Notes; "person" — 248(1); "person whose life was insured" — 148(10)(b); "policy anniversary" — Reg. 310; "policy dividend" — 139.1(8)(a); "policy loan" — 148(9); "pooled registered pension plan" — 147.5(1), 248(1); "premium" — 148(9); "prescribed" — 248(1); "prescribed annuity contract" — Reg. 304; "proceeds of the disposition" (of an interest in a life insurance policy) — 148(9); "property" — 248(1); *Interpretation Act* 35(1); "qualifying trust annuity" — 60.011(2), 248(1); "registered pension plan" — 248(1); "registered retirement savings plan" — 146(1), 248(1); "regulation" — 248(1); "related segregated fund trust" — 138.1(1)(a); "resident in Canada" — 94(3)(a), 250; "segregated fund" — 138.1(1); "segregated fund policy" — 138.1(1)(a); "share" — 248(1); "spouse" — 252(3); "TFSA" — 146.2(5), 248(1); "taxable Canadian corporation" — 89(1), 248(1); "taxable capital gain" — 38(a), 248(1); "taxable dividend" — 89(1), 248(1); "taxable income" — 2(2), 248(1); "taxable income earned in Canada" — 115(1), 248(1); "taxation year" — 249; "taxpayer" — 248(1); "third anniversary" — 12.2(11), 148(9.1); "value" (of an interest in a life insurance policy) — 148(9); "10/8 policy" — 248(1).

Regulations [s. 148]: 300–310.

Eligible Funeral Arrangements

148.1 (1) Definitions — In this section,

"cemetery care trust" means a trust established pursuant to an Act of a province for the care and maintenance of a cemetery;

Related Provisions: 128.1(10)"excluded right or interest"(e)(iii) — No deemed disposition on emigration of individual; 149(1)(s.2) — No tax on cemetery care trust; 248(1)"cemetery care trust" — Definition applies to entire Act; 248(1)"disposition"(f)(vi) — Rollover from one trust to another.

Notes: "Cemetery care trust" added by 1995-97 technical bill, effective for 1993 and later taxation years.

Regulations: 204(3)(d.1) (cemetery care trust need not file T3 return).

Interpretation Bulletins: IT-531: Eligible funeral arrangements.

"cemetery services" with respect to an individual means property (including interment vaults, markers, flowers, liners, urns, shrubs and wreaths) and services that relate directly to cemetery arrangements in Canada in consequence of the death of the individual including, for greater certainty, property and services to be funded out of a cemetery care trust;

Notes: "Cemetery services" added by 1995-97 technical bill, effective for 1993 and later taxation years.

Interpretation Bulletins: IT-531: Eligible funeral arrangements.

"custodian" of an arrangement means

(a) where a trust is governed by the arrangement, a trustee of the trust, and

(b) in any other case, a qualifying person who receives a contribution under the arrangement as a deposit for the provision by the person of funeral or cemetery services;

Related Provisions: 212(1)(v) — Withholding tax on payment by custodian to non-resident person.

Notes: See Notes at end of 148.1. Para. (b) amended by 1995-97 technical bill, retroactive to its introduction, to add reference to cemetery services.

Interpretation Bulletins: IT-87R2: Policyholders' income from life insurance policies; IT-531: Eligible funeral arrangements.

"eligible funeral arrangement" at a particular time means an arrangement established and maintained by a qualifying person solely for the purpose of funding funeral or cemetery services with respect to one or more individuals and of which there is one or more custodians each of whom was resident in Canada at the time the arrangement was established, where

(a) each contribution made before the particular time under the arrangement was made for the purpose of funding funeral or cemetery services to be provided by the qualifying person with respect to an individual, and

(b) for each such individual, the total of all relevant contributions made before the particular time in respect of the individual does not exceed

(i) $15,000, where the arrangement solely covers funeral services with respect to the individual,

(ii) $20,000, where the arrangement solely covers cemetery services with respect to the individual, and

(iii) $35,000, in any other case,

and, for the purpose of this definition, any payment (other than the portion of the payment to be applied as a contribution to a cemetery care trust) that is made in consideration for the immediate acquisition of a right to burial in or on property that is set apart or used as a place for the burial of human remains or of any interest in a building or structure for the permanent placement of human remains, shall be considered to have been made pursuant to a separate arrangement that is not an eligible funeral arrangement;

Related Provisions: 128.1(10)"excluded right or interest"(e)(iv) — No deemed disposition on emigration of individual; 149(1)(s.1) — No tax on EFA; 212(1)(v) — Withholding tax on payment from EFA to non-resident; 248(1)"eligible funeral arrangement" — Definition applies to entire Act; Reg. 9006(i) — EFA not reported to CRA for disclosure to foreign tax authorities.

Notes: See Notes at end of 148.1. Definition amended by 1995-97 technical bill, retroactive to its introduction (effective 1993), to add references to cemetery services, the additional $20,000 for them (previously it was limited to $15,000 for funeral services only), and the closing words.

Regulations: 201(1)(f) (information return on return of funds); 202(2)(m) (information return on payment to non-resident).

Interpretation Bulletins: IT-531: Eligible funeral arrangements.

"funeral or cemetery services" with respect to an individual means funeral services with respect to the individual, cemetery services with respect to the individual or any combination of such services;

Notes: "Funeral or cemetery services" added by 1995-97 technical bill, effective for 1993 and later taxation years.

Interpretation Bulletins: IT-531: Eligible funeral arrangements.

"funeral services" with respect to an individual means property and services (other than cemetery services with respect to the individual) that relate directly to funeral arrangements in Canada in consequence of the death of the individual;

Related Provisions: 255 — "Canada" includes coastal waters.

Notes: See Notes at end of 148.1. Definition "funeral services" amended by 1995-97 technical bill, retroactive to its introduction, to add exclusion of cemetery services and to limit the definition to funeral arrangements.

Interpretation Bulletins: IT-531: Eligible funeral arrangements.

"qualifying person" means a person licensed or otherwise authorized under the laws of a province to provide funeral or cemetery services with respect to individuals;

Notes: See Notes at end of 148.1. Definition "qualifying person" amended by 1995-97 technical bill, retroactive to its introduction, to add reference to cemetery services.

Interpretation Bulletins: IT-531: Eligible funeral arrangements.

"relevant contribution" in respect of an individual under a particular arrangement means

(a) a contribution under the particular arrangement (other than a contribution made by way of a transfer from an eligible funeral arrangement) for the purpose of funding funeral or cemetery services with respect to the individual, or

(b) such portion of a contribution to another arrangement that was an eligible funeral arrangement (other than any such contribution made by way of a transfer from any eligible funeral arrangement) as can reasonably be considered to have subsequently been used to make a contribution under the particular arrangement by way of a transfer from an eligible funeral arrangement for the purpose of funding funeral or cemetery services with respect to the individual.

Related Provisions: 148.1(1)"eligible funeral arrangement"(b) — Dollar limits on relevant contributions.

Notes: Paras. (a) and (b) amended by 1995-97 technical bill, retroactive to their introduction, to add references to cemetery services.

Interpretation Bulletins: IT-531: Eligible funeral arrangements.

(2) Exemption for eligible funeral arrangements — Notwithstanding any other provision of this Act,

(a) no amount that has accrued, is credited or is added to an eligible funeral arrangement shall be included in computing the income of any person solely because of such accrual, crediting or adding;

(b) subject to paragraph (c) and subsection (3), no amount shall be

(i) included in computing a person's income solely because of the provision by another person of funeral or cemetery services under an eligible funeral arrangement, or

(ii) included in computing a person's income because of the disposition of an interest under an eligible funeral arrangement or an interest in a trust governed by an eligible funeral arrangement; and

(c) subparagraph (b)(ii) shall not affect the consequences under this Act of the disposition of any right under an eligible funeral arrangement to payment for the provision of funeral or cemetery services.

Related Provisions: 149(1)(s.1) — No tax on trust governing an eligible funeral arrangement; 149(1)(s.2) — No tax on cemetery care trust.

Notes: See Notes at end of 148.1. 148.1(2)(b) and (c) amended by 1995-97 technical bill, retroactive to their introduction, to add references to cemetery services.

Interpretation Bulletins: IT-531: Eligible funeral arrangements.

(3) Income inclusion on return of funds — Where at any particular time in a taxation year a particular amount is distributed (otherwise than as payment for the provision of funeral or cemetery services with respect to an individual) to a taxpayer from an arrangement that was, at the time it was established, an eligible funeral arrangement and the particular amount is paid from the balance in respect of the individual under the arrangement, there shall be added in computing the taxpayer's income for the year from property the lesser of the particular amount and the amount determined by the formula

$$A + B - C$$

where

A is the balance in respect of the individual under the arrangement immediately before the particular time (determined without regard to the value of property in a cemetery care trust);

B is the total of all payments made from the arrangement before the particular time for the provision of funeral or cemetery services with respect to the individual (other than cemetery services funded by property in a cemetery care trust); and

C is the amount determined by the formula

$$D - E$$

where

D is the total of all relevant contributions made before the particular time in respect of the individual under the arrangement (other than contributions in respect of the individual that were in a cemetery care trust), and

E is the total of all amounts each of which is the amount, if any, by which

(a) an amount relating to the balance in respect of the individual under the arrangement that is deemed by subsection (4) to have been distributed before the particular time from the arrangement

exceeds

(b) the portion of the amount referred to in paragraph (a) that is added, because of this subsection, in computing a taxpayer's income.

Related Provisions: 12(1)(z.4) — Inclusion into income from property; 212(1)(v) — Withholding tax on payment to non-resident; 257 — Formula cannot calculate to less than zero.

Notes: 148.1(3)C amended by 2002-2013 technical bill (Part 5 — technical), effective for amounts that are transferred, credited or added after Dec. 20, 2002, effectively to add element E. Before the amendment, C read as D does now.

148.1(3) amended by 1995-97 technical bill, retroactive to its introduction, to add references to cemetery services and exclusions relating to cemetery care trusts.

Regulations: 201(1)(f) (information return).

Interpretation Bulletins: IT-531: Eligible funeral arrangements.

(4) Deemed distribution on transfer — If at a particular time an amount relating to the balance in respect of an individual (referred to in this subsection and in subsection (5) as the "transferor") under an eligible funeral arrangement (referred to in this subsection and in subsection (5) as the "transferor arrangement") is transferred, credited or added to the balance in respect of the same or another individual (referred to in this subsection and in subsection (5) as the "recipient") under the same or another eligible funeral arrangement (referred to in this subsection and in subsection (5) as the "recipient arrangement"),

(a) the amount is deemed to be distributed to the transferor (or, if the transferor is deceased at the particular time, to the recipient) at the particular time from the transferor arrangement and to be paid from the balance in respect of the transferor under the transferor arrangement; and

(b) the amount is deemed to be a contribution made (other than by way of a transfer from an eligible funeral arrangement) at the particular time under the recipient arrangement for the purpose of funding funeral or cemetery services with respect to the recipient.

Related Provisions: 148.1(5) — No deemed distribution on transfer to same individual.

Notes: 148.1(4) added by 2002-2013 technical bill, effective for amounts transferred, credited or added after Dec. 20, 2002.

(5) Non-application of subsec. (4) — Subsection (4) does not apply if

(a) the transferor and the recipient are the same individual;

(b) the amount that is transferred, credited or added to the balance in respect of the individual under the recipient arrangement is equal to the balance in respect of the individual under the transferor arrangement immediately before the particular time; and

(c) the transferor arrangement is terminated immediately after the transfer.

Notes: 148.1(5) added by 2002-2013 technical bill (Part 5 — technical), effective for amounts transferred, credited or added after Dec. 20, 2002.

Notes [s. 148.1]: 148.1 added by 1994 technical bill and amended by 1995-97 technical bill, both effective 1993. It permits every individual to place up to $35,000 in an eligible funeral arrangement (EFA), defined in 148.1(1), to cover both funeral services ($15,000) and cemetery services ($20,000). Interest earned on the funds is not taxable to the trust (149(1)(s.1), (s.2)). Revenue Canada had allowed these arrangements for many years (IT-246) but had proposed to cancel its administrative policy after 1992. See now IT-531. For detailed discussion see Kingissepp, "Eligible Funeral Arrangements", 43(4) *Canadian Tax Journal* 983-95 (1995).

An EFA can be created by assigning life insurance to the funeral home: VIEWS docs 2003-0042681E5, 2011-0428171R3. Transferring funds from an EFA to an insurer to pay for a life insurance policy to fund a funeral will trigger tax on the accrued income: 2006-0182591E5. An assignment to a funeral home of a death benefit payable under a life insurance policy will not qualify: 2007-0228701R3. When a funeral home sells its business, amounts for prepaid funeral contracts were likely taxed under now-repealed 14(1), not exempt under 148.1(2)(b)(ii): 2013-0480881E5.

Definitions [s. 148.1]: "amount" — 248(1); "Canada" — 255; "cemetery care trust" — 148.1(1), 248(1); "cemetery services", "custodian" — 148.1(1); "eligible funeral arrangement" — 148.1(1), 248(1); "funeral or cemetery services", "funeral services" — 148.1(1); "individual", "property" — 248(1); "province" — *Interpretation Act* 35(1); "qualifying person" — 148.1(1); "recipient", "recipient arrangement" — 148.1(4); "relevant contribution" — 148.1(1); "resident in Canada" — 250; "taxation year" — 249; "taxpayer" — 248(1); "transferor", "transferor arrangement" — 148.1(4); "trust" — 104(1), 248(1), (3).

DIVISION H — EXEMPTIONS

Miscellaneous Exemptions

149. (1) Miscellaneous exemptions — No tax is payable under this Part on the taxable income of a person for a period when that person was

(a) **employees of a country other than Canada** — an officer or servant of the government of a country other than Canada whose duties require that person to reside in Canada

(i) if, immediately before assuming those duties, the person resided outside Canada,

(ii) if that country grants a similar privilege to an officer or servant of Canada of the same class,

(iii) if the person was not, at any time in the period, engaged in a business or performing the duties of an office or employment in Canada other than the person's position with that government, and

(iv) if the person was not during the period a Canadian citizen;

Related Provisions: 94(1)"exempt person"(b) — Exemption from non-resident trust rules; 122.8(2)(d) — 149(1)(a) person ineligible for Climate Action Incentive payment; 125.7(1)"public institution"(a) — 149(1)(a) "organization" ineligible for COVID-19 wage subsidy; 149(1)(b) — Family members and servants; Canada-U.S. Tax Treaty:Art. XIX — Government service; Canada-U.S. Tax Treaty:Art. XXVIII — Diplomatic agents and consular officers; Canada-U.K. Tax Treaty:Art. 25 — Diplomatic and consular officials.

Notes: Foreign governments and their agencies are generally exempt from Canadian tax. See Kam & Lang, "Sovereign Immunity and the Taxation of Foreign Government Entities in Canada", XVII(2) *Corporate Finance* (Federated Press) 1976-80 (2011). Canadian government entities (including many pension plans) are exempt from US tax

by *Internal Revenue Code* s. 892: Seraganian & Devetski, "Recent Developments in US Tax Law", 2012 Cdn Tax Foundation conference report, at 22:16-21.

Foreign doctors employed by a foreign government, receiving a "top-up" amount from a Canadian university under the Post-Graduate Medical Education program, are exempt under 149(1)(a): VIEWS doc 2013-0510061E5.

Foreign diplomats who do not fall within 149(1)(a) are still exempt from tax on foreign-source income under the *Foreign Missions and International Organizations Act* and 81(1)(a): VIEWS doc 2004-0086531I7. A diplomat who has left Canada and later sells Canadian real property without obtaining a s. 116 certificate is liable for a 162(7) penalty: 2013-0498121I7.

Members of armed forces of other countries may effectively be exempt on non-Canadian-source income by being deemed non-resident by the *Visiting Forces Act*. See Notes to 250(1).

For CRA's administrative position exempting the sale of a principal residence by a 149(1)(a) person, see 40(2)(b) Notes.

The US is not considered to fall within 149(1)(a)(ii) merely because of a general exemption on certain kinds of income: VIEWS doc 2006-0189601I7.

(b) **members of the family and servants of employees of a country other than Canada** — a member of the family of a person described in paragraph (a) who resides with that person, or a servant employed by a person described in that paragraph,

(i) if the country of which the person described in paragraph (a) is an officer or servant grants a similar privilege to members of the family residing with and servants employed by an officer or servant of Canada of the same class,

(ii) in the case of a member of the family, if that member was not at any time lawfully admitted to Canada for permanent residence, or at any time in the period engaged in a business or performing the duties of an office or employment in Canada,

(iii) in the case of a servant, if, immediately before assuming his or her duties as a servant of a person described in paragraph (a), the servant resided outside Canada and, since first assuming those duties in Canada, has not at any time engaged in a business in Canada or been employed in Canada other than by a person described in that paragraph, and

(iv) if the member of the family or servant was not during the period a Canadian citizen;

Related Provisions: 94(1)"exempt person"(b) — Exemption from non-resident trust rules; 122.8(2)(d) — 149(1)(b) person ineligible for Climate Action Incentive payment; 125.7(1)"public institution"(a) — 149(1)(b) "organization" ineligible for COVID-19 wage subsidy.

(c) **municipal authorities [and First Nation bands]** — a municipality in Canada, or a municipal or public body performing a function of government in Canada;

Related Provisions: 94(1)"exempt person"(b) — Exemption from non-resident trust rules; 125.7(1)"public institution"(a) — 149(1)(c) organization ineligible for COVID-19 wage subsidy; 149(1)(d)–(d.6) — Municipal or provincial corporations; 149.1(1)"qualified donee"(a)(ii) — Municipality qualifies for charitable donations if registered with CRA; Reg. 205.1(2)(d) — No requirement to file T2 electronically.

Notes: The provinces cannot be taxed by the federal government: *Constitution Act, 1867*, s. 125. 149(1)(c)-(d.6) extend this rule to Crown corporations (subject to 27(2)) and various other bodies, such as municipalities and municipal bodies, that have no constitutional protection from federal taxation. Note that federal Crown corporations are deemed by 27(1) to be subject to the Act, but then exempted by 149(1)(d)!

Municipal or public body performing a function of government (MPBPFG):

An entity does not become a municipality by exercising municipal functions: *Tawich*, 2000 CanLII 9283 (Que. CA), so the MPBPFG term was added. In *Laval Technopole*, 2018 QCCQ 6352, companies promoting municipalities' economies were held to be the municipalities' agents (using the tests for Crown agents), for Quebec health tax.

The Law Society of Ontario is not a MPBPFG because 149(1)(d.5) is intended to exempt only bodies similar to municipalities, as part of preventing intergovernmental taxation: *Lawyers' Professional Indemnity Co.*, 2020 FCA 90 (leave to appeal denied 2021 CarswellNat 865 (SCC)) (though CRA agreed it was a "public body": para. 44). See also "Law societies..." in Notes to 149(1)(l).

For CRA interpretation of MPBPFG see VIEWS docs 2008-0294231R3, 2009-030628117, 2009-031085117, 2011-042849117, 2013-049889115, 2014-052141117, 2015-0568911E5; 2020-0846261E5 ("entity must have the ability and powers to govern, tax, pass by-laws and provide municipal type services"). The following have been held to be a MPBPFG: BC improvement district (2013-050367117); economic development corp making regional investments (2005-0160521R3); Indian bands and councils (see below); parks (2015-053315117, 2015-058493117); Quebec regional county municipality (2015-0568911E5); school board (2013-0500321I7); unidentified "Authority" (2014-055832117). The House of Commons is not a MPBPFG, because it has no executive power: 2014-053228117.

All *Indian Act* bands qualify as MPBPFG: 2016-064503117. (CRA had earlier reviewed each request separately, and issued many rulings approving specific bands (see these Notes up to the 50th ed.), as well as a Society of bands (2005-0113361R3) and a chiefs' council or Tribal Council (2014-054729117 and 2013-0494711R3).) Limited partnership income earned by a band was ruled exempt in 2010-0360361R3, 2010-0362371R3, 2012-0447241R3, 2012-0473041R3, 2013-0478751R3, 2013-0478761R3. A land claim settlement trust may attribute income under 75(2) to the exempt entity: 2010-0372531E5. See also Notes to 81(1)(a).

A 2014-17 pilot project allows rulings on whether an entity is a MPBPFG: tinyurl.com/pubruling-cra.

Donations: a municipality automatically qualifies to issue receipts under 118.1 unless CRA suspends or cancels its registration. A MPBPFG must apply for registration. See 149.1(1)"qualified donee"(a)(ii), (iii).

See also 149(1)(d.5), which exempts a corp owned by a MPBPFG.

Interpretation Bulletins: IT-167R6: Registered pension plans — employee's contributions.

(d) **corporations owned by the Crown** — a corporation, commission or association all of the shares (except directors' qualifying shares) or of the capital of which was owned by one or more persons each of which is Her Majesty in right of Canada or Her Majesty in right of a province;

Related Provisions: 27(2) — Prescribed federal Crown corporations are taxable; 94(1)"exempt person"(b) — Exemption from non-resident trust rules; 125.7(1)"public institution"(a) — 149(1)(d) organization ineligible for COVID-19 wage subsidy; 149(1.1) — No exemption where other person has a right to acquire shares; 149(1.3) — No exemption if 10% ownership or *de facto* control by non-government; 227(14) — Exemption from tax under other Parts; 227(16) — Corporation deemed not private corporation for Part IV tax; Reg. 205.1(2)(d) — No requirement to file T2 electronically.

Notes: For interpretation of 149(1)(d) see VIEWS docs 2009-0310631E5, 2009-0313871E5. For a corporation that has issued shares, only the shares (and not "capital") are considered for 149(1)(d)–(d.4): 2011-0428521E5. See also Richard Yasny, "Province-Controlled Corporation Taxable?", 20(12) *Canadian Tax Highlights* (ctf.ca) 9-10 (Dec. 2012), re BC Credit Union Deposit Insurance Corp.

For corporations owned by *foreign* governments, see Notes to 149(1)(a).

For "directors' qualifying shares", see Notes to 85(1.3).

149(1)(d) amended by 1995-97 technical bill, and by 2001 technical bill to add "one or more persons each of which is", both amendments effective for taxation years and fiscal periods that begin after 1998. The former (d) was expanded and split up into (d)-(d.6). See Notes to 149(1)(c).

Interpretation Bulletins: IT-269R4: Part IV tax on dividends received by a private corporation or a subject corporation; IT-347R2: Crown corporations (cancelled).

(d.1) **corporations 90% owned by the Crown** — a corporation, commission or association not less than 90% of the shares (except directors' qualifying shares) or of the capital of which was owned by one or more persons each of which is Her Majesty in right of Canada or Her Majesty in right of a province;

Related Provisions: 27(2) — Prescribed federal Crown corporations are taxable; 94(1)"exempt person"(b) — Exemption from non-resident trust rules; 125.7(1)"public institution"(a) — 149(1)(d.1) organization ineligible for COVID-19 wage subsidy; 149(1.1) — No exemption where other person has a right to acquire shares; 149(1.3) — No exemption if 10% ownership or *de facto* control by non-government; 227(14) — Exemption from tax under other Parts; 227(16) — Corporation deemed not private corporation for Part IV tax; Reg. 205.1(2)(d) — No requirement to file T2 electronically.

Notes: For interpretation of (d.1) see VIEWS doc 2009-0310631E5 and 149(1)(d) Notes.

149(1)(d.1) added by 1995-97 technical bill, and amended by 2001 technical bill to add "one or more persons each of which is", both effective for taxation years and fiscal periods that begin after 1998. See Notes to 149(1)(c) and (d).

(d.2) **wholly-owned [by Crown corporation] corporations** — a corporation all of the shares (except directors' qualifying shares) or of the capital of which was owned by one or more persons each of which is a corporation, commission or association to which this paragraph or paragraph (d) applies for the period;

Related Provisions: 27(2) — Prescribed federal Crown corporations are taxable; 94(1)"exempt person"(b) — Exemption from non-resident trust rules; 125.7(1)"public institution"(a) — 149(1)(d.2) organization ineligible for COVID-19 wage subsidy; 149(1.1) — No exemption where other person has a right to acquire shares; 149(1.11) — Election for corp that was taxable before 1999 to remain taxable; 149(1.3) — No exemption if 10% ownership or *de facto* control by non-government; 227(14) — Exemption from tax under other Parts; 227(16) — Corporation deemed not

private corporation for Part IV tax; Reg. 205.1(2)(d) — No requirement to file T2 electronically.

Notes: See Notes to 149(1)(d).

149(1)(d.2) added by 1995-97 technical bill, and amended by 2001 technical bill to add "one or more persons each of which is", both effective for taxation years and fiscal periods that begin after 1998. See Notes to 149(1)(c) and (d).

(d.3) **90% [Crown] owned corporations** — a corporation, commission or association not less than 90% of the shares (except directors' qualifying shares) or of the capital of which was owned by

(i) one or more persons each of which is Her Majesty in right of Canada or a province or a person to which paragraph (d) or (d.2) applies for the period, or

(ii) one or more municipalities in Canada in combination with one or more persons each of which is Her Majesty in right of Canada or a province or a person to which paragraph (d) or (d.2) applies for the period;

Related Provisions: 27(2) — Prescribed federal Crown corporations are taxable; 94(1)"exempt person"(b) — Exemption from non-resident trust rules; 125.7(1)"public institution"(a) — 149(1)(d.3) organization ineligible for COVID-19 wage subsidy; 149(1.1) — No exemption where other person has a right to acquire shares; 149(1.11) — Election for corporation that was taxable before 1999 to remain taxable; 149(1.3) — No exemption if 10% ownership or *de facto* control by non-government; 227(14) — Exemption from tax under other Parts; 227(16) — Corporation deemed not private corporation for Part IV tax; Reg. 205.1(2)(d) — No requirement to file T2 electronically.

Notes: The "capital" of a corporation under 149(1)(d.3) generally does not include its indebtedness: VIEWS doc 2002-0168083 (see also Notes to 149(1)(d)).

149(1)(d.3) added by 1995-97 technical bill and amended by 2001 technical bill to add "one or more persons each of which is", both effective for taxation years and fiscal periods that begin after 1998. See Notes to 149(1)(c) and (d).

(d.4) **combined [Crown] ownership** — a corporation all of the shares (except directors' qualifying shares) or of the capital of which was owned by one or more persons each of which is a corporation, commission or association to which this paragraph or any of paragraphs (d) to (d.3) applies for the period;

Related Provisions: 27(2) — Prescribed federal Crown corporations are taxable; 94(1)"exempt person"(b) — Exemption from non-resident trust rules; 125.7(1)"public institution"(a) — 149(1)(d.4) organization ineligible for COVID-19 wage subsidy; 149(1.1) — No exemption where other person has a right to acquire shares; 149(1.11) — Election for corporation that was taxable before 1999 to remain taxable; 149(1.3) — No exemption if 10% ownership or *de facto* control by non-government; 227(14) — Exemption from tax under other Parts; 227(16) — Corporation deemed not private corporation for Part IV tax; Reg. 205.1(2)(d) — No requirement to file T2 electronically.

Notes: A corporation partly owned by the Crown and partly by a Crown corp does not qualify under (d.4): VIEWS doc 2011-0428521E5. See also 149(1)(d) Notes.

149(1)(d.4) added by 1995-97 technical bill, and amended by 2001 technical bill to add "one or more persons each of which is", both effective for tax years and fiscal periods that begin after 1998. See Notes to 149(1)(c) and (d).

(d.5) **[municipally-owned corporation earning] income within boundaries of entities** — subject to subsections (1.2) and (1.3), a corporation, commission or association not less than 90% of the capital of which was owned by one or more entities each of which is a municipality in Canada, or a municipal or public body performing a function of government in Canada, if the income for the period of the corporation, commission or association from activities carried on outside the geographical boundaries of the entities does not exceed 10% of its income for the period;

Related Provisions: 94(1)"exempt person"(b) — Exemption from non-resident trust rules; 125.7(1)"public institution"(a) — 149(1)(d.5) organization ineligible for COVID-19 wage subsidy; 149(1.1) — No exemption where other person has a right to acquire shares; 149(1.2) — Meaning of "outside the geographical boundaries"; 149(1.3) — No exemption if 10% ownership or *de facto* control by non-government; 149(11) — Geographical boundaries of body performing function of government; 227(14) — Exemption from tax under other Parts; 227(16) — Corporation deemed not private corporation for Part IV tax; Reg. 205.1(2)(d) — No requirement to file T2 electronically; Reg. 8901.1 — Aboriginal government (d.5) corps prescribed as eligible employers for COVID-19 Canada Emergency Wage Subsidy.

Notes: See 149(1)(c) and (d) Notes. 149(1)(d.5) overrules *Tawich*, 2000 CanLII 9283 (Que. CA), which held that an entity could not attain the status of municipality simply by exercising municipal functions. It was announced in a Sept. 10, 2002 Finance letter to provincial and territorial officials. See also Notes to 149(1.2) and VIEWS docs

2014-0518651E5; 2015-0578671R3 (limited partnership income of corp owned by First Nation — not subject to 149(1.2)).

For the meaning of "capital" for a non-share corporation, see VIEWS doc 2006-0212801E5. For a ruling that 149(1)(d.5) will not apply see doc 2007-0224741R3. Whether 149(1)(d.5) applies can be determined only after year-end: 2014-0530241E5.

For interpretation of "municipal or public body..." see Notes to 149(1)(c).

"Activities" includes owning and leasing real property, and notwithstanding incidental administrative activities, the principal "activity" in such case is the leasing, which takes place at the location of the property: VIEWS doc 2004-0061221E5.

Income excluded by 149(1.2) from "income from activities carried on outside the geographical boundaries" is to be included in "income for the period" for the 10% test in (d.5) and (d.6): VIEWS doc 2005-011830117. Partnership income can qualify: 2015-0568911E5. For the factors used in determining if capital gains are included in income earned outside the geographical boundaries, see 1999-0006955, 2010-0376961E5. For investment income, see 2011-039552117.

149(1)(d.5) amended by 2002-2013 technical bill, for tax years that begin after May 8, 2000. Added by 1995-97 technical bill.

(d.6) subsidiaries of municipal corporations — subject to subsections (1.2) and (1.3), a particular corporation all of the shares (except directors' qualifying shares) or of the capital of which was owned by one or more entities (referred to in this paragraph as "qualifying owners") each of which is, for the period, a corporation, commission or association to which this paragraph applies, a corporation to which this paragraph applies, a municipality in Canada, or a municipal or public body performing a function of government in Canada, if no more than 10% of the particular corporation's income for the period is from activities carried on outside

(i) if a qualifying owner is a municipality in Canada, or a municipal or public body performing a function of government in Canada, the geographical boundaries of each such qualifying owner,

(ii) if paragraph (d.5) applies to a qualifying owner, the geographical boundaries of the municipality, or municipal or public body, referred to in that paragraph in its application to each such qualifying owner, and

(iii) if this paragraph applies to a qualifying owner, the geographical boundaries of the municipality, or municipal or public body, referred to in subparagraph (i) or paragraph (d.5), as the case may be, in their respective applications to each such qualifying owner;

Related Provisions: 94(1)"exempt person"(b) — Exemption from non-resident trust rules; 125.7(1)"public institution"(a) — 149(1)(d.6) organization ineligible for COVID-19 wage subsidy; 149(1.1) — No exemption where other person has a right to acquire shares; 149(1.2) — Meaning of "outside the geographical boundaries"; 149(1.3) — No exemption if 10% ownership or *de facto* control by non-government; 149(11) — Geographical boundaries of body performing function of government; 227(14) — Exemption from tax under other Parts; 227(16) — Corporation deemed not private corporation for Part IV tax; Reg. 205.1(2)(d) — No requirement to file T2 electronically; Reg. 8901.1 — Aboriginal government (d.6) corps prescribed as eligible employers for COVID-19 Canada Emergency Wage Subsidy.

Notes: See Notes to 149(1)(c) and 149(1).(d.5). For "directors' qualifying shares", see Notes to 85(1.3). Applying 149(1)(d.6) to particular facts, see VIEWS doc 2005-0139031E5.

149(1)(d.6) amended by 2002-2013 technical bill (last change effective for taxation years that begin after May 8, 2000), 2001 and 1995-97 technical bills.

(e) certain organizations — an agricultural organization, a board of trade or a chamber of commerce, no part of the income of which was payable to, or was otherwise available for the personal benefit of, any proprietor, member or shareholder thereof;

Related Provisions: 94(1)"exempt person"(b) — Exemption from non-resident trust rules; 149(2) — Income not to include taxable capital gains; 149(12) — Information returns; 227(14) — Exemption from tax under other Parts; Reg. 205.1(2)(d) — No requirement to file T2 electronically.

Notes: For the meaning of "agricultural organization" see VIEWS docs 2007-0252941E5, 2012-0440121E5.

"No part of the income of which" refers to *net* income; and "personal benefit" could result from one person being able to sign cheques. See Notes to 149(1)(l). For a ruling that certain income will not put an organization offside, see doc 2012-0438831R3. Paying a patronage dividend disqualifies the organization: 2014-0551921E5.

Registered Charities Newsletters: 19 (what is the difference between a registered charity and a non-profit organization?).

(f) registered charities — a registered charity;

Related Provisions: 94(1)"exempt person"(b) — Exemption from non-resident trust rules; 149.1 — Charities; 227(14) — Exemption from tax under Parts IV, IV.1, VI, VI.1; 248(1)"registered charity" — Registration provisions; Reg. 205.1(2)(d) — No requirement to file T2 electronically; Canada-U.S. Tax Treaty:Art. XXI:1 — Religious, literary, scientific, educational or charitable organization — exemption from tax.

Notes: See 149.1 for the rules for charities, and Notes to 248(1)"registered charity".

(g) registered Canadian amateur athletic association — a registered Canadian amateur athletic association;

Related Provisions: Reg. 8901.1(e) — RCAAAs prescribed as eligible employers for COVID-19 Canada Emergency Wage Subsidy.

Notes: 149(1)(g) added by 2011 budget bill #2, effective 2012. (RCAAAs were presumably exempt under 149(1)(l) before 2012.)

Former 149(1)(g), repealed in 1977, exempted a non-profit corporation. See now 149(1)(l).

(h) registered journalism organizations — a registered journalism organization;

Related Provisions: Reg. 8901.1(e) — RJOs prescribed as eligible employers for COVID-19 Canada Emergency Wage Subsidy.

Notes: 149(1)(h) added by 2019 budget bill #1, effective 2020. See Notes to 149.1(1)"qualified donee" re (b.1).

Former 149(1)(h), repealed in 1977, exempted a charitable trust. See now 149(1)(f).

(h.1) Association of Universities and Colleges of Canada — the Association of Universities and Colleges of Canada, incorporated by the *Act to incorporate Association of Universities and Colleges of Canada*, chapter 75 of the Statutes of Canada, 1964-65;

Related Provisions: 227(14) — Exemption from tax under Parts IV, IV.1, VI, VI.1.

(i) certain housing corporations — a corporation that was constituted exclusively for the purpose of providing low-cost housing accommodation for the aged, no part of the income of which was payable to, or was otherwise available for the personal benefit of, any proprietor, member or shareholder thereof;

Related Provisions: 94(1)"exempt person"(b) — Exemption from non-resident trust rules; 149(2) — Income not to include taxable capital gains; 149.1(1)"qualified donee"(a)(i) — Donation to housing corporation can qualify as charitable donation; 227(14) — Exemption from tax under Parts IV, IV.1, VI, VI.1; Reg. 205.1(2)(d) — No requirement to file T2 electronically.

Notes: See Charities Guidance CG-025 for the application process and documentary requirements (but CG-026 for registration as a charity assisting the aged). It states that to fall under 149(1)(i), the corporation must also be *operated* exclusively for providing low-cost housing (this requirement is not explicit in the legislation), and that "aged" means 55 or older. See also VIEWS docs 2007-0256961E5, 2008-0275381C6, 2012-047007117.

"No part of the income of which" refers to *net* income, and "personal benefit" could result from one person being able to sign cheques: see 149(1)(l) Notes.

Charities Guidance: CG-025: Qualified donee: Low-cost housing corporation for the aged.

(j) non-profit corporations for scientific research and experimental development — a corporation that was constituted exclusively for the purpose of carrying on or promoting scientific research and experimental development, no part of whose income was payable to, or was otherwise available for the personal benefit of, any proprietor, member or shareholder thereof, that has not acquired control of any other corporation and that, during the period,

(i) did not carry on any business, and

(ii) expended amounts in Canada each of which is

(A) an expenditure on scientific research and experimental development (within the meaning that would be assigned by paragraph 37(8)(a) if subsection 37(8) were read without reference to paragraph 37(8)(d)) directly undertaken by or on behalf of the corporation, or

(B) a payment to an association, university, college or research institute or other similar institution, described in clause 37(1)(a)(ii)(A) or (B) to be used for scientific research and experimental development, and

the total of which is not less than 90% of the amount, if any, by which the corporation's gross revenue for the period exceeds the total of all amounts paid in the period by the corporation because of subsection (7.1);

Related Provisions: 37(1)(a)(ii)(C), 37(1)(a)(iii) — Deduction for R&D payments to corporation described in 149(1)(j); 94(1)"exempt person"(b) — Exemption from non-resident trust rules; 149(2) — Income not to include taxable capital gains; 149(7) — Prescribed form to be filed; 149(8), (9) — Interpretation rules; 149(9) — Rules; 227(14) — Exemption from tax under other Parts; 256(6)–(9) — Whether control acquired; Reg. 205.1(2)(d) — No requirement to file T2 electronically.

Notes: See Notes to 248(1)"scientific research and experimental development" for the meaning of that phrase. There is no requirement that a 149(1)(j) corp be approved in advance by CRA; for interpretation see VIEWS docs 2006-0168111E5, 2009-0313261R3, 2012-0443751E5. For a ruling that a corp qualified see 2010-0376811R3.

149(1)(j) amended by 1995 Budget, for taxation years that begin after June 1995.

Regulations: 2900(1) (definition of SR&ED, except where work performed pursuant to agreement in writing entered into before Feb. 28, 1995).

Information Circulars: 86-4R3: Scientific research and experimental development.

Application Policies: SR&ED 96-10: Third party payments — approval process.

(k) **labour organizations** — a labour organization or society or a benevolent or fraternal benefit society or order;

Related Provisions: 94(1)"exempt person"(b) — Exemption from non-resident trust rules.

Notes: For interpretation of "benevolent or fraternal society or order", see VIEWS docs 2003-0000187, 2003-0048901E5, 2004-0109131E5, 2011-0427981I7, 2014-0522451E5.

Unlike 149(1)(l), there is no requirement in 149(1)(k) that members not benefit. A union's profit-making activities do not jeopardize 149(1)(k) status: VIEWS doc 2014-0558101E5. Payments by a labour association to its members of its bank balance on annulment do not disqualify it, nor are the payments taxable to the members: 2005-0134441E5. However, on an unincorporated association's windup, distributions to members are capital gains (disposition of membership rights): 2009-0310861I7, 2018-0779221R3.

See Notes to s. 3, at bullet point "union's...", for payments by unions to employees.

Interpretation Bulletins: IT-389R: Vacation pay trusts established under collective agreements.

(l) **non-profit organizations** — a club, society or association that, in the opinion of the Minister, was not a charity within the meaning assigned by subsection 149.1(1) and that was organized and operated exclusively for social welfare, civic improvement, pleasure or recreation or for any other purpose except profit, no part of the income of which was payable to, or was otherwise available for the personal benefit of, any proprietor, member or shareholder thereof unless the proprietor, member or shareholder was a club, society or association the primary purpose and function of which was the promotion of amateur athletics in Canada;

Related Provisions: 94(1)"exempt person"(b) — Exemption from non-resident trust rules; 149(2) — Income not to include taxable capital gains; 149(3) — Application of subsec. (1); 149(5) — Exception re investment income of certain clubs; 149(12) — Information returns; 227(14) — Exemption from tax under other Parts; 248(1) — "person"; 248(1) — "registered Canadian amateur athletic association"; Reg. 205.1(2)(d) — No requirement to file T2 electronically; Reg. 4900(1)(r) — Debt of non-profit corporation as qualified investment for RRSP, etc.

Notes: The 2014 federal Budget (Conservative) announced an intention "to review whether the income tax exemption for NPOs remains properly targeted and whether sufficient transparency and accountability provisions are in place", and to release a consultation paper for comment [Drache, "Non-Profit Consultation Coming", 22(4) *Canadian Not-for-Profit News* (Carswell) 25-27 (April 2014)]. However, nothing further has happened (with Liberal governments elected in Oct. 2015 and Oct. 2019). Finance advised in Nov. 2016 that "the consultation is always possible though it's not a priority at the moment".

The words "club, society or association" are broad enough to include a corporation, and can include a non-resident organization: VIEWS doc 2001-0095285.

A NPO must be not a charity "in the opinion of the Minister". An NPO that chooses not to register as a charity but wants exemption under 149(1)(l) must ensure it is not a charity, e.g. by including in its objects a disqualifying clause such as lobbying for legislative change. See Drache, "Non-Profits: The First Step in Protecting Status", 9(8) *Canadian Not-for-Profit News* (Carswell) 61-63 (Aug. 2001). The entity arguably might have to apply for charity status simply to get an "opinion of the Minister": *L.I.U.N.A. Local 527*, [1992] 2 C.T.C. 2410 (TCC), paras. 73-76. However, CRA states in doc 2009-0329991C6 that no explicit opinion from CRA is needed, and no ruling would be issued anyway because the question depends on how the entity actually operates. See also 2010-0380581I7, 2011-0398661I7, 2011-0425081I7.

Non-profit requirement: Being engaged in commercial activity in a businesslike manner does not disqualify an entity from 149(1)(l) if it is non-profit: *Gulf Log Salvage Cooperative* (1960), 24 Tax A.B.C. 139 (salvaging logs that had gone astray); *Gull Bay Development*, [1984] C.T.C. 159 (FCTD) (logging to provide employment on an Indian reserve); *Canadian Bar Insurance Assn*, [1999] 2 C.T.C. 2833 (TCC) (insurance for lawyers); *BBM Canada*, 2008 TCC 341 (audience measurement data for members, which were broadcasters, advertisers and advertising agencies); *Coop Publicitaire des Concessionaires Chrysler*, 2016 QCCQ 11252 [Quebec provincial tax] (car dealers' advertising co-op, followed *BBM*). However, in *Tourbec (1979) Inc.*, [1988] 2 C.T.C. 2071 (TCC), a company was not an NPO where it used its general travel agency revenues to subsidize tours for students. If the entity's goals cannot be achieved without making a profit, it is not an NPO: *Woodward's Pension Society*, [1962] C.T.C. 11 (SCC), para. 9. A detailed review of the older case law on 149(1)(l) is in VIEWS doc 2002-0153887. See also 2010-0380581I7, 2010-0391311E5, 2011-0398661I7, 2011-0404671I7, 2011-0404731I7, 2011-0410851I7, 2011-0426231I7.

CRA's interpretation of the above cases is that an NPO can engage in commercial activities and earn an "incidental" profit (doc 2010-0389021E5: offering services "at or near" cost is non-profit); but if it "would be unable to undertake its not-for-profit activities but for its profitable activities, the organization cannot be a 149(1)(l) entity because it has a profit purpose"; and "intentionally generating profit in order to finance future capital projects" puts an entity offside: 2009-0337311E5, 2011-0426111C6 [2011 CTF conf]. An NPO wanting to carry on a for-profit business should use a taxable entity and receive after-tax funds from it: 2010-0386301C6 [2010 CTF conf report, p.4:11-13, q.11]; 2011-0412961E5; 2012-0456071E5 (incorporating a Community Contribution Company (C3) is acceptable, but a C3 is not an NPO because it has a profit purpose: 2014-0540031E5). An organization that plans to use an initial donation to earn investment income to fund its non-profit objectives does not qualify: 2010-0366051E5 (though a one-time capital gain from disposing of property does not jeopardize NPO status: 2010-0358021E5). Investment income earned on funds held for periodic distribution to members is acceptable if it is "incidental": 2011-0408851I7. Loans to a taxable subsidiary are offside as they indicate excessive retained earnings: 2011-0429141E5. A community sports team can receive equipment and jerseys from local businesses (2011-0426001I7), but a sports association earning an annual surplus from sponsorships and advertising rights (which it actively pursues) is offside: 2011-0404681I7. A sports club can accept donations for a multi-million dollar capital improvement project: 2012-0454251E5 (investment income will be taxable under 149(5)). A retail operation that intends to earn a profit is offside: 2011-0394251I7, as is the sale of lottery tickets: 2014-0534251I7; but food and beverage sales at an annual festival are not: 2011-0429461I7, 2011-0429471I7. Charging for excess parking spots is normally acceptable: 2014-0542791E5. Fundraising is acceptable as long as its scope is not "so significant that fundraising can be considered a purpose of the organization": 2014-0522451E5, 2019-0809221M4. Building a fibre-optic cable network and charging businesses to access it likely goes too far: 2014-0537941E5. Earning income to reverse past losses may be acceptable: 2011-0392841E5. Accumulating funds, increasing profits, excess revenues, large reserves and/or large retained earnings can put an organization offside: 2011-0427611I7, 2012-0439951I7, 2012-0455501I7, 2012-0458491I7. Funding scholarships suggests the NPO is accumulating too much: 2015-0565601E5. Refunding excess membership fees is allowed, provided they are not mixed with other funds: 2012-0453841E5, 2015-0565601E5. (See also below re condo corporations.) However, this apparent requirement for "zero-based budgeting" *on each activity* may be wrong; see S. Sebastian Elawny & Samantha Iorio, "Hold the Cookies — The CRA Outlaws Bake Sales for Not-For-Profits", 2006 *Tax Topics* (CCH) 1-3 (Aug. 19, 2010); Camille Kam, "NPOs' For-Profit Activities", 18(11) *Canadian Tax Highlights* (ctf.ca) 4-5 (Nov. 2010); Robert Hayhoe & Amanda Stacey, "Charities and Non-Profits Update", 2010 Cdn Tax Foundation conference report at 33:6-12; "Change in CRA Policy — Paragraph 149(1)(l) exemption", in Hayhoe & Gail Black, "Charities and Not-For-Profit Update", 2011 Prairie Provinces Tax Conference (ctf.ca), at 3:6-11.

Condominium corporations: see IT-304R2. A condo corp is normally an NPO, but if not, excess members' fees or "overage" are not taxable: VIEWS docs 2008-0268651E5, 2011-0391921I7; Paul Hickey, "Excess Condo Fees Not Taxable", 19(7) *Canadian Tax Highlights* (ctf.ca) 6 (July 2011). (For a BC strata corporation; the entire corporation is considered as one even if it has different sections: 2011-0424091E5.) A condo corp that makes a profit and thus reduces members' fees is not exempt, e.g. on a public golf course (2010-0379561I7), parking lot, rental suite (2009-0348621E5, 2010-0357831E5), sale or rental of caretaker suite (2012-0468581E5). Solar panel income is not taxable as long as the "profit is incidental and the activity is in support of its not-for-profit objectives": 2010-0380451E5; but otherwise may be income of the unit owners "if this is appropriate under the relevant provincial law": 2014-0528171E5. Cell tower rental income would be taxable if significant, but the income may be income of the unit owners, if they jointly own the common elements under provincial law (e.g., BC, Alberta, Ont.): 2011-0405541I7. Selling or leasing locker space is acceptable if the income is "incidental": 2011-0418691E5. A co-op housing corp was thought exempt in 2008-0268651E5, but taxable in 2011-0394981I7 due to a legal obligation to return revenue surplus to members. A commercial condo corp can be an NPO: 2014-0528701E5.

Law societies, CPA institutes etc. might be exempt under 149(1)(c) even if they make a profit: Richard Yasny, "Professional Regulators", 19(10) *Canadian Tax Highlights* (ctf.ca) 7-9 (Oct. 2011). CPA Canada's (formerly CICA) tax publishing program, competing directly with Carswell and CCH, would seem to be offside 149(1)(l), and since only the provincial CPA institutes regulate members, CPA Canada is not exempt under 149(1)(c). But see Notes to 149(1)(c) re *Lawyers' Professional Indemnity* case.

An NPO that rents space in a building and sublets parts of it is normally not offside, but if it "acquires property considerably in excess of what it might reasonably be expected to need in the foreseeable future", it may be considered to have acquired the property for the purpose of earning income: VIEWS docs 2004-0092851E5, 2007-0248041R3. Short-term income from a tenant occupying a building the NPO has purchased is acceptable: 2007-0224581E5. See also 2005-0142911E5, 2011-0392841E5. See also the rule in 149(5) for income of a dining, recreational or sporting club.

The "no part of the income" requirement refers to net income, so an NPO may pay a member or shareholder a salary or fee that is a reasonable operational expense: IT-496R para. 12; VIEWS doc 2001-0095285 (reasonable honoraria and expenses to directors); Drache, "Remuneration and the Income Tax Act", 17(1) *Canadian Not-for-Profit News [CNfPN]* (Carswell) 4-5 (Jan. 2009). Potential (without actual) distribution of assets to members on dissolution does not violate the identical GST/HST interpretation letter 195314, "Member-funded Societies" (Aug. 21, 2019). Having a single person who can sign cheques could mean all the organization's income is "available" to that person: *Mikkel Dahl Inc.*, [1968] Tax A.B.C. 1033. Distribution of capital including capital gains is allowed (though it may be taxable to the recipient under 15(1)), since 149(2) excludes capital gains: 2010-0358021E5, 2013-0474101E5, 2014-0544201E5, 2015-0593841R3, 2018-0752521R3. Provincial law may also limit payments to directors: Drache, "Remunerating Charitable Trustees", 24(12) *CNfPN* 91-93 (Dec. 2016).

Personal benefits to members: IT-496R paras. 11-13 provide CRA policy. Payments covering expenses to attend meetings or seminars to benefit the association are allowed if this will further its aims and objectives (and see doc 2011-0395201E5). Refunding overpayments to members proportionately is permitted: 2013-0511631R3, 2015-0565601E5 (apparently overruling 2012-0433131E5). Distribution of capital gains to a member or shareholder: see previous para. On whether income is available for personal benefit of members, see also 2003-0053761E5 (providing costumes to dance school students: no, if this furthers the association's objectives and purpose); 2003-0036531E5 (patronage dividend: yes); 2003-0027252R3 and 2006-0194871I7 (cooperative amending bylaws to allow distribution of excess funds to members: yes); 2008-0286681R3 (returns of contributions: no); 2011-0404731I7 (marketing association: unclear); 2011-0404681I7 (yes), 2011-0410851I7 (yes); 2012-0441801E5 (sale of auction items: unclear); 2015-0565601E5 (professional organization reimbursing members for conference fees, unless attending as a delegate: yes); 2015-0565651E5 (on windup, assets go to a municipality which is a "member": yes). Transfer of assets to members may also trigger a 15(1) benefit: 2006-0200451E5.

For more CRA interpretation on NPOs see docs 2005-0142471R3 (amalgamation of NPOs); 2005-0139001R3 (approves a Canadian branch of a foreign university); 2007-0221381E5 (whether organization qualifies as an NPO); 2007-0225861R3 (foreign university extension); 2007-0252941E5 (agricultural organization); 2007-0262861E5 (when is NPO status lost?); 2007-0268941E5 (whether NPO can invest in property and later sell it to members); 2009-0306281I7 (association might qualify); 2009-0310861I7 and 2009-0332161E5 (property received on NPO windup is proceeds of disposition of capital property, per IT-409 paras. 9-11); 2009-0347571E5 (no tax on gain from sale of real property); 2009-0352121R3 (charity can create an NPO to run a business); 2009-0352231E5 (excess assets, and effect of losing NPO status); 2010-0362851E5 (filing requirements); 2010-0383001I7 ("was operated" refers to completed rather than current activities); 2011-0397881E5 (shareholder use of cottages on property owned by NPO is 15(1) taxable benefit); 2011-0410861I7 (bingo hall charities association may qualify); 2012-0471531I7 (distribution of assets to creditor is acceptable); 2014-0516981E5 (CRA will not rule on whether NPO test is met); 2014-0517481E5 (third party fundraising). For amalgamation of NPOs see Notes to 87(1). See also GST/HST Policy P-215, interpreting the similar definition of NPO in the *Excise Tax Act*.

If an unincorporated association is not an NPO, the members are likely taxable on its income: doc 2010-0369701I7; Drache, "Small Treatise on Potential NPO Liability", 18(10) *Canadian Not-for-Profit News* (Carswell) 77-78 (Oct. 2010). If an NPO loses its NPO status, see Notes to 149(10).

CRA has no list of NPOs, except the large ones that file 149(12) returns: doc 2009-0337311E5. (For a full list of Ontario incorporated NPOs and charities, obtained in March 2014 by Mark Blumberg, see tinyurl.com/ont-npos.) Corporate NPOs are asked to file a T2 (150(1)(a)), and large NPOs to file the T1044 (149(12)). CRA undertook a Non-Profit Organization Risk Identification Project from 2010-12, identifying 39,000 NPOs filing T2, T3 and/or T1044s, and randomly selected 1,440 to review. The Feb. 2014 report on the NPORIP (tinyurl.com/cra-NPOreport) states that a "significant portion of incorporated organizations would fail to meet at least one of the requirements in paragraph 149(1)(l) of the Act". For more detail (released under Access to Information) see tinyurl.com/blumb-npo.

CRA wrote "education letters" to many organizations to advise that they might not be NPOs, but stopped in April 2012 after complaints. See Valentine, "NPO Audit Initiative", 5(1) *It's Personal* (Carswell) 10-13 (Feb. 2012); Nychyk, "NPOs' Response to CRA Education Letters", 2(3) *Canadian Tax Focus* (ctf.ca) 8-9 (Aug. 2012); Hickey, "NPO Audit Project", 20(9) *Canadian Tax Highlights* (ctf.ca) 9 (Sept. 2012); VIEWS docs 2011-0426111C6 [2011 CTF conf], 2012-0448531E5.

Choosing incorporation statute: The *Canada Not-for-profit Corporations Act* came into force Oct. 17, 2011; an NFP incorporated under the former *Canada Corporations Act* that did not continue under CNCA by July 31, 2017 was to be dissolved. CNCA is a better choice than the Ontario *Corporations Act*: tinyurl.com/blumberg-why-not-oca. A new Ontario *Not-for-Profit Corporations Act*, passed in 2010, is not yet in force: tinyurl.com/onca-postp. If not in force by end of 2020 it would have been automatically repealed (*Legislation Act*, s. 10.1), but Ont. Legislative Assembly Motion 89, Sept. 21, 2020 (tinyurl.com/OLA-motions) extended it. Draft Regulations were published June

5, 2020: tinyurl.com/npca-regs. See also tinyurl.com/onca-update. It is now targeted to be in force by the end of 2021: tinyurl.com/blumberg-onca.

See also Drache et al., *Charities Taxation, Policy and Practice — Taxation* (Carswell, looseleaf or *Taxnet Pro* Reference Centre), chap. 16, "Non-Profit Organizations" (33pp.); Falk & Morand, "Current Issues Forum", 2011 BC Tax Conference (ctf.ca), 1B:1-61; McMillan, "Noncharitable Nonprofit Organizations in Canada", in *The Quest for Tax Reform Continues* (Carswell, 2013), pp. 310-28; Stevens & Kravetz, "Current Developments in the Application of Paragraph 149(1)(l)", 25(3) *The Philanthropist* (thephilanthropist.ca) 159-197 (2013); Chenier, "Spring Cleaning", 25(3) *Canadian Not-for-Profit News* (Carswell) 19-20 (March 2017) (re complying with bylaws, etc.). Non-tax issues: Seel, *Management of Nonprofit and Charitable Organizations in Canada* (LexisNexis, 4th ed., 2018).

Interpretation Bulletins: IT-83R3: Non-profit organizations — Taxation of income from property; IT-304R2: Condominiums; IT-409: Winding-up of a non-profit organization (cancelled); IT-496R: Non-profit organizations.

I.T. Technical News: 4 (condominium corporations).

Advance Tax Rulings: ATR-29: Amalgamation of social clubs.

Registered Charities Newsletters: 19 (what is the difference between a registered charity and a non-profit organization?); *Charities Connection* 3 (service clubs and fraternal societies).

   (m) **mutual insurance corporations** — a mutual insurance corporation that received its premiums wholly from the insurance of churches, schools or other charitable organizations;

Related Provisions: 94(1)"exempt person"(b) — Exemption from non-resident trust rules; 227(14) — Exemption from tax under other Parts; Reg. 205.1(2)(d) — No requirement to file T2 electronically.

   (n) **housing companies** — a limited-dividend housing company (within the meaning of that expression as defined in section 2 of the *National Housing Act*), all or substantially all of the business of which is the construction, holding or management of low-rental housing projects;

Related Provisions: 94(1)"exempt person"(b) — Exemption from non-resident trust rules; 149.1(1) — Definitions — "non-qualified investment"(d); 227(14) — Exemption from tax under other Parts; Reg. 205.1(2)(d) — No requirement to file T2 electronically.

Notes: *National Housing Act*, R.S.C. 1985, c. N-11, s. 2 provides:

> "limited-dividend housing company" means a company incorporated to construct, hold and manage a low-rental housing project, the dividends payable by which are limited by the terms of its charter or instrument of incorporation to five per cent per annum or less;

CRA considers that "substantially all" means 90% or more.

A 149(1)(n) company can have and use a capital dividend account, but loses it under 89(1.2) if it ceases to be exempt: VIEWS doc 2016-063925117.

   (o) **pension trusts** — a trust governed by a registered pension plan;

Related Provisions: 94(1)"exempt foreign trust"(g) — Foreign pension trust excluded from non-resident trust rules; 94(1)"exempt person"(b) — Exemption from non-resident trust rules; 210(2)(c) — Pension trust not subject to Part XII.2 tax; Canada-U.S. Tax Treaty:Art. XXI:2 — Exemption from tax.

Notes: See Notes to 149(1)(o.2).

   (o.1) **pension corporations** — a corporation

    (i) incorporated and operated throughout the period either

     (A) solely for the administration of a registered pension plan, or

     (B) for the administration of a registered pension plan and for no other purpose other than acting as trustee of, or administering, a trust governed by a retirement compensation arrangement, where the terms of the arrangement provide for benefits only in respect of individuals who are provided with benefits under the registered pension plan, and

    (ii) accepted by the Minister as a funding medium for the purpose of the registration of the pension plan;

Related Provisions: 94(1)"exempt person"(b), (c) — Exemption from non-resident trust rules; 149(1)(q.1) — No tax on RCA trust; 227(14) — Exemption from tax under other Parts; Reg. 205.1(2)(d) — No requirement to file T2 electronically; Reg. 9005(k) — Whether corp reported to CRA for disclosure to foreign tax authorities; Canada-U.S. Tax Treaty:Art. XXI:2 — Exemption from tax.

Notes: For CRA interpretation see VIEWS doc 2008-0274281E5.

149(1)(o.1)(i)(B) added by 1995-97 technical bill, for 1994 and later taxation years.

(o.2) [pension corporation] — a corporation

(i) incorporated before November 17, 1978 solely in connection with, or for the administration of, a registered pension plan,

(ii) that has at all times since the later of November 16, 1978 and the date on which it was incorporated

(A) limited its activities to

(I) acquiring, holding, maintaining, improving, leasing or managing capital property that is real property or an interest in real property — or immovables or a real right in immovables — owned by the corporation, another corporation described by this subparagraph and subparagraph (iv) or a registered pension plan, and

(II) investing its funds in a partnership that limits its activities to acquiring, holding, maintaining, improving, leasing or managing capital property that is real property or an interest in real property — or immovables or a real right in immovables — owned by the partnership,

(B) made no investments other than in real property or an interest in real property — or immovables or a real right in immovables — or investments that a pension plan is permitted to make under the *Pension Benefits Standards Act, 1985* or a similar law of a province, and

(C) borrowed money solely for the purpose of earning income from real property or an interest in real property or from immovables or a real right in immovables,

(ii.1) that throughout the period

(A) limited its activities to

(I) acquiring Canadian resource properties by purchase or by incurring Canadian exploration expense or Canadian development expense, or

(II) holding, exploring, developing, maintaining, improving, managing, operating or disposing of its Canadian resource properties,

(B) made no investments other than in

(I) Canadian resource properties,

(II) property to be used in connection with Canadian resource properties described in clause (A),

(III) loans secured by Canadian resource properties for the purpose of carrying out any activity described in clause (A) with respect to Canadian resource properties, or

(IV) investments that a pension fund or plan is permitted to make under the *Pension Benefits Standards Act, 1985* or a similar law of a province, and

(C) borrowed money solely for the purpose of earning income from Canadian resource properties, or

(iii) that made no investments other than investments that a pension fund or plan was permitted to make under the *Pension Benefits Standards Act, 1985* or a similar law of a province, and

(A) the assets of which were at least 98% cash and investments,

(B) that had not accepted deposits or issued bonds, notes, debentures or similar obligations, and

(C) that had derived at least 98% of its income for the period that is a taxation year of the corporation from, or from the disposition of, investments

if, at all times since the later of November 16, 1978 and the date on which it was incorporated,

(iv) all of the shares, and rights to acquire shares, of the capital stock of the corporation are owned by

(A) one or more registered pension plans,

(B) one or more trusts all the beneficiaries of which are registered pension plans,

(C) one or more related segregated fund trusts (within the meaning assigned by paragraph 138.1(1)(a)) all the beneficiaries of which are registered pension plans, or

(D) one or more prescribed persons, or

(v) in the case of a corporation without share capital, all the property of the corporation has been held exclusively for the benefit of one or more registered pension plans,

and for the purposes of subparagraph (iv), where a corporation has been formed as a result of the merger of two or more other corporations, it shall be deemed to be the same corporation as, and a continuation of, each such other corporation and the shares of the merged corporations shall be deemed to have been altered, in form only, by virtue of the merger and to have continued in existence in the form of shares of the corporation formed as a result of the merger;

Related Provisions: 94(1)"exempt person"(b), (c) — Exemption from non-resident trust rules; 227(14) — Exemption from tax under other Parts; 248(4) — Interest in real property; 248(4.1) — Meaning of "real right in an immovable"; 253.1(1) — Limited partner not considered to carry on partnership business; 259(5)"qualified corporation" — proportional holdings in trust property; Reg. 205.1(2)(d) — No requirement to file T2 electronically; Reg. 9005(l) — Whether corp reported to CRA for disclosure to foreign tax authorities.

Notes: Subpara. (ii) exempts a pension fund real estate corporation that limits its activities "at all times" to *capital* real property (this excludes developing real property for sale). Subpara. (iii) provides for a pension fund investment corp. These corps must be owned by pension plans (subpara. (iv)) or prescribed persons (see Reg. 4802). They operate tax-free and flow earnings up to the pension plans (exempt under 149(1)(o)). Alternatively, pension funds can pool their investments through a small business investment corp (Reg. 5101), exempt under 149(1)(o.3), or a "master trust" (Reg. 4802(1.1)), exempt under 149(1)(o.4). See Heller & Harrison, "Pension Fund Investment in Real Estate", 2002 Cdn Tax Foundation conference report, 31:1-40.

For CRA interpretation see docs 2005-0160571R3 ((o.2)(ii) and (iv) — transfer of assets to REIT); 2005-0164611E5 ((o.2)(ii)(A)); 2020-0854471E5 ((o.2)(ii)(A) — owning furniture in rented apartments is ok); 2013-0490641E5 ((o.2)(ii)(A)(I)); 2012-0453871E5 ((o.2)(ii)(A), (B) [Faye Kravetz, "Pension Fund Investments", 22(10) *Canadian Tax Highlights* (ctf.ca) 8-9 (Oct. 2014)]); 2002-0134885 and 2007-0222661R3 ((o.2)(ii)(C) — borrowed money used to replace capital contributions); 2005-0114481E5 ((o.2)(ii)(C)); 2020-0850981E5 (participating in Canada Emergency Commercial Rent Assistance Program (COVID-19) does not contravene (o.2)(ii)(C)); 2005-0151691E5 ((o.2)(iii)); 2005-0162911E5 ((o.2)(iii) — whether derivatives are "investments"); 2006-0195451R3 ((o.2)(iii) — loan by fund-owned trust is acceptable); 2012-0461151E5 ((o.2)(iii)(B) — advance to pension fund subsidiary); 2013-0508321I7 [Dec. 2016] ((o.2)(iii), (ii)(B) and (ii.1)(B)(IV) — PBSA limit of 10% in any investment applies per pension plan, not to corp [Silverson & Milet, "Investments by Pension Subsidiaries", 25(6) *Canadian Tax Highlights* (ctf.ca) 7 (June 2017)]); 2015-0582901E5 ((o.2)(iv)(B), (C) — shareholder can be a trust with a single RPP beneficiary); 2015-0570381I7 ((o.2)(ii) and (o.2)(iv)(D)). See also Notes to Reg. 4802(1) for (o)(iv)(D).

The quantitative test in (ii) applies per corporation, not at the level of the pension fund, but CRA is discussing with Finance whether this rule should be relaxed: *Income Tax Technical News* 38; 2007 Cdn Tax Foundation conference report at 4:17-18.

149(1)(o.2)(iii)(B) ensures that a pension investment corp does not lose tax-exempt status solely because of 248(26).

See also Silverson & Corcoran, "Issues Affecting Investments by Canadian Pension Plans", 2016 Cdn Tax Foundation conference report, 15:1-40; Joshi & Silverson, "Understanding and Doing Business with Tax-Exempt Entities", 2018 conference report, 29:1-35; Kutsenko, "Pension Plan Taxation in Canada", 38(4) *Estates, Trusts and Pensions Journal* 349 (2019), at 377-82.

149(1)(o.2) amended by 2002-2013 technical bill (last amendment effective June 26, 2013), 2001 technical bill.

Regulations: 4802 (prescribed persons).

I.T. Technical News: 1 (permissible activities of pension fund realty corporations); 38 (pension fund corporations).

(o.3) prescribed small business investment corporations — a corporation that is prescribed to be a small business investment corporation;

Related Provisions: 94(1)"exempt person"(b) — Exemption from non-resident trust rules; 227(14) — Exemption from tax under other Parts; 253.1 — Limited partner not considered to carry on partnership business; Reg. 205.1(2)(d) — No requirement to file T2 electronically.

Notes: See Notes to 149(1)(o.2).

Regulations: 5101.

(o.4) **master trusts** — a trust that is prescribed to be a master trust and that elects to be such a trust under this paragraph in its return of income for its first taxation year ending in the period;

Related Provisions: 94(1)"exempt person"(b) — Exemption from non-resident trust rules; 127.55(f)(iii) — Trust not subject to minimum tax; 210(2)(c) — Exemption from Part XII.2 tax; 248(1)"disposition"(f)(vi) — Rollover from one trust to another; 253.1(1) — Limited partner not considered to carry on partnership business; 259(1) — Election for proportional holdings in trust property; 259(3) — Qualified trusts; Reg. 9005(j) — Whether trust reported to CRA for disclosure to foreign tax authorities.

Notes: See Notes to 149(1)(o.2). For a ruling on a transfer of assets from a unit trust to its beneficiary master trust see VIEWS doc 2005-0151121R3.

Regulations: 4802(1.1) (prescribed master trust).

(p) **trusts under profit sharing plan** — a trust under an employees profit sharing plan to the extent provided by section 144;

Related Provisions: 94(1)"exempt person"(b) — Exemption from non-resident trust rules; 144(2) — No tax while trust governed by plan; 210(2)(c) — Trust not subject to Part XII.2 tax.

(q) **trusts under a registered supplementary unemployment benefit plan** — a trust under a registered supplementary unemployment benefit plan to the extent provided by section 145;

Related Provisions: 94(1)"exempt person"(b) — Exemption from non-resident trust rules; 145(2) — No tax while trust governed by plan; 210(2)(c) — Trust not subject to Part XII.2 tax.

(q.1) **RCA trusts** — an RCA trust (within the meaning assigned by subsection 207.5(1));

Related Provisions: 94(1)"exempt person"(b) — Exemption from non-resident trust rules; 149(1)(o.1)(i)(B) — No tax on corporation administering RCA trust; 207.7(1) — Part XI.3 tax on RCA trust; 210(2)(c) — RCA trust not subject to Part XII.2 tax.

(r) **trusts under registered retirement savings plan** — a trust under a registered retirement savings plan to the extent provided by section 146;

Related Provisions: 94(1)"exempt person"(b) — Exemption from non-resident trust rules; 138.1(7) — Segregated fund rules do not apply to RRSP; 146(4) — No tax while trust governed by plan; 146(10) — Tax on beneficiary when RRSP acquires non-qualified investment; 146(10.1) — Tax on income from non-qualified investments; 207.04 — Tax on annuitant if RRSP acquires non-qualified or prohibited investment; 207.05 — Tax on advantage received from RRSP; 210(2)(c) — RRSP not subject to Part XII.2 tax; 259(5)"specified taxpayer" — Look-through rule available to RRSP.

Interpretation Bulletins: IT-415R2: Deregistration of RRSPs (cancelled).

Information Circulars: 72-22R9: Registered retirement savings plans.

(s) **trusts under deferred profit sharing plan** — a trust under a deferred profit sharing plan to the extent provided by section 147;

Related Provisions: 94(1)"exempt person"(b) — Exemption from non-resident trust rules; 147(7) — No tax while trust governed by plan; 198 — Tax on acquisition of non-qualified investment or use of assets as security; 207.1(2) — Tax on holding non-qualified investment; 210(2)(c) — DPSP not subject to Part XII.2 tax; 259(5)"specified taxpayer" — Look-through rule available to DPSP.

(s.1) **trust governed by eligible funeral arrangement** — a trust governed by an eligible funeral arrangement;

Related Provisions: 94(1)"exempt person"(b) — Exemption from non-resident trust rules; 148.1(2) — No tax on income accruing in funeral arrangement or on provision of funeral or cemetary services; 210(2)(c) — Trust not subject to Part XII.2 tax.

Notes: 149(1)(s.1) added by 1994 technical bill, effective 1993. See Notes to 148.1.

Interpretation Bulletins: IT-531: Eligible funeral arrangements.

(s.2) **cemetery care trust** — a cemetery care trust;

Related Provisions: 94(1)"exempt person"(b) — Exemption from non-resident trust rules; 210(2)(c) — Trust not subject to Part XII.2 tax.

Notes: 149(1)(s.2) added by 1995-97 technical bill, for 1993 and later taxation years.

Interpretation Bulletins: IT-531: Eligible funeral arrangements.

(t) [Repealed]

Notes: 149(1)(t) provided an exemption for insurers of farming and fishing property. It "was introduced in 1954 to encourage provision of insurance in rural districts. With the increased sophistication today of the Canadian financial sector, insurance companies — including mutual companies — are well placed to effectively underwrite farming and fishing risks" [2017 Budget], so 149(1)(t) was repealed by 2017 budget bill #1, for taxation years that begin after 2018. It read:

(t) farmers' and fishermen's insurer — an insurer that, throughout the period, is not engaged in any business other than insurance if, in the opinion of the Minister, on the advice of the Superintendent of Financial Institutions or of the superintendent of insurance of the province under the laws of which the insurer is incorporated, not less than 20% of the total of the gross premium income (net of reinsurance ceded) earned in the period by the insurer and, where the insurer is not a prescribed insurer, by all other insurers that

(i) are specified shareholders of the insurer,

(ii) are related to the insurer, or

(iii) where the insurer is a mutual corporation, are part of a group that controls, directly or indirectly in any manner whatever, or are controlled, directly or indirectly in any manner whatever by, the insurer,

is in respect of insurance of property used in farming or fishing or residences of farmers or fishermen;

149(1)(t) could apply to a non-resident insurer: VIEWS doc 2009-0342671E5. On determining taxable capital of a farm mutual insurer see 2011-0415771E5.

149(1)(t) earlier amended by 1996 Budget.

(u) **registered education savings plans** — a trust governed by a registered education savings plan to the extent provided by section 146.1;

Related Provisions: 94(1)"exempt person"(b) — Exemption from non-resident trust rules; 146.1(5) — Trust not taxable; 207.04 — Tax on subscriber if RESP acquires non-qualified or prohibited investment; 207.05 — Tax on advantage received from RESP; 210(2)(c) — Trust not subject to Part XII.2 tax; 259(5)"specified taxpayer" — Look-through rule available to RESP.

(u.1) **trusts under registered disability savings plans** — a trust governed by a registered disability savings plan to the extent provided by section 146.4;

Related Provisions: 94(1)"exempt person"(b) — Exemption from non-resident trust rules; 146.4(5)(a), (b) — Tax payable by RDSP; 207.04 — Tax on holder if RDSP acquires non-qualified or prohibited investment; 207.05 — Tax on advantage received from RDSP; 210(2)(c) — Trust not subject to Part XII.2 tax; 259(5)"specified taxpayer" — Look-through rule available to RDSP.

Notes: 149(1)(u.1) added by 2007 RDSPs bill, for 2008 and later taxation years.

(u.2) **TFSA trust** — a trust governed by a TFSA to the extent provided by section 146.2;

Related Provisions: 94(1)"exempt person"(b) — Exemption from non-resident trust rules; 146.2(6) — TFSA normally not taxable; 207.01–207.07 — Tax on excess contributions and inappropriate investments; 210(2)(c) — Trust not subject to Part XII.2 tax; 259(5)"specified taxpayer" — Look-through rule available to TFSA.

Notes: 149(1)(u.2) added by 2008 budget bill #1, for 2009 and later taxation years.

(u.3) **PRPP** — a trust governed by a pooled registered pension plan to the extent provided under section 147.5;

Related Provisions: 147.5(8) — Conditions for no tax to apply to PRPP; 210(2)(c) — Trust not subject to Part XII.2 tax.

Notes: 149(1)(u.3) added by 2012 budget bill #2, effective Dec. 14, 2012.

(v) **amateur athlete trust** — an amateur athlete trust;

Related Provisions: 94(1)"exempt person"(b) — Exemption from non-resident trust rules; 143.1 — Rules for amateur athletic trusts; 210.2(2) — Tax payable by amateur athlete trust.

Notes: 149(1)(v) added by 1992 technical bill, effective 1988. See 143.1.

Former 149(1)(v), repealed by 1985 Budget, exempted a registered home ownership savings plan (RHOSP) from tax. See Notes to 146.2.

(w) **trusts to provide compensation** — a trust established as required under a law of Canada or of a province in order to provide funds out of which to compensate persons for claims against an owner of a business identified in the relevant law where that owner is unwilling or unable to compensate a customer or client, if no part of the property of the trust, after payment of its proper trust expenses, is available to any person other than as a consequence of that person being a customer or client of a business so identified;

Related Provisions: 94(1)"exempt person"(b) — Exemption from non-resident trust rules; 210(2)(c) — Trust not subject to Part XII.2 tax.

Notes: An example of a 149(1)(w) trust is the Travel Industry Compensation Fund under s. 41 of the Ontario *Travel Industry Act* to protect clients of travel agents. See also VIEWS docs 9319115 (prepaid funeral services compensation fund established by the Ontario Ministry of Consumer & Commercial Relations may qualify — but see now also 148.1); 2017-0705431E5 (funds held in trust following class action settlement do not qualify, as "relevant law" means legislation).

(x) registered retirement income funds — a trust governed by a registered retirement income fund to the extent provided by section 146.3;

Related Provisions: 94(1)"exempt person"(b) — Exemption from non-resident trust rules; 146.3(3) — No tax while trust governed by fund; 146.3(7) — Tax on beneficiary when RRIF acquires non-qualified investment; 146.3(9) — Tax on income from non-qualified investments; 207.04 — Tax on annuitant if RRIF acquires non-qualified or prohibited investment; 207.05 — Tax on advantage received from RRIF; 210(2)(c) — RRIF not subject to Part XII.2 tax.

(y) trusts to provide vacation pay — a trust established pursuant to the terms of a collective agreement between an employer or an association of employers and employees or their labour organization for the sole purpose of providing for the payment of vacation or holiday pay, if no part of the property of the trust, after payment of its reasonable expenses, is

(i) available at any time after 1980, or

(ii) paid after December 11, 1979

to any person (other than a person described in paragraph (k)) otherwise than as a consequence of that person being an employee or an heir or legal representative thereof;

Related Provisions: 16(2) — Obligation issued at discount; 94(1)"exempt person"(b) — Exemption from non-resident trust rules; 210(2)(c) — Trust not subject to Part XII.2 tax.

Interpretation Bulletins: IT-389R: Vacation pay trusts established under collective agreements.

(z) qualifying environmental trust — a qualifying environmental trust;

Related Provisions: 12(1)(z.1) — Tax on beneficiary; 94(1)"exempt person"(b) — Exemption from non-resident trust rules; 107.3(1) — Tax on beneficiary; 149(1)(z.1), (z.2) — Special Crown-owned environmental trusts; 210(2)(c) — Trust not subject to Part XII.2 tax; 211.6 — Part XII.4 tax on trust.

Notes: 149(1)(z) amended by 1997 Budget, effective for 1997 and later taxation years, to change "mining reclamation trust" to "qualifying environmental trust". (The same change was made throughout the Act.)

149(1)(z) added by 1994 Budget, effective 1994.

(z.1) *Environmental Quality Act* trust — a trust

(i) that was created because of a requirement imposed by section 56 of the *Environment Quality Act*, R.S.Q., c. Q-2,

(ii) that is resident in Canada, and

(iii) in which the only persons that are beneficially interested are

(A) Her Majesty in right of Canada,

(B) Her Majesty in right of a province, or

(C) a municipality (as defined in section 1 of that Act) that is exempt because of this subsection from tax under this Part on all of its taxable income; or

Related Provisions: 94(1)"exempt person"(b) — Exemption from non-resident trust rules; 210(2)(c) — Trust not subject to Part XII.2 tax; 211.6(1) — Exemption from Part XII.4 tax.

Notes: For CRA interpretation see VIEWS doc 2006-0165471E5. Quebec *Environment Quality Act* s. 56 requires certain residual materials elimination facilities to provide financial guarantees by way of establishment of a social trust to cover certain costs after the closure of the facility.

149(1)(z.1) added by 2011 budget bill #2, effective for 1997 and later taxation years (as proposed in a Finance comfort letter, July 17, 2003). This proposal had been in the July 16, 2010 technical package (which later became the 2002-2013 technical bill), but moved to the Budget bill so that amendments to 211.6 that refer to it could be enacted when 211.6 was amended.

(z.2) *Nuclear Fuel Waste Act* trust — a trust

(i) that was created because of a requirement imposed by subsection 9(1) of the *Nuclear Fuel Waste Act*, S.C. 2002, c. 23,

(ii) that is resident in Canada, and

(iii) in which the only persons that are beneficially interested are

(A) Her Majesty in right of Canada,

(B) Her Majesty in right of a province,

(C) a nuclear energy corporation (as defined in section 2 of that Act) all the shares of the capital stock of which are owned by one or more persons described in clause (A) or (B),

(D) the waste management organization established under section 6 of that Act if all the shares of its capital stock are owned by one or more nuclear energy corporations described in clause (C), or

(E) Atomic Energy of Canada Limited, being the company incorporated or acquired in accordance with subsection 10(2) of the *Atomic Energy Control Act*, R.S.C. 1970, c. A-19.

Related Provisions: 94(1)"exempt person"(b) — Exemption from non-resident trust rules; 210(2)(c) — Trust not subject to Part XII.2 tax; 211.6(1) — Exemption from Part XII.4 tax.

Notes: *Nuclear Fuel Waste Act* s. 9(1) requires specified entities to contribute to a trust fund for the management of nuclear fuel waste.

149(1)(z.2) added by 2011 budget bill #2, for 1997 and later tax years (implementing a Finance comfort letter, Nov. 15, 2002).

Interpretation Bulletins [subsec. 149(1)]: IT-465R: Non-resident beneficiaries of trusts.

(1.1) Exception — Where at a particular time

(a) a corporation, commission or association (in this subsection referred to as "the entity") would, but for this subsection, be described in any of paragraphs (1)(d) to (d.6),

(b) one or more other persons (other than Her Majesty in right of Canada or a province, a municipality in Canada or a person which, at the particular time, is a person described in any of subparagraphs (1)(d) to (d.6)) have at the particular time one or more rights in equity or otherwise, either immediately or in the future and either absolutely or contingently to, or to acquire, shares or capital of the entity, and

(c) the exercise of the rights referred to in paragraph (b) would result in the entity not being a person described in any of paragraphs (1)(d.1) to (d.6) at the particular time,

the entity is deemed not to be, at the particular time, a person described in any of paragraphs (1)(d) to (d.6).

Notes: For a ruling that 149(1.1) will not apply see doc 2007-0224741R3.

149(1.1) added by 1995-97 technical bill and amended by 2001 technical bill, both effective for taxation years and fiscal periods that begin after 1998 except that, where a corporation, commission or association elects in writing and files the election with the Minister before 2002, read "at a particular time" as "at any time after November 1999".

(1.11) Election [to remain taxable — 1999 transition] — Subsection (1) does not apply in respect of a person's taxable income for a particular taxation year that begins after 1998 where

(a) paragraph (1)(d) did not apply in respect of the person's taxable income for the person's last taxation year that began before 1999;

(b) paragraph (1)(d.2), (d.3) or (d.4) would, but for this subsection, have applied in respect of the person's taxable income for the person's first taxation year that began after 1998;

(c) there has been no change in the direct or indirect control of the person during the period that

(i) began at the beginning of the person's first taxation year that began after 1998, and

(ii) ends at the end of the particular year;

(d) the person elects in writing before 2002 that this subsection apply; and

(e) the person has not notified the Minister in writing before the particular year that the election has been revoked.

Related Provisions: 149(1.12) — Vertical amalgamation.

Notes: Some entities that were taxable before 1999 became exempt for post-1998 fiscal periods as a result of amendment to 149(1)(d) and the addition of 149(1)(d.2)-(d.4). This result is appropriate from a tax policy standpoint but bad for some entities since it would trigger 149(10), which recognizes gains or losses accrued before the entities become tax-exempt. 149(1.11) allows an entity that became exempt due to 149(1)(d.2)-(d.4) but which was taxable for its last tax year that began before 1999, to elect in writing before 2002 to retain taxable status, provided there has been no change in control of the entity since the beginning of its first tax year that began after 1998.

149(1.11) added by 2001 technical bill, effective for taxation years and fiscal periods that begin after 1998, and an election under 149(1.11) is deemed filed on time if it is filed with the Minister before 2002.

(1.12) Deemed election — If at any time there is an amalgamation (within the meaning assigned by subsection 87(1)) of a corporation (in this subsection referred to as the "parent") and one or more other corporations (each of which in this subsection is referred to as the "subsidiary") each of which is a subsidiary wholly-owned corporation of the parent, and immediately before that time the parent is a person to which subsection (1) does not apply by reason of the application of subsection (1.11), the new corporation is deemed, for the purposes of subsection (1.11), to be the same corporation as, and a continuation of, the parent.

Notes: 149(1.12) added by 2002-2013 technical bill, for amalgamations after Oct. 4, 2004. It implements Finance comfort letters of Dec. 6, 2004 and Sept. 16, 2005.

(1.2) Income test [for municipal corporation] — For the purposes of paragraphs (1)(d.5) and (d.6), income of a corporation, a commission or an association from activities carried on outside the geographical boundaries of a municipality or of a municipal or public body does not include income from activities carried on

(a) under an agreement in writing between

(i) the corporation, commission or association, and

(ii) a person who is Her Majesty in right of Canada or of a province, a municipality, a municipal or public body or a corporation to which any of paragraphs (1)(d) to (d.6) applies and that is controlled by Her Majesty in right of Canada or of a province, by a municipality in Canada or by a municipal or public body in Canada

within the geographical boundaries of,

(iii) if the person is Her Majesty in right of Canada or a corporation controlled by Her Majesty in right of Canada, Canada,

(iv) if the person is Her Majesty in right of a province or a corporation controlled by Her Majesty in right of a province, the province,

(v) if the person is a municipality in Canada or a corporation controlled by a municipality in Canada, the municipality, and

(vi) if the person is a municipal or public body performing a function of government in Canada or a corporation controlled by such a body, the area described in subsection (11) in respect of the person; or

(b) in a province as

(i) a producer of electrical energy or natural gas, or

(ii) a distributor of electrical energy, heat, natural gas or water,

where the activities are regulated under the laws of the province.

Related Provisions: 149(1.3) — Determination of capital ownership; 149(11) — Geographical boundaries of body performing function of government; 256(6), (6.1) — Meaning of "controlled".

Notes: In *Sakitawak Development*, 2008 TCC 529, a municipal bylaw was an "agreement in writing" for 149(1.2) since that term includes "consent in writing"; the corporation was thus exempt under 149(1)(d.5). See case comment by Pierre Letourneau, 19(3) *Taxation Law* (Ontario Bar Assn, oba.org, July 2009).

For interpretation see VIEWS docs 2008-0294231R3 ((1.2)(a) applies); 2009-0311861I7 ((1.2) may apply to First Nation); 2013-0498841E5 (electricity transmitter is not "distributor" for (b)(ii)).

149(1.2) amended to add all references to "municipal or public body" by 2002-2013 technical bill (Part 5 — technical), for taxation years that begin after May 8, 2000 (see Notes to 149(1)(d.5) for late reassessment).

149(1.2) added by 1995-97 technical bill, and para. (b) added by 2001 technical bill (what is now (a)(i)-(v) was paras. (a)-(e)), both effective for taxation years and fiscal periods that begin after 1998.

(1.3) Votes or *de facto* control [by municipality or government] — Paragraphs (1)(d) to (d.6) do not apply in respect of a person's taxable income for a period in a taxation year if at any time during the period

(a) the person is a corporation shares of the capital stock of which are owned by one or more other persons that, in total, give them more than 10% of the votes that could be cast at a meeting of shareholders of the corporation, other than shares that are owned by one or more persons each of which is

(i) Her Majesty in right of Canada or of a province,

(ii) a municipality in Canada,

(iii) a municipal or public body performing a function of government in Canada, or

(iv) a corporation, a commission or an association, to which any of paragraphs (1)(d) to (d.6) apply; or

(b) the person is, or would be if the person were a corporation, controlled, directly or indirectly in any manner whatever, by a person, or by a group of persons that includes a person, who is not

(i) Her Majesty in right of Canada or of a province,

(ii) a municipality in Canada,

(iii) a municipal or public body performing a function of government in Canada, or

(iv) a corporation, a commission or an association, to which any of paragraphs (1)(d) to (d.6) apply.

Related Provisions: 256(5.1), (6) — Meaning of "controlled, directly or indirectly".

Notes: For interpretation of 149(1.3) see VIEWS docs 2007-0224741R3, 2008-0264471E5, 2009-0313871E5.

149(1.3) amended by 2002-2013 technical bill, for tax years that begin after May 8, 2000, with a different version for such years that began before Dec. 21, 2002.

149(1.3) added by 1995-97 technical bill, effective for taxation years and fiscal periods that begin after 1998.

(2) Determination of income — For the purposes of paragraphs (1)(e), (i), (j) and (l), in computing the part, if any, of any income that was payable to or otherwise available for the personal benefit of any person or the total of any amounts that is not less than a percentage specified in any of those paragraphs of any income for a period, the amount of such income shall be deemed to be the amount thereof determined on the assumption that the amount of any taxable capital gain or allowable capital loss is nil.

Notes: 149(2) amended by 1992 technical bill, effective for 1992 and later taxation years, so that allowable capital losses (as well as taxable capital gains) are ignored in determining "income" for the stated purposes.

Interpretation Bulletins: IT-409: Winding-up of a non-profit organization (cancelled); IT-496R: Non-profit organizations.

(3) Application of subsec. (1) — Subsection (1) does not apply in respect of the taxable income of a benevolent or fraternal society or order from carrying on a life insurance business or, for greater certainty, from the sale of property used by it in the year in, or held by it in the year in the course of, carrying on a life insurance business.

Related Provisions: 16(2) — Obligation issued at discount; 149(4) — Computation of taxable income.

(4) Idem — For the purposes of subsection (3), the taxable income of a benevolent or fraternal benefit society or order from carrying on a life insurance business shall be computed on the assumption that it had no income or loss from any other sources.

(4.1)–(4.3) [Repealed]

Notes: 149(4.1)-(4.3) repealed by 2017 budget bill #1, for tax years that begin after 2018, due to repeal of 149(1)(t). They read:

(4.1) Income exempt under 149(1)(t) — Subject to subsection (4.2), subsection (1) applies to an insurer described in paragraph (1)(t) only in respect of the part of its taxable income for a taxation year determined by the formula

$$\frac{(A \times B \times C)}{D}$$

where

A is its taxable income for the year;

B is

(a) ½, where less than 25% of the total of the gross premium income (net of reinsurance ceded) earned in the year by it and, where it is not a prescribed insurer for the purpose of paragraph (1)(t), by all other insurers that

(i) are specified shareholders of the insurer,

(ii) are related to the insurer, or

(iii) where the insurer is a mutual corporation, are part of a group that controls, directly or indirectly in any manner whatever, or are controlled, directly or indirectly in any manner whatever by, the insurer,

is in respect of insurance of property used in farming or fishing or residences of farmers or fishermen; and

(b) 1 in any other case;

C is the part of the gross premium income (net of reinsurance ceded) earned by it in the year that, in the opinion of the Minister, on the advice of the Superintendent of Financial Institutions or of the superintendent of insurance of the province under the laws of which it is incorporated, is in respect of insurance of property used in farming or fishing or residences of farmers or fishermen; and

D is the gross premium income (net of reinsurance ceded) earned by it in the year.

(4.2) Idem — Subsection (4.1) does not apply to an insurer described in paragraph (1)(t) in respect of the taxable income of the insurer for a taxation year where more than 90% of the total of the gross premium income (net of reinsurance ceded) earned in the year by the insurer and, where the insurer is not a prescribed insurer, all other insurers that

(a) are specified shareholders of the insurer,

(b) are related to the insurer, or

(c) where the insurer is a mutual corporation, are part of a group that controls, directly or indirectly in any manner whatever, or are controlled, directly or indirectly in any manner whatever, by the insurer,

is in respect of insurance of property used in farming or fishing or residences of farmers or fishermen.

(4.3) Computation of taxable income of insurer — For the purposes of this Part, in computing the taxable income of an insurer for a particular taxation year, the insurer shall be deemed to have deducted under paragraphs 20(1)(a), 20(7)(c) and 138(3)(a) and section 140 in each taxation year preceding the particular year and in respect of which paragraph (1)(t) applied to the insurer, the greater of

(a) the amount it claimed or deducted under those provisions for that preceding year, and

(b) the greatest amount that could have been claimed or deducted under those provisions to the extent that the total thereof does not exceed the amount that would be its taxable income for that preceding year if no amount had been claimed or deducted under those provisions.

149(4.1) limited the exemption under 149(1)(t) to the portion of the insurer's taxable income that the insurer's gross premium income (net of reinsurance ceded) earned for the year from the insurance of residences of farmers and fishermen, farm and fishing property was of its total gross premium income (net of reinsurance ceded) for the year. This applied to insurers who reached the 25% threshold of total gross premium income (net of reinsurance ceded) of the insurer and certain other insurers that were grouped for this purpose from the insurance of farm risks. For those from 20%-25%, only half the insurer's taxable income attributable to premium income arising from such risks was eligible for exemption. (The 20% threshold was in 149(1)(t).)

For a non-resident insurer, this calculation should be based on the worldwide business: VIEWS doc 2009-0342671E5. For application of 125(5.1) to the small business deduction of a farm mutual insurer see 2011-0401731E5.

149(4.1), (4.2) amended by 1996 Budget, 1991 technical bill. 149(4.3) added by 1991 technical bill.

(5) Exception — investment income of certain clubs — Notwithstanding subsections (1) and (2), where a club, society or association was for any period, a club, society or association described in paragraph (1)(l) the main purpose of which was to provide dining, recreational or sporting facilities for its members (in this subsection referred to as the "club"), a trust is deemed to have been created on the later of the commencement of the period and

the end of 1971 and to have continued in existence throughout the period, and, throughout that period, the following rules apply:

(a) the property of the club shall be deemed to be the property of the trust;

(b) where the club is a corporation, the corporation shall be deemed to be the trustee having control of the trust property;

(c) where the club is not a corporation, the officers of the club shall be deemed to be the trustees having control of the trust property;

(d) tax under this Part is payable by the trust on its taxable income for each taxation year;

(e) the income and taxable income of the trust for each taxation year shall be computed on the assumption that it had no incomes or losses other than

(i) incomes and losses from property, and

(ii) taxable capital gains and allowable capital losses from dispositions of property, other than property used exclusively for and directly in the course of providing the dining, recreational or sporting facilities provided by it for its members;

(f) in computing the taxable income of the trust for each taxation year

(i) there may be deducted, in addition to any other deductions permitted by this Part, $2,000, and

(ii) no deduction shall be made under section 112 or 113; and

(g) the provisions of Subdivision K of Division B (except subsections 104(1) and (2)) do not apply in respect of the trust.

Related Provisions: 16(2) — Obligation issued at discount.

Notes: Interest income from a golf club's surplus funds is taxable under 149(5): *Elm Ridge*, [1999] 3 C.T.C. 163 (FCA), and *Point Grey*, [2000] 2 C.T.C. 312 (FCA). In CRA's view this applies to interest on overdue accounts: doc 2011-0409901E5; but this might be wrong in light of *Irving Oil* and similar cases (see Notes to 9(1) under "Business income vs property income"). CRA remains firmly of the view that all interest, regardless of source, is income from property for 149(5): 2011-0419931I7, 2012-0457611C6, 2012-0462861C6. Unrelated interest expense incurred to renovate a building cannot be deducted against the investment income: 2012-0437651I7.

The deemed trust may need to file a T3 return; see 150(1)(c). It is not eligible for the grandfathering in 122(2): VIEWS doc 2010-0355221E5.

A gain on sale of land used by a recreational club is exempt due to 149(5)(e)(ii): VIEWS docs 2002-0140793, 2005-0148871R3, 2010-0358021E5, 2011-040074 [2011-0400741R3], but only if the land was used "exclusively for and directly in the course of" its activities: 2011-041552117, 2012-0460901E5, 2013-049904117, 2018-0752521R3. An ongoing appeal on this issue was *Mont-Bruno CC*, procedural decisions 2017 CarswellNat 3165 and 2018 TCC 105, consent judgment Dec. 2018 (TCC file 2016-1152(IT)G).

As to whether a club's rental income is income from property (or possibly business income causing it not to be an NPO), see doc 2013-0475041E5.

For a ruling on amalgamation of two clubs see doc 2004-0103121R3. "Recreational" in 149(5) includes "pleasure": 2010-0358021E5. For interpretation of "main purpose is to provide dining, recreational or sporting facilities", see 2011-041205117, 2012-0460901E5.

See also Alexandra Tzannidakis, "The Taxable Income of Non-Profit Organizations", xxxv(12) *The Canadian Taxpayer* (Carswell) 94-95 (June 14, 2013) or 21(8) *Canadian Not-for-Profit News* (Carswell) 57-58 (Aug. 2013).

149(5) opening words amended by 2014 budget bill #2, for 2016 and later taxation years, to change "an *inter vivos* trust shall be" to "a trust is" (in sync with generally replacing "testamentary trust" with "graduated rate estate").

Interpretation Bulletins: IT-83R3: Non-profit organizations — Taxation of income from property; IT-406R2: Tax payable by an *inter vivos* trust; IT-409: Winding-up of a non-profit organization (cancelled); IT-496R: Non-profit organizations.

Advance Tax Rulings: ATR-29: Amalgamation of social clubs.

(6) Apportionment rule — Where it is necessary for the purpose of this section to ascertain the taxable income of a taxpayer for a period that is a part of a taxation year, the taxable income for the period shall be deemed to be the proportion of the taxable income for the taxation year that the number of days in the period is of the number of days in the taxation year.

Related Provisions: 124(3) — Crown agents; 249.1(1)(b)(i) — Exempt individuals not subject to forced calendar year-end.

Interpretation Bulletins: IT-347R2: Crown corporations (cancelled); IT-409: Winding-up of a non-profit organization (cancelled).

(7) [Prescribed form for R&D corporation —] Time for filing — A corporation the taxable income of which for a taxation year is exempt from tax under this Part because of paragraph (1)(j) shall file with the Minister a prescribed form containing prescribed information on or before its filing-due date for the year.

Related Provisions: 149(7.1) — Penalty for late filing.

Notes: 149(7) added by 1995 Budget, for taxation years that end after Feb. 27, 1995.

Former 149(7), repealed in 1977, provided rules dealing with control of a corporation, for purposes of 149(1)(g) and (h), now repealed.

Forms: T661: SR&ED expenditures claim; T1263: Third-party payments for SR&ED; T4088: Claiming scientific research and experimental development expenditures — guide to form T661.

(7.1) Penalty for failure to file on time — Where a corporation fails to file the prescribed form as required by subsection (7) for a taxation year, it is liable to a penalty equal to the amount determined by the formula

$$A \times B$$

where

A   is the greater of

    (a) $500, and

    (b) 2% of its taxable income for the year; and

B   is the lesser of

    (a) 12, and

    (b) the number of months in whole or in part that are in the period that begins on the day on or before which the prescribed form is required to be filed and ends on the day it is filed.

Notes: 149(7.1) added by 1995 Budget, for taxation years that end after Feb. 27, 1995.

See Notes to 239(1).

(8) Interpretation of para. (1)(j) — For the purpose of paragraph (1)(j),

    (a) a corporation is controlled by another corporation if more than 50% of its issued share capital (having full voting rights under all circumstances) belongs to

        (i) the other corporation, or

        (ii) the other corporation and persons with whom the other corporation does not deal at arm's length,

but a corporation shall be deemed not to have acquired control of a corporation if it has not purchased (or otherwise acquired for a consideration) any of the shares in the capital stock of that corporation; and

    (b) there shall be included in computing a corporation's income and in determining its gross revenue the amount of all gifts received by the corporation and all amounts contributed to the corporation to be used for scientific research and experimental development.

Related Provisions: 256(6), (6.1) — Extended meaning of "control".

Notes: 149(8)(b) amended by 1995 Budget, for tax years that begin after June 1995.

(9) Rules for determining gross revenue — In determining the gross revenue of a corporation for the purpose of determining whether it is described by paragraph (1)(j) for a taxation year,

    (a) there may be deducted an amount not exceeding its gross revenue for the year computed without including or deducting any amount under this subsection; and

    (b) there shall be included any amount that has been deducted under this subsection for the preceding taxation year.

Related Provisions: 248(1) — Definition of "gross revenue".

Notes: 149(9) amended by 1995 Budget, for taxation years that begin after June 1995.

(10) Becoming or ceasing to be exempt — If at any time (in this subsection referred to as "that time"), a person — that is a corporation or, if that time is after September 12, 2013, a trust — becomes or ceases to be exempt from tax under this Part on its taxable income, the following rules apply:

    (a) the taxation year of the person that would, but for this paragraph, have included that time is deemed to end immediately before that time, a new taxation year of the person is deemed to begin at that time and, for the purpose of determining the person's fiscal period after that time, the person is deemed not to have established a fiscal period before that time;

    (a.1) for the purpose of computing the person's income for its first taxation year that ends after that time, the person is deemed to have deducted under sections 20, 138 and 140 in computing the person's income for its taxation year that ended immediately before that time, the greatest amount that could have been claimed or deducted by the person for that year as a reserve under those sections;

    (b) the person is deemed to have disposed, at the time (in this subsection referred to as the "disposition time") that is immediately before the time that is immediately before that time, of each property held by the person immediately before that time for an amount equal to its fair market value at that time and to have reacquired the property at that time at a cost equal to that fair market value; and

    (c) for the purposes of applying sections 37, 65 to 66.4, 66.7, 111 and 126, subsections 127(5) to (36) and section 127.3 to the person, the person is deemed to be a new corporation or trust, as the case may be, the first taxation year of which began at that time;

    (d) [Repealed]

Related Provisions: 16(2), (3) — Obligation issued at discount; 54"superficial loss"(c), (g) — Superficial loss rule does not apply; 87(2.1)(b) — Losses of predecessor corporation; 89(1.2) — Capital dividend account of corporation ceasing to be tax-exempt; 100 — Disposition of an interest in a partnership; 107.3(3)(a) — Trust that ceases to be qualifying environmental trust ceases being exempt from Part I tax; 124(3) — Crown agents; 135.2(11) — Application if Cdn Wheat Board Farmers' Trust ceases to be eligible trust; 149(6) — Apportionment rule; 216(1) — Alternative re rents and timber royalties; 219(2) — Exempt corporations; 227(14) — Application of Parts III, IV and VI to certain public corporations.

Notes: The deemed disposition under 149(10)(b) of all property includes goodwill even where not recognized on the balance sheet: VIEWS doc 2002-0126653. Due to the deemed reacquisition at fair market value (para. (b)) on ceasing to be exempt, the entity may have later tax savings from capital cost allowance: *Hydro One*, 2020 ONSC 4331, para. 18.

For interpretation on 149(10) see VIEWS docs 2006-0198211R3 (no avoidance and abuse of "fresh start" rules), 2006-0201621R3 (windup of an NPO), 2007-0262861E5 (determining when NPO ceases to be NPO); 2009-0352231E5 and 2010-0355831I7 (effect of losing NPO status); Drache, "What Happens When a Non-Profit Loses Its Status?", 18(11) *Canadian Not-for-Profit News* (Carswell) 87-88 (Nov. 2010).

149(10) opening words amended by 2017 budget bill #1, for tax years that begin after 2018, to change "on its taxable income otherwise than by reason of paragraph (1)(t)" to "on its taxable income" (due to repeal of 149(1)(t)).

149(10)(d) repealed by 2016 budget bill #2, effective 2017, as part of changing the eligible capital property rules to CCA Class 14.1 (see Notes to 20(1)(b)). Before 2017, read:

    (d) there is to be deducted under paragraph 20(1)(b) in computing the person's income from a business for the taxation year that ended immediately before that time the amount, if any, by which the person's cumulative eligible capital immediately before the disposition time in respect of the business exceeds the total of

        (i) ¾ of the fair market value of the eligible capital property in respect of the business, and

        (ii) the amount otherwise deducted under paragraph 20(1)(b) in computing the person's income from the business for the taxation year that ended immediately before that time.

149(10) amended by 2013 budget bill #2, effective March 21, 2013, essentially to extend the rule to trusts as of Sept. 13, 2013. This links to the "loss restriction event" rules: see Notes to 251.2(2).

149(10)(c) amended by 2002-2013 technical bill (Part 5 — technical), effective for each corporation that after 2006 becomes or ceases to be exempt.

149(10) earlier amended by 1995-97 technical bill and 1992 technical bill.

Interpretation Bulletins: IT-302R3: Losses of a corporation — the effect that acquisitions of control, amalgamations, and windings-up have on their deductibility; IT-409: Winding-up of a non-profit organization (cancelled).

Charities Policies: CPS-017: Effective date of registration.

(11) Geographical boundaries — body performing government functions — For the purpose of this section, the geographical boundaries of a municipal or public body performing a function of government are

(a) the geographical boundaries that encompass the area in respect of which an Act of Parliament or an agreement given effect by an Act of Parliament recognizes or grants to the body a power to impose taxes; or

(b) if paragraph (a) does not apply, the geographical boundaries within which that body has been authorized by the laws of Canada or of a province to exercise that function.

Notes: The Finance Technical Notes to 149(11) state: "if a particular self-governing First Nation meets the definition of 'a public body performing a function of government in Canada', it is intended that the relevant geographic boundary would delineate the area where the self-government agreement, or the statute enacting self-government powers, provides the First Nation authority to impose direct taxes. As a second example, if a particular Indian Band meets the definition of 'a public body performing a function of government in Canada', it is intended that the geographic boundary of the Indian Band be the band's reserves as defined in the *Indian Act*. Similarly, if a particular school board meets the definition of 'a municipal or public body performing a function of government in Canada' it is intended that the geographic boundary of the school board be the area of jurisdiction of the board as defined by provincial legislation or regulation."

149(11) added by 2002-2013 technical bill (Part 5 — technical), for taxation years that begin after May 8, 2000.

Former 149(11) repealed by 1995-97 technical bill, effective June 18, 1998. It prevented 149(10) from applying to a change in control pursuant to an agreement in writing entered into before Nov. 13, 1981.

(12) Information returns — Every person who, because of paragraph (1)(e) or (l), is exempt from tax under this Part on all or part of the person's taxable income shall, within 6 months after the end of each fiscal period of the person and without notice or demand therefor, file with the Minister an information return for the period in prescribed form and containing prescribed information, if

(a) the total of all amounts each of which is a taxable dividend or an amount received or receivable by the person as, on account of, in lieu of or in satisfaction of, interest, rentals or royalties in the period exceeds $10,000;

(b) at the end of the person's preceding fiscal period the total assets of the person (determined in accordance with generally accepted accounting principles) exceeded $200,000; or

(c) an information return was required to be filed under this subsection by the person for a preceding fiscal period.

Related Provisions: 149.1(14) — Charity or RCAAA information return; 162(7)(a) — Penalty for failure to file; 233 — Demand for information return; *Interpretation Act* 27(5) — Meaning of "within 6 months".

Notes: 149(12) imposes a filing requirement on medium to large NPOs, so that CRA can find out who they are and how large they are. See Notes to 149(1)(l), and CRA Guide T4117.

Where new accounting standards require an NPO to record tangible capital assets at FMV on its balance sheet, so total assets exceed $200,000, it must file a T1044: VIEWS doc 2015-0580541E5.

A B.C. strata corporation files a single T1044 even if it has different sections: VIEWS doc 2011-0424091E5.

An NPO's GST/HST refund or rebate can legally be held back if this return is not filed: *Excise Tax Act* ss. 229(2), 263.02 (see David M. Sherman, *The Practitioner's Goods and Services Tax Annotated* (Carswell)). This is enforced for the T1044 but not for an NPO's T2 return: CRA Fact Sheet, April 25, 2012 [*GST & HST Times* 269C].

CRA's policy is not to apply a 162(7) penalty to a first-time late 149(12) return: VIEWS doc 2007-0243291C6. On the consequences of not filing for many years, see 2016-0632811E5. See also Amy Saab, "Late Not-for-Profit Returns", 4(2) *Canadian Tax Focus* (ctf.ca) 6 (May 2014).

An incorporated NPO must also file a T2 return under 150(1)(a) (but not a registered charity: 150(1.1)(a)); and a trust (or deemed trust under 149(5)) may need to file a T3 under 150(1)(c).

149(12) added by 1992 technical bill, effective for fiscal periods that end after 1992.

The Aug. 16/11 draft legislation proposed to add "(other than a registered Canadian amateur athletic association)" to the opening words, but an RCAAA is exempt under 149(1)(g) (not (e) or (l)). 149(1)(14) requires RCAAAs and charities to file an information return.

Interpretation Bulletins: IT-496R: Non-profit organizations.

Forms: T1044: Non-profit organization (NPO) information return; T4117: Income tax guide to the Non-Profit Organization (NPO) information return [guide].

Registered Charities Newsletters: 19 (what is the difference between a registered charity and a non-profit organization?).

Definitions [s. 149]: "allowable capital loss" — 38(b), 248(1); "amateur athlete trust" — 143.1(1.2)(a), 248(1); "amount" — 248(1); "beneficially interested" — 248(25); "business" — 248(1); "Canada" — 255, *Interpretation Act* 35(1); "Canadian resource property" — 66(15), 248(1); "cemetery care trust" — 148.1(1), 248(1); "control" — 149(8); "controlled" — 256(5.1), (6), (6.1); "controlled directly or indirectly" — 256(5.1)–(6); "corporation" — 248(1), *Interpretation Act* 35(1); "cumulative eligible capital" — 14(5), 248(1); "deferred profit sharing plan" — 147(1), 248(1); "depreciable property" — 13(21), 248(1); "direct or indirect control" — 256(5.1)–(6); "disposition time" — 149(10)(b); "dividend", "employed" — 248(1); "eligible capital property" — 54, 248(1); "eligible funeral arrangement" — 148.1(1), 248(1); "employees profit sharing plan" — 144(1), 248(1); "employment" — 248(1); "fair market value" — see 69(1) Notes; "farm loss" — 111(8), 248(1); "farming" — 248(1); "filing-due date" — 150(1), 248(1); "fiscal period" — 249.1; "fishing" — 248(1); "foreign resource property" — 66(15), 248(1); "geographical boundaries" — 149(11); "gross revenue" — 149(8)(b), 149(9), 248(1); "Her Majesty" — *Interpretation Act* 35(1); "immovables" — Quebec *Civil Code* art. 900–907; "income" — 149(1.2), (2); "insurer" — 248(1); "*inter vivos* trust" — 108(1), 248(1); "interest in real property" — 248(4); "life insurance business" — 248(1); "limited partnership loss" — 96(2.1)(e), 248(1); "Minister" — 248(1); "Minister of Finance" — *Financial Administration Act* 14; "month" — *Interpretation Act* 35(1); "net capital loss", "non-capital loss" — 111(8), 248(1); "office" — 248(1); "outside the geographical boundaries" — 149(1.2); "owned" — 149(1.3); "Parliament" — *Interpretation Act* 35(1); "partnership" — see 96(1) Notes; "person" — 248(1); "pooled registered pension plan" — 147.5(1), 248(1); "prescribed", "property" — 248(1); "province" — *Interpretation Act* 35(1); "qualifying environmental trust" — 211.6(1), 248(1); "qualifying owner" — 149(1)(d.6); "qualifying share" — 192(6), 248(1) *[not intended to apply to s. 149]*; "real right in immovables" — 248(4.1); "registered Canadian amateur athletic association" — 248(1); "registered disability savings plan" — 146.4(1), 248(1); "registered journalism organization", "registered pension plan" — 248(1); "registered retirement income fund" — 146.3(1), 248(1); "registered retirement savings plan" — 146(1), 248(1); "registered supplementary unemployment benefit plan" — 145(1), 248(1); "regulation" — 248(1); "related" — 251(2); "related segregated fund trust" — 138.1(1)(a); "resident in Canada" — 250; "restricted farm loss" — 31, 248(1); "retirement compensation arrangement", "scientific research and experimental development" — 248(1), Reg. 2900(1); "servant" — 248(1)"employment"; "share", "shareholder", "specified shareholder", "subsidiary wholly-owned corporation" — 248(1); "TFSA" — 146.2(5), 248(1); "taxable capital gain" — 38(a), 248(1); "taxable income" — 2(2), 248(1); "taxation year" — 249; "taxpayer" — 248(1); "trust" — 104(1), 248(1), (3); "writing" — *Interpretation Act* 35(1).

149.01 [Trade union financial disclosure — Repealed]

Notes: 149.01 repealed by Bill C-4, S.C. 2017, c. 12, effective June 19, 2017, without ever taking effect in practice. It would have required labour unions and labour trusts to make very extensive financial disclosure, as well as information on political, lobbying and other non-labour-relations activities, and would have required CRA to make this information public. It was enacted by Private Member's Bill C-377, S.C. 2015, c. 41, for fiscal periods beginning after Dec. 30, 2015.

Most private members' bills do not make it through the Commons, but Bill C-377 obtained (Conservative) government support and did pass. It was then passed by the Senate in June 2013 but with amendments that would have gutted the bill so that it would apply to only the very largest unions, so it had to return to the Commons for approval. However, the Commons re-passed the original version, ignoring the Senate amendments. The Senate then passed it without further change.

The Liberals proposed in their Oct. 2015 election platform to repeal 149.01, and the new government waived compliance under 220(2.1) pending repeal (CRA news release Dec. 21, 2015). In *Bernard*, 2017 FC 536, a judicial review application challenging the waiver of compliance was stayed until July 1, 2017; at 2017 FC 778, it was struck out, since by then 149.01 had been repealed.

For the text of 149.01, see the 43rd-51st editions.

Qualified Donees [Charities, etc.]

Notes: Heading before 149.1 changed from "Charities" to "Qualified Donees" by 2011 budget bill #2, effective 2012.

149.1 (1) Definitions — In this section and section 149.2,

Related Provisions: 172(6), 187.7 — Application of subsec. 149.1(1).

Notes: 149.1(1) opening words amended by 2007 budget bill #2, effective March 19, 2007, to refer to 149.2. Amended in RSC 1985 (5th Supp) consolidation for tax years ending after Nov. 1991, to delete reference to s. 172 and Part V. These rules of application are now in 172(6) and 187.7.

"Canadian amateur athletic association" means an association that

(a) was created under any law in force in Canada,

(b) is resident in Canada,

(c) has no part of its income payable to, or otherwise available for the personal benefit of, any proprietor, member or shareholder of the association unless the proprietor, member or shareholder was a club, society or association the primary purpose and primary function of which was the promotion of amateur athletics in Canada,

(d) has the promotion of amateur athletics in Canada on a nationwide basis as its exclusive purpose and exclusive function, and

(e) devotes all its resources to that purpose and function;

Related Provisions: 149.1(4.2) — Revocation of RCAAA registration; 149.1(6.01) — Meaning of "devotes all of its resources" — related business; 149.1(6.201) — Meaning of "devotes all of its resources" — political activities; 248(1)"registered Canadian amateur athletic association" — CAAA that is registered.

Notes: See Notes to 248(1)"registered Canadian amateur athletic association". Definition added by 2011 budget bill #2, effective 2012.

"capital gains pool" — [Repealed]

Notes: 149.1(1)"capital gains pool" repealed by 2010 budget bill #2, effective for taxation years that end after March 3, 2010.

"charitable activities" includes public policy dialogue and development activities carried on in furtherance of a charitable purpose;

Proposed Amendment (uncertain) — 149.1(1)"charitable activities"

"charitable activities" includes

(a) public policy dialogue and development activities carried on in furtherance of a charitable purpose; and

(b) making resources — including grants, gifts or transfers — available by transactions, arrangements or collaborations of any kind whatsoever in furtherance of a charitable purpose to a person that is not a qualified donee if those resources are made available by a charity that takes reasonable steps to ensure that those resources are used exclusively for a charitable purpose in accordance with subsection (27).

Application: Private Member's Bill S-222 (First House of Commons Reading June 23, 2021), subsec. 2(1), will amend the definition "charitable activities" in subsec. 149.1(1) to read as above, in force two years after Royal Assent.

S. 6 of the Bill provides:

6. (1) The Minister of National Revenue must, within five years after the day on which this Act comes into force, undertake a review of the provisions enacted by this Act.

(2) The Minister must, within one year after the review is undertaken, cause a report on that review to be laid before each House of Parliament within the first fifteen sitting days of that House after the report is completed.

Notes: This is a private member's bill (Senator Rata Omidvar, Ontario), and such bills usually do not pass. (For background, see Notes to this definition below, at "Foreign spending".) However, the bill has the support of the CRA Advisory Committee on the Charitable Sector, in Report #1 (Jan. 2021, tinyurl.com/char-adv-report1), recommending that the "own activity" test "be replaced with a regime that permits registered charities to operate in furtherance of their charitable purpose". It also has the support of 34 prominent charity lawyers in a Feb. 2021 open letter: tinyurl.com/open-letter-char. Thus, it has more chance of passage (and indeed, it cleared the Senate and received First Reading in the Commons before the House rose for summer break). For a detailed contrary view see Mark Blumberg, "Will changing structured arrangements into a reasonable person test help the charity sector" (4 parts, March 16-17, 2021), blumbergs.ca/blog.

Related Provisions: 149.1(10.1) — Public policy dialogue and development activities considered to be in furtherance of charity's purpose.

Notes: In deciding whether an entity carries on charitable activities (and should be, or remain, registered), CRA need only act "reasonably". See Notes to 172(3).

Due to the word "includes" (see Notes to 188.1(5)), "charitable activities" has its common-law meaning, but is extended to include "public policy dialogue and development activities", provided they are in furtherance of a charitable purpose (and see 149.1(10): this can mean its "stated purposes"). This implements a consultation panel report: see Notes to 149.1(6.1). Note the difference between charitable *activities* and charitable *purposes*, also defined in 149.1(1).

Common-law meaning: the leading case is *Vancouver Society of Immigrant & Visible Minority Women*, [1999] 2 C.T.C. 1 (SCC). The 4 traditional common-law categories (going back to the 17th century) are: relief of poverty, advancement of education, advancement of religion, and other purposes beneficial to the community. "If every or-

ganization that might have beneficial by-products, regardless of its purposes, were found to be charitable, the definition of charity would be much broader than what has heretofore been recognized in the common law": *A.Y.S.A. Amateur Youth Soccer*, 2007 SCC 42, para. 41. The determination of charitable "is a question of public law, not one of property and civil rights to which the private law of Québec is relevant": *Travel Just*, 2006 FCA 343 (leave to appeal denied 2007 CarswellNat 1001 (SCC)), para. 16. Activities that are illegal or against public policy cannot be charitable: *Everywoman's Health*, [1991] 2 C.T.C. 320 (FCA), para. 15.

Poverty: see CRA Guidance CG-029 (Nov. 2020). Preventing poverty (as opposed to relieving it) does not qualify: *Credit Counselling*, 2016 FCA 193 [Drache, "Canadian Charity Law Solidly in the 17th Century", 24(8) *Canadian Not-for-Profit News [CNfPN]* (Carswell) 57-59 (Aug. 2016)]. In *St. Catharines Seniors v. MPAC*, 2015 ONSC 3896, low-income seniors' housing was held to be "for relief of the poor" for municipal property tax; seniors with $22,000 median annual income were "poor", though "not cardboard-box-in-the-park poor" (para. 52). See also Drache, "Relief of Poverty", 26(12) *CNfPN* 89-91 (Dec. 2018).

Education: see CRA Guidance CG-030 (Nov. 2020) for detailed discussion, including criteria for both "content" (educational value, not one-sided unless generally accepted as for public benefit) and "process" (structured teaching). The footnotes cite many Court cases, mostly from outside Canada. In *Hostelling International*, 2008 FCA 396, facilitating travel by providing low-cost accommodation, to provide an opportunity for people to educate themselves, was not charitable [Drache, "FCA Narrows Meaning of Education", 17(2) *CNfPN* 9-11 (Feb. 2009)]. In *Greenpeace*, [2020] NZHC 1999 (New Zealand), para. 117, Greenpeace's research on environmental issues qualified, even though the research was used to support its advocacy.

Religion: see CRA draft guidance, tinyurl.com/religion-advance. In *Fuaran Foundation*, 2004 FCA 181, a foundation set up to operate a Christian retreat centre was denied charity status because its objects were too broad, and workshop attendees would be able to decide not to participate in religious activities. Similarly, in *Humanics Institute*, 2014 FCA 265 (leave to appeal denied 2015 CarswellNat 1114 (SCC)), the applicant's "Oneness of Reality" purposes and objects were broad and vague, and building and maintaining a sanctuary and sculpture park would not advance religion or education. In *Church of Atheism*, 2019 FCA 296 (leave to appeal to SCC requested), atheism was held not to be a religion, as it lacked "a particular and comprehensive system of doctrine and observances" (para. 22). See also Carter, "Advancing Religion as a Head of Charity", 20(4) *The Philanthropist [TPh]* 257-93 (2007); Drache, "Religion and Registration", 18(11) *CnfPN* 81-83 (Nov. 2010); Pellowe, "Religion and Philanthropy: How Does a Place of Worship Really Benefit the Public?", *TPh*, July 15, 2020 (6pp).

Producing and disseminating news is not charitable: *News to You*, 2011 FCA 192; but 149.1(1)"qualified donee"(b.1) now effectively allows charity status for a "248(1)"registered journalism organization".

Human rights and environmental issues: promoting tourism supporting these was not charitable in *Travel Just*, 2006 FCA 343 (leave to appeal denied 2007 CarswellNat 1001 (SCC)): it promoted "commercial activity ... with a strong flavour of private benefit" (para. 9). In *Greenpeace*, [2020] NZHC 1999 (New Zealand), para. 101, environmental advocacy was accepted. See also Cooper, "Environmental Issues under the 4th Head of Charity", tinyurl.com/cooper-enviro; Parachin, "Human Rights and Charity — Regulatory Challenges", *The Philanthropist* (Sept. 2016), tinyurl.com/phil-rights.

For CRA policy on various activities see the "Charities Policies" and "Charities Guidance" annotations below (e.g., promoting volunteerism, promoting animal welfare, upholding human rights, community economic development, arts organizations, promotion of health). CRA provides model language for charitable objects, where it will "not usually need to discuss the wording of the object with the organization", at tinyurl.com/charit-purposes. See also "Factors that will prevent an organization from being registered as a charity", on tinyurl.com/charit-apply; CG-019, "How to Draft Purposes for Charitable Registration" (July 2013); Kerr & Chan, *Charities and Charitable Donations* (*Taxnet Pro* Tax Disputes Centre, Jan. 2018, 82pp); Drache, Hayhoe & Stevens, *Charities Taxation, Policy and Practice — Taxation* (Carswell, looseleaf or *Taxnet Pro* Reference Centre), chap. 3, "Definition of Charity" (72pp). Self-help groups (as opposed to "members' groups" formed to further members' interests) may qualify: Charities Policy CPS-016; Drache, "Self-Help Groups May Be Charitable", 21(10) *CNfPN* 77-78 (Oct. 2013).

The lack of change in the meaning of "charity" for centuries, and CRA's control over charities via the tax system, provoke regular criticism, but no government has been willing to change the rules. See Broder, "The Legal Definition of Charity and CCRA's Charitable Registration Process", 17(3) *The Philanthropist [TPh]* (thephilanthropist.ca) 3-58 (2002); Chan, "Taxing Charities", 55(3) *Canadian Tax Journal* 481-556 (2007); Wyatt, "Modernising Charity Law", 22(2) *TPh* 59-74 (2009); Drache, "C.D. Howe Paper Proposes a Canadian Charities Council", 17(12) *Canadian Not-for-Profit News [CNfPN]* (Carswell) 89-91 (Dec. 2009); Aptowitzer, "Losing the Forest for the Trees", 19(9) *CNfPN* 70-71 (Sept. 2011); Juneau, "Time for a Review: Registered Charities and the ITA", *TPh* (June 12, 2017); Chan & Vander Vies, "The Evolution of the Legal Meaning of Charity", chap. 5 of *Intersections and Innovations* (2021), mut-tart.org/intersections. A new foundation was formed in 2013 to "spur further development of Canadian charity law": Broder, "Pemsel Case Foundation Launched to Foster Canadian Charity Law", 25(4) *TPh* 209-14 (2014). See Maurice Cullity, "Charity and Politics in Canada", 25(4) *TPh* 1-59 (2014); Juneau, "The Canadian *Income Tax Act* and the Concepts of Charitable Purposes and Activities" (tinyurl.com/pemsel-ita); and tinyurl.com/pemsel-all. See also Notes to 149.1(6.1) regarding political activities; and Notes to 168(1) re revocations.

Foreign spending: A charity wishing to send money or goods abroad must enter into an "agency agreement" with a foreign entity, whereby the Canadian charity technically carries out the work and has "direction and control" over the project. Simply giving money to a foreign charity is not permitted, and is grounds for revocation. See Charities Guidance CG-002 (detailed discussion); CG-004 (re using an intermediary); *Canadian Committee for the Tel Aviv Foundation*, 2002 FCA 72; *Canadian Magen David Adom for Israel*, 2002 FCA 323; *Bayit Lepletot*, 2006 FCA 128; *Public Television Assn*, 2015 FCA 170. "It is open for the appellant to carry on its charitable works through an agent but it must be shown that the agent is actually carrying on the charitable works. It is not sufficient to show that the agent is part of another charitable organization which carries on a charitable program": *Bayit Lepletot*, para. 5. In *Promised Land Ministries*, 2019 TCC 145, a charity was suspended because, despite being warned, it did not get receipts for money spent in countries with "cash economies": it could have used a notebook in which the individual receiving funds could sign a receipt. See also Blumberg, "Canadian Charities and Foreign Activities", 21(4) *The Philanthropist* 311-38 (2008) (discusses other options besides agency); "Canadian Charities Conducting International Activities (2015)", tinyurl.com/blumberg-charit-intl; Drache, "Foreign Membership Fees and Similar Payments", 18(2) *CNfPN* 13-14 (Feb. 2010), "CRA Changes the Rules on Donating Foreign Infrastructure", 21(9) 69-70 (Sept. 2013), "Why the Absence of Global Charity HQs in Canada?", 23(1) 5-6 (Jan. 2015), and "A Primer on Agency", 28(4) 30-31 (April 2020); Valentine, "Foreign Activities by Canadian Registered Charities", *The Philanthropist* (Nov. 2016). See also the Bill S-222 Proposed Amendment above.

Privately directed fundraising is not allowed: funds can be raised for a cause but not for a particular needy person or family: Charities Summary Policy CSP-P09; Cooper, "Supporting Syrian Refugees", 24(2) *CNfPN* 14-15 (Feb. 2016).

Complying with the law: see Drache, "Charities in Breach of Local Laws May Retain Status in Canada", 27(4) *Canadian Not-for-Profit News* (Carswell) 30-31 (April 2019).

A workaround if a project does not qualify as charitable is to donate to the local municipality to fund it. However, CRA can cancel a municipality's ability to issue charitable receipts; see Notes to 149.1(1)"qualified donee".

149.1(1)"charitable activities" added by 2018 budget bill #2, effective 2008 in respect of organizations, corporations and trusts that were registered charities on Sept. 14, 2018; and effective Sept. 14, 2018 in any other case.

Registered Charities Newsletters: 11 (consultation on registering organizations that provide rental housing for low-income tenants).

Charities Policies: CPC-003: Umbrella organization (see also July 29, 2005 consultation on proposed guidelines for the registration of umbrella organizations); CPC-004: Housing to the aged; CPC-011: Promotion of employment; CPC-013: Relief of poverty — advancement of education; CPC-022: Administration of registered charities' group insurance; CPS-001: Applicants that are established to hold periodic fundraisers; CPS-005: Festivals and the promotion of tourism; CPS-006: Registered charities making improvements to property leased from others; CPS-008: Organizations established to assist other charities; CPS-009: Holding of property for charities; CPS-010: Registration of arts festivals; CPS-012: Benefits to aboriginal peoples of Canada; CPS-015: Registration of organizations directed at youth; CPS-016: Distinction between self-help and members' groups; CPS-019: What is a related business?; CPS-021: Registering charities that promote racial equality; CPS-023: Applicants assisting ethnocultural communities; CPS-028: Fundraising by registered charities.

Charities Guidance: CG-001: Upholding human rights and charitable registration; CG-002: Canadian registered charities carrying out activities outside Canada; CG-003: Charitable work and ethnocultural groups — information on registering as a charity; CG-004: Using an intermediary to carry out a charity's activities within Canada; CG-011: Promotion of animal welfare and charitable registration; CG-014: Community economic development activities and charitable registration; CG-018: Arts activities and charitable registration; CG-020: Charitable purposes and activities that benefit youth; CG-021: Promotion of health and charitable registration; CG-022: Housing and charitable registration; CG-026: Relieving conditions attributable to being aged and charitable registration; CG-029: Relief of poverty and charitable registration; CG-030: Advancement of education and charitable registration; Draft Guidance on advancement of religion: tinyurl.com/draft-adv.

"charitable foundation" means a corporation or trust that is constituted and operated exclusively for charitable purposes, no part of the income of which is payable to, or is otherwise available for, the personal benefit of any proprietor, member, shareholder, trustee or settlor thereof, and that is not a charitable organization;

Related Provisions: 149 — Exemptions; 149.1(6.1) — Charitable purposes; 149.1(12)(b) — Rules — income; 149.1(22) — Refusal by Minister to register foundation; 188.1(4), (5) — Penalty for conferring undue benefit on a person.

Notes: In general, a charitable organization does direct charitable work while a foundation gives money to charitable organizations. See Drache, "Organization-Linked Foundations", 10(12) *Canadian Not-for-Profit News* (Carswell) 89-91 (Dec. 2002).

On whether a foundation can pay its directors or members a salary or fee, see Notes to 149.1(1)"charitable organization" under "Para. (b)".

For the registration of charities, see 248(1)"registered charity". In *Earth Fund*, 2002 FCA 498, a fund planning to operate a lottery to raise funds for preservation and enhancement of the environment did not qualify as a charitable foundation, as its objects were too broad and the lottery would be a manifestly commercial arrangement.

149.1(1)"charitable foundation" was 149.1(1)(a) before RSC 1985 (5th Supp) consolidation for tax years ending after Nov. 1991.

Interpretation Bulletins: IT-83R3: Non-profit organizations — Taxation of income from property.

Forms: RC4106: Registered charities operating outside Canada [guide]; T2050: Application to register a charity under the ITA; T4063: Registering a charity for income tax purposes [guide].

"charitable organization", at any particular time, means an organization, whether or not incorporated,

  (a) constituted and operated exclusively for charitable purposes,

  (a.1) all the resources of which are devoted to charitable activities carried on by the organization itself,

> **Proposed Amendment (uncertain) —
> 149.1(1)"charitable organization"(a.1)**
>
> **Application**: Private Member's Bill S-222 (First House of Commons Reading June 23, 2021), subsec. 2(2), will amend para. (a.1) of the definition "charitable organization" in subsec. 149.1(1) to delete "carried on by the organization itself", in force two years after Royal Assent (and subject to review after 5 years: see under Proposed Amendment to 149.1(1)"charitable activities").
>
> **Notes**: This is a private member's bill that may not pass. See Notes to Proposed Amendment under 149.1(1)"charitable activities".

  (b) no part of the income of which is payable to, or is otherwise available for, the personal benefit of any proprietor, member, shareholder, trustee or settlor thereof,

  (c) more than 50% of the directors, trustees, officers or like officials of which deal at arm's length with each other and with

    (i) each of the other directors, trustees, officers and like officials of the organization,

    (ii) each person described by subparagraph (d)(i) or (ii), and

    (iii) each member of a group of persons (other than Her Majesty in right of Canada or of a province, a municipality, another registered charity that is not a private foundation, and any club, society or association described in paragraph 149(1)(l)) who do not deal with each other at arm's length, if the group would, if it were a person, be a person described by subparagraph (d)(i), and

  (d) that is not, at the particular time, and would not at the particular time be, if the organization were a corporation, controlled directly or indirectly in any manner whatever

    (i) by a person (other than Her Majesty in right of Canada or of a province, a municipality, another registered charity that is not a private foundation, and any club, society or association described in paragraph 149(1)(l)),

      (A) who immediately after the particular time, has contributed to the organization amounts that are, in total, greater than 50% of the capital of the organization immediately after the particular time, and

      (B) who immediately after the person's last contribution at or before the particular time, had contributed to the organization amounts that were, in total, greater than 50% of the capital of the organization immediately after the making of that last contribution, or

    (ii) by a person, or by a group of persons that do not deal at arm's length with each other, if the person or any member of the group does not deal at arm's length with a person described in subparagraph (i);

Related Provisions: 149 — Exemptions; 149.1(6), (6.2) — Whether resources devoted to charitable activities; 149.1(6.3) — Designation as public foundation, etc.; 149.1(6.4) — Registered national arts service organization deemed to be charitable organization; 149.1(12)(b) — Rules — income; 149.1(22) — Refusal by Minister to register foundation; 188 — Revocation tax; 188.1(4), (5) — Penalty for conferring undue benefit on a person; 256(5.1), (6) — Meaning of "controlled, directly or indirectly".

Notes: See 149.1(2) for restrictions on a charitable organization.

The 1976 legislation that introduced 149.1 provides that an organization that was a registered Canadian charitable organization (as then defined) at the end of 1976 is deemed to be a registered charity unless its registration is revoked.

For registration of charities, see 248(1)"registered charity"; and note that a registered national arts service organization is effectively deemed to be a charity: 149.1(6.4).

There is no federal regulator of charities as many countries have, other than CRA (which as a tax administrator has different goals). Creation of a Charities Commission has been suggested for decades: Drache, "An Independent Regulator of Charities", 24(12) *Canadian Not-for-Profit News* (Carswell) 89-91 (Dec. 2016). Provincial law governs charities, but in practice the level of control by the provinces varies.

CRA's website has services for charities and donors, including public access to charities' financial records: canada.ca/charities-giving. Charities can access their files at tinyurl.com/cra-BusAccount. See also Notes to 248(1)"registered charity".

Audits: T4118, *Auditing Charities*; tinyurl.com/charity-audit ("The audit process for charities"), including statistics on results of audits; Hawara, "CRA Charities Directorate's Approach to Compliance", 2014 Cdn Tax Foundation conference report, 37:1-10.

"Resources" (para. (a.1), formerly (a)): CRA's view is that management and administration costs are "resources devoted to charitable activities": doc 2006-0168601E5. See also Joel Nitikman, "When does a charity devote all of its resources to its charitable activities?" (case comment on *Word Investments*, [2008] HCA 55 (Australia)), 57(1) *Canadian Tax Journal* 79-85 (2009); Drache, "What are the Resources of a Charity?", 26(4) *Canadian Not-for-Profit News* (Carswell) 30-31 (April 2018); Stephen Couchman, "The Administration Paradox", *The Philanthropist* (Oct. 29, 2018), tinyurl.com/admin-pdox. Owning shares can put a charity offside if the relationship between the charity and the corporation "is suggestive of activities that are other than passive in nature": 2009-0306691E5.

Fundraising is usually acceptable, but must meet the "resources" test, and not be an un-"related business" (149.1(2)(a)). See Charities Guidance CG-013 (fundraising costs over 35% of revenues will trigger CRA scrutiny); Policy CPS-019 (related business); Drache, "Fundraising or Related Business", 16(9) *Canadian Not-for-Profit News* (Carswell) 68-69 (Sept. 2008); Manwaring & Valentine, "Comments on CRA Fundraising Guidance", 58(3) *Canadian Tax Journal* 751-70 (2010); Glover, "The CRA's Revised Fundraising Guidelines", 2(3) *Canadian Tax Focus* (ctf.ca) 4-5 (Aug. 2012). In *Opportunities for the Disabled Foundation*, 2016 FCA 94, employing disabled persons as fundraisers was not charitable: "fundraising itself cannot become a raison d'être for a charity" (para. 61).

"Charitable activities" (para. (a.1)): see Notes to 149.1(1)"charitable activities". See also Notes to 168(1).

Para. (b): "No part of the income of which" refers to net income, so a charity can pay directors or members a reasonable salary or fee; but "personal benefit" could result from one person being able to sign cheques. See Notes to 149.1(1)(l); Au, "Personal Benefit for Members?", 15(3) *CNfPN* 22 (March 2007). Examples of charity registrations revoked because a director benefitted: *Humane Society*, 2015 FCA 178; *Ark Angel Foundation*, 2019 FCA 21 (leave to appeal denied 2019 CarswellNat 6296 (SCC)) (same director Michael O'Sullivan, and see also 2019 ONSC 1768 about him). Note also that provincial law (e.g. Ont. Reg. 4/01, *Approved Acts of Executors*) may prohibit or restrict a charity from paying directors: Cooper, "Changes in Ontario to Director Remuneration", 27(3) *Canadian Not-for-Profit News* (Carswell) 3-4 (Jan. 2019).

A charity that does not need to issue donation receipts can consider becoming an NPO instead (see Notes to 149(1)(l)), to avoid compliance costs and CRA control: Drache, "Non-Profit Status as an Option", 22(11) *CNfPN* 81-83 (Nov. 2014). See also the *British Columbia Benefit Companies Act*: a benefit company is a for-profit company committed to conducting business "in a responsible and sustainable manner and promoting one or more public benefits".

For CRA's Charities Advisory Committee see tinyurl.com/charadvis.

Definition amended by 2018 budget bill #2, to renumber para. (a) as (a.1) and add new para. (a), effective on the same basis as 149.1(1)"charitable activities".

Definition amended by 2002-2013 technical bill (Part 5 — technical), last change effective 2005. 149.1(1)"charitable organization" was para. 149.1(1)(b) before RSC 1985 (5th Supp) consolidation for tax years ending after Nov. 1991.

I.T. Application Rules: 69 (meaning of "chapter 148 of ...").

Interpretation Bulletins: IT-83R3: Non-profit organizations — Taxation of income from property. See also at end of s. 149.1.

Registered Charities Newsletters: 11 (consultation on registering organizations that provide rental housing for low-income tenants); 15 (facts and figures about charities and the CRA today; registered charities as internal divisions of other charities; elimination of racial discrimination as a charitable purpose); 17 (new policy statement on promoting racial equality; contact information); 20 (facts and figures; working outside Canada; working with others); 27 (facts and figures about charities and the CRA in 2005); 28 (facts and figures); 31 (disbursement quota — charitable organizations take note); 31 33 (*My Business Account* for charities); *Charities Connection* 5 (the Charities Directorate's guidance documents); *Charities Connection* 8 (golf tournaments).

Charities Policies: CPS-004: Applicants with broad object clauses; See also under 149.1(1)"charitable activities".

Charities Guidance: CG-009: Trust document; CG-017: General requirements for charitable registration; CG-019: How to draft purposes for charitable registration; CG-028: Head bodies and their internal divisions; See also under 149.1(1)"charitable activities".

Forms: RC4106: Registered charities operating outside Canada [guide]; T2050: Application to register a charity under the ITA; T2095: Registered charities — application for re-designation; T4063: Registering a charity for income tax purposes [guide]; T4118: Auditing charities [booklet].

"charitable purposes" includes the disbursement of funds to a qualified donee;

Related Provisions: 149.1(1)"charitable foundation", "charitable organization"(a) — Charitable foundation or organization must be operated exclusively for charitable purposes; 149.1(1)"political activity" — Gift to support donee's political activities; 149.1(6.1) — Charitable purposes can include incidental political activities.

Notes: Note the difference between charitable *purposes* and charitable *activities*, also defined in 149.1(1).

Definition amended by 2018 budget bill #2, to delete (from the end) "other than a gift the making of which is a political activity", effective on the same basis as the amendment to 149.1(6.1) (mostly overriding the 2012 amendment). See Notes to 149.1(6.1).

Definition amended by 2012 budget bill #1, effective June 29, 2012, to add to the end "other than a gift the making of which is a political activity".

149.1(1)"charitable purposes" was 149.1(1)(c) before RSC 1985 (5th Supp) consolidation for tax years ending after Nov. 1991.

Charities Policies: CPC-014: Provision of goods and services. See under 149.1(1)"charitable organization" for Policies on whether the objects of an organization entitle it to registration as a charity.

"charity" means a charitable organization or charitable foundation;

Related Provisions: 149(1)(f) — Exemptions for registered charity; 149(1)(l) — Non-profit organizations; 188 — Revocation tax; 248(1) — "registered charity".

Notes: See Notes to 248(1)"registered charity".

149.1(1)"charity" was 149.1(1)(d) before RSC 1985 (5th Supp) consolidation for tax years ending after Nov. 1991.

Proposed 149.1(1)**"compensation"**, in private member's Bill C-470 (2010), is unlikely to be reintroduced. See Notes to 149.1(15).

Interpretation Bulletins: IT-496R: Non-profit organizations.

Registered Charities Newsletters: See under 248(1)"registered charity".

Forms: T2050: Application to register a charity under the ITA; T2095: Registered charities — application for re-designation; T4063: Registering a charity for income tax purposes [guide].

"designated gift" means that portion of a gift of property made in a taxation year by a particular registered charity, to another registered charity with which it does not deal at arm's length, that is designated by the particular registered charity in its information return for the taxation year;

Related Provisions: 149.1(1.1)(a) — Designated gift (DG) deemed not spent on charitable activities; 149.1(4.1)(d), 188.1(12) — Receiving charity need not disburse DG; 149.1(12)(b)(i) — DG not included in receiving charity's income.

Notes: 149.1(1)"designated gift" added by 2010 budget bill #2, effective for taxation years that end after March 3, 2010. For earlier years see "specified gift" below.

"disbursement quota", for a taxation year of a registered charity, means the amount determined by the formula

$$A \times B \times 0.035/365$$

where

A is the number of days in the taxation year, and

B is

(a) the prescribed amount for the year, in respect of all or a portion of a property owned by the charity at any time in the 24 months immediately preceding the taxation year that was not used directly in charitable activities or administration, if that amount is greater than

(i) if the registered charity is a charitable organization, $100,000, and

(ii) in any other case, $25,000, and

(b) in any other case, nil;

Possible Future Amendment — Disbursement Quota Rules (Consultation)

Federal Budget, Chapter 6, April 19, 2021: *Boosting Charitable Spending in Our Communities*

Every year, charities are required to spend a minimum amount on their charitable programs or on gifts to qualified donees. This is known as the "disbursement quota" and it ensures that charitable donations are being invested into our communities.

While most charities meet or exceed their disbursement quotas, a gap of at least $1 billion in charitable expenditures in our communities exists today. Furthermore, growth in the investment assets of foundations has increased significantly in recent years. In 2019, charitable foundations held over $85 billion in long-term investments. But grant-making and other charitable activities have not kept pace.

[Chart 6.2 omitted — ed.]

Budget 2021 proposes launching public consultations with charities over the coming months on potentially increasing the disbursement quota and updating the tools at the Canada Revenue Agency's disposal, beginning in 2022. This could potentially increase support for the charitable sector and those that rely on its services by between $1 billion and $2 billion annually.

Notes: It is unclear why the government should look only at *increasing* the disbursement quota, when interest rates are so low that spending 3.5% of capital may require dipping into capital. However, there has been pressure for more charitable spending during COVID-19. See Klombies, "Budget 2021: disbursement quota increase on the horizon?", tinyurl.com/drache-dq.

Related Provisions: 149.1(1.2) — Authority of Minister — calculation of pre-scribed amount; 149.1(2)(b) — Charitable organization must expend DQ each year; 149.1(3)(b) — Public foundation must expend DQ each year; 149.1(4)(b) — Private foundation must expend DQ each year; 149.1(4.1) — Anti-avoidance rule re DQ; 149.1(5) — Administrative reduction in DQ; 149.1(8) — If approved by Minister, accumulated property not included in formula; 149.1(12) — Rules; 149.1(20), (21) — Carryforward or carryback of disbursement excess; 248(30)–(33) — Determination of eligible amount of gift; 257 — Formula cannot calculate to less than zero.

Notes: The disbursement quota (DQ) is generally 3.5% of capital: 3.5% of amounts not used directly in 149.1(1)"charitable activities" or administration, if more than $100,000 ($25,000 for a foundation). The DQ must be spent on charitable activities, or the charity's registration can be revoked: 149.1(2)(b), (3)(b), (4)(b). Such activities do not include fund-raising and might not include administrative expenses: Drache, "Administrative Expenses", 15(4) *Canadian Not-for-Profit News* (Carswell) 28-30 (April 2007). Assets for the DQ calculation include those used in a business: Feunekes, "The Disbursement Quota and Related Businesses", 15(2) *Tax Hyperion* (Carswell) 4-5 (March-April 2018). See also Drache et al., *Charities Taxation, Policy and Practice — Taxation* (Carswell, looseleaf or Taxnet Pro Reference Centre), chap. 8, "Disbursement Quota"; Palassio, "Granting During the Pandemic", *The Philanthropist* (thephilanthropist.ca), July 2, 2020 (5pp).

Failure to meet the DQ can be remedied by having a disbursement excess (149.1(21)) the next year and carrying it back: 149.1(20). CRA can also reduce the DQ: 149.1(5).

Even without the DQ, a charity must devote all its resources to charitable activities (charitable organization) or charitable purposes (foundation). See 149.1(1)"charitable organization" Notes. For political activities see 149.1(6.1) Notes.

Definition amended by 2010 budget bill #2, for tax years ending after March 3, 2010. Under the pre-2010 rules, the DQ was essentially 80% of receipted donations (A), amounts received from other charities (B) and 3.5% of capital (B.1). See Mason & Burr, "Registered Charities, the Disbursement Quota", 2010 BC Tax Conference (ctf.ca), 15:1-20; Aptowitzer, "Ghost of Disbursement Quotas Past", 18(4) *Canadian Not-for-Profit News [CNfpN]* (Carswell) 25-27 (April 2010); Drache, "Charities Mulling Disbursement Quota Changes", 18(5) *CNfpN* 33-35 (May 2010) and "Disbursement Quota Changes", 18(12) *CNfpN* 89-90 (Dec. 2010); Lee-Kennedy, "Disbursement Quota Overhaul", 19(3) *Canadian Tax Highlights* (ctf.ca) 6-7 (March 2011).

Definition earlier amended by 2004 Budget (for tax years that began before March 23, 2004), 2002-2013 technical bill (amending pre-2004 version), 1995-97 and 1993 technical bills. 149.1(1)"disbursement quota" was 149.1(1)(e) before RSC 1985 (5th Supp) consolidation for tax years ending after Nov. 1991.

Regulations: 3701 (prescribed amount).

I.T. Application Rules: 69 (meaning of "chapter 148 of ...").

Interpretation Bulletins: IT-244R3: Gifts by individuals of life insurance policies as charitable donations. See also at end of s. 149.1.

Charities Policies: CPC-005: Accumulation of property; CPC-021: Disbursement quota; CPS-009: Holding of property for charities; CPS-028: Fundraising by registered charities.

Registered Charities Newsletters: 4 (issuing receipts for gifts of art); 9 (once a charity has met its DQ); 13 (revised registered charity information return T3010); 18 (how does a charity calculate its DQ if it has received a gift in kind?); 19 (proposed disbursement quota changes); 20 (DQ listed in Notice of Confirmation; working outside Canada — DQ); 31 (disbursement quota — charitable organizations take note; disbursement quota shortfalls); 33 (new fundraising guidance).

Forms: T1259: Capital gains and disbursement quota worksheet; T3010: Registered charity information return; T4033A: Completing the registered charity information return [guide].

"divestment obligation percentage" of a private foundation for a particular taxation year, in respect of a class of shares of the capital stock of a corporation, is the percentage, if any, that is the lesser of

(a) the excess, if any, at the end of the taxation year, of the percentage of issued and outstanding shares of that class that are held by the private foundation over the exempt shares percentage of the private foundation, and

(b) the percentage determined by the formula

$$A + B - C$$

where

A is the percentage determined under this paragraph in respect of the private foundation in respect of the class for the preceding taxation year,

B is the total of all percentages, each of which is the portion of a net increase in the excess corporate holdings percentage of the private foundation in respect of the class for the particular taxation year or for a preceding taxation year that is allocated to the particular taxation year in accordance with subsection 149.2(5), and

C is the total of all percentages, each of which is the portion of a net decrease in the excess corporate holdings percentage of the private foundation in respect of the class for the particular taxation year or for a preceding taxation year that is allocated to the particular taxation year in accordance with subsection 149.2(7);

Related Provisions: 149.2(3) — Net increase in the excess corporate holdings percentage; 149.2(4) — Net decrease in the excess corporate holdings percentage; 188.1(3.1) — Penalty for having divestment obligation percentage; 188.1(3.2)–(3.5) — Avoidance of divestment obligation; 257 — Formula cannot calculate to less than zero.

Notes: A private foundation with a "divestment obligation percentage" (DOP) at year-end is subject to a penalty (188.1(3.1)) and can have its charity status revoked (149.1(4)(c)). The core of the definition is "excess corporate holdings percentage" (ECHP), defined below in 149.1(1). If the foundation holds only an "insignificant interest" of a class of shares (no more than 2%: 149.2(1)(b)), then ECHP is zero (para. (b) of the ECHP definition), so there is no DOP. Otherwise, the ECHP is the excess over 20% of all the issued shares of the class, subject to rules about "entrusted shares". The foundation is required to divest itself of its ECHP over five years.

A net increase in ECHP is allocated under 149.2(5) to DOP for the current year or one of the next 5 years in a specified order. A net decrease to ECHP reduces first the DOP for that year. An unapplied decrease is then applied under 149.2(7) to any later-year DOP.

See Stevens, "The Excess Business Holdings Regime and Investment in Shares by Private Foundations", 1(1) *Personal Tax & Estate Planning* (Federated Press) 13-16 (2008); Drache, "New Excess Holding Rules", 16(8) *Canadian Not-for-Profit News* (Carswell) 59-60 (Aug. 2008); Radu, "Public/Private Foundations", 57(1) *Canadian Tax Journal* 119 at 136-40 (2009); Cheung, "Private Foundations: Exceeding the 20% Limit", 9(2) *Canadian Tax Focus* (ctf.ca) 5 (May 2019).

For more on the Excess Corporate Holdings regime, see Notes to 149.1(1)"exempt shares" and "exempt shares percentage"; 2007 federal Budget Annex 5, under "Private Foundations"; 2008 Budget Annex 4, under "Personal Income Tax Measures" > "Private Foundations".

Definition added by 2007 budget bill #2, effective March 19, 2007, and amended retroactive to its introduction by 2008 budget bill #2.

Forms: T2081: Excess corporate holdings worksheet for private foundations; T2082: Excess corporate holdings regime for private foundations [guide].

"enduring property" — [Repealed]

Notes: 149.1(1)"enduring property" repealed by 2010 budget bill #2, for tax years that end after March 3, 2010. Earlier amended by 2002-2013 technical bill; added by 2004 Budget.

For CRA comments on using a 10-year gift to fund a life insurance policy acquired by a charity, see VIEWS doc 2006-0217931E5. Marketable securities could be enduring property: doc 2008-0268731E5.

Registered Charities Newsletters: 27 (enduring property Q&A).

"entrusted shares percentage" — [Repealed]

Notes: 149.1(1)"entrusted shares percentage" added by 2007 budget bill #2, effective March 19, 2007, and repealed retroactive to its introduction by 2008 budget bill #2. It was replaced by para. (a) of "exempt shares", which applies for "exempt shares percentage".

Forms: T2081: Excess corporate holdings worksheet for private foundations; T2082: Excess corporate holdings regime for private foundations [guide].

"equity percentage" of a person in a corporation has, subject to subsection 149.2(2.1), the same meaning as defined in subsection 95(4);

Related Provisions: 149.2(2.1) — Deemed ownership.

Notes: 149.1(1)"equity percentage" added by 2008 budget bill #2, effective March 19, 2007.

"excess corporate holdings percentage" of a private foundation, in respect of a class of shares of the capital stock of a corporation, at any time means

(a) if the private foundation is not, at that time, a registered charity, 0%,

(b) if the private foundation holds, at that time, an insignificant interest in respect of the class, 0%, and

(c) in any other case, the number of percentage points, if any, by which the total corporate holdings percentage of the private foundation in respect of the class, at that time, exceeds the greater of 20% and the exempt shares percentage, at that time, of the private foundation in respect of the class;

Related Provisions: 149.1(8) — Transitional rule.

Notes: See Notes to 149.1(1)"divestment obligation percentage". An ECHP generally arises from a foundation's acquisitions for consideration or by way of a gift. It may also arise from acquisitions by "relevant persons". The percentage of such holdings can also be affected by the issuance of new shares or the redemption of issued shares.

149.1(1)"excess corporate holdings percentage" added by 2007 budget bill #2, effective March 19, 2007, and para. (c) amended by 2008 budget bill #2, retroactive to its introduction, to change "entrusted shares" to "exempt shares".

Forms: T2081: Excess corporate holdings worksheet for private foundations; T2082: Excess corporate holdings regime for private foundations [guide].

"exempt shares" held by a private foundation at any particular time means shares, of a class of the capital stock of a corporation,

(a) that were acquired by the private foundation by way of a gift that was subject to a trust or direction that the shares are to be held by the private foundation for a period ending not earlier than the particular time, if the gift was made

(i) before March 19, 2007,

(ii) on or after March 19, 2007 and before March 19, 2012

(A) under the terms of a will that was executed by a taxpayer before March 19, 2007 and not amended, by codicil or otherwise, on or after March 19, 2007, and

(B) in circumstances where no other will of the taxpayer was executed or amended on or after March 19, 2007, or

(iii) on or after March 19, 2007, under the terms of a trust created before March 19, 2007, and not amended on or after March 19, 2007,

(b) that were last acquired by the private foundation before March 19, 2007, other than shares that, at the particular time,

(i) are described in paragraph (a),

(ii) are listed on a designated stock exchange, or

(iii) are shares of the capital stock of a particular corporation, which particular corporation has an equity percentage greater than 0% in a public corporation, a class of the shares of the capital stock of which is listed on a designated stock exchange, if

(A) a corporation (in this subparagraph referred to as a "controlled corporation" and which may, for greater certainty, be the particular corporation)

(I) owns one or more shares of a class of the capital stock of the public corporation, and

(II) is controlled, directly or indirectly in any manner whatever, by one or more relevant persons in respect of the private foundation, or by the private foundation alone or together with one or more such relevant persons,

(B) the private foundation, if it held directly the shares described in subclause (A)(I), would have an excess corporate holdings percentage (determined without reference to subsection 149.2(8)) in respect of that class of shares that is greater than 0%, and

(C) the private foundation, alone or together with all controlled corporations, holds more than an insignificant interest in respect of the class of shares described in subclause (A)(I), or

(c) that are substituted shares held by the private foundation;

Related Provisions: 149.2(2.1) — Deemed ownership; 149.2(10) — Shares held through a trust on March 18/07.

Notes: "Exempt shares" applies for purpose of "exempt shares percentage" of a private foundation. In general, under the excess corporate holdings regime, a private foundation need not divest shares (previously called "entrusted shares"), that were

- donated to the foundation before March 19, 2007 subject to a condition that they be retained by the foundation; or

- donated later but before March 19, 2012, under the terms of a will signed, or an *inter vivos* trust settled, before March 19, 2007 that included such a condition and that was not amended after that date.

The new definition also covers shares acquired in exchange for exempt shares (see 149.1(1)"substituted shares").

Exempt shares also include certain unlisted shares held by a private foundation as of March 18, 2007, but this does not extend to unlisted shares in a corporation through which the foundation has, directly or indirectly, an interest in a public corporation.

Unlisted shares that are not exempt shares, and all listed shares, held on March 18, 2007 are subject to the transitional excess corporate holdings rules in 149.2(8).

Subpara. (a)(iii) amended by 2014 budget bill #2, for 2016 and later taxation years, to change "testamentary or *inter vivos* trust" to "trust".

149.1(1)"exempt shares" added by 2008 budget bill #2, effective March 19, 2007.

"exempt shares percentage" of a private foundation at any time, in respect of a class of shares of the capital stock of a corporation, is the total of all amounts, each of which is the percentage of the issued and outstanding shares of that class that are exempt shares held by the private foundation at that time;

Notes: "Exempt shares percentage" applies for calculating a private foundation's "divestment obligation percentage". A private foundation may cease to have an exempt shares percentage if shares that it holds cease to be exempt shares.

If a private foundation holds identical shares of a class of a corporation, some held on March 18, 2007 and others acquired later, the disposition of shares is considered not to reduce the exempt shares percentage except to the extent the number disposed of exceeds the number of shares acquired after March 18, 2007. However, where exempt shares are disposed of, a later acquisition of identical shares will not restore the foundation's exempt shares percentage. [Finance Technical Notes, Dec. 2008]

149.1(1)"exempt shares percentage" added by 2008 budget bill #2, effective March 19, 2007.

"ineligible individual", at any time, means an individual who has been

(a) convicted of a relevant criminal offence unless it is a conviction for which

(i) a pardon has been granted and the pardon has not been revoked or ceased to have effect, or

(ii) a record suspension has been ordered under the *Criminal Records Act* and the record suspension has not been revoked or ceased to have effect,

---

Proposed Amendment — 149.1(1)"ineligible individual"(a)(i), (ii)

(i) a pardon has been granted under Her Majesty's royal prerogative of mercy or under section 748 of the *Criminal Code* and the pardon has not been revoked or ceased to have effect, or

(ii) a pardon *[or pre-2022 record suspension — ed.]* has been granted under the *Criminal Records Act* and the pardon has not been revoked or ceased to have effect,

Application: Bill C-31 (First Reading June 10, 2021), subsec. 47(1), will amend subparas. (a)(i) and (ii) of the definition "ineligible individual" in subsec. 149.1(1) to read as above, in force on a day to be fixed by the Governor in Council.

Notes: A "pardon" in proposed (a)(ii) above appears to include a pre-2022 record suspension. Para. 31(d) of Bill C-31 provides, under "Transitional Provisions":

31. Terminology — Other Acts — If the context so requires, a reference to a pardon in the following provisions, as enacted by this Act, may be read also as a reference to a record suspension: . . .

(d) subparagraph (a)(ii) of the definition "ineligible individual" in subsection 149.1(1) of the *Income Tax Act*;

---

and s. 30(1) of Bill C-31 defines "pardon" and "record suspension" for purposes of s. 31:

> "pardon" has the same meaning as in subsection 2(1) of the *Criminal Records Act*, as amended by subsection 3(2) *[of Bill C-31 — ed.]*, or as in subsection 2(1) of that Act as it read from time to time before March 13, 2012.

> "record suspension" has the same meaning as in subsection 2(1) of the *Criminal Records Act* as it read from time to time after March 12, 2012 but before the coming into force of subsection 3(2) *[of Bill C-31, but note that 3(1), not 3(2), repeals the definition of "record suspension"; this appears to be a drafting error — ed.]*.

(b) convicted of a relevant offence in the five-year period preceding that time,

(c) a director, trustee, officer or like official of a registered charity or a registered Canadian amateur athletic association during a period in which the charity or association engaged in conduct that can reasonably be considered to have constituted a serious breach of the requirements for registration under this Act and for which the registration of the charity or association was revoked in the five-year period preceding that time,

(d) an individual who controlled or managed, directly or indirectly, in any manner whatever, a registered charity or a registered Canadian amateur athletic association during a period in which the charity or association engaged in conduct that can reasonably be considered to have constituted a serious breach of the requirements for registration under this Act and for which its registration was revoked in the five-year period preceding that time,

(e) a promoter in respect of a tax shelter that involved a registered charity or a registered Canadian amateur athletic association, the registration of which was revoked in the five-year period preceding that time for reasons that included or were related to participation in the tax shelter;

(f) a listed terrorist entity, or a member of a listed terrorist entity,

(g) a director, trustee, officer or like official of a listed terrorist entity during a period in which that entity supported or engaged in terrorist activities, including a period prior to the date on which the entity became a listed terrorist entity, or

(h) an individual who controlled or managed, directly or indirectly, in any manner whatever, a listed terrorist entity during a period in which that entity supported or engaged in terrorist activities, including a period prior to the date on which the entity became a listed terrorist entity;

Related Provisions: 149.1(1.01) — Record suspension includes pardon; 149.1(4.1)(e) — Charity registration can be revoked if ineligible individual controls or manages it; 149.1(22) — CRA can refuse to register charity if ineligible individual controls or manages it; 149.1(25) — CRA can refuse to register charity or RCAAA managed by ineligible individual; 188.2(2)(d) — CRA can suspend charity if ineligible individual controls or manages it.

Notes: For discussion and criticism of the "ineligible individual" rules (149.1(4.1)(e), 149.1(25), 188.2) see Mason & Wright, "Ineligible Individuals", National Charity Law Symposium (May 2014), tinyurl.com/mw-inelig; Drache, "New Hurdle for Charity Incorporators", xxxiii(24) *The Canadian Taxpayer* (Carswell) 191-2 (Dec. 23, 2011); Mason, "Charities Update 2014", 2014 Cdn Tax Foundation conference report at 38:8-15; Drache, "Ineligible Individual Rules an Example of Unacceptable Vagueness", 25(4) *Canadian Not-for-Profit News [CNfPN]* (Carswell) 25-27 (April 2017), and "Ineligible Individuals a Target for CRA Compliance", 27(2) 13-15 (Feb. 2019). For very detailed CRA policy see Charities Guidance CG-024 (August 2014); for comment see Drache, "CRA Guidance on Ineligible Individuals", 22(10) *CNfPN* 73-74 (Oct. 2014).

Charities' registrations revoked for reasons (see Notes to 168(1)) that included having ineligible individuals as directors: Jesus of Bethlehem Worship Centre (July 11/14); Friends and Skills Connection Centre (Sept. 13/14).

Para. (h): see 256(5.1) and (6) for "controlled ... directly or indirectly".

Paras. (f)-(h) added by 2021 budget bill #1, effective June 29, 2021. See 149.1(1)"listed terrorist entity".

Para. (a) amended by 2011 budget bill #2, effective March 13, 2012. Definition added by 2011 budget bill #2, effective 2012.

Charities Guidance: CG-024: Ineligible individuals.

"listed terrorist entity", at any time, means a person, partnership, group, fund, unincorporated association or organization that is at that time a "listed entity", as defined in subsection 83.01(1) of the *Criminal Code*;

Related Provisions: 149.1(1)"ineligible individual"(e)–(h) — Person ineligible to be director of charity; 149.1(1.02) — Where entity ceases to be LTE; 168(3.1) — Revocation of charity that is LTE; 188(1) — Deemed year-end on notice of revocation.

Notes: *Criminal Code* s. 83.01(1) defines "listed entity" as "an entity on a list established by the Governor in Council *[i.e., the federal Cabinet]* under section 83.05". See tinyurl.com/canada-lte for the list.

Definition added by 2021 budget bill #1, effective June 29, 2021.

"material transaction" of a private foundation, in respect of a class of shares of the capital stock of a corporation, means a transaction or a series of transactions or events in shares of the class, in respect of which the total fair market value of the shares of the class that are acquired or disposed of by the private foundation or any relevant person in respect of the private foundation as part of the transaction or series (determined at the time of the transaction, or at the end of the series, as the case may be) exceeds the lesser of

(a) $100,000, and

(b) 0.5% of the total fair market value of all of the issued and outstanding shares of the class;

Related Provisions: 149.2(2) — Avoidance transaction deemed to be material transaction.

Notes: This term is used in 149.2(2) and 188.1(3.1)(b)(i).

149.1(1)"material transaction" added by 2007 budget bill #2, effective March 19, 2007.

Forms: T2081: Excess corporate holdings worksheet for private foundations; T2082: Excess corporate holdings regime for private foundations [guide].

"non-qualified investment" of a private foundation means

(a) a debt (other than a pledge or undertaking to make a gift) owing to the foundation by

(i) a person (other than an excluded corporation)

(A) who is a member, shareholder, trustee, settlor, officer, official or director of the foundation,

(B) who has, or is a member of a group of persons who do not deal with each other at arm's length who have, contributed more than 50% of the capital of the foundation, or

(C) who does not deal at arm's length with any person described in clause (A) or (B), or

(ii) a corporation (other than an excluded corporation) controlled by the foundation, by any person or group of persons referred to in subparagraph (i), by the foundation and any other private foundation with which it does not deal at arm's length or by any combination thereof,

(b) a share of a class of the capital stock of a corporation (other than an excluded corporation) referred to in paragraph (a) held by the foundation (other than a share listed on a designated stock exchange or a share that would be a qualifying share within the meaning assigned by subsection 192(6) if that subsection were read without reference to the expression "issued after May 22, 1985 and before 1987"), and

(c) a right held by the foundation to acquire a share referred to in paragraph (b),

and, for the purpose of this definition, an "excluded corporation" is

(d) a limited-dividend housing company to which paragraph 149(1)(n) applies,

(e) a corporation all of the property of which is used by a registered charity in its administration or in carrying on its charitable activities, or

Proposed Amendment (uncertain) — 149.1(1)"non-qualified investment"(e)

Application: Private Member's Bill S-222 (First House of Commons Reading June 23, 2021), subsec. 2(3), will amend para. (e) of the definition "non-qualified investment" in subsec. 149.1(1) to change "in carrying on its" to "for", in force two years after Royal Assent (and subject to review after 5 years: see under Proposed Amendment to 149.1(1)"charitable activities").

Notes: This is a private member's bill that may not pass. See Notes to Proposed Amendment under 149.1(1)"charitable activities".

(f) a corporation all of the issued shares of which are held by the foundation;

Related Provisions: 189 — Tax regarding non-qualified investment; 256(6), (6.1) — Meaning of "controlled".

Notes: For para. (b), 192(6) reads:

(6) **Definition of "qualifying share"** — In this Part, "qualifying share", at any time, means a prescribed share of the capital stock of a taxable Canadian corporation issued after May 22, 1985 and before 1987.

and see Reg. 6203 for prescribed shares.

Para. (b) amended by 2007 budget bill #2, effective Dec. 14, 2007, to change "prescribed stock exchange" to "designated stock exchange".

149.1(1)"non-qualified investment" was 149.1(1)(e.1) before RSC 1985 (5th Supp) consolidation for tax years ending after Nov. 1991. Definition earlier amended by 1991 technical bill.

A proposed definition **"non-qualifying private foundation"** in the Oct. 2, 2007 draft legislation was deleted in the Nov. 13, 2007 revised draft which was enacted by 2007 budget bill #2. See 149.1(1)"divestment obligation percentage" instead.

Registered Charities Newsletters: 27 (what is a non-qualified investment?).

Charities Guidance: CG-006: Non-qualified investment — tax liability.

"original corporate holdings percentage" of a private foundation, in respect of a class of shares of the capital stock of a corporation, means the total corporate holdings percentage of the private foundation, in respect of that class, held on March 18, 2007;

Notes: This term is used in 149.2(8).

149.1(1)"original corporate holdings percentage" added by 2007 budget bill #2, effective March 19, 2007.

Forms: T2081: Excess corporate holdings worksheet for private foundations; T2082: Excess corporate holdings regime for private foundations [guide].

"political activity" — [Repealed]

Related Provisions: 149.1(1)"charitable purposes" — Charitable purposes do not include gift the making of which is a political activity; 149.1(6.1), (6.2), (6.201), (10) — Limits on political activities by charities; 188.2(2)(e)–(g) — Suspension of charity for engaging in political activities.

Notes: See Notes to 149.1(6.1).

149.1(1)"political activity" added by 2012 budget bill #1, effective June 29, 2012; and repealed by 2018 budget bill #2, effective June 29, 2012 for organizations, corporations and trusts that were registered charities on Sept. 14, 2018 and associations that were registered Canadian amateur athletic associations on that date, and effective Sept. 14, 2018 in any other case. It read:

"political activity" includes the making of a gift to a qualified donee if it can reasonably be considered that a purpose of the gift is to support the political activities of the qualified donee;

"private foundation" means a charitable foundation that is not a public foundation;

Related Provisions: 75(3)(b) — Exclusion from reversionary trust rules; 149.1(6.3) — Designation as public foundation, etc.; 149.1(13) — Designation of private foundation as public; 189 — Tax on private foundation with non-qualified investments; 248(1)"private foundation" — Definition applies to entire Act.

Notes: See 149.1(4) for restrictions on a private foundation.

Donations of private company shares to a charity (including a private foundation) are generally non-creditable; see 118.1(13)–(20).

For discussion see the articles cited in Notes to 149.1(1)"public foundation"; Margaret Mason, "Governance Issues for Private Foundations", 2011 STEP Canada conference (contact memberservices@step.ca); Blumbergs, "Top Fallacies about Private Foundations in Canada in 2019", tinyurl.com/foundation-falla; Fontan & Pearson, "Philanthropy in Canada: The Role and Impact of Private Foundations", chap. 12 of *Intersections and Innovations* (2021), muttart.org/intersections.

Practical information for foundation trustees and directors: *Starting a Foundation: A Guide for Philanthropists* (2015), pfc.ca > "Resources".

A foundation typically funds other charities, but it may spend its funds by carrying on charitable activities directly: Drache, "Charity Examiners Get It Wrong Again" 15(10) *Canadian Not-for-Profit News* (Carswell) 73-80 (Oct. 2007). See also Frajman, "A 'Will' for a Private Foundation", xxxvi(16) *The Canadian Taxpayer* (Carswell) 125-26 (Aug. 29, 2014).

As of May 2021, there were 6,215 private foundations registered: tinyurl.com/cra-char-advn (search by Designation).

149.1(1)"private foundation" was 149.1(1)(f) before RSC 1985 (5th Supp) consolidation for tax years ending after Nov. 1991.

Interpretation Bulletins: IT-83R3: Non-profit organizations — Taxation of income from property. See also at end of 149.1.

Forms: T2095: Registered charities — application for re-designation.

Registered Charities Newsletters: 16 (policies: new rules for determining whether a charity is a private foundation); 33 (reminder to file Form T2081, *Excess Corporation Holdings Worksheet for Private Foundations*).

Charities Guidance: CG-006: Non-qualified investment — tax liability; CG-009: Trust document; See also under 149.1(1)"charitable activities".

Charities Policies: See under 149.1(1)"charitable activities".

"promoter" has the meaning assigned by section 237.1;

Notes: Definition "promoter" added by 2011 budget bill #2, effective 2012.

"public foundation", at a particular time, means a charitable foundation

(a) more than 50% of the directors, trustees, officers or like officials of which deal at arm's length with each other and with

(i) each of the other directors, trustees, officers and like officials of the foundation,

(ii) each person described by subparagraph (b)(i) or (ii), and

(iii) each member of a group of persons (other than Her Majesty in right of Canada or of a province, a municipality, another registered charity that is not a private foundation, and any club, society or association described in paragraph 149(1)(l)) who do not deal with each other at arm's length, if the group would, if it were a person, be a person described by subparagraph (b)(i), and

(b) that is not, at the particular time, and would not at the particular time be, if the foundation were a corporation, controlled directly or indirectly in any manner whatever

(i) by a person (other than Her Majesty in right of Canada or of a province, a municipality, another registered charity that is not a private foundation, and any club, society or association described in paragraph 149(1)(l)),

(A) who immediately after the particular time, has contributed to the foundation amounts that are, in total, greater than 50% of the capital of the foundation immediately after the particular time, and

(B) who immediately after the person's last contribution at or before the particular time, had contributed to the foundation amounts that were, in total, greater than 50% of the capital of the foundation immediately after the making of that last contribution, or

(ii) by a person, or by a group of persons that do not deal at arm's length with each other, if the person or any member of the group does not deal at arm's length with a person described in subparagraph (i);

Related Provisions: 149.1(6.3) — Designation as public foundation, etc.; 149.1(13) — Designation of private foundation as public; 248(1)"private foundation" — Definition applies to entire Act.

Notes: See 149.1(3) for restrictions on a public foundation.

The requirement that over 50% of directors or trustees deal with each other at arm's length means that a public foundation cannot have only one trustee: *Sheldon Inwentash & Lynn Factor Charitable Foundation*, 2012 FCA 136.

For detailed discussion see Hoffstein & Roddey, "Private Foundations and Community Foundations", 49(5) *Canadian Tax Journal* 1258-86 (2001); Hoffstein, "Private Foundations and Community Foundations", 2007 Cdn Tax Foundation conference report at 32:24-35; Radu, "Public/Private Foundations: Issues and Planning Opportunities", 57(1) *CTJ* 119-42 (2009); Hayhoe, "Private Foundations and Donor Advised Funds", 2011 STEP Canada conference (contact memberservices@step.ca). See also www.community-fdn.ca, the Community Foundations of Canada.

A foundation typically funds other charities, but it may spend its funds by carrying on charitable activities directly: Arthur Drache, "Charity Examiners Get It Wrong Again" 15(10) *Canadian Not-for-Profit News* (Carswell) 73-80 (Oct. 2007).

As of May 2021, there were 4,953 public foundations registered: tinyurl.com/cra-char-advn (search by Designation).

Definition amended by 2002-2013 technical bill, last change effective 2005. 149.1(1)"public foundation" was 149.1(1)(g) before RSC 1985 (5th Supp) consolidation for tax years ending after Nov. 1991.

I.T. Application Rules: 69 (meaning of "chapter 148 of ...").

Interpretation Bulletins: IT-83R3: Non-profit organizations — Taxation of income from property. See also at end of 149.1.

Registered Charities Newsletters: 16 (policies: new rules for determining whether a charity is a private foundation).

Charities Policies: CPC-002: Related business; CPS-009: Holding of property for charities; CPS-019: What is a related business?; See also under 149.1(1)"charitable activities".

Charities Guidance: CG-009: Trust document; See also under 149.1(1)"charitable activities".

Forms: T2095: Registered charities — application for re-designation.

"qualified donee", at any time, means a person that is

(a) registered by the Minister and that is

(i) a housing corporation resident in Canada and exempt from tax under this Part because of paragraph 149(1)(i) that has applied for registration,

(ii) a municipality in Canada,

(iii) a municipal or public body performing a function of government in Canada that has applied for registration,

(iv) a university outside Canada, the student body of which ordinarily includes students from Canada, that has applied for registration, or

(v) a foreign charity that has applied to the Minister for registration under subsection (26),

(b) a registered charity,

(b.1) a registered journalism organization,

(c) a registered Canadian amateur athletic association, or

(d) Her Majesty in right of Canada or a province, the United Nations or an agency of the United Nations;

Related Provisions: 110.1(1)(a) — Deduction for donation by corporation to qualified donee (QD); 118.1(1)"total charitable gifts", 118.1(3) — Tax credit for donation by individual to QD; 149.1(4.3), 168(1) — Revocation of registration for non-compliance; 149.1(22) — Refusal to register applicant as QD; 230(2) — Requirement to keep records; 248(1)"qualified donee" — Definition applies to entire Act.

Notes: The term "qualified donee" is now used to refer to registered charities and other entities that can receive donations eligible for the donation credit under 118.1 (for corporations, deduction under 110.1).

In addition to the entities listed, U.S. charities qualify for donations up to 3/4 of the taxpayer's U.S.-source income. See Notes to Canada-U.S. tax treaty, Art. XXI:7.

The 2011 Budget changes enable CRA to control whether municipalities, Indian bands and foreign universities can issue receipts valid for Canadian tax donations, even though CRA cannot control them directly. See para. (a) ("registered by the Minister"), 149.1(4.3) (revocation of registration) and 188.2(2) (suspension of receipting privileges). Municipalities and Schedule VIII universities will be automatically registered unless revoked; housing corporations and "municipal or public bodies" must apply for registration (subparas. (a)(i), (iii)). CRA now publishes lists of RCAAAs, municipalities, municipal bodies, universities outside Canada, charities outside Canada that have received Canadian government gifts, and low-cost housing corporations for the aged. See tinyurl.com/qualified-donees.

Para. (a): all entities in para (a) must be registered. CRA can revoke registration (149.1(4.3)) or suspend tax receipting privileges (188.2(2)).

Subpara. (a)(i): see Notes to 149(1)(i). Only housing corporations that register with CRA qualify. See tinyurl.com/cra-housing for the list of registered and revoked corps and the application process.

Subpara. (a)(ii): all Canadian municipalities were registered on Jan. 1, 2012. See tinyurl.com/munici-cra for the list of registered and revoked municipalities. Donations to a municipal election candidate do not qualify: VIEWS doc 2018-0779741M4. A donation to an organization can be routed through a municipality if the municipality "retains discretion as to how the donated funds are to be spent" and is not merely acting as a conduit: 2006-0215921R3, 2008-0304471E5. In *Kérouac*, 2013 TCC 255, the Municipality of Larouche was not allowed to intervene in an appeal by a taxpayer who claimed the municipality was grossly negligent or fraudulent in accepting his donation.

Subpara. (a)(iii): for the meaning of "municipal or public body performing a function of government", see Notes to 149(1)(c). Unlike municipalities, only bodies that have registered with CRA qualify. See tinyurl.com/mpbg-cra for the list of registered and revoked bodies and the application process.

Subpara. (a)(iv): The list of qualifying universities was deleted by 2018 budget bill #1 from Sch. VIII (at end of the Regulations), as it is now maintained by CRA per (a)(iv): see list at tinyurl.com/univs-cra.

The Budget amendment is effective Feb. 27, 2018, except that

(a) if a university applied for registration before that date and is registered by CRA on or after that day, the amendment applies to the university as of the day it applied for registration; and

(b) any university listed in Reg. Sch. VIII as of Feb. 26, 2018 is deemed to have applied for registration. See Notes to Sch. VIII for that list.

The Feb. 27/18 draft of (a)(iv) lacked a transitional rule to grandfather universities prescribed in Reg. Sch. VIII. (It would likely be impossible to find records of applications to get on the list for those prescribed decades ago; the list goes back to 1967.) This was fixed after the author pointed it out to Finance.

A trust for a listed university is exempt from the non-resident trust rules: 94(1)"exempt foreign trust"(c)(ii). These universities are also accepted by CRA for the 118.5(1)(b) tuition credit: Income Tax Folio S1-F2-C2 ¶2.12.

To be added to the list, see CRA publication RC191, and tinyurl.com/blumberg-foreign-univs. CRA says (tinyurl.com/cra-foreign-univs, March 28, 2018) the "criteria for registration as a university outside Canada have not changed", and the RC191 policy still applies. See also "Foreign Universities Applying for Prescribed ... Status: What we have learned" (Sept. 22, 2018), tinyurl.com/blumberg-univs.

CRA can suspend a foreign university's receipting privileges or revoke its registration if it issues receipts not in accordance with the Act: 188.2(2), 149.1(4.3). (This will be done for those accommodating abusive tax shelters: see Notes to 168(1) for Canadian charity revocations.) See Adam Aptowitzer, "Some Light on Terra Incognita for Foreign Universities", 27(2) *Canadian Not-for-Profit News* (Carswell) 15-18 (Feb. 2019).

CRA periodically reviews the list and has institutions removed that have not had significant numbers of Canadian residents attend as students. See Drache, "Schedule VIII Universities Under Review", 7(8) *Canadian Not-for-Profit News* (Carswell) 58-59 (August 1999); Lazier, "Supporting Foreign Universities" (Feb. 2010), tinyurl.com/univs-lazier.

The Regulatory Impact Analysis Statement to the 2014 amendments deleting 36 US and 9 other universities from Sch. VIII states: "The universities that have been removed were contacted and either failed to respond or did not contest the proposed removal.... [they] no longer meet the conditions for prescribed status." Some changes were to update name and/or address information. The RIAS states that to be considered for prescribed status, an institution must: (1) maintain academic entrance requirement of at least secondary school matriculation standing; (2) be organized for teaching, study and research in the higher branches of learning; (3) be empowered, in its own right, to confer degrees of at least baccalaureate level (Bachelor or equivalent), according to academic standards and statutory definitions prevailing in its country; and (4) ordinarily include Canadian students in its student body.

Subpara. (a)(v): For qualifying foreign charities, see Notes to 149.1(26).

Para. (b): See Notes to 149.1(1)"charitable organization", 248(1)"registered charity".

Para. (b.1) applies to non-profit journalism organizations that meet certain criteria. See 248(1)"registered journalism organization", which depends on both 149.1(1)"qualifying journalism organization" and 248(1)"qualified Canadian journalism organization". For a CRA Q&A on para. (b.1) see tinyurl.com/rjo-cra. (For the other 2019 Budget measures supporting journalism see Notes to 248(1)"qualified Canadian journalism organization".) For the list of RJOs see tinyurl.com/cra-rjos; as of June 2021 the only ones are La Presse Inc. and The Narwhal News Society. See also Waddell, "From Media House to Charity Case: New Federal Rules Allowing News Organizations to Become Non-Profits May Not Be Worth the Effort", *The Philanthropist* (thephilanthropist.ca), June 22, 2020 (5pp).

Para. (c): See Notes to 248(1)"registered Canadian amateur athletic association".

Para. (d): The federal and provincial governments and the UN and its agencies are not subject to the revocation and suspension rules in 149.1(4.3) and 188.2(2).

History: Para. (b.1), "a registered journalism organization", added by 2019 budget bill #1 effective 2020. Budget Table 1 predicts this will cost the federal government $6 million in 2019-20, $25m in 2020-21, $32m in 2021-22, $22m in 2022-23 and $11 million in 2023-24.

Subpara. (a)(v) amended by 2015 Budget bill, effective June 23, 2015, to change "foreign organization" to "foreign charity". (See Notes to 149.1(26).)

Subpara. (a)(v) amended by 2012 budget bill #1, effective 2013 (but does not apply re registration of a charitable organization outside Canada made before 2013).

Definition amended by 2011 budget bill #2, effective 2012.

149.1(1)"qualified donee" was 149.1(1)(h) before RSC 1985 (5th Supp) consolidation for tax years ending after Nov. 1991.

Regulations: 3503, Sch. VIII (prescribed universities outside Canada for subpara. (a)(iv)).

Registered Charities Newsletters: 3 (registered national arts service organizations); *Charities Connection* 11 (Budget 2011 changes).

Charities Guidance: CG-010: Qualified donees; CG-015: Charitable organizations outside Canada that have received a gift from Her Majesty in Right of Canada; CG-016: Qualified donees — Consequences of returning donated property; CG-023: Qualified donee: Foreign charities that have received a gift from Her Majesty in right of Canada.

Forms: T624: Application to register a journalism organization under the *Income Tax Act*.

"qualified investment [para. 149.1(1)(i)]" — [Repealed under former Act]

Notes: 149.1(1)(i), repealed in 1984, defined "qualified investment". It was replaced by the definition of "non-qualified investment".

"qualifying journalism organization" means a corporation or trust that meets the following conditions:

(a) it is a qualified Canadian journalism organization,

(b) it is constituted and operated for purposes exclusively related to journalism,

(c) any business activities it carries on are related to its purposes,

(d) it has trustees or a board of directors, each of whom deals at arm's length with each other,

(e) it is not controlled, directly or indirectly in any manner whatever, by a person or by a group of persons that do not deal with each other at arm's length,

(f) it may not, in a taxation year, receive gifts from any one source that represent more than 20% of its total revenues (including donations) for the taxation year, other than a gift

(i) made by way of bequest,

(ii) made within 12 months after the time the organization is first registered, or

(iii) approved, on a case-by-case basis, by the Minister,

(g) no part of its income is payable to, or otherwise available for the personal benefit of, any proprietor, member, shareholder, director, trustee, settlor or like individual, and

(h) it is primarily engaged in the production of original news content;

Notes: This term is used in 248(1)"registered journalism organization", so the conditions here are required to qualify for 149.1(1)"qualified donee"(b.1).

This definition is different from that of the same term in 125.6(1). It is also distinct from 248(1)"*qualified* Canadian journalism organization".

In para. (g), "no part of its income" refers to net income. See Notes to 149(1)(l).

Para. (h) added by 2021 budget bill #1, effective 2019 (which is actually impossible since the definition was originally effective 2020; this has been pointed out to Finance).

Definition added by 2019 budget bill #1, effective 2020.

"related business", in relation to a charity or Canadian amateur athletic association, includes a business that is unrelated to the purposes of the charity or association if substantially all persons employed by the charity or association in the carrying on of that business are not remunerated for that employment;

Related Provisions: 253.1(2) — Owning LP units is not carrying on business.

Notes: This definition and 149.1(2)(a) provide, in effect, permission for charities to operate an unrelated business that is substantially all operated by volunteers. Another option, effective with the increased donation limits in 110.1 since 1997, is for a taxable corporation to be created that donates 75% of its profits to the charity and pays tax on the balance. (However, some provinces have restrictions on charities owning shares in corporations.) See Arthur Drache, "Charities, Non-Profits and Business Activities", 1997 Cdn Tax Foundation conference report, at p. 30:4.

Where funds generated by a business were used for charitable purposes, the business was "related": *Alberta Institute on Mental Retardation*, [1987] 2 C.T.C. 70 (FCA). However, in *Earth Fund*, [2003] 2 C.T.C. 10 (FCA), the Court ruled that this principle does not generally apply: "Alberta Institute was simply soliciting donations of goods which it converted to money. This is somewhat different from the traditional fundraising activities of a foundation, but the difference is only a matter of degree" (para. 30). Selling lottery tickets "in a manifestly commercial arrangement that will, if all goes as planned, result in a profit that will be donated" was an unrelated business (para. 31). Similarly, in *House of Holy God*, 2009 CarswellNat 1223 (FCA) (leave to appeal denied 2009 CarswellNat 3675 (SCC)), a maple syrup business, whose profits were put into an account for future charitable work, was not a related business.

For CRA policy on "related business" see Charities Policy CPS-019. (Para. 19 claims that "employed by the charity" includes independent contractors, which might not be correct: see Notes to to 248(1)"employee".) On fundraising, see also Notes to 149.1(1)"charitable organization".

CRA said that owning limited partnership units constitutes carrying on business and violates 149.1(2)(a): docs 2006-016742117; 2005-016048183. A triple-net lease is usually property income: docs 2003-0024203, 2005-0160481R3. A triple-net lease is usually property income: 2011-0403841E5. Doc 2004-0095001E5 has further policy on leasing real property. For a ruling allowing a charity to lease excess office space or parking space see VIEWS docs 2003-0024203, 2005-0160481R3. A triple-net lease is usually property income: 2011-0403841E5. Doc 2004-0095001E5 has further policy on leasing real property. For a ruling that persons are "not remunerated for that employment" see 2009-0352111R3. For a ruling on a charity using a trust see 2014-0529291R3, 2014-0561281R3.

See Drache, "Related Business: What's Okay", 19(4) *The Philanthropist* (thephilanthropist.ca) 273-79 (2004); Young & Dolson, "Income Tax Consequences of Carrying on an Unrelated Business", XV(1) *Business Vehicles* (Federated Press) 782-87 (2012); Manwaring & Kairys, "Regulating Business Activity", chap. 6 of *Intersections and Innovations* (2021), muttart.org/intersections.

CRA considers that "substantially all" means 90% or more. See Adam Aptowitzer, "Substantially All: Less than Meets the Eye", 25(9) *Canadian Not-for-Profit News* (Carswell) 67-68 (Sept. 2017).

Definition amended by 2011 budget bill #2, effective 2012, to add references to a Canadian amateur athletic association.

149.1(1)"related business" was 149.1(1)(j) before RSC 1985 (5th Supp) consolidation for tax years ending after Nov. 1991.

Registered Charities Newsletters: 13 (related business guidelines); 14 (related business); 15 (court news — related vs. unrelated business); 17 (new policy statement on related business); 27 (legalese for charities: meaning of "substantially all").

Charities Policies: CPC-002: Related business; CPS-001: Applicants that are established to hold periodic fundraisers; CPS-019: What is a related business?.

"relevant criminal offence" means a criminal offence under the laws of Canada, and an offence that would be a criminal offence if it were committed in Canada, that

(a) relates to financial dishonesty, including tax evasion, theft and fraud, or

(b) in respect of a charity or Canadian amateur athletic association, is relevant to the operation of the charity or association;

Related Provisions: 149.1(1)"ineligible individual"(a) — Offence can cause person to be ineligible to manage charity.

Notes: The test of "relevant to the operation of the charity" is very broad, and could include, for example, convictions for assault where the charity deals with children or other vulnerable people.

Definition added by 2011 budget bill #2, effective 2012.

"relevant offence" means an offence, other than a relevant criminal offence, under the laws of Canada or a province, and an offence that would be such an offence if it took place in Canada, that

(a) relates to financial dishonesty, including an offence under charitable fundraising legislation, consumer protection legislation and securities legislation, or

(b) in respect of a charity or Canadian amateur athletic association, is relevant to the operation of the charity or association;

Related Provisions: 149.1(1)"ineligible individual"(b) — Offence can cause person to be ineligible to manage charity.

Notes: Definition added by 2011 budget bill #2, effective 2012.

"relevant person" in respect of a private foundation means a person who, at any time in respect of which the expression is relevant, deals not at arm's length with the private foundation (determined as if subsection 251(2) were applied as if the private foundation were a corporation), but does not include

(a) a person who at that time is considered to deal not at arm's length with the private foundation solely because of a right referred to in paragraph 251(5)(b), or

(b) an individual

(i) who at that time has attained the age of 18 years and lives separate and apart from any other individual (referred to in this definition as a "controlling individual") who would, if the private foundation were a corporation, control, or be a member of a related group that controls, the private foundation, and

(ii) in respect of whom the Minister is satisfied, upon review of an application by the private foundation, that the individual would, if subsection 251(1) were read without reference to its paragraphs (a) and (b), at that time, deal at arm's length with all controlling individuals;

Notes: This term is used in: 149.1(1)"material transaction", "total corporate holdings percentage", 149.1(15)(c)(ii)(B), 149.2(2), 149.2(5)(c)(ii), 188.1(3.1)(b)(i)(B), 188.1(3.2).

149.1(1)"relevant person" added by 2007 budget bill #2, effective March 19, 2007.

Forms: T2082: Excess corporate holdings regime for private foundations [guide].

"specified gift" — [Repealed]

Notes: 149.1(1)"specified gift" repealed by 2010 budget bill #2, effective for taxation years that end after March 3, 2010. See now 149.1(1)"designated gift".

A specified gift (SG) was made from one registered charity to another where the donor charity identified it as such in its information return. A SG did not increase the recipient charity's DQ for the year: former 149.1(1)"disbursement quota"A.1(a), B. The donor charity could not use it to satisfy its own DQ: 149.1(1.1). However, if the recipient charity kept it and did not use the gift in its charitable activities or administration, it might later have to consider the SG when determining the average value of property not used directly in charitable activities or administration for its pre-2010 DQ.

149.1(1)"specified gift" was 149.1(1)(k) before RSC 1985 (5th Supp) consolidation for tax years ending after Nov. 1991.

"substituted shares" held by a private foundation means shares acquired by the private foundation, in exchange for exempt shares held by the private foundation, in the course of a transaction to which section 51, subsection 85.1(1) or section 86 or 87 applies;

Notes: 149.1(1)"substituted shares" added by 2008 budget bill #2, effective March 19, 2007. See Notes to 149.1(1)"exempt shares".

"taxation year" means, in the case of a registered charity or registered Canadian amateur athletic association, a fiscal period;

Related Provisions: 188(1) — Deemed year-end on notice of revocation of charity registration.

Notes: Definition amended by 2011 budget bill #2, effective 2012, to add reference to an RCAAA.

149.1(1)"taxation year" was 149.1(1)(l) before RSC 1985 (5th Supp) consolidation for tax years ending after Nov. 1991.

"total corporate holdings percentage" of a private foundation, in respect of a class of shares of the capital stock of a corporation, at any particular time means the percentage of the issued and outstanding shares of that class that are held at that time by the private foundation, or by a relevant person in respect of the private foundation who holds a material interest in respect of that class;

Notes: This term is used in 149.1(1)"excess corporate holdings percentage"(c), "original corporate holdings percentage", 149.1(15)(c)(ii), 149.2(8), 118.1(3.1)(b)(i)(C).

149.1(1)"total corporate holdings percentage" added by 2007 budget bill #2, effective March 19, 2007.

(1.01) Deeming rule — *Safe Streets and Communities Act* — In this section, a reference to a record suspension is deemed also to be a reference to a pardon that is granted or issued under the *Criminal Records Act*.

Proposed Repeal — 149.1(1.01)

Application: Bill C-31 (First Reading June 10, 2021), subsec. 47(2), will repeal subsec. 149.1(1.01), in force on a day to be fixed by the Governor in Council.

Notes: 149.1(1.01) added by 2011 budget bill #2 (conditional amendment in cl. 103), effective March 13, 2012.

(1.02) Deeming rule — [ceasing to be] listed terrorist entity — If, but for this subsection, a person, partnership, group, fund, unincorporated association or organization becomes a listed terrorist entity at a particular time and ceases to be a listed terrorist entity at a later time further to an application made under subsection 83.05(2) of the *Criminal Code* or as a result of paragraph 83.05(6)(d) of that Act, then the entity is deemed not to have become a listed terrorist entity and to not have been a listed terrorist entity throughout that period.

Notes: 149.1(1.02) added by 2021 budget bill #1 effective June 29, 2021. See 149.1(1)"listed terrorist entity".

(1.1) Exclusions [deemed non-charitable] — For the purposes of paragraphs (2)(b), (3)(b) and (4)(b) and subsection (21), the following shall be deemed to be neither an amount expended in a taxation year on charitable activities nor a gift made to a qualified donee:

(a) a designated gift; and

(b) [Repealed]

(c) a transfer that has, because of paragraph (c) of the description of B in subsection 188(1.1), paragraph 189(6.2)(b) or subsection 189(6.3), reduced the amount of a liability under Part V.

Related Provisions: 149.1(6.1), (6.2) — Political activities that are ancillary and incidental to charitable activities.

Notes: 149.1(1.1)(c) provides that a transfer to another charity that reduces a penalty (188.1) or revocation tax (188) does not help meet the disbursement quota.

149.1(1.1) opening words amended by 2018 budget bill #2, effective Dec. 13, 2018, to change "(21)(a)" to "subsection (21)" and 149.1(1.1)(b) repealed, effective on the same basis as 149.1(1)"charitable activities". Para. (b) read: "an expenditure on political activities made by a charitable organization or a charitable foundation". See now Notes to 149.1(6.1) re political activities.

149.1(1.1) earlier amended by 2010 budget bill #2 (for taxation years ending after March 3, 2010); added by 2004 Budget.

Information Circulars: 87-1: Registered charities — ancillary and incidental political activities.

Registered Charities Newsletters: 1 (partisan political activities); 2 (is participation on a municipal advisory committee a partisan political activity?); 6 (can registered charities average political expenses over time?); 10 (can a charity support or oppose a political party of a candidate?).

(1.2) Authority of Minister — For the purposes of the determination of B in the definition "disbursement quota" in subsection 149.1(1), the Minister may

(a) authorize a change in the number of periods chosen by a registered charity in determining the prescribed amount; and

(b) accept any method for the determination of the fair market value of property or a portion thereof that may be required in determining the prescribed amount.

Notes: 149.1(1.2) opening words and (a) amended by 2010 budget bill #2, effective for taxation years that end after March 3, 2010, to change "D" to "B" and "charitable foundation" to "registered charity".

(2) Revocation of registration of charitable organization — The Minister may, in the manner described in section 168, revoke the registration of a charitable organization for any reason described in subsection 168(1) or where the organization

(a) carries on a business that is not a related business of that charity;

(b) fails to expend in any taxation year, on charitable activities carried on by it and by way of gifts made by it to qualified donees, amounts the total of which is at least equal to the organization's disbursement quota for that year; or

Proposed Amendment (uncertain) — 149.1(2)(b)

Application: Private Member's Bill S-222 (First House of Commons Reading June 23, 2021), subsec. 2(4), will amend para. 149.1(2)(b) to delete "carried on by it", in force two years after Royal Assent (and subject to review after 5 years: see under Proposed Amendment to 149.1(1)"charitable activities").

Notes: This is a private member's bill that may not pass. See Notes to Proposed Amendment under 149.1(1)"charitable activities".

Possible Future Amendment — Disbursement Quota Rules (Consultation)

Federal Budget, Chapter 6, April 19, 2021: See under 149.1(1)"disbursement quota".

(c) makes a disbursement by way of a gift, other than a gift made

(i) in the course of charitable activities carried on by it, or

Proposed Amendment (uncertain) — 149.1(2)(c)(i)

Application: Private Member's Bill S-222 (First House of Commons Reading June 23, 2021), subsec. 2(5), will amend subpara. 149.1(2)(c)(i) to delete "carried on by it", in force two years after Royal Assent (and subject to review after 5 years: see under Proposed Amendment to 149.1(1)"charitable activities").

Notes: This is a private member's bill that may not pass. See Notes to Proposed Amendment under 149.1(1)"charitable activities".

(ii) to a donee that is a qualified donee at the time of the gift.

Related Provisions: 149.1(1.1) — Exclusions; 149.1(4.1), (4.3) — Additional grounds for revoking registration; 149.1(11) — Partnership look-through rule (for "carries on a business"); 168(4) — Objection to proposed revocation; 172(3)(a) — Appeal from refusal to register, revocation of registration, etc.; 188(1) — Deemed year-end on notice of revocation; 188(1.1) — Revocation tax; 188.1(1)(b), 188.1(2)(b) — Penalty for carrying on unrelated business; 188.2(1), (2) — Suspension of charity's receipting privileges; 230(2) — Charity must keep books and records to allow CRA to determine if there are grounds to revoke registration; 248(1)"registered charity" — Application for registration; 253.1(2) — Charity having interest in limited partnership is not carrying on business.

Notes: See Notes to 149.1(1)"charitable activities" and "related business". Note also the grounds in 168(1) and (3) for revoking registration, and the alternatives of penalties under 188.1 and suspension under 188.2.

Note that depending on the reason a charity's registration is revoked, its directors and officers may become "ineligible individuals" (149.1(1)) and unable to run or register another charity (149.1(4.1)(e), 149.1(25)).

For a ruling that a charity does not trigger 149.1(2)(a) by owning shares of a corporation and being represented on its board, but may trigger it by being too involved with the corporation, see VIEWS doc 2011-0431051R3.

149.1(2)(c), along with 149.1(3)(b.1) and (4)(b.1), enacts a longstanding CRA policy that charities must not make gifts to foreign charities that are not qualified donees (149.1(1)"qualified donee"): VIEWS doc 2012-0451231C6. Before para. (c), this policy was conceded to be legally wrong in a settlement with the Wolfe and Millie Goodman Foundation; see Robert Hayhoe, "A Critical Description of the Canadian Tax Treatment of Cross-Border Charitable Giving and Activities", 49(2) *Canadian Tax Journal* 320-44 (2001), at 331-32. Hayhoe suggests at 333-34 that Canada-U.S. Tax Treaty:Art. XXI:7 (formerly XXI:6) can be used by Canadian charities to make gifts to U.S. 501(c)(3) organizations. In *Prescient Foundation*, [2013] 5 C.T.C. 25 (leave to appeal denied 2013 CarswellNat 4462 (SCC)), the FCA agreed with these Notes that before para. (c) was enacted there was no prohibition against a charity giving money to a foreign charity. (The Court declined to address the treaty issue.) Note however that para. (c), although added in June 2013 by the 2002-2013 technical bill (Part 5 — technical), is effective for gifts made after Dec. 20, 2002.

See Drache, "Charitable Goods Policy", 15(3) *Canadian Not-for-Profit News* (Carswell) 17-19 (March 2007), for policy on expending charitable funds outside Canada.

149.1(2)(b) amended by 2004 Budget, for taxation years that begin after March 22, 2004, with grandfathering that prevented the 3.5% disbursement rule (former 149.1(1)"disbursement quota"B.1) from applying to pre-existing charitable organizations (not foundations) until 2009.

149.1(2) earlier amended by 1995-97 technical bill and 1993 technical bill.

Interpretation Bulletins: IT-244R3: Gifts by individuals of life insurance policies as charitable donations. See also at end of 149.1.

Registered Charities Newsletters: 16 (did you know? [voluntary revocation]; why are you sending me these forms (TX11D, TX11E, T2051A, T2051B)?); 28 (new re-registration process).

Charities Policies: CPS-019: What is a related business?.

Proposed Addition (uncertain) — 149.1(2.1)

(2.1) [Charitable foundation may transfer to non-qualified donee] — For greater certainty, a "charitable foundation", as defined in subsection 149.1(1), may make resources — including grants, gifts or transfers — available by transactions, arrangements or collaborations of any kind whatsoever to a person that is not a qualified donee if the charitable foundation takes reasonable steps to ensure that those resources are used exclusively for a charitable purpose in accordance with subsection (27).

Application: Private Member's Bill S-222 (First House of Commons Reading June 23, 2021), subsec. 2(6), will add subsec. 149.1(2.1), in force two years after Royal Assent (and subject to review after 5 years: see under Proposed Amendment to 149.1(1)"charitable activities").

Related Provisions: 149.1(27) — How charity can determine use of resources by non-qualified donee.

Notes: This is a private member's bill that may not pass. See Notes to Proposed Amendment under 149.1(1)"charitable activities".

(3) Revocation of registration of public foundation — The Minister may, in the manner described in section 168, revoke the registration of a public foundation for any reason described in subsection 168(1) or where the foundation

    (a) carries on a business that is not a related business of that charity;

    (b) fails to expend in any taxation year, on charitable activities carried on by it and by way of gifts made by it to qualified donees, amounts the total of which is at least equal to the foundation's disbursement quota for that year;

Proposed Amendment (uncertain) — 149.1(3)(b)

Application: Private Member's Bill S-222 (First House of Commons Reading June 23, 2021), subsec. 2(7), will amend para. 149.1(3)(b) to delete "carried on by it", in force two years after Royal Assent (and subject to review after 5 years: see under Proposed Amendment to 149.1(1)"charitable activities").

Notes: This is a private member's bill that may not pass. See Notes to Proposed Amendment under 149.1(1)"charitable activities".

    (b.1) makes a disbursement by way of a gift, other than a gift made

       (i) in the course of charitable activities carried on by it, or

Proposed Amendment (uncertain) — 149.1(3)(b.1)(i)

Application: Private Member's Bill S-222 (First House of Commons Reading June 23, 2021), subsec. 2(8), will amend subpara. 149.1(3)(b.1)(i) to delete "carried on by it", in force two years after Royal Assent (and subject to review after 5 years: see under Proposed Amendment to 149.1(1)"charitable activities").

Notes: This is a private member's bill that may not pass. See Notes to Proposed Amendment under 149.1(1)"charitable activities".

Possible Future Amendment — Disbursement Quota Rules (Consultation)

Federal Budget, Chapter 6, April 19, 2021: See under 149.1(1)"disbursement quota".

       (ii) to a donee that is a qualified donee at the time of the gift;

    (c) since June 1, 1950, acquired control of any corporation;

    (d) since June 1, 1950, incurred debts, other than debts for current operating expenses, debts incurred in connection with the purchase and sale of investments and debts incurred in the course of administering charitable activities; or

    (e) at any time within the 24 month period preceding the day on which notice is given to the foundation by the Minister pursuant to subsection 168(1) and at a time when the foundation was a private foundation, took any action or failed to expend amounts such that the Minister was entitled, pursuant to subsection (4), to revoke its registration as a private foundation.

Related Provisions: 149.1(1.1) — Exclusions; 149.1(4.1), (4.3) — Additional grounds for revoking registration; 149.1(11) — Partnership look-through rule (for "carries on a business"); 149.1(12)(a) — Meaning of "control"; 149.1(18) — Rules relating to computation of income; 149.1(20) — Rule regarding disbursement excess; 149.2(1) — Material interest; 168(4) — Objection to proposed revocation; 172(3)(a) — Appeal from refusal to register, revocation of registration, etc.; 188(1) — Deemed year-end on notice of revocation; 188(1.1) — Revocation tax; 188.1(1)(b), 188.1(2)(b) — Penalty for carrying on unrelated business; 188.1(3) — Penalty for receiving dividends from controlled corp; 188.2(1), (2) — Suspension of charity's receipting privileges; 230(2) — Charity must keep books and records to allow CRA to determine if there are grounds to revoke registration; 248(1)"registered charity" — Application for registration; 253.1(2) — Charity having interest in limited partnership is not carrying on business; 256(6)–(9) — Whether control acquired.

Notes: See Notes to 149.1(1)"charitable organization" and 149.1(1)"related business". Note also the grounds in 168(1) and (3) for revoking registration, and the alternatives of penalties under 188.1 and suspension under 188.2.

Foundations can incur debt to make investments. See Notes to 149.1(4).

Acquiring 50% of the common shares of a corp is not acquisition of control (and receiving dividends on preferred shares is not carrying on business): VIEWS doc 2007-0218481R3. For a ruling that control was not acquired for 149.1(3)(c) see 2012-0443321R3.

See also Drache, "Charities Holding Shares", 20(1) *Canadian Not-for-Profit News* (Carswell) 2-3 (Jan. 2012).

For discussion of 149.1(3)(b.1) see Notes to 149.1(2). Para. (b.1) added by 2002-2013 technical bill (Part 5 — technical), for gifts made after Dec. 20, 2002.

Registered Charities Newsletters: 27 (debts incurred by charitable foundations).

Charities Policies: CPS-009: Holding of property for charities; CPS-019: What is a related business?.

(4) Revocation of registration of private foundation — The Minister may, in the manner described in section 168, revoke the registration of a private foundation for any reason described in subsection 168(1) or where the foundation

    (a) carries on any business;

    (b) fails to expend in any taxation year, on charitable activities carried on by it and by way of gifts made by it to qualified donees, amounts the total of which is at least equal to the foundation's disbursement quota for that year;

Proposed Amendment (uncertain) — 149.1(4)(b)

Application: Private Member's Bill S-222 (First House of Commons Reading June 23, 2021), subsec. 2(9), will amend para. 149.1(4)(b) to delete "carried on by it", in force two years after Royal Assent (and subject to review after 5 years: see under Proposed Amendment to 149.1(1)"charitable activities").

Notes: This is a private member's bill that may not pass. See Notes to Proposed Amendment under 149.1(1)"charitable activities".

Possible Future Amendment — Disbursement Quota Rules (Consultation)

Federal Budget, Chapter 6, April 19, 2021: See under 149.1(1)"disbursement quota".

(b.1) makes a disbursement by way of a gift, other than a gift made

(i) in the course of charitable activities carried on by it, or

Proposed Amendment (uncertain) — 149.1(4)(b.1)(i)

Application: Private Member's Bill S-222 (First House of Commons Reading June 23, 2021), subsec. 2(10), will amend subpara. 149.1(4)(b.1)(i) to delete "carried on by it", in force two years after Royal Assent (and subject to review after 5 years: see under Proposed Amendment to 149.1(1)"charitable activities").

Notes: This is a private member's bill that may not pass. See Notes to Proposed Amendment under 149.1(1)"charitable activities".

(ii) to a donee that is a qualified donee at the time of the gift;

(c) has, in respect of a class of shares of the capital stock of a corporation, a divestment obligation percentage at the end of any taxation year; [or]

(d) since June 1, 1950, incurred debts, other than debts for current operating expenses, debts incurred in connection with the purchase and sale of investments and debts incurred in the course of administering charitable activities.

Related Provisions: 149.1(1.1) — Exclusions; 149.1(4.1), (4.3) — Additional grounds for revoking registration; 149.1(11) — Partnership look-through rule (for "carries on a business"); 149.1(12)(a) — Meaning of "control"; 149.2(10) — Shares held through a trust on March 18/07; 168(4) — Objection to proposed revocation; 172(3)(a) — Appeal from refusal to register, revocation of registration, etc.; 188(1) — Deemed year-end on notice of revocation; 188(1.1) — Revocation tax; 188.1(3) — Penalty for receiving dividends from controlled corp; 188.2(1), (2) — Suspension of charity's receipting privileges; 230(2) — Charity must keep books and records to allow CRA to determine if there are grounds to revoke registration; 248(1)"registered charity" — Application for registration; 253.1(2) — Charity having interest in limited partnership is not carrying on business; 256(6)–(9) — Whether control acquired.

Notes: See Notes to 149.1(1)"charitable organization" and 149.1(1)"related business". Note also the grounds in 168(1) and (3) for revoking registration, and the alternatives of penalties under 188.1 and suspension under 188.2.

A foundation may incur debt to make investments including construction projects: VIEWS docs 2005-0154751I7, 2009-0343371R3; *Registered Charities Newsletter* 27; *Acorn Foundation*, 2005 CarswellNat 5606 (FC). See Drache, "CRA Reverses Decades-old Policy on Foundation Borrowing", 14(2) *Canadian Not-for-Profit News* (Carswell) 11-12 (Feb. 2006); Robert Hayhoe, "Federal Court Reviews CRA Undertaking Letter", *ibid.*, 13-14. Borrowing to donate to other charities is forbidden, as that is not "charitable activities": 2009-030940117.

For discussion of 149.1(4)(b.1) see Notes to 149.1(2). Para. (b.1) added by 2002-2013 technical bill (Part 5 — technical), for gifts made after Dec. 20, 2002.

149.1(4)(c) changed from "acquired control of any corporation" by 2007 budget bill #2, for foundations' tax years that begin after March 18, 2007. However, the amendment does not apply to a private foundation's tax year if 149.2(8) applies to the foundation in respect of any class of shares of the capital stock of a corporation.

Registered Charities Newsletters: 23 (did you know? golf tournaments); 27 (debts incurred by charitable foundations).

Charities Policies: CPC-023: Private foundations; CPS-009: Holding of property for charities; CPS-019: What is a related business?.

(4.1) Revocation of registration of registered charity —
The Minister may, in the manner described in section 168, revoke the registration

(a) of a registered charity, if it has entered into a transaction (including a gift to another registered charity) and it may reasonably be considered that a purpose of the transaction was to avoid or unduly delay the expenditure of amounts on charitable activities;

(b) of a registered charity, if it may reasonably be considered that a purpose of entering into a transaction (including the acceptance of a gift) with another registered charity to which para-

graph (a) applies was to assist the other registered charity in avoiding or unduly delaying the expenditure of amounts on charitable activities;

(c) of a registered charity, if a "false statement" (as defined in subsection 163.2(1)) was made in circumstances amounting to "culpable conduct" (as defined in subsection 163.2(1)) in the furnishing of information for the purpose of obtaining or maintaining its registration;

(d) of a registered charity, if it has in a taxation year received a gift of property (other than a designated gift) from another registered charity with which it does not deal at arm's length and it has expended, before the end of the next taxation year, in addition to its disbursement quota for each of those taxation years, an amount that is less than the fair market value of the property, on charitable activities carried on by it or by way of gifts made to qualified donees with which it deals at arm's length;

Proposed Amendment (uncertain) — 149.1(4.1)(d)

Application: Private Member's Bill S-222 (First House of Commons Reading June 23, 2021), subsec. 2(11), will amend para. 149.1(4.1)(d) to delete "carried on by it", in force two years after Royal Assent (and subject to review after 5 years: see under Proposed Amendment to 149.1(1)"charitable activities").

Notes: This is a private member's bill that may not pass. See Notes to Proposed Amendment under 149.1(1)"charitable activities".

(e) of a registered charity, if an ineligible individual is a director, trustee, officer or like official of the charity, or controls or manages the charity, directly or indirectly, in any manner whatever; and

(f) of a registered charity, if it accepts a gift from a foreign state, as defined in section 2 of the *State Immunity Act*, that is set out on the list referred to in subsection 6.1(2) of that Act.

Related Provisions: 149.1(23), (24) — Annulment of charity registration; 149.1(25) — CRA can refuse to register charity managed by ineligible individual; 168(4) — Objection to revocation decision; 172(3)(a) — Appeal from refusal to register, revocation of registration, etc.; 188(1) — Deemed year-end on notice of revocation; 188(1.1) — Revocation tax; 188.1(11) — Alternative penalty for making gift for purpose of undue delay; 188.1(12) — Penalty for same facts as 149.1(4.1)(d); 230(2) — Charity must keep books and records to allow CRA to determine if there are grounds to revoke registration.

Notes: *Paras. (a)-(b)* allow revocation for avoiding the annual 149.1(1)"disbursement quota" requirement.

Para. (c) allows revocation for false statements in obtaining charitable registration. Note also the 168(1) grounds for revoking registration, and the alternatives of penalties (188.1) and suspension (188.2).

Para. (d): for interpretation see VIEWS doc 2010-0370841E5.

Para. (e): see 149.1(1)"ineligible individual" Notes.

Para. (f) applies to gifts from **Iran** and **Syria** and their departments and agencies: *Order Establishing a List of Foreign State Supporters of Terrorism*, P.C. 2012-1067 lists them for purposes of *State Immunity Act* s. 6.1, which allows court proceedings against a listed state (and its agencies) for supporting terrorism.

Para. (c) amended by 2021 budget bill #1, effective June 29, 2021, effectively to add "or maintaining". Before that date, read:

(c) of a registered charity, if a false statement, within the meaning assigned by subsection 163.2(1), was made in circumstances amounting to culpable conduct, within the meaning assigned by that subsection, in the furnishing of information for the purpose of obtaining registration of the charity;

149.1(4.1) amended by 2014 budget bill #1 (for gifts accepted after Feb. 10, 2014), 2011 and 2010 budget bills #2, 2004 Budget.

Charities Guidance: CG-024: Ineligible individuals.

(4.2) Revocation of registration of Canadian amateur athletic association — The Minister may, in the manner described in section 168, revoke the registration of a registered Canadian amateur athletic association

(a) for any reason described in subsection 168(1);

(b) if the association carries on a business that is not a related business of that association;

(c) if an ineligible individual is a director, trustee, officer or like official of the association, or controls or manages the association, directly or indirectly, in any manner whatever; or

(d) if the association accepts a gift from a foreign state, as defined in section 2 of the *State Immunity Act*, that is set out on the list referred to in subsection 6.1(2) of that Act.

Related Provisions: 149.1(11) — Partnership look-through rule (for "carries on a business"); 149.1(22) — Refusal to register as RCAAA; 149.1(25) — CRA can refuse to register CAAA managed by ineligible individual; 168(4) — Objection to revocation decision; 172(3)(a) — Appeal of revocation decision.

Notes: 149.1(4.2)(d) added by 2014 budget bill #1, effective for gifts accepted after Feb. 10, 2014. See Notes to 149.1(4.1) re (4.1)(f).

149.1(4.2) added by 2011 budget bill #2, effective 2012.

(4.3) Revocation of a qualified donee — The Minister may, in the manner described in section 168, revoke the registration of a qualified donee referred to in paragraph (a) or (b.1) of the definition "qualified donee" in subsection (1) for any reason described in subsection 168(1).

Related Provisions: 149.1(22) — Refusal to register as qualified donee; 168(4) — Objection to revocation decision; 172(3)(a.2) — Appeal of revocation decision.

Notes: 149.1(4.3) amended by 2019 budget bill #1, effective 2020, to add reference to 149.1(1)"qualified donee"(b.1) (registered journalism organization).

149.1(4.3) added by 2011 budget bill #2, effective 2012.

(5) Reduction — The Minister may, on application made to the Minister in prescribed form by a registered charity, specify an amount in respect of the charity for a taxation year and, for the purpose of paragraph (2)(b), (3)(b) or (4)(b), as the case may be, that amount shall be deemed to be an amount expended by the charity in the year on charitable activities carried on by it.

Proposed Amendment (uncertain) — 149.1(5)

Application: Private Member's Bill S-222 (First House of Commons Reading June 23, 2021), subsec. 2(12), will amend subsec. 149.1(5) to delete "carried on by it", in force two years after Royal Assent (and subject to review after 5 years: see under Proposed Amendment to 149.1(1)"charitable activities").

Notes: This is a private member's bill that may not pass. See Notes to Proposed Amendment under 149.1(1)"charitable activities".

Related Provisions: 241(3.2)(h) — Decision can be disclosed to the public.

Notes: For CRA policy see CPC-029; Drache, "CRA Issues Advice on Disbursement Quota Relief", 17(5) *Canadian Not-for-Profit News* (Carswell) 35-36 (May 2009).

As well as applying for relief from the CRA, a charity hamstrung by low interest rates might apply to a provincial Court to allow changes to the charity's investment and distribution policy. See Rachel Blumenfeld, "Ontario Court Approves a 'Total Return' Approach", 12(4) *Canadian Not-for-Profit News* (Carswell) 26-27 (April 2004).

Forms: T2094: Registered charities — Application to reduce disbursement quota.

Charities Policies: CPC-029: Application for disbursement quota relief; CPS-009: Holding of property for charities.

(6) Devoting resources to charitable activity — A charitable organization shall be considered to be devoting its resources to charitable activities carried on by it to the extent that

Proposed Amendment (uncertain) — 149.1(6) opening words

Application: Private Member's Bill S-222 (First House of Commons Reading June 23, 2021), subsec. 2(12), will amend the opening words of subsec. 149.1(6) to delete "carried on by it", in force two years after Royal Assent (and subject to review after 5 years: see under Proposed Amendment to 149.1(1)"charitable activities").

Notes: This is a private member's bill that may not pass. See Notes to Proposed Amendment under 149.1(1)"charitable activities".

(a) it carries on a related business;

(b) in any taxation year, it disburses not more than 50% of its income for that year to qualified donees; or

(c) it disburses income to a registered charity that the Minister has designated in writing as a charity associated with it.

Related Provisions: 149.1(6.01) — Parallel rule for RCAAAs; 149.1(7) — Designation of associated charities; 149.1(12)(b) — Rules — income.

Notes: See Notes to 149.1(1) re "related business", and 149.1(7) re "associated" charities. For political activities and "public policy dialogue" see Notes to 149.1(6.1).

149.1(6)(b) and (c) amended by 2018 budget bill #2, effective on the same basis as the repeal of 149.1(1)"political activity". Before the amendment read:

(b) it disburses income to qualified donees, other than income disbursed by way of a gift the making of which is a political activity, if the total amount of the

charitable organization's income that is disbursed to qualified donees in a taxation year does not exceed 50% of its income for the year; or

(c) it disburses income to a registered charity that the Minister has designated in writing as a charity associated with it, other than income disbursed by way of a gift the making of which is a political activity.

Paras. (b) and (c) amended by 2012 budget bill #1, effective June 29, 2012.

Information Circulars: 77-6R: Registered charities: designation as associated charities.

Charities Policies: CPS-001: Applicants that are established to hold periodic fundraisers; CPS-019: What is a related business?.

(6.01) Devoting resources to purpose and function — A Canadian amateur athletic association is considered to devote its resources to its exclusive purpose and exclusive function to the extent that it carries on

(a) a related business; or

(b) activities involving the participation of professional athletes, if those activities are ancillary and incidental to its exclusive purpose and exclusive function.

Related Provisions: 149.1(1)"Canadian amateur athletic association"(e) — Requirement to devote resources; 149.1(6) — Parallel rule for charities; 149.1(6.201) — RCAAA — political activities.

Notes: 149.1(6.01) added by 2011 budget bill #2, effective 2012.

(6.1) Charitable purposes [limits to foundation's political activities] — For the purposes of the definition "charitable foundation" in subsection (1), a corporation or trust that devotes any part of its resources to the direct or indirect support of, or opposition to, any political party or candidate for public office shall not be considered to be constituted and operated exclusively for charitable purposes.

Related Provisions: 149.1(1)"political activity" — Extended meaning of term; 188.2(2)(e) — Suspension of receipting privileges.

Notes: This rule is for a charitable *foundation*. 149.1(6.2) applies the same rule to a charitable *organization*. These rules are the product of a long history:

In 1985, *Scarborough Legal Services*, [1985] 1 C.T.C. 98 (FCA) introduced uncertainty as to whether charities could use *any* resources in political activity. In response, 149.1(6.1)-(6.2) were enacted to provide that, as long as a charity devoted substantially all its resources to charitable activities, it could devote a small portion (up to about 10%) to non-partisan political activities that were ancillary and incidental to its purposes. This was intended to be permissive, allowing charities to devote some resources to non-partisan political activities. (See pre-2018 wording of 149.1(6.1) below.)

During 2006-2015 when the Conservatives were in power, media reports claimed CRA was targeting left-wing charities for "political audits". This led the Liberals to promise in their Oct. 2015 election platform: "We will allow charities to do their work on behalf of Canadians free from political harassment...." (This and the other docs summarized here are reproduced in a Proposed Amendment box here, up to the 54th ed.) The Liberals were elected, and the Prime Minister's Nov. 2015 mandate letter to the new Minister of Finance included the same text.

On Jan. 20, 2016, CRA announced the "winding down of the political activities audit program for charities". By then, 30 political-activity audits had been completed; 24 underway would continue. The March 22, 2016 Budget stated that CRA and Finance would undertake "discussions with stakeholder groups and an online consultation to clarify the rules governing the political activities of charities". The consultation began on Oct. 28, 2016, with comments sought by Dec. 14, 2016. A Dec. 21, 2016 news release then stated that CRA had established a 5-person consultation panel, to use feedback obtained and make recommendations to the Minister.

The *Report of the Consultation Panel on the Political Activities of Charities* (tinyurl.com/report-char-polit) was released March 31, 2017. It recommended: (1) Revise CRA policy to allow charities to fully engage in public policy dialogue and development. (2) Implement changes to CRA administration in compliance, appeals, audits, and communication and collaboration, to enhance clarity and consistency. (3) Amend the ITA to delete reference to non-partisan "political activities", to allow charities to fully engage, without limitation, in non-partisan public policy dialogue and development, provided it is subordinate to and furthers their charitable purposes. (4) Modernize the legislative framework governing the charitable sector to focus on charitable *purposes* rather than *activities*, and adopt an inclusive list of acceptable purposes to reflect current social and environmental issues and approaches.

Following the Report, CRA suspended all political audits: Drache, "Government Moves on Charity Political Activities File", xxxix *The Canadian Taxpayer* (Carswell) 83-85 (June 2, 2017).

Meanwhile, on July 16, 2018, in *Canada Without Poverty*, 2018 ONSC 4147, the "substantially all" requirement in 149.1(6.2) [and thus (6.1)] was held to infringe the *Charter of Rights* s. 2(b) right to freedom of expression. (This Ontario decision might not bind the FCA in considering a revocation.) See Drache, "Ontario Court Holds that Political Activities Restrictions Violate Charter Rights", 26(9) *Canadian Not-for-Profit*

News (Carswell) 65-68 (Sept. 2018); Hayhoe & Fitzpatrick, "Canada Without Poverty", 27(2) *Canadian Tax Highlights* (ctf.ca) 3-6 (Feb. 2019).

A CRA/Finance news release Aug 15, 2018 stated the government would appeal *Canada Without Poverty* (but the appeal was dropped: tinyurl.com/cwp-appeal, Feb. 1/19), but also that it would "implement changes consistent with recommendation no. 3 of the *Report*.... The intended amendments will allow charities to pursue their charitable purposes by engaging in non-partisan political activities and in the development of public policy. Charities will still be required to have exclusively charitable purposes, and restrictions against partisan political activities will remain."

Finance then issued a Sept. 14, 2018 news release, with draft legislation for 30-day public consultation, similar to what is now enacted, except 149.1(1)"charitable activities" was not included. Finance described these changes as: (1) Largely removing the provisions relating to charities' political activities, including the one effectively allowing charities to devote 10% of their resources to non-partisan political activities. (2) Maintaining the prohibition on charities providing direct or indirect support of, or opposition to, a political party or candidate for public office. (3) Clarifying that charitable organizations, like charitable foundations, must be constituted and operated for exclusively charitable purposes. "As a result of these changes, the issue of political activities would be largely governed by the common law — meaning that a charity's political activities would continue to be permitted if those activities are ancillary and incidental to the fulfillment of its charitable purposes. At the same time, these changes would leave untouched the common law requirement that a registered charity cannot be established or operated for a political purpose."

2018 budget bill #2 (C-86) was then tabled on Oct. 25, 2018, amending the above by adding 149.1(1)"charitable activities", *overriding* the common law by allowing "public policy dialogue and development" as charitable, provided it is "in furtherance of a charitable purpose". (This follows Report recommendation (3) above.) Also added was 149.1(10.1), ensuring that a charity may always follow its "stated purposes".

149.1(6.1) was thus amended by 2018 budget bill #2 to implement these changes, effective 2008 in respect of organizations, corporations and trusts that were registered charities on Sept. 14, 2018; and effective Sept. 14, 2018 in any other case. The old rule thus applies only in very limited cases. Detailed commentary on that rule can be found in these Notes up to the 54th ed. Where it applies, read:

> (6.1) For the purposes of the definition "charitable foundation" in subsection (1), where a corporation or trust devotes substantially all of its resources to charitable purposes and
>
> > (a) it devotes part of its resources to political activities,
> >
> > (b) those political activities are ancillary and incidental to its charitable purposes, and
> >
> > (c) those political activities do not include the direct or indirect support of, or opposition to, any political party or candidate for public office,
>
> the corporation or trust shall be considered to be constituted and operated for charitable purposes to the extent of that part of its resources so devoted.

Interpretation of the new (2018) rules that apply retroactive to 2008

See *Public policy dialogue and development activities by charities* and Charities Guidance CG-027 (tinyurl.com/cra-pubpol, both Jan. 21, 2019). Advocating and mobilizing support for (or against) a law or policy are specifically allowed, even if the advocacy matches the platform of a particular political party. For criticism of CG-027 see Cdn Bar Association April 18, 2019 letter to CRA.

See also CRA news release, "Government response to the report of the Consultation Panel on the Political Activities of Charities", re CRA changes.

For discussion of these amendments (including at the proposal stage) and the role charities should have in public policy, see articles in *The Philanthropist [TPh]* (thephilanthropist.ca), Feb. 2016; Policy Forum, 65(2) *Canadian Tax Journal* 353-418 (2017); Alalouf-Hall & Grant-Poitras, "Charities Now Welcome in the Political Arena", *The Philanthropist* (thephilanthropist.ca), Oct. 28, 2019 (6pp); Lorino, "Charitable Sector Gradually Adjusting to a New Regulatory World", *TPh*, March 30, 2020 (7pp). For opposition to change see Bernhard, "The Case Against Policy Advocacy Deregulation", *TPh* (March 2017), tinyurl.com/bernhard-dereg; Blumberg, "Finance Changes to Political Activities", tinyurl.com/blumb-politic (Oct. 31, 2018); Dolson, "Democracy Requires Limits on Charities' Political Activities", 8(4) *Canadian Tax Focus* (ctf.ca) 6-7 (Nov. 2018); Drache, "First Indication of CRA's Response to Political Activity Changes", 26(12) *CNfpN* 94 (Dec. 2018); Chenier, "PPPDA, Charitable Purposes and Lobbying Requirements", 27(4) *CNfpN* 25-27 (April 2019).

Note that any charity (or other entity) engaged in lobbying may need to register under the *Lobbying Act*. See Notes to 20(1)(cc).

Note also that during a federal election, the *Canada Elections Act* regulates political advertising. See Drache, "Elections and Third Party Political Advocacy", 23(4) *Canadian Not-for-Profit News [CNfPN]* (Carswell) 29-31 (April 2015); Klombies, "The Charities and the Canada Elections Act Amendments Series", 27(6) *CNfPN* 41-43 (June 2019), 27(7) 49-51 (July 2019), and "Organizations May Face Fines for Third-Party Advertising", xli(16) *The Canadian Taxpayer [TCT]* (Carswell) 127-28 (Aug. 9, 2019) and 27(8) *CNfPN* 61 (Aug. 2019); Prendergast & Carter, "Lobbying and Elections Legislation in Canada", *Charity & NFP Law Bulletin* 453 (Aug. 2019), tinyurl.com/carters-453 (15pp); Drache, "Elections Canada Policies Out of Step with CRA", xli(18) *TCT* 137-39 (Sept. 20, 2019) and 27(10) *CNfPN* 73-75 (Oct. 2019).

See also Notes to 149.1(1)"charitable activities".

Information Circulars: 87-1: Registered charities — ancillary and incidental political activities.

Registered Charities Newsletters: 1 (partisan political activities); 2 (is participation on a municipal advisory committee a partisan political activity?); 6 (can registered charities average political expenses over time?); 14 (new political activity guidelines); 15 (political activities lead to revocation).

Charities Policies: CPC-001: Attendance at a political fundraising dinner; CPC-007: Charging fair market rent to a political party.

Charities Guidance: CG-027: Public policy dialogue and development activities by charities.

(6.2) Charitable purposes — For the purposes of the definition "charitable organization" in subsection (1), an organization that devotes any part of its resources to the direct or indirect support of, or opposition to, any political party or candidate for public office shall not be considered to be constituted and operated exclusively for charitable purposes.

Related Provisions: 149.1(1)"political activity" — Extended meaning of term; 149.1(1.1)(b) — Expenditures on political activities; 149.1(6.201) — Parallel rule for RCAAAs; 188.2(2)(f) — Suspension of receipting privileges.

Notes: See Notes to 149.1(6.1) re political activities, and to 149.1(1)"charitable organization".

149.1(6.2) amended by 2018 budget bill #2, effective on same basis as the amendment to 149.1(6.1), Before the amendment, read:

> (6.2) Charitable activities [limits to charity's political activities] — For the purposes of the definition "charitable organization" in subsection (1), where an organization devotes substantially all of its resources to charitable activities carried on by it and
>
> > (a) it devotes part of its resources to political activities,
> >
> > (b) those political activities are ancillary and incidental to its charitable activities, and
> >
> > (c) those political activities do not include the direct or indirect support of, or opposition to, any political party or candidate for public office,
>
> the organization shall be considered to be devoting that part of its resources to charitable activities carried on by it.

Information Circulars: 87-1: Registered charities — ancillary and incidental political activities.

Registered Charities Newsletters: 1 (partisan political activities); 2 (is participation on a municipal advisory committee a partisan political activity?); 6 (can registered charities average political expenses over time?); 14 (new political activity guidelines); 15 (political activities lead to revocation).

Charities Policies: CPC-001: Partisan political activities — attendance at a political fundraising dinner; CPC-007: Partisan political activity — charging fair market rent to a political party.

Charities Guidance: CG-027: Public policy dialogue and development activities by charities.

(6.201) Activities of Canadian amateur athletic associations — For the purposes of the definition "Canadian amateur athletic association" in subsection (1), an association that devotes any part of its resources to the direct or indirect support of, or opposition to, any political party or candidate for public office shall not be considered to devote that part of its resources to its exclusive purpose and exclusive function.

Related Provisions: 149.1(1)"political activity" — Extended meaning of term; 149.1(6.01) — RCAAA — business activities; 149.1(6.2) — Parallel rule for charities; 188.2(2)(g) — Suspension of receipting privileges.

Notes: See Notes to the parallel rule for charitable foundations in 149.1(6.1).

149.1(6.201) amended by 2018 budget bill #2, effective 2012 in respect of associations that were registered Canadian amateur athletic associations on Sept. 14, 2018, and effective Sept. 14, 2018 in any other case. Before the amendment, read:

> (6.201) Political activities of Canadian amateur athletic association — For the purpose of the definition "Canadian amateur athletic association" in subsection (1), an association that devotes part of its resources to political activities is considered to devote those resources to its exclusive purpose and exclusive function if
>
> > (a) it devotes substantially all its resources to its purpose and function; and
> >
> > (b) those political activities
> >
> > > (i) are ancillary and incidental to its purpose and function, and
> > >
> > > (ii) do not include the direct or indirect support of, or opposition to, any political party or candidate for public office.

See Notes to 149.1(6.1). 149.1(6.201) added by 2011 budget bill #2, effective 2012.

(6.21) Marriage for civil purposes — For greater certainty, subject to subsections (6.1) and (6.2), a registered charity with stated purposes that include the advancement of religion shall not have its registration revoked or be subject to any other penalty under Part V solely because it or any of its members, officials, supporters or adherents exercises, in relation to marriage between persons of the same sex, the freedom of conscience and religion guaranteed under the *Canadian Charter of Rights and Freedoms*.

Notes: 149.1(6.21) added by 2005 same-sex marriage bill, effective July 20, 2005.

(6.3) Designation as public foundation, etc. — The Minister may, by notice sent by registered mail to a registered charity, on the Minister's own initiative or on application made to the Minister in prescribed form, designate the charity to be a charitable organization, private foundation or public foundation and the charity shall be deemed to be registered as a charitable organization, private foundation or public foundation, as the case may be, for taxation years commencing after the day of mailing of the notice unless and until it is otherwise designated under this subsection or its registration is revoked under subsection (2), (3), (4), (4.1) or 168(2).

Related Provisions: 149.1(13) — Designation of private foundation as public; 172(3) — Appeal from refusal to designate; 168(4) — Objection to designation; 241(3.2)(h) — Designation notice may be disclosed to the public; 244(5) — Proof of service by mail; 244(14) — Notice presumed mailed on date of notice; 248(7)(a) — Mail deemed received on day mailed.

Notes: An application referred to in 149.1(6.3), in respect of one or more tax years after 1999, may be made after 1999 and by Sept. 23, 2013. If a designation referred to in 149.1(6.3) for any of those years is made in response to the application, the charity is deemed to be registered as a charitable organization, public foundation or private foundation, as the case may be, for the tax years that the Minister specifies. (2002-2013 technical bill, s. 308(16))

Forms: T2095: Registered charities — application for re-designation.

Charities Policies: CPS-008: Organizations established to assist other charities; CPS-009: Holding of property for charities.

(6.4) National arts service organizations — Where an organization that

(a) has, on written application to the Minister of Communications describing all of its objects and activities, been designated by that Minister on approval of those objects and activities to be a national arts service organization,

(b) has, as its exclusive purpose and its exclusive function, the promotion of arts in Canada on a nation-wide basis,

(c) is resident in Canada and was formed or created in Canada, and

(d) complies with prescribed conditions

applies in prescribed form to the Minister of National Revenue for registration, that Minister may register the organization for the purposes of this Act and, where the organization so applies or is so registered, this section, paragraph 38(a.1), sections 110.1, 118.1, 168, 172, 180 and 230, subsection 241(3.2) and Part V apply, with such modifications as the circumstances require, to the organization as if it were an applicant for registration as a charitable organization or as if it were a registered charity that is designated as a charitable organization, as the case may be.

Related Provisions: 56(1)(z.1) — Benefit from RNASO included in income; 149.1(6.2) — Charitable activities; 149.1(6.5) — Revocation of designation.

Notes: A RNASO is effectively deemed to be a charity for income tax purposes, but CRA considers that this does not apply for GST/HST purposes; *Excise & GST/HST News* 101 (March 2017).

The reference to the Minister of Communications may mean the Minister of Canadian Heritage. See Notes to 8(1)(q).

Closing words of 149.1(6.4) amended by 2001 technical bill (effective June 14, 2001) and 1997 Budget.

149.1(6.4) added by 1991 technical bill, effective July 14, 1990. Where an organization applied to Revenue Canada for registration before Dec. 17, 1991 and Revenue Canada accepted the application as meeting the requirements, the organization is deemed to have become registered on the day the application was made (or, where in the application a later day was specified as the day on which the organization is to become registered, on that later day).

Regulations: 8700 (prescribed conditions for 149.1(6.4)(d)).

Registered Charities Newsletters: 2 (registered national arts service organizations can issue tax receipts); 3 (registered national arts service organizations).

(6.5) Revocation of designation — The Minister of Communications may, at any time, revoke the designation of an organization made for the purpose of subsection (6.4) where

(a) an incorrect statement was made in the furnishing of information for the purpose of obtaining the designation, or

(b) the organization has amended its objects after its last designation was made,

and, where the designation is so revoked, the organization shall be deemed for the purpose of section 168 to have ceased to comply with the requirements of this Act for its registration under this Act.

Notes: The reference to the Minister of Communications may mean the Minister of Canadian Heritage. See Notes to 8(1)(q).

149.1(6.5) added by 1991 technical bill, effective July 14, 1990.

(7) Designation of associated charities — On application made to the Minister in prescribed form, the Minister may, in writing, designate a registered charity as a charity associated with one or more specified registered charities where the Minister is satisfied that the charitable aim or activity of each of the registered charities is substantially the same, and on and after a date specified in such a designation, the charities to which it relates shall, until such time, if any, as the Minister revokes the designation, be deemed to be associated.

Related Provisions: 149.1(6)(c) — Disbursement to associated charity; 241(3.2)(h) — Designation notice may be disclosed to the public.

Notes: CRA has broadened the definition to allow organizations working on a joint project to be associated: Charities Policy CPC-28; Drache, "New Policy on Associated Charities", 15(4) *Canadian Not-for-Profit News* (Carswell) 28 (April 2007).

For a charity filing Quebec returns, the application must be copied to Revenu Québec: *Taxation Act* ss. 985.3, 21.4.6.

Information Circulars: 77-6R: Registered charities: designation as associated charities.

Registered Charities Newsletters: 27 (legalese for charities: meaning of "substantially the same").

Forms: T2050: Application to register a charity under the ITA; T3011: Registered charities — Application for designation as associated charities.

(8) Accumulation of property — A registered charity may, with the approval in writing of the Minister, accumulate property for a particular purpose, on terms and conditions and over any period of time that the Minister specifies in the approval. Any property accumulated after receipt of and in accordance with the approval, including any income earned in respect of the accumulated property, is not to be included in calculating the prescribed amount in paragraph (a) of the description of B in the definition "disbursement quota" in subsection (1) for the portion of any taxation year in the period, except to the extent that the registered charity is not in compliance with the terms and conditions of the approval.

Related Provisions: 241(3.2)(h).— Decision notice may be disclosed to the public.

Notes: 149.1(8) amended by 2010 budget bill #2 (for tax years that end after March 3, 2010), 1993 technical bill.

Registered Charities Newsletters: 22 (permission to accumulate property).

Charities Policies: CPC-005: Accumulation of property; CPS-009: Holding of property for charities.

(9) [Repealed]

Notes: 149.1(9) repealed by 2010 budget bill #2, for taxation years that end after March 3, 2010.

Registered Charities Newsletters: 22 (permission to accumulate property).

(10) Deemed charitable activity — An amount paid by a charitable organization to a qualified donee that is not paid out of the income of the charitable organization is deemed to be a devotion of a resource of the charitable organization to a charitable activity carried on by it.

> **Proposed Amendment (uncertain) — 149.1(10)**
>
> **Application**: Private Member's Bill S-222 (First House of Commons Reading June 23, 2021), subsec. 2(13), will amend subsec. 149.1(10) to delete "carried on by it", in

force two years after Royal Assent (and subject to review after 5 years: see under Proposed Amendment to 149.1(1)"charitable activities").

Notes: This is a private member's bill that may not pass. See Notes to Proposed Amendment under 149.1(1)"charitable activities".

Related Provisions: 149.1(12)(b) — Rules — income.

Notes: 149.1(10) amended by 2018 budget bill #2, to delete (from the end) "unless the amount paid is a gift the making of which is a political activity", effective on the same basis as the repeal of 149.1(1)"political activity". See Notes to 149.1(6.1).

149.1(10) amended by 2012 budget bill #1, effective June 29, 2012, to add everything from "unless".

(10.1) Public policy activities — Subject to subsections (6.1) and (6.2), public policy dialogue and development activities carried on by an organization, corporation or trust in support of its stated purposes shall be considered to be carried on in furtherance of those purposes and not for any other purpose.

Related Provisions: 149.1(1)"charitable activities" — Public policy dialogue and development activities allowed as charitable activities.

Notes: This rule applies to 149.1(1)"charitable activities". See Notes to 149.1(6.1).

149.1(10.1) added by 2018 budget bill #2, effective on the same basis as 149.1(1)"charitable activities".

(11) Partnership look-through rule — For the purposes of this section and sections 149.2 and 188.1, each member of a partnership at any time is deemed at that time to own the portion of each property of the partnership equal to the proportion that the fair market value of the member's interest in the partnership at that time is of the fair market value of all interests in the partnership at that time.

Notes: 149.1(11), added by 2016 budget bill #1 effective April 21, 2015, is consequential on 253.1(2), which provides that a charity can be a limited partner without being considered to carry on a business. Due to 149.1(11), the calculation of a private foundation's excess corporate holdings for 149.1, 149.2 and 188.1 is determined by looking through partnerships of which it is a member.

(12) Rules — For the purposes of this section,

(a) a corporation is controlled by a charitable foundation if more than 50% of the corporation's issued share capital, having full voting rights under all circumstances, belongs to

(i) the foundation, or

(ii) the foundation and persons with whom the foundation does not deal at arm's length,

but, for the purpose of paragraph (3)(c), a charitable foundation is deemed not to have acquired control of a corporation if it has not purchased or otherwise acquired for consideration more than 5% of the issued shares of any class of the capital stock of that corporation;

(b) there shall be included in computing the income of a charity for a taxation year all gifts received by it in the year including gifts from any other charity but not including

(i) a designated gift,

(ii) any gift or portion of a gift in respect of which it is established that the donor is not a charity and

(A) has not been allowed a deduction under paragraph 110.1(1)(a) in computing the donor's taxable income or under subsection 118.1(3) in computing the donor's tax payable under this Part, or

(B) was not taxable under section 2 for the taxation year in which the gift was made, or

(iii) any gift or portion of a gift in respect of which it is established that the donor is a charity and that the gift was not made out of the income of the donor; and

(c) subsections 104(6) and (12) are not applicable in computing the income of a charitable foundation that is a trust.

Related Provisions: 256(6), (6.1) — Control.

Notes: For 149.1(12)(a) to apply, the foundation must own at least one share of the corporation: VIEWS doc 2006-0175081E5. For a ruling applying 149.1(12)(a) see 2012-0443321R3.

149.1(12)(b)(i) amended by 2010 budget bill #2, effective for taxation years that end after March 3, 2010, to change "specified gift" to "designated gift".

149.1(12)(a) closing words amended by 2007 budget bill #2, effective on the same basis as the amendment to 149.1(4), to change "(3)(c) or (4)(c)" to "(3)(c)".

Interpretation Bulletins: IT-244R3: Gifts by individuals of life insurance policies as charitable donations. See also at end of s. 149.1.

(13) Designation of private foundation as public — On application made to the Minister by a private foundation, the Minister may, on such terms and conditions as the Minister considers appropriate, designate the foundation to be a public foundation, and on and after the date specified in such a designation, the foundation to which it relates shall, until such time, if any, as the Minister revokes the designation, be deemed to be a public foundation.

Related Provisions: 149.1(6.3) — Designation as public foundation, etc; 241(3.2)(h) — Designation notice may be disclosed to the public.

Forms: T2095: Registered charities — application for re-designation.

(14) Information returns — Every registered charity and registered Canadian amateur athletic association shall, within six months from the end of each taxation year of the charity or association and without notice or demand, file with the Minister both an information return and a public information return for the year in prescribed form and containing prescribed information.

Related Provisions: 149(12) — NPO information return; 149.1(14.1) — Information return for RJO; 149.1(15) — Public information return may be disclosed to the public; 150(1.1)(a) — Charity not required to file corporate tax return; 168(1)(c) — Revocation of registration for failure to file return; 188.1(3.1) — Penalty for having divestment obligation percentage; 188.1(6) — $500 penalty for failure to file return; 188.2(2.1) — Suspension for failure to provide required information on return; 189(6.1)(a)(ii) — Information returns required when registration revoked; 241(3.2) — Public disclosure of information returns; 241(10)"publicly accessible charity information" — Information in information return; Reg. 204(3)(c) — Annual T3 return not required; Reg. 216 — Information return for RCAAA before 2012; *Interpretation Act* 27(5) — Meaning of "within six months".

Notes: Since Oct. 2018, the T3010 return mailing address is: Charities Directorate, Canada Revenue Agency, 105 - 275 Pope Road, Summerside, PE C1N 6E8. Since June 2019, the T3010 can be filed electronically, under CHAMP (Charities IT Modernization Project): tinyurl.com/champ-cra. CRA now strongly encourages online filing.

See guide T4033, *Completing the Registered Charity Information Return*, for detailed instructions for the T3010 return. See also Drache, "T-3010: Mounting Complexity for Charities", 21(3) *Canadian Not-for-Profit News* (Carswell) 23-24 (March 2013). The T3010 includes a number of specific questions, such as whether the charity compensated its directors; a list of all donations of $10,000 or more from non-resident non-citizens; and details of activities conducted outside Canada. To amend a T3010, use Form T1240. CRA processes about 84,000 charity returns a year, as almost every charity complies.

Guide RC4424 states that if the T3010 is not filed within 5 months after the end of the fiscal period, CRA sends a computer-generated reminder. At 7 months, CRA sends a Notice of Intention to Revoke a Charity's Registration. At 10 months, CRA will begin revocation proceedings with a Notice of Revocation. CRA's *Guidelines for applying sanctions* (tinyurl.com/guide-sanc) state: "The Directorate will continue its zero-tolerance policy for non-filers — if a charity does not file its return after we have reminded it to do so, we will simply revoke its registration. In our view, filing is a fundamental obligation for all registered charities. In its annual return, a charity accounts to donors and Canadians generally for its tax-advantaged status. The return also provides the Directorate with key information needed to administer and enforce the legislation."

Due to COVID-19, the filing deadline for all T3010 returns due March 18 to Dec. 30, 2020 was extended to Dec. 31, 2020: CRA "Charities and giving" email, March 20, 2020 (reproduced here in PITA 59th ed.).

A charity's GST/HST refund or rebate can be held back if this return is not filed: *Excise Tax Act* ss. 229(2), 263.02 (see Notes to 150(1)(a)).

A charity operating in Quebec must also file a Form TP-985.22-v information return with Revenu Québec (*Taxation Act* s. 985.22).

149.1(14) amended by 2011 budget bill #2, effective for fiscal periods that begin after 2011, to add references to an RCAAA.

Information Circulars: 97-2R16: Customized forms.

Registered Charities Newsletters: 1 (annual due date); 2 (revised annual information return); 5 (when does your charity have to file its T3010 return?); 6 (how have we revised the T3010 return that each registered charity has to file annually?); 7 (annual charity information return — frequently asked questions); 8 (increased transparency; changes in departmental policy on applications for re-registration); 11 (renewal in the Charities Directorate; reminder [re charities moving]); 13 (revised registered charity information return T3010; section E — financial information); 14 (form T3010 information online; adjusting T3010 returns); 16 (how can I be certain that my organization's T3010A has been received?; why are you sending me these forms (TX11D, TX11E, T2051A, T2051B)?); 17 (Q&A about the new Form T3010A); 18 (list of companies authorized to produce a customized Form T3010A now available); 19 (reminder: completing the T3010A); 23 (revisions to form T3010A); 27 (reminders: use the correct information returns; where to send your return; use of correct mailing address); 28 (new fillable T3010A); 29 (Guide T4033; tips for completing your annual information return); 31 (avoiding delays in processing returns); 33 (obligation to file financial statements with your Form T3010); *Charities Connection* 5 (the new Form T3010-1); *Charities Connection* 6 (filing a complete T3010); *Charities Connection* 7 (reminder to file your T3010).

Charities Policies: CPC-016: Religious charities — Form T3010; CPS-017: Effective date of registration.

Charities Guidance: CG-008: Confidentiality — public information.

Forms: RC4424: Completing the tax return where registration of a charity is revoked [guide]; T1000-1: Registered journalism organization information return; T1000-2: Completing Form T1000-1, Registered journalism organization information return [guide]; T1000-3: Directors/trustees worksheet for registered journalism organizations; T1235: Directors/trustees and like officials worksheet; T1236: Qualified donees worksheet / amounts provided to other organizations; T1240: Registered charity adjustment request; T3010: Registered charity information return; T4033A: Completing the registered charity information return [guide].

(14.1) Information returns [RJO] — Every registered journalism organization shall, within six months from the end of each taxation year of the organization without notice or demand, file with the Minister both an information return and a public information return for the year in prescribed form and containing prescribed information including, for the public information return, for each donor whose total gifts to the organization in the year exceed $5,000, the name of the donor and the total amount donated.

Related Provisions: 149(12) — NPO information return; 149.1(15), 241(3.2) — Information return may be disclosed to the public; 168(1)(c) — Revocation of registration for failure to file return; 188.1(6) — $500 penalty for failure to file return; 188.2(2.1) — Suspension for failure to provide required information on return; *Interpretation Act* 27(5) — Meaning of "within six months".

Notes: 149.1(14.1) added by 2019 budget bill #1, effective 2020.

(15) Information may be communicated — Notwithstanding section 241,

(a) the information contained in a public information return referred to in subsection 149.1(14) or (14.1) shall be communicated or otherwise made available to the public by the Minister in such manner as the Minister deems appropriate;

(b) the Minister may make available to the public in any manner that the Minister considers appropriate, in respect of each registered, or previously registered, charity, Canadian amateur athletic association, journalism organization and qualified donee referred to in paragraph (a) of the definition "qualified donee" in subsection (1),

(i) its name, address and date of registration,

(ii) in the case of a registered, or previously registered, charity, Canadian amateur athletic association or journalism organization, its registration number, and

(iii) the effective date of any revocation, annulment or termination of registration; and

(c) if, at any time during a taxation year of a private foundation that is a registered charity, the private foundation holds more than an insignificant interest in respect of a class of shares of the capital stock of a corporation, the Minister shall make available to the public in such manner as the Minister deems appropriate,

(i) the name of the corporation, and

(ii) in respect of each class of shares of the corporation, that portion of the total corporate holdings percentage of the private foundation in respect of the class that is attributable to

(A) holdings of shares of that class by the private foundation, and

(B) the total of all holdings of shares of that class by relevant persons in respect of the private foundation;

(d) [Repealed]

Related Provisions: 241(3.2) — Additional disclosure permitted of charity information.

Notes: A list of registered charities, and access to their reported information including financial information and list of directors, is at tinyurl.com/list-charities. 65-70% of charities' revenues come from government, but if one excludes hospitals, universities, colleges and school boards (70% of total charity revenues), then 40% of revenue is from government and 30% from donations: David Lasby, "What T3010 Data Tell Us About Charity Financing", 24(2) *The Philanthropist* (thephilanthropist.ca) 155-60 (2011). See also David D'Onofrio, "Disclosure of Information About Registered Charities", 1(3) *Canadian Tax Focus* (ctf.ca) 8-9 (Nov. 2011).

Bill C-470 (2010) was a private member's bill sponsored by Liberal MP Albina Guarnieri. It would have added 149.1(1)"compensation" and (15.1) and amended 149.1(15)(b), requiring disclosure of each charity employee's compensation exceeding $100,000. (It was substantially changed by the Commons Finance Committee, with MP Guarnieri's agreement, after objection from many charities. The original proposal would have allowed revocation of registration of any charity paying an employee more than $250,000 per year, and would have required disclosure of the five highest employee salaries regardless of quantum. See Drache, "Bill C-470 Passes Committee in a Pale Imitation of the Original", 19(1) *Canadian Not-for-Profit News* (Carswell) 1-2 (Jan. 2011).) As MP Guarnieri retired before the May 2, 2011 election, this proposal is not expected to be reintroduced.

149.1(15) amended by 2019 budget bill #1, effective 2020, to add references to 149.1(14.1) in para. (a) and "journalism organization" in (b).

149.1(15)(d) repealed by 2017 budget bill #1, for gifts made after March 21, 2017 (on repeal of the extra deduction for pharmaceutical donations in 110.1(1)(a.1)). It read:

> (d) the Minister, or a Minister referred to in paragraph 110.1(8)(e), may make available to the public in any manner a listing of the registered charities in respect of which an opinion has been formed for the purpose of paragraph 110.1(8)(e) or revoked under subsection 110.1(9).

149.1(15)(b) amended by 2011 budget bill #2, effective 2012.

149.1(15)(d) added by 2008 budget bill #2, effective March 12, 2009.

149.1(15)(c) added by 2007 budget bill #2, effective for foundations' taxation years that begin after March 18, 2007.

Charities Guidance: CG-008: Confidentiality — public information.

(16)–(19) [Repealed under former Act]

Notes: 149.1(16) and (17), repealed in 1984, enacted penalty taxes that now appear in 188(1) and (2). 149.1(18), repealed effective 1984, provided rules re computing income. 149.1(19), repealed effective 1981, provided an election to allocate disbursements in a foundation's second taxation year to its first year.

(20) Rule regarding disbursement excess — Where a registered charity has expended a disbursement excess for a taxation year, the charity may, for the purpose of determining whether it complies with the requirements of paragraph (2)(b), (3)(b) or (4)(b), as the case may be, for the immediately preceding taxation year of the charity and 5 or less of its immediately subsequent taxation years, include in the computation of the amounts expended on charitable activities carried on by it and by way of gifts made by it to qualified donees, such portion of that disbursement excess as was not so included under this subsection for any preceding taxation year.

Proposed Amendment (uncertain) — 149.1(20)

Application: Private Member's Bill S-222 (First House of Commons Reading June 23, 2021), subsec. 2(14), will amend subsec. 149.1(20) to delete "carried on by it", in force two years after Royal Assent (and subject to review after 5 years: see under Proposed Amendment to 149.1(1)"charitable activities").

Notes: This is a private member's bill that may not pass. See Notes to Proposed Amendment under 149.1(1)"charitable activities".

Related Provisions: 149.1(21) — "Disbursement excess" defined.

Charities Policies: CPS-009: Holding of property for charities.

(21) Definition of "disbursement excess" — For the purpose of subsection (20), "disbursement excess", for a taxation year of a charity, means the amount, if any, by which the total of amounts expended in the year by the charity on charitable activities carried on by it and by way of gifts made by it to qualified donees exceeds its disbursement quota for the year.

Proposed Amendment (uncertain) — 149.1(21)

Application: Private Member's Bill S-222 (First House of Commons Reading June 23, 2021), subsec. 2(14), will amend subsec. 149.1(21) to delete "carried on by it", in force two years after Royal Assent (and subject to review after 5 years: see under Proposed Amendment to 149.1(1)"charitable activities").

Notes: This is a private member's bill that may not pass. See Notes to Proposed Amendment under 149.1(1)"charitable activities".

Related Provisions: 149.1(1.1) — Exclusions; 149.1(20) — Carrying disbursement excess back or forward to another year.

Notes: 149.1(21) amended by 2004 Budget, for tax years that begin after March 22, 2004, with a transitional version for a taxation year that began before 2009 of a charitable organization registered by the Minister before March 23, 2004. Earlier amended by 1995-97 technical bill and 1993 technical bill.

Registered Charities Newsletters: 19 (proposed disbursement quota changes). Also see under 149.1(1)"disbursement quota".

Forms: T3010: Registered charity information return; T4033A: Completing the registered charity information return [guide].

(22) Refusal to register — The Minister may, by registered mail, give notice to a person that the application of the person for registration as a registered charity, registered Canadian amateur athletic association, registered journalism organization or qualified donee referred to in subparagraph (a)(i) or (iii) of the definition "qualified donee" in subsection (1) is refused.

Related Provisions: 149.1(25) — Refusal on grounds ineligible individual is involved; 168(4) — Objection to refusal; 172(3)(a), (a.2) — Appeal of refusal.

Notes: 149.1(22) amended by 2019 budget bill #1, effective 2020, to add "registered journalism organization" [defined in 248(1): see 149.1(1)"qualified donee"(b.1)].

149.1(22) amended by 2011 budget bill #2, effective 2012, to add references to an RCAAA and to a qualified donee under (a)(i) or (iii).

149.1(22) added by 2004 Budget, effective in respect of notices issued by the Minister after June 12, 2005.

(23) Annulment of registration — The Minister may, by registered mail, give notice to a person that the registration of the person as a registered charity is annulled and deemed not to have been so registered, if the person was so registered by the Minister in error or the person has, solely as a result of a change in law, ceased to be a charity.

Related Provisions: 149.1(24) — Receipts issued before annulment; 168(4) — Objection to annulment; 241(3.2)(g) — Annulment letter may be disclosed to the public.

Notes: Annulment is sometimes sought by a charity that CRA proposes to deregister, as a way of avoiding the revocation tax in 188(1.1). This was done by Dying With Dignity Canada, which faced revocation due to political activities: Arthur Drache, "Annulment Offers Second Life to Charity", 23(3) *Canadian Not-for-Profit News* (Carswell) 17-18 (March 2015). See also Drache, "Revocation or Annulment", 16(10) *CNfpN* 73-74 (Oct. 2008).

In *Hostelling International*, 2008 FCA 396, an argument that CRA should have annulled the registration rather than revoking it was rejected. "The record indicates that the Minister was prepared to do so with the consent of the appellant, which was not given" (para. 12).

Unwanted annulment was upheld in *Credit Counselling Services*, 2016 FCA 193.

CRA announced annulment of the Phoenix Community Works Foundation on Feb. 9/09: it had collected $56m in tax shelter donations, and its predominant activity was to receive funds and issue receipts. CRA concluded that it was registered in error.

149.1(23) added by 2004 Budget, effective in respect of notices issued by the Minister after June 12, 2005.

(24) Receipts issued before annulment — An official receipt referred to in Part XXXV of the *Income Tax Regulations* issued, by a person whose registration has been annulled under subsection (23), before that annulment is, if the receipt would have been valid were the person a registered charity at the time the receipt was issued, deemed to be a valid receipt under that Part.

Notes: 149.1(24) added by 2004 Budget, effective in respect of notices issued by the Minister after June 12, 2005.

(25) Refusal to register — ineligible individual — The Minister may refuse to register a charity or Canadian amateur athletic association that has applied for registration as a registered charity or registered Canadian amateur athletic association if

(a) the application for registration is made on its behalf by an ineligible individual;

(b) an ineligible individual is a director, trustee, officer or like official of the charity or association, or controls or manages the charity or association, directly or indirectly, in any manner whatever; or

(c) the charity or association has accepted a gift from a foreign state, as defined in section 2 of the *State Immunity Act*, that is set out on the list referred to in subsection 6.1(2) of that Act.

Related Provisions: 149.1(4.1)(e) — Revocation of registration of charity managed by ineligible individual; 149.1(4.2)(c) — Revocation of registration of RCAAA managed by ineligible individual; 149.1(22) — Notice of refusal.

Notes: See Notes to 149.1(1)"ineligible individual".

149.1(25)(c) added by 2014 budget bill #1, effective for gifts accepted after Feb. 10, 2014. See Notes to 149.1(4.1) re (4.1)(f).

149.1(25) added by 2011 budget bill #2, effective 2012.

Charities Guidance: CG-024: Ineligible individuals.

(26) Foreign charities — For the purposes of subparagraph (a)(v) of the definition "qualified donee" in subsection (1), the Minister may register, in consultation with the Minister of Finance, a foreign charity for a 24-month period that includes the time at which Her Majesty in right of Canada has made a gift to the foreign charity, if

(a) the foreign charity is not resident in Canada; and

(b) the Minister is satisfied that the foreign charity is

(i) carrying on relief activities in response to a disaster,

(ii) providing urgent humanitarian aid, or

(iii) carrying on activities in the national interest of Canada.

Notes: As of 2013, a charity to which Canada has donated must apply rather than qualifying automatically under 149.1(1)"qualified donee"(a)(v). See CG-015 and the list at tinyurl.com/cra-foreignchar.

For interpretation of the criteria in para. (b), see CG-023. An example of a charity acting "in the national interest of Canada" is a hospital in Germany that has treated Canadian soldiers wounded in Afghanistan: Director General, Charities Directorate (Cathy Hawara), speech at National Charity Law Symposium, May 4, 2012.

See also Drache, "Foreign Charities and Gifts from Her Majesty", 24(8) *Canadian Not-for-Profit News* (Carswell) 59-60 (Aug. 2016).

149.1(26) amended by 2015 Budget bill, effective June 23, 2015, to change all instances of "foreign organization" to "foreign charity", and to change "(a) the foreign organization *is a charitable organization* that is not resident" to "the *foreign charity* is not resident". This permits a foreign charitable foundation to qualify, since 149.1(1)"charity" includes both a charitable organization and a charitable foundation.

149.1(26) added by 2012 budget bill #1, effective 2013 (but does not apply in respect of registration of a charitable organization outside Canada made before 2013).

Charities Guidance: CG-023: Qualified donee: Foreign charities that have received a gift from Her Majesty in right of Canada.

Proposed Addition (uncertain) — 149.1(27)

(27) [Reasonable steps to determine use of resources] — A charity is considered to have taken reasonable steps to ensure its resources are used exclusively for a charitable purpose if

(a) before providing resources to a person who is not a qualified donee it collects the information necessary to satisfy a reasonable person that the resources will be used for a charitable purpose by the person who is not a qualified donee, including information on the identity, experience and activities of the person who is not a qualified donee; and

(b) when providing resources to a person who is not a qualified donee, it establishes measures, imposes restrictions or conditions, or otherwise takes actions necessary to satisfy a reasonable person that the resources are being used exclusively for a charitable purpose by the person who is not a qualified donee.

Application: Private Member's Bill S-222 (First House of Commons Reading June 23, 2021), subsec. 2(15), will add subsec. 149.1(27), in force two years after Royal Assent (and subject to review after 5 years: see under Proposed Amendment to 149.1(1)"charitable activities").

Related Provisions: 149.1(2)(b), (2.1), (3)(b) — Charitable foundation may transfer to non-qualified donee when spending funds on charitable activities.

Notes: This is a private member's bill that may not pass. See Notes to Proposed Amendment under 149.1(1)"charitable activities".

Notes [s. 149.1]: See Notes to 149.1(1)"charitable organization".

Definitions [s. 149.1]: "acquired" — 149.1(12)(a), 256(7)–(9); "amount" — 248(1); "arm's length" — 251(1); "associated" — 149.1(7); "business" — 248(1); "Canada" — 255, *Interpretation Act* 35(1); "Canadian amateur athletic association" — 149.1(1); "capital gain" — 39(1)(a), 248(1); "capital gains pool" — 149.1(1); "capital property" — 54, 248(1); "charitable activities" — 149.1(1), (6); "charitable foundation", "charitable organization", "charitable purposes", "charity" — 149.1(1); "class" — 248(6); "control", "controlled" — 149.1(12)(a), 256(5.1)–(9); "corporation" — 248(1), *Interpretation Act* 35(1); "culpable conduct" — 163.2(1); "deferred profit sharing plan" — 147(1), 248(1); "designated gift" — 149.1(1); "designated stock exchange" — 248(1), 262; "devotes" — 149.1(6.01), (6.1), (6.2), (6.201); "disbursement excess" — 149.1(21); "disbursement quota" — 149.1(1); "disposition" — 248(1);

"divestment obligation percentage" — 149.1(1); "eligible amount" — 248(31), (41); "employed", "employment" — 248(1); "enduring property", "equity percentage" — 149.1(1); "excess corporate holdings percentage" — 149.1(1), 149.2(8); "exempt shares", "exempt shares percentage" — 149.1(1); "fair market value" — see 69(1) Notes; "false statement" — 163.2(1); "fiscal period" — 249.1; "Her Majesty" — *Interpretation Act* 35(1); "income" — of charity 149.1(12)(b); "individual" — 248(1); "ineligible individual" — 149.1(1); "*inter vivos* trust" — 108(1), 248(1); "limited-dividend housing company" — 149(1)(n); "listed terrorist entity" — 149.1(1); "material interest" — 149.2(1); "Minister" — 248(1); "Minister of Finance" — *Financial Administration Act* 14; "month" — *Interpretation Act* 35(1); "mutual fund corporation" — 131(8), 248(1); "mutual fund trust" — 132(6)–(7), 132.2(3)(n), 248(1); "net decrease" — 149.2(4); "net increase" — 149.2(3); "non-qualified investment" — 149.1(1); "office", "officer" — 248(1); "own" — 149.2(2.1); "partnership" — see 96(1) Notes; "person", "prescribed" — 248(1); "private foundation" — 149.1(1), 248(1); "promoter" — 149.1(1), 237.1(1); "property" — 248(1); "province" — *Interpretation Act* 35(1); "public corporation" — 89(1), 248(1); "public foundation" — 149.1(1), 248(1); "qualified Canadian journalism organization" — 248(1); "qualified donee" — 149.1(1), 188.2(3)(a), 248(1); "qualifying journalism organization" — 149.1(1); "qualifying share" — 192(6), 248(1); "record suspension" — 149.1(1.01); "registered Canadian amateur athletic association" — 248(1); "registered charity" — 149.1(6.4), 248(1); "registered journalism organization" — 248(1); "related business" — 149.1(1); "related group" — 251(4); "relevant criminal offence", "relevant offence", "relevant person" — 149.1(1); "resident in Canada" — 250; "share", "shareholder" — 248(1); "specified gift" — 149.1(1); "substituted" — 248(5); "substituted shares" — 149.1(1); "tax payable" — 248(2); "tax shelter" — 237.1(1), 248(1); "taxable income" — 2(2), 248(1); "taxation year" — 149.1(1), 249; "taxpayer" — 248(1); "total corporate holdings percentage" — 149.1(1), 248(1), (3); "trust" — 104(1), 248(1); "writing" — *Interpretation Act* 35(1).

149.2 (1) Material and insignificant interests [private foundations] — In this section and section 149.1,

(a) a person has, at any time, a material interest in respect of a class of shares of the capital stock of a corporation if, at that time,

    (i) the percentage of the shares of that class held by the person exceeds 0.5% of all the issued and outstanding shares of that class, or

    (ii) the fair market value of the shares so held exceeds $100,000; and

(b) a private foundation has, at any time, an insignificant interest in respect of a class of shares of the capital stock of a corporation if, at that time, the percentage of shares of that class held by the private foundation does not exceed 2% of all the issued and outstanding shares of that class.

Related Provisions: 149.1(11) — Look through rule for partnerships.

Forms: T2082: Excess corporate holdings regime for private foundations [guide].

(2) Material transaction — anti-avoidance — If a private foundation or a relevant person in respect of the private foundation has engaged in one or more transactions or series of transactions or events, a purpose of which may reasonably be considered to be to avoid the application of the definition "material transaction", each of those transactions or series of transactions or events is deemed to be a material transaction.

(2.1) Ownership — For the purposes of the definition "equity percentage", and subparagraph (b)(iii) of the definition "exempt shares", in subsection 149.1(1), a person who, if paragraph 251(5)(b) applied would be deemed by that paragraph to have the same position in relation to the control of a corporation as if the person owned a share, is deemed to own the share.

Notes: 149.2(2.1) added by 2008 budget bill #2, effective March 19, 2007.

(3) Net increase in excess corporate holdings percentage — The net increase in the excess corporate holdings percentage of a private foundation for a taxation year, in respect of a class of shares of the capital stock of a corporation, is the number of percentage points, if any, determined by the formula

$$A - B$$

where

A is the excess corporate holdings percentage of the private foundation at the end of the taxation year, in respect of the class, and

B is

    (a) 0%, if

        (i) at the beginning of the taxation year the private foundation was not both a private foundation and a registered charity, or

        (ii) the private foundation was both a registered charity and a private foundation on March 18, 2007 and the taxation year is the first taxation year of the private foundation that begins after that date; and

    (b) in any other case, the excess corporate holdings percentage of the private foundation in respect of the class at the end of its preceding taxation year.

Forms: T2081: Excess corporate holdings worksheet for private foundations; T2082: Excess corporate holdings regime for private foundations [guide].

(4) Net decrease in excess corporate holdings percentage — The net decrease in the excess corporate holdings percentage of a private foundation for a taxation year, in respect of a class of shares of the capital stock of a corporation, is the number of percentage points, if any, by which the percentage determined for B in the formula in subsection (3) for the taxation year exceeds the percentage determined for A in that formula for the taxation year.

Forms: T2081: Excess corporate holdings worksheet for private foundations; T2082: Excess corporate holdings regime for private foundations [guide].

(5) Allocation of net increase in excess corporate holdings percentage — For the purpose of the description of B in the definition "divestment obligation percentage" in subsection 149.1(1), the net increase in the excess corporate holdings percentage of a private foundation in respect of a class of shares of the capital stock of a corporation, for a taxation year (in this subsection referred to as the "current year") is to be allocated in the following order:

(a) first to the divestment obligation percentage of the private foundation in respect of that class for the current year, to the extent that the private foundation has in the current year acquired for consideration shares of that class;

(b) then to the divestment obligation percentage of the private foundation in respect of that class for its fifth subsequent taxation year, to the extent of the lesser of

    (i) that portion of the net increase in the excess corporate holdings percentage of the private foundation in respect of that class for the current year that is not allocated under paragraph (a), and

    (ii) the percentage of the issued and outstanding shares of that class that were acquired by the private foundation in the current year by way of bequest;

(c) then to the divestment obligation percentage of the private foundation in respect of that class for its second subsequent taxation year, to the extent of the lesser of

    (i) that portion of the net increase in the excess corporate holdings percentage of the private foundation in respect of that class for the current year that is not allocated under paragraph (a) or (b), and

    (ii) the total of

        (A) the percentage of the issued and outstanding shares of that class that were acquired by the private foundation in the current year by way of gift, other than from a relevant person or by way of bequest, and

        (B) the portion of the net increase in the excess corporate holdings percentage of the private foundation that is attributable to the redemption, acquisition or cancellation of any of the issued and outstanding shares of that class in the current year by the corporation; and

(d) then to the divestment obligation percentage of the private foundation in respect of that class for its subsequent taxation year, to the extent of that portion of the net increase in the excess corporate holdings percentage of the private foundation in respect of that class for the current year that is not allocated under paragraph (a), (b) or (c).

Related Provisions: 149.2(6) — Foundation can apply to CRA to vary allocation.

Notes: 2008 budget bill #2, s. 56(5), provides that if a registered charity was a private foundation on March 19, 2007, in applying 149.2(5)(b) and (c) to the charity's first taxation year that begins after that date, read "in the current year" as "in the period that begins on March 18, 2007 and ends at the end of the current year".

Forms: T2082: Excess corporate holdings regime for private foundations [guide].

(6) Minister's discretion — Notwithstanding subsection (5), on application by a private foundation, the Minister may, if the Minister believes it would be just and equitable to do so, reallocate any portion of the net increase in the excess corporate holdings percentage of the private foundation in respect of a class of shares of the capital stock of a corporation for a taxation year, that would otherwise be allocated under subsection (5) to the private foundation's divestment obligation percentage in respect of that class for a particular taxation year, to the private foundation's divestment obligation percentage in respect of that class for any of the ten taxation years subsequent to the particular taxation year.

Notes: For the meaning of "just and equitable", see Notes to 85(7.1).

Forms: T2082: Excess corporate holdings regime for private foundations [guide].

(7) Allocation of net decrease in excess corporate holdings percentage — For the purpose of the description of C in the definition "divestment obligation percentage" in subsection 149.1(1), the net decrease in the excess corporate holdings percentage of a private foundation in respect of a class of shares of the capital stock of a corporation for a taxation year (in this subsection referred to as the "current year") is to be allocated in the following order:

(a) first, to the divestment obligation percentage of the private foundation in respect of that class for the current year, to the extent of that divestment obligation percentage; and

(b) then to the divestment obligation percentage of the private foundation in respect of that class for a subsequent taxation year of the private foundation (referred to in this paragraph as the "subject year"), to the extent of the lesser of

(i) that portion of the net decrease in the excess corporate holdings percentage of the private foundation in respect of that class for the current year that is not allocated under paragraph (a), or under this paragraph, to the divestment obligation percentage of the private foundation in respect of that class for a taxation year of the private foundation that precedes the subject year, and

(ii) the amount of the divestment obligation percentage of the private foundation in respect of that class for the subject year, calculated as at the end of the current year and without reference to this subsection.

Forms: T2081: Excess corporate holdings worksheet for private foundations; T2082: Excess corporate holdings regime for private foundations [guide].

(8) Transitional rule — If the original corporate holdings percentage of a private foundation in respect of a class of shares of the capital stock of a corporation exceeds 20%, for the purpose of applying the definition "excess corporate holdings percentage" in subsection 149.1(1) to

(a) the first taxation year of the private foundation that begins after March 18, 2007, the reference to 20% in that definition in respect of that class is to be read as the original corporate holdings percentage of the private foundation in respect of that class;

(b) taxation years of the private foundation that are after the taxation year referred to in paragraph (a) and that begin before March 19, 2012, the reference to 20% in that definition in respect of that class is to be read as the greater of

(i) 20%, and

(ii) the lesser of

(A) the total corporate holdings percentage of the private foundation in respect of the class at the end of the immediately preceding taxation year, and

(B) the original corporate holdings percentage in respect of that class;

(c) taxation years of the private foundation that begin after March 18, 2012 and before March 19, 2017, the reference to 20% in that definition in respect of that class is to be read as the greater of

(i) 20%, and

(ii) the lesser of

(A) the total corporate holdings percentage of the private foundation in respect of the class at the end of the preceding taxation year, and

(B) the number of percentage points, if any, by which the private foundation's original corporate holdings percentage in respect of that class exceeds 20%;

(d) taxation years of the private foundation that begin after March 18, 2017 and before March 19, 2022, the reference to 20% in that definition in respect of that class is to be read as the greater of

(i) 20%, and

(ii) the lesser of

(A) the total corporate holdings percentage of the private foundation in respect of the class at the end of the preceding taxation year, and

(B) the number of percentage points, if any, by which the private foundation's original corporate holdings percentage in respect of that class exceeds 40%; and

(e) taxation years of the private foundation that begin after March 18, 2022 and before March 19, 2027, the reference to 20% in that definition in respect of that class is to be read as the greater of

(i) 20%, and

(ii) the lesser of

(A) the total corporate holdings percentage of the private foundation in respect of the class at the end of the preceding taxation year, and

(B) the number of percentage points, if any, by which the private foundation's original corporate holdings percentage in respect of that class exceeds 60%.

Related Provisions: 149.2(10) — Shares held through a trust on March 18/07.

Forms: T2081: Excess corporate holdings worksheet for private foundations; T2082: Excess corporate holdings regime for private foundations [guide].

(9) Where subsec. (10) applies — Subsection (10) applies for the purposes of applying section 149.1 and subsections (8) and 188.1(3.1) to a private foundation at a particular time if, both on March 18, 2007 and at the particular time,

(a) the private foundation was the sole trustee of a trust, or was a majority interest beneficiary (within the meaning assigned by section 251.1) of a trust more than 50% of the trustees of which were the private foundation and one or more relevant persons in respect of the private foundation; and

(b) the trust held one or more shares of a class of the capital stock of a corporation.

Notes: 149.2(9) added by 2008 budget bill #2, effective for private foundations' taxation years that begin after Feb. 25, 2008.

(10) Shares held through a trust on March 18, 2007 — If this subsection applies at a particular time to a private foundation in respect of shares of a class of the capital stock of a corporation held by a trust, the private foundation is deemed to hold at the particular time that number of those shares as is determined by the formula

$$A \times B/C$$

where

A is the lesser of the number of those shares held by the trust on March 18, 2007 and the number so held at the particular time;

B is the total fair market value of all interests held by the private foundation in the trust at the particular time; and

C is the total fair market value of all property held by the trust at the particular time.

Related Provisions: 149.2(9) — Conditions for 149.2(10) to apply; 149.2(11) — Discretionary trusts.

Notes: 149.2(10) added by 2008 budget bill #2, effective for private foundations' taxation years that begin after Feb. 25, 2008.

(11) Discretionary trusts — For the purpose of subsection (10), if the amount of income or capital of a trust that a person may receive as a beneficiary under the trust depends on the exercise by any person of, or the failure by any person to exercise, a discretionary power, that person is deemed to have fully exercised, or to have failed to exercise, the power, as the case may be.

Notes: 149.2(11) added by 2008 budget bill #2, effective for private foundations' taxation years that begin after Feb. 25, 2008.

Notes [s. 149.2]: See Notes to 149.1(1)"divestment obligation percentage". 149.2 added by 2007 budget bill #2, effective for private foundations' taxation years that begin after March 18, 2007.

Definitions [s. 149.2]: "amount" — 248(1); "class of shares" — 248(6); "corporation" — 248(1), *Interpretation Act* 35(1); "divestment obligation percentage", "excess corporate holdings percentage" — 149.1(1); "fair market value" — see 69(1) Notes; "material interest" — 149.2(1); "material transaction" — 149.1(1), 149.2(2); "Minister" — 248(1); "net decrease" — 149.2(4); "net increase" — 149.2(3); "original corporate holdings percentage" — 149.1(1); "person" — 248(1); "private foundation" — 149.1(1), 248(1); "property", "registered charity" — 248(1); "relevant person" — 149.1(1); "share" — 248(1); "taxation year", "total corporate holdings percentage" — 149.1(1); "trust" — 104(1), 248(1), (3).

DIVISION I — RETURNS, ASSESSMENTS, PAYMENT AND APPEALS

Returns

150. (1) Filing returns of income — general rule — Subject to subsection (1.1), a return of income that is in prescribed form and that contains prescribed information shall be filed with the Minister, without notice or demand for the return, for each taxation year of a taxpayer,

Abandoned Proposed Amendment — Mandatory registration of Tax Preparers

Notes: CRA *Registration of Tax Preparers Program Consultation Paper* (Jan. 17, 2014) proposed to require persons preparing returns for a fee to be registered with CRA. See MacKnight, "The CRA and the Registration of Tax Preparers", 14(2) *Tax for the Owner-Manager* (ctf.ca) 1-2 (April 2014); Wen, "CRA's Proposed Registration of Tax Preparers", 5(1) *Canadian Tax Focus* (ctf.ca) 11-12 (Feb. 2015). After consultations, CRA stated in VIEWS doc 2017-0698971C6 [2017 STEP q.15] that "to be effective the program as originally proposed would require significant investments that no longer align with CRA priorities" — bureaucratese for "this idea has been dropped as it would be too expensive".

Announced Administrative Change — COVID-19 — 2021 filing and payment deadlines not extended

CRA notice (tinyurl.com/covid-dates, as of April 2021): *Income tax filing and payment deadlines for the 2020 tax year: CRA and COVID-19*

Here are the current 2020 income tax filing and payment deadlines for individuals, corporations, trusts, and charities:

[All the deadlines shown are the statutory deadlines in 150(1). The extensions provided during 2020 for 2019 returns (see PITA 59th ed. and Notes to the paras. below) are not being extended — ed.]

Notes: Where the deadline for filing a return expires on a weekend or holiday, it is extended administratively by CRA to 11:59 p.m. of the next business day. See also 248(7)(a) and Notes to s. 26 of the *Interpretation Act*.

CRA no longer date-stamps paper returns in the taxpayer's presence, though it still signs for packages sent by courier. In *Saunders*, 2010 TCC 114, the Court accepted evidence of the taxpayer's accountant that a return had been filed on April 29, despite CRA having stamped it May 20: "I do not share the [CRA's] faith in the infallibility of a huge government bureaucracy, especially during its busiest time of the year" (para 13). In *Nacom Inc.*, 2013 TCC 90, the TCC rejected evidence that a T2 had been delivered by a given date.

The prescribed forms for returns (T1, T2, T3) are authorized by CRA and thus are "prescribed"; see 244(16) and Notes to 248(1)"prescribed".

Where no return need be filed, it may still be advisable to file one, to get an assessment and start the 152(3.1) clock running (and, for an individual, to receive various benefits).

A nil or incomplete return may be rejected as invalid and a non-filing penalty assessed: see Notes to 162(7).

The taxpayer is responsible for errors in the return, even if they were made by an accountant or bookkeeper. This liability may or may not extend to penalties for the accountant's gross negligence: see Notes to 163(2).

Amending a return: see Notes to 152(1).

Representations in income tax returns can have external consequences. In *Prince Albert Co-operative v. Rybka*, 2010 SKCA 144, a couple reported income as partners for income-splitting purposes, and the wife was liable to third parties for the husband's debts on the basis that they were in partnership.

Canadian professionals wanting to prepare US tax returns must obtain a US "preparer tax identification number": Brown & Long, "US PTIN a Barrier for Canadian Preparers", 20(2) *Canadian Tax Highlights [CTH]* (ctf.ca) 3-4 (Feb. 2012); but the IRS has been barred from imposing competency testing in *Sabina Loving v. IRS* (US Court of Appeals, Feb. 11, 2014): VIEWS doc 2014-0523051C6 [2014 STEP q.14] (see also Brown, "Choosing a US Tax Adviser", 22(12) *CTH* (ctf.ca) 3-4 (Dec. 2014)). Australia has such rules as well. CRA has dropped a plan to implement a registration system for Canadian tax preparers: see Abandoned Proposed Amendment above.

Opening words of 150(1) amended by 1998 Budget, for taxation years that begin after 1998, and by 1992 Child Benefit bill, for the 1993 taxation year.

See also Related Provisions annotation at end of 150(1).

(a) corporations — in the case of a corporation, by or on behalf of the corporation within six months after the end of the year if

(i) at any time in the year the corporation

(A) is resident in Canada,

(B) carries on business in Canada, unless the corporation's only revenue from carrying on business in Canada in the year consists of amounts in respect of which tax was payable by the corporation under subsection 212(5.1),

(C) has a taxable capital gain (otherwise than from an excluded disposition), or

(D) disposes of a taxable Canadian property (otherwise than in an excluded disposition), or

(ii) tax under this Part

(A) is payable by the corporation for the year, or

(B) would be, but for a tax treaty, payable by the corporation for the year (otherwise than in respect of a disposition of taxable Canadian property that is treaty-protected property of the corporation);

Related Provisions: 115.2(2) — Certain non-residents deemed not carrying on business in Canada; 150(1.1)(a) — Registered charities exempted from filing; 150(5) — Definition of "excluded disposition"; 150.1(2.1) — Corporation with over $1m in revenue must file electronically; 150.1(2.3), (2.4) — Tax preparer who prepares more than 10 corporate returns should file electronically; 162(2.1) — Minimum non-filing penalty for non-resident corporation; 185.2(1) — Part III.1 return required by corporation paying dividends; 235 — Penalty on large corporations for failure to file return even if no balance owing; 236 — Execution of documents by corporations; 250(1) — Meaning of resident in Canada; 253 — Extended meaning of carrying on business in Canada; Reg. 205.1(2)(d) — Most corporations with revenue over $1m required to file electronically; *Interpretation Act* 27(5) — Meaning of "within six months". See also at end of 150(1).

Notes: See Notes to 150(1) opening words; and see Notes to 150.1 re electronic filing of corporate tax returns, which is now mandatory for many corporations.

For T2 returns due after March 18, 2020, the deadline was formally extended due to COVID-19 to June 1 (returns due March 19-May 30) or September 1 (returns due May 31-Aug. 31), and effectively extended to Sept. 30, 2020 (late-filing penalties waived, but since no formal deadline extension, the earlier date applies for calculating the 37(11) SR&ED filing deadline 1 year later). For returns due in 2021 there is no extension: see Announced Administrative Change under 150(1) opening words.

If the corporate year-end is the last day of a month (e.g., Feb. 28), CRA considers the deadline to be the last day of the 6th next month (e.g., Aug. 31): tinyurl.com/corp-file.html. However if a taxpayer has always filed using Feb. 28, even in leap years, CRA will say the deadline is Aug. 28: May 2013 ICAA Roundtable q.23 (tinyurl.com/cra-abtax). See also Notes to *Interpretation Act* s. 26 re extension if the deadline is on a weekend or holiday.

When preparing corporate tax returns, see CRA *T2 Guide* (T4012); Ryan Keey, *Corporate Tax Return and Provisions Guide* (Carswell, annual); *Preparing Your Corporate Tax Returns* (CCH, annual).

Provincial corporate tax: Corporations in Quebec and Alberta file separate returns with the province. In all other provinces/territories, one return for both federal and provincial corp tax is filed with the CRA. For Ontario, this applies to tax years ending after 2008. For CRA policy on Ont. tax see tinyurl.com/cra-onttax; docs 2011-0392901I7 (discretionary adjustments), 2011-0414821E5 (non-resident corp with no PE in Ont. is no longer subject to Ont. tax), 2011-041557117 (Ont. M&P credit and capital tax credit for manufacturers: not for SR&ED corp); 2015-058537117 (corp minimum tax). For Quebec see revenuquebec.ca; Meighen & Ranger, "The Taxation Act (Quebec) Versus the Income Tax Act (Canada)", 2015 Cdn Tax Foundation annual conference. For Alberta see finance.alberta.ca; Dolson, "Alberta to Continue to Run Its Own Corporate Tax", 6(1) *Canadian Tax Focus* (ctf.ca) 2-3 (Feb. 2016).

Ontario annual corporate information returns were filed with CRA, as part of the T2 (Schedule 546), until May 2021. They now go via ontario.ca/businessregistry.

GIFI: Business income must be reported using the General Index of Financial Information, which allows financial details, such as specific types of income and expenses, to be stored on CRA's computers in a way that is easily accessible for audit and sampling purposes. See RC4088 for a full list of GIFI codes, and tinyurl.com/t2return.

A non-resident corp may choose a year-end for Canadian purposes that is different than used in its home country, but once selected it cannot be changed without CRA permission: see 249.1(1) and (7).

A B.C. strata corporation files a single T2 even if it has different sections: VIEWS doc 2011-0424091E5.

T2 Schedule 50 reporting shareholder details: CPA Canada blog (Sept. 17, 2020) advises that CRA has begun asking for these to be completed if they are not, as they are used for risk assessment and business intelligence.

T2 Schedule 88 requires reporting web-based income. A reasonable estimate is acceptable; and only websites "directly" generating revenue need be reported (including bank websites giving online account access that generates fees): VIEWS doc 2014-0538211C6 [2014 APFF q.27]. See instructions on the form.

A corporation that pays any taxable dividends must also file a Part III.1 return to report the extent to which they are "eligible dividends" (eligible for the 45% gross-up under 82(1)(b)(ii) and resulting higher dividend tax credit). See 185.2(1).

An inactive corp must still file returns (see the T2 Short) for periods up to formal dissolution: VIEWS doc 2005-013267117; but is not penalized under 162(7) for not filing: 2010-0386341C6 [2010 CTF q.4], 2017-0708971C6 [2017 APFF q.1]. A corp that is a bare trustee must file: 2007-0251601E5. If a corp's sole shareholder/director dies, 2013-0513191E5 suggests the executor should file the return, but notes this is not a "direct legal obligation" (2006-0201211E5 saying so is incorrect: an executor does not automatically become the corp's officer or director). A Crown corp need not file: 2009-0314301E5, 2014-052154117. On an 88(2) windup, no return need be filed even though the 2013 T2 and T2 Guide say otherwise: VIEWS doc 2013-0480771E5.

Non-resident T2 returns should be sent to the International Tax Services Office, 2204 Walkley Rd., Ottawa K1A 1A8. Inquiries: 613-954-9681 (collect calls accepted) or 1-800-267-5177. See CCRA news release, July 7, 2000. Non-resident corporations claiming tax treaty exemption must file T2 Schedule 91, failing which a penalty of $100 per day, maximum $2,500, may apply: 162(2.1) or (7); VIEWS doc 2018-0748171C6 [2018 IFA q.4]. The CRA uses Sch. 91 to ensure that T4s, T4As and T4A-NRs have been filed for payments to employees and subcontractors. A non-resident corp whose only activity is the sale of partnership interests to Canadian residents need not file: 2009-0341741E5. Corporate members of a partnership carrying on business in Canada must file (no administrative relief: 2011 Cdn Tax Foundation conference report, CRA/RQ Round Table q.5 (p.4:4). A non-resident corp that registers for GST/HST will be automatically registered for income tax and expected to file unless it deregisters on Form RC145: CRA roundtable, Cdn Bar Association Commodity Tax section, Feb. 26, 2015 (cba.org, "Sections"), q.26.

CRA's target (tinyurl.com/cra-standards) for assessing T2 returns is 6 weeks for electronic returns (it no longer has a standard for paper returns), 95% of the time; in 2019-20 it did 96%.

A corporation's GST or HST refund or rebate will be held back if the T2 return is not filed: *Excise Tax Act* ss. 229(2), 263.02 (see David M. Sherman, *Practitioner's Goods and Services Tax Annotated* (Carswell)). For non-profits, federal Crown corporations, native councils, municipalities, universities, schools and hospitals, this is not enforced: CRA Fact Sheet, April 25, 2012 [see *GST & HST Times* 269P]. (Charities do not file T2 returns: 150(1.1)(a); but file an information return under 149.1(14).)

Disclosure of corporations' beneficial shareholders: 2018 budget bill #2 amended the *Canada Business Corporations Act* to add provisions requiring a federal corp to maintain a register listing beneficial owners and those with "direct or indirect control" over shares with 25% or more interest in the corp. See *CBCA* ss. 2.1 ("significant control"), 21.1-21.4 (requirement to prepare and maintain register), 250(4) and 260(1)(c.01)-(c.02) (consequential amendments). Penalties for non-compliance are up to $200,000 fine and 6 months in jail. The rules do not require the register to be sent to CRA, but CRA has access to it when auditing, via 231.1. These rules came into force June 13, 2019. They do not apply to listed companies. See Frajman, "The CBCA's Beneficial Ownership Register", 2446 *Tax Topics* (CCH) 1-4 (Jan. 24, 2019); Ball, "New beneficial ownership rules are coming in June", tinyurl.com/ball-bene (April 9, 2019); Aptowitzer, "Nothing is More Opaque than Absolute Transparency", xli(7) *The Canadian Taxpayer* (Carswell) 54-55 (April 5, 2019); Dy, "Beneficial Ownership Transparency", 1(4) *Perspectives on Tax Law & Policy* (ctf.ca) 6-8 (Dec. 2020). The provinces are following suit with similar rules in their legislation: BC, *Business Corporations Amendment Act, 2019*, S.B.C. 2019, c. 15 (Royal Assent May 16, 2019); Manitoba *Business Registration, Supervision and Ownership Transparency Act* (in force

from 2020; see tinyurl.com/pitblado-brs); Quebec 2020-21 Budget, Additional Information pp. B.35-38, and Bill 78, *An Act mainly to improve the transparency of enterprises*, tabled Dec. 8, 2020 (beneficial ownership to be added to the public "enterprise register": Frajman, "Québec Bill Tabled for Québec's (and Canada's *De Facto*?) Public Ultimate Beneficiary Register", 2549 *Tax Topics* (CCH) 1-5 (Jan. 12, 2021)); Finance Canada and provinces "Joint Statement — Federal, provincial and territorial governments working together to combat money laundering and terrorist financing" (June 14, 2019). The Prime Minister's Dec. 2019 "mandate letter" to the Minister of Finance tells him to: "Support the Minister of Innovation ... in concluding consultations with provinces and territories on the creation of a pan-Canadian public registry for beneficial ownership and in preparing legislation reflecting the outcome of those consultations." See also Proposed Amendment below.

Corporations that fail to file provincial corporate tax returns in provinces requiring them, or annual information returns in several provinces, may be dissolved by the provincial companies regulator. (However, in Saskatchewan, a company struck from the register is not dissolved: *Antifaiff*, 2014 TCC 216, para. 43.) The corp's owner can then be assessed for tax on (what was thought to be) the corp's business income: *Dello*, 2003 TCC 392; *Amerey*, 2005 FCA 428. The corp's assets may be forfeit to the Crown. Revival of a dissolved corp is often possible, with or without retroactive application; see Notes to 227.1(4).

A non-profit with over $10,000 in investment income or $200,000 in assets must file a T1044 information return: 149(12).

150(1)(a) amended by 2008 budget bill #1 (for dispositions of property after 2008), 2001 technical bill, 1998 Budget.

Proposed Amendment — Corporation beneficial ownership registry

Federal Budget, Chapter 10, April 19, 2021: *Beneficial Ownership Transparency*

To catch those who attempt to launder money, evade taxes, or commit other complex financial crimes, law enforcement, tax, and other authorities need access to accurate and up-to-date data on the individuals who own and control corporations. Building on public consultations in 2020:

Budget 2021 proposes to provide $2.1 million over two years to Innovation, Science and Economic Development Canada to support the implementation of a publicly accessible corporate beneficial ownership registry by 2025.

Interpretation Bulletins: IT-243R4: Dividend refund to private corporations; IT-304R2: Condominiums.

Information Circulars: 97-2R16: Customized forms; 00-1R4: Voluntary disclosures program; 12-1: GST/HST compliance refund holds.

I.T. Technical News: 38 (single administration of Ontario corporate tax).

Application Policies: SR&ED 2004-02R5: Filing requirements for claiming SR&ED.

Forms: RC1: Request for a business number; RC321: Delegation of authority number; RC342: Request by an insolvency practitioner for a waiver of the requirement to file a T2 corporation income tax return; RC4088: Guide to the General Index of Financial Information (GIFI) for corporations; T2: Corporation income tax return; T2 Sched. 1: Net income (loss) for income tax purposes; T2 Sched. 97: Additional information on non-resident corporations in Canada; T2 Sched. 150: Net income (loss) for income tax purposes for life insurance companies; T2 Sched. 303: Newfoundland and Labrador direct equity tax credit; T2 Sched. 306: Newfoundland and Labrador capital tax on financial institutions — agreement among related corporations; T2 Sched. 384: Manitoba co-op education and apprenticeship tax credit; T2 Sched. 385: Manitoba odour control tax credit; T2 Sched. 552: Ontario apprenticeship training tax credit; T2 Short: T2 short return; T2WS1: Calculating estimated tax payable and tax credits; T2WS2: Calculating monthly instalment payments; T2WS3: Calculating quarterly instalment payments; T1178: General index of financial information — short; T1219: Provincial alternative minimum tax; T1219-ON: Ontario minimum tax carryover; T2203: Provincial and territorial taxes — multiple jurisdictions; T4012: T2 corporation income tax guide.

(b) deceased individuals — in the case of an individual who dies after October of the year and before the day that would be the individual's filing due date for the year if the individual had not died, by the individual's legal representatives on or before the day that is the later of the day on or before which the return would otherwise be required to be filed and the day that is 6 months after the day of death;

Related Provisions: 70(2) — Return for rights or things; 70(7)(a) — Deadline extended to 18 months after death to untaint spousal trust; 127.55 — Minimum tax not applicable; 150(1)(d)(iii) — Deadline for deceased's cohabiting spouse; 150(4) — Death of partner or proprietor of business; 150.1(2.3), (2.4) — Tax preparer who prepares more than 10 corporate returns should file electronically; 159(1) — Payments on behalf of others. See also at end of 150(1).

Notes: See 70(5) Notes re effects of death. Where a person carrying on business (or whose spouse or common-law partner does: 150(1)(d)(ii)(B)) dies Jan. 1-Dec. 15, the deadline is June 15; death Dec. 16-31, deadline is 6 months after death. For others, death Jan. 1-Oct. 31, deadline is April 30; Nov. 1 to Dec. 31, deadline is 6 months after death.

For the 2019 tax year, due to the COVID-19 pandemic, the deadline was extended to the later of June 1, 2020 and 6 months after death, and effectively to Sept. 30, 2020. For returns due in 2021, no extension is provided. See Announced Administrative Change box under 150(1) opening words.

A copy of the will should be filed with the return: Guide T4011; VIEWS doc 2007-0237141M4. It then does not need to be filed with the estate's first T3 return: May 2013 ICAA Roundtable q.15 (tinyurl.com/cra-abtax).

The executor or estate trustee is personally liable for penalties if the return is filed late: VIEWS doc 2010-0377091E5.

150(1)(b) amended by 1995 Budget (for 1995 and later tax years), 1991 technical bill.

Regulations: 206 (information return).

CRA Audit Manual: 16.1.0: Clearance certificate program; 16.2.2: Estate of a deceased person — non-residents.

Forms: T1 General: Individual income tax and benefit return; T1-BC10, T1-NL01, T1-NT12: Residency information for tax administration agreements; T4011: Preparing returns for deceased persons [guide]. See also under 150(1)(d).

(c) trusts or estates — in the case of an estate or trust, within 90 days from the end of the year;

Proposed Amendment — Additional disclosure required on trust returns

See proposed 150(1.2) and Reg. 204.2.

Related Provisions: 94(3)(a)(vii) — Application to trust deemed resident in Canada; 104(13.4)(c)(i) — Death of beneficiary — spousal and similar trusts; 104(23) — Testamentary trusts; 150(1.2) — Trustees required to file; 150(3) — Trustees in bankruptcy, etc.; 159(1) — Payments on behalf of others; 163(5), (6) — Penalty of 5% of trust assets for failure to file, or false statement in return (as of 2021); 251.2(7)(c) — Deadline extended to regular year's deadline, for short year deemed ended due to change in majority beneficiaries; Reg. 204.2 — All trustees, beneficiaries, settlors and protectors must be identified (as of 2021); *Interpretation Act* 27(5) — Meaning of "within 90 days". See also at end of 150(1).

Notes: The filing deadline for a trust (249(1)(c) determines the taxation year) is normally March 31 (March 30 in a leap year such as 2020), but extended to the next business day on weekends and holidays: see *Interpretation Act* s. 26. For a short year triggered by a change in majority beneficiaries (249(4)(a)), the filing deadline is extended to the ordinary deadline: 251.2(7)(c), 248(1)"balance-due day"(a)(i), (ii). If a trust is wound up mid-year, the deadline does not change, since the "taxation year" remains the calendar year: VIEWS docs 2012-0468101E5, 2018-0744081C6 [STEP 2018 q.3] (deadline for graduated rate estate is 90 days after windup).

For returns due in 2020, due to the COVID-19 pandemic, the deadline was extended to May 1 (year-end Dec. 31, 2019), June 1 (original due date March 31-May 30) or September 1 (original due date May 31-Aug. 31), and effectively to Sept. 30, 2020 (no late-filing penalty). For returns due in 2021, no extension is provided. See Announced Administrative Change box under 150(1) opening words.

The T3 can be filed electronically: CRA news release "Online filing for trust income tax and information returns is here" (Jan. 11, 2018).

See generally Chow & Pryor, *Taxation of Trusts and Estates 2021* (Carswell), chaps. 13-19, on completing the T3 trust return and information slips (those chapters also published annually as *Trust Tax Return Guide*); Frankovic & Spenceley, *Preparing Your Trust Tax Returns* (CCH, annual). For an estate, see 70(5) Notes.

Where to file the T3: tinyurl.com/t3-file-where.

A trust can apply for a trust account number (on Form T3APP) before filing its first T3.

Until 2021, CRA's *T3 Guide* (T4013), chapter 1, says a return is required only if the trust has any of: tax payable; a taxable capital gain [see 150(1.1)(b)(ii)]; total income more than $500; a benefit of more than $100 to any beneficiary (B); income allocated to a non-resident B; holds property that is subject to 75(2); or is a deemed resident trust [see 94(3)(a)]. Where a trust's income is attributed to X under 75(2), a T3 slip should be issued to X: VIEWS docs 2006-0185561C6, 2006-0196201C6, 2007-0234381E5, 2010-0386351C6 [2010 CTF q.10]; 2017-0693371C6 [2017 STEP q.12] (rejects argument that this is contrary to the law); 2019-0798301C6 [2019 STEP q.12] (rejects argument that it is not required due to *Satoma*). 2010-0386351C6 also discusses minimum tax. However, if the 75(2) property generates no revenue, no T3 need be filed: 2010-0373681C6, 2016-0645811C6 [2016 STEP q.13]. A trust holding a principal residence may need to file a T3 only for the year it disposes of it: 2010-0384891E5. A bare trustee need not file a T3, but if it is a corporation must file a T2 (see 150(1)(a)): 2007-0251601E5. A trade union that is trustee of a trust must file: 2011-0415841E5. A class action settlement trust must file: 2017-0705431E5 (IT-129R para. 10 may no longer be current). From tax year 2021, see 150(1.2) and Reg. 204.2 instead.

Where a trust hides a corp's real ownership, see Notes to 150(1)(a) under "Disclosure of corporations' beneficial shareholders".

A T3 return is both a return of income under 150(1)(c) and an information return under Reg. 204(1), so 150(1.1) is not sufficient to exempt a trust from filing a T3 unless the conditions in the T3 Guide are met: 2005 STEP Conference Roundtable q.8 (www.step.ca), VIEWS doc 2006-0196201C6.

The answer to T3 question "Did the trust borrow money" in a non-arm's length (NAL) transaction is "yes" if the trust made income payable to a NAL beneficiary without paying it out: VIEWS doc 2015-0581951C6 [2015 STEP q.14].

CRA's target (tinyurl.com/cra-standards) for assessing T3 returns is 95% within 17 weeks; in 2019-20, it did 99%. For 2018 (most recent data as of Jan. 2021), 259,000 trust returns were assessed, reporting $165 billion total income and paying $5.2 billion in total federal tax: tinyurl.com/stats-cra.

CRA was considering an Auditor General suggestion that trusts be required to file a balance sheet with their returns (but nothing was done): VIEWS doc 2006-0185531C6.

Where a trust cannot get all the necessary information for filing by the 90-day deadline, it should estimate the missing amounts and file: VIEWS doc 2006-0196181C6.

A trust resident in Quebec, or resident in Canada and carrying on business in Quebec, must also file a return with Revenu Québec (RQ). RQ suggests that a trust not required to file, but that has Quebec beneficiaries, should give them Relevé 16 slips and file the slips with RQ, but not file a trust information return.

Regulations: 204 (information return); 204.2 (prescribed information required on trust returns).

Information Circulars: 78-5R3: Communal organizations; 78-14R4: Guidelines for trust companies and other persons responsible for filing T3GR, T3D, T3P, T3S, T3RI, and T3F returns; 97-2R16: Customized forms.

CRA Audit Manual: 16.1.0: Clearance certificate program; 16.2.2: Estate of a deceased person — non-residents.

Forms: T3: Statement of trust income allocations and designations; T3-ADJ: T3 adjustment request; T3APP: Application for trust account number; T3ATH-IND: Amateur athlete trust income tax return; T3D: Income tax return for DPSP or revoked DPSP; T3GR: Group income tax and information return for RRSP, RRIF, RESP, or RDSP trusts (and worksheets); T3MJ: T3 Provincial and territorial taxes — multiple jurisdictions; T3P: Employees' pension plan income tax return; T3RET: Trust income tax and information return; T3 Sched. 11: Federal income tax; T3 SUM: Summary of trust income allocations and designations; T3S: Supplementary unemployment benefit plan — income tax return; T1061: Canadian amateur athletic trust group information return; T1139: Reconciliation of business income for tax purposes.

(d) individuals — in the case of any other person, on or before

(i) the following April 30 by that person or, if the person is unable for any reason to file the return, by the person's guardian, committee or other legal representative (in this paragraph referred to as the person's "guardian"),

(ii) the following June 15 by that person or, if the person is unable for any reason to file the return, by the person's guardian where the person is

(A) an individual who carried on a business in the year, unless the expenditures made in the course of carrying on the business were primarily the cost or capital cost of tax shelter investments (as defined in subsection 143.2(1)), or

(B) at any time in the year a cohabiting spouse or common-law partner (within the meaning assigned by section 122.6) of an individual to whom clause (A) applies, or

(iii) where at any time in the year the person is a cohabiting spouse or common-law partner (within the meaning assigned by section 122.6) of an individual to whom paragraph (b) applies for the year, on or before the day that is the later of the day on or before which the person's return would otherwise be required to be filed and the day that is 6 months after the day of the individual's death; or

Announced Administrative Change — Automatic filing of simple returns

Speech from the Throne, Sept. 23, 2020: The Government will also work to introduce free, automatic tax filing for simple returns to ensure citizens receive the benefits they need.

Notes: Perhaps if a taxpayer does not file by a certain number of days after the deadline, CRA will automatically assess based on all information slips (T4, T5, etc.) that have been filed for that taxpayer.

Related Provisions: 96(1.6) — Members of partnership deemed to carry on business of partnership for purposes of s. 150; 150(1.1)(b) — Individuals exempted from filing; 150.1(2.3), (2.4) — Tax preparer who prepares more than 10 corporate returns should file electronically; 180.2(5) — Return required by residents and non-residents for OAS clawback calculation; 233.3(3) — Foreign property reporting; 237(1) — Application for Social Insurance Number. See also at end of 150(1).

Notes: An individual with low or no income should file a T1 Income Tax and Benefit Return even though no tax is payable, as it provides benefits from "refundable credits" such as the GST/HST Credit (122.5), Canada Child Benefit (122.61) and Climate Action Incentive (122.8).

See Ideias, *Personal Tax Return Guide* (Carswell, annual), and similar guides published by CCH (Wolters Kluwer) and CPA Canada.

Paper filers now get a paper package in the mail the next year, after CRA stopped this for some years: CRA news release, "Do you file your taxes on paper?" (above), Dec. 8, 2020; or download the forms from tinyurl.com/t1package (fillable PDFs can be filled in on-screen). To have them mailed: 1-855-330-3305 or canada.ca/get-cra-forms. For e-filing (now mandatory for most preparers), see Notes to 150.1.

The deadline under 150(1)(d) is defined in 248(1) as the "filing-due date". Non-residents can file by fax: tinyurl.com/where-mail-T1 (note that nothing in the ITA prevents a *resident* filing by fax, as filing is not required "in prescribed manner").

The deadline for individuals who (or whose spouse) carry on business is June 15 rather than April 30 (this includes a limited partner: VIEWS doc 2006-0183751E5). However, interest runs on any balance owing after April 30; see 156.1(4), 161(1) and 248(1)"balance-due day".

The deadline is extended to Monday night when it falls on Saturday or Sunday (per CRA news release issued in April or June). See also Notes to s. 26 of the *Interpretation Act*; and to 220(3) and (3.1) for extensions due to natural disasters. The deadline is not extended for federal government employees affected by the Phoenix payroll disaster (see Notes to 153(3.1)): VIEWS doc 2017-0698801M4.

For the 2019 tax year, due to COVID-19, the deadline was extended to June 1, 2020, and effectively to Sept. 30, 2020. For the 2020 year (returns due in 2021), no extension is provided. See Announced Administrative Change under 150(1) opening words. However, for Quebec provincial returns, Revenu Québec announced on April 15, 2021 an effective extension to May 31, 2021 for both filing and payment: "While the deadline for filing the 2020 income tax return is still 11:59 p.m. on Friday, April 30, 2021, taxpayers who are unable to meet it will not be charged late-filing penalties, and no interest will accrue on unpaid balances of income tax from May 1 to 31, 2021."

For both 2013 and 2014, the deadline for April 30 filers was extended to May 5, 2014 or 2015, due to a CRA online service disruption in 2014 and a mistake in 2015 (see these Notes up to the 54th ed.).

The requirement to file tax returns does not breach the *Charter of Rights*: *Watson*, 2006 BCCA 233. See also Notes to 2(1).

Gyimah, 2010 TCC 621, para. 40, suggested that a return filed by a mentally ill taxpayer might not be a valid return. This was applied in *Ntakos Estate*, 2018 TCC 224, voiding a reassessment implementing an adjustment request from a taxpayer who lacked mental capacity.

CRA's target (tinyurl.com/cra-standards) for processing returns is 2 weeks for electronic returns and 8 weeks for paper returns, 95% of the time in both cases; in the 2019 filing season, it did 97%. (Faster payment of refunds has reduced the number of people using tax rebate discounters; see Notes to 220(6).) However, this excludes late-filed returns and various other categories: in *Sub-standard* (tinyurl.com/sub-standard, Feb. 2020), the Taxpayer's Ombudsman strongly criticized "delays and lack of transparency" in processing T1 returns and adjustments.

To change a filed return, see canada.ca/change-tax-return or file a Form T1-Adj (T1 Adjustment request).

If the taxpayer does not file and CRA issues an arbitrary assessment (based on available information), and the taxpayer files years later after the 152(4) reassessment deadline, a reassessment to reduce tax to reflect the return is considered to have been made under 152(4.2) and cannot be objected to or appealed: *Letendre*, 2011 TCC 577.

If a return is not filed within 4 years of the due date, CPP contributions on self-employment income for the year are deemed to be nil (*Canada Pension Plan* s. 30(5); *Torrance*, 2013 FCA 227), and overpaid employee contributions cannot be refunded (*CPP* s. 38(1); *Jamal*, 2018 TCC 196).

Until 1997, GST and income tax returns could be filed together by individuals who are annual filers under the GST, and a balance owing on one account could be credited with a refund from the other on Form T1124. This "combined annual business return" was eliminated in 1998, as it was not widely used.

See also Notes to opening words of 150(1). For discussion of amounts that can be split on spouses' returns see under "Splitting" in Topical Index.

150(1)(d) amended by 2000 same-sex partners bill (last change effective 2001), 1995-97 technical bill.

Information Circulars: 97-2R16: Customized forms; 00-1R4: Voluntary disclosures program.

Forms: T1 General: Individual income tax and benefit return; T1-ADJ: Adjustment request; T1-KS: T1 keying schedule; T1-BC10, T1-NL01, T1-NT12: Residency information for tax administration agreements; T1256: Manitoba community enterprise development tax credit; T1256-1: Manitoba small business venture capital tax credit (individuals); T1256-2: Manitoba employee share purchase tax credit; T1261: Application for a CRA individual tax number (ITN) for non-residents.

(e) **designated persons** — in a case where no person described by paragraph (a), (b) or (d) has filed the return, by such person as is required by notice in writing from the Minister to file the return, within such reasonable time as the notice specifies.

Related Provisions [subsec. 150(1)]: 149(12) — Non-profit organizations — information return; 149.1(14) — Charity information returns; 150.1 — Electronic filing;

151 — Obligation to estimate tax payable; 152(4)(b.3) — Extended reassessment period where disposition of real property not reported in return; 162(1) — Penalty for late filing; 164(2.01) — All returns must be filed before any refund paid; 220(3) — Extension of time for filing return; 233.1 — Return of transactions with related non-residents; 238(1) — Offence of failing to file return; 248(1) — Definition of "filing-due date"; Reg. 229 — Partnership information returns; Reg. 8409 — Registered pension plan information return; *Interpretation Act* 26 — Extension of deadline where it falls on Sunday or holiday.

Notes [subsec. 150(1)]: See at beginning of 150(1), before para. (a).

Forms: T2203: Provincial and territorial taxes — multiple jurisdictions.

(1.1) Exception [— return not required] — Subsection (1) does not apply to a taxation year of a taxpayer if

Proposed Amendment — 150(1.1) opening words

(1.1) Exception [— return not required] — Subject to subsection (1.2), subsection (1) does not apply to a taxation year of a taxpayer if

Application: The July 27, 2018 draft legislation (Budget), subsec. 7(1), will amend the opening words of subsec. 150(1.1) to read as above, applicable to taxation years that end after Dec. 30, 2021.

Technical Notes: Subsection 150(1) stipulates the tax return requirements and the filing dates for different categories of taxpayers. Subsection 150(1.1) sets out exceptions to subsection 150(1), when the filing of a tax return is not required.

Subsection 150(1.1) is amended to provide that the exceptions from filing a return outlined in that subsection do not apply to an express trust, or for civil law purposes a trust other than a trust that is established by law or by judgement, that is resident in Canada unless the trust meets one of the exceptions outlined in new paragraphs 150(1.2)(a) to (n).

(a) the taxpayer is a corporation that was a registered charity throughout the year; or

(b) the taxpayer is an individual unless

(i) tax is payable under this Part by the individual for the year,

(ii) where the individual is resident in Canada at any time in the year, the individual has a taxable capital gain or disposes of capital property in the year,

(iii) where the individual is non-resident throughout the year, the individual has a taxable capital gain (otherwise than from an excluded disposition) or disposes of a taxable Canadian property (otherwise than in an excluded disposition) in the year, or

(iv) at the end of the year the individual's HBP balance or LLP balance (as defined in subsection 146.01(1) or 146.02(1)) is a positive amount.

Related Provisions: 149.1(14) — Charity must file information return; 150(5) — Definition of "excluded disposition".

Notes: Until 2021, see Notes to 150(1)(c) re application of 150(1.1) to trusts. Starting with the 2021 tax year, see 150(1.2) instead.

Where no return need be filed, it may still be advisable to file one, to get an assessment and start the 152(3.1) clock running.

"Tax is payable" in (b)(i) means tax under 117–127.55, even if no balance is owing due to instalments or source deductions: *Levenson*, 2016 FC 10, para. 43; VIEWS doc 2000-0028651I7.

150(1.1)(b)(iii) amended by 2008 budget bill #1, for dispositions of property after 2008, to refer to excluded dispositions (see 150(5)).

150(1.1) added by 1998 Budget, effective for taxation years that begin after 1998.

Proposed Addition — 150(1.2)

(1.2) Exception [—] trusts — Subsection (1.1) does not apply to a taxation year of a trust if the trust is resident in Canada and is an express trust, or for civil law purposes a trust other than a trust that is established by law or by judgement, unless the trust

(a) had been in existence for less than three months at the end of the year;

(b) holds assets with a total fair market value that does not exceed $50,000 throughout the year, if the only assets held by the trust throughout the year are one or more of

(i) cash,

(ii) a debt obligation described in paragraph (a) of the definition "fully exempt interest" in subsection 212(3),

(iii) a share, debt obligation or right listed on a designated stock exchange,

(iv) a share of the capital stock of a mutual fund corporation,

(v) a unit of a mutual fund trust, and

(vi) an interest in a related segregated fund (within the meaning assigned by paragraph 138.1(1)(a));

(c) is required under the relevant rules of professional conduct or the laws of Canada or a province to hold funds for the purposes of the activity that is regulated under those rules or laws, provided the trust is not maintained as a separate trust for a particular client or clients;

(d) is a registered charity;

(e) is a club, society or association described in paragraph 149(1)(l);

(f) is a mutual fund trust;

(g) is, for greater certainty, a related segregated fund trust, within the meaning assigned by paragraph 138.1(1)(a);

(h) is prescribed to be a master trust;

(i) is, for greater certainty, a graduated rate estate;

(j) is a "qualified disability trust", as defined in subsection 122(3);

(k) is an employee life and health trust;

(l) is a trust described under paragraph 81(1)(g.3);

(m) is a trust under or governed by

(i) a deferred profit sharing plan,

(ii) a pooled registered pension plan,

(iii) a registered disability savings plan,

(iv) a registered education savings plan,

(v) a registered pension plan,

(vi) a registered retirement income fund,

(vii) a registered retirement savings plan, or

(viii) a tax-free savings account; or

(n) a cemetery care trust or a trust governed by an eligible funeral arrangement.

Application: The July 27, 2018 draft legislation (Budget), subsec. 7(2), will add subsec. 150(1.2), applicable to taxation years that end after Dec. 30, 2021.

Technical Notes: New subsection 150(1.2) provides for an exception to subsection 150(1.1) and requires that a trust that is resident in Canada (including trusts that are deemed resident in Canada under section 94) and that is an express trust (or for civil law purposes a trust other than a trust that is established by law or by judgement) file a tax return notwithstanding that it may meet one of the exceptions to filing a return listed in subsection 150(1.1).

Subsection 150(1.2), however, also includes a number of exceptions to the requirement to file a return which are listed in paragraphs (a) to (n). In addition, a trust that meets one of the exceptions listed in paragraphs 150(1.2)(a) to (n) will not be required to provide the additional information set out in new section 204.2 of the Regulations. Trusts that are required to file a return, whether because of current filing requirements under subsection 150(1) or because of new subsection 150(1.2), will be required to provide the additional information outlined in section 204.2 of the Regulations. For more information, see the commentary on section 204.2 of the Regulations.

The exceptions to the reporting requirements in new subsection 150(1.2) are as follows:

• trusts that have been in existence for less than three months;

• trusts that hold assets with a total fair market value that does not exceed $50,000 throughout the year, where the only assets held by the trust throughout the year are one or more of

— cash,

— certain government debt obligations,

— a share, debt obligation or right listed on a designated stock exchange,

— a share of the capital stock of a mutual fund corporation,

— a unit of a mutual fund trust, and

— an interest in a related segregated fund (within the meaning assigned by paragraph 138.1(1)(a));

• trusts that are required under the relevant rules of professional conduct or the laws of Canada or a province to hold funds for the purposes of the activity that is regulated under those rules or laws, provided the trust is not maintained as a separate trust for a particular client or clients (this provides an exception for a lawyer's general trust account, but not for specific client accounts);

• trusts that qualify as non-profit organizations or registered charities;

• mutual fund trusts, segregated funds and master trusts;

• graduated rate estates;

• qualified disability trusts;

• employee life and health trusts;

• certain government funded trusts;

• trusts under or governed by a deferred profit sharing plan, pooled registered pension plan, registered disability savings plan, registered education savings plan, registered pension plan, registered retirement income fund or registered retirement savings plan; and

• cemetery care trusts and trusts governed by eligible funeral arrangements.

Federal Budget, Notice of Ways and Means Motion, Feb. 27, 2018: 17. The Act is modified to give effect to the proposals relating to reporting requirements for trusts described in the budget documents tabled by the Minister of Finance in the House of Commons on February 27, 2018.

Federal Budget, Supplementary Information, Feb. 27, 2018: *Reporting Requirements for Trusts*

Authorities require sufficient information in order to determine taxpayers' tax liabilities and to effectively counter aggressive tax avoidance as well as tax evasion, money laundering and other criminal activities. Some taxpayers have used trusts in complex arrangements to prevent the appropriate authorities from acquiring this required information.

A trust that does not earn income or make distributions in a year is generally not required to file an annual (T3) return of income. A trust is required to file a T3 return if the trust has tax payable or it distributes all or part of its income or capital to its beneficiaries. Even if a trust is required to file a return of income for a year, there is no requirement for the trust to report the identity of all its beneficiaries. Given the absence of an annual reporting requirement, and the limitations with respect to the information collected when reporting is required, there are significant gaps with respect to the information that is currently collected with respect to trusts.

As a consequence, Budget 2017 announced the Government's intention to examine ways to enhance the tax reporting requirements for trusts in order to improve the collection of beneficial ownership information.

Reporting Requirements

To improve the collection of beneficial ownership information with respect to trusts, Budget 2018 proposes to require that certain trusts provide additional information on an annual basis. The new reporting requirements will impose an obligation on certain trusts to file a T3 return where one does not currently exist. This information would be used to help the Canada Revenue Agency assess the tax liability for trusts and its beneficiaries.

The new reporting requirements will apply to express trusts that are resident in Canada and to non-resident trusts that are currently required to file a T3 return. An express trust is generally a trust created with the settlor's express intent, usually made in writing (as opposed to a resulting or constructive trust, or certain trusts deemed to arise under the provisions of a statute). **Exceptions to the additional reporting requirements are proposed for the following types of trusts:**

• mutual fund trusts, segregated funds and master trusts;

• trusts governed by registered plans (i.e., deferred profit sharing plans, pooled registered pension plans, registered disability savings plans, registered education savings plans, registered pension plans, registered retirement income funds, registered retirement savings plans, registered supplementary unemployment benefit plans and tax-free savings accounts);

• lawyers' general trust accounts *[note that this does not exempt lawyers' trust accounts for specific clients, but requiring disclosure of such accounts will likely breach solicitor-client privilege — ed.]*;

• graduated rate estates and qualified disability trusts;

• trusts that qualify as non-profit organizations or registered charities; and

• trusts that have been in existence for less than three months or that hold less than $50,000 in assets throughout the taxation year (provided, in the latter case, that their holdings are confined to deposits, government debt obligations and listed securities).

[It has been suggested to Finance that other regulated trust accounts be added, in addition to those of a lawyer — e.g., real estate brokers, and funeral/cemetery trusts (see 148.1) — ed.]

Where the new reporting requirements apply to a trust, **the trust will be required to report the identity of all trustees, beneficiaries and settlors of the trust,** as well as the identity of each person who has the ability (through the trust terms or a related agreement) to exert control over trustee decisions regarding the appointment of income or capital of the trust (e.g., a **protector**).

In order to implement the new reporting requirements, and to improve the Canada Revenue Agency's audit and administration of trusts and trust returns, Budget 2018 proposes to provide funding of $79 million over a five-year period and $15 million on an ongoing basis to the Canada Revenue Agency in order to support the development of an electronic platform for processing T3 returns.

These proposed new reporting requirements will apply to returns required to be filed for the 2021 and subsequent taxation years.

Penalties

To support these new reporting requirements, Budget 2018 proposes to introduce new penalties for a failure to file a T3 return, including a required beneficial ownership schedule, in circumstances where the schedule is required. The penalty will be equal to $25 for each day of delinquency, with a minimum penalty of $100 and a maximum penalty of $2,500. If a failure to file the return was made knowingly, or due to gross negligence, an additional penalty will apply. The additional penalty will be equal to 5% of the maximum fair market value of property held during the relevant year by the trust, with a minimum penalty of $2,500. As well, existing penalties will continue to apply.

The new penalties will apply in respect of returns required to be filed for the 2021 and subsequent taxation years.

Dept. of Finance news release, Dec. 11, 2017: *Agreement to Strengthen Beneficial Ownership Transparency*

Finance Ministers [at a meeting of federal, provincial and territorial FMs — ed.] agreed on the importance of ensuring appropriate safeguards are in place to prevent the misuse of corporations and other legal entities for tax evasion and other criminal purposes, such as money laundering, corruption and the financing of terrorist activities. To this end:

1. Ministers agreed in principle to pursue legislative amendments to federal, provincial and territorial corporate statutes or other relevant legislation to ensure corporations hold accurate and up to date information on beneficial owners that will be available to law enforcement, and tax and other authorities.

2. Ministers agreed in principle to pursue amendments to federal, provincial and territorial corporate statutes to eliminate the use of bearer shares and bearer share warrants or options and to replace existing ones with registered instruments.

3. Ministers agreed to work with respective Ministers responsible for corporate statutes and through their respective Cabinet processes to make best efforts to put forward these legislative amendments in order to bring these changes into force by July 1, 2019.

4. Ministers agreed to develop a joint outreach and consultation plan for coordinated engagement with the business community and other stakeholders.

5. Ministers agreed to continue existing work assessing potential mechanisms to enhance timely access by competent authorities to beneficial ownership information.

6. Ministers agreed to establish a federal, provincial and territorial working group to combat aggressive tax planning strategies that erode the integrity of the Canadian tax base.

Backgrounder: Tax Fairness and Beneficial Ownership Transparency

The Government of Canada is committed to ensuring all Canadians pay their fair share of taxes.

Appropriate authorities need to know who owns which companies in Canada to counter international tax evasion and avoidance, money laundering, and other criminal activities perpetrated through the misuse of corporate vehicles.

The concealment of corporate ownership information (also called "beneficial ownership") can be part of international webs used to facilitate tax evasion, money laundering, corruption, financing of terrorist activities, and the proliferation of dangerous goods.

Current Legislation

In support of its national and global tax fairness efforts, the federal government has already developed an extensive network of bilateral tax treaties and tax information exchange agreements with international partners. Furthermore, it has recently passed legislation to adopt the Common Reporting Standard, and signed on to the Organisation for Economic Cooperation and Development (OECD)'s Multilateral Convention to Implement Tax Treaty Related Measures to Prevent Base Erosion and Profit Shifting.

However, Canada still has significant blind spots when it comes to knowing the identity of those who own or control a corporation operating in Canada. Addressing this problem requires coordinated action between jurisdictions, given that only 10 per cent of Canadian companies are federally incorporated.

Furthermore, although Canada's anti-money laundering and anti-terrorist financing laws require that beneficial ownership information be provided by corporations when accessing financial services, requirements under federal, provincial and territorial corporate law for corporations to hold beneficial ownership information remain limited.

Addressing the Blind Spots

In Budget 2016 and Budget 2017, the federal government committed to cracking down on tax evasion and tax avoidance. This includes commitments to further strengthening corporate transparency. The information revealed through the recent leaks of the Panama and Paradise Papers reinforces the need for action.

To address current blind spots, action will be taken to improve the available beneficial ownership information to ensure appropriate authorities have timely access to this information in all jurisdictions.

These actions are part of international efforts in that regard. For example, in the United Kingdom, the names of people who have significant control of companies are now included in a central registry.

Federal Budget, Chapter 4, "Tax Fairness for the Middle Class", March 22, 2017: *Strengthening Corporate and Beneficial Ownership Transparency*

The Government of Canada is committed to implementing strong standards for corporate and beneficial ownership transparency that provide safeguards against money laundering, terrorist financing, tax evasion and tax avoidance, while continuing to facilitate the ease of doing business in Canada. Understanding the ownership and control of corporations is vital for good corporate governance and to protect the integrity of the tax and financial systems.

The Government will collaborate with provinces and territories to put in place a national strategy to strengthen the transparency of legal persons and legal arrangements and improve the availability of beneficial ownership information.

The Government is also examining ways to enhance the tax reporting requirements for trusts in order to improve the collection of beneficial ownership information.

These actions will ensure that law enforcement and other authorities have timely access to the information needed to crack down on money laundering, terrorist financing and tax evasion and to combat tax avoidance.

Federal Budget, Supplementary Information, March 19, 2019: *Previously Announced Measures*

Budget 2019 confirms the Government's intention to proceed with the following previously announced tax and related measures, as modified to take into account consultations and deliberations since their release: ...

*   The income tax measures announced in Budget 2018 to implement enhanced reporting requirements for certain trusts to provide additional information on an annual basis;

Federal Budget, Supplementary Information, April 19, 2021: *Previously Announced Measures*

Budget 2021 confirms the government's intention to proceed with the following previously announced tax and related measures, as modified to take into account consultations and deliberations since their release: . . .

*   The income tax measures announced in Budget 2018 to implement enhanced reporting requirements for certain trusts to provide additional information on an annual basis.

Notes: See the editorial notes in the 2018 Budget Supplementary Information text above. Since these rules are for tax years ending after Dec. 30, 2021, they apply to the 2021 (calendar) year for all *inter vivos* trusts: 249(1)(c). Budget Table 1 predicts this change will cost the federal government $12 million in 2018-19, $9m in 2019-20, $10m in 2020-21, $14m in 2021-22 and $34m in 2022-23. (This is the $79m administrative cost stated above. It does not count increased tax collections due to the additional reporting, which are presumably impossible to predict but which one can expect may be substantial.)

The exception in 150(1.2)(c) covers a lawyer's general (mixed) trust account but not trust accounts for specific clients. However, requiring such trusts (for specific clients) to be reported is likely an illegal violation of solicitor-client privilege, so this rule will likely be struck down. See 232(2) Notes. The CBA/CPA Canada Joint Committee has strongly criticized this proposal: see letter to Finance, Sept. 10, 2018.

See proposed Reg. 204.2 for prescribed information to be required on trust returns. See also Mancell, "An Overview of the New Tax Reporting Rules for Trusts", 2434 *Tax Topics* (CCH) 1-4 (Nov. 1, 2018); Sorensen, "Pulling Back the Curtain on Beneficial Ownership", 2019 Cdn Tax Foundation conference report, 9:1-38; Hendry, "New reporting requirements for trusts could be just tip of the iceberg", *Law Times* (tinyurl.com/hendry-rep), Feb. 12, 2020; Harris & Katlai, "New Trust Disclosure Rules", 20(4) *Tax for the Owner-Manager* (ctf.ca) 7-8 (Oct. 2020) (whether contingent beneficiaries must be disclosed under Reg. 204.2(1)(a)); KPMG *TaxNewsFlash* 2020-81, "Prepare for Upcoming Trust Reporting Rules" (Nov. 20, 2020, 5pp); Johnston & Trotta, "Disclosing Persons who Exert Influence on Trustees", 11(2) *Canadian Tax Focus* (ctf.ca) 1-2 (May 2021).

Regulations: 204.2 (prescribed information required on trust returns); 4802(1.1) (prescribed master trust for 150(1.2)(h)).

(2) Demands for returns — Every person, whether or not the person is liable to pay tax under this Part for a taxation year and whether or not a return has been filed under subsection (1) or (3), shall, on demand sent by the Minister, file, within such reasonable time stipulated in the demand, with the Minister in prescribed form and containing prescribed information a return of the income for the taxation year designated in the demand.

Related Provisions: 162(2) — Repeated penalties; 163(5), (6) — Penalty of 5% of trust assets for non-compliance re trust return; 231.2(1)(a) — Generic demand for information or return; 233 — Demand for partnership information return; 238(1) — Fine or imprisonment for failure to file.

Notes: If the taxpayer fails to answer a demand, CRA can issue new demands that create new time periods for compliance, and new offences for failing to comply within those periods: *Grimwood*, [1988] 1 C.T.C. 44 (SCC). A demand to file is not a prerequisite to finding an attempt to evade tax, but is relevant to determining a penalty: *Sorenson*, [1981] C.T.C. 2601 (TRB). In *N.M. Skalbania Ltd.*, [1989] 2 C.T.C. 183 (BC Co. Ct), conviction for failure to comply with a demand was set aside because the demand was made under the wrong section.

150(2) amended by 2012 budget bill #1, effective June 29, 2012, to change "from the Minister, served personally or by registered letter" to "on demand sent by the Minister". Thus, a demand served online (if authorized under 244(14.1)) or by regular mail will be valid and can trigger a 162(2) penalty.

Forms: TX14D: Demand for return.

(3) Trustees, etc. — Every trustee in bankruptcy, assignee, liquidator, curator, receiver, trustee or committee and every agent or other person administering, managing, winding up, controlling or otherwise dealing with the property, business, estate or income of a person who has not filed a return for a taxation year as required by this section shall file a return in prescribed form of that person's income for that year.

Related Provisions: 94(3)(a)(vii) — Application to trust deemed resident in Canada; 150(1)(c) — Trust returns; 159 — Payments on behalf of others; 162(3) — Penalties; 163(1) — Repeated failures.

Notes: See VIEWS doc 2011-0395131I7 re whether a receiver must file a taxpayer's outstanding returns. If a bankruptcy trustee does not file the bankrupt's unfiled returns, refunds must be withheld due to 164(2.01): doc 2011-0422581I7. If the trustee or receiver certifies inability to prepare the return due to a lack of records, on Form RC342, CRA will usually waive the requirement so GST/HST refunds can be released: Information Circular IC100.

Regulations: 204 (information returns).

Information Circulars: 12-1: GST/HST compliance refund holds.

Forms: RC342: Request by an insolvency practitioner for a waiver of the requirement to file a T2 corporation income tax return.

(4) Death of partner or proprietor — Where

(a) subsection 34.1(9) or 34.2(8) applies in computing an individual's income for a taxation year from a business, or

(b) an individual who carries on a business in a taxation year dies in the year and after the end of a fiscal period of the business that ends in the year, another fiscal period of the business (in this subsection referred to as the "short period") ends in the year because of the individual's death, and the individual's legal representative elects that this subsection apply,

the individual's income from businesses for short periods, if any, shall not be included in computing the individual's income for the year and the individual's legal representative shall file an additional return of income for the year in respect of the individual as if the return were filed in respect of another person and shall pay the tax payable under this Part by that other person for the year computed as if

(c) the other person's only income for the year were the amount determined by the formula

$$A + B - C$$

where

A is the total of all amounts each of which is the individual's income from a business for a short fiscal period,

B is the total of all amounts each of which is an amount deducted under subsection 34.2(8) in computing the individual's income for the taxation year in which the individual dies, and

C is the total of all amounts each of which is an amount included under subsection 34.1(9) in computing the individual's income for the taxation year in which the individual dies, and

(d) subject to sections 114.2 and 118.93, that other person were entitled to the deductions to which the individual is entitled under sections 110, 118 to 118.7 and 118.9 for the year in computing the individual's taxable income or tax payable under this Part, as the case may be, for the year.

Related Provisions: 34.1(9)(d)(ii) — Additional income inclusion for off-calendar business year; 70 — Rules for year of death; 114.2 — Deductions in separate returns; 118.93 — Credits in separate returns; 120.2(4)(a) — No minimum tax carryover; 127.1(1)(a) — No refundable investment tax credit; 127.55 — No minimum tax in year of death; 150(1)(b) — Deadline for deceased's return; 162(5) — Penalties — failure to provide information return; 163(1) — Repeated failures; 257 — Formula cannot calculate to less than zero.

Notes: 150(4) amended by 1995-97 technical bill, for 1996 and later taxation years.

Interpretation Bulletins [subsec. 150(4)]: IT-278R2: Death of a partner or of a retired partner; IT-326R3: Returns of deceased persons as "another person".

Forms: T4011: Preparing returns for deceased persons [guide].

(5) Excluded disposition — For the purposes of this section, a disposition of a property by a taxpayer at any time in a taxation year is an excluded disposition if

(a) the taxpayer is non-resident at that time;

(b) no tax is payable under this Part by the taxpayer for the taxation year;

(c) the taxpayer is, at that time, not liable to pay any amount under this Act in respect of any previous taxation year (other than an amount for which the Minister has accepted, and holds, adequate security under section 116 or 220); and

(d) each taxable Canadian property disposed of by the taxpayer in the taxation year is

(i) excluded property within the meaning assigned by subsection 116(6), or

(ii) a property in respect of the disposition of which the Minister has issued to the taxpayer a certificate under subsection 116(2), (4) or (5.2).

Notes: See 150(1)(a)(i)(C)-(D) and 150(1.1)(b)(iii). A non-resident who disposes of taxable Canadian property that is not treaty-protected property must file a return: VIEWS doc 2019-0798861C6 [2019 IFA q.6].

150(5) added by 2008 budget bill #1, for dispositions of property after 2008.

Definitions [s. 150]: "amount", "business" — 248(1); "calendar year" — *Interpretation Act* 37(1)(a); "capital property" — 54, 248(1); "carries on business in Canada", "carrying on business in Canada" — 253; "cemetery care trust" — 148.1(1), 248(1); "cohabiting spouse or common-law partner" — 122.6; "common-law partner" — 248(1); "corporation" — 248(1), *Interpretation Act* 35(1); "deferred profit sharing plan" — 147(1), 248(1); "designated stock exchange" — 248(1), 262; "disposition" — 248(1); "eligible funeral arrangement" — 148.1(1), 248(1); "employee life and health trust" — 144.1(2), 248(1); "estate" — 104(1), 248(1); "excluded disposition" — 150(5); "fair market value" — see 69(1) Notes; "filing-due date" — 248(1); "fiscal period" — 249.1; "graduated rate estate" — 248(1); "HBP balance" — 146.01(1); "individual" — 248(1); "LLP balance" — 146.02(1); "legal representative", "Minister" — 248(1); "month" — *Interpretation Act* 35(1); "mutual fund corporation" — 131(8), 248(1); "mutual fund trust" — 132(6)–(7), 132.2(3)(n), 248(1); "non-resident", "person" — 248(1); "pooled registered pension plan" — 147.5(1), 248(1); "prescribed", "property" — 248(1); "province" — *Interpretation Act* 35(1); "qualified disability trust" — 122(3); "registered charity" — 248(1); "registered disability savings plan" — 146.4(1), 248(1); "registered education savings plan" — 146.1(1), 248(1); "registered pension plan" — 248(1); "registered retirement income fund" — 146.3(1), 248(1); "registered retirement savings plan" — 146(1), 248(1); "related segregated fund" — 138.1(1)(a); "resident in Canada" — 94(3)(a)(vii), 250; "security" — *Interpretation Act* 35(1); "share" — 248(1); "tax payable" — 248(2); "tax treaty", "taxable Canadian property" — 248(1); "taxable capital gain" — 38(a), 248(1); "taxable income" — 2(2), 248(1); "taxation year" — 249; "taxpayer" — 248(1); "trust" — 104(1), 248(1), (3); "writing" — *Interpretation Act* 35(1).

Interpretation Bulletins [s. 150]: IT-109R2: Unpaid amounts.

150.1 (1) Definition of "electronic filing" — For the purposes of this section, "electronic filing" means using electronic media in a manner specified in writing by the Minister.

(2) Filing of return by electronic transmission — A person who meets the criteria specified in writing by the Minister may file a return of income for a taxation year by way of electronic filing.

Related Provisions: 150.1(2.1) — Mandatory e-filing for certain corporations; 150.1(2.3), (2.4) — Mandatory e-filing for certain tax preparers; 244(21) — Proof of e-filing; 244(22) — Electronic filing of information return; Reg. 205.1(2) (prescribed corporation is corporation with gross revenue exceeding $1 million, with certain exceptions).

Notes: See Notes at end of 150.1.

Application Policies: SR&ED 2004-02R5: Filing requirements for claiming SR&ED.

Forms: RC4018: Electronic filers manual [guide]; RC4088: Guide to the General Index of Financial Information (GIFI) for corporations; T183: Information return for electronic filing of an individual's income tax and benefit return; T183 CORP: Information return for corporations filing electronically; T1153: Consent and request form; T4077: EFILE: Electronic filing for individuals [guide].

(2.1) Mandatory filing of return by electronic transmission — If a corporation is, in respect of a taxation year, a prescribed corporation, the corporation shall file its return of income for the taxation year by way of electronic filing.

Related Provisions: 162(7.2) — Penalty for failure to file electronically.

Notes: 150.1(2.1) (added by 2009 budget bill #1 for tax years ending after 2009) requires a corp with annual gross revenue over $1 million to file the T2 return (150(1)(a)) electronically. The return is still valid if filed on paper: VIEWS doc 2012-0445451E5.

Regulations: 205.1(2) (prescribed corporation is corporation with gross revenue exceeding $1 million, with certain exceptions).

(2.2) Definition of "tax preparer" — In this section and subsection 162(7.3), "tax preparer", for a calendar year, means a person or partnership who, in the year, accepts consideration to prepare more than 10 returns of income of corporations or more than 10 returns of income of individuals (other than trusts), but does not include an employee who prepares returns of income in the course of performing their duties of employment.

Related Provisions: 150.1(2.3), (2.4) — Tax preparer required to file electronically.

Notes: 150.1(2.2) added by 2012 budget bill #1, effective for returns for the 2012 and later taxation years that are filed after 2012. See Notes to 150.1(2.3).

(2.3) Electronic filing — tax preparer — A tax preparer shall file any return of income prepared by the tax preparer for consideration by way of electronic filing, except that 10 of the returns of corporations and 10 of the returns of individuals may be filed other than by way of electronic filing.

Proposed Amendment — 150.1(2.3) — 10-return threshold lowered to 5 returns

Federal Budget, Supplementary Information, April 19, 2021: See under 244(14.1), under heading "Tax Preparers".

Related Provisions: 150.1(2.1) — Corporation with over $1 million revenue required to file electronically; 150.1(2.2) — Definition of "tax preparer"; 150.1(2.4) — Exceptions; 162(7.3) — Penalty (fee) for failing to file electronically.

Notes: See tinyurl.com/efile-mandatory. E-filing is not really mandatory; after 10, it merely triggers a $25 penalty under 162(7.3) which can be considered a (non-deductible) "paper filing fee". The return is still validly filed if filed on paper: VIEWS doc 2012-0445451E5.

150.1(2.3) added by 2012 budget bill #1, effective for returns for the 2012 and later taxation years that are filed after 2012.

(2.4) Exceptions — Subsection (2.3) does not apply to a tax preparer for a calendar year in respect of a return of income

(a) of a type for which the tax preparer has applied to the Minister for authority to file by way of electronic filing for the year and for which that authority has not been granted because the tax preparer does not meet the criteria referred to in subsection (2);

(b) of a corporation described in any of paragraphs 205.1(2)(a) to (c) of the *Income Tax Regulations*; or

(c) of a type that the Minister does not accept by way of electronic filing.

Notes: 150.1(2.4) added by 2012 budget bill #1, effective for returns for the 2012 and later taxation years that are filed after 2012.

(3) Deemed date of filing — For the purposes of section 150, where a return of income of a taxpayer for a taxation year is filed by way of electronic filing, it shall be deemed to be a return of income filed with the Minister in prescribed form on the day the Minister acknowledges acceptance of it.

Notes: CRA has an unpublished policy allowing 6 days' grace to refile if a return is rejected. See Notes to 162(1) re the *Bateman* case.

(4) Declaration — Where a return of income of a taxpayer for a taxation year is filed by way of electronic filing by a particular person (in this subsection referred to as the "filer") other than the person who is required to file the return, the person who is required to

file the return shall make an information return in prescribed form containing prescribed information, sign it, retain a copy of it and provide the filer with the information return, and that return and the copy shall be deemed to be a record referred to in section 230 in respect of the filer and the other person.

Forms: RC4018: Electronic filers manual [guide]; T183: Information return for electronic filing of an individual's income tax and benefit return; T183 CORP: Information return for corporations filing electronically.

(5) Application to other Parts — This section also applies to Parts I.2 to XIII, with such modifications as the circumstances require.

Notes: 150.1(5) amended by 2000 Budget to change "Parts I.1 to XIII" to "Parts I.2 to XIII" (due to the repeal of the individual surtax in Part I.1), effective for 2001 and later taxation years.

Announced Temporary Administrative Change — Electronic signature to authorize e-filing

Dept. of Finance Backgrounder, March 18, 2020: See under 241(5).

Notes [s. 150.1]: A tax preparer as defined in 150.1(2.2) (more than 10 individual or corporate returns prepared for compensation) must file electronically (150.1(2.3)) or else pay a fee (penalty under 162(7.3)).

An individual can use canada.ca/my-cra-account for many functions including viewing balances, payments, carryovers, refunds and credits; changing a return; change of address; authorizing a representative; and filing an objection. The former "QuickAccess" system allowing viewing of some balances without signing up was cancelled in Feb. 2015.

A corporation can use tinyurl.com/cra-BusAccount to authorize representatives, file returns and objections, make online requests, request credit transfers, refunds, interest review and CPP/EI rulings, view account information and correspondence, and access various other services. Advisers use canada.ca/taxes-representatives to access corporate and individual accounts for which they are authorized.

The corporate tax return is now inherently electronic, and electronic filing is mandatory for corporations with over $1 million gross revenue (see 150.1(2.1)). Paper filing is still permitted for smaller corporations. Returns are processed electronically, and corporate financial information is gathered and stored using the General Index of Financial Information (GIFI), which includes specific codes for each line of financial information (e.g., each kind of expense). See RC4088 and RC4089 for listings of GIFI codes.

For corporate Internet filing see tinyurl.com/t2-internet. For a Web Access Code call the Corporation Internet Filing Help Desk, 1-800-959-2803.

Notes to the financial statements can be entered electronically at line 100-0001. The transmission format for Internet filing does not recognize PDF files, but HQ is investigating how to accept them: May 2009 ICAA roundtable (tinyurl.com/cra-abtax) q.14.

"Attaching" a document to an electronic return: Some elections or designations are required to be made "in" the return or "attached to" it [e.g., 7(1.31)(b), 12(2.2), 13(4), 13(7.4), 21(1), (2), (3), (4), 28(1)(b), 29(1), 39(4), 40(3.12), 44(1), (6), 45(2), 50(1), 59.1, 60(j)(iii), 60.011, 70(5.2), (6.2), (7), (9.01), (9.2), (9.6), 73(4.1)(c), 84.1(2.1), 86.1(2)(f), 87(8), 88(1)(d), 110(1.1), 164(6)(c), (d), 185.1(2), Reg. 1101(5b.1), (5i), (5l), (5o), (5q), (5u), (5v), 1102(16.1), 1102(25), 1103(2a), (2b), (2c), (2d), (2f), (2h), (2i), 2300]. For an individual, send a paper document to the Tax Centre: tinyurl.com/t1attach, or Guide RC4018 under "Paper documentation". For a corporation, send the document on paper to the Tax Centre, or electronically via "attach a document" in T2 eFile: tinyurl.com/t2software > Attach-a-doc, or Guide T4012. *Dhaliwal*, 2012 TCC 84, held that D had made a valid 50(1) election by claiming an allowable business investment loss, since CRA provided no way to make the election in the electronic return. CRA appears not to accept this decision: 2012-0454041C6 [2012 APFF q.26]. In *Tooth*, [2021] UKSC 17, the UK Supreme Court held that a written explanation provided in the "white space" on an electronically filed return was sufficient to prevent the return having an "inaccuracy" that would permit a late assessment, even though the tax authority's computer could not understand it.

For personal income tax e-filing see canada.ca/efile, and RC4018 e-filer manual. The vast majority of returns are now e-filed (88.6% in the 2019 filing season: Taxpayers' Ombudsman, *Taxpayer Rights in the Digital Age* (May 2020), p. 24. (Most professionally prepared returns must be: 150.1(2.3).)

Some individuals are not permitted to e-file (tinyurl.com/no-efile), e.g. deemed residents, bankrupts, non-residents, and returns with claims such as: election to defer tax on foreign spin-off (86.1); less than maximum foreign tax credit; SR&ED expenses deduction; voluntary disclosure; and others. CRA is studying e-filing for non-residents, but no timeline has been set: VIEWS doc 2014-0538211C6 [2014 APFF q.27].

E-file professionals can use "Express NOA" to get an instant Notice of Assessment upon filing: canada.ca/express-noa. The disadvantage is that CRA does not send the NOA to the taxpayer.

"File my return" (tinyurl.com/cra-phonefile) allows eligible low-income taxpayers to file by phone. (An earlier TELEFILE program allowing filing by phone was discontinued: CRA news release, June 27, 2012.)

NETFILE allows taxpayers to file on the Internet: netfile.gc.ca.

Re verification of the "signed" declaration that an electronic filing is accurate and complete, see VIEWS doc 2009-0338601I7.

Professional return preparers may wish to paper-file T1 returns claiming charitable donations or medical expenses, because these are routinely audited to review the receipts included with the paper return, and there is administrative cost in sending the receipts to CRA later if the return was e-filed. However, there is a $25 penalty for paper-filing each return after 10 per year (unless the preparer loses e-file eligibility: 150.1(2.4)(a)): see 150.1(2.2)–(2.4), 162(7.3). CRA now allows documents to be submitted electronically, and is exploring ways to allow donation receipts to be submitted at time of e-filing: VIEWS doc 2012-0465931C6.

"ReFILE" allows adjustment to a previous return (see also 152(1) Notes re amending a return).

Individuals who can file by Internet may receive an access code printed on their tax return label (but see Notes to 150(1)(d)). The same code is used for other on-line services.

Being an e-File transmitter is a privilege, not a right, and the Courts refused to interfere with CRA's discretion to cut off e-File access to a tax preparer: *Pan-Tax*, [1997] 2 C.T.C. 315 (FCTD); *Paterson*, 2011 FCA 12. However, in *Saber & Sone Group*, 2014 FC 1119, CRA suspension of e-File access (allegedly for not storing T1013s for 6 years, but really related to accessing the accounts of estranged relatives whom the firm had represented) was sent back for reconsideration as not properly supported. The Tax Court does not have jurisdiction to review this issue: *Killam*, 2009 TCC 227. CRA criteria for who can e-File, and grounds for suspension (e.g. "unacceptable cumulative error rate"): tinyurl.com/who-can-efile. (A tax preparer who is refused e-File privileges can prepare and file paper returns without penalty: 150.1(2.4)(a).) In *Larbi*, 2021 ONSC 3240, the Court struck out L's lawsuit claiming that CRA allowed her ex-husband to open an E-File number in her name; it did not raise a valid cause of action.

For paying taxes through a financial institution's Internet or telephone banking services, including by debit or credit card, see tinyurl.com/cra-mypayment.

See also pamphlet RC4358, *Service options for businesses*.

150.1 added by 1992 technical bill (and 150.1(4) amended retroactively by 1993 technical bill), effective for 1992 and later taxation years.

Definitions [s. 150.1]: "calendar year" — *Interpretation Act* 37(1)(a); "corporation" — 248(1), *Interpretation Act* 35(1); "electronic filing" — 150.1(1); "employee", "employment" — 248(1); "filer" — 150.1(4); "individual", "Minister" — 248(1); "partnership" — see 96(1) Notes; "person", "prescribed", "regulation" — 248(1); "tax preparer" — 150.1(2.2); "taxation year" — 249; "trust" — 104(1), 248(1), (3); "writing" — *Interpretation Act* 35(1).

Forms: See under 150.1(2).

Estimate of Tax

151. Estimate of tax — Every person required by section 150 to file a return of income shall in the return estimate the amount of tax payable.

Related Provisions: 104(23) — Testamentary trusts; 150 — Returns; 155, 156 — Instalments required — individuals; 156.1(4) — Payment of balance owing — individuals; 157 — Instalments required — corporations; 162(3) — Penalty — failure to complete return; 183(3) — Provision applicable to Part II; 187(3) — Provision applicable to Part IV; 219(3) — Provision applicable to Part XIV.

Definitions [s. 151]: "amount", "person" — 248(1).

Assessment

152. (1) Assessment — The Minister shall, with all due dispatch, examine a taxpayer's return of income for a taxation year, assess the tax for the year, the interest and penalties, if any, payable and determine

(a) the amount of refund, if any, to which the taxpayer may be entitled by virtue of section 129, 131, 132 or 133 for the year; or

(b) the amount of tax, if any, deemed by subsection 120(2) or (2.2), 122.5(3) or (3.001), 122.51(2), 122.7(2) or (3), 122.8(4), 122.9(2), 122.91(1), 125.4(3), 125.5(3), 125.6(2) or (2.1), 127.1(1), 127.41(3) or 210.2(3) or (4) to be paid on account of the taxpayer's tax payable under this Part for the year.

Announced Administrative Change — Automating T1 Adjustments

Federal Budget, Chapter 10, April 19, 2021: See under 220(1).

Related Provisions: 152(1.4) — Determination of income of partnership; 152(2) — Notice of assessment; 152(4), (5) — Reassessment; 158 — Remainder payable forthwith upon assessment; 160.2(3) — Minister may assess recipient under RRSP or RRIF; 166 — Irregularity or error in assessment; 244(14), (14.1), (15) — Date when assessment made.

Notes: The Minister has no discretion in how to apply the Act: *Harris*, [2000] 3 C.T.C. 220 (FCA; leave to appeal denied 2000 CarswellNat 2664 (SCC)); so (at least in theory) CRA must assess all tax that is payable. In practice, auditors have wide discretion not to reassess; but once a reassessment is issued, Appeals Officers and the Tax Court have no discretion to reduce it unless the change accords with the Act.

Express NOA (Notice of Assessment) immediately on e-filing: see Notes to 150.1.

Due dispatch: For CRA's target times for assessing ("service standards"), see Notes to 150(1)(a), (c) and (d). Although the Minister is supposed to issue an assessment "with all due dispatch", the assessment is valid even if not issued for a long time: *Ginsberg*, [1996] 3 C.T.C. 63 (FCA); *Sabharwal*, 2010 TCC 54, para. 11 (FCA appeal dismissed for delay A-78-10). The obligation is "an elastic standard that gives the Minister sufficient discretion to determine that a particular return should not be assessed until after a detailed review. As long as the necessary review proceeds at a pace that is reasonable in the circumstances, the Minister will not be in default": *Imperial Oil*, 2003 FCA 289. The time limit "purports a discretion to be exercised ... with reason, justice and legal principles": *Jolicoeur*, [1960] C.T.C. 346 (Exch. Ct), para. 47. See also Campbell, *Administration of Income Tax 2020* (Carswell), §9.2; VIEWS doc 2007-0243351C6.

The only remedy is to bring an application for judicial review (JR) in Federal Court for an order of *mandamus* forcing the Minister to assess. However, in *Merlis Investments*, [2001] 1 C.T.C. 57 (FCTD), JR was refused because 18 months delay was not unreasonable for a case that was referred to the GAAR committee for review and to the Dept. of Justice for a legal opinion. GST refund claims delayed by CRA: *Nautica Motors*, 2002 FCT 422 (CRA ordered to process return); *Cambridge Leasing*, 2003 FCT 112 (Court refused to order CRA to process return because interim assessment had been issued and was under objection); *Iris Technologies*, 2020 FCA 117 and *Express Gold*, 2020 FC 614 (Court refused to order CRA to assess and pay refunds because CRA entitled to "a reasonable time" to assess); *Iris Technologies*, 2020 FC 1133 (under appeal to FCA) (later JR application not struck as more time had passed, but no injunction issued as CRA not shown to be delaying audit for improper purpose; further procedural decision 2021 FC 528, aff'd 2021 FC 597 (under appeal to FCA)).

The French for "due dispatch" in 152(1) is "avec diligence", although "due dispatch" is normally thought to mean "promptly". (This was noted in *Ficek* and *McNally*; see next para.) This "diligence" requirement applies only to the initial return, and not to any reassessment under 152(4): *Rio Tinto*, 2017 TCC 67, paras. 163-168 (FCA appeal discontinued A-153-17).

CRA will not assess a return claiming a donation shelter until it has audited the shelter. This was held to be for the improper purpose of discouraging such claims in both *Ficek* and *McNally*: see Notes to 118.1(1)"total charitable gifts".

It is proper for the Minister to issue an initial assessment on filing that merely confirms the calculations, and audit the file later: *Western Minerals*, [1962] C.T.C. 270 (SCC). It is up to the Minister to determine the level of audit detail required: *Rio Tinto* (above), paras. 146-148, and once an initial assessment is issued, 152(4) governs a reassessment and does not require any particular diligence: paras. 165-171.

An assessment should be for one taxation year, but a mistaken assessment of two years is not void and can be cured by reassessment, as long as the tax did not arise in a statute-barred year: *594710 B.C.*, 2018 FCA 166, paras. 94-95 (leave to appeal denied 2019 CarswellNat 434 (SCC)).

Amending a return: see canada.ca/change-tax-return or file a Form T1-Adj. Once a return is assessed, CRA is not required to consider a request to amend it (absent a timely objection under 165(1)): *Imperial Oil (Inco)*, 2003 TCC 46, para. 38 (aff'd without discussing this point 2003 FCA 289); *Armstrong*, 2006 FCA 119, para. 8; *Newfoundland Transshipment*, 2013 TCC 259, paras. 18-21; *Rio Tinto* (above), para. 166 (later SR&ED claim). *Contra*, in *AFD Petroleum*, 2016 FC 547 (FCA appeal discontinued A-215-16), para. 17, the FC held it had jurisdiction to order CRA to reassess to consider an SR&ED claim, but found CRA's refusal to be reasonable; and in *Bakorp Management*, 2019 FCA 195, para. 42, the FCA said the FC can review a CRA refusal to adjust a past return. CRA's view is that a partnership information return cannot be amended after the statute-barred date: doc 2014-0562271I7.

In *Ntakos Estate*, 2018 TCC 224, a reassessment implementing a T1-Adj from N, who lacked mental capacity and did not speak English or authorize the filing, was void.

The Tax Court has jurisdiction to hear an appeal of interest assessed on Part XIII non-resident withholding tax, since 227(7) provides that 152(1) applies: *Cooper*, 2009 TCC 236, paras. 19-22.

To find out whether a personal tax return has been assessed, call TIPS at 1-800-267-6999 or use canada.ca/taxes-representatives or canada.ca/my-cra-account.

A *dissolved corporation* can be assessed for periods before dissolution: VIEWS doc 2012-0455781E5; the shareholders may be liable: *Wesdome Gold*, 2018 QCCA 518, paras. 62-71 (leave to appeal denied 2019 CarswellQue 946 (SCC)); 2011-039919117; and see 84(2) and 159(1). For periods after dissolution, CRA can assess shareholders for continuing to carry on the business: see Notes to 88(2). See also Notes to 169(1) under "Dissolved corporations".

152(1)(b) amended by 2021 budget bill #1 to add 125.6(2) and delete 125.7(2), (2.1) effective 2019 [the latter two are covered by 152(3.4)]; by 2020 COVID bill #5 to add 125.7(2.1) effective Nov. 19, 2020; by 2020 COVID bill #2 to add 125.7(2) effective April 11, 2020; by 2020 COVID bill #1 to add 122.5(3.001) effective March 25, 2020; by 2019 budget bill #1 to add 122.91(1) and 125.6(2) effective 2019; by 2018 budget bill #2 to add 122.8(4) for 2018 and later tax years; by 2016 budget bill #1 to delete "122.8(2) or (3)" for 2017 and later years and add 122.9(2) for 2016 and later; and by

2007 budget bill #2, 1999, 1997, 1995 and 1994 Budgets, 1993 technical bill, 1992 Child Benefit bill, 1990 GST.

CRA Audit Manual: 11.5.9: NIL assessment — notification; 12.1.0: Taxpayer requests (TPR) and general adjustment forms (GAF).

(1.01) Determination of disability tax credit eligibility —
The Minister shall, if an individual requests by prescribed form, determine with all due dispatch whether an amount is deductible, or would if this Act were read without reference to paragraph 118.3(1)(c) be deductible, under section 118.3 in computing the individual's tax payable under this Part for a taxation year and send a notice of the determination to the individual.

Related Provisions: 152(1.2) — Determination can be objected to and appealed.

Notes: In *Tozzi*, 2010 TCC 545, an individual with no tax for the year could not appeal CRA's denial of his eligibility for the Disability Tax Credit [and thus RDSP eligibility], as he was appealing a nil assessment (see Notes to 152(1.1)). David Sherman raised this with Finance and copied James Daw of the *Toronto Star*, who contacted the Minister of Finance: "Star Gets Action: Flaherty vows to 'fix' tax court", *Toronto Star*, Nov. 24, 2010, p. B1. The "fix" is 152(1.01), which allows a request to "determine" eligibility even if no credit is claimed. Under 152(1.2), Divisions I and J apply to the determination, so it can be objected to and appealed to the TCC. See also CRA notice of July 7, 2011, reproduced in Drache, "Disability Tax Credit Appeal Rules Now Changed", xxxiii(17) *The Canadian Taxpayer* (Carswell) 131-33 (Sept. 16, 2011).

152(1.01) added by 2011 budget bill #1, for tax years that end after 2009 in respect of forms filed with the Minister after June 26, 2011, with transitional relief for 2008-10.

(1.1) Determination of losses —
Where the Minister ascertains the amount of a taxpayer's non-capital loss, net capital loss, restricted farm loss, farm loss or limited partnership loss for a taxation year and the taxpayer has not reported that amount as such a loss in the taxpayer's return of income for that year, the Minister shall, at the request of the taxpayer, determine, with all due dispatch, the amount of the loss and shall send a notice of determination to the person by whom the return was filed.

Related Provisions: 111 — Losses deductible; 152(1.2) — Administrative procedures for assessments apply to determinations; 152(1.4) — Determination of loss of partnership; 160.2(3) — Minister may assess recipient under RRSP or RRIF; 244(14), (14.1) — Presumption re date of sending of notice of determination; 244(15) — Determination deemed made on date mailed; 248(7)(a) — Mail deemed received on day mailed.

Notes: A Notice of Determination is treated as an assessment and can be objected to and appealed: 152(1.2) (note references to "this Division and Division J").

If there is a nil assessment (no tax to pay) for year X, with losses but no formal 152(1.1) loss determination, year X cannot be appealed to contest losses or credits denied by CRA: *Okalta Oil*, [1955] C.T.C. 271 (SCC); *Bruner*, 2003 FCA 54; *Bormann*, 2006 FCA 83; *Interior Savings*, 2007 FCA 151; *Hutchinson-Jones*, 2018 FCA 78; *Mosquera*, 2018 FCA 170 (leave to appeal denied 2019 CarswellNat 2912 (SCC)); *Bonev*, 2020 FCA 138, para. 8; *Wilson*, [1996] 3 C.T.C. 203 (FCTD); *Dray*, 2005 TCC 797; *Fotherby*, 2008 TCC 343, para. 37; *Terek*, 2008 TCC 665; *Esesson Canada*, 2009 TCC 336; *Giasson*, 2009 TCC 504; *On-Line Finance*, 2009 TCC 565 (even where CRA told taxpayer to cancel loss determination request); *Grondin*, 2009 TCC 459; *Nicholls*, 2010 TCC 65; *Babich*, 2012 FCA 276; *Tozzi*, 2010 TCC 545 (see Notes to 152(1.01)); *Gallant*, 2012 TCC 119, para. 20; *Algonquin Landscaping*, 2012 TCC 437, para. 13; *Wong*, 2013 TCC 130; *Bérubé*, 2014 TCC 304; *Donaldson*, 2016 TCC 5, para. 10 (terminal loss); *Mockler*, 2016 TCC 241; *Nagel*, 2018 TCC 32 (under appeal to FCA) (unused tuition credits, province of residence); *Keenan*, 2018 TCC 179, paras. 14-17; *Way*, 2018 TCC 198, para. 9; *Mikhail*, 2019 TCC 49, para. 4. (*Contra*, in *Ocean Nutrition*, 2011 NSSC 493, a company was allowed to appeal a nil assessment of Nova Scotia tax to claim provincial R&D credits, despite contrary case law.) The Court also cannot increase tax on appeal: see Notes to 169(1).

A nil assessment cannot be appealed even if the appeal is not about losses but about refundable credits or a credit-union's "preferred-rate amount": *Interior Savings*, 2007 FCA 151 (reversing the TCC and overruling earlier decisions *Joshi* and *Corriveau*). In *Martens*, [1988] 2 C.T.C. 2018 (TCC), an appeal of a refundable investment tax credit was possible because of 152(1)(b) and 152(1.2); the FCA in *Interior Savings* said *Martens* is still good law. The denial of a dividend refund can be disputed on a nil assessment: see Notes to 129(1).

However, one can appeal the assessment of another year in which the loss carryover from year X is denied: *Clibetre Exploration*, 2003 FCA 16; *Aallcann Wood Suppliers*, [1994] 2 C.T.C. 2079 (TCC); *Gestion Raynald Lavoie*, 2008 TCC 204. The loss need not even be reported in year X to be claimed in a later year: *Burleigh*, 2004 TCC 197; *Leola Purdy Sons*, 2009 TCC 21; *On-line Finance*, 2010 TCC 475, para. 67; *Benedict*, 2012 TCC 174, para. 9; *Bérubé* (above), paras. 78-79; VIEWS doc 2013-0514331I7. (Similarly, a capital cost (window replacement) was allowed in computing a capital gain in *Peach*, 2020 TCC 12, para. 67 (under appeal to FCA), even though it may have been wrongly deducted as a current expense in an earlier (statute-barred) year.) [*Contra*, see *Kosek*, 2009 TCC 228, which is likely wrong.] The same solution of appealing a later year applies to non-refundable investment tax credits and other credits: *Marino*,

2020 TCC 50, para. 12 (under appeal to FCA). Refundable credits determined under 152(1)(b) can be appealed in the year they are denied per *Martens*, below. Even a trivial amount of interest assessed means the assessment can be appealed: *Shreedhar*, 2016 TCC 254; but *contra*, see *Nottawasaga Inn*, 2013 TCC 377, para. 32. If what is appealed is income inclusion with an offsetting deduction not sought by the taxpayer, an appeal might be possible: *Shreedhar*, para. 4.

Although a nil assessment cannot be appealed, it operates as an assessment in other respects, including starting a new limitation period: *984274 Alberta*, 2020 FCA 125 (leave to appeal denied 2021 CarswellNat 1167 (SCC)), paras. 57-61, 68, and it **can be issued past the limitation period**: para. 58 [Nitikman, "What is the Effect of a Nil Assessment?", 2531 *Tax Topics* (CCH) 1-7 (Sept. 8, 2020); Vandale & Downie, "Nil Assessments are not a Nothing", XXIII(3) *Tax Litigation* (Federated Press) 8-11 (2020)].

"Although an objection to a notification that no tax is payable is invalid, the CRA follows the practice of reconsidering the issues at the time the objection is filed with a view to resolving them when they are current in the minds of the objector and the CRA auditor": *Appeals Manual* §3.10.1 (§3.10 includes procedures to be followed).

CRA may resist requests to adjust amounts in statute-barred years (VIEWS docs 2010-0352901I7, 2013-0504491I7), as well as carrybacks to a year where the objection period has expired and the carryback is requested in order to open up the year to objection (2010-0374531I7). In *St. Benedict Trust*, 2020 TCC 109 (under appeal to FCA), SBT could not unilaterally reduce old CCA claims so as to extend loss carryforwards. CRA considers that if no Notice of Determination is issued, offsetting adjustments can be made to a year for which no tax is payable, if they do not result in an assessment of tax: 2011-0401241I7; 2012-0459341I7 (business expenses can be substituted for non-capital losses in statute-barred year); 2013-0479161E5 (capital loss in statute-barred year can be amended); 2019 CPA Alberta (tinyurl.com/cra-abtax), income tax q.19 (procedure for corp to amend past capital loss). See also Robson, "Late UCC Additions", 21(12) *Canadian Tax Highlights* (ctf.ca) 6-7 (Dec. 2013).

In *Nottawasaga Inn*, 2013 TCC 377, the TCC held it cannot hear an appeal of interest calculated under 161(7) where the underlying assessment was nil due to loss carrybacks and the basis for the appeal was that CRA wrongly calculated income before applying the carrybacks.

If tax payable for the year is nil, a 152(1.1) loss determination starts the 152(4) 3- or 4-year clock running. Otherwise CRA can assess to deny a loss carryforward in any later year when it is claimed, since that year will not be statute-barred: *New St. James Ltd.*, [1966] C.T.C. 305 (Ex. Ct); *Papier Cascades*, 2006 FCA 419; *3295036 Canada*, 2020 QCCA 1435, para. 22 (leave to appeal denied 2021 CarswellQue 5311 (SCC)). Based on *New St. James*, CRA can challenge factual assumptions about years that are statute-barred: *Atlantic Thermal*, 2016 TCC 135, para. 39. See also IT-512 [cancelled Sept. 30/12]; Income Tax Folio S3-F4-C1 ¶1.113-1.16 and doc 2015-0575921I7 re recalculating UCC balances; docs 9600625, 2008-0284301I7 (CRA can adjust losses or other balances after reassessment deadline where no adjustment results for that year); 2011-0425501E5 (adjustment to statute-barred year's LRIP); *Income Tax Audit Manual* §11.3.3, "Changing the Loss Balance in the Year of Application".

However, 152(1.1) applies only when CRA "ascertains" a loss that was not reported in the return. Therefore, a request for determination of a loss as filed does not fall under 152(1.1), but the determination, if issued, may still start the 152(1.2) clock running since it is arguably a determination "under this Division". 152(1.1) does not require that a nil assessment have been issued: VIEWS doc 2013-0508751I7. Finance thinks CRA can "determine" a loss if that is requested on filing, but CRA disagrees and will do so only if it "ascertains" a different loss than was reported: 2014-0550351C6 [TEI 2014 q.E1].

CRA says a request for an amended loss does not cause the Minister to "ascertain" the loss: VIEWS doc 2011-0401241I7. If CRA "ascertains" the same loss (zero) as claimed in the return, 152(1.1) does not apply: *Petratos*, 2013 TCC 240, para. 38. If CRA "ascertains" a loss different from that filed, it can be compelled to issue a notice of determination of the loss by Federal Court *mandamus* order: *Burnet*, [1999] 3 C.T.C. 60 (FCA); but in *Armstrong*, 2006 FCA 119, *mandamus* was denied after filing an amended return: "An amended income tax return is simply a request that the Minister reassess" (para. 8) [see also Notes to 152(1)].

If no objection is filed to a determination denying or limiting a loss, no objection can be filed for a different year to which the loss was carried over: 152(1.3); *722540 Ontario*, [2002] 1 C.T.C. 2872 (TCC).

In *Inco Ltd.*, 2005 FCA 44 (leave to appeal denied 2005 CarswellNat 2876 (SCC)), a letter from the CRA Tax Centre, answering a query as to what losses a recently-purchased subsidiary had available to claim, was not a 152(1.1) "notice of determination". *Contra*, in *Sterling-Ross*, 2009 TCC 525, SR claimed losses and when the Crown conceded the appeals at the start of trial, the TCC held (para. 16) that CRA thereby made a "determination", so SR could carry the losses over to other years; and in *Hoffman*, 2010 TCC 267, a CRA audit letter rejecting loss claims was held to be a "determination", so an appeal could proceed.

A way to preserve appeal rights for a year to which loss carryovers are applied is to keep a small amount of income (e.g. $100) so some tax is payable. See *407 International*, 2019 TCC 245, para. 8.

See also Michael Lubetsky, "Income Tax Disputes Involving Loss Years", 67(3) *Canadian Tax Journal* 499-531 (2019).

Interpretation Bulletins: IT-488R2: Winding-up of 90%-owned taxable Canadian corporations (cancelled); IT-512: Determination and redetermination of losses.

Information Circulars: 84-1: Revision of capital cost allowance claims and other permissive deductions.

CRA Audit Manual: 11.3.3: Application of losses; 11.5.10: Loss determination.

(1.11) Determination pursuant to subsec. 245(2) — Where at any time the Minister ascertains the tax consequences to a taxpayer by reason of subsection 245(2) with respect to a transaction, the Minister

(a) shall, in the case of a determination pursuant to subsection 245(8), or

(b) may, in any other case,

determine any amount that is relevant for the purposes of computing the income, taxable income or taxable income earned in Canada of, tax or other amount payable by, or amount refundable to, the taxpayer under this Act and, where such a determination is made, the Minister shall send to the taxpayer, with all due dispatch, a notice of determination stating the amount so determined.

Related Provisions: 152(1.111) — Definitions in 245(1) apply; 152(1.12) — Limitation; 152(1.3) — Determination binding; 244(14), (14.1) — Presumption re date of sending of notice of determination; 244(15) — Determination deemed made on date sent; 248(7)(a) — Mail deemed received on day mailed.

Notes: See Notes to 152(1) on the meaning of "all due dispatch".

(1.111) Application of subsec. 245(1) — The definitions in subsection 245(1) apply to subsection (1.11).

Notes: 152(1.111) added in the RSC 1985 (5th Supp) consolidation for tax years ending after Nov. 1991. This rule was formerly in the opening words of 245(1).

(1.12) When determination not to be made — A determination of an amount shall not be made with respect to a taxpayer under subsection (1.11) at a time where that amount is relevant only for the purposes of computing the income, taxable income or taxable income earned in Canada of, tax or other amount payable by, or amount refundable to, the taxpayer under this Act for a taxation year ending before that time.

(1.2) Provisions applicable — Paragraphs 56(1)(l) and 60(o), this Division and Division J, as they relate to an assessment or a reassessment and to assessing or reassessing tax, apply, with any modifications that the circumstances require, to a determination or redetermination under subsection (1.01) and to a determination or redetermination of an amount under this Division or an amount deemed under section 122.61 to be an overpayment on account of a taxpayer's liability under this Part, except that

(a) subsections (1) and (2) do not apply to determinations made under subsections (1.01), (1.1) and (1.11);

(b) an original determination of a taxpayer's non-capital loss, net capital loss, restricted farm loss, farm loss or limited partnership loss for a taxation year may be made by the Minister only at the request of the taxpayer;

(c) subsection 164(4.1) does not apply to a determination made under subsection (1.4); and

(d) if the Minister determines the amount deemed by subsection 122.5(3) or (3.001) to have been paid by an individual for a taxation year to be nil, subsection (2) does not apply to the determination unless the individual requests a notice of determination from the Minister.

Related Provisions: 96(2.1) — Limited partnership losses; 111 — Losses deductible; 160.2(3) — Minister may assess recipient under RRSP or RRIF.

Notes: See Notes to 152(1.1).

Inco Ltd., 2005 FCA 44 (leave to appeal denied 2005 CarswellNat 2876 (SCC)), held that 152(1.2) does not create an independent basis under which the Minister can determine a loss, beyond that allowed under 152(1.1).

Similarly, under 152(1.2), "modifications that the circumstances require" means interpreting the deadline for applying for a Canada Child Benefit as relative to the Minister's determination of eligibility, not the assessment of a past year: *Reynolds*, 2013 TCC 288 (FCA appeal discontinued A-354-13).

Under 152(1.2), 164(1) is to be read so that refunds resulting from a determination can be requested within the "normal *determination* period" rather than the normal reassessment period: *Perfect Fry*, 2007 TCC 133 (aff'd on other grounds 2008 FCA 218). Similarly, it allows redetermination up to 3 years after initial CCB determination: *Jersak (Best)*, 2020 TCC 136, para. 24.

The reference to 152(1.01) means that disability-credit eligibility can be appealed to the Tax Court, overruling *Tozzi*. See Notes to 152(1.01).

152(1.2)(d) (added by 2014 budget bill #1, for 2014 and later tax years and amended to refer to 122.5(3.001) by 2020 COVID bill #1, effective March 25, 2020) relates to an amendment to 122.5(3) under which the GST/HST Credit no longer requires an "application" (by checking a box on the T1 return). CRA will still make a "determination" of whether an individual is entitled to the credit, but is not required to send a Notice of Determination of a nil Credit unless one is requested.

152(1.2) amended by 2011 budget bill #1 to delete reference to 126.1 and add "a determination or redetermination under subsection (1.01)", effective on the same basis as the addition of 152(1.01).

152(1.2)(c) added by 1995-97 technical bill, for determinations after June 18, 1998.

152(1.2) amended by 1992 Economic Statement, effective 1993.

Interpretation Bulletins: IT-488R2: Winding-up of 90%-owned taxable Canadian corporations (cancelled); IT-512: Determination and redetermination of losses.

CRA Audit Manual: 11.5.10: Loss determination.

(1.3) Determination binding — For greater certainty, where the Minister makes a determination of the amount of a taxpayer's non-capital loss, net capital loss, restricted farm loss, farm loss or limited partnership loss for a taxation year or makes a determination under subsection (1.11) with respect to a taxpayer, the determination is (subject to the taxpayer's rights of objection and appeal in respect of the determination and to any redetermination by the Minister) binding on both the Minister and the taxpayer for the purpose of calculating the income, taxable income or taxable income earned in Canada of, tax or other amount payable by, or amount refundable to, the taxpayer, as the case may be, for any taxation year.

Related Provisions: 96(2.1) — Limited partnership loss; 111 — Losses deductible; 160.2(3) — Minister may assess recipient under RRSP or RRIF.

Notes: See Notes to 152(1.1).

Interpretation Bulletins: IT-488R2: Winding-up of 90%-owned taxable Canadian corporations (cancelled); IT-512: Determination and redetermination of losses.

CRA Audit Manual: 11.5.10: Loss determination.

(1.4) Determination in respect of a partnership — The Minister may, within 3 years after the day that is the later of

(a) the day on or before which a member of a partnership is, or but for subsection 220(2.1) would be, required under section 229 of the *Income Tax Regulations* to make an information return for a fiscal period of the partnership, and

(b) the day the return is filed,

determine any income or loss of the partnership for the fiscal period and any deduction or other amount, or any other matter, in respect of the partnership for the fiscal period that is relevant in determining the income, taxable income or taxable income earned in Canada of, tax or other amount payable by, or any amount refundable to or deemed to have been paid or to have been an overpayment by, any member of the partnership for any taxation year under this Part.

Related Provisions: 152(1.2)(c) — Subsec. 164(4.1) does not apply to determination under 152(1.4); 152(1.5), (1.6) — Notice of determination; 152(1.7) — Determination binding; 152(1.8) — Assessment where partnership found not to exist; 152(1.9) — Waiver of limitation period; 163(2.9) — Partnership can be assessed certain penalties as though it were a corporation; 165(1.15) — Objection to determination; 197(6)(b) — Assessment can be made at any time for Part IX.1 distributions tax or tax payable by partner; 244(15) — Determination deemed made on date mailed; *Interpretation Act* 27(5) — Meaning of "within 3 years".

Notes: Before 152(1.4), each partner had to be assessed separately, and assessments could be objected to and appealed separately by each partner. Now a determination of the partnership's income or loss is binding on all partners, and can be objected to by only one partner on behalf of all: 165(1.15).

For 152(1.4)(a), CRA policy does not require a T5013 from some partnerships (see Notes to Reg. 229(1)); this constitutes a 220(2.1) waiver. Such a partnership should consider filing anyway, to start the clock under 152(1.4)(b).

No 152(1.4) determination can be made if the purported partnership is held not to be one: *2078970 Ontario [Lux]*, 2020 FCA 162, paras. 22-33 (if the TCC/FCA so decides, CRA has 1 year to reassess the "partners": 152(1.8)). No determination can be made if the partnership is not required by Reg. 229(1) (not merely exempted by CRA policy) to file a T5013, such as a foreign partnership: VIEWS doc 2018-0768771C6 [2018 APFF q.6].

152(1.4) applies to assessing a partnership a 162(7) or (7.1) penalty: 2011-0397361I7.

152(1.4) is subject to the 152(4) limitation periods, but if time has run, CRA can still assess if there was misrepresentation due to carelessness or neglect (152(4)(a)(i)), since 152(1.2) says "this Division" applies to the determination: 2016-064857I17.

CRA says 152(1.4) allows late assessment of partnership income beyond the normal reassessment period if no partnership return has been filed, due to 152(1.7)(b): 9726115, 2000-0010935, 2008-0285421C6. See also 197(6)(b) to the same effect.

If the time to issue a determination has expired, CRA says it can still directly assess partners whose returns are open: 2005-0111961I7, 2017-073475117; and may but is not required to accept an amendment to a partner's return after the statute-barred date to reflect an amended T5013: 2014-056227I17, 2018-0739141I7. CRA generally permits adjustment to CCA in non-statute-barred years if all partners request it: 2010-0369671E5.

152(1.4) begins "The Minister may"; CRA cannot be forced to issue a determination (unlike 152(1.1)). In doc 2010-035473117, HQ suggests that a local office "decline the taxpayer's invitation to make the determination".

152(1.4) added by 1995-97 technical bill, for determinations made after June 18, 1998.

CRA Audit Manual: 11.5.10: Loss determination.

(1.5) Notice of determination — Where a determination is made under subsection (1.4) in respect of a partnership for a fiscal period, the Minister shall send a notice of the determination to the partnership and to each person who was a member of the partnership during the fiscal period.

Related Provisions: 152(1.6) — Determination valid even if notice not received by partners; 244(14) — Presumption re date of mailing of determination; 244(20) — Notice mailed to partnership deemed provided to all partners; 248(7)(a) — Mail deemed received on day mailed.

Notes: 152(1.5) added by 1995-97 technical bill, for determinations made after June 18, 1998.

(1.6) Absence of notification — No determination made under subsection (1.4) in respect of a partnership for a fiscal period is invalid solely because one or more persons who were members of the partnership during the period did not receive a notice of the determination.

Related Provisions: 244(20) — Notice mailed to partnership deemed provided to all partners.

Notes: This applies only where one or more *partners* have not received the notice. If the *partnership* does not receive the notice, 152(1.6) does not apply, and it can be argued that the determination is invalid because it was never mailed. See Notes to 165(1) under "*Must have been sent*". In such a case, 152(1.7) would not apply, and the partner would have the right to object to a reassessment that was based on CRA's determination of the partnership's income. See also Notes to 152(1.7).

152(1.6) added by 1995-97 technical bill, for determinations made after June 18, 1998.

(1.7) Binding effect of determination — Where the Minister makes a determination under subsection (1.4) or a redetermination in respect of a partnership,

(a) subject to the rights of objection and appeal of the member of the partnership referred to in subsection 165(1.15) in respect of the determination or redetermination, the determination or redetermination is binding on the Minister and each member of the partnership for the purposes of calculating the income, taxable income or taxable income earned in Canada of, tax or other amount payable by, or any amount refundable to or deemed to have been paid or to have been an overpayment by, the members for any taxation year under this Part; and

(b) notwithstanding subsections (4), (4.01), (4.1) and (5), the Minister may, before the end of the day that is one year after the day on which all rights of objection and appeal expire or are determined in respect of the determination or redetermination, assess the tax, interest, penalties or other amounts payable and determine an amount deemed to have been paid or to have been an overpayment under this Part in respect of any member of the partnership and any other taxpayer for any taxation year as may be necessary to give effect to the determination or redetermination or a decision of the Tax Court of Canada, the Federal Court of Appeal or the Supreme Court of Canada.

Notes: In *Cummings*, 2009 TCC 310 (FCA appeal dismissed for delay A-347-09), a waiver of appeal rights in a settlement agreement executed before the formal determination did not cause the appeal rights to "expire" for purposes of 152(1.7)(b). See John Yuan, "Two years for the price of one", 1955 *Tax Topics* (CCH) 3-4 (Aug. 27, 2009).

In *Menzies*, 2016 TCC 73, notification to a tax shelter LP's general partner was binding on the limited partners; 244(20) applied (see also VIEWS doc 2016-0640321I7).

In *Tedesco*, 2019 FCA 235 (reversing *Stewart*, 2018 TCC 75), CRA assessed partners of a limited partnership to deny losses, and issued a Notice of Determination to the LP. The LP appealed but filed a Notice of Discontinuance. The FCA held the partners could continue their own appeals [Studniberg, "A deemed dismissal does not amount to a determination by deeming", 68(1) *Canadian Tax Journal* 251-61 (2020)].

If the purported partnership does not exist, 152(1.7) does not apply: *2078970 Ontario [Lux]*, 2020 FCA 162, para. 33.

152(1.7)(b) amended by 2002 courts administration bill to change "Federal Court of Canada" to "Federal Court of Appeal", effective July 2, 2003. 152(1.7) added by 1995-97 technical bill, for determinations made after June 18, 1998.

(1.8) Time to assess — Where, as a result of representations made to the Minister that a person was a member of a partnership in respect of a fiscal period, a determination is made under subsection (1.4) for the period and the Minister, the Tax Court of Canada, the Federal Court of Appeal or the Supreme Court of Canada concludes at a subsequent time that the partnership did not exist for the period or that, throughout the period, the person was not a member of the partnership, the Minister may, notwithstanding subsections (4), (4.1) and (5), within one year after that subsequent time, assess the tax, interest, penalties or other amounts payable, or determine an amount deemed to have been paid or to have been an overpayment under this Part, by any taxpayer for any taxation year, but only to the extent that the assessment or determination can reasonably be regarded

(a) as relating to any matter that was relevant in the making of the determination made under subsection (1.4);

(b) as resulting from the conclusion that the partnership did not exist for the period; or

(c) as resulting from the conclusion that the person was, throughout the period, not a member of the partnership.

Related Provisions [subsec. 152(1.8)]: 165(1.1)(a), (d) — Limitation of right to object; 169(2)(a), (d) — Limitation of right to appeal; *Interpretation Act* 27(5) — Meaning of "within one year".

Notes: In *Sentinel Hill*, 2014 FCA 161, the Minister had apparently concluded that the partnerships did not exist, by so alleging in the Reply; but the TCC declined to consider under Rule 58 (see 174(1) Notes) whether time had run under 152(1.8), since the partnerships' existence was in dispute. The FCA agreed with the TCC.

If the TCC, FCA or SCC rules that no partnership exists in an appeal from a 152(1.4) determination (not necessarily a later proceeding), 152(1.8) allows CRA a year to reassess the investors: *2078970 Ontario [Lux]*, 2020 FCA 162, para. 35.

Opening words of 152(1.8) amended by 2002 courts administration bill to change "Federal Court of Canada" to "Federal Court of Appeal", effective July 2, 2003.

152(1.8) added by 1995-97 technical bill, for determinations made after June 18, 1998.

(1.9) Waiver of determination limitation period — A waiver in respect of the period during which the Minister may make a determination under subsection (1.4) in respect of a partnership for a fiscal period may be made by one member of the partnership if that member is

(a) designated for that purpose in the information return made under section 229 of the *Income Tax Regulations* for the fiscal period; or

(b) otherwise expressly authorized by the partnership to so act.

Notes: See Notes to 152(4) and (4.01) re waivers. One might think that 152(1.9) should be amended to have 152(4.01) and (4.1) apply to it, so that waivers can be limited in scope and can be revoked. However, Finance's view is that 152(1.9) does not create a new waiver right, as that already exists via 152(1.2); 152(1.9) merely specifies who can sign the waiver. CRA seems to agree: doc 2014-056227I17. If the Courts believe it creates a separate waiver right, then such waiver is not revocable because 152(4.1) does not apply.

152(1.9) added by 2012 budget bill #1, effective June 29, 2012.

Forms: T108: Waiver in respect of the normal determination period for a partnership; T109: Notice of revocation of a waiver in respect of a normal determination period for a partnership.

(2) Notice of assessment — After examination of a return, the Minister shall send a notice of assessment to the person by whom the return was filed.

Proposed Amendment — Electronic notices of assessment

Federal Budget, Supplementary Information, April 19, 2021: See under 244(14.1), under heading "Notices of Assessment".

Related Provisions: 158 — Remainder payable forthwith after assessment mailed; 197(6)(a) — Notice of assessment can be sent to partnership for Part IX.1 distributions tax; 244(14), (15) — Mailing date of assessment; 244(14.1) — Electronic notice.

Notes: A notice of assessment (NoA) is valid only if sent to the taxpayer's correct address in CRA's files, but personal delivery is as good as mailing. See Notes to 165(1) under "Must have been sent".

A NoA need not have any particular form: *Stephens*, [1987] 1 C.T.C. 88 (FCA), and need not specify reasons: *Laurin*, [1960] C.T.C. 194 (Exch. Ct); *Suffolk*, 2010 TCC 295. A NoA "must on its face be made for a taxation year", and if the year is missing the assessment may not be valid: *Sicoli*, 2013 TCC 207, para. 9.

The following are *not* a NoA: interest determination on Statement of Account, with no assessment of tax (*Homa*, 2011 TCC 230 and 2012 TCC 110); letter denying requested adjustment (*Petratos*, 2013 TCC 240, para. 30); letter saying assessment is being issued (*Gordon*, 2009 TCC 271 (FCA appeal discontinued A-140-09); *Jablonski*, 2012 TCC 29; *Newfoundland Transshipment*, 2013 TCC 259).

CRA has been sending taxpayers a "new, simple, easier to read Notice of Assessment" since Feb. 2016, with "streamlined" content. CRA sends out about 29 million NoAs to individuals each year. (The new NoA identifies the taxpayer on the first page only, which can be a challenge for a professional dealing with several Notices.)

CRA Audit Manual: 11.5.7: Notice of assessment, reassessment and notice of return adjustment.

Forms: T67A, T67AC, T67AN, T453, T456, T457, T492: Notices of assessment; T1132: Alternative address authorization.

(3) Liability not dependent on assessment — Liability for the tax under this Part is not affected by an incorrect or incomplete assessment or by the fact that no assessment has been made.

Related Provisions: 152(4), (6), (8) — Assessment and reassessment; 160.2(3) — Minister may assess recipient; 165 — Objections to assessments; 166 — Assessment not to be vacated by reason of improper procedures; 169 — Appeal.

Notes: Based on 152(3), *Burke*, 2012 TCC 378, paras. 41-43, held that CRA has the right to collect on an unmailed notice of assessment that matches what the taxpayer filed. 152(3) is rarely applied, however.

(3.1) Definition of "normal reassessment period" — For the purposes of subsections (4), (4.01), (4.2), (4.3), (5) and (9), the normal reassessment period for a taxpayer in respect of a taxation year is

(a) if at the end of the year the taxpayer is a mutual fund trust or a corporation other than a Canadian-controlled private corporation, the period that ends four years after the earlier of the day of sending of a notice of an original assessment under this Part in respect of the taxpayer for the year and the day of sending of an original notification that no tax is payable by the taxpayer for the year; and

(b) in any other case, the period that ends three years after the earlier of the day of sending of a notice of an original assessment under this Part in respect of the taxpayer for the year and the day of sending of an original notification that no tax is payable by the taxpayer for the year.

Enacted Amendment — *Time Limits and Other Periods Act (COVID-19)* [TLOPA]

[See under 169(1). TLOPA 7(1) permitted the Minister of National Revenue to extend the 152(3.1) deadline by up to 6 months due to the COVID-19 pandemic, but no extension can end after Dec. 31, 2020. See also tinyurl.com/cra-tlopa, reproduced in Notes to TLOPA 7(1) — ed.]

Related Provisions: 136(1) — Cooperative corporation may be private corporation for purposes of s. 152; 137(7) — Credit union may be private corporation; 152(4), (6), (8) — Assessment and reassessment; 160.2(3) — Minister may assess recipient; 165 — Objections to assessments; 166 — Irregularities; 169, 172 — Appeal; 244(14), (14.1) — Date when notice sent; 244(15) — Date when assessment made.

Notes: See Notes to 152(4).

152(3.1)(a) and (b) amended by 2010 budget bill #2, effective Dec. 15, 2010, to change "mailing" to "sending" (4 places), to accommodate electronic notices under 244(14.1).

2001 technical bill, s. 150, provides a transitional rule (reproduced up to the 34th ed.) overriding the normal reassessment period for an individual who became non-resident, or a trust that made a distribution subject to 107(5), from Oct. 2/96 to June 13/99.

152(3.1) amended by 1998 Budget (effective for appeals disposed of after June 17, 1999), 1995-97, 1992 and 1991 technical bills, and 1989 Budget.

(3.2) Determination of deemed overpayment [Canada Child Benefit] — A taxpayer may, during any month, request in writing that the Minister determine the amount deemed by subsection 122.61(1) to be an overpayment on account of the taxpayer's liability under this Part for a taxation year that arose during the month or any of the 11 preceding months.

Related Provisions: 152(3.3) — Notice of determination.

Notes: 152(3.2) added by 1992 Child Benefit bill, effective 1993.

(3.3) Notice of determination [Canada Child Benefit] — On receipt of the request referred to in subsection (3.2), the Minister shall, with all due dispatch, determine the amounts deemed by subsection 122.61(1) to be overpayments on account of the taxpayer's liability under this Part that arose during the months in respect of which the request was made or determine that there is no such amount, and shall send a notice of the determination to the taxpayer.

Related Provisions: 152(1.2) — Determination can be objected to and appealed.

Notes: The regional Tax Centre makes the determination: VIEWS doc 2009-0308031E5.

152(3.3) added by 1992 Child Benefit bill, effective 1993.

(3.4) COVID-19 — notice of determination [CEWS or CERS] — The Minister may at any time determine the amount deemed by any of subsections 125.7(2) to (2.2) to be an overpayment on account of a taxpayer's liability under this Part that arose during a "qualifying period" (as defined in subsection 125.7(1)), or determine that there is no such amount, and send a notice of the determination to the taxpayer.

Related Provisions: 152(1.2) — Determination can be objected to and appealed.

Notes: A CEWS or CERS determination can be appealed via 152(1.2) even if there is no tax to pay for the year.

152(3.4) added by 2020 COVID bill #3, effective April 11, 2020; amended by 2020 COVID bill #5, effective Nov. 19, 2020, to refer to 125.7(2.1) (CERS); and amended by 2021 budget bill #1, effective June 29, 2021, to refer to 125.7(2.2) (CRHP).

See 152(3.5) Notes for former 152(3.4).

(3.5) [Repealed]

Notes: Former 152(3.4) and (3.5) repealed by 2002-2013 technical bill, for forms filed after March 20, 2003. They provided for a "determination" of the UI premium tax credit under 126.1, which applied only for 1993. They were added by the 1992 Economic Statement.

(4) Assessment and reassessment [limitation period] — The Minister may at any time make an assessment, reassessment or additional assessment of tax for a taxation year, interest or penalties, if any, payable under this Part by a taxpayer or notify in writing any person by whom a return of income for a taxation year has been filed that no tax is payable for the year, except that an assessment, reassessment or additional assessment may be made after the taxpayer's normal reassessment period in respect of the year only if

(a) the taxpayer or person filing the return

(i) has made any misrepresentation that is attributable to neglect, carelessness or wilful default or has committed any fraud in filing the return or in supplying any information under this Act, or

(ii) has filed with the Minister a waiver in prescribed form within the normal reassessment period for the taxpayer in respect of the year;

(b) the assessment, reassessment or additional assessment is made before the day that is 3 years after the end of the normal reassessment period for the taxpayer in respect of the year and

(i) is required under subsection (6) or (6.1), or would be so required if the taxpayer had claimed an amount by filing the prescribed form referred to in the subsection on or before the day referred to in the subsection,

(ii) is made as a consequence of the assessment or reassessment pursuant to this paragraph or subsection (6) of tax payable by another taxpayer,

(iii) is made

(A) as a consequence of a "transaction" (as defined in subsection 247(1)) involving the taxpayer and a non-resident person with whom the taxpayer was not dealing at arm's length, or

(B) in respect of any income, loss or other amount in relation to a foreign affiliate of the taxpayer,

(iii.1) is made, if the taxpayer is non-resident and carries on a business in Canada, as a consequence of

(A) an allocation by the taxpayer of revenues or expenses as amounts in respect of the Canadian business (other than revenues and expenses that relate solely to the Canadian business, that are recorded in the books of account of the Canadian business, and the documentation in support of which is kept in Canada), or

(B) a notional transaction between the taxpayer and its Canadian business, where the transaction is recognized for the purposes of the computation of an amount under this Act or an applicable tax treaty.

(iv) is made as a consequence of a payment or reimbursement of any income or profits tax to or by the government of a country other than Canada or a government of a state, province or other political subdivision of any such country,

(v) is made as a consequence of a reduction under subsection 66(12.73) of an amount purported to be renounced under section 66,

(vi) is made in order to give effect to the application of subsection 118.1(15) or (16), or

(vii) is made to give effect to the application of any of sections 94, 94.1 and 94.2;

(b.1) an information return described in subsection 237.1(7) or 237.3(2) that is required to be filed in respect of a deduction or claim made by the taxpayer in relation to a tax shelter, or in respect of a tax benefit (as defined in subsection 245(1)) to the taxpayer from an avoidance transaction (as defined in subsection 245(3)), is not filed as and when required, and the assessment, reassessment or additional assessment is made before the day that is three years after the day on which the information return is filed;

(b.2) the assessment, reassessment or additional assessment is made before the day that is three years after the end of the normal reassessment period for the taxpayer in respect of the year and if

(i) the taxpayer, or a partnership of which the taxpayer is a member, has failed to file for the year a prescribed form as and when required under subsection 233.3(3) or to report on the prescribed form the information required in respect of a specified foreign property (as defined in subsection 233.3(1)) held by the taxpayer at any time during the year, and

(ii) the taxpayer has failed to report, in the return of income for the year, an amount in respect of a specified foreign property that is required to be included in computing the taxpayer's income for the year;

(b.3) the following conditions apply:

(i) the taxpayer, or a partnership of which the taxpayer is a member (directly or indirectly through one or more partnerships), disposes in the year of real or immovable property,

(ii) the taxpayer is not a "real estate investment trust" (as defined in subsection 122.1(1)) for the year,

(iii) if the disposition is by a corporation or partnership, the property is capital property of the corporation or partnership, as the case may be,

(iv) the disposition is not reported in

(A) if the disposition is by the taxpayer, the return of income of the taxpayer under this Part for the year, or

(B) if the disposition is by a partnership, the partnership's return required to be filed for the year under section 229 of the *Income Tax Regulations*, and

(v) in the case that the disposition is not reported in the return described in clause (iv)(A) or (B) and the taxpayer subsequently reports the disposition by filing a prescribed form amending the taxpayer's return of income under this Part for the year, the assessment, reassessment or additional assessment is made before the day that is three years after the day on which the prescribed form amending the return is filed;

(b.4) the assessment, reassessment or additional assessment is made before the day that is six years after the end of the normal reassessment period for the taxpayer in respect of the year if

(i) a reassessment of tax for the year was required under subsection (6), or would have been so required if the taxpayer had claimed an amount by filing the prescribed form referred to in that subsection on or before the day referred to in that subsection, in order to take into account a deduction claimed under section 111 in respect of a loss for a subsequent taxation year,

(ii) an assessment, reassessment, additional assessment of tax or notification that no tax is payable for the subsequent taxation year referred to in subparagraph (i) was made or issued after the normal reassessment period in respect of the subsequent taxation year as a consequence of a transaction involving the taxpayer and a non-resident person with whom the taxpayer was not dealing at arm's length, and

(iii) the assessment, reassessment, additional assessment or notification that no tax is payable referred to in subparagraph (ii) reduced the amount of the loss for the subsequent taxation year;

(c) the taxpayer or person filing the return of income has filed with the Minister a waiver in prescribed form within the additional three-year period referred to in paragraph (b) or (b.1);

(c.1) the taxpayer or person filing the return of income has filed with the Minister a waiver in prescribed form within the additional three-year period referred to in paragraph (b.2); or

(d) as a consequence of a change in the allocation of the taxpayer's taxable income earned in a province as determined under the law of a province that provides rules similar to those prescribed for the purposes of section 124, an assessment, reassessment or additional assessment of tax for a taxation year payable by a corporation under a law of a province that imposes on the corporation a tax similar to the tax imposed under this Part (in this paragraph referred to as a "provincial reassessment") is made, and as a consequence of the provincial reassessment, an assessment, reassessment or additional assessment is made on or before the day that is one year after the later of

(i) the day on which the Minister is advised of the provincial reassessment, and

(ii) the day that is 90 days after the day of sending of a notice of the provincial reassessment.

Enacted Amendment — *Time Limits and Other Periods Act (COVID-19)* [TLOPA]

[See under 169(1). TLOPA 7(1) permits the Minister of National Revenue to extend the 152(4) deadline by up to 6 months due to the COVID-19 pandemic, but no extension can end after Dec. 31, 2020. See also tinyurl.com/cra-tlopa, reproduced in Notes to TLOPA 7(1) — ed.]

Related Provisions

Late reassessment allowed despite 152(4): 12(2.2) — Election re 12(1)(x) inclusion; 21(5) — Election to capitalize interest; 49(4) — Transfer of capital gain from option to underlying property when option exercised; 59.1(b) — Involuntary disposition of resource property; 67.5(2) — Illegal payments; 69(12) — Disposition of property below market value; 74.2(4) — Election for spousal attribution to apply on emigration; 80.04(9) — Transfer of forgiven debt to related person; 86.1(5) — Foreign spinoff; 118.1(11) — Determination of value of cultural property; 127(17) — Agreement to transfer or allocate SR&ED expenditures; 128.1(6)(d), 128.1(7)(i) — Eliminating departure tax paid by taxpayer who returns to Canada; 143.2(15) — Tax shelter investment limitations; 143.4(7) — Denial of contingent amounts in expenditures; 146(8.01) — Home Buyer's Plan or Lifelong Learning Plan withdrawal found not to qualify; 152(1.7) — Assessment of taxpayer following determination of partnership income or loss; 160(2) — Assessment where tax debtor transfers property not arm's length; 160.2(3) — Assessment of recipient of funds under RRSP or RRIF; 161.1(7) — Where corporation claims interest offset from other year; 165(5) — Reassessment following notice of objection; 180.01(2)(e) — Redetermination of net capital loss on election to undo stock option deferral; 184(4)(b)(ii) — Election re excess capital dividend; 185.1(3)(b)(ii) — Election re excess eligible dividend; 191.2(3), 191.3(3) — Election or agreement re taxable preferred shares for Part VI.1 tax; 197(6) — Tax on SIFT partnerships; 220(3.1) — Waiver by CRA of interest or penalty; 220(3.4) — Acceptance by CRA of late or amended election or revocation; 237.1(6.2) — Denial of tax shelter deduction while penalty unpaid; 237.3(7) — Denial of deduction on reportable transaction; 245(8) — Adjustment following application of GAAR. (Many transitional application rules also permit reassessment notwithstanding 152(4) to (5). See Notes to 88(1.8), 88(3), 149(1)(d.5) and 152(4.2) for examples.).

Other issues: 129(1)(b) — Dividend refund where requested by corporation within reassessment deadline; 131(2)(b), 132(1)(b) — Capital gains refund where requested by mutual fund within reassessment deadline; 152(1.9) — Waiver of limitation period for determining partnership income or loss; 152(3.1) — Normal reassessment period; 152(4.01) — Limitation on extended assessments; 152(4.1) — Where waiver revoked; 152(4.2) — Reassessment with taxpayer's consent; 152(4.3) — Consequential assessment; 152(5) — Limitation on assessments; 158 — Payment of balance on assessment; 164(1)(b) — Refund where requested by taxpayer within reassessment deadline; 165(1.1), 169(2) — No right to object or appeal to 152(4)(b)(i) reassessment; 173(2), 174(5)(c) — Reference to Tax Court stops reassessment clock running; 231.6(7) — Time complying with demand for foreign-based information does not count; 231.8 — Time adjudicating demand for information or compliance order does not count; 244(14), (14.1) — Date when notice sent; 244(15) — Date when assessment made; Reg. 1106(1)"application for a certificate of completion"(b) — Waiver required to extend film tax credit application date; *Interpretation Act* 26 — Deadline on Sunday or holiday extended to next business day.

Notes: If a year cannot be assessed due to 152(4), it is **"statute-barred"**, meaning barred by the statute (the Act). The term "prescribed" should not be used for this, nor should the limitation period be called a "prescription"; these are mistranslations from French "prescrit", and correct in English only when referring to Quebec *Civil Code* deadlines (since the official English version of the *Civil Code* uses this word).

The **normal deadline for reassessment** is in 152(4) opening words: 3 or 4 years from the first assessment date (the 152(3.1) "normal reassessment period"). (The date on the notice is normally the assessment date: 244(14)–(15).) It is extended by 3 more years for the reasons in 152(4)(b). (It could also be extended in 2020 by the *Time Limits and Other Periods Act (COVID-19)*, for up to 6 months. See TLOPA s. 7(1), in 169(1) Enacted Amendment.) Thus, for a non-CCPC claiming a loss carryback, the deadline is 7 years: 2010-0364101I7, 2010-0387021I7, 2010-0387441I7. A late reassessment to reduce a loss does not permit reassessment of an earlier year where the loss was claimed: 2010-0388491I7. A 152(4)(b) reassessment can be issued more than once: *Agazarian*, 2004 FCA 32; leave to appeal denied 2004 CarswellNat 4638 (SCC). For a partnership, a CRA "determination" of income or loss is needed to start the clock running for all partners: 152(1.4), (1.7). See 152(1.1) Notes re changing amounts in statute-barred "nil assessment" years to carry forward to later years.

Assessment under a different Part (e.g. Part X.1, RRSP overcontributions), not previously assessed, is not statute-barred even if the Part I assessment was more than 3 years earlier: *Hall*, 2016 TCC 221; *Grenon*, 2021 TCC 30 (under appeal to FCA), paras. 470-472; *Grenon*, paras. 522-536 (Part XI.1 tax on RRSP trust).

"Additional assessment" (AA): An assessment that changes a year's tax from the last assessment is a "reassessment", not an AA: *Rio Tinto*, 2014 TCC 288. In the author's view, since reassessments are always absolute (fixing all tax for the year) and not relative, an AA in 152 can only mean an assessment of penalties (e.g. *684761 B.C.*, 2015 TCC 288, para. 14), or tax under a different Part (e.g. Part X.1: *Hall*, 2016 TCC 221). See also *Rio Tinto*, 2017 TCC 67, paras. 224-278 (FCA appeal discontinued A-153-17).

There is no assessment deadline if no initial assessment has been issued: doc 2011-0399451I7. If an Ontario taxpayer filed and was assessed as resident in another province, CRA says no Ont. assessment has been issued so there is no deadline for assessing Ont. tax: 2013-0476501I7. In *Rousseau*, 2020 QCCA 1308 (leave to appeal denied 2021 CarswellQue 3905), R filed as Alberta-resident and did not file Quebec returns, so Quebec assessments many years later were valid.

If an "arbitrary" assessment is issued without a return being filed, that still starts the clock running, so if the taxpayer files a return more than 3 (or 4) years later, CRA cannot reassess (other than under 152(4.2) for individuals): *6075240 Canada*, 2020 FCA 194 (leave to appeal denied 2021 CarswellNat 2069 (SCC)); *2750-4711 Québec*, 2016 FC 579, paras. 6, 10; *Blackwell*, 2007 TCC 695, para. 40. This is correct in the author's view: 152(1) is subject to the 152(4) deadline; and the reference to "by whom a return... has been filed" in 152(4) opening words applies only to notifying that no tax is payable.

VIEWS docs 2014-0525371I7 and 2014-0526451I7 say failure to file is a "misrepresentation" triggering 152(4)(a)(i), which CRA has advised is based on: a comma in the French wording; the parallel wording in ETA s. 298(4); a common-law principle that when a person has a duty, an omission can be a misrepresentation; and the principle that non-compliance should not give a taxpayer a better result than compliance. In the author's view, not filing is plainly not a misrepresentation, especially given the parallel rule for gross negligence penalties (see Notes to 163(2)); see Sorensen, "CRA's Position on Late Reassessments", 22(11) *Canadian Tax Highlights* (ctf.ca) 5-6 (Nov. 2014).

If no return is filed or assessment issued for 10 years and the tax was payable on March 4, 2004, CRA may be statute-barred from collecting: see Notes to 222(3).

Many provisions in the Act and amending bills provide that assessments can be made "notwithstanding subsections 152(4) to (5)", and so have no limitation period, e.g. 67.5(2) (illegal payments non-deductible), 143.2(15) (tax shelter investment), 143.4(7) (deduction of contingent amount). See Related Provisions annotation above, subheading "Late reassessment allowed". See also Notes to 88(1.8), 88(3), 149(1)(d.5) and 152(4.2) up to PITA 58th ed. for special "late reassessment" rules for the 2002-2013 technical bill. Other assessments can be made "at any time" and so have no limitation period: 159(3) (liability of legal representative), 160(2) (non-arm's length transfer by tax debtor), 160.1(3) (spouse liable for overpaid Canada Child Benefit), 160.2(3) (RRSP payment to non-annuitant), 160.21(4) (RDSP payment), 160.3(2) (RCA payment), 227(10)–(10.1) (assessment re source deductions or non-resident withholding tax, or of corporate director).

A late assessment consequential on that of a related taxpayer is invalid: see 152(4.3) Notes.

If a reassessment is vacated or is held to be void, the previous assessment is reinstated: *Lornport Investments*, [1992] C.T.C. 351 (FCA), para. 8; *Ford*, 2014 FCA 257, para. 16; *Blackburn Radio*, 2012 TCC 255; *Bolton Steel*, 2014 TCC 94, para. 48; *984274 Alberta*, 2019 TCC 85, para. 52 (rev'd on other grounds 2020 FCA 125; leave to appeal denied 2021 CarswellNat 1167 (SCC)).

If the deadline is a Sunday or holiday (and Saturday in most provinces), the reassessment can be issued on the next business day: see Notes to *Interpretation Act* s. 26. See also 244(14) and (15), determining the date of the reassessment.

The reassessment period expires at the end of the 3-year anniversary day, so for an assessment issued on March 16, 1995, a reassessment on March 16, 1998 was valid: *Brunette*, [2001] 1 C.T.C. 2008 (TCC); VIEWS docs 2006-0183801I7, 2015-0614161I7 (see also *Interpretation Act* 27(2)). See Notes to 248(7) re CRA meeting the deadline by mailing or couriering the reassessment on the last day.

In *Trom Electric*, 2004 TCC 727, Trom incorrectly failed to include construction lien holdbacks in income each year, counting them in the next year instead. It was reassessed for 1992-94, at a time when 1991 was statute-barred. Trom successfully argued that the $500,000 it had reported in 1992 had to be removed as it belonged to 1991, even though 1991 could no longer be assessed! The Crown's argument, that Trom was estopped from excluding the amount from 1992 because it had failed to report it in 1991, was rejected. Similarly, in *Heritage Education Funds*, 2010 TCC 161, amounts were excluded from income because they should have been taxed in an earlier year. *Contra* (more or less), see *Jones Development*, 2009 TCC 397, as explained in Bradley Thompson, "Taxpayer not permitted to include year that was statute-barred", 1973 *Tax Topics* (CCH) 7-8 (Dec. 31, 2009).

152(4) does not prevent CRA from fixing the cost of an asset in a statute-barred year for later CCA claims (*Lussier*, [1998] 2 C.T.C. 2794 (TCC)) or for a later transfer-pricing adjustment (VIEWS doc 2016-0631631I7); or to change a statute-barred year's RDTOH under 129(3) (2002-0157005); or to change an old addition to the capital dividend account (2006-0185291E5); or from denying a charitable donation made in a statute-barred year and carried forward (*Okafor*, 2018 TCC 31, para. 23). (See Notes to 152(1.1).) Nor does it apply to initial assessment of a 247(3) transfer pricing penalty: 2016-0631631I7. See 2011-0429991E5, 2018-0768861C6 [2018 APFF q.15] re application to a price adjustment clause.

CRA's view is that the deadline under 152(4) applies only to the "same" return. An individual who filed a return under s. 216 (rental income of a non-resident) and was assessed can still be assessed on other income more than 3 years later: VIEWS doc 2002-0146627.

Treaties also extend time limits for adjustments relating to double taxation (e.g., 6 years in the Canada-U.S. tax treaty, Art. IX:3 and XXVI:2).

CRA will normally reassess on request to reduce tax within the 152(4) deadline (or 152(4.2) for individuals) to correct an amount the taxpayer overlooked, but not for permissive deductions (like CCA) or to benefit from another taxpayer's court decision: Information Circulars 75-7R3 para. 4, 07-1R1 paras. 71-74, VIEWS docs 2004-0085251E5, 2015-0598321C6 [2015 APFF q.25]. The Federal Court can review a CRA refusal to reassess a past year: *Abakhan & Associates (Taylor Ventures)*, 2007 FC 1327 (appeal to FCA dismissed for delay A-30-08).

An assessment that is out of time (and not allowed by 152(4)(a)-(d), discussed below) is void *even if not objected to*, despite 152(8): *Lornport Investments*, [1992] C.T.C. 351 (FCA); *Canadian Marconi*, [1991] 2 C.T.C. 352 (FCA); *Blackburn Radio*, 2012 TCC 255, para. 62; *Cougar Helicopters*, 2017 TCC 126; *984274 Alberta*, 2020 FCA 125 (leave to appeal denied 2021 CarswellNat 1167 (SCC)), para. 55 (holding that *Freitas*, 2018 FCA 110, para. 22 "manifestly overlooked this established line of cases"). This principle does not apply to a nil assessment, which can be issued at any time: *984274 Alberta*, para. 58.

152(4)(a): If there is fraud, or misrepresentation (**MR**) due to "neglect, carelessness or wilful default", there is no time limit on a reassessment relating to the MR or fraud (152(4.01)(a)). The onus is on CRA to prove carelessness or neglect: *Deyab*, 2020 FCA 222, para. 25 (leave to appeal denied 2021 CarswellNat 1815 (SCC)); *Maurice Taylor*, [1961] C.T.C. 211 (Exch. Ct); *Bigayan*, [2000] 1 C.T.C. 2229 (TCC); *Savard*, 2008 TCC 62; *Wachsmann*, 2009 TCC 420; *Papier Domco*, 2011 TCC 441; *Amoako-Boatey*, 2016 TCC 282, para. 13; *Phillip*, 2019 TCC 37, para. 32. The threshold is lower than for a 163(2) penalty: *Deyab* (above), para. 63; VIEWS doc 2013-0509051I7. It is a "real burden of proof, not a mere formality", but "substantially less demanding" than

163(2): *Chaumont*, 2009 TCC 493. It is "not a particularly heavy onus": *Jacobsen*, 2012 TCC 25, para. 24. The onus is not met if the Crown fails to address the issue at the hearing and raises it only in written argument: *D'Andrea*, 2011 TCC 298, para. 47. The onus was not met by showing that many others in the same donor group had admitted to getting kickbacks for their donations: *van der Steen*, 2019 TCC 23, paras. 83-85 (aff'd on other grounds 2020 FCA 168). The Crown has the onus only if the appellant raises the issue in the Notice of Appeal (**NA**): *Naguib*, 2004 FCA 40 (leave to appeal denied 2004 CarswellNat 2825); *DiCosmo*, 2017 FCA 60, paras. 6-9 (consistent with *Farhan*, 2015 TCC 243, para. 19; and overruling *Yunus*, 2015 TCC 272, para. 85) (but see also *Custodio* in Notes to 227.1(2)). *Wood*, 2020 TCC 87, paras. 5-8 (under appeal to FCA), goes further: because the NA did not raise the issue, W could not argue it at trial. Due to the onus, the Crown could in theory be required to present its case first in Tax Court, but not in practice: *Kozar*, 2010 TCC 389, para. 30. The Crown's Reply must allege actual facts that are MR, not restate the legislation as a conclusion of mixed fact and law: *Mont-Bruno*, 2017 CarswellNat 3165 (TCC), para. 19 (the rewrite was acceptable in 2018 TCC 105). The Crown's case must be based on more than "conjecture": *Jencik*, 2004 TCC 295.

The mere existence of misrepresentation (MR) is not enough: *Boucher*, 2004 FCA 46; leave to appeal denied 2004 CarswellNat 3761 (SCC). Many cases say that *any* incorrect statement is MR, so that the only real test is carelessness or neglect: *Foot*, [1964] C.T.C. 317 (SCC); *Maurice Taylor*, [1961] C.T.C. 211 (Ex. Ct); *Nesbitt*, 1996 CarswellNat 1916 (FCA); *Ridge Run*, 2007 TCC 68; *Francis*, 2014 TCC 137, para. 20. *Contra*, see *Bisson*, [1972] C.T.C. 446 (FCTD) (error with no negligence is not MR); *Bondfield Construction*, 2005 TCC 78 (incorrect reporting by taxpayer relying on professionals was not MR); *Petric*, 2006 TCC 306 (*bona fide* belief in valuation meant there was no MR). In *Inwest Investments*, 2015 BCSC 1375, the Court held (para. 126) that a statement of fact on a return can be MR, but a filing position based on law (or mixed fact and law) is not if the position is reasonable. On whether reporting trading gains as capital gains can ever be MR given the French wording "présentation erronée *des faits*", *MacIsaac Consulting*, 2020 TCC 44 left the question open for trial.

The MR must take place *when filing the return*, not at another time: *Vachon*, 2014 FCA 224, paras. 3-4, 9; *Vine Estate*, 2015 FCA 125, para. 33-34; *Aridi*, 2013 TCC 74, para. 34; *Robertson*, 2015 TCC 246, paras. 18, 33 (aff'd without discussing this point 2016 FCA 303). Misrepresentation in supplying information during the audit (not in the return) cannot trigger 152(4)(a)(i): *Ross*, 2013 TCC 333, para. 77; and even if it could, not if the misrepresentation is about a later year rather than the year being reassessed: para. 57. However, note that 152(4)(a)(i) refers to MR "in filing the return or in supplying any information under this Act", so the above cases should be read with caution. CRA says in RC199 that a MR in a Voluntary Disclosure (see Notes to 220(3.1)) allows it to assess all years to which the MR relates. Wrong info in an electronic return that cannot accept the right info might not be MR if a corrective explanation is provided with it, even if CRA's computer cannot understand the explanation: see *Tooth*, [2021] UKSC 17 (UK Supreme Court).

Carelessness or neglect (CN) typically involves failing to make reasonable efforts to comply: *Venne*, [1984] C.T.C. 223 (FCTD); *Froese*, [1981] C.T.C. 2282 (TRB); *Bérubé*, [2002] 4 C.T.C. 2147 (TCC); *Smith*, 2019 TCC 274, para. 21; and included signing a return claiming a substantial loss without verifying it: *Yazdani*, 2012 TCC 371, paras. 24-26. (Neglect is "négligence" in the French version and seems to be equated with negligence, e.g. *Venne*, para. 16; *Mont-Bruno CC*, 2017 CarswellNat 3165 (TCC), paras. 8, 13-14, 18, 24, 27; *Hilderman*, 2020 TCC 58, para. 37.) The "care exercised must be that of a wise and prudent person and [the return filed] ...in a manner that the taxpayer truly believes to be correct": *Regina Shoppers Mall*, [1991] 1 C.T.C. 297 (FCA). An honest but incorrect belief that amounts are not taxable may not be CN: *Can-Am Realty*, [1994] 1 C.T.C. 336 (FCTD). In *Gebhart Estate*, 2008 FCA 206, it was CN for an executor who had received T4As not to deliver them to the estate's lawyer who prepared the return. In *Donato*, 2009 TCC 590 (aff'd on other grounds 2010 FCA 312), it was not CN for a newspaper cartoonist to think his cartoons were personal-use property. In *Cléroux*, 2013 TCC 365, it was CN for C to not report a shareholder benefit on buying a subsidiary of C's company for a nominal amount. In *Bédard*, 2016 TCC 179, RRSP strips had enough alarm bells that 3 of 6 taxpayers had CN. In *Callaghan*, 2020 TCC 28, it was not CN for C to believe his food recipe business was already a business in early years. See also VIEWS docs 2012-0465921C6 [2012 Atlantic conf. q.5]; 2013-0508411I7 (not doing correct circular calculation for Part IV tax and 129(1) dividend refund is CN). In *Kotilainen*, 2017 TCC 7, para. 24, CRA's use of the bank-deposits audit method (see Notes to 231.1(1)) was insufficiently accurate to find CN. CN should not be determined in a Rule 58 hearing (see 174(1) Notes), as it requires the Court to hear the same evidence as is needed to determine tax liability: *Paletta*, 2017 FCA 33.

Executors (estate trustees) have no lower 152(4)(a)(i) standard of care: *Gebhart Estate*, 2008 FCA 206; *Krenbrink Estate*, 2014 FCA 212; *Vine Estate*, 2015 FCA 125; *Lewin Estate*, 2019 TCC 21 (aff'd on other grounds 2020 FCA 104).

Misrepresentation by an employee of X is not an act of X if the employee is defrauding X and thus not acting within the scope of employment: see *Canadian Dredge & Dock*, [1985] 1 S.C.R. 662 at 693; *Cassidy's Ltd.*, [1990] 1 C.T.C. 2043 (TCC).

Mistake of law was CN in *Robertson*, 2015 TCC 246, paras. 26-35 (aff'd without discussing this point 2016 FCA 303) (sophisticated taxpayer not knowing US stock options were taxable).

Reliance on professional advice was not CN in: *Envision Credit Union*, 2010 TCC 576 (aff'd on other grounds 2011 FCA 321, 2013 SCC 48); *Bondfield Construction*, 2005 TCC 78 (reliance on professional comptroller plus external CAs doing full audit); *McKellar*, 2007 TCC 266 (M consulted a CA before claiming Bahamas partnership losses); *Aridi*, 2013 TCC 74 [includes review of the case law] (accountant told A that capital gain need not be reported until a later year). The "person filing the return" was held to mean the taxpayer, not the accountant, in *Aridi*, paras. 20-26; but whether the accountant's negligence is sufficient was left unresolved in *Vine Estate*, 2015 FCA 125, para. 46 (might this change now that accountants file electronically?). Proving reliance on a lawyer risks waiving solicitor-client privilege (see Notes to 232(2)): *Inwest Investments*, 2015 BCSC 1375, paras. 171-177, suggests the content of the advice need not be revealed to establish no CN; but in a lawsuit against CRA for negligence, *Ludmer*, 2018 QCCS 3381, paras. 632-638 (aff'd without addressing this point 2020 QCCA 697; leave to appeal denied 2021 CarswellQue 2160 (SCC)), it was reasonable for CRA to assess late when the legal advice was not disclosed.

Contra, relying on a (possibly) negligent accountant or preparer was CN in: *Snowball*, [1996] 2 C.T.C. 2513 (TCC); *College Park Motors*, 2009 TCC 409 (FCA appeal discontinued A-404-09); *Vine Estate*, 2015 FCA 125 (executors had to review and understand basics of estate return even though they were not tax experts); *Syla*, 2016 TCC 266 (non-English speaking immigrants relied on return preparer who claimed false charitable donations for them); *Thompson*, 2017 TCC 115 (T needed to ask accountant about deferral that had been queried and answered in earlier year); *Ciotola*, 2017 TCC 221 (FCA appeal discontinued A-384-17) (false charitable donation claims); *Gestions Cholette*, 2020 TCC 75 (obvious error in not transferring $920,000 of dividends on T2 Schedule 3 to the return, while claiming 112(1) deduction: CPA, the "person filing the return", was negligent); *Savoie*, 2020 TCC 121 (doctor failed to separate personal from business receipts for accountant). In *Hallmark Ford*, 2010 BCCA 555, para. 46, a company could not rely on "circular" legal advice, where the lawyer told the company it need not remit certain amounts if it held an honest belief the tax was not payable. In *Prima Properties*, 2019 TCC 4, para. 46, it was not negligent for a corp relying on its accountant not to know about a "highly technical provision of the Act" that even CRA at trial was unclear about. *Contra*, in *Levatte Estate*, 2019 TCC 177, paras. 25-29, the estate trustee and accountant should both have known that, since the deceased left property to a spousal trust, there was a deemed disposition on the spouse's death.

Reliance on promoters was held to be CN in: *Johnson*, 2012 FCA 253 (leave to appeal denied 2013 CarswellNat 633 (SCC)) (Ms. J relied on promoter's advice that his family trust had paid the tax on investment income he paid her: "she had no factual basis for assessing the reliability of these assurances, and she failed to do what any reasonable person in her position would have done, which was to seek independent advice"); *Demers*, 2014 TCC 368 (taxpayers relied on fraudulent promoters of scheme to extract RRSP funds); *Bédard*, 2016 TCC 179 (3 of 6 taxpayers in the same situation).

Late reassessment is allowed if there is a large discrepancy between reported and actual income without a "credible" explanation: *Baynham*, [1999] 1 C.T.C. 87 (FCA); *Molenaar*, 2004 FCA 349, para. 4; *Lacroix*, 2008 FCA 241; *Fourney*, 2011 TCC 520, para. 76. In *Labow*, 2010 TCC 408, para. 41 (aff'd on other grounds 2011 FCA 305), hiding contributions to an offshore group insurance trust in "salary expense" crossed the threshold. In CRA's view, not using a CRA published valuation method would constitute neglect: doc 2006-0196001C6. See also 2009-0323991I7, 2009-0352611I7. CRA can rely on a Revenu Québec audit having found carelessness as grounds for a late reassessment: 2012-0436711I7.

Misrepresentation is determined as of when the return is filed, so there is no obligation to file an amended return if the threshold was not crossed at the time and a mistake is discovered later: *Nesbitt*, 1996 CarswellNat 1916 (FCA), VIEWS doc 2005-0113241I7. By the same token, filing a quick correction to a return that crosses the 152(4)(a)(i) threshold does not "cure" the misrepresentation, and the return remains open forever on that issue (see 152(4.01)): *Vine Estate*, 2015 FCA 125, para. 32. The taxpayer's conduct during the audit can be used as evidence of wilful default at time of filing: *Mullen*, 2013 FCA 101, para. 7.

152(4)(a)(i) can possibly be used to *benefit* a taxpayer who overpaid tax due to negligence: *Revera Long Term Care*, 2019 FC 239 (FCA appeal discontinued A-134-19) [Esper, "Minister Did Not Meet SCC Interpretive Test", 27(5) *Canadian Tax Highlights* (ctf.ca) 8-9 (May 2019)]; and note that 152(4.01)(a)(i) must be met.

See also Kopstein & Levi, "When Should the Courts Allow Reassessments Beyond the Limitation Period?", 58(3) *Canadian Tax Journal* 475-527 (2010); Oakey, "Statute-Barred", 13(9) *Tax Hyperion* (Carswell) 1-3 (Sept. 2016); Hogan, "Does a GAAR Assessment Extend the Normal Assessment Period?", 7(2) *Canadian Tax Focus* (ctf.ca) 7-8 (May 2017); Chan, "Reassessment Beyond the Normal Reassessment Period", *Practical Insights*, *Taxnet Pro* Tax Disputes Centre (Nov. 2020, 38pp). For software that assists in determining CN see the *Assessment Period Classifier* at bluejlegal.com.

A voluntary disclosure can lead to a late assessment, as 152(4)(a)(i) is remedial rather than penal: *College Park Motors*, 2009 TCC 409 (FCA appeal discontinued A-404-09).

For CRA interpretation see *Income Tax Audit Manual* §11.3.7, on *TaxPartner* or *Taxnet Pro*. There is no time limit under 152(4)(a)(i), and CRA can wait many years to assess: *Chan*, [2010] 3 C.T.C. 2011 (TCC, affirmed on other grounds [2011] 3 C.T.C. 187 (FCA)). *Taxation Operations Manual* §13(152)5.5(1) formerly stated: "it is the practice of the Department not to reassess returns other than the one for the latest taxation year under review and those for the six immediately preceding years"; but TOM is no longer used and this practice no longer appears to be followed. On processing a change to a later year to allow the taxpayer to carry back a loss to the misrepresentation year, see VIEWS doc 2010-0387701I7.

Waivers [152(4)(a)(ii)]: CRA auditors often ask the taxpayer to sign a waiver of the limitation period to keep the year open. This may be advisable to prevent CRA from assessing immediately, especially if CRA can enforce collection during objection and appeal (e.g. large corporations: see 225.1(7)). A waiver is valid only if filed by the reassessment deadline (152(4)(a)(ii); VIEWS doc 2010-0379511I7), and a reassessment relying on an invalid waiver is void: *984274 Alberta*, 2019 TCC 85, paras. 43, 49 (rev'd on other grounds 2020 FCA 125; leave to appeal denied 2021 CarswellNat 1167 (SCC)). In *Holmes*, 2005 TCC 403, CRA produced a copy of a signed waiver, but was unable to produce the original with a date stamp and so could not prove it had been filed on time: "The onus of proving its filing rests with the Minister." Waiver is done on Form T2029 and should be limited to the specific "matters" CRA has identified, so as not to give CRA *carte blanche* to assess on any issue: see 152(4.01)(a)(ii). CRA normally accepts one filed by fax. A waiver signed without a corporate seal is valid: *Cal Investments*, [1990] 2 C.T.C. 418 (FCTD). A waiver can be revoked on 6 months' notice; see 152(4.1); some practitioners recommend filing a revocation together with the waiver, giving CRA 6 months to reassess; but note that once revoked it cannot be reinstated even with both sides' consent. In *Mitchell*, 2002 FCA 407, taxpayers and CRA agreed to hold appeals in abeyance while one went forward as a test case; a letter from taxpayers' counsel confirming this agreement and stating they would not object to later reassessment beyond the statute-barred period was held to be a waiver. In *Loyens*, 2003 TCC 214, a waiver signed by L's brother was invalid since the brother was not the taxpayer's legal representative, even though it was reasonable for the CRA official to have accepted it. A waiver signed by the taxpayer's accountant was valid in *Ackaoui*, 2006 FCA 315. A waiver signed by a company's vice-president was valid: *Arpeg Holdings*, 2008 FCA 31. See also VIEWS doc 2004-0085251E5 where a waiver is filed and another case succeeds in the courts.

A written request for adjustment will be accepted by CRA as an "implied waiver" if the adjustment favours the taxpayer, the delay in processing the request was not attributable to the taxpayer, and the essential information for a waiver is included: *Audit Manual* §11.4.2. In *Remtilla*, 2015 TCC 200, a T1 adjustment request was held to be a waiver, where the taxpayer reached a settlement with CRA and later tried to say the settlement reassessment was statute-barred. (This will not likely apply more generally against taxpayers, since a waiver must be "in prescribed form".) In *Kerry Canada*, 2019 FC 377, a request to hold objections in abeyance pending consideration by the competent authority (see Notes to 115.1) was held to be an implied waiver, so CRA could reassess late.

A waiver filed after the limitation period has expired should be invalid: 152(4)(a)(ii). 152(4)(c), added in 2009, is intended to apply only in cases where a reassessment could have been issued within the extended period, as per 152(4)(b)(i)-(vi). However, it could be interpreted to allow a blanket 3-year extension to the waiver filing deadline in all cases. This has been brought to Finance's attention. See also Kandev, "Change of Statute of Limitations Should be Welcome to Taxpayers But Contains Technical Glitches", XV(1) *International Tax Planning* (Federated Press) 1030-32 (2009).

There was originally no mechanism for revoking a 152(4)(c) waiver, as 152(4.1) applied only to a 152(4)(a)(ii) waiver. This was fixed with an amendment to 152(4.1) by the 2002-2013 technical bill.

A federal waiver applies to Ontario tax as well, and so applied to a reassessment treating an Alberta trust as resident in Ontario: *Aubrey Dan Family Trust*, 2017 ONCA 875.

Once a waiver is filed, multiple reassessments can be issued based on the same waiver: *Rémillard*, 2011 TCC 327.

A waiver obtained under duress might not be valid, but the Courts have yet to find actual duress: *Placements Marcel Lapointe*, [1993] 1 C.T.C. 2261 (TCC); *Ehrmantraut*, [1995] 2 C.T.C. 2965D (TCC); *Guerette*, [1996] 1 C.T.C. 2780 (TCC); *Radelet*, 2017 TCC 159 (FCA appeal dismissed for delay A-288-18). In *St-Laurent [Simard]*, 2007 TCC 540, para. 398 (aff'd 2009 FCA 379), waivers in a large tax shelter file were valid despite claims they were obtained by false CRA promises. A waiver obtained by trickery from a person who did not understand it was invalid: *Karakas*, 1995 CarswellNat 1946 (TCC); but in *Arpeg Holdings*, 2008 FCA 31, a claim the company's officer was misled and did not know that he was signing a waiver was rejected; and in *Sljivar*, 2009 TCC 581, a largely illiterate taxpayer who did not know what he was signing was bound by the waiver, as he could have asked what it meant before signing (and the Court noted that waivers help the taxpayer since they postpone a reassessment). In *Wiens*, 2011 TCC 152, para. 21, the fact the taxpayer was on medication when he signed the waiver and could not now remember signing it was insufficient to show he lacked capacity to understand what he was signing. See also Notes to 169(2.2) re waiver of right to appeal. Threatening to assess gross-negligence penalties if the taxpayer does not sign a waiver breaches the auditor's duty of care and may make CRA liable for damages: *Leroux*, 2014 BCSC 720, paras. 349-351. In *Loiselle*, 2019 QCCQ 4647, waiver under the parallel Quebec provision was given with "free and informed consent" required by the Quebec *Civil Code* (para. 45, but the test is the same as under the ITA: para 62); and filing a revocation confirmed the waiver's validity (para. 75).

Qureshi, [1992] 1 C.T.C. 2370 (TCC), said that determining a waiver to be a nullity is outside the TCC's jurisdiction, but this is likely incorrect in light of *JP Morgan* (see Notes to 169(1) under "Jurisdiction").

See also Notes to 152(4.01) re the scope of an assessment when a waiver was filed.

It is uncertain whether a treaty limitation period overrides a waiver: it did in *Canwest Mediaworks*, 2006 TCC 579, but the decision was reversed on other grounds 2008 FCA 5 (leave to appeal denied 2008 CarswellNat 1642 (SCC)).

Where the taxpayer refuses to sign a waiver, CRA can issue a protective assessment within the deadline so it can finish the audit: *Golini*, 2013 TCC 293, para. 24; *Karda*, 2006 FCA 238; *Rio Tinto*, 2017 TCC 67 (SR&ED claim) (FCA appeal discontinued A-153-17).

For more on waivers see *Income Tax Audit Manual* §11.4.2 (on *TaxPartner* and *Taxnet Pro*); Tari, "Waivering", 2002 Cdn Tax Foundation conference report, 13:1-13; Campbell, *Administration of Income Tax 2020* (Carswell), §9.10.4.

152(4)(b)(i): see Notes to 152(6).

152(4)(b)(iii) extends the deadline by 3 years for assessments on transactions with a non-arm's length non-resident (and, under (B) added in 2018, amounts involving a foreign affiliate (FA)). This rule applied in: *SMX*, 2003 FCA 479; *Labow*, 2011 FCA 305 (income earned by offshore group sickness insurance trust set up by L and his wife); *1143132 Ontario*, 2009 TCC 477 (transfer-pricing assessment); *Shaw-Almex*, 2009 TCC 538 (FCA appeal discontinued A-479-09) (loan repayment to bank under guarantee of related non-resident company's debt); *Sundog Distributing*, 2010 TCC 392 (FCA appeal discontinued A-327-10) (5-years-from-year-end deadline in Canada-Barbados treaty did not apply because corp's income was taxed by Barbados only as an international business company, not as regular income tax); *Alberta Printed Circuits*, 2011 TCC 232 (same). 152(4)(b)(iii) did not apply in: *Blackburn Radio*, 2009 TCC 155 (deduction of bonus: arrangement with FA was set up many years earlier and the only "transaction" in the year was with arm's-length person; (iii)(B) would now catch this); *Ho*, 2010 TCC 325 (152(4)(b)(iii) did not apply to FAPI imputed to a beneficiary under 75(2) because imputation is not a "transaction"; (iii)(B) would now catch this). CRA considered that 152(4)(b)(iii) applied in docs 2011-0407731E5 (shares of foreign sub distributed to Canadian parent on windup of Canadian sub); 2012-0439301I7 (17(1) income inclusion); 2013-0478121I7 (shares of foreign sub sold to Canadian sister company by Canadian sub); 2016-0651411I7 (attribution of income among provinces); 2018-0763611I7 (capital used by FA to earn FAPI). See also Pandher, "Transfer-Pricing Penalty Update", 7(2) *Canadian Tax Focus* (ctf.ca) 9 (May 2017).

152(4)(b)(iv): For the meaning of "income or profits tax", see Notes to 126(4). For examples of 152(4)(b)(iv) applying see VIEWS docs 2013-0481151I7, 2013-0512601I7, 2016-0641721I7.

CRA must reassess beyond the deadline to allow a claimed carryback: 152(6); and may reassess an individual or testamentary trust beyond the deadline with the taxpayer's consent: 152(4.2).

152(4)(b.1), (b.2): The indefinitely extended reassessment period in (b.1) [until compliance with tax-shelter or reportable-transaction reporting under 237.1 or 237.3] is limited to assessments relating to the information that was not filed: 152(4.01). The 3-year extension in (b.2) [for not filing a T1135 reporting all foreign property] is not so limited; due to (b.2)(ii) it applies only if there is unreported foreign income, but once it applies, *any* matter including domestic income can be reassessed (unless 152(5) prevents it). (See VIEWS doc 2013-0485761C6.) It has been pointed out to Finance that this is unfair: "Sherman Query to Finance", xxxv(20) *The Canadian Taxpayer* (Carswell) 159 (Oct. 25, 2013).

152(4)(b.3): if a sale of real property is not reported (other than inventory of a corporation or partnership), including a principal residence (PR) (see Notes to 40(2)(b)), the reassessment deadline is extended indefinitely for that sale (152(4.01)(c)), or to 3 years after the amount is reported in an amended return ((b.3)(v)). Permitting late assessment for failing to disclose a sale of real property is part of tightening the PR exemption rules, including requiring disclosure of sale of a PR even when exempt under 40(2)(b).

152(4)(c), (c.1): While these say the same thing, they are separated because 152(4.01) applies to (c) but not to (c.1).

152(4)(d) (released as 152(4)(c) on Nov. 28/08) extends the limitation period when an assessment is issued to change the allocation of corporate income to a province. This implements a term of the 2006 *Canada-Ontario Memorandum of Agreement Concerning a Single Administration of Ontario Corporate Tax*, as part of the deal under which CRA took over Ontario corporate tax in 2009.

Unless one of the above exceptions applies, CRA *cannot* reassess a statute-barred corporate return even to reduce tax at the taxpayer's request: see Notes to 152(4.2) and VIEWS doc 2012-0447401I7. (For individuals, see 152(4.2).)

152(4)(b)(iii)(A) amended by 2021 budget bill #1 to add "as defined in subsection 247(1)", for tax years for which the taxpayer's 152(3.1) normal reassessment period ends after March 18, 2019.

152(4)(b)(iii)(B) added by 2018 budget bill #2, for tax years that begin after Feb. 26, 2018.

152(4)(b.4) added by 2018 budget bill #2, effective for a tax year if a reassessment of tax for that year was required under 152(6), or would have been so required if the taxpayer had claimed an amount by filing the prescribed form referred to in 152(6) by the day referred to therein, in order to take into account a deduction claimed under s. 111 in respect of a loss for a subsequent taxation year that ends after Feb. 26, 2018.

152(4)(b.3) added by 2017 budget bill #2, for tax years that end after Oct. 2, 2016.

152(4)(b.1), (b.2) and (c.1) added (and (c) amended to change "return" to "return of income" and add "or (b.1)") by 2013 budget bill #2, effective for 2013 and later taxation years (except (b.1) effective for taxation years ending after March 20, 2013).

152(4)(b)(vii) added by 2002-2013 technical bill (Part 1 — NRTs), for taxation years that end after March 4, 2010.

152(4)(b)(i) amended to add reference to 152(6.1) by 2002-2013 technical bill (Part 2 — FA surplus rules), for tax years that begin after Nov. 1999.

152(4) earlier amended by 2010 budget bill #2 (effective Dec. 15, 2010), 2008 budget bill #2, 2001 and 1995-97 technical bills, 1989 Budget.

I.T. Application Rules: 62(1) (152(4) applies to assessments since Dec. 23, 1971).

Income Tax Folios: S3-F9-C1: Lottery winnings, miscellaneous receipts, and income (and losses) from crime [replaces IT-185R, IT-213R, IT-256R, IT-334R2].

Interpretation Bulletins: IT-109R2: Unpaid amounts; IT-121R3: Election to capitalize cost of borrowed money (cancelled); IT-384R: Reassessment where option exercised in subsequent year.

Information Circulars: 75-7R3: Reassessment of a return of income; 77-11: Sales tax reassessments — deductibility in computing income; 84-1: Revision of capital cost allowance claims and other permissive deductions; 07-1R1: Taxpayer relief provisions.

CRA Audit Manual: 11.3.3: Application of losses; 11.3.7: Assessment after the normal (re)assessment period and penalty for false statements or omissions; 11.4.0: Waivers; 11.5.9: NIL assessment — notification; Appendix A-11.22.25: Assessment after normal (re)assessment period: recommendation report; 12.1.0: Taxpayer requests (TPR) and general adjustment forms (GAF).

Forms: T108: Waiver in respect of the normal determination period for a partnership; T2029: Waiver in respect of the normal reassessment period or extended reassessment period.

(4.01) Extended period assessment — Notwithstanding subsections (4) and (5), an assessment, reassessment or additional assessment to which paragraph (4)(a), (b), (b.1), (b.3), (b.4) or (c) applies in respect of a taxpayer for a taxation year may be made after the taxpayer's normal reassessment period in respect of the year to the extent that, but only to the extent that, it can reasonably be regarded as relating to,

(a) where paragraph (4)(a) applies to the assessment, reassessment or additional assessment,

(i) any misrepresentation made by the taxpayer or a person who filed the taxpayer's return of income for the year that is attributable to neglect, carelessness or wilful default or any fraud committed by the taxpayer or that person in filing the return or supplying any information under this Act, or

(ii) a matter specified in a waiver filed with the Minister in respect of the year;

(b) if paragraph (4)(b), (b.1) or (c) applies to the assessment, reassessment or additional assessment,

(i) the assessment, reassessment or additional assessment to which subparagraph (4)(b)(i) applies,

(ii) the assessment or reassessment referred to in subparagraph (4)(b)(ii),

(iii) the transaction, income, loss or other amount referred to in subparagraph (4)(b)(iii),

(iv) the payment or reimbursement referred to in subparagraph (4)(b)(iv),

(v) the reduction referred to in subparagraph (4)(b)(v),

(vi) the application referred to in subparagraph (4)(b)(vi), or

(vii) the deduction, claim or tax benefit referred to in paragraph (4)(b.1);

(c) if paragraph (4)(b.3) applies to the assessment, reassessment or additional assessment, the disposition referred to in that paragraph; and

(d) if paragraph (4)(b.4) applies to the assessment, reassessment or additional assessment, the reduction under subparagraph (4)(b.4)(iii).

Related Provisions: 152(1.7) — Limitation period re determination of partnership income or loss; 152(3.1) — Normal reassessment period.

Notes: See Notes to 152(4) re waivers.

152(4.01)(a)(i): In *Strum*, 2019 TCC 167, para. 11, carelessness in claiming certain personal expenses as business was enough to open up reassessment of all expenses.

152(4.01)(a)(ii): Reassessments or Crown arguments were rejected as covering matters not in the waiver in: *Honeywell Ltd.*, 2007 FCA 22 (waiver re GAAR and 12(1)(c), motion to amend Reply to argue 95(2)(a)); *Merswolke*, [1995] 1 C.T.C. 2524 (TCC) (waiver re rental income, reassessment for gain on sale of the property); *Mah*, 2003 TCC 720 (waiver re 86(2), reassessment based on 84(3)); *Holmes*, 2005 TCC 403 (waiver re "supporting information relating to the farm operations", reassessment of restricted farm losses); *Loblaw Financial*, 2018 TCC 182 (rev'd on other grounds 2020 FCA 79; SCC appeal heard May 13/21), paras. 279-287 (waiver not mentioning GAAR does not cover GAAR).

Reassessments were valid in *Solberg*, [1992] 2 C.T.C. 208 (FCTD) (technical defect in referring to wrong Part of the Act did not matter where the parties' intentions were clear); *Chafetz (Taylor)*, 2007 FCA 45 (leave to appeal denied 2007 CarswellNat 1882

(SCC)) (waiver re "Canadian Exploration and Development Expenses" applied to Canadian Exploration Expenses); *Jobin*, 2007 FCA 408 (CRA's entitlement to assess penalty did not have to be written onto form); *Fietz*, 2013 FCA 32 (no description of matters being waived, but the waiver responded to CRA's proposal letter, which thus formed part of the waiver); *Brown*, 2006 TCC 381 (waiver referring to Parts XI.3 and XVI of the Act applied to a Part I reassessment, as the taxpayer was not "surprised" by the adjustments made; a waiver is not a contract and evidence of the surrounding circumstances is relevant); *Fagan*, 2011 TCC 523 (waiver referred to renounced expenditures of company one level further down than the one that renounced them; both sides understood what was meant; Court discussed case law in detail); *Gramiak*, 2015 FCA 40, para. 41 (to disallow a waiver "crafted" to include facts the taxpayer disclosed, "but exclude the transaction which he later revealed after the limitation period had expired, would give rise to an absurd result"); *Rio Tinto*, 2017 TCC 67, paras. 236-278 (FCA appeal discontinued A-153-17) (reassessment included amounts previously assessed; Court discussed overlap with 152(5)). In *632738 Alberta*, 2019 TCC 225, aff'd 2021 FCA 43, the TCC rejected a Rule 58 hearing (see 174(1) Notes), finding the reassessment likely valid despite the waiver purporting to limit a reassessment based on 103(1) to income from a specific partnership (para. 81).

In *943372 Ontario*, 2007 TCC 294, para. 10, Bowman CJ speculated that a net worth assessment (see Notes to 152(7)) might not be able to conform to 152(4.01).

152(4.01) opening words amended by 2018 budget bill #2 to add "(b.4)", and 152(4.01)(d) added, effective on the same basis as 152(4)(b.4).

152(4.01)(b)(iii) amended by 2018 budget bill #2, for a taxpayer's taxation years that begin after Feb. 26, 2018, to add "income, loss or other amount" (to match the 152(4)(b)(iii)(B) wording).

152(4.01) amended by 2017 budget bill #2, for taxation years that end after Oct. 2, 2016, to add reference to 152(4)(b.3) in para. (a), and to add para. (c).

152(4.01) opening words and para. (b) opening words amended to refer to 152(4)(b.1), and 152(4.01)(b)(vii) added, by 2013 budget bill #2, for taxation years that end after March 20, 2013.

152(4.01) opening words and (b) amended by 2008 budget bill #2 to add reference to 152(4)(c), in force March 12, 2009.

152(4.01) added/amended by 1995-97 technical bill, last change effective August 1997. 152(4.01)(a) was formerly covered in 152(5)(b) and (c). See Notes to 152(4) and (5).

CRA Audit Manual: 11.4.0: Waivers.

Forms: T2029: Waiver in respect of the normal reassessment period or extended reassessment period.

(4.1) If waiver revoked — If the Minister would, but for this subsection, be entitled to reassess, make an additional assessment or assess tax, interest or penalties by virtue only of the filing of a waiver under subparagraph (4)(a)(ii) or paragraph (4)(c) or (c.1), the Minister may not make such a reassessment, additional assessment or assessment after the day that is six months after the date on which a notice of revocation of the waiver in prescribed form is filed.

Related Provisions: 152(1.7) — Limitation period re determination of partnership income or loss; 152(4.2) — Reassessment with taxpayer's consent; 165(1.2) — No objection permitted where right to object waived; 169(2.2) — No appeal where right to object or appeal waived.

Notes: This is a convoluted way of saying that a waiver can be revoked on 6 months' notice (giving CRA time to issue a reassessment if it wishes). Note that nothing in 152(4.1) requires the revocation to be filed in prescribed *manner* (e.g., at the same Tax Services Office as the waiver is filed), although Form T652 purports to require this.

Some advisors make it a practice to file a revocation with the waiver, thus giving the auditor 6 months to finalize a reassessment. If this is done, the waiver cannot be revived or extended.

In both *236130 British Columbia*, 2006 FCA 352, and *Burstein*, 2009 TCC 103, reassessments were invalid because CRA mailed them only to an incorrect address within the 6-month revocation period. See Notes to 165(1) on mailing to an incorrect address.

After a waiver is revoked, CRA's view is that a new waiver can be filed if the year is not statute-barred: VIEWS doc 2010-037951117.

See also Notes to 152(4) re waivers.

152(4.1) amended by 2013 budget bill #2, effective for 2013 and later taxation years, to add reference to 152(4)(c.1).

152(4.1) amended to add reference to 152(4)(c) by 2002-2013 technical bill (Part 5 — technical), effective June 26, 2013. This corrects an error in that there was originally no mechanism for revoking at 152(4)(c) waiver. However, the amendment is not retroactive to before Royal Assent.

Forms: T109: Notice of revocation of a waiver in respect of a normal determination period for a partnership; T652: Notice of revocation of waiver.

(4.2) Reassessment with taxpayer's consent — Notwithstanding subsections (4), (4.1) and (5), for the purpose of determining — at any time after the end of the normal reassessment period, of a taxpayer who is an individual (other than a trust) or a graduated rate estate, in respect of a taxation year — the amount of any refund to which the taxpayer is entitled at that time for the year, or a reduction of an amount payable under this Part by the taxpayer for the year, the Minister may, if the taxpayer makes an application for that determination on or before the day that is 10 calendar years after the end of that taxation year,

(a) reassess tax, interest or penalties payable under this Part by the taxpayer in respect of that year; and

(b) redetermine the amount, if any, deemed by subsection 120(2) or (2.2), 122.5(3) or (3.001), 122.51(2), 122.7(2) or (3), 122.8(4), 122.9(2), 122.91(1), 127.1(1), 127.41(3) or 210.2(3) or (4) to be paid on account of the taxpayer's tax payable under this Part for the year or deemed by subsection 122.61(1) to be an overpayment on account of the taxpayer's liability under this Part for the year.

Related Provisions: 122.62(2) — 10-year limit to request past Canada Child Benefit; 152(3.1) — Normal reassessment period; 152(4.3) — Consequential assessment; 164(1.5) — Refunds; 164(3.2) — Interest on refunds and repayments; 165(1.2) — Limitation of right to object; 180.01(2)(d) — Election to reduce tax on shares that have dropped in value is deemed to be application under 152(4.2); 225.1(1) — No collection restrictions following assessment.

Notes: 152(4.2) is part of the "Taxpayer Relief" legislation, called "Fairness" from 1991-2007. It permits CRA to reassess an individual (or a "graduated rate estate" — before 2016, a testamentary trust) up to 10 years back, at the taxpayer's request (e.g., to allow a deduction or credit the taxpayer neglected to claim). Without this provision (and as still is the case for corporations), CRA has no jurisdiction to reopen a year that is statute-barred under 152(4) even with the taxpayer's consent: *Canadian Marconi*, [1991] 2 C.T.C. 352 (FCA); *Greenpipe Industries*, 2006 FC 1098; *Building Products*, 2020 FC 784, para. 25; although in *RAR Consultants*, 2017 TCC 214, para. 3, the Court said 152(4.2) had applied to a corp. See also Notes to 164(1) for corps; and note that on settlement of a TCC appeal on consent, any year including one not under appeal can be reassessed under 169(3). Also, a nil assessment (notification that no tax is payable) can be issued at any time (*984274 Alberta*, 2020 FCA 125, para. 58; leave to appeal denied 2021 CarswellNat 1167 (SCC)), so CRA can get to the same result as 152(4.2) for a corp, as long as it eliminates all tax! Tax can also be increased at a corp's request as part of settlement of another year's appeal: *CBS Holdings*, 2020 FCA 4, para. 45.

No rule permits late reassessment at CRA's option, if retroactive amendments are detrimental to the taxpayer. For example, if income from a non-competition agreement, taxable back to 2003 under 56.4(2) as enacted in 2013, was not reported and the years in question are statute-barred, CRA cannot reassess those years. (Not complying with legislation that was not enacted at time of filing the return is not carelessness or neglect for 152(4)(a)(i), and nothing in the Act or any amending legislation requires a taxpayer to refile or correct past years' returns. See 239(1) Notes at "There is no obligation".)

Form RC4288 could be used until about 2015 to seek relief, but that form is now only for 220(3.1) waiver of interest/penalty, so use Form T1-Adj (T1 Adjustment or a letter with explanation: Information Circular 07-1R1 paras. 76-81; Gilmour, "Tricks and Traps in T1 Adjustment Requests", 6(4) *Canadian Tax Focus* (ctf.ca) 6-7 (Nov. 2016).

To request an unclaimed Child Tax Benefit or Canada Child Benefit, use 122.62(2).

If a client's Taxpayer Relief request for reduction of tax in a statute-barred return results in a debit to another statute-barred return, former *Taxation Operations Manual* §1933.1(2)(c) stated: "it is Agency policy to process these reassessments without additional penalty or arrears interest". This does not appear in the current *Taxpayer Relief Procedures Manual*.

Under the 10-year limit, an individual's application for relief for the 2009 taxation year must be filed by Dec. 31, 2019, and so on: *Nicholls*, 2010 FCA 30; *Vidanovic*, 2012 TCC 265. Court delays cannot extend the deadline: VIEWS doc 2014-0530981I7. Relief for earlier years can be granted only by remission order (see Notes to 220(3.1)). A letter asking whether amounts reported as income in a past return are deductible qualified as an "application": 2010-0389831E5. The 10-year limit does not apply to a remission order refund application: 2005-0129791I7.

In *DouangChanh*, 2013 TCC 320, a T1 Adjustment form filed within the normal reassessment period was held not to be a 152(4.2) request, so a reassessment allowing expenses (as requested) was statute-barred and invalid, thus not cancelling an objection filed to a previous disallowance of charitable donations, so that objection could proceed!

In *Letendre*, 2011 TCC 577, the taxpayer filed returns years after CRA issued a notional assessment; CRA's reassessments (reducing tax) to match those returns were held to be under 152(4.2) and thus could not be objected to.

Where a 2001 return was filed in 2011 and then assessed, an adjustment requested in 2013 is within the normal reassessment period and can be reassessed, and 164(1.5) allows a refund to be paid because the return was filed within 10 years: VIEWS docs 2006-020236I17, 2011-042210I17.

152(4.2) cannot be used to increase tax even with the taxpayer's consent, so a pension-splitting election under 60.03, filed after the transferee's normal reassessment period, cannot be accepted despite the net benefit to the two spouses: VIEWS doc 2011-0429921I7. Similarly, in *Freitas*, 2018 FCA 110, para. 15, where a taxpayer requested

a late reassessment for a refund, and CRA assessed him to produce a liability, the assessment was not validly made under 152(4.2).

152(4.2) can be used to reassess without changing the tax owed, to change some other balance: *Ullah*, 2013 TCC 387, para. 14. However, it applies only to income tax, and cannot be used to refund Employment Insurance premiums from more than 3 years back: *McGaw*, 2006 FC 1282.

CRA policy on 152(4.2) is found in Information Circular 07-1R1 and *Taxpayer Relief Procedures Manual*, available on *TaxPartner* and *Taxnet Pro*. No relief is given to benefit from another taxpayer's success in the Courts: IC 75-7R3 para. 4(e); VIEWS doc 2013-0513401M4; *Abraham*, 2012 FCA 266 (leave to appeal denied 2013 CarswellNat 729 (SCC)). Retroactive tax planning is not allowed (e.g., amending past CCA claims to reinstate expired losses: 2013-047411I17). CRA has a duty of procedural fairness but there are no specific rules for this, and no meeting with the taxpayer is required: *Costabile*, 2008 FC 943, para. 37 (FCA appeal dismissed for delay A-437-08).

An employer who has wrongly recorded taxable benefits can issue corrected T4s for up to 10 years back to assist a 152(4.2) request: VIEWS doc 2011-039430I17. However, 152(4.2) cannot be used to reverse a benefit that was correctly recorded at the time: 2014-0524371E5.

CRA agreed to reassess returns of investors defrauded by Earl Jones, to delete reported fictitious income. See Adam Aptowitzer, "Ponzi Schemes and Taxation", xxxii(13) *The Canadian Taxpayer* (Carswell) 97-98 (June 29, 2010).

There is no appeal from a 152(4.2) reassessment or refusal to reassess: 165(1.2), but the Courts may recommend that CRA reassess, e.g. *Osei-Tutu*, 2010 TCC 185, para. 18; *Newcombe*, 2013 FC 955, para. 34; *Mady*, 2017 TCC 112, para. 121; *Tench*, 2018 TCC 192, para. 10. Judicial review (JR) of CRA failure to grant relief under 152(4.2) is available in the Federal Court, but is rarely granted. (The provincial superior court has no jurisdiction: *Gordon*, 2010 SKQB 160.) The FC cannot substitute its own discretion; the standard for JR is the same as under 220(3.1) (see Notes thereto): *Berget*, 2008 FC 1217 (FCA appeal dismissed for delay A-601-08); *Beaulieu*, 2008 FC 1236.

If a requested deduction is rejected because CRA believes the amount was not deductible, misunderstands the facts or acts unreasonably, the Federal Court may grant judicial review and send the matter back for reconsideration. See 220(3.1) Notes re the *Vavilov* standard that applies since Dec. 2019.

Pre-*Vavilov*, judicial review was allowed in: *Lanno*, 2005 FCA 153; *Plattig*, 2003 FC 1074; *Hindle*, 2004 FC 625; *Chisholm*, 2005 FC 303; *Simmonds*, 2006 FC 130 (CRA had incorrectly determined that S was ineligible for ABIL); *Dupuis*, 2006 FC 228 (CRA ordered to reopen past years to determine whether D was employee or independent contractor); *White*, 2011 FC 556 (in denying relief given other taxpayers were treatment of payments to give up fishing, CRA fettered its discretion by applying a "rule" denying relief because W did not file an objection; settlement with other taxpayers must have reflected CRA's understanding of the law); *Radonjic*, 2013 FC 916 (CRA had refused to open past years to delete reported online poker winnings); *Lambert*, 2015 FC 1236 (request was not made solely because of a court case).

However, *Abraham*, 2012 FCA 266 (leave to appeal denied 2013 CarswellNat 729 (SCC)), ruled that it was reasonable for CRA to reject claims for an exemption based on recent case law, when the claims would have been rejected had they been made on time.

Pre-*Vavilov*, judicial review was also refused in *Gagné*, 2007 FCA 399 (leave to appeal denied 2008 CarswellNat 1640 (SCC)); *Hoffman*, 2010 FCA 310 (decision was reasonable); *Fannon*, 2013 FCA 99 (CRA reasonable to deny child care expenses not allowed by s. 63); *Ford*, 2016 FCA 128 (F claimed rental expenses, but failed to provide documents for years, could not use 152(4.2) to circumvent appeals process); *Netupsky*, 2003 FCT 578; *Prsa*, 2003 FC 1495 (CRA's decision was not "patently unreasonable"); *Maloshicky*, 2005 FC 978; *Wyse*, 2007 FC 535 (status Indians' exemption claim was carefully considered based on case law as of that time); *Costabile*, 2008 FC 943 (appeal to FCA dismissed for delay A-437-08) (taxpayer's documentation inadequate); *Berget*, 2008 FC 1217 (appeal to FCA dismissed for delay A-601-08) (CRA review was detailed and reasonable); *Beaulieu*, 2008 FC 1236 (decision was reasonable); *Taylor*, 2008 FC 1317 (decision was reasonable); *Ugro*, 2009 FC 826 (U's invented accounting method unacceptable to CRA); *Caine*, 2011 FC 11 (CRA correct to deny expenses); *Sivadharshan*, 2013 FC 47 (no records to support S's claim he had mistakenly over-reported income); *Sullivan*, 2014 FC 486 (S was not clearly entitled to deductions requested); *Fiorucci*, 2015 FC 223 (documentation to support requested ABIL had not been provided); *Anthony*, 2016 FC 955 (expenses incurred in company's name could not be claimed by owner); *Biles Estate*, 2017 FC 371, paras. 44-47 (CRA refused to change deemed disposition that was based on B's own valuation; and supposed settlement with CRA was unclear); *Abou-Rached*, 2019 FC 750 (insufficient evidence of A-R's income being what he claimed); *Adey*, 2019 FC 1001 (claims based on another taxpayer's successful court case). See also 220(3.1) Notes for case law on similar judicial review re interest waiver.

After an FCA order sending the matter back to CRA, a claim that CRA did not comply with the FCA's reasons must be brought by new application to the FC, not back to the FCA: *Lanno*, 2006 FCA 220. In *Leblanc*, 2010 FC 688, the fact the new decision "re-used" some of the earlier decision was not a breach of procedural fairness, as other documents were considered as well and the earlier decision was not "holistically applied or relied on exclusively".

For other remedies see Sandler & Blackler, "(Can't Get No) Satisfaction?", 2018 Cdn Tax Foundation conference report, 33:1-30.

152(4.2)(b) amended by 2020 COVID bill #1 to refer to 122.5(3.001), effective March 25, 2020.

152(4.2)(b) amended by 2019 budget bill #1 to add "122.91(1)", effective 2019.

152(4.2)(b) amended by 2018 budget bill #2 to add "122.8(4)", for 2018 and later tax years.

152(4.2)(b) amended by 2016 budget bill #1 to add "122.9(2)" for 2016 and later years, and to delete "122.8(2) or (3)" for 2017 and later years.

152(4.2) opening words amended by 2014 budget bill #2, for 2016 and later taxation years, to change "testamentary trust" to "graduated rate estate". (See Notes to 122(1).)

152(4.2)(b) amended to add "122.8(2) or (3)" by 2014 budget bill #2, for 2015 and later taxation years.

152(4.2) amended by 2007 budget bill #2 (for 2007 and later tax years), 2004 Budget (for applications made after 2004, to introduce the 10-year limitation; for applications made before 2005, relief could be granted back to 1985), 1999, 1997 and 1994 Budgets, 1992 Child Benefit bill and 1992 Economic Statement. Added by 1991 technical bill, for assessments and redeterminations in respect of 1985 and later years.

The 2002-2013 technical bill, s. 367, allows reassessment beyond the usual 152(4) reassessment deadline if the taxpayer requests and CRA agrees (changing 152(4.2) to not be limited to individuals), to reflect amendments made by that bill. For CRA confirmation of this rule see VIEWS docs 2012-0432661E5, 2013-0501091I7.

Information Circulars: 75-7R3: Reassessment of a return of income; 07-1R1: Taxpayer relief provisions.

Application Policies: SR&ED 94-01: Retroactive claims for scientific research (TPRs).

CRA Audit Manual: 3.0: Fairness and client rights; 11.6.6 and Appendix A-11.2.24: Fairness report; 12.15.9: Revising capital cost allowance and other permissive deductions; 12.15.10: Unrelated downward adjustments.

Forms: T1-ADJ: Adjustment request; RC376: Taxpayer relief request statement of income and expenses and assets and liabilities for individuals.

(4.3) Consequential assessment

— Notwithstanding subsections (4), (4.1) and (5), if the result of an assessment or a decision on an appeal is to change a particular balance of a taxpayer for a particular taxation year, the Minister may, or if the taxpayer so requests in writing, shall, before the later of the expiration of the normal reassessment period in respect of a subsequent taxation year and the end of the day that is one year after the day on which all rights of objection and appeal expire or are determined in respect of the particular year, reassess the tax, interest or penalties payable by the taxpayer, redetermine an amount deemed to have been paid or to have been an overpayment by the taxpayer or modify the amount of a refund or other amount payable to the taxpayer, under this Part in respect of the subsequent taxation year, but only to the extent that the reassessment, redetermination or modification can reasonably be considered to relate to the change in the particular balance of the taxpayer for the particular year.

Related Provisions: 152(3.1) — Normal reassessment period; 152(4)(b.4) — Consequential assessment of loss carried back; 152(4.4) — Definition of "balance"; 165(1.1) — Limitation of right to object to assessments or determinations; 169(2) — Limitation of right to appeal.

Notes: 152(4.3) allows consequential assessments beyond the normal deadline where a balance (such as a loss carryforward) is changed from an earlier year. See CRA *Appeals Manual* §4.23. A change based on a successful appeal of the same issue for an earlier year is not "consequential": *Sherway Centre*, 2003 FCA 26; *LJP Sales Agency*, 2007 FCA 114. However, on settling a Tax Court appeal, *any* adjustment can be made to *any* year: see 169(3). Where a loss is carried *back*, a consequential assessment may be allowed under 152(4)(b.4).

If CRA refuses to apply 152(4.3) to allow a loss carryforward, judicial review must be sought in the FC, as the TCC has no jurisdiction: *Bakorp Management*, 2019 FCA 195 (leave to appeal dismissed 2020 CarswellNat 19 (SCC)).

CRA was not permitted to use 152(4.3) to recover a s. 129 dividend refund as a result of another year's reassessment, in *Bulk Transfer Systems*, 2005 FCA 94.

In *Ford Credit*, 2016 TCC 1, Ford argued that 152(4.3) did not permit reassessment of 2005 in consequence of 2004 being *vacated* (rather than reassessed). The Court ruled that 2004 had been reassessed, so it did not have to address the issue: para. 36.

If the Tax Court vacates a reassessment, the previous assessment automatically revives (see Notes to 152(4)), so a further reassessment to implement the Court's decision was statute-barred and did not start the 1-year clock under 152(4.3): *Blackburn Radio*, 2012 TCC 255.

152(4.3) was applied in *Hill (Uphill Holdings)*, [1993] 1 C.T.C. 2021 (TCC), and *Hevey*, 2005 TCC 76 (FCA appeal discontinued A-76-05), to allow late reassessment due to reallocation of shareholder loans under 15(2) and repayments under 20(1)(j).

A late assessment consequential on that of a related taxpayer is invalid. CRA accepted this at the objection level (wife W claimed child-care expense; CRA assessed to in-

crease W's income, leading to higher net income than husband H, so child-care expense denied and allowed to H; W's TCC appeal succeeded, so income reduced and child-care expense allowed; CRA assessed H to deny expense since his net income was higher; H successfully objected because this assessment was statute-barred).

See also VIEWS docs 2005-0122381E5 (taxpayer-requested carryforward of loss to statute-barred year); 2011-0404471C6 (procedures for requesting a 152(4.3) reassessment); 2012-046368117 (when 20(1)(m) reserve allowed in year for which waiver filed, parallel inclusion under 12(1)(e) is allowed by 152(4.3)); 2013-0486251I7 (20(1)(m) reserve and s. 111 carryovers do not "reasonably relate" to the balance reassessed under a (later expired) waiver, and are not allowed, because there is no "causal connection" [this might not be correct in the author's view]); 2014-0518641I7 (application to Ontario corporate minimum tax); 2014-0537111E5 (change to closing inventory allows consequential adjustment to next year's opening inventory).

An application for *mandamus* to force CRA to reassess under 152(4.3) should be brought in the Federal Court, not the provincial superior court: *Gordon*, 2010 CarswellSask 267 (Sask. QB). See Notes to 171(1).

See also Chiu & Hosanna, "The Conditions for and Scope of Subsection 152(4.3)", XIX(3) *Tax Litigation* (Federated Press) 1158-66 (2015).

152(4.3) amended by 2002-2013 technical bill, for reassessments, redeterminations and modifications in respect of tax years that relate to changes in balances for other tax years as a result of assessments made, or decisions on appeal rendered, after Nov. 5, 2010, to add "by the taxpayer or modify the amount of a refund or other amount payable to the taxpayer" and "modification".

152(4.3) added by 1992 technical bill and amended by 1993 technical bill.

CRA Audit Manual: 11.5.12: Consequential assessments.

(4.4) Definition of "balance"

— For the purpose of subsection (4.3), a "balance" of a taxpayer for a taxation year is the income, taxable income, taxable income earned in Canada or any loss of the taxpayer for the year, or the tax or other amount payable by, any amount refundable to, or any amount deemed to have been paid or to have been an overpayment by, the taxpayer for the year.

Related Provisions: 152(4.3) — Consequential assessment; 165(1.11)(b) — Balance adjustment to be requested specifically on large corporation's notice of objection.

Notes: 152(4.4) added by 1992 technical bill and amended by 1993 technical bill.

(5) Limitation on assessments

— There shall not be included in computing the income of a taxpayer for a taxation year, for the purpose of an assessment, reassessment or additional assessment made under this Part after the taxpayer's normal reassessment period in respect of the year, any amount that was not included in computing the taxpayer's income for the purpose of an assessment, reassessment or additional assessment made under this Part before the end of the period.

Related Provisions: 12(2.2) — Deemed outlay or expense; 67.5(2) — Reassessments; 127(17) — Assessment re ITC SR&ED pool beyond the deadline; 152(1.7) — Limitation period re determination of partnership income or loss; 152(3.1) — Normal reassessment period; 152(4.01) — Limitation on extended assessments; 152(4.2) — Assessment; 152(4.3) — Consequential assessment; 152(9) — Minister allowed to raise alternative ground of assessment; 160.2(3) — Minister may assess recipient under RRSP or RRIF; 161.1(7) — Late assessment to allow interest offset allocation.

Notes: Many provisions throughout the Act and amending bills provide that assessments can be made "notwithstanding subsections 152(4) to (5)", overriding this rule.

152(5) is a leftover provision that was partly replaced by 152(4.01), but still applies to a reassessment under 165(3) following an objection. (Finance Technical Notes, Dec. 1997) It is rarely cited today but may still be useful for taxpayers. It was held not to apply in *Last*, 2014 FCA 129, paras. 50-53 (leave to appeal denied to Crown 2014 CarswellNat 4451 (SCC)); and *Savics*, 2021 FCA 56, paras. 35-52 (152(5) does not stop CRA from restoring original filing position on cancelling reassessment). It applied in *Foster*, 2015 TCC 334 to permit reassessment of a shareholder benefit at the objection stage with a differently-calculated shareholder benefit, since the "crux" of the reassessments was identical. See also discussion in *Rio Tinto*, 2017 TCC 67, paras. 236-278 (FCA appeal discontinued A-153-17) (interaction with 152(4.01)).

152(5) amended by 1995-97 technical bill, retroactive to April 28, 1989, to delete paras. (b) and (c) and fold what was para. (a) into the body of the subsection. Paras. (b) and (c) are now covered in 152(4.01)(a)(i) and (ii).

152(5) amended by 1989 Budget, effective April 28, 1989, other than for a tax year for which an original notice of assessment (or notification that no tax is payable) was mailed by April 27, 1986. The normal reassessment period was 3 years before the amendment.

I.T. Application Rules: 62(1) (where waiver filed before December 23, 1971).

Interpretation Bulletins: IT-241: Reassessments made after the four-year limit (cancelled).

(6) Reassessment where certain deductions claimed [carrybacks]

— Where a taxpayer has filed for a particular taxation

year the return of income required by section 150 and an amount is subsequently claimed by the taxpayer or on the taxpayer's behalf for the year as

(a) a deduction under paragraph 3(e) of the *Income Tax Act*, chapter 148 of the Revised Statutes of Canada, 1952, by virtue of the taxpayer's death in a subsequent taxation year and the consequent application of section 71 of that Act in respect of an allowable capital loss for the year,

(b) a deduction under section 41 in respect of the taxpayer's listed-personal-property loss for a subsequent taxation year,

(b.1) a deduction under paragraph 60(i) in respect of a premium (within the meaning assigned by subsection 146(1)) paid in a subsequent taxation year under a registered retirement savings plan where the premium is deductible by reason of subsection 146(6.1),

(c) a deduction under section 118.1 in respect of a gift made in a subsequent taxation year or under section 111 in respect of a loss for a subsequent taxation year,

(c.1) [Repealed]

(d) a deduction under subsection 127(5) in respect of property acquired or an expenditure made in a subsequent taxation year,

(e) [Repealed]

(f) a deduction under section 125.3 in respect of an unused Part I.3 tax credit (within the meaning assigned by subsection 125.3(3)) for a subsequent taxation year,

(f.1) a deduction under subsection 126(2) in respect of an unused foreign tax credit (within the meaning assigned by subsection 126(7)), or under subsection 126(2.21) or (2.22) in respect of foreign taxes paid, for a subsequent taxation year,

(f.2) a deduction under subsection 128.1(8) as a result of a disposition in a subsequent taxation year,

(f.3) a deduction (including for the purposes of this subsection a reduction of an amount otherwise required to be included in computing a taxpayer's income) under subsection 146(8.9) or (8.92), 146.3(6.2) or (6.3) or 147.5(14) or (19),

(g) a deduction under subsection 147.2(4) because of the application of subsection 147.2(6) as a result of the taxpayer's death in the subsequent taxation year, or

(h) a deduction by virtue of an election for a subsequent taxation year under paragraph 164(6)(c) or (d) by the taxpayer's legal representative,

by filing with the Minister, on or before the day on or before which the taxpayer is, or would be if a tax under this Part were payable by the taxpayer for that subsequent taxation year, required by section 150 to file a return of income for that subsequent taxation year, a prescribed form amending the return, the Minister shall reassess the taxpayer's tax for any relevant taxation year (other than a taxation year preceding the particular taxation year) in order to take into account the deduction claimed.

Related Provisions: 111 — Losses deductible; 150 — Returns; 152(4)(b)(i) — Reassessment limitation period; 161(7)(b)(iii) — Effect of carryback of loss, etc.; 164(5), (5.1) — No back interest on refund where past year reassessed; 165(1.1) — Limitation of right to object to assessments or determinations; 169(2)(a) — Limitation of right to appeal. See also Related Provisions under 152(4).

Notes: 152(6) extends the period during which CRA can be forced to reassess to allow various carrybacks to an earlier year, since the objection period for the earlier year will normally have expired when the later year's return is filed. (A regular business loss carryback is under 152(6)(c): "a deduction ... under section 111".) CRA's view (Phil Jolie email to Jeffrey Meyers Oct. 8/09) is that 152(6) is subject to a 3-year time limit beyond the usual 3- or 4-year reassessment deadline, as 152(6) is specifically referred to in 152(4)(b)(i) (see also *Income Tax Audit Manual* §11.3.3). This view is likely correct. See also VIEWS doc 2010-0353711E5, to the same effect, re a 128.1(8) election; and 2010-037764117, re reassessment to deny a loss previously carried back. CRA policy allows a loss carryback where a CRA-generated adjustment increases income for a year to which a loss can be applied: *1455257 Ontario*, 2020 TCC 64, para. 53 (FCA appeal heard June 21/21). For a s. 119 credit, the time is extended by 152(6.3). For an option under s. 49, see 49(4).

152(6)(f.3): CRA must reassess up to 6 years back to allow a RRIF or RRSP to claim post-death losses: VIEWS doc 2015-0592681E5.

152(6)(h) "does not require the Estate to file the amended return" [this affects a 152(4)(a) determination of misrepresentation] "but rather addresses the consequences that would flow once the required form has been filed": *Vine Estate*, 2015 FCA 125, para. 31.

See also Ian Crosbie, "Amended Returns, Refunds and Interest", 2012 *Tax Dispute Resolution* conf. report (ctf.ca), 27:1-33.

The closing words "take into account" mean that CRA must consider the claim, but need not accept it if it is not a valid claim: *Greene*, 1995 CarswellNat 1841 (FCA)

Due to the closing words of 152(6), if the later year's return containing the Form T1A is even 1 day late, the taxpayer cannot force CRA to carry back the loss (though for an individual, CRA may do so under 152(4.2)).

After 152(6) is used, CRA can use it again to increase tax even if the 152(4) deadline has passed: *Agazarian*, 2004 FCA 32 (leave to appeal denied 2004 CarswellNat 4638 (SCC)).

For the calculation of interest when loss carrybacks are applied, see VIEWS docs 2006-0189491E5, 2008-029425117.

152(6)(b.1) added by 1990 pension bill, effective 1991.

152(6)(c.1) repealed by 2002-2013 technical bill (Part 5 — technical), for taxation years that end after Oct. 1, 1996. The version in force for taxation years ending after Oct. 1, 1996, as amended by 2000 Budget/2001 technical bill but now deemed never to have been in force, referred to a deduction under s. 119. See now 152(6.3), which provides that credits are available to emigrant taxpayers without regard to the usual reassessment deadlines.

152(6)(e), referring to a deduction under 125.2 for an unused Part VI tax credit under 125.2(3), repealed by 2002-2013 technical bill (Part 5 — technical), for taxation years that begin after Oct. 2011. See Notes to repealed 125.2.

152(6)(f) added by 1989 Budget, effective for taxation years ending after June 1989.

152(6)(f.1) and (f.2) added by 2001 technical bill, effective for taxation years that end after October 1, 1996.

152(6)(f.3) added by 2009 budget bill #1, effective for a RRIF or RRSP from which the last payment is made after 2008; and amended by 2012 budget bill #2 to refer to 147.5(14) and (19), effective Dec. 14, 2012.

152(6)(g) added by 1995-97 technical bill, effective for deaths after 1992.

I.T. Application Rules: 69 (meaning of "chapter 148 of ...").

Income Tax Folios: S5-F2-C1: Foreign tax credit [replaces IT-270R3, IT-395R2, IT-520].

Interpretation Bulletins: IT-124R6: Contributions to registered retirement savings plans; IT-232R3: Losses — their deductibility in the loss year or in other years.

Information Circulars: 75-7R3: Reassessment of a return of income.

CRA Audit Manual: 11.3.3: Application of losses; 11.5.4: Additional assessments.

Forms: T1A: Request for loss carryback; T1-ADJ: Adjustment request; T2 Sched. 4: Corporation loss continuity and application; T67B, T67BCD, T67BD, T458, T459, T493: Notices of reassessment.

(6.1) Reassessment if amount under subsec. 91(1) is reduced [foreign accrual property loss carryback] — If

(a) a taxpayer has filed for a particular taxation year the return of income required by section 150,

(b) the amount included in computing the taxpayer's income for the particular year under subsection 91(1) is subsequently reduced because of a reduction in the foreign accrual property income of a foreign affiliate of the taxpayer for a taxation year (referred to in this paragraph as the "claim year") of the affiliate that ends in the particular year, if

(i) the reduction is

(A) attributable to a foreign accrual property loss (within the meaning assigned by subsection 5903(3) of the *Income Tax Regulations*) of the affiliate for a taxation year of the affiliate that ends in a subsequent taxation year of the taxpayer, and

(B) included in the description of F in the definition "foreign accrual property income" in subsection 95(1) in respect of the affiliate for the claim year, or

(ii) the reduction is

(A) attributable to a foreign accrual capital loss (within the meaning assigned by subsection 5903.1(3) of the *Income Tax Regulations*) of the affiliate for a taxation year of the affiliate that ends in a subsequent taxation year of the taxpayer, and

(B) included in the description of F.1 in the definition "foreign accrual property income" in subsection 95(1) in respect of the affiliate for the claim year, and

(c) the taxpayer has filed with the Minister, on or before the filing-due date for that subsequent taxation year, a prescribed form amending the return,

the Minister shall reassess the taxpayer's tax for any relevant taxation year (other than a taxation year preceding the particular year) in order to take into account the reduction in the amount included under subsection 91(1) in computing the income of the taxpayer for the particular year.

Related Provisions: 152(4)(b)(i) — Reassessment limitation period; 161(7)(a)(xii), (7)(b)(iii), 164(5)(h.4), (k) — Interest calculation on carryback of FAPL; 261(15) — Application of functional currency rules; Reg. 5903(1)(b) — Loss carryback.

Notes: 152(6.1)(b) amended, effectively to add new (b)(ii), by 2002-2013 technical bill, for tax years that end after Aug. 19, 2011.

152(6.1)(b) amended by 2002-2013 technical bill (Part 2 — FA surplus rules), effective for taxation years that begin after Nov. 1999. The amendment reflects the restructuring of Reg. 5903 and 95(1)"foreign accrual property income"F.

152(6.1) added by 2001 technical bill, effective for taxation years of foreign affiliates that begin after Nov. 1999.

(6.2) Extended reassessment period — The Minister shall reassess a taxpayer's tax for a particular taxation year, in order to take into account the application of paragraph (d) of the definition "excluded property" in subsection 142.2(1), or the application of subsection 142.6(1.6), in respect of property held by the taxpayer, if

(a) the taxpayer has filed for the particular taxation year the return of income required by section 150; and

(b) the taxpayer files with the Minister a prescribed form amending the return, on or before the filing-due date for the taxpayer's taxation year that

(i) if the filing is in respect of paragraph (d) of that definition "excluded property", includes the acquisition of control time referred to in that paragraph, and

(ii) if the filing is in respect of subsection 142.6(1.6), immediately follows the particular taxation year.

Notes: 152(6.2) added by 2008 budget bill #2, for tax years that begin after 2001, but

(a) for taxation years that began before Oct. 1, 2006, read 142.2(1)"excluded property"(d) as 142.2(1)"market-to-market property"(d.3); and

(b) a prescribed form in 152(6.2)(b) is deemed filed on time if it is filed by the taxpayer by the "filing-due date" (see 248(1)) for the taxpayer's taxation year that includes March 12, 2009.

(6.3) Reassessment for s. 119 credit — If a taxpayer has filed for a particular taxation year the return of income required by section 150 and an amount is subsequently claimed by the taxpayer, or on the taxpayer's behalf, for the particular year as a deduction under section 119 in respect of a disposition in a subsequent taxation year, and the taxpayer files with the Minister a prescribed form amending the return on or before the filing-due date of the taxpayer for the subsequent taxation year, the Minister shall reassess the taxpayer's tax for any relevant taxation year (other than a taxation year preceding the particular taxation year) in order to take into account the deduction claimed.

Notes: 152(6.3) added by 2002-2013 technical bill (Part 5 — technical), for particular taxation years that end after Oct. 1, 1996. However, if a prescribed form referred to in 152(6.3) is filed with the Minister by the taxpayer's filing-due date for the taxation year that includes June 26, 2013, the form is deemed to have been filed on time. (152(6.3) replaces former 152(6)(c.1), which was narrower in scope.)

(7) Assessment not dependent on return or information — The Minister is not bound by a return or information supplied by or on behalf of a taxpayer and, in making an assessment, may, notwithstanding a return or information so supplied or if no return has been filed, assess the tax payable under this Part.

Related Provisions: 152(4) — Reassessment; 165 — Objections to assessments; 169 — Appeal to Tax Court of Canada.

Notes: Although usual CRA practice is to send a proposal letter before a reassessment (see Notes to 231.1(1)), this is not a legal requirement and CRA can assess any amount at any time (subject to limitation periods such as 152(4)): VIEWS doc 2015-0599851I7 (plan to assess excess TFSA contributions). Where a taxpayer does not file for a long time, CRA may issue an "arbitrary" assessment based on estimates or guesses. This is legally like any other assessment: see 152(4) Notes.

Onus: The burden is on the taxpayer to disprove an assessment: *Johnston*, [1948] C.T.C. 195 (SCC); and see detailed discussion by Webb J.A. in *Sarmadi*, 2017 FCA 131, paras. 18-63 (the other judges did not disagree with his analysis but declined to express an opinion: paras. 16, 71) [Sorenson, "Standard of Proof and Prime Facie Case", 25(11) *Canadian Tax Highlights* (ctf.ca) 5-7 (Nov. 2017)]; and see *Agracity*, 2020 TCC 91, paras. 100-105. On the Crown pleading assumptions of law, or of mixed fact and law, see *Lohas Farm*, 2019 TCC 197, paras. 29-60. If CRA assumes new facts on confirming an assessment following an objection, the taxpayer has the onus of disproving them: *Anchor Pointe*, 2007 FCA 188, paras. 31, 44 (leave to appeal denied 2008 CarswellNat 76 (SCC)). If the taxpayer "demolishes" the Minister's precise assumptions by making a *prima facie* case (on balance of probabilities: *Sarmadi* above), the onus shifts to the Crown, and if the Crown adduces no evidence, the taxpayer is entitled to succeed: *Hickman Motors*, [1998] 1 C.T.C. 213 (SCC), paras. 92-95; *McMillan*, 2012 FCA 126, para. 7; *Last*, 2012 TCC 352, para. 33 (aff'd on other grounds 2014 FCA 129); *Basi*, 2012 TCC 345, para. 7. However, the appellant must also prove the material facts alleged in the Notice of Appeal: *Eisbrenner (Morrison)*, 2020 FCA 93, para. 52 (leave to appeal denied 2021 CarswellNat 72 (SCC)). In *Brewster*, 2012 TCC 187, the Crown pleaded only a conclusion of mixed fact and law (that the taxpayer's RRSP had acquired non-qualified investments): "if the Minister has not made any valid assumptions that would support the reassessment, there are no assumptions for the Appellant to 'demolish' and therefore the Appellant will be successful" (para. 14); the same applied in *Mont-Bruno CC*, 2017 CarswellNat 3165 (TCC). "As a practical matter the onus of proof matters only where, at the end of the hearing on the evidence... the Court is unable to make a finding in respect of one or more material facts": *Keybrand Foods*, 2019 TCC 161, para. 72, footnote 50 (aff'd 2020 FCA 201 without discussing this point).

Northland Properties, 2010 BCCA 177, para. 35, reinterpreted *Hickman* as meaning "(i) What are the assumptions? (ii) Have some or all of the assumptions been disproven (has the taxpayer discharged the initial legal burden)? (iii) If the taxpayer has successfully discharged the initial legal burden, then has the Crown shown that the assessment is valid (has the Crown discharged the conditional legal burden)?". See Innes, "Assumptions Revisited?", XVII(2) *Tax Litigation* (Federated Press) 1038-44 (2010).

For detailed discussion see Kroft & Douglas, "Onus and Standard of Proof in Canadian Tax Litigation", 2012 *Tax Dispute Resolution* conf. report (ctf.ca), 9:1-44; Kroft & Pelletier, "Onus of Proof in Canadian Tax Litigation", *Bennett Jones on Tax Disputes*, *Taxnet Pro* Tax Disputes Centre (Jan. 2021, 17pp).

Oral evidence, if credible, can disprove Crown assumptions: *House*, 2011 FCA 234 (cash not received by taxpayer); *Nelson*, 2017 TCC 178, para. 45 (contract existed); *Dépatie*, 2019 TCC 123, para. 29 (due to trust within family, "contracts, share certificates and agreements are not really of importance" so D had share in company profits); *Anand*, 2019 TCC 119 ("patent ambiguity" or "latent ambiguity" in a contract justifies looking at oral evidence); Yasny, "Demolishing Ministerial Assumptions", 19(9) *Canadian Tax Highlights* (ctf.ca) 5-6 (Sept. 2011). See also 9(1) Notes at "Cash expenses".

Facts not within the taxpayer's knowledge must be proven by the Crown, not merely assumed: *Anchor Pointe*, 2007 FCA 188, para. 36; and (all TCC): *Bell*, [1996] 2 C.T.C. 2191; *Edwards*, [1998] 4 C.T.C. 2906; *Gestion Yvan Drouin*, [2001] 2 C.T.C. 2315; *Simon*, [2002] 4 C.T.C. 2358, paras. 61-80; *Holm*, [2003] 2 C.T.C. 2041, para. 20; *Beaudry*, 2003 TCC 464; *Redash Trading*, 2004 TCC 446; *Calistar Construction*, 2004 TCC 451; *Westborough Place*, 2007 TCC 155; *Ahmad*, 2007 TCC 382, paras. 9-10; *Lavie*, 2006 TCC 655; *Cappadoro*, 2012 TCC 267, para. 34; *Mignardi*, 2013 TCC 67, para. 41; *Monsell*, 2019 TCC 5, paras. 28-31 [Cepparo, "Shifting the Burden of Proof", 27(3) *Canadian Tax Highlights* (ctf.ca) 8-9 (March 2019)]. However, this applies only to facts "solely, exclusively or peculiarly within the Minister's knowledge", not to details about a charity scheme to which the taxpayer donated: *Jensen*, 2018 TCC 60, para. 67; *Morrison (Eisbrenner)*, 2018 TCC 220, paras. 113-120 (aff'd 2020 FCA 93 without addressing this issue; leave to appeal denied 2021 CarswellNat 42 (SCC)).

CRA cannot assess arbitrarily solely to follow a Revenu Québec reassessment: *126632 Canada*, 2008 TCC 132. CRA may also have to show that its audit work was done properly: *Huyen*, [1997] G.S.T.C. 42 (TCC); *Gestion Cheers*, [2001] G.S.T.C. 44 (TCC); *Hsu*, 2006 TCC 304.

Net worth assessment (NWA): CRA can issue a NWA of a taxpayer who appears to have unreported income, by measuring assets at the beginning and end of a period, estimating expenses and presuming the difference to be income. 152(7) confirms that this can be done with cheerful disregard for what the taxpayer has reported. Net worth is called a method of "last resort": *Ramey*, [1993] 2 C.T.C. 2119 (TCC); *Bigayan*, [2000] 1 C.T.C. 2229 (TCC). CRA does not need to specify a theory or income source for a NWA: *Hsu*, 2001 FCA 240, para. 30; *Landry*, 2010 FCA 135, para. 37; *Lee*, 2017 TCC 74, para. 17; even to apply penalties (163(2)) or assess late (152(4)(a)): *Bouromand*, 2015 TCC 320, para. 69 (aff'd 2016 FCA 313). In a NWA, gambling losses reported by casinos can indicate unreported income: *Truong*, 2018 FCA 6, para. 12 (leave to appeal denied 2018 CarswellNat 5785 (SCC)). Income tax debts should not be counted as liabilities: *Duffy*, 2019 TCC 75, paras. 36-43. See also David Graham (now a Tax Court judge), "Anatomy of a Net Worth Assessment", 2007 BC Tax Conference (ctf.ca), 11:1-55; and Webb J (now of the FCA) in *Omer*, 2009 TCC 158, paras. 14-19 (how to apply adjustments to personal expenses when doing a NWA).

NWAs were upheld in *Hsu*, 2001 FCA 240; *Mercier*, 2007 FCA 234; *Sturzer*, 2009 FCA 329; *Lacroix*, 2008 FCA 241; *Ohayon*, 2011 FCA 100; *Pelletier*, 2011 FCA 21; *Korki*, 2011 FCA 287; *Gagnon*, 2012 FCA 328; *Ostroff*, 2013 FCA 79; *Avrams*, 2013

FCA 123; *Boros*, 2014 FCA 147; *Boroumand*, 2016 FCA 313; *Sarmadi*, 2017 FCA 131; *Truong*, 2018 FCA 6 (leave to appeal denied 2018 CarswellNat 5785 (SCC)); *Biron*, [1985] 1 C.T.C. 2014 (TCC)); *Prymych*, 2007 TCC 80; *Vigeant*, 2009 TCC 143; *Nichols*, 2009 TCC 334; *Aubin*, 2009 TCC 600; *Dao*, 2010 TCC 84; *Tam*, 2010 TCC 157; *Samboun*, 2010 TCC 249; *Sanchez*, 2010 TCC 283 (FCA appeal discontinued A-326-10); *Cranston*, 2010 TCC 414 (extension of time to appeal denied 2010 FCA 327 and 2011 FCA 5) (C could not challenge criminal court's findings in Tax Court); *Lawrence*, 2010 TCC 480 (involvement in Ponzi scheme); *Madhollal*, 2010 TCC 524, *Borno*, 2011 TCC 119; *Gingras*, 2011 TCC 439; *Lucas*, 2011 TCC 527; *Le*, 2012 TCC 349; *Desroches*, 2013 TCC 81; *Kalib*, 2013 TCC 134; *Joseph*, 2014 TCC 120; *Gobeil*, 2014 TCC 361; *Okoroze*, 2015 TCC 64 (FCA appeal dismissed for delay A-208-15); *Mehravaran*, 2015 TCC 209; *Agostini*, 2015 TCC 215; *To*, 2016 TCC 176; *Gorev*, 2017 TCC 85; *Auto Maculate*, 2020 TCC 105; and many others.

NWAs were rejected in: *Francisco*, [2003] 2 C.T.C. 2378 (TCC) (spouses' incomes should not be combined to determine their net worth increase and allocate part of income to each); *Mensah*, 2008 TCC 378 (M's records were adequate); *Nguyen*, 2008 TCC 675 (funds came from N's mother in Vietnam); *Quentin*, 2009 TCC 461 (Q lived on cash he kept at home); *Docherty*, 2010 TCC 45 (gifts from family members); *Berezuik*, 2010 TCC 296 (auditor's calculations were "barely comprehensible" and contained "serious errors", including doing 1 net worth calculation for 2 taxpayers and counting value of grain grown on farm as though it were cash); *Kozar*, 2010 TCC 389 (CRA's assumptions of illegal income were unfounded: K had evidence of wedding gifts, loans, assets held for family members and that CRA's expense calculations were inflated; Court awarded K solicitor-client costs, citing "the obligation of CRA employees to act and perform their duties in good faith" (para. 90)); *Swarbrick*, 2010 TCC 605 (S had credible explanation of source of funds and having kept cash at home); *Rail*, 2011 TCC 130 (assessment based on provincial average profit margin for dentists was "fundamentally flawed"); *Virani*, 2011 TCC 236 (assessment methodology was flawed); *Daimsis*, 2014 TCC 118 (D's expenses were paid by her then-fiancé and she worked very little during years under appeal); *Hot Spot*, 2014 TCC 318 (income of deceased who ran business wrongly allocated to his widow).

NWAs were reduced, based on evidence, in: *Cheng*, 1997 CarswellNat 362 (TCC) (loan from parents proven); *Lafond*, 2006 TCC 7; *West*, 2006 TCC 580 (CRA's assumptions about expenses did not correspond to reality of W's lifestyle); *Janda*, 2007 TCC 237; *Seto*, 2007 TCC 489; *Altamimi*, 2007 TCC 553; *Milkowski*, 2007 TCC 680; *Beavies*, 2008 TCC 94; *Wang*, 2008 TCC 308; *Grein*, 2009 FCA 358 (reduction to reflect G's sale of personal belongings and low cost of living); *Brar*, 2008 TCC 647 (FCA appeal discontinued A-620-08) (reduction to reflect undocumented wedding gifts); *Serwatkewich*, 2009 TCC 29 (CRA assumptions were incorrect, and no evidence that taxpayer was selling marijuana); *Corriveau*, 2009 TCC 33 (small reduction because lifestyle expenses were lower than CRA's figures); *Sprio*, 2009 TCC 275 (various adjustments); *Tremblay*, 2009 TCC 313 (one amount was a loan); *Landry*, 2010 FCA 135 (L, nude dancer, received large loan from "X"; but no onus on CRA to investigate X when assessing L); *Tremblay*, 2009 TCC 359 (various adjustments); *Sarwari*, 2009 TCC 357 (calculation incorrectly included gain on principal residence and overstated mortgage; funds also received from family members); *Liang*, 2009 TCC 567 (various adjustments); *Golden*, 2009 TCC 396 (minor adjustments); *Jewett*, 2010 TCC 4 (depreciation allowed on rental properties, and other adjustments); *Shair*, 2011 FCA 315 (various adjustments); *Denisov*, 2010 TCC 101 (adjustment for cash withdrawn for condo purchase); *Garage Gilles Gingras*, 2010 TCC 343 (G had inherited a sum, and his cost of living was lower than CRA calculated); *Guibord*, 2011 FCA 344 (various adjustments); *IPAX Canada*, 2010 TCC 427 (funds came from mortgage loan); *Mann*, 2010 TCC 440 (houses were owned by other family members); *Hanna*, 2010 TCC 442 (reduction for disability insurance payments); *Bogzaran*, 2010 TCC 457 (seized cash was likely crime proceeds from a later year); *Zaki*, 2010 TCC 606 (various adjustments); *Vatchiants*, 2011 TCC 14 (funds received were repayment of investment); *Truong*, 2011 TCC 72 (loans from relatives, and a property was being held for a third party); *Chow*, 2011 TCC 263 (various adjustments); *Ha*, 2011 TCC 271 (amounts were loans, transfers, insurance settlement and RRSP proceeds); *Felske*, 2011 TCC 372; *Phan*, 2011 TCC 392 (gifts from mother in Vietnam, and CRA wrongly calculated expenses as if P were married); *Dompierre*, 2011 TCC 509 (minor adjustments); *Zheng*, 2012 TCC 103 (funds were from family members); *Truong*, 2013 TCC 41 ($50,000 cash belonged to someone else, and $50,000 had been double-counted); *Lenneville*, 2013 TCC 56; *Hedzic*, 2013 TCC 249 (FCA appeal discontinued A-393-13); *McLeod*, 2013 TCC 269 (reduced inclusion in shareholder loan account); *Vicars*, 2013 TCC 329 (FCA appeal discontinued A-386-13); *Dryden*, 2014 TCC 241; *Barbieri*, 2015 TCC 15 (statute-barred assessments, and Crown did not meet onus of proof on some points); *Kang (Tang)*, 2015 FCA 271 (unexplained cash could not simultaneously have been earned by different taxpayers, and cash seized from corp was not income of shareholders); *Yunus*, 2015 TCC 272 (some loans from family members accepted — but the decision may be a nullity due to *Birchcliff Energy* — see Notes to 169(1) under "Replacement by the Chief Justice"); *Kim*, 2016 TCC 150 (one expense item overestimated); *Lee*, 2017 TCC 74 (various adjustments reduced unreported income from $365,000 to $110,000); *Tang*, 2017 TCC 168 (large loans from family members); *Sycheva*, 2018 TCC 180 (loan from friend in Russia); *Owda*, 2019 TCC 46 (son-in-law contributed to family living costs); *Duffy*, 2019 TCC 75, para. 24 (CRA wrongly calculated foreign currency conversion), para. 29 (double counting).

Even if the assessment methodology is upheld, 163(2) penalty may be cancelled without specific proof of gross negligence: *Seto*, 2007 TCC 489; *Milkowski*, 2007 TCC 680; *Omer*, 2009 TCC 158; *Dachkov*, 2009 TCC 403; *Lee*, 2017 TCC 74; *Gorev*, 2017 TCC 85, para. 58; *Owda*, 2019 TCC 46, para. 28; *Fry*, 2019 TCC 236, para. 49. The penalty was upheld in *Liang*, 2009 TCC 567; *Dao*, 2010 TCC 84; *Momperousse*, 2010 TCC 172; *Ohayon*, 2011 FCA 100; *Choi*, 2010 TCC 348; *St-Philippe*, 2011 TCC 284; *Zouaimia*, 2011 TCC 436 (aff'd by FCA without discussing the penalty); *Guan*, 2011 TCC 518; *Le*, 2012 TCC 349; *Truong*, 2013 TCC 41; *Desroches*, 2013 TCC 81; *Kalib*, 2013 TCC 134; *Okoroze*, 2015 TCC 64 (FCA appeal dismissed for delay A-208-15); *Auto Maculate*, 2020 TCC 105, paras. 226-241; and many others. In *Le Tremble*, 2006 TCC 568, "nonchalance, imprudence, negligence, total disinterest and absence of accounting records" were sufficient to establish gross negligence. Some decisions are based on *Molenaar*, 2004 FCA 349, para. 4 and *Lacroix*, 2008 FCA 241: not having a credible explanation for significant unreported income is enough to justify the penalty (see Notes to 163(2)). For convictions based on NWAs see Notes to 239(1).

In *Golden*, 2009 FCA 86, the taxpayers were estopped from contesting a NWA after being convicted of tax evasion. See Notes to 239(1).

Other audit methodologies are also used (and are sometimes incorrectly called "net worth assessments" by the Courts). See Notes to 231.1(1) re the "bank deposits" methodology and others. In both *Medvedev*, 2010 TCC 629 (appeal to FCA allowed in part on consent, A-485-10), and *Schmidt*, 2013 TCC 11 (FCA appeal discontinued A-146-12), the TCC ruled that CRA should have used the net worth method rather than the bank-deposits method (where the taxpayer had a good explanation for the deposits) because it is more reliable and is the preferred method in the *CRA Audit Manual*. In *Dionne*, [2013] G.S.T.C. 34 (TCC), the taxpayer successfully presented a net worth calculation to show that the auditor's "bank deposits" calculation was wrong.

CRA Audit Manual: 11.5.3: Assessments under subsections 152(7) of the ITA and 299(1) of the ETA; 13.2.0: Audit of non-taxable sources of funds; 13.3.0: Indirect verification of income; 13.4.0 and Appendix 13.3.0: Net worth; 13.6.0: Assessments based on projections; 28.4.0: False statements or omissions.

(8) Assessment deemed valid and binding — An assessment shall, subject to being varied or vacated on an objection or appeal under this Part and subject to a reassessment, be deemed to be valid and binding notwithstanding any error, defect or omission in the assessment or in any proceeding under this Act relating thereto.

Related Provisions: 152(3) — Liability for tax not affected by incorrect or incomplete assessment; 152(4) — Reassessment; 158 — Assessed amount payable forthwith; 160(2) — Minister may assess transferee; 160.2(3) — Minister may assess recipient; 165 — Objections to assessments; 166 — Assessment not to be vacated by reason of improper procedures; 172 — Appeal; 225.1 — Collection restrictions while assessment under objection or appeal.

Notes: 152(8) is not absolute. A third party assessed under s. 160 for a transferor's liability can contest the validity of the assessment of the transferor: *Gaucher*, [2001] 1 C.T.C. 125 (FCA), and see #6 in 227.1(1) Notes re a director contesting a corporation's assessment.

152(8) cannot be used to prevent the Crown from taking a position in a Reply that is inconsistent with an earlier, unappealed, assessment: *McAdams*, 2014 FCA 99; *LaBuick*, [1998] G.S.T.C. 122 (TCC); *DenHaan*, 2008 TCC 126; *Landbouwbedrijf Backx*, 2021 TCC 2, para. 65 (under appeal to FCA). More generally, 152(8) is "designed to relieve the Minister from detrimental consequences of errors in his department", and cannot be used to force CRA to honour a wording mistake in a notice of assessment: *Riendeau*, [1990] 1 C.T.C. 141 (FCTD), para. 21; *Karam*, 2015 FC 600, para. 29 (aff'd on other grounds 2016 FCA 86; leave to appeal denied 2016 CarswellNat 4145 (SCC)).

In *Riendeau*, [1991] 2 C.T.C. 64 (FCA), a reference in an assessment to a repealed provision was held not to invalidate the assessment, since the taxpayer was liable on other grounds: "A taxpayer's liability for tax is just the same whether a notice of assessment is mistaken or never sent at all" (para. 2).

See Notes to 152(4) under "If an assessment is out of time" re whether 152(8) applies to a late assessment.

If the notice of assessment contains a substantive error such as assessing the wrong period, it may be invalid despite 152(8): *Horkoff*, [1996] 3 C.T.C. 2737 (TCC); *Cheema Cleaning*, 2009 TCC 145. CRA might disagree: VIEWS doc 2010-037477117. See also McNary, "When Can 'Incorrect or Incomplete' Be Sufficient To Overcome Deemed Validity?", 2015 *Tax Topics* (CCH) 1-3 (Oct. 21, 2010).

See also Notes to 152(2) re the form of a notice of assessment, and to 169(1) and 171(1) re the Federal Court's and Tax Court's powers with respect to assessments.

(9) Alternative basis for assessment — At any time after the normal reassessment period, the Minister may advance an alternative basis or argument — including that all or any portion of the income to which an amount relates was from a different source — in support of all or any portion of the total amount determined on assessment to be payable or remittable by a taxpayer under this Act unless, on an appeal under this Act

(a) there is relevant evidence that the taxpayer is no longer able to adduce without the leave of the court; and

(b) it is not appropriate in the circumstances for the court to order that the evidence be adduced.

Related Provisions: 152(5) — Limitation on income inclusion after normal reassessment period.

Notes: 152(9) was introduced (by 1998 Budget bill, for appeals disposed of after June 17, 1999) to respond to the Supreme Court of Canada ruling in *Continental Bank*, [1998] 4 C.T.C. 77, that the Crown cannot advance a new basis for assessment after the limitation period has expired. It read: "The Minister may advance an alternative argument in support of an assessment at any time after the normal reassessment period unless, on an appeal under this Act". It was then amended by 2016 budget bill #2, for appeals instituted after Dec. 15, 2016, to respond to the ruling in *Last*, 2014 FCA 129, para. 37 (leave to appeal denied 2014 CarswellNat 4451 (SCC)), that the Crown could not raise a new argument that would increase the amount of assessment on one issue, offset by reduction on another issue.

Absent 152(9), CRA cannot take into account transactions other than those that formed the basis of a timely reassessment: *Pedwell*, [2000] 3 C.T.C. 246 (FCA) (but in *Keurig Canada*, 2019 QCCQ 451, a new basis was allowed in a Quebec *Taxation Act* appeal without a 152(9)-like rule, where KC had made a false statement in its return). The same principle applies under 152(5) to prevent CRA from assessing a statute-barred year on a new basis at the objection stage: *Foster*, 2015 TCC 334, paras. 35-36.

(The July 29/16 draft amendment arguably would have allowed CRA to raise any new issue, eviscerating restrictions on reassessments past the limitation period: CBA/CPA Canada Joint Committee on Taxation letter to Finance, Sept. 27, 2016; and arguably did not fix the problem in *Last*: Hosanna, "Alternative Arguments on Appeal", 16(4) *Tax for the Owner-Manager* (ctf.ca) 3-5 (Oct. 2016). The revised version, released Oct. 21, 2016 and now in force, may fix these problems.)

There is no distinction between a new "basis" of assessment and a new "argument" supporting an assessment: *Anchor Pointe Energy*, 2003 FCA 294, para. 38 (the 2016 amendment now allows both). A different reason for the same reassessment is acceptable, but "anything that increases tax payable from what would have been the case prior to expiry of the normal reassessment period would be objectionable": para. 39 (see also 152(5) on this). The Crown can rely on new evidence that supports existing assumptions without amending its pleadings: *Goheen*, 2019 FCA 104, para. 13.

The expiry of the reassessment period does not preclude the Crown from defending an assessment on any ground, subject only to 152(9)(a) and (b), which speak to the prejudice to the taxpayer that may arise if the Crown is permitted to make new factual allegations many years after the event. A new argument asserted by the Crown under 152(9) could include an argument that would justify a higher assessment, but 152(9) does not relieve the Minister from the time limits in 152(4). Therefore, the Minister cannot use 152(9) to reassess outside the 152(4) limitations, or to collect more tax than already assessed: *Loewen*, 2004 FCA 146, para. 22 (leave to appeal denied 2004 CarswellNat 5843 (SCC)).

Where the taxpayer signed a waiver allowing late reassessment, 152(9) cannot be used to allow the Crown to raise a ground not specified in the waiver: *Honeywell Ltd.*, 2007 FCA 22. However, the alternative argument need only "reasonably" relate to the matters specified in the waiver: 152(4.01); and not applying a waiver to an undisclosed transaction would lead to an absurd result: *Gramiak*, 2015 FCA 40, para. 41.

In *Mammone*, 2019 FCA 45, CRA's retroactive revocation of an RPP registration under 147.1(12), after the limitation period expired, changed the factual basis underlying the reassessment and could not be based on 152(9) (before its 2016 amendment): "the Minister was in effect seeking to do away with the limitation period" (para. 39).

Other cases where a new basis for reassessment was allowed: *Hollinger Inc.*, [1999] 4 C.T.C. 61 (FCA); *SmithKline Beecham*, [2000] 2 C.T.C. 329 (FCA) (leave to appeal denied 2000 CarswellNat 2574 (SCC)); *Teck-Bullmoose Coal*, 2002 BCCA 101; *Bradley Holdings*, 2004 TCC 221 (but solicitor-client costs were awarded against the Crown); *Boudreault*, 2005 TCC 660; *Walsh*, 2007 FCA 222 (leave to appeal denied 2007 CarswellNat 4048) (but "the Minister cannot include transactions which did not form the basis of the taxpayer's reassessment"); *Toronto Dominion Bank*, 2008 TCC 284; *McLarty*, 2009 TCC 294 (after taxpayer won at SCC that obligation was not "contingent", Crown amended Reply to allege sham); *Wachsmann*, 2009 TCC 420 (non-reporting of capital gain was statute-barred but interest deduction was disallowed due to taxpayer's neglect); *Teelucksingh*, 2010 TCC 94 (Reply can raise different basis than was used for reassessing); *Greene*, 2010 TCC 162 (FCA appeal discontinued A-191-10) (CRA made wrong argument in confirming assessment but correct argument in Reply); *Lockie*, 2010 TCC 142 (FCA appeal discontinued A-164-10) (but new basis could not increase assessment); *Toronto Dominion Bank*, 2011 FCA 221, paras. 27-30 (written submissions made argument not raised at hearing); *General Electric*, 2012 TCC 564 (FCA appeal discontinued A-498-11); *Global Equity Fund*, 2012 FCA 272, para. 38 (leave to appeal denied 2013 CarswellNat 932) (legal basis for GAAR analysis changed at FCA; costs awarded to taxpayer); *Gill*, 2013 FCA 135 ("US pension" was sufficient basis for assessment of income from US IRA under 56(1)(a)(i)(C.1)); *Terasen International*, 2012 TCC 408 (Crown's appeal to FCA discontinued A-439-12) (amendments to Reply allowed but solicitor-client costs awarded to taxpayer); *Coveley*, 2013 TCC 417, para. 147 (aff'd on other grounds 2014 FCA 281) (new basis for denying ABIL was valid alternative to argument that debt was not bad); *Krenbrink Estate*, 2014 FCA 212 (Crown could argue that 152(4)(a)(i) applied so late assessment was valid); *Levert*, 2017 TCC 208, para. 53 (applying 246(1) instead of 15(1) when L turned out not to be a shareholder); *Aeronautic Development*, 2018 FCA 67, para. 54 (leave to appeal denied 2019 CarswellNat 595) (taxpayer was not taken by surprise by issue); *Thompson*, 2018 TCC 167 (tax shelter non-compliance arguments raised at end of discovery); *Marino*, 2020 TCC 50, paras. 115-128 (Informal Procedure, Crown relying on argument not in Reply; under appeal to FCA).

Cases where the Crown was not allowed to amend its pleadings *during trial*: *Burton*, 2006 FCA 67 (unfair); *Ritonja*, 2006 TCC 346 (Crown cannot raise unpleaded issue at trial); *Adler*, 2009 TCC 613 (at closing argument was too late: this would "circumvent procedural fairness"); *Fourney*, 2011 TCC 520, para. 70 (once trial begins, Crown cannot raise new argument); *Baribeau*, 2011 TCC 544, paras. 40-53 (same). The Crown cannot raise a new issue at the submissions stage that contradicts its admissions: *CanHorizon Inc.*, 2015 TCC 19, para. 35.

Cases where the Crown was not allowed to amend its pleadings *before trial*: *Poulton*, [2002] 2 C.T.C. 2405 (unfair to do so); *Papier Cascades Cabano*, 2005 TCC 396 (reversed on other grounds 2006 FCA 419) (CRA could not use 152(9) to do indirectly what it could not do directly, to deny credits it had already allowed for a statute-barred year); *Walsh*, 2008 TCC 282 (Crown could not argue donation had been overvalued, after assessing on basis there was no donation); *Cheema Cleaning*, 2009 TCC 145 (unreported revenue amounts assessed for 2005 could not be moved to 2004); *Cudmore*, 2010 TCC 318 ("I see no compelling reason to afford the Minister any opportunity to attempt to cooper-up its case with amendments after having the benefit of seeing the Appellant's argument"); *Drouin*, 2011 TCC 519 (pleadings were closed, trial date fixed and new arguments raised new factual questions); *Global Equity Fund*, 2012 FCA 272, para. 37 (leave to appeal denied 2013 CarswellNat 932 (SCC)) (argument raised at FCA that sale was on capital account might have been met with different evidence at TCC); *Last* (see first para. above); *McKay*, 2015 TCC 33 (corporation in receivership so appellant would suffer evidentiary prejudice).

When the Crown raises a new argument in its Reply, the onus is on the Crown to prove the facts supporting that argument: *Anchor Pointe*, 2007 FCA 188; *Swirsky*, 2013 TCC 73, para. 53 (aff'd on other grounds 2014 FCA 36).

The Crown can raise a new argument at the FCA: *594710 B.C.*, 2018 FCA 166, para. 34 (leave to appeal denied 2019 CarswellNat 434 (SCC)) (see also 169(1) Notes).

For discussion see Raphael & Horrigan, "CRA Reassessments and Alternative Arguments beyond the General Limitation Period", XV(1) *Sales Tax, Customs & Trade* (Federated Press) 14-18 (2018). Before the 2016 amendment: Innes & Bissell, "Basis for Assessment, Arguments and Assumptions", 52(1) *Canadian Tax Journal* 59-105 (2004); McMechan, "Alternative Bases for Defending Assessments", 2004 Cdn Tax Foundation conference report, 32:1-18.

See also Notes to 169(1), under "Pleadings".

I.T. Technical News: 16 (*Continental Bank* case).

CRA Audit Manual: 11.3.7: Assessment after the normal (re)assessment period and penalty for false statements or omissions.

(10) Tax deemed not assessed — Notwithstanding any other provision of this section, an amount of tax is deemed, for the purpose of any agreement entered into by or on behalf of the Government of Canada under section 7 of the *Federal-Provincial Fiscal Arrangements Act*, not to have been assessed under this Act until

(a) the end of the period during which the security is accepted by the Minister, if adequate security for the tax is accepted by the Minister under subsection 220(4.5) or (4.6); or

(b) the amount is collected by the Minister, if information relevant to the assessment of the amount was provided to the Canada Revenue Agency under a contract entered into by a person under a program administered by the Canada Revenue Agency to obtain information relating to tax non-compliance.

Related Provisions: 56(1)(z.4) — Payment to informant is taxable.

Notes: The reference to an agreement under s. 7 of the *Federal-Provincial Fiscal Arrangements Act* is to an agreement whereby the CRA is authorized to collect provincial taxes on behalf of a province. The effect of para. (b) is that payments are not made to provinces for amounts assessed under the Offshore Informant Program until the CRA has actually collected the tax assessed to the evader.

Some suggest that the Tax Court should not uphold an assessment on its own motion on a different ground than the Crown claims in its pleadings. The FCA stepped around this question in *Massicotte*, 2008 FCA 60 (leave to appeal denied 2008 CarswellNat 3438 (SCC)), as did the TCC in *Daniel Tremblay*, 2013 TCC 133; but in practice this clearly happens in some cases.

152(10)(b) added by 2014 budget bill #1, effective June 19, 2014.

152(10) added by 2001 technical bill, for taxation years that end after Oct. 1, 1996.

Definitions [s. 152]: "acquisition of control time" — 142.2(1)"excluded property"(d)(i); "allowable capital loss" — 38(b), 248(1); "amount" — 248(1); "arm's length" — 251(1); "assessment" — 248(1); "avoidance transaction" — 245(3); "balance" — 152(4.4); "calendar year" — *Interpretation Act* 37(1)(a); "Canadian-controlled private corporation" — 125(7), 248(1); "capital property" — 54, 248(1); "carries on a business in Canada" — 253; "claim year" — 152(6.1)(b); "corporation" — 248(1), *Interpretation Act* 35(1); "day of sending" — 244(14), (14.1); "disposition" — 248(1); "estate" — 104(1), 248(1); "excluded property" — 142.2(1); "farm loss" — 111(8), 248(1); "Federal Court of Appeal" — *Federal Courts Act* s. 3; "filing-due date" — 248(1); "fiscal period" — 249.1; "foreign accrual property income" — 95(1), (2), 248(1); "foreign accrual property loss" — Reg. 5903(3); "foreign affiliate" — 95(1), 248(1); "graduated rate estate" — 248(1); "immovable" — Quebec *Civil Code* art. 900-907; "income or profits tax" — 126(4); "individual" — 248(1); "limited partnership loss" — 96(2.1)(e), 248(1); "listed personal property" — 54, 248(1); "Minister" — 248(1); "month" — *Interpretation Act* 35(1); "net capital loss", "non-capital loss" — 111(8), 248(1); "non-resident" — 248(1); "normal reassessment period" — 152(3.1); "partnership" — see 96(1) Notes; "person", "prescribed", "property" — 248(1); "province" — *Interpretation Act* 35(1); "provincial reassessment" — 152(4)(d); "qualifying period" — 125.7(1); "real estate investment trust" — 122.1(1); "registered retirement savings plan" — 146(1), 248(1); "restricted farm loss" — 31, 248(1); "security" — *Interpretation Act* 35(1); "share" — 248(1); "specified foreign property" — 233.3(1); "tax benefit" — 245(1); "tax consequences" — 152(1.111), 245(1); "tax shelter" — 237.1(1), 248(1); "taxable income" — 2(2), 248(1); "taxable income earned in Canada" — 115(1), 248(1); "taxation year" — 249; "taxpayer" — 248(1); "transaction" — 152(1.111), 245(1), 247(1); "trust" — 104(1), 108(1), 248(1), (3); "writing" — *Interpretation Act* 35(1).

Payment of Tax

153. (1) Withholding [source deductions] — Every person paying at any time in a taxation year

(a) salary, wages or other remuneration, other than

(i) amounts described in subsection 212(5.1), and

(ii) amounts paid at any time by an employer to an employee if, at that time, the employer is a qualifying non-resident employer and the employee is a qualifying non-resident employee,

(b) a superannuation or pension benefit,

(c) a retiring allowance,

(d) a death benefit,

(d.1) an amount described in subparagraph 56(1)(a)(iv) or (vii),

(d.2) an amount described in paragraph 56(1)(a.3),

(e) an amount as a benefit under a supplementary unemployment benefit plan,

(f) an annuity payment or a payment in full or partial commutation of an annuity,

(g) fees, commissions or other amounts for services, other than amounts described in subsection 115(2.3) or 212(5.1),

(h) a payment under a deferred profit sharing plan or a plan referred to in section 147 as a revoked plan,

(i) a payment from a registered disability savings plan,

(j) a payment out of or under a registered retirement savings plan or a plan referred to in subsection 146(12) as an "amended plan",

(k) an amount as, on account or in lieu of payment of, or in satisfaction of, proceeds of the surrender, cancellation or redemption of an income-averaging annuity contract,

(l) a payment out of or under a registered retirement income fund or a fund referred to in subsection 146.3(11) as an "amended fund",

(m) a prescribed benefit under a government assistance program;

(m.1) [Repealed]

(n) one or more amounts to an individual who has elected for the year in prescribed form in respect of all such amounts,

(o) an amount described in paragraph 115(2)(c.1),

(p) a contribution under a retirement compensation arrangement,

(q) an amount as a distribution to one or more persons out of or under a retirement compensation arrangement,

(r) an amount on account of the purchase price of an interest in a retirement compensation arrangement,

(s) an amount described in paragraph 56(1)(r), (z.2) or (z.4),

(t) a payment made under a plan that was a registered education savings plan, or

(u) a payment out of or under an advanced life deferred annuity

Related Provisions: Reg. 100(1)"remuneration"(p) — Amount payable deemed to be remuneration.

shall deduct or withhold from the payment the amount determined in accordance with prescribed rules and shall, at the prescribed time, remit that amount to the Receiver General on account of the payee's tax for the year under this Part or Part XI.3, as the case may be, and, where at that prescribed time the person is a prescribed person, the remittance shall be made to the account of the Receiver General at a designated financial institution.

Related Provisions: 7(15) — No withholding required on inclusion of deferred stock option benefit; 78(1)(b) — Withholding of tax on unpaid amounts; 125.7(2) — Canada Emergency Wage Subsidy to employers for 2020; 146.3(1.3) — RRIF minimum amount for 2015; 153(1.01) — Withholding from stock option benefits reduced by deductions; 153(1.02)–(1.04) — COVID-19 source deductions subsidy to employers for 2020; 153(1.1) — Undue hardship — reduction in withholding; 153(1.2) — Election to increase withholding; 153(1.3), (1.31) — Pension income splitting stock options cannot reduce source deductions; 153(1.4) — Large remittance through financial institution not required if made one day early; 153(3) — Amount withheld deemed received by payee; 153(6) — Meaning of "designated financial institution", "qualifying non-resident employee", "qualifying non-resident employer""; 153(7) — Certification of qualifying non-resident employer for 153(1)(a)(ii); 154 — Tax transfer payments to provinces; 212 — Withholding tax on payment to non-resident; 221.2 — Transfers of balances from one account to other; 227(1) — No action lies against payor for withholding; 227(8), (9) — 10% penalty for failure to withhold or remit; 227(8.6) — No penalty on qualifying non-resident employer who meets certain conditions for 153(1)(a)(ii); 227(12) — Agreement not to withhold is void; 227.1 — Corporation's directors liable for unremitted source deductions; 238(1) — Offences; 248(7)(b)(i) — Remittance deemed made when received; 252.1(d) — Where union is employer; Reg. 200(1.1) — Exception to information return requirement.

Notes: *153(1) generally*: See 227 for source withholding rules, including their being held in trust for the Crown. Failure to withhold makes an employer or other payor liable for penalty under 227(8) and interest under 227(8.3), but not normally for the tax itself (but see Notes to 227(8.4)). Failure to *remit* withheld amounts: see Notes to 227(4), and director liability under 227.1. Must CRA issue a notice of assessment before enforcing collection on unremitted withholdings? See Notes to 225.1(6). Withholding for non-residents: see s. 212, and (for employees) under 153(1)(a) below.

See Reg. 100-110 for withholding rates; when reading the Regs, note that almost any payor and payee are "employer" and "employee" as defined in Reg. 100(1) (see Reg. 100(1)"remuneration"). Lump sum withholding rates (e.g. RRSP withdrawals, retiring allowances) are in Reg. 103(4).

The amount withheld sits in the employee's CRA account and is automatically credited to the employee on filing their return. The employee cannot sue the employer for withholding; see 227(1). See also 153(3).

No withholding is required for trust income: VIEWS doc 2005-0125271E5.

Recharacterizing salary paid to a shareholder-employee as dividend or shareholder-loan repayment after the fact (to eliminate withholding liability): see Notes to 169(1) under "If there is no rectification".

153(1)(a): As well as for income tax, withholding from wages may be required for employee-side *Canada Pension Plan* contributions and Employment Insurance premiums. To calculate payroll deductions: canada.ca/pdoc. See also Notes to Reg. 102(1).

Payroll withholding of source deductions is required from both resident and non-resident employers: VIEWS docs 2005-0121801E5, 2007-0242081E5; 2010-0383561I7 (withholding can be reduced for foreign tax credit); 2012-0436311I7 (this applies to any Canadian-resident employee, even if all work is performed in the US and the employer is also withholding US income tax!). No withholding is needed from payments to non-resident employees employed outside Canada: Reg. 104(2), 2011-0411711E5, 2012-0437011E5; 2016-0677351E5 (directors attending Canadian board meetings by phone or Internet). A non-resident director is not considered employed in Canada if they do not physically attend meetings or perform functions in Canada: guide T4001, ch. 6, "Director's fees". Long-term disability payments to a non-resident employee: withholding is required, as the payments arise out of the employment relationship: 2014-0531441E5 (but Canada-US tax treaty Art. XVIII:2 may provide partial refund). Incentive payments by manufacturers to retailers' employees for selling warranties are not subject to withholding: 2013-0495611E5.

Salary payments to a non-resident who was formerly resident in Canada, for work outside Canada, may be subject to withholding if the income is not taxed by the foreign country and the payments are not in the ordinary course of a business carried on by the employer: 115(2)(e)(i), Reg. 104(2), VIEWS doc 2008-0276721I7.

A taxpayer who prefers to get a refund on filing can use Form TD1 to ask an employer to withhold more.

Some employers withhold "hypo-tax" (hypothetical tax) for employees posted to overseas branches, and then pay any foreign tax, to leave them the same after-tax income. Doing this was upheld in *Ivandic v. Scotiabank*, 2013 ONCA 214.

Foreign embassies in Canada cannot be forced to withhold and remit source deductions, though CRA asks them to: 2012-0434121E5 (reversing 2008-0298941E5).

153(1)(a) applies to all "office or employment" income due to 248(1)"salary or wages", e.g., taxable benefits [6(1)(a)]; back wages paid under *Companies' Creditors Arrange-*

ment Act settlement even if payor is not the employer [VIEWS doc 2008-0294041E5]; directors' fees [6(1)(c), 2012-0462961C6]; executor and trustee fees that are employment income [see Notes to 6(1)(c)]; wage loss replacement plan benefits [6(1)(f), 2012-0456321I7, T4001 chap. 6; Sanderson, "Tax Reporting on Workplace Disability Insurance Plans", XX(2) *Insurance Planning* (Federated Press) 1279-80 (2014)]; employee benefit plan payments [6(1)(g), 2009-0316621C6]; stock option benefits [7(1), 153(1.01)].

Where non-cash benefits are the employee's only income, withholding is not required: Revenue Canada Roundtable at Cdn Tax Foundation annual conferences, 1988 q.74, 1991 q.47; 2004-0091301E5 (this no longer applies to stock option benefits: 153(1.31)). If cash is being paid as well, withholding on the non-cash benefits should be taken from the cash payment: 2010-0385831E5.

No action can be brought against an employer for withholding tax from a settlement or damage award: 227(1); *Deiana v. Credit Union Central*, 2014 SKQB 79. Nor does a solicitor's lien apply to the amount withheld: *Jenkins Marzban*, 2014 BCSC 1405 (but it can apply to the taxpayer's resulting tax refund: para. 35).

Employers with nil remittances for a period (e.g., seasonal business with no off-season employees) can use TeleReply 1-800-959-2256 to report this by phone. See tinyurl.com/telereply.

Once an amount is withheld and a net salary paid, the amount is credited to the employee even if the employer never remits it: 153(3); *Manke*, [1999] 1 C.T.C. 2186 (TCC). (However, if a net is paid with no other funds available, liability may be only 227(8) penalty for not withholding, not full liability for not remitting: *Coopers & Lybrand*, [1980] C.T.C. 367 (FCA).) For withholding to exist, "all that the law requires is a failure to pay full wages on account of the withholding of source deductions, and not the actual placing of the money into someone's pockets": para. 23. Even if there was no obligation to remit because the taxpayer was an independent contractor, the withholder must remit and the taxpayer gets credit for amounts withheld, due to 153(3): *Suspended Power Lift*, 2007 TCC 519 (FCA appeal dismissed for delay A-449-07) (an earlier decision *contra*, *Liu*, [1995] 2 C.T.C. 2971 (TCC), did not consider 153(3) and is probably wrong). In *Beaudry*, 2013 FC 547, the Court found that no amount had actually been withheld, so the employee got no credit. In *Madore*, 2018 FC 244, an application for judicial review of CRA's refusal to pay a refund was dismissed as premature, as CRA wanted to audit the employer to figure out if $205,000 really was withheld on income of $923. In *Barbe*, 2020 FC 973, B's employer had treated him as self-employed and had not withheld; when CRA assessed him for the unreported income, he sought judicial review but the Federal Court could not require the employer to pay his tax.

The TCC may not have jurisdiction to determine that an amount was paid to an employee net of withholdings that should be credited to the employee's account, as this is a collection issue: *Boucher*, 2004 FCA 46 (leave to appeal denied 2004 CarswellNat 3761 (SCC)); *Beaudry* (above), para. 23; *Manke* (above); *Sutcliffe*, 2012 TCC 347; *Anonby*, 2013 TCC 184. See also 153(3); Notes to 171(1); Richard Yasny, "No Credit for Tax Withheld", 21(7) *Canadian Tax Highlights* (ctf.ca) 5-6 (July 2013).

A taxpayer cannot appeal on the ground the employer failed to withhold tax: *Stein*, 2013 TCC 345.

In *4528957 Manitoba*, 2009 TCC 298, CRA assessed under 153(1) but never explained what the assessment was for. The Court vacated the assessment.

Where doctors or dentists share payroll with one acting as agent for the rest (to avoid GST/HST on re-charging the costs), they can share one payroll account: CRA-Cdn Bar Assn Commodity Tax section meeting, Feb. 25, 2016 (cba.org > "Sections"), q. 7.

Where the employer is not actually paying the salaries, the entity paying is responsible for the withholdings: *G & G Equipment*, 1973 CarswellBC 11 (BCSC); *Coopers & Lybrand*, [1980] C.T.C. 367 (FCA); *Mollenhauer Ltd.*, [1992] 2 C.T.C. 121 (FCTD); *Pratt & Whitney*, 2013 QCCA 706 (leave to appeal denied 2013 CarswellQue 9116 (SCC)) (related corp granted stock options to PW's employees; PW not liable); Reg. 100(1)"employer"; VIEWS docs 2013-0508651E5 (where employee is assigned). The payer is also liable for CPP and EI: *Canada Pension Plan Regulations* s. 8.1; *Insurable Earnings and Collection of Premiums Regulations* ss. 1(2), 10. CRA may also pursue payroll business operators: see *Hennessey v. Eastern Regional Integrated Health*, 2013 CanLII 8492 (Nfld. TD); *Hennessey*, 2014 FC 286 (aff'd 2016 FCA 180); "Former St. John's business owner sentenced for fraud" (CRA, June 4, 2019, re Hennssey's conviction for taking trust funds). However, CRA must not redetermine who the employer is for collection purposes. In *Central Springs*, 2010 TCC 543 (Crown's appeal to FCA discontinued A-454-10), CRA was unable to collect a debt from Humby and instead assessed his companies for payroll deductions, but Humby was the employer. The Court vacated the assessments with harsh words for CRA.

Tips *paid by the employer* (including mandatory service charges, tips paid by credit or debit card, and tips the employer divides up) are subject to payroll withholdings, and included in EI insurable earnings and CPP pensionable earnings: *Tampopo Garden*, 2011 TCC 110; *Andrew Peller Ltd.*, 2015 TCC 329 (FCA appeal discontinued A-30-16); *Ristorante A Mano*, 2021 TCC 22 (under appeal to FCA); VIEWS docs 2005-0163351E5, 2006-0202891E5, 2007-0232621E5. Casino and restaurant tips *not controlled by the employer* were not EI insurable earnings, though they were taxable under the ITA: *Lake City Casinos*, 2007 FCA 100; *BLAJ Hospitality*, 2008 TCC 398. In Quebec see guide IN-250-V, *Tax Measures Respecting Tips* (revenuquebec.ca). See also Wright, "Planning to Avoid Withholding Obligations on Tips", 2(4) *Canadian Tax Focus* (ctf.ca) 2 (Nov. 2012). Casino tips pooled and divided by employees were taxable in *Xia*, 2020 FCA 35.

Where the employer adjusts pay for an injured employee pending Workers' Compensation benefits starting, see Notes to 56(1)(v).

U.S. source withholding may apply to Canadian residents earning wages in the U.S. from a U.S. business. See irs.gov.

The withholding obligation is not affected by an employee changing his name "to include a trademark": VIEWS doc 2010-0380591E5. See Notes to 2(1) and 248(1)"person" for more on the antics of such "tax protesters".

Where an employee incorporates to create a "personal service business" (see Notes to 18(1)(p)), no withholding is required on fees paid to the corporation: VIEWS docs 9611625, 2000-0005305, 2003-0021605, 2012-0455001E5 (the last two say there must be a "*bona fide* contract for service" between the corporation and the payor).

153(1)(a)(ii) exempts from withholding a payment by a "qualifying non-resident employer" (QNEr — 153(6), (7)) to a "qualifying non-resident employee" (153(6)). See tinyurl.com/cra-153-7 and Form RC473. This is much simpler than a Reg. 102 waiver. However, CRA may consider a non-resident that sends employees to Canada for 21 days or more to be carrying on business in Canada and required to register for GST/HST: Caputo, "Payroll Withholding Relief May Cause Sales Tax Pain", 6(4) *Canadian Tax Focus* (ctf.ca) 5-6 (Nov. 2016). See also CBA/CPA Canada Joint Committee on Taxation letter to Finance, May 26, 2015; TEI letters to Finance, June 12 and Oct. 12, 2015; Nevsky, "Update on the Exemption for Non-Residents from Payroll Withholding", 2289 *Tax Topics* (CCH) 1-4 (Jan. 21, 2016); Jung, "New Non-Resident Employer Certification Program", 13(1) *Tax Hyperion* (Carswell) 1-3 (Jan. 2016); Baker & Laher, "Regulation 102 Withholding Relief for Non-Resident Employers", 24(3) *Canadian Tax Highlights* (ctf.ca) 7-8 (March 2016).

When a QNEr is relieved from withholding, it must still issue information slips and report to CRA. Certification under 153(7) does not affect the determination of a non-resident's Canadian tax liability. QNErs continue to be liable for withholding for employees found not to have met the conditions. However, no penalty applies to a QNEr for failing to withhold if, after reasonable inquiry, the employer had no reason to believe, at the time of payment, that the employee did not meet the conditions: 227(8.6).

See also Hegedus & Henel, "Employer Source Deductions: No Ordinary Tax Debts", 9(4) *Canadian Tax Focus* (ctf.ca) 5 (Nov. 2019).

153(1)(b) applies to a RPP forfeiture paid out to an employer: VIEWS docs 2008-0271871E5, 2008-0276471E5.

153(1)(c): on a wrongful dismissal settlement (248(1)"retiring allowance"), no withholding is needed on reimbursement of legal fees identified as such, which is taxable under 56(1)(l.1) and not as a retiring allowance: VIEWS docs 9925615, 2006-0202981E5. A "lump sum pre-retirement leave payment" paid into an ELHT (144.1) is subject to withhholdings, as there is no rollover: 2012-0467221E5.

153(1)(g) ("fees") does not apply to: travel expense reimbursements or allowances for a person who provides no services [VIEWS doc 2010-035911117]; payments to self-employed Canadian residents [2011-0431601E5, Notes to 248(1)"employee"], though a T4A may have to be issued [Reg. 200(1)]; racetrack paying purse winnings to horse owners [2011-0425041R3]. For fees or commissions paid to non-residents, see Reg. 105, Information Circular 75-6R2.

153(1)(h) applies to any payment from a DPSP, including a forfeited amount paid to an employer under 147(2)(i.1): VIEWS docs 2005-0130471E5, 2013-0500511E5.

153(1)(j): RRSP withholding does not change despite spousal attribution of the income under 146(8.3): VIEWS doc 2011-0408251C6 [2011 APFF q.8].

153(1)(n): the only form for self-employed persons to elect to have tax withheld at source appears to be the TD3F for fishers. Form ISP3520 is used to ask for tax to be withheld from Old Age Security or CPP benefits.

153(1)(p): for a ruling that posting collateral under a Credit Facility Agreement is not a contribution to an RCA, see doc 2010-0388761R3.

153(1) closing words force large employers (see Reg. 110) to remit source withholdings through a financial institution (see 153(6)), unless they pay a day early: see 153(1.4). This prevents them from bringing a cheque to a CRA office late on the due date (too late for the funds to get to the bank that day), which would give them an extra day's (or weekend's) interest. In *McNaught Pontiac Buick*, [2007] 1 C.T.C. 179 (FC), a company's in-house courier went to the bank on the deadline but forgot the remittance form, could not pay at the bank, and so took the cheque to the local CRA office instead. The company was assessed a $10,000 penalty under 227(9) which CRA refused to waive. The Court ordered CRA to reconsider its decision.

History: 153(1)(u) added by 2021 budget bill #1, effective 2020. 153(1)(a) amended, effectively to add (a)(ii), by 2016 budget bill #1, for payments made after 2015. 153(1) earlier amended by 2014 budget bill #1 (effective June 19, 2014); 2002-2013 technical bill, S.C. 2012, c. 27; 2010 and 2007 budget bills #2; 2007 RDSPs bill; 2001 technical bill; 1997 Budget; 1995-97, 1993, 1992, 1991 technical bills.

Regulations: 100–108 (withholding and remittance requirements); 103(9) (50% source withholding from informant payment; 30% in Quebec); 110 (prescribed persons for the closing words of 153(1)); 200 (information returns); 5502 (prescribed benefits for 153(1)(m)).

Income Tax Folios: S1-F2-C3: Scholarships, research grants and other education assistance [replaces IT-340R].

Interpretation Bulletins: IT-379R: Employees profit sharing plans — allocations to beneficiaries.

Information Circulars: 75-6R2: Required withholding from amounts paid to non-residents performing services in Canada; 72-22R9: Registered retirement savings plans; 07-1R1: Taxpayer relief provisions. See also "Employers' Guide to Payroll Deductions".

I.T. Technical News: 11 (reporting of amounts paid out of an employee benefit plan).

CRA Audit Manual: 28.7.4: Penalties — failure to deduct or withhold an amount; 28.7.5: Penalties — failure to remit an amount withheld.

Forms: RC1B: Business Number — Payroll Deductions Account; RC473: Non-resident employer certification; RC4004: Seasonal agricultural workers program [guide]; RC4157: Deducting income tax on pension and other income, and filing the T4A slip and summary; RC4163: Employers' guide — remitting payroll deductions; RC4409: Keeping [payroll] records [guide]; T1 General return, Line 43700 [former 437]: Total income tax deducted; TD1: Personal tax credits return; TD3F: Fisher's election to have tax deducted at source; T4A: Statement of pension, retirement, annuity, and other income; T4A Segment; T4A-RCA: Statement of distributions paid from an RCA; T4A-RCA Summ: Return of distributions from an RCA; T735: Application for a remittance number for tax withheld from an RCA; T1213: Request to reduce tax deductions at source; T1213(OAS): Request to reduce OAS recovery tax at source; T1219: Provincial alternative minimum tax; T1219-ON: Ontario minimum tax carryover; T4001: Employers' guide — payroll deductions and remittances [guide]; T4032: Payroll deductions tables [guide]; T4127: Payroll deductions formulas for computer programs [guide]; T4130: Employer's guide — taxable benefits.

(1.01) Withholding — stock option benefits — An amount that is deemed to have been received by a taxpayer as a benefit under or because of any of paragraphs 7(1)(a) to (d.1) is remuneration paid as a bonus for the purposes of paragraph (1)(a), except the portion, if any, of the amount that is

(a) deductible by the taxpayer under paragraph 110(1)(d) in computing the taxpayer's taxable income for a taxation year;

(b) deemed to have been received in a taxation year as a benefit because of a disposition of securities to which subsection 7(1.1) applies; or

(c) determined under paragraph 110(2.1)(b) to be deductible by the taxpayer under paragraph 110(1)(d.01) in computing the taxpayer's taxable income for a taxation year.

Related Provisions: 153(1.31) — Non-cash nature of stock option benefits cannot reduce source deductions.

Notes: See Notes to 153(1.31). CCPC option benefits do not require withholding due to para. (b): VIEWS doc 2017-0709811I7.

153(1.01) says tax must be withheld from stock option benefits (with certain exceptions), but even without it, 153(1)(a) should apply since s. 7 falls into 248(1)"salary or wages". See 153(1) Notes re withholding on benefits.

Finance is willing to consider exempting withholding where the shares are donated to charity: TEI-Finance meeting, Dec. 2017, q.3.

153(1.01) added by 2010 budget bill #2, effective 2011, but it does not apply to benefits arising from rights granted before 2011 to taxpayer T under an agreement to sell or issue securities entered into in writing before 4pm EST, March 4, 2010 that included, at that time, a written condition prohibiting T from disposing of the securities acquired under the agreement for a period of time after exercise.

(1.02) COVID-19 — deemed remittance [10% wage subsidy] — For the purposes of this Act, if an eligible employer pays, at a particular time that is within the eligible period, eligible remuneration in respect of which a particular amount is required to be deducted or withheld under subsection (1), then the eligible employer is deemed to have remitted to the Receiver General at the particular time in respect of the particular amount, an amount equal to the least of

(a) the amount determined by the formula

$$A - B$$

where

A is the prescribed amount, and

B is the total of all amounts, each of which is an amount deemed to have been remitted by the eligible employer under this subsection prior to the particular time (and, if more than one such payment is made at the particular time, the eligible employer may designate the order in which the amounts are considered to have been paid),

(b) the amount determined by the formula

$$C \times D$$

where

C is the prescribed percentage, and

D is the amount of the eligible remuneration, and

(c) the amount determined by the formula

$$E \times F$$

where

E is the prescribed amount, and

F is the total number of eligible employees employed by the eligible employer during the eligible period.

Related Provisions: 125.7(2)B — Canada Emergency Wage Subsidy reduced by this subsidy; 153(1.03) — Definitions; 153(1.04) — COVID-19 emergency benefit to employers deemed not held in trust; 257 — Formula cannot calculate to less than zero.

Notes: 153(1.02)–(1.04) provided a 10% Temporary Wage Subsidy (TWS) from March 18-June 19, 2020, to assist employers during the COVID-19 coronavirus crisis. Amounts the employer is "deemed to have remitted" to CRA are credited to the employer's payroll (RP) account. This rule applies only to income tax remittances, not CPP or EI (but CPP and EI remittances for employees on leave with pay are fully refunded via 125.7(2)D). The prescribed amounts and percentage are $25,000, 10% and $1,375: Reg. 111. This subsidy is separate from the Canada Emergency Wage Subsidy (CEWS) paid by CRA. It reduces CEWS dollar-for-dollar: 125.7(2)B.

153(1.02)–(1.04) added by 2020 COVID bill #1, effective March 25, 2020. For a list of other COVID-19 support measures, see 122.5(3.001) Notes.

For detailed CRA explanation, including reporting on Form PD27, see tinyurl.com/cra-wagesub.

Regulations: 111 (prescribed amounts and percentage for A, C and E: $25,000, 10%, $1,375).

Forms: PD27: 10% temporary wage subsidy self-identification form for employers.

(1.03) Definitions — subsec. (1.02) — The following definitions apply for the purposes of this subsection and subsection (1.02).

"eligible employee" means an individual who is employed in Canada.

"eligible employer" means a person or partnership that

(a) employs one or more eligible employees;

(b) has, on March 18, 2020, a business number in respect of which the person or partnership is registered with the Minister to make remittances required under this section; and

(c) is any of

(i) a Canadian-controlled private corporation for the purposes of section 125 that

(A) would have a business limit for its last taxation year that ended before the start of the eligible period greater than nil, if the amount determined for paragraph 125(5.1)(b) were deemed to be nil, or

(B) if the corporation does not have a taxation year that ended before the start of the eligible period, would meet the condition in clause (A) if its taxation year ended immediately before the start of the eligible period,

(ii) an individual (other than a trust),

(iii) a partnership, all of the members of which are described in subparagraphs (i) to (iii) or (v),

(iv) a person exempt from tax under Part I because of paragraph 149(1)(l), and

(v) a registered charity.

Notes: Para. (b) means the employer has an "RP" (payroll) account with CRA. See also VIEWS doc 2020-0846261E5 (general discussion).

"eligible period" means the period beginning on March 18, 2020 and that ends on June 19, 2020.

"eligible remuneration" means salary, wages or other remuneration paid to an eligible employee during the eligible period.

Notes [153(1.03)]: See Notes to 153(1.02).

(1.04) Deemed remittances under subsec. (1.02) — For greater certainty, amounts deemed under subsection (1.02) to have

been remitted to the Receiver General are deemed to not be held in trust under subsections 227(4) and (4.1).

Notes: See Notes to 153(1.02).

(1.1) Undue hardship

(1.1) Undue hardship — Where the Minister is satisfied that the deducting or withholding of the amount otherwise required to be deducted or withheld under subsection (1) from a payment would cause undue hardship, the Minister may determine a lesser amount and that amount shall be deemed to be the amount determined under that subsection as the amount to be deducted or withheld from that payment.

Related Provisions: 153(1.3) — Pension income splitting cannot reduce source deductions; 153(1.31) — Non-cash stock option benefits cannot reduce source deductions; 164(1.51)–(1.53) — Refund of instalments in cases of undue hardship; 180.2(6) — Reduced withholding available on old age security benefits; 212(5.3) — Parallel rule for withholding on non-resident actor's services; 227(8) — Withholding taxes; 227.1 — Liability of directors.

Notes: An application to permit reduced withholding is made to the local Tax Services Office on Form T1213 and is considered on a case-by-case basis. The request may be accepted for a variety of reasons, including *Indian Act* or tax treaty exemption (VIEWS docs 2008-0302881E5, 2010-0382801E5), minimum tax carryforward (2010-0366801E5), clergy residence deduction (2009-031623117, *Registered Charities Newsletter* 23), 60(n) deduction for pension repayment (2007-0248161E5), interest expense (2003-0020985), or expected reduced tax due to medical expenses, child care expenses, spousal support payments, employment expenses, rental losses, RRSP contributions or charitable donations. (Pension income splitting and non-cash stock option benefits do not qualify: 153(1.3), (1.31).) The CRA does not require demonstration of any actual "hardship" beyond the fact the taxpayer will be owed a refund after filing. (This practice was criticized in the Auditor General's May 1996 report, §11.71-11.76.) An obligation to repay a loan out of the employee's salary does not create "undue hardship" where there is no indication the tax withholding is too high: 2006-0171251E5.

A remission order was granted (*Brian Alm*, P.C. 2002-1970) where authorization under 153(1.1) had been granted based on an interim court order for child support, but the court order had expired and the taxpayer still believed the payments were deductible.

See also Reg. 100(3), which allows automatic reduction of source withholdings to reflect various amounts withheld from payroll by employers, including deductible spousal support and RRSP contributions.

For waiver of withholding on payments to non-residents, see Notes to Reg. 105.

Forms: R105: Regulation 105 waiver application; T1213: Request to reduce tax deductions at source; T1213(OAS): Request to reduce OAS recovery tax at source.

(1.2) Election to increase withholding

(1.2) Election to increase withholding — Where a taxpayer so elects in prescribed manner and prescribed form, the amount required to be deducted or withheld under subsection (1) from any payment to the taxpayer shall be deemed to be the total of

(a) the amount, if any, otherwise required to be deducted or withheld under that subsection from that payment, and

(b) the amount specified by the taxpayer in that election with respect to that payment or with respect to a class of payments that includes that payment.

Related Provisions: 227.1 — Liability of directors.

Notes: A CCRA notice, Jan. 2000, suggests that taxpayers receiving Canada Pension Plan benefits may wish to use 153(1.2) to have tax withheld from the benefits.

Regulations: 109 (prescribed manner for making election, and effect).

Forms: TD1: Personal tax credits return.

(1.3) Reduction not permitted [pension splitting]

(1.3) Reduction not permitted [pension splitting] — A joint election made or expected to be made under section 60.03 is not to be considered a basis on which the Minister may determine a lesser amount under subsection (1.1).

Notes: 153(1.3) provides that pension income splitting (60.03, 60(c), 56(1)(a.2)) is not a ground for reducing payroll withholdings (the transferred amount is deemed withheld on behalf of the transferee spouse: see 153(2)).

CRA says the prohibition against reduced withholdings applies to the Old Age Security clawback under 180.2 due to 180.2(6), but not to withholding reduction for other reasons where the taxpayer happens to be also using 60.03: VIEWS doc 2016-0629341I7.

For 2014-15 when the Family Tax Cut (FTC) pseudo-income-splitting in 119.1 was in force, 153(1.3)(b) provided that the FTC was also not a ground for reducing payroll withholdings. The purpose of this rule (in an election year) was evidently to have the FTC, created by the Conservatives, generate a tax refund that the taxpayer would see in the spring of 2015, rather than being buried into slightly higher weekly take-home pay. (This made no difference: the Liberals won a majority in the Oct. 2015 election.)

153(1.3) amended by 2016 budget bill #1, for 2016 and later tax years.

153(1.3) previously amended by 2015 Budget bill, for 2014 and later tax years. Added by 2007 budget bill #1.

An earlier 153(1.3), repealed by 1995 Budget for payments made after June 20, 1996, was replaced by more general rules in 227(5)-(5.2). Section 227 consolidates all the administrative rules for withholding taxes.

(1.31) Non-cash stock option benefit

(1.31) Non-cash stock option benefit — An amount deemed to have been received as a benefit under or because of any of paragraphs 7(1)(a) to (d.1) shall not be considered a basis on which the Minister may determine a lesser amount under subsection (1.1) solely because it is received as a non-cash benefit.

Notes: Even if no cash is paid on a stock option benefit, the employer must withhold! CRA leaves it to employers to find a solution: docs 2011-0399491E5, 2011-040550117, 2011-0411951C6. (The Courts are unlikely to rule that no withholding is required due to impossibility: see *Folz Vending*, 2008 FCA 160.) The employer can withhold from other cash amounts paid to the employee; or can issue the employee fewer shares, as per 2020-0840681E5, which says 7(3)(b) may prohibit deduction to the employer for the amount withheld. See also Berry, "Properly Structured Charitable Donations May Mitigate Source Deduction Woes", 22(6) *Taxation of Executive Compensation & Retirement [TECR]* (Federated Press) 1367-69 (Feb. 2011); Worndl & Choudhury, "New Stock Option Benefit Withholding Provisions", 22(7) *TECR* 1386-88 (March 2011).

153(1.31) added by 2010 budget bill #2, effective 2011.

(1.4) Exception — remittance to designated financial institution

(1.4) Exception — remittance to designated financial institution — For the purpose of subsection (1), a prescribed person referred to in that subsection is deemed to have remitted an amount to the account of the Receiver General at a designated financial institution if the prescribed person has remitted the amount to the Receiver General at least one day before the day upon which the amount is due.

Notes: 153(1.4) overrides the closing words of 153(1) for large employers if the payment to CRA is made at least one day early. Before 153(1.4) was announced in the Feb. 26/08 Budget, CRA announced that it would strictly enforce the 227(9) penalty for large employers that did not remit through a financial institution: news release, Nov. 24/06. See Notes to 153(1) re the *McNaught Pontiac* case. 153(1.4) is apparently a response to media publicity about Jim McAusland, who remitted $46,000 at a CRA office a week before it was due and was assessed a $4,600 penalty (Don Cayo, "A bizarre tax tale", *Vancouver Sun*, April 1/08).

153(1.4) added by 2008 budget bill #1, effective for remittances by a prescribed person (see Reg. 110) that are first due after February 25, 2008.

Former 153(1.4) repealed by 1995 Budget, effective for payments made after June 20, 1996. It has been replaced by more general rules in 227(5)-(5.2). Section 227 consolidates all the administrative rules relating to withholding taxes.

Regulations: 110 (prescribed person).

(2) Deemed withholding

(2) Deemed withholding — If a pensioner and a pension transferee (as those terms are defined in section 60.03) make a joint election under section 60.03 in respect of a split-pension amount (as defined in that section) for a taxation year, the portion of the amount deducted or withheld under subsection (1) that may be reasonably considered to be in respect of the split-pension amount is deemed to have been deducted or withheld on account of the pension transferee's tax for the taxation year under this Part and not on account of the pensioner's tax for the taxation year under this Part.

Notes: 153(2) provides that when pension income is split between spouses (see 60.03, 60(c), 56(1)(a.2)), the source deductions on the transferred amounts are deemed withheld for the transferee spouse.

153(2) added by 2007 budget bill #1, for 2007 and later taxation years.

Former 153(2), which required an individual to pay the remainder of tax owing for the year by the "balance-due day", repealed by 1995 Budget, effective 1995. This rule is now in 156.1(4). 153(2) earlier amended by 1991 technical bill, effective 1990.

(3) Deemed effect of deduction

(3) Deemed effect of deduction — When an amount has been deducted or withheld under subsection (1), it shall, for all the purposes of this Act, be deemed to have been received at that time by the person to whom the remuneration, benefit, payment, fees, commissions or other amounts were paid.

Related Provisions: 78(1)(b) — Unpaid amounts; 227 — Withholding taxes — rules; 227.1 — Liability of directors.

Notes: This rule means that an amount withheld from employment income is deemed to be employment income. It applies even if the amount withheld was not required to be withheld: *Suspended Power Lift*, 2007 TCC 519 (FCA appeal dismissed for delay A-449-07). See also *Manke*, [1999] 1 C.T.C. 2186 (TCC), and *O'Hara*, 2008 TCC 620. In *Paquet*, 2013 FC 159 (FC), P was not entitled to credit for amounts allegedly withheld at source, due to insufficient evidence. See also Notes to 153(1).

In *Newcombe*, 2013 FC 955, N believed her employer (Justice Canada) should not have issued a T4 and withheld tax from her settlement on termination of employment. The FC agreed the payment was non-taxable but the remedy was to appeal her income tax assessment. The Court also noted that due to 153(3), the employer "is out-of-pocket for the entire sum" (para. 28).

Draft 153(3.1), "Amounts withheld under Part I.2", was included in the drafts of the 1995 Budget legislation released on July 19 and Dec. 12, 1995. It was deleted from the draft of March 28, 1996 which was enacted, and replaced with amendments to 156.1(1)"net tax owing", which include Part I.2 in the base for instalment calculations.

(3.1) Amounts paid in error — For the purposes of this Act, an amount (referred to in this subsection as the "excess amount") is deemed to not have been deducted or withheld under subsection (1) by a person if

(a) the excess amount was, absent the application of this subsection, deducted or withheld by the person under subsection (1);

(b) the excess amount is in respect of an excess payment (referred to in this subsection as the "total excess payment") of an individual's salary, wages or other remuneration by the person to the individual in a particular year, that was paid as a result of a clerical, administrative or system error;

(c) before the end of the third year after the calendar year in which the excess amount is deducted or withheld,

(i) the person elects in prescribed manner to have this subsection apply in respect of the excess amount, and

(ii) the individual has repaid, or made an arrangement to repay, the total excess payment less the excess amount;

(d) an information return correcting for the total excess payment has not been issued by the person to the individual prior to the making of the election in subparagraph (c)(i); and

(e) any additional criteria specified by the Minister have been met.

Related Provisions: 8(1)(n) — Limited deduction for salary repayment.

Notes: 153(3.1) addresses the Phoenix payroll disaster: the federal government employees' new pay system which came online in 2016 and caused hundreds of thousands of pay errors. Parallel amendments in *Canada Pension Plan* 21.01, 38(3.3) and 38(8), and *Employment Insurance Act* 82.01, 96(3.1) and 96(13.1), apply the same rules to CPP and EI source withholdings.

153(3.1), if its conditions are met, allows CRA to directly reimburse employer E for income tax withheld and remitted by E on an erroneous overpayment to an employee. In particular, it provides that an "excess amount" is deemed not withheld under 153(1) if the 153(3.1)(a)-(e) conditions are met. This effectively overrides 153(3), which provides that an amount withheld under 153(1) is deemed received at that time by the person to whom the remuneration was paid. When 153(3.1) applies, since the employee is not deemed to have received the withheld amount, CRA can return the withheld amount to E.

Example (Finance Technical Notes): In 2018, XCo overpays J's salary by $10,000. On this $10,000, XCo withheld and remitted $2,000 in respect of income taxes on behalf of J. In 2020, XCo discovers the error and elects to have new subsection 153(3.1) apply. J makes arrangements to return $8,000 to Xco and new subsection 153(3.1) will allow CRA to reimburse the excess withholding of $2,000 directly to XCo.

See Finance Jan. 15, 2019 news release and accompanying Backgrounder, at tiny-url.com/fin-phoenix. See also CRA Q&A, "Salary overpayments made in error" (Jan. 18, 2019), tinyurl.com/cra-overpay-error. CRA contact number for Phoenix-related tax issues: 1-888-556-5083.

153(3.1) addresses only *withholding*, not income. An employee who is working cannot deduct a repayment to an employer of an overpaid amount: 8(1)(n) allows deduction only for repayments of amounts paid "for a period throughout which the taxpayer *did not* perform the duties of the office or employment". However, CRA accepts the retroactive "undoing" of income if the employer issues a corrected T4.

153(3.1) added by 2019 budget bill #1, for excess payments of salary, wages or other remuneration made after 2015.

(4) Unclaimed dividends, interest and proceeds — Where at the end of a taxpayer's taxation year the person beneficially entitled to an amount received by the taxpayer after 1984 and before the year as or in respect of dividends, interest or proceeds of disposition of property is unknown to the taxpayer, the taxpayer shall remit to the Receiver General on or before the day that is 60 days after the end of the year on account of the tax payable under this Act by that person an amount equal to

(a) in the case of dividends, 33⅓% of the total amount of the dividends,

(b) in the case of interest, 50% of the total amount of the interest, and

(c) in the case of proceeds of disposition of property, 50% of the total of all amounts each of which is the amount, if any, by which the proceeds of disposition of a property exceed the total of any outlays and expenses made or incurred by the taxpayer for the purpose of disposing of the property (to the extent that those outlays and expenses were not deducted in computing the taxpayer's income for any taxation year or attributable to any other property),

except that no remittance under this subsection shall be required in respect of an amount that was included in computing the taxpayer's income for the year or a preceding taxation year or in respect of an amount on which the tax under this subsection was previously remitted.

Related Provisions: 153(5) — Effect of deduction; 227.1 — Liability of directors.

Notes: This rule does not apply to minority shareholders who did not claim shares on a share-exchange takeover: VIEWS doc 2010-0413171E5.

The unclaimed amounts are not included in the payor's income even if they are never claimed and go statute-barred: VIEWS doc 2011-0429031I7.

Regulations: 108(4) (remittance deadline).

Interpretation Bulletins: IT-67R3: Taxable dividends from corporations resident in Canada.

Information Circulars: 71-9R: Unclaimed dividends.

(5) Deemed effect of remittance — An amount remitted by a taxpayer under subsection (4) in respect of dividends, interest or proceeds of disposition of property shall be deemed

(a) to have been received by the person beneficially entitled thereto; and

(b) to have been deducted or withheld from the amount otherwise payable by the taxpayer to the person entitled thereto.

Related Provisions: 227(6), (9) — Withholding taxes; 227(10) — Assessment; 227(13) — Withholding tax; 227.1 — Liability of directors.

(6) Definitions — The following definitions apply in this section.

"designated financial institution" means a corporation that

(a) is a bank, other than an authorized foreign bank that is subject to the restrictions and requirements referred to in subsection 524(2) of the *Bank Act*;

(b) is authorized under the laws of Canada or a province to carry on the business of offering its services as a trustee to the public; or

(c) is authorized under the laws of Canada or a province to accept deposits from the public and carries on the business of lending money on the security of real property or immovables or investing in indebtedness on the security of mortgages on real property or of hypothecs on immovables.

Related Provisions: 153(1) closing words — Large remittances to be made through designated financial institution.

Notes: This definition was simply 153(6) before more definitions were added in 2016.

153(6)(c) amended by 2002-2013 technical bill (Part 4 — bijuralism), effective June 26, 2013.

153(6) added by 2001 technical bill, effective June 28, 1999.

"qualifying non-resident employee", at any time in respect of a payment referred to in paragraph (1)(a), means an employee who

(a) is, at that time, resident in a country with which Canada has a tax treaty;

(b) is not liable to tax under this Part in respect of the payment because of that treaty; and

(c) works in Canada for less than 45 days in the calendar year that includes that time or is present in Canada for less than 90 days in any 12-month period that includes that time.

Notes: 153(6)"qualifying non-resident employee" added by 2016 budget bill #1, for payments made after 2015. See Notes to 153(1) under "153(1)(a)(ii)".

"qualifying non-resident employer", at any time, means an employer

(a) that at that time

(i) in the case of an employer that is not a partnership,

(A) is a resident of a country with which Canada has a tax treaty, or

(B) is a corporation that does not satisfy the condition in clause (A), but would be a resident of a country with which Canada has a tax treaty if the corporation were treated, for the purpose of income taxation in that country, as a body corporate, and

(ii) in the case of an employer that is a partnership, is a partnership in respect of which the total of all amounts, each of which is a share of the partnership's income or loss for the fiscal period that includes that time of a member that, at that time, is a resident of a country with which Canada has a tax treaty (or is a corporation that satisfies the condition in clause (i)(B)), is not less than 90% of the income or loss of the partnership for the period (for the purposes of this subparagraph, where the income and loss of the partnership are nil for the period, the income of the partnership for the period is deemed to be $1,000,000); and

(b) that is at that time certified by the Minister under subsection (7).

Related Provisions: Reg. 200(1.1) — No information return required from QNRE in certain cases.

Notes: 153(6)"qualifying non-resident employer" added by 2016 budget bill #1, for payments made after 2015. See Notes to 153(1) under "153(1)(a)(ii)".

Regulations: 8201 (permanent establishment).

(7) Certification by Minister — The Minister may

(a) certify an employer for a specified period of time if the employer has applied in prescribed form containing prescribed information and the Minister is satisfied that the employer

(i) meets the conditions in paragraph (a) of the definition "qualifying non-resident employer" in subsection (6), and

(ii) meets the conditions established by the Minister; and

(b) revoke an employer's certification if the Minister is no longer satisfied that the employer meets the conditions referred to in subparagraphs (a)(i) or (ii).

Announced Administrative Change — 153(7) — RC473 applications by email

CRA notice (tinyurl.com/cra-internat, April 27, 2021): See under 250(1)(a), sections III and VII.C "Cross-border employment income".

Notes: 153(7) added by 2016 budget bill #1, for payments made after 2015. See Notes to 153(1) under "153(1)(a)(ii)".

Regulations: 8201 (permanent establishment).

Forms: RC473: Non-resident employer certification.

Definitions [s. 153]: "amount", "annuity", "authorized foreign bank", "balance-due day", "bank", "business", "business limit", "business number" — 248(1); "calendar year" — *Interpretation Act* 37(1)(a); "Canada" — 255, *Interpretation Act* 35(1); "Canadian-controlled private corporation" — 125(7), 248(1); "corporation" — 248(1), *Interpretation Act* 35(1); "death benefit" — 248(1); "deferred profit sharing plan" — 147(1), 248(1); "designated financial institution" — 153(6); "disposition", "dividend" — 248(1); "eligible employee", "eligible employer", "eligible period", "eligible remuneration" — 153(1.03); "employed", "employee", "employer" — 248(1); "estate" — 104(1), 248(1); "fiscal period" — 249.1; "hypothecs" — Quebec *Civil Code* art. 2660; "immovables" — Quebec *Civil Code* art. 900–907; "income-averaging annuity contract", "individual" — 248(1); "joint election" — 60.03(1); "Minister", "non-resident" — 248(1); "partnership" — see 96(1) Notes; "pension transferee", "pensioner" — 60.03(1); "permanent establishment" — Reg. 8201; "person", "prescribed" — 248(1); "prescribed benefit" — Reg. 5502; "property" — 248(1); "province" — *Interpretation Act* 35(1); "qualifying non-resident employee", "qualifying non-resident employer" — 153(6); "registered charity" — 248(1); "registered disability savings plan" — 146.4(1), 248(1); "registered education savings plan" — 146.1(1), 248(1); "registered retirement income fund" — 146.3(1), 248(1); "registered retirement savings plan" — 146(1), 248(1); "regulation" — 248(1); "resident" — 250; "retirement compensation arrangement", "retiring allowance" — 248(1); "salary, wages" — 248(1)"salary or wages"; "salary or wages" — 248(1); "security" — *Interpretation Act* 35(1); "split-pension amount" — 60.03(1); "superannuation or pension benefit" — 248(1); "supplementary unemployment benefit plan" — 145(1), 248(1); "tax paya-

ble" — 248(2); "tax treaty", "taxable income" — 248(1); "taxation year" — 249; "taxpayer" — 248(1); "trust" — 104(1), 248(1), (3); "trustee" — 153(1.4).

154. (1) Agreements providing for tax transfer payments — The Minister may, with the approval of the Governor in Council, enter into an agreement with the government of a province to provide for tax transfer payments and the terms and conditions relating to such payments.

(2) Tax transfer payment — Where, on account of the tax for a taxation year payable by an individual under this Part, an amount has been deducted or withheld under subsection 153(1) on the assumption that the individual was resident in a place other than the province in which the individual resided on the last day of the year, and the individual

(a) has filed a return of income for the year with the Minister,

(b) is liable to pay tax under this Part for the year, and

(c) is resident on the last day of the year in a province with which an agreement described in subsection (1) has been entered into,

the Minister may make a tax transfer payment to the government of the province not exceeding an amount equal to the product obtained by multiplying the amount or the total of the amounts so deducted or withheld by a prescribed rate.

Notes: 152(4)(a) amended by 1995-97 technical bill, for 1996 and later tax years.

Regulations: 2607 (individual is resident in province of principal place of residence); 3300 (prescribed rate is 45%).

Income Tax Folios: S5-F1-C1: Determining an individual's residence status [replaces IT-221R3].

(3) Payment deemed received by individual — Where, pursuant to an agreement entered into under subsection (1), an amount has been transferred by the Minister to the government of a province with respect to an individual, the amount shall, for all purposes of this Act, be deemed to have been received by the individual at the time the amount was transferred.

(4) Payment deemed received by Receiver General — Where, pursuant to an agreement entered into under subsection (1), an amount has been transferred by the government of a province to the Minister with respect to an individual, the amount shall, for all purposes of this Act, be deemed to have been received by the Receiver General on account of the individual's tax under this Part for the year in respect of which the amount was transferred.

(5) Amount not to include refund — In this section, an amount deducted or withheld does not include any refund made in respect of that amount.

Related Provisions [s. 154]: 228 — Applying payments under collection agreements.

Definitions [s. 154]: "amount" — 154(5), 248(1); "individual", "Minister", "prescribed" — 248(1); "province" — *Interpretation Act* 35(1); "resident" — Reg 2607; "taxation year" — 249.

155. (1) [Instalments —] Farmers and fishermen — Subject to section 156.1, every individual whose chief source of income for a taxation year is farming or fishing shall, on or before December 31 in the year, pay to the Receiver General in respect of the year, ⅔ of

(a) the amount estimated by the individual to be the tax payable under this Part by the individual for the year, or

(b) the individual's instalment base for the preceding taxation year.

Related Provisions: 31 — Loss from farming where farming not chief source of income; 104(23)(e) — Alternative rule for testamentary trust; 107(5.1) — Trust's gain on distribution to non-resident beneficiary does not increase instalment requirements; 128.1(5) — Deemed disposition on emigration does not increase instalment requirements; 151 — Estimate of tax; 156(1) — Other individuals; 156.1 — No instalment required; 161(2) — Interest on late or insufficient instalments; 161(4) — Limitation on interest — farmers and fishermen; 163.1 — Penalty for late or deficient instalments; 248(7) — Receipt of things mailed.

Notes: 155(1) amended by 1993 Budget (for 1994 and later tax years), 1991 technical bill.

Forms: T1033-WS: Worksheet for calculating instalment payments; T2042: Statement of farming activities; T2121: Statement of fishing activities; T4003: Farming and fishing income [guide].

(2) Definition of "instalment base" — In this section, "instalment base" of an individual for a taxation year means the amount determined in prescribed manner to be the individual's instalment base for the year.

Regulations: 5300 (instalment base).

Definitions [s. 155]: "balance-due day" — 248(1); "farming", "fishing", "individual" — 248(1); "instalment base" — 155(2); "taxable income" — 2(2), 248(1); "taxation year" — 249.

156. (1) [Instalments —] Other individuals — Subject to section 156.1, in respect of each taxation year every individual (other than one to whom section 155 applies for the year) shall pay to the Receiver General

(a) on or before March 15, June 15, September 15 and December 15 in the year, an amount equal to ¼ of

(i) the amount estimated by the individual to be the tax payable under this Part by the individual for the year, or

(ii) the individual's instalment base for the preceding taxation year, or

(b) on or before

(i) March 15 and June 15 in the year, an amount equal to ¼ of the individual's instalment base for the second preceding taxation year, and

(ii) September 15 and December 15 in the year, an amount equal to ½ of the amount, if any, by which

(A) the individual's instalment base for the preceding taxation year

exceeds

(B) ½ of the individual's instalment base for the second preceding taxation year.

Related Provisions: 104(23)(e) — Alternative rule for testamentary trust; 107(5.1) — Trust's gain on distribution to non-resident beneficiary does not increase instalment requirements; 128.1(5) — Deemed disposition on emigration does not increase instalment requirements; 156(4) — No application to SIFT trust; 156.1(2) — Where no instalment required; 156.1(4) — Payment of balance by April 30; 161(2) — Interest on late instalments; 161(4.01) — Minimum instalment payments to avoid interest charges; 163.1 — Penalty for late or deficient instalments; 164(1.51)–(1.53) — Refund of instalments at taxpayer's request; 248(7) — Receipt of things mailed.

Notes: Instalments for individuals may be based on the estimated tax for the year (subpara. (a)(i)), actual tax for the preceding year ((a)(ii)), or the method in para. (b), which uses the second-preceding year for the March and June instalments and the preceding year for the September and December instalments (with adjustments to correct for overpayment or underpayment, so that total instalments for the year equal the tax for the preceding year).

Instalments owing after March 18, 2020 were due on Sept. 30, 2020 due to COVID-19, per tinyurl.com/covid-dates as it read during 2020 (see PITA 59th ed.). This was effectively a promise to waive interest via 220(3.1).

CRA sends taxpayers notices twice a year of the quarterly instalments required using the method in para. (b). Taxpayers who wish to use one of the other methods need not pay the amounts in the notices, but if the taxpayer gets it wrong and tax is unexpectedly higher, interest under 161(2) and (4.01) will apply, and possibly penalty under 163.1: *Elkharadly*, [1995] 1 C.T.C. 2273D (TCC); even if source withholdings for the year exceed the instalment obligation: *Ross*, 2005 TCC 643. See VIEWS docs 2000-0004525, 2007-0259081E5, 2008-0287981E5 for more explanation. Interest also applied in *Bernier*, 2008 TCC 379.

"Instalment interest or penalties are not charged when an instalment reminder has not been sent": CRA May 2007 ICAA roundtable (tinyurl.com/cra-abtax), Q32.

See Notes to 161(2.2) re "contra" interest created by prepaying instalments.

A trust is supposed to pay instalments (other than a GRE: 156.1(2)(c)), but the CRA does not assess interest or penalty if it does not (perhaps its computer system is not yet set up for this): VIEWS docs 2007-0260071E5, 2010-0363181C6, 2014-0526591C6 [2014 STEP conf q.9], 2016-0641461C6 [2016 STEP conf q.6]. Quebec imposes interest on a trust's unpaid provincial tax instalments.

A SIFT partnership is required by 156(1) to pay instalments of Part IX.1 tax, due to 197(6): VIEWS doc 2011-0422731I7.

Under *Canada Pension Plan* s. 33, instalments for CPP contributions on self-employed earnings are due on the same basis as for income tax. In practice, the two instalment requirements are simply added up, with a single remittance to CRA.

For provinces other than Quebec, provincial tax instalments are required on the same basis as s. 156 (e.g. Ontario *Taxation Act, 2007* s. 115). Again, the provincial instalment is simply combined with the federal and a single payment made to CRA. (Quebec instalments are paid to Revenu Québec.)

See also Notes to 158 re paying the final balance.

156(1) amended by 1993 Budget, 1992 and 1991 technical bills.

Forms: P110: Paying your income tax by instalments [pamphlet]; T1 General return, Line 47600 [former 476]: Tax paid by instalments; T1033-WS: Worksheet for calculating instalment payments; T1162A-1: Pre-authorized payment plan (personal quarterly instalment payments).

(2) Payment by mutual fund trusts — Notwithstanding subsection (1), the amount payable by a mutual fund trust to the Receiver General on or before any day referred to in paragraph (1)(a) in a taxation year shall be deemed to be the amount, if any, by which

(a) the amount so payable otherwise determined under that subsection,

exceeds

(b) ¼ of the trust's capital gains refund (within the meaning assigned by section 132) for the year.

Related Provisions: 156(4), 157(2) — Corporate instalment rules apply to SIFT trust instead of s. 156; 156.1 — No instalment required.

(3) Definition of "instalment base" — In this section, "instalment base" of an individual for a taxation year means the amount determined in prescribed manner to be the individual's instalment base for the year.

Related Provisions: 120(2) — Deemed payment of tax; 161(2) — Interest on instalments; 161(4) — Limitation of instalment base.

Regulations: 5300 (instalment base).

(4) Payments by SIFT trusts — Subsections (1) to (3) and section 156.1 do not apply to a SIFT trust.

Related Provisions: 157(2) — Corporate instalment rules apply to SIFT trust.

Notes: See Notes to 157(2). 156(4) added by 2013 budget bill #2, effective for taxation years that begin after July 20, 2011.

Definitions [s. 156]: "amount", "balance-due day" — 248(1); "individual" — 248(1); "instalment base" — 156(3), Reg. 5300(1); "mutual fund trust" — 132(6); "SIFT trust" — 122.1(1), (2), 248(1); "share" — 248(1); "taxable income" — 2(2), 248(1); "taxation year" — 249.

156.1 (1) [Instalments exemption, and annual balance owing —] Definitions — For the purposes of this section,

"instalment threshold" of an individual for a taxation year means

(a) in the case of an individual resident in the Province of Quebec at the end of the year, $1,800, and

(b) in any other case, $3,000;

Notes: The $3,000 includes provincial tax administered by the CRA for all provinces other than Quebec; see B in "net tax owing" below, and Notes at end of 156.1.

Paras. (a) and (b) amended by 2007 budget bill #2 to change $1,200 to $1,800 and $2,000 to $3,000, for 2008 and later taxation years (and, for the purpose of applying 156.1(2) to the 2008 and 2009 taxation years, for the 2006 and 2007 taxation years).

"net tax owing" by an individual for a taxation year means

(a) in the case of an individual resident in the Province of Quebec at the end of the year, the amount determined by the formula

$$A - C - D - F$$

and

(b) in any other case, the amount determined by the formula

$$A + B - C - E - F$$

where

A   is the total of the taxes payable under this Part and Parts I.2, X.5 and XI.4 by the individual for the year,

B   is the total of all income taxes payable by the individual for the year under any law of a province or of an Aboriginal government with which the Minister of Finance has entered into an agreement for the collection of income taxes payable by individuals to the province or Aboriginal government under that law,

C is the total of the taxes deducted or withheld under section 153 and Part I.2 on behalf of the individual for the year,

D is the amount determined under subsection 120(2) in respect of the individual for the year,

E is the total of all amounts deducted or withheld on behalf of the individual for the year under a law of a province or of an Aboriginal government with which the Minister of Finance has entered into an agreement for the collection of income taxes payable by individuals to the province or Aboriginal government under that law, and

F is the amount determined under subsection 120(2.2) in respect of the individual for the year.

Related Provisions: 156.1(1) — Rules for calculating formula elements A and B; 156.1(1.2) — Rule for calculating D; 156.1(1.3) — Rule for calculating F, First Nations Tax; 257 — Formula cannot calculate to less than zero.

Notes: See Notes to 156(1) and Notes at end of 156.1.

Description of A amended to refer to Part XI.4 by 2012 budget bill #2, effective for 2012 and later taxation years.

156.1(1)"net tax owing" amended by 2000 Budget (effective for 2001 and later taxation years), 1999, 1997, 1996, 1995 and 1993 Budgets, 1992 and 1991 technical bills.

Regulations: 2607 (individual is resident in province of principal place of residence).

Forms: P110: Paying your income tax by instalments [pamphlet]; T1033-WS: Worksheet for calculating instalment payments.

(1.1) Values of A and B in "net tax owing" — For the purposes of determining the values of A and B in the definition "net tax owing" in subsection (1), income taxes payable by an individual for a taxation year are determined

(a) before taking into consideration the specified future tax consequences for the year; and

(b) after deducting all tax credits to which the individual is entitled for the year relating to those taxes (other than tax credits that become payable to the individual after the individual's balance-due day for the year, prescribed tax credits and amounts deemed to have been paid because of the application of either subsection 120(2) or (2.2)).

Notes: 156.1(1.1)(b) amended by 1999 Budget, effective for 1999 and later taxation years, to add reference to 120(2.2).

156(1.1) added by 1996 Budget, effective for amounts payable in 1996 or later. For earlier years, see the closing words of 156.1(1)"net tax owing".

(1.2) Value of D in "net tax owing" — For the purpose of determining the value of D in the definition "net tax owing" in subsection (1), the amount deemed by subsection 120(2) to have been paid on account of an individual's tax under this Part for a taxation year is determined before taking into consideration the specified future tax consequences for the year.

Notes: 120(2) refers to the Quebec abatement of tax. 156.1(1.2) added by 1996 Budget, effective for amounts payable in 1996 or later. For earlier years, see the closing words of 156.1(1)"net tax owing".

(1.3) Value of F in "net tax owing" — For the purpose of determining the value of F in the definition "net tax owing" in subsection (1), the amount deemed by subsection 120(2.2) to have been paid on account of an individual's tax under this Part for a taxation year is determined before taking into consideration the specified future tax consequences for the year.

Notes: 120(2.2) refers to First Nations tax paid to an aboriginal government. 156.1(1.3) added by 1999 Budget, effective for 1999 and later taxation years.

(2) No instalment required — Sections 155 and 156 do not apply to an individual for a particular taxation year where

(a) the individual's chief source of income for the particular year is farming or fishing and the individual's net tax owing for the particular year, or either of the 2 preceding taxation years, does not exceed the individual's instalment threshold for that year;

(b) the individual's net tax owing for the particular year, or for each of the 2 preceding taxation years, does not exceed the individual's instalment threshold for that year; or

(c) the individual is a graduated rate estate for the particular year.

Related Provisions: 107(5.1) — Trust's gain on distribution to non-resident beneficiary does not increase instalment requirements; 128.1(5) — Deemed disposition on emigration does not increase instalment requirements; 156(4) — No application to SIFT trust; 157(2.1) — Threshold of $1,000 for corporations; 161(2) — Interest on late or insufficient instalments.

Notes: See Notes at end of 156.1.

156.1(2)(c) added by 2014 budget bill #2, for 2016 and later tax years. See Notes to 248(1)"graduated rate estate".

Forms: T1033-WS: Worksheet for calculating instalment payments.

(3) Idem — Sections 155 and 156 do not require the payment of any amount in respect of an individual that would otherwise become due under either of those sections on or after the day on which the individual dies.

(4) Payment of remainder — Every individual shall, on or before the individual's balance-due day for each taxation year, pay to the Receiver General in respect of the year the amount, if any, by which the individual's tax payable under this Part for the year exceeds the total of

(a) all amounts deducted or withheld under section 153 from remuneration or other payments received by the individual in the year, and

(b) all other amounts paid to the Receiver General on or before that day on account of the individual's tax payable under this Part for the year.

Related Provisions: 104(23)(e) — Alternative rule for testamentary trust; 156(4) — No application to SIFT trust; 161(1) — Interest payable if balance not paid on time.

Notes: See Notes to 107(5.2) and 128.1(5).

Instalments owing after March 18, 2020 were due on Sept. 30, 2020 due to COVID-19, per tinyurl.com/covid-dates as it read during 2020 (see PITA 59th ed. at 156(1)).

Notes [s. 156.1]: In simple terms, if the total payable on filing (i.e., total tax minus source deductions) exceeds $3,000 for both the current year and either of the previous two years, instalments are required. The $3,000 threshold includes provincial tax for all provinces whose personal income taxes are administered by CRA; for residents of Quebec, the threshold is $1,800 and applies to federal tax only. (A separate $1,800 threshold applies to Quebec residents for provincial tax: *Taxation Act* s. 1026.0.2.)

Interest on unpaid instalments applied in *Pereira*, 2017 FCA 238.

Definitions [s. 156.1]: "amount", "balance-due day", "farming", "fishing", "graduated rate estate", "individual" — 248(1); "instalment threshold" — 156.1(1); "Minister of Finance" — *Financial Administration Act* 14; "net tax owing" — 156.1(1); "prescribed" — 248(1); "province" — *Interpretation Act* 35(1); "resident" — Reg 2607; "specified future tax consequence", "taxpayer" — 248(1); "taxation year" — 249.

157. (1) Payment by corporation [monthly instalments and balance] — Subject to subsections (1.1) and (1.5), every corporation shall, in respect of each of its taxation years, pay to the Receiver General

(a) either

(i) on or before the last day of each month in the year, an amount equal to $1/12$ of the total of the amounts estimated by it to be the taxes payable by it under this Part and Parts VI, VI.1 and XIII.1 for the year,

(ii) on or before the last day of each month in the year, an amount equal to $1/12$ of its first instalment base for the year, or

(iii) on or before the last day of each of the first two months in the year, an amount equal to $1/12$ of its second instalment base for the year, and on or before the last day of each of the following months in the year, an amount equal to $1/10$ of the amount remaining after deducting the amount computed pursuant to this subparagraph in respect of the first two months from its first instalment base for the year; and

(b) the remainder of the taxes payable by it under this Part and Parts VI, VI.1 and XIII.1 for the year on or before its balance-due day for the year.

Related Provisions: 87(2)(oo.1) — Effect of amalgamation; 88(1)(e.8), (e.9) — Winding-up; 151 — Estimate of tax; 157(1.1)–(1.5) — Quarterly instalments by small CCPC; 157(2) — Corporate instalment rules apply to SIFT trust; 157(2.1) — No instalments where not more than $3,000 per year; 157(3) — Reduction for dividend refund and capital gains refund; 161(1) — Interest on taxes due; 161(2) — Interest on unpaid tax instalments; 161(2.2) — Interest on instalments; 161(4.1) — Minimum instalment payments to avoid interest charges; 163.1 — Penalty for late or deficient instalments; 164(1.51)–(1.53) — Refund of instalments at taxpayer's request; 197(6) — Corporate instalment rules apply to SIFT partnership; 221.2 — Transfers of instalments to other years' accounts; 248(1)"balance-due day" — Deadline; 248(7) — Receipt of things mailed; 256 — Associated corporations; 261(11) — Where functional currency election made.

Notes: Corporate instalments are due monthly, in contrast to individuals' instalments, which under 156(1) are due quarterly (but small corporations that qualify under 157(1.1)–(1.5) can remit quarterly. The final balance is due 2 or 3 months after year-end (see 248(1)"balance-due day"(d)), even though the return under 150(1)(a) is not due until 6 months after year-end.

Instalments paid earlier than required generate "contra interest" under 161(2.2) to offset interest on late instalments. This can effectively allow a corp to delay its instalment payments until fairly late in the year, to reduce the economic risk of overpaying instalments that may not be needed. See Feltham & Macnaughton, "Optimal Payment Strategy for Corporate Income Tax Instalments", 48(1) *Canadian Tax Journal* 60-89 (2000). The *Taxnet Pro* Corporate Tax Centre has an Instalment Interest Calculator to calculate the catch-up instalment payments required to create contra-interest sufficient to offset interest charges accrued.

The references to "Parts I, VI, VI.1 and XIII.1" allow contra interest for an overpayment under one Part to credit against interest for late payment under another Part.

A corporation can choose any method from (a)(i)-(iii), not necessarily the one that leads to the least total tax, despite 161(4.1): *I.G. (Rockies) Corp.*, 2005 TCC 51; VIEWS doc 2011-039707117. Where a loss carryback is applied and a functional currency election is used, see 2014-054063117.

Instalments owing after March 18, 2020 were due on Sept. 30, 2020 due to COVID-19: tinyurl.com/covid-dates as it read during 2020 (see PITA 59th ed. at 156(1)).

Ontario corporate (but not federal) instalments can be reduced by the Ontario corporation minimum tax credit: doc 2012-0448801E5.

157(1) opening words amended by 2007 budget bill #2, effective for taxation years that begin after 2007, to add reference to 157(1.1)-(1.5); and subpara. (a)(i) and para. (b) amended to delete references to Part I.3.

157(1) earlier amended by 2001 Budget (effective for 2002 and later taxation years), 2001 technical bill, 1996 Budget and 1992 technical bill.

Forms: T7B-CORP: Corporation instalment guide; T2WS1: Calculating estimated tax payable and tax credits; T2WS2: Calculating monthly instalment payments; T2WS3: Calculating quarterly instalment payments.

(1.1) Special case [quarterly instalments] — A small-CCPC may, in respect of each of its taxation years, pay to the Receiver General

(a) one of the following:

(i) on or before the last day of each three-month period in the taxation year (or if the period that remains in a taxation year after the end of the last such three-month period is less than three months, on or before the last day of that remaining period), an amount equal to ¼ of the total of the amounts estimated by it to be the taxes payable by it under this Part and Part VI.1 for the taxation year,

(ii) on or before the last day of each three-month period in the taxation year (or if the period that remains in a taxation year after the end of the last such three-month period is less than three months, on or before the last day of that remaining period), an amount equal to ¼ of its first instalment base for the taxation year, or

(iii) on or before the last day

(A) of the first period in the taxation year not exceeding three months, an amount equal to ¼ of its second instalment base for the taxation year, and

(B) of each of the following three-month periods in the taxation year (or if the period that remains in a taxation year after the end of the last such three-month period is less than three months, on or before the last day of that remaining period), an amount equal to ⅓ of the amount remaining after deducting the amount computed pursuant to clause (A) from its first instalment base for the taxation year; and

(b) the remainder of the taxes payable by it under this Part and Part VI.1 for the taxation year on or before its balance-due day for the taxation year.

Related Provisions: 157(1.2)–(1.4) — Definition of "small-CCPC"; 157(1.5) — Where corporation ceases to qualify; 157(2.1) — No instalments where not more than $3,000 per year; 157(3) — Reduction for dividend refund and capital gains refund; 157(3.1) — Reduction in instalments for dividend refund and certain credits; 161(4.1) — Minimum instalment payment to avoid interest charges; 261(11) — Where functional currency election made.

Notes: 157(1.1) allows quarterly filing, similar to that for individuals, for small Canadian-controlled private corporations that meet certain conditions (see 157(1.2)–(1.4)).

157(1.1) added by 2007 budget bill #2, for taxation years that begin after 2007.

(1.2) Small-CCPC — For the purpose of subsection (1.1), a small-CCPC, at a particular time during a taxation year, is a Canadian-controlled private corporation

(a) for which the amount determined under subsection (1.3) for the taxation year, or for the preceding taxation year, does not exceed $500,000;

(b) for which the amount determined under subsection (1.4) for the taxation year, or for the preceding taxation year, does not exceed $10 million;

(c) in respect of which an amount is deducted under section 125 of the Act in computing the corporation's tax payable for the taxation year or for the preceding taxation year; and

(d) that has throughout the 12-month period that ends at the time its last remittance under this section is due,

(i) remitted, on or before the day on or before which the amounts were required to be remitted, all amounts that were required to be remitted under subsection 153(1), under Part IX of the *Excise Tax Act*, under subsection 82(1) of the *Employment Insurance Act* or under subsection 21(1) of the *Canada Pension Plan*; and

(ii) filed, on or before the day on or before which the returns were required to be filed, all returns that were required to be filed under this Act or under Part IX of the *Excise Tax Act*.

Notes: For application of 157(1.2)-(1.4) following amalgamation or windup, see VIEWS docs 2008-027756117, 2011-0425271E5.

157(1.2)(a) amended by 2009 budget bill #1 to change "$400,000" to "$500,000", effective for taxation years that end after 2008, but prorated for taxation years that end in 2009 to the number of days of the taxation year that are in each of 2008 and 2009.

157(1.2) added by 2007 budget bill #2, for taxation years that begin after 2007.

(1.3) Taxable income — small-CCPC — The amount determined under this subsection in respect of a corporation for a particular taxation year is

(a) if the corporation is not associated with another corporation in the particular taxation year, the amount that is the corporation's taxable income for the particular taxation year; or

(b) if the corporation is associated with another corporation in the particular taxation year, the amount that is the total of all amounts each of which is the taxable income of the corporation for the particular taxation year or the taxable income of a corporation with which it is associated in the particular taxation year for a taxation year of that other corporation that ends in the particular taxation year.

Notes: 157(1.3) added by 2007 budget bill #2, for tax years that begin after 2007.

(1.4) Taxable capital — small-CCPC — The amount determined under this subsection in respect of a corporation for a particular taxation year is

(a) if the corporation is not associated with another corporation in the particular taxation year, the amount that is the corporation's taxable capital employed in Canada (for the purpose of this subsection, within the meaning assigned by section 181.2 or 181.3, as the case may be) for the particular taxation year; or

(b) if the corporation is associated with another corporation in the particular taxation year, the amount that is the total of all amounts each of which is the taxable capital employed in Canada of the corporation for the particular taxation year or the taxable capital employed in Canada of a corporation with which it is associated in the particular taxation year for a taxation year of that other corporation that ends in the particular taxation year.

Notes: 157(1.4)(a), (b) amended by 2002-2013 technical bill, for tax years that begin after 2007. 157(1.4) added by 2007 budget bill #2, for tax years that begin after 2007.

(1.5) No longer a small-CCPC — Notwithstanding subsection (1), where a corporation, that has remitted amounts in accordance with subsection (1.1), ceases at any particular time in a taxation year to be eligible to remit in accordance with subsection (1.1), the corporation shall pay to the Receiver General, the following amounts for the taxation year,

(a) on or before the last day of each month, in the taxation year, that ends after the particular time, either

(i) the amount determined by the formula

$$(A–B)/C$$

where

A is the total of the amounts estimated by the corporation to be the taxes payable by it under this Part and Parts VI, VI.1 and XIII.1 for the taxation year,

B is the total of all payments payable by the corporation in the taxation year in accordance with subsection (1.1), and

C is the number of months that end in the taxation year and after the particular time, or

(ii) the total of

(A) the amount determined by the formula

$$(A–B)/C$$

where

A is the corporation's first instalment base for the taxation year,

B is the total of all payments payable by the corporation in the taxation year in accordance with subsection (1.1), and

C is the number of months that end in the taxation year and after the particular time; and

(B) the amount obtained when the estimated tax payable by the corporation, if any, under Parts VI and XIII.1 for the taxation year is divided by the number of months that end in the taxation year and after the particular time; and

(b) the remainder of the taxes payable by it under this Part and Parts VI, VI.1 and XIII.1 for the taxation year on or before its balance-due day for the year.

Related Provisions: 161(4.1) — Minimum instalment payment to avoid interest charges; 257 — Formula cannot calculate to less than zero.

Notes: 157(1.5) added by 2007 budget bill #2, for tax years that begin after 2007; and corrected retroactively by 2013 budget bill #2 to change "Part" to "Parts" in (a)(ii)(B) and change "balance-due date" to "balance-due day" in (b).

(2) Application to SIFT trusts — Subsections (1), (2.1) and (4) apply to a SIFT trust with any modifications that the circumstances require.

Notes: See Notes to 104(16) re SIFT trusts [defined in 122.1(1)], which are taxed like corporations and thus must pay instalments like corporations.

157(2) added by 2013 budget bill #2, for tax years that begin after July 20, 2011.

Former 157(2) repealed by 2003 Budget, for taxation years that begin after June 2003. It applied to co-ops and credit unions, which are now under 157(1). Earlier amended by 1996 Budget, 1995-97 technical bill, 1992 technical bill.

(2.1) $3,000 threshold — A corporation may, instead of paying the instalments required for a taxation year by paragraph (1)(a) or by subsection (1.1), pay to the Receiver General, under paragraph (1)(b), the total of the taxes payable by it under this Part and Parts VI, VI.1 and XIII.1 for the taxation year, if

(a) the total of the taxes payable under this Part and Parts VI, VI.1 and XIII.1 by the corporation for the taxation year (determined before taking into consideration the specified future tax consequences for the year) is equal to or less than $3,000; or

(b) the corporation's first instalment base for the year is equal to or less than $3,000.

Related Provisions: 156.1(2) — Parallel rule for individuals; 157(2) — Corporate instalment rules apply to SIFT trust; 197(6) — Corporate instalment rules apply to SIFT partnership.

Notes: See Notes to 157(1).

157(2.1) amended by 2007 budget bill #2, for taxation years that begin after 2007. Although completely redrafted, the substantive changes were to add reference to 157(1.1) and to increase the threshold from $1,000 to $3,000.

157(2.1) earlier amended by 2001 technical bill, 1996 Budget, 1992 technical bill, 1992 transportation support bill, 1991 technical bill and 1989 Budget.

(3) Reduced instalments — Notwithstanding subsection[s] (1) and (1.5), the amount payable under subsection (1) or (1.5) for a taxation year by a corporation to the Receiver General on or before the last day of any month in the year is deemed to be the amount, if any, by which

(a) the amount so payable as determined under that subsection for the month

exceeds

(b) where the corporation is neither a mutual fund corporation nor a non-resident-owned investment corporation, $1/12$ of the corporation's dividend refund (within the meaning assigned by subsection 129(1)) for the year,

(c) if the corporation is a mutual fund corporation, $1/12$ of the total of

(i) the corporation's capital gains refund (within the meaning assigned by section 131) for the year, and

(ii) the amount that, because of subsection 131(5) or (11), is the corporation's dividend refund (within the meaning assigned by section 129) for the year,

(d) where the corporation is a non-resident-owned investment corporation, $1/12$ of the corporation's allowable refund (within the meaning assigned by section 133) for the year, and

(e) $1/12$ of the total of the amounts each of which is deemed by subsection 125.4(3), 125.5(3), 125.6(2) or (2.1), 127.1(1) or 127.41(3) to have been paid on account of the corporation's tax payable under this Part for the year.

Related Provisions: 131(5) — Dividend refund to mutual fund corporation; 136 — Cooperative not private corporation — exception.

Notes: 157(3)(e) amended by 2019 budget bill #1, effective 2019, to add 125.6(2); and by 2021 budget bill #1, effective 2019, to add 125.6(2.1).

157(3) earlier amended by 2002-2013 technical bill (for 1999 and later tax years), 2007 budget bill #2, 1995-97 technical bill, 1995 and 1994 Budgets, 1992 technical bill.

Interpretation Bulletins: IT-243R4: Dividend refund to private corporations.

(3.1) Amount of payment — three-month period [reduction for certain credits] — Notwithstanding subsection (1.1), the amount payable under subsection (1.1) for a taxation year by a corporation to the Receiver General on or before the last day of any period in the year is deemed to be the amount, if any, by which

(a) the amount so payable as determined under that subsection for the period

exceeds the total of

(b) $1/4$ of the corporation's dividend refund (within the meaning assigned by subsection 129(1)) for the taxation year, and

(c) $1/4$ of the total of the amounts each of which is deemed by subsection 125.4(3), 125.5(3), 125.6(2) or (2.1), 127.1(1) or 127.41(3) to have been paid on account of the corporation's tax payable under this Part for the taxation year.

Notes: 157(3.1) amended by 2019 budget bill #1, effective 2019, to add 125.6(2); and by 2021 budget bill #1, effective 2019, to add 125.6(2.1).

157(3.1) added by 2007 budget bill #2, for tax years that begin after 2007.

(4) Definitions — In this section, "first instalment base" and "second instalment base" of a corporation for a taxation year have the meanings prescribed by regulation.

Related Provisions: 157(2) — Corporate instalment rules apply to SIFT trust; 197(6) — Corporate instalment rules apply to SIFT partnership; 261(11)(a)(ii), (iii) — Functional currency reporting.

Regulations: 5301 (meaning of "first instalment base", "second instalment base").

Definitions [s. 157]: "amount" — 248(1); "associated" — 256; "balance-due day" — 248(1); "business limit" — 125(2)–(5.1), 248(1); "calendar year" — *Interpretation Act* 37(1)(a); "Canadian-controlled private corporation" — 125(7), 248(1); "capital gain" — 39(1)(a), 248(1); "capital gains refund" — 131(2); "corporation" — 248(1), *Interpretation Act* 35(1); "credit union" — 137(6), 248(1); "dividend refund" — 129(1)(a); "first instalment base" — 157(4), Reg. 5301(1); "month" — *Interpretation Act* 35(1); "mutual fund corporation" — 131(8); "non-resident-owned investment corporation" — 133(8), 248(1); "prescribed", "regulation" — 248(1); "resident in Canada" — 250; "SIFT trust" — 122.1(1), (2), 248(1); "second instalment base" — 157(4), Reg. 5301(2); "share" — 248(1); "small-CCPC" — 157(1.2)–(1.4); "specified future tax consequence" — 248(1); "tax payable" — 248(2); "taxable capital employed in Canada" — 181.2(1), 181.3(1); "taxable income" — 2(2), 248(1); "taxation year" — 249.

157.1 [No longer relevant]

Notes: 157.1 added by 2001 Budget, for 2002 and later tax years. It implements a 6-month deferral of corporate instalments otherwise payable (see 157(1)) in Jan.-March 2002 (other than large corporations). It was introduced in response to the slowdown in the economy following the Sept. 11, 2001 ("9/11") terrorist attacks.

158. Payment of remainder — Where the Minister mails a notice of assessment of any amount payable by a taxpayer, that part of the amount assessed then remaining unpaid is payable forthwith by the taxpayer to the Receiver General.

Related Provisions: 156.1(4) — Obligation of individual to pay balance by balance-due day; 157(1)(b) — Obligation of corporation to pay balance; 161.4(1) — No requirement to pay balance of $2 or less; 164(3) — Interest on overpayments; 220(3.8) — Fee for NSF cheques; 220(4) — Security for taxes; 222–225 — Collection of taxes; 225.1 — Collection restrictions; 248(7)(a) — Mail deemed received on day mailed; 261(11) — Currency in which balance payable when functional currency election made.

Notes: Although the amount assessed is payable "forthwith", it is effectively stopped (except for large corporations and taxpayers claiming donation shelters, both of which must pay half) by filing an objection or Tax Court appeal: 225.1. In general, a taxpayer that can afford to should pay an assessment even if appealing; see Notes to 225.1(1).

Where there is a question as to which taxation year a payment should be allocated to, see Notes to 221.2.

A photocopied remittance voucher does not have the required magnetic ink to be processed at a financial institution. To get remittance vouchers: 1-800-959-5525 (business) or 1-800-959-8281 (individuals). Personalized remittance vouchers can ensure the payment is applied to the right year: VIEWS doc 2010-0373701C6.

CRA no longer accepts cash at local offices; for payment methods see canada.ca/payments. For account access generally: tinyurl.com/myaccount-cra (individuals), /cra-mybusiness (corporations), /cra-represent (for advisers).

Definitions [s. 158]: "assessment", "Minister", "taxpayer" — 248(1).

CRA Audit Manual: 11.5.13: Collection stall code procedures — Form T718.

159. (1) Person acting for another — For the purposes of this Act, where a person is a legal representative of a taxpayer at any time,

(a) the legal representative is jointly and severally, or solidarily, liable with the taxpayer

(i) to pay each amount payable under this Act by the taxpayer at or before that time and that remains unpaid, to the extent that the legal representative is at that time in possession or control, in the capacity of legal representative, of property that belongs or belonged to, or that is or was held for the benefit of, the taxpayer or the taxpayer's estate, and

(ii) to perform any obligation or duty imposed under this Act on the taxpayer at or before that time and that remains outstanding, to the extent that the obligation or duty can reasonably be considered to relate to the responsibilities of the legal representative acting in that capacity; and

(b) any action or proceeding in respect of the taxpayer taken under this Act at or after that time by the Minister may be so taken in the name of the legal representative acting in that capacity and, when so taken, has the same effect as if it had been taken directly against the taxpayer and, if the taxpayer no longer exists, as if the taxpayer continued to exist.

Related Provisions: 150(3) — Obligation to file taxpayer's return; 227.1 — Liability of corporate directors; 248(7)(a) — Mail deemed received on day mailed.

Notes: See Notes to 159(3), and 248(1)"legal representative" (LR). A director of a corp was not liable for distributing its assets: *Groscki*, 2017 TCC 249, paras. 50-69 [Hosanna, "Groscki: Scope for Director's Liability Under Section 159", 18(2) *Tax for the Owner-Manager* (ctf.ca) 9-10 (April 2018)]. On windup of a limited partnership, see VIEWS doc 2011-0410491E5.

By making the LR liable for distributing money from an insolvent estate if CRA is not paid, 159(1) overrides the Nova Scotia *Probate Act* provision that funeral expenses get priority: *Evans Estate*, 2018 NSSC 68.

See also CRA directive RCD-01-01, "Person Acting for Another: Section 159 ITA" (Jan. 1, 2001); docs 2010-0377091E5 (executor or estate trustee is personally liable for penalties if deceased's return is filed late); 2016-0638171E5 (trustee may be liable for value that *was* in a trust ["at any time" per 159(1)(a)(i)], even if value has dropped due to market fluctuations! [Nitikman, "The Trustee's Right to Indemnity and Section 159", *The Tax Advocate* (*Taxnet Pro* Tax Disputes & Resolution Centre), June 2018 (20pp)]).

159(1)(a) opening words amended by 2002-2013 technical bill (Part 4 — bijuralism), effective June 26, 2013, to add "or solidarily".

159(1) earlier amended by 1995-97 technical bill, effective June 18, 1998.

(2) Certificate before distribution — Every legal representative (other than a trustee in bankruptcy) of a taxpayer shall, before distributing to one or more persons any property in the possession or control of the legal representative acting in that capacity, obtain a certificate from the Minister, by applying for one in prescribed form, certifying that all amounts

(a) for which the taxpayer is or can reasonably be expected to become liable under this Act at or before the time the distribution is made, and

(b) for the payment of which the legal representative is or can reasonably be expected to become liable in that capacity

have been paid or that security for the payment thereof has been accepted by the Minister.

Announced Administrative Change — 159(2) — Requesting clearance certificate by email

CRA notice, April 9, 2021 (tinyurl.com/cra-clearance): *CRA and COVID-19: Clearance certificates*

Clearance certificates (Forms TX19 and GST352) continue to be processed. However, as Canada Revenue Agency (CRA) employees are working under certain restrictions for their health and safety during the COVID-19 pandemic, processing times may be increased.

Employees have limited access to the office which may delay receipt of submissions by mail or fax. As a result, any documentation or new clearance request applications sent to the CRA between March 12, 2020 and November 30, 2020, may not have been included in the inventory for processing.

It is recommended that legal representatives who submitted a clearance request by mail between March 12, 2020 and November 30, 2020 resubmit the request and supporting documents online through My Account, Represent a Client, or My Business Account.

For more information go to: *Request a clearance certificate* [tinyurl.com/cra-req-clear — ed.].

NOTE: Submitting documents online through an online portal does not require you to have electronic access to the deceased individuals account.

How to send us your documents by email (available until June 30, 2021)

As part of the response to COVID-19, the CRA has created a temporary procedure which may allow representatives to submit clearance certificate requests and supporting information via email, should they not be able to use one of the online portals. This process for sending documents by email is **temporary and will be cancelled as of June 30, 2021, after which all submissions will need to be submitted via the online portal, mail or fax**.

1. To submit your request for clearance certificate (Forms TX19 and GST352) electronically, send an email to CCTX19G@cra-arc.gc.ca stating that you want to correspond by email with the CRA. In the subject line include the province where the executor lives.

Do not include any sensitive information or attachments in the email.

Example: Sample email from a legal representative

Joe is a legal representative living in the province of Ontario. Joe can submit a request to the CRA via email.

To: CCTX19G@cra-arc.gc.ca

Subject: Clearance certificate (Ontario)

Body: I am the legal representative and need to file a clearance certificate request. Please send instructions.

2. Wait for a CRA officer to respond to your email. The CRA officer will send you the requirements to authorize communication by email, and tell you when/if you are permitted to submit your application or request by email.

NOTE: Please be advised that there are risks involved in sending sensitive and/or personal information over email. The CRA is temporarily allowing applications to be submitted via email as an emergency measure to help stop the spread of COVID-19. This email service will be cancelled as of June 30, 2021.

NOTE: Incomplete applications **will** cause delays in processing.

Related Provisions: 159(3) — Liability where property distributed with no certificate; 159(3.1) — Appropriation of property; 220(4) — Security for taxes; 227.1 — Liability of directors for withholding taxes.

Notes: See Notes to 159(1). The certificate described in 159(2) is commonly referred to as a "clearance certificate". Apply using Form TX19. See Information Circular 82-6R12 for detailed CRA procedures; VIEWS docs 2009-0344351I7, 2012-0464791E5; and Notes to 159(3). This applies to non-resident executors as well: 2002-0117975; and it may apply to a non-resident estate with non-resident beneficiaries: 2017-0717981E5. A general partner winding up a limited partnership needs a certificate for the LP in CRA's view, but does not need one certifying that each limited partner has paid tax on the partnership income: 2012-0432861E5. A corporation can obtain a certificate before dissolution: 2017 CPA Alberta Roundtable (tinyurl.com/cra-abtax), q. 7(b).

CRA's target (tinyurl.com/cra-standards) for clearance certificates is 80% within 120 days; in 2019-20, it did 95%. See also May 2013 ICAA Roundtable q.6 (tinyurl.com/cra-abtax), with "best practices" for advisors to speed up the process; and *Income Tax Audit Manual* §16.1.

A 159(2) certificate relieves the *legal representative* of liability, but does not prevent the CRA from issuing a later reassessment of the taxpayer, in the author's view.

159(2) technically applies to an RRSP trustee before distributing funds from the RRSP, but CRA policy does not require it (though this is being considered where the RRSP beneficiary is non-resident): VIEWS doc 2011-0402391I7. 159(2) applies to a Quebec administration of property created by will: 2014-0537691E5. It also applies to the trustee of a qualified disability trust that owes 122(1)(c) recovery tax after the beneficiary's death: 2016-0651751C6 [2016 APFF q.7].

For discussion see Lamarre et al., *Taxation of Corporate Reorganizations* (Carswell, 3rd ed., 2019), §9.4; Falk & Morand, "Current Issues Forum", 2011 BC Tax Conference (ctf.ca), 1B:1-61; Sorensen, "Executor Liability", 5(2) *BorderCrossings* (Carswell) 1-5 (July 2012).

159(2) amended by 1995-97 technical bill, effective June 18, 1998. See the new definition of "legal representative" in 248(1). Earlier amended by 1991 technical bill.

Interpretation Bulletins: IT-488R2: Winding-up of 90%-owned taxable Canadian corporations (cancelled); CPP-2: Canada pension plan — status of employer where trustee in bankruptcy, receiver or receiver and manager is appointed; UI-3: *Unemployment Insurance Act* — status of employer where trustee in bankruptcy, receiver or receiver and manager is appointed.

Information Circulars: 78-10R5: Books and records retention/destruction; 82-6R12: Clearance certificate; 98-1R5: Tax collection policies.

CRA Audit Manual: 16.1.0: Clearance certificate program.

Forms: TX19: Asking for clearance certificate.

(3) Personal liability — If a legal representative (other than a trustee in bankruptcy) of a taxpayer distributes to one or more persons property in the possession or control of the legal representative, acting in that capacity, without obtaining a certificate under subsection (2) in respect of the amounts referred to in that subsection,

(a) the legal representative is personally liable for the payment of those amounts to the extent of the value of the property distributed;

(b) the Minister may at any time assess the legal representative in respect of any amount payable because of this subsection; and

(c) the provisions of this Division (including, for greater certainty, the provisions in respect of interest payable) apply, with any modifications that the circumstances require, to an assessment made under this subsection as though it had been made under section 152 in respect of taxes payable under this Part.

Related Provisions: 146.2(6.1) — Limit on trustee's liability for tax on TFSA carrying on business; 159(3.1) — Appropriation of property; 222(5)(c) — Restart of 10-year collection limitation period.

Notes: See 159(2) Notes. An executor who distributes property of an estate without obtaining a clearance certificate is personally liable for the deceased's unpaid taxes plus interest. See VIEWS docs 2010-0376441E5, 2010-037684117, 2010-0377041E5, 2010-0390311E5, 2013-0513191E5, 2014-052497117. This is also considered to apply to the parent of a wound-up subsidiary corporation: 2011-039919117. (A GST/HST clearance certificate may also be needed, under s. 270 of the *Excise Tax Act*.) An exec-

utor who finds evidence of unmet tax obligations in the deceased's records may wish to make a voluntary disclosure; see Notes to 220(3.1).

Given the need for an estate to make charitable donations within a limited time to obtain tax relief, CRA is reviewing its clearance-certificate policy (an existing option is to obtain one permitting partial distribution): 2016-0632641C6 [2016 CALU q.5].

CRA may rank ahead of other unsecured debts, based on the common-law "Crown prerogative": *Bank of Nova Scotia* (1885), 11 S.C.R. 1 (SCC); *Household Realty*, [1980] 1 S.C.R. 423 (SCC); *Wright*, [1988] 1 C.T.C. 107 (Ont. Div. Ct); *Royal Bank*, 2012 ABCA 225. An executor who pays debts of the estate (such as the deceased's credit cards) may thus be liable under 159(3): docs 2010-0373611C6, 2012-045725117.

A person winding up a company may be liable for its tax debts that result from retroactive legislation enacted later: VIEWS doc 2011-0401821C6.

Funds put into an estate's bank account by mistake, including life insurance proceeds designated to a beneficiary, are not subject to 159(3): *Nguyen*, 2010 TCC 503.

The words "at any time" in 159(3)(b) mean that there is no time limit for an assessment: see Notes to 160(2) and 227(10), both of which use the same language as 159(3)(b) and (c), and VIEWS doc 2011-0394731E5.

It is uncertain whether the executor can challenge the underlying assessment of the deceased when the executor is assessed. *Parsons*, [1984] C.T.C. 253 (FCA), and *Armstrong*, [1998] 4 C.T.C. 2006 (TCC) suggest not; more recent case law on ss. 160 and 227.1 allows such a challenge: *Gaucher*, [2001] 1 C.T.C. 125 (FCA) and *Duque*, 2020 FCA 73, para. 20; but these cases might not apply if the executor had the legal right to contest the deceased's assessment. See point 6 in Notes to 227.1(1). (CRA says the representative may be liable for using estate assets to fund the dispute!: 2011-0429101C6.) However, the deceased need not be assessed for the legal representative to be assessed: VIEWS doc 2010-037886117. In *Mosher*, 2013 TCC 378, an estate had abandoned its TCC appeal just before trial, and the executor (appealing her 159(3) assessment later) sought to challenge the estate's liability. The TCC considered it premature to strike such challenge from the Notice of Appeal on the basis of estoppel or abuse of process.

159 applies to both federal and provincial tax in the CRA's view but is subject to a creditor's security interest or right of set-off: VIEWS doc 2009-0336911E5. (See also Notes to 227(4) re Crown "super priority" over unremitted source deductions.)

In *Clark*, [1997] 2 C.T.C. 2613 (TCC), a lawyer who distributed funds for an auctioneer was not liable under s. 159. See also *Wesbrook Management*, [1996] 1 C.T.C. 2516 (TCC), on tracing liability through to a person to whom assets were transferred.

159(3) does not preclude RRSP trustee liability under 116(5) for not withholding tax on purchase of taxable Canadian property from a non-resident: *Olympia Trust*, 2015 FCA 279, para. 70.

A director of a corp is not liable for distributing its assets: *Groscki*, 2017 TCC 249, paras. 50-69.

An executor is not necessarily entitled to indemnification from beneficiaries for 159(3) liability: *Muth Estate v. Liesch*, 2019 ABQB 922.

See Notes to 8(1)(b) for the possibility of an estate trustee deducting the costs of passing of accounts.

159(3) amended by 2002-2013 technical bill, for assessments made after Dec. 20, 2002; and by 1995-97 technical bill.

Interpretation Bulletins: IT-488R2: Winding-up of 90%-owned taxable Canadian corporations (cancelled).

Information Circulars: 98-1R5: Tax collection policies.

(3.1) Appropriation of property — For the purposes of subsections (2) and (3), an appropriation by a legal representative of a taxpayer of property in the possession or control of the legal representative acting in that capacity is deemed to be a distribution of the property to a person.

Notes: 159(3.1) added by 1995-97 technical bill, effective June 18, 1998.

(4), (4.1) [Repealed]

Notes: 159(4) and (4.1) repealed by 2001 technical bill, effective for individuals who cease to be resident in Canada after October 1, 1996. See now 220(4.5) and (4.6), which contain more comprehensive and more liberal security rules.

159(4) amended and (4.1) added by 1993 technical bill, effective for changes in residence that occur in 1993 or later.

(5) Election [to spread out payments] where certain provisions applicable [on death] — Where subsection 70(2), (5) or (5.2) of this Act or subsection 70(9.4) of the *Income Tax Act*, chapter 148 of the Revised Statutes of Canada, 1952, is applicable in respect of a taxpayer who has died, and the taxpayer's legal representative so elects and furnishes the Minister with security acceptable to the Minister for payment of any tax the payment of which is deferred by the election, notwithstanding any provision of this Part or the *Income Tax Application Rules* respecting the time within which payment shall be made of the tax payable under this Part by the taxpayer for the taxation year in which the taxpayer died, all or any portion of such part of that tax as is equal to the amount, if any, by which that tax exceeds the amount that that tax would be, if this Act were read without reference to subsections 70(2), (5) and (5.2) and the *Income Tax Act*, chapter 148 of the Revised Statutes of Canada, 1952, were read without reference to subsections 70(2), (5), (5.2) and (9.4) of that Act, may be paid in such number (not exceeding 10) of equal consecutive annual instalments as is specified by the legal representative in the election, the first instalment of which shall be paid on or before the day on or before which payment of that tax would, but for the election, have been required to be made and each subsequent instalment of which shall be paid on or before the next following anniversary of that day.

Related Provisions: 135.2(8)(b)(iii) — Death of farmer owning eligible unit of Cdn Wheat Board Farmers' Trust; 159(5.1) — Pre-1972 professional business; 159(6) — Meaning of "tax payable under this Part"; 159(7) — Form and manner of election, and interest.

Notes: For acceptable security for 159(5) see VIEWS doc 2011-0402761C6.

There is no mechanism for amending a Form T2075 later if asset values are not known when the form is due: Rusak & Kakkar, "Subsection 159(5) Election", 20(2) *Tax for the Owner-Manager* (ctf.ca) 6-7 (April 2020).

Regulations: 1001 (prescribed manner of making election).

I.T. Application Rules: 69 (meaning of "chapter 148 of ...").

Interpretation Bulletins: IT-125R4: Dispositions of resource properties; IT-212R3: Income of deceased persons — rights or things; IT-278R2: Death of a partner or of a retired partner.

Forms: T2075: Election to defer payment of income tax under subsec. 159(5) by a deceased taxpayer's legal representative or trustee; T4011: Preparing returns for deceased persons [guide].

(5.1) Idem [pre-1972 professional business] — Where, in the

taxation year in which a taxpayer dies, an amount is included in computing the taxpayer's income by virtue of paragraph 23(3)(c) of the *Income Tax Application Rules*, the provisions of subsection (5) apply, with such modifications as the circumstances require, as though the amount were an amount included in computing the taxpayer's income for the year by virtue of subsection 70(2) or an amount deemed to have been received by the taxpayer by virtue of subsection 70(5).

Related Provisions: 70(2) — Deceased taxpayer — amounts receivable; 70(5) — Depreciable and other capital property.

Interpretation Bulletins: IT-212R3: Income of deceased persons — rights or things; IT-278R2: Death of a partner or of a retired partner.

(6) Idem — For the purposes of subsection (5), the "tax payable

under this Part" by a taxpayer for the taxation year in which the taxpayer died includes any tax payable under this Part by virtue of an election in respect of the taxpayer's death made by the taxpayer's legal representative under subsection 70(2) or under the provisions of that subsection as they are required to be read by virtue of the *Income Tax Application Rules*.

(6.1) Election where subsec. 104(4) applicable — Where a

time determined under paragraph 104(4)(a), (a.1), (a.2), (a.3), (a.4), (b) or (c) in respect of a trust occurs in a taxation year of the trust and the trust so elects and furnishes to the Minister security acceptable to the Minister for payment of any tax the payment of which is deferred by the election, notwithstanding any other provision of this Part respecting the time within which payment shall be made of the tax payable under this Part by the trust for the year, all or any portion of the part of that tax that is equal to the amount, if any, by which that tax exceeds the amount that that tax would be if this Act were read without reference to paragraph 104(4)(a), (a.1), (a.2), (a.3), (a.4), (b) or (c), as the case may be, may be paid in the number (not exceeding 10) of equal consecutive annual instalments that is specified by the trust in the election, the first instalment of which shall be paid on or before the day on or before which payment of that tax would, but for the election, have been required to be made and each subsequent instalment of which shall be paid on or before the next following anniversary of that day.

Related Provisions: 159(7) — Form and manner of election, and interest.

Notes: 159(6.1) allows a trust to pay tax triggered by the 21-year deemed disposition rule in up to 10 annual instalments (with interest: 159(7)). It can be used on a 104(5.2) deemed disposition: VIEWS doc 2015-0594201E5.

159(6.1) amended by 2001 technical bill, for 2000 and later taxation years. Added by 1992 technical bill.

Forms: T2223: Election under s. 159(6.1) by trust to defer payment of income tax.

(7) Form and manner of election and interest — Every elec-

tion made by a taxpayer under subsection (4) or (6.1) or by the legal representative of a taxpayer under subsection (5) shall be made in prescribed form and on condition that, at the time of payment of any amount payment of which is deferred by the election, the taxpayer shall pay to the Receiver General interest on the amount at the prescribed rate in effect at the time the election was made, computed from the day on or before which the amount would, but for the election, have been required to be paid to the day of payment.

Related Provisions: 221.1 — Application of interest where legislation retroactive; 248(11) — Interest compounded daily.

Notes: 159(7) amended by 1992 technical bill, for 1993 and later taxation years.

Regulations: 4301(a) (prescribed rate of interest).

Forms: T2075: Election to defer payment of income tax under subsec. 159(5) by a deceased taxpayer's legal representative or trustee; T2223: Election under s. 159(6.1) by trust to defer payment of income tax.

Definitions [s. 159]: "amount", "assessment", "balance-due day" — 248(1); "Canada" — 255; "individual", "legal representative", "Minister", "person", "prescribed" — 248(1); "prescribed rate" — Reg. 4301; "property" — 248(1); "taxation year" — 249; "tax payable under this Part" — 159(6); "taxpayer" — 248(1).

160. (1) Tax liability re property transferred not at arm's

length — Where a person has, on or after May 1, 1951, transferred property, either directly or indirectly, by means of a trust or by any other means whatever, to

(a) the person's spouse or common-law partner or a person who has since become the person's spouse or common-law partner,

(b) a person who was under 18 years of age, or

(c) a person with whom the person was not dealing at arm's length,

the following rules apply:

(d) the transferee and transferor are jointly and severally, or solidarily, liable to pay a part of the transferor's tax under this Part for each taxation year equal to the amount by which the tax for the year is greater than it would have been if it were not for the operation of sections 74 to 75.1 of this Act and section 74 of the *Income Tax Act*, chapter 148 of the Revised Statutes of Canada, 1952, in respect of any income from, or gain from the disposition of, the property so transferred or property substituted for it, and

(e) the transferee and transferor are jointly and severally, or solidarily, liable to pay under this Act an amount equal to the lesser of

(i) the amount, if any, by which the fair market value of the property at the time it was transferred exceeds the fair market value at that time of the consideration given for the property, and

(ii) the total of all amounts each of which is an amount that the transferor is liable to pay under this Act (including, for greater certainty, an amount that the transferor is liable to pay under this section, regardless of whether the Minister has made an assessment under subsection (2) for that amount) in or in respect of the taxation year in which the property was transferred or any preceding taxation year,

but nothing in this subsection limits the liability of the transferor under any other provision of this Act or of the transferee for the interest that the transferee is liable to pay under this Act on an assessment in respect of the amount that the transferee is liable to pay because of this subsection.

Proposed Amendments — 160(1)

Federal Budget, Supplementary Information, April 19, 2021: *Avoidance of Tax Debts*

The *Income Tax Act* has an anti-avoidance rule (the "tax debt avoidance rule") that is intended to prevent taxpayers from avoiding their tax liabilities by transferring their assets to non-arm's length persons for insufficient consideration. In these circumstances, the rule causes the transferee to be jointly and severally liable with the transferor for tax debts of the transferor for the current or any prior taxation year, to the extent that the value of the property transferred exceeds the amount of consideration given for the property.

Some taxpayers are engaging in complex transactions that attempt to circumvent the tax debt avoidance rule. This planning seeks to avoid the technical application of the rule by:

- arranging for a tax debt to crystallize after the end of the taxation year in which the property transfer occurs;

- arranging for the transferor to be dealing at arm's length with the transferee at the time of the property transfer; or

- stripping out net asset value of the transferor using a series of transactions that does not breach the point-in-time valuation test for the property transferred and consideration given therefor.

This planning is often packaged with highly aggressive tax plans that attempt to eliminate the underlying tax liability of the transferor so that, if the latter planning fails, the Canada Revenue Agency would be unable to collect the tax debt because the indebted taxpayer has been stripped of their assets.

Budget 2021 proposes a number of measures to address this planning, as well as a penalty for those who devise and promote such schemes. The specific proposals are outlined below.

Deferral of Tax Debts

An anti-avoidance rule would be introduced that would provide that, for the purposes of the tax debt avoidance rule, a tax debt would be deemed to have arisen before the end of the taxation year in which a transfer of property occurs if it is reasonable to conclude that:

- the transferor (or a person that does not deal at arm's length with the transferor) had knowledge (or would have knowledge if they had made reasonable inquiries) that there would be a tax amount owing by the transferor (or there would be a tax amount owing if not for additional tax planning done as part of the series of transactions that includes the transfer) that would arise after the end of the taxation year; and

- one of the purposes for the transfer of property was to avoid the payment of the future tax debt.

Avoidance of Non-Arm's Length Status

Budget 2021 proposes an anti-avoidance rule that would provide that, for the purposes of the tax debt avoidance rule, a transferor and transferee that, at the time of a transfer of property, would otherwise be considered to be dealing with each other at arm's length, would be deemed to have not been dealing with each other at arm's length at that time if:

- at any time within a series of transactions or events that includes the transfer, the transferor and transferee do not deal at arm's length; and

- it is reasonable to conclude that one of the purposes of a transaction or event (or a series of transactions or events) within that series was to cause the transferor and transferee to deal at arm's length at the time of transfer.

Valuations

A rule would be introduced such that, for transfers of property that are part of a series of transactions or events, the overall result of the series would be considered in determining the values of the property transferred and the consideration given for the property, rather than simply using those values at the time of the transfer.

Penalty

A penalty would also be introduced for planners and promoters of tax debt avoidance schemes. The penalty would be equal to the lesser of:

- 50% of the tax that is attempted to be avoided; and

- $100,000 plus the promoter's or planner's compensation for the scheme.

This penalty would mirror an existing penalty in the so-called "third-party civil penalty" rules in the *Income Tax Act* in respect of certain false statements, including the standard for its application.

Application

The rules would apply in respect of transfers of property that occur on or after April 19, 2021.

Other Statutes

Similar amendments would be made to comparable provisions in other federal statutes (e.g., section 325 of the *Excise Tax Act*, section 297 of the *Excise Act, 2001* and section 161 of the *Greenhouse Gas Pollution Pricing Act*).

[See also Proposed Amendment at end of 237.3 — ed.]

Federal Budget, Chapter 10, April 19, 2021: *Combatting Abusive Tax Collection Avoidance Schemes*

A small number of high-net-worth taxpayers are engaging in complex transactions intended to avoid the collection of their tax debts. This is done by transferring their assets to a non-arm's length person — such as a corporation owned by the same person — in

a manner that leaves them without the assets necessary to pay their tax debts while circumventing an existing tax rule that is intended to prevent this type of scheme.

Budget 2021 proposes to introduce a number of amendments to the *Income Tax Act* to address this type of planning, as well as a penalty for those who devise and promote such schemes.

Related Provisions: 74.1–75.1 — Attribution of income on non-arm's length transfers; 160(3.1) — Fair market value of undivided interest in property; 160(4) — Transfer to spouse on breakdown of marriage; 160.2 — Recipient's liability where funds received from deceased's RRSP or RRIF; 188(2) — Liability where revoked charity transfers property; 248(5) — Substituted property.

Notes: 160(1) makes non-arm's length transferee T liable for the value of anything transferred by tax debtor D where D is "liable to pay under this Act" (160(1)(e)(ii): this includes tax of other Parts, source-deduction withholdings, director's liability under 227.1, penalties, and interest). It applies if D transfers assets to a relative and then does not pay D's tax debt. The essence is in 160(1)(e): T is liable for the value of what was transferred, minus anything given in return (at that time, not later: *Hardtke*, 2015 TCC 135, para. 33 (aff'd without discussing this point 2016 FCA 138)), up to a limit (160(1)(e)(ii)) of D's tax liability as of the year of transfer. Typical case: husband H transfers his half interest in the family home to wife W for nothing, leaving H with no assets CRA can seize for his debt (see 160(3.1) to value H's "half"). W can then be assessed for the value transferred, and *any* of her assets (e.g. bank accounts) can be seized for this debt. The value transferred is calculated net of any mortgage on the property, e.g. *Margetts*, 2009 TCC 526; *Truong*, 2011 TCC 380; *Ashworth*, 2018 TCC 76; *Drolet*, 2020 QCCA 636, para. 16. Valuing property: see 69(1) Notes. The value of property transferred is determined in the transferor's hands, and the value of consideration given is determined in the transferee's: *Eyeball Networks*, 2021 FCA 17, para. 67. T need not be a "taxpayer": *Bekkerus*, 2014 TCC 311. For the meaning of "arm's length" see Notes to 251(1). In *Damis Properties (Sabel Investments)*, 2021 TCC 24, 160(1) did not apply because at the time of transfer, the taxpayer corps were at arm's length with their subs. Planning for such avoidance will be stopped by the 2021 Budget amendment above.

Note also 160(1)(d), which makes the transferee liable for the transferor's tax on any income of the transferee that is attributed back to the transferor under 74.1–74.5.

There is no time limit on the assessment: see 160(2).

Services: 160(1) does not apply to services. In *Aitchison Prof. Corp.*, 2018 TCC 131, a lawyer with $2m of tax debt worked as an unpaid employee for his professional corp, and his daughters took salary, plus all profits as dividends. This was "distasteful" (para. 28) but 160(1) did not apply as there was no transfer of "property"; the TCC recommended this be fixed but cautioned against too broad an amendment (paras. 32-36).

Liability applies for any transfer from the *beginning* of the tax year in which the transferor's tax liability arose, even if the transactions creating that liability took place after the transfer: 160(1)(e)(ii). Only if fair value is received in exchange for the transferred property (see 160(1)(e)(i)) is there no liability. The transferee is liable for transfer by a director done before CRA complies with 227.1(2) (i.e., CRA tries to collect from the corp only after the transfer): see 227.1(2) Notes.

Intention: The parties need not intend to defeat the tax debt, or even know of it, for the transferee to be liable, and there is no due diligence defence: *Wannan*, 2003 FCA 423; *Waugh*, 2008 FCA 152; *Livingston*, 2008 FCA 89, para. 19; but "an improper motive, if present, can inform the way the Court views the transactions and assesses their impact": *Eyeball Networks*, 2021 FCA 17, para. 39. (S. 160's "harsh" application, and the fact it creates absolute liability, do not violate principles of fundamental justice: *Goldman*, 2021 TCC 13, para. 10.) In all of *Rose*, 2009 FCA 93, *Viau*, 2011 TCC 193, and *Shulkov*, 2012 TCC 457, wife W was liable where H intended the transfer to defeat creditors, even if they did not intend to change *beneficial* ownership as between them.

Dividends: 160(1) can apply to a dividend paid by a corporation to a shareholder with whom it is not at arm's length: *2753-1359 Québec (Larouche)*, 2010 FCA 32; *Duplessis*, 2016 FCA 264; *Algoa Trust*, [1993] 1 C.T.C. 2294 (TCC); *Delage*, [2002] 1 C.T.C. 2756 (TCC); *Bruneau*, 2010 TCC 145; *Ustel*, 2010 TCC 444; *Hennig*, 2012 TCC 141; *Marcotte*, 2012 TCC 336 (Crown's FCA appeal discontinued A-452-12); *Chau*, 2019 FC 1342; *Gentile Holdings*, 2020 TCC 29, para. 15. Dividends cannot be payment for work done by shareholders: *Neuman*, [1998] 3 C.T.C. 177 (SCC), para. 57; *Piuze*, 2002 CarswellNat 4856 (TCC); *Gazaille*, [2003] 2 C.T.C. 2732 (TCC); *Côté*, [2003] 4 C.T.C. 2064 (TCC); *Gestion André Pomerleau*, 2008 TCC 539 (FCA appeal discontinued A-569-08); *Duchaine*, 2015 TCC 245, para. 5; *Kufsky*, 2019 TCC 254, para. 18; *Valovic*, 2020 TCC 101. *Contra*, *Martel*, 2010 TCC 634, para. 14 (Crown's FCA appeal discontinued A-67-11), held that in Quebec, a dividend can possibly be excluded if paid in consideration of foregone salary (see Notes to *Interpretation Act* s. 8.1 under "Common law vs civil law"). On a stock dividend, see VIEWS doc 2011-0412201C6. 160(1) can apply to a capital dividend: *Neumann*, 2009 TCC 81. It can apply where the dividend recipient is a corporation: *Gestion André Pomerleau* (above); *Mario Côté Inc.*, 2011 TCC 105. It can apply where the recipient is only a 50% shareholder, since "arm's length" is a question of fact: *Fournier*, [1991] 1 C.T.C. 2699 (TCC); *Gosselin*, [1997] 2 C.T.C. 2830 (TCC); *HLB Smith Holdings*, 2018 TCC 83; but did not apply to a minority shareholder not involved in decision-making: *Siracusa*, 2003 TCC 941. The value of the transfer is the actual dividend, not the net after paying tax on it: *Gilbert*, 2007 FCA 136, leave to appeal denied 2007 CarswellNat 2917 (SCC); *Mamdani Trust*, 2020 TCC 93.

Double tax: 160(1) can apply to a shareholder benefit or deemed dividend that is also taxed under 15(1) or 84(2): *Parihar*, 2015 CarswellNat 430 (TCC), para. 45; VIEWS docs 2010-0354691I7, 2010-0358751I7. It can apply to a transfer of a contract from one company to another: 2010-0366821I7. It can apply to a butterfly reorganization (though 160(4) may provide relief): 2012-0442681C6 [2012 STEP q.2].

Joint bank account deposits by a tax debtor triggered 160(1) in *White*, [1995] 1 C.T.C. 2538; *Obadia*, [1998] 4 C.T.C. 2504; *Laframboise*, [2003] 1 C.T.C. 2672 (all TCC); *Heroux*, 2015 TCC 183 (aff'd on other grounds 2015 FCA 240); but in *White*, 2020 TCC 22, this was held to be wrong, except to the extent funds are removed by the other owner. CRA's view is that 160(1) applies: doc 2009-0333851I7.

More examples: 160(1) applied to a bequest by a deceased who had left Canada with taxes owing many years earlier: *Montreuil*, [1996] 1 C.T.C. 2182 (TCC); but did not apply to a bequest in *Homer*, 2009 TCC 219 because the transfer was technically not by the deceased or executor but by the province's *Devolution of Estates Act*. 160(1) applied to a transfer of legal title to be held as bare trustee (and there is no valid trust where the purpose is to avoid creditors): *Parihar*, 2015 TCC 52, paras. 37-39. It applied where the tax debtor: made mortgage payments on the family home: *Medland*, [1999] 4 C.T.C. 293 (FCA) (but in *Menzies*, 2019 TCC 29, M's payments were considered paid for his obligation to the lender, even though by then his wife owned the home); contributed to his spouse's RRSP: *Wannan*, 2003 FCA 423 [the value transferred is the value contributed to the RRSP, as the tax savings received by the transferor are not "consideration" paid by the transferee: *Woodland*, 2009 TCC 434]; transferred pension benefits: *Tétrault*, 2004 TCC 332; transferred funds from his RRSP to his spouse to pay his creditors: *Raphael*, 2002 FCA 23 [though "a legally enforceable promise to pay out monies only on the husband's direction to his creditors" might have avoided 160(1)]; or directed the Ontario Health Insurance Plan to pay his fees to his wife's account: *Klundert*, 2017 FCA 134. It applied where a family trust paid school and summer camp fees for children, who became liable for the trust's tax debt: *Goldberg*, [2003] 2 C.T.C. 2592 (TCC). It applied to a gift from a parent to pay for a child's wedding, albeit done out of moral or cultural obligation: *Gitelman*, 2007 TCC 544. It applied where parents acquired their child's property for less than market value from a bank that had seized it under a mortgage: *St-Fort*, 2009 FCA 188. It applied where a tax debtor endorsed a cheque over to a family friend for no clear consideration: *Banks*, 2011 TCC 415. It applied where L and his corp paid L's brother's corp too much for its assets as part of a sale to another company: *Lupien*, 2016 TCC 2. It can apply to a person receiving funds from a charity owing 188(1.1) revocation tax: VIEWS docs 2010-0380651I7, 2011-0407081I7. It can apply to bank enforcement of a guarantee provided by the tax debtor years before he incurred the tax debt(!): *M. Soutar Decor 2000 Ltd.*, 2016 TCC 62. It did not apply to a 55(3)(a) butterfly and cross-cancellation of promissory notes: *Eyeball Networks*, 2021 FCA 17, as the TCC was wrong to say one note was valuable and the other worthless at the instant of transfer [Kroft & Pelletier, "Section 160", *Bennett Jones on Tax Disputes* (*Taxnet Pro* Tax Disputes Centre, March 2021, 11pp); Awad, "Looking Subsection 160(1) in the Eyeball", 18(1) *Tax Hyperion* (Carswell) 4-6 (Jan-Feb 2021)]. The 2021 Budget amendment above targets planning for 160(1) avoidance.

The transferee is liable even if the transferor went bankrupt before the transferee was assessed: *Heavyside*, [1997] 2 C.T.C. 1 (FCA); *Wannan* (above); *Clause*, 2010 TCC 410 (CRA voted to accept debtor's proposal, but he defaulted on it so went bankrupt); *Nelson*, 2017 TCC 178; *Légaré*, 2019 TCC 106; and can be assessed even if the transferor has not been: VIEWS doc 2008-0300311I7, However, in *Martel*, 2010 TCC 634 (Crown's FCA appeal discontinued A-67-11), CRA's acceptance of a bankruptcy proposal reduced the tax debt to the agreed amount, so the 160(1) assessment was limited to that amount; and in *White*, 2020 TCC 22, para. 4, CRA conceded that transfers after filing a proposal did not fall under 160(1).

The transferee is liable even if the transferee later transfers the property back to the transferor: *Provost*, 2009 TCC 585.

160(1) can apply to a 2-step transfer, from tax debtor to A and from A to B, with B then liable, due to 160(1)(e)(ii) "including an amount that the transferor is liable to pay under this section". Even before this rule was added in 2013 (retroactive to Dec. 21, 2002), the Courts so ruled: *Jurak*, 2003 FCA 58 (leave to appeal denied 2003 CarswellNat 2042 (SCC)); *6149812 Canada [Gauthier Estate, Boivin]*, 2010 FCA 228; *Armenti*, 2007 TCC 389; *Palmer*, 2015 TCC 28 (FCA appeal discontinued A-5-15); *Parihar*, 2015 TCC 52, para. 23; *Manna*, 2019 TCC 70, paras. 26-28 [these decisions overrule *Nanini*, 1994 CarswellNat 2059 (TCC)]. On transfers through a series of family members, all transferees are liable, including those who held the property only briefly and gained nothing therefrom: *Doucet*, 2007 TCC 268 (FCA appeals discontinued A-331-07, A-332-07, A-335-07); and see para. "Accepting funds" below. In *Singh*, 2019 TCC 265 (aff'd 2020 FCA 146), the Court held (the point was not argued) that 160(1) applied in 2 steps to transfer of a family home to trustees who then transferred it to a beneficiary; this is questionable in the author's view in saying the trustees were liable since trustees acquire only *legal* title of no value, so the first step of 160(1) would fail (but 160(1) would apply anyway to the transfer through the trust to the beneficiary, since "directly or indirectly, by means of a trust" in the opening words gets to the same result).

Meaning of "transfer": In *Sokolowski Romar*, 2013 FCA 10 (leave to appeal denied 2013 CarswellNat 1634 (SCC)), sale of the family home from husband to wife for $1 was a "transfer" and not part of the "dissolution of the partnership of acquests" under the Quebec *Civil Code* matrimonial regime (see 248(22)). A company involuntarily dissolved by the government does not "transfer" assets to its shareholders even if they end up with its funds: *Kvas*, 2016 TCC 199, paras. 30-33, 39-40. Dividend or stock dividend: see para. "160(1) can apply to a dividend" above. An indirect transfer is a transfer: 160(1) opening words, *Provost*, 2009 TCC 585; and see Notes to 17.1(1). Where a sole shareholder had his company issue shares to his wife, that was an indirect transfer of part of the company: *Strachan*, 2013 TCC 362, para. 38. See also *Garron [St. Michael Trust Corp.]*, 2010 FCA 309 (aff'd on other grounds as *Fundy Settlement*, 2012 SCC 14), paras. 79-80, finding an acquisition via indirect transfer for purposes of former 94(1). For lengthy discussion of "transfer" see also *Tétrault*, 2004 TCC 332. In *Yu*, 2018 FCA 68, the Court rejected a claim that the transferor had held money in trust for another family member, so that she transferred only legal title and no beneficial interest.

The following are not transfers: disclaimer of pending inheritance causing others to end up with the property (*Biderman*, [2000] 2 C.T.C. 35 (FCA); leave to appeal denied 2000 CarswellNat 3554 (SCC); but in *Baker*, 2016 TCC 120, a waiver signed after the s. 160 assessment was issued did not prevent s. 160 from applying); disclaimer by daughter transferring property back to father once she realized it had been transferred to her (*Leclair*, 2011 TCC 323); loan from parent to child (*Merchant*, 2005 TCC 161, but claims of loans were rejected in *Sauvignon*, 2016 TCC 101 and *Scott*, 2020 TCC 4); death of joint tenant [see Notes to 70(5)], leaving the other owner as 100% owner (VIEWS doc 9520635); corporate amalgamation (2008-0289321I7, but the amalgamated company is liable for the debts of its predecessors anyway). See also Gibney & Gilbert, "Disclaimers in the Canadian Income Tax Context", 6(1) *Personal Tax & Estate Planning* (Federated Press) 7-12 (2018).

Death: A transfer from an RRSP to a spouse as designated beneficiary was a transfer by the deceased "by any other means whatever", but was not subject to 160(1) because the transferor, being dead, was no longer related to his spouse: *Kiperchuk*, 2013 TCC 60. (CRA accepted this result at the objection level in July 2013.) *Contra*, in *Kuchta*, 2015 TCC 289 (FCA appeal discontinued A-551-15 but the decision may be a nullity due to *Birchcliff Energy* — see 169(1) Notes at "Replacement by the Chief Justice"), Graham J ruled after careful analysis that "spouse" in 160(1) includes a deceased tax debtor's spouse and catches transfer on death [for comment see 92 *The Arnold Report* (ctf.ca, Feb. 10, 2016)]. See also 252(2) Notes. In *Dreger*, 2020 TCC 25, the deceased's designation of his daughters as beneficiaries of a life income fund was a transfer, as the parent-child relationship does not end on death: paras. 23-25. In *Higgins*, 2013 TCC 194, the deceased had designated his daughters as beneficiaries of a life insurance seg fund that was a "hybrid comprised of an insurance fund and a regular investment" (para. 29). They were not liable under 160(1) because "the overarching feature was the life insurance component" (para. 34). In *Goldman*, 2021 TCC 13, tax debtor D designated daughter G as her RRSP beneficiary, specifically to use the RRSP funds for certain expenses (such as funeral costs); Graham J held this was a trust that CRA could have separately assessed (with G possibly liable under 159(3): para. 49), and found G liable only for the residue that came to her indirectly (para. 75). See also Doobay, "Designated Beneficiary and Creditors", 22(6) *Canadian Tax Highlights* (ctf.ca) 6-8 (June 2014); Stephens, "Does the Canada Revenue Agency Have the Power to Seize Life Insurance Proceeds to Satisfy the Deceased's Tax Liability?", XXVI(1) *Insurance Planning* (Federated Press) 10-14 (2021), and 146(4) Notes.

Designating a bequest as exempt from seizure under the Quebec *Civil Code* did not make the proceeds of sale of the property exempt from 160(1): *6149812 Canada Inc. [Gauthier Estate, Boivin]*, 2010 FCA 228; *Baker*, 2016 TCC 120, para. 40 [Kreklewetz & Walker, "Section 160's Unexpected Consequences", 16(4) *Tax for the Owner-Manager* (ctf.ca) 5-6 (Oct. 2016)]; *Laliberté*, 2015 TCC 134, paras. 59-64. Similarly, in *Bernier*, 2010 TCC 85, the fact Quebec workers' compensation (CSST) payments were exempt from seizure in the husband's hands did not affect his wife's liability when he deposited the funds in her bank account.

In *Lamothe*, 2008 TCC 13, a transfer of cash from husband to wife to purchase a home was held to be only half subject to 160(1), as the funds came from the husband's father who sought to benefit both spouses.

Accepting funds with obligation to pass them on: Cashing or depositing cheques for a relative or friend, as agent or under a legal obligation to repay, avoided 160(1) in: *Lemire*, 2013 FCA 242 (deposits were under *Civil Code* "mandate" with obligation to return cash to tax debtor, with no knowledge of tax debt being avoided); *Armenti*, 2007 TCC 389; *Gambino*, 2008 TCC 601; *Colborne*, 2012 TCC 198 (funds received under legal commitment to put them into company's account); *Bragg-Smith*, 2012 TCC 252 (daughter used funds from father to pay his creditor under "legally enforceable promise" she made to him); *Lapierre*, 2012 TCC 299 (father transferred funds to daughter's account and out again to new corp; daughter had no control over funds); *Muir*, 2020 TCC 8 (dentist received funds from her corp on sale of business, under obligation to repay trust funds to patients and pay its creditors); *Brown*, 2020 TCC 45 (B deposited husband's paycheques under agreement to pay his credit-card bills, which she did). This issue overlaps with "Consideration" below; e.g., in *Muir* and *Brown*, the obligation to use the funds for the corp's benefit was the consideration provided to the corp.

However, where T deposited cheques payable to related tax debtor D in T's account (to give D access to the funds), without a legal obligation to repay, T was liable under 160(1): *Raphael*, 2002 FCA 23 (husband's RRSP funds went to wife's account so he could pay some creditors, but "a legally enforceable promise to pay out monies only on the husband's direction ...might well have constituted sufficient consideration to avoid 160(1)" (para. 10)); *Livingston*, 2008 FCA 89 (leave to appeal denied 2008 CarswellNat 3336 (SCC)); *Waugh*, 2008 FCA 152; *Yates*, 2009 FCA 50 (discussed below under "Consideration"); *McDonald*, 2016 FCA 23; *Klundert*, 2017 FCA 134 (optometrist directed Ontario Health Insurance Plan to pay his fees to wife's account); *Pickard*, 2010 TCC 535; *Lacroix*, 2011 TCC 111; *Ouellet*, 2012 TCC 77; *Brauer*, 2012 TCC 382 (mother gave tax-debtor son ATM card for her account, and he deposited cheques payable to him and withdrew equal amounts in cash); *Mottle*, 2018 TCC 116 (FCA appeal dismissed for delay A-284-18). Arguably, a transfer can be as a bare trust (see Notes to 104(1)), so that the value received is nil. (See also *3087-8847 Québec Inc.*, in

Notes to 224(1).) A transfer whose purpose is to thwart tax collection by hiding the funds should be caught by 160(1): *9101-2310 Québec Inc.*, 2013 FCA 241, para. 53.

CRA may apply 160(1) to a company that issues preferred shares with a value lower than their subscription cost: Strug, "Section 160 on Share Issue", 12(12) *Canadian Tax Highlights* (ctf.ca) 2 (Dec. 2004). In *594710 B.C.*, 2018 FCA 166, para. 123 (leave to appeal denied 2019 CarswellNat 434 (SCC)), GAAR applied when 160(1) was circumvented by triggering an acquisition of control so that stock dividends were paid in the tax year before the liability arose.

Value transferred: The assessment can be reduced by showing that the value of what was transferred was less than CRA claims. In *Bjornson*, 2010 TCC 337, the value of a van transferred by H to W was held to be less than what W paid, so W was not liable. See Notes to 69(1) re meaning of "fair market value".

Consideration: A transfer from husband **H** to wife **W** was held to be for consideration (so 160(1) did not apply) in *Ducharme*, 2005 FCA 137 (notional "rent" for value of H living in transferred home); *Dupuis*, [1993] 2 C.T.C. 2032 (TCC) (paying share of family expenses); *Michaud*, [1998] 4 C.T.C. 2675 (TCC) (H made mortgage payments under legal obligation to support family, under Quebec *Civil Code*); *Ferracuti*, [1999] 1 C.T.C. 2420 (TCC) (H's legal obligation to support family, under Ontario *Family Law Act*); *Marchand*, 2008 TCC 399; *Miller*, 2011 TCC 412 (consideration was a promise by W to pay H's creditors with funds he transferred to her); *Connolly*, 2016 TCC 139 (money W had advanced to H was loans owing to her); *Konyi*, 2017 TCC 175 (W agreed orally to pay H full value for home over time); *Casolino*, 2020 TCC 99 (consideration for H's 50% interest in home included full amount of mortgage because it secured his business line of credit). *Contra*, W was found liable in: *Logiudice*, 1997 CarswellNat 1079 (TCC) ("genuine contractual arrangement" required); *Tétrault*, 2004 TCC 332 (contribution to family expenses is not for consideration); *Parker*, 2006 TCC 387 (no evidence of "rent" being paid); *Kadola*, 2008 TCC 474; *Cohen*, 2008 TCC 550 (W had paid more of family expenses for years and H had always agreed to equalize); *Yates*, 2009 FCA 50 (varying reasons from different judges: *Ducharme* is specific to its facts; 160(4) cannot apply without marriage breakdown; legal obligation to support the family is not relevant, and TCC cases allowing this argument are wrong; allowing H to live in home was not consideration); *Allen*, 2009 TCC 426 (FCA appeal dismissed for delay A-18-10) (payments made after transfer were not consideration at time of transfer); *Bernier*, 2010 TCC 85; *De Sanctis-Pedro*, 2010 TCC 118; *Crischuk*, 2010 TCC 276; *Ouellet*, 2012 TCC 77, paras. 32-36 (family obligations are insufficient); *MacLeod*, 2012 TCC 379 (H's mortgage payments were not for W's domestic services, and he was not liable to pay them as mortgagor even though he was a guarantor); *Klundert*, 2017 FCA 134 (W paying household expenses was not consideration); *Elander*, 2017 TCC 196, para. 14 (same). Based on *Yates* and the later cases, the *Ducharme* principle is likely dead unless the facts clearly show consideration being given (e.g, *Miller* above). If the transfer is payment of a pre-existing debt owing by the transferor, the transferee is not liable: *Shirafkan*, 2007 TCC 309; *Leblanc*, 2008 TCC 242; *Arsenault*, 2016 FCA 225 (H's transfer was to pay off *inter vivos* gift owing to W under their marriage contract, under the Quebec *Civil Code*); *Nelson*, 2017 TCC 178 (half of earlier joint advances to H's company were loans from W, which H repaid by transferring interest in home to W); *Ashworth*, 2018 TCC 76 (on buying home, W also gave H's company money to pay off line of credit and remove collateral mortgage on home).

Consideration does not include making a loan: *Gentile Holdings*, 2020 TCC 29, para. 32. If the consideration given was assumption of debt or provision of services (e.g., *Menzies*, 2019 TCC 29, paras. 26-28), or the transfer was repayment of a debt, that reduces the assessment, e.g. *Sarkaria*, 2018 TCC 159; but such evidence is often rejected, e.g. *Loates*, 2016 FCA 47; *Nandakumar*, 2012 TCC 338; *Genest*, 2015 TCC 76; *Laliberté*, 2015 TCC 134, paras. 65-69; *Copeland*, 2016 TCC 124; *Shieh*, 2018 TCC 154 (FCA appeal dismissed for delay A-276-18) (parents helping son with education and other costs was not loan with expectation of repayment). In *Jefferson*, 2019 TCC 91 (under appeal to FCA), 26% of $542,000 Gcorp transferred to J was allowed as reimbursement of expenses J had incurred as Gcorp's employee.

However, a transfer can still be offset by the spouse giving up rights to a constructive trust (CT) or resulting trust that the spouse already had in the property: *Savoie*, [1993] 2 C.T.C. 2330 (TCC); *Darte*, 2008 TCC 66; *Warren*, 2008 TCC 674; *VidAmour*, 2009 TCC 414; *Martin*, 2013 TCC 38 [appeal on costs 2015 FCA 95] (doctor's wife had worked without pay for him for years, and provided space rent-free for his medical practice); Bob McCue, "Resulting Trust Still Trumps Section 160", 172 *The Estate Planner* (CCH) 4-5 (May 2009) and "Section 160 and Resulting Trusts", 48 *McCarthy Tétrault on Tax Disputes* (CCH) 5-7 (July 2009). *Contra*, the TCC has held more recently that it cannot find a CT as that is outside the Court's jurisdiction and the parties are not both present and not adversarial; but in these cases there was likely no CT anyway: *Pliskow*, 2013 TCC 283; *Kardaras*, 2014 TCC 135; *Hardtke*, 2016 FCA 138. See also *Markou*, 2016 TCC 137, saying the TCC has jurisdiction to make such findings. In both *Campbell*, 2009 TCC 431 and *Myers*, 2015 TCC 275, there was insufficient evidence to support the taxpayer's claim that her husband held his interest in their home as bare trustee for her before transferring it to her, or that it was registered in his name in error. See also VIEWS docs 2011-0402401I7, 2011-0408371I7. For a recent non-tax CT case see *Mercado Capital v. Qureshi*, 2018 ONCA 711.

Consideration is determined on a "snapshot" at time of transfer, not by looking at the result of a series of transactions: *Eyeball Networks*, 2021 FCA 17, paras. 47-53, 58, 69.

In Quebec, a claim of undisclosed agreed consideration to a transfer (called a "counter letter" in the *Civil Code*) is invalid as a "simulation" that does not bind a third party [the CRA] even if the evidence is believed, due to *Civil Code* art. 1452: *9101-2310 Québec Inc.*, 2013 FCA 241 (reversing the TCC); *Cawthorne*, 2016 TCC 94; *Sauvignon*, 2016 TCC 101. (In common-law provinces, an undisclosed bare trust or agency agreement may be valid.)

Interest owing by the tax debtor can be included in a s. 160 assessment (*Loates*, 2016 FCA 47, para. 11), and interest will run under 161(1) on an amount assessed to the transferee. This is clear from the closing words of 160(1) and 160(2), as amended in 2013; and see *1455257 Ontario*, 2020 TCC 64, paras. 62-82 (FCA appeal heard June 21/21). Even before these amendments, interest was held to apply in *Zen*, 2010 FCA 180 (leave to appeal denied 2011 CarswellNat 47 (SCC)), due to "the provisions of this Division apply" in 160(2); *Gagnon*, 2010 TCC 482; *Richard*, 2011 TCC 136. (Earlier cases had ruled no interest could be assessed: *Algoa Trust*, [1998] 4 C.T.C. 2001 (TCC), *Currie*, 2008 TCC 338 and 2012 TCC 62; *Provost*, 2009 TCC 585; but even those cases seemed to say (per *Gagnon*) only that no interest accrued on the assessment of the transferee once issued, to prevent duplicate interest. (An earlier class action on this point was settled with repayment of interest by CRA: *Ho-A-Shoo*, 2001 CarswellOnt 2114 (Ont. SCJ).) CRA charges the transferee interest from the assessment date, not from the date of transfer, according to VIEWS doc 2008-0287751E5; but the s. 160 assessment is normally for an amount that includes the transferor's interest owing, which comes to the same thing. See also Stirling, "Zen and the Art of Collecting Interest on Directors' Tax Debts", 58(4) *Canadian Tax Journal* 963-72 (2010).

The debt subject to 160(1) may include costs under 223(4) of registering a certificate against the tax debtor: VIEWS doc 2009-0332731I7.

Challenging underlying liability: A person assessed under s. 160 may challenge the underlying assessment of the transferor even if the transferor did not: *Gaucher*, [2001] 1 C.T.C. 125 (FCA); *594710 B.C.*, 2018 FCA 166, paras. 31, 79 (leave to appeal denied 2019 CarswellNat 434 (SCC)); *Smitlener*, 2009 TCC 268; *Martel*, 2010 TCC 634 (Crown's FCA appeal discontinued A-67-11), para. 11; *Benaroch*, 2015 TCC 93; *De Vries*, 2018 TCC 166, para. 44; *Ansems*, 2019 TCC 66 (FCA appeal discontinued A-90-19); *1455257 Ontario*, 2020 TCC 64 (FCA appeal heard June 21/21) (too late for transferor corp to use loss carrybacks to eliminate its tax liability). (However, if the transferor claims to have paid CRA off, that is a "collection issue" that the TCC will not address: *Shieh*, 2018 TCC 154, para. 18 (FCA appeal dismissed for delay A-276-18).) If the transferor's liability arose as a corporate director, the transferee can also challenge the sub-underlying corporate liability: *Cappadoro*, 2012 TCC 267, para. 42.

In any challenge of the underlying liability, the Crown has the onus of proof: *Gestion Yvan Drouin*, [2001] 2 C.T.C. 2315; *Cappadoro*, para. 34; *Beaudry*, 2003 TCC 464; *Arsenault*, 2015 TCC 179 (rev'd on other grounds 2016 FCA 225); *Ellis*, 2015 TCC 285; *Atwill-Morin*, 2016 TCC 127, para. 13; *Monsell*, 2019 TCC 5, paras. 26-28. However, if the transferee is presumed to have access to the information (e.g., the transferor's spouse), this does not apply: *Ansems*, 2019 TCC 66, para. 11 (FCA appeal discontinued A-90-19); *Manna*, 2019 TCC 70, paras. 30-34. See also Tom Boddez, "Derivative Liability: Issues of Estoppel and Onus", X(2) *Tax Litigation* (Federated Press) 619-22 (2002); Kreklewetz & Horrigan, "Onus in Derivative Assessment", 23(7) *Canadian Tax Highlights* (ctf.ca) 1-2 (July 2015). (The Crown normally has the onus of proving facts not within the taxpayer's knowledge: see Notes to 152(7).)

If the underlying liability is reduced after the s. 160 assessment (e.g. CRA waives interest), the assessment must be reduced to match: *Scott*, 2020 TCC 4, para. 38.

See also 160(2) Notes re judicial review of a s. 160 assessment.

For CRA interpretation and procedures see *National Collections Manual* (2015, on *TaxPartner* or *Taxnet Pro*), "Non-Arm's Length Transfer Assessments — Tax programs".

See also David Sherman's *Canada GST Service* analysis to ETA s. 325 (also on *Taxnet Pro*); Woodbury, "The Power to Tax Means Little Without the Power to Collect", 2008 Atlantic Provinces Tax Conference (ctf.ca), 3A:1-22; Graham, "Section 160 Update", 2009 BC Tax Conf. 11:1-32; Tari, "Section 160", 2009 Ontario Tax Conf. 7:1-26; Upshaw, "The Application of Section 160 to Dividends and Shareholder Loans", 9(4) *Tax Hyperion* (Carswell, April 2012); Grower, "Tax Collection", 62(2) *Canadian Tax Journal* 501-21 (2014); Hennessey, "Friends Don't Let Friends Get Assessed Under Section 160", 18(1) *Tax for the Owner-Manager* (ctf.ca) 8-9 (Jan. 2018); Antonello et al., "Tax Accommodation Parties and Novel Applications of Section 160", XXII(3) *Tax Litigation* (Federated Press) 8-16 (2019); Bokenfohr, "When Tax Debts Go Viral", 27(10) *Canadian Tax Highlights* (ctf.ca) 3-5 (Oct. 2019) ("Section 160 has become the tax version of a virus: it can lie dormant for years and spread to transferees at any time"); Corbin, "Joint and Several Tax Liability of Designated Beneficiaries", 35(3) *Money & Family Law* (Carswell) 17-18 (March 2020).

Parallel rules apply for GST/HST (*Excise Tax Act* s. 325), Quebec Sales Tax (QST) and provincial income tax. This can result in double collection, though CRA and Revenu Québec will reduce assessments to prevent this: VIEWS doc 2012-0454241C6; *Ouellet*, 2012 TCC 77, paras. 1, 41-43; *Baker*, 2016 TCC 120, para. 12. The double-tax potential does not violate the *Charter of Rights*: *Ouellet*, paras. 39-59 (but Ouellet "did not argue either the rule of law or s. 10 of the *Charter*": para. 59).

In *Marcotte*, 2012 TCC 336 (Crown's FCA appeal discontinued A-452-12), the reallocation in 2007 of a company's 2004 payment of $500,000, in part to its shareholders' GST and QST accounts, did not revive its debt as of 2004, so dividends it paid in 2005-06 did not attract ETA s. 325 (but M was liable as a director: 2014 FCA 37).

Fraudulent conveyances: A transfer of property that is designed to defeat creditors (including CRA) can be set aside under *Bankruptcy and Insolvency Act* s. 96 or the provincial *Fraudulent Conveyances Act* (in Quebec, *Civil Code* Art. 1631): *Archambault v. Kalandi Anstalt*, [2007] 5 C.T.C. 107 (Ont. SCJ); *Omni Cell Québec*, [1995] G.S.T.C. 30 (FCTD); *Déziel*, 2006 FC 1481; *Abakhan [Botham Holdings] v. Braydon*

Investments, 2009 BCCA 521 (leave to appeal denied 2010 CarswellBC 1574 (SCC)); *Boily*, 2020 FC 490 (FCA appeal discontinued A-113-20). See also Springman, *Frauds on Creditors: Fraudulent Conveyances and Preferences* (Carswell, looseleaf); Yager, "Creditor Proofing is Fraudulent Conveyance", 17(2) *Canadian Tax Highlights [CTH]* (ctf.ca) 6-7 (Feb. 2009); Pantry & Mlynarczyk, "Innocent Attempt to Protect Assets", XIII(2) *Business Vehicles* (Federated Press) 682-85 (2010); Funt, "Asset Protection and Tax Planning", 2010 BC Tax Conference (ctf.ca), 13:1-28; Truster, "The Challenges of Creditor Proofing", 14(3) *Tax for the Owner-Manager* (ctf.ca) 7 (July 2014). A payment to CRA can similarly be attacked as a fraudulent preference: *Cargill Ltd. v. Compton Agro*, 2000 MBCA 29; *Perrette Inc.*, [2001] G.S.T.C. 99 (Que. SC); *Andrews Estate*, 2011 MBQB 50; *Urbancorp*, 2017 ONSC 7156. CRA can also use fraudulent conveyances legislation to collect tax debts: *Transcona Country Club*, 2013 MBQB 216; Bassindale & Kreklewetz, "CRA May Unwind Debtor's Sale", 21(11) *CTH* 3-4 (Nov. 2013). For a different remedy (under the *Business Corporations Act*) see Neil Gurmukh, "Using the Oppression Remedy to Enforce Unpaid Corporate Judgments", 13(2) *Tax for the Owner-Manager* (ctf.ca) 9-10 (April 2013).

160(1)(d) and (e) amended by 2002-2013 technical bill (Part 4 — bijuralism), effective June 26, 2013, to add "or solidarily".

160(1) amended by 2002-2013 technical bill, for assessments after Dec. 20, 2002, to ensure that a 2-step transfer is caught and to ensure interest can be assessed.

160(1) earlier amended by 2000 same-sex partners bill.

I.T. Application Rules: 69 (meaning of "chapter 148 of ...").

Interpretation Bulletins: IT-258R2: Transfer of property to a spouse; IT-260R: Transfer of property to a minor; IT-369R: Attribution of trust income to settlor; IT-510: Transfers and loans of property made after May 22, 1985 to a related minor; IT-511R: Interspousal and certain other transfers and loans of property.

Information Circulars: 98-1R5: Tax collection policies.

I.T. Technical News: 4 (section 160 — the *Davis* case).

CRA Audit Manual: 11.5.11: Joint liability assessments.

(1.1) Joint and several, or solidary, liability — subsec. 69(11)

— If a particular person or partnership is deemed by subsection 69(11) to have disposed of a property at any time, the person referred to in that subsection to whom a benefit described in that subsection was available in respect of a subsequent disposition of the property or property substituted for the property is jointly and severally, or solidarily, liable with each other taxpayer to pay a part of the other taxpayer's liabilities under this Act in respect of each taxation year equal to the amount determined by the formula

$$A - B$$

where

A   is the total of amounts payable under this Act by the other taxpayer in respect of the year, and

B   is the amount that would, if the particular person or partnership were not deemed by subsection 69(11) to have disposed of the property, be determined for A in respect of the other taxpayer in respect of the year,

but nothing in this subsection limits the liability of the other taxpayer under any other provision of this Act or of any person for the interest that the person is liable to pay under this Act on an assessment in respect of the amount that the person is liable to pay because of this subsection.

Related Provisions: 257 — Formula cannot calculate to less than zero.

Notes: 160(1.1) amended by 2002-2013 technical bill (Part 4 — bijuralism), effective June 26, 2013, to add "or solidarily".

160(1.1) closing words amended by 2002-2013 technical bill (Part 5 — technical), for assessments made after Dec. 20, 2002, to add "or of any person for the interest that the person is liable to pay under this Act on an assessment in respect of the amount that the person is liable to pay because of this subsection". See Notes to 160(1) under "Interest owing by the tax debtor".

160(1.1) added by 1995-97 technical bill, effective for dispositions deemed by 69(11) to occur after April 26, 1995.

CRA Audit Manual: 11.5.11: Joint liability assessments.

(1.2) Joint and several, or solidary, liability — tax on split income

— If an amount is required to be added because of subsection 120.4(2) in computing a specified individual's tax payable under this Part for a taxation year and the specified individual has

not attained the age of 24 years before the start of the year, the following rules apply:

(a) subject to paragraph (b), a particular individual is jointly and severally, or solidarily, liable with the specified individual for the amount if

(i) where the specified individual has not attained the age of 17 years before the year, the particular individual is a parent of the specified individual, and

(ii) where the specified individual has attained the age of 17 years before the year,

(A) the particular individual is a source individual in respect of the specified individual,

(B) the amount was derived directly or indirectly from a related business (within the meaning of paragraph 120.4(1.1)(d)) in respect of the specified individual, and

(C) the particular individual meets the conditions in any of paragraphs (a) to (c) in the definition "related business" in subsection 120.4(1) in respect of the related business;

(b) the particular individual's liability under paragraph (a) in respect of the specified individual for the year is to be determined as though the only amounts included in the specified individual's split income for the year are amounts derived from the related business referred to in subparagraph (a)(ii); and

(c) nothing in this subsection limits the liability of

(i) the specified individual under any other provision of this Act, or

(ii) the particular individual for the interest that the particular individual is liable to pay under this Act on an assessment in respect of the amount that the particular individual is liable to pay because of this subsection.

Notes: 160(1.2) makes a parent or other 120.4(1)"source individual" jointly liable for the tax on split income (TOSI) payable by a child or person under 25 at year-end. Assessment of this liability is never statute-barred, due to "at any time" in 160(2).

160(1.2) amended by 2018 budget bill #1, for 2018 and later tax years (in sync with extensive amendments to 120.4). For earlier years, read:

(1.2) A parent of a specified individual is jointly and severally, or solidarily, liable with the individual for the amount required to be added because of subsection 120.4(2) in computing the specified individual's tax payable under this Part for a taxation year if, during the year, the parent

(a) carried on a business that was provided property or services by a partnership or trust all or a portion of the income of which partnership or trust is directly or indirectly included in computing the individual's split income for the year,

(b) was a specified shareholder of a corporation that was provided property or services by a partnership or trust all or a portion of the income of which partnership or trust is directly or indirectly included in computing the individual's split income for the year,

(c) was a specified shareholder of a corporation, dividends on the shares of the capital stock of which were directly or indirectly included in computing the individual's split income for the year;

(d) was a shareholder of a professional corporation that was provided property or services by a partnership or trust all or a portion of the income of which partnership or trust is directly or indirectly included in computing the individual's split income for the year, or

(e) was a shareholder of a professional corporation, dividends on the shares of the capital stock of which were directly or indirectly included in computing the individual's split income for the year,

but nothing in this subsection limits the liability of the specified individual under any other provision of this Act or of the parent for the interest that the parent is liable to pay under this Act on an assessment in respect of the amount that the parent is liable to pay because of this subsection.

Opening words amended by 2002-2013 technical bill (Part 4 — bijuralism), effective June 26, 2013, to add "or solidarily". 160(1.2) earlier amended by same bill effective Dec. 21, 2002, and 1999 Budget.

A different proposed 160(1.2), valuing a fractional interest in property, was moved to 160(3.1) before being enacted in 2000.

(1.3) Joint liability — tax on split-pension income

— Where a pensioner and a pension transferee (as those terms are defined in section 60.03) make a joint election under section 60.03 in respect of a split-pension amount (as defined in that section) for a taxation year, they are jointly and severally, or solidarily, liable for the tax payable by the pension transferee under this Part for the taxation year to the extent that that tax payable is greater than it would have been if no amount were required to be added because of paragraph 56(1)(a.2) in computing the income of the pension transferee under this Part for the taxation year.

Notes: This assessment is never statute-barred, due to "at any time" in 160(2).

160(1.3) added by 2007 budget bill #1, for 2007 and later taxation years.

(1.4) Joint liability — spousal and similar trusts — If subsection 104(13.4) deems an amount to have become payable in a taxation year of a trust to an individual, the individual and the trust are jointly and severally, or solidarily, liable for the tax payable by the individual under this Part for the individual's taxation year that includes the day on which the individual dies to the extent that that tax payable is greater than it would have been if the amount were not included in computing the individual's income under this Part for the taxation year.

Notes: 160(1.4) added by 2014 budget bill #2, for 2016 and later taxation years.

(2) Assessment — The Minister may at any time assess a taxpayer in respect of any amount payable because of this section, and the provisions of this Division (including, for greater certainty, the provisions in respect of interest payable) apply, with any modifications that the circumstances require, in respect of an assessment made under this section as though it had been made under section 152 in respect of taxes payable under this Part.

Related Provisions: 152 — Assessment; 222(5)(c) — Restart of 10-year collection limitation period.

Notes: See Notes to 160(1). The words "at any time" mean there is no limitation period: *Addison & Leyen Ltd.*, 2007 SCC 33, para. 9; *Nandakumar*, 2012 TCC 338, para. 20; *Eyeball Networks*, 2021 FCA 17, para. 11 (assessment 12 years later; point was not in dispute); VIEWS doc 2012-0459421E5. Thus, no 3-year reassessment clock starts from the transfer of property (*Davis*, [1994] 2 C.T.C. 2033 (TCC)), nor from the original income tax assessment for the year (*Sarraf*, [1994] 1 C.T.C. 2519 (TCC); *Bleau*, 2007 FCA 61; *Hennig*, 2012 TCC 141). See also 227(10) Notes. However, once a 160(2) assessment is issued for a transfer of property, the 152(4) 3-year clock starts to run for any later assessment for the same transfer, since "the provisions of this Division" apply. CRA conceded this point to the author in 1998, at the objection stage, and explicitly agreed with these Notes in doc 2010-0357191I7. The 10-year collection limitation period (222(3)) applies; in *Duchaine*, 2015 TCC 245, CRA met the deadline (from introduction of 222(3)) with 12 days to spare; but *Bourgeois*, 2018 TCC 5, says 222(3) applies only if CRA does not contact the tax debtor for 10 years.

A single notice of assessment can cover many transfers (e.g. many payments of money): VIEWS doc 2010-0374761I7, citing extensive supporting case law. CRA takes the view (possibly wrong) that an Informal Procedure appeal (see 169(1) Notes) can reduce the *total* assessment by only $12,000 even if it covers transfers in many years.

In *Addison & Leyen* (above) (reversing the FCA), the Supreme Court of Canada ruled that the Federal Court cannot exercise judicial review over a s. 160 assessment on the grounds of delay, since the Minister can reassess "at any time". Delay in processing an objection could be addressed by an application for *mandamus*.

160(2) amended by 2002-2013 technical bill (Part 5 — technical), for assessments after Dec. 20, 2002, to add "(including, for greater certainty, the provisions in respect of interest payable)" and "in respect of taxes payable under this Part". See Notes to 160(1) under "Interest owing by the tax debtor".

160(2) earlier amended by 1995-97 technical bill, effective June 18, 1998.

CRA Audit Manual: 11.5.11: Joint liability assessments.

(2.1) Assessment — The Minister may at any time assess a taxpayer in respect of any amount payable because of paragraph 94(3)(d) or (e) or subsection 94(17) and the provisions of this Division (including, for greater certainty, the provisions in respect of interest payable) apply, with any modifications that the circumstances require, in respect of an assessment made under this section as though it had been made under section 152 in respect of taxes payable under this Part.

Related Provisions: 160(3) — Discharge of liability.

Notes: This assessment is never statute-barred, due to "at any time". See Notes to 160(2).

160(2.1) added by 2002-2013 technical bill (Part 1 — NRTs), for assessments made after 2006, but ignore the reference to 94(17) for taxation years that end before March 5, 2010; and if amended 94(1) applies to a taxation year of a taxpayer that ends before

2007 (see Notes at end of s. 94), 160(2.1) applies to assessments made on or after the first day of the first such taxation year of the taxpayer to which amended 94(1) applies.

(3) Discharge of liability — If a particular taxpayer has become jointly and severally, or solidarily, liable with another taxpayer under this section or because of paragraph 94(3)(d) or (e) or subsection 94(17) in respect of part or all of a liability under this Act of the other taxpayer,

(a) a payment by the particular taxpayer on account of that taxpayer's liability shall to the extent of the payment discharge their liability; but

(b) a payment by the other taxpayer on account of that taxpayer's liability discharges the particular taxpayer's liability only to the extent that the payment operates to reduce that other taxpayer's liability to an amount less than the amount in respect of which the particular taxpayer is, by this section, made jointly and severally, or solidarily, liable.

Notes: Bankruptcy of the tax debtor does not discharge the third party's liability: *Heavyside*, [1997] 2 C.T.C. 1 (FCA); *Bleau*, 2007 FCA 61.

The words "discharge their liability" are ambiguous. The word "their" could mean the same as "his, her or its", i.e., the "particular taxpayer" (and is used with that meaning in some provisions, e.g. 40(2)(b)D(i)(A), 146.4(1.7)). However, "their liability" replaced the words "the joint liability", and thus refers to the "particular taxpayer" and the "other taxpayer" together. This is confirmed by the French: "leur obligation" (third person plural).

160(3) amended by 2002-2013 technical bill (last change effective June 26, 2013), 1995-97 technical bill.

(3.1) Fair market value of undivided interest or right — For the purposes of this section and section 160.4, the fair market value at any time of an undivided interest, or for civil law an undivided right, in a property, expressed as a proportionate interest or right in that property, is, subject to subsection (4), deemed to be equal to the same proportion of the fair market value of that property at that time.

Notes: 160(3.1) tries to ensure that in the typical situation where husband H and wife W jointly own property (e.g. their home), and H transfers his interest to W, the value of what W receives for 160(1) is 50% of the property's value. (CRA previously applied this rule anyway, as did the TCC without it being legislated, in *Zavos*, [2000] G.S.T.C. 97; *Henderson*, [2000] G.S.T.C. 101; *Warren*, [2002] G.S.T.C. 92; *Arsenau*, 2004 TCC 739. It was also applied without being cited in *Truong*, 2011 TCC 380.) However, in *Gagnon*, 2010 TCC 482, H retained a right to live in the home, so the value of what he transferred was reduced by 5% to reflect this right.

160(3.1) theoretically does not apply to joint tenancy of property in a common-law province (see Notes to 70(5) under "Joint tenants"). If H and W own 100% of their home as joint tenants, each interest is not "expressed" as a 50% "proportionate interest" in the property. In practice the Courts will usually ignore this subtle point.

160(3.1) amended by 2002-2013 technical bill (Part 4 — bijuralism), effective June 26, 2013, to add "or for civil law an undivided right" and "or right".

160(3.1) added by 2000 GST bill, for transfers of property made after June 4, 1999. It was 160(1.2) in the earlier version of the bill released on June 4, 1999.

(4) Special rules re transfer of property to spouse [or common-law partner] — Notwithstanding subsection (1), where at any time a taxpayer has transferred property to the taxpayer's spouse or common-law partner pursuant to a decree, order or judgment of a competent tribunal or pursuant to a written separation agreement and, at that time, the taxpayer and the spouse or common-law partner were separated and living apart as a result of the breakdown of their marriage or common-law partnership, the following rules apply:

(a) in respect of property so transferred after February 15, 1984,

(i) the spouse or common-law partner shall not be liable under subsection (1) to pay any amount with respect to any income from, or gain from the disposition of, the property so transferred or property substituted therefor, and

(ii) for the purposes of paragraph (1)(e), the fair market value of the property at the time it was transferred shall be deemed to be nil, and

(b) in respect of property so transferred before February 16, 1984, where the spouse or common-law partner would, but for this paragraph, be liable to pay an amount under this Act by virtue of subsection (1), the spouse's or common-law partner's liability in respect of that amount shall be deemed to have been discharged on February 16, 1984,

but nothing in this subsection shall operate to reduce the taxpayer's liability under any other provision of this Act.

Related Provisions: 120.4(1)"excluded amount"(b) — Income-splitting tax does not apply to property acquired when 160(4) applies; 248(5) — Substituted property.

Notes: Note the extended definition of "separation agreement" (**SA**) in 248(1).

160(4) did not apply in: *Loates*, 2016 FCA 47 (assertion spouses were separated was not made in notice of appeal and was contradicted by L's evidence); *Carrière*, 2006 TCC 289 (transfer deed noted spouses were separated, but was not SA because it did not provide for support); *Burns*, 2006 TCC 309 and *Viau*, 2011 TCC 193 (spouses not separated at time of transfer, though they were later); *Bashir*, 2013 TCC 6 (Court did not believe marriage had broken down or that transfers were made under SA); *Drolet*, 2020 QCCA 636 (transfer in exchange for wife renouncing support was not recorded as such and was not under SA; retroactive divorce judgment did not fix this). It might apply on a butterfly reorganization: VIEWS doc 2012-0442681C6 [2012 STEP q.2].

160(4) amended by 2000 same-sex partners bill, effective 2001 or earlier.

Information Circulars: 98-1R5: Tax collection policies.

Definitions [s. 160]: "amount", "assessment", "business", "common-law partner", "common-law partnership" — 248(1); "corporation" — 248(1), *Interpretation Act* 35(1); "derived directly or indirectly" — 120.4(1.1)(d); "dividend" — 248(1); "fair market value" — 160(3.1) and see 69(1) Notes; "individual" — 248(1); "Minister" — 248(1); "parent" — 252(2)(a); "person", "professional corporation", "property", "separation agreement", "share", "shareholder" — 248(1); "specified individual" — 120.4(1), 248(1); "specified shareholder" — 248(1); "split income" — 120.4(1), 248(1); "substituted" — 248(5); "taxation year" — 249; "taxpayer" — 248(1); "trust" — 104(1), 248(1), (3).

160.1 (1) Where excess refunded

160.1 (1) Where excess refunded — Where at any time the Minister determines that an amount has been refunded to a taxpayer for a taxation year in excess of the amount to which the taxpayer was entitled as a refund under this Act, the following rules apply:

(a) the excess shall be deemed to be an amount that became payable by the taxpayer on the day on which the amount was refunded; and

(b) the taxpayer shall pay to the Receiver General interest at the prescribed rate on the excess (other than any portion thereof that can reasonably be considered to arise as a consequence of the operation of section 122.5 or 122.61) from the day it became payable to the date of payment.

Related Provisions: 160.1(3) — Assessment; 161.1 — Offset of refund interest against arrears interest; 221.1 — Application of interest where legislation retroactive; 248(11) — Interest compounded daily.

Notes: 160.1(1) can apply to corporation's dividend refund that is reversed by a loss carryback: May 2009 ICAA roundtable (tinyurl.com/cra-abtax) q.5.

160.1(1) applied to recover Child Tax Benefit and GST Credit in *Crete*, 2016 TCC 132.

In *Mario Côté Inc.*, 2011 TCC 105, the fact 160.1(1) could have applied to recover a dividend refund from Xco did not prevent 160(1) being used to recover the funds from Xco's parent corporation to which Xco had paid dividends.

In *984274 Alberta*, 2020 FCA 125 (reversing the TCC; leave to appeal denied 2021 CarswellNat 1167 (SCC)), a nil assessment issued past the statute-barred deadline triggered an "overpayment" to which 164(1) applied, so a refund CRA paid was recoverable via 160.1 when the assessment was reversed. The refund need not have been claimed by the taxpayer to be recovered: para. 80.

See Notes to 122.62(4) for cases where CRA sought to recover an allegedly overpaid Canada Child Benefit.

160.1(1) does not apply to cashing a duplicate CRA cheque: VIEWS doc 2009-033435117.

160.1(1)(b) amended by 1991 technical bill, effective 1989, and by 1992 Child Benefit bill, effective 1993, to add the references to 122.5 and 122.61(1), so that no interest is charged on the portion of a refund that represents a repayment of the GST Credit or the Canada Child Benefit.

Regulations: 4301(a) (prescribed rate of interest).

Remission Orders: See under 122.5(3) and 122.62(4).

(1.1) Liability for refund by reason of s. 122.5 [GST credit]

(1.1) Liability for refund by reason of s. 122.5 [GST credit] — If a person is a qualified relation of an individual (within the meaning assigned by subsection 122.5(1)), in relation to one or more months specified for a taxation year, the person and the individual are jointly and severally, or solidarily, liable to pay the lesser of

(a) any excess described in subsection (1) that was refunded in respect of the taxation year to, or applied to a liability of, the

individual as a consequence of the operation of section 122.5, and

(b) the total of the amounts deemed by subsection 122.5(3) to have been paid by the individual during those specified months.

Related Provisions: 160.1(2) — Liability still exists under other provisions; 160.1(3) — Assessment.

Notes: 160.1(1.1) amended by 2001 Budget, effective with the July 2002 payment.

160.1(1.1) added by 1990 GST, effective 1989.

(2) Liability under other provisions

(2) Liability under other provisions — Subsection (1.1) does not limit a person's liability under any other provision of this Act.

Notes: 160.1(2) added by 2001 Budget, effective with the July 2002 payment.

Former 160.1(2) repealed by 1992 Child Benefit bill. It made both parents liable for overpayment of the former Child Tax Credit in 122.2.

(2.1) [Spouse's] Liability for refunds by reason of s. 122.61 [Canada Child Benefit]

(2.1) [Spouse's] Liability for refunds by reason of s. 122.61 [Canada Child Benefit] — If a person was a cohabiting spouse or common-law partner (within the meaning assigned by section 122.6) of an individual at the end of a taxation year, the person and the individual are jointly and severally, or solidarily, liable to pay any excess described in subsection (1) that was refunded in respect of the year to, or applied to a liability of, the individual as a consequence of the operation of section 122.61 if the person was the individual's cohabiting spouse or common-law partner at the time the excess was refunded, but nothing in this subsection is deemed to limit the liability of any person under any other provision of this Act.

Related Provisions: 160.1(3) — Assessment.

Notes: See Notes to 122.62(4) for cases where the CRA seeks to recover a Canada Child Benefit allegedly overpaid to a spouse who had left the home.

160.1(2.1) amended by 2002-2013 technical bill (Part 4 — bijuralism), effective June 26, 2013, to add "or solidarily".

160.1(2.1) amended by 2000 same-sex partners bill, effective 2001 or earlier. Added by 1992 Child Benefit bill, effective for 1991 and later tax years. Earlier version repealed by 1990 GST effective 1991. For 1986-90, it related to the FST credit in 122.4.

(2.2) [No longer relevant]

(2.2) [No longer relevant]

Notes: 160.1(2.2) relates to the UI premium tax credit (126.1), which was for 1993.

(3) Assessment

(3) Assessment — The Minister may at any time assess a taxpayer in respect of any amount payable by the taxpayer because of subsection (1) or (1.1) or for which the taxpayer is liable because of subsection (2.1) or (2.2), and the provisions of this Division (including, for greater certainty, the provisions in respect of interest payable) apply, with any modifications that the circumstances require, in respect of an assessment made under this section, as though it were made under section 152 in respect of taxes payable under this Part, except that no interest is payable on an amount assessed in respect of an excess referred to in subsection (1) that can reasonably be considered to arise as a consequence of the operation of section 122.5 or 122.61.

Notes: See 160.1(1) Notes; and see 160(2) Notes re assessment "at any time". Note also that no interest runs on overpayment of the GST Credit or Canada Child Benefit (122.5, 122.61).

160.1(3) amended by 2002-2013 technical bill (for assessments made after Dec. 20, 2002), 1992 Child Benefit bill, 1992 Economic Statement.

(4) Where amount applied to liability

(4) Where amount applied to liability — Where an amount is applied to a liability of a taxpayer to Her Majesty in right of Canada in excess of the amount to which the taxpayer is entitled as a refund under this Act, this section applies as though that amount had been refunded to the taxpayer on the day on which it was so applied.

Notes [subsec. 160.1(4)]: 160.1(4) amended by 1991 technical bill, effective 1990.

Definitions [s. 160.1]: "amount", "assessment" — 248(1); "child" — 252(1); "cohabiting spouse or common-law partner" — 122.6; "common-law partner", "common-law partnership" — 248(1); "Her Majesty" — *Interpretation Act* 35(1); "individual", "Minister" — 248(1); "months specified" — 122.5(4); "partnership" — see 96(1) Notes; "person" — 248(1); "prescribed rate" — Reg. 4301; "qualified relation" — 122.5(1); "taxation year" — 249; "taxpayer" — 248(1).

160.2 (1) Joint and several liability in respect of amounts received out of or under RRSP — Where

(a) an amount is received out of or under a registered retirement savings plan by a taxpayer other than an annuitant (within the meaning assigned by subsection 146(1)) under the plan, and

(b) that amount or part thereof would, but for paragraph (a) of the definition "benefit" in subsection 146(1), be received by the taxpayer as a benefit (within the meaning assigned by that definition),

the taxpayer and the last annuitant under the plan are jointly and severally, or solidarily, liable to pay a part of the annuitant's tax under this Part for the year of the annuitant's death equal to that proportion of the amount by which the annuitant's tax for the year is greater than it would have been if it were not for the operation of subsection 146(8.8) that the total of all amounts each of which is an amount determined under paragraph (b) in respect of the taxpayer is of the amount included in computing the annuitant's income because of that subsection, but nothing in this subsection limits the liability of the annuitant under any other provision of this Act or of the taxpayer for the interest that the taxpayer is liable to pay under this Act on an assessment in respect of the amount that the taxpayer is liable to pay because of this subsection.

Notes: In *O'Callaghan*, 2016 TCC 169, O was the beneficiary of her deceased brother's RRSP. She was liable for his terminal year tax even without his estate having been assessed. See also Notes to 160.2(2) and 160(1).

160.2(1) closing words amended by 2002-2013 technical bill, for assessments made after Dec. 20, 2002.

Interpretation Bulletins: IT-500R: RRSPs — death of an annuitant.

(2) Joint and several liability in respect of amounts received out of or under RRIF — Where

(a) an amount is received out of or under a registered retirement income fund by a taxpayer other than an annuitant (within the meaning assigned by subsection 146.3(1)) under the fund, and

(b) that amount or part thereof would, but for paragraph 146.3(5)(a), be included in computing the taxpayer's income for the year of receipt pursuant to subsection 146.3(5),

the taxpayer and the annuitant are jointly and severally, or solidarily, liable to pay a part of the annuitant's tax under this Part for the year of the annuitant's death equal to that proportion of the amount by which the annuitant's tax for the year is greater than it would have been if it were not for the operation of subsection 146.3(6) that the amount determined under paragraph (b) is of the amount included in computing the annuitant's income because of that subsection, but nothing in this subsection limits the liability of the annuitant under any other provision of this Act or of the taxpayer for the interest that the taxpayer is liable to pay under this Act on an assessment in respect of the amount that the taxpayer is liable to pay because of this subsection.

Notes: On payment of a deceased annuitant's RRIF to a beneficiary, the estate must be assessed first so that the annuitant's tax can be determined, before the beneficiary can be assessed under 160.2(2): *Bélanger*, 2007 TCC 502.

In *Higgins*, 2013 TCC 194, daughters received payments from a life insurance RRIF on the death of their tax-debtor father. They were "liable only to the correct amount of income tax attributable to the specific sum each received from the RRIF" (para. 11).

See also VIEWS doc 2010-0376841I7 (how to calculate 160.2(2) liability and interest), and Notes to 160.2(1).

160.2(2) closing words amended by 2002-2013 technical bill (Part 5 — technical), for assessments made after Dec. 20, 2002.

(2.1) Joint and several liability in respect of a qualifying trust annuity — If a taxpayer is deemed by section 75.2 to have received at any time an amount out of or under an annuity that is a qualifying trust annuity with respect to the taxpayer, the taxpayer, the annuitant under the annuity and the policyholder are jointly and severally, or solidarily, liable to pay the part of the taxpayer's tax under this Part for the taxation year of the taxpayer that includes that time that is equal to the amount, if any, determined by the formula

$$A - B$$

where

A is the amount of the taxpayer's tax under this Part for that taxation year; and

B is the amount that would be the taxpayer's tax under this Part for that taxation year if no amount were deemed by section 75.2 to have been received by the taxpayer out of or under the annuity in that taxation year.

Related Provisions: 160.2(2.2) — No limitation on liability; 160.2(5) — Rules applicable when (2.1) applies.

Notes: 160.2(2.1) added by 2002-2013 technical bill (Part 5 — technical), for assessments made after 2005.

(2.2) No limitation on liability — Subsection (2.1) limits neither

(a) the liability of the taxpayer referred to in that subsection under any other provision of this Act; nor

(b) the liability of an annuitant or policyholder referred to in that subsection for the interest that the annuitant or policyholder is liable to pay under this Act on an assessment in respect of the amount that the annuitant or policyholder is liable to pay because of that subsection.

Notes: 160.2(2.2) added by 2002-2013 technical bill (Part 5 — technical), for assessments made after 2005.

(3) Assessment — The Minister may at any time assess a taxpayer in respect of any amount payable because of this section, and the provisions of this Division (including, for greater certainty, the provisions in respect of interest payable) apply, with any modifications that the circumstances require, in respect of an assessment made under this section as though it had been made under section 152 in respect of taxes payable under this Part.

Notes: See Notes to 160(2) re assessment "at any time".

160.2(3) amended by 2002-2013 technical bill (Part 5 — technical), for assessments made after Dec. 20, 2002.

(4) Rules applicable — If a taxpayer and an annuitant have, by virtue of subsection (1) or (2), become jointly and severally, or solidarily, liable in respect of part or all of a liability of the annuitant under this Act, the following rules apply:

(a) a payment by the taxpayer on account of the taxpayer's liability shall to the extent thereof discharge their liability; but

(b) a payment by the annuitant on account of the annuitant's liability discharges the taxpayer's liability only to the extent that the payment operates to reduce the annuitant's liability to an amount less than the amount in respect of which the taxpayer was, by subsection (1) or (2), as the case may be, made jointly and severally, or solidarily, liable.

Notes: See Notes to 160(3) re meaning of "their liability" in 160.2(4)(a).

160.2(4) amended by 2002-2013 technical bill (Part 4 — bijuralism), effective June 26, 2013, to add "or solidarily" (opening words and para. (b)) and to change "the joint liability" to "their liability" (para. (a)).

(5) Rules applicable — qualifying trust annuity — If an annuitant or policyholder has, because of subsection (2.1), become jointly and severally, or solidarily, liable with a taxpayer in respect of part or all of a liability of the taxpayer under this Act, the following rules apply:

(a) a payment by the annuitant on account of the annuitant's liability, or by the policyholder on account of the policyholder's liability, shall to the extent of the payment discharge their liability, but

(b) a payment by the taxpayer on account of the taxpayer's liability only discharges the annuitant's and the policyholder's liability to the extent that the payment operates to reduce the taxpayer's liability to an amount less than the amount in respect of which the annuitant and the policyholder were, by subsection (2.1), made liable.

Notes: 160.2(5) added by 2002-2013 technical bill (Part 5 — technical), for assessments made after 2005.

Definitions [s. 160.2]: "amount", "annuity", "assessment" — 248(1); "fair market value" — see 69(1) Notes; "Minister" — 248(1); "qualifying trust annuity" — 60.011(2), 248(1); "registered retirement income fund" — 146.3(1), 248(1); "registered retirement savings plan" — 146(1), 248(1); "taxation year" — 249; "taxpayer" — 248(1).

Interpretation Bulletins [s. 160.2]: IT-500R: RRSPs — death of an annuitant.

160.21 (1) Joint and several liability — registered disability savings plan — Where, in computing income for a taxation year, a taxpayer is required to include an amount in respect of a disability assistance payment (as defined in subsection 146.4(1)) that is deemed by subsection 146.4(10) to have been made at any particular time from a registered disability savings plan, the taxpayer and each holder (as defined in subsection 146.4(1)) of the plan immediately after the particular time are jointly and severally, or solidarily, liable to pay the part of the taxpayer's tax under this Part for that taxation year that is equal to the amount, if any, determined by the formula

$$A - B$$

where

A is the amount of the taxpayer's tax under this Part for that taxation year; and

B is the amount that would be the taxpayer's tax under this Part for that taxation year if no disability assistance payment were deemed by subsection 146.4(10) to have been paid from the plan at the particular time.

Related Provisions: 160.21(2) — No limitation on liability; 160.21(3) — Discharge of holder's liability; 160.21(4) — Assessment.

Notes: See at end of 160.21.

(2) No limitation on liability — Subsection (1) limits neither

(a) the liability of the taxpayer referred to in that subsection under any other provision of this Act, nor

(b) the liability of any holder referred to in that subsection for the interest that the holder is liable to pay under this Act on an assessment in respect of the amount that the holder is liable to pay because of that subsection.

(3) Rules applicable — registered disability savings plans — Where a holder (as defined in subsection 146.4(1)) of a registered disability savings plan has, because of subsection (1), become jointly and severally, or solidarily, liable with a taxpayer in respect of part or all of a liability of the taxpayer under this Act, the following rules apply:

(a) a payment by the holder on account of the holder's liability shall to the extent of the payment discharge the holder's liability, but

(b) a payment by the taxpayer on account of the taxpayer's liability only discharges the holder's liability to the extent that the payment operates to reduce the taxpayer's liability to an amount less than the amount in respect of which the holder was, by subsection (1), made liable.

(4) Assessment — The Minister may at any time assess a taxpayer in respect of any amount payable because of this section, and the provisions of this Division (including, for greater certainty, the provisions in respect of interest payable) apply, with any modifications that the circumstances require, in respect of an assessment made under this section as though it had been made under section 152 in respect of taxes payable under this Part.

Notes: See Notes to 160(2) re assessment "at any time".

160.21 added by 2007 RDSPs bill, effective for 2008 and later taxation years.

Definitions [s. 160.21]: "amount", "assessment", "Minister" — 248(1); "registered disability savings plan" — 146.4(1), 248(1); "taxation year" — 249; "taxpayer" — 248(1).

Information Circulars: 99-1R2: Registered disability savings plans.

160.3 (1) Liability in respect of amounts received out of or under RCA trust — If an amount required to be included in the income of a taxpayer because of paragraph 56(1)(x) is received by a person with whom the taxpayer is not dealing at arm's length, that person is jointly and severally, or solidarily, liable with the taxpayer to pay a part of the taxpayer's tax under this Part for the taxation year in which the amount is received equal to the amount by which the taxpayer's tax for the year exceeds the amount that would be the taxpayer's tax for the year if the amount had not been received, but nothing in this subsection limits the liability of the taxpayer under any other provision of this Act or of the person for the interest that the person is liable to pay under this Act on an assessment in respect of the amount that the person is liable to pay because of this subsection.

Notes: 160.3(1) amended by 2002-2013 technical bill (Part 5 — technical), for assessments made after Dec. 20, 2002.

(2) Assessment — The Minister may at any time assess a person in respect of any amount payable because of this section, and the provisions of this Division (including, for greater certainty, the provisions in respect of interest payable) apply, with any modifications that the circumstances require, in respect of an assessment made under this section as though it had been made under section 152 in respect of taxes payable under this Part.

Notes: See Notes to 160(2) re assessment "at any time".

160.3(2) amended by 2002-2013 technical bill (Part 5 — technical), for assessments made after Dec. 20, 2002.

(3) Rules applicable — If a taxpayer and another person have, by virtue of subsection (1), become jointly and severally, or solidarily, liable in respect of part or all of a liability of the taxpayer under this Act, the following rules apply:

(a) a payment by the other person on account of the other person's liability shall to the extent thereof discharge their liability; but

(b) a payment by the taxpayer on account of the taxpayer's liability discharges the other person's liability only to the extent that the payment operates to reduce the taxpayer's liability to an amount less than the amount in respect of which the other person was, by subsection (1), made jointly and severally, or solidarily, liable.

Notes: See Notes to 160(3) re meaning of "their liability" in 160.3(3)(a).

160.3(3) opening words and (b) amended by 2002-2013 technical bill (Part 4 — bijuralism), effective June 26, 2013.

Related Provisions [s. 160.3]: Part XI.3 — Tax in respect of retirement compensation arrangements.

Definitions [s. 160.3]: "amount" — 248(1); "arm's length" — 251(1); "assessment", "Minister", "person" — 248(1); "taxation year" — 249; "taxpayer" — 248(1).

160.4 (1) Liability in respect of transfers by insolvent corporations — If property is transferred at any time by a corporation to a taxpayer with whom the corporation does not deal at arm's length at that time and the corporation is not entitled because of subsection 61.3(3) to deduct an amount under section 61.3 in computing its income for a taxation year because of the transfer or because of the transfer and one or more other transactions, the taxpayer is jointly and severally, or solidarily, liable with the corporation to pay the lesser of the corporation's tax payable under this Part for the year and the amount, if any, by which the fair market value of the property at that time exceeds the fair market value at that time of the consideration given for the property, but nothing in this subsection limits the liability of the corporation under any other provision of this Act or of the taxpayer for the interest that the taxpayer is liable to pay under this Act on an assessment in respect of the amount that the taxpayer is liable to pay because of this subsection.

Related Provisions: 160(3.1) — Fair market value of undivided interest in property.

Notes: 160.4(1) is of very limited application. For discussion of the remedies CRA has to pursue assets when a corporation winds up without paying its tax debt (15(1), 84(2) and 160(1)), see VIEWS doc 2010-0358751I7 and Notes to those provisions.

See Notes to 61.3(1) and at end of 160.4.

160.4(1) amended by 2002-2013 technical bill, for assessments after Dec. 20, 2002.

(2) Indirect transfers — Where

(a) property is transferred at any time from a taxpayer (in this subsection referred to as the "transferor") to another taxpayer (in this subsection referred to as the "transferee") with whom the transferor does not deal at arm's length,

(b) the transferor is liable because of subsection (1) or this subsection to pay an amount of the tax of another person (in this subsection referred to as the "debtor") under this Part, and

(c) it can reasonably be considered that one of the reasons of the transfer would, but for this subsection, be to prevent the enforcement of this section,

the transferee is jointly and severally, or solidarily, liable with the transferor and the debtor to pay an amount of the debtor's tax under this Part equal to the lesser of the amount of that tax that the transferor was liable to pay at that time and the amount, if any, by which the fair market value of the property at that time exceeds the fair market value at that time of the consideration given for the property, but nothing in this subsection limits the liability of the debtor or the transferor under any provision of this Act or of the transferee for the interest that the transferee is liable to pay under this Act on an assessment in respect of the amount that the transferee is liable to pay because of this subsection.

Notes: 160.4(2) amended by 2002-2013 technical bill (Part 5 — technical), for assessments made after Dec. 20, 2002.

(3) Assessment — The Minister may at any time assess a person in respect of any amount payable by the person because of this section, and the provisions of this Division (including, for greater certainty, the provisions in respect of interest payable) apply, with any modifications that the circumstances require, in respect of an assessment made under this section, as though it had been made under section 152 in respect of taxes payable under this Part.

Notes: See Notes to 160(2) re assessment "at any time".

160.4(3) amended by 2002-2013 technical bill (Part 5 — technical), for assessments made after Dec. 20, 2002.

(4) Rules applicable — If a corporation and another person have, because of subsection (1) or (2), become jointly and severally, or solidarily, liable in respect of part or all of a liability of the corporation under this Act

(a) a payment by the other person on account of that person's liability shall to the extent thereof discharge their liability; and

(b) a payment by the corporation on account of the corporation's liability discharges the other person's liability only to the extent that the payment operates to reduce the corporation's liability to an amount less than the amount in respect of which the other person was, by subsection (1) or (2), as the case may be, made jointly and severally, or solidarily, liable.

Notes: See Notes to 160(3) re meaning of "their liability" in 160.4(4)(a).

160.4(4) amended by 2002-2013 technical bill, effective June 26, 2013.

Notes [s. 160.4]: 160.4 added by 1994 technical bill, effective for transfers that occur after December 20, 1994.

Definitions [s. 160.4]: "amount" — 248(1); "arm's length" — 251(1); "corporation" — 248(1), *Interpretation Act* 35(1); "debtor" — 160.4(2)(b); "fair market value" — 160(3.1) and see 69(1) Notes; "Minister", "person", "property" — 248(1); "taxation year" — 249; "taxpayer" — 248(1); "transferee", "transferor" — 160.4(2)(a).

Interest

161. (1) General [interest on late balances] — Where at any time after a taxpayer's balance-due day for a taxation year

(a) the total of the taxpayer's taxes payable under this Part and Parts I.3, VI and VI.1 for the year

exceeds

(b) the total of all amounts each of which is an amount paid at or before that time on account of the taxpayer's tax payable and applied as at that time by the Minister against the taxpayer's liability for an amount payable under this Part or Part I.3, VI or VI.1 for the year,

the taxpayer shall pay to the Receiver General interest at the prescribed rate on the excess, computed for the period during which that excess is outstanding.

Related Provisions: 12.6(4) — SIFTs — interest on temporary unstapling of securities; 18(1)(t) — Interest is non-deductible; 156.1(4) — Due date for paying balance; 160(1)(e)(ii) — Third party can be liable for interest; 161(5), (6.1), (7) — Special rules; 161.1 — Offset of refund interest against arrears interest; 161.2 — No interest if balance paid within 20-day grace period; 161.3 — Interest and penalty up to $25 may be cancelled if tax paid; 164(3) — Interest on refunds paid by CRA; 220(3.1) — Waiver or cancellation of interest; 220(4.5)(b)(i) — No interest on unpaid departure tax if security provided; 220(4.6)(d)(i) — No interest on unpaid tax on distribution by trust to non-resident beneficiary where security provided; 221.1 — Application of interest where legislation retroactive; 227(8.3), (9.3) — Interest on certain unpaid withholding taxes; 248(11) — Interest compounded daily.

Notes: Interest under 161(1) runs on regular tax assessments, and compounds daily (248(11)) at a prescribed rate which changes quarterly (see list of rates in Notes to Reg. 4301). It also runs on s. 227.1 director-liability assessments, due to the words "Divisions I and J apply with any modifications that the circumstances require" in 227(10): *Zen*, 2010 FCA 180 (leave to appeal denied 2011 CarswellNat 47 (SCC)). It also runs on s. 160 third-party liability assessments, due to the closing words of 160(1) (and the FCA's comments in *Zen*). Interest runs on a GAAR assessment before CRA has assessed: see Notes to 245(7).

There is no due-diligence defence to interest: *Tuck*, 2012 TCC 332, para. 25.

Interest paid to CRA is non-deductible (18(1)(t)), except for a repayment of refund interest (20(1)(ll)). Because of this, one who can afford to should often pay an assessment even if objecting or appealing: see Notes to 225.1(1).

Interest runs from the "balance-due day", defined in 248(1) as April 30 for living individuals, 90 days after year-end for trusts, and two or three months after year-end for corporations. During 2020 (COVID-19), interest is automatically waived on certain balances: see Announced Administrative Change under 150(1) opening words.

Tax can be prepaid in advance of a reassessment, to prevent interest from running: VIEWS doc 2007-0239491E5.

Determination of interest on a Statement of Account, without assessment of tax, is not an "assessment" that can be appealed: *Homa*, 2011 TCC 230 and 2012 TCC 110 (see Notes to 152(1.1)). The TCC can consider a wrong *calculation* of interest on an assessment: *Moledina*, 2007 TCC 354, para. 5; *Nottawasaga Inn*, 2013 TCC 377, para. 25; *Isah*, 2018 TCC 28, para. 17. Otherwise, the only relief is by CRA waiver under 220(3.1). In *Hoffman*, 2010 FCA 310, CRA's calculation was held correct in the absence of evidence to the contrary.

CRA statements of account normally give a due date by which the balance on the statement may be paid (usually 20 days after the statement date). If it is paid in full by that date, no interest applies: see 161.2.

See also Ian Crosbie, "Amended Returns, Refunds and Interest", 2012 *Tax Dispute Resolution* conf. report (ctf.ca), 27:1-33.

Loss carryback effect on interest calculation: see Notes to 161(7).

161(1) amended by 1983 Budget, 1988 tax reform, 1992 technical bill and 1996 Budget. The current version applies to 1996 and later taxation years, but is substantively identical to that which applies to 1992-95. For tax payable for 1989-91, ignore the references in paras. (a) and (b) to Parts I.3, VI and VI.1, and ignore the words "(or would be so required if a remainder of such tax were payable)" in the opening words. For earlier interest, calculated from April 20, 1983 and on, read the opening words as:

> 161. (1) Where at any time after the day on or before which a return of a taxpayer's income was required under this Part to be filed for a taxation year,

For interest relating to any period before April 20, 1983, read 161(1) as follows:

> 161. (1) Where the amount paid on account of tax payable by a taxpayer under this Part for a taxation year before the expiration of the time allowed for filing the return of the taxpayer's income is less than the amount of tax payable for the year under this Part, the person liable to pay the tax shall pay interest at a prescribed rate per annum on the difference between those two amounts from the expiration of the time for filing the return of income to the day of payment.

Note also that daily compounding of interest under 248(11) applies only since January 1, 1987; interest accrued since before 1987 is compounded from that date only.

Regulations: 4301(a) (prescribed rate of interest).

I.T. Application Rules: 62(2) (subsec. 161(1) applies to interest payable in respect of any period after December 23, 1971).

Information Circulars: 07-1R1: Taxpayer relief provisions.

(2) Interest on instalments — In addition to the interest payable under subsection (1), where a taxpayer who is required by this Part to pay a part or instalment of tax has failed to pay all or any part thereof on or before the day on or before which the tax or instalment, as the case may be, was required to be paid, the taxpayer shall pay to the Receiver General interest at the prescribed rate on the amount that the taxpayer failed to pay computed from the day on or before which the amount was required to be paid to the day of payment, or to the beginning of the period in respect of which the taxpayer is required to pay interest thereon under subsection (1), whichever is earlier.

Related Provisions: 18(1)(t) — Interest is non-deductible; 107(5.1) — Trust's gain on distribution to non-resident beneficiary does not increase instalment requirements; 128.1(5) — Deemed disposition on emigration does not increase instalment requirements; 155–157 — Times for instalments; 161(4) — Limitation — farmers and fishermen; 161(4.01) — Limitation — other individuals; 161(4.1) — Limitation — corporations; 161(5), (6.1), (7) — Special rules; 161(8) — Deemed instalments; 161(10) — When amount deemed paid; 163.1 — Penalty for late or deficient instalments; 211.5(2) — Interest on instalments of Part XII.3 tax; 220(3.1) — Waiver or cancellation of interest; 221.1 — Application of interest where legislation retroactive; 248(11) — Interest compounded daily.

Notes: See Notes to 156(1) (individuals) and 157(1) (corporations); and to 163.1 re how instalment interest and penalty are calculated. Instalment interest was upheld in: *Strain*, 1997 CarswellNat 1588 (TCC); *Wieckowski*, 1998 CarswellNat 3675 (TCC); *Ross*, 2005 TCC 643; *Bhachu*, 2021 FCA 12 (foreign source deductions do not reduce instalment obligation).

In *Emcon Services*, 2008 TCC 501, a corporation could not contest interest charges resulting from delay in CRA applying a prior-year refund to its instalment account, as this was outside the TCC's jurisdiction.

No interest is payable under 161(2) in respect of any amount payable before July 1995 because of 190.1(1.2): 1995 Budget bill s. 49(4).

Regulations: 4301(a) (prescribed rate of interest).

I.T. Application Rules: 62(2) (subsec. 161(2) applies to interest payable in respect of any period after December 23, 1971.

Interpretation Bulletins: IT-243R4: Dividend refund to private corporations.

Information Circulars: 07-1R1: Taxpayer relief provisions.

(2.1) [Repealed]

Notes: 161(2.1) repealed by 2003 Budget, for taxation years that end after June 2003. See now 161.3 instead re small amounts of interest.

161(2.1) amended by 1991 technical bill, effective December 17, 1991.

(2.2) Contra interest [offset interest] — Notwithstanding subsections (1) and (2), the total amount of interest payable by a taxpayer (other than a graduated rate estate) under those subsections, for the period that begins on the first day of the taxation year for which a part or instalment of tax is payable and ends on the taxpayer's balance-due day for the year, in respect of the taxpayer's tax or instalments of tax payable for the year shall not exceed the amount, if any, by which

(a) the total amount of interest that would be payable for the period by the taxpayer under subsections (1) and (2) in respect of the taxpayer's tax and instalments of tax payable for the year if no amount were paid on account of the tax or instalments

exceeds

(b) the amount of interest that would be payable under subsection 164(3) to the taxpayer in respect of the period on the amount that would be refunded to the taxpayer in respect of the year or applied to another liability if

(i) no tax were payable by the taxpayer for the year,

(ii) no amount had been remitted under section 153 to the Receiver General on account of the taxpayer's tax for the year,

(iii) the rate of interest prescribed for the purpose of subsection (1) were prescribed for the purpose of subsection 164(3), and

(iv) the latest of the days described in paragraphs 164(3)(a), (b) and (c) were the first day of the year.

Related Provisions: 161.1 — Offset of refund interest and arrears interest of different years.

Notes: 161(2.2) allows "offset" interest (also called "contra" interest) to be earned on early or overpaid instalments at the "high" rate for late payments, to reduce the interest charge resulting from late or insufficient instalments for the same year. Thus, as long as interest rates do not go down, a single instalment payment at the midpoint of all instalment due dates for the year will result in no instalment interest being assessed. See Notes to 157(1) for discussion. See also 161.1.

For CRA application of 161(2.2) where corporate instalments are late but a reassessment reduces tax, see VIEWS doc 2004-0063651E5.

161(2.2) opening words amended by 2014 budget bill #2, for 2016 and later taxation years, to change "testamentary trust" to "graduated rate estate". (See Notes to 248(1) "graduated rate estate".)

161(2.2) earlier amended by 1996 Budget (for 1996 and later taxation years), 1995 Budget, 1991 technical bill.

Regulations: Reg. 4301(a) (prescribed rate of interest).

(3) [Repealed]

Notes: 161(3) repealed by 1991 technical bill, effective 1988. It imposed an extra 3% interest on a cooperative corporation or credit union in certain cases.

(4) Limitation — farmers and fishermen — For the purposes of subsection (2) and section 163.1, where an individual is required to pay a part or instalment of tax for a taxation year computed by reference to a method described in subsection 155(1), the individual shall be deemed to have been liable to pay on or before the day referred to in subsection 155(1) a part or instalment computed by reference to

(a) the amount, if any, by which

(i) the tax payable under this Part by the individual for the year, determined before taking into consideration the specified future tax consequences for the year,

exceeds

(ii) the amounts deemed by subsections 120(2) and (2.2) to have been paid on account of the individual's tax under this Part for the year, determined before taking into consideration the specified future tax consequences for the year,

(b) the individual's instalment base for the preceding taxation year, or

(c) the amount stated to be the amount of the instalment payable by the individual for the year in the notice, if any, sent to the individual by the Minister,

whichever method gives rise to the least amount required to be paid by the individual on or before that day.

Related Provisions: 107(5.1) — Trust's gain on distribution to non-resident beneficiary does not increase instalment requirements; 128.1(5) — Deemed disposition on emigration does not increase instalment requirements.

Notes: 161(4)(a)(ii) amended by 1999 Budget, effective for 1999 and later taxation years, to add reference to 120(2.2). See also Notes to 161(4.01).

(4.01) Limitation — other individuals — For the purposes of subsection (2) and section 163.1, where an individual is required to pay a part or instalment of tax for a taxation year computed by reference to a method described in subsection 156(1), the individual shall be deemed to have been liable to pay on or before each day referred to in subsection 156(1) a part or instalment computed by reference to

(a) the amount, if any, by which

(i) the tax payable under this Part by the individual for the year, determined before taking into consideration the specified future tax consequences for the year,

exceeds

(ii) the amounts deemed by subsections 120(2) and (2.2) to have been paid on account of the individual's tax under this Part for the year, determined before taking into consideration the specified future tax consequences for the year,

(b) the individual's instalment base for the preceding taxation year,

(c) the amounts determined under paragraph 156(1)(b) in respect of the individual for the year, or

(d) the amounts stated to be the amounts of instalments payable by the individual for the year in the notices, if any, sent to the individual by the Minister,

reduced by the amount, if any, determined under paragraph 156(2)(b) in respect of the individual for the year, whichever method gives rise to the least total amount of such parts or instalments required to be paid by the individual by that day.

Related Provisions: 107(5.1) — Trust's gain on distribution to non-resident beneficiary does not increase instalment requirements; 128.1(5) — Deemed disposition on emigration does not increase instalment requirements.

Notes: 161(4.01)(a)(ii) amended by 1999 Budget, effective for 1999 and later taxation years, to add reference to 120(2.2).

161(4)(a) and (4.01)(a) both amended by 1996 Budget, effective for 1996 and later taxation years, to add the exclusion of specified future tax consequences in place of the existing exclusion. ("Specified future tax consequences" (see 248(1)) refers to adjustments from the carryback of losses or similar amounts or because of corrections of certain amounts renounced in connection with the issuance of flow-through shares.)

161(4) amended and (4.01) added by 1992 technical bill, and (4.01) amended retroactively by 1993 technical bill, all effective for 1992 and later taxation years. However, for instalments payable on or before June 10, 1993, ignore the references to 163.1 (so that 161(4) and (4.01) do not apply for purposes of that section).

(4.1) Limitation — corporations — For the purposes of subsection (2) and section 163.1, where a corporation is required to pay a part or instalment of tax for a taxation year computed by reference to a method described in subsection 157(1), (1.1) or (1.5), as the case may be, the corporation is deemed to have been liable to pay on or before each day on or before which subparagraph 157(1)(a)(i), (ii) or (iii), subparagraph 157(1.1)(a)(i), (ii) or (iii), or subparagraph 157(1.5)(a)(i) or (ii), as the case may be, requires a part or instalment to be made equal to the amount, if any, by which

    (a) the part or instalment due on that day computed in accordance with whichever allowable method in the circumstances gives rise to the least total amount of such parts or instalments of tax for the year, computed by reference to

        (i) the total of the taxes payable under this Part and Parts VI, VI.1 and XIII.1 by the corporation for the year, determined before taking into consideration the specified future tax consequences for the year,

        (ii) its first instalment base for the year, or

        (iii) its second instalment base and its first instalment base for the year,

exceeds

    (b) the amount, if any, determined under any of paragraphs 157(3)(b) to (e) or under paragraph 157(3.1)(b) or (c), as the case may be, in respect of that instalment.

Notes: See Notes to 157(1) re *I.G. (Rockies) Corp.* case.

161(4.1) amended by 2007 budget bill #2 (for tax years that begin after 2007), 1993 and 1992 technical bills.

Regulations: 5301(7), (9) (instalment obligations of parent after windup of subsidiary).

(5) [Repealed]

Notes: 161(5) repealed by 2012 budget bill #1, effective June 29, 2012 (consequential on the *Marketing Freedom for Grain Farmers Act*; see Notes to 135.2). It dealt with Canadian Wheat Board participation certificates.

(6) Income of resident from a foreign country in blocked currency — Where the income of a taxpayer for a taxation year, or part thereof, is from sources in another country and the taxpayer by reason of monetary or exchange restrictions imposed by the law of that country is unable to transfer it to Canada, the Minister may, if the Minister is satisfied that payment as required by this Part of the whole of the additional tax under this Part for the year reasonably attributable to income from sources in that country would impose extreme hardship on the taxpayer, postpone the time for payment of the whole or a part of that additional tax for a period to be determined by the Minister, but no such postponement may be granted if any of the income for the year from sources in that country has been

    (a) transferred to Canada,

    (b) used by the taxpayer for any purpose whatever, other than payment of income tax to the government of that other country on income from sources in that country, or

    (c) disposed of by the taxpayer,

and no interest is payable under this section in respect of that additional tax, or part thereof, during the period of postponement.

Related Provisions: 91(2) — FAPI reserve for blocked currency.

Interpretation Bulletins: IT-351: Income from a foreign source — blocked currency (cancelled).

(6.1) Foreign tax credit adjustment — Notwithstanding any other provision in this section, where the tax payable under this Part by a taxpayer for a particular taxation year is increased because of

    (a) an adjustment of an income or profits tax payable by the taxpayer to the government of a country other than Canada or to the government of a state, province or other political subdivision of such a country, or

    (b) a reduction in the amount of foreign tax deductible under subsection 126(1) or (2) in computing the taxpayer's tax otherwise payable under this Part for the particular year, as a result of the application of subsection 126(4.2) in respect of a share or debt obligation disposed of by the taxpayer in the taxation year following the particular year,

no interest is payable, in respect of the increase in the taxpayer's tax payable, for the period

    (c) that ends 90 days after the day on which the taxpayer is first notified of the amount of the adjustment, if paragraph (a) applies, and

    (d) before the date of the disposition, if paragraph (b) applies.

Related Provisions: 248(1)"specified future tax consequence"(c) — Adjustment under 161(6.1) is a specified future tax consequence.

Notes: See VIEWS doc 2011-0411121I7 (general explanation).

For the meaning of "income or profits tax" in para. (a), see Notes to 126(4).

161(6.1)(b) and (d) added by 1998 Budget, for 1998 and later tax years.

(6.2) Flow-through share renunciations — Where the tax payable under this Part by a taxpayer for a taxation year is more than it otherwise would be because of a consequence for the year described in paragraph (b) of the definition "specified future tax consequence" in subsection 248(1) in respect of an amount purported to be renounced in a calendar year, for the purposes of the provisions of this Act (other than this subsection) relating to interest payable under this Act, an amount equal to the additional tax payable is deemed

    (a) to have been paid on the taxpayer's balance-due day for the taxation year on account of the taxpayer's tax payable under this Part for the year; and

    (b) to have been refunded on April 30 of the following calendar year to the taxpayer on account of the taxpayer's tax payable under this Part for the taxation year.

Notes: 161(6.2) added by 1996 Budget, for 1996 and later tax years. It applies where tax payable under Part I is more than it otherwise would be because of 248(1)"specified future tax consequence"(b). That results from reduction under 66(12.73) of an amount purported to be renounced under 66(12.6) or (12.601) because of 66(12.66). Where 161(6.2) applies, the Part I tax account for the year is, on the balance-due day, credited with an amount equal to such additional tax payable. The account is subsequently debited, on April 30 of the calendar year that follows the year of the renunciation, with the same amount.

The main purpose of this rule, in conjunction with amendments to 156.1 and 157 and Reg. 5300–5301, is to avoid arrears interest being payable by an investor because of adjustments to renunciations made due to the 1-year look-back rule under 66(12.66). In effect, the taxpayer has a grace period until April 30 of the year after the year in which the renunciation was made. 161(6.2) is also relevant in determining refund interest under 164 because of its effect on a taxpayer's "overpayment"; see 164(7).

(7) Effect of carryback of loss, etc. — For the purpose of computing interest under subsection (1) or (2) on tax or a part of an instalment of tax for a taxation year, and for the purpose of section 163.1,

    (a) the tax payable under this Part and Parts I.3, VI and VI.1 by the taxpayer for the year is deemed to be the amount that it would be if the consequences of the deduction, reduction or exclusion of the following amounts were not taken into consideration:

        (i) any amount deducted under section 119 in respect of a disposition in a subsequent taxation year,

        (ii) any amount deducted under section 41 in respect of the taxpayer's listed-personal-property loss for a subsequent taxation year,

(iii) any amount excluded from the taxpayer's income for the year by virtue of section 49 in respect of the exercise of an option in a subsequent taxation year,

(iv) any amount deducted under section 118.1 in respect of a gift made in a subsequent taxation year or under section 111 in respect of a loss for a subsequent taxation year,

(iv.1) any amount deducted under subsection 126(2) in respect of an unused foreign tax credit (within the meaning assigned by subsection 126(7)), or under subsection 126(2.21) or (2.22) in respect of foreign taxes paid, for a subsequent taxation year,

(iv.2) any amount deducted in computing the taxpayer's income for the year by virtue of an election in a subsequent taxation year under paragraph 164(6)(c) or (d) by the taxpayer's legal representative,

(v) any amount deducted under subsection 127(5) in respect of property acquired or an expenditure made in a subsequent taxation year,

(vi) [Repealed]

(vi.1) [Repealed under former Act]

(vii) any amount deducted under section 125.3 in respect of an unused Part I.3 tax credit (within the meaning assigned by subsection 125.3(3)) for a subsequent taxation year,

(viii) any amount deducted, in respect of a repayment under subsection 68.4(7) of the *Excise Tax Act* made in a subsequent taxation year, in computing the amount determined under subparagraph 12(1)(x.1)(ii),

(viii.1) any amount deducted under subsection 147.2(4) in computing the taxpayer's income for the year because of the application of subsection 147.2(6) as a result of the taxpayer's death in the subsequent taxation year,

(ix) any amount deducted under subsection 181.1(4) in respect of any unused surtax credit (within the meaning assigned by subsection 181.1(6)) of the taxpayer for a subsequent taxation year,

(x) any amount deducted under subsection 190.1(3) in respect of any unused Part I tax credit (within the meaning assigned by subsection 190.1(5)) of the taxpayer for a subsequent taxation year;

(xi) any amount deducted under any of subsections 128.1(6) to (8) from the taxpayer's proceeds of disposition of a property because of an election made in a return of income for a subsequent taxation year; and

(xii) any amount by which the amount included under subsection 91(1) for the year is reduced because of a reduction referred to in paragraph 152(6.1)(b) in the foreign accrual property income of a foreign affiliate of the taxpayer for a taxation year of the affiliate that ends in the year; and

(b) the amount by which the tax payable under this Part and Parts I.3, VI and VI.1 by the taxpayer for the year is reduced as a consequence of the deduction or exclusion of amounts described in paragraph (a) is deemed to have been paid on account of the taxpayer's tax payable under this Part for the year on the day that is 30 days after the latest of

(i) the first day immediately following that subsequent taxation year,

(ii) the day on which the taxpayer's or the taxpayer's legal representative's return of income for that subsequent taxation year was filed,

(iii) if an amended return of the taxpayer's income for the year or a prescribed form amending the taxpayer's return of income for the year was filed under subsection 49(4) or 152(6) or (6.1) or paragraph 164(6)(e), the day on which the amended return or prescribed form was filed, and

(iv) where, as a consequence of a request in writing, the Minister reassessed the taxpayer's tax for the year to take into account the deduction or exclusion, the day on which the request was made.

Related Provisions: 162(11) — Effect of carryback of losses etc.; 248(1)"specified future tax consequence"(a) — Deduction or exclusion of amount referred to in 161(7)(a) is a specified future tax consequence.

Notes: Under 161(7), if tax payable for a year is reduced because of certain deductions or exclusions arising from carryback of losses or credits or from events in later years, interest on any unpaid tax for the year is calculated without regard to the reduction until 30 days after the latest of several dates.

Where no tax was payable for a year, and a loss carryback is used to replace a credit or a different loss, no interest is charged even though 161(7) technically requires it: VIEWS docs 2005-0141251C6, 2017-0736291E5. However, this does not apply where a loss is carried back to a year where discretionary deductions were unclaimed, as "tax payable" in 161(7) means tax payable on the basis of the way the taxpayer chooses to compute taxable income: doc 9733167; *Connaught Laboratories*, [1995] 1 C.T.C. 216 (FCTD); *Amirix Systems*, 2011 TCC 60.

See also docs 2006-0189491E5, 2008-0275501I7, 2008-0294251I7, 2009-0313781I7, 2009-0319471I7 [Cyna, "Interest Charges and Loss Carry-backs", 6(12) *Tax Hyperion* (Carswell, Dec. 2009)], 2009-0331501I7 (arrears interest should be calculated before effects of loss carryback), 2009-0337341I7, 2009-0348481E5, 2009-0351721E5, 2010-0371691I7, 2010-0360181E5, 2011-042070I17, 2012-044506I17, 2012-045279I17; and Remission Orders annotation below.

In *Slau Ltd.*, 2009 FCA 270, CRA had not properly calculated interest after applying loss carrybacks, and was ordered to reconsider the case.

In *Nottawasaga Inn*, 2013 TCC 377, the TCC ruled it cannot hear an appeal of interest where the underlying tax calculated was nil due to loss carrybacks and the basis for the appeal was that CRA wrongly calculated income before applying the carrybacks [Mc-Donnell, "Loss Carrybacks and Nil Assessments", 14(2) *Tax for the Owner-Manager* (ctf.ca) 5-6 (April 2014)].

161(7)(a)(iv) and (b)(iii)-(iv) applied in *Zandi*, 2012 TCC 259.

A somewhat similar rule under the pre-2009 Ontario *Corporations Tax Act* did not apply to deny refund interest in *Stonehouse Group*, 2021 ONCA 10.

161(7) amended by 2002-2013 technical bill (last change effective for tax years that begin after Oct. 2011), 2003 Budget, 2001 technical bill, 1997 and 1996 Budgets, 1995-97 and 1992 technical bills, 1992 transportation support bill, 1989 Budget.

I.T. Application Rules: 69 (meaning of "chapter 148 of ...").

Remission Orders: *Jerry Mathews Remission Order*, P.C. 2006-446 (1980-85 returns filed in 2000, balance for 1983 eliminated by loss carryback; resulting interest cancelled by remission order).

(8) Certain amounts deemed to be paid as instalments — For the purposes of subsection (2), where in a taxation year an amount has been paid by a non-resident person pursuant to subsection 116(2) or (4) or an amount has been paid on that person's behalf by another person in accordance with subsection 116(5), the amount shall be deemed to have been paid by that non-resident person in the year as an instalment of tax on the first day on which the non-resident person was required under this Act to pay an instalment of tax for that year.

(9) Definitions of "instalment base", etc. — In this section,

(a) "instalment base" of an individual for a taxation year means the amount determined in prescribed manner to be the individual's instalment base for the year; and

(b) "first instalment base" and "second instalment base" of a corporation for a taxation year have the meanings prescribed by regulation.

Regulations: 5300 (instalment base); 5301 (first instalment base, second instalment base).

(10) When amount deemed paid — For the purposes of subsection (2), where an amount has been deducted by virtue of paragraph 127.2(1)(a) or 127.3(1)(a) in computing the tax payable under this Part by a taxpayer for a taxation year, the amount so deducted shall be deemed to have been paid by the taxpayer

(a) in the case of a taxpayer who has filed a return of income under this Part for the year as required by section 150, on the last day of the year; and

(b) in any other case, on the day on which the taxpayer filed the taxpayer's return of income under this Part for the year.

(11) Interest on penalties — Where a taxpayer is required to pay a penalty, the taxpayer shall pay the penalty to the Receiver

General together with interest thereon at the prescribed rate computed,

(a) in the case of a penalty payable under section 162, 163 or 235, from the day on or before which

(i) the taxpayer's return of income for a taxation year in respect of which the penalty is payable was required to be filed, or would have been required to be filed if tax under this Part were payable by the taxpayer for the year, or

(ii) the information return, return, ownership certificate or other document in respect of which the penalty is payable was required to be made,

as the case may be, to the day of payment;

(b) in the case of a penalty payable for a taxation year because of section 163.1, from the taxpayer's balance-due day for the year to the day of payment of the penalty;

(b.1) in the case of a penalty under subsection 237.1(7.4) or 237.3(8), from the day on which the taxpayer became liable to the penalty to the day of payment; and

(c) in the case of a penalty payable by reason of any other provision of this Act, from the day of sending of the notice of original assessment of the penalty to the day of payment.

Related Provisions: 18(1)(t) — Interest and penalty are non-deductible; 161.1 — Offset of refund interest against arrears interest; 163(2.9) — Partnership liable to interest on penalty re tax shelters; 189(9) — No interest on charity revocation tax or penalties to extent reduced by charitable transfer; 221.1 — Application of interest where legislation retroactive; 244(14), (14.1) — Date when notice sent; 248(11) — Interest compounded daily.

Notes: For an example of 161(11) imposing interest on penalty see *Pereira-Jennings*, 2009 TCC 330 (failure to report RRSP overcontributions). See also VIEWS docs 2009-0335321E5 (interest on a penalty when a T106 is filed late), 2010-0380641I7 (interest on 162(7.02) penalty re not filing information returns electronically).

161(11)(b.1) amended to add reference to 237.3(8) by 2002-2013 technical bill (Part 5 — technical), effective on the same basis as 237.3 applies.

161(11)(c) amended by 2010 budget bill #2, effective Dec. 15, 2010, to change "mailing" to "sending" (to accommodate electronic notices under 244(14.1)).

161(11) amended by 1996 Budget (effective for 1996 and later taxation years), 1995-97 technical bill (effective Dec. 2, 1994) and 1991 technical bill.

Regulations: 4301(a) (prescribed rate of interest).

Interpretation Bulletins: IT-407R4: Dispositions of cultural property to designated Canadian institutions.

Information Circulars: 07-1R1: Taxpayer relief provisions.

(12) [Repealed]

Notes: 161(12) added by 1995-97 technical bill, effective December 2, 1994, and repealed by 1999 Budget, effective June 29, 2000. It made a partnership liable to administrative rules, including interest, on a 237.1(7.4) penalty. See now 163(2.9).

This rule is needed because a partnership is not a "person" as defined in 248(1). See Notes to 96(1).

Definitions [s. 161]: "allowable capital loss" — 38(b), 248(1); "amount", "assessment", "balance-due day" — 248(1); "calendar year" — *Interpretation Act* 37(1)(a); "corporation" — 248(1), *Interpretation Act* 35(1); "day of sending" — 244(14), (14.1); "foreign accrual property income", "foreign affiliate" — 95(1), 248(1); "foreign tax" — 126(4.2); "graduated rate estate" — 248(1); "income or profits tax" — 126(4); "individual" — 248(1); "instalment base" — 161(9); "Minister" — 123(1); "non-resident" — 248(1); "partnership" — see 96(1) Notes; "person", "prescribed" — 248(1); "prescribed rate" — Reg. 4301; "property" — 248(1); "province" — *Interpretation Act* 35(1); "regulation", "share", "specified future tax consequence" — 248(1); "tax payable" — 248(2); "taxable income" — 2(2), 248(1); "taxation year" — 249; "taxpayer" — 248(1); "writing" — *Interpretation Act* 35(1).

Offset of Refund Interest and Arrears Interest

161.1 (1) Definitions — The definitions in this subsection apply in this section.

"accumulated overpayment amount", of a corporation for a period, means the overpayment amount of the corporation for the period together with refund interest (including, for greater certainty, compound interest) that accrued with respect to the overpayment amount before the date specified under paragraph (3)(b) by the corporation in its application for the period.

"accumulated underpayment amount", of a corporation for a period, means the underpayment amount of the corporation for the period together with arrears interest (including, for greater certainty, compound interest) that accrued with respect to the underpayment amount before the date specified under paragraph (3)(b) by the corporation in its application for the period.

"arrears interest" means interest computed under paragraph (5)(b), 129(2.2)(b), 131(3.2)(b), 132(2.2)(b), 133(7.02)(b) or 160.1(1)(b), subsection 161(1) or (11), paragraph 164(3.1)(b) or (4)(b) or subsection 187(2).

"overpayment amount", of a corporation for a period, means the amount referred to in subparagraph (2)(a)(i) that is refunded to the corporation, or the amount referred to in subparagraph (2)(a)(ii) to which the corporation is entitled.

"refund interest" means interest computed under subsection 129(2.1), 131(3.1), 132(2.1), 133(7.01) or 164(3) or (3.2).

"underpayment amount", of a corporation for a period, means the amount referred to in paragraph (2)(b) payable by the corporation on which arrears interest is computed.

(2) Concurrent refund interest and arrears interest — A corporation may apply in writing to the Minister for the reallocation of an accumulated overpayment amount for a period that begins after 1999 on account of an accumulated underpayment amount for the period if, in respect of tax paid or payable by the corporation under this Part or Part I.3, II, IV, IV.1, VI, VI.1 or XIV,

(a) refund interest for the period

(i) is computed on an amount refunded to the corporation, or

(ii) would be computed on an amount to which the corporation is entitled, if that amount were refunded to the corporation; and

(b) arrears interest for the period is computed on an amount payable by the corporation.

Related Provisions: 161.1(3) — Contents of and deadline for application; 161.1(5) — Where refund previously paid.

Notes: See Notes at end of 161.1.

(3) Contents of application — A corporation's application referred to in subsection (2) for a period is deemed not to have been made unless

(a) it specifies the amount to be reallocated, which shall not exceed the lesser of the corporation's accumulated overpayment amount for the period and its accumulated underpayment amount for the period;

(b) it specifies the effective date for the reallocation, which shall not be earlier than the latest of

(i) the date from which refund interest is computed on the corporation's overpayment amount for the period, or would be so computed if the overpayment amount were refunded to the corporation,

(ii) the date from which arrears interest is computed on the corporation's underpayment amount for the period, and

(iii) January 1, 2000; and

(c) it is made on or before the day that is 90 days after the latest of

(i) the day of sending of the first notice of assessment giving rise to any portion of the corporation's overpayment amount to which the application relates,

(ii) the day of sending of the first notice of assessment giving rise to any portion of the corporation's underpayment amount to which the application relates,

(iii) if the corporation has served a notice of objection to an assessment referred to in subparagraph (i) or (ii), the day of sending of the notification under subsection 165(3) by the Minister in respect of the notice of objection,

(iv) if the corporation has appealed, or applied for leave to appeal, from an assessment referred to in subparagraph (i) or (ii) to a court of competent jurisdiction, the day on which the court dismisses the application, the application or appeal is discontinued or final judgment is pronounced in the appeal, and

(v) the day of sending of the first notice to the corporation indicating that the Minister has determined any portion of the corporation's overpayment amount to which the application relates, if the overpayment amount has not been determined as a result of a notice of assessment sent before that day.

Related Provisions: 161.1(4) — Amount reallocated is deemed to have been refunded; 244(14), (14.1) — Date when notice sent.

Notes: 161.1(3)(c)(i)-(iii) and (v) amended by 2010 budget bill #2, effective Dec. 15, 2010, to change "mail" to "send" (to accommodate electronic notices under 244(14.1)).

(4) Reallocation — The amount to be reallocated that is specified under paragraph (3)(a) by a corporation is deemed to have been refunded to the corporation and paid on account of the accumulated underpayment amount on the date specified under paragraph (3)(b) by the corporation.

Related Provisions: 161.1(6) — Consequential reallocations.

(5) Repayment of refund — If an application in respect of a period is made under subsection (2) by a corporation and a portion of the amount to be reallocated has been refunded to the corporation, the following rules apply:

(a) a particular amount equal to the total of

(i) the portion of the amount to be reallocated that was refunded to the corporation, and

(ii) refund interest paid or credited to the corporation in respect of that portion

is deemed to have become payable by the corporation on the day on which the portion was refunded; and

(b) the corporation shall pay to the Receiver General interest at the prescribed rate on the particular amount from the day referred to in paragraph (a) to the date of payment.

Related Provisions: 248(11) — Interest compounded daily.

(6) Consequential reallocations — If a particular reallocation of an accumulated overpayment amount under subsection (4) results in a new accumulated overpayment amount of the corporation for a period, the new accumulated overpayment amount shall not be reallocated under this section unless the corporation so applies in its application for the particular reallocation.

(7) Assessments — Notwithstanding subsections 152(4), (4.01) and (5), the Minister shall assess or reassess interest and penalties payable by a corporation in respect of any taxation year as necessary in order to take into account a reallocation of amounts under this section.

Related Provisions: 165(1.1) — Limitation of right to object to assessment.

Proposed Amendment — Extension of s. 161.1 to individuals

Federal Budget, Notice of Ways and Means Motion, Feb. 28, 2000: *Offsetting of Interest on Personal Tax Overpayments and Underpayments*

(23) That, for individuals other than trusts, the taxable amount of refund interest accruing over any period after 1999 on overpayments of income tax be reduced by the amount of any arrears interest accruing over the same period on unpaid income tax.

Federal Budget, Supplementary Information, Feb. 28, 2000: *Offsetting of Interest on Personal Tax Overpayments and Underpayments*

An individual who has made an overpayment of income tax may be entitled to receive refund interest from the government on the overpayment. Refund interest is included in income for tax purposes, in the same manner as interest from other sources.

If, on the other hand, an individual has failed to pay an amount of income tax when due, the individual is required to pay arrears interest to the government. Arrears interest is not deductible in computing a taxpayer's income for tax purposes.

The taxation of refund interest and non-deductibility of arrears interest can produce inappropriate results in situations where an individual who owes interest on unpaid tax from one taxation year is concurrently owed interest on a tax overpayment from a different taxation year. In this circumstance, the cost of the non-deductible interest paya-

ble by the individual exceeds the after-tax value of the taxable interest receivable by the individual. In many instances, this difference results from the non-deductibility of interest paid and the inclusion in income of interest received.

This budget proposes a relieving mechanism for these individuals. Refund interest accruing over a period will be taxable only to the extent that it exceeds any arrears interest that accrued over the same period to which the refund interest relates. As under current practice, the individual's notice of assessment will indicate the full amount of refund interest. In addition, the Canada Customs and Revenue Agency will issue an information slip indicating the amount, if any, of the refund interest that must be included in the individual's income for tax purposes.

This measure will apply to individuals other than trusts in respect of arrears and refund interest amounts that accrue concurrently after 1999, regardless of the taxation year to which the amounts relate.

Dept. of Finance news release 2000-101 Backgrounder, Dec. 21, 2000: *Offset Interest*

The 2000 budget proposed an interest offset mechanism in respect of overpayments and underpayments of tax by individuals. The Department of Finance and the Canada Customs and Revenue Agency are working to develop a mechanism under which this proposal can be given effect, for implementation at the earliest opportunity.

Notes: See Notes to 161.1 below.

Notes [s. 161.1]: 161.1 added by 1999 Budget, effective 2000. It allows a corporation to net interest payable to the CRA for one taxation year against interest on refunds for another taxation year, where they accrue over the same period. It is needed because interest on unpaid tax is non-deductible under 18(1)(t) and applies at a high rate under Reg. 4301(a), while refund interest is taxable under 12(1)(c) and applies at 2% less under Reg. 4301(b)). See Madden, "Interest Offset", 14(6) *Canadian Tax Highlights* (ctf.ca) 3-4 (June 2006).

161.1 cannot apply to offset Part I refund interest against Part XIII withholding tax interest, because Part XIII is not listed in 161.1(2): VIEWS doc 2008-0294031I7. (Nor can 161.1 be used to offset income tax with GST/HST.) Where a parent and subsidiary amalgamated, and sought to apply 161.1 to reduce interest on their pre-amalgamation accounts, CRA suggested using 221.2 instead: 2011-0396021I7.

This rule is supposedly to be extended to individuals as proposed in the Feb. 2000 budget, but as per the Dec. 2000 announcement above, implementation has been postponed while the mechanism is developed. It appears this may never happen; VIEWS doc 2007-0243311C6 confirms that CRA does not allow the offset to individuals. Finance confirmed in May 2017 that this proposal is still pending.

Definitions [s. 161.1]: "accumulated overpayment amount", "accumulated underpayment amount" — 161.1(1); "amount" — 248(1); "arrears interest" — 161.1(1); "assessment" — 248(1); "corporation" — 248(1), *Interpretation Act* 35(1); "day of sending" — 244(14), (14.1); "Minister" — 248(1); "overpayment amount" — 161.1(1); "prescribed" — 248(1); "refund interest" — 161.1(1); "sent" — 244(14), (14.1); "taxation year" — 249; "underpayment amount" — 161.1(1); "writing" — *Interpretation Act* 35(1).

161.2 Period where interest not payable — Notwithstanding any other provision of this Act, if the Minister notifies a taxpayer that the taxpayer is required to pay a specified amount under this Act and the taxpayer pays the specified amount in full before the end of the period that the Minister specifies with the notice, interest is not payable on the specified amount for the period.

Notes [s. 161.2]: 161.2 added by 2003 Budget, effective July 2003. It legislates a long-standing administrative practice (announced in a March 24, 1994 Revenue Canada Fact Sheet). When CRA provides a Statement of Account to T showing an amount payable, T normally has 20 days from the statement date to pay the amount in full, in which case no interest applies during the payment period. If T does not pay the balance in full by the deadline, interest is payable for the period.

Definitions [s. 161.2]: "amount", "Minister", "taxpayer" — 248(1).

Small Amounts Owing

161.3 Interest and penalty amounts of $25 or less — If, at any time, a person pays an amount not less than the total of all amounts, other than interest and penalty, owing at that time to Her Majesty in right of Canada under this Act for a taxation year of the person and the total amount of interest and penalty payable by the person under this Act for that year is not more than $25.00, the Minister may cancel the interest and penalty.

Notes: 161.3 added by 2003 Budget, effective for taxation years that end after June 2003. It allows the CRA discretion to cancel up to $25 of interest and/or penalty when the tax is paid (and thus overlaps with 220(3.1), which administratively is only used for "Taxpayer Relief" situations). For earlier years, see 161(2.1).

Definitions [s. 161.3]: "amount" — 248(1); "Her Majesty" — *Interpretation Act* 35(1); "Minister", "person" — 248(1); "taxation year" — 249.

161.4 (1) Taxpayer [owing $2 or less] — If the Minister determines, at any time, that the total of all amounts owing by a person to Her Majesty in right of Canada under this Act does not exceed two dollars, those amounts are deemed to be nil.

(2) Minister [owing $2 or less] — If, at any time, the total of all amounts payable by the Minister to a person under this Act does not exceed two dollars, the Minister may apply those amounts against any amount owing, at that time, by the person to Her Majesty in right of Canada. However, if the person, at that time, does not owe any amount to Her Majesty in right of Canada, those amounts payable are deemed to be nil.

Notes [s. 161.4]: An amount of up to $2 is neither paid nor refunded. In practice, a taxpayer paying a balance in full can pay the total minus $2.00, and the CRA will cancel the remainder.

The same rule for various other payments by (but not owing to) the federal government (but 99¢ for CPP, EI, OAS) is in the *Low-value Amounts Regulations*, SOR/2015-68.

161.4(2) amended by 2006 budget bill #1, for amounts owing after March 2007.

161.4 added by 2003 Budget, effective for amounts owing or payable, as the case may be, after June 2003. This was previously $1, applying to refund interest only, in the closing words of 164(3).

Definitions [s. 161.4]: "amount" — 248(1); "Her Majesty" — *Interpretation Act* 35(1); "Minister", "person", "taxpayer" — 248(1).

Penalties

162. (1) Failure to file return of income — Every person who fails to file a return of income for a taxation year as and when required by subsection 150(1) is liable to a penalty equal to the total of

(a) an amount equal to 5% of the person's tax payable under this Part for the year that was unpaid when the return was required to be filed, and

(b) the product obtained when 1% of the person's tax payable under this Part for the year that was unpaid when the return was required to be filed is multiplied by the number of complete months, not exceeding 12, from the date on which the return was required to be filed to the date on which the return was filed.

Related Provisions: 94(3)(a)(vii) — Application to trust deemed resident in Canada; 161.3 — Interest and penalty up to $25 may be cancelled if tax paid; 162(2.1) — Minimum penalty for non-resident corporation; 162(11) — Effect of carryback of losses, etc.; 189(8)(a) — 162(1) does not apply to charity revocation tax return; 220(3) — No penalty if return filed by extended deadline; 235 — Additional penalty on large corporation for late filing even where no balance owing. See additional Related Provisions and Definitions at end of s. 162.

Notes: The late-filing penalty under 162(1) (maximum 17% unless 162(2) applies) is based on the tax unpaid as of the return due date (April 30 or June 15 for individuals; 6 months after year-end for corporations; 90 days after year-end for trusts). Interest also applies, under 161(1), from the "balance-due day". If the return is not ready, it is thus wise to guess at the amount owing and make a payment by the return due date. If no tax is owing, there is no 162(1) penalty, and CRA practice is not to apply 162(7) to a resident corporation: see Notes to 162(7).

Due to COVID-19, no penalty is imposed on late 2019-2020 returns filed by Sept. 30, 2020: tinyurl.com/covid-dates.

A nil or incomplete return may be rejected as invalid and a 162(1) penalty assessed: see Notes to 162(7).

The penalty is based on the amount actually owing on the due date, and is not reduced by the carryback of a loss from a later year: *Cloud*, [1995] 1 C.T.C. 2726 (TCC); and 162(11), and Notes to 162(7).

See Notes to 162(10) re the onus of proof for penalties.

Unfairness: See Notes to 162(7), and to 163(1) re disproportionate penalties.

162(1) applies to failure to file a T1-OVP return to pay the 204.1 "penalty tax" for RRSP over-contributions, due to 204.3(2): *Pereira-Jennings*, 2009 TCC 330; *Wilson*, 2009 TCC 475; *McNamee*, 2009 TCC 630; *Lans*, 2011 FCA 290; *Dimovski*, 2011 FC 721; *Friedlander*, 2012 TCC 163 (penalty cancelled; see below).

The penalty was upheld because the return was filed late in *Pont Rouge*, 2013 TCC 224. In *Sherrick*, 2009 TCC 148, the taxpayer's evidence was insufficient to prove the return had been sent on time.

Due diligence defence: The Tax Court will cancel the penalty if there was due diligence. See *Consolidated Canadian Contractors*, [1998] G.S.T.C. 91 (FCA) and *École Polytechnique*, 2004 FCA 127. The TCC found due diligence and cancelled income tax penalties in: *Ford*, [1994] 2 C.T.C. 2395; *Katepwa Park*, [2000] 3 C.T.C. 2043; *Carlisi*, [2001] 1 C.T.C. 2734; *Gregg*, [2002] 4 C.T.C. 2670; *Bateman*, 2006 TCC 635

(return was filed electronically but CRA rejected it because surname had changed); *Jay*, 2010 TCC 122; *Friedlander*, 2012 TCC 163 (immigrant went to bank to set up investment account and got an RRSP by mistake); *Deschesnes*, 2015 TCC 177 (D tried to contact provincial pension plan and insurer to clarify tax liability); *Chiang*, 2017 TCC 165 (C reasonably believed he had unused RRSP deduction room); *Levatte Estate*, 2019 TCC 177, para. 44 (trustee's husband was dying; return filed 1 day late); *Rousseau*, 2018 QCCQ 7340 (aff'd on other grounds 2020 QCCA 1308; leave to appeal denied 2021 CarswellQue 3905 (SCC)) (R relied on accountant in reporting he was resident in AB, not QC). The TCC accepted the defence as valid but found no due diligence in: *Feuiltault*, 1994 CarswellNat 1148; *Bennett*, [1995] 2 C.T.C. 2308; *Ogden Palladium*, 2002 FCA 336; *Quantz*, [2003] 1 C.T.C. 2714; *Stuart Estate*, 2003 TCC 171, *Gosselin*, 2004 TCC 544; *Alsayegh*, 2005 TCC 544; *Tuck*, 2012 TCC 332; *830480 Alberta Inc.*, 2012 TCC 424. CPP/EI penalties were cancelled for due diligence in *Gutierrez*, 2012 TCC 234. See Tassé, "The Due Diligence Defence in Tax Matters", 2001 Cdn Tax Foundation conference report, 36:1-41; Russell & Stilwell, "Aspects of Fixing Mistakes in Tax Context", 2009 Atlantic Provinces Tax Conference (ctf.ca), 6A:1-46; Sohmer & Costom, "Should taxpayers be penalized for their accountant's lack of due diligence?", xxxiv(14), (15) *The Canadian Taxpayer* (Carswell) 105-07 and 113-16 (July 13 and Aug. 3, 2012).

Where the taxpayer provided her information on time but her preparer filed the return late, no relief was given as "this is an issue between the Appellant and her tax preparers": *Ross*, 2014 TCC 317, para. 51.

In *La Souveraine v. Autorité des marchés financiers*, 2013 SCC 63, the Supreme Court of Canada stated at paras. 56-57: "The due diligence defence is available if the defendant reasonably believed in a mistaken set of facts that, if true, would have rendered his or her act or omission innocent. A defendant can also avoid liability by showing that he or she took all reasonable steps to avoid the particular event (*Sault Ste. Marie*, at p. 1326). The defence of due diligence is based on an objective standard: it requires consideration of what a reasonable person would have done in similar circumstances. However, this defence will not be available if the defendant relies solely on a mistake of law." This may limit the use of the defence; although the case dealt with regulatory offences (like s. 238) rather than administrative penalties, the due-diligence defence to tax penalties came from the cited *Sault Ste. Marie* case (*Pillar Oilfield*, [1993] G.S.T.C. 49 (TCC)). See also *R. v. Legrande*, 2014 ABCA 192 on mistake of fact vs. mistake of law as a defence to a strict liability penalty.

The penalty can also be cancelled at CRA's discretion, but only if requested within 10 years: see Notes to 220(3.1).

In *Saunders*, 2010 TCC 114, the Court accepted evidence that a return had been filed on time (see Notes to 150(1) opening words).

See Notes to 239(1) on the difference between an administrative penalty and criminal prosecution for an offence. See end of Notes to 163(1) for articles discussing penalties.

Information Circulars: 00-1R4: Voluntary disclosures program; 07-1R1: Taxpayer relief provisions.

CRA Audit Manual: 28.2.2: Late filing of income tax return.

(2) Repeated failure to file — Every person

(a) who fails to file a return of income for a taxation year as and when required by subsection 150(1),

(b) to whom a demand for a return for the year has been sent under subsection 150(2), and

(c) by whom, before the time of failure, a penalty was payable under this subsection or subsection (1) in respect of a return of income for any of the 3 preceding taxation years

is liable to a penalty equal to the total of

(d) an amount equal to 10% of the person's tax payable under this Part for the year that was unpaid when the return was required to be filed, and

(e) the product obtained when 2% of the tax payable under this Part for the year that was unpaid when the return was required to be filed is multiplied by the number of complete months, not exceeding 20, from the date on which the return was required to be filed to the date on which the return was filed.

Related Provisions: 162(2.1) — Minimum penalty for non-resident corporation; 162(11) — Effect of carryback of losses, etc. See also at end of s. 162.

Notes: See Notes to 239(1). This penalty tops out at 50% (10% + (2 × 20%)). See Notes to 162(10) re the onus of proof for penalties.

When reading a VIEWS doc or article in French about 162(2), note that the para. numbers differ in French from English!

162(2)(b) in English has one less condition than the French, which requires failure to file *within the reasonable period set out in the demand*. The French version was held correct: *Hughes*, 2017 TCC 95, paras. 37, 64, so the penalty did not apply because CRA had not proven this fact or pleaded it as an assumption: para. 75. See also Michelle Moriartey, "Repeated Failure-To-File Penalty", 7(3) *Canadian Tax Focus* (ctf.ca) 2-3 (Aug. 2017), re questions *Hughes* left unresolved.

A penalty is not "payable" under 162(2)(c) until it is assessed, so if several returns are filed at once, 162(2) does not apply: *Wichartz*, [1995] 1 C.T.C. 2866 (TCC); VIEWS doc 2002-0178707.

When F made a payment but did not specify where to allocate it, she could not later claim that it applied to the year for which tax was "unpaid" under 162(2): *Fuerth*, 2007 TCC 588.

In *Nedza Enterprises*, 2010 FC 435, CRA's decision not to waive 162(2) was held reasonable, and an extension of time to comply with a Demand to File did not stop the penalty from applying; but the FCA allowed the company's appeal on consent, after the Court drew the parties' attention to the 2006 amendment to 220(3): A-199-10. (A consent judgment has no precedential value: see Notes to 221.2.)

162(2)(b) amended by 2012 budget bill #1, effective June 29, 2012, to change "on" to "to" and "served" to "sent", so that the penalty can apply following a demand served by regular mail or online (see Notes to 150(2)). Under the old rule: in *Kikot*, 2008 TCC 38, 162(2)(b) did not apply because demands sent to the taxpayer had been returned as unclaimed and so had not been "served"; in *Kreuz*, 2012 TCC 238, paras. 84-85, the penalty was cancelled because the CRA did not prove the demand was served personally or by registered mail; in *Bailey*, 2017 TCC 24, the CRA proved a demand to file for 2010 was sent by registered mail, so the penalty was upheld, while for 2012, there was insufficient proof of mailing procedures, so 162(1) applied instead.

Information Circulars: 00-1R4: Voluntary disclosures program; 07-1R1: Taxpayer relief provisions.

CRA Audit Manual: 28.2.2: Late filing of income tax return.

(2.1) Failure to file — non-resident corporation — Notwithstanding subsections (1) and (2), if a non-resident corporation is liable to a penalty under subsection (1) or (2) for failure to file a return of income for a taxation year, the amount of the penalty is the greater of

(a) the amount computed under subsection (1) or (2), as the case may be, and

(b) an amount equal to the greater of

(i) $100, and

(ii) $25 times the number of days, not exceeding 100, from the day on which the return was required to be filed to the day on which the return is filed.

Related Provisions: 150(1)(a)(i), (ii) — Obligation on non-resident to file return.

Notes: If no penalty is payable under 162(1)-(2), the 162(2.1) penalty does not apply: *Exida.com*, 2010 FCA 159 (reversing the TCC [and VIEWS doc 2006-0195531E5] on this point and agreeing with *Goar*, 2009 TCC 174). However, a parallel penalty under 162(7)(b) applies instead. In *Cogesco Services*, 2013 FC 1238, the CRA refused to waive a 162(2.1) penalty, citing this case law and saying that 162(7) imposed the same amount of penalty. The Court ordered the CRA to reconsider its decision, as the decision did not respond to the request.

The Non-Resident Operations Division has confirmed an administrative policy of not applying the 162(2.1) penalty to first-time filers claiming treaty-based exemptions: 5(1) *Toronto West Tax Practitioners Consultation Group Newsletter* (Jan. 2004), p. 4. This "one chance" policy has not yet been withdrawn despite being withdrawn for various other penalties (see Notes to 162(10)), because it was published.

162(2.1) added by 1998 Budget, effective for taxation years that begin after 1998.

(3) Failure to file by trustee — Every person who fails to file a return as required by subsection 150(3) is liable to a penalty of $10 for each day of default but not exceeding $50.

Related Provisions: See Related Provisions at end of s. 162.

Notes: See Notes to 239(1).

Information Circulars: 00-1R4: Voluntary disclosures program; 07-1R1: Taxpayer relief provisions.

(4) Ownership certificate — Every person who

(a) fails to complete an ownership certificate as required by section 234,

(b) fails to deliver an ownership certificate in the manner prescribed at the time prescribed and at the place prescribed by regulations made under that section, or

(c) cashes a coupon or warrant for which an ownership certificate has not been completed pursuant to that section,

is liable to a penalty of $50.

Related Provisions: See Related Provisions at end of s. 162.

Notes: See Notes to 239(1).

Information Circulars: 00-1R4: Voluntary disclosures program; 07-1R1: Taxpayer relief provisions.

(5) Failure to provide information on form — Every person who fails to provide any information required on a prescribed form made under this Act or a regulation is liable to a penalty of $100 for each such failure, unless

(a) in the case of information required in respect of another person or partnership, a reasonable effort was made by the person to obtain the information from the other person or partnership; or

(b) in the case of a failure to provide a Social Insurance Number on a return of income, the person had applied for the assignment of the Number and had not received it at the time the return was filed.

Related Provisions: 162(8.1) — Where partnership liable to penalty. See also at end of s. 162.

Notes: See Notes to 239(1) on penalties vs. criminal punishment.

If a form is substantially incomplete, it may be considered invalid and a 162(7) penalty imposed instead or as well: see Notes to 162(7).

162(5)(a) amended by 1995-97 technical bill to add references to a partnership, effective June 18, 1998. 162(5) earlier amended by 1991 technical bill.

Information Circulars: 82-2R2: SIN legislation that relates to the preparation of information slips; 00-1R4: Voluntary disclosures program.

Registered Plans Compliance Bulletins: 6 (penalty will apply to pension adjustment on T4, PSPA on T215 and PAR on T10); 7 (application of penalties).

(5.1) Failure to provide [SR&ED] claim preparer information — Every person or partnership who makes, or participates in, assents to or acquiesces in the making of, a false statement or omission in respect of claim preparer information required to be included in an SR&ED form is jointly and severally, or solidarily, liable, together with any claim preparer of the form, to a penalty equal to $1,000.

Related Provisions: 37(11)(b) — Requirement to provide information on SR&ED claim form; 37(11.1) — Expenditures not disallowed due to failure to provide claim preparer information; 162(5.2) — Due-diligence defence; 162(5.3) — Definitions.

Notes: 162(5.1) added by 2013 budget bill #2, effective 2014.

(5.2) Due diligence — A claim preparer of an SR&ED form is not liable for a penalty under subsection (5.1) in respect of a false statement or omission if the claim preparer has exercised the degree of care, diligence and skill to prevent the making of the false statement or omission that a reasonably prudent person would have exercised in comparable circumstances.

Related Provisions: 162(5.3) — Definitions.

Notes: This due-diligence defence uses the same wording as 227.1(3), so the jurisprudence under 227.1(3) (and *Excise Tax Act* 323(3) — GST/HST) applies.

162(5.2) added by 2013 budget bill #2, effective 2014.

(5.3) Definitions — The following definitions apply in this subsection and subsections (5.1) and (5.2).

"**claim preparer**", of an SR&ED form, means a person or partnership who agrees to accept consideration to prepare, or assist in the preparation of, the form but does not include an employee who prepares, or assists in the preparation of, the form in the course of performing their duties of employment.

"**claim preparer information**" means prescribed information regarding

(a) the identity of the claim preparer, if any, of an SR&ED form, and

(b) the arrangement under which the claim preparer agrees to accept consideration in respect of the preparation of the form.

Notes: "Prescribed" is defined in 248(1), for information to be given on a form, as "authorized by the Minister", so this allows CRA to define what information triggers a penalty if not provided. The T661 Q&A q. 1 (tinyurl.com/qa-t661) says the following must be included: name and business number of claim preparer; billing arrangement code (list of codes is provided); billing rate (percentage, hourly/daily rate or flat fee); other billing arrangements; total fee paid, payable or expected to be paid. If a claim preparer has concerns about the confidentiality of the information requested in Part 9 (fees), Part 9 can be filed separately.

"**SR&ED form**" means a prescribed form required to be filed under subsection 37(11).

Notes: 162(5.3) added by 2013 budget bill #2, effective 2014.

Forms: T661: SR&ED expenditures claim.

(6) Failure to provide identification number — Every person or partnership who fails to provide on request their business number, their Social Insurance Number, their trust account number or their U.S. federal taxpayer identifying number to a person required under this Act or the Regulations to make an information return requiring the number is liable to a penalty of $100 for each such failure, unless

(a) an application for the assignment of the number is made within 15 days (or, in the case of a U.S. federal taxpayer identifying number, 90 days) after the request was received; and

(b) the number is provided to the person who requested the number within 15 days after the person or partnership received it.

Related Provisions: 162(8.1) — Where partnership liable to penalty; 237(1), (1.1), (2) — Obligation to apply for and provide Social Insurance Number on information return; *Interpretation Act* 27(5) — Meaning of "within 15 days". See additional Related Provisions at end of s. 162.

Notes: See Notes to 239(1) (re penalties vs offences) and to 248(1)"business number".

162(6) opening words amended by 2018 budget bill #1, for 2018 and later tax years, to refer to a trust account number.

162(6) amended by 2014 budget bill #1, effective June 27, 2014, to apply to a U.S. federal taxpayer identifying number (see Notes to 269). Earlier amended by 1995-97 technical bill (to apply to a business number), 1991 technical bill.

Information Circulars: 82-2R2: SIN legislation that relates to the preparation of information slips; 00-1R4: Voluntary disclosures program.

(7) Failure to comply — Every person (other than a registered charity) or partnership who fails

(a) to file an information return as and when required by this Act or the regulations, or

(b) to comply with a duty or obligation imposed by this Act or the regulations

is liable in respect of each such failure, except where another provision of this Act (other than subsection (10) or (10.1) or 163(2.22)) sets out a penalty for the failure, to a penalty equal to the greater of $100 and the product obtained when $25 is multiplied by the number of days, not exceeding 100, during which the failure continues.

Related Provisions: 149(4.1), 188 — Revocation of registration and penalty tax for registered charity; 162(7.01), (7.02) — Penalty for failure to file information return correctly; 162(7.2) — Penalty for failure to file corporate return electronically; 162(8.1) — Where partnership liable to penalty; 188.1 — Penalties for registered charities (reducible under 189(6.3)); 237.1(7.5) — Penalty for promoter's failure to file tax shelter information return after demand; Reg. 205.1(1) — Forms of which more than 50 must be filed by Internet. See also at end of s. 162.

Notes: When reading a VIEWS doc or article in French about 162(7), note that in French it is all one subsection, with no paras. (a) and (b).

Once 100 days have passed, the 162(7) penalty is $2,500. See Notes to 162(10) re the onus of proof for penalties. See end of Notes to 163(1) for articles about penalties.

Diligence: This penalty is subject to a due-diligence defence (see Notes to 162(1)): VIEWS doc 2009-0335321E5. No due diligence was found in *Samson*, 2016 TCC 115; *Apex City Homes*, 2018 TCC 247 (ACH chose to disagree with CRA position that Reg. 238 applied to a business that hired a contractor to build condos it sold).

Unfairness: In *Lipson*, 2012 TCC 20, the TCC had harsh words for CRA assessing a $19,000 penalty for failing to send a s. 116 notice where no tax was payable (the Court also held the notice was not required). VIEWS doc 2013-0498121I7 suggests the penalty should be waived if there was no gain. In *Hok Ltd.*, [2012] UKUT 363, the UK tax authority failed to notify HL of a filing obligation for 4 months so a £500 penalty applied. The Upper Tribunal ruled the First-Tier Tribunal had no jurisdiction to cancel the penalty on the basis of disproportionality or unfairness. See also Notes to 163(1) for cases mostly upholding disproportionate penalties.

Incomplete forms: If information is missing from a form (or return), a 162(5) penalty may apply, but if what is missing is "substantial", the form may be invalid and a 162(7) or 162(1) penalty imposed instead: VIEWS docs 2012-045840I7, 2014-051970117; or *both* 162(5) and (7) may apply if the form is both incomplete and late: 2019-0791541I7 (but care should be taken to ensure a double penalty is "appropriate" and "equitable"). CRA will not penalize taxpayers who make "reasonable estimates based on the best available information": 2015-0595461E5, 162(5)(a).

162(7)(a) applies only to an information return, not a return of income. It applies to failure to file a T1134, T1135 or other foreign property forms; see Notes to 162(10), 233.1(2), 233.3(3) and 233.4(4). On the interaction of 162(7), (10) and (10.1) re foreign asset reporting, see 2013-049723117 (the total of these penalties cannot exceed the largest penalty).

CRA policy is not to apply 162(7)(a) to a non-profit organization's first late T1044 (149(12)): doc 2007-0243291C6. In *7547978 Canada*, 2015 TCC 112, it applied to an employer that filed T4As instead of T4s for workers it wrongly thought were independent contractors.

162(7)(a) does not apply where 162(7.01) or (7.02) applies, due to the words "except where another provision ...": VIEWS docs 2009-034405117, 2010-038976117; nor to a partnership information return required under Reg. 229, since 162(7.1) applies.

Can 162(7) apply to a T3 trust return, which is also an information return? It should not, since the T3 is a return of income, for which 162(1) already provides a different penalty. However, if the 162(1) penalty is $0 because no tax is owing on a late-filed T3, the answer is unclear. The author has asked CRA Rulings (May 2021) for an interpretation: the anwer will be in doc 2021-0895261E5.

Time limit: The penalty (including for an unfiled T1134 or T1135) must be assessed within the 152(4) reassessment period: VIEWS docs 2013-049723117, 2014-053770117, 2015-057277117, 2016-0645001C6 (the 152(4)(a)(i) exception still applies); 2017-0708511C6 [2017 APFF q.14] (CRA says it must apply the penalty automatically and cannot waive it under 220(3.1) for more than 10 years back); and see *RAR Consultants*, 2017 TCC 214, paras. 22-25. 152(4)(b.2) extends the reassessment period if there is unreported foreign income. For the deadline for assessing a partnership under 162(7), see 2011-039736117.

Tax returns: 162(7)(b) applies to a non-resident's failure to file a tax return on which no tax is owing, since no other penalty is payable due to 162(2.1) being badly drafted: *Exida.com*, 2010 FCA 159. Despite *Exida*, CRA does not apply 162(7) to resident corporations' tax returns: VIEWS doc 2010-0386341C6 [2010 CTF q.4], 2017-0708971C6 [2017 APFF q.1]; Jin Wen, "Late-Filing Penalties Without Unpaid Tax", 5(4) *Canadian Tax Focus* (ctf.ca) 6-7 (Nov. 2015).

Disposing of TCP: 162(7)(b) applies to a non-resident's failure to report a disposition of taxable Canadian property under 116(3): *Serge Côté Family Trust*, 2009 FC 69, and *Suissa*, 2013 FC 897. See also under "Unfairness" above.

162(7) amended by 1996 Budget, 1993 technical bill.

Information Circulars: 89-4: Tax shelter reporting; 00-1R4: Voluntary disclosures program; 07-1R1: Taxpayer relief provisions.

Registered Plans Compliance Bulletins: 3 (penalties); 6 (penalty will apply to PSPA on Form T215 and PAR on T10, and to failure to file T1007 or T244); 7 (application of penalties); 8 (prescribed information to register an education savings plan).

Registered Plans Directorate Newsletters: 16-2 (RPP annual information return).

CRA Audit Manual: 15.7.5: Foreign reporting requirements — penalties.

(7.01) Late filing penalty — prescribed information returns — Every person (other than a registered charity) or partnership who fails to file, when required by this Act or the regulations, one or more information returns of a type prescribed for the purpose of this subsection is liable to a penalty equal to the greater of $100 and

(a) where the number of those information returns is less than 51, $10 multiplied by the number of days, not exceeding 100, during which the failure continues;

(b) where the number of those information returns is greater than 50 and less than 501, $15 multiplied by the number of days, not exceeding 100, during which the failure continues;

(c) where the number of those information returns is greater than 500 and less than 2,501, $25 multiplied by the number of days, not exceeding 100, during which the failure continues;

(d) where the number of those information returns is greater than 2,500 and less than 10,001, $50 multiplied by the number of days, not exceeding 100, during which the failure continues; and

(e) where the number of those information returns is greater than 10,000, $75 multiplied by the number of days, not exceeding 100, during which the failure continues.

Related Provisions: 162(8.1) — Where partnership liable to penalty. See also at end of 162.

Notes: For the forms this penalty applies to (instead of the higher 162(7) penalty), see Reg. 205(3). "Each slip is an information return": tinyurl.com/cra-late. CRA's view is that "the number of those information returns" refers to the "type" in the opening words, so if there are 40 late T4As and 40 late T5s, that is only 40 of each type and para. (a) applies (VIEWS doc 2013-0515121E5, addressed to the author).

CRA says "the failure continues" until all slips are filed, so if 73 T5s are filed 8 days late and 1 is filed 56 days late, para. (b) applies and the penalty is $15 × 56: doc 2018-074844117 (this might not be correct).

For CRA administrative reduction in the penalty for the NR4, T4, T4A, T4E, T5 and T5018, see tinyurl.com/penalty-late.

In *7547978 Canada*, 2015 TCC 112, penalty under 162(7) rather than (7.01) applied to failure to file T4s.

This penalty can apply cumulatively with that under 162(7.02) but not 162(7): VIEWS doc 2010-038976I7. If a 162(7.01) penalty is assessed and 3-4 years have run, no further penalty under 162(7.01) or (7.02) can be assessed due to 152(4): 2011-040385I17. See also 2009-034405I17.

162(7.01) added by 2009 budget bill #1, effective for returns required to be filed after 2009, but really effective 2012 based on Reg. 205(3). Failure to comply in earlier years falls under 162(7).

Regulations: 205(3) (list of prescribed information returns).

(7.02) Failure to file in appropriate manner [electronically] — prescribed information returns — Every person (other than a registered charity) or partnership who fails to file, in the manner required by the regulations, one or more information returns of a type prescribed for the purpose of this subsection is liable to a penalty equal to

(a) where the number of those information returns is greater than 50 and less than 251, $250;

(b) where the number of those information returns is greater than 250 and less than 501, $500;

(c) where the number of those information returns is greater than 500 and less than 2,501, $1,500;

(d) where the number of those information returns is greater than 2,500, $2,500; and

(e) in any other case, nil.

Related Provisions: 162(8.1) — Where partnership liable to penalty. See also at end of 162.

Notes: 162(7.02) requires electronic filing of certain information returns (listed in Reg. 205.1(1)) if more than 50 are required. CRA's view is that "the number of those information returns" refers to the "type" in the opening words, so if there are 150 paper T4As and 200 paper T5s, that is less than 251 of each type and para. (a) applies (VIEWS doc 2013-0515121E5, addressed to the author).

See also VIEWS doc 2009-034405I17. Interest applies on top of the penalty: 2010-038064I17. This penalty can apply cumulatively with that under 162(7.01) but not 162(7): 2010-038976I17. Once a 162(7.01) penalty has been assessed and 3-4 years have run, no penalty under 162(7.02) can be assessed due to 152(4): 2011-040385I17.

At approximately $1 per paper-filed information return, this penalty is really just a filing fee, though it is non-deductible (18(1)(t), 67.6).

162(7.02) added by 2009 budget bill #1, effective for returns due after 2013 (technically after 2009, but Reg. 205.1(1) is effective only for returns due after 2013). Earlier failure to comply falls under 162(7).

Regulations: 205.1(1) (prescribed information returns).

(7.1) Failure to make partnership information return — Where a member of a partnership fails to file an information return as a member of the partnership for a fiscal period of the partnership as and when required by this Act or the regulations and subsection (10) does not set out a penalty for the failure, the partnership is liable to a penalty equal to the greater of $100 and the product obtained when $25 is multiplied by the number of days, not exceeding 100, during which the failure continues.

Related Provisions: 96(1) — Taxation of partnership; 162(8.1) — Rules where partnership is liable to penalty; Reg. 205.1(1) — Forms of which more than 50 must be filed by Internet. See also at end of s. 162.

Notes: See Notes to 239(1) on assessed penalties vs offences.

For the deadline for assessing a partnership a 162(7.1) penalty, see VIEWS doc 2011-039736I17.

162(7.1) amended by 1996 Budget (for returns required to be filed in 1998 or later); added by 1991 technical bill.

(7.2) Failure to file in appropriate manner [electronically] — [corporate] return of income — Every person who fails to file a return of income for a taxation year as required by subsection 150.1(2.1) is liable to a penalty equal to $1,000.

Related Provisions: See at end of 162.

Notes: This is the penalty for not filing corporate tax returns electronically, for corporations with gross revenue over $1 million. It might be considered a $1,000 filing fee for filing on paper, though it is non-deductible (18(1)(t), 67.6).

The penalty applied in *Kokanee Placer*, 2016 TCC 63, despite the corp having no tax payable for the year and despite a claim that it had mistakenly reported gross revenue exceeding $1m. (A due-diligence defence exists but there was no due diligence.)

162(7.2) is worded "fails to file ... as required by subsection 150.1(2.1)". This applies to a corporation that files on paper when required to file electronically. Although the wording could cover a *lack* of filing, the CRA will not apply this penalty to an unfiled or late return: VIEWS doc 2012-0445451E5.

162(7.2) added by 2009 budget bill #1, effective for taxation years that end after 2010 except that, in its application to the 2011 and 2012 taxation years, read "$1,000" as "$250" for the 2011 taxation year, and "$500" for the 2012 taxation year.

(7.3) Failure to file in appropriate manner [electronically] — tax preparer — Every tax preparer who fails to file a return of income as required by subsection 150.1(2.3) is liable to a penalty equal to

(a) $25 for each such failure in respect of a return of an individual; and

(b) $100 for each such failure in respect of a return of a corporation.

Proposed Amendment — 162(7.3) — 10-return threshold lowered to 5 returns

Federal Budget, Supplementary Information, April 19, 2021: See under 244(14.1), under heading "Tax Preparers".

Related Provisions: 150.1(2.2) — Definition of "tax preparer"; 162(5.1)-(5.3) — Penalty for not providing details regarding SR&ED claim preparer fees; 162(8.1) — Where partnership liable to penalty. See also at end of 162.

Notes: For a tax preparer who prefers paper filing (e.g., to prevent wasted time dealing with CRA requests for supporting documents by filing them with the return), this penalty is just a filing fee, though it is non-deductible (18(1)(t), 67.6). Such a preparer can avoid the penalty by becoming ineligible to e-File (see criteria in Notes to 150.1), in which case no penalty applies: 150.1(2.4)(a). See also 2017 CPA Alberta (tiny-url.com/cra-abtax), q. 8, denying a due-diligence defence if the preparer could not E-file because no T183 was signed.

If the taxpayer rather than the tax preparer files the return on paper, the penalty still applies: VIEWS doc 2012-0445451E5. If the return is *never* filed, CRA will apparently not apply the penalty (same doc).

162(7.3) added by 2012 budget bill #1, effective 2013.

(8) Repeated failure to file — Where

(a) a penalty was payable under subsection (7.1) in respect of a failure by a member of a partnership to file an information return as a member of the partnership for a fiscal period of the partnership,

(b) a demand for the return or for information required to be contained in the return has been served under section 233 on the member, and

(c) a penalty was payable under subsection (7.1) in respect of the failure by a member of a partnership to file an information return as a member of the partnership for any of the 3 preceding fiscal periods,

the partnership is liable, in addition to the penalty under subsection (7.1), to a penalty of $100 for each member of the partnership for each month or part of a month, not exceeding 24 months, during which the failure referred to in paragraph (a) continues.

Related Provisions: 162(8.1) — Rules where partnership is liable to penalty. See also at end of s. 162.

(8.1) Rules — partnership liable to a penalty — If a partnership is liable to a penalty under any of subsections (5) to (7.1), (7.3), (8) and (10), then sections 152, 158 to 160.1, 161 and 164 to 167 and Division J apply, with any modifications that the circumstances require, to the penalty as if the partnership were a corporation.

Notes: 162(8.1) is needed because a partnership is not a "person" as defined in 248(1) and could not otherwise be assessed a penalty. See 96(1)(a).

162(8.1) extended to apply to 162(7.01), (7.02) and (7.3) by 2012 budget bill #1, effective 2013 (by changing "under subsection (5), (6), (7), (7.1), (8) or (10)" to "under any of subsections (5) to (7.1), (7.3), (8) and (10)").

162(8.1) amended by 1995-97 technical bill (effective for returns required to be filed after 1997) and 1996 Budget; added by 1991 technical bill.

(9) [Repealed]

Notes: 162(9) repealed by 1995-97 technical bill, effective Dec. 2, 1994. It was replaced by a penalty in 237.1(7.4), relating to tax shelter identification numbers. See Notes to 237.1(7.4).

(10) Failure to furnish foreign-based information — Every person or partnership who,

(a) knowingly or under circumstances amounting to gross negligence, fails to file an information return as and when required by any of sections 233.1 to 233.4 and 233.8, or

(b) where paragraph (a) does not apply, knowingly or under circumstances amounting to gross negligence, fails to comply with a demand under section 233 to file a return

is liable to a penalty equal to the amount determined by the formula

$$(\$500 \times A \times B) - C$$

where

A is

(c) where paragraph (a) applies, the lesser of 24 and the number of months, beginning with the month in which the return was required to be filed, during any part of which the return has not been filed, and

(d) where paragraph (b) applies, the lesser of 24 and the number of months, beginning with the month in which the demand was served, during any part of which the return has not been filed,

B is

(e) where the person or partnership has failed to comply with a demand under section 233 to file a return, 2, and

(f) in any other case, 1, and

C is the penalty to which the person or partnership is liable under subsection (7) in respect of the return.

Related Provisions: 162(7) — Initial calculation of penalty; 162(8.1) — Where partnership liable to penalty; 162(10.1) — Additional penalty; 163(2.4)–(2.91) — Penalty for false statement or omission in return; 233.2(4.1) — Foreign arrangements similar to trusts; 233.5 — Due diligence defence; 257 — Formula cannot calculate to less than zero. See also at end of s. 162.

Notes: The onus of proof for a 163(2) gross-negligence penalty is on the Crown, per 163(3). Arguably this also applies to 162(10), and perhaps to any penalty: see *Alex Excavating*, [1995] G.S.T.C. 57 (TCC), para. 64 (163(3) rule applied to GST without being enacted); *Weisz, Rocchi*, 2001 TCC 821, para. 16 (any penalty puts the onus on the Crown).

CRA had an administrative "one chance" policy to not apply a 162(7) or 162(10) penalty to a taxpayer's first late voluntary filing of a foreign property form T106, T1134, T1135, T1141 or T1142 (233.1–233.6): VIEWS doc 2004-0086681C6. This policy was withdrawn in Jan. 2006; the taxpayer must apply via the Voluntary Disclosure Program for relief from the penalty: 2006-0185642C6, 2007-0243291C6; *Leclerc*, 2010 TCC 99.

This penalty can be assessed past the normal reassessment period, due to 152(4)(a)(i): VIEWS docs 2013-0497231I7, 2014-0537701I7.

See also Notes to 162(7).

162(10)(a) amended to add reference to 233.8 by 2016 budget bill #2, effective Dec. 15, 2016.

162(10) amended by 1996 Budget, effective for returns required to be filed by April 30, 1998 or later.

CRA Audit Manual: 15.7.5: Foreign reporting requirements — penalties.

(10.1) Additional penalty — Where

(a) a person or partnership is liable to a penalty under subsection (10) for the failure to file a return (other than an information return required to be filed under section 233.1),

(b) if paragraph (10)(a) applies, the number of months, beginning with the month in which the return was required to be filed, during any part of which the return has not been filed exceeds 24, and

(c) if paragraph (10)(b) applies, the number of months, beginning with the month in which the demand referred to in that paragraph was served, during any part of which the return has not been filed exceeds 24,

the person or partnership is liable, in addition to the penalty determined under subsection (10), to a penalty equal to the amount determined by the formula

$$A - B$$

where

A is

(d) if the return is required to be filed under section 233.2 in respect of a trust, 5% of the total of all amounts each of which is the fair market value, at the time it was made, of a contribution of the person or partnership made to the trust before the end of the last taxation year of the trust in respect of which the return is required,

(e) where the return is required to be filed under section 233.3 for a taxation year or fiscal period, 5% of the greatest of all amounts each of which is the total of the cost amounts to the person or partnership at any time in the year or period of a specified foreign property (as defined by subsection 233.3(1)) of the person or partnership, and

(f) where the return is required to be filed under section 233.4 for a taxation year or fiscal period in respect of a foreign affiliate of the person or partnership, 5% of the greatest of all amounts each of which is the total of the cost amounts to the person or partnership at any time in the year or period of a property of the person or partnership that is a share of the capital stock or indebtedness of the affiliate, and

B is the total of the penalties to which the person or partnership is liable under subsections (7) and (10) in respect of the return.

Related Provisions: 162(7) — Initial calculation of penalty; 162(10.11) — Application to trust contribution; 162(10.2) — Shares or debt owned by controlled foreign affiliate; 162(10.3) — Application to partnership; 162(10.4) — Application to non-resident trust; 163(2.4)–(2.91) — Penalty for false statement or omission in return; 233.2(4.1) — Foreign arrangements similar to trusts; 233.5 — Due diligence defence to penalty; 257 — Formula cannot calculate to less than zero.

Notes: See Notes to 162(7). This penalty can be assessed past the normal reassessment period, due to 152(4)(a)(i): VIEWS docs 2013-0497231I7, 2014-0537701I7. The calculation for (e) should use the one day in the year where the total is the highest, not total the highest cost of each property during the year: 2015-0590681I7.

162(10.1)A(d) amended by 2002-2013 technical bill (Part 1 — NRTs), effective for returns in respect of taxation years that end after 2006, and also for returns in respect of an earlier taxation year of a taxpayer if amended 94(1) applies to that earlier taxation year (see Notes at end of s. 94).

162(10.1) added by 1996 Budget, effective for returns required to be filed by April 30, 1998 or later.

CRA Audit Manual: 15.7.5: Foreign reporting requirements — penalties.

(10.11) Application to trust contributions — In paragraph (d) of the description of A in subsection (10.1), subsections 94(1), (2) and (9) apply.

Notes: 162(10.11) added by 2002-2013 technical bill (Part 1 — NRTs), effective on the same basis as the amendment to 162(10.1)A(d).

(10.2) Shares or debt owned by controlled foreign affiliate — For the purpose of paragraph (f) of the description of A in subsection (10.1),

(a) shares or indebtedness owned by a controlled foreign affiliate of a person or partnership are deemed to be owned by the person or partnership; and

(b) the cost amount at any time of such shares or indebtedness to the person or partnership is deemed to be equal to 20% of the cost amount at that time to the controlled foreign affiliate of the shares or indebtedness.

Related Provisions: 162(10.3) — Application to partnerships; 162(10.4) — Application to non-resident trusts.

Notes: 162(10.2) added by 1996 Budget, effective for returns required to be filed by April 30, 1998 or later.

(10.3) Application to partnerships — For the purposes of paragraph (f) of the description of A in subsection (10.1) and subsection (10.2), in determining whether a non-resident corporation or trust is a foreign affiliate or a controlled foreign affiliate of a partnership,

(a) the definitions "direct equity percentage" and "equity percentage" in subsection 95(4) shall be read as if a partnership were a person; and

(b) the definitions "controlled foreign affiliate" and "foreign affiliate" in subsection 95(1) shall be read as if a partnership were a taxpayer resident in Canada.

Notes: The non-resident trusts draft legislation of 2000-09 had proposed to delete "or trust" from the opening words of 162(10.3) and 163(2.6) and to repeal 162(10.4) and 163(2.91), but these changes were dropped in 2010 (and from the eventual enactment by 2002-2013 technical bill (Part 1 — NRTs)), because some trusts are still treated as foreign affiliates by new 94.2, and thus references to trusts are still needed.

162(10.3) added by 1996 Budget, for returns required to be filed after April 29, 1998.

(10.4) Application to non-resident trusts — For the purposes of this subsection, paragraph (f) of the description of A in subsection (10.1) and subsection (10.2),

(a) a non-resident trust is deemed to be a controlled foreign affiliate of each beneficiary of which the trust is a controlled foreign affiliate for the purpose of section 233.4;

(b) the trust is deemed to be a non-resident corporation having a capital stock of a single class divided into 100 issued shares;

(c) each beneficiary under the trust is deemed to own at any time the number of the issued shares of the corporation that is equal to the proportion of 100 that

(i) the fair market value at that time of the beneficiary's beneficial interest in the trust

is of

(ii) the fair market value at that time of all beneficial interests in the trust; and

(d) the cost amount to a beneficiary at any time of a share of the corporation is deemed to be equal to the amount determined by the formula

$$\frac{A}{B}$$

where

A   is the fair market value at that time of the beneficiary's beneficial interest in the trust, and

B   is the number of shares deemed under paragraph (c) to be owned at that time by the beneficiary in respect of the corporation.

Notes: See Notes to 162(10.3).

162(10.4) added by 1996 Budget, effective for returns required to be filed by April 30, 1998 or later.

(11) Effect of subsequent events — For the purpose of computing a penalty under subsection (1) or (2) in respect of a person's return of income for a taxation year, the person's tax payable under this Part for the year shall be determined before taking into consideration the specified future tax consequences for the year.

Notes: 162(11) provides that, in computing penalties under 161(1)–(2), tax is determined without reference to deductions from later-year events such as loss carrybacks or unused foreign tax credits. It applied in *Zandi*, [2012] 6 C.T.C. 2062 (TCC).

162(11) amended by 1996 Budget (for 1996 and later taxation years), due to the new definition "specified future tax consequence" in 248(1). Added by 1991 technical bill, for carrybacks from taxation years ending after July 13, 1990.

A former 162(11), enacted in 1988 but never proclaimed in force and repealed in 1991, would have imposed a penalty for NSF cheques. See now 220(3.8).

CRA Audit Manual: 28.2.2: Late filing of income tax return.

Related Provisions [s. 162]: 18(1)(t), 67.6 — Penalties are non-deductible; 161(11) — Interest on penalty; 180.01(4), 180.2(6), 183(3), 183.2(2), 185.2(2), 187(3), 187.6, 189(8), 190.21, 191.4(2), 196(4), 202(3), 204.3(2), 204.7(3), 204.87, 204.93, 204.94(4), 207.07(3), 207.2(3), 207.4(2), 207.7(4), 207.8(5), 209(5), 210.2(7), 211.5, 211.6(5), 211.82, 211.91(3), 218.2(5), 218.3(10), 219(3), 247(11) — Provisions of s. 162 apply for purposes of Parts I.01, I.2, II, II.1, III.1, IV, IV.1, V, VI, VI.1, VII, VIII, IX, IX.1, X, X.1, X.2, X.3, X.4, X.5, XI, XI.01, XI.1, XI.2, XI.3, XI.4, XII.1, XII.2, XII.3, XII.4, XII.5, XII.6, XIII.1, XIII.2, XIV and XVI.1 respectively; 220(3.1) — Waiver or cancellation of penalty; 227(10.01), (10.1) — Provisions of s. 162 apply to withholding taxes under Parts XII.5 and XIII; 238(1), (3) — Offences; 239(3) — Penalty assessment cannot be issued after charge laid if person convicted.

Definitions [s. 162]: "amount", "business number" — 248(1); "claim preparer", "claim preparer information" — 162(5.3); "controlled foreign affiliate" — 95(1), 248(1); "corporation" — 162(10.4)(b), 248(1), *Interpretation Act* 35(1); "employee", "employment" — 248(1); "fair market value" — see 69(1) Notes; "fiscal period" — 249.1; "foreign affiliate" — 95(1), 162(10.3), 248(1); "individual", "Minister", "non-resident" — 248(1); "owned" — 162(10.2); "partnership" — see 96(1) Notes; "person", "prescribed", "property" — 248(1); "received" — 248(7); "registered charity", "regulation" — 248(1); "resident in Canada" — 250; "SR&ED form" — 162(5.3);

"specified foreign property" — 233.3(1); "specified future tax consequence" — 248(1); "tax preparer" — 150.1(2.2); "tax shelter" — 237.1(1), 248(1); "taxation year" — 249; "trust" — 104(1), 248(1), (3); "trust account number" — 248(1).

Information Circulars [s. 162]: 00-1R4: Voluntary disclosures program.

CRA Audit Manual [s. 162]: 28.0: Penalties.

163. (1) Repeated failure to report income — Every person is liable to a penalty who

(a) fails to report an amount, equal to or greater than $500, required to be included in computing the person's income in a return filed under section 150 for a taxation year (in this subsection and subsection (1.1) referred to as the "unreported amount");

(b) had failed to report an amount, equal to or greater than $500, required to be included in computing the person's income in any return filed under section 150 for any of the three preceding taxation years; and

(c) is not liable to a penalty under subsection (2) in respect of the unreported amount.

Related Provisions: 163(1.1) — Amount of penalty; 163(3) — Burden of proof. See also Related Provisions at end of s. 163.

Notes: See Notes to 239(1) on the difference between a penalty and a fine. This penalty applies to a taxpayer that fails to report an amount of income in two years out of any four.

This penalty has always been understood to apply to unreported *gross* revenue, but see Froh & Kessler, "Is the Omissions Penalty Based on Gross Income or Net Income?", 11(1) *Canadian Tax Focus* (ctf.ca) 8-9 (Feb. 2021).

The 10% penalty in 163(1.1)(a) is 20% if the CRA imposes a parallel 10% penalty under the provincial *Income Tax Act*, as it often does (in Ontario this is automatic per *Taxation Act, 2007* s. 113). The provincial portion cannot be appealed to the Tax Court of Canada: *Raboud*, 2009 TCC 99; *Norlock*, 2012 TCC 121; *Polubiec*, 2019 TCC 146, para. 15; but usually (e.g., in Ontario) the provincial penalty will be adjusted automatically to be consistent with the federal result. The TCC may recommend CRA cancel it: *Dunlop*, 2009 TCC 177.

The Crown has the onus of making a *prima facie* case that the income was earned: *Raboud*, 2009 TCC 99. Once that is done, 163(1) is a strict liability penalty, but a "due diligence" defence (see Notes to 162(1)) is available, and is accepted by the CRA: VIEWS docs 2010-035636I7, 2012-0462921C6 [2012 Ont. Tax Conf. Q13].

2015 and later: the penalty is much less harsh than before. First, it now applies only when each year's unreported amount was $500 or more. Second, while the penalty is still 10% of the unreported revenue (163(1.1)(a)), it is limited to 50% of the tax resulting from that income, minus any tax withheld on it (163(1.1)((b)B), and taking 163(2.1) into account (VIEWS doc 2018-078610I7). If enough tax was withheld, the penalty is nil.

These changes, announced in the 2015 Budget and enacted in 2016, were overdue and are very welcome. 2015 Budget Table A5.1 forecast that they will cost the federal government $10 million in each of 2016-17 through 2018-19 and $15m in 2019-20.

Since the changes, the penalty was upheld in *Greenstreet*, 2019 TCC 237.

For dividend income, the penalty applies to the 125% or 138% grossed-up dividend under 82(1): *Chan*, 2012 TCC 168, para. 14; *Tacilauskas*, 2012 TCC 288.

CRA interpretation: 163(1) applies only to amounts not reported in a filed return, not where no return was filed: VIEWS docs 2005-0133411I7, 2012-0462921C6 [2012 Ont. Tax Conf. q.13]. It does not apply to false expense claims: 2009-0328171I7. It applies where the reassessment to add income to an earlier year comes after the reassessment of the later year: 2009-034495117. It does not apply if a Form T1-Adj, increasing a past year's income, is filed before the CRA discovers the error and reassesses: May 2007 ICAA Roundtable (tinyurl.com/cra-abtax), Q29.

Even if the penalty is upheld by the Tax Court as legally correct and the due-diligence defence is rejected, CRA may still cancel it under Taxpayer Relief (220(3.1)), e.g. *Lemieux*, 2016 FC 798.

"If the income from a particular slip was overlooked or under reported and the slip is received after the tax return is filed, an adjustment request should be submitted in a timely manner. Under these circumstances, the CRA will generally not consider the original omission to be failure under subsection 163(1) as the taxpayer has made reasonable efforts to report the income. A failure to report income from an information slip would be detected in the Agency's Matching Program, for which the peak period is September to March. Therefore, even if a slip is received during the first or second week of April, this would still leave plenty of time for the taxpayer to make an adjustment request before the Matching Program begins in September. In this way, the original omission would not contribute to a 163(1) penalty." (ICABC/CRA Pacific Region meeting, Jan. 22, 2013, q.9) Note also that information slips are now available online when preparing the return, on canada.ca/my-cra-account or canada.ca/taxes-representatives.

Cases on the pre-2015 penalty, generally still relevant except as to penalty amount: 163(1) applied in: *Spence*, 2012 FCA 58 (taxpayer who engages a third party to prepare return remains responsible for its accuracy, even though $7,600 penalty was disproportionate to unpaid tax of $124); *Saunders*, 2006 TCC 51 (S failed to report RRSP withdrawal due to missing T5, and next year failed to report employment income due to not getting T4 and providing accountant only employment record); *Lestage Giguère*, 2005 TCC 201 (G failed to declare unrelated amounts in consecutive years due to husband's mistake in interpreting two almost identical T5s); *Paul*, 2008 TCC 159 (P did not check returns carefully after they were prepared by accountant); *Belliveau*, 2009 TCC 374 (FCA appeal dismissed for delay A-330-09) (failure to report 2005 employment income, and 2006 income for which no T4A received); *Smith*, 2009 FC 694 (failure to report 2003 investment income and 2006 severance pay); *Porter*, 2010 TCC 251 (not all T4 slips reported); *Ciobanu*, 2011 TCC 319 (no due diligence (**DD**)); *Mignault*, 2011 TCC 500 (RRSP withdrawal); *Knight*, 2012 TCC 118 (K failed to report substantial income on missing T4 slips); *Norlock*, 2012 TCC 121 (N did not take "all reasonable precautions" to report all income); *Chendrean*, 2012 TCC 205 (C received 2 T4s from same employer, reported only 1); *Tacilauskas*, 2012 TCC 288 (T did not take sufficient care to report private-company dividends); *Jack*, 2013 TCC 1 (J was reckless or careless about reporting all income); *Morgan*, 2013 TCC 232 (no DD in failing to report lump-sum pension income, even though tax withheld at source; but CRA later waived the penalty under Taxpayer Relief); *Strimaitis*, 2013 TCC 274 (no DD in failing to send one of three T4s to accountant); *Chiasson*, 2014 TCC 158 (no DD); *Dhanoa*, 2015 TCC 164 (D not credible: no DD); *Whissell*, 2016 TCC 133 (no DD); *Morrison*, 2018 FC 141 (FCA appeal dismissed for delay A-61-18) (M's accountant missed including a T4); *Polubiec*, 2019 TCC 146 (well-educated investor failed to report $700,000 of RRSP income from which tax was withheld plus two other items in 2014, after missing several items of income each year 2007-11: no DD; Court recommended waiver of penalty); *Zhang*, 2020 TCC 49 (not reporting kickback from realtor was mistake of law, not DD). Cases may be in the FC as applications for judicial review of CRA's failure to waive the penalty under Taxpayer Relief (see Notes to 220(3.1)).

163(1) did not apply because of taxpayer *due diligence* in: *Khalil [Khail]*, [2003] 1 C.T.C. 2263 (TCC) (K failed to report employment income on which source deductions had been taken, believing this meant the income need not be reported); *Iszcenko*, 2009 TCC 229 (Isz had failed to report $278 in investment income 3 years earlier, and thought $40,000 dividend from company was return of capital, relying on her deceased husband's father who told her he need not report it); *Dunlop*, 2009 TCC 177 (where T4 slip not received, D noted fact on return and stated it would be provided when available); *Thompson*, 2010 TCC 381 (T did not receive one T5 slip and had confirmed with investment manager that they had sent all slips); *Cooper*, 2010 TCC 403 (C had faxed the necessary information to H&R Block; Crown's failure to introduce the return in evidence led to a negative inference); *Paquette*, 2011 TCC 208 (P had learning difficulties and relied on his father to prepare returns; T4s had not been received, and tax had been withheld at source); *Franck*, 2011 TCC 179 (F thought CRA would complete his return since T4s had been filed; $7,000 penalty exceeded his tax for the year, which had already been withheld at source); *Symonds*, 2011 TCC 274 (amount of first failure to report was small; negative inference drawn from Crown's failure to introduce first return in evidence); *Chan*, 2012 TCC 168 (some tax slips had not been received by March 31 and the unreported income was only 1% of total income); *Morgan*, 2013 TCC 232 (due diligence in failing to report lump-sum pension withdrawal that was transferred directly to RRSP).

Most TCC judges say due diligence can be shown for either year of unreported income: *Franck*, 2011 TCC 179, para. 2; *Symonds*, 2011 TCC 274, para. 23; *Chan*, 2012 TCC 168, para. 21; *Norlock*, 2012 TCC 121; *Galachiuk*, 2014 TCC 188, paras. 8-10; *Greenstreet*, 2019 TCC 237, para. 25; *Zhang*, 2020 TCC 49, para. 34. Some judges say due diligence can only be in the later year: *Chendrean*, 2012 TCC 205, para. 13; *Chiasson*, 2014 TCC 158, para. 37; *Dhanoa*, 2015 TCC 164, para. 5. This question will have to be resolved by the FCA.

163(1) did not apply *on other grounds* in: *Villanueva*, 2009 TCC 86 (filing blank return with T4 slip constituted reporting employment income); *Raboud*, 2009 TCC 99 (mailing T4 slips to CRA constituted reporting the income); *Alcala*, 2010 TCC 198 (tax had been withheld at source, no T4 received, and prior year's amount was small yet triggered large penalty for later year).

Where a taxpayer had unreported amounts in 2006, 2007 and 2009, 163(1) applied to both 2007 and 2009: *Morgan*, 2013 TCC 232, para. 22.

Pre-2015 penalty:

The penalty for years beginning before 2015 is 10% (20% including the provincial penalty) of unreported revenue, even if tax was withheld at source so no tax was unpaid.

Pre-2015 163(1) was acknowledged by the Courts as "harsh" (*Sheppard*, 2011 TCC 407, para. 11) if the first failure to report income involved minimal or no unpaid tax, or if tax was withheld at source on the unreported income. The pre-2015 penalty plus provincial penalty (total 20% of unreported income) was higher in most cases than the 163(2) gross-negligence penalty (50% of the tax). Because of this, the Court recommended waiver of the penalty in *Knight*, 2012 TCC 118. (The unfairness was pointed out to Finance (2012 Ontario Tax Conf. Q13) and led to the amendments.) When appealing such a case, consider arguing that the taxpayer knowingly made a false statement so that 163(2) applies instead! (As long as that does not compromise the taxpayer's position on the penalty for 2015 and later years.)

CRA may waive the pre-2015 penalty under 220(3.1) if it is unfair: May 2008 ICAA Roundtable (tinyurl.com/cra-abtax) q. 40; but the usual Taxpayer Relief criteria apply even though the 163(1) penalty is harsh: May 2010 ICAA q. 5, doc 2012-0462921C6. The CRA refuses to consider reducing the penalty even when it is harsh and exceeds

the 163(2) penalty, claiming that whether it is "just and equitable" is up to Finance: May 2013 ICAA q.4. In the author's view, this is unreasonable, but since the penalty was amended only from 2015, the CRA's views on the pre-2015 penalty will be maintained: 2016 Alberta CPA (tinyurl.com/cra-abtax), q. 4.

For case law on the pre-2015 penalty see under the current penalty, above. Cases specific to the pre-2015 penalty: *Nixon*, 2008 FC 917 (unreasonable for CRA not to cancel penalty when taxpayer inadvertently missed $4,000 of income, then later failed to report $184,000 of dividend, leading to a $36,796 penalty [the CRA cancelled the penalty: see Notes to 220(3.1)]); *Sheppard*, 2011 TCC 407 ($837 unreported in 2005, $14,071 unreported in 2008 led to $1,407 penalty); *Perusco*, 2011 TCC 409 (163(1) does not violate the *Charter of Rights* even where penalty is higher than under 163(2)). See also Notes to 220(3.1) for judicial review of refusal to waive the penalty.

See also Karsan, "Subsection 163(1) Penalties", 12(3) *Tax for the Owner-Manager* (ctf.ca) 8-9 (July 2012); Burbank et al., "Comprehensive Discussion on Penalties", 2013 Prairie Provinces Tax Conference (ctf.ca), 9:1-40; Sorensen et al., "Non-Criminal Penalties Under the *Income Tax Act*", 2013 Ontario Tax Conf. 12:1-50.

163(1) amended and 163(1.1) added by 2016 budget bill #1, for tax years that begin after 2014. For earlier years, read:

> (1) Every person who
>
> (a) fails to report an amount required to be included in computing the person's income in a return filed under section 150 for a taxation year, and
>
> (b) had failed to report an amount required to be so included in any return filed under section 150 for any of the three preceding taxation years
>
> is liable to a penalty equal to 10% of the amount described in paragraph (a), except where the person is liable to a penalty under subsection (2) in respect of that amount.

Information Circulars: 73-10R3: Tax evasion; 00-1R4: Voluntary disclosures program.

CRA Audit Manual: 28.3.0: Repeated failures — subsection 163(1) ITA.

(1.1) Amount of penalty — The amount of the penalty to which the person is liable under subsection (1) is equal to the lesser of

(a) 10% of the unreported amount, and

(b) the amount determined by the formula

$$0.5 \times (A - B)$$

where

A is the total of the amounts that would be determined under paragraphs (2)(a) to (g) if subsection (2) applied in respect of the unreported amount, and

B is any amount deducted or withheld under subsection 153(1) that may reasonably be considered to be in respect of the unreported amount.

Related Provisions: 257 — Formula cannot calculate to less than zero.

Notes: See Notes to 163(1).

(2) False statements or omissions — Every person who, knowingly, or under circumstances amounting to gross negligence, has made or has participated in, assented to or acquiesced in the making of, a false statement or omission in a return, form, certificate, statement or answer (in this section referred to as a "return") filed or made in respect of a taxation year for the purposes of this Act, is liable to a penalty of the greater of $100 and 50% of the total of

(a) the amount, if any, by which

(i) the amount, if any, by which

(A) the tax for the year that would be payable by the person under this Act

exceeds

(B) the amounts that would be deemed by subsections 120(2) and (2.2) to have been paid on account of the person's tax for the year

if the person's taxable income for the year were computed by adding to the taxable income reported by the person in the person's return for the year that portion of the person's understatement of income for the year that is reasonably attributable to the false statement or omission and if the person's tax payable for the year were computed by subtracting from the deductions from the tax otherwise payable by the person for the year such portion of any such deduction as may reasonably be attributable to the false statement or omission

exceeds

(ii) the amount, if any, by which

(A) the tax for the year that would have been payable by the person under this Act

exceeds

(B) the amounts that would be deemed by subsections 120(2) and (2.2) to have been paid on account of the person's tax for the year

had the person's tax payable for the year been assessed on the basis of the information provided in the person's return for the year,

(b) [Repealed]

(c) the total of all amounts each of which is the amount, if any, by which

(i) the amount that would be deemed by subsection 122.61(1) to be an overpayment on account of the person's liability under this Part for the year that arose during a particular month or, where that person is a cohabiting spouse or common-law partner (within the meaning assigned by section 122.6) of an individual at the end of the year and at the beginning of the particular month, of that individual's liability under this Part for the year that arose during the particular month, as the case may be, if that total were calculated by reference to the information provided

exceeds

(ii) the amount that is deemed by subsection 122.61(1) to be an overpayment on account of the liability of that person or that individual, as the case may be, under this Part for the year that arose during the particular month,

(c.1) the amount, if any, by which

(i) the total of all amounts each of which is an amount that would be deemed by section 122.5 to be paid by that person during a month specified for the year or, where that person is the qualified relation of an individual in relation to that specified month (within the meaning assigned by subsection 122.5(1)), by that individual, if that total were calculated by reference to the information provided in the person's return of income (within the meaning assigned by subsection 122.5(1)) for the year

exceeds

(ii) the total of all amounts each of which is an amount that is deemed by section 122.5 to be paid by that person or by an individual of whom the person is the qualified relation in relation to a month specified for the year (within the meaning assigned to subsection 122.5(1)),

(c.2) the amount, if any, by which

(i) the amount that would be deemed under subsection 122.51(2) to be paid on account of the person's tax payable under this Part for the year if the amount were calculated by reference to the information provided in the return

exceeds

(ii) the amount that is deemed under subsection 122.51(2) to be paid on account of the person's tax payable under this Part for the year,

(c.3) the amount, if any, by which

(i) the total of all amounts each of which is an amount that would be deemed by subsection 122.7(2) or (3) to be a payment on account of the person's tax payable under this Part or another person's tax payable under this Part for the year if those amounts were calculated by reference to the information provided in the return

exceeds

(ii) the total of all amounts each of which is an amount that is deemed by subsection 122.7(2) or (3) to be a payment on account of the person's tax payable under this Part and, where applicable, the other person's tax payable under this Part for the year,

(c.4) the amount, if any, by which

(i) the total of all amounts each of which is an amount that would be deemed by section 122.8 to be paid by that person for the year or, where that person is the "qualified relation" of an individual for that year (within the meaning assigned by subsection 122.8(1)), by that individual, if that total were calculated by reference to the information provided in the person's "return of income" (within the meaning assigned by subsection 122.8(1)) for the year

exceeds

(ii) the total of all amounts each of which is an amount that is deemed by section 122.8 to be paid by that person or by an individual of whom the person is the "qualified relation" for the year (within the meaning assigned by subsection 122.8(1)),

(c.5) the amount, if any, by which

(i) the total of all amounts each of which is an amount that would be deemed by subsection 122.9(2) to have been paid on account of the person's tax payable under this Part for the year if that amount were calculated by reference to the person's claim for the year under the subsection

exceeds

(ii) the total of all amounts each of which is the amount that the person is entitled to claim for the year under subsection 122.9(2),

(c.6) the amount, if any, by which

(i) the total of all amounts each of which is an amount that would be deemed by subsection 122.91(1) to have been paid on account of the person's tax payable under this Part for the year if those amounts were calculated by reference to the information provided in the return

exceeds

(ii) the total of all amounts each of which is an amount that is deemed by subsection 122.91(1) to be a payment on account of the person's tax payable under this Part for the taxation year,

(d) the amount, if any, by which

(i) the amount that would be deemed by subsection 127.1(1) to be paid for the year by the person if that amount were calculated by reference to the information provided in the return or form filed for the year pursuant to that subsection

exceeds

(ii) the amount that is deemed by that subsection to be paid for the year by the person,

(e) the amount, if any, by which

(i) the amount that would be deemed by subsection 127.41(3) to have been paid for the year by the person if that amount were calculated by reference to the person's claim for the year under that subsection

exceeds

(ii) the maximum amount that the person is entitled to claim for the year under subsection 127.41(3),

(f) the amount, if any, by which

(i) the amount that would be deemed by subsection 125.4(3) to have been paid for the year by the person if that amount were calculated by reference to the information provided in the return filed for the year pursuant to that subsection

exceeds

(ii) the amount that is deemed by that subsection to be paid for the year by the person,

(g) the amount, if any, by which

(i) the amount that would be deemed by subsection 125.5(3) to have been paid for the year by the person if that amount were calculated by reference to the information provided in the return filed for the year pursuant to that subsection

exceeds

(ii) the amount that is deemed by that subsection to be paid for the year by the person,

(h) the amount, if any, by which

(i) the amount that would be deemed by subsection 125.6(2) or (2.1) to have been paid for the year by the person if that amount were calculated by reference to the information provided in the return filed for the year pursuant to that subsection

exceeds

(ii) the amount that is deemed by that subsection to be paid for the year by the person, and

(i) the amount, if any, by which

(i) the amount that would be deemed by any of subsections 125.7(2) to (2.2) to have been an overpayment by the person or partnership if that amount were calculated by reference to the information provided in the application filed pursuant to paragraph (a) of the definition "qualifying entity" in subsection 125.7(1), paragraph (a) of the definition "qualifying renter" in subsection 125.7(1) or paragraph (a) of the definition "qualifying recovery entity" in subsection 125.7(1), as the case may be

exceeds

(ii) the amount that is deemed by that subsection to be an overpayment by the person or partnership.

Related Provisions: 94(3)(a)(vii) — Application to trust deemed resident in Canada; 163(2.1) — Interpretation; 163(2.901) — Penalty for manipulating COVID-19 wage subsidy (separate from 163(2)(i) for misrepresentation); 163(3) — Burden of proof; 163.2 — Penalty for acts of a third party; 163.2(15)(b) — Conduct of employee deemed to be conduct of employer; 163.3 — Penalty for using, owning, making or selling zapper software; 239(1) — Offence — false statements. See also Related Provisions at end of s. 163.

Notes: See Notes to 239(1) on the difference between an administrative penalty (such as 163(2)) and criminal prosecution for an offence.

Timing: "Whether or not there is misrepresentation through neglect or carelessness in the completion of a return is determinable at the time the return is filed": *Nesbitt*, 1996 CarswellNat 1916 (FCA), para. 8. The same rule should apply to a 163(2) penalty, and there is no obligation in the ITA to correct a past error (see Notes to 239(1) under "There is no obligation"), so deliberately failing to correct an inadvertent error (that was not gross negligence when made and is discovered later) should not give rise to the penalty. Similarly, "a 2003 misrepresentation on a return cannot reopen a 2001 tax return": *Ross*, 2013 TCC 333, para. 53. However, conduct during the audit can be an indicator of the taxpayer's mindset at time of filing: *Mullen*, 2013 FCA 101, para. 7; *Gray*, 2016 TCC 54, para. 38(h).

No return filed: No 163(2) penalty applies to failing to report income by not filing, since no false statement or omission was made *on a return*: *Lee*, 2010 TCC 400, para. 61; *Calandra*, 2011 TCC 7, para. 20; *Khan*, 2011 TCC 481, para. 16; *Last*, 2012 TCC 352, para. 127 (aff'd on other grounds 2014 FCA 129). However, penalties can apply to related false statements, e.g., "they provided false information to the Minister to cause the partnership to be deregistered for GST" (*Kion*, 2009 TCC 447, para. 12).

Kinds of statement: 163(2) does not apply to an oral statement, as "answer" in 163(2) opening words means a written answer: VIEWS doc 2011-0421151E5; or to false statements made to an auditor (when requesting additional expenses that were false): 2010-035651117. The penalty applied to a false claim in a T1-Adj seeking adjustment to past years' returns to generate refunds, even though the refunds were never paid: *Morton*, 2014 CarswellNat 590 (TCC).

Onus: The onus of proof of a 163(2) penalty is on the Crown (163(3)) and is a "heavy" burden: *Corriveau*, [1999] 2 C.T.C. 2580 (TCC). If the Crown does not plead facts sufficient to justify the penalty, it will be cancelled: *Lubega-Matovu*, 2011 FCA 265. Because of the onus, an appeal of the penalty normally cannot be struck out without a trial: see Notes to 163(3). The onus is "greater than on a balance of probabilities, and closer to the criminal onus under the *Criminal Code*": *Lust*, 2009 TCC 577, para. 23 (FCA appeal discontinued A-435-09). See also *Roy*, 2011 TCC 299, para. 16. In *Rail*, 2011 TCC 130, the CRA officer who testified was not the auditor, so his evidence was hearsay and gross negligence was not proven. In *Semenov*, 2018 TCC 58, CRA's assumptions about S taking funds from his corp were insufficient to support penalties [MacKnight, "Facts, Not Assumptions", 18(3) *Tax for the Owner-Manager* (ctf.ca) 4-5

(July 2018)]. However, the taxpayer may need a "credible" explanation for failing to report income: *Baynham*, [1999] 1 C.T.C. 87 (FCA). Where a large sum is unreported and the taxpayer is found not credible, that discharges the Crown's burden: *Lacroix*, 2008 FCA 241. Campbell J in *Dao*, 2010 TCC 84, para. 44, says *Lacroix* leaves her "bewildered" because it seems to eliminate the *mens rea* requirement for "conduct bordering on criminal behaviour for which [the taxpayer] may be slammed with the punishment of gross negligence penalties". In *Fourney*, 2011 TCC 520, para. 76, Hogan J saw *Lacroix* as applying if the facts imply gross negligence with no other reasonable explanation. *Deyab*, 2020 FCA 222, para. 68 (leave to appeal denied 2021 CarswellNat 1815 (SCC)), clarifies that *Lacroix* does not mean that, to set aside the penalty, the taxpayer must "identify the source of the income and show that is not taxable": shareholder appropriations were taxable under 15(1) but D may have thought he was repaying shareholder loans so no penalty applied. See also Ho, "Reverse Onus?", 18(4) *Canadian Tax Highlights* (ctf.ca) 11-12 (April 2010). *Lacroix* has been followed in many cases including *Nowak*, 2011 TCC 3 (aff'd 2012 FCA 1 without discussing *Lacroix*); *St-Philippe*, 2011 TCC 284; *Boroumand*, 2015 TCC 239 (aff'd 2016 FCA 313); *Auto Maculate*, 2020 TCC 105, para. 132 (net worth assessment; see also 152(7) Notes). Where there were "multiple instances of fraud and fabrication", journal entries transferring funds from one company to another were sufficient evidence to establish unreported revenue: *Coombs*, 2015 TCC 148, para. 25. Where large charitable donations were implausible (Global Prosperity scheme), the Court inferred the taxpayers knew they would get back benefits, and upheld the penalties: *Jensen*, 2018 TCC 60 and *Goheen*, 2019 FCA 104.

"A taxpayer should be given every reasonable opportunity to defend himself" against a 163(2) penalty: *Bygrave*, 2017 FCA 124, para. 22, so extension of time to appeal was allowed.

Materiality: The penalty applied in: *Hougassian*, 2007 TCC 293 (businessman with $3 million total income reported $985 interest income instead of the $275,000 for which he received a T5); *Boyer*, 2008 TCC 88 (not reporting a large capital gain was "wilful blindness"); *Lapalme*, 2011 TCC 396 (not reporting $58,000 in "gifts" from the insurance broker after the taxpayers' company bought life insurance on the shareholders); *Griffin*, 2011 TCC 531 (large discrepancy in couple's income: $86,000 of $240,000 reported); *Melman*, 2017 FCA 83 (experienced banker had $15m of dividends, yet signed without reviewing a return prepared by his accountants showing $367,000 tax liability). *Contra*, in *Murugesu*, 2013 TCC 21, para. 48, the magnitude of unreported income was not by itself sufficient reason for imposing the penalty; and in *Cantin*, 2014 TCC 116, a lawyer who failed to declare a $65,000 dividend from his firm was not liable, where he thought the dividend had gone to his Holdco, the Court believed him, and his annual income fluctuated by more than $100,000.

Amount of penalty: The penalty under 163(2) relates to the undeclared income, and can apply even if the income could have been offset by additional discretionary deductions such as CCA: *MacDonald*, [1997] 3 C.T.C. 2195 (TCC); *Bolay*, [2002] 4 C.T.C. 2401 (TCC); *Chopp*, [1987] 2 C.T.C. 2071 (TCC). See 163(2.1)(a)(ii). Where a false donation credit is claimed, the penalty is calculated as 50% of that credit: VIEWS doc 2011-0423781I7. It can apply to a requested adjustment that was not processed, since it is based on the false information *filed*: doc 2005-012913117. See also Notes to 163(2.1).

Once 163(2) applies, the Tax Court cannot reduce the quantum of the penalty for mitigating circumstances: *Simard*, [2004] 3 C.T.C. 269 (FCA). The penalty can be waived by the CRA under Taxpayer Relief, though this will rarely happen; see discussion of *Cayer* in Notes to 220(3.1).

"Knowingly" is conceptually different from "gross negligence". Being wilfully blind is deliberate ignorance (and falls under "knowingly"): "if the wilfully blind taxpayer knew better, the grossly negligent taxpayer ought to have known better": *Wynter*, 2017 FCA 195, paras. 17-20. "Knowingly" does not require intention to defraud the system, as long as the person knows the statement is false: *Bellil*, 2017 FCA 104.

Gross negligence definition: "Gross negligence must be taken to involve greater neglect than simply a failure to use reasonable care. It must involve a high degree of negligence tantamount to intentional acting, an indifference as to whether the law is complied with or not": *Venne*, [1984] C.T.C. 223 at 234 (FCTD); *Findlay*, [2000] 3 C.T.C. 152 (FCA); approved in *Guindon*, 2015 SCC 41, para. 60 ("It is akin to burying one's head in the sand". Per *Wynter*, 2017 FCA 195 at para. 21, the issue is "whether the conduct ... is such a marked departure from what would be expected that it constitutes a high degree of negligence sufficient to be characterized as a marked departure from the standards, practices, and due diligence expected of a responsible taxpayer.... these penalties are meant to capture serious conduct, not ordinary negligence or simple mistakes". In *Smith*, 2019 TCC 274, para. 27, amounts that "were not extraordinary, they simply remained unprovable and therefore misstated" did not justify a penalty.

CRA overstepping: CRA was excoriated by Bowman J. for applying the gross-negligence penalty without evidence, in *897366 Ontario*, [2000] G.S.T.C. 13 (TCC), para. 19: "The imposition of [such] penalties ...requires a serious and deliberate consideration by the taxing authority of the taxpayer's conduct to determine whether it demonstrates a degree of wilfulness or gross negligence justifying the penalty.... penalties may only be imposed in the clearest of cases, and after an assiduous scrutiny of the evidence." On the same point, see also *Drozdzik*, [2003] 2 C.T.C. 2183 (TCC), paras. 289-291; *Chaloux*, 2015 TCC 284 (FCA appeal discontinued A-540-15), para. 52. The test is not "ought to have known": *Fourney*, 2011 TCC 520, para. 73. CRA must be "extremely cautious" in imposing the penalty: *Farm Business Consultants*, [1994] 2 C.T.C. 2450 (TCC), para. 27, approved in *Lacroix*, 2008 FCA 241, para. 28 and *Deyab*, 2020 FCA 222, para. 73 (leave to appeal denied 2021 CarswellNat 1815 (SCC)); *Hine*, 2012 TCC 295, para. 26 (H relied on wife to prepare returns, they were otherwise compliant, inadvertent claim of large loss did not stand out, and no indication of intention to reduce tax).

Conviction of tax evasion on the same facts should in theory be conclusive proof of the facts required to support the penalty, but see Notes to 239(1).

Experience and education: The penalty applied to all of: former CGA with accounting experience who did not keep proper records (*Nguyen*, 2015 TCC 7, paras. 20-23); CRA auditor who claimed losses to offset employment income without proper records (*Lubega-Matovu*, 2016 FCA 315, para. 41); experienced businessman with financial background who directed Ponzi scheme commissions to non-Canadian cash cards (*Carphin*, 2015 TCC 158, para. 43); former financial advisor working at casino who did not report tips (*Xia*, 2020 FCA 35); experienced businessman who took funds from foundation he ran (*Hamel*, 2020 TCC 48); tax-savvy investment advisor and his corp deducted personal expenses (*Hilderman*, 2020 TCC 58, paras. 89-90); experienced real estate investor who sold unit in building he lived in without reporting it (*Mandel*, 2020 TCC 76). See also *Melman* under "Materiality" above. *Contra*, it did not apply in *Mason*, 2014 TCC 297 (aff'd on other grounds 2016 FCA 15) (accountant with 25 years' experience who "intended to implement effective tax planning" in claiming his income was earned by trusts but "did not do it particularly well" (para. 61)).

Reliance: The penalty was cancelled in all of: *Klotz*, 2004 TCC 147 (art flip where the taxpayer relied on appraiser's valuation when donating art; this issue not appealed to FCA); *Nash (Tolley, Quinn)*, 2004 TCC 651 (same, conceded by the Crown); *Robichaud*, 2004 TCC 661 (stamps flip where R, a CA, relied on published catalogue for stamps' values); *Julian*, 2004 TCC 330 (J, a lawyer, was "aggressive, if not cavalier" not to have questioned donation scheme that "in hindsight looked outrageous", but he relied on his firm's tax expert); *Mady*, 2017 TCC 112 (reorganization on sale of dental practice was so complex the CRA auditor got the analysis wrong); *DaCosta*, 2017 TCC 235, paras. 16-18 (21-year-old selling condo, relying on father and grandmother real estate agents). See also detailed discussion of reliance in *Gray*, 2016 TCC 54, paras. 39-51, and the para. below.

Even if the accountant or tax return preparer was grossly negligent (see 163.2 for preparer liability), if taxpayer TP was not aware of this, TP was not liable: *Findlay*, [2000] 3 C.T.C. 152 (FCA) (TP was not privy to tax preparer's omissions); *Udell*, [1969] C.T.C. 704 (Exch. Ct); *Venne*, [1984] C.T.C. 223 (FCTD) (TP did not notice bookkeeper's errors); *Gagnon*, 2005 TCC 311 (TP unaware son was claiming fraudulent refunds); *Murugesu*, 2013 TCC 21 (credible witness with limited English had to rely on accountant); *Vachon*, 2013 TCC 330 (aff'd on other grounds 2014 FCA 224) (experienced TP was negligent in being defrauded by tax preparer who stole his tax payments, but not wilfully blind); *Phénix*, 2018 TCC 204 (T5 mixup between accountant and external auditor); *Frank-Fort Construction*, 2020 TCC 6 (reliance on CPA firm by corp whose owner had no knowledge of accounting or tax).

Contra, the TP was liable (where the accountant was negligent) in: *Columbia Enterprises*, [1983] C.T.C. 204 (FCA) (accountant "was a vital organ of the corporation and virtually its directing mind" in preparing its returns); *DeCosta*, 2005 TCC 545 (TP could not turn blind eye to accountant's omission of an amount almost twice what he reported); *Jackson*, 2008 TCC 188 (TP should have noticed false charitable donations on her return, and not blindly entrusted her tax affairs to preparer); *Brochu*, 2011 TCC 75 (TP claimed she did not understand "business income" and "credit" on her return, but if so was wilfully blind in not asking); *Melman* (see under "Materiality" above); *McLeod*, 2017 TCC 192, para. 31 (accountant recommended M take share sale proceeds as consulting income of his company); *Heno*, 2020 TCC 127, para. 74 (preparer created refunds via false charitable donations, TP did not ask questions). See also discussion of this issue in Notes to 152(4) re "carelessness or neglect". For a TP suing an accountant for negligence, the lawsuit limitation period might not start running until negligence has been proven by the tax appeal failing: see Notes to 118.1(1)"total charitable gifts" under "The shelters have led to lawsuits".

Spouses: In *Mehravaran*, 2015 TCC 209, a Muslim wife who was subservient to her husband and left everything in his control, giving him a Power of Attorney over her affairs, was liable for the penalty. Similarly, in *Bonhomme*, 2016 TCC 152, para. 56 (FCA appeal dismissed for delay A-321-16), a wife who relied on her husband could not use him "as a shield" for her negligence.

Fiscal Arbitrators (FA) claimed fictitious "agent" business losses for 241 taxpayers, and responded to CRA inquiries with absurd "tax protester" language (see Notes to 2(1)). The penalty was upheld for taxpayers claiming the losses despite relying on FA or its promoters or preparers [Larry Watts, Amed Solutions, DSC Lifestyle Solutions, Carlton Branch, Pierre Joanisse, Roual McGann, Muntaz Rasool, Tom Thomson, "Roger", "Lloyd", "Mr. Morley"]: *Maynard*, 2016 FCA 251; *Lauzon*, 2016 FCA 298 (blind reliance on a "trusted advisor"); *Engel*, 2017 FCA 122; *Grier*, 2017 FCA 129; *Wynter*, 2017 FCA 195 (gross negligence is a lower standard than wilfully blind; a finding of WB ("deliberate ignorance") implies GN); *Kim*, 2019 FCA 210 (even though K was misled by TCC into trying to prove his case); *Chénard*, 2012 TCC 211; *Janovsky*, 2013 TCC 140; *Bhatti*, 2013 TCC 143; *McLeod*, 2013 TCC 228; *Brisson*, 2013 TCC 235; *Torres*, 2013 TCC 380 (most FCA appeals discontinued A-2-14 to A-8-14; one aff'd as *Strachan*, 2015 FCA 60); *Chartrand*, 2015 TCC 298; *Spurvey*, 2015 TCC 300; *Taylor*, 2015 TCC 335; *Atutornu*, 2014 TCC 174; *Khattar*, 2015 TCC 338; *Robichaud*, 2016 TCC 19; *Ramlal*, 2016 TCC 26; *Mallette*, 2016 TCC 27; *Brathwaite*, 2016 TCC 29 (one spouse liable); *Daszkiewicz*, 2016 TCC 44; *Gray*, 2016 TCC 54; *Sledge*, 2016 TCC 100; *De Gennaro*, 2016 TCC 108; *Mayne*, 2016 TCC 212; *Tomlinson*, 2016 TCC 246; *Rowe*, 2017 TCC 122; *Bradshaw*, 2017 TCC 123; *Arbuckle*, 2017 TCC 181; *Hogg*, 2017 TCC 231; *Rousseau*, 2018 TCC 9 (FCA appeal discontinued A-55-18); *Peck*, 2018 TCC 52; *Manhue*, 2018 TCC 71; *Tavernier*, 2018 TCC 173; *Brad-

shaw*, 2019 TCC 1; *Mior*, 2019 FC 321 and 322; *Wardlaw*, 2019 TCC 199; *Strachan*, 2020 TCC 37 (under appeal to FCA). The factors in these cases are: education and experience of the taxpayer; suspicion or need to make an inquiry; fee structure and anonymity of the preparer; blatantness of the false statement; lack of inquiries of other professionals or the CRA. See also *Bolduc*, 2014 TCC 128 (FCA appeal discontinued A-247-14). The penalty was cancelled in all of: *Lavoie*, 2015 TCC 228 (taxpayers relied on their long-time lawyer saying the scheme worked); *Sam*, 2016 TCC 98 (reliance on sister-in-law with accounting training who had done returns for many years, and no red flags); *Morrison*, 2016 TCC 99 (reliance on friend of many years, and no documents that would raise red flags); *Brathwaite*, 2016 TCC 29 (no proof one spouse signed or approved her return); *Anderson*, 2016 TCC 93 (preparer added false information after A signed return); *Boateng*, 2017 CarswellNat 7260 (TCC) (no proof B signed return, and other documents were clearly forged); *Kajtor*, 2018 TCC 6 (K, unsophisticated, saw boyfriend's brother's $50,000 tax refund cheque to confirm scheme was genuine); *Mahdi*, 2018 TCC 149 (reliance on apparently reliable long-term tax preparer, and taxpayers asked questions); *Pimentel*, 2012-4863(IT)G and 2012-4864(IT)G (July 18, 2019, unreported). Lawrence Watts, Aurelius Branch and Muntaz Rasool were charged criminally: *Windsor Star*, "CRA charges tax preparers who led Windsorites to financial ruin" (Feb. 21, 2013). Watts was convicted of fraud by a jury and sentenced to 6 years, plus 2 years if he does not pay a $149,000 fine: 2018 ONCA 148 (leave to appeal denied 2018 CarswellOnt 16100 (SCC), and see 2019 FC 1321, Watts' attempt to relitigate issues). Branch was extradited from Costa Rica (with assistance from Interpol), convicted and sentenced to 4.5 years plus a fine: CRA, "Brampton tax preparer sentenced fraud" (Feb. 28, 2020). See also Carolyn Hogan, "Escaping Penalties After Admitting False Statements", 6(3) *Canadian Tax Focus* (ctf.ca) 7-8 (Aug. 2016).

Similar to FA, Solutions 21 (S21) claimed fictitious losses for taxpayers, but in *Bolduc*, 2017 TCC 203, the penalty was cancelled: B and relatives had dealt with S21 for years and trusted them; S21 ("organized and sophisticated tax schemers": para. 164) had professional offices and appeared to be tax experts; and B had queried the losses and other "red flags" and had been given answers that satisfied him. DeMara Consulting and Serge Frechette promoted similar schemes; penalties were upheld in *Saunders*, 2019 TCC 39, and *St-Yves*, 2019 TCC 186; but were cancelled in: *Rattai*, 2020 TCC 55 (under appeal by Crown to FCA) (CRA did not bring to Court copy of R's return as filed: para. 81; Mrs. R relied on husband and was not wilfully blind: para. 159); and *Bowker*, 2021 TCC 14 (B did not authorize DeMara to file for her, and relied on her husband to handle her tax affairs). Another was C&M Tax (*Stone*, 2019 TCC 253: penalty upheld).

Detaxers arguing that "sovereign persons" are not subject to the Act (see Notes to 248(1)"person") or that a person can choose not to pay tax (see Notes to 2(1)) were subject to the penalty in: *Stein*, 2017 FCA 71; *Meerman*, 2019 FCA 119, leave to appeal denied 2020 CarswellNat 370 (SCC); *Turnnir*, 2011 TCC 495 (accountant had warned T against this position); *McLeod*, 2013 TCC 228; *Romaker*, 2017 TCC 241; *Tyskerud*, 2019 TCC 84, para. 39.

In *Villeneuve*, 2004 FCA 20 and *Savard*, 2004 FCA 150 (both reversing the TCC), the penalty applied to taxpayers who participated in a scheme by CRA employees to get them false refunds in exchange for a commission.

Excuses: In *Rohani*, 2009 TCC 88, R's "major depressive disorder" was reason for the penalty not to apply to overclaimed charitable donations. In *De Couto*, 2013 TCC 198, paras. 19-20, the penalty was cancelled due to the appellants' "limited business acumen, language facility, education and managerial background. They were clearly confused and failed to understand their obligations ...lack of culpable intention, manifest inaugural business ignorance and the absence of any overt act to mislead". In *Bandula*, 2013 TCC 282, para. 44, the penalty was cancelled for the first 2 years of business of a new immigrant, due to his limited English and not having the "experience, knowledge or insight" to keep proper records, given his experience in Hungary of "operating within a cash system". In *Chaloux*, 2015 TCC 284 (FCA appeal discontinued A-540-15), para. 53, taxpayers with "minimal" accounting knowledge were not grossly negligent by reporting on a cash basis.

Not receiving a T4 slip for substantial stock options was insufficient grounds for avoiding the penalty: *Panini*, 2005 TCC 151 and parallel appeals (*Klapka, Riendeau, Riordan, Southin, Whitzman*), all aff'd 2006 FCA 224.

Post-filing actions: In *Gosselin*, [2004] 2 C.T.C. 3019 (TCC), the penalty applied to a taxpayer who received a false $7,000 refund claimed for him by a CRA employee, because he deposited the cheque and did not advise CRA about it. (This seems wrong, since depositing the cheque cannot be tied to a statement made in a return or statement filed. See the second para. at beginning of these Notes.)

Net worth assessments: See Notes to 152(7) re applying the penalty on NWAs.

Auditor rules: Detailed rules on what the auditor *must* consider before applying 163(2) are in *Income Tax Audit Manual* §§11.6.2, 28.4.4 and 28.4.8, but many auditors ignore these rules and their managers back them up: see David Sherman, "GST Tidbits — Official CRA Policy Is To Ignore Its Audit Manual In Assessing Gross Negligence Penalties", *GST & HST Times* 281P (Carswell) 4-6 (April 2013). See also Information Circular 73-10R3 paras. 45-47. Merely disagreeing with a CRA published position on GAAR is not gross negligence: VIEWS doc 2006-0196021C6. For calculation of the penalty see Notes to 163(2.1).

163(2) is normally applied only after the auditor prepares a "penalty report" justifying it. The report can be obtained under the *Privacy Act* (individuals) or *Access to Information Act* (corps). See 241(1) Notes. ATIP staff may assist in getting the auditor to release the report informally: see 231.1(1) Notes. The report is finalized only after one is given an opportunity to reply to the proposal letter, and "the auditor must fully apprise the taxpayer ... the reason(s) for the application of the penalty": May 2011 ICAA roundtable (tinyurl.com/cra-abtax), q.9 (also discusses criteria used in assessing the penalty); May 2013 roundtable (*Member Advisory*, April 2014), q.4. In practice, many CRA auditors do not follow this rule, especially when assessing individuals. Note that for a 2nd year of unreported income, the 20% penalty under 163(1) (including provincial penalty), which does not require gross negligence, can exceed the 163(2) penalty.

Quebec also imposes penalties for engaging in or advising on a sham: see Notes to 245(2) under "Sham transactions"; and for not disclosing a nominee (bare trustee) agreement to Revenu Québec: see Notes to 54"capital property" under "Bare trustee".

CRA standard of care: In *Leroux*, 2014 BCSC 720, paras. 339-355, CRA negligently breached its duty of care to the taxpayer in assessing excessive penalties, but (paras. 385-386) this did not cause Leroux's damages because he could have prevented collection action by filing timely objections and appeals and providing information to the CRA. Threatening to assess penalties if the taxpayer does not sign a waiver breaches the duty of care and may make the CRA liable for damages: paras. 349-351. In *9016-9202 Québec Inc.*, 2014 TCC 281 (FCA appeal discontinued A-469-14), the TCC cancelled penalties that it found (para. 97) were imposed solely to force the taxpayers to stop using an independent-contractor structure for garbage collectors.

See also Campbell, *Administration of Income Tax 2020* (Carswell), §11.2, "False Statements or Omissions"; Clarke, "Civil Penalties", 2012 *Tax Dispute Resolution* conf. report (ctf.ca), 20:1-33; Sarna & Barnett, "Just Plain Gross", XIV(1) *Sales and Use Tax* (Federated Press) 5-10 (2017); Wallace, "Gross Negligence Penalties", 14(4) *Tax Hyperion* (Carswell) 3-6 (July-Aug. 2017). See also the *Gross Negligence Classifier* software model at bluejlegal.com, described in Velez, "Gross Negligence Pursuant to Subsection 163(2)", *Taxnet Pro* Tax Disputes Centre (Dec. 2017, 12pp). See also articles at end of Notes to 163(1).

163(2)(h)(i) amended by 2021 budget bill #1, effective 2019, to refer to 125.6(2.1).

163(2)(i)(i) amended by 2021 budget bill #1, effective June 29, 2021, to apply to 125.7(2.2). From Nov. 19, 2020 until that date, read:

> (i) the amount that would be deemed by subsection 125.7(2) or (2.1) to have been an overpayment by the person or partnership if that amount were calculated by reference to the information provided in the application filed pursuant to paragraph (a) of the definition "qualifying entity" in subsection 125.7(1) or paragraph (a) of the definition "qualifying renter" in subsection 125.7(1), as the case may be

163(2)(i) added by 2020 COVID bill #2, effective April 11, 2020, and amended by 2020 COVID bill #5, effective Nov. 19, 2020, to refer to 125.7(2.1) and the CERS application. From April 11-Nov. 18, read subpara. (i)(i) as:

> (i) the amount that would be deemed by subsection 125.7(2) to have been an overpayment by the person or partnership if that amount were calculated by reference to the information provided in the application filed pursuant to section 125.7

163(2)(c.6) and (h) added by 2019 budget bill #1, effective 2019.

163(2)(c.4) added by 2018 budget bill #2, for 2018 and later tax years.

Former 163(2)(c.4) repealed by 2016 budget bill #1, for 2017 and later taxation years. For 2015-2016, read:

> (c.4) the amount, if any, by which
>
> > (i) the total of all amounts each of which is an amount that would be deemed by subsections 122.8(2) or (3) to have been paid on account of the person's tax payable under this Part for the year if that amount were calculated by reference to the person's claim for the year under those subsections
>
> exceeds
>
> > (ii) the total of all amounts each of which is the amount that the person is entitled to claim for the year under subsections 122.8(2) or (3),

163(2)(c.5) added by 2016 budget bill #1, for 2016 and later taxation years.

163(2)(c.4) added by 2014 budget bill #2, for 2015 and later taxation years.

163(2)(c.1) amended by 2002-2013 technical bill (Part 5 — technical), for amounts deemed paid during months specified for the 2001 and later taxation years.

163(2) earlier amended by 2007 budget bill #2 (for 2007 and later taxation years), 2000 same-sex partners bill, 1999 and 1997 Budgets, 1995-97 technical bill, 1995 and 1994 Budgets, 1992 Economic Statement, 1992 Child Benefit bill and 1990 GST.

Income Tax Folios: S3-F9-C1: Lottery winnings, miscellaneous receipts, and income (and losses) from crime [replaces IT-185R, IT-213R, IT-256R, IT-334R2].

Information Circulars: 73-10R3: Tax evasion; 00-1R4: Voluntary disclosures program.

Application Policies: SR&ED 96-05: Penalties under subsec. 163(2).

Registered Plans Compliance Bulletins: 4 (abusive schemes — RRSP stripping).

CRA Audit Manual: 11.3.3: Application of losses; 11.3.7: Assessment after the normal (re)assessment period and penalty for false statements or omissions; 11.6.2 and Appendix A-11.2.21: Penalty recommendation report; 28.4.0: False statements or omissions.

(2.1) Interpretation — For the purposes of subsection (2), the taxable income reported by a person in the person's return for a taxa-

tion year shall be deemed not to be less than nil and the "understatement of income" for a year of a person means the total of

(a) the amount, if any, by which

> (i) the total of all amounts that were not reported by the person in the person's return and that were required to be included in computing the person's income for the year

exceeds

> (ii) the total of such of the amounts deductible by the person in computing the person's income for the year under the provisions of this Act as were wholly applicable to the amounts referred to in subparagraph (i) and were not deducted by the person in computing the person's income for the year reported by the person in the person's return,

(b) the amount, if any, by which

> (i) the total of all amounts deducted by the person in computing the person's income for the year reported by the person in the person's return

exceeds

> (ii) the total of such of the amounts referred to in subparagraph (i) as were deductible by the person in computing the person's income for the year in accordance with the provisions of this Act, and

(c) the amount, if any, by which

> (i) the total of all amounts deducted by the person (otherwise than by virtue of section 111) from the person's income for the purpose of computing the person's taxable income for the year reported by the person in the person's return

exceeds

> (ii) the total of all amounts deductible by the person (otherwise than by virtue of section 111) from the person's income for the purpose of computing the person's taxable income for the year in accordance with the provisions of this Act.

Related Provisions: 163(3) — Burden of proof; 163(4) — Effect of carryback of losses etc.

Notes: Deductions may not be claimable under 163(2.1) to reduce a penalty unless they apply *entirely* to the undeclared income: *MacDonald*, [1997] 3 C.T.C. 2195 (TCC). If some (rather than none) of the income was declared, 163(2.1) does not reduce the penalty, even though this result is "absurd": *Roy*, [2001] 3 C.T.C. 226 (FCA).

Where false losses were claimed leading to false carryback claims, then "Under the formula, which is based on the tax that is sought to be avoided, the tax is computed at a relatively high tax rate which does not take into account that the actual tax savings would be spread over four taxation years and computed at lower tax rates": *McLeod*, 2013 TCC 228, para. 30; *Wardlaw*, 2019 TCC 199, paras. 12-13 (penalty was effectively 70%); *Stone*, 2019 TCC 253, para. 78.

In *Leroux*, 2014 BCSC 720, an action for damages, the Court found it unreasonable for CRA to assess a $50,000 penalty on income of $5,000, but the penalty was calculated on a claimed $100,000 loss. L argued that "the taxable income reported by a person shall be deemed not to be less than nil" means that 163(2.1) does not apply to losses (the Court did not resolve this issue). In the author's view, since a business loss claim does not result in taxable income of less than nil, that phrase is irrelevant. 163(2.1)(b) imposes a penalty for overclaimed expenses, whether or not they result in a loss claim.

See also VIEWS docs 2009-0344291I7 (social benefits repayment under 60(v.1) is deductible from unreported EI benefits before applying 163(2)); 2012-0442021I7, 2012-0454821I7 and 2012-0459581I7 (calculation of penalty on overclaimed Child Tax Benefits, GST Credits and similar credits); 2012-0452151I7 and 2013-0485161I7 (calculation of penalty on fictitious business losses).

(2.2) False statement or omission — Every person who, knowingly or under circumstances amounting to gross negligence, has made or has participated in, assented to or acquiesced in the making of, a false statement or omission in a renunciation that was to have been effective as of a particular date and that is purported to have been made under any of subsections 66(10) to (10.3), (12.6), (12.601) and (12.62), otherwise than because of the application of subsection 66(12.66), is liable to a penalty of 25% of the amount, if any, by which

(a) the amount set out in the renunciation in respect of Canadian exploration expenses, Canadian development expenses or Canadian oil and gas property expenses

exceeds

(b) the amount in respect of Canadian exploration expenses, Canadian development expenses or Canadian oil and gas property expenses, as the case may be, that the corporation was entitled under the applicable subsection to renounce as of that particular date.

Related Provisions: 163(2.21) — Penalty relating to 66(12.66); 163(3) — Burden of proof. See also Related Provisions at end of s. 163.

Notes: 163(2.2) amended by 1996 Budget (last change effective for purported renunciations made after 1998), 1992 Economic Statement.

Information Circulars: 00-1R4: Voluntary disclosures program.

(2.21) False statement or omissions with respect to look-back rule [flow-through shares] — A person is liable to the penalty determined under subsection (2.22) where the person,

(a) knowingly or under circumstances amounting to gross negligence has made or has participated in, assented to or acquiesced in the making of, a false statement or omission in a document required to be filed under subsection 66(12.73) in respect of a renunciation purported to have been made because of the application of subsection 66(12.66); or

(b) fails to file the document on or before the day that is 24 months after the day on or before which it was required to be filed.

Related Provisions: 163(3) — Burden of proof.

Notes: 163(2.21) added by 1996 Budget, effective April 25, 1997.

(2.22) Penalty — For the purpose of subsection (2.21), the penalty to which a person is liable in respect of a document required to be filed under subsection 66(12.73) is equal to 25% of the amount, if any, by which

(a) the portion of the excess referred to in subsection 66(12.73) in respect of the document that was known or that ought to have been known by the person

exceeds

(b) where paragraph (2.21)(b) does not apply, the portion of the excess identified in the document, and

(c) in any other case, nil.

Related Provisions: 162(7) — Additional penalty. See also at end of s. 163.

Notes: 163(2.22) added by 1996 Budget, effective April 25, 1997.

(2.3) Idem — Every person who, knowingly or under circumstances amounting to gross negligence, makes or participates in, assents to or acquiesces in the making of, a false statement or omission in a prescribed form required to be filed under subsection 66(12.691) or (12.701) is liable to a penalty of 25% of the amount, if any, by which

(a) the assistance required to be reported in respect of a person or partnership in the prescribed form

exceeds

(b) the assistance reported in the prescribed form in respect of the person or partnership.

Related Provisions: 163(3) — Burden of proof. See also at end of s. 163.

Notes: 163(2.3) added by 1991 technical bill, effective Dec. 17, 1991.

(2.4) False statement or omission [re foreign asset reporting] — Every person or partnership who, knowingly or under circumstances amounting to gross negligence, makes or participates in, assents to or acquiesces in, the making of a false statement or omission in a return is liable to a penalty of

(a) where the return is required to be filed under section 233.1, $24,000;

(b) if the return is required to be filed under section 233.2 in respect of a trust, the greater of

(i) $24,000, and

(ii) 5% of the total of all amounts each of which is the fair market value, at the time it was made, of a contribution of the person or partnership made to the trust before the end of the

last taxation year of the trust in respect of which the return is required;

(c) where the return is required to be filed under section 233.3 for a taxation year or fiscal period, the greater of

(i) $24,000, and

(ii) 5% of the greatest of all amounts each of which is the total of the cost amounts to the person or partnership at any time in the year or period of a specified foreign property (as defined by subsection 233.3(1)(a)) of the person or partnership in respect of which the false statement or omission is made;

(d) where the return is required to be filed under section 233.4 for a taxation year or fiscal period, the greater of

(i) $24,000, and

(ii) 5% of the greatest of all amounts each of which is the total of the cost amounts to the person or partnership at any time in the year or period of a property of the person or partnership that is a share of the capital stock or indebtedness of the foreign affiliate in respect of which the return is being filed; and

(e) where the return is required to be filed under section 233.6 for a taxation year or fiscal period, the greater of

(i) $2,500, and

(ii) 5% of the total of

(A) all amounts each of which is the fair market value of a property that is distributed to the person or partnership in the year or period by the trust and in respect of which the false statement or omission is made, and

(B) all amounts each of which is the greatest unpaid principal amount of a debt that is owing to the trust by the person or partnership in the year or period and in respect of which the false statement or omission is made.

Related Provisions: 162(10), (10.1) — Penalty for failure to file return; 163(2.41) — Application to trust contributions; 163(2.5) — Shares or debt owned by controlled foreign affiliate; 163(2.6), (2.7) — Application to partnerships; 163(2.9) — Where partnership liable to penalty; 163(2.91) — Application to non-resident trusts; 163(3) — Burden of proof; 233.2(4.1) — Foreign arrangements similar to trusts; 233.5 — Due diligence defence to penalty. See also at end of s. 163.

Notes: A deliberate or grossly negligent failure to file a return required under 233.1–233.6 should not trigger this penalty, since there is no false statement or omission "in" the return. See the third para. of Notes to 163(2).

In *Ludmer*, 2018 QCCS 3381, paras. 182-200 (aff'd on other grounds 2020 QCCA 697; leave to appeal denied 2021 CarswellQue 2160 (SCC)), CRA was not liable for threatening this penalty. Filing the wrong form triggers 163(2.4): QCCS para. 197 (filing *no* form does not: see 163(2) Notes).

163(2.4)(b) amended by 2002-2013 technical bill, for taxation years that end after 2006 (earlier years in some cases).

163(2.4) added by 1996 Budget, for returns required to be filed by April 30, 1998 or later.

Information Circulars: 00-1R4: Voluntary disclosures program.

CRA Audit Manual: 15.7.5: Foreign reporting requirements — penalties.

(2.41) Application to trust contributions — In subparagraph (2.4)(b)(ii), subsections 94(1), (2) and (9) apply.

Notes: 163(2.41) added by 2002-2013 technical bill (Part 1 — NRTs), effective on the same basis as the amendment to 163(2.4)(b).

(2.5) Shares or debt owned by controlled foreign affiliate — For the purpose of paragraph (2.4)(d),

(a) shares or indebtedness owned by a controlled foreign affiliate of a person or partnership are deemed to be owned by the person or partnership; and

(b) the cost amount at any time of such shares or indebtedness to the person or partnership is deemed to be equal to 20% of the cost amount at that time to the controlled foreign affiliate of the shares or indebtedness.

Related Provisions: 163(2.6) — Application to partnerships; 163(2.91) — Application to non-resident trusts.

Notes: 163(2.5) added by 1996 Budget, effective for returns required to be filed by April 30, 1998 or later.

(2.6) Application to partnerships — For the purposes of paragraph (2.4)(d) and subsection (2.5), in determining whether a non-resident corporation or trust is a foreign affiliate or a controlled foreign affiliate of a partnership

(a) the definitions "direct equity percentage" and "equity percentage" in subsection 95(4) shall be read as if a partnership were a person; and

(b) the definitions "controlled foreign affiliate" and "foreign affiliate" in subsection 95(1) shall be read as if a partnership were a taxpayer resident in Canada.

Notes: See Notes to 162(10.3).

163(2.6) added by 1996 Budget, effective for returns required to be filed by April 30, 1998 or later.

(2.7) Application to partnerships — For the purpose of subsection (2.4), each act or omission of a member of a partnership in respect of an information return required to be filed by the partnership under section 233.3, 233.4 or 233.6 is deemed to be an act or omission of the partnership in respect of the return.

Related Provisions: 163(2.8) — Tiers of partnerships.

Notes: 163(2.7) added by 1996 Budget, effective for returns required to be filed by April 30, 1998 or later.

(2.8) Application to members of partnerships — For the purposes of this subsection and subsection (2.7), a person who is a member of a partnership that is a member of another partnership is deemed to be a member of the other partnership.

Notes: 163(2.8) added by 1996 Budget, effective for returns required to be filed by April 30, 1998 or later. This rule looks through tiers of partnerships.

(2.9) Partnership liable to penalty — If a partnership is liable to a penalty under paragraph (2)(i), subsection (2.4) or (2.901) or section 163.2, 237.1 or 237.3, sections 152, 158 to 160.1, 161 and 164 to 167 and Division J apply, with any changes that the circumstances require, in respect of the penalty as if the partnership were a corporation.

Notes: This rule is needed because a partnership is not a "person" as defined in 248(1). See Notes to 96(1).

163(2.9) amended to add reference to 163(2)(i) and 163(2.901) by 2020 COVID bill #2, effective April 11, 2020. Earlier amended by 2002-2013 technical bill (generally effective 2011), 1999 Budget. Added by 1996 Budget.

(2.901) Penalty — COVID-19 [CEWS] — Every eligible entity that is deemed by subsection 125.7(6) to have an amount of qualifying revenue — for a current reference period for a qualifying period — is liable to a penalty equal to 25% of the amount that would be deemed by subsection 125.7(2) or (2.1) to have been an overpayment by the eligible entity during that qualifying period if that amount were calculated by reference to the information provided in the application filed pursuant to paragraph (a) of the definition "qualifying entity" in subsection 125.7(1) or paragraph (a) of the definition "qualifying renter" in subsection 125.7(1), as the case may be.

Related Provisions: 125.7(1) — Definitions apply to 163(2.901); 163(2)(i) — Penalty for false statement re same subsidy; 163(2.9) — Application to partnership; 163(3) — Burden of proof; 239(1) — Offence — false statements.

Notes: See 125.7(6) for conditions triggering this anti-avoidance penalty, of 25% of the excess Canada Emergency Wage Subsidy or Canada Emergency Rent Subsidy received. This penalty applies to manipulating revenue under 125.7(6) to get CEWS or CERS, while 163(2)(i) imposes a penalty for a false statement made to get it. An individual making a false statement on the 125.7(1)"qualifying entity" or "qualifying renter" attestation can also be liable for a third-party penalty under 163.2(4) (significant shareholders only: 163.2(15)).

163(2.901) added by 2020 COVID bill #2, effective April 11, 2020, and amended by 2020 COVID bill #5, effective Nov. 19, 2020, to apply to CERS (125.7(2.1) and "qualifying renter"). From April 11-Nov. 18, read:

(2.901) Every eligible entity that is deemed by subsection 125.7(6) to have an amount of qualifying revenue — for a current reference period for a qualifying period — is liable to a penalty equal to 25% of the amount that would be deemed by subsection 125.7(2) to have been an overpayment by the eligible entity during

that qualifying period if that amount were calculated by reference to the information provided in the application filed pursuant to paragraph (a) of the definition "qualifying entity" in subsection 125.7(1).

(2.902) Penalty — COVID-19 — Every eligible entity that is deemed by subsection 125.7(6.1) to have an amount of total current period remuneration for a qualifying period is liable to a penalty equal to 25% of the amount that would be deemed by subsection 125.7(2.2) to have been an overpayment by the eligible entity during that qualifying period if that amount were calculated by reference to the information provided in the application filed pursuant to paragraph (a) of the definition "qualifying recovery entity" in subsection 125.7(1).

Notes: 163(2.902) added by 2021 budget bill #1, effective June 29, 2021.

(2.91) Application to non-resident trusts — For the purposes of this subsection, paragraph (2.4)(d) and subsection (2.5),

(a) a non-resident trust is deemed to be a controlled foreign affiliate of each beneficiary of which the trust is a controlled foreign affiliate for the purpose of section 233.4;

(b) the trust is deemed to be a non-resident corporation having a capital stock of a single class divided into 100 issued shares;

(c) each beneficiary under the trust is deemed to own at any time the number of the issued shares of the corporation that is equal to the proportion of 100 that

(i) the fair market value at that time of the beneficiary's beneficial interest in the trust

is of

(ii) the fair market value at that time of all beneficial interests in the trust; and

(d) the cost amount to a beneficiary at any time of a share of the corporation is deemed to be equal to the amount determined by the formula

$$\frac{A}{B}$$

where

A   is the fair market value at that time of the beneficiary's beneficial interest in the trust, and

B   is the number of shares deemed under paragraph (c) to be owned at that time by the beneficiary in respect of the corporation.

Notes: See Notes to 162(10.3).

163(2.91) added by 1996 Budget, effective for returns required to be filed by April 30, 1998 or later. For purposes of the penalty under 163(2.4), it treats non-resident trusts as foreign affiliates or controlled foreign affiliates of their beneficiaries, if they are treated as such for the reporting requirements in 233.4. As well, a cost amount is ascribed to shares deemed to be issued by such trusts to beneficiaries. The cost amount is based on the fair market value of beneficiaries' interests in the trust.

(3) Burden of proof in respect of penalties — Where, in an appeal under this Act, a penalty assessed by the Minister under this section or section 163.2 is in issue, the burden of establishing the facts justifying the assessment of the penalty is on the Minister.

Related Provisions: 163.2(10) — Exception where valuation wrong by more than prescribed percentage.

Notes: See Notes to 163(2) and 239(1). Where penalties are the only issue in dispute so that the onus is on the Crown, the Crown may be required to present its case first in TCC, but this is not automatic: *Kim*, 2019 FCA 210, para. 28 and *Kozar*, 2010 TCC 389, para. 30. Because of the onus, an appeal of the penalty normally cannot be struck out without a trial: *Brown*, 2014 FCA 301, para. 21. However, in *Russell*, 2016 TCC 122, para. 28, the notice of appeal admitted the taxpayer (a "de-taxer") knowingly did not report his income, so the appeal was struck out. In *Kim*, K was misled by the TCC into trying to prove his case; despite this, the FCA dismissed his appeal because the Crown could have compelled him to testify.

163(3) amended by 1999 Budget, for 1999 and later taxation years.

CRA Audit Manual: 28.4.8: Burden of proof.

(4) Effect of carryback of losses etc. — In determining under subsection (2.1) the understatement of income for a taxation year of a person, the following amounts shall be deemed not to be deductible or excludable in computing the person's income for the year:

(a) any amount that may be deducted under section 41 in respect of the person's listed-personal-property loss for a subsequent taxation year;

(b) any amount that may be excluded from the person's income because of section 49 in respect of the exercise of any option in a subsequent taxation year;

(b.1) any amount that may be deducted under subsection 147.2(4) in computing the person's income for the year because of the application of subsection 147.2(6) as a result of the person's death in the subsequent taxation year; and

(c) any amount that may be deducted in computing the person's income for the year because of an election made under paragraph 164(6)(c) or (d) in a subsequent taxation year by the person's legal representative.

Notes: 163(4)(b.1) added by 1995-97 technical bill, effective for deaths after 1992.

163(4) added by 1991 technical bill, effective where the "subsequent taxation year" referred to ends after July 13, 1990.

Proposed Addition — 163(5), (6)

(5) False statement or omission — trust return — A person or partnership is liable to a penalty if the person or partnership

(a) knowingly or under circumstances amounting to gross negligence

(i) makes — or participates in, assents to or acquiesces in, the making of — a false statement or omission in a return of income of a trust that is not subject to one of the exceptions listed in paragraphs 150(1.2)(a) to (n) for a taxation year, or

(ii) fails to file a return described in subparagraph (i); or

(b) fails to comply with a demand under subsection 150(2) or 231.2(1) to file a return described in subparagraph (a)(i).

Related Provisions: 163(3) — Burden of proof. See also at end of s. 163.

Notes: See Notes to 163(6).

(6) False statement or omission — trust return — The amount of the penalty to which the person or partnership is liable under subsection (5) is equal to the greater of

(a) $2,500; and

(b) 5% of the highest amount at any time in the year that is equal to the total fair market value of all the property held by the trust referred to in subsection (5) at that time.

Application: The July 27, 2018 draft legislation (Budget), s. 8, will add subsecs. 163(5) and (6), applicable to taxation years that end after Dec. 30, 2021.

Technical Notes: New subsection 150(1.2) and section 204.2 of the Regulations introduce reporting requirements for certain trusts to file a return of income and to provide additional information. New subsection 163(5) introduces a penalty for a failure to comply with these new reporting requirements, including the additional information requested in section 204.2 of the Regulations.

New subsection 163(5) imposes a penalty on any person or partnership that is subject to the reporting requirements in section 204.2 and who fails to file a return for a trust or who knowingly or under circumstances amounting to gross negligence either makes — or participates in, assents to or acquiesces in, the making of — a false statement or omission in the return.

In addition, the penalty will apply if the person or partnership fails to comply with a demand by the Canada Revenue Agency under subsection 150(2) or 231.2(1) to file the return.

New subsection (6) sets out the amount of the penalty in respect of a trust for the purposes of subsection (5) as the greater of

• $2,500; and

• 5% of the highest total fair market value of all the property held by the trust in the year.

Notes: This penalty will not take effect until 2021, but will be severe: 5% of trust assets, minimum $2,500. If a trust with $100 million in assets mis-reports income by $500 and the accountant who files the return is considered to have acted with gross negligence, the accountant is subject to a penalty of $5 million. Based on *Guindon*, 2015 SCC 41, that would not be a *Charter* violation. The same penalty will apply if any one beneficiary's name is omitted due to gross negligence (new Reg. 204.2 will require disclosure of all beneficiaries, trustees, settlers and protectors). What happens if the beneficiaries are "all the grandchildren of person X" and the accountant fails to ask

if any new grandchildren have been born in the past year? If that is considered gross negligence, the penalty will again be 5% of the trust's assets. See also Joint Committee letter to Finance, Sept. 10, 2018, pp. 6-7.

Related Provisions [s. 163]: 18(1)(t) — Penalty is non-deductible; 161(11) — Interest on penalty; 180.01(4), 180.2(6), 183(3), 183.2(2), 185.2(2), 187(3), 187.6, 189(8), 190.21, 191.4(2), 196(4), 197(6), 202(3), 204.3(2), 204.7(3), 204.87, 204.93, 204.94(4), 207.07(3), 207.2(3), 207.4(2), 207.7(4), 207.8(5), 209(5), 210.2(7), 211.5, 211.6(5), 211.82, 211.91(3), 218.2(5), 218.3(10), 219(3), 247(11) — Provisions of s. 163 apply for purposes of Parts I.01, I.2, II, II.1, III.1, IV, IV.1, V, VI, VI.1, VII, VIII, IX, IX.1, X, X.1, X.2, X.3, X.4, X.5, XI, XI.01, XI.1, XI.2, XI.3, XI.4, XII.1, XII.2, XII.3, XII.4, XII.5, XII.6, XIII.1, XIII.2, XIV and XVI.1 respectively; 220(3.1) — Waiver of penalty; 227(10.01), (10.1) — Provisions of s. 163 apply to withholding taxes under Parts XII.5 and XIII; 239(3) — Penalty assessment cannot be issued after charge laid if person convicted.

Definitions [s. 163]: "amount", "assessment" — 248(1); "Canadian development expense" — 66.2(5), 248(1); "Canadian exploration expense" — 66.1(6), 248(1); "Canadian oil and gas property expense" — 66.4(5), 248(1); "child" — 252(1); "cohabiting spouse or common-law partner" — 122.6; "common-law partner" — 248(1); "controlled foreign affiliate" — 95(1), 248(1); "corporation" — 163(2.91)(b), 248(1), *Interpretation Act* 35(1); "eligible entity" — 125.7(1); "fair market value" — see 69(1) Notes; "fiscal period" — 249.1; "individual", "Minister" — 248(1); "net capital loss", "non-capital loss" — 111(8), 248(1); "non-resident" — 248(1); "owned" — 163(2.5); "partnership" — see 96(1) Notes; "person", "prescribed", "property" — 248(1); "qualified relation" — 122.8(1); "qualifying period", "qualifying revenue" — 125.7(1); "restricted farm loss" — 31, 248(1); "return" — 163(2); "return of income" — 122.8(1); "specified foreign property" — 233.3(1); "tax payable" — 248(2); "taxable income" — 2(2), 248(1); "taxation year" — 249; "trust" — 104(1), 248(1), (3); "understatement of income" — 163(2.1); "unreported amount" — 163(1)(a).

163.1 Penalty for late or deficient instalments — Every person who fails to pay all or any part of an instalment of tax for a taxation year on or before the day on or before which the instalment is required by this Part to be paid is liable to a penalty equal to 50% of the amount, if any, by which

(a) the interest payable by the person under section 161 in respect of all instalments for the year

exceeds the greater of

(b) $1,000, and

(c) 25% of the interest that would have been payable by the person under section 161 in respect of all instalments for the year if no instalment had been made for that year.

Related Provisions: 18(1)(t) — Penalty is non-deductible; 161(2.2) — Offset interest from prepaying instalments; 161(4) — Interest — limitation — farmers and fishermen; 161(4.01) — Limitation — other individuals; 161(4.1) — Limitation — corporations; 161(7) — Effect of carryback of loss, etc.; 161(11) — Interest on penalties; 211.5(2) — Interest on instalments of Part XII.3 tax; 220(3.1) — Waiver or cancellation of interest. See also at end of s. 163.

Notes: This penalty applies only if the interest on late instalments exceeds $1,000 and also exceeds 25% of the interest that would be payable if no instalments were paid for the year. Under 161(2), such interest stops running once regular interest starts under 161(1), from the "balance-due day" (April 30 for individuals).

For example, if $25,000 of instalments are required from an individual each quarter and nothing is paid; and the prescribed rate is 5% (compounded daily, about 5.13% annually); then 161(2) interest from the March 15 instalment date would be for 13.5 months (about 5.77% or $1,442); from June 15, 10.5 months (about 4.49% or $1,122); from Sept. 15, 7.5 months (about 3.21% or $802); from Dec. 15, 4.5 months (about 1.92% or $480), total $3,847, minus the greater of $1,000 and 25% of $3,847 ($961), or about $2,837; and the penalty would be 50% of that, or about $1,418.

See Notes to 156(1) and 239(1).

163.1 added by 1988 tax reform, effective for taxation years beginning after June 1989.

Definitions [s. 163.1]: "amount" — 248(1); "instalment" — 155–157; "person" — 248(1); "taxation year" — 249.

Information Circulars: 00-1R4: Voluntary disclosures program; 07-1R1: Taxpayer relief provisions.

Misrepresentation of a Tax Matter by a Third Party

163.2 [Third party civil penalties] — **(1) Definitions** — The definitions in this subsection apply in this section.

"culpable conduct" means conduct, whether an act or a failure to act, that

(a) is tantamount to intentional conduct;

(b) shows an indifference as to whether this Act is complied with; or

(c) shows a wilful, reckless or wanton disregard of the law.

Related Provisions: 149.1(4.1)(c), 188.2(2)(f) — Definition applies for revoking or suspending charity's registration; 188.1(9) — Definition applies to charity false-statement penalty.

Notes: The "culpable conduct" (CC) standard is a legislated version of the judicial definition of "gross negligence" in *Venne* (see Notes to 163(2)). However, the word "or" suggests that each of the three tests is a standalone test, so the threshold for culpable conduct is merely "indifference", potentially a much lower standard than *Venne*. Arguably, despite the use of "or", the definition applies the *Venne* standard whereby some elements of all three of (a), (b) and (c) must be present. The Supreme Court of Canada ruled in *Guindon*, 2015 SCC 41, para. 61, that "the standard must be at least as high as gross negligence under s. 163(2). The third party penalties are meant to capture serious conduct, not ordinary negligence or simple mistakes".

In *Guindon* (above), a lawyer who was president of a charity gave a misleading legal opinion about a tax shelter involving the charity, and issued false receipts. She was found to have engaged in CC and was liable for the penalty.

In *Ploughman*, 2017 TCC 64, paras. 42-62, a promoter of the same donation scheme committed CC, as he knew there were major problems with the scheme and was indifferent as to whether the Act was complied with.

"entity" includes an association, a corporation, a fund, a joint venture, an organization, a partnership, a syndicate and a trust.

Notes: See Notes to 188.1(5) re meaning of "includes".

"excluded activity", in respect of a false statement, means the activity of

(a) promoting or selling (whether as principal or agent or directly or indirectly) an arrangement, an entity, a plan, a property or a scheme (in this definition referred to as the "arrangement") where it can reasonably be considered that

(i) subsection 66(12.68) applies to the arrangement,

(ii) the definition "tax shelter" in subsection 237.1(1) applies to a person's interest in the arrangement, or

(iii) one of the main purposes for a person's participation in the arrangement is to obtain a tax benefit; or

(b) accepting (whether as principal or agent or directly or indirectly) consideration in respect of the promotion or sale of an arrangement.

Notes: For the meaning of "indirectly" in para. (a) opening words and (b), see Notes to 17.1(1). For "one of the main purposes" in (a)(iii), see Notes to 83(2.1).

"false statement" includes a statement that is misleading because of an omission from the statement.

Related Provisions: 149.1(4.1)(c) — Definition applies for revoking charity's registration; 188.1(9) — Definition applies to charity false-statement penalty.

Notes: Since the definition uses "includes" rather than "means", the ordinary meaning of "false statement" applies as well (see Notes to 188.1(5)).

"gross compensation" of a particular person at any time, in respect of a false statement that could be used by or on behalf of another person, means all amounts to which the particular person, or any person not dealing at arm's length with the particular person, is entitled, either before or after that time and either absolutely or contingently, to receive or obtain in respect of the statement.

Related Provisions: 163.2(12)(c) — Exclusion of penalty assessed to another person under subsec. (5).

"gross entitlements" of a person at any time, in respect of a planning activity or a valuation activity of the person, means all amounts to which the person, or another person not dealing at arm's length with the person, is entitled, either before or after that time and either absolutely or contingently, to receive or obtain in respect of the activity.

Related Provisions: 163.2(12) — Special rules re gross entitlements.

"participate" includes

(a) to cause a subordinate to act or to omit information; and

(b) to know of, and to not make a reasonable attempt to prevent, the participation by a subordinate in an act or an omission of information.

"person" includes a partnership.

"planning activity" includes

(a) organizing or creating, or assisting in the organization or creation of, an arrangement, an entity, a plan or a scheme; and

(b) participating, directly or indirectly, in the selling of an interest in, or the promotion of, an arrangement, an entity, a plan, a property or a scheme.

Notes: See Notes to 188.1(5) re meaning of "includes" in the opening words. For "indirectly" in (b), see Notes to 17.1(1).

"subordinate", in respect of a particular person, includes any other person over whose activities the particular person has direction, supervision or control whether or not the other person is an employee of the particular person or of another person, except that, if the particular person is a member of a partnership, the other person is not a subordinate of the particular person solely because the particular person is a member of the partnership.

"tax benefit" means a reduction, avoidance or deferral of tax or other amount payable under this Act or an increase in a refund of tax or other amount under this Act.

"valuation activity" of a person means anything done by the person in determining the value of a property or a service.

(2) Penalty for misrepresentations in tax planning arrangements — Every person who makes or furnishes, participates in the making of or causes another person to make or furnish a statement that the person knows, or would reasonably be expected to know but for circumstances amounting to culpable conduct, is a false statement that could be used by another person (in subsections (6) and (15) referred to as the "other person") for a purpose of this Act is liable to a penalty in respect of the false statement.

Related Provisions: 18(1)(t) — Penalty is non-deductible; 161(11) — Interest on penalty; 163(2.9) — Where partnership is liable to penalty; 163(3) — Burden of proof of penalty is on CRA; 163.2(3) — Amount of penalty; 163.2(4) — Alternative penalty; 163.2(6) — Reliance in good faith on information provided; 163.2(8) — Multiple false statements in one arrangement; 163.2(12) — Special rules re gross entitlements; 163.2(14) — Where penalty applies under both (2) and (4); 163.2(15) — Transfer of liability of certain employees to employer; 188.1(9), (10) — Alternative penalty relating to charity receipt; 220(3.1) — Waiver of penalty; 239(3) — Penalty cannot be assessed after charge laid if person convicted. See also at end of s. 163 re application to other Parts.

Notes: See Notes at end of 163.2.

Information Circulars: 00-1R4: Voluntary disclosures program; 01-1: Third-party civil penalties.

Registered Charities Newsletters: 18 (charitable donation tax shelter arrangements).

Registered Plans Compliance Bulletins: 4 (abusive schemes — RRSP stripping).

(3) Amount of penalty — The penalty to which a person is liable under subsection (2) in respect of a false statement is

(a) where the statement is made in the course of a planning activity or a valuation activity, the greater of $1,000 and the total of the person's gross entitlements, at the time at which the notice of assessment of the penalty is sent to the person, in respect of the planning activity and the valuation activity; and

(b) in any other case, $1,000.

(4) Penalty for participating in a misrepresentation — Every person who makes, or participates in, assents to or acquiesces in the making of, a statement to, or by or on behalf of, another person (in this subsection and subsections (5) and (6), paragraph 12(c) and subsection (15) referred to as the "other person") that the person knows, or would reasonably be expected to know but for circumstances amounting to culpable conduct, is a false statement that could be used by or on behalf of the other person for a purpose of this Act is liable to a penalty in respect of the false statement.

Related Provisions: 18(1)(t) — Penalty is non-deductible; 161(11) — Interest on penalty; 163(2.9) — Where partnership is liable to penalty; 163(3) — Burden of proof of penalty is on CRA; 163.2(2) — Alternative penalty; 163.2(5) — Amount of penalty; 163.2(6) — Reliance in good faith on information provided; 163.2(14) — Where penalty applies under both (2) and (4); 163.2(15) — Transfer of liability of certain employees to employer; 188.1(9), (10) — Alternative penalty relating to charity receipt;

220(3.1) — Waiver of penalty; 239(3) — Penalty cannot be assessed after charge laid if person convicted. See also at end of s. 163 re application to other Parts.

Notes: See Notes at end of 163.2.

Employees are not liable for the penalty when filing for their employer unless they are non-arm's length with the employer, or own at least 10% of the shares of any class of the employer, or are involved in promotion or sale of a scheme: see 163.2(15).

Information Circulars: 00-1R4: Voluntary disclosures program; 01-1: Third-party civil penalties.

Registered Charities Newsletters: 18 (charitable donation tax shelter arrangements).

Registered Plans Compliance Bulletins: 4 (abusive schemes — RRSP stripping).

(5) Amount of penalty — The penalty to which a person is liable under subsection (4) in respect of a false statement is the greater of

(a) $1,000, and

(b) the lesser of

(i) the penalty to which the other person would be liable under subsection 163(2) if the other person made the statement in a return filed for the purposes of this Act and knew that the statement was false, and

(ii) the total of $100,000 and the person's gross compensation, at the time at which the notice of assessment of the penalty is sent to the person, in respect of the false statement that could be used by or on behalf of the other person.

Related Provisions: 163.2(4) — Meaning of "other person".

(6) Reliance in good faith — For the purposes of subsections (2) and (4), a person (in this subsection and in subsection (7) referred to as the "advisor") who acts on behalf of the other person is not considered to have acted in circumstances amounting to culpable conduct in respect of the false statement referred to in subsection (2) or (4) solely because the advisor relied, in good faith, on information provided to the advisor by or on behalf of the other person or, because of such reliance, failed to verify, investigate or correct the information.

Related Provisions: 163.2(2), (4) — Meaning of "other person"; 163.2(7) — No application to "excluded activity" such as selling tax shelters.

Notes: This defence does not apply unless (1) the information relied on is provided by the taxpayer, and (2) the advisor is acting on *behalf* of the taxpayer: *Ploughman*, 2017 TCC 64, para. 64. The Court doubted that "information" in 163.2(6) "extends to a statement of one's future conduct": para. 84.

(7) Non-application of subsec. (6) — Subsection (6) does not apply in respect of a statement that an advisor makes (or participates in, assents to or acquiesces in the making of) in the course of an excluded activity.

(8) False statements in respect of a particular arrangement — For the purpose of applying this section (other than subsections (4) and (5)),

(a) where a person makes or furnishes, participates in the making of or causes another person to make or furnish, two or more false statements, the false statements are deemed to be one false statement if the statements are made or furnished in the course of

(i) one or more planning activities that are in respect of a particular arrangement, entity, plan, property or scheme, or

(ii) a valuation activity that is in respect of a particular property or service; and

(b) for greater certainty, a particular arrangement, entity, plan, property or scheme includes an arrangement, an entity, a plan, a property or a scheme in respect of which

(i) an interest is required to have, or has, an identification number issued under section 237.1 that is the same number as the number that applies to each other interest in the property,

(ii) a selling instrument in respect of flow-through shares is required to be filed with the Minister because of subsection 66(12.68), or

(iii) one of the main purposes for a person's participation in the arrangement, entity, plan or scheme, or a person's acquisition of the property, is to obtain a tax benefit.

Notes: For the meaning of "one of the main purposes" in (b)(iii), see Notes to 83(2.1).

(9) Clerical services — For the purposes of this section, a person is not considered to have made or furnished, or participated in, assented to or acquiesced in the making of, a false statement solely because the person provided clerical services (other than bookkeeping services) or secretarial services with respect to the statement.

(10) Valuations — Notwithstanding subsections (6) and 163(3), a statement as to the value of a property or a service (which value is in this subsection referred to as the "stated value"), made by the person who opined on the stated value or by a person in the course of an excluded activity is deemed to be a statement that the person would reasonably be expected to know, but for circumstances amounting to culpable conduct, is a false statement if the stated value is

(a) less than the product obtained when the prescribed percentage for the property or service is multiplied by the fair market value of the property or service; or

(b) greater than the product obtained when the prescribed percentage for the property or service is multiplied by the fair market value of the property or service.

Proposed Amendment — 163.2(10)

Letter from Dept. of Finance, July 11, 2000:

Dear [xxx]

Thank you for your letter of February 4, 2000 concerning our meeting of November 4, 1999 regarding the 1999 budget proposal to introduce a civil penalty in respect of misrepresentations of tax matters by third parties. As you may know, the legislation implementing this proposal received Royal Assent on June 29, 2000 (i.e., S.C. 2000, c. 19).

Your letter replies to our request for input from the [xxx] on the appropriate prescribed percentages for the purpose of establishing a deviation range under new subsection 163.2(10) of the *Income Tax Act* (the "Act"). In your letter, you have indicated that the Institute has concluded that, if a percentage threshold is to-be set by the government, it should be the 200% test adopted by the U.S. under section 6700 of the Internal Revenue Code (the "IRC"). The Institute is also of the view that providing separate prescribed percentages for different industries would be inappropriate because it would be unworkable from a practical perspective — diversifications and business combinations defeat industry classification.

We agree with your observation that it may be impractical to have prescribed percentages that differ for various industries. However, we remain of the view that the deviation range established by prescribed percentages should be narrower than that which would exist under a range that is based upon a 200% standard.

It is our understanding that the U.S. 200% test for gross overstatements results in an automatic application of the penalty under section 6700 of the IRC, subject only to an exception for valuations for which there is a reasonable basis, which were made in good faith and then only if the Secretary of the Treasury waives the penalty under the authority of subsection 6700(b)(2) of the IRC. In contrast, section 163.2 of the Act merely provides a reverse onus. That is to say, in the case of valuations outside of the range, the onus is on the valuator to establish to the Minister of National Revenue or the judiciary that the valuation was reasonable in the circumstances, was made in good faith and was not based on a misleading assumption. The Canadian approach favours Canadian valuators.

The objective of the reverse onus rule in the Canadian provisions is to ensure that valuators and tax shelter promoters justify a substantial deviation from actual value. We would expect that a *bona fide* professional valuator would be prepared to substantiate that a particular valuation is reasonable in the circumstances (regardless of whether it is, on an ex post facto basis, proven to be inaccurate), that the valuation was made in good faith and that it is not based upon misleading assumptions. In this regard, therefore, it would be inappropriate to permit valuators to refuse to justify valuations that are proven to be inaccurate by a wide margin.

We anticipate a deviation range for all valuations that is narrower than 200%. However, consideration will be given within this parameter as to whether the deviation range for valuations used in a non-tax shelter context should differ from valuations used in a tax-shelter context and, if so, the appropriate percentages. If you wish to make further presentations to the Department on this issue, please contact Mr. Kerry Harnish at (613) 992-4385.

Finally, you should be aware that we intend to recommend that the percentages, which are "prescribed" for the purpose of applying new subsection 163.2(10) of the Act, be effective only for statements made after the day on which they are announced.

Thank you again for bringing your concerns to our attention.

Yours sincerely,

Len Farber
General Director, Tax Legislation Division, Tax Policy Branch

Related Provisions: 163.2(11) — Exception where valuation was reasonable and made in good faith.

Notes: No regulations have been proposed for 163.2(10), and the issue is not actively under consideration by Finance. Any regulations proposed will apply only from the date of announcement, as per Finance letter of July 11/00 reproduced above.

Registered Charities Newsletters: 18 (charitable donation tax shelter arrangements).

(11) Exception — Subsection (10) does not apply to a person in respect of a statement as to the value of a property or a service if the person establishes that the stated value was reasonable in the circumstances and that the statement was made in good faith and, where applicable, was not based on one or more assumptions that the person knew or would reasonably be expected to know, but for circumstances amounting to culpable conduct, were unreasonable or misleading in the circumstances.

(12) Special rules — For the purpose of applying this section,

(a) where a person is assessed a penalty that is referred to in subsection (2) the amount of which is based on the person's gross entitlements at any time in respect of a planning activity or a valuation activity and another assessment of the penalty is made at a later time,

(i) if the person's gross entitlements in respect of the activity are greater at that later time, the assessment of the penalty made at that later time is deemed to be an assessment of a separate penalty, and

(ii) in any other case, the notice of assessment of the penalty sent before that later time is deemed not to have been sent;

(b) a person's gross entitlements at any time in respect of a planning activity or a valuation activity, in the course of which the person makes or furnishes, participates in the making of or causes another person to make or furnish a false statement, shall exclude the total of all amounts each of which is the amount of a penalty (other than a penalty the assessment of which is void because of subsection (13)) determined under paragraph (3)(a) in respect of the false statement for which notice of the assessment was sent to the person before that time; and

(c) where a person is assessed a penalty that is referred to in subsection (4), the person's gross compensation at any time in respect of the false statement that could be used by or on behalf of the other person shall exclude the total of all amounts each of which is the amount of a penalty (other than a penalty the assessment of which is void because of subsection (13)) determined under subsection (5) to the extent that the false statement was used by or on behalf of that other person and for which notice of the assessment was sent to the person before that time.

Related Provisions: 163.2(4) — Meaning of "other person".

(13) Assessment void — For the purposes of this Act, if an assessment of a penalty that is referred to in subsection (2) or (4) is vacated, the assessment is deemed to be void.

(14) Maximum penalty — A person who is liable at any time to a penalty under both subsections (2) and (4) in respect of the same false statement is liable to pay a penalty that is not more than the greater of

(a) the total amount of the penalties to which the person is liable at that time under subsection (2) in respect of the statement, and

(b) the total amount of the penalties to which the person is liable at that time under subsection (4) in respect of the statement.

(15) Employees — Where an employee (other than a specified employee or an employee engaged in an excluded activity) is employed by the other person referred to in subsections (2) and (4),

(a) subsections (2) to (5) do not apply to the employee to the extent that the false statement could be used by or on behalf of the other person for a purpose of this Act; and

(b) the conduct of the employee is deemed to be that of the other person for the purposes of applying subsection 163(2) to the other person.

Related Provisions: 163.2(2), (4) — Meaning of "other person".

Notes [s. 163.2]: 163.2 added by 1999 Budget, for statements made after June 29, 2000. It implements a civil penalty for third parties such as tax preparers, advisors, shelter promoters and valuators who cause others to misrepresent their tax owing. There are two separate penalties, in 163.2(2) and (4), with different calculations as set out in 163.2(3) and (5) respectively. See also Notes to 163.2(1)"culpable conduct").

Concerns have been expressed that any assessment of this penalty against lawyers would put them in conflict with their clients. A lawyer might not be able to defend against assessment of the penalty without breaching solicitor-client privilege by revealing client communications. Brian Nichols, in "Third Party Penalties", 2000 Ontario Tax Conference proceedings (Cdn Tax Foundation), tab 3, suggests that 163.2 could be contrary to fundamental principles of law in that tax advisors are required to act in their clients' best interests, per *Hodgkinson v. Simms*, 95 D.T.C. 5135 (SCC); and that it could be contrary to the *Charter of Rights*, given that a very onerous penalty can be equivalent to a criminal fine, per *R. v. Wigglesworth*, [1987] 2 S.C.R. 541 (SCC).

The Supreme Court of Canada held in *Guindon*, 2015 SCC 41, that even if the penalty under 163.2(4) is very large (it was $546,000), it is still an administrative penalty, not a criminal fine, so it does not require conviction by a provincial court, with *Charter of Rights* protection and proof beyond a reasonable doubt.

The only other reported decision is *Ploughman*, 2017 TCC 64, on the same donation scheme as *Guindon*. Ploughman was liable under both 163.2(2) and (4); the Court disbelieved his claim he was only a marketer and not a creator/promoter of the scheme.

In *Glatt*, 2019 FC 738, CRA settled an appeal by conceding the penalty did not apply; CRA was ordered to pay interest on $1m of the penalty that G had paid.

Assessments under 163.2 are issued only on approval of the Third-Party Penalty Review Committee (VIEWS doc 2008-0278801C6 q.12), which as of fall 2020 was composed of: Ted Gallivan [Chair, 613-946-9684, ted.gallivan@cra.gc.ca] (Assistant Commissioner, Compliance Programs Branch (ILBI)); Christopher Bowen (Director General, High Net Worth & Compliance Directorate [HNW], CPB); Holly Brant (Director, Audit Division, HNW); Guy Lafrance (Director, Collections Enforcement, Collections Directorate); Sylvain Lessard (Director, Aggressive GST/HST Planning & Refund Integrity Division, GST/HST Directorate); Melinda Shaughnessy (A/Director, Compliance Division, Charities Directorate); Len Lubbers (Director, Abusive Tax Avoidance); Patrizia Fontanarosa (Asst Director Audit, Eastern Quebec TSO); Sean Vlasman (Asst Director Audit, London/Windsor TSO); Patricia Moran-Kelly (Asst Director Audit, PEI TSO); Catherine Berry (Asst Director Audit, Southern Alberta TSO); Stacey Cera (Asst Director Audit, Southern Interior BC TSO); Danny Gagnon (Manager, Corp Income Tax Legislative Amendments); Joanne Verkerk (Manager, Technical Application Section); Mihaela Scarlet (A/Manager, Tax Promoter & Advisor Compliance); Christine Morris and Caroline Ebata (Legal Services Branch); and a Finance representative.

Criteria for assessing the penalty are in Information Circular 01-1 and Communiqué AD-03-1. As of March 31, 2020, the Committee had considered 141 cases, and had recommended the penalty in 109 of them, to assess preparers a total of $7.6 million and promoters $266m. (*Access to Information Act* disclosure)

CRA can consider waiving the penalty under 220(3.1): 2016 Alberta CPA (tinyurl.com/cra-abtax) q.13.

Where a scheme has been found not to work by the SCC (*Lipson*), CRA might apply 163.2 to users of the same scheme: VIEWS doc 2009-0327071C6.

See also Carr & Pereira, "The Defence Against Civil Penalties", 48(6) *Canadian Tax Journal* 1737-92 (2000); various authors, "Civil Penalties: Case Studies", 2000 Cdn Tax Foundation conference report, 19:1-29; McNary, "The New Civil Penalty Provisions", 2000 Prairie Provinces Tax Conference (ctf.ca), 4:1-42; Innes & Williams, "Penalizing Tax Planners", 2001 Ontario Tax Conf., 7:1-33; Innes & Burke, "Adviser Penalties", 2001 conference report, 37:1-48; Keey, "Third Party Penalty Assessments on the Rise", *General Corporate Tax* newsletter (Carswell), Nov. 2012, pp. 1-2; Blachford & Gurfinkel, "Third-Party Civil Penalties for Accountants", *Taxnet Pro* Tax Disputes Centre (Nov. 2017, 9pp).

Definitions [s. 163.2]: "advisor" — 163.2(6); "amount" — 248(1); "arm's length" — 251(1); "assessment" — 248(1); "corporation" — 248(1), *Interpretation Act* 35(1); "culpable conduct" — 163.2(1); "employee" — 248(1); "entity", "excluded activity" — 163.2(1); "fair market value" — see 69(1) Notes; "false statement" — 163.2(1); "flow-through share" — 66(15), 248(1); "gross compensation" — 163.2(1), (12)(c); "gross entitlements" — 163.2(1); "Minister" — 248(1); "other person" — 163.2(2), (4); "participates" — 163.2(1); "partnership" — see 96(1) Notes; "person" — 163.2(1), 248(1); "planning activity" — 163.2(1); "prescribed", "property", "specified employee" — 248(1); "subordinate", "tax benefit" — 163.2(1); "trust" — 104(1), 248(1), (3); "valuation activity" — 163.2(1).

Information Circulars [s. 163.2]: 01-1: Third-party civil penalties.

I.T. Technical News [s. 163.2]: 32 (application of penalties); 34 (third party penalties).

CRA Audit Manual [s. 163.2]: 28.5.0: Third-party civil penalties.

163.3 [Zappers] — **(1) Definitions** — The following definitions apply in this section.

"electronic cash register" means a device that keeps a register or supporting documents through the means of an electronic device or computer system designed to record transaction data or any other electronic point-of-sale system.

"electronic suppression of sales device" means

(a) a software program that falsifies the records of electronic cash registers, including transaction data and transaction reports; or

(b) a hidden programming option, whether preinstalled or installed at a later time, embedded in the operating system of an electronic cash register or hardwired into the electronic cash register that

(i) may be used to create a virtual second till, or

(ii) may eliminate or manipulate transaction records, which may or may not be preserved in digital formats, in order to represent the actual or manipulated record of transactions in the electronic cash register.

"service" has the same meaning as in subsection 123(1) of the *Excise Tax Act*.

Notes: *Excise Tax Act* s. 123(1), which applies for GST/HST purposes, provides:

"service" means anything other than

(a) property,

(b) money, and

(c) anything that is supplied to an employer by a person who is or agrees to become an employee of the employer in the course of or in relation to the office or employment of that person;

ETA 123(1) also has definitions of "property", "money", "employer" and "person",

(2) Penalty — use [of zapper software or device] — Every person that uses, or that knowingly, or under circumstances attributable to neglect, carelessness or wilful default, participates in, assents to or acquiesces in the use of, an electronic suppression of sales device or a similar device or software in relation to records that are required to be kept by any person under section 230 is liable to a penalty of

(a) unless paragraph (b) applies, $5,000; or

(b) $50,000 if the action of the person occurs after the Minister has assessed a penalty payable by the person under this section or section 285.01 of the *Excise Tax Act*.

Related Provisions: See at end of 163.3.

Notes: See Notes at end of 163.3. For the meaning of "neglect" and "carelessness", see Notes to 152(4) re 152(4)(a)(i).

(3) Penalty — possession [of zapper software or device] — Every person that acquires or possesses an electronic suppression of sales device or a right in respect of an electronic suppression of sales device that is, or is intended to be, capable of being used in relation to records that are required to be kept by any person under section 230 is liable to a penalty of

(a) unless paragraph (b) applies, $5,000; or

(b) $50,000 if the action of the person occurs after the Minister has assessed a penalty payable by the person under this section or section 285.01 of the *Excise Tax Act*.

Related Provisions: See at end of 163.3.

Notes: See Notes at end of 163.3. This rule is subject to a due-diligence defence: 163.3(8).

(4) Penalty — manufacturing or making available [zapper software or device] — Every person that designs, develops, manufactures, possesses for sale, offers for sale, sells, transfers or otherwise makes available to another person, or that supplies installation, upgrade or maintenance services for, an electronic suppression of sales device that is, or is intended to be, capable of being used in relation to records that are required to be kept by any person under section 230 is liable to a penalty of

(a) unless paragraph (b) or (c) applies, $10,000;

(b) unless paragraph (c) applies, $50,000 if the action of the person occurs after the Minister has assessed a penalty payable by the person under subsection (2) or (3) or subsection 285.01(2) or (3) of the *Excise Tax Act*; or

(c) $100,000 if the action of the person occurs after the Minister has assessed a penalty payable by the person under this subsection or subsection 285.01(4) of the *Excise Tax Act*.

Related Provisions: See at end of 163.3.

Notes: See Notes at end of 163.3. This rule is subject to a due-diligence defence: 163.3(8).

(5) Assessment — The Minister may at any time assess a taxpayer in respect of any penalty payable by a person under subsections (2) to (4), and the provisions of this Division apply, with any modifications that the circumstances require, in respect of an assessment made under subsections (2) to (4) as though it had been made under section 152.

(6) Limitation — Despite section 152, if at any time the Minister assesses a penalty payable by a person under subsections (2) to (4), the Minister is not to assess, at or after that time, another penalty payable by the person under subsections (2) to (4) that is in respect of an action of the person that occurred before that time.

(7) Certain defences not available — Except as otherwise provided in subsection (8), a person does not have a defence in relation to a penalty assessed under subsections (2) to (4) by reason that the person exercised due diligence to prevent the action from occurring.

Notes: See Notes to 163.3(8).

(8) Due diligence — A person is not liable for a penalty under subsection (3) or (4) in respect of an action of the person if the person exercised the degree of care, diligence and skill that a reasonably prudent person would have exercised in comparable circumstances to prevent the action from occurring.

Notes: This due-diligence defence uses the same wording as 227.1(3), so the jurisprudence under 227.1(3) (and *Excise Tax Act* 323(3) — GST/HST) applies, and the person will need to show positive efforts to prevent the action. Due to 163.3(7), the regular due-diligence defence against penalties (see Notes to 162(1)) is not available. However, 163.3(2) applies only "knowingly or under neglect, carelessness or wilful default", and does not have this due-diligence defence.

(9) Assessment vacated — For the purposes of subsections (2) to (8), if an assessment of a penalty under subsections (2) to (4) is vacated, the penalty is deemed to have never been assessed.

Notes: This rule prevents an assessment that was vacated (whether on objection or by the Tax Court) from counting "against" a person to result in the $50,000 or $100,000 penalties under 163.3(2)(b), (3)(b), (4)(b) or (4)(c).

Related Provisions [s. 163.3]: 18(1)(t) — Penalty is non-deductible; 161(11) — Interest on penalty; 220(3.1) — Waiver of penalty; 222(1)"tax debt" — Penalty collectible as tax debt, subject to 10-year collection limitation period; 239(3) — Penalty cannot be assessed after charge laid if person convicted; 239.1(1) — Definitions in 163.3(1) apply to 239.1; 239.1(2) — Criminal offence — use, possession, sale, etc. of zapper software or device; 239.1(4) — Whether person convicted under 239.1 is also liable for penalty under 163.3.

Notes [s. 163.3]: 163.3 imposes a penalty on the use (163.3(2)), possession (163.3(3)), manufacture or sale (163.3(4)) of "zapper" software (or hardware) that suppresses a portion of cash-register sales. 163.3(2) has a "knowingly or neglect or carelessness" test; the others have a due-diligence defence.

The penalty for use or possession is $5,000, with CRA having no discretion to assess a smaller penalty. For manufacture or sale, the penalty is $10,000. For a second infraction (where the person had previously been assessed the penalty under either 163.3 or ETA 285.01 before the new action), the penalty is $50,000, or $100,000 for manufacture or sale. There appears to be no time limit for assessing a penalty under 163.3: the limitations in 152(4) apply only to an assessment of *tax*.

Excise Tax Act s. 285.01 provides a parallel penalty, so each penalty is actually *double* the amount stated above (except in the rare case of a business with no GST/HST record-keeping obligations, such as a provider of exempt heath care). If the provinces enact parallel penalties (as may be required under their tax collection agreements with Canada, and as Quebec and Ontario have already announced), the possible penalties will be *triple* the amounts shown. (See Notes to 163(1) for cases of both federal and provincial penalties being imposed for the same act.)

The penalty can be waived or cancelled by CRA under 220(3.1). (The penalty under ETA 285.01 cannot be waived or cancelled, though of course CRA can choose not to assess it in the first place, or can cancel it by concluding that the facts do not support the imposition of the penalty.)

The person can also be charged criminally with an offence under 239.1 and/or ETA 327.1 (max fine $1 million and 5 years' imprisonment; minimum fine $10,000). See Notes to 239(1) re distinction between an administrative penalty and a criminal charge.

See Notes to 239.1 for Quebec's requirement for restaurants and bars to provide customers with SRM receipts, and Ontario's consideration of this issue.

163.3 added by 2013 budget bill #2, effective 2014.

Definitions [s. 163.3]: "assessment" — 248(1); "electronic cash register", "electronic suppression of sales device" — 163.3(1); "Minister", "person", "record" — 248(1); "service" — 163.3(1).

Refunds

164. (1) Refunds — If the return of a taxpayer's income for a taxation year has been made within 3 years from the end of the year, the Minister

(a) may,

(i) before sending the notice of assessment for the year, where the taxpayer is, for any purpose of the definition "refundable investment tax credit" (as defined in subsection 127.1(2)), a qualifying corporation (as defined in that subsection) and claims in its return of income for the year to have paid an amount on account of its tax payable under this Part for the year because of subsection 127.1(1) in respect of its refundable investment tax credit (as defined in subsection 127.1(2)), refund all or part of any amount claimed in the return as an overpayment for the year, not exceeding the amount by which the total determined under paragraph (f) of the definition "refundable investment tax credit" in subsection 127.1(2) in respect of the taxpayer for the year exceeds the total determined under paragraph (g) of that definition in respect of the taxpayer for the year,

(ii) before sending the notice of assessment for the year, where the taxpayer is a "qualified corporation" (as defined in subsection 125.4(1)), an "eligible production corporation" (as defined in subsection 125.5(1)) or a "qualifying journalism organization" (as defined in subsection 125.6(1)) and an amount is deemed under subsection 125.4(3), 125.5(3) or 125.6(2) or (2.1) to have been paid on account of its tax payable under this Part for the year, refund all or part of any amount claimed in the return as an overpayment for the year, not exceeding the total of those amounts so deemed to have been paid, and

(iii) on or after sending the notice of assessment for the year, refund any overpayment for the year, to the extent that the overpayment was not refunded pursuant to subparagraph (i) or (ii); and

(b) shall, with all due dispatch, make the refund referred to in subparagraph (a)(iii) after sending the notice of assessment if application for it is made in writing by the taxpayer within the period within which the Minister would be allowed under subsection 152(4) to assess tax payable under this Part by the taxpayer for the year if that subsection were read without reference to paragraph 152(4)(a).

Related Provisions: 160.1 — Where excess refunded; 161.4(2) — No refund of $2 or less; 164(1.5) — Late refund of overpayment; 164(1.52) — Refund of instalments on request; 164(1.8) — Request to pay refund to prescribed province; 164(2) — Refund applied to other debt; 164(2.01) — No refund paid until all income tax and GST returns filed; 164(2.3) — Canada Child Benefit form deemed to be a return of income; 164(3) — Interest on refund; 220(6) — Assignment of corporation's tax refund; 244(14), (14.1) — Date notice sent; *Interpretation Act* 27(5) — Meaning of "within 3 years"; *Tax Rebate Discounting Act* — Assignment of personal income tax refund to tax return preparer.

Notes: Refunds can be made by direct deposit (DD): tinyurl.com/cra-deposit. Use Form T1-DD(1) (individuals), T2-DD (corps), or online; "tell us once" means direct-deposit details can be shared among CRA, CPP and esdc.gc.ca (CRA news release, Feb. 14, 2018). Frauds have been committed by changing taxpayers' DD information; those signed up for email notification are advised if it changes: VIEWS doc 2019-0816111C6 [2019 CPTS], q.7. CRA had planned to eliminate cheques and use only DD from April 2016, but this was dropped: May 2015 ICAA roundtable (tinyurl.com/cra-abtax), q. 6. Uncashed refund cheques are listed online, on My Account, since March 2020. A refund is non-taxable, except for any interest included: 2016-0641771E5.

For the status of a personal tax refund, go to canada.ca/my-cra-account or call the Tax Information Phone Service (TIPS) at 1-800-267-6999 (see tinyurl.com/cra-tips).

See Notes to 152(1) on the meaning of "all due dispatch", and CRA refusing to assess (and pay a refund) until it finishes its audit.

A corporate tax refund can be assigned under 220(6), and a personal income tax refund can be assigned under the *Tax Rebate Discounting Act*. See Notes to 220(6).

A refund for the year of bankruptcy vests in the bankruptcy trustee, due to *Bankruptcy and Insolvency Act* s. 67(1)(c): VIEWS doc 2008-030490117. The refund is normally a family asset on divorce, unless the parties have agreed otherwise: *Hutton v. Hutton*, 2010 BCSC 923.

Refunds can be applied to other federal or provincial debts of any kind: see 164(2). Since April 2007, refunds can be withheld from taxpayers who have outstanding unpaid assessments under objection or appeal, due to the repeal of 225.1(1)(e). Refunds are not paid to a taxpayer who has any overdue income tax or GST returns: see 164(2.01). See also Notes to 224.1.

Where the 3-year deadline in the opening words is not met (e.g., *715476 Alberta*, 2006 TCC 93, or *Landmark Auto*, 2008 TCC 121), CRA said it cannot waive or extend the deadline via 220(2.1) or (3) (VIEWS doc 2008-026958117, but in light of *Bonnybrook Industrial*, 2018 FCA 136, ruling on the same issue for 129(1), 220(3) *can* be used to extend the 3-year deadline. For an individual or graduated rate estate, CRA can also provide relief under 164(1.5), subject to a 10-year limitation period.

One can also ask CRA to transfer an unrefunded instalment balance under 221.2 to another year for which tax is or will be owing. CRA now has a harsh "extraordinary circumstances" requirement (Form RC431) for this (see Notes to 221.2), after these Notes from 2000-2014 described the author's success in having several such transfers done. As the policy is unfair, the author and CPA Canada asked Finance in 2015 (tinyurl.com/ds-cpa-fin) to change 164(1) to always permit refund of a corp's money, with a penalty for very late filing; the current rule is a "confiscation of the taxpayer's property" that is "abusive" and "deplorable": *Chalifoux*, [1991] 2 C.T.C. 2243 (TCC), paras. 10-12. (At the 2017 Cdn Tax Foundation annual conference (conf. report, 32:11), CRA's Ted Gallivan agreed that "the status quo is not acceptable" and said "there will be clarity on this issue in 2018", but that did not happen.)

The TCC has no jurisdiction to hear an appeal of the refund not being paid out: *3735851 Canada*, 2010 TCC 24.

If the 3-year deadline is missed and CRA issues an arbitrary assessment, and the corporation then files (or objects) and gets a reduced assessment, the overpayment cannot be refunded (other than by applying 221.2): *Clover International*, 2013 FC 676; VIEWS doc 2014-0538901E5.

However, if a corp objects to or appeals its assessment, a refund can possibly be paid under 164(1.1) or (4.1) despite the missed deadline.

Where the deadline in 164(1)(b) is missed, having filed a waiver under 152(4)(a)(ii) does not entitle the taxpayer to the refund: VIEWS doc 2012-046808117, but does if the waiver "contains an implicit request for a refund for the particular issue outlined in the waiver": 2015-058308117.

"Overpayment": Where CRA Collections seizes too much from the taxpayer to pay a tax debt, there is arguably no "overpayment" under (a)(iii) (see 164(7)) that is subject to the 3-year limitation; but without 164(1) it is unclear what authority provides for refund of the overseized amount (perhaps general debtor-creditor principles). In *984274 Alberta*, 2020 FCA 125 (reversing the TCC; leave to appeal denied 2021 CarswellNat 1167 (SCC)), a nil assessment issued past the statute-barred deadline triggered an "overpayment" to which 164(1) applied, so the refund CRA paid was recoverable via 160.1 when the assessment was reversed.

If CRA claims a refund cheque was sent but cannot produce the cancelled cheque, the Federal Court can order a Statement of Account adjusted to delete the refund: *Workum*, 2005 FC 991. In *Madore*, 2018 FC 244, CRA refused to pay a refund of $205,000 allegedly withheld by IBM on employment income of $923 without doing a payroll audit of IBM; an application to order CRA to pay the refund was dismissed as premature.

See also Ian Crosbie, "Amended Returns, Refunds and Interest", 2012 *Tax Dispute Resolution* conf. report (ctf.ca), 27:1-33.

164(1)(a)(ii) amended by 2021 budget bill #1, effective 2019, to refer to 125.6(2.1).

164(1)(a)(ii) amended by 2019 budget bill #1, effective 2019, to add references to a qualifying journalism organization and 125.6(2).

164(1)(a), (b) amended by 2010 budget bill #2, effective Dec. 15, 2010, to change "mailing" to "sending" (4 places), to accommodate electronic notices under 244(14.1).

164(1) earlier amended by 2004 Budget (for taxation years ending after March 22, 2004), 2001 and 1995-97 technical bills, 1989 Budget.

Information Circulars: 75-7R3: Reassessment of a return of income; 01-1: Third-party civil penalties; 07-1R1: Taxpayer relief provisions.

Forms: RC431: Request for re-appropriation of T2 statute-barred credits; T1-DD: Direct deposit request — individuals; T1132: Alternative address authorization.

(1.1) Repayment on objections and appeals — Subject to subsection (1.2), where a taxpayer

(a) has under section 165 served a notice of objection to an assessment and the Minister has not within 120 days after the day of service confirmed or varied the assessment or made a reassessment in respect thereof, or

(b) has appealed from an assessment to the Tax Court of Canada,

and has applied in writing to the Minister for a payment or surrender of security, the Minister shall, where no authorization has been granted under subsection 225.2(2) in respect of the amount assessed, with all due dispatch repay all amounts paid on account of that amount or surrender security accepted therefor to the extent that

(c) the lesser of

(i) the total of the amounts so paid and the value of the security, and

(ii) the amount so assessed

exceeds

(d) the total of

(i) the amount, if any, so assessed that is not in controversy, and

(ii) ½ of the amount so assessed that is in controversy if

(A) the taxpayer is a large corporation (within the meaning assigned by subsection 225.1(8)), or

(B) the amount is in respect of a particular amount claimed under section 110.1 or 118.1 and the particular amount was claimed in respect of a tax shelter.

Related Provisions: 164(1.7) — 164(1.1) does not apply to security under s. 116; 225.1(7) — Limitation on collection restrictions — large corporations; *Interpretation Act* 27(5) — Meaning of "within 120 days".

Notes: 164(1.1) is consistent with 225.1(1), which permits most taxpayers to withhold payment of tax under dispute. See Notes to 158.

If a 225.2(2) jeopardy order is cancelled, the resulting refund (pending the taxpayer's TCC appeal) bears interest: *Grenon*, 2017 FCA 167 (reversing the FC).

164(1.1)(d)(ii)(B), added by 2013 budget bill #1 for amounts assessed for taxation years that end after 2012, implements a Budget proposal (along with 225.1(7)) to require payment of half the amount in dispute when a donation credit based on a tax shelter is denied. See Notes to 118.1(1)"total charitable gifts".

164(1.1) amended by 1992 technical bill, effective June 11, 1993.

(1.2) Collection in jeopardy — Notwithstanding subsection (1.1), where, on application by the Minister made within 45 days after the receipt by the Minister of a written request by a taxpayer for repayment of an amount or surrender of a security, a judge is satisfied that there are reasonable grounds to believe that the collection of all or any part of an amount assessed in respect of the taxpayer would be jeopardized by the repayment of the amount or the surrender of the security to the taxpayer under that subsection, the judge shall order that the repayment of the amount or a part thereof not be made or that the security or part thereof not be surrendered or make such other order as the judge considers reasonable in the circumstances.

Related Provisions: 225.2(2) — Lifting of collection restrictions where collection of tax in jeopardy; *Interpretation Act* 27(5) — Meaning of "within 45 days".

Notes: The test for 164(1.2) is different than for jeopardy collection orders under 225.2(2); "delay is not an issue because the funds are held by the government and are not at risk of being dissipated": *Chabot*, 2010 FC 574, para. 21; *Clarke*, 2011 FC 838; *0741449 B.C. Ltd.*, 2016 FC 530 (refunds ordered held back in all 3 cases).

CRA Audit Manual: 11.5.5: Jeopardy assessments.

(1.3) Notice of application — The Minister shall give 6 clear days notice of an application under subsection (1.2) to the taxpayer in respect of whom the application is made.

Related Provisions: *Interpretation Act* 27(1) — Calculation of "clear days".

(1.31) Application of subsecs. 225.2(4), (10), (12) and (13) — Where an application under subsection (1.2) is made by the Minister, subsections 225.2(4), (10), (12) and (13) are applicable in respect of the application with such modifications as the circumstances require.

(1.4) Provincial refund — Where, at any time, a taxpayer is entitled to a refund or repayment on account of taxes imposed by a province or as a result of a deduction in computing the taxes imposed by a province and the Government of Canada has agreed to make the refund or repayment on behalf of the province, the amount thereof shall be a liability of the Minister of National Revenue to the taxpayer.

(1.5) Exception [Late refund of overpayment] — Notwithstanding subsection (1), the Minister may, on or after sending a notice of assessment for a taxation year, refund all or any portion of any overpayment of a taxpayer for the year

(a) if the taxpayer is an individual (other than a trust) or a graduated rate estate for the year and the taxpayer's return of income under this Part for the year was filed on or before the day that is 10 calendar years after the end of the year;

(b) where an assessment or a redetermination was made under subsection 152(4.2) or 220(3.1) or (3.4) in respect of the taxpayer; or

(c) to the extent that the overpayment relates to an assessment of another taxpayer under subsection 227(10) or (10.1) (in this paragraph referred to as the "other assessment"), if the taxpayer's return of income under this Part for the taxation year is filed on or before the day that is two years after the date of the other assessment and if the other assessment relates to

(i) in the case of an amount assessed under subsection 227(10), a payment to the taxpayer of a fee, commission or other amount in respect of services rendered in Canada by a non-resident person or partnership, and

(ii) in the case of an amount assessed under subsection 227(10.1), an amount payable under subsection 116(5) or (5.3) in respect of a disposition of property by the taxpayer.

Related Provisions: 152(4.2) — Reassessment with taxpayer's consent; 164(3.2) — Interest on refunds and repayments; 244(14), (14.1) — Date when notice sent.

Notes: 164(1.5) is part of the "Taxpayer Relief" legislation, called "Fairness" from 1991 to 2007. It permits an overpayment by an individual or GRE (248(1)"graduated rate estate") (such as from instalments or source withholdings) to be refunded past the 3-year limit in 164(1), provided the return is filed within 10 years of year-end (even if an adjustment to the return, creating the refund, is requested after the 10 years: VIEWS docs 2006-020236117, 2011-042210117). 164(1.5) does not apply to BC and Manitoba provincial refundable credits: 2017-0699781E5. For corporations, see Notes to 164(1).

Relief under 164(1.5) is at CRA discretion: VIEWS doc 2008-026958117. Policy on granting relief is in Information Circular 07-1R1 paras. 67-75. As with 152(4.2), it is a generous policy: normally relief is given if the taxpayer neglected to claim a refund that was available, provided it is not due to an optional claim (like CCA) or another taxpayer's success in the Courts. If relief is refused, judicial review is available in the Federal Court: see Notes to 220(3.1).

The 10-year deadline applies to returns filed after 2004. Relief for earlier years can still be granted under the pre-2005 version of 164(1.5)!

164(1.5)(a) amended by 2014 budget bill #2, for 2016 and later tax years, to change "is a testamentary trust" to "a graduated rate estate for the year". (See Notes to 122(1).)

164(1.5) opening words amended by 2010 budget bill #2, effective Dec. 15, 2010, to change "mailing" to "sending" (to accommodate electronic notices under 244(14.1)).

164(1.5)(c) added by 2010 budget bill #1, effective for overpayments in respect of which applications for refunds are made after March 4, 2010. Finance says that it is needed because there is no deadline for CRA to assess a payor who fails to withhold taxes, while the non-resident's refund application deadline may have passed (for an illustration see the trial decision in *FMC Technologies*, 2008 FC 871, para. 32). See also Ernst, "Canada Moves to Eliminate Timing Problem for Refunds to Nonresidents", 58(10) *Tax Notes International* (taxnotes.com) 827-29 (June 7, 2010).

164(1.5)(a) amended by 2004 Budget, for returns filed after 2004, to introduce the 10-year limit.

164(1.5) added by 1991 technical bill and amended retroactively by 1992 technical bill, for refunds for 1985 and later taxation years.

Information Circulars: 75-7R3: Reassessment of a return of income; 07-1R1: Taxpayer relief provisions.

CRA Audit Manual: 3.0: Fairness and client rights; 11.6.6 and Appendix A-11.2.24: Fairness report.

Forms: RC376: Taxpayer relief request statement of income and expenses and assets and liabilities for individuals; RC4288: Request for taxpayer relief.

(1.51) When subsec. (1.52) applies — Subsection (1.52) applies to a taxpayer for a taxation year if, at any time after the beginning of the year

(a) the taxpayer has, in respect of the tax payable by the taxpayer under this Part (and, if the taxpayer is a corporation, Parts I.3, VI, VI.1 and XIII.1) for the year, paid under any of sections 155 to 157 one or more instalments of tax;

(b) it is reasonable to conclude that the total amount of those instalments exceeds the total amount of taxes that will be payable by the taxpayer under those Parts for the year; and

(c) the Minister is satisfied that the payment of the instalments has caused or will cause undue hardship to the taxpayer.

Notes: 164(1.51) added by 2002-2013 technical bill, effective June 26, 2013.

(1.52) Instalment refund — If this subsection applies to a taxpayer for a taxation year, the Minister may refund to the taxpayer all or any part of the excess referred to in paragraph (1.51)(b).

Related Provisions: 164(1.51) — Conditions for 164(1.52) to apply; 164(1.53) — Refunded instalment deemed not paid for penalty/interest purposes.

Notes: Although there was no explicit authority, CRA policy for many years has been to refund personal income tax instalments on request.

164(1.52) added by 2002-2013 technical bill, effective June 26, 2013.

(1.53) Penalties, interest not affected — For the purpose of the calculation of any penalty or interest under this Act, an instalment is deemed not to have been paid to the extent that all or any part of the instalment can reasonably be considered to have been refunded under subsection (1.52).

Notes: 164(1.53) is too primitive. No credit is given for the period during which the instalments were held by CRA. Contra interest should be applied under 161(2.2). Even without 164(1.53), however, the author's experience is that where CRA has refunded instalments that would have generated contra interest, the resulting interest will be cancelled under 220(3.1) if a Taxpayer Relief request is made.

164(1.53) added by 2002-2013 technical bill, effective June 26, 2013.

(1.6) COVID-19 refunds — Notwithstanding subsection (2.01), at any time after the beginning of a taxation year of a taxpayer in which an overpayment is deemed to have arisen under any of subsections 125.7(2) to (2.2), the Minister may refund to the taxpayer all or any part of the overpayment.

Related Provisions: 164(1.61) — Application to partnership.

Notes: 164(1.6) added by 2020 COVID bill #2, effective April 11, 2020; amended by 2020 COVID bill #5, effective Nov. 19, 2020, to apply to 125.7(2.1) (CERS); and amended by 2021 budget bill #1, effective June 29, 2021, to apply to 125.7(2.2). It allows the Canada Emergency Wage Subsidy, Canada Emergency Rent Subsidy or Canada Recovery Hiring Program to be paid without waiting for a return to be filed after year-end. 2020 COVID bill #2 s.7 provides that for purposes of 164(1.6), CRA "may make payments to a person or partnership out of the Consolidated Revenue Fund, at the times and in the manner that the Minister considers appropriate".

Former 164(1.6), repealed by 2002-2013 technical bill, effective March 21, 2003, provided for refund of the 126.1 UI premium tax credit, which was only for 1993. Added by 1992 Economic Statement. A different proposed 164(1.6) was enacted as 164(1.7).

(1.61) COVID-19 refunds — partnerships — For the purposes of subsection (1.6), references to a taxpayer include a partnership and the reference to a taxation year includes a fiscal period.

(1.7) Limitation of repayment on objections and appeals — Subsection (1.1) does not apply in respect of an amount paid or security furnished under section 116 by a non-resident person.

Notes: 164(1.7) added by 1993 Budget bill, effective May 12, 1994.

(1.8) Request to pay refund to province — An individual (other than a trust) may, in the individual's return of income for a taxation year, request the Minister to pay to Her Majesty in right of a prescribed province all or any part of a refund for the year claimed by the individual in the return and, where the individual makes such a request,

(a) the Minister may make the payment to Her Majesty in right of the province in accordance with the request; and

(b) the amount of the payment is deemed to have been refunded under this section to the individual at the time a notice of an

original assessment of tax payable under this Part by the individual for the year, or a notification that no tax is payable under this Part by the individual for the year, is sent to the individual.

Related Provisions: 241(4)(m) — Disclosure of information by CRA to prescribed province.

Notes: 164(1.8) added by 1995-97 technical bill, for requests made in returns for 1997 and later tax years that are filed after 1997. It allows Ontario residents to designate any amount of their tax refund (on the last page of the T1 return) to the Ontario Opportunities Fund. About $1 million was donated 1996-2004: tinyurl.com/oof-2006.

Regulations: Prop. amend., but s. 190(12) of the 1995-97 technical bill (1998, c. 19) deems Ontario to be a prescribed province until Regulations are provided. Ontario is to be prescribed in the Regulations (Department of Finance Technical Notes, Dec. 1997).

(2) Application to other debts — Instead of making a refund or repayment that might otherwise be made under this section, the Minister may, where the taxpayer is, or is about to become, liable to make any payment to Her Majesty in right of Canada or in right of a province, apply the amount of the refund or repayment to that other liability and notify the taxpayer of that action.

Related Provisions: 164(2.1) — Application of GST credit; 164(2.2) — Application to refunds under s. 122.61; 164(3.2) — Interest on refunds and repayments; 164(7) — Overpayment defined; 165 — Objections to assessments; 169 — Appeals; 172 — Appeals; 203 — Set-off of Part X refund; 222(1)"action" — Ten-year limitation period applies to 164(2); 224.1 — Set-off of tax debt against other amount owing by the Crown to the taxpayer; 227 — Withholding taxes; 241(4)(d)(xiii)(B) — Disclosure of information by CRA to provincial officials for set-off purposes.

Notes: 164(2) allows an income tax refund to be set off against another liability (e.g., a GST assessment). 224.1 allows another refund (e.g. a GST refund) to be offset against an income tax liability. This is done automatically where the Business Number is the same, e.g. corporate income tax refund applied to GST/HST balance, which can lead to errors: 2019 CPA Alberta (tinyurl.com/cra-abtax), Plenary q.6.

The words "is about to become" apply only if the debt is "imminently pending", *Creative Graphic*, 1975 CarswellNat 117 (FCA); VIEWS doc 2009-032693117. A non-resident's failure to post GST security as required by *Excise Tax Act* 240(6) is not grounds for withholding a refund; VIEWS doc 2013-0483031E5. Outside Quebec, it appears that posting security is not "payment": *Industries Perron*, 2013 FCA 176, paras. 39-40.

In *Simon*, 2011 FCA 6 (leave to appeal denied 2012 CarswellNat 3748 (SCC)), CRA had used the taxpayer's refund to pay a claim British Columbia had for social assistance paid to the taxpayer's wife, whom he had sponsored into Canada. The FCA ruled that the taxpayer could bring action in Federal Court to challenge CRA's action.

In *Hérold*, 2013 FCA 19, CRA was held to have been correct in applying the taxpayer's income tax refunds to her Canada Student Loan debt (which was found not to be statute-barred).

"There is a large number of Crown or federally-administered debts that may be set-off from personal or corporate income tax refunds. Any federal, provincial or territorial department, agency or Crown corporation may participate in the Refund Set-Off (RSO) program.... A list of RSO partners is not available for distribution": CRA May 2007 ICAA roundtable (tinyurl.com/cra-abtax), Q28. The author obtained the list in 2008 via Access to Information: it lists 63 federal programs and 101 provincial and territorial programs (none in NB, Quebec, Nunavut or Yukon). The Ontario budget of March 27, 2012 proposes to have *Provincial Offences Act* unpaid fines (including speeding tickets) set off against CRA tax refunds.

CRA also collects certain non-tax government debts, such as defaulted Canada Student Loans [e.g., *Cisse*, 2016 ONSC 7217]; EI, CPP and OAS overpayments; and Labour Program receivables. See Information Circular 13-2R1.

164(2) amended by 1995-97 technical bill (effective June 18, 1998), 1991 technical bill.

Information Circulars: 13-2R1: Government programs collection policies.

(2.01) Withholding of refunds — The Minister shall not, in respect of a taxpayer, refund, repay, apply to other debts or set-off amounts under this Act at any time unless all returns of which the Minister has knowledge and that are required to be filed by the taxpayer at or before that time under this Act, the *Air Travellers Security Charge Act*, the *Excise Act, 2001* and the *Excise Tax Act* have been filed with the Minister.

Related Provisions: 164(1.6) — COVID-19 wage subsidy payable despite 164(2.01).

Notes: This rule prevents income tax refunds (other than the Canada Emergency Wage Subsidy) from being paid to a taxpayer who has any overdue income tax or GST/HST returns. Similarly, *Excise Tax Act* ss. 229(2) and 263.02 (see David M. Sherman, *The Practitioner's Goods and Services Tax, Annotated*) prevent GST/HST refunds and rebates from being paid to a taxpayer who has any such returns unfiled (CRA does not enforce this for tax-exempt corporations such as charities and NPOs: Fact Sheet, April 25, 2012 [see *GST & HST Times* 269P]).

164(2.01) does not apply to a non-resident's failure to file Form GST114 and post security for GST/HST under *Excise Tax Act* 240(6), as that form is not a "return": VIEWS doc 2013-0483031E5.

164(2.01) applies to a trustee in bankruptcy if the bankrupt has unfiled returns, which the trustee is required by 150(3) to file: VIEWS doc 2011-0422581I7.

164(2.01) added by 2006 budget bill #1, effective April 2007.

(2.1) Application respecting refunds under s. 122.5 [GST/HST credit] — Where an amount deemed under section 122.5 to be paid by an individual during a month specified for a taxation year is applied under subsection (2) to a liability of the individual and the individual's return of income for the year is filed on or before the individual's balance-due day for the year, the amount is deemed to have been so applied on the day on which the amount would have been refunded if the individual were not liable to make a payment to Her Majesty in right of Canada.

Notes: 164(2.1) amended by 1995-97 technical bill, effective June 18, 1998.

164(2.1) added by 1990 GST, effective 1989. It relates to the GST credit.

(2.2) Application respecting refunds re section 122.61 [Canada Child Benefit] — Subsection (2) does not apply to a refund to be made to a taxpayer and arising because of section 122.61 except to the extent that the taxpayer's liability referred to in that subsection arose from the operation of paragraph 160.1(1)(a) with respect to an amount refunded to the taxpayer in excess of the amount to which the taxpayer was entitled because of section 122.61.

Notes: 164(2.2) added by 1992 Child Benefit bill, for overpayments arising in 1993 or later.

(2.3) [Canada Child Benefit] Form deemed to be return of income — For the purpose of subsection (1), where a taxpayer files the form referred to in paragraph (b) of the definition "return of income" in section 122.6 for a taxation year, the form is deemed to be a return of the taxpayer's income for that year and a notice of assessment in respect of that return is deemed to have been sent by the Minister.

Notes: 164(2.3) amended by 2010 budget bill #2, effective Dec. 15, 2010, to change "mailed" to "sent" to accommodate electronic notices under 244(14.1).

164(2.3) added by 1992 Child Benefit bill, for overpayments arising in 1993 or later.

(3) Interest on refunds and repayments — If, under this section, an amount in respect of a taxation year (other than an amount, or a portion of the amount, that can reasonably be considered to arise from the operation of section 122.5, 122.61 or 125.7) is refunded or repaid to a taxpayer or applied to another liability of the taxpayer, the Minister shall pay or apply interest on it at the prescribed rate for the period that begins on the day that is the latest of the days referred to in the following paragraphs and that ends on the day on which the amount is refunded, repaid or applied:

(a) if the taxpayer is an individual, the day that is 30 days after the individual's balance-due day for the year;

(b) if the taxpayer is a corporation, the day that is 120 days after the end of the year;

(c) if the taxpayer is

(i) a corporation, the day that is 30 days after the day on which its return of income for the year was filed under section 150, unless the return was filed on or before the corporation's filing-due date for the year, and

(ii) an individual, the day that is 30 days after the day on which the individual's return of income for the year was filed under section 150;

(d) in the case of a refund of an overpayment, the day on which the overpayment arose; and

(e) in the case of a repayment of an amount in controversy, the day on which an overpayment equal to the amount of the repayment would have arisen if the total of all amounts payable on account of the taxpayer's liability under this Part for the year were the amount by which

(i) the lesser of the total of all amounts paid on account of the taxpayer's liability under this Part for the year and the total

of all amounts assessed by the Minister as payable under this Part by the taxpayer for the year

exceeds

(ii) the amount repaid.

Related Provisions: 12(1)(c) — Interest is taxable; 20(1)(ll) — Deduction for refund interest repaid; 129(2.1) — Interest on dividend refund; 131(3.1), 132(2.1) — Interest on capital gains refund; 161.1 — Offset of refund interest against arrears interest; 221.1 — Application of interest where legislation retroactive; 248(11) — Interest compounded daily.

Notes: Refund interest (at the rate in Reg. 4301(b)) is taxable under 12(1)(c), but in some cases may instead be taxable as business income (and thus eligible for the s. 125 small business deduction). See 12(1)(c) Notes.

The date the return "was filed" (para. (c)) means the original return; an overpayment "arises" (para. (d) and 164(7)) once payments on account exceed tax payable (except where 164(5) applies): VIEWS doc 2005-0151221E5.

In *Glatt*, 2019 FC 738, CRA was ordered to pay interest on G's $1m payment of a 163.2 penalty; the "reassessment" cancelling the penalty triggered 164(3) (CRA argued it was merely a notice of refund and did not apply to any tax year).

Refund interest is payable on tax prepaid for an anticipated reassessment, but only (in CRA's view) if there is a *bona fide* possibility of reassessment: VIEWS doc 2008-0301761E5. Formerly CRA allowed corps to keep total $4 billion on deposit with no pending reassessment, which led to $30 million in excessive interest per year: Auditor General 2009 report Chapter 4 (oag-bvg.gc.ca). The 2010 federal budget announced a 2-point reduction in the refund interest rate for corps, from July 2010, to address this problem. See Reg. 4301(b)(ii).

As a further response (now unnecessary) to the Auditor General's report, CRA issued a Sept. 2010 Fact Sheet and Q&A (tinyurl.com/cra-prepay), stating that a business anticipating a reassessment for a previous year may make an advance deposit to reduce interest charges, using Form RC159, indicating the payment is an advance deposit and specifying the year(s) to which it applies. CRA will review advance deposits on a regular basis to ensure there is risk of reassessment for those years and that the amount is reasonable; if this is not confirmed, the deposit will be returned. Advance deposits can be transferred to other years on request. An overpayment can be held as an advance deposit only for the tax year the overpayment occurred, not transferred to another year as an advance deposit. See also doc 2011-0427281C6 for detailed discussion.

Refund interest on Part XIII non-resident withholding tax: see VIEWS docs 2007-0228081E5, 2009-032474I7; *Lord Rothermere Donation*, 2009 TCC 70.

Refund interest is not payable on a remission order, even if CRA pays the remission by crediting the taxpayer's Part I tax: *Imperial Oil Resources*, 2016 FCA 139.

Refund interest is not payable on funds seized under a 225.2(2) jeopardy order and refunded when the order is cancelled: *Grenon*, 2016 FC 604.

164(3) amended by 2020 COVID bill #2 (effective April 11, 2020, to exclude 125.7), 2002-2013 technical bill (for forms filed after March 20, 2003), 2003, 1995 and 1992 Budgets, 1992 Child Benefit bill, 1992 Economic Statement, 1990 GST.

Regulations: 4301(b) (prescribed rate of interest).

I.T. Application Rules: 62(2) (subsec. 164(3) applies to interest payable in respect of any period after December 23, 1971).

(3.1) Idem — Where at a particular time interest has been paid to, or applied to a liability of, a taxpayer under subsection (3) or (3.2) in respect of an overpayment and it is determined at a subsequent time that the actual overpayment was less than the overpayment in respect of which interest was paid or applied,

(a) the amount by which the interest that has been paid or applied exceeds the interest, if any, computed in respect of the amount that is determined at the subsequent time to be the actual overpayment shall be deemed to be an amount (in this subsection referred to as "the amount payable") that became payable under this Part by the taxpayer at the particular time;

(b) the taxpayer shall pay to the Receiver General interest at the prescribed rate on the amount payable computed from that particular time to the day of payment; and

(c) the Minister may at any time assess the taxpayer in respect of the amount payable and, where the Minister makes such an assessment, the provisions of this Division are applicable, with such modifications as the circumstances require, in respect of the assessment as though it had been made under section 152.

Related Provisions: 20(1)(ll) — Deduction on repayment of interest; 161.1 — Offset of refund interest against arrears interest; 221.1 — Application of interest where legislation retroactive; 248(11) — Interest compounded daily.

Notes: In *984274 Alberta*, 2020 FCA 125 (reversing the TCC; leave to appeal denied 2021 CarswellNat 1167 (SCC)), a nil assessment issued past the statute-barred deadline triggered an "overpayment" to which 164(1) and (3.1) applied.

Opening words of 164(3.1) amended by 1991 technical bill, effective for refunds for 1985 and later years.

Regulations: 4301(a) (prescribed rate of interest).

(3.2) Interest where amounts cancelled — Notwithstanding subsection (3), if an overpayment of a taxpayer for a taxation year is determined because of an assessment made under subsection 152(4.2) or 220(3.1) or (3.4) and an amount in respect of the overpayment is refunded to, or applied to another liability of, the taxpayer under subsection (1.5) or (2), the Minister shall pay or apply interest on the overpayment at the prescribed rate for the period beginning on the day that is 30 days after the day on which the Minister received a request in a manner satisfactory to the Minister to apply those subsections and ending on the day on which the amount is refunded or applied.

Related Provisions: 161.1 — Offset of refund interest against arrears interest; 221.1 — Application of interest where legislation retroactive; 248(11) — Interest compounded daily.

Notes: 164(3.2) amended by 2003 Budget, effective for requests received by the Minister of National Revenue after June 2003, primarily to add 30 days to the date on which interest starts being payable.

164(3.2) added by 1991 technical bill (as part of the "Fairness Package" (now called Taxpayer Relief); see 164(1.5)) and amended retroactively by 1992 technical bill, effective for refunds for 1985 and later taxation years.

Regulations: 4301(b) (prescribed rate of interest).

(4) Interest on interest repaid — Where at any particular time interest has been paid to, or applied to a liability of, a taxpayer pursuant to subsection (3) in respect of the repayment of an amount in controversy made to, or applied to a liability of, the taxpayer and it is determined at a subsequent time that the repayment or a part thereof is payable by the taxpayer under this Part, the following rules apply:

(a) the interest so paid or applied on that part of the repayment that is determined at the subsequent time to be payable by the taxpayer under this Part shall be deemed to be an amount (in this subsection referred to as the "interest excess") that became payable under this Part by the taxpayer at the particular time;

(b) the taxpayer shall pay to the Receiver General interest at the prescribed rate on the interest excess computed from the particular time to the day of payment; and

(c) the Minister may at any time assess the taxpayer in respect of the interest excess and, where the Minister makes such an assessment, the provisions of this Division and Division J are applicable, with such modifications as the circumstances require, in respect of the assessment as though it had been made under section 152.

Related Provisions: 12(1)(c) — Interest is taxable; 20(1)(ll) — Deduction for interest repaid; 161.1 — Offset of refund interest against arrears interest; 221.1 — Application of interest where legislation retroactive; 248(11) — Interest compounded daily.

Regulations: 4301(a) (prescribed rate of interest).

I.T. Application Rules: 62(2) (subsec. 164(4) applies to interest payable in respect of any period after December 23, 1971).

(4.1) Duty of Minister — Where the Tax Court of Canada, the Federal Court of Appeal or the Supreme Court of Canada has, on the disposition of an appeal in respect of taxes, interest or a penalty payable under this Act by a taxpayer resident in Canada,

(a) referred an assessment back to the Minister for reconsideration and reassessment, or

(b) varied or vacated an assessment,

the Minister shall with all due dispatch, whether or not an appeal from the decision of the Court has been or may be instituted,

(c) where the assessment has been referred back to the Minister, reconsider the assessment and make a reassessment in accordance with the decision of the Court, unless otherwise directed in writing by the taxpayer, and

(d) refund any overpayment resulting from the variation, vacation or reassessment,

and the Minister may repay any tax, interest or penalties or surrender any security accepted therefor by the Minister to that taxpayer or any other taxpayer who has filed another objection or instituted another appeal if, having regard to the reasons given on the disposition of the appeal, the Minister is satisfied that it would be just and equitable to do so, but for greater certainty, the Minister may, in accordance with the provisions of this Act, the *Tax Court of Canada Act*, the *Federal Courts Act* or the *Supreme Court Act* as they relate to appeals from decisions of the Tax Court of Canada or the Federal Court of Appeal, appeal from the decision of the Court notwithstanding any variation or vacation of any assessment by the Court or any reassessment made by the Minister under paragraph (c).

Related Provisions: 152(1.2)(c) — Subsec. 164(4.1) does not apply to determination under 152(1.4); 169(2)(a) — Limitation of right to appeal.

Notes: For the meaning of "just and equitable" in the closing words, see Notes to 85(7.1).

164(4.1) amended by 2002 courts administration bill, effective July 2, 2003.

164(4.1) amended by 1988 Tax Court bill, effective January 1, 1991.

CRA Audit Manual: 11.5.10: Loss determination.

(5) Effect of carryback of loss, etc. — For the purpose of subsection (3), the portion of any overpayment of the tax payable by a taxpayer for a taxation year that arose as a consequence of

(a) the deduction of an amount, in respect of a repayment under subsection 68.4(7) of the *Excise Tax Act* made in a subsequent taxation year, in computing the amount determined under subparagraph 12(1)(x.1)(ii),

(a.1) any amount deducted under section 119 in respect of the disposition of a taxable Canadian property in a subsequent taxation year,

(b) the deduction of an amount under section 41 in respect of the taxpayer's listed-personal-property loss for a subsequent taxation year,

(c) the exclusion of an amount from the taxpayer's income for the year by virtue of section 49 in respect of the exercise of an option in a subsequent taxation year,

(d) the deduction of an amount under section 118.1 in respect of a gift made in a subsequent taxation year or under section 111 in respect of a loss for a subsequent taxation year,

(e) the deduction of an amount under subsection 126(2) in respect of an unused foreign tax credit (within the meaning assigned by subsection 126(7)), or under subsection 126(2.21) or (2.22) in respect of foreign taxes paid, for a subsequent taxation year,

(f) the deduction of an amount under subsection 127(5) in respect of property acquired or an expenditure made in a subsequent taxation year,

(g) [Repealed]

(h) the deduction of an amount under section 125.3 in respect of an unused Part I.3 tax credit (within the meaning assigned by subsection 125.3(3)) for a subsequent taxation year,

(h.01) the deduction of an amount under subsection 147.2(4) in computing the taxpayer's income for the year because of the application of subsection 147.2(6) as a result of the taxpayer's death in the following taxation year,

(h.02) the deduction under any of subsections 128.1(6) to (8) of an amount from the taxpayer's proceeds of disposition of a property, because of an election made in a return of income for a subsequent taxation year,

(h.1) the deduction of an amount in computing the taxpayer's income for the year by virtue of an election for a subsequent taxation year under paragraph (6)(c) or (d) by the taxpayer's legal representative,

(h.2) the deduction of an amount under subsection 181.1(4) in respect of an unused surtax credit (within the meaning assigned by subsection 181.1(6)) of the taxpayer for a subsequent taxation year, (h.3) the deduction of an amount under subsection 190.1(3) in respect of an unused Part I tax credit (within the meaning assigned by subsection 190.1(5)) of the taxpayer for a subsequent taxation year, or

(h.4) the reduction of the amount included under subsection 91(1) for the year because of a reduction referred to in paragraph 152(6.1)(b) in the foreign accrual property income of a foreign affiliate of the taxpayer for a taxation year of the affiliate that ends in the year,

is deemed to have arisen on the day that is 30 days after the latest of

(i) the first day immediately following that subsequent taxation year,

(j) the day on which the taxpayer's or the taxpayer's legal representative's return of income for that subsequent taxation year was filed,

(k) if an amended return of a taxpayer's income for the year or a prescribed form amending the taxpayer's return of income for the year was filed under paragraph (6)(e) or subsection 49(4) or 152(6) or (6.1), the day on which the amended return or prescribed form was filed, and

(l) where, as a consequence of a request in writing, the Minister reassessed the taxpayer's tax for the year to take into account the deduction or exclusion, the day on which the request was made.

Related Provisions: 161(7) — Effect of loss carryback.

Notes: A somewhat similar rule under the pre-2009 Ontario *Corporations Tax Act* did not apply to deny refund interest in *Stonehouse Group*, 2021 ONCA 10.

164(5) amended by 2002-2013 technical bill (last change effective for tax years that begin after Oct. 2011), 2003 Budget, 2001 technical bill, 1997 Budget, 1995-97 technical bill, 1992 transportation support bill, 1992 technical bill, 1989 Budget.

(5.1) Interest — disputed amounts

(5.1) Interest — disputed amounts — Where a portion of a repayment made under subsection (1.1) or (4.1), or an amount applied under subsection (2) in respect of a repayment, can reasonably be regarded as being in respect of a claim made by the taxpayer in an objection to or appeal from an assessment of tax for a taxation year for a deduction or exclusion described in subsection (5) in respect of a subsequent taxation year, interest shall not be paid or applied on the portion for any part of a period that is before the latest of the dates described in paragraphs (5)(i) to (l).

Notes: 164(5.1) amended by 2001 technical bill (for tax years that end after Oct. 1, 1996), 1995-97 and 1992 technical bills, 1992 transportation support bill, 1989 Budget.

(6) Disposition by legal representative of deceased [loss carried back from estate to deceased]

(6) Disposition by legal representative of deceased [loss carried back from estate to deceased] — If in the course of administering the graduated rate estate of a taxpayer, the taxpayer's legal representative has, within the first taxation year of the estate,

(a) disposed of capital property of the estate so that the total of all amounts each of which is a capital loss from the disposition of a property exceeds the total of all amounts each of which is a capital gain from the disposition of a property, or

(b) disposed of all of the depreciable property of a prescribed class of the estate so that the undepreciated capital cost to the estate of property of that class at the end of the first taxation year of the estate is, by virtue of subsection 20(16) or any regulation made under paragraph 20(1)(a), deductible in computing the income of the estate for that year,

notwithstanding any other provision of this Act, the following rules apply:

(c) such parts of one or more capital losses of the estate from the disposition of properties in the year (the total of which is not to exceed the excess referred to in paragraph (a)) as the legal representative so elects, in prescribed manner and within a prescribed time, are deemed (except for the purpose of subsection 112(3) and this paragraph) to be capital losses of the deceased taxpayer from the disposition of the properties by the taxpayer in the taxpayer's last taxation year and not to be capital losses of the estate from the disposition of those properties,

(d) such part of the amount of any deduction described in paragraph (b) (not exceeding the amount that, but for this subsection,

would be the total of the non-capital loss and the farm loss of the estate for its first taxation year) as the legal representative so elects, in prescribed manner and within a prescribed time, shall be deductible in computing the income of the taxpayer for the taxpayer's taxation year in which the taxpayer died and shall not be an amount deductible in computing any loss of the estate for its first taxation year,

(e) the legal representative shall, at or before the time prescribed for filing the election referred to in paragraphs (c) and (d), file an amended return of income for the deceased taxpayer for the taxpayer's taxation year in which the taxpayer died to give effect to the rules in those paragraphs, and

(f) in computing the taxable income of the deceased taxpayer for a taxation year preceding the year in which the taxpayer died, no amount may be deducted in respect of an amount referred to in paragraph (c) or (d).

Related Provisions: 40(3.61) — Application of 40(3.4) and (3.6) to loss carried back; 91(2) — FAPI reserve for blocked currency; 152(1) — Assessment; 152(6)(h) — Reassessment to give effect to election; 161(7)(b)(iii) — Effect of carryback of loss, etc.; 220(3.2), Reg. 600(b) — Late filing or revocation of election.

Notes: 164(6) can be used to carry estate losses back to a deceased's terminal return, to reduce tax in that year including tax on the 70(5) deemed disposition on death. For example, following death a company owned by the deceased might eliminate its value by distributing dividends, then be sold for a nominal amount, giving the estate a capital loss to carry back under 164(6). Note that to use 164(6), the loss must be realized during the estate's first tax year (CRA cannot extend this for COVID-19: VIEWS docs 2020-0839951C6 [2020 STEP q.15], 2020-0865071E5), and (since 2016) the estate must be a GRE (see Notes to 248(1)"graduated rate estate"). The election can be filed late, per 220(3.2) and Reg. 600(b). The estate T3 must be assessed before the loss is allowed on the deceased's T1 (unlike Revenu Québec practice), so the T1 should be amended (para. (e)) rather than claiming the carryback up front: 2020-0852161C6 [2020 APFF q.4].

On a 164(6)(c) election, probate fees and legal fees incurred to enable the estate to sell the property are added to the cost base (or are expenses of disposition): *Brosamler Estate*, 2012 TCC 204. CRA says *Brosamler* is "based on the unique facts of the case" and not precedential: docs 2012-0457521C6 [2012 BC Tax Conf. q.2], 2012-0462831C6 [2012 Ontario Tax Conf. q.18], 2013-0480411C6 [2012 STEP q.10] (but see Corbin, "Estate Administration Tax and Capital Gains Calculation", 35(1) *Money & Family Law* (Carswell) 1-2 (Jan. 2020) and "Estate Administration Tax and Capital Loss Carrybacks", 35(8) 57-59 (Aug. 2020)).

For planning using 164(6) (also note the "graduated rate estate" requirement as of 2016, which does not really change anything), see Cadesky, *Taxation of Real Estate in Canada* (Carswell, looseleaf or *Taxnet Pro* Reference Centre), §10.3.2, "Mechanisms for Reducing or Eliminating Double Taxation"; Chow & Cadesky, *Taxation at Death: A Practitioner's Guide 2016* (Carswell), chap. 16; Rees, "Testamentary Planning to Avoid Double Taxation", 48(1) *Canadian Tax Journal* 155-72 (2000); Truster, "Stock Dividends and GAAR", 6(4) *Tax for the Owner-Manager [TfOM]* (ctf.ca) 2-3 (Oct. 2006) and "Redeeming Shares Below FMV", 10(4) 7-8 (Oct. 2010); Faccone & Gehlen, "Post-Mortem Estate Planning", 2006 B.C. Tax Conf. (ctf.ca), 12:1-34; Cyna, "Post-Mortem Losses on Former Principal Residence", 6(4) *Tax Hyperion [TH]* (Carswell, April 2009); Moraitis & Kakkar, "Potential Circularity Problem with Estate Loss Carryback", 6(3) *TfOM* 5-6 (July 2006) (interaction with 40(3.61); see next para. re CRA review of this circularity); Yull, "Post Mortem Planning Where Investments Decline in Value", 7(3) *TH* (March 2010); Brubacher, "Dealing with Private Company Shares at Death", XVII(1) *Insurance Planning* (Federated Press) 1058-66 (2010), and "... Part III", XVII(2) 1081-88 (2011); Benjamin & Martini, "Post Mortem Planning", 2011 Ontario Tax Conf. 5:1-28. For the "pipeline" strategy, see Notes to 84(2).

For CRA discussion of 164(6) see docs September 1990-131 (application to non-residents); 2002-0130065 (several situations); 2004-0088061I7 (loss on QSBC shares carried back to deceased's return must be netted against gain under 110.6(2.1)(d) for capital gains exemption); 2004-0100621E5 (164(6) can apply to shares that are the object of a Quebec "legacy by particular title"); 2008-0280751E5 (deceased taxpayer's residence sold by estate: Jim Yager, "Estate's Loss on Principal Residence Carried Back", 18(3) *Canadian Tax Highlights* (ctf.ca) 10-11 (March 2010)); 2009-0349411I7 (interaction with 107(2) and (2.001)); 2005 STEP Conference Roundtable q. 6, www.step.ca (164(6) can be used by personal representative even if taxpayer dies without a will); 2010-0384531E5 (164(6) can apply to a non-resident estate, but not to its shares of a private corp whose value is no longer primarily Canadian real property); 2012-0437211I7 (application to non-resident estate); 2020-0847181C6 [2020 STEP q.5] (circularity with 40(3.61) and 164(6) applying iteratively leads to inappropriate result, so 40(3.61) will not apply; reverses 2012-0444911C6 [2012 Prairie Conf q.5], 2012-0449801C6 [2012 STEP q.5] and 2012-0462941C6 [2012 Ont. Conf q.14] [Nichols & Horning, "Shift in CRA Position on Circularity", 2548 *Tax Topics* (CCH) 1-2 (Jan. 5, 2021)]).

If the deceased was resident in Quebec, an election under 164(6)(c) or (d) must be copied to Revenu Québec: *Taxation Act* ss. 1054, 21.4.6.

164(6) opening words amended by 2014 budget bill #2, for 2016 and later tax years, to change "estate" to "graduated rate estate".

164(6)(c) amended by 1995-97 technical bill, for deaths after 1993.

Regulations: 1000 (prescribed manner, prescribed time).

Income Tax Folios: S4-F8-C1: Business investment losses [replaces IT-484R2].

Interpretation Bulletins: IT-140R3: Buy-sell agreements.

Information Circulars: 07-1R1: Taxpayer relief provisions.

I.T. Technical News: 34 (GAAR and audit issues/concerns, q.2).

Forms: T1-ADJ: Adjustment request.

(6.1) Realization of deceased employees' options — Notwithstanding any other provision of this Act, if a right to acquire securities (as defined in subsection 7(7)) under an agreement in respect of which a benefit was deemed by paragraph 7(1)(e) to have been received by a taxpayer (in this subsection referred to as "the right") is exercised or disposed of by the taxpayer's legal representative within the first taxation year of the graduated rate estate of the taxpayer and the representative so elects in prescribed manner and on or before a prescribed day,

(a) the amount, if any, by which

(i) the amount of the benefit deemed by paragraph 7(1)(e) to have been received by the taxpayer in respect of the right

exceeds the total of

(ii) the amount, if any, by which the value of the right immediately before the time it was exercised or disposed of exceeds the amount, if any, paid by the taxpayer to acquire the right, and

(iii) where in computing the taxpayer's taxable income for the taxation year in which the taxpayer died an amount was deducted under paragraph 110(1)(d) in respect of the benefit deemed by paragraph 7(1)(e) to have been received by the taxpayer in that year by reason of paragraph 7(1)(e) in respect of that right, ½ of the amount, if any, by which the amount determined under subparagraph (i) exceeds the amount determined under subparagraph (ii),

shall be deemed to be a loss of the taxpayer from employment for the year in which the taxpayer died;

(b) there shall be deducted in computing the adjusted cost base to the estate of the right at any time the amount of the loss that would be determined under paragraph (a) if that paragraph were read without reference to subparagraph (a)(iii); and

(c) the legal representative shall, at or before the time prescribed for filing the election under this subsection, file an amended return of income for the taxpayer for the taxation year in which the taxpayer died to give effect to paragraph (a).

Related Provisions: 53(2)(t) — Deduction from adjusted cost base of right to acquire shares or units; 220(3.2), Reg. 600(b) — Late filing or revocation of election.

Notes: 164(6.1) amended by 2014 budget bill #2, for 2016 and later taxation years, to change "estate" to "graduated rate estate". Earlier amended by 2000 and 1998 Budgets; added by 1992 technical bill.

Regulations: 1000.1 (prescribed manner and day for making election).

(7) Definition of "overpayment" — In this section, "overpayment" of a taxpayer for a taxation year means

(a) where the taxpayer is not a corporation, the total of all amounts paid on account of the taxpayer's liability under this Part for the year minus all amounts payable in respect thereof; and

(b) where the taxpayer is a corporation, the total of all amounts paid on account of the corporation's liability under this Part or Parts I.3, VI or VI.1 for the year minus all amounts payable in respect thereof.

Notes: See 164(1) Notes. In *984274 Alberta*, 2020 FCA 125 (leave to appeal denied 2021 CarswellNat 1167 (SCC)), paras. 64-65, an "overpayment" resulted from a nil assessment issued late (no limitation period applies to such an assessment: para. 58).

A 224(1) garnishment payment returned because the taxpayer is in bankruptcy is not an "overpayment" and thus not subject to interest: VIEWS doc 2009-0331681I7.

164(7)(b) added by 1992 technical bill, effective 1992 and later taxation years.

Related Provisions [s. 164]: 144(9) — Refunds — employees profit sharing plans. See also at end of s. 163.

Definitions [s. 164]: "allowable capital loss" — 38(b), 248(1); "amount", "assessment", "balance-due day" — 248(1); "calendar year" — *Interpretation Act* 37(1)(a); "Canada" — 255; "capital loss" — 39(1)(b), 248(1); "capital property" — 54, 248(1); "clear days" — *Interpretation Act* 27(1); "corporation" — 248(1), *Interpretation Act* 35(1); "depreciable property" — 13(21), 248(1); "eligible production corporation" — 125.5(1); "estate" — 104(1), 248(1); "farm loss" — 111(8); "Federal Court of Appeal" — *Federal Courts Act* s. 3; "filing-due date", "graduated rate estate" — 248(1); "Her Majesty" — *Interpretation Act* 35(1); "individual" — 248(1); "investment tax credit" — 127(9), 248(1); "large corporation" — 225.1(8); "legal representative" — 248(1); "listed personal property" — 54, 248(1); "Minister" — 248(1); "net capital loss", "non-capital loss" — 111(8), 248(1); "non-resident" — 248(1); "overpayment" — 164(7); "prescribed" — 248(1); "prescribed rate" — Reg. 4301; "property" — 248(1); "province" — *Interpretation Act* 35(1); "qualified corporation" — 125.4(1); "qualifying journalism organization" — 125.6(1); "regulation" — 248(1); "resident in Canada" — 94(3)(a)(vii), 250; "security" — *Interpretation Act* 35(1); "share" — 248(1); "tax shelter" — 237.1(1), 248(1); "taxable income" — 2(2), 248(1); "taxation year" — 249; "taxpayer" — 164(1.61), 248(1); "trust" — 104(1), 248(1), (3); "writing" — *Interpretation Act* 35(1).

164.1 [Repealed]

Notes: 164.1 repealed by 1992 Child Benefit bill. Until 1992, it allowed Revenue Canada to prepay up to ⅔ of the refundable Child Tax Credit provided certain conditions were met. See now 122.61(1) for the Canada Child Benefit.

Objections to Assessments

165. (1) Objections to assessment — A taxpayer who objects to an assessment under this Part may serve on the Minister a notice of objection, in writing, setting out the reasons for the objection and all relevant facts,

(a) if the assessment is in respect of the taxpayer for a taxation year and the taxpayer is an individual (other than a trust) or a graduated rate estate for the year, on or before the later of

(i) the day that is one year after the taxpayer's filing-due date for the year, and

(ii) the day that is 90 days after the day of sending of the notice of assessment; and

(b) in any other case, on or before the day that is 90 days after the day of sending of the notice of assessment.

Related Provisions: 152(1.2) — Administrative procedures for assessments apply to determinations; 164(1.1) — Repayment or surrender of security while objection outstanding; 164(4) — Interest on overpayments; 165(1.2) — Limitations on right to object; 165(1.11) — Large corporations — detail required on notice of objection; 165(2) — Service of notice of objection; 165(2.1) — Application of 165(1)(a); 165(3) — Duties of Minister on receipt of notice of objection; 166.1, 166.2 — Applications for extension of time to object; 167(1) — Application to Tax Court of Canada for time extension; 168(4) — Objection procedures apply to charity revocations, annulments, designations and refusals to register; 173(2), 174(5) — Time during consideration not to count; 189(8) — Objection to charity penalties and to receipting suspensions; 225.1(2) — Collection restrictions; 244(10) — Proof that no notice of objection filed; 244(14), (14.1) — Date when notice sent; *Interpretation Act* 26 — Deadline on Sunday or holiday extended to next business day.

Notes: 165 provides for an "objection", which is an administrative appeal within CRA, and is considered by an Appeals Officer: see 165(3). An alternative to filing an objection, if CRA is certain to accept the request or if the objection deadline has passed, is to file an adjustment request (for an individual, Form T1-Adj or canada.ca/change-tax-return), which is at CRA discretion to accept (see 152(4.2)).

If the taxpayer is unhappy with CRA's decision, the next level of appeal is to the Tax Court of Canada (TCC): see 169(1).

In cases of wrong CRA action, a Service Complaint (see 220(1) Notes) or contacting the Ombudsman can *sometimes* work as an alternative, e.g. *Taxpayers' Ombudsman Annual Report 2019-2020*, pp. 17-19, but beware of letting the objection deadline expire.

Once filed, an objection cannot legally be withdrawn. See 165(3) Notes.

Consider whether to appeal directly to the TCC under 169(1)(b) after 90 days from filing an objection, without waiting for the objection to be considered, especially if the Appeals Officer is likely to confirm the assessment anyway. This can speed up the process, as objections often take >1 year to be considered; and it allows access to the Court's process and timelines, which can encourage settlement. It also avoids giving CRA more time to examine the file and come up with additional support for its case (though 152(9) allows CRA to change its grounds during the appeal process).

See Notes to 165(2) re what constitutes a valid objection, and Notes to 165(3) re how objections are handled by CRA. An individual can use canada.ca/my-cra-account, and a corporation can use tinyurl.com/cra-BusAccount, to "register a formal dispute", which appears to be accepted by CRA as a valid objection.

The 90-day period for filing an objection begins from the date of mailing (or electronic sending — 244(14.1)) of the assessment, which is also deemed to be the date of the assessment; see Notes to 244(15). It is advisable to keep the envelope showing the postmark, if it was not mailed until a later date than the date shown on the notice. See also Notes to 244(14) re CRA's possible inability to prove the date the assessment was sent; and Notes to 152(2) re validity of the notice of assessment to start the 90-day clock running. If the deadline is missed, see 166.1 and 166.2 for extension of time. If no extension application is filed, missing the deadline by even a day or two makes the objection invalid, so no Tax Court appeal can be filed: *Girmay*, 2019 TCC 288. However *CRA Appeals Manual* §6.4.1 says that if reasons for filing late are included with the objection, it will be considered as an application for extension of time; and if the objection is less than 31 days late without saying why, the objector should be contacted by phone and an extension considered, or reasons sought in writing if the reasons given by phone are inadequate.

For an individual or a GRE (see 248(1)"graduated rate estate"), 165(1)(a)(i) extends the deadline for a recent year. An individual's deadline to object to 2015 is April 30, 2017 or June 15, 2017: see 248(1)"filing-due date", 150(1)(d). Where CRA has extended the filing deadline for all taxpayers, this alternate objection deadline is also extended: VIEWS doc 2015-0598301C6 [2015 APFF q.22]. Thus, for the 2014 year (see Notes to 150(1)(d)), the April 30 objection deadline is extended to May 5, 2016.

If the deadline expires on a Saturday, Sunday or holiday, it is extended to the next business day: CRA *Appeals Manual* §3.3.2.3; *Interpretation Act* s. 26.

Must have been sent: An assessment (or other CRA notice) is invalid if it was never mailed (the onus is on CRA to show it was mailed), so the 90-day clock does not start: *Aztec Industries*, [1995] 1 C.T.C. 327 (FCA); *Kovacevic*, 2003 FCA 293; *Gray*, 2008 FCA 284; *Mpamugo*, 2017 FCA 136; *Boroumend*, 2017 FCA 245; *Gratl*, 2019 FCA 3 (leave to appeal denied 2019 CarswellNat 6300 (SCC)); *Sykes*, [1998] 1 C.T.C. 2639 (TCC); *Massarotto*, [2000] G.S.T.C. 19 (TCC); *Giannakouras*, 2005 TCC 225; *741290 Ontario*, 2008 TCC 55; *Barrington Lane Developments*, 2010 TCC 388 (CRA's evidence of its mailing procedures was sufficient); *Nicholls*, 2011 TCC 39, para. 15 (FCA appeal discontinued A-209-11); *Carcone*, 2011 TCC 550 (CRA witness was unable to testify to mailing procedures); *Hamer*, 2014 TCC 218 (CRA affidavit evidence of mailing procedures was inadequate); *Oddi*, 2016 TCC 102 (Crown led no evidence that notices of reassessment had been sent); *Bailey*, 2017 TCC 24, para. 18; *Duncan*, 2020 TCC 89 (CRA witness was relying on another official's review); *Luxury Home*, 2021 TCC 4 (CRA did not prove it had sent 165(3) notice of confirmation by registered mail). An allegation of non-receipt must be credible to require the Crown to prove mailing; *Mpamugo*, para. 12; for the "steps" to follow when non-receipt is alleged, see *DaSilva*, 2018 TCC 74, para. 4 and *Afkari*, 2019 TCC 173. A taxpayer who files an application for extension of time is presumed to have notice of the assessment, but this does not mean the notice was sent when CRA thinks it was: *Burke*, 2012 TCC 378, paras. 27, 35-36.

An assessment is also invalid if it was mailed to an incorrect address: *236130 British Columbia*, 2006 FCA 352; *Corsi*, 2008 TCC 472; *Burstein*, 2009 TCC 103; *Gyimah*, 2010 TCC 621; *Lambo*, 2011 TCC 293; or lacks the suite number in a large building: *Le Sage au Piano*, 2014 TCC 319; *Pilgrim*, 2015 TCC 302. In *Kirschke*, 2019 TCC 68, K had told CRA about her address change for income tax, but not GST/HST (that account was inactive, with nil returns); the GST/HST assessment was held not validly mailed. Delivery to the taxpayer's accountant, when the taxpayer had left the country with no forwarding address, was valid in *Gebele*, 2006 FCA 333, and delivery was valid when the taxpayer had deliberately tried to confuse the CRA by providing various addresses: *Consultation Next Step*, 2009 TCC 410, or when the taxpayer had failed to provide the CRA with his current address: *Carvalho*, 2007 TCC 709, *Newell*, 2010 TCC 196; *Austin*, 2010 TCC 452. Delivery by registered mail (unclaimed) to an old address was valid in *Roy*, 2009 TCC 573, where the taxpayer had moved and notified Revenu Québec but not CRA. See Notes to 171(1) re the TCC having jurisdiction to address this issue; in *Burke* at paras. 41-43, the TCC agreed that CRA is not entitled to pursue collection of an unmailed assessment that increases tax, but ruled that assessment matching what the taxpayer filed is not a prerequisite to collection. Personal delivery is as good as mailing: *Grunwald*, 2005 FCA 421 (leave to appeal denied [2006] G.S.T.C. 44 (SCC)).

If the Crown can show that the assessment was likely mailed, it is deemed by 248(7) to have been received even if it was not received: *Bowen*, [1991] 2 C.T.C. 266 (FCA); *Schafer*, [2000] G.S.T.C. 82 (FCA); *McLelland*, 2004 FCA 315; *Rossi*, 2015 FCA 267; *Abraham*, 2004 TCC 380; *Lai*, 2005 TCC 636; *Skalbania*, 2009 TCC 576. The taxpayer's ability to comprehend the assessment is irrelevant: *Gyimah*, 2010 TCC 621, para. 39; *Jablonski*, 2012 TCC 29; but at para. 40 of *Gyimah*, the Court suggested that a return filed by a mentally ill person might be invalid, thus invalidating the resulting assessment even if it was correctly mailed! See also Notes to 167(1) under "If the Court finds that an objection or appeal was filed on time".

See Notes to 152(2) re what constitutes a notice of assessment that can be objected to. An objection before the reassessment, responding to a letter advising that a reassessment will be issued, was invalid in *Jablonski*, 2012 TCC 29; but was held valid in *Persaud*, 2013 TCC 405, para. 15, and *Ihama-Anthony*, 2018 TCC 262, paras. 34-35. A reassessment displaces an earlier assessment and makes it a nullity, so the earlier assessment can no longer be objected to: *Abrahams*, [1966] C.T.C. 690 (Exch. Ct), para. 9; *Yarmoloy*, 2014 TCC 27; *Nagel*, 2018 TCC 32, para. 11.

When CRA issues an "arbitrary assessment" because no return was filed, filing a return will normally get CRA to reassess; but filing an objection is also advisable as it protects the appeal right.

Objection to own filing: A taxpayer can object to the assessment issued on filing, even though it matches what was filed: *Imperial Oil (Inco)*, 2003 FCA 289; *Ntakos Estate*, 2012 TCC 409; *Abenaim*, 2017 TCC 223, para. 99; *Scott*, 2017 TCC 224, para. 2.

After a series of reassessments and objections, the taxpayer can in the last objection raise any issue even if it was not raised in a prior objection: VIEWS doc 2012-0435571I7.

An arbitrary assessment issued because no return was filed can be objected to (though some CRA officials wrongly think otherwise), since legally it is an "assessment". See VIEWS doc 2014-0538901E5 for an example.

In *Carlson*, 2002 FCA 145, the Court held that the 90 days for objecting started when the assessment was issued, even though the taxpayer did not understand the significance of the assessment. The common-law "discoverability" rule did not apply (see also *Al-Rubaiy*, 2020 TCC 34). See also Notes to 167(1).

No objection can be brought against a nil assessment (e.g., to change a loss calculation); see Notes to 152(1.1). However if CRA has issued a Notice of Determination of Loss, or correspondence treated as a determination of loss (see Notes to 152(1.1)), then under 152(1.2), an objection can be filed as if the determination were an assessment.

While a person is bankrupt, only the trustee can object to that person's assessment: see Notes to 128(2).

The determination of interest on a Statement of Account, without an assessment of tax, is not an "assessment" that can be objected to: *Homa*, 2011 TCC 230, 2012 TCC 110.

Where double tax results from tax by another country with which Canada has a tax treaty, an objection can be filed and put on hold, and the matter referred to CRA's "Competent Authority" (see Notes to 115.1) to negotiate with the other country's tax administration under the treaty (which may have a deadline for such referral). In *Kerry Canada*, 2019 FC 377, a request to hold objections in abeyance this way was held to be a 152(4)(a)(ii) waiver, so CRA could reassess late.

In general, a taxpayer that can afford to should pay an assessment even if objecting. See Notes to 225.1(1).

See also Ashton, Leung & Martini, "Objections", *Practical Insights*, *Taxnet Pro* Tax Disputes Centre (Dec. 2020, 32pp); Campbell, *Administration of Income Tax 2020* (Carswell), chap. 10, "Objections"; Brown & Taylor, "A Practical Guide to the Audit and Audit Issues", 2007 Cdn Tax Foundation conference report, 17:1-12; Gibson & Misutka, "The Art of Resolving Tax Disputes", 2011 Prairie Provinces Tax Conference (ctf.ca), 5:1-25; Briggs, "Notice of Objection", 2011 Atlantic Provinces Tax Conf. [APTC] 5A:1-14; Walse, "Notice of Objections", *ibid.* 5B:1-12; Boddez et al, "Notices of Objection", 2012 *Tax Dispute Resolution* conf. report (ctf.ca), 12:1-24; Arkin, "Understanding Tax Disputes", 2018 APTC 6:1-27; Tomlinson, "Objections to Income Tax Assessments", 2478 *Tax Topics* (CCH) 1-5 (Sept. 5, 2019); Marcil & Tassé, "De la vérification à l'opposition", 2019 Cdn Tax Foundation conference report, 6:1-34; David Sherman's Analysis to *Excise Tax Act* s. 301 in the *Canada GST Service* or *Taxnet Pro*; and tinyurl.com/cra-objections.

A taxpayer unsatisfied with CRA service can complain using Form RC193 (see tinyurl.com/cra-complaints), or to the Ombudsman (oto-boc.gc.ca), but not if the problem is that the assessment is wrong.

An administrative appeal (equivalent to an objection) of a CPP or EI assessment is made using Form CPT100 or CPT101. The 90-day appeal period runs from receipt of notice (CPP s. 27.1; EIA s. 92), not from date of mailing: *742190 Ontario [Van Del Manor]*, 2010 FCA 162, para. 20. A single Notice of Objection can possibly be filed together for income tax, EI and CPP: *Holmes*, [2000] 3 C.T.C. 2235 (TCC), paras. 6-7; *4528957 Manitoba*, 2009 TCC 298, para. 29.

165(1)(a) opening words amended by 2014 budget bill #2, for 2016 and later tax years, to change "testamentary trust" to "graduated rate estate for the year". (See 122(1) Notes.)

165(1)(a)(ii) and (b) amended by 2010 budget bill #2, effective Dec. 15, 2010, to change "mailing" to "sending" (to accommodate electronic notices under 244(14.1)).

165(1)(a)(i) amended to change "balance-due day" to "filing-due date" by 1995 Budget, effective for 1995 and later taxation years.

165(1) amended by 1991 technical bill, for objections made after Dec. 17, 1991.

Information Circulars: 98-1R5: Tax collection policies.

I.T. Technical News: 32 (taxpayer's opportunities to respond to assessments).

Application Policies: SR&ED 2000-02R: Guidelines for resolving claimants' SR&ED concerns.

Registered Charities Newsletters: 28 (objections and appeals on issues relating to charities).

CRA Audit Manual: 19.2.0: objections.

Forms: ON100: Notice of Objection — Ontario *Corporations Tax Act*; P148: Resolving your dispute: objections and appeal rights under the *Income Tax Act* [pamphlet]; T400A: Objection — *ITA*. (The prescribed form does not have to be used, however. See 165(2)).

(1.1) Limitation of right to object to assessments or determinations — Notwithstanding subsection (1), where at any time the Minister assesses tax, interest, penalties or other amounts payable under this Part by, or makes a determination in respect of, a taxpayer

(a) under subsection 67.5(2) or 152(1.8), subparagraph 152(4)(b)(i) or subsection 152(4.3) or (6), 161.1(7), 164(4.1), 220(3.4) or 245(8) or in accordance with an order of a court vacating, varying or restoring an assessment or referring the assessment back to the Minister for reconsideration and reassessment,

(b) under subsection (3) where the underlying objection relates to an assessment or a determination made under any of the provisions or circumstances referred to in paragraph (a), or

(c) under a provision of an Act of Parliament requiring an assessment to be made that, but for that provision, would not be made because of subsections 152(4) to (5),

the taxpayer may object to the assessment or determination within 90 days after the day of sending of the notice of assessment or determination, but only to the extent that the reasons for the objection can reasonably be regarded

(d) where the assessment or determination was made under subsection 152(1.8), as relating to any matter or conclusion specified in paragraph 152(1.8)(a), (b) or (c), and

(e) in any other case, as relating to any matter that gave rise to the assessment or determination

and that was not conclusively determined by the court, and this subsection shall not be read or construed as limiting the right of the taxpayer to object to an assessment or a determination issued or made before that time.

Related Provisions: 169(2) — Limitation of right to appeal; 244(14), (14.1) — Date when notice sent; *Interpretation Act* 27(5) — Meaning of "within 90 days".

Notes: 165(1.1) provides that if a reassessment is made after the normal deadline under a special provision (such as those allowing for a consequential assessment), the taxpayer cannot use that as an excuse to open up a return that was otherwise statute-barred (to the taxpayer) and claim additional deductions or credits beyond those that are the subject of the special reassessment. (See 169(2) for the same rule as it applies to appeals.) For more on 165(1.1), see *Chevron Canada*, [1999] 3 C.T.C. 140 (FCA), and the commentaries on *Chevron* by Sharlow in VI(4) *Tax Litigation* (Federated Press) 394-97 (1998) and by Galway & Spiro, pp. 398-400. *Res judicata* may also apply: *Chevron* (see Notes to 169(2)). See also 165(1.2) for a similar rule for certain other reassessments, such as those issued at the taxpayer's request to reduce tax.

In *Hoffman*, 2010 TCC 267, the TCC thought an objection was under 165(1.1), but since it was to a 152(1.1) loss determination, it was under 165(1) via 152(1.2) deeming the determination to be an assessment, not under 165(1.1).

165(1.1) also applies to a reassessment resulting from an appeal to the Tax Court. Effectively this is a statutory rule of *res judicata*, which rule would apply anyway; see *Ahmad*, 2004 TCC 149; *Davitt*, 2012 FCA 27 (leave to appeal denied 2012 CarswellNat 2185 (SCC)).

165(1.1) does not allow a taxpayer to appeal a reassessment made under 152(4.3), on a ground on which 152(4.3) does not permit the Minister to reassess: *Sherway Centre*, 2003 FCA 26.

165(1.1) does not apply to an ordinary determination of loss (other than of a partnership under 152(1.8)). Such a determination, under 152(1.1), is treated as an assessment by 152(1.2) and therefore can be objected to under 165(1).

165(1.1) amended by 2010 budget bill #2, effective Dec. 15, 2010, to change "mailing" to "sending" (to accommodate electronic notices under 244(14.1)).

165(1.1)(a) amended by 1999 Budget, effective 2000. Earlier amended by 1995-97 technical bill, 1992 technical bill and 1991 technical bill.

(1.11) Objections by large corporations — Where a corporation that was a large corporation in a taxation year (within the meaning assigned by subsection 225.1(8)) objects to an assessment under this Part for the year, the notice of objection shall

(a) reasonably describe each issue to be decided;

(b) specify in respect of each issue, the relief sought, expressed as the amount of a change in a balance (within the meaning assigned by subsection 152(4.4)) or a balance of undeducted outlays, expenses or other amounts of the corporation; and

(c) provide facts and reasons relied on by the corporation in respect of each issue.

Related Provisions: 165(1.12) — Late compliance with 165(1.11); 165(1.13) — Corporation may only object on grounds raised; 169(2.1)(a) — Appeal only on grounds raised in objection.

Notes: 165(1.11) requires large corporations to provide extensive detail on their notices of objection. It was introduced after *Gulf Canada*, [1992] 1 C.T.C. 183 (FCA) allowed resource companies unexpected deductions, and other companies that had objections outstanding on unrelated issues amended their objections to include the *Gulf* issue, costing the federal government $2 billion. (See Robert Beith, "Draft Legislation on Income Tax Objections and Appeals", 1994 Cdn Tax Foundation conference report, p. 34:2.) A TCC appeal cannot include issues not properly raised as required by 165(1.11): see 169(2.1).

The parallel GST/HST rules in *Excise Tax Act* (ETA) 301(1.2) and 306.1(1) are essentially the same, and should be interpreted in sync, so the ETA case law applies here: *Ford Motor*, 2015 TCC 39, para. 50.

The amount specified is the maximum relief the Tax Court can grant, under the closing words of 169(2.1): *Potash* (below), para. 27. Thus, if there is uncertainty as to the quantum, a large corp should overestimate the 165(1.11)(b) amount.

169(2.1) prevented new issues from being raised in: *Potash Corp.*, 2003 FCA 471 (leave to appeal denied 2004 CarswellNat 4079 (SCC)) (large corp appealing resource allowance could not add 5 types of income that had been excluded from resource profits eligible for the resource allowance); *Newmont Canada*, 2006 FCA 431; *Telus Communications*, 2005 FCA 139 (objection to GST assessment "along with the associated penalty" did not allow Telus to assert due-diligence defence to penalty); *Bakorp Management*, 2014 FCA 104 (objection indicated issue was amount of deemed dividend but appeal sought to shift deemed dividend to other year); *Rio Tinto*, 2016 TCC 172, paras. 191-200 (aff'd on other grounds 2018 FCA 124) (notice of appeal argued deductibility under 20(1)(g), (bb) and (cc); 20(1)(e) could not be argued as well); *Jayco Inc.*, 2018 TCC 34, para. 68 (objection to GST/HST assessment on basis goods were supplied outside Canada did not allow argument that transportation service was zero-rated).

Contra, new arguments were allowed in: *Ford Motor*, 2015 TCC 39 (it was sufficient that the objection could be understood by CRA, which had already received submissions during the audit; a sufficient description "is one that will allow the Minister to determine what is actually in dispute": para. 55); *Devon Canada*, 2015 FCA 214 (DC could not normally change its claim of a deduction under 9(1) to be under 20(1)(b) or 20(1)(e), but since it made submissions to the CRA on these issues, and the Appeals Officer considered them, the issues became part of the objection and DC could appeal on them!); *Heritage Education*, 2010 TCC 161 (company that lost on question of whether amounts were "receivable" in the year was entitled to deduct amounts it had included from earlier years, even though it had not raised this argument in its objection, as it could be "inferred from the pleadings" that the company did not accept CRA's method of income calculation); *General Motors*, 2015 QCCQ 386 (GM specified its issue sufficiently for the parallel Quebec rule); *Loblaw Financial*, 2018 TCC 182 (rev'd on other grounds 2020 FCA 79; SCC appeal heard May 13/21), paras. 186-191 (objection to FAPI on basis of foreign bank exception did not need to specify every detail, such as number of full-time employees).

In *Roberge Transport*, 2010 TCC 155, a motion had been granted allowing an amendment to the Notice of Appeal; the Court held that this was a final decision, so the Crown could not later object to the new argument on the ground it was not in the Notice of Objection.

New grounds based on different legislative provisions, but not changing the amount claimed, were allowed in *British Columbia Transit*, 2006 TCC 437, and *Canadian Imperial Bank of Commerce*, 2013 TCC 170. However, these cases might now be overruled by *Devon* and *Rio Tinto*.

In *Potash*, the FCA acknowledged that the result was harsh, but was "the result that Parliament intended". Each issue must be described "reasonably", not "exactly". In *Devon* at para. 33, the FCA declined to address the argument that the CRA cannot refuse to consider new issues raised within the original 90-day objection period.

For CRA's administrative views on these rules, see Beith (first para. above), 34:1-5. CRA confirmed at the 2004 conference (p. 5A:7) that these guidelines are still valid in light of *Potash*.

165(1.12) allows CRA to permit the objector to rectify an omission, but not in respect of 165(1.11)(a). Where a reassessment does not provide enough detail for the corporation to specify its objection, the corporation should object with the information it has, Appeals will explain the adjustments, and the corporation then has 60 days under 165(1.12) to comply with 165(1.11): VIEWS doc 2005-0164681C6.

If the corporation may wish to make elective claims (e.g., CCA claims or using loss carryforwards) if it loses on the main issue, these additional issues should be put into the notice of objection.

See also Kroft, "Large Corporation Objections and Appeals — How Much Detail is Enough?", XII(1) *Tax Litigation* (Federated Press) 726-29 (2004); Haymour and Munoz, "Objection and Appeal Process for Large Corporations in Canada: What Is Wrong with This Picture?", 2016 Cdn Tax Foundation conference report, 36:1-34; Kroft, "Recent Caselaw regarding Objections and their Compliance with the Large Corporation Rules", *Blakes on Cdn Tax Controversy* (Taxnet Pro Tax Disputes Centre, Nov. 2018, 6pp).

165(1.11) added by 1994 technical bill, effective Sept. 27, 1994 except where an appeal of the assessment was instituted by June 22, 1995.

I.T. Technical News: 32 (notice of objection of large corporation: impact of the *Potash Corp.* case).

(1.12) Late compliance — Notwithstanding subsection (1.11), where a notice of objection served by a corporation to which that subsection applies does not include the information required by paragraph (1.11)(b) or (c) in respect of an issue to be decided that is described in the notice, the Minister may in writing request the corporation to provide the information, and those paragraphs shall be deemed to be complied with in respect of the issue if, within 60 days after the request is made, the corporation submits the information in writing to a Chief of Appeals referred to in subsection (2).

Related Provisions: *Interpretation Act* 27(5) — Meaning of "within 60 days".

Notes: 165(1.12) added by 1994 technical bill, effective after September 26, 1994 for notices of objection filed at any time, except where an appeal of the assessment has been instituted by June 22, 1995.

(1.13) Limitation on objections by large corporations — Notwithstanding subsections (1) and (1.1), where under subsection (3) a particular assessment was made for a taxation year pursuant to a notice of objection served by a corporation that was a large corporation in the year (within the meaning assigned by subsection 225.1(8)), except where the objection was made to an earlier assessment made under any of the provisions or circumstances referred to in paragraph (1.1)(a), the corporation may object to the particular assessment in respect of an issue

(a) only if the corporation complied with subsection (1.11) in the notice with respect to that issue; and

(b) only with respect to the relief sought in respect of that issue as specified by the corporation in the notice.

Related Provisions: 165(1.14) — Application.

Notes: 165(1.13) added by 1994 technical bill, effective after September 26, 1994 for notices of objection filed at any time, except where an appeal of the assessment has been instituted by June 22, 1995.

(1.14) Application of subsec. (1.13) — Where a particular assessment is made under subsection (3) pursuant to an objection made by a taxpayer to an earlier assessment, subsection (1.13) does not limit the right of the taxpayer to object to the particular assessment in respect of an issue that was part of the particular assessment and not part of the earlier assessment.

Notes: 165(1.14) added by 1994 technical bill, effective after September 26, 1994 for notices of objection filed at any time, except where an appeal of the assessment has been instituted by June 22, 1995.

(1.15) Partnership — Notwithstanding subsection (1), where the Minister makes a determination under subsection 152(1.4) in respect of a fiscal period of a partnership, an objection in respect of the determination may be made only by one member of the partnership, and that member must be either

(a) designated for that purpose in the information return made under section 229 of the *Income Tax Regulations* for the fiscal period; or

(b) otherwise expressly authorized by the partnership to so act.

Notes: 165(1.15) added by 1995-97 technical bill, effective for determinations made after June 18, 1998. See Notes to 152(1.4).

Partnerships will generally wish to determine who is the "tax matters partner" for dealing with CRA.

(1.2) Limitation on objections — Notwithstanding subsections (1) and (1.1), no objection may be made by a taxpayer to an assessment made under subsection 118.1(11), 152(4.2), 169(3) or 220(3.1) nor, for greater certainty, in respect of an issue for which the right of objection has been waived in writing by the taxpayer.

Related Provisions: 169(2.2) — No appeal permitted where right to object or appeal waived.

Notes: For CRA interpretation and procedures see Communiqué AD-19-01, *Audit Agreement and Waiver of Objection Rights Guidelines* (Feb. 19, 2019); *Appeals Manual* §§3.3.2.4, 4.8.1.

Since an assessment under 152(4.2) to reduce tax is made at CRA discretion (as "Taxpayer Relief"), no objection can be made to it. See *Groulx*, 2009 FCA 10; *Kubbernus*, 2010 FCA 50 (adjustment stated to be under "the fairness provisions" could only have been under 152(4.2)); *Yaremy*, [2000] 1 C.T.C. 2393 (TCC); *Haggart*, 2003 TCC 925;

Chou, 2005 TCC 408; *Mellish*, 2007 TCC 228; *Letendre*, 2011 TCC 577 (reassessment to match return filed years after arbitrary assessment could only have been under 152(4.2) — but see next para.); *Yee*, 2012 TCC 275. In *Palin*, 2007 TCC 255, 165(1.2) was held to apply to an appeal of denial of interest relief under 220(3.1) (technically, this seems wrong as no assessment was issued).

However, in *St-Germain*, 2009 TCC 518, the taxpayer could appeal years CRA had reassessed after the 3-year deadline, as his filing of amended returns to replace arbitrary assessments was not a 152(4.2) request; and in *Ullah*, 2013 TCC 387, para. 3, CRA did not prove the original assessment date, so it was not clear the reassessment was under 152(4.2).

No objection can be made where the taxpayer has waived the right to object. See Notes to 169(2.2), which provides the same rule for appeals.

165(1.2) added by 1991 technical bill effective 1991, and amended by 1995 cultural property bill, in force July 12, 1996.

Transfer Pricing Memoranda: TPM-02: Repatriation of funds by non-residents — Part XIII assessments.

CRA Audit Manual: 11.5.10: Loss determination.

(2) Service — A notice of objection under this section shall be served by being addressed to the Chief of Appeals in a District Office or a Taxation Centre of the Canada Revenue Agency and delivered or mailed to that Office or Centre.

Related Provisions: 165(6) — Acceptance of notice of objection; 189(8)(b) — Objection by charity to penalties or suspension of receipting privileges must be addressed to Assistant Commissioner, Appeals Branch; 248(7)(a) — Mail deemed received on day mailed.

Notes: A Notice of Objection can be sent to any Chief of Appeals, but will be forwarded to the Intake Centre: Sudbury (for Ontario eastward) or Burnaby/Fraser (Manitoba westward, and the territories). After intake, it may be considered by any Tax Services Office (TSO) or Tax Centre based on workload availability, regardless of which office issued the assessment. To have the office changed, see the Appeals File Transfer Policy, reproduced in David Sherman's commentary to *Excise Tax Act* s. 301 in the *Canada GST Service*, *GST Partner* or *Taxnet Pro*.

An objection need not use any particular form, but must be in writing to be valid: *Natarajan*, 2010 TCC 582. It can simply be a letter saying the taxpayer objects to the assessment: *Randall*, 2008 TCC 621. A letter requesting reconsideration of the assessment may qualify: *Lester*, 2004 TCC 179; *Schneidmiller*, 2009 TCC 354; *Johnson*, 2019 TCC 13, para. 15 (under appeal to FCA); but an adjustment request addressed to "Disability Tax Credit Assessor, Surrey Tax Centre" did not: *Dionne*, 2012 TCC 197. Nor did T1 Adjustment requests or letters sending documents to auditors or requesting more time to provide information: *870 Holdings*, 2003 FCA 460; *Petratos*, 2013 TCC 240, para. 24; *Ihama-Anthony*, 2018 TCC 262, paras. 17-18. Unless 165(1.1) applies, an objection is not invalid by lacking detailed facts and reasons: CRA *Appeals Manual* §3.3.1.2.1.

An objection filed online using "Register my formal dispute" is legally valid: tinyurl.com/online-obj; CRA reply to TEI, Dec. 4, 2018, q. C.2.

An objection not addressed to a Chief of Appeals is invalid unless CRA accepts it under 165(6): *Mohammed*, 2006 TCC 265; *Fidelity Global*, 2010 TCC 108; *Dionne*, 2012 TCC 197; *Ihama-Anthony*, 2018 TCC 262, para. 24. However, this requirement was ignored in *Lester* and *Schneidmiller* (above). *Hoffman*, 2010 TCC 267, distinguished *Fidelity Global* because the taxpayer had written "Notice of Objection" and sent it to his local TSO; this was enough even though he had not specified "Chief of Appeals".

In *Blackburn*, 2010 TCC 69, the Crown could not argue that no objection had been filed, because it had not raised this issue in its (Informal Procedure) Reply, although it had done so in correspondence.

Objections to assessments of provincial taxes administered by CRA are filed with CRA, even though any later appeal would have to go to the provincial court (see Notes to 169(1) under "Jurisdiction").

For CRA's handling of an objection see Notes to 165(3).

165(2) amended by 2004 CRA/CBSA bill (effective Dec. 12, 2005), *CCRA Act* (1999), in 1994, and by 1991 technical bill.

Forms: ON100: Notice of Objection — Ontario *Corporations Tax Act*; P148: Resolving your dispute: objections and appeal rights under the *Income Tax Act* [pamphlet]; T400A: Objection — *ITA*. (The prescribed form does not have to be used, however. See 165(2)).

(2.1) Application — Notwithstanding any other provision of this Act, paragraph (1)(a) shall apply only in respect of assessments, determinations and redeterminations under this Part and Part I.2.

Notes: 165(2.1) is needed because s. 165 is deemed by other provisions (e.g. 202(3)) to apply for the purposes of the taxes under various Parts.

165(2.1) amended by 2000 Budget, effective for 2001 and later taxation years. Added by 1991 technical bill, for objections made after Dec. 17, 1991.

(3) Duties of Minister — On receipt of a notice of objection under this section, the Minister shall, with all due dispatch, reconsider the assessment and vacate, confirm or vary the assessment or reassess, and shall thereupon notify the taxpayer in writing of the Minister's action.

Related Provisions: 152(9) — Minister may raise new basis for assessment during appeal process; 165(5) — Normal reassessment limitations do not apply to reassessment under 165(3); 169 — Appeals; 189(8) — Suspension of charity's receipting privileges can be confirmed or vacated, but not varied; 244(5) — Proof of service by mail; 244(14) — Date of mailing presumed to be date of notification; 248(7)(a) — Mail deemed received on day mailed.

Notes: For detailed CRA procedures see the Appeals Manual, on *Taxnet Pro* or *TaxPartner*.

Timeline: CRA normally sends out a first contact letter acknowledging the objection as validly filed within 30 days. Instead of saying it will be X months before the objection is assigned to an Appeals Officer, the letter now refers to tinyurl.com/obj-timelines to check the current backlog; that page shows which objections are currently being assigned. CRA's target (tinyurl.com/cra-standards) for processing the objection is 180 days for a low-complexity (LC) objection and 365 days for medium complexity (MC), 80% of the time; in 2019-20 it did 97% for LC and 83% for MC. Large-file objections averaged 690 days as of Nov. 2018 (CRA reply to TEI, Dec. 4, 2018, q. D.2). The Auditor General's 2016 Report 2 (oag-bvg.gc.ca) identified delays and other problems in the objection process and recommended changes, to which CRA agreed, including providing feedback to auditors of the results of the objection. In 2017-18, CRA resolved 93,577 objections (income tax and GST/HST combined): *Departmental Results Report*, tinyurl.com/cra-results, p. 29 (no data in 2018-19 or 2019-20 Reports). See VIEWS doc 2018-0779901C6 [2018 CTF q.6] for an update on progress.

A Notice of Objection is considered by an Appeals Officer (AO), who is a CRA employee, independent of the Audit branch. Files are assigned based on workload availability rather than to the local Tax Services Office, and face-to-face meetings are discouraged: *Appeals Manual* §4.1.4.2. See May 2008 ICAA roundtable (tinyurl.com/cra-abtax), q. 33.

There is no formal "hearing"; discussions are informal, and the AO will usually indicate his or her thoughts, so the taxpayer or representative can respond to specific concerns or correct any misunderstood facts. Some AOs insist that all documents and submissions be provided without delay, and will give only one 30-day extension. (The author's practice is to always do a full submission with all documents when first filing the Notice of Objection.)

The AO will provide the taxpayer or taxpayer's representative with copies of the auditor's report and all supporting documents that the AO is considering, although more reliably complete information is available under the Access to Information procedures (see Notes to 241(1)). See VIEWS doc 2008-0285441C6. (A Federal Court application was started to force CRA to give taxpayers a copy of the audit file automatically when they are reassessed. The Court's Prothonotary refused to strike out the application: *Hanna and Dorion*, 2010 CarswellNat 4344 (FC), but the application was discontinued: T-1495-09.) The auditor should release the information informally: see Notes to 231.1(1). As well, any meeting between the AO and the auditor must be documented, and the minutes of the meeting made available to the taxpayer or representative.

Information should not be "held back" from the auditor to use on objection. If facts or documents are provided to the AO that were requested at audit and not provided, the AO *must* send them back to Audit for review: RC4067, *Protocol between the Appeals Branch and the Compliance Programs Branch*.

CRA can increase tax during an objection: *Edmonton v. Edmonton East*, 2016 SCC 47, para. 61 (*contra*, see dissent at para. 95). For cases where this may be done see *CRA Appeals Manual* §4.22. See Doucette, "Filing a Notice of Objection Could Result in Increased Assessed Tax Payable", *Canadian Tax Focus* (ctf.ca) 6-7 (Nov. 2014). About 0.5% of objections result in increases: Auditor General 2016 Report 2 p. 22, Exh. 2.4.

Once filed, an objection cannot legally be withdrawn. Normally CRA will confirm an assessment on request, but if tax is to be increased (see above), CRA will do that even if the objector wants to withdraw the objection: *Appeals Manual* §4.22.1.

If criminal charges are laid, an objection to an assessment issued by the Criminal Investigations Program (including if the file started in Audit and was referred to Investigations) will be put in abeyance by the AO, and not considered until all charges have been resolved: *CRA Appeals Manual* §4.31.1. See also 239(4). If the assessment was not issued by Investigations, this does not apply, e.g. *Elbaz*, 2017 TCC 177.

A settlement with Appeals can be reached only if there is legal authority for the position finally reached. See Notes to 169(3).

CRA's failure to consider an objection "with all due dispatch" is not grounds for overturning the assessment: *Bolton*, [1996] 3 C.T.C. 3 (FCA); *James*, [2001] 1 C.T.C. 227 (FCA); *Shabani*, 2004 TCC 235; *Santerre*, 2005 TCC 606; *Angell*, 2005 FC 782; *Vert-Dure Plus*, 2007 TCC 379; *Cassa*, 2013 TCC 43, para. 5; *Ford*, 2014 FCA 257; but CRA may need to waive interest under 220(3.1): see under "Delay" in Notes to 220(3.1). See also Notes to 152(1) on the meaning of "all due dispatch". The taxpayer's remedy is to appeal to the TCC under 169(1)(b) without waiting for a decision, or to bring a FC application for *mandamus* (*Addison & Leyen*, 2007 SCC 33, but the Dept. of Justice believes this *obiter* comment is incorrect: Johanne D'Auray, 2007 Cdn Tax Foundation annual conference, Nov. 27/07). (The taxpayer can also consider bankruptcy: see *Baran*, 2012 ONSC 240.)

The AO should not finalize the objection (unless allowing it in full) without discussing it with the objector or representative: VIEWS doc 2010-0373711C6. The AO should

give reasons when confirming an assessment, so the taxpayer can know whether to appeal to the TCC: Taxpayers' Ombudsman Aug. 2010 report *The Right to Know* (oto-boc.gc.ca). CRA agrees (news release, Nov. 9, 2010), and was to start issuing decisions in a new format in Sept. 2011 (May 2011 ICAA roundtable (tinyurl.com/cra-abtax), q. 22). However, a confirmation issued without explanation is valid: *Sui*, 2011 TCC 342 (FCA appeal dismissed for delay A-354-11).

Since 2015, an AO must consider a Taxpayer Relief request with the objection, if the taxpayer qualifies (see Notes to 220(3.1)), and may issue a "decision letter" cancelling interest and/or penalty, but will not issue a reassessment to do so until the objection is resolved. Financial hardship relief must wait until any appeal is finally resolved. (Asst. Commissioner Appeals, 2015 Cdn Tax Foundation annual conf. roundtable; see also Information Circular 07-1R1 paras. 109-110.1.)

Time to reassess continues to run while an objection is being considered. Therefore, CRA cannot increase tax payable, after the 152(4) reassessment deadline, at the objection stage: *Anchor Pointe Energy*, 2003 FCA 294. Similarly, if a reassessment is statute-barred, a second reassessment in response to an objection is equally statute-barred: *943372 Ontario Inc.*, 2007 TCC 294. However, a changed assessment for the same amount, under a different ITA provision, was permitted in *Gilbert*, 2009 TCC 328, since "as soon as there is a reassessment, it necessarily has a new basis" (para. 21). CRA can restore the original filing position when reassessing under 165(3): *Savics*, 2021 FCA 56, para. 51. See also 152(9) and 165(5); and Samtani, "Revisiting the Limits: the Powers of the Minister Post-objection", XVIII(3) *Tax Litigation* (Federated Press) 1106-15 (2012).

If CRA assumes facts on confirming the assessment that were not assumed by the auditor on assessing, the taxpayer still has the onus of disproving those facts: *Anchor Pointe Energy*, 2007 FCA 188; leave to appeal denied 2008 CarswellNat 76 (SCC).

"Notify the taxpayer": In *Charendoff*, 2005 TCC 300 (FCA appeal discontinued A-245-05), CRA was found to have "notified the taxpayer" by sending confirmation to the accountant's address used for filing the returns, even though another representative had filed the objection years earlier. In *Air Canada*, 2016 QCCA 710 (a Quebec tax case), the Court said Revenu Québec should have notified the lawyer *as well as* the taxpayer, but still, Air Canada was negligent and did not get an extension of time to appeal. In *Ford Credit*, 2016 TCC 1, a CRA Appeals Officer's letter saying "we are vacating the 2004 reassessment" did not actually vacate the assessment, as it was part of a settlement offer that was declined. In *Luxury Home*, 2021 TCC 4, CRA did not prove it had sent a confirmation notice by registered mail, so the 169(1) appeal deadline did not run.

Once CRA sends a Notice of Confirmation or Notice of Decision, it has completed its work and a subsequent "Revised" Notice of Confirmation clarifying that penalties were also confirmed was of no legal effect, and was not a substitute for the original: *Danada Enterprises*, 2012 FC 403.

The Appeals Advisory Committee met twice a year with CRA officials from 1997 to 2005, to provide input from the profession re the objection and appeal process. It was disbanded along with all other CRA advisory committees on Sept. 25, 2006, as part of a Conservative government cost-cutting measure.

For detailed discussion see David Sherman's Analysis of *Excise Tax Act* s. 301 in the *Canada GST Service*, *GST Partner* or *Taxnet Pro*. For SR&ED objections see Notes to 127(9)"SR&ED qualified expenditure pool".

165(3) amended by 1992 technical bill, effective June 10, 1993.

I.T. Application Rules: 62(4).

Interpretation Bulletins: IT-241: Reassessments made after the four-year limit (cancelled).

Information Circulars: 98-1R5: Tax collection policies.

Registered Charities Newsletters: 28 (objections and appeals on issues relating to charities).

CRA Audit Manual: 3.4.0: Privacy and confidentiality; 19.2.3: Objections — review process.

Forms: RC4067: Protocol between the verification . . . branch and the appeals branch of the CRA.

(3.1), (3.2), (4) [Repealed]

Notes: 165(3.1) and (3.2), which related to decisions by the Minister of National Health and Welfare, added by 1992 Child Benefit bill effective 1993, and repealed by 1995-97 technical bill effective August 28, 1995, as a result of the transfer of all responsibility for the Child Tax Benefit to Revenue Canada.

165(4) repealed by 1992 technical bill, effective June 10, 1993, in conjunction with the repeal of 165(3)(b).

(5) Validity of reassessment — The limitations imposed under subsections 152(4) and (4.01) do not apply to a reassessment made under subsection (3).

Notes: As long as tax is not increased, a reassessment made in response to an objection is valid: *Gilbert*, 2009 TCC 328; but not if it is based on different transactions than formed the basis of the original assessment: *Viterra Inc.*, 2018 TCC 29, para. 34 (on the parallel GST/HST rule).

If a reassessment is statute-barred, a second reassessment in response to an objection is not "cured" by 165(5): *943372 Ontario*, 2007 TCC 294; *Klemen*, 2014 TCC 244, paras. 23-24. See also Notes to 165(3) above, under "Time to reassess".

165(5) amended by 1995-97 technical bill, effective April 28, 1989.

Interpretation Bulletins: IT-241: Reassessments made after the four-year limit (cancelled).

(6) Validity of notice of objection — The Minister may accept a notice of objection served under this section that was not served in the manner required by subsection (2).

Notes: 165(6) allows the Minister to waive compliance with 165(2), but not 165(1): *Jones*, [2004] 2 C.T.C. 339 (FC). See also Notes to 165(2).

165(6) amended by 1991 technical bill to substitute "in the manner" for "in duplicate or in the manner", effective for objections made after Jan. 16, 1992.

(7) Notice of objection not required — Where a taxpayer has served in accordance with this section a notice of objection to an assessment and thereafter the Minister reassesses the tax, interest, penalties or other amount in respect of which the notice of objection was served or makes an additional assessment in respect thereof and sends to the taxpayer a notice of the reassessment or of the additional assessment, as the case may be, the taxpayer may, without serving a notice of objection to the reassessment or additional assessment,

> (a) appeal therefrom to the Tax Court of Canada in accordance with section 169; or

> (b) amend any appeal to the Tax Court of Canada that has been instituted with respect to the assessment by joining thereto an appeal in respect of the reassessment or the additional assessment in such manner and on such terms, if any, as the Tax Court of Canada directs.

Related Provisions: 169(2.1)(b) — Grounds for appeal by large corporation.

Notes: 165(7) allows an appeal to the Tax Court without filing another objection if a reassessment or new assessment is received in response to an objection: *Ivens*, 2003 TCC 910. 165(7) does not permit appeal from a reassessment issued under 169(3) on consent: *TransCanada Pipelines*, 2001 FCA 314, para. 20. See beginning of Notes to 152(4) for the meaning of "additional assessment".

An amendment under this rule gives the Crown 60 days to file a new Reply, not the 10 days normally allowed: *Rybakov*, 2020 FCA 169. (The TCC (2019 TCC 209) also discussed the effect of an amendment bumping the appeal from Informal to General Procedure.)

In (under appeal to FCA; stay issued 2019 TCC 284), when R amended the existing notice of appeal, the Crown had 60 days to file a new Reply. The case also discusses the impact of the amendment bumping the appeal from Informal to General Procedure.

In *Stone*, 2019 TCC 253, CRA reassessed S to reduce tax by a small amount after he filed his appeal. He did not amend his appeal to be from the new assessment. The Court did so on its "own motion" (paras. 73, 76) to let the appeal continue.

If the taxpayer does not appeal under 165(7)(a) within 90 days of the reassessment, the appeal right expires: *Blackwell*, 2016 TCC 155 (FCA appeal discontinued A-265-16) (there was no pre-existing appeal that could be amended).

In *102751 Canada v. Quebec*, 2019 QCCQ 7378, a Quebec reassessment did not change the expenses being contested, and the Court said the existing appeal remained valid (it is not clear whether this would apply federally).

165(7) amended by 1991 technical bill, for 1986 and later taxation years.

Definitions [s. 165]: "amount", "assessment" — 248(1); "balance" — 152(4.4); "Canada Revenue Agency" — *Canada Revenue Agency Act* s. 4(1); "day of sending" — 244(14), (14.1); "filing-due date" — 150(1), 248(1); "graduated rate estate", "individual", "Minister", "prescribed" — 248(1); "large corporation" — 225.1(8); "Parliament" — *Interpretation Act* 35(1); "taxation year" — 249; "taxpayer" — 248(1); "trust" — 104(1), 108(1), 248(1), (3); "writing" — *Interpretation Act* 35(1).

General

166. Irregularities — An assessment shall not be vacated or varied on appeal by reason only of any irregularity, informality, omission or error on the part of any person in the observation of any directory provision of this Act.

Related Provisions: 152(3) — Liability for tax not affected by incorrect or incomplete assessment; 152(8) — Assessment valid despite error; 158 — Assessment payable forthwith; 165(3) — Objections — duties of Minister; 168(4) — S. 166 applies to charity revocations etc. See also at end of s. 163.

Notes: 166 or its predecessor was used to uphold assessments challenged as procedurally wrong in *Western Minerals*, [1962] C.T.C. 270 (SCC) (initial assessment took only

15 minutes, audit came later); *Ginsberg*, [1996] 3 C.T.C. 63 (FCA) (long delay in issuing initial assessment); *Rio Tinto*, 2017 TCC 67, paras. 177-191 (FCA appeal discontinued A-153-17) (reassessment of SR&ED claim without audit since limitation period was expiring).

A "directory" provision is something less than a "mandatory" provision. See Notes to 63(1) and 227.1(2).

Definitions [s. 166]: "assessment", "person" — 248(1).

166.1 (1) Extension of time [to object] by Minister — Where no notice of objection to an assessment has been served under section 165, nor any request under subsection 245(6) made, within the time limited by those provisions for doing so, the taxpayer may apply to the Minister to extend the time for serving the notice of objection or making the request.

Related Provisions: 168(4) — Application to charity revocations, annulments, designations and refusals to register; 244(10) — Proof that no notice of objection filed.

Notes: 166.1 allows CRA to extend the time to file an objection. If CRA refuses, 166.2 allows the Tax Court to extend the time. (Extension of time to *appeal* is in 167.) CRA allowed 90-92% of applications every year from 2011-2014 (*Access to Information Act* disclosure), though it is unclear whether those disallowed include applications filed too late under 166.1(7)(a).

The four conditions in 166.1(7) are mandatory. An application brought past the one-year extension cannot be granted; see Notes to 167(1). Note that it is only necessary to have *either* been unable to object or had an intention to object, not both.

CRA *Appeals Manual* §3.8.1 states: "When it is OBVIOUS that the issue in a late-filed objection should be adjusted in full, Appeals will process the adjustment without reference to a time extension."

Appeals Manual §6.3 (formerly *Taxation Operations Manual* §7036) sets out the criteria CRA uses in considering the application. See excerpts reproduced in the commentary to ETA s. 303 in the *Canada GST Service, GST Partner* or on *Taxnet Pro*.

If the taxpayer never received the notice of (re)assessment, CRA may have to prove that it was sent. See Notes to 165(1).

If an objection has already been filed once, 166.1(1) may not be used to attempt to file a second objection: *Mansukh*, [2003] 2 C.T.C. 2526 (TCC).

Forms: P148: Resolving your dispute: objections and appeal rights under the *Income Tax Act* [pamphlet].

(2) Contents of application — An application made under subsection (1) shall set out the reasons why the notice of objection or the request was not served or made, as the case may be, within the time otherwise limited by this Act for doing so.

Notes: The word "shall" in 166.1(2) is "mandatory", so omitting the reasons is fatal: *Pereira*, [2009] 2 C.T.C. 17 (FCA) (ruling that *Haight*, [2000] 4 C.T.C. 2546 (TCC), was wrongly decided). However, an objection inadvertently filed late may be understood by the Courts as implicitly being an application for extension of time. "The words 'I am late because' do not have to appear in an application to satisfy the requirements of subsection 166.1(2)": *Melanson*, 2011 TCC 569, para. 14.

(3) How application made — An application under subsection (1) shall be made by being addressed to the Chief of Appeals in a District Office or a Taxation Centre of the Canada Revenue Agency and delivered or mailed to that Office or Centre, accompanied by a copy of the notice of objection or a copy of the request, as the case may be.

Related Provisions: 248(7)(a) — Mail deemed received on day mailed.

Notes: The application can be sent to the local Tax Services Office, even if a different office issued the assessment. It is valid if filed at any Tax Services Office or Taxation Centre, and under 166.1(4) may be accepted even if sent in some other way (e.g. by fax, or addressed to another person such as a Collections officer). There is no fee for filing an objection or an application for extension of time.

Although "shall" is mandatory (see Notes to 166.1(2)), this does not mean CRA cannot use 166.1(4): "I do not see the subject legislative provisions or the decision in *Pereira* as going to far as to say to a CRA officer: you must return an application to an applicant with an instruction to send it to the officer upstairs because the statute says you cannot walk it up the stairs yourself": *Melanson*, 2011 TCC 569, para. 15.

166.1(3) amended by *CCRA Act*, effective Nov. 1, 1999, to change "Department of National Revenue" to "Canada Customs and Revenue Agency"; and by 2004 CRA/CBSA bill, effective December 12, 2005, to "Canada Revenue Agency". Previously changed from "Department of National Revenue, Taxation" by *Department of National Revenue Act* amending bill, effective May 12, 1994.

(4) Idem — The Minister may accept an application under this section that was not made in the manner required by subsection (3).

Notes: See Notes to 166.1(3).

(5) Duties of Minister — On receipt of an application made under subsection (1), the Minister shall, with all due dispatch, consider the application and grant or refuse it, and shall thereupon notify the taxpayer in writing of the Minister's decision.

Related Provisions: 166.2(1) — Extension of time by Tax Court; 244(14) — Date of mailing presumed to be date of notification.

Notes: 166.1(5) amended by 1992 technical bill, effective June 10, 1993. Before, the Minister was required to notify the taxpayer by registered mail rather than simply "in writing".

See Notes to 166.1(1), and to 165(3) re "all due dispatch".

(6) Date of objection or request if application granted — If an application made under subsection (1) is granted, the notice of objection or the request, as the case may be, is deemed to have been served or made on the day on which the decision of the Minister is sent to the taxpayer.

Related Provisions: 244(14), (14.1) — Date when decision sent.

Notes: 166.1(6) amended by 2010 budget bill #2, effective Dec. 15, 2010, to change "mailed" to "sent" (to accommodate electronic notices under 244(14.1)).

(7) When order to be made — No application shall be granted under this section unless

(a) the application is made within one year after the expiration of the time otherwise limited by this Act for serving a notice of objection or making a request, as the case may be; and

(b) the taxpayer demonstrates that

(i) within the time otherwise limited by this Act for serving such a notice or making such a request, as the case may be, the taxpayer

(A) was unable to act or to instruct another to act in the taxpayer's name, or

(B) had a *bona fide* intention to object to the assessment or make the request,

(ii) given the reasons set out in the application and the circumstances of the case, it would be just and equitable to grant the application, and

(iii) the application was made as soon as circumstances permitted.

Related Provisions: 248(7)(a) — Mail deemed received on day mailed; *Interpretation Act* 27(5) — Meaning of "within one year".

Notes: The 166.1(7) deadline could be extended by up to 6 months during 2020 under TLOPA 7(1). See Enacted Amendment under 169(1).

Notes [s. 166.1]: See Notes to 166.1(1) and 166.2(1). 166.1 added by 1991 technical bill, effective for applications filed after Jan. 16, 1992.

Definitions [s. 166.1]: "assessment" — 248(1); "Canada Revenue Agency" — *Canada Revenue Agency Act* s. 4(1); "Minister" — 248(1); "sent" — 244(14), (14.1); "taxpayer" — 248(1); "writing" — *Interpretation Act* 35(1).

166.2 (1) Extension of time [to object] by Tax Court — A taxpayer who has made an application under subsection 166.1[(1)] may apply to the Tax Court of Canada to have the application granted after either

(a) the Minister has refused the application, or

(b) 90 days have elapsed after service of the application under subsection 166.1(1) and the Minister has not notified the taxpayer of the Minister's decision,

but no application under this section may be made after the expiration of 90 days after the day on which notification of the decision was mailed to the taxpayer.

Related Provisions: 168(4) — Application to charity revocations, annulments, designations and refusals to register.

Notes: Electronic filing of a 166.2 application can be done at tinyurl.com/tcc-file.

If no application was filed with CRA under 166.1, an application to the TCC under 166.2 is invalid: *McKernan*, [2003] 1 C.T.C. 2275 (TCC); *Boyko*, 2010 TCC 534; *Asiedu*, 2011 TCC 150.

The 166.2(1) deadline could be extended by up to 6 months during 2020 under TLOPA 6(1). See Enacted Amendment under 169(1).

If one misses the 90-day deadline to apply to the TCC after CRA rejects a 166.1 application, the TCC has no jurisdiction to hear the application: *Lemieux*, 2003 TCC 855; *9848-3173 Québec*, 2003 TCC 217; *Maman*, 2007 TCC 429; *de Lucia*, 2010 TCC 479; *Burke*, 2012 TCC 378, para. 28.

See Notes to 167(1) for case law on 166.2 (the two sections have the same conditions except an extra condition in 167(5)(b)(iv) that there be reasonable grounds for the appeal). The four conditions in 166.2(5) are mandatory; if the original application to CRA did not meet the one-year deadline extension, the extension cannot be granted. Note that it is only necessary to have *either* been unable to object or had an intention to object, not both.

See Cases annotation to s. 304 in David M. Sherman, *Practitioner's Goods and Services Tax Annotated*, for extensive case law on the parallel GST/HST rule.

166.2 can be circumvented by the Court finding that an earlier request for reassessment was actually a Notice of Objection: *Schneidmiller*, 2009 TCC 354.

If the taxpayer claims not to have received the assessment, the onus is on CRA to prove it was sent: see Notes to 165(1).

See Notes to *Interpretation Act* s. 26 if the deadline expires on a weekend. See Notes to 244(14) re determining when the assessment was mailed (or sent electronically — 244(14.1)) to start the 90-day clock running.

The Federal Court has no jurisdiction to review a CRA refusal to extend time: *Moise*, 2012 FC 1468.

Forms: P148: Resolving your dispute: objections and appeal rights under the *Income Tax Act* [pamphlet].

(2) How application made — An application under subsection (1) shall be made by filing in the Registry of the Tax Court of Canada, in accordance with the provisions of the *Tax Court of Canada Act*, three copies of the documents referred to in subsection 166.1(3) and three copies of the notification, if any, referred to in subsection 166.1(5).

Related Provisions: 248(7)(a) — Mail deemed received on day mailed.

Notes: 166.2(2) amended by 2000 GST bill, effective October 20, 2000, to change "or by sending by registered mail addressed to an office of the Registry" to "in accordance with the provisions of the *Tax Court of Canada Act*".

(3) Copy to Commissioner — The Tax Court of Canada shall send a copy of each application made under this section to the office of the Commissioner of Revenue.

Notes: 166.2(3) amended by *CCRA Act*, effective November 1, 1999, to change "Deputy Minister of National Revenue" to "Commissioner of Customs and Revenue"; and by 2004 CRA/CBSA bill, effective December 12, 2005, to change to "Commissioner of Revenue". Previously changed from "Deputy Minister of National Revenue for Taxation" by *Department of National Revenue Act* amending bill, effective May 12, 1994.

(4) Powers of Court — The Tax Court of Canada may grant or dismiss an application made under subsection (1) and, in granting an application, may impose such terms as it deems just or order that the notice of objection be deemed to have been served on the date of its order.

Notes: The Court is never obligated to grant the extension of time, no matter what facts it finds: 166.2(4) provides that it "may" grant the application. However, unless all the conditions in 166.2(5) are met, the Court cannot grant it.

The Court may treat a Notice of Objection as being an application for extension of time, and grant the extension: *Fagbemi*, [2005] 3 C.T.C. 2470 (TCC).

(5) When application to be granted — No application shall be granted under this section unless

(a) the application was made under subsection 166.1(1) within one year after the expiration of the time otherwise limited by this Act for serving a notice of objection or making a request, as the case may be; and

(b) the taxpayer demonstrates that

(i) within the time otherwise limited by this Act for serving such a notice or making such a request, as the case may be, the taxpayer

(A) was unable to act or to instruct another to act in the taxpayer's name, or

(B) had a *bona fide* intention to object to the assessment or make the request,

(ii) given the reasons set out in the application and the circumstances of the case, it would be just and equitable to grant the application, and

(iii) the application was made under subsection 166.1(1) as soon as circumstances permitted.

Related Provisions: *Interpretation Act* 27(5) — Meaning of "within one year".

Notes: The 166.2(5) deadline could be extended by up to 6 months during 2020 under TLOPA 7(1). See Enacted Amendment under 169(1).

Related Provisions [s. 166.2]: 169 — Appeals.

Notes [s. 166.2]: See Notes to 166.2(1). 166.2 added by 1991 technical bill (replacing former 167), for applications filed after Jan. 16, 1992.

Definitions [s. 166.2]: "Commissioner of Revenue" — *Canada Revenue Agency Act* s. 25; "Minister", "taxpayer" — 248(1).

167. (1) Extension of time to appeal — Where an appeal to the Tax Court of Canada has not been instituted by a taxpayer under section 169 within the time limited by that section for doing so, the taxpayer may make an application to the Court for an order extending the time within which the appeal may be instituted and the Court may make an order extending the time for appealing and may impose such terms as it deems just.

Notes: Electronic filing of a 167(1) application can be done at tinyurl.com/tcc-file. For extension of the deadline during COVID-19 see *Time Limits and Other Periods Act* s. 6(1), in Enacted Amendment under 169(1).

Note that it is only necessary under 167(5)(b)(i) to have *either* been unable to appeal or had an intention to appeal, not both. "Unable to act" was held to include not having enough information to make an informed decision to object, in *Patterson Dental*, 2014 TCC 62. If the application does not disclose reasonable grounds for the appeal to be allowed, it does not meet the test in 167(5)(b)(ii) and will be dismissed: *Ferrara*, [2002] G.S.T.C. 18 (TCC); *Delage*, 2011 FCA 274 (but this requirement is only in 167 and not in 166.2). If no application was first made to CRA, the application will be dismissed: *McKernan*, [2003] 1 C.T.C. 2275 (TCC).

For more on the meaning of "just and equitable" (used in 166.1(7)(b)(ii), 166.2(5)(b)(ii), 167(5)(b)(ii)), see Notes to 85(7.1).

A "failure to meet any one of the conditions is fatal to the application": *Dewey*, 2004 FCA 82, para. 3. A notice of appeal filed within the deadline for applying for an extension of time, but not meeting the other conditions, failed in *Guled*, 2010 TCC 387. However, a defence to a Crown motion to dismiss an appeal as filed too late was treated as an application for extension of time in *Pardiak*, 2011 TCC 375.

If the Court finds the notice of assessment or confirmation was not properly sent (see Notes to 165(1)), it should not allow the application for extension of time (as it sometimes does — e.g., *Girard*, *Poulin* and *Pylatuke* above), but should dismiss it with a ruling that the objection or appeal is valid and can proceed: *Aztec Industries*, [1995] 1 C.T.C. 327 (FCA), para. 23. The TCC did this in *Rick Pearson Auto*, [1996] G.S.T.C. 44; *Massarotto*, [2000] G.S.T.C. 19; *John Moore*, 2013 CarswellNat 1466; *Sicoli*, 2013 TCC 207; *Reynolds*, 2013 TCC 288 (FCA appeal discontinued A-354-13); *DouangChanh*, 2013 TCC 320 (see Notes to 152(4.2)); *Kirschke*, 2019 TCC 68. In *Duncan*, 2020 TCC 89, D likely first saw the notice 10 months before filing the application for extension of time (para. 18), so the application was allowed.

The Tax Court is more stringent than CRA in granting extensions of time (see Notes to 166.1(1)). For TCC cases denying an extension to object or appeal because the applicant could have acted sooner, see *106850 Canada*, [2001] G.S.T.C. 141; *Groulx*, [2002] G.S.T.C. 109; *Di Modica*, [2002] 1 C.T.C. 2299; *Sauvageau*, 2008 TCC 166; *Carrier*, 2005 TCC 182 (accountant was too busy to file objection during tax filing season); *Charette*, 2007 TCC 567 (FCA appeal discontinued); *Ritter*, 2008 TCC 514; *Esesson Canada*, 2009 TCC 336 (no evidence of compliance with 167(5)(b)); *Cloutier*, 2010 FCA 96; *Haines*, 2010 TCC 450 (no reasonable grounds for appeal); *Bouganim*, 2010 TCC 560 (delaying in retaining new lawyer and filing application); *M.P.N. Holdings*, 2011 TCC 181 (late appeal sought to take advantage of Tax Court decision in unrelated case, changing interpretation of Canada-US tax treaty); *Sampson*, 2012 TCC 156 (taxpayer chose not to appeal because of filing fee charged at the time); *Tcheng*, 2012 TCC 276 (representative had first consulted with MP and filed complaint with Ombudsman); *Hamilton*, 2013 TCC 192 (application only 7 days late, but H not present in Court to testify why it was late); *Haynes*, 2013 TCC 229 (frivolous tax-protester arguments); *Esmezyan*, 2015 TCC 213 (evidence that wife did not give applicant notice she signed for was rejected, even though they were in divorce proceedings); *Shabitai*, 2016 TCC 20 (explanations not credible); *Sapi*, 2016 TCC 239 (not "just and equitable": S trusted an agent to file appeals but did not follow up); *Gionet*, 2017 TCC 97 (FCA appeal discontinued A-138-17) (no evidence conditions met); *Amrite*, 2018 TCC 11 (A intended to appeal denial of donation credits but relied on promoter to file appeal as promised; A was responsible for representative's negligence); *Bergevin*, 2021 FCA 9 (leave to appeal to SCC requested) (criteria not met).

In *Stein*, 2013 TCC 345, the TCC dismissed an application to extend time to appeal because the appeal would have no chance of success (see 167(5)(b)(iv); note this is not a condition for an *objection* extension under 166.2(5)(b)).

The deadline is not extended by it being "impossible" to act, despite the Quebec *Civil Code* providing such a rule: *Larocque*, 2016 QCCA 556; *Andreou*, 2018 QCCA 695 (leave to appeal denied 2019 CarswellQue 1547 (SCC)); *Gauthier*, 2019 TCC 115.

If the one-year deadline extension in 166.1(7)(a), 166.2(5)(a) or 167(5)(a) is missed, the application must be dismissed, even if the delay was because of extenuating circumstances such as: ongoing discussions with CRA officials (*Banque Nationale*, [2003] G.S.T.C. 44 (TCC); *Vescio*, 2007 TCC 690; *Gordon Moffat Welding*, 2009 TCC 69; *Bush*, 2014 TCC 97); taxpayer filed GST appeal and neglected to file parallel income tax appeal (*Aumuller*, [2001] 3 C.T.C. 2665 (TCC)); taxpayer did not understand meaning of notice of assessment (*Carlson*, 2002 FCA 145; *Johnson*, 2009 TCC 496; *Anderson*, 2015 TCC 229); taxpayer thought accountant had filed objection or appeal (*Lamothe*, [2003] 2 C.T.C. 2791 (TCC); *Gauthier*, 2019 TCC 115); taxpayer did not receive notice of assessment or confirmation (248(7)(a); *Vigier*, 2004 TCC 763; *Odebala-Fregene*, 2015 TCC 44 (FCA appeal dismissed for delay A-145-15); *Vo*, 2015 FCA 246; *Afkari*, 2019 TCC 173); criminal lawyer advised that objecting could compromise evidence for upcoming criminal trial (*Cameron*, 2006 TCC 588); taxpayer had not provided CRA with his current address (*Carvalho*, 2007 TCC 709); unfairness on CRA's part (*Bouari*, 2008 TCC 431); confusion when multiple years were assessed (*Gollner*, 2009 TCC 346; *Azzopardi*, 2016 TCC 194, para. 27); taxpayer had moved and advised Revenu Québec but not CRA (*Roy*, 2009 TCC 573); former tax counsel failed to file appeal (*Woodworth*, 2010 TCC 220 (FCA appeal discontinued A-201-10)); objection made only orally and amount acknowledged by CRA as being in dispute (*Natarajan*, 2010 TCC 582); taxpayer objected within 1 year but did not apply for extension of time (*Moon*, 2010 TCC 393; *Thangarajah*, 2017 TCC 72; *Roland*, 2011 TCC 202); deadline missed by 1 day or 1 week (*Vatasescu*, 2011 TCC 149; *Edgelow*, 2011 TCC 255 (FCA appeal struck A-164-11)); taxpayer relying on accountant who was ill (*Sutherland*, 2011 TCC 170); relief previously granted to wife did not apply to husband (*Hess*, 2011 TCC 387 (FCA appeal dismissed for delay A-361-11)); notice of confirmation contained no explanation (*Sui*, 2011 TCC 342 (FCA appeal dismissed for delay A-354-11)); objection filed on time for one year but not another (*Johnson*, 2011 TCC 401; *Shy Brothers*, 2011 TCC 419; *Schoenne*, 2011 TCC 189); TCC had suggested CRA reassess the year to allow appeal (*Kuszka*, 2011 TCC 578); wrong information received from CRA (*Michaud*, 2011 TCC 573); taxpayer's former fiancé had withheld her mail so she did not receive notice (*Campbell*, 2012 TCC 363); CRA auditor refused to meet with taxpayer and issued unreasonable assessment (*Hansen*, 2013 TCC 142); husband called CRA to change his address but wife's address not changed on CRA records (*Brando*, 2013 TCC 223); taxpayer had signed objection and tax shelter promoter told him it would be filed (*Hanson*, 2013 TCC 341); request to adjust CCA claims in returns had been made years earlier (*Newfoundland Transshipment*, 2013 TCC 259); tax authority waited until just after the year expired to start collection (*Bellemare*, 2013 TCC 381); taxpayer claimed accountants told him he did not need to object to GST assessment until his income tax objections were resolved (*Sahibi*, 2014 TCC 79); taxpayer's accountant sent objection to "pending" reassessments in response to proposal letter (*Poot*, 2014 TCC 295); assessments were "notional" assessments and taxpayer could not find a lawyer to take her case (*Carpenter*, 2016 TCC 201 (FCA appeal dismissed without reasons A-396-16)); taxpayer asked counsel to appeal 2 years but only 1 was appealed (*Pietrovito*, 2017 TCC 119); letter rejecting objection as too late was not confirmation of assessment (*Jiahua Car Rental*, 2019 TCC 258); CRA issued Notice of Confirmation, then a few days later an erroneous letter saying CRA had received objection and would contact taxpayer when it was assigned (*Dutka*, 2020 TCC 21). The same result applied in *O'Byrne*, 2015 FCA 239; *Denney*, 2021 FCA 15; *Nicholls*, 2011 TCC 39; *Gu*, 2011 TCC 397; *Winters*, 2011 TCC 417; *Reimer*, 2011 TCC 426; *Ross*, 2011 TCC 538 (FCA appeal dismissed for delay A-435-11); *Sampson*, 2012 TCC 156; *Monsef*, 2012 TCC 189; *Sedlak*, 2012 TCC 190; *Riley*, 2012 TCC 208; *Yankey*, 2012 TCC 266; *Vidanovic*, 2012 TCC 265; *Hewstan*, 2012 TCC 292; *Petratos*, 2013 TCC 240; *Palubjak*, 2013 TCC 285; *Topping*, 2013 TCC 346; *Roopchand*, 2016 TCC 279; *Mockler*, 2016 TCC 240; *M.R.E. Developments*, 2019 TCC 151; *McBrearty*, 2019 TCC 268. The TCC can avoid this result by finding that the reassessment or confirmation was not properly mailed (see Notes to 165(1)): *Lambo*, 2011 TCC 293. The TCC ruled in *Haight*, [2000] 4 C.T.C. 2546 and *1682320 Ontario Ltd.*, 2013 TCC 126, that a notice of objection filed within the 1-year period could be considered as an application for extension of time; but the FCA stated in *Pereira*, 2008 FCA 264 that *Haight* "was wrongly decided and ought not to be followed".

If the deadline is missed, CRA can be asked to reassess under 152(4.2) (for an individual or graduated rate estate) if it agrees the assessment is wrong and there were "exceptional circumstances" that prevented objecting or appealing on time: Information Circular 07-1R1 ¶73.2.

Extension granted: In *Bygrave*, 2017 FCA 124 (reversing the TCC), the FCA allowed an extension: B had instructed a CA to file the appeal but the CA thought he could not until he had all the documentation. The test of "as soon as circumstances permitted" applies to the *application*, not the *notice of appeal*: para. 16. Also, a taxpayer should have "every reasonable opportunity to defend himself" from a gross negligence penalty: para. 22. The TCC granted extensions in: *Haight*, [2000] 4 C.T.C. 2546 (health problems; but held wrongly decided in *Pereira*, 2008 FCA 264); *Multi-Point Enterprises*, [1995] G.S.T.C. 72 (applicant should appear at hearing, even if CRA consents); *Meer*, [2001] 3 C.T.C. 2537 (8-month delay after finding out deadline missed was OK); *Yates*, [2002] 2 C.T.C. 2835 (Y did not receive CRA letter setting out his appeal rights); *Gorenko*, [2002] 4 C.T.C. 2044 (lawyer acted with reasonable degree of diligence); *Industries Bonneville*, [2002] G.S.T.C. 99 (lawyer thought file was still under discussion with government officials when assessment had been issued); *Wells*, [2001] 4 C.T.C. 2950 (W mistakenly appealed only 1 taxation year instead of 2; Court held Notice of Appeal could be amended to refer to second year); *Paquet*, 2003 TCC 841 (illiterate taxpayer relied on accountants); *Bourdages*, 2008 TCC 623 (B did not receive notice of confirmation and always intended to appeal); *Big Bad Voodoo Daddy*, 2010 TCC 12 (accountant misled corp in not advising confirmation had been issued, and corp acted immediately once it knew); *Busque*, 2010 TCC 80 (B received confirmation but no statement of account from CRA, and always intended to appeal);

Spectrol Inc., 2010 TCC 390 (corp always intended to object and had not received notice of assessment); *Rock*, 2010 TCC 607 (Indian employees of Native Leasing Services; although appeals would likely fail, they could be joined with others scheduled for trial); *Mehta*, 2011 TCC 38 (M duped by representative who did not file appeal for him); *Miniotas*, 2011 TCC 43 (unclear why now-deceased accountant did not file application sooner, but letter accepted as being application for extension of time); *Gamble*, 2011 TCC 244 (health problems, and due to separation G did not receive confirmation for many months); *Lambo*, 2011 TCC 293 (unconscionable for CRA to send letter saying objection would be assigned to an officer, then to write months later to say it was filed too late); *Chénard*, 2011 TCC 344 (tax shelter promoter failed to file appeal but C had intended to); *Pardiak*, 2011 TCC 375 (P always intended to appeal and did not receive Notice of Confirmation); *Girard*, 2012 TCC 343 (G testified he filled out objection form at tax office and dropped it into box provided, and Revenu Québec lost it); *Poulin*, 2013 TCC 104 (P's evidence of mailing objection on time was credible); *1682320 Ontario*, 2013 TCC 126 (corp formed intention to object before the deadline); *Pylatuke*, 2013 TCC 364 (CRA's claim assessment sent by registered mail required more evidence); *Apic*, 2015 TCC 192 (A thought deadline was 18 months; "I am generally loath to deny an application to extend time on the grounds set out in clauses (b)(i) and (iii) unless non-compliance is clear ...it is not appropriate to set the bar too high" (para. 4)); *Azzopardi*, 2016 TCC 194, para. 3 (conditions met and Crown did not oppose application); *Bureau Barrister*, 2020 TCC 119 (lawyer held off seeking extension until near 12-month deadline because he thought CRA was issuing reassessment following consent judgment).

Extended deadline missed: In *Burke*, 2010 TCC 398, extension of time to appeal was granted but the notice of appeal was filed past the new deadline. The Court extended the deadline further "in the interests of justice." However, in *Ward*, 2008 TCC 510, on similar facts, the Court ruled it had no jurisdiction to extend time by modifying the earlier Order. In *Kamangar*, 2013 TCC 385, extension was granted subject to a "proper Notice of Appeal" being filed; when that was not done, the Court file was closed, and the taxpayer would have had to apply within 180 days to set aside the dismissal.

Possible creative workarounds: *Hoffman*, 2010 TCC 267 (appeal of nil assessment was actually appeal of loss determination); *Melanson*, 2011 TCC 569, para. 21 (Minister can waive requirement of 166.1 to file application for extension of time); *Breathe E-Z Homes*, 2014 TCC 122 (taxpayer instructed lawyer to file appeal and lawyer made errors; Court deemed objection filed with CRA to be a notice of appeal filed with the Court); *Azzopardi*, 2016 TCC 194, para. 27 ("making some effort [to object], however unfocused, ill-addressed or malformed may still have allowed a cleft which the Court could grasp"); *Ntakos Estate*, 2018 TCC 224 (reassessment implementing adjustment request from mentally deficient taxpayer was void, so no objection needed); *Phillip*, 2019 TCC 37, para. 2 (Notice of Appeal treated as application to extend time); *Persaud*, 2013 TCC 405 (objection filed after CRA letter saying reassessment would be issued, but before reassessment, was valid). See also Notes to 165(2) (*Lester* and *Schneidmiller* cases) re a letter being held to be a Notice of Objection. The TCC only rarely assists in this way, however. CRA cannot use 220(2.1) to extend time to object even if it wants to: *Conocophillips*, 2017 FCA 243. The FC has no jurisdiction to review a CRA decision to enforce an assessment where the objection deadline was missed: *Newton*, 2018 FC 343 (see Notes to 169(1) under "Jurisdictional issues").

In both *Hickerty*, 2007 TCC 482 and *Cheam Tours*, 2008 TCC 18, the taxpayer had mistakenly sent a Notice of Appeal to CRA rather than the Court, and the Court held the one-year period excludes time "during which the taxpayer is under a reasonable but mistaken belief that she has validly instituted an appeal." The *Hickerty* principle was doubted, but distinguished, in *Castle*, [2008] 3 C.T.C. 2370 (TCC), and *Chu*, 2009 TCC 444. This "discoverability" defence had been rejected in *Carlson*, 2002 FCA 145 (though the FCA left open the slight hope it might apply on different facts) and *Al-Rubaiy*, 2020 TCC 34, and *Hickerty* was explicitly rejected in *Odebala-Fregene*, 2015 TCC 44, para. 17 (FCA appeal dismissed for delay A-145-15), and *Andreou*, 2018 QCCA 695. In *Govender*, 2010 TCC 486, on the same facts, the Court found the appeal not validly filed, without discussing *Hickerty*. In *Gidda*, 2013 TCC 190 (FCA appeal dismissed for delay A-245-13), the taxpayer alleged he had filed appeals with CRA instead of the Court, but the Court did not believe him.

In *Larson*, 2018 TCC 242, L did not show up for the hearing of her application for extension of time to appeal (part of a tax shelter group). Her application was dismissed, and her motion to set aside that judgment, filed almost 7 months later, was denied.

The *Indian Act* exemption (see Notes to 81(1)(a)) does not extend taxpayers' rights if the deadline is missed: *Johnston*, 2009 TCC 327 (appeal to FCA dismissed for delay: A-293-09). Nor does the Crown's duty to consult and accommodate before deciding aboriginal claims: *Diome*, 2012 TCC 9.

If the taxpayer never received the notice of assessment or confirmation denying the objection, CRA may have to prove that it was sent. See Notes to 165(1).

A reassessment displaces an earlier assessment and makes it a nullity, so an extension of time can no longer be sought to object to the earlier assessment: *Yarmoloy*, 2014 TCC 27.

For extension of time to appeal TCC decisions to the FCA, see end of Notes to 169(1).

The rules in 167(1) apply to an extension of time to appeal a decision under *Canada Pension Plan* s. 28 and *Employment Insurance Act* s. 103, but the final deadline is 90+90 days, instead of 90 days + 1 year (e.g., *Covic*, 2014 TCC 105; *Breathe E-Z Homes*, 2014 TCC 122).

Forms: P148: Resolving your dispute: objections and appeal rights under the *Income Tax Act* [pamphlet].

(2) Contents of application — An application made under subsection (1) shall set out the reasons why the appeal was not instituted within the time limited by section 169 for doing so.

(3) How application made — An application made under subsection (1) shall be made by filing in the Registry of the Tax Court of Canada, in accordance with the provisions of the *Tax Court of Canada Act*, three copies of the application accompanied by three copies of the notice of appeal.

Related Provisions: 165(2) — Service.

Notes: 167(3) amended by 2000 GST bill, effective October 20, 2000.

(4) Copy to Deputy Attorney General — The Tax Court of Canada shall send a copy of each application made under this section to the office of the Deputy Attorney General of Canada.

(5) When order to be made — No order shall be made under this section unless

(a) the application is made within one year after the expiration of the time limited by section 169 for appealing; and

(b) the taxpayer demonstrates that

(i) within the time otherwise limited by section 169 for appealing the taxpayer

(A) was unable to act or to instruct another to act in the taxpayer's name, or

(B) had a *bona fide* intention to appeal,

(ii) given the reasons set out in the application and the circumstances of the case, it would be just and equitable to grant the application,

(iii) the application was made as soon as circumstances permitted, and

(iv) there are reasonable grounds for the appeal.

Related Provisions: 169 — Appeal; *Interpretation Act* 27(5) — Meaning of "within one year".

Notes: See Notes to 167(1). The 167(5)(a) deadline could be extended by up to 6 months during 2020 under TLOPA 6(1). See Enacted Amendment under 169(1).

Notes [s. 167]: 167 rewritten by 1991 technical bill, effective for applications filed after January 16, 1992.

Definitions [s. 167]: "taxpayer" — 248(1).

Revocation of Registration of Certain Organizations and Associations

168. (1) Notice of intention to revoke registration — The Minister may, by registered mail, give notice to a person described in any of paragraphs (a) to (c) of the definition "qualified donee" in subsection 149.1(1) that the Minister proposes to revoke its registration if the person

(a) applies to the Minister in writing for revocation of its registration;

(b) ceases to comply with the requirements of this Act for its registration;

(c) in the case of a registered charity, registered Canadian amateur athletic association or registered journalism organization, fails to file an information return as and when required under this Act or a regulation;

(d) issues a receipt for a gift otherwise than in accordance with this Act and the regulations or that contains false information;

(e) fails to comply with or contravenes any of sections 230 to 231.5; or

(f) in the case of a registered Canadian amateur athletic association or registered journalism organization, accepts a gift the granting of which was expressly or implicitly conditional on the association or organization making a gift to another person, club, society, association or organization.

Related Provisions: 149.1(2) — Revocation of registration of charity; 149.1(3) — Revocation of public foundation registration; 149.1(4.1) — Revocation of charity registration for contraventions or involvement of ineligible individual; 149.1(4.2) —

Revocation of RCAAA registration; 149.1(4.3) — Revocation of qualified-donee registration; 149.1(6.4), (6.5) — Application of s. 168 to registered national arts service organizations; 149.1(23), (24) — Annulment of charity registration as alternative to revocation; 168(3) — Deemed revocation when certificate issued claiming charity supports terrorism; 168(4) — Objection to proposed revocation; 172(3)(a) — Appeal from revocation; 188(1) — Deemed year-end on notice of revocation; 188(1.1) — Revocation tax; 188.1(6)–(10) — Alternative penalties for failing to file information return and for incorrect receipts; 188.2(1), (2) — Suspension of charity's receipting privileges; 230(2) — Charity must keep records to allow CRA to determine if there are grounds to revoke registration; 241(3.2)(g) — Revocation letter may be disclosed to the public; 244(5) — Proof of service by mail; 248(1)"registered Canadian amateur athletic association", "registered charity" — Application for registration; 248(7)(a) — Mail deemed received on day mailed.

Notes [s. 168(1)]: Note also the grounds in 149.1(2)-(4.1) for revoking registration, the annulment option in 149.1(23), and the alternatives of penalties under 188.1 and suspension under 188.2. A charity engaging in political activities is no longer grounds for revocation: see Notes to 149.1(6.1).

CRA's *Guidelines for applying sanctions* (tinyurl.com/guide-sanc) state: "In cases of aggravated non-compliance, we will likely move directly to revoking the charity's registration. These include cases where one or more of the following factors are present: the organization has a previous record of serious non-compliance, and the current form of non-compliance is both serious and intentional; the non-compliance has resulted in a substantial adverse impact on others (beneficiaries, donors, or funders), particularly where the organization cannot or will not remedy the harm done; and the organization cannot or will not bring itself into compliance.

"There are two other cases where we are likely to move directly to revocation. The first is when a charity does not file its annual return.... The second are serious cases for which there is no appropriate sanction, such as engaging in non-charitable activities. However, we intend to exercise some discretion in these instances, as it is not our intention to move directly to revocation in those cases where it is possible and appropriate to work with the charity to get its operations back onside." See also Cathy Hawara, "The CRA Charities Directorate's Approach to Compliance", 2014 Cdn Tax Foundation conference report, at 37:3-8.

In 2015, about 800 charities were revoked voluntarily; 700 for failure to file; 1 for losing corporate status; 23 after audit: Yvonne Chenier, "Why Some Charities Lost Their Status", 24(3) *Canadian Not-for-Profit News* (Carswell) 20-22 (March 2016).

See Notes to 149.1(1)"charitable organization" and 149.1(14); and Guide RC4424, *Completing the Tax Return Where Registration of a Charity is Revoked*.

Depending on the reason a charity's registration is revoked, its directors and officers may become "ineligible individuals" (149.1(1)) and unable to manage or register another charity (149.1(4.1)(e), 149.1(25)).

Appealing a revocation successfully is almost impossible due to the FCA: see Notes to 172(3). Before appealing a revocation, the charity must first object under 168(4).

Where a revoked charity wishes to re-register, see Notes to 188(2.1).

In *Canadian Magen David Adom*, 2002 FCA 323, revocation of a charity that bought ambulances for the Israeli equivalent of the Red Cross was upheld on the grounds the Canadian charity did not exercise sufficient control over the ambulances through an agency agreement, and thus was not engaged in charitable activities(!). However, the real reason for CRA's notice of revocation, that the ambulances were operating in the West Bank and east Jerusalem so that the charity was acting against Canadian public policy (because those territories are under dispute), was rejected by the Court, which ruled that this alleged "public policy" does not exist. (CRA policy prohibited only Jewish charities from operating in these areas.) An application for leave to appeal to the SCC was dropped when CMDA reached a settlement with CRA that allowed it to be de-registered and immediately re-registered as a charity. See also Adam Aptowitzer, "Beware of Operating Contrary to Public Policy", 24(4) *Canadian Not-for-Profit News* (Carswell) 27-28 (April 2016).

See Notes to 149.1(1)"charitable organization" re agency arrangements for a charity's foreign activities.

Charity revocations were also upheld by the FCA in *Human Life International*, [1998] 3 C.T.C. 126 (leave to appeal to SCC denied Jan. 1999); *Alliance for Life*, [1999] 3 C.T.C. 1 (charity resources spent on political activities re abortion); *Canadian Committee for the Tel Aviv Foundation*, 2002 FCA 72 (failing to keep proper records, plus other infractions); *Lord's Evangelical Church of Deliverance*, 2004 FCA 397 (violations included giving $150,000 to pastor's children); *House of Holy God*, 2009 FCA 148 (leave to appeal denied 2009 CarswellNat 3675) (charity's maple syrup business was not related business); *Triumphant Church of Christ*, 2009 FCA 161 (CRA had advised charity of its concerns about poor record-keeping); *Christ Apostolic Church*, 2009 FCA 162 (CRA entitled to unilaterally withdraw "compliance agreement" and revoke registration); *Holy Alpha and Omega Church of Toronto*, 2009 FCA 265 (numerous contraventions; Court would not prohibit CRA from publishing Notice of Intent to Revoke since no "irreparable harm"); *Faith Assemblies Mission International*, 2009 FCA 318 (appeal deadline expired); *International Pentecostal Ministry Fellowship of Toronto*, 2010 FCA 51 (CRA's regulation of charities is constitutionally valid as part of taxation; CRA's decision within range of acceptable outcomes); *World Job and Food Bank*, 2013 FCA 65 (CRA's conclusions were reasonable); *Trinity Global Support*, 2013 FCA 109 (no proof of irreparable harm); *Prescient Foundation*, 2013 FCA 120 (leave to appeal denied 2013 CarswellNat 4462) (gifts to foreign charities OK, but adequate records not maintained re donation to US charity); *Gateway City Church*,

2013 FCA 126 (no proof of irreparable harm); *Public Television Assn of Quebec*, 2015 FCA 170 (PTAQ served as fundraiser for US public TV station and did not actually exercise control and direction over it despite agency agreement); *Humane Society of Canada for the Protection of Animals*, 2015 FCA 178 (leave to appeal denied 2016 CarswellNat 601) (charity reimbursed $251,000 of officer's expenses including $70,000 personal expenses); *Jaamiah al Uloom al Islamiyyah*, 2016 FCA 49 (leave to appeal denied 2016 CarswellNat 3372) (failing to issue T4s, lending receipting privileges to another entity, not keeping proper books and records); *Opportunities for the Disabled Foundation*, 2016 FCA 94 (non-compliance with previous compliance agreement; 70% of donations went to fundraising costs; a T3010 with many inaccuracies was not a properly filed return); *Galerie Fôkus*, 2018 FCA 198 (gallery was selling paintings for artists, not promoting art, and issued receipts for donations to non-charities); *Ark Angel Foundation*, 2019 FCA 21 (leave to appeal denied 2019 CarswellNat 6296) (consulting fees to director not shown to be for charitable purposes); *Many Mansions*, 2019 FCA 189 (leave to appeal denied 2020 CarswellNat 54) (inadequate records; and pastor thrice used charity's meeting room for his personal business); *Ark Angel Fund*, 2020 FCA 99 (same as *Ark Angel Foundation*).

For CRA letters detailing reasons for hundreds of charity revocations see tinyurl.com/char-revoked (Blumberg). Revocations announced since 2008 for participating in abusive tax shelters (CRA news release date and details in parentheses): ACTLAP Children's Foundation (July 8/16: $64m in receipts for Pharma Gifts International shelter); African Computer and Technology Literacy Awareness Program ($8.6m in receipts for Mission Life shelter); Alberta Distribution Relief Agency Aid Society International (Sept. 14/09: $106m in receipts for Canadian Humanitarian Trust (CHT) shelter); The Animals' Charity (Nov. 9/12: issued $9m in receipts under Innovative Gifting (IG) shelter, and over 90% of $1m cash went to promoter); Banyan Tree Foundation (Oct. 20/08: issued $210m in improper receipts, and failed to show that $10m paid to directors and their corporations was bona fide); Cdn Friends of Pearl Children (July 17/15: $167m in receipts for Mission Life shelter); Children's Emergency Foundation (May 11/09: $57.8m in receipts and devoted $3.2m to charitable activities); Choson Kallah Fund (Nov. 3/08: $177m in receipts under CHT) [attempt to delay revocation failed: 2008 FCA 311; leave to appeal denied 2009 CarswellNat 935 (SCC)]; Destiny Health and Wellness Foundation (April 19/10: $42m in receipts for Universal Donation Program (UDP) and Destiny Gifting Program shelters, of which 98% went elsewhere); Ecotecture Centre for Ecological Art (Dec. 12/14: $200m in receipts for vintage photographs under Vintage Iconic Archives shelter); Escarpment Biosphere Foundation (Feb. 10/12: $407m in receipts under CHT and redistributed 99% of cash to other parties); Francis Jude Wilson Foundation (March 5/08: received net $100,000 donations and issued receipts >$10m); Funds for Canada Foundation (Aug. 10/09: $176m in receipts for Donations for Canada shelter, of which 90% went offshore); Giving Tree Foundation (CBC news report, May 14/15: EquiGenesis shelter [see *Cassan*, 2017 TCC 174 (FCA appeal settled A-304-17)]); Glooscap Heritage Society (Oct. 19/12: $11m in receipts under Global Learning (GL) shelter [$117m according to FCA reasons], and over 90% of cash received went to shelter's promoters or another charity in the shelter) [attempt to delay revocation failed: 2012 FCA 255]; H.B. Arts Foundation (Dec. 8/08: $13m in receipts and reported $15,300 in charitable activity); Healing and Assistance not Dependence Canada (June 8/09: funds raised were circulated in a shelter); Help Eliminate Disease and Addiction Canada (May 4/12: $113m in receipts under Relief Lending Group shelter, spending $138,000 on charitable purposes); Henvey Inlet First Nation Community Support Organization (May 10/10: $44m in receipts for shelters, of which 99% went elsewhere); International Fellowship Mission Inc. (Jan. 11/13: $1.1m in receipts for non-gifts in Universal Barter Group shelter); Jesus El Buen Pastor Spanish Pentecostal Church of Toronto (Aug. 10/09: $18m in receipts for Insured Giving Donation Program [IGDP] and earned only $56,000 for use in charitable activities); Liberty Wellness Initiative (April 19/10: $89m in receipts for UDP, of which over 90% went elsewhere); Living Waters Ministry Trust (June 8/09: $40.7m of $41.6m raised was directed to another charity as part of a shelter, and most was paid out to promoters); Malvern Rouge Valley Youth Services (Nov. 15/11: $103m in receipts for GL; over 80% of cash went to shelter's promoters); Marketplace Ministries International (March 15/13: $23m in receipts for IGDP, with only $125,000 retained for use in charitable activities); Millennium Charitable Foundation (Jan. 12/09: $169m in receipts and spent $2,200 on charitable activity) [attempt to delay revocation failed 2008 FCA 414]; New Hope Ministries Institute (Sept. 8/09: $100m in receipts for pharmaceuticals for CHT); Orion Foundation (May 10/10: $91m in receipts for medicine for Cdn International Aid Program shelter, of which over 99% went elsewhere); Pinnacle Foundation (Nov. 17/08: $6.7m in receipts under shelters and used only $18,000 for charitable purposes); Le Refuge des Rescapés (Dec. 4/15: $2m in receipts for Foncière AgroTerre shelter); Trinity Divine Outreach Ministries (Jan. 11/13: issued $1.1m in receipts for IG); Trinity Global Support Foundation (May 3/13: $17.1m in receipts for Mission Life Financial pharmaceuticals shelter, and $7.8m for Canadians Care leveraged donations); Word of Christ Ministry and Hope Church of God Deliverance Ministries (Jan. 20/12: participated in promoted donation arrangements).

Revocations for providing funds to entities listed as terrorist organization: Canadian Foundation for Tamil Refugee Rehabilitation (Dec. 12/11: $722,000 to organizations supporting Tamil Tigers terrorism); Canadian Islamic Trust Foundation, ISNA Development Foundation and ISNA Islamic Services of Canada (tinyurl.com/isna-revoked and -revoked2: funds provided to Relief Organization for Kashmiri Muslims, connected to Hizbul Mujahideen, listed as a terrorist entity by the EU and India). Tamil (Sri Lanka) Refugee-Aid Society of Ottawa (July 19/10: $713,000).

Other revocations: Canadian Quadraplegic *[sic]* Assn (Sept. 14/12: failed to maintain books and records to support charitable activities or to maintain duplicate copies of receipts); Christ Apostolic Church [see also FCA decision above] (Aug. 20/10: false invoices); Friends and Skills Connection Centre (Sept. 13/14: issued false receipts, did not maintain proper records, and a director was an ineligible individual); Jesus of Bethlehem Worship Centre (July 11/14: issued $156,000 in receipts for donations not made, and directors included ineligible individuals); Latitude Foundation (Nov. 9/12: issued $15m in receipts used through Univ. of the West Indies to buy life insurance for charity's directors); Life Centre Word of Faith Ministries (May 3/13: undue benefits conferred on director, and improper investments); Metro Street Focus Organization (Dec. 10/10: inadequate records for $1m in donations, and cash used for director's personal benefit); The Mission Against Poverty Shelter (July 27/09: issued $265,000 in receipts for $36,000 in donations); New Flame Deliverance Ministries (Dec. 7/12: $430,000 in receipts for $64,000 in donations); Operation Save Canada's Teenagers and Revival Time Ministries International and (Jan. 7/11: receipting discrepancies, falsified bank statements); Organ Donation & Transplant Assn of Canada (Feb. 25/11) and Pediatric AIDS Canada/USA (Feb. 18/11: most resources spent on fundraising and administrative expenses, and international donation arrangement to artificially inflate charitable activities); Power Zone Outreach Ministries (May 4/12: acted as conduit for non-qualified donee and did not control resources used in foreign programs); Skyway Foundation of Canada (Oct. 17/14: issued receipts for donations of publicly traded shares whose value was artificially inflated by market transactions); Universal Aide Society (April 27/09: personal benefits to employees, and unsubstantiated fees to employees and directors) [attempt to delay revocation failed 2009 FCA 107]; Universal Community Help (Nov. 9/12: books and records not kept properly; $450,000 more revenues than bank deposits); The Voice of the Cerebral Palsied of Greater Vancouver (Feb. 8/13: 93% of funds raised by third party fundraisers remained with the fundraiser, and less than 15% of income devoted to charitable activities); Beth Oloth (Jan./19: tinyurl.com/beth-oloth; lack of control over foreign activities).

CRA will also revoke registration for long-term inactivity: globalphilanthropy.ca/blog, Dec. 12, 2015; Drache, "CRA Looking at Inactive Charities", 17(4) *Canadian Not-for-Profit News* (Carswell) 29-30 (April 2009).

For CRA revocation letters for hundreds of charities going back to 1995, see Drache et al., *Charities Taxation, Policy and Practice — Government Publications* (Carswell, looseleaf or *Taxnet Pro* Reference Centre), binders 1-2, chap. 4A. See also tinyurl.com/blumberg-revocletters and tinyurl.com/blumberg-revocletters2 for recent letters.

See Notes to 149.1(23) re annulments of registration, and to 248(1)"registered Canadian amateur athletic association" for RCAAA revocations.

See also Drache, "CRA Playing Hardball on Revocations", 16(12) *Canadian Not-for-Profit News* (Carswell) 89-90 (Dec. 2008), Chenier, "Revocations!", 2012(22) *Tax Times* (Carswell) 1-2 (Nov. 23, 2012); Harris, "Revocation of Charitable Registration", 11(11) *Tax Hyperion* (Carswell) 1-2 (Nov. 2014); Awad, "Registered Charities ... Revocation of Registration", 16(4) *Tax Hyperion* (Carswell) 3-5 (July-Aug. 2019). See 118.1(1)"total charitable gifts" Notes for more on charity tax shelters and criminal convictions for providing false receipts.

168(1) amended by 2019 budget bill #1, effective 2020, to add "registered journalism organization" [defined in 248(1)] in paras. (c) and (f) and "or organization" in (f).

168(1) amended by 2011 budget bill #2, effective 2012, to change the opening words, to limit para. (c) to registered charities and RCAAAs, and to change "impliedly" to "implicitly" in para. (f).

Interpretation Bulletins: IT-496R: Non-profit organizations.

Forms: RC4424: Completing the tax return where registration of a charity is revoked [guide]; T1189: Application to register a Canadian amateur athletic association under the ITA; T2050: Application to register a charity under the ITA; T2052: Registered Canadian amateur athletic association information return; T4063: Registering a charity for income tax purposes [guide].

Registered Charities Newsletters: 4 (issuing receipts for gifts of art); 11 (audit of tax preparer lands registered charities and executive director in hot water); 13 (charities operating abroad: lessons from the court; about auditing charities); 23 (court news: procedural fairness when a result is inevitable); 28 (new re-registration process; objections and appeals on issues relating to charities); 33 (tax shelter-related revocations).

Charities Policies: CPS-007: RCAAAs: Receipts — issuing policy.

(2) Revocation of registration — If the Minister gives notice under subsection (1) to a registered charity, to a registered Canadian amateur athletic association or to a registered journalism organization,

(a) if it has applied to the Minister in writing for the revocation of its registration, the Minister shall, forthwith after the mailing of the notice, publish a copy of the notice in the *Canada Gazette*, and on that publication of a copy of the notice, the registration is revoked; and

(b) in any other case, the Minister may, after the expiration of 30 days from the day of mailing of the notice, or after the expiration of such extended period from the day of mailing of the notice as the Federal Court of Appeal or a judge of that Court, on application made at any time before the determination of any appeal pursuant to subsection 172(3) from the giving of the no-

tice, may fix or allow, publish a copy of the notice in the *Canada Gazette*, and on that publication of a copy of the notice, the registration is revoked.

Related Provisions: 149.1(4) — Revocation of registration of private foundation; 168(3) — Deemed revocation when certificate issued claiming charity supports terrorism; 172(3) — Appeal from refusal to register or revocation of registration; 180 — Appeals to Federal Court of Appeal; 188(1) — Revocation tax.

Notes [s. 168(2)]: Once notice is published in the *Canada Gazette* and the registration is revoked, the charity cannot apply for stay of the revocation or to reinstate the registration, but an objection and appeal under 168(4) and 172(3) is possible: *Operation Save Canada's Teenagers*, 2011 FCA 71; *International Relief Fund for the Afflicted*, 2011 FCA 206.

In *Cheder Chabad*, 2013 FCA 196, a temporary injunction was issued to prevent CRA from publishing a revocation notice in the *Canada Gazette* for 4 months, since the charity operated a school whose term was about to begin and the children would be affected if the school closed or could not issue tax receipts. A similar injunction was denied in *Ahlul-Bayt Centre*, 2018 FCA 61, as the evidence did not establish "irreparable harm".

168(2) amended by 2019 budget bill #1, effective 2020, to cover a registered journalism organization. Before 2020, read:

(2) Where the Minister gives notice under subsection (1) to a registered charity or to a registered Canadian amateur athletic association,

(a) if the charity or association has applied to the Minister in writing for the revocation of its registration, the Minister shall, forthwith after the mailing of the notice, publish a copy of the notice in the *Canada Gazette*, and

(b) in any other case, the Minister may, after the expiration of 30 days from the day of mailing of the notice, or after the expiration of such extended period from the day of mailing of the notice as the Federal Court of Appeal or a judge of that Court, on application made at any time before the determination of any appeal pursuant to subsection 172(3) from the giving of the notice, may fix or allow, publish a copy of the notice in the *Canada Gazette*,

and on that publication of a copy of the notice, the registration of the charity or association is revoked.

Registered Charities Newsletters: 11 (audit of tax preparer lands registered charities in hot water).

Forms: RC4424: Completing the tax return where registration of a charity is revoked [guide].

(3) Charities Registration (Security Information) Act [revocation for supporting terrorism] — Notwithstanding subsections (1), (2) and (4), if a registered charity is the subject of a certificate that is determined to be reasonable under subsection 7(1) of the *Charities Registration (Security Information) Act*, the registration of the charity is revoked as of the making of that determination.

Related Provisions: 172(3.1) — No appeal for charity that has certificate issued; 172(4.1) — Regular appeal suspended when certificate issued; 188(1) — Deemed year-end upon determination.

Notes [s. 168(3)]: 168(3) allows revocation of a charity's registration for supporting terrorist activity. The *Charities Registration (Security Information) Act* (CRSIA), enacted by the same bill, permits the Solicitor General and Minister of National Revenue to sign a certificate that it is their opinion, based on security or criminal intelligence reports, that there are reasonable grounds to believe that a registered charity has made (or will make) available any of its resources, directly or indirectly, to an entity engaged in terrorist activities or support of such activities. The charity's registration is then revoked; the certificate is "conclusive proof" that the charity does not comply with the requirements to be a charity, subject to review by the Federal Court. The CRSIA can be found on canlii.org and in this annotation in the 21st-25th editions.

See Terrance Carter, "Charities and Compliance with Anti-Terrorism Legislation: The Shadow of the Law", 19(1) *The Philanthropist* (thephilanthropist.ca) 43-79 (2004), and "...: A Due Diligence Response", 19(2) 109-115 (2004).

168(3) amended by 2004 Budget (for notices issued by the Minister after June 12, 2005) and 2001 anti-terrorism bill.

Registered Charities Newsletters: 12 (the new anti-terrorism law).

(3.1) Listed terrorist entities — Notwithstanding subsections (1), (2) and (4), if a qualified donee is a listed terrorist entity for the purposes of section 149.1, the registration of the qualified donee is revoked as of the date on which it became a listed terrorist entity.

Related Provisions: 188(1) — Deemed year-end on notice of revocation.

Notes: 168(3.1) added by 2021 budget bill #1, effective June 29, 2021.

(4) Objection to proposal or designation — A person may, on or before the day that is 90 days after the day on which the notice was mailed, serve on the Minister a written notice of objection in the manner authorized by the Minister, setting out the reasons for the objection and all the relevant facts, and the provisions of subsections 165(1), (1.1) and (3) to (7) and sections 166, 166.1 and 166.2 apply, with any modifications that the circumstances require, as if the notice were a notice of assessment made under section 152, if

(a) in the case of a person that is or was registered as a registered charity or is an applicant for such registration, it objects to a notice under any of subsections (1) and 149.1(2) to (4.1), (6.3), (22) and (23);

(b) in the case of a person that is or was registered as a registered Canadian amateur athletic association or is an applicant for such registration, it objects to a notice under any of subsections (1) and 149.1(4.2) and (22); or

(c) in the case of a person described in any of subparagraphs (a)(i) to (v) and paragraph (b.1) of the definition "qualified donee" in subsection 149.1(1), that is or was registered by the Minister as a qualified donee or is an applicant for such registration, it objects to a notice under any of subsections (1) and 149.1(4.3) and (22).

Related Provisions: 172(3)(a.1) — Appeal to Federal Court of Appeal where objection rejected or not answered; 189(8.1)(a) — Objection to revocation is not an objection to revocation tax; 189(8.1)(b) — No appeal to Tax Court of Canada.

Notes: 168(4) extends the objection review process of s. 165 (CRA review by an Appeals Officer) to charity, RCAAA and other "qualified donee" revocations, which can thereafter be appealed only to the Federal Court of Appeal (172(3)). See Notes to 149.1(1)"qualified donee".

An objection is made by addressing a letter to the Assistant Commissioner, Appeals Branch of the Canada Revenue Agency and delivering or mailing it to the Assistant Commissioner's office (25 Nicholas St., Ottawa K1A 0L5). This is the "manner authorized by the Minister", as signed by Jeanne Flemming, Assistant Commissioner Appeals on July 11, 2005, under delegation of the Minister's powers signed Sept. 27, 1999.

168(4)(c) amended by 2019 budget bill #1, effective 2020, to add reference to 149.1(1)"qualified donee"(b.1) (registered journalism organization).

168(4) amended by 2011 budget bill #2, effective 2012. Added by 2004 Budget, effective in respect of notices issued by the Minister after June 12, 2005.

Registered Charities Newsletters: 19 (appeals process); 28 (objections and appeals on issues relating to charities).

Definitions [s. 168]: "assessment" — 248(1); "contravene" — *Interpretation Act* 35(1); "Federal Court of Appeal" — *Federal Courts Act* s. 3; "listed terrorist entity" — 149.1(1); "Minister", "person" — 248(1); "qualified donee" — 149.1(1), 188.2(3)(a), 248(1); "registered Canadian amateur athletic association", "registered charity", "registered journalism organization", "regulation" — 248(1); "writing", "written" — *Interpretation Act* 35(1)"writing".

Designation of Qualified Canadian Journalism Organizations

168.1 (1) Date of designation — If an organization is designated for the purpose of the definition "qualified Canadian journalism organization" in subsection 248(1), the organization is deemed to have become designated on the date that the application for designation of the organization was made, unless otherwise specified by the Minister.

(2) Revocation of designation — The Minister may, at any time, revoke the designation of an organization made for the purpose of the definition "qualified Canadian journalism organization" in subsection 248(1) and, for that purpose, the Minister shall take into account any recommendations of a body established for the purpose of that definition and referred to in paragraph (b) of that definition.

(3) Notice and date of revocation — If the designation of an organization is revoked under subsection (2),

(a) the Minister shall provide notice of the revocation to the organization in writing; and

(b) the revocation is deemed to be effective as of the date on which the notice in paragraph (a) is sent, unless the Minister specifies an earlier date.

Related Provisions: 118.02(4) — CRA can de-list digital subscriptions that no longer qualify for credit; 118.02(5) — Organization must tell subscribers if digital subscription credit ceases to be available.

Notes: Since no appeal procedure is provided, judicial review of a revocation is available in Federal Court. See Notes to 220(3.1).

Notes [s. 168.1]: 168.1 (added by 2021 budget bill #1, effective 2019) permits revocation of designation as a 248(1)"qualifying Canadian journalism organization" (QCJO). An Advisory Board (248(1)"qualified Canadian journalism organization"(b)) makes recommendations to CRA on whether an organization meets the criteria. In deciding to revoke a designation, CRA is required to consider any advice provided by the Advisory Board.

Definitions [s. 168.1]: "Minister", "qualified Canadian journalism organization" — 248(1); "writing" — *Interpretation Act* 35(1).

DIVISION J — APPEALS TO THE TAX COURT OF CANADA AND THE FEDERAL COURT OF APPEAL

169. (1) Appeal — Where a taxpayer has served notice of objection to an assessment under section 165, the taxpayer may appeal to the Tax Court of Canada to have the assessment vacated or varied after either

(a) the Minister has confirmed the assessment or reassessed, or

(b) 90 days have elapsed after service of the notice of objection and the Minister has not notified the taxpayer that the Minister has vacated or confirmed the assessment or reassessed,

but no appeal under this section may be instituted after the expiration of 90 days from the day notice has been sent to the taxpayer under section 165 that the Minister has confirmed the assessment or reassessed.

Enacted Amendment — *Time Limits and Other Periods Act (COVID-19)* [TLOPA]

Notes: See Notes to TLOPA 6(1) and 7(1) below.

Time Limits and Other Periods Act (COVID-19)

An Act respecting the suspension or extension of time limits and the extension of other periods as part of the response to the coronavirus disease 2019

Short title

1. Short title — This Act may be cited as the *Time Limits and Other Periods Act (COVID-19)*.

Interpretation and Application

2. Definition of "period" — In this Act, "period" includes the time during which a licence, permit or other authorization is valid.

3. Effect of suspension or extension — If a time limit is suspended or extended or a period is extended under this Act, then, during the period that the suspension or extension is in effect, every reference in any Act of Parliament or its regulations to that time limit or period is to be read as a reference to the time limit or period as it is suspended or extended.

4. (1) Non-application — offences — This Act does not apply in respect of the investigation of an offence or in respect of a proceeding respecting an offence.

(2) Non-application — *Corrections and Conditional Release Act* — This Act does not apply in respect of a time limit or other period that is established by or under the *Corrections and Conditional Release Act*.

Notes: 4(2) was not in the May 19, 2020 draft of TLOPA.

Purpose

5. (1) Purpose — The purpose of this Act is

(a) to temporarily suspend certain time limits and to temporarily authorize, in a flexible manner, the suspension or extension of other time limits in order to prevent any exceptional circumstances that may be produced by coronavirus disease 2019 (COVID-19) from making it difficult or impossible to meet those time limits; and

(b) to temporarily authorize, in a flexible manner, the extension of other periods in order to prevent any unfair or undesirable effects that may result from the expiry of those periods due to those exceptional circumstances.

(2) For greater certainty — For greater certainty, this Act is to be interpreted in a manner that provides certainty in relation to proceedings and that respects the rule of law and the *Canadian Charter of Rights and Freedoms*.

Time Limits Related to Proceedings

6. (1) Suspensions — The following time limits are, if established by or under an Act of Parliament, suspended for the period that starts on March 13, 2020 and that ends on September 13, 2020 or on any earlier day fixed by order of the Governor in Council made on the recommendation of the Minister of Justice:

(a) any limitation or prescription period for commencing a proceeding before a court;

(b) any time limit in relation to something that is to be done in a proceeding before a court; and

(c) any time limit within which an application for leave to commence a proceeding or to do something in relation to a proceeding is to be made to a court.

Related Provisions: 11(1) — Order must be tabled in Parliament within 3 days.

Notes: 6(1) extends the 90-day period in 169(1) for filing a Tax Court Notice of Appeal, as well as all deadlines in the *Tax Court of Canada Act* (see Announced Administrative Change shaded box below for other Tax Court deadlines that are controlled by the Court). The extension is for 6 months unless an Order-in-Council (by the federal Cabinet) makes it shorter. It can be varied by the Court, but cannot exceed 6 months: 6(2). The Court has further flexibility under 6(3).

6(1) also extends:

• the 90-day period for filing an application in the Tax Court for extension of time to object (166.2(1) closing words)

• the 1-year period for filing an application in the Tax Court for extension of time to appeal (167(5)(a))

• the 30-day period for filing an appeal to the Federal Court of Appeal (*Federal Courts Act* s. 27(2)(b), and see near end of 169(1) Notes; for charity and similar registration or revocation appeals, see 180(1))

• the 30-day period for filing a Federal Court judicial-review application (*Federal Courts Act* s. 18.1(2), and see Notes to 171(1)).

The word "prescription" in 6(1)(a) means a limitation period under Quebec law that applies in a federal court. See second para. of 152(4) Notes.

TLOPA applies only to *federal* courts. Limitations periods in the provinces' courts are governed by provincial law. The provinces have provided COVID-19 extensions in various forms.

The Government's view was that "time limits ... established by or under an Act of Parliament" includes orders and directives issued by the Courts for procedural steps in Court proceedings. In *Re section 6 of TLOPA*, 2020 FCA 137, the FCA held that this is wrong, and that "this Court's Practice Directions, Judgments, orders and directions remain in full force and effect" (para. 11). The quoted words from 6(1) refer only to time limits set in Acts of Parliament, and do not cover the *Federal Courts Rules* (para. 18). For the Tax Court of Canada, the Aug. 14, 2020 Practice Direction (reproduced under "Announced Administrative Change" below) excludes March 13-Sept. 13, 2020 from the computation of time in earlier court orders, to be consistent with TLOPA.

(2) Court orders — variation — The court may, by order, vary the suspension of a time limit as long as the commencement date of the suspension remains the same and the duration of the suspension does not exceed six months.

(3) Court orders — effects — The court may make orders respecting the effects of a failure to meet a suspended time limit, including orders that cancel or vary those effects.

(4) Orders in council — The Governor in Council may, by order made on the recommendation of the Minister of Justice, lift a suspension in circumstances specified in the order.

Related Provisions: 11(1) — Order must be tabled in Parliament within 3 days.

Other Time Limits and Periods

7. (1) Ministerial orders — Acts and regulations — The minister who is responsible for an Act of Parliament set out in column 1 of the schedule or a relevant portion of the Act may make an order

(a) suspending or extending a time limit that is established by or under any provision of the Act that is set out in column 2;

(b) extending any other period that is established by or under any provision of the Act that is set out in column 2;

(c) if a regulation is set out in column 2 in respect of the Act,

(i) suspending or extending a time limit that is established by or under that regulation, or

(ii) extending any other period that is established by or under that regulation; or

(d) extending a suspension or extension.

CRA Ministerial Order, Aug. 31, 2020: *Order Respecting Time Limits and Other Periods under the Income Tax Act (COVID-19)*

Interpretation

1. Definition of Act — In this Order, Act means the *Income Tax Act*.

Extension

2. (1) Extension — six months — Subject to subsection (2), the following time limits and periods are extended by six months or until December 31, 2020 if that day is before the end of those six months:

(a) the time limit of 12 months set out in subsection 37(11) of the Act;

(b) the time limit of one year set out in paragraph (m) of the definition "investment tax credit" in subsection 127(9) of the Act;

(c) the period of four years set out in paragraph 152(3.1)(a) of the Act;

(d) the period of three years set out in paragraph 152(3.1)(b) of the Act;

(e) the period of three years set out in paragraph 152(4)(b) of the Act;

(f) the period of three years set out in paragraph 152(4)(b.1) of the Act;

(g) the period of three years set out in paragraph 152(4)(b.2) of the Act;

(h) the time limit of three years set out in subparagraph 152(4)(b.3)(v) of the Act;

(i) the time limit of six years set out in paragraph 152(4)(b.4) of the Act;

(j) the time limit of one year set out in paragraph 152(4)(d) of the Act;

(k) the time limit of one year set out in paragraph 166.1(7)(a) of the Act; and

(l) the time limit of one year set out in paragraph 166.2(5)(a) of the Act.

(2) Application — The extension applies in each of the following circumstances:

(a) with respect to the time limits in paragraphs (1)(a), (b), (k) and (l), if the time limit would otherwise expire during the period beginning on March 13, 2020 and ending on December 30, 2020; and

(b) with respect to the time limits and periods in paragraphs (1)(c) to (j), if the time limit or period would otherwise expire during the period beginning on May 20, 2020 and ending on December 30, 2020.

Coming into Force

3. March 13, 2020 — This Order is deemed to have come into force on March 13, 2020.

Explanatory Note (CRA, Aug. 31, 2020): *Background*

As per subsections 7(1) and 7(5) of the *Time Limits and Other Periods Act (COVID-19)*, the Minister of National Revenue may make a Ministerial Order for the purpose of mitigating unintended consequences brought on as a result of the coronavirus disease 2019 (COVID-19).

Due to the COVID-19 pandemic, many Canadians, businesses and other organizations, including the Canada Revenue Agency, may be unable to meet time limits set out in federal legislation. The *Time Limits and Other Periods Act (COVID-19)*, enacted through Bill C-20, allows federal ministers to make temporary orders to extend or suspend time limits in specific federal legislation for which they are responsible.

Implications

This Ministerial Order, in respect of the *Income Tax Act*, temporarily extends:

1. The time limit for the filing of certain prescribed forms for the purposes of the Scientific Research and Experimental Development Tax Incentive Program (expenditures and investment tax credit) [37(11) and 127(9)"investment tax credit"(m), per 2(1)(a)-(b) of the Order — ed.] for a maximum of six months beginning on or after March 13, 2020 and not beyond December 31, 2020.

2. The time limits on the Minister's ability to make an assessment, reassessment or additional assessment [152(3.1) and (4), per 2(1)(c)-(j) of the Order — ed.], which would otherwise have expired on or after May 20, 2020, for a maximum of six months and not beyond December 31, 2020.

3. The time limit by which the Minister may grant an extension of time to a taxpayer to file a Notice of Objection to an assessment [166.1(7)(a), per 2(1)(k) of the Order — ed.], which would otherwise have expired on or after March 13, 2020, for a maximum of six months and not beyond December 31, 2020.

4. The time limit by which a taxpayer or registrant may apply to the Tax Court of Canada for an extension of time to object to an assessment, which would otherwise have expired on or after March 13, 2020, for a maximum of six months and not beyond December 31, 2020. [This is an incorrect description: 166.2(5)(a), extended by 2(1)(l) of the Order, refers to the *original* application to the Minister for an extension of time that is later sought from the Tax Court. This extension allows that original application to have been more than one year late. The time limit *to apply to the Tax Court* is extended by TLOPA 6(1), not by 7(1) and Ministerial Order — ed.]

All provisions made under this Ministerial Order will cease to apply on the earlier of December 31, 2020, or the day on which the order that enacted the provision is repealed.

Related Provisions: 11(1) — Order must be tabled in Parliament within 3 days.

Notes: The Schedule lists 37(11) and 127(9)"investment tax credit"(m), allowing the Minister of National Revenue to extend (by up to 6 months beginning March 13, 2020) the Form T661 SR&ED application filing deadline, normally 1 year past the regular filing date (i.e., 18 months after year-end for corporations). (This deadline cannot otherwise be extended by CRA: 220(2.2).)

The Schedule also lists 152(3.1) and 152(4), allowing the Minister to extend both the "normal reassessment period" (NRP) *and* the deadline for CRA to reassess after the NRP. However, the combined extension cannot exceed 6 months, and the extended deadline cannot go past Dec. 31, 2020: see 7(4) below. *Example 1*: personal tax return filed April 2018, assessed May 14, 2018. Normal reassessment deadline is May 14, 2021. Since this is after Dec. 31, 2020, it is not extended by TLOPA: see 7(4). *Example 2*: assessment issued Oct. 14, 2017. Normal reassessment deadline is Oct. 14, 2020. TLOPA 7(1) can extend the deadline, but only to Dec. 31, 2020. TLOPA does not extend limitation periods specified in tax treaties: 2020 IFA Roundtable q.4.

The Schedule also lists 166.1(7) and 166.2(5), so that CRA can extend the 1-year deadline (166.1(7)(a), 166.2(5)(a)) for filing an application for extension of time to file an objection (this has been done by the Ministerial Order above).

CRA webpage "Time Limits and Other Periods Act (COVID-19)" (tinyurl.com/cra-tlopa, as of Feb. 17, 2021) states:

The *Time Limits and Other Periods Act (COVID-19)* (TLOPA), enacted under Bill C-20, received Royal Assent July 27, 2020.

Overview

Under the TLOPA, the Canada Revenue Agency (CRA) has been given a temporary authority to extend certain deadlines imposed under the *Income Tax Act* and *Excise Tax Act* through the issuance of a Ministerial Order. The period of extension is a maximum of six months and can begin as early as March 13, 2020 and ending no later than December 31, 2020.

As a result, the TLOPA impacts taxpayers and registrants whose tax filings would otherwise be statute-barred [because the TLOPA Schedule lists 152(3.1) and (4) — ed.] and it may also impact certain requests for an extension of time to file an objection where the deadline would have normally expired [the Schedule lists 166.1(7) and 166.2(5) — ed.]. "Statute-barred" in general terms means immune from reassessment due to the passage of time, except in certain situations such as gross negligence [actually any "carelessness or neglect", not only gross negligence — ed.] or intentional misrepresentations.

The TLOPA also impacts taxpayers who file scientific research and experimental development (SR&ED) claims with the CRA, by extending their SR&ED reporting deadline by the maximum allowed by this legislation [the Schedule lists 37(11) and 127(9)"investment tax credit"(m) — ed.]. For more information on the deadline extension see *What's new — SR&ED Program* [under 127(9)"investment tax credit" — ed.].

Frequently asked questions

Why does the CRA need to have certain deadlines extended?

Like many individuals and organizations, the CRA has been impacted by the COVID-19 pandemic. For the past several months, the CRA has focused on delivering critical services, including benefits, to Canadians and businesses facing hardship as a result of the global COVID-19 outbreak. Additionally, taxpayers needed extra time to respond to CRA compliance questions. As a result, the CRA may need additional time to finalize compliance activities, including reviews and audits.

When does the extension apply in the context of an income tax compliance audit?

The extension to the statute-barred date applies where a taxpayer's income tax return would have otherwise become statute-barred [152(4) — ed.] from assessment, reassessment or additional assessment on or after May 20, 2020 [see Ministerial Order 2(2)(b) — ed.] and before December 31, 2020.

When does the extension apply in the context of a GST/HST compliance audit?

The extension applies where a GST/HST reporting period would otherwise become statute-barred from assessment, reassessment or additional assessment [ETA 298(1) — ed.] on a day that is on or after May 20, 2020 and before December 31, 2020.

What about reporting periods or taxation years that have already become statute-barred since the start of the pandemic in March 2020?

Similar to the coming into force of many tax provisions, the temporary authority under the TLOPA takes into consideration the date on which the draft legislation was announced, which was May 19, 2020. Therefore, reporting periods and taxation years which became statute-barred on or before May 19, 2020 are not covered under the Ministerial Orders [see Ministerial Order 2(2)(b) — ed.].

How long are the statute-barred deadlines extended for?

The legislation allows for the extension of these deadlines for a maximum of six months but not beyond December 31, 2020. For example, a tax return that would normally become statute-barred on September 30, 2020 will not become statute-barred until December 31, 2020. In contrast, a return that would otherwise have been statute-barred on May 31, 2020, will become statute-barred on November 30, 2020.

Will I know if a CRA auditor is relying on a Ministerial Order in my situation?

Generally, taxpayers would be informed of the details of a potential (re)assessment, including whether or not the CRA is applying an extension to a (re)assessment period under the Ministerial Order, by the auditor. Any questions about the timing or reasons for a (re)assessment should be addressed with the CRA auditor/employee or their direct supervisor.

How does the extension of time allowed under the Ministerial Orders apply to requests for an extension of time to file a Notice of Objection with the CRA [166.1 — ed.]?

A request to CRA for an extension of time can generally be made up to one year after the deadline to file the objection [166.1(7)(a) — ed.]. Under the TLOPA, taxpayers and registrants whose deadline to request an extension of time to file a Notice of Objection to a (re)assessment expired between March 13, 2020 and December 30, 2020 will have up to six additional months, but not beyond December 31, 2020, to make their request. For example, a taxpayer or registrant whose deadline to make a request for an extension of time to object to a (re)assessment was March 13, 2020 will now have until September 13, 2020 to make their request. Similarly, a taxpayer or registrant with a September 30, 2020 deadline will have until December 31, 2020 to make their request.

Taxpayers and registrants whose deadline to request an extension of time to file a Notice of Objection to an assessment or reassessment expires after December 30, 2020 will not receive an extension of time to make their request.

How does the extension of time allowed under the Ministerial Orders apply to requests to the Tax Court of Canada for an extension of time to object to a (re)assessment [166.2 — ed.]?

Taxpayers and registrants whose deadline to apply to the Tax Court of Canada for an extension of time to object to a (re)assessment expired between March 13, 2020 and December 30, 2020 will have up to six additional months, but not beyond December 31, 2020, to make their request. [This happens under TLOPA 6(1), not the Ministerial Order under 7(1) — ed.] For example, a taxpayer or registrant whose deadline to make a request for an extension of time to object to a (re)assessment was March 13, 2020 will have until September 13, 2020 to make their request. Similarly, a taxpayer or registrant with a September 30, 2020 deadline will have until December 31, 2020 to make their request.

Taxpayers and registrants whose deadline to request an extension of time to file a Notice of Objection to an assessment or reassessment expires after December 30, 2020 will not receive an extension of time to make their request.

Does this extension apply to the time limits found under Canada's tax treaties?

No, the legislation does not apply to Canada's tax treaties and does not allow for the extension of any time limit to raise an adjustment that may be contained in Canada's tax treaties. For the same reason, the legislation also does not allow for the extension of any time limit that may apply for notifying a treaty partner of the (potential) double tax arising from an adjustment. Similarly, the legislation does not extend the period during which a request for competent authority assistance can be made under the Mutual Agreement Procedure of Canada's treaties.

(2) Ministerial orders — regulations — The minister who is responsible for a regulation set out in column 1 of the schedule or a relevant portion of the regulation may make an order

(a) suspending or extending a time limit that is established by or under any provision of the regulation that is set out in column 2;

(b) extending any other period that is established by or under any provision of the regulation that is set out in column 2; or

(c) extending a suspension or extension.

Related Provisions: 11(1) — Order must be tabled in Parliament within 3 days.

(3) Non-application — An order under subsection (1) or (2) does not apply in respect of a time limit or other period that ends on or after December 31, 2020.

Notes: See Notes to 7(1) above and to 7(4) below.

(4) Duration — The total duration of a suspension or extension must not exceed six months. However, a suspension must not have the effect of allowing a time limit to continue after December 31, 2020 and an extended time limit or period must end on or before that day.

Notes: See Notes to 7(1) above. 7(3), and the second sentence of 7(4), were not in the May 19, 2020 draft of TLOPA. They ensure that an extended time limit cannot go past Dec. 31, 2020. Thus, if a 152(4) reassessment deadline expires for CRA on Jan. 15, 2021, it is not extended. A deadline that expires Oct. 15, 2020 may be extended, but not past Dec. 31, 2020. A deadline that expired March 15, 2020 can be extended only to Sept. 15, 2020.

(5) Retroactivity — An order under subsection (1) or (2) may, if it so provides, have retroactive effect, but not before March 13, 2020, and it may also include provisions respecting the effects of a failure to meet the time limit or of the expiry of the period before the day on which the order was made, including provisions that cancel or vary those effects.

Notes: This was 7(4) in the May 19, 2020 draft of TLOPA.

(6) Additional content — An order under subsection (1) or (2) may provide that

(a) a suspension or extension does not apply in respect of any circumstance specified in the order without the consent of a person, court or body specified in the order;

(b) a suspension or extension applies in respect of any circumstance specified in the order unless a person, court or body specified in the order decides otherwise; or

(c) a person, court or body specified in the order may vary the effects of the order in relation to any circumstance specified in the order.

Notes: This was 7(5) in the May 19, 2020 draft of TLOPA.

(7) Regulations — The Governor in Council may, on the recommendation of the Minister of Justice, make regulations restricting, or imposing conditions on, a power to make an order under subsection (1) or (2).

Notes: This was 7(6) in the May 19, 2020 draft of TLOPA.

General

8. *Statutory Instruments Act* — The *Statutory Instruments Act* does not apply to an order made under subsection 6(1), (2), (3) or (4) or 7(1) or (2).

9. Sunset provision — A power conferred on the Governor in Council or a minister under this Act is not to be exercised after September 30, 2020.

Transparency and Parliamentary Oversight

10. (1) Publication on website — An order made under subsection 6(1) or (4) or 7(1) or (2), together with the reasons for making it, must be published, as soon as feasible after the day on which it is made but no later than five days after the day on which it is made, on a Government of Canada website for a period of at least six months.

(2) Publication in *Canada Gazette* — An order referred to in subsection (1) must be published in Part I of the *Canada Gazette* within 14 days after the day on which it is made.

11. (1) Tabling in Parliament — An order made under subsection 6(1) or (4) or 7(1) or (2) must be tabled in each House of Parliament within three days after the day on which it is made, unless a House is not sitting within those three days, in which case the order is to be tabled in that House at the earliest opportunity.

Related Provisions: 11(2) — Order must be referred to committee.

(2) Referral to committee — An order that is tabled in a House of Parliament must be referred to a committee of that House.

SCHEDULE
(Subsections 7(1) and (2))

Acts, Regulations and Provisions

Column 1	Column 2
Acts	Provisions and Regulations
Excise Tax Act	subsections 298(1) and (2), 303(7) and 304(5) of the Act
Income Tax Act	subsection 37(11), paragraph (m) of the definition "investment tax credit" in subsection 127(9) and subsections 152(3.1) and (4), 166.1(7) and 166.2(5) of the Act

[19 non-tax statutes and 22 non-tax regulations omitted — ed.]

Notes: See Notes to TLOPA 7(1) above. ITA 166.1(7) and 166.2(5) were not included in the May 19, 2020 draft of TLOPA. TLOPA enacted by 2020 COVID bill #3, effective July 27, 2020.

Explanatory Note (May 2020): *Explanation:*

Many provisions in federal legislation set time limits to accomplish certain things, like payment of fees or filing reports. Federal legislation also sets out periods during which certain things can be done, for example, periods of validity for licences, permits or other authorizations allowing the holder to perform specified things. With respect to civil proceedings before the courts, at the federal level alone, there are hundreds of deadlines that are fixed by statute.

Due to the current COVID-19 pandemic, there is a risk that many will be unable to meet the numerous time limits set out in Canadian federal legislation through no fault of their own. If there is no discretion in a given statute to extend time periods, then Canadians may begin to experience serious negative circumstances.

In order to respond to this problematic situation, the proposal would provide for measures to extend limitation periods in civil proceedings before courts as well as measures to address pressing regulatory time limits.

Description

Purpose

The legislative proposals would aim to address the need for flexibility in time limits and other periods under federal legislation because of exceptional circumstances due to COVID-19.

Their purpose would therefore be to temporarily suspend some time limits and allow others to be suspended or extended where these circumstances may make compliance difficult or impossible, and to extend other periods so that their expiration does not produce unfair or undesirable effects.

The legislative proposals would indicate that they should be interpreted in a manner that would bring certainty to proceedings and respects both the rule of law and the *Canadian Charter of Rights of Freedoms*.

Sections 6 and 7

In particular, the legislative proposals would:

- suspend, as of March 13, 2020 and until September 13, 2020 or an earlier date set by the Governor in Council, certain time limits concerning proceedings, other than proceedings concerning offences, before the courts;
- allow courts to vary the suspension within certain limits and take measures regarding the effects of a failure to meet a suspended time limit;
- allow the Governor in Council to lift such suspensions in certain circumstances;
- allow ministers, in respect of specified legislation, to suspend or extend time limits and extend other periods for no more than six months, and to give such suspensions or extensions retroactive effect to March 13, 2020; and
- allow ministers in the case described in the previous point to give specified persons, bodies or tribunals some flexibility in applying these suspensions or extensions.

The proposals would allow the Governor in Council to restrict or impose conditions on the powers granted to ministers.

Sections 8 and 9

Orders made under subsection 6(1), (3) or (4) or 7(1) or (2) would be exempted from the application of the *Statutory Instruments Act*

The legislative proposals would also state that these powers cannot be exercised after September 30, 2020.

Sections 10 and 11

The proposals would require that orders, along with a statement explaining the reason for their making, be published on a Government of Canada website no later than five days after they are made, for a period of at least six months, followed by publication in the *Canada Gazette*.

The proposals would also provide that orders would be tabled before each House of Parliament within three days of their being made or, if a House is not sitting, as soon as possible, and that such orders would be referred to a committee of each House.

Schedule

List of acts, regulations and provisions for which Ministers can make orders suspending or extending time limits.

Bill C-20 Summary for Parliament: Part 3 [of Bill C-20] enacts the *Time Limits and Other Periods Act (COVID-19)* which addresses the need for flexibility in relation to certain time limits and other periods that are established by or under Acts of Parliament and that are difficult or impossible to meet as a result of the exceptional circumstances produced by COVID-19. In particular, the enactment

(a) suspends, for a maximum of six months, certain time limits in relation to proceedings before courts [TLOPA s. 6 — ed.];

(b) temporarily enables ministers to suspend or extend time limits and to extend other periods in relation to specified Acts and regulations for a maximum of six months [TLOPA s. 7 — ed.]; and

(c) provides for the transparent exercise of the powers it confers and for Parliamentary oversight over the exercise of those powers [TLOPA ss. 10-11 — ed.].

Dept. of Finance news release, July 20, 2020. *Government introduces legislation to support Canadian workers, businesses and persons with disabilities*

[First part of news release discusses amendments to the Canada Emergency Wage Subsidy. See 125.7(2) Notes — ed.]

[Second part of news release discusses providing payments of $600 to persons with disabilities. See Announced Administrative Change under 118.3(1) — ed.]

In these exceptional circumstances, many Canadians, businesses and other organizations may be unable to meet numerous time limits currently set out in federal legislation, including those for civil court cases and some key regulatory matters. That is why the legislation proposes to enact a new Act *[now enacted — ed.]* that would suspend limitation periods in civil litigation proceedings as well as enable the extension or suspension of select regulatory time limits. The *Time Limits and Other Periods Act (COVID-19)* would ensure the continued protection of Canadians' rights in the context of civil legal proceedings, by ensuring that individuals are not prevented from asserting their rights because of the passage of a time limit. It would also ensure that Canadians,

Canadian businesses and the government are able to avoid irreversible legal consequences.

The government continues to assess and respond to the impacts of COVID-19, and stands ready to take additional actions as needed to stabilize the economy and mitigate the impacts of the pandemic.

Announced Administrative Change — Tax Court reopening, re-closing and deadlines

Tax Court of Canada, May 27, 2020: *Amended Practice Direction and Order*

[Replaces previous Practice Directions, and superseded by later ones below — ed.]

WHEREAS the Tax Court of Canada has further cancelled its judicial sittings and conference calls until July 17th, 2020 inclusively;

AND WHEREAS the Tax Court of Canada including all its offices in Canada shall not be open for the transaction of any business pertaining to matters under the jurisdiction of the Tax Court of Canada, pursuant to section 12 of the *Tax Court of Canada Act*, until further notice;

AND WHEREAS given the extraordinary circumstances which exist today by virtue of the spread of the COVID-19 virus, it is in the interests of justice, for all matters under the jurisdiction of the Tax Court of Canada pursuant to section 12 of the *Tax Court of Canada Act*, that I dispense with compliance of certain Rules;

AND WHEREAS it is in the interests of justice given the extraordinary circumstances to provide specific direction for the streamlining of Notices of Appeal and Applications for an Extension of Time to Appeal;

PURSUANT to:

Rules 9 and 12 of the *Tax Court of Canada Rules (General Procedure)*,

Any and all analogous provisions in all other Rules made under the *Tax Court of Canada Act* governing the conduct of matters under the Tax Court of Canada's jurisdiction, and

The Tax Court of Canada's power to control its own process,

I HEREBY EXCLUDE the period beginning on March 16th, 2020, and ending on the day that is 60 days after the Court and its offices reopen for the transaction of business, from the computation of time under:

The *Tax Court of Canada Rules (General Procedure)*,

All other Rules made under the *Tax Court of Canada Act* governing the conduct of matters under the Tax Court of Canada's jurisdiction pursuant to section 12 of the Tax Court of Canada Act, and

An Order or Direction of this Court made prior to March 16th, 2020,

[Note that this does not extend the deadline for appeals, which is in legislation the Court does not control such as ITA 169(1) (though the next paragraph addresses the issue in part). That is handled by the Time Limits and Other Periods Act (TLOPA). See Enacted Amendment above — ed.]

IT IS ALSO ORDERED that all Notices of Appeal filed during the period beginning March 16, 2020, and ending on the day that is 60 days after the Court and its offices reopen for the transaction of business shall be treated as including an Application for Extension of Time to Appeal brought on the exceptional grounds that the COVID-19 pandemic and the closure of the Registry prevented the timely filing of a Notice of Appeal;

[Note that if the deemed included Application for Extension of Time to Appeal is itself too late, TLOPA extends the deadline to file it by up to 6 months. See 7(1) under Enacted Amendment (TLOPA) above — ed.]

IT IS ALSO ORDERED that upon being advised of this fact by the Registry when served with a Notice of Appeal, the Respondent will confirm to the Registry within 60 days of service that the appeal was filed:

1. in a timely manner and no extension is necessary;

2. after the statutory deadline but that the Respondent consents to the application; or

3. after the statutory deadline and that the Respondent opposes the application.

IT IS FURTHER ORDERED that to the extent that this Amended Practice Direction and Order conflicts with the Practice Directions and Orders issued since March 16, 2020, this Amended Practice Direction and Order shall prevail.

DIRECTED AND ORDERED at the City of Ottawa, this 27th day of May, 2020

Eugene P. Rossiter, Chief Justice

Tax Court of Canada, May 27, 2020: *Notice to the Public and the Profession*

[Replaces previous Practice Directions, and superseded by later ones below — ed.]

Further to the Notices to the Public and the Profession issued on March 13th, March 23rd, April 17th and May 20th, 2020, and in light of the exceptional circumstances evolving constantly, the Tax Court of Canada is further restricting its judicial sittings and operations.

Cancellation of Sittings

The Chief Justice has further cancelled all Tax Court of Canada sittings and conference calls scheduled between July 6th, 2020 and up to July 17th, 2020, inclusively. Parties affected by these cancellations will be contacted directly by the Registry staff in the coming days.

At this time, sittings that are scheduled beyond August 17th, 2020 will proceed.

Please note that should circumstances allow for the resumption of the Court's operations in the coming weeks, the Court will sit during the 4-week summer recess and appeals will be scheduled between July 20th and August 13th, 2020. Parties whose hearings were interrupted in March by the closure of the Court or whose general appeals were adjourned in March and April can expect to be contacted in priority to schedule the continuation or hearing of their appeal.

At this time, the Court is also looking into conducting proceedings related to litigation process, such as Case Management Conferences and Status Hearings, by phone or online before the resumption of in-person Court sittings.

The Chief Justice will continue to monitor the situation closely and reassess on or before June 15, 2020, whether the judicial sittings schedule will have to be further altered.

Closure of Registry Offices

The Court and its Registry offices across the country remain closed for the transaction of business until further notice.

Please refer to the Notice to the Public and the Profession dated April 17, 2020 for information pertaining to the suspension of timelines, applications for extensions of time to file notices of appeal and rescheduling.

Updates and Return to Regular Operations

The Court is monitoring this situation very closely. Parties are encouraged to check the Court's website for updates and for information regarding the Court's return to regular operations and transaction of business.

Dated this 27th day of May, 2020.

Eugene P. Rossiter, Chief Justice

Tax Court of Canada, July 3, 2020: *Practice Direction and Order*

WHEREAS the Tax Court of Canada including all its offices in Canada have not been open for the transaction of any business pertaining to matters under the jurisdiction of the Tax Court of Canada, pursuant to section 12 of the *Tax Court of Canada Act*, since March 16, 2020;

AND WHEREAS the Tax Court of Canada is ready to reopen for the transaction of business;

IT IS ORDERED pursuant to Rule 14 of the *Tax Court of Canada Rules (General Procedure)* and the general power of the Court to control its own process, that the Tax Court of Canada and its Registry offices across the country, with the exception of the Hamilton office, shall reopen on July 6, 2020, for the transaction of any business pertaining to matters under the jurisdiction of the Tax Court of Canada pursuant to section 12 of the *Tax Court of Canada Act*.

DIRECTED AND ORDERED at the City of Ottawa, this 3rd day of July, 2020.

Eugene P. Rossiter, Chief Justice

Tax Court of Canada, July 3, 2020: *Notice to the Public and the Profession*

Reopening of the Tax Court of Canada

The Tax Court of Canada will reopen for the transaction of business on July 6, 2020.

The Court's Registry offices across the country will be open, with the exception of the Hamilton office.

The Court will provide a notice next week outlining multiple aspects of the Court's reopening process, including an updated exclusion period regarding the computation of time and a list of locations where sittings will proceed.

Dated this 3rd day of July, 2020.

Eugene P. Rossiter, Chief Justice

Tax Court of Canada, July 10, 2020: *Practice Direction and Order*

WHEREAS the Tax Court of Canada cancelled its judicial sittings and conference calls between March 16, 2020 and July 17, 2020, inclusively;

AND WHEREAS the Tax Court of Canada including all its offices in Canada was closed for the transaction of any business pertaining to matters under the jurisdiction of the Tax Court of Canada, pursuant to section 12 of the *Tax Court of Canada Act*, between March 16, 2020 and July 5, 2020, inclusively;

AND WHEREAS the Tax Court of Canada is ready to resume judicial sittings and conference calls;

AND WHEREAS given the extraordinary circumstances which exist today by virtue of the spread of the COVID-19 virus, it is in the interest of justice, for all matters under the jurisdiction of the Tax Court of Canada pursuant to section 12 of the *Tax Court of Canada Act*, that I dispense with compliance of certain Rules;

PURSUANT to

Rules 9 and 12 of the *Tax Court of Canada Rules (General Procedure)*,

Any and all analogous provisions in all other Rules made under the *Tax Court of Canada Act* governing the conduct of matters under the Tax Court of Canada's jurisdiction, and

The Tax Court of Canada's power to control its own process,

I HEREBY EXCLUDE the period beginning on March 16, 2020, and ending on September 4, 2020, inclusively, from the computation of time under

The *Tax Court of Canada Rules (General Procedure)*,

All other Rules made under the *Tax Court of Canada Act* governing the conduct of matters under the Tax Court of Canada's jurisdiction pursuant to section 12 of the *Tax Court of Canada Act*, and

An Order or Direction of this Court made prior to March 16, 2020.

IT IS ALSO ORDERED that all Notices of Appeal filed after the statutory deadline during the period beginning March 16, 2020, and ending on September 4, 2020, shall be treated as including an Application for Extension of Time to Appeal brought on the exceptional grounds that the COVID-19 pandemic and the closure of the Registry prevented the timely filing of a Notice of Appeal;

IT IS ALSO ORDERED that upon being advised of this fact by the Registry when served with a Notice of Appeal, the Respondent will confirm to the Registry within 60 days of service that the appeal was filed:

1. after the statutory deadline but that the Respondent consents to the application; or

2. after the statutory deadline and that the Respondent opposes the application.

IT IS FURTHER ORDERED that to the extent that this Practice Direction and Order conflicts with the Practice Directions and Orders issued between March 16, 2020 and May 27, 2020, this Practice Direction and Order shall prevail.

DIRECTED AND ORDERED at the City of Ottawa, this 8th day of July, 2020

Eugene P. Rossiter, Chief Justice

Tax Court of Canada, Aug. 14, 2020: *Notice to the Public and the Profession*

The Time Limits and Other Periods Act (COVID-19)

On July 27, 2020, the federal *Time Limits and Other Periods Act (COVID-19)* (the "Act") came into force. The Act contains provisions that suspend certain time limits established by or under an Act of Parliament and that relate to court proceedings. The Act suspends these time limits from March 13, 2020 to September 13, 2020.

The Act suspends time limits relating to Tax Court of Canada proceedings that are contained in the *Income Tax Act, Excise Tax Act, Tax Court of Canada Act, Tax Court of Canada Rules (General Procedure), Tax Court of Canada Rules (Informal Procedure)*, and other statutes and regulations.

Suspension of time

In order to align with the Act, and to provide clarity, consistency and certainty, the Court is issuing a new Order regarding the suspension of time.

The period beginning on March 13, 2020 and ending on September 13, 2020, inclusively, will be excluded from the computation of time under the *Tax Court of Canada Rules (General Procedure)*; all other Rules made under the *Tax Court of Canada Act* governing the conduct of matters that, pursuant to 12 of the *Tax Court of Canada Act*, are under the Tax Court of Canada's jurisdiction; or an Order or Direction of this Court issued on or prior to March 13, 2020.

The full length of the updated exclusion period is 185 days, compared to the previous exclusion period length of 173 days.

Extensions of time to file Notices of Appeal

The Act's effects include the suspension of time limits for filing Notices of Appeal if the time limits fall between March 13, 2020 and September 13, 2020, inclusively. In the Court's Practice Direction and Order dated July 8, 2020, the Court ordered that certain Notices of Appeal filed after the statutory deadline would be treated as including an Application for an extension of time to appeal. The Act's coming into force means that these Notices of Appeal will no longer be considered to be filed after the statutory deadline. As such, the Registry will not be treating these Notices of Appeal as including an Application for an extension of time to appeal. The Registry will serve these Notices of Appeal on the Respondent.

Timetables

The Court will not be issuing Orders for new timetables with adjusted dates. Parties are asked to adjust the timetable issued by the Court on or before March 13, 2020 in their proceedings by adding 185 days to all dates scheduled in the timetable. This will result in a shift forward of all outstanding steps as of March 13, 2020. Parties can determine their adjusted dates using the chart in Appendix I of this Notice. An example scenario is also contained in Appendix II of this Notice.

If an adjusted timetable is no longer acceptable to the parties, parties may apply to the Court for direction.

Response deadlines to Registry

Correspondence issued by the Registry often requires the parties to provide responses by certain dates. These dates will be extended and updated in the same manner as the suspension of time described above, meaning that the period beginning on March 13, 2020 and ending on September 13, 2020, inclusively, will not be included in the computation of time for the response deadline.

To determine the new response dates, parties should use the chart in Appendix I of this Notice. Neither the Court nor the Registry will be issuing new correspondence with adjusted dates.

If the adjusted date are not acceptable to the parties, parties should contact the Registry.

Dated this 14th day of August, 2020.

Eugene P. Rossiter, Chief Justice

Appendix I: Adjusted Dates

[Not reproduced — ed.]

Appendix II: Example of adjusted timetable

Litigation step	Original date	Adjusted date
List of documents	May 1, 2020	November 2, 2020
Completion of examinations for discovery	August 1, 2020	February 22, 2021
Satisfaction of undertakings	September 1, 2020	March 23, 2021
Communicate with Hearings Coordinator	December 15, 2020	July 6, 2021

Tax Court of Canada, Aug. 14, 2020: *Practice Direction and Order*

[Replaces and supersedes previous Practice Directions above — ed.]

WHEREAS the *Time Limits and Other Periods Act (COVID-19)* (the "Act") came into force on July 27, 2020;

AND WHEREAS given the extraordinary circumstances which exist today by virtue of the spread of the COVID-19 virus, it is in the interest of justice, for all matters under the jurisdiction of the Tax Court of Canada pursuant to section 12 of the *Tax Court of Canada Act*, that I dispense with compliance of certain Rules;

PURSUANT to

Rules 9 and 12 of the *Tax Court of Canada Rules (General Procedure)*,

Any and all analogous provisions in all other Rules made under the *Tax Court of Canada Act* governing the conduct of matters under the Tax Court of Canada's jurisdiction, and

The Tax Court of Canada's power to control its own process,

I HEREBY EXCLUDE the period beginning on March 13, 2020, and ending on September 13, 2020, inclusively, from the computation of time under

The *Tax Court of Canada Rules (General Procedure)*,

All other Rules made under the *Tax Court of Canada Act* governing the conduct of matters under the Tax Court of Canada's jurisdiction pursuant to section 12 of the *Tax Court of Canada Act*, and

An Order or Direction of this Court made on or prior to March 13, 2020.

IT IS FURTHER ORDERED that to the extent that this Practice Direction and Order conflicts with the Practice Directions and Orders issued between March 16, 2020 and July 8, 2020, this Practice Direction and Order shall prevail.

DIRECTED AND ORDERED at the City of Ottawa, this 14th day of August, 2020

Eugene P. Rossiter, Chief Justice

Tax Court of Canada, Nov. 26, 2020: *Notice to the Public and the Profession*

Cancellation of Sittings

Due to the increased prevalence of COVID-19 in cities where the Tax Court of Canada currently holds proceedings, and the associated impact of travel on the health and safety of all involved in these proceedings, the Chief Justice has cancelled all in-person Court sittings scheduled between November 30th, 2020 and January 15, 2021, inclusively.

Please note that select appeals underway this week in Montreal and scheduled to conclude on November 30th and December 1st, 2020, will proceed. The parties involved in these appeals have already been advised accordingly.

Conference calls are not affected by this cancellation and will proceed as scheduled.

Parties affected by these cancellations will be contacted directly by the Registry staff in the coming days.

The Chief Justice will continue to monitor the situation closely and will reassess the week of January 4, 2021, whether the judicial sittings schedule will have to be further altered.

The Court and its Registry offices remain open, with the exception of the Hamilton office.

Dated this 26th day of November, 2020.

Eugene P. Rossiter, Chief Justice

Tax Court of Canada, Jan. 11, 2021: *Notice to the Public and the Profession*

Cancellation of Sittings

Due to the prevalence of COVID-19 in cities where the Tax Court of Canada is scheduled to hold proceedings, the Chief Justice has cancelled all in-person Court sittings scheduled between January 18, 2021 and February 12, 2021, inclusively.

Some conference calls scheduled to proceed between January 18, 2021 and February 12, 2021, inclusively, may also need to be cancelled.

Parties affected by the cancellation of in-person sittings or conference calls will be contacted directly by the Registry staff in the coming days.

The Chief Justice will continue to monitor the situation closely and will reassess the week of February 1, 2021, whether the judicial sittings schedule will have to be further altered.

The Court and its Registry offices remain open, with the exception of the Hamilton office.

Dated this 11th day of January, 2021.

Eugene P. Rossiter, Chief Justice

Tax Court of Canada, Feb. 8, 2021: *Notice to the Public and the Profession*

Cancellation of Sittings

Due to the prevalence of COVID-19 in cities where the Tax Court of Canada is scheduled to hold proceedings, the Chief Justice has cancelled all in-person Court sittings scheduled between February 15, 2021 and March 12, 2021, inclusively.

Some conference calls scheduled to proceed between February 15, 2021 and March 12, 2021, inclusively, may also need to be cancelled.

Parties affected by the cancellation of in-person sittings or conference calls will be contacted directly by the Registry staff in the coming days.

The Chief Justice will continue to monitor the situation closely and will reassess the week of March 1st, 2021, whether the judicial sittings schedule will have to be further altered.

The Court and its Registry offices remain open, with the exception of the Hamilton office.

Dated this 8th day of February, 2021.

Eugene P. Rossiter, Chief Justice

Tax Court of Canada, March 9, 2021: *Notice to the Public and the Profession*

Update on Sittings Schedule

The Chief Justice has cancelled all in-person sittings of the Tax Court of Canada scheduled between March 15, 2021 and March 26, 2021.

Starting March 29, 2021 and until July 16, 2021, a reduced number of in-person Court sittings will proceed in Toronto, Montreal and Vancouver, with a small number proceeding in other cities during that period. All other in-person Court sittings scheduled between March 29, 2021 and July 16, 2021 will be cancelled.

All parties affected by the sittings schedule described herein have been or will be contacted directly by the Registry staff in the coming weeks.

Conference calls scheduled to proceed as of March 15, 2021 will proceed as scheduled.

The Chief Justice will continue to monitor the situation closely and may further alter this schedule as circumstances require.

The Court and its Registry offices remain open, with the exception of the Hamilton office.

Dated this 9th day of March, 2021.

Eugene P. Rossiter, Chief Justice

Tax Court of Canada, April 29, 2021: *Notice to the Public and the Profession*

Update on Registry Services

In light of the evolving circumstances surrounding the pandemic, the Tax Court of Canada's Registry offices are operating with significantly reduced staff on-site. While some Registry functions can be carried out remotely, the reduction in on-site staff will impact the speed with which the Registry can perform its services.

The impacts of reduced on-site staff may include the following:

- The Registry may be delayed in sending newly filed notices of appeal to the Canada Revenue Agency and Department of Justice.
- The Registry may be delayed in sending documents to parties.
- The Registry may send some documents to parties by e-mail only. In these cases, the Registry may ask the parties to confirm receipt.
- There may be a delay in the processing of other documents.

In the case of timetables, the Court expects parties to adhere to the self-imposed deadlines submitted even if the Court has not yet approved the proposed timetable.

The Court does not expect any delays to prejudice parties' positions in their respective proceedings. The Court will also continue to meet its statutory obligations regarding documents that must be sent by mail.

All Registry offices remain open except for Hamilton.

Dated this 29th day of April, 2021.

Eugene P. Rossiter, Chief Justice

Tax Court of Canada, June 1, 2021: *Notice to the Public and the Profession*

Update on Sittings Schedule

In light of the evolving circumstances surrounding the pandemic, the Chief Justice has **cancelled all in-person sittings of the Tax Court of Canada scheduled between August 16, 2021 and September 10, 2021**, inclusively.

In the coming weeks, the Court will continue to endeavour to conduct virtual hearings for some proceedings previously scheduled to occur in person between August 16, 2021 and September 10, 2021, inclusively. The Court will identify appeals for virtual hearings and will contact parties to determine with them if the hearing could proceed virtually. All parties affected by the sittings schedule described herein have been or will be contacted directly by the Registry staff in the coming weeks.

Conference calls and virtual hearings previously scheduled to proceed between August 16, 2021 and September 10, 2021, inclusively, will proceed as scheduled.

The Court and its Registry offices remain open with reduced staff. The Hamilton office remains closed.

Dated this 1st day of June 2021.

Eugene P. Rossiter, Chief Justice

Notes: Tax Court Chief Justice Eugene Rossiter gave a video presentation on May 15, 2020, describing the challenges in reopening the Court. Among other things, its staff and resources all come from the government's Courts Administration Service, and the Court has no control over any of it, including when and how quickly any staff will return. The Court is unable to operate digitally because it is still largely a paper-based Court, and the files must stay at the Registry. As a result, it shut down completely during the pandemic.

Chief Justice Rossiter gave a further video update on June 25, 2020. The first Court staff returned on June 22 (about 25% of Registry staff), and the Court anticipated restarting hearings on July 20, but sitting only in Vancouver, Edmonton, Calgary, Toronto, Hamilton, Ottawa, Montreal, Quebec City and Halifax. Sittings scheduled in smaller cities through the end of 2020 are generally cancelled, to allow more judges to hear cases in the larger centres. General Procedure appeals will get priority over Informal Procedure (IP), but IP appeals in certain categories also get priority, including those on the GST/HST Credit [see 122.5], Canada Child Benefit [122.61], Disability Tax Credit [118.3], "employee vs independent contractor" [see 248(1)"employee" Notes] and SR&ED credits [127(9)"SR&ED qualified expenditure pool" Notes]. At hearings, four copies of exhibits must be submitted ahead of time (90 minutes before the hearing for Informal Procedure, 7 days for General Procedure), as well as provided to opposing counsel, to avoid documents having to be passed around in Court. A "fast track settlement conference" procedure is also being introduced to increase the number of settlements. Details on these matters are available on the Court's website, and see shaded box below "Announced Administrative Change — COVID-19 — TCC hearings".

Over 3,000 documents received by the Court during the shutdown had to be uploaded into the system. On March 16, 52 appeals already underway were adjourned; 1,191 appeals scheduled from then to June 30 were also adjourned; and 210 conference calls were cancelled. The Court lost 202 "sitting weeks" (judges in Court), but has scheduled 78 new sitting weeks from July 20 to Oct. 1 beyond those previously scheduled, to start dealing with the backlog.

Chief Justice Rossiter gave a further video update on February 9, 2021. He noted that because of COVID-19 restrictions, staff on-site at the Court at any time are only 22% of the full workforce. The Court was still hoping for three new judges and prothonotaries, as requested before the pandemic [2021 Budget bill #1, tabled later in April, provides for an increase of 2 judges]. The Court is not yet capable of video trials and it may be some years before it will be ready, though it has begun the process of digitizing its files.

The Chief Justice noted that the "fast track" settlement process described above had only two cases volunteer, and only one of those was suitable for the procedure.

Announced Administrative Change — More funding for the Tax Court

Federal Budget Plan, Feb. 27, 2018, Chapter 1: To ensure that Canada's federal courts, including the Tax Court of Canada, receive adequate support to address a growing and increasingly complex caseload, the Government will provide $41.9 million over five years, and $9.3 million per year ongoing, to the Courts Administration Service. This investment includes support for new front-line registry and judicial staff, most of whom are expected to support the Tax Court of Canada.

Notes: The Chief Justice of the Tax Court has complained publicly for years, speaking at the Canadian Tax Foundation annual conference, that the Court is underfunded and unable to modernize its IT system. This announcement will help to some extent.

Announced Administrative Change — COVID-19 — TCC hearings

Tax Court of Canada, Aug. 5, 2020: *Tax Court of Canada Guidance for attending in-person hearings*

The health and safety of all who participate in in-person hearings at the Tax Court of Canada (the "Court") is our top priority. Below are some of the measures and directives in place for in-person hearings during the COVID-19 pandemic. Please read them carefully and note that preventive measures and directives could differ in some cities or provinces in light of local and provincial guidelines and legislation in effect at the time of your hearing:

- If you are experiencing any symptoms of COVID-19, or have been advised by public health officials or your doctor to self-isolate, do not present yourself to the Court's facilities. If you are unable to attend your hearing for this reason, please contact the opposing party(ies) and the Court's Registry as soon as possible.

  You will be asked to answer questions about your health and recent travel at a screening site before entering the court facilities. You may be denied entry based on health and security considerations.

- You must wear the appropriate PPE (mask and/or gloves) inside the court facilities where two-metre physical distancing is not possible. This includes courtrooms and indoor common areas. Masks and gloves will be available.

- You cannot bring any bags into the courtroom except briefcases and documents required for your hearing. You may also bring your valuables into the courtroom.

- Disposable water bottles will be provided on request.

- If you plan on introducing documents (exhibits) into evidence or jurisprudence at the hearing, please note the following protocols:

  General Procedure hearings:

  Four (4) bound and paginated copies of your book(s) of documents and of your book(s) of authorities shall be filed at least seven (7) days before the hearing with the local Registry office where the hearing will take place. Copies may be filed in person or by mail at the address of the hearing location in the attached Order.

  Informal Procedure hearings:

  If your hearing is scheduled to be heard in the morning, you must file one (1) copy of your documents and jurisprudence to the Registry counter at 8:30 a.m.

  If your hearing is scheduled to be heard in the afternoon, you must file one (1) copy of your documents and jurisprudence to the Registry counter at 12:30 p.m.

- Regularly consult the Tax Court of Canada website at www.tcc-cci.gc.ca for additional information and any updated guidance on in-person hearings before you attend your hearing.

Proposed Amendment — More Tax Court judges

Federal Budget, Chapter 9, April 19, 2021: *Enhancing the Capacity of Superior Courts*

An accessible justice system requires efficient court processes that help Canadians obtain timely resolutions to their legal disputes. That is why the government has committed to creating new judicial positions. To help reduce court delays and enhance access to justice across Canada's superior courts:

Budget 2021 proposes to amend the *Judges Act*, the *Federal Courts Act*, and the *Tax Court of Canada Act* to add 13 new superior court positions, including an Associate Chief Justice position for the Supreme Court of Newfoundland and Labrador. Budget 2021 also proposes to provide $49.3 million over five years, starting in 2021-22, and $10.4 million ongoing, for these 13 additional superior court judicial positions.

Notes: 2021 budget bill #1, clause 260 amends *Tax Court of Canada Act* s. 4(1)(c) to increase the total number of judges from 22 to 24.

Related Provisions: 152(1.01), (1.2) — appeal of eligibility for disability credit; 152(9) — Minister may raise new basis for assessment during appeal; 167 — Application for time extension; 170 — Informal procedure appeals; 173(2), 174(5) — Time during consideration not to count; 175 — General procedure appeals; 179.1 — Where no reasonable grounds for appeal; 189(8) — Appeals of charity penalties and of suspension of charity's receipting privileges; 225.1(3) — Collection restrictions; 244(14), (14.1) — Date when notice sent; *Interpretation Act* 26 — Deadline on Sunday or holiday extended to next business day.

Notes: Electronic filing of a TCC appeal can be done at tinyurl.com/tcc-file.

The FCA's interpretation of *Vavilov* in *Ark Angel Fund* could mean a Tax Court appellant must show CRA made a "palpable and overriding error", to contest CRA's view of the facts of an appeal, but the Crown has never taken this position. See 172(3) Notes.

Appeals are governed by the *Tax Court of Canada Act* (TCCA). Under TCCA s. 18(1), an appellant may use the Court's "Informal Procedure" if the total *federal* income tax + penalty [FT+P] (excluding interest) at issue is $25,000 or less or $50,000 in losses. (The limit applies per tax year under appeal and per appellant, and excludes interest and provincial tax, so the real amount at stake can be far higher, e.g. $200,000 in *Callaghan*, 2021 TCC 35, para. 21 footnote.) The taxpayer automatically loses any right to amounts above the cap (TCCA s. 18.1): *Innovations & Intégrations Brassicoles*, 2009 FCA 302; *Berezuik*, 2010 TCC 296; *Lirette*, 2010 TCC 633; *1726437 Ontario [AirMax]*, 2012 TCC 376; *Hughes*, 2017 TCC 95, para. 91; but a case can be bumped up to General Procedure mid-hearing: TCCA s. 18.13; *Hennig*, 2012 TCC 141, para. 3. FT+P is counted for each assessment of one year, so a single appeal of several $25,000 assessments (plus the provincial tax) can be made under the Informal Procedure: *Maier*, 1994 CarswellNat 3242 (TCC); *Pink Elephant*, 2011 TCC 395; *Auto Maculate*, 2020 TCC 105, para. 185; but CRA's view is that this does not apply to a s. 160 assessment. (Carryovers to other years are not counted as part of FT+P, so a multimillion-dollar dispute was Informal Procedure in *407 International*, 2019 TCC 245, para. 13.) An Informal Procedure appeal is not subject to the strict rules of evidence (see "Evidence" below), but is still a formal Court hearing with evidence by each side, then argument by each side. The taxpayer may be represented by a non-lawyer agent, though the Court expects some competence from an agent: *Giguère*, 2018 TCC 211 (FCA appeal discontinued A-386-18). Costs awards are lower: see 171(1) Notes. Above the threshold, the Court's "General Procedure" normally requires a lawyer (see "Lawyer required" below) and follows formal rules of court (oral discovery normally only if FT+P exceeds $50,000: TCCA s. 17.3(1); *Fullum*, 2017 TCC 140). An Informal and a General Procedure appeal may be heard together, or not; see Notes to 174(1).

Filing an appeal usually prevents CRA from collecting on the assessment, but in many cases it is advisable to pay while the appeal is pending. See Notes to 225.1(1).

An ongoing challenge for the Court is thousands of pending "tax shelter" cases (see Notes to 118.1(1)"total charitable gifts" and 237.1(1)"tax shelter"); the Court has no class action mechanism, but the 2013 amendments to s. 174 allow a determination of an issue in one taxpayer's appeal to be binding on others, with minimal notice requirements (174(2)(b)). As well, new 171(2)–(4) (2013) allow a Court ruling to apply to an "issue" rather than an assessment (some taxpayers will have other issues under appeal for the same taxation year).

The Dept. of Justice represents CRA as its counsel, and does not charge CRA (2015-16 value of litigation $63 million, all services $77m: *Access to Information Act* disclosure).

Taxpayer T need not appear in Court personally if counsel and witnesses can present the appeal: *Krauss*, 2009 TCC 597, para. 4 (aff'd on other grounds 2010 FCA 284). T's appeal may be put on hold if the evidence may incriminate T in pending criminal proceedings: *Long*, 2010 FCA 254 (leave to appeal denied 2011 CarswellNat 3999).

The filing deadline is 90 days from CRA sending its decision on the objection (plus any *Time Limits and Other Periods Act (COVID-19)* extension: see Proposed Amendment above). See Notes to 165(1) if CRA's decision was not received. The Notice of Appeal must be *received* by the Court (rather than mailed) by the deadline: *Tax Court of Canada Act* 17.2(2), 18.15(2). It can be filed online: tinyurl.com/tcc-file. Only General Procedure appeals require a fee; for the Informal Procedure, a $100 fee was eliminated Dec. 10, 2008. An appeal mistakenly mailed to CRA is validly filed only if CRA forwards it to the Court: *Hickerty*, 2007 TCC 482 (and see Notes to 167(1)).

If the filing deadline expires on a Sunday or holiday (and Saturday in most provinces), it is extended to the next business day: see Notes to *Interpretation Act* s. 26. The deadline is not extended by a provision in the *Tax Court of Canada Rules* that excludes the December holiday period from the calculation of time: *Haynes*, 2013 TCC 185, para. 6.

169(1)(b) can be used to jump to the TCC without waiting for a decision on the objection; see Notes to 165(1). It does not give the taxpayer any other rights due to CRA's non-response; see Notes to 165(3).

Adjournment is at a Court's discretion, and refusal to adjourn is not normally grounds for appeal: *Rybka*, 2011 TCC 191 (despite Crown's consent, taxpayers "are not entitled to waste [Court] days that could be used by other taxpayers"); *Liddle*, 2011 FCA 159 (L had "ample opportunity to retain counsel before the trial"); *Sarrazin*, 2014 TCC 127 (no second adjournment to allow expert report to be filed); *Montana*, 2017 FCA 194 (unrepresented litigants retained counsel last-minute); *Yu*, 2018 FCA 68, paras. 17-20 (counsel sought adjournment to speak with client mid-testimony); *6260268 Canada*, 2018 FCA 70 (FCA would not intervene on emergency basis in TCC's refusal to adjourn hearing when new counsel appointed); *9194-2359 Québec*, 2019 TCC 179 (no adjournment where appellant advised by Court to retain counsel 2 years earlier, met with lawyer 3 days before hearing). In *McNicholas*, 2019 TCC 171, adjournment was granted but with $2,000 costs for abuse of process, as M waited 7 months to tell the Court he had a flight booked abroad on the trial date. See also "Judges' Panel", 2019 Cdn Tax Foundation conference report, at 2:6-9.

Ambiguity in tax legislation: if unresolved, there is a "residual presumption" in favour of the taxpayer: *Notre-Dame de Bon-Secours*, 1994 CarswellQue 86 (SCC); *Placer Dome*, 2006 SCC 20, para. 24; *Fortnum*, 2018 TCC 126, para. 24, but this should not overrule interpretive discretion given to a tax authority: *Pong Marketing*, 2018 ONCA 555, para. 52; *Stonehouse Group*, 2021 ONCA 10 (para. 26 also says legislation should not be interpreted to operate "illogically"). More common now is the "text, context and purpose" analysis set out by the Supreme Court of Canada in *Canada Trustco*, 2005 SCC 54 (e.g., *Bonnybrook Industrial*, 2018 FCA 136). A provision's purpose may "reveal ambiguity in apparently plain language": *Canada Trustco*, para. 47.

Bankrupt persons can appeal only through the trustee: see Notes to 128(2).

Bias of judge: see "Recusal" below.

CRA publications cannot legally be relied on: see "Estoppel" below.

Conflict of interest: In *Woessner*, 2017 TCC 124, counsel could not act on a file where his firm had promoted the software shelter claimed and a firm partner would likely be called as a witness. Where multiple appellants may have conflicting interests (e.g., directors assessed under 227.1) and have not waived the conflict, the same lawyer cannot act for all: *Attisano*, 2016 CarswellNat 966 (TCC).

Contract interpretation: the Court was traditionally prohibited from looking beyond a contract's words unless they were ambiguous (the "parol evidence" rule), but it may now look at extrinsic evidence of the "factual matrix" to determine the true nature of a payment for tax purposes: *Sattva Capital v. Crestron*, 2014 SCC 53 (SCC); *Henco Industries*, 2014 TCC 192, paras. 79-107; *Invesco Canada*, 2014 TCC 375, paras. 40-45, 75.

Costs: see Notes to 171(1).

Delay: see "Status hearing" below.

Disclosure: The auditor and appeals officer should provide their file to the appellant even without a formal Access to Information request: see Notes to 231.1(1) and 165(3).

Discontinuance of an appeal cannot be reversed absent fraud, even if the parties consent: *Scarola*, 2003 FCA 157; *Davies*, 2016 TCC 104, para. 10 (aff'd 2019 FCA 191; leave to appeal denied 2020 CarswellNat 52 (SCC)); *Stover*, 2016 TCC 235; *Heath*, 2018 TCC 119; *Supavititpatana*, 2020 TCC 46. See also 169(3) Notes re settlements.

Discovery: for a thorough review see Chan, "Discovery", *Practical Insights*, *Taxnet Pro* Tax Disputes Centre (July 2020, 51pp); Sorensen, "Document Demands on Audit and at Discovery", 2019 Cdn Tax Foundation conference report, 12:1-50. "Discovery fails when the parties are engaged in obfuscation... Every effort should therefore be made to allow for full and proper disclosure": *Canadian Imperial Bank of Commerce*, 2015 TCC 280, para. 271. Paras. 14-18 of this case discuss the key principles of discovery; and see also *1716790 Ontario*, 2016 TCC 189, paras. 35-75; *506913 N.B.*, 2016 TCC 286, para. 11. Discovery of CRA: *Burlington Resources*, 2015 TCC 71; *Paletta*, 2017 TCC 233; varied 2018 CarswellNat 12392 (FCA); *DiLalla*, 2018 FCA 28 (broad, vague fishing expedition denied) and 2018 TCC 178 (discovery is "not about witnesses, evidence or arguments for trial"); *Canadian Western Trust [Ahamed TFSA]*, 2020 FCA 213 (unpublished Dept of Finance drafts during legislative design did not have "institutional quality" so as to represent government's position on the legislation, so were irrelevant: para. 31); *Thompson Bros.*, 2021 TCC 15 (under appeal to FCA) (key question is relevance). If an appellant fails to respond properly to questions on discovery or fulfil undertakings, the appeal can be dismissed, e.g. *Harris*, 2014 TCC 110; *Kelly*, 2016 FCA 25; *Djelebian*, 2016 FCA 26; *Lynch*, 2017 FCA 248. (Undertakings answered by counsel may be deemed to be answers given by the witness: Rule 97; Kreklewetz & Bassindale, "Undertakings", *Tax Advocate* (Taxnet Pro Tax Disputes Centre), Sept. 2020, 8pp.) On "proportionality" and the level of effort a party must make to find answers, see *Burlington Resources*, 2017 TCC 144, paras. 23-47 (also noting that questions should not be taken "under advisement": para. 80); Jacyk & Mihailovich, "Proportionality and the Train of Inquiry in Tax Court Discovery", 66(4) *Canadian Tax Journal* 809-46 (2018). A party cannot be required to consult experts to answer a question: *Burlington Resources*, 2019 TCC 143, para. 26. Counsel should not lead their witness or intervene to prevent a damaging answer: *Enterprise Rent-A-Car*, 2020 ONSC 5339, paras. 47, 53-54. Answers given on discovery are subject to an "implied undertaking" that the information will not be used elsewhere without the Court's permission: *Juman v. Doucette*, 2008 SCC 8, para. 27; *506913 N.B.*, 2012 TCC 210, paras. 69-82; *Silver Wheaton*, 2019 TCC 170 (FCA appeal discontinued A-304-19) (detailed discussion; class action plaintiffs were denied access to SW's TCC discovery); but in *Rennie Produce*, [2018] FCAFC 38, the Australia Full Federal Court held such information disclosable under a 231.2-like Requirement. It is unclear whether information disclosed in TCC discovery can be used by CRA for a further assessment: in *Fio Corp.*, 2015 FCA 236, the TCC ruled it cannot be, but the FCA allowed it to be used, but only because the same documents had earlier been provided to the auditor; arguably, a taxpayer should not gain an advantage by withholding documents from CRA on audit and providing them only on discovery. A party's expert may be allowed to attend discovery, to assist counsel silently: *Blenk Development*, 2014 TCC 185. Being forced to answer questions on discovery is not "torture" that entitles a taxpayer to refuse to answer (duh!): *McCarthy*, 2016 TCC 45 (FCA appeal discontinued A-57-16); *Oberkirsch*, 2016 TCC 84. Discovery in a GAAR appeal: see Notes to 245(2). If a Court orders disclosure that would violate foreign law, see *Bank Mellat*, [2019] EWCA Civ 449 (England).

Dissolved corporations can be assessed but cannot appeal without being revived: *1455257 Ontario*, 2016 FCA 100 (leave to appeal denied 2016 CarswellNat 4147 (SCC)) [corp given 60 days to get revived so it could continue appeal]; *1218395 Ontario*, 2017 FCA 121 (Ontario refused to revive corp until it paid its provincial tax debt); *Lilyfield Development*, 2020 TCC 16 (FCA appeal dismissed for delay A-71-20). [These overrule older cases *495187 Ontario*, [1993] 2 C.T.C. 113 (FCA); *460354 Ontario*, [1992] 2 C.T.C. 287 (FCTD).] A dissolved corp cannot bring a motion: *GMC Distribution*, 2012 TCC 262; but see *Sickinger v. Krek*, 2016 ONCA 459, para. 16, re "continuing" an existing action. If appellant X has ceased to exist, Rule 29 of the *Tax Court of Canada Rules* permits person Y to continue X's appeal at the TCC's discretion, if Y is liable for X's tax debt, e.g. under 159(3), 160(1) or 227.1(1): *Clearwater Seafoods*, 2013 FCA 180 (but Y can also just appeal Y's assessment and challenge the underlying assessment of X: *Gaucher*, 2000 CarswellNat 2656 (FCA); *Duque*, 2020 FCA 73, para. 20). See also Notes to 152(1).

Double tax should be avoided in deciding an appeal: see Notes to 248(28).

Estoppel: The fact CRA promised not to assess, or provided misinformation regarding the law, does not create estoppel and is irrelevant to an appeal: *Klassen*, 2007 FCA 339; *Goldstein*, [1995] 2 C.T.C. 2036 (TCC); *Chitalia*, 2017 TCC 227, para. 20; *Farm Credit Canada*, 2017 FCA 244, para. 28; *International Hi-Tech*, 2018 TCC 107, para. 13; *Ellaway*, 2019 TCC 118, para. 15; *Ghumman*, 2019 TCC 125; but it can be grounds for waiver of interest (220(3.1)), extending a filing deadline (*Lounsbury*, 2019 TCC 109, para. 32) or possibly for suing CRA (see Notes to 171(1)). CRA's acceptance of a filing position for some years is not binding on CRA for those years or other years: see "Inconsistent assessments" below. However, see Notes to 169(3) re *Rosenberg* and *Sifto Canada*, where settlements prevented CRA from reassessing a given year; and Notes to 220(2.1) re CRA waiver of filing deadlines. See also Ruby, "Estoppel and Res Judicata in Tax Litigation", 2012 Tax Dispute Resolution conf. report (ctf.ca), 2:1-21; Handfield, "Relying on Incorrect CRA Information", 3(2) *Canadian Tax Focus* (ctf.ca) 3 (May 2013); Tonkovich & Bezarkewich, "Striking a Balance: Exploring Legitimate Expectations", XXXII(2) *Tax Litigation* (Federated Press) 2-9 (2019). In *Agnico-Eagle v. Nunavut*, 2016 NUCA 2, a Gazetted regulatory change to a fuel tax rebate deadline, affecting only AE, applied even though Nunavut did not advise AE of it; promissory estoppel did not apply. In *BP Canada*, 2017 FCA 61, para. 105, CRA wrongly "acted in defiance of published policy" in demanding tax-risk information from BP. A taxpayer is not estopped from arguing that designation of marital status in a return is incorrect, if CRA "has not acted on it to [its] detriment": *Kelner*, 1995 CarswellNat 1207, para. 17. In *Mikhail*, 2019 TCC 49, taxpayers were not bound by having reported income that the Court found was earned by their corporation.

Evidence is governed by the rules of the province in which the hearing takes place: *Canada Evidence Act* s. 40; *Hardy*, 2018 FCA 103, para. 13. An Informal Procedure

appeal is not subject to the strict rules of evidence (*TCCA* s. 18.15(3)), and it is an error of law to exclude hearsay without considering its reliability: *Suchon*, 2002 FCA 282, para. 32; *Selmeci*, 2002 FCA 293, paras. 6-9; *Madison*, 2012 FCA 80, para. 11; *De Santis*, 2015 TCC 95, para. 24. If no objection is raised to evidence at trial, it cannot be challenged on appeal: *Dow & Duggan*, 2021 FCA 66. If no objection to hearsay evidence is raised in an appeal in Quebec, it must be allowed: *Hardy*, para. 14. See also Sopinka et al., *The Law of Evidence* (LexisNexis, 5th ed., 2018, 1547pp); Atkinson, *Proof: Canadian Rules of Evidence* (LexisNexis, 4th ed., 2018, 265pp) (very readable); Ummat, "No Witnesses?", XXIII(3) *Tax Litigation* (Federated Press) 16-19 (2020) (alternatives to live testimony); and "Expert evidence" and "Judicial notice" below.

Expert evidence: see Rule 145. An expert witness must be independent and non-partisan, and has a primary duty to the Court to be objective: *White Burgess v. Abbott*, 2015 SCC 23; *Advanced Agricultural Testing*, 2009 TCC 190, para. 13; *Glubis*, 2015 SKPC 143, para. 138; *Logix Data*, 2021 TCC 36, paras. 14-21 (under appeal to FCA). However, having close social ties to the appellants in a small community did not exclude expert witnesses in *Lichtman*, 2017 TCC 252 (FCA appeal discontinued A-35-18), paras. 65-76, though it did go to weight: para. 137. A Crown valuation expert who failed to disclose that he had seen CRA's internal valuation report had his independence "compromised" so his testimony was unreliable: *Vine Estate*, 2014 TCC 64, para. 55 (aff'd on other grounds 2015 FCA 125). A CRA SR&ED advisor acting as expert witness must not determine facts or follow CRA guidelines, or the evidence will be rejected as not impartial: *Abeilles Services*, 2014 TCC 313, paras. 89-97. Similarly, in *He*, 2010 BCPC 457, para. 31, CRA investigators who had seized a restaurant's records could not be expert witnesses. The expert's main duty is to assist the Court, and a CRA expert who worked on the file throughout the audit lacked detachment and could not testify as expert: *HLP Solution*, 2015 TCC 41. An expert report will be excluded if it does not state the facts and reasoning relied on (including any quantitative data) in reaching its conclusions: *Bekesinski*, 2014 TCC 35, paras. 27-32. An expert whose report failed to disclose the data he relied on violated Rule 145(3) and his report was given no weight: *Gerbro Holdings*, 2016 TCC 173, paras. 140-152 (aff'd without discussing this point 2018 FCA 197). Experts should "not be permitted to usurp the functions of the trier of fact": *Mohan*, [1994] 2 S.C.R. 9; *Exxonmobil*, 2019 TCC 108, para. 62. It is not inappropriate for counsel to review and comment on draft expert reports: *Moore v. Getahun*, 2015 ONCA 55 [Hassan, "Moore v. Getahun: Lessons for Tax Litigators", XIX(4) *Tax Litigation* (Federated Press) 1170-73 (2015)]. A "participant expert" who was involved in the transaction can be allowed to testify: *Kaur*, 2017 TCC 55 (and 2019 TCC 17, para. 4; aff'd 2019 FCA 313); *Imeson v. Maryvale*, 2018 ONCA 888. Rule 145(4) normally limits a party to 5 expert witnesses: *General Electric*, 2009 TCC 246; *Canadian Imperial Bank of Commerce*, 2018 TCC 248. TCC Practice Note 22 encourages "hot tubbing", where the judge seeks consensus among the experts once the factual evidence is in ["Expert Witness Panels" in Sorensen, "Tax Court Update", 27(4) *Canadian Tax Highlights* (ctf.ca) 10-12 (April 2019)]. See also *Tax and Expert Witnesses* (ctf.ca, 2019); Doobay, "Expert Witness and the Tax Court", *Practical Insights*, Taxnet Pro Tax Disputes Centre (Nov. 2020), 37pp.

An expert can testify as to how *foreign law* applies: e.g. *Jayco Inc.*, 2018 TCC 34, para. 83. However, an expert normally cannot testify in a Canadian court as to *Canadian* law, as that is for the judge to determine: *Syrek*, 2009 FCA 53, paras. 28-30; *Brandon (City)*, 2010 FCA 244, para. 27; *Shulkov*, 2012 TCC 457, para. 98; *Charette v. Trinity Capital*, 2012 ONSC 2824, para. 45; *Walsh v. BDO Dunwoody*, 2013 BCSC 1463, paras. 23-89 (detailed discussion; there is no "blanket exclusionary rule" against such evidence, but cases allowing it "will be rare"); *Henco Industries*, 2014 TCC 278, para. 24; *Agnico-Eagle Mines*, 2014 TCC 324, para. 33 (rev'd on unrelated grounds 2016 FCA 130). In a lawsuit against CRA for negligence, *Ludmer*, 2018 QCCS 3381, para. 608 (aff'd without discussing this point 2020 QCCA 697; leave to appeal denied 2021 CarswellQue 2160 (SCC)), opinions of retired judges were filed on the correctness of CRA assessing positions, but were not treated by the Court as expert opinions. Whether "international law" (if such law exists) can be the subject of expert evidence is unclear: *Boily*, 2021 FCA 23, paras. 22, 25.

Where there are many documents (such as expense invoices) and the numbers are in dispute, an accountant or other competent witness should prepare summaries and testify, to simplify the evidence: *Merchant*, [1998] 3 C.T.C. 2505 (TCC), para 7 (aff'd 2001 FCA 19); *897366 Ontario*, 2000 CanLII 246 (TCC), para. 8; *378733 Ontario (Robson)*, 2001 CarswellNat 2499 (TCC), para. 6; *Chrabalowski*, 2004 TCC 644, para. 10; *Montréal Timbres*, 2005 TCC 186, para. 5; *Rail*, 2011 TCC 130, para. 33; *Porisky*, 2012 BCSC 67, para. 24 (rev'd on other grounds 2014 BCCA 146); *Amiripour*, 2015 TCC 187, para. 16. However, such a report might not be accepted as an "expert" report: *Belley*, 2019 QCCQ 1411. A CRA official can testify to calculations of business income without being qualified as an expert: *Mahmood*, 2012 ONSC 6487.

In camera proceedings or publication ban: See Notes to s. 179.

Inconsistent assessments of different taxpayers are legal (except where s. 174 brings them together): *Hawkes*, [1997] 2 C.T.C. 133 (FCA), paras. 7-9; *Fagan*, 2011 TCC 523, para. 83; *Tennant*, 2013 ABCA 81 (leave to appeal to SCC denied 2013 CarswellAlta 1179 (SCC)); *Michael Hill Finance*, [2016] NZCA 276 (New Zealand); *Mullings*, 2017 TCC 133, footnote 19 (to heading before para. 33); *Archibald*, 2018 FCA 2, para. 12; *Thompson Bros.*, 2021 TCC 15, para. 50 (under appeal to FCA). However, see Bruce Russell, "White — Taxpayer Equal Treatment", 9(11) *Tax Hyperion* (Carswell) 1-4 (Nov. 2012) and "Tried and True Tips", 2014 Cdn Tax Foundation conference report at 29:2 (Russell is now a Tax Court judge); and since CRA policy is to be evenhanded, CRA senior officials can be pushed to assess consistently (see CRA reply to TEI, Dec. 4, 2018, q. D.4). See also Auditor General's fall 2018 report #7 (oag-bvg.gc.ca). Inconsistent assessments of the same taxpayer for different years are permitted, and the fact CRA allows a claim one year does not require allowing it in a later year: *Landbouwbedrijf Backx*, 2019 FCA 310, para. 14 (or even changing its assessment of the earlier year: 2021 TCC 2, paras. 50-56); *Roywood Investments*, 1979 CarswellNat 515 (FCTD), para. 24 (aff'd [1981] C.T.C. 206 (FCA)); *Harris*, 2018 TCC 148, para. 13.

Increasing tax: The Court cannot increase tax on appeal, since the "Minister cannot appeal his own assessment": *Continental Bank*, [1998] 4 C.T.C. 77 (SCC), para. 10; *Hollinger Inc.*, [1999] 4 C.T.C. 61 (FCA), para. 23; *Pedwell*, [2000] 3 C.T.C. 246 (FCA), para. 18; *Valdis*, [2001] 1 C.T.C. 2827; *Rogic*, [2002] 1 C.T.C. 2236 (TCC), para. 31; *R. Marcoux & Fils Inc.*, 2005 TCC 507, para. 30; *Skinner*, 2009 TCC 269; *Papp*, 2009 TCC 621, para. 7; *McIntosh*, 2011 TCC 147 (taxpayer wanted increased credit for source withholdings); *Katz*, 2012 TCC 232 (FCA appeal discontinued A-412-12), para. 26; *Longo*, 2013 TCC 213, para. 2; *Bolton Steel*, 2014 TCC 94, paras. 30-35; *Last*, 2014 FCA 129, para. 37 (application of the rule to each issue under appeal, overturned by 2016 amendment) (leave to appeal denied to Crown 2014 CarswellNat 4451 (SCC)); *Nazih*, 2016 TCC 70, para. 12; *Club Intrawest*, 2016 TCC 149, para. 323; *Golini*, 2016 TCC 174, para. 141 (FCA appeal discontinued A-349-16); *Farm Credit Canada*, 2017 TCC 29, para. 22 (aff'd on other grounds 2017 FCA 244); *Peach*, 2020 TCC 12, para. 36 (under appeal to FCA). However, the Court can increase revenue where the increase is offset by a larger deduction: *Bobic*, 2017 TCC 107, para. 53 footnote; and the Court can increase tax at the taxpayer's request (as part of a settlement reducing another year's tax): *CBS Canada*, 2020 FCA 4, para. 45.

Issue estoppel and *res judicata* (relitigating a resolved issue): see Notes to 169(2). On whether conviction of evasion is proof the tax is owing, see Notes to 239(1).

Judicial notice can be taken by a judge of information that is very well-known. See Jeffrey Miller, *The Law of Judicial Notice* (Carswell, 2017, 258pp).

Jurisdiction of the Tax Court and other courts: see "Jurisdiction" heading below.

Language: witnesses can testify in English or French as they prefer, even if they speak the other official language: *Mazraani [Industrielle Alliance]*, 2018 SCC 50 (quashing a TCC decision). Translated documents were allowed in evidence where done by a Taiwan translation service and accompanied by a notarized affidavit, without the Crown being able to examine the translator (the Crown had seen the documents before): *Tang*, 2017 TCC 168, paras. 17-33.

Lawyer required in General Procedure: An individual can always represent themself, but cannot have anyone other than a lawyer appear: *Sutlej Foods*, 2019 TCC 20, para. 23; *Hazan*, 2019 TCC 152. (Counsel cannot normally be a witness: *Pluri Vox*, 2012 FCA 18; but a non-lawyer agent in Informal Procedure can testify.) A corporation cannot appear "in person" in General Procedure (TCCA s. 17.1), and cannot be represented by a non-lawyer officer or agent (even though TCC Rule 30(2) purports to say the Court can allow it, which the Court did in many past cases): *BCS Group*, 2020 FCA 205 (resolving conflicting TCC cases *Masa Sushi*, *Suchocki Accounting*, *1532099 Ontario*, *Sutlej Foods*, *Groupe Nepveu* and *BCS*). The Federal Court and FCA can allow a non-lawyer to act: *Federal Courts Rules* r. 120; *TPG Technology*, 2011 FCA 345; *Kennedy*, 2012 FC 1050, paras. 12-18; *Shantakumar*, 2018 FC 677, para. 4; *Gittens*, 2019 FCA 256, para. 2.

Objection required: If no (timely) objection was filed, no appeal can be brought and the TCC will quash a notice of appeal: *Bormann*, 2006 FCA 83; *Goguen*, 2007 FCA 67; *Ballantyne*, 2013 FCA 30; *Hokhold*, 2013 FCA 86; *Mpamugo*, 2017 FCA 136; and many TCC decisions. (See Notes to 165(1) if the notice of assessment or confirmation was not sent or not received.) An intervening reassessment on an unrelated issue cancels an objection, and no appeal can be filed without a new objection: *Nicksy*, 2017 TCC 116 (but see also 165(7)).

Onus: the taxpayer normally has the burden of proving the assessment wrong, but there are exceptions; see Notes to 152(7).

Pleadings: the appellant files a notice of appeal (NA) and the Crown files a Reply. In the Informal Procedure, the Reply is usually prepared by a CRA litigation officer, and this is legal: *Narivontchik*, 2020 TCC 60. A General Procedure (GP) NA must properly plead the facts and issues and cite the relevant legislative provisions: *Nolasco (Zurowski)*, 2015 TCC 318; *Adebogun*, 2018 TCC 181. If the Crown does not file a Reply within 60 days, the facts alleged in the NA are presumed true (*Tax Court Rules* 44(2) for GP, TCCA 18.16(4) for Informal Procedure (IP); *Gratl*, 2019 TCC 9, para. 47), but not if the TCC has not yet ruled on a Crown request to extend time to reply: *Boroumend*, 2017 FCA 245. (Where the Crown *filed* the Reply on time but failed to serve it within 5 days as required by the Rules, J's motion for summary judgment was "totally without merit": *Jackson*, 2019 TCC 63.) If CRA agrees the appeal is well-founded, it may consent to the appeal and reassess without filing a Reply. Either side's failure to plead an issue may mean that issue cannot be raised at trial: *Jayco Inc.*, 2018 TCC 34, paras. 63, 66; *Hollinger Estate*, 2013 TCC 252, para. 23 [this can apply to the Crown even in IP: *Blackburn*, 2010 TCC 69; *Ahmad*, 2017 TCC 195, para. 27; *Andersen*, 2020 TCC 51 (assumptions did not support the assessment)]. Assumptions pleaded in the Reply cannot be changed at trial, but the Crown can lead evidence to show an assumption was wrong: *Sud*, 2017 TCC 106 (IP), paras. 8-10. The Reply cannot say the Minister made a given "assumption" when assessing if CRA did not make it until later: *Loewen*, 2004 FCA 146, para. 10; *Banque Laurentienne*, 2020 TCC 73, para. 92. An admission in a pleading does not bind the Court if it is contrary to the facts: *Hammill*, 2005 FCA 252, para. 31; *Paletta*, 2019 TCC 205, paras. 105-107 (under appeal to FCA); *9178-3472 Québec*, 2020 FCA 15, para. 9; *Leonard*, 2021 TCC 33 (under appeal to FCA), para. 80. An admission can be withdrawn with the Court's consent: Rule 132; but only formal admissions of fact are binding anyway: *Burlington Resources*, 2020 TCC 32, paras. 71-84 (appeal conditionally settled at FCA A-72-20). Judgment is not issued based on admissions if there is dispute over other facts or doubt on the law: *Georgeson Shareholder*, 2020 FCA 139, paras. 9-10. The Reply can have inconsistent pleadings with respect to different appellants: *Agracity*, 2015 FCA 288; but otherwise, inconsistent pleadings must clearly state they are "in the alternative": Rule 51(2); *Husky Oil*, 2019 TCC 136, paras. 32-34. CRA allegations about the taxpayer's criminal conviction for acts related to the business assessed may be allowed in a Reply: *Heron*, 2017 FCA 229. A motion to strike a pleading (or part of one) can succeed only if it is "plain and obvious" the pleading cannot succeed, or is vexatious or an abuse of process: *Canadian Imperial Bank of Commerce*, 2013 FCA 122, para. 7; *Mont-Bruno CC*, 2018 TCC 105, paras. 17-20; *Mudge*, 2020 TCC 77. Such motion must be brought within a "reasonable time" of becoming aware of the issue, and before taking other procedural steps: Rule 8; *Dilalla*, 2020 FCA 39; *Drazin-Bendheim*, 2018 TCC 30, para. 37. If a NA is defective and the appellant fails to fix it when ordered to, the appeal may be dismissed, e.g. *Wilson*, 2019 FCA 155. Paragraphs of pleadings may be struck for repetition and redundancy: *Husky Oil*, para. 31. *Amending pleadings*: Rule 54 allows amendment on consent, or with the Court's leave, which is generally granted unless injustice would result that cannot be compensated with costs: *Canderel Ltd.*, 1993 CarswellNat 949 (FCA), para. 10; *Thompson*, 2018 TCC 167, para. 22; *6075240 Canada*, 2018 FC 1044. The Crown may be allowed to raise a new issue: see 152(9). See also Chan, "Drafting Pleadings", *Practical Insights*, *Taxnet Pro* Tax Disputes Centre (Nov. 2020, 47pp).

Precedent (previous cases): See the Introduction, under subheading "Precedent".

Recusal by a judge is rare, but was done by Bocock J (as case management judge) in *Cooper*, 2017 TCC 36, due to absurd claims by the CBC that his attending a Cdn Tax Foundation reception sponsored by Dentons was wrong when the firm had some involvement with the appeal. See also *McKesson Canada*, 2014 TCC 266 (discussed in Notes to 247(2)), where Boyle J issued a decision, then recused himself from the remaining issues (including costs) because he was offended by accusations against him in McKesson's FCA factum. A judge will not recuse him/herself merely because a party alleges bias due to that judge's earlier decisions: *Olumide*, 2017 FCA 42, para. 6; *Gordon*, 2017 FC 454, para. 6; *Faas v. CAMH*, 2018 ONSC 3323 (aff'd on other grounds 2019 ONCA 192). Allegations of judge bias "are serious allegations which should not be made lightly": *Truong*, 2018 FCA 6, para. 20 (leave to appeal denied 2018 CarswellNat 5785 (SCC)), and the test for finding bias is high: *Lee*, 2018 FC 504, para. 17 (aff'd on other grounds 2020 FCA 17); *Hokhold*, 2018 FCA 163, para. 7; and can trigger costs as being "scandalous": *Chin*, 2021 FCA 16, para. 8.

Replacement by the Chief Justice of a TCC judge who takes too long to issue a decision is invalid, and the second judge's decision is a nullity: *High-Crest*, 2017 FCA 88; *Birchcliff Energy*, 2017 FCA 89. (It would seem that unappealed decisions in the same situation, such as *Yunus*, 2015 TCC 272, *Kuchta*, 2015 TCC 289 and *Romanza Soins Capillaires*, 2015 TCC 328, are also nullities.)

Rule 58 hearings (to shorten a trial): see Notes to 174(1).

Security for costs may be required from a non-resident appellant under the General Procedure: Rule 160; *Mathias*, 2017 FCA 19 (appealing a $9,000 order resulted in it increasing to $13,850); *Sweetman*, 2020 TCC 36 ($19,375 required to continue appeal of donation shelter TCC previously rejected); or from an insolvent appellant: *CO2 Solution (Bresse Syndic)*, 2020 FCA 153.

Self-represented appellants: the judge and Dept. of Justice counsel should provide some assistance: *Alex Excavating*, [1995] G.S.T.C. 57 (TCC), footnote 2; *Poulton*, [2002] 2 C.T.C. 2405 (TCC), para. 18; *Pytel*, 2009 TCC 615, para. 42; *Sugnanam*, 2012 TCC 100. paras. 12, 15; *Kotilainen*, 2017 TCC 7, paras. 5, 35; *Johnson*, 2018 TCC 201, paras. 100-115 (FCA appeal [as *The Butler Did It*] discontinued A-363-18) (judges are traditionally passive in Canada's adversarial (not inquisitorial) judicial system, but can intervene to see justice done, especially if taxpayer is self-represented). See also André Gallant, "The Tax Court's Informal Procedure and Self-Represented Litigants", 53(2) *Canadian Tax Journal* 333-66 (2005); Associate Chief Justice Lamarre & Ranxi, "Taxpayer Rights and Voluntary Compliance", 84(1) *Tax Notes International* (taxnotes.com) 61-68 (Oct. 3, 2016).

Settlement conferences: see Notes to 169(3).

Status hearing: If an appeal does not move forward or a taxpayer does not comply with ongoing Orders to complete steps, the Court will schedule a "status hearing" or "show cause" hearing (General Procedure) or schedule the trial (Informal Procedure), and if the taxpayer does not provide sufficient explanation or appear, the appeal may be dismissed for delay or "want of prosecution": e.g., *Ghaffar*, 2016 FCA 33; *Samson*, 2016 FCA 169; *Paradissis*, 2019 FCA 70; *Di Mauro*, 2019 FCA 106; *Pike*, 2019 FCA 164; *McGuire*, 2019 FCA 242; *Sher-E-Punjab Radio*, 2020 FCA 206; *Blais*, 2014 TCC 354; *Wolsey*, 2016 TCC 236 (FCA appeal dismissed for delay A-438-16); *Exacte*, 2018 TCC 137; *Nott Estate*, 2019 TCC 107. Dismissal can be set aside on motion if the taxpayer gives good reason, e.g. *Izumi*, 2014 TCC 108 (Izumi had moved and provided new address to CRA but not the TCC); *Akanda Innovation*, 2018 FCA 200 (allowed extension of time to apply to set aside dismissal); or if the TCC breached natural justice: *Kibalian*, 2019 FCA 160, para. 11 (dismissal for failing to pay outstanding costs award, without hearing submissions).

Summary judgment is not available in the TCC, although a motion can be brought to dismiss an appeal as frivolous and vexatious: *Cockeram*, 2003 TCC 510, para. 20; *Morissette*, 2019 TCC 103, para. 30.

Transitional rules in the Act should be interpreted in the taxpayer's favour: *Bow River*, [1997] 3 C.T.C. 397 (FCA), para. 31; *Trade Investments*, 1996 CarswellNat 2771 (FCA), paras. 7-8; *Imapro*, 1992 CarswellNat 337 (FCTD), para. 29.

Vexatious litigant (VL): In any court, a person who repeatedly brings meritless proceedings can be declared a VL and barred from filing anything without leave of the Court, e.g. *Prefontaine*, 2004 TCC 775; *Shannon*, 2016 TCC 255; *Mehedi*, 2019 ONSC 1774; *Industrial Alliance v. Morrissette*, 2020 ONSC 5177; *Green v. Univ. of Winnipeg*, 2020 MBCA 49 (leave to appeal denied 2021 CarswellMan 77 (SCC)); *Hayden*, 2020 ABCA 37 (leave to appeal denied 2021 CarswellAlta 657). This is much easier since *Olumide*, 2017 FCA 42: e.g. *Wilson*, 2017 FC 817; *Desrosiers*, 2018 TCC 251 (FCA appeal dismissed for delay A-51-19); *Simon*, 2019 FCA 28; *Bernard*, 2019 FCA 144; *Lessard-Gauvin*, 2021 FCA 94; *Coady*, 2020 FCA 154. (On the criteria for granting leave see *Bernard*.) Such a finding does not automatically apply to other Courts, but a Court may more strictly "regulate" a person found to be a VL by another Court: *Fabrikant*, 2018 FCA 206, 2018 FCA 224, 2019 FCA 198. In *Virgo*, 2019 FCA 167, Olumide's spouse filed an appeal that was really his. It was dismissed, and both were warned that future attempts to circumvent the VL order would risk imprisonment for contempt of Court.

Who can appeal: in *Straessle*, 2018 TCC 144, a non-executor beneficiary could appeal an assessment of a Quebec deceased's (wound-up) estate, since 248(1)"person" include heirs. See also "Bankrupt persons" and "Dissolved corporations" above.

Wrong appeal procedure: An appeal that should have been filed under another statute within TCC jurisdiction (GST, EI, CPP) can possibly be amended by the Court so it is still valid: *Toole*, 2010 TCC 270 and *Brown*, 2010 TCC 229; but the Court may refuse: *Aumuller*, [2001] 3 C.T.C. 2665 (TCC); *Holte*, [2003] 2 C.T.C. 2060 (TCC); *Neptune Service*, 2017 TCC 248 (extension of time for EI/CPP appeal could not be obtained with ITA appeal). A single Notice of Appeal can possibly be filed together for income tax, EI and CPP: *Holmes*, [2000] 3 C.T.C. 2235 (TCC), paras. 6-7; *4528957 Manitoba Ltd.*, 2009 TCC 298, para. 29. Where a taxpayer appealed 2 years and the second year was still under objection, but CRA confirmed the assessment before trial, the TCC ordered that the second year was validly under appeal: *Verones*, 2012 TCC 291, para. 3 (aff'd on other grounds 2013 FCA 69); but declined to do this in *Li*, 2011 TCC 416, when only one year was under appeal.

A "quick assessment" issued automatically on filing can be appealed, even though the CRA has not yet audited the return: *Imperial Oil*, [2003] 4 C.T.C. 177 (FCA).

A nil assessment cannot be appealed (e.g., to change a loss calculation); see Notes to 152(1.1). An earlier assessment cannot be appealed after a reassessment, as the earlier assessment is a nullity: *Abrahams*, [1966] C.T.C. 690 (Exch. Ct.), para. 9; *Yarmoloy*, 2014 TCC 27; *Nagel*, 2018 TCC 32, para. 11. The taxpayer's options on reassessment of a year already under appeal are: file an objection, appeal the reassessment to the TCC, or amend the existing appeal: *Fio Corp.*, 2014 TCC 58, para. 43 (rev'd without discussing this point 2015 FCA 236). If a reassessment is vacated, the previous assessment is revived: *Lornport Investments*, [1992] C.T.C. 3512 (FCA), para. 8; *Bolton Steel*, 2014 TCC 94, para. 48; *984274 Alberta*, 2019 TCC 85, para. 52 (rev'd on other grounds 2020 FCA 125; leave to appeal denied 2021 CarswellNat 1167 (SCC)).

See Notes to 152(2) re what constitutes a notice of assessment that can be appealed.

Where a corporation succeeds in an appeal of some taxation years but failed to file an objection for later years while the appeal was proceeding, the corporation cannot appeal those later years despite its court success: *Canadian Marconi*, [1991] 2 C.T.C. 352 (FCA); *LJP Sales Agency*, 2007 FCA 114 (see Notes to 152(4.2)).

More on appeals: McMechan & Bourgard, *Tax Court Practice* (Carswell, 2 vols. looseleaf or *Taxnet Pro* Reference Centre); Campbell, *Administration of Income Tax 2020* (Carswell), chap. 13; Gadbois et al., *Le litige fiscal au Québec et au Canada* (Carswell, 2015, 750pp.); Barsalou, "Preparing and Arguing a Tax Appeal", 45(2) *Canadian Tax Journal [CTJ]* 223-59 (1997); Samtani & Kutyan, "Tax Litigation Demystified", 59(3) *CTJ* 527-45 (2011); McNary et al., "Tax Dispute Resolution", 2010 Cdn Tax Foundation conference report, 14:1-16; Samtani, "The Possibilities and Perils of Tax Litigation", 2013 conference report, 38:1-20; Kroft, "Adviser's Toolbox", 2014 conference report, 27:1-14; Samtani, "Litigation", *ibid*, 30:1-9; Belley & Shaughnessey, "Evidence and Procedure", 2015 conference report, 43:1-25; Nurmohamed, "Attending TCC Hearings", 9(1) *Canadian Tax Focus* (ctf.ca) 6-7 (Feb. 2019). See also David Sherman's *Canada GST Service* commentary to *Excise Tax Act* s. 306 (also on *Taxnet Pro*); CRA Appeals Manual chaps. 7, 12.

Rectification

If an appeal would fail because a transaction was not correctly executed, consider seeking "rectification" from a provincial superior court *before* asking CRA or the Tax Court for a decision. (The Tax Court cannot provide rectification or recharacterize transactions: *Kufsky*, 2019 TCC 254, para. 26 (under appeal to FCA).) Provincial law determines the legal relationships to which tax law applies, so CRA is effectively bound by such a retroactive order: *Archambault (Services Environnementaux AES, Riopel)*, 2013 SCC 65, end of para. 45; *Dale*, [1997] 2 C.T.C. 286 (FCA); *Sussex Square*, [2000] 4 C.T.C. 203 (FCA); *Interpretation Act* s. 8.1. No collateral attack on another Court's order is permitted in the TCC: *Dale*; *Yourkin*, 2008 TCC 686 and 2011 TCC 557. However, the TCC may be unwilling to put a case on hold ("hoist into judicial never-never-land") pending an as-yet unfiled rectification application: *Kovarik*, [2001] 2 C.T.C. 2503. A foreign court's rectification order is relevant in Canada but the Tax Court must determine how much weight to give it: *Canadian Forest Navigation*, 2017 FCA 39.

Rectification was severely restricted by the Supreme Court of Canada in *Fairmont Hotels*, 2016 SCC 56. Before *Fairmont*, rectification was often granted where the transaction would have been different if the parties had not been mistaken about the tax consequences. Now it is "limited to cases where the agreement between the parties was not correctly recorded", and "it may not change the agreement in order to salvage what a party hoped to achieve" (para. 3). "Rectification is not equity's version of a mulligan": para. 39. A party seeking rectification must bring "clear, convincing and cogent" evi-

dence "that the true substance of its unilateral intention or agreement with another party was not accurately recorded in the instrument to which it nonetheless subscribed", and this requires "evidence exhibiting a high degree of clarity, persuasiveness and cogency": para. 36. What must be shown is (para. 38): (1) a prior agreement whose terms are definite and ascertainable; (2) the agreement was still in effect when the instrument was executed; (3) the instrument fails to accurately record the agreement; (4) the instrument, if rectified, would carry out the parties' prior agreement; (5) for a unilateral mistake, the party seeking rectification must show the other party knew or ought to have known about the mistake and that permitting it to take advantage of the erroneously drafted agreement would amount to fraud or its equivalent.

Pre-*Fairmont* rectification case law (see these Notes up to the 50th ed.) is irrelevant now. The SCC explicitly (para. 16) overruled *Juliar*, [2001] 4 C.T.C. 45 (Ont CA). However, *5551928 Manitoba* and *Crean* (below) have somewhat revived the doctrine.

Since *Fairmont*, **rectification was granted** in: *Buyting*, 2017 NBQB 190 (B always intended to transfer one property to his son's corp, not his son); *5551928 Manitoba*, 2019 BCCA 376 (capital dividend was intended to be the amount of the capital dividend account); *Crean*, 2019 BCSC 146 (parties intended sale to be for capital gain but advisor overlooked 84.1 [Vukovic, "Rectification Allowed", 27(4) *Canadian Tax Highlights* (ctf.ca) 1-2 (April 2019)]); *2484234 Ontario v. Hanley Park*, 2020 ONCA 273 (non-tax real estate dispute); *Bunton v. FTA*, 2020 ONSC 5463 (B never agreed to be director of FTA; Court declared she never was one, to prevent liability under 227.1).

Since *Fairmont*, **rectification was denied** in: *BC Trust*, 2017 BCSC 209 (retroactive allocation of trust income to beneficiaries); *Greither Estate*, 2017 BCSC 994 (request to change transaction to avoid 212.1); *Buyting* (above) (intention not clear re second property); *Harvest Operations*, 2017 ABCA 393 (parties had agreed to make transaction tax-neutral, but last-minute change triggered capital gain); *Canada Life*, 2018 ONCA 562 (leave to appeal denied 2019 CarswellOnt 3325 (SCC)) (tax plan overlooked 98(5); the requested "equitable remedy" was merely rectification under another name; alternative remedies were to sue the tax advisors or to seek a remission order); *Mandel v. 1909975 Ontario*, 2020 ONSC 5343 (parties' intention was to issue shares they now sought to have declared invalid); *RJ McLeod Investments*, 2021 ABQB 439 (capital dividend declared, intended to be tax-free, but CDA was miscalculated).

Rescission to nullify a contract was granted before *Fairmont*, e.g. *Stone's Jewellery v. Arora*, 2009 ABQB 656 (transaction done under belief it would be tax-free was void *ab initio*); *Pallen Trust*, 2015 BCCA 222 (dividends were expected to be subject to 75(2) but were not due to new case law); *0741508 B.C.*, 2014 BCSC 1791 (land sale to entity that was inadvertently not GST-registered was voided so it could be redone without collecting HST). One expected these cases would no longer apply in light of *Fairmont*; indeed, in *Canada Life* (above), partial rescission was rejected as a way of "fixing" a tax plan that overlooked an ITA provision, as this was just rectification under another name; and in *RJ McLeod Investments*, 2021 ABQB 439, rescission could not be used to nullify capital dividend that was based on a miscalculation. However, in *Collins Family Trust*, 2020 BCCA 196 (leave to appeal to SCC granted to Crown March 25/21, file 39383), on the same facts as *Pallen* (also discussed in 75(2) Notes), rescission was allowed on the basis that *Fairmont* applies only to rectification, not rescission. (See also 9(1) Notes at "Diverting income" re void vs voidable contracts.)

Rectification of a *will* is possible to fix a clerical error, or if the testator's instructions were misunderstood or not carried out by the drafter: *Bank of Nova Scotia Trust v. Haugrud*, 2016 ONSC 8150, para. 15.

In Quebec, rectification (a common-law remedy) was thought unavailable, and only nullification possible under the *Civil Code*. However, the SCC held in *Archambault* (above) that rectification is possible; and in *Jean Coutu Group*, 2016 SCC 55 (issued together with *Fairmont*), that the rules for Quebec are the same as under the common law: there must be a mistake in the way the transaction was expressed, not in the choice of transaction. Again, the pre-*Coutu* case law is now mostly irrelevant; but in *9069-1841 Québec v. Filtrum*, 2011 QCCS 1570, a remedy was available under Quebec *Business Corporations Act* s. 458, "Correction of mistakes".

For Quebec, in *Archambault* (above), para. 50, the SCC stated: "since the parties could not turn back time, they changed the 'legal time' applicable to their agreements... Such a stipulation, although once again subject to the rights of third parties, was valid as between the parties". It thus seems that to be valid against CRA, a Court Order is required as in common-law provinces. The SCC warned at para. 54: "Taxpayers should not view this recognition of the primacy of the parties' internal will — or common intention — as an invitation to engage in bold tax planning on the assumption that it will always be possible for them to redo their contracts retroactively should that planning fail." (This will be even more so since *Coutu*.) In *Fournier*, 2018 QCCQ 786, para. 107, a corrected notarial deed was accepted as reflecting ownership of a condo as originally intended.

CRA should be notified of a rectification application, and the Courts will allow it to participate: *Columbia North Realty*, 2005 NSSC 212; *Aim Funds*, [2009] G.S.T.C. 169 (Ont. SC) (by issuing an assessment CRA becomes a "creditor" of the taxpayer with an interest in the case); *Lau*, 2014 BCSC 2384, paras. 163-182. However, *Brogan Family Trust*, 2014 ONSC 6354, held that if no assessment has been issued, CRA is not yet a creditor and need not be notified; and 10 months' delay from when CRA learned about the rectification order meant it did not act "forthwith" in moving to set it aside. If no notice was given, CRA may still be bound to accept the facts determined by the order (it might be able to obtain leave to appeal it). However, in Quebec, CRA must be made a party (*Archambault* (above), para. 51), as otherwise it is not bound by a declaratory judgment: *A v. B*, 2013 QCCS 575; *Bourgault*, 2019 TCC 6, para. 55. See also Bruce

Russell [before he became a TCC judge], "Rectification Applications — Notice or Not?", 11(11) *Tax Hyperion* (Carswell) 6-7 (Nov. 2014).

Court applications for rectification are reviewed (to decide whether to oppose them) by the Dept. of Justice's Rectification Committee. As of June 2019, its members are: Christa Akey (Vancouver); Valerie Meyer (Edmonton); Anne Jinnouchi (Saskatoon); Larissa Benham (Winnipeg); Diana Aird [National Coordinator] and Alisa Apostle (Toronto); Chris Kitchen (Ottawa); Antonia Paraherakis [National Coordinator] (Montreal); Greg King (Halifax). The committee considered 23 cases in 2004, 28 in 2005, 28 in 2006, 36 in 2007 and 51 in Jan.-Aug. 2008 (*Access to Information Act* disclosure; "no records exist" for later years). Most requests relate to simple mistakes in documents, such as mathematical errors, and are not opposed.

CRA generally accepts a rectification order, but may challenge it if the order was obtained without notifying CRA or if rectification is used to "fix aggressive tax plans that are uncovered on audit": *Income Tax Technical News* 22; VIEWS doc 2010-0381961E5 (in light of *Fairmont*, this should no longer arise). In *Slate Management*, 2017 ONCA 763, rectification was ordered and the Crown appealed but neglected to seek a stay of the order; the provincial corporation authority's cancelling an amalgamation and changing articles of incorporation were valid, so the Crown's appeal was dismissed as moot.

CRA settlement offers may ask the taxpayer to promise not to seek rectification, in addition to waiving appeal rights (see 169(2.2)): e.g. *Remtilla*, 2015 TCC 200, para. 21.

Discontinuing a rectification application and then bringing a different one was not prohibited by "cause of action estoppel" in *Lau*, 2014 BCSC 2384, paras. 28-58.

Rectification does not always accomplish its goal: see Notes to 18(1)(e) re *General Motors*. In *Demers*, 2014 TCC 368, amounts extracted from the taxpayers' RRSPs were taxed even though the contracts under which this was done were nullified by the Quebec Superior Court. In *Foster*, 2015 TCC 334, rectification during the objection stage solved a problem, but CRA was allowed by 152(5) to reassess to apply tax calculated differently, since the crux of the reassessment was the same. In *Anderson v. Benson Trithardt*, 2016 SKCA 120 (leave to appeal denied 2017 CarswellSask 79 (SCC)), rectification was granted but not retroactively, so it did not solve the taxpayers' problem. In *St-Pierre*, 2018 FCA 144, a capital dividend was overpaid due to miscalculation of the capital dividend account; after the Quebec Superior Court nullified the dividend, the TCC held the cash paid was included in S's income under 15(2), and created deemed interest under 80.4; but the FCA overruled this (apparently ignoring the retroactive effect of the QSC order).

For a trust, see David Thompson, "Nullifying Catastrophic Trustee Decisions", 4(4) *Tax for the Owner-Manager* (ctf.ca) 6-7 (Oct. 2004); *Futter v. HMRC*, [2013] UKSC 26 (UK Supreme Court: conditions for setting aside a trust). In *Sheila Holmes Spousal Trust*, 2013 ABQB 489, the Court declined to issue a declaration on a trust's validity, as this was the core issue in a dispute over which the TCC would have jurisdiction. On whether a person with Power of Attorney can use it to create a trust without a Court order, see VIEWS doc 2014-0523331C6 [2014 CALU q.6]. The provincial *Variation of Trusts Act* or similar legislation may allow a change, by Court order or by amending the trust document: Roth et al., *Canadian Taxation of Trusts* (ctf.ca, 2016), pp. 625-67; *Waters' Law of Trusts in Canada* (Carswell, 4th ed., 2012), chap. 27 "Variation of Trusts"; *Oosterhoff on Trusts* (Carswell, 9th ed., 2019), §6.5; Crowell, "Variations of Trusts", 9(6) *Tax Hyperion* (Carswell) 5-6 (June 2012); Gilbert, "Variations of Personal Trusts", 2013 Prairie Provinces Tax Conf. (ctf.ca), 3B:1-17. In *Fishleigh-Eaton v. Eaton-Kent*, 2013 ONSC 7985, non-retroactive variation of a trust was ordered to allow encroachment on capital, so that a 107(2) rollout could be used to avoid a 104(4)-triggered capital gain. In *Shinewald*, 2014 MBQB 254, a trust was varied to make X an income beneficiary where he was not originally intended to be, so the variation was non-retroactive. In *Kaleidescape v. Computershare*, 2014 ONSC 4983, a trust deed was rectified to fit the parties' original intention that a company not be controlled by non-residents so that it would be a CCPC (this would not be done now due to *Fairmont*). Rectification of a trust "appointment" (distribution to the settlor) was allowed in *Kennedy*, [2014] EWHC 4129 (England, Chancery Divn).

Rectification may also be allowed by statute, e.g. "Remedying corporate mistakes" in BC *Business Corporations Act* s. 229; but in *Greither Estate*, 2017 BCSC 994, the s. 229 conditions were not met.

For more on rectification since *Fairmont*, see MacDougall, *Mistake in Contracting* (LexisNexis, 2018), chap. 5, "Rectification"; Swan et al., *Canadian Contract Law* (4th ed., LexisNexis, 2018), §8.3.2; Sandler & Chen, "Make No Mistake About It", 65(1) *Canadian Tax Journal* 147-58 (2017); Sharlow & Cook, "Equitable Remedies and Fixing Corporate Mistakes Under the British Columbia *Business Corporations Act*", 2017 BC Tax Conference (ctf.ca); Agioritis, "Is Rectification Still a Remedy?", 2017 Prairie Provinces Tax Conf.; O'Brien, "Rectification in Tax Law", *Income Tax at 100 Years* (ctf.ca, 2017), pp. 14:1-22; Fitzsimmons & Roth, "Rectification, Rescission and Other Equitable Remedies", 2017 Cdn Tax Foundation conference report, 30:1-63; Aird, "Limitations of Equitable Remedies", *ibid*, 31:1-9; Pandher, "Rectification: Where Are We Now?", 9(2) *Canadian Tax Focus* (ctf.ca) 2 (May 2019). [Articles listed here up to the 50th ed. are no longer useful due to *Fairmont*.]

If there is no rectification, CRA will not accept backdating: VIEWS docs 9613507 (changing owner-manager salary to loan repayment after year-end), 2008-0269671E5, 2009-0338861E5. Retroactive change by journal entry is invalid if it is "creating out of airy nothing transactions ... that were not even a gleam in anybody's eye", but may be valid if a "quantification of taxable benefits for a prior year of a manager/shareholder": *King*, [1995] 1 C.T.C. 2353 (TCC); *Kaiser*, 2008 TCC 84. *Maxi Maid*, 2012 TCC 178, allowed a retroactive change from dividend to salary and cancelled the penalty as-

sessed: "It is not uncommon for small businesses to sort out at year end how the owner/manager is to be paid. The Minister's position would require that this decision be made at the time of each and every draw made by a company to its owner/manager. That is not in line with commercial reality" (para. 14). *Contra*, post-year-end recharacterizations of payments were rejected in: *Wood*, [1988] 1 C.T.C. 2312 (TCC) (dividend declared after year-end); *Irmen*, 2006 TCC 475; *Gestion Foret-Dale Inc.*, 2009 TCC 255; *Bibby*, 2009 TCC 588; *Johnson*, 2012 TCC 399, para. 48 (expenses could not be reclassified after audit); *Trower*, 2019 TCC 77 (corp's payments to joint bank account were not dividends to separated spouse); *Park Avenue Furniture*, 2019 TCC 94 (salary payments to family members, recharacterized as draws on shareholder loan account late in the year to reclaim cash flow from withholdings, were still salary). See also "Backdating" in Ruby & Roth, "Fixing Mistakes", 2009 Ontario Tax Conference (ctf.ca), 14:1-46; Gill, "Documenting Transactions: Backdating and Rectification", 2009 BC Tax Conference (ctf.ca), 15:1-23; Beaubier et al., "Some Do's and Don'ts in Documenting Transactions and Fixing Mistakes", 2010 Prairie Provinces Tax Conf. 6:1-42; Nightingale & Sorensen, "Backdating of Dividends", 2392 *Tax Topics* (CCH) 1-4 (Jan. 11, 2018). In *Twomey*, 2012 TCC 310, inadvertent issuance of only 1 share when 100 shares were intended to be issued was corrected by directors' resolution and retroactively met the holding period required by 110.6(14)(f) for the capital gains exemption, without needing a rectification order. This seems counter to other case law: Studniberg, "Self-Help Versus Rectification", 2(4) *Canadian Tax Focus* (ctf.ca) 3-4 (Nov. 2012).

Recognizing an oral contract can be another solution. Most contracts can be oral: Fridman, *The Law of Contracts in Canada* (Carswell, 6th ed., 2011), chapter 6, "Writing". Oral agreements were accepted as credible without written contracts in *Mountain v. TD*, 2012 ONCA 806; *Connolly*, 2016 TCC 139, paras. 27-30; *Black*, 2019 TCC 135, para. 129; *Brown*, 2020 TCC 45, paras. 24, 67. See also "Oral evidence" in 152(7) Notes. An oral contract can be buttressed by being "reduced to writing" later (advisable when dealing with CRA): *McClain Industries*, [1978] C.T.C. 511 (FCTD), para. 90; *Dilorenzo*, [1982] C.T.C. 151 (FCTD), para. 12; *Bouchard*, [1983] C.T.C. 173 (FCTD); *Van Der Haegen*, [1987] 1 C.T.C. 2193 (TCC), para. 14; *Spence*, [1995] 2 C.T.C. 2911 (TCC), para. 2; *UBS Securities v. Sands Bros.*, 2009 ONCA 328; *MRR v. JM*, 2017 ONSC 2655 (pre-conception oral contract, documented post-birth).

Jurisdiction

Federal Courts Act s. 18.5 prohibits an application for judicial review in Federal Court (see Notes to 171(1)) if an appeal is available to the TCC, which has exclusive jurisdiction over assessment appeals under *Tax Court of Canada Act* s. 12: *Addison & Leyen Ltd.*, 2007 SCC 33 (reversing the FCA). (152(8) may be another reason the FC cannot vacate an assessment.) The SCC stated at para. 8: "Judicial review is available, provided the matter is not otherwise appealable. It is also available to control abuses of power, including abusive delay" (para. 8).

However, judicial review is unavailable even to address abuse by CRA, if the abuse relates to issuing an assessment; the only remedy is to appeal the assessment or sue later for damages (see Notes to 171(1)). "The Federal Court does not have the jurisdiction to order the Minister to vacate tax assessments": *Redeemer Foundation*, 2008 SCC 46, para. 28. The leading case analyzing this issue in detail is *JP Morgan Asset Management*, 2013 FCA 250.

Other cases where the FC had no jurisdiction: *Webster*, 2003 FCA 388; *Roitman*, 2006 FCA 266 (leave to appeal denied 2006 CarswellNat 4148 (SCC)); *FMC Technologies*, 2009 FCA 217 (leave to appeal denied 2010 CarswellNat 33); *Tele-Mobile*, 2011 FCA 89 (leave to appeal denied [2012] G.S.T.C. 29) (FC has no jurisdiction to prevent CRA issuing an assessment for the wrong reasons or contrary to CRA guidelines); *Rusnak*, 2011 FCA 181 (FCA) (leave to appeal denied 2011 CarswellNat 4791) (even if no procedural fairness at objection stage); *Conocophillips*, 2014 FCA 297 (leave to appeal denied 2015 CarswellNat 4941) (FC order that CRA reconsider rejection of objection as filed too late was reversed, as this was TCC's jurisdiction); *Johnson*, 2015 FCA 51 (large assessment without factual basis in order to seize cash); *Karam*, 2016 FCA 86 (leave to appeal denied 2016 CarswellNat 4145) (FC could not rule that notice of confirmation set a cap on amount CRA could collect from taxpayer); *Horseman*, 2016 FCA 252 (claim for damages for Requirement to Pay was challenging the assessment); *Valero Energy*, 2020 FCA 68 (FC cannot stop CRA from issuing Requirement under 231.2 or from assessing contrary to prior administrative practice); *Beaudry*, 2001 FCT 1347; *Twentieth Century Fox*, [2001] 2 C.T.C. 63 (FCTD) (aff'd on other grounds 2002 FCA 232); *Angell*, 2005 FC 782; *Verdicchio*, 2010 FC 117 (leave to appeal to SCC denied 2010 CarswellNat 4499); *Moise*, 2012 FC 1468; *General Motors*, 2013 FC 1219; *ColasCanada Inc.*, 2014 FC 452; *Sood*, 2015 FC 857 (FC had no jurisdiction to force CRA to adhere to settlement agreement by issuing an assessment); *Garbutt*, 2016 FC 1292 (FCA dismissed for delay A-450-16) (CRA issued payroll assessment of lawyer who refused to provide files for audit, claiming solicitor-client privilege); *Newton*, 2018 FC 343 (director claimed assessment issued too late but she had not objected in time); *Bjorkman*, 2018 FC 721 (challenge to Child Tax Benefit); *Kerry Canada*, 2019 FC 377, paras. 31-35 (question of whether objection remained valid after a reassessment); *Ghazi*, 2019 FC 860 (attempt to force CRA to change auditors due to alleged bias); *Holland*, 2019 FC 1433 (challenging CRA decision that H was resident in Canada); *Westminster Savings*, 2019 FC 1496 (CRA determination that WS was not a credit union); *MS*, 2020 FC 982 (under appeal to FCA) (attempted class action for parents denied Canada Child Benefit and GST/HST Credit); *Dow Chemical*, 2020 TCC 139 (under appeal by Crown to FCA) (TCC can review CRA 247(10) decision not to make downward transfer-pricing adjustment).

Even FC action to restrain collection on the ground that the assessment is invalid is prohibited by s. 18.5, since the TCC can decide that issue: *Walker*, 2005 FCA 393;

Ritter, 2013 FC 411; *Mason*, 2015 FC 926 (FCA appeal discontinued A-369-15). In *Newcombe*, 2013 FC 955, the taxpayer believed her employer (Justice Canada) should not have issued a T4 and withheld tax from her settlement on termination of employment. The FC agreed the payment was non-taxable but the remedy was to appeal her income tax assessment, as the real issue was within the TCC's jurisdiction (para. 27).

Contra, the FC was held to have jurisdiction in: *Canadian Pacific Railway*, 2013 FC 161 (CP could contest fuel taxes and Large Corporations Tax in the FC on the basis that a historic exemption made such taxes on CP *ultra vires* and in breach of contract); *Sifto Canada*, 2014 FCA 140 (Sifto could proceed with FC application for order that CRA cannot breach agreement not to assess penalties under Voluntary Disclosure Program (but Sifto later won in Tax Court: 2017 TCC 37)); *AFD Petroleum*, 2016 FC 547 (FCA appeal discontinued A-215-16) (CRA refusal to consider amendment to filed return to add SR&ED claim); *Safe Workforce*, 2019 FC 645 (FC refused to strike application for injunction to prevent CRA from finalizing audit before Access to Information disclosure released, but also refused interlocutory injunction); *Iris Technologies*, 2020 FCA 117, para. 51 and 2021 FC 597 (under appeal to FCA) (if CRA assesses for improper purpose or abuses its power); and the bullets listed in Notes to 171(1).

The *JP Morgan* case (2013 FCA 250) has put strict limits on judicial review in the FC, leaving no remedy in many cases. See Russell, "*JP Morgan*", 10(11) *Tax Hyperion* (Carswell) 3-4 (Nov. 2013); Murray, "JP Morgan", 2178 *Tax Topics* (CCH) 1-6 (Dec. 5, 2013); Kreklewetz & Siu, "Judicial Review", 21(12) *Canadian Tax Highlights* (ctf.ca) 2-3 (Dec. 2013); Nitikman, "JP Morgan", 2184 *Tax Topics* 1-5 (Jan. 16, 2014); Studniberg case comment, 62(1) *Canadian Tax Journal* 183-92 (2014); Diep & Marshall, "The Continued Pursuit by Taxpayers for Judicial Review", *Blakes on Canadian Tax Controversy & Tax Litigation* (Carswell) 1-6 (June 2016).

Provincial courts usually refuse to address a matter that can be appealed to the TCC, to which *Tax Court of Canada Act* s. 12 gives exclusive jurisdiction: *422252 Alberta*, 2003 BCSC 1362, *GLP NT Corp.*, [2004] 1 C.T.C. 58 (Ont. SCJ); *Prefontaine v. Paris*, 2007 ABQB 77; *Deep*, 2010 ONCA 678; *Tennant*, 2013 ABCA 81 (leave to appeal denied 2013 CarswellAlta 1179 (SCC)); *Stephkan Holdings*, 2013 QCCA 1651; *Baxter*, 2013 ONSC 3153; *Sheila Holmes Spousal Trust*, 2013 ABQB 489; *JAFT Corp.*, 2014 MBQB 59, para. 26; *Nixon v. Nixon*, 2014 SKQB 264; *Scotia Mortgage v. Gladu*, 2017 BCSC 1182; *Fehrman v. Goodlife*, 2017 ONSC 4348, para. 18; *Grenon*, 2017 ABCA 96, para. 36 (leave to appeal denied 2017 CarswellAlta 1714); *Ludmer*, 2020 QCCA 697, paras. 133-145 (leave to appeal denied 2021 CarswellQue 2160 (SCC)); *Siemens v. Baker*, 2019 SKQB 99, paras. 33-39 (lawsuit was disguised attack on tax assessments); *Mandel v. 1909975 Ontario*, 2020 ONSC 5343 (declaration sought on validity of share issue). (Similarly, a provincial court will decline to address CRA collections or withholding issues, which are FC jurisdiction: *Fazakas*, 2018 NBQB 12; *Rousseau*, 2020 QCCA 1308, paras. 19-27 (leave to appeal denied 2021 CarswellQue 3905 (SCC)).) This is often wise: non-tax judges can err in tax cases by being unfamiliar with the ITA and tax practice (e.g., *Iskander* — see Notes to Reg. 103(4); *CCI Industries*, 2005 ABQB 675, holding an audit proposal letter to be a notice of assessment; *Aim Funds*, [2009] G.S.T.C. 169 (Ont. SCJ), stating that CRA could make itself a company's "creditor", entitled to be notified of a rectification application, by issuing a "ruling"). However, in a civil dispute, a provincial court may need to determine a matter as between the parties (e.g., *RJM56 v. Kurnik*, 2016 ONCA 821); and rectification applications (see above) are within provincial superior court jurisdiction. In unusual cases on whether an entity is subject to tax at all, a provincial court may accept jurisdiction: *British Columbia Investment Management*, 2019 SCC 63, paras. 33-42. Also, rectification cases (see above) involve provincial court declarations affecting tax assessments, e.g. *Danso-Coffey*, 2010 ONCA 171 (declaration that person was not a director); *Orman v. Marnat*, 2012 ONSC 549 (declaration that Ponzi scheme income was return of capital). See also Awad, "Jurisdictional Overlap Between the Tax Court and Provincial Superior Courts", 14(6) *Tax Hyperion* 3-5 (Nov-Dec 2017).

For which court has jurisdiction to hear an appeal of Part XIII non-resident withholding tax or interest thereon, see Notes to 227(7).

If an issue involves double tax imposed by both Canada and another country, consider competent-authority relief instead of an appeal. See Notes to 115.1.

Where tax cannot be legally appealed (e.g. because the assessment is correct or it is too late to appeal) but CRA would like to help, see Notes to 220(3.1) re Remission Orders.

An appeal of only *provincial tax*, such as a provincial tax credit, provincial penalty or provincial tax assessed against a person who claims not to be resident in the province, can be taken only to the provincial court under the province's *Income Tax Act*, even though CRA administers the provincial tax (for Ontario, see CRA Form ON201, Notice of Appeal; an objection must have first been filed with CRA): e.g. *Inwest Investments*, 2015 BCSC 1375; *Karim*, 2016 TCC 91, para. 4. The TCC has ruled it has no jurisdiction to hear such appeals: *Stiege*, [1991] 2 C.T.C. 2005 (ON); *Hennick*, [1998] 4 C.T.C. 2855 (ON); *Gardner*, 2001 FCA 401, leave to appeal denied 2002 CarswellNat 2541 (SCC) (ON); *Wittmer*, [2002] 2 C.T.C. 2097 (BC); *Joshi*, 2003 TCC 615 (SK); *Sutcliffe*, 2004 FCA 376 (all provinces); *Marwaha*, 2004 TCC 781 (ON); *Gray*, 2005 CarswellNat 5053 (ON); *Hiscock*, 2006 TCC 560 [rev'd on other grounds 2007 FCA 382] (NS); *Little*, 2006 TCC 627 (NS); *Boudali*, 2007 TCC 270 (ON); *McKim*, 2007 TCC 351 (NL); *Baluyot*, 2007 TCC 682 (FCA appeal discontinued A-566-07) (ON foreign tax credit); *Ding (Lin)*, 2009 FCA 355; leave to appeal denied 2010 CarswellNat 1227 (SCC) (ON); *Young*, 2009 TCC 423 (AB Royalty Rebate, despite mistake made by CRA); *Quigley*, 2009 FCA 287 (residence in NL vs AB); *Buckingham*, 2010 TCC 247 [aff'd on other grounds 2011 FCA 142] (director liability for source deductions of provincial income tax); *Weinberg Family Trust*, 2016 TCC 37 (FCA appeal on hold pending ONSC decision: A-59-16); *Perron*, 2017 TCC 220 (AB); *Lavrinenko*, 2017 TCC

230, para. 3 (aff'd on other grounds 2019 FCA 51) (ON Child Benefit, Trillium Benefit); *Nagel*, 2018 TCC 32 (under appeal to FCA); *Polubiec*, 2019 TCC 146 (provincial side of 163(1) penalty); *Jersak (Best)*, 2020 TCC 136 (AB Family Employment Tax Credit and Climate Leadership Adjustment Rebate). In *Fontana*, 2008 FCA 172, the appeal was not quashed, as it was not certain that it would affect only ON tax. An appeal of provincial tax should name "Her Majesty the Queen" as respondent: *Smale*, 2009 SKQB 114.

See also Notes to 171(1) re which matters go to the Federal Court instead of the TCC.

Federal Court of Appeal

TCC decisions can be appealed to the FCA, but TCC findings of fact, or mixed fact and law where there is no "extricable legal question", can be overturned only if there is "palpable and overriding error" (*Housen v. Nikolaisen*, 2002 SCC 33; *Vavilov*, 2019 SCC 65, para. 37). "An error is palpable if it is readily apparent and it is overriding if it changes the result": *Fio Corp.*, 2015 FCA 236, para. 10; "it is not enough to pull at leaves and branches and leave the tree standing. The entire tree must fall": *South Yukon Forest*, 2012 FCA 165, para. 46. (There is no appeal from an interlocutory [interim procedural] decision in the Informal Procedure: *Federal Courts Act* s. 27(1.2); *742190 Ontario*, 2010 FCA 162, para. 27; and in general, there is no appeal from a ruling that is not a judgment or Order: *Rahmatian v. HFH Video*, 1991 CanLII 1453 (BCCA); *NB Telephone v. Maryon*, 1980 CanLII 2521 (NBCA).) In rare cases the FCA may substitute its own findings of fact based on the record: see *Carmichael v. GlaxoSmithKline*, 2020 ONCA 447, para. 135 for criteria.

The FCA appeal deadline is 30 days (not including July/August, or any *Time Limits and Other Periods Act (COVID-19)* extension during 2020: see Enacted Amendment above) from the judgment date (*Federal Courts Act* s. 27(2)), not 30 days from when the judgment is sent to the appellant: *Canada Trustco*, 2008 FCA 382; and the date is the oral judgment date, not when a later written judgment is issued: *2786885 Canada*, 2011 FCA 197. Under s. 27(2)(b), the FCA may consider a motion for extension of time to appeal even years later: *Thom*, 2007 FCA 249; *Kane*, 2012 FCA 309. Extension of time requires consideration of "(1) whether there is an arguable case on appeal, (2) whether there are special circumstances that justify the delay in commencing the appeal, (3) whether there was a continuing intention to appeal, (4) whether the delay has been excessive, and (5) whether the respondent will be prejudiced if the extension of time is granted": *Abbott Laboratories*, 2003 FCA 333, followed in many tax cases such as *Canada Trustco* (above); *Faith Assemblies*, 2009 FCA 318; *Cranston*, 2010 FCA 327 and 2011 FCA 5; *Kaur*, 2011 FCA 292; *Doray*, 2014 FCA 87; *Toby Creek*, 2014 FCA 94. The FCA has discretion to waive the $50 appeal fee: *Fabrikant*, 2014 FCA 89. On whether a non-lawyer can represent a party at the FCA, see para. "Lawyer required" above.

On an FCA appeal, the Court will admit new evidence (*Federal Courts Rules* r. 351) only if it is credible, "practically conclusive" of the appeal, and could not with due diligence have been led at the TCC: *Shire Canada v. Apotex*, 2011 FCA 10; *Barry*, 2014 FCA 280, para. 6; *Archibald*, 2018 FCA 2, para. 3; *Coady*, 2019 FCA 102, para. 3; *Iris Technologies*, 2020 FCA 117, paras. 25-30; *Pomeroy Acquireco*, 2020 FCA 221 (new evidence allowed). The FCA *may* entertain a new argument not raised at the TCC if no further evidence is required: *Zhu*, 2016 FCA 113, para. 4; *Revcon Oilfield*, 2017 FCA 22, para. 4; *SCDA*, 2017 FCA 177, para. 18; *Eli Lilly v. Teva*, 2018 FCA 53, paras. 44-45; *Atlantic Packaging*, 2020 FCA 75 (new case law may justify a new argument: para. 32) (leave to appeal denied 2020 CarswellNat 4337 (SCC)). Counsel on an FCA appeal should be prepared to discuss the French wording of the legislation, as the 3-judge panel will likely include a francophone (about half of the judges), and FCA decisions always quote both French and English text. See end of Notes to *Interpretation Act* s. 8.1. Each side normally has only 1 hour to present their argument. For further practical advice see Pooja Samtani, "Appellate Litigation", 2012 Tax Dispute Resolution conf. report (ctf.ca), 10:1-15.

See Notes to 247(2) re *McKesson Canada*, where the TCC judge criticized the appellant's FCA factum and recused himself from further dealings on the case.

The Crown appeals a decision only if the CRA Adverse Decision Committee so recommends: *CRA Appeals Manual* §7.18. As of fall 2020, the committee members for income tax appeals were: Cathy Hawara [Chair, 613-960-2388] (Assistant Commissioner Appeals); Sue Murray, Annie Crousset, Nicole Mondou, plus the manager and appeals officer in the case (Appeals Branch); Frank Vermaeten, Ted Gallivan, Marc Lemieux, Geoff Trueman and Lorraine Redekop (other CRA); Brian Ernewein (Finance); Shalene Curtis-Micallef, Daniel Bourgeois and Patrick Vezina (Justice). The committee considered 8 cases in the year ended March 31, 2020, deciding to appeal none and seek leave to appeal in 1. From April-Oct. 2020 it considered 2 cases, deciding to seek leave in 1 and not to seek leave in 1.

For more on this committee see *GST Times* 251C (Carswell, Oct. 2010); Padina, "Canada Revenue Agency Clarifies Position in Deciding Not to Appeal", 67(5) *Tax Notes International* (taxnotes.com) 453-56 (July 30, 2012) (discusses why CRA did not appeal *Velcro*, *Lipson*, *Messar-Splinter*, *Transalta* and *McClarty Family Trust*). If the Crown appeals an Informal-Procedure decision, it must pay the taxpayer's "reasonable and proper" (meaning actual: *Furukawa*, 2003 FCA 183) legal fees: *Tax Court of Canada Act* s. 18.25. See, e.g., *Tallon*, 2015 FCA 156, para. 45; *770373 Ontario*, [1997] G.S.T.C. 1 (FCA), para. 3.

From the Federal Court of Appeal, appeal to the Supreme Court of Canada is permitted only with leave. An application for leave to appeal must be filed within 60 days, excluding days in July: *Supreme Court Act* s. 58 (TLOPA extends this during 2020: see Enacted Amendment above). An FCA ruling cannot be appealed to the FCA itself: *Raincoast Conservation*, 2019 FCA 259.

See also Chan, "Federal Appellate Courts", *Practical Insights*, *Taxnet Pro* Tax Disputes Centre (Nov. 2020, 54pp).

169(1) closing words amended by 2010 budget bill #2, effective Dec. 15, 2010, to change "mailed" to "sent" (to accommodate electronic notices under 244(14.1)).

Information Circulars: 98-1R5: Tax collection policies.

CRA Audit Manual: 10.5.0: Audit evidence; 19.3.0: Appeals.

Forms: ON200: Notice of appeal (Ontario tax); P148: Resolving your dispute: objections and appeal rights under the *Income Tax Act* [pamphlet]; T400A: Objection — ITA. (The prescribed form does not have to be used, however. See 165(2)).

(1.1) Ecological gifts — Where at any particular time a taxpayer has disposed of a property, the fair market value of which has been confirmed or redetermined by the Minister of the Environment under subsection 118.1(10.4), the taxpayer may, within 90 days after the day on which that Minister has issued a certificate under subsection 118.1(10.5), appeal the confirmation or redetermination to the Tax Court of Canada.

Related Provisions: 171(1.1) — Powers of Tax Court on appeal; 244(14), (14.1) — Date when notice sent; *Interpretation Act* 27(5) — Meaning of "within 90 days".

Notes: 169(1.1) added by 2000 Budget, for gifts after Feb. 27, 2000.

(2) Limitation of right to appeal from assessments or determinations — Notwithstanding subsection (1), where at any time the Minister assesses tax, interest, penalties or other amounts payable under this Part by, or makes a determination in respect of, a taxpayer

(a) under subsection 67.5(2) or 152(1.8), subparagraph 152(4)(b)(i) or subsection 152(4.3) or (6), 164(4.1), 220(3.4) or 245(8) or in accordance with an order of a court vacating, varying or restoring the assessment or referring the assessment back to the Minister for reconsideration and reassessment,

(b) under subsection 165(3) where the underlying objection relates to an assessment or a determination made under any of the provisions or circumstances referred to in paragraph (a), or

(c) under a provision of an Act of Parliament requiring an assessment to be made that, but for that provision, would not be made because of subsections 152(4) to (5),

the taxpayer may appeal to the Tax Court of Canada within the time limit specified in subsection (1), but only to the extent that the reasons for the appeal can reasonably be regarded

(d) where the assessment or determination was made under subsection 152(1.8), as relating to any matter specified in paragraph 152(1.8)(a), (b) or (c), and

(e) in any other case, as relating to any matter that gave rise to the assessment or determination

and that was not conclusively determined by the Court, and this subsection shall not be read or construed as limiting the right of the taxpayer to appeal from an assessment or a determination issued or made before that time.

Related Provisions: 165(1.1) — Limitation of right to object to assessments or determinations.

Notes: 169(2) provides that, where a reassessment is made after the normal deadline under a special provision (such as those allowing for consequential assessment), the taxpayer cannot use that as an excuse to open up a return that was otherwise statute-barred and claim additional deductions or credits beyond those that are the subject of the special reassessment. (See 165(1.1) for the same rule as it applies to objections.)

169(2) also provides that once a matter has gone to Court, new issues cannot be raised. "Once an appeal has been commenced it is for the appellant's entire taxation year ...there has to be an end somewhere": *Armstrong*, 2004 TCC 348; aff'd 2006 FCA 119. "The right of appeal in subsection 169(2) does not displace or diminish the doctrine of *res judicata*": *Armstrong* (FCA), para. 28. In the same vein, see also *Coutre*, 2009 TCC 456; *Jenner*, 2010 TCC 523 ("chose jugée", in Quebec: *Charbonneau*, "Préclusion, *res judicata* et préclusion", 93 *Canadian Bar Review* 373-409 (2015)); *Mailloux*, 2012 FCA 331 (after consent judgment); *Lytle*, 2012 TCC 368. See also Spiro, "Should the Crown Move to Strike Out Judicial Review Applications in the Federal Court when the Impugned Decision Culminates in an Assessment?", 2012 Tax Dispute Resolution conf. report (ctf.ca), 4:1-19; Chasson, "A Challenge to a Reassessment Masquerading as an Application for Judicial Review", *ibid.*, 5:1-12.

In *Struck*, 2017 FCA 69, a consent judgment determining "taxable capital gains" (TCG) for a year precluded claiming a 40(1)(a)(iii) reserve, since TCG is based on the gain in 40(1). In *MacDonald*, 2021 FCA 6, an FCA costs award of TCC costs could not

be revisited after further appeal to the SCC, due to *res judicata* (the parties should have advised the FCA about separate costs proceedings underway).

Even without 169(2), issue estoppel, *res judicata* or "abuse of process" prevents an issue being relitigated: *Chevron Canada*, [1999] 3 C.T.C. 140 (FCA); *Goodfellow*, 2010 FCA 23, para. 5 (Court's determination of tax liability is final and precludes raising new arguments not raised at first trial); *742190 Ontario*, 2010 FCA 162, para. 44 (TCC Informal Procedure interlocutory decision is binding on the parties even if it has "no precedential value" for other cases); *Laquerre*, 2016 FCA 62, paras. 66-68 (related creditor affected by FC order charging property, but who chose not to participate in hearing, could not challenge order years later); *Lee*, 2020 FCA 17 (lawsuit re previously decided tax appeals); *Boily*, 2021 FCA 23 (*res judicata*, issue estoppel, collateral attack and abuse of process are "complementary and interrelated, and more than one doctrine may support a particular outcome": para. 41); *Wilson*, 2013 FC 39 (extension of time to appeal denied, 13-A-20 (FCA), leave to appeal denied 2014 CarswellOnt 13767 (SCC)) (where appeal dismissed due to unfulfilled discovery undertakings so substantive issue never litigated, it would abuse Court's process to let appellant try again); *Watts*, 2019 FC 1321; *Modlivco Inc.*, 1996 CarswellNat 1625 (TCC) (CRA cannot reassess on issue not addressed by TCC in appeal); *Rogic*, [2001] G.S.T.C. 107 (TCC) (GST consent judgment was binding for income tax); *Greenstreet*, 2004 TCC 194; *McFadyen*, 2008 TCC 441 (FCA appeal discontinued A-479-08); *Yee*, 2012 TCC 275; *Klundert*, 2013 TCC 208; *Mosher*, 2013 TCC 378 (premature to strike issue from notice of appeal); *Abrametz*, 2014 TCC 227 (arguments not raised on initial appeal could not be raised on appeal of reassessment implementing Court's judgment). A partnership discontinuing an appeal of denied losses did not stop the partners from appealing their assessments: see Notes to 152(1.7) re *Tedesco*. In *Accurso (Bruno)*, 2020 QCCQ 3001, the Court of Quebec refused to revisit a *Jarvis* decision (see 231.2(1) Notes) despite a new, contrary Court of Appeal judgment on the same facts. See also Lange, *The Doctrine of Res Judicata in Canada* (LexisNexis, 4th ed., 2015, 588pp); Handley, *Res Judicata* (LexisNexis UK, 5th ed., 2019, 446pp); Turnell, "Second Chances in Tax Litigation", 2(4) *Canadian Tax Focus* (ctf.ca) 9-10 (Nov. 2012). See Notes to 239(1) re the impact of a tax evasion criminal conviction or acquittal on a TCC appeal. The Supreme Court of Canada addressed issue estoppel in (non-tax cases) *Danyluk v. Ainsworth Technologies*, 2001 SCC 44; *Penner v. Niagara*, 2013 SCC 19; and the Ont. CA discussed abuse of process in *Wright v. Urbanek*, 2019 ONCA 823 (leave to appeal denied 2020 CarswellOnt 4940).

Some cases have said that a decided issue can be raised for a different year and must be considered anew, especially if new evidence can be led: *Victoriaville (Commission Scolaire)*, [2002] G.S.T.C. 49 (TCC); *Merrins*, 2006 TCC 281; *General Electric*, 2011 TCC 564; *Kreuz*, 2012 TCC 238; *Peach*, 2020 TCC 12, para. 8 (under appeal to FCA); Siegal, "Court Permits Pleading of Previously Rejected Arguments", XVII(3) *Tax Litigation* (Federated Press) 1116-20 (2012). *Contra*, see *Leduc*, [2002] 2 C.T.C. 2735 (TCC), where a finding of permanent disability was binding on CRA for a later year; *Yevzeroff*, 2014 TCC 145, where denied GST input tax credits could not be claimed for a later year (thus, a denied income tax loss cannot be relitigated as a carryforward in a later year); *Yourkin*, 2014 TCC 48 and 2016 TCC 111, where the deduction (for support) being claimed had failed in earlier appeals. Whether an appeal of the same issue is barred for a later year was to be considered under Rule 58 (see 174(1) Notes), in *Ironside*, 2015 TCC 116 (but TCC appeal discontinued Sept. 2016: 2014-1619(IT)G).

In *Priftis*, 2012 TCC 414, para. 20, an out-of-court settlement did not bind P for a future directors' liability appeal (see also Notes to 227.1(1) re a director contesting the underlying corporate liability). A consent judgment has no precedential value for other cases: see Notes to 221.2. An Agreed Statement of Facts in a prosecution plea bargain did not bind CRA (and issue estoppel did not apply), as CRA could reassess for more tax than the evasion conviction: *McIntyre*, 2014 TCC 111.

Where the identical issue was decided by a different court (e.g., Court of Quebec on an appeal under parallel provincial tax law), the TCC will refuse to rehear the issue, based on "abuse of process" and judicial comity, and the Quebec court will normally do the same for a TCC decision: *Houda International*, 2010 TCC 622; *Congiu*, 2014 FCA 73 (leave to appeal denied 2014 CarswellQue 8554 (SCC)); *Construction S.Y.L. Tremblay*, 2018 QCCA 552; *Carrier*, 2017 QCCQ 7738; *TricomCanada*, 2020 QCCQ 8827; but in *Menasse*, 2020 QCCQ 1829, the TCC's oral reasons were not sufficiently detailed for this to apply. (In earlier cases, issues were relitigated: *Victoriaville (Commission Scolaire)*, [2003] G.S.T.C. 122 (TCC); *Invera Inc.*, 2005 TCC 72; *Passucci*, 2007 FCA 155 (leave to appeal denied [2007] G.S.T.C. 129); *Ross*, 2010 FC 921; *Patterson Dental*, 2014 TCC 62, paras. 41-45. In *Bombardier Inc.*, 2013 QCCA 947, para. 3, an FCA decision on Part I.3 tax applied to Quebec capital tax, but only because the Quebec court adopted it.) See also the Introduction under subheading "Precedent".

See Notes to 239(1) re whether conviction of evasion is proof that the tax is owing.

A decision on the same facts with a *different* taxpayer does not bind the taxpayer (absent an agreement to follow the result in the case): *228262 Alberta*, [1996] 1 C.T.C. 2416 (TCC).

169(2) amended by 1995-97 technical bill, effective for determinations made after June 18, 1998, by 1992 technical bill and by 1991 technical bill.

(2.1) Limitation on appeals by large corporations — Notwithstanding subsections (1) and (2), where a corporation that was a large corporation in a taxation year (within the meaning assigned by subsection 225.1(8)) served a notice of objection to an assessment under this Part for the year, the corporation may appeal to the Tax

Court of Canada to have the assessment vacated or varied only with respect to

(a) an issue in respect of which the corporation has complied with subsection 165(1.11) in the notice, or

(b) an issue described in subsection 165(1.14) where the corporation did not, because of subsection 165(7), serve a notice of objection to the assessment that gave rise to the issue

and, in the case of an issue described in paragraph (a), the corporation may so appeal only with respect to the relief sought in respect of the issue as specified by the corporation in the notice.

Related Provisions: 171(1) — Jurisdiction of Tax Court on appeal.

Notes: See case law in Notes to 165(1.11). See also Notes to 171(1), and *Chevron Canada Resources*, [1999] 3 C.T.C. 140 (FCA). 169(2.1) does not explicitly limit the grounds on which a case can be appealed from the TCC to the FCA, but if certain grounds of appeal are unavailable at the TCC, its decision is not "wrong" in not considering those grounds and thus likely cannot be appealed.

169(2.1) added by 1994 technical bill, for appeals instituted after June 22, 1995.

I.T. Technical News: 32 (notice of objection of large corporation: impact of the *Potash Corp.* case).

(2.2) Waived issues — Notwithstanding subsections (1) and (2), for greater certainty a taxpayer may not appeal to the Tax Court of Canada to have an assessment under this Part vacated or varied in respect of an issue for which the right of objection or appeal has been waived in writing by the taxpayer.

Related Provisions: 165(1.2) — No objection permitted where right to object waived.

Notes: The word "or" in the phrase "right of objection or appeal" is ambiguous. If a taxpayer waived the right of objection but not of appeal, does 169(2.2) apply? Arguably, in such case, the condition that the "right of objection or appeal has been waived" is not met. (In practice CRA requests a waiver of both rights at the same time.) The required elements for waiver are full knowledge of one's rights, and unequivocal and conscious intention to abandon them, communicated to CRA: *Abdalla*, 2019 FCA 5, para. 4 (leave to appeal to SCC requested).

Note, however, that 169(2.2) is "for greater certainty" only. The Supreme Court of Canada confirmed the validity of a waiver of appeal rights in *Smerchanski*, [1976] C.T.C. 488. See also Notes to 169(3) re settlements reached before trial.

A taxpayer who waives appeal rights cannot then sue CRA for wrongfully issuing the assessment: *Roitman*, 2006 FCA 266; leave to appeal denied 2006 CarswellNat 4148 (SCC). Signing a 169(2.2) waiver when settling a 15(1) shareholder-benefit dispute did not estop CRA from assessing the taxpayer under 160(1) on the same transfer: *Parihar*, 2015 TCC 52, paras. 42-45.

169(2.2) was applied to quash appeals in: *Pearce*, 2005 TCC 38 (taxpayer claimed he was forced to sign the waiver by threat of imprisonment, but his claim was disbelieved); *Nguyen*, 2005 TCC 697 (educated taxpayer could not prove he was unable to understand consequences of signing waiver); *Anthony*, 2007 TCC 606 (A claimed duress, but the pressure on him to settle had been from his own accountant); *McGonagle*, 2010 FCA 108 (threatening to close file unless waiver was given was not coercion; the fact the "bottom line" effect of the settlement was costlier than expected did not invalidate the waiver); *M.P.N. Holdings*, 2011 TCC 181 (waiver reserved right to object if retroactive change was made to the Canada-US tax treaty to provide relief to LLCs; change in Tax Court's interpretation of how existing treaty applied to LLCs did not qualify); *Taylor*, 2012 FCA 148 (no "unconscionable bargain", and Court did not believe that T felt "lost" or "devastated" when signing settlement); *Hill*, 2012 TCC 202 (FCA appeal dismissed for delay A-384-12) (H wrote "signed under duress" but his advisor removed those words before sending waiver to CRA and taxpayer ratified that; CRA pressure to settle case was not duress); *Noran West Developments*, 2012 TCC 434 (settlement reached and FCA appeal discontinued, A-552-12) (waiver agreement did not name the parties but it was clear enough and not unconscionable; legality of assessment preceding waiver reassessment not relevant; taxpayer's claimed mistake in agreement's meaning rejected; *Burg Properties*, 2014 FCA 154 (leave to appeal denied 2014 CarswellNat 5185 (SCC)) (basis for adjustments in settlement agreement was the last reassessment, not the original return); *Abdalla*, 2019 FCA 5 (agreement to abide by result in Global Learning [GLGI] lead case was not obtained by coercion and was valid without consideration despite being poorly worded); *Oddleifson*, 2021 TCC 26 (under appeal to FCA) (GLGI: O had agreed to be bound by lead case). In *Savics*, 2019 TCC 71 (aff'd on this point 2021 FCA 56, para. 28), CRA and S reached a settlement allowing deductions on the basis that certain limited partnerships did exist; CRA's assessment of a later-year capital gain was a "consequential adjustment" (of the LPs' existence) per the settlement, so 169(2.2) applied.

169(2.2) was held not to apply in *Rainville*, [2002] 2 C.T.C. 2786 (TCC), because the reassessments did not entirely match the agreement signed; but this does not mean "that any inconsistency between the reassessment and the waiver agreement allows a taxpayer to appeal any aspect of the reassessment as if no waiver had been given" (*Noran West* (above), para. 65).

In *Remtilla*, 2015 TCC 200, the parties reached a settlement and R (an experienced accountant) signed a waiver of appeal rights, then claimed that part of the resulting reassessment was statute-barred under 152(4). The Court undercut him by ruling that a T1 adjustment request R had filed was a 152(4)(c) waiver!

See CRA Communiqué AD-19-01, *Audit Agreement and Waiver of Objection Rights Guidelines* (Feb. 19, 2019). CRA will request a waiver under 169(2.2) when applying the incremental costs approach of calculating scientific research expenditures, "because this approach is not founded in law and is only allowed on an administrative basis": SR&ED Application Policy 2004-03.

Once a taxpayer signs a settlement waiving the right of appeal, the CRA will not pursue competent-authority relief under a tax treaty (see 115.1).

For commentary on the CRA's practice of insisting on a waiver, whether this is consistent with the Minister's duty to assess correctly, and the effect of the waiver, see Bruce Russell, "Waiving Objection/Appeal Rights: Art of the Deal", 3(6) *Tax Hyperion* (Carswell), June 2006. (Russell is now a TCC judge.)

A settlement can also lead to facts being assumed true even without 169(2.2): *Pugh*, [2008] 2 C.T.C. 183 (FCA), and see Notes to 169(2) re issue estoppel.

See also Notes to 165(1.2).

169(2.2) added by 1994 technical bill, effective after June 22, 1995 for waivers signed at any time.

Application Policies: SR&ED 2002-02R2: Experimental production and commercial production with experimental development work — allowable SR&ED expenditures; SR&ED 2004-03: Prototypes, Pilot Plants/Commercial Plants, Custom Products and Commercial Assets.

Transfer Pricing Memoranda: TPM-02: Repatriation of funds by non-residents — Part XIII assessments.

(3) Disposition of appeal on consent — Notwithstanding section 152, for the purpose of disposing of an appeal made under a provision of this Act, the Minister may at any time, with the consent in writing of the taxpayer, reassess tax, interest, penalties or other amounts payable under this Act by the taxpayer.

Related Provisions: 165(1.2) — Limitation of right to object; 169(4) — Provisions applicable; 225.1(1) — No collection restrictions following assessment.

Notes: 169(3) permits *any* tax year to be reassessed on consent to settle a Tax Court appeal, even a year that was not under appeal. It does not appear to apply to a settlement at the FCA, since such appeal is not made "under a provision of this Act" but under the *Federal Courts Act* (unless it was a 171(4) appeal of a partial disposition of a Tax Court appeal, or a 172(3) charity registration/revocation appeal).

"Consent in writing of the taxpayer" applies only to the parties to the appeal, not to a third party (3P) that signs the settlement: *984274 Alberta*, 2019 TCC 85, paras. 20, 60; but 2020 FCA 125, paras. 51-52 (leave to appeal denied 2021 CarswellNat 1167 (SCC)), noted the 3P's agreement was required for the settlement, implying but not ruling that 3P should be bound by it. *Pirart*, 2016 TCC 291, para. 19, said the Crown "could not reasonably accept" an offer that allocated income to a third party without their consent.

"Taxpayer" in 169(3) means only the appellant, and cannot justify reassessment of other parties: VIEWS doc 2010-0378981A11.

The TCC may schedule a settlement conference: Rule 126.2. The conference is hosted by a judge who will give frank views on what might happen at trial (and will not be the trial judge). See Marta & Brown, "Settlement Conferences in the Tax Court of Canada", *Bennett Jones on Tax Disputes* (Taxnet Pro Tax Disputes Centre, Nov. 2019), pp. 1-8; IFA Canada presentation by Justice Hogan, June 24, 2020, slides at tinyurl.com/tcc-setconf. (See 169(2.2) re settlement at the audit or objection stage.)

CRA must not maintain a position for settlement negotiations that it knows is wrong and that it will drop: *Ludmer*, 2018 QCCS 3381, paras. 657, 668, 702; aff'd 2020 QCCA 697, para. 52 (leave to appeal denied 2021 CarswellQue 2160 (SCC)). For Quebec provincial tax, Revenu Québec has been unfair in pushing settlements on taxpayers without "free and informed consent": Quebec Ombudsman report *So that taxpayers' rights are upheld* (Feb. 27, 2020).

Although a case may be settled on consent, there must still be a legal basis for the final reassessment: *Galway*, [1974] C.T.C. 313 (FCTD); *Cohen*, [1980] C.T.C. 318 (FCA); *CIBC World Markets*, 2012 FCA 3 (as Crown could not accept taxpayer's offer to settle for 90%, no costs consequences even though result exceeded offer); *Transalta Corp.*, 2013 FCA 285 (leave to appeal denied 2014 CarswellNat 1703 (SCC)); *Bolton Steel*, 2014 TCC 94; *Sood*, 2015 FC 857; *Biles Estate*, 2017 FC 371, para. 47; *Quebec Fonte*, 2020 TCC 126 (repeated letters from Crown counsel to QF's counsel explaining that the settlement can cover only the issues under appeal). Thus, for example, a midpoint valuation can be agreed on as part of a settlement; but if there is a yes/no issue whose outcome is uncertain, the CRA has no authority to "split the difference" and agree to settle for half the tax owing. However, if the taxpayer is insolvent, a compromise settlement is arguably allowed so that CRA can collect, based on *Dept. of Justice Act* s. 5(d): *Galway* (above), para. 12; Walker & Kreklewetz, "Deals with the CRA", 25(3) *Canadian Tax Highlights* (ctf.ca) 9-10 (March 2017).

A settlement cannot be read as imposing tax higher than originally assessed: *Bolton Steel* (above), para. 34, unless the taxpayer is seeking the increase, e.g. to reduce another year's tax: *CBS Canada*, 2020 FCA 4, para. 45.

For CRA interpretation and procedures see CRA *Appeals Manual* §7.15, "Settlements".

In *Biles Estate* (above), para. 46, the parties did not agree what a supposed settlement actually meant, so there was no agreement.

On reaching settlement, the taxpayer can discontinue the appeal with (confidential) minutes of settlement (**MOS**) specifying the real result, or the parties can have the Court issue a consent judgment (**CJ**), which binds them by issue estoppel (see Notes to 169(2)). A CJ requires CRA to apply 164(4.1); if the reassessment does not match the CJ, it can be objected to, e.g. *Fono*, 2020 TCC 81; or appealed under 169(1). For an example of a CJ one can cite to CRA, see 60(o) Notes. However, a CJ legally has no precedential value: see 221.2 Notes. A CJ applies only to the years under appeal, while MOS can include other years. See also Sorensen, "The 'Cone of Silence' in Tax Settlements", XIX(2) *Tax Litigation* (Federated Press) 1150-52 (2013).

The basis from which adjustments in a settlement agreement apply is the last reassessment, not the original return: *Burg Properties*, 2014 CarswellNat 3556 (FCA) (leave to appeal denied 2014 CarswellNat 5185 (SCC)).

Costs: Settlement is encouraged by TCC General Procedure Rules, Rule 147(3.1) and Practice Note #18. From the time a formal settlement offer is made, 80% of solicitor-client costs are to be awarded if the offeror does at least as well at trial (in *ACSIS EHR*, 2016 TCC 50, the award was 95% because of the Crown's "refusal to participate in a meaningful way in the settlement negotiation process"!). See Tonkovich, "New Tax Court Rules", XVII(1) *Tax Litigation* (Federated Press) 1030-36 (2010); Novoselac & Sorensen, "TCC Settlements", 19(3) *Canadian Tax Highlights* (ctf.ca) 1-2 (March 2011); *AON Inc.*, 2018 TCC 111. However, the offer must be one that CRA can legally accept: see *CIBC World Markets* above. Also, an offer that the appeal be allowed in full might not be a real offer, as a genuine offer must include an "element of compromise": *Allen v. Mueller*, 2006 ABCA 101, para. 15; *Imperial Oil*, 2011 FC 652; *McKenzie*, 2012 TCC 329; *Hine*, 2012 TCC 295; but see also *Walsh*, 2010 TCC 125; *O'Dwyer*, 2014 TCC 90, para. 19 (costs proposal is part of the offer; on this point see also *SCDA (2005) Inc.*, 2017 FCA 177, paras. 28-30; *Chaplin*, 2017 TCC 257, paras. 9-10). In *Blackburn Radio*, 2013 TCC 98, CRA rejected an offer to allow the appeal in full; since CRA's case was "weak", higher costs were awarded, but the Court declined to rule on whether a settlement offer needs to have an element of compromise (paras. 18-23). Where X was awarded less than X's settlement offer but came close, higher costs than Tariff were awarded: *1378055 Ontario*, 2020 TCC 133, para. 19. The Court cannot order CRA to re-make an expired settlement offer: *Amoroso*, 2013 FC 157, para. 71; *Wiegers (Weigers)*, 2019 TCC 260.

Settlements should be reached early; one reached less than 30 days before trial leaves an unfillable hole in the Court's trial calendar. The Court plans to have a rule imposing costs on both parties, payable to the Court, for late settlements: Chief Justice Rossiter, 2019 Cdn Tax Foundation annual conference, Dec. 3, 2019.

In *Prévost Car*, 2014 FCA 86, the Crown conceded the case a few weeks before the TCC hearing. Each party was required to bear its own costs. For criticism see Sorensen, "The Cost of Folly or a Folly of Costs?", 2202 *Tax Topics* (CCH) 1-4 (May 22, 2014).

Whether there is a settlement: the TCC has jurisdiction to determine this issue, since the result is a 171(1) reassessment; *CBS Canada*, 2020 FCA 4, para. 53 (even if settlement increases tax in a later year). It enforced settlements in: *Oberoi*, 2006 TCC 293; *1390758 Ontario*, 2010 TCC 572 (noted that settlements should be encouraged); *Huppe*, 2010 TCC 644; *SoftSim Technologies*, 2012 TCC 181; *Davies*, 2016 TCC 104 (aff'd 2019 FCA 191; leave to appeal denied 2020 CarswellNat 52 (SCC)); *Granofsky*, 2017 FCA 119; *University Hill*, 2017 FCA 232 (leave to appeal denied 2018 CarswellNat 4689 (SCC)) (settlement with one Sentinel Hill film LP applied to other LPs); *CBS Canada* (above) (Crown bound by settlement allowing $24m loss carryforward despite later finding the loss did not exist; parties should be bound by their agreements); *Supavititpatana*, 2020 TCC 46 (claim, that agent consented to judgments to which appellants had not agreed, was not supported). In *Oberoi*, *SoftSim* and *Granofsky*, clients who authorized counsel to accept offers, then changed their minds, were bound to the settlements. In *Davies*, the client claimed he had not authorized counsel to settle, but his remedy was to sue counsel: para. 24. Absent fraud, a Notice of Discontinuance is final: see Notes to 169(1) under "Discontinuance". Solicitor-client privilege does not apply when determining whether the client authorized the lawyer to accept a settlement: *SoftSim*, paras. 16-20. The "consent in writing of the taxpayer" in 169(3) can be given by counsel: *SoftSim*, paras. 71-82; *Granofsky*, para. 6. See also Elwany et al., "Deal or no Deal?", 2032 *Tax Topics* (CCH) 1-4 (Feb. 17, 2011); Sorensen, "Cautionary Tales for Counsel When Settling", 65(1) *Canadian Tax Journal* 167-72 (2017) (re *Granofsky* and *Davies*). In *Quebec Fonte*, 2020 TCC 126, the settlement was limited to what was in the settlement agreement (not earlier correspondence). See also 162(2.2) Notes.

A lawyer in the firm representing the taxpayer can swear an affidavit to prove a settlement: *CBS Canada*, 2017 FCA 65, paras. 34-42.

In *Rosenberg*, 2014 QCCA 1651, the parties reached a settlement in which CRA agreed not to assess certain years, and CRA then demanded new information about those years. The Quebec courts had no jurisdiction over this issue, as it had to go to Federal Court. At 2016 FC 1376, the settlement was held binding and CRA was prohibited from seeking this information. (For related background see *Furguiele*, 2017 FC 268.)

In *Sifto Canada*, 2017 TCC 37, a settlement reached under the Canada-US tax treaty competent authority provisions to prevent double tax (on a transfer pricing adjustment) was held to prevent the CRA from reassessing inconsistent with the settlement.

The Dept. of Justice has legal carriage of Crown litigation, and can apparently repudiate a settlement reached by the CRA: *Garber*, [2006] 4 C.T.C. 135 (FCA). See Notes to

169(2.2) re settlements being binding on the taxpayer. But see *Consoltex Inc.*, [1997] 2 C.T.C. 2846 (TCC), paras. 30-38 (if the Minister is not bound by an "illegal settlement", the taxpayer should also not be bound by a settlement).

See also MacGregor & Goulard, "The Future of Tax Administration", 1997 Cdn Tax Foundation conference report, 57:4-5; Junkin, "Mechanisms To Implement a Settlement", 44 *McCarthy Tétrault on Tax Disputes* (CCH) 3-4 (Dec. 2008); Bass et al., "Trends in Sales Tax Litigation", 2008 conference report at 35:20-23; Sandler & Campbell, "Catch-22: A Principled Basis for the Settlement of Tax Appeals", 57(4) *Canadian Tax Journal* 762-86 (2009); Macdonell, "Settlement of Tax Disputes", 2012 *Tax Dispute Resolution* conf. report (ctf.ca), 6:1-14; Chan, "Negotiating Tax Settlements", *Taxnet Pro* Tax Disputes Centre (July 2018, 10pp); "Judges' Panel", 2019 Cdn Tax Foundation conference report, at 2:6-7 and 2:10-11; Hogan et al., "All About Settlements", *ibid.*, 14:1-19; Bassindale & Loo, "Settling Tax Disputes", *Tax Advocate* (*Taxnet Pro* Tax Disputes Centre), April 2021 (5pp).

169(3) added by 1992 technical bill, effective June 10, 1993.

(4) Provisions applicable — Division I applies, with such modifications as the circumstances require, in respect of a reassessment made under subsection (3) as though it had been made under section 152.

Notes: 169(4) added by 1992 technical bill, effective June 10, 1993.

Definitions [s. 169]: "assessment" — 248(1); "fair market value" — see 69(1) Notes; "Minister" — 248(1); "Parliament" — *Interpretation Act* 35(1); "sent" — 244(14), (14.1); "taxpayer" — 248(1); "writing" — *Interpretation Act* 35(1).

I.T. Application Rules [ss. 169–180]: 62(5).

170. (1) [Informal Procedure appeals —] Notice to Commissioner — Where an appeal is made to the Tax Court of Canada under section 18 of the *Tax Court of Canada Act*, the Court shall forthwith send a copy of the notice of the appeal to the office of the Commissioner of Revenue.

Notes: See Notes to 169(1) re Informal Procedure appeals.

(2) [Repealed]

Notes: 170(2) repealed by 2002-2013 technical bill (Part 5 — technical), effective June 26, 2013. It is no longer needed because the *Tax Court of Canada Act* provides the necessary rules. It required CRA to forward to the Tax Court, for an Informal Procedure appeal, the relevant returns, notices of assessment and objections.

170(1) and (2) amended by *CCRA Act*, effective Nov. 1, 1999, and by 2004 CRA/CBSA bill, effective Dec. 12, 2005.

Definitions [s. 170]: "Commissioner of Revenue" — *Canada Revenue Agency Act* s. 25.

I.T. Application Rules [s. 170]: 62(5).

171. (1) Disposal of appeal — The Tax Court of Canada may dispose of an appeal by

(a) dismissing it; or

(b) allowing it and

(i) vacating the assessment,

(ii) varying the assessment, or

(iii) referring the assessment back to the Minister for reconsideration and reassessment.

Related Provisions: 152(1.01) — appeal of eligibility for disability credit; 152(1.2) — Assessment — provisions applicable; 152(9) — Minister may raise new basis for assessment during appeal process; 164(4.1) — Minister's duty following Court judgment; 169 — Appeal; 171(2)–(4) — Disposition of specific issue rather than entire assessment; 202(3) Returns and payment of estimated tax — provisions applicable; 222.1 — Costs awarded to Crown by Court become part of tax debt; 227(7) — Withholding taxes; 227(10) — Assessment.

Notes: The TCC is limited by 171(1) and cannot award damages: *Way*, 2018 TCC 198; *Roy*, 2019 TCC 110 (see further below re suing CRA). Once the TCC issues a judgment, CRA must apply 164(4.1) in following it.

CRA's conduct in issuing an assessment is irrelevant on an appeal of the assessment: *Main Rehabilitation*, 2004 FCA 403 (leave to appeal denied 2005 CarswellNat 1110 (SCC)); *Webster*, 2003 FCA 388; *St-Laurent [Simard]*, 2009 FCA 379, para. 19; *Ereiser*, 2013 FCA 20 (leave to appeal denied 2013 CarswellNat 2353 (SCC)) (even egregious misfeasance on CRA's part, reassessing to coerce a guilty plea to a criminal charge, would not invalidate the assessment); *Johnson*, 2015 FCA 52; *Brooks*, 2019 FCA 293; *Bonev*, 2010 FCA 138, para. 10; *Kearsey*, 2008 TCC 590; *Uddin*, 2009 TCC 471; *MacLeod*, 2010 TCC 38; *French*, 2010 TCC 258; *Dial Drug Stores*, 2011 TCC 303, para. 15; *Magnus*, 2011 TCC 404, para. 6; *Bruce*, 2012 TCC 52, para. 16 (FCA appeal discontinued A-93-12); *Bauer*, 2016 TCC 136 (aff'd on other grounds 2018 FCA 62); *Kowalczyk*, 2018 TCC 190, para. 18; *Keenan*, 2019 TCC 259 (substantial costs for repeatedly pursuing unsubstantiated claims); *881751 Ontario*, 2021 TCC 9, para. 22. See also Notes to 169(1) re the FC's inability to address CRA conduct due to *Federal Courts Act* s. 18.5.

The TCC is required to give adequate reasons, including stating which theory of the winning side the Court agrees with: *SRI Homes*, 2012 FCA 208.

Costs:

Costs are normally awarded to the winning party in the General Procedure (but in *Loblaw Financial*, 2018 TCC 263, CRA won the case due to one point, but got no costs because it lost many other issues; LF's appeal was allowed anyway at 2020 FCA 79 [SCC appeal heard May 13/21]). Costs are "taxed" or "assessed" by the Court. Historically TCC costs were based on the Tariff (tinyurl.com/tcc-tariff), which covers only a small fraction of actual legal costs, but a judge fixing costs (as opposed to a Registrar) has never been bound by the Tariff. Costs are now often 50% or more of actual legal fees, and no special reason is needed to depart from the Tariff: *Univar Holdco*, 2020 TCC 15, paras 7, 50 and cases cited there; *Duffy*, 2020 TCC 135, para. 21. Large TCC awards in taxpayers' favour include: *Cameco*, 2019 TCC 92 [aff'd on other grounds 2020 FCA 112: see paras. 26, 96; leave to appeal denied 2021 CarswellNat 377 (SCC)] ($10.5 million [=35% of counsel fees] + disbursements: huge transfer-pricing case); *Paletta*, 2021 TCC 41 ($2.24 million including $726,000 disbursements: foreign exchange trading straddles); *Loblaw Financial*, 2020 FCA 79 ($1.8 million plus disbursements) (SCC appeal heard May 13/21); *CIT Group*, 2017 TCC 86 ($1.1m + disbursements); *Alta Energy*, 2018 TCC 235 ($1.19m); *General Electric Capital*, 2010 TCC 490 ($1.13m); *Bank of Montreal*, 2021 TCC 3 ($871,000); *Sommerer*, 2011 CarswellNat 6998 ($658,000); *Henco Inc.*, 2014 TCC 278 ($576,000); *Repsol Canada*, 2015 TCC 154 (aff'd on other grounds 2017 FCA 193) ($560,000); *Rio Tinto*, 2016 TCC 258 ($553,000 — 30% of actual legal fees); *MacDonald*, 2018 TCC 55 ($433,000, but reversed on substantive issue 2018 FCA 128; SCC appeal heard Oct. 17, 2019); *Jayco Inc.*, 2018 TCC 239 ($427,222); *Spruce Credit Union*, 2014 TCC 42 (FCA appeal discontinued A-96-14) ($410,000 minus certain amounts; includes detailed review of the case law, and strongly rejects Crown argument that Tariff applies except in very limited circumstances: para. 56); *Univar Holdco*, 2020 TCC 15 ($305,000 for 1-day hearing on $40m GAAR issue); *Scavuzzo*, 2006 TCC 181 ($275,000). The Rules allow broad discretion in awarding costs, so "the Tariff is an item for referral only if the Court so chooses": *Velcro Canada*, 2012 TCC 273, para. 10. Disbursements can be awarded if "essential to the conduct of the proceedings": *Jayco Inc.*, 2018 TCC 239, para. 44 (denying $1.4 million paid for a letter of credit to post as security to prevent collection of a GST/HST assessment, while it was under appeal). In *Buday*, 2019 TCC 164, the Court gave reasons why costs should go against B, invited the parties to settle costs, then penalized B for arguing against a costs award. Provincial superior courts award costs in tax appeals as they do in other civil litigation, typically far higher than TCC Tariff, e.g. *Inter-Leasing*, 2014 ONCA 683 ($925,000).

"Solicitor-client costs", usually awarded only if there was reprehensible, scandalous or outrageous conduct in the litigation (*Lacombe*, 2010 SCC 38, para. 67), or in some cases where an offer was made but rejected, may approach actual legal fees (plus GST/HST if not otherwise recoverable as input tax credits). There may be a distinction between such costs and "solicitor and *own* client costs" (actual fees): *Goldstick Estate*, 2019 ABCA 508, para. 25 (leave to appeal denied 2020 CarswellAlta 945 (SCC)).

In *Kotilainen*, 2017 TCC 7, para. 35, no costs were awarded to K because Dept. of Justice counsel had assisted him in presenting his case. A rejected settlement offer may result in higher costs: see Notes to 169(3). The Court may also award no costs despite a win or substantial win, e.g. *Pirart*, 2016 TCC 291. A self-represented taxpayer is not normally allowed costs for their own time: *Mittal*, 2013 TCC 355; but in *David M. Sherman*, 2004 FCA 29, a self-represented lawyer who showed he "incurred an opportunity cost by foregoing remunerative activity" was entitled to a "moderate allowance" for time and effort; similarly, see *Fong v. Chan*, 1999 CanLII 2052 (Ont. CA); *Mitchinson v. Marshall*, 2018 ONSC 7419; *Benarroch v. Fred Tayar*, 2019 ONCA 228; *McMahon (Foroglou)*, 2020 TCC 104, paras. 61-70. The TCC awarded solicitor-client costs against the Crown for alleging a tax shelter's promoters had been charged criminally: *Simard*, 2015 TCC 2. In *Martin*, 2015 FCA 95 (leave to appeal denied 2015 CarswellNat 5255 (SCC)), the TCC was held wrong to award extra costs due to CRA conduct at the audit and objection stage (the TCC also did this for sloppy audit work in *Kozar*, 2010 TCC 389, para. 90, and *Salaison Lévesque*, 2015 TCC 247). Dropping an issue, at a second hearing scheduled for that issue, led to solicitor-client costs against Revenu Québec in *Delia*, 2018 QCCQ 9487, para. 137 (under Quebec law); however, the Crown's dropping an issue in a complex case, after discovery, did not justify costs against it: *Burlington Resources*, 2020 TCC 32, para. 117 (appeal conditionally settled at FCA A-72-20).

Costs to Crown: For large TCC awards *against* taxpayers see *Golini*, 2016 TCC 247 (FCA appeal discontinued A-426-16) ($531,000 — Crown had made settlement offer); *Mariano*, 2016 TCC 161 ($491,000 (mostly expert witness disbursements) minus a small adjustment — leveraged donation scheme was a sham); *Standard Life*, 2015 TCC 97, aff'd as *SCDA*, 2017 FCA 177 ($475,000, including 80% of solicitor-client (SC) fees after CRA's settlement offer: offer with no element of compromise does not trigger automatic 80%-SC costs but can still justify enhanced costs; also, appellant's "window dressing" conduct was reprehensible); *Elbadawi*, 2016 FCA 57 ($86,000: taxpayer ignored judge's repeated warnings that CRA conduct was irrelevant, and his abuse of TCC to advance civil action was "reprehensible": para. 30). (SC costs in *Cameco Inc.*, 2014 TCC 367 were set aside at 2015 FCA 143.) It is unclear how SC cost awards to the Crown should be calculated, since the Dept. of Justice does not charge CRA for lawyers' time and the lawyers are on fixed salary; but note that costs can be awarded where counsel act *pro bono*: *Roby*, 2013 FCA 251, paras. 24-28. See the 7 factors in Rule 147 of the TCC General Procedure Rules. Ability to pay is not a relevant factor in

awarding costs: *Martinez*, 2020 FCA 150, paras. 13-15. In *Promised Land Ministries*, 2019 TCC 282, the Crown was awarded *less* than tariff despite winning, for no stated reason, and despite the Court rejecting (para. 26) PLM's argument that it was a small charity that would have difficulty paying. If the Crown is awarded costs in the General Procedure, lengthy delay in having the costs fixed can lead to them being reduced or cancelled: *Bailey*, 2012 TCC 101. A 10% charge (non-deductible due to 18(1)(t)) can be assessed for a groundless appeal filed to delay collection action: 179.1. See also Horrigan & Kreklewetz, "TCC Costs Awards", 23(10) *Canadian Tax Highlights* (ctf.ca) 1-2 (Oct. 2015).

If an appeal is 80% successful, the Court sometimes awards 80% costs, but in the author's view it should be 60% since the Crown should get an offsetting 20% award for the 20% it won.

Extension of time to make costs submissions: *MacDonald*, 2018 TCC 55, paras. 29-41.

Costs should not be awarded if they are not requested, and the Court must explain "costs of a punitive nature": *Kibalian*, 2019 FCA 160, paras. 16-17.

Informal Procedure (IP) — costs to appellant: the taxpayer can be awarded costs if more than 50% successful: *Tax Court of Canada Act* s. 18.26; but the low Tariff numbers are the starting point, not a percentage of actual costs: *Callaghan*, 2021 TCC 35, paras. 25-27, 68. *Chitalia*, 2017 TCC 227, para. 25, awarded costs to a losing appellant who had relied on a misleading CRA publication. In *Roy*, 2019 TCC 50, paras. 26-27 and 2019 TCC 110, costs of $1,000 were awarded against CRA for making arguments based on fairness with no "clear legal position". In *Wachal*, 2020 TCC 78, para. 32, costs of $300 were awarded due to "pleading deficiencies" in the Reply.

The Court also has inherent jurisdiction to award costs to either side to prevent abuse of its process: *Fournier*, 2005 FCA 131, para. 8; *Levy*, 2021 FCA 93; *Caribbean Queen*, 2009 TCC 566, para. 16.

IP — costs against appellant: the Crown is not normally awarded costs, but *Tax Court of Canada Rules (Informal Procedure)* s. 10(2) permits costs against a taxpayer who has "unduly delayed the prompt and effective resolution of the appeal". Surprisingly, in *Lichtman*, 2018 TCC 82, bringing a clergy residence IP appeal which required expert testimony without arranging for an expert triggered this rule; $22,200 costs were awarded to the Crown. Costs were awarded against IP tax-protester appellants in: *Tuck*, 2007 TCC 418 ($100 each); *Dillon*, 2013 TCC 242 ($1,000); *Davis*, 2015 TCC 79 ($1,185); *Brown*, 2014 TCC 91 ($1,000, but rev'd 2014 FCA 301 because gross-negligence penalties could not be upheld without a trial); and against other IP appellants in: *Foster (Atherton)*, 2007 TCC 659 ($3,000: calling irrelevant witnesses in SR&ED appeal); *Nicholls*, aff'd 2012 FCA 243 ($1,000: multiple motions trying to relitigate issues); *Graham*, 2013 TCC 294 ($375: RRSP deduction arguments were "vacuous and devoid of merit"); *Yourkin*, 2014 TCC 48 and 2016 TCC 111 ($628 and $1,850: repeated appeals of same issue for different years); *Hassan*, 2014 TCC 144 ($300: false donation claim); *Yevzeroff*, 2014 TCC 145 ($1,000: false claims in Court while relitigating issue decided for earlier period); *Amyan*, 2014 TCC 175 (false statements in Notice of Appeal); *Doncaster*, 2015 TCC 127 (tariff amount: proceedings delayed a year to allow appellant to subpoena Bell Canada to prove GST on expenses, but he never did); *Mentor*, 2015 TCC 190 ($250: taxpayer did not show up for appeal hearing); *Garmeco Canada*, 2015 TCC 194, para. 50 ($1,000: appellant's "lengthy, rambling explanations and argumentative manner"); *Smith*, 2015 TCC 234 ($625: taxpayer did not show up for appeal hearing after adjournment at his request); *Blackwell*, 2016 TCC 155 (FCA appeal discontinued A-265-16) ($625: dishonest agents missed part of hearing); *Mazo*, 2016 TCC 232 ($375: delay caused by using vexatious agent); *Pakzad*, 2017 TCC 83 ($1,000: threatening the Court unless it granted a publication ban); *Jackson*, 2019 TCC 63, para. 11 (wasteful motion for summary judgment when Crown filed Reply but failed to serve it within 5 days). The TCC refused to award costs against IP appellants in *McIvor*, 2009 TCC 469, para. 120 (Indians paid by Native Leasing Services were legitimately seeking to reduce their tax liability by appealing); *RAR Consultants*, 2016 TCC 206 (claiming amount previously denied did not unduly delay proceedings) and 2017 TCC 214, paras. 47-49 (case was complex and company's rep was courteous and respectful); *Poirier*, 2016 TCC 231, para. 17 (no undue delay); *Flavor Net*, 2017 TCC 179 (SR&ED unproven); *Lappan*, 2017 TCC 240 (no undue delay).

Costs to losing party may be awarded in "highly exceptional" cases raising an important issue of public law, but this is rare: *Goodwin v. BC*, 2015 SCC 46, para. 90; *Sherman*, 2002 FCT 586, para. 24 (rev'd on other grounds 2003 FCA 202); *Deegan (Highton)*, 2019 FC 1176 (under appeal to FCA).

Costs against or to third party: in *Mazraani*, 2016 TCC 65, para. 304, a life insurer that intervened to oppose an insurance agent's EI (IP) appeal was ordered to pay him $2,000 for drawing out the appeal with evidence the Court found misleading; but new trial ordered on unrelated grounds 2018 SCC 50. The TCC can award costs to or against a non-party: *Mariano*, 2016 TCC 161 (tax shelter promoter jointly liable with appellants for costs); *Di Mauro*, 2016 TCC 234 (DM ordered to pay $50 to each of 7 appellants waiting in Court for unrelated appeals, for delaying their hearings by raising irrelevant issues). See also non-tax cases *1318847 Ontario v. Laval Tool*, 2017 ONCA 184 (detailed review of the issue; Court has inherent jurisdiction to award costs against non-party for abuse of process); *Hunt v. Worrod*, 2019 ONCA 540 (leave to appeal denied 2020 CarswellOnt 816 (SCC)) (Legal Aid Ontario not liable for not monitoring litigation it was funding to ensure position taken was reasonable); *Cornerstone Properties v. Southside Construction*, 2020 ONCA 380.

Costs against counsel personally can be awarded for causing delay or abusing the Court's process: *Quebec v. Jodoin*, 2017 SCC 26 (non-tax case); *9128-8456 Québec*, 2014 TCC 84; *Breathe E-Z Homes*, 2014 TCC 201; *McCarthy*, 2016 TCC 86 ("wasting resources needs to be determined cautiously, charitably and generously to ensure that the courts do not discourage counsel from fearlessly representing their client's interest including putting forward novel, unpopular or heretofore unrecognized positions": para. 11); *Blackwell*, 2016 TCC 155 (FCA appeal discontinued A-265-16) (costs can be awarded against agent who is not a lawyer); *Beatty v. Wei*, 2017 ONSC 2922 (non-tax case); *DiGiuseppe v. Evanov*, 2019 ONSC 910 (non-tax case: lawyer took untenable positions, missed hearings and breached Court orders). Ineffectiveness did not justify costs against counsel: *Children's Aid*, 2017 ONCA 931, paras. 95, 98 (non-tax case); *CC Gold*, 2018 TCC 155, para. 64.

Costs apportionment: the TCC can apportion an award against a group of appellants among them: *Makuz*, 2006 CarswellNat 3375 (TCC); *Bailey*, 2012 TCC 101, para. 24. If this is not done, the usual litigation rule that plaintiffs are jointly and severally liable may not apply "where we have numerous appellants each with their own appeal against their own assessments and arguably different evidence with respect to their reasons for the investment": *Makuz*, para. 4.

See also Wallace, "To the Victor Go the Spoils: A Look at Costs Awards in Tax Court Proceedings", 17(5) *Tax Hyperion* (Carswell) 4-6 (Sept-Oct 2020).

Effect of Tax Court decision:

If the Tax Court vacates a reassessment, the assessment before it automatically revives, so a further reassessment to implement the Court's decision is void if it is statute-barred: *Blackburn Radio*, 2012 TCC 255. Therefore, if the Tax Court varies (or vacates) a reassessment (rather than sending it back to the Minister for reassessment with particular instructions), the Minister cannot reassess to give effect to that decision: VIEWS doc 2013-0489471I7.

The TCC cannot increase tax from what was assessed, since the Minister "cannot appeal his own assessment": see Notes to 169(1) under "The Court cannot increase tax on appeal". Therefore, the TCC cannot vacate a reassessment if that would reinstate a higher previous assessment: *Ford*, 2014 FCA 257, para. 17.

The Tax Court has jurisdiction to dismiss an appeal where a costs order has not been paid: *Roper*, 2013 FCA 245.

The TCC claims it can vacate an assessment without finding it invalid or incorrect, "under its implied jurisdiction to control its own process and ensure its proper functioning as a court of law" (to address breach of an undertaking): *Fio Corp.*, 2014 TCC 58, para. 69 (rev'd without discussing this point 2015 FCA 236).

The Tax Court cannot hear an appeal of a nil assessment. See 152(1.1) Notes.

The TCC can determine whether parties reached a settlement: see 169(3) Notes.

Jurisdiction — TCC vs Federal Court:

Certain matters are outside the Tax Court's jurisdiction and are therefore taken to the Federal Court (called Federal Court–Trial Division until July 2, 2003). These include:

- application for judicial review of the CRA's failure to waive interest or penalty under 220(3.1), failure to accept a late election under 220(3.2) or 85(7.1), failure to issue a discretionary reassessment under 152(4.2) [all called "Taxpayer Relief", formerly "Fairness"], failure to pay an amount owing to the taxpayer under a remission order, or failure to provide a waiver of Reg. 105 withholding

- application for an order of *mandamus* when CRA has failed to assess a return "with all due dispatch" under 152(1)

- application for *mandamus* to force CRA to assess to refund overpaid non-resident withholding tax after the 2-year deadline in 227(6): *CGI Holding*, 2016 FC 1086

- application to force CRA to reassess a past year to allow a deduction: *9027-4218 Québec [3087-1883 Québec]*, 2019 FC 785

- application to force CRA to pay a refund after the three-year limitation period in 164(1): *3735851 Canada*, 2010 TCC 24; *Sterritt*, 2018 TCC 117

- disputes over collection issues such as whether an amount was paid or has been properly credited to the taxpayer's account: *Neuhaus*, 2002 FCA 391; *Boucher*, 2004 FCA 47; *Alciné*, 2010 FCA 325; *Curwen*, 2005 TCC 226; *Pintendre Autos*, 2003 TCC 818; *Surikov*, 2008 TCC 161; *Welford*, 2009 TCC 464; *Forrester*, 2010 TCC 608; *Sutcliffe*, 2012 TCC 347; *Beaudry*, 2013 FC 547, para. 23

- (maybe) dispute over the amount withheld as source deductions by an employer: *Brooks*, [1995] 1 C.T.C. 2880 (TCC), *Liu*, 1995 CarswellNat 635 (TCC), and *McIntosh*, 2011 TCC 147; but *contra*, saying the Tax Court has jurisdiction, see *Ashby*, 1995 CarswellNat 956 (TCC), *Manke*, 1998 CarswellNat 1676 (TCC), and *Caday*, 2011 TCC 61, para. 9

- application to correct alleged errors in taxpayer's payroll account: *Associated Mechanical*, 2014 FC 732

- request for a refund of excess CPP contributions (*Freitas*, 2018 FCA 110, para. 7)

- application to restrain CRA from proceeding with collection action (but not on the basis the assessment is invalid: *Walker*, 2005 FCA 393), or to quash a CRA seizure of assets or garnishment order

- application to quash a Requirement for Information (RFI) issued under 231.2

- application to quash a search warrant issued under 231.3 or *Criminal Code* s. 487: *Lawson*, 2012 FCA 77; *Blerot (Lewry, Sigglekow)*, 2012 FCA 124 (leave to appeal denied *Lewry*, [2012] G.S.T.C. 118)

- application to force CRA to allow business to E-file client returns: *Pan-Tax*, [1997] 2 C.T.C. 315 (FCTD); *Killam*, 2009 TCC 227

- action to force CRA to follow the Act in assessing other taxpayers: *Harris*, [2000] 3 C.T.C. 220 (FCA); leave to appeal denied 2000 CarswellNat 2664 [and see *783783 Alberta* below]

- review of CRA decision to apply transfer pricing adjustment under Canada-US tax treaty Art. IX: *Chrysler Canada*, 2008 FC 1049 [McNary, "A 'New' Way to Challenge Decisions of the Minister?", 1923 *Tax Topics* (CCH) 1-4 (Jan. 15, 2009)]

- application for declaration of taxpayer's marital status: *Kostiuk*, 2010 TCC 630

- determination of disability credit entitlement for someone paying no tax, to qualify for RDSP: *Tozzi*, 2010 TCC 545 (fixed in 2011 with 152(1.01), (1.2))

- suing CRA for improper conduct of the audit (see below)

- other disputes outside the TCC's jurisdiction (see below).

The following also have been held to be outside TCC jurisdiction: claim for tax credits for CPP and EI contributions that was really a claim the employer had collected and not remitted CPP and EI (*Curwen*, 2005 TCC 226); claim that CRA failed to inform P that business under investigation was not remitting P's source deductions (*Pintendre*, 2003 TCC 818); claim that CRA wrongly set off tax refund with debt owed from another year (*Marchand*, 2004 TCC 205; leave to appeal denied 2006 CarswellNat 1632 (SCC)); claim that CRA statements of account do not match reassessment that correctly implemented TCC decision (*Miller*, 2007 TCC 207); claim that CRA should use s. 221.2 to change date of transferring instalments to a later year (*Emcon Services*, 2008 TCC 501; dispute over whether amount was paid to employee net of tax withholdings (*Boucher*, 2004 FCA 46 (leave to appeal denied 2004 CarswellNat 3761 (SCC)) and *Sutcliffe*, 2012 TCC 347; but see *Suermondt*, 2001 FCA 155, and 153(3)); request to review CRA's accounting systems (*Esesson Canada*, 2009 TCC 336).

See also Notes to 169(1) under "*Jurisdiction*".

The tax profession has sought amendments to expand the TCC's jurisdiction. The Cdn Bar Association (March 13/08) asked the Minister of Justice to extend it to various matters currently under FC or FCA jurisdiction, so all tax disputes could be dealt with by the same court. See "Sherman Writes to Justice Minister re Tax Court Jurisdiction", xxxiii(21) *The Canadian Taxpayer* (Carswell) 166-68 (Nov, 11, 2011). However, the Minister's response (Dec. 2011) was "the timing for such an ambitious set of legislative amendments is not opportune". (The FC is opposed to reduction of its jurisdiction.)

The deadline to apply for judicial review is 30 days (plus any *Time Limits and Other Periods Act (COVID-19)* extension during 2020: see Enacted Amendment under 169(1)) after the decision is "first communicated": *Federal Courts Act* s. 18.1. This can be extended if there is: (1) continuing intention to pursue the application; (2) some merit to it; (3) a reasonable explanation for missing the deadline; and (4) no prejudice to CRA: *Imperial Oil Resources*, 2016 FCA 139, paras. 59-62 (pursuing objection did not extend time); *Sharma*, 2020 FCA 203 (no reasonable explanation given); *Zen*, 2008 FC 371; *Matsui*, 2014 FC 553, para. 8; *Rosenberg*, 2015 FC 549, para. 61; *Dun-Rite Plastics*, 2018 FC 892 (counsel's 15-month delay was unreasonable); *Glatt*, 2019 FC 738, para. 44. It is not always clear when the clock starts running: Jonathan Bitran, "Limitation Period Considerations", 55 *McCarthy Tétrault on Tax Disputes* (CCH) 2-3 (Sept. 2010); *9027-4218 Québec [3087-1883 Québec]*, 2019 FC 785 (CRA letters sent after decision were "courtesy" letters that did not extend deadline).

The CRA is under no obligation to advise a taxpayer, when issuing a discretionary decision, that JR is available: *R & S Industries*, 2016 FC 275, paras. 37, 39. See also Notes to 220(3.1) for more on JR.

See also Ed Kroft, "Challenging the Actions of Tax Authorities: Guidelines on the Appropriate Use of Judicial Review in the Federal Court", *Blakes on Canadian Tax Controversy* (Taxnet Pro), Nov. 2013, pp. 1-15.

Where an issue is of broad interest but CRA tries to avoid judicial review by solving the particular taxpayer's complaint before the hearing, the FC may hear the case even though it is moot: *Ficek*, 2013 FC 430 (complaint about CRA's refusal to assess returns claiming donation shelters).

The provincial superior courts should not be used for *mandamus* applications or injunctions against collection or audit action, which should be left to the FC: *Gordon*, 2010 SKQB 160; *Burkes*, 2010 ONSC 6059; *861808 Ontario*, 2013 ONCA 604; *S. Suite Property Management*, 2013 ONSC 5249 (declaration sought, that CRA cannot seize trust account and must return funds, was equivalent to an injunction); *Rosenberg*, 2014 QCCA 1651 (CRA reopening audit after settlement reached in TCC appeal); *Smith*, 2016 ONSC 489 (s. 224.1 offset of Canadian Forces pension against tax debt).

For discussion of the "inherent jurisdiction" of superior courts, see *Meads v. Meads*, 2012 ABQB 571, paras. 351-378.

The TCC can hear a dispute over whether a notice of assessment (or confirmation) was validly mailed to a taxpayer to start the objection (or appeal) clock running (see Notes to 165(1)): *Aztec Industries*, [1995] 1 C.T.C. 327 (FCA); *Rick Pearson Auto Transport*, [1996] G.S.T.C. 44; *Massarotto*, [2000] G.S.T.C. 19 (TCC); *Simard*, 2009 TCC 131; *9122-5789 Québec*, 2008 TCC 279; *Pilgrim*, 2015 TCC 302. The author asked for this to be addressed at the Nov. 2009 TCC Bench and Bar Committee meeting; the Dept. of Justice stated that it will not oppose the TCC addressing the issue, since Justice "is of the view that the assessment is deemed by s. 152(8) to be valid unless or until a Court decides otherwise" (Committee Minutes, para. 59). The legal efficacy of a notice of assessment is a matter to be determined by the TCC: *Walker*, 2005 FCA 393, para. 13; *Danada Enterprises*, 2012 FC 403, para. 26. (In *Carter*, 2009 FC 846, the FC ruled that it had jurisdiction, but this was overturned on consent (2009 CarswellNat 3443) when the Crown agreed to refer the issue to the TCC [a consent judgment has no precedential value: see Notes to 221.2].)

For discussion of the jurisdictional quagmire facing a Canadian magazine trying (unsuccessfully) to force CRA to deny deductions under 19.01 to advertisers in a competing magazine that it said was not Canadian, see *783783 Alberta* [*7837783 Alberta*], 2010 ABCA 226.

The TCC has jurisdiction to find a person in contempt (see Notes to 231.7), but this will rarely apply to CRA failure to comply with a TCC order: *Currie*, 2012 TCC 62, paras. 45-52 (FCA appeal dismissed for delay A-85-12).

Where an assessment can be (or has been) appealed to the TCC, the FC cannot address its validity: *Federal Courts Act* s. 18.5, *Tax Court of Canada Act* s. 12 (see Notes to 169(1)).

Charter of Rights:

The Tax Court "has jurisdiction to decide *Charter* challenges to the validity of a provision in the ITA or its application to particular facts, or of administrative action purportedly taken pursuant to it, when necessary to dispose of an appeal otherwise within its jurisdiction": *Campbell*, 2005 FCA 420, para. 23. No relief is possible under *Charter* s. 7 (life, liberty, security of the person) or s. 12 (cruel and unusual punishment), as income tax affects only "economic interests": *Siemens v. Manitoba*, 2003 SCC 3, paras. 45-46; *Gratl*, 2012 FCA 88, para. 8 (leave to appeal denied 2012 CarswellNat 3282 (SCC)); *Goldman*, 2021 TCC 13, paras. 3-8. A corporation cannot claim *Charter* protection under s. 7 (life, liberty and security: *Main Rehabilitation*, 2004 FCA 403; leave to appeal denied 2005 CarswellNat 1110) or s. 12 (cruel and unusual punishment: *9147-0732 Québec*, 2020 SCC 32; *Prairies Tubulars*, 2021 FC 36). A non-profit corp cannot claim s. 15 protection (equality rights): *Church of Atheism*, 2019 FCA 296, para. 13 (leave to appeal denied 2020 CarswellNat 4487). The FC cannot hear a *Charter* issue that is within TCC jurisdiction: *Grenier*, 2015 FCA 292 (leave to appeal to SCC denied 2016 CarswellNat 1945 (SCC)).

A challenge to an ITA provision under the *Charter* requires an advance "Notice of Constitutional Question" served on the federal and each province's Attorney General: *TCC Act* s. 19.2; *Federal Courts Act* s. 57; *Guindon*, 2015 SCC 41.

Not counting criminal prosecutions, the *Charter* has applied only rarely in tax cases. In *Gernhart*, [2000] 1 C.T.C. 192 (FCA), disclosure of the taxpayer's personal income tax returns under 176(1) was held to violate s. 8. In *Chua*, [2000] 4 C.T.C. 159 (FCTD), Art. XXVI-A of the Canada-US tax treaty (cross-border collection) violated the *Charter* in applying to a tax debtor who was not a Canadian citizen when the debt arose but later became a citizen.

The Supreme Court of Canada rejected *Charter* arguments in *Symes*, [1994] 1 C.T.C. 40 (child care expenses); *Del Zotto*, [1999] 1 C.T.C. 113 (inquiries under 231.4); and *Thibaudeau*, [1995] 1 C.T.C. 382 (taxable child support under former 56(1)(b) — but legislative amendments followed).

The FCA rejected *Charter* arguments in: *Lister*, [1994] 2 C.T.C. 365; *McFadyen*, [2001] 1 C.T.C. 140; *Campbell* (above); *McFadyen*, 2006 FCA 11 (leave to appeal denied 2006 CarswellNat 1230 (SCC)); *Ali*, 2008 FCA 190; *Tall*, 2009 FCA 342; *Pilette*, 2009 FCA 367; *Ray*, 2010 FCA 17; *Gratl* (above); *Maheux*, 2012 FCA 283; *Lessard*, 2012 FCA 311; *Fannon*, 2013 FCA 99; *Romanuk*, 2013 FCA 133; *Grenier* (above); *Grenon*, 2016 FCA 4 (leave to appeal denied 2016 CarswellNat 2619 (SCC)); *Filion*, 2017 FCA 67; *Engel*, 2017 FCA 122; *Grier*, 2017 FCA 129, para. 16; *Kim*, 2019 FCA 210, paras. 31-32; *Brooks*, 2019 FCA 293. The FC rejected *Charter* arguments in: *Mercier*, 1996 CarswellNat 3187; *Moors*, 2015 FC 446; *Almadhoun*, 2018 FCA 112, para. 28; *Campbell*, 2018 FC 683.

The TCC rejected *Charter* arguments in: *Wells*, [1998] 1 C.T.C. 2118; *Troupe*, [2002] 2 C.T.C. 2449; *Noddin*, 2004 TCC 687; *Wetzel*, 2004 TCC 767; *Alibhai*, 2005 TCC 574; *Donovan*, 2005 TCC 667; *Sulcs*, 2007 TCC 637; *Chevalier*, 2008 TCC 11; *Calogeracos*, 2008 TCC 389; *Bradley*, 2009 TCC 15; *Neault*, 2009 TCC 586; *Sears*, 2009 TCC 22; *Nightingale*, 2010 TCC 1; *Hotte*, 2010 TCC 611; *Chiasson*, 2014 TCC 158; *Stogrin*, 2011 TCC 532; *Perusco*, 2011 TCC 409; *Ouellet*, 2012 TCC 77; *Sarophim*, 2012 TCC 92; *Vegh*, 2012 TCC 95; *Astley*, 2012 TCC 155; *Johnston*, 2012 TCC 177; *Hall*, 2013 TCC 314; *Konecny*, 2013 TCC 334; *D'Ambrosio*, 2014 TCC 70 (FCA appeal discontinued A-187-14); *Dubuc*, 2014 TCC 115; *Zanatta*, 2014 TCC 293, para. 22; *Bleiler*, 2014 TCC 296; *Leeper*, 2015 TCC 82; *Bradshaw*, 2017 TCC 123; *Lawson*, 2017 TCC 131; *Tyskerud*, 2019 TCC 84, para. 26; *881751 Ontario*, 2021 TCC 9, paras. 25-31; *Goldman*, 2021 TCC 13, paras. 1-8.

The TCC had no jurisdiction to apply the *Charter* to a CRA policy of taxing pre-judgment interest (PJI) on a pay equity award when the policy exempted other PJI: *Burrows*, 2005 TCC 761 (FCA appeal discontinued A-19-06).

See also Alison Scott Butler, "Making Charter Arguments in Civil Tax Cases", 41(5) *Canadian Tax Journal* 847-80 (1993).

The *Universal Declaration of Human Rights* was rejected as overriding the ITA in: *MacIver*, 2002 FCT 877, para. 15; *Girard*, 2014 TCC 107; *Oberkirsch*, 2016 TCC 84, paras. 19-22; *Di Mauro*, 2016 TCC 87; *Reyes*, 2019 FCA 7, para. 6. Similarly, the *Canadian Bill of Rights* was rejected in many cases. For the CRA's *Taxpayer Bill of Rights*, see Notes to 220(1).

See also Jacyk, "The Dividing Line Between the Jurisdictions of the Tax Court and Other Superior Courts", 56(3) *Canadian Tax Journal* 661-707 (2008); Bass et al., "Trends in Sales Tax Litigation", 2008 Cdn Tax Foundation conference report at 35:25-29; Jacyk, "The Jurisdiction of the Tax Court", 60(1) *CTJ* 55-92 (2012); Du Pont & Lubetsky, "The Power to Audit is the Power to Destroy", 61(Supp.) *CTJ* 103-21 (2013).

An appeal from the TCC goes to the FCA: see end of Notes to 169(1).

Suing CRA:

A lawsuit for negligent or malicious acts can be brought in either Federal Court or the province's superior court: *Crown Liability and Proceedings Act*; *Federal Courts Act* s. 17(2)(d); *TeleZone*, 2010 SCC 62. See Rennie et al., *The 2019 Annotated Crown Liability and Proceedings Act* (Carswell, 240pp). An assignment of a plaintiff's claims to its lawyers for legal fees may be invalid: *Dupuis Paquin*, 2013 QCCA 637 (leave to appeal denied [2013] G.S.T.C. 158 (SCC)); *Financial Administration Act* s. 67 [see Notes to 220(6)] (and in the common-law provinces, under the doctrines of champerty and maintenance). A lawsuit claiming the taxpayer should have been assessed consistently with other taxpayers will fail: *Tennant*, 2013 ABCA 81 (leave to appeal denied 2013 CarswellAlta 1179). In *Konyi*, 2018 FC 1030, an unjust enrichment claim that K had paid instalments for 1997 was rejected as unsupported by the evidence and past the 6-year limitation period.

Does CRA have a duty of care to taxpayers, so it can be liable for negligence? The cases in common-law provinces (i.e., all but Quebec) are conflicting but tend to "No": *Canus Fisheries*, 2005 NSSC 283; *Foote*, 2011 BCSC 1062; *Grenon*, 2017 ABCA 96 (leave to appeal denied 2017 CarswellAlta 1714 (SCC)), paras. 8-25 (due to the "inherently adverse relationship between auditors and taxpayers", disagreeing with *Leroux* below, and limiting *McCreight* below to criminal investigations); *Jayco Inc.*, 2021 ONSC 2120; *Signal Hill*, 2021 ABQB 460, para. 75 (CRA Collections). *Leroux*, 2014 BCSC 720, paras. 304-311, says there is a duty of care if there is "proximity" due to a "close and direct relationship" between auditor and taxpayer (but on the facts, the breach did not cause damages). Cases leaving the question open: *Gordon*, 2013 FC 597; *McCreight*, 2013 ONCA 483; *Grand River Enterprises*, 2017 ONCA 526 (leave to appeal denied 2018 CarswellOnt 7925), paras. 100-166. (Investigators of tax *evasion* do have a duty of care: *Gordon*, 2019 FC 853, paras. 140-162 (under appeal to FCA); *Softcom Solutions*, 2020 ONSC 3290, paras. 195-199.) In Quebec, *Civil Code* ss. 1376 and 1457 allow a claim for negligence (civil fault): *Groupe Enico*, 2016 QCCA 76, paras. 97-101; *Ludmer*, 2018 QCCS 3381, paras. 134-151 ("*Taxpayer Bill of Rights* helps define what a reasonable auditor would do"); aff'd 2020 QCCA 697, paras. 41, 43 (leave to appeal denied 2021 CarswellQue 2160).

Misfeasance in public office requires that the official engaged in unlawful conduct in the exercise of a public duty, *and* the official was aware the conduct was unlawful and likely to injure the plaintiff: *Odhavji v. Woodhouse*, 2003 SCC 69; *Trillium Power v. Ontario*, 2013 ONCA 683. (Since 2020, a misfeasance claim against Ontario requires leave of the Court: *Crown Liability and Proceedings Act, 2019* (Ont.), s. 17(2).)

Lawsuit limitation period: The cases (both common-law provinces and Quebec) say the deadline for a lawsuit does not start running until the Tax Court allows the plaintiff's appeal and rules CRA acted wrongly: *Gardner*, 2013 ONCA 423; *Grenon*, 2016 ABQB 260, para. 97 (aff'd on other grounds 2017 ABCA 96; leave to appeal denied 2017 CarswellAlta 1714 (SCC)); *Restaurant Le Relais*, 2020 QCCA 823, paras. 43-52 (leave to appeal denied 2021 CarswellQue 5277 (SCC)) (TCC's views about the auditor are relevant but not binding in finding liability: para. 57). See also 118.1(1)"total charitable gifts" Notes at "For more on a lawsuit limitation clock" for the time limit on suing advisors for failed tax schemes, where the same issue arises.

Lawsuits *in common-law provinces* succeeded in: *Luo* (1997), 33 O.R. (3d) 300 (Ont. Div. Ct) (Unemployment Insurance Commission liable where employee negligently provided wrong information about benefits); *Chhabra*, [1989] 2 C.T.C. 13 (FCTD) (malicious actions by Collections officials); *Hamel* (1999), 175 D.L.R. (4th) 323 (FCA) (Canada Customs liable for seizing horses based on incorrect tip they were being used for drug smuggling); *Longley*, [1999] 4 C.T.C. 108 (BCSC) (CRA refusal to approve Rhinoceros Party plan to abuse political donation credit was misfeasance in public office; the BCCA at [2000] 2 C.T.C. 382 implied the decision was wrong but did not reverse it because the Crown had inexplicably abandoned its appeal).

Lawsuits in Quebec (under the *Civil Code*) succeeded in: *Joncas*, 2012 QCCQ 5096 (abusive assessments by Revenu Québec (RQ)); *Groupe Enico (Archambault)*, 2016 QCCA 76 (RQ abuse of audit and collection powers: $3 million award including $1m punitive damages [David Sherman, 233 *GST & HST Case Notes* (Carswell) 4-7 (March 2016)]); *Ludmer*, 2018 QCCS 3381; aff'd 2020 QCCA 697 (leave to appeal denied 2021 CarswellQue 2160 (SCC)) ($4.8m for negligence in taking unreasonable assessing positions to gain leverage for a settlement; damages were for part of professional fees, lost interest on tax required to be paid, damage to reputation, stress, trouble and inconvenience, but no punitive damages: QSSC paras. 702, 820-832; QCCA paras. 20-25, 90-105).

Lawsuits proceeded in: *Swift*, 2004 FCA 316 (suit for fraudulent assessment, even though TCC dismissed appeal of assessment); *Heckendorn*, 2009 BCSC 952 (claims for negligence and defamation); *Grand River Enterprises*, 2017 ONCA 526 (leave to appeal to SCC requested) ("forced incorporation" for Indians to obtain tobacco licence, requiring payment of excise tax they would not have had to pay; misfeasance claim can also proceed); *506913 NB Ltd. v. McIntyre*, 2012 NBQB 225 (suit for abuse of process and malicious prosecution); *Foote*, 2013 BCCA 135 (much of claim struck out as challenging correctness of assessments or as being statute-barred, but claim for misfeasance could proceed); *Gordon*, 2013 FC 597 (claims for negligence and intentional interference with contractual relations); *Gardner*, 2013 ONCA 423 (claim that CRA officials deliberately misapplied the law in assessing); *McCreight*, 2013 ONCA 483 (claim of malicious prosecution struck out, but claims of negligent investigation, abuse of process and misfeasance in public office could proceed); *Grenon*, 2017 ABCA 96 (leave to appeal denied 2017 CarswellAlta 1714 (SCC)) (negligence claim struck; attacks on CRA reassessment and jeopardy order action struck; misfeasance claim allowed to proceed but stayed pending TCC appeal of assessments); *Hociung*, 2019 FCA 215 (suing

CBSA for seizing precious coins not declared at border: claim only partly dismissed); *Myers*, 2021 BCSC 432 (claim of unfair audit method struck as collateral attack on FC jurisdiction; claims of misfeasance and negligence stayed pending TCC decision).

Lawsuits by nonsense tax-protester and "natural person" cases: see Notes to 2(1). Lawsuits claiming CRA should have taken action to prevent use of donation shelters: see Notes to 118.1(1)"total charitable gifts".

Lawsuits in Quebec failed in: *Construction MDGG v. Quebec*, 2014 QCCA 858 (Revenu Québec not liable for collecting penalty that lower court had ordered cancelled); *Duchesne v. Québec*, 2014 QCCA 1052 (leave to appeal denied 2015 Carswell-Que 834) (government gave employee wrong information as to how much pension she would receive on retirement: not proven what was wrong); *Passucci v. Quebec*, 2014 QCCQ 3802 (*res judicata*, as plaintiff's tax liability had been determined through TCC appeal process and she had previously tried to sue Quebec); *Bouthillier*, 2014 QCCQ 11562 (Court of Quebec can award damages, but not in a tax appeal); *Orsini*, 2016 QCCA 1579 (leave to appeal denied 2017 CarswellQue 2063) (claim struck for *res judicata* and being out of time); *3092-8949 Québec*, 2018 QCCA 967 (delay in moving lawsuit forward); *3092-8949 Québec v. ARQ*, 2018 QCCA 967 (leave to appeal denied 2019 CarswellQue 2691 (delay in moving claim forward); *Naples Pizza*, 2019 QCCS 710 (action was statute-barred, and RQ's use of alternative audit methodology not shown to be unreasonable); *Restaurant Le Relais*, 2020 QCCA 823 (leave to appeal denied 2021 CarswellQue 5277 (SCC)) (auditor errors were not malicious or so unreasonable as to create "fault" under *Civil Code*: paras. 40, 72).

Lawsuits in other provinces failed in: *Merchant Law Group*, 2010 FCA 184 (attempted class action over GST on disbursements); *Neumann*, 2011 BCCA 313 (leave to appeal denied [2012] G.S.T.C. 28 (SCC)) (CRA committed no tort in executing valid search warrant, so BCCA overturned jury award of $1.3m for infringing homeowner's rights); *Maheux*, 2011 FC 901 (aff'd on other grounds 2012 FCA 283) (claim struck but could be refiled for damages for CRA allegedly fabricating documents [but plaintiff did not do so]); *Nicholls*, 2012 ONSC 1842 (attempting to revive tax claims was abusive); *Leighton*, 2012 BCSC 961 (claim for abuse of process and defamation struck out: no duty of care owed, and counsel's statements in Court are privileged); *Weninger Farms*, 2012 ONSC 4544 (tobacco growers could not sue government for not enforcing tobacco legislation against illegal vendors); *Lawson* (Ont. Small Claims, Nov. 7, 2012, SC-12-226-0000) (taxpayer could not sue for costs of legal proceedings since Tax Court had sole jurisdiction to award costs); *Hérold*, 2013 FCA 19 (income tax refunds correctly applied against Canada Student Loan debt); *Deep*, 2013 FCA 228 (leave to appeal denied 2014 CarswellNat 566) (action was collateral attack on Tax Court judgment); *Leroux*, 2014 BCSC 720 (CRA breached duty of care in assessing excessive penalties, but the cause of destruction of L's business was his failure to respond to assessment proposals or provide proper documentation for years); *Compucare v. Ontario*, 2015 ONSC 1987 (plaintiff corp had been dissolved; *Proceedings Against the Crown Act* requirements not followed); *Humby*, 2015 FCA 266 (leave to appeal denied [2017] G.S.T.C. 26) (CRA collection action was valid); *Brown*, 2015 BCCA 102 and 2015 BCSC 1910 (claims were statute-barred; later claim was *res judicata*); *Foote*, 2015 BCSC 849 (auditor and investigator were just doing their jobs: no deliberately unlawful acts); *Total Energy v. Alberta*, 2015 ABQB 439 (claim for damages for cost of contesting assessments that were later withdrawn, and for alleged lies by Alberta officials); *Collins*, 2015 FCA 281 (lawsuit by former CRA employee alleging CRA had permitted unauthorized persons to access her account); *Beima*, 2015 FC 1367 (wild claims against the government and Tax Court judges); *Scheuer*, 2016 FCA 7 (claim struck out that CRA should have warned taxpayers that the Global Learning donation shelter would fail; leave to amend granted); *Hennessey*, 2016 FCA 180 (unfounded claim that CRA acted maliciously and unlawfully in enforcing collection of payroll remittance arrears owed by plaintiff's clients); *Smith*, 2016 ONSC 489 (claim for damages was "inextricably linked" with injunction sought against collection action, which was solely FC jurisdiction); *Bouchard*, 2016 FC 983 (alleged harm was done not to plaintiff but his corporations, and essential elements of misfeasance not pleaded); *Keay*, 2016 FCA 281 (leave to appeal denied 2017 CarswellNat 2224) (no evidence that CRA officials committed any tort); *Holterman*, 2017 ONCA 769 (leave to appeal denied 2018 CarswellOnt 11225) (parties settled and plaintiffs discontinued action, then sought to set aside discontinuance when reassessments showed they were not liable for tax); *Lee*, 2020 FCA 17 (attempt to relitigate previously decided tax appeals); *Samaroo*, 2019 BCCA 113 (leave to appeal denied 2019 CarswellBC 2946) (claim for malicious prosecution won at trial but lost on appeal: CRA had "reasonable and probable cause" to prosecute); *Siemens v. Baker*, 2019 SKQB 99 (no material facts pled, and claim in effect challenged tax assessments); *Gordon*, 2019 FC 853 (under appeal to FCA) (claim for malicious prosecution: CRA had reasonable grounds to prosecute); *Softcom Solutions*, 2020 ONSC 3290, paras. 200-218 (CRA acted reasonably in audit and investigation; $273,000 costs awarded against taxpayers at 2020 ONSC 5385); *Jayco Inc.*, 2021 ONSC 2120 (CRA has no duty of care when auditing, and no obligation to indemnify agent for cost of collecting HST); *De Vries*, 2021 BCSC 527 (lawsuit was attempt to relitigate Tax Court dispute); *Larbi*, 2021 ONSC 3240 (claim that CRA allowed L's ex-husband to open an E-File number in her name did not raise a valid cause of action); *Lauzon*, 2021 FC 431 (claim that L never received CRA refund cheques was likely incorrect, and limitation period had expired); *Signal Hill*, 2021 ABQB 460, para. 75 (collection action, including issuing Requirements to Pay to SH's customers).

For CRA comment on such lawsuits see doc 2018-0779951C6 [2018 CTF q.7].

Shareholders normally have no claim for harm to their corporation, as only the corp can sue: *Foss v. Harbottle* (1843), 67 E.R. 189 (England, House of Lords); *Brunette v. Legault Joly*, 2018 SCC 55; *Naples Pizza*, 2019 QCCS 710, para. 21; *Restaurant Le Relais*, 2017 QCCS 5397 (aff'd without addressing this point 2020 QCCA 823; leave to appeal denied 2021 CarswellQue 5277 (SCC)).

Lawsuits against CRA employees acting within the scope of their employment will be struck without a trial: *Heckendorn*, 2006 FCA 407 and 2009 BCSC 952; *Humby*, 2009 FC 1238; *Deluca*, 2016 ONSC 3865, paras. 67-73. So will claims against Dept. of Justice lawyers: *Nicholls*, 2012 ONSC 1842; *Beima v. McPherson*, 2015 FC 1368; and claims against judges for anything they do in exercising judicial functions: *Prefontaine v. Paris*, 2007 ABCA 245; *Collins v. Heneghan*, 2011 ONCA 461 (leave to appeal denied [2012] G.S.T.C. 3 (SCC)); *McPherson v. Campbell*, 2019 NSCA 23 (leave to appeal denied 2019 CarswellNS 898); *Taha v. Clements*, 2021 PECA 5. In *Dickson*, 2017 FCA 198, a claim was allowed to proceed against CRA employees for allegedly acting *outside* their authority (refusing to renew a tobacco licence). Crown Attorneys have "prosecutorial immunity" from lawsuits: *Smith*, 2019 ONCA 651, paras. 96-98.

See also Nitikman, "To Sue or Not to Sue?", 2088 *Tax Topics* (CCH) 1-4 (March 15, 2012); Nanji, "Can Taxpayers Successfully Sue the CRA for Negligence?", 2013 *Tax Topics* (CCH) 1-4 (Oct. 17, 2013); Bevacqua, "Suing Canadian Tax Officials for Negligence", 61(4) *Canadian Tax Journal* 893-914 (2013); Feldthusen, "Public Authority Immunity from Negligence Liability", 92 *Canadian Bar Review* 211-34 (2013-14); Purse, "How to Sue the CRA", 8(2) *Taxes & Wealth Management* (Carswell) 4-9 (May 2015); Fazel, "Suing the Canada Revenue Agency in Tort", 67(3) *Canadian Tax Journal* 581-611 (2019).

See Notes to 237.1(1)"tax shelter" for lawsuits against tax advisers and promoters of tax shelters.

(1.1) Ecological gifts — On an appeal under subsection 169(1.1), the Tax Court of Canada may confirm or vary the amount determined to be the fair market value of a property and the value determined by the Court is deemed to be the fair market value of the property determined by the Minister of the Environment.

Notes: 171(1.1) added by 2000 Budget, effective for gifts made after Feb. 27, 2000.

(2) Partial disposition of appeal — If an appeal raises more than one issue, the Tax Court of Canada may, with the consent in writing of the parties to the appeal, dispose of a particular issue by

    (a) dismissing the appeal with respect to the particular issue; or

    (b) allowing the appeal with respect to the particular issue and

        (i) varying the assessment, or

        (ii) referring the assessment back to the Minister for reconsideration and reassessment.

Related Provisions: 171(3) — Disposal of remaining issues; 171(4) — Appeal of specific issue to Federal Court of Appeal.

Notes: 171(2)-(4) are part of a package announced in June 2012 (along with 174(1)–(4.2) and amendments to the *Tax Court of Canada Act*) to improve the Tax Court's caseload management with thousands of tax shelter appeals looming. They allow part of an appeal to go forward without resolving other issues the taxpayer has for the same taxation year. However, the notice of appeal still needs to raise all issues. See "Tax Litigation" panel, 2012 Cdn Tax Foundation conference report, at 31:2-4.

In *Patel*, 2020 FCA 27, the TCC was wrong to say 171(2) could not apply. If both parties agree to bifurcate an appeal, that is "highly relevant, although not determinative": para. 3.

171(2), (3) and (4) added by 2013 budget bill #1, for issues disposed of by the Tax Court of Canada after June 26, 2013.

(3) Disposal of remaining issues — If a particular issue has been disposed of under subsection (2), the appeal with respect to the remaining issues may continue.

Notes: See Notes to 171(2).

Former 171(3), repealed in 1984, prohibited the Tax Court from awarding costs. Costs are now provided under by the *Tax Court of Canada Act*.

(4) Appeal to Federal Court of Appeal — If the Tax Court of Canada has disposed of a particular issue under subsection (2), the parties to the appeal may, in accordance with the provisions of the *Tax Court of Canada Act* or the *Federal Courts Act*, as they relate to appeals from decisions of the Tax Court of Canada, appeal the disposition to the Federal Court of Appeal as if it were a final judgment of the Tax Court of Canada.

Notes: See Notes to 171(2). 171(4) added by 2013 budget bill #1, for issues disposed of by the Tax Court after June 26, 2013.

Former 171(4), repealed by 1993 GST bill effective June 10, 1993, required the Tax Court to send its decision to the parties by registered mail (see now *Tax Court of Canada Act* s. 18.22(3)).

Definitions [s. 171]: "assessment" — 248(1); "fair market value" — see 69(1) Notes; "Federal Court" — *Federal Courts Act* s. 4; "Minister" — 248(1); "writing" — *Interpretation Act* 35(1).

172. (1), (2) [Repealed under former Act]

Notes: 172(1), (2), repealed by 1988 Tax Court bill (for appeals launched after 1990), permitted an appeal to the Federal Court — Trial Division. The only first appeal now is to the Tax Court.

(3) Appeal from refusal to register [charity], revocation of registration, etc. — Where the Minister

(a) confirms a proposal or decision in respect of which a notice was issued under any of subsections 149.1(4.2) and (22) and 168(1) by the Minister, to a person that is or was registered as a registered Canadian amateur athletic association or is an applicant for registration as a registered Canadian amateur athletic association, or does not confirm or vacate that proposal or decision within 90 days after service of a notice of objection by the person under subsection 168(4) in respect of that proposal or decision,

(a.1) confirms a proposal, decision or designation in respect of which a notice was issued by the Minister to a person that is or was registered as a registered charity, or is an applicant for registration as a registered charity, under any of subsections 149.1(2) to (4.1), (6.3), (22) and (23) and 168(1), or does not confirm or vacate that proposal, decision or designation within 90 days after service of a notice of objection by the person under subsection 168(4) in respect of that proposal, decision or designation,

(a.2) confirms a proposal or decision in respect of which a notice was issued under any of subsections 149.1(4.3) and (22) and 168(1) by the Minister, to a person that is a person described in any of subparagraphs (a)(i) to (v) and paragraph (b.1) of the definition "qualified donee" in subsection 149.1(1) that is or was registered by the Minister as a qualified donee or is an applicant for such registration, or does not confirm or vacate that proposal or decision within 90 days after service of a notice of objection by the person under subsection 168(4) in respect of that proposal or decision,

(b) refuses to accept for registration for the purposes of this Act any retirement savings plan,

(c) refuses to accept for registration for the purposes of this Act any profit sharing plan or revokes the registration of such a plan,

(d) [Repealed]

(e) refuses to accept for registration for the purposes of this Act an education savings plan,

(e.1) sends notice under subsection 146.1(12.1) to a promoter that the Minister proposes to revoke the registration of an education savings plan,

(f) refuses to register for the purposes of this Act any pension plan or gives notice under subsection 147.1(11) to the administrator of a registered pension plan that the Minister proposes to revoke its registration,

(f.1) refuses to accept an amendment to a registered pension plan,

(g) refuses to accept for registration for the purposes of this Act any retirement income fund,

(h) refuses to accept for registration for the purposes of this Act any pooled pension plan or gives notice under subsection 147.5(24) to the administrator of a pooled registered pension plan that the Minister proposes to revoke its registration, or

(i) refuses to accept an amendment to a pooled registered pension plan,

the person described in paragraph (a), (a.1) or (a.2), the applicant in a case described in paragraph (b), (e) or (g), a trustee under the plan or an employer of employees who are beneficiaries under the plan, in a case described in paragraph (c), the promoter in a case described in paragraph (e.1), the administrator of the plan or an employer who participates in the plan, in a case described in paragraph (f) or (f.1), or the administrator of the plan in a case described in paragraph (h) or (i), may appeal from the Minister's decision, or from the giving of the notice by the Minister, to the Federal Court of Appeal.

Related Provisions: 147.1(13) — Revocation of registration; 149.1(6.4) — Application to registered national arts service organizations; 168(2) — Revocation of registration of certain organizations; 172(3.1) — No appeal for charity that has registration revoked or refused for supporting terrorism; 172(4), (5) — Deemed refusal to register; 172(4.1) — Appeal suspended when certificate issued that charity supports terrorism; 180(1) — Appeal to Federal Court of Appeal; 189(8.1)(b) — Revocation of registration cannot be appealed to Tax Court of Canada; 204.81(9) — Right of appeal; *Interpretation Act* 27(5) — Meaning of "within 90 days".

Notes: This section deals *only* with appeals of registrations and revocations of registered charities, RCAAAs, other qualified donees (see Notes to 149.1(1)"qualified donee"), pension plans and other registered plans. Normal appeals from the TCC to the FCA are under the *Federal Courts Act*; see Notes to 169(1).

See Notes to 168(1) for cases on the *reasons* for charity revocations, and to 248(1)"registered Canadian amateur athletic association" for RCAAAs. The discussion below is about the appeal process and procedure.

FCA appeals under 172(3) (after the CRA audit and objection process) are based on the written record only, with no evidence given. Before *Vavilov*, 2019 SCC 65, the standard of review was "reasonableness" (e.g., *1346687 Ontario*, 2007 FCA 262, para. 33 (leave to appeal denied (SCC)); *Loba Ltd.*, 2004 FCA 342 (leave to appeal denied 2005 CarswellNat 848)). Now, per *Vavilov* para. 17, the standard is "correctness", but per para. 37, in applying the law to questions of fact (as is almost always the case for charity appeals), there must be "palpable and overriding error" on CRA's part to overturn the decision: *Ark Angel Fund*, 2020 FCA 99, para. 4. This is very unfair in the author's view, as it makes appeals virtually impossible to win, giving CRA total control over the revocation process. (*Quaere* whether the same test must now apply to Tax Court appeals!) See D'Aoust & Luu, "Revoking a Charity's Registration: The Standard of Review", 10(3) *Canadian Tax Focus [CTFo]* (ctf.ca) 10-11 (Aug. 2020); Luu & Sherman, "Appeals of Charity Revocations", 10(4) *CTFo* 9 (Nov. 2020).

No charity appeals have succeeded in over 20 years (since *Vancouver Regional Freenet*, [1996] 3 C.T.C. 102). The lack of an oral hearing during the revocation process, and CRA's failure to provide the charity with audit reports and working papers, do not violate a charity's right to fair treatment: *Canadian Committee for the Tel Aviv Foundation*, 2002 FCA 72. As the only issue is whether the Minister's decision was reasonable, the charity generally cannot introduce evidence that was not before the Minister: *International Relief Fund for the Afflicted and Needy (IRFAN)*, 2013 FCA 178, paras. 9-10. For criticism of this approach, see Kathryn Chan, "The Function (or Malfunction) of Equity in the Charity Law of Canada's Federal Courts", ssrn.com/abstract=2847202.

For review of the procedures required before filing an appeal (notice, publication, objection, confirmation), see *International Charity Association Network (ICAN)*, 2008 FCA 62. Appeal of a revocation is invalid unless a 168(4) objection is filed first: *Liberty Assembly*, 2008 FCA 319; *Israelite Church*, 2010 FCA 93; *Christ Apostolic Church*, 2010 FCA 252. In *1344746 Ontario Inc.*, 2008 FCA 314, the Court refused to extend time to file a 172(3) appeal when counsel missed the deadline.

Charity *registration* refusal was upheld in *Sagkeening Memorial Arena*, 2012 FCA 171 (Minister's request for more information was reasonable); and several cases discussed in Notes to 149.1(1)"charitable activities". Refusing to register a charity does not interfere with its members' *Charter* rights more than trivially or insubstantially: *Church of Atheism*, 2019 FCA 296, para. 16 (leave to appeal to SCC requested).

There has been pressure on the Dept. of Finance to introduce legislation to allow charity registration and revocation appeals to be taken to the Tax Court. See Arthur Drache, "Revised Appeal Procedure Offers Hope", 10(8) *Canadian Not-for-Profit News [CNfpN]* (Carswell) 57-59 (Aug. 2002), and "Regulatory Table Reports Now Available", 11(6) 41-43 (June 2003). The 2004 Budget provided a partial response, introducing an objection process for revocations, as well as intermediate penalties that can be objected to and appealed to the TCC. See 168(4), 188.1 and 189(8). However, it seems nothing else will change: Drache, "Why Finance Says Charity Appeals Go to the Federal Court of Appeal", 20(3) *CNfpN* 21-22 (March 2012), and "Another Appeal Rejected Out of Hand", 20(8) 60 (Aug. 2012).

172(3)(a.2) amended by 2019 budget bill #1, effective 2020, to add reference to 149.1(1)"qualified donee"(b.1) (registered journalism organization).

172(3) amended by 2012 budget bill #2 (effective Dec. 14, 2012), 2011 budget bill #2, 2004 and 1997 Budgets, 1991 technical bill, 1990 pension bill.

I.T. Application Rules: 69 (meaning of "chapter 148 of ...").

(3.1) Exception — *Charities Registration (Security Information) Act* — Paragraphs (3)(a) and (a.1) do not apply to an applicant or a registered charity that is the subject of a certificate that has been determined to be reasonable under subsection 7(1) of the *Charities Registration (Security Information) Act*.

Notes: 172(3.1) added by 2001 anti-terrorism bill, proclaimed in force December 24, 2001, and amended to change "paragraph 6(1)(d)" to "subsection 7(1)" by S.C. 2001, c. 27 (*Immigration and Refugee Protection Act*), effective June 28, 2002 (per P.C. 2002-996). See Notes to 168(3).

Registered Charities Newsletters: 12 (the new anti-terrorism law).

(4) Deemed refusal to register — For the purposes of subsection (3), the Minister shall be deemed to have refused

(a) to register an applicant for registration as a Canadian amateur athletic association,

(a.1) [Repealed]

(b) to accept for registration for the purposes of this Act any retirement savings plan or profit sharing plan,

(c) [Repealed]

(d) to accept for registration for the purposes of this Act any education savings plan, or

(e) [Repealed under former Act]

(f) to accept for registration for the purposes of this Act any retirement income fund,

where the Minister has not notified the applicant of the disposition of the application within 180 days after the filing of the application with the Minister, and, in any such case, subject to subsection (3.1), an appeal from the refusal to the Federal Court of Appeal pursuant to subsection (3) may, notwithstanding subsection 180(1), be instituted under section 180 at any time by filing a notice of appeal in the Court.

Related Provisions: 167(4) — Application for time extension; 172(4.1) — Appeal suspended when certificate issued that charity supports terrorism; 180 — Appeals to Federal Court of Appeal; *Interpretation Act* 27(5) — Meaning of "within 180 days".

Notes: 172(4)(c), "to issue a certificate of exemption under subsection 212(14)", repealed by 2011 budget bill #2, effective 2012.

172(4)(a) amended and (a.1) repealed by 2004 Budget, effective in respect of notices issued by the Minister after June 12, 2005. Charity revocations are now covered under 168(4) and 172(3). (See "Letter from CRA Corrects Errors in Article", 17(10) *Canadian Not-for-Profit News* (Carswell) 76-77 (Oct. 2009).)

Closing words of 172(4) amended by 2001 anti-terrorism bill to add "subject to subsection (3.1)", proclaimed in force December 24, 2001.

I.T. Application Rules: 69 (meaning of "chapter 148 of ...").

(4.1) Exception — *Charities Registration (Security Information) Act* — An appeal referred to in subsection (3) or (4) is suspended when an applicant or a registered charity is, under subsection 5(1) of the *Charities Registration (Security Information) Act*, served with a copy of a certificate that has been signed under that Act, whether the appeal was instituted before or after the certificate was so signed, and the appeal is

(a) discontinued on the determination, under subsection 7(1) of that Act, that the certificate is reasonable; or

(b) reinstated as of the date the certificate is, under subsection 7(2) of that Act, quashed.

Notes: See Notes to 168(3). 172(4.1) added by 2001 anti-terrorism bill and amended by S.C. 2001, c. 27 (*Immigration and Refugee Protection Act*), effective June 28, 2002 (per P.C. 2002-996).

Registered Charities Newsletters: 12 (the new anti-terrorism law).

(5) Idem — For the purposes of subsection (3), the Minister shall be deemed to have refused

(a) to register for the purposes of this Act any pension plan or pooled pension plan, or

(b) to accept an amendment to a registered pension plan or a pooled registered pension plan

where the Minister has not notified the applicant of the Minister's disposition of the application within 1 year after the filing of the application with the Minister, and, in any such case, an appeal from the refusal to the Federal Court of Appeal pursuant to subsection (3) may, notwithstanding anything in subsection 180(1), be instituted under section 180 at any time by filing a notice of appeal in the Court.

Related Provisions: *Interpretation Act* 27(5) — Meaning of "within 1 year".

Notes: 172(5)(a) and (b) amended by 2012 budget bill #2, effective Dec. 14, 2012, to add references to pooled pension plan and PRPP.

172(5) added by 1990 pension bill, effective 1989.

(6) Application of subsec. 149.1(1) — The definitions in subsection 149.1(1) apply to this section.

Notes: 172(6) added in the RSC 1985 (5th Supp) consolidation for tax years ending after Nov. 1991. This rule was formerly in the opening words of 149.1(1).

Definitions [s. 172]: "administrator" — 147.1(1), 147.5(1); "Canadian amateur athletic association" — 110(8), 248(1); "charitable foundation", "charitable organization", "charitable purposes", "charity" — 149.1(1); "employee", "employer" — 248(1); "Federal Court of Appeal" — *Federal Courts Act* s. 3; "Minister", "person" — 248(1); "pooled pension plan" — 147.5(1), 248(1); "private foundation" — 149.1(1), 248(1); "profit sharing plan" — 147(1); "promoter" — 146.1(1); "public foundation" — 149.1(1), 248(1); "qualified donee" — 149.1(1), 188.2(3)(a), 248(1); "registered Canadian amateur athletic association", "registered charity" — 248(1); "registered education savings plan" — 146.1(1), 248(1); "registered pension plan" — 248(1); "retirement income fund" — 146.3(1), 248(1); "retirement savings plan" — 146(1), 248(1); "taxpayer" — 248(1).

173. (1) References to Tax Court of Canada — Where the Minister and a taxpayer agree in writing that a question of law, fact or mixed law and fact arising under this Act, in respect of any assessment, proposed assessment, determination or proposed determination, should be determined by the Tax Court of Canada, that question shall be determined by that Court.

Related Provisions: 174 — Reference of common questions to Tax Court; 225.1(4) — Collection by the Minister.

Notes: Note that this procedure can be used (with CRA's consent) for a *proposed* assessment, at the Audit stage. The TCC General Procedure applies: *Tax Court of Canada Act* s. 18.31. CRA policy on when to use 173(1): *Appeals Manual* §7.19.4. See also "Judges' Panel", 2018 Cdn Tax Foundation conference report, at pp. 2:7-9. For Rule 58, another way to resolve an issue without a full TCC hearing, see 174(1) Notes.

For examples of s. 173 references, see *Nova Scotia Power*, 2004 SCC 51; *Syspro Software*, 2003 TCC 498; *236130 British Columbia*, 2006 FCA 352; *Fagan*, 2011 TCC 523; *Taylor*, 2012 FCA 148 (whether taxpayer had validly waived right of appeal); *Moules Industriels*, 2018 TCC 85 (under appeal to FCA) (whether corporations owned by trusts were associated due to 256(1.2)(f)(ii)). See also Colin Campbell, *Administration of Income Tax 2020* (Carswell), §14.1.1.

CRA refusal to agree to a reference was not grounds for civil liability: *Ludmer*, 2018 QCCS 3381, paras. 207-226 (aff'd on other grounds 2020 QCCA 697; leave to appeal denied 2021 CarswellQue 2160 (SCC)).

173(1) amended by 1988 Tax Court bill, effective January 1, 1991, to change "Federal Court" to "Tax Court of Canada".

(2) Time during consideration not to count — The time between the day on which proceedings are instituted in the Tax Court of Canada to have a question determined pursuant to subsection (1) and the day on which the question is finally determined shall not be counted in the computation of

(a) the periods determined under subsection 152(4),

(b) the time for service of a notice of objection to an assessment under section 165, or

(c) the time within which an appeal may be instituted under section 169,

for the purpose of making an assessment of the tax payable by the taxpayer who agreed in writing to the determination of the question, for the purpose of serving a notice of objection thereto or for the purpose of instituting an appeal therefrom, as the case may be.

Notes: 173(2) amended by 1988 Tax Court bill, effective January 1, 1991, to change "Federal Court" to "Tax Court of Canada".

Definitions [s. 173]: "assessment", "Minister", "taxpayer" — 248(1); "writing" — *Interpretation Act* 35(1).

174. (1) Common questions [bringing multiple taxpayers to Tax Court] — The Minister may apply to the Tax Court of Canada for a determination of a question if the Minister is of the opinion that the question is common to assessments or proposed assessments in respect of two or more taxpayers and is a question of law, fact or mixed law and fact arising out of

(a) one and the same transaction or occurrence or series of transactions or occurrences; or

(b) substantially similar transactions or occurrences or series of transactions or occurrences.

Related Provisions: 174(2) — Application to Tax Court for common question to be determined; 174(4) — Determination of question is binding on all taxpayers.

Notes: The 2013 amendments to s. 174 are part of a package announced in June 2012 (along with 171(2)–(4) and amendments to the *Tax Court of Canada Act*) to improve the Court's caseload management with thousands of tax shelter appeals looming.

174(1) now allows "substantially similar" appeals to be based on a lead case even if they are not the same transaction. See "Tax Litigation" panel, 2012 Cdn Tax Foundation conference report, at 31:4-8. Rossiter ACJ noted (p. 31:8) that taxpayers will always be given an opportunity to say why their case should not be part of the group. (The Court can decide an appeal's other issues but defer the common issue to the lead case: *Auto Maculate*, 2020 TCC 105, paras. 10, 248.) In *Morrison*, 2016 FCA 256, a "lead case" appellant was denied contact information for other investors in the same shelter because they were still at the objection stage. A "lead case" (*Tax Court Rules* s. 146.1) binds only parties (including the Crown) who agree to be bound: *Mariano*, 2016 TCC 161; *4092325 Investments*, 2018 TCC 228; aff'd 2019 FCA 225 (Abacus Group appeals; but see also *Negus*, 2019 FCA 159, holding related cases in abeyance). However, CRA was wrong to try to use 174(1) for 17,000 taxpayers who used the Global Learning shelter (see 118.1(1)"total charitable gifts" Notes), as each person subject to s. 174 must be able to participate: *McMahon (Foroglou)*, 2020 TCC 104, paras. 41-45.

Rule 26 of the TCC General Procedure Rules can also be used to consolidate two or more appeals [Mackey & Novotny, "Orders for Consolidation and Common Hearings Under Tax Court Rule 26", 2019(3) *Tax Times* (Carswell) 1-4 (Feb. 8, 2019)]. See *407 International*, 2019 TCC 245, joining an Informal with a General Procedure appeal. In *Boguski*, 2018 TCC 236, aff'd 2021 FCA 118, the TCC refused to join appeals of a large group of unrelated taxpayers with a similar issue [Royal Crown Gold Reserve mining rights], because: (1) it had already ruled that two lead cases should proceed and others should be held in abeyance; (2) s. 174 does not apply to taxpayers who have been assessed and have not objected [but see below under "Who is bound"]; (3) self-represented Informal Procedure appellants should not be forced to take part in a General Procedure appeal, or to travel to the hearing from a different province; (4) discovery and trial involving 42 parties would be impractical.

Rule 58 can also shorten an appeal, with a TCC hearing to address a legal issue without a full trial. See, e.g. *Quinco Financial*, 2018 FCA 137; *Hunt*, 2020 FCA 118; *2078970 Ontario [Lux]*, 2017 TCC 173 (Rule 58 ruling rev'd 2020 FCA 162); *Devon Canada*, 2013 TCC 4; *Rio Tinto*, 2017 TCC 67 (FCA appeal discontinued A-153-17); *Cougar Helicopters*, 2017 TCC 126; *Dow Chemical*, 2020 TCC 139 (under appeal to FCA). The TCC may **refuse a Rule 58 hearing** if it would not shorten the trial: e.g. *Paletta*, 2017 FCA 33; *McCartie*, 2020 FCA 18; *632738 Alberta*, 2021 FCA 43 (TCC should not make findings at Rule 58 Stage 1 that may conflict with trial findings); *HBSC Bank*, 2011 TCC 37; *Aitchison Prof. Corp.*, 2016 TCC 281; *Lehigh Hanson*, 2017 TCC 205; *Hillman*, 2018 TCC 122; *MacIsaac Consulting*, 2020 TCC 44; *Jovic Developments*, 2021 TCC 19; *Fiducie Historia*, 2021 TCC 38. See also Innes, "The Pitfalls, Perils and Enigmas of Applications under Rule 58", XX(3) *Tax Litigation* (Federated Press) 6-11 (2017); Toaze & Brown, "Post-*Paletta* — Recent Trends in Rule 58", *Blakes on Canadian Tax Controversy* (*Taxnet Pro* Tax Disputes Centre), Jan. 2018, pp. 1-7; Canning, "TCC's Rule 58", 11(2) *Canadian Tax Focus* (ctf.ca) 9 (May 2021); and discussion in *Ludmer*, 2018 QCCS 3381, paras. 217-225 (aff'd 2020 QCCA 697 without discussing Rule 58; leave to appeal denied 2021 CarswellQue 2160 (SCC)).

Other ways to streamline appeals include: Rule 126 (case management); Rule 146.1 (lead cases); Rule 170.1 (judgment without trial, but only if there is "nothing in controversy": *Georgeson Shareholder*, 2020 FCA 139). Also a "preliminary ruling docket" hearing: 2-year TCC pilot project in 2020-21 for cases up to $300,000: if the parties agree, a judge hears the case for up to 2 days and gives a non-binding ruling to which the parties can consent, with higher costs for a non-consenting party that later loses; Sorensen, "Tax Court Update", 27(4) *Canadian Tax Highlights* (ctf.ca) 10-12 (April 2019); "Judges' Panel", 2019 Cdn Tax Foundation conference report at 2:1-4; TCC Practice Note 23.

Under pre-2013 174(1), the TCC heard joined appeals on the tax status of support payments between ex-spouses, where payments are either taxable to the recipient + deductible to the payor, or neither, e.g., *Artes*, [2003] 2 C.T.C. 2135; *Levy*, 2003 TCC 349; *Howard*, 2004 TCC 69; *Tossell*, 2004 FCA 30; *Peterson*, 2005 FCA 263; *Defina*, 2005 TCC 404; *Callwood*, 2006 FCA 188; *Sebag*, 2006 FCA 312; *Clement*, 2007 TCC 296, *Thorlakson*, 2007 TCC 576, *Boisvert*, 2008 TCC 323; *Poirier*, 2011 TCC 311; *Maheu*, 2013 TCC 279. For more examples see *Hassanali Estate*, [1996] 2 C.T.C. 123 (FCA); *Bourret*, 2008 TCC 108 (which spouse got the Child Tax Benefit); *Lauzon*, 2014 TCC 3 (FCA appeal discontinued A-87-14) (determining whether a business actually paid cash payments it claimed to another business); *ACI Properties*, 2014 FCA 45 (allocation of sale price among assets, to bind both vendor and purchaser).

In *ACI Properties* (above), the Crown's request was allowed where the issue was characterization of a $1.95m payment; the fact CRA had knowingly accepted the payee's characterization of the payment in question for 6 years was not relevant.

In *Dalton*, 2004 FCA 173, a woman appealed an assessment relating to child support, and her ex-husband wrote to the Dept. of Justice and the Tax Court denying that the signature on the child support election form was his. He was added as a party under s. 174. The TCC concluded the signature was the ex-husband's but that he did not remember signing the form. The TCC awarded costs to the woman but not against the ex-husband since he did not initiate the proceeding. The FCA overturned this and ordered the ex-husband to reimburse the Crown for the costs paid to the woman, since his denials caused the appeal to have to be filed.

Who is bound: If the TCC issues separate s. 174 judgments and only one party appeals, the FCA can rule on both judgments: 174(4.2); *Tossell*, 2005 FCA 263, para. 29. The TCC can order a person joined to an appeal even if an assessment of the person would be statute-barred (and see also 174(5)(c)): *Miller*, 2005 FCA 394. However, in *Brenneur*, 2010 TCC 610, the Court refused the Crown's request to apply s. 174 to join X to

B's appeal, because X (a subcontractor of B) had not yet been reassessed, was past the limitation period, might not be reassessed, and spoke only English while B's hearing was to be in French or bilingual.

See also Colin Campbell, *Administration of Income Tax 2020* (Carswell), §14.2.

174(1) amended by 2013 budget bill #1, effective for applications made after June 26, 2013. (The amendments to s. 174 were originally in the June 8, 2012 draft legislation, but were included in the Budget bill.)

(2) Application to Court — An application under subsection (1)

(a) shall set out

(i) the question in respect of which the Minister requests a determination,

(ii) the names of the taxpayers that the Minister seeks to have bound by the determination of the question, and

(iii) the facts and reasons on which the Minister relies and on which the Minister based or intends to base assessments of tax payable by each of the tax-payers named in the application; and

(b) shall be served by the Minister on each of the taxpayers named in the application and on any other persons who, in the opinion of the Tax Court of Canada, are likely to be affected by the determination of the question,

(i) by sending a copy to each taxpayer so named and each other person so likely to be affected, or

(ii) on *ex parte* application by the Minister, in accordance with the directions of the Court.

Related Provisions: 174(3) — Court order defining who will be bound by decision.

Notes: See Notes to 174(1). 174(2) amended by 2013 budget bill #1, for applications made after June 26, 2013, effectively to add subpara. (b)(ii).

(3) Determination of question by Tax Court — If the Tax Court of Canada is satisfied that a question set out in an application under this section is common to assessments or proposed assessments in respect of two or more taxpayers who have been served with a copy of the application, the Tax Court of Canada may

(a) make an order naming the taxpayers in respect of whom the question will be determined;

(b) if one or more of the taxpayers so served has or have appealed an assessment to the Tax Court of Canada in respect of which the question is relevant, make an order joining a party or parties to that or those appeals as it considers appropriate; and

(c) proceed to determine the question in such manner as it considers appropriate.

Notes: See Notes to 174(1). 174(3) amended by 2013 budget bill #1, for applications made after June 26, 2013.

(4) Determination final and conclusive — Subject to subsection (4.1), if a question set out in an application under this section is determined by the Tax Court of Canada, the determination is final and conclusive for the purposes of any assessments of tax payable by the taxpayers named in the order made under paragraph (3)(a).

Related Provisions: 174(4.1) — Who can appeal Tax Court's determination of common question.

Notes: A determination by the TCC under 174 "is a judgment of the Court and the determination is binding in any appeal by taxpayers named in the application for the determination of an assessment or proposed assessment affected by the determination": *Giglio*, [1999] 2 C.T.C. 2591 (TCC).

See Notes to 174(1). 174(4) amended by 2013 budget bill #1, for applications made after June 26, 2013, to change "taxpayers named by it pursuant to subsection (3)" to "taxpayers named in the order made under paragraph (3)(a)".

(4.1) Appeal — If a question set out in an application under this section is determined by the Tax Court of Canada, an appeal from the determination may, in accordance with the provisions of the *Tax Court of Canada Act* or the *Federal Courts Act*, as they relate to appeals from decisions of the Tax Court of Canada to the Federal Court of Appeal, be made by

(a) the Minister; or

(b) any taxpayer named in an order of the Court made under paragraph (3)(a) if

(i) the question arises out of one and the same transaction or occurrence or series of transactions or occurrences,

(ii) the taxpayer has appealed an assessment to the Tax Court of Canada in respect of which the question is relevant, or

(iii) the taxpayer has been granted leave by a judge of the Federal Court of Appeal.

Related Provisions: 174(4.2) — Determination by appeal court is binding on all taxpayers.

Notes: See Notes to 174(1). 174(4.1) amended by 2013 budget bill #1, for applications made after June 26, 2013. Earlier amended by 2002 courts administration bill, effective July 2, 2003.

(4.2) Binding to appeal — Any taxpayer named in an order made under paragraph (3)(a) in respect of a question is bound by any determination in respect of the question under an appeal made to the Federal Court of Appeal or the Supreme Court of Canada.

Notes: See Notes to 174(1). 174(4.2) added by 2013 budget bill #1, for applications made after June 26, 2013.

(5) Time during consideration of question not counted — The time between the day on which an application under this section is served on a taxpayer pursuant to subsection (2) and

(a) in the case of a taxpayer named in an order of the Tax Court of Canada pursuant to subsection (3), the day on which the determination becomes final and conclusive and not subject to any appeal, or

(b) in the case of any other taxpayer, the day on which the taxpayer is served with notice that the taxpayer has not been named in an order of the Tax Court of Canada pursuant to subsection (3),

shall not be counted in the computation of

(c) the periods determined under subsection 152(4),

(d) the time for service of a notice of objection to an assessment under section 165, or

(e) the time within which an appeal may be instituted under section 169,

for the purpose of making an assessment of the tax, interest or penalties payable by the taxpayer, serving a notice of objection thereto or instituting an appeal therefrom, as the case may be.

Notes: 174 amended by 1988 Tax Court bill, effective 1991, to change "Federal Court" to "Tax Court of Canada" and to make related amendments.

Definitions [s. 174]: "assessment" — 248(1); "Federal Court" — *Federal Courts Act* s. 4; "Minister", "person" — 248(1); series of transactions — 248(10); "taxpayer" — 248(1).

175. Institution of appeals — An appeal to the Tax Court of Canada under this Act, other than one referred to in section 18 of the *Tax Court of Canada Act*, shall be instituted in the manner set out in that Act or in any rules made under that Act.

Related Provisions: 170(1) — Informal procedure appeals.

Notes: This refers to General Procedure appeals. Section 18 of the *Tax Court of Canada Act* provides for the Court's "informal procedure". See Notes to 169(1).

175(1)(b), 175(2) and 175(3) repealed by 1992 technical bill, effective June 10, 1993. These rules were moved to the *Tax Court of Canada Act*.

Definitions [s. 175]: "Minister", "taxpayer" — 248(1).

176. [Repealed]

Notes: 176 repealed by 2002-2013 technical bill, effective June 26, 2013. It is no longer needed because the *Tax Court of Canada Act* and *Federal Courts Act* provide the rules. It required CRA to forward relevant documents to the Tax Court once an appeal was filed. 176(1) had been struck down anyway in *Gernhart*, [2000] 1 C.T.C. 192 (FCA): disclosure of the taxpayer's personal income tax returns under 176(1) was an unreasonable seizure in violation of s. 8 of the *Charter of Rights*. 176(2) earlier amended by 2002 courts administration bill, effective July 2, 2003.

177, 178 [Repealed under former Act]

Notes: 177 and 178 repealed by 1988 Tax Court bill, effective 1991. They provided powers to the Federal Court on a pre-1991 appeal. Appeals now go only to the TCC.

179. Hearings *in camera* — Proceedings in the Federal Court of Appeal under this Division may, on the application of the taxpayer, be held *in camera* if the taxpayer establishes to the satisfaction of the Court that the circumstances of the case justify *in camera* proceedings.

Notes: A s. 179 order will rarely be granted, and can possibly be challenged under *Charter of Rights* para. 2(b). See *Roseland Farms*, [1996] 1 C.T.C. 176 (FCA). The "open court" principle allows anyone access to most Court files, to protect the public's freedom of expression: *Sierra Club*, 2002 SCC 41, para. 36; *Rémillard*, 2020 FC 1061, para. 27 (under appeal to FCA); but see Notes to s. 176 re disclosure of personal income tax returns.

Tax Court of Canada Act s. 16.1 permits *in camera* TCC hearings, and ITA 225.2(10), 232(5) and 241(4.1)(a) specifically contemplate them. In *Abenaim*, 2015 TCC 242, the TCC ordered one to keep an employee's termination settlement confidential. For detailed discussion of grounds for a publication ban of a TCC decision, see *Pakzad*, 2017 TCC 83 (denied since no good reason provided). A reported decision may suppress the taxpayer name to avoid disclosing "sensitive personal information": *KC*, 2021 FC 222, para. 1 (but this has been done very rarely).

179 amended by 2002 courts administration bill, effective July 2, 2003.

Definitions [s. 179]: "Federal Court of Appeal" — *Federal Courts Act* s. 3; "taxpayer" — 248(1).

179.1 No reasonable grounds for appeal [— penalty] — Where the Tax Court of Canada disposes of an appeal by a taxpayer in respect of an amount payable under this Part or where such an appeal has been discontinued or dismissed without trial, the Court may, on the application of the Minister and whether or not it awards costs, order the taxpayer to pay to the Receiver General an amount not exceeding 10% of any part of the amount that was in controversy in respect of which the Court determines that there were no reasonable grounds for the appeal, if in the opinion of the Court one of the main purposes for instituting or maintaining any part of the appeal was to defer the payment of any amount payable under this Part.

Related Provisions: 18(1)(t) — No deduction for payments under Act.

Notes: 179.1 applied in *Raynier*, [1990] 2 C.T.C. 2379 (TCC), and *Chin*, 1996 CarswellNat 2873 (TCC), where appeals were held to have been filed only to delay payment via 225.1 (in *Chin*, the penalty was only 5%). In *Rouleau*, 2007 TCC 338, para. 44 (aff'd 2008 FCA 288), the TCC declined to apply 179.1 as the taxpayer, though misguided, was serious about his appeal. In *Foster (Atherton)*, 2007 TCC 659, the TCC did not apply 179.1 but did award costs against A in the Informal Procedure for wasting the Court's time by calling irrelevant witnesses. (See also Notes to 171(1) re awarding costs against taxpayers.)

The same rule appears to apply to the provincial tax component of the appeal, due to provincial legislation providing that 179.1 applies (e.g., Ontario *Taxation Act, 2007* s. 125(8), though arguably that may apply only to appeals in the provincial superior Court; it is unclear whether the TCC has jurisdiction to impose a penalty under that provincial legislation). The author asked CRA for its views: doc 2014-0556221E5 would have an answer if CRA ever replied.

For the meaning of "one of the main purposes" see Notes to 83(2.1).

179.1 amended by 1992 technical bill, effective June 11, 1993, with respect to appeals instituted after June 1992.

Definitions [s. 179.1]: "amount", "Minister", "taxpayer" — 248(1).

CRA Audit Manual: 28.8.1: Penalties — unfounded appeal.

180. (1) Appeals to Federal Court of Appeal [filing deadline] — An appeal to the Federal Court of Appeal pursuant to subsection 172(3) may be instituted by filing a notice of appeal in the Court within 30 days from

(a) the day on which the Minister notifies a person under subsection 165(3) of the Minister's action in respect of a notice of objection filed under subsection 168(4),

(b) [Repealed]

(c) the mailing of notice to the administrator of the registered pension plan under subsection 147.1(11),

(c.1) the sending of a notice to a promoter of a registered education savings plan under subsection 146.1(12.1),

(c.2) the mailing of notice to the administrator of the pooled registered pension plan under subsection 147.5(24), or

(d) the time the decision of the Minister to refuse the application for acceptance of the amendment to the registered pension plan or pooled registered pension plan was mailed, or otherwise communicated in writing, by the Minister to any person,

as the case may be, or within such further time as the Court of Appeal or a judge thereof may, either before or after the expiration of those 30 days, fix or allow.

> **Enacted Amendment — 180(1) — *Time Limits and Other Periods Act (COVID-19)* [TLOPA]**
>
> [See Enacted Amendment under 169(1). TLOPA 6(1) extended the 180(1) 30-days deadline by up to 6 months during the COVID-19 pandemic — ed.]

Related Provisions: 172(4) — Deemed refusal to register; 248(7)(a) — Mail deemed received on day mailed; *Interpretation Act* 27(5) — Meaning of "within 30 days".

Notes: This section deals with charity registration appeals. Normal appeals from the TCC to the FCA are under the *Tax Court of Canada Act* and the *Federal Courts Act*. See 169(1) Notes.

180(1) amended by 2012 budget bill #2 (effective Dec. 14, 2012), 2011 budget bill #2, 2004 and 1997 Budgets, 1991 technical bill, 1990 pension bill.

(2) No jurisdiction in Tax Court of Canada or Federal Court — Neither the Tax Court of Canada nor the Federal Court has jurisdiction to entertain any proceeding in respect of a decision of the Minister from which an appeal may be instituted under this section.

Notes: 180(2) amended by 2002 courts administration bill, effective July 2, 2003.

(3) Summary disposition of appeal — An appeal to the Federal Court of Appeal instituted under this section shall be heard and determined in a summary way.

Related Provisions: 172(4) — Deemed refusal to register.

Definitions [s. 180]: "administrator" — 147.1(1), 147.5(1); "Federal Court" — *Federal Courts Act* s. 4; "Federal Court of Appeal" — *Federal Courts Act* s. 3; "Minister", "person" — 248(1); "pooled registered pension plan" — 147.5(1), 248(1); "profit sharing plan" — 147(1); "promoter" — 146.1(1); "registered charity", "registered pension plan" — 248(1); "writing" — *Interpretation Act* 35(1).

PART I.01 — TAX IN RESPECT OF STOCK OPTION BENEFIT DEFERRAL

180.01 [No longer relevant]

Notes [s. 180.01]: 180.01 (added by 2010 budget bill #2, effective March 4, 2010 for dispositions before 2015) provided relief until 2014 for taxpayers who elected under former 7(8) to defer a stock option benefit from publicly-traded shares, where the shares later dropped in value (see 7(1) Notes re "underwater" options). It replaced the deferred income inclusion with a deemed capital gain, which could be offset by a capital loss on selling the shares. For the text see up to PITA 58th ed. The mechanics are: 180.01(2)(a) reverses the 7(1) income inclusion by converting the 110(1)(d) 50% offsetting deduction (assuming it is available) to a 100% deduction. 180.01(2)(b) then deems the benefit to be a capital gain, which carries over via 40(3.21) to 38-40 as an ordinary capital gain, offsettable by capital losses. 180.01(2)(c) applies a 100% tax on the proceeds of disposition (although 73(1) does not apply, 69(1) might). 180.01(2)(d) deems the election to be a 152(4.2) application for adjustment of a past year's return, but this does not mean that the election can be filed up to 10 years late, since 180.01(1)(c) must be satisfied before 180.01(2) applies. See also Ziesmann, "Relief for the Stock Option Capital Loss Trap", 22(2) *Taxation of Executive Compensation & Retirement* (Federated Press) 1319-24 (Sept. 2010). Corporate bankruptcy does not create a disposition of the shares for 180.01, since 50(1) applies only for purposes of ss. 38-55: VIEWS doc 2011-0420241E5.

PART I.1 — INDIVIDUAL SURTAX

180.1 [Repealed]

Notes: 180.1 imposed a surtax on individuals. (The corporate surtax in 123.2 was repealed in 2008.) 180.1 amended by 1989 Budget, 1991 and 1992 technical bills, 1993 and 1998 Budgets, 2000 Budget/2001 technical bill (which repealed Part I.1 effective for 2001 and later years). For 1989, basic surtax (BS) was 4% and additional surtax (AS) was 1.5% of basic federal tax (BFT) over $15,000. For 1990, BS was 5% and AS was 3% of BFT over $15,000. 1991: BS 5%, AS 5% of BFT over $12,500. 1992: BS 4.5%, AS 5% of BFT over $12,500. 1993-97: BS 3%, AS 5% of BFT over $12,500. 1998: BS 3% but 1.5% for lower-income taxpayers, AS 5% of BFT over $12,500.

1999: BS 1.5% for all taxpayers, AS 5% of BFT over $12,500. 2000: BS nil and high-income surtax 5% of BFT over $15,500. As of 2001, all surtaxes are gone.

The Aug. 27/10 draft legislation (Part 3) proposed a new s. 180.1, which was changed to and enacted as 180.01 by 2010 budget bill #2.

PART I.2 — TAX [CLAWBACK] ON OLD AGE SECURITY BENEFITS

180.2 (1) Definitions — The definitions in this subsection apply in this Part.

"adjusted income" of an individual for a taxation year means the amount that would be the individual's income under Part I for the year if in computing that income no amount were

(a) included

(i) under paragraph 56(1)(q.1) or subsection 56(6),

(ii) in respect of a gain from a disposition of property to which section 79 applies, or

(iii) in respect of a gain described in subsection 40(3.21), or

(b) deductible under paragraph 20(1)(ww) or 60(w), (y) or (z);

Notes: Due to the references to 56(1)(q.1) and 60(z), RDSP income is excluded from the income base on which the OAS clawback is calculated.

Para. (b) amended by 2018 budget bill #1 to add reference to 20(1)(ww), for 2018 and later tax years. Definition earlier amended by 2007 RDSPs bill (for 2008 and later years), 2010 budget bill #2 (for 2000 and later years), 2006 budget bill #1.

"base taxation year", in relation to a month, means

(a) where the month is any of the first 6 months of a calendar year, the taxation year that ended on December 31 of the second preceding calendar year, and

(b) where the month is any of the last 6 months of a calendar year, the taxation year that ended on December 31 of the preceding calendar year.

"return of income" in respect of an individual for a taxation year means

(a) where the individual was resident in Canada throughout the year, the individual's return of income (other than a return of income filed under subsection 70(2) or 104(23), paragraph 128(2)(e) or subsection 150(4)) that is filed or required to be filed under Part I for the year, and

(b) in any other case, a prescribed form containing prescribed information.

Related Provisions: 60(v.1) — UI benefit repayment; 60(w) — Other deductions — tax under Part I.2.

Notes: See Notes at end of 180.2.

(2) Tax payable — Every individual shall pay a tax under this Part for each taxation year equal to the amount determined by the formula

$$A(1 - B)$$

where

A is the lesser of

(a) the amount, if any, by which

(i) the total of all amounts each of which is the amount of any pension, supplement or spouse's or common-law partner's allowance under the *Old Age Security Act* included in computing the individual's income under Part I for the year

exceeds

(ii) the amount of any deduction allowed under subparagraph 60(n)(i) in computing the individual's income under Part I for the year, and

(b) 15% of the amount, if any, by which the individual's adjusted income for the year exceeds $50,000[27]; and

---

[27] Indexed by 117.1 — ed.

B is the rate of tax payable by the individual under Part XIII on amounts described in paragraph (a) of the description of A.

Related Provisions: 60(w) — Deduction for amounts clawed back to avoid double tax; 117.1(2)(t) — Indexing for inflation; 156.1(1)"net tax owing"(b)A — Part I.2 tax included in determining instalments required; 180.2(3) — Withholding of tax from OAS benefits.

Notes: This tax is known as the "clawback" of OAS benefits. The benefits are simply not paid to high-income individuals or couples, rather than clawed back; see 180.2(3). To request reduction of the OAS withholding, use Form T1213(OAS). For reporting amounts on the T4(OAS), see VIEWS doc 2011-0400281M4.

The $50,000 figure is $79,054 for 2020 and $79,845 for 2021. See table after s. 117.1.

For details on the OAS see tinyurl.com/oas-canada.

See also Notes at end of 180.2.

180.2(2)(a)(i) amended by 2000 same-sex partners bill to refer to "common-law partner", effective as per Notes to 248(1)"common-law partner".

Remission Orders: *Dane Pocrnic Remission Order*, P.C. 2005-624 (remission where taxable lump sum paid all in one year due to government agency delay led to OAS clawback applying); *Keith Kirby Remission Order*, P.C. 2005-1533 (same); *Josephine Pastorious Remission Order*, P.C. 2005-1534 (same); *Jacques Beauvais Remission Order*, P.C. 2006-406 (same); *Wesley Kool Remission Order*, P.C. 2006-1277 (same); *Murray Chalmers Remission Order*, P.C. 2007-254 (same); *Bela Revi Tax Remission Order*, P.C. 2011-1140 (same, without indication of government agency delay).

Forms: T1 General return, Lines 235, 422; T1136: OAS return of income; T4155: Old age security return of income guide for non-residents.

(3) Withholding

(3) Withholding — Where at any time Her Majesty pays an amount described in paragraph (a) of the description of A in subsection (2) in respect of a month to an individual, there shall be deducted or withheld from that amount on account of the individual's tax payable under this Part for the year the amount determined under subsection (4) in respect of that amount.

Related Provisions: 227 — Rules applicable to withholding.

Notes: See Notes to 180.2(2) and at end of 180.2.

Forms: T1213(OAS): Request to reduce OAS recovery tax at source.

(4) Determination of amount to be withheld

(4) Determination of amount to be withheld — The amount determined in respect of a particular amount described in subsection (3) is

(a) where the individual has filed a return of income for the base taxation year in relation to the month in which the particular amount is paid, the lesser of

(i) the amount by which the particular amount exceeds the amount of tax payable under Part XIII by the individual on the particular amount, and

(ii) the amount determined by the formula

$$(0.0125A - \$665^{27})(1-B)$$

where

A is the individual's adjusted income for the base taxation year, and

B is the rate of tax payable under Part XIII by the individual on the particular amount;

(b) where the individual has not filed a return of income for the base taxation year in relation to the month and

(i) the Minister has demanded under subsection 150(2) that the individual file the return, or

(ii) the individual was non-resident at any time in the base taxation year,

the amount by which the particular amount exceeds the amount of tax payable under Part XIII by the individual on the particular amount; and

(c) in any other case, nil.

Related Provisions: 117.1(2)(t) — Indexing for inflation; 180.2(5) — Obligation to file return; 257 — Formula cannot calculate to less than zero.

Notes: The $665 figure is 1/12 of $7,982, which is 15% of $53,215, the figure as of 1999 before inflation adjustment (see 117.1(1)) in 180.2(2).

The effect of 180.2(4)(b)(ii) is that for a non-resident who does not file a return under 180.2(5)(a)(ii) showing total income, no OAS benefits are paid.

180.2(4)(a)(ii) amended by 2001 technical bill to change $625 to $665, for amounts paid after November 1999.

See also Notes at end of 180.2.

Forms: T1213(OAS): Request to reduce OAS recovery tax at source.

(5) Return

(5) Return — Every individual liable to pay tax under this Part for a taxation year shall

(a) file with the Minister, without notice or demand therefor,

(i) where the individual is resident in Canada throughout the taxation year, a return for the year under this Part in prescribed form and containing prescribed information on or before the individual's filing-due date for the year, and

(ii) in any other case, a return of income for the year on or before the individual's balance-due day for the year; and

(b) pay the individual's tax payable under this Part for the year on or before the individual's balance-due day for the year.

Related Provisions: 180.2(4)(b)(ii) — No OAS benefits paid to non-resident who does not file return.

Notes: See Notes at end of 180.2.

Forms: T4155: Old age security return of income guide for non-residents.

(6) Provisions applicable to this Part

(6) Provisions applicable to this Part — Subsection 150(3), sections 150.1, 151 and 152, subsections 153(1.1), (1.2) and (3), sections 155 to 156.1 and 158 to 167 and Division J of Part I apply to this Part with any modifications that the circumstances require.

Notes: See Notes to 153(1.3) re application of 180.2(6).

Notes [s. 180.2]: The tax under 180.2(2) is informally known as the "clawback" of old age security benefits. See Notes to 180.2(2).

Workers' compensation payments (including a retroactive tribunal award), although effectively not taxed (see 56(1)(v), 110(1)(f)(ii)) and even if in respect of many years, can cause 180.2 to claw back OAS: *Butler*, 2016 FCA 65; *Miner Estate*, 2003 TCC 599; *Fenner*, 2006 TCC 396; *Stoddard*, 2007 TCC 380; *Pelletier*, 2010 TCC 454. See also VIEWS doc 2018-0762381M4. Similarly, in *Burchill*, 2010 FCA 145, and *Parisée*, 2009 TCC 132, a lump sum of pension arrears made the clawback apply, even though most of the income was subject to 110.2 averaging. Relief is sometimes provided by remission order: see Remission Orders annotation to 180.2(2).

Per Guide T4155, non-residents are not subject to the clawback if they are resident in Argentina, Australia, Azerbaijan, Bangladesh, Barbados, Brazil [Brazilian nationals only], Bulgaria, Colombia, Cyprus, Dominican Republic, Ecuador, Finland, Germany, Greece, Hungary, Ireland, Israel, Ivory Coast, Kenya, Malaysia, Malta, Mexico, New Zealand, Norway, Papua New Guinea, Peru, Philippines [if total Canadian pensions do not exceed $5,000 for the year] Poland, Portugal, Romania, Senegal, Serbia, Spain, Sri Lanka, Switzerland, Taiwan, Tanzania, Trinidad & Tobago, Turkey, United Kingdom, United States, Zambia or Zimbabwe. Any other non-resident must file a T1136 showing world income to receive OAS payments: VIEWS doc 2012-0444821E5.

In *Swantje*, [1994] 2 C.T.C. 382 (FCA); aff'd [1996] 1 C.T.C. 355 (SCC), the clawback was held not to be a tax on (treaty-exempt) German pension income when it took that income into account, since the purpose of 180.2 was to require repayment of social benefits. Nor can the Tax Court apply principles of equity to provide relief: *Dubois*, 2006 TCC 403. (For U.S. residents, see Canada-U.S. Tax Treaty:Art. XXIV:10.) See also Notes to 118(2).

Similarly, the dividend gross-up under 82(1)(b) is included in the 180.2 calculation: VIEWS doc 2016-0667301M4.

180.2 is not a violation of the *Charter of Rights*: *Alibhai*, 2005 TCC 574; or the *Bill of Rights*: *Kieling*, 2006 TCC 222. Nor can the Tax Court apply principles of equity to provide relief: *Dubois* (above).

The clawback is not adjusted merely because the individual receives the OAS benefit for only a few months of the year: VIEWS doc 2009-0352331E5.

See also Macnaughton, "Defer OAS to Avoid Clawback", 21(7) *Canadian Tax Highlights* (ctf.ca) 2-3 (July 2013); Veall, "Cash RRSPs Early, Avoid Clawback", 22(1) *CTH* 2-3 (Jan. 2014).

180.2 amended by 1995 Budget, 1992 Child Benefit bill, 1991 technical bill. Added by 1989 Budget.

Definitions [s. 180.2]: "adjusted income" — 180.2(1); "amount", "balance-due day" — 248(1); "base taxation year" — 180.2(1); "calendar year" — *Interpretation Act* 37(1)(a); "common-law partner" — 248(1); "filing-due date" — 150(1), 248(1); "Her Majesty" — *Interpretation Act* 35(1); "individual" — 248(1); "Minister", "non-resident" — 248(1); "resident in Canada" — 250; "return of income" — 180.2(1); "tax payable" — 248(2); "taxation year" — 249.

---

27 Indexed by 117.1 — ed.

PART I.3 — TAX ON LARGE CORPORATIONS [PRE-2006]

Notes: The Large Corporations Tax has been eliminated, but the rules in Part I.3 are still used for various purposes. See Notes to 181.1(1).

181. (1) Definitions — For the purposes of this Part,

"financial institution", in respect of a taxation year, means a corporation that at any time in the year is

(a) a bank or credit union,

(b) an insurance corporation that carries on business in Canada,

(c) authorized under the laws of Canada or a province to carry on the business of offering its services as a trustee to the public,

(d) authorized under the laws of Canada or a province to accept deposits from the public and carries on the business of lending money on the security of real property or immovables or investing in indebtedness on the security of mortgages on real property or of hypothecs on immovables,

(e) a registered securities dealer,

(f) a mortgage investment corporation, or

(g) a corporation

(i) listed in the schedule *[reproduced after s. 281 — ed.]*, or

(ii) all or substantially all of the assets of which are shares or indebtedness of financial institutions to which the corporation is related;

Related Provisions: 142.2(1)"financial institution"(a)(i), 248(1)"restricted financial institution"(e.1), "specified financial institution"(e.1) — Corporation under para. (g) deemed to be FI, RFI and SFI.

Notes: CRA considers that "substantially all", used in subpara. (g)(ii), means 90% or more, based on the cost of the assets for accounting purposes: doc 2002-0150325.

Definition amended by 2002-2013 technical bill (bijuralism amendment effective June 26, 2013; last substantive amendment was for tax years ending after Dec. 19, 2002); 2001 *Civil Code* harmonization bill; 1994 technical bill; 1991 technical bill.

"long-term debt" means,

(a) in the case of a bank, its subordinated indebtedness (within the meaning assigned by section 2 of the *Bank Act*) evidenced by obligations issued for a term of not less than 5 years,

(b) in the case of an insurance corporation, its subordinated indebtedness (within the meaning assigned by section 2 of the *Insurance Companies Act*) evidenced by obligations issued for a term of not less than 5 years, and

(c) in the case of any other corporation, its subordinated indebtedness (within the meaning that would be assigned by section 2 of the *Bank Act* if the definition of that expression in that section were applied with such modifications as the circumstances require) evidenced by obligations issued for a term of not less than 5 years,

but does not include, where the corporation is a prescribed federal Crown corporation for the purpose of section 27, any indebtedness evidenced by obligations issued to and held by Her Majesty in right of Canada;

Notes: Preferred shares that are not retractable within 5 years and are a liability on the balance sheet are considered long-term debt: VIEWS doc 2010-0353081I7.

Definition "long-term debt" amended by 1993 technical bill, effective June 1, 1992. Previously amended by 1992 technical bill.

I.T. Technical News: 28 (large corporations tax — long-term debt).

"reserves", in respect of a corporation for a taxation year, means the amount at the end of the year of all of the corporation's reserves, provisions and allowances (other than allowances in respect of depreciation or depletion) and, for greater certainty, includes any provision in respect of deferred taxes.

Related Provisions: 181.2(3) — Reserves included in capital tax base.

Notes: Unamortized or deferred portions of an insurer's gains on disposition of investments were not "reserves" and thus not included in capital: *Manufacturers Life Insurance Co.*, 2001 FCA 213; VIEWS doc 2010-035481117.

Future income tax liability, recorded under CICA *Handbook* §3465, is considered to be a provision for deferred taxes and therefore "reserves": VIEWS doc 2001-0080075.

See also Notes to 181(3).

Interpretation Bulletins: IT-532: Part I.3 — tax on large corporations.

I.T. Technical News: 18 (*Oerlikon Aérospatiale* case).

(2) Prescribed expressions — For the purposes of this Part, the expressions "attributed surplus", "Canadian assets", "Canadian premiums", "Canadian reserve liabilities", "permanent establishment", "total assets", "total premiums" and "total reserve liabilities" have such meanings as may be prescribed.

Regulations: 8600 (prescribed meanings of expressions).

(3) Determining values and amounts — For the purposes of determining the carrying value of a corporation's assets or any other amount under this Part in respect of a corporation's capital, investment allowance, taxable capital or taxable capital employed in Canada for a taxation year or in respect of a partnership in which a corporation has an interest,

(a) the equity and consolidation methods of accounting shall not be used; and

(b) subject to paragraph (a) and except as otherwise provided in this Part, the amounts reflected in the balance sheet

(i) presented to the shareholders of the corporation (in the case of a corporation that is neither an insurance corporation to which subparagraph (ii) applies nor a bank) or the members of the partnership, as the case may be, or, where such a balance sheet was not prepared in accordance with generally accepted accounting principles or no such balance sheet was prepared, the amounts that would be reflected if such a balance sheet had been prepared in accordance with generally accepted accounting principles, or

(ii) accepted by the Superintendent of Financial Institutions, in the case of a bank or an insurance corporation that is required by law to report to the Superintendent, or the superintendent of insurance or other similar officer or authority of the province under whose laws the corporation is incorporated, in the case of an insurance corporation that is required by law to report to that officer or authority,

shall be used.

Related Provisions: 190(2) — Rules in 181(3) apply to Part VI also.

Notes: See Notes to 181.1(1). The definitions in Part I.3 are generally to be interpreted in accordance with accounting principles rather than legal terminology: *Oerlikon Aérospatiale*, [1999] 4 C.T.C. 358 (FCA); leave to appeal denied 2000 CarswellNat 865 (SCC); *Ford Credit*, 2007 FCA 225 (shares were treated as debt on the balance sheet). "The proper interpretation of subsec. 181(3) must be determined in the context of its ... history... In enacting the LCT as a deficit reduction measure, Parliament must have intended the tax to be temporary in nature... in enacting subsec. 181(3), Parliament basically chose to adopt a method of computing capital for the purpose of the temporary new tax that was well known to large corporations. The financial statements of large corporations are routinely prepared on an audited basis in accordance with GAAP, and therefore, adopting GAAP as the principal determinant of the capital tax base for most corporations ensured that the new and temporary tax would be relatively simple to implement and administer. However, a complete adoption of GAAP did not occur." (*Ford Credit*, FCA para. 20)

The term "reflected on the balance sheet" should be given its accounting meaning, the same as "recorded" or "included in": *Royal Trust Co.*, [2001] 3 C.T.C. 2268 (TCC). However, in *Inco Ltd.*, 2007 TCC 1, calling share options "contingently issuable equity" did not exclude them from capital: "unless GAAP requires the use of particular labels on the balance sheet, it is doubtful that Parliament would have intended s. 181(3) to be interpreted [so that the label on the balance sheet is determinative] because the tax could so readily be avoided" (para. 26).

GAAP determines both characterization and amounts of items in the financial statements; unamortized or deferred portions of an insurer's gains on disposition of investments were excluded from capital as they were not reflected on the balance sheet for accounting purposes as reserves or surpluses: *Manufacturers Life*, 2001 FCA 213. In *SNC Technologies*, 2008 TCC 461 (FCA appeal discontinued A-447-08), 181(3) applied to progress payments on a Dept. of Defence contract. In *Bombardier Inc.*, 2012 FCA 46, advances toward construction of airplanes were counted only to the extent they were liabilities on Bombardier's balance sheet.

In *FCMI Financial*, 2007 ONCA 316, a company was allowed to revise its financial statements for Ontario capital tax purposes to be in accordance with GAAP.

CRA's view is that if consolidated financial statements are in accordance with GAAP, the same method must be used for unconsolidated statements rather than another method that is also in accordance with GAAP: docs 2004-0104301I7, 2005-0136961I7.

GAAP referred to in 181(3) is Canadian GAAP, not US GAAP, even for a subsidiary of a US company: VIEWS doc 2004-0091181I7.

Partnership earnings for the fiscal period of a partnership ended in a corporate partner's taxation year are included in the partner's capital based on allocation of partnership income. Stub period earnings (both income and losses) are included only to the extent the partner has received a distribution of such earnings: VIEWS docs 2003-0181695, 2004-0064701E5.

See also VIEWS docs 2008-0305241I7 (application to 181.2(3)(a)), 2009-0313311I7 (cash transfers within corporate group under Central Banking Arrangement), 2011-0415771E5 (taxable capital of farm mutual insurer).

Interpretation Bulletins: IT-532: Part I.3 — tax on large corporations.

I.T. Technical News: 18 (*Oerlikon Aérospatiale* case); 22 (large corporation tax — capital tax cases); 29 (large corporations tax — outstanding cheques).

(4) Limitations respecting inclusions and deductions —
Unless a contrary intention is evident, no provision of this Part shall be read or construed to require the inclusion or to permit the deduction, in computing the amount of a corporation's capital, investment allowance, taxable capital or taxable capital employed in Canada for a taxation year, of any amount to the extent that that amount has been included or deducted, as the case may be, in computing the first-mentioned amount under, in accordance with or by reason of any other provision of this Part.

Interpretation Bulletins: IT-532: Part I.3 — tax on large corporations.

Related Provisions: 190(2) — Rules in 181(4) apply to Part VI also; 248(28) — Similar rule for the Act as a whole.

Definitions [s. 181]: "amount" — 248(1); "bank" — 248(1), *Interpretation Act* 35(1); "business" — 248(1); "Canada" — 255; "carrying on business in Canada" — 253; "corporation" — 248(1), *Interpretation Act* 35(1); "credit union" — 137(6), 248(1); "financial institution" — 181(1); "Her Majesty" — *Interpretation Act* 35(1); "hypothecs" — Quebec *Civil Code* art. 2660; "immovables" — Quebec *Civil Code* art. 900–907; "insurance corporation" — 248(1); "investment allowance" — 181.2(4), 181.3(4); "mortgage investment corporation" — 130.1(6), 248(1); "province" — *Interpretation Act* 35(1); "registered securities dealer" — 248(1); "related" — 251(2); "taxation year" — 249.

181.1 (1) Tax payable — Every corporation shall pay a tax under this Part for each taxation year equal to the amount obtained by multiplying the corporation's specified percentage for the taxation year by the amount, if any, by which

(a) its taxable capital employed in Canada for the year

exceeds

(b) its capital deduction for the year.

Related Provisions: 132.2(3)(l)(ii) — Deemed taxation year of mutual fund corporation on reorganization; 161(1) — Interest; 161(4.1) — Interest — limitation; 181.1(1.1) — Specified percentage; 190.1(1) — Financial institutions capital tax.

Notes: The Large Corporations Tax has been eliminated. It applied at 0.225% of taxable capital employed in Canada from Feb. 28, 1993 through 2003; 0.2% for 2004, 0.175% for 2005 and zero since Jan. 2006 (see 181.1(1.1)).

The LCT was payable only to the extent Part I surtax was not payable, and thus did not affect most profitable corporations. See 181.1(4)(a).

The LCT rules are still relevant for: calculating unused surtax credits (161(7)(a)(ix), 164(5)(h.2)); the small business deduction (125(5.1)(a), 181.1(1.2), 181.5(1.1)); the requirement for full details in a notice of objection (165(1.11)); the Part VI financial institutions capital tax (190.1(2)); the requirement that a large corporation pay half the tax in dispute (225.1(8)); the penalty for large corporations that file returns late (235); and the definitions 248(1)"restricted financial institution"(e.1) and 248(1)"specified financial institution"(e.1) (these terms are used in numerous places in the Act).

See Notes to 27(1) re *Canadian Pacific Railway* case.

181.1(1) amended by 2003 Budget, effective for 2004 and later taxation years, to change "0.225%" to the "specified percentage" (see 181.1(1.1)). Earlier amended by 1995 Budget and 1991 technical bill; added by 1989 Budget.

Interpretation Bulletins: IT-532: Part I.3 — tax on large corporations.

(1.1) Specified percentage — For the purpose of subsection (1), the specified percentage of a corporation for a taxation year that ends after 2003 is the total of

(a) that proportion of 0.225% that the number of days in the taxation year that are before 2004 is of the number of days in the taxation year,

(b) that proportion of 0.200% that the number of days in the taxation year that are in 2004 is of the number of days in the taxation year, and

(c) that proportion of 0.175% that the number of days in the taxation year that are in 2005 is of the number of days in the taxation year.

(d), (e) [Repealed]

Notes: 181.1(1.1)(d) and (e) repealed by 2006 budget bill #1, for 2006 and later tax years. This repeals Large Corporations Tax. A 3-year carryback of the credit from later years is still allowed under 181.1(4).

181.1(1.1) added by 2003 Budget, for 2004 and later tax years. See Notes to 181.1(1).

(1.2) Exceptions — Notwithstanding subsection (1.1), for the purposes of applying subsection 125(5.1) and the definitions "unused surtax credit" in subsections (6) and 190.1(5), the amount of tax in respect of a corporation under subsection (1) for a taxation year is to be determined as if the specified percentage of the corporation for the taxation year were 0.225%.

Notes: 181.1(1.2) added by 2003 Budget, for 2004 and later tax years. It ensures that various provisions that use Part I.3 tax as a measure of a corporation being "large" continue to work as they did before the 2003 Budget amendment to 181.1(1).

(2) Short taxation years — Where a taxation year of a corporation is less than 51 weeks, the amount determined under subsection (1) for the year in respect of the corporation shall be reduced to that proportion of that amount that the number of days in the year is of 365.

Related Provisions: 132.2(3)(l)(ii) — Deemed taxation year of mutual fund corporation on reorganization.

Notes: 181.1(2) amended by 1992 technical bill, for 1992 and later tax years.

(3) Where tax not payable — No tax is payable under this Part for a taxation year by a corporation

(a) that was a non-resident-owned investment corporation throughout the year;

(b) that was a bankrupt at the end of the year;

(c) that was throughout the year exempt from tax under section 149 on all of its taxable income;

(d) that neither was resident in Canada nor carried on business through a permanent establishment in Canada at any time in the year;

(e) that was throughout the year a deposit insurance corporation (within the meaning assigned by subsection 137.1(5)) or a corporation deemed by subsection 137.1(5.1) to be a deposit insurance corporation; or

(f) that was throughout the year a corporation described in subsection 136(2) the principal business of which was marketing (including processing incidental to or connected therewith) natural products belonging to or acquired from its members or customers.

Related Provisions: 132.2(3)(l)(ii) — Deemed taxation year of mutual fund corporation on reorganization.

Notes: For the meaning of "principal business" in para. (f) see Notes to 20(1)(bb).

181.1(3)(b) amended by 2017 budget bill #2, for bankruptcies after April 26, 1995, to delete "(within the meaning assigned by subsection 128(3))" after "bankrupt". ("Bankrupt" is now defined in 248(1).)

181.1(3)(e) added by 1991 technical bill and (f) added by 1992 technical bill, both retroactive to the introduction of the tax (taxation years ending after June 1989).

Interpretation Bulletins: IT-347R2: Crown corporations (cancelled); IT-496R: Non-profit organizations; IT-532: Part I.3 — tax on large corporations.

(4) Deduction — There may be deducted from a corporation's tax otherwise payable under this Part for a taxation year an amount equal to the total of

(a) its Canadian surtax payable for the year, and

(b) such part as the corporation claims of its unused surtax credits for its 7 immediately preceding and 3 immediately following taxation years,

to the extent that that total does not exceed the amount by which

(c) the amount that would, but for this subsection, be its tax payable under this Part for the year

exceeds

(d) the total of all amounts each of which is the amount deducted under subsection 125.3(1) in computing the corporation's tax payable under Part I for a taxation year ending before 1992 in respect of its unused Part I.3 tax credit (within the meaning assigned by section 125.3) for the year.

Related Provisions: 87(2)(j.91) — Amalgamation; 87(2.11) — Vertical amalgamations; 161(7)(a)(ix), 164(5)(h.1), 164(5.1)(h.2) — Effect of carryback of loss etc.; 181.6 — Return; 261(7)(a), 261(15) — Functional currency reporting.

Notes: 181.1(4) added by 1992 technical bill and amended by 1993 technical bill for 1992 and later tax years. See Notes to 125.3.

Interpretation Bulletins: IT-532: Part I.3 — tax on large corporations.

Forms: T2 Sched. 37: Calculation of unused surtax credit.

(5) Idem — For the purposes of this subsection and subsections (4), (6) and (7),

(a) an amount may not be claimed under subsection (4) in computing a corporation's tax payable under this Part for a particular taxation year in respect of its unused surtax credit for another taxation year until its unused surtax credits, if any, for taxation years preceding the other year that may be claimed under this Part for the particular year have been claimed; and

(b) an amount in respect of a corporation's unused surtax credit for a taxation year may be claimed under subsection (4) in computing its tax payable under this Part for another taxation year only to the extent that it exceeds the total of all amounts each of which is an amount claimed in respect of that unused surtax credit in computing its tax payable under this Part or Part VI for a taxation year preceding that other year.

Related Provisions: 87(2.11) — Vertical amalgamations.

Notes: 181.1(5) added by 1992 technical bill, for 1992 and later taxation years.

(6) Definitions — For the purposes of this subsection and subsections (4), (5) and (7),

"Canadian surtax payable" of a corporation for a taxation year has the meaning assigned by subsection 125.3(4);

Notes: The definition in 125.3(4) reads:

"Canadian surtax payable" of a corporation for a taxation year means

(a) in the case of a corporation that is non-resident throughout the year, the lesser of

(i) the amount determined under section 123.2 in respect of the corporation for the year, and

(ii) its tax payable under this Part for the year, and

(b) in any other case, the lesser of

(i) the prescribed proportion of the amount determined under section 123.2 in respect of the corporation for the year, and

(ii) its tax payable under this Part for the year;

"unused surtax credit" for a taxation year ending after 1991

(a) of a corporation (other than a corporation that was throughout the year a financial institution, within the meaning assigned by section 190) means the amount, if any, by which

(i) its Canadian surtax payable for the year

exceeds the total of

(ii) the amount that would, but for subsection (4), be its tax payable under this Part for the year, and

(iii) the amount, if any, deducted under section 125.3 in computing the corporation's tax payable under Part I for the year, and

(b) of a corporation that was throughout the year a financial institution (within the meaning assigned by section 190) means the lesser of

(i) the amount, if any, by which

(A) its Canadian surtax payable for the year

exceeds the total of

(B) the amount that would, but for subsection (4), be its tax payable under this Part for the year, and

(C) the amount, if any, deducted under section 125.3 in computing the corporation's tax payable under Part I for the year, and

(ii) the amount, if any, by which its tax payable under Part I for the year exceeds the amount that would, but for subsection (4) and subsection 190.1(3), be the total of its taxes payable under Parts I.3 and VI for the year.

Related Provisions: 87(2.11) — Vertical amalgamations; 181.1(1.2) — Calculation to be based on tax rate of 0.225%; 181.5(1.1), (4.1) — Calculation to be based on threshold of $10 million; 256(9) — Date of acquisition of control.

Notes: 181.1(6) added by 1992 technical bill, for 1992 and later taxation years.

(7) Acquisition of control — Where at any time control of a corporation has been acquired by a person or group of persons, no amount in respect of its unused surtax credit for a taxation year ending before that time is deductible by the corporation for a taxation year ending after that time and no amount in respect of its unused surtax credit for a taxation year ending after that time is deductible by the corporation for a taxation year ending before that time, except that

(a) the corporation's unused surtax credit for a particular taxation year that ended before that time is deductible by the corporation for a taxation year that ends after that time (in this paragraph referred to as the "subsequent year") to the extent of that proportion of the corporation's Canadian surtax payable for the particular year that

(i) the amount, if any, by which

(A) the total of all amounts each of which is

(I) its income under Part I for the particular year from a business that was carried on by the corporation throughout the subsequent year for profit or with a reasonable expectation of profit, or

(II) where properties were sold, leased, rented or developed or services were rendered in the course of carrying on that business before that time, its income under Part I for the particular year from any other business all or substantially all of the income of which was derived from the sale, leasing, rental or development, as the case may be, of similar properties or the rendering of similar services

exceeds

(B) the total of all amounts each of which is an amount deducted under paragraph 111(1)(a) or (d) in computing its taxable income for the particular year in respect of a non-capital loss or a farm loss, as the case may be, for a taxation year in respect of any business referred to in clause (A)

is of the greater of

(ii) the amount determined under subparagraph (i), and

(iii) the corporation's taxable income for the particular year; and

(b) the corporation's unused surtax credit for a particular taxation year that ends after that time is deductible by the corporation for a taxation year that ended before that time (in this paragraph referred to as the "preceding year") to the extent of that proportion of the corporation's Canadian surtax payable for the particular year that

(i) the amount, if any, by which

(A) the total of all amounts each of which is

(I) its income under Part I for the particular year from a business that was carried on by the corporation in the preceding year and throughout the particular year for profit or with a reasonable expectation of profit, or

(II) where properties were sold, leased, rented or developed or services were rendered in the course of carrying on that business before that time, the corporation's income under Part I for the particular year from any other business all or substantially all of the income of which was derived from the sale, leasing, rental or development, as the case may be, of similar properties or the rendering of similar services

exceeds

(B) the total of all amounts each of which is an amount deducted under paragraph 111(1)(a) or (d) in computing the corporation's taxable income for the particular year in respect of a non-capital loss or a farm loss, as the case may be, for a taxation year in respect of any business referred to in clause (A)

is of the greater of

(ii) the amount determined under subparagraph (i), and

(iii) the corporation's taxable income for the particular year.

Related Provisions: 87(2.11) — Vertical amalgamations; 256(6)–(9) — Anti-avoidance — deemed exercise of right to increase voting power; 256.1 — Deemed change in control if 75% FMV acquired.

Notes: See Notes to 111(5), which has the same general purpose.

181.1(7) amended by 1995-97 technical bill (for acquisitions of control after April 26, 1995) and 1992 technical bill.

I.T. Technical News: 7 (control by a group — 50/50 arrangement).

Interpretation Bulletins: IT-532: Part I.3 — tax on large corporations.

Definitions [s. 181.1]: "acquired" — 256(7)–(9); "amount" — 181(3), 248(1); "bankrupt", "business" — 248(1); "capital deduction" — 181.5(1); "Canadian surtax payable" — 125.3(4), 181.1(6); "carrying on business in Canada" — 253; "control" — 256(6)–(9), 256.1(3); "corporation" — 248(1), *Interpretation Act* 35(1); "deposit insurance corporation" — 137.1(5); "farm loss" — 111(8); "financial institution" — 190(1); "non-capital loss" — 111(8), 248(1); "non-resident-owned investment corporation" — 133(8), 248(1); "permanent establishment" — 181(2); "property" — 248(1); "resident in Canada" — 250; "specified percentage" — 181.1(1.1); "taxable capital employed in Canada" — 181.2(1), 181.3(1), 181.4; "taxable income" — 2(2), 248(1); "taxation year" — 249; "unused surtax credit" — 181.1(6).

181.2 (1) Taxable capital employed in Canada — The taxable capital employed in Canada of a corporation for a taxation year (other than a financial institution or a corporation that was throughout the year not resident in Canada) is the prescribed proportion of the corporation's taxable capital for the year.

Related Provisions: 66(12.6012) — Definition used for limitation on renunciation of Canadian development expenses to flow-through shareholder as Canadian exploration expense; 181(4) — Limitations respecting inclusions and deductions; 181.3(1) — Taxable capital employed in Canada of financial institution.

Notes: A charity or non-profit organization can have TCEC, even though it did not pay Part I.3 tax before the tax was eliminated (181.1(3)(c)), since the calculation does not depend on 181.1. See VIEWS docs 2008-0285371C6, 2012-0468831E5.

Regulations: 8601 (prescribed proportion).

(2) Taxable capital — The taxable capital of a corporation (other than a financial institution) for a taxation year is the amount, if any, by which its capital for the year exceeds its investment allowance for the year.

Related Provisions: 181(4) — Limitations respecting inclusions and deductions.

(3) Capital — The capital of a corporation (other than a financial institution) for a taxation year is the amount, if any, by which the total of

(a) the amount of its capital stock (or, in the case of a corporation incorporated without share capital, the amount of its members' contributions), retained earnings, contributed surplus and any other surpluses at the end of the year,

(b) the amount of its reserves for the year, except to the extent that they were deducted in computing its income for the year under Part I,

(b.1) the amount of its deferred unrealized foreign exchange gains at the end of the year,

(c) the amount of all loans and advances to the corporation at the end of the year,

(d) the amount of all indebtedness of the corporation at the end of the year represented by bonds, debentures, notes, mortgages, hypothecary claims, banker's acceptances or similar obligations,

(e) the amount of any dividends declared but not paid by the corporation before the end of the year,

(f) the amount of all other indebtedness (other than any indebtedness in respect of a lease) of the corporation at the end of the year that has been outstanding for more than 365 days before the end of the year, and

(g) the total of all amounts, each of which is the amount, if any, in respect of a partnership in which the corporation held a membership interest at the end of the year, either directly or indirectly through another partnership, determined by the formula

$$(A - B) \times C/D$$

where

A is the total of all amounts that would be determined under paragraphs (b) to (d) and (f) in respect of the partnership for its last fiscal period that ends at or before the end of the year if

(a) those paragraphs applied to partnerships in the same manner that they apply to corporations, and

(b) those amounts were computed without reference to amounts owing by the partnership

(i) to any corporation that held a membership interest in the partnership either directly or indirectly through another partnership, or

(ii) to any partnership in which a corporation described in subparagraph (i) held a membership interest either directly or indirectly through another partnership,

B is the partnership's deferred unrealized foreign exchange losses at the end of the period,

C is the share of the partnership's income or loss for the period to which the corporation is entitled either directly or indirectly through another partnership, and

D is the partnership's income or loss for the period

exceeds the total of

(h) the amount of its deferred tax debit balance at the end of the year,

(i) the amount of any deficit deducted in computing its shareholders' equity (including, for this purpose, the amount of any provision for the redemption of preferred shares) at the end of the year,

(j) any amount deducted under subsection 135(1) in computing its income under Part I for the year, to the extent that the amount can reasonably be regarded as being included in the amount determined under any of paragraphs (a) to (g) in respect of the corporation for the year.

(k) the amount of its deferred unrealized foreign exchange losses at the end of the year.

Related Provisions: 132.2(1)(o) — Deemed year-end of mutual fund corporation on reorganization; 181(4) — Limitations respecting inclusions and deductions; 257 — Formula cannot calculate to less than zero.

Notes: *Para. (a)*: In *Inco Ltd.*, 2007 TCC 1, share options labelled "contingently issuable equity" were "surplus". See also VIEWS docs 2008-0285381C6 ("any other surpluses" is not limited to accounting surpluses); 2008-0305241I7 (effect of GAAP and

181(3)(b)(i)); 2016-0663781E5 ("retained earnings" has ASPE meaning if taxpayer uses ASPE).

Para. (b): Future Income Tax Liability under CICA Handbook §3465 is "reserves": VIEWS doc 2001-0080075. See also 2005-0159721E5 below.

Para. (c): "advance" and "loan" were given their ordinary meaning in *FCMI Financial*, 2007 ONCA 316. Progress payments on a Dept. of Defence contract were "loans" or "advances": *SNC Technologies*, 2008 TCC 461 (FCA appeal discontinued A-447-08). The following were not: outstanding cheques not yet cashed (*Canadian Forest Products*, 2004 TCC 405); funds ADP received from clients in advance for payroll payments (*ADP Canada*, 2009 FCA 117). In *Bombardier*, 2012 FCA 46, amounts paid toward construction of airplanes were "advances" only to the extent they were liabilities on Bombardier's balance sheet, excluding amounts that reduced the value of inventory. This decision was applied to Bombardier's Quebec capital tax in 2013 QCCA 947 (leave to appeal denied 2014 CarswellQue 30 (SCC)).

In *PCL Construction*, [2001] 1 C.T.C. 2132 (TCC), a construction company's "unearned revenues and contract advances" were excluded from capital, where they related to outstanding cheques and portions of unearned amounts not received by year-end. Although they were liabilities, they did not fall within 181.2(3)(a)-(g) unless they were advances. It was permissible to look behind the balance sheet to divide unearned amounts into what had and had not been received by year-end. CRA accepts this decision, and also states that "holdbacks receivable" are not included in capital: VIEWS doc 2002-0163545, but see also 2009-0313311I7 re netting offsetting amounts.

Government assistance amortized into income under GAAP and shown as a "deferred credit" on the balance sheet is generally not a "reserve", "provision", "allowance" or "advance", even if it may be repayable: VIEWS doc 2005-0159721E5. Payments under construction contracts are normally "advances": 2006-0191831E5. So are travel agency customer deposits held in trust: 2007-0229191E5. Liabilities on interest rate and currency swap contracts are not "loans or advances": 2003-0027201I7.

Para. (f): "Indebtedness" is based on legal form, not accounting principles: 1996 Corporate Management Tax Conference q.6, pp. 24:7-9; VIEWS doc 9530990. See also Notes to 79(1)"debt". In *Autobus Thomas*, 2001 SCC 64, a bus dealer purchased school buses from manufacturers by way of conditional sales contracts. The debts owing to the bank were "indebtedness". In *Gaz Métro*, 2017 QCCQ 3664, mirrored debt (lent to another entity which paid the interest) was still "debt" because GM had not been legally released from it.

Para. (g): see VIEWS docs 2005-0131771E5, 2009-0347511I7.

Para. (i): See doc 2005-0159721E5 above re "provision".

Other: In *Kruger Inc.*, 2016 FCA 186, para. 17, accrued losses on foreign exchange option contracts were reflected in taxable capital.

In *Northland Properties*, 2012 BCSC 721, leave to appeal denied 2012 BCCA 494, non-GAAP-compliant statements were rejected for BC capital tax.

181.2(3) amended by 2002-2013 technical bill, last change effective for 2012 and later taxation years. Earlier amended by 2001 *Civil Code* harmonization bill, 1995-97, 1992 and 1991 technical bills.

Interpretation Bulletins: IT-532: Part I.3 — tax on large corporations.

I.T. Technical News: 18 (*Oerlikon Aérospatiale* case); 29 (large corporations tax — outstanding cheques).

(4) Investment allowance — The investment allowance of a corporation (other than a financial institution) for a taxation year is the total of all amounts each of which is the carrying value at the end of the year of an asset of the corporation that is

(a) a share of another corporation,

(b) a loan or advance to another corporation (other than a financial institution),

(c) a bond, debenture, note, mortgage, hypothecary claim or similar obligation of another corporation (other than a financial institution),

(d) long-term debt of a financial institution,

(d.1) a loan or advance to, or a bond, debenture, note, mortgage, hypothecary claim or similar obligation of, a partnership each member of which was, throughout the year,

(i) another corporation (other than a financial institution) that was not exempt from tax under this Part (otherwise than because of paragraph 181.1(3)(d)), or

(ii) another partnership described in this paragraph,

(e) an interest in a partnership, or

(f) a dividend payable to the corporation at the end of the year on a share of the capital stock of another corporation,

other than a share of the capital stock of, a dividend payable by, or indebtedness of, a corporation that is exempt from tax under this Part (otherwise than because of paragraph 181.1(3)(d)).

Related Provisions: 181(4) — Limitations re inclusions and deductions; 181.2(6) — Deemed amount of loan.

Notes: In *Imperial Oil*, [2003] 2 C.T.C. 2754 (TCC), loans structured to fall within 181.2(4)(b) reduced Part I.3 tax, and GAAR in 245(2) did not apply. In *9199-3899 Québec*, 2017 QCCA 1524, an interest-free loan to the parent corp before year-end, so as to reduce Quebec capital tax by claiming the investment allowance, triggered Quebec GAAR.

For CRA interpretation see VIEWS docs 2000-005117 (loan to foreign affiliate, recorded in affiliate's books as contributed surplus); 2006-0174951I7 (direct financing lease); 2011-0421911I7 (stock options issued to employees of indirect subsidiaries).

The term "bond, debenture, note, mortgage, hypothecary claim or similar obligation" in 181.2(4)(c) does not include bankers' acceptances: *Federated Co-operatives*, 2001 FCA 217; leave to appeal denied 2001 CarswellNat 1788 (SCC).

VIEWS doc 2002-0162255: "for there to be a loan at law ... there [must] be a delivery of the subject of the loan by the lender to the borrower and that there be an obligation on behalf of the borrower to return the subject matter of the loan ... According to ... *Federated Co-Operatives* ... whether the funds have been advanced to the recipient depends upon whether the funds represent a payment made by the corporation in return for the agreement of the recipient to provide goods or services in the future. In *Oerlikon Aérospatiale*, [1999] 4 C.T.C. 358 (FCA); leave to appeal denied 2000 CarswellNat 865 (SCC), the Court stated 'the effect of an advance, be it in the sense of a payment on account or a loan, is to make the amount of money it represents available to the person or corporation which receives it.' "

181.2(4)(d.1)(ii) added by 2002-2013 technical bill (Part 5 — technical), for 2004 and later taxation years.

Per 2002-2013 technical bill s. 325(10), special rules apply in applying 181.2(4)(b), (c) and (d.1) to a particular corporation in respect of an asset that is a loan or an advance to, or an obligation of, another corp or partnership that the particular corp holds at the end of a taxation year of the particular corporation that began before Dec. 20, 2002.

181.2(4) amended by 2001 *Civil Code* harmonization bill (effective June 14, 2001) and by 1992 and 1991 technical bills.

Interpretation Bulletins: IT-532: Part I.3 — tax on large corporations.

I.T. Technical News: 28 (large corporations tax — long-term debt).

(5) Value of interest in partnership — For the purposes of subsection (4) and this subsection, the carrying value at the end of a taxation year of an interest of a corporation or of a partnership (each of which is referred to in this subsection as the "member") in a particular partnership is deemed to be the member's specified proportion, for the particular partnership's last fiscal period that ends at or before the end of the taxation year, of the amount that would, if the particular partnership were a corporation, be the particular partnership's investment allowance at the end of that fiscal period.

Related Provisions: 248(1) — Definition of "specified proportion".

Notes: For CRA interpretation see VIEWS doc 2005-0131771E5.

Under the 2013 amendment, a corporate partner can claim investment allowance for the carrying value of its interest in a partnership that lends money to another partnership, provided the requirements of 181.2(4)(d.1) are met: VIEWS doc 2004-0079251E5.

181.2(5) amended by 2002-2013 technical bill, for tax years that begin after Dec. 20, 2002.

181.2(5)(a) amended by 1991 technical bill, retroactive to the introduction of the tax (taxation years ending after June 1989).

Interpretation Bulletins: IT-532: Part I.3 — tax on large corporations.

(6) Loan — For the purpose of subsection (4), where a corporation made a particular loan to a trust that neither

(a) made any loans or advances to nor received any loans or advances from, nor

(b) acquired any bond, debenture, note, mortgage, hypothecary claim or similar obligation of nor issued any bond, debenture, note, mortgage, hypothecary claim or similar obligation to

a person not related to the corporation, as part of a series of transactions in which the trust made a loan to another corporation (other than a financial institution) to which the corporation is related, the least of

(c) the amount of the particular loan,

(d) the amount of the loan from the trust to the other corporation, and

(e) the amount, if any, by which

(i) the total of all amounts each of which is the amount of a loan from the trust to any corporation

exceeds

(ii) the total of all amounts each of which is the amount of a loan (other than the particular loan) from any corporation to the trust

at any time shall be deemed to be the amount of a loan from the corporation to the other corporation at that time.

Related Provisions: 248(10) — Series of transactions.

Notes: References to "hypothecary claim" added to 181.2(6)(b) by 2001 *Civil Code* harmonization bill, effective June 14, 2001. The change is non-substantive; see *Interpretation Act* s. 8.2.

181.2(6) added by 1992 technical bill, retroactive to the introduction of the tax (effective July 1989).

Interpretation Bulletins: IT-532: Part I.3 — tax on large corporations.

Definitions [s. 181.2]: "amount" — 181(3), 181.2(6), 248(1); "carrying value" — 181(3); "corporation" — 248(1), *Interpretation Act* 35(1); "financial institution" — 181(1); "fiscal period" — 249(2)(b), 249.1; "investment allowance" — 181.2(4); "long-term debt" — 181(1); "partnership" — see 96(1) Notes; "permanent establishment" — 181(2); "preferred share" — 248(1); "reserves" — 181(1); "resident in Canada" — 250; "series of transactions" — 248(10); "share", "specified proportion" — 248(1); "taxation year" — 249.

181.3 (1) Taxable capital employed in Canada of financial institution

— The taxable capital employed in Canada of a financial institution for a taxation year is the total of

(a) the total of all amounts each of which is the carrying value at the end of the year of an asset of the financial institution (other than property held by the institution primarily for the purpose of resale that was acquired by the financial institution, in the year or the preceding taxation year, as a consequence of another person's default, or anticipated default, in respect of a debt owed to the institution) that is tangible, or for civil law corporeal, property used in Canada and, in the case of a financial institution that is an insurance corporation, that is non-segregated property, within the meaning assigned by subsection 138(12),

(b) the total of all amounts each of which is an amount in respect of a partnership in which the financial institution has an interest at the end of the year equal to that proportion of

(i) the total of all amounts each of which is the carrying value of an asset of the partnership, at the end of its last fiscal period ending at or before the end of the year, that is tangible, or for civil law corporeal, property used in Canada

that

(ii) the financial institution's share of the partnership's income or loss for that period

is of

(iii) the partnership's income or loss for that period, and

(c) an amount that is equal to

(i) in the case of a financial institution other than an insurance corporation, that proportion of its taxable capital for the year that its Canadian assets at the end of the year is of its total assets at the end of the year,

(ii) in the case of an insurance corporation that was resident in Canada at any time during the year and carried on a life insurance business at any time in the year, the total of

(A) that proportion of the amount, if any, by which the total of

(I) its taxable capital for the year, and

(II) the amount prescribed for the year in respect of the corporation

exceeds

(III) the amount prescribed for the year in respect of the corporation

that its Canadian reserve liabilities as at the end of the year is of the total of

(IV) its total reserve liabilities as at the end of the year, and

(V) the amount prescribed for the year in respect of the corporation, and

(B) [Repealed]

(iii) in the case of an insurance corporation that was resident in Canada at any time in the year and throughout the year did not carry on a life insurance business, that proportion of its taxable capital for the year that the total amount of its Canadian premiums for the year is of its total premiums for the year, and

(iv) in the case of an insurance corporation that was throughout the year not resident in Canada and carried on an insurance business in Canada at any time in the year, its taxable capital for the year.

Related Provisions: 181(4) — Limitations respecting inclusions and deductions; 190.11 — Taxable capital employed in Canada for Part VI tax.

Notes: For CRA interpretation of 181.3(1)(a) and 181.3(1)(c)(ii)(A)(I) see VIEWS doc 2004-0086751C6. For former 181.3(1)(c)(ii)(B) for a life insurer: 2002-0168217.

181.3(1)(a), (b)(i) amended by 2002-2013 technical bill (Part 4 — bijuralism), effective June 26, 2013, to add "or for civil law corporeal".

181.3(1)(c)(ii)(B) repealed by 2008 budget bill #2, for tax years that begin after Sept. 2006. The "reserve adjustment" added to taxable capital employed in Canada was considered unnecessary due to demutualization of the insurance industry: Finance news release 2006-091 (Dec. 28/06). (Although the Large Corporations Tax is zero since 2006, some of its calculations are used for other purposes: see Notes to 181.1(1).)

181.3(1) earlier amended by 1993 technical bill (last change effective for taxation years that end after Feb. 25, 1992) and 1992 technical bill.

Regulations: 8605 (prescribed amounts for 181.3(1)(c)(ii)(A)(II), (III) and (V)).

Interpretation Bulletins: IT-532: Part I.3 — tax on large corporations.

(2) Taxable capital of financial institution

— The taxable capital of a financial institution for a taxation year is the amount, if any, by which its capital for the year exceeds its investment allowance for the year.

Related Provisions: 181(4) — Limitations respecting inclusions and deductions; 190.12 — Taxable capital for Part VI tax.

(3) Capital of financial institution

— The capital of a financial institution for a taxation year is

(a) in the case of a financial institution, other than an authorized foreign bank or an insurance corporation, the amount, if any, by which the total at the end of the year of

(i) the amount of its long-term debt,

(ii) the amount of its capital stock (or, in the case of an institution incorporated without share capital, the amount of its members' contributions), retained earnings, contributed surplus and any other surpluses, and

(iii) the amount of its reserves for the year, except to the extent that they were deducted in computing its income under Part I for the year,

exceeds the total of

(iv) the amount of its deferred tax debit balance at the end of the year,

(v) the amount of any deficit deducted in computing its shareholders' equity (including, for this purpose, the amount of any provision for the redemption of preferred shares) at the end of the year, and

(vi) any amount deducted under subsection 130.1(1) or 137(2) in computing its income under Part I for the year, to the extent that the amount can reasonably be regarded as being included in the amount determined under subparagraph (i), (ii) or (iii) in respect of the institution for the year;

(b) in the case of an insurance corporation that was resident in Canada at any time in the year and carried on a life insurance business at any time in the year, the amount, if any, by which the total at the end of the year of

(i) the amount of its long-term debt, and

(ii) the amount of its capital stock (or, in the case of an insurance corporation incorporated without share capital, the amount of its members' contributions), retained earnings, contributed surplus and any other surpluses

exceeds the total of

(iii) the amount of its deferred tax debit balance at the end of the year, and

(iv) the amount of any deficit deducted in computing its shareholders' equity (including, for this purpose, the amount of any provision for the redemption of preferred shares) at the end of the year;

(c) in the case of an insurance corporation that was resident in Canada at any time in the year and throughout the year did not carry on a life insurance business, the amount, if any, by which the total at the end of the year of

(i) the amount of its long-term debt,

(ii) the amount of its capital stock (or, in the case of an insurance corporation incorporated without share capital, the amount of its members' contributions), retained earnings, contributed surplus and any other surpluses, and

(iii) the amount of its reserves for the year, except to the extent that they were deducted in computing its income under Part I for the year,

exceeds the total of

(iv) the amount of its deferred tax debit balance at the end of the year,

(v) the amount of any deficit deducted in computing its shareholders' equity (including, for this purpose, the amount of any provision for the redemption of preferred shares) at the end of the year,

(vi) the total amount of its deferred acquisition expenses in respect of its property and casualty insurance business in Canada, to the extent that it can reasonably be attributed to an amount included in the amount determined under subparagraph (iii), and

(vii) any amount recoverable through reinsurance, to the extent that it can reasonably be regarded as being included in the amount determined under subparagraph (iii) in respect of a claims reserve;

(d) in the case of an insurance corporation that was throughout the year not resident in Canada and carried on an insurance business in Canada at any time in the year, the total at the end of the year of

(i) the amount that is the greater of

(A) the amount, if any, by which

(I) the corporation's surplus funds derived from operations (as defined in subsection 138(12)) as of the end of the year, computed as if no tax were payable under this Part or Part VI for the year

exceeds the total of all amounts each of which is

(II) an amount on which the corporation was required to pay, or would but for subsection 219(5.2) have been required to pay, tax under Part XIV for a preceding taxation year, except the portion, if any, of the amount on which tax was payable, or would have been payable, because of subparagraph 219(4)(a)(i.1), and

(III) an amount on which the corporation was required to pay, or would but for subsection 219(5.2) have been required to pay, tax under subsection 219(5.1) for the year because of the transfer of an insurance business to which subsection 138(11.5) or (11.92) has applied, and

(B) the corporation's attributed surplus for the year,

(ii) any other surpluses relating to its insurance businesses carried on in Canada,

(iii) the amount of its long-term debt that may reasonably be regarded as relating to its insurance businesses carried on in Canada, and

(iv) the amount, if any, by which

(A) the amount of its reserves for the year (other than its reserves in respect of amounts payable out of segregated funds) that may reasonably be regarded as having been established in respect of its insurance businesses carried on in Canada

exceeds the total of

(B) the total of all amounts each of which is the amount of a reserve (other than a reserve described in subparagraph 138(3)(a)(i)) to the extent that it was included in the amount determined under clause (A) and was deducted in computing its income under Part I for the year,

(C) the total of all amounts each of which is the amount of a reserve described in subparagraph 138(3)(a)(i) to the extent that it was included in the amount determined under clause (A) and was deductible under subparagraph 138(3)(a)(i) in computing its income under Part I for the year,

(D) the total of all amounts each of which is the amount outstanding (including any interest accrued thereon) as at the end of the year in respect of a policy loan (within the meaning assigned by subsection 138(12)) made by the corporation, to the extent that it was deducted in computing the amount determined under clause (C),

(E) the total amount of its deferred acquisition expenses in respect of its property and casualty insurance business in Canada, to the extent that it can reasonably be attributed to an amount included in the amount determined under clause (A), and

(F) the total of all amounts each of which is an amount recoverable through reinsurance, to the extent that it can reasonably be regarded as being included in the amount determined under clause (A) in respect of a claims reserve; and

(e) in the case of an authorized foreign bank, the total of

(i) 10% of the total of all amounts, each of which is the risk-weighted amount at the end of the year of an on-balance sheet asset or an off-balance sheet exposure of the bank in respect of its Canadian banking business that the bank would be required to report under the OSFI risk-weighting guidelines if those guidelines applied and required a report at that time, and

(ii) the total of all amounts, each of which is an amount at the end of the year in respect of the bank's Canadian banking business that

(A) if the bank were a bank listed in Schedule II to the *Bank Act*, would be required under the risk-based capital adequacy guidelines issued by the Superintendent of Financial Institutions and applicable at that time to be deducted from the bank's capital in determining the amount of capital available to satisfy the Superintendent's requirement that capital equal a particular proportion of risk-weighted assets and exposures, and

(B) is not an amount in respect of a loss protection facility required to be deducted from capital under the Superintendent's guidelines respecting asset securitization applicable at that time.

Related Provisions: 181(4) — Limitations respecting inclusions and deductions; 190.13 — Capital for Part VI tax.

Notes: See Notes to 181(3). For interpretation of "reasonably be attributed" in (c)(vi) and (d)(iv)(E), see *729658 Alberta Ltd.*, 2004 TCC 474.

Unamortized or deferred portions of an insurer's gains on disposition of investments were excluded from capital by 181(3): *Manufacturers Life*, 2001 FCA 213.

Preferred shares that are not retractable within 5 years and are a liability on the balance sheet are long-term debt, not capital stock under 181.3(3): VIEWS doc 2010-035308I7.

181.3(3)(c)(vii) and (d)(iv)(F) added, and (a)(v), (b)(iv) and (c)(v) amended, for tax years that begin after 1995.

181.3(3) amended by 2001 technical bill (effective June 28, 1999), and by 1995-97, 1993 and 1991 technical bills.

I.T. Technical News: 28 (large corporations tax — long-term debt).

(4) Investment allowance of financial institution — The investment allowance for a taxation year of a corporation that is a financial institution is

(a) in the case of a corporation that was resident in Canada at any time in the year, the total of all amounts each of which is the carrying value at the end of the year of an eligible investment of the corporation;

(b) in the case of an insurance corporation that was throughout the year not resident in Canada, the total of all amounts each of which is the carrying value at the end of the year of an eligible investment of the corporation that was used or held by it in the year in the course of carrying on an insurance business in Canada;

(c) in the case of an authorized foreign bank, the total of all amounts each of which is the amount at the end of the year, before the application of risk weights, that the bank would be required to report under the OSFI risk-weighting guidelines if those guidelines applied and required a report at that time, of an eligible investment used or held by the bank in the year in the course of carrying on its Canadian banking business; and

(d) in any other case, nil.

Related Provisions: 181(4) — Limitations re inclusions and deductions; 181.3(5) — Meaning of "eligible investment"; 181.5(6) — Whether corporations related.

Notes: 181.3(4) amended by 2001 technical bill (effective June 28, 1999), 1991 technical bill.

(5) Interpretation — For the purpose of subsection (4),

(a) an eligible investment of a corporation is a share of the capital stock or long-term debt (and, where the corporation is an insurance corporation, is non-segregated property within the meaning assigned by subsection 138(12)) of a financial institution that at the end of the year

(i) is related to the corporation,

(ii) is not exempt from tax under this Part, and

(iii) is resident in Canada or can reasonably be regarded as using the proceeds of the share or debt in a business carried on by the institution through a permanent establishment (as defined by regulation) in Canada; and

(b) a credit union and another credit union of which the credit union is a shareholder or member are deemed to be related to each other.

Notes: 181.3(5) does not apply where a credit union invests in a wholly-owned subsidiary of another credit union: VIEWS doc 2004-0091071E5.

181.3(5) added by 2001 technical bill, effective June 28, 1999, except that in its application to taxpayers other than authorized foreign banks for taxation years that end before 2002, ignore 181.3(5)(a)(iii).

Regulations: 8201 (meaning of "permanent establishment" for 181.3(5)(a)(iii)).

Definitions [s. 181.3]: "amount" — 181(3), 248(1); "attributed surplus" — 181(2); "authorized foreign bank", "bank", "business" — 248(1); "Canada" — 255, *Interpretation Act* 35(1); "Canadian assets" — 181(2), Reg. 8602; "Canadian banking business" — 248(1); "Canadian premiums", "Canadian reserve liabilities" — 181(2), Reg. 8602; "carrying on business in Canada" — 253; "carrying value" — 181(3); "corporation" — 248(1), *Interpretation Act* 35(1); "corporeal" — Quebec *Civil Code* art. 899, 906; "credit union" — 137(6), 248(1); "eligible investment" — 181.3(5); "financial institution" — 181(1); "fiscal period" — 249, 249.1; "insurance corporation" — 248(1); "investment allowance" — 181.3(4); "life insurance business" — 248(1); "long-term debt" — 181(1); "OSFI risk-weighting guidelines" — 248(1); "permanent establishment" — Reg. 8201; "preferred share", "property", "regulation" — 248(1); "related" — 181.3(5)(b), 181.5(6), (7), 251(2); "reserves" — 181(1); "resident in Canada" — 250; "share", "shareholder", "subsidiary wholly-owned corporation" — 248(1); "taxation year" — 249; "total assets", "total premiums", "total reserve liabilities" — 181(2), Reg. 8602.

181.4 Taxable capital employed in Canada of non-resident — The taxable capital employed in Canada for a taxation year of a corporation (other than a financial institution) that was throughout the year not resident in Canada is the amount, if any, by which

(a) the total of all amounts each of which is the carrying value at the end of the year of an asset of the corporation used by it in the year in, or held by it in the year in the course of, carrying on any business carried on by it during the year through a permanent establishment in Canada

exceeds the total of

(b) the amount of the corporation's indebtedness at the end of the year (other than indebtedness described in any of paragraphs 181.2(3)(c) to (f)) that may reasonably be regarded as relating to a business carried on by it during the year through a permanent establishment in Canada,

(c) the total of all amounts each of which is the carrying value at the end of the year of an asset described in subsection 181.2(4) of the corporation that was used by it in the year in, or held by it in the year in the course of, carrying on any business carried on by it during the year through a permanent establishment in Canada, and

(d) the total of all amounts each of which is the carrying value at the end of the year of an asset of the corporation that

(i) is a ship or aircraft operated by the corporation in international traffic or is personal or movable property used in its business of transporting passengers or goods by ship or aircraft in international traffic, and

(ii) was used by the corporation in the year in, or held by it in the year in the course of, carrying on any business during the year through a permanent establishment in Canada,

if the country in which the corporation is resident imposed neither a capital tax for the year on similar assets nor a tax for the year on the income from the operation of a ship or aircraft in international traffic, of any corporation resident in Canada during the year.

Notes: 181.4(d)(i) amended by 2002-2013 technical bill (Part 4 — bijuralism), effective June 26, 2013, to add "or movable".

181.4 earlier amended by 1995-97 technical bill (for 1995 and later tax years), 1991 technical bill.

Definitions [s. 181.4]: "amount" — 181(3), 248(1); "business" — 248(1); "Canada" — 255; "carrying on business in Canada" — 253; "carrying value" — 181(3); "corporation" — 248(1), *Interpretation Act* 35(1); "financial institution" — 181(1); "international traffic" — 248(1); "movable" — Quebec *Civil Code* art. 900–907; "permanent establishment" — 181(2); "resident in Canada" — 250.

Interpretation Bulletins [s. 181.4]: IT-532: Part I.3 — tax on large corporations.

181.5 (1) Capital deduction — Subject to subsection (1.1), the capital deduction of a corporation for a taxation year is $50 million unless the corporation is related to another corporation at any time in the taxation year, in which case, subject to subsection (4), its capital deduction for the year is nil.

Notes: For how the capital deduction works see VIEWS doc 2004-0080271E5.

181.5(1) amended by 2003 Budget, effective for 2004 and later taxation years, to change the capital deduction from $10 million to $50 million and to add "Subject to subsection (1.1)". See Notes to 181.1(1).

(1.1) Exceptions — For the purposes of applying subsection 125(5.1), the definitions "unused surtax credit" in subsections 181.1(6) and 190.1(5), and subsection 225.1(8), the amount of tax in respect of a corporation under subsection 181.1(1) for a taxation year is to be determined as if the reference to "$50 million" in subsection (1) were a reference to "$10 million".

Related Provisions: 181.5(4.1) — Parallel rule re allocation of $10 million among associated corporations.

Notes: 181.5(1.1) added by 2003 Budget, for 2004 and later tax years. It ensures that various places in the Act that use Part I.3 tax as a measure of a corporation being "large" continue to work as they did before the 2003 amendment to 181.5(1).

(2) Related corporations — Subject to subsection (4.1), a corporation that is related to any other corporation at any time in a taxation year of the corporation that ends in a calendar year may file with the Minister in prescribed form an agreement on behalf of the related group of which the corporation is a member under which an amount that does not exceed $50 million is allocated among all corporations that are members of the related group for each taxation year of each such corporation ending in the calendar year and at a time when it was a member of the related group.

Related Provisions: 181.5(4) — Amount allocated; 181.5(6) — Corporations deemed not related.

Notes: 181.5(2) amended by 2003 Budget, for 2004 and later tax years, to change $10 million to $50 million and to add "Subject to subsection (4.1)".

Interpretation Bulletins: IT-532: Part I.3 — tax on large corporations.

Forms: T2 Sched. 36: Agreement among related corporations — Part I.3 tax.

(3) Allocation by Minister — Subject to subsection (4.1), the Minister may request a corporation that is related to any other corporation at the end of a taxation year to file with the Minister an agreement referred to in subsection (2) and, if the corporation does not file such an agreement within 30 days after receiving the request, the Minister may allocate an amount among the members of the related group of which the corporation is a member for the taxation year not exceeding $50 million.

Notes: 181.5(3) amended by 2003 Budget, effective for 2004 and later taxation years, to change $10 million to $50 million and to add "Subject to subsection (4.1)".

(4) Idem — The least amount allocated for a taxation year to a member of a related group under an agreement described in subsection (2) or by the Minister pursuant to subsection (3) is the capital deduction of that member for that taxation year.

(4.1) Exceptions — For the purposes of applying subsection 125(5.1), the definitions "unused surtax credit" in subsections 181.1(6) and 190.1(5), and subsection 225.1(8), subsections (2) to (4) are to be read as if the amount determined under subsection (2) or (3), as the case may be, in respect of the corporation for the taxation year were that proportion of $10 million that the amount otherwise determined in respect of the corporation for the taxation year under that subsection is of $50 million.

Notes: 181.5(4.1) added by 2003 Budget, for 2004 and later taxation years. It ensures that various references in the Act to Part I.3 tax as a measure of a corporation being "large" continue to work as they did before the 2003 Budget amendments to 181.5(1)–(3).

(5) Idem — Where a corporation (in this subsection referred to as the "first corporation") has more than one taxation year ending in the same calendar year and is related in 2 or more of those taxation years to another corporation that has a taxation year ending in that calendar year, the capital deduction of the first corporation for each such taxation year at the end of which it is related to the other corporation is an amount equal to its capital deduction for the first such taxation year.

(6) Idem — Two corporations that would, but for this subsection, be related to each other by reason only of

(a) the control of any corporation by Her Majesty in right of Canada or a province, or

(b) a right referred to in paragraph 251(5)(b),

are, for the purposes of this section and subsection 181.3(4), deemed not to be related to each other except that, where at any time a taxpayer has a right referred to in paragraph 251(5)(b) with respect to shares and it can reasonably be considered that one of the main purposes for the acquisition of the right was to avoid any limitation on the amount of a corporation's capital deduction for a taxation year, for the purpose of determining whether a corporation is related to any other corporation, the corporations are, for the purposes of this section, deemed to be in the same position in relation to each other as if the right were immediate and absolute and as if the taxpayer had exercised the right at that time.

Related Provisions: 256(6), (6.1) — Meaning of "control".

Notes: For the meaning of "one of the main purposes" see Notes to 83(2.1).

Closing words of 181.5(6) amended by 1995-97 technical bill, effective April 27, 1995.

(7) Related corporations that are not associated — For the purposes of subsection 181.3(4) and this section, a Canadian-controlled private corporation and another corporation to which it would, but for this subsection, be related at any time shall be deemed not to be related to each other at that time where the corporations are not associated with each other at that time.

Notes: 181.5(7) added by 1991 technical bill, effective 1991 (and effective for 1989 and 1990 if an election was filed by Dec. 10/93).

Definitions [s. 181.5]: "amount" — 181(3), 248(1); "associated" — 256; "calendar year" — *Interpretation Act* 37(1)(a); "Canadian-controlled private corporation" — 125(7), 248(1); "control" — 256(6), (6.1); "corporation" — 248(1), *Interpretation Act* 35(1); "Her Majesty" — *Interpretation Act* 35(1); "Minister", "prescribed" — 248(1); "province" — *Interpretation Act* 35(1); "related" — 181.5(6), (7), 251(2); "related group" — 251(4); "share" — 248(1); "taxation year" — 249; "taxpayer" — 248(1).

181.6 Return — Every corporation that is or would, but for subsection 181.1(4), be liable to pay tax under this Part for a taxation year shall file with the Minister, not later than the day on or before which the corporation is required by section 150 to file its return of income for the year under Part I, a return of capital for the year in prescribed form containing an estimate of the tax payable under this Part by it for the year.

Related Provisions: 150.1(5) — Electronic filing; 235 — Penalty for failure to file return even where no balance owing.

Notes: 181.6 amended by 1992 technical bill, for 1992 and later taxation years.

Definitions [s. 181.6]: "corporation" — 248(1), *Interpretation Act* 35(1); "Minister" — 248(1); "prescribed" — 248(1); "taxation year" — 249.

Forms: T2 Sched. 33: Taxable capital employed in Canada — large corporations; T2 Sched. 34: Part I.3 tax on financial institutions; T2 Sched. 35: Part I.3 tax on large insurance corporations; T2 Sched. 342: Nova Scotia tax on large corporations; T2 Sched. 343: Nova Scotia tax on large corporations — agreement among related corporations; T2 Sched. 37: Calculation of unused surtax credit; T2 Sched. 361: New Brunswick tax on large corporations; T2 Sched. 362: New Brunswick tax on large corporations — agreement among related corporations.

181.7 Provisions applicable to Part — Sections 152, 158 and 159, subsection 161(11), sections 162 to 167 and Division J of Part I apply to this Part with such modifications as the circumstances require and, for the purpose of this section, paragraph 152(6)(a) shall be read as follows:

"(a) a deduction under section 181.1(4) in respect of any unused surtax credit (within the meaning assigned by subsection 181.1(6)) for a subsequent taxation year,"

Related Provisions: 157(1), (2), (2.1) — Instalment and payment obligations; 161(1), (4.1) — Interest.

Notes: 181.7 enacted to replace 181.7, 181.8 and 181.9 by 1992 technical bill, for 1992 and later tax years. Former 181.7 and 181.8 dealt specifically with payment of tax, payment of instalments, and interest; 181.9 caused various other provisions of the Act to apply, as 181.7 does now. Earlier amended by 1991 technical bill. Part I.3 (181 to 181.9) added by 1989 Budget, for tax years that end after June 1989.

Definitions [s. 181.7]: "unused surtax credit" — 181.1(6).

Interpretation Bulletins [s. 181.7]: IT-532: Part I.3 — tax on large corporations.

181.71 Provisions applicable — Crown corporations — Section 27 applies to this Part with any modifications that the circumstances require.

Notes: 181.71 added by 1995-97 technical bill, for taxation years that end after June 1989.

Interpretation Bulletins [s. 181.71]: IT-532: Part I.3 — tax on large corporations.

PART II — TOBACCO MANUFACTURERS' SURTAX

182, 183 [Repealed]

Notes [s. 182, 183]: Part II (182-183) repealed by 2017 budget bill #1, for tax years that begin after March 22, 2017. It was a 50% surtax on tobacco manufacturers' profits. It was added in 1994 to offset part of the revenue given up by drastic reductions in excise taxes and duties on tobacco products, in response to extensive tobacco smuggling. Finance has now reversed itself, replacing the surtax with higher excise duties on tobacco products. For tax years that include March 22, 2017, read:

182. (1) **Surtax** — Every corporation shall pay a tax under this Part for the corporation's taxation year equal to the amount determined by the formula

$$0.5A(B/C)$$

where

A   is the corporation's Part I tax on tobacco manufacturing profits for the year;

B   is the number of days in the year that are before March 23, 2017; and

C   is the number of days in the year.

Related Provisions [Former 182(1)]: 182(2) — Calculation of tax; 183 — Return and payment.

(2) **Definitions** — In this Part,

"exempt activity", of a particular corporation, means

    (a) farming; or

    (b) processing leaf tobacco, if

        (i) that processing is done by, and is the principal business of, the particular corporation,

        (ii) the particular corporation does not manufacture any tobacco product, and

        (iii) the particular corporation is not related to any other corporation that carries on tobacco manufacturing (determined, in respect of the other corporation, as if the particular corporation did not exist and the definition "tobacco manufacturing" were read without reference to the words "in Canada");

"Part I tax on tobacco manufacturing profits" of a corporation for a taxation year means 21% of the amount determined by the formula

$$\left(\frac{A \times B}{C}\right) - D$$

where

A   is the amount that would be the corporation's Canadian manufacturing and processing profits for the year, within the meaning assigned by subsection 125.1(3), if the total of all amounts, each of which is the corporation's loss for the year from an active business, other than tobacco manufacturing, carried on by it in Canada, were equal to the lesser of

    (a) that total otherwise determined, and

    (b) the total of all amounts, each of which is the amount of the corporation's income for the year from an active business, other than tobacco manufacturing, carried on by it in Canada,

B   is the corporation's tobacco manufacturing capital and labour cost for the year,

C   is the total of the corporation's cost of manufacturing and processing capital for the year and its cost of manufacturing and processing labour for the year, within the meanings assigned by regulations made for the purposes of section 125.1, and

D   is

    (a) where the corporation is a Canadian-controlled private corporation throughout the year, the corporation's business limit for the year as determined for the purpose of section 125, and

    (b) in any other case, nil;

Related Provisions [Former 182(2)"Part I tax on tobacco manufacturing profits"]: 257 — Formula cannot calculate to less than zero.

Regulations [Former 182(2)"Part I tax on tobacco manufacturing profits"]: 5202, 5204 (cost of manufacturing and processing capital, cost of manufacturing and processing labour).

"tobacco manufacturing" means any activity, other than an exempt activity, relating to the manufacture or processing in Canada of tobacco or tobacco products in or into any form that is, or would after any further activity become, suitable for smoking;

"tobacco manufacturing capital and labour cost" of a corporation for a taxation year means the total of the amounts that would be the corporation's cost of manufacturing and processing capital for the year and its cost of manufacturing and processing labour for the year, within the meanings assigned by regulations made for the purpose of section 125.1, if the manufacturing or processing referred to in the definition "qualified activities" in those regulations were tobacco manufacturing.

Regulations [Former 182(2)"tobacco manufacturing capital and labour cost"]: 5202, 5204 (cost of manufacturing and processing capital, cost of manufacturing and processing labour).

183. (1) **Return** — Every corporation that is liable to pay tax under this Part for a taxation year shall file with the Minister a return for the year in prescribed form not later than the day on or before which the corporation is required by section 150 to file its return of income for the year under Part I.

Related Provisions [Former 183(1)]: 150(1)(a) — Deadline for return; 150.1(5) — Electronic filing.

(2) **Payment** — Every corporation shall pay to the Receiver General on or before its balance-due day for each taxation year its tax payable under this Part for the year.

(3) **Provisions applicable** — Subsections 150(2) and (3), sections 151, 152, 158 and 159, subsections 161(1) and (11), sections 162 to 167 and Division J of Part I apply to this Part with such modifications as the circumstances require.

For taxation years that ended before March 22, 2017, read 182(1) as:

(1) Every corporation shall pay a tax under this Part for each taxation year equal to 50% of the corporation's Part I tax on tobacco manufacturing profits for the year.

182(1) amended by S.C. 2001, c. 16 to change the rate from 40% to 50%, for taxation years ending after April 5, 2001, prorated to April 6, 2001. Earlier amended by 2000 GST bill, for taxation years ending after Feb. 8, 2000, to extend the surtax indefinitely (as announced by Dept. of Finance news release, Nov. 5, 1999); and by 1997 Budget (first bill) to extend the surtax by 3 years, as announced Nov. 28, 1996.

182(2)"exempt activity" added by 2007 budget bill #2 for 2007 and later taxation years. It was apparently targeted to Simcoe Leaf Tobacco: Drache, "Surprise!", xxix(5) *The Canadian Taxpayer* (Carswell) 34-35 (Feb. 27, 2007). For "principal business" in (b)(i) see Notes to 20(1)(bb). For "farming" see Notes to 248(1)"farming".

182(2)"tobacco manufacturing" amended by 2007 budget bill #2, for 2007 and later taxation years, to change "farming" to "an exempt activity".

Former Part II (181, 182) repealed in 1986. From 1982-86, it imposed a tax on a corporation that paid dividends out of income subject to the small business deduction, to bring the effective tax rate up from 25% to 33.33% (including provincial tax).

Before 1978, a different Part II (181-183) imposed a tax when a corporation redeemed or acquired certain of its shares at a premium.

PART II.1 — TAX ON CORPORATE DISTRIBUTIONS

183.1 (1) Application of Part — This Part applies to a corporation (other than a mutual fund corporation) for a taxation year in which the corporation, at any time in the year,

    (a) was a public corporation; or

    (b) was resident in Canada and had a class of shares outstanding that were purchased and sold in the manner in which such shares normally are purchased and sold by any member of the public in the open market.

(2) Tax payable — Where, as a part of a transaction or series of transactions or events,

    (a) a corporation, or any person with whom the corporation was not dealing at arm's length, has, at any time, paid an amount, directly or indirectly, to any person as proceeds of disposition of any property, and

    (b) all or any portion of the amount may reasonably be considered, having regard to all the circumstances, to have been paid as a substitute for dividends that would otherwise have been paid in the normal course by the corporation,

the corporation shall, on or before its balance-due day for its taxation year that includes that time, pay tax of 45% of that amount or portion of it, as the case may be.

Related Provisions: 183.1(5) — Indirect payment; 248(10) — Series of transactions.

Notes: For the meaning of "indirectly" in para. (a), see 183.1(5) and Notes to 17.1(1).

183.1(2) amended by 2003 Budget, for tax years that begin after June 2003.

(3) Stock dividend — Where, as a part of a transaction or series of transactions or events,

    (a) a share was issued by a corporation as a stock dividend and the amount of the stock dividend was less than the fair market value of the share at the time that it was issued, and

    (b) the share or any other share of the capital stock of the corporation was purchased, directly or indirectly, by the corporation, or by a person with whom the corporation was not dealing at arm's length, for an amount in excess of its paid-up capital, that excess shall, for the purposes of subsection (2), be deemed to have been paid as a substitute for dividends that would otherwise have been paid in the normal course by the corporation.

(4) Purchase of shares — Where, as a part of a transaction or series of transactions or events,

(a) a share of the capital stock of a corporation was purchased, directly or indirectly, by the corporation, or any person with whom the corporation was not dealing at arm's length, and

(b) any portion of the amount paid for the share may reasonably be considered, having regard to all the circumstances, as consideration for a dividend that had been declared, but not yet paid, on the share,

that portion of the amount shall, for the purposes of subsection (2), be deemed to have been paid as a substitute for dividends that would otherwise have been paid in the normal course by the corporation notwithstanding that the dividend was actually paid thereafter.

Notes: For the meaning of "indirectly" in para. (a), see Notes to 17.1(1).

(5) Indirect payment — Where, as a part of a transaction or series of transactions or events, a person received a payment from a corporation, or from any person with whom the corporation was not dealing at arm's length, in consideration, in whole or in part, for paying an amount to any other person as proceeds of disposition of any property, the corporation shall, for the purposes of subsection (2), be deemed to have paid the amount indirectly to the other person.

(6) Where subsec. (2) does not apply — Subsection (2) does not apply if none of the purposes of the transaction or series of transactions or events referred to therein may reasonably be considered, having regard to all the circumstances, to have been to enable shareholders of a corporation who are individuals or non-resident persons to receive an amount, directly or indirectly, as proceeds of disposition of property rather than as a dividend on a share that was of a class that was listed on a stock exchange or that was purchased and sold in the manner in which shares are normally purchased and sold by any member of the public in the open market.

Notes: For the meaning of "indirectly", see Notes to 17.1(1).

(7) Where subsec. 110.6(8) does not apply — Where this section has been applied in respect of an amount, subsection 110.6(8) does not apply to the capital gain in respect of which the amount formed all or a part of the proceeds of disposition.

Definitions [s. 183.1]: "adjusted cost base" — 54, 248(1); "amount" — 248(1); "arm's length" — 251(1); "balance-due day" — 248(1); "Canada" — 255; "capital gain" — 39(1)(a), 248(1); "class of shares" — 248(6); "corporation" — 248(1), *Interpretation Act* 35(1); "dividend", "employee" — 248(1); "fair market value" — see 69(1) Notes; "indirectly" — 183.1(5); "individual" — 248(1); "mutual fund corporation" — 131(8), 248(1); "non-resident" — 248(1); "paid an amount" — 183.1(5); "paid-up capital" — 89(1), 248(1); "person", "prescribed", "property" — 248(1); "public corporation" — 89(1), 248(1); "resident in Canada" — 250; "series of transactions" — 248(10); "share", "shareholder" — 248(1); "substituted property" — 248(5); "taxation year" — 249.

183.2 (1) Return — Every corporation liable to pay tax under this Part for a taxation year shall, on or before the day on or before which it is required to file its return of income under Part I for the year, file with the Minister a return for the year under this Part in prescribed form.

Related Provisions: 150.1(5) — Electronic filing.

Forms: T2141: Part II.1 tax return — tax on corporate distributions.

(2) Provisions applicable to Part — Subsections 150(2) and (3), sections 152, 158 and 159, subsections 160.1(1) and 161(1) and (11), sections 162 to 167 and Division J of Part I are applicable to this Part with such modifications as the circumstances require.

Definitions [s. 183.2]: "corporation" — 248(1), *Interpretation Act* 35(1); "Minister", "prescribed" — 248(1); "taxation year" — 249.

PART III — ADDITIONAL TAX ON EXCESSIVE ELECTIONS

184. (1) [Repealed under former Act]

Notes: 184(1), repealed as of 1979, imposed a tax on excessive elections under former 83(1), which provided an election for a dividend to be deemed paid out of "tax-paid undistributed surplus" or "1971 capital surplus on hand".

(2) Tax on excessive [capital dividend] elections — If a corporation has elected in accordance with subsection 83(2), 130.1(4) or 131(1) in respect of the full amount of any dividend payable by it on shares of any class of its capital stock (in this section referred to as the "original dividend") and the full amount of the original dividend exceeds the portion of the original dividend deemed by that subsection to be a capital dividend or capital gains dividend, as the case may be, the corporation shall, at the time of the election, pay a tax under this Part equal to $^3/_5$ of the excess.

Related Provisions: 18(1)(t) — Tax is non-deductible; 87(2)(z.2) — Amalgamation — continuing corp; 184(3) — Election to treat excess as separate dividend.

Notes: See Notes to 83(2) and 184(3).

184(2) amended by 2002-2013 technical bill (Part 5 — technical) to change the tax from 3/4 to 3/5 and add the term "original dividend", effective for original dividends paid by a corporation after its 1999 taxation year.

Income Tax Folios: S3-F2-C1: Capital Dividends [replaces IT-66R6].

(2.1) [Repealed]

Notes: 184(2.1) repealed by 2002-2013 technical bill, for original dividends (as defined in 184(2)) paid by a corporation after its 1999 taxation year. It was a transitional rule for certain dividends paid before 1988.

(3) Election to treat excess as separate dividend — If, in respect of an original dividend payable at a particular time, a corporation would, but for this subsection, be required to pay a tax under this Part in respect of an excess referred to in subsection (2), and the corporation elects in prescribed manner on or before the day that is 90 days after the day of sending of the notice of assessment in respect of the tax that would otherwise be payable under this Part, the following rules apply:

(a) the portion of the original dividend deemed by subsection 83(2), 130.1(4) or 131(1) to be a capital dividend or capital gains dividend, as the case may be, is deemed for the purposes of this Act to be the amount of a separate dividend that became payable at the particular time;

(b) if the corporation identifies in its election any part of the excess, that part is, for the purposes of any election under subsection 83(2), 130.1(4) or 131(1) in respect of that part, and, where the corporation has so elected, for all purposes of this Act, deemed to be the amount of a separate dividend that became payable immediately after the particular time;

(c) the amount by which the excess exceeds any portion deemed by paragraph (b) to be a separate dividend for all purposes of this Act is deemed to be a separate taxable dividend that became payable at the particular time; and

(d) each person who held any of the issued shares of the class of shares of the capital stock of the corporation in respect of which the original dividend was paid is deemed

(i) not to have received any portion of the original dividend, and

(ii) to have received, at the time that any separate dividend determined under any of paragraphs (a) to (c) became payable, the proportion of that dividend that the number of shares of that class held by the person at the particular time is of the number of shares of that class outstanding at the particular time except that, for the purpose of Part XIII, the separate dividend is deemed to be paid on the day that the election in respect of this subsection is made.

Related Provisions: 184(4) — Concurrence with election; 184(5) — Exception for non-taxable shareholders; 220(3.2), Reg. 600(b) — Late filing or revocation of election; 244(14), (14.1) — Date when notice sent.

Notes: See Income Tax Folio S3-F2-C1 ¶1.86-1.93. A dividend must all qualify (i.e., the "capital dividend account" in 89(1) must be high enough) to be a capital dividend under 83(2). Where it does not (typically due to miscalculation of the CDA), 184(3) allows the two parts to be split into separate dividends, provided the requirements of Reg. 2106 are followed. (The excess dividend is then deemed "paid" proportionally, for 12(1)(j), 82(1) and 184(3)(d): VIEWS doc 2007-022943117.) Where a reassessment creates an excess and the company appeals the reassessment, if it eventually loses, CRA will not automatically allow a late election: docs 2007-022121117, 2008-0285131C6, 2010-0373261C6; but CRA will now allow an election to be filed on time and held in abeyance until the appeal is resolved (and withdrawn if the appeal succeeds): 2013-0504951E5.

Subpara. (d)(ii) deems the separate dividend "received" even if the original dividend was never paid (184(2) applies to a dividend "payable"). This anomaly has been raised with Finance: VIEWS doc 2017-0709081C6 [2017 APFF q.10a].

Administratively, CRA accepts a 184(3) election before the assessment of Part III tax: May 2009 ICAA roundtable (tinyurl.com/cra-abtax) q.3.

The Short Cut Method is an administrative practice allowing a corp that has filed an excessive election to treat the excess as a taxable dividend without requiring assessment and reversal of Part III tax or the Reg. 2106 documentation. CRA generally allows it if it is "appropriate": VIEWS docs 2011-0412071C6, 2017-0709031C6 [2017 APFF q.5]. However, in *Morissette*, 2019 TCC 103, a company made the Short Cut election to avoid Part III tax, but also appealed the assessment, claiming the excess really was a capital dividend. The appeal was allowed to proceed to trial [see *Naiken & Templeton* case comment, 67(3) *Canadian Tax Journal* 784-88 (2019)].

If corp C "paid" the excess capital dividend to shareholder S by increasing "Loan from shareholder", CRA Headquarters approves a "carry on the books option". C can elect under 184(3) to avoid Part III tax, and S can avoid including in income the "separate" taxable portion, as long as C records a liability for the unpaid dividend on its balance sheet. S recognizes the income only when (and if) this liability is paid. The rationale for this position (which appears in several audit proposal letters) is that 184(3)(d) opening words requires the original dividend to have been "paid" to deem the separate dividend received. (This liability seems not to create a 15(1) shareholder benefit: see *Chaplin*, 2017 TCC 194, para. 118.)

If a subsidiary declares an excessive capital dividend and then winds up, the parent can make the 184(3) election via 87(2)(z.2) and 88(1)(e.2).

Where the paying corporation's year is statute-barred, see Notes to 184(4).

184(3) amended by 2002-2013 technical bill, for original dividends (as defined in 184(2)) paid by a corp after its 1999 taxation year; but for notices of assessments sent before Dec. 15, 2010 (when 244(14.1) came into force), read "sending" as "mailing".

184(3) opening words amended by 2010 budget bill #2, effective Dec. 15, 2010, to change "mailing" to "sending" (to accommodate electronic notices under 244(14.1)) and delete "the day that is the later of December 15, 1977 and" before "the day".

Regulations: 2106 (prescribed manner).

I.T. Application Rules: 69 (meaning of "chapter 148 of ...").

Income Tax Folios: S3-F2-C1: Capital Dividends [replaces IT-66R6].

Information Circulars: 07-1R1: Taxpayer relief provisions.

(3.1), (3.2) [Repealed]

Notes: 184(3.1), (3.2) repealed by 2002-2013 technical bill (Part 5 — technical), effective for original dividends (as defined in 184(2)) paid by a corporation after its 1999 taxation year. They applied to certain dividends paid before 1986.

(4) **Concurrence with election** — An election under subsection (3) is valid only if

(a) it is made with the concurrence of the corporation and all its shareholders

(i) who received or were entitled to receive all or any portion of the original dividend, and

(ii) whose addresses were known to the corporation; and

(b) either

(i) it is made on or before the day that is 30 months after the day on which the original dividend became payable, or

(ii) each shareholder described in subparagraph (a)(i) concurs with the election, in which case, notwithstanding subsections 152(4) to (5), any assessment of the tax, interest and penalties payable by each of those shareholders for any taxation year shall be made that is necessary to take the corporation's election into account.

Related Provisions: 185 — Assessment of tax.

Notes: Where a 184(3) election is made and the payor corporation's year is statute barred, the recipient corporation can be assessed Part IV tax due to 184(4)(b)(ii), but the payor cannot be reassessed to get its dividend refund, so its RDTOH may become "trapped": VIEWS doc 2003-005121117. A submission has been made to Finance to fix this: Louis Provenzano & Sheryl Mapa, "Dividends Exceeding CDA", 12(4) *Canadian Tax Highlights* (ctf.ca) 5-6 (April 2004).

Where the 184(4) conditions cannot be met because one of the dividend recipients has been dissolved, CRA will not accept the election and the payer should seek to undo the capital dividend: VIEWS doc 2007-0220471E5. See however Ed Kroft, "CRA Policy on Excessive CDA Elections", 43 *McCarthy Tétrault on Tax Disputes* (CCH) 1 (Nov. 2008), suggesting CRA's interpretation is wrong.

184(4) amended by 2002-2013 technical bill (Part 5 — technical), effective for original dividends (as defined in 184(2)) paid by a corporation after its 1999 taxation year.

184(4)(b) added by 1991 technical bill, effective July 14, 1990.

Income Tax Folios: S3-F2-C1: Capital Dividends [replaces IT-66R6].

(5) **Exception for non-taxable shareholders** — If each person who, in respect of an election made under subsection (3), is deemed by subsection (3) to have received a dividend at a particular time is also, at the particular time, a person all of whose taxable income is exempt from tax under Part I,

(a) subsection (4) does not apply to the election; and

(b) the election is valid only if it is made on or before the day that is 30 months after the day on which the original dividend became payable.

Related Provisions: 18(1)(t) — Penalty is non-deductible; 220(3.1) — Waiver of penalty by CRA.

Notes: 184(5) replaced by 2002-2013 technical bill, for original dividends (as defined in 184(2)) paid by a corp after its 1999 tax year. The previous 184(5) provided a penalty for an election under 184(3.1) or (3.2), re certain dividends paid before 1986.

Definitions [s. 184]: "amount", "assessment" — 248(1); "capital dividend" — 83(2)-(2.4), 248(1); "capital gain" — 39(1)(a), 248(1); "class of shares" — 248(6); "corporation" — 248(1), *Interpretation Act* 35(1); "dividend" — 248(1); "month" — *Interpretation Act* 35(1); "original dividend" — 184(2); "person", "prescribed", "share", "shareholder" — 248(1); "taxable dividend" — 89(1), 248(1); "taxable income" — 2(2), 248(1); "taxation year" — 249.

185. (1) Assessment of tax — The Minister shall, with all due dispatch, examine each election made by a corporation in accordance with subsection 83(2), 130.1(4) or 131(1), assess the tax, if any, payable under this Part in respect of the election and send a notice of assessment to the corporation.

Related Provisions: 184 — Tax on excessive election; 227(14) — No application to corporation exempt under s. 149.

(2) Payment of tax and interest — Where an election has been made by a corporation in accordance with subsection 83(2), 130.1(4) or 131(1) and the Minister mails a notice of assessment under this Part in respect of the election, that part of the amount assessed then remaining unpaid and interest thereon at the prescribed rate computed from the day of the election to the day of payment is payable forthwith by the corporation to the Receiver General.

Related Provisions: 221.1 — Application of interest where legislation retroactive; 248(7) — Mail deemed received on day mailed; 248(11) — Interest compounded daily.

Notes: See Notes to s. 158.

Regulations: 4301(a) (prescribed rate of interest).

(3) Provisions applicable to Part — Subsections 152(3), (4), (5), (7) and (8) and 161(11), sections 163 to 167 and Division J of Part I are applicable to this Part with such modifications as the circumstances require.

(4) Joint and several, or solidary, liability from excessive elections — Each person who has received a dividend from a corporation in respect of which the corporation elected under subsection 83(2), 130.1(4) or 131(1) is jointly and severally, or solidarily, liable with the corporation to pay that proportion of the corporation's tax payable under this Part because of the election that

(a) the amount of the dividend received by the person

is of

(b) the full amount of the dividend in respect of which the election was made,

but nothing in this subsection limits the liability of any person under any other provision of this Act.

Related Provisions: 185(5) — Assessment; 185(6) — Rules applicable.

Notes: 185(4) opening words amended by 2002-2013 technical bill (Part 4 — bijuralism), effective June 26, 2013, to add "or solidarily".

185(4) added by 1991 technical bill, for dividends paid after July 13, 1990.

Income Tax Folios: S3-F2-C1: Capital Dividends [replaces IT-66R6].

(5) Assessment — The Minister may, at any time after the last day on which a corporation may make an election under subsection 184(3) in respect of a dividend, assess a person in respect of any amount payable under subsection (4) in respect of the dividend, and the provisions of Division I of Part I apply, with such modifications as the circumstances require, to an assessment made under this subsection as though it were made under section 152.

Notes: Interest accrues on a 185(5) assessment: VIEWS doc 2009-0313301I7.

185(5) added by 1991 technical bill, for dividends paid after July 13, 1990.

(6) Rules applicable — If under subsection (4) a corporation and another person have become jointly and severally, or solidarily, liable to pay part or all of the corporation's tax payable under this Part in respect of a dividend described in that subsection,

(a) a payment at any time by the other person on account of the liability shall, to the extent of the payment, discharge their liability after that time; and

(b) a payment at any time by the corporation on account of its liability shall discharge the other person's liability only to the extent of the amount determined by the formula

$$(A - B) \times C / D$$

where

A is the total of

(i) the amount of the corporation's liability, immediately before that time, under this Part in respect of the full amount of the dividend, and

(ii) the amount of the payment,

B is the amount of the corporation's liability, immediately before that time, under this Act,

C is the amount of the dividend received by the other person, and

D is the full amount of the dividend.

Related Provisions: 257 — Formula cannot calculate to less than zero.

Notes: See Notes to 160(3) re meaning of "their liability" in 185(6)(a).

185(6) amended by 2002-2013 technical bill, effective June 26, 2013. Added by 1991 technical bill.

Definitions [s. 185]: "assessment" — 248(1); "corporation" — 248(1), *Interpretation Act* 35(1); "dividend", "Minister", "person", "prescribed" — 248(1); "prescribed rate" — Reg. 4301.

PART III.1 — ADDITIONAL TAX ON EXCESSIVE ELIGIBLE DIVIDEND DESIGNATIONS

185.1 (1) Tax on excessive eligible dividend designations — A corporation that has made an excessive eligible dividend designation in respect of an eligible dividend paid by it at any time in a taxation year shall, on or before the corporation's balance-due day for the taxation year, pay a tax under this Part for the taxation year equal to the total of

(a) 20% of the excessive eligible dividend designation, and

(b) if the excessive eligible dividend designation arises because of the application of paragraph (c) of the definition "excessive eligible dividend designation" in subsection 89(1), 10% of the excessive eligible dividend designation.

Related Provisions: 87(2)(z.2) — Amalgamation — continuing corporation; 185.1(2) — Election to treat excess as ordinary dividend; 185.2(1) — Return required; 185.2(3), (5) — Joint and several liability.

Notes: See Notes at end of 185.1.

(2) Election to treat excessive eligible dividend designation as an ordinary dividend — If, in respect of an excessive eligible dividend designation that is not described in paragraph (1)(b) and that is made by a corporation in respect of an eligible dividend (in this subsection and subsection (3) referred to as the "original dividend") paid by it at a particular time, the corporation would, if this Act were read without reference to this subsection, be required to pay a tax under subsection (1), and it elects in prescribed manner on or before the day that is 90 days after the day of sending the notice of assessment in respect of that tax that would otherwise be payable under subsection (1), the following rules apply:

(a) notwithstanding the definition "eligible dividend" in subsection 89(1), the amount of the original dividend paid by the corporation is deemed to be the amount, if any, by which

(i) the amount of the original dividend, determined without reference to this subsection

exceeds

(ii) the amount claimed by the corporation in the election not exceeding the excessive eligible dividend designation, determined without reference to this subsection;

(b) an amount equal to the amount claimed by the corporation in the election is deemed to be a separate taxable dividend (other than an eligible dividend) that was paid by the corporation immediately before the particular time;

(c) each shareholder of the corporation who at the particular time held any of the issued shares of the class of shares in respect of which the original dividend was paid is deemed

(i) not to have received the original dividend, and

(ii) to have received at the particular time

(A) as an eligible dividend, the shareholder's pro rata portion of the amount of any dividend determined under paragraph (a), and

(B) as a taxable dividend (other than an eligible dividend) the shareholder's pro rata portion of the amount of any dividend determined under paragraph (b); and

(d) a shareholder's pro rata portion of a dividend paid at any time on a class of the shares of the capital stock of a corporation is that proportion of the dividend that the number of shares of that class held by the shareholder at that time is of the number of shares of that class outstanding at that time.

Related Provisions: 87(2)(z.2) — Amalgamation — continuing corporation; 185.1(3) — Election requires consent of all shareholders, and consequences to them; 244(14), (14.1) — Date when notice sent.

Notes: See tinyurl.com/elect-excess for the prescribed manner of making the election: VIEWS doc 2015-0598311C6 [2015 APFF q.23]. No Regulations like Reg. 2106 are needed: see 248(1)"prescribed"(a.1). See also Notes to 185.2(1).

Where excessive eligible dividends were paid on different share classes, the designation cannot be all made for one class but must be prorated to each excess dividend: doc 2016-0626371E5.

Administratively, CRA accepts a 185.1(2) election before the assessment of Part III.1 tax: May 2009 ICAA roundtable (tinyurl.com/cra-abtax) q.3. The 90-day filing deadline cannot be extended under 220(3.2), so the election should be filed even if the assessment is being appealed: VIEWS doc 2010-0383801E5.

185.1(2) opening words amended by 2010 budget bill #2, effective Dec. 15, 2010, to change "mailing" to "sending" (to accommodate electronic notices under 244(14.1)).

Forms: T2 Sched. 55: Tax on excessive eligible dividend designations.

(3) Concurrence with election — An election under subsection (2) in respect of an original dividend is valid only if

(a) it is made with the concurrence of the corporation and all its shareholders

(i) who received or were entitled to receive all or any portion of the original dividend, and

(ii) whose addresses were known to the corporation; and

(b) either

(i) it is made on or before the day that is 30 months after the day on which the original dividend was paid, or

(ii) each shareholder described in subparagraph (a)(i) concurs with the election, in which case, notwithstanding subsections

152(4) to (5), any assessment of the tax, interest and penalties payable by each of those shareholders for any taxation year shall be made that is necessary to take the corporation's election into account.

Related Provisions: 185.1(4) — Exception for non-taxable shareholders.

(4) Exception for non-taxable shareholders
— If each shareholder who, in respect of an election made under subsection (2), is deemed by subsection (2) to have received a dividend at a particular time is also, at the particular time, a person all of whose taxable income is exempt from tax under Part I,

(a) subsection (3) does not apply to the election; and

(b) the election is valid only if it is made on or before the day that is 30 months after the day on which the original dividend was paid.

Notes: See Notes to 89(1)"eligible dividend" re eligible dividends. 185.1 added by 2006 budget bill #2, for 2006 and later tax years.

Definitions [s. 185.1]: "amount", "assessment", "balance-due day" — 248(1); "class of shares" — 248(6); "corporation" — 248(1), *Interpretation Act* 35(1); "day of sending" — 244(14), (14.1); "dividend" — 248(1); "eligible dividend", "excessive eligible dividend designation" — 89(1), 248(1); "month" — *Interpretation Act* 35(1); "person", "prescribed", "share", "shareholder" — 248(1); "taxable dividend" — 89(1), 248(1); "taxable income" — 248(1); "taxation year" — 249.

185.2 (1) Return — Every corporation resident in Canada that pays a taxable dividend (other than a capital gains dividend within the meaning assigned by subsection 130.1(4) or 131(1)) in a taxation year shall file with the Minister, not later than the corporation's filing-due date for the taxation year, a return for the year under this Part in prescribed form containing an estimate of the taxes payable by it under this Part for the taxation year.

Related Provisions: 87(2)(z.2) — Amalgamation — continuing corporation.

Notes: This "return" is part of the T2 return: T2 Schedule 55.

CRA can adjust the LRIP of a statute-barred year using 185.2(1): VIEWS doc 2011-0425501E5.

(2) Provisions applicable to Part
— Subsections 150(2) and (3), sections 151, 152, 158 and 159, subsections 161(1) and (11), sections 162 to 167 and Division J of Part I are applicable to this Part with such modifications as the circumstances require.

Related Provisions: 87(2)(z.2) — Amalgamation — continuing corporation.

(3) Joint and several liability from excessive eligible dividend designations
— Without limiting the liability of any person under any other provision of this Act, if a Canadian-controlled private corporation or a deposit insurance corporation pays an eligible dividend in respect of which it has made an excessive eligible dividend designation to a shareholder with whom it does not deal at arm's length, the shareholder is jointly and severally, or solidarily, liable with the corporation to pay that proportion of the corporation's tax payable under this Part because of the designation that the amount of the eligible dividend received by the shareholder is of the total of all amounts each of which is a dividend in respect of which the designation was made.

Related Provisions: 185.2(4) — Assessment; 185.2(5) — Rules applicable.

(4) Assessment
— The Minister may, at any time after the last day on which a corporation may make an election under subsection 185.1(2) in respect of an excessive eligible dividend designation, assess a person in respect of any amount payable under subsection (3) in respect of the designation, and the provisions of Division I of Part I (including, for greater certainty, the provisions in respect of interest payable) apply, with any modifications that the circumstances require, to an assessment made under this subsection as though it were made under section 152.

Related Provisions: 87(2)(z.2) — Amalgamation — continuing corporation.

(5) Rules applicable
— If under subsection (3) a corporation and a shareholder have become jointly and severally, or solidarily, liable to pay part or all of the corporation's tax payable under this Part

in respect of an excessive eligible dividend designation described in subsection (3),

(a) a payment at any time by the shareholder on account of the liability shall, to the extent of the payment, discharge their liability after that time; and

(b) a payment at any time by the corporation on account of its liability shall discharge the shareholder's liability only to the extent of the amount determined by the formula

$$(A - B) \times C/D$$

where

A is the total of

   (i) the amount of the corporation's liability, immediately before that time, under this Part in respect of the designation, and

   (ii) the amount of the payment,

B is the amount of the corporation's liability, immediately before that time, under this Act,

C is the amount of the eligible dividend received by the shareholder, and

D the total of all amounts each of which is a dividend in respect of which the designation was made.

Related Provisions: 87(2)(z.2) — Amalgamation — continuing corporation; 257 — Formula cannot calculate to less than zero.

Notes: 185.2 added by 2006 budget bill #2 (Part 2 — eligible dividends), effective for 2006 and later taxation years.

Definitions [s. 185.2]: "amount" — 248(1); "arm's length" — 251(1); "assessment" — 248(1); "Canadian-controlled private corporation" — 125(7), 248(1); "capital gain" — 39(1)(a), 248(1); "corporation" — 248(1), *Interpretation Act* 35(1); "dividend" — 248(1); "eligible dividend", "excessive eligible dividend designation" — 89(1), 248(1); "filing-due date", "insurance corporation", "Minister" — 248(1); "original dividend" — 185.2(2); "person", "prescribed" — 248(1); "resident in Canada" — 250; "shareholder" — 248(1); "taxable dividend" — 89(1), 248(1); "taxation year" — 249.

PART IV — TAX ON TAXABLE DIVIDENDS RECEIVED BY PRIVATE CORPORATIONS

186. (1) [Refundable] Tax on assessable dividends — Every corporation (in this section referred to as the "particular corporation") that is at any time in a taxation year a private corporation or a subject corporation shall, on or before its balance-due day for the year, pay a tax under this Part for the year equal to the amount, if any, by which the total of

(a) 38⅓% of all assessable dividends received by the particular corporation in the year from corporations other than payer corporations connected with it, and

(b) all amounts, each of which is an amount in respect of an assessable dividend received by the particular corporation in the year from a private corporation or a subject corporation that was a payer corporation connected with the particular corporation, equal to that proportion of the payer corporation's dividend refund (within the meaning assigned by paragraph 129(1)(a)) for its taxation year in which it paid the dividend that

   (i) the amount of the dividend received by the particular corporation

is of

   (ii) the total of all taxable dividends paid by the payer corporation in its taxation year in which it paid the dividend and at a time when it was a private corporation or a subject corporation

exceeds 38⅓% of the total of

(c) such part of the particular corporation's non-capital loss and farm loss for the year as it claims, and

(d) such part of the particular corporation's

(i) non-capital loss for any of its 20 taxation years immediately preceding or 3 taxation years immediately following the year, and

(ii) farm loss for any of its 20 taxation years immediately preceding or 3 taxation years immediately following the year

as it claims, not exceeding the portion thereof that would have been deductible under section 111 in computing its taxable income for the year if subparagraph 111(3)(a)(ii) were read without reference to the words "the particular taxation year and" and if the corporation had sufficient income for the year.

Related Provisions: 18(1)(t) — Part IV tax is non-deductible; 87(2.11) — Losses, etc., on amalgamation with subsidiary wholly-owned corporation; 88(1.1) — Non-capital losses, etc., of subsidiary; 88(1.3) — Computation of income and tax of parent; 129(1) — Part IV tax is refundable; 129(4)"eligible refundable dividend tax on hand"(a) — Refund of Part IV tax; 129(4.1), (4.2) — Allocation of losses that reduce Part IV tax; 131(5) — Dividend refund to mutual fund corporation; 186(6) — Partnerships; 186.1 — Exempt corporations; 186.2 — Exempt dividends; 227(14) — No tax on corporation exempt under s. 149; 227(16) — Municipal or provincial corporation excepted.

Notes: The Part IV tax is refundable to a private corporation under 129(1), once it pays out sufficient dividends. The amount of Part IV tax paid goes into ERDTOH in 129(4)"eligible refundable dividend tax on hand". Under 129(1)(a), the RDTOH is fully refunded if 2.61 times the RDTOH (legislated as 100 / 38.33) is paid out as taxable dividends. Since 2016, the Part IV tax is 38.33%; if it is $38.33 on $100, then by paying out $100 in dividends — the $61.67 left after Part IV tax plus the $38.33 to be refunded — the $38.33 can be recovered, or simply not remitted. Before 2016, the rate was 33.33% but the principle was the same. The refund rate in 129(1) was adjusted in sync with the 2016 change, which was consequential on the increase in the top marginal rate in 117(2) from 29% to 33%. See also Notes to 129(1).

Part IV tax is imposed on two kinds of dividends: (a) portfolio dividends (that is, dividends from corporations not "connected" with the recipient corporation, as defined in 186(4), at the time the dividend is received [VIEWS doc 2004-0057821E5]); and (b) dividends that entitle the payer corporation to a dividend refund under 129(1) (even if the payer corporation did not want the refund: doc 2003-0049015). That dividend refund arises if the payer corporation has an RDTOH balance. The RDTOH arises under 129(4)"eligible refundable dividend tax on hand" and "non-eligible refundable dividend tax on hand" (before 2019, under 129(3)), from Part IV tax paid and from 26²/₃% (see Notes to 129(1)) of a corporation's investment income (thus reducing the corporate tax on investment income that is flowed out to a shareholder to a rate that achieves integration; see 82(1) and 121).

Available non-capital losses and farm losses (see 111(8)) can reduce Part IV tax: 186(1)(c), (d).

On a share redemption, Part IV tax may apply even if the shareholder was "connected" and the corporation had no RDTOH, since RDTOH is calculated at the end of the year and can arise from investment income after the redemption. See Purkey, "Unexpected Part IV Tax Liability", VI(4) *Corporate Structures & Groups* (Federated Press) 343-344 (2001).

On a cross-redemption of shares, the 129(1) and 186(1) calculations may be circular: VIEWS docs 2003-0030085 [2003 APFF q.13], 2018-0771831E5.

Dividends paid through a trust and allocated out to a corporate beneficiary under 104(19) will retain the flow-through and 186(1)(b) will apply: VIEWS doc 2005-0121931E5. Dividends paid to a partnership are counted proportionately for the partners, due to 186(6)(a): 2013-0485691E5. On the effect of 55(2) see 2013-0498191E5. On the interaction with 112(4) see doc 2008-0265311E5. On the timing when the "connected" status is broken before the trust's year-end, see Notes to 104(19).

In *Ottawa Air Cargo*, 2008 FCA 54, Part IV tax applied even though no payment was ultimately required because of an offsetting dividend refund. See also VIEWS docs 2008-0266191E5, 2008-0294631E5 on the interaction of 186(1) and 55(2).

Para. (a) and words before (c) amended by 2016 tax-rate bill to change "1/3" to "38 1/3%" for tax years ending after 2015, with transitional rules for years beginning before 2016. The increase from 33.33% to 38.33% approximates the extra tax individuals pay on dividends under the new 33% (from 29%) bracket in 117(2).

186(1) amended by 2006 budget bill #1 (for losses arising in 2006 and later tax years, to change "10" to "20" in (d)(i), (ii)); 2004, 2003, 1995 Budgets; 1992 technical bill.

Interpretation Bulletins: IT-232R3: Losses — their deductibility in the loss year or in other years; IT-269R4: Part IV tax on taxable dividends received by a private corporation or a subject corporation; IT-328R3: Losses on shares on which dividends have been received.

Information Circulars: 88-2, para. 14: General anti-avoidance rule — section 245 of the *Income Tax Act*.

Advance Tax Rulings: ATR-32: Rollover of fixed assets from Opco into Holdco; ATR-35: Partitioning of assets to get specific ownership — "butterfly".

Forms: T2 Sched. 3: Dividends received, taxable dividends paid, and Part IV tax calculation.

(1.1) Reduction where Part IV.1 tax payable — Notwithstanding subsection (1), where an assessable dividend was received by a corporation in a taxation year and was included in an amount in respect of which tax under Part IV.1 was payable by the corporation for the year, the tax otherwise payable under this Part by the corporation for the year shall be reduced

(a) where the assessable dividend is described in paragraph (1)(a), by 10% of the assessable dividend, and

(b) where the assessable dividend is described in paragraph (1)(b), by 30% of the amount determined under that paragraph in respect of the assessable dividend.

Notes: Part IV.1 (187.1–187.61) levies a 10% tax on certain dividends received by certain corporations. Both Part IV tax and Part IV.1 tax may apply to the same dividend. To relieve this duplication, 186(1.1) in effect deducts from Part IV tax the Part IV.1 tax payable on any dividend figuring in the Part IV tax base.

186(1.1) amended by 1995 Budget, effective for taxation years that end after June 1995, with a transitional rule for 1995.

Interpretation Bulletins: IT-269R4: Part IV tax on taxable dividends received by a private corporation or a subject corporation.

(2) When corporation controlled — For the purposes of this Part, other than for the purpose of determining whether a corporation is a subject corporation, one corporation is controlled by another corporation if more than 50% of its issued share capital (having full voting rights under all circumstances) belongs to the other corporation, to persons with whom the other corporation does not deal at arm's length, or to the other corporation and persons with whom the other corporation does not deal at arm's length.

Related Provisions: 88(1)(d.2) — Winding-up — when taxpayer last acquired control; 111(3)(a) — Limitation on deductibility; 112(1) — Deduction of dividends received by corporation resident in Canada; 113(1) — Deduction re dividend received from foreign affiliate; 186(7) — 186(2) applies to all uses of the term "connected" based on 186(4).

Notes: Where Xco and Yco are controlled equally by Aco and Bco, which are owned by unrelated A and B, CRA will presume Xco and Yco are connected absent evidence to the contrary: doc 2019-0812711C6 [2019 APFF q.12].

100% control through a trust is "control": VIEWS doc 2007-0252231E5. Ownership through a partnership is counted, due to 186(6)(b): 2013-0485691E5. On the meaning of "full voting rights" see Notes to 186(4).

Interpretation Bulletins: IT-243R4: Dividend refund to private corporations; IT-269R4: Part IV tax on taxable dividends received by a private corporation or a subject corporation; IT-302R3: Losses of a corporation — the effect that acquisitions of control, amalgamations, and windings-up have on their deductibility; IT-489R: Non-arm's length sale of shares to a corporation.

(3) Definitions — The definitions in this subsection apply in this Part.

"assessable dividend" means an amount received by a corporation at a time when it is a private corporation or a subject corporation as, on account of, in lieu of payment of or in satisfaction of, a taxable dividend from a corporation, to the extent of the amount in respect of the dividend that is deductible under section 112, paragraph 113(1)(a), (a.1), (b) or (d) or subsection 113(2) in computing the recipient corporation's taxable income for the year.

Notes: Definition amended by 2002-2013 technical bill, effective Aug. 20, 2011. "Assessable dividend" added by 1995 Budget, for tax years that end after June 1995.

"subject corporation" means a corporation (other than a private corporation) resident in Canada and controlled, whether because of a beneficial interest in one or more trusts or otherwise, by or for the benefit of an individual (other than a trust) or a related group of individuals (other than trusts).

Notes: Definition "subject corporation" added by 1995 Budget, for tax years that end after June 1995.

Former 186(3), repealed by 1985 technical bill, defined "dividend refund", a term defined by 129(1) for purposes of the entire Act.

(4) Corporations connected with particular corporation — For the purposes of this Part, a payer corporation is connected with a particular corporation at any time in a taxation year (in this subsection referred to as the "particular year") of the particular corporation if

(a) the payer corporation is controlled (otherwise than by virtue of a right referred to in paragraph 251(5)(b)) by the particular corporation at that time; or

(b) the particular corporation owned, at that time,

(i) more than 10% of the issued share capital (having full voting rights under all circumstances) of the payer corporation, and

(ii) shares of the capital stock of the payer corporation having a fair market value of more than 10% of the fair market value of all of the issued shares of the capital stock of the payer corporation.

Related Provisions: 186(7) — 186(2) applies to all uses of the term "connected" in the Act.

Notes: "Owned" means direct legal ownership: VIEWS doc 2002-0141295, though one includes ownership through a partnership due to 186(6)(b): 2013-0485691E5. Common shares have "full voting rights" (FVR) even where there are pref shares with a veto right: docs 2006-0204901E5. FVR are measured by number of shares regardless of how many votes each share carries: 2010-0359551I7, 2014-0538081C6 [2014 APFF q.18] [this seems wrong in the author's view: "full" should refer to the maximum number of votes possible per share].

If A is connected with B, is B connected with A? One would think so, but the legislation does not explicitly say so.

The words defining "particular year" in the opening words of 186(4) are superfluous, as the term "particular year" is not otherwise used in the subsection. They are left over from earlier wording that has been repealed.

See also VIEWS docs 2009-0330061C6 (applying 186(4)(b)(ii) if share value is nil); 2011-0426081E5 (shares in (b)(i) and (ii) can be different shares).

See also Léger and Neilson, "Family Trusts and the 'Connected' Status Rules", 11(2) *Tax for the Owner-Manager [TfOM]* (ctf.ca) 8-9 (April 2011); Carolin & Kakkar, "Estate Plans, Trusts, and Dividends: Is There a Gap Here?", 21(1) *TfOM* 1-2 (Jan. 2021) (Part IV tax deferral or saving due to CRA's view that a 104(19)-designated dividend is not received the trust's year-end).

Interpretation Bulletins: IT-269R4: Part IV tax on taxable dividends received by a private corporation or a subject corporation; IT-302R3: Losses of a corporation — the effect that acquisitions of control, amalgamations, and windings-up have on their deductibility; IT-489R: Non-arm's length sale of shares to a corporation.

Advance Tax Rulings: ATR-42: Transfer of shares; ATR-55: Amalgamation followed by sale of shares.

(5) Deemed private corporation — A corporation that is at any time in a taxation year a subject corporation shall, for the purposes of paragraph 87(2)(aa) and section 129, be deemed to be a private corporation at that time, except that its "non-eligible refundable dividend tax on hand" (as defined in subsection 129(4)) at the end of the year shall be determined without reference to paragraph (a) of that definition.

Notes: 186(5) provides that a subject corporation (see 186(3)) is treated as a private corporation for the purposes of 129. This ensures that a subject corporation may claim a dividend refund, under 129, of Part IV tax paid on its dividend income and included in its RDTOH under 129(3) (starting 2019-2020, its eligible and non-eligible RDTOH under 129(4)).

186(5) amended by 2018 budget bill #1 to change RDTOH reference to "non-eligible" RDTOH (see 129(4)), effective on the same basis as 87(2)(aa) amendment (taxation years that begin after 2018, but earlier if planning was used to try to trigger a year-end before 125(5.1)(b) applied). Earlier amended by 1995 Budget, 1992 technical bill.

Interpretation Bulletins: IT-269R4: Part IV tax on taxable dividends received by a private corporation or a subject corporation; IT-302R3: Losses of a corporation — the effect that acquisitions of control, amalgamations, and windings-up have on their deductibility.

(6) Partnerships — For the purposes of this Part,

(a) all amounts received in a fiscal period by a partnership as, on account or in lieu of payment of, or in satisfaction of, taxable dividends shall be deemed to have been received by each member of the partnership in the member's fiscal period or taxation year in which the partnership's fiscal period ends, to the extent of that member's share thereof; and

(b) each member of a partnership shall be deemed to own at any time that proportion of the number of the shares of each class of the capital stock of a corporation that are property of the partnership at that time that the member's share of all dividends re-

ceived on those shares by the partnership in its fiscal period that includes that time is of the total of all those dividends.

Notes: For an example of 186(6) applying see VIEWS doc 2013-0485691E5.

(7) Interpretation — For greater certainty, where a provision of this Act or the regulations indicates that the term "connected" has the meaning assigned by subsection 186(4), that meaning shall be determined by taking into account the application of subsection 186(2) unless the provision expressly provides otherwise.

Notes: 186(7) is designed to overrule *Olsen*, [2000] 3 C.T.C. 2299 (TCC; later reversed 2002 FCA 3, leave to appeal denied 2002 CarswellNat 2193 (SCC)), where the TCC held that for purposes of 84.1(1), 186(2) did not apply to define "controlled" when determining the meaning of "connected" under 186(4). This rule applies to 84(11), 84.1(1), 110.6(1)"qualified small business corporation share"(c)(ii) and (d)(i), 110.6(15), 212.1(1), 248(1)"small business corporation"(b) and Reg. 6205(3).

186(7) added by 2001 technical bill, effective March 16, 2001, with an election for grandfathering for an agreement signed by that date.

Definitions [s. 186]: "amount" — 248(1); "assessable dividend" — 186(3); "balance-due day" — 248(1); "Canada" — 255; "class of shares" — 248(6); "connected" — 186(4); "controlled" — 186(2); "corporation" — 248(1), *Interpretation Act* 35(1); "dividend" — 248(1); "dividend refund" — 129(1); "fair market value" — see 69(1) Notes; "farm loss" — 111(8); "fiscal period" — 249(2), 249.1; "individual" — 248(1); "insurance corporation" — 248(1); "non-capital loss" — 111(8), 248(1); "non-eligible refundable dividend tax on hand" — 129(4); "non-resident-owned investment corporation" — 133(8), 248(1); "particular corporation" — 186(1); "partnership" — see 96(1) Notes; "person" — 248(1); "private corporation" — 89(1), 186(5), 227(16), 248(1); "related group" — 251(4); "resident in Canada" — 250; "share" — 248(1); "subject corporation" — 186(3); "taxable dividend" — 89(1), 186.2, 248(1); "taxable income" — 2(2), 248(1); "taxation year" — 249; "trust" — 104(1), 248(1).

Interpretation Bulletins [s. 186]: IT-269R4: Part IV tax on taxable dividends received by a private corporation or a subject corporation.

186.1 Exempt corporations — No tax is payable under this Part for a taxation year by a corporation

(a) that was, at any time in the year, a bankrupt; or

(b) that was, throughout the year,

(i) a bank,

(ii) a corporation licensed or otherwise authorized under the laws of Canada or a province to carry on in Canada the business of offering to the public its services as a trustee,

(iii) an insurance corporation,

(iv) a prescribed labour-sponsored venture capital corporation,

(v) a prescribed investment contract corporation,

(vi) a non-resident-owned investment corporation, or

(vii) a registered securities dealer that was throughout the year a member, or a participating organization, of a designated stock exchange in Canada.

Related Provisions: 131(11)(d) — Rules re prescribed labour-sponsored venture capital corporations; 227(14) — Application to exempt corporations; 227(16) — Application to municipal and provincial corporations.

Notes: 186.1(a) amended by 2017 budget bill #2, for bankruptcies after April 26, 1995, to delete "(within the meaning assigned by subsection 128(3))" after "bankrupt". ("Bankrupt" is now defined in 248(1).)

186.1 amended by 2007 budget bill #2 (effective Dec. 14, 2007), 1995-97 technical bill.

Definitions [s. 186.1]: "bank" — 248(1), *Interpretation Act* 35(1); "bankrupt", "business" — 248(1); "corporation" — 248(1), *Interpretation Act* 35(1); "designated stock exchange" — 248(1), 262; "insurance corporation" — 248(1); "non-resident-owned investment corporation" — 133(8), 248(1); "prescribed" — 248(1); "prescribed labour-sponsored venture capital corporation" — Reg. 6701; "province" — *Interpretation Act* 35(1); "taxation year" — 249.

Regulations [s. 186.1]: 6701 (prescribed labour-sponsored venture capital corporation); 6703 (prescribed investment contract corporation).

Interpretation Bulletins [s. 186.1]: IT-269R4: Part IV tax on dividends received by a private corporation or a subject corporation.

186.2 Exempt dividends — For the purposes of subsection 186(1), dividends received in a taxation year by a corporation that was, throughout the year, a prescribed venture capital corporation from a corporation that was a prescribed qualifying corporation with respect to those dividends shall be deemed not to be taxable dividends.

Definitions [s. 186.2]: "corporation" — 248(1), *Interpretation Act* 35(1); "dividend", "prescribed" — 248(1); "prescribed venture capital corporation" — Reg. 6700; "taxable dividend" — 89(1), 248(1); "taxation year" — 249.

Regulations [s. 186.2]: 6700 (prescribed venture capital corporation); 6704 (prescribed qualifying corporation).

Interpretation Bulletins [s. 186.2]: IT-269R4: Part IV tax on dividends received by a private corporation or a subject corporation; IT-328R3: Losses on shares on which dividends have been received.

187. (1) Information return — Every corporation that is liable to pay tax under this Part for a taxation year in respect of a dividend received by it in the year shall, on or before the day on or before which it is required to file its return of income under Part I for the year, file a return for the year under this Part in prescribed form.

Related Provisions: 150(1)(a) — Corporations — Part I return; 150.1(5) — Electronic filing; 186 — Tax payable on certain taxable dividends.

Interpretation Bulletins: IT-269R4: Part IV tax on dividends received by a private corporation or a subject corporation.

Forms: T2: Corporation income tax return, "Part IV Tax on Taxable Dividends Received"; T2 Sched. 50: Shareholder information.

(2) Interest — Where a corporation is liable to pay tax under this Part and has failed to pay all or any part thereof on or before the day on or before which the tax was required to be paid, it shall pay to the Receiver General interest at the prescribed rate on the amount that it failed to pay computed from the day on or before which the tax was required to be paid to the day of payment.

Related Provisions: 161.1 — Offset of refund interest against arrears interest; 221.1 — Application of interest where legislation retroactive; 248(11) — Interest compounded daily.

Notes: In *Bakorp Management*, 2016 FCA 74, an overpayment of Part IV tax for 1995 could not be used to offset an underpayment for 1993 (absent a "re-appropriation" under 221.2) to stop interest running, until 2000 when CRA assessed and applied it. The same payment could not both reduce interest owing and generate refund interest.

Regulations: 4301(a) (prescribed rate of interest).

(3) Provisions applicable to Part — Sections 151, 152, 158 and 159, subsections 161(7) and (11), sections 162 to 167 and Division J of Part I are applicable to this Part with such modifications as the circumstances require.

Notes: In *Gestion Forêt-Dale Inc.*, 2009 CarswellNat 1311 (TCC), 152(4) and 163(2) applied to a Part IV assessment due to 187(3).

Definitions [s. 187]: "amount" — 248(1); "corporation" — 248(1), *Interpretation Act* 35(1); "dividend", "prescribed" — 248(1); "prescribed rate" — Reg. 4301; "taxation year" — 249.

PART IV.1 — TAXES ON DIVIDENDS ON CERTAIN PREFERRED SHARES RECEIVED BY CORPORATIONS

187.1 Definition of "excepted dividend" — In this Part, "excepted dividend" means a dividend

(a) received by a corporation on a share of the capital stock of a foreign affiliate of the corporation, other than a dividend received by a specified financial institution on a share acquired in the ordinary course of the business carried on by the institution;

(b) received by a corporation from another corporation (other than a corporation described in any of paragraphs (a) to (f) of the definition "financial intermediary corporation" in subsection 191(1)) in which it has or would have, if the other corporation were a taxable Canadian corporation, a substantial interest (as determined under section 191) at the time the dividend was paid;

(c) received by a corporation that was, at the time the dividend was received, a private corporation or a financial intermediary corporation (within the meaning assigned by subsection 191(1));

(d) received by a corporation on a short-term preferred share of the capital stock of a taxable Canadian corporation other than a

dividend described in paragraph (b) or (c) of the definition "excluded dividend" in subsection 191(1); or

(e) received by a corporation on a share (other than a taxable RFI share or a share that would be a taxable preferred share if the definition "taxable preferred share" in subsection 248(1) were read without reference to paragraph (a) of that definition) of the capital stock of a mutual fund corporation.

Related Provisions: 191(4)(d) — Deemed excepted dividend.

Notes: 187.1(a) amended by 1991 technical bill, effective 1988.

Definitions [s. 187.1]: "business" — 248(1); "carrying on business" — 253; "corporation" — 248(1), *Interpretation Act* 35(1); "dividend" — 248(1); "foreign affiliate" — 248(1); "mutual fund corporation" — 131(8), 248(1); "private corporation" — 89(1), 248(1); "received" — 248(7); "share", "short-term preferred share", "specified financial institution" — 248(1); "substantial interest" — 191(2), (3); "taxable Canadian corporation" — 89(1), 248(1); "taxable preferred share", "taxable RFI share" — 248(1).

187.2 Tax on dividends on taxable preferred shares — Every corporation shall, on or before its balance-due day for a taxation year, pay a tax under this Part for the year equal to 10% of the total of all amounts each of which is a dividend, other than an excepted dividend, received by the corporation in the year on a taxable preferred share (other than a share of a class in respect of which an election under subsection 191.2(1) has been made) to the extent that an amount in respect of the dividend was deductible under section 112 or 113 or subsection 138(6) in computing its taxable income for the year or under subsection 115(1) in computing its taxable income earned in Canada for the year.

Related Provisions: 18(1)(t) — Tax is non-deductible; 87(4.2) — Exchanged shares; 186(1.1) — Reduction in tax; 187.4 — Amounts received by partnerships; 187.5 — Information return; 191(3) — Substantial interest; 191(4)(d) — Deemed dividends; 227(14) — No tax on corporation exempt under s. 149.

Notes: To the extent 55(2) applies, Part IV.1 tax will not: VIEWS doc 2007-0250831E5.

187.2 amended by 2003 Budget to require payment on the "balance-due day" (as defined in 248(1)), for taxation years that begin after June 2003.

Definitions [s. 187.2]: "amount", "balance-due day" — 248(1); "corporation" — 248(1), *Interpretation Act* 35(1); "dividend" — 248(1); "excepted dividend" — 187.1; "received" — 248(7); "share" — 248(1); "taxable income" — 2(2), 248(1); "taxable income earned in Canada" — 115(1), 248(1); "taxable preferred share" — 248(1); "taxation year" — 249.

Interpretation Bulletins: IT-88R2: Stock dividends.

Advance Tax Rulings: ATR-46: Financial difficulty.

Forms: T2 Sched. 43: Calculation of Parts IV.1 and VI.1 taxes.

187.3 (1) Tax on dividends on taxable RFI shares — Every restricted financial institution shall, on or before its balance-due day for a taxation year, pay a tax under this Part for the year equal to 10% of the total of all amounts each of which is a dividend, other than an excepted dividend, received by the institution at any time in the year on a share acquired by any person before that time and after 8:00 p.m. Eastern Daylight Saving Time, June 18, 1987 that was, at the time the dividend was paid, a taxable RFI share to the extent that an amount in respect of the dividend was deductible under section 112 or 113 or subsection 138(6) in computing its taxable income for the year or under subsection 115(1) in computing its taxable income earned in Canada for the year.

Related Provisions: 87(4.2) — Exchanged shares; 186(1.1) — Reduction in tax; 187.3(2) — Time of acquisition of share; 187.4 — Partnerships; 187.5 — Information return; 191(3) — Substantial interest.

Notes: See Notes to 187.2.

187.3(1) amended by 2003 Budget to require payment on the "balance-due day" (as defined in 248(1)), effective for taxation years that begin after June 2003.

Advance Tax Rulings: ATR-46: Financial difficulty.

(2) Time of acquisition of share — For the purposes of subsection (1),

(a) a share of the capital stock of a corporation acquired by a person after 8:00 p.m. Eastern Daylight Saving Time, June 18, 1987 pursuant to an agreement in writing entered into before that time shall be deemed to have been acquired by that person before that time;

(b) a share of the capital stock of a corporation acquired by a person after 8:00 p.m. Eastern Daylight Saving Time, June 18, 1987 and before 1988 as part of a distribution to the public made in accordance with the terms of a prospectus, preliminary prospectus, registration statement, offering memorandum or notice filed before 8:00 p.m. Eastern Daylight Saving Time, June 18, 1987 with a public authority pursuant to and in accordance with the securities legislation of the jurisdiction in which the shares are distributed shall be deemed to have been acquired by that person before that time;

(c) a share (in this paragraph referred to as the "new share") of the capital stock of a corporation that is acquired by a person after 8:00 p.m. Eastern Daylight Saving Time, June 18, 1987 in exchange for

(i) a share of a corporation that was issued before 8:00 p.m. Eastern Daylight Saving Time, June 18, 1987 or is a grandfathered share, or

(ii) a debt obligation of a corporation that was issued before 8:00 p.m. Eastern Daylight Saving Time, June 18, 1987, or issued after that time pursuant to an agreement in writing entered into before that time,

where the right to the exchange for the new share and all or substantially all the terms and conditions of the new share were established in writing before that time shall be deemed to have been acquired by that person before that time;

(d) a share of a class of the capital stock of a Canadian corporation listed on a designated stock exchange in Canada that is acquired by a person after 8:00 p.m. Eastern Daylight Saving Time, June 18, 1987 on the exercise of a right

(i) that was issued before that time and listed on a prescribed stock exchange in Canada, and

(ii) the terms of which at that time included the right to acquire the share,

where all or substantially all the terms and conditions of the share were established in writing before that time shall be deemed to have been acquired by that person before that time;

(e) where a share that was owned by a particular restricted financial institution at 8:00 p.m. Eastern Daylight Saving Time, June 18, 1987 has, by one or more transactions between related restricted financial institutions, been transferred to another restricted financial institution, the share shall be deemed to have been acquired by the other restricted financial institution before that time unless at any particular time after 8:00 p.m. Eastern Daylight Saving Time, June 18, 1987 and before the share was transferred to the other restricted financial institution the share was owned by a shareholder who, at that particular time, was a person other than a restricted financial institution related to the other restricted financial institution; and

(f) where, at any particular time, there has been an amalgamation within the meaning assigned by section 87, and

(i) each of the predecessor corporations was a restricted financial institution throughout the period from 8:00 p.m. Eastern Daylight Saving Time, June 18, 1987 to the particular time and the predecessor corporations were related to each other throughout that period, or

(ii) each of the predecessor corporations and the new corporation is a corporation described in any of paragraphs (a) to (d) of the definition "restricted financial institution" in subsection 248(1),

a taxable RFI share acquired by the new corporation from a predecessor corporation on the amalgamation shall be deemed to have been acquired by the new corporation at the time it was acquired by the predecessor corporation.

Notes: CRA considers that "substantially all", used in 187.3(2)(c) and (d)(ii), means 90% or more.

187.3(2)(d) opening words amended by 2007 budget bill #2, effective Dec. 14, 2007, to change "prescribed stock exchange" to "designated stock exchange".

Regulations: 3200 (repealed — for "prescribed stock exchange in Canada" in 187.3(2)(d)(i)).

Definitions [s. 187.3]: "amount", "balance-due day" — 248(1); "class of shares" — 248(6); "designated stock exchange" — 248(1), 262; "dividend" — 248(1); "excepted dividend" — 187.1; "grandfathered share", "person" — 248(1); "prescribed stock exchange in Canada" — Reg. 3200; "related" — 251(2); "restricted financial institution", "share", "specified financial institution — 248(1); "taxable income" — 2(2), 248(1); "taxable income earned in Canada" — 115(1), 248(1); "taxable RFI share" — 248(1); "taxation year" — 249; "writing" — *Interpretation Act* 35(1).

Regulations [s. 187.3]: 6201 (prescribed shares).

Interpretation Bulletins [s. 187.3]: IT-88R2: Stock dividends.

187.4 Partnerships — For the purposes of this Part,

(a) all amounts received in a fiscal period by a partnership as, on account or in lieu of payment of, or in satisfaction of, dividends shall be deemed to have been received by each member of the partnership in the member's fiscal period or taxation year in which the partnership's fiscal period ends, to the extent of that member's share thereof;

(b) each member of a partnership shall be deemed to own at any time that proportion of the number of the shares of each class of the capital stock of a corporation that are property of the partnership at that time that the member's share of all dividends received on those shares by the partnership in its fiscal period that includes that time is of the total of all those dividends; and

(c) a reference to a person includes a partnership.

Definitions [s. 187.4]: "amount" — 248(1); "class of shares" — 248(6); "dividend" — 248(1); "fiscal period" — 249(2), 249.1; "partnership" — see 96(1) Notes; "person" — 187.4(c), 248(1); "share" — 248(1); "taxation year" — 249.

187.5 Information return — Every corporation liable to pay tax under this Part for a taxation year shall file with the Minister, not later than the day on or before which it is required by section 150 to file its return of income for the year under Part I, a return for the year under this Part in prescribed form containing an estimate of the taxes payable by it under sections 187.2 and 187.3 for the year.

Related Provisions: 150.1(5) — Electronic filing.

Definitions [s. 187.5]: "corporation" — 248(1), *Interpretation Act* 35(1); "Minister", "prescribed" — 248(1); "taxation year" — 249.

Forms: T2 Sched. 43: Calculation of Parts IV.1 and VI.1 taxes.

187.6 Provisions applicable to Part — Sections 152, 158 and 159, subsections 161(1), (2) and (11), sections 162 to 167 and Division J of Part I are applicable to this Part with such modifications as the circumstances require.

187.61 Provisions applicable — Crown corporations — Section 27 applies to this Part with any modifications that the circumstances require.

Notes: 187.61 added by 1995-97 technical bill, retroactive to 1988. It confirms that a prescribed federal Crown corporation is liable to Part IV.1 tax. See Notes to 181.71.

PART V — TAX AND PENALTIES IN RESPECT OF QUALIFIED DONEES

Notes: "Registered Charities" in heading changed to "Qualified Donees" by 2011 budget bill #2, effective 2012; "and Penalties" added by 2004 Budget, effective March 23, 2004.

187.7 Application of subsec. 149.1(1) — The definitions in subsection 149.1(1) apply to this Part.

Notes: 187.7 added in the RSC 1985 (5th Supp) consolidation for tax years ending after Nov. 1991. This rule was formerly in the opening words of 149.1(1).

188. (1) Deemed year-end on notice of revocation [of charity] — If on a particular day the Minister issues a notice of intention to revoke the registration of a taxpayer as a registered charity under any of subsections 149.1(2) to (4.1) and 168(1), it becomes a listed terrorist entity or it is determined, under subsection 7(1) of the *Charities Registration (Security Information) Act*, that a certificate served in respect of the charity under subsection 5(1) of that

Act is reasonable on the basis of information and evidence available,

(a) the taxation year of the charity that would otherwise have included that day is deemed to end at the end of that day;

(b) a new taxation year of the charity is deemed to begin immediately after that day; and

(c) for the purpose of determining the charity's fiscal period after that day, the charity is deemed not to have established a fiscal period before that day.

Related Provisions: 188(2.1) — Conditions for 188(1) not to apply.

Notes: Where a revoked charity wishes to re-register, see Notes to 188(2.1).

188(1) opening words amended by 2021 budget bill #1, effective June 29, 2021, to add "it becomes a listed terrorist entity". 188(1) earlier amended by 2004 Budget.

Forms: RC4424: Completing the tax return where registration of a charity is revoked [guide].

(1.1) Revocation tax — A charity referred to in subsection (1) is liable to a tax, for its taxation year that is deemed to have ended, equal to the amount determined by the formula

$$A - B$$

where

A is the total of all amounts, each of which is

(a) the fair market value of a property of the charity at the end of that taxation year,

(b) the amount of an appropriation (within the meaning assigned by subsection (2)) in respect of a property transferred to another person in the 120-day period that ended at the end of that taxation year, or

(c) the income of the charity for its winding-up period, including gifts received by the charity in that period from any source and any income that would be computed under section 3 as if that period were a taxation year; and

B is the total of all amounts (other than the amount of an expenditure in respect of which a deduction has been made in computing income for the winding-up period under paragraph (c) of the description of A), each of which is

(a) a debt of the charity that is outstanding at the end of that taxation year,

(b) an expenditure made by the charity during the winding-up period on charitable activities carried on by it, and

---

Proposed Amendment (Uncertain) — 188(1.1)B(b)

Application: Private Member's Bill S-222 (First House of Commons Reading June 23, 2021), s. 3, will amend para. (b) of the description of B in subsec. 188(1.1) to delete "carried on by it", in force two years after Royal Assent (and subject to review after 5 years: see under Proposed Amendment to 149.1(1)"charitable activities").

Notes: This is a private member's bill that may not pass. See Notes to Proposed Amendment under 149.1(1)"charitable activities".

(c) an amount in respect of a property transferred by the charity during the winding-up period and not later than the latter[28] of one year from the end of the taxation year and the day, if any, referred to in paragraph (1.2)(c), to a person that was at the time of the transfer an eligible donee in respect of the charity, equal to the amount, if any, by which the fair market value of the property, when transferred, exceeds the consideration given by the person for the transfer.

Related Provisions: 149.1(1.1)(c) — Amount transferred under B(c) deemed not expended on charitable activities; 149.1(6.4) — Application to registered national arts service organizations; 188(1.2), (1.3) — "Winding-up period", "eligible donee"; 188(2) — Transferee of property liable for tax; 188(2.1) — Conditions for 188(1.1) not to apply; 189(6.1) — Return and payment required within one year; 189(6.2) — Reduction of revocation tax liability; 189(7) — Assessment of revocation tax; 225.1(1.1)(a) — No collection action for one year; 257 — Formula cannot calculate to less than zero.

---
[28] *Sic.* Should be "later" — ed.

Notes: If a charity's registration is revoked, all its assets are forfeited as a 100% "revocation tax", but it has one year (or longer — see 188(1.2)) to distribute assets to "eligible donees" (see B(c), 188(1.3), 189(6.2)(b)) or use them on charitable activities (see B(b), 189(6.2)(a) and Notes to 149.1(1)"charitable activities"). During that year the tax cannot be collected (225.1(1.1)(a)), unless a Court order is obtained because collection is in jeopardy (225.2(2)).

No interest accrues on revocation tax: 189(8), VIEWS doc 2009-033272117; Drache, "Revocation Tax Liability Clarification", 18(2) *Canadian Not-for-Profit News* (Carswell) 15-16 (Feb. 2010).

Access to Information disclosure to the author shows that the number of organizations subject to the revocation tax was about 1,400 per year for 2014-15 through 2016-17. Total tax assessed (where after one year the charity has not distributed all assets) was $425,000 in 2014-15, $9.7 million in 2015-16 and $6.2m in 2016-17.

188(1.1) added by 2004 Budget, effective in respect of notices issued and certificates served by the Minister after June 12, 2005. It replaces former 188(1) [whose description of B was amended retroactively by s. 328 of 2002-2013 technical bill to change "amount" to "eligible amount" effective Dec. 21, 2002 — see 248(31)].

Former 188(1) previously amended by 2001 anti-terrorism bill and 1993 technical bill.

Remission Orders: *Quebec Domestic Help Charities Remission Order* (P.C. 2011-1323) (remission of 188(1.1) tax on charities participating in the Programme d'exonération financière pour les services d'aide domestique to provide subsidized domestic help services to Quebec residents).

Forms: RC4424: Completing the tax return where registration of a charity is revoked [guide].

Charities Policies: CPC-020: Revocation tax.

(1.2) Winding-up period — In this Part, the winding-up period of a charity is the period that begins immediately after the day on which the Minister issues a notice of intention to revoke the registration of a taxpayer as a registered charity under any of subsections 149.1(2) to (4.1) and 168(1) (or, if earlier, immediately after the day on which it is determined, under subsection 7(1) of the *Charities Registration (Security Information) Act*, that a certificate served in respect of the charity under subsection 5(1) of that Act is reasonable on the basis of information and evidence available), and that ends on the day that is the latest of

(a) the day, if any, on which the charity files a return under subsection 189(6.1) for the taxation year deemed by subsection (1) to have ended, but not later than the day on which the charity is required to file that return,

(b) the day on which the Minister last issues a notice of assessment of tax payable under subsection (1.1) for that taxation year by the charity, and

(c) if the charity has filed a notice of objection or appeal in respect of that assessment, the day on which the Minister may take a collection action under section 225.1 in respect of that tax payable.

Notes: 188(1.2) added by 2004 Budget, effective in respect of notices issued and certificates served by the Minister after June 12, 2005.

(1.3) Eligible donee [for revoked charity] — In this Part, an eligible donee in respect of a particular charity is

(a) a registered charity

(i) of which more than 50% of the members of the board of directors or trustees of the registered charity deal at arm's length with each member of the board of directors or trustees of the particular charity,

(ii) that is not the subject of a suspension under subsection 188.2(1),

(iii) that has no unpaid liabilities under this Act or under the *Excise Tax Act*,

(iv) that has filed all information returns required by subsection 149.1(14), and

(v) that is not the subject of a certificate under subsection 5(1) of the *Charities Registration (Security Information) Act* or, if it is the subject of such a certificate, the certificate has been determined under subsection 7(1) of that Act not to be reasonable; or

(b) a municipality in Canada that is approved by the Minister in respect of a transfer of property from the particular charity.

Related Provisions: 188(1.4) — Eligible donee of RCAAA.

Notes: Para. (b) added (former paras. (a)-(e) renumbered (a)(i)-(iv)) by 2018 budget bill #1, for transfers after Feb 26, 2018, to permit a revoked charity to transfer its assets to a municipality. The Budget explains: "In some circumstances, a charity may not be able to locate an eligible donee that is willing or able to assume ownership of one or more of its assets. For example, a charity may operate in a rural area where there are very few charities or it may own assets that are of importance to the community, such as a fire hall or a cemetery. In such cases, a municipality may be the most appropriate recipient of such property even though it is not a charity."

188(1.3) added by 2004 Budget, for notices issued and certificates served by the Minister after June 12, 2005.

Forms: RC4424: Completing the tax return where registration of a charity is revoked [guide].

(1.4) Eligible donee [for RCAAA] — In this Part, an eligible donee in respect of a particular Canadian amateur athletic association is a registered Canadian amateur athletic association

(a) of which more than 50% of the members of the board of directors or trustees of the registered Canadian amateur athletic association deal at arm's length with each member of the board of directors or trustees of the particular Canadian amateur athletic association;

(b) that is not the subject of a suspension under subsection 188.2(1);

(c) that has no unpaid liabilities under this Act or under the *Excise Tax Act*; and

(d) that has filed all information returns required by subsection 149.1(14).

Related Provisions: 188(1.3) — Eligible donee of charity.

Notes: 188(1.4) added by 2011 budget bill #2, effective 2012.

(2) Shared liability — revocation tax — A person who, after the time that is 120 days before the end of the taxation year of a charity that is deemed by subsection (1) to have ended, receives property from the charity, is jointly and severally, or solidarily, liable with the charity for the tax payable under subsection (1.1) by the charity for that taxation year for an amount not exceeding the total of all appropriations, each of which is the amount by which the fair market value of such a property at the time it was so received by the person exceeds the consideration given by the person in respect of the property.

Related Provisions: 160(1) — General rule making transferee of property liable.

Notes: 188(2) is similar to 160(1), which makes a non-arm's length transferee of property liable for any tax debt of the transferor. However, 160(1), which is broader (no 120-day limit), can apply also: VIEWS doc 2010-0380651I7.

188(2) amended by 2004 Budget, effective in respect of notices issued and certificates served by the Minister after June 12, 2005. 188(2) previously amended by 1993 technical bill.

Charities Policies: CPC-020: Revocation tax.

(2.1) Non-application of revocation tax — Subsections (1) and (1.1) do not apply to a charity in respect of a notice of intention to revoke given under any of subsections 149.1(2) to (4.1) and 168(1) if the Minister abandons the intention and so notifies the charity or if

(a) within the one-year period that begins immediately after the taxation year of the charity otherwise deemed by subsection (1) to have ended, the Minister has registered the charity as a charitable organization, private foundation or public foundation; and

(b) the charity has, before the time that the Minister has so registered the charity,

(i) paid all amounts, each of which is an amount for which the charity is liable under this Act (other than subsection (1.1)) or the *Excise Tax Act* in respect of taxes, penalties and interest, and

(ii) filed all information returns required by or under this Act to be filed on or before that time.

Related Provisions: *Interpretation Act* 27(5) — Meaning of "within the one-year period".

Notes: A charity seeking to re-register after revocation must file a new application along with all required documents, any missing past returns, financial statements from the past 4 fiscal periods, and must pay any amounts owing plus a $500 late filing penalty: CRA notice, Aug. 25, 2006; Drache, "Charities Directorate Imposes Re-registration fee", 14(10) *Canadian Not-for-Profit News* (Carswell) 78 (Oct. 2006). See also "How to apply for re-registration" and "What an organization should know about re-registration" at canada.ca/charities-registration > Re-Registration.

188(2.1) added by 2004 Budget, effective in respect of notices issued and certificates served by the Minister after June 12, 2005.

(3) Transfer of property tax — Where, as a result of a transaction or series of transactions, property owned by a registered charity that is a charitable foundation and having a net value greater than 50% of the net asset amount of the charitable foundation immediately before the transaction or series of transactions, as the case may be, is transferred before the end of a taxation year, directly or indirectly, to one or more charitable organizations and it may reasonably be considered that the main purpose of the transfer is to effect a reduction in the disbursement quota of the foundation, the foundation shall pay a tax under this Part for the year equal to the amount by which 25% of the net value of that property determined as of the day of its transfer exceeds the total of all amounts each of which is its tax payable under this subsection for a preceding taxation year in respect of the transaction or series of transactions.

Related Provisions: 149.1(6.4) — Application to registered national arts service organizations; 188(3.1) — 188(3) does not apply to gift to which penalty under 188.1(11) or (12) applies; 248(10) — Series of transactions.

Notes: For the meaning of "indirectly", see Notes to 17.1(1).

(3.1) Non-application of subsec. (3) — Subsection (3) does not apply to a transfer that is a gift to which subsection 188.1(11) or (12) applies.

Notes: 188(3.1) amended to refer to 188.1(12) by 2010 budget bill #2, effective for taxation years that end after March 3, 2010.

188(3.1) added by 2004 Budget, for taxation years that begin after March 22, 2004.

(4) Joint and several, or solidary, liability — tax transfer — If property has been transferred to a charitable organization in circumstances described in subsection (3) and it may reasonably be considered that the organization acted in concert with a charitable foundation for the purpose of reducing the disbursement quota of the foundation, the organization is jointly and severally, or solidarily, liable with the foundation for the tax imposed on the foundation by that subsection in an amount not exceeding the net value of the property.

Notes: 188(4) amended by 2002-2013 technical bill (Part 4 — bijuralism), effective June 26, 2013, to add "or solidarily".

(5) Definitions — In this section,

"net asset amount" of a charitable foundation at any time means the amount determined by the formula

$$A - B$$

where

A is the fair market value at that time of all the property owned by the foundation at that time, and

B is the total of all amounts each of which is the amount of a debt owing by or any other obligation of the foundation at that time;

Related Provisions: 257 — Formula cannot calculate to less than zero.

Notes: 188(5)"net asset amount" was 188(5)(a) before RSC 1985 (5th Supp) consolidation for tax years ending after Nov. 1991. The previous version was in descriptive rather than formula form.

"net value" of property owned by a charitable foundation, as of the day of its transfer, means the amount determined by the formula

$$A - B$$

where

A is the fair market value of the property on that day, and

B is the amount of any consideration given to the foundation for the transfer.

Related Provisions: 257 — Formula cannot calculate to less than zero.

Notes: 188(5)"net value" was 188(5)(b) before RSC 1985 (5th Supp) consolidation for tax years ending after Nov. 1991. The previous version was in descriptive rather than formula form.

Definitions [s. 188]: "amount" — 248(1); "arm's length" — 251(1); "assessment" — 248(1); "Canada" — 255, *Interpretation Act* 35(1); "Canadian amateur athletic association" — 149.1(1), 187.7; "charitable foundation", "charitable organization", "charitable purposes", "charity", "disbursement quota" — 149.1(1), 187.7; "eligible amount" — 248(31), (41); "eligible donee" — 188(1.3); "fair market value" — see 69(1) Notes; "fiscal period" — 249.1; "listed terrorist entity" — 149.1(1), 187.7; "Minister" — 248(1); "net asset amount", "net value" — 188(5); "non-qualified investment" — 149.1(1), 187.7; "person", "prescribed" — 248(1); "private foundation" — 149.1(1), 248(1); "property" — 248(1); "public foundation" — 149.1(1), 248(1); "qualified donee", "qualified investment" — 149.1(1), 187.7; "registered Canadian amateur athletic association", "registered charity" — 248(1); "related business" — 149.1(1), 187.7; "series of transactions" — 248(10); "specified gift" — 149.1(1), 187.7; "taxation year" — 149.1(1), 187.7; "taxpayer" — 248(1); "valuation day" — 188(1)(a)A; "winding-up period" — 188(1.2).

188.1 (1) Penalty — carrying on business — Subject to subsection (2), a person is liable to a penalty under this Part equal to 5% of its gross revenue for a taxation year from any business that it carries on in the taxation year, if

(a) the person is a registered charity that is a private foundation;

(b) the person is a registered charity that is not a private foundation and the business is not a related business in relation to the charity; or

(c) the person is a registered Canadian amateur athletic association and the business is not a related business in relation to the association.

Related Provisions: 149.1(2)(a) — Revocation of charitable organization for carrying on unrelated business; 149.1(3)(a) — Revocation of public foundation for carrying on unrelated business; 149.1(4)(a) — Revocation of private foundation for carrying on any business; 149.1(11) — Look through rule for partnerships; 188.1(2) — Increased penalty on second assessment; 189(6.3) — Reduction of penalty if funds transferred to an eligible donee; 189(7), (8) — Assessment of penalty and administrative procedures; 241(3.2)(g) — Penalty notice may be disclosed to the public; 253.1(2) — Charity having interest in limited partnership is not carrying on business.

Notes: See Notes at end of 188.1.

A much higher penalty applies (100% instead of 5% of revenue) if the charity continues to carry on the business after being assessed: 188.1(2).

188.1(1) amended by 2011 budget bill #2, effective for taxation years that begin after 2011, effectively to add para. (c).

(2) Increased penalty for subsequent assessment — A person that, less than five years before a particular time, was assessed a liability under subsection (1) or this subsection, for a taxation year, is liable to a penalty under this Part equal to its gross revenue for a subsequent taxation year from any business that, after that assessment and in the subsequent taxation year, it carries on at the particular time if

(a) the person is a registered charity that is a private foundation;

(b) the person is a registered charity that is not a private foundation and the business is not a related business in relation to the charity; or

(c) the person is a registered Canadian amateur athletic association and the business is not a related business in relation to the association.

Related Provisions: 188.2(1)(a) — Mandatory one-year suspension of charity's ability to issue receipts; 189(6.3) — Reduction of penalty if funds transferred to an eligible donee; 189(7), (8) — Assessment of penalty and administrative procedures; 241(3.2)(g) — Penalty notice may be disclosed to the public; 253.1(2) — Charity having interest in limited partnership is not carrying on business.

Notes: 188.1(2) amended by 2011 budget bill #2, effectively to add para. (c).

(3) Control of corporation by a charitable foundation — If at a particular time a charitable foundation has acquired control (within the meaning of subsection 149.1(12)) of a particular corporation, the foundation is liable to a penalty under this Part for a taxation year equal to

(a) 5% of the total of all amounts, each of which is a dividend received by the foundation from the particular corporation in the taxation year and at a time when the foundation so controlled the particular corporation, except if the foundation is liable under paragraph (b) for a penalty in respect of the dividend; or

(b) if the Minister has, less than five years before the particular time, assessed a liability under paragraph (a) or this paragraph for a preceding taxation year of the foundation in respect of a dividend received from any corporation, the total of all amounts, each of which is a dividend received, after the particular time, by the foundation, from the particular corporation, in the taxation year and at a time when the foundation so controlled the particular corporation.

Related Provisions: 149.1(3)(c) — Revocation of public foundation for acquiring control of a corporation; 149.1(4)(c) — Revocation of private foundation for acquiring control of a corporation; 189(6.3) — Reduction of penalty if funds transferred to an eligible donee; 189(7), (8) — Assessment of penalty and administrative procedures; 241(3.2)(g) — Penalty notice may be disclosed to the public.

Notes: See Notes at end of 188.1.

The 5% safe harbour rule in 149.1(12)(a) applies for 188.1(3): VIEWS doc 2006-0217041E5.

(3.1) Penalty for excess corporate holdings — A private foundation is liable to a penalty under this Part for a taxation year, in respect of a class of shares of the capital stock of a corporation, equal to

(a) 5% of the amount, if any, determined by multiplying the divestment obligation percentage of the private foundation for the taxation year in respect of the class by the total fair market value of all of the issued and outstanding shares of the class, except if the private foundation is liable for the taxation year under paragraph (b) for a penalty in respect of the class; or

(b) 10% of the amount, if any, determined by multiplying the divestment obligation percentage of the private foundation for the taxation year in respect of the class by the total fair market value of all of the issued and outstanding shares of the class, if

(i) the private foundation has failed to disclose, in its return required under subsection 149.1(14) for the taxation year,

(A) a material transaction, in the taxation year, of the private foundation in respect of the class,

(B) a material interest held at the end of the taxation year by a relevant person in respect of the private foundation, or

(C) the total corporate holdings percentage of the private foundation in respect of the class at the end of the taxation year, unless at no time in the taxation year the private foundation held greater than an insignificant interest in respect of the class, or

(ii) the Minister has, less than five years before the end of the taxation year, assessed a liability under paragraph (a) or this paragraph for a preceding taxation year of the private foundation in respect of any divestment obligation percentage.

Related Provisions: 149.2(10) — Shares held through a trust on March 18/07; 188.1(3.2)–(3.5) — Avoidance of divestment obligation.

Notes: The first 188.1(3.1) penalty imposed was on the Radcliffe Foundation, for $147,749 (*Globe & Mail*, Nov. 17, 2010).

188.1(3.1) added by 2007 budget bill #2, effective Dec. 14, 2007. It imposes a penalty on a private foundation for having a divestment obligation percentage (see Notes to 149.1(1)"divestment obligation percentage".

Forms: T2082: Excess corporate holdings regime for private foundations [guide].

(3.2) Avoidance of divestiture — If, at the end of a taxation year, a private foundation would — but for a transaction or series of transactions entered into by the private foundation or a relevant person in respect of the private foundation (in this subsection referred to as the "holder") a result of which is that the holder holds, directly or indirectly, an interest (or for civil law, a right), in a corporation other than shares — have a divestment obligation percentage for that taxation year in respect of the private foundation's holdings of a class of shares of the capital stock of the corporation, and it can reasonably be considered that a purpose of the transaction or series is to avoid that divestment obligation percentage by substituting

shares of the class for that interest or right, for the purposes of applying this section, subsection 149.1(1) and section 149.2,

(a) each of those interests or rights is deemed to have been converted, immediately after the time it was first held, directly or indirectly by the holder, into that number of shares of that class that would, if those shares were shares of the class that were issued by the corporation, have a fair market value equal to the fair market value of the interest or right at that time;

(b) each such share is deemed to be a share that is issued by the corporation and outstanding and to continue to be held by the holder until such time as the holder no longer holds the interest or right; and

(c) each of those shares is deemed to have a fair market value, at the particular time, equal to the fair market value, at the particular time, of a share of the class issued by the corporation, determined without reference to this subsection.

Related Provisions: 188.1(3.3)–(3.5) — Anti-avoidance rule re ownership through trust.

Notes: See Notes to 149.1(1)"divestment obligation percentage".

188.1(3.2)(c) amended by 2008 budget bill #2, for private foundations' tax years that begin after Feb. 25, 2008.

188.1(3.2) added by 2007 budget bill #2, effective Dec. 14, 2007.

Forms: T2082: Excess corporate holdings regime for private foundations [guide].

(3.3) Where subsec. (3.5) applies — Subsection (3.5) applies to a private foundation at a particular time in a taxation year if

(a) at the particular time, a person (in this subsection and subsection (3.5) referred to as an **"insider"** of the private foundation) that is the private foundation, or is a relevant person in respect of the private foundation, is a beneficiary under a trust;

(b) at or before the particular time

(i) the insider acquired an interest in or under the trust, or

(ii) the trust acquired a property;

(c) it may reasonably be considered that a purpose of the acquisition described in paragraph (b) was to hold, directly or indirectly, shares of a class of the capital stock of a corporation (referred to in subsection (3.5) as the "subject corporation");

(d) the shares described in paragraph (c) would, if they were held by the insider, cause the private foundation to have a divestment obligation percentage for the taxation year; and

(e) at the particular time, the insider holds the interest described in subparagraph (b)(i), or the trust holds the property described in subparagraph (b)(ii), as the case may be.

Related Provisions: 188.1(3.4) — Interpretation.

Notes: For CRA interpretation see VIEWS doc 2018-0745861C6 [2018 CALU Q.5] (188.1(3.3) may apply where private foundation is beneficiary of *alter ego* trust).

188.1(3.3) added by 2008 budget bill #2, effective for private foundations' taxation years that begin after Feb. 25, 2008.

(3.4) Rules applicable — For the purpose of subsections (3.3) and (3.5),

(a) interests (or, for civil law, rights), other than shares, of a trust in a corporation that entitle the trust to a right described in paragraph 251(5)(b) in respect of a class of the capital stock of the corporation, are deemed to be converted into shares of that class in the manner described by paragraph (3.2)(a); and

(b) if the amount of income or capital of the trust that a person may receive as a beneficiary under the trust depends on the exercise by any person of, or the failure by any person to exercise, a discretionary power, that person is deemed to have fully exercised, or to have failed to exercise, the power, as the case may be.

Notes: 188.1(3.4) added by 2008 budget bill #2, effective for private foundations' taxation years that begin after Feb. 25, 2008.

(3.5) Avoidance of divestiture — If this subsection applies to a private foundation at a particular time in respect of an interest of an insider of the private foundation in a trust, for the purposes of applying this section, subsection 149.1(1) and section 149.2,

(a) the insider is deemed to hold at the particular time, in addition to any shares of the capital stock of the subject corporation that it holds otherwise than because of this subsection, the number of shares, of the class of shares referred to in paragraph (3.3)(c), determined by the formula

$$A \times B / C$$

where

A   is the number of shares of that class that are held, directly or indirectly, by the trust at the particular time,

B   is the total fair market value of all interests held by the insider in the trust at the particular time, and

C   is the total fair market value of all property held by the trust at the particular time;

(b) each of those shares is deemed to be a share that is issued by the subject corporation and outstanding and to continue to be held by the holder until such time as the holder no longer holds the interest or right; and

(c) each of those shares is deemed to have a fair market value, at the particular time, equal to the fair market value, at the particular time, of a share of the class issued by the subject corporation, determined without reference to this subsection.

Related Provisions: 188.1(3.3) — Conditions for 188.1(3.5) to apply; 188.1(3.4) — Interpretation.

Notes: 188.1(3.5) added by 2008 budget bill #2, effective for private foundations' taxation years that begin after Feb. 25, 2008.

(4) Undue benefits — A registered charity or registered Canadian amateur athletic association that, at a particular time in a taxation year, confers on a person an undue benefit is liable to a penalty under this Part for the taxation year equal to

(a) 105% of the amount of the benefit, except if the charity or association is liable under paragraph (b) for a penalty in respect of the benefit; or

(b) if the Minister has, less than five years before the particular time, assessed a liability under paragraph (a) or this paragraph for a preceding taxation year of the charity or association and the undue benefit was conferred after that assessment, 110% of the amount of the benefit.

Related Provisions: 149.1(1)"charitable foundation", 149.1(1)"charitable organization"(b) — No benefit to be available to any member, shareholder, etc.; 188.1(5) — Meaning of "undue benefit"; 188.2(1)(b) — One-year suspension of charity's ability to issue receipts; 189(6.3) — Reduction of penalty if funds transferred to an eligible donee; 189(7), (8) — Assessment of penalty and administrative procedures; 241(3.2)(g) — Penalty notice may be disclosed to the public.

Notes: This catches a gift made to a non-qualified donee (see 188.1(5)(c)). See Notes at end of 188.1.

A loan by a private foundation (to family members) at the prescribed rate in Reg. 4301(c) (e.g., 1% or 2%) may be an "undue benefit" despite not triggering 189(1): VIEWS doc 2017-0683831I7.

CRA applied 188.1(4) to penalize Reimer Express Foundation $174,228 (July 20, 2011); [Richmond Hill] Hindu Temple Society of Canada $139,520 (Jan. 13/12) and Hindu Mission of Mississauga [also under 188.1(9)] $301,869 (April 23/12), for giving funds to "TRO Sri Lanka, an organization that formed part of the support network for the LTTE, a listed entity under the *Criminal Code*". A penalty was proposed instead of revocation because of "extenuating circumstances of the tsunami disaster and the fact that the payments in question appeared to be outside the normal operations of the Mission" (CRA letter, April 23, 2012).

188.1(4) amended by 2011 budget bill #2, effective for taxation years that begin after 2011, to add references to an RCAAA.

(5) Meaning of undue benefits — For the purposes of this Part, an undue benefit conferred on a person (referred to in this Part as the "beneficiary") by a registered charity or registered Canadian amateur athletic association includes a disbursement by way of a gift or the amount of any part of the income, rights, property or resources of the charity or association that is paid, payable, assigned or otherwise made available for the personal benefit of any person who is a proprietor, member, shareholder, trustee or settlor of the charity or association, who has contributed or otherwise paid into the charity or association more than 50% of the capital of the charity or association, or who deals not at arm's length with such a person or with the charity or association, as well as any benefit conferred on a beneficiary by another person, at the direction or with the consent of the charity or association, that would, if it were not conferred on the beneficiary, be an amount in respect of which the charity or association would have a right, but does not include a disbursement or benefit to the extent that it is

(a) an amount that is reasonable consideration or remuneration for property acquired by or services rendered to the charity or association;

(b) a gift made, or a benefit conferred,

(i) in the case of a registered charity, in the course of a charitable act in the ordinary course of the charitable activities carried on by the charity, unless it can reasonably be considered that the eligibility of the beneficiary for the benefit relates solely to the relationship of the beneficiary to the charity, and

Proposed Amendment (Uncertain) — 188.1(5)(b)(i)

Application: Private Member's Bill S-222 (First House of Commons Reading June 23, 2021), subsec. 4(1), will amend subpara. 188.1(5)(b)(i) to delete "carried on by it", in force two years after Royal Assent (and subject to review after 5 years: see under Proposed Amendment to 149.1(1)"charitable activities").

Notes: This is a private member's bill that may not pass. See Notes to Proposed Amendment under 149.1(1)"charitable activities".

(ii) in the case of a registered Canadian amateur athletic association, in the ordinary course of promoting amateur athletics in Canada on a nationwide basis; or

(c) a gift to a qualified donee.

Related Provisions: 149.1(1)"charitable foundation", 149.1(1)"charitable organization"(b) — No benefit to be available to any member, shareholder, etc.

Notes: Since 188.1(5) uses "includes" rather than "means", the ordinary meaning of "undue benefit" applies as well. See *Storrow*, [1978] C.T.C. 792 (FCTD) at 795; *R. v. McLeod* (1950), 97 C.C.C. 366 (BCCA), para. 14; *Pacific Abrasives*, 2010 BCCA 369; *Lethbridge (County)*, 2005 TCC 809, para. 95; *Canadian Legal Information Institute*, 2020 TCC 56, para. 39. (However, in *Canada 3000*, 2006 SCC 24, paras. 46-53, "includes" was held to be exhaustive in a particular case.)

Conversely, "means" is exhaustive: *Blackmore*, 2013 TCC 264, para. 30; aff'd 2014 FCA 210, para. 7. See however Notes to 120(3) for a "means" that is non-exhaustive.

Where "includes" is followed by a list, that list can restrict the scope of the definition: *Igloo Vikski*, 2016 SCC 38, para. 50.

See also Murphy, " 'Means and Includes' — Interpreting Internal Contradictions in Defined Terms", VII(2) *Resource Sector Taxation* (Federated Press) 517-19 (2009).

For "charitable activities" in (b)(i) see Notes to 149.1(1)"charitable activities".

188.1(5) amended by 2011 budget bill #2, for taxation years that begin after 2011.

(6) Failure to file information returns

— Every registered charity, registered Canadian amateur athletic association and registered journalism organization that fails to file a return for a taxation year as and when required by subsection 149.1(14) or (14.1) is liable to a penalty equal to $500.

Related Provisions: 168(1)(c) — Revocation of registration for failing to file information return; 189(6.3) — Reduction of penalties exceeding $1,000 per taxation year if funds transferred to an eligible donee; 189(7), (8) — Assessment of penalty and administrative procedures; 241(3.2)(g) — Penalty notice may be disclosed to the public.

Notes: See Notes at end of 188.1.

188.1(6) amended by 2019 budget bill #1, effective 2020, to add references to "registered journalism organization" [defined in 248(1)] and 149.1(14.1).

188.1(6) amended by 2011 budget bill #2, for tax years that begin after 2011, to add reference to an RCAAA.

Registered Charities Newsletters: 28 (new re-registration process).

Forms: RC4424: Completing the tax return where registration of a charity is revoked [guide].

(7) Incorrect information

— Except where subsection (8) or (9) applies, every registered charity, registered Canadian amateur athletic association and registered journalism organization that issues, in a taxation year, a receipt for a gift otherwise than in accordance

with this Act and the regulations is liable for the taxation year to a penalty equal to 5% of the amount reported on the receipt as representing the amount in respect of which a taxpayer may claim a deduction under subsection 110.1(1) or a credit under subsection 118.1(3).

Related Provisions: 168(1)(d) — Revocation of registration for issuing incorrect receipt; 188.1(8) — Increased penalty for subsequent assessment; 188.1(9) — Penalty for false statement relating to receipt; 189(6.3) — Reduction of penalty if funds transferred to an eligible donee; 189(7), (8) — Assessment of penalty and administrative procedures; 225.1(1)(b) — No collection action for one year from assessment; 241(3.2)(g) — Assessment notice may be disclosed to the public.

Notes: See Notes at end of 188.1.

188.1(7) amended by 2019 budget bill #1, effective 2020, to add "registered journalism organization" [defined in 248(1)].

188.1(7) amended by 2011 budget bill #2, for tax years that begin after 2011, to add reference to an RCAAA.

(8) Increased penalty for subsequent assessment

— Except where subsection (9) applies, if the Minister has, less than five years before a particular time, assessed a penalty under subsection (7) or this subsection for a taxation year of a registered charity, registered Canadian amateur athletic association or registered journalism organization and, after that assessment and in a subsequent taxation year, it issues, at the particular time, a receipt for a gift otherwise than in accordance with this Act and the regulations, it is liable for the subsequent taxation year to a penalty equal to 10% of the amount reported on the receipt as representing the amount in respect of which a taxpayer may claim a deduction under subsection 110.1(1) or a credit under subsection 118.1(3).

Related Provisions: 189(6.3) — Reduction of penalty if funds transferred to an eligible donee; 189(7), (8) — Assessment of penalty and administrative procedures.

Notes: 188.1(8) amended by 2019 budget bill #1, effective 2020, to add "registered journalism organization" [defined in 248(1)] and change [2x] "the charity or association" to "it".

188.1(8) amended by 2011 budget bill #2, for tax years that begin after 2011, to add references to an RCAAA.

(9) False information

— If at any time a person makes or furnishes, participates in the making of or causes another person to make or furnish a statement that the person knows, or would reasonably be expected to know but for circumstances amounting to "culpable conduct" (as defined in subsection 163.2(1)), is a "false statement" (as defined in subsection 163.2(1)) on a receipt issued by, on behalf of or in the name of another person for the purposes of subsection 110.1(2) or 118.1(2), the person (or, where the person is an officer, employee, official or agent of a registered charity, registered Canadian amateur athletic association or registered journalism organization, the charity, association or organization) is liable for their taxation year that includes that time to a penalty equal to 125% of the amount reported on the receipt as representing the amount in respect of which a taxpayer may claim a deduction under subsection 110.1(1) or a credit under subsection 118.1(3).

Related Provisions: 163.2(2), (4) — Alternative penalties; 188.1(10) — No double penalty under 163.2 and 188.1(9); 188.2(1)(b) — Mandatory one-year suspension of charity's ability to issue receipts if penalties exceed $25,000; 189(6.3) — Reduction of penalty if funds transferred to an eligible donee; 189(7), (8) — Assessment of penalty and administrative procedures.

Notes: The words "is liable for their taxation year that includes that time" attribute the penalty to a year, but the Part I return for that year is not reopened to assess the penalty, so there is no limitation period: VIEWS doc 2007-0239941I7. 188.1(9) can apply to a municipality: 2013-0497791I7.

Hindu Mission of Mississauga was penalized under 188.1(9); see Notes to 188.1(4).

See also Notes at end of 188.1.

188.1(9) amended by 2019 budget bill #1, effective 2020, to add "registered journalism organization" [defined in 248(1)] and "or organization".

188.1(9) amended by 2011 budget bill #2, for tax years that begin after 2011, to add references to an RCAAA.

(10) Maximum amount

— A person who is liable at any time to penalties under both section 163.2 and subsection (9) in respect of the same false statement is liable to pay only the greater of those penalties.

(11) Delay of expenditure — If, in a taxation year, a registered charity has entered into a transaction (including a gift to another registered charity) and it may reasonably be considered that a purpose of the transaction was to avoid or unduly delay the expenditure of amounts on charitable activities, the registered charity is liable to a penalty under this Act for its taxation year equal to 110% of the amount of expenditure avoided or delayed, and in the case of a gift to another registered charity, both charities are jointly and severally, or solidarily, liable to the penalty.

Related Provisions: 149.1(4.1) — Revocation for making gift for purpose of undue delay; 188(3.1) — 188(3) does not apply to gift where 188.1(11) applies; 189(6.3) — Reduction of penalty if funds transferred to an eligible donee; 189(7), (8) — Assessment of penalty and administrative procedures.

Notes: For meaning of "charitable activities" see Notes to 149.1(1)"charitable activities".

188.1(11) amended by 2010 budget bill #2, effective for taxation years that end after March 3, 2010.

(12) Gifts not at arm's length — If a registered charity has in a taxation year received a gift of property (other than a designated gift) from another registered charity with which it does not deal at arm's length and it has expended, before the end of the next taxation year, in addition to its disbursement quota for each of those taxation years, an amount that is less than the fair market value of the property, on charitable activities carried on by it or by way of gifts made to qualified donees with which it deals at arm's length, the registered charity is liable to a penalty under this Act for that subsequent taxation year equal to 110% of the difference between the fair market value of the property and the additional amount expended.

Proposed Amendment (Uncertain) — 188.1(12)

Application: Private Member's Bill S-222 (First House of Commons Reading June 23, 2021), subsec. 4(2), will amend subsec. 188.1(12) to delete "carried on by it", in force two years after Royal Assent (and subject to review after 5 years: see under Proposed Amendment to 149.1(1)"charitable activities").

Notes: This is a private member's bill that may not pass. See Notes to Proposed Amendment under 149.1(1)"charitable activities".

Related Provisions: 188(3.1) — 188(3) does not apply to gift where 188.1(12) applies.

Notes: For meaning of "charitable activities" see Notes to 149.1(1)"charitable activities".

188.1(12) added by 2010 budget bill #2, for tax years that end after March 3, 2010.

Notes [s. 188.1]: 188.1 imposes penalties on registered charities for breaches of the Act. Before 188.1 was introduced in 2004, the only remedy available to the CRA was to revoke the charity's registration. However, the CRA still uses revocation rather than penalties: Drache, "Intermediate Sanctions: A Failed Initiative", 24(4) *Canadian Not-for-Profit News* (Carswell) 25-27 (April 2016).

Like other administrative penalties, charity penalties are imposed by assessment (189(7)), can be objected to and appealed to the Tax Court (189(8)), and are distinct from fines for offences (see Notes to 239(1)). Charity penalties differ from other penalties (e.g., 163(2) for gross negligence) in that a charity can escape penalties over $1,000 per taxation year by transferring assets to another charity (189(6.3)). This recognizes that charities' funds were donated by the public for the public good and, as a policy matter, should not be seized for general government use even if the charity is non-compliant. The revocation tax in 188 follows the same principle (see 189(6.2)).

The non-filing penalty in 188.1(6) was imposed on 308 charities in 2014, 201 in 2015 and 141 in 2016. All the other penalties combined (only 188.1(3.1), (4), (5), (7)) were imposed on only 10 charities from 2013-16 (*Access to Information Act* disclosure).

See also Manwaring & Hayhoe, "Charities Update", 2004 Cdn Tax Foundation conference report, 8:12-25; Hayhoe & Owens, "The New Tax Sanctions for Canadian Charities: Learning from the US Experience", 54(1) *Canadian Tax Journal* 57-81 (2006); and 188.1(3.1) Notes.

CRA's *Guidelines for applying sanctions* (tinyurl.com/guide-sanc) state: "As a general rule, the Directorate intends to start with educational methods to obtain compliance, and then move progressively through compliance agreements, sanctions, and the ultimate sanction of revocation, if necessary. However, ... in serious cases of non-compliance, we are prepared to move directly to a sanction or revocation." The *Guidelines* continue with detail about each sanction in 188.1 and when it will be imposed.

CRA states that penalties for carrying on an unrelated business "would only be considered after non-compliance with the policy [in CPS-019], and even then only after having had the opportunity to voluntarily comply": Drache, "CRA Policy on Related Business", 13(2) *Canadian Not-for-Profit News* 16 (Feb. 2005).

188.1 added by 2004 Budget, for tax years that begin after March 22, 2004.

Definitions [s. 188.1]: "amount" — 248(1); "arm's length" — 251(1); "assessment" — 248(1); "beneficiary" — 188.1(5); "business" — 248(1); "Canada" — 255, *Interpretation Act* 35(1); "charitable foundation", "charity" — 149.1(1), 187.7; "class" — 248(6); "control" — 149.1(12), 256(5.1); "corporation" — 248(1), *Interpretation Act* 35(1); "culpable conduct" — 163.2(1); "designated gift" — 149.1(1); "disbursement quota" — 149.1(1), 187.7; "divestment obligation percentage" — 149.1(1); "dividend", "employee" — 248(1); "fair market value" — see 69(1) Notes; "false statement" — 163.2(1); "gross revenue" — 248(1); "insider" — 188.1(3.3)(a); "material interest" — 149.2(1); "material transaction" — 149.1(1), 149.2(2); "Minister", "officer", "person" — 248(1); "private foundation" — 149.1(1), 248(1); "property" — 248(1); "qualified donee" — 149.1(1), 188.2(3)(a), 248(1); "registered Canadian amateur athletic association", "registered charity", "registered journalism organization", "regulation" — 248(1); "related business" — 149.1(1), 187.7; "relevant person" — 149.1(1); "series of transactions" — 248(10); "share", "shareholder" — 248(1); "subject corporation" — 188.1(3.3)(c); "taxation year" — 149.1(1), 187.7; "taxpayer" — 248(1); "total corporate holdings percentage" — 149.1(1); "trust" — 104(1), 248(1), (3); "undue benefit" — 188.1(5).

Registered Charities Newsletters: 19 (introduction of intermediate sanctions); 27 (introducing guidelines for applying the new sanctions); 28 (objections and appeals on issues relating to charities).

Forms: T4118: Auditing charities [booklet].

188.2 (1) Notice of suspension with assessment — The Minister shall, with an assessment referred to in this subsection, give notice by registered mail to a registered charity, registered Canadian amateur athletic association or registered journalism organization that its authority to issue an official receipt referred to in Part XXXV of the *Income Tax Regulations* is suspended for one year from the day that is seven days after the day on which the notice is mailed, if the Minister has assessed the charity, association or organization for a taxation year for

(a) a penalty under subsection 188.1(2);

(b) a penalty under paragraph 188.1(4)(b) in respect of an undue benefit, other than an undue benefit conferred by the charity or association by way of a gift; or

(c) a penalty under subsection 188.1(9) if the total of all such penalties for the taxation year exceeds $25,000.

Related Provisions: 188.2(3) — Effect of suspension; 188.2(4) — Application to Tax Court to postpone suspension; 189(8) — Notice of objection (s. 165) may be filed against suspension; 241(3.2)(g) — Suspension letter may be disclosed to the public.

Notes: See Notes at end of 188.2.

If the conditions in (a), (b) or (c) are satisfied, the suspension is mandatory, due to word "shall".

188.2(1) opening words amended by 2019 budget bill #1, effective 2020, to add "registered journalism organization" [defined in 248(1)], to change "the authority of the charity or association to issue" to "its authority to issue" and "charity or association" to "charity, association or organization".

188.2(1) amended by 2011 budget bill #2, for tax years that begin after 2011.

Registered Charities Newsletters: 28 (objections and appeals on issues relating to charities).

(2) Notice of suspension — general — The Minister may give notice by registered mail to a person referred to in any of paragraphs (a) to (c) of the definition "qualified donee" in subsection 149.1(1) that the authority of the person to issue an official receipt referred to in Part XXXV of the *Income Tax Regulations* is suspended for one year from the day that is seven days after the day on which the notice is mailed

(a) if the person contravenes any of sections 230 to 231.5;

(b) if it may reasonably be considered that the person has acted, in concert with another person that is the subject of a suspension under this section, to accept a gift or transfer of property on behalf of that other person;

(c) in the case of a person referred to in paragraph (a) of the definition "qualified donee" in subsection 149.1(1), if the person has issued a receipt for a gift otherwise than in accordance with this Act and the regulations;

(d) in the case of a person that is a registered charity or registered Canadian amateur athletic association, if an ineligible individual is a director, trustee, officer or like official of the person, or controls or manages the person, directly or indirectly, in any manner whatever;

(e) in the case of a person that is a registered charity or registered Canadian amateur athletic association, if the person devotes any part of its resources to the direct or indirect support of, or opposition to, any political party or candidate for public office; or

(f) in the case of a person that is a registered charity, if a "false statement" (as defined in subsection 163.2(1)) was made in circumstances amounting to "culpable conduct" (as defined in subsection 163.2(1)) in the furnishing of information for the purpose of maintaining its registration.

(g) [Repealed]

Related Provisions: 188.2(3) — Effect of suspension; 188.2(4) — Application to Tax Court to postpone suspension; 189(8) — Notice of objection (s. 165) may be filed against suspension; 241(3.2)(g) — Suspension letter may be disclosed to the public.

Notes: See Notes at end of 188.2.

188.2(2)(f) added by 2021 budget bill #1, effective June 29, 2021.

188.2(2)(e) amended and (f)-(g) repealed by 2018 budget bill #2, effective June 29, 2012 for organizations, corporations and trusts that were registered charities on Sept. 14, 2018 and for associations that were registered Canadian amateur athletic associations on that date, and effective Sept. 14, 2018 in any other case. (See Notes to 149.1(6.1).) Before the amendment, read:

> (e) in the case of a registered charity that is a charitable foundation, if the foundation devotes resources to political activities that are not considered under subsection 149.1(6.1) to be devoted to charitable purposes;
>
> (f) in the case of a registered charity that is a charitable organization, if the organization devotes resources to political activities that are not considered under subsection 149.1(6.2) to be devoted to charitable activities; or
>
> (g) in the case of a registered Canadian amateur athletic association, if the association devotes resources to political activities that are not considered under subsection 149.1(6.201) to be devoted to its exclusive purpose and exclusive function.

188.2(2) earlier amended by 2012 budget bill #1 (effective June 29, 2012), 2011 budget bill #2.

Registered Charities Newsletters: 26 (books and records — Q10); 28 (objections and appeals on issues relating to charities).

Charities Guidance: CG-024: Ineligible individuals.

(2.1) Suspension — failure to report

(2.1) Suspension — failure to report — If a registered charity, a registered Canadian amateur athletic association or a registered journalism organization fails to report information that is required to be included in a return filed under subsection 149.1(14) or (14.1), the Minister may give notice by registered mail to the charity, association or organization that its authority to issue an official receipt referred to in Part XXXV of the *Income Tax Regulations* is suspended from the day that is seven days after the day on which the notice is mailed until such time as the Minister notifies the charity, association or organization that the Minister has received the required information in prescribed form.

Related Provisions: 188.2(3) — Effect of suspension; 188.2(4) — Application for postponement.

Notes: 188.2(2.1) amended by 2019 budget bill #1, effective 2020, to add references to "registered journalism organization" [defined in 248(1)] and 149.1(14.1), and to change "charity or association" to "charity, association or organization".

188.2(2.1) added by 2012 budget bill #1, effective June 29, 2012.

(3) Effect of suspension

(3) Effect of suspension — If the Minister has issued a notice to a qualified donee under any of subsections (1) to (2.1), subject to subsection (4),

(a) the qualified donee is deemed, in respect of gifts made and property transferred to the qualified donee within the one-year period that begins on the day that is seven days after the day on which the notice is mailed, not to be a qualified donee for the purposes of subsections 110.1(1) and 118.1(1) and Part XXXV of the *Income Tax Regulations*; and

(b) if the qualified donee is, during that period, offered a gift from any person, the qualified donee shall, before accepting the gift, inform that person that

(i) it has received the notice,

(ii) no deduction under subsection 110.1(1) or credit under subsection 118.1(3) may be claimed in respect of a gift made to it in the period, and

(iii) a gift made to it in the period is not a gift to a qualified donee.

Related Provisions: 188.2(2)(b) — Suspension for charity that accepts gift on behalf of suspended charity.

Notes: 188.2(3) opening words amended by 2012 budget bill #1 to change "(1) or (2)" to "(1) to (2.1)", effective June 29, 2012.

188.2(3) amended by 2011 budget bill #2, for tax years that begin after 2011.

(4) Application for postponement

(4) Application for postponement — If a notice of objection to a suspension under any of subsections (1) to (2.1) has been filed by a qualified donee, the qualified donee may file an application to the Tax Court of Canada for a postponement of that portion of the period of suspension that has not elapsed until the time determined by the Court.

Related Provisions: 188.2(5) — Grounds for postponement by Tax Court; 189(8) — Notice of objection (s. 165) may be filed against suspension.

Notes: 188.2 does not explicitly provide for a Notice of Objection to be filed; this is covered by 189(8), which provides that 162-167 (including 165) apply to a suspension.

188.2(4) amended by 2012 budget bill #1 to change "(1) or (2)" to "(1) to (2.1)", effective June 29, 2012.

188.2(4) amended by 2011 budget bill #2, for tax years that begin after 2011.

Registered Charities Newsletters: 28 (objections and appeals on issues relating to charities).

(5) Grounds for postponement

(5) Grounds for postponement — The Tax Court of Canada may grant an application for postponement only if it would be just and equitable to do so.

Notes: For the meaning of "just and equitable", see Notes to 85(7.1).

Notes [188.2]: 188.2 provides for suspension of a charity's tax-receipting privileges on assessment of certain penalties under 188.1 (or, under 188.2(2.1), for not filing an information return under 149.1(14)). For the 1-year period beginning 7 days after the assessment date (or until the return is filed, for suspension under 188.2(2.1)), donations to a suspended charity are not valid donations for tax purposes, nor may other charities give it gifts: 188.2(3).

Guidelines for applying sanctions (tinyurl.com/cra-sanctions) state: "... while under suspension, a charity is obliged to inform anyone (including other registered charities) planning to donate to it of its suspended status. It can still receive gifts, but it cannot issue an official donation receipt for them. We intend to revoke the registration of any suspended charity that issues an official donation receipt for a gift made to it during the suspension period. If the suspended charity arranges for another charity to receive and receipt gifts on its behalf, we intend to suspend the other charity as well."

International Charity Association Network (ICAN) was suspended for a year starting Nov. 28, 2007 (and revocation proceedings were begun), for failing to maintain and provide access to books and records relating to its involvement in tax shelter arrangements (CRA news release, Nov. 29/07). An application to have the suspension postponed was dismissed on Jan. 3/08: 2008 TCC 3 (FCA appeal discontinued A-21-08). The Court called ICAN's "Global Learning" tax shelter arrangements "disturbing" (para. 69). The CRA is denying all Global Learning donations: *Ficek*, 2013 FC 502, paras. 6-10. ICAN's registration was revoked effective Aug. 9, 2008 (CRA news release, Aug. 11, 2008). See Notes to 168(1).

The Court stated in *ICAN* (paras. 6-8) that since 188.2(5) "is essentially a statutory injunction", the applicable tests are those for an injunction: (1) serious question to be tried; (2) irreparable harm; (3) balance of convenience. See also Shayne Saskiw, "Suspending the Suspension", XV(4) *Tax Litigation* (Federated Press) 960-65 (2008).

A motion to defer publication of ICAN's revocation notice failed: 2008 FCA 114.

Congregation Adath Israel (Montreal) was suspended for a year, with a $500,000 fine, effective March 19, 2008: Drache, "The Value of a Right", 16(5) *Canadian Not-for-Profit News* (Carswell) 37-38 (May 2008); Carr, "A Fate Worse Than Death (Revocation)?", *Charities and Not-for-Profit Newsletter* (millerthomson.com), May 2008.

International Relief Fund for the Afflicted and Needy-Canada (IRFAN) was suspended for a year on April 13, 2010, for failing to maintain proper records and failing to provide documents on audit and under a Requirement. IRFAN's registration was revoked on April 9, 2011 and it was designated a terrorist entity on April 29, 2014.

In *Promised Land Ministries*, 2019 TCC 145, a 1-year suspension was upheld for not keeping adequate records of cash expenses outside Canada. The TCC likely misstated the test as being whether CRA's decision was reasonable: Adam Aptowitzer, "No Equity in Tax Court", 27(9) *Canadian Not-for-Profit News* (Carswell) 70-71 (Sept. 2019).

188.2 added by 2004 Budget, for taxation years that begin after March 22, 2004.

Definitions [s. 188.2]: "assessment" — 248(1); "Canada" — 255, *Interpretation Act* 35(1); "charity" — 149.1(1), 187.7; "contravene" — *Interpretation Act* 35(1); "culpable conduct", "false statement" — 163.2(1); "ineligible individual" — 149.1(1), 187.7; "Minister", "officer", "person", "prescribed", "property" — 248(1); "qualified donee" — 149.1(1), 188.2(3)(a), 248(1); "registered Canadian amateur athletic association", "registered charity", "registered journalism organization", "regulation" — 248(1); "taxation year" — 149.1(1), 187.7.

189. (1) Tax regarding non-qualified investment — Where at any particular time in a taxation year a debt (other than a debt in respect of which subsection 80.4(1) applies or would apply but for subsection 80.4(3)) is owing by a taxpayer to a registered charity that is a private foundation and at that time the debt was a non-qualified investment of the foundation, the taxpayer shall pay a tax under this Part for the year equal to the amount, if any, by which

(a) the amount that would be payable as interest on that debt for the period in the year during which it was outstanding and was a non-qualified investment of the foundation if the interest were payable at such prescribed rates as are in effect from time to time during the period

exceeds

(b) the amount of interest for the year paid on that debt by the taxpayer not later than 30 days after the end of the year.

Related Provisions: 149.1(6.4) — Application to registered national arts service organizations.

Notes: For an example of 189(1) applying see VIEWS doc 2011-0422811I7. Even where it does not apply, a loan may be an "undue benefit" triggering the 188.1(4) penalty: 2017-0683831I7.

Regulations: 4301(c) (prescribed rate of interest).

Charities Guidance: CG-006: Non-qualified investment — tax liability.

(2) Computation of interest on debt — For the purpose of paragraph (1)(a), where a debt in respect of which subsection (1) applies (other than a share or right that is deemed by subsection (3) to be a debt) is owing by a taxpayer to a private foundation, interest on that debt for the period referred to in that paragraph shall be computed at the least of

(a) such prescribed rates as are in effect from time to time during the period,

(b) the rate per annum of interest on that debt that, having regard to all the circumstances (including the terms and conditions of the debt), would have been agreed on, at the time the debt was incurred, had the taxpayer and the foundation been dealing with each other at arm's length and had the ordinary business of the foundation been the lending of money, and

(c) where that debt was incurred before April 22, 1982, a rate per annum equal to 6% plus 2% for each calendar year after 1982 and before the taxation year referred to in subsection (1).

Regulations: 4301(c) (prescribed rate of interest).

(3) Share deemed to be debt — For the purpose of subsection (1), where a share, or a right to acquire a share, of the capital stock of a corporation held by a private foundation at any particular time during the corporation's taxation year was at that time a non-qualified investment of the foundation, the share or right shall be deemed to be a debt owing at that time by the corporation to the foundation

(a) the amount of which was equal to,

(i) in the case of a share or right last acquired before April 22, 1982, the greater of its fair market value on April 21, 1982 and its cost amount to the foundation at the particular time, or

(ii) in any other case, its cost amount to the foundation at the particular time,

(b) that was outstanding throughout the period for which the share or right was held by the foundation during the year, and

(c) in respect of which the amount of interest paid in the year is equal to the total of all amounts each of which is the amount of a dividend received on the share by the foundation in the year,

and the reference in paragraph (1)(a) to "such prescribed rates as are in effect from time to time during the period" shall be read as a reference to "⅔ of such prescribed rates as are in effect from time to time during the period".

(4) Computation of interest with respect to a share — For the purposes of subsection (3), where a share or right in respect of which that subsection applies was last acquired before April 22, 1982, the reference therein to "⅔ of such prescribed rates as are in

effect from time to time during the period" shall be read as a reference to "the lesser of

(a) a rate per annum equal to 4% plus 1% for each 5 calendar years contained in the period commencing after 1982 and ending before the particular time, and

(b) a rate per annum equal to ⅔ of such prescribed rates as are in effect from time to time during the year".

(5) Share substitution — For the purpose of subsection (3), where a share or right is acquired by a charity in exchange for another share or right in a transaction after April 21, 1982 to which section 51, 85, 85.1, 86 or 87 applies, it shall be deemed to be the same share or right as the one for which it was substituted.

(6) Taxpayer to file return and pay tax — Every taxpayer who is liable to pay tax under this Part (except a charity that is liable to pay tax under [sub]section 188(1)) for a taxation year shall, on or before the day on or before which the taxpayer is, or would be if tax were payable by the taxpayer under Part I for the year, required to file a return of income or an information return under Part I for the year,

(a) file with the Minister a return for the year in prescribed form and containing prescribed information, without notice or demand therefor;

(b) estimate in the return the amount of tax payable by the taxpayer under this Part for the year; and

(c) pay to the Receiver General the amount of tax payable by the taxpayer under this Part for the year.

Related Provisions: 150.1(5) — Electronic filing.

Notes: 189(6) amended by 1993 technical bill, effective 1993.

Forms: T2046: Tax return where registration of a charity is revoked; T2140: Part V tax return — tax on non-qualified investments of a registered charity.

(6.1) Revoked charity to file returns — Every taxpayer who is liable to pay tax under subsection 188(1.1) for a taxation year shall, on or before the day that is one year from the end of the taxation year, and without notice or demand,

(a) file with the Minister

(i) a return for the taxation year, in prescribed form and containing prescribed information, and

(ii) both an information return and a public information return for the taxation year, each in the form prescribed for the purpose of subsection 149.1(14); and

(b) estimate in the return referred to in subparagraph (a)(i) the amount of tax payable by the taxpayer under subsection 188(1.1) for the taxation year; and

(c) pay to the Receiver General the amount of tax payable by the taxpayer under subsection 188(1.1) for the taxation year.

Related Provisions: 188(1) — Deemed year-end on notice of revocation.

Notes: 189(6.1) added by 2004 Budget, effective in respect of notices issued by the Minister after June 12, 2005.

Forms: RC4424: Completing the tax return where registration of a charity is revoked [guide]; T2046: Tax return where registration of a charity is revoked.

(6.2) Reduction of revocation tax liability — If the Minister has, during the one-year period beginning immediately after the end of a taxation year of a person, assessed the person in respect of the person's liability for tax under subsection 188(1.1) for that taxation year, has not after that period reassessed the tax liability of the person, and that liability exceeds $1,000, that liability is, at any particular time, reduced by the total of

(a) the amount, if any, by which

(i) the total of all amounts, each of which is an expenditure made by the charity, on charitable activities carried on by it, before the particular time and during the period (referred to in this subsection as the "post-assessment period") that begins immediately after a notice of the latest such assessment was sent and ends at the end of the one-year period

exceeds

(ii) the income of the charity for the post-assessment period, including gifts received by the charity in that period from any source and any income that would be computed under section 3 if that period were a taxation year, and

(b) all amounts, each of which is an amount, in respect of a property transferred by the charity before the particular time and during the post-assessment period to a person that was at the time of the transfer an eligible donee in respect of the charity, equal to the amount, if any, by which the fair market value of the property, when transferred, exceeds the consideration given by the person for the transfer.

Related Provisions: 149.1(1.1)(c) — Amount transferred under (b) deemed not expended on charitable activities; 189(9)(a) — No interest on revocation tax to extent reduced by 189(6.2); 244(14), (14.1) — Date when notice sent.

Notes: 189(6.2) applies when a charity's registration is revoked, if CRA assesses more than $1,000 revocation tax under 188(1.1) less than 1 year after the notice is issued. The charity can reduce the revocation tax during the balance of the 1-year period (post-assessment period), by spending funds on charitable activities or transferring property (which can include money: 248(1)"property") to an "eligible donee" (188(1.3)). See also Notes at end of 188.1.

For meaning of "charitable activities" in (a) see Notes to 149.1(1)"charitable activities".

189(6.2)(a)(i) amended by 2010 budget bill #2, effective Dec. 15, 2010, to change "mailed" to "sent" (to accommodate electronic notices under 244(14.1)).

189(6.2) added by 2004 Budget, effective in respect of notices issued by the Minister after June 12, 2005.

(6.3) Reduction of liability for penalties — If the Minister has assessed a particular person in respect of the particular person's liability for penalties under section 188.1 for a taxation year, and that liability exceeds $1,000, that liability is, at any particular time, reduced by the total of all amounts, each of which is an amount, in respect of a property transferred by the particular person after the day on which the Minister first assessed that liability and before the particular time to another person that was at the time of the transfer an eligible donee described in paragraph 188(1.3)(a) in respect of the particular person, equal to the amount, if any, by which the fair market value of the property, when transferred, exceeds the total of

(a) the consideration given by the other person for the transfer, and

(b) the part of the amount in respect of the transfer that has resulted in a reduction of an amount otherwise payable under subsection 188(1.1).

Related Provisions: 149.1(1.1)(c) — Amount transferred under (b) deemed not expended on charitable activities; 188(1.3) — Eligible donee of charity; 188(1.4) — Eligible donee of RCAAA; 189(9)(b) — No interest on penalties to extent reduced by 189(6.3).

Notes: A charity or other "qualified donee" (see 149.1(1)) assessed for penalties over $1,000 under 188.1 can reduce the liability by transferring property (which can include money: 248(1)"property") to an "eligible donee" (188(1.3)(a)). See Notes at end of 188.1 for the rationale.

189(6.3) opening words amended by 2018 budget bill #1 to add "described in paragraph 188(1.3)(a)", for transfers after Feb. 26, 2018. This preserved the existing 189(6.3) rule as applying only to charities, as 188(1.3) was expanded to include municipalities, and charities are now under 188(1.3)(a).

189(6.3) amended by 2011 budget bill #2, for tax years that begin after 2011. Added by 2004 Budget.

(7) Minister may assess — Without limiting the authority of the Minister to revoke the registration of a registered charity or registered Canadian amateur athletic association, the Minister may also at any time assess a taxpayer in respect of any amount that a taxpayer is liable to pay under this Part.

Related Provisions: 189(8) — Objection to penalty and other administrative procedures; 221.1 — Application of interest where legislation retroactive; 248(11) — Interest compounded daily.

Notes: 189(7) allows assessment of revocation tax (188) and charity penalties (188.1).

189(7) amended by 2011 budget bill #2 (for tax years that begin after 2011), 2004 Budget.

Regulations: 4301 (prescribed rate of interest).

(8) Provisions applicable to Part — Subsections 150(2) and (3), sections 152 and 158, subsection 161(11), sections 162 to 167 and Division J of Part I apply in respect of an amount assessed under this Part and of a notice of suspension under subsection 188.2(1) or (2) as if the notice were a notice of assessment made under section 152, with any modifications that the circumstances require including, for greater certainty, that a notice of suspension that is reconsidered or reassessed may be confirmed or vacated, but not varied, except that

(a) section 162 does not apply in respect of a return required to be filed under paragraph (6.1)(a); and

(b) the reference in each of subsections 165(2) and 166.1(3) to the expression "Chief of Appeals in a District Office or a Taxation Centre" is to be read as a reference to the expression "Assistant Commissioner, Appeals Branch".

Related Provisions: 189(8.1)(a) — Objection to revocation is not an objection to revocation tax; 189(8.1)(b) — Revocation of registration cannot be appealed to Tax Court of Canada; 189(9) — No interest on revocation tax or penalties to extent reduced by 189(6.2) or (6.3).

Notes: 189(8) allows an objection to be filed to the revocation tax (188), charity penalties (188.1) and suspension of a charity's receipting privileges (188.2). It also allows appeals of these matters to the Tax Court (since Division J of Part I includes s. 169).

189(8) amended by 2004 Budget, for notices issued by the Minister after June 12, 2005.

Registered Charities Newsletters: 19 (appeals process); 28 (objections and appeals on issues relating to charities).

(8.1) Clarification re objections under subsec. 168(4) — For greater certainty, in applying the provisions referred to in subsection (8), with any modifications that the circumstances require,

(a) a notice of objection referred to in subsection 168(4) does not constitute a notice of objection to a tax assessed under subsection 188(1.1); and

(b) an issue that could have been the subject of a notice of objection referred to in subsection 168(4) may not be appealed to the Tax Court of Canada under subsection 169(1).

Related Provisions: 172(3)(a.1) — Appeal of revocation to Federal Court of Appeal.

Notes: 189(8.1) added by 2004 Budget, for notices issued by the Minister after June 12, 2005.

Registered Charities Newsletters: 19 (appeals process).

(9) Interest — Subsection 161(11) does not apply to a liability of a taxpayer for a taxation year

(a) under subsection 188(1.1) to the extent that the liability is reduced by subsection (6.2), or paid, before the end of the one-year period that begins immediately after the end of the taxation year deemed to have ended by paragraph 188(1)(a); or

(b) under section 188.1 to the extent that the liability is reduced by subsection (6.3), or paid, before the end of the one-year period that begins immediately after the liability was first assessed.

Notes: 189(9) added by 2004 Budget, for notices CRA issues after June 12, 2005.

Definitions [s. 189]: "amount" — 248(1); "arm's length" — 251(1); "assessment", "business" — 248(1); "calendar year" — *Interpretation Act* 37(1)(a); "charitable foundation", "charitable organization", "charitable purposes", "charity" — 149.1(1), 187.7; "corporation" — 248(1), *Interpretation Act* 35(1); "disbursement quota", "dividend" — 248(1); "eligible donee" — 188(1.3), (1.4); "fair market value" — see 69(1) Notes; "Minister" — 248(1); "non-qualified investment" — 149.1(1), 187.7; "person", "prescribed" — 248(1); "prescribed rate" — Reg. 4301; "private foundation" — 149.1(1), 187.7, 248(1); "property" — 248(1); "public foundation", "qualified donee", "qualified investment" — 149.1(1), 187.7; "registered Canadian amateur athletic association", "registered charity" — 248(1); "related business" — 149.1(1), 187.7; "sent" — 244(14), (14.1); "share" — 248(1); "specified gift", "taxation year" — 149.1(1), 187.7; "taxpayer" — 248(1).

PART VI — TAX ON CAPITAL OF FINANCIAL INSTITUTIONS

Notes: Life insurers are also subject to Part XII.3 tax. See 211–211.5.

190. (1) Definitions — For the purposes of this Part,

"financial institution" means a corporation that

(a) is a bank,

(b) is authorized under the laws of Canada or a province to carry on the business of offering its services as a trustee to the public,

(c) is authorized under the laws of Canada or a province to accept deposits from the public and carries on the business of lending money on the security of real property or immovables or investing in indebtedness on the security of mortgages on real property or of hypothecs on immovables,

(d) is a life insurance corporation that carries on business in Canada, or

(e) is a corporation all or substantially all of the assets of which are shares or indebtedness of corporations described in any of paragraphs (a) to (d) or this paragraph to which the corporation is related;

Related Provisions: 253 — Extended meaning of "carrying on business in Canada".

Notes: CRA considers that "substantially all", in para. (e), means 90% or more.

Para. (c) amended by 2002-2013 technical bill, effective June 26, 2013.

Definition earlier amend by 2001 *Civil Code* harmonization bill (effective June 14, 2001) and 1990 Budget/1991 technical bill.

"long-term debt" means

(a) in the case of a bank, its subordinated indebtedness (within the meaning assigned by section 2 of the *Bank Act*) evidenced by obligations issued for a term of not less than 5 years,

(b) in the case of an insurance corporation, its subordinated indebtedness (within the meaning assigned by section 2 of the *Insurance Companies Act*) evidenced by obligations issued for a term of not less than 5 years, and

(c) in the case of any other corporation, its subordinated indebtedness (within the meaning that would be assigned by section 2 of the *Bank Act* if the definition of that expression in that section were applied with such modifications as the circumstances require) evidenced by obligations issued for a term of not less than 5 years;

Notes: "Long-term debt" amended by 1993 technical bill, effective June 1, 1992.

"reserves", in respect of a financial institution for a taxation year, means the amount at the end of the year of all of the institution's reserves, provisions and allowances (other than allowances in respect of depreciation or depletion) and, for greater certainty, includes any provision in respect of deferred taxes.

Notes: See Notes to 181(1)"reserves" and to 190.11.

"Reserves" added by 1993 technical bill, effective for 1992 and later taxation years.

(1.1) Prescribed meanings — For the purposes of this Part, the expressions "attributed surplus", "Canadian assets", "Canadian reserve liabilities", "total assets" and "total reserve liabilities" have the meanings that are prescribed.

Regulations: 8603 (prescribed meanings of expressions).

(2) Application of subsecs. 181(3) and (4) — Subsections 181(3) and (4) apply to this Part with such modifications as the circumstances require.

Notes: 190(2) amended by 1993 technical bill, effective for 1992 and later taxation years. The rule formerly in 190(2) is now in 248(24).

Definitions [s. 190]: "amount" — 248(1); "bank" — 248(1), *Interpretation Act* 35(1); "business" — 248(1); "Canada" — 255; "carrying on business in Canada" — 253; "corporation" — 248(1), *Interpretation Act* 35(1); "immovables" — Quebec *Civil Code* art. 900–907; "hypothecs" — Quebec *Civil Code* art. 2660; "life insurance corporation", "prescribed" — 248(1); "province" — *Interpretation Act* 35(1).

Calculation of Capital Tax

190.1 (1) Tax payable — Every corporation that is a financial institution at any time during a taxation year shall pay a tax under this Part for the year equal to 1.25% of the amount, if any, by which its taxable capital employed in Canada for the year exceeds its capital deduction for the year.

Related Provisions: 18(1)(t) — Tax is non-deductible; 157(1) — Instalment and payment obligations; 161(1), (4.1) — Interest; 181.1(1) — Large Corporations Tax (pre-2006); 190.1(3)(a) — Tax reduced by Part I surtax paid; 190.15 — Capital deduction; 227(14) — No tax on corporation exempt under s. 149.

Notes: See Notes to 190.15(1) re the effective rate of tax.

For corporations to which this tax applies, see 190(1)"financial institution". See also Part I.3 (ss. 181-181.71), which imposed the Large Corporations Tax before 2006, and still has some rules that apply here.

(1.1), (1.2) [Repealed]

Notes: 190.1(1.1) and (1.2) repealed by 2006 budget bill #2, for tax years that end after June 2006. They imposed surtaxes on life insurance corps (expired end of 2000) and deposit-taking financial institutions (expired Oct. 31, 2000). 190.1(1.1) previously amended by 2001 technical bill, 1996 Budget and 1993 technical bill. 190.1(1.2) previously amended by 1999, 1998, 1997, 1996 and 1995 Budgets.

(2) Short taxation years — Where a taxation year of a corporation is less than 51 weeks, the amount determined under subsection (1) for the year in respect of the corporation shall be reduced to that proportion of that amount that the number of days in the year is of 365.

Notes: 190.1(2) amended by 1992 technical bill, for 1992 and later tax years.

(3) Deduction — There may be deducted in computing a corporation's tax payable under this Part for a taxation year an amount equal to the total of

(a) the corporation's tax payable under Part I for the year; and

(b) such part as the corporation claims of its unused Part I tax credits and unused surtax credits for its 7 taxation years immediately before and its 3 taxation years immediately after the year.

(c), (d) [Repealed]

Related Provisions: 87(2)(j.91) — Amalgamation — continuing corporation; 87(2.11) — Vertical amalgamations; 161(7)(a)(x), 164(5)(h.2), 164(5.1)(h.3) — Effect of carryback of loss etc.; 190.2 — Return; 261(7)(a), 261(15) — Functional currency reporting.

Notes [subsec. 190.1(3)–(6)]: For the rationale of 190.1(3) to (6), see Notes to 125.2. Under 190.1(3), a financial institution can reduce its Part VI tax by the total of its Part I tax liability for the year, plus such amount as it chooses of its unused Part I tax credits and unused surtax credits for the 7 preceding and 3 following taxation years.

190.1(3) amended by 2002-2013 technical bill (for tax years that begin after 2007), 2006 budget bill #2, 1995 Budget. 190.1(3)-(6) added by 1992 technical bill.

Forms: T2 Sched. 42: Calculation of unused Part I tax credit; T921: Calculation of unused Part VI tax credit and unused Part I tax credit.

(4) Idem — For the purposes of this subsection and subsections (3), (5) and (6),

(a) an amount may not be claimed under subsection (3) in computing a corporation's tax payable under this Part for a particular taxation year

(i) in respect of its unused Part I tax credit for another taxation year, until its unused Part I tax credits for taxation years preceding the other year that may be claimed under this Part for the particular year have been claimed, and

(ii) in respect of its unused surtax credit for another taxation year, until its unused surtax credits for taxation years preceding the other year that may be claimed under Part I.3 or this Part for the particular year have been claimed;

(b) an amount may be claimed under subsection (3) in computing a corporation's tax payable under this Part for a particular taxation year

(i) in respect of its unused Part I tax credit for another taxation year, only to the extent that it exceeds the total of all amounts each of which is the amount claimed in respect of that unused Part I tax credit in computing its tax payable under this Part for a taxation year preceding the particular year, and

(ii) in respect of its unused surtax credit for another taxation year, only to the extent that it exceeds the total of all amounts each of which is the amount claimed in respect of the unused surtax credit

(A) in computing its tax payable under this Part for a taxation year preceding the particular year, or

(B) in computing its tax payable under Part I.3 for the particular year or a taxation year preceding the particular year; and

(c) an amount may be claimed under paragraph (3)(b) in computing a corporation's tax payable under this Part for a taxation year that ends before July 1, 2006 in respect of its unused Part I tax credit for a taxation year that ends after July 1, 2006 (referred to in this paragraph as the "credit taxation year") only to the extent that the unused Part I tax credit exceeds the amount, if any, by which

(i) the amount that would, if this Part were read as it applied to the 2005 taxation year, be the corporation's tax payable under this Part for the credit taxation year

exceeds

(ii) the corporation's tax payable under this Part for the credit taxation year.

Related Provisions: 87(2.11) — Vertical amalgamations.

Notes: 190.1(4)(c) added by 2006 budget bill #2, for tax years that end after June 2006. This transitional rule restricts a financial institution's ability to carry back unused Part I tax credits under 190.1(3)(b). Under 190.1(4)(c), unused Part I tax credits for taxation years ending after June 2006 that are carried back under 190.1(3)(b) to earlier years are computed as if the Part VI tax were still levied at a rate of 1% on taxable capital employed in Canada of $200m–$300m, and 1.25% over $300m.

See Notes to 190.1(3).

(5) Definitions — For the purposes of subsections (3), (4) and (6),

"unused Part I tax credit", of a corporation for a taxation year, means the amount, if any, by which

(a) the corporation's tax payable under Part I for the year

exceeds

(b) the amount that would, but for subsection (3), be its tax payable under this Part for the year;

Notes: Definition amended by 2002-2013 technical bill, for tax years that begin after 2007.

"unused surtax credit" of a corporation for a taxation year has the meaning assigned by subsection 181.1(6).

Related Provisions: 181.1(1.2) — Calculation to be based on tax rate of 0.225%; 181.5(1.1), (4.1) — Calculation to be based on capital deduction of $10 million.

Related Provisions [subsec. 190.1(5)]: 87(2.11) — Vertical amalgamations.

Notes [subsec. 190.1(5)]: See Notes to 190.1(3).

(6) Acquisition of control — Where at any time control of a corporation was acquired by a person or group of persons, no amount in respect of its unused Part I tax credit or unused surtax credit for a taxation year ending before that time is deductible by the corporation for a taxation year ending after the time and no amount in respect of its unused Part I tax credit or unused surtax credit for a taxation year ending after that time is deductible by the corporation for a taxation year ending before that time, except that

(a) the corporation's unused Part I tax credit and unused surtax credit for a particular taxation year that ended before that time is deductible by the corporation for a taxation year that ends after that time (in this paragraph referred to as the "subsequent year") to the extent of that proportion of the corporation's tax payable under Part I for the particular year that

(i) the amount, if any, by which

(A) the total of all amounts each of which is

(I) its income under Part I for the particular year from a business that was carried on by the corporation for

profit or with a reasonable expectation of profit throughout the subsequent year, or

(II) where properties were sold, leased, rented or developed or services were rendered in the course of carrying on that business before that time, its income under Part I for the particular year from any other business all or substantially all of the income of which was derived from the sale, leasing, rental or development, as the case may be, of similar properties or the rendering of similar services

exceeds

(B) the total of all amounts each of which is an amount deducted under paragraph 111(1)(a) or (d) in computing its taxable income for the particular year in respect of a non-capital loss or a farm loss, as the case may be, for a taxation year in respect of any business referred to in clause (A)

is of the greater of

(ii) the amount determined under subparagraph (i), and

(iii) the corporation's taxable income for the particular year; and

(b) the corporation's unused Part I tax credit and unused surtax credit for a particular taxation year that ends after that time is deductible by the corporation for a taxation year (in this paragraph referred to as the "preceding year") that ended before that time to the extent of that proportion of the corporation's tax payable under Part I for the particular year that

(i) the amount, if any, by which

(A) the total of all amounts each of which is

(I) its income under Part I for the particular year from a business that was carried on by the corporation in the preceding year and throughout the particular year for profit or with a reasonable expectation of profit, or

(II) where properties were sold, leased, rented or developed or services were rendered in the course of carrying on that business before that time, its income under Part I for the particular year from any other business all or substantially all of the income of which was derived from the sale, leasing, rental or development, as the case may be, of similar properties or the rendering of similar services

exceeds

(B) the total of all amounts each of which is an amount deducted under paragraph 111(1)(a) or (d) in computing its taxable income for the particular year in respect of a non-capital loss or a farm loss, as the case may be, for a taxation year in respect of any business referred to in clause (A)

is of the greater of

(ii) the amount determined under subparagraph (i), and

(iii) the corporation's taxable income for the particular year.

Related Provisions: 87(2.11) — Vertical amalgamations; 256(6)–(9) — Anti-avoidance — deemed exercise of right to increase voting power; 256.1 — Deemed change in control if 75% FMV acquired.

Notes: 190.1(6)(a) and (b) amended by 1995-97 technical bill, for acquisitions of control after April 26, 1995. See Notes to 190.1(3).

I.T. Technical News: 7 (control by a group — 50/50 arrangement).

Definitions [s. 190.1]: "acquired" — 256(7)–(9); "amount" — 181(3), 190(2), 248(1); "business" — 248(1); "Canadian surtax payable" — 125.3(4); "capital deduction" — 190.15; "control" — 256(6)–(9), 256.1(3); "corporation" — 248(1), *Interpretation Act* 35(1); "farm loss" — 111(8), 248(1); "financial institution" — 190(1); "non-capital loss" — 111(8), 248(1); "property" — 248(1); "tax payable" — 248(2); "taxable capital employed in Canada" — 190.11; "taxation year" — 249; "unused Part I credit", "unused surtax credit" — 190.1(5).

190.11 Taxable capital employed in Canada — For the purposes of this Part, the taxable capital employed in Canada of a financial institution for a taxation year is,

(a) in the case of a financial institution other than a life insurance corporation, that proportion of its taxable capital for the year that its Canadian assets at the end of the year is of its total assets at the end of the year;

(b) in the case of a life insurance corporation that was resident in Canada at any time in the year, the total of

(i) that proportion of the amount, if any, by which the total of

(A) its taxable capital for the year, and

(B) the amount prescribed for the year in respect of the corporation

exceeds

(C) the amount prescribed for the year in respect of the corporation

that its Canadian reserve liabilities as at the end of the year is of the total of

(D) its total reserve liabilities as at the end of the year, and

(E) the amount prescribed for the year in respect of the corporation, and

(ii) [Repealed]

(c) in the case of a life insurance corporation that was non-resident throughout the year, its taxable capital for the year.

Related Provisions: 181.3(1) — Taxable capital employed in Canada for Part I.3 tax; 257 — Formula cannot calculate to less than zero [applies to amending legislation by virtue of *Interpretation Act* subsec. 42(3)].

Notes: In *London Life*, [2000] 3 C.T.C. 2622 (TCC), deferred income taxes were held not to be part of "reserves" under 190.11(b)(ii)(A).

190.11(b)(ii) repealed by 2008 budget bill #2, for tax years that begin after Sept. 2006. The "reserve adjustment" added to TCEC (also 190.13(c)(iv)) was considered unnecessary due to the demutualization of the insurance industry: Finance news release 2006-091 (Dec. 28/06).

190.11 earlier amended by 1995-97 technical bill (rule of application to 2001), 1993 technical bill and 1990 Budget/1991 technical bill.

Definitions [s. 190.11]: "amount" — 181(3), 190(2), 248(1); "authorized foreign bank" — 248(1); "Canadian assets" — 190(1.1), Reg. 8603(a); "Canadian reserve liabilities" — 190(1.1), Reg. 2405(3), 8600, 8602, 8603(b), 8603(c); "corporation" — 248(1), *Interpretation Act* 35(1); "financial institution" — 190(1); "life insurance corporation" — 248(1); "reserves" — 190(1); "resident in Canada" — 250; "taxable capital" — 190.12; "taxation year" — 249; "total assets" — 190(1.1), Reg. 8602, 8603(a), 8603(b); "total reserve liabilities" — 190(1.1), Reg. 2405(3), 8600, 8602, 8603(b), 8603(c).

Regulations: 8605 (prescribed amounts for 190.11(b)(i)(B), (C) and (E)).

190.12 Taxable capital — For the purposes of this Part, the taxable capital of a corporation for a taxation year is the amount, if any, by which its capital for the year exceeds the total determined under section 190.14 in respect of its investments for the year in financial institutions related to it.

Related Provisions: 181.3(2) — Taxable capital for Part I.3 tax.

Definitions [s. 190.12]: "amount" — 181(3), 190(2), 248(1); "capital" — 190.13; "corporation" — 248(1), *Interpretation Act* 35(1); "financial institution" — 190(1); "investments in financial institutions" — 190.14; "taxation year" — 249.

190.13 Capital — For the purposes of this Part, the capital of a financial institution for a taxation year is,

(a) in the case of a financial institution, other than an authorized foreign bank or a life insurance corporation, the amount, if any, by which the total at the end of the year of

(i) the amount of its long-term debt,

(ii) the amount of its capital stock (or, in the case of an institution incorporated without share capital, the amount of its members' contributions), retained earnings, contributed surplus and any other surpluses, and

(iii) the amount of its reserves, except to the extent that they were deducted in computing its income under Part I for the year,

exceeds the total at the end of the year of

(iv) the amount of its deferred tax debit balance, and

(v) the amount of any deficit deducted in computing its shareholders' equity (including, for this purpose, the amount of any provision for the redemption of preferred shares);

(b) in the case of a life insurance corporation that was resident in Canada at any time in the year, the amount, if any, by which the total at the end of the year of

(i) the amount of its long-term debt, and

(ii) the amount of its capital stock (or, in the case of an insurance corporation incorporated without share capital, the amount of its members' contributions), retained earnings, contributed surplus and any other surpluses

exceeds the total at the end of the year of

(iii) the amount of its deferred tax debit balance, and

(iv) the amount of any deficit deducted in computing its shareholders' equity (including, for this purpose, the amount of any provision for the redemption of preferred shares);

(c) in the case of a life insurance corporation that was non-resident throughout the year, the total at the end of the year of

(i) the amount that is the greater of

(A) the amount, if any, by which

(I) its surplus funds derived from operations (as defined in subsection 138(12)) as of the end of the year, computed as if no tax were payable under Part I.3 or this Part for the year

exceeds the total of all amounts each of which is

(II) an amount on which it was required to pay, or would but for subsection 219(5.2) have been required to pay, tax under Part XIV for a preceding taxation year, except the portion, if any, of the amount on which tax was payable, or would have been payable, because of subparagraph 219(4)(a)(i.1), and

(III) an amount on which it was required to pay, or would but for subsection 219(5.2) have been required to pay, tax under subsection 219(5.1) for the year because of the transfer of an insurance business to which subsection 138(11.5) or (11.92) has applied, and

(B) its attributed surplus for the year,

(ii) any other surpluses relating to its insurance businesses carried on in Canada,

(iii) the amount of its long-term debt that can reasonably be regarded as relating to its insurance businesses carried on in Canada, and

(iv) [Repealed]

(d) in the case of an authorized foreign bank, the total of

(i) 10% of the total of all amounts, each of which is the risk-weighted amount at the end of the year of an on-balance sheet asset or an off-balance sheet exposure of the bank in respect of its Canadian banking business that the bank would be required to report under the OSFI risk-weighting guidelines if those guidelines applied and required a report at that time, and

(ii) the total of all amounts, each of which is an amount at the end of the year in respect of the bank's Canadian banking business that

(A) if the bank were a bank listed in Schedule II to the *Bank Act*, would be required under the risk-based capital adequacy guidelines issued by the Superintendent of Financial Institutions and applicable at that time to be deducted from the bank's capital in determining the amount of capital available to satisfy the Superintendent's requirement that capital equal a particular proportion of risk-weighted assets and exposures, and

(B) is not an amount in respect of a loss protection facility required to be deducted from capital under the Superintendent's guidelines respecting asset securitization applicable at that time.

Related Provisions: 181.3(3) — Capital for Part I.3 tax.

Notes: CRA considers that "debt" for Part VI is based on legal form, not accounting principles: 1996 Corporate Management Tax Conf. q.6, pp. 24:7-9; VIEWS doc 9530990.

Discretionary surplus appropriations of a life insurer are included in capital under 190.13(b)(ii) in CRA's view: doc 2015-060629117.

The words "computed as if no tax were payable by it under Part I.3 or this Part for the year" in 190.13(c)(i) avoid a circularity problem, since "surplus funds from operations" in 138(12) depends in part on the corporation's Part I.3 and VI liability.

For calculation of a credit union's capital for provincial capital tax purposes, see *Coast Capital*, 2009 BCSC 1768; aff'd 2011 BCCA 20.

190.13(a)(v) and (b)(iv) amended by 2002-2013 technical bill, for tax years that begin after 1995.

190.13 earlier amended by 2008 budget bill #2, 2001, 1995-97, 1993 and 1991 technical bills.

Definitions [s. 190.13]: "amount" — 181(3), 190(2), 248(1); "attributed surplus" — 190(1.1), 190(2), Reg. 2405(3), 8600, 8602, 8603(b), (c); "authorized foreign bank", "Canadian banking business" — 248(1); "corporation" — 248(1), *Interpretation Act* 35(1); "financial institution" — 190(1); "insurance corporation", "life insurance corporation" — 248(1); "long-term debt" — 190(1); "preferred share" — 248(1); "reserves" — 190(1); "taxation year" — 249.

190.14 (1) Investment in related institutions — A corporation's investment for a taxation year in a financial institution related to it is

(a) in the case of a corporation that was resident in Canada at any time in the year, the total of all amounts each of which is the carrying value (or in the case of contributed surplus, the amount) at the end of the year of an eligible investment of the corporation in the financial institution;

(b) in the case of a life insurance corporation that was non-resident throughout the year, the total of all amounts each of which is the carrying value (or is, in the case of contributed surplus, the amount) at the end of the year of an eligible investment of the corporation in the financial institution that was used or held by the corporation in the year in the course of carrying on an insurance business in Canada (or that, in the case of contributed surplus, was contributed by the corporation in the course of carrying on that business); and

(c) in the case of a corporation that is an authorized foreign bank, the total of all amounts each of which is the amount at the end of the year, before the application of risk weights, that would be required to be reported under the OSFI risk-weighting guidelines if those guidelines applied and required a report at that time, of an eligible investment of the corporation in the financial institution that was used or held by the corporation in the year in the course of carrying on its Canadian banking business or, in the case of an eligible investment that is contributed surplus of the financial institution at the end of the year, the amount of the surplus contributed by the corporation in the course of carrying on that business.

Related Provisions: 190.14(2) — Meaning of "eligible investment".

Notes: 190.14 renumbered as 190.14(1) and amended by 2001 technical bill, effective June 28, 1999. 190.14 earlier amended by 1993 and 1991 technical bills.

(2) Interpretation — For the purpose of subsection (1), an eligible investment of a corporation in a financial institution is a share of the capital stock or long-term debt (and, where the corporation is an insurance corporation, is non-segregated property within the meaning assigned by subsection 138(12)) of the financial institution or any surplus of the financial institution contributed by the corporation (other than an amount otherwise included as a share or debt) if the financial institution at the end of the year is

(a) related to the corporation; and

(b) resident in Canada or can reasonably be regarded as using the surplus or the proceeds of the share or debt in a business carried on by the financial institution through a permanent establishment (as defined by regulation) in Canada.

Notes: 190.14(2) added by 2001 technical bill, effective June 28, 1999.

Regulations: 8201 (meaning of "permanent establishment" for 190.14(2)(b)).

Related Provisions: 190.15(6) — Related financial institution.

Definitions [s. 190.14]: "amount", "authorized foreign bank", "business" — 248(1); "Canada" — 255, *Interpretation Act* 35(1); "Canadian banking business" — 248(1); "carrying value" — 181(3), 190(2); "corporation" — 248(1), *Interpretation Act* 35(1); "eligible investment" — 190.14(2); "insurance corporation", "life insurance corporation", "non-resident", "OSFI risk-weighting guidelines" — 248(1); "permanent establishment" — Reg. 8201; "property", "regulation" — 248(1); "related" — 251(2)–(6); "resident in Canada" — 250; "share" — 248(1); "taxation year" — 249.

190.15 (1) Capital deduction — For the purposes of this Part, the capital deduction of a corporation for a taxation year during which it was at any time a financial institution is $1 billion unless the corporation was related to another financial institution at the end of the year, in which case, subject to subsection (4), its capital deduction for the year is nil.

Notes: 190.15(1) amended by 2006 budget bill #2, for tax years ending after June 2006.

(2) Related financial institution — A corporation that is a financial institution at any time during a taxation year and that was related to another financial institution at the end of the year may file with the Minister an agreement in prescribed form on behalf of the related group of which the corporation is a member under which an amount that does not exceed $1 billion is allocated among the members of the related group for the taxation year.

Related Provisions: 190.15(6) — Where corporations deemed not related; 190.16(2) — Transitional rule — proportionate allocation.

Notes: 190.15(2) amended by 2006 budget bill #2, effective for taxation years that end after June 2006.

Forms: T2 Sched. 39: Agreement among related financial institutions Part VI tax; T2 Sched. 306: Newfoundland and Labrador capital tax on financial institutions — agreement among related corporations.

(3) Allocation by Minister — The Minister may request a corporation that is a financial institution at any time during a taxation year and that was related to any other financial institution at the end of the year to file with the Minister an agreement referred to in subsection (2) and, if the corporation does not file such an agreement within 30 days after receiving the request, the Minister may allocate an amount among the members of the related group of which the corporation is a member for the year not exceeding $1 billion.

Related Provisions: 190.16(2) — Transitional rule — proportionate allocation; *Interpretation Act* 27(5) — Meaning of "within 30 days".

Notes: 190.15(3) amended by 2006 budget bill #2 (for taxation years that end after June 2006), 1991 technical bill.

190.15(1)(b), (2)(b) and (3)(b) amended by 1991 technical bill, effective 1990.

(4) Idem — For the purposes of this Part, the least amount allocated for a taxation year to each member of a related group under an agreement described in subsection (2) or by the Minister pursuant to subsection (3) is the capital deduction for the taxation year of that member, but, if no such allocation is made, the capital deduction of each member of the related group for that year is nil.

(5) Idem — Where a corporation (in this subsection referred to as the "first corporation") has more than one taxation year ending in the same calendar year and is related in 2 or more of those taxation years to another corporation that has a taxation year ending in that calendar year, the capital deduction of the first corporation for each such taxation year at the end of which it is related to the other corporation is, for the purposes of this Part, an amount equal to its capital deduction for the first such taxation year.

Related Provisions: 190.16(3) — Transitional rule — deemed capital deduction.

(6) Idem — Two corporations that would, but for this subsection, be related to each other solely because of

(a) the control of any corporation by Her Majesty in right of Canada or a province, or

(b) a right referred to in paragraph 251(5)(b),

are, for the purposes of this section and section 190.14, deemed not to be related to each other except that, where at any time a taxpayer has a right referred to in paragraph 251(5)(b) with respect to shares and it can reasonably be considered that one of the main purposes for the acquisition of the right was to avoid any limitation on the amount of a corporation's capital deduction for a taxation year, for the purpose of determining whether a corporation is related to any other corporation, the corporations are, for the purpose of this section, deemed to be in the same position in relation to each other as if the right were immediate and absolute and as if the taxpayer had exercised the right at that time.

Related Provisions: 256(6), (6.1) — Meaning of "control".

Notes: For the meaning of "one of the main purposes" see Notes to 83(2.1).

Closing words of 190.15(6) amended by 1995-97 technical bill, effective April 27, 1995. 190.15(6) added by 1992 technical bill, effective 1989 and later tax years.

Definitions [s. 190.15]: "amount" — 181(3), 190(2), 248(1); "calendar year" — *Interpretation Act* 37(1)(a); "capital deduction" — 190.15, 190.16(3); "control" — 256(6), (6.1); "corporation" — 248(1), *Interpretation Act* 35(1); "financial institution" — 190(1); "Her Majesty" — *Interpretation Act* 35(1); "Minister", "prescribed" — 248(1); "province" — *Interpretation Act* 35(1); "related" — 190.15(6), 251; "related group" — 251(4); "taxation year" — 249.

190.16, 190.17 [Repealed]

Notes: 190.16 repealed by 2002-2013 technical bill (Part 5 — technical), for taxation years that begin after Oct. 2011. It provided transitional rules for 2005-06. It was added by 2006 budget bill #2, replacing a previous 190.16 (added by 1993 technical bill), which provided the capital deduction for financial institutions (see now 190.15(1)).

190.17 repealed by 2006 budget bill #2, for tax years that end after June 2006. Added by 1995 Budget, it provided an enhanced capital deduction for 190.1(1.2), a surtax which expired in 2000.

An earlier 190.17-190.19, repealed by 1989 Budget, applied to pre-1990 Part VI tax.

Administrative Provisions

190.2 Return — A corporation that is or would, but for subsection 190.1(3), be liable to pay tax under this Part for a taxation year shall file with the Minister, not later than the day on or before which the corporation is required by section 150 to file its return of income for the year under Part I, a return of capital for the year in prescribed form containing an estimate of the tax payable under this Part by it for the year.

Related Provisions: 150.1(5) — Electronic filing; 235 — Penalty for late filing of return even where no balance owing.

Notes: 190.2 amended by 1992 technical bill, effective for 1991 and later taxation years, so that a return must still be filed if no Part VI tax is payable only because it is fully credited against Part I tax.

Definitions [s. 190.2]: "corporation" — 248(1), *Interpretation Act* 35(1); "Minister", "prescribed" — 248(1); "tax payable" — 248(2); "taxation year" — 249.

Forms [s. 190.2]: T2 Sched. 38: Part VI tax on capital of financial institutions; T2 Sched. 42: Calculation of unused Part I tax credit; T2 Sched. 305: Newfoundland and Labrador capital tax on financial institutions.

190.21 Provisions applicable to Part — Sections 152, 158 and 159, subsection 161(11), sections 162 to 167 and Division J of Part I apply to this Part with such modifications as the circumstances require and, for the purpose of this section, paragraph 152(6)(a) shall be read as follows:

"(a) a deduction under subsection 190.1(3) in respect of any unused surtax credit or unused Part I tax credit (within the meanings assigned by subsection 190.1(5)) for a subsequent taxation year,".

Notes: 190.21 enacted to replace 190.21 to 190.24 by 1992 technical bill, effective for 1992 and later taxation years.

For years before the above amendments, 190.21 dealt with payment of instalments; 190.22 defined the instalment bases; 190.23 dealt with interest; and 190.24 was similar to the present 190.21.

The definition "financial institution" in 190(1) was amended by 1990 Budget/1991 technical bill to add life insurance corporations and certain holding companies. For taxation years commencing before February 21, 1990 of such corporations, payment of Part VI tax was prorated to begin on February 21, 1990 by reading 190.21 differently.

190.211 Provisions applicable — Crown corporations — Section 27 applies to this Part with any modifications that the circumstances require.

Notes: 190.211 added by 1995-97 technical bill, effective May 24, 1985. It confirms that a prescribed federal Crown corp is liable to Part VI tax. See 181.71 Notes.

PART VI.1 — TAX ON CORPORATIONS PAYING DIVIDENDS ON TAXABLE PREFERRED SHARES

191. (1) Definitions — In this Part,

"excluded dividend" means a dividend

(a) paid by a corporation to a shareholder that had a substantial interest in the corporation at the time the dividend was paid,

(b) paid by a corporation that was a financial intermediary corporation or a private holding corporation at the time the dividend was paid,

(c) paid by a particular corporation that would, but for paragraphs (h) and (i) of the definition "financial intermediary corporation" in this subsection, have been a financial intermediary corporation at the time the dividend was paid, except where the dividend was paid to a controlling corporation in respect of the particular corporation or to a specified person (within the meaning assigned by paragraph (h) of the definition "taxable preferred share" in subsection 248(1)) in relation to such a controlling corporation,

(d) paid by a mortgage investment corporation, or

(e) that is a capital gains dividend within the meaning assigned by subsection 131(1);

Related Provisions: 191(4)(d) — Deemed excluded dividend; 191(6) — Where corporation pays dividend to partnership.

"financial intermediary corporation" means a corporation that is

(a) a corporation described in subparagraph (b)(ii) of the definition "retirement savings plan" in subsection 146(1),

(b) an investment corporation,

(c) a mortgage investment corporation,

(d) a mutual fund corporation,

(e) a prescribed venture capital corporation, or

(f) a prescribed labour-sponsored venture capital corporation,

but does not include

(g) a prescribed corporation,

(h) a corporation that is controlled by or for the benefit of one or more corporations (each of which is referred to in this subsection as a "controlling corporation") other than financial intermediary corporations or private holding corporations unless the controlling corporations and specified persons (within the meaning assigned by paragraph (h) of the definition "taxable preferred share" in subsection 248(1)) in relation to the controlling corporations do not own in the aggregate shares of the capital stock of the corporation having a fair market value of more than 10% of the fair market value of all of the issued and outstanding shares of the capital stock of the corporation (those fair market values being determined without regard to any voting rights attaching to those shares), or

(i) any particular corporation in which another corporation (other than a financial intermediary corporation or a private holding corporation) has a substantial interest unless the other corporation and specified persons (within the meaning assigned by paragraph (h) of the definition "taxable preferred share" in subsection 248(1)) in relation to the other corporation do not own in the aggregate shares of the capital stock of the particular corporation having a fair market value of more than 10% of the fair market value of all of the issued and outstanding shares of the capital stock of the particular corporation (those fair market values being determined without regard to any voting rights attaching to those shares);

Related Provisions: 256(6), (6.1) — Meaning of "controlled".

Regulations: 6700 (prescribed venture capital corporation); 6701 (prescribed labour-sponsored venture capital corporation).

"private holding corporation" means a private corporation the only undertaking of which is the investing of its funds, but does not include

(a) a specified financial institution,

(b) any particular corporation that owns shares of another corporation in which it has a substantial interest, except where the other corporation would, but for that substantial interest, be a financial intermediary corporation or a private holding corporation, or

(c) any particular corporation in which another corporation owns shares and has a substantial interest, except where the other corporation would, but for that substantial interest, be a private holding corporation.

Notes: Para. (b) amended by 1991 technical bill, retroactive to 1988, to correct a circularity problem.

Related Provisions: 253.1(1) — Limited partner not considered to carry on partnership business.

(2) Substantial interest — For the purposes of this Part, a shareholder has a substantial interest in a corporation at any time if the corporation is a taxable Canadian corporation and

(a) the shareholder is related (otherwise than by reason of a right referred to in paragraph 251(5)(b)) to the corporation at that time; or

(b) the shareholder owned, at that time,

(i) shares of the capital stock of the corporation that would give the shareholder 25% or more of the votes that could be cast under all circumstances at an annual meeting of shareholders of the corporation,

(ii) shares of the capital stock of the corporation having a fair market value of 25% or more of the fair market value of all the issued shares of the capital stock of the corporation,

and either

(iii) shares (other than shares that would be taxable preferred shares if the definition "taxable preferred share" in subsection 248(1) were read without reference to subparagraph (b)(iv) thereof and if they were issued after June 18, 1987 and were not grandfathered shares) of the capital stock of the corporation having a fair market value of 25% or more of the fair market value of all those shares of the capital stock of the corporation, or

(iv) in respect of each class of shares of the capital stock of the corporation, shares of that class having a fair market value of 25% or more of the fair market value of all the issued shares of that class,

and for the purposes of this paragraph, a shareholder shall be deemed to own at any time each share of the capital stock of a corporation that is owned, otherwise than by reason of this paragraph, at that time by a person to whom the shareholder is related (otherwise than by reason of a right referred to in paragraph 251(5)(b)).

Related Provisions: 191(3) — Substantial interest.

Notes: If shares are redeemed so that 84(3) deems a dividend, CRA's view is that the "substantial interest" test is applied immediately before the redemption: VIEWS doc 2005-0118531E5.

(3) Idem — Notwithstanding subsection (2),

(a) where it can reasonably be considered that the principal purpose for a person acquiring an interest that would, but for this

subsection, be a substantial interest in a corporation is to avoid or limit the application of Part I or IV.1 or this Part, the person shall be deemed not to have a substantial interest in the corporation;

(b) where it can reasonably be considered that the principal purpose for an acquisition of a share of the capital stock of a corporation (in this paragraph referred to as the "issuer") by any person (in this paragraph referred to as the "acquirer") who had, immediately after the time of the acquisition, a substantial interest in the issuer from another person who did not, immediately before that time, have a substantial interest in the issuer, was to avoid or limit the application of Part I or IV.1 or this Part with respect to a dividend on the share, the acquirer and specified persons (within the meaning assigned by paragraph (h) of the definition "taxable preferred share" in subsection 248(1)) in relation to the acquirer shall be deemed not to have a substantial interest in the issuer with respect to any dividend paid on the share;

(c) a corporation described in paragraphs (a) to (f) of the definition "financial intermediary corporation" in subsection (1) shall be deemed not to have a substantial interest in another corporation unless it is related (otherwise than by reason of a right referred to in paragraph 251(5)(b)) to the other corporation;

(d) any partnership or trust, other than

(i) a partnership all the members of which are related to each other otherwise than by reason of a right referred to in paragraph 251(5)(b),

(ii) a trust in which each person who is beneficially interested is

(A) related (otherwise than because of a right referred to in paragraph 251(5)(b)) to each other person who is beneficially interested in the trust and who is not a registered charity, or

(B) a registered charity

and, for the purpose of this subparagraph, where a particular person who is beneficially interested in the trust is an aunt, uncle, niece or nephew of another person, the particular person and any person who is a child or descendant of the particular person shall be deemed to be related to the other person and to any person who is the child or descendant of the other person, or

(iii) a trust in which only one person (other than a registered charity) is beneficially interested,

shall be deemed not to have a substantial interest in a corporation; and

(e) where at any time a shareholder holds a share of the capital stock of a corporation to which paragraph (g) of the definition "taxable preferred share" in subsection 248(1) or paragraph (e) of the definition "taxable RFI share" in that subsection applies to deem the share to be a taxable preferred share or a taxable RFI share, the shareholder shall be deemed not to have a substantial interest in the corporation at that time.

Related Provisions: 248(25) — Beneficially interested.

Notes: The reference in 191(3)(a) to avoiding Part I tax by creating a "substantial interest" may refer to avoiding 258(5) and thus 12(1)(c).

For a CRA interpretation that 191(3) does not apply see doc 2013-0511101E5 [Chalmers, "Quebec Corporate Law: Voting Shares", 22(7) *Canadian Tax Highlights* (ctf.ca) 1-2 (July 2014)].

191(3) last amended by 1992 technical bill.

(4) Deemed dividends — Where at any particular time

(a) a share of the capital stock of a corporation is issued,

(b) the terms or conditions of a share of the capital stock of a corporation are changed, or

(c) an agreement in respect of a share of the capital stock of a corporation is changed or entered into, and the terms or conditions of the share or the agreement in respect of the share specify an amount in respect of the share, including an amount for which the share is to be redeemed, acquired or cancelled (together with, where so provided, any accrued and unpaid dividends thereon) and where paragraph (a) applies, the specified amount does not exceed the fair market value of the consideration for which the share was issued, and where paragraph (b) or (c) applies, the specified amount does not exceed the fair market value of the share immediately before the particular time, the amount of any dividend deemed to have been paid on a redemption, acquisition or cancellation of the share to which subsection 84(2) or (3) applies shall

(d) for the purposes of this Part and section 187.2, be deemed to be an excluded dividend and an excepted dividend, respectively, unless

(i) where paragraph (a) applies, the share was issued for consideration that included a taxable preferred share, or

(ii) where paragraph (b) or (c) applies, the share was, immediately before the particular time, a taxable preferred share, and

(e) be deemed not to be a dividend to which subsection 112(2.1) or 138(6) applies to deny a deduction with respect to the dividend in computing the taxable income of a corporation under subsection 112(1) or (2) or 138(6), unless

(i) where paragraph (a) applies, the share was issued for consideration that included a term preferred share or for the purpose of raising capital or as part of a series of transactions or events the purpose of which was to raise capital, and

(ii) where paragraph (b) or (c) applies, the share was, immediately before the particular time, a term preferred share, or the terms or conditions of the share were changed, or the agreement in respect of the share was changed or entered into for the purpose of raising capital or as part of a series of transactions or events the purpose of which was to raise capital.

Related Provisions: 87(2)(rr) — Amalgamation — continuing corporation; 87(4.2)(f) — Amalgamations — where amount specified for purposes of 191(4); 248(10) — Series of transactions.

Notes: See VIEWS docs 2007-0243101C6 (re 191(4)(d)); 2016-0634551E5 (effect of price adjustment clause on specified amount [Cepparo, "TPS Price Reduction May Eliminate Excluded Dividend", 24(11) *Canadian Tax Highlights* (ctf.ca) 7-8 (Nov. 2016)]).

(5) Where subsec. (4) does not apply — Subsection (4) does not apply to the extent that the total of

(a) the amount paid on the redemption, acquisition or cancellation of the share, and

(b) all amounts each of which is an amount (other than an amount deemed by subsection 84(4) to be a dividend) paid, after the particular time and before the redemption, acquisition or cancellation of the share, on a reduction of the paid-up capital of the corporation in respect of the share

exceeds the specified amount referred to in subsection (4).

(6) Excluded dividend — partner — If at any time a corporation pays a dividend to a partnership, the corporation is, for the purposes of this subsection and paragraph (a) of the definition "excluded dividend" in subsection (1), deemed to have paid at that time to each member of the partnership a dividend equal to the amount determined by the formula

$$A \times B$$

where

A is the amount of the dividend paid to the partnership; and

B is the member's specified proportion for the last fiscal period of the partnership that ended before that time (or, if the partnership's first fiscal period includes that time, for that first fiscal period).

Related Provisions: 248(1) — Definition of "specified proportion".

Notes: 191(6) added by 2002-2013 technical bill, for dividends paid after Dec. 20, 2002.

Definitions [s. 191]: "amount" — 248(1); "aunt" — 252(2)(e); "beneficially interested" — 248(25); "capital gain" — 39(1)(a), 248(1); "child" — 252(1); "class of shares" — 248(6); "control" — 256(6), (6.1); "corporation" — 248(1), *Interpretation Act* 35(1); "dividend" — 248(1); "excluded dividend" — 191(1); "fair market value" — see 69(1) Notes; "financial intermediary corporation" — 191(1); "fiscal period" — 249.1; "grandfathered share" — 248(1); "investment corporation" — 130(3)(a), 248(1); "mortgage investment corporation" — 130.1(6), 248(1); "mutual fund corporation" — 131(8), 248(1); "nephew", "niece" — 252(2)(g); "paid-up capital" — 89(1), 248(1); "partnership" — see 96(1) Notes; "person", "prescribed" — 248(1); "prescribed labour-sponsored venture capital corporation" — Reg. 6701; "prescribed venture capital corporation" — Reg. 6700; "private corporation" — 89(1), 248(1); "private holding corporation" — 191(1); "registered charity" — 248(1); "related" — 251(2); "series of transactions or events" — 248(10); "share", "shareholder", "specified financial institution" — 248(1); "specified person" — 248(1)"taxable preferred share"(h); "specified proportion" — 248(1); "substantial interest" — 191(2), (3); "taxable Canadian corporation" — 89(1), 248(1); "taxable income" — 2(2), 248(1); "taxable preferred share", "taxable RFI share", "term preferred share" — 248(1); "trust" — 104(1), 248(1), (3); "uncle" — 252(2)(e).

191.1 (1) Tax on taxable dividends — Every taxable Canadian corporation shall pay a tax under this Part for each taxation year equal to the amount, if any, by which

(a) the total of

(i) the amount determined by multiplying the amount by which the total of all taxable dividends (other than excluded dividends) paid by the corporation in the year and after 1987 on short-term preferred shares exceeds the corporation's dividend allowance for the year, by

(A) 50% for dividends paid in a taxation year that ends before 2010,

(B) 45% for dividends paid in a taxation year that ends after 2009 and before 2012,

(C) 40% for dividends paid in a taxation year that ends after 2011,

(ii) 40% of the amount, if any, by which the total of all taxable dividends (other than excluded dividends) paid by the corporation in the year and after 1987 on taxable preferred shares (other than short-term preferred shares) of all classes in respect of which an election under subsection 191.2(1) has been made exceeds the amount, if any, by which the corporation's dividend allowance for the year exceeds the total of the dividends referred to in subparagraph (i),

(iii) 25% of the amount, if any, by which the total of all taxable dividends (other than excluded dividends) paid by the corporation in the year and after 1987 on taxable preferred shares (other than short-term preferred shares) of all classes in respect of which an election under subsection 191.2(1) has not been made exceeds the amount, if any, by which the corporation's dividend allowance for the year exceeds the total of the dividends referred to in subparagraphs (i) and (ii), and

(iv) the total of all amounts each of which is an amount determined for the year in respect of the corporation under paragraph 191.3(1)(d)

exceeds

(b) the total of all amounts each of which is an amount determined for the year in respect of the corporation under paragraph 191.3(1)(c).

Related Provisions: 18(1)(t) — Tax is non-deductible; 87(4.2) — Exchanged shares; 110(1)(k) — Deduction of 3.5 × Part VI.1 tax (less before 2012) from taxable income; 157(1)–(3) — Payment of Part VI.1 tax; 161(4.1) — Interest — corporations; 191.3(6) — Payment by transferor corporation; 227(14) — No tax on corporation exempt under s. 149.

Notes: Part VI.1 (ss. 191 to 191.4) provides for a special tax on dividends, other than excluded dividends, paid by corporations on taxable preferred shares. Its purpose is to make the tax system more neutral as between debt and preferred share financing. Part VI.1 tax can be offset against tax payable under Part I by 110(1)(k) deduction so that the overall tax liability for corps with Part I tax payable is largely unaffected. A $500,000 annual dividend allowance (191.1(2)(a)) exempts dividends on preferred shares paid by most small corporations.

For CRA interpretation see VIEWS docs 2007-0236821R3 (191.1(1) did not apply to a dividend paid in the course of a spinoff); 2007-0250831E5 (where 55(2) applies, Part VI.1 tax may still apply); 2007-0241561R3 and 2008-0283681R3 (no Part VI.1 tax because a stock dividend is deemed by 137(4.1) to be interest); 2010-0354391I7 (no Part VI.1 tax because share is not short-term preferred share).

See also Austin del Rio, "Part VI.1 Tax on Dividend Paid Through Family Trust", 19(3) *Tax for the Owner-Manager* (ctf.ca) 9-10 (July 2019).

191.1(1)(a)(i) amended by 2002-2013 technical bill, for 2003 and later tax years.

Interpretation Bulletins: IT-88R2: Stock dividends.

Advance Tax Rulings: ATR-46: Financial difficulty.

Forms: T2 Sched. 43: Calculation of Parts IV.1 and VI.1 taxes.

(2) Dividend allowance — For the purposes of this section, a taxable Canadian corporation's "dividend allowance" for a taxation year is the amount, if any, by which

(a) $500,000

exceeds

(b) the amount, if any, by which the total of taxable dividends (other than excluded dividends) paid by it on taxable preferred shares, or shares that would be taxable preferred shares if they were issued after June 18, 1987 and were not grandfathered shares, in the calendar year immediately preceding the calendar year in which the taxation year ended exceeds $1,000,000,

unless the corporation is associated in the taxation year with one or more other taxable Canadian corporations, in which case, except as otherwise provided in this section, its dividend allowance for the year is nil.

Related Provisions: 87(2)(rr) — Amalgamation — continuing corporation.

Interpretation Bulletins: IT-88R2: Stock dividends.

(3) Associated corporations — If all of the taxable Canadian corporations that are associated with each other in a taxation year and that have paid taxable dividends (other than excluded dividends) on taxable preferred shares in the year have filed with the Minister in prescribed form an agreement whereby, for the purposes of this section, they allocate an amount to one or more of them for the taxation year, and the amount so allocated or the total of the amounts so allocated, as the case may be, is equal to the total dividend allowance for the year of those corporations and all other taxable Canadian corporations with which each such corporation is associated in the year, the dividend allowance for the year for each of the corporations is the amount so allocated to it.

Forms: T2 Sched. 43: Calculation of Parts IV.1 and VI.1 taxes.

(4) Total dividend allowance — For the purposes of this section, the "total dividend allowance" of a group of taxable Canadian corporations that are associated with each other in a taxation year is the amount, if any, by which

(a) $500,000

exceeds

(b) the amount, if any, by which the total of taxable dividends (other than excluded dividends) paid by those corporations on taxable preferred shares, or shares that would be taxable preferred shares if they were issued after June 18, 1987 and were not grandfathered shares, in the calendar year immediately preceding the calendar year in which the taxation year ended exceeds $1,000,000.

Related Provisions: 87(2)(rr) — Amalgamation — continuing corporation.

Interpretation Bulletins: IT-88R2: Stock dividends.

(5) Failure to file agreement — If any of the taxable Canadian corporations that are associated with each other in a taxation year and that have paid taxable dividends (other than excluded dividends) on taxable preferred shares in the year has failed to file with the Minister an agreement as contemplated by subsection (3) within 30 days after notice in writing by the Minister has been forwarded to any of them that such an agreement is required for the purpose of any assessment of tax under this Part, the Minister shall, for the purpose of this section, allocate an amount to one or more of them for the taxation year, which amount or the total of which amounts,

as the case may be, shall equal the total dividend allowance for the year for those corporations and all other taxable Canadian corporations with which each such corporation is associated in the year, and the dividend allowance for the year of each of the corporations is the amount so allocated to it.

Related Provisions: *Interpretation Act* 27(5) — Meaning of "within 30 days".

(6) Dividend allowance in short years — Notwithstanding any other provision of this section,

(a) where a corporation has a taxation year that is less than 51 weeks, its dividend allowance for the year is that proportion of its dividend allowance for the year determined without reference to this paragraph that the number of days in the year is of 365; and

(b) where a taxable Canadian corporation (in this paragraph referred to as the "first corporation") has more than one taxation year ending in a calendar year and is associated in two or more of those taxation years with another taxable Canadian corporation that has a taxation year ending in that calendar year, the dividend allowance of the first corporation for each taxation year in which it is associated with the other corporation ending in that calendar year is, subject to the application of paragraph (a), an amount equal to the amount that would be its dividend allowance for the first such taxation year if the allowance were determined without reference to paragraph (a).

Definitions [s. 191.1]: "amount" — 248(1); "associated" — 256; "calendar year" — *Interpretation Act* 37(1)(a); "corporation" — 248(1), *Interpretation Act* 35(1); "dividend" — 248(1); "dividend allowance" — 191.1(2); "excluded dividend" — 191(1); "grandfathered share", "Minister", "prescribed", "share", "short-term preferred share" — 248(1); "taxable Canadian corporation", "taxable dividend" — 89(1), 248(1); "taxable preferred share" — 248(1); "taxation year" — 249; "total dividend allowance" — 191.1(4); "writing" — *Interpretation Act* 35(1).

191.2 (1) Election — For the purposes of determining the tax payable by reason of subparagraphs 191.1(1)(a)(ii) and (iii), a taxable Canadian corporation (other than a financial intermediary corporation or a private holding corporation) may make an election with respect to a class of its taxable preferred shares the terms and conditions of which require an election to be made under this subsection by filing a prescribed form with the Minister

(a) not later than the day on or before which its return of income under Part I is required by section 150 to be filed for the taxation year in which shares of that class are first issued or first become taxable preferred shares; or

(b) within the 6 month period commencing on any of the following days, namely,

(i) the day of sending of any notice of assessment of tax payable under this Part or Part I by the corporation for that year,

(ii) where the corporation has served a notice of objection to an assessment described in subparagraph (i), the day of sending of a notice that the Minister has confirmed or varied the assessment,

(iii) where the corporation has instituted an appeal in respect of an assessment described in subparagraph (i) to the Tax Court of Canada, the day of mailing of a copy of the decision of the Court to the taxpayer, and

(iv) where the corporation has instituted an appeal in respect of an assessment described in subparagraph (i) to the Federal Court of Appeal or the Supreme Court of Canada, the day on which the judgment of the Court is pronounced or delivered or the day on which the corporation discontinues the appeal.

Related Provisions: 87(4.2)(e) — Amalgamation; 187.2 — Tax on dividends on taxable preferred shares; 244(14), (14.1) — Date when notice sent; *Interpretation Act* 27(5) — Meaning of "within the 6 month period".

Notes: 191.2(1)(b)(i) and (ii) amended by 2010 budget bill #2, effective Dec. 15, 2010, to change "mailing" to "sending" (see 244(14.1) re electronic notices).

191.2(1)(b)(iv) amended by 2002 courts administration bill to change "Federal Court of Canada" to "Federal Court of Appeal", effective July 2, 2003.

Forms: T769: Election under section 191.2 by an issuer of taxable preferred shares to pay Part VI.1 tax at a rate of 40%.

(2) Time of election — An election with respect to a class of taxable preferred shares filed in accordance with subsection (1) shall be deemed to have been filed before any dividend on a share of that class is paid.

(3) Assessment — Where an election has been filed under subsection (1), the Minister shall, notwithstanding subsections 152(4) and (5), assess or reassess the tax, interest or penalties payable under this Act by any corporation for any relevant taxation year in order to take into account the election.

Definitions [s. 191.2]: "assessment" — 248(1); "class" — 248(6); "corporation" — 248(1), *Interpretation Act* 35(1); "day of sending" — 244(14), (14.1); "dividend" — 248(1); "Federal Court of Appeal" — *Federal Courts Act* s. 3; "financial intermediary corporation" — 191(1); "Minister", "prescribed" — 248(1); "private holding corporation" — 191(1); "share" — 248(1); "tax payable" — 248(2); "taxable Canadian corporation" — 89(1), 248(1); "taxable preferred share" — 248(1); "taxation year" — 249; "taxpayer" — 248(1).

Interpretation Bulletins [s. 191.2]: IT-88R2: Stock dividends.

191.3 (1) Agreement respecting liability for tax — Where a corporation (in this section referred to as the **"transferor corporation"**) and a taxable Canadian corporation (in this section referred to as the **"transferee corporation"**) that was related (otherwise than because of a right referred to in paragraph 251(5)(b) or because of the control of any corporation by Her Majesty in right of Canada or a province) to the transferor corporation

(a) throughout a particular taxation year of the transferor corporation (or, where the transferee corporation came into existence in that year, throughout the part of that year in which the transferee corporation was in existence), and

(b) throughout the last taxation year of the transferee corporation ending at or before the end of the particular taxation year (or, where the transferor corporation came into existence in that last taxation year of the transferee corporation, throughout that part of that last year in which the transferor corporation was in existence)

file as provided in subsection (2) an agreement or amended agreement with the Minister under which the transferee corporation agrees to pay all or any portion, as is specified in the agreement, of the tax for that taxation year of the transferor corporation that would, but for the agreement, be payable under this Part by the transferor corporation (other than any tax payable by the transferor corporation by reason of another agreement made under this section), the following rules apply, namely,

(c) the amount of tax specified in the agreement is an amount determined for that taxation year of the transferor corporation in respect of the transferor corporation for the purpose of paragraph 191.1(1)(b),

(d) the amount of tax specified in the agreement is an amount determined in respect of the transferee corporation for its last taxation year ending at or before the end of that taxation year of the transferor corporation for the purpose of subparagraph 191.1(1)(a)(iv), and

(e) the transferor corporation and the transferee corporation are jointly and severally, or solidarily, liable to pay the amount of tax specified in the agreement and any interest or penalty in respect thereof.

Related Provisions: 87(2)(ss) — Amalgamation — continuing corporation; 110(1)(k) — Part VI.1 tax; 191.3(1.1) — Consideration for entering into agreement deemed to be nil; 191.3(6) — Payment by transferor corporation; 256(6), (6.1) — Meaning of "control".

Notes: 191.3(1)(e) amended by 2002-2013 technical bill (Part 4 — bijuralism), effective June 26, 2013, to add "or solidarily".

191.3(1) earlier amended by 1995-97 technical bill (last change effective for taxation years of the transferor ending after April 26, 1995).

Forms: T2 Sched. 45: Agreement respecting liability for Part VI.1 tax.

(1.1) Consideration for agreement — For the purposes of Part I of this Act, where property is acquired at any time by a transferee corporation as consideration for entering into an agreement with a transferor corporation that is filed under this section,

(a) where the property was owned by the transferor corporation immediately before that time,

(i) the transferor corporation shall be deemed to have disposed of the property at that time for proceeds equal to the fair market value of the property at that time, and

(ii) the transferor corporation shall not be entitled to deduct any amount in computing its income as a consequence of the transfer of the property, except any amount arising as a consequence of subparagraph (i);

(b) the cost at which the property was acquired by the transferee corporation at that time shall be deemed to be equal to the fair market value of the property at that time;

(c) the transferee corporation shall not be required to add an amount in computing its income solely because of the acquisition at that time of the property; and

(d) no benefit shall be deemed to have been conferred on the transferor corporation as a consequence of the transferor corporation entering into an agreement filed under this section.

Notes: 191.3(1.1) added by 1994 technical bill. It is similar to 80.04(5).

(2) Manner of filing agreement — An agreement or amended agreement referred to in subsection (1) between a transferor corporation and a transferee corporation shall be deemed not to have been filed with the Minister unless

(a) it is in prescribed form;

(b) it is filed on or before the day on or before which the transferor corporation's return for the year in respect of which the agreement is filed is required to be filed under this Part or within the 90-day period beginning on the day of sending of a notice of assessment of tax payable under this Part or Part I by the transferor corporation for the year or by the transferee corporation for its taxation year ending in the calendar year in which the taxation year of the transferor corporation ends or the sending of a notification that no tax is payable under this Part or Part I for that taxation year;

(c) it is accompanied by,

(i) where the directors of the transferor corporation are legally entitled to administer its affairs, a certified copy of their resolution authorizing the agreement to be made,

(ii) where the directors of the transferor corporation are not legally entitled to administer its affairs, a certified copy of the document by which the person legally entitled to administer the corporation's affairs authorized the agreement to be made,

(iii) where the directors of the transferee corporation are legally entitled to administer its affairs, a certified copy of their resolution authorizing the agreement to be made, and

(iv) where the directors of the transferee corporation are not legally entitled to administer its affairs, a certified copy of the document by which the person legally entitled to administer the corporation's affairs authorized the agreement to be made; and

(d) where the agreement is not an agreement to which subsection (4) applies, an agreement amending the agreement has not been filed in accordance with this section.

(e) [Repealed]

Related Provisions: 244(14), (14.1) — Date when notice sent.

Notes: 191.3(2)(b) amended by 2010 budget bill #2, effective Dec. 15, 2010, to change "mailing" to "sending" (to accommodate electronic notices under 244(14.1)).

191.3(2)(e), repealed by 1991 technical bill effective 1989, required that the transferor corporation have no Part I tax liability for the year.

(3) Assessment — Where an agreement or amended agreement between a transferor corporation and a transferee corporation has been filed under this section with the Minister, the Minister shall, notwithstanding subsections 152(4) and (5), assess or reassess the tax, interest and penalties payable under this Act by the transferor corporation and the transferee corporation for any relevant taxation year in order to take into account the agreement or amended agreement.

Notes: Although the transferor may be liable under 191.3(3), only the transferee includes the Part VI.1 tax in its base for determining instalments under s. 157: VIEWS docs 2011-0406831I7, 2012-045535117.

(4) Related corporations — Where, at any time, a corporation has become related to another corporation and it may reasonably be considered, having regard to all the circumstances, that the main purpose of the corporation becoming related to the other corporation was to transfer, by filing an agreement or an amended agreement under this section, the benefit of a deduction under paragraph 110(1)(k) to a transferee corporation, the amount of the tax specified in the agreement shall, for the purposes of paragraph (1)(c), be deemed to be nil.

(5) Assessment of transferor corporation — The Minister may at any time assess a transferor corporation in respect of any amount for which it is jointly and severally, or solidarily, liable by reason of paragraph (1)(e) and the provisions of Division I of Part I are applicable in respect of the assessment as though it had been made under section 152.

Notes: 191.3(5) amended by 2002-2013 technical bill (Part 4 — bijuralism), effective June 26, 2013, to add "or solidarily".

(6) Payment by transferor corporation — If a transferor corporation and a transferee corporation are by reason of paragraph (1)(e) jointly and severally, or solidarily, liable in respect of tax payable by the transferee corporation under subparagraph 191.1(1)(a)(iv) and any interest or penalty in respect thereof, the following rules apply:

(a) a payment by the transferor corporation on account of the liability shall, to the extent thereof, discharge their liability; and

(b) a payment by the transferee corporation on account of its liability discharges the transferor corporation's liability only to the extent that the payment operates to reduce the transferee corporation's liability under this Act to an amount less than the amount in respect of which the transferor corporation was, by paragraph (1)(e), made jointly and severally, or solidarily, liable.

Notes: See Notes to 160(3) re meaning of "their liability" in 191.3(6)(a).

191.3(6) amended by 2002-2013 technical bill (Part 4 — bijuralism), effective June 26, 2013, to add "or solidarily" (opening words and para. (b)) and to change "the joint liability" to "their liability" (para. (a)).

Definitions [s. 191.3]: "amount", "assessment" — 248(1); "calendar year" — *Interpretation Act* 37(1)(a); "control" — 256(6)–(9); "corporation" — 248(1), *Interpretation Act* 35(1); "day of sending" — 244(14), (14.1); "fair market value" — see 69(1) Notes; "Her Majesty" — *Interpretation Act* 35(1); "Minister", "prescribed" — 248(1); "province" — *Interpretation Act* 35(1); "related" — 251(2); "tax payable" — 248(2); "taxable Canadian corporation" — 89(1), 248(1); "taxation year" — 249; "transferee corporation", "transferor corporation" — 191.3(1).

Interpretation Bulletins [s. 191.3]: IT-88R2: Stock dividends.

191.4 (1) Information return — Every corporation that is or would, but for section 191.3, be liable to pay tax under this Part for a taxation year shall, not later than the day on or before which it is required by section 150 to file its return of income for the year under Part I, file with the Minister a return for the year under this Part in prescribed form containing an estimate of the tax payable by it under this Part for the year.

Related Provisions: 150.1(5) — Electronic filing; 157(1) — Payment of Part VI.1 tax; 157(2.1) — Special cases; 161(4.1) — Limitation respecting corporations.

Forms: T2 Sched. 43: Calculation of Parts IV.1 and VI.1 taxes.

(2) Provisions applicable to Part — Sections 152, 158 and 159, subsection 161(11), sections 162 to 167 and Division J of Part I apply to this Part with such modifications as the circumstances require.

Notes: 191.4(2) amended by 1992 technical bill, effective for 1992 and later taxation years, to delete reference to 161(1) and (2). The change results from the integration of the interest provisions for Parts I, I.3, VI and VI.1 in section 161. See Notes to 157(1).

(3) Provisions applicable — Crown corporations — Section 27 applies to this Part with any modifications that the circumstances require.

Notes: 191.4(3) added by 1995-97 technical bill, retroactive to 1988. It confirms that a prescribed federal Crown corporation is liable to tax under Part VI.1.

Definitions [s. 191.4]: "corporation" — 248(1), *Interpretation Act* 35(1); "Minister", "prescribed" — 248(1); "tax payable" — 248(2); "taxation year" — 249.

PART VII — REFUNDABLE TAX ON CORPORATIONS ISSUING QUALIFYING SHARES

192, 193 [Tax on pre-1987 share-purchase tax credit — No longer relevant.]

Notes: Part VII (192, 193) effectively expired at the end of 1986. It allowed a corporation to designate an amount for purpose of the shareholders' share-purchase tax credit under 127.2. The corporation then became liable for a refundable tax. See Notes to 127.2, and 227.1(1) regarding liability of corporate directors for unpaid Part VII tax.

For 192(4.1), still relevant for computing PUC of an SPTC share, see these Notes up to the 42nd ed.; for 192(6), see Notes to 149.1(1)"non-qualified investment".

An earlier Part VII was repealed in 1977. It imposed a tax on the recipient of a dividend paid out of "designated surplus".

PART VIII — REFUNDABLE TAX ON CORPORATIONS IN RESPECT OF SCIENTIFIC RESEARCH AND EXPERIMENTAL DEVELOPMENT TAX CREDIT

194, 195 [Tax on pre-1986 scientific research tax credit — No longer relevant.]

Notes: Part VIII (194, 195) effectively expired at the end of 1985, with the repeal of the scientific research tax credit (SRTC) due to widespread abuse: see for example *Cancor Software (Corr)*, [1994] 1 C.T.C. 237 (Ont CA) (prison term of 2 years less a day + $750,000 fine); *Wilder*, 2006 BCCA 1 (leave to appeal denied 2007 CarswellBC 366 (SCC)); W sentenced to 9 years in prison and restitution of $5 million: *Wilder*, 2008 BCCA 370 (leave to appeal denied 2009 CarswellBC 572). See 127.3 Notes.

194(4.1) is still relevant for computing PUC of an SRTC share. It is reproduced in these Notes up to the 42nd ed.

An earlier Part VIII was repealed in 1977. It imposed a tax on a corporation paying a dividend out of "designated surplus".

PART IX — TAX ON DEDUCTION UNDER SECTION 66.5

196. [No longer relevant]

Notes [Part IX]: Part IX (s. 196) relates to payments under the *Petroleum and Gas Revenue Tax Act* and thus has not applied since 1986: Carr & Calverley, *Canadian Resource Taxation* (Carswell, looseleaf or *Taxnet Pro* Reference Centre), chap. 12.

Previous Part IX (196-197), repealed in 1977, taxed a corporation's "1971 undistributed income on hand" in certain cases.

PART IX.1 — TAX ON SIFT PARTNERSHIPS

197. (1) Definitions — The following definitions apply in this Part and in section 96.

"non-portfolio earnings", of a SIFT partnership for a taxation year, means the total of

(a) the amount, if any, by which

(i) the total of all amounts each of which is the SIFT partnership's income for the taxation year from a business carried on by it in Canada or from a non-portfolio property, other than income that is a taxable dividend received by the SIFT partnership,

exceeds

 (ii) the total of all amounts each of which is the SIFT partnership's loss for the taxation year from a business carried on by it in Canada or from a non-portfolio property, and

(b) the amount, if any, by which all taxable capital gains of the SIFT partnership from dispositions of non-portfolio properties during the taxation year exceeds the total of the allowable capital losses of the SIFT partnership for the taxation year from dispositions of non-portfolio properties during the taxation year.

Related Provisions: 122.1(1)"non-portfolio earnings" — Parallel definition for SIFT trusts.

Notes: See Notes at end of s. 197. For CRA interpretation see doc 2010-0377081E5.

"SIFT partnership", being a specified investment flow-through partnership, for any taxation year, means a partnership other than an excluded subsidiary entity (as defined in subsection 122.1(1)) for the taxation year that meets the following conditions at any time during the taxation year:

 (a) the partnership is a Canadian resident partnership;

 (b) investments (as defined in subsection 122.1(1)) in the partnership are listed or traded on a stock exchange or other public market; and

 (c) the partnership holds one or more non-portfolio properties.

Related Provisions: 85.1(8) — Rollover of partnership units to corporation; 122.1(1)"SIFT trust" — Parallel definition for trust; 197(6), 157(1) — SIFT partnership pays same instalments as a corporation; 197(8) — Application of definition for 2006–2010; 248(1)"SIFT partnership" — Definition applies to entire Act.

Notes: See Notes to 104(16) and 122.1(1)"SIFT trust"; Rumball, "The Specified Investment Flow-Through Partnership Rules", XI(3) *Business Vehicles* (Federated Press) 586-91 (2007); Miller, "Private Partnerships and the SIFT Rules", XII(4) *BV* 659-61 (2009).

See CRA letter to CBA/CICA Joint Committee, May 3, 2010 (VIEWS doc 2009-0309281E5), discussing cases where a partnership with no publicly listed units might be a SIFT due to the broad definitions of "investment" and "security" in 122.1(1); Russell, "SIFT Rules", 18(10) *Canadian Tax Highlights* (ctf.ca) 4-5 (Oct. 2010); Marchand, "The Canada Revenue Agency Issues Guidance on the Application of the SIFT Rules to Private Partnerships", XII(2) *Corporate Structures & Groups* (Federated Press) 660-65 (2010); Sherman, "Application of the SIFT Rules to Private Partnerships", XVI(4) *Corporate Finance* (Federated Press) 1892-95 (2010).

See also VIEWS docs 2007-0261591E5 (subsidiary entity of an income trust); 2010-0385581E5 and 2010-0386841E5 (application of "security test" and "replicate test").

197(1)"SIFT partnership" opening words amended by 2008 budget bill #2 to add exception for an excluded subsidiary entity, effective Oct. 31, 2006 (i.e., retroactive to introduction of the definition). See Finance news release 2007-106 (Dec. 20/07).

"taxable non-portfolio earnings" of a SIFT partnership, for a taxation year, means the lesser of

 (a) the amount that would, if the SIFT partnership were a taxpayer for the purposes of Part I and if subsection 96(1) were read without reference to its paragraph (d), be its income for the taxation year as determined under section 3; and

 (b) its non-portfolio earnings for the taxation year.

(2) Tax on partnership income — Every partnership that is a SIFT partnership for a taxation year is liable to a tax under this Part equal to the amount determined by the formula

$$A \times (B + C)$$

where

A is the taxable non-portfolio earnings of the SIFT partnership for the taxation year;

B is the net corporate income tax rate in respect of the SIFT partnership for the taxation year; and

C is the provincial SIFT tax rate of the SIFT partnership for the taxation year.

Related Provisions: 96(1.11)(b) — Taxable non-portfolio earnings reduced by Part IX.1 tax paid by SIFT partnership; 104(16), 122(1)(b) — Parallel taxation of SIFT trust distributions; 197(4) — Partnership to file return; 197(6) — Application of Part I rules to Part IX.1 tax (and see 157(1) for instalments).

Notes: The "net corporate income tax rate" (248(1)) is 21% for 2007, 19.5% for 2008, 19% for 2009, 18% for 2010, 16.5% for 2011 and 15% since 2012: see 123.4(1)"gen-

eral rate reduction percentage" and 123.4(2). The "provincial SIFT tax rate" is defined in 248(1). There is no additional provincial tax: see 120(3)(d).

For interpretation see VIEWS doc 2007-0245281R3 (income trust windup). See also Notes to 96(1.11) and 104(16).

It has been suggested that the words "is liable to a tax" do not actually impose tax: Bloom & Wiener, "Has Parliament Failed to Charge the Tax on SIFT Partnerships?", 59(1) *Canadian Tax Journal* 1-23 (2011); but *contra* see Campbell, 59(4) *CTJ* 709-29 (2011); and *recontra* see Bloom & Wiener's reply, 60(1) *CTJ* 93-100 (2012); and Nitikman, Correspondence, 60(2) *CTJ* 529-31 (2012).

197(2)C amended by 2008 budget bill #1, to change "provincial SIFT tax factor" to "provincial SIFT tax rate of the SIFT partnership", for 2009 and later tax years and any earlier year in which 248(1)"provincial SIFT tax rate" applies to the partnership.

(3) Ordering — This Part and section 122.1 are to be applied as if this Act were read without reference to subsection 96(1.11).

(4) Partnership to file return — Every member of a partnership that is liable to pay tax under this Part for a taxation year shall — on or before the day on or before which the partnership return is required to be filed for the year under section 229 of the *Income Tax Regulations* — file with the Minister a return for the taxation year under this Part in prescribed form containing an estimate of the tax payable by the partnership under this Part for the taxation year.

Related Provisions: 197(5) — Who has authority to file return; Reg. 229 — Information return for partnerships.

Forms: T5013-1: Part IX.1 income tax calculation — SIFT partnership.

(5) Authority to file return — For the purposes of subsection (4), if, in respect of a taxation year of a partnership, a particular member of the partnership has authority to act for the partnership,

 (a) if the particular member has filed a return as required by this Part for a taxation year, each other person who was a member of the partnership during the taxation year is deemed to have filed the return; and

 (b) a return that has been filed by any other member of the partnership for the taxation year is not valid and is deemed not to have been filed by any member of the partnership.

(6) Provisions applicable to Part — Subsection 150(2), section 152, subsections 157(1), (2.1) and (4), sections 158, 159 and 161 to 167 and Division J of Part I apply to this Part, with any modifications that the circumstances require, and for greater certainty,

 (a) a notice of assessment referred to in subsection 152(2) in respect of tax payable under this Part is valid notwithstanding that a partnership is not a person; and

 (b) notwithstanding subsection 152(4), the Minister may at any time make an assessment or reassessment of tax payable under this Part or Part I to give effect to a determination made by the Minister under subsection 152(1.4), including the assessment or reassessment of Part I tax payable in respect of the disposition of an interest in a SIFT partnership by a member of the partnership.

Notes: 197(6) opening words amended by 2013 budget bill #2, for tax years that begin after July 20, 2011, to delete reference to 156 and 156.1 and add 157(1), (2.1) and (4). This is because SIFTs now pay instalments like corporations: see 157(2) Notes. Before this amendment, a SIFT partnership was required by 156(1) to pay quarterly instalments of Part IX.1 tax: VIEWS doc 2011-0422731I7.

(7) Payment — Every SIFT partnership shall pay to the Receiver General, on or before its SIFT partnership balance-due day for each taxation year, its tax payable under this Part for the taxation year.

(8) Application of definition "SIFT partnership" — The definition "SIFT partnership" applies to a partnership for a taxation year of the partnership that ends after 2006, except that if the partnership would have been a SIFT partnership on October 31, 2006 had that definition been in force and applied to the partnership as of that date, that definition does not apply to the partnership for a taxation year of the partnership that ends before the earlier of

 (a) 2011, and

 (b) the first day after December 15, 2006 on which the partnership exceeds normal growth as determined by reference to the normal growth guidelines issued by the Department of Finance on December 15, 2006, as amended from time to time, unless that excess arose as a result of a prescribed transaction.

Related Provisions: 122.1(2) — Parallel rules for trusts.

Notes: See Notes here and to 122.1(2) up to PITA 48th ed. for the guidelines.

Notes [s. 197]: 197 added by 2007 budget bill #1, effective Oct. 31, 2006 (but for actual effective dates see 197(8) above). It implements the rules for SIFT partnerships. See Notes to 96(1.11) and 104(16).

Definitions [s. 197]: "allowable capital loss" — 38(b), 248(1); "amount", "assessment", "business" — 248(1); "Canada" — 255, *Interpretation Act* 35(1); "Canadian resident partnership", "disposition" — 248(1); "excluded subsidiary entity", "investment" — 122.1(1); "Minister", "net corporate income tax rate" — 248(1); "non-portfolio earnings" — 197(1); "non-portfolio property" — 122.1(1), 248(1); "partnership" — see 96(1) Notes; "person", "prescribed", "provincial SIFT tax rate" — 248(1); "public market" — 122.1(1), 248(1); "SIFT partnership" — 197(1), (8), 248(1); "SIFT partnership balance-due day" — 248(1); "specified investment flow-through partnership" — 197(1)"SIFT partnership"; "taxable capital gain" — 38(a), 248(1); "taxable dividend" — 89(1), 248(1); "taxable non-portfolio earnings" — 197(1); "taxation year" — 249; "taxpayer" — 248(1).

PART X — TAXES ON DEFERRED PROFIT SHARING PLANS AND REVOKED PLANS

198. (1) Tax on non-qualified investments and use of assets as security — Every trust governed by a deferred profit sharing plan or revoked plan that

(a) acquires a non-qualified investment, or

(b) uses or permits to be used any property of the trust as security for a loan,

shall pay a tax equal to the fair market value of

(c) the non-qualified investment at the time it was acquired by the trust, or

(d) the property used as security at the time it commenced to be so used.

Related Provisions: 147(14) — DPSP — revocation of registration; 198(4), (5) — Refund of tax on disposition of investment or release of security; 199–204 — Taxes on deferred profit sharing plans; 207.1(2) — Tax payable while non-qualifying investment held by DPSP; 259(1) — Proportional holdings in trust property.

(2) Payment of tax — A trustee of a trust liable to pay tax under subsection (1) shall remit the amount of the tax to the Receiver General within 10 days of the day on which the non-qualified investment is acquired or the property is used as security for a loan, as the case may be.

Related Provisions: *Interpretation Act* 27(5) — Meaning of "within 10 days".

(3) Trustee liable for tax — Where a trustee of a trust liable to pay tax under subsection (1) does not remit to the Receiver General the amount of the tax within the time specified in subsection (2), the trustee is personally liable to pay on behalf of the trust the full amount of the tax and is entitled to recover from the trust any amount paid by the trustee as tax under this section.

(4) Refund of tax on disposition of non-qualified investment — Where a trust disposes of a property that, when acquired, was a non-qualified investment, the trust is, on application in accordance with section 202, entitled to a refund of an amount equal to the lesser of

(a) the amount of the tax imposed under this section as a result of the acquisition of the property, and

(b) the proceeds of disposition of the property.

Related Provisions: 198(6) — Special rules re life insurance policies; 200 — Distribution deemed disposition; 202(4) — Application to certain provisions of Part I; 203 — Application to other taxes.

(5) Refund of tax on recovery of property given as security — Where a loan, for which a trust has used or permitted to be used trust property as security, ceases to be extant, the trust is, on application in accordance with section 202, entitled to a refund of an amount equal to the amount remaining, if any, when

(a) the net loss (exclusive of payments by the trust as or on account of interest) sustained by the trust in consequence of its

using or permitting to be used the property as security for the loan and not as a result of a change in the fair market value of the property

is deducted from

(b) the tax imposed under this section in consequence of the trust's using or permitting to be used the property as security for the loan.

Related Provisions: 202(4) — Application of certain provisions of Part I; 203 — Application to other taxes.

(6) Special rules relating to life insurance policies — For the purposes of this section,

(a) the acquisition of an interest in or the payment of an amount under a life insurance policy shall be deemed not to be the acquisition of a non-qualified investment, and

(b) the disposition of an interest in a life insurance policy shall be deemed not to be the disposition of a non-qualified investment,

except that where a trust governed by a deferred profit sharing plan or revoked plan makes a payment under or to acquire an interest in a life insurance policy, other than a life insurance policy under which

(c) the trust is, or by virtue of the payment about to become, the only person entitled to any rights or benefits under the policy (other than the rights or benefits of the insurer),

(d) the cash surrender value of the policy (exclusive of accumulated dividends) is or will be, at or before the end of the year in which the insured person attains 71 years of age, if all premiums under the policy are paid, not less than the maximum total amount (exclusive of accumulated dividends) payable by the insurer under the policy, and

(e) the total of the premiums payable in any year under the policy is not greater than the total of the amounts that, if the annual premiums had been payable in monthly instalments, would have been payable as such instalments in the 12 months commencing with the date the policy was issued,

the making of the payment shall be deemed to be the acquisition of a non-qualified investment at a cost equal to the amount of the payment.

Related Provisions: 139.1(13) — No application to conversion benefit on demutualization of insurer; 146(11) — RRSP — life insurance policies.

Notes: A life insurance policy is not a qualified investment, but under 146(11) and 198(6), if it meets certain conditions it is deemed not to be a non-qualified investment for an RRSP. The RRSP must be the only person entitled to any rights or benefits under the policy. It is a question of fact whether or not any particular segregated fund contract will be a qualified investment under 146(1)"qualified investment"(c.1)–(c.2) or a life insurance policy falling under 146(11): VIEWS doc 9823075. See also 2003-0035905.

198(6)(d) amended by 2007 budget bill #1, effective 2007, to change "69" to "71" (in conjunction with the increase in RRSP age limit in 146(2)(b.4)).

198(6)(d) amended by 1996 Budget to change "at a time before the 71st anniversary of the birth of the insured person" to "at or before the end of the year in which the insured person attains 69 years of age". The change is effective 1997, except that

(a) the amendment does not apply to a policy held by a trust where the trust acquired the policy before 1997;

(b) the amendment does not apply to a policy where the insured person turned 70 before 1997; and

(c) in applying it to a policy where the insured person turned 69 in 1996, read "70 years" in place of "69 years".

Similar grandfathering was provided for the RRSP rules in 146(13.2) and for DPSPs in 147(10.6). See also 146(2)(b.4) (RRSPs) and 147(2)(k) (DPSPs).

Interpretation Bulletins: IT-408R: Life insurance policies as investments of RRSPs and DPSPs (cancelled).

(6.1) Idem — A life insurance policy giving an option to the policyholder to receive annuity payments that otherwise complies with paragraph (6)(d) shall be deemed,

(a) where the option has not been exercised, to comply with that paragraph; and

(b) where at a particular time the option is exercised, to have been disposed of at that time for an amount equal to the cash surrender value of the policy immediately before that time, and an annuity contract shall be deemed to have been acquired at that time at a cost equal to that amount.

Interpretation Bulletins: IT-408R: Life insurance policies as investments of RRSPs and DPSPs (cancelled).

(7) Idem — Notwithstanding subsection (6), where the total of all payments made in a year by a trust governed by a deferred profit sharing plan or revoked plan under or to acquire interests in life insurance policies in respect of which the trust is the only person entitled to any rights or benefits (other than the rights or benefits of the insurer) does not exceed an amount equal to 25% of the total of all amounts paid by employers to the trust in the year under the plan for the benefit of beneficiaries thereunder, the making of the payments under or to acquire interests in such policies shall be deemed, for the purposes of this section, not to be the acquisition of non-qualified investments.

Interpretation Bulletins: IT-408R: Life insurance policies as investments of RRSPs and DPSPs (cancelled).

(8) Idem — Where a trust surrenders, cancels, assigns or otherwise disposes of its interest in a life insurance policy,

(a) the trust shall be deemed, for the purposes of subsection (4), to have disposed of each non-qualified investment that, by virtue of payments under the policy, it was deemed by subsection (6) to have acquired; and

(b) the proceeds of the disposition shall be deemed to be the amount, if any, by which

(i) the amount received by the trust in consequence of the surrender, cancellation, assignment or other disposition of its interest in the policy

exceeds the total of

(ii) each amount paid by the trust under or to acquire an interest in the policy, the payment of which is deemed by this section not to be the acquisition of a non-qualified investment, and

(iii) the cash surrender value on December 21, 1966 of the interest of the trust in the policy on that date.

Related Provisions: 146(11) — RRSP — life insurance policies; 202(5) — Interest; 204 — "Qualified investment".

Definitions [s. 198]: "amount", "annuity" — 248(1); "deferred profit sharing plan" — 147(1), 248(1); "disposition" — 198(6)(b), 200; "dividend", "employer" — 248(1); "fair market value" — see 69(1) Notes; "insurer" — 248(1); "life insurance policy" — 138(12), 248(1); "non-qualified investment" — 204; "person", "property" — 248(1); "revoked plan" — 204; "trust" — 104(1), 248(1), (3).

Information Circulars [s. 198]: 77-1R4: Deferred profit sharing plans.

199. (1) Tax on initial non-qualified investments not disposed of — Every trust governed by a deferred profit sharing plan or revoked plan shall pay a tax

(a) for 1967, equal to the amount, if any, by which 20% of the initial base of the trust exceeds the proceeds of disposition of its initial non-qualified investments disposed of after December 21, 1966 and before 1968;

(b) for 1968, equal to the amount, if any, by which 40% of the initial base of the trust exceeds the total of

(i) the proceeds of disposition of its initial non-qualified investments disposed of after December 21, 1966 and before 1969, and

(ii) the tax payable by the trust determined under paragraph (a);

(c) for 1969, equal to the amount, if any, by which 60% of the initial base of the trust exceeds the total of

(i) the proceeds of disposition of its initial non-qualified investments disposed of after December 21, 1966 and before 1970, and

(ii) the tax payable by the trust determined under paragraphs (a) and (b); and

(d) for 1970, equal to the amount, if any, by which 100% of the initial base of the trust exceeds the total of

(i) the proceeds of disposition of its initial non-qualified investments disposed of after December 21, 1966 and before 1971, and

(ii) the tax payable by the trust determined under paragraphs (a), (b) and (c).

Related Provisions: 201 — Tax on forfeitures.

(2) Refund — Where at the end of a year,

(a) the total of all taxes paid by a trust under subsection (1)

exceeds

(b) the total of

(i) all refunds made to the trust under this subsection, and

(ii) the amount, if any, by which the initial base of the trust exceeds the proceeds of disposition of its initial non-qualified investments disposed of after December 21, 1966 and before the end of the year,

the trust is, on application in accordance with section 202, entitled to a refund equal to the amount by which the total described in paragraph (a) exceeds the total described in paragraph (b).

Related Provisions: 201 — Tax on forfeitures; 202(2) — Returns and payment of estimated tax; 202(4) — Application of certain provisions of Part I; 203 — Application to other taxes.

Definitions [s. 199]: "amount" — 248(1); "deferred profit sharing plan" — 147(1), 248(1); "disposition" — 198(6)(b), 200; "initial base" — 204; "initial non-qualified investment" — 204; "revoked plan" — 204; "trust" — 104(1), 248(1), (3).

Information Circulars [s. 199]: 77-1R4: Deferred profit sharing plans.

200. Distribution deemed disposition — For the purposes of this Part, a distribution by a trust of a non-qualified investment to a beneficiary of the trust shall be deemed to be a disposition of that non-qualified investment and the proceeds of disposition of that non-qualified investment shall be deemed to be its fair market value at the time of the distribution.

Definitions [s. 200]: "fair market value" — see 69(1) Notes; "non-qualified investment" — 204; "trust" — 104(1), 248(1), (3).

201. Tax where inadequate consideration on purchase or sale — Every trust governed by a deferred profit sharing plan or a revoked plan shall, for each calendar year after 1990, pay a tax equal to 50% of the total of all amounts each of which is, by reason of subsection 147(18), an amount taxable under this section for the year.

Notes: 201 amended by 1990 pension bill, effective 1991.

Definitions [s. 201]: "amount" — 248(1); "calendar year" — *Interpretation Act* 37(1)(a); "deferred profit sharing plan" — 147(1), 248(1); "revoked plan" — 204; "trust" — 104(1), 248(1), (3).

Information Circulars: 77-1R4: Deferred profit sharing plans.

202. (1) Returns and payment of estimated tax — Within 90 days from the end of each year after 1965, a trustee of every trust governed by a deferred profit sharing plan or revoked plan shall

(a) file with the Minister a return for the year under this Part in prescribed form and containing prescribed information, without notice or demand therefor;

(b) estimate in the return the amount of tax payable by the trust under this Part for the year;

(c) estimate in the return the amount of any refund to which the trust is entitled under this Part for the year; and

(d) pay to the Receiver General the unpaid balance of the trust's tax for the year minus any refund to which it is entitled under this Part, or apply in the return for any amount owing to it.

Related Provisions: 150.1(5) — Electronic filing; *Interpretation Act* 27(5) — Meaning of "within 90 days".

Forms: T3D: Income tax return for DPSP or revoked DPSP.

(2) Consideration of application for refund — Where a trustee of a trust has made application for an amount owing to it pursuant to subsection (1), the Minister shall

(a) consider the application;

(b) determine the amount of any refund; and

(c) send to the trustee a notice of refund and any amount owing to the trust, or a notice that no refund is payable.

Related Provisions: 198(4) — Refund of tax on disposition of non-qualified investment; 198(5) — Refund of tax on recovery of property given as security.

(3) Provisions applicable to Part — Subsection 150(2), sections 152 and 158, subsections 161(1) and (11), sections 162 to 167 and Division J of Part I are applicable to this Part with such modifications as the circumstances require and, for the purposes of the application of those provisions to this Part, a notice of refund under this section shall be deemed to be a notice of assessment.

(4) Provisions applicable to refunds — Subsections 164(3) to (4) are applicable, with such modifications as the circumstances require, to refunds of tax under subsection 198(4) or (5) or 199(2).

Related Provisions: 198 — Tax on non-qualified investments and use of assets as security; 199 — Tax on initial non-qualified investments not disposed of.

(5) Interest — In addition to the interest payable under subsection 161(1), where a taxpayer is required by section 198 to pay a tax and has failed to pay all or any part thereof on or before the day on or before which the tax was required to be paid, the taxpayer shall pay to the Receiver General interest at the prescribed rate on the amount that the taxpayer failed to pay computed from the day on or before which the amount was required to be paid to the day of payment or to the beginning of the period in respect of which the taxpayer is required by subsection 161(1) to pay interest thereon, whichever is earlier.

Related Provisions: 202(6) — Deemed payment of tax; 221.1 — Application of interest where legislation retroactive; 248(11) — Interest compounded daily.

Regulations: 4301(a) (prescribed rate of interest).

I.T. Application Rules: 62(2) (subsec. 202(5) applies to interest payable in respect of any period after December 23, 1971).

(6) Deemed payment of tax — For the purposes of subsections 161(1) and 202(5), where a trust is liable to pay tax under this Part on the acquisition by it of a non-qualified investment or on the use of its property as security for a loan, it shall, except to the extent that the tax has previously been paid, be deemed to have paid tax on the date on which the property is disposed of or on which the loan ceases to be extant, as the case may be, in an amount equal to the refund referred to in subsection 198(4) in respect of that property or subsection 198(5) in respect of the loan, as the case may be.

Related Provisions: 161(1) — Interest; 198(4) — Refund of tax on disposition of non-qualified investment; 198(5) — Refund of tax on recovery of property given as security.

Definitions [s. 202]: "amount", "assessment" — 248(1); "deferred profit sharing plan" — 147(1), 248(1); "Minister" — 248(1); "non-qualifying investment" — 204; "prescribed" — 248(1); "prescribed rate" — Reg. 4301; "property" — 248(1); "revoked plan" — 204; "taxpayer" — 248(1); "trust" — 104(1), 248(1), (3).

203. Application to other taxes — Instead of making a refund to which a trust is entitled under subsection 198(4) or (5) or 199(2), the Minister may, where the trust is liable or about to become liable to make another payment under this Act, apply the amount of the refund or any part thereof to that other liability and notify a trustee of the trust of that action.

Related Provisions: 164(2) — Set-off of Part I refund; 222(1)"action" — Ten-year limitation period applies to s. 203; 224.1 — Recovery by set-off.

Definitions [s. 203]: "amount", "Minister" — 248(1); "trust" — 104(1), 248(1), (3).

204. Definitions — In this Part,

"debt obligation" means a bond, debenture, note or similar obligation;

Notes: "Debt obligation" added by 2007 budget bill #1, effective in determining whether a property is, at any time after March 18, 2007, a qualified investment. It is used in 204"qualified investment"(b)-(c.1).

"equity share" means

(a) a share, other than an excluded share or a non-participating share, the owner of which has, as owner thereof, a right

(i) to a dividend, and

(ii) to a part of the surplus of the corporation after repayment of capital and payment of dividend arrears on the redemption of the share, a reduction of the capital of the corporation or the winding-up of the corporation,

at least as great, in any event, as the right of the owner of any other share, other than a non-participating share, of the corporation, when the magnitude of the right in each case is expressed as a rate based on the paid-up capital value of the share to which the right relates, or

(b) a share, other than an excluded share or a non-participating share, the owner of which has, as owner thereof, a right

(i) to a dividend, after a dividend at a rate not in excess of 12% per annum of the paid-up capital value of each share has been paid to the owners of shares of a class other than the class to which that share belongs, and

(ii) to a part of the surplus of the corporation after repayment of capital and payment of dividend arrears on the redemption of the share, a reduction of the capital of the corporation or the winding-up of the corporation, after a payment of a part of the surplus at a rate not in excess of 10% of the paid-up capital value of each share has been made to the owners of shares of a class other than the class to which that share belongs,

at least as great, in any event, as the right of the owner of any other share, other than a non-participating share, of the corporation, when the magnitude of the right in each case is expressed as a rate based on the paid-up capital value of the share to which the right relates;

Notes: 204"equity share" was 204(a) before RSC 1985 (5th Supp) consolidation, effective for 1991 and later calendar years.

"excluded property", in relation to a trust governed by a deferred profit sharing plan or revoked plan, means a debt obligation or bankers' acceptance issued by

(a) an employer by whom payments are made in trust to a trustee under the plan for the benefit of beneficiaries under the plan, or

(b) a corporation with whom that employer does not deal at arm's length;

Notes: "Excluded property" added by 2007 budget bill #1, effective in determining whether a property is, at any time after March 18, 2007, a qualified investment. See opening words of 204"qualified investment".

"excluded share" means each share of the capital stock of a private corporation where

(a) the paid-up capital of the corporation that is represented by all its issued and outstanding shares that would, but for this definition, be equity shares is less than 50% of the paid-up capital of the corporation that is represented by all its issued and outstanding shares other than non-participating shares, or

(b) a non-participating share of the corporation is issued and outstanding and the owner of which has, as owner thereof, a right to a dividend

(i) at a fixed annual rate in excess of 12%, or

(ii) at an annual rate not in excess of a fixed maximum annual rate, if the fixed maximum annual rate is in excess of 12%,

when the right to the dividend is expressed as a rate based on the paid-up capital value of the share to which the right relates;

Notes: 204"excluded share" was 204(a.1) before RSC 1985 (5th Supp) consolidation, effective for 1991 and later calendar years.

"initial base" of a trust means the total of the values of all initial non-qualified investments held by the trust on December 21, 1966 when each such investment is valued at the lower of

(a) its cost to the trust, and

(b) its fair market value on December 21, 1966;

Notes: 204"initial base" was 204(b) before RSC 1985 (5th Supp) consolidation, effective for 1991 and later calendar years.

"initial non-qualified investment" of a trust means an investment held by the trust on December 21, 1966 that was, on that date, a non-qualified investment but does not include

(a) any interest in a life insurance policy, or

(b) an equity share that would be a qualified investment if the date of acquisition of the share were December 21, 1966;

Notes: 204"initial non-qualified investment" was 204(c) before RSC 1985 (5th Supp) consolidation, effective for 1991 and later calendar years.

"non-participating share" means

(a) in the case of a private corporation, a share the owner of which is not entitled to receive, as owner thereof, any dividend, other than a dividend, whether cumulative or not,

(i) at a fixed annual rate or amount, or

(ii) at an annual rate or amount not in excess of a fixed annual rate or amount, and

(b) in the case of a corporation other than a private corporation, any share other than a common share;

Notes: 204"non-participating share" was 204(a.2) before RSC 1985 (5th Supp) consolidation, effective for 1991 and later calendar years.

"non-qualified investment" means property that is not a qualified investment for a trust governed by a deferred profit sharing plan or revoked plan within the meaning of the definition "qualified investment" in this subsection;

Notes: See Notes to 204"qualified investment".

204"non-qualified investment" was 204(d) before RSC 1985 (5th Supp) consolidation, effective for 1991 and later calendar years.

Information Circulars: 77-1R4: Deferred profit sharing plans.

"paid-up capital value" of a share means the amount determined by the formula

$$A / B$$

where

A is the paid-up capital of the corporation that is represented by the shares of the class to which that share belongs, and

B is the number of shares of that class that are in fact issued and outstanding;

Notes: 204"paid-up capital value" was 204(a.3) before RSC 1985 (5th Supp) consolidation, effective for 1991 and later calendar years.

"qualified investment" for a trust governed by a deferred profit sharing plan or revoked plan means, with the exception of excluded property in relation to the trust,

(a) money (other than money the fair market value of which exceeds its stated value as legal tender in the country of issuance or money that is held for its numismatic value) and deposits (within the meaning assigned by the *Canada Deposit Insurance Corporation Act* or with a branch in Canada of a bank) of such money standing to the credit of the trust,

(b) debt obligations described in paragraph (a) of the definition "fully exempt interest" in subsection 212(3),

(c) debt obligations issued by

(i) a corporation, mutual fund trust or limited partnership the shares or units of which are listed on a designated stock exchange in Canada,

(ii) a corporation the shares of which are listed on a designated stock exchange outside Canada, or

(iii) an authorized foreign bank and payable at a branch in Canada of the bank,

(c.1) debt obligations that meet the following criteria, namely,

(i) any of

(A) the debt obligations had, at the time of acquisition by the trust, an investment grade rating with a prescribed credit rating agency,

(B) the debt obligations have an investment grade rating with a prescribed credit rating agency, or

(C) the debt obligations were acquired by the trust in exchange for debt obligations that satisfied the condition in clause (A) and as part of a proposal to, or an arrangement with, the creditors of the issuer of the debt obligations that has been approved by a court under the *Bankruptcy and Insolvency Act* or the *Companies' Creditors Arrangement Act*, and

(ii) either

(A) the debt obligations were issued as part of a single issue of debt of at least $25 million, or

(B) in the case of debt obligations that are issued on a continuous basis under a debt issuance program, the issuer of the debt obligations had issued and outstanding debt under the program of at least $25 million,

(d) securities (other than futures contracts or other derivative instruments in respect of which the holder's risk of loss may exceed the holder's cost) that are listed on a designated stock exchange,

(e) equity shares of a corporation by which, before the date of acquisition by the trust of the shares, payments have been made in trust to a trustee under the plan for the benefit of beneficiaries thereunder, if the shares are of a class in respect of which

(i) there is no restriction on their transferability, and

(ii) in each of 4 taxation years of the corporation in the period of the corporation's 5 consecutive taxation years that ended less than 12 months before the date of acquisition of the shares by the trust, and in the corporation's last taxation year in that period, the corporation

(A) paid a dividend on each share of the class of an amount not less than 4% of the cost per share of the shares to the trust, or

(B) had earnings attributable to the shares of the class of an amount not less than the amount obtained when 4% of the cost per share to the trust of the shares is multiplied by the total number of shares of the class that were outstanding immediately after the acquisition,

(f) guaranteed investment certificates issued by a trust company incorporated under the laws of Canada or of a province,

(g) investment contracts described in subparagraph (b)(ii) of the definition "retirement savings plan" in subsection 146(1) and issued by a corporation approved by the Governor in Council for the purposes of that subparagraph, and

(h) prescribed investments;

(i) [Repealed]

Related Provisions: 87(10) — New share issued on amalgamation of public corp deemed listed; 132.2(3)(h) — Where share ceases to be QI due to mutual fund reorg; 135.2(4)(f) — Unit of Cdn Wheat Board Farmers' Trust deemed not to be QI; 146(1)"qualified investment"(a), 146.1(1)"qualified investment"(a), 146.3(1)"qualified investment"(a) — Certain investments in s. 204 are QIs for RRSPs, RESPs and RRIFs; 248(1)"qualifying environmental trust"(e) — Trust must acquire only certain QIs.

Notes: Many qualified investments are listed in Reg. 4900. See Notes to Reg. 4900(1) and Income Tax Folio S3-F10-C1. See also 146(1)"qualified investment", 146.3(1)"qualified investment", etc.

For (c), "listed" means only an *unconditional* listing in CRA's view: Income Tax Folio S3-F10-C1, ¶1.20; but "the shares of which are listed" does not mean *all* classes of shares need be listed: VIEWS doc 2000-0054365.

Linked notes issued by an authorized foreign bank qualify under (c)(iii) [former 146(1)"qualified investment"(b)(ii)]: docs 2004-0060891R3, 2004-0097561R3. Bank GICs and term deposits in any currency qualify: 2005-0161541C6.

For (c.1)(i), an investment grade rating assigned to a debt issuer's debt issuance program rather than to a specific tranche of debt can be sufficient, if it is clear "that all debt obligations issued under the debt issuance program will have the investment grade rating": VIEWS doc 2012-0444371E5.

CRA does not provide a list of qualified investments; "security" in para. (d) should be given broad application and interpreted using the plain-meaning approach to refer to any security (other than future contracts or similar derivatives that are specifically excluded) listed on a prescribed stock exchange in or outside Canada: VIEWS doc 2007-0251981C6. For options traded on the Montreal Stock Exchange see 2008-0272681E5. Securities traded on the Alternative Investment Market of the London Stock Exchange do not qualify under para. (d): 2007-0253561E5. A BATS exchange-traded fund does not qualify: 2014-0519461M4. It is uncertain whether a listing as an investment fund on the Irish Stock Exchange qualifies: 2008-0280951E5. For a ruling that a particular bond qualifies, see 2006-217661R3.

Definition amended by 2008 budget bill #2 (effective March 19, 2007), 2007 budget bills #1 and #2 (last change effective 2008), 2001 technical bill and 2001 *Civil Code* harmonization bill. 204"qualified investment" was 204(e) before RSC 1985 (5th Supp) consolidation for 1991 and later calendar years.

Regulations: 221 (information return where mutual fund etc. claims its shares are QI); 4900(1)–(3), (7), (11), 4901(2) (investments prescribed as qualified investments).

Income Tax Folios: S3-F10-C1: Qualified investments — RRSPs, RESPs, RRIFs, RDSPs and TFSAs [replaces IT-320R3].

Information Circulars: 77-1R4: Deferred profit sharing plans.

Forms: T3F: Investments prescribed to be qualified information return.

"revoked plan" means a deferred profit sharing plan the registration of which has been revoked by the Minister pursuant to subsection 147(14) or (14.1).

Notes: 204"revoked plan" was 204(f) before RSC 1985 (5th Supp) consolidation, effective for calendar years ending after Nov. 1991.

Definitions [s. 204]: "amount", "authorized foreign bank" — 248(1); "arm's length" — 251(1); "Canada" — 255, *Interpretation Act* 35(1); "common share" — 248(1); "corporation" — 248(1), *Interpretation Act* 35(1); "debt obligation" — 204; "deferred profit sharing plan" — 147(1), 248(1); "designated stock exchange" — 248(1), 262; "dividend", "employer" — 248(1); "equity share", "excluded share", "excluded property" — 204; "fair market value" — see 69(1) Notes; "fully exempt interest" — 212(3); "initial non-qualified investment" — 204; "investment corporation" — 130(3), 248(1); "life insurance policy" — 138(12), 248(1); "listed" — 87(10); "Minister" — 248(1); "mutual fund trust" — 132(6)–(7), 132.2(3)(n), 248(1); "non-participating share", "non-qualified investment", "paid-up capital value" — 204; "partnership" — see 96(1) Notes; "prescribed" — 248(1); "private corporation" — 89(1), 248(1); "property" — 248(1); "province" — *Interpretation Act* 35(1); "qualified investment" — 204; "regulation" — 248(1); "revoked plan" — 204; "share" — 248(1); "taxation year" — 249; "trust" — 104(1), 248(1), (3).

PART X.1 — TAX IN RESPECT OF OVER-CONTRIBUTIONS TO DEFERRED INCOME PLANS

204.1 (1), (2) Tax payable by individuals [before 1991] — [No longer relevant.]

Notes: 204.1(2.1) applies instead of 204.1(1)-(2) now. See 204.2(1)(a).

(2.1) Tax payable by individuals — contributions after 1990 [RRSP overcontributions] — Where, at the end of any month after December, 1990, an individual has a cumulative excess amount in respect of registered retirement savings plans, the individual shall, in respect of that month, pay a tax under this Part equal to 1% of that cumulative excess amount.

Related Provisions: 18(1)(t) — Tax is non-deductible; 146(2)(c.1) — RRSP must permit payment to taxpayer to reduce overcontributions; 146(8.2) — Withdrawal of RRSP overcontributions; 146(21.1) — Contribution to Saskatchewan Pension Plan deemed to be RRSP premium for purposes of Part X.1; 204.1(4) — Waiver of tax by CRA; 204.3 — Return and payment of tax.

Notes: See Notes to 204.2(1.1). 204.1(2.1) added by 1990 pension bill.

Advance Tax Rulings: ATR-24: RRSP damages suit against investment management companies.

Forms: T1-OVP: Individual tax return for RRSP, SPP and PRPP excess contributions; T1-OVP-S: Simplified individual tax return for RRSP, SPP and PRPP excess contributions; T4040: RRSPs and other registered plans for retirement [guide].

(3) Tax payable by deferred profit sharing plan — Where, at the end of any month after May, 1976, a trust governed by a deferred profit sharing plan has an excess amount, the trust shall, in respect of that month, pay a tax under this Part equal to 1% of the excess amount.

Related Provisions: 204.2(4) — Definition of "excess amount" for a DPSP.

(4) Waiver of tax — Where an individual would, but for this subsection, be required to pay a tax under subsection (1) or (2.1) in respect of a month and the individual establishes to the satisfaction of the Minister that

(a) the excess amount or cumulative excess amount on which the tax is based arose as a consequence of reasonable error, and

(b) reasonable steps are being taken to eliminate the excess,

the Minister may waive the tax.

Notes: Form RC2503 can be used to apply for waiver, but a letter is just as valid, as no "prescribed form" is required. For CRA guidelines on waiver see May 2007 ICAA roundtable (tinyurl.com/cra-abtax), Q29; VIEWS doc 2020-0852131C6 [2020 APFF q.1]; and *Connolly*, 2019 FCA 161.

See 220(3.1) Notes on the *Vavilov* "transparent, intelligible and justified" standard for determining if CRA refusal to waive the tax is reasonable. It was held **unreasonable** in *Kerr*, 2008 FC 1073 (CRA repeatedly provided wrong information to K; Court directed the tax be waived). Refusal was **reasonable** in: *Connolly*, 2019 FCA 161 (CRA guidelines are unreasonably restrictive, but on the facts no waiver was justified); *Lepiarczyk*, 2008 FC 1022 (L confused by Notice of Assessment (NoA) wording "unused RRSP contributions" and contributed more); *Fleet*, 2010 FC 609; *Gagné*, 2010 FC 778 (G had outstanding overcontributions for many years); *Ferron*, 2011 FC 481; *Dimovski*, 2011 FC 721; *Kapil*, 2011 FC 1373 (K got inconsistent advice, chose to follow advice saying he could contribute in first year of employment); *Levenson*, 2016 FC 10 (L filed returns late so NoA RRSP information was wrong); *Pouchet*, 2018 FC 473 (P did not take reasonable steps to eliminate excess contribution [Hirji, "RRSP Overcontributions: CRA Continues to Punish", 18(4) *Tax for the Owner-Manager* (ctf.ca) 8-9 (Oct. 2018)]). See also 207.06(1) Notes for similar TFSA cases.

The TCC cannot waive the tax, but "strongly" encouraged CRA to waive it in *Friedlander*, 2012 TCC 163, where an immigrant went to a bank to open an investment account and got an RRSP by mistake; and recommended waiver in *Hall*, 2016 TCC 221, para. 37.

In *Roy*, 2019 TCC 50, CRA waiver under 204.1(4) did not disentitle R from deducting the excess as he built up new contribution room in later years.

See also McDonnell, "RRSP Overcontributions: Unreasonably Harsh and Disproportionate Penalties", 18(1) *Tax for the Owner-Manager* (ctf.ca) 6-8 (Jan. 2018).

204.1(4) added by 1990 pension bill, effective June 27, 1990.

Forms: RC2503: Request for waiver or cancellation of Part X.1 tax — RRSP, PRPP and SPP excess contribution tax.

Definitions [s. 204.1]: "amount" — 248(1); "cumulative excess amount" — 204.2(1.1); "deferred profit sharing plan" — 147(1), 248(1); "excess amount" — 204.2(1), (4); "individual", "Minister" — 248(1); "registered retirement savings plan" — 146(1), 248(1); "trust" — 104(1), 248(1), (3).

Interpretation Bulletins [s. 204.1]: IT-124R6: Contributions to registered retirement savings plans.

204.2 (1) Definition of "excess amount for a year in respect of registered retirement savings plans" [before 1991] — "Excess amount for a year in respect of registered retirement savings plans" of an individual at a particular time means,

(a) where the excess amount is for a year after 1990, nil; and

(b) [No longer relevant.]

Notes: For excess RRSP contributions after 1990, see 204.2(1.1).

(1.1) Cumulative excess amount in respect of RRSPs — The cumulative excess amount of an individual in respect of registered retirement savings plans at any time in a taxation year is the amount, if any, by which

(a) the amount of the individual's undeducted RRSP premiums at that time

exceeds

(b) the amount determined by the formula

$$A + B + R + C + D + E$$

where

A is the individual's unused RRSP deduction room at the end of the preceding taxation year,

B is the amount, if any, by which

> (i) the lesser of the RRSP dollar limit for the year and 18% of the individual's earned income (as defined in subsection 146(1)) for the preceding taxation year

exceeds the total of all amounts each of which is

> (ii) the individual's pension adjustment for the preceding taxation year in respect of an employer, or

> (iii) a prescribed amount in respect of the individual for the year,

C is, where the individual attained 18 years of age in a preceding taxation year, $2,000, and in any other case, nil,

D is the group plan amount in respect of the individual at that time,

E is, where the individual attained 18 years of age before 1995, the individual's transitional amount at that time, and in any other case, nil, and

R is the individual's total pension adjustment reversal for the year.

Related Provisions: 146(21.1) — Contribution to Saskatchewan Pension Plan deemed to be RRSP premium for purposes of Part X.1; 147.5(33) — Part X.1 applies to PRPP overcontributions out of an Indian's exempt income; 204.1(2.1) — Tax payable by individuals — Contributions after 1990; 204.1(4) — Waiver of tax by CRA; 204.2(1.2) — Undeducted RRSP premiums; 204.2(1.3) — Group plan amount; 204.2(1.5) — Transitional amount.

Notes: 204.1(2.1) imposes a 1% monthly tax (informally called a "penalty tax") on RRSP overcontributions exceeding $2,000 (204.2(1.1)C). CRA can waive it: 204.1(4). If a T1-OVP return under 204.3(1) is not filed, there is no deadline for CRA to assess the tax: *Hall*, 2016 TCC 221, paras. 17-24. Overcontributions can be withdrawn tax-free if the conditions of 146(8.2) are met.

Both *Gagné*, 2010 FC 778 and *Kapil*, 2011 FC 1373 wrongly stated that this penalty is limited to 60 months. It is not.

Formula element C allows a $2,000 cumulative overcontribution "cushion" for those who may make a mistake. The overcontribution is not deductible but is not subject to the penalty tax. Some people use the $2,000 for a one-time non-deductible contribution that can grow tax-free in the RRSP. It is not available for children under 18.

For 204.2(1.1)(a), note the surprising definition of "undeducted RRSP premiums" in 204.2(1.2): element J includes all taxable RRSP, RRIF and PRPP withdrawals. This should include an overcontribution withdrawal that is deductible under 146(8.2), since the amount is first included in income (248(28) would not appear to apply).

Where an RRSP has been converted to a RRIF, the RRSP may be deemed by 204.2(2) to continue to exist so that Part X.1 tax is payable forever. However, as per above, RRIF withdrawals will reduce the tax over time. See also VIEWS docs 9025045, 9429215; Yvette Kapoor, "RRSP Overcontributions: What Happens on Maturity", II(3) *RRSP Planning* (Federated Press) 140-43 (1995).

For an example with the Court providing detailed calculations over many years, see *Chiang*, 2017 TCC 165. For pension adjustment reversals (formula element R), see Notes to 146(1)"RRSP deduction limit", and Reg. 8304.1.

See also Notes to 204.1(4) re waiver of the tax, and to 162(1) re penalty for failing to file the T1-OVP to report the excess.

The overcontributions tax applied in: *Neubauer*, 2006 TCC 457; *Larose*, 2002 FCA 151 (leave to appeal denied 2002 CarswellNat 3772 (SCC)); *Lennox*, 2009 TCC 360; *Rezler*, 2009 TCC 609; *McNamee*, 2009 TCC 630; *Lans*, 2011 FCA 290; *Dimovski*, 2011 FC 721; *Bruce*, 2012 TCC 52 (FCA appeal discontinued A-93-12) (CRA conceded reductions; there was "confusion on the part of both parties as to the proper application of these provisions": para. 15); *Chiang* (above); *Turcotte*, 2017 TCC 243 (CRA agreed to cancel penalty); *Nolis*, 2018 TCC 127; *Gontovnick*, 2019 TCC 140.

The tax did not apply in *Grenon*, 2021 TCC 30, paras. 447-454 (under appeal to FCA on other grounds) ($186 million distributed to RRSP by invalidly-created mutual funds was not excess contribution).

CRA's view is that this tax is not an exempt "tax on capital" under Canada-US tax treaty Art. XXIII: VIEWS doc 2009-0308711E5.

See also Drache, "Is There a CRA Project on RRSP Over-Contributions?", xxix(5) *The Canadian Taxpayer* 39-40 (Feb. 27, 2007).

204.2(1.1)(b)D amended by 2012 budget bill #2, effective Dec. 14, 2012.

Formula element R added by 1997 Budget, for 1998 and later taxation years.

204.2(1.1)(b) amended by 1995 Budget, for 1996 and later taxation years, to reduce the "free" overcontribution room from $8,000 to $2,000.

204.2(1.1) added by 1990 pension bill, effective 1989.

Regulations: 8308(2), 8308.2, 8308.4(2), 8309 (prescribed amounts for "B").

Interpretation Bulletins: IT-124R6: Contributions to registered retirement savings plans; IT-307R4: Spousal or common-law registered retirement savings plans.

Advance Tax Rulings: ATR-24: RRSP damages suit against investment management companies.

Forms: T1-OVP: Individual tax return for RRSP, SPP and PRPP excess contributions; T1-OVP-S: Simplified individual tax return for RRSP, SPP and PRPP excess contributions.

(1.2) Undeducted RRSP premiums — For the purposes of subsection (1.1) and the description of K in paragraph (1.3)(a), the amount of undeducted RRSP premiums of an individual at any time in a taxation year is the amount determined by the formula

$$H + I - J$$

where

H is, for taxation years ending before 1992, nil, and for taxation years ending after 1991, the amount, if any, by which

> (a) the amount of the individual's undeducted RRSP premiums at the end of the immediately preceding taxation year

exceeds

> (b) the total of the amounts deducted under subsections 146(5) and (5.1) in computing the individual's income for the immediately preceding taxation year, to the extent that each amount was deducted in respect of premiums paid under registered retirement savings plans in or before that preceding year,

I is the total of all amounts each of which is

> (a) a premium (within the meaning assigned by subsection 146(1)) paid by the individual in the year and before that time under a registered retirement savings plan under which the individual or the individual's spouse or common-law partner was the annuitant (within the meaning assigned by subsection 146(1)) at the time the premium was paid, other than

>> (i) an amount paid to the plan in the first 60 days of the year and deducted in computing the individual's income for the immediately preceding taxation year,

>> (ii) an amount paid to the plan in the year and deducted under paragraph 60(j), (j.1), (j.2) or (l) in computing the individual's income for the year or the immediately preceding taxation year,

>> (iii) an amount transferred to the plan on behalf of the individual in accordance with any of subsections 146(16), 147(19), 147.3(1) and (4) to (7) and 147.5(21) or in circumstances to which subsection 146(21) applies,

>> (iv) an amount deductible under subsection 146(6.1) in computing the individual's income for the year or a preceding taxation year,

>> (v) where the individual is a non-resident person, an amount that would, if the individual were resident in Canada throughout the year and the immediately preceding taxation year, be deductible under paragraph 60(j), (j.1), (j.2) or (l) in computing the individual's income for the year or the immediately preceding taxation year, or

>> (vi) an amount paid to the plan in the year that is not deductible in computing the individual's income for the year because of subparagraph 146(5)(a)(iv.1) or (5.1)(a)(iv),

> (b) a gift made in the year and before that time to a registered retirement savings plan under which the individual is the annuitant (within the meaning assigned by subsection 146(1)), other than a gift made thereto by the individual's spouse or common-law partner, or

> (c) an amount contributed in the year and before that time by an employer or former employer of the individual to an account of the individual under a pooled registered pension plan, and

J is the amount, if any, by which

> (a) the total of all amounts each of which is an amount (other than the portion of it that reduces the amount on which tax is payable by the individual under subsection 204.1(1)) re-

ceived by the individual in the year and before that time out of or under a pooled registered pension plan, a registered retirement savings plan, a registered retirement income fund or a specified pension plan and included in computing the individual's income for the year

exceeds

(b) the amount deducted under paragraph 60(l) in computing the individual's income for the year.

Related Provisions: 146(21.1) — Contribution to Saskatchewan Pension Plan deemed to be RRSP premium for purposes of Part X.1; 147.5(11) — Pooled registered pension plan contribution deemed to be RRSP premium; 204.2(1.4) — Deemed receipt where RRSP or RRIF amended; 204.2(3) — When retirement savings plan deemed to be registered plan; 257 — Formula cannot calculate to less than zero.

Notes: For discussion of formula element J see VIEWS doc 2010-0367021E5.

204.2(1.2)J(a) amended by 2017 budget bill #2 to add "a specified pension plan", effective 2010.

204.2(1.2) earlier amended by 2012 budget bill #2 (effective Dec. 14, 2012 — PRPP changes), 2000 same-sex partners bill, 1995 and 1994 Budgets, 1993 technical bill, 1990 pension bill.

(1.3) Group plan amount — For the purposes of this section, the group plan amount in respect of an individual at any time in a taxation year is the lesser of

(a) the lesser of the value of F and the amount determined by the formula

$$F - (G - K)$$

where

F   is the lesser of

(i) the total of all amounts each of which is a qualifying group plan amount in respect of the individual, to the extent that the amount is included in determining the value of I in subsection (1.2) in respect of the individual at that time, and

(ii) the RRSP dollar limit for the following taxation year,

G   is the amount that would be determined under paragraph (1.1)(b) in respect of the individual at that time if the values of C, D and E in that paragraph were nil, and

K   is

(i) where the year is the 1996 taxation year, the amount, if any, by which the amount of the individual's undeducted RRSP premiums at the beginning of the year exceeds the individual's cumulative excess amount in respect of registered retirement savings plans at the end of the 1995 taxation year, and

(ii) in any other case, the group plan amount in respect of the individual at the end of the preceding taxation year, and

(b) the amount that would be the individual's cumulative excess amount in respect of registered retirement savings plans at that time if the value of D in paragraph (1.1)(b) were nil.

Related Provisions: 146(1) — Meaning of "net past service pension adjustment" for RRSP rules; 204.2(1.2) — Undeducted RRSP premiums; 204.2(1.31) — Qualifying group plan amount"; 257 — Formula amounts cannot calculate to less than zero.

Notes: 204.2(1.3) opening words and (a)K(ii) amended to change "group RRSP amount" to "group plan amount", and (a)F(i) amended to change "qualifying group RRSP premium paid by" to "qualifying group plan amount in respect of", by 2012 budget bill #2, all effective Dec. 14, 2012.

204.2(1.3) amended by 1995 Budget, for 1996 and later tax years. Added by 1990 pension bill; amended by 1992 technical bill to eliminate a deduction for PSPA transfers.

Regulations: 8303(2) (accumulated PSPA before 1996); 8307(5) (individual's PSPA withdrawals before 1996).

(1.31) Qualifying group plan amount — For the purposes of the description of F in paragraph (1.3)(a), a qualifying group plan amount in respect of an individual is a premium paid under a registered retirement savings plan or an amount contributed by an employer or former employer of the individual to an account of the individual under a pooled registered pension plan if

(a) the plan is part of a qualifying arrangement or is a pooled registered pension plan,

(b) the premium or contribution is an amount to which the individual is entitled for services rendered by the individual (whether or not as an employee), and

(c) the premium or contribution was remitted to the plan on behalf of the individual by the person or body of persons that is required to remunerate the individual for the services, or by an agent for that person or body,

but does not include the part, if any, of a premium or contribution that, by making (or failing to make) an election or exercising (or failing to exercise) any other right under the plan after beginning to participate in the plan and within 12 months before the time the premium was paid or the contribution was made, the individual could have prevented the premium or contribution and that would not as a consequence have been required to be remitted on behalf of the individual to another registered retirement savings plan or pooled registered pension plan or to a money purchase provision of a registered pension plan.

Related Provisions: 204.2(1.32) — Qualifying arrangement.

Notes: 204.2(1.31) amended by 2012 budget bill #2, effective Dec. 14, 2012, generally to change "qualifying group RRSP premium" to "qualifying group plan amount" and add reference to PRPP contributions.

204.2(1.31) added by 1995 Budget, effective for 1996 and later taxation years.

(1.32) Qualifying arrangement — For the purpose of paragraph (1.31)(a), a qualifying arrangement is an arrangement under which premiums that satisfy the conditions in paragraphs (1.31)(b) and (c) are remitted to registered retirement savings plans on behalf of two or more individuals, but does not include an arrangement where it is reasonable to consider that one of the main purposes of the arrangement is to reduce tax payable under this Part.

Notes: For the meaning of "one of the main purposes" see Notes to 83(2.1).

204.2(1.32) added by 1995 Budget, effective for 1996 and later taxation years.

(1.4) Deemed receipt where RRSP or RRIF amended — For the purposes of subsection (1.2),

(a) where an amount in respect of a registered retirement savings plan has been included in computing an individual's income pursuant to paragraph 146(12)(b), that amount shall be deemed to have been received by the individual out of the plan at the time referred to in that paragraph; and

(b) where an amount in respect of a registered retirement income fund has been included in computing an individual's income pursuant to paragraph 146.3(11)(b), that amount shall be deemed to have been received by the individual out of the fund at the time referred to in that paragraph.

Notes: 204.2(1.4) added by 1990 pension bill, effective 1989.

(1.5) Transitional amount — For the purpose of the description of E in paragraph (1.1)(b), an individual's transitional amount at any time in a taxation year is the lesser of

(a) $6,000, and

(b) where the value of L is nil, nil, and in any other case, the amount determined by the formula

$$L - M$$

where

L   is the amount, if any, by which

(i) the amount that would be determined under subsection (1.2) to be the amount of the individual's undeducted RRSP premiums at that time if

(A) the value of I in that subsection were determined for the 1995 taxation year without including premiums paid after February 26, 1995,

(B) the value of I in that subsection were nil for the 1996 and subsequent taxation years, and

(C) the value of J in that subsection were determined for the 1995 and subsequent taxation years without including the part, if any, of an amount received by the individual out of or under a registered retirement savings plan or registered retirement income fund that can reasonably be considered to be in respect of premiums paid after February 26, 1995 by the individual under a registered retirement savings plan

exceeds

(ii) the total of all amounts each of which is an amount deducted under subsection 146(5) or (5.1) in computing the individual's income for a preceding taxation year, to the extent that the amount was deducted in respect of premiums paid after that year (other than premiums paid before February 27, 1995), and

M is the amount that would be determined by the formula in paragraph (1.1)(b) in respect of the individual at that time if the values of D and E in that paragraph were nil and section 257 did not apply to that formula.

Related Provisions: 257 — Formula cannot calculate to less than zero.

Notes: 204.2(1.5) added by 1995 Budget, for 1996 and later tax years. The transitional amount provides an exemption from Part X.1 tax for RRSP contributions made before Feb. 27, 1995 that would otherwise become subject to the tax after 1995 because of the reduction in the overcontribution margin from $8,000 to $2,000 (see 204.2(1.1)(b)). The exemption applies until an individual has sufficient RRSP deduction room to deduct the contributions.

In general terms, an individual's transitional amount for a year is the lesser of $6,000 (the amount by which the margin has been reduced) and the amount needed to ensure that there is no penalty tax on the portion of the individual's pre-February 27, 1995 RRSP contributions that have not been deducted before the year. For this purpose, contributions are treated as being deducted in the order in which they are made.

(2) Where terminated plan deemed to continue to exist — Notwithstanding paragraph 146(12)(a), for the purposes of this Part, where a registered retirement savings plan ceases to exist and a payment or transfer of funds out of that plan has been made to which subsection 146(16) applied, if an individual's excess amount for a year in respect of registered retirement savings plans would have been greater had that plan not ceased to exist, for the purpose of computing the excess amount for a year in respect of registered retirement savings plans for so long as the individual or the individual's spouse or common-law partner is the annuitant under any registered retirement savings plan under which an annuity has not commenced to be paid to the annuitant, the plan that ceased to exist shall be deemed to remain in existence and the individual or the individual's spouse or common-law partner, as the case may be, shall be deemed to continue to be the annuitant thereunder.

Notes: See Notes to 204.2(1.1).

204.2(2) amended by 2000 same-sex partners bill to refer to "common-law partner", effective as per Notes to 248(1)"common-law partner".

(3) When retirement savings plan deemed to be a registered plan — Where a retirement savings plan under which an individual or the individual's spouse or common-law partner is the annuitant (within the meaning assigned by subsection 146(1)) is accepted by the Minister for registration, for the purpose of determining

(a) the amount of undeducted RRSP premiums of the individual at any time, and

(b) the excess amount for a year in respect of registered retirement savings plans of the individual at any time,

the retirement savings plan shall be deemed to have become a registered retirement savings plan on the later of the day on which the plan came into existence and May 25, 1976.

Notes: 204.2(3) amended by 2000 same-sex partners bill to refer to "common-law partner", effective as per Notes to 248(1)"common-law partner".

204.2(3)(a) added by 1990 pension bill, effective 1989.

(4) Definition of "excess amount" for a DPSP — "Excess amount" at any time for a trust governed by a deferred profit sharing plan means the total of all amounts each of which is

(a) such portion of the total of all contributions made to the trust before that time and after May 25, 1976 by a beneficiary under the plan, other than

(i) contributions that have been deducted by the beneficiary under paragraph 60(k) of the *Income Tax Act*, chapter 148 of the Revised Statutes of Canada, 1952,

(ii) amounts transferred to the plan on behalf of the beneficiary in accordance with subsection 147(19), or

(iii) the portion of the contributions (other than contributions referred to in subparagraphs (i) and (ii)) made by the beneficiary in each calendar year before 1991 not in excess of $5,500,

as has not been returned to the beneficiary before that time; or

(b) a gift received by the trust before that time and after May 25, 1976.

Related Provisions: 147(2)(a.1) — Acceptance of plan for registration.

Notes: 204.2(4)(a) amended by 1990 pension bill, effective 1989, to add subpara. (ii) and limit (iii) to pre-1991 contributions.

I.T. Application Rules: 69 (meaning of "chapter 148 of ...").

(5) PRPP withdrawals — Notwithstanding the *Pooled Registered Pension Plans Act* or any similar law of a province, a member of a PRPP may withdraw an amount from the member's account under the PRPP to reduce the amount of tax that would otherwise be payable by the member under this Part, to the extent that the reduction cannot be achieved by withdrawals from plans other than PRPPs.

Notes: 204.2(5) added by 2012 budget bill #2, effective Dec. 14, 2012.

Definitions [s. 204.2]: "amount", "annuity" — 248(1); "calendar year" — *Interpretation Act* 37(1)(a); "Canada" — 255; "common-law partner" — 248(1); "cumulative excess amount" — 204.2(1.1); "deferred profit sharing plan" — 147(1), 248(1); "earned income" — 146(1); "employer" — 248(1); "excess amount" — 204.2(1), (4); "amount" — 248(1); "group plan amount", "group RRSP amount" — 204.2(1.3); "individual", "Minister" — 248(1); "money purchase provision" — 147.1(1); "net past service pension adjustment" — 204.2(1.3); "past service pension adjustment" — 248(1), Reg. 8303; "pension adjustment" — 248(1), Reg. 8301(1); "pooled registered pension plan" — 147.5(1), 248(1); "premium" — 146(1); "prescribed" — 248(1); "qualifying arrangement" — 204.2(1.32); "qualifying group plan amount" — 204.2(1.31); "qualifying group RRSP premium" — 204.2(1.31); "registered pension plan" — 248(1); "registered retirement income fund" — 146.3(1), 248(1); "registered retirement savings plan" — 146(1), 248(1); "RRSP dollar limit" — 146(1), 248(1); "resident in Canada" — 250; "retirement savings plan" — 146(1); "specified pension plan" — 248(1), Reg. 7800; "taxation year" — 249; "taxpayer" — 104(1), 248(1); "total pension adjustment reversal" — 248(1); "transitional amount" — 204.2(1.5); "trust" — 104(1), 248(1), (3); "undeducted RRSP premiums" — 204.2(1.2); "unused RRSP deduction room" — 146(1), 248(1).

204.3 (1) Return and payment of tax — Within 90 days after the end of each year after 1975, a taxpayer to whom this Part applies shall

(a) file with the Minister a return for the year under this Part in prescribed form and containing prescribed information, without notice or demand therefor;

(b) estimate in the return the amount of tax, if any, payable by the taxpayer under this Part in respect of each month in the year; and

(c) pay to the Receiver General the amount of tax, if any, payable by the taxpayer under this Part in respect of each month in the year.

Related Provisions: 150.1(5) — Electronic filing; *Interpretation Act* 27(5) — Meaning of "within 90 days".

Notes: See Notes to 204.2(1.1) and 204.3(2).

Information Circulars: 78-14R4: Guidelines for trust companies and other persons responsible for filing T3GR, T3D, T3P, T3S, T3RI, and T3F returns.

Forms: T1-OVP: Individual tax return for RRSP, SPP and PRPP excess contributions; T1-OVP-S: Simplified individual tax return for RRSP, SPP and PRPP excess contributions; T1-OVP Sched.: Calculating the amount of RRSP contributions made before 1991 that are subject to tax; T3D: Income tax return for DPSP or revoked DPSP.

(2) Provisions applicable to Part — Subsections 150(2) and (3), sections 152 and 158, subsections 161(1) and (11), sections 162 to 167 and Division J of Part I are applicable to this Part with such modifications as the circumstances require.

Notes: Due to 204.3(2), penalty under 162(1), and interest on it under 161(11), apply to failure to file a T1-OVP return: See Notes to 162(1).

Definitions [s. 204.3]: "amount", "Minister" — 248(1); "month" — *Interpretation Act* 35(1); "prescribed", "taxpayer" — 248(1).

Interpretation Bulletins [s. 204.3]: IT-124R6: Contributions to registered retirement savings plans.

PART X.2 — TAX IN RESPECT OF REGISTERED INVESTMENTS

204.4 (1) Definition of "registered investment" — In this Part, "registered investment" means a trust or a corporation that has applied in prescribed form as of a particular date in the year of application and has been accepted by the Minister as of that date as a registered investment for one or more of the following:

(a) registered retirement savings plans,

(b) [Repealed under former Act]

(c) registered retirement income funds, and

(d) deferred profit sharing plans

and that has not been notified by the Minister that it is no longer registered under this Part.

Related Provisions: 248(1)"registered investment" — Definition applies to entire Act; Reg. 4900(1)(a), (5) — RI is qualified investment for various plans.

Notes: A registered investment (RI) is a pooled investment vehicle pre-approved by the CRA based on a submission by investment professionals to set up a trust or corporation, units or shares of which are marketed to deferred income plans such as RRSPs and DPSPs (see Reg. 4900(1)(a), 4900(5)). There are 4 types of RI: mutual fund trust (MFT), pooled fund trust, mutual fund corp and investment corp. There are also "quasi" versions, and for MFTs, distinction between redeemable and non-redeemable. See tinyurl.com/faqs-cra > "Registered Investments". See Notes to 204.5 re published list of RIs.

204.4(1)(b), "registered home ownership savings plans", repealed after 1985. See end of Notes to 146.2.

(2) Acceptance of applicant for registration — The Minister may accept for registration for the purposes of this Part any applicant that is

(a) a trust that has as its sole trustee a corporation licensed or otherwise authorized under the laws of Canada or a province to carry on in Canada the business of offering to the public its services as trustee if, on the particular date referred to in subsection (1),

  (i) all the property of the applicant is held in trust for the benefit of not fewer than 20 beneficiaries and

    (A) not fewer than 20 beneficiaries are taxpayers described in any of paragraphs 149(1)(o) to (o.2), (o.4) or (s), or

    (B) not fewer than 100 beneficiaries are taxpayers described in paragraph 149(1)(r) or (x),

  (ii) the total of

    (A) the fair market value at the time of acquisition of its

      (I) shares, marketable securities and cash, and

      (II) bonds, debentures, mortgages, hypothecary claims, notes and other similar obligations, and

    (B) the amount by which the fair market value at the time of acquisition of its real or immovable property that may reasonably be regarded as being held for the purpose of producing income from property exceeds the total of all amounts each of which is owing by it on account of its acquisition of the real or immovable property

is not less than 80% of the amount by which the fair market value at the time of acquisition of all its property exceeds the total of all amounts each of which is owing by it on account of its acquisition of real or immovable property,

    (iii) the fair market value at the time of acquisition of its shares, bonds, mortgages, hypothecary claims and other securities of any one corporation or debtor (other than bonds, mortgages, hypothecary claims and other securities of or guaranteed by Her Majesty in right of Canada or a province or Canadian municipality) is not more than 10% of the amount by which the fair market value at the time of acquisition of all its property exceeds the total of all amounts each of which is an amount owing by it on account of its acquisition of real or immovable property,

    (iv) the amount by which

      (A) the fair market value at the time of acquisition of any one of its real or immovable properties

exceeds

      (B) the total of all amounts each of which is owing by it on account of its acquisition of the real or immovable property

is not more than 10% of the amount by which the fair market value at the time of acquisition of all its property exceeds the total of all amounts each of which is owing by it on account of its acquisition of real or immovable property,

    (v) not less than 95% of the income of the applicant for its most recently completed fiscal period, or where no such period exists, that part of its current fiscal period before the particular date, was derived from investments described in subparagraph (ii),

    (vi) the total value of all interests in the applicant owned by all trusts or corporations described in any of paragraphs 149(1)(o) to (o.2), (o.4) or (s) to which any one employer, either alone or together with persons with whom the employer was not dealing at arm's length, has made contributions does not exceed 25% of the value of all its property,

    (vii) the total value of all interests in the applicant owned by all trusts described in paragraph 149(1)(r) or (x) to which any one taxpayer, either alone or together with persons with whom the taxpayer was not dealing at arm's length, has made contributions does not exceed 25% of the value of all its property, and

    (viii) the applicant does not hold property acquired by it after May 26, 1975 that is

      (A) a mortgage or hypothecary claim (other than a mortgage or hypothecary claim insured under the *National Housing Act* or by a corporation that offers its services to the public in Canada as an insurer of mortgages or hypothecary claims and that is approved as a private insurer of mortgages or hypothecary claims by the Superintendent of Financial Institutions pursuant to the powers assigned to the Superintendent under subsection 6(1) of the *Office of the Superintendent of Financial Institutions Act*), or an interest therein, or for civil law a right therein, in respect of which the mortgagor or hypothecary debtor is the annuitant under a registered retirement savings plan or registered retirement income fund, or a person with whom the annuitant is not dealing at arm's length, if any of the funds of a trust governed by such a plan or fund have been used to acquire an interest in the applicant, or

      (B) a bond, debenture, note or similar obligation issued by a cooperative corporation (within the meaning assigned by subsection 136(2)) or a credit union that has granted any benefit or privilege to any annuitant or beneficiary under a plan or fund referred to in subsection (1) that is dependent on or related to

        (I) ownership by a trust governed by any such plan or fund of shares, bonds, debentures, notes or similar obligations of the cooperative corporation or credit union, or

(II) ownership by the applicant of shares, bonds, debentures, notes or similar obligations of the cooperative corporation or credit union if the trust governed by any such plan or fund has used any of its funds to acquire an interest in the applicant;

(b) a trust that

(i) would be a trust described in paragraph (a) if that paragraph were read without reference to subparagraphs (a)(i), (vi) and (vii), and

(ii) holds only prescribed investments for the type of plan or fund in respect of which it has applied for registration;

(c) a mutual fund trust;

(d) a trust that

(i) would be a mutual fund trust if paragraph 132(6)(c) were not applicable, and

(ii) holds only prescribed investments for the type of plan or fund in respect of which it has applied for registration;

(e) a mutual fund corporation or investment corporation; or

(f) a corporation that

(i) would be a mutual fund corporation or investment corporation if it could have elected to be a public corporation under paragraph (b) of the definition "public corporation" in subsection 89(1) had the conditions prescribed therefor required only that a class of shares of its capital stock be qualified for distribution to the public, and

(ii) holds only prescribed investments for the type of plan or fund in respect of which it has applied for registration.

Related Provisions: 204.6(1), (2), (3) — Tax payable.

Notes: CRA's Registered Plans Division announced on July 4, 2005 that it now accepts photocopies (rather than only originals) of RI registration documents.

204.4(2) amended by 2002-2013 technical bill (effective June 26, 2013), 2005 budget bill #1, 2001 *Civil Code* harmonization bill.

Regulations: 4900, 4901 (prescribed investments).

Forms: T3RI: Registered investment income tax return; T2217: Application for registration as a registered investment.

(3) Revocation of registration — The Minister shall notify a registered investment that it is no longer registered

(a) on being satisfied that, at a date subsequent to its registration date, it no longer satisfies one or more of the conditions necessary for it to be acceptable for registration under this Part, other than a condition the failure of which to satisfy would make it liable for tax under section 204.6; or

(b) within 30 days after receipt of a request in prescribed form from the registered investment for termination of its registration.

Related Provisions: *Interpretation Act* 27(5) — Meaning of "within 30 days".

(4) Suspension of revocation — Notwithstanding a notification to a taxpayer under subsection (3), for the purposes of sections 204.6 and 204.7, the taxpayer is deemed to be a registered investment for each month or part of a month after the notification during which an interest in, or a share of the capital stock of, the taxpayer continues, by virtue of having been a registered investment, to be a qualified investment for a plan or fund referred to in subsection (1).

Notes: 204.4(4) amended by 2005 budget bill #1, effective for taxation years that begin after 2004, to no longer apply for purposes of (repealed) Part XI.

(5) Cancellation of revocation — Where a registered investment has been notified pursuant to paragraph (3)(a) and within 3 months from the date of notification it satisfies the Minister that it is acceptable for registration under this Part, the Minister may declare the notification to be a nullity.

Related Provisions: *Interpretation Act* 27(5) — Meaning of "within 3 months".

(6) Successor trust — Where at any time in a year a particular trust described in paragraph (2)(a) or (b) has substantially the same beneficiaries and can reasonably be regarded as being a continuation of another trust that was a registered investment in the year or the immediately preceding year, for the purposes of this Part, the particular trust shall be deemed to be the same trust as the other trust.

(7) Deemed registration of registered investment — Where at the end of any month a registered investment could qualify for acceptance at that time under subsection (2), it shall be deemed for the purposes of section 204.6 to have been registered under the first of the following paragraphs under which it is registrable regardless of the paragraph under which it was accepted for registration by the Minister:

(a) paragraph (2)(c) or (e), as the case may be;

(b) paragraph (2)(a);

(c) paragraph (2)(d) or (f), as the case may be; and

(d) paragraph (2)(b).

Definitions [s. 204.4]: "amount" — 248(1); "arm's length" — 251(1); "business" — 248(1); "Canada" — 255, *Interpretation Act* 35(1); "class of shares" — 248(6); "cooperative corporation" — 136(2); "corporation" — 248(1), *Interpretation Act* 35(1); "credit union" — 137(6), 248(1); "deferred profit sharing plan" — 147(1), 248(1); "employer" — 248(1); "fiscal period" — 249.1; "Her Majesty" — *Interpretation Act* 35(1); "hypothecary" — *Quebec Civil Code* art. 2660; "immovable" — *Quebec Civil Code* art. 900–907; "insurer" — 248(1); "investment corporation" — 130(3), 248(1); "Minister" — 248(1); "month" — *Interpretation Act* 35(1); "mutual fund corporation" — 131(8), 248(1); "mutual fund trust" — 132(6)–(7), 248(1); "person", "prescribed", "property" — 248(1); "province" — *Interpretation Act* 35(1); "public corporation" — 89(1), 248(1); "registered investment" — 204.4(1), 248(1); "registered retirement income fund" — 146.3(1), 248(1); "registered retirement savings plan" — 146(1), 248(1); "related" — 251(2)–(6); "share", "taxpayer" — 248(1); "trust" — 104(1), 248(1), (3).

204.5 Publication of list in *Canada Gazette* — Each year the Minister shall cause to be published in the *Canada Gazette* a list of all registered investments as of December 31 of the preceding year.

Notes: For the current list of registered investments see Table G-10 on *TaxPartner* or *Taxnet Pro* (under "Tax Rates and Reference Tables" in the Table of Contents); or search gazette.gc.ca for "registered investments".

Definitions [s. 204.5]: "Minister" — 248(1); "registered investment" — 204.4(1), 248(1).

204.6 (1) Tax payable — Where at the end of any month a taxpayer that is a registered investment described in paragraph 204.4(2)(b), (d) or (f) holds property that is not a prescribed investment for that taxpayer, it shall, in respect of that month, pay a tax under this Part equal to 1% of the fair market value at the time of its acquisition of each such property.

Proposed Amendment — 204.6(1)

(1) Tax payable — If at the end of any month a taxpayer that is a registered investment described in paragraph 204.4(2)(b), (d) or (f) holds property that is not a prescribed investment for that taxpayer, it shall, in respect of that month, pay a tax under this Part equal to the total of all amounts each of which is an amount determined in respect of such a property by the formula

$$0.01(A \times B/C)$$

where

A is the fair market value of the property at the time of its acquisition by the taxpayer;

B is the total number of issued units or issued and outstanding shares of the capital stock of the registered investment held at the end of the month by

(a) registered retirement savings plans,

(b) deferred profit sharing plans,

(c) registered retirement income funds, or

(d) registered investments described in paragraphs 204.4(2)(b), (d) or (f); and

C is the total number of issued units or issued and outstanding shares of the capital stock of the registered investment at the end of the month.

Application: The April 19, 2021 Notice of Ways and Means Motion, s. 10, will amend subsec. 204.6(1) to read as above, applicable in respect of months after 2020; it also applies to a taxpayer in respect of a month before 2021 if, before April 20, 2021,

(a) no notice of assessment in respect of an amount payable under subsec. 204.6(1) for the month has been sent to the taxpayer in respect of the month, or

(b) if such a notice of assessment has been sent to the taxpayer in respect of the month, it is not the case that the taxpayer has no further right of objection and appeal in respect of the assessment.

Federal Budget, Supplementary Information, April 19, 2021: *Taxes Applicable to Registered Investments*

A trust or corporation that satisfies certain requirements can apply to the Canada Revenue Agency to be a registered investment for registered retirement savings plans (RRSPs), registered retirement income funds or deferred profit sharing plans. The units of a trust, or shares of a corporation, that is a registered investment are qualified investments for the types of plans for which it is registered.

Certain categories of registered investments (e.g., mutual fund trusts and mutual fund corporations) must have a minimum number of investors. A trust or corporation that is a registered investment and is not sufficiently widely held (e.g., a trust that does not have the 150 unit holders required to qualify as a mutual fund trust) is limited to holding investments that would be qualified investments for the types of registered plans for which it is registered. For example, if a trust or corporation is a registered investment for RRSPs, it can hold only investments that are qualified investments for an RRSP.

If a registered investment that is subject to this investment restriction holds property that is not a qualified investment for the type of registered plans for which it is registered, the registered investment is liable to pay a tax under Part X.2 of the *Income Tax Act*. This tax is equal to 1% of the property's fair market value, at the time it was acquired, for each month that the registered investment holds the property. However, in some cases the effect of the tax can be disproportionate because the tax applies without regard to the proportion of the shares or units of the registered investment that are held by investors that are themselves subject to the qualified investment rules.

Budget 2021 proposes that the tax imposed under Part X.2 of the *Income Tax Act* be pro-rated based on the proportion of shares or units of the registered investment that are held by investors that are themselves subject to the qualified investment rules. For example, if a registered investment is registered for RRSPs and 20% of its units are held by RRSPs while 80% of its units are held by individuals via their non-registered accounts, the monthly tax imposed under Part X.2 would now be 20% of 1% of the fair market value of a non-qualified investment at the time it was acquired.

This measure would apply to taxes imposed under Part X.2 of the *Income Tax Act* in respect of months after 2020. However, the measure would also apply to taxpayers whose tax liability under Part X.2 in respect of months before 2021 has not been finally determined by the Canada Revenue Agency as of April 19, 2021.

Notes: Budget Table 1 projects that these measures will cost the federal government $2 million in 2020-21, and $6m in each of 2021-22 through 2025-26.

Related Provisions: 204.4(3) and (4) — Revocation of registration; 259 — Proportional holdings in trust property.

Regulations: 4901 (prescribed investment).

(2) Tax payable — Where at the end of any month a taxpayer that is a registered investment described in paragraph 204.4(2)(a) or (b) holds property that is a share, bond, mortgage, hypothecary claim or other security of a corporation or debtor (other than bonds, mortgages, hypothecary claims and other securities of or guaranteed by Her Majesty in right of Canada or a province or Canadian municipality), it shall, in respect of that month, pay a tax under this Part equal to 1% of the amount, if any, by which

(a) the total of all amounts each of which is the fair market value of such a property at the time of its acquisition

exceeds

(b) 10% of the amount by which

(i) the total of all amounts each of which is the fair market value, at the time of acquisition, of one of its properties

exceeds

(ii) the total of all amounts each of which is an amount owing by the trust at the end of the month in respect of the acquisition of real property or immovables.

Related Provisions: 259 — Proportional holdings in trust property.

Notes: 204.6(2)(b)(ii) amended by 2002-2013 technical bill (Part 4 — bijuralism), effective June 26, 2013, to add "or immovables".

204.6(2) amended by 2001 *Civil Code* harmonization bill, effective June 14, 2001.

(3) Tax payable — real property or immovables — If at the end of any month a taxpayer that is a registered investment described in paragraph 204.4(2)(a) holds real or immovable property, it shall, in respect of that month, pay a tax under this Part equal to 1% of the total of all amounts each of which is the amount by which the excess of

(a) the fair market value at the time of its acquisition of any one real or immovable property of the taxpayer

over

(b) the total of all amounts each of which was an amount owing by it at the end of the month on account of its acquisition of the real or immovable property

was greater than 10% of the amount by which the total of all amounts each of which is the fair market value at the time of its acquisition of a property held by it at the end of the month exceeds the total of all amounts each of which was an amount owing by it at the end of the month on account of its acquisition of real or immovable property.

Notes: 204.6(3) amended by 2002-2013 technical bill (Part 4 — bijuralism), effective June 26, 2013, to add "or immovable".

Definitions [s. 204.6]: "amount" — 248(1); "corporation" — 248(1), *Interpretation Act* 35(1); "deferred profit sharing plan" — 147(1), 248(1); "fair market value" — see 69(1) Notes; "Her Majesty" — *Interpretation Act* 35(1); "immovable" — Quebec *Civil Code* art. 900–907; "month" — *Interpretation Act* 35(1); "prescribed"; "property" — 248(1); "registered investment" — 204.4(1), 248(1); "registered retirement income fund" — 146.3(1), 248(1); "registered retirement savings plan" — 146(1), 248(1); "share", "taxpayer" — 248(1); "trust" — 104(1), 248(1), (3).

204.7 (1) Return and payment of tax — Within 90 days from the end of each taxation year commencing after 1980, a registered investment shall

(a) file with the Minister a return for the year under this Part in prescribed form and containing prescribed information, without notice or demand therefor;

(b) estimate in the return the amount of tax, if any, payable by it under this Part for the year; and

(c) pay to the Receiver General the amount of tax, if any, payable by it under this Part for the year.

Related Provisions: 150.1(5) — Electronic filing; 251.2(7)(d) — Deadline extended to regular year's deadline, for trust year deemed ended due to change in majority beneficiaries; *Interpretation Act* 27(5) — Meaning of "within 90 days".

Notes: Due to COVID-19, Part X.2 tax owing from March 18-Sept. 29, 2020 was due on Sept. 30, 2020: see PITA 59th ed. at 150(1) opening words.

A registered investment need not use a Dec. 31 year-end for the T3RI return (e.g., a mutual fund that has elected Dec. 15 under 132.11(1)): VIEWS doc 2004-0064661I7.

Forms: T3RI: Registered investment income tax return.

(2) Liability of trustee — Where the trustee of a registered investment that is liable to pay tax under this Part does not remit to the Receiver General the amount of the tax within the time specified in subsection (1), the trustee is personally liable to pay on behalf of the registered investment the full amount of the tax and is entitled to recover from the registered investment any amount paid by the trustee as tax under this section.

(3) Provisions applicable to Part — Subsections 150(2) and (3), sections 152 and 158, subsections 161(1) and (11), sections 162 to 167 and Division J of Part I are applicable to this Part with such modifications as the circumstances require.

Definitions [s. 204.7]: "amount", "Minister", "prescribed" — 248(1); "registered investment" — 204.4(1), 248(1); "taxation year" — 249.

PART X.3 — LABOUR-SPONSORED VENTURE CAPITAL CORPORATIONS

204.8 (1) Definitions — In this Part,

Notes [204.8(1)]: 204.8 renumbered as 204.8(1) by 1999 Budget, effective for 1999 and later taxation years.

"annuitant" has the meaning assigned by subsection 146(1);

"eligible business entity", at any time, means a particular entity that is

(a) a prescribed corporation, or

(b) a Canadian partnership or a taxable Canadian corporation, all or substantially all of the fair market value of the property of which is, at that time, attributable to

(i) property used in a specified active business carried on by the particular entity or by a corporation controlled by the particular entity,

(ii) shares of the capital stock or debt obligations of one or more entities that, at that time, are eligible business entities related to the particular entity, or

(iii) any combination of properties described in subparagraph (i) or (ii);

Related Provisions: 256(6), (6.1) — Meaning of "controlled".

Notes: CRA considers that "substantially all" means 90% or more.

"204.8(1)"eligible business entity" amended by 1999 Budget, effective for 1999 and later taxation years, to add para. (a).

Regulations: 4801.02 (prescribed corporation for para. (a)).

"eligible investment" of a particular corporation means

(a) a share that was issued to the particular corporation and that is a share of the capital stock of a corporation that was an eligible business entity at the time the share was issued,

(b) a particular debt obligation that was issued to the particular corporation by an entity that was an eligible business entity at the time the particular debt obligation was issued where

(i) the entity is not restricted by the terms of the particular debt obligation or by the terms of any agreement related to that obligation from incurring other debts,

(ii) the particular debt obligation, if secured, is secured solely by a floating charge on the assets of the entity or by a guarantee referred to in paragraph (c), and

(iii) the particular debt obligation, by its terms or any agreement relating to that obligation, is subordinate to all other debt obligations of the entity, except that, where the entity is a corporation, the particular debt obligation need not be subordinate to

(A) a debt obligation, issued by the entity, that is prescribed to be a small business security, or

(B) a debt obligation owing to a shareholder of the entity or to a person related to any such shareholder,

(c) a guarantee provided by the particular corporation in respect of a debt obligation that would, if the debt obligation had been issued to the particular corporation at the time the guarantee was provided, have been at that time an eligible investment because of paragraph (b), or

(d) an option or a right granted by an eligible business entity that is a corporation, in conjunction with the issue of a share or debt obligation that is an eligible investment, to acquire a share of the capital stock of the eligible business entity that would be an eligible investment if that share were issued at the time that the option or right was granted,

if the following conditions are satisfied:

(e) immediately after the time the share or debt obligation was issued, the guarantee was provided or the option or right was granted, as the case may be, the total of the costs to the particular corporation of all shares, options, rights and debt obligations of the eligible business entity and all corporations related to it and 25% of the amount of all guarantees provided by the particular corporation in respect of debt obligations of the eligible business entity and the related corporations does not exceed the lesser of $15,000,000 and 10% of the shareholders' equity in the particular corporation, determined in accordance with generally accepted accounting principles, on a cost basis and without taking into account any unrealized gains or losses on the investments of the particular corporation, and

(f) immediately before the time the share or debt obligation was issued, the guarantee was provided or the option or right was granted, as the case may be,

(i) the carrying value of the total assets of the eligible business entity and all corporations (other than prescribed labour-sponsored venture capital corporations) related to it (determined in accordance with generally accepted accounting principles on a consolidated or combined basis, where applicable) did not exceed $50,000,000, and

(ii) the total of

(A) the number of employees of the eligible business entity and all corporations related to it who normally work at least 20 hours per week for the entity and the related corporations, and

(B) ½ of the number of other employees of the entity and the related corporations,

did not exceed 500;

Related Provisions: 204.81(4) — Determination of cost.

Notes: Cl. (b)(iii)(A) amended by 2005 budget bill #1, for tax years that begin after 2004, due to repeal of Part XI (foreign property).

Everything after para. (d) to end of the definition amended by 1997 Budget, effective for property acquired after Feb. 18, 1997. For property acquired up to that date, see these Notes up to the 57th ed.

Para. (a) amended by 1992 Economic Statement, effective Dec. 3, 1992, to delete a requirement that the share be prescribed for purposes of 110.6(8) and (9) (i.e., a prescribed share under Reg. 6205). The effect is that preferred shares issued by qualifying small and medium-sized businesses are included in the definition.

Para, (f) of "eligible investment" amended by 1992 Budget/technical bill, for 1992 and later tax years, to raise the limit from $35 million to $50 million.

Regulations: 5100(2) (prescribed small business security for (b)(iii)(A)); 6701 (prescribed labour-sponsored venture capital corporation, for (f)(i)).

"eligible labour body" means a trade union, as defined in the *Canada Labour Code*, that represents employees in more than one province, or an organization that is composed of 2 or more such unions;

Notes: Definition "eligible labour body" added by 1992 Budget/technical bill, effective for 1992 and later taxation years. It replaces "national central labour body".

"labour-sponsored funds tax credit" — [Repealed]

Notes: Definition "labour-sponsored funds tax credit" repealed by 1996 Budget, effective 1996. It simply referred to the definition in 127.4(1), and is no longer needed due to amendments to 204.8"specified individual".

"national central labour body" — [Repealed]

Notes: Definition "national central labour body" repealed by 1992 Budget/technical bill, effective for 1992 and later taxation years. See "eligible labour body" above.

"original acquisition" of a share has the meaning assigned by subsection 127.4(1);

Notes: Definition "original acquisition" added by 1996 Budget, effective 1996.

"original purchaser" — [Repealed]

Notes: Definition "original purchaser" repealed by 1996 Budget, effective 1996. It is no longer needed due to an amendment to 204.81(1)(c)(v)(A)(I).

"registered labour-sponsored venture capital corporation" — [Repealed]

Notes: Definition revised and moved to 248(1) by 1996 Budget, effective 1996.

"reserve" means

(a) property described in any of paragraphs (a), (b), (c), (f) and (g) of the definition "qualified investment" in section 204, and

(b) deposits with a credit union that is a "member institution" in relation to a deposit insurance corporation (within the meaning assigned by subsection 137.1(5));

Notes: Para. (b) added by 2002-2013 technical bill, for tax years that end after 2006. It implements a May 22, 2008 Finance comfort letter to GrowthWorks.

"revoked corporation" means a corporation the registration of which has been revoked under subsection 204.81(6);

Related Provisions: 211.7(1)"revoked corporation" — Definition for Part XII.5.

"specified active business", at any time, means an active business that is carried on in Canada where

(a) at least 50% of the full-time employees employed at that time in respect of the business are employed in Canada, and

(b) at least 50% of the salaries and wages paid to employees employed at that time in respect of the business are reasonably attributable to services rendered in Canada by the employees;

Notes: It is not clear whether the definition "salary or wages" in 248(1) is intended to apply to the phrase "salaries and wages" in para. (b).

Definition amended by 1995-97 technical bill, retroactive to 1989.

"specified individual", in respect of a share, means an individual (other than a trust) whose labour-sponsored funds tax credit (as defined by subsection 127.4(6)) in respect of the original acquisition of the share is not nil or would not be nil if this Act were read without reference to paragraphs 127.4(6)(b) and (d).

Notes: This definition accounts for the fact that under 127.4(1)"qualifying trust" and 127.4(3), the LSVCC share can be purchased either by an individual or by that individual's RRSP.

Definition "specified individual" added by 1992 Economic Statement, effective December 3, 1992, and amended by 1996 Budget, effective 1996.

"start-up period" of a corporation means

(a) subject to paragraph (c), in the case of a corporation that first issued Class A shares before February 17, 1999, the corporation's taxation year in which it first issued those shares and the four following taxation years,

(b) subject to paragraph (c), in the case of a corporation that first issues Class A shares after February 16, 1999, the corporation's taxation year in which it first issues those shares and the following taxation year, or

(c) where a corporation files an election with its return under this Part for a particular taxation year of the corporation that ends after 1998 and that is referred to in paragraph (a) or (b), the period, if any, consisting of the taxation years referred to in paragraph (a) or (b), as the case may be, other than the particular year and all taxation years following the particular year.

Notes: 204.8(1)"start-up period" added by 1999 Budget, effective 1998.

"terminating corporation" in respect of a particular corporation means a predecessor corporation in circumstances where

(a) subsection 204.85(3) applies to a merger of the particular corporation and the predecessor corporation,

(b) Class A shares of the particular corporation have been issued to the predecessor corporation in exchange for property of the predecessor corporation, and

(c) within a reasonable period of time after the exchange, Class A shareholders of the predecessor corporation receive all of the Class A shares of the particular corporation issued to the predecessor corporation in the course of a wind-up of the predecessor corporation.

Related Provisions: 204.81(1)(c)(ii)(A) — Class A shares can be issued to terminating corporation.

Notes: Definition added by 2002-2013 technical bill, effective 2005. This term (see 204.81(1)(c)(ii)(A)) and 211.7(2) implement an Oct. 17, 2005 Finance comfort letter.

(2) When venture capital business discontinued — For the purposes of section 127.4, this Part and Part XII.5, a corporation discontinues its venture capital business

(a) at the time its articles cease to comply with paragraph 204.81(1)(c) and would so cease to comply if it had been incorporated after December 5, 1996;

(b) at the time it begins to wind-up, and for the purpose of this paragraph a corporation is not to be considered to have begun to wind up solely because it discontinues its venture capital business under prescribed wind-up rules;

(c) immediately before the time it amalgamates or merges with one or more other corporations to form one corporate entity (other than an entity deemed by paragraph 204.85(3)(d) to have been registered under this Part);

(d) at the time it becomes a revoked corporation, if one of the grounds on which the Minister could revoke its registration for the purposes of this Part is set out in paragraph 204.81(6)(a.1); or

(e) at the first time after the revocation of its registration for the purposes of this Part that it fails to comply with any of the provisions of its articles governing its authorized capital, the management of its business and affairs, the reduction of paid-up capital or the redemption or transfer of its Class A shares.

Related Provisions: 127.4(1.1) — Application to labour-sponsored funds tax credit; 204.841 — Penalty tax on discontinuance of venture capital business; 211.8(1.1) — Rule applies to 211.8(1).

Notes: 204.8(2)(b) changed by 2002-2013 technical bill to add everything after "it begins to wind-up", effective Oct. 24, 2012. See the prescribed wind-up rules in Reg. 6708.

204.8(2) added by 1999 Budget, effective Feb. 17, 1999.

Regulations: 6708 (prescribed wind-up rule for para. (b)).

(3) Date of issue of Class A shares — For the purposes of this Part and subsection 211.8(1), in determining the time of the issue or the original acquisition of Class A shares, identical Class A shares held by a person are deemed to be disposed of by the person in the order in which the shares were issued.

Related Provisions: 211.8(1.1) — Rule applies to 211.8(1).

Notes: 204.8(3) added by 1999 Budget, effective February 17, 1999.

Definitions [s. 204.8]: "active business", "amount", "business" — 248(1); "Canada" — 255, *Interpretation Act* 35(1); "Canadian partnership" — 102(1), 248(1); "controlled" — 256(6), (6.1); "corporation" — 248(1), *Interpretation Act* 35(1); "credit union" — 137(6), 248(1); "deposit insurance corporation" — 137.1(5); "eligible business entity", "eligible investment" — 204.8(1); "employed", "employee", "individual", "insurance corporation", "Minister" — 248(1); "original acquisition" — 127.4(1), 204.8(1); "paid-up capital" — 89(1), 248(1); "person", "prescribed" — 248(1); "prescribed labour-sponsored venture capital corporation" — Reg. 6701; "property" — 248(1); "province" — *Interpretation Act* 35(1); "related" — 251(2)–(6); "revoked corporation" — 204.8(1); "security" — *Interpretation Act* 35(1); "share", "shareholder" — 248(1); "specified active business" — 204.8(1); "taxable Canadian corporation" — 89(1), 248(1); "taxation year" — 249; "trust" — 104(1), 248(1), (3).

204.81 (1) Conditions for registration [before March 21/13] — The Minister may register a corporation for the purposes of this Part if the corporation's application for registration was received before March 21, 2013 and if, in the opinion of the Minister, it complies with the following conditions:

(a) the corporation has applied in prescribed form to the Minister for registration;

(b) the corporation was caused to be incorporated under the *Canada Business Corporations Act* by an eligible labour body; and

(c) the articles of the corporation provide that

(i) the business of the corporation is restricted to assisting the development of eligible business entities and to creating, maintaining and protecting jobs by providing financial and managerial advice to such entities and by investing funds of the corporation in eligible investments and reserves,

(ii) the authorized capital of the corporation shall consist only of

(A) Class A shares that are issuable only to individuals (other than trusts), terminating corporations in respect of the corporation and trusts governed by registered retirement savings plans or by TFSAs and that entitle their holders

(I) to receive notice of and, subject to the *Canada Business Corporations Act*, to attend and vote at all meetings of the shareholders of the corporation,

(II) to receive dividends at the discretion of the board of directors of the corporation, and

(III) to receive, on dissolution of the corporation, all the assets of the corporation that remain after payment of all amounts payable to the holders of all other classes of shares of the corporation,

(B) Class B shares that are issuable only to and may be held only by eligible labour bodies, that entitle each of those shareholders

(I) to receive notice of and, subject to the *Canada Business Corporations Act*, to attend and vote at all meetings of the shareholders of the corporation, and

(II) to receive, on dissolution of the corporation, an amount equal to the amount of the consideration received by the corporation on the issue of the Class B shares,

but that do not entitle them to receive dividends, and

(C) any additional classes of shares that are authorized, if the rights, privileges, restrictions and conditions attached to the shares are approved by the Minister of Finance,

(iii) the business and affairs of the corporation shall be managed by a board of directors, at least ½ of whom are appointed by the Class B shareholders,

(iv) the corporation shall not reduce its paid-up capital in respect of a class of shares (other than Class B shares) otherwise than by way of

(A) a redemption of shares of the corporation, or

(B) a reduction in its paid-up capital attributable to a class of shares for which no shares have been issued in the eight-year period ending at the time of the reduction,

(v) the corporation shall not redeem a Class A share in respect of which an information return described in paragraph (6)(c) has been issued unless

(A) if the share is held by the specified individual in respect of the share, a spouse or common-law partner or former spouse or common-law partner of that individual or a trust governed by a registered retirement savings plan, TFSA or registered retirement income fund under which that individual, spouse or common-law partner is the annuitant,

(I) a request in writing to redeem the share is made by the holder to the corporation and the information return referred to in paragraph (6)(c) has been returned to the corporation, or

(II) [Repealed]

(III) the corporation is notified in writing that the specified individual in respect of the share became disabled and permanently unfit for work or terminally ill after the share was issued,

(B) there is no specified individual in respect of the share,

(C) [Repealed]

(D) the corporation is notified in writing that the share is held by a person on whom the share has devolved as a consequence of the death of

(I) a holder of the share, or

(II) an annuitant under a trust governed by a registered retirement savings plan, TFSA or registered retirement income fund that was a holder of the share,

(E) the redemption occurs

(I) more than eight years after the day on which the share was issued, or

(II) if the day that is eight years after that issuance is in February or March of a calendar year, in February or on March 1st of that calendar year but not more than 31 days before that day, or

(F) the holder of the share has satisfied such other conditions as are prescribed,

(vi) [Repealed]

(vii) the corporation shall not register a transfer of a Class A share by the specified individual in respect of the share, a spouse or common-law partner of the specified individual or a trust governed by a registered retirement savings plan, TFSA or registered retirement income fund under which the specified individual or spouse or common-law partner is the annuitant, unless

(A) no information return has been issued under paragraph (6)(c) in respect of the share,

(B) the transfer occurs more than eight years after the day on which the share was issued,

(C) the transfer is to the specified individual, a spouse or common-law partner or former spouse or common-law partner of the specified individual or a trust governed by a registered retirement savings plan, TFSA or registered retirement income fund under which the specified individual or the spouse or common-law partner or former spouse or common-law partner of the specified individual is the annuitant,

(D) the corporation is notified in writing that the transfer occurs as a consequence of the death of the specified individual or a spouse or common-law partner of the specified individual,

(E) the corporation is notified in writing that the transfer occurs after the specified individual dies,

(F) [Repealed]

(G) the corporation is notified in writing that the specified individual became disabled and permanently unfit for work or terminally ill after the share was issued and before the transfer, or

(H) such other conditions as are prescribed are satisfied;

(viii) the corporation shall not pay any fee or remuneration to a shareholder, director or officer of the corporation unless the payment was approved by a resolution of the directors of the corporation, and

(ix) the corporation shall not make any investment in an eligible business entity with which the corporation or any of the directors of the corporation does not deal at arm's length unless

(A) the corporation would deal at arm's length with the eligible business entity but for the corporation's interest as the holder of eligible investments in such entity, or

(B) the investment was approved by special resolution of the shareholders of the corporation before the investment was made.

Related Provisions: 131(8) — Prescribed LSVCC deemed to be a mutual fund corporation; 131(11) — Rules respecting prescribed LSVCCs; 204.81(1.1), (1.2) — Application before 2004; 204.81(6)(a), (a.1) — Revocation of registration for failure to comply with conditions; 204.81(8.3), (8.4) — Where province discontinues LSVCC credit program; 211.7 — Recovery of credit from provincial LSVCCs; 211.8(1) — Clawback of credit on disposition of approved share; 248(1)"registered labour-sponsored venture capital corporation" — Definition of RLSVCC for entire Act; 248(8) — Meaning of "consequence" of death.

Notes: Labour-sponsored venture capital corps were to be phased out by 2017 (2013 budget bill #2), but were reinstated, for *provincially*-registered LSVCCs only, by the 2016 Liberal Budget: see amendments to 127.4(2), (5), (6), 211.7(1), Reg. 6701.1. A credit is available under 127.4(6). LSVCCs can no longer be federally registered: 204.81(1) opening words.

204.81(1) amended by 2013 budget bill #2 (effective March 21, 2013), 2002-2013 technical bill, 2010 and 2008 budget bills #2, 2000 same-sex partners bill, 1997 and 1996 Budgets, 1992 technical bill, 1992 Economic Statement. Some of these amendments apply only to corps incorporated after March 5, 1996 (see up to PITA 58th ed. for wording).

Regulations: 6706 (prescribed conditions for 204.81(1)(c)(v)(G)).

Forms: T5005: Application to register a labour-sponsored venture capital corporation.

(1.1) Corporations incorporated before March 6, 1996 — In applying clause (1)(c)(v)(E) in relation to any time before 2004 in respect of a corporation incorporated before March 6, 1996, the references in that clause to "eight" are replaced with references to "five" if, at that time, the relevant statements in the corporation's articles refer to "five".

Notes: 204.81(1.1) added by 2002-2013 technical bill (Part 5 — technical), effective Feb. 7, 2000. This change was announced in a Feb. 7, 2000 Finance news release, reproduced under 211.7(3) up to PITA 43rd ed.

(1.2) Deemed provisions in articles — In applying subsection (1) in relation to any time before 2004, to a corporation incorporated before February 7, 2000, if the articles of the corporation comply with subclause (1)(c)(v)(E)(I) (as modified, where relevant, by subsection (1.1)), those articles are deemed to provide the statement required by subclause (1)(c)(v)(E)(II).

Notes: 204.81(1.2) added by 2002-2013 technical bill (Part 5 — technical), effective Feb. 7, 2000. This change was announced in a Feb. 7, 2000 Finance news release, reproduced under 211.7(3) up to PITA 43rd ed.

(2) Registration number — On registering a corporation under subsection (1), the Minister shall assign to it a registration number.

(3) Successive registrations — Where an eligible labour body causes more than one corporation to be registered under this Part, for the purposes of paragraph (6)(h) and section 204.82, each of those corporations shall be deemed

(a) to have issued a Class A share at the earliest time any such corporation issued a Class A share,

and, where the corporation did not exist at the time referred to in paragraph (a),

(b) to have been in existence during the particular period beginning immediately before that time and ending immediately after the corporation was incorporated, and

(c) to have had, throughout the particular period, fiscal periods ending on the same calendar day in each year in the particular period as the calendar day on which its first fiscal period after it was incorporated ended.

Notes: 204.81(3) amended by 1992 technical bill, for 1992 and later taxation years.

(4) Determination of cost — For the purposes of this Part, the cost at any time to a corporation of an eligible investment that is a guarantee shall be deemed to be 25% of the amount of the debt obligation subject to the guarantee at that time.

(5) Registration date — Where the Minister registers a corporation for the purposes of this Part, the corporation shall be deemed to have become so registered on the later of

(a) the day the application for registration of the plan is received by the Minister, and

(b) where in the application for registration a day is specified as the day on which the registration is to take effect, that day.

(6) Revocation of registration — The Minister may revoke the registration of a corporation for the purposes of this Part where

(a) the articles of the corporation do not comply with paragraph (1)(c) and would not comply with that paragraph if the corporation had been incorporated after December 5, 1996;

(a.1) the corporation does not comply with any of the provisions of its articles described in paragraph (1)(c), except where there would be no failure to comply if the provisions of its articles were consistent with the articles of a corporation that would be permitted to be registered under this Part if it had been incorporated after December 5, 1996;

(b) an individual acquires or irrevocably subscribes and pays for a Class A share of the capital stock of the corporation in the period beginning on the 61st day of a calendar year and ending on the 60th day of the following calendar year and the corporation fails to file with the Minister an information return in prescribed form containing prescribed information before April of that following calendar year;

(c) an individual acquires or irrevocably subscribes and pays for a Class A share of the capital stock of the corporation in the period beginning on the 61st day of a calendar year and ending on the 60th day of the following calendar year and the corporation fails to issue to the individual before April of that following

calendar year an information return in prescribed form stating the amount of the consideration paid for the share in that period;

(d) the corporation issues more than one information return described in paragraph (c) in respect of the same acquisition of or subscription for a Class A share;

(e) the financial statements of the corporation presented to its shareholders are not prepared in accordance with generally accepted accounting principles;

(f) the corporation fails within 6 months after the end of any taxation year to have an independent valuation of its shares made as of the end of that year;

(g) [Repealed]

(h) the corporation does not pay the tax or penalty payable under section 204.82 by it on or before the day on or before which that tax or penalty is required to be paid;

(i) tax was payable under subsection 204.82(3) by the corporation for 3 or more taxation years;

(j) the corporation provides a guarantee that is an eligible investment and fails to maintain, at any time during the term of the guarantee, a reserve equal to the cost to the corporation of the guarantee at that time;

(k) the corporation pays a fee or commission in excess of a reasonable amount in respect of the offering for sale, or the sale, of its shares; or

(l) the corporation has a monthly deficiency in 18 or more months in any 36-month period.

Related Provisions: 127.4(6)(b) — No labour-sponsored funds tax credit unless return under 204.81(6)(c) filed with tax return; 204.8(1)"revoked corporation", 211.7(1)"revoked corporation" — Corporations whose registration has been revoked; 204.81(4) — Determination of cost; 204.81(7), (8) — Notice of intent to revoke registration; 204.81(8.1) — Voluntary de-registration; *Interpretation Act* 27(5) — Meaning of "within 6 months".

Notes: For a ruling that CRA will not revoke a registration when one LSVCC temporarily holds shares of another in the course of a merger, see doc 2006-0171471R3.

204.81(6)(g) repealed by 1999 Budget, effective Feb. 17, 1999 (it required the corporation to keep minimum eligible investments or reserves). 204.81(6) earlier amended by 1996 Budget and 1992 Economic Statement.

Forms: T2152: Part X.3 tax return for an LSVCC; T2152 Sched. 1: Calculating tax under subsec. 204.82(2); T2152 Sched. 2: Calculating tax under subsecs. 204.82(3) and (6) and s. 204.841; T2152A: Part X.3 tax return and request for a refund for an LSVCC; T5006: Statement of registered LSVCC class A shares; T5006 Summ: Summary of registered LSVCC Class A shares.

(7) Notice of intent to revoke registration — Where the Minister proposes to revoke the registration of a corporation under subsection (6), the Minister shall, by registered mail, give notice to the corporation of the proposal.

Related Provisions: 244(5) — Proof of service by mail; 248(7)(a) — Mail deemed received on day mailed; 204.81(9) — Appeal of decision to revoke registration.

(8) Idem — Where the Minister gives notice under subsection (7) to a registered labour-sponsored venture capital corporation, the Minister may, after the expiration of 30 days after the day of mailing of the notice, or after the expiration of such extended period after the day of mailing as the Federal Court of Appeal or a judge thereof, on application made at any time before the determination of any appeal under subsection (9) from the giving of the notice, may fix or allow, publish a copy of the notice in the *Canada Gazette* and, on the publication of a copy of the notice, the registration of the corporation is revoked.

(8.1) Voluntary de-registration — Where at any time the Minister receives a certified copy of a resolution of the directors of a corporation seeking the revocation of the corporation's registration under this Part,

(a) the registration is revoked at that time; and

(b) the Minister shall, with all due dispatch, give notice in the *Canada Gazette* of the revocation.

Related Provisions: 204.81(6) — Revocation of registration; 204.81(8.2) — Actual date of receipt applies.

Notes: 204.81(8.1) added by 1999 Budget, effective for resolutions received by the Minister of National Revenue after June 29, 2000.

(8.2) Application of subsec. 248(7) — Subsection 248(7) does not apply for the purpose of subsection (8.1).

Notes: 204.81(8.2) added by 1999 Budget, effective for resolutions received by the Minister of National Revenue after June 29, 2000.

(8.3) Transitional rules — If a registered labour-sponsored venture capital corporation notifies the Minister in writing of its intent to revoke its registration under this Part, the following rules apply:

(a) the corporation shall not, on or after the day the notice is provided to the Minister (referred to in this subsection and subsection (8.4) as the "notification date"), issue any tax credit certificates, other than duplicate certificates to replace certificates issued before that day;

(b) section 204.841 does not apply on the discontinuance of its venture capital business;

(c) subsections 204.82(1) to (4) do not apply to taxation years of the corporation that begin on or after the notification date; and

(d) subsection 204.83(1) does not apply in respect of a period, referred to in that subsection as the "second period", that ends after the notification date.

Related Provisions: 204.81(8.4) — Conditions for subsec. (8.3) to apply; 204.85(3)(d)(vi) — Amalgamation or merger.

Notes: 204.81(8.3) opening words amended by 2014 budget bill #1, effective Nov. 27, 2013.

204.81(8.3) and (8.4) added by 2002-2013 technical bill, effective 2005.

Regulations: 6701 (prescribed labour-sponsored venture capital corporation); 6708 (prescribed wind-up rule).

(8.4) Discontinuance of provincial program — Subsection (8.3) applies to a corporation only if,

(a) on the notification date, the percentage determined in respect of the corporation by the following formula is less than 20 per cent:

$$A/(B - C) \times 100$$

where

A is the amount of equity capital received by the corporation on the issue of Class A shares that were issued in the 24 months immediately preceding the notification date and are still outstanding on that date,

B is the total amount of equity capital received by the corporation on the issue of Class A shares that are still outstanding on the notification date, and

C is the amount of equity capital received by the corporation on the issue of Class A shares that, as of the notification date, have been outstanding for at least eight years.

(b) the corporation has revoked its registration before the third anniversary of the notification date.

Notes: See Notes to 204.81(8.3).

(9) Right of appeal — Where the Minister refuses to accept a corporation for registration under subsection (1) or gives notice of a proposal to revoke the registration of a corporation under subsection (7), the corporation may appeal to the Federal Court of Appeal from the decision or from the giving of the notice.

Related Provisions: 168(3) — Parallel rule for appeal of revocation of charity registration.

Definitions [s. 204.81]: "amount" — 248(1); "annuitant" — 146(1), 204.8(1); "arm's length" — 251(1); "business" — 248(1); "calendar year" — *Interpretation Act* 37(1)(a); "Canada" — 255, *Interpretation Act* 35(1); "class of shares" — 248(6); "common-law partner" — 248(1); "consequence of the death" — 248(8); "corporation" — 248(1), *Interpretation Act* 35(1); "dividend" — 248(1); "eligible business entity", "eligible investment", "eligible labour body" — 204.8(1); "Federal Court of Appeal" — *Federal Courts Act* s. 3; "fiscal period" — 249.1; "individual", "Minister" — 248(1); "Minister of Finance" — *Financial Administration Act* 14; "month" — *Interpretation Act* 35(1); "notification date" — 204.81(8.3)(a); "officer" — 248(1); "paid-up capital" — 89(1), 248(1); "person", "prescribed" — 248(1); "province" — *Interpretation Act* 35(1); "registered labour-sponsored venture capital corporation" — 248(1);

"registered retirement income fund" — 146.3(1), 248(1); "registered retirement savings plan" — 146(1), 248(1); "reserve" — 204.8(1); "share", "shareholder" — 248(1); "specified individual" — 204.8(1); "TFSA" — 146.2(5), 248(1); "taxation year" — 249; "terminating corporation" — 204.8(1); "trust" — 104(1), 248(1), (3); "writing" — *Interpretation Act* 35(1).

204.82 (1) Recovery of credit — Where, at any time that is both in a taxation year included in the start-up period of a corporation that was registered under this Part and before its venture capital business is first discontinued,

(a) 80% of the amount, if any, by which the total consideration received by it for Class A shares issued by it before that time exceeds the total of all amounts paid by it before that time to its shareholders as a return of capital on such shares

exceeds

(b) the total of all amounts each of which is the cost to the corporation of an eligible investment or reserve of the corporation at that time,

the corporation shall pay a tax under this Part for the year equal to the amount determined by the formula

$$(A \times 20\%) - B$$

where

A is the greatest amount by which the amount determined under paragraph (a) exceeds the amount determined under paragraph (b) for the year, and

B is the total of all taxes payable under this subsection by the corporation for preceding taxation years.

Related Provisions: 204.81(4) — Determination of cost; 204.81(8.3)(b) — 204.82(1)–(4) do not apply to provincial LSVCC that deregisters after province cancels credit program; 257 — Formula cannot calculate to less than zero.

Notes: Opening words of 204.82(1) amended by 1999 Budget, effective for 1999 and later taxation years.

(2) Liability for tax — Each corporation that has been registered under this Part shall, in respect of each month that ends before its venture capital business is first discontinued and in a particular taxation year of the corporation that begins after the end of the corporation's start-up period (or, where the corporation has no start-up period, that begins after the time the corporation first issues a Class A share), pay a tax under this Part equal to the amount obtained when the greatest investment shortfall at any time that is in the month and in the particular year (in this section and sections 204.81 and 204.83 referred to as the "monthly deficiency") is multiplied by $\frac{1}{60}$ of the prescribed rate of interest in effect during the month.

Related Provisions: 204.82(2.1), (2.2) — Investment shortfall.

Notes: 204.82(2) amended by 1999 Budget, effective for 1999 and later taxation years. Earlier amended by 1997 Budget.

Regulations: 4301 (prescribed rate of interest).

Forms: T2152 Sched. 1: Calculating tax under subsec. 204.82(2).

(2.1) Determination of investment shortfall — Subject to subsection (2.2), a corporation's investment shortfall at any time in a particular taxation year is the amount determined by the formula

$$A - B - C$$

where

A is 60% of the lesser of

(a) the amount, if any, by which the amount of the shareholders' equity in the corporation at the end of the preceding taxation year exceeds the specified adjustment in respect of the shareholders' equity in the corporation at the end of that year, and

(b) the amount, if any, by which the amount of the shareholders' equity in the corporation at the end of the particular taxation year exceeds the specified adjustment in respect of the shareholders' equity in the corporation at the end of the particular year;

B is the greater of

(a) the total of all amounts each of which is the adjusted cost to the corporation of an eligible investment of the corporation at that time, and

(b) 50% of the total of all amounts each of which is

(i) the adjusted cost to the corporation of an eligible investment of the corporation at the beginning of the particular year, or

(ii) the adjusted cost to the corporation of an eligible investment of the corporation at the end of the particular year; and

C is 60% of the amount, if any, by which

(a) the total of all amounts each of which is a tax or penalty under subsection (3) or (4), or a prescribed tax or penalty, paid before that time by the corporation (other than the portion, if any, of that tax or penalty the liability for which resulted in a reduction in the amount of the shareholders' equity at the end of any preceding taxation year)

exceeds

(b) the total of all amounts each of which is a refund before that time of any portion of the total described in paragraph (a).

Notes: See Notes to 127.4(5) re parallel Ontario changes.

Related Provisions: 257 — Formula cannot calculate to less than zero.

Notes: 204.82(2.1) amended by 1998 Budget, effective for taxation years that begin after 1997.

204.82(2.1) added by 1997 Budget, for taxation years that end after February 1997.

(2.2) Investment shortfall — For the purpose of this subsection and for the purpose of computing a corporation's investment shortfall under subsection (2.1) at any time in a taxation year (in this subsection referred to as the "relevant year"),

(a) unrealized gains and losses in respect of its eligible investments shall not be taken into account in computing the amount of the shareholders' equity in the corporation;

(b) where

(i) the relevant year ends after 1998, and

(ii) it is expected that a redemption of its Class A shares will occur after the end of a particular taxation year and, as a consequence, the amount of the shareholders' equity in the corporation at the end of the particular year would otherwise be reduced to take into account the expected redemption,

subject to paragraph (c), the amount (or, where the relevant year ends in 1999, 2000, 2001 or 2002, 20%, 40%, 60% or 80%, respectively of the amount) expected to be redeemed shall not be taken into account in determining the amount of the shareholders' equity in the corporation at the end of the particular year;

(c) paragraph (b) does not apply to a redemption expected to be made after the end of a taxation year where

(i) the redemption is made within 60 days after the end of the year, and

(ii) either

(A) tax under Part XII.5 became payable as a consequence of the redemption, or

(B) tax under Part XII.5 would not have become payable as a consequence of the redemption if the redemption had occurred at the end of the year; and

(c.1) the specified adjustment in respect of shareholders' equity in the corporation at the end of a taxation year is the amount determined by the formula

$$(A \times (B/C)) - D$$

where

A is the shareholders' equity at the end of the year,

B is the total of

(i) the fair market value at the end of the year of all Class A shares issued by it before March 6, 1996 and more than five years before the end of the year,

(ii) the fair market value at the end of the year of all Class A shares issued by it after March 5, 1996 and more than eight years before the end of the year,

(iii) the fair market value at the end of the year of all Class A shares issued by it in the last 60 days of the year, and

(iv) if the corporation so elects in writing filed with the Minister not more than six months after the end of the year and is not a revoked corporation at the end of the year, the fair market value at the end of the year of all shares of classes, of the capital stock of the corporation, to which clause 204.81(1)(c)(ii)(C) applies,

C is the fair market value at the end of the year of all shares issued by it, and

D is the amount by which the shareholders' equity in the corporation at the end of the year has been reduced to take into account the expected subsequent redemption of shares of the capital stock of the corporation; and

(d) the adjusted cost to the corporation of an eligible investment of the corporation at any time is

(i) 150% of the cost to the corporation of the eligible investment at that time where the eligible investment is

(A) a property acquired by the corporation after February 18, 1997 (other than a property to which subparagraph (i.1) applies) that would be an eligible investment of the corporation if the reference to "$50,000,000" in paragraph (f) of the definition "eligible investment" in subsection 204.8(1) were read as "$10,000,000", or

(B) a share of the capital stock of a prescribed corporation,

(i.1) 200% of the cost to the corporation of the eligible investment at that time where the eligible investment is a property acquired by the corporation after February 16, 1999 (other than a property described in clause (i)(B)) that would be an eligible investment of the corporation if the reference to "$50,000,000" in paragraph (f) of the definition "eligible investment" in subsection 204.8(1) were read as "$2,500,000", and

(ii) in any other case, the cost to the corporation of the eligible investment of the corporation at that time.

Related Provisions: 257 — Formula cannot calculate to less than zero; Reg. 5100(1)"eligible corporation"(f) — Corporation that makes election under (c.1) does not qualify for foreign property exception.

Notes: 204.82(2.2) amended by 1999 Budget (for 1999 and later taxation years), 1998 and 1997 Budgets.

Regulations: 4801.02 (prescribed corporation for 204.82(2.2)(d)(i)(B)).

(3) Recovery of credit — Where a corporation is liable under subsection (2) to pay a tax in respect of 12 consecutive months (in this subsection referred to as the "particular period"), the corporation shall pay a tax under this Part for a taxation year in respect of each particular period that ends in the year equal to the total of the amounts determined by the formula

$$\left(\frac{A}{12} \times 20\%\right) - (B - C)$$

where

A is the total of the monthly deficiencies for each month in the particular period;

B is the total of all taxes payable by the corporation under subsection (1) for preceding taxation years and taxes payable by it under this subsection in respect of a period ending before the end of the particular period; and

C is the total of all amounts refunded under section 204.83 in respect of the tax paid under this subsection by the corporation for preceding taxation years.

Related Provisions: 204.82(4) — Penalty; 204.83(1) — Refund of amount paid; 257 — Formula cannot calculate to less than zero.

Forms: T2152 Sched. 2: Calculating tax under subsecs. 204.82(3) and (6) and s. 204.841.

(4) Penalty — Where a corporation is liable under subsection (3) to pay a tax for a taxation year, the corporation shall pay, in addition to the tax payable under that subsection, a penalty for the year equal to that tax.

Related Provisions: 18(1)(t) — Penalty is non-deductible; 204.83(1) — Refund of 80% of penalty; 211.7 — Recovery of credit from shareholder where share redeemed or disposed of.

Notes: See Notes to 239(1).

(5) Provincially registered LSVCCs — Where

(a) an amount (other than interest on an amount to which this subsection applies or an amount payable under or as a consequence of a prescribed provision of a law of a province) is payable to the government of a province by a corporation,

(b) the amount is payable as a consequence of a failure to acquire sufficient properties of a character described in the law of the province,

(c) the corporation has been prescribed for the purpose of the definition "approved share" in subsection 127.4(1), and

(d) the corporation is not a registered labour-sponsored venture capital corporation or a revoked corporation,

the corporation shall pay a tax under this Part for the taxation year in which the amount became payable equal to that amount.

Related Provisions: 204.83(2) — Refund; 204.86(2) — Return and payment of tax.

Notes: 204.82(5) added by 1997 Budget, for liabilities arising after Feb. 18, 1997. It imposes a tax on LSVCCs that have been prescribed under the Regulations for the purpose of 127.41(1)"approved share" and that were not registered under Part X.3. See Finance Technical Notes, or these Notes up to the 57th ed., for detail.

Regulations: 6707 (prescribed provision of a law of a province (Ontario)).

(6) Further matching of amounts payable to a province — Where

(a) a particular amount is payable (other than interest on an amount to which this subsection applies) by a registered labour-sponsored venture capital corporation or a revoked corporation to the government of a province as a consequence of a failure of a prescribed corporation to acquire sufficient properties of a character described in a law of the province, and

(b) the particular amount became payable before the corporation first discontinued its venture capital business,

the corporation shall pay a tax under this Part for the taxation year in which the particular amount became payable equal to that amount.

Related Provisions: 204.83(2) — Refund of tax paid under 204.82(6).

Notes: 204.82(6) added by 1999 Budget, effective for 1999 and later taxation years.

Regulations: 4801.02 (prescribed corporation for 204.82(6)(a)).

Forms: T2152 Sched. 2: Calculating tax under subsecs. 204.82(3) and (6) and s. 204.841.

Definitions [s. 204.82]: "adjusted cost" — 204.82(2.2)(d); "amount" — 248(1); "corporation" — 248(1), *Interpretation Act* 35(1); "eligible investment" — 204.8(1); "fair market value" — see 69(1) Notes; "investment shortfall" — 204.82(2.1), (2.2); "Minister" — 248(1); "month" — *Interpretation Act* 35(1); "particular period" — 204.82(3); "prescribed" — 248(1); "prescribed rate" — Reg. 4301; "property" — 248(1); "province" — *Interpretation Act* 35(1); "registered labour-sponsored venture capital corporation" — 248(1); "relevant year" — 204.82(2.2); "reserve", "revoked corporation" — 204.8(1); "share", "shareholder" — 248(1); "shareholders' equity" — 204.82(2.2)(a), (b); "specified adjustment" — 204.82(2.2)(c.1); "start-up period" — 204.8(1); "taxation year" — 249; "writing" — *Interpretation Act* 35(1).

204.83 (1) Refunds for federally registered LSVCCs — If a corporation is required, under subsections 204.82(3) and (4), to pay a tax and a penalty under this Part for a taxation year, it has no monthly deficiency throughout any period of 12 consecutive months (in this section referred to as the "second period") that begins after the 12-month period in respect of which the tax became payable (in this section referred to as the "first period") and it so requests in an application filed with the Minister in prescribed form, the Minister shall refund to it an amount equal to the total of the amount that was paid under subsection 204.82(3) and 80% of the amount that was paid under subsection 204.82(4) in respect of the first period on or before the later of

(a) the 30th day after receiving the application, and

(b) the 60th day after the end of the second period.

Related Provisions: 204.81(8.3)(b) — 204.83(1) does not apply to provincial LSVCC that deregisters after province cancels credit program.

Notes: 204.83(1) amended by 1998 Budget, effective June 17, 1999, but applications received before that day are deemed to have been received on that day.

204.83 renumbered as 204.83(1) by 1997 Budget, effective February 19, 1997, to accommodate the introduction of 204.83(2).

Forms: T2152A: Part X.3 tax return and request for a refund for an LSVCC.

(2) Refunds of amounts payable to provinces — Where

(a) the government of a province refunds, at any time, an amount to a corporation,

(b) the refund is of an amount that had been paid in satisfaction of a particular amount payable in a taxation year of the corporation, and

(c) tax was payable under subsection 204.82(5) or (6) by the corporation for a taxation year because the particular amount became payable,

the corporation is deemed to have paid at that time an amount equal to the refund on account of its tax payable under this Part for the year.

Notes: 204.83(2) added by 1997 Budget, effective Feb. 19, 1997. 204.83(2)(c) amended by 1999 Budget, effective for 1999 and later taxation years.

Definitions [s. 204.83]: "amount" — 248(1); "corporation" — 248(1), *Interpretation Act* 35(1); "first period" — 204.83(1); "Minister" — 248(1); "month", "province" — *Interpretation Act* 35(1); "second period" — 204.83(1); "taxation year" — 249.

204.84 Penalty — Every corporation that for a taxation year issues an information return described in paragraph 204.81(6)(c) in respect of

(a) the issuance of a share when the corporation was a revoked corporation, or

(b) a subscription in respect of a share if the share is not issued on or before the day that is 180 days after the day the information return was issued,

is liable to a penalty for the year equal to the amount of the consideration for which the share was or was to be issued.

Related Provisions: 18(1)(t) — Penalty is non-deductible.

Notes: See Notes to 239(1).

Definitions [s. 204.84]: "amount" — 248(1); "corporation" — 248(1), *Interpretation Act* 35(1); "revoked corporation" — 204.8(1); "share" — 248(1); "taxation year" — 249.

204.841 Penalty tax where venture capital business discontinued — Where, at a particular time in a taxation year, a particular corporation that is a registered labour-sponsored venture capital corporation or a revoked corporation first discontinues its venture capital business, the particular corporation shall pay a tax under this Part for the year equal to the total of all amounts each of which is the amount in respect of a Class A share of the capital stock of the particular corporation outstanding immediately before the particular time that is determined by the formula

$$A \times B$$

where

A is

(a) if the original acquisition of the share was before March 6, 1996 and less than five years before the particular time,

4% of the consideration received by the particular corporation for the issue of the share,

(b) if the original acquisition of the share was after March 5, 1996 and less than eight years before the particular time, 1.875% of the consideration received by the particular corporation for the issue of the share, and

(c) in any other case, nil; and

B is

(a) if the original acquisition of the share was before March 6, 1996, the number obtained when the number of whole years throughout which the share was outstanding before the particular time is subtracted from five, and

(b) in any other case, the number obtained when the number of whole years throughout which the share was outstanding is subtracted from eight.

Related Provisions: 204.8(2) — Determining when an RLSVCC discontinues its business; 204.81(8.3)(b) — 204.841 does not apply to provincial LSVCC that deregisters after province cancels credit program.

Notes: 204.841 added by 1999 Budget, effective for businesses discontinued after February 16, 1999.

Definitions [s. 204.841]: "amount", "business" — 248(1); "corporation" — 248(1), *Interpretation Act* 35(1); "discontinues" — 204.8(2); "original acquisition" — 127.4(1), 204.8(1); "registered labour-sponsored venture capital corporation" — 248(1); "revoked corporation" — 204.8(1); "share" — 248(1); "taxation year" — 249.

Forms: T2152 Sched. 2: Calculating tax under subsecs. 204.82(3) and (6) and s. 204.841.

204.85 (1) Dissolution of federally registered LSVCCs — A

registered labour-sponsored venture capital corporation or a revoked corporation that has issued any Class A shares shall send written notification of any proposed amalgamation, merger, liquidation or dissolution of the corporation to the Minister at least 30 days before the amalgamation, merger, liquidation or dissolution, as the case may be.

Notes: 204.85(1) amended by 1999 Budget, effective for amalgamations, mergers, liquidations and dissolutions that occur after July 29, 2000. It previously prohibited such amalgamation, liquidation, etc., without written permission of the Minister of Finance.

204.85 renumbered as 204.85(1) effective for taxation years that end after February 19, 1997 to accommodate the introduction of 204.85(2), and amended effective August 1997, both by 1997 Budget.

(2) Dissolution of other LSVCCs — Where

(a) an amount (other than interest on an amount to which this subsection applies or an amount payable under or as a consequence of a prescribed provision of a law of a province) is payable to the government of a province by a corporation,

(b) the amount is payable as a consequence of the amalgamation or merger of the corporation with another corporation, the winding-up or dissolution of the corporation or the corporation ceasing to be registered under a law of the province,

(c) the corporation has been prescribed for the purpose of the definition "approved share" in subsection 127.4(1), and

(d) the corporation is not a registered labour-sponsored venture capital corporation or a revoked corporation,

the corporation shall pay a tax under this Part for the taxation year in which the amount became payable equal to that amount.

Notes: 204.85(2) added by 1997 Budget, effective for taxation years that end after February 19, 1997.

(3) Amalgamations and mergers — For the purposes of sec-

tion 127.4, this Part and Part XII.5, where two or more corporations (each of which is referred to in this subsection as a "predecessor corporation") amalgamate or merge to form one corporate entity (in this subsection referred to as the "new corporation") and at least one of the predecessor corporations was, immediately before the amalgamation or merger, a registered labour-sponsored venture capital corporation or a revoked corporation,

(a) subject to paragraphs (d) and (e), the new corporation is deemed to be the same corporation as, and a continuation of, each predecessor corporation;

(b) where a predecessor corporation was authorized to issue a class of shares to which clause 204.81(1)(c)(ii)(C) applies, the new corporation is deemed to have received approval from the Minister of Finance to issue substantially similar shares at the time of the amalgamation or merger;

(c) where a share of a predecessor corporation (in this paragraph referred to as the "predecessor share") is replaced on the amalgamation or merger by a new share of the new corporation,

(i) the new share

(A) is deemed not to have been issued on the amalgamation or merger, and

(B) is deemed to have been issued by the new corporation at the time the predecessor corporation issued the predecessor share, and

(ii) if the new share was issued to a person who acquired the predecessor share as a consequence of a transfer the registration of which by the predecessor corporation was permitted under paragraph 204.81(1)(c), the issuance of the new share is deemed to be in compliance with the conditions described in paragraph 204.81(1)(c);

(d) the Minister is deemed to have registered the new corporation for the purposes of this Part unless

(i) the new corporation is not governed by the *Canada Business Corporations Act*,

(ii) one or more of the predecessor corporations was a registered labour-sponsored venture capital corporation the venture capital business of which was discontinued before the amalgamation or merger,

(iii) one or more of the predecessor corporations was, immediately before the amalgamation or merger, a revoked corporation,

(iv) immediately after the amalgamation or merger, the articles of the new corporation do not comply with paragraph 204.81(1)(c),

(v) shares other than Class A shares of the capital stock of the new corporation were issued to any shareholder of the new corporation in satisfaction of any share (other than a share to which clause 204.81(1)(c)(ii)(B) or (C) applied) of a predecessor corporation, or

(vi) immediately before the amalgamation or merger, one or more of the predecessor corporations is a corporation that has given notification under subsection 204.81(8.3) and one or more of the predecessor corporations is a registered labour-sponsored venture capital corporation that has not given notification under that subsection;

(e) where paragraph (d) does not apply, the new corporation is deemed to be a revoked corporation;

(f) subsection 204.82(1) does not apply to the new corporation; and

(g) subsection 204.82(2) shall, in its application to the new corporation, be read without reference to the words "that begins after the end of the corporation's start-up period (or, where the corporation has no start-up period, that begins after the time the corporation first issues a Class A share)".

Related Provisions: 87 — General rules for amalgamations; 127.4(1.1) — Rule applies to labour-sponsored funds tax credit; 204.8(1) "terminating corporation" — Definition; 211.7(2) — Effect of amalgamation on Part XII.5 tax; 211.8(1.1) — Rule applies to 211.8(1).

Notes: See Notes to 204.8(1) "terminating corporation".

For rulings that transactions are a "merger" for 204.85(3) see VIEWS docs 2006-0171471R3, 2006-0184981R3, 2008-0286001R3, 2009-0315031R3, 2010-0381371R3, 2011-0412341R3.

204.85(3)(d)(vi) added by 2014 budget bill #1, effective Nov. 27, 2013.

204.85(3) added by 1999 budget, for amalgamations and mergers after Feb. 16, 1999.

Definitions [s. 204.85]: "amount", "business" — 248(1); "Canada" — 255, *Interpretation Act* 35(1); "class of shares" — 248(6); "corporation" — 248(1), *Interpretation Act* 35(1); "Minister" — 248(1); "Minister of Finance" — *Financial Administration*

Act 14; "prescribed" — 248(1); "province" — Interpretation Act 35(1); "registered labour-sponsored venture capital corporation" — 248(1); "revoked corporation" — 204.8(1); "share", "shareholder" — 248(1); "start-up period" — 204.8(1); "taxation year" — 249; "written" — Interpretation Act 35(1)"writing".

204.86 (1) Return and payment of tax for federally-registered LSVCCs — Every registered labour-sponsored venture capital corporation and every revoked corporation shall

(a) on or before its filing-due date for a taxation year, file with the Minister a return for the year under this Part in prescribed form and containing prescribed information, without notice or demand therefor;

(b) estimate in the return the amount of tax and penalties, if any, payable under this Part by it for the year; and

(c) on or before its balance-due day for the year, pay to the Receiver General the amount of tax and penalties, if any, payable under this Part by it for the year.

Related Provisions: 150.1(5) — Electronic filing.

Notes: 204.86(1)(c) amended by 2003 Budget to require payment on the "balance-due day" (as defined in 248(1)), effective for taxation years that begin after June 2003.

204.86 renumbered as 204.86(1) by 1997 Budget (and amended to use the new term "filing-due date", with no substantive change), effective February 19, 1997, to accommodate the introduction of 204.86(2).

Forms: T2152: Part X.3 tax return for an LSVCC; T2152 Sched. 1: Calculating tax under subsec. 204.82(2); T2152 Sched. 2: Calculating tax under subsecs. 204.82(3) and (6) and s. 204.841; T2152A: Part X.3 tax return and request for a refund for an LSVCC.

(2) Return and payment of tax for other LSVCCs — Where tax is payable under this Part for a taxation year by a corporation because of subsection 204.82(5) or 204.85(2), the corporation shall

(a) on or before its filing-due date for the year, file with the Minister a return for the year under this Part in prescribed form and containing prescribed information, without notice or demand therefor;

(b) estimate in the return the amount of tax payable under this Part by it for the year; and

(c) on or before its balance-due day for the year, pay to the Receiver General the amount of tax payable under this Part by it for the year.

Related Provisions: 150.1(5) — Electronic filing.

Notes: 204.86(2)(c) amended by 2003 Budget to require payment on the "balance-due day" (as defined in 248(1)), effective for taxation years that begin after June 2003.

204.86(2) added by 1997 Budget, effective February 19, 1997.

Forms [subsec. 204.86(2)]: T2152: Part X.3 tax return for an LSVCC; T2152 Sched. 1: Calculating tax under subsec. 204.82(2); T2152 Sched. 2: Calculating tax under subsecs. 204.82(3) and (6) and s. 204.841; T2152A: Part X.3 tax return and request for a refund for an LSVCC.

Definitions [s. 204.86]: "amount", "balance-due day" — 248(1); "corporation" — 248(1), Interpretation Act 35(1); "filing-due date", "Minister", "prescribed", "registered labour-sponsored venture capital corporation" — 248(1); "revoked corporation" — 204.8(1); "taxation year" — 249.

204.87 Provisions applicable to Part — Subsection 150(3), sections 152 and 158, subsections 161(1) and (11), sections 162 to 164 and 165 to 167, Division J of Part I and section 227.1 apply to this Part, with such modifications as the circumstances require.

Notes [Part X.3]: Part X.3 (204.8–204.87) added by 1991 technical bill, effective 1989.

PART X.4 — TAX IN RESPECT OF OVERPAYMENTS TO REGISTERED EDUCATION SAVINGS PLANS

204.9 (1) Definitions — The definitions in this subsection apply in this Part.

"excess amount" for a year at any time in respect of an individual means

(a) for years before 2007, the amount, if any, by which the total of all contributions made after February 20, 1990 in the year and before that time into all registered education savings plans by or on behalf of all subscribers in respect of the individual exceeds the lesser of

(i) the RESP annual limit for the year; and

(ii) the amount, if any, by which the RESP lifetime limit for the year exceeds the total of all contributions made into registered education savings plans by or on behalf of all subscribers in respect of the individual in all preceding years; and

(b) for years after 2006, the amount, if any, by which the total of all contributions made in the year and before that time into all registered education savings plans by or on behalf of all subscribers in respect of the individual exceeds the amount, if any, by which

(i) the RESP lifetime limit for the year exceeds

(ii) the total of all contributions made into registered education savings plans by or on behalf of all subscribers in respect of the individual in all preceding years.

Related Provisions: 146.1(2)(k) — Limit on annual RESP contributions; 204.9(2)(a) — Where agreement entered into before February 21, 1990.

Notes: Definition amended by 2007 budget bill #1, effectively to add para. (b), effective for determining tax under Part X.4 for months that are after 2006. The lifetime limit is now $50,000. For CRA interpretation see VIEWS doc 2013-047636117 (application where beneficiary is replaced).

"Excess amount" amended by 1997 Budget, effective for determining Part X.4 tax for months that are after 1996.

Paras. (a) and (b) amended by 1996 Budget, effective for months that end after 1995. For initial enactment see Notes after 204.93.

Registered Plans Compliance Bulletins: 1 (educational assistance payments (EAP) and RESP contributions).

"RESP lifetime limit" for a year means

(a) for 1990 to 1995, $31,500;

(b) for 1996 to 2006, $42,000; and

(c) for 2007 and subsequent years, $50,000.

Notes: Para. (b) amended (to stop at 2006) and para. (c) added, by 2007 budget bill #1, effective for determining tax under Part X.4 for months that are after 2006.

"RESP lifetime limit" added by 1997 Budget, effective for determining Part X.4 tax for months that are after 1996.

Registered Plans Compliance Bulletins: 1 (educational assistance payments (EAP) and RESP contributions).

"subscriber's gross cumulative excess" at any time in respect of an individual means the total of all amounts each of which is the subscriber's share of the excess amount for a relevant year at that time in respect of the individual and, for the purpose of this definition, a relevant year at any time is a year that began before that time.

Notes: "Subscriber's gross cumulative excess" added by 1997 Budget, effective for determining Part X.4 tax for months that are after 1996.

"subscriber's share of the excess amount" for a year at any time in respect of an individual means the amount determined by the formula

$$(A/B) \times C$$

where

A is the total of all contributions made after February 20, 1990, in the year and before that time into all registered education savings plans by or on behalf of the subscriber in respect of the individual;

B is the total of all contributions made after February 20, 1990, in the year and before that time into all registered education savings plans by or on behalf of all subscribers in respect of the individual; and

C is the excess amount for the year at that time in respect of the individual.

Related Provisions: 204.9(2)(b) — Agreement entered into before Feb. 21, 1990.

Notes: "Subscriber's share of the excess amount" amended by 1997 Budget, effective for determining Part X.4 tax for months that are after 1996, to add "after February 20, 1990" in the descriptions of A and B.

For initial enactment see Notes to 204.93.

(1.1) Application of subsec. 146.1(1) — The definitions in subsection 146.1(1) apply to this Part.

Notes: 204.9(1.1) added in revised version of 1991 technical bill that is consistent with the R.S.C. (5th Supp.) consolidation. This rule was formerly contained in the opening words of 146.1(1).

(2) Agreements before February 21, 1990 — Where a subscriber is required, pursuant to an agreement in writing entered into before February 21, 1990, to make payments of specified amounts on a periodic basis into a registered education savings plan in respect of a beneficiary, and the subscriber makes at least one payment under the agreement before that day,

(a) the excess amount for a year in respect of the beneficiary shall be deemed not to exceed the excess amount for the year that would be determined under subsection (1) if the total of all such payments made in the year and, where the agreement so provides, amounts paid in the year in satisfaction of the requirement to make such payments under all such agreements by all such subscribers in respect of the beneficiary were equal to the lesser of the amounts described in paragraphs (a) and (b) of the definition "excess amount" in subsection (1); and

(b) in determining a subscriber's share of an excess amount for a year, any payment included in the total described in paragraph (a) in respect of the year shall be excluded in determining the values for A and B in the definition "subscriber's share of the excess amount" in subsection (1).

(3) Refunds from unregistered plans — For the purposes of subsection (1) and section 146.1, where an individual entered into an education savings plan before February 21, 1990, pursuant to a preliminary prospectus issued by a promoter, and the promoter refunds all payments made into the plan and all income accrued thereon to the individual, each payment made by the individual into a registered education savings plan before December 31, 1990 shall be deemed to be a payment made before February 21, 1990, to the extent that the total of all such payments does not exceed the amount so refunded to the individual.

(4) New beneficiary — For the purposes of this Part, if at any particular time an individual (in this subsection referred to as the "new beneficiary") becomes a beneficiary under a registered education savings plan in place of another individual (in this subsection referred to as the "former beneficiary") who ceased at or before the particular time to be a beneficiary under the plan,

(a) except as provided by paragraph (b), each contribution made at an earlier time by or on behalf of a subscriber into the plan in respect of the former beneficiary is deemed also to have been made at that earlier time in respect of the new beneficiary;

(b) except for the purpose of applying this subsection to a replacement of a beneficiary after the particular time, applying subsection (5) to a distribution after the particular time and applying subsection 204.91(3) to events after the particular time, paragraph (a) does not apply as a consequence of the replacement at the particular time of the former beneficiary if

(i) the new beneficiary had not attained 21 years of age before the particular time and a parent of the new beneficiary was a parent of the former beneficiary, or

(ii) both beneficiaries were connected by blood relationship or adoption to an original subscriber under the plan and neither had attained 21 years of age before the particular time; and

(c) except where paragraph (b) applies, each contribution made by or on behalf of a subscriber under the plan in respect of the former beneficiary under the plan is, without affecting the determination of the amount withdrawn from the plan in respect of the new beneficiary, deemed to have been withdrawn at the particular time from the plan to the extent that it was not withdrawn before the particular time.

Related Provisions: 251(6) — Connected by blood relationship, etc.

Notes: 204.9(4)(b)(ii) added by 1998 Budget, effective for replacements of beneficiaries that occur after 1997.

204.9(4) amended by 1997 Budget, effective for replacements of beneficiaries and distributions that occur after 1996.

For initial enactment see Notes after 204.93.

(5) Transfers between plans — For the purposes of this Part, if property held by a trust governed by a registered education savings plan (in this subsection referred to as the "transferor plan") is distributed at a particular time to a trust governed by another registered education savings plan (in this subsection referred to as the "transferee plan"),

(a) except as provided by paragraphs (b) and (c), the amount of the distribution is deemed not to have been contributed into the transferee plan;

(b) subject to paragraph (c), each contribution made at any earlier time by or on behalf of a subscriber into the transferor plan in respect of a beneficiary under the transferor plan is deemed also to have been made at that earlier time by the subscriber in respect of each beneficiary under the transferee plan;

(c) except for the purpose of applying this subsection to a distribution after the particular time, applying subsection (4) to a replacement of a beneficiary after the particular time and applying subsection 204.91(3) to events after the particular time, paragraph (b) does not apply as a consequence of the distribution where

(i) any beneficiary under the transferee plan was, immediately before the particular time, a beneficiary under the transferor plan, or

(ii) a parent of a beneficiary under the transferee plan was a parent of an individual who was, immediately before the particular time, a beneficiary under the transferor plan and

(A) the transferee plan is a plan that allows more than one beneficiary under the plan at any one time, or

(B) in any other case, the beneficiary under the transferee plan had not attained 21 years of age at the time the transferee plan was entered into;

(d) where subparagraph (c)(i) or (ii) applies in respect of the distribution, the amount of the distribution is deemed not to have been withdrawn from the transferor plan; and

(e) each subscriber under the transferor plan is deemed to be a subscriber under the transferee plan.

Related Provisions: 146.1(2)(g.2), (i.2) — Restrictions on transfers between RESPs; 146.1(6.1) — Effect of transfers between RESPs.

Notes: 204.9(5)(c)(ii) amended by 2011 budget bill #2, for property transferred after 2010, effectively to add cl. (A). This implements a Budget proposal to provide subscribers of separate individual plans with the same flexibility to allocate assets among siblings as exists for subscribers of family plans, without tax penalties and without triggering the repayment of Canada Education Savings Grants. The *Canada Education Savings Regulations* were amended to give effect to the CESGs change.

204.9(5) added by 1997 Budget, effective for replacements of beneficiaries and distributions that occur after 1996.

Definitions [s. 204.9]: "adoption" — 251(6)(c); "amount" — 248(1); "beneficiary" — 146.1(1), 204.9(1.1); "blood relationship" — 251(6)(a); "connected" — 251(6); "contribution" — 146.1(1), 204.9(1.1); "excess amount" — 204.9(1); "individual" — 248(1); "parent" — 252(2)(a); "property" — 248(1); "registered education savings plan" — 146.1(1), 204.9(1.1), 248(1); "RESP annual limit" — 146.1(1), 204.9(1.1); "RESP lifetime limit" — 204.9(1); "share" — 248(1); "subscriber" — 146.1(1), 204.9(1.1); "subscriber's share of the excess amount" — 204.9(1); "trust" — 146.1(1), 204.9(1.1); "writing" — *Interpretation Act* 35(1).

204.91 (1) Tax payable by subscribers — Every subscriber under a registered education savings plan shall pay a tax under this

Part in respect of each month equal to 1% of the amount, if any, by which

(a) the total of all amounts each of which is the subscriber's gross cumulative excess at the end of the month in respect of an individual

exceeds

(b) the total of all amounts each of which is the portion of such an excess that has been withdrawn from a registered education savings plan before the end of the month.

Notes: 204.91 amended and renumbered as 204.91(1) by 1997 Budget, effective for determining Part X.4 tax for months that are after 1996.

For initial enactment see Notes after 204.93.

Regulations: 103(8) (withholding of tax at source).

(2) Waiver of tax — If a subscriber under a registered education savings plan would, but for this subsection, be required to pay a tax in respect of a month under subsection (1) in respect of an individual, the Minister may waive or cancel all or part of the tax where it is just and equitable to do so having regard to all the circumstances, including

(a) whether the tax arose as a consequence of reasonable error;

(b) whether, as a consequence of one or more transactions or events to which subsection 204.9(4) or (5) applies, the tax is excessive; and

(c) the extent to which further contributions could be made into registered education savings plans in respect of the individual before the end of the month without causing additional tax to be payable under this Part if this Part were read without reference to this subsection.

Notes: For the meaning of "just and equitable", see Notes to 85(7.1).

204.91(2) added by 1997 Budget, effective for determining Part X.4 tax for months that are after January 1990.

(3) Marriage [or common-law partnership] breakdown — If at any time an individual (in this subsection referred to as the "former subscriber") ceases to be a subscriber under a registered education savings plan as a consequence of the settlement of rights arising out of, or on the breakdown of, the marriage or common-law partnership of the former subscriber and another individual (in this subsection referred to as the "current subscriber") who is a subscriber under the plan immediately after that time, for the purpose of determining tax payable under this Part in respect of a month that ends after that time, each contribution made before that time into the plan by or on behalf of the former subscriber is deemed to have been made into the plan by the current subscriber and not by or on behalf of the former subscriber.

Notes: 204.91(3) amended by 2000 same-sex partners bill to refer to "common-law partnership", effective as per Notes to 248(1)"common-law partner".

204.91(3) added by 1997 Budget, effective for determining Part X.4 tax for months that are after 1997.

(4) Deceased subscribers — For the purpose of applying this section where a subscriber has died, the subscriber's estate is deemed to be the same person as, and a continuation of, the subscriber for each month that ends after the death.

Notes: 204.91(4) added by 1997 Budget, effective for determining Part X.4 tax for months that are after 1997.

Related Provisions [s. 204.91]: 18(1)(t) — Tax is non-deductible.

Definitions [s. 204.91]: "amount", "common-law partnership" — 248(1); "contribution" — 146.1(1), 204.9(1.1); "estate" — 104(1), 248(1); "individual", "Minister" — 248(1); "month" — *Interpretation Act* 35(1); "person" — 248(1); "registered education savings plan" — 146.1(1), 204.9(1.1), 248(1); "subscriber" — 146.1(1), 204.9(1.1); "subscriber's gross cumulative excess" — 204.9(1).

204.92 Return and payment of tax — Every person who is liable to pay tax under this Part in respect of a month in a year shall, within 90 days after the end of the year,

(a) file with the Minister a return for the year under this Part in prescribed form and containing prescribed information, without notice or demand therefor;

(b) estimate in the return the amount of tax, if any, payable under this Part by the person in respect of each month in the year; and

(c) pay to the Receiver General the amount of tax, if any, payable by the person under this Part in respect of each month in the year.

Related Provisions: 150.1(5) — Electronic filing; *Interpretation Act* 27(5) — Meaning of "within 90 days".

Notes: Due to COVID-19, Part X.4 tax owing from March 18-Sept. 29, 2020 was due on Sept. 30, 2020: see PITA 59th ed. at 150(1) opening words.

Definitions [s. 204.92]: "amount", "Minister" — 248(1); "month" — *Interpretation Act* 35(1); "person", "prescribed" — 248(1).

Regulations: 103(8) (withholding of tax at source).

Forms: T1E-OVP: Individual tax return for RESP excess contributions.

204.93 Provisions applicable to Part — Subsections 150(2) and (3), sections 152, 158 and 159, subsections 161(1) and (11), sections 162 to 167 and Division J of Part I are applicable to this Part, with such modifications as the circumstances require.

Notes [Part X.4]: Part X.4 (204.9-204.93) added by 1990 Budget, effective Feb. 1990.

PART X.5 — PAYMENTS UNDER REGISTERED EDUCATION SAVINGS PLANS

204.94 (1) Definitions — The definitions in subsection 146.1(1) apply for the purposes of this Part, except that the definition "subscriber" in that subsection shall be read without reference to paragraph (c).

Notes: See Notes at end of 204.94.

(2) Charging provision — Every person (other than a public primary caregiver that is exempt from tax under Part I) shall pay a tax under this Part for each taxation year equal to the amount determined by the formula

$$(A + B - C) \times D$$

where

A is the total of all amounts each of which is an accumulated income payment made at any time that is

(a) either

(i) under a registered education savings plan under which the person is a subscriber at that time, or

(ii) under a registered education savings plan under which there is no subscriber at that time, where the person has been a spouse or common-law partner of an individual who was a subscriber under the plan, and

(b) included in computing the person's income under Part I for the year;

B is the total of all amounts each of which is an accumulated income payment that is

(a) not included in the value of A in respect of the person for the year, and

(b) included in computing the person's income under Part I for the year;

C is the lesser of

(a) the lesser of the value of A in respect of the person for the year and the total of all amounts each of which is an amount deducted under subsection 146(5) or (5.1) in computing the person's income under Part I for the year, and

(b) the amount, if any, by which $50,000 exceeds the total of all amounts each of which is an amount determined under paragraph (a) in respect of the person for a preceding taxation year; and

D is

(a) where a tax, similar to the tax provided under this Part, is payable by the person for the year under a law of the province of Quebec, 12%, and

(b) in any other case, 20%.

Related Provisions: 146(21.1) — Contribution to Saskatchewan Pension Plan deemed to be RRSP premium for purposes of Part X.5; 147.5(11) — Pooled registered pension plan contribution deemed to be RRSP premium for purposes of C(a); 156.1(1)"net tax owing"A — Part X.5 tax included in determining instalments; 257 — Formula cannot calculate to less than zero.

Notes: See Notes at end of 204.94.

204.94(2) opening words amended to add "(other than a public primary caregiver that is exempt from tax under Part I)" by 2002-2013 technical bill (Part 5 — technical), for 2007 and later taxation years. See 146.1(1)"public primary caregiver". This implements a Jan. 7/08 Finance comfort letter to Human Resources & Social Development Canada.

204.94(2)A(a)(ii) amended by 2000 same-sex partners bill to refer to "common-law partner", effective as per Notes to 248(1)"common-law partner".

Formula in 204.94(2) amended by 1998 Budget to change "0.2" to "D" and add description for D, effective for 1998 and later taxation years. The rate is 12% instead of 20% in Quebec because Quebec imposes its own 8% tax (*Taxation Act* s. 1129.64).

204.94(2)C(b) amended by 1998 Budget to change $40,000 to $50,000, effective for 1999 and later taxation years.

Regulations: 103(8) (withholding of 20% at source).

(3) Return and payment of tax — Every person who is liable to pay tax under this Part for a taxation year shall, on or before the person's filing-due date for the year,

(a) file with the Minister a return for the year under this Part in prescribed form and containing prescribed information, without notice or demand therefor;

(b) estimate in the return the amount of tax payable under this Part by the person for the year; and

(c) pay to the Receiver General the amount of tax payable under this Part by the person for the year.

Related Provisions: 156.1(1)"net tax owing"(b)A — Part X.5 tax included in calculation of instalment threshold.

Notes: See Notes at end of 204.94. Due to COVID-19, Part X.5 tax owing from March 18-Sept. 29, 2020 was due on Sept. 30, 2020: see PITA 59th ed. at 150(1) opening words.

(4) Administrative rules — Subsections 150(2) and (3), sections 152, 155 to 156.1 and 158 to 167 and Division J of Part I apply with any modifications that the circumstances require.

Related Provisions: 156.1(1)"net tax owing"(b)A — Part X.5 tax included in calculation of instalment threshold.

Notes: 204.94 added by 1997 Budget, for 1998 and later tax years. It imposes a special 20% tax on "accumulated income payments" from RESPs. This tax can generally be reduced to the extent the recipient makes deductible RRSP contributions under 146(5) or (5.1) for the year in which the payment is made. The purpose of this tax is to discourage the use of RESPs strictly for their tax deferral advantages, particularly by individuals who already maximize their tax savings through RRSP contributions. See also Notes at end of 146.1; and VIEWS doc 2012-0466091E5.

Part X.5 tax applies to pre-1990 RESPs, even though it was not introduced until 1998. This is an intentional response to those who used RESPs solely for tax deferral: VIEWS doc 2006-0182811E5.

Regulations: 103(8) (withholding of 20% at source).

Definitions [s. 204.94]: "accumulated income payment" — 146.1(1), 204.94(1); "amount", "common-law partner", "filing-due date", "individual", "Minister", "person", "prescribed" — 248(1); "public primary caregiver" — 146.1(1); "registered education savings plan" — 146.1(1), 204.94(1), 248(1); "subscriber" — 204.94; "tax payable" — 248(2); "taxation year" — 249.

PART XI — TAX IN RESPECT OF ADVANCED LIFE DEFERRED ANNUITY

205. (1) Definitions — The following definitions apply in this section.

"ALDA dollar limit", for a calendar year, means

(a) for 2020, $150,000; and

(b) for each year after 2020, the amount (rounded to the nearest multiple of $10,000, or if that amount is equidistant from two such consecutive multiples, to the higher multiple) that is equal to $150,000 adjusted for each year after 2020 in the manner set out in section 117.1.

Related Provisions: 205(1)"cumulative excess amount"A(b)D, 205(2) — Exceeding dollar limit triggers tax.

Notes: Indexing from 2020 to 2021 is 1.0%, so the $150,000 is indexed to $151,500, which rounded to the nearest $10,000 is still $150,000.

"cumulative excess amount", of an individual at any particular time in a calendar year, means the amount determined by the formula

$$A - B$$

where

A is the greater of

(a) the total of all amounts each of which is an excess ALDA transfer of the individual at or before the particular time, and

(b) the amount determined by the formula

$$C - D$$

where

C is the total of all amounts each of which is the amount of a transfer at or before the particular time to acquire an advanced life deferred annuity on behalf of the individual, and

D is the ALDA dollar limit for the calendar year; and

B is the total of all amounts each of which is the amount of a refund described in paragraph (g) of the definition "advanced life deferred annuity" in subsection 146.5(1) made at or before the particular time on behalf of the individual.

Related Provisions: 205(2) — Tax on cumulative excess amount; 257 — Formula cannot calculate to less than zero.

"excess ALDA transfer", of an individual, means the portion of the amount of a transfer, made from a transferor plan under any of subsections 146(16) and 146.3(14.1) and paragraphs 147(19)(d), 147.3(1)(c) and 147.5(21)(c) to acquire an advanced life deferred annuity on behalf of the individual, determined by the formula

$$A - B$$

where

A is the amount of the transfer; and

B is the amount determined by the formula

$$0.25(C + D) - E$$

where

C is the total value of the property held for the benefit of the individual under the transferor plan at the end of the calendar year preceding the calendar year in which the transfer is made, other than

(a) if the transferor plan is a registered pension plan, property held in connection with

(i) a "defined benefit provision" (as defined in subsection 147.1(1)) of the transferor plan, or

(ii) a VPLA fund, as described in subsection 8506(13) of the *Income Tax Regulations*,

(b) if the transferor plan is a pooled registered pension plan, property held in connection with benefits that would be described in paragraph 147.5(5)(a) if the reference in that paragraph to "8506(1)(e.1) or (e.2)" were read as a reference to "8506(1)(e.2)",

(c) if the transferor plan is a registered retirement income fund, contracts for annuities held in connection with the fund other than annuities described in paragraph (b.1) of the definition "qualified investment" in subsection 146.3(1), and

(d) if the transferor plan is a registered retirement savings plan, contracts for annuities held in connection with the plan other than annuities described in paragraph (c.1) of the definition "qualified investment" in subsection 146(1),

D   is the total of all amounts each of which is the amount transferred from the transferor plan, in a calendar year preceding the calendar year in which the transfer is made, to acquire an advanced life deferred annuity on behalf of the individual, and

E   is the total of all amounts each of which is the amount of a previous transfer from the transferor plan to acquire an advanced life deferred annuity on behalf of the individual.

Related Provisions: 205(1)"cumulative excess amount" — Amount to which tax applies; 205(2) — Tax on excess transfer; 257 — Formula cannot calculate to less than zero.

(2) Tax payable by individuals — If at the end of any month an individual has a cumulative excess amount, the individual shall, in respect of that month, pay a tax under this Part equal to 1% of that cumulative excess amount.

Related Provisions: 205(3) — Waiver of tax; 206(1) — Obligation to file return and report tax.

Notes: 205(2) imposes a 1% monthly tax (informally called a "penalty tax") on excessive transfers to an ALDA (205(1)"cumulative excess amount"). CRA can waive it: 205(3). If a return under 206(1) is not filed, there is no deadline for CRA to assess the tax: see Notes to 204.2(1.1).

(3) Waiver of tax — If an individual would, but for this subsection, be required to pay a tax under subsection (2) in respect of a month, the Minister may waive or cancel all or part of the tax if the individual establishes to the satisfaction of the Minister that

(a) the cumulative excess amount on which the tax is based arose as a consequence of reasonable error; and

(b) reasonable steps are being taken to eliminate the cumulative excess amount.

Notes: See 204.1(4) Notes re waiver of the similar RRSP overcontributions tax.

Notes [s. 205]: See Notes at end of s. 206.

Definitions [s. 205]: "ALDA dollar limit — 205(1); "advanced life deferred annuity" — 146.5(1), 248(1); "amount", "annuity" — 248(1); "calendar year" — *Interpretation Act* 37(1)(a); "cumulative excess amount" — 205(1); "defined benefit provision" — 147.1(1); "excess ALDA transfer" — 205(1); "individual", "Minister" — 248(1); "month" — *Interpretation Act* 35(1); "pooled registered pension plan" — 147.5(1), 248(1); "property" — 248(1); "qualified investment" — 146(1), 146.3(1); "registered pension plan" — 248(1); "registered retirement income fund" — 146.3(1), 248(1); "registered retirement savings plan" — 146(1), 248(1); "VPLA fund" — Reg. 8506(13).

206. (1) Return and payment of tax — Every person who is liable to pay tax under this Part for all or part of a calendar year shall,

(a) on or before the person's filing-due date for the year, file with the Minister a return for the year under this Part in prescribed form and containing prescribed information, without notice or demand; and

(b) on or before the person's balance-due day for the year, pay to the Receiver General the amount of tax payable under this Part by the person for the year.

Notes: See Notes to 206(2).

(2) Provisions applicable to Part — Subsections 150(2) and (3), sections 152 and 158 to 167 and Division J of Part I apply with any modifications that the circumstances require.

Notes: Due to 206(2), the 162(1) penalty, and interest on it under 161(11), apply to failure to file a 206(1) return: see Notes to 162(1).

Notes [s. 206]: Part XI (205, 206) added by 2021 budget bill #1, effective 2020.

Definitions [s. 206]: "amount", "balance-due day" — 248(1); "calendar year" — *Interpretation Act* 37(1)(a); "filing-due date" — 150(1), 248(1); "Minister", "person", "prescribed" — 248(1).

206.1–207 [Repealed]

Notes [former ss. 205-207]: Former Part XI (205-207) repealed by 2017 budget bill #2, for transactions and events occurring, income earned, capital gains accruing and

investments acquired after March 22, 2017. See now 207.01–207.07 instead. They read:

205. (1) Definitions — The following definitions apply in this Part.

"advantage", in relation to a registered disability savings plan, means any benefit or loan that is conditional in any way on the existence of the plan other than

(a) a disability assistance payment;

(b) a contribution made by, or with the written consent of, a holder of the plan;

(c) a transfer in accordance with subsection 146.4(8);

(d) an amount paid under or because of the *Canada Disability Savings Act* or a designated provincial program as defined in subsection 146.4(1);

(e) a benefit derived from the provision of administrative or investment services in respect of the plan; or

(f) a loan

(i) made in the ordinary course of the lender's ordinary business of lending money if, at the time the loan was made, *bona fide* arrangements were made for repayment of the loan within a reasonable time, and

(ii) whose sole purpose was to enable a person to make a contribution to the plan.

Related Provisions [Former 205(1)"advantage"]: 206.2 — Tax on advantage; 207.5(1)"advantage" — Parallel definition for RCA.

Notes [Former 205(1)"advantage"]: See VIEWS docs 2009-0319871I7 (RDSP paying doctor's fee to complete Form T2201 is an "advantage"); 2009-0322761I7 (whether certain undisclosed promotions are an advantage).

Para. (d) changed from "an amount paid under the *Canadian Disability Savings Act*" by 2010 budget bill #1, effective for 2009 and later taxation years.

"allowable refund" of a person for a calendar year means the total of all amounts each of which is a refund to which the person is entitled under subsection 206.1(4) for the year.

Related Provisions [Former 205(1)"allowable refund"]: 207(2) — Refund of allowable refund.

"benefit", in relation to a registered disability savings plan, includes any payment or allocation of an amount to the plan that is represented to be a return on investment in respect of property held by the plan trust, but which cannot reasonably be considered, having regard to all the circumstances, to be on terms and conditions that would apply to a similar transaction in an open market between parties dealing with each other at arm's length and acting prudently, knowledgeably and willingly.

Related Provisions [Former 205(1)"benefit"]: 206.2(2)(a) — Tax on benefit.

"qualified investment" for a trust governed by a registered disability savings plan means

(a) an investment that would be described by any of paragraphs (a) to (d), (f) and (g) of the definition "qualified investment" in section 204 if the reference in that definition to "a trust governed by a deferred profit sharing plan or revoked plan" were read as a reference to "a trust governed by a registered disability savings plan" and if that definition were read without reference to the words "with the exception of excluded property in relation to the trust";

(b) a contract for an annuity issued by a licensed annuities provider where

(i) the trust is the only person who, disregarding any subsequent transfer of the contract by the trust, is or may become entitled to any annuity payments under the contract, and

(ii) the holder of the contract has a right to surrender the contract at any time for an amount that would, if reasonable sales and administration charges were ignored, approximate the value of funds that could otherwise be applied to fund future periodic payments under the contract;

(c) a contract for an annuity issued by a licensed annuities provider where

(i) annual or more frequent periodic payments are or may be made under the contract to the holder of the contract,

(ii) the trust is the only person who, disregarding any subsequent transfer of the contract by the trust, is or may become entitled to any annuity payments under the contract,

(iii) neither the time nor the amount of any payment under the contract may vary because of the length of any life, other than the life of the beneficiary under the plan,

(iv) the day on which the periodic payments began or are to begin is not later than the end of the later of

(A) the year in which the beneficiary under the plan attains the age of 60 years, and

(B) the year following the year in which the contract was acquired by the trust,

(v) the periodic payments are payable for the life of the beneficiary under the plan and either there is no guaranteed period under the contract or there is a guaranteed period that does not exceed 15 years,

(vi) the periodic payments

    (A) are equal, or

    (B) are not equal solely because of one or more adjustments that would, if the contract were an annuity under a retirement savings plan, be in accordance with subparagraphs 146(3)(b)(iii) to (v) or that arise because of a uniform reduction in the entitlement to the periodic payments as a consequence of a partial surrender of rights to the periodic payments, and

(vii) the contract requires that, in the event the plan must be terminated in accordance with paragraph 146.4(4)(p), any amounts that would otherwise be payable after the termination be commuted into a single payment; and

(d) a prescribed investment.

Related Provisions [Former 205(1)"qualified investment"]: 87(10) — New share issued on amalgamation of public corporation deemed listed; 206.1 — Tax on non-qualified investments; Reg. 221(2) — Information return reporting that securities are qualified investments.

Notes [Former 205(1)"qualified investment"]: Reg. 4900(5) provides that any "registered investment" for RRSP purposes (see 204.4) is a qualified investment (QI). See also lists of QIs in 204"qualified investment" [not all qualify] and Reg. 4900(1).

Regulations [Former 205(1)"qualified investment"]: 4900(1), (5) (prescribed investments for para. (d)).

Income Tax Folios [Former 205(1)"qualified investment"]: S3-F10-C1: Qualified investments — RRSPs, RESPs, RRIFs, RDSPs and TFSAs [replaces IT-320R3].

(2) **Definitions in subsec. 146.4(1)** — The definitions in subsection 146.4(1) apply in this Part.

Notes [Former 205]: 205 added by 2007 RDSPs bill, effective for 2008 and later taxation years.

For pre-2005 s. 205, see Notes after s. 207 up to PITA 36th ed.

Definitions [Former 205]: "amount", "annuity" — 248(1); "arm's length" — 251(1); "benefit" — 205(1); "business" — 248(1); "calendar year" — *Interpretation Act* 37(1)(a); "Canada" — 255, *Interpretation Act* 35(1); "deferred profit sharing plan" — 147(1), 248(1); "designated provincial program" — 146.4(1); "disability assistance payment" — 146.4(1), 205(2); "holder" — 146.4(1), 205(2); "licensed annuities provider" — 147(1), 248(1); "listed" — 87(10); "person" — 248(1); "plan trust" — 146.4(1), 205(2); "prescribed", "property" — 248(1); "registered disability savings plan" — 146.4(1), 248(1); "retirement savings plan" — 146(1), 248(1); "trust" — 104(1), 248(1), (3); "written" — *Interpretation Act* 35(1)"writing".

206. (1) Tax payable where inadequate consideration — A tax is payable under this Part for a calendar year in connection with a registered disability savings plan if, in the year, a trust governed by the plan

(a) disposes of property for consideration less than the fair market value of the property at the time of the disposition, or for no consideration; or

(b) acquires property for consideration greater than the fair market value of the property at the time of the acquisition.

Related Provisions [Former 206(1)]: 206(2) — Amount of tax; 206(4) — Payment of tax by Minister to new plan; 206.4 — Waiver of tax by Minister; 207(1) — Return and payment of tax.

(2) **Amount of tax payable** — The amount of tax payable in respect of each disposition or acquisition described in subsection (1) is

(a) the amount by which the fair market value differs from the consideration; or

(b) if there is no consideration, the amount of the fair market value.

(3) **Liability for tax** — Each person who is a holder of a registered disability savings plan at the time that a tax is imposed under subsection (1) in connection with the plan is jointly and severally, or solidarily, liable to pay the tax.

(4) **Payment of amount collected to RDSP** — Where a tax has been imposed under subsection (1) in connection with a registered disability savings plan of a beneficiary, the Minister may pay all or part of any amount collected in respect of the tax to a trust governed by a registered disability savings plan of the beneficiary (referred to in this subsection as the "current plan") if

(a) it is just and equitable to do so having regard to all circumstances; and

(b) the Minister is satisfied that neither the beneficiary nor any existing holder of the current plan was involved in the transaction that gave rise to the tax.

Related Provisions [Former 206(4)]: 206(5) — Payment deemed not to be a contribution.

Notes [Former 206(4)]: For the meaning of "just and equitable" in para. (a), see Notes to 85(7.1).

(5) **Deemed not to be contribution** — A payment under subsection (4) is deemed not to be a contribution to a registered disability savings plan for the purposes of section 146.4.

Notes [Former 206]: 206 added by 2007 RDSPs bill, effective for 2008 and later taxation years.

For pre-2005 s. 206, see Notes after s. 207 up to PITA 36th ed.

Definitions [Former 206]: "amount" — 248(1); "calendar year" — *Interpretation Act* 37(1)(a); "disposition" — 248(1); "fair market value" — see Notes to 69(1); "holder" — 146.4(1), 205(2); "Minister", "person", "property" — 248(1); "registered disability savings plan" — 146.4(1), 248(1); "trust" — 104(1), 248(1), (3).

206.1 (1) Tax payable on non-qualified investment — A tax is payable under this Part for a calendar year in connection with a registered disability savings plan if, in the year,

(a) the trust governed by the plan acquires property that is not a qualified investment for the trust; or

(b) property held by the trust governed by the plan ceases to be a qualified investment for the trust.

Related Provisions [Former 206.1(1)]: 206.1(2) — Amount of tax; 206.1(4) — Refund of tax on disposition of investment; 206.4 — Waiver of tax by Minister; 207(1) — Return and payment of tax.

(2) **Amount of tax payable** — The amount of tax payable,

(a) in respect of each property described in paragraph (1)(a), is 50% of the fair market value of the property at the time it was acquired by the trust; and

(b) in respect of each property described in paragraph (1)(b), is 50% of the fair market value of the property at the time immediately before the time it ceased to be a qualified investment for the trust.

Income Tax Folios [Former 206.1(2)]: S3-F10-C1: Qualified investments — RRSPs, RESPs, RRIFs, RDSPs and TFSAs [replaces IT-320R3].

(3) **Liability for tax** — Each person who is a holder of a registered disability savings plan at the time that a tax is imposed under subsection (1) in connection with the plan is jointly and severally, or solidarily, liable to pay the tax.

(4) **Refund of tax on disposition of non-qualified investment** — Where in a calendar year a trust governed by a registered disability savings plan disposes of a property in respect of which a tax is imposed under subsection (1), the person or persons who are liable to pay the tax are entitled to a refund for the year of an amount equal to

(a) except where paragraph (b) applies, the lesser of

    (i) the amount of the tax so imposed, and

    (ii) the proceeds of disposition of the property; and

(b) nil,

    (i) if it is reasonable to expect that any of those persons knew or ought to have known at the time the property was acquired by the trust that it was not, or would cease to be, a qualified investment for the trust, or

    (ii) if the property is not disposed of by the trust before the end of the calendar year following the calendar year in which the tax arose, or any later time that the Minister considers reasonable in the circumstances.

Related Provisions [Former 206.1(4)]: 206.1(5) — Apportionment of refund.

(5) **Apportionment of refund** — Where more than one person is entitled to a refund under subsection (4) for a calendar year in respect of the disposition of a property, the total of all amounts so refundable shall not exceed the amount that would be so refundable for the year to any one of those persons in respect of that disposition if that person were the only person entitled to a refund for the year under that subsection in respect of the disposition. If the persons cannot agree as to what portion of the refund each can so claim, the Minister may fix the portions.

(6) **Deemed disposition and reacquisition** — For the purposes of this Act, where at any time property held by a plan trust in respect of which a tax was imposed under subsection (1) subsequently becomes a qualified investment for the trust, the trust is deemed to have disposed of the property at that time for proceeds of disposition equal to its fair market value at that time and to have reacquired it immediately after that time at a cost equal to that fair market value.

Income Tax Folios [Former 206.1(6)]: S3-F10-C1: Qualified investments — RRSPs, RESPs, RRIFs, RDSPs and TFSAs [replaces IT-320R3].

Notes [Former 206.1]: 206.1 added by 2007 RDSPs bill, effective for 2008 and later taxation years.

For pre-2005 s. 206.1, see Notes after s. 207 up to PITA 36th ed.

Definitions [Former 206.1]: "amount" — 248(1); "calendar year" — *Interpretation Act* 37(1)(a); "disposition" — 248(1); "fair market value" — see Notes to 69(1); "holder" — 146.4(1), 205(2); "Minister", "person" — 248(1); "plan trust" — 146.4(1), 205(2); "property" — 248(1); "qualified investment" —

205(1); "registered disability savings plan" — 146.4(1), 248(1); "trust" — 104(1), 248(1), (3).

206.2 (1) Tax payable where advantage extended — A tax is payable under this Part for a calendar year in connection with a registered disability savings plan if, in the year, an advantage in relation to the plan is extended to a person who is, or who does not deal at arm's length with, a beneficiary under, or a holder of, the plan.

Related Provisions [Former 206.2(1)]: 206.2(2) — Amount of tax; 206.4 — Waiver of tax by Minister; 207(1) — Return and payment of tax.

Notes [Former 206.2(1)]: See Notes to 205(1)"advantage".

(2) Amount of tax payable — The amount of tax payable in respect of an advantage described in subsection (1) is

    (a) in the case of a benefit, the fair market value of the benefit; and

    (b) in the case of a loan, the amount of the loan.

(3) Liability for tax — Each person who is a holder of a registered disability savings plan at the time that a tax is imposed under subsection (1) in connection with the plan is jointly and severally, or solidarily, liable to pay the tax. If, however, the advantage is extended by the issuer of the plan or by a person not dealing at arm's length with the issuer, the issuer is liable to pay the tax and not the holders.

Notes [Former 206.2]: 206.2 added by 2007 RDSPs bill, effective for 2008 and later taxation years.

Definitions [Former 206.2]: "advantage" — 205(1); "amount" — 248(1); "arm's length" — 251(1); "benefit" — 205(1); "calendar year" — *Interpretation Act* 37(1)(a); "fair market value" — see Notes to 69(1); "holder" — 146.4(1), 205(2); "person" — 248(1); "registered disability savings plan" — 146.4(1), 248(1).

206.3 (1) Tax payable on use of property as security — Every issuer of a registered disability savings plan shall pay a tax under this Part for a calendar year if, in the year, with the consent or knowledge of the issuer, a trust governed by the plan uses or permits to be used any property held by the trust as security for indebtedness of any kind.

Related Provisions [Former 206.3(1)]: 206.3(2) — Amount of tax; 206.4 — Waiver of tax by Minister; 207(1) — Return and payment of tax.

(2) Amount of tax payable — The amount of tax payable in respect of each property described in subsection (1) is equal to the fair market value of the property at the time the property commenced to be used as security.

Notes [Former 206.3]: 206.3 added by 2007 RDSPs bill, effective for 2008 and later taxation years.

Definitions [Former 206.3]: "amount" — 248(1); "calendar year" — *Interpretation Act* 37(1)(a); "fair market value" — see Notes to 69(1); "property" — 248(1); "registered disability savings plan" — 146.4(1), 248(1); "security" — *Interpretation Act* 35(1); "trust" — 104(1), 248(1), (3).

206.4 Waiver of liability — If a person would otherwise be liable to pay a tax under this Part for a calendar year, the Minister may waive or cancel all or part of the liability where it is just and equitable to do so having regard to all the circumstances, including

    (a) whether the tax arose as a consequence of reasonable error; and

    (b) the extent to which the transaction which gave rise to the tax also gave rise to another tax under this Part.

Notes [Former 206.4]: This rule is parallel to 220(3.1), which applies to interest and penalties. Without 206.4, Part XI tax could not be waived even in extenuating circumstances, since the Act provides no general authority to waive tax. See Notes to 220(3.1) for conditions where waiver may be granted.

For the meaning of "just and equitable", see Notes to 85(7.1).

206.4 added by 2007 RDSPs bill, effective for 2008 and later taxation years.

Definitions [Former 206.4]: "calendar year" — *Interpretation Act* 37(1)(a); "Minister", "person" — 248(1).

Income Tax Folios [Former 206.4]: S3-F10-C1: Qualified investments — RRSPs, RESPs, RRIFs, RDSPs and TFSAs [replaces IT-320R3].

207. (1) Return and payment of tax — Every person who is liable to pay tax under this Part for a calendar year shall within 90 days after the end of the year

    (a) file with the Minister a return for the year under this Part in prescribed form and containing prescribed information including

        (i) an estimate of the amount of tax payable under this Part by the person for the year, and

        (ii) an estimate of the amount of any refund to which the person is entitled under this Part for the year; and

    (b) pay to the Receiver General the amount, if any, by which the amount of the person's tax payable under this Part for the year exceeds the person's allowable refund for the year.

Related Provisions [Former 207(1)]: Interpretation Act 27(5) — Meaning of "within 90 days".

Forms [Former 207(1)]: RC4532: Individual tax return for registered disability savings plan (RDSP).

(2) Refund — Where a person has filed a return under this Part for a calendar year within three years after the end of the year, the Minister

    (a) may, on sending the notice of assessment for the year, refund without application any allowable refund of the person for the year, to the extent that it was not applied against the person's tax payable under paragraph (1)(b); and

    (b) shall, with all due dispatch, make the refund referred to in paragraph (a) after sending the notice of assessment if an application for it has been made in writing by the person within three years after the sending of an original notice of assessment for the year.

Related Provisions [Former 207(2)]: 244(14), (14.1) — Date when notice sent; *Interpretation Act* 27(5) — Meaning of "within three years".

Notes [Former 207(2)]: 207(2)(a) and (b) amended by 2010 budget bill #2, effective Dec. 15, 2010, to change "mailing" to "sending" (3 places), to accommodate electronic notices under 244(14.1).

(3) Multiple holders — Where two or more holders of a registered disability savings plan are jointly and severally, or solidarily, liable with each other to pay a tax under this Part for a calendar year in connection with the plan,

    (a) a payment by any of the holders on account of that tax liability shall to the extent of the payment discharge the joint liability; and

    (b) a return filed by one of the holders as required by this Part for the year is deemed to have been filed by each other holder in respect of the joint liability to which the return relates.

(4) Provisions applicable to Part — Subsections 150(2) and (3), sections 152 and 158 to 167 and Division J of Part I apply to this Part with any modifications that the circumstances require.

Notes [Former 207]: 207 added by 2007 RDSPs bill, effective for 2008 and later taxation years.

Definitions [Former 207]: "allowable refund" — 205(1); "amount", "assessment" — 248(1); "calendar year" — *Interpretation Act* 37(1)(a); "holder" — 146.4(1), 205(2); "Minister", "person", "prescribed" — 248(1); "registered disability savings plan" — 146.4(1), 248(1); "writing" — *Interpretation Act* 35(1).

Earlier Part XI (205-207) repealed by 2005 budget bill #1, for tax years that begin after 2004; but former 206.1 became 207.1(5). Part XI limited the "foreign property" that pension plans, RRSPs, RRIFs and DPSPs could hold to 30% of assets (50% in some cases). Any excess was subject to 1% tax per month.

PART XI.01 — TAXES IN RESPECT OF REGISTERED PLANS

Notes: Heading changed from "Taxes in Respect of RRIFs, RRSPs and TFSAs" by 2017 budget bill #2, effective March 23, 2017 (to apply to RESPs and RDSPs). "RRIFs, RRSPs and" added by 2011 budget bill #2, effective March 23, 2011.

207.01 (1) Definitions — The following definitions and the definitions in subsections 146(1) (other than the definition "benefit"), 146.1(1), 146.2(1), 146.3(1) and 146.4(1) apply in this Part and Part XLIX of the *Income Tax Regulations*.

Notes: 207.01(1) opening words amended by 2017 budget bill #2 to add reference to 146.1(1) and 146.4(1), for transactions and events occurring, income earned, capital gains accruing and investments acquired after March 22, 2017. Generally, Part XI.01 (207.01-207.07) was extended to apply to RESPs and RDSPs in addition to TFSAs, RRSPs and RRIFs.

Opening words earlier amended by 2013 and 2011 budget bills #2, both effective March 23, 2011.

"advantage", in relation to a registered plan, means

    (a) any benefit, loan or indebtedness that is conditional in any way on the existence of the registered plan, other than

        (i) a benefit derived from the provision of administrative or investment services in respect of the registered plan,

        (ii) a loan or an indebtedness (including, in the case of a TFSA, the use of the TFSA as security for a loan or an indebtedness) the terms and conditions of which are terms and conditions that persons dealing at arm's length with each other would have entered into,

        (iii) a payment out of or under the registered plan in satisfaction of all or part of a beneficiary's or controlling individual's interest in the registered plan,

        (iv) the payment or allocation of any amount to the registered plan by the issuer, carrier or promoter, (iv.1) an amount paid under or because of the *Canada Disability Savings Act*, the *Canada Education Savings Act* or under a designated provincial program, and

(v) a benefit provided under an incentive program that is — in a normal commercial or investment context in which parties deal with each other at arm's length and act prudently, knowledgeably and willingly — offered to a broad class of persons, if it is reasonable to conclude that none of the main purposes of the program is to enable a person or partnership to benefit from the exemption from tax under Part I of any amount in respect of the plan;

(b) a benefit that is an increase in the total fair market value of the property held in connection with the registered plan if it is reasonable to consider, having regard to all the circumstances, that the increase is attributable, directly or indirectly, to

(i) a transaction or event or a series of transactions or events that

(A) would not have occurred in a normal commercial or investment context in which parties deal with each other at arm's length and act prudently, knowledgeably and willingly, and

(B) had as one of its main purposes to enable a person or a partnership to benefit from the exemption from tax under Part I of any amount in respect of the registered plan,

(ii) a payment received as, on account or in lieu of, or in satisfaction of, a payment

(A) for services provided by a person who is, or who does not deal at arm's length with, the controlling individual of the registered plan, or

(B) of interest, of a dividend, of rent, of a royalty or of any other return on investment, or of proceeds of disposition, in respect of property (other than property held in connection with the registered plan) held by a person who is, or who does not deal at arm's length with, the controlling individual of the registered plan,

(iii) a swap transaction, or

(iv) specified non-qualified investment income that has not been paid from the registered plan to its controlling individual within 90 days of receipt by the controlling individual of a notice issued by the Minister under subsection 207.06(4);

Proposed Amendment —
207.01(1)"advantage"(b) — Investment management fees paid by taxpayer

Letter from Dept. of Finance, Aug. 26, 2019: Mr. Geoff Trueman, Assistant Commissioner, Legislative Policy and Regulatory Affairs, Canada Revenue Agency

Dear Mr. Trueman:

I am writing in regard to discussions between officials of the Canada Revenue Agency and the Department of Finance Canada regarding the definition "advantage" in subsection 207.01(1) of the *Income Tax Act* (the Act).

Investment management fees of registered plans, such as a Tax-Free Savings Account or a Registered Retirement Savings Plan, are normally expected to be paid using funds from within the plan. If the fees are paid directly by the holder/annuitant using funds outside of the plan, the resulting indirect increase in the value of the plan assets might be viewed as an advantage under the Act, if one of the main purposes is to benefit from the tax-exempt status of the plan.

Even so, we have no tax policy concerns with respect to the payment of investment management fees directly by the annuitant/holder of the registered plan. It is not evident that plan holders are tax-motivated when entering into arrangements to directly pay the investment management fees of their financial service providers. Generally, the direct payment of fees results in either a net loss, or negligible gain, for the plan holder. We are therefore prepared to recommend to the Minister of Finance that the Act be amended to clarify that the payment by a controlling individual (as defined in subsection 207.01(1)) of investment management fees that pertain to a registered plan does not constitute an advantage for the plan.

Specifically, we are prepared to recommend that paragraph (b) of the definition "advantage" in subsection 207.01(1) be amended such that it does not apply to payments by a controlling individual of a registered plan, not exceeding a reasonable amount, of fees described in paragraph 20(1)(bb) of the Act.

We also intend to recommend that the proposed amendment apply in respect of the 2018 and subsequent taxation years.

Thank you for engaging with us on this matter.

Yours sincerely,

Brian Ernewein, Assistant Deputy Minister — Legislation, Tax Policy Branch

Notes: See Notes to definition, below, at "Paying fees".

(c) a benefit that is income (determined without reference to paragraph 82(1)(b)), or a capital gain, that is reasonably attributable, directly or indirectly, to

(i) a prohibited investment in respect of the registered plan or any other registered plan of the controlling individual,

(ii) in the case of a registered plan that is not a TFSA, an amount received by the controlling individual of the registered plan, or by a person who does not deal at arm's length with the controlling individual (if it is reasonable to consider, having regard to all the circumstances, that the amount was paid in relation to, or would not have been paid but for, property held in connection with the registered plan) and the amount was paid as, on account or in lieu of, or in satisfaction of, a payment

(A) for services provided by a person who is, or who does not deal at arm's length with, the controlling individual of the registered plan, or

(B) of interest, of a dividend, of rent, of a royalty or of any other return on investment, or of proceeds of disposition, or

(iii) a deliberate over-contribution;

(d) a registered plan strip in respect of the registered plan; and

(e) a prescribed benefit.

Related Provisions: 135.2(4)(g) — Unit of Cdn Wheat Board Farmers' Trust deemed to be advantage if acquired by TFSA; 207.01(1)"specified distribution"(a)(i) — Distribution attributable to advantage is specified distribution; 207.05 — Tax payable where advantage extended; 207.06(4) — CRA may notify TFSA holder that distribution required within 90 days; 207.5(1)"advantage" — Parallel definition for RCA.

Notes: "Advantage" is defined very broadly, to include any benefit that would not have been received in the open market, a swap transaction ((b)(iii)) and a registered plan strip (para. (d)). An advantage is forfeited to the government by being taxed at 100%: 207.05(2). These rules were introduced for TFSAs in 2009, extended to RRSPs and RRIFs in 2011, and to RESPs and RDSPs in 2017.

In *Louie*, 2019 FCA 255 (leave to appeal denied 2020 CarswellNat 1258 (SCC)), (b)(i) applied to swap transactions (using the market daily low price going into the TFSA and the high coming out, turning $5,000 in Jan. 2009 into $206,000 at year-end), even before (b)(iii) applied. Later years' gains (due to market increases) from the $206,000 were also caught as "indirectly" attributable to the 2009 swaps. See also Notes to 17.1(1) for more on "indirectly".

If a company issues shares to minority shareholders' TFSAs after a freeze, this is an "advantage" under (b)(i): VIEWS docs 2009-0339051R3, 2009-0351931R3. This is still the case after the 2011 amendments: 2015-0574481E5.

Detailed CRA interpretation: see Income Tax Folio S3-F10-C3, with many examples.

Paying plan fees outside the plan was to have been considered an "advantage" starting 2018 (VIEWS doc 2016-0670801C6 [2016 CTF q.5]), but this was deferred, first to 2019 (2017-0722391E5) and then indefinitely pending review by Finance (2018-0779261E5, Folio S3-F10-C3 ¶3.35, 2018-0785021C6 [2018 CTF q.12]). This has now been resolved by the Aug. 26, 2019 comfort letter above.

CRA says that a "TFSA maximizer scheme", using a mortgage investment company to invest in mortgages, with low-dividend MIC shares in an RRSP and high-dividend shares in a TFSA, creates an "advantage": tinyurl.com/tfsa-maximizer (May 13, 2021).

See also VIEWS docs 2012-0437821E5 (transfer of credit union shares); 2012-0438701E5 (paying discretionary dividend to RRSP falls under (b)(i)); 2012-0451801E5 (84(3) deemed dividend on redemption of share is "advantage"; sale of prohibited investment at FMV is not); 2012-0457011E5 (shares of cooperative corp held in RRSP); 2012-0460611E5 (swap of securities between registered plans is advantage); 2013-0486111E5 (prohibited investment exchanged under 51(1): no advantage due to 207.01(13)); 2013-0504191E5 (RRSP uses asset of a corp of which it is a shareholder; May 2013 ICAA Roundtable q.10 (tinyurl.com/cra-abtax) (TFSA assessing policy); 2017-0731541E5, 2018-0739751E5 (third-party payment to TFSA at owner O's direction or with O's concurrence is not "advantage"); 2019-0830101E5 (interpretation of (a)(v) — promotional incentives); 2020-0865641I7 (settlement paid to plan for actionable loss is not advantage).

See also Ball & Welch, "Update on the Prohibited Investment and Advantage Rules", 2012 Cdn Tax Foundation conference report, 34:1-25.

Definition amended by 2017 budget bill #2, effective on the same basis as amendment to 207.01(1) opening words (generally March 23, 2017), to add "beneficiary's or" in (a)(iii), "or promoter" in (a)(iv), to add (a)(iv.1), and to change "RRIF and RRSP" to "registered plan that is not a TFSA" in (c)(ii) opening words and "RRSP strip" to "registered plan strip" in (d).

Definition earlier amended by 2013 and 2011 budget bills #2 (both effective March 23, 2011), 2008 budget bill #2.

Regulations: No prescribed benefits yet for para. (e).

Income Tax Folios: S3-F10-C3: Advantages — RRSPs, RESPs, RRIFs, RDSPs and TFSAs.

I.T. Technical News: 44 (key employee TFSA).

Forms: RC298: Advantage tax return for RRSP or TFSA issuers or RRIF carriers.

"allowable refund" of a person for a calendar year means the total of all amounts each of which is a refund, for the year, to which the person is entitled under subsection 207.04(4).

Related Provisions: 207.07(2) — Refund payable by Minister; 207.05 — Tax payable where advantage extended.

"controlling individual", of a registered plan, means

(a) the holder of a TFSA;

(b) a holder of a RDSP;

(c) a subscriber of a RESP; or

(d) the annuitant of a RRIF or RRSP.

Notes: Definition changed from "controlling individual, of a registered plan, means the holder of a TFSA or the annuitant of a RRIF or RRSP, as the case may be" by 2017 budget bill #2, effective on the same basis as amendment to 207.01(1) opening words (generally March 23, 2017).

Definition added by 2011 budget bill #2, effective March 23, 2011.

"deliberate over-contribution" of an individual means a contribution made under a TFSA by the individual that results in, or increases, an excess TFSA amount, unless it is reasonable to conclude that the individual neither knew nor ought to have known that the contribution could result in liability for a penalty, tax or similar consequence under this Act.

Related Provisions: 207.01(1)"advantage"(c)(iii) — Benefit attributable to deliberate over-contribution is "advantage".

Notes: A benefit from a DOC falls into 207.01(1)"advantage"(c)(iii), and is 100% taxed by 207.05, plus monthly 1% tax under 207.02.

Definition added by 2010 budget bill #2, for contributions made after Oct. 16, 2009.

"equity", of a corporation, trust or partnership, means

(a) in the case of a corporation, a share of the capital stock of the corporation;

(b) in the case of a trust, an income or capital interest in the trust; and

(c) in the case of a partnership, an interest as a member of the partnership.

Notes: Definition added by 2013 budget bill #2, effective March 23, 2011.

"excess TFSA amount" of an individual at a particular time in a calendar year means the amount, if any, determined by the formula

$$A - B - C - D - E$$

where

A is the total of all amounts each of which is a contribution made under a TFSA by the individual in the calendar year and at or before the particular time, other than a contribution that is

(a) a qualifying transfer, or

(b) an exempt contribution;

B is the individual's unused TFSA contribution room at the end of the preceding calendar year;

C is the total of all amounts each of which was a distribution made in the preceding calendar year under a TFSA of which the individual was the holder at the time of the distribution, other than a distribution that is

(a) a qualifying transfer, or

(b) a specified distribution;

D is

(a) the TFSA dollar limit for the calendar year if, at any time in the calendar year, the individual is resident in Canada, and

(b) nil, in any other case; and

E is the total of all amounts each of which is the qualifying portion of a distribution made in the calendar year and at or before the particular time under a TFSA of which the individual was the holder at the time of the distribution and, for this purpose, the qualifying portion of a distribution is

(a) nil, if the distribution is a qualifying transfer or a specified distribution, and

(b) in any other case, the lesser of

(i) the amount of the distribution, and

(ii) the amount that would be the individual's excess TFSA amount at the time of the distribution if the amount of the distribution were nil.

Related Provisions: 207.01(1) — Definitions of "deliberate over-contribution", "qualifying transfer" and "unused TFSA contribution room"; 207.02 — Tax on excess TFSA amount; 207.06(4) — CRA may notify TFSA holder that distribution of certain amounts required within 90 days.

Notes: The words "if any" in the opening words of the definition are unnecessary: see s. 257. Finance has indicated that these words were added to give meaning to 207.01(2)(d)(iii), but they will likely be deleted and that provision reworded.

In simple terms, the "excess TFSA amount" (1% monthly tax under 207.02) is the total of all contributions to TFSAs (A), minus all distributions from TFSAs (C and E), in excess of the unused contribution room and the cumulative dollar limit ($5,000 for 2009-2012, $5,500 for 2013-14, $10,000 starting 2015) (B and D — see 207.01(1)"TFSA dollar limit").

"Qualifying transfers" (to another TFSA or to a spouse/partner's TFSA on marriage breakdown) are ignored in both directions: C(a) and E(a). "Exempt contributions" (see 207.01(2)) are also ignored: A(b).

See Notes to 207.02 as to how the penalty on excess TFSA amounts is applied.

C(b) and E(a) amended by 2010 budget bill #2, effective Oct. 17, 2009, to change "prescribed distribution" to "specified distribution".

207.01(1)"excess TFSA amount"E amended by 2008 budget bill #2, for 2009 and later tax years (i.e., retroactive to the introduction of 207.01). The former version, now deemed never to have been in force, is in PITA 34th-36th ed.

Forms: RC240: Designation of an exempt contribution TFSA; RC243 Sched. B: Schedule B — Non-resident contributions to a TFSA.

"excluded property", at any time for a trust governed by a registered plan, means

(a) property described in paragraph 4900(1)(j.1) of the *Income Tax Regulations*;

(b) an equity of a mutual fund corporation, mutual fund trust or registered investment if

(i) either

(A) the equity is equity of a mutual fund corporation or mutual fund trust that derives all or substantially all its value from one or more mutual funds that are subject to, and substantially comply with, the requirements of *National Instrument 81-102 Mutual Funds*, as amended from time to time, of the Canadian Securities Administrators, or

(B) the corporation, trust or registered investment follows a reasonable policy of investment diversification,

(ii) the time is

(A) during the 24-month period that begins on the day on which the first taxation year of the corporation, trust or registered investment begins,

(B) during the 24-month period that ends on the day on which the last taxation year of the corporation, trust or registered investment ends, or

(C) where the equity is a share of the capital stock of a mutual fund corporation and the share derives all or substantially all its value from a particular mutual fund,

(I) during the 24-month period that begins on the day on which the particular mutual fund is established, or

(II) during the 24-month period that ends on the day on which the particular mutual fund is terminated,

(iii) it is reasonable to conclude that none of the main purposes of the structure of the corporation, trust or registered investment, or of the terms and conditions of the equity, is to accommodate transactions or events that could affect the fair market value of the property held by the trust governed by the registered plan in a manner that would not occur in a normal commercial or investment context in which parties deal with each other at arm's length and act prudently, knowledgeably and willingly, and

(iv) it is reasonable to conclude that none of the main purposes of the incorporation, establishment or operation of the corporation, trust or registered investment, or of the particular mutual fund, is to benefit from this paragraph; or

(c) equity of a corporation, partnership or trust (in this paragraph referred to as the "investment entity") if at that time

(i) the fair market value of the equity (in this paragraph referred to as the "arm's length equity") of the investment entity that is owned by persons who deal at arm's length with the controlling individual of the registered plan is at least 90% of the fair market value of all the equity of the investment entity,

(ii) the total fair market value of the arm's length equity and the debt of the investment entity that is owned by persons who deal at arm's length with the controlling individual is at least 90% of the total fair market value of all the equity and debt of the investment entity,

(iii) the controlling individual, either alone or together with persons with whom the controlling individual does not deal at arm's length, does not have the right to cast at least 10% of the votes, if any, that could be cast regarding the governance of the investment entity,

(iv) the specific terms and conditions of each share or unit of equity of the investment entity held by the trust governed by the registered plan are the same as, or substantially similar to, the terms and conditions of particular equity that is included in the arm's length equity,

(v) the fair market value of the particular equity referred to in subparagraph (iv) is equal to at least 10% of the total fair market value of all equity of the investment entity having the specific terms and conditions referred to in subparagraph (iv) or terms and conditions that are substantially similar to those terms and conditions,

(vi) the controlling individual deals at arm's length with the investment entity, and

(vii) it is reasonable to conclude that none of the main purposes of the structure of the investment entity, or of the terms and conditions of the equity, is to accommodate transactions or events that could affect the fair market value of the property held by the trust governed by the registered plan in a manner that would not occur in a normal commercial or investment context in which parties deal with each other at arm's length and act prudently, knowledgeably and willingly.

Notes: "Excluded property" (added by 2013 budget bill #2 effective March 23, 2011) is an investment that is excluded from being a prohibited investment for a TFSA, RRSP or RRIF. This definition replaces, and expands on, "prescribed excluded property" in former Reg. 5000.

In CRA's view, votes "regarding the governance" in (c)(iii) include board votes, so being a director can put a person offside: Income Tax Folio S3-F10-C2 ¶2.18; doc 2014-0545041E5.

Income Tax Folios: S3-F10-C2: Prohibited investments — RRSPs, RRIFs and TFSAs.

"exempt contribution" means a contribution made in a calendar year under a TFSA by the survivor of an individual if

(a) the contribution is made during the period (in this definition referred to as the "rollover period") that begins when the individual dies and that ends at the end of the first calendar year that begins after the individual dies (or at any later time that is acceptable to the Minister);

(b) a payment (in this definition referred to as the "survivor payment") was made to the survivor during the rollover period, as a consequence of the individual's death, directly or indirectly out of or under an arrangement that ceased, because of the individual's death, to be a TFSA;

(c) the survivor designates, in prescribed form filed in prescribed manner within 30 days after the day on which the contribution is made (or at any later time that is acceptable to the Minister), the contribution in relation to the survivor payment; and

(d) the amount of the contribution does not exceed the least of

(i) the amount, if any, by which

(A) the amount of the survivor payment

exceeds

(B) the total of all other contributions designated by the survivor in relation to the survivor payment,

(ii) the amount, if any, by which

(A) the total proceeds of disposition that would, if section 146.2 were read without reference to subsection 146.2(9), be determined in respect of the arrangement under paragraph 146.2(8)(a), (10)(a) or (11)(a), as the case may be,

exceeds

(B) the total of all other exempt contributions in respect of the arrangement made by the survivor at or before the time of the contribution, and

(iii) if the individual had, immediately before the individual's death, an excess TFSA amount or if payments described in paragraph (b) are made to more than one survivor of the individual, nil or the greater amount, if any, allowed by the Minister in respect of the contribution.

Related Provisions: 146.2(9) — Effect of death on TFSA; 207.01(3) — Survivor as successor holder; 248(8) — Meaning of "consequence" of death; *Interpretation Act* 27(5) — Meaning of "within 30 days".

Notes: "Survivor payment" in para. (b) can include paying off a family-law debt owed by the deceased: VIEWS doc 2015-0617331E5; an amount the executor *chooses* to pay to the survivor from the deceased's (former) TFSA; and an amount paid from a deceased's TFSA to a spousal trust and then distributed to the spouse: 2020-0851601C6 [2020 APFF Financial q.5]. See also 2019-0813421C6 [2019 APFF Financial q.4] (FMV of TFSA property decreases after death); 2019-0821701C6 [2019 APFF Financial q.7] (CRA may accept payment made after end of year after death); 248(8) for "consequence" of death; and 17.1(1) Notes on the meaning of "indirectly".

A survivor's contribution within the para. (d) limits can be an "exempt contribution" even if made before receiving a "survivor payment": VIEWS doc 2019-0820901C6 [2019 APFF Financial q.5]. CRA may allow an amount under (d)(iii) if a deceased has both a surviving spouse and a surviving common-law partner: 2010-0371961C6.

Para. (c) amended by 2013 budget bill #2, retroactive to March 23, 2011, to add "(or at any later time that is acceptable to the Minister)".

207.01(1)"exempt contribution" added by 2008 budget bill #2, for 2009 and later taxation years. This definition was formerly in 207.01(2).

Forms: RC240: Designation of an exempt contribution TFSA.

"non-qualified investment" for a trust governed by a registered plan means property that is not a qualified investment for the trust.

Related Provisions: 146(1)"qualified investment" — Definition for RRSP; 146(10.1) — Tax on RRSP's income from NQI; 146.2(6) — Tax on TFSA's income from non-qualified investment (NQI); 146.3(1)"qualified investment" — Definition for RRIF; 146.3(9) — Tax on RRIF's income from NQI; 207.01(1)"qualified investment" — Definition for TFSA; 207.01(1)"prohibited investment" — Definitions; 207.01(5) — Obligation of TFSA issuer; 207.01(6) — Deemed disposition and reacquisition on property becoming or ceasing to be QI; 207.04(1) — Tax on acquisition of NQI; 207.04(3) — Where NQI is also prohibited investment.

Notes: "Qualified investment" is defined in 146(1), 146.3(1) and 207.01(1) for an RRSP, RRIF and TFSA respectively (see opening words of 207.01(1)).

Definition amended by 2011 budget bill #2 to change "TFSA" to "registered plan" (i.e., extended to RRSPs and RRIFs), effective for transactions occurring, income earned, capital gains accruing and investments acquired after March 22, 2011.

Regulations: 223(3) (notification to holder of non-qualified investments).

"prohibited investment", at any time for a trust governed by a registered plan, means property (other than excluded property for the trust) that is at that time

(a) a debt of the controlling individual of the registered plan;

(b) a share of the capital stock of, an interest in, or a debt of

(i) a corporation, partnership or trust in which the controlling individual has a significant interest, or

(ii) a person or partnership that does not deal at arm's length with the controlling individual;

(c) an interest (or, for civil law, a right) in, or a right to acquire, a share, interest or debt described in paragraph (a) or (b); or

(d) prescribed property.

Related Provisions: 207.01(1)"advantage"(c)(ii) — Benefit attributable to prohibited investment is "advantage"; 207.01(1)"non-qualified investment"; 207.01(1)"transitional prohibited investment benefit" — Grandfathering; 207.01(4) — Significant interest; 207.01(6) — Deemed disposition and reacquisition on property becoming or ceasing to be PI; 207.01(7) — Grandfathering of FMV of PI; 207.01(8)–(13) — Transitional rules; 207.04(1), (6) — Tax on acquisition of prohibited investment (PI); 207.04(3) — Where PI is also non-qualified investment; 207.5(1)"prohibited investment" — Parallel definition for RCA.

Notes: See Notes to 207.04(1). A publicly-traded mutual fund or mortgage investment corporation is a prohibited investment (PI) if the TFSA holder and non-arm's length parties own 10% or more of its value: 207.01(4), VIEWS docs 2008-0304051E5 (also describes the consequences of holding a PI), 2009-0308231E5, 2010-0369031E5.

CRA's view is that the controlling individual is responsible for compliance with the PI rules; plan trustees "generally have no obligation" to identify a PI, but "the CRA expects that trustees will not knowingly facilitate" acquisition or holding of PIs: Income Tax Folio S3-F10-C2 ¶2.4.

See also VIEWS docs 2011-0426041E5 (pre-March/11 investment that was QI under Reg. 4900(12) retains its status); 2012-0438701E5 (corporation ceasing to be specified small business corp does not make the share a PI); 2012-0457011E5 and 2012-0441781E5 (whether shares of a cooperative corp are PI); 2012-0467151E5 (mortgage under Reg. 4900(1)(j.1) is prescribed excluded property [see now 207.01(1)"excluded property"(a)] and so is not PI).

See also Kabouchi & White, "Qualified Investment and Prohibited Investment Rules", 2017 Ontario Tax Conference (ctf.ca).

Definition amended by 2013 budget bill #2, effective March 23, 2011 for investments acquired at any time, to change "prescribed excluded property" to "excluded property for the trust" in opening words, and to delete from the end of (b)(ii) "or with a person or partnership described in subparagraph (i)" [as per Finance letter of June 12/12 to the CBA/CICA Joint Committee].

Definition amended by 2011 budget bill #2, effective March 23, 2011 in respect of investments acquired at any time, to change all instances of "TFSA" to "registered plan", "holder" to "controlling individual" and "prescribed property" to "prescribed excluded property". (This extends the rules for TFSAs to apply to RRSPs and RRIFs.) For transitional relief see 207.01(1)"transitional prohibited investment benefit" and VIEWS doc 2011-0418161E5.

207.01(1)"prohibited investment" amended by 2008 budget bill #2, for 2009 and later tax years (i.e., retroactive to the introduction of 207.01), to change "prescribed property in relation to a trust" to "prescribed property" in opening words and "restricted property" to "prescribed property" in para. (d).

Regulations: 4900(15) (prescribed property for para. (d)).

Income Tax Folios: S3-F10-C1: Qualified investments — RRSPs, RESPs, RRIFs, RDSPs and TFSAs [replaces IT-320R3]; S3-F10-C2: Prohibited investments — RRSPs, RRIFs and TFSAs.

"qualified investment" for a trust governed by a TFSA means

(a) an investment that would be described by any of paragraphs (a) to (d), (f) and (g) of the definition "qualified investment" in section 204 if the reference in that definition to "a trust governed by a deferred profit sharing plan or revoked plan" were read as a reference to "a trust governed by a TFSA" and if that definition were read without reference to the words "with the exception of excluded property in relation to the trust";

(b) a contract for an annuity issued by a licensed annuities provider if

(i) the trust is the only person who, disregarding any subsequent transfer of the contract by the trust, is or may become entitled to any annuity payments under the contract, and

(ii) the holder of the contract has a right to surrender the contract at any time for an amount that would, if reasonable sales and administration charges were ignored, approximate the value of funds that could otherwise be applied to fund future periodic payments under the contract; and

(c) a prescribed investment.

Related Provisions: 87(10) — New share issued on amalgamation of public corporation deemed listed; 132.2(3)(h) — Where share ceases to be QI due to mutual fund reorganization; 146.2(4) — Tax on TFSA's income from non-QI; 207.01(5) — Obligation of TFSA issuer; 207.01(6) — Deemed disposition and reacquisition on property becoming or ceasing to be QI; 207.04 — Tax on acquisition of non-QI.

Notes: This follows essentially the same rules as for RRSPs. See Notes to 146(1)"qualified investment". But see also 207.01(1)"prohibited investment", 207.04, and VIEWS docs 2009-0305501E5 (general discussion), 2010-0381031E5 (foreign exchange contract is not QI), 2013-0504191E5 (owning shares in a private company).

See also Kabouchi & White, "Qualified Investment and Prohibited Investment Rules", 2017 Ontario Tax Conference (ctf.ca).

"Qualified investment" for an RRSP, RESP, RRIF or RDSP is defined in 146(1), 146.1(1), 146.3(1) and 146.5(1) respectively.

Regulations: 221 (information return where mutual fund etc. claims its shares are QI); 4900 (prescribed investments — and note 4900(14) specifically for TFSAs).

Income Tax Folios: S3-F10-C1: Qualified investments — RRSPs, RESPs, RRIFs, RDSPs and TFSAs [replaces IT-320R3].

"qualifying transfer" means the transfer of an amount from a TFSA of which a particular individual is the holder if

(a) the amount is transferred directly to another TFSA, the holder of which is the particular individual; or

(b) the amount is transferred directly to another TFSA, the holder of which is a spouse or common-law partner or former spouse or common-law partner of the particular individual, and the following conditions are satisfied:

(i) the individuals are living separate and apart at the time of the transfer, and

(ii) the transfer is made under a decree, order or judgment of a competent tribunal, or under a written separation agreement, relating to a division of property between the individuals in settlement of rights arising out of, or on the breakdown of, their marriage or common-law partnership.

Related Provisions: 146.2(2)(e) — Transfer to another TFSA permitted; 207.01(1)"excess TFSA amount"A(a), C(a), E(a), 207.01(1)"unused TFSA contribution room"(b)B(i), D(i) — Qualifying transfers ignored in determining contribution limit; 248(1)"disposition"(f)(vi) — Transfer from TFSA to TFSA is not a disposition; 252(3) — Extended meaning of "spouse".

Notes: See Notes to 118.8 for the meaning of "separate and apart" in (b)(i).

"RRSP strip" — [Repealed]

Related Provisions: 207.01(1)"advantage"(d), 207.05(2)(c) — RRSP strip is an "advantage" taxed at 100%; 207.5(1)"RCA strip" — Parallel definition for retirement compensation arrangement.

Notes: Definition repealed by 2017 budget bill #2, effective on the same basis as amendment to 207.01(1) opening words (generally March 23, 2017). See now "registered plan strip". It read:

"RRSP strip", in respect of a RRIF or RRSP, means the amount of a reduction in the fair market value of property held in connection with the RRIF or RRSP, if the value is reduced as part of a transaction or event or a series of transactions or events one of the main purposes of which is to enable the controlling individual of the RRIF or RRSP, or a person who does not deal at arm's length with the controlling individual, to obtain a benefit in respect of property held in connection with the RRIF or RRSP or to obtain a benefit as a result of the reduction, but does not include an amount that is

(a) included in the income of the controlling individual or their spouse or common-law partner under section 146 or 146.3;

(b) an excluded withdrawal under section 146.01 or 146.02; or

(c) described in subsection 146(16) or 146.3(14.2).

(d) [Repealed]

See Notes to 207.01(1)"advantage" and 207.05(1). Note that this definition applied to a RRIF as well as an RRSP!

The sale of a prohibited investment to the annuitant for cash equal to its fair market value is not an RRSP strip: VIEWS docs 2012-0439151E5, 2012-0439211E5, 2012-0445851E5. An in-kind transfer to an IPP under 146(16)(a) is excluded by para. (c): 2015-060549117.

For the meaning of "one of the main purposes" see Notes to 83(2.1).

For case law on RRSP strips before this definition and 207.05(2)(c) were introduced, see Notes to 146(10).

Definition added by 2011 budget bill #2, effective March 23, 2011, and amended retroactive to its introduction by 2013 budget bill #2.

"registered plan" means a RDSP, RESP, RRIF, RRSP or TFSA.

Notes: Definition amended to add reference to RDSP and RESP by 2017 budget bill #2, effective on the same basis as amendment to 207.01(1) opening words (generally March 23, 2017).

Definition added by 2011 budget bill #2, effective March 23, 2011. The rules in Part X.01 were extended from TFSAs to cover RRSPs and RRIFs as well.

"registered plan strip", in respect of a registered plan that is not a TFSA, means the amount of a reduction in the fair market value of property held in connection with the registered plan, if the value is reduced as part of a transaction or event or a series of transactions or events one of the main purposes of which is to enable the controlling individual of the registered plan, or a person who does not deal at arm's length with the controlling individual, to obtain a benefit in respect of property held in connection with the registered plan or to obtain a benefit as a result of the reduction, but does not include an amount that is

(a) included in the income of a person under section 146, 146.1, 146.3 or 146.4;

(b) an excluded withdrawal under section 146.01 or 146.02;

(c) described in subsection 146(16), 146.3(14.2) or 146.4(8);

(d) a distribution to a trust governed by a RESP under circumstances to which subparagraph 204.9(5)(c)(i) or (ii) applies;

(e) an accumulated income payment made to a RDSP under circumstances to which subsection 146.1(1.2) applies;

(f) a refund of payments under a RESP; or

(g) the non-taxable portion of a disability assistance payment made from a RDSP.

Notes: This term replaces "RRSP strip", as it now applies to a RRSP, RRIF, RESP or RDSP. For interpretation before 2017 see Notes to 207.01(1)"RRSP strip".

Definition added by 2017 budget bill #2, effective on the same basis as amendment to 207.01(1) opening words (generally March 23, 2017). It replaces "RRSP strip".

"restricted property" — [Repealed]

Notes: 207.01(1)"restricted property" repealed by 2008 budget bill #2, effective for 2009 and later taxation years (i.e., retroactive to the introduction of 207.01). It defined the term as having "the meaning assigned by regulation", but no regulations were proposed. 207.01(1)"prohibited investment"(d) now refers to "prescribed property".

"specified distribution" means

(a) a distribution made under a TFSA to the extent that it is, or is reasonably attributable to, an amount that is

(i) an advantage in respect of the TFSA or any other TFSA of the holder,

(ii) specified non-qualified investment income,

(iii) an amount in respect of which tax was payable under Part I by a trust governed by the TFSA or any other TFSA of the holder, or

(iv) an amount described in subparagraph 207.06(1)(b)(ii); or

(b) a prescribed distribution.

Related Provisions: 207.01(1)"excess TFSA amount"C(b), E(a) — Specified distribution does not reduce excess TFSA amount; 207.01(1)"unused TFSA contribution room"(b)B(ii) — Specified distribution does not increase contribution room; 207.061 — Amount under "specified distribution"(a)(ii) included in TFSA holder's income.

Notes: 207.01(1)"specified distribution" added by 2010 budget bill #2, effective for distributions that occur after Oct. 16, 2009, other than the portion of a distribution that is, or is reasonably attributable to, an advantage that was extended, or income earned, before Oct. 17, 2009. See Notes to 207.01(1)"advantage".

Regulations: No prescribed distributions yet for para. (b).

"specified non-qualified investment income", in respect of a registered plan and its controlling individual, means income (determined without reference to paragraph 82(1)(b)), or a capital gain, that is reasonably attributable, directly or indirectly, to an amount in respect of which tax was payable under Part I by a trust governed by the registered plan or by any other registered plan of the controlling individual.

Related Provisions: 146.2(6) — When tax payable under Part I by TFSA; 207.01(1)"advantage"(b)(vi) — Benefit attributable to SNQII is "advantage" if not distributed after notice under 207.06(4); 207.01(1)"specified distribution"(a)(ii) — Distribution attributable to SNQII is specified distribution; 207.06(4) — CRA may notify TFSA holder that distribution of SNQII required within 90 days.

Notes: For the meaning of "indirectly", see Notes to 207.01(1)"advantage".

Definition amended by 2013 budget bill #2, retroactive to March 23, 2011, to change "income (including a capital gain)" to "income (determined without reference to paragraph 82(1)(b)), or a capital gain".

Definition amended by 2011 budget bill #2 to change "TFSA" to "registered plan" and "holder" to "controlling individual", for transactions occurring, income earned, capital gains and investments acquired after March 22, 2011. (This extends the rules for TFSAs to apply to RRSPs and RRIFs.)

207.01(1)"specified non-qualified investment income" added by 2010 budget bill #2, effective for 2010 and later taxation years. See Notes to 207.01(1)"advantage".

"swap transaction", in respect of a registered plan, means a transfer of property between the registered plan and its controlling individual or a person with whom the controlling individual does not deal at arm's length, but does not include

(a) a payment out of or under the registered plan in satisfaction of all or part of the controlling individual's interest in the registered plan;

(b) a payment into the registered plan that is

(i) a contribution, a premium or an amount transferred in accordance with paragraph 146.3(2)(f),

(ii) described in paragraph (a) or (b) of the definition "contribution" in subsection 146.1(1), or

(iii) described in any of paragraphs (a) to (d) of the definition "contribution" in subsection 146.4(1);

(c) a transfer of a prohibited investment or a non-qualified investment from the registered plan for consideration, in circumstances where the controlling individual is entitled to a refund under subsection 207.04(4) on the transfer;

(d) a transfer of property from one registered plan of a controlling individual to another registered plan of the controlling individual if

(i) both registered plans are RRIFs or RRSPs,

(ii) both registered plans are TFSAs,

(iii) both registered plans are RDSPs, or

(iv) both registered plans are RESPs;

(e) a transfer of a prohibited investment from the registered plan for consideration, if subsection (13) applies in respect of all or part of the consideration received by the registered plan;

(f) a transfer of property from the registered plan in consideration for the issuance of a debt obligation that is an excluded property for the trust governed by the registered plan; or

(g) a payment into the registered plan that is a payment of, or in satisfaction of, the principal amount of, or interest on, a debt obligation that is an excluded property for the trust governed by the registered plan.

Related Provisions: 207.01(1)"advantage"(b)(iii) — Benefit attributable to swap transaction is "advantage".

Notes: A swap transaction (ST) with an RRSP, RRIF, TFSA, RESP or RDSP is effectively prohibited, as it falls into 207.01(1)"advantage"(b)(iii), so any income from the property swapped into the plan is 100% taxed under 207.05. Even before this definition applied effective Oct. 17, 2009, swap transactions created an "advantage" in *Louie*, 2019 FCA 255 (leave to appeal denied 2020 CarswellNat 1258 (SCC)).

Since 248(1)"property"(b) includes money unless there is a contrary intention, this catches a swap in either direction, i.e., a transfer of money both to and from a registered plan in exchange for securities. However, a distribution from a plan (for nothing) and a contribution to a plan (for nothing), even of securities, are not STs due to paras. (a) and (b): VIEWS doc 2010-0359001E5.

Converting an RRSP to a RRIF when the annuitant turns 71 (see Notes to 146(2)) is not a ST due to para. (b).

See VIEWS docs 2010-0367511M4 (transfer of GICs to TFSA can only be done as a contribution); 2011-0413291E5 (TFSA rules for STs extended to RRSPs and RRIFs); 2011-0416621E5 (swap between investment account and RRSP is caught even if done at FMV); 2011-0429561M4 and 2012-0432611E5 (since rules effectively prohibit all STs, CRA expects RRSP issuers and RRIF carriers to stop processing swaps); 2012-

0437821E5 (transfer of credit union shares); 2012-0460611E5 (swap between two plans with same tax attributes, e.g. RRSP to RRSP/RRIF, is not a ST); 2015-0605491I7 (in-kind transfer from RRSP to IPP is not a ST).

Subparas. (b)(ii)-(iii) and (d)(iii)-(iv) added by 2017 budget bill #2, effective

(a) after 2021 in relation to transactions undertaken to remove a property from a RDSP or RESP if it is reasonable to conclude that tax would be payable under Part XI.01 if the property were retained in the RDSP or RESP;

(b) after 2027 in relation to transactions undertaken to remove a transitional prohibited property (as defined in 207.01(1)) from a RDSP or RESP if it is reasonable to conclude that tax would be payable under Part XI.01 of the Act if the property were retained in the RDSP or RESP; and

(c) in any other case, after June 2017.

Para. (c) amended to add "for consideration", and paras. (e)-(g) added, by 2013 budget bill #2, effective on the same basis as the 2011 amendment below.

Definition amended by 2011 budget bill #2 (s. 95), effective [in-force rule as modified by 2013 budget bill #2, s. 95]

(a) after 2021 in relation to a swap transaction undertaken to remove a property from a RRIF or RRSP if it is reasonable to conclude that tax would be payable under Part XI.01 if 207.05(4) did not apply and the property were retained in the RRIF or RRSP; and

(b) in any other case, after June 2011.

Before this amendment, read:

"swap transaction", in respect of a trust governed by a TFSA, means a transfer of property (other than a transfer that is a distribution or a contribution) occurring between the trust and the holder of the TFSA or a person with whom the holder does not deal at arm's length.

207.01(1)"swap transaction" added by 2010 budget bill #2, effective for transfers after Oct. 16, 2009.

Income Tax Folios: S3-F10-C2: Prohibited investments — RRSPs, RRIFs and TFSAs.

"TFSA dollar limit" for a calendar year means,

(a) for 2009 to 2012, $5,000;

(b) for 2013 and 2014, $5,500;

(c) for 2015, $10,000; and

(d) for each year after 2015, the amount (rounded to the nearest multiple of $500, or if that amount is equidistant from two such consecutive multiples, to the higher multiple) that is equal to $5,000 adjusted for each year after 2009 in the manner set out in section 117.1.

Related Provisions: 207.01(1)"excess TFSA amount"D(a) — Effect of contributions that exceed dollar limit.

Notes: See Notes to 146.2. The annual contribution limit (for a person 18 or over) is: $5,000 (2009-12), $5,500 (2013-14 and 2016-18); $10,000 (2015, Conservative election-year budget increase); $6,000 (2019-21).

The $5,500 continues to be indexed under 117.1(1) as though it had been $5,000 in 2009, rounded to the nearest $500: see para. (d) above.

The cumulative limit for taxpayers born before 1992 is $75,500 as of Jan. 2021. (Funds withdrawn from a TFSA restore contribution room as of the following Jan. 1: 207.01(1)"unused TFSA contribution room"B, "excess TFSA amount"C.)

Since TFSA eligibility starts at age 18 and TFSAs started in 2009, the cumulative TFSA contribution limit *during 2021* is, based on the taxpayer's **birthdate**:

before 1992 (2009-2021)	$75,500
1992 (2010-2021)	70,500
1993 (2011-2021)	65,500
1994 (2012-2021)	60,500
1995 (2013-2021)	55,500
1996 (2014-2021)	50,000
1997 (2015-2021)	44,500
1998 (2016-2021)	34,500
1999 (2017-2021)	29,000
2000 (2018-2021)	23,500
2001 (2019-2021)	18,000
2002 (2020-2021)	12,000
2003 (2021 only)	6,000
2004 or later (age <18 at year-end)	0

Para. (c) changed from "for each year after 2014, $10,000", and para. (d) added, by 2016 tax-rate bill effective 2016. This implements the Liberals' 2015 election proposal to undo the Conservatives' increase in the limit to $10,000, but leaves the rate at $10,000 for 2015. As of 2016, the limit is back to $5,500 but indexing is restored.

Definition amended by 2015 Budget bill, effective June 23, 2015, to introduce the $10,000 (non-indexed) limit for 2015 and later years.

Forms: RC343: Worksheet — TFSA contribution room.

"transitional prohibited investment benefit", of a controlling individual for a taxation year, means the amount determined by the formula

$$A - B$$

where

A is the total of all amounts each of which is income (determined without reference to paragraph 82(1)(b)) earned, or a capital gain realized, in the taxation year by a trust governed by a RRIF or RRSP of the controlling individual that

(a) is reasonably attributable, directly or indirectly, to a property that is a prohibited investment, and a transitional prohibited property, for the trust, and

(b) in the case of income, is earned after March 22, 2011 and, in the case of a capital gain, accrues after March 22, 2011; and

B is the total of all amounts each of which is a capital loss (determined without reference to subparagraph 40(2)(g)(i) and subsection 40(3.4)) realized in the taxation year by a trust governed by a RRIF or RRSP of the controlling individual that

(a) is reasonably attributable, directly or indirectly, to a property that is a prohibited investment, and a transitional prohibited property, for the trust, and

(b) accrues after March 22, 2011.

Related Provisions: 207.01(7) — Grandfathering of FMV of prohibited investment; 207.05(4) — No Part XI.01 tax on RRSP or RRIF transitional benefit; 207.05(5) — No Part XI.01 tax on RESP or RDSP transitional benefit; 257 — Formula cannot calculate to less than zero.

Notes: For the meaning of "indirectly", see Notes to 207.01(1)"advantage".

A proposed amendment to "transitional prohibited investment benefit", in the March 22, 2017 draft Budget legislation, was dropped.

Definition amended by 2013 budget bill #2, retroactive to March 23, 2011. The previous version is now deemed never to have been in force.

Definition added by 2011 budget bill #2, effective March 23, 2011. See Notes to 207.01(1)"prohibited investment".

Income Tax Folios: S3-F10-C2: Prohibited investments — RRSPs, RRIFs and TFSAs.

Forms: RC341: Election on transitional prohibited investment benefit for RRSPs or RRIFs.

"transitional prohibited property", at any time for a particular trust governed by a registered plan (other than a TFSA) of a controlling individual, means a property that is held by the particular trust at that time, that was held

(a) on March 22, 2011 by a trust governed by a RRIF or RRSP of the controlling individual and that was a prohibited investment for that trust on March 23, 2011; or

(b) on March 22, 2017 by a trust governed by a RDSP or RESP of the controlling individual and that was a prohibited investment for that trust on March 23, 2017.

Related Provisions: 207.01(7) — ACB of transitional prohibited property; 207.01(8), (9) — Prohibited investment status; 207.01(10), (11) — Marriage or common-law partnership breakdown; 207.01(12), (13) — Exchange of property.

Notes: Opening words amended to change "RRIF or RRSP" to "registered plan (other than a TFSA)", and para. (b) added, by 2017 budget bill #2, effective on the same basis as amendment to 207.01(1) opening words (generally March 23, 2017).

Definition added by 2013 budget bill #2, effective March 23, 2011.

Income Tax Folios: S3-F10-C2: Prohibited investments — RRSPs, RRIFs and TFSAs.

"unused TFSA contribution room" of an individual at the end of a calendar year means,

(a) if the year is before 2009, nil;

(a.1) in circumstances where the Minister has, in accordance with section 207.06, waived or cancelled all or part of the liability imposed on the individual, the amount determined by the Minister; and

(b) in any other case, the positive or negative amount determined by the formula

$$A + B + C - D$$

where

A   is the individual's unused TFSA contribution room at the end of the preceding calendar year,

B   is the total of all amounts each of which was a distribution made in the preceding calendar year under a TFSA of which the individual was the holder at the time of the distribution, other than a distribution that is

     (i) a qualifying transfer, or

     (ii) a specified distribution,

C   is

     (i) the TFSA dollar limit for the calendar year, if at any time in the calendar year the individual is 18 years of age or older and resident in Canada, and

     (ii) nil, in any other case, and

D   is the total of all amounts each of which is a contribution made under a TFSA by the individual in the calendar year, other than a contribution that is

     (i) a qualifying transfer, or

     (ii) an exempt contribution.

Related Provisions: 207.01(1)"excess TFSA amount"B — Unused contribution room can be contributed in a later year; 207.01(1)"qualifying transfer".

Notes: See Notes at end of 146.2 and to 207.01(1)"excess TFSA amount". The words "positive or negative amount" in para. (b) override the rule in s. 257.

Subpara. (a.1) added, and (b)B(ii) amended to change "prescribed distribution" to "specified distribution", by 2010 budget bill #2, effective Oct. 17, 2009.

Forms: RC343:Worksheet — TFSA contribution room.

(2) [Repealed]

Notes: 207.01(2) repealed by 2008 budget bill #2, effective for 2009 and later taxation years (i.e., retroactive to the introduction of 207.01). It defined an exempt contribution. See now 207.01(1)"exempt contribution".

(3) Survivor as successor holder

— If an individual's survivor becomes the holder of a TFSA as a consequence of the individual's death and, immediately before the individual's death, the individual had an excess TFSA amount, the survivor is deemed (other than for the purposes of the definition "exempt contribution") to have made, at the beginning of the month following the individual's death, a contribution under a TFSA equal to the amount, if any, by which

     (a) that excess TFSA amount

exceeds

     (b) the total fair market value immediately before the individual's death of all property held in connection with arrangements that ceased, because of the individual's death, to be TFSAs.

Notes: 207.01(3) amended by 2008 budget bill #2, for 2009 and later taxation years (i.e., retroactive to the introduction of 207.01).

Income Tax Folios: S3-F10-C1: Qualified investments — RRSPs, RESPs, RRIFs, RDSPs and TFSAs [replaces IT-320R3].

(4) Significant interest

— An individual has a significant interest in a corporation, partnership or trust at any time if

     (a) in the case of a corporation, the individual would, at that time, be a specified shareholder of the corporation if the references in the portion of the definition "specified shareholder" in subsection 248(1) before paragraph (a) to "in a taxation year" and "at any time in the year" were read as "at any time" and "at that time", respectively;

     (b) in the case of a partnership, the individual, or the individual together with persons and partnerships with which the individual does not deal at arm's length, holds at that time interests as a member of the partnership that have a fair market value of 10%

or more of the fair market value of the interests of all members in the partnership; and

     (c) in the case of a trust, the individual, or the individual together with persons and partnerships with which the individual does not deal at arm's length, holds at that time interests as a beneficiary (in this paragraph, as defined in subsection 108(1)) under the trust that have a fair market value of 10% or more of the fair market value of the interests of all beneficiaries under the trust.

Related Provisions: 207.01(1)"prohibited investment"(b)(i) — Effect of holding significant interest; 207.5(1)"significant interest" — Definition applies to RCAs.

Notes: 207.01(4)(a) changed from "in the case of a corporation, the individual is a specified shareholder of the corporation at that time" by 2013 budget bill #2, retroactive to 2009 (the introduction of 207.01).

Income Tax Folios: S3-F10-C2: Prohibited investments — RRSPs, RRIFs and TFSAs.

(5) Obligation of issuer

— The issuer, carrier or promoter of a registered plan shall exercise the care, diligence and skill of a reasonably prudent person to minimize the possibility that a trust governed by the registered plan holds a non-qualified investment.

Notes: For case law on this "due diligence" test, which is the same as that for corporate directors liable for payroll withholdings, see Notes to 227.1(3).

207.01(5) amended by 2017 budget bill #2, effective March 23, 2017, to add "or promoter" (so as to apply to a RESP).

207.01(5) amended by 2011 budget bill #2, effective March 23, 2011, to change "TFSA" to "registered plan" and to change "issuer" to "issuer or carrier".

Income Tax Folios: S3-F10-C1: Qualified investments — RRSPs, RESPs, RRIFs, RDSPs and TFSAs [replaces IT-320R3].

(6) Deemed disposition and reacquisition of investments

— If, at any time, a property held by a trust governed by a registered plan becomes, or ceases to be, a prohibited investment or non-qualified investment for the trust, the trust is deemed to have disposed of the property immediately before that time for proceeds of disposition equal to the fair market value of the property at that time and to have reacquired the property at that time at a cost equal to that fair market value.

Related Provisions: 207.01(7) — Grandfathering of FMV of prohibited investment; 207.01(8), (9) — Election to have subsec. (6) not apply; 207.04(1) — Tax on deemed reacquisition of property by trust; 207.04(3) — Where investment is both prohibited and non-qualified.

Notes: This rule replaces 207.04(5).

Where shares are delisted and so become a non-qualifying investment, 207.01(6) deems the RRSP/RRIF to dispose of and reacquire the shares at current value; so there is no recognition for the drop in value to that point, but any later gain is taxed under 146(10.1) or 146.3(9): VIEWS doc 2012-0447191E5.

207.01(6) added by 2013 budget bill #2, effective March 23, 2011.

Income Tax Folios: S3-F10-C1: Qualified investments — RRSPs, RESPs, RRIFs, RDSPs and TFSAs [replaces IT-320R3].

(7) Adjusted cost base

— For the purpose of computing the adjusted cost base to a trust governed by a registered plan (other than a TFSA) of a property that is a transitional prohibited property for the trust, the cost to the trust of the property until the property is disposed of by the trust is deemed to be equal to the fair market value of the property,

     (a) in the case of a RRIF or RRSP, at the end of March 22, 2011; and

     (b) in the case of a RDSP or RESP, at the end of March 22, 2017.

Notes: 207.01(7) amended by 2017 budget bill #2, effective March 23, 2017, to change "RRIF or RRSP" to "registered plan (other than a TFSA)" and add para. (b).

207.01(7) added by 2013 budget bill #2, effective March 23, 2011.

Income Tax Folios: S3-F10-C2: Prohibited investments — RRSPs, RRIFs and TFSAs.

(8) Prohibited investment status

— Subsection (9) applies in respect of a property if

     (a) the property would, in the absence of subsection (9), have ceased at any time (in this subsection and subsection (9) referred to as the "relevant time") to be a prohibited investment for a trust governed by a registered plan (other than a TFSA) of a controlling individual;

(b) the property is a transitional prohibited property for the trust immediately before the relevant time;

(c) in the case of a property held under a RRIF or RRSP, the controlling individual elected under subsection 207.05(4); and

(d) the controlling individual elects in prescribed form that subsection (9) apply in respect of the property and the election is filed with the Minister on or before the day that is 90 days after the end of the taxation year of the controlling individual that includes the relevant time.

Notes: The 2011 Budget extended the taxes on "advantages" and "prohibited investments" from TFSAs to RRSPs and RRIFs; and in the 2017 Budget extended them to RESPs and RDSPs. 207.01(8) and (9) are relieving changes, allowing an election to prevent a deemed disposition of a "transitional prohibited property" (207.01(1)), so the taxpayer will not be subject to the advantage tax or be forced to withdraw the gain from the plan to take advantage of the transitional relief under 207.05(4) even though the plan did not receive any actual proceeds.

207.01(8) amended by 2017 budget bill #2, effective March 23, 2017, to change "RRIF or RRSP" to "registered plan (other than a TFSA)" in para. (a), and to add "in the case of a property held under a RRIF or RRSP" to para. (c).

207.01(8) added by 2013 budget bill #2, effective March 23, 2011, except that an election referred to in 207.01(8)(d) is deemed filed on time if it is filed with the Minister by March 12, 2014.

Income Tax Folios: S3-F10-C2: Prohibited investments — RRSPs, RRIFs and TFSAs.

(9) Prohibited investment status — If this subsection applies in respect of a property, the property is deemed to be a prohibited investment at and after the relevant time for every trust governed by a registered plan (other than a TFSA) of the controlling individual referred to in paragraph (8)(a).

Related Provisions: 207.01(8) — Conditions for subsec. (9) to apply.

Notes: See Notes to 207.01(8). 207.01(9) added by 2013 budget bill #2, effective March 23, 2011; and amended by 2017 budget bill #2 effective March 23, 2017 to change "RRIF or RRSP" to "registered plan (other than a TFSA)" [extending it to RESPs and RDSPs].

Income Tax Folios: S3-F10-C2: Prohibited investments — RRSPs, RRIFs and TFSAs.

(10) Breakdown of marriage or common-law partnership — Subsection (11) applies in respect of a property if

(a) the property is transferred at any time (in this subsection and subsection (11) referred to as the "transfer time") by a trust (in this subsection and subsection (11) referred to as the "transferor trust") governed by a RRIF or RRSP of a controlling individual (in this subsection and subsection (11) referred to as the "transferor") under paragraph 146(16)(b) or subsection 146.3(14) to a trust (in subsection (11) referred to as the "recipient trust") governed by a RRIF or RRSP of which the spouse or common-law partner or former spouse or common-law partner (in this subsection and subsection (11) referred to as the "recipient") of the transferor is the controlling individual;

(b) the property is a prohibited investment, and a transitional prohibited property, for the transferor trust immediately before the transfer time;

(c) the transferor elected under subsection 207.05(4); and

(d) the transferor and the recipient jointly elect in prescribed form that subsection (11) apply in respect of the property and the election

(i) is filed with the Minister on or before the day that is 90 days after the end of the taxation year of the transferor that includes the transfer time; and

(ii) designates an amount (in subsection (11) referred to as the "designated amount") in respect of the property that

(A) is not less than the adjusted cost base to the transferor trust of the property immediately before the transfer time, and

(B) does not exceed the greater of the amount determined under clause (A) and the fair market value of the property at the transfer time.

Notes: 207.01(10) and (11) allow the controlling individual of an RRSP or RRIF and their (current or former) spouse or common-law partner to make a joint election in certain circumstances in respect of property that is transferred directly to the controlling individual's RRSP or RRIF from the spouse's RRSP or RRIF tax-free under 146(16)(b) or 146.3(14), so as to not penalize parties financially where spouses are required to reallocate assets between their RRSPs as a result of marriage breakdown. This implements a July 9, 2013 Finance comfort letter.

207.01(10) added by 2013 budget bill #2, effective March 23, 2011, and an election in 207.01(10)(d) could be filed by March 12, 2014.

Income Tax Folios: S3-F10-C2: Prohibited investments — RRSPs, RRIFs and TFSAs.

(11) Breakdown of marriage or common-law partnership — If this subsection applies in respect of a property,

(a) the property is deemed to be, at and after the transfer time, a property that was held on March 22, 2011 by a trust governed by a RRIF or RRSP of the recipient and that was a prohibited investment for the trust on March 23, 2011;

(b) where the property would, in the absence of this paragraph, not be a prohibited investment for the recipient trust immediately after the transfer time, the property is deemed to be a prohibited investment at and after the transfer time for every trust governed by a RRIF or RRSP of the recipient;

(c) the recipient is deemed to have elected under subsection 207.05(4); and

(d) notwithstanding any other provision of this Act, the designated amount is deemed to be

(i) the proceeds of disposition to the transferor trust from the transfer described in paragraph (10)(a), and

(ii) the cost of the property to a trust governed by a RRIF or RRSP of the recipient until the property is disposed of by the trust.

Related Provisions: 207.01(10) — Conditions for subsec. (11) to apply.

Notes: See Notes to 207.01(10). 207.01(11) added by 2013 budget bill #2, effective March 23, 2011.

Income Tax Folios: S3-F10-C2: Prohibited investments — RRSPs, RRIFs and TFSAs.

(12) Exchange of property — Subsection (13) applies in respect of a property other than money if

(a) the property is acquired at any time (in this subsection and subsection (13) referred to as the "exchange time") by a trust (in this section and subsection (13) referred to as the "exchanging trust") governed by a registered plan (other than a TFSA) of a controlling individual in exchange for another property (in this subsection referred to as the "exchanged property") in a transaction to which any of section 51, subsection 85(1) and sections 85.1, 86 and 87 apply;

(b) the exchanged property is a prohibited investment, and a transitional prohibited property, for the exchanging trust immediately before the exchange time;

(c) the property is, or would be, if subsection 4900(14) of the *Income Tax Regulations* were read without reference to its paragraph (b), a qualified investment for the exchanging trust immediately after the exchange time; and

(d) in the case of a property held under a RRIF or RRSP, the controlling individual elected under subsection 207.05(4).

Notes: 207.01(12) amended by 2017 budget bill #2, effective March 23, 2017, to change "RRIF or RRSP" to "registered plan (other than a TFSA)" in para. (a) [to extend it to RESPs and RDSPs] and to add "in the case of a property held under a RRIF or RRSP" to para. (d).

207.01(12) and (13) (added by 2013 budget bill #2 effective March 23, 2011) extend the transitional relief from the prohibited investment and advantage rules (for "transitional prohibited property" held by an RRSP or RRIF) to non-cash property acquired by the trust in the course of a reorganization or exchange under 51, 85(1), 85.1, 86 and 87. This implements a Feb. 12, 2013 Finance comfort letter. No election is required. For an example see VIEWS doc 2013-0486111E5.

Income Tax Folios: S3-F10-C2; Prohibited investments — RRSPs, RRIFs and TFSAs.

(13) Exchange of property — If this subsection applies in respect of a property,

(a) other than for the purposes of subsection (7), the property is deemed to be, at and after the exchange time, a property,

(i) in the case of a trust governed by a RRIF or RRSP, that was

(A) held on March 22, 2011 by a trust governed by a RRIF or RRSP of the controlling individual referred to in subsection (12), and

(B) a prohibited investment for the trust on March 23, 2011, and

(ii) in the case of a trust governed by a RDSP or RESP, that was

(A) held on March 22, 2017 by a trust governed by a RDSP or RESP of the controlling individual referred to in subsection (12), and

(B) a prohibited investment for the trust on March 23, 2017; and

(b) if the property would, in the absence of this paragraph, not be a prohibited investment for the exchanging trust immediately after the exchange time, the property is deemed to be a prohibited investment at and after the exchange time for every trust governed by a registered plan (other than a TFSA) of the controlling individual.

Related Provisions: 207.01(1)"swap transaction"(e) — Deemed swap transaction where subsec. (13) applies; 207.01(12) — Conditions for subsec. (13) to apply.

Notes: See Notes to 207.01(12).

207.01(13)(a), (b) amended by 2017 budget bill #2, effective March 23, 2017, to cover RESPs and RDSPs. Before that date, read:

(a) other than for the purposes of subsection (7), the property is deemed to be, at and after the exchange time, a property that was held on March 22, 2011 by a trust governed by a RRIF or RRSP of the controlling individual referred to in subsection (12) and that was a prohibited investment for the trust on March 23, 2011; and

(b) where the property would, in the absence of this paragraph, not be a prohibited investment for the exchanging trust immediately after the exchange time, the property is deemed to be a prohibited investment at and after the exchange time for every trust governed by a RRIF or RRSP of the controlling individual.

Income Tax Folios: S3-F10-C2: Prohibited investments — RRSPs, RRIFs and TFSAs.

Notes [s. 207.01]: 207.01 added by 2008 budget bill #1, effective for 2009 and later taxation years. See Notes at end of 146.2. It originally covered only TFSAs but was expanded to RRSPs and RRIFs in 2011 (see Notes to 207.04(1)). For the parallel rules for RCAs, see 207.5–207.65.

Definitions [s. 207.01]: "accumulated income payment" — 146.1(1), 207.01(1); "adjusted cost base" — 54, 248(1); "advantage" — 207.01(1); "amount" — 248(1); "annuitant" — 146(1), 146.3(1), 207.01(1); "annuity" — 248(1); "arm's length" — 251(1); "beneficiary" — 146.1(1), 207.01(1); "calendar year" — Interpretation Act 37(1)(a); "capital gain" — 39(1)(a), 248(1); "capital interest" — 108(1), 248(1); "capital loss" — 39(1)(b), 248(1); "carrier" — 146.3(1), 207.01(1); "common-law partner", "common-law partnership" — 248(1); "consequence" — 248(8); "contribution" — 146.1(1), 146.4(1), 207.01(1); "controlling individual" — 207.01(1); "corporation" — 248(1), Interpretation Act 35(1); "deferred profit sharing plan" — 147(1), 248(1); "deliberate over-contribution" — 207.01(1); "designated provincial program" — 146.1(1), 207.01(1); "disability assistance payment" — 146.4(1), 207.01(1); "disposition" — 248(1); "distribution" — 146.2(1), 207.01(1); "dividend" — 248(1); "equity", "excess TFSA amount" — 207.01(1); "exchanging trust" — 207.01(12)(a); "excluded property", "exempt contribution" — 207.01(1); "fair market value" — see 69(1) Notes; "holder" — 146.2(1), 207.01(1); "individual" — 248(1); "issuer" — 146(1), 146.2(1), 146.4(1), 207.01(1); "licensed annuities provider" — 147(1), 248(1); "listed" — 87(10); "Minister" — 248(1); "month" — Interpretation Act 35(1); "mutual fund corporation" — 131(8), 248(1); "mutual fund trust" — 132(6)–(7), 132.2(3)(n), 248(1); "non-qualified investment" — 207.01(1); "partnership" — see 96(1) Notes; "person" — 248(1); "premium" — 146(1), 207.01(1); "prescribed", "principal amount" — 248(1); "prohibited investment" — 207.01(1); "promoter" — 146.1(1), 207.01(1); "property" — 248(1); "property held" — 146.3(1), 207.01(1); "qualified investment" — 146(1), 146.3(1), 207.01(1); "qualifying transfer" — 207.01(1); "RDSP" — 248(1)"registered disability savings plan"; "RESP" — 248(1)"registered education savings plan"; "RRIF" — 248(1)"registered retirement income fund"; "RRSP" — 248(1)"registered retirement savings plan"; "RRSP strip" — 207.01(1); "refund of pay-

ments" — 146.1(1), 207.01(1); "registered investment" — 204.4(1), 248(1); "registered plan", "registered plan strip" — 207.01(1); "regulation" — 248(1); "related" — 251(2)–(6); "relevant time" — 207.01(8)(a); "resident in Canada" — 250; "security" — Interpretation Act 35(1); "separation agreement" — 248(1); "series of transactions" — 248(10); "share" — 248(1); "significant interest" — 207.01(4); "specified distribution", "specified non-qualified investment income" — 207.01(1); "specified shareholder" — 248(1); "spouse" — 252(3); "subscriber" — 146.1(1), 207.01(1); "survivor" — 146.2(1); "survivor payment" — 207.01(1)"exempt contribution"(b); "swap transaction" — 207.01(1); "TFSA" — 146.2(5), 248(1); "TFSA dollar limit" — 207.01(1); "taxation year" — 249; "transitional prohibited investment benefit", "transitional prohibited property" — 207.01(1); "trust" — 104(1), 146.1(1), 207.01(1), 248(1), (3); "unused TFSA contribution room" — 207.01(1); "written" — Interpretation Act 35(1)"writing".

207.02 Tax payable on excess TFSA amount — If, at any time in a calendar month, an individual has an excess TFSA amount, the individual shall, in respect of that month, pay a tax under this Part equal to 1% of the highest such amount in that month.

Related Provisions [s. 207.02]: 207.06(1) — Minister may waive tax under certain conditions; 207.062 — Tax under 207.05 reduced by amount payable under 207.02 for same contribution; 207.07 — Return and payment of tax.

Notes: 207.02 imposes a tax on an individual's "excess TFSA amount" (see 207.01(1)) of 1% each month of the individual's highest excess TFSA amount in that month. Excess contributions are not determined separately for each TFSA, but cumulatively for all TFSAs to which the individual has contributed. 207.06(1) allows CRA to waive this tax if satisfied that the excess arose because of reasonable error and the individual arranges, without delay, for it to be withdrawn. See also VIEWS doc 2020-0843071E5 (deliberate overcontribution), Notes to 146.2.

CRA initially applied this penalty strictly, if a taxpayer withdraws funds and recontributes in the same year. See Griffin & Provenzano, "TFSA Penalties and Tax", 17(1) Canadian Tax Highlights (ctf.ca) 6-7 (Jan. 2009). Due to public uproar, CRA has become more lenient. See also Notes to 207.06(1) re waiver of the tax.

Since 2016, CRA will send a warning letter to a first-time excess contributor; if they do not remove the excess from the TFSA, they will be assessed. After the first time, taxpayers will be assessed without notice: VIEWS doc 2015-0599851I7. This happened in Robitaille, 2019 TCC 200: R was warned for overcontributing in one year, and the next year mistakenly deposited a $40,000 cheque to his TFSA at an ATM (the Court recommended CRA waive the tax under 207.06(1)).

Where the tax applies, CRA will also assess a penalty for not filing the return to report the tax: Robitaille, para. 2.

Additional penalty taxes: If taxpayer T knew or ought to have known the contribution was not allowed, then it is a 207.01(1)"deliberate over-contribution", and any resulting benefit is 100% taxed: 207.01(1)"advantage"(c)(iii), 207.05. If T is non-resident when contributing, 207.03 applies (but see Notes thereto).

Income or gains earned on excess contributions are not taxed beyond 207.02, but if the 207.02 tax is waived, such amounts must be withdrawn and included in income: VIEWS doc 2017-0732391E5 (see 207.06(1), 207.061).

207.02 added by 2008 budget bill #1, for 2009 and later tax years.

Definitions [s. 207.02]: "amount" — 248(1); "excess TFSA amount" — 207.01(1); "individual" — 248(1); "month" — Interpretation Act 35(1).

Forms: RC243: TFSA return; RC243 Sched. A: Schedule A — Excess TFSA amounts; RC243 Sched. B: Schedule B — Non-resident contributions to a TFSA; RC257: Request for an information return program account (RZ); RC376: Taxpayer relief request statement of income and expenses and assets and liabilities for individuals; RC4288: Request for taxpayer relief.

207.03 Tax payable on non-resident contributions — If, at a particular time, a non-resident individual makes a contribution under a TFSA (other than a contribution that is a qualifying transfer or an exempt contribution), the individual shall pay a tax under this Part equal to 1% of the amount of the contribution in respect of each month that ends after the particular time and before the earlier of

(a) the first time after the particular time at which the amount of the contribution is equalled or exceeded by the total of all amounts each of which is a distribution

(i) that is made after the particular time under a TFSA of which the individual is the holder, and

(ii) that the individual designates in prescribed manner to be a distribution in connection with the contribution and not in connection with any other contribution, and

(b) the time at which the individual becomes resident in Canada.

Related Provisions [s. 207.03]: 207.06(1) — Minister may waive or cancel tax under certain conditions; 207.062 — Tax under 207.05 reduced by amount payable under 207.03 for same contribution; 207.07 — Return and payment of tax.

Notes: *Double tax*: A non-resident who contributes to a TFSA is usually a former resident who did not realize they had become non-resident (perhaps due to application of a tax treaty). CRA practice is to assess under *both* 207.02 and 207.03. But the same contribution triggers both: the non-resident gets no new contribution room (207.01(1)"unused TFSA contribution room"(b)C(i)), triggering 207.02; and is non-resident, triggering 207.03. In the author's view, this violates the principle against double tax: see 248(28) Notes. (Consider: *Excise Tax Act* 165(2) says the tax it imposes [provincial portion of the HST] is "*in addition to* the tax payable under subsection (1)" [the federal portion]; the omission of these words suggests 207.03 should not apply in addition to 207.02.)

See Notes to 207.06(1) re waiver of the tax. 207.03 added by 2008 budget bill #1 and amended by 2008 budget bill #2, both for 2009 and later tax years.

Definitions [s. 207.03]: "amount" — 248(1); "distribution" — 146.2(1); "exempt contribution" — 207.01(1); "holder" — 146.2(1); "individual" — 248(1); "month" — *Interpretation Act* 35(1); "non-resident", "prescribed" — 248(1); "qualifying transfer" — 207.01(1); "resident in Canada" — 250; "TFSA" — 146.2(5), 248(1).

207.04 (1) Tax payable on prohibited or non-qualified investment

— The controlling individual of a registered plan that governs a trust shall pay a tax under this Part for a calendar year if, at any time in the year, the trust acquires property that is a prohibited investment, or a non-qualified investment, for the trust.

Related Provisions: 146(1)"benefit"(b.1) — Amount subject to Part XI.01 tax is not an RRSP benefit; 146(10.1) — RRSP — tax on income from non-qualified investment; 146.2(6) — TFSA also pays regular tax on income from non-qualified investment; 146.3(5)(d) — Amount subject to Part XI.01 tax is not a RRIF benefit; 146.3(9) — RRIF — tax on income from non-qualified investment; 207.01(6) — Deemed acquisition of property when it becomes PI or NQI; 207.04(2) — Amount of tax; 207.04(3) — Where investment both prohibited and non-qualified; 207.04(4) — Refund of tax on disposition of investment; 207.04(6) — RDSP holders and RESP subscribers liable for the tax; 207.06(2) — Minister may waive tax; 207.07 — Return and payment of tax; 207.61(1) — Parallel rule for prohibited investment of RCA; 259(1) — Election for proportional holdings in trust property.

Notes: See generally Income Tax Folios S3-F10-C1 and -C2. If the acquisition of the prohibited investment is inadvertent, this tax is not particularly onerous as it can generally be refunded under 207.04(4).

Before 2011, 146(10) and 146.3(7) taxed the annuitant if an RRSP or RRIF acquired a non-qualified investment. As well, 207.1(1) and (4) imposed a monthly tax on an RRSP or RRIF holding a non-qualified investment.

The 2011 amendments extended the TFSA "prohibited investment" and "non-qualified investment" rules (see Notes to 146.2) to RRSPs and RRIFs. There was substantial criticism, and Finance announced relieving amendments in a June 12, 2012 letter (available in PITA 42nd-44th ed. and in *Dept. of Finance Technical Notes*), later incorporated into Dec. 12, 2012 draft legislation, which was enacted by 2013 budget bill #2.

Since the June 2012 announcement, see Coburn, "One Size Fits All?", 2012 BC Tax Conference (ctf.ca), 13:1-23; Ball & Welch, "Update on the Prohibited Investment and Advantage Rules", 2012 Cdn Tax Foundation conference report, 34:1-25; Jones, "Prohibited Investments", XVIII(3) *Corporate Finance* (Federated Press) 2134-35 (2012); Wong, "Prohibited Investment Rules", 3(1) *Canadian Tax Focus* (ctf.ca) 10 (May 2013); De Lisser & Krieger, "Registered Savings Plans", 61(3) *Canadian Tax Journal* 769-96 (2013); Frydberg, "Top Technical Bill Issues", 2013 Prairie Provinces Tax Conference (ctf.ca), 11:1, §11.

207.04(1) applies to the exercise of a warrant or conversion right (that is a PI) acquired before March 23/11 to acquire a new PI: VIEWS docs 2012-0446031E5, 2012-0453301C6. It does not apply to a PI exchanged under s. 51, due to 207.01(13): 2013-0486111E5. See also 2014-0518601M4 (207.04(1) applies when QI becomes NQI).

207.04(1) amended by 2013 budget bill #2, retroactive to March 23, 2011.

207.04(1) opening words amended by 2011 budget bill #2, to change "holder" to "controlling individual" and "TFSA" to "registered plan", effective

(a) in respect of any investment acquired after March 22, 2011, except in the case of a prohibited investment acquired after that date by a RRIF or RRSP of an annuitant if the investment was a prohibited investment for another RRIF or RRSP of the same annuitant; and

(b) in respect of any investment acquired before March 23, 2011 that first becomes

(i) a prohibited investment after October 4, 2011, or

(ii) a non-qualified investment after March 22, 2011.

Regulations: 214(2) (information return for RRSP); 215(3) (information return for RRIF); 223(3) (notification for TFSA).

Income Tax Folios: S3-F10-C1: Qualified investments — RRSPs, RESPs, RRIFs, RDSPs and TFSAs [replaces IT-320R3]; S3-F10-C2: Prohibited investments — RRSPs, RRIFs and TFSAs.

Forms: RC339: Individual return for certain taxes for RRSPs or RRIFs.

(2) Amount of tax payable

— The amount of tax payable in respect of each property described in subsection (1) is 50% of the fair market value of the property at the time referred to in that subsection.

Income Tax Folios: S3-F10-C2: Prohibited investments — RRSPs, RRIFs and TFSAs.

(3) Both prohibited and non-qualified investment

— For the purposes of this section and subsections 146(10.1), 146.1(5), 146.2(6), 146.3(9), 146.4(5) and 207.01(6), if a trust governed by a registered plan holds property at any time that is, for the trust, both a prohibited investment and a non-qualified investment, the property is deemed at that time not to be a non-qualified investment, but remains a prohibited investment, for the trust.

Notes: See VIEWS doc 2018-0750591I7 (207.04(3) applies to RRSP and RRIF investments acquired before March 23/11: earlier doc 2011-0426041E5 no longer applies).

207.04(3) amended by 2017 budget bill #2, effective March 23, 2017, to add reference to 146.1(5) and 146.4(5) (as part of extending Part XI.01 to RESPs and RDSPs).

207.04(3) amended to add reference to 207.01(6) by 2013 budget bill #2, retroactive to March 23, 2011.

207.04(3) amended by 2011 budget bill #2, effective on the same basis as the amendments to 207.04(1), to add reference to 146(10.1) and 146.3(9) and to change "TFSA" to "registered plan".

207.04(3) amended by 2008 budget bill #2, effective for 2009 and later taxation years (i.e., retroactive to the introduction of 207.04), to change "146.2(4)" to "146.2(6)" (due to renumbering of 146.2).

Income Tax Folios: S3-F10-C1: Qualified investments — RRSPs, RESPs, RRIFs, RDSPs and TFSAs [replaces IT-320R3]; S3-F10-C2: Prohibited investments — RRSPs, RRIFs and TFSAs.

(4) Refund of tax on disposition of investment

— If in a calendar year a trust governed by a registered plan disposes of a property in respect of which a tax is imposed under subsection (1) on the controlling individual of the registered plan, the controlling individual is entitled to a refund for the year of an amount equal to

(a) except where paragraph (b) applies, the amount of the tax so imposed; or

(b) nil,

(i) if it is reasonable to consider that the controlling individual knew, or ought to have known, at the time the property was acquired by the trust, that it was, or would become, a property described in subsection (1), or

(ii) if the property is not disposed of by the trust before the end of the calendar year following the calendar year in which the tax arose, or any later time that the Minister considers reasonable in the circumstances.

Related Provisions: 207.01(1) — Definition of "allowable refund"; 207.04(5) — Apportionment of refund where more than one person is entitled; 207.07(2) — Refund payable by Minister.

Notes: 207.04(4) opening words and subpara. (b)(i) amended by 2011 budget bill #2, effective on the same basis as the amendments to 207.04(1), to change all instances of "TFSA" to "registered plan" and "holder" to "controlling individual".

Regulations: 214(2) (information return for RRSP); 215(3) (information return for RRIF); 223(3) (notification for TFSA).

(5) Apportionment of refund

— If more than one person is entitled to a refund under subsection (4) for a calendar year in respect of the disposition of a property, the total of all amounts so refundable shall not exceed the amount that would be so refundable for the year to any one of those persons in respect of that disposition if that person were the only person entitled to a refund for the year under that subsection in respect of the disposition. If the persons cannot agree as to what portion of the refund each can so claim, the Minister may fix the portions.

Notes: 207.04(5) added by 2017 budget bill #2, effective March 23, 2017.

Former 207.04(5) repealed by 2013 budget bill #2, effective March 23, 2011.

(6) Liability for tax

— Each person who is a holder of a RDSP or a subscriber of a RESP at the time that a tax is imposed under subsection (1) in connection with the plan is jointly and severally, or solidarily, liable to pay the tax.

Notes: 207.04(6) added by 2017 budget bill #2, effective March 23, 2017.

Former 207.04(6), (7) repealed by 2010 budget bill #2, effective Oct. 17, 2009. They imposed a tax on a TFSA holding a prohibited investment. The 207.02 tax on an "advantage" now applies instead.

207.04(7) amended by 2008 budget bill #2, for 2009 and later taxation years (i.e., retroactive to the introduction of 207.04).

(7) [Repealed]

Notes: See under 207.04(6).

Notes [s. 207.04]: 207.04 added by 2008 budget bill #1, effective for 2009 and later taxation years.

Definitions [s. 207.04]: "allowable capital loss" — 38(b), 248(1); "amount" — 248(1); "calendar year" — *Interpretation Act* 37(1)(a); "capital gain" — 39(1)(a), 248(1); "capital loss" — 39(1)(b), 248(1); "controlling individual" — 207.01(1); "disposition", "dividend" — 248(1); "fair market value" — see 69(1) Notes; "holder" — 146.2(1), 207.01(1); "Minister" — 248(1); "non-qualified investment" — 207.01(1); "person" — 248(1); "prohibited investment" — 207.01(1); "property" — 248(1); "RDSP" — 248(1)"registered disability savings plan"; "RESP" — 248(1)"registered education savings plan"; "registered plan" — 207.01(1); "subscriber" — 146.1(1), 207.01(1); "TFSA" — 146.2(5), 248(1); "taxable capital gain" — 38(a), 248(1); "taxation year" — 249; "trust" — 104(1), 146.1(1), 207.01(1), 248(1), (3).

207.05 (1) Tax payable in respect of advantage

— A tax is payable under this Part for a calendar year if, in the year, an advantage in relation to a registered plan is extended to, or is received or receivable by, the controlling individual of the registered plan, a trust governed by the registered plan, or any other person who does not deal at arm's length with the controlling individual.

Related Provisions: 146(1)"benefit"(b.1) — Amount subject to Part XI.01 tax is not an RRSP benefit; 146.3(5)(d) — Amount subject to Part XI.01 tax is not a RRIF benefit; 207.05(2) — Amount of tax; 207.05(3) — Who liable for tax; 207.06(2) — Minister may waive tax; 207.07 — Return and payment of tax; 207.62(1) — Parallel rule for RCA.

Notes: See Notes to 207.01(1)"advantage" and "swap transaction".

See Income Tax Folio S3-F10-C3 ¶3.43-3.47; Demner, "TFSA Project Audit", 21(1) *Canadian Tax Highlights* (ctf.ca) 2-3 (Jan. 2013).

207.05(1) amended by 2011 budget bill #2, effective March 23, 2011, to apply to RRSPs and RRIFs (as well as TFSAs).

207.05(1) amended by 2010 budget bill #2, effective Oct. 17, 2009.

Income Tax Folios: S3-F10-C1: Qualified investments — RRSPs, RESPs, RRIFs, RDSPs and TFSAs [replaces IT-320R3]; S3-F10-C2: Prohibited investments — RRSPs, RRIFs and TFSAs; S3-F10-C3: Advantages — RRSPs, RESPs, RRIFs, RDSPs and TFSAs.

Forms: RC339: Individual return for certain taxes for RRSPs or RRIFs.

(2) Amount of tax payable

— The amount of tax payable in respect of an advantage described in subsection (1) is

(a) in the case of a benefit, the fair market value of the benefit;

(b) in the case of a loan or an indebtedness, the amount of the loan or indebtedness; and

(c) in the case of a registered plan strip, the amount of the registered plan strip.

Related Provisions: 207.05(4) — Transitional rule for RRSPs and RRIFs; 207.062 — Tax reduced by amount payable under 207.02 or 207.03 for same contribution.

Notes: The 100% tax in 207.05 is not unconstitutional by infringing on provincial jurisdiction, or by having the rate delegated to CRA due to the 207.06 waiver discretion: *Hunt*, 2020 FCA 118.

207.05(2)(c) amended by 2017 budget bill #2, effective March 23, 2017, to change "RRSP strip" to "registered plan strip" (2x).

207.05(2)(c) added by 2011 budget bill #2, effective March 23, 2011.

(3) Liability for tax

— Each controlling individual of a registered plan in connection with which a tax is imposed under subsection (1) is jointly and severally, or solidarily, liable to pay the tax except that, if the advantage is extended by the issuer, carrier or promoter of the registered plan or by a person with whom the issuer, carrier or promoter is not dealing at arm's length, the issuer, carrier or promoter, and not the controlling individual, is liable to pay the tax.

Notes: 207.05(3) amended by 2017 budget bill #2, effective March 23, 2017 (mostly adding "promoter" to cover RESPs). Before that date, read:

(3) The controlling individual of a registered plan in connection with which a tax is imposed under subsection (1) is liable to pay the tax except that, if the advan-

tage is extended by the issuer or carrier of the registered plan or by a person with whom the issuer or carrier is not dealing at arm's length, the issuer or carrier, and not the controlling individual, is liable to pay the tax.

207.05(3) amended by 2011 budget bill #2, effective March 23, 2011, to change all instances of "TFSA" to "registered plan" and "holder" to "controlling individual", and to add all instances of "or carrier".

Forms: RC243: TFSA return; RC298: Advantage tax return for RRSP or TFSA issuers or RRIF carriers; RC339: Individual return for certain taxes for RRSPs or RRIFs.

(4) Transitional rule

— If an individual so elects before March 2, 2013 in prescribed form, subsection (1) does not apply in respect of any advantage that is an amount included in the calculation of the transitional prohibited investment benefit of the individual for a taxation year provided that the transitional prohibited investment benefit

(a) is paid to the individual, from a RRIF or RRSP of the individual, on or before the later of April 2, 2013 and the day that is 90 days after the end of the taxation year; and

(b) is not paid by way of transfer to another RRIF or RRSP of the individual.

Related Provisions: 207.01(7) — Grandfathering of FMV of prohibited investment; 207.01(8)–(13) — Transitional rules; *Interpretation Act* 27(5) — Meaning of "within 90 days".

Notes: For an example of 207.05(4) applying see VIEWS doc 2013-0486111E5.

Where the prohibited investment is in a locked-in RRSP, VIEWS doc 2012-0456601I7 suggests solutions: (a) make the withdrawal from another RRSP; (b) swap out the PI from the locked-in plan; (c) transfer funds to a locked-in RRIF, where they are partly accessible; (d) consult the pension benefits authority, as some jurisdictions now allow some unlocking.

An amount extracted from a RRIF under 207.05(4) counts toward the minimum withdrawal required by 146.3(1)"minimum amount": VIEWS doc 2012-0453161C6.

207.05(4) amended by 2013 budget bill #2, effective March 23, 2011, to change "before July 2012" to "before March 2, 2013" and "within 90 days after" to "on or before the later of April 2, 2013 and the day that is 90 days after".

207.05(4) added by 2011 budget bill #2, effective March 23, 2011.

A proposed **207.05(5)** in the March 22, 2017 Notice of Ways and Means Motion, "Transitional rule — RDSP or RESP", will not be enacted.

Income Tax Folios: S3-F10-C2: Prohibited investments — RRSPs, RRIFs and TFSAs.

Forms: RC341: Election on transitional prohibited investment benefit for RRSPs or RRIFs.

Notes [s. 207.05]: 207.05 added by 2008 budget bill #1, for 2009 and later tax years.

Definitions [s. 207.05]: "advantage" — 207.01(1); "amount" — 248(1); "arm's length" — 251(1); "calendar year" — *Interpretation Act* 37(1)(a); "carrier" — 146.3(1), 207.01(1); "controlling individual" — 207.01(1); "fair market value" — see 69(1) Notes; "holder" — 146.2(1); "individual" — 248(1); "issuer" — 146(1), 146.2(1), 146.4(1), 207.01(1); "person", "prescribed" — 248(1); "promoter" — 146.1(1), 207.01(1); "RDSP" — 248(1)"registered disability savings plan"; "RESP" — 248(1)"registered education savings plan"; "RRIF" — 248(1)"registered retirement income fund"; "RRSP" — 248(1)"registered retirement savings plan"; "RRSP strip" — 207.01(1); "registered plan", "registered plan strip" — 207.01(1); "TFSA" — 146.2(5), 248(1); "taxation year" — 249; "transitional prohibited investment benefit" — 207.01(1); "trust" — 104(1), 248(1), (3).

207.06 (1) Waiver of tax payable [TFSA overcontribution or non-resident contribution]

— If an individual would otherwise be liable to pay a tax under this Part because of section 207.02 or 207.03, the Minister may waive or cancel all or part of the liability if

(a) the individual establishes to the satisfaction of the Minister that the liability arose as a consequence of a reasonable error; and

(b) one or more distributions are made without delay under a TFSA of which the individual is the holder, the total amount of which is not less than the total of

(i) the amount in respect of which the individual would otherwise be liable to pay the tax, and

(ii) income (including a capital gain) that is reasonably attributable, directly or indirectly, to the amount described in subparagraph (i).

Related Provisions: 207.01(1)"specified distribution"(a)(iv) — Amount in 207.06(1)(b)(ii) is a specified distribution; 207.01(1)"unused TFSA contribution room"(a.1) — CRA determines unused contribution room after waiver; 207.061 — Amount under 207.06(1)(b)(ii) included in TFSA holder's income.

Notes: If conditions (a) and (b) are not both met, CRA has no authority to waive or cancel the tax. (Tax already assessed is *cancelled*; tax not yet assessed is *waived*.)

For where to send waiver requests (TFSA Processing Unit, Box 9788 Station T, Ottawa K1G 3X9) and what must be included, see VIEWS doc 2012-0462901C6 [2012 Ontario Tax Conf. q.17]. For CRA guidelines on waiver see VIEWS doc 2020-0852131C6 [2020 APFF q.1].

In *Robitaille*, 2019 TCC 200, the Court recommended CRA waive the tax (R mistakenly deposited a cheque to his TFSA at a bank machine); but in *Deshaies*, 2019 FCA 300, para. 7, the FCA said this is inadvisable because it "creates expectations".

See 220(3.1) Notes on the *Vavilov* "transparent, intelligible and justified" standard for determining if CRA refusal to waive the tax is reasonable. It was held **unreasonable** in: *Gekas*, 2019 FC 1031 (TFSA overcontributions were caused by financial institution's mistakes); *Sangha*, 2020 FC 712 (CRA decision lacked analysis and justification, and ignored evidence submitted; CRA assessed S for overcontributions predating its warning letter, when he overcontributed again); *Ifi*, 2020 FC 1150 (CRA had not advised Ifi that she could not contribute while non-resident, yet found she "continued" to contribute after being advised of overcontribution made *while resident*). See also 204.1(4) Notes for similar cases on RRSP overcontributions.

CRA refusal to waive was held **reasonable** in: *Jiang*, 2019 FC 629 (J did not realize she could not make TFSA contributions while non-resident); *Weldegebriel*, 2019 FC 1565 (Canadian Forces member did not receive overcontribution notices, as he repeatedly failed to advise CRA of address changes); *Perinpanayagam*, 2020 FC 1111 (P, allegedly acting on bank's advice, replaced $19,000 lost on TFSA's investment in bankrupt corp, and did not withdraw excess after CRA told him to do so); *Messenger*, 2021 FC 95 (CRA erred in telling M he had more contribution room than he did, but M failed to withdraw full overcontribution after CRA told him to); *Badesha*, 2021 FC 215 (B failed to withdraw excess despite repeated CRA letters telling him to); *Rempel*, 2021 FC 337 and *Posmyk*, 2021 FC 393 (taxpayers who had signed up for email correspondence did not check for notices from CRA).

For the meaning of "indirectly" in (b)(ii), see Notes to 207.01(1)"advantage".

207.06(1)(b) amended by 2010 budget bill #2, effective Oct. 17, 2009.

(2) Waiver of tax payable — If a person would otherwise be liable to pay a tax under this Part because of subsection 207.04(1) or section 207.05, the Minister may waive or cancel all or part of the liability where the Minister considers it just and equitable to do so having regard to all the circumstances, including

(a) whether the tax arose as a consequence of reasonable error;

(b) the extent to which the transaction or series of transactions that gave rise to the tax also gave rise to another tax under this Act; and

(c) the extent to which payments have been made from the person's registered plan.

Related Provisions: 207.01(1)"unused TFSA contribution room"(a.1) — CRA determines unused contribution room after waiver.

Notes: For examples where CRA may waive the tax, see VIEWS doc 2011-0430141E5. For TFSAs, see Notes to 207.06(1). A 2015 Access to Information request for the criteria used when considering a request for waiver produced only blacked-out documents. Income Tax Folio S3-F10-C2 ¶2.36-2.38 and S3-F10-C3 ¶3.51-3.53 say the factors taken into account include "reasonable error, the extent to which the transactions that gave rise to the tax also gave rise to another tax, and the extent to which payments were made from the taxpayer's registered plan"; that each waiver request is considered on its own merits; and "CRA administers the waiver provisions in a fair and flexible manner". The request should be made to the address shown on Form RC339 (RRSP, RRIF) or RC243 (TFSA).

For the meaning of "just and equitable", see Notes to 85(7.1).

CRA sometimes waives only a portion of the 207.05 tax: *Hunt*, 2020 FCA 118 (this did not make the tax unconstitutional).

207.06(2)(c) added by 2013 budget bill #2, effective March 23, 2011.

207.06(2)(b) amended by 2011 budget bill #2, effective March 23, 2011, to add "or series of transactions" and to change "this Part" to " this Act" (thus covering RRSP and RRIF income inclusions under 146 and 146.3).

207.06(2) opening words amended by 2008 budget bill #2, effective for 2009 and later taxation years (i.e., retroactive to its introduction), to change "207.04" to "207.04(1)".

Income Tax Folios: S3-F10-C1: Qualified investments — RRSPs, RESPs, RRIFs, RDSPs and TFSAs [replaces IT-320R3]; S3-F10-C2: Prohibited investments — RRSPs, RRIFs and TFSAs; S3-F10-C3: Advantages — RRSPs, RESPs, RRIFs, RDSPs and TFSAs.

(3) [Repealed]

Related Provisions: 207.061 — Amount under 207.06(3) included in TFSA holder's income.

Notes: 207.06(3) repealed by 2013 budget bill #2, effective March 23, 2011; see now 207.06(2)(c). Now deemed never to have been in force for RRSPs and RRIFs, it provided that CRA could not waive a 207.05(3) liability unless the plan paid out "without delay" an equivalent amount to the individual. Earlier amended by 2011 budget bill #2, effective March 23, 2011, to apply to RRSPs and RRIFs; added by 2010 budget bill #2 effective Oct. 17, 2009.

(4) Other powers of Minister — The Minister may notify the controlling individual of a registered plan that the controlling individual must cause a payment to be made from the registered plan to the controlling individual within 90 days of receipt of the notice, the amount of which is not less than the amount of specified non-qualified investment income in respect of the registered plan.

Related Provisions: 207.01(1)"advantage"(b)(iv) — Benefit constitutes "advantage" if certain amounts not distributed after notice; *Interpretation Act* 27(5) — Meaning of "within 90 days".

Notes: 207.06(4) amended by 2011 budget bill #2, effective March 23, 2011, to change "holder" to "controlling individual", "TFSA" to "registered plan" and "under the TFSA" to "from the registered plan to the controlling individual".

207.06(4) added by 2010 budget bill #2, effective Oct. 17, 2009.

Notes [s. 207.06]: 207.06 added by 2008 budget bill #1, effective for 2009 and later taxation years.

Definitions [s. 207.06]: "amount" — 248(1); "advantage" — 207.01(1); "capital gain" — 39(1)(a), 248(1); "controlling individual" — 207.01(1); "distribution" — 146.2(1); "holder" — 146.2(1); "individual", "Minister", "person" — 248(1); "registered plan" — 207.01(1); "series of transactions" — 248(10); "specified non-qualified investment income" — 207.01(1); "TFSA" — 146.2(5), 248(1).

207.061 Income inclusion — A holder of a TFSA shall include in computing the holder's income for a taxation year under Part I any portion of a distribution made in the year that is described in subparagraph (a)(ii) of the definition "specified distribution" in subsection 207.01(1) or subparagraph 207.06(1)(b)(ii) or that is specified by the Minister as part of an agreement to waive or cancel a liability for tax under this Part.

Related Provisions: 12(1)(z.5) — Inclusion in holder's income from property under Part I.

Notes: 207.061 amended by 2013 budget bill #2, effective March 23, 2011. Added by 2010 budget bill #2, effective Oct. 17, 2009.

Definitions [s. 207.061]: "amount" — 248(1); "distribution", "holder" — 146.2(1); "taxation year" — 249; "TFSA" — 146.2(5), 248(1).

207.062 Special limit on tax payable — If an individual is liable to pay an amount of tax under section 207.05 and under sections 207.02 or 207.03 in respect of the same contribution for the same calendar year, the tax payable under section 207.05 for the year shall be reduced by the amount of the tax payable under section 207.02 or 207.03, as the case may be, for the year.

Notes: 207.062 added by 2010 budget bill #2, effective Oct. 17, 2009.

Definitions [s. 207.062]: "amount" — 248(1); "calendar year" — *Interpretation Act* 37(1)(a); "individual" — 248(1).

207.07 (1) Return and payment of tax — A person who is liable to pay tax under this Part for all or any part of a calendar year shall before July of the following calendar year

(a) file with the Minister a return for the year under this subsection in prescribed form and containing prescribed information including

(i) an estimate of the amount of tax payable under this Part by the person in respect of the year, and

(ii) an estimate of the amount of the person's allowable refund, if any, for the year; and

(b) pay to the Receiver General the amount, if any, by which the amount of the person's tax payable under this Part in respect of the year exceeds the person's allowable refund, if any, for the year.

Related Provisions: *Interpretation Act* 27(5) — Meaning of "within 90 days".

Notes: See Notes to 207.02.

207.07(1) opening words amended by 2013 budget bill #2, effective Dec. 12, 2013.

Forms: RC243: TFSA return; RC243 Sched. A: Schedule A — Excess TFSA amounts; RC243 Sched. B: Schedule B — Non-resident contributions to a TFSA;

RC339: Individual return for certain taxes for RRSPs or RRIFs; RC4532: Individual tax return for RDSP.

(1.1) Multiple holders or subscribers — If two or more holders of a RDSP, or two or more subscribers of a RESP, are jointly and severally, or solidarily, liable with each other to pay a tax under this Part for a calendar year in connection with the plan,

(a) a payment by any of the holders, or any of the subscribers, on account of that tax liability shall to the extent of the payment discharge the joint liability; and

(b) a return filed by one of the holders, or one of the subscribers, as required by this Part for the year is deemed to have been filed by each other holder, or each other subscriber, in respect of the joint liability to which the return relates.

Notes: 207.07(1.1) added by 2017 budget bill #2, effective March 23, 2017.

(2) Refund — If a person has filed a return under this Part for a calendar year within three years after the end of the year, the Minister

(a) may, on sending the notice of assessment for the year, refund without application any allowable refund of the person for the year, to the extent that it was not applied against the person's tax payable under paragraph (1)(b); and

(b) shall, with all due dispatch, make the refund referred to in paragraph (a) after sending the notice of assessment if an application for it has been made in writing by the person within three years after the sending of an original notice of assessment for the year.

Related Provisions: 164(1) — Parallel rule for corporate income tax refund; 244(14), (14.1) — Date when notice sent; *Interpretation Act* 27(5) — Meaning of "within three years".

Notes: 207.07(2)(a) and (b) amended by 2010 budget bill #2, effective Dec. 15, 2010.

(3) Provisions applicable to Part — Subsections 150(2) and (3), sections 152 and 158 to 167 and Division J of Part I apply to this Part with any modifications that the circumstances require.

Related Provisions: 150(2) — Demands for returns; 150(3) — Trustees, etc. required to file returns; 161(1) — Interest on late payment; 161(11) — Interest on penalties.

Notes [s. 207.07]: 207.07 added by 2008 budget bill #1, for 2009 and later tax years.

Definitions [s. 207.07]: "allowable refund" — 207.01(1); "amount", "assessment" — 248(1); "calendar year" — *Interpretation Act* 37(1)(a); "Minister", "person", "prescribed" — 248(1); "writing" — *Interpretation Act* 35(1).

PART XI.1 — TAX IN RESPECT OF DEFERRED INCOME PLANS AND OTHER TAX EXEMPT PERSONS

207.1 (1) [Repealed]

Notes: See Notes to 207.04, which as of March 23, 2011 has replaced this tax for RRSPs acquiring non-qualified investments.

207.1(1) applied when an existing investment became non-qualified: VIEWS doc 2010-0354681E5.

207.1(1) repealed by 2011 budget bill #2, effective in respect of any investment acquired after March 22, 2011, and any investment acquired earlier that first becomes a non-qualified investment after March 22, 2011. (See now 207.04 instead.) It read:

(1) Tax payable by trust under registered retirement savings plan [holding non-qualified investment] — Where, at the end of any month, a trust governed by a registered retirement savings plan holds property that is neither a qualified investment (within the meaning assigned by subsection 146(1)) nor a life insurance policy in respect of which, but for subsection 146(11), subsection 146(10) would have applied as a consequence of its acquisition, the trust shall, in respect of that month, pay a tax under this Part equal to 1% of the fair market value of the property at the time it was acquired by the trust of all such property held by it at the end of the month, other than

(a) property, the fair market value of which was included, by virtue of subsection 146(10), in computing the income, for any year, of an annuitant (within the meaning assigned by subsection 146(1)) under the plan; and

(b) property acquired by the trust before August 25, 1972.

(2) Tax payable by trust under deferred profit sharing plan [holding non-qualified investment] — Where, at the end of

any month, a trust governed by a deferred profit sharing plan holds property that is neither a qualified investment (within the meaning assigned by section 204) nor a life insurance policy (referred to in paragraphs 198(6)(c) to (e) or subsection 198(6.1)), the trust shall, in respect of that month, pay a tax under this Part equal to 1% of the fair market value of the property at the time it was acquired by the trust of all such property held by it at the end of the month, other than

(a) property in respect of the acquisition of which the trust has paid or is liable to pay a tax under subsection 198(1); and

(b) property acquired by the trust before August 25, 1972.

Related Provisions: 198(1) — Tax on acquisition of non-qualified investment; 207.2 — Return and payment of tax; 259(1) — Proportional holdings in trust property.

(3) [Repealed]

Related Provisions: 207.2 — Return and payment of tax.

Notes: 207.1(3) imposed a 1% monthly tax on non-"qualified investments" (as defined in 146.1(1)) held by a RESP. Note that property that a RESP acquired by Oct. 27, 1998 is a qualified investment under para. (d) of the definition.

207.1(3) repealed by 2017 budget bill #2, effective for any investment acquired after March 22, 2017 and any investment acquired earlier that ceases to be a 146.1(1)"qualified investment" after March 22, 2017. (207.04 now applies to a RESP that acquires a non-QI.) It read:

(3) Tax payable by trust under registered education savings plan [holding non-qualified investment] — Every trust governed by a registered education savings plan shall, in respect of any month, pay a tax under this Part equal to 1% of the total of all amounts each of which is the fair market value of a property, at the time it was acquired by the trust, that

(a) is not a qualified investment (as defined in subsection 146.1(1)) for the trust; and

(b) is held by the trust at the end of the month.

Holding non-qualified investments can also cause the RESP to be revoked, although CRA will not normally issue a revocation notice unless there is abuse. See 146.1(2.1) and (12.1).

207.1(3) added by 1998 Budget, for 1999 and later taxation years.

Former 207.1(3), repealed by 1985 Budget, imposed a similar tax on registered home ownership savings plans. See Notes to 146.2.

Income Tax Folios: S3-F10-C1: Qualified investments — RRSPs, RESPs, RRIFs, RDSPs and TFSAs [replaces IT-320R3].

(4) [Repealed]

Notes: See Notes to 207.04, which as of March 23, 2011 has replaced this tax for RRIFs acquiring non-qualified investments.

207.1(4) repealed by 2011 budget bill #2, effective in respect of any investment acquired after March 22, 2011, and any investment acquired earlier that first becomes a non-qualified investment after March 22, 2011. (See now 207.04 instead.) It read:

(4) Tax payable by trust under registered retirement income fund [holding non-qualified investment] — Where, at the end of any month after 1978, a trust governed by a registered retirement income fund holds property that is not a qualified investment (within the meaning assigned by subsection 146.3(1)), the trust shall, in respect of that month, pay a tax under this Part equal to 1% of the fair market value of the property at the time it was acquired by the trust of all such property held by it at the end of the month other than property, the fair market value of which was included by virtue of subsection 146.3(7) in computing the income for any year of an annuitant (within the meaning assigned by subsection 146.3(1)) under the fund.

(5) Tax payable in respect of agreement to acquire shares — Where at any time a taxpayer whose taxable income is exempt from tax under Part I makes an agreement (otherwise than as a consequence of the acquisition or writing by it of an option listed on a designated stock exchange) to acquire a share of the capital stock of a corporation (otherwise than from the corporation) at a price that may differ from the fair market value of the share at the time the share may be acquired, the taxpayer shall, in respect of each month during which the taxpayer is a party to the agreement, pay a tax under this Part equal to the total of all amounts each of which is the amount, if any, by which the amount of a dividend paid on the share at a time in the month at which the taxpayer is a party to the agreement exceeds the amount, if any, of the dividend that is received by the taxpayer.

Notes: 207.1(5) (formerly 206.1 until Part XI was repealed) imposes a penalty tax on a tax-exempt entity (see 149 — this includes an RRSP or pension fund) that enters into an agreement to purchase shares at a price different from their value. This is intended to discourage tax-exempt entities from temporarily transferring shares to persons who may be able to receive dividends on those shares on a tax-favoured basis. It is also intended to apply where the same result could be achieved by a delay in the acquisition of a share by the tax-exempt entity. However, the policy underlying this provision is respected when no dividends are paid while the agreement to purchase is outstanding or when the dividends paid are actually received by the tax-exempt entity.

207.1(5) amended by 2007 budget bill #2, effective Dec. 14, 2007, to change "prescribed stock exchange" to "designated stock exchange".

207.1(5) added by 2005 budget bill #1, effective for months that end after 2004.

Former 207.1(5) repealed by 1992 Economic Statement, retroactive to its introduction in 1985. It imposed a tax on excessive small business property holdings.

Forms [s. 207.1(5)]: T2000: Calculation of tax on agreements to acquire shares.

Related Provisions [s. 207.1]: 207.2 — Return and payment of tax; 259(1) — Proportional holdings in trust property.

Definitions [s. 207.1]: "amount" — 248(1); "annuitant" — 146.3(1); "corporation" — 248(1), *Interpretation Act* 35(1); "deferred profit sharing plan" — 147(1), 248(1); "designated stock exchange" — 248(1), 262; "dividend" — 248(1); "fair market value" — see 69(1) Notes; "life insurance policy" — 138(12), 248(1); "month" — *Interpretation Act* 35(1); "property" — 248(1); "qualified investment" — 146(1), 146.1(1), 146.3(1), 204; "registered education savings plan" — 146.1(1), 248(1); "registered retirement income fund" — 146.3(1), 248(1); "registered retirement savings plan" — 146(1), 248(1); "share", "taxable income", "taxpayer" — 248(1); "trust" — 104(1), 248(1), (3); "writing" — *Interpretation Act* 35(1).

Regulations [s. 207.1]: 4901(1.1) (prescribed property).

Information Circulars [s. 207.1]: 77-1R4: Deferred profit sharing plans.

207.2 (1) Return and payment of tax — Within 90 days after the end of each year, a taxpayer to whom this Part applies shall

(a) file with the Minister a return for the year under this Part in prescribed form and containing prescribed information, without notice or demand therefor;

(b) estimate in the return the amount of tax, if any, payable by it under this Part in respect of each month in the year; and

(c) pay to the Receiver General the amount of tax, if any, payable by it under this Part in respect of each month in the year.

Related Provisions: 150.1(5) — Electronic filing; *Interpretation Act* 27(5) — Meaning of "within 90 days".

Interpretation Bulletins: IT-320R3: Qualified investments — Trusts governed by RRSPs, RESPs and RRIFs.

Information Circulars: 78-14R4: Guidelines for trust companies and other persons responsible for filing T3GR, T3D, T3P, T3S, T3RI, and T3F returns.

Registered Plans Compliance Bulletins: 4 (abusive schemes — RRSP stripping).

Forms: T3D: Income tax return for DPSP or revoked DPSP; T3GR: Group income tax and information return for RRSP, RRIF, RESP, or RDSP trusts (and worksheets).

(2) Liability of trustee — Where the trustee of a trust that is liable to pay tax under this Part does not remit to the Receiver General the amount of the tax within the time specified in subsection (1), the trustee is personally liable to pay on behalf of the trust the full amount of the tax and is entitled to recover from the trust any amount paid by the trustee as tax under this section.

Registered Plans Compliance Bulletins: See under 146(1)"qualified investment".

(3) Provisions applicable to Part — Subsections 150(2) and (3), sections 152 and 158, subsections 161(1) and (11), sections 162 to 167 and Division J of Part I are applicable to this Part with such modifications as the circumstances require.

Definitions [s. 207.2]: "amount", "Minister", "prescribed", "taxpayer" — 248(1); "trust" — 104(1), 248(1), (3).

PART XI.2 — TAX IN RESPECT OF DISPOSITIONS OF CERTAIN PROPERTIES

207.3 Tax payable by institution or public authority — Every institution or public authority that, at any time in a year, disposes of an object within 10 years after the object became an object described in subparagraph 39(1)(a)(i.1) shall pay a tax under this Part, in respect of the year, equal to 30% of the object's fair market value at that time, unless the disposition was made to another institution or public authority that was, at that time, designated under

subsection 32(2) of the *Cultural Property Export and Import Act* either generally or for a specified purpose related to that object.

Related Provisions: 39(1)(a)(i.1) — No capital gain on gift of cultural property (CP); 118.1(7.1)(a) — Gift of CP by artist or artist's estate.

Notes: 207.3 is an incentive to galleries, museums and other charities to keep cultural property for 10 years, in light of the special relief under 39(1)(a)(i.1), 118.1(1)"total gifts"(c) and 118.1(7.1)(a).

207.3 amended by 1998 Budget (for dispositions after Feb. 23, 1998), 1991 technical bill.

Definitions [s. 207.3]: "fair market value" — see 69(1) Notes.

Interpretation Bulletins: IT-407R4: Dispositions of cultural property to designated Canadian institutions.

207.31 (1) Ecological gift — tax payable — A charity, municipality in Canada or municipal or public body performing a function of government in Canada (each of which is referred to in this section as the "recipient") shall, in respect of a property, pay a tax under this Part in respect of a taxation year if

(a) at any time in the year, the recipient

(i) disposes of the property, or

(ii) in the opinion of the Minister of the Environment, or a person designated by that Minister, changes the use of the property;

(b) the property is described in paragraph 110.1(1)(d) or in the definition "total ecological gifts" in subsection 118.1(1); and

(c) the disposition or change is made without the authorization of the Minister of the Environment or a person designated by that Minister.

(2) Ecological gift — amount of tax — The amount of tax to be paid under subsection (1) is equal to 50% of the amount that would be determined for the purposes of section 110.1 or 118.1, if this Act were read without reference to subsections 110.1(3) and 118.1(6), to be the fair market value of the property referred to in subsection (1) if the property were given to the recipient immediately before the disposition or change referred to in paragraph (1)(a).

Related Provisions: 110.1(5), 118.1(12) — Fair market value of ecological servitude, covenant or easement; 118.1(10.1)–(10.5) — Determination of fair market value by Minister of the Environment; 207.4(1) — Return and payment of tax.

Notes: See Notes to 118.1(1)"total ecological gifts"; VIEWS docs 2014-0539731E5 (tax is based on FMV of property at time of change in use, likely applies on a property-by-property basis, and can apply to multiple changes in use); 2016-0625241I7 (tax can apply even if donor claimed no 110.1(1)(d) deduction for the gift).

For the meaning of "municipal or public body...", see Notes to 149(1)(c).

207.31 amended by 2017 budget bill #2, effective in respect of dispositions made, and changes that occur, after March 21, 2017. The substantive changes were to delete the words "given to the recipient", so 207.31 can apply to any later transferee, and to add "in the opinion of the Minister of the Environment" in (1)(a)(ii), giving that Minister "the ability to determine whether proposed changes to the use of lands would degrade conservation protections" (2017 Budget Supplementary Information). Before the amendment, read:

> 207.31 Tax payable by recipient of an ecological gift — Any charity, municipality in Canada or municipal or public body performing a function of government in Canada (referred to in this section as the "recipient") that at any time in a taxation year, without the authorization of the Minister of the Environment or a person designated by that Minister, disposes of or changes the use of a property described in paragraph 110.1(1)(d) or in the definition "total ecological gifts" in subsection 118.1(1) and given to the recipient shall, in respect of the year, pay a tax under this Part equal to 50% of the amount that would be determined for the purposes of section 110.1 or 118.1, if this Act were read without reference to subsections 110.1(3) and 118.1(6), to be the fair market value of the property if the property were given to the recipient immediately before the disposition or change.

207.31 amended by 2002-2013 technical bill (effective July 19, 2005), 2001 technical bill, 1995 Budget.

Definitions [s. 207.31]: "amount" — 248(1); "Canada" — 255, *Interpretation Act* 35(1); "disposition" — 248(1); "fair market value" — 110.1(5) and see 69(1) Notes; "Minister", "person", "property" — 248(1); "recipient" — 207.31; "taxation year" — 249.

207.4 (1) Return and payment of tax — Any institution, public authority, charity or municipality that is liable to pay a tax under subsection 207.3 or 207.31 in respect of a year shall, within 90 days after the end of the year,

(a) file with the Minister a return for the year under this Part in prescribed form and containing prescribed information without notice or demand therefor;

(b) estimate in the return the amount of tax payable by it under this Part in respect of the year; and

(c) pay to the Receiver General the amount of tax payable by it under this Part in respect of the year.

Related Provisions: 150.1(5) — Electronic filing; *Interpretation Act* 27(5) — Meaning of "within 90 days".

Notes: 207.4(1) amended by 1995 Budget, effective February 28, 1995, to add "charity or municipality" and reference to 207.31.

Forms: T913: Part XI.2 tax return — tax for the disposition of certain properties.

(2) Provisions applicable to Part — Subsections 150(2) and (3), sections 152 and 158, subsections 161(1) and (11), sections 162 to 167 and Division J of Part I are applicable to this Part with such modifications as the circumstances require.

Definitions [s. 207.4]: "Minister", "prescribed" — 248(1).

PART XI.3 — TAX IN RESPECT OF RETIREMENT COMPENSATION ARRANGEMENTS

207.5 (1) Definitions — In this Part,

"advantage", in relation to a retirement compensation arrangement, means

(a) any benefit, loan or indebtedness that is conditional in any way on the existence of the arrangement, other than

(i) a benefit derived from the provision of administrative or investment services in respect of the arrangement,

(ii) a loan or an indebtedness the terms and conditions of which are terms and conditions that persons dealing at arm's length with each other would have entered into, and

(iii) a payment out of or under the arrangement that is included in computing a taxpayer's income under Part I, and

(b) a benefit that is an increase in the total fair market value of the subject property of the arrangement if it is reasonable to consider, having regard to all the circumstances, that the increase is attributable, directly or indirectly, to a transaction or event or a series of transactions or events one of the main purposes of which was to enable a person or a partnership to benefit from a provision of this Part, or from the exemption from tax under paragraph 149(1)(q.1), if the transaction, event or series

(i) would not have occurred in a normal commercial or investment context in which parties deal with each other at arm's length and act prudently, knowledgeably and willingly, or

(ii) included a payment received as, on account or in lieu of, or in satisfaction of, a payment

(A) for services provided by a person who is, or does not deal at arm's length with, a specified beneficiary of the arrangement, or

(B) of interest, of a dividend, of rent, of a royalty or of any other return on investment, or of proceeds of disposition, in respect of property (other than subject property of the arrangement) held by a person who is, or does not deal at arm's length with, a specified beneficiary of the arrangement,

(c) a benefit that is income or a capital gain that is reasonably attributable, directly or indirectly, to

(i) a prohibited investment in respect of the arrangement,

(ii) an amount received by a specified beneficiary of the arrangement, or by a person who does not deal at arm's length

with the specified beneficiary, if it is reasonable to consider, having regard to all the circumstances, that the amount was paid in relation to, or would not have been paid but for, subject property of the arrangement and the amount was paid as, on account or in lieu of, or in satisfaction of, a payment

(A) for services provided by a person who is, or who does not deal at arm's length with, the specified beneficiary, or

(B) of interest, of a dividend, of rent, of a royalty or of any other return on investment, or of proceeds of disposition,

(d) an RCA strip in respect of the arrangement, and

(e) a prescribed benefit;

Related Provisions: 207.01(1)"advantage" — Parallel definition for RRSP, RRIF or TFSA; 207.5(3) — Limitation on RCA election where decline in value of property attributable to advantage; 207.62 — Tax on advantage.

Notes: See Notes to 207.61(1). For the meaning of "one of the main purposes" in para. (b), see Notes to 83(2.1). For "indirectly" in (b) and (c), see Notes to 207.01(1)"advantage".

"Advantage" added by 2012 budget bill #2, effective March 29, 2012, but does not apply in respect of transactions or events that relate to subject property of an RCA acquired before March 29, 2012

(a) if the amount of what would otherwise be an advantage is included in computing the income of a beneficiary of the arrangement, or an employer in respect of the arrangement, for the taxation year in which the amount arose or the immediately following taxation year; or

(b) if the subject property is a promissory note or similar debt obligation, commercially reasonable payments of principal and interest are made at least annually after 2012 in respect of the note or obligation and no RCA strip arises after March 28, 2012 in respect of the arrangement. For purposes of this para., an amendment to the terms of the note or obligation to provide for such payments is deemed not to be a disposition or an acquisition of the note or obligation.

Regulations: No prescribed benefits yet for para. (e).

"prohibited investment", for a retirement compensation arrangement at any time, means property (other than prescribed excluded property) that is at that time

(a) a debt of a specified beneficiary of the arrangement,

(b) a share of the capital stock of, an interest in, or a debt of

(i) a corporation, partnership or trust in which the specified beneficiary has a significant interest, or

(ii) a person or partnership that does not deal at arm's length with, or is affiliated with, the specified beneficiary,

(c) an interest (or, for civil law, a right) in, or a right to acquire, a share, interest or debt described in paragraph (a) or (b), or

(d) prescribed property;

Related Provisions: 207.01(1)"prohibited investment" — Parallel definition for RRSP, RRIF or TFSA; 207.5(3) — Limitation on RCA election where decline in value of property attributable to prohibited investment; 207.61 — Tax on prohibited investment.

Notes: Definition added by 2012 budget bill #2, effective March 29, 2012.

Regulations: No prescribed excluded property proposed for opening words, or prescribed property for para. (d).

"RCA strip", in respect of a retirement compensation arrangement, means the amount of a reduction in the fair market value of subject property of the arrangement, if the value is reduced as part of a transaction or event or a series of transactions or events one of the main purposes of which is to enable a specified beneficiary of the arrangement, or a person or a partnership who does not deal at arm's length with the specified beneficiary, to benefit from a provision of this Part or to obtain a benefit in respect of subject property of the arrangement or as a result of the reduction, but does not include an amount that is included in computing the income of the specified beneficiary or of an employer or former employer of the specified beneficiary;

Notes: See 207.01(1)"registered plan strip". For the meaning of "one of the main purposes" see Notes to 83(2.1). Finance's Technical Notes say that an example of an RCA strip is "where an RCA has directly or indirectly made a loan to, or acquired a debt of, a specified beneficiary or a person who does not deal at arm's length with the beneficiary, and steps are undertaken to ensure that the loan cannot be repaid. The definition is not limited to loan-back transactions, however, and could apply in other circumstances (such as dilution of share value) where the basic operation of the RCA regime would otherwise be circumvented."

Definition added by 2012 budget bill #2, effective March 29, 2012.

"RCA trust" under a retirement compensation arrangement means

(a) any trust deemed by subsection 207.6(1) to be created in respect of subject property of the arrangement, and

(b) any trust governed by the arrangement;

Notes: See Notes to 207.7(2).

"refundable tax" of a retirement compensation arrangement at the end of a taxation year of an RCA trust under the arrangement means the amount, if any, by which the total of

(a) 50% of all contributions made under the arrangement while it was a retirement compensation arrangement and before the end of the year, and

(b) 50% of the amount, if any, by which

(i) the total of all amounts each of which is the income (determined as if this Act were read without reference to paragraph 82(1)(b)) of an RCA trust under the arrangement from a business or property for the year or a preceding taxation year or a capital gain of the trust for the year or a preceding taxation year,

exceeds

(ii) the total of all amounts each of which is a loss of an RCA trust under the arrangement from a business or property for the year or a preceding taxation year or a capital loss of the trust for the year or a preceding taxation year,

exceeds

(c) 50% of all amounts paid as distributions to one or more persons (including amounts that are required by paragraph 12(1)(n.3) to be included in computing the recipient's income) under the arrangement while it was a retirement compensation arrangement and before the end of the year, other than a distribution paid where it is established, by subsequent events or otherwise, that the distribution was paid as part of a series of payments and refunds of contributions under the arrangement;

Related Provisions: 207.5(2) — Deemed refundable tax on election; 207.6(7)(c) — Where amount transferred from one RCA to another; 207.65 — Tax paid under 207.61 or 207.62 is deemed to be a distribution; 207.7(2) — Refund of refundable tax in later year; 248(10) — Series of payments and refunds. See additional Related Provisions at end of Part XI.3.

Notes: For CRA interpretation see VIEWS docs 2008-0301151E5 (amount includable under (b)(i)); 2010-0388761R3 (ruling that posting collateral under a Credit Facility Agreement is not a contribution); 2013-0511051E5 (whether amount paid by employer to RCA is contribution or loan); 2017-0692331C6 [CLHIA 2017 q.3] (post-retirement benefits paid directly by employer to retired employees under SERP do not fall into para. (c)); 2017-0720901R3 (securing obligations with a surety bond).

"significant interest" has the same meaning as in subsection 207.01(4);

Notes: Definition added by 2012 budget bill #2, effective March 29, 2012.

"specified beneficiary", of a retirement compensation arrangement, means an individual who has an interest or a right in respect of the arrangement and who has or had a significant interest in an employer or former employer in respect of the arrangement;

Notes: Definition added by 2012 budget bill #2, effective March 29, 2012.

"subject property of a retirement compensation arrangement" means property that is held in connection with the arrangement.

(2) Election — Notwithstanding the definition "refundable tax" in subsection (1), where the custodian of a retirement compensation arrangement so elects in the return under this Part for a taxation year of an RCA trust under the arrangement and all the subject property, if any, of the arrangement (other than a right to claim a refund under subsection 164(1) or 207.7(2)) at the end of the year consists only of cash, debt obligations, shares listed on a designated stock exchange, or any combination thereof, an amount equal to the total of

(a) the amount of that cash at the end of the year,

(b) the total of all amounts each of which is the greater of the principal amount of such a debt obligation outstanding at the end of the year and the fair market value of the obligation at the end of the year, and

(c) the fair market value of those shares at the end of the year

shall be deemed for the purposes of this Part to be the refundable tax of the arrangement at the end of the year.

Related Provisions: 207.5(3) — Limitation where decline in value attributable to advantage or prohibited investment. See also at end of Part XI.3.

Notes: For discussion of this election see Montgomery, "Executive Retirement Arrangements", 2003 Cdn Tax Foundation conference report at 16:15-16. For calculation of the refundable tax for the year following the election, see VIEWS docs 2004-0068231I7, 2015-0617341E5. Foreign tax paid by an RCA can be deducted under 20(11) or (12) in the calculation: 2009-0316841E5. Where the only property an RCA trust holds is an exempt insurance policy with underlying investments, the election cannot be made: 2013-0493741E5. However, it may be possible after distributing a life insurance policy to the beneficiary, where the only property held at year-end is the right to claim a refund under 164(1) or 207.7(1): 2015-0580461E6.

207.5(2) amended by 2007 budget bill #2, effective Dec. 14, 2007, to change "prescribed stock exchange" to "designated stock exchange".

(3) Limitation on election — Subsection (2) does not apply in respect of an RCA trust if any part of a decline in the fair market value of subject property of the retirement compensation arrangement is reasonably attributable to a prohibited investment for, or an advantage in relation to, the RCA trust unless the Minister is satisfied that it is just and equitable to allow the election to be made, having regard to all the circumstances, in which case, the Minister may adjust the amount deemed by subsection (2) to be the refundable tax of the arrangement to take into account all or part of the decline in the fair market value of the subject property.

Notes: For the meaning of "just and equitable", see Notes to 85(7.1).

207.5(3) added by 2012 budget bill #2, effective for elections in respect of tax paid under 207.7(1) in respect of contributions made to an RCA after March 28, 2012 and income earned, capital gains realized and losses incurred, in respect of such contributions.

Definitions [s. 207.5]: "advantage" — 207.5(1); "affiliated" — 251.1; "amount" — 248(1); "arm's length" — 251(1); "capital gain" — 39(1)(a), 248(1); "capital loss" — 39(1)(b), 248(1); "corporation" — 248(1), *Interpretation Act* 35(1); "custodian" — 248(1)"retirement compensation arrangement"; "designated stock exchange" — 248(1), 262; "disposition", "dividend", "employer" — 248(1); "fair market value" — see 69(1) Notes; "individual", "Minister" — 248(1); "partnership" — see 96(1) Notes; "person", "prescribed" — 248(1); "prohibited investment" — 207.5(1); "property" — 248(1); "RCA strip", "RCA trust" — 207.5(1); "refundable tax" — 207.5(1), (2); "retirement compensation arrangement" — 248(1); "series", "series of transactions" — 248(10); "share" — 248(1); "significant interest" — 207.01(4), 207.5(1); "specified beneficiary" — 207.5(1); "subject property" — 207.5(1); "taxation year" — 249; "taxpayer" — 248(1); "trust" — 104(1), 248(1), (3).

207.6 (1) Creation of trust — In respect of the subject property of a retirement compensation arrangement, other than subject property of the arrangement held by a trust governed by a retirement compensation arrangement, for the purposes of this Part and Part I, the following rules apply:

(a) a trust is deemed to be created on the day that the arrangement is established;

(b) the subject property of the arrangement is deemed to be property of the trust and not to be property of any other person; and

(c) the custodian of the arrangement is deemed to be the trustee having ownership or control of the trust property.

Related Provisions: 207.6(7) — Transfer from RCA to another RCA. See also Related Provisions at end of Part XI.3.

Notes: 207.6(1)(a) amended by 2014 budget bill #2, for 2016 and later taxation years, to change "an *inter vivos* trust" to "a trust" (in sync with generally replacing "testamentary trust" with "graduated rate estate").

Forms: T733: Application for an RCA account number; T4041: Retirement compensation arrangements guide.

(2) Life insurance policies — For the purposes of this Part and Part I, where by virtue of a plan or arrangement an employer is obliged to provide benefits that are to be received or enjoyed by any person on, after or in contemplation of any substantial change in the services rendered by a taxpayer, the retirement of a taxpayer or the loss of an office or employment of a taxpayer, and where the employer, former employer or a person or partnership with whom the employer or former employer does not deal at arm's length acquires an interest in a life insurance policy that may reasonably be considered to be acquired to fund, in whole or in part, those benefits, the following rules apply in respect of the plan or arrangement if it is not otherwise a retirement compensation arrangement and is not excluded from the definition "retirement compensation arrangement", in subsection 248(1), by any of paragraphs (a) to (l) and (n) thereof:

(a) the person or partnership that acquired the interest is deemed to be the custodian of a retirement compensation arrangement;

(b) the interest is deemed to be subject property of the retirement compensation arrangement;

(c) an amount equal to twice the amount of any premium paid in respect of the interest or any repayment of a policy loan thereunder is deemed to be a contribution under the retirement compensation arrangement; and

(d) any payment received in respect of the interest, including a policy loan, and any amount received as a refund of refundable tax is deemed to be an amount received out of or under the retirement compensation arrangement by the recipient and not to be a payment of any other amount.

Notes: For interpretation see VIEWS docs 2007-0244651C6, 2012-0435771C6.

(3) Incorporated employee — For the purpose of the provisions of this Act relating to retirement compensation arrangements, where

(a) a corporation that at any time carried on a personal services business, or an employee of the corporation, enters into a plan or arrangement with a person or partnership (referred to in this subsection as the "employer") to whom or which the corporation renders services, and

(b) the plan or arrangement provides for benefits to be received or enjoyed by any person on, after or in contemplation of the cessation of, or any substantial change in, the services rendered by the corporation, or an employee of the corporation, to the employer,

the following rules apply:

(c) the employer and the corporation are deemed to be an employer and employee, respectively, in relation to each other, and

(d) any benefits to be received or enjoyed by any person under the plan or arrangement are deemed to be benefits to be received or enjoyed by the person on, after or in contemplation of a substantial change in the services rendered by the corporation.

Related Provisions: 18(1)(p) — Limitation on deductions re incorporated employees. See additional Related Provisions at end of Part XI.3.

Notes: See Notes to 125(7)"personal services business" for discussion of incorporated employees.

(4) Deemed contribution — Where at any time an employee benefit plan becomes a retirement compensation arrangement as a consequence of a change of the custodian of the plan or as a consequence of the custodian ceasing either to carry on business through a fixed place of business in Canada or to be licensed or otherwise authorized under the laws of Canada or a province to carry on in Canada the business of offering to the public its services as trustee,

(a) for the purposes of this Part and Part I, the custodian of the plan is deemed to have made a contribution to the arrangement immediately after that time, in an amount equal to the fair market value at that time of all the properties of the plan; and

(b) for the purposes of section 32.1, that amount is deemed to be a payment made at that time out of or under the plan to or for the benefit of employees or former employees of the employers who contributed to the plan.

Related Provisions: See Related Provisions and Definitions at end of Part XI.3.

(5) Resident's arrangement — For the purposes of this Act, where a resident's contribution has been made under a plan or arrangement (in this subsection referred to as the "plan"),

(a) the plan is deemed, in respect of its application to all resident's contributions made under the plan and all property that can reasonably be considered to be derived from those contributions, to be a separate arrangement (in this subsection referred to as the "residents' arrangement") independent of the plan in respect of its application to all other contributions and property that can reasonably be considered to derive from those other contributions;

(b) the residents' arrangement is deemed to be a retirement compensation arrangement; and

(c) each person and partnership to whom a contribution is made under the residents' arrangement is deemed to be a custodian of the residents' arrangement.

Related Provisions: 207.6(5.1) — Resident's contribution; 252.1 — Where union is employer. See additional Related Provisions at end of Part XI.3.

Notes: For CRA views see docs 2010-0388731E5; 2012-044068117 (deemed RCA is subject to all RCA rules, including withholding and information return).

207.6(5) amended by 1993 technical bill, retroactive to October 9, 1986.

Regulations: 6804(4)–(6) (prescribed contribution).

(5.1) Resident's contribution — For the purpose of subsection (5), "resident's contribution" means such part of a contribution made under a plan or arrangement (in this subsection referred to as the "plan") at a time when the plan would, but for paragraph (l) of the definition "retirement compensation arrangement" in subsection 248(1), be a retirement compensation arrangement as

(a) is not a prescribed contribution; and

(b) can reasonably be considered to have been made in respect of services rendered by an individual to an employer in a period

(i) throughout which the individual was resident in Canada and rendered services to the employer that were primarily services rendered in Canada or services rendered in connection with a business carried on by the employer in Canada (or a combination of such services), and

(ii) at the beginning of which the individual had been resident in Canada throughout at least 60 of the 72 preceding calendar months, where the individual was non-resident at any time before the period and became a member of the plan before the end of the month after the month in which the individual became resident in Canada,

and, for the purpose of this paragraph, where benefits provided to an individual under a particular plan or arrangement are replaced by benefits under another plan or arrangement, the other plan or arrangement shall be deemed, in respect of the individual, to be the same plan or arrangement as the particular plan or arrangement.

Related Provisions: 252.1 — Where union is employer.

Notes: For a ruling that 207.6(5.1) does not apply see VIEWS doc 2007-0220151R3.

207.6(5.1) added by 1993 technical bill, retroactive to October 9, 1986 (i.e., to the introduction of Part XI.3). See Notes to 207.6(5).

Regulations: 6804(4)–(6) (prescribed contribution).

(6) Prescribed plan or arrangement — For the purposes of the provisions of this Act relating to retirement compensation arrangements, the following rules apply in respect of a prescribed plan or arrangement:

(a) the plan or arrangement shall be deemed to be a retirement compensation arrangement;

(b) an amount credited at any time to the account established in the accounts of Canada or a province in connection with the plan or arrangement shall be, except to the extent that it is in respect of a refund determined under subsection 207.7(2), deemed to be a contribution under the plan or arrangement at that time;

(c) the custodian of the plan or arrangement shall be deemed to be

(i) where the account is established in the accounts of Canada, Her Majesty in right of Canada, and

(ii) where the account is established in the accounts of a province, Her Majesty in right of that province; and

(d) the subject property of the plan or arrangement, at any time, shall be deemed to include an amount of cash equal to the balance at that time in the account.

Related Provisions: See at end of Part XI.3.

Notes: 207.6(6) added by 1992 technical bill, effective 1992.

Regulations: 103(7)(a)(ii) (no withholding on transfer under 207.6(6)); 6802 (prescribed plan or arrangement).

(7) Transfers — Where an amount (other than an amount that is part of a series of periodic payments) is transferred directly to a retirement compensation arrangement (other than an arrangement the custodian of which is non-resident or which is deemed by subsection (5) to be a retirement compensation arrangement) from another retirement compensation arrangement,

(a) the amount shall not, solely because of the transfer, be included in computing a taxpayer's income under Part I;

(b) no deduction may be made in respect of the amount in computing a taxpayer's income under Part I; and

(c) the amount is considered, for the purpose of the definition "refundable tax" in subsection 207.5(1), to be paid as a distribution to one or more persons under the arrangement from which the amount is transferred and to be a contribution made under the arrangement to which the amount is transferred.

Related Provisions: 60(t)(ii)(A), (A.1), (E), 60(u)(ii)(A), (A.1), (E) — Whether amounts transferred under 207.6(7) deductible; 212(1)(j) — Transfer not subject to non-resident withholding tax.

Notes: 207.6(7) added by 1995-97 technical bill, for amounts transferred after 1995. It provides for a tax-neutral transfer from RCA plan R1 to plan R2. The employer does not include the payment from R1 in income under 12(1)(n.3) or 56(1)(x)-(z), there is no deduction under 8(1)(m.2) or 20(1)(r), and the individual gets no 60(t) deduction, though 60(t) and (u) allow deduction when payments are ultimately received from R2. There is no withholding on the transferred amount: Reg. 103(7)(a). For Part XI.3 tax, the 207.6(7) transfer amount is considered a distribution from R1 and a contribution to R2, transferring the obligation for the tax from R1 to R2.

For a ruling approving a transfer see VIEWS doc 2019-0803761R3. If what is transferred is shares with accrued gain, the "amount" is the shares' market value: 2016-0645471E5.

Regulations: 103(7)(a)(iii) (no withholding on transfer under 207.6(7)); 6802.1(2) (prescribed plans and arrangements).

Definitions [s. 207.6]: "amount" — 248(1); "arm's length" — 251(1); "business" — 248(1); "Canada" — 255; "carrying on business" — 253; "corporation" — 248(1), *Interpretation Act* 35(1); "custodian" — 248(1)"retirement compensation arrangement"; "employee", "employee benefit plan", "employer", "employment" — 248(1); "fair market value" — see 69(1) Notes; "Her Majesty" — *Interpretation Act* 35(1); "individual" — 248(1); "*inter vivos* trust" — 108(1), 248(1); "life insurance policy" — 138(12), 248(1); "non-resident", "office", "person", "prescribed" — 248(1); "prescribed plan or arrangement" — Reg. 6801, 6802, 6802.1, 6803; "property" — 248(1); "province" — *Interpretation Act* 35(1); "refundable tax" — 207.5(1); "resident in Canada" — 250; "residents' arrangement" — 207.6(5)(b); "resident's contribution" — 207.6(5.1); "retirement compensation arrangement" — 248(1); "subject property" — 207.5(1); "taxpayer" — 248(1); "trust" — 104(1), 248(1), (3).

207.61 (1) Tax payable on prohibited investment — A custodian of a retirement compensation arrangement shall pay a tax under this Part for a calendar year if, at any time in the year,

(a) the arrangement acquires property that is a prohibited investment for the arrangement; or

(b) subject property of the arrangement becomes a prohibited investment for the arrangement after March 29, 2012.

Related Provisions: 207.04(1) — Parallel rule for RRSP, RRIF or TFSA; 207.61(2) — Amount of tax payable; 207.61(3) — Refund of tax on disposition of investment; 207.61(4) — Deemed disposition on property becoming or ceasing to be PI; 207.63 — Custodian and specified beneficiary jointly liable; 207.64 — CRA may waive or cancel tax; 207.65 — Tax paid under 207.61 is deemed to be a distribution.

Notes: See Ball & Welch, "Update on the Prohibited Investment and Advantage Rules", 2012 Cdn Tax Foundation conference report, at 34:16-22; Singh & Welch,

"Retirement Compensation Arrangements and the Prohibited Investment and Advantage Rules", XVIII(4) *Insurance Planning* [*IP*] (Federated Press) 1170-72 (2012); Welch, "Retirement Compensation Arrangements: an Update", XIX(4) *IP* 1239-45 (2013). See also Notes to 207.01(1)"advantage" and "prohibited investment" for the parallel rules for registered plans; and Notes at end of 207.61.

See also VIEWS docs 2012-0453141C6 [2012 APFF q.5] (whether split-dollar arrangement creates an "advantage"); 2012-0470181E5 (various questions on the RCA advantage rules); 2013-0499501E5 and 2014-0544211E5 (RCA trust owns universal life policy on life of RCA beneficiary); 2013-0500581I7 (advantage where specified beneficiary of RCA assigns RCA right to secure a debt); 2013-0501941E5 (questions on the transitional rules).

(2) Amount of tax payable — The amount of tax payable in respect of each property described in subsection (1) is 50% of the fair market value of the property at the time referred to in that subsection.

Related Provisions: 207.63 — Custodian and specified beneficiary jointly liable; 207.64 — CRA may waive or cancel tax.

(3) Refund — If in a calendar year an RCA trust disposes of a property in respect of which a tax is imposed under subsection (1) on the custodian of the retirement compensation arrangement, the custodian is entitled to a refund for the year of an amount equal to

(a) the amount of the tax so imposed, unless paragraph (b) applies; or

(b) nil,

(i) if it is reasonable to consider that the custodian, or a specified beneficiary of the arrangement, knew, or ought to have known, at the time the property was acquired by the arrangement, that it was, or would become, a property described in subsection (1), or

(ii) if the property is not disposed of by the arrangement before the end of the calendar year following the calendar year in which the tax arose, or any later time that the Minister considers reasonable in the circumstances.

(4) Deemed disposition and reacquisition — If, at any time, a property held by an RCA trust ceases to be, or becomes, a prohibited investment for the RCA trust, the RCA trust is deemed to have disposed of the property immediately before that time for proceeds of disposition equal to the fair market value of the property at that time and to have reacquired the property at that time at a cost equal to that fair market value.

Notes: The deemed reacquisition when property becomes a PI triggers tax under 207.61(1).

Notes [s. 207.61]: 207.61 added by 2012 budget bill #2, effective March 29, 2012. For purposes of 207.61, an amendment to the terms of a promissory note, or similar debt obligation, that is subject property of an RCA acquired before March 29, 2012 to provide for commercially reasonable payments of principal and interest is deemed not to be a disposition or an acquisition of the note or obligation (bill s. 45(2)).

Definitions [s. 207.61]: "amount" — 248(1); "calendar year" — *Interpretation Act* 37(1)(a); "custodian" — 248(1)"retirement compensation arrangement"; "disposition" — 248(1); "fair market value" — see 69(1) Notes; "Minister" — 248(1); "prohibited investment" — 207.5(1); "property", "retirement compensation arrangement" — 248(1); "specified beneficiary" — 207.5(1); "trust" — 104(1), 248(1), (3).

207.62 (1) Tax payable in respect of advantage — A custodian of a retirement compensation arrangement shall pay a tax under this Part for a calendar year if, in the year, an advantage in relation to the arrangement is extended to, or is received or receivable by, an RCA trust under the arrangement, a specified beneficiary of the arrangement or any person who does not deal at arm's length with the specified beneficiary.

Related Provisions: 207.05(1) — Parallel rule for RRSP, RRIF or TFSA; 207.62(2) — Amount of tax; 207.63 — Custodian and specified beneficiary jointly liable; 207.64 — CRA may waive or cancel tax; 207.65 — Tax paid under 207.62 is deemed to be a distribution.

Notes: See Notes to 207.61(1).

(2) Amount of tax payable — The amount of tax payable in respect of an advantage described in subsection (1) is

(a) in the case of a benefit, the fair market value of the benefit;

(b) in the case of a loan or an indebtedness, the amount of the loan or indebtedness; and

(c) in the case of an RCA strip, the amount of the RCA strip.

Related Provisions: 207.63 — Custodian and specified beneficiary jointly liable; 207.64 — CRA may waive or cancel tax.

Notes: 207.62 added by 2012 budget bill #2, effective March 29, 2012.

Definitions [s. 207.62]: "advantage" — 207.5(1); "amount" — 248(1); "arm's length" — 251(1); "calendar year" — *Interpretation Act* 37(1)(a); "custodian" — 248(1)"retirement compensation arrangement"; "fair market value" — see 69(1) Notes; "person" — 248(1); "RCA strip" — 207.5(1); "retirement compensation arrangement" — 248(1); "specified beneficiary" — 207.5(1); "trust" — 104(1), 248(1), (3).

207.63 Joint liability — If a custodian of a retirement compensation arrangement is liable to pay a tax under section 207.61 or 207.62, a specified beneficiary of the arrangement is jointly and severally, or solidarily, liable for that tax to the extent that the specified beneficiary participated in, assented to or acquiesced in the making of, the transaction or event or series of transactions or events that resulted in the liability.

Related Provisions: 207.64 — CRA may waive or cancel liability.

Notes: 207.63 added by 2012 budget bill #2, effective March 29, 2012.

Definitions [s. 207.63]: "custodian" — 248(1)"retirement compensation arrangement"; "retirement compensation arrangement" — 248(1); "series of transactions" — 248(10); "specified beneficiary" — 207.5(1).

207.64 Waiver of tax payable — If a person would otherwise be liable to pay a tax under this Part because of any of sections 207.61 to 207.63, the Minister may waive or cancel all or part of the liability if the Minister considers it just and equitable to do so having regard to all the circumstances, including

(a) whether the tax arose as a consequence of reasonable error; and

(b) the extent to which the transaction or event or series of transactions or events that gave rise to the tax also gave rise to another tax under this Act.

Notes: For the meaning of "just and equitable", see Notes to 85(7.1).

207.64 added by 2012 budget bill #2, effective March 29, 2012.

Definitions [s. 207.64]: "Minister", "person" — 248(1); "series of transactions" — 248(10).

207.65 Deemed distribution — For the purposes of the definition "refundable tax" in subsection 207.5(1), tax paid under section 207.61 or 207.62 by a custodian of a retirement compensation arrangement out of property held in connection with the arrangement is deemed to be a distribution under the arrangement for the taxation year in which the tax is paid to the extent that the tax has not been refunded, waived or cancelled.

Notes: 207.65 added by 2012 budget bill #2, effective March 29, 2012.

Definitions [s. 207.65]: "custodian" — 248(1)"retirement compensation arrangement"; "disposition", "property", "retirement compensation arrangement" — 248(1); "taxation year" — 249.

207.7 (1) Tax payable — Every custodian of a retirement compensation arrangement shall pay a tax under this Part for each taxation year of an RCA trust under the arrangement equal to the amount, if any, by which the refundable tax of the arrangement at the end of the year exceeds the refundable tax of the arrangement at the end of the immediately preceding taxation year, if any.

Related Provisions: See at end of Part XI.3.

Forms: T4041: Retirement compensation arrangements guide.

(2) Refund — Where the custodian of a retirement compensation arrangement has filed a return under this Part for a taxation year within three years after the end of the year, the Minister

(a) may, on sending the notice of assessment for the year or a notification that no tax is payable for the year, refund without application an amount equal to the amount, if any, by which the refundable tax of the arrangement at the end of the immediately preceding year exceeds the refundable tax of the arrangement at the end of the year; and

(b) shall, with all due dispatch, make such a refund after sending the notice of assessment if application for it has been made in writing by the custodian within three years after the day of sending of a notice of an original assessment for the year or of a notification that no tax is payable for the year.

Related Provisions: 207.6(6) — Prescribed plan or arrangement; 244(14), (14.1) — Date when notice sent. See additional Related Provisions at end of Part XI.3; *Interpretation Act* 27(5) — Meaning of "within three years".

Notes: Where refundable tax builds up and cannot be refunded, replacing the RCA trust with a new one will not trigger the refund: VIEWS doc 2013-0511061E5.

207.7(2)(a) and (b) amended by 2010 budget bill #2, effective Dec. 15, 2010, to change "mailing" to "sending" (3 places), to accommodate electronic notices under 244(14.1).

(3) Payment of tax — Every custodian of a retirement compensation arrangement shall, within 90 days after the end of each taxation year of an RCA trust under the arrangement,

(a) file with the Minister a return for the year under this Part in prescribed form and containing prescribed information, without notice or demand therefor;

(b) estimate in the return the amount of tax, if any, payable by the custodian under this Part for the year; and

(c) pay to the Receiver General the amount of tax, if any, payable by the custodian under this Part for the year.

Related Provisions: 147.1(3) — Postponement of filing deadline where RCA is registered as pension plan; 150.1(5) — Electronic filing; 248(7) — Return deemed received on day mailed; *Interpretation Act* 27(5) — Meaning of "within 90 days". See additional Related Provisions at end of Part XI.3.

Forms: T3-RCA: Part XI.3 tax return — retirement compensation arrangement; T4041: Retirement compensation arrangements guide.

(4) Provisions applicable to Part — Subsections 150(2) and (3), sections 152 and 158, subsections 161(1) and (11), sections 162 to 167 and Division J of Part I are applicable to this Part with such modifications as the circumstances require.

Definitions [s. 207.7]: "amount", "assessment" — 248(1); "custodian" — 248(1)"retirement compensation arrangement"; "day of sending" — 244(14), (14.1); "Minister", "prescribed" — 248(1); "RCA trust", "refundable tax" — 207.5(1); "retirement compensation arrangement" — 248(1); "tax payable" — 248(2); "taxation year" — 249; "trust" — 104(1), 248(1), (3); "writing" — *Interpretation Act* 35(1).

Forms [s. 207.7]: T4A-RCA: Statement of distributions from an RCA; T4A-RCA Summ: Information return of distributions from an RCA; T735: Application for a remittance number for tax withheld from an RCA; T737-RCA: Statement of contributions paid to a custodian of an RCA.

Related Provisions [Part XI.3]: 8(1)(m.2) — Deduction for employee RCA contributions; 87(2)(j.3) — Amalgamation — continuation of corporation; 107.2 — Distribution by RCA to beneficiary; 149(1)(q.1) — RCA trust exempt from Part I tax; 153(1)(p)–(r) — Withholding of tax at source on contribution to RCA, distribution out of RCA, and purchase of interest in RCA; 160.3 — Joint and several liability — RCA benefits; 227(8.2) — Liability for failure to withhold.

PART XI.4 — TAX ON EXCESS EPSP AMOUNTS

207.8 (1) Excess EPSP amount — In this Part, "excess EPSP amount", of a specified employee for a taxation year in respect of an employer, means the amount determined by the formula

$$A - (20\% \times B)$$

where

A is the portion of the total of all amounts paid by the employer of the specified employee (or by a corporation with which the employer does not deal at arm's length) to a trust governed by an employees profit sharing plan that is allocated for the year to the specified employee; and

B is the specified employee's total income for the year from an office or employment with the employer computed without reference to paragraph 6(1)(d) and sections 7 and 8.

Related Provisions: 257 — Formula cannot calculate to less than zero.

Notes: See Notes at end of 207.8. An excess EPSP amount is "compensation" under 147.1(1): VIEWS doc 2013-0380911E5.

(2) Tax payable — If a specified employee has an excess EPSP amount for a taxation year, the specified employee shall pay a tax for the year equal to the amount determined by the formula

$$(A + B) \times C$$

where

A is the highest individual percentage for the year;

B is

    (a) if the specified employee is resident in Quebec at the end of the year, 0%,

    (b) if the specified employee is resident in a province other than Quebec at the end of the year, the highest percentage rate of tax, including surtaxes but not taxes that are limited to a maximum amount, imposed by the province for the year on the income of an individual who is a resident of the province, or

    (c) in any other case, 14%; and

C is the total of all excess EPSP amounts of the specified employee for the year.

Related Provisions: 8(1)(o.2) — Deduction from income to prevent double tax; 156.1(1)"net tax owing"A — Part XI.4 tax included in determining instalments required; 207.8(3) — Waiver or cancellation of tax; 207.8(4) — Return and payment of tax; Reg. 2607 — Determination of "resident" in a province.

Notes: For CRA interpretation see VIEWS doc 2012-0412181E5 (general discussion).

207.8(2)A changed from "29%" by 2016 budget bill #1, for 2016 and later taxation years.

(3) Waiver or cancellation — If a specified employee would otherwise be liable to pay a tax under subsection (2), the Minister may waive or cancel all or part of the liability if the Minister considers it just and equitable to do so having regard to all the circumstances.

Notes: For the meaning of "just and equitable", see Notes to 85(7.1).

(4) Return and payment of tax — Every person who is liable to pay tax under this Part for a taxation year shall

    (a) on or before the person's filing-due date for the year, file with the Minister a return for the year under this Part in prescribed form and containing prescribed information; and

    (b) on or before the person's balance-due day for the year, pay to the Receiver General the amount of tax payable under this Part by the person for the year.

Related Provisions: 207.8(5) — Administrative provisions applicable.

Forms: RC359: Tax on excess employees profit-sharing plan amounts.

(5) Provisions applicable to this Part — Subsections 150(2) and (3), sections 152, 155 to 156.1, 158 to 160.1, 161 and 161.2 to 167 and Division J of Part I apply to this Part with any modifications that the circumstances require.

Related Provisions: 156.1(1)"net tax owing"(b)A — Part XI.4 tax included in calculation of instalment threshold.

Notes [s. 207.8]: Part XI.4 (207.8) added by 2012 budget bill #2, for 2012 and later taxation years, but it does not apply in respect of payments made to a trust governed by an EPSP

    (a) before March 29, 2012, or

    (b) before 2013 pursuant to an obligation arising under a written agreement or arrangement entered into before March 29, 2012.

Definitions [s. 207.8]: "amount" — 248(1); "arm's length" — 251(1); "corporation" — 248(1), *Interpretation Act* 35(1); "employees profit sharing plan" — 144(1), 248(1); "employer", "employment" — 248(1); "excess EPSP amount" — 207.8(1); "highest individual percentage", "Minister" — 248(1); "province" — *Interpretation Act* 35(1); "resident" — Reg 2607; "specified employee" — 248(1); "taxation year" — 249; "trust" — 104(1), 248(1), (3).

PART XI.5 — TAX IN RESPECT OF EMPLOYEE LIFE AND HEALTH TRUST

207.9 (1) Definitions — The following definitions apply in this Part.

"participating employer" of an employee life and health trust means an employer that provides designated employee benefits for its employees through a trust that meets the conditions described in subsection 144.1(2).

"prohibited investment", at any time for an employee life and health trust, means property that is at that time

    (a) a share of the capital stock of, an interest in or a debt of

        (i) a participating employer of the employee life and health trust, or

        (ii) a person or partnership that does not deal at arm's length with a participating employer of the employee life and health trust; or

    (b) an interest (or, for civil law, a right) in, or a right to acquire, a share, interest or debt described in paragraph (a).

Related Provisions: 207.9(2)–(3) — Tax on PI; 207.9(5) — Where property ceases to be PI.

(2) Tax payable on prohibited investment — A trust shall pay a tax under this Part for a calendar year if, at any time in the year while the trust is an employee life and health trust,

    (a) the trust acquires property that is a prohibited investment for the trust; or

    (b) income is received or becomes receivable by the trust from, or the trust has a taxable capital gain from the disposition of, a prohibited investment for the trust.

Related Provisions: 207.9(3) — Amount of tax; 207.9(4) — Refund on disposition of investment.

Notes: Part XI.5 tax (207.9) applies on an ELHT's acquiring a prohibited investment. The tax is 50% of the value of the property when acquired, and 50% of any income or gains: 207.9(3). This tax is consequential on repeal of 144.1(2)(h), as per a Dec. 19, 2012 Finance comfort letter to GM Canada.

(3) Amount of tax payable — The amount of tax payable under subsection (2) is

    (a) if paragraph (2)(a) applies, 50% of the fair market value of the property at the time it is acquired; and

    (b) if paragraph (2)(b) applies, 50% of the income or the taxable capital gain.

(4) Refund — If in a calendar year a trust disposes of a property in respect of which a tax is imposed on the trust under subsection (2), the trust is entitled to a refund for the year of an amount equal to

    (a) the amount of the tax so imposed, unless paragraph (b) applies; or

    (b) nil, if

        (i) it is reasonable to consider that the trustees knew, or ought to have known, at the time the property was acquired that it was, or would become, a property described in subsection (2), or

        (ii) the property is not disposed of by the trust before the end of the calendar year following the calendar year in which the tax arose, or any later time that the Minister considers reasonable in the circumstances.

(5) Deemed disposition and reacquisition — If, at any time, a property held by an employee life and health trust ceases to be, or becomes, a prohibited investment for the employee life and health trust, the employee life and health trust is deemed to have disposed of the property immediately before that time for proceeds of disposition equal to the fair market value of the property at that time and to have reacquired the property at that time at a cost equal to that fair market value.

Notes [s. 207.9]: Finance advises that it will add administrative provisions to Part XI.5, similar to 207.8(4)-(5), to cover returns, objections, appeals, penalties, etc. Given the discretion built into the refund mechanism in 207.9(4)(b)(ii), a separate provision permitting waiver of the tax (like 207.8(3)) may not be needed.

See 207.9(2) Notes. Part XI.5 added by 2021 budget bill #1, for 2014 and later tax years.

Definitions [s. 207.9]: "amount" — 248(1); "arm's length" — 251(1); "calendar year" — *Interpretation Act* 37(1)(a); "disposition", "employee" — 248(1); "employee life and health trust" — 144.1(2), 248(1); "employer" — 248(1); "fair market value" — see 69(1) Notes; "Minister" — 248(1); "partnership" — see 96(1) Notes; "person", "property", "share" — 248(1); "taxable capital gain" — 38(a), 248(1); "taxation year" — 249; "trust" — 104(1), 248(1), (3).

PART XII — TAX IN RESPECT OF CERTAIN ROYALTIES, TAXES, LEASE RENTALS, ETC., PAID TO A GOVERNMENT BY A TAX EXEMPT PERSON [REPEALED]

208. [Repealed]

Notes: 208 (Part XII) repealed by 2003 resource bill, for tax years that begin after 2006 (with the repeal of 12(1)(o) and 18(1)(m)). It imposed a penalty tax on certain resource property in which both taxable and tax-exempt persons had an interest. Previously amended by 2003 and 1996 Budgets, 1991 technical bill.

An earlier Part XII (208, 209), which imposed a tax on investment income of life insurers, was repealed in 1977 but re-enacted in 1988 as Part XII.3 (211-211.5).

PART XII.1 — TAX ON CARVED-OUT INCOME

209. (1) Definitions — For the purposes of this Part,

"carved-out income" of a person for a taxation year from a carved-out property means the amount, if any, by which

(a) the person's income for the year attributable to the property computed under Part I on the assumption that in computing income no deduction was allowed under section 20, Subdivision E of Division B of Part I or section 104,

exceeds the total of

(b) the amount deducted under subsection 66.4(2) in computing the person's income for the year to the extent that it may reasonably be considered to be attributable to the property, and

(c) to the extent that the property is an interest in a bituminous sands deposit or oil shale deposit, the amount deducted under subsection 66.2(2) in computing the person's income for the year to the extent that it can reasonably be considered to be attributable to the cost of that interest;

Related Provisions: 66(14.6) — Deduction of carved-out income; 209(6) — Partnerships.

Notes: Part XII.1 tax on "carved-out income" discourages use of tax-exempt persons and loss corporations for holding profitable resource property, where a profitable person retains an economic interest. Tax under 209(2) is 50% of carved-out income. In a typical carve-out arrangement, a profitable resource company transfers a temporary interest in a producing oil or gas well (i.e., the "carving-out" of income) to another corp which has accumulated losses or is tax-exempt. After a period of tax-free income, the resource properties are reconveyed to the resource company.

When Part XII.1 tax applies, 66(14.6) allows a deduction for the carved-out income, to prevent double tax.

Para. (a) amended by 2003 resource bill, for taxation years that begin after 2006. Definition earlier amended by 1996 Budget.

"carved-out property" of a person means

(a) a Canadian resource property where

(i) all or substantially all of the amount that the person is or may become entitled to receive in respect of the property may reasonably be considered to be limited to a maximum amount or to an amount determinable by reference to a stated quantity of production from a mineral resource or an accumulation of petroleum, natural gas or related hydrocarbons,

(ii) the period of time during which the person's interest in the income attributable to the property may reasonably be expected to continue is

(A) where the property is a head lease or may reasonably be considered to derive from a head lease, less than the lesser of 10 years and the remainder of the term of the head lease, and

(B) in any other case, less than 10 years,

(iii) the person's interest in the income attributable to the property, expressed as a percentage of production for any period, may reasonably be expected to be reduced substantially,

(A) where the property is a head lease or may reasonably be considered to derive from a head lease, at any time before

(I) the expiration of a period of 10 years commencing when the property was acquired, or

(II) the expiration of the term of the head lease,

whichever occurs first, and

(B) in any other case, at any time before the expiration of a period of 10 years commencing when the property was acquired, or

(iv) another person has a right under an arrangement to acquire, at any time, the property or a portion thereof or a similar property from the person and it is reasonable to consider that one of the main reasons for the arrangement, or any series of transactions or events that includes the arrangement, was to reduce or postpone tax that would, but for this subparagraph, be payable under this Part, or

(b) an interest in a partnership or trust that holds a Canadian resource property where it is reasonable to consider that one of the main reasons for the existence of the interest is to reduce or postpone the tax that would, but for this paragraph, be payable under this Part,

but does not include

(c) an interest, or for civil law a right, in respect of a property that was acquired by the person solely in consideration of the person's undertaking under an agreement to incur Canadian exploration expense or Canadian development expense in respect of the property and, where the agreement so provides, to acquire gas or oil well equipment (as defined in subsection 1104(2) of the *Income Tax Regulations*) in respect of the property,

(c.1) an interest, or for civil law a right, in respect of a property that was retained by the person under an agreement under which another person obtained an absolute or conditional right to acquire another interest, or for civil law another right, in respect of the property, if the other interest or right is not carved-out property of the other person because of paragraph (c),

(d) a particular property acquired by the person under an arrangement solely as consideration for the sale of a Canadian resource property (other than a property that, immediately before the sale was a carved-out property of the person) that relates to the particular property except where it is reasonable to consider that one of the main reasons for the arrangement, or any series of transactions or events that includes the arrangement, was to reduce or postpone tax that would, but for this paragraph, be payable under this Act,

(e) a property retained or reserved by the person out of a Canadian resource property (other than a property that, immediately before the transaction by which the retention or reservation is made, was a carved-out property of the person) that was disposed of by the person except where it is reasonable to consider that one of the main reasons for the retention or reservation, or any series of transactions or events in which the property or interest was retained or reserved, was to reduce or postpone tax that would, but for this paragraph, be payable under this Act,

(f) a property acquired by the person from a taxpayer with whom the person did not deal at arm's length at the time of the acquisition and the property was acquired by the taxpayer or a person with whom the taxpayer did not deal at arm's length

(i) pursuant to an agreement in writing to do so entered into before July 20, 1985, or

(ii) under the circumstances described in this paragraph or paragraph (d) or (e),

except where it is reasonable to consider that one of the main reasons for the acquisition of the property, or any series of transactions or events in which the property was acquired, was to reduce or postpone tax that would, but for this paragraph, be payable under this Act,

(f.1) where the taxable income of the person is exempt from tax under Part I, a property of the person that

(i) does not relate to property of a person whose taxable income is not exempt from tax under Part I, and

(ii) is not, and does not relate to, property that was at any time a carved-out property of any other person, or

(g) a prescribed property;

Related Provisions: 209(6) — Partnerships; 248(10) — Series of transactions.

Notes: See Notes to 209(1)"carved-out income". Generally, a carved-out property is a Canadian resource property in which the taxpayer has a temporary interest.

CRA considers that "substantially all", used in (a)(i), means 90% or more. For "one of the main reasons" in (a)(iv), (b), (d), (e) and (f), see Notes to 83(2.1).

Paras. (c), (c.1) amended by 2002-2013 technical bill, effective June 26, 2013.

Definition "carved-out property" earlier amended by 1991 technical bill.

Regulations: 7600 (prescribed property).

"head lease" means a contract under which

(a) Her Majesty in right of Canada or a province grants, or

(b) an owner in fee simple, other than Her Majesty in right of Canada or a province, grants for a period of not less than 10 years

any right, licence or privilege to explore for, drill for or take petroleum, natural gas or related hydrocarbons in Canada or to prospect, explore, drill or mine for minerals in a mineral resource in Canada;

Notes: For the meaning of "right, licence or privilege", see Notes to 66(15)"Canadian resource property".

"term" of a head lease includes all renewal periods in respect of the head lease.

(2) Tax — Every person shall pay a tax under this Part for each taxation year equal to 45% of the total of the person's carved-out incomes for the year from carved-out properties.

Related Provisions: 18(1)(t) — Tax is non-deductible; 66(14.6) — Deduction of carved-out income.

Notes: See Notes to 209(1)"carved-out income".

Tax rate in 209(2) changed from 50% to 45% by 1993 technical bill, effective for 1992 and later taxation years, to more closely approximate the combined federal/provincial corporate tax rate.

(3) Return — Every person liable to pay tax under this Part for a taxation year shall file with the Minister, not later than the day on or before which the person is or would be, if the person were liable to pay tax under Part I for the year, required under section 150 to file a return of the person's income for the year under Part I, a return for the year under this Part in prescribed form containing an estimate of the amount of tax payable by the person under this Part for the year.

Related Provisions: 150.1(5) — Electronic filing.

Forms: T2096: Part XII.1 tax return — tax on carved-out income.

(4) Payment of tax — Where a person is liable to pay tax for a taxation year under this Part, the person shall pay in respect of the year, to the Receiver General

(a) on or before the last day of each month in the year, an amount equal to 1/12 of the amount of tax payable by the person under this Part for the year; and

(b) the remainder, if any, of the tax payable by the person under this Part for the year, on or before the person's balance-due day for the year.

Notes: Due to COVID-19, Part XII.1 tax owing from March 18-Sept. 29, 2020 was due on Sept. 30, 2020: see PITA 59th ed. at 150(1) opening words.

209(4)(b) amended by 2003 Budget to require payment on the "balance-due day" (as defined in 248(1)), effective for taxation years that begin after June 2003.

(5) Provisions applicable to Part — Subsections 150(2) and (3) and sections 152, 158 and 159, subsections 161(1), (2) and (11), sections 162 to 167 and Division J of Part I are applicable to this Part with such modifications as the circumstances require.

(6) Partnerships — For the purposes of subsection (1), a partnership shall be deemed to be a person and its taxation year shall be deemed to be its fiscal period.

Definitions [s. 209]: "amount" — 248(1); "arm's length" — 251(1); "balance-due day", "bituminous sands" — 248(1); "Canada" — 255; "Canadian development expense" — 66.2(5), 248(1); "Canadian exploration expense" — 66.1(6), 248(1); "Canadian resource property" — 66(15), 248(1); "carved-out income", "carved-out property" — 209(1); "fiscal period" — 249(2)(b), 249.1; "head lease" — 209(1); "Her Majesty" — *Interpretation Act* 35(1); "mineral resource", "mineral", "Minister" — 248(1); "partnership" — see 96(1) Notes; "person" — 209(6), 248(1); "prescribed", "property" — 248(1); "province" — *Interpretation Act* 35(1); "series of transactions" — 248(10); "tax payable" — 248(2); "taxable income" — 2(2), 248(1); "taxation year" — 209(6), 249; "taxpayer" — 248(1); "term" — 209(1); "trust" — 104(1), 248(1), (3); "writing" — *Interpretation Act* 35(1).

PART XII.2 — TAX ON DESIGNATED INCOME OF CERTAIN TRUSTS

210. (1) Definitions — The following definitions apply in this Part.

"designated beneficiary", under a particular trust at any time, means a beneficiary, under the particular trust, who is at that time

(a) a non-resident person;

(b) [Repealed]

(c) a person who is, because of subsection 149(1), exempt from tax under Part I on all or part of their taxable income and who acquired an interest as a beneficiary under the particular trust after October 1, 1987 directly or indirectly from a beneficiary under the particular trust except if

(i) the interest was, at all times after the later of October 1, 1987 and the day on which the interest was created, held by persons who were exempt from tax under Part I on all of their taxable income because of subsection 149(1), or

(ii) the person is a trust, governed by a registered retirement savings plan or a registered retirement income fund, who acquired the interest, directly or indirectly, from an individual or the spouse or common-law partner, or former spouse or common-law partner, of the individual who was, immediately after the interest was acquired, a beneficiary under the trust governed by the fund or plan;

(d) another trust (in this paragraph referred to as the "other trust") that is not a graduated rate estate, a mutual fund trust or a trust that is exempt because of subsection 149(1) from tax under Part I on all or part of its taxable income, if any beneficiary under the other trust is at that time

(i) a non-resident person,

(ii) [Repealed]

(iii) a trust that is not

(A) a graduated rate estate,

(B) a mutual fund trust,

(C) a trust that is exempt because of subsection 149(1) from tax under Part I on all or part of its taxable income, or

(D) a trust

(I) whose interest, at that time, in the other trust was held, at all times after the day on which the interest was created, either by it or by persons who were exempt because of subsection 149(1) from tax under Part I on all of their taxable income, and

(II) none of the beneficiaries under which is, at that time, a designated beneficiary under it, or

(iv) a person or partnership that

(A) is a designated beneficiary under the other trust because of paragraph (c) or (e), or

(B) would be a designated beneficiary under the particular trust because of paragraph (c) or (e) if, instead of being a beneficiary under the other trust, the person or partnership were at that time a beneficiary, under the particular trust, whose interest as a beneficiary under the particular trust were

(I) identical to its interest (referred to in this clause as the "particular interest") as a beneficiary under the other trust,

(II) acquired from each person or partnership from whom it acquired the particular interest, and

(III) held, at all times after the later of October 1, 1987 and the day on which the particular interest was created, by the same persons or partnerships that held the particular interest at those times; or

(e) a particular partnership any of the members of which is at that time

(i) another partnership, except if

(A) each such other partnership is a Canadian partnership,

(B) the interest of each such other partnership in the particular partnership is held, at all times after the day on which the interest was created, by the other partnership or by persons who were exempt because of subsection 149(1) from tax under Part I on all of their taxable income,

(C) the interest of each member, of each such other partnership, that is a person exempt because of subsection 149(1) from tax under Part I on all or part of its taxable income was held, at all times after the day on which the interest was created, by that member or by persons who were exempt because of subsection 149(1) from tax under Part I on all of their taxable income, and

(D) the interest of the particular partnership in the particular trust was held, at all times after the day on which the interest was created, by the particular partnership or by persons who were exempt because of subsection 149(1) from tax under Part I on all of their taxable income,

(ii) a non-resident person,

(iii) [Repealed]

(iv) another trust that is, under paragraph (d), a designated beneficiary of the particular trust or that would, under paragraph (d), be a designated beneficiary of the particular trust if the other trust were at that time a beneficiary under the particular trust whose interest as a beneficiary under the particular trust were

(A) acquired from each person or partnership from whom the particular partnership acquired its interest as a beneficiary under the particular trust, and

(B) held, at all times after the later of October 1, 1987 and the day on which the particular partnership's interest as a beneficiary under the particular trust was created, by the same persons or partnerships that held that interest of the particular partnership at those times, or

(v) a person exempt because of subsection 149(1) from tax under Part I on all or part of its taxable income except if the interest of the particular partnership in the particular trust was held, at all times after the day on which the interest was created, by the particular partnership or by persons who were exempt because of subsection 149(1) from tax under Part I on all of their taxable income.

Related Provisions: 104(7) — No deduction to non-resident trust for income paid to designated beneficiary (DB); 132.2(3)(g)(v) — Effect of mutual fund rollover; 135.2(4)(b)(ii) — Deemed DBs for Cdn Wheat Board Farmers' Trust; 210.2(1) — Part XII.2 tax on trust with DBs; 210.2(2) — Tax on amateur athlete trust; 210.2(3) — Designation of Part XII.2 tax to non-DBs for credit; 210.3(1) — No Part XII.2 tax where no DBs; 210.3(2) — Non-resident beneficiary taxed in Canada deemed not to be DB; 252(3) — Extended meaning of "spouse" and "former spouse".

Notes: Part XII.2 (210-210.3) imposes tax on a trust (generally excluding a non-resident, mutual fund, tax-exempt or testamentary trust) if it has a "designated beneficiary" (DB) and "designated income" (DI), and if the trust has claimed a 104(6)(b) deduction

for income paid or payable in the year to any beneficiary. In general, a DB is a non-resident entity (except for certain non-residents subject to Part I tax: 210.3(2)) or certain tax-exempt trusts. DI (210(1)) is generally income that would be taxable under 2(3) if earned by a non-resident, plus amounts arising from certain pre-emigration planning. A trust with DBs (210.3(1)) must pay Part XII.2 tax (210.2(1)) on its DI if it distributes the DI and claims a 104(6)(b) deduction, but can designate an amount of that tax as being paid on the account of beneficiaries who are not DBs, to the extent of their income inclusion under 104(13) in respect of DI they receive (210.2(3)), so the beneficiaries get credit for the trust's Part XII.2 tax on their Part I tax return, though that tax is also included in their income under 104(31).

The tax is 40% of the DI [210.2(1)(a)], capped at 40% of the trust's income (before deducting amounts payable to beneficiaries under 104(6) and the Part XII.2 tax itself deductible under 104(30)) [210.2(1)(b)], and also capped at 40% of 100/60ths of the 104(6)(b) deduction [210.2(1)(c)]. This limits the tax based on the amount distributed to DBs and deducted by the trust: if the trust's income is $100 and is all DI, and the full after-tax amount is paid out to DBs, the tax is $40, leaving $60 to pay out, so 210.2(1)(c) grosses this back up to $100 to apply the $40 cap. If no 104(6)(b) deduction is claimed, no Part XII.2 tax is payable regardless of the amount of DI, the existence of DBs or the trust's distributions.

Before 2016, 40% and 60% above were 36% and 64%. The change for 2016 was consequential to the top personal marginal rate increase in 117(2).

The Part XII.2 tax is also deductible to the trust for Part I tax purposes under 104(30), to avoid double tax. The combination of these rules is intended to be the same as if the Canadian beneficiaries were taxed on their income from the trust, and the trust received a corresponding deduction, so that at the end of the day, it is the non-resident and exempt beneficiaries who bear the burden of the 36% Part XII.2 tax, plus non-resident withholding tax under 212(1)(c).

A non-resident trust is not subject to Part XII.2 and gets no 104(6) deduction for paying income to a DB: 104(7); a trust deemed resident in Canada under 94(3)(a) is not deemed resident for Part XII.2 so this tax does not apply, and the 104(6) deduction is limited by 104(7.01) to a level of tax similar to what would be payable if Part XII.2 had applied to the trust and 212(1)(c) to its distributions to non-resident beneficiaries.

Part XII.2 also applies to amateur athlete trusts, imposing a 56.25% tax on distributions to DBs: 210.2(2).

For more on Part XII.2 tax see Roth et al., *Canadian Taxation of Trusts* (ctf.ca, 2016), pp. 910-26; Stephen Bowman, "Sophisticated Estate Planning Techniques", 1993 Cdn Tax Foundation conference report, at 38:28-30 (before the amendments retroactive to 1996 were proposed); Audrey Gibeault, "Unexpected Application of Part XII.2 Tax to a Canadian Personal Trust", 3(2) *Canadian Tax Focus* (ctf.ca) 10-11 (May 2013).

The 2013 Budget extended the thin-capitalization rule in 18(4) to deem certain trusts to have made payments to non-resident beneficiaries, which may trigger Part XII.2 tax.

See also VIEWS docs 2004-0091961R3, 2006-0201361R3 (rulings that Indian band that maintains a trust for on-reserve housing loans or a mining project is not a DB); 2016-0657531E5 (non-resident trust deemed resident by 94(3)(a) is a DB).

For "indirectly" in para. (c), see Notes to 17.1(1).

Para. (d) opening words and (d)(iii)(A) amended by 2014 budget bill #2, for 2016 and later taxation years, to change "testamentary trust" to "graduated rate estate". (See Notes to 122(1).)

Each of (b), (d)(ii) and (e)(iii), "a non-resident-owned investment corporation", repealed by 2014 budget bill #2, effective Dec. 16, 2014. (NROs are gone: see s. 133.)

Former 210, which defined "designated beneficiary", replaced by 210(1) (including this definition) and (2) by 2002-2013 technical bill, for 1996 and later tax years. Former 210 earlier amended by 2000 same-sex partners bill (effective 2001) and 1993 technical bill.

"designated income", of a trust for a taxation year, means the amount that would be the income of the trust for the year determined under section 3 if

(a) this Act were read without reference to subsections 104(6), (12) and (30);

(b) the trust had no income other than taxable capital gains from dispositions described in paragraph (c) and incomes from

(i) real or immovable properties in Canada (other than Canadian resource properties),

(ii) timber resource properties,

(iii) Canadian resource properties (other than properties acquired by the trust before 1972), and

(iv) businesses carried on in Canada;

(c) the only taxable capital gains and allowable capital losses referred to in paragraph 3(b) were from

(i) dispositions of taxable Canadian property, and

(ii) dispositions of particular property (other than property described in any of subparagraphs 128.1(4)(b)(i) to (iii)), or property for which the particular property is substituted, that was transferred at any particular time to a particular trust in circumstances in which subsection 73(1) or 107.4(3) applied, if

(A) it is reasonable to conclude that the property was so transferred in anticipation that a person beneficially interested at the particular time in the particular trust would subsequently cease to reside in Canada, and a person beneficially interested at the particular time in the particular trust did subsequently cease to reside in Canada, or

(B) when the property was so transferred, the terms of the particular trust satisfied the conditions in subparagraph 73(1.01)(c)(i) or (iii), and it is reasonable to conclude that the transfer was made in connection with the cessation of residence, on or before the transfer, of a person who was, at the time of the transfer, beneficially interested in the particular trust and a spouse or common-law partner, as the case may be, of the transferor of the property to the particular trust; and

(d) the only losses referred to in paragraph 3(d) were losses from sources described in any of subparagraphs (b)(i) to (iv).

Related Provisions: 104(7.01)(b)(i) — Effect on deduction available to trust deemed resident in Canada; 135.2(4)(b)(i) — Deemed designated income (DI) for Cdn Wheat Board Farmers' Trust; 210.2(1) — Tax on DI; 210.2(2) — Tax on amateur athlete trusts; 252(3) — Extended meaning of "spouse" and "former spouse"; 253 — Extended meaning of carrying on business.

Notes: See Notes to 210(1)"designated beneficiary".

Before the 2002-2013 technical bill amendments effective for 1996 and later tax years, this definition was in 210.2(2) (see Notes thereto). Paras. (a), (b), (c)(i), (d) are largely unchanged from former 210.2(2) opening words, (a), (b), (c) respectively; (c)(ii) is new, applying to dispositions after Dec. 20, 2002. Former 210, which only defined "designated beneficiary", replaced by 210(1) (including this definition) and (2) by 2002-2013 technical bill, for 1996 and later tax years, but read "designated income"(c) differently before Dec. 21, 2002.

(2) Tax not payable — No tax is payable under this Part for a taxation year by a trust that was throughout the year

(a) a graduated rate estate;

(b) a mutual fund trust;

(c) exempt from tax under Part I because of subsection 149(1);

(d) a trust to which paragraph (a), (a.1) or (c) of the definition "trust" in subsection 108(1) applies; or

(e) non-resident.

Related Provisions: 132(6.2) — Retention of status as mutual fund trust.

Notes: 210(2)(a) amended by 2014 budget bill #2, for 2016 and later taxation years, to change "testamentary trust" to "graduated rate estate". (See Notes to 122(1).)

210(2) added by 2002-2013 technical bill (Part 5 — technical), for 1996 and later taxation years. This rule was previously in s. 210.1.

Definitions [s. 210]: "allowable capital loss" — 38(b), 248(1); "amount" — 248(1); "beneficially interested" — 248(25); "beneficiary" — 248(25) [Notes]; "business" — 248(1); "Canada" — 255, *Interpretation Act* 35(1); "Canadian partnership" — 102(1), 248(1); "Canadian resource property" — 66(15), 248(1); "common-law partner" — 248(1); "designated beneficiary", "designated income" — 210; "disposition", "graduated rate estate" — 248(1); "identical" — 248(12); "immovable" — Quebec *Civil Code* art. 900-907; "individual" — 248(1); "mutual fund trust" — 132(6)-(7), 132.2(3)(n), 248(1); "non-resident" — 248(1); "partnership" — see 96(1) Notes; "person", "property" — 248(1); "registered retirement income fund" — 146.3(1), 248(1); "registered retirement savings plan" — 146(1), 248(1); "spouse" — 252(3); "substituted" — 248(5); "taxable Canadian property" — 248(1); "taxable capital gain" — 38(a), 248(1); "taxable income" — 2(2), 248(1); "taxation year" — 249; "timber resource property" — 13(21), 248(1); "trust" — 104(1), 248(1), (3).

210.1 [Repealed]

Notes: 210.1 repealed and moved to 210(2) by 2002-2013 technical bill, for 1996 and later tax years (superseding earlier amendments).

210.2 (1) Tax on income of trust — Subject to section 210.3, if a trust deducts an amount under paragraph 104(6)(b) in computing its income under Part I for a taxation year, the trust shall pay a tax under this Part in respect of the year equal to 40% of the least of

(a) the designated income of the trust for the year,

(b) the amount that, but for subsections 104(6) and (30), would be the income of the trust for the year, and

(c) 100/60 of the amount deducted.

Related Provisions: 18(1)(t), 104(30) — Part XII.2 tax deductible in computing income of trust; 210.1, 210.3 — Where no tax payable.

Notes: For discussion of Part XII.2 tax, see Notes to 210(1)"designated beneficiary".

210.2(1) opening words and (c) amended by 2016 budget bill #1, for 2016 and later taxation years.

Information Circulars: 77-16R4: Non-resident income tax.

(1.1) [Repealed]

Notes: 210.2(1.1) repealed by 2002-2013 technical bill (Part 5 — technical), for 1996 and later taxation years. This rule was revised and moved to 210.2(2).

Forms: T3ATH-IND: Amateur athlete trust income tax return.

(2) Amateur athlete trusts — Notwithstanding subsection 210(2), a trust shall pay a tax under this Part in respect of a particular taxation year of the trust equal to $2/3$ of the amount that is required by subsection 143.1(2) to be included in computing the income under Part I for a taxation year of a beneficiary under the trust, if

(a) the beneficiary is at any time in the particular taxation year a designated beneficiary under the trust; and

(b) the particular taxation year ends in that taxation year of the beneficiary.

Related Provisions: 104(7.01)(b)(i) — No deduction under 104(6) for designated income of trust.

Notes: 210.2(2) opening words amended by 2016 budget bill #1, for 2016 and later taxation years, to change "56.25%" to "2/3". See Finance Technical Notes for explanation of the tax rate.

210.2(2) replaced by 2002-2013 technical bill (Part 5 — technical), for 1996 and later tax years. Former 210.2(2), defining "designated income", was moved to 210(1). The rule for amateur athlete trusts, now in 210.2(2), was formerly in 210.2(1.1).

Forms: T3ATH-IND: Amateur athlete trust income tax return.

(3) Tax deemed paid by beneficiary — Where an amount (in this subsection and subsection 210.3(2) referred to as the "income amount") in respect of the income of a trust for a taxation year is, by reason of subsection 104(13) or 105(2), included in computing

(a) the income under Part I of a person who was not at any time in the year a designated beneficiary under the trust, or

(b) the income of a non-resident person (other than a person who, at any time in the year, would be a designated beneficiary under the trust if section 210 were read without reference to paragraph (a) of the definition "designated beneficiary" in that section) that is subject to tax under Part I by reason of subsection 2(3) and is not exempt from tax under Part I by reason of a provision contained in a tax treaty,

an amount determined by the formula

$$A \times B / C$$

where

A is the tax paid under this Part by the trust for the year,

B is the income amount in respect of the person, and

C is the total of all amounts each of which is an amount that is or would be, if all beneficiaries under the trust were persons resident in Canada to whom Part I was applicable, included in computing the income under Part I of a beneficiary under the trust by reason of subsection 104(13) or 105(2) in respect of the year,

shall, if designated by the trust in respect of the person in its return for the year under this Part, be deemed to be an amount paid on account of the person's tax payable under Part I for the person's taxation year in which the taxation year of the trust ends, on the day that is 90 days after the end of the taxation year of the trust.

Related Provisions: 104(31) — Amount deemed payable by trust to beneficiary; 152(1)(b) — Minister's determination of tax deemed paid on account by 210.2(3); 152(4.2)(b) — Redetermination of credit at taxpayer's request; 210.3(2) — Where non-resident beneficiary already taxed in Canada; 210.2(4) — Where amount is designated in respect of partnership.

Notes: See Notes to 210(1)"designated beneficiary". The amount deemed paid by the beneficiary is credited against the beneficiary's tax obligations, and creates a refund to the extent the beneficiary had no tax to pay.

In *Bui*, 2013 TCC 326, no refund was allowed because no tax had been paid by a trust.

210.2(3)(b) amended by 2002-2013 technical bill, this version for 1998 and later tax years.

Interpretation Bulletins: IT-342R: Trusts — Income payable to beneficiaries.

Forms: T1 General return, Line 45600 [former 456].

(4) Designations in respect of partnerships — Where a taxpayer is a member of a partnership in respect of which an amount is designated by a trust for a taxation year of the trust (in this subsection referred to as the "particular year") under subsection (3),

(a) no amount shall be deemed to be paid on account of the partnership's tax payable under Part I by reason of subsection (3) except in the application of that subsection for the purposes of subsection 104(31), and

(b) an amount determined by the formula

$$A \times B / C$$

where

A is the amount so designated,

B is the amount that may reasonably be regarded as the share of the taxpayer in the designated income of the trust received by the partnership in the fiscal period of the partnership in which the particular year ends (that fiscal period being referred to in this subsection as the "partnership's period"), and

C is the designated income received by the partnership from the trust in the partnership's period,

shall be deemed to be an amount paid on account of the taxpayer's tax payable under Part I for the person's taxation year in which the partnership's period ends, on the last day of that year.

Related Provisions: 152(1)(b) — Minister's determination of tax deemed paid on account by 210.2(4); 152(4.2)(b) — Redetermination of credit at taxpayer's request.

(5) Returns — A trust shall, within 90 days after the end of each taxation year,

(a) file with the Minister a return for the year under this Part in prescribed form and containing prescribed information, without notice or demand therefor;

(b) estimate in the return the amount of tax, if any, payable by it under this Part for the year; and

(c) pay to the Receiver General the tax, if any, payable by it under this Part for the year.

Related Provisions: 150.1(5) — Electronic filing; 251.2(7)(e) — Deadline extended to regular year's deadline, for trust year deemed ended due to change in majority beneficiaries; *Interpretation Act* 27(5) — Meaning of "within 90 days".

Forms: T3 Sched. 10: Part XII.2 tax and Part XIII non-resident withholding tax.

(6) Liability of trustee — A trustee of a trust is personally liable to pay to the Receiver General on behalf of the trust the full amount of any tax payable by the trust under this Part to the extent that the amount is not paid to the Receiver General within the time specified in subsection (5), and the trustee is entitled to recover from the trust any such amount paid by the trustee.

(7) Provisions applicable to Part — Subsections 150(2) and (3), sections 152 and 158, subsections 161(1) and (11), sections 162 to 167 and Division J of Part I are applicable to this Part with such modifications as the circumstances require.

Definitions [s. 210.2]: "amount" — 248(1); "beneficiary" — 248(25) [Notes]; "designated beneficiary", "designated income" — 210(1); "fiscal period" — 249.1; "Minister", "non-resident" — 248(1); "partnership" — see 96(1) Notes; "person", "prescribed" — 248(1); "resident in Canada" — 94(3)(a), 250; "share", "tax treaty" — 248(1); "taxation year" — 249; "taxpayer" — 248(1); "trust" — 104(1), 248(1), (3).

210.3 (1) Where no designated beneficiaries — No tax is payable under this Part by a trust for a taxation year in respect of which the trustee has certified in the trust's return under this Part for the year that no beneficiary under the trust was a designated beneficiary in the year.

Notes: See Notes to 210(1)"designated beneficiary".

(2) Where beneficiary deemed not designated — Where a trust would, if the trust paid tax under this Part for a taxation year, be entitled to designate an amount under subsection 210.2(3) in respect of a non-resident beneficiary and the income amount in respect of the beneficiary is included in computing the income of the beneficiary which is subject to tax under Part I by reason of subsection 2(3) and is not exempt from tax under Part I by reason of a provision contained in a tax convention or agreement with another country that has the force of law in Canada, for the purposes of subsection (1), the beneficiary shall be deemed not to be a designated beneficiary of the trust at any time in the year.

Definitions [s. 210.3]: "amount" — 248(1); "beneficiary" — 248(25) [Notes]; "Canada" — 255, *Interpretation Act* 35(1); "non-resident" — 248(1); "taxation year" — 249; "trust" — 104(1), 248(1), (3).

Notes [Part XII.2]: Part XII.2 added by 1988 tax reform.

PART XII.3 — TAX ON INVESTMENT INCOME OF LIFE INSURERS

Notes: Life insurance companies are also subject to the financial institutions capital tax under Part VI (190–190.211). See also Notes at end of s. 138.

211. (1) Definitions — For the purposes of this Part,

"existing guaranteed life insurance policy", at any time, means a non-participating life insurance policy in Canada in respect of which

(a) the amount of every premium that became payable before that time and after December 31, 1989,

(b) the number of premium payments under the policy, and

(c) the amount of each benefit under the policy at that time

were fixed and determined on or before December 31, 1989;

"life insurance policy" includes a benefit under

(a) a group life insurance policy, and

(b) a group annuity contract

but does not include

(c) that part of a policy in respect of which the policyholder is deemed by paragraph 138.1(1)(e) to have an interest in a related segregated fund trust, or

(d) a reinsurance arrangement;

Notes: Definition "life insurance policy" amended by 1996 Budget, for 1996 and later taxation years. The substantive change was to extend the definition to include benefits under both group life insurance policies and group annuity contracts.

"life insurance policy in Canada" means a life insurance policy issued or effected by an insurer on the life of a person resident in Canada at the time the policy was issued or effected;

Notes: Definition "life insurance policy in Canada" amended by 1996 Budget, for 1996 and later taxation years. For earlier years, see Notes to "life insurance policy" above. The new definition is needed because it has been repealed from 138(12).

"net interest rate", in respect of a liability, benefit, risk or guarantee under a life insurance policy of an insurer for a taxation year, is the positive amount, if any, determined by the formula

$$(A - B) \times C$$

where

A is the simple arithmetic average determined as of the first day of the year of the average yield (expressed as a percentage per year rounded to 2 decimal points) in each of the 60 immediately preceding months prevailing on all domestic Canadian-dollar Government of Canada bonds outstanding on the last Wednesday of that month that have a remaining term to maturity of more than 10 years,

B is

(a) in the case of a guaranteed benefit provided under the terms and conditions of the policy as they existed on March 2, 1988, other than a policy where, at any time after March 2,

1988, its terms and conditions relating to premiums and benefits were changed (otherwise than to give effect to the terms and conditions that were determined before March 3, 1988), the greater of

(i) the rate of interest (expressed as a percentage per year) used by the insurer in determining the amount of the guaranteed benefit, and

(ii) 4%, and

(b) in any other case, nil, and

C is

(a) in the case of a guaranteed benefit to which paragraph (a) of the description of B applies, 65%, and

(b) in any other case, 55%;

Related Provisions: 257 — Formula cannot calculate to less than zero.

"non-participating life insurance policy" means a life insurance policy that is not a participating life insurance policy;

"participating life insurance policy" has the meaning assigned by subsection 138(12);

"policy loan" has the meaning assigned by subsection 138(12);

Notes: "policy loan" was included together with "participating life insurance policy" above, before RSC 1985 (5th Supp) consolidation.

"registered life insurance policy" means a life insurance policy issued or effected as or under a pooled registered pension plan, a registered retirement savings plan, a deferred profit sharing plan or a registered pension plan;

Related Provisions: 211(1)"taxable life insurance policy"(c) — RLIP not taxable.

Notes: Definition amended by 2012 budget bill #2, effective Dec. 14, 2012, effectively to add reference to a PRPP.

Para. (a) amended by 2008 budget bill #1, for 2009 and later tax years, to refer to a TFSA, and then amended by 2008 budget bill #2 to remove the reference, effective on the same basis. (The reference was redundant, because an annuity contract, which is the only insurance product eligible to be issued as a TFSA, is excluded from Part XII.3 tax by 211(1)"taxable life insurance policy"(b).)

"reinsurance arrangement" does not include an arrangement under which an insurer has assumed the obligations of the issuer of a life insurance policy to the policyholder;

"segregated fund" has the meaning given that expression in subsection 138.1(1);

Notes: "segregated fund" was included under "participating life insurance policy" above, before RSC 1985 (5th Supp) consolidation.

"specified transaction or event", in respect of a life insurance policy, means

(a) a change in underwriting class,

(b) a change in premium because of a change in frequency of premium payments within a year that does not alter the present value, at the beginning of the year, of the total premiums to be paid under the policy in the year,

(c) an addition under the terms of the policy as they existed on

(i) in the case of an existing guaranteed life insurance policy, December 31, 1989,

(ii) in any other case, March 2, 1988,

of accidental death, dismemberment, disability or guaranteed purchase option benefits,

(d) the deletion of a rider,

(e) redating lapsed policies within the reinstatement period referred to in paragraph (g) of the definition "disposition" in subsection 148(9) or redating for policy loan indebtedness,

(f) a change in premium because of a correction of erroneous information,

(g) the payment of a premium after its due date, or no more than 30 days before its due date, as established on or before

(i) in the case of an existing guaranteed life insurance policy, December 31, 1989, and

(ii) in any other case, March 2, 1988, and

(h) the payment of an amount described in paragraph (a) of the definition "premium" in subsection 148(9);

"taxable life insurance policy" of an insurer at any time means a life insurance policy in Canada issued by the insurer (or in respect of which the insurer has assumed the obligations of the issuer of the policy to the policyholder), other than a policy that is at that time

(a) an existing guaranteed life insurance policy,

(b) an annuity contract (including a settlement annuity),

(c) a registered life insurance policy,

(d) a registered pension plan, or

(e) a retirement compensation arrangement.

(2) Riders and changes in terms — For the purposes of this Part,

(a) any rider added at any time after March 2, 1988 to a life insurance policy shall be deemed to be a separate life insurance policy issued and effected at that time; and

(b) a change in the terms or conditions of a life insurance policy resulting from a specified transaction or event shall be deemed not to have occurred and not to be a change.

Notes: 211(1) completely rewritten by 1991 technical bill.

Definitions [s. 211]: "amount", "annuity" — 248(1); "Canada" — 255, *Interpretation Act* 35(1); "deferred profit sharing plan" — 147(1), 248(1); "existing guaranteed life insurance policy" — 211(1); "insurance policy", "insurer" — 248(1); "life insurance policy" — 138(12), 211(1), 248(1); "life insurance policy in Canada" — 211(1); "month" — *Interpretation Act* 35(1); "non-participating life insurance policy" — 138(12), 211(1); "participating life insurance policy" — 211(1); "person" — 248(1); "policy loan" — 211(1); "pooled registered pension plan" — 147.5(1), 248(1); "registered life insurance policy" — 211(1); "registered pension plan" — 248(1); "registered retirement savings plan" — 146(1), 248(1); "reinsurance arrangement" — 211(1); "related segregated fund trust" — 138.1(1); "resident in Canada" — 250; "retirement compensation arrangement" — 248(1); "segregated fund", "specified transaction or event" — 211(1); "taxation year" — 249; "trust" — 104(1), 248(1), (3).

211.1 (1) Tax payable — Every life insurer shall pay a tax under this Part for each taxation year equal to 15% of its taxable Canadian life investment income for the year.

Related Provisions: 18(1)(t) — Tax is non-deductible; 138(3)(g) — Part XII.3 tax deductible by insurer.

Notes: The 2012 federal Budget proposed that the Part XII.3 Investment Income Tax (IIT) "be recalibrated where appropriate to neutralize impacts of the proposed technical improvements on the IIT base". This was done by enacting Reg. 1401(5) in 2014.

See also Notes at beginning of Part XII.3 (before s. 211).

(2) Taxable Canadian life investment income — For the purposes of this Part, the taxable Canadian life investment income of a life insurer for a taxation year is the amount, if any, by which its Canadian life investment income for the year exceeds the total of its Canadian life investment losses for the 20 taxation years immediately preceding the year, to the extent that those losses were not deducted in computing its taxable Canadian life investment income for any preceding taxation year.

Related Provisions: 87(2.2) — Amalgamation of insurance corporations; 138(11.5)(k) — Transfer of business by non-resident insurer.

Notes: 211.1(2) amended by 2006 budget bill #1 (implementing a Nov. 14/05 proposal), effective for losses that arise in 2006 and later taxation years, to change "10 taxation years" to "20 taxation years". See Notes to 111(1)(a).

211.1(2) amended to change "7 taxation years immediately preceding the year that begin after 1989" to "10 taxation years immediately preceding the year" by 2004 Budget, effective in respect of losses that arise in taxation years that end after March 22, 2004.

211.1(2) amended by 1991 technical bill to limit the carryforward of Canadian life investment losses to losses arising in 1990 and later years, in view of the significant changes to the design of the Part XII.3 tax.

(3) Canadian life investment income — For the purposes of this Part, the Canadian life investment income or loss of a life insurer for a taxation year is the positive or negative amount determined by the formula

$$A + B - C$$

where

A is, subject to subsection (4), the total of all amounts, each of which is in respect of a liability, benefit, risk or guarantee under a life insurance policy that was at any time in the year a taxable life insurance policy of the insurer, determined by multiplying the net interest rate in respect of the liability, benefit, risk or guarantee for the year by ½ of the total of

(a) the maximum amount that would be determined under paragraph 1401(1)(a), (c) or (d) of the *Income Tax Regulations* (other than an amount that would be determined under subparagraph 1401(1)(d)(ii) of those Regulations in respect of a disabled life) in respect of the insurer for the year in respect of the liability, benefit, risk or guarantee if subsection 1401(1) of those Regulations applied to all life insurance policies and if that amount were determined without reference to any policy loan or reinsurance arrangement, and

(b) the maximum amount that would be determined under paragraph 1401(1)(a), (c) or (d) of the *Income Tax Regulations* (other than an amount that would be determined under subparagraph 1401(1)(d)(ii) of those Regulations in respect of a disabled life) in respect of the insurer for the preceding taxation year in respect of the liability, benefit, risk or guarantee if subsection 1401(1) of those Regulations applied to all life insurance policies and if that amount were determined without reference to any policy loan or reinsurance arrangement;

B is the total of all amounts, each of which is the positive or negative amount in respect of a life insurance policy that was at any time in the year a taxable life insurance policy of the insurer, determined by the formula

$$D - E$$

where

D is, subject to subsection (4), the amount determined by multiplying the percentage determined in the description of A in the definition "net interest rate" in subsection 211(1) in respect of the year by ½ of the total of

(a) the maximum amount that would be determined under paragraph 1401(1)(c.1) of the *Income Tax Regulations* in respect of the insurer for the year in respect of the policy if subsection 1401(1) of those Regulations applied to all life insurance policies and if that amount were determined without reference to any policy loan or reinsurance arrangement, and

(b) the maximum amount that would be determined under paragraph 1401(1)(c.1) of the *Income Tax Regulations* in respect of the insurer for the preceding taxation year in respect of the policy if subsection 1401(1) of those Regulations applied to all life insurance policies and if that amount were determined without reference to any policy loan or reinsurance arrangement, and

E is the amount, if any, by which

(a) the total of all amounts determined in respect of the insurer under the description of D in respect of the policy for the year and any preceding taxation years ending after 1989

exceeds the total of

(b) all amounts determined in respect of the insurer under the description of E in respect of the policy for taxation years ending before the year, and

(c) the amount, if any, by which

(i) the maximum amount that would be determined under paragraph 1401(1)(c.1) of the *Income Tax Regulations* in respect of the insurer for the year in respect of the policy if subsection 1401(1) of those Regulations applied to all life insurance policies and if that amount were determined without reference to any policy loan or reinsurance arrangement

exceeds

(ii) the maximum amount that would be determined under paragraph 1401(1)(c.1) of the *Income Tax Regulations* in respect of the insurer for its last 1989 taxation year in respect of the policy if subsection 1401(1) of those Regulations applied to all life insurance policies and if that amount were determined without reference to any policy loan or reinsurance arrangement; and

C is the total of all amounts each of which is 100% of the amount required to be included in computing the income of a policyholder under section 12.2 or paragraph 56(1)(j) for which the insurer is required by regulation to prepare an information return in respect of the calendar year ending in the taxation year, in respect of a taxable life insurance policy of the insurer, except that the reference in this description to 100% shall be read as a reference to,

(a) where paragraph (a) of the description of B in the definition "net interest rate" in subsection 211(1) applies for any taxation year in respect of a guaranteed benefit under the policy,

0% for calendar years before 1991,
5% for 1991,
10% for 1992,
15% for 1993,
20% for 1994,
25% for 1995,
30% for 1996,
35% for 1997,
40% for 1998,
45% for 1999, and
50% for calendar years after 1999,

and

(b) where the policy was at any time after 1989 an existing guaranteed life insurance policy,

0% for the calendar year in which it became a taxable life insurance policy of the insurer,
0% for the first following calendar year,
0% for the second following calendar year,
5% for the third following calendar year,
10% for the fourth following calendar year,
15% for the fifth following calendar year,
20% for the sixth following calendar year,
25% for the seventh following calendar year,
30% for the eighth following calendar year,
35% for the ninth following calendar year,
40% for the tenth following calendar year,
45% for the eleventh following calendar year, and
50% for the twelfth following and subsequent calendar years.

Related Provisions: 257 — Formula amounts cannot calculate to less than zero; Reg. 1401(5) — Application rules for life insurance policy.

Notes: 211.1(3) amended by 1995-97 technical bill, for 1992 and later years. 211.1(3) earlier amended by 1996 Budget and 1991 technical bill.

Regulations: 1401(1) (amounts determined).

(4) Short taxation year — Where a taxation year of a life insurer is less than 51 weeks, the values of A and D in subsection (3) for the year are that proportion of those values otherwise so determined that the number of days in the year (other than February 29) is of 365.

Notes: 211.1(4) added by 1995-97 technical bill, effective for 1992 and later years.

Definitions [s. 211.1]: "amount" — 248(1); "calendar year" — *Interpretation Act* 37(1)(a); "existing guaranteed life insurance policy" — 211(1); "insurer" — 248(1); "life insurance policy" — 138(12), 211(1), 248(1); "life insurer" — 248(1); "net interest rate", "policy loan" — 211(1); "regulation" — 248(1); "reinsurance arrangement", "taxable life insurance policy" — 211(1); "taxation year" — 249.

211.2 Return — Every life insurer shall file with the Minister, not later than the day on or before which it is required by section 150 to file its return of income for a taxation year under Part I, a return of taxable Canadian life investment income for that year in prescribed form containing an estimate of the tax payable by it under this Part for the year.

Related Provisions: 150.1(5) — Electronic filing.

Definitions [s. 211.2]: "life insurer", "Minister", "prescribed" — 248(1); "taxation year" — 249.

Forms: T2142: Part XII.3 tax return — tax on investment income of life insurers.

211.3 (1) Instalments — Every life insurer shall, in respect of each of its taxation years, pay to the Receiver General on or before the last day of each month in the year, an amount equal to $1/12$ of the lesser of

(a) the amount estimated by the insurer to be the annualized tax payable under this Part by it for the year, and

(b) the annualized tax payable under this Part by the insurer for the immediately preceding taxation year.

Notes: See Notes at end of 211.3.

(2) Annualized tax payable — For the purposes of subsections (1) and 211.5(2), the annualized tax payable under this Part by a life insurer for a taxation year is the amount determined by the formula

$$(365/A) \times B$$

where

A is

(a) if the year is less than 357 days, the number of days in the year (other than February 29), and

(b) otherwise, 365; and

B is the tax payable under this Part by the insurer for the year.

Notes: 211.3 replaced by 211.3(1) and (2) by 1995-97 technical bill, effective for taxation years that begin after 1995.

Definitions [s. 211.3]: "amount" — 248(1); "annualized tax payable" — 211.3(2); "insurer", "life insurer" — 248(1); "month" — *Interpretation Act* 35(1); "taxation year" — 249.

211.4 Payment of remainder of tax — Every life insurer shall pay, on or before its balance-due day for a taxation year, the remainder, if any, of the tax payable under this Part by the insurer for the year.

Notes: Due to COVID-19, Part XII.3 tax owing from March 18-Sept. 29, 2020 was due on Sept. 30, 2020: see PITA 59th ed. at 150(1) opening words.

211.4 amended by 2003 Budget to require payment on the "balance-due day" (as defined in 248(1)), effective for taxation years that begin after June 2003.

Definitions [s. 211.4]: "balance-due day", "insurer", "life insurer" — 248(1); "taxation year" — 249.

211.5 (1) Provisions applicable to Part — Section 152, subsection 157(2.1), sections 158 and 159, subsections 161(1), (2), (2.1), (2.2) and (11), sections 162 to 167 and Division J of Part I apply to this Part, with such modifications as the circumstances require.

Notes: 211.5 renumbered as 211.5(1) by 1995-97 technical bill, effective for taxation years that begin after 1995.

211.5 amended and 211.6 repealed by 1991 technical bill, effective 1990. 211.5 formerly dealt only with interest (now covered by the references to 161), while 211.6 provided the rest of what is now 211.5.

(2) Interest on instalments — For the purposes of subsection 161(2) and section 163.1 as they apply to this Part, a life insurer is, in respect of a taxation year, deemed to have been liable to pay, on or before the last day of each month in the year, an instalment equal to $1/12$ of the lesser of

(a) the annualized tax payable under this Part by the insurer for the year, and

(b) the annualized tax payable under this Part by the insurer for the immediately preceding taxation year.

Related Provisions: 211.3(2) — Annualized tax payable.

Notes: 211.5(2) added by 1995-97 technical bill, effective for taxation years that begin after 1995.

Definitions [s. 211.5]: "annualized tax payable" — 211.3(2); "insurer", "life insurer" — 248(1); "month" — *Interpretation Act* 35(1); "taxation year" — 249.

PART XII.4 — TAX ON QUALIFYING ENVIRONMENTAL TRUSTS

211.6 (1) Definitions — The definitions in this section apply for the purposes of this Part.

"excluded trust", at any time, means a trust that

(a) relates at that time to the reclamation of a well;

(b) is not maintained at that time to secure the reclamation obligations of one or more persons or partnerships that are beneficiaries under the trust;

(c) borrows money at that time;

(d) if the trust is not a trust to which paragraph (e) applies, acquires at that time any property that is not described by any of paragraphs (a), (b) and (f) of the definition "qualified investment" in section 204;

(e) if the trust is created after 2011 (or if the trust was created before 2012, it elects in writing filed with the Minister on or before its filing-due date for a particular taxation year to have subparagraphs (i) and (ii) apply to it for the particular taxation year and all subsequent taxation years, and that election is made jointly with Her Majesty in right of Canada or a particular province, depending upon the qualifying law or qualifying contract in respect of the trust),

(i) acquires at that time any property that is not described by any of paragraphs (a), (b), (c), (c.1), (d) and (f) of the definition "qualified investment" in section 204, or

(ii) holds at that time a prohibited investment;

(f) elected in writing filed with the Minister, before 1998 or before April of the year following the year in which the first contribution to the trust was made, never to have been a qualifying environmental trust; or

(g) was at any previous time during its existence not a qualifying environmental trust (as determined under the definition "qualifying environmental trust" in subsection 248(1) as it applied at that previous time).

Notes: For a trust filing a Quebec return, a para. (e) or (f) election must be copied to Revenu Québec: *Taxation Act* ss. 1129.51, 21.4.6.

"prohibited investment", of a trust at any time, means a property that

(a) at the time it was acquired by the trust, was described by any of paragraphs (c), (c.1) or (d) of the definition "qualified investment" in section 204; and

(b) was issued by

(i) a person or partnership that has contributed property to, or that is a beneficiary under, the trust,

(ii) a person that is related to, or a partnership that is affiliated with, a person or partnership that has contributed property to, or that is a beneficiary under, the trust, or

(iii) a particular person or partnership if

(A) another person or partnership holds a significant interest (within the meaning assigned by subsection 207.01(4) with any modifications that the circumstances require) in the particular person or partnership, and

(B) the holder of that significant interest has contributed property to, or is a beneficiary under, the trust.

Notes: Securities of a U.S. ETF that fall under 204"qualified investment"(d) are allowed: VIEWS docs 2018-0787071R3, 2018-0787081R3, 2018-0787091R3.

"QET income tax rate", for a trust's taxation year, means the amount, expressed as a decimal fraction, by which

(a) the percentage rate of tax provided under paragraph 123(1)(a) for the taxation year

exceeds

(b) the total of

(i) the percentage that would, if the trust were a corporation, be its general rate reduction percentage, within the meaning assigned by subsection 123.4(1), for the taxation year, and

(ii) the percentage deduction from tax provided under subsection 124(1) for the taxation year.

"qualifying contract", in respect of a trust, means a contract entered into with Her Majesty in right of Canada or a province on or before the later of January 1, 1996 and the day that is one year after the day on which the trust was created.

"qualifying environmental trust" means a trust

(a) each trustee of which is

(i) Her Majesty in right of Canada or a province, or

(ii) a corporation resident in Canada that is licensed or otherwise authorized under the laws of Canada or a province to carry on in Canada the business of offering to the public its services as trustee;

(b) that is maintained for the sole purpose of funding the reclamation of a qualifying site;

(c) that is, or may become, required to be maintained under

(i) the terms of a qualifying contract, or

(ii) a qualifying law; and

(d) that is not an excluded trust.

Notes: Before the 2012 taxation year, the substantive definition of QET was in 248(1). See Notes to 248(1)"qualifying environmental trust".

"qualifying law", in respect of a trust, means

(a) a law of Canada or a province that was enacted on or before the later of January 1, 1996 and the day that is one year after the day on which the trust was created; and

(b) if the trust was created after 2011, an order made

(i) by a tribunal constituted under a law described by paragraph (a), and

(ii) on or before the day that is one year after the day on which the trust was created.

"qualifying site", in respect of a trust, means a site in Canada that is or has been used primarily for, or for any combination of,

(a) the operation of a mine,

(b) the extraction of clay, peat, sand, shale or aggregates (including dimension stone and gravel),

(c) the deposit of waste, or

(d) if the trust was created after 2011, the operation of a pipeline.

Notes: For the meaning of "used primarily" see Notes to 73(3).

Notes [subsec. 211.6(1)]: See at end of 211.6.

(2) Charging provision — Every trust that is a qualifying environmental trust at the end of a taxation year (other than a trust that is at that time described by paragraph 149(1)(z.1) or (z.2)) shall pay a tax under this Part for the year equal to the amount determined by the formula

$$A \times B$$

where

A is the trust's income (computed as if this Act were read without reference to subsections 104(4) to (31) and sections 105 to 107) under Part I for the year; and

B is the QET income tax rate for the year.

Related Provisions: 127.41 — Part XII.4 tax credit to beneficiary; 149(1)(z) — No Part I tax on trust.

(3) Return — Every trust that is a qualifying environmental trust at the end of a taxation year shall file with the Minister on or before its filing-due date for the year a return for the year under this Part in prescribed form containing an estimate of the amount of its tax payable under this Part for the year.

Related Provisions: 150.1(5) — Electronic filing.

Forms: T3M: Environmental trust income tax return.

(4) Payment of tax — Every trust shall pay to the Receiver General its tax payable under this Part for each taxation year on or before its balance-due day for the year.

(5) Provisions applicable to Part — Subsections 150(2) and (3), sections 152, 158 and 159, subsections 161(1) and (11), sections 162 to 167 and Division J of Part I apply to this Part, with such modifications as the circumstances require.

Notes [s. 211.6]: See Notes to 248(1)"qualifying environmental trust".

211.6(1) and (2) amended (with the charging provision moved from (1) to (2), and all the definitions in (1) added) by 2011 budget bill #2, effective for 2012 and later taxation years.

211.6 amended by 1997 Budget, for 1997 and later taxation years. (Before then, "mining reclamation trust" was used in place of "qualifying environmental trust".)

211.6 (Part XII.4) added by 1994 Budget, effective 1994.

For former 211.6, see Notes to 211.5.

Definitions [s. 211.6]: "affiliated" — 251.1; "amount", "balance-due day" — 248(1); "beneficiary" — 248(25) [Notes]; "business" — 248(1); "Canada" — 255, *Interpretation Act* 35(1); "corporation" — 248(1), *Interpretation Act* 35(1); "excluded trust" — 211.6(1); "filing-due date" — 248(1); "Her Majesty" — *Interpretation Act* 35(1); "Minister" — 248(1); "partnership" — see 96(1) Notes; "person", "prescribed" — 248(1); "prohibited investment" — 211.6(1); "property" — 248(1); "province" — *Interpretation Act* 35(1); "QET income tax rate", "qualifying contract" — 211.6(1); "qualifying environmental trust" — 211.6(1), 248(1); "qualifying site" — 211.6(1); "related" — 251(2)–(6); "resident in Canada" — 250; "taxation year" — 249; "trust" — 104(1), 248(1); "trust's year" — 107.3(1); "writing" — *Interpretation Act* 35(1).

PART XII.5 — RECOVERY OF LABOUR-SPONSORED FUNDS TAX CREDIT

211.7 (1) Definitions — The definitions in this section apply for the purposes of this Part.

Notes: 211.7 renumbered as 211.7(1) by 1999 Budget, effective February 17, 1999.

"approved share" has the meaning assigned by subsection 127.4(1).

"labour-sponsored funds tax credit" in respect of a share is

(a) where the original acquisition of the share occurred before 1996, 20% of the net cost of the share on that acquisition;

(b) in any other case, the amount that would be determined under subsection 127.4(6) in respect of the share if this Act were read without reference to its paragraphs (b) and (d).

(c) [Repealed]

Notes: The Part XII.5 tax on disposition of a share is essentially a recovery of the labour-sponsored funds tax credit granted on the original acquisition of the share, as calculated in this definition.

Paras. (b)-(c) replaced with (b) by 2016 budget bill #1, for 2016 and later tax years. Since the credit was restored in 2016 for provincially prescribed LSVCCs (see Notes to 127.4(5)), the amendment provides that for LSVCC shares acquired after 1996, the credit is based on the credit that was potentially available in 127.4(6) for the share. The amendment ensures that the penalty in 211.8(1) will apply to a provincially prescribed LSVCC that was eligible for the credit in 127.4(6) for the 2017 and subsequent tax years. (Finance Technical Notes)

Para. (b) replaced with (b)-(c) by 2013 budget bill #2, effective March 21, 2013.

"net cost" has the meaning assigned by subsection 127.4(1).

"original acquisition" has the meaning assigned by subsection 127.4(1).

"qualifying exchange" means an exchange by a taxpayer of an approved share, that is part of a series of Class A shares of the capital stock of a corporation, for another approved share, that is part of another series of Class A shares of the capital stock of the corporation, if

(a) the only consideration received by the taxpayer on the exchange is the other share; and

(b) the rights in respect of the series are identical except for the portion of the reserve (within the meaning assigned by subsection 204.8(1)) of the corporation that is attributable to each series.

Related Provisions: 211.7(3) — Exchangeable shares; 211.8(1) — Disposition of approved share.

Notes: See Notes to 211.7(3). Definition added by 2002-2013 technical bill (Part 5 — technical), effective 2004.

"qualifying trust" has the meaning assigned by subsection 127.4(1).

"revoked corporation" means a corporation the registration of which has been revoked under subsection 204.81(6).

(2) Amalgamations and mergers — For the purposes of this Part, where two or more corporations (each of which is referred to in this subsection as a "predecessor corporation") amalgamate or merge to form a corporate entity deemed by paragraph 204.85(3)(d) to have been registered under Part X.3, the shares of each predecessor corporation are deemed not to be redeemed, acquired or cancelled by the predecessor corporation on the amalgamation or merger.

Notes: 211.7(2) added by 1999 Budget, effective February 17, 1999.

(3) Exchangeable shares — For the purposes of this Part and Part X.3, if an approved share of the capital stock of a corporation (referred to in this subsection as the "new share") has been issued in exchange for another approved share (referred to in this subsection as the "original share") in a qualifying exchange, the new share is deemed not to have been issued on the exchange and is deemed to have been issued at the time the corporation issued the original share.

Related Provisions: 127.4(6)(e) — No labour-sponsored funds credit on exchange of shares.

Notes: 211.7(3) added by 2002-2013 technical bill (Part 5 — technical), effective 2004. It implements an Oct. 17, 2005 Finance comfort letter. For CRA rulings based on that comfort letter, see VIEWS docs 2005-0129801R3, 2005-0130171R3.

Notes [s. 211.7]: 211.7 added by 1996 Budget, effective on the same basis as 211.8(1).

Definitions [s. 211.7]: "amount" — 248(1); "corporation" — 248(1); *Interpretation Act* 35(1); "net cost", "original acquisition" — 127.4(1), 211.7(1); "qualifying exchange" — 211.7(1); "share" — 248(1).

211.8 (1) Disposition of approved share — If an approved share of the capital stock of a registered labour-sponsored venture capital corporation or a revoked corporation is, before the first discontinuation of its venture capital business, redeemed, acquired or cancelled by the corporation less than eight years after the day on which the share was issued (other than in circumstances described in subclause 204.81(1)(c)(v)(A)(I) or (III) or clause 204.81(1)(c)(v)(B) or (D) or other than if the share is a Class A share of the capital stock of the corporation that is exchanged for another Class A share of the capital stock of the corporation as part of a qualifying exchange) or any other share that was issued by any other labour-sponsored venture capital corporation is disposed of, the person who was the shareholder immediately before the redemption, acquisition, cancellation or disposition shall pay a tax under this Part equal to the lesser of

(a) the amount determined by the formula

$$A \times B$$

where

A is

  (i) where the share was issued by a registered labour-sponsored venture capital corporation or a revoked corporation, the labour-sponsored funds tax credit in respect of the share, and

  (ii) where the share was issued by any other labour-sponsored venture capital corporation and was at any time an approved share, the amount, if any, required to be remitted to the government of a province as a consequence of

the redemption, acquisition, cancellation or disposition (otherwise than as a consequence of an increase in the corporation's liability for a penalty under a law of the province), and

B is

  (i) nil, where the share was issued by a registered labour-sponsored venture capital corporation or a revoked corporation, the original acquisition of the share was before March 6, 1996 and the redemption, acquisition, cancellation or disposition is

    (A) more than 2 years after the day on which it was issued, where the redemption, acquisition, cancellation or disposition is permitted under the articles of the corporation because an individual attains 65 years of age, retires from the workforce or ceases to be resident in Canada,

    (B) more than five years after its issuance, or

    (C) if the day that is five years after its issuance is in February or March of a calendar year, in February or on March 1st of that calendar year but not more than 31 days before that day,

  (i.1) nil, where the share was issued by a registered labour-sponsored venture capital corporation or a revoked corporation, the original acquisition of the share was after March 5, 1996 and the redemption, acquisition or cancellation is in February or on March 1st of a calendar year but is not more than 31 days before the day that is eight years after the day on which the share was issued,

  (ii) one, in any other case where the share was issued by a registered labour-sponsored venture capital corporation or a revoked corporation, and

  (iii) in any other case, the quotient obtained when the labour-sponsored fund tax credit in respect of the share is divided by the tax credit provided under a law of a province in respect of any previous acquisition of the share, and

(b) the amount that would, but for subsection (2), be payable to the shareholder because of the redemption, acquisition, cancellation or disposition (determined after taking into account the amount determined under subparagraph (ii) of the description of A in paragraph (a)).

Related Provisions: 127.4(6)(e) — No labour-sponsored funds credit on exchange of shares; 204.8(2) — Determining when an RLSVCC discontinues its business; 204.8(3) — Order of disposition of shares; 211.8(1.1) — Rules of application; 211.82(2) — Withholding and remittance of tax; 211.82 — Administration of Part XII.5 tax; 227(10.01) — Assessment of amount payable by resident of Canada; 227(10.1)(c) — Assessment of amount payable by non-resident; Reg. 6706 — Repayment of credit by national LSVCCs.

Notes: 211.8 provides a mechanism for CRA to recover a 127.4 credit obtained on acquiring a share issued by a labour-sponsored venture capital corp (LSVCC). The mechanism is Part XII.5 tax, all or part of which may be refundable. This tax applies to: (1) disposition of a share issued by an LSVCC, other than a "federally-registered LSVCC" (FRL) that was never registered under 204.81; (2) disposition of a share issued by a FRL due to the LSVCC purchasing or acquiring the share for cancellation without redeeming it; (3) redemption of a share issued by a FRL. See Finance Technical Notes (or these Notes up to the 57th ed.) for detailed explanation, and VIEWS docs 2005-013372117, 2008-0299171R3.

211.8(1) amended by 2002-2013 technical bill (for shares redeemed, acquired or cancelled after 2003), 1999 Budget. Added by 1996 Budget. It was 211.7 in the November 15, 1995 draft legislation.

(1.1) Rules of application — Subsections 204.8(2) and (3) and 204.85(3) apply for the purpose of subsection (1).

Notes: 211.8(1.1) added by 1999 Budget, effective for redemptions, acquisitions, cancellations and dispositions that occur after February 16, 1999.

(2) Withholding and remittance of tax — Where a person or partnership (in this section referred to as the "transferee") redeems, acquires or cancels a share and, as a consequence, tax is payable under this Part by the person who was the shareholder immediately before the redemption, acquisition or cancellation, the transferee shall

(a) withhold from the amount otherwise payable on the redemption, acquisition or cancellation to the shareholder the amount of the tax;

(b) within 30 days after the redemption, acquisition or cancellation, remit the amount of the tax to the Receiver General on behalf of the shareholder; and

(c) submit with the remitted amount a statement in prescribed form.

Related Provisions: 211.8(3) — Liability for failure to withhold; 227 — Withholding taxes — administration and enforcement; 227(5)(a.1) — Person who has influence over payment may be liable for failure to withhold; 227(6) — Application of excess amount withheld; 227(8.3)(c) — Interest on amounts not withheld; *Interpretation Act* 27(5) — Meaning of "within 30 days".

Notes: Due to COVID-19, Part XII.5 tax owing from March 18-Sept. 29, 2020 was due on Sept. 30, 2020: see PITA 59th ed. at 150(1) opening words.

For a ruling that 211.8(2) does not apply see VIEWS doc 2008-0299171R3.

211.8(2) added by 1996 Budget, effective for redemptions, acquisitions and cancellations that occur after April 25, 1997 (Royal Assent).

Forms: T1149: Remittance form for labour-sponsored funds tax credits withheld on redeemed shares.

(3) Liability for tax — Where a transferee has failed to withhold any amount as required by subsection (2) from an amount paid or credited to a shareholder, the transferee is liable to pay as tax under this Part on behalf of the shareholder the amount the transferee failed to withhold, and is entitled to recover that amount from the shareholder.

Related Provisions: 227(10.01) — Assessment of amount payable by resident of Canada; 227(10.1)(c) — Assessment of amount payable by non-resident.

Notes: 211.8(3) added by 1996 Budget, effective for redemptions, acquisitions and cancellations that occur after April 25, 1997 (Royal Assent).

Definitions [s. 211.8]: "approved share" — 127.4(1), 211.7(1); "business" — 248(1); "corporation" — 248(1), *Interpretation Act* 35(1); "discontinuation" — 204.8(2); "disposition", "individual" — 248(1); "labour-sponsored funds tax credit" — 211.7(1); "original acquisition" — 127.4(1), 211.7(1); "partnership" — see 96(1) Notes; "person", "prescribed" — 248(1); "province" — *Interpretation Act* 35(1); "qualifying exchange" — 211.7(1); "registered labour-sponsored venture capital corporation" — 248(1); "resident in Canada" — 250; "revoked corporation" — 211.7(1); "share", "shareholder" — 248(1); "transferee" — 211.8(2).

211.81 Tax for failure to reacquire certain shares [— Quebec] — If a particular amount is payable under a prescribed provision of a provincial law for a taxation year of an individual as determined for the purposes of that provincial law (referred to in this section as the "relevant provincial year"), and an amount has been included in the computation of the labour-sponsored funds tax credit of the individual under subsection 127.4(6) in respect of an approved share that has been disposed of by a qualifying trust in respect of the individual, the individual shall pay a tax for the taxation year in which the relevant provincial year ends equal to the amount deducted by the individual under subsection 127.4(2) in respect of the share.

Related Provisions: 211.82 — Return required.

Notes: 211.81 added by 2002-2013 technical bill and amended by 2013 budget bill #2, both effective Oct. 24, 2012.

Definitions [s. 211.81]: "amount" — 248(1); "approved share" — 127.4(1), 211.7(1); "individual" — 248(1); "labour-sponsored funds tax credit" — 211.7(1); "prescribed" — 248(1); "provincial" — *Interpretation Act* 33(3), 35(1)"province"; "qualifying trust" — 127.4(1), 211.7(1); "relevant provincial year" — 211.81; "share" — 248(1); "taxation year" — 249; "trust" — 104(1), 248(1), (3).

Regulations: 6709 (Quebec *Taxation Act* ss. 1086.14 and 1086.20 are prescribed provisions).

211.82 (1) Return — Every person that is liable to pay tax under this Part for a taxation year shall, not later than the day on or before which the person is required by section 150 to file a return of income for the year under Part I, file with the Minister a return for the year under this Part in prescribed form containing an estimate of the tax payable by the person for the year.

(2) Provisions applicable to this Part — Subsections 150(2) and (3), sections 152, 158 and 159, subsections 161(1) and (11), sections 162 to 167 and Division J of Part I apply to this Part, with any modifications that the circumstances require.

Notes: 211.82 added by 2002-2013 technical bill, for tax years that end after Oct. 24, 2012.

Definitions [s. 211.82]: "Minister", "person", "prescribed" — 248(1); "taxation year" — 249.

211.9 [Repealed]

Notes: 211.9 repealed by 2002-2013 technical bill, for tax years that end after Oct. 24, 2012. For Part XII.5 administrative provisions, see now 211.82.

The March 21, 2013 Budget Notice of Ways and Means Motion included a proposed amendment to 211.9(b) that would have taken effect in 2015. Since 211.9 has been repealed, that amendment will not proceed.

PART XII.6 — TAX ON FLOW-THROUGH SHARES

211.91 (1) Tax imposed — Every corporation shall pay a tax under this Part in respect of each month (other than January) in a calendar year equal to the amount determined by the formula

$$\left(A + \frac{B}{2} - C - \frac{D}{2}\right) \times \left(\frac{E}{12} + \frac{F}{10}\right)$$

where

A   is the total of all amounts each of which is an amount that the corporation purported to renounce in the year under subsection 66(12.6) or (12.601) because of the application of subsection 66(12.66) (other than an amount purported to be renounced in respect of expenses incurred or to be incurred in connection with production or potential production in a province where a tax, similar to the tax provided under this Part, is payable by the corporation under the laws of the province as a consequence of the failure to incur the expenses that were purported to be renounced);

B   is the total of all amounts each of which is an amount that the corporation purported to renounce in the year under subsection 66(12.6) or (12.601) because of the application of subsection 66(12.66) and that is not included in the value of A;

C   is the total of all expenses described in paragraph 66(12.66)(b) that are

(a) made or incurred by the end of the month by the corporation, and

(b) in respect of the purported renunciations in respect of which an amount is included in the value of A;

D   is the total of all expenses described in paragraph 66(12.66)(b) that are

(a) made or incurred by the end of the month by the corporation, and

(b) in respect of the purported renunciations in respect of which an amount is included in the value of B;

E   is the rate of interest prescribed for the purpose of subsection 164(3) for the month; and

F   is

(a) one, where the month is December, and

(b) nil, in any other case.

Related Provisions: 18(1)(t), 20(1)(nn) — Part XII.6 tax is deductible; 66(18) — Members of partnerships; 87(4.4)(e)–(h) — Amalgamation of principal-business corps; 211.91(2) — Return and payment of tax; 211.91(2.1) — COVID-19 extension for agreement made in 2019-20; 257 — Formula cannot calculate to less than zero.

Notes: See Notes at end of 211.91.

Regulations: 4301(b) (prescribed rate of interest under 164(3), for 211.91(1)E).

(2) Return and payment of tax — A corporation liable to tax under this Part in respect of one or more months in a calendar year shall, before March of the following calendar year,

(a) file with the Minister a return for the year under this Part in prescribed form containing an estimate of the tax payable under this Part by it in respect of each month in the year; and

(b) pay to the Receiver General the amount of tax payable under this Part by it in respect of each month in the year.

Related Provisions: 211.91(2.1) — COVID-19 extension for agreement made in 2019-20.

Forms: T100: Instructions for the flow-through share program [guide]; T101C: Part XII.6 tax return.

(2.1) COVID-19 — expenses deemed incurred earlier — If an agreement referred to in subsection 66(12.66) was made in 2019 or 2020,

(a) the reference in subsection (2) to "the following calendar year" is to be read as a reference to "the second following calendar year"; and

(b) for the purposes of this section and, where subparagraph (iii) applies, paragraph 66(12.66)(a), Canadian exploration expenses incurred by a corporation in respect of the agreement in a particular month in a calendar year are deemed to have been incurred

(i) in January 2020, if the expenses were incurred in 2020 and the agreement was entered into in 2019,

(ii) in January 2021, if the expenses were incurred in 2021 and the agreement was entered into in 2020, and

(iii) 12 months earlier, in any other case.

Notes: See also the COVID-19 extensions in 66(12.6001) and 66(12.731). For CRA interpretation see VIEWS doc 2021-0870401I7.

211.91(2.1) added by 2021 budget bill #1, effective June 29, 2021. It provides relief, due to COVID-19, for flow-through share agreements entered into in 2019-2020. 211.91(2.1)(a) extends the Part XII.6 filing and payment deadline by one year. 211.91(2.1)(b) deems certain expenditures to be incurred earlier than they were, to reduce Part XII.6 tax.

(3) Provisions applicable to Part — Subsections 150(2) and (3), sections 152, 158 and 159, subsections 161(1) and (11), sections 162 to 167 and Division J of Part I apply to this Part, with any modifications that the circumstances require.

Notes [211.91]: Part XII.6 levies a tax on flow-through share issuers that use the 1-year look-back rule under 66(12.66), under which certain CEE and CDE incurred in Year 2 can be flowed out to an investor and deducted as if incurred in Year 1. The monthly E/12 in 211.91(1) compensates for the 66(12.6) acceleration of the deduction, effectively imposing interest at the rate for corporate refunds. A further annual 10% tax (F/10) applies if the flow-through share funds are not spent by the end of the calendar year. Part XII.6 tax is deductible to the issuer: 18(1)(t)(i), 20(1)(nn). For an example (incorporating 211.91(2.1)), see VIEWS doc 2021-0870401I7.

See Angelo Toselli, "Flow-Through Shares: An Update", 10 *Canadian Petroleum Tax Journal* (1997), under heading "New Part XII.6 Tax".

Where the look-back renunciation was invalid because the issuer and shareholders were not at arm's length, 211.91 still applied because "purported to renounce" in 211.91(1)B refers to an amount the issuer "stated in the forms that it filed that it was renouncing": *Tusk Exploration*, 2018 FCA 121, para. 28.

211.91 (Part XII.6) added by 1996 Budget, for 1997 and later calendar years.

Definitions [s. 211.91]: "amount" — 248(1); "calendar year" — *Interpretation Act* 37(1)(a); "Canadian exploration expense" — 66.1(6), 248(1); "corporation" — 248(1), *Interpretation Act* 35(1); "Minister" — 248(1); "month" — *Interpretation Act* 35(1); "prescribed" — 248(1); "province" — *Interpretation Act* 35(1).

PART XIII — TAX ON INCOME FROM CANADA OF NON-RESIDENT PERSONS

212. (1) Tax — Every non-resident person shall pay an income tax of 25% on every amount that a person resident in Canada pays or credits, or is deemed by Part I to pay or credit, to the non-resident person as, on account or in lieu of payment of, or in satisfaction of,

Related Provisions: 94(3)(a)(viii), (ix), 104(7.01) — Application to trust deemed resident in Canada; 212(13.1) — Application where payor or payee is a partnership; 212(13.3)(a) — Authorized foreign bank deemed resident in Canada; 214(1) — No deductions from tax; 214(3) — Various amounts deemed paid for purposes of Part XIII;

215(1) — Requirement to withhold and remit; 216 — Election to pay tax on net income from rents and timber royalties; 217 — Election to file return under Part I in respect of certain kinds of income; 218.3(2)(c) — Withholding tax on mutual fund distributions to non-residents; 227 — Withholding taxes — administration and enforcement; 244.2 — Banks, etc. required to report international transfers of $10,000 or more; Reg. 105 — Withholding on payments to non-residents for services; Reg. 805 — No tax where income attributable to permanent establishment or taxable under 115(1)(a)(iii.3).

Notes: The 25% withholding tax rate under 212(1) (212(2) for dividends) is reduced by Canada's tax treaties, for various kinds of payments to residents of many countries. The tax on interest, dividends, royalties, pension benefits, and occasionally trust income and management fees is often reduced to 15%, 10%, zero or some other rate. (Whether or not withholding is required, in most cases the payer must file an NR4 information return: Reg. 202(1).) See Table O-5 in the introductory pages; CRA guide T4061; Information Circular 76-12R6; tinyurl.com/partxiii-calc (CRA); VIEWS doc 2018-0743891M4; and the Canada-US and Canada-UK treaties reproduced near the end of the book. See also ITAR 10(6), which limits the tax rate under s. 212 to the limit provided by the treaty. CRA phone number for Part XIII withholding tax issues: 1-855-284-5946 (613-940-8499).

However, where the treaty partner has signed and ratified the Multilateral Instrument (MLI), relief may be denied if "one of the principal purposes of any arrangement or transaction" was to obtain the benefit, "unless it is established that granting that benefit ... would be in accordance with the object and purpose" of the treaty (MLI Art. 7:1). This rule is aimed at treaty shopping and other schemes that tax authorities consider to be misusing treaties. For the MLI, see the pages before the Canada-US tax treaty.

See Vidal, *Introduction to International Tax in Canada* (Carswell, 8th ed., 2020), chap. 10; Li & Cockfield, *International Taxation in Canada* (4th ed., LexisNexis, 2018), chap. 9; Brown, "An Introduction to ... Part XIII Tax", 2004 Cdn Tax Foundation conference report, at 38:10-23.

Before withholding less than 25%, the payer should obtain a completed Form NR301 (NR302 from a partnership, NR303 from a hybrid entity such as a US LLC), as evidence the payee qualifies for treaty relief. A non-resident with no Social Insurance Number can apply on Form T1261 for an Individual Tax Number for this purpose. The CRA advises that if no form is provided, the full 25% should be withheld, but this is not a legal requirement. For a partnership with both resident and non-resident partners, 212(13.1)(b) requires full withholding as though the payee were non-resident (IT-81R para. 7; VIEWS doc 2012-0450491E5); however, where treaty relief applies, Form NR302 allows a blended withholding rate calculation based on the non-resident partners. CRA has confirmed (email from Rulings, Dec. 27, 2013) that this applies *only* where there is treaty relief, and 2012-0450491E5 applies otherwise. See also Steve Suarez, "Canada Extends Transition Period for Treaty-Reduced Nonresident Withholding", 65(9) *Tax Notes International* (taxnotes.com) 687-89 (Feb. 27, 2012); Harry Chana, "Part XIII Withholding Adequate?", 20(11) *Canadian Tax Highlights* (ctf.ca) 3-4 (Nov. 2012); CRA, "More information on forms NR301, NR302, and NR303" (May 1, 2012); VIEWS doc 2012-0444051C6.

An amount is "credited" even if not "paid", if it is set aside and unconditionally available to the creditor; a mere journal entry is not enough: Information Circular 77-16R4 para. 5; *Income Tax Technical News* 14; *Cie minière Québec Cartier*, [1984] C.T.C. 2408 (TCC). In *North Shore Power*, 2018 FCA 9, an insolvent corp's unilateral "credit memo" (never paid) did not mean the corp "credited" an amount to NSP for GST purposes. An amount applied to reduce a promissory note is "credited": VIEWS doc 2013-0499621E5. In *Lewin [Herbert Family Trust]*, 2012 FCA 279, a trustee declaration that an amount was "payable" to a beneficiary did not make it paid or credited for 212(1); this is now overruled by 214(3)(f)(i)(C) for a trust that later becomes non-resident. An amount, paid to a trust that was void for uncertainty (so that there was a resulting trust), was still "paid" in *Clark*, [2020] EWCA Civ 204 (England).

Where an agreement requires that an amount be grossed up to yield a particular after-tax amount, the total including the gross-up is subject to withholding tax: VIEWS doc 2006-021429I7. If only non-cash assets are being paid (e.g., shares distributed on a windup), the payor is still required to remit the tax: May 2010 ICAA roundtable (tinyurl.com/cra-abtax), q.9.

The amount withheld must be remitted "forthwith" (215(1)), and late payment interest legally applies after the day of payment to the non-resident (227(8.3)(b) or (9.2)); but CRA charges interest only after the 15th of the next month: Guide T4061 (unchanged for COVID-19: tinyurl.com/covid-dates).

A payer who fails to withhold is liable under 215(6) and can be assessed under 227(10). The non-resident is also liable under 212(1) (for tax) and 227(8.1) (for interest) and can be assessed under 227(10.1), e.g. *Solomon*, 2007 TCC 654. (There is no form for a non-resident to report Part XIII tax owing.) See Notes to Canada-US treaty Art. XXVI-A:1 re using the IRS or other countries' authorities to collect Canadian tax.

Exemptions can be available to: foreign diplomatic missions and organizations, per the *Foreign Missions and International Organizations Act* and related Orders-in-Council (VIEWS doc March 1991-6); US charitable organizations and pension trusts (Canada-US tax treaty Art. XXI; Guide T4016). Taxpayers exempt under 149(1) are exempt only from Part I tax, so not from 212(1), though few are non-resident. For interest see 212(3)"fully exempt interest".

No return is filed by non-residents for tax withheld under 212, except where an election is made under section 216 or 217 to file a return and pay regular tax on the net rather than withholding tax on the gross. If tax is wrongly withheld or overwithheld, a refund application may be made under 227(6), but only by the non-resident.

There is no deadline for an assessment for failing to withhold and remit Part XIII tax: see Notes to 227(10). On the lack of detail provided on Part XIII assessments, see VIEWS doc 2011-0427251C6.

The withholding tax raised about $6.5 billion in calendar 2015. Of this, about $4b was from dividends, $630m from interest, $750m from royalties and $180m rents. (*Access to Information Act* disclosure; the breakdown shows all codes on the NR4 slip.)

I.T. Application Rules [subsec. 212(1)]: 10(4) (application to debts issued before 1976); 10(6) (reduction of 25% rate by treaty).

Interpretation Bulletins [subsec. 212(1)]: IT-77R: Securities in satisfaction of income debt (cancelled); IT-360R2: Interest payable in a foreign currency.

Information Circulars [subsec. 212(1)]: 76-12R6: Applicable rate of Part XIII tax on amounts paid or credited to persons in countries with which Canada has a tax convention; 77-16R4: Non-resident income tax.

I.T. Technical News [subsec. 212(1)]: 11 (reporting of amounts paid out of an employee benefit plan); 14 (meaning of "credited" for purposes of Part XIII withholding tax).

CRA Audit Manual [subsec. 212(1)]: 10.11.13: Consultation and referrals regarding non-residents; 15.2.0: Income of a non-resident; 15.3.0: Part XIII tax on income from Canada of non-resident persons.

Forms [subsec. 212(1)]: NR4: Statement of amounts paid or credited to non-residents of Canada; NR4 Segment; NR4 Summ: Return of amounts paid or credited to non-residents of Canada; NR4(OAS): Statement of OAS pension paid or credited to non-residents of Canada; NR7R: Application for refund of Part XIII tax withheld; NR301: Declaration of eligibility for benefits under a tax treaty for a non-resident taxpayer; NR302: Declaration of eligibility for benefits (reduced tax) under a tax treaty for a partnership with non-resident partners; NR303: Declaration of eligibility for benefits (reduced tax) under a tax treaty for a hybrid entity; NR304: Direct deposit request for non-resident account holders and NR7-R refund applicants; NR601: Non-resident ownership certificate — withholding tax; NR602: Non-resident ownership certificate — no withholding tax; NR603: Remittance of non-resident tax on income from film or video acting services; T1136: OAS return of income; T1141: Information return re transfers or loans to a non-resident trust; T1142: Information return re distributions from and indebtedness to a non-resident trust; T4061: Non-resident withholding tax guide.

(a) management fee — a management or administration fee or charge;

Related Provisions: 212(4) — Meaning of "management or administration fee or charge"; Reg. 105 — Withholding tax on payments to non-residents for services. See also at beginning of subsec. 212(1).

Notes: See Notes to 212(1) opening words above.

Meaning of management or administration fee: "an amount paid in respect of managerial services in connection with the direction or supervision of business activities": *Peter Cundill & Associates*, [1991] 1 C.T.C. 197 (FCTD); aff'd [1991] 2 C.T.C. 221 (FCA). However, 212(4)(a) excludes arm's-length fees for services provided in the ordinary course of business (if services are rendered in Canada, Reg. 105 may require withholding); it applied in VIEWS doc 2011-0416891R3.

212(4)(b) excludes reimbursement of a "specific expense", which must be an "explicit and identifiable expense": *Agricultural & Industrial*, [1991] 2 C.T.C. 2721 (TCC), and which CRA says in IT-468R para. 8 must be with no markup. An NR4 slip is required: doc 2011-0402791E5. 212(4)(b) applied in 2008-0280131R3. See also Yau, "How Specific is a Specific Expense?", XXIV(4) *International Tax Planning* (Federated Press) 2-7 (2020).

Tax treaties: some (Barbados, Guyana, Jamaica, Trinidad & Tobago) reduce the 212(1)(a) withholding tax rate. But under all treaties, reasonable management fees paid to non-resident N are considered business profits and not taxed by Canada if N does not have a permanent establishment (PE) in Canada: IT-468R; Information Circular 77-16R4 para. 15. (212(1)(a) does not apply because Art. 7 says that, absent a PE, Canada cannot tax the profits.)

See also VIEWS docs 2008-0271251R3 (212(1)(a) did not apply to certain mutual fund dealers' fees); 2016-0636721I7 (212(1)(a) did not apply to "consent fees" paid to lenders to assist in sale of a business: "the provision [is not] interpreted as broadly as the words would otherwise clearly permit").

See also Woltersdorf & Posey, "Payment of Management or Administration Fees to a Non-Resident", 2409 *Tax Topics* (CCH) 1-7 (May 10, 2018). For fees charged by a NR parent to a Canadian sub, see Purdy & Zanchelli, "Calculating and Supporting Management Fees", 44(1) *Canadian Tax Journal* 157–87 (1996). For criticism of 212(1)(a) as outdated, see Wilson, Plecko & Alary, "Paragraph 212(1)(a): The Perils of an Obsolete Tax Provision", tinyurl.com/gowling-212-1a (2011).

In *JP Morgan*, 2013 FCA 250, a judicial review application of a CRA decision to assess 7 years of management fees under 212(1)(a), contrary to CRA guidelines, was struck out.

Regulations: 202(1)(a) (information return); 805 (no tax where income attributable to permanent establishment).

Interpretation Bulletins: IT-468R: Management or administrative fees paid to non-residents. See also at beginning of s. 212.

Information Circulars: 87-2R: International transfer pricing (archived). See also at beginning of subsec. 212(1).

Forms: See at beginning of subsec. 212(1).

(b) interest — interest that

(i) is not fully exempt interest and is paid or payable

(A) to a person with whom the payer is not dealing at arm's length, or

(B) in respect of a debt or other obligation to pay an amount to a person with whom the payer is not dealing at arm's length, or

(ii) is participating debt interest;

Related Provisions: 18(6.1) — Back-to-back loans — deemed interest; 125.21 — Credit to offset withholding tax on bank's upstream deposits; 142.7(8)(d) — Application of 212(1)(b)(vii) on conversion of foreign bank subsidiary to branch; 212(3) — Meaning of "fully exempt interest" and "participating debt interest"; 212(3.1)–(3.81) — Back-to-back rules; 212(6)–(8) — Reduced tax on interest on pre-1961 provincial bonds; 212(9)(c) — Exemption for interest received by mutual fund trust and paid to non-resident; 212(13.3)(a) — Authorized foreign bank deemed resident in Canada; 212(15) — CDIC-insured obligations deemed not guaranteed by Canada; 212(18) — Return by financial institutions; 212(19) — Tax on dealers re excess amount exempted under securities lending arrangement; 214(2) — Income and capital combined; 214(3)(e) — Deemed payments; 214(4) — Securities; 214(6) — Deemed interest; 214(7), (7.1) — Sale of obligation; 214(15) — Deemed interest; 214(16), (17) — Thin capitalization — interest deemed to be dividend taxed by 212(2); 218 — Loan to wholly-owned subsidiary; 240(2) — Interest coupon to be identified; 251(1) — Arm's length; 260(8) — Securities lending arrangement — deemed payment of interest; Canada-U.S. Tax Treaty:Art. XI — Taxation of interest. See additional Related Provisions at beginning of 212(1).

Notes: See Notes to 212(1) opening words above. See 12(1)(c) Notes on the meaning of "interest".

Withholding tax on *arm's-length* interest (paid to a non-resident in any country) has been eliminated, except for 212(3) "participating debt interest". This was announced in conjunction with the Fifth Protocol amending the Canada-US tax treaty (see Art. XI:1). Although the Protocol did not come into force until Dec. 2008, the change to 212(1)(b) was made effective Jan. 2008. Using the Canada-US treaty to eliminate withholding tax that would be payable by a related company in another country may be acceptable, but see Notes to treaty Art. X:2 and XXIX-A:1 re "treaty shopping".

Withholding tax still applies on *non-arm's length* interest (see Notes to 251(1) on the meaning of arm's length), unless it is "fully exempt interest" (212(3)); and still applies to "participating debt interest" (212(3)). Art. XI of the Canada US tax treaty also eliminates tax on interest paid to US residents in many cases. For residents of most other countries, the rate is reduced by tax treaty: see Table O-5 at beginning of book.

Note the "back-to-back" rules in 212(3.1)-(3.81), which impose tax on schemes designed to avoid the tax.

For interpretation of post-2007 212(1)(b) see VIEWS docs 2007-0241391E5; 2007-0248031E5 (no withholding tax (WT) on payment considered to be repayment of principal); 2008-0268281E5; 2008-0301391E5 (EBITDA calculation measures creditworthiness and is not participating debt interest); 2009-0326881R3 and 2009-0348861R3 (no WT on notes payable via delivery of gold); 2011-0407301R3 (interest is "fully exempt interest"); 2012-0465651E5 (non-resident corp that owns 27% of Cdn corp might be non-arm's length); 2013-0475701R3 (mortgage investment corporation's payments to non-resident shareholders are taxable); 2013-0494211I7 (15% rate applies under Canada-US treaty Art. XI:6 where interest is computed by reference to a public commodity index); 2014-0523691R3 (non-viable contingent capital debt — interest is exempt [Sherman & Jamal, "Cuckoo for CoCos", XX(2) *International Tax Planning* (Federated Press) 1388-91 (2015)]); 2014-0539791R3, 2014-0563221R3 (interest paid under CCAA plan of arrangement); 2015-0602711R3 (interest not based on profit participation features); 2016-0636721I7 (no WT on "consent fees" paid to lenders to assist in the sale of a business, calculated as a percentage of the principal owing); 2016-0664041R3 (additional contingent payment did not taint periodic interest payment [Lang & Kabouchi, "Participating Debt Interest Once Payable Taints Future Interest Payments", XXI(3) *Corporate Finance* (Federated Press) 20-22 (2018)]); 2017-071330117 (assumption of accrued interest creates novation and payment in kind that triggers tax); 2016-0635081R3 (interest on notes is not based on profit); 2016-0649061R3, 2017-0732001R3 (notes not subject to 212(1)(b)); 2018-0766771R3 (commodity-linked notes not sufficiently linked to profitability to be subject to 212(1)(b)); 2018-0776381R3 (negative repo spread in "reverse repo" securities repurchase is not interest for 212(1)(b)); 2019-0798741C6 [2019 IFA q.3] (participating amount taints later payments, but Canada-US Treaty provides relief due to CRA interpretation of Art. XI:6(b) [Wang, "Tainting of Non-Participating Interest", 9(3) *Canadian Tax Focus* (ctf.ca) 12 (Aug. 2019)]); 2020 IFA Roundtable q.2 (mismatched swap payments are not interest: legal character of amount paid must be preserved). See also Notes to 212(3) "participating debt interest" for docs re convertible debt.

See also Jonathan Willson, "Canada's New Interest Withholding Tax Regime — Some Interpretive Issues", XV(2) *Corporate Finance* (Federated Press) 1645-55 (2008).

The elimination of withholding tax on interest led to immigrants depositing money in Canadian banks in an offshore friend or relative's name. Now an NR4 is required even if no tax is withheld (see Notes to Reg. 202(1)), and large deposits will normally be reported to the foreign tax authority (ss. 270-281).

On whether interest has been "paid or credited" see Notes at beginning of 212(1).

Before paying interest or dividends to a financial intermediary acting as agent for non-resident owners, payers must either withhold 25% or get certification of where the beneficial owner is resident: Information Circular 76-12R6 para. 12. (This should no longer apply to arm's-length interest.)

212(1)(b) can apply to payments by non-residents operating in Canada: 212(13.2).

212(1)(b)(i)(B) addresses the situation raised under the pre-2008 rules in *Lehigh Cement*, 2010 FCA 124 (leave to appeal denied 2010 CarswellNat 4035 (SCC)), where interest coupons were stripped and sold to a third party. See Grant Russell, "Department of Finance Draft Legislative Proposals a Response to Recent Federal Court of Appeal Decision in Lehigh", XVI(3) *International Tax Planning* (Federated Press) 1129-32 (2011).

212(1)(b)(i)(B) added by 2002-2013 technical bill (Part 5 — technical), effective for interest paid or payable by a person or partnership (the "payer") to a person or partnership (the "recipient") after March 15, 2011, unless

(a) the interest is paid in respect of a debt or obligation incurred by the payer before March 16, 2011; and

(b) the recipient acquired the entitlement to the interest as a consequence of an agreement or other arrangement entered into by the recipient, and evidenced in writing, before March 16, 2011.

Before the amendment, read 212(1)(b)(i) as:

(i) is not fully exempt interest, and is paid or payable to a person with whom the payer is not dealing at arm's length, or

212(1)(b) amended by 2007 Budget, effective 2008 (and then the effective-2008 version restored by 2002-2013 technical bill s. 347(4), after amending the pre-2008 version). Former 212(1)(b)(iii) and 212(1)(b)(vii), which still apply due to 214(8)(a) (see Notes to 212(3)"participating debt interest"), read:

(b) ...

(iii) [foreign currency debt] — interest payable in a currency other than Canadian currency to a person with whom the payer is dealing at arm's length, on

(A) any obligation where the evidence of indebtedness was issued on or before December 20, 1960,

(B) any obligation where the evidence of indebtedness was issued after December 20, 1960, if the obligation was entered into under an agreement in writing made on or before that day, under which the obligee undertook to advance, on or before a specified day, a specified amount at a specified rate of interest or a rate of interest to be determined as provided in the agreement, to the extent that the interest payable on the obligation is payable

(I) in respect of a period ending not later than the earliest day on which, under the terms of the obligation determined as of the time it was entered into, the obligee would be entitled to demand payment of the principal amount of the obligation or the amount outstanding as or on account of the principal amount thereof, as the case may be, if the terms of the obligation determined as of that time provided for that payment on or after a specified day, or

(II) in respect of a period ending not later than one year after the time the obligation was entered into, in any other case,

(C) any bond, debenture or similar obligation issued after December 20, 1960, for the issue of which arrangements were made on or before that day with a dealer in securities, if the existence of the arrangements for the issue of the bond, debenture or similar obligation can be established by evidence in writing given or made on or before that day,

(D) an amount not repayable in Canadian currency deposited with an institution that was at the time the amount was deposited or at the time the interest was paid or credited a prescribed financial institution,

(E) any obligation entered into in the course of carrying on a business in a country other than Canada, to the extent that the interest payable on the obligation is deductible in computing the income of the payer under Part I from a business carried on by the payer in such a country, or that, but for subsection 18(2) or section 21, would have been so deductible, or

(F) any obligation entered into by the payer after December 20, 1960, on assuming an obligation referred to in clause (A) in consideration or partial consideration for the purchase by the payer of property of the vendor that constituted security for that obligation, if the payer on entering into the obligation undertook to pay the same amount of money on or before the same date and at the same rate of interest as the vendor of the property had undertaken in respect of the obligation under which the vendor was the obligor,

(for the purpose of this subparagraph, interest expressed to be computed by reference to Canadian currency shall be deemed to be payable in Canadian currency),

(vii) [5-year corporate debt] — interest payable by a corporation resident in Canada to a person with whom that corporation is dealing at arm's length on any obligation where the evidence of indebtedness was issued by that corporation after June 23, 1975 if under the terms of the obligation or any agreement relating thereto the corporation may not under any circumstances be obliged to pay more than 25% of

(A) where the obligation is one of a number of obligations that comprise a single debt issue of obligations that are identical in respect of all rights (in equity or otherwise, either immediately or in the future and either absolutely or contingently) attaching thereto, except as regards the principal amount thereof, the total of the principal amount of those obligations, or

(B) in any other case, the principal amount of the obligation,

within 5 years from the date of issue of that single debt issue or that obligation, as the case may be, except

(C) in the event of a failure or default under the said terms or agreement,

(D) if the terms of the obligation or any agreement relating thereto become unlawful or are changed by virtue of legislation or by a court, statutory board or commission,

(E) if the person exercises a right under the terms of the obligation or any agreement relating thereto to convert the obligation into, or exchange the obligation for, a prescribed security, or

(F) in the event of the person's death;

(G) in the event that a change to this Act or to a tax treaty has the effect of relieving the non-resident person from liability for tax under this Part in respect of the interest;

Commentary on pre-2008 212(1)(b)(iii): For rulings that 212(1)(b)(iii)(D) exempts the return on foreign denominated index-linked notes, see VIEWS docs 2005-0139661R3, 2006-0178791R3.

The exemption in 212(1)(b)(iii)(E) applied in *Kinguk Trawl*, 2003 FCA 85. Kinguk operated a fishing trawler, financed by a Danish company in a way that made it Kinguk's agent when selling the fish, so Kinguk was carrying on business in Denmark.

Commentary on pre-2008 212(1)(b)(vii): The "5/25" exemption in 212(1)(b)(vii) applies if the conditions are met for "the" debt. As to whether a new debt has been created (novation), see *General Electric Capital*, [2002] 1 C.T.C. 217 (FCA); leave to appeal denied 2002 CarswellNat 2539 (SCC). The fundamental terms of a note are: (a) the debtor's identity; (b) the principal amount of the note; (c) the amount of interest under the note; and (d) the note's maturity date. "Where substantial changes have been made to the fundamental terms of an obligation which materially alter the terms of that obligation, then a new obligation is created" for 212(1)(b)(vii). This overrides IT-448 and *Technical News* 14. See also Biringer, "When Is an Obligation New?", IX(4) *Corporate Finance* (Federated Press) 906-10 (2001); Schwartz & Rosebrugh, "The Interpretation of Legal Terms Undefined in Tax Legislation", 2002 Cdn Tax Foundation conference report, 37:1-18; VIEWS docs 2002-0178455, 2005-0156081I7, 2009-032259117 [Quebec], 2017-071330117; *Technical News* 30; GST Policy Statement P-249, "Agreements and Novation".

In *Lehigh Cement*, 2010 FCA 124, leave to appeal denied 2010 CarswellNat 4035 (SCC), GAAR did not apply to a loan restructuring done to access the 5/25 exemption. (See now 212(1)(b)(i)(B).)

For more on 212(1)(b)(vii) and valid "events of default" see IT-361R3; *Technical News* 9; VIEWS docs 2005-01200761R3, 2005-0124081R3, 2005-0133561R3, 2006-0174101E5, 2006-0191881R3, 2007-0223521R3, 2007-0225751R3, 2007-0240951R3, 2007-0241271R3; Oliver, "Defaults and Triggers under 212(1)(b)(vii)", 16(1) *Taxation Law* (Ontario Bar Assn, oba.org) 9-11 (Nov. 2005); Kopstein & Pantry, "Subparagraph 212(1)(b)(vii) Withholding Tax Exemption", 2005 Cdn Tax Foundation conference report, 15:1-48; Choudhury, "Moving the Goalposts", 17(2) *Taxation Law* 16-19 (April 2007). A "material adverse effect" clause that gives the lender discretion to recall the debt will prevent 212(1)(b)(vii) from applying: 2001-0087185, but see 2006-0218931R3 allowing the exemption.

In CRA's view, it is acceptable for the general partner of a limited partnership operating a business in Canada, that qualifies for the 212(1)(b)(vii) exemption, to borrow and on-loan the funds (at a positive spread) to a limited partnership: docs 2003-0039243, 2004-0092731R3, 2004-0093591R3, 2005-0114100R3, 2005-0127241R3, 2005-01268141R3 (and supp. 2005-0144551R3), 2005-0145911R3, 2005-0153641R3, 2006-0171011R3, 2006-0195501R3, 2006-0211781R3, 2006-0213101R3. 2004-0094751R3 allows a back-to-back loan by a new corporation to a securitization trust. See also John Jakolev, "Back-to-Back Withholding Relief", 12(12) *Canadian Tax Highlights* (ctf.ca) 5 (Dec. 2004); David Glicksman & Margaret Nixon, "Back-to-back Loans for Non-corporate Borrowers", XII(3) *Corporate Finance* 1220-22 (2005).

See also 2004-0094741R3 and 2006-0180251R3 (accepting a minimum EBITDA for 212(1)(b)(vii)), 2005-0134621E5 (non-resident payor is a partnership of corporations), 2006-0194191R3 (one financing agreement with 2 tranches is one debt issue for the 5/25 rule); 2007-0226281R3 (using a Finco owned by a charity trust); 20070244561R3 (loans to Finco under 3P project); 2007-0252491R3 (assumption of debt for assets).

Regulations: 202(1)(b) (information return).

Information Circulars: See at beginning of subsec. 212(1).

I.T. Technical News: 44 (convertible debentures and Part XIII).

Forms: See at beginning of subsec. 212(1).

(c) **estate or trust income** — income of or from an estate or a trust to the extent that the amount

(i) is included in computing the income of the non-resident person under subsection 104(13), except to the extent that the amount is deemed by subsection 104(21) to be a taxable capital gain of the non-resident person, or

(ii) can reasonably be considered (having regard to all the circumstances including the terms and conditions of the estate or trust arrangement) to be a distribution of, or derived from, an amount received by the estate or trust as, on account of, in lieu of payment of or in satisfaction of, a dividend on a share of the capital stock of a corporation resident in Canada, other than a taxable dividend;

Related Provisions: 94(1)"exempt amount"(c)(ii) — Exemption from non-resident trust rules; 94(3)(a)(ix) — Application to trust deemed resident in Canada; 104(16)(d) — SIFT trust distribution deemed to be dividend; 132(5.1), (5.2) — Deemed dividend on distribution of gain derived from taxable Canadian property by mutual fund trust; 212(2)(b) — Withholding tax on capital dividends; 212(9) — Exemptions; 212(10) — Trust established before 1949; 212(11) — Payment to a beneficiary as income of trust; 212(13) — Non-resident payor deemed resident in Canada; 212(17) — No withholding tax on payments from employee benefit plan or employee trust; 214(3)(f), (f.1) — Deemed payments; 218.3(2)(c) — Withholding tax on mutual fund distributions to non-residents; 250.1(b) — Calculation of income of non-resident person; Canada-U.S. Tax Treaty:Art. XXII:2 — Estate or trust income. See additional Related Provisions at beginning of subsec. 212(1).

Notes: Tax under 212(1)(c) may be reduced by treaty, e.g. to 15% under Canada-US treaty Art. XXII:2; 15% to a resident of Sweden: VIEWS doc 2014-0522271E5. See Notes at beginning of 212(1).

18(5.4) deems certain trust income to have been paid to non-resident beneficiaries, which can trigger 212(1)(c).

104(16) deems a SIFT income trust distribution to be a dividend, subject to withholding tax under 212(2). (122.1(1)"SIFT trust" excludes a REIT, which is subject to 212(1)(c) at the applicable treaty rate: 2013-0497381E5.)

Part XII.2 tax on income from Canadian trusts: see Notes to 210(1)"designated beneficiary".

Estate income paid to non-resident beneficiaries: 212(1)(c) applies to the payment unless the estate trustee elects under 104(13.1) to retain the income for tax purposes (VIEWS doc 2010-0385771E5).

A *capital distribution* to a beneficiary may be deemed by 212(11) to be paid out of the trust's income for withholding tax purposes. If the distribution is of capital but relates to a prior year's capital dividend, withholding tax applies under 212(1)(c)(ii). See VIEWS doc 2003-0020695. (A distribution of capital may also be subject to s. 116 if it is in satisfaction of part of the beneficiary's interest in the trust.) A capital dividend distributed by an estate to non-resident beneficiaries is taxed under 212(1)(c) (2011-0422441E5) rather than 212(2) due to 212(11), so the Canada-US treaty reduction is under Art. XXII:2, not Art. X: 2009-0327001C6. (Even a non-taxable capital distribution must be reported on an NR4, due to 212(11): see Reg. 202(1) Notes.) See also Shew & Cho, "Withholding Tax on Capital Distributions to Non-Residents", 7(3) *Canadian Tax Focus* (ctf.ca) 11 (Aug. 2017)

Where trustees pass a resolution entitling a non-resident beneficiary to the trust's income for the year, but do not pay the amount until the next year, withholding tax need not be remitted until after the amount is paid: doc 2003-0009211E5. However, if the trust becomes non-resident, 214(3)(f)(i)(C) triggers immediate withholding tax.

See also Fernando, "Non-resident Beneficiaries", 10(7) *Tax Hyperion* (Carswell) 4-5 (July 2013).

212(1)(c)(i) amended by 2001 technical bill for amounts paid or credited after Dec. 17, 1999. 212(1)(c)(ii) added by 1991 technical bill.

Regulations: 202(1)(c) (information return).

Interpretation Bulletins: IT-342R: Trusts — income payable to beneficiaries; IT-465R: Non-resident beneficiaries of trusts; IT-500R: RRSPs — death of an annuitant; IT-531: Eligible funeral arrangements. See also at beginning of s. 212.

Information Circulars: See at beginning of subsec. 212(1).

CRA Audit Manual: 15.3.6: Non-resident beneficiaries of trusts; 16.2.2: Estate of a deceased person — non-residents.

Forms: See at beginning of subsec. 212(1).

(d) **rents, royalties, etc.** — rent, royalty or similar payment, including, but not so as to restrict the generality of the foregoing, any payment

(i) for the use of or for the right to use in Canada any property, invention, trade-name, patent, trade-mark, design or model, plan, secret formula, process or other thing whatever,

(ii) for information concerning industrial, commercial or scientific experience where the total amount payable as consideration for that information is dependent in whole or in part on

(A) the use to be made of, or the benefit to be derived from, that information,

(B) production or sales of goods or services, or

(C) profits,

(iii) for services of an industrial, commercial or scientific character performed by a non-resident person where the total amount payable as consideration for those services is dependent in whole or in part on

(A) the use to be made of, or the benefit to be derived from, those services,

(B) production or sales of goods or services, or

(C) profits,

but not including a payment made for services performed in connection with the sale of property or the negotiation of a contract,

(iv) unless paragraph (i) applies to the amount, made pursuant to an agreement between a person resident in Canada and a non-resident person under which the non-resident person agrees not to use or not to permit any other person to use any thing referred to in subparagraph (i) or any information referred to in subparagraph (ii), or

(v) that was dependent on the use of or production from property in Canada whether or not it was an instalment on the sale price of the property, but not including an instalment on the sale price of agricultural land,

but not including

(vi) a royalty or similar payment on or in respect of a copyright in respect of the production or reproduction of any literary, dramatic, musical or artistic work,

(vii) a payment in respect of the use by a railway company or by a person whose principal business is that of a common carrier of property that is railway rolling stock as defined in the definition "rolling stock" in section 2 of the *Railway Act*

(A) if the payment is made for the use of that property for a period or periods not expected to exceed in the aggregate 90 days in any 12 month period, or

(B) in any other case, if the payment is made pursuant to an agreement in writing entered into before November 19, 1974;

(viii) a payment made under a *bona fide* cost-sharing arrangement under which the person making the payment shares on a reasonable basis with one or more non-resident persons research and development expenses in exchange for an interest, or for civil law a right, in any or all property or other things of value that may result therefrom,

(ix) a rental payment for the use of or the right to use outside Canada any tangible, or for civil law corporeal, property,

(x) any payment made to a person with whom the payer is dealing at arm's length, to the extent that the amount thereof is deductible in computing the income of the payer under Part I from a business carried on by the payer in a country other than Canada,

(xi) a payment made to a person with whom the payer is dealing at arm's length for the use of or the right to use property that is

(A) an aircraft,

(B) furniture, fittings or equipment attached to an aircraft,

(C) a spare part for property described in clause (A) or (B);

(D) air navigation equipment utilized in the provision of services under the *Civil Air Navigation Services Commer-*

cialization Act or computer software the use of which is necessary for the operation of that equipment that is used by the payer for no other purpose; or

(xii) an amount to which subsection (5) would apply if that subsection were read without reference to "to the extent that the amount relates to that use or reproduction";

Proposed Amendment — Additional tax on vacant housing owned by non-residents

Federal Budget, April 19, 2021: See under 115(1)(b).

Related Provisions: 212(3.9)–(3.94) — Back-to-back rules for 212(1)(d); 212(5) — Motion picture films; 212(9)(b) — Exemption for royalty payment received by trust and paid to non-resident; 216 — Alternative re rents and timber royalties; Canada-U.S. Tax Treaty:Art. VI — Income from real property; Art. XII — Royalties. See additional Related Provisions at beginning of subsec. 212(1).

Notes: See Notes to 212(1) opening words above.

Royalty and rental payments to residents of countries with which Canada has a tax treaty are subject to a lower rate such as 15%. See Table O-5 (treaty withholding rates) at beginning of the book. Treaty relief applies when the "beneficial owner" of the royalties is resident in the treaty country: see Notes to Canada-US Treaty Art. X:2 for the meaning of this term; and see the "back-to-back" rules in 212(3.9)-(3.94).

The federal government announced in its 1993 budget that it was prepared to eliminate withholding tax, in its tax treaties, on arm's length payments for rights to use patented information or information concerning scientific experience, and on payments made for the use of software. This has now been done in many treaties or Protocols, e.g. Algeria, Australia, Austria, Belgium, Denmark, Finland, Germany, Ireland [for an example see doc 2011-0399581I7], Israel, Kyrgyzstan, Luxembourg, Namibia, The Netherlands, Norway, Oman, United Arab Emirates, the UK and the US. See Notes to Canada-US treaty Art. XII:3 and Canada-UK treaty Art. 12(3). New treaties with Azerbaijan, Italy, Madagascar, New Zealand and Romania reduce the rate to 5% instead of zero.

For detailed discussion of 212(1)(d) see *Hasbro Canada*, [1999] 1 C.T.C. 2512 (TCC) (payments to purchasing agents were not caught).

Rents: One can elect to pay regular tax on net rental income from real property, rather than withholding tax on the gross. See 216(1). For more on real estate rental payments to non-residents see VIEWS docs 2009-0311311E5, 2011-0414341E5. Where the tenant pays property taxes directly to the municipality, that is part of the rent and is subject to 212(1)(d): *Burland Properties*, 1968 CarswellNat 349 (SCC).

Rental payments to a non-resident that are attributed to the NR's permanent establishment in Canada are exempt due to Reg. 805(1): VIEWS doc 2007-0225861R3. But see Ian MacInnis, "Potential Double Taxation of Rental Income to Non-Residents?", 1965 *Tax Topics* (CCH) 1-2 (Nov. 5, 2009); Manu Kakkar, "Rental Equipment Used in Canada and Part XIII Tax", 10(3) *Tax for the Owner-Manager* (ctf.ca) 9 (July 2010).

Rent (paid to a relative) that is less than market value is still rent subject to 212(1)(d), as are payments of property taxes on the owner's behalf: VIEWS doc 2014-053205117. Payments to settle breach of a rental contract fall within 212(1)(d) as "in lieu of" rent despite the French being "au titre" ["as" rent]: *Transocean Offshore*, 2005 FCA 104 (leave to appeal denied 2005 CarswellNat 3125 (SCC)); VIEWS docs 2015-057429117, 2015-0570011E5.

Payments for "participation rights" from mine production are not rent, royalties or similar payments: VIEWS doc 2005-0157901R3. Payments under aircraft lease agreements fall under various provisions of 212(1)(d): doc 2005-0161381I7.

Royalties: In *Zainul & Shazma Holdings*, 2004 TCC 527, an initial franchise one-time licence fee did not fall under 212(1)(d) because it was an application fee paid before the grant of franchise, to compensate the franchisor for reviewing the franchisee's qualifications. In *Blais*, 2010 TCC 361, payments by a satellite TV reseller for access to satellite channels were for services, not "rent, royalty or similar payments". The following can be royalties: franchise fees, depending on the facts (2007-0253321E5, 2011-0416821R3, 2013-0512921E3 [renewal fee]); procurement licence fee under franchise agreement (2011-043187117, but see *Zainul* above); payment to settle patent infringement action (2004-0081521R3). See also "212(1)(d)(vi)" below; Johnson & Mackey, "Inbound Investment in Canadian Oil and Gas Royalties", XIV(2) *Resource Sector Taxation* (Federated Press) 1-21 (2020).

For motion picture films, see also 212(5). Payment for (or for an option to acquire) motion picture rights to a script does not fall under 212(1)(d) because it is payment for the purchase of the property, not its use: VIEWS doc 2006-017937117.

212(1)(d)(i) covered a lump-sum payment for a trade name (but not payment for the right to buy and sell a machine) in *Farmparts Distributing*, [1980] C.T.C. 205 (FCA). *Contra*, in *Saint John Shipbuilding*, [1979] C.T.C. 380 (FCTD) (aff'd without resolving this issue [1980] C.T.C. 352 (FCA)), a lump-sum payment for computerized information used in shipbuilding did not fall under 212(1)(d)(i).

CRA says that payments for the following fall under 212(1)(d)(i): "know-how" (IT-303, VIEWS doc 2009-0331791E5); right to broadcast an artistic work (2006-0196191C6); trademark, despite *Trade Marks Act* s. 4 (2009-0349481E5); right to manufacture and sell a trademarked product, allocated to use in Canada (2007-0246981E5); right to use a patent (2014-0549281E5). The following do not: payment for right to use digital property (2011-0422781E5); exclusive distribution rights (2017-070129117).

212(1)(d)(ii): Payment for customer information falls under (d)(ii) but is exempted by Canada-US treaty Art. XII:3(c): doc 2012-0457951E5. A procurement licence fee under a franchise agreement was considered to fall partly under 212(1)(d)(ii): 2011-043187117. Payment for engineering services or know-how could fall under any of (i), (ii) or (iii). See also docs 9404997, 9419675, 2013-0475751E5 and next para.

212(1)(d)(iii): the exemption in the closing words can apply to payments for use of an electronic trading system: 2002-0158753. Where payment for finding a buyer is for *information* rather than *services*, it falls under 212(1)(d)(ii) which has no similar exemption: doc 9323355. Incentive payments by manufacturers to retailers' employees for selling warranties are exempted by 212(1)(d)(iii) closing words: 2013-0495611E5. Payment to advertising on a US website falls under (d)(iii) but is exempt if the USCo has no permanent establishment in Canada, due to Canada-US treaty Art. VII:6, XII:4 and VII:1: 2011-0416181E5. See also under "Royalties:" above.

212(1)(d)(iv) covers non-compete payments, but only if 212(1)(i) does not catch them (so if they are taxed under 212(1)(i), treaty reductions to the rate under 212(1)(d) do not apply). See also VIEWS doc 2003-0044351E5. A procurement licence fee under a franchise agreement was considered to fall partly under 212(1)(d)(iv): 2011-043187117.

212(1)(d)(v) will not apply to a share sale earn-out provision if the shares are taxable Canadian property and the conditions in IT-426R (see Notes to 12(1)(g)) are met: docs 2005-0145311C6 [2005 APFF q.30], 2006-0196211C6 [2006 APFF q.17], 2019-0824461C6 [2019 CTF q.10]. Gravel extraction payments and oil & gas royalties are taxable and not reduced by treaty: 2010-038223117, 2011-0431571E5, 2013-0509771E5 [but could fall under 115(1)(a)]. 212(1)(d)(v) applies to payments for client or customer lists: 2013-0494251E5, 2014-0525501E5 (but Canada-US treaty Art. XII:3(c) or Canada-UK treaty Art. 12:3(b) can exempt them).

212(1)(d)(vi) exempts musical and dramatic works, but this can be overridden by 212(5), which taxes payments for films and TV shows: docs 2011-0404511E5, 2011-042422117, 2012-0443561E5, 2013-0506191E5, 2013-0514291E5. On tax issues for musicians, see Paul Sanderson, *Musicians and the Law in Canada* (Carswell, 4th ed., 2014), pp. 517-557.

"Literary work" includes virtually anything covered by copyright law, including software: *Angoss International*, [1999] 2 C.T.C. 2259 (TCC), para. 21; *Syspro Software*, 2003 TCC 498, paras. 12, 20; *Apple Computer v. Mackintosh Computers*, 1987 CarswellNat 720 (FC), para. 42 (literary quality is irrelevant); *Bulman Group v. Alpha One-Write*, 1981 CarswellNat 737 (FC), para. 10; *CCH Canadian v. Law Society of Upper Canada*, 2004 SCC 13.

Software: The exemption for "literary" works in 212(1)(d)(vi) applies to the right to reproduce and distribute copies of software. The exemption does not apply to payments by end-users to non-residents. See Revenue Canada Round Table, 1988 Cdn Tax Foundation conference report, Q. 41, pp. 53:89-90; and 1993 conference report, Q. 29, p. 58:15. A royalty exempted under 212(1)(d)(vi) can be based on the number of copies made, the number sold or the license fees earned: VIEWS doc 2002-0147545. See also 2010-0354921E5 (royalties for a play); 2011-0399141R3 (212(1)(d)(vi) applies to payments for right to distribute software in various forms); 2011-0427181E5 (payments for software distribution, upgrades and support); 2012-0441091E5 (payments under software licensing agreement); 2012-0462801R3 (custom software distribution fees are considered copyright royalties).

Payment for a right to use packaged or "shrink-wrapped" software is considered payment for sale of goods rather than royalties: docs 9319685, 9425035, 9500705, 2003-0016791E5; *Engineering Analysis* (Supreme Court of India, 2021, tinyurl.com/india-eng). (The same principle applies to GST/HST: Technical Information Bulletin B-037R.) Payments for custom software are royalties. Reasonable fees for related services such as maintenance are not caught by 212(1)(d), but can be subject to Reg. 105 withholding.

CRA's view is that payment for software downloaded from a web site is not payment of a royalty: *Income Tax Technical News* 25. (As per above, many of Canada's treaties now exempt software royalties from withholding tax anyway.)

The reference in 212(1)(d)(vi) to *production* of a work does not mean the payor must manufacture or produce it: doc 2017-0697811E5.

Payments under the Public Lending Right Program of the Canada Council for the Arts are considered to be for independent personal services, not royalties, so they do not fall under 212(1)(d)(vi): VIEWS doc 2014-052790117.

For detailed discussion of 212(1)(d) and electronic commerce see Pierre Gonthier, "Les déclinaisons de la notion de redevance selon l'impôt de la partie XIII: Restrictions au concept élargi de redevance", 51(6) *Canadian Tax Journal* 2119-90 (2003); VIEWS doc 2008-0279141E5 (discusses the issues and several additional sources).

CRA considers that distribution of satellite video signals by a bar owner to TV screens in the bar is not the "reproduction" of a work, and so is not exempted by 212(1)(d)(vi): VIEWS doc 2003-0018975.

A royalty based on net sales of reproduced artwork is exempt under 212(1)(d)(vi), but if the payment is for an exclusive right, it is partly taxable under 212(1)(d)(iv): VIEWS doc 2004-0086631E5.

212(1)(d)(vii): for the meaning of "principal business" see Notes to 20(1)(bb). See Notes to 212(13) re "rolling stock".

212(1)(d)(viii): for an example see VIEWS doc 2011-039958117.

212(1)(d)(ix): Payments under a bareboat charter are for "use of corporeal property", though they may be exempt by treaty: VIEWS docs 2005-0127961R3, 2006-0211991R3, 2008-0267201E5.

212(1)(d)(xi) extends the exemption from withholding tax for lease payments on aircraft, which applies under 212(1)(d)(ix) to aircraft used in international traffic, to aircraft used in domestic flights. For the meaning of "aircraft" see Notes to 8(1)(j).

212(1)(d)(xii) ensures that 212(5) is the only provision that taxes payment for rights in or to use a film or video that is used or reproduced in Canada. (Dept. of Finance Technical Notes)

See also Jovicic, Seidner & Sorensen, "Blurred Lines: Cross-Border Rents and Royalties", 2013 Cdn Tax Foundation annual conference, 22:1-36.

212(1)(d) amended by 2002-2013 technical bill (Part 4 — bijuralism), effective June 26, 2013, to add "or for civil law a right" ((d)(viii)) and change "corporeal" to "tangible, or for civil law corporeal" ((d)(ix)). Other amendments by that bill were effective 2000 or 2003. Earlier amended by 1992 transportation support bill.

Regulations: 202(1)(d) (information return).

Interpretation Bulletins: IT-303: Know-how and similar payments to non-residents; IT-393R2: Elections re tax on rents and timber royalties — non-residents; IT-438R2: Crown charges — resource properties in Canada; IT-494: Hire of ships and aircraft from non-residents. See also at beginning of s. 212.

Information Circulars: See at beginning of subsec. 212(1).

I.T. Technical News: 23 (computer software); 25 (e-commerce — payments for digital products not royalties).

Forms: See at beginning of subsec. 212(1).

(e) **timber royalties** — a timber royalty in respect of a timber resource property or a timber limit in Canada (which, for the purposes of this Part, includes any consideration for a right under or pursuant to which a right to cut or take timber from a timber resource property or a timber limit in Canada is obtained or derived, to the extent that the consideration is dependent on, or computed by reference to, the amount of timber cut or taken);

Related Provisions: 13(21) — Timber resource property defined; 212(13) — Non-resident payor deemed resident in Canada; 216 — Alternative re rents and timber royalties. See additional Related Provisions at beginning of subsec. 212(1).

Notes: Timber harvesting by third parties on non-commercial woodlots owned by non-residents may fall under 212(1)(e), if the amount paid is based on the amount of timber taken: VIEWS doc 2002-0173367, which also reviews the relevant case law on "dependent on or computed by referenced to".

For the meaning of "timber limit" see Notes to 13(21)"timber resource property".

Regulations: 202(1)(e) (information return).

Interpretation Bulletins: IT-393R2: Election re tax on rents and timber royalties — non-residents. See also at beginning of s. 212.

Information Circulars: See at beginning of subsec. 212(1).

Forms: See at beginning of subsec. 212(1).

(f) [Repealed]

Notes: 212(1)(f) repealed by 1996 Budget, for amounts paid and (or) credited after April 1997. It imposed withholding tax on alimony and support payments that were taxable under Canada under former 56(1)(b), (c) or (c.1).

This withholding tax was repealed at the same time as amendments to 56(1)(b) and 60(b) that eliminated the income inclusion and deduction for certain child support payments. (See Notes to 56(1)(b).) However, the repeal of 212(1)(f) goes much further than was done with domestic payments, which are only non-taxable if they are child (not spousal) support, and only if the agreement was made or varied after April 1997. For payments to non-residents, *all* child and spousal support is now non-taxable. (Under the Canada-U.S. tax treaty Art. XVIII:6(a), such payments were already exempt when paid to a U.S. resident. The same applied to residents of several other countries.)

For a chart showing US and Canadian tax deductibility and inclusion of child and spousal support, see Martin Pont & Julie Hannaford, "Cross-Border Support Payments", 19(5) *Money & Family Law* (Carswell) 37-39 (May 2004).

(g) **patronage dividend** — a patronage dividend, that is, a payment made pursuant to an allocation in proportion to patronage as defined by section 135 or an amount that would, under subsection 135(7), be included in computing the non-resident person's income if that person were resident in Canada;

Related Provisions: See at beginning of subsec. 212(1).

Regulations: 202(1)(g) (information return).

Interpretation Bulletins: IT-362R: Patronage dividends. See also at beginning of s. 212.

Information Circulars: See at beginning of subsec. 212(1).

Forms: See at beginning of subsec. 212(1).

(h) **pension benefits** — a payment of a superannuation or pension benefit, other than

(i) [Repealed]

(ii) an amount distributed from a pooled registered pension plan that has been designated by the administrator of the plan in accordance with subsection 147.5(18),

(iii) an amount or payment referred to in subsection 81(1) to the extent that that amount or payment would not, if the non-resident person had been resident in Canada throughout the taxation year in which the payment was made, be included in computing that person's income,

(iii.1) the portion of the payment that is transferred by the payer on behalf of the non-resident person, pursuant to an authorization in prescribed form, to a pooled registered pension plan, registered pension plan, registered retirement savings plan, registered retirement income fund or specified pension plan and that

(A) because of any of subsections 146(21), 147.3(9) and 147.5(22) would not, if the non-resident person had been resident in Canada throughout the taxation year in which the payment was made, be included in computing the non-resident person's income, or

(B) by reason of paragraph 60(j) or (j.2) would, if the non-resident person had been resident in Canada throughout the year, be deductible in computing the non-resident person's income for the year,

(iii.2) an amount referred to in paragraph 110(1)(f) to the extent that the amount would, if the non-resident person had been resident in Canada throughout the taxation year in which the amount was paid, be deductible in computing that person's taxable income or that of the spouse or common-law partner of that person,

(iv) in the case of a payment described in section 57, that portion of the payment that would, by virtue of that section, not be included in the recipient's income for the taxation year in which it was received, if the recipient were resident in Canada throughout that year, or

(iv.1) the portion of the payment that is transferred by the payer on behalf of the non-resident person, pursuant to an authorization in prescribed form, to acquire an annuity contract in circumstances to which subsection 146(21) applies,

except such portion, if any, of the payment as may reasonably be regarded as attributable to services rendered by the person, to or in respect of whom the payment is made, in taxation years

(v) during which the person at no time was resident in Canada, and

(vi) throughout which the person was not employed, or was only occasionally employed, in Canada;

Related Provisions: 128.1(10)"excluded right or interest"(a)(viii), (g) — No deemed disposition of pension rights on emigration; 180.2(2)B — Reduction in OAS clawback to reflect non-resident withholding tax; 180.2(4)(b)(ii), 180.2(5)(a)(ii) — No OAS benefits paid to non-resident who has not filed return; 215(5) — Regulations reducing amount to be deducted or withheld; 217 — Election to pay tax under Part I instead of withholding tax; Canada-U.S. Tax Treaty:Art. XVIII — Pensions and annuities. See additional Related Provisions at beginning of subsec. 212(1).

Notes: See Notes to 212(1) opening words above. For a "periodic pension payment", withholding tax may be reduced by treaty, e.g. to 15% by Canada-US Treaty Art. XVIII:2(a), or to zero by Canada-UK Treaty Art. 17:1.

If the non-resident has little income other than the Canadian pension, or has unused Canadian loss carryforwards, it may be better to file a Part I return. See s. 217.

For CRA interpretation see VIEWS docs 2014-0525491E5 (various pension payments to emigrant subject to 25% tax, but reduced by treaty); 2014-0541961E5 and 2014-0553351E5 (payments to non-resident former embassy/consulate employees: exempt under (v) and (vi)).

See CRA, "Changes to the Taxation of Social Security Benefits for Residents of Certain Countries with Which Canada has an Income Tax Convention" (2010), tiny-url.com/cra-ssb-treaty, for residents of Bangladesh, Bulgaria, Cyprus, Dominican Republic, Senegal, Tanzania, Trinidad & Tobago.

OAS/CPP: Former 212(1)(h)(i) and (ii), repealed by 1995 Budget for payments made after 1995, excluded Old Age Security, Canada Pension Plan and Quebec Pension Plan payments. These are all now subject to withholding tax, even if they are arrears for prior years: *Pope*, 2009 TCC 498. The change related to the 1995 Protocol to the Canada-US tax treaty, which amended Art. XVIII:5 so that cross-border social security benefits (including OAS and CPP) became taxed only by the paying country, not the recipient's country of residence. The 1997 Protocol then retroactively reversed that rule, so Canada no longer taxes OAS and CPP payments to US residents. Nevertheless, the repeal of 212(1)(h)(i) and (ii) remained, so Canada now taxes such payments to residents of other countries, except where a treaty provides relief: VIEWS doc 2011-0420111E5. (The treaty with Germany limits Canadian tax to the portion of the pension payments that Germany would tax if the individual were resident there: CRA news release, Dec. 18, 2003.)

A $50 payment to US social security recipients in lieu of interest, to compensate for the time tax was withheld during the above flip-flop, was first proposed as 122.7, but was enacted as 1998 Budget bill Part 2; see under treaty Art. XVIII:5.

QPP disability payments were taxable as "pension" payments in *Blauer*, 2007 TCC 706 (see also Notes to 115(1)).

The words "only occasionally employed in Canada" in 212(1)(h)(vi) applied to players on US NHL teams who played only a small fraction of their games in Canada: *Lou Nanne & Stan Mikita*, [2000] 1 C.T.C. 2776 (TCC). See VIEWS docs 2001-0114463, 2003-0038011R3. See also Notes to 115(1) re the *Austin* case.

212(1)(h)(iii.1) opening words amended by 2017 budget bill #2, to add "specified pension plan" effective 2010. 212(1)(h) earlier amended by 2012 budget bill #2 (effective Dec. 14, 2012, to refer to a PRPP), 2000 same-sex partners bill, 1993 and 1992 technical bills, 1990 pension bill.

Regulations: 202(2)(a) (information return).

Interpretation Bulletins: IT-76R2: Exempt portion of pension when employee has been a non-resident; IT-397R: Amounts excluded from income — statutory exemptions and certain pensions, allowances and compensations; IT-451R: Deemed disposition and acquisition on ceasing to be or becoming resident in Canada. See also at beginning of s. 212.

Information Circulars: See at beginning of 212(1).

Forms: NRTA1: Authorization for non-resident tax exemption. See also at beginning of subsec. 212(1).

(i) **restrictive covenant [non-competition agreement] amount** — an amount that would, if the non-resident person had been resident in Canada throughout the taxation year in which the amount was received or receivable, be required by paragraph 56(1)(m) or subsection 56.4(2) to be included in computing the non-resident person's income for the taxation year;

Related Provisions: 212(13)(g) — Where non-resident makes payment in respect of restrictive covenant.

Notes: 212(1)(i) applied in *Pangaea One*, 2020 FCA 21.

Non-compete payments can also fall under 212(1)(d)(iv) if 212(1)(i) does not apply (and see VIEWS doc 2003-0044351E5). The Canada-Luxembourg treaty does not reduce this tax: 2014-0539631I7, but no tax applies if the payment is business profit with no PE in Canada (any treaty Article 7): 2017-0701291I7.

212(1)(i) added by 2002-2013 technical bill, for amounts paid or credited after Oct. 7, 2003.

(j) **[RCA] benefits** — any benefit described in any of subparagraphs 56(1)(a)(iii) to (vi), any amount described in paragraph 56(1)(x) or (z) (other than an amount transferred under circumstances in which subsection 207.6(7) applies) or the purchase price of an interest in a retirement compensation arrangement;

Related Provisions: 128.1(10)"excluded right or interest"(a)(ix), (h) — No deemed disposition of rights on emigration; 214(3)(b.1) — Deemed payments; 215(5) — Regulations reducing amount to be deducted or withheld; 217 — Election to pay tax under Part I instead of withholding tax. See also at beginning of subsec. 212(1).

Notes: See Ross, "Withholding Taxes on Retirement Compensation Arrangements", 20(4) *Taxation of Executive Compensation & Retirement* (Federated Press) 1074-76 (Nov. 2008), arguing that payments from an RCA to a US resident should be subject to 15% tax under Canada-US treaty Art. XXII:2 (trust income) rather than under Art. XVIII (pensions).

Parenthetical exclusion relating to 207.6(7) added to 212(1)(j) by 1995-97 technical bill, effective for amounts paid or credited after 1995.

Regulations: 202(2)(b) (information return).

Interpretation Bulletins: IT-451R: Deemed disposition and acquisition on ceasing to be or becoming resident in Canada. See also at beginning of s. 212.

Information Circulars: See at beginning of subsec. 212(1).

Forms: T735: Application for a remittance number for tax withheld from an RCA; See also at beginning of subsec. 212(1).

(j.1) **retiring allowances** — a payment of any allowance described in subparagraph 56(1)(a)(ii), except

(i) such portion, if any, of the payment as may reasonably be regarded as attributable to services rendered by the person, to or in respect of whom the payment is made, in taxation years

(A) during which the person at no time was resident in Canada, and

(B) throughout which the person was not employed, or was only occasionally employed, in Canada, and

(ii) the portion of the payment transferred by the payer on behalf of the non-resident person pursuant to an authorization in prescribed form to a registered pension plan or to a registered retirement savings plan under which the non-resident person is the annuitant (within the meaning assigned by subsection 146(1)) that would, if the non-resident person had been resident in Canada throughout the year, be deductible in computing the income of the non-resident person by virtue of paragraph 60(j.1);

Related Provisions: 128.1(10)"excluded right or interest"(d) — No deemed disposition of right to retiring allowance on emigration; 146(21.2), 147.5(12) — Sask. Pension Plan and PRPP deemed to be RRSP for purposes of 212(1)(j.1); 212(1)(h) — Tax on PRPP payments; 212(1)(l) — Tax on RRSP payments; 215(5) — Regulations reducing deduction or withholding; 217 — Election to pay tax under Part I instead of withholding tax. See also at beginning of subsec. 212(1).

Notes: This applies to termination pay and severance as well as amounts paid on retirement: VIEWS doc 2010-0377821E5. See 248(1)"retiring allowance" and Notes to 212(1) opening words. A treaty can exempt the payment depending on the circumstances: 2014-0534301E5.

Where the non-resident has little income other than from the "retiring allowance", or has unused Canadian loss carryforwards, it may be better to file a Part I return. See Notes to s. 217.

Regulations: 202(2)(b) (information return).

Interpretation Bulletins: IT-451R: Deemed disposition and acquisition on ceasing to be or becoming resident in Canada. See also at beginning of s. 212.

Information Circulars: See at beginning of subsec. 212(1).

Forms: NRTA1: Authorization for non-resident tax exemption. See also at beginning of subsec. 212(1).

(k) **supplementary unemployment benefit plan payments** — a payment by a trustee under a registered supplementary unemployment benefit plan;

Related Provisions: 128.1(10)"excluded right or interest"(a)(xi) — No deemed disposition of rights on emigration; 212(13)(e) — Payment by non-resident deemed made by resident of Canada; 215(5) — Regulations reducing amount to be deducted or withheld; 217 — Election to pay tax under Part I instead of withholding tax. See also at beginning of 212(1).

Regulations: 202(2)(c) (information return).

Interpretation Bulletins: IT-451R: Deemed disposition and acquisition on ceasing to be or becoming resident in Canada. See also at beginning of s. 212.

Information Circulars: See at beginning of subsec. 212(1).

Forms: See at beginning of subsec. 212(1).

(l) **registered retirement savings plan payments** — a payment out of or under a registered retirement savings plan or a plan referred to in subsection 146(12) as an "amended plan" that would, if the non-resident person had been resident in Canada throughout the taxation year in which the payment was made, be required by section 146 to be included in computing the income of the non-resident person for the year, other than the portion thereof that

(i) has been transferred by the payer on behalf of the non-resident person pursuant to an authorization in prescribed form

(A) to a registered retirement savings plan under which the non-resident person is the annuitant (within the meaning assigned by subsection 146(1)),

(B) to acquire an annuity described in subparagraph 60(l)(ii) under which the non-resident person is the annuitant, or

(C) to a carrier (within the meaning assigned by subsection 146.3(1)) as consideration for a registered retirement income fund under which the non-resident person is the annuitant (within the meaning assigned by subsection 146.3(1)), and

(ii) would, if the non-resident person had been resident in Canada throughout the year, be deductible in computing the income of the non-resident person for the year by virtue of paragraph 60(l);

Related Provisions: 128.1(10)"excluded right or interest"(a)(i) — No deemed disposition of rights on emigration; 146(16) — RRSP — deduction on transfer of funds; 212(1)(h) — Tax on PRPP payments; 212(13)(e) — Payment by non-resident deemed made by resident of Canada; 214(3)(c) — Deemed payments; 215(5) — Regulations reducing amount to be deducted or withheld; 217 — Election to pay tax under Part I instead of withholding tax; *Income Tax Conventions Interpretation Act* 5.1 — Definition of "pension" for tax treaty purposes. See also at beginning of subsec. 212(1); Canada-U.S. Tax Treaty:Art. XXIX:5 — Election for income accruing in RRSP not to be taxed until paid out.

Notes: See Notes to 212(1) opening words above. A withdrawal from an RRSP may not be protected by tax treaty provisions that limit withholding tax on pension payments, depending on the wording and the definition of "pension" in the treaty: VIEWS doc 2014-0525491E5. See the definitions "pension" and "periodic pension payment" in s. 5 of the *Income Tax Conventions Interpretation Act* (reproduced before the treaties). Where "pension" is defined in the treaty to include a "retirement arrangement", as in Canada-U.S. Tax Treaty:Art. XVIII:3 and Canada-U.K. Tax Treaty:Art. 17:3, an RRSP falls into ITCIA 5"pension"(b).

Growth within the RRSP may be taxed in the foreign country. US citizens or residents: see Notes to Canada-US tax treaty Art. XVIII:7.

Only the amount that would be taxed to a resident beneficiary under s. 146 is subject to withholding: 212(1)(l) opening words. Where a deceased's RRSP is paid out to a non-resident beneficiary (not a spouse or financially-dependent child or grandchild), no withholding applies since the amount was already taxed to the estate under 146(8.8). A transfer to a UK pension is subject to 25% tax in CRA's view (unless a s. 217 election is made): VIEWS docs 2009-0317041M4, 2013-0479901E5. On a lump sum RRSP payment to a resident of New Zealand, see 2013-0509751E5.

Where the non-resident has little income other than from the RRSP, or has unused Canadian loss carryforwards, it is often better to file a Part I return. See Notes to s. 217.

The tax-free transfers in 212(1)(l)(i) and 212(1)(q)(i) require the non-resident to provide a Social Insurance Number: VIEWS doc 2014-0534821C6 [2014 APFF q.2]. (Presumably the 248(1)"prescribed" form is not satisfied if the SIN is not provided.)

On the death of a non-resident RRIF annuitant or one with a non-resident spouse, see VIEWS docs 2002-0141355, 2013-0495281C6 [2013 APFF q. 9].

212(1)(l)(i)(C) added by 1990 pension bill, for payments made after June 27, 1990.

Regulations: 202(2)(d) (information return).

Interpretation Bulletins: IT-451R: Deemed disposition and acquisition on ceasing to be or becoming resident in Canada; IT-500R: RRSPs — death of an annuitant. See also at beginning of s. 212.

Information Circulars: 72-22R9: Registered retirement savings plans. See also at beginning of subsec. 212(1).

Registered Plans Compliance Bulletins: 4 (abusive schemes — RRSP stripping).

Forms: NRTA1: Authorization for non-resident tax exemption. See also at beginning of subsec. 212(1).

(l.1) **advanced life deferred annuity payment** — a payment of an amount described in paragraph 56(1)(z.5);

Notes: See 146.5 re ALDAs. Withholding tax on annuities is often reduced to 15% or 10% by Art. 18 of Canada's tax treaty with the payee's country of residence (Art. 17 of the Canada-UK treaty).

212(1)(l.1) added by 2021 budget bill #1, effective 2020. It was 212(1)(y) in the July 30, 2019 draft legislation.

(m) **deferred profit sharing plan payments** — a payment under a deferred profit sharing plan or a plan referred to in subsection 147(15) as a "revoked plan" that would, if the non-resident person had been resident in Canada throughout the taxation year in which the payment was made, be required by section 147, if it were read without reference to subsections 147(10.1) and (20), to be included in computing the non-resident person's income for the year, other than the portion thereof that is transferred by the payer on behalf of the non-resident person, pursuant to an authorization in prescribed form, to a registered pension plan or registered retirement savings plan and that

(i) by reason of subsection 147(20) would not, if the non-resident person had been resident in Canada throughout the

year, be included in computing the non-resident person's income, or

(ii) by reason of paragraph 60(j.2) would, if the non-resident person had been resident in Canada throughout the year, be deductible in computing the non-resident person's income for the year;

Related Provisions: 128.1(10)"excluded right or interest"(a)(iv) — No deemed disposition of rights on emigration; 146(21.2), 147.5(12) — Sask. Pension Plan and PRPP deemed to be RRSP for purposes of 212(1)(m); 212(13)(e) — Payment by non-resident deemed made by resident of Canada; 214(3)(d) — Deemed payments; 215(5) — Regulations reducing amount to be deducted or withheld; 217 — Election to pay tax under Part I instead of withholding tax. See also at beginning of subsec. 212(1).

Notes: 212(1)(m) amended by 1990 pension bill, for payments after June 27, 1990.

Regulations: 202(2)(e) (information return).

Interpretation Bulletins: IT-451R: Deemed disposition and acquisition on ceasing to be or becoming resident in Canada. See also at beginning of s. 212.

Information Circulars: See at beginning of subsec. 212(1).

Forms: NRTA1: Authorization for non-resident tax exemption. See also at beginning of subsec. 212(1).

(n) **income-averaging annuity contract payments** — [No longer relevant]

Notes: IAACs were dropped in 1981 and no longer exist.

(o) **other annuity payments** — a payment under an annuity contract (other than a payment in respect of an annuity issued in the course of carrying on a life insurance business in a country other than Canada) to the extent of the amount in respect of the interest of the non-resident person in the contract that, if the non-resident person had been resident in Canada throughout the taxation year in which the payment was made,

(i) would be required to be included in computing the income of the non-resident person for the year, and

(ii) would not be deductible in computing that income;

Related Provisions: 56(1)(d) — Annuity payments required to be included in income of resident; 128.1(10)"excluded right or interest"(f)(i) — No deemed disposition of rights on emigration; 240(1) — Taxable and non-taxable obligations defined. See also at beginning of 212(1).

Notes: For application of 212(1)(o) to a non-resident holder of a charitable annuity see VIEWS doc 2005-0145141E5.

Regulations: 202(2)(g) (information return).

Interpretation Bulletins: IT-451R: Deemed disposition and acquisition on ceasing to be or becoming resident in Canada. See also at beginning of s. 212.

Information Circulars: See at beginning of subsec. 212(1).

Forms: See at beginning of subsec. 212(1).

(p) **former TFSA** — an amount that would, if the non-resident person had been resident in Canada at the time at which the amount was paid, be required by paragraph 12(1)(z.5) to be included in computing the non-resident person's income for the taxation year that includes that time;

Notes: 212(1)(p) replaced by 2008 budget bill #2, for 2009 and later taxation years. Former 212(1)(p) applied to a (pre-1986) registered home ownership savings plan (see Notes at end of 146.2).

Regulations: 202(2)(h) (information return).

Interpretation Bulletins: See at beginning of s. 212.

Information Circulars: See at beginning of subsec. 212(1).

Forms: See at beginning of subsec. 212(1).

(q) **registered retirement income fund payments** — a payment out of or under a registered retirement income fund that would, if the non-resident person had been resident in Canada throughout the taxation year in which the payment was made, be required by section 146.3 to be included in computing the non-resident person's income for the year, other than the portion thereof that

(i) has been transferred by the payer on behalf of the non-resident person pursuant to an authorization in prescribed form

(A) to a registered retirement savings plan under which the non-resident person is the annuitant (within the meaning assigned by subsection 146(1)),

(B) to acquire an annuity described in subparagraph 60(l)(ii) under which the non-resident person is the annuitant, or

(C) to a carrier (within the meaning assigned by subsection 146.3(1)) as consideration for a registered retirement income fund under which the non-resident person is the annuitant (within the meaning assigned by subsection 146.3(1)), and

(ii) would, if the non-resident person had been resident in Canada throughout the year, be deductible in computing the non-resident person's income for the year by reason of paragraph 60(l);

Related Provisions: 128.1(10)"excluded right or interest"(a)(ii) — No deemed disposition of rights on emigration; 212(13)(e) — Payment by non-resident deemed made by resident of Canada; 214(3)(i) — Deemed payments; 215(5) — Regulations reducing amount to be deducted or withheld; 217 — Election to pay tax under Part I instead of withholding tax. See also at beginning of 212(1).

Notes: See Notes to 212(1) opening words. For examples of 212(1)(q) applying to RRIF payments to non-residents see VIEWS docs 2012-0438961E5 (Mexico), 2013-0509751E5 (New Zealand).

A RRIF withdrawal in excess of twice the "minimum amount" for the year may not be protected by tax treaty provisions that limit withholding tax on pension payments, due to 5"pension" and 5"periodic pension payment"(c)(i) of the *Income Tax Conventions Interpretation Act* (reproduced before the Canada-U.S. tax treaty). Such a lump-sum payment cannot be bifurcated into separate parts taxed at 25% and 15% in CRA's view: VIEWS doc 2007-0248991E5.

See Notes to 212(1)(l) re the 212(1)(q)(i) exception, as well as the limitation in the opening words that only amounts that would be taxed to a Canadian resident are subject to withholding tax.

Where the non-resident has little income other than from the RRIF, or has unused Canadian loss carryforwards, it may be better to file a Part I return. See Notes to s. 217.

Exceptions in 212(1)(q)(i) and (ii) added by 1990 pension bill, effective for payments made after June 27, 1990.

Regulations: 202(2)(i) (information return).

Interpretation Bulletins: IT-451R: Deemed disposition and acquisition on ceasing to be or becoming resident in Canada. See also at beginning of s. 212.

Information Circulars: See at beginning of subsec. 212(1).

Forms: NRTA1: Authorization for non-resident tax exemption. See also at beginning of subsec. 212(1).

(r) **registered education savings plan** — a payment that is

(i) required by paragraph 56(1)(q) to be included in computing the non-resident person's income under Part I for a taxation year, and

(ii) not required to be included in computing the non-resident person's taxable income or taxable income earned in Canada for the year;

Related Provisions: See at beginning of subsec. 212(1).

Notes: See VIEWS doc 2013-0504641E5 (if RESP is a trust, withholding tax on educational assistance payments can be reduced by treaty; no s. 217 election is possible).

212(1)(r) amended by 1997 Budget, for amounts paid or credited after Feb. 1979.

Regulations: 202(2)(j) (information return).

Information Circulars: See at beginning of subsec. 212(1).

Forms: See at beginning of subsec. 212(1).

(r.1) **registered disability savings plan [payments]** — an amount that would, if the non-resident person had been resident in Canada throughout the taxation year in which the amount was paid, be required by paragraph 56(1)(q.1) to be included in computing the non-resident person's income for the taxation year;

Related Provisions: See at beginning of subsec. 212(1).

Notes: 212(1)(r.1) imposes tax on payments from an RDSP to a non-resident that would be taxable (see 146.4(6)) if paid to a resident of Canada.

212(1)(r.1) added by 2007 RDSPs bill, effective for 2008 and later taxation years.

Regulations: 202(2)(n) (information return).

(s) **home insulation or energy conversion grants** — a grant under a prescribed program of the Government of Canada relating to home insulation or energy conversion;

Related Provisions: See at beginning of subsec. 212(1).

Regulations: 202(2)(k) (information return).

Information Circulars: See at beginning of subsec. 212(1).

Forms: See at beginning of subsec. 212(1).

(t) **NISA Fund No. 2 payments** — a payment out of a NISA Fund No. 2 to the extent that that amount would, if Part I applied, be required by subsection 12(10.2) to be included in computing the person's income for a taxation year;

Related Provisions: 128.1(10)"excluded right or interest"(i) — No deemed disposition on emigration; 214(3)(l) — Deemed payments. See also at beginning of subsec. 212(1).

Notes: 212(1)(t) added by 1992 technical bill, for payments made in 1991 or later.

Regulations: 202(2.1) (information return).

Information Circulars: See at beginning of subsec. 212(1).

Forms: See at beginning of subsec. 212(1).

(u) **amateur athlete trust payments** — a payment in respect of an amateur athlete trust that would, if Part I applied, be required by section 143.1 to be included in computing the person's income for a taxation year;

Related Provisions: 214(3)(k) — Deemed payments. See also at beginning of subsec. 212(1).

Notes: 212(1)(u) added by 1992 technical bill, for payments made in 1992 or later.

Information Circulars: See at beginning of subsec. 212(1).

(v) **payments under an eligible funeral arrangement** — a payment made by a custodian (within the meaning assigned by subsection 148.1(1)) of an arrangement that was, at the time it was established, an eligible funeral arrangement, to the extent that such amount would, if the non-resident person were resident in Canada, be included because of subsection 148.1(3) in computing the person's income;

Related Provisions: 212(13)(e) — Payment by non-resident deemed made by resident of Canada. See also at beginning of subsec. 212(1).

Notes: 212(1)(v) added by 1994 technical bill, effective for amounts paid or credited after October 21, 1994. See Notes to 148.1.

Regulations: 202(2)(m) (information return); 204(3)(d.1) (cemetery care trust need not file T3 return).

Information Circulars: IT-531: Eligible funeral arrangements. See at beginning of subsec. 212(1).

(w) **[payment from ELHT]** — a payment out of a trust that is, or was, at any time, an employee life and health trust, except to the extent that it is a payment of a designated employee benefit (as defined by subsection 144.1(1)); or

Notes: 212(1)(w) added by 2010 budget bill #2, effective 2010.

(x) **tax informant program** — a payment of an amount described in paragraph 56(1)(z.4).

Related Provisions: 56(1)(z.4), 153(1)(s) — Tax and withholding on payment to informant in Canada; Reg. 202(2)(m) — Information return to be filed.

Notes: See 56(1)(z.4) Notes. 212(1)(x) added by 2014 budget bill #1, effective June 19, 2014.

Proposed **212(1)(y)** in the July 30/19 draft legislation was moved to 212(1)(l.1).

Related Provisions, Notes, I.T. Application Rules, Interpretation Bulletins, Information Circulars, I.T Technical News, Forms [subsec. 212(1)]: See at beginning of subsec. 212(1), before para. (a).

(2) Tax on dividends — Every non-resident person shall pay an income tax of 25% on every amount that a corporation resident in Canada pays or credits, or is deemed by Part I or Part XIV to pay or credit, to the non-resident person as, on account or in lieu of payment of, or in satisfaction of,

(a) a taxable dividend (other than a capital gains dividend within the meaning assigned by subsection 130.1(4), 131(1) or 133(7.1)), or

(b) a capital dividend.

Related Provisions: 40(3.7) — Stop-loss rule where non-resident has received dividends; 84 — Deemed dividends; 94(3)(a)(ix) — Application to trust deemed resident in Canada; 104(16)(d) — SIFT trust distribution deemed to be dividend paid by corporation resident in Canada; 128.1(1)(c.1) — Deemed dividend to non-resident corporation before it becomes resident in Canada; 131(5.1), (5.2) — Deemed dividend on distribution of gain derived from taxable Canadian property by mutual fund corporation; 139.1(4)(f)(ii) — Dividend deemed received on demutualization of insurance corporation; 212(1)(c)(ii) — Estate or trust income derived from capital dividend; 212(2.1) — Securities lending arrangement — no tax on dividend compensation payments and deemed dividends; 212(3.1)–(3.94) — Back-to-back rules; 212(13.3)(a) — Authorized foreign bank deemed resident in Canada; 212.1, 212.2 — Deemed dividends on surplus strips by non-resident; 212.3(2) — Deemed dividend on foreign-affiliate dumping; 213(1) — Tax not payable — mining or public utilities; 214(1) — No deductions; 214(3)(a) — Deemed payments; 214(16), (17) — Thin capitalization — interest deemed to be dividend; 215(1), (1.1) — Requirement to withhold and remit; 218.3(2)(c) — Withholding tax on mutual fund distributions to non-residents; 219 — Branch tax; 227(10), (10.1) — Assessment; 247(12) — Deemed dividend resulting from transfer pricing adjustment; 250(5) — Person deemed non-resident by treaty is non-resident; 257 — Formula cannot calculate to less than zero; Canada-U.S. Tax Treaty:Art. X — Taxation of dividends.

Notes: See Notes to 212(1) opening words about s. 212 generally. 212(2) imposes withholding tax on both regular dividends and 83(2) capital dividends.

Dividend payments to residents of countries with which Canada has a tax treaty are usually limited by the treaty to a lower rate, such as 15%. See ITAR 10(6) and Table O-5 (treaty withholding rates) at the beginning of this book, and VIEWS doc 2012-0464381E5. "Direct" intercorporate dividends (where the recipient owns at least 10% of the voting shares) are reduced to 5% in at least 55 of Canada's treaties, but MLI (Multilateral Instrument) Article 8:1 requires the shares to have been held for 365 days to get the low rate, if the other country has signed on to the MLI (reproduced before the Canada-US treaty) and has accepted Art. 8 (e.g., the UK has not accepted it).

Treaty relief applies when the "beneficial owner" of the dividends is resident in the treaty country: see Notes to Canada-US Treaty Art. X:2 for the meaning of this term. However, if the treaty partner has ratified the MLI, treaty relief will be denied if "one of the principal purposes of any arrangement or transaction" was to obtain the benefit, "unless it is established that granting that benefit ... would be in accordance with the object and purpose" of the treaty (MLI Art. 7:1).

A benefit from a corporation to a non-resident shareholder is subject to 212(2) due to 15(1) and 214(3)(a). See Notes to 214(3). An increase in paid-up capital causing an 84(1) deemed dividend triggers 212(2): VIEWS doc 2011-0399121R3.

The words "or is deemed by Part I or Part XIV to pay or credit" are unnecessary, since once something is deemed, it is treated as existing (see Notes to 244(15)). Thus, 214(3) or 214(16) deeming a dividend for purposes of Part XIII applies for 212(2) even though it is not "deemed by Part I or Part XIV". A deemed dividend is treated as a dividend for tax treaty purposes: see Notes to Canada-US treaty Art. X:3.

An interest-free loan to a non-resident parent creates a 212(2) obligation via 15(1), 15(9) and 214(3): VIEWS docs 2007-0241991R3, 2007-0243331C6, 2008-0280041R3, 2011-0418711R3.

Where a dividend is paid to a partnership with members resident in a treaty country, the partnership is disregarded and withholding tax depends on the residence of the partners. However, the 10% "direct dividend" ownership test cannot be met by corporate partners, since under partnership law a particular partner does not own any of the partnership's property: VIEWS docs 2004-0072231C6, 2004-0074241E5. See also Notes to 212(1) opening words on payments to a partnership.

Dividends paid to a trust in a non-treaty country whose beneficiary is in a treaty country are taxed at 25% unless the trust is acting as agent of the beneficiary: VIEWS doc 2004-0099401I7. Where dividends are paid to a foreign financial intermediary for a Canadian resident, see Notes to 215(3).

A SIFT income trust or publicly-traded partnership distribution is deemed by 104(16)(d) to be a dividend for purposes of 212(2).

See also Kelly, "Hybrid Debt Instruments", XXIII(1) *Corporate Finance* (Federated Press) 8-13 (2020) (payments on "perpetual debt": dividends or interest?).

Regulations: 202(1)(g) (information return); 805 (where no withholding tax).

Interpretation Bulletins: IT-96R6: Options granted by corporations to acquire shares, bonds, or debentures and by trusts to acquire trust units; IT-119R4: Debts of shareholders and certain persons connected with shareholders; IT-421R2: Benefits to individuals, corporations and shareholders from loans or debt; IT-430R3: Life insurance proceeds received by a private corporation or a partnership as a consequence of death; IT-465R: Non-resident beneficiaries of trusts; IT-468R: Management or administration fees paid to non-residents. See also at end of s. 212.

Information Circulars: 77-16R4: Non-resident income tax; 88-2 Supplement, para. 7: General anti-avoidance rule — section 245 of the *Income Tax Act*.

I.T. Technical News: 14 (meaning of "credited" for purposes of Part XIII withholding tax).

Transfer Pricing Memoranda: TPM-02: Repatriation of funds by non-residents — Part XIII assessments.

CRA Audit Manual: 24.12.5: Section 80.4 — benefit on interest-free or low-interest loans — non-residents.

Forms: NR4: Statement of amounts paid or credited to non-residents of Canada; NR4 Segment; NR4 Summ: Return of amounts paid or credited to non-residents of Canada; NR4(OAS): Statement of OAS pension paid or credited to non-residents of Canada; NR601: Non-resident ownership certificate — withholding tax; NR602: Non-resident ownership certificate — no withholding tax; NR603: Remittance of non-resident tax on income from film or video acting services; T2 Sched. 19: Non-resident shareholder information; T1136: OAS return of income; T4061: Non-resident withholding tax guide.

(2.1) Exempt dividends — Subsection (2) does not apply to an amount paid or credited, by a borrower, under a securities lending arrangement or a specified securities lending arrangement if

(a) the amount is deemed by subparagraph 260(8)(a)(ii) to be a dividend;

(b) either

(i) the arrangement is a fully collateralized arrangement, or

(ii) the borrower and the lender are dealing at arm's length; and

(c) the security that is transferred or lent to the borrower under the securities lending arrangement is a share of a class of the capital stock of a non-resident corporation.

Related Provisions: 260(1.2) — Interpretation of "borrower" and "lender" for specified securities lending arrangement.

Notes: 212(2.1), as originally enacted, implements a Feb. 18, 2002 Finance comfort letter. See Paul Tamaki, "The Slow Expansion of the Securities Lending Rules", X(4) *Corporate Finance* (Federated Press) 993-96 (2003).

212(2.1) amended by 2021 budget bill #1, for amounts paid or payable or credited after March 18, 2019. For earlier amounts, read opening words and (a)-(b) as:

(2.1) Subsection (2) does not apply to an amount paid or credited, by a borrower, under a securities lending arrangement if

(a) the amount is deemed by subparagraph 260(8)(c)(i) to be a dividend;

(b) the securities lending arrangement was entered into by the borrower in the course of carrying on a business outside Canada; and

212(2.1) added by 2002-2013 technical bill, last change effective for securities lending arrangements entered into after 2001.

(3) Interest — definitions — The following definitions apply for the purpose of paragraph (1)(b).

"fully exempt interest" means

(a) interest that is paid or payable on a bond, debenture, note, mortgage, hypothecary claim or similar debt obligation

(i) of, or guaranteed (otherwise than by being insured by the Canada Deposit Insurance Corporation) by, the Government of Canada,

(ii) of the government of a province,

(iii) of an agent of a province,

(iv) of a municipality in Canada or a municipal or public body performing a function of government in Canada,

(v) of a corporation, commission or association to which any of paragraphs 149(1)(d) to (d.6) applies, or

(vi) of an educational institution or a hospital if repayment of the principal amount of the obligation and payment of the interest is to be made, or is guaranteed, assured or otherwise specifically provided for or secured by the government of a province;

(b) interest that is paid or payable on a mortgage, hypothecary claim or similar debt obligation secured by, or on an agreement for sale or similar obligation with respect to, real property situated outside Canada or an interest in any such real property, or to immovables situated outside Canada or a real right in any such immovable, except to the extent that the interest payable on the obligation is deductible in computing the income of the payer under Part I from a business carried on by the payer in Canada or from property other than real or immovable property situated outside Canada;

(c) interest that is paid or payable to a prescribed international organization or agency; or

(d) an amount paid or payable or credited under a securities lending arrangement, or a specified securities lending arrangement, that is deemed by subparagraph 260(8)(a)(i) to be a payment made by a borrower to a lender of interest, if the arrangement is a fully collateralized arrangement, and

(i) the following conditions are met:

(A) the arrangement was entered into by the borrower in the course of carrying on a business outside Canada, and

(B) the security that is transferred or lent to the borrower under the arrangement is described in paragraph (b) of the definition "qualified security" in subsection 260(1) and issued by a non-resident issuer,

(ii) the security that is transferred or lent to the borrower under the arrangement is described in paragraph (c) of the definition "qualified security" in subsection 260(1), or

(iii) the security that is transferred or lent to the borrower under the arrangement is described in paragraph (a) or (b).

Related Provisions: 260(1.2) — Interpretation of "borrower" and "lender" for specified securities lending arrangement.

Notes: See Notes to 212(1)(b). For the meaning of "municipal or public body..." in (a)(iv), see Notes to 149(1)(c).

Para. (d) amended by 2021 budget bill #1, for amounts paid or payable or credited after March 18, 2019. For earlier amounts, read:

(d) an amount paid or payable or credited under a securities lending arrangement that is deemed by subparagraph 260(8)(c)(i) to be a payment made by a borrower to a lender of interest, if

(i) the securities lending arrangement was entered into by the borrower in the course of carrying on a business outside Canada, and

(ii) the security that is transferred or lent to the borrower under the securities lending arrangement is described in paragraph (b) or (c) of the definition "qualified security" in subsection 260(1) and issued by a non-resident issuer.

212(3)"fully exempt interest" added by 2007 budget bill #2, effective 2008, and para. (d) amended retroactive to 2008 by 2002-2013 technical bill (Part 5 — technical).

"participating debt interest" means interest (other than interest described in any of paragraphs (b) to (d) of the definition "fully exempt interest") that is paid or payable on an obligation, other than a prescribed obligation, all or any portion of which interest is contingent or dependent on the use of or production from property in Canada or is computed by reference to revenue, profit, cash flow, commodity price or any other similar criterion or by reference to dividends paid or payable to shareholders of any class of shares of the capital stock of a corporation.

Related Provisions: 204"qualified investment"(b) — Debt obligations qualify for deferred income plans; 214(7) — Deemed payment of interest on sale of obligation.

Notes: "Participating debt interest" (PDI) is, very generally, interest that depends on the success of the payer's business or investments (similar to 12(1)(g) for Canadian residents). The definition draws from the former 212(1)(b) closing words, and is intended to have the same effect. See Notes to 212(1)(b).

The pre-2008 "5/25" exemption in former 212(1)(b)(vii) (see 212(1)(b) Notes) is still relevant due to 214(8)(a): Tkachenko, "Convertible Debt: 5/25 Alive?", XIV(4) *Corporate Finance* (Federated Press) 1567 (2008). See also Lang & Tkachenko, "Withholding Tax Implications of Participating Interest and Convertible Debt", 1916 *Tax Topics* (CCH) 1-5 (Nov. 27, 2008); Kwan & Zitlau, "Participating Debt Interest and the Canada-U.S. Tax Treaty", XIX(1) *International Tax Planning* (Federated Press) 1298-1302 (2013); and Notes to 214(8) re convertible debt.

See Notes to 212(1)(b) for more CRA interpretation of this definition. See also Notes to Canada-US treaty Art. XI:6.

212(3)"participating debt interest" added by 2007 budget bill #2, replacing former 212(3) effective 2008 (and then the effective-2008 version restored by 2002-2013 technical bill s. 347(13), after changing the pre-2008 version as per below). See Notes to 212(1)(b). Former 212(3), relevant only to the pre-2008 212(1)(b), provided (after 2002-2013 technical bill s. 347(12) repealed 212(3)(b) for replacement obligations issued after 2000, implementing a June 11, 2001 Finance comfort letter):

(3) Replacement obligations — For the purpose of subparagraph (1)(b)(vii), an obligation (in this subsection referred to as the "replacement obligation") issued by a corporation resident in Canada wholly or in substantial part and either directly or indirectly in exchange or substitution for an obligation or a part of an obligation (in this subsection referred to as the "former obligation") shall, where

(a) the replacement obligation was issued

(i) as part of a proposal to, or an arrangement with, its creditors that was approved by a court under the *Bankruptcy and Insolvency Act*,

(ii) at a time when all or substantially all of its assets were under the control of a receiver, receiver-manager, sequestrator or trustee in bankruptcy, or

(iii) at a time when, because of financial difficulty, the issuing corporation or another corporation resident in Canada with which it does not deal at arm's length was in default, or could reasonably be expected to default, on the former obligation,

(b) [Repealed.]

(c) all interest on the former obligation was (or would be, if the person to whom that interest was paid or credited were non-resident) exempt from tax under this Part because of subparagraph (1)(b)(vii),

be deemed to have been issued when the former obligation was issued.

Former 212(3) added by 1993 technical bill, effective for replacement obligations issued after June 1993. It allowed a corporation in financial difficulty to restructure long-term debt by issuing replacement debt, keeping the 212(1)(b)(vii) exemption (see IT-361R3 para. 2).

An earlier 212(3), repealed by 1981 Budget, reduced the withholding tax on dividends to non-residents paid by corporations with a "degree of Canadian ownership".

Regulations: 806.2 (prescribed obligation).

I.T. Technical News: 41 (convertible debt); 44 (convertible debentures and Part XIII).

(3.1) Back-to-back loan arrangement [conditions for 212(3.2) to apply] — Subsection (3.2) applies at any time in respect of a taxpayer if

(a) the taxpayer pays or credits a particular amount at that time as, on account or in lieu of payment of, or in satisfaction of, interest (determined without reference to paragraph 18(6.1)(b) and subsection 214(16)) in respect of a particular debt or other obligation to pay an amount to a person or partnership (in this subsection and subsection (3.2) referred to as the "immediate funder");

(b) the immediate funder is not

(i) a person resident in Canada that does not deal at arm's length with the taxpayer, or

(ii) a partnership each member of which is a person described in subparagraph (i);

(c) at any time in the period during which the interest accrued (in this subsection and subsections (3.2) and (3.3) referred to as the "relevant period"), a relevant funder, in respect of a particular relevant funding arrangement,

(i) has an amount outstanding as or on account of a debt or other obligation to pay an amount to a person or partnership that meets any of the following conditions:

(A) recourse in respect of the debt or other obligation is limited in whole or in part, either immediately or in the future and either absolutely or contingently, to a relevant funding arrangement, or

(B) it can reasonably be concluded that all or a portion of the particular relevant funding arrangement was entered into, or was permitted to remain in effect, because

(I) all or a portion of the debt or other obligation was entered into or was permitted to remain outstanding, or

(II) the relevant funder anticipated that all or a portion of the debt or other obligation would become owing or remain outstanding, or

(ii) has a specified right in respect of a particular property that was granted directly or indirectly by a person or partnership and

(A) the existence of the specified right is required under the terms and conditions of the particular relevant funding arrangement, or

(B) it can reasonably be concluded that all or a portion of the particular relevant funding arrangement was entered into, or was permitted to remain in effect, because

(I) the specified right was granted, or

(II) the relevant funder anticipated that the specified right would be granted;

(d) the tax that would be payable under this Part in respect of the particular amount, if the particular amount were paid or credited to any ultimate funder rather than the immediate funder, is greater than the tax payable under this Part (determined without reference to this subsection and subsection (3.2)) in respect of the particular amount; and

(e) at any time during the relevant period, the total of all amounts — each of which is an amount outstanding as or on account of a debt or other obligation owed by the immediate funder that is a relevant funding arrangement or the fair market value of a particular property in respect of which the immediate funder is granted a specified right that is a relevant funding arrangement — is equal to at least 25% of the total of

(i) the amount outstanding as or on account of the particular debt or other obligation, and

(ii) the total of all amounts each of which is an amount (other than the amount described in subparagraph (i)) that the taxpayer, or a person or partnership that does not deal at arm's length with the taxpayer, has outstanding as or on account of a debt or other obligation to pay an amount to the immediate funder under the agreement, or an agreement that is connected to the agreement, under which the particular debt or other obligation was entered into where

(A) the immediate funder is granted a "security interest" (as defined in subsection 18(5)) in respect of a property that is the debt or other obligation owed by the immediate funder or the particular property, as the case may be, and the security interest secures the payment of two or more debts or other obligations that include the debt or other obligation and the particular debt or other obligation, and

(B) each security interest that secures the payment of a debt or other obligation referred to in clause (A) secures the payment of every debt or other obligation referred to in that clause.

Related Provisions: 212(3.8) — Definitions.

Notes: See Notes to 212(3.2). For "indirectly" in (c)(ii), see Notes to 207.01(1)"advantage".

212(3.1) amended by 2016 budget bill #2, for amounts paid or credited after 2016. For amounts paid or credited in 2015-2016, read:

(3.1) Subsections (3.2) and (3.3) apply at any time in respect of a taxpayer if

(a) the taxpayer pays or credits a particular amount at that time on account or in lieu of payment of, or in satisfaction of, interest (determined without reference to paragraph 18(6.1)(b) and subsection 214(16)) in respect of a particular debt or other obligation to pay an amount to a person or partnership (in this subsection referred to as the "intermediary");

(b) the intermediary is not

(i) a person resident in Canada that does not deal at arm's length with the taxpayer, or

(ii) a partnership each member of which is a person described in subparagraph (i);

(c) at any time in the period during which the interest accrued (in subsections (3.2) and (3.3) referred to as the "relevant period"), the intermediary, or a person or partnership that does not deal at arm's length with the intermediary,

(i) has an amount outstanding as or on account of a debt or other obligation to pay an amount to a non-resident person that meets any of the following conditions (in this subsection and subsection (3.2) referred to as the "intermediary debt"):

(A) recourse in respect of the debt or other obligation is limited in whole or in part, either immediately or in the future and either absolutely or contingently, to the particular debt or other obligation, or

(B) it can reasonably be concluded that all or a portion of the particular debt or other obligation became owing, or was permitted to remain owing, because

(I) all or a portion of the debt or other obligation was entered into or was permitted to remain outstanding, or

(II) the intermediary anticipated that all or a portion of the debt or other obligation would become owing or remain outstanding, or

(ii) has a specified right (as defined in subsection 18(5)) in respect of a particular property that was granted directly or indirectly by a non-resident person and

(A) the existence of the specified right is required under the terms and conditions of the particular debt or other obligation, or

(B) it can reasonably be concluded that all or a portion of the particular debt or other obligation became owing, or was permitted to remain owing, because

(I) the specified right was granted, or

(II) the intermediary anticipated that the specified right would be granted;

(d) the tax that would be payable under this Part in respect of the particular amount, if the particular amount were paid or credited to the non-resident person rather than the intermediary, is greater than the tax payable under this Part (determined without reference to this subsection and subsection (3.2)) in respect of the particular amount; and

(e) the total of all amounts — each of which is, in respect of the particular debt or other obligation, an amount outstanding as or on account of an intermediary debt or the fair market value of a particular property described in subparagraph (c)(ii) — is equal to at least 25% of the total of

(i) the amount outstanding as or on account of the particular debt or other obligation, and

(ii) the total of all amounts each of which is an amount (other than the amount described in subparagraph (i)) that the taxpayer, or a person or partnership that does not deal at arm's length with the taxpayer, has outstanding as or on account of a debt or other obligation to pay an amount to the intermediary under the agreement, or an agreement that is connected to the agreement, under which the particular debt or other obligation was entered into where

(A) the intermediary is granted a security interest (as defined in subsection 18(5)) in respect of a property that is the intermediary debt or the particular property, as the case may be, and the security interest secures the payment of two or more debts or other obligations that include the debt or other obligation and the particular debt or other obligation, and

(B) each security interest that secures the payment of a debt or other obligation referred to in clause (A) secures the payment of every debt or other obligation referred to in that clause.

212(3.1) added by 2014 budget bill #2, for amounts paid or credited after 2014. Para. (b) was not in the Aug. 29/14 draft legislation; what became (c)-(e) were (b)-(d).

(3.2) Back-to-back loan arrangement — If this subsection applies at any time in respect of a taxpayer, then for the purposes of paragraph (1)(b), the taxpayer is deemed, at that time, to pay interest to each ultimate funder, the amount of which is determined for each particular ultimate funder by the formula

$$(A - B) \times C/D \times (E - F)/E$$

where

A is the particular amount referred to in paragraph (3.1)(a);

B is the portion, if any, of the particular amount deemed by subsection 214(16) to have been paid by the taxpayer as a dividend;

C is the average of all amounts each of which is, at a particular time in the relevant period, the amount determined by the formula

$$G - H$$

where

G is the lesser of the following amounts:

(a) the amount of the particular debt or other obligation referred to in paragraph (3.1)(a) outstanding at the particular time, and

(b) the total of all amounts each of which is at that particular time

(i) an amount outstanding as or on account of a debt or other obligation that is owed to the particular ultimate funder under a relevant funding arrangement,

(ii) the fair market value of a particular property referred to in subparagraph (3.1)(c)(ii) in respect of which the particular ultimate funder has granted a specified right under a relevant funding arrangement, or

(iii) if neither subparagraph (i) nor (ii) applies at that particular time, nil, and

H is the total of all amounts each of which is, at the particular time, the amount that is

(a) an amount outstanding as or on account of a debt or other obligation that is owed by the particular ultimate funder under a relevant funding arrangement,

(b) the fair market value of a particular property referred to in subparagraph (3.1)(c)(ii) in respect of which the particular ultimate funder has a specified right under a relevant funding arrangement, or

(c) if neither paragraph (a) nor (b) applies at that particular time, nil;

D   is the average of all amounts each of which is the amount of the particular debt or other obligation outstanding at a time in the relevant period;

E   is the rate of tax (determined without reference to subsection 214(16)) that would be imposed under this Part on the particular amount if the particular amount were paid by the taxpayer to the particular ultimate funder at that time; and

F   is the rate of tax (determined without reference to subsection 214(16)) imposed under this Part on the immediate funder in respect of all or the portion of the particular amount paid or credited to the immediate funder.

Related Provisions: 15(2.16)–(2.192) — Shareholder loans — back-to-back arrangements; 212(3.1) — Conditions for 212(3.2) to apply; 212(3.8) — Definitions; 212(3.81) — Rules for specified shares; 257 — Formula amounts cannot calculate to less than zero.

Notes: 212(3.1)-(3.81) provide "back-to-back" rules preventing taxpayers from interposing a third party between a Canadian borrower and a foreign lender to avoid 212(1)(b) withholding tax on certain cross-border payments. The 2016 budget bill #2 amendments extend the rules to rents and royalties taxed by 212(1)(d) [212(3.9)-(3.94)], multiple funding arrangements [212(3.5) and add character substitution rules [212(3.6), (3.7), (3.92), (3.93)]; and provide an election to reduce the compliance burden where a taxpayer is deemed to make interest payments to two or more ultimate funders [212(3.21), (3.22)]. Back-to-back loan rules were also added to the domestic shareholder-loan rules [15(2.16)-(2.192)]. See also the similar back-to-back thin capitalization rules under 18(6)-(6.1).

See Suarez, "An Analysis of Canada's Latest International Tax Proposals", 75(13) *Tax Notes International [TNI]* (taxnotes.com) 1131 (Sept. 29, 2014) at 1132-36 and "Canada Releases Revised Back-to-Back Loan Rules", 76(4) 357-63 (Oct. 27, 2014); Lorito & O'Brien, "International Finance: Cash-Pooling Arrangements", 2014 Cdn Tax Foundation conference report at 20:4-10; Kandev, "Canadian Interest Anti-Conduit Rule Soon to Be Law", 76(11) *TNI* 1027-30 (Dec. 15, 2014).

For the 2016 amendments see O'Neill, "Significant Expansion of Back-to-Back Loan Rules", *International Tax Newsletter* (*Taxnet Pro*), June 2016, pp. 3-6; Wong, "Bill C-29 Amendments to the Back-to-Back Rules", 91 *International Tax* (CCH) 5-11 (Dec. 2016); Boland and Montes, "A Detailed Review of the Back-to-Back Loan Rules", 2016 Cdn Tax Foundation conference report at 26:9-17 and 25-27; Kandev, "Canada Expands Back-to-Back Regime", 86(12) *Tax Notes International* (taxnotes.com) 1087-92 (June 19, 2017); Diksic & Wong, "Cross-Border Lending Practices", 2017 Cdn Tax Foundation conference report, 21:1-30. For criticism of the amendments (and 15(2.16)-(2.192)) as being too broad, see CBA/CPA Canada Joint Committee letter to Finance, Sept. 27, 2016; Bradley et al., "Is the Back-to-Back Withholding Tax Regime an Effective Anti-Treaty-Shopping Measure?", 64(4) *Canadian Tax Journal* 833-58 (2016).

For CRA interpretation before the 2016 amendments see VIEWS doc 2014-0521831R3 (Canada-US treaty Art. XI:1 exempts payments); and Notes to 18(6.1).

212(3.2) amended by 2016 budget bill #2, for amounts paid or credited after 2016. For amounts paid or credited in 2015-2016, read:

(3.2) If this subsection applies at any time in respect of a taxpayer, then for the purposes of paragraph (1)(b), the taxpayer is deemed, at that time, to pay interest to a non-resident person referred to in subparagraph (3.1)(c)(i) or (ii), the amount of which is determined by the formula

$$[(A \times B/C) - D] \times (E - F)/E$$

where

A   is the particular amount referred to in paragraph (3.1)(a);

B   is the average of all amounts each of which is the lesser of

(i) the amount of the particular debt or other obligation referred to in paragraph (3.1)(a) outstanding at a particular time in the relevant period; and

(ii) the total of all amounts each of which is at that particular time

(A) an amount outstanding as or on account of an intermediary debt, in respect of the particular debt or other obligation, that is owed to the non-resident person,

(B) the fair market value of a particular property referred to in subparagraph (3.1)(c)(ii) in respect of the particular debt or other obligation, or

(C) if neither clause (A) nor (B) applies at that particular time, nil;

C   is the average of all amounts each of which is the amount of the particular debt or other obligation outstanding at a time in the relevant period;

D   is the portion, if any, of the particular amount deemed by subsection 214(16) to have been paid by the taxpayer as a dividend;

E   is the rate of tax (determined without reference to subsection 214(16)) that would be imposed under this Part on the particular amount if the particular amount were paid by the taxpayer to the non-resident person at that time; and

F   is the rate of tax (determined without reference to subsection 214(16)) imposed under this Part on the intermediary in respect of all or the portion of the particular amount paid or credited to the intermediary.

212(3.1)-(3.3) added by 2014 budget bill #2, for amounts paid or credited after 2014.

(3.21) Back-to-back arrangement — election [conditions for (3.22) to apply] — Subsection (3.22) applies in respect of a taxpayer and two or more ultimate funders (referred to in this subsection and subsection (3.22) as the **"electing ultimate funders"**) at any time if

(a) at that time, subsection (3.2) applies in respect of the taxpayer;

(b) prior to that time, the taxpayer and the electing ultimate funders have jointly filed an election under this subsection;

(c) the election designates one of the electing ultimate funders to be the recipient of interest payments that are deemed to be made by the taxpayer under subsection (3.22);

(d) at that time, the tax that would be payable under this Part in respect of an interest payment by the taxpayer to the designated ultimate funder is not less than the tax that would be payable under this Part if the interest payment were made by the taxpayer to any of the other electing ultimate funders; and

(e) the election has not been revoked prior to that time.

Notes: 212(3.21) and (3.22) provide an election to relieve the compliance burden where 212(3.2) deems taxpayer T to make interest payments to two or more ultimate funders (UFs). This effectively relieves the reporting requirements for the separate interest payments otherwise deemed by 212(3.2) to be made by T to each UF. In general, the election allows T and two or more of the UFs to elect that the interest payments are deemed made by T to one of them, provided the withholding tax rate on interest paid to the designated UF is not less than the rate for any of the electing UFs.

212(3.21) added by 2016 budget bill #2, for amounts paid or credited after 2016.

(3.22) Back-to-back arrangement — election — If this subsection applies at any time in respect of a taxpayer and two or more electing ultimate funders, then each interest payment that would, in the absence of this subsection, have been deemed under subsection (3.2) to have been made at that time by the taxpayer to an electing ultimate funder, and received by the electing ultimate funder from the taxpayer, is deemed to have instead been

(a) made by the taxpayer to the designated ultimate funder; and

(b) received by the designated ultimate funder from the taxpayer.

Related Provisions: 212(3.21) — Conditions for 212(3.22) to apply.

Notes: See Notes to 212(3.21). 212(3.22) added by 2016 budget bill #2, for amounts paid or credited after 2016.

(3.3) Excess funding [conditions for 212(3.4) to apply] — Subsection (3.4) applies in respect of a particular relevant funder if the amount determined by the following formula is greater than nil:

$$A - B$$

where

A   is the total of all amounts each of which is the amount owing by the particular relevant funder, or is the fair market value of a property in respect of which the particular relevant funder has a specified right, under a relevant funding arrangement; and

B   is the total of all amounts each of which is the amount owed to the particular relevant funder, or is the fair market value of a property in respect of which the particular relevant funder has granted a specified right, under a relevant funding arrangement.

Related Provisions: 212(3.8) — Definitions; 257 — Formula cannot calculate to less than zero.

Notes: 212(3.3) and (3.4) are intended to ensure that 212(3.2) deems interest payments to ultimate funders (UFs) in the appropriate amounts in cases where a relevant funder (RF) has received *more* funding under relevant funding arrangements (RFAs, which are, by their definition in 212(3.8), part of the back-to-back arrangement that includes the particular debt or other obligation) than the RF has provided under RFAs (i.e., the funding "into" the RF exceeds the funding "out"). In such case, absent 212(3.3) and (3.4), the total for 212(3.2)C in respect of UFs (generally representing the funding that UFs are, collectively, considered to contribute, under RFAs, to the debt) would generally exceed the amount outstanding on the debt. As a result, the total interest those UFs would be deemed to receive under 212(3.2) would exceed the interest referred to in 212(3.1)(a). This would be an inappropriate result.

If 212(3.4) applies in respect of a RF, then, for the purposes of 212(3.2)-(3.4) (to avoid circularity, other than for the purpose of applying 212(3.3) and (3.4) in respect of that RF), each amount owed by the RF under a RFA, or that is the value of property in respect of which the particular RF has been granted a specified right under a RFA, is deemed to be the amount determined by the formula C/D × E. The end result is that the total funding *received* by the RF under RFAs is deemed to be equal to the total funding *provided* by the RF under RFAs. (Finance Technical Notes)

212(3.3) amended by 2016 budget bill #2, for amounts paid or credited after 2016. For amounts paid or credited in 2015-2016, read:

(3.3) Back-to-back loan arrangement — If subsection (3.2) applies at any time to deem a taxpayer to pay interest at that time to more than one non-resident person referred to in subparagraph (3.1)(c)(i) or (ii) in respect of a particular debt or other obligation and the total of all amounts determined (without reference to this subsection) for B in subsection (3.2) in respect of the particular debt or other obligation exceeds the average of all amounts each of which is the amount of the particular debt or other obligation outstanding at a time in the relevant period, then the taxpayer may reduce the amount determined for B in respect of one or more of the non-resident persons by one or more amounts designated by the taxpayer, as is reasonable in the circumstances, the total of which designated amounts shall not be greater than that excess.

(3.4) Excess funding — deemed funding allocation

— If this subsection applies in respect of a particular relevant funder, for the purposes of subsections (3.2) to (3.4) (other than for the purpose of applying subsections (3.3) and (3.4) in respect of the particular relevant funder), each amount that is owed by the particular relevant funder, or that is the fair market value of a property in respect of which the particular relevant funder has been granted a specified right, under a relevant funding arrangement, is deemed to be the amount determined by the formula

$$C/D \times E$$

where

C is the amount owing or the fair market value of the property, as the case may be;

D is the amount determined for A in subsection (3.3); and

E is the amount determined for B in subsection (3.3).

Related Provisions: 212(3.3) — Conditions for 212(3.4) to apply; 212(3.8) — Definitions.

Notes: See Notes to 212(3.3). 212(3.4) added by 2016 budget bill #2, effective for amounts paid or credited after 2016.

(3.5) Multiple funding arrangements

— If an amount owing by a relevant funder or a specified right held by the relevant funder is a relevant funding arrangement in respect of more than one particular debt or other obligation referred to in paragraph (3.1)(a), for the purposes of applying subsections (3.2) to (3.4) in respect of each of the particular debts or other obligations, the amount owing, or the fair market value of the property in respect of which the specified right was granted, as the case may be, is deemed, in respect of each particular debt or other obligation, to be the amount determined by the formula

$$A/B \times C$$

where

A is the total of all amounts each of which is an amount owing to the relevant funder, or the fair market value of a property in respect of which the relevant funder has granted a specified right, under a relevant funding arrangement, in respect of the particular debt or other obligation;

B is the total of all amounts each of which is an amount owing to the relevant funder, or the fair market value of a property in respect of which the relevant funder has granted a specified right, under a relevant funding arrangement, in respect of all of the particular debts or other obligations; and

C is the amount owing by the relevant funder or the fair market value of the property in respect of which the relevant funder holds the specified right.

Related Provisions: 212(3.8) — Definitions.

Notes: See Notes to 212(3.2).

212(3.5) addresses cases where a debt, or a specified right granted in respect of property, funds (indirectly, through back-to-back arrangements) more than one particular debt referred to in 212(3.1)(a). This can occur where the debt or the specified right is a "relevant funding arrangement" in respect of more than one debt — in other words, where it is part of more than one back-to-back loan arrangement. To ensure the full amount of the debt (or the full value of the property in respect of which the specified right is granted), is not considered (for 212(3.2)-(3.4)) to fund each of the debts, 212(3.5) effectively allocates the amount of the particular debt (or the value of the property) between the debts on a *pro rata* basis (i.e., based on the value of the particular debt relative to all particular debts owing to the relevant funder).

212(3.5) added by 2016 budget bill #2, for amounts paid or credited after 2016.

(3.6) Back-to-back loan arrangement — character substitution

— Subsection (3.7) applies in respect of

(a) shares (other than specified shares) of the capital stock of a particular relevant funder, in respect of a particular relevant funding arrangement, if — at any time at or after the time when the particular debt or other obligation referred to in paragraph (3.1)(a) was entered into — the particular relevant funder has an obligation to pay or credit an amount as, on account or in lieu of payment of, or in satisfaction of, a dividend on the shares, either immediately or in the future and either absolutely or contingently, to a person or partnership, and any of the following conditions is met:

(i) the amount of the dividend is determined, in whole or in part, by reference to an amount of interest paid or credited, or an obligation to pay or credit interest, under a relevant funding arrangement, or

(ii) it can reasonably be concluded that the particular relevant funding arrangement was entered into or was permitted to remain in effect, because

(A) the shares were issued or were permitted to remain issued and outstanding, or

(B) it was anticipated that the shares would be issued or would be permitted to remain issued and outstanding; or

(b) a specified royalty arrangement, if — at any time at or after the time when the particular debt or other obligation referred to in paragraph (3.1)(a) was entered into — a particular relevant funder, in respect of a particular relevant funding arrangement, is a specified licensee that has an obligation to pay or credit an amount under the specified royalty arrangement, either immediately or in the future and either absolutely or contingently, to a person or partnership, and any of the following conditions is met:

(i) the amount is determined, in whole or in part, by reference to an amount of interest paid or credited, or an obligation to pay or credit interest, under a relevant funding arrangement, or

(ii) it can reasonably be concluded that the particular relevant funding arrangement was entered into or was permitted to remain in effect, because

(A) the specified royalty arrangement was entered into or was permitted to remain in effect, or

(B) it was anticipated that the specified royalty arrangement would be entered into or remain in effect.

Related Provisions: 212(3.8) — Definitions.

Notes: See Notes to 212(3.7). 212(3.6) added by 2016 budget bill #2, for amounts paid or credited after 2016.

(3.7) Back-to-back loan arrangement — character substitution

— If this subsection applies in respect of a specified royalty arrangement (under which a particular relevant funder is a specified licensee) or shares of the capital stock of a particular relevant funder, then, for the purposes of subsections (3.1) to (3.8),

(a) the specified royalty arrangement or the holding of the shares, as the case may be, is deemed to be a relevant funding arrangement;

(b) the specified licensor or shareholder, as the case may be, in respect of the relevant funding arrangement, is deemed to be a relevant funder, in respect of the relevant funding arrangement;

(c) the conditions in paragraph (3.1)(c) are deemed to be met in respect of the relevant funding arrangement; and

(d) the relevant funder is deemed to be owed, under the relevant funding arrangement and by the particular relevant funder, an amount as or on account of a debt, the outstanding amount of which is determined by the formula

$$(A - B) \times C/D$$

where

A   is the total of all amounts each of which is at the particular time,

(i) an amount outstanding as or on account of a debt or other obligation that is owed to the particular relevant funder under a relevant funding arrangement,

(ii) the fair market value of a particular property referred to in subparagraph (3.1)(c)(ii) in respect of which the particular relevant funder has granted a specified right under a relevant funding arrangement, or

(iii) if neither subparagraph (i) nor (ii) applies at that particular time, nil,

B   is the total of all amounts each of which is, at the particular time, in respect of a relevant funding arrangement (other than a relevant funding arrangement deemed under paragraph (a)) and is

(i) an amount outstanding as or on account of a debt or other obligation that is owed by the particular relevant funder under the relevant funding arrangement,

(ii) the fair market value of a particular property referred to in subparagraph (3.1)(c)(ii) in respect of which the particular relevant funder has been granted a specified right under a relevant funding arrangement, or

(iii) if neither subparagraph (i) nor (ii) applies at that particular time, nil,

C   is the fair market value, at the particular time, of

(i) if the relevant funding arrangement is described in paragraph (3.6)(a), the shares, or

(ii) if the relevant funding arrangement is described in paragraph (3.6)(b), the specified royalty arrangement, and

D   is the total of all amounts each of which is, in respect of a relevant funding arrangement referred to in the description of C, the amount determined for C at the particular time.

Related Provisions: 212(3.6) — Conditions for 212(3.7) to apply; 212(3.8) — Definitions; 257 — Formula cannot calculate to less than zero.

Notes: 212(3.6)-(3.7) and (3.92)-(3.93) are "character substitution" rules. They apply to prevent a taxpayer from avoiding the back-to-back (BB) loan rules for interest (212(3.1)-(3.3)) and for royalties (212(3.9)-(3.94)) by substituting arrangements that provide payments economically similar to interest or royalty payments. Specifically, a BB arrangement may exist in situations where

• interest is paid by a Canadian resident to an intermediary and there is an agreement that provides royalty payments from the intermediary to a non-resident;

• royalties are paid by a Canadian resident to an intermediary and there is a loan from a non-resident to the intermediary; or

• interest or royalties are paid by a Canadian resident to an intermediary and a non-resident holds shares of the intermediary that include certain obligations to pay dividends or that satisfy certain other conditions (e.g., they are redeemable or cancellable).

Under these character substitution rules, a BB arrangement will exist where a sufficient connection is established between the arrangement under which an interest or royalty payment is made from Canada and the intermediary's obligations. The presence of such a connection is determined by applying tests similar to those used for BB loans and BB royalty arrangements, but adapted to reflect the particular circumstances of these arrangements. Where a BB arrangement exists under these rules, an additional payment of the same character as that paid by the Canadian resident to the intermediary is deemed to be made directly by the Canadian resident payor to the other non-residents. (Finance Technical Notes)

Finance said at 2017 IFA q.7 that "obligation" to pay a dividend in 212(3.6)(a) was intended to apply to common shares, as declaration of a dividend creates an obligation to pay it.

See also Peter Lee, "The Character Substitution Rules", 94 *International Tax* (CCH) 10-16 (June 2017).

212(3.7) added by 2016 budget bill #2, for amounts paid or credited after 2016.

(3.8) Back-to-back loan arrangement — definitions — The following definitions apply in this subsection and subsections (3.1) to (3.7) and (3.81).

"relevant funder", in respect of a relevant funding arrangement, means

(a) if the relevant funding arrangement is described in paragraph (a) of the definition "relevant funding arrangement", the immediate funder referred to in paragraph (3.1)(a);

(b) if the relevant funding arrangement is described in paragraph (b) of the definition "relevant funding arrangement", the creditor in respect of the debt or other obligation or the grantor of the specified right, as the case may be; or

(c) a person or partnership that does not deal at arm's length with a person or partnership that is referred to in paragraph (a) or (b) and that deals at arm's length with the taxpayer.

"relevant funding arrangement" means

(a) the particular debt or other obligation referred to in paragraph (3.1)(a); and

(b) each debt or other obligation or specified right, owing by or granted to a relevant funder, in respect of a particular relevant funding arrangement, if the debt or other obligation or specified right meets the conditions in subparagraph (3.1)(c)(i) or (ii) in respect of a relevant funding arrangement.

"specified licensee" means

(a) a lessee, licensee or grantee of a right similar to a right granted under a lease or licence, under a specified royalty arrangement;

(b) an assignee under a specified royalty arrangement; or

(c) a purchaser under a specified royalty arrangement.

"specified licensor" means

(a) a lessor, licensor or grantor of a right similar to a right granted under a lease or licence, under a specified royalty arrangement;

(b) an assignor under a specified royalty arrangement; or

(c) a seller under a specified royalty arrangement.

"specified right" has the same meaning as in subsection 18(5).

"specified royalty arrangement" has the same meaning as in subsection (3.94).

"specified share" means a share of the capital stock of a corporation if, under the terms or conditions of the share, or any agreement or arrangement relating to the share,

(a) the holder of the share may cause the share to be redeemed, acquired or cancelled;

(b) the issuing corporation is, or may be, required to redeem, acquire or cancel the share at a specific time; or

(c) the share is convertible or exchangeable into a share that meets the conditions in paragraph (a) or (b).

Related Provisions: 212(3.81) — Rules for specified shares.

"ultimate funder" means a relevant funder, in respect of a relevant funding arrangement (other than the immediate funder) that either

(a) is not a debtor, or a holder of a specified right, under a relevant funding arrangement; or

(c) is a debtor, or a holder of a specified right, under a relevant funding arrangement, if the amount that would — if the relevant funder were an ultimate funder — be determined for C in the formula in subsection (3.2) is greater than nil.

Related Provisions: 212(3.21), (3.22) — Election by ultimate funders.

Notes: A relevant funder (RF) is an ultimate funder (UF) under a relevant funding arrangement (RFA) if it is the ultimate source of funding under a back-to-back arrangement (BB). A RF can be an UF under two situations: first, where the RF has provided funding under a RFA, but without having received any funding connected to the BB (para (a)). Second (para. (b)), although the RF is a debtor (or holder of a specified right), under a RFA, the total funding provided by the RF under RFAs is greater than the total funding the RF received under RFAs. A RF that acts solely as an intermediary (conduit) for funding originating from another RF is not a UF.

Notes [subsec. 212(3.8)]: 212(3.8) added by 2016 budget bill #2, for amounts paid or credited after 2016.

(3.81) Specified shares — For the purposes of subsections (3.1) to (3.8),

(a) specified shares of a relevant funder, in respect of a relevant funding arrangement, held at any time by a person or partnership are deemed to be a debt of the relevant funder owing to the person or partnership; and

(b) the amount outstanding at that time as or on account of the debt is deemed to be equal to the fair market value of the specified shares at that time.

Notes: 212(3.81) added by 2016 budget bill #2, for amounts paid or credited after 2016. This was not in the July 29/16 draft legislation.

(3.9) Back-to-back arrangement — rents, royalties, similar payments — Subsection (3.91) applies at any time in respect of a taxpayer if

(a) the taxpayer pays or credits a particular amount at that time as, on account or in lieu of payment of, or in satisfaction of, rent, royalty or similar payment, in respect of a particular lease, licence or similar agreement, to a non-resident person or a partnership any member of which is a non-resident person (in this subsection and subsections (3.91) to (3.94) referred to as the **"immediate licensor"**);

(b) at any time at or after the time when the particular lease, licence or similar agreement was entered into,

(i) a relevant licensor in respect of a particular relevant royalty arrangement has an obligation to pay or credit an amount, either immediately or in the future and either absolutely or contingently, to a person or partnership, in respect of a specified royalty arrangement, and either of the following additional conditions is met:

(A) the amount is determined, in whole or in part, by reference to

(I) an amount paid or credited, or an obligation to pay or credit an amount, in respect of a relevant royalty arrangement, or

(II) one or more of the fair market value of, any revenue, profits, income, or cash flow from, or any other similar criteria in respect of, a particular property, if a right in respect of the property is granted under the particular lease, licence or similar agreement, or

(B) it can reasonably be concluded that the particular relevant royalty arrangement was entered into, or was permitted to remain in effect, because

(I) the specified royalty arrangement was entered into or was permitted to remain in effect, or

(II) it was anticipated that the specified royalty arrangement would be entered into or remain in effect, and

(ii) either the person or partnership

(A) does not deal at arm's length with the taxpayer, or

(B) deals at arm's length with the taxpayer, if it can reasonably be concluded that one of the main purposes of the specified royalty arrangement was

(I) to reduce or avoid the tax payable under this Part in respect of the particular amount, or

(II) to avoid the application of subsection (3.91); and

(c) the tax that would be payable under this Part in respect of the particular amount, if the particular amount were paid or credited to an ultimate licensor rather than the immediate licensor, is greater than the tax payable under this Part (determined without reference to this subsection and subsection (3.91)) in respect of the particular amount.

Related Provisions: 212(3.94) — Definitions.

Notes: 212(3.9)-(3.94) extend the back-to-back rules (see Notes to 212(3.2) to rents and royalties subject to 212(1)(d) withholding tax. If the ultimate licensor deals at arm's length with the Canadian resident, the rules apply only if it can reasonably be concluded that one of the main purposes of the relevant royalty arrangement was to reduce or avoid Part XIII tax on the royalty or to avoid the application of the rules: 212(3.9)(b)(ii)(B). As well, the rules apply only if the back-to-back arrangement results in a reduction of Part XIII tax that would be payable if the payment were made directly to the ultimate licensor instead of the immediate licensor: 212(3.9)(c).

See Gheorgiu, "Back-to-Back Royalty and Character Substitution Rules", 6(4) *Canadian Tax Focus* (ctf.ca) 1-15 (Nov. 2016); Boland and Montes, "A Detailed Review of the Back-to-Back Loan Rules", 2016 Cdn Tax Foundation conference report at 26:17-23, 25-27.

212(3.9) added by 2016 budget bill #2, for amounts paid or credited after 2016.

(3.91) Back-to-back arrangement — rents, royalties, similar payments — If this subsection applies at any time in respect of a taxpayer, then, for the purposes of paragraph (1)(d), the taxpayer is deemed, at that time, to pay to each ultimate licensor an amount — of the same character as the particular amount referred to in paragraph (3.9)(a) — determined for each particular ultimate licensor by the formula

$$(A \times B/C) \times (D - E)/D$$

where

A   is the particular amount referred to in paragraph (3.9)(a);

B   is

(a) the portion of the amount referred to in paragraph (3.9)(a) that is demonstrated, to the satisfaction of the Minister, to be reasonably allocable to the particular ultimate licensor, and

(b) if an amount is not demonstrated, to the satisfaction of the Minister, to be reasonably allocable to each particular ultimate licensor, one;

C   is

(a) the total of all amounts, each of which is the portion of the amount referred to in paragraph (3.9)(a) that is demonstrated, to the satisfaction of the Minister, to be reasonably allocable to each ultimate licensor, and

(b) if an amount is not demonstrated, to the satisfaction of the Minister, to be reasonably allocable to each particular ultimate licensor, the number of ultimate licensors;

D   is

(a) if an amount is not demonstrated, to the satisfaction of the Minister, to be reasonably allocable to each particular ultimate licensor, the highest rate of tax that would be imposed under this Part on the particular amount referred to in paragraph (3.9)(a) if the particular amount were paid by the taxpayer to any of the ultimate licensors at that time, and

(b) in any other case, the rate of tax that would be imposed under this Part on the particular amount referred to in paragraph (3.9)(a) if the particular amount were paid by the taxpayer to the particular ultimate licensor at that time; and

E   is the rate of tax imposed under this Part at that time on the immediate licensor in respect of the particular amount, referred to in paragraph (3.9)(a), paid or credited to the immediate licensor.

Related Provisions: 212(3.9) — Conditions for 212(3.91) to apply; 212(3.94) — Definitions; 257 — Formula cannot calculate to less than zero.

Notes: See Notes to 212(3.9). 212(3.91) added by 2016 budget bill #2, effective for amounts paid or credited after 2016.

(3.92) Back-to-back arrangement — character substitution — Subsection (3.93) applies in respect of

(a) shares of the capital stock of a particular relevant licensor, in respect of a particular relevant royalty arrangement, if — at any time at or after the time when a particular lease, license or similar agreement referred to in paragraph (3.9)(a) was entered into — the particular relevant licensor has an obligation to pay or credit an amount as, on account or in lieu of payment of, or in satisfaction of, a dividend on the shares, either immediately or in the future and either absolutely or contingently, to a person or partnership, and

(i) either of the following conditions is met:

(A) the amount of the dividend is determined, in whole or in part, by reference to

(I) an amount of rent, royalty or similar payment paid or credited, or an obligation to pay or credit rent, royalty or similar payment, under a relevant royalty arrangement, or

(II) one or more of the fair market value of, any revenue profits, income or cash flow from, or any other similar criteria in respect of a particular property, if a right in respect of the property is granted under the particular lease, licence or similar agreement, or

(B) it can reasonably be concluded that the particular relevant royalty arrangement was entered into or was permitted to remain in effect, because

(I) the shares were issued or were permitted to remain issued and outstanding, or

(II) it was anticipated that the shares would be issued or would be permitted to remain issued and outstanding, and

(ii) either the person or partnership

(A) does not deal at arm's length with the taxpayer referred to in paragraph (3.9)(a), or

(B) deals at arm's length with that taxpayer, if it can reasonably be concluded that one of the main purposes of the issuance of the shares was

(I) to reduce or avoid the tax payable under this Part in respect of the particular amount referred to in paragraph (3.9)(a), or

(II) to avoid the application of subsection (3.91); and

(b) an amount outstanding as or on account of a debt or other obligation to pay an amount, if — at any time at or after the time when a particular lease, license or similar agreement referred to in paragraph (3.9)(a) was entered into — a particular relevant licensor, in respect of a particular relevant royalty arrangement, has an obligation to pay or credit an amount as, on account or in lieu of payment of, or in satisfaction of, interest under the debt or other obligation, either immediately or in the future and either absolutely or contingently, to a person or partnership, and

(i) either of the following conditions is met:

(A) the amount of the interest is determined, in whole or in part, by reference to

(I) an amount of rent, royalty or similar payment paid or credited, or an obligation to pay or credit rent, royalty or similar payment, under a relevant royalty arrangement, or

(II) one or more of the fair market value of, any revenue profits, income or cash flow from, or any other similar criteria in respect of a particular property, if a right in respect of the property is granted under the particular lease, licence or similar agreement, or

(B) it can reasonably be concluded that the particular relevant royalty arrangement was entered into or was permitted to remain in effect, because

(I) the debt or other obligation was entered into or was permitted to remain in effect, or

(II) it was anticipated that the debt or other obligation would be entered into or remain in effect, and

(ii) either the person or partnership

(A) does not deal at arm's length with the taxpayer referred to in paragraph (3.9)(a), or

(B) deals at arm's length with that taxpayer, if it can reasonably be concluded that one of the main purposes of entering into the debt or other obligation was

(I) to reduce or avoid the tax payable under this Part in respect of the particular amount referred to in paragraph (3.9)(a), or

(II) to avoid the application of subsection (3.91).

Related Provisions: 212(3.94) — Definitions.

Notes: See Notes to 212(3.7). 212(3.92) added by 2016 budget bill #2, effective for amounts paid or credited after 2016.

(3.93) Back-to-back arrangement — character substitution — If this subsection applies in respect of a debt or other obligation to pay an amount (under which a particular relevant licensor is a borrower) or shares of the capital stock of a particular relevant licensor, then, for the purposes of subsections (3.9) to (3.94),

(a) the debt or other obligation or the holding of the shares, as the case may be, is deemed to be a relevant royalty arrangement;

(b) the creditor or shareholder, as the case may be, in respect of the relevant royalty arrangement, is deemed to be a relevant licensor, in respect of the relevant royalty arrangement; and

(c) the relevant royalty arrangement is deemed to be a specified royalty arrangement in respect of which the conditions in paragraph (3.9)(b) are met.

Related Provisions: 212(3.92) — Conditions for 212(3.93) to apply; 212(3.94) — Definitions.

Notes: See Notes to 212(3.7). 212(3.93) added by 2016 budget bill #2, effective for amounts paid or credited after 2016.

(3.94) Back-to-back arrangement — definitions — The following definitions apply in this subsection and subsections (3.9) to (3.93).

"lease, licence or similar agreement" means an agreement under which a rent, royalty or similar payment is or could be made.

"relevant licensor", in respect of a relevant royalty arrangement, means

(a) if the relevant royalty arrangement is described in paragraph (a) of the definition "relevant royalty arrangement", the immediate licensor referred to in paragraph (3.9)(a);

(b) if the relevant royalty arrangement is described in paragraph (b) of the definition "relevant royalty arrangement", a person or partnership that is the lessor, the licensor or the grantor of a right similar to a right granted under a lease or licence, the assignor or the seller, as the case may be; or

(c) a person or partnership that does not deal at arm's length with a relevant licensor referred to in paragraph (a) or (b).

"relevant royalty arrangement" means

(a) the particular lease, licence or similar agreement referred to in paragraph (3.9)(a); and

(b) each specified royalty arrangement that

(i) meets, in respect of a relevant royalty arrangement, the conditions in clause (3.9)(b)(i)(A) or (B), and

(ii) is an arrangement in respect of which the person or partnership referred to in subparagraph (3.9)(b)(ii) meets the conditions in clause (3.9)(b)(ii)(A) or (B).

"rent, royalty or similar payment" means a rent, royalty or similar payment described in paragraph (1)(d) and, for greater certainty, includes any payment described in subparagraphs (1)(d)(i) to (v) but does not include any payment described in subparagraphs (1)(d)(vi) to (xii).

"specified royalty arrangement" means a lease, license or similar agreement, an assignment or an instalment sale.

"ultimate licensor" means a relevant licensor (other than the immediate licensor), in respect of a relevant royalty arrangement, that is not, under a relevant royalty arrangement,

(a) a lessee, a licensee or a grantee of a right similar to a right granted under a lease or licence;

(b) an assignee; or

(c) a purchaser.

Notes: 212(3.94) added by 2016 budget bill #2, for amounts paid or credited after 2016.

(4) Interpretation of "management or administration fee or charge" — For the purpose of paragraph (1)(a), "management or administration fee or charge" does not include any amount paid or credited or deemed by Part I to have been paid or credited to a non-resident person as, on account or in lieu of payment of, or in satisfaction of,

(a) a service performed by the non-resident person if, at the time the non-resident person performed the service

(i) the service was performed in the ordinary course of a business carried on by the non-resident person that included the performance of such a service for a fee, and

(ii) the non-resident person and the payer were dealing with each other at arm's length, or

(b) a specific expense incurred by the non-resident person for the performance of a service that was for the benefit of the payer,

to the extent that the amount so paid or credited was reasonable in the circumstances.

Notes: See Notes to 212(1)(a).

Interpretation Bulletins: IT-468R: Management or administration fees paid to non-residents. See also at end of s. 212.

(5) Motion picture films — Every non-resident person shall pay an income tax of 25% on every amount that a person resident in Canada pays or credits, or is deemed by Part I to pay or credit, to the non-resident person as, on account or in lieu of payment of, or in satisfaction of, payment for a right in or to the use of

(a) a motion picture film, or

(b) a film, video tape or other means of reproduction for use in connection with television (other than solely in connection with and as part of a news program produced in Canada),

that has been, or is to be, used or reproduced in Canada to the extent that the amount relates to that use or reproduction.

Related Provisions: 212(1)(d) — Withholding tax — royalties; 214(1) — No deduction; 215(1) — Requirement to withhold and remit.

Notes: Copyright royalties for production and reproduction of motion pictures and other works for private home use are exempt under Canada-US tax treaty Art. XII:3, but this is based on the 1984 Technical Explanation, and similar treaty wording does *not* give rise to exemption under the treaties with the UK, France and Thailand in CRA's view: doc 2010-0374421E5. Certain payments by film distributors are exempt under the Canada-US and Canada-France treaties: 2011-0392761E5. For a ruling exempting fees for digital content provided to home users, see 2011-0416891R3.

CRA says streamed movies and TV shows (used by Canadian subscribers) fall under 212(5): doc 2017-0715561E5.

Payment for (or for an option to acquire) motion picture rights to a script does not fall under 212(5) because it is payment for the purchase of the property, not its use: VIEWS doc 2006-017937117. Similarly, payment for the use of photos or music in a TV program is exempt under 212(1)(d)(vi) and not excluded by 212(5): 2013-0506191E5, 2013-0514291E5.

Sports news is not "news" according to CRA: VIEWS doc 2010-0379021E5.

See also Notes to 212(1)(d), under "212(1)(d)(vi)".

212(5) closing words amended by 2002-2013 technical bill (Part 5 — technical), for 2000 and later taxation years, to add "to the extent that the amount relates to that use or reproduction". Even before this amendment, CRA would consider excluding the portion relating to use outside Canada on a case-by-case basis: Revenue Canada Round Table, 1993 Cdn Tax Foundation conference report, p. 58E:16, q.30.

Regulations: 202(1)(h) (information return).

Forms: NR4: Statement of amounts paid or credited to non-residents of Canada; NR4 Segment; NR4 Summ: Return of amounts paid or credited to non-residents of Canada.

(5.1) Acting services — Notwithstanding any regulation made under paragraph 214(13)(c), every person who is either a non-resident individual who is an actor or that is a corporation related to such an individual shall pay an income tax of 23% on every amount paid or credited, or provided as a benefit, to or on behalf of the person for the provision in Canada of the acting services of the actor in a film or video production.

Related Provisions: 115(2.1) — Actor's income not considered earned in Canada unless election made; 115(2.2) — Where corporation makes payment to actor in later year; 150(1)(a)(i)(B) — No requirement for actor to file Canadian tax return; 153(1)(a), (g) — No Part I withholding on payments to actor; 212(5.2) — Relief from double tax on corporation payment; 212(5.3) — Reduction in withholding for undue hardship; 212(13.1)(a.1) — Where payor is a partnership; 215(1) — Payor's requirement to withhold and remit tax; 216.1 — Election by actor to be taxed under Part I.

Notes: The actor can elect under 216.1 to file a return and pay regular tax on net income, rather than the 23% withheld on the gross. See tinyurl.com/nonres-actors; Jadd, Bacal & Leung, "Performing in Canada: Taxation of Non-Resident Artists, Athletes and Other Service Providers", 56(3) *Canadian Tax Journal* 589-638 (2008).

212(5.1) added by 2001 technical bill, for amounts paid, credited or provided after 2000.

Regulations: 202(1.1) (information return).

Remission Orders: *Maniganses, Festival International des arts de la Marionette Remission Order*, P.C. 2005-708 (waiver of tax not withheld on payments to international puppet troupes).

(5.2) Relief from double taxation — Where a corporation is liable to tax under subsection (5.1) in respect of an amount for acting services of an actor (in this subsection referred to as the "corporation payment") and the corporation pays, credits or provides as a benefit to the actor an amount for those acting services (in this subsection referred to as the "actor payment"), no tax is payable under subsection (5.1) with respect to the actor payment except to the extent that it exceeds the corporation payment.

Notes: 212(5.2) added by 2001 technical bill, effective for amounts paid, credited or provided after 2000.

(5.3) Reduction of withholding — If the Minister is satisfied that the deduction or withholding otherwise required by section 215 from an amount described in subsection (5.1), would cause undue hardship, the Minister may determine a lesser amount to be deducted or withheld and that lesser amount is deemed to be the amount so required to be deducted or withheld.

Related Provisions: 153(1.1) — Parallel rule for withholding generally.

Notes: 212(5.3) added by 2001 technical bill, for amounts paid, credited or provided after 2000.

See also Notes to 153(1.1).

Forms: T1213: Request to reduce tax deductions at source; T1213(OAS): Request to reduce OAS recovery tax at source.

(6) Interest on provincial bonds from wholly-owned subsidiaries — Where an amount described by subsection (1) relates to interest on bonds or other obligations of or guaranteed by Her Majesty in right of a province or interest on bonds or other obligations provision for the payment of which was made by a statute of a provincial legislature, the tax payable under subsection (1) is 5% of that amount.

Related Provisions: 212(7) — Application of subsec. 212(6); 240(1) — Taxable and non-taxable obligations defined.

Notes: There is no withholding tax on provincial bonds issued after April 15, 1966. See 212(1)(b)(ii)(C)(II) and (IV).

(7) Where subsec. (6) does not apply — Subsection (6) does not apply to interest on any bond or other obligation described therein that was issued after December 20, 1960, except any such bond or other obligation for the issue of which arrangements were made on or before that day with a dealer in securities, if the existence of the arrangements for the issue of the bond or other obligation can be established by evidence in writing given or made on or before that day.

Related Provisions: 212(8) — Bonds issued in exchange for earlier bonds.

(8) Bonds issued after December 20, 1960 in exchange for earlier bonds — For the purposes of this Part, where any bond, except a bond to which clause (1)(b)(ii)(C) applies, was issued after December 20, 1960 in exchange for a bond issued on or before that day, it shall, if the terms on which the bond for which it was exchanged was issued conferred on the holder thereof the right to make the exchange, be deemed to have been issued on or before December 20, 1960.

Interpretation Bulletins: IT-360R2: Interest payable in a foreign currency. See also at end of s. 212.

(9) Exemptions — Where

(a) a dividend or interest is received by a trust from a non-resident-owned investment corporation,

(b) an amount (in this subsection referred to as the "royalty payment") is received by a trust as, on account of, in lieu of payment of or in satisfaction of, a royalty on or in respect of a copyright in respect of the production or reproduction of any literary, dramatic, musical or artistic work,

(c) interest is received by a mutual fund trust maintained primarily for the benefit of non-resident persons, or

(d) a dividend or interest is received by a trust that is created under a reinsurance trust agreement

(i) to which a regulatory authority — being the Superintendent of Financial Institutions or a provincial regulatory authority having powers similar to those of the Superintendent — is a party, and

(ii) that accords with guidelines issued by the regulatory authority relating to reinsurance arrangements with unregistered insurers

and a particular amount is paid or credited to a non-resident person as income of or from the trust and can reasonably be regarded as having been derived from the dividend, interest or royalty payment, as the case may be, no tax is payable because of paragraph (1)(c) as a consequence of the payment or crediting of the particular amount if no tax would have been payable under this Part in respect of the dividend, interest or royalty payment, as the case may be, if it had been paid directly to the non-resident person instead of to the trust.

Notes: 212(9) implements a June 8, 2011 Finance comfort letter. It was reworded to include reference to a provincial regulatory authority when revised on Oct. 24, 2012.

212(9)(d) added by 2002-2013 technical bill for amounts paid or credited after 2000. CRA would not apply 212(9)(d) before it was enacted: VIEWS docs 2004-0098591E5, 2010-0373501C6, and 227(6) normally has a 2-3 year deadline for refunds. However, per 2002-2013 technical bill s. 347(31), a written application under 227(6) was deemed filed on time if filed by Dec. 23, 2013, and the amount is one on which tax is not payable because of 212(9) (ignoring paras. (a)-(c)).

212(9) earlier amended by 1995-97 technical bill.

Interpretation Bulletins: IT-465R: Non-resident beneficiaries of trusts. See also list at end of s. 212.

(10) Trust beneficiaries residing outside of Canada — Where all the beneficiaries of a trust established before 1949 reside, during a taxation year, in one country other than Canada and all amounts included in computing the income of the trust for the taxation year were received from persons resident in that country, no tax is payable under paragraph (1)(c) on an amount paid or credited in the taxation year to a beneficiary as income of or from the trust.

Interpretation Bulletins: IT-465R: Non-resident beneficiaries of trusts. See also list at end of s. 212.

(11) Payment to beneficiary as income of trust — An amount paid or credited by a trust or an estate to a beneficiary or other person beneficially interested therein shall be deemed, for the purpose of paragraph (1)(c) and without limiting the generality thereof, to have been paid or credited as income of the trust or es-

tate, regardless of the source from which the trust or estate derived it.

Related Provisions: 107(5) — Distribution to non-resident; 248(25) — Meaning of "beneficially interested".

Notes: Although 212(11) appears to apply withholding tax to capital distributions, it does not, because it only deems them to be income for 212(1)(c), and neither of subparas. 212(1)(c)(i) or (ii) applies: VIEWS doc 9409560.

See Notes to 212(1)(c) on the distribution of a capital dividend by an estate.

212(11) amended by 1991 technical bill, effective July 14, 1990, to remove an exclusion for "a distribution or payment of capital", so that 212(1)(c)(ii) can be operative.

Interpretation Bulletins: IT-465R: Non-resident beneficiaries of trusts. See also list at end of s. 212.

(11.1), (11.2) [Repealed under former Act]

Notes: 212(11.1) and (11.2), repealed by 1988 tax reform, dealt with distributions by a trust before 1988. See 212(1)(c) now.

(12) Deemed payments to spouse, etc. — Where by reason of subsection 56(4) or (4.1) or any of sections 74.1 to 75 of this Act or section 74 of the *Income Tax Act*, chapter 148 of the Revised Statutes of Canada, 1952, there is included in computing a taxpayer's income under Part I for a taxation year an amount paid or credited to a non-resident person in the year, no tax is payable under this section on that amount.

Notes: 212(12) prevents double tax from applying when the attribution rules deem a payment to a non-resident to be income to a Canadian resident.

I.T. Application Rules: 69 (meaning of "chapter 148 of ...").

Interpretation Bulletins: IT-369R: Attribution of trust income to settlor; IT-438R2: Crown charges — resource properties in Canada; IT-440R2: Transfer of rights to income. See also at end of s. 212.

(13) Rent and other payments — For the purposes of this section, where a non-resident person pays or credits an amount as, on account or in lieu of payment of, or in satisfaction of,

(a) rent for the use in Canada of property (other than property that is rolling stock as defined in section 2 of the *Railway Act*),

(b) a timber royalty in respect of a timber resource property or a timber limit in Canada,

(c) a payment of a superannuation or pension benefit under a registered pension plan or of a distribution to one or more persons out of or under a retirement compensation arrangement,

(d) a payment of a retiring allowance or a death benefit to the extent that the payment is deductible in computing the payer's taxable income earned in Canada,

(e) a payment described in any of paragraphs (1)(k) to (n), (q) and (v),

(f) interest on any mortgage, hypothecary claim or other indebtedness entered into or issued or modified after March 31, 1977 and secured by real property situated in Canada or an interest therein, or by immovables situated in Canada or real rights therein, to the extent that the amount so paid or credited is deductible in computing the non-resident person's taxable income earned in Canada or the amount on which the non-resident person is liable to pay tax under Part I, or

(g) an amount to which paragraph (1)(i) would apply if the amount paid or credited were paid or credited by a person resident in Canada, and that amount affects, or is intended to affect, in any way whatever,

(i) the acquisition or provision of property or services in Canada,

(ii) the acquisition or provision of property or services outside Canada by a person resident in Canada, or

(iii) the acquisition or provision outside Canada of a taxable Canadian property,

the non-resident person shall be deemed in respect of that payment to be a person resident in Canada.

Related Provisions: 13(21) — Timber resource property defined; 56.4 — Restrictive covenant rules parallel to 212(13)(g); 212(1)(d) — Withholding tax on rent; 248(4.1) — Meaning of "real rights" in 212(13)(f).

Notes: 212(13)(a) imposes withholding tax on payments by non-residents to non-residents, for property located in Canada, by deeming the payer to be resident in Canada so that 212(1)(d) or another provision of 212(1) will apply. Where the property is a vehicle, Canada-U.S. Tax Treaty Art. VIII:6 may provide relief. See also VIEWS docs 2000-0022277 (retirement compensation arrangement), 2002-0120785 (retiring allowance), 2005-0134621E5 (non-resident partnership whose members fall within 212(13)(f)), 2006-0211991R3 and 2008-0267201E5 (bareboat charters); Manu Kakkar, "Rental Equipment Used in Canada and Part XIII Tax", 10(3) *Tax for the Owner-Manager* (ctf.ca) 9 (July 2010).

The *Railway Act*, referred to in 212(13)(a), was repealed by s. 185 of the *Canada Transportation Act* (S.C. 1996, c. 10), s. 6 of which provides (and this definition now applies here: see *Interpretation Act* para. 44(h)):

> 6. **"rolling stock"** includes a locomotive, engine, motor car, tender, snow-plough, flanger and any car or railway equipment that is designed for movement on its wheels on the rails of a railway;

212(13)(f) amended by 2002-2013 technical bill (Part 4 — bijuralism), effective June 26, 2013, to add "or by immovables situated in Canada or real rights therein".

212(13)(g) added by 2002-2013 technical bill (Part 5 — technical), for amounts paid or credited after Oct. 7, 2003, but read (g) opening words before July 16, 2010 as:

> (g) an amount to which paragraph (1)(i) applies if that amount affects, or is intended to affect, in any way whatever,

(The words "would apply if the amount paid or credited were paid or credited by a person resident in Canada" (rather than simply "applies") were first added in the July 16, 2010 draft, and so were made effective that day.)

212(13) earlier amended by 1994 technical bill (for amounts paid or credited after Oct. 21, 1994), 2001 *Civil Code* harmonization bill.

Regulations: 202(4) (information return).

(13.1) Application of Part XIII tax where payer or payee is a partnership — For the purposes of this Part, other than section 216,

(a) where a partnership pays or credits an amount to a non-resident person, the partnership shall, in respect of the portion of that amount that is deductible, or that would but for section 21 be deductible in computing the amount of the income or loss, as the case may be, referred to in paragraph 96(1)(f) or (g) if the references therein to "a particular place" and "that particular place" were read as references to "Canada", be deemed to be a person resident in Canada;

(a.1) where a partnership pays, credits or provides to a non-resident person an amount described in subsection (5.1), the partnership is deemed in respect of the amount to be a person; and

(b) where a person resident in Canada pays or credits an amount to a partnership (other than a Canadian partnership within the meaning assigned by section 102), the partnership shall be deemed, in respect of that payment, to be a non-resident person.

Related Provisions: 212(13.3)(b) — Authorized foreign bank deemed resident for purposes of meaning of "Canadian partnership" in para. (b); 227(15) — Partnership included in "person".

Notes: In *Gillette Canada*, 2003 FCA 22, the conversion of an existing promissory note into indebtedness payable to Gillette by a French partnership was held not to be a "loan" by Gillette to the partnership, and thus was not a "payment or credit" under 212(13.1). (See also Notes at beginning of 212(1).)

For CRA interpretation see VIEWS docs 2003-0039231E5, 2004-0072131C6, 2017-0713301I7 (para. (a)); 2009-0340031E5 (para. (b)). See also Notes to 212(2) re dividends paid to partnerships, and to 212(1) opening words re payments to partnerships generally.

See also Jesse Brodlieb, "Payments to a Partnership with a Non-Resident Member", 5(2) *Canadian Tax Focus* (ctf.ca) 3-4 (May 2015).

212(13.1)(a.1) added by 2001 technical bill, for amounts paid, credited or provided after 2000.

Regulations: 202(5) (information return).

Interpretation Bulletins: IT-81R: Partnerships — income of non-resident partners. See also at end of s. 212.

Forms: NR302: Declaration of eligibility for benefits (reduced tax) under a tax treaty for a partnership with non-resident partners.

(13.2) Application of Part XIII tax — non-resident operates in Canada — For the purposes of this Part, a particular non-resident person, who in a taxation year pays or credits to another non-resident person an amount other than an amount to which subsection (13) applies, is deemed to be a person resident in Canada in respect of the portion of the amount that is deductible in computing the particular non-resident person's taxable income earned in Canada for any taxation year from a source that is neither a treaty-protected business nor a treaty-protected property.

Notes: See Barry Segal, "Canadian Withholding Tax on Loans between Non-Residents", 16(2) *Taxation Law* (Ontario Bar Assn, oba.org) 28-32 (April 2006).

In *Easter Law Trust (Eastern Success)*, 2004 TCC 689 (Crown's FCA appeal discontinued A-600-04), amounts that became part of the cost of inventory were held not deductible in computing taxable income earned in Canada, so not subject to 212(13.2).

If 247(2) reduces the amount deductible by a Canadian branch on a payment to a related non-resident, 247(12) does not create a secondary adjustment to reduce withholding tax: VIEWS doc 2014-0530911I7.

212(13.2) amended by 2002-2013 technical bill (Part 5 — technical), for amounts paid or credited under obligations entered into after Dec. 20, 2002 (originally planned to be amounts paid or credited after that date, but changed as per Finance comfort letters, May 14, 2003 and Sept. 30, 2003).

Regulations: 202(6) (information return).

(13.3) Application of Part XIII to authorized foreign bank — An authorized foreign bank is deemed to be resident in Canada for the purposes of

(a) this Part, in respect of any amount paid or credited to or by the bank in respect of its Canadian banking business; and

(b) the application in paragraph (13.1)(b) of the definition "Canadian partnership" in respect of a partnership interest held by the bank in the course of its Canadian banking business.

Related Provisions: 218.2 — Branch interest tax on authorized foreign banks.

Notes: A 2001 Finance comfort letter reproduced here up to PITA 57th ed. proposed adjustments to s. 116 and Part XIII tax to accommodate authorized foreign banks. These were addressed by 116(6)(f), Reg. 105(2)(c) and (for 1999-2009) Reg. 803.1.

212(13.3) added by 2001 technical bill, effective June 28, 1999.

(14) [Repealed]

Notes: 212(14) repealed by 2007 budget bill #2, effective 2008, due to changes to 212(1)(b). It permitted the Minister to issue a certificate of exemption to a non-resident that was exempt from income tax in the foreign country and would be exempt in Canada. Certificates under 212(14) were generally issued by CRA to foreign pension entities, charities and certain other tax-exempt entities. With the repeal of most withholding tax on arm's length interest in 212(1)(b), they are no longer needed.

212(14)(c)(ii) amended by 1998 Budget, last change effective for applications for certificates of exemption made after 1998.

(15) Certain obligations — For the purposes of subparagraph (1)(b)(ii), after November 18, 1974 interest on a bond, debenture, note, mortgage, hypothecary claim or similar obligation that is insured by the Canada Deposit Insurance Corporation is deemed not to be interest with respect to an obligation guaranteed by the Government of Canada.

Notes: Reference to "hypothecary claim" added to 212(15) by 2001 *Civil Code* harmonization bill, effective June 14, 2001. The change is non-substantive; see *Interpretation Act* s. 8.2.

Interpretation Bulletins: IT-155R3: Exemption from non-resident tax on interest payable on certain bonds, debentures, notes, hypothecs or similar obligations. See also at end of s. 212.

(16) Payments for temporary use of rolling stock — Clause (1)(d)(vii)(A) does not apply to a payment in a year for the temporary use of railway rolling stock by a railway company to a person resident in a country other than Canada unless that country grants substantially similar relief for the year to the company in respect of payments received by it for the temporary use by a person resident in that country of railway rolling stock.

(17) Exception — This section is not applicable to payments out of or under an employee benefit plan or employee trust.

Interpretation Bulletins: IT-502: Employee benefit plans and employee trusts. See also at end of s. 212.

(17.1) Payments to the International Olympic Committee and the International Paralympic Committee — [No longer relevant]

Notes: 212(17.1) exempts the IOC and IPC from non-resident withholding tax on pre-2011 payments in respect of the 2010 Vancouver Winter Olympics and Paralympics. Added by 2007 budget bill #2, effective Dec. 14, 2007.

(18) Undertaking — Every person who in a taxation year is a prescribed financial institution or a person resident in Canada who is a registered securities dealer shall on demand from the Minister, served personally or by registered letter, file within such reasonable time as may be stipulated in the demand, an undertaking in prescribed form relating to the avoidance of payment of tax under this Part.

Related Provisions: 150.1(5) — Electronic filing; 212(19) — Tax on securities traders; 248(7)(a) — Mail deemed received on day mailed.

Notes: 212(18) amended by 2007 budget bill #2, effective 2008, to change "prescribed financial institution for the purpose of clause (1)(b)(iii)(D)" to "prescribed financial institution" and delete what was para. (a).

Regulations: 7900 (prescribed financial institutions; needs to be amended to apply to 212(18), as it applied to 212(1)(b)(iii)(D) before 2008).

Forms: NR4: Statement of amounts paid or credited to non-residents of Canada; NR4 Segment; NR4 Summ: Return of amounts paid or credited to non-residents of Canada; NR601: Non-resident ownership certificate — withholding tax; NR602: Non-resident ownership certificate — no withholding tax; T4061: Guide for payers of non-resident tax.

(19) Tax on registered securities dealers — Every taxpayer who is a registered securities dealer resident in Canada shall pay a tax under this Part equal to the amount determined by the formula

$$1/365 \times .25 \times (A - B) \times C$$

where

A is the total of all amounts each of which is the amount of money provided before the end of a day to the taxpayer (and not returned or repaid before the end of the day) by or on behalf of a non-resident person as collateral or as consideration for a security that was lent or transferred under a designated securities lending arrangement,

B is the total of

(a) all amounts each of which is the amount of money provided before the end of the day by or on behalf of the taxpayer (and not returned or repaid before the end of the day) to a non-resident person as collateral or as consideration for a security that is described in paragraph (a) of the definition "fully exempt interest" in subsection (3), or that is an obligation of the government of any country, province, state, municipality or other political subdivision, and that was lent or transferred under a securities lending arrangement, and

(b) the greater of

(i) 10 times the greatest amount determined, under the laws of the province or provinces in which the taxpayer is a registered securities dealer, to be the capital employed by the taxpayer at the end of the day, and

(ii) 20 times the greatest amount of capital required, under the laws of the province or provinces in which the taxpayer is a registered securities dealer, to be maintained by the taxpayer as a margin in respect of securities described in paragraph (a) of the definition "fully exempt interest" in subsection (3), or that is an obligation of the government of any country, province, state, municipality or other political subdivision, at the end of the day, and

C is the prescribed rate of interest in effect for the day,

and shall remit that amount to the Receiver General on or before the 15th day of the month after the month in which the day occurs.

Related Provisions: 212(18) — Return by securities traders; 212(20) — Designated securities lending arrangement; 227(9) — Penalty on tax not paid; 227(9.3) — Interest on tax not paid; 257 — Formula cannot calculate to less than zero.

Notes: 212(19) amended by 2007 budget bill #2, effective 2008 (and earlier version amended retroactive to introduction of 212(19) by 2002-2013 technical bill (Part 5 — technical)).

212(19) added by 1993 technical bill (and amended by 1994 technical bill to use the new term "registered securities dealer"), effective for securities lending arrangements entered into after May 28, 1993. See Notes to 212(1)(b)(xii).

(20) Designated SLA — For the purpose of subsection (19), a designated securities lending arrangement is a securities lending arrangement

(a) under which

(i) the lender is a prescribed financial institution or a registered securities dealer resident in Canada,

(ii) the particular security lent or transferred is an obligation described in paragraph (a) of the definition "fully exempt interest" in subsection (3) or an obligation of the government of any country, province, state, municipality or other political subdivision,

(iii) the amount of money provided to the lender at any time during the term of the arrangement either as collateral or as consideration for the particular security does not exceed 110% of the fair market value at that time of the particular security; and

(b) that was neither intended, nor made as a part of a series of securities lending arrangements, loans or other transactions that was intended, to be in effect for more than 270 days.

Notes: 212(20) added by 2007 budget bill #2, effective 2008.

Definitions [s. 212]: "active business" — 248(1); "amateur athlete trust" — 143.1(1.2)(a), 248(1); "amount" — 248(1); "annuitant" — 146(1), 146.3(1); "annuity", "authorized foreign bank" — 248(1), *Interpretation Act* 35(1); "bank" — 248(1), *Interpretation Act* 35(1); "beneficially interested" — 248(25); "business" — 248(1); "Canada" — 255, *Interpretation Act* 35(1); "Canadian banking business" — 248(1); "Canadian partnership" — 102(1), 248(1); "capital dividend" — 83(2), 248(1); "capital gain" — 39(1)(a), 248(1); "capital property" — 54, 248(1); "class" — 248(6); "common-law partner" — 248(1); "corporation" — 248(1), *Interpretation Act* 35(1); "corporeal" — Quebec *Civil Code* art. 899, 906; "credit union" — 137(6), 248(1); "custodian" — 148.1(1); "death benefit" — 248(1); "deferred profit sharing plan" — 147(1), 248(1); "designated employee benefit" — 144.1(1; "designated securities lending arrangement" — 212(20); "dividend" — 248(1); "electing ultimate funders" — 212(3.21); "eligible funeral arrangement" — 148.1(1), 248(1); "employed", "employee benefit plan" — 248(1); "employee life and health trust" — 144.1(2), 248(1); "employee trust" — 248(1); "estate" — 104(1), 248(1); "fair market value" — see 69(1) Notes; "fully collateralized arrangement" — 248(1); "fully exempt interest" — 212(3); "Her Majesty" — *Interpretation Act* 35(1); "identical" — 248(12); "immediate funder" — 212(3.1)(a); "immovable" — Quebec *Civil Code* art. 900–907; "income-averaging annuity contract" — 61(4), 248(1); "individual", "insurer" — 248(1); "interest in any such real property" — 248(4); "land" — see 70(5.2) Notes; "lease, license or similar agreement" — 212(3.94); "legislature" — *Interpretation Act* 35(1)"legislative assembly"; "management or administration fee or charge" — 212(4); "mineral resource", "Minister" — 248(1); "month" — *Interpretation Act* 35(1); "NISA Fund No. 2", "non-resident" — 248(1); "non-resident-owned investment corporation" — 133(8), 248(1); "OSFI risk-weighting guidelines", "oil or gas well" — 248(1); "participating debt interest" — 212(3); "partnership" — see 96(1) Notes; "person" — 248(1); "pooled registered pension plan" — 147.5(1), 248(1); "prescribed" — 248(1); "prescribed rate" — Reg. 4301; "principal amount" — 248(1), (26); "property" — 248(1); "province" — *Interpretation Act* 35(1); "provincial" — *Interpretation Act* 33(3), 35(1)"province"; "real rights" — 248(4.1); "registered education savings plan" — 146.1(1), 248(1); "registered pension plan" — 248(1); "registered retirement income fund" — 146.3(1), 248(1); "registered retirement savings plan" — 146(1), 147.5(12), 248(1); "registered securities dealer" — 248(1); "registered supplementary unemployment benefit plan" — 145(1), 248(1); "regulation" — 248(1); "related" — 251(2)–(6); "relevant funder", "relevant funding arrangement" — 212(3.8); "relevant licensor" — 212(3.94); "relevant period" — 212(3.1)(c); "relevant royalty arrangement" — 212(3.94); "rent, royalty or similar payment" — 212(3.94); "replacement obligation" — 212(3); "resident in Canada" — 212(13.3), 250; "retirement compensation arrangement", "retiring allowance" — 248(1); "securities lending arrangement" — 248(1), 260(1); "security interest" — 18(5); "series", "series of transactions" — 248(10); "share", "shareholder" — 248(1); "specified licensee", "specified licensor" — 212(3.8); "specified pension plan" — 248(1), Reg. 7800; "specified right" — 18(5), 212(3.8); "specified royalty arrangement" — 212(3.8), (3.94); "specified securities lending arrangement" — 248(1), 260(1); "specified share" — 212(3.8); "subsidiary wholly-owned corporation" — 248(1); "superannuation or pension benefit", "tax treaty" — 248(1); "taxable capital gain" — 38(a), 248(1); "taxable dividend" — 89(1), 248(1); "taxable income" — 2(2), 248(1); "taxable income earned in Canada" — 115(1), 248(1); "taxation year" — 249; "taxpayer" — 248(1); "timber resource property" — 13(21), 248(1); "treaty-protected business", "treaty-protected property" — 248(1); "trust" — 104(1), 248(1), (3); "ultimate funder" — 212(3.8); "ultimate licensor" — 212(3.94); "writing" — *Interpretation Act* 35(1).

Income Tax Folios [s. 212]: S5-F1-C1: Determining an individual's residence status [replaces IT-221R3].

Interpretation Bulletins [s. 212]: IT-88R2: Stock dividends; IT-109R2: Unpaid amounts; IT-168R3: Athletes and players employed by football, hockey and similar clubs; IT-280R: Employees profit sharing plans — payments computed by reference to profits. See also at beginning of 212(1).

212.1 (1) Non-arm's length sales of shares by non-residents — Subsection (1.1) applies if a non-resident person disposes of shares (in this section referred to as the **"subject shares"**) of any class of the capital stock of a corporation resident in Canada (in this section referred to as the **"subject corporation"**) to another corporation resident in Canada (in this section referred to as the **"purchaser corporation"**) with which the non-resident person does not (otherwise than because of a right referred to in paragraph 251(5)(b)) deal at arm's length and, immediately after the disposition, the subject corporation is connected (within the meaning that would be assigned by subsection 186(4) if the references in that subsection to "payer corporation" and "particular corporation" were read as "subject corporation" and "purchaser corporation", respectively, and if section 186 were read without reference to its subsection (6)) with the purchaser corporation.

Related Provisions: 212.1(1.2) — Deemed consideration; 212.1(5) — Tiered trusts and partnerships; 212.1(6) — Trusts and partnerships look-through rule.

Notes: The object of 212.1 is the same as 84.1 (taxing surplus stripping), but where the shareholder is non-resident. In general, 212.1(1.1) deems the excess sale proceeds over paid-up capital (PUC), on a non-arm's length sale, to be a deemed dividend subject to withholding tax under 212(2). See Notes to 84.1(1); Vidal, *Introduction to International Tax in Canada* (Carswell, 8th ed., 2020), chap. 11; Shew, "Post Mortem Pipeline Fails for Non-Resident Beneficiaries", 9(1) *Canadian Tax Focus* (ctf.ca) 1-2 (Feb. 2019); Nichols & Horning,. "Non-Resident Beneficiaries, Pipelines, and Section 212.1", 2530 *Tax Topics* (CCH) 1-3 (Sept. 1, 2020). 212.1 was extended in 2018 to add look-through rules for partnerships and trusts: 212.1(5), (6).

As to whether avoiding 212.1 triggers GAAR, see Notes to 245(2) and (4), and Cdn Tax Foundation 2014 conference roundtable q.4 [VIEWS doc 2014-0547401C6]. In *Collins & Aikman Products*, 2010 FCA 251, GAAR did not apply to a reorganization followed by a return of capital to the non-resident shareholder, which did not fall within 212.1 (the "limited scope" of 212.1 was "a deliberate policy choice by Parliament") (today it would be caught by 212.3). In *Univar Holdco*, 2017 FCA 207, GAAR did not apply to a reorganization done to fall within the 212.1(4) exception (see Notes to 212.1(4)). For rulings that GAAR does not apply to a sale that avoids 212.1(1) [now (1.1)], see VIEWS docs 2005-0133571R3, 2006-0211381R3, 2019-0794571R3 [2019-0833091R3]. See also Biringer, "Surplus Stripping After Copthorne", 2012 Cdn Tax Foundation conference report, 14:1-25.

For interpretation that 212.1(1) [now (1.1)] does apply see docs 2006-0192101E5; 2011-0425441R3, 2012-0459781R3, 2018-0761621R3 (cross-border butterfly — 212.1(1)(b) applies).

212.1(1) amended by 2018 budget bill #2, for dispositions after Feb. 26, 2018, to change "a non-resident person or designated partnership (in this subsection and subsections (1.1) and (1.2) referred to as the "non-resident person")" to "a non-resident person", and to add "and if section 186 were read without reference to its subsection (6)". (See now the look-through rules for partnerships in 212.1(5)-(7).)

212.1(1) amended by 2016 budget bill #2, for dispositions after March 21, 2016, moving the substantive rule to 212.1(1.1). For earlier dispositions, read:

(1) If a non-resident person, a designated partnership or a non-resident-owned investment corporation (in this section referred to as the "non-resident person") disposes of shares (in this section referred to as the "subject shares") of any class of the capital stock of a corporation resident in Canada (in this section referred to as the "subject corporation") to another corporation resident in Canada (in this section referred to as the "purchaser corporation") with which the non-resident person does not (otherwise than because of a right referred to in paragraph 251(5)(b)) deal at arm's length and, immediately after the disposition, the subject corporation is connected (within the meaning that would be assigned by subsection 186(4) if the references in that subsection to "payer corporation" and "particular corporation" were read as "subject corporation" and "purchaser corporation", respectively) with the purchaser corporation,

(a) the amount, if any, by which the fair market value of any consideration (other than any share of the capital stock of the purchaser corporation) received by the non-resident person from the purchaser corporation for the subject shares exceeds the paid-up capital in respect of the subject shares immediately before the disposition shall, for the purposes of this Act, be deemed to be a dividend paid at the time of the disposition by the purchaser corporation to the non-resident person and received at that time by the non-resident person from the purchaser corporation; and

(b) in computing the paid-up capital at any particular time after March 31, 1977 of any particular class of shares of the capital stock of the purchaser corporation, there shall be deducted that proportion of the amount, if any, by which the increase, if any, by virtue of the disposition in the paid-up capital, computed without reference to this section as it applies to the disposition, in respect of all of the shares of the capital stock of the purchaser corporation exceeds the amount, if any, by which

(i) the paid-up capital in respect of the subject shares immediately before the disposition

exceeds

(ii) the fair market value of the consideration described in paragraph (a),

that the increase, if any, by virtue of the disposition, in the paid-up capital, computed without reference to this section as it applies to the disposition, in respect of the particular class of shares is of the increase, if any, by virtue of the disposition, in the paid-up capital, computed without reference to this section as it applies to the disposition, in respect of all of the issued shares of the capital stock of the purchaser corporation.

212.1(1) opening words amended by 1998 Budget, effective February 24, 1998.

Interpretation Bulletins: See at end of s. 212.1.

Information Circulars: 77-16R4: Non-resident income tax.

(1.1) Non-arm's length sales of shares by non-residents — If this subsection applies,

(a) the amount, if any, by which the fair market value of any consideration (other than any share of the capital stock of the purchaser corporation) received by the non-resident person referred to in subsection (1) from the purchaser corporation for the subject shares exceeds the paid-up capital in respect of the subject shares immediately before the disposition shall, for the purposes of this Act, be deemed to be a dividend

(i) in the case that, immediately before the disposition, the purchaser corporation controlled the non-resident person,

(A) paid at the time of the disposition by the subject corporation to the non-resident person, and

(B) received at that time by the non-resident person from the subject corporation, and

(ii) in any other case,

(A) paid at the time of the disposition by the purchaser corporation to the non-resident person, and

(B) received at that time by the non-resident person from the purchaser corporation; and

(b) in computing the paid-up capital at any particular time after March 31, 1977 of any particular class of shares of the capital stock of the purchaser corporation, there shall be deducted that proportion of the amount, if any, by which the increase, if any, by virtue of the disposition, in the paid-up capital, computed without reference to this section as it applies to the disposition, in respect of all of the shares of the capital stock of the purchaser corporation exceeds the amount, if any, by which

(i) the paid-up capital in respect of the subject shares immediately before the disposition

exceeds

(ii) the fair market value of the consideration described in paragraph (a),

that the increase, if any, by virtue of the disposition, in the paid-up capital, computed without reference to this section as it applies to the disposition, in respect of the particular class of shares is of the increase, if any, by virtue of the disposition, in the paid-up capital, computed without reference to this section as it applies to the disposition, in respect of all of the issued shares of the capital stock of the purchaser corporation.

Related Provisions: 54"proceeds of disposition"(k) — Exclusion of deemed dividend from proceeds; 84(7) — When dividend payable; 84.1 — Similar rule for residents of Canada; 186(7) — Interpretation of "connected"; 212.1(1) — Conditions for 212.1(1.1) to apply; 212.1(1.2) — Deemed consideration; 212.1(4) — Exception on disposition to parent; 212.1(5) — Tiered trusts and partnerships; 212.1(6) — Trusts and partnerships look-through rule; 212.2 — Deemed dividend on surplus strip to non-resident insurer.

Notes: See Notes to 212.1(1).

212.1(1.1)(a) opening words amended by 2018 budget bill #2, for dispositions after Feb. 26, 2018, to change "non-resident person" to "non-resident person referred to in subsection (1)".

212.1(1.1) added by 2016 budget bill #2, for dispositions after March 21, 2016. (This rule was previously in 212.1(1).)

(1.2) Deemed consideration — For the purposes of subsections (1) and (1.1), if, in the absence of this subsection, no consideration would be received by the non-resident person referred to in subsection (1) from the purchaser corporation for the subject shares, the non-resident person is deemed to receive consideration other than shares of the capital stock of the purchaser corporation from the purchaser corporation for the subject shares, the fair market value of which is equal to the amount, if any, by which the fair market value of the subject shares disposed of by the non-resident person exceeds the amount of any increase because of the disposition in the fair market value of the shares of the capital stock of the purchaser corporation.

Notes: 212.1(1.2) amended by 2018 budget bill #2, for dispositions after Feb. 26, 2018, to change "non-resident person" to "non-resident person referred to in subsection (1)".

212.1(1.2) added by 2016 budget bill #2, for dispositions after March 21, 2016.

(2) Idem [PUC addition] — In computing the paid-up capital at any particular time after March 31, 1977 of any particular class of shares of the capital stock of a corporation, there shall be added an amount equal to the lesser of

(a) the amount, if any, by which

(i) the total of all amounts each of which is an amount deemed by subsection 84(3), (4) or (4.1) to be a dividend on shares of the particular class paid after March 31, 1977 and before the particular time by the corporation and received by a non-resident-owned investment corporation or by a person who is not a corporation resident in Canada

exceeds

(ii) the total that would be determined under subparagraph (i) if this Act were read without reference to paragraph (1.1)(b), and

(b) the total of all amounts each of which is an amount required by paragraph (1.1)(b) to be deducted in computing the paid-up capital in respect of the particular class of shares after March 31, 1977 and before the particular time.

Notes: 212.1(2)(a)(ii) and (b) amended by 2016 budget bill #2, for dispositions after March 21, 2016, to change "212.1(1)(b)" to "212.1(1.1)(b)".

(3) Idem [relationship rules] — For the purposes of this section,

(a) a non-resident person shall, for greater certainty, be deemed not to deal at arm's length with a purchaser corporation at the time of a disposition described in subsection (1) if the non-resident person was,

(i) immediately before the disposition, one of a group of less than 6 persons that controlled the subject corporation, and

(ii) immediately after the disposition, one of a group of less than 6 persons that controlled the purchaser corporation, each member of which was a member of the group referred to in subparagraph (i);

(b) for the purposes of determining whether or not a non-resident person referred to in paragraph (a) was a member of a group of less than six persons that controlled a corporation at any time, any shares of the capital stock of that corporation owned at that time by any of the following persons shall be deemed to be owned at that time by the non-resident person and not by the person who actually owned the shares at that time:

(i) the non-resident person's "child" (within the meaning assigned by subsection 70(10)), who is under 18 years of age, or the non-resident person's spouse or common-law partner,

(ii) a trust of which the non-resident person, a person described in subparagraph (i) or a corporation described in subparagraph (iii) is a beneficiary,

(iii) a corporation controlled by the non-resident person, a person described in subparagraph (i), a trust described in subparagraph (ii) or any combination thereof, and

(iv) a partnership of which the non-resident person or a person described in one of subparagraphs (i) to (iii) is a majority-interest partner or a member of a "majority-interest group of partners" (as defined in subsection 251.1(3));

(c) a trust and a beneficiary of the trust or a person related to a beneficiary of the trust shall be deemed not to deal with each other at arm's length;

(d) for the purpose of paragraph (a),

(i) a group of persons in respect of a corporation means any 2 or more persons each of whom owns shares of the capital stock of the corporation,

(ii) a corporation that is controlled by one or more members of a particular group of persons in respect of that corporation shall be considered to be controlled by that group of persons, and

(iii) a corporation may be controlled by a person or a particular group of persons notwithstanding that the corporation is also controlled or deemed to be controlled by another person or group of persons; and

(e) [Repealed]

(f) in this subsection, a person includes a partnership.

Related Provisions: 256(6), (6.1) — Meaning of "controlled".

Notes: 212.1(3)(a) opening words amended by 2018 budget bill #2, for dispositions after Feb. 26, 2018, to change "non-resident person or designated partnership" to "non-resident person" (2x). See now the look-through rules for partnerships in 212.1(5)-(7).

212.1(3)(b) amended by 2018 budget bill #2, for dispositions after Feb. 26, 2018, to change "a particular non-resident person or designated partnership (in this paragraph referred to as the "taxpayer")" to "a non-resident person"; to add "by any of the following persons shall be deemed to be owned at that time by the non-resident person and not by the person who actually owned the shares at that time" in opening words; and to change "taxpayer" to "non-resident person" in paras. (i)-(iv).

212.1(3)(e) repealed by 2018 budget bill #2, for dispositions after Feb. 26, 2018. It read:

(e) a "designated partnership" means a partnership of which either a majority-interest partner or every member of a majority-interest group of partners (as defined in subsection 251.1(3)) is a non-resident person; and

212.1(3)(a) opening words amended, and (b) opening words amended to add "or designated partnership", by 2016 budget bill #2, for dispositions after March 21, 2016. For earlier dispositions, read (a) opening words as:

(a) in respect of any disposition described in subsection (1) by a non-resident person of shares of the capital stock of a subject corporation to a purchaser corporation, the non-resident person shall, for greater certainty, be deemed not to deal at arm's length with the purchaser corporation if the non-resident person was,

212.1(3)(b)(iv) and (e) amended by 2013 budget bill #2, effective Dec. 12, 2013, to change "majority interest" to "majority-interest" (with a hyphen).

212.1(3)(b)(i) amended by 2000 same-sex partners bill to refer to "common-law partner", effective as per Notes to 248(1)"common-law partner".

212.1(3) amended by 1978 Budget, by 1991 technical bill, by 1992 technical bill and by 1998 Budget. Current version effective February 24, 1998.

(4) Where section does not apply — Notwithstanding subsection (1), subsection (1.1) does not apply in respect of a disposition by a non-resident corporation of shares of a subject corporation to a purchaser corporation if

(a) immediately before the disposition, the purchaser corporation controlled the non-resident corporation; and

(b) it is not the case that, at the time of the disposition, or as part of a transaction or event or series of transactions or events that includes the disposition, a non-resident person

(i) holds, directly or indirectly, shares of the capital stock of the purchaser corporation, and

(ii) does not deal at arm's length with the purchaser corporation.

Related Provisions: 256(6), (6.1) — Meaning of "controlled".

Notes: A reorganization so as to fall within pre-2016 212.1(4) did not trigger GAAR (245(2)) in *Univar Holdco*, 2017 FCA 207, as 212.1 does not apply to an arm's-length sale (para. 19). The 2016 amendment did not make the 2007 transaction abusive (para. 29). See Aiken & Kopstein case comment, 66(1) *Canadian Tax Journal* 111-18 (2018).

For discussion of the 2016 amendment (adding para. (b)), see Angelo Nikolakakis, "Cross-Border Surplus Stripping", 87 *International Tax* (CCH) 4-8 (May 2016); CBA/CPA Canada Joint Committee letter to Finance, July 25, 2016, pp. 13-31.

In VIEWS doc 2013-0483771C6 [2013 IFA q.4], CRA considered 3 scenarios that used (pre-2016) 212.1(4) to avoid 212.1, and concluded 212.3 now applies to each one [see Calvert & Mar, "Recent Transactions", 2013 Cdn Tax Foundation conference report at 7:12-14; and Notes to 212.3].

212.1(4)(b) amended by 2018 budget bill #2, for dispositions after Feb. 26, 2018, to delete "or designated partnership" at end of opening words and to change "owns" to "holds" in (b)(i).

212.1(4) amended by 2016 budget bill #2, for dispositions after March 21, 2016. For earlier dispositions, read:

> (4) Notwithstanding subsection (1), this section does not apply in respect of a disposition by a non-resident corporation of shares of a subject corporation to a purchaser corporation that immediately before the disposition controlled the non-resident corporation.

(5) Tiered trusts and partnerships — For the purposes of this section and paragraph (k) of the definition "proceeds of disposition" in section 54, a person or partnership that is, at any time, a beneficiary under a trust (other than a trust that is the non-resident person referred to in subsection (1)), or a member of a partnership (such trust or partnership referred to in this subsection as the "particular conduit"), that is a beneficiary under a trust or member of a partnership (such trust or partnership referred to in this subsection as the "other conduit") is deemed

(a) to be a beneficiary under or member of, as the case may be, the other conduit; and

(b) to hold the interest in the other conduit that is held by the particular conduit in the proportion expressed by the formula

$$A/B$$

where

A is the portion of the fair market value, at that time, of the person or partnership's interest in the particular conduit that is attributable to the interest in the other conduit held by the particular conduit, and

B is the total fair market value, at that time, of all direct interests (determined without reference to this subsection) in the other conduit.

Related Provisions: 212.1(7) — Anti-avoidance rule.

Notes: 212.1(5) added by 2018 budget bill #2, for dispositions after Feb. 26, 2018.

(6) Trusts and partnerships look-through rule — The following rules apply for the following purposes:

(a) for the purposes of this subsection and subsections (1) and (1.1), if at any time an interest (in this paragraph referred to as the "pertinent interest") in a trust or a partnership (each referred to in this subsection as a "conduit") is disposed of by a person or partnership with an interest as a beneficiary under the conduit or that is a member of the conduit (each referred to in this subsection as a "holder"), as the case may be, to a purchaser and any portion of the fair market value of the pertinent interest is attributable to shares of the capital stock of a corporation resident in Canada held, directly or indirectly (unless all of the shares are held indirectly through one or more non-resident corporations), by the conduit (in this paragraph referred to as the "shares held by the conduit"), then

(i) the holder is deemed, on a class-by-class basis, to have disposed, at that time, of the shares held by the conduit to the purchaser, and the purchaser is deemed to have acquired the shares, in the proportion expressed by the formula

$$A/B$$

where

A is the portion of the fair market value, at that time, of the pertinent interest that is attributable to the shares held by the conduit, and

B is the total fair market value, at that time, of the shares held by the conduit, and

(ii) the holder is deemed to have received from the purchaser and the purchaser is deemed to have paid to the holder, as consideration for the shares deemed to have been disposed of in subparagraph (i), consideration (other than any share of the capital stock of the purchaser corporation) in an amount determined by the formula

$$A \times B/C$$

where

A is the fair market value of the consideration (other than any share of the capital stock of the purchaser corporation) that is received by the holder from the purchaser for the pertinent interest,

B is the amount determined for A in subparagraph (i), and

C is the total fair market value of the pertinent interest;

(b) for the purposes of subsections (1) and (1.1) and paragraph (c), if at any time a conduit (other than a non-resident trust) disposes of shares of the capital stock of a corporation resident in Canada to a purchaser, then

(i) each holder of an interest in the conduit is deemed, on a class-by-class basis, to have disposed, at that time, of the shares to the purchaser in the proportion expressed by the formula

$$A/B$$

where

A is the fair market value, at that time, of the holder's interest in the conduit, and

B is the total fair market value, at that time, of all direct interests (determined without reference to subsection (5)) in the conduit, and

(ii) each holder of an interest in the conduit is deemed to have received from the purchaser and the purchaser is deemed to have paid to each such holder, as consideration for the shares deemed to have been disposed of in subparagraph (i), consideration (other than any share of the capital stock of the purchaser corporation) in an amount determined by the formula

$$A \times B/C$$

where

A is the fair market value of the consideration (other than any share of the capital stock of the purchaser corporation) that is received by the conduit from the purchaser for the shares,

B is the amount determined for A in subparagraph (i), and

C is the amount determined for B in subparagraph (i);

In Budget 2018 (February 27, 2018), the Government proposed measures to ensure that this rule could not be frustrated by transactions involving partnerships or trusts. Draft legislative proposals were released for public consultation on July 27, 2018. In this consultative draft, a partnership's disposition of shares of a corporation resident in Canada was to be allocated to its members, based on the relative fair market value of their interests. Legislative amendments were included in *Budget Implementation Act, 2018, No. 2*, and, effective for dispositions after February 26, 2018, the look-through rule for dispositions of shares, enacted in paragraph 212.1(6)(b) of the Act, is applicable to dispositions of shares by partnerships as well as by Canadian resident trusts, including graduated rate estates.

In communications with officials of the Tax Legislation Division, concerns were expressed regarding the application of the look-through rule in paragraph 212.1(6)(b) to a Canadian resident graduated rate estate with one or more non-resident beneficiaries. Specifically, there is concern that this look-through rule will reduce the ability of such an estate to implement certain post-mortem tax planning transactions that are commonly undertaken.

We understand that this post-mortem tax planning is generally implemented by the graduated rate estate selling the shares of a Canadian resident corporation ("Canco") held at death to a new Canadian corporation ("NewCanco") in exchange for a promissory note equal to the graduated rate estate's adjusted cost base ("ACB") in the Canco shares (which ACB is generally equal to the fair market value of the Canco shares at the deceased's date of death). Our further understanding is that, under this post-mortem tax planning, tax is generally payable in respect of the deemed disposition of the Canco shares on the deceased's death, and not payable in respect of the corporate surplus that is eventually extracted by the graduated rate estate through the repayment of the promissory note.

With the application of paragraph 212.1(6)(b), when the graduated rate estate disposes of the Canco shares to the NewCanco, each holder of an interest in the trust (i.e., each beneficiary) is deemed, for the purposes of subsections 212.1(1) and (1.1), to have disposed of their proportionate interest in the Canco shares to the NewCanco and to have received their proportionate share of consideration from the NewCanco. In general, under paragraph 212.1(6)(b) of the Act, each beneficiary of the graduated rate estate that implements this post-mortem tax planning is treated, for the purposes of subsections 212.1(1) and (1.1), as having implemented it directly, based on the relative fair market value of their interest in the estate.

Where the conditions of subsection 212.1(1) are satisfied, each non-resident beneficiary is deemed to have received a dividend from the NewCanco to the extent that the non-resident beneficiary's proportionate share of the promissory note from the New-Canco exceeds the PUC of the non-resident beneficiary's proportionate interest in the Canco shares transferred to the NewCanco. As a result, tax is payable in respect of this deemed dividend to the non-resident beneficiary.

Our Comments

We agree that the application of paragraph 212.1(6)(b) of the Act can give rise to results in the context of graduated rate estates that are not consistent with current tax policy. Therefore, we are prepared to recommend to the Minister of Finance that the Act be amended to exclude, from the application of paragraph 212.1(6)(b), dispositions of shares by a Canadian resident graduated rate estate of an individual who was resident in Canada immediately before the individual's death, provided that those shares were acquired by the estate on and as a consequence of the individual's death. We also intend to recommend that this proposed amendment apply to dispositions after February 26, 2018.

While we cannot offer any assurances that either the Minister of Finance or Parliament will agree with our recommendations, we hope that this statement of our intention is helpful.

Yours sincerely,

Brian Ernewein, Assistant Deputy Minister — Legislation, Tax Policy Branch

[Identical letters TL-26, TL-27 and TL-28 issued to Jehad Haymour & Marshall Haughey (Bennett Jones, Calgary); Grace Chow & Henry Shew (Cadesky Tax, Toronto); Alexander Demner & Kyle Lamothe, Thorsteinssons (Toronto) — ed.]

Notes: See Lamothe & Demner, "Section 212.1 Post Mortem Pipeline Comfort Letter", 20(2) *Tax for the Owner-Manager* (ctf.ca) 8-9 (April 2020).

(c) for the purposes of subsections (1) and (1.1), if at any time a conduit acquires shares of the capital stock of a corporation resident in Canada from a vendor, then

(i) each holder of an interest in the conduit is deemed to have acquired, at that time, the shares from the vendor, on a class-by-class basis, in the proportion expressed by the formula

$$A/B$$

where

A is the fair market value, at that time, of the holder's interest in the conduit and

B is the total fair market value, at that time, of all direct interests (determined without reference to subsection (5)) in the conduit, and

(ii) each holder of an interest in the conduit is deemed to have paid to the vendor and the vendor is deemed to have received from each such holder, as consideration for the shares deemed to have been acquired in subparagraph (i), consideration (other than any share of the capital stock of the purchaser corporation) in an amount determined by the formula

$$A \times B/C$$

where

A is the fair market value of the consideration (other than any share of the capital stock of the purchaser corporation) that is paid by the conduit to the vendor for the shares,

B is the amount determined for A in subparagraph (i), and

C is the amount determined for B in subparagraph (i); and

(d) for the purpose of determining whether the subject corporation is connected with the purchaser corporation for the purposes of subsection (1) at any time, if at that time a conduit owns shares of the capital stock of the subject corporation, each holder of an interest in the conduit is deemed to own, at that time, the shares of each class of the capital stock of the subject corporation that are owned by the conduit the number of which is determined by the formula

$$A \times B/C$$

where

A is the total number of shares of the class of the capital stock of the subject corporation that are owned by the conduit at that time,

B is the fair market value, at that time, of the holder's interest in the conduit, and

C is the total fair market value, at that time, of all direct interests (determined without reference to subsection (5)) in the conduit.

Related Provisions: 212.1(7) — Anti-avoidance rule.

Notes: See Demner & Lamothe, "Section 212.1 Lookthrough Rules Create Issues for Trusts with Non-Resident Beneficiaries", 19(2) *Tax for the Owner-Manager* (ctf.ca) 2-4 (April 2019).

212.1(6) can apply to a post-mortem "pipeline" (see Notes to 84(2)), but Finance's Dec. 2, 2019 comfort letter (above) will provide relief in many cases: CRA, 2019-0824561C6 [2019 CTF q.5].

212.1(6) added by 2018 budget bill #2, for dispositions after Feb. 26, 2018.

(7) Avoidance of subsecs. (5) and (6) — The amounts determined for A and B in paragraph (5)(b), for A and B in subparagraph (6)(c)(i) and for B and C in paragraph (6)(d) are, in respect of an interest as a beneficiary under a trust held by a person or partnership deemed to be equal to one if

(a) the person or partnership's share of the accumulating income or capital of the trust depends on the exercise by any person of, or the failure by any person to exercise, any discretionary power; and

(b) it can reasonably be considered that one of the reasons for the discretionary power is to avoid or limit the application of subsection (1.1).

Notes: 212.1(7) added by 2018 budget bill #2, for dispositions after Feb. 26, 2018.

Definitions [s. 212.1]: "amount" — 248(1); "arm's length" — 212.1(3)(c), 251(1), 260(9.1); "beneficiary" — 248(25) [Notes]; "Canada" — 255; "Canadian corporation" — 89(1), 248(1); "child" — 70(10), 252(1); "class of shares" — 248(6); "common-law partner" — 248(1); "connected" — 186(4), (7); "control" — 212.1(3)(d); "controlled" — 256(6), (6.1); "corporation" — 248(1), *Interpretation Act* 35(1); "disposition", "dividend" — 248(1); "fair market value" — see 69(1) Notes; "group" — 212.1(3)(c); "majority-interest partner", "non-resident" — 248(1); "non-resident-owned investment corporation" — 133(8), 248(1); "owned" — 212.1(3)(b); "paid-up capital" — 89(1), 248(1); "partnership" — see 96(1) Notes; "person" — 212.1(3)(f), 248(1); "purchaser corporation" — 212.1(1); "received" — 248(7); "resident in Canada" — 250; "series of transactions" — 248(10); "share" — 248(1); "subject corporation" — 212.1(1); "subject shares" — 212.1(1); "taxpayer" — 248(1); "trust" — 104(1), 108(1), 248(1), (3).

Interpretation Bulletins [s. 212.1]: IT-88R2: Stock dividends; IT-109R2: Unpaid amounts; IT-489R: Non-arm's length sale of shares to a corporation.

212.2 (1) Application [demutualization surplus stripping] — This section applies where

(a) a taxpayer disposes at a particular time of a share of the capital stock of a corporation resident in Canada (or any property more than 10% of the fair market value of which can be attributed to shares of the capital stock of corporations resident in Canada) to

   (i) a person resident in Canada,

   (ii) a partnership in which any person resident in Canada has, directly or indirectly, an interest, or

   (iii) a person or partnership that acquires the share or the property in the course of carrying on a business through a permanent establishment in Canada, as defined in the *Income Tax Regulations*;

(b) subsection 212.1(1.1) does not apply in respect of the disposition;

(c) the taxpayer is non-resident at the particular time;

(d) it is reasonable to conclude that the disposition is part of an expected series of transactions or events that includes the issue after December 15, 1998 of a particular share of the capital stock of a particular insurance corporation resident in Canada on the demutualization (within the meaning assigned by subsection 139.1(1)) of the particular corporation and

   (i) after the particular time, the redemption, acquisition or cancellation of the particular share, or a share substituted for the particular share, by the particular corporation or the issuer of the substituted share, as the case may be,

   (ii) after the particular time, an increase in the level of dividends declared or paid on the particular share or a share substituted for the particular share, or

   (iii) the acquisition, at or after the particular time, of the particular share or a share substituted for the particular share by

      (A) a person not dealing at arm's length with the particular corporation or with the issuer of the substituted share, as the case may be, or

      (B) a partnership any direct or indirect interest in which is held by a person not dealing at arm's length with the particular corporation or with the issuer of the substituted share, as the case may be; and

(e) at the particular time, the person described in subparagraph (a)(i) or (iii) or any person who has, directly or indirectly, an interest in the partnership described in subparagraph (a)(ii) or (iii) knew, or ought reasonably to have known, of the expected series of transactions or events described in paragraph (d).

Related Provisions: 248(10) — Series of transactions.

Notes: See Notes at end of 212.2.

212.2(1)(b) amended by 2016 budget bill #2, for dispositions after March 21, 2016, to change "212.1(1)" to "212.1(1.1)".

Regulations: No regulation defining "permanent establishment" as yet (though Reg. 8201 would be the logical choice).

(2) Deemed dividend — For the purposes of this Part, where property is disposed of at any time by a taxpayer to a person or partnership in circumstances in which this section applies,

(a) a taxable dividend is deemed to be paid at that time by the person or partnership to the taxpayer and received at the time by the taxpayer;

(b) the amount of the dividend is deemed to be equal to the amount determined by the formula

$$A - ((A/B) \times C)$$

where

A is the portion of the proceeds of disposition of the property that can reasonably be attributed to the fair market value of

shares of a class of the capital stock of a corporation resident in Canada,

B is the fair market value immediately before that time of shares of that class, and

C is the paid-up capital immediately before that time of that class of shares; and

(c) in respect of the dividend, the person or partnership is deemed to be a corporation resident in Canada.

Related Provisions [subsec. 212.2(2)]: 54"proceeds of disposition"(k) — Exclusion of deemed dividend from proceeds; 257 — Formula cannot calculate to less than zero.

Notes [212.2]: 212.2 added by 1999 Budget, effective Dec. 16, 1998. It is an antiavoidance "surplus stripping" rule designed, in the context of the demutualization of insurance corps (see 139.1), to discourage transactions designed to allow Canadian corporate surplus to be distributed to non-residents free of Part XIII withholding tax.

For interpretation of "reasonably be attributed" in A, see *729658 Alberta Ltd.*, 2004 TCC 474.

Definitions [s. 212.2]: "amount" — 248(1); "arm's length" — 251(1), 260(9.1); "business" — 248(1); "Canada" — 255, *Interpretation Act* 35(1); "class of shares" — 248(6); "corporation" — 248(1), *Interpretation Act* 35(1); "demutualization" — 139.1(1); "disposition", "dividend" — 248(1); "fair market value" — see 69(1) Notes; "insurance corporation", "non-resident" — 248(1); "paid-up capital" — 89(1), 248(1); "partnership" — see 96(1) Notes; "person", "property" — 248(1); "resident in Canada" — 250; "series of transactions" — 248(10); "share" — 248(1); "substituted" — 248(5); "taxable dividend" — 89(1), 248(1); "taxpayer" — 248(1).

212.3 (1) Foreign affiliate dumping — conditions for application — Subsection (2) applies to an investment in a non-resident corporation (in this section referred to as the "subject corporation") made at any time (in this section referred to as the "investment time") by a corporation resident in Canada (in this section referred to as the "CRIC") if

(a) the subject corporation is immediately after the investment time, or becomes as part of a transaction or event or series of transactions or events that includes the making of the investment, a foreign affiliate of

   (i) the CRIC, or

   (ii) a corporation that does not deal at arm's length with the CRIC (if the condition in this paragraph is satisfied because of this subparagraph and not because of subparagraph (i), such a corporation is referred to in paragraph (b) as an "other Canadian corporation");

(b) the CRIC or an other Canadian corporation is immediately after the investment time, or becomes after the investment time and as part of a transaction or event or series of transactions or events that includes the making of the investment, controlled by one non-resident person or, if no single non-resident person controls the CRIC, by a group of non-resident persons not dealing with each other at arm's length (in this section, that one non-resident person, or each member of the group of non-resident persons, as the case may be, is referred to as a "parent", and the group of non-resident persons, if any, is referred to as the "group of parents"), and any of the following conditions is satisfied:

   (i) if, at the investment time, a parent owned all shares of the capital stock of the CRIC and the other Canadian corporation, if applicable, that are owned — determined without reference to paragraph (25)(b) in the case of partnerships referred to in this subparagraph and as if all rights referred to in paragraph 251(5)(b), of the parent, each person that does not deal at arm's length with the parent and all of those partnerships, were immediate and absolute and the parent and each of the other persons and partnerships had exercised those rights at the investment time — by the parent, persons that are not dealing at arm's length with the parent and partnerships of which the parent or a person that is not dealing at arm's length with the parent is a member (other than a limited partner within the meaning assigned by subsection

96(2.4)), the parent would own shares of the capital stock of the CRIC or the other Canadian corporation that

(A) give the holders of those shares 25% or more of all of the votes that could be cast at any annual meeting of the shareholders in respect of all shares of the capital stock of the CRIC or the other Canadian corporation, as the case may be, or

(B) have a fair market value of 25% or more of the fair market value of all of the issued and outstanding shares of the capital stock of the CRIC or the other Canadian corporation, as the case may be,

(ii) the investment is an acquisition of shares of the capital stock of a subject corporation by a CRIC to which this subparagraph applies because of subsection (19), or

(iii) under an arrangement entered into in connection with the investment, a person or partnership, other than the CRIC or a person related to the CRIC, has in any material respect the risk of loss or opportunity for gain or profit in respect of a property that can reasonably be considered to relate to the investment; and

(c) neither subsection (16) nor (18) applies in respect of the investment.

Related Provisions: 93.1(1) — Shares held by a partnership; 93.3(3), (4)(c) — Special rule for certain Australian trusts; 128.1(1)(c.3) — Foreign affiliate dumping — corporate immigration; 212.3(10)–(14) — Meaning of "investment" in a subject corporation; 212.3(15) — Restricted meaning of "controlled"; 212.3(19) — Preferred shares; 212.3(23) — Indirect investment; 212.3(25) — Application to partnerships; 219.1(2) — Foreign affiliate dumping — corporate emigration; 248(10) — Series of transactions.

Notes: See Notes at end of 212.3.

212.3(1)(b) before (i)(A amended by 2021 budget bill #1, for transactions or events after March 18, 2019, to cover control by non-resident groups or individuals. Before then, read:

(b) the CRIC or an other Canadian corporation is immediately after the investment time, or becomes after the investment time and as part of a transaction or event or series of transactions or events that includes the making of the investment, controlled by a non-resident corporation (in this section referred to as the "parent"), and any of the following conditions is satisfied:

(i) if, at the investment time, the parent owned all shares of the capital stock of the CRIC and the other Canadian corporation, if applicable, that are owned — determined without reference to paragraph (25)(b) in the case of partnerships referred to in this subparagraph and as if all rights referred to in paragraph 251(5)(b), of the parent, each person that does not deal at arm's length with the parent and all of those partnerships, were immediate and absolute and the parent and each of the other persons and partnerships had exercised those rights at the investment time — by the parent, persons that are not dealing at arm's length with the parent and partnerships of which the parent or a non-resident person that is not dealing at arm's length with the parent is a member (other than a limited partner within the meaning assigned by subsection 96(2.4)), the parent would own shares of the capital stock of the CRIC or the other Canadian corporation that

212.3(1) amended by 2017 budget bill #2, to add (a)(ii) and to add each reference to "the other Canadian corporation" in (b), effective in respect of transactions or events that occur after Sept. 15, 2016. For this purpose, a portion of a particular amount owing by, or debt obligation of, a particular subject corporation is deemed to be a separate amount owing or debt obligation that became owing or was acquired, as the case may be, on Jan. 1, 2017 in the same manner and on the same terms as the particular amount owing or debt obligation if

(a) 212.3(2) would not apply in respect of the separate amount owing or debt obligation absent these amendments;

(b) the particular amount owing or debt obligation became owing to, or was acquired by, a CRIC

(i) after March 28, 2012 and before Sept. 16, 2016, or

(ii) before March 29, 2012, if its maturity date was extended after March 28, 2012 and before Sept. 16, 2016; and

(c) the portion is the amount outstanding in respect of the particular amount owing or debt obligation on Jan. 1, 2017.

212.3(1)(b) opening words amended by 2014 budget bill #2, retroactive to transactions and events that occur after March 28, 2012, effectively to add subparas. (i)-(iii).

The Aug. 16, 2013 draft legislation proposed a **212.3(1.1)** to define "dividend time". That definition is now in 212.3(4).

(2) Foreign affiliate dumping — consequences — If this subsection applies to an investment in a subject corporation made by a CRIC,

(a) for the purposes of this Part and subject to subsections (3) and (7), the CRIC is deemed to have paid to each parent, and each parent is deemed to have received from the CRIC, at the dividend time, a dividend in an amount determined by the formula

$$A \times B/C$$

where

A is the total of all amounts each of which is the portion of the fair market value at the investment time of any property (not including shares of the capital stock of the CRIC) transferred, any obligation assumed or incurred, or any benefit otherwise conferred, by the CRIC, or of any property transferred to the CRIC which transfer results in the reduction of an amount owing to the CRIC, that can reasonably be considered to relate to the investment,

B is

(i) if there is one parent, one, and

(ii) if there is a group of parents, the fair market value at the dividend time of the shares of the capital stock of the CRIC that are held, directly or indirectly, by the parent, and

C is

(i) if there is one parent, one, and

(ii) if there is a group of parents, the total of all amounts each of which is the fair market value at the dividend time of the shares of the capital stock of the CRIC that are held, directly or indirectly, by a parent; and

(b) in computing the paid-up capital in respect of any class of shares of the capital stock of the CRIC at any time that is at or after the investment time, there is to be deducted the amount of any increase in the paid-up capital in respect of the class, determined without reference to this section, that can reasonably be considered to relate to the investment.

Related Provisions: 212(2) — Withholding tax on deemed dividend; 212.3(1) — Application of 212.3(2); 212.3(3) — Election for substituted dividend; 212.3(4) — Meaning of "dividend time"; 212.3(5) — Effect of modification of terms under 212.3(10)(e); 212.3(5.1) — Sequential investments; 212.3(7) — Reduction of deemed dividend; 212.3(8), (9) — Adjustments to paid-up capital; 212.3(10)–(14) — Meaning of "investment" in a subject corporation; 212.3(16), (17) — Exception — more closely connected business activities; 212.3(18)–(21) — Exception — corporate reorganization; 212.3(22) — Effect of amalgamation or windup; 212.3(23) — Indirect investment; 212.3(24) — Exception — indirect funding; 212.3(25) — Application to partnerships; 219.1(3)(b) — PUC reinstatement of emigrating corporation after 212.3(2)(b) applies; 247(15) — No application to transfer pricing amount deemed to be dividend for non-resident withholding tax.

Notes: See Notes at end of 212.3.

212.3(2)(a) amended by 2021 budget bill #1, for transactions or events after March 18, 2019, to cover control by non-resident groups or individuals. Before then, read:

(a) for the purposes of this Part and subject to subsections (3) and (7), the CRIC is deemed to have paid to the parent, and the parent is deemed to have received from the CRIC, at the dividend time, a dividend equal to the total of all amounts each of which is the portion of the fair market value at the investment time of any property (not including shares of the capital stock of the CRIC) transferred, any obligation assumed or incurred, or any benefit otherwise conferred, by the CRIC, or of any property transferred to the CRIC which transfer results in the reduction of an amount owing to the CRIC, that can reasonably be considered to relate to the investment; and

212.3(2)(a) amended by 2014 budget bill #2, retroactive to transactions and events that occur after March 28, 2012.

(3) Dividend substitution election — If a CRIC (or a CRIC and a corporation that is a qualifying substitute corporation in respect of the CRIC at the dividend time) and a parent (or a parent and another non-resident person that at the dividend time is related to the parent) jointly elect in writing under this subsection in respect of an investment, and the election is filed with the Minister on or before the filing-due date of the CRIC for its taxation year that includes the dividend time, then the dividend that would, in the absence of this subsection, be deemed under paragraph (2)(a) to have been paid by the CRIC to the parent and received by the parent from the CRIC is deemed to have instead been

(a) paid by the CRIC or the qualifying substitute corporation, as agreed on in the election; and

(b) paid to, and received by, the parent or the other non-resident person, as agreed on in the election.

Related Provisions: 212.3(4)"dividend time", "qualifying substitute corporation" — Definitions; 212.3(7) — Reduction of deemed dividend; 212.3(12), (13) — Late-filed election; 212.3(15) — Restricted meaning of "controlled".

Notes: 212.3(3) amended by 2021 budget bill #1, for transactions or events after March 18, 2019, to cover control by non-resident groups or individuals. Before then, read:

(3) If a CRIC (or a CRIC and a corporation that is a qualifying substitute corporation in respect of the CRIC at the dividend time) and the parent (or the parent and another non-resident corporation that at the dividend time does not deal at arm's length with the parent) jointly elect in writing under this subsection in respect of an investment, and the election is filed with the Minister on or before the filing-due date of the CRIC for its taxation year that includes the dividend time, then the dividend that would, in the absence of this subsection, be deemed under paragraph (2)(a) to have been paid by the CRIC to the parent and received by the parent from the CRIC is deemed to have instead been

(a) paid by the CRIC or the qualifying substitute corporation, as agreed on in the election; and

(b) paid to, and received by, the parent or the other non-resident corporation, as agreed on in the election.

Earlier amended by 2014 budget bill #2, for transactions/events after March 28, 2012.

(4) Definitions — The following definitions apply in this section.

"cross-border class", in respect of an investment, means a class of shares of the capital stock of a CRIC or qualifying substitute corporation if, immediately after the dividend time in respect of the investment,

(a) a parent, or a non-resident person that does not deal at arm's length with a parent, owns at least one share of the class; and

(b) no more than 30% of the issued and outstanding shares of the class are owned by one or more persons resident in Canada that do not deal at arm's length with a parent.

Related Provisions: 212.3(6) — Anti-avoidance rule.

Notes: Paras. (a), (b) amended by 2021 budget bill #1, for transactions/events after March 18, 2019, to cover control by non-resident groups or individuals. Before then, read:

(a) the parent, or a non-resident corporation that does not deal at arm's length with the parent, owns at least one share of the class; and

(b) no more than 30% of the issued and outstanding shares of the class are owned by one or more persons resident in Canada that do not deal at arm's length with the parent.

Definition added by 2014 budget bill #2, for transactions and events after March 28, 2012, except that for those before Aug. 29, 2014, ignore para. (b).

"dividend time", in respect of an investment, means

(a) if the CRIC is controlled by a parent or group of parents at the investment time, the investment time; and

(b) in any other case, the earlier of

(i) the first time, after the investment time, at which the CRIC is controlled by a parent or group of parents, as the case may be, and

(ii) the day that is one year after the day that includes the investment time.

Related Provisions: 212.3(1) — Meaning of "investment time"; 212.3(15) — Restricted meaning of "controlled".

Notes: "Dividend time" amended by 2021 budget bill #1, for transactions/events after March 18, 2019, to cover control by non-resident groups or individuals. Before then, read:

"dividend time", in respect of an investment, means

(a) if the CRIC is controlled by the parent at the investment time, the investment time; or

(b) in any other case, the earlier of

(i) the first time, after the investment time, at which the CRIC is controlled by the parent, and

(ii) the day that is one year after the day that includes the investment time.

Definition added by 2014 budget bill #2, effective for transactions and events that occur after March 28, 2012.

"qualifying substitute corporation", at any time in respect of a CRIC, means a corporation resident in Canada

(a) that is, at that time, controlled by

(i) a parent,

(ii) a group of parents, or

(iii) a non-resident person that does not deal at arm's length with a parent;

(b) that has, at that time, an "equity percentage" (as defined in subsection 95(4)) in the CRIC; and

(c) shares of the capital stock of which are, at that time, owned by a parent or another non-resident person with which the parent does not, at that time, deal at arm's length.

Related Provisions: 212.3(15) — Restricted meaning of "controlled"; 251(1) — Arm's length.

Notes: For a ruling that entities fall into this definition see VIEWS doc 2014-0541951R3.

Paras. (a)-(c) amended by 2021 budget bill #1, for transactions/events after March 18, 2019, to cover control by non-resident groups or individuals. Before then, read:

(a) that is, at that time, controlled by the parent or by a non-resident corporation that does not deal at arm's length with the parent;

(b) that has, at that time, an equity percentage (as defined in subsection 95(4)) in the CRIC; and

(c) shares of the capital stock of which are, at that time, owned by the parent or another non-resident corporation with which the parent does not, at that time, deal at arm's length.

Para. (a) amended by 2014 budget bill #2, effective for transactions and events that occur after March 28, 2012, to add "or by a non-resident...".

(5) Modification of terms — para. (10)(e) — In the case of an investment described in paragraph (10)(e), the CRIC is deemed for the purposes of paragraph (2)(a) to transfer to the subject corporation property that relates to the investment, the fair market value of which property is

(a) if the investment is described in subparagraph (10)(e)(i), the amount owing in respect of the debt obligation referred to in that subparagraph immediately after the investment time, or

(b) if the investment is described in subparagraph (10)(e)(ii), the fair market value of the shares referred to in that subparagraph immediately after the investment time.

Notes: This was 212.3(3) in the draft legislation of Aug. 14, 2012.

(5.1) Sequential investments — para. (10)(f) — In the case of an investment (in this subsection referred to as the "second investment") in a subject corporation by a CRIC described in paragraph (10)(f), the amount determined for A in paragraph (2)(a) in respect of the second investment is to be reduced by the amount determined for A in paragraph (2)(a) in respect of a prior investment (in this subsection referred to as the "first investment") in the subject corporation by another corporation resident in Canada if

(a) the first investment is an investment that is described in paragraph (10)(a) or (b) and to which paragraph (2)(a) applies;

(b) immediately after the investment time in respect of the first investment, the other corporation is not controlled by

(i) if there is one parent in respect of the CRIC, the parent, and

(ii) if there is a group of parents in respect of the CRIC, the group of parents; and

(c) the other corporation becomes, after the time that is immediately after the investment time in respect of the first investment and as part of a transaction or event or series of transactions or events that includes the making of the first investment, controlled by the parent or group of parents, as the case may be, because of the second investment.

Notes: 212.3(5.1) amended by 2021 budget bill #1, for transactions/events after March 18, 2019, to cover control by non-resident groups or individuals. Before then, read:

(5.1) In the case of an investment (in this subsection referred to as the "second investment") in a subject corporation by a CRIC described in paragraph (10)(f), the total referred to in paragraph (2)(a) in respect of the second investment is to be reduced by the total referred to in paragraph (2)(a) in respect of a prior investment (in this subsection referred to as the "first investment") in the subject corporation by another corporation resident in Canada if

(a) the first investment is an investment that is described in paragraph (10)(a) or (b) and to which paragraph (2)(a) applies;

(b) immediately after the investment time in respect of the first investment, the other corporation is not controlled by the parent; and

(c) the other corporation becomes, after the time that is immediately after the investment time in respect of the first investment and as part of a transaction or event or series of transactions or events that includes the making of the first investment, controlled by the parent because of the second investment.

212.3(5.1) added by 2014 budget bill #2, for transactions and events that occur after March 28, 2012.

(6) Anti-avoidance rule — cross-border class — A particular class of shares of the capital stock of a CRIC or a qualifying substitute corporation that, in the absence of this subsection, would be a cross-border class in respect of an investment is deemed not to be a cross-border class in respect of the investment if

(a) a particular corporation resident in Canada that does not deal at arm's length with a parent

(i) acquires shares of the particular class (or shares that are substituted for those shares) as part of a transaction or event or series of transactions or events that includes the investment, or

(ii) owns shares of the particular class (or shares that are substituted for those shares) and, as part of a transaction or event or series of transactions or events that includes the investment,

(A) the paid-up capital in respect of the particular class is increased otherwise than as a result of an acquisition described in subparagraph (i), and

(B) the increase in paid-up capital in respect of the particular class can reasonably be considered to be connected to funding provided to the particular corporation or another corporation resident in Canada (other than the corporation that issued the particular class) by a parent or a non-resident person that does not deal at arm's length with a parent, unless

(I) the funding results in an increase, equal to the amount funded, in the paid-up capital of shares of a class of the capital stock of the particular corporation, or the other corporation, that is a cross-border class in respect of the investment, and

(II) the increase referred to in subclause (I) occurred at or before the time of the increase to the paid-up capital in respect of the particular class; and

(b) it can reasonably be considered that one of the main reasons for the acquisition or for the funding, as the case may be, was to increase the amount of a deduction required under paragraph (7)(b) or (c) in computing the paid-up capital in respect of shares of the particular class held by the particular corporation.

Notes: 212.3(6)(a) amended by 2021 budget bill #1 to change "the parent" to "a parent" (3 places), for transactions or events after March 18, 2019, to cover control by non-resident groups or individuals.

212.3(6) added by 2014 budget bill #2, for transactions/events after Aug. 28, 2014.

(7) Reduction of deemed dividend — If paragraph (2)(a) applies to an investment in a subject corporation made by a CRIC,

(a) where the CRIC demonstrates — in respect of one or more classes of shares of the capital stock of the CRIC, or of a qualifying substitute corporation, all the issued and outstanding shares of which are owned, immediately after the dividend time in respect of the investment, by persons that deal at arm's length with the CRIC — that an amount of paid-up capital in respect of

each of the classes arose as a consequence of one or more transfers of property, directly or indirectly, to the CRIC and that all of the property transferred was used by the CRIC to make, in whole or in part, the investment (or, in the case of an investment described in paragraph (10)(f), the direct acquisition referred to in that paragraph), then

(i) the amount determined, without reference to this subsection, for A in paragraph (2)(a), is reduced by the lesser of

(A) that amount, and

(B) the total of all amounts of paid-up capital so demonstrated by the CRIC, and

(ii) in computing the paid-up capital in respect of each class described in this paragraph, at any time after the dividend time, there is to be deducted an amount equal to the portion of the amount determined under subparagraph (i) that can reasonably be considered to relate to that class;

(b) where the amount determined, without reference to this paragraph, for A in paragraph (2)(a) is equal to or greater than the total of all amounts each of which is an amount of paid-up capital immediately after the dividend time, determined without reference to this paragraph, of a cross-border class in respect of the investment, then

(i) the amount determined, without reference to this paragraph, for A in paragraph (2)(a) is reduced by the total referred to in this paragraph, and

(ii) in computing, at any time after the dividend time, the paid-up capital in respect of each cross-border class in respect of the investment, there is to be deducted an amount equal to the paid-up capital in respect of that class immediately after the dividend time, determined without reference to this paragraph;

(c) where paragraph (b) does not apply and there is at least one cross-border class in respect of the investment,

(i) the amount determined, without reference to this paragraph, for A in paragraph (2)(a) is reduced to nil,

(ii) in computing, at any time after the dividend time, the paid-up capital in respect of a particular cross-border class in respect of the investment, there is to be deducted the amount, if any, that when added to the total of all amounts that are deducted under this paragraph in computing the paid-up capital of other cross-border classes, results in the greatest total reduction because of this paragraph, immediately after the dividend time, of the paid-up capital in respect of shares of cross-border classes that are owned by a parent or another non-resident person with which a parent does not, at the dividend time, deal at arm's length,

(iii) if the proportion of the shares of a particular class owned, in aggregate, by parents and non-resident persons that do not deal at arm's length with parents is equal to the proportion so owned of one or more other cross-border classes (in this subparagraph all those classes, together with the particular class, referred to as the "relevant classes"), then the proportion that the reduction under subparagraph (ii) to the paid-up capital in respect of the particular class is of the paid-up capital, determined immediately after the dividend time and without reference to this paragraph, in respect of that class is to be equal to the proportion that the total reduction under subparagraph (ii) to the paid-up capital in respect of all the relevant classes is of the total paid-up capital, determined immediately after the dividend time and without reference to this paragraph, of all the relevant classes, and

(iv) the total of all amounts each of which is an amount to be deducted under subparagraph (ii) in computing the paid-up capital of a cross-border class is to be equal to the amount by which the amount determined for A in paragraph (2)(a) is reduced under subparagraph (i); and

(d) if the amount determined for A in paragraph (2)(a) is reduced because of any of subparagraphs (a)(i), (b)(i) and (c)(i),

(i) the CRIC shall file with the Minister in prescribed manner a form containing prescribed information and the amounts of the paid-up capital, determined immediately after the dividend time and without reference to this subsection, of each class of shares that is described in paragraph (a) or that is a cross-border class in respect of the investment, the paid-up capital of the shares of each of those classes that are owned by a parent or another non-resident person that does not, at the dividend time, deal at arm's length with a parent, and the reduction under any of subparagraphs (a)(ii), (b)(ii) and (c)(ii) in respect of each of those classes, and

(ii) if the form is not filed on or before the CRIC's filing-due date for its taxation year that includes the dividend time, the CRIC is deemed to have paid to each parent, and each parent is deemed to have received from the CRIC, on the filing-due date, a dividend equal to the total of all amounts each of which is the amount of a reduction because of any of subparagraphs (a)(i), (b)(i) and (c)(i) in the amount the CRIC is deemed under paragraph (2)(a) to have paid to the parent.

Related Provisions: 212.3(4) — Meaning of "dividend time"; 212.3(7.1) — Election to not reduce deemed dividend (re investment in 2012-13); 212.3(8), (9) — Adjustments to paid-up capital; 212.3(22) — Effect of amalgamation or windup; 212.3(25) — Application to partnerships; 219.1(3)(b) — PUC reinstatement of emigrating corporation after 212.3(7)(b) applies; 227(6.2) — Late-filed form under (d)(ii) — refund payable by Minister; 227(8.5) — No penalty for failing to withhold tax on 212.3(7)(d)(ii) deemed dividend.

Notes: 212.3(7)(a)(i) opening words, (b) before (ii), (c) and (d) amended by 2021 budget bill #1, for transactions or events after March 18, 2019, to cover control by non-resident groups or individuals. Before then, read:

(a) ...

(i) the amount, determined without reference to this subsection, of the dividend deemed under paragraph (2)(a) to have been paid and received, is reduced by the lesser of

[...]

(b) where the amount, determined without reference to this paragraph, of the dividend deemed under paragraph (2)(a) to have been paid and received is equal to or greater than the total of all amounts each of which is an amount of paid-up capital immediately after the dividend time, determined without reference to this paragraph, of a cross-border class in respect of the investment, then

(i) the amount of the dividend is reduced by the total referred to in this paragraph, and

[...]

(c) where paragraph (b) does not apply and there is at least one cross-border class in respect of the investment,

(i) the amount, determined without reference to this paragraph, of the dividend is reduced to nil,

(ii) in computing, at any time after the dividend time, the paid-up capital in respect of a particular cross-border class in respect of the investment, there is to be deducted the amount, if any, that when added to the total of all amounts that are deducted under this paragraph in computing the paid-up capital of other cross-border classes, results in the greatest total reduction because of this paragraph, immediately after the dividend time, of the paid-up capital in respect of shares of cross-border classes that are owned by the parent or another non-resident corporation with which the parent does not, at the dividend time, deal at arm's length,

(iii) if the proportion of the shares of a particular class owned, in aggregate, by the parent and non-resident corporations that do not deal at arm's length with the parent is equal to the proportion so owned of one or more other cross-border classes (in this subparagraph all those classes, together with the particular class, referred to as the "relevant classes"), then the proportion that the reduction under subparagraph (ii) to the paid-up capital in respect of the particular class is of the paid-up capital, determined immediately after the dividend time and without reference to this paragraph, in respect of that class is to be equal to the proportion that the total reduction under subparagraph (ii) to the paid-up capital in respect of all the relevant classes is of the total paid-up capital, determined immediately after the dividend time and without reference to this paragraph, of all the relevant classes, and

(iv) the total of all amounts each of which is an amount to be deducted under subparagraph (ii) in computing the paid-up capital of a cross-border class is to be equal to the amount by which the dividend is reduced under subparagraph (i); and

(d) if the amount of the dividend is reduced because of any of subparagraphs (a)(i), (b)(i) and (c)(i),

(i) the CRIC shall file with the Minister in prescribed manner a form containing prescribed information and the amounts of the paid-up capital, determined immediately after the dividend time and without reference to this subsection, of each class of shares that is described in paragraph (a) or that is a cross-border class in respect of the investment, the paid-up capital of the shares of each of those classes that are owned by the parent or another non-resident corporation that does not, at the dividend time, deal at arm's length with the parent, and the reduction under any of subparagraphs (a)(ii), (b)(ii) and (c)(ii) in respect of each of those classes, and

(ii) if the form is not filed on or before the CRIC's filing-due date for its taxation year that includes the dividend time, the CRIC is deemed to have paid to the parent, and the parent is deemed to have received from the CRIC, on the filing-due date, a dividend equal to the total of all amounts each of which is the amount of a reduction because of any of subparagraphs (a)(i), (b)(i) and (c)(i).

For comment on the 2014 amendments see Barnicke & Ong, "FA Dumping", 22(10) *Canadian Tax Highlights* (ctf.ca) 5-6 (Oct. 2014). See also VIEWS doc 2015-0583821E5 (prescribed form and information for (d)(i)). For "indirectly" in para. (a), see Notes to 17.1(1).

212.3(7) amended by 2014 budget bill #2, for transactions and events after March 28, 2012, with transitional rules to 2015. It was 212.3(5) in the Aug. 14, 2012 draft legislation.

(7.1) Election to not reduce deemed dividend [2012-13 investment] — Subsection (7) does not apply in respect of an investment made by a CRIC if

(a) the investment was made after March 28, 2012 and before August 16, 2013;

(b) at the investment time, each share of the capital stock of the CRIC, and each qualifying substitute corporation in respect of the CRIC, that was not owned by the parent was owned by persons or partnerships with which the parent did not deal at arm's length; and

(c) the CRIC files an election with the Minister before 2017 to have this subsection apply in respect of the investment.

Notes: 212.3(7.1) added by 2017 budget bill #2, effective March 29, 2012.

(8) Paid-up capital adjustment — In computing the paid-up capital at any time after March 28, 2012 in respect of a class of shares of the capital stock of a corporation, there is to be added an amount equal to the lesser of

(a) the amount, if any, by which

(i) the total of all amounts deemed by subsection 84(3), (4) or (4.1) to be a dividend on shares of the class paid after March 28, 2012 and before that time by the corporation

exceeds

(ii) the total that would be determined under subparagraph (i) if this Act were read without reference to paragraph (2)(b) and subsections (7) and (9), and

(b) the amount, if any, by which

(i) the total of all amounts required by paragraph (2)(b) or subsection (7) to be deducted in computing the paid-up capital in respect of the class before that time

exceeds

(ii) the total of all amounts required by subsection (9) to be added in computing the paid-up capital in respect of the class before that time.

Related Provisions: 212.3(9.2) — Continuity of paid-up capital reinstatement.

Notes: See Notes at end of 212.3.

212.3(8)(a)(ii) and (b)(i) both amended by 2014 budget bill #2, retroactive to transactions and events that occur after March 28, 2012.

This was 212.3(6) in the draft legislation of Aug. 14, 2012.

(9) Paid-up capital reinstatement — If, in respect of an investment in a subject corporation made by a CRIC that is described in any of paragraphs (10)(a) to (f), an amount is deducted under paragraph (2)(b) or subsection (7) in computing the paid-up capital in respect of a class of shares of the capital stock of a particular corporation and, at a time subsequent to the investment time, there is a reduction of paid-up capital referred to in subparagraph (b)(i) or a receipt of property referred to in the description of A in subparagraph (b)(ii), then the paid-up capital in respect of the class is to be increased, immediately before the subsequent time, by the lesser of

(a) the amount, if any, by which

(i) the total of all amounts deducted, before the subsequent time, under paragraph (2)(b) or subsection (7), in respect of the investment, in computing the paid-up capital in respect of the class

exceeds

(ii) the total of all amounts added under this subsection, in respect of the investment, to the paid-up capital in respect of the class before the time that is immediately before the subsequent time, and

(b) an amount that

(i) if the investment is described in paragraph (10)(a), (b) or (f), the paid-up capital in respect of the class is reduced at the subsequent time as part of or because of a distribution of property by the particular corporation and the property (in this paragraph referred to as the "distributed shares") is shares of the capital stock of the subject corporation or shares of the capital stock of a foreign affiliate of the particular corporation that were substituted for shares of the capital stock of the subject corporation, is equal to the amount determined by the formula

$$A/B$$

where

A is

(A) if the investment is described in paragraph (10)(b), the portion of the fair market value, immediately before the subsequent time, of the distributed shares that can reasonably be considered to relate to the contribution of capital that is the investment, and

(B) if the investment is described in paragraph (10)(a) or (f), the lesser of

(I) the portion of the fair market value, immediately before the subsequent time, of the distributed shares that can reasonably be considered to relate to the shares (in this paragraph referred to as the "acquired shares") of the capital stock of the subject corporation that were acquired on the investment (other than any portion described in clause (A)), and

(II) the proportion of the amount determined under subparagraph (a)(i) that the amount determined under subclause (I) is of the fair market value, immediately before the subsequent time, of the acquired shares, or the portion of the fair market value of shares that were substituted for the acquired shares that can reasonably be considered to relate to the acquired shares, and

B is

(A) if the particular corporation is, immediately after the dividend time, a qualifying substitute corporation in respect of the CRIC, the particular corporation's equity percentage (as defined in subsection 95(4)) in the CRIC immediately after the dividend time, and

(B) in any other case, 100%, and

(ii) in any other case, is equal to the amount determined by the formula

$$A \times B/C$$

where

A is the amount that is equal to the fair market value of property that the particular corporation demonstrates has been received at the subsequent time by it or by a corpo-

ration resident in Canada that was not dealing at arm's length with the particular corporation at that time (in this subparagraph referred to as the "recipient corporation")

(A) as proceeds from the disposition of the acquired shares, or other shares to the extent that the proceeds from the disposition of those other shares can reasonably be considered to relate to the acquired shares or to shares of the capital stock of the subject corporation in respect of which an investment described in paragraph (10)(b) was made, other than

(I) the fair market value of shares of the capital stock of another foreign affiliate of the taxpayer acquired by the recipient corporation as consideration for the disposition and as an investment to which subsection (16) or (18) applies, and

(II) proceeds from a disposition of shares to a corporation resident in Canada for which the acquisition of the shares is an investment to which subsection (16) or (18) applies,

(B) as a reduction of paid-up capital or dividend in respect of a class of shares of the capital stock of the subject corporation or the portion, of a reduction of paid-up capital or dividend in respect of a class of shares of the capital stock of a foreign affiliate of the particular corporation that were substituted for shares of the capital stock of the subject corporation, that can reasonably be considered to relate to the subject shares, or

(C) if the investment is described in paragraph (10)(c) or (d) or subparagraph (10)(e)(i),

(I) as a repayment of or as proceeds from the disposition of the debt obligation or amount owing, other than

1. if the debt obligation or amount owing was acquired by another foreign affiliate of the taxpayer, the portion of the fair market value of property received by the particular corporation as a result of an investment by the particular corporation that is described in paragraphs (10)(a) to (f) to which subsection (16) or (18) applies, or

2. as proceeds from a disposition to a corporation resident in Canada and that is affiliated with the particular corporation, and where subsection (16) or (18) applies to the other corporation in respect of its acquisition, or

(II) as interest on the debt obligation or amount owing,

B is the amount determined under paragraph (a) in respect of the class, and

C is the total of all amounts each of which is an amount determined under paragraph (a) in respect of all classes of shares of the capital stock of the particular corporation or of any corporation that does not deal at arm's length with the particular corporation.

Related Provisions: 212.3(9.1) — Exchange of debt obligation for shares; 212.3(9.2) — Continuity of paid-up capital reinstatement; 219.1(3)–(5) — PUC reinstatement rules for emigrating corporation.

Notes: This was 212.3(7) in the draft legislation of Aug. 14, 2012.

For rulings that distributions meet the conditions of 212.3(9)(b)(ii)A(B), see VIEWS docs 2014-0541951R3, 2016-0629011R3. Circular transactions that reinstate PUC will trigger GAAR: 2020 IFA Roundtable q.6.

212.3(9) amended by 2014 budget bill #2, for transactions and events after March 28, 2012 (or Aug. 15, 2013 by election). 212.3(9)(c)(ii)(B) amended by 2002-2013 technical bill, retroactive to introduction of s. 212.3.

(9.1) Exchange of debt obligation for shares — For the purposes of subsection (9), if at any time a debt obligation that relates to a particular investment described in paragraph (10)(c) or (d) or subparagraph (10)(e)(i) is exchanged for shares of a subject corporation and as part of the exchange there is an acquisition of shares described in subparagraph (18)(b)(i) or paragraph 18(d), then all amounts, in respect of the particular investment, deducted under paragraph (2)(b) or subsection (7) from, or added under subsection (9) to, the paid-up capital in respect of a class of shares before that time are deemed to have been deducted or added, as the case may be, in respect of the acquisition of the shares and not the particular investment.

Notes: 212.3(9.1) added by 2014 budget bill #2, for transactions and events after March 28, 2012.

(9.2) Continuity for paid-up capital reinstatement — If at any particular time shares (in this subsection referred to as the "new shares") of a class of the capital stock of a corporation resident in Canada are acquired, in a transaction to which any of sections 51, 85, 85.1, 86 and 87 apply, in exchange for a share (in this subsection referred to as the "old share") of a class of the capital stock of a particular corporation that is either the corporation or another corporation resident in Canada, then for the purposes of subsections (8) and (9),

(a) if the corporation that issues the new shares is not the particular corporation, it is deemed to be the same corporation as, and a continuation of, the particular corporation;

(b) the new shares are deemed to be the same share, and of the same class of the capital stock of the particular corporation, as the old share; and

(c) if the old share remains outstanding after the exchange, it is deemed to be a share of a different class of the capital stock of the particular corporation.

Notes: 212.3(9.2) added by 2014 budget bill #2, for transactions and events that occur after March 28, 2012.

(10) Investment in subject corporation — In this section, "investment", in a subject corporation made by a CRIC, means any of

(a) an acquisition of shares of the capital stock of the subject corporation by the CRIC;

(b) a contribution of capital to the subject corporation by the CRIC, which is deemed to include any transaction or event under which a benefit is conferred on the subject corporation by the CRIC;

(c) a transaction under which an amount becomes owing by the subject corporation to the CRIC, other than an amount owing

(i) that arises in the ordinary course of the business of the CRIC and that is repaid, other than as part of a series of loans or other transactions and repayments, within 180 days after the day on which the amount becomes owing,

(ii) that is a pertinent loan or indebtedness immediately after the time of the transaction, or

(iii) because a dividend has been declared, but not yet paid, by the subject corporation;

(d) an acquisition of a debt obligation of the subject corporation by the CRIC from a person, other than

(i) if the acquisition is made in the ordinary course of the business of the CRIC, a debt obligation acquired from a person with which the CRIC deals at arm's length at the time of the acquisition, or

(ii) a debt obligation that is a pertinent loan or indebtedness immediately after the time of the acquisition;

(e) an extension of

(i) the maturity date of a debt obligation (other than a debt obligation that is a pertinent loan or indebtedness immediately after the time of the extension) owing by the subject corporation to the CRIC, or

(ii) the redemption, acquisition or cancellation date of shares of the capital stock of the subject corporation owned by the CRIC;

(f) an indirect acquisition by the CRIC of shares of the capital stock of the subject corporation that results from a direct acquisition by the CRIC of shares of the capital stock of another corporation resident in Canada, of which the subject corporation is a foreign affiliate, if the total fair market value of all the shares that are held directly or indirectly by the other corporation and are shares of foreign affiliates of the other corporation exceeds 75% of the total fair market value (determined without reference to debt obligations of any corporation resident in Canada in which the other corporation has a direct or indirect interest) of all of the properties owned by the other corporation; and

(g) an acquisition by the CRIC of an option in respect of, or an interest in, or for civil law a right in, shares of the capital stock of, an amount owing by (other than an amount owing described in subparagraph (c)(i) or (ii)), or a debt obligation of (other than a debt obligation described in subparagraph (d)(i) or (ii)), the subject corporation.

Related Provisions: 93.3(3), (4)(c) — Special rule for certain Australian trusts; 212.3(5) — Effect of modification of terms under (10)(e); 212.3(5.1) — Sequential investments — para. (10)(f); 212.3(9) — Paid-up capital reinstatement; 212.3(11) — Meaning of "pertinent loan or indebtedness"; 212.3(14) — Rules for para. (10)(f); 212.3(22) — Effect of amalgamation or windup; 212.3(25) — Application to partnerships.

Notes: Note that an "acquisition" for purposes of 212.3(10) does not require the CRIC to have paid any consideration.

See the Serabi Gold acquisition of Kenai Resources, discussed in Calvert & Mar, "Recent Transactions", 2013 Cdn Tax Foundation conference report at 7:3-5.

212.3(10)(c)(iii) added by 2014 budget bill #2, for transactions and events after March 28, 2012.

This was 212.3(8) in the draft legislation of Aug. 14, 2012, and 212.3(3) in the draft of March 29, 2012. See also Notes at end of 212.3.

(11) Pertinent loan or indebtedness — For the purposes of subsection (10) and subject to subsection 17.1(3), "pertinent loan or indebtedness", at any time, means an amount owing at that time by the subject corporation to the CRIC in respect of which all of the following apply:

(a) either

(i) the amount became owing after March 28, 2012, or

(ii) the amount became owing before March 29, 2012 and is a debt obligation for which the maturity date was extended after March 28, 2012 and at or before that time;

(b) the amount owing is not an amount owing described in subparagraph (10)(c)(i) or a debt obligation described in subparagraph (10)(d)(i); and

(c) the CRIC and each parent jointly elect in writing under this paragraph in respect of the amount owing and file the election with the Minister on or before the filing-due date of the CRIC

(i) in the case of an amount owing described in subparagraph (a)(i), for the year in which the amount became owing, or

(ii) in the case of an amount owing described in subparagraph (a)(ii), for the year in which the extension was made.

Related Provisions: 15(2.11) — Definition of PLOI for shareholder-loan rules; 17.1(1) — Deemed interest income on pertinent loan or indebtedness; 18(5)"outstanding debts to specified non-residents"(b)(ii) — Exclusion from thin capitalization rules; 212.3(12), (13) — Late-filed election under (11)(c).

Notes: For a corporation filing a Quebec return, a 212.3(11)(c) election must be copied to Revenu Québec: *Taxation Act* ss. 127.16, 21.4.6.

For CRA interpretation see VIEWS docs 2014-0517151E5 (application of 17.1(1) where PLOI is denominated in foreign currency); 2014-0534541I7 (one document can make multiple elections; partners, not partnership, file the election).

212.3(11)(c) amended by 2021 budget bill #1 to change "the parent" to "each parent", for transactions/events after March 18, 2019, to cover control by non-resident groups or individuals.

(12) Late-filed elections — Where an election referred to in subsection (3) or paragraph (11)(c) was not made on or before the day on or before which the election was required by that paragraph to be made, the election is deemed to have been made on that day if the election is made on or before the day that is three years after that day and the penalty in respect of the election is paid by the CRIC when the election is made.

Related Provisions: 212.3(13) — Penalty for late-filed election.

Notes: This provision was not in the draft legislation of Aug. 14, 2012.

(13) Penalty for late-filed election — For the purposes of subsection (12), the penalty in respect of an election referred to in that subsection is the amount equal to the product obtained by multiplying $100 by the number of months each of which is a month all or part of which is during the period commencing with the day on or before which the election is required by subsection (3) or paragraph (11)(c), as the case may be, to be made and ending on the day on which the election is made.

Notes: On calculating the penalty when there are multiple "amounts" owing from different transactions, see VIEWS doc 2016-0642031C6 [2016 IFA q.11].

This provision was not in the draft legislation of Aug. 14, 2012.

(14) Rules for para. (10)(f) — For the purposes of paragraph (10)(f),

(a) the condition in that paragraph is deemed to be satisfied at the time of the acquisition if

(i) any property (other than shares of foreign affiliates of the other corporation that is referred to in that paragraph) held directly or indirectly by that other corporation is disposed of, after the time of the acquisition, directly or indirectly by that corporation as part of a series of transactions or events that includes the acquisition, and

(ii) at any time that is subsequent to the time of the acquisition and that is in the period during which the series occurs, the condition in that paragraph would have been satisfied had the acquisition occurred at the subsequent time; and

(b) the fair market value of properties held directly or indirectly by the other corporation is not to be taken into account more than once in determining whether the condition in that paragraph is satisfied.

Notes: This was 212.3(10) in the draft legislation of Aug. 14, 2012.

(15) Control — For the purposes of this section and paragraph 128.1(1)(c.3),

(a) a CRIC or a taxpayer to which paragraph 128.1(1)(c.3) applies (in this subsection referred to as the "specific corporation"), that would, in the absence of this subsection, be controlled at any time

(i) by more than one non-resident person, is deemed not to be controlled at that time by any such person that controls at that time another non-resident person that controls at that time the specific corporation, unless the application of this paragraph would otherwise result in no non-resident person controlling the specific corporation, and

(ii) by a particular non-resident corporation is deemed not to be controlled at that time by the particular non-resident corporation if the particular non-resident corporation is controlled at that time by another corporation that is at that time

(A) resident in Canada, and

(B) not controlled by any non-resident person or group of non-resident persons not dealing with each other at arm's length; and

(b) a non-resident person is deemed not to be a member of a particular group of non-resident persons not dealing with each other at arm's length that controls the specific corporation if

(i) the non-resident person would, absent the application of this paragraph, be a member of the particular group, and

(ii) the non-resident person is a member of the particular group solely because it controls, or is a member of a group that controls, another member of the particular group.

Notes: 212.3(15)(a)-(b) amended by 2021 budget bill #1, for transactions/events after March 18, 2019, to cover control by non-resident groups or individuals. Before then, read:

(a) a CRIC or a taxpayer to which paragraph 128.1(1)(c.3) applies (in this paragraph referred to as the "specific corporation"), that would, in the absence of this subsection, be controlled at any time

(i) by more than one non-resident corporation is deemed not to be controlled at that time by any such non-resident that controls at that time another non-resident corporation that controls at that time the specific corporation, unless the application of this paragraph would otherwise result in no non-resident corporation controlling the specific corporation, and

(ii) by a particular non-resident corporation is deemed not to be controlled at that time by the particular corporation if the particular corporation is controlled at that time by another corporation that is at that time

(A) resident in Canada, and

(B) not controlled by any non-resident person; and

(b) if at any time a corporation would not, in the absence of this subsection, be controlled by any non-resident corporation, and a related group (determined without reference to paragraph 251(5)(b)), each member of which is a non-resident corporation, is in a position to control the corporation, the corporation is deemed to be controlled at that time by

(i) the member of the group that has the greatest direct equity percentage (within the meaning assigned by subsection 95(4)) in the corporation at that time, or

(ii) where no member of the group has a direct equity percentage in the corporation that is greater than that of every other member, the member determined by the corporation or, if the corporation does not make a determination, by the Minister.

212.3(15) amended by 2014 budget bill #2, effectively to use the term "specific corporation" in (a)(i) (retroactive to transactions and events that occur after March 28, 2012), and to add para. (b) for transactions and events after Aug. 15, 2013.

(16) Exception — more closely connected business activities — Subject to subsection (19), subsection (2) does not apply to an investment in a subject corporation made by a CRIC if the CRIC demonstrates that all of the following conditions are met:

(a) the business activities carried on by the subject corporation and all other corporations (those other corporations in this subsection and subsection (17) referred to as the "**subject subsidiary corporations**") in which the subject corporation has, at the investment time, an "equity percentage" (as defined in subsection 95(4)) are at the investment time, and are expected to remain, on a collective basis, more closely connected to the business activities carried on in Canada by the CRIC, or by any corporation resident in Canada with which the CRIC does not, at the investment time, deal at arm's length, than to the business activities carried on by any non-resident person with which the CRIC, at the investment time, does not deal at arm's length, other than

(i) the subject corporation,

(ii) the subject subsidiary corporations, and

(iii) any corporation that is, immediately before the investment time, a controlled foreign affiliate of the CRIC for the purposes of section 17,

(b) officers of the CRIC, or of a corporation resident in Canada that did not, at the investment time, deal at arm's length with the CRIC, had and exercised the principal decision-making authority in respect of the making of the investment and a majority of those officers were, at the investment time, persons each of whom was resident, and working principally,

(i) in Canada, or

(ii) in a country in which a particular corporation is resident if the particular corporation (in this subsection and subsection (17) referred to as a "connected affiliate") is a controlled foreign affiliate of the CRIC for the purposes of section 17 and carries on business activities that are, at the investment time, and are expected to remain, at least as closely connected to those of the subject corporation and the subject subsidiary corporations, on a collective basis, as the business activities carried on in Canada by the CRIC, or any corporation resident in Canada with which the CRIC does not, at the investment time, deal at arm's length, as the case may be, are to those of the subject corporation and the subject subsidiary corporations, on a collective basis; and

(c) at the investment time, it is reasonably expected that

(i) officers of the CRIC, or of a corporation resident in Canada that does not deal at arm's length with the CRIC, will have and exercise the ongoing principal decision-making authority in respect of the investment,

(ii) a majority of those officers will be persons each of whom will be resident, and working principally, in Canada or in a country in which a connected affiliate is resident, and

(iii) the performance evaluation and compensation of the officers of the CRIC, or of the corporation resident in Canada that does not deal at arm's length with the CRIC, who are resident, and work principally, in Canada, or in a country in which a connected affiliate is resident, will be based on the results of operations of the subject corporation to a greater extent than will be the performance evaluation and compensation of any officer of a non-resident corporation (other than the subject corporation, a corporation controlled by the subject corporation or a connected affiliate) that does not deal at arm's length with the CRIC.

Related Provisions: 212.3(15) — Restricted meaning of "controlled"; 212.3(17) — Dual officers; 212.3(19) — 212.3(16) does not apply to most preferred shares; 212.3(22) — Effect of amalgamation or windup; 212.3(23) — Indirect investment; 212.3(25) — Application to partnerships.

Notes: See Morier & Grigoriu, "Foreign Affiliate Dumping: The Strategic Business Expansion", XXI(3) *International Tax Planning* (Federated Press) 14-22 (2017).

212.3(16)(a) opening words amended by 2021 budget bill #1 to change "any non-resident corporation" to "any non-resident person", for transactions/events after March 18, 2019, to cover control by non-resident groups or individuals.

212.3(16)(b), (c)(i) and (c)(iii) amended by 2014 budget bill #2, retroactive to transactions and events that occur after March 28, 2012.

(17) Dual officers — For the purposes of paragraphs (16)(b) and (c), any person who is an officer of the CRIC, or of a corporation resident in Canada that does not deal at arm's length with the CRIC, and of a non-resident corporation that does not, at the investment time, deal at arm's length with the CRIC (other than the subject corporation, a subject subsidiary corporation or a connected affiliate) is deemed to not be resident, and to not work principally, in a country in which a connected affiliate is resident.

Notes: This provision was not in the draft legislation of Aug. 14, 2012.

212.3(17) amended by 2014 budget bill #2, retroactive to transactions and events that occur after March 28, 2012.

(18) Exception — corporate reorganizations — Subject to subsections (18.1) to (20), subsection (2) does not apply to an investment in a subject corporation made by a CRIC if

(a) the investment is described in paragraph (10)(a) or (d) and is an acquisition of shares of the capital stock, or a debt obligation, of the subject corporation

(i) from a corporation resident in Canada (in this paragraph referred to as the "disposing corporation") to which the CRIC is, immediately before the investment time, related (determined without reference to paragraph 251(5)(b)), and

(A) each shareholder of the disposing corporation immediately before the investment time is

(I) if there is only one parent in respect of the CRIC,

1 either the CRIC or a corporation resident in Canada that is, immediately before the investment time, related to the parent, and

2 at no time that is in the period during which the series of transactions or events that includes the making of the investment occurs and that is before the investment time, dealing at arm's length (determined without reference to paragraph 251(5)(b)) with the parent or a non-resident person that participates in the series and is, at any time that is in the

period and that is before the investment time, related to the parent, and

(II) if there is a group of parents in respect of the CRIC,

1 either the CRIC or a corporation resident in Canada that is, immediately before the investment time, controlled by the group of parents, and

2 at all times that are in the period during which the series of transactions or events that includes the making of the investment occurs and that are before the investment time, controlled by the group of parents, or

(B) the disposing corporation is,

(I) if there is only one parent in respect of the CRIC, at no time that is in the period and that is before the investment time, dealing at arm's length (determined without reference to paragraph 251(5)(b)) with the parent or a non-resident person that participates in the series and is, at any time that is in the period and that is before the investment time, related to the parent, and

(II) if there is a group of parents in respect of the CRIC, at all times that are in the period during which the series of transactions or events that includes the making of the investment occurs and that are before the investment time, controlled by the group of parents, or

(ii) on an amalgamation described in subsection 87(1) of two or more corporations (each of which is in this subparagraph referred to as a "predecessor corporation") to form the CRIC if all of the predecessor corporations are, immediately before the amalgamation, related to each other (determined without reference to paragraph 251(5)(b)) and

(A) either

(I) if there is only one parent in respect of the CRIC, none of the predecessor corporations are, at any time that is in the period during which the series of transactions or events that includes the making of the investment occurs and that is before the investment time, dealing at arm's length (determined without reference to paragraph 251(5)(b)) with the parent or a non-resident person that participates in the series and is, at any time that is in the period and that is before the investment time, related to the parent, or

(II) if there is a group of parents in respect of the CRIC, all of the predecessor corporations are, at all times that are in the period during which the series of transactions or events that includes the making of the investment occurs and that are before the investment time, controlled by the group of parents, or

(B) if the condition in clause (A) is not satisfied in respect of a predecessor corporation, each shareholder of that predecessor immediately before the investment time is

(I) if there is only one parent in respect of the CRIC,

1 either the CRIC or a corporation resident in Canada that is, immediately before the investment time, related to the parent, and

2 at no time that is in the period and that is before the investment time, dealing at arm's length (determined without reference to paragraph 251(5)(b)) with the parent or a non-resident person that participates in the series and is, at any time that is in the period and that is before the investment time, related to the parent, and

(II) if there is a group of parents in respect of the CRIC,

1 either the CRIC or a corporation resident in Canada that is, immediately before the investment time, controlled by the group of parents, and

2 at all times that are in the period during which the series of transactions or events that includes the making of the investment occurs and that are before the investment time, controlled by the group of parents;

(b) the investment is described in paragraph (10)(a) and is an acquisition of shares of the capital stock of the subject corporation in which the shares are acquired by the CRIC

(i) in an exchange to which subsection 51(1) applies,

(ii) as consideration for a disposition of shares to which subsection 85.1(3) applies (determined without reference to subsection 85.1(4)),

(iii) in the course of a reorganization of the capital of the subject corporation to which subsection 86(1) applies,

(iv) as a result of a foreign merger (as defined in subsection 87(8.1)) under which the subject corporation was formed,

(v) on a liquidation and dissolution to which subsection 88(3) applies,

(vi) on a redemption of shares of another non-resident corporation that is, immediately before the investment time, a foreign affiliate of the CRIC,

(vii) as a dividend or a qualifying return of capital, within the meaning assigned by subsection 90(3), in respect of the shares of another non-resident corporation that is, immediately before the investment time, a foreign affiliate of the CRIC, or

(viii) as a result of a disposition of the shares by the CRIC to a partnership and to which subsection 97(2) applies;

(c) the investment is an indirect acquisition referred to in paragraph (10)(f) that results from a direct acquisition of shares of the capital stock of another corporation resident in Canada

(i) from a corporation (in this paragraph referred to as the "disposing corporation") to which the CRIC is, immediately before the investment time, related (determined without reference to paragraph 251(5)(b)) and

(A) each shareholder of the disposing corporation immediately before the investment time is

(I) if there is only one parent in respect of the CRIC,

1 either the CRIC or a corporation resident in Canada that, immediately before the investment time, is related to the parent, and

2 at no time that is in the period during which the series of transactions or events that includes the making of the investment occurs and that is before the investment time, dealing at arm's length (determined without reference to paragraph 251(5)(b)) with the parent or a non-resident person that participates in the series and is, at any time that is in the period and that is before the investment time, related to the parent, and

(II) if there is a group of parents in respect of the CRIC,

1 either the CRIC or a corporation resident in Canada that is, immediately before the investment time, controlled by the group of parents, and

2 at all times that are in the period during which the series of transactions or events that includes the making of the investment occurs and that are

before the investment time, controlled by the group of parents, or

(B) the disposing corporation is

(I) if there is only one parent in respect of the CRIC, at no time that is in the period and that is before the investment time, dealing at arm's length (determined without reference to paragraph 251(5)(b)) with the parent or a non-resident person that participates in the series and is, at any time that is in the period and that is before the investment time, related to the parent, and

(II) if there is a group of parents in respect of the CRIC, at all times that are in the period during which the series of transactions or events that includes the making of the investment occurs and that are before the investment time, controlled by the group of parents, or

(ii) on an amalgamation described in subsection 87(1) of two or more corporations (each of which is in this subparagraph referred to as a "predecessor corporation") to form the CRIC, or a corporation of which the CRIC is a shareholder, if all of the predecessor corporations are, immediately before the amalgamation, related to each other (determined without reference to paragraph 251(5)(b)) and

(A) either

(I) if there is only one parent in respect of the CRIC, none of the predecessor corporations are, at any time that is in the period during which the series of transactions or events that includes the making of the investment occurs and that is before the investment time, dealing at arm's length (determined without reference to paragraph 251(5)(b)) with the parent or a non-resident person that participates in the series and is, at any time that is in the period and that is before the investment time, related to the parent, or

(II) if there is a group of parents in respect of the CRIC, all of the predecessor corporations are, at all times that are in the period during which the series of transactions or events that includes the making of the investment occurs and that are before the investment time, controlled by the group of parents, or

(B) if the condition in clause (A) is not satisfied in respect of a predecessor corporation, each shareholder of that predecessor immediately before the investment time is

(I) if there is only one parent in respect of the CRIC,

1 either the CRIC or a corporation resident in Canada that is, immediately before the investment time, related to the parent, and

2 at no time that is in the period and that is before the investment time, dealing at arm's length (determined without reference to paragraph 251(5)(b)) with the parent or a non-resident person that participates in the series and is, at any time that is in the period and that is before the investment time, related to the parent, and

(II) if there is a group of parents in respect of the CRIC,

1 either the CRIC or a corporation resident in Canada that is, immediately before the investment time, controlled by the group of parents, and

2 at all times that are in the period during which the series of transactions or events that includes the making of the investment occurs and that are before the investment time, controlled by the group of parents;

(iii) in an exchange to which subsection 51(1) applies,

(iv) in the course of a reorganization of the capital of the other corporation to which subsection 86(1) applies,

(v) to the extent that an investment (other than one described in paragraph (10)(f)) is made in the subject corporation by the other corporation, or by a particular corporation resident in Canada to which the CRIC and the other corporation are related at the investment time, using property transferred, directly or indirectly, by the CRIC to the other corporation or the particular corporation, as the case may be, if the two investments

(A) occur within 90 days of each other, and

(B) are part of the same series of transactions or events, or

(vi) as a result of a disposition of the shares by the CRIC to a partnership and to which subsection 97(2) applies; or

(d) the investment is an acquisition of shares of the capital stock of the subject corporation that is described in paragraph (10)(a), or an indirect acquisition referred to in paragraph (10)(f) that results from a direct acquisition of shares of the capital stock of another corporation resident in Canada, if

(i) the shares are acquired by the CRIC in exchange for a bond, debenture or note, and

(ii) subsection 51(1) would apply to the exchange if the terms of the bond, debenture or note conferred on the holder the right to make the exchange.

Related Provisions: 212.3(18.1) — Exception — repayment or settlement of PLOI; 212.3(19) — Paras. (b) and (d) do not apply to most preferred shares; 212.3(20), (21) — Exceptions to 212.3(18); 212.3(22) — Effect of amalgamation or windup.

Notes: *Cl. (a)(i)(A)* implements a July 9, 2013 Finance comfort letter to Brian Bloom.

Subpara. (c)(v): for the meaning of "indirectly" see Notes to 17.1(1).

212.3(18)(a) and (c)(i)-(ii) amended by 2021 budget bill #1, for transactions/events after March 18, 2019, to cover control by non-resident groups or individuals. Before then, read:

(a) the investment is described in paragraph (10)(a) or (d) and is an acquisition of shares of the capital stock, or a debt obligation, of the subject corporation

(i) from a corporation resident in Canada (in this paragraph referred to as the "disposing corporation") to which the CRIC is, immediately before the investment time, related (determined without reference to paragraph 251(5)(b)), and

(A) each shareholder of the disposing corporation immediately before the investment time is

(I) either the CRIC or a corporation resident in Canada that is, immediately before the investment time, related to the parent, and

(II) at no time that is in the period during which the series of transactions or events that includes the making of the investment occurs and that is before the investment time, dealing at arm's length (determined without reference to paragraph 251(5)(b)) with the parent or a non-resident corporation that participates in the series and is, at any time that is in the period and that is before the investment time, related to the parent, or

(B) the disposing corporation is, at no time that is in the period and that is before the investment time, dealing at arm's length (determined without reference to paragraph 251(5)(b)) with the parent or a non-resident corporation that participates in the series and is, at any time that is in the period and that is before the investment time, related to the parent, or

(ii) on an amalgamation described in subsection 87(1) of two or more corporations (each of which is in this subparagraph referred to as a "predecessor corporation") to form the CRIC if

(A) all of the predecessor corporations are, immediately before the amalgamation, related to each other (determined without reference to paragraph 251(5)(b)), and

(B) either

(I) none of the predecessor corporations are, at any time that is in the period during which the series of transactions or events that includes the making of the investment occurs and that is before the investment time, dealing at arm's length (determined without reference to paragraph 251(5)(b)) with the parent or a non-resident corporation that participates in the series and is, at any time that is in the period and that is before the investment time, related to the parent, or

(II) if the condition in subclause (I) is not satisfied in respect of a predecessor corporation, each shareholder of that predecessor immediately before the investment time is

1. either the CRIC or a corporation resident in Canada that is, immediately before the investment time, related to the parent, and

2. at no time that is in the period and that is before the investment time, dealing at arm's length (determined without reference to paragraph 251(5)(b)) with the parent or a non-resident corporation that participates in the series and is, at any time that is in the period and that is before the investment time, related to the parent;

[...]

(c) ...

(i) from a corporation (in this paragraph referred to as the "disposing corporation") to which the CRIC is, immediately before the investment time, related (determined without reference to paragraph 251(5)(b)), and

(A) each shareholder of the disposing corporation immediately before the investment time is

(I) either the CRIC or a corporation resident in Canada that, immediately before the investment time, is related to the parent, and

(II) at no time that is in the period during which the series of transactions or events that includes the making of the investment occurs and that is before the investment time, dealing at arm's length (determined without reference to paragraph 251(5)(b)) with the parent or a non-resident corporation that participates in the series and is, at any time that is in the period and that is before the investment time, related to the parent, or

(B) the disposing corporation is, at no time that is in the period and that is before the investment time, dealing at arm's length (determined without reference to paragraph 251(5)(b)) with the parent or a non-resident corporation that participates in the series and is, at any time that is in the period and that is before the investment time, related to the parent,

(ii) on an amalgamation described in subsection 87(1) of two or more corporations (each of which is in this subparagraph referred to as a "predecessor corporation") to form the CRIC, or a corporation of which the CRIC is a shareholder, if

(A) all of the predecessor corporations are, immediately before the amalgamation, related to each other (determined without reference to paragraph 251(5)(b)), and

(B) either

(I) none of the predecessor corporations are, at any time that is in the period during which the series of transactions or events that includes the making of the investment occurs and that is before the investment time, dealing at arm's length (determined without reference to paragraph 251(5)(b)) with the parent or a non-resident corporation that participates in the series and is, at any time that is in the period and that is before the investment time, related to the parent, or

(II) if the condition in subclause (I) is not satisfied in respect of a predecessor corporation, each shareholder of that predecessor immediately before the investment time is

1. either the CRIC or a corporation resident in Canada that, immediately before the investment time, is related to the parent, and

2. at no time that is in the period and that is before the investment time, dealing at arm's length (determined without reference to paragraph 251(5)(b)) with the parent or a non-resident corporation that participates in the series and is, at any time that is in the period and that is before the investment time, related to the parent,

212.3(18) amended by 2014 budget bill #2 (last change effective for transactions and events after Aug. 15, 2013), 2002-2013 technical bill.

(18.1) Exchange — pertinent loan or indebtedness — Subsection (18) does not apply to an investment that is an acquisition of property if the property can reasonably be considered to have been received by the CRIC as repayment in whole or in part, or in settlement, of a pertinent loan or indebtedness.

Notes: 212.3(18.1) added by 2014 budget bill #2, effective for transactions and events that occur after Aug. 15, 2013

(19) Preferred shares — Subparagraph (1)(b)(ii) applies, and subsection (16) and paragraphs (18)(b) and (d) do not apply, to an acquisition of shares of the capital stock of a subject corporation by a CRIC if, having regard to all the terms and conditions of the shares and any agreement in respect of the shares, the shares cannot reasonably be considered to fully participate in the profits of the subject corporation and any appreciation in the value of the subject corporation, unless the subject corporation would be a subsidiary wholly-owned corporation of the CRIC throughout the period during which the series of transactions or events that includes the acquisition occurs if the CRIC owned all of the shares of the capital stock of the subject corporation that are owned by any of

(a) the CRIC;

(b) a corporation resident in Canada that is a subsidiary wholly-owned corporation of the CRIC; and

(c) a corporation resident in Canada of which the CRIC is a subsidiary wholly-owned corporation.

Notes: 212.3(19) opening words amended by 2014 budget bill #2, retroactive to transactions and events that occur after March 28, 2012.

This was 212.3(14) in the draft legislation of Aug. 14, 2012.

(20) Assumption of debt on liquidation or distribution — Subsection (2) applies to an investment in a subject corporation made by a CRIC that is an acquisition of shares of the capital stock of the subject corporation described in any of subparagraphs (18)(b)(v) to (vii) to the extent of the lesser of

(a) the total of all amounts each of which is the amount of a debt obligation assumed by the CRIC in respect of the liquidation and dissolution, redemption, dividend or qualifying return of capital, as the case may be, and

(b) the fair market value of the shares at the investment time.

Notes: This was 212.3(15) in the draft legislation of Aug. 14, 2012.

212.3(20)(a) amended by 2002-2013 technical bill, retroactive to introduction of 212.3.

(21) Persons deemed not to be related — If it can reasonably be considered that one of the main purposes of one or more transactions or events is to cause two or more persons to be related to each other, or a person or group of persons to control another person, so that, in the absence of this subsection, subsection (2) would not apply because of subsection (18) to an investment in a subject corporation made by a CRIC, those persons are deemed not to be related to each other, or that person or group of persons is deemed not to control that other person, as the case may be, for the purposes of subsection (18).

Notes: For the meaning of "one of the main purposes" see Notes to 83(2.1).

212.3(21) amended by 2021 budget bill #1, for transactions/events after March 18, 2019, to cover control by non-resident groups or individuals. Before then, read:

(21) If it can reasonably be considered that one of the main purposes of one or more transactions or events is to cause two or more persons to be related to each other so that, in the absence of this subsection, subsection (2) would not apply because of subsection (18) to an investment in a subject corporation made by a CRIC, those persons are deemed not to be related to each other for the purposes of subsection (18).

(22) Mergers — For the purposes of this section and subsections 219.1(3) and (4),

(a) if there has been an amalgamation to which subsection 87(11) applies,

(i) the new corporation referred to in that subsection is deemed to be the same corporation as, and a continuation of, the parent and each subsidiary referred to in that subsection,

(ii) the new corporation is deemed not to acquire any property of the parent, or of any subsidiary, as a result of the amalgamation, and

(iii) each shareholder of the new corporation is deemed not to acquire indirectly any shares as a result of the amalgamation; and

(b) if there has been a winding-up to which subsection 88(1) applies,

(i) the parent referred to in that subsection is deemed to be the same corporation as, and a continuation of, the subsidiary referred to in that subsection, and

(ii) the parent is deemed not to acquire any property of the subsidiary as a result of the winding-up.

Notes: 212.3(22)(a)(iii) added by 2014 budget bill #2, retroactive to transactions and events that occur after March 28, 2012.

This was 212.3(16) in the draft legislation of Aug. 14, 2012.

(23) Indirect investment — Subsection (2) applies to an investment in a subject corporation made by a CRIC to which, in the absence of this subsection, subsection (2) would not apply because of subsection (16) or (24), to the extent that one or more properties received by the subject corporation from the CRIC as a result of the investment, or property substituted for any such property, may reasonably be considered to have been used by the subject corporation, directly or indirectly as part of a series of transactions or events that includes the making of the investment, in a transaction or event to which subsection (2) would have applied if the CRIC had entered into the transaction, or participated in the event, as the case may be, instead of the subject corporation.

Notes: For the meaning of "indirectly", see Notes to 17.1(1).

212.3(23) amended to add reference to 212.3(24) by 2014 budget bill #2, for transactions and events after March 28, 2012. This was 212.3(17) in the draft legislation of Aug. 14, 2012, and 212.3(6) in the draft of March 29, 2012. See also Notes at end of 212.3.

(24) Indirect funding — Subsection (2) does not apply to an investment in a subject corporation made by a CRIC to which, in the absence of this subsection, subsection (2) would apply, if the CRIC demonstrates that

(a) all the properties received by the subject corporation from the CRIC as a result of the investment were used, at a particular time that is within 30 days after the investment time and at all times after the particular time, by the subject corporation

(i) to derive income from activities that can reasonably be considered to be directly related to active business activities carried on by a particular corporation and all of the income is income from an active business because of subparagraph 95(2)(a)(i), or

(ii) to make a loan or acquire a property, all or substantially all of the income from which is, or would be, if there were income from the loan or property, derived from amounts paid or payable, directly or indirectly, to the subject corporation by a particular corporation and is, or would be, income from an active business because of subparagraph 95(2)(a)(ii);

(b) the particular corporation was, at the particular time, a controlled foreign affiliate of the CRIC for the purposes of section 17; and

(c) the particular corporation is, throughout the period that begins at the investment time and during which the series of transactions or events that includes the activities of, or the making of the loan or acquisition of property by, the subject corporation occurs, a corporation in which an investment made by the CRIC would not be subject to subsection (2) because of subsection (16).

Related Provisions: 212.3(23) — Indirect investment.

Notes: For the meaning of "indirectly" in (a)(ii), see Notes to 17.1(1).

Paras. (a)-(c) amended by 2014 budget bill #2, retroactive to transactions and events that occur after March 28, 2012.

This provision was not in the draft legislation of Aug. 14, 2012.

(25) Partnerships — For the purposes of this section, subsection 17.1(1) (as it applies in respect of a pertinent loan or indebtedness as defined in subsection (11)), paragraph 128.1(1)(c.3) and subsection 219.1(2),

(a) any transaction entered into, or event participated in, by a partnership is deemed to have been entered into, or participated in, as the case may be, by each member of the partnership in the proportion that the fair market value, at the time of the transaction or event, of the member's interest — held directly or indirectly through one or more other partnerships — in the partnership is of the fair market value, at that time, of all direct interests in the partnership;

(b) if at any time, based on the assumptions contained in paragraph 96(1)(c), property would be owned by a partnership, that property is deemed to be owned at that time by each member of the partnership in the proportion that the fair market value, at that time, of the member's interest — held directly or indirectly through one or more other partnerships — in the partnership is of the fair market value, at that time, of all direct interests in the partnership;

(c) if at any time there is an increase (including, for greater certainty, as a result of a particular acquisition of an interest in a partnership in which, immediately prior to the particular acquisition, the member did not have an interest) in the portion of a property that is deemed under paragraph (b) to be owned by a member of a partnership, the member is deemed at that time

(i) to acquire the additional portion of the property, and

(ii) to transfer property that relates to the acquisition of the additional portion and that has a fair market value equal to the fair market value at that time of the additional portion;

(d) if at any time, based on the assumptions contained in paragraph 96(1)(c), an amount would be owing by a partnership, that amount is deemed to be owed by each member of the partnership in the proportion that the fair market value, at that time, of the member's interest — held directly or indirectly through one or more other partnerships — in the partnership is of the fair market value, at that time, of all direct interests in the partnership;

(e) if a member of a partnership enters into a transaction, or participates in an event, with the partnership, paragraph (a) does not apply to the transaction or event to the extent that the transaction or event would, in the absence of this paragraph, be deemed by paragraph (a) to have been entered into, or participated in, as the case may be, by the member; and

(f) a person or partnership that is (or is deemed by this paragraph to be) a member of a particular partnership that is a member of another partnership is deemed to be a member of the other partnership.

Notes: This was 212.3(18) in the draft legislation of Aug. 14, 2012, and 212.3(7) in the draft of March 29, 2012.

For transitional 212.3(25), see Notes at end of 212.3.

(26) [Determining "related" and "control" for] Trusts — For the purposes of this section, subsection 17.1(1) (as it applies in respect of a "pertinent loan or indebtedness" as defined in subsection (11)), paragraph 128.1(1)(c.3) and subsection 219.1(2), and for the purpose of paragraph 251(1)(a) as it applies for the purposes of those provisions,

(a) in determining, at any time, whether two persons are related to each other or whether any person is controlled by any other person or group of persons, it shall be assumed that

(i) each trust is a corporation having a capital stock of a single class of voting shares divided into 100 issued shares, and

(ii) each beneficiary under a trust owned at that time the number of issued shares of that class determined by the formula

$$A/B \times 100$$

where

A is the fair market value at that time of the beneficiary's interest in the trust, and

B is the total fair market value at that time of all beneficiaries' interests in the trust;

(b) in determining, at any time, the extent to which any person owns shares of the capital stock of a corporation, if at that time a trust resident in Canada owns (determined without reference to this paragraph) shares of the capital stock of the corporation, each beneficiary of the trust is deemed to own, and the trust is deemed not to own, at that time, the shares of each class of the capital stock of the corporation that are owned (determined without reference to this paragraph) by the trust, the number of which is determined by the formula

$$A \times B/C$$

where

A is the total number of shares of the class of the capital stock of the corporation that are owned (determined without reference to this paragraph) by the trust at that time,

B is the fair market value, at that time, of the beneficiary's interest in the trust, and

C is the total fair market value, at that time, of all beneficiaries' interests in the trust; and

(c) if a beneficiary's share of the income or capital of a trust depends on the exercise by any person of, or the failure by any person to exercise, any discretionary power, then the amounts determined for A and B in paragraph (a), and for B and C in paragraph (b), in respect of the beneficiary are deemed to be equal to one, unless

(i) the trust is resident in Canada, and

(ii) it cannot reasonably be considered that one of the main reasons for the discretionary power is to avoid or limit the application of paragraph 128.1(1)(c.3) or subsection 212.3(2) or 219.1(2).

Notes: 212.3(26) added by 2021 budget bill #1, for transactions or events after March 18, 2019 (part of extending 212.3 to control by non-resident groups or individuals).

Notes [s. 212.3]: 212.3 addresses "foreign affiliate dumping", where a foreign owner causes a profitable Canadian sub to borrow to acquire shares of an active foreign corp in the group, to create deductible interest to offset Canadian profits, while dividends from the foreign corp are tax-free due to 113(1).

Simplified, 212.3(2)(a) deems the Canadian sub to have paid a dividend to the foreign parent (or group of parents), triggering 212(2) withholding tax, at the time of the investment (see "dividend time" in 212.3(4) and "investment time" in 212.3(1) opening words); and 212.3(2)(b) grinds down the paid-up capital (PUC) of the shares of the Canadian sub resulting from the investment, resulting in higher capital gain on their eventual sale.

Exceptions to 212.3(2) are found in 212.3(16) (closely connected business — narrow exception) and (18) (reorganizations); and 212.3(7) allows a PUC grind-down to reduce the deemed dividend in many cases. If the ultimate parent is Canadian, 212.3(15)(a)(ii) prevents 212.3(2) from applying. See also 18(5)"equity amount"(a)(ii) (effect on thin capitalization rules) and 84(1)(c.1)-(c.3) (effect on surplus-stripping rules).

For detailed discussion (some before the 2021 amendments) see Vidal, *Introduction to International Tax in Canada* (Carswell, 8th ed., 2020), chap. 11; Anderson & Maduke, "Practical Implementation Issues Arising from the Foreign Affiliate Dumping Rules", 2014 Cdn Tax Foundation conference report, 19:1-49; Kraus & O'Connor, "Foreign Affiliate Dumping", 2017 conference report, 20:1-39; Trossman, "The Foreign Affiliate Dumping Rules", XV(1) *Corporate Structures & Groups* (Federated Press) 10-22 (2019).

Shorter articles (see also Notes to the 212.3 subsections): Armstrong & Glicklich, "Recent Transactions of Interest"; 2016 conference report at 7:3-5, 9-10; Kjellander, "Options to Acquires Shares and the Foreign Affiliate Dumping Rules", XII(2) *Resource Sector Taxation [RST]* (Federated Press) 17-20 (2018); Shew, "Foreign Affiliate Dumping and Estates with Non-Resident Beneficiaries", 10(1) *Canadian Tax Focus* (ctf.ca) 9-10 (Feb. 2020); Chan & Prystal, "The Foreign Affiliate Dumping Rules and Private Equity Investments", XIV(1) *RST* 14-20 (2020); Murdoch & Ji, "Foreign Affiliate Dumping Rules", IX(2) *Personal Tax & Estate Planning* (Federated Press) 10-16 (2020).

212.3 was substantially changed from March 29 and Aug. 14, 2012 drafts to what was enacted in 2012, and changed again in 2014 retroactive to its introduction. On the 2014 changes see Suarez, "An Analysis of Canada's Latest International Tax Proposals", 75(13) *Tax Notes International* (taxnotes.com) 1131 (Sept. 29, 2014) at 1136-43; Nikolakakis, "Foreign Affiliate Dumping", 78 *International Tax* (CCH) 1-6 (Oct. 2014). On the 2016 amendments see CBA/CPA Canada Joint Committee letter to Finance, Nov. 15, 2016, pp. 7-14.

On the 2019 proposals enacted in 2021 (expanding 212.3 to non-resident individual owners), see Keung & Moody, "Surprise! Foreign Affiliate Dumping Rules Coming to a Private Business Near You", 2019(7) *Tax Times* (Carswell) 2-3 (April 12, 2019); CBA/CPA Canada Joint Committee letter to Finance, May 24, 2019, pp. 1-15; Rodrigues, "2019 Proposed Amendments to the Foreign Affiliate Dumping Rules", 12(2) *Taxes & Wealth Management* (Carswell) 2-5 (June 2019); Loney & Denny, "Proposed Changes to Foreign Affiliate Dumping Rules", tinyurl.com/loney-denny (Sept. 11, 2019); Watson & Wong, "Recent Legislative Proposals to the FAD Rules", 108 *International Tax* (CCH, Oct. 2019).

For CRA interpretation see VIEWS docs 2014-0526691C6 [IFA 2014 q.1] (CRIC guarantees of debt for no fee); 2015-0581641C6 [IFA 2015 q.10] (whether 111(4)(e) designation triggers 212.3); 2016-0643931R3 [Wang & Lee, "Buy, Bump and Emigrate?", 26(8) *Canadian Tax Highlights* (ctf.ca) 8-9 (Aug. 2018)].

(Earlier docs should be read with caution due to the 2014 changes: 2011-0425441R3 (no 212.3(2) on cross-border butterfly); 2012-0451421R3 (purchase of target and bump); 2012-0452291R3 (double-dip financing structure); 2013-0474671E5 (meaning of "more closely connected business activities" in 212.3(16)); 2013-0483751C6 [IFA 2013 q.6] (numerous questions on 212.3(3), (9)-(11), (16)); 2013-0483771C6 [IFA 2013 q.4] (GAAR in scenarios using Canadian holdco to acquire shares of FA); 2013-0491061R3 (no 212.3(2) due to 212.3(18), (25)).)

For the pre-212.3 rules see Bunn, "Debt Dumping", 2(2) *Canadian Tax Focus* (ctf.ca) 2 (May 2012).

212.3 added by 2012 budget bill #2, for transactions/events after March 28, 2012 (Aug. 13 or Dec. 31, 2012 in some cases). It reflects changes proposed in Finance comfort letters of May 31 and Sept. 4, 2012 (see David M. Sherman, *Department of Finance Technical Notes*).

Definitions [s. 212.3]: "active business", "amount" — 248(1); "affiliated" — 251.1; "arm's length" — 251(1); "beneficiary" — 248(25) [Notes]; "business" — 248(1); "CRIC" — 212.3(1); "Canada" — 255, *Interpretation Act* 35(1); "Canadian corporation" — 89(1), 248(1); "class of shares" — 248(6); "connected affiliate" — 212.3(16)(b)(ii); "control", "controlled" — 212.3(15), (26), 256(6)–(9), 256.1(3); "controlled foreign affiliate" — 95(1), 248(1); "controls" — 212.3(15); "corporation" — 248(1), *Interpretation Act* 35(1); "cross-border class" — 212.3(4), (6); "direct equity percentage" — 95(4); "disposition" — 248(1); "dividend" — 212.3(2), (3), 248(1); "dividend time" — 212.3(4); "equity percentage" — 95(4); "fair market value" — see 69(1) Notes; "filing-due date" — 150(1), 248(1); "foreign affiliate" — 95(1), 248(1); "group of parents" — 212.3(1)(b); "indirect acquisition" — 212.3(10)(f); "investment" — 212.3(10); "investment time" — 212.3(1); "limited partner" — 96(2.4); "Minister" — 248(1); "month" — *Interpretation Act* 35(1); "non-resident", "officer" — 248(1); "other Canadian corporation" — 212.3(1)(a)(ii); "paid-up capital" — 89(1), 248(1); "parent" — 212.3(1)(b); "partnership" — see 96(1) Notes; "person" — 248(1); "pertinent loan or indebtedness" — 212.3(11); "predecessor corporation" — 212.3(18)(a)(ii), 212.3(18)(c)(ii); "prescribed", "property" — 248(1); "qualifying return of capital" — 90(3); "qualifying substitute corporation" — 212.3(4); "related" — 212.3(21), (26), 251(2)–(6); "related group" — 251(4); "resident" — 250; "resident in Canada" — 94(3)(a), 250; "series of transactions" — 248(10); "share", "shareholder" — 248(1); "specific corporation" — 212.3(15)(a); "subject corporation" — 212.3(1); "subject subsidiary corporation" — 212.3(16)(a); "subsidiary wholly-owned corporation" — 248(1); "substituted" — 248(5); "taxation year" — 249; "taxpayer" — 248(1); "trust" — 104(1), 248(1), (3); "writing" — *Interpretation Act* 35(1).

213. (1) Tax non-payable by non-resident person — Tax is not payable by a non-resident person under subsection 212(2) on a dividend in respect of a share of the capital stock of a foreign business corporation if not less than 90% of the total of the amounts received or receivable by it that are required to be included in computing its income for the taxation year in which the dividend was paid was received or receivable in respect of the operation by it of public utilities or from mining, transporting and processing of ore in a country in which

(a) if the non-resident person is an individual, the non-resident person resides; or

(b) if the non-resident person is a corporation, individuals who own more than 50% of its share capital (having full voting rights under all circumstances) reside.

Forms: T4061: Non-resident withholding tax guide.

(2) Idem — For the purposes of this section, if 90% of the total of the amounts received or receivable by a corporation that are required to be included in computing its income for a taxation year was received or receivable in respect of the operation by it of public utilities or from the mining, transporting and processing of ore, an amount received or receivable in that year from that corporation by another corporation shall, if it is required to be included in computing the receiving corporation's income for the year, be deemed to have been received by the receiving corporation in respect of the operation by it of public utilities or from the mining, transporting and processing of ore by it in the country in which the public utilities were operated or the mining, transporting and processing of ore was carried out by the payer corporation.

(3) Corporation deemed to be foreign business corporation — For the purposes of this section, a corporation shall be deemed to be a foreign business corporation at a particular time if it would have been a foreign business corporation within the meaning of section 71 of the *Income Tax Act*, chapter 148 of the Revised Statutes of Canada, 1952 (as that section read in its application to the 1971 taxation year), for the taxation year of the corporation in which the particular time occurred, if that section had been applicable to that taxation year.

I.T. Application Rules: 69 (meaning of "chapter 148 of ...").

Definitions [s. 213]: "amount" — 248(1); "corporation" — 248(1), *Interpretation Act* 35(1); "dividend" — 248(1); "foreign business corporation" — 213(3); "individual", "non-resident", "person" — 248(1); "taxation year" — 249.

Interpretation Bulletins [s. 213]: IT-109R2: Unpaid amounts.

214. (1) No deductions — The tax payable under section 212 is payable on the amounts described therein without any deduction from those amounts whatever.

Related Provisions: 216 — Option to pay tax on the net rather than the gross.

I.T. Application Rules: 10(6) (tax limited to treaty rate).

Interpretation Bulletins: IT-88R2: Stock dividends; IT-109R2: Unpaid amounts; IT-438R2: Crown charges — resource properties in Canada; IT-465R: Non-resident beneficiaries of trusts.

(2) Income and capital combined — Where paragraph 16(1)(b) would, if Part I were applicable, result in a part of an amount being included in computing the income of a non-resident person, that part of the amount shall, for the purposes of this Part, be deemed to have been paid or credited to the non-resident person in respect of property, services or otherwise, depending on the nature of that part of the amount.

Related Provisions: 214(12) — Application.

Interpretation Bulletins: IT-88R2: Stock dividends; IT-265R3: Payments of income and capital combined (cancelled).

(3) Deemed payments — For the purposes of this Part,

(a) where section 15 or subsection 56(2) would, if Part I were applicable, require an amount to be included in computing a taxpayer's income, that amount shall be deemed to have been paid to the taxpayer as a dividend from a corporation resident in Canada;

(b) where paragraph 56(1)(f) would, if Part I were applicable, require an amount to be included in computing an individual's income, that amount shall be deemed to have been paid to the individual under an income-averaging annuity contract;

(b.1) where paragraph 56(1)(y) would, if Part I were applicable, require an amount to be included in computing a taxpayer's income, that amount shall be deemed to have been paid to the taxpayer to acquire an interest in a retirement compensation arrangement;

(c) where, because of subsection 146(8.1), (8.8), (8.91), (9), (10) or (12), an amount would, if Part I applied, be required to be included in computing a taxpayer's income, that amount shall be deemed to have been paid to the taxpayer as a payment under a registered retirement savings plan or an amended plan (within the meaning assigned by subsection 146(12)), as the case may be;

(d) where, by virtue of subsection 147(10), (13) or (15), an amount would, if Part I were applicable, be required to be included in computing a taxpayer's income, that amount shall be deemed to have been paid to the taxpayer as a payment under a deferred profit sharing plan or a plan referred to in subsection 147(15) as a "revoked plan", as the case may be;

(e) where subsection 130.1(2) would, if Part I were applicable, deem an amount received by a shareholder of a mortgage investment corporation to have been received by the shareholder as interest, that amount shall be deemed to have been paid to the shareholder as interest on a bond issued after 1971;

(f) where subsection 104(13) would, if Part I were applicable, require any part of an amount payable by a trust in its taxation year to a beneficiary to be included in computing the income of the non-resident person who is a beneficiary of the trust, that part is deemed to be an amount paid or credited to that person as income of or from the trust

(i) on, or at, the earliest of

(A) the day on which the amount was paid or credited,

(B) the day that is 90 days after the end of the taxation year, and

(C) if the taxation year is deemed by subparagraph 128.1(4)(a)(i) to end after July 25, 2012, the time that is immediately before the end of the taxation year, and

(ii) not at any later time;

(f.1) where paragraph 132.1(1)(d) would, if Part I were applicable, require an amount to be included in computing a taxpayer's income for a taxation year by reason of a designation by a mutual fund trust under subsection 132.1(1), that amount shall be deemed to be an amount paid or credited to that person as income of or from the trust on the day of the designation;

(g) [no longer relevant: applies on death of owner of pre-1986 registered home ownership savings plan — ed.]

(h) [Repealed under former Act]

(i) where, because of subsection 146.3(4), (6), (6.1), (7) or (11), an amount would, if Part I applied, be required to be included in computing a taxpayer's income, that amount shall be deemed to have been paid to the taxpayer as a payment under a registered retirement income fund;

(j) [Repealed]

(k) where, because of subsection 143.1(2), an amount distributed at any time by an amateur athlete trust would, if Part I were applicable, be required to be included in computing an individual's income, that amount shall be deemed to have been paid at that time to the individual as a payment in respect of an amateur athlete trust; and

(l) where, because of subsection 12(10.2), an amount would at any particular time, if Part I were applicable, be required to be included in computing a taxpayer's income, that amount shall be deemed to have been paid by Her Majesty in right of Canada at that time to the taxpayer out of the taxpayer's NISA Fund No. 2.

Related Provisions: 94(3)(a)(iii), 104(7.01) — Trusts that are deemed resident in Canada; 214(3.1) — Time of deemed payment; 218.3(10) — 214(3)(f) applies to mutual fund distributions withholding tax; 227(6.1) — Repayment of non-resident shareholder loan; 247(12) — Deemed dividend resulting from transfer pricing adjustment.

Notes: In both *Axa Canada*, 2006 TCC 4, and *General Electric Capital*, 2010 FCA 344, 214(3) was held not to apply as, on the facts, no 15(1) benefit had been conferred.

Where a trust becomes non-resident [see 128.1(4)], 214(3)(f)(i)(C) effectively overrules *Lewin [JJ Herbert Family Trust]*, 2012 FCA 279, where a trustee declaration that an amount was "payable" to a beneficiary did not make it paid or credited for purposes of 212(1). See Finance news release, July 25, 2012.

214(3) makes the non-resident liable for Part XIII tax, but arguably does not impose liability on the payor to withhold under 215(1). For example, if 56(2) applies to a payment that X (an individual) instructs Y to pay to Z, 214(3)(a) deems the amount to have been paid "as a dividend from a corporation resident in Canada", but arguably does not deem either X or Z to be a corporation that paid the dividend (though 214(3.1) deems a time of payment).

The deemed dividend may be eligible for a reduced tax-treaty rate only if the treaty so provides, as Canada-US Treaty Art. X:3 and Canada-UK Treaty Art. 10:5 do (e.g., "income treated in the same way as income from shares").

For examples of 214(3)(a) applying see VIEWS docs 2006-0196241C6, 2007-0241991R3, 2007-0243331C6, 2008-0280041R3, 2011-039792I17, 2013-0486011E5; *Canadian Winesecrets*, 2011 TCC 390 (unclear as to why tax applied).

See also Notes to 15(2).

214(3) amended by 2013 budget bill #2 (adding (f)(i)(C) effective July 25, 2012), 1997 Budget, 1993 and 1992 technical bills, 1990 pension bill.

I.T. Application Rules: 69 (meaning of "chapter 148 of ...").

Interpretation Bulletins: IT-88R2: Stock dividends; IT-96R6: Options to acquire shares, bonds or debentures and by trusts to acquire trust units; IT-109R2: Unpaid amounts; IT-119R4: Debts of shareholders, certain persons connected with shareholders, etc.; IT-335R2: Indirect payments; IT-421R2: Benefits to individuals, corporations and shareholders from loans or debt; IT-432R2: Benefits conferred on shareholders; IT-465R: Non-resident beneficiaries of trusts; IT-468R: Management or administration fees paid to non-residents; IT-500R: RRSPs — death of an annuitant.

Information Circulars: 77-16R4: Non-resident income tax; 72-22R9: Registered retirement savings plans.

Registered Plans Compliance Bulletins: 4 (abusive schemes — RRSP stripping).

Transfer Pricing Memoranda: TPM-02R: Secondary transfer pricing adjustments, repatriation and Part XIII tax assessments.

(3.1) Time of deemed payment — Except as otherwise expressly provided, each amount deemed by subsection (3) to have

been paid shall be deemed to have been paid at the time of the event or transaction as a consequence of which the amount would, if Part I were applicable, be required to be included in computing a taxpayer's income.

Transfer Pricing Memoranda: TPM-02R: Secondary transfer pricing adjustments, repatriation and Part XIII tax assessments.

(4) Securities — Where, if section 76 were applicable in computing a non-resident person's income, that section would require an amount to be included in computing the income, that amount shall, for the purpose of this Part, be deemed to have been, at the time the non-resident person received the security, right, certificate or other evidence of indebtedness, paid to the non-resident person on account of the debt in respect of which the non-resident person received it.

Related Provisions: 214(5) — Interpretation.

Interpretation Bulletins: IT-77R: Securities in satisfaction of an income debt (cancelled); IT-88R2: Stock dividends; IT-109R2: Unpaid amounts.

(5) Interpretation — Subsection (4) is enacted for greater certainty and shall not be construed as limiting the generality of the other provisions of this Part defining amounts on which tax is payable.

(6) Deemed interest — Where, in respect of interest stipulated to be payable, on a bond, debenture, bill, note, mortgage, hypothecary claim or similar obligation that has been assigned or otherwise transferred by a non-resident person to a person resident in Canada, subsection 20(14) would, if Part I were applicable, require an amount to be included in computing the transferor's income, that amount is, for the purposes of this Part, deemed to be a payment of interest on that obligation made by the transferee to the transferor at the time of the assignment or other transfer of the obligation, if

(a) the obligation was issued by a person resident in Canada;

(b) the obligation was not an obligation described in paragraph (8)(a) or (b); and

(c) the assignment or other transfer is not an assignment or other transfer referred to in paragraph (7.1)(b).

Related Provisions: 214(7.1) — Sale of obligation; 214(9) — Deemed resident; 214(14) — Deemed assignment of obligation; 214(17) — Interest deemed paid for thin-capitalization withholding tax.

Notes: The term "bond, debenture, bill, note, mortgage, hypothecary claim or similar obligation" in 214(6) may not include bankers' acceptances: *Federated Co-operatives*, 2001 FCA 217; leave to appeal denied 2001 CarswellNat 1788 (SCC).

Reference to "hypothecary claim" added to 214(6) opening words by 2001 *Civil Code* harmonization bill, effective June 14, 2001. The change is non-substantive; see *Interpretation Act* s. 8.2.

214(6) amended in 1973, effective for bonds, debentures, bills, notes or similar obligations issued after July 27, 1973. For obligations issued earlier, see up to the 28th edition of this book.

214(6) amended by 1991 technical bill, effective for obligations assigned or transferred after July 13, 1990, to conform to numbering changes in 214(8).

Interpretation Bulletins: IT-410R: Debt obligations — accrued interest on transfer (cancelled).

Information Circulars: 77-16R4: Non-resident income tax.

(7) Sale of obligation — Where

(a) a non-resident person has at any time assigned or otherwise transferred to a person resident in Canada a bond, debenture, bill, note, mortgage, hypothecary claim or similar obligation issued by a person resident in Canada,

(b) the obligation was not an excluded obligation, and

(c) the assignment or other transfer is not an assignment or other transfer referred to in paragraph (7.1)(b),

the amount, if any, by which

(d) the price for which the obligation was assigned or otherwise transferred at that time,

exceeds

(e) the price for which the obligation was issued,

shall, for the purposes of this Part, be deemed to be a payment of interest on that obligation made by the person resident in Canada to the non-resident person at that time.

Related Provisions: 16(6) — Indexed debt obligations; 214(7.1) — Sale of obligation; 214(8) — Meaning of "excluded obligation"; 214(9) — Deemed resident; 214(10) — Reduction of tax; 214(14) — Deemed assignment of obligation; 214(17) — Interest deemed paid for thin-capitalization withholding tax; 215(5) — Regulations reducing amount to be deducted or withheld.

Notes: See Notes to 212(3)"participating debt interest" and 214(8). For an example of deemed interest subject to withholding tax, see discussion of TimberWest Forest acquisition in Carrie Smit, "Recent Transactions of Interest", 2011 Cdn Tax Foundation conference report, 10:10-15. See also Michael Kandev & John Lennard, "Interpreting and Applying Deeming Provisions", 60(2) *Canadian Tax Journal* 275 (2012) at 295-302.

"Hypothecary claim" added to 214(7)(a) by 2001 *Civil Code* harmonization bill, effective June 14, 2001 (non-substantive change: *Interpretation Act* s. 8.2).

214(7) amended in 1973, effective for bonds, debentures, bills, notes or similar obligations issued after July 27, 1973. For obligations issued earlier, see up to the 28th edition of this book.

Interpretation Bulletins: IT-88R2: Stock dividends; IT-109R2: Unpaid amounts; IT-360R2: Interest payable in a foreign currency.

Information Circulars: 77-16R4: Non-resident income tax.

I.T. Technical News: See under 214(8).

(7.1) Idem — Where

(a) a person resident in Canada has at a particular time assigned or otherwise transferred an obligation to a non-resident person,

(b) the non-resident person has at a subsequent time assigned or otherwise transferred the obligation back to the person resident in Canada, and

(c) subsection (6) or (7) would apply with respect to the assignment or other transfer referred to in paragraph (b), if those subsections were read without reference to paragraphs (6)(c) and (7)(c),

the amount, if any, by which

(d) the price for which the obligation was assigned or otherwise transferred at the subsequent time,

exceeds

(e) the price for which the obligation was assigned or otherwise transferred at the particular time,

shall, for the purposes of this Part, be deemed to be a payment of interest on that obligation made by the person resident in Canada to the non-resident person at the subsequent time.

Related Provisions: 214(14) — Deemed assignment of obligation.

Notes: 214(7.1) deems an amount to be interest but does not impose withholding tax, which is done by 212(1)(b) (only in limited cases, since 2008). See VIEWS doc 2000-0046375 re pre-2008 interest computed by reference to a stock index.

214(7.1) added in 1973, effective for bonds, debentures, bills, notes or similar obligations issued after July 27, 1973.

Interpretation Bulletins: IT-88R2: Stock dividends; IT-109R2: Unpaid amounts; IT-410R: Debt obligations — accrued interest on transfer (cancelled).

Information Circulars: 77-16R4: Non-resident income tax.

(8) Meaning of "excluded obligation" — For the purposes of subsection (7), "excluded obligation" means any bond, debenture, bill, note, mortgage, hypothecary claim or similar obligation

(a) that is described in paragraph (a) of the definition "fully exempt interest" in subsection 212(3), or on which the interest would have been exempt under subparagraph 212(1)(b)(iii) or (vii) as they applied to the 2007 taxation year;

(b) that is prescribed to be a public issue security; or

(c) that is not an indexed debt obligation and that was issued for an amount not less than 97% of the principal amount thereof, and the yield from which, expressed in terms of an annual rate on the amount for which the obligation was issued (which annual rate shall, if the terms of the obligation or any agreement relating thereto conferred on the holder thereof a right to demand payment of the principal amount of the obligation or the amount outstanding as or on account of the principal amount thereof, as the case may be, before the maturity of the obligation, be calculated on the basis of the yield that produces the

highest annual rate obtainable either on the maturity of the obligation or conditional on the exercise of any such right) does not exceed $\frac{4}{3}$ of the interest stipulated to be payable on the obligation, expressed in terms of an annual rate on

(i) the principal amount thereof, if no amount is payable on account of the principal amount before the maturity of the obligation, and

(ii) the amount outstanding from time to time as or on account of the principal amount thereof, in any other case.

Notes: For interpretation see VIEWS docs 2004-0098601E5, 2008-0268281E5; 2011-0431891R3 (mortgage pool).

For convertible debt (using 214(7) and 214(8)(c)) see *Income Tax Technical News* 41 [2008 CTF conf. p.3:14-16] and 44 ("convertible debentures and Part XIII"); VIEWS docs 2008-0300101R3, 2008-0300102R3, 2009-0320231C6 [2009 IFA q.12], 2013-0514551R3, 2014-0536001R3 [Lang, "Make-Whole Amounts After Withholding", 23(4) *Canadian Tax Highlights* (ctf.ca) 6 (April 2015)]. CRA was reviewing convertible debentures and discussing this with Finance: 2011-0426171C6 [2011 CTF conf. p.4:13-14, q.17]; 2013-0483781C6 [2013 IFA q.9]. At the 2013 CTF annual conference Roundtable, CRA (Mark Symes) stated that standard convertible debentures are now accepted as not being "participating debt interest" under 212(3) (now doc 2013-0509061C6, with some qualifications). This position was applied in 2014-0532411R3 (amending 2011-0418721R3); as of Aug. 2020, there was no change in CRA's position: International Fiscal Assn CRA Q&A (Aug. 6, 2020), tinyurl.com/ifa-covid-qa, q.16. However, doc 2013-0515631E5 (March 2014) says there is no general policy and issuers should apply for advance rulings. See also Glicksman & Lille, "Convertible Debt Obligations", XVI(1) *Corporate Finance [CF]* (Federated Press) 1747-49 (2009); Tamaki & Eastwood, "Convertible Debt: a Legislative Fix Needed Quickly", XVI(1) *CF* 1750-52; Gravelle & Chan, "Financing with Convertible Debt", VII(1) *Resource Sector Taxation* (Federated Press) 493-96 (2009); Gabrielle Richards, "Canada Revenue Agency Revises Its Position on Convertible and Exchangeable Debt", XI(3) *Corporate Structures & Groups* (Federated Press) 627-30 (2009); Sherman & Saddington, "Standard Convertible Debentures", XIX(4) *CF* 2681-84 (2015).

214(8) amended by 2007 budget bill #2 (effective 2008), 2001 *Civil Code* harmonization bill, 1992 and 1991 technical bills.

Regulations: No prescribed public issue security yet under 214(8)(b).

I.T. Technical News: 41 (convertible debt); 44 (convertible debentures and Part XIII).

(9) Deemed resident — Where

(a) the assignment or other transfer of an obligation to a non-resident person carrying on business in Canada would be described in subsection (6) or (7) if those subsections were read without reference to paragraphs (6)(c) and (7)(c) and if that non-resident person were a person resident in Canada, and

(b) that non-resident person

(i) may deduct, under subsection 20(14), in computing the non-resident person's taxable income earned in Canada for a taxation year an amount in respect of interest on the obligation, or

(ii) may deduct, under Part I, in computing the non-resident person's taxable income earned in Canada for a taxation year an amount in respect of any amount paid on account of the principal amount of the obligation,

the non-resident person shall, with respect to the assignment or other transfer of the obligation, be deemed, for the purposes of this Part, to be a person resident in Canada.

Related Provisions: 214(14) — Assignment of obligation.

Notes: 214(9) amended in 1973, effective for bonds, debentures, bills, notes or similar obligations issued after July 27, 1973. For obligations issued earlier, see up to the 28th edition of this book.

Interpretation Bulletins: IT-88R2: Stock dividends; IT-109R2: Unpaid amounts; IT-410R: Debt obligations — accrued interest on transfer (cancelled).

(10) Reduction of tax — Where a non-resident person has assigned or otherwise transferred to a person resident in Canada an obligation

(a) on which an amount of interest was deemed by subsection (6) or (7) to have been paid, and

(b) that the non-resident person had previously acquired from a person resident in Canada,

the amount of the tax under this Part that the non-resident person is liable to pay in respect thereof shall be deemed, for the purpose of subsection 227(6), to be that proportion of the tax the non-resident person would otherwise have been liable to pay in respect thereof that

(c) the number of days in the period commencing with the day the obligation was last acquired by the non-resident person from a person resident in Canada and ending with the day the obligation was last assigned or otherwise transferred by the non-resident person to a person resident in Canada

is of

(d) the number of days in the period commencing with the day the obligation was issued and ending with the day the obligation was last assigned or otherwise transferred by the non-resident person to a person resident in Canada.

Related Provisions: 214(14) — Deemed assignment of obligation.

Notes: 214(10) amended in 1973, effective for bonds, debentures, bills, notes or similar obligations issued after July 27, 1973. For obligations issued earlier, see up to the 28th edition of this book.

Interpretation Bulletins: IT-88R2: Stock dividends; IT-109R2: Unpaid amounts; IT-410R: Debt obligations — accrued interest on transfer (cancelled).

(11) [Repealed]

Notes: 214(11) repealed by 2007 budget bill #2, effective 2008. It applied to the pre-2008 212(1)(b).

(12) Where subsec. (2) does not apply — Subsection (2) does not apply in respect of a payment to a non-resident person under any obligation in respect of which that person is liable to pay tax under this Part by reason of subsection (7) or (7.1).

Notes: 214(12) amended in 1973, effective for bonds, debentures, bills, notes or similar obligations issued after July 27, 1973. For earlier ones see up to 50th ed.

(13) Regulations respecting residents — The Governor in Council may make general or special regulations, for the purposes of this Part, prescribing

(a) who is or has been at any time resident in Canada;

(b) where a person was resident in Canada as well as in some other place, what amounts are taxable under this Part; and

(c) where a non-resident person carried on business in Canada, what amounts are taxable under this Part or what portion of the tax under this Part is payable by that person.

Regulations: 802 (amounts taxable). None for paras. (a), (b).

(14) Assignment of obligation — For the purposes of this section, any transaction or event by which an obligation held by a non-resident person is redeemed in whole or in part or is cancelled shall be deemed to be an assignment of the obligation by the non-resident person.

Notes: 214(14) added in 1973, effective for bonds, debentures, bills, notes or similar obligations issued after July 27, 1973.

Interpretation Bulletins: IT-88R2: Stock dividends; IT-109R2: Unpaid amounts; IT-360R2: Interest payable in a foreign currency.

(15) Standby charges and guarantee fees — For the purposes of this Part,

(a) where a non-resident person has entered into an agreement under the terms of which the non-resident person agrees to guarantee the repayment, in whole or in part, of the principal amount of a bond, debenture, bill, note, mortgage, hypothecary claim or similar obligation of a person resident in Canada, any amount paid or credited as consideration for the guarantee is deemed to be a payment of interest on that obligation; and

(b) where a non-resident person has entered into an agreement under the terms of which the non-resident person agrees to lend money, or to make money available, to a person resident in Canada, any amount paid or credited as consideration for so agreeing to lend money or to make money available shall, if the non-resident person would be liable to tax under this Part in respect of interest payable on any obligation issued under the terms of the agreement on the date it was entered into, be deemed to be a payment of interest.

Related Provisions: Canada-U.S. Tax Treaty:Art. XXII:4 — No withholding tax on guarantee fee.

Notes: For examples of 214(15)(a) applying see *General Electric Capital*, 2010 FCA 344, and VIEWS doc 2008-0280131R3. Where a letter of credit is used to provide security between a Canadian purchaser and a non-resident supplier, and is payable on proof of shipment of the goods, the fee for the letter of credit does not fall under 214(15)(b): docs 2003-0014145, 2006-0210641R3.

214(15) amended by 2001 *Civil Code* harmonization bill, effective March 1994, to add reference to "hypothecary claim" (change is non-substantive; see *Interpretation Act* s. 8.2), and to change "repayment of interest" to "payment of interest".

Advance Tax Rulings: ATR-49: Long-term foreign debt.

(16) Deemed dividends [on thin capitalization interest] — For the purposes of this Part,

(a) an amount paid or credited as interest by a corporation resident in Canada, or by a partnership, in a taxation year of the corporation to a non-resident person is deemed to have been paid by the corporation as a dividend, and not to have been paid or credited by the corporation or the partnership as interest, to the extent that an amount in respect of the interest

(i) is not deductible in computing the income of the corporation for the year because of subsection 18(4), or

(ii) is included in computing the income of the corporation for the year under paragraph 12(1)(l.1); and

(b) to the extent that amounts paid or credited to a non-resident person in the year are deemed by paragraph (a) to have been paid by a corporation as dividends, the corporation may designate in its return of income under Part I for the year which amounts paid or credited as interest to the non-resident person in the year are deemed to have been paid as dividends and not as interest.

Related Provisions: 18(6.1) — Back-to-back loans — deemed interest; 212(2) — Withholding tax on deemed dividend; 214(17) — Interest payable deemed paid; 227(8.5) — No penalty for failing to withhold tax unless it would have applied to payment of interest; Canada-U.S. Tax Treaty:Art. XXII:4 — No withholding tax on guarantee fee.

Notes: Interest is subject to withholding tax under 212(1)(b) only in limited circumstances. 214(16) deems interest disallowed as a deduction under the thin-capitalization rules (18(4)), or subject to the add-back for partners (12(1)(l.1)), to be a dividend, and thus subject to withholding tax under 212(2). (This deeming applies only for Part XIII, so it has no impact on LRIP, GRIP or FAPI: VIEWS doc 2015-0614021I7.) No penalty applies to failure to withhold unless withholding would have applied to the payment of interest anyway: 227(8.5). See also 214(17); and Carrie Smit, "Thin Capitalization Amendments — Denied Interest May be Subject to Tax", 2114 *Tax Topics* (CCH) 1-4 (Sept. 13, 2012); 2013-0483731C6 [2013 IFA] (gives examples).

214(16)(b) allows post-year-end allocation of specific interest payments as dividends; otherwise "the appropriate portion of each interest payment is deemed to be a dividend" (Finance Technical Notes). This allows a corp some flexibility as to its withholding obligations: VIEWS doc 2018-0768721C6 [2018 APFF q.1] (also notes that a corp that withholds too much can recover the excess via 227(6)).

214(16) added by 2012 budget bill #2, for tax years that end after March 28, 2012, with a transitional calculation for years that include that day.

(17) Deemed interest payments — For the purposes of subsection (16),

(a) interest payable (other than interest payable pursuant to a legal obligation to pay interest on an amount of interest) by a corporation resident in Canada, or by a partnership, in respect of a taxation year of the corporation, but that has not been paid or credited in the year, is deemed to have been paid immediately before the end of the year and not to have been paid or credited at any other time; and

(b) if subsection (6) or (7) deems a payment of interest to have been made to a non-resident person in respect of a debt or other obligation of a corporation, interest that, at the time of the transfer or assignment, is payable by the corporation in respect of the debt or other obligation and has not been paid or credited is deemed to have been paid by the corporation immediately before that time to the non-resident person.

Related Provisions: 18(6.1) — Back-to-back loans — deemed interest.

Notes: See Notes to 214(16). 214(17) added by 2012 budget bill #2, this version effective Aug. 14, 2012.

Definitions [s. 214]: "amateur athlete trust" — 143.1(1.2)(a), 248(1); "amount" — 248(1); "assignment" — 214(14); "beneficiary" — 248(25) [Notes]; "business" — 248(1); "Canada" — 255; "carried on business in Canada" — 253; "corporation" — 248(1), *Interpretation Act* 35(1); "deferred profit sharing plan" — 147(1), 248(1); "dividend" — 248(1); "excluded obligation" — 214(8); "fair market value" — see 69(1) Notes; "fully exempt interest" — 212(3); "Governor in Council", "Her Majesty" — *Interpretation Act* 35(1); "income-averaging annuity contract" — 61(4), 248(1); "indexed debt obligation", "individual" — 248(1); "mutual fund trust" — 132(6)–(7), 132.2(3)(n), 248(1); "NISA Fund No. 2", "non-resident" — 248(1); "non-resident-owned investment corporation" — 133(8), 248(1); "partnership" — see 96(1) Notes; "person", "prescribed", "principal amount", "property" — 248(1); "registered education savings plan" — 146.1(1), 248(1); "registered retirement income fund" — 146.3(1), 248(1); "registered retirement savings plan" — 146(1), 248(1); "regulation" — 248(1); "resident in Canada" — 250; "retirement compensation arrangement", "shareholder" — 248(1); "taxable income earned in Canada" — 115(1), 248(1); "taxation year" — 249; "taxpayer" — 248(1); "trust" — 104(1), 248(1), (3).

215. (1) Withholding and remittance of tax

— When a person pays, credits or provides, or is deemed to have paid, credited or provided, an amount on which an income tax is payable under this Part, or would be so payable if this Act were read without reference to subparagraph 94(3)(a)(viii) and to subsection 216.1(1), the person shall, notwithstanding any agreement or law to the contrary, deduct or withhold from it the amount of the tax and forthwith remit that amount to the Receiver General on behalf of the non-resident person on account of the tax and shall submit with the remittance a statement in prescribed form.

Related Provisions: 94(3)(a)(ix), 94(4)(c) — Application of rule deeming non-resident trust to be resident in Canada; 94(3)(g) — Amount withheld for non-resident trust deemed resident in Canada is considered paid on account; 215(1.1) — Exception on corporate immigration; 215(5) — Regulations reducing deduction or withholding; 215(6) — Liability for tax; 227 — Withholding taxes — administration and enforcement; 227.1 — Liability of directors; 248(7)(b)(i) — Remittance deemed made when received.

Notes: See 227(8.3) Notes re remittance being required "forthwith".

215(1) requires a tenant to withhold tax on rent paid to a non-resident landlord: *Dorey*, 2003 FC 1241. Due to the wording of 94(3)(a)(viii), it applies where the landlord is a non-resident trust deemed resident in Canada by 94(3), even though the trust is not liable for Part XIII tax.

215(1) amended to add reference to 94(3)(a)(viii) by 2002-2013 technical bill, for trust taxation years that end after 2006, and also for each earlier taxation year of a trust to which amended 94(1) applies (see Notes at end of s. 94).

215(1) earlier amended by 2001 technical bill.

Regulations: 105 (withholding of 15% on fees for services); 202 (information return); 800, 803.1 (no withholding on amounts paid or credited to authorized foreign bank [before Aug. 8/09] or non-resident insurer); 805 (where withholding not required); 805.1 (certificate confirming compliance with Reg. 805); 809 (reduction in withholding).

Interpretation Bulletins: IT-88R2: Stock dividends; IT-465R: Non-resident beneficiaries of trusts.

Information Circulars: 77-16R4: Non-resident income tax.

I.T. Technical News: 14 (meaning of "credited" for purposes of Part XIII withholding tax).

CRA Audit Manual: 15.3.3: Withholding and reporting obligations of the payer.

Advance Tax Rulings: ATR-49: Long-term foreign debt; ATR-69: Withholding tax on interest paid to non-resident persons.

Forms: NR4 Segment; NR4 Summ: Return of amounts paid or credited to non-residents of Canada; NR7R: Application for refund of Part XIII tax withheld; NR304: Direct deposit request for non-resident account holders and NR7-R refund applicants; NR603: Remittance of non-resident tax on income from film or video acting services; T3 Sched. 10: Part XII.2 tax and Part XIII non-resident withholding tax.

(1.1) Exception — corporate immigration

— Subsection (1) does not apply in respect of a dividend deemed to be paid under paragraph 128.1(1)(c.1) by a corporation to a non-resident corporation with which the corporation was dealing at arm's length.

Notes: 215(1.1) added by 1998 Budget, effective February 24, 1998. See Notes to 128.1(1) re 128.1(1)(c.1).

(2) Idem [amount paid by agent]

— Where an amount on which an income tax is payable under this Part is paid or credited by an agent or other person on behalf of the debtor either by way of redemption of bearer coupons or warrants or otherwise, the agent or other person by whom the amount was paid or credited shall, notwithstanding any agreement or law to the contrary, deduct or withhold and remit the amount of the tax and shall submit therewith a

statement in prescribed form as required by subsection (1) and shall thereupon, for purposes of accounting to or obtaining reimbursement from the debtor, be deemed to have paid or credited the full amount to the person otherwise entitled to payment.

Related Provisions: 94(3)(a)(ix), 94(4)(c) — Application of rule deeming non-resident trust to be resident in Canada; 215(5) — Regulations reducing deduction or withholding; 215(6) — Liability for tax; 227(8)–(8.4) — Liabilities arising from failure to withhold or deduct amount; 227.1 — Liability of directors.

Notes: See Notes to 215(3).

Regulations: 202(2) (information return); 800, 803.1 (no withholding on amounts paid or credited to authorized foreign bank [before Aug. 8/09] or non-resident insurer); 805 (where withholding not required); 805.1 (certificate confirming compliance with Reg. 805); 809 (reduction in withholding).

I.T. Technical News: 14 (meaning of "credited" for purposes of Part XIII withholding tax).

(3) Idem [amount paid to agent]

— Where an amount on which an income tax is payable under this Part was paid or credited to an agent or other person for or on behalf of the person entitled to payment without the tax having been deducted or withheld under subsection (1), the agent or other person shall, notwithstanding any agreement or law to the contrary, deduct or withhold therefrom the amount of the tax and forthwith remit that amount to the Receiver General on behalf of the person entitled to payment in payment of the tax and shall submit therewith a statement in prescribed form, and the agent or other person shall thereupon, for purposes of accounting to the person entitled to payment, be deemed to have paid or credited that amount to that person.

Related Provisions: 94(3)(a)(ix), 94(4)(c) — Application of rule deeming non-resident trust to be resident in Canada; 215(5) — Regulations reducing deduction or withholding; 215(6) — Liability for tax; 216(4), (4.1) — Optional method of payment; 227(8)–(8.4) — Liabilities arising from failure to withhold or deduct amount; 227.1 — Liability of directors.

Notes: See 212(1)(b) Notes re interest and dividend payments to agents in the UK.

215(3) typically applies to a property manager who collects rents on behalf of a non-resident landlord. The property manager is required to withhold and remit 25% withholding tax under 212(1)(d) if the tenant did not withhold. However, see 216(1) and (4) for an election that allows the withholding requirement to be reduced or eliminated.

215(3) does not apply to the operator of a web site where non-resident owners advertise properties in Canada for rent, since the vacationers pay the rent directly to the owners: VIEWS doc 2004-0103641R3. Similarly, an Irish Common Contractual Fund, Luxembourg fonds commun de placement (FCP) and similar are look-through co-ownership arrangements so that amounts are considered paid directly to the unitholders for purposes of withholding tax: docs 2006-0199741R3, 2007-0231581R3, 2012-0432341R3, 2013-0496831R3, 2015-0605161R3, 2017-0738041R3.

Where an amount is paid to a foreign financial intermediary for a Canadian resident, CRA says tax should be withheld: doc 2011-0419191E5; Slade, "Part XIII Withholding on Payments to Foreign Intermediaries", XVIII(1) *Corporate Finance* (Federated Press) 2082-83 (2012).

Regulations: 202(3) (information return); 800, 803.1 (no withholding on amounts paid or credited to authorized foreign bank [before Aug. 8/09] or non-resident insurer); 805 (where withholding not required); 805.1 (certificate confirming compliance with Reg. 805); 809 (reduction in withholding).

Interpretation Bulletins: IT-393R2: Election re tax on rents and timber royalties — non-residents.

I.T. Technical News: 14 (meaning of "credited" for purposes of Part XIII withholding tax).

Forms: NR7R: Application for refund of Part XIII tax withheld; NR304: Direct deposit request for non-resident account holders and NR7-R refund applicants.

(4) Regulations creating exceptions

— The Governor in Council may make regulations with reference to any non-resident person or class of non-resident persons who carries or carry on business in Canada, providing that subsections (1) to (3) are not applicable to amounts paid to or credited to that person or those persons and requiring the person or persons to file an annual return on a prescribed form and to pay the tax imposed by this Part within a time limited in the regulations.

Related Provisions: 162(7) — Penalty for failure to comply with regulation; 227(9) — Penalty on tax not paid; 227(9.3) — Interest on tax not paid; 227.1 — Liability of directors; 235 — Penalty for failure to make returns.

Regulations: 800, 801, 803, 805, 805.1.

Forms: T2016: Part XIII tax return — tax on income from Canada of approved non-resident insurers.

(5) Regulations reducing deduction or withholding — The Governor in Council may make regulations in respect of any non-resident person or class of non-resident persons to whom any amount is paid or credited as, on account of, in lieu of payment of or in satisfaction of, any amount described in any of paragraphs 212(1)(h), (j) to (m) and (q) reducing the amount otherwise required by any of subsections (1) to (3) to be deducted or withheld from the amount so paid or credited.

Related Provisions: 190.15(6) — Related financial institution; 212(1) — Tax on Canadian income of non-residents; 212(2) — Tax on dividends; 227.1 — Liability of directors.

Notes: 215(5) amended by 2001 technical bill (effective May 1997), 1991 technical bill.

Regulations: 805 (where withholding not required); 809 (reduction in withholding on s. 217 election).

Forms: NR5: Application by a non-resident of Canada for a reduction in the amount of non-resident tax required to be withheld; NR7R: Application for refund of Part XIII tax withheld; NR304: Direct deposit request for non-resident account holders and NR7-R refund applicants.

(6) Liability for tax — Where a person has failed to deduct or withhold any amount as required by this section from an amount paid or credited or deemed to have been paid or credited to a non-resident person, that person is liable to pay as tax under this Part on behalf of the non-resident person the whole of the amount that should have been deducted or withheld, and is entitled to deduct or withhold from any amount paid or credited by that person to the non-resident person or otherwise recover from the non-resident person any amount paid by that person as tax under this Part on behalf thereof.

Related Provisions: 94(3)(a)(ix), 94(4)(c) — Application of rule deeming non-resident trust to be resident in Canada; 227(8.4) — Parallel provision for other withholding taxes; 227.1 — Liability of directors where corporation fails to withhold.

Notes: See Notes to 212(1) opening words.

A 215(6) assessment of withholding tax on a benefit (deemed dividend) conferred on a foreign parent via transfer pricing was not subject to the limitation period in the Canada-Luxembourg tax treaty for transfer-pricing assessments: *McKesson Canada*, 2013 TCC 404, para. 396 (FCA appeal discontinued A-48-14).

CRA Audit Manual: 15.3.3: Withholding and reporting obligations of the payer.

Definitions [s. 215]: "amount" — 248(1); "arm's length" — 251(1), 260(9.1); "business" — 248(1); "Canada" — 255; "carry on business in Canada" — 253; "corporation" — 248(1), *Interpretation Act* 35(1); "dividend" — 248(1); "Governor in Council" — *Interpretation Act* 35(1); "non-resident", "person", "prescribed", "regulation" — 248(1).

Interpretation Bulletins [s. 215]: IT-88R2: Stock dividends; IT-109R2: Unpaid amounts; IT-362R: Patronage dividends.

216. (1) Alternatives re rents and timber royalties — If an amount has been paid during a taxation year to a non-resident person or to a partnership of which that person was a member as, on account of, in lieu of payment of or in satisfaction of, rent on real or immovable property in Canada or a timber royalty, that person may, within two years (or, if that person has filed an undertaking described in subsection (4) in respect of the year, within six months) after the end of the year, file a return of income under Part I for that year in prescribed form. On so filing and without affecting the liability of the non-resident person for tax otherwise payable under Part I, the non-resident person is, in lieu of paying tax under this Part on that amount, liable to pay tax under Part I for the year as though

(a) the non-resident person were a person resident in Canada and not exempt from tax under section 149;

(b) the non-resident person's income from the non-resident person's interest in real property, or real right in immovables, in Canada and interest in, or for civil law right in, timber resource properties and timber limits in Canada, and the non-resident person's share of the income of a partnership of which the non-resident person was a member from its interest in real property, or real right in immovables, in Canada and interest in, or for civil law right in, timber resource properties and timber limits in Canada, were the non-resident person's only income;

(c) the non-resident person were entitled to no deductions from income for the purpose of computing the non-resident person's taxable income; and

(d) the non-resident person were entitled to no deductions under sections 118 to 118.9 in computing the non-resident person's tax payable under Part I for the year.

Proposed Amendment — Additional tax on vacant housing owned by non-residents

Federal Budget, April 19, 2021: See under 115(1)(b).

Related Provisions: 13(21) — "Timber resource property"; 18(5)"equity amount"(c)(i)(B) — Application of thin-capitalization rules where 216(1) election made; 96 — Partnerships and their members; 120(1) — Additional tax on income not earned in a province; 150.1(5) — Electronic filing; 216(8) — Restriction on deduction; 220(3) — Extension of time for making return; 248(4) — Interest in real property; 248(4.1) — Meaning of "real right in immovables"; 250.1(b) — Calculation of income of non-resident person; *Interpretation Act* 27(5) — Meaning of "within 2 years" or "within 6 months".

Notes: 216 allows a non-resident (NR) to file a return (T1159) and pay regular (Part I) tax on the *net* income from real property in Canada (or a timber royalty), rather than paying a flat 25% (or 15% or whatever other rate applies by treaty) on the *gross* income. (Similar mechanisms are provided for other kinds of income in 216.1, 217 and 218.3.) See CRA Guide T4144. See also 216(4), which then allows the NR's agent in Canada to elect to withhold 25% of the net rather than of the gross. Losses from prior or later years cannot be deducted against 216(1) income. If the NR dies, see VIEWS doc 2020-0847201C6 [2020 STEP q.13] re the estate and NR heirs using 216(1). See also Ranger & Rudick, "Federal and Provincial Tax Considerations Relating to Non-Resident Investment in Canadian Real Estate", 2019 Cdn Tax Foundation conference report, 32:1-39.

Under 216(1)(d), personal credits are not allowed on such a return; but the graduated tax rates under 117(2) do apply if the non-resident is an individual. Note also that deductions under s. 60, including RRSP contributions and deductible alimony or support, *are* deductible for purposes of 216(1). (They are specifically listed on Form T1159.)

For a corporation, the thin-cap rules in 18(4)-(8) apply to a 216(1) return: VIEWS doc 2015-0599161I7. No 10% provincial abatement is allowed under 124(1), even if Quebec will tax the rent: 2006-0196171C6 [2006 APFF q.37].

The election applies only to amounts actually paid, not those accrued: VIEWS doc 2004-0095441E5. Interest capitalized under s. 21 cannot be deducted against the capital gain when selling the building in the CRA's view, effective 2011: 2010-0386071C6 [2010 CTF conf report, p.4:23-24, q.24]. The election can be made on income allocated through a two-tier partnership structure: 2004-0075721E5; and on compensation payments for loss of rental income: 2015-0570011E5.

CRA policy on late filing is at tinyurl.com/cra-late216: a non-resident gets one chance to file late, unless: (1) CRA previously advised the taxpayer about its Part XIII obligations re rental income or timber royalties; (2) "we have already initiated action because of your failure to comply with Part XIII"; or (3) "you have submitted and we approved Form NR6". CRA will not apply penalties but may charge interest for failure to deduct and remit Part XIII tax and on Part I tax liability. In *Kutlu*, 1997 CanLII 5990 (FCTD, Crown's FCA appeal discontinued), the Court ruled that Revenue Canada could not refuse a late 216(1) return where it had accepted them late in the past.

Interest under 227(8.3) for not withholding and remitting runs on a s. 216 return, even though tax is being paid under Part I: *Pechet*, 2009 FCA 341, effectively overruling *Wright*, [2001] 3 C.T.C. 2426 (TCC); and see VIEWS doc 2013-0506151I7.

216(1)(b) amended by 2002-2013 technical bill, last change effective June 26, 2013.

216(1) earlier amended by 1991 technical bill.

Interpretation Bulletins: IT-81R: Partnerships — income of non-resident partners; IT-88R2: Stock dividends; IT-109R2: Unpaid amounts; IT-121R3: Election to capitalize cost of borrowed money (cancelled); IT-393R2: Election re tax on rents and timber royalties — non-residents; IT-434R: Rental of real property by individual.

Information Circulars: 77-16R4: Non-resident income tax; 00-1R4: Voluntary disclosures program.

CRA Audit Manual: 15.3.5: Election by a non-resident to be taxed under Part I.

Forms: T1 General income tax return; T2: Corporation income tax return; T2 Sched. 97: Additional information on non-resident corporations in Canada; T3: Statement of trust income allocations and designations; NR6: Undertaking to file an income tax return by a non-resident receiving rent from real property or receiving a timber royalty; T1159: Income tax return for electing under s. 216; T4144: Income tax guide for electing under section 216.

(2) Idem — Where a non-resident person has filed a return of income under Part I as permitted by this section, the amount deducted under this Part from

(a) rent on real or immovable property or from timber royalties paid to the person, and

(b) the person's share of the rent on real or immovable property or from timber royalties paid to a partnership of which the person is a member

and remitted to the Receiver General shall be deemed to have been paid on account of tax under this section and any portion of the amount so remitted to the Receiver General in a taxation year on the person's behalf in excess of the person's liability for tax under this Act for the year shall be refunded to the person.

Notes: 216(2)(a), (b) amended by 2002-2013 technical bill (Part 4 — bijuralism), effective June 26, 2013, to add "or immovable".

(3) Idem — Part I is applicable, with such modifications as the circumstances require, to payment of tax under this section.

Notes: An overpaid amount under s. 216 might not generate refund interest, due to the wording of 164(3): VIEWS doc 9203916.

(4) Optional method of payment — If a non-resident person or, in the case of a partnership, each non-resident person who is a member of the partnership files with the Minister an undertaking in prescribed form to file within six months after the end of a taxation year a return of income under Part I for the year as permitted by this section, a person who is otherwise required by subsection 215(3) to remit in the year, in respect of the non-resident person or the partnership, an amount to the Receiver General in payment of tax on rent on real or immovable property or on a timber royalty may elect under this section not to remit under that subsection, and if that election is made, the elector shall,

(a) when any amount is available out of the rent or royalty received for remittance to the non-resident person or the partnership, as the case may be, deduct 25% of the amount available and remit the amount deducted to the Receiver General on behalf of the non-resident person or the partnership on account of the tax under this Part; and

(b) if the non-resident person or, in the case of a partnership, a non-resident person who is a member of the partnership

(i) does not file a return for the year in accordance with the undertaking, or

(ii) does not pay under this section the tax the non-resident person or member is liable to pay for the year within the time provided for payment,

pay to the Receiver General, on account of the non-resident person's or the partnership's tax under this Part, on the expiration of the time for filing or payment, as the case may be, the full amount that the elector would otherwise have been required to remit in the year in respect of the rent or royalty minus the amounts that the elector has remitted in the year under paragraph (a) in respect of the rent or royalty.

Possible Future Amendment — Requirement for non-resident to post security

Letter from Dept. of Finance, June 17, 1996:

Mr. Donald H. Watkins, Chair, Taxation Section, The Canadian Bar Association

Mr. Robert Spindler, C.A., Chair, Taxation Committee, Canadian Institute of Chartered Accountants

Dear Messrs. Watkins and Spindler:

At our recent meeting we discussed the possibility of revising the Canadian income tax rules governing the taxation of rental income earned by non-resident owners of Canadian real estate. This letter outlines a proposal that would, if implemented, place the risk of a non-resident's non-compliance with the Canadian tax system on the non-resident rather than the non-resident's Canadian property agent.

In general, Part XIII of the *Income Tax Act* levies a withholding tax of 25% on rental payments made by Canadians to non-resident owners of Canadian real property. Where the non-resident collects the rent through a Canadian agent (who is typically a building or property manager), the agent is responsible for ensuring that 25% of the gross rental payments are remitted to Revenue Canada. An exception to this general rule exists where a non-resident elects, under section 216 of the Act, to file a Canadian income tax return in respect of the rental income and pay tax on the net property income.

To make the election the non-resident and the non-resident's Canadian agent are required to provide an undertaking to Revenue Canada to file an income tax return for the rental income within six months of the end of the relevant year. Where an election is made, the rule requiring the Canadian agent to remit 25% of the gross rental payments to Revenue Canada does not apply; instead, only 25% of the net amount of rent re-

ceived by the agent need be remitted. However, if the non-resident fails to either file an income tax return or pay his tax liability within the time required under the election, the Canadian agent becomes liable for the amount that the agent would ordinarily have been required to withhold under Part XIII of the Act (ie., 25% of the gross rental payments) less the amount of tax actually remitted. The non-resident's tax liability is placed on the Canadian agent in an attempt to protect the government from the loss of any tax revenue arising from the non-resident's failure to pay the required tax. This mechanism is necessary because, in practice, it would be very difficult to enforce a tax liability on non-resident property owners.

We are considering alternatives to the current system which may reduce the liability of Canadian agents while at the same time protecting Canada's tax base. To achieve these objectives, we are prepared to consider a system which would require non-resident property owners to post security with Revenue Canada in order to take advantage of the election to file an income tax return and avoid having tax withheld on the gross amount of the rental payments. Where the non-resident fails to pay the required amount of tax within the specified time, the government would be able to look to the security; accordingly, the Canadian agent's exposure to tax could be reduced. In this context, acceptable security could be similar to that which is required under section 116 of the Act.

Finance is not, however, committed to this proposal; it remains our view that the current system works reasonably well from the government's viewpoint, and implementation of the alternative proposal would be considered only if it were thought to provide a better system from the taxpayer's perspective. This alternative has been outlined to a number of real estate organizations and other interested parties from whom we hope to gather comments over the course of the coming months.

I would also note that at our recent meeting you raised the possibility of considering changes to the existing time limits for filing a Part I income tax return under subsection 216(4). We would be pleased to receive written comments on your suggestion for modifying those time limits or on the alternative system outlined above.

Yours sincerely,

Len Farber, Director, Tax Legislation Division

Notes: Finance advised in Jan. 2018 that this matter is still pending.

Related Provisions: 96 — Partnerships and their members; 216(1) — Alternative re rents and timber royalties; *Interpretation Act* 27(5) — Meaning of "within six months".

Notes: For discussion of 216(4) see Maureen Berry, "Section 216 Shortfall", 1904 *Tax Topics* (CCH) 1-3 (Sept. 4, 2008).

CRA interprets "amount available out of the rent or royalty" as after the agent pays the non-resident's expenses, so withholding can be on net rental income: VIEWS doc 2014-0520701E5 [Tollstam, "Section 216: Net Rental Income", 22(1) *Canadian Tax Highlights* (ctf.ca) 11-12 (Oct. 2014)].

If the return is not filed within the 6-month period, tax applies on the gross rather than the net, even if there was a good reason for the late filing: *Stellwaag*, 2013 TCC 111.

CRA can extend the 6-month deadline under 220(3): *Sailsman*, 2014 FC 1033; tiny-url.com/216late. Due to COVID-19, the June 30, 2020 filing deadline for non-resident individuals was extended to Sept. 1, and for corps, a March 18-May 30 deadline was extended to June 1 and May 31-Aug. 31 deadline extended to Sept. 1, 2020; for all taxpayers, the payment deadline for tax owing from March 18-Sept. 29 was extended to Sept. 30, 2020. See PITA 59th ed. at 150(1) opening words.

If the Canadian agent files an NR6 undertaking, but the non-resident does not file the 216(4) return by the following June 30, CRA will assess the agent the full 25% withholding requirement on the gross rental income, plus interest (less any payments received): ICABC/CRA Pacific Region liaison meeting, Jan. 22, 2013, q.24.

216(4) opening words amended by 2002-2013 technical bill, effective June 26, 2013, to add "or immovable". 216(4) earlier amended by 1995-97 technical bill.

Forms: NR6: Undertaking to file an income tax return by a non-resident receiving rent from real property or receiving a timber royalty; T1159: Income tax return for electing under s. 216; T2 Sched. 97: Additional information on non-resident corporations in Canada; T4144: Income tax guide for electing under section 216.

(4.1) Optional method of payment [by deemed-resident trust] — If a trust is deemed by subsection 94(3) to be resident in Canada for a taxation year for the purpose of computing the trust's income for the year, a person who is otherwise required by subsection 215(3) to remit in the year, in respect of the trust, an amount to the Receiver General in payment of tax on rent on real or immovable property or on a timber royalty may elect in prescribed form filed with the Minister under this subsection not to remit under subsection 215(3) in respect of amounts received after the election is made, and if that election is made, the elector shall,

(a) when any amount is available out of the rent or royalty received for remittance to the trust, deduct 25% of the amount available and remit the amount deducted to the Receiver General on behalf of the trust on account of the trust's tax under Part I; and

(b) if the trust does not file a return for the year as required by section 150, or does not pay the tax that the trust is liable to pay under Part I for the year within the time required by that Part, on the expiration of the time for filing or payment, as the case may be, pay to the Receiver General, on account of the trust's tax under Part I, the amount by which the full amount that the elector would otherwise have been required to remit in the year in respect of the rent or royalty exceeds the amounts that the elector has remitted in the year under paragraph (a) in respect of the rent or royalty.

Notes: 216(4.1) added by 2002-2013 technical bill, for trust tax years that end after 2006, or earlier in some cases.

(5) Disposition by non-resident — If a person or a trust under which a person is a beneficiary has filed a return of income under Part I for a taxation year as permitted by this section or as required by section 150 and, in computing the amount of the person's income under Part I an amount has been deducted under paragraph 20(1)(a), or is deemed by subsection 107(2) to have been allowed under that paragraph, in respect of property that is real property in Canada — or an interest therein — or an immovable in Canada — or a real right therein — , a timber resource property or a timber limit in Canada, the person shall file a return of income under Part I in prescribed form on or before the person's filing-due date for any subsequent taxation year in which the person is non-resident and in which the person, or a partnership of which the person is a member, disposes of that property or any interest, or for civil law any right, in it. On so filing and without affecting the person's liability for tax otherwise payable under Part I, the person is, in lieu of paying tax under this Part on any amount paid, or deemed by this Part to have been paid, in that subsequent taxation year in respect of any interest in, or for civil law any right in, that property to the person or to a partnership of which the person is a member, liable to pay tax under Part I for that subsequent taxation year as though

(a) the person were a person resident in Canada and not exempt from tax under section 149;

(b) the person's income from the person's interest in real property, or real right in immovables, in Canada or interest in, or for civil law right in, timber resource properties and timber limits in Canada, and the person's share of the income of a partnership of which the person was a member from its interest in real property, or real right in immovables, in Canada or interest in, or for civil law right in, timber resource properties and timber limits in Canada, were the person's only income;

(c) the person were entitled to no deductions from income for the purpose of computing the person's taxable income; and

(d) the person were entitled to no deductions under sections 118 to 118.9 in computing the person's tax payable under Part I for the year.

Related Provisions: 110.1(3), 118.1(6) — Election for reduced proceeds on donation of property; 150.1(5) — Electronic filing; 216(6) — Saving provision; 216(8) — Restriction on deduction; 248(4) — Interest in real property; 248(4.1) — Meaning of "real right in immovables".

Notes: For the meaning of "timber limit" see 13(21)"timber resource property" Notes.

216(5)(b) amended by 2002-2013 technical bill, effective June 26, 2013.

216(5) opening words amended by 2002-2013 technical bill (Part 5 — technical), for taxation years that end after Dec. 20, 2002. Most of the changes were stylistic; the reference to the Part I return was updated to reflect the introduction of a special return for these non-residents.

(6) Saving provision — Subsection (5) does not apply to require a non-resident person

(a) to file a return of income under Part I for a taxation year unless, by filing that return, there would be included in computing the non-resident person's income under Part I for that year an amount by virtue of section 13; or

(b) to include in computing the non-resident person's income for a taxation year any amount to the extent that that amount has been included in computing the non-resident person's taxable income earned in Canada for that taxation year by virtue of any provision of this Act other than subsection (5).

Related Provisions: 13(1) — Recaptured depreciation.

(7) [Repealed]

Notes: 216(7) repealed by 2002-2013 technical bill (Part 5 — technical), effective June 26, 2013. It dealt with income-averaging annuity contracts under s. 61; they were discontinued in 1981.

(8) Restriction on deduction — For greater certainty, in determining the amount of tax payable by a non-resident person under Part I for a taxation year by reason of subsection (1) or (5), no deduction in computing the non-resident person's income or tax payable under Part I for the year shall be made to the extent that such a deduction by non-resident persons is not permitted under Part I.

Definitions [s. 216]: "amount" — 248(1); "Canada" — 255, *Interpretation Act* 35(1); "filing-due date" — 248(1); "immovable" — Quebec *Civil Code* art. 900–907; "interest in real property" — 248(4); "Minister" — 248(1); "month" — *Interpretation Act* 35(1); "non-resident" — 248(1); "partnership" — see 96(1) Notes; "person", "prescribed", "property" — 248(1); "real right" — 248(4.1); "resident in Canada" — 250; "tax payable" — 248(2); "taxable income" — 2(2), 248(1); "taxation year" — 249; "timber resource property" — 13(21), 248(1); "trust" — 104(1), 248(1), (3).

Interpretation Bulletins [s. 216]: See under subsec. 216(1).

216.1 (1) Alternative re acting services — No tax is payable under this Part on any amount described in subsection 212(5.1) that is paid, credited or provided to a non-resident person in a taxation year if the person

(a) files with the Minister, on or before the person's filing-due date for the year, a return of income under Part I for the year; and

(b) elects in the return to have this section apply for the year.

Related Provisions: 215(1) — Payor required to withhold even if election filed; 216.1(2) — Amounts withheld and remitted credited against Part I obligation; 216.1(3) — Where corporation makes payment to actor.

Notes: 216.1(1) allows non-resident NR who receives income from the provision of acting services to elect not to be taxed under 212(5.1) on that income. Instead, NR includes this income in "taxable income earned in Canada" under 115 (or in taxable income, if NR was resident in Canada for part of the year). This income is then subject to tax at ordinary rates under Part I, instead of the flat 23% under 212(5.1).

The election cannot be filed late, even by a US resident invoking the Canada-US tax treaty: VIEWS doc 2015-0603271E5.

Forms: T1287: Application by a non-resident of Canada (individual) for a reduction in the amount of non-resident tax required to be withheld on income earned from acting in a film or video production; T1288: Application by a non-resident of Canada (corporation) for a reduction in the amount of non-resident tax required to be withheld on income earned from acting in a film or video production.

(2) Deemed Part I payment — If in respect of a particular amount paid, credited or provided in a taxation year, a non-resident person has complied with paragraphs (1)(a) and (b), any amount deducted or withheld and remitted to the Receiver General on behalf of the person on account of tax under subsection 212(5.1) in respect of the particular amount is deemed to have been paid on account of the person's tax under Part I.

(3) Deemed election and restriction — Where a corporation payment (within the meaning assigned by subsection 212(5.2)) has been made to a non-resident corporation in respect of an actor and at any time the corporation makes an actor payment (within the meaning assigned by subsection 212(5.2)) to or for the benefit of the actor, if the corporation makes an election under subsection (1) for the taxation year in which the corporation payment is made, the actor is deemed to make an election under subsection (1) for the taxation year of the actor in which the corporation makes the actor payment.

Notes: 216.1(3) applies to non-resident actors who use a related corporation to provide their acting services in Canada. If the corporation has elected under 216.1(1) to be taxed under Part I in respect of a corporation payment, the actor is deemed to have made the same election in respect of the related actor payment. (See 212(5.2) for definitions of "corporation payment" and "actor payment".)

Notes: [216.1]: 216.1 added by 2001 technical bill, effective for 2001 and later taxation years.

Definitions [s. 216.1]: "actor payment" — 212(5.2); "amount" — 248(1); "corporation" — 248(1), *Interpretation Act* 35(1); "corporation payment" — 212(5.2); "filing-due date", "Minister", "non-resident", "person" — 248(1); "taxation year" — 249.

217. (1) Alternative [reporting] re Canadian benefits — In this section, a non-resident person's "Canadian benefits" for a taxation year is the total of all amounts each of which is an amount paid or credited in the year and in respect of which tax under this Part would, but for this section, be payable by the person because of any of paragraphs 212(1)(h), (j) to (m) and (q).

(2) Part I return — No tax is payable under this Part in respect of a non-resident person's Canadian benefits for a taxation year if the person

(a) files with the Minister, within 6 months after the end of the year, a return of income under Part I for the year; and

(b) elects in the return to have this section apply for the year.

Related Provisions: 150.1(5) — Electronic filing; 217(3)–(6) — Part I tax payable when election made; *Interpretation Act* 27(5) — Meaning of "within 6 months".

Notes: See at end of s. 217. Due to COVID-19, the June 30 filing deadline was extended to Sept. 1, 2020, and the payment deadline for 2019 tax was extended to Sept. 30, 2020. See PITA 59th ed. at 150(1) opening words.

Regulations: 809 (reduced withholding tax).

CRA Audit Manual: 15.3.5: Election by a non-resident to be taxed under Part I.

Forms: See at end of s. 217.

(3) Taxable income earned in Canada — Where a non-resident person elects under paragraph (2)(b) for a taxation year, for the purposes of Part I

(a) the person is deemed to have been employed in Canada in the year; and

(b) the person's taxable income earned in Canada for the year is deemed to be the greater of

(i) the amount that would, but for subparagraph (ii), be the person's taxable income earned in Canada for the year if

(A) paragraph 115(1)(a) included the following subparagraph after subparagraph (i):

"(i.1) the non-resident person's Canadian benefits for the year, within the meaning assigned by subsection 217(1),", and

(B) paragraph 115(1)(f) were read as follows:

"(f) such of the other deductions permitted for the purpose of computing taxable income as can reasonably be considered wholly applicable to the amounts described in subparagraphs (a)(i) to (vi).", and

(ii) the person's income (computed without reference to subsection 56(8)) for the year minus the total of such of the deductions permitted for the purpose of computing taxable income as can reasonably be considered wholly applicable to the amounts described in subparagraphs 115(1)(a)(i) to (vi).

Related Provisions: 2(3) — Tax payable under Part I as a result of being deemed employed in Canada; 250.1(b) — Calculation of income of non-resident person.

Notes: See Notes at end of 217. 217(3) describes how a non-resident person who elects to have 217 apply computes taxable income earned in Canada (TIEC). The person is deemed to have been employed in Canada, and is deemed to have TIEC equal to the greater of two amounts. The first amount (217(3)(b)(i)) is essentially the amount that would be the person's TIEC if s. 115 included the person's Canadian benefits in TIEC. The second amount (217(3)(b)(ii)) is net worldwide income, less any deductions in computing taxable income that can reasonably be considered wholly applicable to the Canadian-source Part I income (not including the Canadian benefits).

This means, for example, that a non-resident person who has $10,000 in Canadian benefits for a year, and $60,000 in foreign-source income, will be deemed under 217(3) to have TIEC of $70,000 (assuming no deductions in computing taxable income). This does not mean that the non-resident will pay Canadian tax on the $60,000 of foreign income: 217(6) provides a special credit to offset the Canadian tax on such income. The effect of this rule is that the Part I tax on the $10,000 applies at high rates.

217(3)(b)(ii) amended by 1997 Budget, for 1997 and later tax years, to add "(computed without reference to subsection 56(8))". Thus, withholding tax applies to the full amount of any CPP/QPP lump sum payment for purposes of the s. 217 calculation.

CRA Audit Manual: 15.3.5: Election by a non-resident to be taxed under Part I.

(4) Tax credits — limitation — Sections 118 to 118.91 and 118.94 do not apply in computing the tax payable under Part I for a taxation year by a non-resident person who elects under paragraph (2)(b) for the year, unless

(a) where section 114 applies to the person for the year, all or substantially all of the person's income for the year is included in computing the person's taxable income for the year; or

(b) in any other case, all or substantially all of the person's income for the year is included in computing the amount determined under subparagraph (3)(b)(i) in respect of the person for the year.

Notes: CRA considers that "substantially all" means 90% or more.

(5) Tax credits allowed — In computing the tax payable under Part I for a taxation year by a non-resident person to whom neither paragraph (4)(a) nor paragraph (4)(b) applies for the year there may, notwithstanding section 118.94 and subsection (4), be deducted the lesser of

(a) the total of

(i) such of the amounts that would have been deductible under any of section 118.2, subsections 118.3(2) and (3) and sections 118.8 and 118.9 in computing the person's tax payable under Part I for the year if the person had been resident in Canada throughout the year, as can reasonably be considered wholly applicable, and

(ii) the amounts that would have been deductible under any of sections 118 and 118.1, subsection 118.3(1) and sections 118.5 and 118.7 in computing the person's tax payable under Part I for the year if the person had been resident in Canada throughout the year, and

(b) the appropriate percentage for the year of the person's Canadian benefits for the year.

Notes: 217(5)(a)(i) amended to delete reference to 118.6 by 2016 budget bill #1, for 2017 and later taxation years.

(6) Special credit — In computing the tax payable under Part I for a taxation year by a non-resident who elects under paragraph (2)(b) for the year, there may be deducted the amount determined by the formula

$$A \times [\,(B - C)\,/\,B\,]$$

where

A is the amount of tax under Part I that would, but for this subsection, be payable by the person for the year;

B is the amount determined under subparagraph (3)(b)(ii) in respect of the person for the year; and

C is the amount determined under subparagraph (3)(b)(i) in respect of the person for the year.

Related Provisions: 257 — Formula cannot calculate to less than zero.

Notes: 217(6) provides a special credit in computing tax payable by a non-resident under Part I for a year as a result of a s. 217 election. The effect of the credit is to exclude foreign-source (and non-Part I) income from Canadian tax, while maintaining the appropriate rate of tax on the non-resident's Part I income, including Canadian benefits. See 217(4) Notes.

Notes [s. 217]: 217 allows a non-resident to elect to pay tax on worldwide net income instead of withholding tax on gross Canadian-source income. See CRA pamphlet T4145 and Notes to 217(3) as well as below.

Withholding tax can be reduced under Reg. 809 with the filing of a Form NR5. Since 2011, this needs to be filed only once every 5 years once approved (CRA notice, July 30, 2010; "CRA's Five-Year Administrative Policy Regarding Form NR5", 2004 *Tax Topics* (CCH) 1-2 (Aug. 5, 2010)).

In determining the Part I tax rate that applies where a non-resident elects under the section, the non-resident's non-Canadian income (and Canadian-source income subject to Part XIII but not eligible for the s. 217 election) is taken into consideration. This will not mean that Canada will tax that other income under Part I, but only that the foreign income may increase the rate of tax that applies to the non-resident's Canadian-source Part I income. See Notes to 217(3).

As well, the requirement that more than half a non-resident's income be included in the non-resident's taxable income earned in Canada, in order for any Part I tax credits to be available, was deleted.

A former Canadian resident with losses that are expiring can receive income (e.g., from an RRSP) and offset it with the losses under s. 217: VIEWS doc 2004-0079041E5. See also docs 2009-0315041M4 (general comments); 2013-0504641E5 (s. 217 cannot apply to RESP educational assistance payment under 212(1)(r)).

In *Merrins*, 2003 FCA 147, a resident of Ireland had Canadian pension income, Old Age Security and CPP. He did not elect under s. 217 but was assessed as though he had, as this was better for him. The Court held that the pension income exemption under the Canada-Ireland tax treaty did not apply once the s. 217 calculation was being used. 217 gave him the benefit of non-refundable tax credits as well as the special credit under 217(6). A taxpayer cannot "pick and choose" between application of a tax treaty and domestic tax laws on different kinds of income. M got the same result in *Merrins*, 2005 TCC 470 and 2006 TCC 281, both aff'd 2007 FCA 295 (both TCC decisions discussed further the application of s. 217).

See *Pope*, 2009 TCC 498, for a case where the election was not beneficial.

217 amended by 1996 Budget (effective 1997), 1995 Budget and 1991 technical bill.

Definitions [s. 217]: "amount", "appropriate percentage" — 248(1); "Canada" — 255; "Canadian benefits" — 217(1); "individual", "Minister", "non-resident", "person" — 248(1); "resident in Canada" — 250; "tax payable" — 248(2); "taxable income" — 2(2), 248(1); "taxable income earned in Canada" — 115(1), 248(1); "taxation year" — 249.

Regulations [s. 217]: 809 (reduced withholding tax).

Interpretation Bulletins [s. 217]: IT-88R2: Stock dividends; IT-109R2: Unpaid amounts; IT-171R2: Non-resident individuals — computation of taxable income earned in Canada and non-refundable tax credits (cancelled); IT-337R2: Retiring allowances.

Forms [s. 217]: 5013-R: T1 General 2016 — Income tax and benefit return for non-residents and deemed residents of Canada; NR5: Application by a non-resident of Canada for a reduction in the amount of non-resident tax required to be withheld; NR7R: Application for refund of Part XIII tax withheld; NR304: Direct deposit request for non-resident account holders and NR7-R refund applicants; T4056: Emigrants and income tax [guide]; T4145: Electing under section 217 of the *Income Tax Act* [guide].

218. (1) Loan to wholly-owned subsidiary — For the purposes of this Act, where

(a) a non-resident corporation (in this section referred to as the **"parent corporation"**) is indebted to

    (i) a person resident in Canada, or

    (ii) a non-resident insurance corporation carrying on business in Canada,

(in this section referred to as the **"creditor"**) under an arrangement whereby the parent corporation is required to pay interest in Canadian currency, and

(b) the parent corporation has lent the money in respect of which it is so indebted, or a part thereof, to a subsidiary wholly-owned corporation resident in Canada whose principal business is the making of loans (in this section referred to as the "subsidiary corporation") under an arrangement whereby the subsidiary corporation is required to repay the loan to the parent corporation with interest at the same rate as is payable by the parent corporation to the creditor,

the amount so lent by the parent corporation to the subsidiary corporation shall be deemed to have been borrowed by the parent corporation as agent of the subsidiary corporation and interest paid by the subsidiary corporation to the parent corporation that has been paid by the parent corporation to the creditor shall be deemed to have been paid by the subsidiary corporation to the creditor and not by the subsidiary corporation to the parent corporation or by the parent corporation to the creditor.

Notes: 218 allows exemption from withholding tax where funds are loaned to a non-resident for use by its Canadian subsidiary, if the conditions in 218(1) are met and a 218(3) election is filed. Since the interest payments are going out of Canada and then back into Canada, they are exempt from 212(1)(b) when paid by the Canadian sub to its non-resident parent.

For the meaning of "principal business" in 218(1)(b) see Notes to 20(1)(bb).

(2) Idem — Where a parent corporation has lent money to a subsidiary wholly-owned corporation resident in Canada whose principal business is not the making of loans and the money has been lent by that corporation to a subsidiary corporation wholly-owned by it and resident in Canada whose principal business is the making of loans, the loan by the parent corporation shall be deemed, for the purpose of subsection (1), to have been a loan to a subsidiary wholly-owned corporation whose principal business is the making of loans.

Notes: For the meaning of "principal business" see Notes to 20(1)(bb).

(3) Election — This section does not apply in respect of any payment of interest unless the parent corporation and the creditor have executed, and filed with the Minister, an election in prescribed form.

Forms: T2023: Election in respect of loans from non-residents.

(4) Application of election — An election filed under subsection (3) does not apply in respect of any payment of interest made more than 12 months before the date on which the election was filed with the Minister.

Related Provisions: 17 — Inclusion of deemed interest in income of corporation resident in Canada.

Definitions [s. 218]: "business" — 248(1); "carrying on business in Canada" — 253; "corporation" — 248(1), *Interpretation Act* 35(1); "creditor" — 218(1)(a); "insurance corporation", "Minister", "non-resident" — 248(1); "parent corporation" — 218(1)(a); "person", "prescribed" — 248(1); "resident in Canada" — 250; "subsidiary corporation" — 218(1)(b); "subsidiary wholly-owned corporation" — 248(1).

Interpretation Bulletins [s. 218]: IT-88R2: Stock dividends; IT-109R2: Unpaid amounts.

218.1 Application of s. 138.1 — In respect of life insurance policies for which all or any part of an insurer's reserves vary in amount depending on the fair market value of a specified group of properties, the rules contained in section 138.1 apply for the purposes of this Part.

Notes: 218.1 added in RSC 1985 (5th Supp) consolidation. It was previously contained in the opening words of 138.1(1), which applied "for the purposes of this Part and Part XIII". Part XIII is sections 212 to 218.1.

Definitions [s. 218.1]: "amount" — 248(1); "fair market value" — see 69(1) Notes; "insurer", "life insurance policy" — 248(1).

PART XIII.1 — ADDITIONAL TAX ON AUTHORIZED FOREIGN BANKS

218.2 (1) Branch interest tax — Every authorized foreign bank shall pay a tax under this Part for each taxation year equal to 25% of its taxable interest expense for the year.

Related Provisions: 157(1)(a)(i) — Monthly instalments required; 218.2(2) — Taxable interest expense; 218.2(3), (4) — Effect of treaties on tax rate; 218.2(5) — Administration of Part XIII.1 tax.

Notes: See Notes at end of 218.2.

(2) Taxable interest expense — The taxable interest expense of an authorized foreign bank for a taxation year is 15% of the amount, if any, by which

(a) the total of all amounts on account of interest that are deducted under section 20.2 in computing the bank's income for the year from its Canadian banking business

exceeds

(b) the total of all amounts that are included in paragraph (a) and that are in respect of a liability of the bank to another person or partnership.

(3) Where tax not payable — No tax is payable under this Part for a taxation year by an authorized foreign bank if

(a) the bank is resident in a country with which Canada has a tax treaty at the end of the year; and

(b) no tax similar to the tax under this Part would be payable in that country for the year by a bank resident in Canada carrying on business in that country during the year.

(4) Rate limitation — Despite any other provision of this Act, the reference in subsection (1) to 25% shall, in respect of a taxation year of an authorized foreign bank that is resident in a country with which Canada has a tax treaty on the last day of the year, be read as a reference to,

(a) if the treaty specifies the maximum rate of tax that Canada may impose under this Part for the year on residents of that country, that rate;

(b) if the treaty does not specify a maximum rate as described in paragraph (a) but does specify the maximum rate of tax that Canada may impose on a payment of interest in the year by a person resident in Canada to a related person resident in that country, that rate; and

(c) in any other case, 25%.

(5) Provisions applicable to Part — Sections 150 to 152, 158, 159, 160.1 and 161 to 167 and Division J of Part I apply to this Part with any modifications that the circumstances require.

Related Provisions: 157(1)(a)(i) — Monthly instalments required.

Notes [s. 218.2]: 218.2 applies a special branch interest tax, in lieu of Part XIII withholding tax, to certain notional interest payments by an "authorized foreign bank" (AFB) (see 248(1)). Its operation is tied to the interest-deductibility rules for AFBs. Generally, 20.2 allows an AFB to deduct as interest expense of its Canadian banking business one or more of three amounts; see Notes at end of 20.2.

212(1)(b) applies withholding tax to certain payments of interest by Canadian residents to non-residents. 212(13.3) treats an AFB, in respect of its Canadian banking business, as resident in Canada for purposes of Part XIII. Thus, its actual interest payments to non-residents may attract Part XIII tax.

218.2 complements Part XIII by ensuring the appropriate tax results in respect of an AFB's notional and residual interest expenses. Specifically, 218.2(1) imposes a 25% tax (same as 212(1)) of an AFB's "taxable interest expense" for a year. This is defined in 218.2(2) as 15% of the amount by which the bank's interest expense deduction for the year exceeds that part of the deduction that relates to actual liabilities to other persons or partnerships.

218.2 may in practice be inoperative due to 218.2(3)(b) and (4)(b), since it does not apply if the bank's home country is a treaty country that would not impose a comparable tax, and since Canada-US treaty Art. XI:1 now reduces withholding on most interest to zero (it could still apply to non-arm's length or profit-dependent interest). No other AFB appears to be in a country that triggers the tax.

218.2 added by 2001 technical bill, for taxation years that end after June 27, 1999.

Definitions [s. 218.2]: "amount", "authorized foreign bank", "bank", "business" — 248(1); "Canada" — 255, *Interpretation Act* 35(1); "Canadian banking business" — 248(1); "partnership" — see 96(1) Notes; "person" — 248(1); "related" — 251(2)–(6); "resident", "resident in Canada" — 250; "tax treaty" — 248(1); "taxable interest expense" — 218.2(2); "taxation year" — 249.

Forms: T2 Sched. 97: Additional information on non-resident corporations in Canada.

PART XIII.2 — NON-RESIDENT INVESTORS IN CANADIAN MUTUAL FUNDS

218.3 (1) Definitions — The following definitions apply in this Part.

"assessable distribution", in respect of a Canadian property mutual fund investment, means the portion of any amount that is paid or credited (otherwise than as a SIFT trust wind-up event), by the mutual fund that issued the investment, to a non-resident investor who holds the investment, and that is not otherwise subject to tax under Part I or Part XIII.

Related Provisions: 53(2)(h)(i.1)(B)(III) — Assessable distribution not deducted from adjusted cost base of capital interest in trust; 132.2(3)(g)(iii) — Effect of mutual fund reorganization.

Notes: See Notes at end of 218.3.

218.3(1)"assessable distribution" amended by 2008 budget bill #2, effective July 15, 2008, to add the exclusion for a SIFT trust wind-up event (see Notes to 85.1(8)).

Regulations: 202(1)(f) (information return required).

"Canadian property mutual fund investment" means a share of the capital stock of a mutual fund corporation, or a unit of a mutual fund trust, if

(a) the share or unit is listed on a designated stock exchange; and

(b) more than 50% of the fair market value of the share or unit is attributable to one or more properties each of which is real property in Canada, a Canadian resource property or a timber resource property.

Notes: The designated stock exchange in para. (a) may be in Canada or outside Canada (see Notes to s. 262). For the meaning of "real property" see Notes to 248(4).

218.3(1)(a) amended by 2007 budget bill #2, effective Dec. 14, 2007, to change "prescribed stock exchange" to "designated stock exchange".

"Canadian property mutual fund loss" — of a non-resident investor for a taxation year for which the non-resident investor has filed, on or before their filing-due date for the taxation year, a return of income under this Part in prescribed form, in respect of a Canadian property mutual fund investment — means the lesser of

(a) the non-resident investor's loss (for greater certainty as determined under section 40) for the taxation year from the disposition of the Canadian property mutual fund investment, and

(b) the total of all assessable distributions that were paid or credited on the Canadian property mutual fund investment after the non-resident investor last acquired the investment and at or before the time of the disposition.

"non-resident investor" means a non-resident person or a partnership other than a Canadian partnership.

"unused Canadian property mutual fund loss", of a non-resident investor for a taxation year, means the portion of the total of the non-resident investor's Canadian mutual fund property losses for preceding taxation years that has neither reduced under subsection (3) the amount of tax payable, nor increased under subsection (5) the amount of a refund of tax paid, under this Part for any preceding taxation year.

(2) Tax payable — If at any time a person (referred to in this section as the "payer") pays or credits, to a non-resident investor who holds a Canadian property mutual fund investment, an amount as, on account of, in lieu of payment of or in satisfaction of, an assessable distribution,

(a) the non-resident investor is deemed for the purposes of this Act, other than section 150, to have disposed at that time, for proceeds equal to the amount of the assessable distribution, of a property

(i) that is a taxable Canadian property the adjusted cost base of which to the non-resident investor immediately before that time is nil, and

(ii) that is in all other respects identical to the Canadian property mutual fund investment;

(b) the non-resident investor is liable to pay an income tax of 15% on the amount of any gain (for greater certainty as determined under section 40) from the disposition; and

(c) the payer shall, notwithstanding any agreement or law to the contrary,

(i) deduct or withhold 15% from the amount paid or credited,

(ii) immediately remit that amount to the Receiver General on behalf of the non-resident investor on account of the tax, and

(iii) submit with the remittance a statement in prescribed form.

Related Provisions: 115(1)(b) — Deemed disposition excluded from non-resident's taxable income earned in Canada; 218.3(2) — Non-resident may file return to reduce losses; 218.3(10), 227.1 — Directors of corporation liable for unremitted tax.

Notes: See Notes at end of 218.3. The mechanism of paying tax on the "net" rather than the "gross" is similar to that in s. 216 for real property rents.

Regulations: 202(1)(f), 210 (information return).

(3) Use of losses — If a non-resident investor files, on or before their filing-due date for a taxation year, a return of income under this Part in prescribed form for the taxation year, the non-resident investor is liable, instead of paying tax under paragraph (2)(b) in respect of any amount paid or credited in the taxation year, to pay an income tax of 15% for the taxation year on the amount, if any, by which

(a) the total of the non-resident investor's gains under subsection (2) for the taxation year

exceeds

(b) the total of the non-resident investor's Canadian property mutual fund losses for the year and the non-resident investor's unused Canadian property mutual fund loss for the taxation year.

Related Provisions: 218.3(4) — Tax deemed paid; 218.3(5)-(7) — Refund and carryback; 218.3(8), (9) — Application to partnership.

Forms: T1262: Part XIII.2 tax return for non-resident's investments in Canadian mutual funds.

(4) Deemed tax paid — If a non-resident investor files, on or before their filing-due date for a taxation year, a return of income under this Part in prescribed form for the taxation year, any amount that is remitted to the Receiver General in respect of an assessable distribution paid or credited to the non-resident investor in the taxation year is deemed to have been paid on account of the non-resident investor's tax under subsection (3) for the taxation year.

Forms: T1262: Part XIII.2 tax return for non-resident's investments in Canadian mutual funds.

(5) Refund — The amount, if any, by which the total of all amounts paid on account of a non-resident investor's tax under subsection (3) for a taxation year exceeds the non-resident investor's liability for tax under this Part for the taxation year shall be refunded to the non-resident investor.

(6) Excess loss — carryback — If a non-resident investor files, on or before their filing-due date for a taxation year, a return of income under this Part in prescribed form for the taxation year, the Minister shall refund to the non-resident investor an amount equal to the lesser of

(a) the total amount of tax under this Part paid by the non-resident investor in each of the three preceding taxation years, to the extent that the Minister has not previously refunded that tax, and

(b) 15% of the amount, if any, by which

(i) the total of the non-resident investor's Canadian property mutual fund losses for the taxation year and the non-resident investor's unused Canadian property mutual fund loss for the taxation year

exceeds

(ii) the total of all assessable distributions paid or credited to the non-resident investor in the taxation year.

Related Provisions: 218.3(7) — Ordering.

(7) Ordering — In applying subsection (6), amounts of tax are to be considered to be refunded in the order in which they were paid.

(8) Partnership filing-due date — For the purposes of this Part, the taxation year of a partnership is its fiscal period and the filing-due date for the taxation year is to be determined as if the partnership were a corporation.

(9) Partnership — member resident in Canada — If a non-resident investor is a partnership a member of which is resident in Canada, the portion of the tax paid by the partnership under this Part in respect of an assessable distribution paid or credited to the partnership in a particular taxation year of the partnership (or, if the partnership files a return of income for the particular taxation year in accordance with subsection (3), the portion of the tax paid by the partnership under that subsection for the taxation year) that can reasonably be considered to be the member's share is deemed

(a) to be an amount paid on account of that member's liability for tax under Part I for that member's taxation year in which the particular taxation year of the partnership ends; and

(b) except for the purposes of this subsection, to be neither a tax paid on account of the partnership's tax under this Part nor a tax paid by the partnership.

(10) Provisions applicable — Section 150.1, subsections 161(1), (7) and (11), sections 162 to 167, Division J of Part I, paragraph 214(3)(f), subsections 215(2), (3) and (6) and sections 227 and 227.1 apply to this Part with any modifications that the circumstances require.

Notes [s. 218.3]: 218.3 (Part XIII.2) applies a 15% income tax, as a tax on gains, to distributions that are not otherwise subject to tax under Part I or XIII, paid or credited by a mutual fund to non-resident investors, where the fund's value is primarily from Canadian real property (or resource or timber property): 218.3(1)"Canadain property

mutual fund investment". Where the non-resident investor realizes a loss on the disposition of the mutual fund investment (218.3(1)"Canadian property mutual fund loss"), the loss may in some cases be applied against the gain on similar investments. In general, the loss may be carried back 3 taxation years and forward indefinitely.

For CRA interpretation see VIEWS doc 2006-0187461E5.

218.3 added by 2004 Budget, effective for distributions paid or credited after 2004.

Definitions [s. 218.3]: "adjusted cost base" — 54, 248(1); "amount" — 248(1); "assessable distribution" — 218.3(1); "Canada" — 255, *Interpretation Act* 35(1); "Canadian partnership" — 102(1), 248(1); "Canadian property mutual fund investment", "Canadian property mutual fund loss" — 218.3(1); "Canadian resource property" — 66(15), 248(1); "corporation" — 248(1), *Interpretation Act* 35(1); "designated stock exchange" — 248(1), 262; "disposition" — 248(1); "fair market value" — see 69(1) Notes; "filing-due date" — 218.3(8), 248(1); "fiscal period" — 249.1; "Minister" — 248(1); "mutual fund corporation" — 131(8), 248(1); "mutual fund trust" — 132(6)–(7), 132.2(3)(n), 248(1); "non-resident" — 248(1); "non-resident investor" — 218.3(1); "partnership" — see 96(1) Notes; "payer" — 218.3(2); "person", "prescribed" — 248(1); "property" — 248(1); "resident in Canada" — 250; "SIFT trust wind-up event", "share", "taxable Canadian property" — 248(1); "taxation year" — 218.3(8), 249; "timber resource property" — 13(21), 248(1); "unused Canadian property mutual fund loss" — 218.3(1).

PART XIV — ADDITIONAL TAX [BRANCH TAX] ON NON-RESIDENT CORPORATIONS

219. (1) Additional tax [branch tax] — Every corporation that is non-resident in a taxation year shall, on or before its balance-due day for the year, pay a tax under this Part for the year equal to 25% of the amount, if any, by which the total of

(a) the corporation's taxable income earned in Canada for the year (in this subsection referred to as the corporation's "base amount"),

(b) the amount deducted because of section 112 and paragraph 115(1)(e) in computing the corporation's base amount,

(c) [Repealed]

(d) the amount, if any, by which the total of all amounts each of which is a taxable capital gain of the corporation for the year from a disposition of a taxable Canadian property exceeds the total of all amounts each of which is

(i) an allowable capital loss of the corporation for the year from a disposition of a taxable Canadian property, or

(ii) an amount deductible because of paragraphs 111(1)(b) and 115(1)(d) in computing the corporation's base amount,

(e) the total of all amounts each of which is an amount in respect of a grant or credit that

(i) can reasonably be considered to have been received by the corporation in the year as a reimbursement or repayment of, or as indemnification or compensation for, an amount deducted because of paragraph (j), as it read in its application to the 1995 taxation year, in computing the amount determined under this subsection for a preceding taxation year that began before 1996, and

(ii) was not included in computing the corporation's base amount for any taxation year,

(f) where, at any time in the year, the corporation has made one or more dispositions described in paragraph (l) of qualified property, the total of all amounts each of which is an amount in respect of one of those dispositions equal to the amount, if any, by which the fair market value of the qualified property at the time of the disposition exceeds the corporation's proceeds of disposition of the property, and

(g) the amount, if any, claimed for the immediately preceding taxation year under paragraph (j) by the corporation,

exceeds the total of

(h) that proportion of the total of

(i) the total of the taxes payable under Parts I, I.3 and VI for the year by the corporation, determined without reference to subsection (1.1), and

(ii) the total of the income taxes payable to the government of a province for the year by the corporation, determined without reference to subsection (1.1),

that the corporation's base amount is of the amount that would, if this Act were read without reference to subsection (1.1), be the corporation's base amount,

(i) the total of all amounts each of which is the amount of interest or a penalty paid by the corporation in the year

(i) under this Act, or

(ii) on or in respect of an income tax payable by it to the government of a province under a law of the province relating to income tax,

to the extent that the interest or penalty was not deductible in computing its base amount for any taxation year,

(j) where the corporation was carrying on business in Canada at the end of the year, the amount claimed by the corporation for the year, not exceeding the amount prescribed to be its allowance for the year in respect of its investment in property in Canada, and

(k) [Repealed]

(l) where the corporation has at any time in the year disposed of property (in this paragraph and paragraph (f) referred to as "qualified property") used by it immediately before that time for the purpose of gaining or producing income from a business carried on by it in Canada to a Canadian corporation (in this paragraph referred to as the "purchaser corporation") that was, immediately after the disposition, a qualified related corporation of the corporation for consideration that includes a share of the capital stock of the purchaser corporation, the total of all amounts each of which is an amount in respect of a disposition in the year of a qualified property equal to the amount, if any, by which

(i) the fair market value of the qualified property at the time of the disposition

exceeds the total of

(ii) the amount, if any, by which the paid-up capital in respect of the issued and outstanding shares of the capital stock of the purchaser corporation increased because of the disposition, and

(iii) the fair market value, at the time of receipt, of the consideration (other than shares) given by the purchaser corporation for the qualified property.

Related Provisions: 18(1)(t) — Tax is non-deductible; 18(4) — Thin capitalization rule applies to non-resident corporation; 52(7) — Cost of shares of subsidiary; 115.2 — Non-resident investment or pension fund deemed not to be carrying on business in Canada; 142.7(10)(b) — Addition under 219(1)(g) for branch-establishment dividend of foreign entrant bank; 218.2 — Branch interest tax on foreign banks; 219(1.1) — Excluded gains; 219(2) — Exempt corporations; 219.1(1) — Corporate emigration — 25% tax; 219.1(2) — Foreign affiliate dumping; 219.2 — Limitation on rate of Part XIV tax to dividend rate under treaties; Canada-U.K. Tax Treaty:Art. 22:3 — Limitation on branch tax; Canada-U.S. Tax Treaty:Art. X:6(d) — Exemption for first $500,000 of earnings and rate limited to 5%.

Notes: Part XIV tax is known informally as the "branch tax". It parallels the withholding tax in 212(2) by taxing a non-resident's Canadian branch profits not reinvested in Canada at the same rate as dividends. The measurement of "not reinvested in Canada" (see 219(1)(j) and Reg. 808) is intended to approximate the funds remitted to the home base; Canada having no exchange controls or currency controls, there is no other way to measure the actual funds "sent home". Filing and administration of the tax follow the same rules as Part I tax: see 219(3).

Where the rate on dividends is reduced by treaty, as is usually the case, the branch tax rate is normally correspondingly reduced: see 219.2. (Until 1985, the rule in 219.2 was in ITAR 11(4).)

Note that some of Canada's tax treaties exempt the first $500,000 of a non-resident corporation's income: e.g., Canada-US treaty Art. X:6(d). As well, under the treaty this tax applies only if the US company has a permanent establishment in Canada: Art. X:6; VIEWS doc 2007-026237I7; and Art. X:6 applies to S corporations, limited partnership income and sometimes LLCs: 2009-0339951E5, 2012-0440101E5, 2013-0466091E5, 2017-073653I7; and to income earned through hybrid partnerships: 2012-0444151C6. (See also 2012-0458841M4 re Canada-Ireland treaty Art. 10:6.) As a result, Part XIV tax raised only $263m from 751 corporations in 2010 and $194m from 813 corporations in 2011 (*Access to Information Act* disclosure).

In *TD Securities (USA) LLC*, 2010 TCC 186, a US LLC was held entitled to the 5% Canada-US treaty Art. X:6 rate on branch tax, even before the amendments adding Art. IV:6 to the treaty. The CRA changed its assessing policy as a result, but its refusal to refund the extra tax was upheld in *CGI Holding LLC*, 2016 FC 1086, where the refund request was made late and the CRA considered the facts to be different.

In *Big Bad Voodoo Daddy*, 2011 TCC 226 (FCA appeal discontinued A-206-11), Part XIV tax applied to small amounts of a US LLC's income with no indication as to why the $500,000 treaty exemption did not apply.

The 2013 Budget extended the thin-capitalization rule in 18(4) to non-resident corporations; this may increase the branch tax.

See also Vidal, *Introduction to International Tax in Canada* (Carswell, 8th ed., 2020), chap. 10; Kakkar, "Branch Tax Exigible When There Is No Canadian Establishment", 9(4) *Tax for the Owner-Manager* (ctf.ca) 7-8 (Oct. 2009) (notes example where s. 219 can apply even with no PE in Canada); Chong, "LLCs and Canadian Branch Tax", 20(9) *Canadian Tax Highlights* (ctf.ca) 5-6 (Sept. 2012); VIEWS doc 2008-0298011E5 (capital gains on real property used in business in Canada can be subject to branch tax).

219(1)(d)(ii) amended to change 115(1) reference from (e) to (d) by 2013 budget bill #2, effective for 1998 and later taxation years.

219(1)(e) amended, and (c) and (k) repealed, by 2003 resource bill, effective for taxation years that begin after 2006.

219(1) earlier amended by 2003 Budget (for taxation years beginning after June 2003), 2001 technical bill, 2000 Budget, and 1995-97, 1992 and 1991 technical bills.

Regulations: 808 (allowance in respect of investment in property in Canada).

Interpretation Bulletins: See list at end of s. 219.

CRA Audit Manual: 15.2.0: Income of a non-resident.

Forms: T2 Sched. 20: Part XIV — additional tax on non-resident corporations.

(1.1) Excluded gains — For the purposes of subsection (1), the definition "taxable Canadian property" in subsection 248(1) shall be read without reference to paragraphs (a) and (c) to (e) of that definition and as if the only options, interests or rights referred to in paragraph (f) of that definition were those in respect of property described in paragraph (b) of that definition.

Notes: See VIEWS doc 2008-0298011E5.

219(1.1) amended by 2002-2013 technical bill (Part 4 — bijuralism, effective June 26, 2013), 2013 budget bill #2, 2001 technical bill. Added by 1995-97 technical bill.

(2) Exempt corporations — No tax is payable under this Part for a taxation year by a corporation that was, throughout the year,

(a) [Repealed]

(b) a corporation whose principal business was

(i) the transportation of persons or goods,

(ii) communications, or

(iii) mining iron ore in Canada; or

(c) a corporation exempt from tax under section 149.

Notes: Film distribution is not "communications" for (b)(ii): *Twentieth Century Fox*, 2002 FCA 232. For the meaning of "principal business" see Notes to 20(1)(bb).

219(2)(a), "a bank", repealed by 2001 technical bill for tax years that end after June 27, 1999. Authorized foreign banks (defined in 248(1)) are now subject to the branch tax. See Reg. 808(8).

(3) Provisions applicable to Part — Sections 150 to 152, 154, 158, 159 and 161 to 167 and Division J of Part I are applicable to this Part with such modifications as the circumstances require.

Notes: Due to 219(3), the reassessment deadlines in 152(4) apply to a Part XIV tax reassessment: VIEWS doc 2011-042660I7.

Interpretation Bulletins: See list at end of s. 219.

(4) Non-resident insurers — No tax is payable under subsection (1) for a taxation year by a non-resident insurer, but where it elects, in prescribed manner and within the prescribed time, to deduct, in computing its Canadian investment fund as of the end of the immediately following taxation year, an amount not greater than the amount, if any, by which

(a) the amount, if any, by which the total of

(i) the insurer's surplus funds derived from operations as of the end of the year, and

(i.1) where, in any particular taxation year that began before the end of the year, the insurer transferred to a taxable Canadian corporation with which it did not deal at arm's length any designated insurance property of the insurer for the particular year, and

(A) the property was transferred before December 16, 1987 and subsection 138(11.5) of the *Income Tax Act*, chapter 148 of the Revised Statutes of Canada, 1952, applied in respect of the transfer, or

(B) the property was transferred before November 22, 1985 and subsection 85(1) of that Act applied in respect of the transfer,

the amount, if any, by which

(C) the total of the fair market value, at the time of the transfer, of all such property

exceeds

(D) the total of the insurer's proceeds of disposition of all such property,

exceeds the total of

(ii) each amount on which the insurer has paid tax under this Part for a previous taxation year,

(iii) the amount, if any, by which the insurer's accumulated 1968 deficit exceeds the amount of the insurer's maximum tax actuarial reserves for its 1968 taxation year for its life insurance policies in Canada,

(iv) the insurer's loss, if any, for each of its 5 consecutive taxation years ending with its 1968 taxation year, from all insurance businesses (other than its life insurance business) carried on by it in Canada (computed without reference to section 30 of the *Income Tax Act*, chapter 148 of the Revised Statutes of Canada, 1952, as it read in its application to those years), except to the extent that any such loss was deductible in computing its taxable income for any of its taxation years ending before 1969, and

(v) the total of all amounts in respect of which the insurer has filed an election under subsection (5.2) for a previous taxation year in accordance with that subsection,

exceeds

(b) the amount of the insurer's attributed surplus for the year,

the insurer shall, on or before the day on or before which it is required to file a return under Part I for the year, pay a tax for the year equal to 25% of the amount, if any, by which the amount it has so elected to deduct exceeds the amount in respect of which it filed an election under subsection (5.2) for the year in accordance with that subsection.

Related Provisions: 181.3(3)(d)(i)(A), 190.13(c)(i)(A) — Effect on capital tax.

Notes: 219(4)(a)(i.1) amended by 1996 Budget, for 1997 and later tax years.

Regulations: 2403(1) (prescribed manner and time).

I.T. Application Rules: 69 (meaning of "chapter 148 of ...").

Interpretation Bulletins: See list at end of s. 219.

(5) [Repealed under former Act]

(5.1) Additional tax on insurer — Where a non-resident insurer ceases in a taxation year to carry on all or substantially all of an insurance business in Canada, it shall, on or before its filing-due date for the year, pay a tax for the year equal to 25% of the amount, if any, by which

(a) that portion of the amount determined under paragraph (4)(a) for the year in respect of the insurer that can reasonably be attributed to the business, including the disposition by it of property that was its designated insurance property in respect of the business for the year in which the disposition occurred,

exceeds

(b) the amount the insurer and a qualified related corporation of the insurer jointly elect in accordance with subsection (5.2) for the year in respect of the business.

Related Provisions: 18(1)(t) — Tax is non-deductible.

Notes: For interpretation of "reasonably be attributed" in para. (a), see *729658 Alberta Ltd.*, 2004 TCC 474.

CRA considers that "substantially all" means 90% or more.

219(5.1) amended by 1996 Budget, effective for 1997 and later taxation years, to reflect the new definition of "designated insurance property" in 138(12), and use the new term "filing-due date" (defined in 248(1)).

(5.2) Election by non-resident insurer — Where

(a) a non-resident insurer has ceased to carry on all or substantially all of an insurance business in Canada in a taxation year, and

(b) the insurer has transferred the business to a qualified related corporation of the insurer and the insurer and the corporation have elected to have subsection 138(11.5) apply in respect of the transfer,

the insurer and the corporation may elect, in prescribed manner and within prescribed time, to reduce the amount in respect of which the insurer would otherwise be liable to pay tax under subsection (5.1) by an amount not exceeding the lesser of

(c) the amount determined under paragraph (5.1)(a) in respect of the insurer in respect of the business, and

(d) the total of the paid-up capital of the shares of the capital stock of the corporation received by the insurer as consideration for the transfer of the business and any contributed surplus arising on the issue of those shares.

Related Provisions: 138(11.9) — Computation of contributed surplus; 190.13(c)(i)(A) — Effect on capital tax.

Notes: CRA considers that "substantially all", used in 219(5.2)(a), means 90% or more.

Regulations: 2403(2) (prescribed manner and time).

Interpretation Bulletins: See list at end of s. 219.

(5.3) Deemed payment of dividend — Where, at any time in a taxation year,

(a) a qualified related corporation of a non-resident insurer ceases to be a qualified related corporation of that insurer, or

(b) the tax deferred account of a qualified related corporation of a non-resident insurer exceeds the total of the paid-up capital in respect of all the shares of the capital stock of the corporation and its contributed surplus,

the corporation shall be deemed to have paid, immediately before that time, a dividend to the insurer in an amount equal to

(c) where paragraph (a) is applicable, the balance of the tax deferred account of the corporation at that time, or

(d) where paragraph (b) is applicable, the amount of the excess referred to in that paragraph at that time.

Related Provisions: 138(11.9) — Computation of contributed surplus.

Notes: CRA's view is that a non-resident insurer that defers branch tax under 219(5.2) should treat the deemed dividend under 219(5.3), for purposes of the Canada-US tax treaty, as a dividend (15% withholding tax in the absence of 10% share ownership) and not branch tax (5% withholding tax in all cases): VIEWS doc 2001-0106695.

Interpretation Bulletins: See list at end of s. 219.

(6) [Repealed under former Act]

Notes: 219(6), which related to non-resident insurers, was repealed in 1978.

(7) Definitions — In this Part,

"accumulated 1968 deficit" of a life insurer means such amount as can be established by the insurer to be its deficit as of the end of its 1968 taxation year from carrying on its life insurance business in Canada on the assumption that the amounts of its assets and liabilities (including reserves of any kind)

(a) as of the end of any taxation year before its 1968 taxation year, were the amounts thereof determined for the purposes of the Superintendent of Insurance for Canada or other similar officer, and

(b) as of the end of its 1968 taxation year, were

(i) in respect of depreciable property, the capital cost thereof as of the first day of its 1969 taxation year,

(ii) in respect of policy reserves, the insurer's maximum tax actuarial reserves for its 1968 taxation year for life insurance policies issued by it in the course of carrying on its life insurance business in Canada, and

(iii) in respect of other assets and liabilities, the amounts thereof determined as of the end of that year for the purpose of computing its income for its 1969 taxation year;

Notes: Definition "accumulated 1968 deficit" amended by 1996 Budget, effective for 1997 and later taxation years. It was previously defined by reference to the definition in 138(12). That definition was repealed, so the substantive definition was moved here.

219(7)"accumulated 1968 deficit" was 219(7)(b) before RSC 1985 (5th Supp) consolidation for tax years ending after Nov. 1991.

"attributed surplus" of an insurer for a taxation year has the meaning assigned by regulation;

Notes: Term changed from "attributed surplus for the year" to "attributed surplus" by 1996 Budget, effective for 1997 and later taxation years.

219(7)"attributed surplus for the year" was 219(7)(a) before RSC 1985 (5th Supp) consolidation for tax years ending after Nov. 1991.

Regulations: 2400(4)(b).

"Canadian investment fund" has the meaning prescribed for that expression;

Notes: 219(7)"Canadian investment fund" was 219(7)(a) before RSC 1985 (5th Supp) consolidation for tax years ending after Nov. 1991.

Regulations: 2400(4)(b).

"maximum tax actuarial reserves" has the meaning assigned by subsection 138(12);

Notes: 219(7)"maximum tax actuarial reserves" was 219(7)(b.1) before RSC 1985 (5th Supp) consolidation for tax years ending after Nov. 1991.

"surplus funds derived from operations" has the meaning assigned by subsection 138(12);

Notes: 219(7)"surplus funds derived from operations" was 219(7)(b.2) before RSC 1985 (5th Supp) consolidation for tax years ending after Nov. 1991.

"tax deferred account" of a qualified related corporation at any time means the amount determined by the formula

$$A - B$$

where

A is the total of all amounts each of which is an amount in respect of which the qualified related corporation and a non-resident insurer have elected jointly before that time in accordance with subsection (5.2), and

B is the total of all amounts each of which is the amount of a dividend deemed by subsection (5.3) to have been paid by the qualified related corporation before that time.

Related Provisions: 257 — Formula cannot calculate to less than zero.

Notes: 219(7)"tax deferred account" was 219(7)(c) before RSC 1985 (5th Supp) consolidation for tax years ending after Nov. 1991.

Interpretation Bulletins: See list at end of s. 219.

(8) Meaning of "qualified related corporation" — For the purposes of this Part, a corporation is a "qualified related corporation" of a particular corporation if it is resident in Canada and all of the issued and outstanding shares (other than directors' qualifying shares) of its capital stock (having full voting rights under all circumstances) are owned by

(a) the particular corporation,

(b) a subsidiary wholly-owned corporation of the particular corporation,

(c) a corporation of which the particular corporation is a subsidiary wholly-owned corporation,

(d) a subsidiary wholly-owned corporation of a corporation of which the particular corporation is also a subsidiary wholly-owned corporation, or

(e) any combination of corporations each of which is a corporation described in paragraph (a), (b), (c) or (d),

and, for the purpose of this subsection, a subsidiary wholly-owned corporation of a particular corporation includes any subsidiary wholly-owned corporation of a corporation that is a subsidiary wholly-owned corporation of the particular corporation.

Notes: 219(8) amended by 1995-97 technical bill, effective for taxation years that begin in 1996 or later. The former version was identical in effect but was worded throughout in terms of a "non-resident insurer" rather than a "particular corporation". The amendment extends its application beyond corporations related to insurers, to apply for other purposes of Part XIV as well. This is relevant to the transfer of Canadian business property by a non-resident under amended 219(1)(f) and (l), which require that the transfer be to a qualified related corporation.

For "directors' qualifying shares", see Notes to 85(1.3).

Definitions [s. 219]: "accumulated 1968 deficit" — 138(12), 219(7); "allowable capital loss" — 38(b), 248(1); "amount" — 248(1); "arm's length" — 251(1); "attributed surplus" — 219(7), Reg. 2400(4)(b); "balance-due day" — 248(1); "base amount" — 219(1)(a); "business" — 248(1); "Canada" — 255; "Canadian corporation" — 89(1), 248(1); "Canadian investment fund" — 219(7), Reg. 2400(4)(b); "carrying on business" — 253; "corporation" — 248(1), *Interpretation Act* 35(1); "depreciable property" — 13(21), 248(1); "designated insurance property" — 138(12), 248(1); "dividend" — 248(1); "fair market value" — see 69(1) Notes; "filing-due date" — 248(1); "insurer" — 248(1); "life insurance policy" — 138(12), 248(1); "life insurer" — 248(1); "maximum tax actuarial reserve" — 138(12), 219(7); "non-resident" — 248(1); "paid-up capital" — 89(1), 248(1); "person", "prescribed", "property" — 248(1); "province" — *Interpretation Act* 35(1); "qualified property" — 219(1)(l); "qualified related corporation" — 219(8); "qualifying share" — 192(6), 248(1) *[not intended to apply to s. 219]*; "regulation" — 248(1); "resident in Canada" — 250; "share" — 248(1); "subsidiary wholly-owned corporation" — 219(8), 248(1); "surplus funds derived from operations" — 138(12), 219(7); "tax deferred account" — 219(7); "taxable Canadian corporation" — 89(1), 248(1); "taxable Canadian property" — 219(1.1), 248(1); "taxable capital gain" — 38(a), 248(1); "taxable income" — 2(2), 248(1); "taxable income earned in Canada" — 248(1); "taxation year" — 249.

Interpretation Bulletins [s. 219]: IT-137R3: Additional tax on certain corporations carrying on business in Canada; IT-393R2: Election re tax on rents and timber royalties — non-residents.

219.1 (1) Corporate emigration — If a taxation year of a corporation (in this subsection and subsection (2) referred to as the "emigrating corporation") is deemed by paragraph 128.1(4)(a) to have ended at any time, the emigrating corporation shall, on or before its filing-due date for the year, pay a tax under this Part for the year equal to the amount determined by the formula

$$25\% \times (A - B)$$

where

A is the fair market value of all the property owned by the emigrating corporation immediately before that time; and

B is the total of

(a) the paid-up capital in respect of all the shares of the capital stock of the emigrating corporation immediately before that time,

(b) all amounts (other than amounts payable by the emigrating corporation in respect of dividends and amounts payable under this section) each of which is a debt owing by the emigrating corporation, or an obligation of the emigrating corporation to pay an amount, that is outstanding at that time, and

(c) if a tax was payable by the emigrating corporation under subsection 219(1) or this section for a preceding taxation year that began before 1996 and after the emigrating corporation last became resident in Canada, four times the total of all amounts that would, but for sections 219.2 and 219.3 and any tax treaty, have been so payable.

Related Provisions: 219.1(2) — Foreign affiliate dumping; 219.3 — Limitation of tax under 219.1(1) to rate under treaty; 257 — Formula cannot calculate to less than zero; Canada-U.S. Tax Treaty:Art. IV:3 — Continuance in other jurisdiction.

Notes: 219.1(1) applies when a corporation resident in Canada becomes non-resident. This may happen by moving "central management and control" (CM&C: see Notes to 250(4)) to another country, but note that a corp *incorporated* in Canada after April 26, 1965 is deemed to remain resident in Canada, and an earlier-incorporated corp may be so deemed: see 250(4). Also, some of Canada's tax treaties, such as with the US (Art IV:3), provide that a corp incorporated in Canada is deemed resident in Canada if it would otherwise be resident in both countries.

A corp can also be "continued" in another jurisdiction, which deems it to have been incorporated there: 250(5.1); so if its CM&C is not in Canada (or if a treaty tie-breaker rule so provides), it will become non-resident.

219.1(1) renumbered from 219.1 to be a subsection and amended by 2012 budget bill #2, effective for corporations that cease to be resident in Canada after March 28, 2012, to use the term "emigrating corporation" throughout and to change the wording to a formula (non-substantive changes).

(2) Foreign affiliate dumping — emigrating corporation —
The paid-up capital referred to in paragraph (a) of the description of B in subsection (1) is deemed to be nil if

(a) one or more shares of the emigrating corporation are, at the time the emigrating corporation ceases to be resident in Canada, owned by another corporation resident in Canada;

(b) the other corporation is controlled, at that time, by a non-resident person or a group of non-resident persons not dealing with each other at arm's length; and

(c) the emigrating corporation is, immediately after that time — or becomes, as part of a transaction or event or series of transactions or events that includes the emigrating corporation ceasing to be resident in Canada — a foreign affiliate of the other corporation.

Related Provisions: 93.1(1) — Shares held by a partnership; 128.1(1(c.3) — Foreign affiliate dumping — corporate immigration; 212.3(2)(a) — Foreign affiliate dumping — deemed dividend; 212.3(25) — Application to partnerships; 212.3(26) — Determining "related" and "control" for a trust for certain purposes.

Notes: 219.1(2) was added to deter certain corporate emigration strategies that could be used as substitutes for transactions addressed by the foreign affiliate (FA) dumping rules in 212.3. 219.1(2) applies where shares of the emigrating corp are owned by a Canadian-resident corp that is controlled by a non-resident corp, and the emigrating corp is a FA of the shareholder immediately after the emigration. In such a case, emigration would lead to a result similar to what 212.3 is aimed at preventing. Thus, if these conditions are met, any PUC the emigrating corporation would otherwise have is deemed to be nil, so it will pay higher departure tax.

The look-through rules in 93.1(1) and 212.3(25) apply to 219.1(2), if one or more partnerships are in the ownership structure.

219.1(2)(b) amended by 2021 budget bill #1, for transactions or events after March 18, 2019, to change "by a non-resident corporation" to "by a non-resident person or a..." (to end) to align with amendments to 212.3(1)(b).

219.1(2) added by 2012 budget bill #2, for corporations that cease to be resident in Canada after March 28, 2012.

(3) Application of subsec. (4) — Subsection (4) applies if

(a) a corporation ceases to be resident in Canada at any time (referred to in subsection (4) as the "emigration time");

(b) an amount is required by paragraph 212.3(2)(b) or subsection 212.3(7) to be deducted in computing the paid-up capital in respect of a class of shares of the capital stock of the corporation because of an investment in a subject corporation made by a CRIC that is described in any of paragraphs 212.3(10)(a) to (f);

(c) subsection 212.3(9) has not applied in respect of any reduction of the paid-up capital in respect of a class of shares of the capital stock of the corporation or a specified predecessor corporation (as defined in subsection 95(1)) of the corporation; and

(d) subsection (2) does not apply in respect of the cessation of residence.

Related Provisions: 212.3(22) — Effect of amalgamation or windup; 219.1(5) — Meaning of "CRIC", "subject corporation" and "investment".

Notes: 219.1(3)(b) amended by 2014 budget bill #2, retroactive to corporations that cease to be resident in Canada after March 28, 2012, to change reference from 212.3(7)(b) to 212.3(7) and effectively add reference to 212.3(10)(c)-(e).

219.1(3) added by 2012 budget bill #2, for corporations that cease to be resident in Canada after March 28, 2012. This provision was not in the Dec. 14, 2011 draft legislation.

(4) Paid-up capital reinstatement — If this subsection applies,
the paid-up capital referred to in paragraph (a) of the description of B in subsection (1) is to be increased, immediately before the time that is immediately before the emigration time, by the lesser of

(a) the total of all amounts each of which is an amount by which the paid-up capital of a class of shares of the capital stock of the corporation was required by paragraph 212.3(2)(b) or subsection 212.3(7) to be reduced in respect of an investment in a subject

corporation made by the CRIC that is described in any of paragraphs 212.3(10)(a) to (f), and

(b) the total of all amounts each of which is

(i) the fair market value of a share of the capital stock of a subject corporation that is owned by the corporation immediately before the emigration time,

(ii) the portion of the fair market value of a particular share of the capital stock of a foreign affiliate of the corporation owned by the corporation immediately before the emigration time that may reasonably be considered to relate to a share of the capital stock of a subject corporation that was previously owned by the corporation and for which the particular share was substituted, or

(iii) the fair market value of a debt obligation, other than a pertinent loan or indebtedness (as defined in subsection 212.3(11)), of a subject corporation that is owned by the corporation immediately before the emigration time.

Related Provisions: 212.3(22) — Effect of amalgamation or windup; 219.1(3) — Conditions for 219.1(4) to apply; 219.1(5) — Meaning of "CRIC", "subject corporation" and "investment".

Notes: For a ruling on 219.1(4) see VIEWS doc 2016-0643931R3 [Wang & Lee, "Buy, Bump and Emigrate?", 26(8) *Canadian Tax Highlights* (ctf.ca) 8-9 (Aug. 2018)].

219.1(4) amended by 2014 budget bill #2, retroactive to its introduction: (b)(iii) added, and (a) amended to change reference from 212.3(7)(b) to 212.3(7) and effectively add reference to 212.3(10)(c)-(e).

219.1(4) added by 2012 budget bill #2, for corporations that cease to be resident in Canada after March 28, 2012. It was not in the draft legislation of Dec. 14, 2011.

(5) Assigned meanings from s. 212.3 — For the purposes of
subsections (3) and (4), **"CRIC"** and **"subject corporation"** have the meaning assigned to those terms by subsection 212.3(1) and **"investment"** has the same meaning as in subsection 212.3(10).

Notes: 219.1(5) added by 2012 budget bill #2, effective for corporations that cease to be resident in Canada after March 28, 2012. It was not in the draft legislation of Dec. 14, 2011.

Notes [s. 219.1]: 219.1 amended by 1995-97 technical bill, for 1996 and later tax years.

219.1 earlier amended by 1993 technical bill, effective 1993, or, by election (see Notes to 250(5.1)), effective from the corporation's earlier "time of continuation". With the amendment, the scope of 219.1 was widened. Before 1993, it applied only to a corporation becoming non-resident by moving to a treaty country.

Definitions [s. 219.1]: "amount" — 248(1); "arm's length" — 251(1); "class of shares" — 248(6); "controlled" — 212.3(26), 256(6)-(9); "corporation" — 248(1), *Interpretation Act* 35(1); "CRIC" — 219.1(5), 212.3(1); "dividend" — 248(1); "emigrating corporation" — 219.1(1); "emigration time" — 219.1(3)(a); "fair market value" — see 69(1) Notes; "filing-due date" — 150(1), 248(1); "foreign affiliate" — 95(1), 248(1); "investment" — 219.1(5), 212.3(10); "non-resident" — 248(1); "paid-up capital" — 89(1), 248(1); "person" — 248(1); "pertinent loan or indebtedness" — 212.3(11); "property" — 248(1); "resident in Canada" — 94(3)(a), 250; "series of transactions" — 248(10); "share" — 248(1); "subject corporation" — 219.1(5), 212.3(1); "substituted" — 248(5); "tax treaty" — 248(1); "taxation year" — 249.

Interpretation Bulletins: IT-137R3: Additional tax on certain corporations carrying on business in Canada; IT-451R: Deemed disposition and acquisition on ceasing to be or becoming resident in Canada.

219.2 Limitation on rate of branch tax — Notwithstanding any
other provision of this Act, where an agreement or convention between the Government of Canada and the government of another country that has the force of law in Canada

(a) does not limit the rate of tax under this Part on corporations resident in that other country, and

(b) provides that, where a dividend is paid by a corporation resident in Canada to a corporation resident in that other country that owns all of the shares of the capital stock of the corporation resident in Canada, the rate of tax imposed on the dividend shall not exceed a specified rate,

any reference in section 219 to a rate of tax shall, in respect of a taxation year of a corporation to which that agreement or convention applies on the last day of that year, be read as a reference to the specified rate.

Related Provisions: Canada-U.S. Tax Treaty:Art. X:2 — Limit on withholding tax rate on dividends.

Notes: This rule applied in *TD Securities*; see Notes to 219(1).

"Another country" includes Hong Kong, with which Canada has a tax treaty but is not a country: *Canada-Hong Kong Tax Agreement Act, 2013*, s. 4.1 (enacted Dec. 2016, but CRA previously applied this rule administratively: doc 2014-0560351E5). The tax "arrangement" with Taiwan (which is not a treaty, presumably so as not to offend China) is also effectively deemed to be a "treaty" with a "country": *Canada and Taiwan Territories Tax Arrangement Act*, s. 5.

219.2 amended by 1993 technical bill, for 1985 and later taxation years, so that the rate limitation used is the rate that applies under treaties to wholly-owned corporations rather than the treaty rate that applies to dividends generally. The rate for such so-called "direct dividends" is sometimes lower, and never higher, than the regular rate. See Notes to 212(2) and 219(1).

The rule in 219.2 was originally in ITAR 11(4).

Definitions [s. 219.2]: "Canada" — 255; "corporation" — 248(1), *Interpretation Act* 35(1); "dividend" — 248(1); "property" — 248(1); "resident in Canada" — 250; "share" — 248(1); "taxation year" — 249.

Interpretation Bulletins: IT-137R3: Additional tax on certain corporations carrying on business in Canada.

219.3 Effect of tax treaty — For the purpose of section 219.1, where an agreement or convention between the Government of Canada and the government of another country that has the force of law in Canada provides that the rate of tax imposed on a dividend paid by a corporation resident in Canada to a corporation resident in the other country that owns all of the shares of the capital stock of the corporation resident in Canada shall not exceed a specified rate, the reference in section 219.1 to "25%" shall, in respect of a corporation that ceased to be resident in Canada and to which the agreement or convention applies at the beginning of its first taxation year after its taxation year that is deemed by paragraph 128.1(4)(a) to have ended, be read as a reference to the specified rate unless it can reasonably be concluded that one of the main reasons that the corporation became resident in the other country was to reduce the amount of tax payable under this Part or Part XIII.

Notes: 219.3 reduces the departure tax imposed under 219.1(1), where the corporation has become resident in a country whose tax treaty with Canada limits the rate of Canadian tax on dividends paid by a wholly-owned subsidiary in Canada to its parent in that country. 219.3 limits the departure tax to that rate for dividends, unless it can reasonably be concluded that one of the main reasons the corporation became resident in that country was to reduce the tax payable under Parts XIII or XIV. For the meaning of "one of the main reasons" see Notes to 83(2.1).

"Country" includes Hong Kong and Taiwan: see Notes to 219.2.

219.3 amended by 1995-97 technical bill, for 1996 and later taxation years. Added by 1993 technical bill.

Definitions [s. 219.3]: "Canadian corporation" — 89(1), 248(1); "corporation" — 248(1), *Interpretation Act* 35(1); "dividend" — 248(1); "resident in Canada" — 250; "share" — 248(1); "taxation year" — 249.

PART XV — ADMINISTRATION AND ENFORCEMENT

Administration

220. (1) Minister's duty — The Minister shall administer and enforce this Act and the Commissioner of Revenue may exercise all the powers and perform the duties of the Minister under this Act.

Announced Administrative Changes — COVID-19

CRA notice (tinyurl.com/cra-resuming), as of April 19, 2021: *CRA and COVID-19 — Resuming business activities*

The Government temporarily suspended some programs and services, including many collection and compliance activities, to support Canadians through the COVID-19 pandemic.

In a commitment to resuming business activities, some of the CRA's programs and services will return as of September 2020.

As a result, you may receive a call or letter from us, with a specific call to action.

Protect yourself against fraud

As business is resuming, it is important to remind you that the CRA will never use aggressive language, threaten you with jail time, or demand payment by gift cards.

Learn how to recognize a scam and protect yourself from fraud.

Programs that are returning — April 2021

Compliance activities

Who is affected: Businesses

What we're doing: The CRA will be resuming certain post-assessment reviews of T2 Corporation Income Tax Returns to determine if they are accurate and complete. During these reviews, we will be looking for errors and inconsistencies and will make adjustments to them accordingly.

What this means for you:

If your return is selected by the CRA and you are contacted for review, you may need to provide the following:

- your business number, case number, and other account information to verify your identity
- receipts or documents to support a claim or deduction on your return

If you are experiencing negative impacts from the COVID-19 pandemic on your business, you may request a reasonable extension of time to submit this information.

Once the review is complete, you will be advised of the outcome in writing.

Learn more:

- CARP–Reviewing your corporate income tax return and common mistakes *[link available on webpage — ed.]*

Programs that are returning — March 2021

Compliance activities

Who is affected: Businesses, GST/HST Registrants

What we're doing: The CRA is resuming examinations of payroll accounts to ensure employers are deducting, remitting, and reporting taxes, CPP contributions, and EI premiums from salaries, wages, taxable benefits, and other income paid to employees.

In addition, the CRA is resuming examinations of non-compliant GST/HST accounts to ensure registrants are charging, collecting, and filing GST/HST on applicable revenues.

What this means for you:

If you are contacted by the CRA in regard to your payroll accounts, you may need to provide the following books and records:

- payroll journals showing deductions and remittances (including CPP, EI, and income tax)
  - in both detailed and summary form
- taxable benefits information for all employees that receive them (reporting obligations)
- bank statements and cancelled cheques
- additional items as required

For GST/HST returns, if you have not filed you may receive a call or letter from the CRA.

If you are contacted by the CRA in regard to your GST/HST return, you may need to provide the following books and records:

- completed outstanding GST/HST returns
- sales invoices and sales ledgers
- purchase receipts and purchase journals
- bank statements and cancelled cheques
- additional items as required

Learn more *[links available on webpage — ed.]*:

- What to expect during a Payroll Examination
- What to expect during a GST/HST trust accounts examination

Programs that are returning — February 2021

Compliance activities

Who is affected: Individuals, Businesses

What we're doing: As we fully resume our collections activities, collections staff will work with clients to address their individual needs on a case-by-case basis. We understand that for many organizations face financial hardships during these challenging times. If you receive a phone call or letter indicating that you owe money and can't pay your balance in full, give us a call. We're here to help.

What this means for you:

- You may receive a call or a letter from us about an outstanding balance.
- Should you owe money, we may be able help by setting up a payment arrangement.
- If you cannot meet your tax obligations, contact the CRA.
- If you do not contact the CRA or refuse to cooperate, the CRA may take legal action such as issuing a garnishment or proceeding with the seizure or sale of assets.

Learn more:

- When you owe money–collections at the CRA *[link available on webpage — ed.]*

Programs that are returning — January 2021

Audit

Who is affected: Businesses

What we're doing: Starting in January 2021, the CRA is resuming excise audit activities such as:

- audits for excise duty, excise tax, air travellers security charge and fuel charge

What this means for you:

- Business locations of the excise duty and excise tax licensees or the ATSC and fuel charge registrants may receive a telephone call to indicate that they have been selected for an audit.
- A follow up audit confirmation letter will be sent to outline the audit details, including the audit period, books and records to be reviewed and to schedule a time for the initial audit interview.
- If an auditor requests copies of books or records or samples of source documents, a business would submit these items electronically through their My Business Account portal.

Learn more:

- Excise taxes and duties, and other levies *[link available on webpage — ed.]*

Programs that are returning — November 2020

Audits

Who is affected: Individuals, Businesses

What we're doing: Starting in November 2020, the CRA is resuming audit activities such as:

- all small business audits, specifically related to income tax and GST/HST, as well as GST/HST desk audits.
- registered plans, including employee pension plans, retirement savings plans, retirement income funds, deferred profit sharing plans, supplementary unemployment benefit plans, education savings plans, disability savings plans, tax-free savings accounts, registered investments and pooled pension plans.

What this means for you:

- Small business enterprises and individual holders may receive a letter to inform and educate them on common areas of non-compliance.
- Plan providers may receive a letter to educate them on common areas of non-compliance.
- Errors found may not result in a re-assessment, but rather in an information review with the business, and be revisited for correction in future years. Others may result in a re-assessment.

Learn more *[links available on webpage — ed.]*:

- Business audits
- Savings and pension plans
- Compliance Bulletin No. 9 — what to expect during a registered pension plan audit

Compliance activities

Who is affected: Businesses/Exporters

What we're doing: Effective immediately, the CRA will accept applications for GST/HST Export Relief Programs via email. This is a temporary alternative for new or renewal applicants after February 15, 2020.

What this means for you: If you have submitted your application after February 15, 2020, send an email to CPGSTWKLDG@cra-arc.gc.ca with the following information:

- Your name and phone number
- The name of the program you are applying for:
  - Export Distribution Centre Program
  - Export Trading House Program
  - Exporter of Processing Services Program

Do *not include* any confidential information such as detailed financial information.

Learn more:

- GST/HST–Imports and exports *[link available on webpage — ed.]*

Programs that are returning — October 2020

Audits

Who is affected: Businesses

What we're doing: Starting in October, medium business audits will resume, except for audits in the GST/HST Special Audits Program, which include non-profit organizations and charities, and MUSH sectors (Municipalities, Universities, Schools and Hospitals).

What this means for you:

- Medium enterprises may receive a letter to inform and educate them on common areas of non-compliance.
- Errors found may not result in a re-assessment, but rather in an information review with the business, and be revisited for correction in future years.

Learn more:

- Business audits *[link available on webpage — ed.]*

Benefits validation

Who is affected: Individuals, Businesses

What we're doing: The CRA will conduct benefits validation review to make sure that Canadians are receiving benefits they are entitled to.

Throughout the COVID-19 pandemic, the Government of Canada has been committed to ensuring Canadians had the financial support they needed. In addition to administering emergency support benefits like the Canada Emergency Response Benefit, Canada Emergency Student Benefit and Canada Emergency Wage Subsidy, the CRA continued to issue benefit and credit payments to individuals who had not yet filed their 2019 tax return.

We based payment amounts on information from 2018 tax returns if the 2019 tax return had not been filed or assessed yet.

What this means for you:

- If you still haven't filed your 2019 tax return, you need to do so as soon as possible to avoid any future interruptions to your CCB and/or GST/HST credit payments.
- Once your 2019 tax return is filed and assessed, your payments will be reinstated if you're still eligible for the CCB and/or the GST/HST credit.
- If you are a benefit recipient, we may contact you to ask for information to validate your claim.
- If you are applying for the Canada Emergency Response Benefit or Canada Emergency Student Benefit and receive a notification that your application can't be processed, you may have to provide further information to validate your application. Once the supporting information is provided, the CRA will conduct a review of your benefits application, and send you a determination letter with the decision.
- Should you have to repay your benefits, we may be able help by setting up a repayment arrangement.

Learn more *[links available on webpage — ed.]*:

- Benefits being reviewed? Here's what you need to know
- Benefits, credits and financial support

Compliance activities

Who is affected: Businesses

What we're doing: The GST/HST Delinquent Filer program will begin, which will hold refunds on non-compliant GST/HST registrants, and address chronic and high-risk delinquent filers.

What this means for you: If you are identified as a GST/HST Delinquent Filer, you may be assessed by the CRA.

Learn more:

- When you owe money — collections at the CRA *[link available on webpage — ed.]*

September 2020

Appeals

Who is affected: Individuals, Businesses, Charities

What we're doing: The CRA's dispute resolution and taxpayer relief programs are resuming operations. We are currently contacting taxpayers who filed objections or CPP/EI appeals to the Minister, or who applied for relief of penalties and interest. We will also be activating CPP/EI rulings.

We will strive to be flexible with deadlines to submit supporting documents, recognizing taxpayers' unique circumstances. Taxpayers are encouraged to use the CRA's electronic portals to submit documents.

What this means for you: You may be contacted about a filed:

- objection
- CPP/EI appeal
- application for relief of penalties and interest

There may be delays finalizing your request due to COVID-19. We appreciate your patience as we address all requests.

Learn more

- Service feedback, objections, appeals, disputes, and relief measures *[link available on webpage — ed.]*

Audits

Who is affected: Businesses, Charities

What we're doing: Earlier this summer, the CRA resumed a full range of audit work, adapting our practices to reflect the health and economic impacts of COVID-19. We are prioritizing actions that benefit the taxpayer, including situations where a taxpayer indicates it is urgent to advance their audit.

We are also focusing on:

- higher dollar audits first
- audits close to completion
- audits with a strategic importance to the Government of Canada, provinces and territories, or our tax treaty partners
- efforts to combat suspected fraud and other criminal activity

Beginning in September, the CRA's business audits will focus on:

- complex and aggressive tax planning arrangements using partnerships and trusts by sophisticated and high income earners
- Audits in the real estate sector aim to combat offensive non-compliance prevalent in Vancouver and Toronto areas.

The CRA's Charities Directorate will also begin contacting charities to:

- resume ongoing charity audits
- begin Canada Emergency Wage Subsidy post-payment audits
- begin new audits to address highest risk areas

What this means for you:

- Small and medium enterprises may receive a letter to educate them on common areas of non-compliance.
- Errors found may not result in a re-assessment, but rather in an information review with the business, and be revisited for correction in future years.

Learn more *[links available on webpage — ed.]*:

- Business audits
- The audit process for charities

Charity revocations

Who is affected: Charities

What we're doing: The CRA's Charities Directorate will begin processing revocations for failure to comply with the requirements of charity registration. This is a longstanding practice that helps to ensure charities meet their filing and reporting obligations. Where a charity has consistently failed to file and has not responded to notices from the CRA, their registration may be revoked. The revocations will relate to reporting periods that predate the COVID-19 pandemic.

What this means for you: Your charity may receive a letter by registered mail explaining the reasons why we intend to revoke your charity's registration. The letter will also include your objection and appeal rights.

Learn more:

- Revoking registered status *[link available on webpage — ed.]*

Collections

Who is affected: Individuals, Businesses

What we're doing: Collections officers or agents from the debt management call centre will begin contacting individuals and businesses with a balance owing to discuss and re-evaluate their financial situation. The officer may request payment of the debt, or offer a payment arrangement, where possible.

What this means for you:

- You may receive a call or a letter from us about an outstanding balance.
- Should you owe money, we may be able help by setting up a payment arrangement.

Learn more *[links available on webpage — ed.]*:

- When you owe money — collections at the CRA
- Slam the scam — Protect yourself against fraud

Compliance activities

Who is affected: Individuals, Businesses, Charities

What we're doing: As an agency, we are committed to providing a fair tax administration to Canadians. To ensure all taxpayers comply with their tax obligations, we will contact individuals and businesses that have not filed, or may have improperly filed their tax returns. Our compliance activities include:

- individual income tax reviews
- business compliance reviews
- information audits
- non-resident compliance activities

What this means for you:

- If you have not filed your individual or business tax return, or may have filed improperly, you may receive a call or letter from the CRA.
- We are taking an educational approach to help you file and correct your return.

- Errors found may not result in a re-assessment, but rather in an information review where we can review any errors with you, so that they are corrected in future years.
- In-person services are available virtually, like:
  - free tax clinics for individuals
  - the liaison officer service for businesses
- You may receive an automated call from the CRA to remind you of upcoming business filing requirements.

Learn more *[links available on webpage — ed.]*:

- Review of your tax return
- Reassessments — Adjustments to your T2 return

Outreach activities

Who is affected: Individuals, Businesses, Charities

What we're doing: Outreach activities will continue but will follow physical distancing guidelines. Some of these activities include:

- free virtual tax clinics
- virtual meetings with our outreach officers
- virtual liaison officer service
- the individual tax filing assistance initiative
- the Charities Education Program (CEP)

What this means for you:

- Activities may be offered virtually.
- If you have not filed your 2019 income tax and benefit return, you may receive a phone call from a CRA employee to assist you in filing your return.
- Your charity may receive a call from the CRA for a CEP virtual visit.
- The CRA may reach out to your business with information to assist you in meeting your compliance obligations.

Learn more *[links available on webpage — ed.]*:

- Outreach activities
- Charities Education Program

Notes: See also tinyurl.com/cra-covid-plan (June 2020 COVID-19 Business Continuity Plan); Alexandra MacLean, "Tax Administration During and After a Crisis", 1(3) *Perspectives on Tax Law & Policy* (ctf.ca) 14-16 (Sept. 2020).

CRA officials can now use email to communicate with taxpayers and representatives, provided a waiver is given acknowledging security risks: International Fiscal Assn CRA Q&A (Aug. 6, 2020), tinyurl.com/ifa-covid-qa, q.13. However, CRA requires either Level 3 authorization (see 241(5) Notes) or the *taxpayer's* consent to this (not just that of the representative).

Proposed Amendments — Electronic filing and communications

Federal Budget, Supplementary Information, April 19, 2021: See under 244(14.1).

Announced Administrative Change — More money for CRA, including for automated T1 Adjustments

Federal Budget, Chapter 10, April 19, 2021: *Modernizing CRA Services*

To modernize CRA services and help people quickly and easily access the tax credits and benefits they are entitled to:

Budget 2021 proposes to provide $41.7 million over three years, starting in 2021-22, to the CRA to reduce processing time for T1 adjustments (i.e. corrections to people's general income tax return) by making online self-service more user-friendly and improving automated processing of T1 adjustments. Faster processing of T1 adjustments will provide Canadians with more timely access to their credits and benefits.

The CRA has created a simplified credit and benefit return and Canada Child Benefit form for First Nations individuals, and will be expanding this project to make these forms more widely available to more Indigenous people. The improved forms take into account Indigenous experience — such as community care and nurturing of children — and remove information that is not applicable to Indigenous peoples.

[See also additional CRA funding proposals under 224(1), 241(1) and 239(1) — ed.]

Related Provisions: 166 — Assessment not to be vacated by reason of CRA failure to follow proper procedures; 220(2.01) — Delegation of powers; *Canada Revenue Agency Act* — Establishment of CRA; *Interpretation Act* 24(2) — Power of others to act for Minister; *Interpretation Act* 31(2) — Ancillary powers granted to enable work to be done.

Notes: *Agent of the Crown*: CRA is deemed by *Canada Revenue Agency Act* s. 4(2) to be "for all purposes an agent of Her Majesty in right of Canada"; see *Interpretation Act* s. 17 and Notes to 27(1).

Audits: see Notes to 231.1(1).

Collections: see Note to 223(2), 223(3) and 224(1).

Commissioners (appointed under *CRA Act* s. 25) have been: Rob Wright (Deputy Minister of National Revenue from Jan./97; Commissioner from CCRA's creation Nov. 1/99); Alan Nymark (from June 2/03); Michel Dorais (from Dec. 20/04); Bill Baker (from April 2/07); Linda Lizotte-MacPherson (from Oct. 13/09); Andrew Treusch (from Jan. 14/13); Bob Hamilton (since Aug. 1/16). See Notes to 220(2.01) re delegation to other officials.

Complaints: A taxpayer unsatisfied with CRA service can complain using Form RC193 (see tinyurl.com/cra-complaints and Guide RC4420), or to the Ombudsman (otoboc.gc.ca).

Contacting CRA: canada.ca/cra-contact, or CRA Directory at beginning of this book. See also tinyurl.com/cra-wait-times.

Corruption: While CRA is overwhelmingly honest, there was an RCMP investigation into corruption in the Montreal Tax Services Office, "Operation Coche": tinyurl.com/cra-corrup1 and /cra-corrup2; *Bruno*, 2019 QCCS 65, para. 20; *Accurso*, 2019 QCCQ 3705 and 2020 QCCQ 3001; *Iammarone*, 2019 QCCQ 7836 (jail term of 2 years less a day for auditor accepting bribe to "fix" an audit); *BT Céramiques (Bruno)*, 2020 QCCA 402 (leave to appeal denied 2020 CarswellQue 8842 (SCC)). There is also an ongoing investigation of the Laval TSO ("Operation Critique").

Cost: CRA cost $7.2 billion to run in 2019-20, with 41,753 full-time employee equivalents: *Departmental Results Report 2019-20* (tinyurl.com/cra-results), pp. 54, 57. See also the annual Corporate Business Plan, tinyurl.com/cra-busplans.

Delegation of the Minister's powers: see 220(2.01) Notes.

Electronic systems: CRA's website moved from cra.gc.ca to canada.ca/revenue-agency (canada.ca/tax) in 2017, and almost all links to the old pages stopped working April 1, 2019. Online access to accounts: canada.ca/my-cra-account (My Account — individuals), tinyurl.com/cra-mybusiness (My Business Account — corps), canada.ca/taxes-representatives (advisors). E-filing: see 150.1. Possible system improvements are discussed in 2019 CPA Alberta (tinyurl.com/cra-abtax), income tax q.21. See also Taxpayers' Ombudsman, *Taxpayer Rights in the Digital Age* (May 2020) (re assisting vulnerable persons), and "Taxpayers' Ombudsman launches review into the lack of communications regarding access to CRA My Account" (news release, Feb. 23, 2021).

Fairness (now called Taxpayer Relief): see Notes to 220(3.1).

Manuals used by CRA are on *Taxnet Pro* (obtained via Access to Information). Several are in CRA's "virtual reading room", tinyurl.com/cra-reading.

Objections and Appeals: see Notes to 165(3) and 169(1).

Obligations of CRA: The fact the Minister "shall" administer the Act does not prevent CRA from being bound by an agreement not to assess an issue: *Rosenberg*, 2016 FC 1376, para. 76. See also Notes to 169(3) re settlements, and re CRA needing a legal basis for an assessment, even on consent.

Payment: see canada.ca/payments and Notes to 229.1.

Phone line for accountants: CRA has a "dedicated telephone service" (DTS) for technical inquiries to Rulings (the phone agents do not have access to taxpayer accounts): dts-str@cra.gc.ca [for inquiries about DTS, not tax questions]. From a 2017 pilot project, this is now offered to "all small and medium-sized income tax service providers across Canada" who are E-Filers: Form RC562; "Canada Revenue Agency is making improvements for small and medium businesses" (June 10, 2019); VIEWS docs 2018-0744381C6 [2018 STEP q.1], 2019-0809731C6 [2019 STEP q.18], 2019-0825031C6 [2019 APFF q.19]. CRA is considering whether to allow escalation of complex client issues, as with the IRS "Practitioners' Gate": 2019 CPA Alberta (tinyurl.com/cra-abtax), income tax q.16.

Processing times: See tinyurl.com/cra-standards for "service standards" for various tasks, and tinyurl.com/cra-proctime for expected processing times. The Auditor General reported (2017 Fall Report 2, ¶2.24) that CRA was blocking more than 50% of calls to its call centre so it could claim it was meeting phone inquiry targets; for CRA's response see Minister's letter, June 12, 2018, tinyurl.com/call-centre-letter.

Provincial programs: CRA administers many provincial programs including personal income tax for all provinces other than QC, corporate income tax for all other than QC and AB (see Notes to 150(1)(a)), and various benefits.

Publications: Aside from information on the website, the main technical publication is now Income Tax Folios, which are replacing the Interpretation Bulletins: VIEWS doc 2017-0724261C6 [2017 CTF q.7]. "Archived" bulletins and Technical News can still be relied on as accurate as of their publication date: 2018-0744171C6 [2018 STEP q.18]. Information Circulars and Guides are also issued. CRA publications are not law, and are not binding on taxpayers or the Courts, but "are entitled to weight and can be an important factor": *Nowegijick*, [1983] C.T.C. 20 (SCC). Errors in CRA publications do not give the taxpayer any rights beyond Taxpayer Relief waiver of penalty (see Notes to 220(3.1)): see Notes to 169(1) under "Estoppel".

Rulings and interpretations: CRA charges nothing for interpretation letters, but they are not binding. No interpretation is given if the matter is under audit: Information Circular 70-6R11 para. 7(c); VIEWS doc 2018-0753161E5. A binding Advance Income Tax Ruling costs (since April 2021) $104.04/hr for the first 10 hours, $161.26/hr after that: IC70-6R11, para. 43. This increases to $221.24/hr (same rate for all work) April 2022, and $281.22/hr April 2023: proposed *Order Amending the Advance Income Tax Ruling Fees Order* (*Canada Gazette* Part I, Vol. 155 No. 16, April 17/21). If the fee is not paid, CRA can recover it by filing a claim in Federal Court, and will not work on further rulings or interpretations for that firm: 2009-0324721X0, 2011-0414681E2, 2011-0418311E2, 2011-0418321E2, 2011-0418331E2, 2011-0418341E2, 2011-0418351E2, 2011-0418361E2, 2011-0418371E2, 2011-0418391E2, 2011-0418401E2.

See also 2017-0734831C6 [2017 TEI q.B5] (2017-18 changes to the rulings process); Adams & Sinclair, "What, When, Why and How to Request an Income Tax Ruling", 2005 BC Tax Conference (ctf.ca), 11:1-14; Bernstein, "Advance Income Tax Rulings", 20(10) *Canadian Tax Highlights* (ctf.ca) 9-11 (Oct. 2013); "CRA Session on Advance Tax Rulings", 2017 Cdn Tax Foundation conference report, 34:1-15. CRA also offers a "Pre-Ruling Consultation" for a fee, aiming to respond within 3 weeks by phone as to how Rulings will likely treat a ruling request: IC70-6R11 paras. 30-40.

Service and culture: A new position of Chief Service Officer (currently Mireille Laroche) was created in 2018, to lead CRA's "service transformation to be trusted, fair and helpful by putting people first". See also 2018 Budget chap. 1 and 2019 Budget chap 4, both at heading "Improving Client Service" (reproduced here up to the 57th ed.); "Canada Revenue Agency announces the creation of an external advisory panel on service" (Dec. 13, 2018). See also *Serving You Better* report (June 2019), tinyurl.com/cra-serving; Taxpayer's Ombudsman annual report 2018-2019, *Breaking Down Barriers to Service*.

Suing CRA for negligence or malicious acts: see Notes to 171(1).

Taxpayer Bill of Rights (TBR; canada.ca/taxpayer-rights) sets out standards CRA seeks to follow. It provides no legal rights outside Quebec: *Barrons*, 1996 CarswellNat 1597 (FCTD), para. 7; *Plachcinski*, 2016 CarswellNat 10234 (FC), para. 22; *Gordon*, 2019 FC 853, para. 168 (under appeal to FCA); Mirandola & Kaur, "Struggling with Taxpayers' Rights", XXI(2) *Tax Litigation* (Federated Press) 2-8 (2018); but in *Ludmer*, 2018 QCCS 3381, paras. 151, 465; aff'd 2020 QCCA 697 [leave to appeal denied 2021 CarswellQue 2160 (SCC)], paras. 17, 43, 62, 67, treating a taxpayer inconsistently with others, in violation of TBR, was a reason to award damages against CRA in Quebec (see 171(1) Notes). The Taxpayer's Ombudsman, in *Back to Basics: Taxpayers Have Rights* (June 2020, 62pp; tinyurl.com/tbr-ombud) suggests CRA should have taxpayer rights "embedded at every level" of CRA's business, and should treat the TBR as one of its "foundational documents" (p. 50).

There is a move to encourage governments worldwide to adopt standards for taxpayer dealings. Cadesky et al., *Towards Greater Fairness in Taxation: A Model Taxpayer Charter* (2nd ed., 2016, 240pp, ibfd.org and step.ca), surveys how 41 countries deal with many policy, administration and practice issues, and suggests a Taxpayer Charter for governments to adopt.

Waiver of interest (Taxpayer Relief): see Notes to 220(3.1).

220(1) amended by *Canada Customs & Revenue Agency Act*, effective Nov. 1, 1999, to change "Deputy Minister" to "Commissioner of Customs and Revenue"; and by 2004 CRA/CBSA bill, effective Dec. 12, 2005, to change to "Commissioner of Revenue".

Regulations: 900 (delegation of powers and duties to other officials).

I.T. Technical News: 8 (publication of advance tax rulings); 9 (electronic publication of severed rulings); 14 (the Income Tax rulings and Interpretations Directorate — common deficiencies or omissions in requests for advance rulings); 18 (The advance income tax rulings process — practical problems and possible solutions).

CRA Audit Manual: 2.0: The Canada Revenue Agency; 5.0: Human resource issues; 7.0: Compliance programs branch; 10.11.14: Referrals to technical application and valuations division — compliance programs branch — headquarters.

Forms: RC17: Taxpayer Bill of Rights guide: Understanding your rights as a taxpayer; RC193: Service feedback; RC459: Reprisal complaint.

(2) Officers, clerks and employees — Such officers, clerks and employees as are necessary to administer and enforce this Act shall be appointed or employed in the manner authorized by law.

Related Provisions: 220(2.01) — Delegation of powers; *Interpretation Act* 23(1) — Public officers hold office during pleasure; *Interpretation Act* 31(2) — Ancillary powers granted to enable work to be done.

(2.01) Delegation — The Minister may authorize an officer or a class of officers to exercise powers or perform duties of the Minister under this Act.

Related Provisions: *Interpretation Act* 23(1) — Public officers hold office during pleasure; *Interpretation Act* 31(2) — Ancillary powers granted to enable work to be done.

Notes: 220(2.01) provides that the Minister of National Revenue may administratively delegate his/her powers and duties under the Act or Regulations to an officer or class of officers in CRA. This replaces the requirement under 221(1)(f) that delegation be done by regulation (former Reg. 900), and allows more timely revision of the delegation of the Minister's powers and duties.

The Commissioner is authorized under *Canada Revenue Agency Act* 8(1) to act for the Minister. The Commissioner then delegates to other officials. For lists of delegated officials (all include the Deputy Commissioner, Assistant Commissioners and Deputy Assistant Commissioners), see tinyurl.com/deleg-cra. These are unofficial consolidations; for a certified true copy to use in Court (*Canada Evidence Act* para. 21(e)), ask the Dept. of Justice to obtain one from CRA's Remissions and Delegations Section, Legislative Policy Directorate.

Where delegation is in place, sub-delegation is invalid: *Murphy*, 2009 FC 1226. Thus, requirements for information (RFIs) under 231.2 were quashed when issued by a Team Leader (TL), where the Director of the Tax Services Office had purported to delegate to the TL her delegated authority to issue RFIs and the TL issued them using the Director's signature stamp.

Delegation by the Minister was permitted even where no specific official was authorized by the regulations: *Doyle*, [1989] 2 C.T.C. 270 (FCTD). The Minister need not sign a notice of assessment personally: *Mailhot*, 2005 TCC 132.

Delegation to a provincial official would likely be valid, as it was found to be for purposes of the GST: *Ricken Leroux Inc.*, [1998] G.S.T.C. 1 (Que. CA), leave to appeal denied [1998] G.S.T.C. 24 (SCC).

Judicial review of a delegation under 220(2.01) was refused in *VR Interactive*, 2005 FC 273. See also Notes to 220(3.1) re judicial review of CRA discretion.

220(2.01) added by 1995-97 technical bill, effective June 18, 1998. The amending bill provided that any power or duty of the Minister delegated to an officer or a class of officers by a regulation made under 221(1)(f) before June 18, 1998 continues until an authorization by the Minister made under 220(2.01) changes the delegation of that power or duty. (The above authorization has now done so.)

Transfer Pricing Memoranda: TPM-03: Downward transfer pricing adjustments under subsec. 247(2).

(2.1) Waiver of filing of documents — Where any provision of this Act or a regulation requires a person to file a prescribed form, receipt or other document, or to provide prescribed information, the Minister may waive the requirement, but the person shall provide the document or information at the Minister's request.

Related Provisions: 220(2.2) — No extension or waiver allowed for SR&ED claims.

Notes: If a CRA publication says a document need not be filed, that is waiver under 220(2.1): *Leith*, 2015 TCC 314, para. 7. Examples are: Form T2200 for 8(10) (*Leith*); Form T2091 before 2016 if principal residence exemption eliminated the gain (see Notes to 40(2)(b)); child care expense receipts (Notes to 63(1)); RC435 for rollover from RESP to RDSP (Notes to 146.1(1.2)); T1134 for inactive foreign affiliates (Notes to 233.4(4)); some partnerships need not file T5013 information return (Notes to Reg. 229(1)). The requirements of 149.01 pending its repeal were explicitly waived under 220(2.1) by CRA news releases, Dec. 21, 2015 and Dec. 19, 2016.

See Notes to 80.1(4) and 220(3.2) re the difference between *making* an election and *filing* an election form.

The deadline for SR&ED claims cannot be extended: see 220(2.2). Before, limited relief was available from the Courts if the deadline was missed: *Sixgraph Informatique*, 2005 FCA 86 (no relief); *Dorothea Knitting*, 2005 FC 318 (relief granted); *Greenpipe Industries*, 2006 FC 1098 (no relief, and CRA had no discretion to allow late filing of return because year was statute-barred).

In *Bul River Mineral*, 2006 FC 41, CRA was not allowed to revoke a waiver granted under 220(2.1) for a provincial tax credit refund claim.

220(2.1) cannot be used to extend time to file an objection under 165(1), because 165-167 provide detailed rules for late filing of objections: *Conocophillips*, 2017 FCA 243 (effectively overruling *Melanson*, 2011 TCC 569, para. 21; *Poulin*, 2013 TCC 104, paras. 33-41; *Petratos*, 2013 TCC 240, footnote 3).

CRA says 220(2.1) cannot be used to waive filing a return so that a dividend refund can be paid under 129(1) if the return is filed late, but this is uncertain: *Bonnybrook Industrial*, 2018 FCA 136, para. 30.

220(2.1) added by 1992 technical bill, effective for 1992 and later taxation years.

Income Tax Folios: S1-F3-C1: Child care expense deduction [replaces IT-495R3].

Information Circulars: 12-1: GST/HST compliance refund holds.

Charities Policies: CPC-016: Religious charities — Form T3010.

Application Policies: SR&ED 2000-02R: Guidelines for resolving claimants' SR&ED concerns.

Forms: RC342: Request by an insolvency practitioner for a waiver of the requirement to file a T2 corporation income tax return; T3010: Registered charity information return.

(2.2) Exception [SR&ED claims] — Subsection (2.1) does not apply in respect of a prescribed form, receipt or document, or prescribed information, that is filed with the Minister on or after the day specified, in respect of the form, receipt, document or information, in subsection 37(11) or paragraph (m) of the definition "investment tax credit" in subsection 127(9).

Notes: 220(2.2) overrides *Alex Parallel*, [1999] 2 C.T.C. 180 (FCTD), where the Court instructed Revenue Canada not to honour a directive in Application Policy SR&ED 96-01 stating that 220(2.1) could not be used for late SR&ED filings; and *Dorothea Knitting Mills*, 2005 FC 318, overriding CRA's decision not to extend the deadline. See also Notes to 37(11).

The deadlines that 220(2.2) prevents CRA from extending were legislatively extended during 2020, for COVID-19, by *Time Limits and Other Periods Act (TLOPA)* 7(1). See Enacted Amendment under 169(1).

220(2.2) added by 2002-2013 technical bill, effective for a prescribed form, receipt or document, and prescribed information, filed with the Minister after Nov. 16, 2005, except where a waiver request was made in writing to the Minister by that date.

(3) Extensions for returns — The Minister may at any time extend the time for making a return under this Act.

Related Provisions: 127.4(5.1) — Authorization for late LSVCC investments; 146(22) — Authorization for late RRSP contributions; 220(3.2) — Late filing of elections.

Notes: See 220(1), and TLOPA Enacted Amendment under 169(1), for extensions provided in 2020 for COVID-19.

In *Kutlu*, 1997 CanLII 5990 (FCTD; Crown's appeal to FCA discontinued), the Court ruled that Revenue Canada could not refuse to accept a late-filed 216(1) return when it had accepted such returns late in the past.

CRA can use 220(3) to extend the return filing deadline for a 129(1) dividend refund (and thus no doubt a 164(1) refund, which has identical wording): *Bonnybrook Industrial*, 2018 FCA 136 (reversing *Binder Capital*, 2017 FC 642); see 129(1) Notes.

If CRA refuses to extend a filing deadline, the Federal Court will rarely intervene: see *Sixgraph Informatique*, 2005 FCA 86; *Sailsman*, 2014 FC 1033. See Notes to 220(3.1); the same judicial-review principles apply.

220(3) cannot be used to extend a statute-barred reassessment period: VIEWS doc 2013-0487181I7.

Filing deadlines for spring 2003 were extended on a case-by-case basis due to the SARS virus: CCRA news release, April 29/03. Filing deadlines for 2008 personal returns were extended to June 1/09 for Manitoba residents in flood areas: CRA news release, April 17/09. See also bullet list in Notes to 220(3.1).

This 220(3) applies to extensions of time granted after March 2007, as amended by 2006 budget bill #1. For earlier extensions granted from Feb. 19, 2003 (as amended by 2003 Budget), read in addition: "However, the extension does not apply for the purpose of calculating a penalty that a person is liable to pay under section 162 if the person fails to make the return within the period of the extension." Since April 2007, extending the deadline means no s. 162 penalty if the extended deadline is met: *Hughes*, 2017 TCC 95, para. 86. Interest continues to run on unpaid balances, which are unrelated to filing deadlines.

(3.1) Waiver [or cancellation] of penalty or interest — The Minister may, on or before the day that is ten calendar years after the end of a taxation year of a taxpayer (or in the case of a partnership, a fiscal period of the partnership) or on application by the taxpayer or partnership on or before that day, waive or cancel all or any portion of any penalty or interest otherwise payable under this Act by the taxpayer or partnership in respect of that taxation year or fiscal period, and notwithstanding subsections 152(4) to (5), any assessment of the interest and penalties payable by the taxpayer or partnership shall be made that is necessary to take into account the cancellation of the penalty or interest.

Announced Administrative Change — Interest waiver on income tax debt arising from COVID-19 support

CRA news release, Feb. 9, 2021: *Government of Canada addresses CERB repayments for self-employed individuals and announces interest relief on 2020 income tax debt due to COVID-19 related income support*

Since the beginning of the COVID-19 pandemic, the Government of Canada has provided urgently-needed income support to millions of Canadians, which has helped them put food on the table and keep a roof over their heads during this crisis. The federal government is committed to continuing to support Canadians throughout this crisis.

Today, the Government of Canada announced that self-employed individuals who applied for the Canada Emergency Response Benefit (CERB) and would have qualified based on their gross income will not be required to repay the benefit, provided they also met all other eligibility requirements. The same approach will apply whether the individual applied through the Canada Revenue Agency or Service Canada.

This means that, self-employed individuals whose net self-employment income was less than $5,000 and who applied for the CERB will not be required to repay the CERB, as long as their gross self-employment income was at least $5,000 and they met all other eligibility criteria.

Some self-employed individuals whose net self-employment income was less than $5,000 may have already voluntarily repaid the CERB. The CRA and Service Canada will return any repaid amounts to these individuals. Additional details will be available in the coming weeks.

In addition, today, the Honourable Diane Lebouthillier, Minister of National Revenue, announced that the Government of Canada will provide targeted interest relief to Canadians who received COVID-related income support benefits. Once individuals have filed their 2020 income tax and benefit return, they will **not be required to pay interest on any outstanding income tax debt for the 2020 tax year until April 30, 2022**. This will give Canadians more time and flexibility to pay if they have an amount owing.

To qualify for targeted interest relief, individuals must have had a **total taxable income of $75,000 or less in 2020 and have received income support in 2020 through one or more of the following COVID-19 measures**:

- the Canada Emergency Response Benefit (CERB);
- the Canada Emergency Student Benefit (CESB);
- the Canada Recovery Benefit (CRB);
- the Canada Recovery Caregiving Benefit (CRCB);
- the Canada Recovery Sickness Benefit (CRSB);
- Employment Insurance benefits; or
- similar provincial emergency benefits.

The Canada Revenue Agency (CRA) will **automatically apply the interest relief** measure for individuals who meet these criteria.

Additionally, any CRA-administered credits and benefits normally paid monthly or quarterly, such as the Canada Child Benefit and the goods and services tax/harmonized sales tax credit will not be applied to reduce individuals' tax debt owing for the 2020 tax year. Canadians are strongly encouraged to file their tax returns by the filing deadline to ensure that their benefit payments continue without interruption.

The Government of Canada recognizes that many Canadians continue to face serious financial impacts as a result of the ongoing pandemic. The interest relief measure announced today will provide an estimated 4.5 million low- and middle-income Canadians with the flexibility required to feel confident about accessing the COVID-19 income support without facing additional stress at tax time.

Quick facts

- All individuals are encouraged to file their income tax returns.
- Any amounts owing are determined based on an individual's personal circumstances and the credits and benefits they may receive.
- Like Employment Insurance (EI) benefits, the COVID-19 emergency and recovery benefits, including similar provincial benefits, are taxable. Although 10% of the benefit amount for the three Canada Recovery Benefits (CRB, CRCB, and CRSB) is withheld at source, many other emergency benefits, including the CERB and the CESB did not withhold tax at source. Today's announcement will give those Canadians who owe any taxes as a result of accessing these benefits more time and flexibility to pay those amounts.
- The CRA has not extended the tax filing deadline. Canadians should complete and submit their tax returns by April 30, 2021, the filing due date for most individuals. Canadians are strongly encouraged to file their tax returns to ensure that their benefit payments continue uninterrupted.

Contacts: Jeremy Bellefeuille, Press Secretary, Office of the Minister of National Revenue, 613-995-2960; Marielle Hossack, Press Secretary, Office of the Minister of Employment, Workforce Development and Disability Inclusion, marielle.hossack@canada.ca; Media Relations, Canada Revenue Agency, 613-948-8366, cra-arc.media@cra-arc.gc.ca; Media Relations Office, Employment and Social Development Canada, 819-994-5559, media@hrsdc-rhdcc.gc.ca.

Related Provisions: 161.3 — CRA discretion to cancel interest and penalty up to $25; 164(1.5) — Late refund of overpayment; 164(3.2) — Interest on refunds and repayments; 165(1.2) — Limitation of right to object; 206.4 — Waiver of Part XI taxes on registered disability savings plans; 207.06 — Waiver of Part XI.01 tax re TFSA; 225.1(1) — No collection restrictions following assessment.

Notes: 220(3.1) is part of the "Taxpayer Relief" legislation, called "Fairness" legislation from 1991 to June 2007. It allows CRA to waive (technically, "cancel" if already assessed) any penalty or interest under the Act, but not "penalty taxes" that are enacted as taxes rather than as penalties, such as Part III tax on excessive capital dividends (184(2)) (some have their own waiver provisions: 204.1(4), 204.91(2), 206.4, 207.06). Use Form RC4288, or simply a letter marked "Taxpayer Relief", to apply for relief. Address it to "Taxpayer Relief" at the applicable tax centre (see addresses at beginning of book): Burnaby-Fraser for BC, Yukon; Winnipeg for AB, SK, MB, NWT; Shawinigan-Sud for QC; Summerside for ON, NB, NS, PEI, NL and Nunavut. If relief is denied, a "second administrative review" can be requested; it need not be a more senior official and is no longer called a "second-*level* review". CRA will sometimes agree to a third or even a fourth review, e.g. *Simmons*, 2021 FC 202 (under appeal to FCA) [and the author's experience]; or may reply that it is done reviewing and confirm its previous decisions, which reply may be a "decision" triggering a new 30-day judicial review deadline: *Cheeseman*, 2021 FC 273, para. 10.

Taxpayer Relief requests take too long: Taxpayers' Ombudsman report, *Without Delay* (Nov. 2017), tinyurl.com/ombud-delay. CRA now seeks (tinyurl.com/cra-standards) to resolve requests within 180 days, 85% of the time (with certain exceptions); in 2019-20, it did 90.8%; and accepts "in principle" the Ombudsman's recommendation to "advise the taxpayer whether their request is routine or complex, and provide the taxpayer a clear and accurate estimated processing time" starting April 2019: news release "Updates on CRA Service Improvements" (Sept. 7, 2018).

The 10-year limit refers to years *during which* the interest accrued, not the year for which the tax was originally payable: Information Circular 07-1R1 paras. 15-15.4, based on *Bozzer*, 2011 FCA 186 (confirming the view expressed for many years in these Notes, and overruling CRA policy in former IC 07-1 para. 39 and doc 2008-0273391I7 as well as *Telfer*, 2008 FC 218). Thus, for interest accrued starting 2008 on a liability from the 2007 or earlier tax year, a waiver request made up to the end of

2018 is valid; but if the request is filed only in 2021, interest accruing after 2010 on the 2007 debt can still be cancelled. The new rule applied in *Pavage St-Eustache Inc.*, 2013 FCA 14, and *Société Angelo Colatosti*, 2012 FC 124, para. 22.

CRA accepts *Bozzer*: Information Circular 00-1R6 para. 18; VIEWS doc 2014-0530571C6 [2014 STEP conf. q.13]. If a matter is still under objection or appeal, one should make the request to meet the deadline, and ask for it to be put on hold until the appeal is resolved.

CRA policy (tinyurl.com/10year-cra) now states:

> For requests made before June 2, 2011, that were considered late-filed beyond 10 years after the end of the tax year under the previous interpretation of the limitation period, the CRA may grant relief from the interest that accrued within the last 10 calendar years effective from the 2011 year or the year in which the new request is made, whichever is later. The revised 10-year limitation period will not be applied from the 2010 or prior calendar year in which the initial late-filed request was made.

This is likely a wrongful fettering of CRA discretion, since the June 2011 date of the *Bozzer* decision is not relevant to CRA's legal authority to waive interest back for 10 years. The FCA did not change the law; it determined what the law had always been. Arguably, the 10-year limit could also be bypassed by the CRA using 220(2.1) to extend the time for filing an application under 220(3.1). However, the CRA does not believe it can do this, as an application is not "required" by the Act or regulations. (See *Conocophillips*, 2017 FCA 243.)

It can also be argued that the CRA cannot collect if the tax was payable on March 4, 2004 and no return was filed for >10 years; see Notes to 222(3).

After the introduction of the 10-year rule, Cabinet reverted to issuing Remission Orders (discussed further below) to waive interest and penalty more than 10 years back, as it did before 220(3.1) was enacted. See under the Remission Orders annotation below (e.g., *Speakman, Carlson, Doskoch, Warden, Gill, Jacobs*). In light of *Bozzer*, the CRA has reverted to waiving interest, except where it *accrued* more than 10 years before the application, in which case a remission order is needed (e.g., *Bacci, McGowan*).

Despite *Bozzer*, the 10-year rule is still nonsensical when it prevents CRA from waiving interest and penalty more than 10 years back under the Voluntary Disclosure Program (VIEWS docs 2011-0401922IC6, 2012-0462951C6), as that defeats the purpose of the VDP. A way to avoid this problem is to ask the CRA to agree to assess no more than 10 years back. See below re voluntary disclosures. Gross negligence penalty under 163(2), unlike "mandatory" late-filing penalties, does not have to be applied in the first place even past 10 years: 2012-0462951C6.

Guidelines: Information Circular 07-1R1 sets out the administrative guidelines for Taxpayer Relief. In general, waiver will be granted only for (1) events beyond taxpayer control, such as death or natural disaster; (2) reliance on incorrect information from CRA; (3) delay on CRA's part; or (4) inability to pay, where waiver will enable the account to be paid, or where loss of employment and financial hardship have caused collection actions to be suspended [use Form RC376 to apply for waiver on ground (4)]. Events beyond taxpayer control need not be "extraordinary" to qualify under the guidelines: *3500772 Canada*, 2008 FC 554. The Circular's guidelines are "only guidelines" (para. 6); it is an error for CRA to say that it "cannot" provide relief in a situation outside them: *Alex Parallel Computers*, [1999] 2 C.T.C. 180 (FCTD); *Spence*, 2010 FC 52. "The Minister does not have a free hand to do whatever she wants, act on whim, or unthinkingly rubber-stamp her earlier penalty assessment ...Her discretion must be genuinely exercised and must not be fettered or dictated by policy statements such as Information Circular 07-1": *Guindon*, 2013 FCA 153, paras. 57-58 (aff'd without discussing this issue 2015 SCC 41); see also *Toronto Dominion Bank v. BC*, 2017 BCCA 159, para. 59; *1092072 Ontario*, 2017 QCCS 5369; *Dickinson*, [2018] EWCA Civ 2798 (England), paras. 55-56.

The following qualify for relief as events beyond taxpayers' control, so waiver can be requested (date in parentheses is date of Revenue Canada/CRA news release):

- January 1998 ice storm (Feb. 18, 1998)
- spring 1998 forest fires in Alberta and Northern Ontario (May 19, 1998)
- spring 1999 service of Canadian military and police personnel in the Serbia-Kosovo NATO action (April 23, 1999)
- June 2000 E.coli water contamination in Walkerton, Ont. (June 29, 2000)
- 2003 SARS (Severe Acute Respiratory Syndrome) virus (April 29, 2003)
- August 14, 2003 blackout in Ontario, if source deduction remittances were late due to lack of power (Aug. 17, 2003)
- summer 2003 forest fires (Sept. 4, 2003)
- Hurricane Juan in Nova Scotia and PEI (Oct. 1, 2003)
- spring 2008 flooding in New Brunswick (April 30, 2008)
- spring 2009 flooding in Manitoba (April 17, 2009)
- alleged fraud involving financial advisor Earl Jones (July 31, 2009: to be addressed "on a case-by-case basis"; for some results see Adam Aptowitzer, "Ponzi Schemes and Taxation", xxxii(13) *The Canadian Taxpayer* (Carswell) 97-98 (June 29, 2010))
- earthquakes in Haiti and Chile, for Canadians participating in relief efforts: call 1-800-267-5177, or 613-952-3741 collect (March 8, 2010)
- Hurricane Igor in Newfoundland & Labrador (Sept. 23, 2010)

- earthquakes, tsunami and nuclear crisis in Japan and other disasters, including for Canadians participating in relief efforts (April 28, 2011)
- spring flooding (April 28, 2011)
- tornado in Goderich, Ont. and Hurricane Irene (Sept. 1, 2011)
- flooding and severe wind in BC, Yukon and Saskatchewan (July 29, 2012)
- spring flooding (April 30, 2013)
- flooding in Fort McMurray, Alberta (June 18, 2013)
- flooding in Calgary and southern Alberta (June 22 and 26, 2013; affected business taxpayers have until August 2, 2013 to file on time, and "the CRA offers to expedite taxpayer relief requests through its general enquiries line at 1-800-959-8281 or the business enquiries line at 1-800-959-5525. Taxpayer relief requests can also be made in writing using the Form RC4288.")
- Lac-Mégantic July 6/13 train disaster (July 25, 2013)
- power outages caused by Dec. 2013 ice storms in Ontario, Quebec and Atlantic Canada (Jan. 9, 2014)
- "extreme weather conditions", such as flooding in Ontario and Alberta (June 27, 2014)
- wildfires in BC, the Prairie provinces and Ontario (July 21, 2015)
- wildfires in Fort McMurray and environs (May 6, 2016)
- flooding in Quebec and Ontario (May 8, 2017)
- flooding in New Brunswick and BC (May 24, 2018)
- wildfires in BC and Ontario (Aug. 28, 2018)
- flooding (April 26, 2019)

Postal strikes apparently no longer qualify (since filing and payment can be done online): "Important Notice About a Postal Disruption", CRA, Oct. 24, 2018.

A CRA news release, May 19, 2009, states that enquiries agents at CRA call centres will now provide their first name and employee ID number when answering the phone. This could improve taxpayers' ability to demonstrate that they were given wrong information by CRA officials for 220(3.1) purposes.

Objection/appeal plus waiver request: Interest will not be waived for purposes of settling an appeal, but CRA announced at the 2014 Cdn Tax Foundation annual conference (through Deen Olsen, Dept. of Justice) that CRA now will consider waiver requests during settlement discussions, to facilitate settling an appeal (see Notes to 169(3)), and the amount of interest and penalty to be cancelled will be included in Minutes of Settlement. Waiver is "not a negotiating tool" (the Taxpayer Relief criteria still apply), but taxpayers can predict the effect of a settlement. Where a taxpayer appeals a penalty based on due diligence and applies for Taxpayer Relief at the same time, the Appeals Officer will now address both: May 2015 ICAA roundtable (tinyurl.com/cra-abtax), q. 3. Gross negligence penalties can be waived as part of a settlement: *Taylor*, 2010 TCC 246, para. 34 (aff'd 2012 FCA 148).

CRA policy on 220(3.1) is found in the *Taxpayer Relief Procedures Manual*, available on *Taxnet Pro*. In 2018-19, CRA waived $577m in penalties and interest (on 318,865 requests, many of which were automated): *Departmental Results Report* (tinyurl.com/cra-results), p. 16 (no data in 2019-20 Report).

Tax Appeals Evaluation Final Report (May 2012: tinyurl.com/cra-appeals-eval) shows that 12% of taxpayers losing at Tax Court applied for Taxpayer Relief, and relief was granted in 36% of such cases.

No Tax Court appeal is available from a 220(3.1) decision not to waive (or not waiving enough): 165(1.2); *Neathly*, 2011 FCA 275; *Raby*, 2006 TCC 406; *Hrynkiewicz*, 2007 TCC 154; *Moledina*, 2007 TCC 354, *Beauregard*, 2008 TCC 224; *Ugro*, 2011 TCC 317. The Court sometimes recommends or suggests that interest or penalty be waived: e.g., *Breault*, [1997] G.S.T.C. 25; *Hrenchuk*, [2005] G.S.T.C. 136; *Johnston*, 2006 TCC 367; *McNamee*, 2009 TCC 630; *Duchaine*, 2015 TCC 245, para. 50; *Duplessis*, 2016 FCA 264, para. 5; *Bolduc*, 2017 TCC 104 (employer issued wrong T4); *Polubiec*, 2019 TCC 146, para. 51; *Wardlaw*, 2019 TCC 199, para. 41; *Wiegers (Weigers)*, 2019 TCC 260; *Morrisseau*, 2020 TCC 5, para. 100; *Ambs*, 2020 TCC 62, para. 45; *Fono*, 2020 TCC 81, paras. 11-16; *Kyei*, 2021 TCC 10, para. 29; but in *Deshaies*, 2019 FCA 300, para. 7, the FCA said that to recommend CRA waive interest (done at 2018 FC 699) is inadvisable because it "creates expectations". The TCC cannot *direct* CRA to consider waiver: *Almadhoun*, 2018 FCA 112, para. 33.

Judicial review of CRA refusal to grant relief under 220(3.1) is available in the Federal Court [apply within 30 days: see 171(1) Notes], but only if the decision is unreasonable. **The Supreme Court of Canada, in *Vavilov***, 2019 SCC 65, overturned past law (including *Dunsmuir*, 2008 SCC 9) and gives new rules for determining when to apply "reasonableness" rather than "correctness". For 220(3.1), "reasonableness" will still apply, and the same test should apply to CRA discretion under 85(7.1), 122.62(2), 152(4.2), 204.1(4), 204.91(2), 206.4, 207.06 and 220(2.1), (3) and (3.201); but *Vavilov*'s framework for determining "reasonableness" is new.

Under *Vavilov*, "courts intervene in administrative matters only where it is truly necessary to do so in order to safeguard the legality, rationality and fairness of the administrative process" (para. 13). However, "administrative decision makers *[i.e., CRA]* must adopt a culture of justification and demonstrate that their exercise of delegated public power can be justified" (para. 14). The Court must ensure the "decision as a whole is **transparent, intelligible and justified**" (para. 15). The Court does not ask what decision it would have made, ascertain the range of possible conclusions, conduct a new analysis or seek the correct solution; but must consider only whether CRA's decision, including both rationale and outcome, was unreasonable (para. 83). Two fundamental flaws that can render a decision unreasonable (para. 101) are a "failure of rationality internal to the reasoning process" (e.g. irrational chain of analysis, or if the reasons in conjunction with the record do not make it possible to understand the reasoning on a critical point, or exhibit clear logical fallacies: paras. 103-104) and "when a decision is in some respect untenable in light of the relevant factual and legal constraints", taking into account the governing statutory scheme, other relevant statutory or common law, the principles of statutory interpretation (including text, context and purpose: para. 120), the evidence before CRA and facts of which CRA may take notice, the parties' submissions, CRA past practices and decisions, and the decision's potential impact on the taxpayer (para. 106). However, "reasonableness review is not a line-by-line treasure hunt for error": para. 102. CRA must consider the evidentiary record and the general factual matrix, and its decision must be reasonable in light of them (para. 126). Whether a particular decision is consistent with past CRA decisions is also a constraint the court should consider (para. 131); but in *Bank of Montreal*, 2020 FC 1014, paras. 154-158, CRA could reject a GST calculation method it had allowed the previous year, as it gave clear reasons. Finally, individuals are entitled to greater procedural protection when the decision involves potentially significant personal impact or harm, including threatening one's "livelihood" (para. 133), and if the impact is severe, CRA's reasons must explain why the decision best reflects the legislature's intention (this new factor will likely be cited in applications under 220(3.1): note that there is relatively little information about Parliament's intention on introducing 220(3.1) in 1991).

Successful judicial review normally means sending the matter back to CRA for a new decision; but the Court may order a result if a particular outcome is "inevitable" (*Vavilov*, para. 142). For an interesting non-tax example (guns, helicopters and bears) where the FCA declined to order a specific result but told the government to be reasonable, see *Sexsmith*, 2021 FCA 111.

Post-decision answers to questions about the decision can help comply with *Vavilov*, if they explain the decision and are not after-the-fact justification: *KIK Custom Products*, 2020 FC 462, paras. 65, 69.

Due to *Vavilov*, CRA may be required not to depart from longstanding administrative practice without reasonable explanation: *Honey Fashions*, 2020 FCA 64, para. 46.

If CRA has incorrect facts, it is not "reasonable" for an official to rely on that information: *Posmyk*, 2021 FC 393, para. 21.

Vavilov has been applied since 2020, e.g. *Grewal*, 2020 FC 356 (under appeal to FCA) (VDP); *Neyedly*, 2020 FC 678 (interest waiver); *Bayer Inc.*, 2020 FC 750 (CRA demand for information was too broad); *Carpenter*, 2020 FC 753 (interest waiver).

See also Neilson, Singh & Lang, "*Vavilov* and the New Framework for Judicial Review", XXIII(1) *Tax Litigation* (Federated Press) 1-7 (2020); Kutsenko, "Judicial Review of CRA Decisions after Vavilov", *Bennett Jones on Tax Disputes* (*Taxnet Pro* Tax Disputes Centre), March 23, 2020, pp. 7-14.

When the FC sends a decision back to CRA, a fresh review must be "reached with an open mind, based on an entirely new assessment of the case and its merits" and a "truly independent new appraisal": *Dobson Estate*, 2007 FC 565. Thus, a denial letter that was an edited version of the previous letter meant no fresh review was done, so the matter was sent back yet again. Similarly, in *Jaka Holdings*, 2011 FC 518, the fact the decision under review had been copied from earlier decisions was a "breach of procedural fairness", and it was sent back.

Can the Court order that interest and penalty be waived? In *Galetzka*, 2004 FC 672, based on new information that CRA had not seen, the Court referred the case back to CRA "with directions that the only fair and reasonable decision is that the interest and penalty be waived upon the applicant paying $500 as a reasonable payment arrangement." Similarly, in *Maarsman*, 2003 FC 1234, the Court sent the case back "to CRA for new decision based on these reasons". In *Liddar*, 2007 FCA 323, the FCA ruled that *Federal Courts Act* s. 18.1 allows the FC to order CRA (effectively a *mandamus* order) to "do any act or thing it has unlawfully failed or refused to do" (para. 7). Thus, such orders are valid, and perhaps the matter need not always be sent back for new exercise of CRA discretion. In *Kerr*, 2008 FC 1073, the Court directed that Part X.1 tax be waived under 204.1(4). However, in *Slau Ltd.*, 2009 FCA 270, the FC had sent the file back to CRA with directions to cancel interest after a particular date and declare the amount owing to be $X, but the FCA ruled that "the exercise of the Minister's discretion could lead to outcomes other than the one stipulated", and ordered the matter back to CRA for redetermination. In *Borel Christen*, 2017 FC 1022, BC sought a "directed verdict" that a disclosure should be accepted as "voluntary"; CRA consented only to review the matter again, and sought an order allowing the application on that basis, but the Court held the matter should be heard.

Where a judicial review application was stayed because CRA agreed to review the file again, and the taxpayer disputed the new decision, the stay could not be lifted; instead, a new JR application had to be brought: *Lazaridis*, 2007 FC 19.

Parallel GST/HST waiver is available under *Excise Tax Act* s. 281.1 (see David M. Sherman, *Practitioner's Goods and Services Tax Annotated*). Income tax and GST/HST waivers need not be done consistently, as each is considered on its own merit: *Price*, 2016 FC 906, para. 23; *Parmar*, 2018 FC 912.

In the judicial review application, the Court must not consider evidence that were not before the CRA decision-maker: *Robinson*, 2009 FC 795; *Formosi*, 2010 FC 326; *Butlin*, 2011 FC 616; *Levenson*, 2016 FC 10, para. 9; *Anthony*, 2016 FC 955, para. 15; *Coley*, 2017 FC 210, paras. 11, 22-23; *Dougal*, 2017 FC 1075, para. 3; *Al-Quq*, 2018 FC 574, paras. 22-26; *Mokrycke*, 2020 FC 1027, para. 8; *Perinpanayagam*, 2020 FC

1111, para. 18; *Schillaci*, 2021 FC 27, para. 30; *Allen*, 2021 FC 364, para. 22. Nor can arguments not put to CRA be considered: *Building Products*, 2020 FC 784, para. 28; *Schillaci*, para. 41 (in the author's view this should not always be true: if CRA made a legal error on the issue before it, it should not matter what arguments had been made). However, affidavits can provide evidence of: procedural defects not in the evidentiary record; a complete absence of evidence before the decision-maker; and general background: *Anthony*, para. 17. As well, "evidence that could show that the CRA possessed pertinent information that it did not consider potentially has probative value": *Bird*, 2014 FC 843, para. 41.

The FC ruled CRA decisions on *financial hardship* to be reasonable in (**pre-*Vavilov***): *Grundy*, 2005 FC 1312; *Grosh*, 2007 FC 654; *McIntosh*, 2007 FC 723; *Tomaszewski*, 2010 FC 145 (FCA appeal discontinued A-176-10); *Chwaiewsky*, 2010 FC 1178 (CRA's considering taxpayer's interest in jointly-owned property as part of his assets was reasonable); *Kidzugane*, 2011 FC 40; *Williamson*, 2011 FC 383 (insufficient hardship); *Inline Fibreglass*, 2011 FC 1506; *Desjardins*, 2011 FC 1490; *Amoroso*, 2013 FC 157, para. 72; *Kotel*, 2013 FC 1015; *Bird*, 2014 FC 843; *Robinson*, 2015 FC 117; *MacDonald*, 2015 FC 177; *Muir*, 2016 FC 362; *Coley*, 2017 FC 210. **Post-*Vavilov***: none yet.

Judicial review was also denied in (**pre-*Vavilov***): *Mueller*, [2000] 4 C.T.C. 242; *Chapman*, [2002] 3 C.T.C. 563 (FCTD); *Légaré*, 2003 FC 1047; *Case*, 2004 FC 825; *Tywriwskyi*, 2004 FC 542; *Neilans*, 2004 FC 716; *Downey*, 2004 FC 1143; *Tadross*, 2004 FC 1698; *Mandate Erectors*, 2005 FC 832 (penalty for late payroll deductions); *Babin*, 2005 FC 972 (penalty for filing returns late); *Groleau*, 2005 FC 1713 (no exceptional circumstances or circumstances beyond G's control, and no evidence that his right to a fair, objective and unbiased decision was violated); *Latour*, 2005 FC 1720 (interest on amount that CRA mistakenly credited to L's account); *Fetterly*, 2006 TCC 94 (no evidence discretion exercised unreasonably); *Sutherland*, 2006 FC 154; *Wax*, 2006 FC 675 (CRA's partial waiver was not an admission of mistake); *K-Bel Holdings*, 2006 FC 825 ($25,000 penalty upheld when payroll remittance for management bonus was 7 days late and taxpayer had always been compliant) [*contra*, see *NRT Technology* 4 paras. down]; *Young*, 2006 FC 1164 (taxpayers chose to channel resources into business and into supporting ill parents); *Tedford*, 2006 FC 1334 (past events too remote to prevent late filing); *Jenkins*, 2007 FC 295 (deaths in family occurred 8 months before return was due); *PPSC Enterprises*, 2007 FC 784 (director wrongly paid CPP contributions as self-employed person, and corporation liable for failing to remit); *Kreklewich*, 2007 FC 892 (CRA had not provided a breakdown of interest calculations); *Christie*, 2007 FC 1014 (unclear for years whether deceased's RRIF would go to estate or widow, and estate became liable for tax and interest); *Jaholkowski*, 2007 FC 736 (J did not make significant efforts to pay off tax debt over extended period); *McLean*, 2007 FC 1072 (M's failure to comply was largely because of his choices and priorities); *Zylka*, 2007 FC 1198 (no evidence decision unreasonable); *3651541 Canada*, 2008 FCA 262 (reasonable for CRA "to not consider what the applicant did not raise"); *Panchyshyn*, 2008 FC 996 (CRA had taken factors into account and provided some relief); *Northview Apartments*, 2009 FC 74; *Knie*, 2009 FC 183 (error by K's accountant); *Solomenescu*, 2009 FC 544 (taxpayer's confusion was his own problem); *Jones Estate*, 2009 FC 646 (CRA had considered circumstances); *Serge Côté Family Trust*, 2009 FC 698 (information circular's failure to state penalty for 116(3) non-compliance was not CRA action justifying relief); *Hi-Tech Seals*, 2009 FC 901 (controller away on holiday when payroll remittances missed); *Smith*, 2009 FC 694 (penalty for failing to report severance pay); *Ugro*, 2009 FC 825 and 826 (FCA appeal discontinued A-396-09) (dissatisfaction with accountant was not circumstance beyond taxpayer's control); *Cooke* and *Lesage*, 2009 FC 1161 and 1162 (economic downturn was not reason not to pay interest); *Peter Pond Holdings*, 2010 FC 5 (CRA official did not fetter discretion in applying guidelines); *Lemerise*, 2010 FC 116 (insufficient evidence of health problems); *Gangnon*, 2010 FC 155 (but costs of $1,200 awarded due to CRA's delay in dealing with the matter); *Formosi*, 2010 FC 326; *Osborne*, 2010 FC 673 (taxpayer relied unduly on accountant to deal with CRA); *Couch*, 2010 FC 1130 (CRA correctly applied its Guidelines); *Spence*, 2012 FCA 58 (errors in return prepared by third party); *Rosenberg Estate*, 2011 FC 445 (complexity of estate should not have prevented filing of return); *Butlin*, 2011 FC 616 (taxpayer with PTSD could have hired accountant to complete returns); *Toastmaster Inc.*, 2012 FCA 317 (CRA decision was reasonable even though after carryback $600,000 interest was assessed on $42,000 tax balance); *Mytting*, 2012 FC 465 (taxpayer not misled by CRA Statements of Account that did not show full amount owing); *Taylor*, 2012 FC 994 (no breach of procedural fairness); *T & S First Choice*, 2012 FC 1146; *CPNI Inc.*, 2013 FC 96 (global financial crisis was not "man-made disaster"); *1148902 Ontario*, 2013 FC 703 (company had been told by CRA to treat its owner as employee and not independent contractor, and ignored that advice); *Suissa*, 2013 FC 897 (disposition of 4 properties by 6 related co-owners and not notifying under 116(3) led to 162(7) penalties of $60,000 [$2,500 × 4]; each of 6 CRA refusal decisions was reasonable); *Kotel*, 2013 FC 1015 (wrong advice from accountant was not "extraordinary circumstance" justifying relief); *Tremblay*, 2013 FC 1049 (late filings not justified by accountant's delay that resulted from T not paying accountant's fees); *Higgins*, 2014 FC 100 (CRA decision addressed relevant factors); *Gilbert*, 2014 FC 890; *Taylor*, 2014 FC 894 (T non-compliant over many years); *Larouche*, 2015 FC 232 (L could have paid balance while appealing); *Muir*, 2016 FC 362 (errors were by accountant, not CRA); *Price*, 2016 FC 906 (CRA gave partial relief for various family tragedies; P had not provided CRA with better documentation); *Herrington*, 2016 FC 953 (163(1) penalty where bank lost H's change of address and did not send him T5 slips); *Walsh*, 2018 FCA 229 (inconsistent assessments of "departure trade" resulting in 2 levels of tax was not extraordinary circumstance); *Dougal & Co.*, 2017 FC 1075; *Norris*, 2018 FC 1; *Morrison*, 2018 FC 141 (FCA appeal dismissed for delay A-61-18) (large unreported T4 amount led to 163(1) penalty); *Al-Quq*, 2018 FC 574 (taxpayers could not claim errors in assessments when they did not appeal to TCC); *Martineau*, 2018 FC 595; *Robinson*, 2018 FC 825; *Klopak*, 2019 FC 235; *Pathak*, 2019 FC 252; *1680169 Ontario*, 2019 FC 562 (company took years to recover from accountant's errors and filed returns late; CRA's duty of procedural fairness did not require disclosing its calls to accountant or to set out a "case to meet"); *Bifano*, 2019 FC 742 (death of son and divorce did not explain inability to remit source deductions when B continued to run business); *Chekosky*, 2019 FC 841; *Chau*, 2019 FC 1342; *Macintosh*, 2019 FC 1343. **Post-*Vavilov***: *Neyedly*, 2020 FC 678; *Carpenter*, 2020 FC 753 (personal misfortunes did not prevent C from filing returns); *Building Products*, 2020 FC 784 (CRA had not followed policy to offer to apply loss carryovers, and BP failed to object to reassessment on time); *Allstaff Inc.*, 2021 FC 52 (under appeal to FCA) (AI had no money for its payroll remittances until it was paid by clients); *Shea*, 2021 FC 54 (S failed to provide details of his financial situation); *Simmons*, 2021 FC 202 (under appeal to FCA) (S took no steps to pay balance when his objection re charitable donation scheme was put on hold while test case litigated); *KC*, 2021 FC 222 (neurological disorder did not prevent C from filing); *Cheeseman*, 2021 FC 273 (financial hardship not proven, and C's medical issues were not in the non-compliance timeframe).

An application challenging a first decision is "premature", as a second review should be requested first: *Tomaszewski*, 2010 FC 145, para. 21 (FCA appeal discontinued A-176-10).

In *Stemijon Investments [Canwest Communications, Leonard Asper Holdings]*, 2011 FCA 299, 6 related companies failed to file the T1135 re foreign property and were penalized under 233.3(3). CRA saying "I cannot grant your request" for relief was an "unreasonable" fettering of discretion; however, the FCA ruled that the matter should not be sent back because CRA reached the only reasonable outcome! (The FCA thus overrode 220(3.1) by narrowing the reasons for which relief can be granted to what is in CRA policy rather than what is in 220(3.1). In the author's view this is seriously wrong.) For more cases on CRA refusal to waive the penalty on a late T1135, see Notes to 233.3(3). CRA is studying whether it has power to waive the penalty for a T1135: doc 2015-0588971C6 [2015 APFF q.4].

Delay was accepted as reason to overturn CRA decisions in (**pre-*Vavilov***): *Hillier*, 2001 FCA 197 (31 months to consider objection); *Dort Estate*, 2005 FC 1201 (delay while test case proceeded); *Cole*, 2005 FC 1445 (delay in the Courts); *Lalonde*, 2008 FC 183 and 2010 FC 531 (5-year delay while criminal charges proceeded against other parties); *Stover*, 2019 FC 1599 (3 years to consider objection). In *Gangnon*, 2010 FC 155, $1,200 costs were awarded to unrepresented taxpayers to compensate for CRA delay in dealing with the file.

Delay was rejected as a reason in (**pre-*Vavilov***): *Comeau*, 2005 FCA 271 (objection put in abeyance during criminal proceedings); *Telfer*, 2009 FCA 23 (leave to appeal denied 2009 CarswellNat 1538 (SCC)) and *Gestions Bussey*, 2019 FC 17 (delay while awaiting court decision in similar case: CRA decision was "within a range of possible acceptable outcomes"); *Jewett*, 2020 FCA 187 (CRA had granted partial relief); *Belchetz (Brandimarte)*, 2020 FCA 225 (30-year dispute re Overseas Credit shelter; CRA had granted partial relief for lengthy delays); *Metro-Can Construction*, 2002 FCT 1171 (22 months to confirm objection, reasonable given file's complexity); *Khanna*, 2004 FC 1606 (2-year delay in reconsidering application regrettable but not procedurally unfair); *Wax*, 2006 FC 675 (CRA delays were reasonable); *Phillips*, 2011 FC 448 (criminal prosecution made delay reasonable); *Amoroso*, 2013 FC 157, para. 68 (delay was not imputable to CRA); *APL Properties*, 2013 FC 449 (some relief had been granted, and decision was within range of reasonable outcomes); *Shea*, 2019 FC 787 (S was responsible for part of delay); *Martel*, 2019 FC 840 (CRA granted partial relief and had warned M that interest would continue to accrue if unpaid). **Post-*Vavilov***: *Schillaci*, 2021 FC 27 (CRA did not enforce collection for many years).

(Delay in the Court appeal process would not permit the Tax Court to reduce interest: cf. *Schwartz*, 2019 QCCA 2068, ruling that the Court of Quebec could not cancel Quebec interest.)

Depression was accepted as a medical ground (for non-compliance over several years) that CRA had not properly considered in: *McLeod Estate*, 2007 FC 1111; *Laflamme*, 2008 FC 1403; *Cayer*, 2009 FC 1195; *Holmes*, 2010 FC 809, *Yachimec*, 2010 FC 1333. CRA accepted this principle and cancelled many years of interest in a 2018 application the author was involved with.

Financial hardship was accepted as basis for judicial review in (**pre-*Vavilov***): *Galetzka*, 2004 FC 672 (CRA's belief about G's ability to pay was patently unreasonable); *Vitellaro*, 2005 FCA 166; *Dick*, 2005 FC 560; *Lund*, 2006 FC 640 ("sloppiness and imprecision" in CRA's review of claim); *Gandy*, 2006 FC 862 (accountant's error was beyond G's control, and penalty caused financial hardship; "hardship is not the equivalent of impossibility"); *3500772 Canada Inc.*, 2008 FC 554 (CRA misunderstood basis for corp's claim of hardship); *Meier*, 2011 FC 840 (unreasonable for CRA to criticize M for buying groceries and a trailer to live in when expenses exceeded income: "CRA thought that the Applicant should move from poverty to abject poverty and would not forgive her interest unless she took that step"). **Post-*Vavilov***: none yet.

Taxpayers succeeded on other grounds in (**pre-*Vavilov***): *Edison*, [2001] 3 C.T.C. 233 (FCTD) and *Robertson*, [2001] 4 C.T.C. 38 (FCTD) (official who made initial decision to deny waiver was involved in reviewing the decision); *Isaac*, [2002] G.S.T.C. 36 (FCTD); *Robertson*, 2003 FCT 16; *Brickenden*, 2003 FC 929; *Johnston*, 2003 FCT 713; *Maarsman*, 2003 FC 1234 ("astronomical" sum of interest when no tax was payable due to loss carrybacks; CRA should treat the request with "common sense" [the FCA later somewhat overruled this in *Toastmaster Inc.*, 2012 FCA 317]); *Miller*, 2004 FC 46; *Comeau*, 2004 FC 961; *Elwell*, 2004 FC 943; *Beacock*, 2005 FC 567; *Singh*,

2005 FC 1457; *Rahey*, 2005 FC 86 (CRA had warned the taxpayers only that interest would continue accruing during an objection; refusal to cancel penalties was unjustified); *Carter-Smith*, 2006 FC 1175 (CS's emotional stress and physical disability not properly considered); *1373997 Ontario Inc.*, 2006 FC 1251 (CRA had already agreed to reconsider the matter but applicant wanted Court to issue reasons on the merits); *McNaught Pontiac*, 2006 FC 1296 (in-house courier mistakenly took payment to CRA office because he had forgotten remittance form, so did not make payment through financial institution as required); *LaFramboise*, 2008 FC 196 (house-destroying fire affected L's ability to address his tax affairs); *Nixon*, 2008 FC 917 ("extraordinary circumstances" not required for relief); *MacKay*, 2008 FC 1074 (M's submissions had been misunderstood); *Slau Ltd.*, 2009 FCA 270 (CRA did not properly consider loss carryback request); *Peddle*, 2009 FC 348 (decision was based on incorrect information); *Adams*, 2009 FC 995 (CRA did not provide adequate reasons); *Spence*, 2010 FC 52 (H&R Block failed to include information provided by S; it was error for CRA to say that "the Taxpayer Relief provisions do not allow for cancellation of interest in these types of situations"; but on reconsideration, S lost again: 2012 FCA 58); *Moodley*, 2011 FC 238 (CRA conceded discretion not properly exercised, and also agreed to consider due-diligence defence); *Sherry*, 2011 FC 1208 (FCA appeal dismissed for delay A-443-11) (decision did not provide adequate reasons, but applicant now had Taxpayer Relief Report so no further remedy); *Kelley Estate*, 2011 FC 1335 and 2012 FC 1202 (insufficient information was available to file estate's return on time; decision on reconsideration failed to apply first FC ruling); *Société Angelo Colatosti*, 2012 FC 124 (interest payable due to accountant's error; terse CRA decision did not indicate facts reviewed and appeared to fetter CRA's discretion); *3563537 Canada Inc.*, 2012 FC 1290 (decision ignored that advisor's fraud made it impossible for corp to prepare return on time); *NRT Technology*, 2013 FC 200 (one-time bonus outside payroll system; company remitted source deductions 11 days late, 1 day after CRA advised it was required [*contra*, see *K-Bel Holdings* 4 paras. up]); *Cogesco Services*, 2013 FC 1238 (CRA refusal to waive 162(2.1) penalty on the basis a parallel penalty applied did not respond to the request); *Finanders*, 2015 FC 448 (CRA decision based on mistake of fact); *Pavage St-Eustache Inc.*, 2015 FC 477 (CRA did not take into account errors it had made and that it was reasonable for corp to ignore statements of account as not yet reflecting settlement agreement); *2750-4711 Québec Inc.*, 2016 FC 579 (CRA misunderstood timing of when company's owner had been ill); *Lemieux*, 2016 FC 798 (CRA had misunderstood medical evidence); *Morrison*, 2016 FC 1145 (M's rejection of settlement offers was not valid factor to consider); *Pylatuik*, 2016 FC 1394 (P's father had filed P's return and wrongly reported income; CRA gave no "intelligible explanation" for waiving only part of interest); *Shantakumar*, 2018 FC 677 (CRA failed to consider totality of evidence); *Loyer (Succession)*, 2019 FC 1528 (CRA did not consider agreement with Revenu Québec to waive penalties). **Post-*Vavilov***: *Allen*, 2021 FC 364 (inability to comply due to debilitating mental illness over many years; CRA reasons were not sufficiently transparent, intelligible and justified, and did not take A's submissions into account).

In *Bremer*, 2006 FC 91, it was unreasonable for CRA to apply a late filing penalty where B filed his return 5 months late, but had paid the total amount owing two weeks after the balance-due day.

See also Notes to 152(4.2) for similar case law on late reassessments, and to 204.1(4) for case law on waiver of the RRSP overcontributions tax.

Refusal to consider waiving 163(2) gross-negligence penalty is wrong: *Cayer*, 2009 FC 1195. It is acceptable to say it may only be appropriate to waive it in "exceptional circumstances" [see Information Circular 07-1R1 para. 37, and 2016 Alberta CPA (tinyurl.com/cra-abtax) q.13], but not that "the courts should decide", since the legal correctness of the penalty is a different issue from whether it should be waived.

For more on Taxpayer Relief waiver **pre-*Vavilov***, see: Campbell, *Administration of Income Tax 2020* (Carswell), §11.8; Campbell, "Fairness, Taxpayer Relief and Voluntary Disclosures", 2009 BC Tax Conference (ctf.ca), 14:1-27; Watson, "Taxpayer Relief", 2010 Atlantic Provinces Tax Conf. [APTC] 10A:1-17; Wright, "Judicial Review of Ministerial Decisions", 2012 APTC 6:1-29; Lareau et al., "L'annulation ou la renonciation aux intérêts et aux pénalités", 60(4) *Canadian Tax Journal* 837-65 (2012); Sorensen, "Comprehensive Review of Penalty and Interest Relief", 2015 Cdn Tax Foundation conference report, 41:1-49; Sittler, "Review of Penalty and Interest Relief Requests", *ibid.*, 42:1-12; Lubetsky, "Interest Relief Under the Federal and Provincial Regimes", XX(1) *Tax Litigation* (Federated Press) 1182-92 (2015) (relief in Quebec and Alberta). **Post-*Vavilov***: "Interest Relief on Income Tax Debts: Canada Versus the United States", 68(4) *Canadian Tax Journal* (2020) 931-86. See also 171(1) Notes for more on FC judicial review applications.

Voluntary Disclosures Program (VDP):

Since March 2018: see Information Circular 00-1R6 (Dec. 2017), new Form RC199, and tinyurl.com/vdp-cra. All VDP is now handled in the Shawinigan Tax Centre. If a disclosure qualifies, CRA will not prosecute criminally (see Notes to 239(1)), will waive gross-negligence penalties (163(2)), and may waive other penalties and some interest. Five conditions to qualify (00-1R6 para. 28): the disclosure must be "voluntary" [see below]; "complete" [below]; involve a penalty; include information at least 1 year past due; and include payment of the estimated tax (para. 26), though a payment arrangement may be accepted if this is impossible (para. 40). VDP is "generally" not allowed for: elections; advance pricing arrangements; competent authority issues; post-assessment relief of penalty/interest; a bankrupt or person in receivership: para. 23. A second disclosure is permitted only in limited cases: para. 25. For GST/HST VDP, see GST/HST Memorandum 16-5.

The Limited Program (**LPGM**) waives only criminal prosecution and gross-negligence penalties. LPGM applies to intentional conduct, and "generally" to all corps with gross revenue >$250m in 2 of the past 5 years: IC 00-1R6 paras. 20-21. Intentional conduct is evidenced by: efforts made to avoid detection; large dollar amounts; multiple years of non-compliance; sophisticated taxpayer; disclosure after CRA announcement of focus on the taxpayer's area.

The General Program waives criminal prosecution, all penalties (e.g. late filing, instalment penalties, source-deduction penalties), and 50% of the interest older than the most recent 3 years being corrected: IC 00-1R6 para. 15. Penalties and interest over 10 years old cannot be waived under 220(3.1); but due to *Bozzer* (see third para. of these Notes), CRA can waive interest *accrued* during the past 10 years, even on older years' tax.

If VDP treatment is refused, one may apply for second administrative review, as with Taxpayer Relief above (IC 00-1R6 para. 59), and then judicial review in the FC, as above (paras. 61-64); but the FC will not issue an injunction to stop the assessment being issued: *Prince*, 2020 FCA 32, para. 17.

"Voluntary": there must be no existing or pending CRA enforcement action that would lead to the unreported information, such as requesting returns or starting an audit; and CRA must not have received detail that names the taxpayer, such as offshore banking info (IC 00-1R6 para. 29). This test is more stringent than pre-2018, when the taxpayer could be unaware of CRA's action or information (*Brown*, 2007 FCA 26; *334156 Alberta*, 2008 FCA 228; *L'Heureux*, 2006 FC 1180; *Robinson*, 2009 FC 795; *Livaditis*, 2010 FC 950 (aff'd on other grounds 2012 FCA 55); *Amour International*, 2010 FC 1070; *Charky*, 2010 FC 1327; *Williams*, 2011 FC 766 (FCA appeal dismissed for delay A-348-11); *Bontje*, 2012 FCA 53). See now *4053893 Canada*, 2021 FC 218 (CRA had asked shareholder about corp). Rejection of VDP treatment was sent back because CRA had not explained why a demand to file, or audit of, a corp would have led to discovery of non-compliance by a shareholder, or vice versa, in all of: *Poon*, 2009 FC 432; *Worsfold*, 2012 FC 644; *4053893 Canada*, 2019 FC 51 [Sorensen, "Successful Judicial Review", 27(2) *Canadian Tax Highlights* (ctf.ca) 11-12 (Feb. 2019)]. In *Ludmer*, 2018 QCCS 3381, paras. 162-172 (aff'd on other grounds 2020 QCCA 697; leave to appeal denied 2021 CarswellQue 2160 (SCC)), CRA refusal to accept a disclosure was reasonable because it appeared L knew another shareholder was being audited. CRA's "self-review" letters (see 231.1(1) Notes at "Letter campaign") are not "enforcement action"; nor is an unrelated audit (e.g. GST vs payroll): IC 00-1R6 para. 31.

In *Matthew Boadi Prof. Corp.*, 2018 FC 53, CRA's decision that a disclosure was not "voluntary" was sent back as unreasonable: demands to file recent returns, followed by MBPC filing those returns showing foreign property over $100,000, would not likely have triggered review of *older* years for missing T1135s (233.3(3)).

Voluntarily filing T1 adjustments without requesting VDP treatment led to late-filing penalties not being waived in *Klopak*, 2019 FC 235.

"Complete": the taxpayer must disclose everything relevant for all years (IC 00-1R6 paras. 29-34; para. 43 says all returns, forms and schedules *must* be included with the application). Disclosures were not "complete" in: *Palonek*, 2007 FCA 281; *Peintres Filmar*, 2007 FC 560; *Grewal*, 2020 FC 356 (under appeal to FCA) (later audit identified that amounts reported under VDP as loans were taxable benefits; penalties applied to these amounts). In *McCracken*, 2009 FC 1189, eBay's failure to provide the taxpayer his sales records did not make it unreasonable for CRA to refuse to extend the deadline to provide complete information. CRA says that for disclosure of FAPI to be complete, full T1134s as well as amended returns must be filed for all years, and working papers calculating the surplus accounts of the foreign affiliate may be requested: VIEWS doc 2014-0537701I7.

Under the new program, CRA will not limit assessments to only 6 or 10 years as it generally did before, but may assess *all* past years: Ted Gallivan letter to David Sohmer, Oct. 4, 2018 (on TaxPartner or *Taxnet Pro*).

"No-names" disclosure protection is no longer offered; instead, one can have a non-binding "pre-disclosure discussion" to get a "better understanding of the risks involved in remaining non-compliant and the relief available under the VDP" (IC 00-1R6 paras. 41-42).

Discussion of the new (2018) VDP: *Voluntary Disclosure — Checklist* (*Taxnet Pro* Tax Disputes Centre, 2020, 8pp); Vanasse & Bertolas, "Revised VDP Applies on March 1, 2018", 26(2) *Canadian Tax Highlights* (ctf.ca) 4-5 (Feb. 2018); Sorensen & Arrigo, "Two-Tier Justice in the CRA's New VDP", XXI(1) *Corporate Finance* (Federated Press) 23-28 (2018) (re large corporations being forced into the LPGM); Chernier, "Voluntary disclosure and the Difference Between Non-Profits and Registered Charities", 26(5) *Canadian Not-for-Profit News* (Carswell) 33-35 (May 2018); Rabinovitch & Dusablon, "Voluntary Disclosures", *Taxnet Pro* Tax Disputes Centre (June 2018, 26pp); Sohmer, "Transparency and the Voluntary Disclosure Program", xl(23) *The Canadian Taxpayer* (Carswell) 177-79 (Nov. 30, 2018) (quantifies the relative cost of disclosing under the new VDP).

For articles criticizing the June 2017 draft IC which (mostly) became the current rules, see these Notes up to the 57th ed.

VDP applications filed before March 2018 did not have the LPGM (all penalties were waived in all cases) and did not require payment of the tax upon disclosure. As well, "voluntary" was based on what the taxpayer was aware of CRA doing, not on what CRA was actually doing; and "no-names" disclosure could provide protection from the date of such disclosure.

In *Khan*, 2015 ONSC 7283, paras. 584-605, a false voluntary disclosure was evidence of tax fraud.

Where CRA sought to assess penalties in breach of a VDP agreement, a judicial-review application was allowed to proceed in *Sifto Canada*, 2014 FCA 140.

How many years will be assessed under VDP? Before 2012, CRA would usually limit assessments to 6-10 years, and thus not assess years for which penalty could not be waived. In *Gauthier*, 2017 FC 1173, G put $300,000 in a Bahamas bank account in 1978, and made a voluntary disclosure in 2015. CRA accepted the disclosure for 2005-2014 (the years for which penalty could be waived), and later proposed to assess penalties for 1980-2004! The Court refused an injunction preventing the assessment. See David Sohmer, "A CRA All Star Tag Team v. Gaston Gauthier", xli *The Canadian Taxpayer* (Carswell) 17-19 (Feb. 8, 2019).

In 2018-19, CRA received 9,835 voluntary disclosures (down from over 19,000 due to the 2018 changes), reporting $1 billion in previously unreported income (down from $1.3b), of which $435m (down from $573m) was from offshore: *Departmental Results Report* (tinyurl.com/cra-results), p. 24 (no data in 2019-20 Report).

CRA has no jurisdiction to waive *tax*; the waiver applies only to penalty and (sometimes) interest. However, see David M. Sherman, "Revenue Canada Comes Through With Tax Waiver", X(4) *GST & Commodity Tax* (Carswell) 25-26 (May 1996). Tax can be "written off" by Collections when it is uncollectible, but it still remains legally owing (see s. 222, which provides a minimum 10-year collection limitation period). Note also that even when VDP applies, the remaining interest charges can be very high, e.g., *Toastmaster Inc.*, 2012 FCA 317. Bankruptcy eliminates a tax debt (see Notes to 128(2)) but not criminal fines.

Remission orders: Where 220(3.1) cannot apply (e.g., because the 10-year deadline has passed, or because the taxpayer seeks cancellation of tax rather than interest), Cabinet can grant a remission order under the *Financial Administration Act*. For detailed discussion and case law see Notes at the beginning of the Remission Orders, reproduced after the Regulations. See also the Remission Orders annotation below.

220(3.1) amended by 2004 Budget (essentially to add the 10-year limitation), effective 2005 with grandfathering for applications filed before 2005.

220(3.1) added by 1991 technical bill and amended by 1992 technical bill, both effective for penalty and interest in respect of 1985 and later tax years.

Remission Orders

Remission of interest and penalty more than 10 years back (i.e., waiver not possible): *Laura Speakman Remission Order*, P.C. 2010-1593; *Cynthia Carlson Remission Order*, P.C. 2010-1594; *Jacqueline Doskoch Remission Order*, P.C. 2010-1595; *Evan Warden Remission Order*, P.C. 2010-1596; *Susan Gill Remission Order*, P.C. 2011-279; *Mildred Jacobs Remission Order*, P.C. 2011-482; *Alfo Bacci Tax Remission Order*, P.C. 2012-33; *Ron Adams Remission Order*, P.C. 2014-1129; *Estates of Kathleen and William McGowan Remission Order*, P.C. 2014-1477; *Mary Duncan Remission Order*, P.C. 2016-821; *Rita Sweet Remission Order*, P.C. 2016-1052.

Other: *Léopold Bouchard Remission Order*, P.C. 2007-562 (remission of tax where paying debt would cause extreme hardship); *Doina-Florica Calin Remission Order*, P.C. 2007-563 (tax refunded where deadline missed due to health problems); *Yvonne Townshend Remission Order*, P.C. 2007-1776 (remission of tax and interest based on extreme hardship); *Eugene Skripkariuk Remission Order*, P.C. 2009-169 (remission of tax where filing error would have been detected by CRA "if proper procedures had been followed", and payment of amount would cause extreme hardship); *Catherine Bland Remission Order*, P.C. 2009-170 (remission of tax where interest charges "increased the debt to a level where paying it would cause extreme hardship"); *Jared Torgerson Remission Order*, P.C. 2009-878 (tax and interest remitted due to CRA error); *Pierre Gosselin Remission Order*, P.C. 2009-951 (remission due to circumstances not within taxpayer's control); *Keith Phillips Remission Order*, P.C. 2013-40 (unwarranted refund when identity stolen).

Information Circulars: 98-1R5: Tax collection policies; 00-1R4: Voluntary disclosures program; 07-1R1: Taxpayer relief provisions.

CRA Audit Manual: 3.0: Fairness and client rights; 11.6.6 and Appendix A-11.2.24: Fairness report.

Forms: RC199: Voluntary disclosures program (VDP) — taxpayer agreement; RC376: Taxpayer relief request statement of income and expenses and assets and liabilities for individuals; RC4288: Request for taxpayer relief; T4060: Collections policies [guide].

(3.2) Late, amended or revoked elections — The Minister may extend the time for making an election or grant permission to amend or revoke an election if

(a) the election was otherwise required to be made by a taxpayer or by a partnership, under a prescribed provision, on or before a day in a taxation year of the taxpayer (or in the case of a partnership, a fiscal period of the partnership); and

(b) the taxpayer or the partnership applies, on or before the day that is ten calendar years after the end of the taxation year or the fiscal period, to the Minister for that extension or permission.

Related Provisions: 60(l), 60(l)(iv) — Minister may accept late rollover of RRSP after death to spouse, child or grandchild; 127.4(5.1) — Authorization for late LSVCC investments; 146(22) — Authorization for late RRSP contributions; 220(3) — Late filing allowed by extending time for return; 220(3.21) — Certain designations deemed to be elections; 220(3.3) — Date of late election, amended election or revocation;

220(3.4) — Consequential assessment; 220(3.5) — Penalty for late filed, amended or revoked elections.

Notes: 220(3.2) allows late filing, amendment or revocation of certain elections (Reg. 600) or designations (220(3.21)), but only with CRA permission, and only if a penalty is paid (220(3.5)). For the pension income splitting election (no penalty payable), see 220(3.201).

220(3.2) is part of the Taxpayer Relief (formerly called "Fairness") legislation. See 220(3.1) Notes re CRA discretion and judicial review, including the *Vavilov* standard.

CRA does accept some late-filed election forms that are not specifically listed in Reg. 600. There is a distinction between *making* an election (where 220(3.2) applies) and *filing* an election form, for which CRA can apply 220(2.1) to waive the requirement. A 37(10) election cannot be revoked because it is not listed in Reg. 600: *Advanced Agricultural Testing*, 2009 TCC 190.

CRA administrative policy is found in the *Taxpayer Relief Procedures Manual*, available on *TaxPartner* and *Taxnet Pro*. See also docs 2007-0220471E5 (cancelling excessive capital dividend election that cannot be repaired); 2008-0277991E5 (late filed replacement property election); 2008-026574117, 2011-039622117 (late 45(2) election).

If CRA refuses, the Federal Court on judicial review (see Notes to 220(3.1)) may allow late filing of *designations*, but likely not *elections* not listed in Reg. 600: *Nassau Walnut*, [1998] 1 C.T.C. 33 (FCA); *Terminal Norco*, 2006 TCC 139. See also Notes to 220(3) re *Kutlu* (late-filed s. 216 *return*); VIEWS docs 2010-0381311E5 (discusses the case law), 2015-0573861C6 [2015 CLHIA q.3]; Tompkins, "Fixing Income Tax Elections and Designations", 1995 Cdn Tax Foundation conference report, at pp. 9:1-10.

In *Gjernes*, 2007 FC 609, CRA was ordered to reconsider its disallowance of a late 45(2) election, but there were no "extraordinary circumstances" justifying a direction from the Court for a specific result.

See also 85(7.1) Notes for case law on the same issue (for s. 85 elections).

220(3.2) amended by 2004 Budget, for applications made after 2004, effectively to add the 10-year limitation. Added by 1991 technical bill, for elections in respect of 1985 and later years.

Regulations: 600 (prescribed provisions).

Income Tax Folios: S1-F3-C2: Principal residence [replaces IT-120R6, IT-437R].

Information Circulars: 07-1R1: Taxpayer relief provisions.

CRA Audit Manual: 12.4.5: Late filed elections; 28.6.3: Fairness provisions — late, amended or revoked elections; 28.12.0: Cancellation/waiver of penalties under the fairness provisions.

(3.201) Joint election — pension income split — On application by a taxpayer, the Minister may extend the time for making an election, or grant permission to amend or revoke an election, under section 60.03 if

(a) the application is made on or before the day that is three calendar years after the taxpayer's filing-due date for the taxation year to which the election applies; and

(b) the taxpayer is resident in Canada

(i) if the taxpayer is deceased at the time of the application, at the time that is immediately before the taxpayer's death, or

(ii) in any other case, at the time of the application.

Notes: 220(3.201) is part of the Taxpayer Relief (formerly called "Fairness") legislation. See Notes to 220(3.1) and (3.2). However, this rule has a 3-year application deadline, unlike the 10-year rule elsewhere.

A request to amend the amount elected is made with a new Form T1032; a request to revoke the election or split income should be made by letter to the local tax services office, signed by both parties: May 2010 ICAA (tinyurl.com/cra-abtax), q.15.

Where the election is filed after the transferee's normal reassessment period, CRA cannot accept it because 152(4.2) does not permit an increase in tax payable (despite the net benefit to the two spouses): VIEWS doc 2011-042992117.

220(3.201) added by 2007 budget bill #2, for 2007 and later taxation years.

(3.21) Designations and allocations — For the purpose of subsection (3.2),

(a) a designation in any form prescribed for the purpose of paragraph 80(2)(i) or any of subsections 80(5) to (11) or 80.03(7) is deemed to be an election under a prescribed provision of this Act;

(a.1) a designation is deemed to be an election under a prescribed provision of this Act if the designation is made under the definition "principal residence" in section 54; and

(b) a designation or allocation under subsection 132.11(6) is deemed to be an election under a prescribed provision of this Act.

Related Provisions: 220(3.2), (3.5) — Late filing of principal residence designation allowed with penalty.

Notes: 220(3.21)(a.1) added by 2017 budget bill #2, for tax years that end after Oct. 2, 2016. This allows late filing of a principal-residence designation (with a penalty: 220(3.5)). CRA permits this for 2016 and 2017 dispositions except in the most serious cases.

220(3.21)(b) added by 1998 Budget, effective June 17, 1999.

220(3.21) added by 1994 technical bill, effective June 22, 1995.

(3.3) Date of late election, amended election or revocation — Where, under subsection (3.2), the Minister has extended the time for making an election or granted permission to amend or revoke an election,

(a) the election or the amended election, as the case may be, shall be deemed to have been made on the day on or before which the election was otherwise required to be made and in the manner in which the election was otherwise required to be made, and, in the case of an amendment to an election, that election shall be deemed, otherwise than for the purposes of this section, never to have been made; and

(b) the election that was revoked shall be deemed, otherwise than for the purposes of this section, never to have been made.

Related Provisions: 220(3.4) — Assessment to take late filing into account.

Notes: 220(3.3) added by 1991 technical bill, effective for elections in respect of 1985 and later years.

(3.4) Assessments — Notwithstanding subsections 152(4), (4.01), (4.1) and (5), such assessment of the tax, interest and penalties payable by each taxpayer in respect of any taxation year that began before the day an application is made under subsection (3.2) to the Minister shall be made as is necessary to take into account the election, the amended election or the revocation, as the case may be, referred to in subsection (3.3).

Related Provisions: 164(1.5) — Refunds; 164(3.2) — Interest on refunds and repayments; 165(1.1) — Limitation of right to object to assessment or determination; 169(2)(a) — Limitation of right to appeal.

Notes: 220(3.4) added by 1991 technical bill, effective for elections in respect of 1985 and later years; and amended retroactive to its introduction by 1995-97 technical bill.

(3.5) Penalty for late filed, amended or revoked elections — Where, on application by a taxpayer or a partnership, the Minister extends the time for making an election or grants permission to amend or revoke an election (other than an extension or permission under subsection (3.201)), the taxpayer or the partnership, as the case may be, is liable to a penalty equal to the lesser of

(a) $8,000, and

(b) the product obtained when $100 is multiplied by the number of complete months from the day on or before which the election was required to be made to the day the application was made in a form satisfactory to the Minister.

Related Provisions: 220(3.6) — Assessment of penalty.

Notes: 220(3.5) amended by 2007 budget bill #2, for 2007 and later tax years, to exclude 220(3.201): late elections for pension splitting are not subject to a penalty.

220(3.5) added by 1991 technical bill, for elections in respect of 1985 and later years.

CRA Audit Manual: 28.6.3: Fairness provisions — late, amended or revoked elections.

(3.6) Unpaid balance of penalty — The Minister shall, with all due dispatch, examine each election, amended election and revoked election referred to in subsection (3.3), assess any penalty payable and send a notice of assessment to the taxpayer or the partnership, as the case may be, and the taxpayer or the partnership, as the case may be, shall pay forthwith to the Receiver General the amount, if any, by which the penalty so assessed exceeds the total of all amounts previously paid on account of that penalty.

Related Provisions: 161(11)(c) — Interest on penalties.

Notes: 220(3.6) added by 1991 technical bill, for elections in respect of 1985 and later years.

(3.7) Idem — The provisions of Divisions I and J of Part I apply, with such modifications as the circumstances require, to an assess-

ment made under this section as though it had been made under section 152.

Notes: 220(3.7) added by 1991 technical bill, for elections in respect of 1985 and later years.

(3.8) Dishonoured instruments — For the purposes of this Act and section 155.1 of the *Financial Administration Act*

(a) any charge that becomes payable at any time by a person under the *Financial Administration Act* in respect of an instrument tendered in payment or settlement of an amount that is payable or remittable under this Act is deemed to be an amount that becomes payable or remittable by the person at that time under this Act;

(b) sections 152, 158 and 159, subsections 161(1), (2) and (11), sections 162 to 167 and Division J of this Part are applicable to the amount deemed to become payable or remittable by this subsection with any modifications that the circumstances require;

(c) Part II of the *Interest and Administrative Charges Regulations* does not apply to the charge; and

(d) any debt under subsection 155.1(3) of the *Financial Administration Act* in respect of the charge is deemed to be extinguished at the time the total of the amount and any applicable interest under this Act is paid.

Notes: 220(3.8) makes the administrative charge for NSF cheques part of the tax debt. *Financial Administration Act* s. 155.1(2) makes this charge payable if, in making a payment due to Her Majesty, a person "tenders an instrument that is subsequently dishonoured", or "has authorized the direct debiting at a specified time of an account at a financial institution and the debit is not made at the specified time". *Interest and Administrative Charges Regulations* s. 10 sets the charge at $15, plus $10 for payment by the Crown to the financial institution, plus whatever the institution charges. However, s. 10 is in Part II of the Regulations, which 220(3.8)(c) says does not apply, so arguably there are no regulations setting the charge for 220(3.8)!

220(3.8) added by 2006 Budget first bill, for instruments dishonoured after March 2007.

(4) Security — The Minister may, if the Minister considers it advisable in a particular case, accept security for payment of any amount that is or may become payable under this Act.

Related Provisions: 222(8)(b) — Extension of 10-year limitation period on collection action while security held; 222.1 — Application to awards of court costs.

Notes: Note that interest continues to run when security has been posted to stop collection action.

CRA uses 220(4) to accept security for tax on a gain to be eliminated by acquiring replacement property under 44(1): Income Tax Folio S3-F3-C1 ¶1.16, VIEWS doc 2008-0283901I7.

See also Clifford Rand, "Managing the Minister's Collection Powers on Behalf of Large Corporations", 2014 Cdn Tax Foundation conference report, 28:1-12, on posting security to prevent collection action.

Regulations: 2200 (Minister may discharge security).

(4.1) Idem — Where a taxpayer has objected to or appealed from an assessment under this Act, the Minister shall, while the objection or appeal is outstanding, accept adequate security furnished by or on behalf of the taxpayer for payment of the amount in controversy except to the extent that the Minister may collect the amount because of subsection 225.1(7).

Related Provisions: 222(8)(b) — Extension of 10-year limitation period on collection action while security held.

Notes: A CRA refusal to accept a particular security can be challenged via judicial review in the Federal Court (see Notes to 220(3.1)).

220(4.1) amended by 1992 technical bill, effective June 10, 1993.

(4.2) Surrender of excess security — Where at any time a taxpayer requests in writing that the Minister surrender any security accepted by the Minister under subsection (4) or (4.1), the Minister shall surrender the security to the extent that the value of the security exceeds the total of amounts payable under this Act by the taxpayer at that time.

Related Provisions: 222.1 — Application to awards of court costs.

(4.3) Security furnished by a member institution of a deposit insurance corporation — The Minister shall accept adequate security furnished by or on behalf of a taxpayer that is a member institution in relation to a deposit insurance corporation (within the meaning assigned by subsection 137.1(5)) for payment of

(a) the tax payable under this Act by the taxpayer for a taxation year, to the extent that the amount of that tax exceeds the amount that that tax would be if no amount that the taxpayer is obliged to repay to the corporation were included under paragraph 137.1(10)(a) or (b) in computing the taxpayer's income for the year or a preceding taxation year, and

(b) interest payable under this Act by the taxpayer on the amount determined under paragraph (a),

until the earlier of

(c) the day on which the taxpayer's obligation referred to in paragraph (a) to repay the amount to the corporation is settled or extinguished, and

(d) the day that is 10 years after the end of the year.

Notes: 220(4.3)(a) amended by 1991 technical bill, effective July 14, 1990, to add the words "or a preceding taxation year" at the end.

(4.4) Additional security — The adequacy of security furnished by or on behalf of a taxpayer under subsection (4.3) shall be determined by the Minister and the Minister may require additional security to be furnished from time to time by or on behalf of the taxpayer where the Minister determines that the security that has been furnished is no longer adequate.

(4.5) Security for departure tax — If an individual who is deemed by subsection 128.1(4) to have disposed of a property (other than a right to a benefit under, or an interest in a trust governed by, an employee benefit plan) at any particular time in a taxation year (in this section referred to as the individual's "emigration year") elects, in prescribed manner on or before the individual's balance-due day for the emigration year, that this subsection and subsections (4.51) to (4.54) apply in respect of the emigration year,

(a) the Minister shall, until the individual's balance-due day for a particular taxation year that begins after the particular time, accept adequate security furnished by or on behalf of the individual on or before the individual's balance-due day for the emigration year for the lesser of

(i) the amount determined by the formula

$$A - B - [((A - B)/A) \times C]$$

where

A   is the total amount of taxes under Parts I and I.1 that would be payable by the individual for the emigration year if the exclusion or deduction of each amount referred to in paragraph 161(7)(a) were not taken into account,

B   is the total amount of taxes under those Parts that would have been so payable if each property (other than a right to a benefit under, or an interest in a trust governed by, an employee benefit plan) deemed by subsection 128.1(4) to have been disposed of at the particular time, and that has not been subsequently disposed of before the beginning of the particular year, were not deemed by subsection 128.1(4) to have been disposed of by the individual at the particular time, and

C   is the total of all amounts deemed under this or any other Act to have been paid on account of the individual's tax under this Part for the emigration year, and

(ii) if the particular year immediately follows the emigration year, the amount determined under subparagraph (i), and in any other case, the amount determined under this paragraph in respect of the individual for the taxation year that immediately precedes the particular year; and

(b) except for the purposes of subsections 161(2), (4) and (4.01),

(i) interest under this Act for any period that ends on the individual's balance-due day for the particular year and throughout which security is accepted by the Minister, and

(ii) any penalty under this Act computed with reference to an individual's tax payable for the year that was, without reference to this paragraph, unpaid

shall be computed as if the particular amount for which adequate security has been accepted under this subsection were an amount paid by the individual on account of the particular amount.

Related Provisions: 128.1(6) — Tax cancelled if emigrant returns to Canada; 128.3 — Shares acquired on rollover deemed same shares for 220(4.5); 152(10) — Posted security deemed not to be tax assessed for purposes of administration of provincial tax; 220(4.51) — Exemption for first $25,000 of security; 220(4.52) — Security effective only for departure tax; 220(4.53) — Where security proves inadequate; 220(4.54) — Extension of time for making election; 220(4.7) — Reduction in security for undue hardship; 257 — Formula cannot calculate to less than zero.

Notes: 220(4.5)-(4.54) permit an individual to elect, on giving security acceptable to CRA, to defer payment of departure tax under 128.1(4)(b). Interest, and any penalty calculated by reference to the unpaid tax, do not run on the amount secured.

For CRA interpretation see VIEWS docs 2006-0215891E5, 2008-0299841E5, 2012-0454231C6; 2015-0608051E5 (election can be made by a trust).

220(4.5) added by 2001 technical bill, for dispositions and distributions after Oct. 1, 1996.

This was 220.1(1) in the draft legislation (migration) of Dec. 23/98.

Forms: T1244: Election, under subsec. 220(4.5) of the *ITA*, to defer the payment of tax on income re deemed disposition of property.

(4.51) Deemed security — If an individual (other than a trust) elects under subsection (4.5) that that subsection apply in respect of a taxation year, for the purposes of this subsection and subsections (4.5) and (4.52) to (4.54), the Minister is deemed to have accepted at any time after the election is made adequate security for a total amount of taxes payable under Parts I and I.1 by the individual for the emigration year equal to the lesser of

(a) the total amount of those taxes that would be payable for the year by a trust resident in Canada (other than a graduated rate estate or a qualified disability trust as defined in subsection 122(3)) the taxable income of which for the year is $50,000, and

(b) the greatest amount for which the Minister is required to accept security furnished by or on behalf of the individual under subsection (4.5) at that time in respect of the emigration year,

and that security is deemed to have been furnished by the individual before the individual's balance-due day for the emigration year.

Notes: This is a convoluted way of saying that security need not be provided for the first $16,500 of federal tax (top federal rate of 33% on up to $50,000 of income, or $100,000 of capital gain). See VIEWS doc 2014-0561391I7. This relief is not available for a trust, due to the opening words of (4.51): 2015-0608051E5.

220(4.51)(a) amended by 2014 budget bill #2, for 2016 and later tax years, to change "an *inter vivos*" trust" to "a trust" and "a trust described in subsection 122(2)" to "a graduated rate estate or a qualified disability trust as defined in subsection 122(3)".

220(4.51) added by 2001 technical bill, last change effective for emigration after 2000.

This was 220.1(2) in the draft legislation (migration) of Dec. 23, 1998.

(4.52) Limit — Notwithstanding subsections (4.5) and (4.51), the Minister is deemed at any time not to have accepted security under subsection (4.5) in respect of an individual's emigration year for any amount greater than the amount, if any, by which

(a) the total amount of taxes that would be payable by the individual under Parts I and I.1 for the year if the exclusion or deduction of each amount referred to in paragraph 161(7)(a), in respect of which the day determined under paragraph 161(7)(b) is after that time, were not taken into account

exceeds

(b) the total amount of taxes that would be determined under paragraph (a) if this Act were read without reference to subsection 128.1(4).

Notes: This is a convoluted way of saying that the security is effective only with respect to the departure tax under 128.1(4).

220(4.52) added by 2001 technical bill, for dispositions and distributions after Oct. 1, 1996. It was 220.1(3) in the draft legislation (migration) of Dec. 23, 1998.

(4.53) Inadequate security — Subject to subsection (4.7), if it is determined at any particular time that security accepted by the Minister under subsection (4.5) is not adequate to secure the particular amount for which it was furnished by or on behalf of an individual,

(a) subject to a subsequent application of this subsection, the security shall be considered after the particular time to secure only the amount for which it is adequate security at the particular time;

(b) the Minister shall notify the individual in writing of the determination and shall accept adequate security, for all or any part of the particular amount, furnished by or on behalf of the individual within 90 days after the day of notification; and

(c) any security accepted in accordance with paragraph (b) is deemed to have been accepted by the Minister under subsection (4.5) on account of the particular amount at the particular time.

Related Provisions: 220(4.54)(c) — Extension of 90-day period under (4.53)(b); *Interpretation Act* 27(5) — Meaning of "within 90 days".

Notes: 220(4.53) added by 2001 technical bill, for dispositions and distributions after Oct. 1, 1996. It was 220.1(4) in the draft legislation (migration) of Dec. 23, 1998.

(4.54) Extension of time

(4.54) Extension of time — If in the opinion of the Minister it would be just and equitable to do so, the Minister may at any time extend

(a) the time for making an election under subsection (4.5);

(b) the time for furnishing and accepting security under subsection (4.5); or

(c) the 90-day period for the acceptance of security under paragraph (4.53)(b).

Notes: For the meaning of "just and equitable", see Notes to 85(7.1).

220(4.54) added by 2001 technical bill, for dispositions and distributions after Oct. 1, 1996. It was 220.1(5) in the draft legislation (migration) of Dec. 23, 1998.

(4.6) Security for tax on distributions of taxable Canadian property to non-resident beneficiaries

(4.6) Security for tax on distributions of taxable Canadian property to non-resident beneficiaries — Where

(a) solely because of the application of subsection 107(5), paragraphs 107(2)(a) to (c) do not apply to a distribution by a trust in a particular taxation year (in this section referred to as the trust's "distribution year") of taxable Canadian property, and

(b) the trust elects, in prescribed manner on or before the trust's balance-due day for the distribution year, that this subsection and subsections (4.61) to (4.63) apply in respect of the distribution year,

the following rules apply:

(c) the Minister shall, until the trust's balance-due day for a subsequent taxation year, accept adequate security furnished by or on behalf of the trust on or before the trust's balance-due day for the distribution year for the lesser of

(i) the amount determined by the formula

$$A - B - [((A - B)/A) \times C]$$

where

A   is the total amount of taxes under Parts I and I.1 that would be payable by the trust for the distribution year if the exclusion or deduction of each amount referred to in paragraph 161(7)(a) were not taken into account,

B   is the total amount of taxes under those Parts that would have been so payable if the rules in subsection 107(2) (other than the election referred to in that subsection) had applied to each disposition by the trust in the distribution year of property (other than property subsequently disposed of before the beginning of the subsequent year) to which paragraph (a) applies, and

C   is the total of all amounts deemed under this or any other Act to have been paid on account of the trust's tax under this Part for the distribution year, and

(ii) where the subsequent year immediately follows the distribution year, the amount determined under subparagraph (i), and in any other case, the amount determined under this paragraph in respect of the trust for the taxation year that immediately precedes the subsequent year, and

(d) except for the purposes of subsections 161(2), (4) and (4.01),

(i) interest under this Act for any period ending on the trust's balance-due day for the subsequent year and throughout which security is accepted by the Minister, and

(ii) any penalty under this Act computed with reference to the trust's tax payable for the year that was, without reference to this paragraph, unpaid

shall be computed as if the particular amount for which adequate security has been accepted under this subsection were an amount paid by the trust on account of the particular amount.

Related Provisions: 128.3 — Shares acquired on rollover deemed to be same shares for 220(4.6); 152(10) — Posted security deemed not to be tax assessed for purposes of administration of provincial tax; 220(4.61) — Security effective only for tax caused by 107(5); 220(4.62) — Where security proves inadequate; 220(4.63) — Extension of time for making election; 220(4.7) — Reduction in security for undue hardship; 257 — Formula cannot calculate to less than zero.

Notes: 220(4.6)–(4.63) are parallel to 220(4.5)–(4.54) (see Notes to 220(4.5)), but apply to a trust to defer payment of tax that it owes as a result of the distribution of a taxable Canadian property to a non-resident beneficiary.

220(4.6) added by 2001 technical bill, effective for dispositions and distributions after Oct. 1, 1996, except that if a distribution by a trust occurred to which 220(4.6)(a) applies in respect of the trust before June 14, 2001, an election was made on time, or security furnished on time, if it was done by the filing-due date for the taxation year that included June 14, 2001.

This was 220.2(1) in the draft legislation (migration) of Dec. 23, 1998.

(4.61) Limit

(4.61) Limit — Notwithstanding subsection (4.6), the Minister is deemed at any time not to have accepted security under that subsection in respect of a trust's distribution year for any amount greater than the amount, if any, by which

(a) the total amount of taxes that would be payable by the trust under Parts I and I.1 for the year if the exclusion or deduction of each amount referred to in paragraph 161(7)(a), in respect of which the day determined under paragraph 161(7)(b) is after that time, were not taken into account

exceeds

(b) the total amount of taxes that would be determined under paragraph (a) if paragraphs 107(2)(a) to (c) had applied to each distribution by the trust in the year of property to which paragraph (1)(a) applies.

Notes: 220(4.61) added by 2001 technical bill, for dispositions and distributions after Oct. 1, 1996. It was 220.2(2) in the draft legislation (migration) of Dec. 23, 1998.

(4.62) Inadequate security

(4.62) Inadequate security — Subject to subsection (4.7), where it is determined at any particular time that security accepted by the Minister under subsection (4.6) is not adequate to secure the particular amount for which it was furnished by or on behalf of a trust,

(a) subject to a subsequent application of this subsection, the security shall be considered after the particular time to secure only the amount for which it is adequate security at the particular time;

(b) the Minister shall notify the trust in writing of the determination and shall accept adequate security, for all or any part of the particular amount, furnished by or on behalf of the trust within 90 days after the notification; and

(c) any security accepted in accordance with paragraph (b) is deemed to have been accepted by the Minister under subsection (4.6) on account of the particular amount at the particular time.

Related Provisions: *Interpretation Act* 27(5) — Meaning of "within 90 days".

Notes: 220(4.62) added by 2001 technical bill, for dispositions and distributions after Oct. 1, 1996. It was 220.2(3) in the draft legislation (migration) of Dec. 23, 1998.

(4.63) Extension of time

(4.63) Extension of time — Where in the opinion of the Minister it would be just and equitable to do so, the Minister may at any time extend

(a) the time for making an election under subsection (4.6);

(b) the time for furnishing and accepting security under subsection (4.6); or

(c) the 90-day period for the acceptance of the security under paragraph (4.62)(b).

Notes: For the meaning of "just and equitable", see Notes to 85(7.1).

220(4.63) added by 2001 technical bill, effective for dispositions and distributions after Oct. 1, 1996. It was 220.2(4) in the draft legislation (migration) of Dec. 23/98.

(4.7) Undue hardship — If, in respect of any period of time, the Minister determines that an individual who has made an election under either of subsection (4.5) or (4.6)

> (a) cannot, without undue hardship, pay or reasonably arrange to have paid on the individual's behalf, an amount of taxes to which security under that subsection would relate, and

> (b) cannot, without undue hardship, provide or reasonably arrange to have provided on the individual's behalf, adequate security under that subsection,

the Minister may, in respect of the election, accept for the period security different from, or of lesser value than, that which the Minister would otherwise accept under that subsection.

Related Provisions: 220(4.71) — Transactions entered into to create hardship to be ignored.

Notes: The term "undue hardship" is interpreted very liberally for purposes of 153(1.1). It may be interpreted more strictly for 220(4.7).

220(4.7) added by 2001 technical bill, effective for dispositions and distributions after Oct. 1, 1996.

(4.71) Limit — In making a determination under subsection (4.7), the Minister shall ignore any transaction that is a disposition, lease, encumbrance, mortgage, hypothec, or other voluntary restriction by a person or partnership of the person's or partnership's rights in respect of a property, if the transaction can reasonably be considered to have been entered into for the purpose of influencing the determination.

Notes: 220(4.71) added by 2001 technical bill, effective for dispositions and distributions after Oct. 1, 1996.

(5) Administration of oaths — Any officer or servant employed in connection with the administration or enforcement of this Act, if designated by the Minister for the purpose, may, in the course of that employment, administer oaths and take and receive affidavits, declarations and affirmations for the purposes of or incidental to the administration or enforcement of this Act or regulations made thereunder, and every officer or servant so designated has for those purposes all the powers of a commissioner for administering oaths or taking affidavits.

Related Provisions: *Interpretation Act* 19 — Administration of oaths.

(6) Assignment by corporation — Notwithstanding section 67 of the *Financial Administration Act* and any other provision of a law of Canada or a province, a corporation may assign any amount payable to it under this Act.

Related Provisions: 220(7) — Assignment not binding on federal government.

Notes: In *Marzetti v. Marzetti*, [1994] 2 S.C.R. 765, the Supreme Court of Canada ruled that an income tax refund could not be assigned, due to s. 67 of the *Financial Administration Act* (FAA). Similarly, in *Profitt v. Wasserman*, 2002 CanLII 44914 (ONCA), and *Bief des Seigneurs c. Fortin*, 1996 CarswellQue 321 (Que. CA), a federal sales tax refund or rebate could not be assigned under a security agreement. (However, a direction by X to CRA to pay a refund to X's lawyer in trust does not violate s. 67, because this is still for X's benefit: *1074022 B.C. v. Li*, 2020 BCSC 65, para. 15.) See also VIEWS doc 2008-0282481E5. 220(6) gets around this prohibition for corporations, if CRA consents (see 220(7)). Since the assignment is not binding on CRA, it is only effective to the extent allowed by CRA administrative discretion (see doc 2009-0322511M6). It was introduced to permit assignments of film tax credits under 125.4 and R&D investment tax credits under 127(5). In *Grant Forest Products*, 2010 ONCA 355, GFP breached its agreement to transfer its tax refunds to G, and the Court awarded G ownership in the refunds without mentioning 220(7); the problem of unenforceability as against the Crown was solved by requiring GFP to hold the refund in trust for G. CRA was not aware of the arrangement and paid the refund to GFP.

In *Freeport Financial v. PRACS*, 2016 ONSC 5026, 220(6) justified the assignment of a loss carry-back refund.

See also the *Assignment of Crown Debt Regulations* (CanLII.org, or *Practitioner's Goods and Services Tax Annotated*), permitting certain federal government debts to be assigned.

Tax rebate discounting: The *Tax Rebate Discounting Act* permits assignment of personal income tax refunds to tax return preparers, who charge a fee for paying the refund up-front on filing (CRA Guide T4163, Form RC76). For the 2018 filing season, there were 2,509 "active discounting locations" [up from 2,342 for 2010], and CRA processed 639,107 discounted returns [down from 1,068,395 for 2010] and paid out $1.04 billion in refunds to discounters [down from $1.18b]. (*Access to Information Act* disclosure) See also CRA news release "Tax preparer fined for overcharging discounted tax returns" (July 19, 2011) (Yasmena Hamid and ACCTAX Services pled guilty to 50 counts of overcharging clients on discounted returns); *Ashton*, 2012 TCC 353, para. 7 (discounting is "fraught with risk of false T4s and identity theft").

220(6)-(7) added by 1996 Budget, for assignments made after March 5, 1996.

Forms: RC71: Statement of discounting transaction; RC72: Notice of the actual amount of the refund of tax; RC76: Application and agreement to obtain a discounter code/discounter direct deposit enrolment; T4163: Guide for discounters.

(7) Effect of assignment — An assignment referred to in subsection (6) is not binding on Her Majesty in right of Canada and, without limiting the generality of the foregoing,

> (a) the Minister is not required to pay to the assignee the assigned amount;

> (b) the assignment does not create any liability of Her Majesty in right of Canada to the assignee; and

> (c) the rights of the assignee are subject to all equitable and statutory rights of set-off in favour of Her Majesty in right of Canada.

Notes: See Notes to 220(6).

Definitions [s. 220]: "amount", "assessment", "balance-due day" — 248(1); "calendar year" — *Interpretation Act* 37(1)(a); "Commissioner of Revenue" — *Canada Revenue Agency Act* s. 25; "corporation" — 248(1), *Interpretation Act* 35(1); "deposit insurance corporation" — 137.1(5); "disposition" — 248(1); "distribution year" — 220(4.6)(a); "emigration year" — 220(4.5); "employed", "employee benefit plan", "employment", "filing-due date" — 248(1); "fiscal period" — 249.1; "graduated rate estate" — 248(1); "Her Majesty" — *Interpretation Act* 35(1); "individual", "insurance corporation" — 248(1); "*inter vivos* trust" — 108(1), 248(1); "Minister", "non-resident" — 248(1); "oath" — *Interpretation Act* 35(1); "officer" — 248(1)"office"; "partnership" — see 96(1) Notes; "person", "prescribed", "property" — 248(1); "province" — *Interpretation Act* 35(1); "qualified disability trust" — 122(3); "regulation" — 248(1); "resident in Canada" — 250; "security" — *Interpretation Act* 35(1); "servant" — 248(1)"employment"; "tax payable" — 248(2); "taxable Canadian property", "taxable income" — 248(1); "taxation year" — 249; "taxpayer" — 248(1); "trust" — 104(1), 248(1), (3); "undue hardship" — 220(4.71); "writing" — *Interpretation Act* 35(1).

221. (1) Regulations — The Governor in Council may make regulations

> (a) prescribing anything that, by this Act, is to be prescribed or is to be determined or regulated by regulation;

> (b) prescribing the evidence required to establish facts relevant to assessments under this Act;

> (c) to facilitate the assessment of tax where deductions or exemptions of a taxpayer have changed in a taxation year;

> (d) requiring any class of persons to make information returns respecting any class of information required in connection with assessments under this Act;

> (d.1) requiring any person or partnership to provide any information — including their name, address, business number, Social Insurance Number or trust account number — to any class of persons required to make an information return containing that information;

> (d.2) requiring any class of persons to make information available to the public for the purpose of making information returns respecting any class of information required in connection with assessments under this Act;

> (e) requiring a person who is, by a regulation made under paragraph (d), required to make an information return to supply a copy of the information return or of a prescribed part thereof to the person to whom the information return or part thereof relates;

> (f) [Repealed]

> (g) providing for the retention by way of deduction or set-off of the amount of a taxpayer's income tax or other indebtedness under this Act out of any amount or amounts that may be or become payable by Her Majesty to the taxpayer in respect of salary or wages;

(h) defining the classes of persons who may be regarded as dependent for the purposes of this Act;

(i) defining the classes of non-resident persons who may be regarded for the purposes of this Act

(i) as a spouse or common-law partner supported by a taxpayer, or

(ii) as a person dependent or wholly dependent on a taxpayer for support,

and specifying the evidence required to establish that a person belongs to any such class; and

(j) generally to carry out the purposes and provisions of this Act.

Related Provisions: 65(2) — Regulations permitting resource allowances; 147.1(18) — Authority for regulations re registered pension plans; 214(13), 215(4), (5) — Regulations re non-resident withholding tax; 221(2) — Effect of regulations; 221(3) — Regulations binding Crown; 233 — Demands for information returns; 244(12) — Judicial notice to be taken of regulations; *Interpretation Act* 31(4) — Power to repeal, amend or vary regulations.

Notes: Regulations are theoretically easier to pass (by Cabinet) than legislation (by Parliament), but since Budget bills are passed twice-yearly and do not require the same paperwork justifying regulations, legislation is often easier, and tax bills now often amend the regulations directly. See Xiao Jin Chen, "Regulations: An Outmoded Idea?", 3(3) *Canadian Tax Focus* (ctf.ca) 3 (Aug. 2013).

221(1)(d.1) amended by 2018 budget bill #1 to add reference to a trust account number, for 2018 and later tax years.

221(1)(d.2) added by 2007 budget bill #2, effective for information in respect of taxpayers' taxation years and partnerships' fiscal periods that end after July 3, 2007.

221(1)(f), repealed in 1998, allowed regulations (former Reg. 900) authorizing designated officers to exercise the Minister's powers or duties. 220(2.01) now authorizes delegation without regulations.

221(1) earlier amended by 2000 same-sex partners bill and 1995-97 technical bill.

Regulations: Parts I–XCIV and Schedules I to VIII. For regulations under paras. 221(1)(d), (e), see Part II; under para. (g), see Part XXV; 204.1, 229.1 (required disclosure for 221(1)(d.2) by publicly traded trusts and partnerships).

Information Circulars: 82-2R2: SIN legislation that relates to the preparation of information slips.

(2) Effect — A regulation made under this Act shall have effect from the date it is published in the *Canada Gazette* or at such time thereafter as may be specified in the regulation unless the regulation provides otherwise and it

(a) has a relieving effect only;

(b) corrects an ambiguous or deficient enactment that was not in accordance with the objects of this Act or the *Income Tax Regulations*;

(c) is consequential on an amendment to this Act that is applicable before the date the regulation is published in the *Canada Gazette*; or

(d) gives effect to a budgetary or other public announcement, in which case the regulation shall not, except where paragraph (a), (b) or (c) applies, have effect

(i) before the date on which the announcement was made, in the case of a deduction or withholding from an amount paid or credited, and

(ii) before the taxation year in which the announcement is made, in any other case.

(3) Regulations binding Crown — Regulations made under paragraph (1)(d) or (e) are binding on Her Majesty in right of Canada or a province.

Notes: 221(3) added by 1991 technical bill, effective 1991.

(4) Incorporation by reference — A regulation made under this Act may incorporate by reference material as amended from time to time.

Notes: 221(4) added by 1995-97 technical bill, effective since June 18, 1998 for any regulation, even if it was made before that date. It allows regulations to give legal effect to documents not included directly in the Regulations but that are incorporated as amended from time to time.

Definitions [s. 221]: "amount", "assessment", "business number", "common-law partner" — 248(1); "Governor in Council", "Her Majesty" — *Interpretation Act* 35(1); "Minister", "non-resident" — 248(1); "partnership" — see 96(1) Notes; "person",

"prescribed" — 248(1); "province" — *Interpretation Act* 35(1); "regulation", "salary or wages" — 248(1); "taxation year" — 249; "taxpayer", "trust account number" — 248(1).

221.01 Providing information returns in electronic format — A person may provide an information return electronically under subsection 209(5) of the *Income Tax Regulations* if the criteria specified by the Minister are met.

Notes: 221.01 added by 2017 budget bill #1, effective 2018. It authorizes electronic provision of T4s and similar slips. See Notes to Reg. 209(5).

Definitions [s. 221.01]: "Minister", "person" — 248(1).

221.1 Application of interest — For greater certainty, where an amendment to this Act or an amendment or enactment that relates to this Act applies to or in respect of any transaction, event or time, or any taxation year, fiscal period or other period of time or part thereof (in this section referred to as the "application time") occurring, or that is, before the day on which the amendment or enactment is assented to or promulgated, for the purposes of the provisions of this Act that provide for payment of, or liability to, any interest, the amendment or enactment shall, unless a contrary intention is evident, be deemed to have come into force at the beginning of the last taxation year beginning before the application time.

Notes: 221.1 added by 1991 technical bill, effective 1990. It allows interest to be assessed where legislation is retroactive.

Definitions [s. 221.1]: "application time" — 221.1; "fiscal period" — 249(2)(b), 249.1; "taxation year" — 11(2), 249.

CRA Audit Manual: 12.3.0: Application of proposed legislative amendments.

221.2 (1) Re-appropriation of amounts — Where a particular amount was appropriated to an amount (in this section referred to as the "debt") that is or may become payable by a person under any enactment referred to in paragraphs 223(1)(a) to (d), the Minister may, on application by the person, appropriate the particular amount, or a part thereof, to another amount that is or may become payable under any such enactment and, for the purposes of any such enactment,

(a) the later appropriation shall be deemed to have been made at the time of the earlier appropriation;

(b) the earlier appropriation shall be deemed not to have been made to the extent of the later appropriation; and

(c) the particular amount shall be deemed not to have been paid on account of the debt to the extent of the later appropriation.

(2) Re-appropriation of amounts — Where a particular amount was appropriated to an amount (in this section referred to as the "debt") that is or may become payable by a person under this Act, the *Excise Tax Act*, the *Air Travellers Security Charge Act* or the *Excise Act, 2001*, the Minister may, on application by the person, appropriate the particular amount, or a part of it, to another amount that is or may become payable under any of those Acts and, for the purposes of any of those Acts,

(a) the later appropriation is deemed to have been made at the time of the earlier appropriation;

(b) the earlier appropriation is deemed not to have been made to the extent of the later appropriation; and

(c) the particular amount is deemed not to have been paid on account of the debt to the extent of the later appropriation.

Related Provisions: 161.1 — Offsetting of refund interest and arrears interest.

Notes [s. 221.2]: 221.2(1) allows CRA to transfer amounts between different tax accounts, such as instalments, arrears of tax owing, and employer remittances (payroll deductions), including amounts for CPP, EI and provincial tax withholdings. (221.2(2) allows transfers to GST and other accounts as well.) Where an amount is so transferred at the taxpayer's request, it is treated as though it had never been paid on account of the first account, and had initially been a payment on the second. Thus, interest that would otherwise accumulate on a deficient account can be reduced or eliminated by using a surplus balance from another account.

CRA often misallocates payments: see Taxpayers' Ombudsman special report, *Getting it Right* (July 2012), oto-boc.gc.ca.

221.2 could not apply to offset Part I refund interest against Part XIII tax interest where the taxpayer had not made a "payment" that could be moved: VIEWS doc 2008-029403117. Where a payor over-withheld Part XIII tax so a non-resident has overpaid, and it is too late to claim a 227(6) refund, 221.2 can move the refund to another year, but since nothing relieves a payor from withholding in future, it is only useful against Part I tax: 2012-0463421E5. Similarly for 227(6.1): 2013-0482991E5.

Allocation of a payment when made: A general principle of contract law, applicable to CRA, is that a debtor has the right to specify the account to be credited when making a payment. See: *Agricultural Insurance v. Sargeant* (1896), 26 S.C.R. 29; *Andrew Paving*, 1984 CarswellNat 303 (TCC); *Polish Combattants' Association v. Moge*, 1984 CanLII 3013 (Man. CA); *Frankel*, [1984] C.T.C. 259 (FCTD). CRA accepts this rule: *Danada Enterprises*, 2012 FC 403, paras. 38-39. Even without 221.2, a taxpayer can ask that an overpayment be transferred to another year, and CRA must honour the request: *Koenig*, [1997] 2 C.T.C. 3077 (TCC), para. 13. However, if the debtor (taxpayer) does not specify what debt is being paid at time of payment, the right of application moves to the creditor (CRA): *Waisman v. Crown Trust*, [1970] S.C.R. 553 at 560; *Fuerth*, 2007 TCC 588, but this rule does not apply to trust funds under s. 227: *Andrew Paving*, paras. 6-8. (In Quebec, see Art. 1572 of the *Civil Code*, as interpreted in *Yvan Lessard*, 2001 CarswellNat 3802 (TCC).) Thus, if a corp has not filed several returns and CRA issues arbitrary assessments and is enforcing collection, the corp may wish to notify CRA as to how amounts collected should be applied.

Two related companies cannot transfer balances between them (i.e., use one's refund to offset the other's debt); CRA has this policy "to avoid situations where one legal entity is making decisions for another" (CRA-TEI liaison meeting, Dec. 4, 2012, q.16). CRA might allow transfer of a refund balance to another corporation in very unusual circumstances. Sometimes this can be done by a direction from one corporation to CRA to pay its refund to the other. See 220(6), which permits a corporation's refund to be assigned.

221.2(1) provided a way around the 3-year limit on refunds where a corporation's return is filed late (see 164(1)). For years after the author first used this method in 1998 and publicized it here, CRA was willing to apply 221.2 to transfer instalments, provided there was an existing or anticipated tax liability for the year to which a balance was transferred: VIEWS docs 2008-026958117, 2010-0384921E5, 2011-039602117, 2011-041096117. Since 2014, however, Form RC431 (sent to T2 Re-appropriation, Business Returns Division, Winnipeg Tax Centre) requires a Taxpayer-Relief-like explanation (see Notes to 220(3.1)) as to why the taxpayer was "unable" to file the return within the 3 years, and CRA refuses a transfer absent "extraordinary circumstances that prevent the timely filing". This is unfair: the Tax Court described the 3-year limit as a "confiscation of the appellant's property" that was "deplorable" (*Chalifoux*, [1991] 2 C.T.C. 2243). However, CRA on review has confirmed this policy. See also CRA's "Re-appropriations of T2 Statute-barred credits" user guide, on *Taxnet Pro* and *TaxPartner*. The author and CPA Canada made a submission to Finance in Oct. 2015 to request an amendment to 164(1): tinyurl.com/ds-cpa-fin. See also Cepparo, "Accessing Statute-Barred Refunds", 22(9) *Canadian Tax Highlights* (ctf.ca) 1 (Sept. 2014). In *Cybernius Medical*, 2017 FC 226, it was "unreasonable" for CRA not to apply 221.2 when it had taken collection action in violation of 225.1 (para. 47); and also because "It would be counter to the purpose of the ITA" not to apply the refund to a payroll debt "given the importance of source deductions" (para. 53). Similarly, in *Pomeroy's Masonry*, 2017 FC 952, PM did not file for 5 years, was assessed, paid the balance, filed its returns and was owed a refund which it sought to apply to its HST arrears. CRA's refusal to apply 221.2 was held unreasonable as not considering all the factors PM had raised. Application of a refund to pay tax debts is an important factor to take into account (para. 25), as is hardship (the HST debt might put PM into bankruptcy). CRA later allowed the re-appropriation. In light of *Cybernius* and *Pomeroy's*, CRA stated at the 2017 Cdn Tax Foundation annual conference that it will review the RC431 criteria. Similarly, in *Referred Realty*, 2018 FC 59, CRA failed to consider RR's efforts to comply, and rejected the request due to non-compliance over many years; the decision was found unreasonable and was sent back. (As well, CRA referred to RR's late GST filings without allowing RR to respond to this point: para. 10.) Similarly, in *Forbes Painting*, 2019 FC 160, CRA's decision was unreasonable because it did not consider FP's financial hardship, and was sent back.

In *Clover International*, 2013 FC 676, the Court agreed with CRA that the transfer can be made only to the extent the transfer-to year has a balance owing. 221.2 cannot be used to transfer a 129(1) dividend refund to another year if the return was filed late: see Notes to 129(1).

In *Bakorp Management*, 2016 FCA 74, an overpayment of Part IV tax for 1995 could not be used to offset an underpayment for 1993, absent a 221.2 re-appropriation, until 2000 when CRA assessed and applied it. (The provision charging interest, 187(2), did not refer as 161(1) does to amounts the Minister "applied" to other years.)

In *Emcon Services*, 2008 TCC 501, a corporation could not challenge interest charges caused by delay in CRA applying its prior-year refund to its instalment account, as forcing CRA to apply 221.2 was outside the TCC's jurisdiction.

See also the inexplicable decision in *Forest Oil*, 1998 CarswellNat 3526 (FCA), reversing *on consent* a FCTD decision ordering a $400,000 refund for an overpayment under the *Petroleum and Gas Revenue Tax Act*. However, a consent judgment has no precedential value: *Uppal*, [1987] 3 F.C. 565 (FCA), para. 18; *Markou*, 2019 FCA 299 (leave to appeal denied 2020 CarswellNat 1486), para. 61 ("it is hazardous to draw any inference"); *Collins*, [2001] G.S.T.C. 60 (TCC), para. 11; *Brown*, 2012 TCC 452, para. 11; and see discussion in *Surrey City Centre Mall*, 2010 TCC 619, at paras. 46-47. A consent judgment may be binding on the parties by way of issue estoppel: *Rogic*, [2001] G.S.T.C. 107 (TCC) (see Notes to 169(2)).

221.2(2) added by 2006 budget bill #1, for re-appropriation applications made after March 2007. 221.2 added by 1992 technical bill, effective June 10, 1993.

Definitions [s. 221.2]: "amount" — 248(1); "debt" — 221.2(1), (2); "Minister", "person" — 248(1).

Forms: RC431: Request for re-appropriation of T2 statute-barred credits.

Collection

222. (1) Definitions — The following definitions apply in this section.

"action" means an action to collect a tax debt of a taxpayer and includes a proceeding in a court and anything done by the Minister under subsection 129(2), 131(3), 132(2) or 164(2), section 203 or any provision of this Part.

Notes: See Notes to 222(3) re the *Thandi* case.

"tax debt" means any amount payable by a taxpayer under this Act.

Notes [subsec. 222(1)]: 222(1) added by 2004 budget bill #1 (former 222 became 222(2)), effective May 14, 2004.

(2) Debts to Her Majesty — A tax debt is a debt due to Her Majesty and is recoverable as such in the Federal Court or any other court of competent jurisdiction or in any other manner provided by this Act.

Announced Administrative Change — More money for CRA Collections

Federal Budget, Chapter 10, April 19, 2021: *Strengthening the CRA*

The success of the CRA's work in combatting aggressive tax planning, the underground economy, and tax evasion depends on the CRA's ability to collect outstanding taxes in a timely way.

Budget 2021 proposes to provide $230 million over five years, starting in 2021-22, for the CRA to improve its ability to collect outstanding taxes. It is anticipated that this proposal will lead to the collection of an additional $5 billion in outstanding taxes over five years.

Related Provisions: 220(4), (4.1) — CRA may accept security, and must accept security while assessment under objection or appeal; 225.1 — Collection restrictions.

Notes: 222 renumbered as 222(2) and amended by 2004 budget bill #1, effective May 14, 2004.

CRA collection action generally: see IC98-1R7; tinyurl.com/cra-collection; CRA *National Collections Manual* (on *Taxnet Pro* or TaxPartner). See also Taxpayers' Ombudsman, "Fair Warning: an examination into service issues related to legal warnings issued by the CRA during debt collection procedures" (March 2019, re not explaining to taxpayers what "we may take legal action" really means and whether a payment arrangement is binding; it includes detailed explanation of collection procedures). Legal warning before collection action is required by the common law: *R.E. Lister v. Dunlop Canada*, 1982 CanLII 19 (SCC).

For collection from non-residents, see Notes to 223(3). For collection without assessment see Notes to 225.1(6). Where there is a question as to which tax year an amount paid should be allocated to, see Notes to 221.2. Fraudulent conveyance claims: see near end of 160(1) Notes.

Outside Quebec, jointly-owned property (e.g., a bank account or home) cannot be seized for the debt of one owner unless CRA as creditor obtains an order of partition (but execution against the tax debtor can be registered on real property). See *DaimlerChrysler v. Mega Pets*, 2002 BCCA 242; *Wachsmann-Zahler*, 2007 FC 1254; *Duval*, 2012 FC 480. However, see also *Merchant Law*, 2019 ABCA 360 (joint account of related corporations — unresolved). In *White*, 2020 TCC 22, para. 29, the TCC said CRA could garnish a joint account and that a third party had done this; this might be wrong. (Whether a spouse can be assessed under 160(1) for a tax debtor's contributions to a joint account is uncertain: see 160(1) Notes.) CRA's *National Collections Manual* (2015), under "Garnishment — Tax programs", says that AB, SK, MB, ON and NL "allow for garnishment of a joint bank account even when some of the signatories are not indebted to the CRA", *provided* a garnishment order is obtained from the provincial court; and that a Requirement to Pay can be used to garnish a joint bank account in Quebec.

CRA collection action can be challenged in Federal Court, not Tax Court (see Notes to 169(1) under "Jurisdiction", and to 171(1)), and not a provincial superior court: *Mpamugo*, 2017 ONSC 406; *Fazakas*, 2018 NBQB 12. In practice the FC almost never stops collection action: no collateral attack on the assessment is allowed as this is TCC jurisdiction (*Walker*, 2005 FCA 393; *Ritter*, 2013 FC 411; *Mason*, 2015 FC 926 (FCA appeal discontinued A-369-15); *Davis*, 2019 FC 1222 (FCA appeal dismissed for delay A-406-19)). See also *Couverture C.G.L.*, [1995] G.S.T.C. 16 (FCTD); *Omni Cell*, [1995] G.S.T.C. 30 (FCTD); *Thrust Marketing*, 1996 CanLII 3482 (BCSC); *Brant*, [1998] G.S.T.C. 38 and [1998] G.S.T.C. 101 (FCTD); *Nibron Restaurants*, [1999] G.S.T.C. 99 (FCTD); *Canadian Aggregate*, [2001] G.S.T.C. 117 (FCTD); *9099-3262*

Québec, [2002] G.S.T.C. 35 (FCTD); *Vu*, 2005 FC 788; *Lemieux*, [2005] G.S.T.C. 166 (Que. SC); *893134 Ontario [Mega Distributors]*, 2008 FC 715; *Diabo*, 2010 QCCS 6476; *Burkes*, 2011 FC 166; *Danada Enterprises*, 2012 FC 403; *Matsui*, 2014 FC 553 (no basis for injunction); *Associated Mechanical*, 2014 FC 732 (alleged errors in AM's payroll and GST accounts). However, in *Swiftsure Taxi*, 2005 FCA 136, CRA was ordered to leave legally-seized assets in ST's hands pending a judicial review application to determine the amount of tax debt; and in *Duval*, 2012 FC 480, CRA was ordered to repay to D money it took from a joint account for D's spouse's tax debt.

Arguably, in cases of hardship CRA has discretion not to collect a tax debt, based on *Surdivall v. Ontario*, 2014 ONCA 240.

CRA also collects certain non-tax government debts directly. See Notes to 164(2).

For more on CRA collection action see Hamilton et al., "Government Collection of Tax in the Insolvency Context", 2012 *Tax Dispute Resolution* conf. report (ctf.ca), 18:1-31; Chan, "Collection", *Practical Insights, Taxnet Pro* Tax Disputes Centre (Nov. 2020, 35pp); Venton et al., "A Primer on CRA's Collection Powers", tinyurl.com/fogler-collect; CRA, *Payment Tax Gap and Collection Efforts* (Dec. 2020, 42pp).

Information Circulars: 98-1R5: Tax collection policies; 13-2R1: Government programs collection policies; 13-3: Customs collections policies.

I.T. Technical News: 22 (limitation laws on collection actions).

CRA Audit Manual: 10.11.7: Referral of files and information to revenue collections.

(3) No actions after limitation period — The Minister may not commence an action to collect a tax debt after the end of the limitation period for the collection of the tax debt.

Related Provisions: 222(4), (5) — Limitation period; 225.1 — Collection restrictions.

Notes: 222(3) (added by 2004 budget bill #1 effective May 14, 2004) overrules *Markevich*, 2003 SCC 9, which held that collection proceedings on an old tax debt were invalid because of the 6-year limitation period in *Crown Liability and Proceedings Act* s. 32. 222(5) provides that any collection efforts during the limitation period restart the clock. 222(8) provides more ways for the period to be extended. The rule was held valid in *Kennedy*, 2012 FC 1050 and *Glazer*, 2019 FC 436; and is retroactive: see Notes to 222(10). In *Duchaine*, 2015 TCC 245, CRA met the deadline with 12 days to spare. See VIEWS doc 2012-0438471I7 (general discussion).

In *Thandi*, 2017 BCSC 1201, paras. 32-33, the limitation period was restarted when CRA filed an Appearance in foreclosure proceedings, and also when CRA received correspondence from the tax debtor's lawyer, as both of these were 222(1)"action". In *Harrison*, 2020 FC 772, an old debt expired March 4, 2014 as per 222(10), and was not revived by H appealing in 2011 or by reassessment in Dec. 2014.

222(3) does not apply to a s. 160 assessment unless CRA has taken no collection action against the tax debtor for 10 years: *Bourgeois*, 2018 TCC 5 (see Notes to 160(2)).

In *Matthew*, 2017 FC 538, para. 3, CRA withheld "credits and refunds as they may become payable", despite being barred from collection action. This is puzzling, since 222(1)"action" refers to 164(2); perhaps the "credits" were the GST/HST credit refunded under 164(2.1).

For very detailed discussion see Vigeant, "Tax Debt: O Time! Stop Your Flight No More!", *The Harmonization of Federal Legislation with Quebec Civil Law: Second Collection of Studies in Tax Law* (2005, apff.org), 7:1-90. See also Murdoch, "New Limitation Periods Added Post-Markevich", XII(3) *Tax Litigation* (Federated Press) 768-75 (2004).

The extended limitation in s. 222 overrides the provincial limitation period on discharge of a bankruptcy trustee: *Dyrland*, 2008 ABQB 356. It also applies to a certificate registered in the Federal Court for a tax debt, so the certificate can be re-registered if it has lapsed: *Ryckman*, 2010 BCSC 669.

It is argued that 222(3) applies to a year for which no return was filed if the tax was payable on March 4, 2004 (222(4)(a)(ii)), since 152(3) says liability for tax is not affected by the fact no assessment has been issued: MacEachern, "Ten-Year Limitation Period for Tax Debts Arising Prior to 2004", 14(3) *Tax for the Owner-Manager* (ctf.ca) 8-9 (July 2014). CRA disagrees, claiming (doc 2014-0556211E5) that 248(2), defining "tax payable" as tax fixed by assessment, determines "amount payable" in 222(1)"tax debt". (Why "tax payable" should define "amount payable" is not explained, other than to get to the result CRA wants.) 222(4)(a)(i) on its face says that once CRA issues an assessment of the year, a new 10-year period starts running, suggesting CRA may be right; but it can also be argued that "the" limitation period under 222(3) expired on March 4, 2014 and issuing a notice of assessment cannot start a new one (per *Markevich* para. 41 saying the debt has been "extinguished").

CRA can still collect a debt it has "written off", if it is not statute-barred: VIEWS doc 2013-0501521I7.

An order awarding costs to the Crown can apparently be enforced many years later even without 222(3): *Hay*, 2008 FCA 327. However, *Markevich* still applies to non-tax Crown debts: *Simone Sherman*, 2008 TCC 487 (CRA claim against employee for overpaid salary lapsed after 6 years).

Collection efforts (222(5)) restart the clock for s. 222, but not for a private debt, where a debtor does not pay a creditor, the limitation period expires, and CRA assesses the

debtor under 224(4) for not honouring a garnishment notice in respect of the creditor's tax debt: *Browning*, 2010 TCC 487.

Doig, 2012 FCA 28 (leave to appeal denied 2012 CarswellNat 990 (SCC)) refused a declaration that Doig did not have any tax debt for 1971-84, and ruled that the deadline for a taxpayer to bring an application against CRA is 6 years under the *Crown Liability and Proceedings Act*, as 222(3) applies only to CRA collection action. In *Ruh*, 2017 FC 272, the Court refused to rule that R could cash out insurance policies without being subject to 20-year-old garnishment.

The Tax Court has no jurisdiction to address the application of 222(3): *O'Byrne*, 2014 TCC 136 and 249 (aff'd on other grounds 2015 FCA 239); and see Notes to 171(1).

Note that there is no time limit on collecting Ontario tax, even by CRA: Ont. *Limitations Act, 2002*, s. 16(1)(i); *Gibson*, 2005 FCA 180, para. 19.

On whether CRA can collect without issuing an assessment, see Notes to 225.1(6).

(4) Limitation period — The limitation period for the collection of a tax debt of a taxpayer

(a) begins

(i) if a notice of assessment, or a notice referred to in subsection 226(1), in respect of the tax debt is sent to or served on the taxpayer, after March 3, 2004, on the day that is 90 days after the day on which the last one of those notices is sent or served, and

(ii) if subparagraph (i) does not apply and the tax debt was payable on March 4, 2004, or would have been payable on that date but for a limitation period that otherwise applied to the collection of the tax debt, on March 4, 2004; and

(b) ends, subject to subsection (8), on the day that is 10 years after the day on which it begins.

Related Provisions: 222(5) — Restart of limitation period; 222(8) — Extension of limitation period; 244(14), (14.1) — Date when notice sent.

Notes: See Notes to 222(3). 222(4) added by 2004 budget bill #1, effective May 14, 2004, and (a)(i) amended by 2010 budget bill #2, effective Dec. 15, 2010, to change "mailed" to "sent" (2 places), to accommodate electronic notices under 244(14.1).

(5) Limitation period restarted — The limitation period described in subsection (4) for the collection of a tax debt of a taxpayer restarts (and ends, subject to subsection (8), on the day that is 10 years after the day on which it restarts) on any day, before it would otherwise end, on which

(a) the taxpayer acknowledges the tax debt in accordance with subsection (6);

(b) the Minister commences an action to collect the tax debt; or

(c) the Minister, under subsection 159(3) or 160(2) or paragraph 227(10)(a), assesses any person in respect of the tax debt.

Related Provisions: 222(6), (7) — Meaning of "acknowledges".

Notes: See Notes to 222(3). 222(5) added by 2004 budget bill #1, effective May 14, 2004.

(6) Acknowledgement of tax debts — A taxpayer acknowledges a tax debt if the taxpayer

(a) promises, in writing, to pay the tax debt;

(b) makes a written acknowledgement of the tax debt, whether or not a promise to pay can be inferred from the acknowledgement and whether or not it contains a refusal to pay; or

(c) makes a payment, including a purported payment by way of a negotiable instrument that is dishonoured, on account of the tax debt.

Related Provisions: 222(7) — Acknowledgment by agent or legal representative.

Notes: Appealing a reassessment is not an acknowledgment of the debt: *Harrison*, 2020 FC 772, paras. 62-97.

222(6) added by 2004 budget bill #1, effective May 14, 2004.

(7) Agent or legal representative — For the purposes of this section, an acknowledgement made by a taxpayer's agent or legal representative has the same effect as if it were made by the taxpayer.

Notes: 222(7) added by 2004 budget bill #1, effective May 14, 2004.

(8) Extension of limitation period — In computing the day on which a limitation period ends, there shall be added the number of days on which one or more of the following is the case:

(a) the Minister may not, because of any of subsections 225.1(2) to (5), take any of the actions described in subsection 225.1(1) in respect of the tax debt;

(b) the Minister has accepted and holds security in lieu of payment of the tax debt;

(c) if the taxpayer was resident in Canada on the applicable date described in paragraph (4)(a) in respect of the tax debt, the taxpayer is non-resident; or

(d) an action that the Minister may otherwise take in respect of the tax debt is restricted or not permitted by any provision of the *Bankruptcy and Insolvency Act*, of the *Companies' Creditors Arrangement Act* or of the *Farm Debt Mediation Act*.

Notes: 222(8)(a) did not apply to the amount not "in controversy" where only part of a reassessment was appealed: *Harrison*, 2020 FC 772, para. 110.

222(8)(c) deals with a situation like *Montreuil*, [1996] 1 C.T.C. 2182 (TCC), where an individual left Canada with taxes owing (in that case, his children were assessed under 160(1) when he died years later and left them his money).

222(8)(d) extends the limitation period for a bankrupt until discharge of the trustee.

222(8) added by 2004 budget bill #1, effective May 14, 2004.

(9) Bar to claims — Notwithstanding any law of Canada or a province, Her Majesty is not liable for any claim that arises because the Minister collected a tax debt after the end of any limitation period that applied to the collection of the tax debt and before March 4, 2004.

Notes: 222(9) added by 2004 budget bill #1, effective May 14, 2004.

(10) Orders after March 3, 2004 and before effect — Notwithstanding any order or judgment made after March 3, 2004 that declares a tax debt not to be payable by a taxpayer, or that orders the Minister to reimburse to a taxpayer a tax debt collected by the Minister, because a limitation period that applied to the collection of the tax debt ended before royal assent to any measure giving effect to this section, the tax debt is deemed to have become payable on March 4, 2004.

Notes: 222(10) (added by 2004 budget bill #1) overrides court decisions based on *Markevich*, 2003 SCC 9 and issued after March 3, 2004, the date Finance announced the amendments that became 222(3)-(8). 222(10) also re-awakened old tax debts that expired before 2004 due to *Markevich*; they went statute-barred only in 2014. For criticism see Vigeant paper cited in Notes to 222(3).

The retroactivity of 222(10) was accepted in *Gibson*, 2005 FCA 180 (leave to appeal denied 2005 CarswellNat 3624 (SCC)); *Collins*, 2005 FC 1431; *Rose*, 2005 FC 1731; *Wax*, 2006 FC 675; *Bleau*, 2007 FCA 61; *Leeado Enterprises*, 2009 BCSC 625 (leave to appeal denied 2009 BCCA 501). See also *Harrison* case in 222(3) Notes. See also VIEWS doc 2005-0133061E5.

In extreme cases, the amount owing may be cancelled by remission order; see Remission Orders annotation below.

Remission Orders [subsec. 222(10)]: *Ram Sewak Remission Order*, P.C. 2006-445 (cancels $990 tax debt from 1977, which grew with interest while taxpayer was away from Canada 1978-2001).

Definitions [s. 222]: "acknowledges" — 222(6); "action" — 222(1); "amount", "assessment" — 248(1); "Canada" — 255, *Interpretation Act* 35(1); "Federal Court" — *Federal Courts Act* s. 4; "Her Majesty" — *Interpretation Act* 35(1); "legal representative" — 248(1); "limitation period" — 222(4); "Minister", "non-resident", "person" — 248(1); "province" — *Interpretation Act* 35(1); "resident in Canada" — 250; "security" — *Interpretation Act* 35(1); "sent" — 244(14), (14.1); "tax debt" — 222(1); "taxpayer" — 248(1); "writing" — *Interpretation Act* 35(1); "written" — *Interpretation Act* 35(1)"writing".

222.1 Court costs — Where an amount is payable by a person to Her Majesty because of an order, judgment or award of a court in respect of the costs of litigation relating to a matter to which this Act applies, subsections 220(4) and (4.2) and sections 223, 224 to 225 and 226 apply to the amount as if the amount were a debt owing by the person to Her Majesty on account of tax payable by the person under this Act.

Notes: 222.1 added by 1995-97 technical bill, for amounts payable after June 18, 1998, including amounts that became payable before that date. It allows CRA to use its collection powers to recover court costs awarded against a taxpayer. "Litigation relating to a matter to which this Act applies" is broader than just a Tax Court appeal, and includes Federal Court applications for judicial review of a CRA decision (e.g., under 220(3.1)). The TCC has no jurisdiction to vacate such costs awarded by the FC or FCA: *Olumide*, 2016 FCA 10.

Definitions [s. 222.1]: "amount" — 248(1); "Her Majesty" — *Interpretation Act* 35(1); "person" — 248(1).

223. (1) Definition of "amount payable" — For the purposes of subsection (2), an "amount payable" by a person means any or all of

(a) an amount payable under this Act by the person;

(a.1) [Repealed]

(b) an amount payable under the *Employment Insurance Act* by the person;

(b.1) an amount payable under the *Unemployment Insurance Act* by the person;

(c) an amount payable under the *Canada Pension Plan* by the person; and

(d) an amount payable by the person under an Act of a province with which the Minister of Finance has entered into an agreement for the collection of taxes payable to the province under that Act.

Related Provisions: 221.2 — Transfers of balances between accounts; 223.1(1) — Application.

Notes: 223(1)(a.1), which referred to the *Wage Claim Payment Act*, was never proclaimed in force and was repealed retroactive to its introduction. That Act would have imposed a small payroll tax on all employers to create a fund for unpaid wages of employees of bankrupt corporations.

Reference in 223(1)(b) changed from *Unemployment Insurance Act* to *Employment Insurance Act* by 1996 EI bill, effective June 20, 1996. 223(1)(b.1) then added by 1995-97 technical bill, effective June 30, 1996, because proceedings under the UI Act are still underway in respect of past years.

(2) Certificates — An amount payable by a person (in this section referred to as a "debtor") that has not been paid or any part of an amount payable by the debtor that has not been paid may be certified by the Minister as an amount payable by the debtor.

Related Provisions: 222(3) — Ten-year limitation on collection action; 222.1 — Application to awards of court costs; 225.1 — No collection action for 90 days or if objection filed; 231.2(1) — requirement to provide information or documents for collection purposes; 231.6(1) — foreign-based documents sought for collection purposes.

Information Circulars: 98-1R5: Tax collection policies.

(3) Registration in court — On production to the Federal Court, a certificate made under subsection (2) in respect of a debtor shall be registered in the Court and when so registered has the same effect, and all proceedings may be taken thereon, as if the certificate were a judgment obtained in the Court against the debtor for a debt in the amount certified plus interest thereon to the day of payment as provided by the statute or statutes referred to in subsection (1) under which the amount is payable and, for the purpose of any such proceedings, the certificate shall be deemed to be a judgment of the Court against the debtor for a debt due to Her Majesty, enforceable in the amount certified plus interest thereon to the day of payment as provided by that statute or statutes.

Related Provisions: 161(1) — Interest; 161(11) — Interest on penalties; 222(3) — Ten-year limitation on collection action; 222.1 — Application to awards of court costs; 223.1(1) — Application; 225.1 — No collection action for 90 days or if objection filed; 227.1(2)(a) — Liability of directors; 248(11) — Compound interest.

Notes: *Collection from non-residents*: Unlike most court judgments, a judgment based on a tax debt is normally not enforceable in a foreign jurisdiction. Thus, CRA cannot enforce collection against a non-resident with no assets in Canada (unless it can issue a 224(1) Requirement to Pay to a Canadian resident that owes or will owe money to the non-resident). See *United States v. Harden*, [1963] C.T.C. 450 (SCC); this "revenue rule" is generally followed in other countries (e.g., *R.J. Reynolds Tobacco* (2001), 268 F.3d 103 (US Court of Appeals, 2nd Circuit)). See Debenham, "From the Revenue Rule," 56(1) *Canadian Tax Journal* 1-66 (2008). (In *Prince v. ACE Aviation*, 2014 ONCA 285, the rule was extended to mean that a Canadian court should not consider whether US tax law was being wrongly applied in Canada until US remedies were exhausted.) However, some of Canada's tax treaties permit CRA to use the foreign tax authority to collect (but the IRS cannot collect Canadian tax from a US citizen or US-incorporated company): see Canada-US treaty Art. XXVI-A:1 Notes.

A foreign penal judgment is also unenforceable in Canada: *Pro Swing v. Elta Golf*, 2006 SCC 52. In *Pasquantino* (tinyurl.com/pasq-ussc, 2005), the US Supreme Court convicted P of US wire fraud for evading Canadian customs duties.

CRA collection action generally: see Notes to 222(2).

Under 223(3), "the certificate of the Minister registered in the Court has the same effect as if the certificate were a judgment obtained in the Court. It is deemed to be a judgment of the Court. All proceedings may be taken thereon as if the certificate were a judgment obtained in the Court": *Gadbois*, 2002 FCA 228 (leave to appeal denied 2003 CarswellNat 960 (SCC)); *McDonald*, 2010 FC 340. See also *Piccott*, 2004 FCA 291, ruling that no writ of seizure and sale from the provincial court was needed to charge the provincial sheriff to seize a tax debtor's assets; *Laquerre*, 2008 FC 460, 2016 FCA 62, 2018 FC 919 (FCA appeal dismissed for delay A-332-18), 2018 FC 1012. Taxpayers cannot contest the certificate in Federal Court, because their right was to object to the assessment under s. 165 and appeal to the Tax Court under 169: *Klassen*, 2007 SKQB 393. In *Herbison*, 2014 BCCA 461, a "tax protester" challenge against the validity of the deemed judgment was dismissed as vexatious and significant costs awarded.

The provincial *Exemptions Act* (in Quebec, the *Civil Code*) governs enforcement of the certificate: *Federal Court Rules* r. 448; *Investors Group v. Eckhoff*, 2008 SKCA 18 (taxpayer's home and household goods); *London Life*, 2014 FCA 106 (leave to appeal denied 2015 CarswellNat 95 (SCC)). (However, see also 225(5) and Notes to 224(1).)

In *Greenslades Northern*, 2014 FC 904, GN was found in contempt for failing to deliver up specific assets (vehicles) to satisfy its debt to CRA, per a Court order.

A certificate does not become invalid through the assessment being replaced by a second assessment, as long as tax is still owing: *Lambert*, [1976] C.T.C. 611 (FCA); *Optical Recording*, [1990] 2 C.T.C. 524 (FCA).

In *Swiftsure Taxi*, 2005 FCA 136, CRA was ordered to leave legally-seized assets in ST's hands pending the outcome of a judicial review application challenging a certificate. In *Malachowski*, 2011 FC 413, CRA was allowed an interim charging order against tax debtor M's equitable interest in a property that was allegedly only rented by M, but in which M appeared to have an ownership interest. In *Baroud*, 2011 FC 508, a certificate registered against real property gave CRA priority over a third party's garnishment before judgment, which is "a conservatory measure that protects an eventual right to any claim. It does not confer any rights of ownership on the seizing party" (para. 7). In *Hagen*, 2009 FC 510, and *Zieffle*, 2011 FC 800, the Court agreed to extend a 6-year Writ of Seizure and Sale by a further 6 years, to enable CRA to continue collection action.

The fact that an assessment is registered in the Court as a judgment does not entitle a tax debtor to pay the *Federal Courts Act* rate of interest, which is lower than the rate under s. 161: *Prodor*, [1997] 3 C.T.C. 179 (FCTD).

See also Jeff Oldewening, "Certification of Unpaid Income Taxes Under Section 223 in Federal Court", 43 *McCarthy Tétrault on Tax Disputes* (CCH) 2-3 (Nov. 2008).

See also Notes to 223(5) and (6); 222(3) re the 10-year limitation on collection proceedings; and 158 re payment of balances owing. Where there is a question as to which tax year an amount paid should be allocated to, see Notes to 221.2.

223(3) amended by 1992 technical bill, effective June 10, 1993.

Information Circulars: See under 222(2).

(4) Costs — All reasonable costs and charges incurred or paid in respect of the registration in the Court of a certificate made under subsection (2) or in respect of any proceedings taken to collect the amount certified are recoverable in like manner as if they had been included in the amount certified in the certificate when it was registered.

Notes: CRA states that these costs can be traced through a 160(1) assessment: VIEWS doc 2009-0332731I7.

(5) Charge on property — A document issued by the Federal Court evidencing a certificate in respect of a debtor registered under subsection (3), a writ of that Court issued pursuant to the certificate or any notification of the document or writ (such document, writ or notification in this section referred to as a "memorial") may be filed, registered or otherwise recorded for the purpose of creating a charge, lien or priority on, or a binding interest in, property in a province, or any interest in, or for civil law any right in, such property, held by the debtor in the same manner as a document evidencing

(a) a judgment of the superior court of the province against a person for a debt owing by the person, or

(b) an amount payable or required to be remitted by a person in the province in respect of a debt owing to Her Majesty in right of the province

may be filed, registered or otherwise recorded in accordance with or pursuant to the law of the province to create a charge, lien or priority on, or a binding interest in, the property or interest.

Related Provisions: 222(3) — Ten-year limitation on collection action; 223(11.1) — Where charge registered under *Bankruptcy and Insolvency Act*; 223.1(1) — Application; 225.1 — No collection action for 90 days or if objection filed; 248(4) — Interest in real property.

Notes: The "memorial" under 223(5) is commonly called a "lien" on property.

223(5) was applied in *Piccott*, 2004 FCA 291, so no writ of seizure and sale from the provincial court was required to charge the sheriff to seize a tax debtor's assets. The charge under 223(5) can apply to an RRSP: *Keith G. Collins Ltd.*, 2008 MBCA 92.

A CRA claim has priority over other unsecured claims, but not a mortgage: *Edgar*, 2018 ABQB 202. In *Trang v. Nguyen*, 2012 ONCA 885, CRA liens on real property under 223(5) were held subordinate to an unregistered equitable interest (constructive trust or equitable mortgage); but the Court suggested that if 223(6) had been argued, the result might have been different. See Yasny, "Section 223 Lien's Priority", 21(2) *Canadian Tax Highlights* (ctf.ca) 8-10 (Feb. 2013). See also *Digiuseppe*, 2018 FC 1095.

In *McCullough-Greiff*, 2014 ABCA 202, a CRA lien was subject to a spouse's earlier claim under a certificate of *lis pendens* filed under Alberta *Matrimonial Property Act*.

In *Noble*, 2016 FC 1126, a memorial was cancelled because it was challenged under the New Brunswick *Land Titles Act* and CRA did not obtain a Court order within 30 days extending it!

223(5) is subject to provincial exemptions: see Notes to 223(3).

223(5) opening words amended by 2002-2013 technical bill (Part 4 — bijuralism), effective June 26, 2013, to add "or for civil law any right in".

223(5) amended by 1995-97 technical bill, effective June 18, 1998.

(6) Creation of charge — If a memorial has been filed, registered or otherwise recorded under subsection (5),

(a) a charge, lien or priority is created on, or a binding interest is created in, property in the province, or any interest in, or for civil law any right in, such property, held by the debtor, or

(b) such property, or interest or right in the property, is otherwise bound,

in the same manner and to the same extent as if the memorial were a document evidencing a judgment referred to in paragraph (5)(a) or an amount referred to in paragraph (5)(b), and the charge, lien, priority or binding interest created shall be subordinate to any charge, lien, priority or binding interest in respect of which all steps necessary to make it effective against other creditors were taken before the time the memorial was filed, registered or otherwise recorded.

Related Provisions: 223(11.1) — Where charge registered under *Bankruptcy and Insolvency Act*; 223.1(1) — Application; 248(4) — Interest in real property.

Notes: The writ binds property "in the same manner and to the same extent" as a provincial superior court judgment, but that does not detract from the Crown prerogative of payment, as provincial law cannot compel the Crown to share *pro rata* with other creditors. Filing the writ at the Land Titles office (using the provincial system) did not waive the prerogative: *Liberty Mortgage (Royal Bank v. Samra)*, 2012 ABCA 225. See also Notes to 223(5).

223(6) amended by 2002-2013 technical bill (effective June 26, 2013, to add references to a "right"), 1995-97 technical bill.

(7) Proceedings in respect of memorial — If a memorial is filed, registered or otherwise recorded in a province under subsection (5), proceedings may be taken in the province in respect of the memorial, including proceedings

(a) to enforce payment of the amount evidenced by the memorial, interest on the amount and all costs and charges paid or incurred in respect of

(i) the filing, registration or other recording of the memorial, and

(ii) proceedings taken to collect the amount,

(b) to renew or otherwise prolong the effectiveness of the filing, registration or other recording of the memorial,

(c) to cancel or withdraw the memorial wholly or in respect of any of the property, or interests or rights, affected by the memorial, or

(d) to postpone the effectiveness of the filing, registration or other recording of the memorial in favour of any right, charge, lien or priority that has been or is intended to be filed, registered or otherwise recorded in respect of any property, or interest or right, affected by the memorial, in the same manner and to the same extent as if the memorial were a document evidencing a judgment referred to in paragraph (5)(a) or an amount referred to in paragraph (5)(b), except that if in any such proceeding or as a condition precedent to any such proceeding any order, consent or ruling is required under the law of the province to be made or given by the superior court of the province or a judge or official of the court, a like order, consent or ruling may be made or given by the Federal Court or a judge or official of the Federal Court and, when so made or given, has the same effect for the purposes of the proceeding as if it were made or given by the superior court of the province or a judge or official of the court.

Related Provisions: 222(3) — Ten-year limitation on collection action; 225.1 — No collection action for 90 days or if objection filed.

Notes: 223(7) is subject to provincial exemptions: see Notes to 223(3).

In *Vallelunga*, 2016 FC 1329, a memorial was put on V's home due to a s. 160 liability, and CRA later issued a statement showing he owed no income tax. This did not create estoppel, and a 223(7)(c) application to cancel the memorial was dismissed.

223(7)(c), (d) amended by 2002-2013 technical bill (Part 4 — bijuralism), effective June 26, 2013, to add "or rights" and "or right".

223(7) amended by 1995-97 technical bill, effective June 18, 1998.

(8) Presentation of documents — If

(a) a memorial is presented for filing, registration or other recording under subsection (5) or a document relating to the memorial is presented for filing, registration or other recording for the purpose of any proceeding described in subsection (7) to any official in the land registry system, personal property or movable property registry system, or other registry system, of a province, it shall be accepted for filing, registration or other recording, or

(b) access is sought to any person, place or thing in a province to make the filing, registration or other recording, the access shall be granted

in the same manner and to the same extent as if the memorial or document relating to the memorial were a document evidencing a judgment referred to in paragraph (5)(a) or an amount referred to in paragraph (5)(b) for the purpose of a like proceeding, as the case may be, except that, if the memorial or document is issued by the Federal Court or signed or certified by a judge or official of the Court, any affidavit, declaration or other evidence required under the law of the province to be provided with or to accompany the memorial or document in the proceedings is deemed to have been provided with or to have accompanied the memorial or document as so required.

Related Provisions: 223.1(1) — Application.

Notes: 223(8)(a) amended by 2002-2013 technical bill, effective June 26, 2013, to add reference to movable property.

223(8) amended by 1995-97 technical bill, effective June 18, 1998.

(9) Sale, etc. — Notwithstanding any law of Canada or of a province, a sheriff or other person shall not, without the written consent of the Minister, sell or otherwise dispose of any property, or publish any notice or otherwise advertise in respect of any sale or other disposition of any property pursuant to any process issued or charge, lien, priority or binding interest created in any proceeding to collect an amount certified in a certificate made under subsection (2), interest on the amount and costs, but if that consent is subsequently given, any property that would have been affected by such a process, charge, lien, priority or binding interest if the Minister's consent had been given at the time the process was issued or the charge, lien, priority or binding interest was created, as the case may be, shall be bound, seized, attached, charged or otherwise affected as it would be if that consent had been given at the time the process was issued or the charge, lien, priority or binding interest was created, as the case may be.

Related Provisions: 223.1(1) — Application.

Notes: 223(9) amended by 1995-97 technical bill, effective June 18, 1998.

(10) Completion of notices, etc. — If information required to be set out by any sheriff or other person in a minute, notice or document required to be completed for any purpose cannot, by reason of subsection (9), be so set out, the sheriff or other person shall com-

plete the minute, notice or document to the extent possible without that information and, when the consent of the Minister is given under that subsection, a further minute, notice or document setting out all the information shall be completed for the same purpose, and the sheriff or other person having complied with this subsection is deemed to have complied with the Act, regulation or rule requiring the information to be set out in the minute, notice or document.

Related Provisions: 223.1(1) — Application.

Notes: 223(10) amended by 1995-97 technical bill, effective June 18, 1998 (non-substantive changes).

(11) Application for an order — A sheriff or other person who is unable, by reason of subsection (9) or (10), to comply with any law or rule of court is bound by any order made by a judge of the Federal Court, on an *ex parte* application by the Minister, for the purpose of giving effect to the proceeding, charge, lien, priority or binding interest.

Related Provisions: 223.1(1) — Application.

Notes: 223(11) amended by 1995-97 technical bill, effective June 18, 1998, to add "priority or binding interest" at the end.

(11.1) Deemed security — When a charge, lien, priority or binding interest created under subsection (6) by filing, registering or otherwise recording a memorial under subsection (5) is registered in accordance with subsection 87(1) of the *Bankruptcy and Insolvency Act*, it is deemed

(a) to be a claim that is secured by a security and that, subject to subsection 87(2) of that Act, ranks as a secured claim under that Act; and

(b) to also be a claim referred to in paragraph 86(2)(a) of that Act.

Notes: CRA's deemed security under 223(11.1) can apply to an RRSP: *Keith G. Collins Ltd.*, 2008 MBCA 92. It survives bankruptcy discharge and is not *ultra vires* Parliament: *Barr*, 2009 BCSC 1433, para. 87. It applied in *Gidda*, 2020 BCSC 121 (trustee argued that it was contrary to intent of *Bankruptcy & Insolvency Act*).

For CRA interpretation see VIEWS docs 2009-0316521I7 (post-bankruptcy refund cannot be applied as setoff against deemed security interest), 2009-0338291E5 (227(4.1) does not create security interest if 223(11.1) does not apply).

223(11.1) added by 1995-97 technical bill, effective June 18, 1998, and corrected retroactively by 2000 GST bill.

(12) Details in certificates and memorials — Notwithstanding any law of Canada or of a province, in any certificate made under subsection (2) in respect of a debtor, in any memorial evidencing the certificate or in any writ or document issued for the purpose of collecting an amount certified, it is sufficient for all purposes

(a) to set out, as the amount payable by the debtor, the total of amounts payable by the debtor without setting out the separate amounts making up that total; and

(b) to refer to the rate of interest to be charged on the separate amounts making up the amount payable in general terms as interest at the rate prescribed under this Act applicable from time to time on amounts payable to the Receiver General without indicating the specific rates of interest to be charged on each of the separate amounts or to be charged for any particular period of time.

Related Provisions [subsec. 223(12)]: 223.1(1) — Application; 225.1 — Collection restrictions.

Definitions [s. 223]: "amount" — 223(1), 248(1); "debtor" — 223(2); "Federal Court" — *Federal Courts Act* s. 4; "Her Majesty" — *Interpretation Act* 35(1); "interest" — in real property 248(4); "memorial" — 223(5); "Minister" — 248(1); "Minister of Finance" — *Financial Administration Act* 14; "movable" — Quebec Civil Code art. 900–907; "person", "property" — 248(1); "province" — *Interpretation Act* 35(1); "superior court" — *Interpretation Act* 35(1).

Regulations [s. 223]: 4301 (prescribed rate of interest).

223.1 (1) Application of subsecs. 223(1) to (8) and (12) — Subsections 223(1) to (8) and (12) are applicable with respect to certificates made under section 223 or section 223 of the *Income Tax Act*, chapter 148 of the Revised Statutes of Canada, 1952, after 1971 and documents evidencing such certificates that were issued by the Federal Court and that were filed, registered or otherwise

recorded after 1977 under the laws of a province, except that, where any such certificate or document was the subject of an action pending in a court on February 10, 1988 or the subject of a court decision given on or before that date, section 223 shall be read, for the purposes of applying it with respect to that certificate or document, as section 223 of the *Income Tax Act*, chapter 148 of the Revised Statutes of Canada, 1952, read at the time the certificate was registered or the document was issued, as the case may be.

(2) Application of subsecs. 223(9) to (11) — Subsections 223(9) to (11) are applicable with respect to certificates made under section 223, or section 223 of the *Income Tax Act*, chapter 148 of the Revised Statutes of Canada, 1952, after September 13, 1988.

Notes: 223.1 added in the RSC 1985 (5th Supp) consolidation, effective Dec. 1991. This rule was formerly in a 1988 tax reform application rule (1988, c. 55, s. 168(2)).

I.T. Application Rules: 69 (meaning of "chapter 148 of ...").

Definitions [s. 223.1]: "Federal Court" — *Federal Courts Act* s. 4; "province" — *Interpretation Act* 35(1).

224. (1) Garnishment — Where the Minister has knowledge or suspects that a person is, or will be within one year, liable to make a payment to another person who is liable to make a payment under this Act (in this subsection and subsections (1.1) and (3) referred to as the "tax debtor"), the Minister may in writing require the person to pay forthwith, where the moneys are immediately payable, and in any other case as and when the moneys become payable, the moneys otherwise payable to the tax debtor in whole or in part to the Receiver General on account of the tax debtor's liability under this Act.

Announced Administrative Change — More money for CRA Collections
Federal Budget, Chapter 10, April 19, 2021: See under 222(2).

Related Provisions: 222(3) — Ten-year limitation on collection action; 222.1 — Application to awards of court costs; 224(4) — Liability on failure to comply; 224(5), (6) — Service of garnishee; 225.1 — No collection action for 90 days or if objection filed; 231.2(1) — requirement to provide information or documents for collection purposes; 231.6(1) — foreign-based documents sought for collection purposes; 244(5), (6) — Proof of service by mail or personal service; 248(7)(a) — Mail deemed received on day mailed.

Notes: CRA collection action generally: see Notes to 222(2).

The garnishment notice under 224(1) or (1.1) is called a Requirement to Pay (**R2P**) or a Third Party Demand. No Court action is needed. CRA usually issues R2Ps to the taxpayer's bank to clean out bank accounts, and often sends them to employers, clients and other income sources, though it generally takes only a percentage of certain types (e.g. 20% of pension income); see also below under "Scope of garnishment". A R2P can apply to ongoing payments past one year: 224(3). CRA phone number to discuss a R2P: 1-800-675-6184.

Garnishment cannot start for regular tax until objection/appeal rights expire: see 225.1(1). It can start immediately for unremitted source deductions. For collection without a Notice of Assessment, see Notes to 225.1(6).

Parallel GST/HST garnishment is under *Excise Tax Act* s. 317(1) (with no stay during objection/appeal): see the *Practitioner's Goods and Services Tax Annotated* (Carswell). Case law under 224(1) or ETA 317(1) generally applies to both.

Detailed CRA information for a recipient of a R2P is at tinyurl.com/cra-garnish; internal procedures are in the *National Collections Manual*, under "Garnishment — Tax programs".

A R2P can be challenged in the Federal Court (see Notes to 171(1)), but in practice the Court never orders CRA to halt collection action: see Notes to 222(2).

No warning to the taxpayer is needed before garnishment: *Dingman*, 2009 FC 395, para. 29; but CRA must give reasons for refusing a payment proposal before taking collection action, though little formality is required: *Burkes*, 2011 FC 166.

Designated branch: *Bank Act* s. 462(2.1) (see CanLii.org) provides that notice to a bank can be sent to the bank's "designated office" rather than the specific branch. Thus, CRA can issue a R2P to the "designated office" of the major banks, to scoop up a delinquent taxpayer's accounts at any branch. Parallel provisions are *Bank Act* s. 579(2.1) (for authorized foreign banks), *Cooperative Credit Associations Act* s. 385.32(2.1) (credit unions), *Trust and Loan Companies Act* s. 448(2.1). However, CRA's *National Collections Manual* says: "Do not use designated branches to search for bank accounts. You must have a reason to believe the debtor deals with that bank."

Meaning of "liable to pay" [L2P] the tax debtor: A lawyer holding funds in a trust account is normally L2P the client, but not if the client is subject to a Court order directing the funds elsewhere: *Berry Creek v. KYJO*, 2006 ABQB 384. In *Inch Hammond v. Richter LLP (Big Truck TV)*, 2015 ONCA 567, funds received by a law

firm in trust under an irrevocable direction to pay were not a "debt" subject to garnishment by a (non-CRA) creditor. A Court Clerk holding funds to be distributed to a tax debtor under a Court Order is not "liable to make a payment" and cannot be garnisheed (and for CRA to send the Clerk a garnishment notice could be contempt of Court): *HSBC Bank v. 410086 Alberta Ltd.*, 2010 ABQB 403.

A life insurer is L2P the policy's surrender value to the policyholder, so garnishment can apply (at least in Quebec, but likely common-law provinces too): *London Life*, 2014 FCA 106 (leave to appeal denied 2015 CarswellNat 95 (SCC)); *Ruh*, 2017 FC 272 (once garnishment is fixed by Court order, no time limitation runs). *Contra*, an unmatured policy does not represent an amount the insurer is L2P if the taxpayer has not requested a cash payout: *Maritime Life*, [2000] 4 C.T.C. 98 (FCA).

A partner is not considered to be making a payment to another partner when partnership profits are distributed, and so a garnishment of the partner or partnership was invalid: *Yvan Lessard*, [2003] 3 C.T.C. 2824 (TCC). A partnership's obligation to CRA (or any other third party) is effectively an obligation of the individual partners; thus, 224(6) provides that the partnership can be served the garnishment notice. In *Gordon Feil CGA*, 2015 TCC 140, members of an accounting firm joint venture were each liable for the firm having paid tax debtor G by paying his Nevada "corporation sole"; the Court ruled that it was merely a conduit for G.

A garnishee with right of setoff against the tax debtor was not L2P: *PCL Constructors v. Norex*, 2009 BCSC 95; *Caisse Desjardins*, 2014 FCA 279 (Quebec *Civil Code*).

See also *Bélair*, [1996] 2 C.T.C. 2374 (TCC) (insurance company paying for cleaning after a fire was not L2P the cleaning company); *Hudon*, [1997] 3 C.T.C. 2983 (TCC) (notary holding construction financing was not L2P the contractor); *Kowalski*, [1998] G.S.T.C. 23 (TCC) (garnishee had received funds from tax debtor as fees, not as loan, so was not L2P); *Champagne*, [1998] G.S.T.C. 108 (Que. SC) (garnishee G owed tax debtor, not his corp, so G was L2P); *Absolute Bailiffs*, 2003 FCA 397 (bailiff seizing assets for landlord's lien was not L2P the tenant); *Browning*, 2010 TCC 487 (mortgage debt became unenforceable due to limitation period, so garnishee was not L2P); *Maclean v. Ryan*, 2007 ABQB 453 (matrimonial property judgment was declaration of wife's existing interest in property, not order for husband to pay); *Mpamugo*, 2016 ONSC 7569 (CRA used R2P to collect cash seized by banks under *Mareva* injunction in civil litigation); *De Vries*, 2018 TCC 166 (company was not L2P a loan to H, who had agreed to postpone his right to repayment until a third-party lawsuit concluded).

Scope of garnishment: 224(1) is not subject to the rule in 225(5) preventing seizures of goods exempt under provincial law, and provincial law cannot bind Canada: *Bruyère (Quebec v. Canada)*, 2011 SCC 60; *Sun Life*, [1992] 2 C.T.C. 315 (Sask. QB); *Wainio*, [2000] 2 C.T.C. 513 (Ont. SCJ); *Marcoux*, 2001 FCA 92; *Mutter (Meyers Norris)*, 2014 ABCA 176, para. 24; Richard Yasny, "Federal Tax Garnishment", 20(1) *Canadian Tax Highlights* (ctf.ca) 10-11 (Jan. 2012). CRA's *National Collections Manual* (2015) states that it is not bound by provincial exemptions, and does not say, as the 2012 version did, that CRA voluntarily applies them, though it lists restrictions due to memoranda of understanding with Ontario and Nova Scotia. (Seizures were subject to provincial exemptions without discussing constitutionality in *Belliard*, [1998] G.S.T.C. 30 (FCA) (lawyer's computer and files); *Fegol*, [1999] G.S.T.C. 52 (FCA) (farmer's equipment); *Investors Group v. Eckhoff*, 2008 SKCA 18 (taxpayer's home and household goods); *Affinity Credit v. Renz*, 2019 SKQB 301 (per provincial *Administration of Estates Act*, estate administration costs paid first).) On conflict with provincial garnishment for spousal support see Milan Legris, "Federal/Provincial Collection Priorities — A s. 224(1) Garnishment and an Ontario Support Deduction Order", 11(2) *Tax Law Update* (Ont. Bar Assn) 9-11 (March 2001).

On whether an RRSP or RRIF can be garnished, see Notes to 146(4).

A joint bank account may be immune from seizure due to the spouse's interest: see Notes to 222(2). However, as noted in those Notes, a spouse can be assessed under 160(1) for half the tax debtor's contributions to a joint account.

Garnishment cannot apply to a lawyer's trust account for the lawyer's own debts: *Canada Trustco*, 2011 SCC 36, paras. 9, 28, 53; Kreklewetz & Bassindale, "Some Cheques Not Subject to Requirements to Pay", 19(8) *Canadian Tax Highlights* (ctf.ca) 9-10 (Aug. 2011). Similarly, if an insurance broker, real estate broker or other person holds funds in trust, the account should be immune from seizure, but to avoid risk of seizure the bank branch's manager should be advised of its trust status.

A R2P does not become invalid if the assessment is replaced by a reassessment: *Lambert*, [1976] C.T.C. 611 (FCA); *Optical Recording*, [1990] 2 C.T.C. 524 (FCA); *Jus d'Or Inc.*, 2007 FC 754; *Mason*, 2015 FC 926 (FCA appeal discontinued A-369-15).

In *Location D'Autos Niveau Plus*, [1998] G.S.T.C. 73 (FCTD), Revenu Québec was allowed to attach a notice to a civil lawsuit so that any proceeds to the plaintiff could be seized for the defendant's GST debt. The Crown can also intervene in Quebec civil judgment-debtor proceedings to issue a R2P: *Gadbois*, 2002 FCA 228 (leave to appeal denied 2003 CarswellNat 960 (SCC)). In *Dunn*, 2016 ONSC 6533, CRA had seized from a tax debtor money that the claimants said was stolen from them; the Court declined to order the money paid into Court, in part because it was secure in the government's hands.

Priority: A garnishment order issued before a builder's lien was registered took priority over the lien: *APM Construction*, 2012 NSSC 277 (aff'd but explicitly not resolving this issue 2013 NSCA 62, para. 33). See also 224(1.2) for "super-priority" over source withholdings.

Bankruptcy takes priority over 224(1) (but not 224(1.2)), and CRA will return to the bankruptcy trustee any funds received from third parties (except for post-bankruptcy debt: see *Mutter (Meyers Norris)*, 2014 ABCA 176), but no longer pays interest on these amounts: VIEWS doc 2009-0331681I7. In *Paine Edmonds*, 2017 BCSC 2275, an undischarged bankrupt (whose trustee had been discharged 10 years earlier) received personal injury damages in his lawyer's trust account; CRA's R2P applied to the damages for past wage loss, but not to those for pain and suffering, cost of future care and future wage loss, which were protected due to the bankruptcy.

Garnishee liability: Garnishee G receiving a R2P for tax debtor D is liable under 224(4) for failing to pay CRA, and can be assessed under 227(10), if G is liable to pay D, even if G pays nothing to D. See *Encan Construction*, 2007 TCC 579; *Imperial Pacific Greenhouses*, 2011 FCA 79; *607730 B.C.*, 2007 TCC 748; *Westwood Floors*, 2010 TCC 632 (intercompany loan created the liability); *Fiducie Alex Trust*, 2014 FCA 123; *602960 Alberta*, 2017 TCC 228 (under appeal to FCA). The Crown need not prove D's debt if G appeals: *Browning*, 2004 TCC 414, para. 8 (holding that *Cyrus J. Moulton Ltd.*, [1976] C.T.C. 416 (FCTD) does not apply to a TCC appeal).

Where a tax debtor used a bank account in his company's name to keep funds out of CRA's reach, the company was liable for not honouring R2Ps for funds the tax debtor withdrew: *3087-8847 Québec*, 2007 TCC 302. CRA's view is that any corporate debt to a shareholder can thus be garnished: VIEWS doc 2012-0441141I7. (See also 160(1) Notes, para. "Accepting funds".) A shareholder is not subject to garnishment for a corporation's debt where the corporation's charter is cancelled and the shareholder continues the business: VIEWS doc 2009-032870I17.

A R2P is not defective if it names two garnishees and only one is liable to the tax debtor: *PCL Constructors v. Norex*, 2009 BCSC 95, para. 81.

Where there is a question as to which tax year an amount paid should be allocated to, see Notes to 221.2.

An employee has no claim against an employer for withholding wages and paying them under a R2P: 224(2); 227(1); *Coulbeck v. Univ. of Toronto*, [2005] 5 C.T.C. 65 (Ont. SCJ); *Korkut v. Kinloch*, 2014 BCSC 1576. A bank honouring a R2P has no obligation to the debtor to determine whether the assessment is correct: *Drosdovech*, 2010 FC 858, para. 11.

Further discussion: Lamer, *Priority of Crown Claims in Insolvency* (Carswell, supplemented book); Campbell, *Administration of Income Tax 2020* (Carswell), §8.5; Schulze, "The Legality of Administrative Garnishments Under the *Income Tax Act*", 50(5) *Canadian Tax Journal* 1597-1622 (2002); Brown & Andrea, "Garnishment, Pensions and Support Orders", *Taxation of Executive Compensation & Retirement* (Federated Press) 1535-41 (May 2012); Hamilton et al., "Government Collection of Tax in the Insolvency Context", 2012 *Tax Dispute Resolution* conf. report (ctf.ca), 18:1-31.

See also s. 222 re the 10-year limitation period on collection proceedings, and Notes to 158 re payment of balances owing.

As an alternative to 224(1), the Crown can register a certificate in Federal Court (s. 223) and use the Court's collection mechanisms for garnishment: e.g., *Lizotte*, 2003 FC 1508 and 1509; *Avard*, 2009 FC 315.

224(1) amended by 1993 technical bill, for requirements and notifications made after June 15, 1994.

Information Circulars: See under 222(2).

(1.1) Idem — Without limiting the generality of subsection (1), where the Minister has knowledge or suspects that within 90 days

(a) a bank, credit union, trust company or other similar person (in this section referred to as the "institution") will lend or advance moneys to, or make a payment on behalf of, or make a payment in respect of a negotiable instrument issued by, a tax debtor who is indebted to the institution and who has granted security in respect of the indebtedness, or

(b) a person, other than an institution, will lend or advance moneys to, or make a payment on behalf of, a tax debtor who the Minister knows or suspects

(i) is employed by, or is engaged in providing services or property to, that person or was or will be, within 90 days, so employed or engaged, or

(ii) where that person is a corporation, is not dealing at arm's length with that person,

the Minister may in writing require the institution or person, as the case may be, to pay in whole or in part to the Receiver General on account of the tax debtor's liability under this Act the moneys that would otherwise be so lent, advanced or paid and any moneys so paid to the Receiver General shall be deemed to have been lent, advanced or paid, as the case may be, to the tax debtor.

Related Provisions: 222(3) — Ten-year limitation on collection action; 222.1 — Application to awards of court costs; 224(4.1) — Liability on failure to comply; 224(5), (6) — Service of garnishee; 225.1 — No collection action for 90 days or if objection filed; 231.2(1) — requirement to provide information or documents for collection purposes; 231.6(1) — foreign-based documents sought for collection purposes; 244(5), (6) — Proof of service by mail or personal service; 248(7)(a) — Mail deemed received on day mailed.

Notes: See Notes to 224(1). 224(1.1) allows a R2P to be issued to a financial institution or other person that *will loan* or advance money to a tax debtor who owes money to the institution *and* who has granted security in respect of the debt. Typically this is an advance on a credit line. 224(1.1) is invoked by CRA adding its "paragraph 4" to the R2P: *National Collections Manual*. The R2P is valid for 90 days.

The parallel GST rule in *Excise Tax Act* 317(2) applied in *Royal Bank*, [1999] G.S.T.C. 2 (TCC), to amounts to be advanced by the bank to Mastercraft, which had granted security and whose shareholder had personally guaranteed its loan. At the time of the R2P, Mastercraft had used its full line of credit. The bank advanced funds, taking the position that this was on the shareholder's guarantee, not Mastercraft's security. The bank was liable for not honouring the R2P.

Closing words of 224(1.1) amended by 1993 technical bill, for R2Ps issued in 1993 or later, to change "by registered letter or letter served personally" to "in writing".

Information Circulars: 98-1R5: Tax collection policies.

(1.2) Garnishment — Notwithstanding any other provision of this Act, the *Bankruptcy and Insolvency Act*, any other enactment of Canada, any enactment of a province or any law, but subject to subsections 69(1) and 69.1(1) of the *Bankruptcy and Insolvency Act* and section 11.09 of the *Companies' Creditors Arrangement Act*, if the Minister has knowledge or suspects that a particular person is, or will become within one year, liable to make a payment

(a) to another person (in this subsection referred to as the "tax debtor") who is liable to pay an amount assessed under subsection 227(10.1) or a similar provision, or

(b) to a secured creditor who has a right to receive the payment that, but for a security interest in favour of the secured creditor, would be payable to the tax debtor,

the Minister may in writing require the particular person to pay forthwith, where the moneys are immediately payable, and in any other case as and when the moneys become payable, the moneys otherwise payable to the tax debtor or the secured creditor in whole or in part to the Receiver General on account of the tax debtor's liability under subsection 227(10.1) or the similar provision, and on receipt of that requirement by the particular person, the amount of those moneys that is so required to be paid to the Receiver General shall, notwithstanding any security interest in those moneys, become the property of Her Majesty to the extent of that liability as assessed by the Minister and shall be paid to the Receiver General in priority to any such security interest.

Announced Administrative Change — Deferral of source deduction-related payments under bankruptcy proposal

CRA notice [tinyurl.com/cra-bia60], April 23, 2020: *Pending Default of a Proposal under the BIA where the Canada Revenue Agency is a majority creditor*

The Canada Revenue Agency (CRA) is taking a people-first approach in realigning its resources to ensure that all Canadians and businesses are supported if they are experiencing financial hardship due to the COVID-19 outbreak.

The CRA has heard from Licensed Insolvency Trustees (LITs) and the Office of the Superintendent of Bankruptcy (OSB) about debtors who have suffered a loss of employment or a reduction of income as a result the COVID-19 outbreak and their concerns over defaulting on their proposals.

The CRA is proposing a solution to assist taxpayers and LITs in circumstances where the CRA *is a creditor* and the debtor is experiencing financial hardship.

For proposals filed under Division 1 of the *Bankruptcy and Insolvency Act* (BIA), the CRA is offering a waiver of the default pursuant to section 62.1 of the BIA and granting a deferral of payments to the estate up to *September 1, 2020*. This will also apply to any amounts subject to section 60(1.1) of the BIA as per our existing Administrative Agreement policy with LITs.

For consumer proposals under the BIA, the CRA offers the acceptance of an amended proposal that calls for a deferral of payments up to *September 1, 2020*.

Hopefully, this will offer taxpayers the time to focus on other aspects of their financial wellbeing without having to file for bankruptcy.

Further notifications will be provided to stakeholders through the Canadian Association of Insolvency and Restructuring Professionals and through updates to the CRA information page on the OSB website.

[BIA forms for deferral of payments and adjournment of creditors' meeting — not reproduced — ed.]

Related Provisions: 222(3) — Ten-year limitation on collection action; 224(4) — Liability on failure to comply; 224(5), (6) — Service of garnishee; 244(5), (6) — Proof of service by mail or personal service; 248(7)(a) — Mail deemed received on day mailed.

Notes: See Notes to 224(1). 224(1.2) provides "enhanced garnishment" or "super priority" confiscation of funds owing by a third party to a tax debtor who is liable to the CRA for unremitted source deductions (which under s. 227 are deemed held in trust for the Crown). 224(1.2) applies to many kinds of tax withholdings (plus related interest and penalty) listed in 227(10.1), including employee payroll deductions (227(9.4)). The same rule applies to withholdings of CPP contributions (*Canada Pension Plan* 23(2)(b)), EI premiums (*Employment Insurance Act* 99(b)) and GST/HST (*Excise Tax Act* 317(3)), but the GST rule is subject to the *Bankruptcy and Insolvency Act* (BIA)). For CRA interpretation and procedures see *National Collections Manual* (on *TaxPartner* or *Taxnet Pro*), "Garnishment — Tax programs — Enhanced Requirement to Pay". See also the related "deemed trust" priority in 227(4), (4.1).

224(1.2) debts must be paid under a bankruptcy proposal. See 128(2) Notes.

224(1.2) is constitutionally valid and does not infringe provincial jurisdiction: *TransGas v. Mid-Plains Contractors [Non-Labour Lien Claimants]*, [1994] 3 S.C.R. 753 (SCC). 224(1.2) was also applied in *Caisse Populaire Desjardins*, 2009 SCC 29, on the basis that Parliament intended it to apply broadly; see Notes to 224(1.3).

Due to "notwithstanding ... any law", 224(1.2) supersedes the common-law doctrine of "marshalling", which requires a creditor with two sources available to satisfy a claim to use them in the order that will benefit a secondary creditor: *Nova Scotia Business Development v. Wandlyn Inn*, [2000] 2 C.T.C. 402 (NSSC)).

The words "notwithstanding any security interest in those moneys, become the property of Her Majesty" ensure the super-priority operates against secured creditors: *Canada Trustco Mortgage Corp. v. Port O'Call Hotel*, [1996] G.S.T.C. 17 (also cited as *Province of Alberta Treasury Branches*, as *Re Country Inns*, and as *Pigott Project Management*, [1996] 1 C.T.C. 395). The Supreme Court of Canada ruled 3-2 that a general assignment of book debts is a security interest, not an absolute assignment, so it remains subject to 224(1.2) garnishment, which takes priority over the bank to whom the assignment was made. However, an absolute assignment of book debts overrides the garnishment, since the tax debtor no longer has any interest in the property: *First Vancouver Finance*, 2002 SCC 49 (see also Notes to 227(4)).

The super-priority took priority over other creditors with assignment of book debts or rents in: *Canoe Cove*, [1994] G.S.T.C. 36 (BCSC); *National Bank* (1994), 2 G.T.C. 7348 (FCTD); *Bonavista v. Atlantic Technologists*, [1994] 2 C.T.C. 234 (Nfld SC); *Metal Fabricating v. Husky Oil* (1995), 35 C.B.R. (3d) 162 (Sask. QB); *Encor Energy*, [1995] G.S.T.C. 54 (Sask. CA); *Coopers & Lybrand v. Bank of Montreal*, [1993] G.S.T.C. 36 (Nfld. TD); *Montreal Trust*, [1999] G.S.T.C. 58 (Que. CA); *Pointe-Verte v. Frizzell*, 2000 CarswellNB 170 (NBQB); *Phase Atlantic*, 2001 NBQB 54; *Winnipeg Enterprises*, 2008 MBCA 23; *CanaDream v. Garmeco*, 2016 BCSC 2426.

The super-priority took priority over construction liens and other liens in: *TransGas* (SCC, above); *Montreal Trust v. Powell Lane*, [1994] G.S.T.C. 66 (BCSC); *Polyco Window v. Prudential*, [1994] 2 C.T.C. 399 (Sask. QB) (lien for unpaid wages); *Bonavista v. Atlantic Technologists*, [1994] 2 C.T.C. 234 (Nfld. SC); *Japan Canada Oil v. Stoney Mountain*, 2001 CarswellAlta 732 (Alta. QB); *Absolute Bailiffs*, 2003 FCA 397 (landlord's lien); *Community Expansion*, 2005 CarswellOnt 214 (Ont CA) (landlord's right to distrain); *Ledcor Construction*, 2006 BCSC 2097; *South Rock*, 2007 ABCA 115; *Manitoba Hydro v. Chartrand*, 2007 MBQB 196; *Polymere Epoxy-Pro*, 2009 FC 912 (workers' hypothecary claims under Quebec *Civil Code*); *Mullner Trucking v. Baer Enterprises*, 2010 BCCA 90 (woodworker liens); *Canadian Western Bank v. 702348 Alberta*, 2012 ABQB 305; *APM Construction v. Caribou Island*, 2012 NSSC 277; *Van T. Holdings v. KCS Equipment*, 2013 ABQB 154; *Okanagan Regional Library v. Isaak Electrical*, 2013 BCSC 953; *Canadian Natural Resources v. Thermal Energy*, 2017 ABQB 698; *Guarantee Co. v. Manitoba Housing*, 2018 MBCA 32 (leave to appeal denied 2019 CarswellMan 12 (SCC)).

In *GlassCell Isofab*, 2011 ONSC 2660, 224(1.2) took priority over funds seized by the Sheriff from the tax debtor in a garnishment to satisfy a civil judgment.

The super-priority failed against BIA s. 69(3)(a) in *Hamachi House*, 2016 NSSC 58, the Court finding that source deductions that had been withheld were "due" when withheld, not on the remittance due date, so that there was no default on payment of an amount "due" following a notice of intention to file a proposal. (This seems wrong.)

See also Notes to 224(1.3) for 224(1.2) taking priority over a security interest; and Notes to 224(1) for cases on "liable to pay".

224(1.2) applies to penalties and interest: *Dav-Jor Contracting*, 2006 BCCA 330.

See also Campbell, *Administration of Income Tax 2020* (Carswell), §8.5.2.

224(1.2) amended by S.C. 2005, c. 47, in force Sept. 18, 2009 (per P.C. 2009-1207), to change "section 11.4" to "section 11.09". Earlier amended by 1997 CCAA amending bill, 1993 technical bill, 1992 technical bill and 1990 garnishment/collection bill.

Companies' Creditors Arrangement Act

CCAA s. 11.09 provides:

> 11.09 (1) Stay — Her Majesty — An order made under section 11.02 may provide that
>
> (a) Her Majesty in right of Canada may not exercise rights under subsection 224(1.2) of the *Income Tax Act* or any provision of the *Canada Pension Plan* or of the *Employment Insurance Act* that refers to subsection 224(1.2) of the *Income Tax Act* and provides for the collection of a contribution, as defined in the *Canada Pension Plan*, or an employee's premium, or employer's premium, as defined in the *Employment Insurance Act*, or a premium under Part VII.1 of that Act, and of any related interest, penalties or

other amounts, in respect of the company if the company is a tax debtor under that subsection or provision, for the period that the court considers appropriate but ending not later than

> (i) the expiry of the order,
>
> (ii) the refusal of a proposed compromise by the creditors or the court,
>
> (iii) six months following the court sanction of a compromise or an arrangement,
>
> (iv) the default by the company on any term of a compromise or an arrangement, or
>
> (v) the performance of a compromise or an arrangement in respect of the company; and
>
> (b) Her Majesty in right of a province may not exercise rights under any provision of provincial legislation in respect of the company if the company is a debtor under that legislation and the provision has a purpose similar to subsection 224(1.2) of the *Income Tax Act*, or refers to that subsection, to the extent that it provides for the collection of a sum, and of any related interest, penalties or other amounts, and the sum
>
> (i) has been withheld or deducted by a person from a payment to another person and is in respect of a tax similar in nature to the income tax imposed on individuals under the *Income Tax Act*, or
>
> (ii) is of the same nature as a contribution under the *Canada Pension Plan* if the province is a "province providing a comprehensive pension plan" as defined in subsection 3(1) of the *Canada Pension Plan* and the provincial legislation establishes a "provincial pension plan" as defined in that subsection,
>
> for the period that the court considers appropriate but ending not later than the occurrence or time referred to in whichever of subparagraphs (a)(i) to (v) that may apply.
>
> (2) When order ceases to be in effect — The portions of an order made under section 11.02 that affect the exercise of rights of Her Majesty referred to in paragraph (1)(a) or (b) cease to be in effect if
>
> (a) the company defaults on the payment of any amount that becomes due to Her Majesty after the order is made and could be subject to a demand under
>
> (i) subsection 224(1.2) of the *Income Tax Act*,
>
> (ii) any provision of the *Canada Pension Plan* or of the *Employment Insurance Act* that refers to subsection 224(1.2) of the *Income Tax Act* and provides for the collection of a contribution, as defined in the *Canada Pension Plan*, or an employee's premium, or employer's premium, as defined in the *Employment Insurance Act*, or a premium under Part VII.1 of that Act, and of any related interest, penalties or other amounts, or
>
> (iii) any provision of provincial legislation that has a purpose similar to subsection 224(1.2) of the *Income Tax Act*, or that refers to that subsection, to the extent that it provides for the collection of a sum, and of any related interest, penalties or other amounts, and the sum
>
> (A) has been withheld or deducted by a person from a payment to another person and is in respect of a tax similar in nature to the income tax imposed on individuals under the *Income Tax Act*, or
>
> (B) is of the same nature as a contribution under the *Canada Pension Plan* if the province is a "province providing a comprehensive pension plan" as defined in subsection 3(1) of the *Canada Pension Plan* and the provincial legislation establishes a "provincial pension plan" as defined in that subsection; or
>
> (b) any other creditor is or becomes entitled to realize a security on any property that could be claimed by Her Majesty in exercising rights under
>
> (i) subsection 224(1.2) of the *Income Tax Act*,
>
> (ii) any provision of the *Canada Pension Plan* or of the *Employment Insurance Act* that refers to subsection 224(1.2) of the *Income Tax Act* and provides for the collection of a contribution, as defined in the *Canada Pension Plan*, or an employee's premium, or employer's premium, as defined in the *Employment Insurance Act*, or a premium under Part VII.1 of that Act, and of any related interest, penalties or other amounts, or
>
> (iii) any provision of provincial legislation that has a purpose similar to subsection 224(1.2) of the *Income Tax Act*, or that refers to that subsection, to the extent that it provides for the collection of a sum, and of any related interest, penalties or other amounts, and the sum
>
> (A) has been withheld or deducted by a person from a payment to another person and is in respect of a tax similar in nature to the income tax imposed on individuals under the *Income Tax Act*, or
>
> (B) is of the same nature as a contribution under the *Canada Pension Plan* if the province is a "province providing a comprehensive pension plan" as defined in subsection 3(1) of the *Canada Pension Plan* and the provincial legislation establishes a "provincial pension plan" as defined in that subsection.

(3) **Operation of similar legislation** — An order made under section 11.02, other than the portions of that order that affect the exercise of rights of Her Majesty referred to in paragraph (1)(a) or (b), does not affect the operation of

(a) subsections 224(1.2) and (1.3) of the *Income Tax Act*,

(b) any provision of the *Canada Pension Plan* or of the *Employment Insurance Act* that refers to subsection 224(1.2) of the *Income Tax Act* and provides for the collection of a contribution, as defined in the *Canada Pension Plan*, or an employee's premium, or employer's premium, as defined in the *Employment Insurance Act*, or a premium under Part VII.1 of that Act, and of any related interest, penalties or other amounts, or

(c) any provision of provincial legislation that has a purpose similar to subsection 224(1.2) of the *Income Tax Act*, or that refers to that subsection, to the extent that it provides for the collection of a sum, and of any related interest, penalties or other amounts, and the sum

(i) has been withheld or deducted by a person from a payment to another person and is in respect of a tax similar in nature to the income tax imposed on individuals under the *Income Tax Act*, or

(ii) is of the same nature as a contribution under the *Canada Pension Plan* if the province is a "province providing a comprehensive pension plan" as defined in subsection 3(1) of the *Canada Pension Plan* and the provincial legislation establishes a "provincial pension plan" as defined in that subsection,

and for the purpose of paragraph (c), the provision of provincial legislation is, despite any Act of Canada or of a province or any other law, deemed to have the same effect and scope against any creditor, however secured, as subsection 224(1.2) of the *Income Tax Act* in respect of a sum referred to in subparagraph (c)(i), or as subsection 23(2) of the *Canada Pension Plan* in respect of a sum referred to in subparagraph (c)(ii), and in respect of any related interest, penalties or other amounts.

For discussion of the CCAA generally see Janis Sarra, *Rescue! The Companies' Creditors Arrangement Act* (Carswell, 2nd ed., 2013, 1050pp.). See also Beaudry & Kraus, "Selected Income Tax Considerations in Court-Approved Debt Restructuring and Liquidations", 2015 Cdn Tax Foundation annual conference.

Information Circulars: See under 222(2).

I.T. Technical News: 6 (enhanced garnishment takes priority over builders' lien claimants).

(1.3) Definitions — In subsection (1.2),

"secured creditor" means a person who has a security interest in the property of another person or who acts for or on behalf of that person with respect to the security interest and includes a trustee appointed under a trust deed relating to a security interest, a receiver or receiver-manager appointed by a secured creditor or by a court on the application of a secured creditor, a sequestrator, or any other person performing a similar function;

Related Provisions: 227(5.1)(h) — Secured creditor jointly liable for unremitted withholding tax.

"security interest" means any interest in, or for civil law any right in, property that secures payment or performance of an obligation and includes an interest, or for civil law a right, created by or arising out of a debenture, mortgage, hypothec, lien, pledge, charge, deemed or actual trust, assignment or encumbrance of any kind whatever, however or whenever arising, created, deemed to arise or otherwise provided for;

Notes: See Notes to 224(1.2). The meaning of "security interest" in 224(1.3) is not determined by provincial law: *Caisse Populaire Desjardins de l'Est de Drummond / du Bon Conseil*, 2009 SCC 29, paras. 12-13. "Parliament has chosen an expansive definition... to enable maximum recovery by the Crown under its deemed trust for unremitted income tax... The definition ...does not require that the agreement between the creditor and debtor take any particular form... So long as the creditor's interest in the debtor's property secures payment or performance of an obligation, there is a 'security interest' ...While Parliament has provided a list of 'included' examples, these examples do not diminish the broad scope of the words 'any interest in property'." (paras. 14-15)

The following cases found a security interest: *Caisse Populaire Desjardins* (above) (agreement to use term deposit as security for loan); *United Used Auto*, 2000 BCSC 1708 (purchase money security interest used to secure loan with vehicles purchased by borrower); *Allianz Insce.*, 2004 BCSC 566 (purchase of debtor's accounts receivable under security agreement); *Community Expansion*, 2005 CarswellOnt 214 (Ont CA) (landlord's exercise of right to distrain); *Pointe-Verte v. Alexander Frizzell Construction*, 2000 CarswellNB 170 (NBQB) (assignment of book debts to bank as "continuing collateral security"); *South Rock*, 2007 ABCA 115 (builders' lien); *W. Mullner Trucking*, 2010 BCCA 90 (woodworker liens).

The following cases found no security interest: *Bank of Nova Scotia v. Turyders Trucking*, 2001 CarswellOnt 4945 (Ont. SCJ) (lease); *Absolute Bailiffs*, [2002] G.S.T.C. 116 (TCC, aff'd on other grounds 2003 FCA 397) (landlord's lien right under B.C. *Rent*

Distress Act); *DaimlerChrysler Financial v. Mega Pets*, 2002 BCCA 242 (conditional sale agreement); *Schwab Construction*, 2002 SKCA 6 (vehicle leases with buyout option — i.e., conditional sale contracts); *PCL Constructors v. Norex*, 2009 BCSC 95 (holdbacks not owed to tax debtor subcontractors because holdback funds had been used to complete their unfinished work); *Travelers Canada v. Elite Builders*, 2017 NLTD(G) 214 (standard mortgage clause for lender with mortgage on insured property created a separate insurance contract).

Definition amended by 2002-2013 technical bill (Part 4 — bijuralism), effective June 26, 2013; and by 2001 *Civil Code* harmonization bill.

"similar provision" means a provision, similar to subsection 227(10.1), of any Act of a province that imposes a tax similar to the tax imposed under this Act, where the province has entered into an agreement with the Minister of Finance for the collection of the taxes payable to the province under that Act.

(1.4) Garnishment [applies to the Crown] — Provisions of this Act that provide that a person who has been required to do so by the Minister must pay to the Receiver General an amount that would otherwise be lent, advanced or paid to a taxpayer who is liable to make a payment under this Act, or to that taxpayer's secured creditor, apply to Her Majesty in right of Canada or a province.

Notes: 224(1.4) added by 1993 technical bill, effective June 15, 1994. It and 227(4.3) overrule *Brant*, [1998] G.S.T.C. 101 (FCTD), where a garnishment notice was held not to apply to a province.

(2) Minister's receipt discharges original liability — The receipt of the Minister for moneys paid as required under this section is a good and sufficient discharge of the original liability to the extent of the payment.

Notes: Payment to CRA under a garnishment notice discharges the payor's liability to the tax debtor: *Dias v. MacLean*, [1994] 1 C.T.C. 127 (NSSC), para. 32; *Imperial Pacific Greenhouses*, 2010 TCC 431, para. 46 (aff'd 2011 FCA 79); *APM Construction*, 2013 NSCA 62, para. 29.

(3) Idem — Where the Minister has, under this section, required a person to pay to the Receiver General on account of a liability under this Act of a tax debtor moneys otherwise payable by the person to the tax debtor as interest, rent, remuneration, a dividend, an annuity or other periodic payment, the requirement applies to all such payments to be made by the person to the tax debtor until the liability under this Act is satisfied and operates to require payments to the Receiver General out of each such payment of such amount as is stipulated by the Minister in the requirement.

Related Provisions: 224(4) — Liability on failure to comply.

Notes: 224(3) amended by 1993 technical bill, for requirements and notifications made in 1993 or later.

(4) Failure to comply with subsec. (1), (1.2) or (3) requirement — Every person who fails to comply with a requirement under subsection (1), (1.2) or (3) is liable to pay to Her Majesty an amount equal to the amount that the person was required under subsection (1), (1.2) or (3), as the case may be, to pay to the Receiver General.

Related Provisions: 227(10) — Assessment.

Notes: See Notes to 224(1).

In *Encan Construction*, 2007 TCC 579, EC had mailed a cheque to its supplier, postdated by a week to one day after a garnishment notice was received by ordinary mail. EC was liable for the amount paid (even though its controller did not see the notice), because it could have stopped payment on the cheque.

(4.1) Failure to comply with subsec. (1.1) requirement — Every institution or person that fails to comply with a requirement under subsection (1.1) with respect to moneys to be lent, advanced or paid is liable to pay to Her Majesty an amount equal to the lesser of

(a) the total of moneys so lent, advanced or paid, and

(b) the amount that the institution or person was required under that subsection to pay to the Receiver General.

Related Provisions: 227(10) — Assessments.

(5) Service of garnishee — Where a person carries on business under a name or style other than the person's own name, notification to the person of a requirement under subsection (1), (1.1) or (1.2) may be addressed to the name or style under which the person carries on business and, in the case of personal service, shall be deemed to be validly served if it is left with an adult person employed at the place of business of the addressee.

Notes: 224(5) amended by 1993 technical bill, effective for requirements and notifications made in 1993 or later.

(6) Idem — Where persons carry on business in partnership, notification to the persons of a requirement under subsection (1), (1.1) or (1.2) may be addressed to the partnership name and, in the case of personal service, shall be deemed to be validly served if it is served on one of the partners or left with an adult person employed at the place of business of the partnership.

Related Provisions: 244(20)(b) — Service of documents on partnerships.

Notes: 224(6) amended by 1993 technical bill, for requirements and notifications made in 1993 or later.

Notes [s. 224]: 224 amended by 1990 garnishment/collection bill, effective June 27, 1990.

Definitions [s. 224]: "amount", "annuity" — *Interpretation Act* 35(1); "bank" — 248(1), *Interpretation Act* 35(1); "business" — 248(1); "Canada" — 255; "carrying on business" — 253; "credit union" — 137(6), 248(1); "dividend", "employed", "employee", "employer" — 248(1); "Her Majesty" — *Interpretation Act* 35(1); "institution" — 224(1.1)(a); "Minister" — 248(1); "Minister of Finance" — *Financial Administration Act* 14; "person", "property" — 248(1); "province" — *Interpretation Act* 35(1); "secured creditor", "security interest", "similar provision" — 224(1.3); "tax debtor" — 224(1); "tax payable" — 248(2); "trust" — 104(1), 248(1), (3); "writing" — *Interpretation Act* 35(1).

224.1 Recovery by deduction or set-off — Where a person is indebted to Her Majesty under this Act or under an Act of a province with which the Minister of Finance has entered into an agreement for the collection of the taxes payable to the province under that Act, the Minister may require the retention by way of deduction or set-off of such amount as the Minister may specify out of any amount that may be or become payable to the person by Her Majesty in right of Canada.

Related Provisions: 164(2) — Set-off of refund against other amount owing by the taxpayer to the Crown or a province; 203 — Set-off of Part X refunds; 222(3) — Ten-year limitation on collection action; 222.1 — Application to awards of court costs; 225.1 — Before April 2007, no collection action for 90 days or if objection filed; 231.2(1) — requirement to provide information or documents for collection purposes; 231.6(1) — foreign-based documents sought for collection purposes.

Notes: GST/HST refunds and rebates are automatically offset against income tax debts, and vice versa, for corporations (based on the Business Number). For individuals (whose income tax account is the Social Insurance Number), this is done only manually. 224.1 can be used to apply setoff even where an assessment is under objection or appeal, due to the repeal of 225.1(1)(e).

164(2) also provides a set-off, specific to the payment of refunds under s. 164.

Where there is a question as to which taxation year a payment should be allocated to, see Notes to 221.2.

In *Ultramar Canada*, [2000] 2 C.T.C. 505 (FCTD), a set-off notice under 224.1 under which CRA retained Ultramar's federal fuel tax rebates was quashed. Although the rebates arose from Ultramar's sales of fuel to Socanav (the tax debtor), Ultramar was not indebted to Socanav and could not be subject to a 224(1.2) garnishment order.

In *Bouchard*, 2009 FCA 321, set-off of 30% of B's CPP benefits was upheld despite the Quebec *Civil Code*. In *Glazer*, 2019 FC 436, paras. 36-39, withholding of Alberta refunds was upheld. Since set-off is not a "seizure", no *Charter* protection applies: *Maheux*, 2012 FCA 283. Set-off under 224.1 can be challenged only in the FC, not the provincial courts: *Smith*, 2016 ONSC 489.

Where a debt is legally set off against income payable to a taxpayer, the income is still considered received and so is taxable: *Tessier*, 2005 TCC 677 (see also Notes to 5(1)).

Income tax refunds will be offset against Saskatchewan provincial traffic fines (Sask. Justice news release, Feb. 12, 2008).

Definitions [s. 224.1]: "amount" — 248(1); "Her Majesty" — *Interpretation Act* 35(1); "Minister" — 248(1); "Minister of Finance" — *Financial Administration Act* 14; "person" — 248(1); "province" — *Interpretation Act* 35(1).

Information Circulars: See under 222(2).

224.2 Acquisition of debtor's property — For the purpose of collecting debts owed by a person to Her Majesty under this Act or under an Act of a province with which the Minister of Finance has entered into an agreement for the collection of taxes payable to the province under that Act, the Minister may purchase or otherwise acquire any interest in, or for civil law any right in, the person's property that the Minister is given a right to acquire in legal pro-

ceedings or under a court order or that is offered for sale or redemption and may dispose of any interest or right so acquired in such manner as the Minister considers reasonable.

Related Provisions: 222(3) — Ten-year limitation on collection action; 222.1 — Application to awards of court costs; 231.2(1) — requirement to provide information or documents for collection purposes; 231.6(1) — foreign-based documents sought for collection purposes.

Notes: 224.2 amended by 2002-2013 technical bill (Part 4 — bijuralism), effective June 26, 2013, to add "or for civil law any right in" and "or right".

Definitions [s. 224.2]: "Her Majesty" — *Interpretation Act* 35(1); "Minister" — 248(1); "Minister of Finance" — *Financial Administration Act* 14; "person" — 248(1); "province" — *Interpretation Act* 35(1).

224.3 (1) Payment of moneys seized from tax debtor — Where the Minister has knowledge or suspects that a particular person is holding moneys that were seized by a police officer in the course of administering or enforcing the criminal law of Canada from another person (in this section referred to as the "tax debtor") who is liable to make a payment under this Act or under an Act of a province with which the Minister of Finance has entered into an agreement for the collection of taxes payable to the province under that Act and that are restorable to the tax debtor, the Minister may in writing require the particular person to turn over the moneys otherwise restorable to the tax debtor in whole or in part to the Receiver General on account of the tax debtor's liability under this Act or under the Act of the province, as the case may be.

Related Provisions: 222(3) — Ten-year limitation on collection action; 222.1 — Application to awards of court costs; 225.1 — No collection action for 90 days or if objection filed; 231.2(1) — requirement to provide information or documents for collection purposes; 231.6(1) — foreign-based documents sought for collection purposes; 244(5), (6) — Proof of service by mail or personal service; 248(7)(a) — Mail deemed received on day mailed.

Notes: In *Millar*, 2007 BCCA 401 (leave to appeal denied [2008] G.S.T.C. 11 (SCC)), the Court ordered cash seized illegally by the police to be turned over to CRA under 224.3. CRA was not tainted by the police's wrongful actions in seizing the funds.

224.3(1) is an enforcement tool available to CRA, and a Court will not order CRA to use it to benefit a taxpayer: *Zins*, 2007 FC 1358.

224.3(1) amended by 1993 technical bill, for requirements made in 1993 or later, so that the requirement need not be sent by registered mail or served personally.

Information Circulars: See under 222(2).

(2) Receipt of Minister — The receipt of the Minister for moneys turned over as required by this section is a good and sufficient discharge of the requirement to restore the moneys to the tax debtor to the extent of the amount so turned over.

Definitions [s. 224.3]: "Minister" — 248(1); "Minister of Finance" — *Financial Administration Act* 14; "person" — 248(1); "province" — *Interpretation Act* 35(1); "tax debtor" — 224.3(1); "writing" — *Interpretation Act* 35(1).

225. (1) Seizure of goods, chattels or movable property — If a person has failed to pay an amount as required by this Act, the Minister may give 30 days notice to the person by registered mail addressed to the person's latest known address of the Minister's intention to direct that the person's goods and chattels, or movable property, be seized and sold, and, if the person fails to make the payment before the expiration of the 30 days, the Minister may issue a certificate of the failure and direct that the person's goods and chattels, or movable property, be seized.

Related Provisions: 222(3) — Ten-year limitation on collection action; 222.1 — Application to awards of court costs; 225.1 — No collection action for 90 days or if objection filed; 231.2(1) — requirement to provide information or documents for collection purposes; 231.6(1) — foreign-based documents sought for collection purposes; 244(5) — Proof of service by mail; 248(7) — Mail deemed received on day mailed.

Notes: Goods can also be seized by a sheriff acting under the authority of the Federal Court, once an assessment is registered in that Court (see 223(3)), without using s. 225. In *Humby Enterprises*, 2007 FC 1085 (Crown's FCA appeal discontinued), CRA was not entitled to force the sheriff to sell goods for below their appraised value, and the sheriff returned the goods to the tax debtors.

In *Matvieshen*, 2014 FC 633, attempts to argue that a seized tractor and snowmobiles belonged to people other than the tax debtors (and so should not have been seized) were rejected as unproven, as "strong evidence" is needed for such a claim (para. 13).

225(1) amended by 2002-2013 technical bill (Part 4 — bijuralism), effective June 26, 2013, to add "or movable property" (twice).

Information Circulars: See under 222(2).

(2) Sale of seized property — Property seized under this section shall be kept for 10 days at the cost and charges of the owner and, if the owner does not pay the amount owing together with the costs and charges within the 10 days, the property seized shall be sold by public auction.

Related Provisions: *Interpretation Act* 27(5) — Meaning of "within the 10 days".

(3) Notice of sale — Except in the case of perishable goods, notice of the sale setting out the time and place thereof, together with a general description of the property to be sold shall, a reasonable time before the goods are sold, be published at least once in one or more newspapers of general local circulation.

(4) Surplus returned to owner — Any surplus resulting from the sale after deduction of the amount owing and all costs and charges shall be paid or returned to the owner of the property seized.

(5) Exemptions from seizure — Goods and chattels, or movable property, of any person in default that would be exempt from seizure under a writ of execution issued out of a superior court of the province in which the seizure is made are exempt from seizure under this section.

Related Provisions: 226(2) — Taxpayer leaving Canada or defaulting.

Notes: The Courts apply the same rule to certificates and garnishments: see Notes to 223(3) and 224(1). However, 225(5) does not directly apply to a garnishment under 224(1): *Marcoux*, [2000] 4 C.T.C. 143 (FCTD).

225(5) amended by 2002-2013 technical bill (Part 4 — bijuralism), effective June 26, 2013, to add "or movable property" and change "as would" to "that would".

Definitions [s. 225]: "assessment", "Minister" — 248(1); "movable" — Quebec *Civil Code* art. 900–907; "person", "property" — 248(1); "province", "superior court" — *Interpretation Act* 35(1).

225.1 (1) Collection restrictions [90 days or while under dispute] — If a taxpayer is liable for the payment of an amount assessed under this Act, other than an amount assessed under subsection 152(4.2), 169(3) or 220(3.1), the Minister shall not, until after the collection-commencement day in respect of the amount, do any of the following for the purpose of collecting the amount:

(a) commence legal proceedings in a court,

(b) certify the amount under section 223,

(c) require a person to make a payment under subsection 224(1),

(d) require an institution or a person to make a payment under subsection 224(1.1),

(e) [set-off under 224.1 — repealed effective April 2007]

(f) require a person to turn over moneys under subsection 224.3(1), or

(g) give a notice, issue a certificate or make a direction under subsection 225(1).

[Closing words repealed]

Related Provisions: 164(1.1) — Refund to taxpayer of amount under objection or appeal; 179.1 — 10% penalty for appealing without reasonable grounds to delay collection; 220(4.1) — CRA must accept security while objection or appeal is outstanding; 222(3) — Ten-year limitation on collection action; 225.1(1.1) — Collection-commencement day; 225.1(6), (7) — Limitations on collection restrictions; 225.2 — Immediate collection on jeopardy assessment.

Notes: 225.1 effectively means that most taxpayers (but see 225.1(6), (7)) need not pay an assessment during the 90-day objection period (not the extended period of 1 year from filing deadline for individuals, in 165(1)(a)(i)), or while an assessment is under objection or a Tax Court appeal, though interest will continue to accrue under 161(1). If the amount in dispute has already been paid, it can be retrieved by the taxpayer under 164(1.1). However, if an appeal is filed to delay collection and there were no reasonable grounds to appeal, the Tax Court can penalize the taxpayer under 179.1. On CRA collection powers generally, see 222(2) Notes.

In general, a taxpayer that can afford to should pay an assessment even if objecting or appealing (unless bankruptcy is a possibility: see 128(2) Notes). Payment is not admission of liability and is not considered relevant by CRA or the Courts in deciding the objection or appeal. Payment stops non-deductible (18(1)(t)) high-rate arrears interest (161(1), Reg. 4301(a)) from accruing if the appeal fails, though refund interest after winning will be at a low rate (164(3), Reg. 4301(b)) and taxable (12(1)(c)). If a corporation's original return for the year assessed was filed more than 3 years after year-end,

the assessment should *not* be paid, as it may not be refundable if the appeal succeeds: 164(1) (subject to 164(4.1) and 221.2). In *Ludmer*, 2020 QCCA 697, paras. 120-126, taxpayers who paid unreasonable assessments (for which CRA was liable in negligence) could not recover, as damages, lost interest on their voluntary payments (leave to appeal denied 2021 CarswellQue 2160 (SCC)).

If the taxpayer obtains an extension of time and files an objection or TCC appeal after collection action begins, collection action must be stopped but past actions need not be reversed: *Alessandro*, 2006 FC 895; *Leroux*, 2014 BCSC 720, paras. 155, 392 (but see also 164(1.1)).

In *Cybernius Medical*, 2017 FC 226, collection action taken within 90 days of the reassessment, or afterwards while an objection was underway, was held to be "statute-barred" and grounds for requiring CRA to reappropriate under 221.2 a non-payable refund and apply it against the debt (paras. 46-47).

225.1(1)(e) has been repealed, so CRA can withhold income tax (or GST or other) refunds as a set-off against amounts that are under objection or appeal, or during the first 90 days after assessment. This means that a taxpayer with an appeal before the Courts (e.g., a tax shelter), who overpays instalments or who has deductions reducing tax below the level of source withholdings, might not receive a refund. CRA has said that this action will only be taken by collections officers when recovery is considered to be in jeopardy; and that if the taxpayer requests repayment of the amount withheld under 164(1.1), CRA would have to obtain a Court order to retain the refund (this was done in *Chabot*, 2010 FC 574).

The collection restrictions do not apply to tax that has been or should have been withheld at source (both from employees and from non-residents), as well as certain other amounts. See 225.1(6), as well as the opening words of 225.1(1). They also do not apply to GST/HST remittances under the *Excise Tax Act*, which CRA can collect as soon as they are assessed even if the assessment is under appeal (and even if it is for GST or HST that was never collected, rather than collected and not remitted). See Kreklewetz & Bassindale, "No Statutory Stay of GST Collection", 20(3) *Canadian Tax Highlights* (ctf.ca) 9-10 (March 2012). They also do not apply if a 225.2 jeopardy order is issued. See Information Circular 98-1R7 for administrative policies re collection action. The restrictions only half-apply to large corporations and to disputes over charitable donation shelters: 225.1(7).

Another way to stop collection action is to issue a notice of intention to file a Proposal under the *Bankruptcy and Insolvency Act*. See Notes to 128(2).

See also s. 222 re the 10-year limitation period on collection proceedings, and Notes to 158 re payment of balances owing.

In *Swiftsure Taxi*, 2005 FCA 136, CRA was ordered to leave legally-seized assets in ST's hands pending the outcome of a judicial review application challenging a certificate.

See also Notes to Canada-U.S. Tax Treaty:Art. XXVI-A:1 and to 223(2), re collection of cross-border tax debts.

225.1(1)(e) repealed by 2006 budget bill #1, effective April 2007. It read: "(e) require the retention of the amount by way of deduction or set-off under section 224.1,".

225.1(1) opening words amended and closing words repealed by 2004 Budget, for notices issued by the Minister after June 12, 2005. The change introduces the term "collection-commencement day", defined in 225.1(1.1).

Opening words of 225.1(1) amended by 1995-97 technical bill, effective June 18, 1998, to add reference to assessments under 152(4.2), 169(3) and 220(3.1). These are relieving assessments that cannot be objected to.

Closing words of 225.1(1) amended by 1992 technical bill, effective June 10, 1993, to change "before" to "until after", so that collection proceedings cannot start on day 90.

Information Circulars: 98-1R5: Tax collection policies.

CRA Audit Manual: 10.11.7: Referral of files and information to revenue Collections; 11.5.13: Collection stall code procedures — Form T718.

(1.1) Collection-commencement day — The collection-commencement day in respect of an amount is

(a) in the case of an amount assessed under subsection 188(1.1) in respect of a notice of intention to revoke given under subsection 168(1) or any of subsections 149.1(2) to (4.1), one year after the day on which the notice was mailed;

(b) in the case of an amount assessed under section 188.1, one year after the day on which the notice of assessment was sent; and

(c) in any other case, 90 days after the day on which the notice of assessment was sent.

Related Provisions: 225.2 — Immediate collection on jeopardy assessment; 244(14), (14.1) — Date when notice sent.

Notes: 225.1(1.1)(b) and (c) amended by 2010 budget bill #2, effective Dec. 15, 2010, to change "mailed" to "sent" (to accommodate electronic notices under 244(14.1)).

225.1(1.1) added by 2004 Budget, effective in respect of notices issued by the Minister after June 12, 2005. Para. (c) was formerly in the closing words of 225.1(1). Paras. (a) and (b) are new, consequential on new rules for charities in 188-188.1.

(2) No action by Minister — If a taxpayer has served a notice of objection under this Act to an assessment of an amount payable under this Act, the Minister shall not, for the purpose of collecting the amount in controversy, take any of the actions described in paragraphs (1)(a) to (g) until after the day that is 90 days after the day on which notice is sent to the taxpayer that the Minister has confirmed or varied the assessment.

Related Provisions: 222(8)(a) — Extension of 10-year limitation period on collection action while 225.1(2) applies; 225.1(6), (7) — Limitations on collection restrictions; 244(14), (14.1) — Date when notice sent.

Notes: See Notes to 225.1(1). 225.1(2) amended by 2010 budget bill #2, effective Dec. 15, 2010, to change "mailed" to "sent" (to accommodate electronic notices under 244(14.1)). Earlier amended by 1992 technical bill.

(3) Idem [while under appeal to TCC] — Where a taxpayer has appealed from an assessment of an amount payable under this Act to the Tax Court of Canada, the Minister shall not, for the purpose of collecting the amount in controversy, take any of the actions described in paragraphs (1)(a) to (g) before the day of mailing of a copy of the decision of the Court to the taxpayer or the day on which the taxpayer discontinues the appeal, whichever is the earlier.

Related Provisions: 179.1 — Penalty applied by Court where appeal filed solely for delay; 222(8)(a) — Extension of 10-year limitation period on collection action while 225.1(3) applies; 225.1(6), (7) — Limitations on collection restrictions.

Notes: Once a Tax Court decision is reached against the taxpayer, CRA can enforce collection even if a FCA appeal is filed: *Ostroff*, 2012 FCA 235. In *Langlois (Faraggi)*, 2009 FCA 69, the FCA refused to stay a decision dismissing a TCC appeal, partly because even if it did, collection could proceed due to the TCC decision.

(4) Idem [while under reference to TCC] — Where a taxpayer has agreed under subsection 173(1) that a question should be determined by the Tax Court of Canada, or where a taxpayer is served with a copy of an application made under subsection 174(1) to that Court for the determination of a question, the Minister shall not take any of the actions described in paragraphs (1)(a) to (g) for the purpose of collecting that part of an amount assessed, the liability for payment of which will be affected by the determination of the question, before the day on which the question is determined by the Court.

Related Provisions: 222(8)(a) — Extension of 10-year limitation period on collection action while 225.1(4) applies; 225.1(6), (7) — Limitations on collection restrictions.

(5) Idem [waiting for test case] — Notwithstanding any other provision in this section, where a taxpayer has served a notice of objection under this Act to an assessment or has appealed to the Tax Court of Canada from an assessment and agrees in writing with the Minister to delay proceedings on the objection or appeal, as the case may be, until judgment has been given in another action before the Tax Court of Canada, the Federal Court of Appeal or the Supreme Court of Canada in which the issue is the same or substantially the same as that raised in the objection or appeal of the taxpayer, the Minister may take any of the actions described in paragraphs (1)(a) to (g) for the purpose of collecting the amount assessed, or a part thereof, determined in a manner consistent with the decision or judgment of the Court in the other action at any time after the Minister notifies the taxpayer in writing that

(a) the decision of the Tax Court of Canada in that action has been mailed to the Minister,

(b) judgment has been pronounced by the Federal Court of Appeal in that action, or

(c) judgment has been delivered by the Supreme Court of Canada in that action,

as the case may be.

Related Provisions: 222(8)(a) — Extension of 10-year limitation period on collection action while 225.1(5) applies.

Notes: Where many cases depend on the same issue (e.g., certain kinds of investments or tax shelters), CRA may write to all taxpayers involved, asking them to agree to hold their objections or appeals "in abeyance" pending resolution of a test case by the courts. Once the test case has been decided, 225.1(5) gives CRA the right to proceed with collection action based on that decision — without prejudicing one's right to proceed with one's own appeal (possibly on the basis of distinguishable facts, or by pursu-

ing the case to a higher court). See CRA *Appeals Manual* §4.28.3. See also Notes to 169(1) and 174(1).

Where 225.1(5) applies to an objection held in abeyance, collection action is not resuspended by filing a Tax Court appeal: *Webster*, 2003 FCA 442. Furthermore, the Court will not decide whether the issues in the other case were indeed "substantially the same" as the taxpayer's case, if the parties agreed in writing that they were.

225.1(5) amended by 1991 technical bill, effective January 1, 1991, to delete a reference to the Federal Court–Trial Division.

(6) Where subsecs. (1) to (4) do not apply — Subsections (1) to (4) do not apply with respect to

(a) an amount payable under Part VIII *[ss. 194-195: pre-1986 scientific research tax credit — ed.]*;

(a.1) an amount payable under section 281;

(b) an amount required to be deducted or withheld, and required to be remitted or paid, under this Act or the Regulations;

(c) an amount of tax required to be paid under section 116 or a regulation made under subsection 215(4) but not so paid;

(d) the amount of any penalty payable for failure to remit or pay an amount referred to in paragraph (b) or (c) as and when required by this Act or a regulation made under this Act; and

(e) any interest payable under a provision of this Act on an amount referred to in this paragraph or any of paragraphs (a) to (d).

Related Provisions: 225.2 — Collection in jeopardy.

Notes: 225.1(6) allows CRA to enforce collection, even though an objection or appeal can be or has been filed, on: source deductions, non-resident withholding tax and other amounts withheld (and held in trust) or required to be withheld; s. 116 and 215(4) liability; the penalty under 281(3) for failing to provide a Taxpayer Identification Number; and penalty and interest on the above.

There are also no collection restrictions on a GST/HST assessment under the *Excise Tax Act* (ETA), which is considered analogous to an assessment of a taxpayer who fails to withhold and remit tax on payments to employees (amounts held in trust) — even if the GST or HST was never collected.

Being required to pay tax in order to file a Court appeal under the *Special Import Measures Act* (not the same as 225.1(6), which requires payment even if appealing but is not a condition of appealing) was held not to violate the rule of law or *Constitution Act, 1867* s. 96 in *Prairies Tubulars*, 2021 FC 36.

It is uncertain whether 225.1(6) applies to a director's liability for unremitted source deductions. It might, since under 227.1(1) the director is jointly liable with the corp for the withholdings, not merely liable because the corp did not pay (though *assessment* of the director requires that the corp not have paid: 227.1(2)).

In *Coombs*, 2012 FC 1499, the FC refused judicial review of a CRA decision to enforce collection of a payroll debt, due to 225.1(6).

Collection without assessment: Due to 225.1(6), CRA need not issue a notice of assessment before enforcing collection on unremitted payroll withholdings: *Dupont Roofing*, 2011 FC 160! This is wrong in the author's view. Liability arises under 227(9.4) and an assessment must be issued under 227(10.1) before collection can begin. Otherwise the entire mechanism for objecting to and appealing assessments would not be possible. 225.1 was introduced in 1985 as a collections-timing rule to *protect* taxpayers, so where it does not apply (due to 225.1(6)), it should not be used *against* taxpayers. When a 227(10.1) assessment is issued, "sections 150 to 153 apply", so the usual rules for assessments apply; and s. 158 states that "when the Minister mails a notice of assessment", the unpaid amount is "payable forthwith". See also 248(2), which defines "tax payable" (though not "amount") as "fixed by assessment". For liability to be enforceable without an assessment runs contrary to the entire scheme of the Act. See David Sherman, "Payroll Withholding Notice of Assessment?", 19(6) *Canadian Tax Highlights* (ctf.ca) 9-10 (June 2011). See also *Oroville Reman*, 2016 TCC 75, paras. 18-20 (softwood lumber charge likely cannot be enforced without assessment). In *Johnson*, 2015 FCA 51, para. 50, no collection action was allowed before assessment, but that was based on the GST/HST rule in ETA 315(1) that says this explicitly.

225.1(6) does not allow immediate collection of tax from a non-resident where the payor did not withhold tax: VIEWS doc 2012-0460181I7.

225.1(6)(a.1) added by 2016 budget bill #2, effective July 2017.

225.1(6)(b) amended by 2001 technical bill, effective June 14, 2001 (Royal Assent), to change "an amount deducted or withheld" to "an amount required to be deducted or withheld". Thus, there are no collection restrictions on source deductions even if they were not withheld.

See also Notes to 225.1(1).

Information Circulars: 98-1R5: Tax collection policies.

(7) One-half collection [large corporations and donation shelters] — If an amount has been assessed under this Act in respect of a corporation for a taxation year in which it was a large corporation, or in respect of a particular amount claimed under section 110.1 or 118.1 where the particular amount was claimed in respect of a tax shelter, then subsections (1) to (4) do not limit any action of the Minister to collect

(a) at any time on or before the particular day that is 90 days after the day of the sending of the notice of assessment, $\frac{1}{2}$ of the amount so assessed; and

(b) at any time after the particular day, the amount, if any, by which the amount so assessed exceeds the total of

(i) all amounts collected before that time with respect to the assessment, and

(ii) $\frac{1}{2}$ of the amount in controversy at that time.

Related Provisions: 164(1.1) — Repayment on objection or appeal; 220(4.1) — CRA must accept security for other half while objection or appeal is outstanding; 244(14), (14.1) — Date when notice sent.

Notes: 225.1(7) and (8) require payment of half the amount in dispute, even if an objection or appeal is underway, by (a) large corporations, and (b) taxpayers assessed for donation shelters (see Notes to 118.1(1)"total charitable gifts"). (Based on the wording of 225.1(7), if a large corporation is disputing a donation shelter assessment, it will still only have to pay half.)

Although a trust company is a large corp, when it acts as trustee of a trust it is considered a separate person, so 225.1(7) does not apply to the trust: VIEWS doc 2011-0405811R11.

225.1(7) opening words amended by 2013 budget bill #1, for amounts assessed for taxation years that end after 2012, to add "or in respect of a particular amount claimed under section 110.1 or 118.1 where the particular amount was claimed in respect of a tax shelter, then" (i.e., the rule for donation shelters).

225.1(7)(a) amended by 2010 budget bill #2, effective Dec. 15, 2010, to change "mailing" to "sending" (to accommodate electronic notices under 244(14.1)).

225.1(7) added by 1992 technical bill, effective June 10, 1993. (The proceeds from this rule were supposedly used to finance aid to Canadian farmers: Finance news release, Dec. 2, 1991.)

Information Circulars: 98-1R5: Tax collection policies.

(8) Definition of "large corporation" — For the purposes of this section and section 235, a corporation (other than a corporation described in subsection 181.1(3)) is a "large corporation" in a particular taxation year if the total of the taxable capital employed in Canada of the corporation, at the end of the particular taxation year, and the taxable capital employed in Canada of any other corporation, at the end of the other corporation's last taxation year that ends at or before the end of the particular taxation year, if the other corporation is related (within the meaning assigned for the purposes of section 181.5) to the corporation at the end of the particular taxation year, exceeds $10 million, and, for the purpose of this subsection, a corporation formed as a result of the amalgamation or merger of 2 or more predecessor corporations is deemed to be the same corporation as, and a continuation of, each predecessor corporation.

Related Provisions: 164(1.1) — Repayment on objections and appeals; 165(1.11), (1.13), 169(2.1) — Limitations on objections and appeals by large corporations; 181.5(1.1), (4.1) — Application of Part I.3 tax for purposes of 225.1(8); 220(4.1) — Security; 225.1(8) — Definition of "large corporation".

Notes: See Notes to 225.1(7) and 181.1(1). 225.1(8) amended by 2006 budget bill #1 (for 2006 and later taxation years), 1993 technical bill. Added by 1992 technical bill.

Notes [s. 225.1]: 225.1 amended by 1990 garnishment/collection bill, effective June 27, 1990.

Definitions [s. 225.1]: "amount", "assessment" — 248(1); "collection-commencement day" — 225.1(1.1); "corporation" — 248(1), *Interpretation Act* 35(1); "day of the sending" — 244(14), (14.1); "Federal Court of Appeal" — *Federal Courts Act* s. 3; "large corporation" — 225.1(8); "Minister", "person" — 248(1); "regulation" — 248(1); "related" — 181.5(6), (7); "sent" — 244(14), (14.1); "tax shelter" — 237.1(1), 248(1); "taxable capital employed in Canada" — 181.2(1), 181.3(1), 181.4 [technically do not apply]; "taxation year" — 249; "taxpayer" — 248(1); "writing" — *Interpretation Act* 35(1).

225.2 [Jeopardy orders] — (1) Definition of "judge" — In this section, "judge" means a judge or a local judge of a superior court of a province or a judge of the Federal Court.

Notes: An application under 225.2(2) can be brought in either Federal Court or a provincial "superior court" (*Interpretation Act* s. 35(1)).

In *Abu-Taha*, 2001 FCT 76, the Federal Court denied CRA's application for a 225.2 order because the Ontario Court would be hearing the taxpayer's application to have

funds seized by the RCMP paid out to him for living expenses. The Court ruled that it would be better to have the Ontario Court deal with both issues.

(2) Authorization to proceed forthwith [jeopardy order] — Notwithstanding section 225.1, where, on *ex parte* application by the Minister, a judge is satisfied that there are reasonable grounds to believe that the collection of all or any part of an amount assessed in respect of a taxpayer would be jeopardized by a delay in the collection of that amount, the judge shall, on such terms as the judge considers reasonable in the circumstances, authorize the Minister to take forthwith any of the actions described in paragraphs 225.1(1)(a) to (g) with respect to the amount.

Related Provisions: 164(1.2) — Delay of refund where collection of tax in jeopardy.

Notes: The order issued under 225.2(2) is called a "jeopardy order" or a "jeopardy assessment". See Notes to 225.2(1) re what court may issue it. The order cannot be appealed to the FCA, as an application must be made under 225.2(8) instead: *Tennina*, 2010 FCA 25; leave to appeal to SCC denied 2011 CarswellNat 280.

The taxpayer has no right to be given notice and allowed to make representations before a jeopardy order is issued. "The question was whether, on the basis of the material put before the Court, it appeared that the Minister had reasonable grounds for believing that the taxpayer would waste, liquidate or otherwise transfer his assets so as to become less able to pay the amount assessed and thereby jeopardizing the Minister's debt": *Golbeck*, [1990] 2 C.T.C. 438 (FCA).

"The evidence must show, on a balance of probability, that it is more likely than not that collection would be jeopardized by delay. The test is not whether the evidence shows beyond all reasonable doubt that the time allowed to the taxpayer would jeopardize the Minister's debt.... The Minister may certainly act not only in cases of fraud or situations amounting to fraud, but also where the taxpayer may waste, liquidate or otherwise transfer his property to escape the tax authorities: in short, to meet any situation in which the taxpayer's assets may vanish in thin air because of the passage of time. However, the mere suspicion or concern that delay may jeopardize collection is not sufficient *per se*.... An *ex parte* collection order is an extraordinary remedy. Revenue Canada must exercise utmost good faith and insure full and frank disclosure": *Services M.L. Marengère Inc.*, [2000] 1 C.T.C. 229 (FCTD); this includes disclosing unhelpful facts and reasonably foreseeable weaknesses in its case: *Grenon RRSP Trust*, 2015 FC 1050, para. 5.

A 225.2(8) application cannot be used to challenge the correctness of an assessment, as there is a TCC appeal procedure (see 169(1)): *Papa (Gallo)*, 2009 FC 49, para. 27.

Jeopardy orders were **set aside** in *Steele*, [1996] 2 C.T.C. 279 (Sask. QB) (tax debtor transferring assets to her husband; since husband could be assessed under s. 160, collection would not be jeopardized!); *Naber*, 2003 SKQB 563 (reasonable doubt raised that collection would be prejudiced; the reason for the reassessment (e.g., tax avoidance or evasion) is not relevant); *Sagman*, 2004 FC 1630 (taxpayer testified he had paid his taxes under a corporate name, and undertook to "administer his affairs in a conservative manner" until his tax litigation was resolved); *Gravel*, 2005 FC 1252 (Crown's evidence had gaps); *Abergel*, 2008 FC 589 (taxpayer received cash from her father who had large tax debt, but no evidence of fraud on her part); *Alexander*, 2008 FC 902 (no evidence that sale of property was reaction to assessment; taxpayer was innocent of US fraud charges until proven guilty); *Douville*, 2009 FC 986 (evidence of taxpayer and advisers showed his alleged non-cooperation was caused by CRA auditor's actions); *Robarts*, 2010 FC 875 (CRA affidavit omitted key facts; mere suspicion or concern was not reasonable grounds); *Proulx*, 2011 FC 1231 (CRA did not make full and fair disclosure to Court; taxpayer showed he intended to remain in Canada); *Patry*, 2012 FC 977 (no clear indication of unorthodox behaviour; taxpayers' home was not listed for sale and even if sold, not clear proceeds would be placed beyond CRA's reach); *Grenon RRSP Trust*, 2015 FC 1050 (taxpayer had moved to New Zealand and withdrawal of $55m from RRSP was to deregister it in advance of increase in withholding tax rate; no evidence of criminality, and CIBC as trustee would be liable for RRSP's debt); *684761 BC Ltd.*, 2016 FC 791 (owner had equity in family home, and no evidence he attempted to evade payment or moved assets out of Canada).

Jeopardy orders were **approved** in: *Moss*, [1998] 1 C.T.C. 283 (FCTD); *Thériault-Sabourin*, 2003 FCT 124; *514659 B.C.*, 2003 FCT 148; *Fabrication GMCA*, 2002 FCT 1260; *Blouin*, 2003 FCT 178; *Greenwood*, 2003 BCSC 1045; *Paryniuk*, 2003 FC 1505; *Arab*, 2005 FC 264; *1384405 Ontario*, 2005 FC 912; *Goldland Jewelers*, 2006 ABQB 108; *Mann*, 2006 FC 1358 ("unorthodox behaviour which raises a reasonable apprehension that it would be difficult to trace funds or recover them to satisfy a tax debt"); *Chamas*, 2006 FC 1548 (history of "unorthodox banking practices" and filing false financial information); *Delaunière*, 2007 FC 636 ("unorthodox behaviour", and sale of residence); *Wachsmann-Zahler*, 2007 FC 1254 (distills applicable principles from earlier case law); *Reddy*, 2008 FC 208 ($600,000 transferred to incapacitated mother's account by son who was tax debtor; her only assets were two homes which she was refinancing); *Tran*, 2008 FC 297 (application for review filed late); *Lachapelle*, 2007 FC 1161 (corporation was merely *alter ego* of individual); *Laquerre*, 2008 FC 458 (evidence showed that L intended to liquidate assets to avoid creditors); *Hazan*, 2008 FC 1075 (evidence sufficient to trigger 225.2); *Hernandez*, 2008 FC 1105 and *Lepine*, 2008 FC 1106 (CRA's fears of dissipation of assets were well-founded); *Papa (Gallo)*, 2009 FC 49 [no appeal possible due to 225.2(13): 2009 FCA 112] (CRA did not fail to make full and frank disclosure); *Dauphin*, 2009 FC 346 [judicial review refused 2009

FCA 257] (D had history of fraud and not paying taxes); *Imbeault*, 2009 FC 499 (I's only major asset was $580,000 in a bank account, she owed $406,000 to CRA, and her husband, who had a history of tax evasion, had transferred the funds to her to avoid paying CRA); *Douville*, 2009 FC 986; *Ross*, 2010 FC 594 and 921 (risk that R would sell his business; Quebec decision cancelling provincial assessment did not justify reversing decision); *Mulé*, 2010 FC 1125 (M had $172,000 tax debt and had liquidated most assets); *Dauphin*, 2010 FC 1144 (Crown need not prove fraud); *Park*, 2011 FC 263 (family was known to move significant funds offshore and had history of unorthodox behaviour); *Arif*, 2011 FC 1000 (police found large amount of cocaine in home, and A had recently liquidated property); *Tehrani*, 2011 FC 1232 (T had liquidated assets and made numerous misrepresentations); *Friends of Googolplexion*, 2011 FC 1270 (past "unorthodox behaviour" intended to thwart collection — discusses the case law); *Accredited Home Lenders*, 2012 FC 461 (Canadian sub of bankrupt US subprime mortgage lender was liquidating assets to transfer to parent's bankruptcy trustee); *Deschênes*, 2013 FC 87 ("double accounts, not declaring all income, a lifestyle that does not correspond to a declared income and the provision of false statements"); *Tassone*, 2013 FC 1100 (unorthodox behaviour included substantial unreported income and transferring funds offshore, and T's only asset of value was the home); *Prospera Developments*, 2015 FC 291 (company with $1.3m tax debt and only one known bank account was trying to transfer $928,000 to Turks & Caicos; CRA made "full and frank disclosure"); *9183-4507 Québec*, 2015 FC 901 (FCA appeal discontinued A-371-15) (value shift left shell company with insufficient assets to pay $10m GAAR assessment); *Izmirlian*, 2019 FC 63 (I sold home, gave $1.5m to his children and depleted his bank account); *Moise*, 2021 FC 452 (225.2(8) application requires showing reasonable grounds to doubt the 225.2(2) test was met).

In *S & D International*, 2009 ABQB 536, a jeopardy order was upheld but the terms were varied to allow the company to sell properties provided it paid 65% of the proceeds to CRA, so that it could stay in business. In *I. Waxman & Sons*, 2010 ONCA 447, a jeopardy order was not an "interim" order and took effect before bankruptcy, so it had priority.

In *Klundert*, 2014 FCA 156 (leave to appeal denied 2014 CarswellNat 4957 (SCC)), CRA was not required to apply monies collected under a jeopardy order to K's criminal fines (which would survive bankruptcy).

In *Comber*, 2009 TCC 72, where CRA had already seized assets under a jeopardy order, the Court declined to order C to post security for costs in his appeal, as that would deprive him of his only avenue to recover the amounts seized.

Moss, 2009 FCA 92 (leave to appeal to SCC discontinued May 25/09), dismissed a lawsuit against CRA for proceeding with jeopardy collection, preventing M from converting insurance policies into annuities exempt from seizure.

For earlier discussion see Elaine Sibson, "Revenue Canada's Long Collection Arm", 1998 Cdn Tax Foundation conference report, 26:1-13.

Interest is not payable on funds seized under a jeopardy order if they are refunded to the taxpayer: *Grenon*, 2016 FC 604.

For CRA interpretation and procedures see *National Collections Manual* (2015, on *TaxPartner* or *Taxnet Pro*), "Jeopardy — Tax programs", though some of the information is suppressed.

Information Circulars: 98-1R5: Tax collection policies.

CRA Audit Manual: 11.5.5: Jeopardy assessments.

(3) Notice of assessment not sent — An authorization under subsection (2) in respect of an amount assessed in respect of a taxpayer may be granted by a judge notwithstanding that a notice of assessment in respect of that amount has not been sent to the taxpayer at or before the time the application is made where the judge is satisfied that the receipt of the notice of assessment by the taxpayer would likely further jeopardize the collection of the amount, and for the purposes of sections 222, 223, 224, 224.1, 224.3 and 225, the amount in respect of which an authorization is so granted shall be deemed to be an amount payable under this Act.

(4) Affidavits — Statements contained in an affidavit filed in the context of an application under this section may be based on belief with the grounds therefor.

(5) Service of authorization and of notice of assessment — An authorization granted under this section in respect of a taxpayer shall be served by the Minister on the taxpayer within 72 hours after it is granted, except where the judge orders the authorization to be served at some other time specified in the authorization, and, where a notice of assessment has not been sent to the taxpayer at or before the time of the application, the notice of assessment shall be served together with the authorization.

(6) How service effected — For the purposes of subsection (5), service on a taxpayer shall be effected by

(a) personal service on the taxpayer; or

(b) service in accordance with directions, if any, of a judge.

Related Provisions: 244(6) — Proof of personal service.

(7) Application to judge for direction — Where service on a taxpayer cannot reasonably otherwise be effected as and when required under this section, the Minister may, as soon as practicable, apply to a judge for further direction.

(8) Review of authorization — Where a judge of a court has granted an authorization under this section in respect of a taxpayer, the taxpayer may, on 6 clear days notice to the Deputy Attorney General of Canada, apply to a judge of the court to review the authorization.

Related Provisions: *Interpretation Act* 27(1) — Calculation of clear days.

Notes: See Notes to 225.2(2) for cases under 225.2(8).

The words "a judge of *the* court" indicate that a judge of the same court must be approached for a review of the first judge's order.

(9) Limitation period for review application — An application under subsection (8) shall be made

(a) within 30 days from the day on which the authorization was served on the taxpayer in accordance with this section; or

(b) within such further time as a judge may allow, on being satisfied that the application was made as soon as practicable.

Related Provisions: *Interpretation Act* 27(5) — Meaning of "within 30 days".

(10) Hearing *in camera* — An application under subsection (8) may, on the application of the taxpayer, be heard *in camera*, if the taxpayer establishes to the satisfaction of the judge that the circumstances of the case justify *in camera* proceedings.

Notes: See Notes to 179.

(11) Disposition of application — On an application under subsection (8), the judge shall determine the question summarily and may confirm, set aside or vary the authorization and make such other order as the judge considers appropriate.

Related Provisions: 225.2(13) — No appeal from judge's decision.

(12) Directions — Where any question arises as to the course to be followed in connection with anything done or being done under this section and there is no direction in this section with respect thereto, a judge may give such direction with regard thereto as, in the opinion of the judge, is appropriate.

(13) No appeal from review order — No appeal lies from an order of a judge made pursuant to subsection (11).

Notes: One might wonder whether, if the judge made an error of law, there could be judicial review (JR) under *Federal Courts Act* s. 28 or equivalent provincial legislation; but see *Papa (Gallo)*, 2009 FCA 112 (appeal quashed), and *Dauphin*, 2009 FCA 257 (no JR as it would subvert 225.2(13)).

Definitions [s. 225.2]: "amount", "assessment" — 248(1); "clear days" — *Interpretation Act* 27(1); "Federal Court" — *Federal Courts Act* s. 4; "Minister" — 248(1); "province" — *Interpretation Act* 35(1); "superior court" — *Interpretation Act* 35(1); "taxpayer" — 248(1).

Information Circulars [s. 225.2]: 73-10R3: Tax evasion.

226. (1) Taxpayer leaving Canada — Where the Minister suspects that a taxpayer has left or is about to leave Canada, the Minister may, before the day otherwise fixed for payment, by notice served personally or by registered letter addressed to the taxpayer's latest known address, demand payment of the amount of all taxes, interest and penalties for which the taxpayer is liable or would be liable if the time for payment had arrived, and that amount shall be paid forthwith by the taxpayer notwithstanding any other provision of this Act.

Related Provisions: 128.1(4) — Tax effects of ceasing to be resident in Canada; 222(4)(a)(i) — Beginning of limitation period for collection action; 222.1 — Application to awards of court costs; 225.2 — Immediate collection of amounts owing; 231.2(1) — requirement to provide information or documents for collection purposes; 231.6(1) — foreign-based documents sought for collection purposes; 248(7)(a) — Notice deemed received on day mailed.

Notes: 226(1) amended by 1991 technical bill to include the case where the taxpayer has already left Canada, effective December 17, 1991.

See Notes to 223(3).

Information Circulars: 98-1R5: Tax collection policies.

(2) Seizure in case of default of payment — If a taxpayer fails to pay, as required, any tax, interest or penalties demanded under this section, the Minister may direct that the goods and chattels, or movable property, of the taxpayer be seized and subsections 225(2) to (5) apply, with respect to the seizure, with any modifications that the circumstances require.

Related Provisions: 222(3) — Ten-year limitation on collection action; 222.1 — Application to awards of court costs; 231.2(1) — requirement to provide information or documents for collection purposes; 231.6(1) — foreign-based documents sought for collection purposes.

Notes: 226(2) amended by 2002-2013 technical bill (Part 4 — bijuralism), effective June 26, 2013, to add "or movable property" and change "as the circumstances require" to "that the circumstances require".

Definitions [s. 226]: "Minister" — 248(1); "movable" — Quebec *Civil Code* art. 900–907; "taxpayer" — 248(1).

227. (1) Withholding taxes — No action lies against any person for deducting or withholding any sum of money in compliance or intended compliance with this Act.

Related Provisions: 224(2) — Minister's receipt discharges tax debtor's liability under Requirement to Pay.

Notes: Once an amount is withheld it must be remitted, even if it did not need to be withheld, and 227(1) applies: *Suspended Power*, 2007 TCC 519 (FCA appeal dismissed for delay). Since the employee (or other person) from whom tax is withheld gets full credit for the amount withheld when filing their return, even if an action is possible the only damages are the use of the funds until April when the year's tax is due: *RJM56 v. Kurnik*, 2016 ONCA 821, para. 30; *Fehrman v. Goodlife*, 2017 ONSC 4348, para. 14. See also Notes to 9(1) under "Damages" re *Kennett* case.

Employers were held to be right to withhold funds from settlements (though 227(1) was not cited) in: *Schneider v. Electrohome*, [1990] O.J. No. 182; *Scharf v. Freure Homes*, [1996] 1 C.T.C. 70 (Ont. CJ); *Ahmad v. Northstar Motors*, 2006 ABQB 616; *Deiana v. Credit Union Central*, 2014 SKQB 79. See also *RJM56* (above).

In *Marquest Asset v. Stone Investment*, 2021 ONSC 1476, MA sold an investment business to SI, and the parties agreed to have SI report the entire year's taxes withheld (presumably non-resident withholding tax) to CRA. SI claimed that MA was required to transfer funds from its CRA withholding tax account to MA's account. The Court found no breach of contract.

The same rule applies to CPP withholding (*Canada Pension Plan* 26(1)), EI (*Employment Insurance Act* 89(1)) and GST/HST (*Excise Tax Act* 224.1).

(2) Return filed with person withholding — Where a person (in this subsection referred to as the "payer") is required by regulations made under subsection 153(1) to deduct or withhold from a payment to another person an amount on account of that other person's tax for the year, that other person shall, from time to time as prescribed, file a return with the payer in prescribed form.

Related Provisions: 162(7) — Failure to comply with regulation; 227(3) — Where return is not filed.

Regulations: 107 (deadline for employee to file TD1 return).

Forms: TD1: Personal tax credits return.

(3) Failure to file return — Every person who fails to file a return as required by subsection (2) is liable to have the deduction or withholding under section 153 on account of the person's tax made as though the person were a person who is neither married nor in a common-law partnership and is without dependants.

Notes: 227(3) amended by 2000 same-sex partners bill, effective for 2001 and later taxation years, or earlier by election (see Notes to 248(1)"common-law partner").

(4) Trust for moneys deducted — Every person who deducts or withholds an amount under this Act is deemed, notwithstanding any security interest (as defined in subsection 224(1.3)) in the amount so deducted or withheld, to hold the amount separate and apart from the property of the person and from property held by any secured creditor (as defined in subsection 224(1.3)) of that person that but for the security interest would be property of the person, in trust for Her Majesty and for payment to Her Majesty in the manner and at the time provided under this Act.

Related Provisions: 153(1.04) — COVID-19 emergency benefit to employers deemed not held in trust; 227(4.1) — Extension of trust; 227(4.2) — Meaning of security interest; 227(4.3) — Application to the Crown.

Notes: Failing to remit employee source deductions withheld is considered by the CRA to be theft of trust moneys. Where a corporation fails to remit, its directors are normally liable under 227.1. A lawyer failing to remit may be committing professional misconduct: see Law Society of Upper Canada, "Invitations to Attend: for the information of the profession", *Ontario Reports*, Sept. 11, 2015, p. lxxxviii.

227(4)-(4.2) and 224(1.2)-(1.3) give CRA a "super priority" over source deductions. A parallel rule for GST/HST collected but not remitted is in *Excise Tax Act* s. 222, but that rule is subject to the *Bankruptcy and Insolvency Act*. See the *Practitioner's GST Annotated* for case law under that section.

The super-priority applied in: *Ontario v. NRS Mississauga*, 2003 CarswellOnt 1239 (Ont CA) (over a real estate brokerage trust account holding deposits for closings, as no "constructive trust" was proven for those deposits); *HSBC Bank*, 2004 FC 467 (bank's redemption of GIC under security agreement, when debtor was in default on its source deductions — CRA need not send notice for priority to be effective); *National Bank*, 2004 FCA 92 (leave to appeal denied 2004 CarswellNat 3585 (SCC)) (bank liable for customer's unremitted source deductions when bank seized property subject to chattel mortgages); *Newcourt Financial*, 2004 FCA 91 (same); *Canadian Western Bank v. 702348 Alberta*, 2012 ABQB 89 and 2012 ABQB 305 (tax debtor paid money into Court to clear builders' liens, but since payment was made unilaterally, funds remained the tax debtor's and became Crown property under 227(4.1)); *Royal Bank v. Galmar Electrical*, 2015 ONSC 5561 (priority over union's claim on behalf of employees); *PriceWaterhouseCoopers v. Bank of Montreal*, 2017 NLTD(G) 43; *Rosedale Farms*, 2017 NSSC 160 (debtor-in-possession financing). The same super-priority under the Ontario *Retail Sales Tax Act* was upheld in *Toronto-Dominion Bank v. Comrie*, 2014 ONSC 1924. See also cases in Notes to 224(1.2).

CRA's priority did not apply to an absolute assignment of accounts receivable to a factoring company (since the receivables no longer belonged to the tax debtor), in *First Vancouver Finance*, 2002 SCC 49 and *Saskatchewan Power v. Mainline*, 2018 SKQB 222 (aff'd on other grounds as *Liquid Capital v. Mainline*, 2019 SKCA 66).

CRA's priority also did not apply in: *DaimlerChrysler v. Mega Pets*, 2002 BCCA 242 (seized vehicle had not belonged solely to tax debtor; creditor of joint owner cannot seize jointly-owned property without obtaining order of partition); *Canada North*, 2019 ABCA 314 (SCC appeal heard Dec. 1/20, file 38871) (*Companies' Creditors Arrangement Act* priority over interim financing); *Nortip Development [Travelers Canada v. Elite Builders]*, 2019 NLCA 34 (standard mortgage clause re insurance protected lender with mortgage on insured property because it created a separate insurance contract, not a security interest).

See also CRA *National Collections Manual* under "Deemed trust", on *Taxnet Pro* and *TaxPartner*; VIEWS docs 2008-0289321I7, 2009-0338291E5. CRA can be aggressive in asserting its 227(4)-(4.2) rights, such as over mortgagees where the unremitted source deductions or GST existed before the mortgage was granted (Reg. 2201): see *MCAP Service v. Hunter*, 2007 ONCA 83; *Toronto-Dominion Bank*, 2020 FCA 80 (leave to appeal to SCC requested); 2011-0413081C6 (application on sale to *bona fide* third party).

See also 227(4.1) Notes.

227(4) amended and (4.1), (4.2) added by 1995-97 technical bill, effective June 15, 1994, to overturn *Royal Bank v. Sparrow Electric*, 1997 CarswellAlta 113 (SCC) and give CRA stronger powers of recovery of source deductions. Earlier amended by 1993 technical bill, effective June 15, 1994.

Information Circulars: 98-1R5: Tax collection policies.

(4.1) Extension of trust — Notwithstanding any other provision of this Act, the *Bankruptcy and Insolvency Act* (except sections 81.1 and 81.2 of that Act), any other enactment of Canada, any enactment of a province or any other law, where at any time an amount deemed by subsection (4) to be held by a person in trust for Her Majesty is not paid to Her Majesty in the manner and at the time provided under this Act, property of the person and property held by any secured creditor (as defined in subsection 224(1.3)) of that person that but for a security interest (as defined in subsection 224(1.3)) would be property of the person, equal in value to the amount so deemed to be held in trust is deemed

    (a) to be held, from the time the amount was deducted or withheld by the person, separate and apart from the property of the person, in trust for Her Majesty whether or not the property is subject to such a security interest, and

    (b) to form no part of the estate or property of the person from the time the amount was so deducted or withheld, whether or not the property has in fact been kept separate and apart from the estate or property of the person and whether or not the property is subject to such a security interest

and is property beneficially owned by Her Majesty notwithstanding any security interest in such property and in the proceeds thereof, and the proceeds of such property shall be paid to the Receiver General in priority to all such security interests.

Related Provisions: 153(1.04) — COVID-19 emergency benefit to employers deemed not held in trust; 223(11.1) — Deemed security interest where registered under

Bankruptcy and Insolvency Act s. 87(1); 227(4.2) — Meaning of security interest; 227(4.3) — Application to the Crown.

Notes: See Notes to 227(4). On application to a bankrupt limited partnership, see Notes to 227(15).

A landlord's right to distrain is a "security interest" covered by 227(4.1): *Community Expansion*, 2005 CarswellOnt 214 (Ont CA) (but see *Absolute Bailiffs*, [2002] G.S.T.C. 116 (TCC); aff'd on other grounds 2003 FCA 397). 227(4.1) also applied in *Caisse Populaire Desjardins de l'Est de Drummond (Caisse Populaire du Bon Conseil)*, 2009 SCC 29; *Caisse populaire de la Vallée de l'Or*, 2005 FC 948; *Toronto Dominion Bank*, 2007 FC 313 (227(4.1) took priority over a mortgage); *CanaDream v. Garmeco*, 2016 BCSC 2426 (priority over rent payments). See also *Banque Nationale*, 2009 QCCQ 8079, on the parallel Quebec provision.

On an arm's length asset sale, the deemed trust stays with the vendor (the sale proceeds), not the assets: CRA, Cdn Bar Assn Commodity Tax section meeting, March 6, 2014 (cba.org > "Sections"), q. 3 (for the GST/HST rule in *Excise Tax Act* s. 222(3)).

227(4.1) added by 1995-97 technical bill, effective June 15, 1994.

(4.2) Meaning of security interest — For the purposes of subsections (4) and (4.1), a security interest does not include a prescribed security interest.

Related Provisions: 227(4.3) — Application to the Crown.

Notes: 227(4.2) added by 1995-97 technical bill, effective June 15, 1994.

Regulations: 2201 (prescribed security interest).

(4.3) Application to Crown — For greater certainty, subsections (4) to (4.2) apply to Her Majesty in right of Canada or a province where Her Majesty in right of Canada or a province is a secured creditor (within the meaning assigned by subsection 224(1.3)) or holds a security interest (within the meaning assigned by that subsection).

Notes: 227(4.3) added by 2001 technical bill, effective June 14, 2001 (Royal Assent). It and 224(1.4) overrule *Brant*, [1998] G.S.T.C. 101 (FCTD), where the Court ruled that the Ontario government was not a "person" to whom a Requirement to Pay could be issued.

(5) Payments by trustees, etc. — Where a specified person in relation to a particular person (in this subsection referred to as the "payer") has any direct or indirect influence over the disbursements, property, business or estate of the payer and the specified person, alone or together with another person, authorizes or otherwise causes a payment referred to in subsection 135(3), 135.1(7) or 153(1), or on or in respect of which tax is payable under Part XII.5 or XIII, to be made by or on behalf of the payer, the specified person

(a) is, for the purposes of subsections 135(3) and 153(1), section 215 and this section, deemed to be a person who made the payment;

(a.1) is, for the purposes of subsections 135.1(7) and 211.8(2), deemed to be a person who redeemed, acquired or cancelled a share and made the payment as a consequence of the redemption, acquisition or cancellation;

(b) is jointly and severally, or solidarily, liable with the payer to pay to the Receiver General

(i) all amounts payable by the payer because of any of subsections 135(3), 135.1(7), 153(1) and 211.8(2) and section 215 in respect of the payment, and

(ii) all amounts payable under this Act by the payer because of any failure to comply with any of those provisions in respect of the payment; and

(c) is entitled to deduct or withhold from any amount paid or credited by the specified person to the payer or otherwise recover from the payer any amount paid under this subsection by the specified person in respect of the payment.

Related Provisions: 227(5.1) — Specified person; 227(5.2) — "Person" includes partnership; 227.1 — Liability of corporate directors.

Notes: In *Roll*, [2001] 1 C.T.C. 143 (FCA), a bare trustee of a corporation was not liable for the corp's failure to withhold source deductions. In *Lewin [JJ Herbert Family Trust]*, 2011 TCC 476 (aff'd on other grounds 2012 FCA 279: "we are not to be taken as endorsing the judge's reasons with respect to subsection 227(5)"), a trustee was not liable for the trust's failure to withhold non-resident tax because he resigned before an amount payable to a beneficiary was paid out.

227(5)(b) opening words amended by 2002-2013 technical bill (Part 4 — bijuralism), effective June 26, 2013, to add "or solidarily".

227(5) earlier amended by 2006 budget bill #1 (effective 2006), 1996 Budget. Added by 1995 Budget. Former 227(5) repealed by 1993 technical bill.

(5.1) Definition of "specified person" — In subsection (5), a "specified person" in relation to a particular person means a person who is, in relation to the particular person or the disbursements, property, business or estate of the particular person,

(a) a trustee;

(b) a liquidator;

(c) a receiver;

(d) an interim receiver;

(e) a receiver-manager;

(f) a trustee in bankruptcy or other person appointed under the *Bankruptcy and Insolvency Act*;

(g) an assignee;

(h) a secured creditor (as defined in subsection 224(1.3));

(i) an executor, a liquidator of a succession or an administrator;

(j) any person acting in a capacity similar to that of a person referred to in any of paragraphs (a) to (i);

(k) a person appointed (otherwise than as an employee of the creditor) at the request of, or on the advice of, a secured creditor in relation to the particular person to monitor, or provide advice in respect of, the disbursements, property, business or estate of the particular person under circumstances such that it is reasonable to conclude that the person is appointed to protect or advance the interests of the creditor; or

(l) an agent of a specified person referred to in any of paragraphs (a) to (k).

Notes: Reference to a liquidator of a succession added to 227(5.1)(i) by 2001 *Civil Code* harmonization bill, effective June 14, 2001. The change is non-substantive; see *Interpretation Act* s. 8.2.

227(5.1) added by 1995 Budget, effective June 20, 1996 (Royal Assent).

(5.2) "Person" includes partnership — For the purposes of this section, references in subsections (5) and (5.1) to persons include partnerships.

Related Provisions: 227(15) — "Person" includes partnerships for certain purposes throughout s. 227.

Notes: 227(5.2) added by 1995 Budget, effective June 20, 1996 (Royal Assent).

Proposed **227(5.2)-(5.4)** (Dec. 12, 1995) would have made a secured creditor with influence over clearing cheques or payments (such as a bank) liable for refusing to clear (or otherwise interfering with) remittances of withholdings, unless *all* payments were being stopped. (Similar proposals for GST remittances were in proposed *Excise Tax Act* s. 323.1.) However, the banks and other financial institutions promised to comply voluntarily, and the proposals were put on hold to allow CRA to monitor this compliance. They were officially withdrawn in Nov. 2014. For the text, see PITA 9th-36th ed.

(6) Excess withheld, returned or applied — Where a person on whose behalf an amount has been paid under Part XII.5 or XIII to the Receiver General was not liable to pay tax under that Part or where the amount so paid is in excess of the amount that the person was liable to pay, the Minister shall, on written application made no later than 2 years after the end of the calendar year in which the amount was paid, pay to the person the amount so paid or such part of it as the person was not liable to pay, unless the person is or is about to become liable to make a payment to Her Majesty in right of Canada, in which case the Minister may apply the amount otherwise payable under this subsection to that liability and notify the person of that action.

Notes: 227(6) provides for a refund of non-resident withholding tax (Part XIII): VIEWS doc 2007-0253901E5; or Part XII.5 tax (re labour-sponsored funds tax credit). For payroll source withholding, the employee claims amounts withheld at source as a refundable credit on page 4 of the T1 General tax return, and can do so even if the employer never remits the amount withheld: see 153(3) and Notes to 153(1).

227(6) could be used by US LLCs seeking refunds based on the *TD Securities* case; see VIEWS doc 2010-0369271C6 and Notes to Canada-US tax treaty Art. IV:6. (However, relief was denied in *CGI Holding*, 2016 FC 1086, as CRA considered the facts to be different from *TD* and the 2-year limit was missed.) It can also be used to recover Part

XIII tax withheld on payment to a deemed resident trust via 94(3)(g): 2014-0517511E5; and tax payable on thin capitalization interest due to 214(16).

The application form is NR7R, but it need not be used and a letter will suffice, since 227(6) does not say "in prescribed form".

The 2-year deadline is extended for a refund based on enactment of 212(9)(d) in 2013: 2002-2013 technical bill s. 347(31). See Notes to 212(9). It may also be extended by treaty provisions (e.g., Canada-Singapore treaty Art. XXI): VIEWS doc 2011-0425911C6 [2011 CTF conf. q.4]. Where the deadline is missed, see Notes to 221.2.

Only the non-resident can apply for the refund, even if the Canadian payor bore the cost of the tax due to a gross-up agreement: *Sentinel Hill*, 2008 ONCA 132 (leave to appeal denied 2008 CarswellOnt 5023 (SCC)); *FMC Technologies*, 2009 FCA 217 (leave to appeal denied 2010 CarswellNat 33).

For refund interest see Notes to 164(3).

227(6) amended by 1996 Budget (effective April 25, 1997) and 1993 technical bill.

Forms: NR7R: Application for refund of Part XIII tax withheld; NR302: Declaration of eligibility for benefits (reduced tax) under a tax treaty for a partnership with non-resident partners; NR303: Declaration of eligibility for benefits (reduced tax) under a tax treaty for a hybrid entity; NR304: Direct deposit request for non-resident account holders and NR7-R refund applicants.

(6.1) Repayment of non-resident shareholder loan —

Where, in respect of a loan from or indebtedness to a corporation or partnership, a person on whose behalf an amount was paid to the Receiver General under Part XIII because of subsection 15(2) and paragraph 214(3)(a) repays the loan or indebtedness or a portion of it and it is established by subsequent events or otherwise that the repayment was not made as part of a series of loans or other transactions and repayments, the Minister shall, on written application made no later than 2 years after the end of the calendar year in which the repayment is made, pay to the person an amount equal to the lesser of

(a) the amount so paid to the Receiver General in respect of the loan or indebtedness or portion of it, as the case may be, and

(b) the amount that would be payable to the Receiver General under Part XIII if a dividend described in paragraph 212(2)(a) equal in amount to the amount of the loan or indebtedness repaid were paid by the corporation or partnership to the person at the time of the repayment,

unless the person is or is about to become liable to make a payment to Her Majesty in right of Canada, in which case the Minister may apply the amount otherwise payable under this subsection to that liability and notify the person of that action.

Related Provisions: 227(7.1) — Determination of amount under subsec. (6.1); 248(10) — Series of transactions.

Notes: For examples of 227(6.1) applying see VIEWS docs 2011-0397921I7, 2014-0560401E5. Where the repaid loan was in a foreign currency that has fluctuated, see 2010-0381061I7. Where the 2-year deadline is missed, see 2013-0482991E5 re applying 221.2.

227(6.1) added by 1993 technical bill, effective June 15, 1994.

Interpretation Bulletins: IT-119R4: Debts of shareholders and certain persons connected with shareholders.

Transfer Pricing Memoranda: TPM-02: Repatriation of funds by non-residents — Part XIII assessments.

(6.2) Foreign affiliate dumping — late-filed form —

If, in respect of an investment described in subsection 212.3(10), a corporation is deemed by subparagraph 212.3(7)(d)(ii) to pay a dividend and the corporation subsequently complies with the requirements of subparagraph 212.3(7)(d)(i) in respect of the investment,

(a) subject to paragraph (b), the Minister shall, on written application made on a particular day that is, or is no more than two years after, the day on which the form described in subparagraph 212.3(7)(d)(i) is filed, pay to the corporation an amount equal to the lesser of

(i) the total of all amounts, if any, paid to the Receiver General, on or prior to the particular day, on behalf of a person and in respect of the liability of the person to pay an amount under Part XIII in respect of the dividend, and

(ii) the amount that the person was liable to pay in respect of the dividend under Part XIII;

(b) where the corporation or the person is or is about to become liable to make a payment to Her Majesty in right of Canada, the Minister may apply the amount otherwise payable under paragraph (a) to that liability and notify the corporation, and, if applicable, the person, of that action; and

(c) for the purposes of this Part (other than subparagraph (a)(i)), if the amount described in subparagraph (a)(ii) exceeds the amount described in subparagraph (a)(i), the corporation is deemed to pay that excess to the Receiver General on the day on which the form described in subparagraph 212.3(7)(d)(i) is filed.

Notes: 227(6.2) added by 2014 budget bill #2, effective for transactions and events that occur after March 28, 2012.

(7) Application for assessment —

Where, on application under subsection (6) by or on behalf of a person to the Minister in respect of an amount paid under Part XII.5 or XIII to the Receiver General, the Minister is not satisfied

(a) that the person was not liable to pay any tax under that Part, or

(b) that the amount paid was in excess of the tax that the person was liable to pay,

the Minister shall assess any amount payable under that Part by the person and send a notice of assessment to the person, and sections 150 to 163, subsections 164(1) and (1.4) to (7), sections 164.1 to 167 and Division J of Part I apply with any modifications that the circumstances require.

Notes: Due to 227(7), the Tax Court has jurisdiction to hear an appeal of interest assessed on Part XIII tax: *Cooper*, 2009 TCC 236; but where an application to refund such tax is made after the 2-year deadline, the Federal Court has jurisdiction: *CGI Holding LLC*, 2016 FC 1086. For calculation of interest on a Part XIII refund, see Notes to 164(3).

227(7) amended by 1996 Budget (effective April 25, 1997) and 1993 technical bill.

(7.1) Application for determination —

Where, on application under subsection (6.1) by or on behalf of a person to the Minister in respect of an amount paid under Part XIII to the Receiver General, the Minister is not satisfied that the person is entitled to the amount claimed, the Minister shall, at the person's request, determine, with all due dispatch, the amount, if any, payable under subsection (6.1) to the person and shall send a notice of determination to the person, and sections 150 to 163, subsections 164(1) and (1.4) to (7), sections 164.1 to 167 and Division J of Part I apply with such modifications as the circumstances require.

Notes: 227(7.1) added by 1993 technical bill, effective June 15, 1994.

(8) Penalty —

Subject to subsection (9.5), every person who in a calendar year has failed to deduct or withhold any amount as required by subsection 153(1) or section 215 is liable to a penalty of

(a) 10% of the amount that should have been deducted or withheld; or

(b) where at the time of the failure a penalty under this subsection was payable by the person in respect of an amount that should have been deducted or withheld during the year and the failure was made knowingly or under circumstances amounting to gross negligence, 20% of that amount.

Related Provisions: 147.1(3) — Deemed registration; 161(11) — Interest on penalties; 227(8.3) — Interest on amounts not deducted or withheld; 227(8.4) — Non-resident employees and patronage dividends; 227(8.5) — No penalty for failing to withhold tax on deemed dividend due to thin-cap rules or transfer-pricing adjustment; 227(8.6) — No penalty on qualifying non-resident employer who meets certain conditions; 227(9) — Penalty; 227(9.5) — Each establishment considered a separate person; 227(10) — Assessment; 227(10.2) — Joint and several liability re contributions to RCA; 252.1 — Where union is employer.

Notes: 227(8), (8.3) and (8.4) deal with failure to withhold tax, while 227(9), (9.2) and (9.4) deal with a failure to remit amounts (trust funds) that have been withheld: *United Used Auto*, [2000] 3 C.T.C. 338 (BCSC). See Notes to 239(1) and 227(10).

Onus of proof for a penalty: see Notes to 162(10).

For CRA examples of "common remittance form errors that would result in the late remitting penalty being cancelled once the payment is properly allocated", see May 2013 ICAA Roundtable q.19 (tinyurl.com/cra-abtax).

CRA administrative policy is not to impose penalties on a First Nation for failing to withhold taxes, but the policy "can be revoked if the First Nation abuses the exemption privilege": VIEWS doc 2014-0533091I7.

227(8) amended by 2002-2013 technical bill (effective June 26, 2013), 1992 technical bill.

I.T. Application Rules: 62(2) (subsec. 227(8) applies to interest payable in respect of any period after December 23, 1971).

Interpretation Bulletins: IT-494: Hire of ships and aircraft from non-residents.

Information Circulars: 77-16R4: Non-resident income tax; 07-1R1: Taxpayer relief provisions.

Transfer Pricing Memoranda: TPM-02: Repatriation of funds by non-residents — Part XIII assessments; TPM-06: Bundled transactions.

CRA Audit Manual: 28.7.4: Penalties — failure to deduct or withhold an amount.

(8.1) Joint and several, or solidary, liability — If a particular person has failed to deduct or withhold an amount as required under subsection 153(1) or section 215 in respect of an amount that has been paid to a non-resident person, the non-resident person is jointly and severally, or solidarily, liable with the particular person to pay any interest payable by the particular person pursuant to subsection (8.3) in respect thereof.

Related Provisions: 227(10) — Assessment.

Notes: See Notes to 216(1) re interest applying under 227(8.1) when Part XIII liability is eliminated by filing s. 216 return.

227(8.1) amended by 2002-2013 technical bill (Part 4 — bijuralism), effective June 26, 2013, to add "or solidarily".

(8.2) Retirement compensation arrangement deductions — Where a person has failed to deduct or withhold any amount as required under subsection 153(1) in respect of a contribution under a retirement compensation arrangement, that person is liable to pay to Her Majesty an amount equal to the amount of the contribution, and each payment on account of that amount is deemed to be, in the year in which the payment is made,

(a) for the purposes of paragraph 20(1)(r), a contribution by the person to the arrangement; and

(b) an amount on account of tax payable by the custodian under Part XI.3.

Related Provisions: 147.1(3) — Deemed registration; 153(1)(p) — Withholding required; 227(10) — Assessment; 227(10.2) — Joint and several liability re contributions to RCA; 252.1 — Where union is employer.

(8.3) Interest on amounts not deducted or withheld — A person who fails to deduct or withhold any amount as required by subsection 135(3), 135.1(7), 153(1) or 211.8(2) or section 215 shall pay to the Receiver General interest on the amount at the prescribed rate, computed

(a) in the case of an amount required by subsection 153(1) to be deducted or withheld from a payment to another person, from the fifteenth day of the month immediately following the month in which the amount was required to be deducted or withheld, or from such earlier day as may be prescribed for the purposes of subsection 153(1), to,

(i) where that other person is not resident in Canada, the day of payment of the amount to the Receiver General, and

(ii) where that other person is resident in Canada, the earlier of the day of payment of the amount to the Receiver General and April 30 of the year immediately following the year in which the amount was required to be deducted or withheld;

(b) in the case of an amount required by subsection 135(3) or 135.1(7) or section 215 to be deducted or withheld, from the day on which the amount was required to be deducted or withheld to the day of payment of the amount to the Receiver General; and

(c) in the case of an amount required by subsection 211.8(2) to be withheld, from the day on or before which the amount was required to be remitted to the Receiver General to the day of the payment of the amount to the Receiver General.

Related Provisions: 221.1 — Application of interest where legislation retroactive; 227(8.1) — Joint and several liability; 227(10) — Assessment; 227(10.2) — Joint and several liability re contributions to RCA; 248(11) — Compound interest; 252.1 — Where union is employer.

Notes: For non-resident withholding tax, remittable "forthwith" under 215(1), interest under 227(8.3)(b) applies after the day of payment to the non-resident, but CRA requires remittance by (and charges interest after) the 15th of the next month: Guide T4061 (unchanged for COVID-19: tinyurl.com/covid-dates).

See also Notes to 227(8) and (8.4).

227(8.3) amended by 2006 budget bill #1 (implementing a 2005 Budget proposal), effective 2006, to refer to 135.1(7). Earlier amended by 1996 Budget, 1991 technical bill.

Regulations: 4301(a) (prescribed rate of interest).

Information Circulars: 07-1R1: Taxpayer relief provisions.

(8.4) Liability to pay amount not deducted or withheld — A person who fails to deduct or withhold any amount as required under subsection 135(3) or 135.1(7) in respect of a payment made to another person or under subsection 153(1) in respect of an amount paid to another person who is non-resident or who is resident in Canada solely because of paragraph 250(1)(a) is liable to pay as tax under this Act on behalf of the other person the whole of the amount that should have been so deducted or withheld and is entitled to deduct or withhold from any amount paid or credited by the person to the other person or otherwise to recover from the other person any amount paid by the person as tax under this Part on behalf of the other person.

Related Provisions: 215(6) — Parallel provision for non-resident withholding tax; 227(10) — Assessment.

Notes: 227(8.4) does not impose liability for tax not withheld at source from an employee who is resident in Canada (e.g., where the "employer" thought that the "employee" was an independent contractor). Similarly, 227(8.1) applies only to withholdings from non-residents. There are penalty and interest provisions, but no provision in 227 appears to impose liability for the unwithheld tax itself. (This is different from tax withheld but not remitted, for which 227(9.4) imposes liability.) If the entity not withholding is a corporation, 227.1(1) appears to impose liability on both corporation and directors, although it was designed specifically to catch the directors. See however VIEWS docs 9810975, 2003-0051261E5, and *Storrie*, [1996] 2 C.T.C. 2596 (TCC).

See also Notes to 227(8) and (10).

227(8.4) amended by 2006 budget bill #1 (implementing a 2005 Budget proposal), effective 2006, to add reference to 135.1(7). (The references to 135(3) and 153(1) were formerly broken out into paras. (a) and (b).)

227(8.4) amended by 1991 technical bill, effective July 14, 1990.

CRA Audit Manual: 15.2.11: Withholding of Part I tax — income from carrying on a business in Canada.

(8.5) No penalty — certain deemed payments — Subsection (8) does not apply to a corporation in respect of

(a) an amount of interest deemed by subsection 214(16) to have been paid as a dividend by the corporation unless, if the Act were read without reference to subsection 214(16), a penalty under subsection (8) would have applied in respect of the amount; and

(b) an amount deemed by subparagraph 212.3(7)(d)(ii) or subsection 247(12) to have been paid as a dividend by the corporation.

Notes: 227(8.5) provides that there is no penalty for failing to withhold tax on a deemed dividend resulting from the thin-capitalization rules (18(4), 12(1)(l.1), triggering tax under 214(16) and 212(2) — provided 212(1)(b) withholding was not already required on the interest) or a transfer-pricing adjustment (247(12) and 212(2)). This is presumably because these rules' application may not be known until after year-end.

227(8.5)(b) amended by 2014 budget bill #2 to add reference to 212.3(7)(d)(ii), effective for transactions and events that occur after March 28, 2012.

227(8.5) added by 2012 budget bill #2, for tax years that end after March 28, 2012.

Former 227(8.5) repealed by 1992 technical bill, effective 1993. It and 227(9.5) were replaced with new 227(9.5).

(8.6) No penalty — qualifying non-resident employers — Subsection (8) does not apply to a "qualifying non-resident employer" (as defined in subsection 153(6)) in respect of a payment made to an employee if, after reasonable inquiry, the employer had no reason to believe at the time of the payment that the employee was not a "qualifying non-resident employee" (as defined in subsection 153(6)).

Notes: 227(8.6) added by 2016 budget bill #1, for payments made after 2015. See Notes to 153(1) under "153(1)(a)(ii)".

(9) Penalty — Subject to subsection (9.5), every person who in a calendar year has failed to remit or pay as and when required by this Act or a regulation an amount deducted or withheld as required by this Act or a regulation or an amount of tax that the person is, by section 116 or by a regulation made under subsection 215(4), required to pay is liable to a penalty of

(a) subject to paragraph (b), if

(i) the Receiver General receives that amount on or before the day it was due, but that amount is not paid in the manner required, 3% of that amount,

(ii) the Receiver General receives that amount

(A) no more than three days after it was due, 3% of that amount,

(B) more than three days and no more than five days after it was due, 5% of that amount, or

(C) more than five days and no more than seven days after it was due, 7% of that amount, or

(iii) that amount is not paid or remitted on or before the seventh day after it was due, 10% of that amount; or

(b) where at the time of the failure a penalty under this subsection was payable by the person in respect of an amount that should have been remitted or paid during the year and the failure was made knowingly or under circumstances amounting to gross negligence, 20% of that amount.

Related Provisions: 227(8) — Penalty; 227(9.1) — Exclusion of first $500 of withholdings; 227(9.3) — Interest on certain tax not paid; 227(9.5) — Each establishment considered a separate person; 227(10.1) — Assessment; 227(10.2) — Joint and several liability re contributions to RCA; 248(7) — Receipt of things mailed; 252.1 — Where union is employer.

Notes: 227(9) applies only to amounts withheld and not remitted, not to amounts that *should have been* withheld but were not (227(8) applies to such amounts): *Maxi Maid*, 2012 TCC 178.

The 227(9)(a) graduated penalties, enacted in 2008, match a CRA administrative policy in effect since 2003 (news release, June 20, 2003). Originally a pilot project, the 2003 policy replaced an earlier "one free late remittance" policy (Directive 92-25; see *K-Bel*, 2006 FC 825, paras. 6, 10).

See Notes to 153(1) re the *McNaught Pontiac* case.

Onus of proof for a penalty: See Notes to 162(10).

Due diligence: Where a firm mailed its remittance a week before the deadline, but CRA allegedly received it late, the penalty was cancelled: *Weisz, Rocchi*, 2001 TCC 821. The due-diligence defence for this penalty is more stringent than for a director under 227.1(3), so in *741290 Ontario*, 2011 TCC 91, para. 17 (aff'd 2011 FCA 361), a successful directors' appeal did not relieve the company of the penalty.

See also Notes to 227(8).

227(9)(a) amended by 2008 budget bill #1, for payments and remittances that are required to be first made after Feb. 25, 2008. Before the amendment, read "10% of that amount".

227(9)(b) amended by 1992 technical bill, effective 1993.

Regulations: Part I (amount required to be withheld).

I.T. Application Rules: 62(2) (subsec. 227(9) applies to interest payable in respect of any period after December 23, 1971).

Information Circulars: 07-1R1: Taxpayer relief provisions.

Registered Plans Compliance Bulletins: 4 (abusive schemes — RRSP stripping).

CRA Audit Manual: 28.7.5: Penalties — failure to remit an amount withheld.

(9.1) Penalty — Notwithstanding any other provision of this Act, any other enactment of Canada, any enactment of a province or any other law, the penalty for failure to remit an amount required to be remitted by a person on or before a prescribed date under subsection 153(1), subsection 21(1) of the *Canada Pension Plan*, subsection 53(1) of the *Unemployment Insurance Act* and subsection 82(1) of the *Employment Insurance Act* shall, unless the person who is required to remit the amount has, knowingly or under circumstances amounting to gross negligence, delayed in remitting the amount or has, knowingly or under circumstances amounting to gross negligence, remitted an amount less than the amount required, apply only to the amount by which the total of all amounts so required to be remitted on or before that date exceeds $500.

Notes: For the meaning of "gross negligence" see Notes to 163(2).

227(9.1) amended by 1996 EI bill and 1995-97 technical bill (both effective June 30, 1996), 1992 technical bill.

CRA Audit Manual: 28.7.5: Penalties — failure to remit an amount withheld.

(9.2) Interest on amounts deducted or withheld but not remitted — Where a person has failed to remit as and when required by this Act or a regulation an amount deducted or withheld as required by this Act or a regulation, the person shall pay to the Receiver General interest on the amount at the prescribed rate computed from the day on which the person was so required to remit the amount to the day of remittance of the amount to the Receiver General.

Related Provisions: 221.1 — Application of interest where legislation retroactive; 227(10.1) — Assessment; 227(10.2) — Joint and several liability re contributions to RCA; 248(11) — Compound interest; 252.1 — Where union is employer.

Notes: See Notes to 227(8). For non-resident withholding tax, remittable "forthwith" under 215(1), interest under 227(9.2) applies after the day of payment to the non-resident, but CRA requires remittance by (and charges interest after) the 15th of the next month: Guide T4061 (unchanged for COVID-19: tinyurl.com/covid-dates).

Regulations: 4301(a) (prescribed rate of interest).

Information Circulars: 07-1R1: Taxpayer relief provisions.

(9.3) Interest on certain tax not paid — Where a person fails to pay an amount of tax that, because of section 116, subsection 212(19) or a regulation made under subsection 215(4), the person is required to pay, as and when the person is required to pay it, the person shall pay to the Receiver General interest on the amount at the prescribed rate computed from the day on or before which the amount was required to be paid to the day of payment of the amount to the Receiver General.

Related Provisions: 221.1 — Application of interest where legislation retroactive; 227(10.1) — Assessment; 248(11) — Compound interest.

Notes: 227(9.3) amended by 1993 technical bill, effective May 29, 1993.

Regulations: 4301 (prescribed rate of interest).

(9.4) Liability to pay amount not remitted — A person who has failed to remit as and when required by this Act or a regulation an amount deducted or withheld from a payment to another person as required by this Act or a regulation is liable to pay as tax under this Act on behalf of the other person the amount so deducted or withheld.

Related Provisions: 227(10.1) — Assessment; 227(10.2) — Joint and several liability re contributions to RCA; 252.1 — Where union is employer.

Notes: 227(9.4) applies to amounts withheld but not remitted. See Notes to 227(8) and (8.4).

Must CRA issue a notice of assessment before enforcing collection on a 227(9.4) liability? See Notes to 225.1(6).

In *Marché Lambert*, 2007 TCC 466, ML was liable under 227(9.4) when a payroll processing company paid ML's employees but failed to remit the tax withheld.

(9.5) Payment from same establishment — In applying paragraphs (8)(b) and (9)(b) in respect of an amount required by paragraph 153(1)(a) to be deducted or withheld, each establishment of a person shall be deemed to be a separate person.

Notes: 227(9.5) amended by 1992 technical bill, effective 1993.

Information Circulars: 07-1R1: Taxpayer relief provisions.

(10) Assessment — The Minister may at any time assess any amount payable under

(a) subsection (8), (8.1), (8.2), (8.3) or (8.4) or 224(4) or (4.1) or section 227.1 or 235 by a person,

(b) subsection 237.1(7.4) or (7.5) or 237.3(8) by a person or partnership,

(c) subsection (10.2) by a person as a consequence of a failure of a non-resident person to deduct or withhold any amount, or

(d) Part XIII by a person resident in Canada,

and, where the Minister sends a notice of assessment to that person or partnership, Divisions I and J of Part I apply with any modifications that the circumstances require.

Related Provisions: 164(1.5)(c)(i) — Late refund of amount overpaid due to 227(10) assessment under Reg. 105; 222(5)(c) — Restart of 10-year collection limitation period.

Notes: Due to the words "at any time", there is no limitation period on a 227(10) assessment: *Dagenais*, 2006 TCC 209; *McKesson Canada*, 2013 TCC 404, para. 396

(FCA appeal discontinued A-48-14); *Grant*, 2017 TCC 121, paras. 18-20 (no obligation on CRA to act "with all due dispatch"); VIEWS doc 2013-0481581I7. See also Notes to 160(2). Tax Executives Institute (TEI) has asked that Part XIII tax be subject to initial assessment and a 3-4 year reassessment limit: submissions to Finance, Dec. 6, 2017 and Dec. 5, 2018.

227(10) is the basis for assessing a director's liability under 227.1, and interest runs on the assessment, due to the words "Divisions I and J apply ...": *Zen*, 2010 FCA 180 (leave to appeal denied 2011 CarswellNat 47 (SCC)).

In *JP Morgan Asset Management*, 2013 FCA 250, an application for judicial review of a CRA decision to assess 7 years of Part XIII tax under 227(10), allegedly contrary to CRA guidelines, was struck out.

227(10) amended by 2002-2013 technical bill (effective June 26, 2013, to refer to 237.3(8)); 2012 budget bill #1 (to refer to 237.1(7.5)); 1995-97, 1993 and 1991 technical bills.

Information Circulars: 89-2R3: Directors' liability — s. 227.1 of the *Income Tax Act*, s. 323 of the *Excise Tax Act*, s. 81 of the *Air Travellers Security Charge Act*, subsec. 295(1) of the *Excise Act, 2001*, and section 95 of the *Softwood Lumber Products Export Charge Act, 2006*.

(10.01) Part XII.5 [assessment] — The Minister may at any time assess any amount payable under Part XII.5 by a person resident in Canada and, where the Minister sends a notice of assessment to that person, Divisions I and J of Part I apply with any modifications that the circumstances require.

Notes: 227(10.01) added by 1996 Budget, effective April 25, 1997 (Royal Assent). It implements the same rules for Part XII.5 (special tax in respect of the labour-sponsored funds tax credit) as does 227(10) for Part XIII non-resident withholding tax.

(10.1) Idem — The Minister may at any time assess

(a) any amount payable under section 116 or subsection (9), (9.2), (9.3) or (9.4) by any person,

(b) any amount payable under subsection (10.2) by any person as a consequence of a failure by a non-resident person to remit any amount, and

(c) any amount payable under Part XII.5 or XIII by any non-resident person,

and, where the Minister sends a notice of assessment to the person, sections 150 to 163, subsections 164(1) and (1.4) to (7), sections 164.1 to 167 and Division J of Part I apply with such modifications as the circumstances require.

Related Provisions: 164(1.5)(c)(ii) — Late refund of amount overpaid due to 227(10.1) assessment under 116(5) or (5.3); 224(1.2) — Garnishment of payments redirected to secured creditors.

Notes: 227(10.1), which triggers 224(1.2) garnishment super-priority, applies to payroll deductions withheld but not remitted (227(9.4)), as well as all the other amounts listed.

See Notes to 160(2) re assessment "at any time".

Interest under 164(3) applies to a Part XIII tax refund: see 164(3) Notes.

See Notes to 225.1(6) re whether a 227(10.1) assessment for unremitted payroll deductions must be issued before collection can be enforced.

See Notes to 223(3) re CRA enforcing collection against a non-resident.

227(10.1) amended by 1996 Budget (effective April 25, 1997) and 1993 technical bill.

(10.2) Joint and several, or solidary, liability re contributions to RCA — If a non-resident person fails to deduct, withhold or remit an amount as required by subsection 153(1) in respect of a contribution under a retirement compensation arrangement that is paid on behalf of the employees or former employees of an employer with whom the non-resident person does not deal at arm's length, the employer is jointly and severally, or solidarily, liable with the non-resident person to pay any amount payable under subsection (8), (8.2), (8.3), (9), (9.2) or (9.4) by the non-resident person in respect of the contribution.

Related Provisions: 227(10)(c) — Assessment for failure to deduct or withhold; 227(10.1)(c) — Assessment for failure to remit tax.

Notes: 227(10.2) amended by 2002-2013 technical bill (Part 4 — bijuralism), effective June 26, 2013, to add "or solidarily".

227(10.2) added by 1993 technical bill, effective June 15, 1994.

(10.3)–(10.9) [Repealed]

Notes: Former 227(10.2) to (10.9), never proclaimed into force, repealed by 1992 technical bill. They would have created a priority in favour of the Crown in respect of

amounts owing under the Act by a person as unremitted source deductions. The enhanced garnishment in 224(1.2)–(1.3) is now used instead for this purpose.

(11) Withholding tax — Provisions of this Act requiring a person to deduct or withhold an amount in respect of taxes from amounts payable to a taxpayer are applicable to Her Majesty in right of Canada or a province.

(12) Agreement not to deduct void — Where this Act requires an amount to be deducted or withheld, an agreement by the person on whom that obligation is imposed not to deduct or withhold is void.

(13) Minister's receipt discharges debtor — The receipt of the Minister for an amount deducted or withheld by any person as required by or under this Act is a good and sufficient discharge of the liability of any debtor to the debtor's creditor with respect thereto to the extent of the amount referred to in the receipt.

(14) Application of other Parts — Parts IV, IV.1, VI and VI.1 do not apply to any corporation for any period throughout which it is exempt from tax because of section 149.

Related Provisions: 186.1 — Part IV tax — exempt corporations; 219(2) — Part XIV tax — exempt corps; 227(16) — Part IV tax — municipal or provincial corp.

Notes: For a ruling applying 227(14) see VIEWS doc 2010-0376811R3.

227(14) amended by 1991 technical bill, effective 1990, to delete reference to Part III. An exempt corporation can thus be liable for Part III tax by making an election under 83(2) where the dividend payable exceeds its capital dividend account.

Interpretation Bulletins: IT-269R4: Part IV tax on taxable dividends received by a private corporation or a subject corporation; IT-347R2: Crown corporations (cancelled); IT-496R: Non-profit organizations.

(15) Partnership included in "person" — In this section, a reference to a "person" with respect to any amount deducted or withheld or required to be deducted or withheld is deemed to include a partnership.

Related Provisions: 96 — Partnerships and their members; 212(13.1) — Application of Part XIII tax to partnership; 227(5.2) — "Person" includes partnership for purposes of certain provisions.

Notes: Due to 227(15) and the "super priority" rule in 227(4.1), source deductions are recoverable from a bankrupt limited partnership: VIEWS doc 2009-033643I7.

227(15) amended by 1996 Budget, effective April 25, 1997, so that it applies for all purposes of withholding (including Part XII.5), rather than just Part XIII.

Forms: NR302: Declaration of eligibility for benefits (reduced tax) under a tax treaty for a partnership with non-resident partners.

(16) Municipal or provincial corporation excepted — A corporation that at any time in a taxation year would be a corporation described in any of paragraphs 149(1)(d) to (d.6) but for a provision of an appropriation Act is deemed not to be a private corporation for the purposes of Part IV with respect to that year.

Notes: 227(16) amended by 2001 technical bill, effective for taxation years that begin after 1998, to change "(d)" to "(d) to (d.6)" and add "with respect to that year".

Interpretation Bulletins [subsec. 227(16)]: IT-269R4: Part IV tax on taxable dividends received by a private corporation or a subject corporation; IT-347R2: Crown corporations (cancelled).

Definitions [s. 227]: "Act" — *Interpretation Act* 35(1); "amount", "assessment" — 248(1); "calendar year" — *Interpretation Act* 37(1)(a); "common-law partnership" — 248(1); "corporation" — 248(1), *Interpretation Act* 35(1); "custodian" — 248(1)"retirement compensation arrangement"; "dividend", "employee", "employer" — 248(1); "estate" — 104(1), 248(1); "Her Majesty" — *Interpretation Act* 35(1); "Minister", "non-resident" — 248(1); "person" — 227(5.2), (15), 248(1); "prescribed" — 248(1); "prescribed rate" — Reg. 4301; "private corporation" — 89(1), 248(1); "property" — 248(1); "province" — *Interpretation Act* 35(1); "public corporation" — 89(1), 248(1); "qualifying non-resident employer" — 153(6); "regulation" — 248(1); "resident in Canada" — 250; "retirement compensation arrangement", "salary or wages" — 248(1); "secured creditor" — 224(1.3); "security interest" — 224(1.3), 227(4.2); "series" — 248(10); "specified person" — 227(5.1); "tax payable" — 248(2); "taxation year" — 249; "taxpayer" — 248(1); "trust" — 104(1), 248(1), (3); "writing", "written" — *Interpretation Act* 35(1)"writing".

227.1 (1) Liability of directors for failure to deduct — Where a corporation has failed to deduct or withhold an amount as required by subsection 135(3) or 135.1(7) or section 153 or 215, has failed to remit such an amount or has failed to pay an amount of tax for a taxation year as required under Part VII or VIII, the directors of the corporation at the time the corporation was required to deduct, withhold, remit or pay the amount are jointly and severally, or solidarily, liable, together with the corporation, to pay that amount and any interest or penalties relating to it.

Related Provisions: 159(2) — Requirement for clearance certificate before distributing property; 204.87 — S. 227.1 applies to Part X.3 tax; 222(5)(c) — Restart of 10-year collection limitation period when director assessed under 227(10)(a); 227(10) — Assessment; 236 — Execution of documents by corporations; 242 — Officers and directors guilty of corporation's offences.

Notes: Directors are liable for a corporation's source withholdings (withheld but not remitted — see next para.), such as employee payroll deductions (s. 153), unremitted non-resident withholding tax (s. 215) including on mutual fund distributions (218.3(10)), withholding relating to patronage (135(3)), Part X.3 tax payable by labour-sponsored venture capital corporations (204.87) and the expired share-purchase and scientific research tax credit taxes (Parts VII and VIII). (This includes directors of non-profit corporations: *Wheeliker and Corsano*, [1999] 2 C.T.C. 395 (FCA); VIEWS doc 2008-029563117.) The liability is assessed under 227(10), and also applies to post-assessment interest: *Zen*, [2010] 6 C.T.C. 28 (FCA) (leave to appeal denied 2011 CarswellNat 47 (SCC)). For the amount recoverable from the director see 227.1(5). For CRA administrative policy see Information Circular 89-2R3. Directors of a corp that is a general partner can be liable for source deductions of the limited partnership: *Laxton*, [1989] 2 C.T.C. 2407 (TCC); VIEWS doc 2014-053125117.

Where a corp fails to *withhold* source deductions (rather than withholding and failing to *remit*), the words of 227.1(1) seem to apply; but in light of 227(8) (which imposes only a penalty, not liability for the amount not withheld) and 227(8.4) (which imposes liability for failing to remit s. 153 deductions, but only for non-resident employees), neither director nor corp is liable for the amount not withheld: *Storrie*, [1996] 2 C.T.C. 2596 (TCC); VIEWS docs 9810975, 2003-0051261E5.

Directors are also liable for unremitted CPP and EI withholdings; see *Canada Pension Plan* s. 21.1 and *Employment Insurance Act* s. 83, which covers both employee and employer premiums: *Matossian*, [2005] 2 C.T.C. 2503 (TCC). They are also liable for unremitted GST or HST (and overpaid GST/HST net tax refunds), whether or not collected from purchasers (*Excise Tax Act* s. 323 — see *Practitioner's Goods and Services Tax, Annotated* and the *Canada GST Service*); for excise duties (*Excise Act, 2001*, s. 295); and in some provinces, for unremitted sales taxes (e.g., Ontario *Retail Sales Tax Act* s. 43, for sales before July 2010).

Directors are not liable for ordinary unpaid tax of a corporation under Part I, or under other Parts (such as Part IV) — but they *can* be assessed under 160(1) if as shareholders they have received dividends from the company (see Notes to 160(1)). Where directors or shareholders have taken funds from a corp that owes tax, see also Carolyn Hogan, "Provincial Oppression Remedies and Unpaid Corporate Tax", 11(4) *Taxes & Wealth Management* (Carswell) 16-22 (Nov. 2018). Directors are not liable for interest accruing on remittances that became due before they became directors: VIEWS doc 2011-0412471E5.

Provincial tax: A director is normally assessed for the corp's federal + provincial liability. *Buckingham*, 2010 TCC 247 [aff'd on other grounds 2011 FCA 142], paras. 5-10, and *Seier*, 2010 TCC 495, para. 5, held that the TCC cannot consider the provincial tax (see Notes to 169(1)), so a parallel appeal is theoretically needed in the provincial superior court; but CRA will always adjust or cancel to match the federal appeal result (VIEWS doc 2012-0446051E5), so this is not needed in practice other than in Quebec and possibly Alberta. (In *Helgesen*, 2017 FCA 21, para. 1, the FCA said the TCC upheld the Alberta liability, but this seems wrong.) Also, in some provinces the provincial result now follows the federal automatically and cannot be appealed separately, e.g. Ontario *Taxation Act, 2007*, s. 140(4), (5).

Defences directors have against a 227.1 assessment are:

1. Denying that the Notice of Assessment was ever mailed. See Notes to 165(1).

2. Non-compliance by CRA with the technicalities of 227.1(2).

3. "Due diligence" — see 227.1(3).

4. Ceasing to be a director more than two years before the assessment (and not continuing as a *de facto* director: see below) — see 227.1(4). (There is no other limitation period: see Notes to 227(10).)

5. Not being either a legally-appointed or a *de facto* director. If X is on the public register of directors, CRA will presume X is a director, but this can be overcome with evidence that X never consented in writing to be one: *Lau*, [2003] G.S.T.C. 1 (TCC); *Netupsky*, [2003] G.S.T.C. 15 (TCC); *Colbran*, 2003 TCC 154; *Lambert*, 2003 TCC 557; *Bisaillon*, 2010 TCC 44; *Hay*, 2004 TCC 51; *Mikloski Estate*, 2004 TCC 253; *Pereira*, 2007 TCC 737, paras. 12-13; *Danso-Coffey*, 2010 ONCA 171; *MacDonald*, 2014 TCC 308; *Le*, 2018 TCC 65; *Bunton v. FTA*, 2020 ONSC 5463 (see also 227.1(4) Notes). Often the Court will conclude from the evidence that X was a director, e.g. *Gagné*, 2020 TCC 111 (under appeal to FCA).

Rectification can be sought from the province's superior court, deeming a person not to have been a director: *Danso-Coffey* (above), paras. 43-49; *Bunton v. FTA* (granted because B never consented to be one); Ontario *Business Corporations Act* s. 250. Such court might not have jurisdiction to rule that a person was not a *de facto* director for ITA purposes.

De facto directors (DFD): in *Wheeliker (Corsano)*, [1999] 2 C.T.C. 395 (FCA, leave to appeal denied 2000 CarswellNat 679 (SCC)), DFDs were liable even though not tech-

nically legal directors. This might be limited to persons who purport to be directors but technically are not: *Mosier*, [2001] G.S.T.C. 124 (TCC) (President & CEO who ran company but never purported to be director was not DFD); *Netupsky*, [2003] G.S.T.C. 15 (TCC) (former director was found to have continued to operate corp in capacity of shareholder); *Walsh*, 2009 TCC 557 (former director's discussions with CRA were largely in his personal capacity); *Macdonald*, 2014 TCC 308 (M had always been clear in his intention not to be a director, and was not DFD despite having signed 10-12 documents (at the direction of others) as director or officer); *Le*, 2018 TCC 65 (L never held herself out as director). *Koskocan*, 2016 TCC 277, distinguishes the actions of a *director* from those of an *officer or manager*, and rules convincingly that the latter do not make a person a DFD. *Contra: Hartrell*, 2008 FCA 59 (man who "played a key role" in corp and "had ultimate decision-making authority" was DFD even though he had never purported to be one); *McDonald*, 2014 TCC 315 (service manager who got contracts for the business, did bids and supervised employees was DFD despite never purporting to be one); *Ustel*, 2010 TCC 444 (former director who signed corp returns as director in 2003-04 was held to be DFD in 2008 because he had not otherwise notified CRA!); *Robin*, 2019 TCC 172 (R admitted he was DFD). DFDship, once established, "must be considered to endure at least as long as that person manages or supervises the management of the business and affairs of the corp": *Bremner*, 2009 FCA 146. See also Brian Studniberg, "Identifying the *De Facto* Director", 63(4) *Canadian Tax Journal* 1073-95 (2015).

If the last director resigns and no new director is appointed, that person may be a "deemed" director (whether or not they are a *de facto* director). In both *Goicoechea*, 2010 TCC 539, and *Snively*, 2011 TCC 196, the sole shareholder's resignation as director triggered Ontario *Business Corporations Act* (OBCA) s. 115(4), whereby "any person who manages or supervises the management of the business and affairs of the corporation" is deemed to be a director, and he remained liable. In all of *Zwierschke*, [1991] 2 C.T.C. 2783 (TCC), *Savoy*, 2011 TCC 35, paras. 52-57, *Doncaster*, 2015 TCC 127, and *Soulliere*, 2020 TCC 67 (under appeal to FCA), a first director could not validly resign without a replacement being appointed, due to OBCA 119(2); while in *Netupsky*, [2003] G.S.T.C. 15 (TCC), the absence of this rule in BC made the resignation valid.

6. Contesting the underlying corporate liability where the corporation did not. This can now definitely be done: *Duque*, 2020 FCA 73, para. 20. (Earlier, the TCC was conflicted on this, but the FCA allowed appeals on this basis in *Abrametz*, 2009 FCA 70, *Doncaster*, 2012 FCA 38 and *Gougeon*, 2012 FCA 294, without discussing the point.) CRA may have the onus of proving the liability, especially if CRA has this information and the director does not: *Simon*, [2002] 4 C.T.C. 2358 (TCC), paras. 61-80; *Mignardi*, 2013 TCC 67, para. 41; *Monsell*, 2019 TCC 5, paras. 28-31. A director can be assessed even if CRA does not prove it assessed the corp: *Siow*, 2010 TCC 594, but CRA *does* have to prove it attempted collection: 227.1(2).

7. If the corporation has filed a proposal or a Notice of Intention under the *Bankruptcy and Insolvency Act* (BIA), then arguably neither assessment or collection action can be taken against directors until the Court approves the proposal or the corporation goes bankrupt: BIA s. 69.31. (BIA 50(13) also allows a proposal to include a "compromise of claims against directors".)

If the corporation is bankrupt so interest does not accrue on its liability, interest still runs on the director's liability: VIEWS doc 2009-0311161E5.

The meaning of "deduct or withhold" in 227.1(1) may be unclear: *Storrie*, [1996] 2 C.T.C. 2596 (TCC).

The cost of contesting a 227.1 assessment is deductible under 60(o), but not if the assessment is solely for unremitted GST: *Shapiro*, 2011 TCC 79.

Counsel may be prohibited from acting for multiple directors if they do not waive the automatic conflict of interest: *Attisano*, 2016 CarswellNat 966 (TCC).

Rudan v. Chapman (procedural decision 2019 ONSC 6247) is a lawsuit claiming it was negligent for lawyer C to admit to CRA that his client R was a director. (One would think that the subsequent CRA assessment succeeded because R actually was a director, not because of anything C admitted.)

See also Stilwell, "Directors' Personal Liability", *Taxnet Pro* Tax Disputes Centre (July 2017, 25pp.); Rorabeck, "Directors' Liability for Unremitted Taxes: An Update", 2008 Atlantic Provinces Tax Conference (ctf.ca), 3B:1-18; Doobay & Markson, "Risky Business", 2011 Ontario Tax Conf. 3:1-26; "Directors' Liability", in Aron, *Tax Aspects of Litigation* (Carswell, looseleaf or *Taxnet Pro* Reference Centre), pp. 11:1-43; Lewy & Nevsky, "Directors' Liability", 22(10) *Canadian Tax Highlights* (ctf.ca) 10-11 (Oct. 2014).

Non-tax liability: Daley & Bieber, *Directors' and Officers' Liability in Canada* (LexisNexis, 2015, 301pp.); Nathan & Stuchberry, *The Directors' Handbook* (LexisNexis, 2019, 204pp).

227.1(1) amended by 2006 budget bill #1, effective 2006, to change "severally liable" to "severally, or solidarily, liable" and "relating thereto" to "relating to it", and to add reference to 135.1(7).

Information Circulars: 89-2R3: Directors' liability — s. 227.1 of the *Income Tax Act*, s. 323 of the *Excise Tax Act*, s. 81 of the *Air Travellers Security Charge Act*, subsec. 295(1) of the *Excise Act, 2001*, and section 95 of the *Softwood Lumber Products Export Charge Act, 2006*; 98-1R5: Tax collection policies.

CRA Audit Manual: 28.7.6: Directors liability — failure to deduct, remit GST/HST or income tax.

(2) Limitations on liability — A director is not liable under subsection (1), unless

(a) a certificate for the amount of the corporation's liability referred to in that subsection has been registered in the Federal Court under section 223 and execution for that amount has been returned unsatisfied in whole or in part;

(b) the corporation has commenced liquidation or dissolution proceedings or has been dissolved and a claim for the amount of the corporation's liability referred to in that subsection has been proved within six months after the earlier of the date of commencement of the proceedings and the date of dissolution; or

(c) the corporation has made an assignment or a bankruptcy order has been made against it under the *Bankruptcy and Insolvency Act* and a claim for the amount of the corporation's liability referred to in that subsection has been proved within six months after the date of the assignment or bankruptcy order.

Related Provisions: *Interpretation Act* 27(5) — Meaning of "within six months".

Notes: Since directors cannot be assessed until execution against the corp has been attempted, one can check the FC website at tinyurl.com/files-fc to see if a certificate has been issued against the corp.

There is no requirement that a bailiff's report for 227.1(2)(a) be in any particular form, such as endorsing the writ of execution *"nulla bona"*: *Turner*, 2006 TCC 130. If the company's directors hide its assets, they cannot later object that the bailiff should have found some: *Miotto*, 2008 TCC 128. CRA as creditor need not make reasonable efforts to collect the debt, but only act in good faith: *Barrett*, 2012 FCA 33; *Tjelta*, 2017 TCC 187.

"Unless" in 227.1(2) does not mean "until"; the director's liability arises when the corp fails to remit, so 160(1) applied to a transfer of property from a director to his wife before 227.1(2) was satisfied: *Colitto*, 2020 FCA 70 [leave to appeal denied 2020 CarswellNat 4006 (SCC)] (reversing the TCC, upholding *Filippazzo*, [2000] 3 C.T.C. 2691 (TCC), *Pliskow*, 2013 TCC 283 and *Sheck*, 2018 TCC 125, and despite *obiter* comments in *Worrell*, [2001] 1 C.T.C. 79 (FCA), para. 74).

In *Walsh*, 2009 TCC 557, a director's appeal was allowed where the Crown did not prove that the writ of execution was returned unsatisfied, because the Sheriff's letter to that effect had been omitted from the Crown's list of documents. Similarly, in *Benaroch*, 2015 TCC 91 and 93, Crown counsel thought the issue was not in dispute, and failed to lead evidence of 227.1(2)(a) execution having been returned unsatisfied; the Court refused to reopen the hearing to allow the evidence, and found the director not liable; and in *Custodio*, 2018 TCC 47, the Crown failed to file the Federal Court certificate in evidence, so the director was not liable even though the Notice of Appeal did not raise this issue. In both *Cherniak*, 2015 TCC 53 and *Maxwell*, 2015 TCC 74, the director's liability was limited to the amount in the certificate that was returned unsatisfied. In *Archambault*, 2018 QCCQ 3291, the parallel Quebec condition was not met where the writ of execution had the wrong address for the corporation.

"Proof of claim" in 227.1(2)(b) means a proof of claim in liquidation or dissolution proceedings, and "does not apply where a corporation is dissolved under a procedure that does not require the appointment of a liquidator or the submission of proofs of claim", so CRA can meet the test under 227.1(2)(a) instead: *Madison*, 2012 FCA 80, paras. 20-21 (overruling *Savoy*, 2011 TCC 35 on this point). CRA notes that "liquidation" in (2)(b) refers to proceedings under company law, not insolvency law, and a proof of claim need not be on the prescribed form: docs 2009-0311441I7, 2010-0358761I7.

The "proof of claim" for a bankrupt company's liability for 227.1(2)(c) is satisfied by CRA advising the trustee of the liability even if no Notice of Assessment is issued: *Matossian*, 2006 FCA 55; *Tehrani*, 2007 FCA 12.

The para. (c) requirement to issue a Proof of Claim in the correct amount is only "directory", not mandatory, so a wrong figure does not prevent CRA from proving the correct amount after the 6 months: *Kyte*, [1997] 2 C.T.C. 14 (FCA); *Moriyama*, 2005 FCA 207; *Grant*, 2017 TCC 121, paras. 36-41. See Notes to 63(1) for more on "directory" vs. "mandatory".

The preconditions in 227.1(2)(a)-(c) operate disjunctively, and only one applies in any given case: *Madison* (above), para. 18.

227.1(2)(c) amended by 2004 *Civil Code* harmonization bill to change "receiving order" to "bankruptcy order" (no substantive change), effective December 15, 2004.

Information Circulars: 89-2R3: Directors' liability — s. 227.1 of the *Income Tax Act*, s. 323 of the *Excise Tax Act*, s. 81 of the *Air Travellers Security Charge Act*, subsec. 295(1) of the *Excise Act, 2001*, and section 95 of the *Softwood Lumber Products Export Charge Act, 2006*.

(3) Idem [due diligence defence] — A director is not liable for a failure under subsection (1) where the director exercised the degree of care, diligence and skill to prevent the failure that a reasonably prudent person would have exercised in comparable circumstances.

Related Provisions

Parallel due-diligence wording: 146.4(13)(d) — RDSP issuer obligations; 147.5(9) — PRPP administrator obligations; 162(5.2) — Penalty for failing to provide SR&ED claim preparer information; 163.3(8) — Penalty for possessing, manufacturing or selling zapper software; 207.01(5) — RRSP etc. holding non-qualified investment; 237.3(11) — Reportable transactions.

Notes: There is extensive case law on this "due diligence" defence, going both ways. (Much of the recent case law is under s. 323 of the *Excise Tax Act*, in the *Canada GST Cases*; see the summary in David M. Sherman, *Practitioner's Goods and Services Tax Annotated*, at s. 323. *Buckingham*, 2011 FCA 142, para. 47, confirms that the standard is the same under the ITA and the ETA.) Generally the director must have taken active steps to ensure that the corporation will make its source deduction remittances. Attempting (even valiantly) to "cure" the default after the corp fails to remit cannot relieve a director from liability: *Buckingham*, paras. 48-58; *Ahmar*, 2020 FCA 65, para. 27. An outside director will not be held to the same standard as an inside director (and may not be required to take any specific action if there is no indication the company is in financial trouble), but a director's background and experience in business will be given great weight in determining whether the director has met the due-diligence test.

Until 2004, the most authoritative and complete statement of the law on this issue was in *Soper*, [1997] 3 C.T.C. 242 (FCA). The Supreme Court of Canada overruled *Soper*'s "objective subjective" test in *Peoples Department Stores v. Wise*, 2004 CarswellQue 2863 at paras. 63-67, interpreting the same wording in *Canada Business Corporations Act* 122(1)(b): "We prefer to describe it as an objective standard. To say that the standard is objective makes it clear that the factual aspects of the circumstances surrounding the actions of the director or officer are important in the case of the s. 122(1)(b) duty of care, as opposed to the subjective motivation of the director or officer, which is the central focus of the statutory fiduciary duty of s. 122(1)(a) of the CBCA.

"The contextual approach dictated by s. 122(1)(b) of the CBCA not only emphasizes the primary facts but also permits prevailing socio-economic conditions to be taken into consideration. The emergence of stricter standards puts pressure on corporations to improve the quality of board decisions. The establishment of good corporate governance rules should be a shield that protects directors from allegations that they have breached their duty of care. However, even with good corporate governance rules, directors' decisions can still be open to criticism from outsiders.... directors and officers often have business expertise that courts do not. Many decisions made in the course of business, although ultimately unsuccessful, are reasonable and defensible at the time they are made. Business decisions must sometimes be made, with high stakes and under considerable time pressure, in circumstances in which detailed information is not available. It might be tempting for some to see unsuccessful business decisions as unreasonable or imprudent in light of information that becomes available ex post facto. Because of this risk of hindsight bias, Canadian courts have developed a rule of deference to business decisions called the 'business judgment rule', adopting the American name for the rule....

"Directors and officers will not be held to be in breach of the duty of care under s. 122(1)(b) of the CBCA if they act prudently and on a reasonably informed basis. The decisions they make must be reasonable business decisions in light of all the circumstances about which the directors or officers knew or ought to have known. In determining whether directors have acted in a manner that breached the duty of care, it is worth repeating that perfection is not demanded. Courts are ill-suited and should be reluctant to second-guess the application of business expertise to the considerations that are involved in corporate decision making, but they are capable, on the facts of any case, of determining whether an appropriate degree of prudence and diligence was brought to bear in reaching what is claimed to be a reasonable business decision at the time it was made."

Although *Peoples* interprets wording identical to 227.1(3), it was uncertain whether it would apply to source deduction and GST assessments, because there is no provision parallel to CBCA 122(1)(a) to deal with the "subjective motivation". TCC decisions were conflicting, but *Buckingham*, 2011 FCA 142, para. 34, ruled explicitly that the *Soper* "objective subjective" standard "has been replaced by the objective standard" in *Peoples*.

The FCA also stated in *Buckingham* (para. 45) that directors' liability under 227.1 "is not conditional on the existence of sufficient cash in the corporation to pay the remittances", and (para. 51) that the due-diligence defence relates only to attempts to *prevent* the failure to remit, not to attempts to remedy the failure after the fact. A director does not exercise due diligence "where he condones the continued operation of the corporation by diverting employee source deductions to other purposes ... This is precisely the mischief which section 227.1 seeks to avoid."

The standard is reasonableness, not perfection: *Smith*, 2001 FCA 84. The director has the onus to prove due diligence on a balance of probabilities: *Borduas*, 2010 FCA 102, para. 26 (same as TCC appeals generally: see 152(7) Notes).

Reliance on another person who is managing the company can be due diligence if there are no red flags indicating the company is in financial difficulty, and there is systemic compliance. Reliance based on the director's "lack of experience or knowledge" will likely no longer work due to *Buckingham*: see *McKenzie*, 2013 TCC 239, para. 106; *Kaur*, 2013 CarswellNat 2477 (TCC, FCA appeal dismissed for delay A-326-13).

Directors who cannot act because they have lost control of the company to a creditor may have a due-diligence defence: *Worrell*, [2001] 1 C.T.C. 79 (FCA); *Liddle*, 2011 FCA 159; but this applies only if the creditor can legally prevent the directors from remitting: *Chriss (Gariepy)*, 2016 FCA 236, para. 29 (leave to appeal denied 2017 CarswellNat 1823 (SCC)).

Directors who thought they had resigned but did not sign a written resignation were not excused from liability: *Chriss (Gariepy)*, para. 19; but in *Cybulski*, 1988 CarswellNat 426, a director who had resigned in writing was excused (the resignation was invalid because no replacement had been appointed).

See also Gray, "Due diligence defence", 68(1) *CTJ* 281-312 (2020). For software to assist in determining due diligence see *Directors' Liability Classifier* at bluejlegal.com.

Information Circulars: 89-2R3: Directors' liability — s. 227.1 of the *Income Tax Act*, s. 323 of the *Excise Tax Act*, s. 81 of the *Air Travellers Security Charge Act*, subsec. 295(1) of the *Excise Act, 2001*, and section 95 of the *Softwood Lumber Products Export Charge Act, 2006*.

CRA Audit Manual: 28.11.0: Due diligence — cancellation or waiver of penalty.

(4) **Limitation period** — No action or proceedings to recover any amount payable by a director of a corporation under subsection (1) shall be commenced more than two years after the director last ceased to be a director of that corporation.

Notes: There is no time limit on a 227.1 assessment other than this one, regardless of CRA delay in assessing a director: *Kern*, 2006 FCA 257, paras. 8-9; *Jarrold*, 2010 FCA 278; *Peterson*, 2005 TCC 745; *Asadollah*, 2007 TCC 333; *Mueller*, 2018 TCC 260. However, it can be argued that since 227(10)(a) provides for 227.1 assessment, and 227(10) states that "Divisions I and J of Part I apply" (and 152(4) is in Division I), 152(4) should apply in some way (such as from final determination of the corporate liability). This argument was rejected in *Siow*, 2011 TCC 301, but in the author's view the Court did not fully address the issue.

To use this defence, the person must have *legally* ceased to be a director more than 2 years before the Notice of Assessment date. Merely losing control of the corporation due to its going into bankruptcy or receivership does not start the clock running: *Kalef*, [1996] 2 C.T.C. 1 (FCA); *Drover*, [1998] G.S.T.C. 45 (FCA); *Butterfield*, 2010 FCA 330; *Grant*, 2017 TCC 121, paras. 21-26; *Tozer*, 2018 TCC 56, paras. 52-70. However, in practice no new liability arises after losing control, due to 227.1(3): *Worrell (McKinnon)*, [2000] G.S.T.C. 91 (FCA); *Mosier*, [2001] G.S.T.C. 124 (TCC); *Savard*, 2008 TCC 309; *Trajkovich*, 2008 TCC 402; *Bourabaa*, 2018 TCC 245, para. 39.

CRA confirmed to the author in VIEWS doc 2011-0412471E5 that if the directors resign and a new director takes over, the new director is not liable for interest accruing on the earlier failure to remit.

The deadline expires at the end of the anniversary day (if X ceased to be a director on May 15, 2016, an assessment on May 15, 2018 is valid): *Larocque*, [1991] 2 C.T.C. 2151 (TCC); *Brunette*, [2001] 1 C.T.C. 2008 (TCC); *Priftis*, 2012 TCC 414; VIEWS doc 2009-033735117; and see *Interpretation Act* s. 27(5).

The clock starts running if the corporation is dissolved: *Aujla*, 2008 FCA 304; *Butterfield*, 2009 TCC 575, para. 5 [aff'd on other grounds 2010 FCA 330]; *Madison*, 2011 TCC 201, para. 62 (rev'd on other grounds 2012 FCA 80); *Priftis*, 2012 TCC 414. (However, in Saskatchewan, being struck off the provincial register is not the same as being dissolved: see *Thomas*, 2011 TCC 421 and *Antifaiff*, 2014 TCC 216.) Revival does not restart an expired director's liability unless the Court Order reviving the corp specifically says so: *Aujla* (FCA, above); *Leger*, 2007 TCC 322; VIEWS doc 2009-0320991I7; May 2009 ICAA roundtable (tinyurl.com/cra-abtax), q. 13; *contra*, *Cadorette*, 2008 TCC 416, paras. 13-16 (appeal to FCA discontinued A-452-08) says the director's liability reappears retroactively under the relevant *Business Corporations Act*, and the director is not protected by a provision saying this is "subject to rights acquired" during the period of dissolution (this is incorrect in the author's view). In *Blackwater Marine*, 2010 BCSC 340, the Court refused to retroactively reinstate the director because the CRA had "slept on its rights", and after two years the director "had a reasonable expectation that he would not be called upon to account for any liability".

A failure to follow the strict formalities of a resignation may not be fatal to its validity: *Kantonen*, [2004] 2 C.T.C. 2261 (TCC). However, a resignation that did not meet the requirements of Ontario *Business Corporations Act* s. 119(2) was invalid: *Zwierschke*, [1991] 2 C.T.C. 2783 (TCC); *Shepherd*, 2008 TCC 361 (FCA appeal discontinued A-241-08). In *Chriss (Gariepy)*, 2016 FCA 236 (reversing the TCC) (leave to appeal denied 2017 CarswellNat 1823 (SCC)), written resignations were never signed and oral resignations were invalid: "the status of directors must be capable of objective verification" (para. 14). In most cases the resignation need not be accepted by the Board: e.g., Ontario *BCA* s. 121(2); *Adams v. Professional Engineers*, 2012 ONSC 3850; *Kandolo v. Kabelu*, 2012 ONSC 4420. In *Marra*, 2016 TCC 24, sending a resignation letter to the company's lawyer was sufficient. The resignation need not be placed in the company's minute book to be valid: *Walsh*, 2009 TCC 557, para. 38. A sole director can resign, provided any requirements of the corporate legislation are followed: *Campbell*, 2010 TCC 100, para. 20; but see Notes to 227.1(1) (item 5) re "deemed" or *de facto* director if there are no directors left. Evidence of resignation was insufficient in *Campbell*; but in *Létourneau*, 2011 FCA 354 (reversing the TCC) the evidence before the TCC judge was held sufficient. See also the GST cases listed in the Cases annotation to s. 323 in the *Practitioner's Goods and Services Tax Annotated*; Carol Hansell, *Directors and Officers in Canada* (Carswell, looseleaf), chap. 5, "Ceasing to Hold Office".

In *Bekesinski*, 2014 TCC 245 (FCA appeal discontinued A-424-14), the Court believed the director's resignation was likely backdated, but due to poor Crown pleadings and failure to properly introduce forensic report, the resignation was held valid.

Even with a valid resignation, the clock will not start running if the person continues as a *de facto* director; see item 5 in Notes to 227.1(1).

Must a director's resignation be recorded with the provincial corporate registry to start the clock running? No: *Lau*, [2003] G.S.T.C. 1 (TCC); *Netupsky*, [2003] G.S.T.C. 15 (TCC); *Moll*, 2008 TCC 234 (but the director must be sure not to continue as a *de facto* director: para. 18); *Singh*, 2019 TCC 120. Yes: *Birchard*, 2003 TCC 90; *Hattem*, 2008 TCC 32 (based on Quebec *Companies Act* s. 123.30 providing that a document relating to a company is not presumed known to third parties unless filed, and stating that this result would be the same for all provinces and under the CBCA); *Goicoechea*, 2010 TCC 539. See also *Milani*, 2011 TCC 488, for discussion of the case law. In *Chriss*, 2016 FCA 236, para. 10, the FCA stated a written resignation is effective when "received by the corporation", but the point about notifying the government authorities was not raised. (Note that a director who has resigned no longer represents the company and has no legal obligation to file the form, even if it *may* be filed by an "individual having knowledge of the affairs of the corporation".)

Information Circulars: 89-2R3: Directors' liability — s. 227.1 of the *Income Tax Act*, s. 323 of the *Excise Tax Act*, s. 81 of the *Air Travellers Security Charge Act*, subsec. 295(1) of the *Excise Act, 2001*, and section 95 of the *Softwood Lumber Products Export Charge Act, 2006*.

(5) **Amount recoverable** — Where execution referred to in paragraph (2)(a) has issued, the amount recoverable from a director is the amount remaining unsatisfied after execution.

Notes: For CRA interpretation of the amount recoverable in various situations, see VIEWS doc 2008-0300111I7.

(6) **Preference** — Where a director pays an amount in respect of a corporation's liability referred to in subsection (1) that is proved in liquidation, dissolution or bankruptcy proceedings, the director is entitled to any preference that Her Majesty in right of Canada would have been entitled to had that amount not been so paid and, where a certificate that relates to that amount has been registered, the director is entitled to an assignment of the certificate to the extent of the director's payment, which assignment the Minister is hereby empowered to make.

(7) **Contribution** — A director who has satisfied a claim under this section is entitled to contribution from the other directors who were liable for the claim.

Notes: In *Adams v. Anderson*, 2011 ONCA 381, Adams' claim for contribution failed against one defendant because he had never been a director even though the provincial corporate registry showed he had been; and failed against another because she had resigned and Adams did not prove that the corp's liability he paid arose before she resigned. The Court ruled that the sued directors' liability is conclusively determined by whether they were assessed by CRA; this seems incorrect. In *Paria Enterprises v. 829194 Ontario*, 2018 ONSC 124, para. 74, a claim for contribution was adjourned until final determination of liability by the TCC/FCA.

Definitions [s. 227.1]: "amount" — 248(1); "corporation" — 248(1), *Interpretation Act* 35(1); "Federal Court" — *Federal Courts Act* s. 4; "Her Majesty" — *Interpretation Act* 35(1); "Minister" — 248(1).

228. Applying payments under collection agreements — Where a payment is made to the Minister on account of tax under this Act, an Act of a province that imposes a tax similar to the tax imposed under this Act, or any two or more such Acts, such part of that payment as is applied by the Minister in accordance with the provisions of a collection agreement entered into under Part III of the *Federal-Provincial Fiscal Arrangements Act* against the tax payable by a taxpayer for a taxation year under this Act discharges the liability of the taxpayer for that tax only to the extent of the part of the payment so applied, notwithstanding that the taxpayer directed that the payment be applied in a manner other than that provided in the collection agreement or made no direction as to its application.

Related Provisions: 154 — Tax transfer payments.

Notes: CRA can legally assess and collect provincial tax under tax collection agreements: *Gendis Inc.*, 2006 MBCA 58; leave to appeal denied 2007 CarswellMan 33.

Definitions [s. 228]: "Minister" — 248(1); "province" — *Interpretation Act* 35(1); "taxation year" — 249; "taxpayer" — 248(1).

229. [Repealed]

Notes: See Notes to 229.1.

229.1 (1) Section 229 is repealed.

(2) Subsection (1) shall come into force on a day to be fixed by proclamation.

Notes: 229 repealed by 229.1, proclaimed in force March 1, 1994 with all of the current ITA (RSC 1985, c. 1 (5th Supp)) by P.C. 1994-196. It provided that a "chartered bank in Canada shall receive for deposit, without any charge for discount or commission, any cheque made payable to the Receiver General in payment of tax, interest or penalty imposed by this Act..." *Financial Administration Act* 159(2) now provides that a bank or financial institution must not *charge* for accepting a cheque or payment for the Government of Canada, but it does not say the bank must *accept* the cheque. Most banks no longer accept cheques from non-customers for CRA payments.

CRA payment methods: see canada.ca/payments.

Definitions [s. 229.1]: "proclamation" — *Interpretation Act* 35(1).

General

230. (1) Records and books [of business]
— Every person carrying on business and every person who is required, by or pursuant to this Act, to pay or collect taxes or other amounts shall keep records and books of account (including an annual inventory kept in prescribed manner) at the person's place of business or residence in Canada or at such other place as may be designated by the Minister, in such form and containing such information as will enable the taxes payable under this Act or the taxes or other amounts that should have been deducted, withheld or collected to be determined.

Related Provisions: 150.1(4) — Record of return filed electronically; 230(4.1) — Requirement to keep electronic records; 238(1) — Punishment for failing to comply; 267, 279 — Record-keeping required for financial institution account reporting for foreign tax authorities.

Notes: See Information Circulars 05-1R1 and 78-10R5 (both June 2010) for policy on keeping and backing-up records that are stored on computer. Paper records can be destroyed as long as digital images are kept: VIEWS docs 2014-0526121E5, 2014-0538211C6 [2014 APFF q.27]. Tax Executives Institute (Nov. 19, 2014 submission) has asked CRA to eliminate its stated requirement (IC 05-1R1 para. 9) that records be on a server in Canada, in light of cloud-computing developments.

238(1) makes non-compliance with 230(1) a criminal offence, and corporate directors and officers can be charged due to s. 242.

Records not required by 230(1) are not entitled to extra protection from seizure: *SPE Valeur*, 2019 TCC 174, para. 64 (under appeal to FCA).

Contravening 230(1) does not mean expenses or claims *must* be disallowed; oral evidence of a credible taxpayer can be accepted. See 9(1) Notes under "Cash expenses". However, 230(1) is often cited in reasons disallowing appeals due to lack of records, e.g. *Pierre Juneau Rénovations*, 2020 TCC 54, paras. 43-46 (under appeal to FCA).

For discussion of s. 230 see Keey, "Books & Records", *Practical Insights*, Taxnet Pro Tax Disputes Centre (Jan. 2021, 30pp); Quigley, "Controlling Tax Information", 47(1) *Canadian Tax Journal* 1-48 (1999); Cronkwright and Loranger, *Records and Information Management* (Carswell, 3 vols. looseleaf or ProView); Drache, "What are 'Books and Records'?", 17(8) *Canadian Not-for-Profit News* (Carswell) 61-64 (Aug. 2009); Kalamut, "Record Retention Policies as a Strategy to Limit Exposure on Audit", 2043 *Tax Topics* (CCH) 1-3 (May 5, 2011); Aptowitzer, "Do Record Keeping Time Limits Mean Anything Anymore?", xli(4) *The Canadian Taxpayer* (Carswell) 25-27 (Feb. 22, 2019) [notes that for certain purposes, records must be kept longer].

See Notes to 8(1)(h.1) re whether a log must be kept of vehicle travel for business or employment.

Some commentators suggest that the requirement to keep records "in Canada" is modified by *eBay Canada* (see Notes to 231.2(1), 231.6(1)): e.g., Desmarais, "eBay", xxxi(2) *The Canadian Taxpayer* (Carswell) 14-15 (Jan. 20, 2009). CRA does not accept this: "Administrative Follow-Up on *eBay* Decision", xxxi(11) *TCT* 87-88 (May 26, 2009); Charities Guidance CG-002, Q.3 ("It is still the CRA's position that charities must keep their books and records at an address in Canada.").

CRA as employer considers employees' RC500 and RC509 timesheet forms not to be payroll records and disposes of them after 2 years: ATIP disclosure A-061011 to Clint Kimery, Sept. 14, 2012. (These records may be relevant to a *Jarvis* defence: see Notes to 231.2(1).) However, due to *Interpretation Act* s. 17, 230(1) may not be binding on CRA even *qua* employer.

See also VIEWS doc 2007-0246241E5 re records to be kept for a rental property; and tinyurl.com/cra-records generally.

Regulations: 1800 (prescribed manner of keeping inventory).

Information Circulars: 77-9R: Books, records and other requirements for taxpayers having foreign affiliates; 78-10R5: Books and records retention/destruction; 05-1R1: Electronic record keeping.

CRA Audit Manual: 10.2.0: Books and records; 10.3.0: Maintaining records; 10.8.11: Requirement to keep specific records and books of account.

Forms: RC4409: Keeping records [guide].

(1.1) [Repealed under former Act]

Notes: 230(1.1), repealed by 1985 Budget, required books and records to be kept by the administrator of an indexed security investment plan.

(2) Records and books [of charity, etc.]
— Every qualified donee referred to in paragraphs (a) to (c) of the definition "qualified donee" in subsection 149.1(1) shall keep records and books of account — in the case of a qualified donee referred to in any of subparagraphs (a)(i) and (iii) and paragraphs (b), (b.1) and (c) of that definition, at an address in Canada recorded with the Minister or designated by the Minister — containing

(a) information in such form as will enable the Minister to determine whether there are any grounds for the revocation of its registration under this Act;

(b) a duplicate of each receipt containing prescribed information for a donation received by it; and

(c) other information in such form as will enable the Minister to verify the donations to it for which a deduction or tax credit is available under this Act.

Related Provisions: 149.1(6.4) — Rules apply to registered national arts service organizations; 168(1)(e) — Revocation of charity registration for failing to comply; 188.2(2)(a) — Suspension of charity's receipting privileges for failing to comply; 238(1) — Punishment for failing to comply.

Notes: 230(2)(a) is "vague", and for a charity registration to be revoked for not complying, CRA must clearly identify the records the charity failed to keep, and explain why this justifies revocation: *Prescient Foundation*, 2013 FCA 120, paras. 47, 50 (leave to appeal denied 2013 CarswellNat 4462 (SCC)). Revocation was upheld because Prescient did not keep records of directors' meetings re certain transactions, or records showing that a gift was to a US charity. In *Ark Angel Foundation*, 2019 FCA 21 (leave to appeal denied 2019 CarswellNat 6296 (SCC)), failure to justify a director's consulting services provided to the charity meant the records were insufficient.

CRA can demand records from a charity that does not keep proper lists of donors: *Redeemer Foundation*, 2008 SCC 46.

Since the 2015 tax year, churches must keep their envelopes for 6 years: CRA, "New Books and Records Position for Church Offering Envelopes", July 22, 2016.

See also Tzannidakis, tinyurl.com/tzan-records (how to comply); Registered Charities Newsletter 26; Arthur Drache, "What are 'Books and Records'?", 17(8) *Canadian Not-for-Profit News* (Carswell) 61-64 (Aug. 2009), "Minutes of Meetings", 19(2) 15-16 (Feb. 2011), and "Books, Records and Minutes", 24(10) 75-77 (Oct. 2016).

See Notes to 230(1) re requirement to keep records "in Canada".

230(2) opening words amended by 2019 budget bill #1, effective 2020, to add reference to 149.1(1)"qualified donee"(b.1) (registered journalism organization).

230(2) opening words amended by 2011 budget bill #2, effective 2012 (extended from charities to most other qualified donees; see Notes to 149.1(1)"qualified donee").

230(2) amended by 1993 technical bill, effective Dec. 22, 1992.

Regulations: 216 (information return); 3502 (prescribed information for receipts).

Information Circulars: 78-10R5: Books and records retention/destruction.

Registered Charities Newsletters: 5 (where and why does the Department require your registered charity to keep books and records?); 10 (books and records); 13 (about auditing charities); 20 (financial controls — books and records [when operating outside Canada]); 26 (books and records Q&A).

Charities Policies: CPS-007: RCAAAs: Receipts — issuing policy; CPS-014: Computer-generated official donation receipts.

(2.1) Idem, lawyers
— For greater certainty, the records and books of account required by subsection (1) to be kept by a person carrying on business as a lawyer (within the meaning assigned by subsection 232(1)) whether by means of a partnership or otherwise, include all accounting records of the lawyer, including supporting vouchers and cheques.

(3) Minister's requirement to keep records, etc.
— Where a person has failed to keep adequate records and books of account for the purposes of this Act, the Minister may require the person to keep such records and books of account as the Minister may specify and that person shall thereafter keep records and books of account as so required.

Related Provisions: 230.1(3) — Application to political party's or candidate's records; 238(1) — Punishment for failing to comply.

Notes: This provision applies only where the person has first failed to keep adequate records, meaning sufficient to enable tax to be determined. That determination is a question of fact to be decided by the courts, but the onus is on the taxpayer to show that the Minister did not have a basis for reaching such a determination. See *Empire House (London) Ltd.*, [1966] C.T.C. 681 (Ont. SC), and *Merchant (2000) Ltd.*, [2000] 3 C.T.C. 291 (FCTD); rev'd [2001] 4 C.T.C. 181 (FCA).

Information Circulars: 78-10R5: Books and records retention/destruction; 05-1R1: Electronic record keeping.

(4) Limitation period for keeping records, etc. — Every person required by this section to keep records and books of account shall retain

(a) the records and books of account referred to in this section in respect of which a period is prescribed, together with every account and voucher necessary to verify the information contained therein, for such period as is prescribed; and

(b) all other records and books of account referred to in this section, together with every account and voucher necessary to verify the information contained therein, until the expiration of six years from the end of the last taxation year to which the records and books of account relate.

Related Provisions: 150.1(4) — Record of return filed electronically; 168(1)(e) — Revocation of charity registration for failing to comply; 188.2(2)(a) — Suspension of charity's receipting privileges for failing to comply; 230(4.1) — Requirement to keep electronic records; 230.1(3) — Application to political party's or candidate's records; 238(1) — Punishment for failing to comply; 244.7(3) — Five-year period for keeping records of large international electronic funds transfers; 267(3) — Time limit for financial institution to keep records of US persons having interests in accounts.

Notes: The words "six years from the end of the last taxation year to which the records and books of account relate", for documenting the cost of property, refer to the year the property is *sold*, since that year is when the tax must be calculated: *Tibilla*, 2013 TCC 215, para. 38 (aff'd without discussing this point 2014 FCA 227); *Hill Fai Investments*, 2015 TCC 167, para. 66. Similarly, *Kueviakoe*, 2021 FCA 64, para. 7, held that business records from a year in which losses are claimed must be kept for 6 years from the year in which the loss carryforward is used.

This rule requires a trustee in bankruptcy to keep a bankrupt corporation's records: VIEWS doc 2009-0352341I7. See also 2012-0461301E5; 2014-0548841E5 (interaction between 230(4) and Reg. 5800).

Regulations: 5800 (required retention periods).

Information Circulars: 78-10R5: Books and records retention/destruction; 05-1R1: Electronic record keeping.

Forms: T137: Request for destruction of records.

(4.1) Electronic records — Every person required by this section to keep records who does so electronically shall retain them in an electronically readable format for the retention period referred to in subsection (4).

Related Provisions: 230(4.2) — Exemption from requirement; 238(1) — Punishment for failing to comply.

Notes: 230(4.1) added by 1995-97 technical bill, effective June 18, 1998.

Information Circulars: 78-10R5: Books and records retention/destruction; 05-1R1: Electronic record keeping.

Registered Charities Newsletters: 26 (books and records Q6).

CRA Audit Manual: 13.1.0: Computer-assisted audit techniques.

(4.2) Exemptions — The Minister may, on such terms and conditions as are acceptable to the Minister, exempt a person or a class of persons from the requirement in subsection (4.1).

Notes: 230(4.2) added by 1995-97 technical bill, effective June 18, 1998.

Information Circulars: 78-10R5: Books and records retention/destruction; 05-1R1: Electronic record keeping.

(5) Exception — Where, in respect of any taxation year, a person referred to in subsection (1) has not filed a return with the Minister as and when required by section 150, that person shall retain every record and book of account that is required by this section to be kept and that relates to that taxation year, together with every account and voucher necessary to verify the information contained therein, until the expiration of six years from the day the return for that taxation year is filed.

Related Provisions: 238(1) — Punishment for failing to comply.

(6) Exception where objection or appeal — Where a person required by this section to keep records and books of account serves a notice of objection or where that person is a party to an appeal to the Tax Court of Canada under this Act, that person shall retain every record, book of account, account and voucher necessary for dealing with the objection or appeal until, in the case of the serving of a notice of objection, the time provided by section 169 to appeal has elapsed or, in the case of an appeal, until the appeal is disposed

of and any further appeal in respect thereof is disposed of or the time for filing any such further appeal has expired.

Notes: In *Hill Fai Investments*, 2015 TCC 167, para. 67, a company that wanted to claim losses should have kept records during its appeal process to justify its claims.

In *Ampratwum-Duah*, 2020 TCC 18, a church leader's donations to the church were denied due to lack of evidence beyond the receipts; over 6 years had passed but the church should have kept the records while AD's assessment was under objection and appeal.

230(6) amended by 1988 Tax Court bill, effective 1991.

Information Circulars: 78-10R5: Books and records retention/destruction.

(7) Exception where demand by Minister — Where the Minister is of the opinion that it is necessary for the administration of this Act, the Minister may, by registered letter or by a demand served personally, require any person required by this section to keep records and books of account to retain those records and books of account, together with every account and voucher necessary to verify the information contained therein, for such period as is specified in the letter or demand.

Related Provisions: 244(5), (6) — Proof of service by mail or personal service; 248(7)(a) — Mail deemed received on day mailed.

Information Circulars: 78-10R5: Books and records retention/destruction.

(8) Permission for earlier disposal — A person required by this section to keep records and books of account may dispose of the records and books of account referred to in this section, together with every account and voucher necessary to verify the information contained therein, before the expiration of the period in respect of which those records and books of account are required to be kept if written permission for their disposal is given by the Minister.

Related Provisions: 230.1(3) — Application to political party's or candidate's records; 238(1) — Offences.

Forms: T137: Request for destruction of records.

Definitions [s. 230]: "allowable capital loss" — 38(b), 248(1); "amount", "business" — 248(1); "Canada" — 255; "inventory" — 248(1); "lawyer" — 232(1); "Minister", "person", "prescribed" — 248(1); "qualified donee" — 149.1(1); "record" — 150.1(4), 248(1); "registered Canadian amateur athletic association", "registered charity" — 248(1); "taxable capital gain" — 38(a), 248(1); "taxation year" — 249; "taxpayer" — 248(1).

230.1 (1) Records re monetary contributions — *Canada Elections Act* — Every agent authorized under the *Canada Elections Act* to accept monetary contributions referred to in that Act shall keep records, sufficient to enable each monetary contribution within the meaning assigned by subsection 127(4.1) that they receive and the expenditures that they make to be verified, including a duplicate of the receipt referred to in subsection 127(3) for each of those monetary contributions) at

(a) in the case of an agent other than an official agent of a candidate, the address recorded in the registry of political parties or of electoral district associations referred to in the *Canada Elections Act*; and

(b) in the case of an official agent of a candidate, the agent's address set out in the nomination papers filed under that Act with the returning officer when the candidate was a prospective candidate or any other address that the Minister designates.

Related Provisions: 127(3)–(4.2) — Credit for political contributions; 238(1) — Punishment for failing to comply.

Notes: 230.1(1)(a) amended by S.C. 2014, c. 12 to change "parties" to "political parties", effective Dec. 19, 2014. 230.1(1) earlier amended by 2003 election financing bill, 1992 technical bill.

Regulations: 2000, 2002 (contents of receipts).

Information Circulars: 75-2R9: Contributions to a registered party, a registered association or to a candidate at a federal election; 05-1R1: Electronic record keeping.

(2) Information return — Each agent to whom subsection (1) applies shall file with the Minister an information return in prescribed form and containing prescribed information. The return is to be filed within the period for the filing of a financial transactions return or an electoral campaign return, as the case may be, under the *Canada Elections Act*.

Related Provisions: 230.1(4) — Reports to chief electoral officer; 238(1) — Punishment for failing to comply.

Notes: 230.1(2) amended by 2003 election financing bill (effective 2004), 1992 technical bill.

Regulations: 2001 (time for filing return).

Information Circulars: 75-2R9: Contributions to a registered party, a registered association or to a candidate at a federal election.

Forms: T2092: Contributions to a registered party or to a registered association — information return; T2093: Contributions to a candidate at an election — information return.

(3) Application of subsecs. 230(3) to (8) — Subsections 230(3) to (8) apply, with any modifications that the circumstances require, in respect of the keeping of records by agents as required by subsection (1).

Notes: 230.1(3) amended by 2003 election financing bill, effective 2004.

Regulations: 5800(2) (retention period for records and books of account).

Information Circulars: 78-10R5: Books and records retention/destruction; 05-1R1: Electronic record keeping.

(4)–(7) [Repealed]

Notes: 230.1(4) and (5) repealed by 1993 technical bill, effective June 15, 1994. In view of the extensive public reporting requirements imposed on political parties and candidates by the *Canada Elections Act*, reporting requirements by Revenue Canada to the Chief Electoral Officer were considered redundant.

230.1(4) earlier amended by 1992 technical bill, effective 1992.

230.1(6) and (7) repealed by 2003 election financing bill, effective 2004.

See Notes to 127(3) and (4) for definitions in the *Canada Elections Act*.

Definitions [s. 230.1]: "amount contributed" — 127(4.1), 230.1(7); "candidate" — 230.1(6); "Minister" — 248(1); "monetary contribution" — 127(4.1); "official agent" — 230.1(6); "person", "prescribed", "record" — 248(1); "registered agent", "registered party" — 230.1(6).

231. Definitions — In sections 231.1 to 231.8,

Notes: 231 opening words amended by 2018 budget bill #2 to change "231.1 to 231.7" to "231.1 to 231.8", effective Dec. 13, 2018.

Opening words amended by 2001 technical bill to change "231.1 to 231.6" to "231.1 to 231.7", effective June 14, 2001.

"authorized person" means a person authorized by the Minister for the purposes of sections 231.1 to 231.5;

"document" includes money, a security and a record;

Notes: Definition "document" enacted to replace "documents" by 1995-97 technical bill, effective June 18, 1998. The previous wording is incorporated in 248(1)"record".

"dwelling-house" means the whole or any part of a building or structure that is kept or occupied as a permanent or temporary residence and includes

(a) a building within the curtilage of a dwelling-house that is connected to it by a doorway or by a covered and enclosed passageway, and

(b) a unit that is designed to be mobile and to be used as a permanent or temporary residence and that is being used as such a residence;

Notes: "Curtilage" in para. (a) means "a courtyard, field of land including any buildings on it lying near and belonging to a dwelling" (*Dictionary of Canadian Law*).

"judge" means a judge of a superior court having jurisdiction in the province where the matter arises or a judge of the Federal Court.

Notes: "Judge" in legislation does not include a deputy judge: *Bruyea*, 2019 ONCA 599.

Due to the *Federal Courts Act*, since 2003 this definition no longer includes a judge of the Federal Court of Appeal. The "Federal Court" is now only the court that was formerly the Federal Court–Trial Division.

Definitions [s. 231]: "Federal Court" — *Federal Courts Act* s. 4; "Minister", "person" — 248(1); "province" — *Interpretation Act* 35(1); "record" — 248(1); "superior court" — *Interpretation Act* 35(1).

231.1 (1) [Audits,] inspections — An authorized person may, at all reasonable times, for any purpose related to the administration or enforcement of this Act,

(a) inspect, audit or examine the books and records of a taxpayer and any document of the taxpayer or of any other person that relates or may relate to the information that is or should be in the books or records of the taxpayer or to any amount payable by the taxpayer under this Act, and

(b) examine property in an inventory of a taxpayer and any property or process of, or matter relating to, the taxpayer or any other person, an examination of which may assist the authorized person in determining the accuracy of the inventory of the taxpayer or in ascertaining the information that is or should be in the books or records of the taxpayer or any amount payable by the taxpayer under this Act,

and for those purposes the authorized person may

(c) subject to subsection (2), enter into any premises or place where any business is carried on, any property is kept, anything is done in connection with any business or any books or records are or should be kept, and

(d) require the owner or manager of the property or business and any other person on the premises or place to give the authorized person all reasonable assistance and to answer all proper questions relating to the administration or enforcement of this Act and, for that purpose, require the owner or manager to attend at the premises or place with the authorized person.

Proposed Amendment — 231.1(1)(c), (d)

(c) require the owner or manager of a property or business of a taxpayer — and any particular person on the premises or place where the business is carried on, the property is kept, anything is done in connection with the business or any books or records of the taxpayer are or should be kept — to give the authorized person all reasonable assistance and to answer all proper questions and, for those purposes, the authorized person may require

(i) the owner or manager to attend at the premises or place with the authorized person, and

(ii) the owner, manager or the particular person to answer those questions orally or in writing, in any form specified by the authorized person.

Application: The April 19, 2021 Budget Notice of Ways and Means Motion, subsec. 28(1), will amend para. 231.1(1)(c) to read as above and repeal para. (d), in force on Royal Assent.

Federal Budget, Supplementary Information, April 19, 2021: *Audit Authorities*

The *Income Tax Act* provides the Canada Revenue Agency (CRA) with the authority to audit taxpayers and otherwise ensure compliance with the *Income Tax Act*. The scope of this authority was the subject of a recent court decision [*Cameco*, 2019 FCA 67 — ed.] which called into question the extent to which CRA officials can require persons to answer all proper questions and to provide all reasonable assistance relating to the administration or enforcement of the *Income Tax Act*. The decision also called into question the extent to which CRA officials can require that questions be answered orally.

To ensure that the CRA has the authority it needs to conduct audits and undertake other compliance activities, Budget 2021 proposes amendments to the *Income Tax Act*, the *Excise Tax Act*, the *Excise Act, 2001*, the *Air Travellers Security Charge Act* and Part 1 of the *Greenhouse Gas Pollution Pricing Act*. These amendments would confirm that CRA officials have the authority to require persons to answer all proper questions, and to provide all reasonable assistance, for any purpose related to the administration or enforcement of the relevant statute. They would also provide that CRA officials have the authority to require persons to respond to questions orally or in writing, including in any form specified by the relevant CRA official. These amendments would allow the CRA to undertake audit and other compliance activities in the same manner as it did prior to the decision.

These measures would come into force on Royal Assent.

Notes: This amendment appears to allow CRA to demand answers from a particular person even if they are not an "owner or manager", and even if the person is not already "on the premises", if the person is in a "place where ... anything is done in connection with the business" (including their own home).

CRA refuses to allow recording of its interviews: Aptowitzer, "Compelling Oral Interviews Without Recording Is a Recipe for a Disaster", tinyurl.com/apto-interv.

Announced Administrative Change — Audits in real estate sector

Federal Budget, March 19, 2019, Chapter 1, Part 1: *Taking Action to Enhance Tax Compliance in the Real Estate Sector*

The Canada Revenue Agency (CRA) helps contribute to a healthy, competitive and stable Canadian housing market through its efforts to address tax non-compliance in real estate transactions.

Through the use of advanced risk assessment tools, analytics and third-party data, as well as collaboration with the provinces and territories to share information and access to data, the CRA is continuously enhancing its ability to detect, and take action whenever it finds, real estate transactions where parties have failed to pay the required taxes.

Recent efforts have uncovered more than $100 million of additional taxes assessed due to increasingly complex real estate transactions, which can only be addressed by auditors and business intelligence officers with specific knowledge, training, and expertise.

Budget 2019 proposes to provide the CRA with $50 million over five years, starting in 2019-20, to create four new dedicated residential and commercial real estate audit teams in high-risk regions, notably in British Columbia and Ontario. These teams will work to ensure that tax provisions regarding real estate are being followed, with a focus on ensuring that:

- Taxpayers report all sales of their principal residence on their tax returns;

- Any capital gain derived from a real estate sale, where the principal residence tax exemption does not apply, is identified as taxable;

- Money made on real estate flipping is reported as income;

- Commissions earned are reported as taxable income; and

- For Goods and Services Tax/Harmonized Sales Tax (GST/HST) purposes, builders of new residential properties remit the appropriate amount of tax to the CRA.

The expected revenue from this initiative is $68 million over five years, starting in 2019-20.

Notes: See Notes to 40(2)(b) for discussion of these audits.

Announced Administrative Change — More resources to combat tax avoidance

Federal Budget, Chapter 4, March 19, 2019; Federal Economic Statement, Chapter 4, Nov. 30, 2020; Federal Budget, Chapter 10, April 19, 2021: See under 239(1).

Proposed Amendment — Electronic correspondence with business

Federal Budget, Supplementary Information, April 19, 2021: See under 244(14.1).

Related Provisions: 56(1)(z.4) — Offshore Informant Program — payments to informers taxable; 168(1)(e) — Revocation of charity registration for failing to comply; 188.2(2)(a) — Suspension of charity's receipting privileges for failing to comply; 230 — Requirement to keep books and records; 231.2 — Requirements for information; 231.3 — Search warrants; 231.5(1) — Auditor may copy documents; 231.5(2) — Obligation to comply with auditor; 231.7 — Court order for compliance with audit; 232(3.1) — Examination of documents where privilege claimed; 237.1(8) — Application to tax shelter disclosure rules; 237.3(13) — Audit of reportable avoidance transaction before return filed; 238(1) — Punishment for failing to comply; 244.2 — Banks, etc. required to report international transfers of $10,000 or more; *Interpretation Act* 31(2) — Ancillary powers granted to enable work to be done; Canada-U.S. Tax Treaty:Art. XXVII:7 — Auditors permitted to enter US to inspect records with taxpayer's consent.

Notes: See canada.ca/taxes-audit. At the local Tax Services Office, Verification and Enforcement is now again called Audit since 2006; the senior official in charge of all local audit work (formerly Chief of Audit, then Assistant Director V&E) is now Assistant Director, Income Tax Audit.

Large portions of the *Income Tax Audit Manual* are available on *TaxPartner* and *Taxnet Pro*. For detailed CRA instructions to its auditors see the chapters listed in the "Income Tax Audit Manual" annotation below. Chapter 8, "Audit Selection — Risk Assessment" includes information on how registrants are selected for audit.

CRA auditor behaviour is irrelevant when appealing an assessment. See 171(1) Notes.

The April 21, 2015 Budget (pp. 347-48) announced additional audit resources for the CRA over 5 years: $118.2 million for underground economy audits; $25.3m for offshore tax evasion and aggressive tax avoidance, and $58.2m for avoidance by large complex entities.

Large business audits (over $250m revenue): since 2010, large corps are not automatically audited, as CRA found that 89% of adjusted tax came from 20% of them. In 2018-19, CRA's large-business and multinational-enterprise audits resulted in $8.6 billion in federal "fiscal impact": *Departmental Results Report 2018-19* (tinyurl.com/cra-results), p. 19 (no data in 2019-20 Report). CRA uses an "integrated risk-based approach" (Approach to Large Business Compliance — ALBC)) to identify and address the highest risk cases: VIEWS doc 2018-0779961C6 [2018 CTF q.8]. There are 20,000 legal entities within the large business population. Main risk factors: audit history; corporate governance (tax/audit committee, oversight); corporate structure (controls, etc.);

openness and transparency (relationship with CRA); past participation in aggressive tax schemes; unusual and/or complex transactions; major acquisitions and disposals; industry sector issues; international transactions. CRA's algorithm considers 200 variables: Commons Finance Committee Sixth Report, Oct. 2016 (tinyurl.com/fin6rep), p. 11. Audits in certain sectors are co-ordinated through specific TSOs (oil & gas: Calgary; automotive: Windsor; financial institutions: Toronto North; pharmaceuticals: Laval), which participate in risk assessment, consult during the audit, advise HQ of national issues and do post-assessment reviews (Lyse Ricard, Cdn Tax Foundation annual conference, Nov. 24/09). See also CRA Round Table, 2010 conference report, q.28, p. 4:26-27; 2011-0427271C6 [2011 TEI q.7]; 2019-0816111C6 [2019 CPTS], q.4; Hickey, "Risk-Based Audits", 19(4) *Canadian Tax Highlights* (ctf.ca) 1-2 (April 2011); Misutka & MacEachern, "The CRA's Tax Transparency Initiatives", 61(3) *Canadian Tax Journal* 829-55 (2013); Abrary et al., "CRA Audits of Large Corporations", 2018 Cdn Tax Foundation conference report, 34:1-25 (criticizes how CRA audits large corps). The old "Audit Protocol" (see 1998 conference report, pp. 20:1-18, 21:1-17, 22:1-23) is now little used: Larry Jacobson, CTF annual conference, Nov. 28/11.

Quotas: CRA is emphatic that auditors are not graded or compensated based on the amount they reassess. TEBA ("tax earned by audit") or Additional Tax Assessed by Audit is measured, but only to determine audit quality and whether CRA is best selecting which files to audit (Jeff Sadrian, 2013 Cdn Tax Foundation annual conference; VIEWS doc 2019-0816111C6 [2019 CPTS], q.4). (In *Ludmer*, 2018 QCCS 3381, paras. 198, 711; aff'd 2020 QCCA 697, paras. 19, 95, 98 [leave to appeal denied 2021 CarswellQue 2160 (SCC)], the trial judge found that TEBA had some impact on bonuses but did not motivate CRA officials to assess a high amount.) A BC pilot project that used a risk-based approach was found to raise more dollars than TEBA targets (Richard Montroy, 2011 conference). See also 2012-0439491C6 [2011 TEI q.8]; Montroy, "CRA Update on Compliance Programs and Communications", 2012 Tax Dispute Resolution conf. report (ctf.ca), 16:1-15. In *Groupe Enico*, 2013 QCCS 5189, a lawsuit against Revenu Québec for damages for abusive assessment action, the Superior Court found that despite its denials, RQ had a quota system giving auditors bonuses for assessing higher amounts; and see TVA news report at tinyurl.com/rq-quotas confirming this. However, the Court of Appeal ruled at 2016 QCCA 76 that this was an internal issue for RQ's management, not relevant to the case; and in *Pellerin*, 2017 QCCA 1339, the existence of a bonus to a RQ auditor for assessing did not change the onus of proof. CRA (Alexandra MacLean) acknowledged at the 2018 Cdn Tax Foundation conference that TEBA leads to assessments that are reversed on appeal, and CRA wants to move away from that (TEBA does not currently count later reversals: CRA reply to TEI, Dec. 4, 2018, q. D.6).

For "employer compliance audits", see Notes to 6(1)(a).

Small business audits: CRA auditors will often search for relevant information on the Internet, and a taxpayer's Web site or other "Google-able" sources may contradict what the taxpayer tells the auditor. On a full audit of a small business, CRA will often request full bank records and other financial information of all owners and spouses, to ensure business revenues are deposited only in the business account: VIEWS docs 2015-0572151C6 [2015 STEP q.15], 2020-0852141C6 [2020 APFF q.2]; Oakey, "CRA's New Audit Policy — Guilty Until Proven Innocent", 13(5) *Tax Hyperion* (Carswell) 6-8 (May 2016). Restaurants and bars are a particular CRA target: tinyurl.com/cbc-cra-bars. CRA obtained an order to access Ontario Beer Store 2017-2022 sales: *Brewers Retail*, 2018 CarswellNat 7577 (FC), so it can presume a markup from alcohol purchases to meal sales (see "Audit methodologies" below). Incentives paid by drug companies to pharmacies have been an audit target: *Mikhail*, 2019 TCC 49, para. 10. CRA is now targeting social media influencers and others in the "platform economy": tinyurl.com/cra-platform; Kamboj, "Taxation of the Digital Economy", 14(1) *Taxes and Wealth Management* (Carswell) 9-11 (March 2021).

See also "Disclosure of corporations' beneficial shareholders" in Notes to 150(1)(a).

Letter campaign: CRA sends 30,000 "educational and intent-to-audit" letters annually to randomly-selected taxpayers claiming business or rental losses or employment expenses, inviting them to correct their returns before they are audited. Voluntary Disclosure (see Notes to 220(3.1)) is permitted. See tinyurl.com/letters-cra. (A similar project uses overseas electronic funds transfer information from 244.2: see sample letter in *GST & HST Times* 329C (Carswell, April 2017).) CRA also has "Liaison Officers", who contact small and medium-sized businesses to help them comply with their obligations: canada.ca/cra-liaison-officer.

For CRA audits of trusts, see Notes to 104(1). A national project to develop an audit strategy was completed in 2007-08: VIEWS doc 2010-0373601C6.

All loss carryback claims over $200,000 are internally referred for audit: *Posteraro*, 2014 BCPC 31, para. 15.

High net worth families (Related Party Initiative, or Billionaires' Audit): CRA is (since 2011) auditing high net worth individuals and families (over $50 million net worth), sending questionnaires asking for information about all companies, trusts, etc. that they control (for a copy of the questionnaire see *Plachcinski*, 2016 CarswellNat 10234 (FC), para. 22; Lidder, "Current Issues Forum", 2011 BC Tax Conference (ctf.ca), paper 1A, Appendix A). The questionnaire was held to be enforceable in *Plachcinski*. See Summerhill, "CRA Targets 'High Net Worth' Individuals", 2053 *Tax Topics* (CCH) 1-2 (July 14, 2011); Ranot & DeBresser, "Canada Revenue Agency's Related Party Initiative", 26(10) *Money & Family Law* (Carswell) 73-74 (Oct. 2011); docs 2011-0398351C6; 2011-0401901C6 (audit of all individuals who together with related economic entities have net worth over $50m); 2012-0442991C6; CRA Round Table, 2010 Cdn Tax Foundation conference report, q.37, p. 4:33; May 2013 ICAA Roundtable q.3 (tinyurl.com/cra-abtax); 2018-0779961C6 [2018 CTF q.8] (over 30 audit teams across

Canada); *Departmental Results Report 2019-20* (tinyurl.com/cra-results: 200 files, $361 million "fiscal impact"); *Ghermezian*, 2020 FC 1137, para. 131. The CRA work is based on OECD, *Engaging with high net worth individuals on tax compliance*, tinyurl.com/oecd-hnw. In 2017-18, CRA was also conducting a postal code audit project, checking homes in wealthy neighbourhoods to ensure income is being reported: CBC report, tinyurl.com/cra-postal.

CRA's "matching" program automatically picks up cases where numbers on information slips (e.g., T3, T4, T4A, T5, T5008) are not included in the appropriate line's total on the taxpayer's return. See CRA May 2006 ICAA roundtable (tinyurl.com/cra-abtax), q. 4; May 2008 roundtable, q. 28; May 2010 roundtable, q.12; VIEWS doc 2011-0412211C6; Reg. 230(2) Notes re T5008. Unfortunately, reassessments are often sent without prior contact. This is a deliberate choice because "Statistically, matching reassessments reflect an accuracy rate of 97%" (letter from Ontario Region Service Complaints Office, Feb. 1, 2012), but that is in part because many people do not have the expertise or energy to correct errors; and even 3% error means 50,000 wrong assessments a year. CRA does process correction requests within 30 days (May 2011 roundtable, q. 18 and the author's experience), so a Notice of Objection may not be needed (but should be filed if the 90-day deadline is approaching).

Taxpayers must report business income earned from the Internet (individuals: on Form T2125; corporations: T2 Sched. 88). Presumably CRA will cross-match this data against websites advertising goods and services, and audit taxpayers who do not report such income. See Notes to 150(1)(a) for more on Sched. 88.

For the most common adjustments for individuals, see tinyurl.com/common-adj.

For discussion of CRA audits to find non-filers, see Auditor General, spring 2012 report (oag-bvg.gc.ca), Chap. 3.

In theory, CRA has no discretion in applying the Act and must "follow it absolutely" by assessing: *JP Morgan*, 2013 FCA 250, para. 78. In practice, auditors have wide discretion not to assess an amount; once it is correctly assessed, an Appeals Officer or Tax Court judge cannot cancel it on grounds of equity, fairness or compassion (see 169(3) Notes). Audit consults Rulings for technical advice but should not "bully" Rulings into getting the desired answer, or ignore Rulings' advice: *Ludmer*, 2018 QCCS 3381, paras. 456-458, 531; aff'd 2020 QCCA 697, para. 60 (leave to appeal denied 2021 CarswellQue 2160 (SCC)). In *Rosenberg*, 2016 FC 1376, CRA's agreement to not assess year X (in exchange for R agreeing to stop using a tax plan) was binding and meant CRA could not re-audit that year.

Requests for information: 231.1 entitles auditors to request and examine documents including computer records (see 248(1)"record"). 231.2 is a more formal provision whereby a "requirement" is issued, but is not needed if 231.1 suffices: *Redeemer Foundation*, 2008 SCC 46; *Vert-Dure Plus*, 2007 TCC 379. See Notes to 231.2(1), (2). In *Romanuk*, 2012 TCC 58 (aff'd 2013 FCA 133 without discussing this issue; leave to appeal denied 2013 CarswellNat 4317 (SCC)), the TCC treated an audit request as less compelling than a demand, but in light of 231.5(2) this may be incorrect. Some of the *Jarvis* cases discussed in Notes to 231.2(1) were 231.1(1) demands (e.g., *Campbell*, 2018 FC 683). *Chad*, 2019 FC 1456, was also a demand under 231.1 (and 231.6), upheld on the basis of relevance and content; whether C could actually comply with the demand was not yet at issue, as CRA had not yet sought a 231.7 compliance order.

Labelling a document "Without Prejudice" will not keep it out of Court if it is provided to CRA in response to an audit inquiry rather than as part of settlement negotiations: *Woodland*, 2009 TCC 434, para. 66.

In *R. v. He*, 2012 BCCA 318, records seized in a CRA pilot project researching the adequacy of businesses' electronic records could not be used in prosecuting the owner of a restaurant because there was no "genuine and serious inquiry into the tax liability" of the owner, so this was an unreasonable seizure.

For CRA policy on audit requests for information, including access to accountants' working papers and tax-risk documents, see Notes to 231.2(1).

One of the largest current audit issues is transfer pricing. See Notes to 247(2). Other current "hot" audit issues include (per CRA, Toronto Centre TSO Professionals Group seminar, Nov. 14, 2012): artificial capital losses; loss trading; surplus strips; use of offshore bank accounts; donation arrangements; international transactions; 85(1) rollovers; RRSP appropriations; and abuse of TFSAs.

Foreign bank account information is available to auditors: see Notes to 281.

Real estate (property flipping) audits: see Notes to 40(2)(b).

Tax shelter audits: see Notes to 237.1(1)"tax shelter".

Statistics from CRA 2019-20 *Departmental Results Report* (tinyurl.com/cra-results): p. 30: 85,000 audits [calculated as $12.7b/$142,000] (down from 127,000 audits in 2014-15) generated $12.7 billion in federal tax and penalties (up from $11.7b), suggesting either that audits are better targeted, as CRA says, or that auditors are getting harsher, as some practitioners find. (The 2018-19 Report showed 98,000 audits completed; COVID-19 sending everyone home March 13 will have meant that many audits that would have been finished by March 31 year-end were not.)

Scope of CRA audit power (see also Notes to 231.2(1)): CRA can choose to audit anyone, but this discretion does not permit a vexatious audit made for capricious reasons: *Duval*, 2012 FC 480, para. 13. See Notes to 171(1) for lawsuits against CRA for audit abuse. There is no time limit on CRA requesting records from years back: *Stankovic*, 2018 FC 462, para. 34; *Lin*, 2019 FC 646, para. 25; but 230(4) requires keeping only 6 years of most records.

Oral interviews before the 2021 Budget proposals: Taxpayer T is entitled to choose representative R to answer questions (*Taxpayer Bill of Rights*, Article 15 — not a legal right but CRA respects it). If T asks the auditor to deal only with R, the auditor cannot insist on interviewing T personally. The right to audit does not entitle CRA to compel oral interviews, and 231.1(1)(d) applies to questions about where to find records: *Cameco*, 2019 FCA 67, paras. 20-21 (though the FCA left open the question of whether (d) provides an "independent power to compel attendance and answer questions") [Sorenson, case comment, 67(3) *Canadian Tax Journal* 775-83 (2019)]. CRA sort of accepted this decision (and did not seek leave to appeal), but noted ominously: "Refusal to participate in oral interviews ... indicates a lack of openness and transparency, and potentially a higher risk of non-compliance", and that declining interviews can lead CRA to make "assumptions about the nature of the taxpayer's business activities": "Statement from the [CRA re] *Cameco*", May 31, 2019, tinyurl.com/cra-cameco; Communiqué AD-19-02R, *Obtaining Information for Audit Purposes* (June 3, 2019). CRA is not entitled to visit a home without the occupant's permission or a search warrant: 231.1(2); *Income Tax Audit Manual* §4.5.1 (and §4.6.5 re CRA "borrowing" taxpayer records). For a business operated at home, review at the accountant's office may be preferable.

Oral interviews since the 2021 Budget proposals: See proposed 231.1(1)(c) above, which, once enacted, will allow CRA to demand that an owner, manager or "particular person" answer questions, both orally and in writing.

CRA may need to show its audit work was done properly. See for example *Huyen*, [1997] G.S.T.C. 42; *Gestion Cheers*, [2001] G.S.T.C. 44; *Hsu*, 2006 TCC 304. For a case rejecting an auditor's interpretation of the facts (re whether a taxpayer appropriated money from a corporation), see *Osinski*, 2013 TCC 71.

"It is not for the Court or anyone else to prescribe what the intensity of the examination of a taxpayer's return in any given case should be. That is exclusively a matter for the Minister": *Western Minerals*, [1962] C.T.C. 270 (SCC), para. 12. *Stukanov*, 2021 FC 49, upheld the Human Rights Commission's refusal to consider S's claim that CRA auditing him 3 times was discrimination on the basis of his ethnicity.

Audit methodologies: Where books and records are unavailable or inadequate, CRA uses various methods. See *Income Tax Audit Manual* chap. 13. **Net worth assessments**: see Notes to 152(7). **Application of funds** method (similar to net worth but focused only on personal expenditures): *Zhang*, 2013 TCC 19. **Bank deposits** method (assuming all deposits represent income earned) is accepted if the taxpayer cannot demonstrate otherwise: e.g., *Chow*, 2009 TCC 90, *Hébert*, 2009 TCC 124; *Henriques*, 2010 TCC 173; *Mulvaney*, 2010 TCC 182; *Malik*, 2011 TCC 224; *Khandwala*, 2011 TCC 466; *Nowak*, 2012 FCA 1; *Zeljkovic*, 2013 TCC 48; *Crichton*, 2013 TCC 96; *Arif*, 2014 TCC 73; *Narula*, 2014 TCC 371; *Bachmann*, 2015 TCC 51; *Pouliot*, 2014 TCC 273; *Farhan*, 2015 TCC 243; *Bonhomme*, 2016 TCC 152 (FCA appeal dismissed for delay A-321-16); *Aimurie*, 2016 TCC 164; *Liu*, 2017 TCC 117 (under appeal to FCA); *Carlini*, 2017 TCC 259; *Buday*, 2019 TCC 128; *Wood*, 2020 TCC 87 (under appeal to FCA); *Carpino*, 2020 TCC 88; but the TCC will accept credible evidence of another source of deposits, such as transfers from another account, including by cheque (*Cantore*, 2010 TCC 367; *Hemmati*, 2013 TCC 66, para. 19; *Chettabi*, 2020 TCC 19; *Tong*, 2020 TCC 70, paras. 34-35 [but unsupported claim of funds coming from repeated back-and-forth currency exchange was rejected]) or loans from family members (*2187028 Ontario*, 2016 TCC 216; *Semenov*, 2018 TCC 58); and it is wrong for an auditor to simply treat bank deposits as income when the records show transfers and other sources: *Pépin*, 2011 TCC 424, para. 21 (FCA appeal discontinued A-381-11); *Lee*, 2012 TCC 17; *9081-2769 Québec*, 2019 TCC 14 (deposits were in company's shareholder's spouse's account); *Robinson*, 2019 TCC 181, paras. 9-18. In both *Medvedev*, 2010 TCC 629 (FCA appeal allowed in part on consent A-485-10), and *Schmidt*, 2013 TCC 11 (FCA appeal discontinued A-146-12), the TCC rejected the bank-deposits method because the net worth method, though hard to do, would have been more accurate! **Employee hours-worked** method was accepted in *Langheit*, 2017 TCC 250. **Industry average markup** method was rejected in *Hemmati* (above), para. 12, and in *2741-2568 Québec*, 2016 TCC 207 (auditor's method based on price of 10 key food items was unreliable); but accepted by the TCC in many Revenu Québec GST audit cases: *Lady Elle*, [1999] G.S.T.C. 14; *9001-9159 Québec*, 2002 CarswellNat 4437; *Modes Crossfire*, 2002 CarswellNat 4651; *Bordeleau*, 2003 TCC 209; *2760-3125 Québec*, 2004 TCC 183; *Old Western Pizza*, 2004 TCC 452; *9022-8891 Québec*, 2006 TCC 60; *9010-9869 Québec*, 2007 TCC 365 (FCA appeal discontinued A-442-07); *9030-2340 Québec*, 2007 TCC 759; *Restaurant Place Romaine*, 2010 TCC 347; *9100-8649 Québec*, 2013 TCC 160 (aff'd 2014 FCA 20); *125319 Canada*, 2013 TCC 368; *9120-1616 Québec*, 2014 TCC 4; *Syed*, 2014 TCC 307; *9103-4348 Québec*, 2015 TCC 220; *Gouskos*, 2020 TCC 110, para. 41. **Marijuana yield** method was accepted in *Hole*, 2016 TCC 55 and *Clermont*, 2017 TCC 32. **Projection** method based on taxicab mileage was accepted in *Zouaimia*, 2012 FCA 248; a "labour/materials ratio" projection was rejected due to auditor errors in *Post*, 2016 TCC 92, paras. 12, 21. For detailed discussion and case law on these and other methodologies, see David Sherman's Analysis to *Excise Tax Act* s. 288 in the *Canada GST Service*, *GST Partner* or *Taxnet Pro*.

CRA auditors reportedly use casino records to treat all deposits and withdrawals as income the taxpayer must have earned, even though the same funds may be reused: tinyurl.com/cra-casinos.

An auditor, on completing the initial work, will normally send the taxpayer a "proposal letter" with details of a proposed reassessment, and allow 30 days to reply. (Such a letter is not a "decision" that the Federal Court can review to stop the assessment: *Prince*, 2020 FCA 32, para. 21; *Chekosky*, 2019 FC 841.) This deadline is informal and will generally be extended on request. Unless the auditor appears to have made up his or her mind and to be unwilling to listen, it is usually worthwhile making written submissions at this stage rather than waiting for a reassessment and objecting under s. 165. If it is important not to have the assessment issued (e.g., a public corp where disclosure of the assessment will affect share price), the taxpayer can call Headquarters; see CRA Roundtable q.17, 2009 Cdn Tax Foundation conference report, 3:16-17 (*Income Tax Technical News* 44); one option may be a pre-assessment s. 173 referral to the Tax Court. If CRA promises to give notice before reassessing and then does not, it can be liable in Quebec: *Ludmer*, 2018 QCCS 3381, paras. 548-553; aff'd 2020 QCCA 697, para. 81 (leave to appeal denied 2021 CarswellQue 2160 (SCC)) (see 171(1) Notes re suing CRA).

If the taxpayer disagrees with the proposal but negotiates to concede some issues while the auditor concedes other issues, the auditor will seek a 165(1.2) waiver of appeal rights. See CRA Communiqué AD-19-01, *Audit Agreement and Waiver of Objection Rights Guidelines* (Feb. 19, 2019).

Mandatory referrals to Headquarters: see RC478, *CPB National Early Warning System referral form* (on *Taxnet Pro* or *TaxPartner*). Adjustment to income exceeding $100 million must be referred to HQ before assessing; also (based on judgment) if the file is contentious or sensitive under various categories (financial hardship; impact on an industry; material amount of SR&ED or film claim disallowed; media sensitivity; non-compliance with other federal Acts; potential impact on policy or legislation; potential escalation to senior CRA officials; or public figure).

Disclosure of information by CRA: the auditor should provide a copy of the T20 Audit Report with the analysis underlying the proposal without an Access to Information (see Notes to 241(1)) request: CRA brochure P148 under "What is available to you?"; *Income Tax Audit Manual* §3.4.7, TEI/CRA Dec. 6, 2017 meeting q. 4(b) (see tiny-url.com/cra-informal for what can be released informally). The ATIP office will assist in asking the auditor to provide informal disclosure: VIEWS doc 2011-0403751C6. CRA officially encourages informal requests for disclosure rather than formal ATIP requests: Taxpayers' Ombudsman special report, *Acting on ATIP* (March 2012), oto-boc.gc.ca, pp. 20-21. Since 2018, CRA will not provide audit working papers and other CRA records (even under Access to Information) until the audit is finished (Perry Dirksen, Dept. of Justice, 2019 Cdn Tax Foundation conference, Dec. 2, 2019).

Years to audit: CRA has an internal policy that audits should normally be limited to "one plus one" years: the most recent year for which a return has been filed and assessed, plus one year back, with limited exceptions: *CRA Audit Manual* §9.12.3. This policy can be quoted to an auditor to limit the scope of audit requests, but it has no legal status and cannot be used to contest an assessment.

If an income tax audit identifies issues that are relevant to GST/HST, the auditor may issue a "workload referral" to trigger a GST/HST audit: *Income Tax Audit Manual* §9.13.0; and vice-versa: *GST/HST Audit and Examination Manual* §11.1.2.1.

CRA conducts some "simultaneous audits" with the U.S. Internal Revenue Service, exchanging information as they proceed. Q. 5, CCRA comments at IFA seminar, May 13, 2002 (search on ifacanada.org). CRA was conducting a pilot project of "joint audits" where Canadian and US auditors audit together: Scott Wilkie, "International Tax: Joint Audits", 2012 Cdn Tax Foundation conference report, 6:1-11.

CRA's audit powers cannot be used to collect information for purposes of a criminal investigation and prosecution. See Notes to 231.2(1) re the *Jarvis* case. Once the threshold of investigation has been crossed, accountants are not compelled to answer CRA inquiries, and due to client confidentiality normally should not do so without the client's permission.

One concern expressed by practitioners about auditors is that there is no accountability if an audit assessment is overturned on appeal; some auditors appear determined to issue assessments even where they will likely be overturned.

See also Chan, "Audits", *Practical Insights*, *Taxnet Pro* Tax Disputes Centre (Dec. 2020, 55pp); Campbell, *Administration of Income Tax 2020* (Carswell), chap. 7, "Audit and Investigation"; Quigley, "Controlling Tax Information", 47(1) *Canadian Tax Journal* 1 at 28-48 (1999); Henry & Kingisepp, "Managing the Confidentiality of Tax Accrual Working Papers", 2009 Cdn Tax Foundation conference report, 29:1-34; Kroft, "Recent Developments in CRA's Reach for Information", 2011 BC Tax Conference (ctf.ca), 5:1-88 and 2011 Ontario Tax Conf. 4:1-88; Mar et al., "Hot Audit Issues", 2011 conference report, 3:1-20; Goyette et al., "What To Do When an Audit Goes Wrong", *ibid.*, 32:1-24; Sorensen et al., "The CRA's New and Aggressive Tax Enforcement Powers", XVIII(4) *International Tax Planning* (Federated Press) 1270-74 (2013); Doobay, "The MNR's Audit Powers", 27(3) *Canadian Tax Highlights* (ctf.ca) 10-12 (March 2019).

Information Circulars: 71-14R3: The tax audit; 78-10R5: Books and records retention/destruction; 94-4R: International transfer pricing — advance pricing arrangements (APAs); 94-4R-SR: APAs for small businesses.

I.T. Technical News: 32 (taxpayer's opportunities to respond to assessments); 34 (enhanced CRA audits); 38 (CRA auditors' access to audit working papers); 44 (assessments; consistency in audit practice; update on committees).

Transfer Pricing Memoranda: TPM-04: Third-party information.

Registered Plans Compliance Bulletins: 8 (requirements to provide information under s. 231.2).

Registered Charities Newsletters: 13 (about auditing charities).

CRA Audit Manual: All chapters, including 8.0: Audit selection — risk assessment; 9.0: Audit planning and preparation; 10.0: Conducting the audit; 11.0: Finalizing the audit; 12.0: Specific audit techniques and checklists; 13.0: Audit techniques; and 40.0.0: Sector profiles.

Forms: RC4024: Enhancing service for large businesses: the audit protocol; real-time audit, concurrent audit, single-window focus [guide]; RC4188: What you should know about audits [pamphlet]; RC4409: Keeping records [guide].

(2) Prior authorization — Where any premises or place referred to in paragraph (1)(c) is a dwelling-house, an authorized person may not enter that dwelling-house without the consent of the occupant except under the authority of a warrant under subsection (3).

Proposed Amendment — 231.1(2)

(2) Entry to premises — For the purposes of subsection (1), an authorized person may enter into the premises or place where any business is carried on, any property is kept, anything is done in connection with any business or any books or records are or should be kept, except if the premises or place is a dwelling-house, the authorized person may enter the dwelling-house without the consent of the occupant only under the authority of a warrant under subsection (3).

Application: The April 19, 2021 Budget Notice of Ways and Means Motion, subsec. 28(2), will amend subsec. 231.1(2) to read as above, in force on Royal Assent.

Federal Budget, Supplementary Information, April 19, 2021: [See under 231.1(1)(c), though that proposal does not describe this amendment — ed.]

(3) Application — Where, on *ex parte* application by the Minister, a judge is satisfied by information on oath that

(a) there are reasonable grounds to believe that a dwelling-house is a premises or place referred to in paragraph (1)(c),

(b) entry into the dwelling-house is necessary for any purpose relating to the administration or enforcement of this Act, and

(c) entry into the dwelling-house has been, or there are reasonable grounds to believe that entry will be, refused,

the judge may issue a warrant authorizing an authorized person to enter the dwelling-house subject to such conditions as are specified in the warrant but, where the judge is not satisfied that entry into the dwelling-house is necessary for any purpose relating to the administration or enforcement of this Act, the judge may

(d) order the occupant of the dwelling-house to provide to an authorized person reasonable access to any document or property that is or should be kept in the dwelling-house, and

(e) make such other order as is appropriate in the circumstances to carry out the purposes of this Act,

to the extent that access was or may be expected to be refused and that the document or property is or may be expected to be kept in the dwelling-house.

Notes [subsec. 231.1(3)]: A warrant under 231.1(3) was issued in *Muller*, 2015 FC 262; aff'd 2016 FCA 260 (leave to appeal denied 2017 CarswellNat 1036 (SCC)). See Notes to 231.3(1) re search warrants generally.

231.1(3) amended by 1993 technical bill, effective June 15, 1994, to change "shall" to "may" in two places between paras. (c) and (d). See Notes to 231.3(3).

Definitions [s. 231.1]: "amount" — 248(1); "authorized person" — 231; "business" — 248(1); "documents", "dwelling-house" — 231; "inventory" — 248(1); "judge" — 231; "Minister" — 248(1); "oath" — *Interpretation Act* 35(1); "person", "property", "record", "taxpayer" — 248(1); "writing" — *Interpretation Act* 35(1).

231.2 (1) Requirement to provide documents or information — Notwithstanding any other provision of this Act, the Minister may, subject to subsection (2), for any purpose related to the administration or enforcement of this Act (including the collection of any amount payable under this Act by any person), of a listed international agreement or, for greater certainty, of a tax treaty with another country, by notice sent or served in accordance with subsection (1.1), require that any person provide, within such reasonable time as is stipulated in the notice,

(a) any information or additional information, including a return of income or a supplementary return; or

(b) any document.

Announced Administrative Change — Requirements for Information during COVID-19 pandemic

CRA information notice, April 20, 2020: *COVID-19 Update: Additional measures from the Canada Revenue Agency for businesses*

[Full text reproduced in PITA 59th ed. under 220(1) — ed.]

Requirements for information (RFI): Generally, taxpayers who have received a RFI can choose to defer acting on the requirement until further notice.

Notes: Presumably taxpayers who have not received a followup to an early-2020 RFI can rely on this statement.

Related Provisions: 150(2) — Demand to file income tax return; 163(5), (6) — Penalty of 5% of trust assets for non-compliance with demand re trust (as of 2021); 168(1)(e) — Revocation of charity's registration for failure to comply; 188.2(2)(a) — Suspension of charity's receipting privileges for failing to comply; 231.1(1)(b) — Examination of inventory; 231.5(1) — Copy of taxpayer's document may be used in court proceedings; 231.5(2) — Obligation to comply with auditor; 231.7 — Court order for compliance with requirement; 231.8 — Time contesting demand for information does not count towards reassessment clock; 232(2) — Solicitor-client privilege defence; 232(3.1) — Examination of documents where privilege claimed; 237.1(8) — Application to tax shelter disclosure; 237.3(13) — Audit of reportable avoidance transaction before return filed; 238(1) — Punishment for failure to comply; 244(5), (6) — Proof of service by mail or personal service; 244(9) — Copy of taxpayer's document may be used in court proceedings; 248(7)(a) — Mail deemed received on day mailed.

Notes: This is called a Requirement for Information (RFI), Demand for Information or Requirement Letter. For CRA interpretation and procedures on use of RFIs by Audit, see *Income Tax Audit Manual* §10.8; by Collections, *National Collections Manual*, "Requirements and requests for information — Tax programs". CRA normally allows 30 days for a reply: *Audit Manual* §10.8.6. (A demand can also be made under 231.1, e.g. *Chad*, 2019 FC 1456.)

For the meaning of "reasonable time" see *Joseph*, [1985] 2 C.T.C. 164 (Ont. HCJ) (7-10 days is normally reasonable); *1013808 Ontario*, [1994] 1 C.T.C. 401 (Ont. Gen. Div) (24 hours was reasonable for a company's minute book); *MacDonald*, 2005 BCPC 398 (30 days was insufficient time to produce all financial documentation for a year recently ended); *Brochu*, 2018 QCCS 722 ("immediately" was illegal use of a Requirement to seize documents, justifying punitive damages).

An extension of time to comply with a demand to file a return did not prevent s. 162 penalties from applying to late filing: *Nedza Enterprises*, 2010 FC 435; but the FCA allowed the company's appeal on consent, after drawing the parties' attention to the 2006 amendment to 220(3): A-199-10. (A consent judgment has no precedential value: see Notes to 221.2.) In *Patry*, 2011 FC 1032, para. 69, the Ps resisted demands to file returns because they believed CRA would use the information in criminal proceedings, but this was not reason to stay the demands, as "requiring them to comply with their statutory obligations does not constitute irreparable harm".

A demand for "information" in 231.2(1)(a) can require a person to answer a questionnaire; also, a requirement is valid if the information is relevant to the named taxpayer's tax liability, and this is a "low threshold": *Tower (Kitsch)*, 2003 FCA 307; *1144020 Ontario*, 2005 FC 813; *Nadler Estate*, 2005 FCA 385. However, one cannot be forced to create a record in a particular form: *Amdocs Canadian*, 2015 FC 1234 (organizational chart); *Developpements Béarence*, 2019 FC 22 (Excel spreadsheet, general ledger; CRA already had the information in other forms (CRA appears to accepts this: doc 2019-0816111C6 [2019 CPTS], q.1)). Nor can one be forced to conduct legal analysis (to provide information relevant to a particular ITA section applying): *Ghermezian*, 2020 FC 1137, para. 161. See also Taylor, "Requirements for Information and Documents", XII(2) *Tax Litigation* (Federated Press) 742-50 (2004); Zabolotney, "Can an Auditor Compel a Taxpayer to Create a New Document?", 8(4) *Canadian Tax Focus* (ctf.ca) 15-16 (Nov. 2018). A requirement may be used to determine whether collection is at risk even though collection is suspended by 225.1 pending an appeal: *Stanfield*, 2008 FC 605; *Carriero*, 2016 FC 1296. A demand can be made to obtain information for another country under Canada's tax treaty with that country, e.g. *Roch*, 2018 FC 340; *Blue Bridge*, 2021 FCA 62 (leave to appeal to SCC requested; stay of judgment denied 2021 FCA 114) (same matter as *Roch*); in *Levett*, 2021 FC 295 (under appeal to FCA), CRA was entitled under the Canada-Switzerland tax treaty to ask Switzerland for information about L. See also 231.1(1) Notes at "Oral interviews". There is no time limit on CRA demanding records from even 21 years back: *Ghermezian* (above), para. 141; but 230(4) requires keeping only 6 years of most records. CRA need not tell the taxpayer the purpose of the RFI: *Ghermezian*, para. 152.

Foreign-based information is subject to 231.6, but if it may be within X's "power, possession and control", CRA can demand it from X under 231.2 (if X does not have it, 231.6 will then apply): *Ghermezian*, 2020 FC 1137, paras. 86-111. In *eBay*, 2008 FCA 348, eBay Canada was required to release Canadian-address customer information it had access to, though it did not own the data, which was on servers outside Canada. (eBay was also ordered to disclose it while appealing from the FC: 2008 FCA 141.) [A province's superior court may not have jurisdiction to order a foreign non-party to disclose documents that are outside the province: *Lockwood Financial v. China Blue*, 2015 BCSC 839; but in *Jiminez*, [2019] EWCA Civ 51 (England), the UK tax authority could demand information from a non-resident, "provided no steps are taken to seek to enforce the penalty in a foreign state" (para. 54): see Notes to 223(3).] For convictions of eBay sellers see Notes to 239(1). For failed appeals by eBay sellers see *Zhang*, 2013 TCC 19; *Osaduke*, 2016 TCC 209.

231.2(1) is a tool for the Minister to administer and enforce the Act, and is not available to examine for discovery a non-party in a Tax Court appeal: *Advantex Marketing*, 2014 TCC 21, para. 31.

The scope of 231.2(1) "has been reduced ...to situations where the information sought by the Minister is relevant to the tax liability of some specific person or persons, and when the tax liability of such person or persons is the subject of a genuine and serious inquiry": *AGT Ltd.*, [1997] 2 C.T.C. 275 (FCA), para. 27 (but see Notes to 231.2(2)). In *Murphy*, 2009 FC 1226, CRA appeared to be using 231.2 to collect information for the police rather than in a genuine inquiry into tax liability, so RFIs were quashed (and costs of $214,000 awarded: 2010 FC 448). However, CRA no longer needs to prove "genuine and serious inquiry" but only a real audit, so a "fishing expedition" through the taxpayer's records is allowed: *Plachcinski*, 2016 CarswellNat 10234 (FC), para. 14.

Having bankruptcy protection does not protect X from having to disclose information under 231.2, as the demand is not a seizure of X's property: *Stern*, 2004 FC 763; *Fabi*, 2006 FCA 22; *Stanfield*, 2008 FC 605.

In *Fraser Milner Casgrain*, 2002 FCT 912, information on a transaction's purpose had to be disclosed to allow CRA to determine whether it was an avoidance transaction under GAAR.

231.2(1) is unconstitutional in its application to lawyers and Quebec notaries in their capacity as legal advisers, because it violates solicitor-client privilege (and civil law "professional secrecy"): *Chambre des notaires*, 2016 SCC 20, para. 93 (see 232(2) Notes).

Accountants' communications are not protected by privilege: see 232(2) Notes.

Demands for roadmaps: In *BP Canada*, 2017 FCA 61, BP did not have to disclose its "uncertain tax positions" analysis (prepared for its external auditors) to give CRA a roadmap on what to audit: CRA "cannot compel taxpayers to reveal their soft spots" and "self-audit" (paras. 82, 83); this would cause public companies to not disclose tax risks to external auditors and "imperil the integrity of the financial reporting system put in place by the provinces" (para. 98). CRA did not seek leave to appeal to the SCC. For CRA's revised policy on *BP* and tax accrual working papers, see Communiqué AD-19-02R, *Obtaining Information for Audit Purposes* (June 3, 2019); VIEWS doc 2018-0779971C6 [2018 CTF q.11]. In *Atlas Tube*, 2018 FC 1086 (CPA Canada added as intervenor 2019 FCA 120 but FCA appeal discontinued A-396-18), CRA was entitled to a draft tax due-diligence report prepared in advance of an acquisition, on the basis that *BP* prevents giving CRA a roadmap for *future* audits, and this was for audit of a specific transaction. See also Clark, "BP, Atlas Tube and Roofmart", 1(4) *Perspectives on Tax Law & Policy* (ctf.ca) 8-10 (Dec. 2020); Sorenson, "CRA Powers to Compel Production", *ibid*. 10-12. The April 2021 Budget's proposed expansion of the "reportable transaction" rules (see at end of 237.3) will force certain companies to disclose their "uncertain tax positions" to CRA.

As to whether a demand can be sent to a province, see Notes to 248(1)"person".

CRA may have a duty to notify X when sending a requirement for information about X to someone else: *Dwyer v. Shevkenek*, 2004 FC 130.

CRA may use 231.2 to check a taxpayer's credit where a large balance is owing even before the April 30 due date: VIEWS doc 2005-0141121C6.

Where a person does not comply with an RFI, CRA may prosecute under 238(1) (e.g., *Carter*, 2011 BCPC 253; *Logan*, 2014 BCCA 240 (leave to appeal denied 2015 CarswellBC 75 (SCC)), but usually seeks a 237.1 compliance order, so that non-compliance is contempt of Court. The RFI need not be in both official languages to be valid: *Brewer*, 2009 NBPC 5. See 238(1) Notes for convictions and acquittals. A charity that does not comply may be suspended; see 188.2 Notes.

Challenging an RFI is done by application for judicial review in Federal Court (see 171(1) Notes). The *Vavilov* "reasonableness" test applies (see 220(3.1) Notes): *Ghermezian*, 2020 FC 1137, paras. 13-18. If only one request in an RFI is invalid, the Court might sever it and enforce the rest: *Ghermezian*, paras. 164-5. One can also ignore the RFI and raise defences in a 238(1) prosecution for failure to comply, or, since CRA usually seeks a 231.7 compliance order before prosecuting, raise the defences in the 231.7(2) hearing. See also Kroft & Lipetz, "How Does a Taxpayer Contest a Requirement for Information...?", VIII(2) *Tax Litigation [TL]* (Federated Press) 502-03 (2000); Oldewening & Chua, "Effective Strategies for Dealing With Requirements", XVII(4) *TL* 1066-74 (2010); and 232(2) Notes re solicitor-client privilege defence.

See Notes to 231.2(2) re demands for information about unnamed persons.

Jarvis defence: The Supreme Court of Canada drew the line between tax audits and investigations in *Jarvis*, 2002 SCC 73, and *Ling*, 2002 SCC 74. Once the "predominant purpose" of an inquiry is investigation for purposes of prosecution rather than assessment (see Notes to 239(1)), the 231.1 and 231.2 audit powers can no longer be used, and if they are, the information collected cannot be used in a prosecution due to *Charter of Rights* protections against self-incrimination (s. 7) and unreasonable search and seizure (s. 8 — see Notes to 231.3(1)). To determine if an audit "crossed the Rubicon" into an investigation, one must look at all factors, including but not limited to:

(a) Did the authorities have reasonable grounds to lay charges? Could a decision to proceed with a criminal investigation have been made?

(b) Was the general conduct of the authorities consistent with the pursuit of a criminal investigation?

(c) Had the auditor transferred his or her files and materials to the investigators?

(d) Was the conduct of the auditor such that he or she was effectively acting as an agent for the investigators?

(e) Does it appear that the investigators intended to use the auditor as their agent in the collection of evidence?

(f) Is the evidence sought relevant to taxpayer liability generally, or only to criminal liability?

(g) Are there any other circumstances or factors that can lead the judge to the conclusion that the audit had in reality become a criminal investigation?

See Kiselbach & Brooks, "From Tax Audit to Criminal Investigation", xxix(16-18) *The Canadian Taxpayer* (Carswell) 113-16, 121-24, 129-30 (July-Sept. 2007); Lindsay, "Tax Sensitive Document Management", 20 *Canadian Petroleum Tax Journal* (2007); Boddez & DelBigio, "Criminal Tax Evasion", 2012 Cdn Tax Foundation conference report, 38:1-28.

Post-*Jarvis*, evidence was held inadmissible or requirements were quashed (because the predominant purpose had become a criminal investigation) in *Bining*, 2003 FCA 286; *Kligman [Plastiques Algar]*, 2004 FCA 152; *Foy*, [2005] G.S.T.C. 31 (Ont. SCJ); *Stanfield*, 2005 FC 1010; *Chen*, 2007 ONCJ 177; *Borg*, 2007 ONCJ 451; *Tiffin*, 2008 ONCA 306 (mixed decision but new trial ordered); *Lombardo*, 2011 BCPC 177 (CRA audit was triggered by Special Enforcement Program); *McCartie*, 2015 BCPC 66 and 69 (CRA auditor had lost notes that might show she was used as a tool by Investigations); *Mori*, 2015 ONCJ 810 (once auditor's suspicions that taxpayer was not reporting income were confirmed, he had investigative intent). *BT Céramiques (Bruno)*, 2020 QCCA 402 (leave to appeal denied 2020 CarswellQue 8842 (SCC)) (purpose of audit was to investigate corruption within CRA, which related to taxpayers' evasion); *Goldberg (Bouclair Inc.)*, 2020 QCCQ 4548 (CRA could not use RQ's audit records for prosecution, in a case where RQ could have prosecuted but had chosen to continue to audit so as to assess).

Evidence was held admissible in: *Anderson*, 2003 SKCA 27 (inquiries were routine audit); *Bjellebo [Bellfield]*, 2003 CarswellOnt 3955 (Ont CA; leave to appeal denied 2004 CarswellNat 1760 (SCC)) (evidence was otherwise discoverable); *Dial Drug Stores*, [2003] 3 C.T.C. 207 (Ont. SC) (evidence admissible up to point where auditor formally referred file to Investigations); *Aviscar Inc.*, 2003 CarswellQue 3562 and 2004 CarswellQue 8389 (Que. SC); *Wilder*, 2003 BCSC 859 (facts predated *Jarvis*, Revenue Canada did not act in bad faith or recklessly, evidence was non-prescriptive, and allegations amounted to a very serious offence); *Pomerleau*, 2005 QCCA 364 (leave to appeal denied 2005 CarswellQue 9987 (SCC)); *Lempen*, 2006 NBQB 131 (file referred to Investigations only after evidence obtained; focus of audit was determining entitlement to input tax credits); *Chahine-Badr*, [2006] 2 C.T.C. 243 (Ont. SCJ) (audit became criminal investigation only later); *Ellingson*, 2006 FCA 202 (leave to appeal denied 2006 CarswellNat 4271 (SCC)) (audit and criminal inquiries can proceed in parallel); *Brigham*, 2007 ONCJ 445 (even though auditor had enough information to refer to Investigations, she did not decide to do so until later); *Weinstein & Gavino Fabrique*, 2007 QCCS 6339 (project seeking to find "zapper" software by eating in restaurants and later demanding records to look for the purchases was purely audit project); *DiGiuseppe*, 2008 ONCJ 126 (police investigation of strip club was focused on prostitution and proceeds-of-crime offences, and Revenue Canada involvement was purely audit); *Ostrowski*, [2008] G.S.T.C. 147 (Ont. SCJ) (auditor had no contact with Investigations and was not their agent); *Bath*, 2011 BCSC 251 (requests to banks for records predated *Jarvis*, at a time when CRA policy permitted audit action up until charges were laid); *McMahon*, 2012 ABPC 296 (CRA official's demands for returns were made to verify tax liability, and she had no contact with Investigations); *Smith*, 2013 ONCJ 316 (auditor was in "audit" mode throughout his work, and audit of false claims by company whose ID was stolen by S had not even identified S yet); *Giroux*, 2014 BCPC 24 (auditor was considering 163(2) penalties, and ceased work once she had enough information to refer file to Investigations); *Posteraro*, 2014 BCPC 31 (auditor was in "audit mode" throughout, including when determining whether to assess 163(2) penalties); *Hilcoff*, 2014 SKPC 28 (auditor did not have enough information to refer file to Investigations until she completed net worth analysis); *Martin*, 2015 NSSC 8 (admission that amounts were deliberately left off GST returns did not turn CRA audit into investigation); *Gunner Industries*, 2015 SKQB 349 (SKCA denied leave to appeal; SCC denied leave to appeal 2019 CarswellSask 116) (audit had not yet become investigation); *Berger*, 2016 QCCA 226 (RQ demand for Swiss bank account information was valid); *Muller*, 2016 FCA 260 (leave to appeal denied 2017 CarswellNat 1036 (SCC)) (no investigation underway); *Mori*, 2017 ONSC 1551, para. 33; *Patry*, 2018 BCSC 591 (no reasonable basis to conduct a *Jarvis* inquiry); *Mariani*, 2019 ONCJ 128 (auditor had suspicions but was still considering civil penalties); *Accurso (Bruno)*, 2019 QCCQ 3705 (investigation into CRA corruption did not change nature of audit; refusal to revisit decision 2020 QCCQ 3001). (The GST decisions are under *Excise Tax Act* s. 289, which contains the same rules: see David M. Sherman, *Practitioner's Goods and Services Tax Annotated*.)

The tension between *Jarvis* (accused's right to know when matter was referred to Investigations) and the Crown's right to keep informer tips confidential is considered in four decisions in *McCartie*, 2013 BCPC 150, 174, 221 and 289.

To better distinguish between auditors and investigators in light of *Jarvis*, CRA investigators have been given ID badges: news release, March 28/07.

CRA employee time records can be a way for an accused to show that CRA had begun investigation as of a given date (but CRA destroys RC500 and RC509 timesheet records after 2 years: see Notes to 230(1)). Clint Kimery, "Predominant Purpose" (on davidsherman.ca/files), discusses CRA internal operations and claims that once an AIMS (Audit Information Management System) "Case Number" is assigned, the file is an investigation, not an audit (which uses the Social Insurance Number or Business Number). See CRA *Criminal Investigations Manual* (CIM) §15.8. Kimery claims that the T133 (Project Information or Tax Lead) form is effectively the referral cover sheet to initiate a Stage 2 investigation, rather than the official T134 fraud referral form, but CIM §3.14 suggests otherwise. (CRA is not legally required to use a T134: *Gordon*, 2019 FC 853, para. 233 (under appeal to FCA).)

Unrelated to *Jarvis*, a restaurant's records were inadmissible in *He*, 2012 BCCA 318, because they were seized as part of an electronic records compliance research and "awareness-raising" project that was not an audit of the restaurant, and this was an unreasonable seizure under the *Charter*.

Information obtained in violation of *Jarvis* can be used in assessing the taxpayer and in Tax Court: *Dwyer*, 2003 FCA 322; *Warawa*, 2005 FCA 34; *Kiwan (Nassar)*, 2006 FCA 58; *Romanuk*, 2013 FCA 133 (leave to appeal denied 2013 CarswellNat 4317 (SCC)); *Breau*, 2013 FCA 215 (RFIs were valid even though criminal and audit action were both underway with the two CRA groups talking to each other); *Piersanti*, 2014 FCA 243 (leave to appeal denied 2015 CarswellNat 1024); *Bauer*, 2018 FCA 62; *Campbell*, 2018 FC 683; *Abinader*, 2007 TCC 111 (FCA appeal discontinued A-144-07); *Keenan*, 2019 TCC 259, para. 36. More generally, *Jarvis* does not operate in reverse, so documents seized in a criminal investigation can be used for assessment purposes: *SPE Valeur*, 2016 FC 56. Older cases said that evidence obtained by illegal search could be disallowed in Tax Court: *O'Neill Motors*, [1998] 3 C.T.C. 385 (FCA), and *Fritz Marketing*, 2009 FCA 62, para. 36 [for the *Customs Act*]; and this rule is still theoretically valid, though it applies only to an illegal search warrant, not to information given voluntarily (in violation of the *Jarvis* rule which is based on *Charter* protection against illegal search!): *Romanuk* (above), para. 9. In *Klundert*, 2013 TCC 208, the issue could not be raised because the taxpayer did not raise it in his criminal trial and appeals; and in *506913 N.B.*, 2013 TCC 209 (FCA appeal discontinued on consent A-278-13), the TCC refused to consider whether the search warrant was illegal, as that would be a collateral attack on orders of the provincial courts that issued and approved the warrant. See also Kirby, "Is O'Neill Motors Out of Gas?", XII(1) *Tax Litigation* (Federated Press) 730-34 (2004). A corporation cannot claim *Charter* relief in a tax appeal: *Main Rehabilitation*, 2004 FCA 403 (leave to appeal denied 2005 CarswellNat 1110 (SCC)); *SPE Valeur*, 2019 TCC 174 (under appeal to FCA).

Some "tax protesters" have made the spurious argument that demands for information under 231.2 are valid only if made to the taxpayer's legal representative. This argument has been soundly rejected: *Camplin*, 2007 FC 183; *Becelaere*, 2007 FC 409.

Where CRA seeks information from a third party such as a bank, it may obtain a "production order" under *Criminal Code* s. 487.012 or 487.013 rather than 231.2. See CRA *Criminal Investigations Manual* §6.2.5.

In *1068754 Alberta [Bitton Trust]*, 2019 SCC 37, Revenu Québec could validly send an RFI to National Bank's Calgary branch at which a Quebec taxpayer had an account, as the bank carried on business in Quebec.

See also: 231.1(1) Notes; Heddema & Russell, "CRA Requests for Information", 2008 BC Tax Conference (ctf.ca), 1:1-18; Schmidt, "Limits on the CRA's Power to Access Information", 20(4) *Canadian Tax Highlights* (ctf.ca) 3-4 (April 2012); Nitikman, "Everything You Always Wanted To Know About Requirements", 2018 Cdn Tax Foundation conference report, 30:1-33; Sorensen, "Document Demands", 2019 Cdn Tax Foundation conference report, 12:1-50; David Sherman's Analysis of *Excise Tax Act* ss. 289, 290 in *Canada GST Service* or *Taxnet Pro*.

231.2(1) opening words amended by 2021 budget bill #1, effective June 29, 2021, to change "notice served personally or by registered mail" to "notice sent or served in accordance with subsection (1.1)".

231.2(1) amended by 2002-2013 technical bill (effective June 26, 2013), 2007 budget bill #2, 2000 GST bill.

Information Circulars: 78-10R5: Books and records retention/destruction; 05-1R1: Electronic record keeping.

I.T. Technical News: 32 (CRA access to accountants' or auditors' working papers); 38 (CRA auditors' access to audit working papers).

Registered Plans Compliance Bulletins: 8 (requirements to provide information under s. 231.2).

CRA Audit Manual: 10.6.0: Obtaining information from third parties; 10.8.0: Requirement guidelines; Appendix A-10.1.0: Letters [sample requirement letters].

(1.1) Notice — A notice referred to in subsection (1) may be

(a) served personally;

(b) sent by registered or certified mail; or

(c) sent electronically to a bank or credit union that has provided written consent to receive notices under subsection (1) electronically.

Related Provisions: 231.6(3.1) — Parallel rule for requirement to provide foreign-based information; 244(6.1) — Proof of electronic delivery.

Notes: See also "Proposed Amendments — Electronic filing and communications" under 244(14.1). It seems likely that, once those changes are in place, consent from the financial institution will not be needed for a Requirement to be deliverable electronically.

231.2(1.1) added by 2021 budget bill #1, effective June 29, 2021 (adding para. (c) to what had been in 231.2(1)), as proposed in 2019 Budget.

(2) Unnamed persons — The Minister shall not impose on any person (in this section referred to as a **"third party"**) a requirement under subsection (1) to provide information or any document relating to one or more unnamed persons unless the Minister first obtains the authorization of a judge under subsection (3).

Notes: 231.2(2) provides that CRA needs judicial authorization under 231.2(3) to obtain information about a third party. This goes back to a tradition of limiting "fishing expeditions": *James Richardson & Sons Ltd.*, [1984] C.T.C. 345 (SCC). See Notes to 231.2(3) re relaxation of the restrictions in 1995.

"Unnamed" appears to mean "not known to the Minister", not "not named in the Requirement": *Ghermezian*, 2020 FC 1137, paras. 67-74. Unnamed persons not sought for their own tax liability do not trigger this rule: in *Artistic Ideas*, 2005 FCA 68, CRA could demand from an art flip promoter the names of charities involved in the scheme, but not the donors, since the audit sought to reassess the donors; and in *Zeifmans LLP*, 2021 FC 363, para. 32 (under appeal to FCA), a demand for information about unnamed entities owned or controlled by the Ghermezian family did not trigger 231.2(2), as this was to audit the Ghermezians (even though CRA might audit one of those entities in the future). In *Toronto Dominion Bank*, 2004 FCA 359, a tax debtor deposited a cheque to X's bank account; the Court held that 231.2(2) applied to a demand for X's name, but later cases limit *TD*'s scope: see *Ghermezian* para. 40 and *Zeifmans* paras. 39-42.

Most recent cases have ordered such information released: *Artistic Ideas*, 2005 FCA 68 (names and addresses of donors demanded from art flip promoter); *Greater Montreal Real Estate Board (Chambre immobilière du Grand Montréal)*, 2007 FCA 346 (leave to appeal denied 2008 CarswellNat 1116 (SCC)) (list of real estate agents and properties sold); *Advantage Credit Union*, 2008 FC 853 (banking details to enforce collection against tax debtor); *eBay Canada*, 2008 FCA 348 (see Notes to 231.2(1)); *Amex Bank*, 2008 FC 972 (details about primary cardholder on a credit-card account); *Whitewater Golf Club*, 2009 FC 739 (list of members of golf club and fees paid); *D'Alma (Municipalité)*, 2011 CarswellNat 2782 (FC); *Pointe-Calumet*, 2011 CarswellNat 2783 (FC); *Arrondissement Greenfield Park*, 2011 CarswellNat 2784 (FC); *KPMG*, 2016 FC 1322 (clients using KPMG offshore tax structure); *Rona Inc.*, 2017 FCA 118 (leave to appeal to SCC requested) (customers who were construction contractors); *Paypal Canada*, 2017 CarswellNat 6671 (FC) (all business accounts in Canada [Kreklewetz & Raphael, "CRA RFI Powers", 25(12) *Canadian Tax Highlights* (ctf.ca) 6-7 (Dec. 2017)]); *Brewers Retail*, 2018 CarswellNat 7577 (FC); *Roofmart*, 2020 FCA 85 ("sector wide" audits are allowed, as "pending or existing tax audit of a particular individual is not a precondition": paras. 40, 45); *Coinsquare*, 2021 CarswellNat 1193 (FC) (cryptocurrency exchange, order issued on consent: tinyurl.com/coinsq-cra). In *S&V Service Centers*, 2014 CarswellOnt 18860 (Ont. CJ), a demand for banking information about X revealed information about Y, and that information was used to obtain a search warrant against Y, which was held to be valid.

Contra: *Hydro-Québec*, 2018 FC 622, denied CRA a demand for a list of all HQ's commercial customers, as this was an artificial "ascertainable" group and was a "fishing expedition" invading taxpayers' privacy (but this was partly overruled by the FCA in *Roofmart*). *Derakhshani*, 2009 FCA 190, upheld the FC's refusal to order a company preparing taxi drivers' tax returns to release information, as CRA's affidavit was inadequate. See also Notes to 231.2(3).

See Notes to 231.2(3) re CRA's obligation to make "full and frank disclosure" in *ex parte* applications made before June 27, 2013.

See also Yuan, "Section 8 of the Charter and Requirements", 2126 *Tax Topics [TT]* (CCH) 1-4 (Dec. 6, 2012); Antel, "Disclosing Information to the CRA About Unnamed Non-Target Persons", 3(1) *Canadian Tax Focus* (ctf.ca) 4 (Feb. 2013); Roberge, "Unnamed Person Requirement", 2489 *TT* 1-5 (Nov. 21, 2019).

CRA can bypass 231.2(2) by making a demand under 231.1 during an audit, "to verify the compliance of the taxpayer being audited": *Redeemer Foundation*, 2008 SCC 46, so a charity was required to disclose details about its donors. This arguably applies only to charities and not generally: David Spiro, "Charity Donor Lists", XVI(1) *Tax Litigation* (Federated Press) 970-974 at 973 (2008). It supersedes earlier cases on disclosure of charity donors: *National Foundation for Christian Leadership*, 2005 FCA 246; *John McKellar Charitable Foundation*, 2006 FCA 235; *All Saints Greek Orthodox Church*, 2006 FC 374 (FCA appeal discontinued due to *Redeemer*: A-167-06).

Similarly, in *Bernick*, 2002 CarswellOnt 2356 (Ont. SCJ), a demand for information about a partnership's other partners was valid without 231.2(2) because CRA was auditing B, and nothing suggested CRA was seeking to audit the other partners; and in *London Life*, 2009 FC 956 (FCA appeal discontinued A-465-09), an insurance company was required to disclose information about a broker's clients where only the broker was under audit. In *Van Egmond*, 2002 BCCA 226, CRA was allowed to use 231.2(1) to demand a GST consultant's sales records so as to audit his clients.

A former director or officer of a dissolved corporation is not a "third party" for purposes of 231.2(2): *Morton*, 2007 FC 503.

Orders under 231.2(3) were upheld under former 231.2(5) in: *Sand Exploration*, [1995] 2 C.T.C. 140 (FC); *Welton Parent*, 2006 FC 67 (actuarial firm records re valuations of health and welfare trusts, but not employer names).

(3) Judicial authorization — A judge of the Federal Court may, on application by the Minister and subject to any conditions that the judge considers appropriate, authorize the Minister to impose on a third party a requirement under subsection (1) relating to an unnamed person or more than one unnamed person (in this section

referred to as the **"group"**) if the judge is satisfied by information on oath that

(a) the person or group is ascertainable; and

(b) the requirement is made to verify compliance by the person or persons in the group with any duty or obligation under this Act.

(c), (d) [Repealed]

Related Provisions: 168(1)(e) — Revocation of charity's registration for failure to comply; 188.2(2)(a) — Suspension of charity's receipting privileges for failing to comply; 231.2(5), (6) — Judicial review of authorization; 232(2), (3.1) — Solicitor-client privilege defence; 237.1(8) — Application to tax shelter disclosure; 238(1) — Punishment for failure to comply.

Notes: See Notes to 231.2(2).

Applications made after June 26, 2013 are no longer *ex parte* (without notice to the taxpayer). Before this change, "The fact that the Minister may obtain a court authorization *ex parte* places an obligation on the Minister to act in the utmost good faith and ensure full and frank disclosure of information": *Sand Exploration Ltd.*, [1995] 2 C.T.C. 140 (FC); *All Saints Greek Orthodox Church*, [2006] 3 C.T.C. 87 (FC) (FCA appeal discontinued A-167-06). If the CRA did not make "full and frank disclosure" of the reasons for seeking an order, the order would be struck down on later review. See *Lordco Parts*, 2013 FCA 49 (order for information about promotional cruises given to customers' employees — CRA "failed to disclose alternative sources of the information" and "provided an inaccurate and misleading description of the circumstances justifying the authorization"); *RBC Life Insurance [BMO Life Insurance]*, 2013 FCA 50 (requirement for information on life insurance "10-8" plans — the FC believed the reason for requiring the order was not to audit participants but to "send a message to the industry" to chill the use of such plans, and the Crown did not disclose internal documentation accepting that 10-8 plans comply with the Act). [The tax benefits of these policies were later eliminated by the 2013 Budget: see 248(1)"10/8 policy".] However, in *Cormark Securities*, 2011 FC 1472, the Court refused to strike down an *ex parte* order for information on "Tech Wreck" restructurings (see *Income Tax Technical News* 34 and Notes to 111(5)), as the information could not be obtained another way and was required to verify compliance with the Act.

The 2013 amendment below, eliminating the *ex parte* nature of the application, also means that if the third party wants to contest the order, it must do so at the application hearing, rather than seeking a later review under former 231.2(5), which would delay the audit process.

231.2(3) opening words amended by 2013 budget bill #1, effective for applications made by the Minister after June 26, 2013. Before the amendment, read:

(3) On *ex parte* application by the Minister, a judge may, subject to such conditions as the judge considers appropriate, authorize the Minister to impose on a third party a requirement under subsection (1) relating to an unnamed person or more than one unnamed person (in this section referred to as the "group") where the judge is satisfied by information on oath that

231.2(3)(c) and (d) repealed by 1995 Budget, effective June 20, 1996 (Royal Assent). They provided additional conditions:

(c) it is reasonable to expect, based on any grounds, including information (statistical or otherwise) or past experience relating to the group or any other persons, that the person or any person in the group may have failed or may be likely to fail to provide information that is sought pursuant to the requirement or to otherwise comply with this Act; and

(d) the information or document is not otherwise more readily available.

This change means that the CRA can now go on judicially-authorized "fishing expeditions" by demanding information from various sources. The Department of Finance Technical Notes explain the change as follows: "Paragraphs 231.2(3)(c) and (d) are repealed in order to simplify those conditions." However, the 1995 Budget papers put it this way:

These restrictions, which make it difficult for Revenue Canada to obtain timely information in order to verify compliance with the Act, are being eliminated. This proposed measure will improve Revenue Canada's ability to verify compliance with the self-assessment system with respect to transactions where no information reporting is required.

(4)–(7) [Repealed]

Notes: See Notes to 231.3(3) re elimination of *ex parte* hearings. 231.2(4)-(6) repealed by 2013 budget bill #1, effective for applications made by the Minister after June 26, 2013. They read:

(4) Service of authorization — Where an authorization is granted under subsection (3), it shall be served together with the notice referred to in subsection (1).

(5) Review of authorization — Where an authorization is granted under subsection (3), a third party on whom a notice is served under subsection (1) may, within 15 days after the service of the notice, apply to the judge who granted the authorization or, where the judge is unable to act, to another judge of the same court for a review of the authorization.

(6) Powers on review — On hearing an application under subsection (5), a judge may cancel the authorization previously granted if the judge is not then satisfied that the conditions in paragraphs (3)(a) and (b) have been met and the judge may confirm or vary the authorization if the judge is satisfied that those conditions have been met.

231.2(6) earlier amended by 1995 Budget, effective June 20, 1996.

231.2(7), repealed by 1988 tax reform effective Sept. 13, 1988, allowed the court to make further compliance orders. It was repealed on the introduction of a general power in 238(2) to make compliance orders.

Definitions [s. 231.2]: "amount", "bank" — 248(1); "credit union" — 137(6), 248(1); "document" — 231; "group" — 231.2(3); "listed international agreement", "Minister" — 248(1); "oath" — *Interpretation Act* 35(1); "person", "tax treaty" — 248(1); "third party" — 231.2(2); "written" — *Interpretation Act* 35(1)"writing".

Information Circulars [s. 231.2]: 73-10R3: Tax evasion.

231.3 (1) Search warrant

231.3 (1) Search warrant — A judge may, on *ex parte* application by the Minister, issue a warrant in writing authorizing any person named therein to enter and search any building, receptacle or place for any document or thing that may afford evidence as to the commission of an offence under this Act and to seize the document or thing and, as soon as practicable, bring it before, or make a report in respect of it to, the judge or, where the judge is unable to act, another judge of the same court to be dealt with by the judge in accordance with this section.

Related Provisions: 232(3) — Seizure of certain documents where privilege claimed; 237.1(8) — Application to tax shelter disclosure rules; 237.3(13) — Audit of reportable avoidance transaction before return filed; 238(1) — Punishment for failing to comply.

Notes: Instead of 231.3, CRA now gets search warrants under *Criminal Code* s. 487: *Criminal Investigations Manual* §2.4(1), §6.1(3), so a single Information can allege offences under the *Code*, ITA and *Excise Tax Act* (GST/HST); *Watts*, 2019 FC 1321, para. 23. Also, s. 487 needs only a JP or provincial court judge (*Code* s. 2"justice") rather than a superior court judge (ITA 231"judge"). The SCC held in *Multiform Manufacturing*, [1990] 2 S.C.R. 624 at 631 that s. 487 can be used in enforcing any federal Act, even one with its own search-warrant provisions. Based on *Multiform*, tax-protester challenges of s. 487 warrants were rejected in: *Porisky*, 2012 BCSC 68; *Sigglekow*, 2013 ABQB 116 and 2014 ABQB 101; *Amell*, 2013 SKCA 48; *Anderson*, 2014 BCSC 2002, 2021 BCCA 101; *Watts*, 2015 ONSC 5597. CRA executed 172 search warrants in 2017-18: *Departmental Results Report*, p. 39 (no data in 2018-19 or 2019-20 Reports).

The language of a warrant must be specific, not general or vague: *Hawkins Truck Mart*, 2007 NBQB 370. Search warrants were upheld and the seized evidence was admissible in *Witen*, 2014 ONCA 694 (extension of time to file leave to appeal denied by SCC Dec. 10/15, file 36533)), and *Martin*, 2010 ONSC 7235. Having someone not named in the search warrant invited to participate by the officer in charge does not invalidate the seizure: *Coombs*, 2009 FCA 74, paras. 6-8, 2014 FCA 222 (leave to appeal denied 2015 CarswellNat 694 (SCC)), 2015 FC 869 (FCA appeal discontinued A-328-15) and 2015 FC 1321; *Select Travel*, 2013 TCC 93, para. 15.

Eddy, 2016 ABQB 42, held: (1) CRA can use records obtained in its (valid) search of X's home to prosecute Y (paras. 23, 82-93); (2) the Crown's report to a justice after seizure need not be made within any fixed deadline (para. 52); (3) the Crown has the right to keep copies of documents and computer data seized (paras. 42, 46); (4) once a computer is validly seized, electronic searches of the computer are valid (paras 107-110). On point (4), see also *Uber Canada*, 2016 QCCS 2158, paras. 241-84 (leave to appeal denied 2016 QCCA 1303); *Muller*, 2015 FC 262, paras. 49-53 (aff'd 2016 FCA 260; leave to appeal denied 2017 CarswellNat 1036 (SCC)). In *Mariani*, 2019 ONCJ 128, the warrant allowed seizing computers but not a full search of them; data from their disk drives was allowed in evidence, as "CRA officers limited their search to banking records, tax forms, invoices and similar documents" (para. 80).

In *McCartie*, 2015 BCPC 233, refusing to give the home's occupant a requested copy of the warrant *before* entering violated the *Charter*, and the evidence seized was excluded: 2015 BCPC 254.

Where CRA's conduct in wrongly obtaining a search warrant was "serious and egregious", costs were still not awarded against the Crown (although CRA might be liable in damages): *Taylor*, 2008 NSCA 5. In *Neumann*, 2011 BCCA 313 (leave to appeal denied [2012] G.S.T.C. 28 (SCC)), a jury had awarded a homeowner $1.3m damages for infringing his rights when executing a search warrant investigating a third party, but the BCCA ruled there is no tort in executing a properly-obtained warrant even if third party suffers damage. In *Gerlitz*, 2013 ABQB 624, the RCMP and CRA were held to have used only the force necessary to do the search, and the fact the search ended past the timeframe stated in the warrant did not require the evidence to be excluded.

CRA can examine documents seized under a search warrant by another government agency without CRA having its own "reasonable and probable grounds": *CRA v. CBSA*, 2013 BCSC 594; *CRA v. RCMP*, 2016 BCSC 2275; Plumridge, "CRA's Access to Taxpayer Documents Expanded", 21(5) *Canadian Tax Highlights* (ctf.ca) 11-12 (May 2012). (However, more recently see *QW*, 2017 SKPC 85, para. 16, though other factors were also relevant in that case.) CRA can also give copies of seized documents

to Revenu Québec, even if no charges are laid: *SPE Valeur*, 2016 FC 56. A valid search of X may generate records that can be used to prosecute Y: *Siggelkow*, 2014 ABQB 101, para. 77; unless Y has a "reasonable expectation of privacy" in the records: *Anderson*, 2014 BCSC 2002, paras. 90-92. Seizing past emails does not require a wiretap authorization, which is for future communications: *Siggelkow*, para. 94.

See also 231.3(7) and (8) below re CRA keeping the seized materials.

See also Notes to 231.2(1) re limitations on using information obtained via CRA's audit powers, and to 232(3) re searches of lawyers' offices. In *9229-0188 Québec (Saramac)*, 2018 QCCA 1039 (leave to appeal denied 2019 CarswellQue 3023 (SCC)), a search warrant was cancelled where Revenu Québec had not disclosed to the judge that a lawyer and notary worked at the search location.

See CRA *Criminal Investigations Manual* §1.5.1 and Chapter 6. See also Fontana & Keeshan, *The Law of Search & Seizure in Canada* (LexisNexis, 11th ed., 2019, 1696pp); Hasan et al., *Search and Seizure* (emond.ca, 2021, 762pp); Boddez & DelBigio, "Criminal Tax Evasion", 2012 Cdn Tax Foundation conference report, 38:1-28; Chodikoff & Perumal, "Search and Seizure", *Practical Insights* (*Taxnet Pro* Tax Dispute & Resolutions Centre), Oct. 2019 (32pp).

Information Circulars: 73-10R3: Tax evasion.

(2) Evidence in support of application — An application under subsection (1) shall be supported by information on oath establishing the facts on which the application is based.

(3) Evidence — A judge may issue the warrant referred to in subsection (1) where the judge is satisfied that there are reasonable grounds to believe that

    (a) an offence under this Act was committed;

    (b) a document or thing that may afford evidence of the commission of the offence is likely to be found; and

    (c) the building, receptacle or place specified in the application is likely to contain such a document or thing.

Related Provisions: See at end of 231.3.

Notes: Opening words of 231.3(3) amended by 1993 technical bill, effective June 15, 1994, to change "shall" to "may". This responded to the Supreme Court of Canada's ruling, in *Baron*, [1993] 1 C.T.C. 111, that 231.3(3) violated s. 8 of the *Charter of Rights* because it allowed the judge no discretion as to whether to issue a warrant.

(4) Contents of warrant — A warrant issued under subsection (1) shall refer to the offence for which it is issued, identify the building, receptacle or place to be searched and the person alleged to have committed the offence and it shall be reasonably specific as to any document or thing to be searched for and seized.

(5) Seizure of document — Any person who executes a warrant under subsection (1) may seize, in addition to the document or thing referred to in that subsection, any other document or thing that the person believes on reasonable grounds affords evidence of the commission of an offence under this Act and shall as soon as practicable bring the document or thing before, or make a report in respect thereof to, the judge who issued the warrant or, where the judge is unable to act, another judge of the same court to be dealt with by the judge in accordance with this section.

Related Provisions: 231.5(1) — Copy of document seized may be used in court proceedings; 231.5(2) — Compliance; 232(3) — Seizure of certain documents where privilege claimed; 244(9) — Copy of document seized may be used in court proceedings.

Information Circulars: 73-10R3: Tax evasion.

(6) Retention of things seized — Subject to subsection (7), where any document or thing seized under subsection (1) or (5) is brought before a judge or a report in respect thereof is made to a judge, the judge shall, unless the Minister waives retention, order that it be retained by the Minister, who shall take reasonable care to ensure that it is preserved until the conclusion of any investigation into the offence in relation to which the document or thing was seized or until it is required to be produced for the purposes of a criminal proceeding.

(7) Return of things seized — Where any document or thing seized under subsection (1) or (5) is brought before a judge or a report in respect thereof is made to a judge, the judge may, of the judge's own motion or on summary application by a person with an interest in the document or thing on three clear days notice of application to the Deputy Attorney General of Canada, order that the document or thing be returned to the person from whom it was seized or the person who is otherwise legally entitled thereto if the judge is satisfied that the document or thing

(a) will not be required for an investigation or a criminal proceeding; or

(b) was not seized in accordance with the warrant or this section.

Related Provisions: *Interpretation Act* 27(1) — Meaning of "clear days".

Notes: In *Yang*, 2020 CarswellAlta 2621 (Alta. QB), the Crown was given 18 months past the initial detention period to keep the records (under *Criminal Code* s. 490(3)), but then was ordered to return them despite Crown claims of delay due to complexity.

(8) Access and copies — The person from whom any document or thing is seized pursuant to this section is entitled, at all reasonable times and subject to such reasonable conditions as may be imposed by the Minister, to inspect the document or thing and to obtain one copy of the document at the expense of the Minister.

Notes: CRA policy is that this rule applies to items seized under *Criminal Code* s. 487 as well: *Criminal Investigations Manual* §1.5.4(1).

Information Circulars [subsec. 231.3(8)]: 73-10R3: Tax evasion.

Definitions [s. 231.3]: "clear days" — *Interpretation Act* 27(1); "documents", "judge" — 231; "Minister" — 248(1); "oath" — *Interpretation Act* 35(1); "person" — 248(1); "writing" — *Interpretation Act* 35(1).

231.4 (1) Inquiry — The Minister may, for any purpose related to the administration or enforcement of this Act, authorize any person, whether or not the person is an officer of the Canada Revenue Agency, to make such inquiry as the person may deem necessary with reference to anything relating to the administration or enforcement of this Act.

Related Provisions: 231.5(2) — Compliance. See also Related Provisions and Definitions at end of 231.4.

Notes: Inquiries under 231.4 were found not to violate the *Charter of Rights* in *Del Zotto*, [1999] 1 C.T.C. 113 (SCC). See also Innes & Williams, "Protection Against Self-Incrimination", 49(6) *Canadian Tax Journal* 1459-95 (2001).

A CRA audit was not a *de facto* 231.4 inquiry: *Keenan*, 2019 TCC 259, para. 27.

231.4(1) amended by *CCRA Act*, effective Nov. 1, 1999, to change "Department of National Revenue" to "Canada Customs and Revenue Agency"; and by 2004 CRA/CBSA bill, effective Dec. 12, 2005, to "Canada Revenue Agency".

(2) Appointment of hearing officer — Where the Minister, pursuant to subsection (1), authorizes a person to make an inquiry, the Minister shall forthwith apply to the Tax Court of Canada for an order appointing a hearing officer before whom the inquiry will be held.

(3) Powers of hearing officer — For the purposes of an inquiry authorized under subsection (1), a hearing officer appointed under subsection (2) in relation thereto has all the powers conferred on a commissioner by sections 4 and 5 of the *Inquiries Act* and that may be conferred on a commissioner under section 11 thereof.

Notes: *Inquiries Act* ss. 4-5 (see CanLii.org) provide that a commissioner has power to summon witnesses, require them to give evidence under oath (orally or in writing) and produce relevant documents, and the same power as a court to compel witnesses to attend and give evidence.

(4) When powers to be exercised — A hearing officer appointed under subsection (2) in relation to an inquiry shall exercise the powers conferred on a commissioner by section 4 of the *Inquiries Act* in relation to such persons as the person authorized to make the inquiry considers appropriate for the conduct thereof but the hearing officer shall not exercise the power to punish any person unless, on application by the hearing officer, a judge of a superior or county court certifies that the power may be exercised in the matter disclosed in the application and the applicant has given to the person in respect of whom the applicant proposes to exercise the power 24 hours notice of the hearing of the application or such shorter notice as the judge considers reasonable.

(5) Rights of witness at inquiry — Any person who gives evidence in an inquiry authorized under subsection (1) is entitled to be represented by counsel and, on request made by the person to the Minister, to receive a transcript of the evidence given by the person.

(6) Rights of person whose affairs are investigated — Any person whose affairs are investigated in the course of an inquiry

authorized under subsection (1) is entitled to be present and to be represented by counsel throughout the inquiry unless the hearing officer appointed under subsection (2) in relation to the inquiry, on application by the Minister or a person giving evidence, orders otherwise in relation to the whole or any part of the inquiry on the ground that the presence of the person and the person's counsel, or either of them, would be prejudicial to the effective conduct of the inquiry.

Related Provisions [s. 231.4]: 168(1)(e) — Revocation of charity registration for failing to comply; 188.2(2)(a) — Suspension of charity's receipting privileges for failing to comply; 238(1) — Punishment for failing to comply.

Definitions [s. 231.4]: "Canada Revenue Agency" — *Canada Revenue Agency Act* s. 4(1); "judge" — 231; "Minister", "person" — 248(1).

Information Circulars [s. 231.4]: 73-10R3: Tax evasion.

231.5 (1) Copies — Where any document is seized, inspected, audited, examined or provided under any of sections 231.1 to 231.4, the person by whom it is seized, inspected, audited or examined or to whom it is provided or any officer of the Canada Revenue Agency may make, or cause to be made, one or more copies thereof and, in the case of an electronic document, make or cause to be made a print-out of the electronic document, and any document purporting to be certified by the Minister or an authorized person to be a copy of the document, or to be a print-out of an electronic document, made pursuant to this section is evidence of the nature and content of the original document and has the same probative force as the original document would have if it were proven in the ordinary way.

Related Provisions: 244(9) — Copy of taxpayer's document may be used in court proceedings.

Notes: 231.5(1) amended by *CCRA Act*, effective Nov. 1, 1999, to change "Department of National Revenue" to "Canada Customs and Revenue Agency"; and by 2004 CRA/CBSA bill, effective Dec. 12, 2005, to "Canada Revenue Agency".

231.5(1) amended by 1995-97 technical bill, for copies and print-outs made after June 18, 1998.

CRA Audit Manual: 10.5.4: Type and source of evidence [procedures for using photocopies as evidence].

(2) Compliance — No person shall, physically or otherwise, interfere with, hinder or molest an official (in this subsection having the meaning assigned by subsection 241(10)) doing anything that the official is authorized to do under this Act or attempt to interfere with, hinder or molest any official doing or prevent or attempt to prevent an official from doing, anything that the official is authorized to do under this Act, and every person shall, unless the person is unable to do so, do everything that the person is required to do by or under subsection (1) or sections 231.1 to 231.4.

Related Provisions [subsec. 231.5(2)]: 168(1)(e) — Revocation of charity registration for failing to comply; 188.2(2)(a) — Suspension of charity's receipting privileges for failing to comply; 231.7 — Court order for compliance with audit or demand; 238(1) — Punishment for failing to comply.

Notes: 231.5(2) amended by 2000 Budget, effective June 14, 2001, effectively to extend the provision to apply to persons interfering with Collections officers rather than just auditors or investigators.

Definitions [s. 231.5]: "authorized person", "documents" — 231; "Canada Revenue Agency" — *Canada Revenue Agency Act* s. 4(1); "Minister" — 248(1); "official" — 241(10); "person" — 248(1).

Information Circulars [s. 231.5]: 73-10R3: Tax evasion.

231.6 (1) Definition of "foreign-based information or document" — For the purposes of this section, "foreign-based information or document" means any information or document that is available or located outside Canada and that may be relevant to the administration or enforcement of this Act, including the collection of any amount payable under this Act by any person.

Notes: Data stored on a server outside Canada but routinely accessed from Canada is not "foreign-based information": *eBay Canada*, 2008 FCA 348; Ed Kroft, "Requirement Letters and Technology", 46 *McCarthy Tétrault on Tax Disputes* (CCH) 2-7 (March 2009).

231.6(1) amended by 2000 GST bill, effective Oct. 20, 2000.

CRA Audit Manual: 15.5.0 and Appendix 15.13.1: Foreign-based information and documentation.

(2) Requirement to provide foreign-based information — Notwithstanding any other provision of this Act, the Minister may, by notice sent or served in accordance with subsection (3.1), require that a person resident in Canada or a non-resident person carrying on business in Canada provide any foreign-based information or document.

Related Provisions: 231.6(4) — Application for review by court; 231.6(8) — Consequences of failure to comply; 233.1–233.7 — Requirement to file annual information returns with respect to non-resident dealings; 244(5) — Proof of service by mail; 248(7)(a) — Mail deemed received on day mailed.

Notes: See 231.2(1) Notes re CRA using 231.2 to demand foreign-based information.

If the Requirement is not substantially complied with, the taxpayer cannot use any of the requested information in Court: 231.6(8). CRA is of the view that, in addition, "it is an offence not to produce any foreign-based information, as and when required" (IC 78-10R4), though it could be argued that 231.6(8) provides a remedy that is a "complete code".

In *Bernick*, 2002 CarswellOnt 2356 (Ont. SCJ), the taxpayer was a member of a Bahamas partnership from which he claimed losses. A requirement under 231.6 for the identity of the other partners and their equity positions was held to be valid.

A provision similar to 231.6, under U.S. *Internal Revenue Code* §982, was upheld in *Flying Tigers Oil* (1989), 92 T.C. 1261. As well as refusing to allow the taxpayer to introduce any foreign-based documents, the US Tax Court also excluded the taxpayer's domestic documentation which it found was either based on or prepared in reliance on such foreign documents.

See also Notes to 231.6(5); Innes & McCart, "Transfer-Pricing Disputes", 43(4) *Canadian Tax Journal* 821 at 840-52 (1995); Barsalou, "Transfer-Pricing Audits", 2003 Cdn Tax Foundation conference report, 12:2-9; Reid, "Documents Not Produced", 19(5) *Canadian Tax Highlights* (ctf.ca) 2-3 (May 2011); Kroft, "Recent Developments in CRA's Reach for Information", 2011 BC Tax Conference (ctf.ca), 5:1-88 and 2011 Ontario Tax Conf. 4:1-88.

231.6(2) amended by 2021 budget bill #1, effective June 29, 2021, to change "notice served personally or by registered mail" to "notice sent or served in accordance with subsection (3.1)".

Information Circulars: 77-9R: Books, records and other requirements for taxpayers having foreign affiliates; 78-10R5: Books and records retention/destruction.

CRA Audit Manual: 15.5.0 and Appendix 15.13.1: Foreign-based information and documentation.

(3) Notice — The notice referred to in subsection (2) shall set out

(a) a reasonable period of time of not less than 90 days for the production of the information or document;

(b) a description of the information or document being sought; and

(c) the consequences under subsection (8) to the person of the failure to provide the information or documents being sought within the period of time set out in the notice.

Related Provisions: *Interpretation Act* s. 27 — Computation of time.

CRA Audit Manual: 15.5.0: Foreign-based information and documentation.

(3.1) Notice — A notice referred to in subsection (2) may be

(a) served personally;

(b) sent by registered or certified mail; or

(c) sent electronically to a bank or credit union that has provided written consent to receive notices under subsection (2) electronically.

Related Provisions: 231.2(1.1) — Parallel rule for ordinary Requirement for Information; 244(6.1) — Proof of electronic delivery.

Notes: 231.6(3.1) added by 2021 budget bill #1, effective June 29, 2021 (adding para. (c) to what had been in 231.6(2)), as proposed in 2019 Budget (in sync with 231.2(1.1)).

(4) Review of foreign information requirement — The person who is sent or served with a notice of a requirement under subsection (2) may, within 90 days after the notice is sent or served, apply to a judge for a review of the requirement.

Related Provisions: *Interpretation Act* 27(5) — Meaning of "within 90 days".

Notes: See Notes to 231.6(5) below; and Notes to 165(1) re time limits and weekends.

231.6(4) amended by 2021 budget bill #1, effective June 29, 2021, to add references to a notice being "sent" (to accommodate electronic delivery under (3.1)(c)). Before that date, read:

> (4) The person on whom a notice of a requirement is served under subsection (2) may, within 90 days after the service of the notice, apply to a judge for a review of the requirement.

CRA Audit Manual: 15.5.0: Foreign-based information and documentation.

(5) Powers on review — On hearing an application under subsection (4) in respect of a requirement, a judge may

(a) confirm the requirement;

(b) vary the requirement as the judge considers appropriate in the circumstances; or

(c) set aside the requirement if the judge is satisfied that the requirement is unreasonable.

Notes: Parliament intended 231.6 to give CRA far-reaching powers: *Merko*, [1990] 2 C.T.C. 518 (FCTD). CRA need only show that the information sought is relevant to administration or enforcement of the Act. The taxpayer is protected from abusive use of 231.6 through the judge's power to review the Requirement. The Requirement in *Merko* was neither an abuse of process nor unreasonable.

CRA's Requirement (as part of a transfer-pricing audit) was found unreasonably broad in *Bayer Inc.*, 2020 FC 750, as CRA did not explain why it had greatly expanded from earlier audit queries. The Court varied the Requirement to match the audit queries.

Challenges to 231.6 Requirements were rejected in *European Marine Contractors*, 2004 FC 114, and *Saipem Luxembourg*, 2005 FCA 218 (leave to appeal denied 2005 CarswellNat 3949 (SCC)), involving audits of non-resident companies to determine whether they had a permanent establishment in Canada. The correct test was whether the information sought was relevant to administration of the Act, not whether it was relevant to the company's Canadian tax liability. CRA was not required to use other information-gathering techniques such as making a request to a tax treaty partner.

Challenges were also rejected in: *Fidelity Investments*, 2006 FC 551 (FI argued that CRA had not undertaken to keep the information confidential, but s. 241 protected it); *Soft-Moc Inc.*, 2014 FCA 10 (CRA entitled to demand detailed information about offshore suppliers for transfer-pricing purposes); *Chad*, 2019 FC 1456 (demand to individual for info about offshore trusts).

The Court on review will not declare that a taxpayer has complied with the requirement; this will be left to when the taxpayer introduces evidence or a document that CRA says was covered by the Requirement: *1144020 Ontario*, 2005 FC 813.

In *CA Canada*, 2019 CarswellNat 48 (FC), a judicial review application was struck out with leave to amend, as it did not provide any basis for saying the Requirement was inappropriate.

CRA Audit Manual: 15.5.0: Foreign-based information and documentation.

(6) Unreasonableness — For the purposes of paragraph (5)(c), the requirement to provide the information or document shall not be considered to be unreasonable because the information or document is under the control of or available to a non-resident person that is not controlled by the person who is sent or served with the notice of the requirement under subsection (2) if that person is related to the non-resident person.

Related Provisions: 256(6), (6.1) — Meaning of "controlled".

Notes: 231.6(6) amended by 2021 budget bill #1, effective June 29, 2021, to add "who is sent or" (to accommodate electronic delivery under (3.1)(c)).

CRA Audit Manual: 15.5.0: Foreign-based information and documentation.

(7) Time period not to count — The period of time between the day on which an application for review of a requirement is made pursuant to subsection (4) and the day on which the application is finally disposed of shall not be counted in the computation of

(a) the period of time set out in the notice of the requirement; and

(b) the period of time within which an assessment may be made pursuant to subsection 152(4).

Related Provisions: 231.8 — Same rule applies to Requirements for Information and compliance orders.

Notes: 231.6(7) opening words amended by 2018 budget bill #2 to change "the review is decided" to "the application is finally disposed of" (consistent with new 231.8), effective Dec. 13, 2018.

CRA Audit Manual: 15.5.0: Foreign-based information and documentation.

(8) Consequence of failure — If a person fails to comply substantially with a notice sent or served under subsection (2) and if the notice is not set aside by a judge pursuant to subsection (5), any court having jurisdiction in a civil proceeding relating to the administration or enforcement of this Act shall, on motion of the Minister, prohibit the introduction by that person of any foreign-based information or document covered by that notice.

Related Provisions [subsec. 231.6(8)]: 143.2(13), (14) — Effect of information outside Canada on tax shelter investments.

Notes: Absent substantial compliance, the taxpayer cannot introduce *any* foreign-based information or document (FBID) in Court, even information that was provided to the CRA. See *Soft-Moc Inc.*, 2014 FCA 10.

In *Glaxo SmithKline*, 2003 TCC 258, Glaxo failed to comply with a 231.6(2) requirement for information from its affiliates in other countries, and did not show reasonable cause why. The Court rejected the absolute language of 231.6(8) that allows the judge no discretion: there must be "a residual discretion with the trial judge to admit evidence that would otherwise be excluded, where it can be shown that the evidence is required in order to prevent injustice." However, Glaxo was prohibited from introducing any FBID covered by the 231.6 notice, other than as rebuttal evidence or in cross-examination, and only with leave of the trial judge.

231.6(8) amended by 2021 budget bill #1, effective June 29, 2021, to add "sent or" (to accommodate electronic delivery under (3.1)(c)).

See also Notes to 231.6(2).

CRA Audit Manual: 15.5.0: Foreign-based information and documentation.

Definitions [s. 231.6]: "assessment", "bank", "business" — 248(1); "Canada" — 255; "carrying on business" — 253; "controlled" — 256(6), (6.1); "credit union" — 137(6), 248(1); "document", "judge" — 231; "Minister", "non-resident", "person" — 248(1); "related" — 251(2)–(6); "resident in Canada" — 250; "written" — *Interpretation Act* 35(1)"writing".

231.7 (1) Compliance order

231.7 (1) Compliance order — On summary application by the Minister, a judge may, notwithstanding subsection 238(2), order a person to provide any access, assistance, information or document sought by the Minister under section 231.1 or 231.2 if the judge is satisfied that

(a) the person was required under section 231.1 or 231.2 to provide the access, assistance, information or document and did not do so; and

(b) in the case of information or a document, the information or document is not protected from disclosure by solicitor-client privilege (within the meaning of subsection 232(1)).

Related Provisions: 231.5(2) — Compliance with audit or demand required; 231.7(2) — Five clear days' notice required; 231.7(3) — Conditions can be imposed; 231.7(4) — Contempt of court for failure to comply; 231.7(5) — Appeal of order; 231.8 — Time adjudicating order does not count towards reassessment clock.

Notes: See Notes at end of 231.7.

Information Circulars: 78-10R5: Books and records retention/destruction.

Registered Plans Compliance Bulletins: 8 (requirements to provide information under s. 231.2).

(2) Notice required

(2) Notice required — An application under subsection (1) must not be heard before the end of five clear days from the day the notice of application is served on the person against whom the order is sought.

Notes: See *Interpretation Act* 27(1) for the meaning of "clear days", and Notes at end of 231.7.

(3) Judge may impose conditions

(3) Judge may impose conditions — A judge making an order under subsection (1) may impose any conditions in respect of the order that the judge considers appropriate.

(4) Contempt of court

(4) Contempt of court — If a person fails or refuses to comply with an order, a judge may find the person in contempt of court and the person is subject to the processes and the punishments of the court to which the judge is appointed.

Notes: See Notes at end of 231.7.

(5) Appeal

(5) Appeal — An order by a judge under subsection (1) may be appealed to a court having appellate jurisdiction over decisions of the court to which the judge is appointed. An appeal does not suspend the execution of the order unless it is so ordered by a judge of the court to which the appeal is made.

Notes: Under 231.7(5), a compliance order can be appealed to the same court as can other decisions of the court issuing the order. Thus, for example, an order issued by the Manitoba Court of Queen's Bench can be appealed only to the Manitoba Court of Appeal. Until the appeal has been dealt with, the compliance order continues in force, unless a judge of the *appeal* court issues an order staying the compliance order.

See also Notes at end of 231.7.

Notes [s. 231.7]: 231.7 allows CRA to apply for a Court order relating to an audit or a Requirement for Information (RFI). The advantage of a Court order over a legislative obligation is that violation is contempt of Court (231.7(4); see below). See also 238(2). For CRA administrative policy see *Income Tax Audit Manual* §10.9.0, "Compliance Order Guidelines".

231.7 is unconstitutional in its application to lawyers and Quebec notaries in their capacity as legal advisers, because it violates solicitor-client privilege (and civil law "professional secrecy"): *Chambre des notaires*, 2016 SCC 20, para. 93; but this does not automatically extend to a compliance order issued to a taxpayer for documents received from a law firm: *Revcon Oilfield*, 2017 FCA 22 (privilege can still be asserted, of course). See also Notes to 232(2).

The procedure for the Crown to use to institute proceedings under 231.7 was set out in *Norris*, [2002] 3 C.T.C. 346 (FCTD, Prothonotary).

Contempt of Court can be punished by any amount of jail time the Court chooses. See Jeffrey Miller, *The Law of Contempt in Canada* (Carswell, 2nd ed., 2016). Conditions for contempt: (1) the order states clearly and unequivocally what must be done; (2) the person disobeys deliberately and wilfully; (3) the evidence shows contempt beyond reasonable doubt, and any doubt must be resolved in the person's favour: *Black Sun Rising*, 2013 FC 773, para. 7; (4) the Court issues a Show Cause order (inviting the person to show why they should not be held in contempt), which must be served personally: *Pintea v. Johns*, 2017 SCC 23; *Gray*, 2018 FC 549, para. 10.

Convictions for contempt of Court for failing to comply: *Wigemyr*, 2004 FC 930 ($2,000 fine + $2,500 costs); *Iwaschuk*, 2004 FC 1602 ($2,500 fine); *Robertson*, 2005 FC 242, 2005 FC 850 ($3,000 fine + $1,500 solicitor-client (S-C) costs); *McMordie*, 2006 FC 209 (accused had only partly complied; $1,000 fine + $800 costs); *Middleton*, 2006 FC 455 ($2,000 fine + $1,000 costs; when unpaid, warrant of committal issued at 2007 FC 1269); *9093-4134 Québec Inc.*, 2006 FC 683 ($1,000 fine + $500 costs); *Marshall*, 2006 FC 788 ($3,000 fine + $2,000 costs + 10 days' jail if information not provided); *Bjornstad*, 2006 FC 818 ($2,000 fine + $4,090 S-C costs, since "a party who assists the Court in the enforcement of its orders and in ensuring respect for its orders should not be put out of pocket"); *Camplin*, 2007 FC 183 ($3,000 fine + $2,000 costs); *Becelaere*, 2007 FC 409; *757746 Alberta*, 2007 FC 834 (taxpayers ignored Court orders); *Group EC*, 2007 FC 1083 (failure to provide records); *Jourdain*, 2007 FC 739 ($1,500 fine + $2,238 costs); *Humphreys*, 2008 FC 38 (taxpayer's evidence of inability to comply disbelieved); *Cha*, 2007 FC 917 and 2008 FC 120 ($3,000 fine + $4,000 costs); *Kerby*, 2008 FC 452 ($4,000 fine husband + $1,000 fine wife + $6,500 S-C costs, citing *Bjornstad*); *Stanchfield*, 2009 FC 72 and 61 ($5,000 fine and $3,000 costs, plus 6 months jail if order not obeyed); *Cunliffe*, 2009 FC 184 (mental element of contempt can be inferred from non-compliance); *Jackson*, 2009 FC 1197 (taxpayer ignored orders and provided irrelevant documents); *Kocsis*, 2009 FC 1216 (administrative burden in complying and alleged mould contamination were not lawful excuses; $3,000 fine + $10,000, per CRA news release Feb. 16/10); *Money Stop*, 2013 FC 133 ($5,000 fine, $19,900 S-C costs, and 3 years prison if no compliance within 30 days; release from prison ordered at 2013 FC 684 because documents had been filed); *Bosnjak*, 2013 FC 399 ($3,000 fine + $1,000 costs for ignoring order to provide information about assets to Collections); *Marangoni*, 2013 FC 1154 ($500 fine + $1,000 S-C costs); *Vallelonga*, 2013 FC 1155 ($3,000 fine + $14,700 S-C costs for ignoring order and sending tax-protester correspondence; up to 3 years prison if he continues not to comply); *Bélanger*, 2014 FC 127 ($1,500 fine + $2,500 S-C costs) and 2015 FC 35 ($2,000 fine + $3,000 costs for continued non-compliance); *Cameron*, 2014 FC 482 ($5,000 fine + $5,822 S-C costs, with 30 days in jail if unpaid); *Ryder*, 2014 FC 519 ($1,250 fine + $1,100 S-C costs, with jail for not paying or continued non-compliance); *Dundas [Biokinetic Energy]*, 2015 BCPC 74 ($4,000 fine + 1 day in jail; accused had eventually complied); *Schimpf*, 2015 FC 1354 ($3,000 fine + $7,000 S-C costs); *Blake*, 2017 FC 901 ($3,000 fine + $4,000 costs); *Ciciarelli [Cicarelli]*, 2018 FC 644 (under appeal to FCA) ($6,000 fine + $4,560 S-C costs, + 30 days if continued non-compliance); *Chi*, 2018 FC 897 ($2,000 fine + $3,500 costs: 15 days if continued non-compliance); *Gray*, 2018 FC 549 and 2019 FC 352 ($3,000 fine + costs; 30 days in jail if continued non-compliance); *Beima*, 2019 FCA 280 (stay issued by FC expired when FCA upheld compliance order; $5,000 + $500 costs, no fine).

Acquittal on contempt or non-compliance charges: *Black Sun Rising*, 2013 FC 773 (because taxpayers had made efforts to comply, Crown had not yet "proven beyond a reasonable doubt that [they] deliberately and wilfully disobeyed a court order"); *Strong*, 2014 SKQB 119 (no evidence Court order was served on the accused or that he had knowledge of its terms); *Gray*, 2018 FC 549 (corp acquitted, as Crown failed to prove G was director of corp when served).

Compliance orders were issued or upheld in *Cornfield*, 2008 FCA 156 (lawyer ordered to disclose transaction documents); *Zen*, 2010 FCA 180 (taxpayer ordered to disclose assets to permit collection); *Lee*, 2016 FCA 53 (even if RFI addressed to L required information about his corporations, it was valid, as scope and breadth of RFI are up to the Minister); *Beima*, 2017 FCA 85 (leave to appeal to SCC denied 2019 CarswellNat 31) (taxpayer uncooperative with auditor); *Montana*, 2017 FCA 194 (leave to appeal denied 2018 CarswellNat 3402 (SCC)) (no adjournment of FC hearing where taxpayers retained counsel late); *Blue Bridge*, 2021 FCA 62 (leave to appeal to SCC requested; stay of judgment denied 2021 FCA 114) (info requested by France under tax treaty); *Friedman*, 2021 FCA 101 (despite *Lin* (below), RFIs were directed to the Fs, not their corporations, and there was no evidence of criminal investigation); *Stern*, 2004 FC 763; *Singh Lyn*, 2005 FC 1538; *Reddy*, 2006 FC 277 (see Notes to 232(3)); *Marshall*, 2006 FC 279; *Watson*, 2006 BCCA 233; *Castros Cuban Cigar*, 2006 FC 1049; *GMAC Location*, 2006 CanLII 42088 (FC); *Vlug*, 2006 FC 86 (lawyer ordered to disclose transaction documents); *Morton*, 2007 FC 503; *Dropsy*, 2007 FC 932; *Comtax International*, 2008 FC 175; *Currie*, 2008 FC 237; *Stanchfield*, 2009 FC 72 (taxpayer's FCA appeal discontinued A-108-09) (person charged and person ordered to comply were same person); *Winter*, 2009 CarswellNat 6000 (FC); *Moodys LLP and Nerland*, 2011 FC 713, 714 and 715 (solicitor-client privilege did not apply to most documents involved in creating trusts); *Hanes*, 2011 FC 1271 (H ordered to disclose files for audit); *Clark*,

2012 FC 950 (lawyer ordered to provide company's accounting and banking records); *BP Canada*, 2015 FC 714 (under appeal to FCA; CPA Canada granted leave to intervene April 7/16) (BP ordered to disclose its "uncertain tax positions" working papers to expedite CRA audits); *Carriero*, 2016 FC 1296 (CRA can seek info for Collections purposes even if collection is suspended by 225.1); *Stankovic*, 2018 FC 462 (inquiry based on "Falciani List" of Swiss HSBC accounts; no evidence that this was for criminal rather than audit purposes); *2276230 Canada*, 2021 FC 242 (ongoing GST/HST audit: detailed demands were not abusive or oppressive, and taxpayer need not have "refused" to comply for order to be issued).

In *Edward Enterprise*, 2020 FC 1044, the Court issued a compliance order, refusing EE's requests for a condition prohibiting CRA from sharing the information with foreign officials (where otherwise lawfully allowed), and for a condition requiring CRA to give EE notice before sharing it with others outside CRA.

In *Ciciarelli [Cicarelli] (Montana)*, 2019 FC 900, a compliance order to "provide" documents was amended to add "deliver"; given C&M's "extraordinary" non-cooperation over 5 years, it was insufficient to simply make 30 boxes of documents available for CRA inspection in an accountant's office; after non-compliance, the same "deliver" was ordered in *CN Construction [Ciciarelli]*, 2020 FC 775.

Compliance orders were refused in: *Banque Toronto Dominion*, 2004 FCA 359 (see Notes to 231.2(2)); *SML Operations*, 2003 FC 868 (unclear whether RFI was addressed to individual or corp, and "given the partial production of some documents, and the severe penalties for non-compliance under the Act, I am unable to conclude the respondent was uncooperative"); *Grant Thornton*, 2012 FC 1313 (solicitor-client privilege applied); *Chamandy*, 2014 FC 354 (earlier RFI had not clearly been addressed to corp's director in his personal capacity); *Amdocs Canadian*, 2015 FC 1234 (info sought for transfer-pricing audit, including detailed organization chart of group and basis for charges to Canadian subsidiary, was not in AC's possession or available to it); *Lin*, 2019 FC 646 (unclear whether RFI was addressed to individuals or their connected entities).

Where a compliance order application was withdrawn because CRA no longer needed it, costs but not solicitor-client costs were payable by CRA: *Prince*, 2017 CarswellNat 6672 (FC).

231.7 added by 2001 technical bill, effective June 14, 2001.

Definitions [s. 231.7]: "clear days" — *Interpretation Act* 27(1); "document", "judge" — 231; "Minister", "person" — 248(1).

CRA Audit Manual: 10.9.0: Compliance order guidelines.

231.8 Time period [contesting requirement or application] not to count [for reassessment clock]

— The following periods of time shall not be counted in the computation of the period of time within which an assessment may be made for a taxation year of a taxpayer under subsection 152(4):

(a) where the taxpayer is sent or served with a notice of a requirement under subsection 231.2(1), the period of time between the day on which an application for judicial review in respect of the requirement is made and the day on which the application is finally disposed of; and

(b) where an application is commenced by the Minister under subsection 231.7(1) to order the taxpayer to provide any access, assistance, information or document, the period of time between the day on which the taxpayer files a notice of appearance, or otherwise opposes the application, and the day on which the application is finally disposed of.

Notes: 231.8 "stops the clock" for reassessment while a Requirement or compliance order is being contested. The reassessment deadline is extended for all purposes, not just those relating to the information CRA seeks [Pantaleo & Wyse, "Power to Lengthen Assessment Period", 26(5) *Canadian Tax Highlights* (ctf.ca) 1-2 (May 2018)].

Para. (a) amended by 2021 budget bill #1, effective June 29, 2021, to change "served" to "sent or served with", to accommodate electronic delivery under 231.2(1.1)). 231.8 added by 2018 budget bill #2, effective Dec. 13, 2018.

Definitions [s. 231.8]: "assessment" — 248(1); "document" — 231; "Minister" — 248(1); "taxation year" — 249; "taxpayer" — 248(1).

232. (1) [Solicitor-client privilege] Definitions — In this section,

"custodian" means a person in whose custody a package is placed pursuant to subsection (3);

Related Provisions: 230(2.1) — Books and records.

Notes: 232(1)"custodian" was 232(1)(b) before RSC 1985 (5th Supp) consolidation for tax years ending after Nov. 1991.

"judge" means a judge of a superior court having jurisdiction in the province where the matter arises or a judge of the Federal Court;

Notes: Due to the *Federal Courts Act*, in force July 2, 2003, this definition no longer includes a judge of the Federal Court of Appeal. The "Federal Court" is now only the court which was formerly the Federal Court–Trial Division.

232(1)"judge" was 232(1)(a) before RSC 1985 (5th Supp) consolidation, effective December 1, 1991.

"lawyer" means, in the province of Quebec, an advocate or notary and, in any other province, a barrister or solicitor;

Related Provisions: 248(1)"lawyer" — Definition applies to entire Act.

Notes: 232(1)"lawyer" was 232(1)(c) before RSC 1985 (5th Supp) consolidation, effective December 1, 1991.

"officer" means a person acting under the authority conferred by or under sections 231.1 to 231.5;

Notes: 232(1)"officer" was 232(1)(d) before RSC 1985 (5th Supp) consolidation, effective December 1, 1991.

"solicitor-client privilege" means the right, if any, that a person has in a superior court in the province where the matter arises to refuse to disclose an oral or documentary communication on the ground that the communication is one passing between the person and the person's lawyer in professional confidence, except that for the purposes of this section an accounting record of a lawyer, including any supporting voucher or cheque, shall be deemed not to be such a communication.

Related Provisions: 237.3(1)"solicitor-client privilege" — Definition applies to reportable-transaction rules.

Notes: The exclusion of accounting records in this definition is "unconstitutional and invalid" (*Chambre des notaires*, 2016 SCC 20, para. 94), as it violates common-law solicitor-client privilege (and civil law "professional secrecy"). See also Notes to 232(2).

232(1)"solicitor-client privilege" was 232(1)(e) before RSC 1985 (5th Supp) consolidation, effective December 1, 1991.

(2) Solicitor-client privilege defence — Where a lawyer is prosecuted for failure to comply with a requirement under section 231.2 with respect to information or a document, the lawyer shall be acquitted if the lawyer establishes to the satisfaction of the court

(a) that the lawyer, on reasonable grounds, believed that a client of the lawyer had a solicitor-client privilege in respect of the information or document; and

(b) that the lawyer communicated to the Minister, or some person duly authorized to act for the Minister, the lawyer's refusal to comply with the requirement together with a claim that a named client of the lawyer had a solicitor-client privilege in respect of the information or document.

Notes: S. 232 is more limited than common-law solicitor-client privilege (SCP), and is superseded by invoking SCP. For example, 232(3) purports to apply only to documents in the lawyer's possession; it requires the lawyer to name the client to assert privilege; 232(4) requires the lawyer to make a Court application within 14 days, failing which the client supposedly loses the privilege; and 232(1)"solicitor-client privilege" does not apply to all documents that might be privileged. None of these limitations applies: in *Chambre des notaires*, 2016 SCC 20, the Supreme Court of Canada ruled that these statutory rules are insufficient protection of SCP. Where computers are seized under search warrant and SCP is claimed on some of the contents, an independent expert (not CRA's forensic analysts) must examine the disks to isolate SCP material: *Solicitor-Client Privilege of Things Seized*, 2019 BCSC 91.

SCP (also called legal advice privilege) has quasi-constitutional status and is a substantive rule of law, not just of evidence: *Descôteaux v. Mierzwinski*, [1982] 1 S.C.R. 860 at 875 (SCC); and can be set aside "only by legislative language that is clear, explicit and unequivocal": *Alberta v. Univ. of Calgary*, 2016 SCC 53, para. 2. It "must be as close to absolute as possible to ensure public confidence and retain relevance": *Ontario v. Criminal Lawyers' Assn*, 2010 SCC 23. The same applies to "professional secrecy" under Quebec civil law, which covers both lawyers and notaries: *Chambre des notaires*, 2016 SCC 20, para. 42. SCP is also protected under the *Charter of Rights*: *Lavallee, Rackel & Heintz*, 2002 SCC 61; *Chambre des notaires*. It can include client names: *Federation of Law Societies*, 2015 SCC 7; *Chambre des notaires*, para. 74 (and see under "SCP in tax disputes" below). It does not cover the *lawyer's* identity except in unusual situations: *Métaux Kitco*, 2016 QCCQ 12090, paras. 68-72. SCP requires that the client have been seeking legal advice and have intended that the communication be in confidence.

SCP covers in-house counsel (provided the advice given is legal advice): *Pritchard*, 2004 SCC 31. It applies to advice from Dept. of Justice lawyers to CRA: *Métaux Kitco*, 2016 QCCQ 12090; *Ludmer*, 2018 QCCS 3381, para. 127 (aff'd without discussing privilege 2020 QCCA 697; leave to appeal denied 2021 CarswellQue 2160 (SCC)); *British Columbia*, 2021 BCSC 266. In a criminal prosecution, SCP applies to communication between the investigating officer and the prosecutor: *Ciurcovich*, 2016 CarswellOnt 3349 (Ont. SCJ). Other Supreme Court cases include *Maranda v. Richer*, 2003 SCC 67 and *Foster Wheeler v. SIGED*, 2004 SCC 18. SCP belongs to the client and can be waived only by the client: see "Waiver" below.

Requirements under 231.2(1) and compliance orders under 231.7 are unconstitutional in their application to lawyers and Quebec notaries in their capacity as legal advisers: *Chambre des notaires*, 2016 SCC 20, para. 93. See John Sorensen, "Privilege Affirmed, but What's Next?", 64(3) *Canadian Tax Journal* 619-29 (2016). In any event, a client must be given a chance to contest disclosure of the information (*Thompson*, 2016 SCC 21, para. 40), so disclosing client names to CRA without their permission is prohibited (and may be professional misconduct: see "Law Society codes" below). The *Chambre des notaires* rule applies only to demands made of law firms; in *Levett*, 2021 FC 295 (under appeal to FCA), para. 141, SCP did not apply to trust account records that were requested *from the taxpayers* and provided by their representatives: privilege was waived, and the records were not privileged anyway.

The 3 conditions for SCP (*Solosky*, [1980] 1 S.C.R. 821) are: (i) communication between solicitor and client; (ii) which entails seeking or giving legal advice; (iii) intended by the parties to be confidential. The principles are reviewed in *Donell v. GJB Enterprises*, 2012 BCCA 135; *Slansky*, 2013 FCA 199, paras. 65-79. Lawyers' bills are presumptively privileged, but the presumption may be rebutted if there is no reasonable possibility disclosure will reveal protected communications. Other financial records of lawyers do not have this presumption, but if they relate to communications to obtain legal advice, may be privileged.

SCP in tax disputes: for the rules see *Copthorne Holdings*, 2005 TCC 491; *Canadian Imperial Bank of Commerce ("CIBC")*, 2015 TCC 280, paras. 23-42. Privilege applied to deny documents to CRA in *Imperial Tobacco*, 2013 TCC 144, and *Chambre des notaires* (above). Since client information is *prima facie* privileged, clients must be able to claim privilege before their identity is revealed to CRA (it is insufficient that the lawyer can assert privilege): *Thompson*, 2016 SCC 21. For CRA interpretation and procedures in a criminal context, see *Criminal Investigations Manual* (on *TaxPartner* or *Taxnet Pro*), chap. 8 (but note that *Chambre des notaires* and *Thompson* may now override these). The *Income Tax Audit Manual* has very little on SCP in an audit context. If SCP is claimed on documents CRA demands from X or X's accountant, the Court may appoint an independent reviewer to identify unprivileged docs, and X's counsel can contest that person's decisions: e.g. *Gong*, 2019 ONSC 5899 (tinyurl.com/gong-onsc), leave to appeal denied 2020 CarswellOnt 5336 (SCC); appeal quashed 2020 ONCA 587, leave to appeal denied 2021 CarswellOnt 3166.

In *Welton Parent Inc.*, 2006 FC 67, actuarial firm records re health and welfare trust valuations provided to lawyers for unnamed employers had to be disclosed, but the names of the employers were protected by SCP (and this could not be bypassed by seeking accounting and banking records from the lawyer's management company to identify his clients: *Nesathurai*, 2008 FC 177). (In *Taxpro Professional Corp. and Nesathurai*, 2011 FC 224; aff'd 2011 FCA 306, the Court examined 31 documents CRA sought from that lawyer and ruled that 27 (including invoices for legal services) were privileged, while a Deed of Settlement and certain financial discussions were not.) However, in *Ouellette*, 2008 FC 594, a lawyer was unable to prevent release of bank records that would reveal his clients' names. In *Moodys LLP and Nerland*, 2011 FC 713, SCP did not apply to most documents involved in creating trusts for tax planning. In *Redhead Equipment*, 2016 SKCA 115, some tax planning documents were held privileged; SCP "extends only to third party communications that are in furtherance of a function essential to the existence or operation of the solicitor-client relationship" (para. 43), or where the third party is a "conduit of advice" from the lawyer or "conduit of instructions" to the lawyer, or employs expertise in assembling client information and explaining it to the solicitor (para. 41).

Revcon Oilfield, 2015 FC 524 (aff'd 2017 FCA 22), paras. 20-21, says "Tax planning communications are not privileged" and that privilege does not extend to "Advice given ... by a lawyer for accounting or tax planning purposes", but these statements cannot be correct (the Court must have meant business advice, not legal advice). In *Atlas Tube*, 2018 FC 1086 (under appeal; CPA Canada added as intervenor 2019 FCA 120), paras. 31-36, a draft tax due-diligence report prepared for an acquisition, and possibly provided to counsel, was not privileged as its "dominant purpose" (DP) was to inform the purchase decision [for strong criticism see Suarez, "FCA to Hear Atlas Tube Appeal", 27(12) *Canadian Tax Highlights* (ctf.ca) 2-4 (Dec. 2019)]. In *Jet2.com*, [2020] EWCA Civ 35 (England), in-company emails seeking input from various executives including in-house counsel were not protected, as the DP was not obtaining legal advice. In light of *Atlas Tube*, DP may be the test in Canada (it clearly is for litigation privilege, discussed below under "Other forms").

Factual documents: Until June 2016, the view was that SCP "does not apply to documents relating to monies flowing through a solicitor's accounts to or from a client or to documents relating to real estate transactions": *Heath*, [1990] 2 C.T.C. 28 (BCSC); *Reddy*, 2006 FC 277; *Singh Lyn LLP*, 2005 FC 1538; *Vlug*, 2006 FC 86; *Cornfield*, 2008 FCA 156; *Banque Nationale*, 2008 FC 594 (funds paid or received on behalf of clients); *Jakabfy*, 2013 FC 706 (destination of lawyer's trust account funds following client's sale of property); *J.G.C.*, 2014 BCSC 557; *Revcon Oilfield*, 2015 FC 524, paras. 33-35 (aff'd 2017 FCA 22); *Clark*, 2012 FC 950. Similarly it was held that SCP does not apply to: solicitors' reporting letters on transactions and corporate financing (*Defehr*, 2011 BCSC 1548); a corporation's minute book and similar records in the lawyer's office (*1013808 Ontario Inc.*, [1994] 1 C.T.C. 401 (Ont. Gen. Div.)); documents that are merely deposited with a solicitor (*1496956 Ontario Ltd.*, [2009] 5 C.T.C. 101 (Ont. SCJ)); ordinary accounting records regarding the lawyer's tax liability: *Lipkowski*, 2014 FCA 171. The fact a lawyer is present at meetings is not sufficient to create SCP without evidence that legal advice was being sought: *Zeldap Corp.*, 2015 TCC 78 (FCA appeal discontinued A-191-15). **However,** the Supreme Court of Canada ruled in *Thompson*, 2016 SCC 21, para. 20, that financial records are *prima facie* privileged absent proof to the contrary, and ruled in *Chambre des notaires*, 2016 SCC 20, para. 94, that requirements for information and compliance orders issued to lawyers and Quebec notaries are unconstitutional and invalid (although para. 73 says not all documents are privileged). This leaves all the above cases up in the air. It is possible that many documents are not privileged, but that there is currently no legal mechanism by which CRA can demand to see them!

Workplace accident investigation records were not covered by SCP merely because legal counsel requested an investigation that was required by statute: *Suncor*, 2017 ABCA 221; leave to appeal denied 2018 CarswellAlta 882 (SCC).

Fraud exception: SCP does not apply to communications for the purpose of committing a crime or fraud: *Solosky*, 1979 CanLII 9 (SCC); *Descôteaux v. Mierzwinski*, 1982 CanLII 22 (SCC); *Campbell*, 1999 CanLII 676 (SCC), para. 55; *Industrial Alliance v. Kunicyn*, 2020 ONSC 3393 (it is a narrow exception, to be invoked only when absolutely necessary: paras. 4, 27); *Addlesee v. Dentons Europe*, [2020] EWHC 238 (Ch) (England). This can apply to tax evasion planning.

Third parties: SCP is normally lost (deemed waived) on documents shared with third parties: *Revcon Oilfield*, 2015 FC 524, para. 24 (aff'd 2017 FCA 22). Legal advice circulated or summarized within the client is still privileged: in *Global Cash Access*, 2010 TCC 493, a CRA internal memo summarizing Dept. of Justice legal advice was privileged. In *Glencore International*, [2019] HCA 26, Australia's High Court denied an injunction to prevent use of "Paradise Papers" stolen from a law firm (see 239(1) Notes under "Offshore accounts"); it is unclear how this would be treated in Canada.

Waiver: Inadvertent disclosure of a privileged document may or may not result in waiver of SCP: *Chapelstone Developments*, 2004 NBCA 96 (leave to appeal denied [2005] G.S.T.C. 95 (SCC)); *MIL (Investments)*, 2006 TCC 208; *506913 N.B.*, 2012 TCC 210; *CIBC* (above), paras. 47-53. Express intention should be stated to not waive SCP (provision to external auditors implies such intention): *Philip Services v. Ont. Securities Commission*, 2005 CanLII 30328 (Ont. SCJ). In *Grant Thornton*, 2012 FC 1313, memos from a lawyer/CA were protected, and inadvertent disclosure to the company's auditor did not waive SCP. Proving reliance on a lawyer's advice to avoid a 163(2) penalty or non-carelessness for 152(4)(a) (statute-barred assessment) risks waiving SCP, but *Inwest Investments*, 2015 BCSC 1375, paras. 171-77, suggests the *content* of the advice might not have to be revealed. In *Hart*, [2017] FCA 571 (Fed. Ct. Australia), a detailed summary of a legal opinion, provided to the Tax Office to show the taxpayer had relied on it, constituted waiver. Deliberate waiver for part of a communication, or part of legal advice, waives it for all of the communication or advice: *Imperial Tobacco*, 2013 TCC 144, para. 86; *Abenaim*, 2015 TCC 242, para. 61; however, waiver of *corporate* legal advice in discovery did not necessarily waive privilege on *tax* advice from the same firm: *Superior Plus*, 2015 FCA 241. In *Morris*, 2019 QCCQ 7635 (a tax prosecution), a Revenu Québec (RQ) auditor sent M an audit report containing part of a legal opinion provided to RQ; this was done without authority so it did not waive privilege over the rest of the advice. Waiver may be implied: *Gerbro Inc.*, 2014 TCC 179; *Youvarajah*, 2011 ONCA 654, paras. 147, 153; *Ferrara v. Lorenzetti*, 2012 ONCA 851, paras. 77-79; *CIBC* (above), paras. 54-73. An auditor saying CRA has a legal opinion is arguably a waiver; Éthier & Sohmer, "CRA Audit Says it has a Justice Opinion", 2532 *Tax Topics* (CCH) 1-2 (Sept. 15, 2020).

Common interest privilege (CIP) defence to waiver: Legal advice given to multiple parties on a complex transaction whose interests are not adverse has long been considered protected: *Pitney Bowes*, 2003 FCT 214 (even though there was disclosure to other parties); *Barrick Gold v. Goldcorp*, 2011 ONSC 1325, para. 4 (documents circulated to the team "whose input was necessary and appropriate to the consideration, structuring, planning and implementation of very complex transactions"); *Bank of Montreal v. Tortora*, 2010 BCSC 1430 (lawyer consulting with other advisors); *CIBC* (above), paras. 210-212; *Imperial Tobacco*, 2013 TCC 144, paras. 62-68; *IGGillis Holdings*, 2018 FCA 51 (leave to appeal denied 2018 CarswellNat 5994 (SCC)) (tax opinions shared where lawyers cooperated on deal between their clients; FCA reversed the FC, which had valiantly tried to undo this privilege); Michael Wong, "Asserting Privilege over Third-Party Communications", 1(2) *Canadian Tax Focus* (ctf.ca) 4 (Aug. 2011); Henry Gluch, "Common Interest Privilege", 2012 Tax Dispute Resolution conf. report (ctf.ca), 8:1-18; Joel Nitikman, "Who Can Waive Common Interest Privilege?", 2466 *Tax Topics* (CCH) 1-3 (June 13, 2019).

Taxpayers claiming deductions for legal fees must be willing to disclose to CRA some detail about the legal services, without providing specifics of the advice or waiving privilege: *Richard A. Kanan Corp.*, 2014 TCC 124; *Dr. Mike Orth Inc. (371501 B.C. Ltd.)*, 2014 FCA 34, para. 13; *Kyard*, 2019 QCCQ 1617, paras. 129-144. Consider seeking an undertaking from CRA, before disclosure, not to use the information for any purpose other than determining deductibility of the fees; or providing the information only on Tax Court discovery, so that the "implied undertaking" rule (see Notes to 169(1)) applies; but evidence given in open Court is not protected. See also Hosanna, "Legal Invoices: Maintaining Privilege While Supporting Deductibility", 15(3) *Tax for the Owner-Manager* (ctf.ca) 9-10 (July 2015). The quantum of fees paid to a lawyer is not always protected by SCP: *Kalogerakis*, 2017 QCCA 1253.

More on SCP [the pre-2016 articles are partly superseded by new case law above]: see David Sherman's *Canada GST Service* commentary to ETA s. 293 (also on *Taxnet Pro*); Campbell, *Administration of Income Tax 2020* (Carswell), §7.8; Krishna, "Legal Privilege", *Taxnet Pro* Tax Disputes Centre (Jan. 2021, 32pp); Geddes, "The Fragile Privilege", 47(4) *Canadian Tax Journal* 799-843 (1999); Yaskowich, "Privilege ... in a

Cross-Border Context", 2006 Cdn Tax Foundation conference report, 23:1-42; Lindsay, "Tax Sensitive Document Management", 20 *Canadian Petroleum Tax Journal* (2007); Carr, "Solicitor-Client Privilege", 2010 conference report, 7:1-36; Kroft, "Recent Developments in CRA's Reach for Information", 2011 BC Tax Conf. (ctf.ca) 5:1-88 and Ontario Tax Conf. 4:1-88; Misutka, "Select Issues Relating to Solicitor-Client Privilege", 2012 Tax Dispute Resolution conf. report (ctf.ca), 7:1-15; Kreklewetz & Horrigan, "Privilege in a TCC Discovery", 24(1) *Canadian Tax Highlights* (ctf.ca) 5-6 (Jan. 2016) (*CIBC* case); Gibson and Goldbach, "Tax Disputes and Litigation", 2016 conference report, at 16:2-10; Mirandola & Kabouchi, "Document Production in Tax Disputes", XX(4) *Tax Litigation* (Federated Press) 8-15 (2017); Goldbach & James, "Protecting Privilege", 2018 BC Tax Conf. 5:1-29; Ewens, "Privilege where Legal Advice Rendered by a Law Firm of Collaborating Lawyers and Accountants" (April 2021), tinyurl.com/moodys-priv.

Law Society codes of conduct (and other professions) require client confidentiality; see Malcolm Mercer, "Professional Conduct Rules and Confidential Information Versus Solicitor-Client Privilege", 92 *Canadian Bar Review* 595-609 (2013-14). This confidentiality requirement does not create privilege: *Clark*, 2012 FC 950, para. 22.

Other forms of privilege:

Accountant-client privilege (ACP) does not exist in Canada: *Susan Hosiery*, [1969] C.T.C. 353 (Exch.); *Tower (Kitsch)*, 2003 FCA 307; *Redhead Equipment*, 2016 SKCA 115, para. 44; *Atlas Tube*, 2018 FC 1086 (under appeal; CPA Canada added as intervenor 2019 FCA 120). (The US has a limited privilege for accountants: *Textron* (2009), 577 F.3d 21 (1st Circuit CA, leave to appeal to USSC denied May 24, 2010); *Deloitte LLP*, 2010 TNT 125-11 (DC CA); Sorensen, "Protecting Tax Accrual Workpapers", 6(2) *BorderCrossings* (Carswell) 1-6 (Oct. 2013) (re *Wells Fargo* case).) Unless SCP can be claimed on documents in an accountant's files, CRA can seize them; but due to *BP Canada* (see Notes to 231.2(1)), public companies' tax-risk memos are exempt. SCP is available for accountant-client correspondence if the accountant is retained to act as the client's agent in obtaining legal advice, or to assist the client's lawyer in providing legal advice: *Susan Hosiery* (above); *Telus Communications*, 2004 FCA 380; Watson, "The Client, Accountant and Lawyer", 16(5) *Tax Hyperion* (Carswell) 7-10 (Sept-Oct 2019). In *Chancey v. Dharmadi*, 2007 CanLII 28332 (ONSC), paralegal-client privilege applied where the client retained a paralegal to defend a traffic ticket; might this apply to CPAs who act for clients in Tax Court? See also Nitikman, "Accountant's Privilege", VI(3) *Tax Litigation* (Federated Press) 382-4 (1998); Lawlor, "Extending Privilege to Accountants", 1998 Cdn Tax Foundation conference report, 4:1-22; TEI Dec. 7, 2011 submission to Finance, q. 7; Arnold, *The Arnold Report* (ctf.ca) #056 (Sept. 10, 2013); Studniberg, case comment on *Prudential plc* ([2013] UKSC 1), 61(2) *Canadian Tax Journal* 444-60 (2013); Colapinto, "A necessary privilege?", *CPA Magazine*, June/July 2014, 39-42 (describes developments in other countries and recommends Canada adopt ACP); Ideias, "Accountant-Client Privilege: What a Tax Planner Needs to Know" (*Taxnet Pro* Tax & Estate Planning Centre, 2021, 9pp); Nitikman, "Everything You Always Wanted To Know About Requirements", 2018 conference report, at 30:21-23.

Crown privileges: "Informer privilege" or "informant privilege" protects the identity of someone providing a lead to CRA or the police: *Basi*, 2009 SCC 52; *McCartie*, 2013 BCPC 150, 174, 221 and 289; *Gunner Industries*, 2015 SKQB 349, para. 143. "Public interest privilege": audit and investigation techniques need not be disclosed in judicial review of an audit demand: *Chad*, 2018 FC 556; or in tax evasion prosecutions: *Gunner*, para. 85; *Construction Frank Catania*, 2015 QCCQ 9735. "Prosecutorial immunity" protects the Attorney General's documents discussing whether to lay charges: *Davies*, 2009 BCCA 337; *Foote*, 2014 BCSC 526.

Litigation privilege is a "fundamental principle of the administration of justice": *Lizotte v. Aviva Insurance*, 2016 SCC 52, para. 4. It applies to documents produced in contemplation of litigation and whose "dominant purpose" is to aid in the conduct of litigation (e.g., expert reports): *Blank*, 2006 SCC 39; *Moore v. Getahun*, 2015 ONCA 55, paras. 68-77; *Suncor*, 2017 ABCA 221 (leave to appeal denied 2018 CarswellAlta 882 (SCC)). It expires when the litigation ends, but may still apply during closely related litigation: *CIBC* (above), paras. 175-186 (possible "apprehended" related litigation does not keep privilege alive); *Pederson v. Allstate*, 2020 ABCA 65. It applies to documents prepared for mediation: *Ontario v. Magnotta Winery*, 2010 ONCA 681. It applied in *Defehr*, 2011 BCSC 1548, para. 13; *General Accident v Chrusz*, 1999 CanLII 7320 (Ont CA). It did not apply in *Zeldap Corp.*, 2015 TCC 78 (FCA appeal discontinued A-191-15), to meetings 3 years before reassessments were issued. In *General Motors Acceptance*, [1999] 3 C.T.C. 2056 (TCC), para. 29, Bell J. suggested that CRA's Appeals file might always be protected: "Potential litigation respecting income tax assessments is always present because every assessment is subject to litigation procedures contained in the very statute that authorizes assessments". Litigation privilege in a criminal law context: *Métaux Kitco*, 2016 QCCQ 12090, paras. 138-157, 181-185. See also Leah Plumridge, "Litigation Privilege in Tax Disputes", 2(4) *Canadian Tax Focus* (ctf.ca) 12 (Nov. 2012).

Patent and trademark agents are effectively given SCP by *Patent Act* s. 16.1 and *Trade-marks Act* s. 51.13, enacted in 2015.

Physician-patient privilege is limited: see *College of Physicians v. SJO*, 2020 ONSC 1047.

Quality assurance privilege can apply to a law firm's review of its own work so as to avoid mistakes: *Lipson v. Cassels Brock*, 2019 ONSC 5483, paras. 46-56. (It also applies to hospitals: para. 45.)

Settlement privilege allows settlement discussions to remain confidential, and includes documents prepared for mediation: *CIBC* (above), paras. 118-174. In *Abenaim*, 2015

TCC 242, lawyers were permitted to testify (albeit *in camera*) to allow the Court to determine the tax treatment of an employee's termination settlement. See also Whaley, "Mediation Confidentiality and Settlement Privilege", 36(3) *Money & Family Law* (Carswell) 23-24 (March 2021).

Aside from the above, *case-by-case privilege* may apply where a Court considers it appropriate: *B*, 2020 ONSC 7563, paras. 20-24.

CRA Audit Manual: 10.6.8: Obtaining information from lawyers and notaries; 10.7.0: Solicitor-client privilege.

(3) Seizure of certain documents where privilege claimed — Where, pursuant to section 231.3, an officer is about to seize a document in the possession of a lawyer and the lawyer claims that a named client of the lawyer has a solicitor-client privilege in respect of that document, the officer shall, without inspecting, examining or making copies of the document,

(a) seize the document and place it, together with any other document in respect of which the lawyer at the same time makes the same claim on behalf of the same client, in a package and suitably seal and identify the package; and

(b) place the package in the custody of the sheriff of the district or county in which the seizure was made or, if the officer and the lawyer agree in writing on a person to act as custodian, in the custody of that person.

Notes: See Notes to 232(2). 232(3) is presumably unconstitutional as it applies to evidence to be used in appeals of tax assessments. The parallel rule in s. 488.1 of the *Criminal Code* was held to violate the *Charter of Rights* in the context of criminal law, in *Lavallee, Rackel & Heintz*, 2002 SCC 61. The reason the provision is unconstitutional is that if the lawyer does not take action within 14 days (see 232(4)), and provide the client's name, solicitor-client privilege is lost. This is more than the minimum interference with privilege that could have been legislated.

A search of a law office was quashed in *9162-4676 Québec Inc. [Trimax]*, 2016 QCCA 962 (there must be no other reasonable alternative).

Although 232(3) refers to documents "in the possession of the lawyer", CRA and the Dept. of Justice acknowledge that the privilege extends to documents in the possession of the client, if they are otherwise protected by privilege. See also Notes to 231.3(1).

No costs could be recovered by the law firm where documents were seized, privilege was claimed, and CRA eventually returned the documents without examining them: *Shea Nerland Calnan LLP*, 2009 CarswellAlta 1840 (Alta. QB).

(3.1) Examination of certain documents where privilege claimed — Where, pursuant to section 231.1, an officer is about to inspect or examine a document in the possession of a lawyer or where, pursuant to section 231.2, the Minister has required provision of a document by a lawyer, and the lawyer claims that a named client or former client of the lawyer has a solicitor-client privilege in respect of the document, no officer shall inspect or examine the document and the lawyer shall

(a) place the document, together with any other document in respect of which the lawyer at the same time makes the same claim on behalf of the same client, in a package and suitably seal and identify the package or, if the officer and the lawyer agree, allow the pages of the document to be initialed and numbered or otherwise suitably identified; and

(b) retain it and ensure that it is preserved until it is produced to a judge as required under this section and an order is issued under this section in respect of the document.

Notes: 232(3.1) is probably unconstitutional. See Notes to 232(3).

Opening words of 232(3.1) amended by 1995-97 technical bill, effective June 18, 1998.

(4) Application to judge — Where a document has been seized and placed in custody under subsection (3) or is being retained under subsection (3.1), the client, or the lawyer on behalf of the client, may

(a) within 14 days after the day the document was so placed in custody or commenced to be so retained apply, on three clear days notice of motion to the Deputy Attorney General of Canada, to a judge for an order

(i) fixing a day, not later than 21 days after the date of the order, and place for the determination of the question whether the client has a solicitor-client privilege in respect of the document, and

(ii) requiring the production of the document to the judge at that time and place;

(b) serve a copy of the order on the Deputy Attorney General of Canada and, where applicable, on the custodian within 6 days of the day on which it was made and, within the same time, pay to the custodian the estimated expenses of transporting the document to and from the place of hearing and of safeguarding it; and

(c) if the client or lawyer has proceeded as authorized by paragraph (b), apply at the appointed time and place for an order determining the question.

Related Provisions: *Interpretation Act* 27(1), (2) — Calculation of days; *Interpretation Act* 27(5) — Meaning of "within 14 days" or "within 6 days".

Notes: The restrictions in 232(4) are superseded by the common-law protection of privilege. See Notes to 232(2).

(5) Disposition of application — An application under paragraph (4)(c) shall be heard *in camera*, and on the application

(a) the judge may, if the judge considers it necessary to determine the question, inspect the document and, if the judge does so, the judge shall ensure that it is repackaged and resealed; and

(b) the judge shall decide the matter summarily and,

(i) if the judge is of the opinion that the client has a solicitor-client privilege in respect of the document, shall order the release of the document to the lawyer, and

(ii) if the judge is of the opinion that the client does not have a solicitor-client privilege in respect of the document, shall order

(A) that the custodian deliver the document to the officer or some other person designated by the Commissioner of Revenue, in the case of a document that was seized and placed in custody under subsection (3), or

(B) that the lawyer make the document available for inspection or examination by the officer or other person designated by the Commissioner of Revenue, in the case of a document that was retained under subsection (3.1),

and the judge shall, at the same time, deliver concise reasons in which the judge shall identify the document without divulging the details thereof.

Notes: 232(5) amended by *Canada Customs & Revenue Agency Act*, effective Nov. 1, 1999, to change "Deputy Minister of National Revenue" to "Commissioner of Customs and Revenue"; and by 2004 CRA/CBSA bill, effective December 12, 2005, to change to "Commissioner of Revenue".

(6) Order to deliver or make available — Where a document has been seized and placed in custody under subsection (3) or where a document is being retained under subsection (3.1) and a judge, on the application of the Attorney General of Canada, is satisfied that neither the client nor the lawyer has made an application under paragraph (4)(a) or, having made that application, neither the client nor the lawyer has made an application under paragraph (4)(c), the judge shall order

(a) that the custodian deliver the document to the officer or some other person designated by the Commissioner of Revenue, in the case of a document that was seized and placed in custody under subsection (3); or

(b) that the lawyer make the document available for inspection or examination by the officer or other person designated by the Commissioner of Revenue, in the case of a document that was retained under subsection (3.1).

Notes: 232(6) amended by *Canada Customs & Revenue Agency Act*, effective Nov. 1, 1999, and 2004 CRA/CBSA bill, effective Dec. 12, 2005.

(7) Delivery by custodian — The custodian shall

(a) deliver the document to the lawyer

(i) in accordance with a consent executed by the officer or by or on behalf of the Deputy Attorney General of Canada or the Commissioner of Revenue, or

(ii) in accordance with an order of a judge under this section; or

(b) deliver the document to the officer or some other person designated by the Commissioner of Revenue

(i) in accordance with a consent executed by the lawyer or the client, or

(ii) in accordance with an order of a judge under this section.

Notes: 232(7) amended by *Canada Customs & Revenue Agency Act*, effective Nov. 1, 1999, and 2004 CRA/CBSA bill, effective Dec. 12, 2005.

(8) Continuation by another judge — Where the judge to whom an application has been made under paragraph (4)(a) cannot for any reason act or continue to act in the application under paragraph (4)(c), the application under paragraph (4)(c) may be made to another judge.

(9) Costs — No costs may be awarded on the disposition of any application under this section.

(10) Directions — Where any question arises as to the course to be followed in connection with anything done or being done under this section, other than subsection (2), (3) or (3.1), and there is no direction in this section with respect thereto, a judge may give such direction with regard thereto as, in the judge's opinion, is most likely to carry out the object of this section of allowing solicitor-client privilege for proper purposes.

(11) Prohibition — The custodian shall not deliver a document to any person except in accordance with an order of a judge or a consent under this section or except to any officer or servant of the custodian for the purposes of safeguarding the document.

(12) Idem — No officer shall inspect, examine or seize a document in the possession of a lawyer without giving the lawyer a reasonable opportunity of making a claim under this section.

(13) Authority to make copies — At any time while a document is in the custody of a custodian under this section, a judge may, on an *ex parte* application of the lawyer, authorize the lawyer to examine or make a copy of the document in the presence of the custodian or the judge by an order that shall contain such provisions as may be necessary to ensure that the document is repackaged and that the package is resealed without alteration or damage.

(14) Waiver of claim of privilege — Where a lawyer has, for the purpose of subsection (2), (3) or (3.1), made a claim that a named client of the lawyer has a solicitor-client privilege in respect of information or a document, the lawyer shall at the same time communicate to the Minister or some person duly authorized to act for the Minister the address of the client last known to the lawyer so that the Minister may endeavour to advise the client of the claim of privilege that has been made on the client's behalf and may thereby afford the client an opportunity, if it is practicable within the time limited by this section, of waiving the claim of privilege before the matter is to be decided by a judge or other tribunal.

(15) Compliance — No person shall hinder, molest or interfere with any person doing anything that that person is authorized to do by or pursuant to this section or prevent or attempt to prevent any person doing any such thing and, notwithstanding any other Act or law, every person shall, unless the person is unable to do so, do everything the person is required to do by or pursuant to this section.

Related Provisions: 238(1) — Punishment for failing to comply.

Definitions [s. 232]: "clear days" — *Interpretation Act* 27(1); "Commissioner of Revenue" — *Canada Agency Act* s. 25; "county" — *Interpretation Act* 35(1); "custodian" — 232(1); "Federal Court" — *Federal Courts Act* s. 4; "judge", "lawyer" — 232(1); "Minister" — 248(1); "officer" — 232(1); "person" — 248(1); "province" — *Interpretation Act* 35(1); "record" — 248(1); "servant" — 248(1) (under "employment"); "solicitor-client privilege" — 232(1); "superior court", "writing" — *Interpretation Act* 35(1).

Information Circulars [s. 232]: 73-10R3: Tax evasion.

233. (1) Information return — Every person shall, on written demand from the Minister served personally or otherwise, whether or not the person has filed an information return as required by this Act or the regulations, file with the Minister, within such reasonable time as is stipulated in the demand, the information return if it has not been filed or such information as is designated in the demand.

Related Provisions: 150(2) — Demands for returns; 162 — Penalties; 237.1(7.5) — Penalty for promoter's failure to file tax shelter information return on demand; 244(5) — Proof of service by mail; 244(6) — Proof of personal service; 248(7)(a) — Mail deemed received on day mailed.

Regulations: 200–233 (information returns).

(2) Partnerships — Every partnership shall, on written demand from the Minister served personally or otherwise on any member of the partnership, file with the Minister, within such reasonable time as is stipulated in the demand, an information return required under section 233.3, 233.4 or 233.6.

Related Provisions: 150(2) — Demands for returns; 162 — Penalties; 233(3) — Tiers of partnerships; 244(5) — Proof of service by mail; 244(6) — Proof of personal service; 244(20)(b) — Service of documents on partnerships; 248(7)(a) — Mail deemed received on day mailed.

(3) Application to members of partnerships — For the purposes of this subsection and subsection (2), a person who is a member of a partnership that is a member of another partnership is deemed to be a member of the other partnership.

Notes: 233 amended by 1996 Budget (effective for returns required to be filed by April 30, 1998 or later) and 1992 technical bill.

Definitions [s. 233]: "Minister" — 248(1); "partnership" — see 96(1) Notes; "person", "regulation" — 248(1).

Information Circulars [s. 233]: 77-9R: Books, records and other requirements for taxpayers having foreign affiliates.

233.1 [Reporting transactions with related non-residents] — (1) Definitions — The definitions in this subsection apply in this section.

"reportable transaction" means

(a) in the case of

(i) a reporting person for a taxation year who is not resident in Canada at any time in the year, or

(ii) a reporting partnership for a fiscal period no member of which is resident in Canada in the period,

a transaction or series of transactions that relate in any manner whatever to a business carried on in Canada by the reporting person or partnership in the year or period or a preceding taxation year or period; and

(b) in any other case, a transaction or series of transactions that relate in any manner whatever to a business carried on by a reporting person (other than a business carried on by a reporting person as a member of a partnership) or partnership in a taxation year or fiscal period.

Related Provisions: 248(10) — Series of transactions.

"reporting partnership" for a fiscal period means a partnership

(a) a member of which is resident in Canada in the period; or

(b) that carries on a business in Canada in the period.

"reporting person" for a taxation year means a person who, at any time in the year,

(a) is resident in Canada; or

(b) is non-resident and carries on a business (other than a business carried on as a member of a partnership) in Canada.

Notes: CRA considers a foreign company that carries on business in Canada (see s. 253) to be a "reporting person" (RP) even if its business income is not taxed in Canada due to a tax treaty and not having a permanent establishment in Canada: VIEWS doc 2009-0352151E5. A federal or provincial Crown corporation that is acting as a Crown agent is not an RP: 2014-054970I17.

"transaction" includes an arrangement or event.

Related Provisions [233.1(1)"transaction"]: 245(1)"transaction" — Parallel definition under GAAR; 247(1) — Parallel definition re transfer pricing.

(2) Reporting person's information return [T106] — Subject to subsection (4), a reporting person for a taxation year shall, on or before the reporting person's filing-due date for the year, file with the Minister, in respect of each non-resident person with whom the reporting person does not deal at arm's length in the year and each partnership of which such a non-resident person is a member, an information return for the year in prescribed form containing prescribed information in respect of the reportable transactions in which the reporting person and the non-resident person or the partnership, as the case may be, participated in the year.

Related Provisions: 152(4)(b)(iii) — Reassessment period extended by 3 years re non-arm's length transactions with non-residents; 162(7), (10) — Penalty for failure to file; 163(2.4)(a) — Penalty of $24,000 for false statement or omission; 233.2–233.7 — Foreign reporting requirements; 247 — Transfer pricing rules; Canada-U.S. Tax Treaty:Art. IX — Adjustments on non-arm's length transactions.

Notes: See the Instructions section on Form T106.

CRA will typically use the T106 to initiate a transfer pricing audit. See Notes to 247(2). Information collected under 233.1 is "entered into the Foreign Reporting Requirements Management System ... [which] provides the main risk assessment tool for Aggressive Tax Planning and international auditors": VIEWS doc 2012-045840I17.

Charges by a non-resident corporation to its Canadian branch do not fall under 233.1, since there is no transaction with a different person: VIEWS docs 2006-020368I17, 2009-033358I17. A provincial Crown corp need not file a T106: 2009-0314301E5. A corporation with 2 short years (due to change in control) that do not exceed 12 months can file 1 T106 for both: 2016-0652771C6 [2016 APFF q.1(c)].

For penalty and interest (162(7), 162(10), 161(11)) for not filing the T106, see VIEWS docs 2009-031252117, 2009-0335321E5. For CRA's former administrative "one chance" policy of not applying the penalty see Notes to 162(10). Allowing e-filing of the T106 is not a high priority: 2011-0427241C6.

The IRS requires Form 5472 from a "reporting corporation" (which includes a foreign corporation engaged in a trade or business within the US), reporting transactions with related parties. Non-filing can lead to an automatic US$25,000 penalty [Turkovich, "Penalty Increased for Failure to Timely File Form 5472", 26(8) *Canadian Tax Highlights* (ctf.ca) 3-4 (Aug. 2018)].

See also Jack Bernstein & Ron Choudhury, "Expanded Form T106", 18(7) *Canadian Tax Highlights* (ctf.ca) 2-3 (July 2010).

CRA Audit Manual: 15.8.0: Non-arm's length transactions with non-residents; 15.10.7: T106 audit guide.

Forms: T106: Information return of non-arm's length transactions with non-residents.

(3) Reporting partnership's information return — Subject to subsection (4), a reporting partnership for a fiscal period shall, on or before the day on or before which a return is required by section 229 of the *Income Tax Regulations* to be filed in respect of the period or would be required to be so filed if that section applied to the reporting partnership, file with the Minister, in respect of each non-resident person with whom the reporting partnership, or a member of the reporting partnership, does not deal at arm's length in the period and each partnership of which such a non-resident person is a member, an information return for the period in prescribed form containing prescribed information in respect of the reportable transactions in which the reporting partnership and the non-resident person or the partnership, as the case may be, participated in the period.

Related Provisions: 152(4)(b)(iii) — Reassessment period extended by 3 years re non-arm's length transactions with non-residents; 162(7), (10), (10.1) — Penalty for failure to file; 163(2.4)(a) — Penalty of $24,000 for false statement or omission; 233.1(5) — Tiers of partnerships; 233.2–233.7 — Foreign reporting requirements; 247 — Transfer pricing rules; Canada-U.S. Tax Treaty:Art. IX — Adjustments on non-arm's length transactions.

Forms: T106: Information return of non-arm's length transactions with non-residents.

(4) *De minimis* exception — A reporting person or partnership that, but for this subsection, would be required under subsection (2) or (3) to file an information return for a taxation year or fiscal period is not required to file the return unless the total of all amounts, each of which is the total fair market value of the property or services that relate to a reportable transaction in which the reporting person or partnership and any non-resident person with whom the reporting person or partnership, or a member of the reporting partnership, does not deal at arm's length in the year or period, or a partnership of which such a non-resident person is a member, as the case may be, participated in the year or period, exceeds $1,000,000.

(5) Deemed member of partnership — For the purposes of this section, a person who is a member of a partnership that is a member of another partnership is deemed to be a member of the other partnership.

Notes [subsec. 233.1(5)]: This rule looks through tiers of partnerships.

Notes [s. 233.1]: 233.1 replaced by 1995-97 technical bill, for tax years and fiscal periods that begin after 1997.

Definitions [s. 233.1]: "amount" — 248(1); "arm's length" — 251(1); "business" — 248(1); "Canada" — 255; "carries on a business in Canada", "carry on business in Canada" — 253; "fair market value" — see 69(1) Notes; "filing-due date" — 248(1); "fiscal period" — 249.1; "Minister", "non-resident" — 248(1); "partnership" — see 96(1) Notes; "person", "prescribed", "property" — 248(1); "reportable transaction", "reporting partnership", "reporting person" — 233.1(1); "resident in Canada" — 250; "series" — 248(10); "taxation year" — 249; "transaction" — 233.1(1).

Information Circulars [s. 233.1]: 87-2R: International transfer pricing (archived); 77-9R: Books, records and other requirements for taxpayers having foreign affiliates.

233.2 [Reporting transfers or loans to foreign trusts] — (1) Definitions — The definitions in this subsection apply in this section.

"exempt trust" means

(a) a trust that is governed by a foreign retirement arrangement;

(b) a trust that

(i) is resident in a country under the laws of which an income tax is imposed,

(ii) is exempt under the laws referred to in subparagraph (i) from the payment of income tax to the government of that country,

(iii) is established principally in connection with, or the principal purpose of which is to administer or provide benefits under, one or more superannuation, pension or retirement funds or plans or any funds or plans established to provide employee benefits, and

(iv) is either

(A) maintained primarily for the benefit of non-resident individuals, or

(B) governed by an employees profit sharing plan; or

(c) a trust

(i) where the interest of each beneficiary under the trust is described by reference to units, and

(ii) that complies with prescribed conditions.

Related Provisions: 233.6(2)(a) — No reporting required on distribution from certain exempt trusts.

Notes: A Roth IRA can effectively be an exempt trust (ET) if an election under Canada-US Treaty Art. XVIII:7 has been filed: Income Tax Folio S5-F3-C1 ¶1.22.

In VIEWS doc 2014-0527921E5, CRA refused to say whether the Australian "ipac select superwrap personal super plan" is an ET. In 2018-0753611E5, a US qualified pension plan taken over by Pension Benefit Guaranty Corp was an ET (for 233.3(1)"specified foreign property"(n)).

"Exempt trust"(b)(iv)(B) added by 1995-97 technical bill, retroactive to the introduction of 233.2 (see Notes at end of 233.2).

Regulations: Reg. 4801.1 (prescribed conditions for subpara. (c)(ii)).

"specified beneficiary" — [Repealed]

Related Provisions: 248(10) — Series of transactions; 248(25) — Extended meaning of "beneficially interested".

Notes: "Specified beneficiary" repealed by 2002-2013 technical bill (Part 1 — NRTs) (in consequence of new s. 94), for returns in respect of trust taxation years that end after 2006, and also for returns in respect of an earlier taxation year if amended 94(1) applies to the trust for that earlier year (see Notes at end of s. 94).

"specified foreign trust" — [Repealed]

Related Provisions: 248(25) — Extended meaning of "beneficially interested".

Notes: Definition repealed by 2002-2013 technical bill (Part 1 — NRTs), effective on the same basis as the repeal of "specified beneficiary" above.

"Specified foreign trust"(b) opening words and (b)(i) amended by 1995-97 technical bill, effective December 1997.

(2) Rule of application — In this section and paragraph 233.5(c.1), subsections 94(1), (2) and (10) to (13) apply, except that the reference to the expression "(other than restricted property)" in the definition "arm's length transfer" in subsection 94(1) is to be read as a reference to the expression "(other than property to which paragraph 94(2)(g) applies but not including a unit of a mutual fund trust or of a trust that would be a mutual fund trust if section 4801 of the *Income Tax Regulations* were read without reference to paragraph 4801(b), a share of the capital stock of a mutual fund corporation, or a particular share of the capital stock of a corporation (other than a closely held corporation) which particular share is identical to a share that is, at the transfer time, of a class that is listed on a designated stock exchange)".

Related Provisions: 248(12) — Identical properties.

Notes: 233.2(2) amended by 2002-2013 technical bill (Part 1 — NRTs) (in consequence of new s. 94), effective on the same basis as the repeal of 233.2(1)"specified beneficiary".

(3) [Repealed]

Notes: 233.2(3) repealed by 2002-2013 technical bill (in consequence of new s. 94), effective on the same basis as the repeal of 233.2(1)"specified beneficiary".

(4) Filing information on foreign trusts [T1141] — A person shall file an information return in prescribed form, in respect of a taxation year of a particular trust (other than an exempt trust or a trust described in any of paragraphs (c) to (h) of the definition "exempt foreign trust" in subsection 94(1)) with the Minister on or before the person's filing-due date for the person's taxation year in which the particular trust's taxation year ends if

(a) the particular trust is non-resident at a specified time in that taxation year of the particular trust;

(b) the person is a contributor, a connected contributor or a resident contributor to the particular trust; and

(c) the person

(i) is resident in Canada at that specified time, and

(ii) is not, at that specified time,

(A) a mutual fund corporation,

(B) an exempt person,

(C) a mutual fund trust,

(D) a trust described in any of paragraphs (a) to (e.1) of the definition "trust" in subsection 108(1),

(E) a registered investment,

(F) a trust in which all persons beneficially interested are persons described in clauses (A) to (E), or

(G) a contributor to the particular trust by reason only of being a contributor to another trust that is resident in Canada and is described in any of clauses (B) to (F).

Related Provisions: 94(7)(b) — Limitation on person's liability for trust's tax when return filed; 162(7), (10), (10.1) — Penalty for failure to file; 163(2.4)(b) — Minimum $24,000 penalty for false statement or omission; 220(2.1) — Waiver of filing requirement; 220(3) — Extension of time to file return; 233.2(2) — Application of non-resident trust rules; 233.2(4.1) — Similar arrangements; 233.2(5) — Election to use other person's information return; 233.3(3) — Requirement to file return re foreign property; 233.5 — Due diligence exception; 233.6(2)(b) — No return required on distribution from trusts where return required under 233.2; 233.7 — No requirement to file in first year of immigration; 248(25.1) — Transfer to non-resident bare trust.

Notes: See Notes to 162(10) and 233.7. Information collected under 233.2 is "entered into the Foreign Reporting Requirements Management System ... [which] provides the main risk assessment tool for Aggressive Tax Planning and international auditors": VIEWS doc 2012-0458401I7.

The reference on Form T1141 to "person with whom the trustee must consult before exercising discretionary powers" and "persons who have any powers relating to the trust" includes a protector: VIEWS doc 2006-0185642C6.

233.2(4) amended by 2002-2013 technical bill (Part 1 — NRTs), effective on same basis as repeal of 233.2(1)"specified beneficiary".

233.2(4)(c) amended by 1995-97 technical bill, effective December 1997.

I.T. Technical News: 43 (taxation of Roth IRAs).

CRA Audit Manual: 15.7.0: Foreign reporting requirements; 15.10.8: Foreign reporting audit guide; 28.2.4: Foreign reporting — penalties and offences.

Forms: T1141: Information return re transfers or loans to a non-resident trust.

(4.1) Similar arrangements — In this section and sections 162, 163 and 233.5, a person's obligations under subsection (4) (except to the extent that they are waived in writing by the Minister) are to be determined as if a contributor described in paragraph (4)(b) were any person who had transferred or loaned property, an arrangement or entity were a non-resident trust throughout the calendar year that includes the time referred to in paragraph (a) and that calendar year were a taxation year of the arrangement or entity, if

(a) the person at any time, directly or indirectly, transferred or loaned the property to be held

(i) under the arrangement and the arrangement is governed by the laws of a country or a political subdivision of a country other than Canada or exists, was formed or organized, or was last continued under the laws of a country or a political subdivision of a country other than Canada, or

(ii) by the entity and the entity is a non-resident entity (as defined by subsection 94.1(2));

(b) the transfer or loan is not an arm's length transfer;

(c) the transfer or loan is not solely in exchange for property that would be described in paragraphs (a) to (i) of the definition "specified foreign property" in subsection 233.3(1) if that definition were read without reference to paragraphs (j) to (q);

(d) the arrangement or entity is not a trust in respect of which the person would, if this Act were read without reference to this subsection, be required to file an information return for a taxation year that includes that time; and

(e) the arrangement or entity is, for a taxation year or fiscal period of the arrangement or entity that includes that time, not

(i) an exempt foreign trust (as defined in subsection 94(1)),

(ii) a foreign affiliate in respect of which the person is a reporting entity (within the meaning assigned by subsection 233.4(1)), or

(iii) an exempt trust.

Notes: For the meaning of "indirectly" in para. (a), see Notes to 17.1(1).

233.2(4.1) added by 2002-2013 technical bill (in consequence of new s. 94), effective on same basis as repeal of 233.2(1)"specified beneficiary".

(5) Joint filing — Where information returns in respect of a trust's taxation year would, but for this subsection, be required to be filed under subsection (4) by a particular person and another person, and the particular person identifies the other person in an election filed in writing with the Minister, for the purposes of applying this Act to the particular person

(a) the information return filed by the other person shall be treated as if it had been filed by the particular person;

(b) the information required to be provided with the return by the particular person shall be deemed to be the information required to be provided by the other person with the return;

(c) the day on or before which the return is required to be filed by the particular person is deemed to be the later of the day on or before which

(i) the return would, but for this subsection, have been required to have been filed by the particular person, and

(ii) the return is required to have been filed by the other person; and

(d) each act and omission of the other person in respect of the return is deemed to be an act or omission of the particular person.

Notes [s. 233.2]: 233.2 added by 1996 Budget, effective for returns in respect of trusts' taxation years that begin after 1995.

See also Notes to 233.7.

Definitions [s. 233.2]: "arm's length transfer" — 233.2(2); "arm's length" — 251(1); "beneficially interested" — 248(25); "beneficiary" — 248(25) [Notes]; "calendar year" — *Interpretation Act* 37(1)(a); "Canada" — 255, *Interpretation Act* 35(1); "connected contributor", "contributor" — 94(1), 233.2(2); "corporation" — 248(1), *Interpretation Act* 35(1); "designated stock exchange" — 248(1), 262; "employee" —

248(1); "employees profit sharing plan" — 144(1), 248(1); "exempt foreign trust" — 94(1); "exempt person" — 94(1), 233.2(2); "exempt trust" — 233.2(1); "filing-due date" — 150(1), 248(1); "fiscal period" — 249.1; "foreign affiliate" — 95(1), 248(1); "foreign retirement arrangement" — 248(1), Reg 6803; "identical" — 248(12); "individual", "Minister" — 248(1); "mutual fund corporation" — 131(8), 248(1); "mutual fund trust" — 132(6)–(7), 132.2(3)(n), 248(1); "non-resident" — 248(1); "non-resident entity" — 94.1(2); "person", "prescribed", "property" — 248(1); "registered investment" — 204.4(1), 248(1); "reporting entity" — 233.4(1); "resident" — 250; "resident contributor" — 94(1), 233.2(2); "resident in Canada" — 94(3)(a), 250; "share" — 248(1); "specified time" — 94(1), 233.2(2); "taxation year" — 249; "trust" — 104(1), 248(1), (3); "writing" — *Interpretation Act* 35(1).

233.3 [Reporting foreign property: T1135] — **(1) Definitions** — The definitions in this subsection apply in this section.

"reporting entity" for a taxation year or fiscal period means a specified Canadian entity for the year or period where, at any time (other than a time when the entity is non-resident) in the year or period, the total of all amounts each of which is the cost amount to the entity of a specified foreign property of the entity exceeds $100,000.

Related Provisions: 233.6(2)(c) — No return required on distribution from certain trusts to reporting entity.

Notes: A deceased person's return may need a T1135 because of the "any time ... in the year" test, but at year-end the deceased owns no property so the form should report $0: VIEWS doc 2014-0527611E5.

The settlor of a non-resident trust can generally answer "no" to the foreign-property question, but may have to file a T1141 under 233.2 or T1142 under 233.6: VIEWS doc 2002-0133035.

Reporting is not affected by the attribution rules: if X gives spouse Y $75,000 and they jointly buy a $150,000 SFP (and they have no other SFP), they need not file as each has cost of $75,000: VIEWS docs 2015-0610641C6 [2015 CTF conf q.12]; 2016-0639481E5 (beneficial owner should report); 2016-0669081E5 (income from property should be reported without applying attribution rules).

For more CRA interpretation see docs 2009-0319881E5 (determination of which of 2 partnerships is the reporting entity); 2010-0361681E5 (see 248(1)"cost amount" in determining cost); 2011-0399441C6, 2012-0444711C6 (cost of life insurance policy); 2014-0547721E5 (trust whose beneficiaries are all tax-exempt need not file); 2014-0532061E5 (94(3)(f) trust need not file).

See also Jacqueline Huang, "Partnership Interests and Form T1135: Which Party Should File?", *Canadian Tax Focus* (ctf.ca) 3-4 (Nov. 2014).

"specified Canadian entity" for a taxation year or fiscal period means

(a) a taxpayer resident in Canada in the year that is not

(i) a mutual fund corporation,

(ii) a non-resident-owned investment corporation,

(iii) a person (other than a trust) all of whose taxable income for the year is exempt from tax under Part I,

(iv) a trust all of the taxable income of which for the year is exempt from tax under Part I,

(v) a mutual fund trust,

(vi) a trust described in any of paragraphs (a) to (e.1) of the definition "trust" in subsection 108(1),

(vii) a registered investment, nor

(viii) a trust in which all persons beneficially interested are persons described in subparagraphs (i) to (vii); and

(b) a partnership (other than a partnership all the members of which are taxpayers referred to in any of subparagraphs (a)(i) to (viii)) where the total of all amounts, each of which is a share of the partnership's income or loss for the period of a non-resident member, is less than 90% of the income or loss of the partnership for the period, and, where the income and loss of the partnership are nil for the period, the income of the partnership for the period is deemed to be $1,000,000 for the purpose of determining a member's share of the partnership's income for the purpose of this paragraph.

Related Provisions: 94(3)(a)(vi) — Certain trusts deemed resident in Canada; 248(25) — Meaning of "beneficially interested".

Notes: See Notes to 233.3(1)"reporting entity".

"specified foreign property" of a person or partnership means any property of the person or the partnership that is

(a) funds or intangible property, or for civil law incorporeal property, situated, deposited or held outside Canada,

(b) tangible property, or for civil law corporeal property, situated outside Canada,

(c) a share of the capital stock of a non-resident corporation,

(d) an interest in a non-resident trust,

(e) an interest in a partnership that owns or holds specified foreign property,

(f) an interest in, or right with respect to, an entity that is non-resident,

(g) indebtedness owed by a non-resident person,

(h) an interest in, or for civil law a right in, or a right — under a contract in equity or otherwise either immediately or in the future and either absolutely or contingently — to, any property (other than any property owned by a corporation or trust that is not the person) that is specified foreign property, and

(i) property that, under the terms or conditions thereof or any agreement relating thereto, is convertible into, is exchangeable for or confers a right to acquire, property that is specified foreign property,

but does not include

(j) property that is used or held exclusively in the course of carrying on an active business of the person or partnership (determined as if the person or partnership were a corporation resident in Canada),

(k) a share of the capital stock or indebtedness of a non-resident corporation that is a foreign affiliate of the person or partnership for the purpose of section 233.4,

(l) an interest in, or indebtedness of, a non-resident trust that is a foreign affiliate of the person or partnership for the purpose of section 233.4,

(m) an interest in a non-resident trust that was not acquired for consideration by either the person or partnership or a person related to the person or partnership,

(n) an interest in a trust described in paragraph (a) or (b) of the definition "exempt trust" in subsection 233.2(1),

(o) an interest in a partnership that is a specified Canadian entity,

(o.1) a right with respect to, or indebtedness of, an authorized foreign bank that is issued by, and payable or otherwise enforceable at, a branch in Canada of the bank.

(p) personal-use property of the person or partnership, and

(q) an interest in, or for civil law a right in, or a right to acquire, a property that is described in any of paragraphs (j) to (p).

Notes: When reading a VIEWS doc or article in French about this definition, note that the para. numbering is totally different in French than in English!

Specified foreign property (SFP) includes: American life annuity (VIEWS doc 2010-0361681E5); Australian Superannuation Fund (2015-0595461E5) [Tollstam, "T1135: Right to Amounts Under Foreign Retirement Plan", 24(10) *Canadian Tax Highlights* (ctf.ca) 6-7 (Oct. 2016)]; Bitcoins, and a foreign partnership holding them (2014-0561061E5); Canadian shares held at a foreign broker (tinyurl.com/qa-t1135); debt owed to a partner by partnership that includes non-resident (NR) partners (2013-0484461I7); debt owing by a NR, if it is not personal-use property (2013-0513361E5); employee stock options in foreign corp (2014-0529281E5); mineral right outside Canada (2014-052224117, 2016-063118117); Swiss "Libre Passage" pension account (2010-0360171E5); UK Individual Savings Account with foreign investments (2013-0485661E5); a vacant rental apartment building (2015-0614371E5).

SFP **does not include**: property held through a subsidiary (2014-0517021E5); property in an RRSP or personal-use property (2015-0614371E5); interest in a US qualified pension plan taken over by Pension Benefit Guaranty Corp (2018-0753611E5, due to para. (n)); Roth IRA, if an election under Canada-US Treaty Art. XVIII:7 has been filed and no contribution is made while resident in Canada (Income Tax Folio S5-F3-C1 ¶1.22).

Para. (k) excludes a loan owed by a foreign affiliate, but this does not apply to a FA owned through a Canadian sub, due to 233.4(2)(a), so such a loan must be reported on

the T1135, not the T1134: Mark Dumalski, "T1135 Filing Required for Certain Intercompany Debts", 4(3) *Canadian Tax Focus* (ctf.ca) 2 (Aug. 2014).

On whether an interest in a life insurance policy issued by a non-resident insurer is SFP (and how to report it if it is), see T.E. McDonnell, "Recent Changes in the Taxation of Insurance Policies", 2014 STEP Canada conference (contact memberservices@step.ca).

94(3)(a)(vi) can deem a non-resident trust to be resident in Canada so that it must file a 233.3 return, but not for purposes of other persons reporting on the trust, so an interest in a non-resident trust deemed resident in Canada is SFP under para. (d).

See also CRA Q&A at tinyurl.com/qa-t1135; Jason Kujath, "Uncommon Scenarios for T1135 Reporting", 15(2) *Tax for the Owner-Manager* (ctf.ca) 2-3 (April 2015).

Arguably, SFP does not include shares in an investment account that are actually "security entitlements", which are contractual rights, not property. See David Sohmer, "Margin Trading, Short Selling and My Client-Broker Agreement", xl(10) *The Canadian Taxpayer* (Carswell) 75-76 (May 18, 2018) and "Do Shares of an American Company Credited to An Account with a Canadian Broker Constitute Specified Foreign Property?", xl(16) 121-123 (Aug. 10, 2018), and "The *Securities Transfer Act*", 2556 *Tax Topics* (CCH) 1-4 (March 2, 2021). By analogy, consider that CRA says that foreign currency held in an account at a financial institution is not actually foreign currency for 39(1.1): VIEWS doc 2017-0712621C6 [2017 APFF q.8].

Definition amended by 2002-2013 technical bill, last change effective June 26, 2013.

(2) Application to members of partnerships — For the purpose of this section, a person who is a member of a partnership that is a member of another partnership

(a) is deemed to be a member of the other partnership; and

(b) the person's share of the income or loss of the other partnership is deemed to be equal to the amount of that income or loss to which the person is directly or indirectly entitled.

Notes: This rule looks through tiers of partnerships. For the meaning of "indirectly" in para. (b), see Notes to 17.1(1).

(3) Returns respecting foreign property [T1135] — A reporting entity for a taxation year or fiscal period shall file with the Minister for the year or period a return in prescribed form on or before the day that is

(a) where the entity is a partnership, the day on or before which a return is required by section 229 of the *Income Tax Regulations* to be filed in respect of the fiscal period of the partnership or would be required to be so filed if that section applied to the partnership; and

(b) where the entity is not a partnership, the entity's filing-due date for the year.

Related Provisions: 94(3)(a)(vi) — Application to trust deemed resident in Canada; 152(4)(b.2) — Reassessment deadline extended by 3 years if T1135 not correctly filed or foreign income not reported; 162(7), (10), (10.1) — Penalty for failure to file; 163(2.4)(c) — Minimum $24,000 penalty for false statement or omission; 220(2.1) — Waiver of filing requirement; 220(3) — Extension of time to file return; 233(2) — Demand for return by partnership; 233.2(4) — Requirement to file return re transfers to foreign trusts; 233.7 — No requirement to file in year of immigration.

Notes: The T1135 requires reporting of "specified foreign property" (SFP: see Notes to definition in 233.3(1)) if total cost exceeds $100,000 [233.1(1)"reporting entity"]. The form can be filed electronically. The T1 General tax return, p. 2, has a check-box question on whether the taxpayer owns SFP costing over $100,000. A first-year resident need not file (but must still check the box): 233.7.

See tinyurl.com/t1135-cra and tinyurl.com/t1135-qa for CRA explanation and Q&A.

CRA considers that beneficial ownership must be reported, and income must be reported without applying the attribution rules. See Notes to 233.3(1)"reporting entity".

Total cost under $250,000: a simplified "tick the box for each type of property" reporting is allowed. Gross income from SFP and gains from SFP dispositions must also be reported. This method, though introduced for 2015-year filing, can be used to file or amend earlier returns: tinyurl.com/t1135-qa, q.17.

$250,000 or more: For accounts at a 248(1)"registered securities dealer" or Canadian trust company, the total value of all SFP can be reported on a country-by-country basis in Category 7 of the form (rather than details of each property), showing highest value at the end of any month and year-end value. For SFP not in such accounts, each property as well as gross income/gain from it must be reported separately.

Note that, under FATCA, the IRS automatically reports to CRA assets in US brokerage or bank accounts. See Notes to 269.

See also VIEWS docs 2006-0211121E5, 2008-0288441E5, 2008-030144117; 2014-0527611E5 (deceased's return should report $0 since deceased owns nothing at year-end); 2014-0529371E5 (emigrant need report only up to date of emigration); 2014-0532601E5 (94(3)(f) election: neither deemed trust needs to file); 2015-0611141E5 (former resident returning to Canada must file for entire year); tinyurl.com/cpa-t1135

(CPA Canada webinar Q&A with CRA answers, updated to April 2016); Vance, "T1135 — The Saga Continues", 2248 *Tax Topics* (CCH) 1-3 (April 9, 2015).

Information collected under 233.3 is "entered into the Foreign Reporting Requirements Management System ... [which] provides the main risk assessment tool for Aggressive Tax Planning and international auditors": VIEWS doc 2012-0458401I7.

A penalty ($2,500 after 100 days) applies under 162(7) for not filing the T1135 on time. It can be cancelled for due diligence (see Notes to 162(1)) or waived by the CRA (220(3.1)). The penalty (or CRA's refusal to waive it) was upheld in: *Seabrook*, 2009 TCC 532 (Hawaii condominium); *Leclerc*, 2010 TCC 99 (French condo); *Sandler*, 2010 FC 459; *Canwest Communications [Leonard Asper Holdings, Stemijon Investments]*, 2011 FCA 299 (conscious decision not to file because all income was being reported); *Edwards*, 2012 TCC 430 (taxpayer knew she was resident in Canada; no due diligence); *Fung*, 2014 FC 934 (taxpayer unaware she had to file T1135 even if no tax payable for the year); *Chen*, 2019 FC 1435 (C had been assessed same penalty the previous year). *Contra*, the penalty was cancelled in *Douglas*, 2012 TCC 73, where a low-income taxpayer filed his return late and included the form with the return as per the instructions on the form; in *Moore*, 2019 TCC 141, where CRA's Guide was unclear and M voluntarily disclosed with his 2016 return his non-filing for 2015; and likely would have been cancelled based on due diligence in *Fiset*, 2017 TCC 63, para. 9, had CRA not already agreed to cancel it; and in *Takenaka*, 2018 FC 347, CRA was ordered to revisit its decision not to waive the penalty in a similar case. (The taxpayer did the same in *Biswal*, 2017 FC 529, but the Federal Court had no grounds to overturn CRA's decision not to waive the penalty and recommended Ms. B appeal to the TCC!) CRA did not change its assessing policy in response to *Douglas* (2012-0453211C6), but has added a warning in the T1 Guide about filing the T1135 even if no return is required (CRA meeting with Institute of CAs of BC, Jan. 22/13, q.3). In *Chen* (above), paras. 9 and 20, CRA and the Court both said that if records are unavailable, one should file an estimate and amend it later. See also Notes to 162(7), and to 220(3.1) re voluntary disclosures (*Matthew Boadi* case).

For discussion of CRA efforts re Swiss bank accounts and other offshore funds, see Notes to 239(1).

US filing: US citizens (including merely because a parent was born in the US), residents (including dual residents who are Canadian-resident under Canada-US tax treaty Art. IV:2) and green card holders must file US income tax returns: see 128.1(1) Notes. If no US tax is payable due to the Foreign Earned Income Exclusion, foreign tax credit and/or Canada-US tax treaty, late returns can often be filed with no penalty, but some forms have severe late-filing penalties even if no tax is owed. Form 8938 requires detailed disclosure of non-US accounts and other foreign financial assets over US$200,000 at year-end or $300,000 any time in the year (for filers outside the US; $400K/$600K for joint filers) with minimum US$10,000 penalty for non-filing. Forms 3520 and 3520-A require reporting distributions from, contributions to or ownership of a non-US trust or estate (including a TFSA or an inheritance), or receipt of a foreign gift over US$100K, with substantial non-reporting penalty (5% of trust's value, minimum $10,000, or 35% of transfers in or out if that is higher) [and see Bandoblu, "Due Date for IRS Form 3520 for Non-Residents", 27(3) *Canadian Tax Highlights* (ctf.ca) 3-4 (March 2018)]. Relief is provided for RRSPs, RRIFs, RESPs and RDSPs in most cases: IRS Rev. Proc. 2020-17; Hirji & Silvius, "Reporting Relief for US Citizens Residing in Canada", tinyurl.com/moodys-3520 (March 8, 2020); Sheppard, "Foreign Retirement and Savings Plans, Waiver of Forms 3520 and 3520-A", 2514 *Tax Topics* (CCH) 6-19 (May 12, 2020). Other forms possibly required: 926 (transfer to foreign corp), 8865 (owning foreign partnership), 5471 (certain foreign corps), 8833 (treaty-based return disclosure), 8621 (shareholder of passive foreign investment company). Form 8891 is no longer needed for Canadian retirement accounts: IRS Rev. Proc. 2014-55. See also Marino & Sloan, "Typical Issues When a US Person is Part of the Mix", 2015 Prairie Provinces Tax Conference (ctf.ca) at 3:11-18; Tennyson & MacRae, "Taxation of US Citizens Resident in Canada", 13(6) *Tax Hyperion* (Carswell) 1-3 (June 2016); Glicklich & Benson, "Onerous US Reporting Requirements for US Members of Non-US Family-Controlled Entities", 64(4) *Canadian Tax Journal* 929-39 (2016).

On June 17/14, the IRS announced changes to the "Streamlined Program", for non-US-resident taxpayers physically outside the US at least 330 full days in one of the previous 3 years, eliminating a limit of no more than $1,500 US tax per year and completion of a "risk questionnaire"; and merely requiring participants to certify that previous failures to comply were not wilful. Taxpayers using these new rules will pay no penalties (unlike the OVDP).

See also Wiltse, "New US Reporting for Foreign Assets", 20(3) *Canadian Tax Highlights [CTH]* (ctf.ca) 4-5 (March 2012); Peace and Snelgrove, "US Persons Living in Canada", 2012 Prairie Provinces Tax Conf. (ctf.ca), 8:1-20; Waiss, "US Tax Information Reporting", 25(9) *CTH* 3-4 (Sept. 2017).

US FBAR (foreign bank account reporting): US persons with signature authority on non-US financial accounts (including Canadian brokerage accounts and RRSPs) totalling over US$10,000 at any time must also file Form FinCEN 114 electronically, at bsaefiling.fincen.treas.gov (Dept. of the Treasury) by each Oct. 15, with penalty of US$10,000 per violation (limited to 6 years) for inadvertent non-filing (much higher for wilful failure). This is under the *Bank Secrecy Act*, not the *Internal Revenue Code*. This obligation also applies if the US person has signing power over an account (such as of a corporate employer) in which the US person has no beneficial interest. Bitcoin and other virtual currencies in an account are not subject to FBAR, though this may change: FinCEN Notice 2020-2. An amnesty under the Offshore Voluntary Disclosure Program (OVDP) applied until Sept. 28, 2018; penalties can still be reduced or eliminated through the Streamlined Program. See Bercovici, "It's Not Too Late to Come

Clean", 12(2) *Taxes & Wealth Management* (Carswell) 12-15 (June 2019). FBAR penalties cannot be collected by CRA: see Notes to Canada-US tax treaty Art. XXVI-A:1; but see Reed & Ko, "IRS Sues Non-US Resident for FBAR Penalties", 25(4) *Canadian Tax Highlights* (ctf.ca) 3-4 (April 2017), re *Pomerantz* case.

See also Seraganian & Devetski, "Recent Developments in US Tax Law", 2012 Cdn Tax Foundation conference report, at 22:11-13; Bonham, "FATCA and FBAR Reporting by Individuals: Enforcement Considerations from a Canadian Perspective", 60(2) *Canadian Tax Journal* 305-54 (2012); Bandoblu, "IRS Guidance of FBAR Penalties", 23(7) *Canadian Tax Highlights* (ctf.ca) 7-8 (July 2015); Miller, "Look before you leap", 65(2) *CTJ* 531-39 (2017).

US FATCA: For reporting required by Canadian financial institutions to the CRA of accounts of US citizens and other US persons, see Notes to s. 269.

I.T. Technical News: 43 (taxation of Roth IRAs).

CRA Audit Manual: 15.7.0: Foreign reporting requirements; 15.10.8: Foreign reporting audit guide; 28.2.4: Foreign reporting — penalties and offences.

Forms: T1 General return, p. 2, Line 26600 [former 266]; T1135: Foreign income verification statement.

Notes [s. 233.3]: 233.3 added by 1996 Budget (as amended by 1998 Budget bill), effective for returns for taxation years and fiscal periods that begin after 1997, except that such a return for a taxation year or fiscal period that ended in 1998 could be filed until April 30, 1999 (or the due date if later).

See also Notes to 233.7.

Definitions [s. 233.3]: "active business", "amount", "authorized foreign bank", "bank" — 248(1); "beneficially interested" — 248(25); "Canada" — 255, *Interpretation Act* 35(1); "corporation" — 248(1), *Interpretation Act* 35(1); "corporeal property" — Quebec *Civil Code* art. 899, 906; "cost amount", "filing-due date" — 248(1); "fiscal period" — 249.1; "foreign affiliate" — 95(1), 248(1); "incorporeal property" — Quebec *Civil Code* art. 899, 906; "insurance policy", "Minister" — 248(1); "mutual fund corporation" — 131(8), 248(1); "mutual fund trust" — 132(6)–(7), 248(1); "non-resident" — 248(1); "non-resident-owned investment corporation" — 133(8), 248(1); "partnership" — see 96(1) Notes; "person" — 248(1); "personal-use property" — 54, 248(1); "prescribed", "property" — 248(1); "registered investment" — 204.4(1), 248(1); "related" — 251(2)–(6); "reporting entity" — 233.3(1); "resident in Canada" — 94(3)(a)(vi), 250; "share" — 248(1); "specified Canadian entity", "specified foreign property" — 233.3(1); "taxable income" — 248(1); "taxation year" — 249; "taxpayer" — 248(1); "trust" — 104(1), 248(1), (3).

233.4 [Reporting foreign affiliates: T1134] — (1) Reporting entity — For the purpose of this section, "reporting entity" for a taxation year or fiscal period means

(a) a taxpayer resident in Canada (other than a taxpayer all of whose taxable income for the year is exempt from tax under Part I) of which a non-resident corporation is a foreign affiliate at any time in the year;

(b) a taxpayer resident in Canada (other than a taxpayer all of whose taxable income for the year is exempt from tax under Part I) of which a non-resident trust is a foreign affiliate at any time in the year; and

(c) a partnership

(i) where the total of all amounts, each of which is a share of the partnership's income or loss for the period of a member that is not resident in Canada or that is a taxpayer all of whose taxable income for the year in which the period ends is exempt from tax under Part I, is less than 90% of the income or loss of the partnership for the period, and, where the income and loss of the partnership are nil for the period, the income of the partnership for the period is deemed to be $1,000,000 for the purpose of determining a member's share of the partnership's income for the purpose of this subparagraph, and

(ii) of which a non-resident corporation or trust is a foreign affiliate at any time in the fiscal period.

Related Provisions: 93.1(1) — Shares owned by partnership deemed owned proportionately by partners; 93.3(3), (4)(b) — Special rule for certain Australian trusts; 94(3)(a)(vi) — Certain trusts deemed resident in Canada; 95(11) — Deemed separate corp for tracking class.

Notes: Where a US corp is owned by a US partnership that has a 94(3)(a) deemed-resident trust as a partner, there is no "reporting entity": VIEWS doc 2015-0608671E5.

233.4(1)(c)(i) amended by 2014 budget bill #2, for taxation years that end after July 11, 2013, to change "of a non-resident member" to "of a member ... under Part I".

233.4(1)(c)(ii) amended to delete superfluous "of which" (after "affiliate") by 2002-2013 technical bill (Part 5 — technical), effective June 26, 2013. The non-resident trust proposals (Part 1 of the bill) had proposed to amend 233.4(1)(c)(ii), as well as other provisions of 233.4, to delete references to trusts. This was dropped in 2010 because new 94.2 deems certain trusts to be subject to FAPI, but the correction proceeded in the "technical" part of the bill.

(2) Rules of application — For the purpose of this section, in determining whether a non-resident corporation or trust is a foreign affiliate or a controlled foreign affiliate of a taxpayer resident in Canada or of a partnership

(a) paragraph (b) of the definition "equity percentage" in subsection 95(4) shall be read as if the reference to "any corporation" were a reference to "any corporation other than a corporation resident in Canada";

(b) the definitions "direct equity percentage" and "equity percentage" in subsection 95(4) shall be read as if a partnership were a person;

(c) the definitions "controlled foreign affiliate" and "foreign affiliate" in subsection 95(1) shall be read as if a partnership were a taxpayer resident in Canada; and

(d) if the taxpayer is a member of one or more partnerships described in subparagraph (1)(c)(i) of which a non-resident corporation or trust is a foreign affiliate, and the taxpayer does not have any direct or indirect interest (determined without reference to subsection 93.1(1)) in the non-resident corporation or trust other than through its interest in the partnerships, then the non-resident corporation or trust is deemed not to be a foreign affiliate of the taxpayer.

Related Provisions: 93.3(3), (4)(b) — Special rule for certain Australian trusts.

Notes: See Notes to 233.3(1)"specified foreign property".

233.4(2)(d) added by 2014 budget bill #2, effective for taxation years that end after July 11, 2013.

(3) Application to members of partnerships — For the purpose of this section, a person who is a member of a partnership that is a member of another partnership

(a) is deemed to be a member of the other partnership; and

(b) the person's share of the income or loss of the other partnership is deemed to be equal to the amount of that income or loss to which the person is directly or indirectly entitled.

Related Provisions: 93.1(1) — Shares owned by partnership deemed owned proportionately by partners; 162(7), (10), (10.1) — Penalty for failure to file.

Notes: This rule looks through tiers of partnerships. For the meaning of "indirectly" in para. (b), see Notes to 17.1(1).

(4) Returns respecting foreign affiliates [T1134] — A reporting entity for a taxation year or fiscal period shall file with the Minister for the year or period a return in prescribed form in respect of each foreign affiliate of the entity in the year or period within 10 months after the end of the year or period.

Related Provisions: 95(11) — Deemed separate corp for tracking class; 162(7), (10), (10.1) — Penalty for failure to file; 163(2.4)(d) — Minimum $24,000 penalty for false statement or omission; 220(2.1) — Waiver of filing requirement; 220(3) — Extension of time to file return; 233(2) — Demand for return by partnership; 233.6(2)(d) — No return required on distribution from trust where return required under 233.4; 233.7 — No requirement to file in first year of immigration; *Interpretation Act* 27(5) — Meaning of "within 15 months".

Notes: Form T1134 need not be filed for a foreign affiliate (FA) with gross receipts under $25,000 that at no time in the year had assets over $1m value (a "dormant" or "inactive" company), provided the reporting person has total cost of FAs under $100,000. See instructions on the form, which are a waiver under 220(2.1). A new 15-page T1134 applies since Feb. 2021, requiring far more detail.

Where multiple related taxpayers are in a tiered structure so an FA appears more than once, repetitive reporting was required (VIEWS docs 2009-0316721C6, 2013-0481401C6, 2013-0483811C6 [2013 IFA q.8]). However, CRA now "will accept information limited only to each foreign affiliate of the reporting entity that has a *direct* equity percentage in any other foreign affiliate of the reporting entity": tinyurl.com/cra-t1134. CRA may consider in the future whether there is duplication with 233.8 CbC reporting: 2018-0748151C6 [2018 IFA q.9].

See also Income Tax Folio S5-F3-C1 ¶1.22 (no T1134 needed for Roth IRA if election under Canada-US Treaty Art. XVIII:7 has been filed and no contribution made while resident in Canada); docs 2012-0456491E5 (even if the FA has no year ending in the taxpayer's tax year, T1134 must be filed); 2012-0458601E5 (in determining $25,000 gross receipts for "dormant or inactive FA" where an FA is general partner of an LP, the LP's gross receipts must be counted); 2014-0520091E5 (reporting required for for-

eign corp in process of dissolution); 2017-0691241C6 [2017 IFA q.6] (no relief from duplicate reporting after an amalgamation).

In *Desmarais*, 2013 TCC 356, a 162(7) penalty for not filing the T1134 was cancelled because the FA (a private Russian company 3 levels down through minority interests) was not known to be worth over $1m until it was sold. The penalty was upheld in *RAR Consultants*, 2017 TCC 214.

Information collected under 233.4 is "entered into the Foreign Reporting Requirements Management System ...[which] provides the main risk assessment tool for Aggressive Tax Planning and international auditors": VIEWS doc 2012-045840I17.

See also Paul Hickey, "New Foreign Information Reporting Form", 21(2) *Canadian Tax Highlights* (ctf.ca) 1 (Feb. 2013).

A US citizen with a "controlled foreign corporation" may have to file a Form 5471 (see irs.gov) with the IRS.

233.4(4) amended by 2018 Budget second bill to change "15 months" to "12 months", for tax years and partnership fiscal periods that begin after 2019; and to "10 months" for those beginning after 2020.

I.T. Technical News: 43 (taxation of Roth IRAs).

CRA Audit Manual: 15.7.0: Foreign reporting requirements; 15.10.8: Foreign reporting audit guide; 28.2.4: Foreign reporting — penalties and offences.

Forms: RC257: Request for an information return program account (RZ); T1134: Information return relating to controlled and not-controlled foreign affiliates; T1134-1: Supplement package — reporting entity and information sheet.

Notes [s. 233.4]: 233.4 added by 1996 Budget, effective for returns for taxation years and fiscal periods that begin after 1995 (the first returns were due June 30/98).

See also Notes to 162(10) and 233.7.

Definitions [s. 233.4]: "amount" — 248(1); "Canada" — 255; "controlled foreign affiliate" — 95(1), 248(1); "corporation" — 248(1), *Interpretation Act* 35(1); "direct equity percentage", "equity percentage" — 95(4); "filing-due date" — 248(1); "fiscal period" — 249.1; "foreign affiliate" — 95(1), 233.4(2), 248(1); "non-resident" — 248(1); "partnership" — see 96(1) Notes; "person" — 248(1); "reporting entity" — 233.4(1); "resident in Canada" — 94(3)(a)(vi), 250; "taxation year" — 249; "trust" — 104(1), 248(1), (3).

233.5 Due diligence exception — The information required in a return filed under section 233.2 or 233.4 does not include information that is not available, on the day on which the return is filed, to the person or partnership required to file the return where

(a) there is a reasonable disclosure in the return of the unavailability of the information;

(b) before that day, the person or partnership exercised due diligence in attempting to obtain the information;

(c) if the return is required to be filed under section 233.2 in respect of a trust, at the time of each transaction, if any, entered into by the person or partnership after March 5, 1996 and before June 23, 2000 that gave rise to the requirement to file a return for a taxation year of the trust that ended before 2007 or that affects the information to be reported in the return, it was reasonable to expect that sufficient information would be available to the person or partnership to comply with section 233.2 in respect of each taxation year of the trust that ended before 2007;

(c.1) if the return is required to be filed under section 233.2, at the time of each contribution (determined with reference to subsection 233.2(2)) made by the person or partnership after June 22, 2000 that gives rise to the requirement to file the return or that affects the information to be reported in the return, it was reasonable to expect that sufficient information would be available to the person or partnership to comply with section 233.2;

(c.2) if the return is required to be filed under section 233.4 by a person or partnership in respect of a corporation that is a controlled foreign affiliate for the purpose of that section of the person or partnership, at the time of each transaction, if any, entered into by the person or partnership after March 5, 1996 that gives rise to the requirement to file the return or that affects the information to be reported in the return, it was reasonable to expect that sufficient information would be available to the person or partnership to comply with section 233.4; and

(d) if the information subsequently becomes available to the person or partnership, it is filed with the Minister not more than 90 days after it becomes so available.

Related Provisions: 233.2(2) — Application of non-resident trust rules to 233.5(c.1); 233.2(4.1) — Foreign arrangements similar to trusts.

Notes: If a foreign affiliate has not prepared financial statements because the due date is before its year-end, the information to be filed will be minimal, but the Disclosure section of the form should still be completed to meet the due-diligence test: VIEWS doc 2012-0456491E5.

233.5(c) amended and (c.1) and (c.2) added by 2002-2013 technical bill (Part 1 — NRTs), effective for returns in respect of trust taxation years that end after 2006, and also in respect of an earlier taxation year of a trust if amended 94(1) applies to that earlier taxation year (see Notes at end of s. 94).

233.5 added by 1996 Budget, effective for returns required to be filed by April 30, 1998 or later.

Definitions [s. 233.5]: "corporation" — 248(1), *Interpretation Act* 35(1); "controlled foreign affiliate" — 95(1), 248(1); "Minister" — 248(1); "partnership" — see 96(1) Notes; "person" — 248(1).

CRA Audit Manual: 15.7.5: Foreign reporting requirements — penalties; 15.10.8: Foreign reporting audit guide; 28.2.4: Foreign reporting — penalties and offences; 28.11.3: Due diligence — section 233.5.

233.6 (1) Returns respecting distributions from non-resident trusts [T1142] — Where a specified Canadian entity (as defined by subsection 233.3(1)) for a taxation year or fiscal period receives a distribution of property from, or is indebted to, a non-resident trust (other than a trust that was an excluded trust in respect of the year or period of the entity or an estate that arose on and as a consequence of the death of an individual) in the year or period and the entity is beneficially interested in the trust at any time in the year or period, the entity shall file with the Minister for the year or period a return in prescribed form on or before the day that is

(a) where the entity is a partnership, the day on or before which a return is required by section 229 of the *Income Tax Regulations* to be filed in respect of the fiscal period of the partnership or would be required to be so filed if that section applied to the partnership; and

(b) where the entity is not a partnership, the entity's filing-due date for the year.

Related Provisions: 162(7) — Penalty for failure to file; 163(2.4)(e) — Minimum $2,500 penalty for false statement or omission; 220(2.1) — Waiver of filing requirement; 220(3) — Extension of time to file return; 233.6(2) — Meaning of "excluded trust"; 233.7 — No requirement to file in first year of immigration; 248(8) — Meaning of "consequence" of death; 248(25) — Extended meaning of "beneficially interested".

Notes: See Notes to 162(10) and 233.7.

The exception for "an estate that arose on and as a consequence of the death" applied to income from a non-resident testamentary trust in *Hess*, 2011 TCC 360 (effectively overruling VIEWS docs 2007-0233741C6, 2009-0332521I7).

A dual resident must file a T1142: VIEWS doc 2011-0407681E5. A T1142 may have to be filed by beneficiaries of a foreign exchange-traded fund that is a trust: 2008-02842161C6. It is not needed by a Roth IRA, if a Canada-US Treaty Art. XVIII:7 election has been filed and no contribution is made while resident in Canada: Income Tax Folio S5-F3-C1 ¶1.22.

Information collected under 233.6 is "entered into the Foreign Reporting Requirements Management System ... [which] provides the main risk assessment tool for Aggressive Tax Planning and international auditors": VIEWS doc 2012-045840117.

CRA Audit Manual: 15.7.0: Foreign reporting requirements; 15.10.8: Foreign reporting audit guide; 28.2.4: Foreign reporting — penalties and offences.

Forms: T1142: Information return re distributions from and indebtedness to a non-resident trust.

(2) Excluded trust defined — For the purpose of subsection (1), an excluded trust in respect of the taxation year or fiscal period of an entity means

(a) a trust described in paragraph (a) or (b) of the definition "exempt trust" in subsection 233.2(1) throughout the portion of the year or period during which the trust was extant;

(b) a trust in respect of which the entity is required by section 233.2 to file a return in respect of each taxation year of the trust that ends in the entity's year;

(c) a trust an interest in which is at any time in the year or period specified foreign property (as defined by subsection 233.3(1)) of the entity, where the entity is a reporting entity (as defined by subsection 233.3(1)) for the year or period; and

(d) a trust in respect of which the entity is required by section 233.4 to file a return for the year or period.

Related Provisions [subsec. 233.6(2)]: 233(1) — Demand for return by partnership.

Notes [s. 233.6]: 233.6 added by 1996 Budget, effective for returns for taxation years and fiscal periods that begin after 1995, with transitional rules (as amended by 1998 Budget bill, s. 91) for periods that ended before 1999.

See also Notes to 233.7.

Definitions [s. 233.6]: "beneficially interested" — 248(25); "consequence of the death" — 248(8); "excluded trust" — 233.6(2); "specified Canadian entity" — 233.3(1).

233.7 Exception for first-year residents — Notwithstanding sections 233.2, 233.3, 233.4 and 233.6, a person who, but for this section, would be required under any of those sections to file an information return for a taxation year, is not required to file the return if the person is an individual (other than a trust) who first became resident in Canada in the year.

Notes: 233.7 added by 1996 Budget, effective for returns required to be filed by April 30, 1998 or later (i.e., all returns under 233.2–233.6).

CRA's view is that "first became resident" applies only to a person who was never previously Canadian resident: VIEWS doc 2009-0315911E5.

For review of 233.2–233.7 see Joel Nitikman, "The New Foreign Property Reporting Rules", 44(2) *Canadian Tax Journal* 425-50 (1996); Colin Campbell, *Administration of Income Tax 2020* (Carswell), §3.6; VIEWS doc 2006-0185642C6.

Definitions [s. 233.7]: "individual", "person" — 248(1); "resident in Canada" — 250; "taxation year" — 249; "trust" — 104(1), 248(1), (3).

233.8 Country-by-country report [large multinationals] — definitions — (1) The following definitions apply in this section.

"business entity" means

(a) a person (other than an individual that is not a trust) or partnership; and

(b) a business that is carried on through a permanent establishment, if a separate financial statement for the business is prepared for financial reporting, regulatory, tax reporting or internal management control purposes.

Notes: See Notes at end of 233.8.

"consolidated financial statements" means financial statements in which the assets, liabilities, income, expenses and cash flows of the members of a group are presented as those of a single economic entity.

Related Provisions: 110(0.1)"consolidated financial statements" — Definition applies to stock option limits.

"constituent entity", of an MNE group, means

(a) any business entity of the MNE group that

(i) is included in the consolidated financial statements of the MNE group for financial reporting purposes, or

(ii) would be required to be included if equity interests in any of the business entities in the MNE group were traded on a public securities exchange; and

(b) any business entity that is excluded from the MNE group's consolidated financial statements solely because of size or materiality.

"excluded MNE group" means two or more business entities that meet the conditions in paragraphs (a) and (b) of the definition "MNE group", if, with respect to a particular fiscal year of the MNE group, it has a total consolidated group revenue of less than €750 million during the fiscal year immediately preceding the particular fiscal year, as reflected in its consolidated financial statements for the preceding fiscal year.

"fiscal year", of an MNE group, means an annual accounting period with respect to which the ultimate parent entity of the MNE group prepares its financial statements.

"multinational enterprise group" or **"MNE group"** means two or more business entities, if

(a) they are either required to prepare consolidated financial statements for financial reporting purposes under applicable accounting principles or would be so required if equity interests in any of the business entities were traded on a public securities exchange;

(b) one of the business entities is resident in a particular jurisdiction and

(i) another business entity resides in a different jurisdiction, or

(ii) is subject to tax in a different jurisdiction with respect to a business carried on by it through a business entity — described in paragraph (b) of the definition "business entity" — in that other jurisdiction; and

(c) they are not an excluded MNE group.

"permanent establishment" has the meaning assigned by regulation.

Regulations: 8201 (meaning of permanent establishment).

"qualifying competent authority agreement" means an agreement that

(a) is between authorized representatives of those jurisdictions that are parties to a listed international agreement; and

(b) requires the automatic exchange of country-by-country reports between the party jurisdictions.

"reporting fiscal year" means a fiscal year, if the financial and operational results of the fiscal year are reflected in the country-by-country report.

"surrogate parent entity" means a constituent entity of an MNE group that has been appointed by the MNE group — in substitution for the ultimate parent entity — to file the country-by-country report on behalf of the MNE group, if one or more of the conditions in subparagraph (3)(b)(ii) applies.

"systemic failure" means, with respect to a jurisdiction, that the jurisdiction has a qualifying competent authority agreement in effect with Canada, but

(a) has suspended automatic exchange (for reasons other than those that are in accordance with the terms of the agreement); or

(b) has persistently failed to automatically provide country-by-country reports in its possession — in respect of MNE groups that have constituent entities in Canada — to Canada.

"ultimate parent entity" means a constituent entity of an MNE group that meets the following conditions:

(a) the constituent entity holds directly or indirectly a sufficient interest in one or more constituent entities of the MNE group so that it is required to prepare consolidated financial statements under accounting principles generally applied in its jurisdiction of residence, or would be so required if its equity interests were traded on a public securities exchange in its jurisdiction of residence; and

(b) no other constituent entity of the MNE group holds, directly or indirectly, an interest in it that is described in paragraph (a).

Related Provisions: 233.8(2) — Determination of ultimate parent entity's residence.

(2) Determination of residence — ultimate parent entity — For the purposes of this section, if an ultimate parent entity is a partnership, it is deemed to be resident

(a) if it is, under the laws of another jurisdiction, resident in that other jurisdiction for tax purposes, in that other jurisdiction; and

(b) in any other case, in the jurisdiction under the laws of which it was organized.

(3) Filing obligations — A report in prescribed form (this report, along with each substantially similar report required to be filed in a jurisdiction other than Canada, collectively referred to in this section as a **"country-by-country report"**), in respect of a reporting fiscal year of an MNE group, shall be filed in prescribed manner

with the Minister on or before the date specified in subsection (6) by

(a) the ultimate parent entity of the MNE group, if it is resident in Canada in the reporting fiscal year; or

(b) a constituent entity of the MNE group — which is not the ultimate parent entity of the MNE group — with respect to the reporting fiscal year of the MNE group, if the following conditions are satisfied:

(i) the constituent entity is resident in Canada in the reporting fiscal year, and

(ii) one of the following conditions applies:

(A) the ultimate parent entity of the MNE group is not obligated to file a country-by-country report in its jurisdiction of residence,

(B) the jurisdiction of residence of the ultimate parent entity of the MNE group does not have a qualifying competent authority agreement in effect to which Canada is a party on or before the time specified in subsection (6) for filing the country-by-country report for the reporting fiscal year, or

(C) there has been a systemic failure of the jurisdiction of residence of the ultimate parent entity and the Minister has notified the constituent entity of the systemic failure.

Related Provisions: 162(10)(a) — Penalty for failure to file; 233.8(4) — Designation of which constituent entity will file; 233.8(5) — Filing not required if surrogate parent files elsewhere residence.

Notes: See Notes at end of 233.8.

Forms: RC4649: Country-by-country report.

(4) Designation for multiple constituent entities — If more than one constituent entity of an MNE group is described in paragraph (3)(b) in respect of a reporting fiscal year, one of those constituent entities may be designated — on or before the date specified in subsection (6) in respect of the reporting fiscal year — so that it is entitled to file a country-by-country report for the reporting fiscal year with the Minister on behalf of all such constituent entities in the MNE group.

(5) Surrogate filing — Notwithstanding subsection (3), a constituent entity of an MNE group described in paragraph (3)(b) is not required to file a country-by-country report with the Minister with respect to a reporting fiscal year if

(a) a surrogate parent entity of the MNE group files a country-by-country report in respect of the reporting fiscal year with the tax authority of its jurisdiction of residence on or before the date specified in subsection (6); and

(b) the jurisdiction of residence of the surrogate parent entity

(i) requires filing of country-by-country reports,

(ii) has a qualifying competent authority agreement in effect to which Canada is a party on or before the time specified in subsection (6) for filing the country-by-country report in respect of the reporting fiscal year,

(iii) is not in a position of systemic failure, and

(iv) has been notified by the surrogate parent entity that it is the surrogate parent entity.

(6) Time for filing — A country-by-country report in respect of a reporting fiscal year of an MNE group that is required to be filed by a constituent entity under this section shall be filed on or before the later of

(a) if notification of systemic failure has been received by the constituent entity, 30 days after receipt of the notification, and

(b) 12 months after the last day of the reporting fiscal year.

Notes [s. 233.8]: 233.8 implements "country-by-country" (CbC) reporting of transfer pricing information, required by multinational enterprises (MNEs) with more than €750 million annual revenues [see 233.8(1)"excluded MNE group"], as per OECD BEPS project Action 13 (see Proposed Amendments box at end of s. 95). CRA expected about 120 country-by-country reports to be filed by Canadian multinationals in 2017. For Canada's transfer pricing rules see 247(2).

See RC4651, *Guidance on Country-by-Country Reporting in Canada*; OECD Guidance (Dec. 2019) at tinyurl.com/oecd-cbc-guide. Form RC4649 must be filed [233.8(3)] with the tax administration of the country in which the MNE's "ultimate parent entity" [233.8(1)] resides. A CbC report includes the global allocation, by country, of key variables for the MNE including: revenue, profit, tax paid, stated capital, accumulated earnings, number of employees and tangible assets, as well as the main activities of each of its subsidiaries.

A country receiving a CbC report will automatically exchange it with other countries in which the MNE operates, where the other country has implemented CbC reporting, the two countries have a legal framework in place for automatic exchange of information [233.8(1)"qualifying competent authority agreement"], and they have entered into a competent authority agreement relating to CbC reporting. If country S where a subsidiary resides cannot obtain the CbC report from the parent's country automatically, then in certain cases S's tax administration may require the subsidiary to file the CbC report. An MNE can avoid having this filing requirement imposed on multiple subsidiaries in multiple countries by designating one subsidiary to be a "surrogate" for filing purposes [233.8(5)]. As long as the surrogate is in a country that has implemented CbC reporting, the surrogate would file the CbC report for the MNE as a whole.

Where an MNE's ultimate parent entity is resident in Canada (or a Canadian resident subsidiary in the circumstances set out above), it must file a CbC report with the CRA within 1 year of fiscal year-end [233.8(6)]. First exchanges between countries of CbC reports are expected by June 2018. Before any exchange with another country, the CRA will formalize an exchange arrangement that ensures the country has appropriate safeguards in place to protect confidentiality of the reports.

Canada and the US signed an "arrangement" on the exchange of CbC reports on June 7, 2017 (CRA news release, June 8/17). Reports will first be exchanged for the fiscal years of multinational groups that begin on or after Jan. 1, 2016. Reports will be exchanged no later than 15 months after the last day of the fiscal year of the group (for the 2016 year, 18 months). Under the arrangement, the information can be used only to assess high-level transfer pricing risks and risks related to BEPS. Where appropriate, it can also be used for economic and statistical analysis. The data from a report may be used to make further enquiries into the affairs of multinational groups in the course of an audit and, then, to make adjustments to taxable income. The information cannot be used as a substitute for a detailed transfer pricing analysis of individual transactions and prices based on a full functional and comparability analysis.

See CRA, "Statement by the Minister of National Revenue on Canada's successful first exchange of the Country-by-Country Reporting initiative" (July 10, 2018).

The OECD concluded in *Country-by-Country Reporting — Compilation of Peer Review Reports (Phase 2)* (Sept. 2019), p. 113, that "Canada's implementation ... meets all applicable terms of reference".

In the US, reporting is required on Form 8975: Reg. TD 9773 (tinyurl.com/us-irs-cbc).

See also Cockfield & MacArthur, "Country-by-Country Reporting and Commercial Confidentiality", 63(3) *Canadian Tax Journal* 627-60 (2015); Zorzi & Spencer, "BEPS Action 13", 2015 Cdn Tax Foundation annual conference report, pp. 27:1-26; Baker & Dujsic, "Country-by-Country Reporting", 25(3) *Canadian Tax Highlights [CTH]* (ctf.ca) 2-3 (March 2017); Doobay, "US Country-by-Country Reporting", 25(4) *CTH* 6-7 (April 2017); Hu, "CRA Form for Country-by-Country Reporting", 7(2) *Canadian Tax Focus* (ctf.ca) 8 (May 2017); Davis, "CRA and IRS to Begin Country-By-Country Exchanges", *Transfer Pricing Newsletter*, Taxnet Pro Corporate Tax Centre (Sept. 2017); Williams, "Country-by-Country Reporting", 2016 conference report, 22:1-20; "The CbC Challenge", 2450 *Tax Topics* (CCH) 1-3 (Feb. 21, 2019).

See also VIEWS doc 2016-0669801C6 [2016 CTF q.9] (233.8 addresses BEPS Action 13 but does not include a requirement to produce a "local file" or "master file").

233.8 added by 2016 budget bill #2, for reporting fiscal years of MNE groups that begin after 2015.

Definitions [s. 233.8]: "business" — 248(1); "business entity" — 233.8(1); "Canada" — 255, *Interpretation Act* 35(1); "consolidated financial statements", "constituent entity" — 233.8(1); "country-by-country report" — 233.8(3); "excluded MNE group" — 233.8(1); "fiscal year" — 233.8(1); "individual", "listed international agreement" — 248(1); "MNE group" — 233.8(1)"multinational enterprise group"; "Minister" — 248(1); "month" — *Interpretation Act* 35(1); "multinational enterprise group" — 233.8(1); "partnership" — see 96(1) Notes; "permanent establishment" — 233.8(1), Reg. 8201; "person", "prescribed" — 248(1); "qualifying competent authority agreement" — 233.8(1); "regulation" — 248(1); "reporting fiscal year" — 233.8(1); "resident" — 250; "resident in Canada" — 94(3)(a), 250; "surrogate parent entity", "systemic failure" — 233.8(1); "trust" — 104(1), 248(1), (3); "ultimate parent entity" — 233.8(1).

234. (1) Ownership certificates — Before a bearer coupon or warrant representing either interest or dividends payable by any debtor or cheque representing dividends or interest payable by a non-resident debtor is negotiated by or on behalf of a resident of Canada, there shall be completed by or on behalf of the resident an ownership certificate in prescribed form.

Related Provisions: 162(4) — Failure to complete ownership certificate.

Forms: NR601: Non-resident ownership certificate — withholding tax; NR602: Non-resident ownership certificate — no withholding tax; T600: Ownership certificate; T600B: Ownership certificate.

(2) Idem — An ownership certificate completed pursuant to subsection (1) shall be delivered in such manner, at such time and at such place as may be prescribed.

Regulations: 207 (prescribed time).

Forms: NR601: Non-resident ownership certificate — withholding tax; NR602: Non-resident ownership certificate — no withholding tax.

(3) Idem — The operation of this section may be extended by regulation to bearer coupons or warrants negotiated by or on behalf of non-resident persons.

(4)–(6) [Repealed under former Act]

Notes: 234(4), repealed by 1988 tax reform, provided a fine for failure to deliver an ownership certificate. See now 162(4)(b).

234(5) and (6), repealed by 1980 Budget, imposed a requirement to withhold 25% of amounts paid on bearer bonds and warrants (such as Canada Savings Bonds) where the ownership certificate did not disclose a Social Insurance Number.

Definitions [s. 234]: "amount", "dividend", "individual", "non-resident", "person", "prescribed", "regulation" — 248(1); "resident of Canada" — 94(3)(a), 250; "trust" — 104(1), 248(1), (3).

234.1 [Repealed under former Act]

Notes: 234.1, repealed in 1983, required fuel certificates for aviation turbine fuel.

235. Penalty for failing to file corporate returns [large corporations] — Every large corporation (within the meaning assigned by subsection 225.1(8)) that fails to file a return for a taxation year as and when required by section 150 or 190.2 is liable, in addition to any penalty otherwise provided, to a penalty for each such failure equal to the amount determined by the formula

$$A \times B$$

where

A is the total of

    (a) 0.0005% of the corporation's taxable capital employed in Canada at the end of the taxation year, and

    (b) 0.25% of the tax that would be payable under Part VI by the corporation for the year if this Act were read without reference to subsection 190.1(3); and

B is the number of complete months, not exceeding 40, from the day on or before which the return was required to be filed to the day on which the return is filed.

Related Provisions: 18(1)(t) — No deduction for penalties; 161(11) — Interest on unpaid penalties; 220(3.1) — Waiver of penalty by CRA; 227(10)(a) — Assessment.

Notes: 235 imposes a penalty on large corporations that fail to file their returns on time, even if no tax remains unpaid (see 162(1)). See Notes to 239(1). With the repeal of the Large Corporations Tax as of 2006, 235 no longer applies to a failure to file a Part I.3 return, but the penalty continues to be calculated by reference to Part I.3's "taxable capital employed in Canada", as well as tax payable under Part VI.

235 amended by 2006 Budget, for 2006 and later tax years. Earlier amended by 1992 technical bill; added by 1991 technical bill.

Definitions [s. 235]: "amount" — 248(1); "corporation" — 248(1), *Interpretation Act* 35(1); "large corporation" — 225.1(8); "month" — *Interpretation Act* 35(1); "taxable capital employed in Canada" — 181.2(1), 181.3(1), 181.4 [technically do not apply]; "taxation year" — 249.

Information Circulars: 00-1R4: Voluntary disclosures program.

CRA Audit Manual: 28.2.3: Penalties — failure to file certain corporate returns.

236. Execution of documents by corporations — A return, certificate or other document made by a corporation pursuant to this Act or a regulation shall be signed on its behalf by the President, Secretary or Treasurer of the corporation or by any other officer or person thereunto duly authorized by the Board of Directors or other governing body of the corporation.

Related Provisions: 227.1 — Liability of directors; 242 — officers and directors of corporation guilty of corporate offences.

Definitions [s. 236]: "corporation" — 248(1), *Interpretation Act* 35(1); "officer", "person", "regulation" — 248(1).

237. (1) Social Insurance Number — Every individual (other than a trust) who was resident or employed in Canada at any time in

a taxation year and who files a return of income under Part I for the year, or in respect of whom an information return is to be made by a person pursuant to a regulation made under paragraph 221(1)(d), shall,

(a) on or before the first day of February of the year immediately following the year for which the return of income is filed, or

(b) within 15 days after the individual is requested by the person to provide his[29] Social Insurance Number,

apply to the Canada Employment Insurance Commission in prescribed form and manner for the assignment to the individual of a Social Insurance Number unless the individual has previously been assigned, or made application to be assigned, a Social Insurance Number.

Related Provisions: 162(6) — Penalty for failure to provide Social Insurance Number; 221(1)(d.1) — Regulations may require disclosure of Social Insurance Number; 237(1.1), (2) — Obligations re Social Insurance Number; 239(2.3) — Offence re Social Insurance Number; *Interpretation Act* 27(5) — Meaning of "within 15 days".

Notes: See Notes to 248(1)"business number".

There is no statutory requirement for an RRSP annuitant to have a SIN, but the CRA requires it before registering the RRSP: VIEWS doc 2007-0240191C6.

Non-resident individuals who have no SIN must apply for an Individual Tax Number (ITN) on Form T1261 to do business with CRA: VIEWS doc 2008-0278801C6 q.7. However, s. 237 does not apply to the ITN: CRA Registered Plans Directorate, 2008 *Specialty Products Practitioners' Forum* q.6 (doc 2009-05-08B on *TaxPartner* or *Taxnet Pro*).

Closing words of 237(1) amended to change "Minister of Human Resources Development" to "Canada Employment Insurance Commission" by S.C. 2005, c. 34, proclaimed in force Oct. 5, 2005. 237(1) earlier amended by 1995-97 technical bill (effective June 18, 1998) and S.C. 1996, c. 11.

Regulations: 3800 (how Social Insurance Number to be applied for).

Information Circulars: 82-2R2: SIN legislation that relates to the preparation of information slips.

Forms: T600: Ownership certificate; T1261: Application for a CRA individual tax number (ITN) for non-residents.

(1.1) Production of number — Every person and partnership shall provide their designated number

(a) in any return filed under this Act; and

(b) to another person or partnership at the request of the other person or partnership, if the other person or partnership is required to make an information return pursuant to this Act or the Regulations requiring the designated number.

Related Provisions: 237(1.2) — Designated number; 237(2) — Obligations of person required to obtain number.

Notes: An investor must provide his/her SIN to a payer to enable preparation of a T5: VIEWS doc 2011-0419251E5.

237(1.1) amended by 2018 budget bill #1, for 2018 and later tax years, effectively to add reference to a trust account number (see 237(1.2)(b)). For earlier years, read:

(1.1) Every person and partnership shall provide

(a) in the case of an individual (other than a trust), the individual's Social Insurance Number, and

(b) in any other case, the person's or partnership's business number

in any return filed under this Act or, at the request of any person required to make an information return pursuant to this Act or the regulations requiring either number, to that person.

237(1.1) added by 1995-97 technical bill, effective June 18, 1998. This requirement (but only in respect of a SIN) was formerly in the closing words of 237(1).

(1.2) Designated number — For the purpose of subsection (1.1), "designated number", of a person or partnership, means

(a) in the case of an individual (other than a trust), their Social Insurance Number;

(b) in the case of a trust, its trust account number; and

(c) in any other case, the person's or partnership's business number.

Notes: 237(1.2) added by 2018 budget bill #1, for 2018 and later tax years. See Notes to 237(1.1).

(2) Number required in information returns — For the purposes of this Act and the Regulations, a person or partnership required to make an information return requiring a business number, Social Insurance Number or trust account number of another person or partnership

(a) shall make a reasonable effort to obtain the number from the other person or partnership; and

(b) shall not knowingly use, communicate or allow to be communicated, otherwise than as required or authorized under this Act or a regulation, the number without the written consent of the other person or partnership.

Related Provisions: 162(6) — Failure to provide Social Insurance Number; 237(3) — Communication to related person allowed; 237(4) — Communication allowed to agent during insurance demutualization; 239(2.3) — Offence re Social Insurance Number or business number.

Notes: 237(2) amended by 2018 budget bill #1, for 2018 and later tax years, to change "a person" to "a person or partnership" and add reference to a trust account number. Earlier amended by 1999 Budget, 1995-97 technical bill.

Information Circulars: 82-2R2: SIN legislation that relates to the preparation of information slips.

Registered Plans Compliance Bulletins: 8 (prescribed information to register an education savings plan).

Forms: T1204: Government service contract payments.

(3) Authority to communicate number — A particular person may communicate, or allow to be communicated, a business number, Social Insurance Number or trust account number to another person related to the particular person where the other person is required, by this Act or the Regulations, to make an information return that requires the number.

Notes: An employer may not disclose employees' SINs to a union, even under a negotiated term of a collective agreement, unless required for some purpose by the Act: VIEWS docs 2005-0148331E5, 2011-0422501E5.

237(3) amended by 2018 budget bill #1, for 2018 and later tax years, to add reference to a trust account number.

237(3) added by 1999 Budget, effective June 29, 2000.

(4) Authority to communicate number [for demutualization] — An insurance corporation may communicate, or allow to be communicated, to another person the business number, Social Insurance Number or trust account number of a particular person or partnership if

(a) the other person became the holder of a share of the capital stock of the insurance corporation, or of a holding corporation (in this subsection having the meaning assigned by subsection 139.1(1)) in respect of the insurance corporation, on the share's issuance in connection with the demutualization (as defined by subsection 139.1(1)) of the insurance corporation;

(b) the other person became the holder of the share in the other person's capacity as nominee or agent for the particular person or partnership pursuant to an arrangement established by the insurance corporation or a holding corporation in respect of the insurance corporation; and

(c) the other person is required, by this Act or the Regulations, to make an information return, in respect of the disposition of the share or income from the share, that requires the number.

Notes: 237(4) amended by 2018 budget bill #1, for 2018 and later tax years, to add reference to a trust account number.

237(4) added by 1999 Budget, effective June 29, 2000.

Definitions [s. 237]: "business number" — 248(1); "Canada" — 255; "demutualization" — 139.1(1); "designated number" — 237(1.2); "employed" — 248(1); "holding corporation" — 139.1(1); "individual" — 248(1); "partnership" — see 96(1) Notes; "person", "prescribed", "regulation" — 248(1); "related" — 251(1)–(6); "taxation year" — 249; "trust" — 104(1), 248(1), (3); "trust account number" — 248(1); "written" — *Interpretation Act* 35(1)"writing".

237.1 [Tax shelters] — (1) Definitions — In this section,

---

[29] *Sic*. Should be "the individual's".

"gifting arrangement" means any arrangement under which it may reasonably be considered, having regard to statements or representations made or proposed to be made in connection with the arrangement, that if a person were to enter into the arrangement, the person would

(a) make a gift to a qualified donee, or a contribution referred to in subsection 127(4.1), of property acquired by the person under the arrangement; or

(b) incur a limited-recourse debt, determined under subsection 143.2(6.1), that can reasonably be considered to relate to a gift to a qualified donee or a monetary contribution referred to in subsection 127(4.1);

Related Provisions: 225.1(7) — Charitable donation shelter assessment can be half-collected while under appeal; 248(35)–(37) — Value of gift limited to cost if acquired within 3 years or as gifting arrangement.

Notes: This definition is broad and does not require the existence of an agreement to acquire property: VIEWS doc 2004-0098191E5.

For gifting arrangements with favourable rulings, see Notes to 38 re 38(a.1) flow-through share donations. For discussion of "bad" donation shelters, see Notes to 118.1(1)"total charitable gifts". The CRA will not assess returns claiming donation shelters until it has audited the shelter.

The Strategic Gifting scheme was held to be a gifting arrangement: *Murji*, 2018 TCC 7.

Para. (b) amended by 2002-2013 technical bill (Part 5 — technical), effective for gifts and monetary contributions made after 6pm EST on Dec. 5, 2003.

Definition "gifting arrangement" added by 2003 Budget (see Notes to 237.1(1)"tax shelter"), effective as follows: opening words are effective February 19, 2003; para. (a) is effective in respect of property acquired, and statements and representations made, after February 18, 2003; and para. (b) is effective in respect of property acquired, and gifts, contributions, statements and representations made, after February 18, 2003.

I.T. Technical News: 41 (donation of flow-through shares).

Registered Charities Newsletters: 29 (tax shelter gifting arrangements).

"person" includes a partnership;

Notes: Definition "person" added by 1995-97 technical bill, effective December 1994.

"promoter" in respect of a tax shelter means a person who in the course of a business

(a) sells or issues, or promotes the sale, issuance or acquisition of, the tax shelter,

(b) acts as an agent or adviser in respect of the sale or issuance, or the promotion of the sale, issuance or acquisition, of the tax shelter, or

(c) accepts, whether as a principal or agent, consideration in respect of the tax shelter,

and more than one person may be a tax shelter promoter in respect of the same tax shelter;

Related Provisions: 149.1(1)"promoter" — Definition applies for purposes of 149.1(1); 163.2 — Penalty for false statement by tax shelter promoter.

Notes: For discussion of the meaning of "promoter" see CRA instructions to Form T5001, and the Kepes article in Notes to 237.1(1)"tax shelter". In *Kinglon Investments*, 2014 TCC 131; rev'd 2015 FCA 134, portions of the Crown's Reply were initially struck (with leave to amend) because it did not clearly specify facts that would lead to a finding that statements or representations had been made by a "promoter"; but this was reversed as it is a possible interpretation that "a tax shelter can exist regardless of who makes the statements or representations so long as they are made to the taxpayer" (FCA, para. 18). See Gislason, "A Further Revision to the Definition of Tax Shelters", 2266 *Tax Topics* (CCH) 1-4 (Aug. 13, 2015).

For discussion of lawyers' obligations to promoters (and some history of film shelter deals) see *Strother*, 2007 SCC 24.

Definition "promoter" amended by 1995-97 technical bill, effective Dec. 2, 1994.

Forms: T5001: Application for a tax shelter identification number and undertaking to keep books and records; T5001-INSTR: Instructions for applying for a tax shelter identification number [instructions guide].

"tax shelter" means

(a) a gifting arrangement described by paragraph (b) of the definition "gifting arrangement"; and

(b) a gifting arrangement described by paragraph (a) of the definition "gifting arrangement", or a property (including any right to income) other than a flow-through share or a prescribed property, in respect of which it can reasonably be considered, having regard to statements or representations made or proposed to be made in connection with the gifting arrangement or the property, that, if a person were to enter into the gifting arrangement or acquire an interest in the property, at the end of a particular taxation year that ends within four years after the day on which the gifting arrangement is entered into or the interest is acquired,

(i) the total of all amounts each of which is

(A) an amount, or a loss in the case of a partnership interest, represented to be deductible in computing the person's income for the particular year or any preceding taxation year in respect of the gifting arrangement or the interest in the property (including, if the property is a right to income, an amount or loss in respect of that right that is stated or represented to be so deductible), or

(B) any other amount stated or represented to be deemed under this Act to be paid on account of the person's tax payable, or to be deductible in computing the person's income, taxable income or tax payable under this Act, for the particular year or any preceding taxation year in respect of the gifting arrangement or the interest in the property, other than an amount so stated or represented that is included in computing a loss described in clause (A),

would equal or exceed

(ii) the amount, if any, by which

(A) the cost to the person of the property acquired under the gifting arrangement, or of the interest in the property at the end of the particular year, determined without reference to section 143.2,

would exceed

(B) the total of all amounts each of which is the amount of any prescribed benefit that is expected to be received or enjoyed, directly or indirectly, in respect of the property acquired under the gifting arrangement, or of the interest in the property, by the person or another person with whom the person does not deal at arm's length.

Related Provisions: 18.1(1)"tax shelter" — Definition for purposes of matchable expenditure rules; 53(2)(c)(i.3) — Tax shelter excluded from certain ACB reductions; 127.52(1)(c.3) — Minimum tax on tax shelter deductions; 143.2(1)"tax shelter investment"(a) — Definition includes a tax shelter under 237.1(1); 143.2(6), (6.1) — Limitations on cost of tax shelter; 163.2(1)"excluded activity"(a)(i) — No good-faith reliance defence for advisor assessed third-party penalty re tax shelter; 174 — All taxpayers in same shelter can be bound by one Tax Court decision; 225.1(7) — Charitable donation shelter assessment can be half-collected while under appeal; 237.1(6) — Deductions and claims denied if form not filed; 237.1(7) — Information reporting required for tax shelter; 237.3 — Information reporting required for "reportable transaction"; 248(1)"tax shelter" — Definition applies to entire Act; 249.1(5) — Election for non-calendar year-end not permitted for tax shelters; Reg. 1100(20.1), (20.2) — Limitation on CCA claim for computer tax shelter property.

Notes: The federal government cannot regulate tax shelters directly (e.g., shut them down) because that is provincial jurisdiction under the *Constitution Act, 1867*. Regulation is done by requiring taxpayers claiming tax shelter benefits to provide the shelter number on a T5004 with their return. See also the disclosure requirements in 237.3.

The core of the definition (other than for donation schemes) is in para. (b) after the first few words: "or a property ... in respect of which it can reasonably be considered...". The test should be applied separately to each property acquired, not including related interest expense: *Lee*, 2020 QCCQ 780, paras. 544-560 (parallel Quebec rule).

Form T5001 has been expanded to require detailed information before a tax shelter number is issued, thus giving CRA extensive audit assistance.

In CRA's view, "cost" in (b)(ii)(A) likely does not include interest expense: 2006 Cdn Tax Foundation annual conference roundtable (Nov. 28, 2006, slides available). The elimination of capital gain on donated securities (38(a.1)) could create a tax shelter, but 248(37)(d) will prevent 248(35) applying to deny the donation credit: VIEWS doc 2006-01970521C6.

For the meaning of "indirectly" in (b)(ii)(B), see Notes to 17.1(1).

A packaged purchase and donation of flow-through shares is a tax shelter: *Income Tax Technical News* 41, VIEWS doc 2008-0289451C6 (see Notes to 38 re 38(a.1)).

The determination of "tax shelter" is always a question of fact, so CRA may refrain from expressing an opinion: VIEWS doc 2009-0339761E5.

The "prescribed benefits" that can cause there to be a tax shelter include revenue guarantees and situations where the indebtedness will still be outstanding after many years. See Reg. 3100(1)(b)(ii) and VIEWS doc 2008-0302981E5.

For discussion see Kepes, "Tax Shelter Application Form Requires Full Disclosure and Targets Tax Advisers", 16(3) *Taxation Law* (Ontario Bar Assn, oba.org) 7-14 (June 2006); McGowan, "Tax Shelters", 2006 Cdn Tax Foundation conference report, 37:1-17; Campbell, *Administration of Income Tax 2020* (Carswell), §3.5. See also 143.2.

Investments were found to be a "tax shelter" and deductions were denied under 237.1(6) in: *Baxter*, 2007 FCA 172 (leave to appeal denied 2007 CarswellNat 3625 (SCC)); *Krumm*, 2021 FCA 78 (software; the tax shelter rules are not limited to publicly marketed transactions); *Haggarty*, 2003 TCC 358; *Labelle*, 2003 TCC 905; *Malo*, 2012 TCC 75 (FCA appeal discontinued A-98-12) (Maya tree-planting); *Gleig*, 2015 TCC 191 (para. 42: holder never demanded payment on promissory notes so this was prescribed benefit under [now] Reg. 3100); *Murji*, 2018 TCC 7 (Strategic Gifting scheme); *Paletta*, 2019 TCC 205 (under appeal to FCA), paras. 260-271 (film investment); *Lee*, 2020 QCCQ 780, paras. 351-400 (Prospector Networks software: parallel Quebec rule; at paras. 441-445 deductions disallowed included all interest expense; at paras. 418-430, deductions were allowed to investors who received an ID number and filed the prescribed form for certain years). Investments were found to be a "tax shelter" and penalty was applied under 237.1(7.4) (or its predecessor 162(9)) in: *Bernier*, 2004 FCA 236; *Maya Inc.*, 2003 TCC 502; *Hexalog*, 2005 TCC 67; *Dagenais*, 2006 TCC 209. A tax shelter registration does not mean the deductions or credits will be allowed: 237.1(5)(c); *St-Laurent [Simard]*, 2007 TCC 540, para. 257, aff'd 2009 FCA 379. An appeal was settled in *Kopstein*, 2010 TCC 448 (discontinued 2008-2468(IT)G). See also Notes to 237.1(7.4).

To be a "tax shelter", statements or representations must be "announced, communicated or make known, by or on behalf of a promoter to prospective purchasers", but not necessarily to the taxpayer who is appealing, so the subjective knowledge of the purchaser is irrelevant: *Baxter* (above), paras. 45, 54. In *Baxter*, statements in a tax opinion and appraisals, considered together, created a tax shelter. Similarly, in *Jevremovic (Maege)*, 2007 FCA 125, the absence of actual representations (to sophisticated investors) did not matter; there was a tax shelter despite the appellants' evidence that no tax benefits were represented to them. The shelter arises based on the calculation under the definition, rather than based on any particular investor's reliance on the representations. Similarly, in *Krumm* (above), statements in a private transaction valuation report that software was Class 12 and "available for use" (with nothing about deductions) were sufficient to create a tax shelter. For detailed discussion and criticism of *Maege*, see Wertschek & Wilson, "Shelter from the Storm", 56(2) *Canadian Tax Journal* 285-336 (2008). For CRA comments on *Maege* and *Baxter* see *Income Tax Technical News* 41. Infrastructure projects can inadvertently trigger the rules: Tobin, "Infrastructure and P3 Projects", 2017 Cdn Tax Foundation conference report, 10:1-31, footnote 35.

The "amount" in subpara. (a)(i) should be the acquisition cost of the property assumed to have been acquired by the prospective purchaser, so CCA claims were included in the calculation: *Baxter* (FCA), para. 50.

CRA will not assess returns claiming donation shelters until it has audited the shelter. See Notes to 118.1(1)"total charitable gifts".

In VIEWS doc 2009-0340381R3, CRA ruled that purchasing life insurance and using it as security to borrow from a bank to acquire an annuity was not a tax shelter.

CRA considered it "totally unacceptable" for a promoter to use a draft ruling as a marketing tool, when it had been sent out for the sole purpose of verifying that the facts were correctly stated: VIEWS doc 2006-0203321R3. In 2012-0440191R3, CRA refused to rule on a limited partnership financing arrangement, as the result depended on the future intentions of the parties.

Lawsuits against tax advisers and shelter promoters succeeded in: *Felty v. Ernst & Young*, 2015 BCCA 445 (E&Y was negligent, but engagement letter limited its liability to fees paid); *Ozerdinc Family Trust v. Gowling Lafleur*, 2017 ONSC 6 (lawyer liable for not advising clients about trust 21-year deemed disposition rule [later settled: see 2019 ONSC 6818, para. 3]); *Barker v. Baxendale Walker*, [2017] EWCA Civ 2056 (England) (tax solicitor negligent in not advising of risk that his advice was wrong); *Lindsay v. Aird & Berlis*, 2018 ONSC 7424 (amateur athlete trust was wound up with donation to charity that lawyer knew had been revoked, and using plan lawyer knew would violate GAAR and bordered on evasion). See also 118.1(1)"total charitable gifts" Notes re suits over donation shelters and re when a lawsuit limitation period starts. Non-tax lawyers may also be liable re tax issues, e.g. *Tellini v. Bell*, 2021 BCSC 549 (real estate firm liable for erroneous advice on BC Foreign Buyers Tax and property transfer tax).

Lawsuits against tax advisors and shelter promoters were allowed to proceed in: *Sigma Capital v. KPMG*, 2014 ONSC 3997 (alleged negligent advice on how to qualify for a refundable investment tax credit: matter settled in 2019); *Mason v. Perras*, 2018 ONCA 978 (tax advisor has obligation to ensure his advice is understood by the client: paras. 25-29); *Kaye v. Fogler Rubinoff*, 2019 ONSC 1289 (action stayed until Tax Court appeal decided).

Lawsuits against tax advisers and shelter promoters failed in: *Quinney v. Orr*, 2012 SKCA 53 (taxpayers sued accountant for setting up corporation for Romanian business rather than partnership that would allow them to claim losses; claim failed because profits had been expected and because Romania required corporate ownership); *Addison & Leyen Ltd. v. Fraser Milner*, 2014 ABCA 230 (tax advisors not liable to clients if opinion or advice is wrong but not negligent); *Akagi v. Synergy Group*, 2015 ONCA 368 (limits on how far receiver can go in investigating shelter); *Holmes v. Schonfeld Inc.*, 2016 ONCA 148 (persons whose assets were being managed could not sue receiver for not repaying loan from corp to prevent inclusion); *Altus Group v. Baker Tilly*, [2015] EWHC 12 (Chancery Divn) [Ip, "UK Denies Tax-Planning Negligence Award", 5(2) *Canadian Tax Focus* (ctf.ca) 10 (May 2015)]; *Taiga Building*

Products, 2014 BCSC 1083 (claim dismissed in part because Taiga settled with CRA without appealing its assessment); *Schneider v. Royal Crown*, 2016 SKQB 380 (under appeal to SKCA) (McMillan LLP not liable for negligent misrepresentation re fraudulent gold mining shelter [and awarded $309,000 costs: 2017 SKQB 222]); *Biancaniello v. DMCT LLP*, 2017 ONCA 386 (broadly worded release signed when settling CA firm's claim for unpaid fees meant client could not sue firm for butterfly transaction done wrong); *Brunette v. Legault Joly*, 2018 SCC 55 (shareholder cannot sue for damage to corp caused by bad tax planning — both Quebec and common-law provinces [Lubetsky, "SCC on Suing Tax Advisers", 27(1) *Canadian Tax Highlights* (ctf.ca) 2-3 (Jan. 2019)]); *Halsall v. Champion Consulting*, [2017] EWHC 1079 (England) (accountant negligent in telling lawyer-investors that donation shelter was "no-brainer", but claim statute-barred); *422252 Alberta v. Messenger*, 2018 ABQB 576 (claim that 1990 opinion that no tax would be payable was wrong; action dismissed due to delay); *McPeake v. Cadesky*, 2018 ONCA 554 (on motion for summary judgment, expert evidence may be needed to show adviser fell below standard of care); *McMahon v. Grant Thornton*, [2020] CSOH 50 (Scotland, Court of Session) (accountant failed to advise business owner on exit strategy that would take a year to implement, but owner likely would not have used it).

Lawsuits: see also Boyd & Ludwin, "Professional Liability in the Tax Context", XXI(3) *Tax Litigation* (Federated Press) 13-18 (2018); Purse, "Referring Clients to Other Professionals", 9(2) *Canadian Tax Focus* (ctf.ca) 14 (May 2019) (re *Salomon v. Matte-Thompson*, 2019 SCC 14 — lawyer liable for referring client to investment advisor who was running Ponzi scheme); Mickelson & Gartner, "Liability and Practice Precautions for Tax Advisors", 2019 British Columbia Tax Conference (ctf.ca) 11:1-18.

A person marketing a tax shelter may need to be licensed under securities law to do so: e.g., *Furtak v. Ont. Securities Commission*, 2018 ONSC 6616.

Definition amended by 2003 Budget to include schemes that use the charitable donation credit as a tax shelter (see 237.1(1)"gifting arrangement"), generally effective Feb. 19, 2003.

Definition amended by 1995-97 technical bill (effective Dec. 1994), 1991 technical bill.

Regulations: 3100 (prescribed benefit for (b)(ii)(B)); 3101 (prescribed property for para. (b)).

Income Tax Folios: S7-F1-C1: Split-receipting and deemed fair market value.

I.T. Technical News: 34 (future directions — novel tax planning disclosure; review of the advance income tax rulings process: q.3); 41 (definition of "tax shelter"; donation of flow-through shares).

Registered Charities Newsletters: 29 (tax shelter gifting arrangements).

Forms: T5001: Application for tax shelter identification number and undertaking to keep books and records; T5001-INSTR: Instructions for applying for a tax shelter identification number; T5004: Claim for tax shelter loss or deduction. See also under 237.1(7).

(2) Application — A promoter in respect of a tax shelter shall apply to the Minister in prescribed form for an identification number for the tax shelter unless an identification number therefor has previously been applied for.

Related Provisions: 237.1(4) — Sale without identification number prohibited; 237.1(7.4) — Penalty for false information or selling shelter without number.

Information Circulars: 89-4: Tax shelter reporting.

Forms: T5001: Application for tax shelter identification number and undertaking to keep books and records; T5001-INSTR: Instructions for applying for a tax shelter identification number.

(3) Identification — On receipt of an application under subsection (2) for an identification number for a tax shelter, together with prescribed information and an undertaking satisfactory to the Minister that books and records in respect of the tax shelter will be kept and retained at a place in Canada that is satisfactory to the Minister, the Minister shall issue an identification number for the tax shelter.

Related Provisions: 237.1(5) — Number is for administrative purposes only.

Information Circulars: 89-4: Tax shelter reporting.

(4) Sales prohibited — A person may, at any time, whether as a principal or an agent, sell or issue, or accept consideration in respect of, a tax shelter only if

(a) the Minister has issued before that time an identification number for the tax shelter; and

(b) that time is during the calendar year designated by the Minister as being applicable to the identification number.

Related Provisions: 237.1(7.4) — Penalty for false information or selling shelter without number.

Notes: This prohibition is arguably an infringement on provincial jurisdiction under the *Constitution Act, 1867*.

237.1(4) amended twice by 2012 budget bill #1, this version effective for any tax shelter for which an application for an identification number was made after March 28, 2012. Otherwise, since March 29, 2012, read para. (b) as "that time is before 2014".

237.1(4) amended by 1995-97 technical bill, effective December 2, 1994, to change "towards the acquisition of, an interest in a tax shelter" to "in respect of, a tax shelter".

Information Circulars: 89-4: Tax shelter reporting.

(5) Providing tax shelter number — Every promoter in respect of a tax shelter shall

(a) make reasonable efforts to ensure that all persons who acquire or otherwise invest in the tax shelter are provided with the identification number issued by the Minister for the tax shelter;

(b) prominently display on the upper right-hand corner of any statement of earnings prepared by or on behalf of the promoter in respect of the tax shelter the identification number issued for the tax shelter; and

(c) on every written statement made after 1995 by the promoter that refers either directly or indirectly and either expressly or impliedly to the issuance by the Canada Revenue Agency of an identification number for the tax shelter, as well as on the copies of the portion of the information return to be forwarded pursuant to subsection (7.3), prominently display

(i) where the statement or return is wholly or partly in English, the following:

"The identification number issued for this tax shelter shall be included in any income tax return filed by the investor. Issuance of the identification number is for administrative purposes only and does not in any way confirm the entitlement of an investor to claim any tax benefits associated with the tax shelter."

(ii) where the statement or return is wholly or partly in French, the following:

"Le numéro d'inscription attribué à cet abri fiscal doit figurer dans toute déclaration d'impôt sur le revenu produite par l'investisseur. L'attribution de ce numéro n'est qu'une formalité administrative et ne confirme aucunement le droit de l'investisseur aux avantages fiscaux découlant de cet abri fiscal."

and

(iii) where the statement includes neither English nor French, the following:

"The identification number issued for this tax shelter shall be included in any income tax return filed by the investor. Issuance of the identification number is for administrative purposes only and does not in any way confirm the entitlement of an investor to claim any tax benefits associated with the tax shelter.

Le numéro d'inscription attribué à cet abri fiscal doit figurer dans toute déclaration d'impôt sur le revenu produite par l'investisseur. L'attribution de ce numéro n'est qu'une formalité administrative et ne confirme aucunement le droit de l'investisseur aux avantages fiscaux découlant de cet abri fiscal."

Related Provisions: 163.2 — Penalty for false statement by tax shelter promoter; 239(2.1) — Incorrect identification number.

Notes: A tax shelter number cannot be used for a similar plan; each arrangement must have its own number: *Glover*, 2015 TCC 199, para. 26.

237.1(5)(c) amended by *CCRA Act*, effective Nov. 1, 1999, to change "Department of National Revenue" to "Canada Customs and Revenue Agency"; and by 2004 CRA/CBSA bill, effective Dec. 12, 2005, to "Canada Revenue Agency".

237.1(5) amended by 1995-97 technical bill, effective December 2, 1994, effectively to add paras. (b) and (c); these requirements were formerly in Reg. 231(5).

Regulations: 231(5) (disclosure requirements in providing identification number; now incorporated into ITA 237.1(5)).

Information Circulars: 89-4: Tax shelter reporting.

(6) Deductions and claims disallowed — No amount may be deducted or claimed by a person in respect of a tax shelter unless the person files with the Minister a prescribed form containing pre-

scribed information, including the identification number for the tax shelter.

Related Provisions: 143.2 — Limitation on tax shelter expenditure; 237.3(2)(a) — Taxpayer must file information return for reportable transaction.

Notes: 237.1(6) prohibits deductions for a tax shelter unless a prescribed form is filed, but it does not require the form to be filed by any particular date. Arguably it could be filed during audit or even during the objection or appeal stage. See Notes to 220(3.2). However, the correct interpretation may be that the form must be filed no later than the filing of the return in which the amount is claimed. This appears to be the CRA's view: May 2007 ICAA roundtable (tinyurl.com/cra-abtax), Q20. This was also the interpretation in the *Baxter* and *Malo* cases. For cases where 237.1(6) was applied, see Notes to 237.1(1)"tax shelter". See also Notes to 237.1(5).

"Field 6765 from the T5004 can be transmitted electronically via EFILE/NETFILE. There is no need to send a paper copy of the form": May 2010 roundtable (*Member Advisory*, Oct. 2010), q.17.

237.1(6) amended by 1995-97 technical bill (effective Dec. 2, 1994), 1991 technical bill.

Information Circulars: 89-4: Tax shelter reporting.

Forms: T5004: Claim for tax shelter loss or deduction. See also under subsec. 237.1(7).

(6.1) Deductions and claims disallowed — No amount may be deducted or claimed by any person for any taxation year in respect of a tax shelter of the person where any person is liable to a penalty under subsection (7.4) or 162(9) in respect of the tax shelter or interest on the penalty and

(a) the penalty or interest has not been paid; or

(b) the penalty and interest have been paid, but an amount on account of the penalty or interest has been repaid under subsection 164(1.1) or applied under subsection 164(2).

Related Provisions: 237.1(6.2) — No time limit on assessment; 237.1(7.4) — Penalty for false information or selling shelter without number.

Notes: It is unclear whether paying the penalty late can "cure" the default so that the deduction can be allowed on objection or appeal.

237.1(6.1) added by 1995-97 technical bill, effective Dec. 2, 1994.

(6.2) Assessments — Notwithstanding subsections 152(4) to (5), such assessments, determinations and redeterminations may be made as are necessary to give effect to subsection (6.1).

Related Provisions: 143.2(15) — Late assessment to implement tax shelter deduction rules.

Notes: 237.1(6.2) added by 1995-97 technical bill, effective Dec. 2, 1994.

(7) Information return — Every promoter in respect of a tax shelter who accepts consideration in respect of the tax shelter or who acts as a principal or agent in respect of the tax shelter in a calendar year shall, in prescribed form and manner, file an information return for the year containing

(a) the name, address and the business number, Social Insurance Number or trust account number of each person who so acquires or otherwise invests in the tax shelter in the year,

(b) the amount paid by each of those persons in respect of the tax shelter, and

(c) such other information as is required by the prescribed form

unless an information return in respect of the tax shelter has previously been filed.

Related Provisions: 152(4)(b.1) — Extended reassessment deadline if information return not filed on time; 237.1(7.1)–(7.3) — Administrative requirements for returns; 237.1(7.5) — Penalty for failure to file information return after demand made; 237.3(14)(a), (16) — No information return required for reportable avoidance transaction if return filed under 237.1(7).

Notes: 237.1(7)(a) amended by 2018 budget bill #1, for 2018 and later tax years, to add reference to a trust account number.

237.1(7) amended by 1995-97 technical bill, last change effective June 18, 1998.

Regulations: 231(2)–(4) (prescribed manner).

Information Circulars: 89-4: Tax shelter reporting.

Forms: T5003: Statement of tax shelter information; T5003 Summ: Tax shelter information return; T5004: Claim for tax shelter loss or deduction; T5013A, T5013A-INST: Statement of partnership income for tax shelters and renounced resource expenses (plus instructions for recipient).

(7.1) Time for filing return — An information return required under subsection (7) to be filed in respect of the acquisition of an interest in a tax shelter in a calendar year shall be filed with the Minister on or before the last day of February of the following calendar year.

Related Provisions: 152(4)(b.1) — Extended reassessment deadline if information return not filed on time; 237.1(7.2) — Return required within 30 days of discontinuing business or activity.

Notes: 237.1(7.1) added by 1995-97 technical bill, effective Dec. 2, 1994.

(7.2) Time for filing — special case — Notwithstanding subsection (7.1), where a person is required under subsection (7) to file an information return in respect of a business or activity and the person discontinues that business or activity, the return shall be filed on or before the earlier of

(a) the day referred to in subsection (7.1); and

(b) the day that is 30 days after the day of the discontinuance.

Notes: 237.1(7.2) added by 1995-97 technical bill, effective Dec. 2, 1994.

(7.3) Copies to be provided — Every person required to file a return under subsection (7) shall, on or before the day on or before which the return is required to be filed with the Minister, forward to each person to whom the return relates 2 copies of the portion of the return relating to that person.

Notes: 237.1(7.3) added by 1995-97 technical bill, effective Dec. 2, 1994.

(7.4) Penalty — Every person who files false or misleading information with the Minister in respect of an application under subsection (2) or, whether as a principal or as an agent, sells, issues or accepts consideration in respect of a tax shelter before the Minister has issued an identification number for the tax shelter is liable to a penalty equal to the greater of

(a) $500, and

(b) 25% of the greater of

(i) the total of all amounts each of which is the consideration received or receivable from a person in respect of the tax shelter before the correct information is filed with the Minister or the identification number is issued, as the case may be, and

(ii) the total of all amounts each of which is an amount stated or represented to be the value of property that a particular person who acquires or otherwise invests in the tax shelter could donate to a qualified donee, if the tax shelter is a gifting arrangement and consideration has been received or is receivable from the particular person in respect of the tax shelter before the correct information is filed with the Minister or the identification number is issued, as the case may be.

Related Provisions: 161(11)(b.1) — Interest on penalty; 163(2.9) — Where partnership is liable to penalty; 227(10)(b) — Assessment of penalty at any time; 237.1(6.1) — No deduction allowed while tax shelter penalty unpaid.

Notes: See Notes to 237.1(1)"tax shelter" for cases where this penalty was applied.

There is no time limit on a 237.1(7.4) penalty (227(10)(b)), which is quite distinct from a regular gross-negligence penalty: *Hexalog Ltée*, 2005 TCC 67.

In *O'Dwyer*, 2013 FCA 200, a $2.3 million penalty was cancelled because the Crown did not identify what statements or representations were made to meet the definition of "tax shelter".

Repayment of a loan is not "consideration" under 237.1(7.4): VIEWS doc 2004-0072531I7.

237.1(7.4)(b)(ii) added by 2012 budget bill #1, effective for any application for an identification number made, any sale or issuance of a tax shelter made and any consideration in respect of a tax shelter accepted, after June 28, 2012.

237.1(7.4) added by 1995-97 technical bill, effective Dec. 2, 1994.

CRA Audit Manual: 28.2.3: Penalties — failure to file in respect of tax shelters.

(7.5) Penalty — Every person who is required under subsection (7) to file an information return and who fails to comply with a demand under section 233 to file the return, or to report in the return information required under paragraph (7)(a) or (b), is liable to a penalty equal to 25% of the greater of

(a) the total of all amounts each of which is the consideration received or receivable by the person in respect of the tax shelter

from a particular person in respect of whom information required under paragraph (7)(a) or (b) had not been reported at or before the time that the demand was issued or the return was filed, as the case may be, and

(b) if the tax shelter is a gifting arrangement, the total of all amounts each of which is an amount stated or represented to be the value of property that the particular person could donate to a qualified donee.

Related Provisions: 152(4)(b.1) — Extended reassessment deadline if information return not filed on time; 163(2.9) — Where partnership is liable to penalty; 227(10)(b) — Assessment of penalty at any time.

Notes: 237.1(7.5) added by 2012 budget bill #1, effective in respect of any demand made, and any information return filed, after June 28, 2012.

(8) Application of sections 231 to 231.3 — Without restricting the generality of sections 231 to 231.3, where an application under subsection (2) with respect to a tax shelter has been made, notwithstanding that a return of income has not been filed by any taxpayer under section 150 for the taxation year of the taxpayer in which an amount is claimed as a deduction in respect of the tax shelter, sections 231 to 231.3 apply, with such modifications as the circumstances require, for the purpose of permitting the Minister to verify or ascertain any information in respect of the tax shelter.

Information Circulars [subsec. 237.1(8)]: 89-4: Tax shelter reporting.

Notes [s. 237.1]: 237.1 added by 1988 tax reform, effective for interests acquired after August 1989 (see 237.2).

Definitions [s. 237.1]: "amount" — 248(1); "arm's length" — 251(1); "assessment", "business", "business number" — 248(1); "calendar year" — *Interpretation Act* 37(1)(a); "flow-through share" — 66(15), 248(1); "gifting arrangement" — 237.1(1); "limited-recourse amount" — 143.2(1), 248(1); "limited-recourse debt" — 143.2(6.1); "Minister" — 248(1); "partnership" — see 96(1) Notes; "person" — 237.1(1), 248(1); "prescribed" — 248(1); "prescribed benefit" — Reg. 3100; "prescribed property" — Reg. 3101; "promoter" — 237.1(1); "property" — 248(1); "qualified donee" — 149.1(1), 248(1); "record", "share" — 248(1); "tax shelter" — 237.1(1), 248(1); "taxable income" — 2(2), 248(1); "taxable income earned in Canada" — 115(1), 248(1); "taxation year" — 249; "trust account number" — 248(1); "written" — *Interpretation Act* 35(1)"writing".

237.2 Application of section 237.1 — Section 237.1 is applicable with respect to interests acquired after August 31, 1989.

Notes: 237.2 added in the RSC 1985 (5th Supp) consolidation, effective Dec. 1, 1991. This rule was formerly in the 1988 tax reform bill (S.C. 1988, c. 55, s. 180).

237.3 [Reportable transactions] — **(1) Definitions** — The following definitions apply in this section.

Notes: See Notes at end of 237.3 for in-force rules.

"advisor", in respect of a transaction or series of transactions, means each person who provides, directly or indirectly in any manner whatever, any contractual protection in respect of the transaction or series, or any assistance or advice with respect to creating, developing, planning, organizing or implementing the transaction or series, to another person (including any person who enters into the transaction for the benefit of another person).

Related Provisions: 237.3(2)(c) — Advisor must file information return for reportable transaction; 237.3(8), (15) — Penalty for advisor not filing information return.

Notes: For the meaning of "indirectly", see Notes to 17.1(1).

"avoidance transaction" has the meaning assigned by subsection 245(3).

Related Provisions: 237.3(1)"reportable transaction" — Avoidance transaction that meets certain conditions.

"confidential protection", in respect of a transaction or series of transactions, means anything that prohibits the disclosure to any person or to the Minister of the details or structure of the transaction or series under which a tax benefit results, or would result but for section 245, but for greater certainty, the disclaiming or restricting of an advisor's liability shall not be considered confidential protection if it does not prohibit the disclosure of the details or structure of the transaction or series.

Notes: See Notes at end of 237.3 if the series of transactions began before 2011.

"contractual protection", in respect of a transaction or series of transactions, means

(a) any form of insurance (other than standard professional liability insurance) or other protection, including, without limiting the generality of the foregoing, an indemnity, compensation or a guarantee that, either immediately or in the future and either absolutely or contingently,

(i) protects a person against a failure of the transaction or series to achieve any tax benefit from the transaction or series, or

(ii) pays for or reimburses any expense, fee, tax, interest, penalty or similar amount that may be incurred by a person in the course of a dispute in respect of a tax benefit from the transaction or series; and

(b) any form of undertaking provided by a promoter, or by any person who does not deal at arm's length with a promoter, that provides, either immediately or in the future and either absolutely or contingently, assistance, directly or indirectly in any manner whatever, to a person in the course of a dispute in respect of a tax benefit from the transaction or series.

Related Provisions: 60(o) — Costs of disputing assessment are deductible by whoever pays them; 237.3(2)(c)(ii) — Advisor or promoter entitled to fee subject to contractual protection must report transaction.

"fee", in respect of a transaction or series of transactions, means any consideration that is, or could be, received or receivable, directly or indirectly in any manner whatever, by an advisor or a promoter, or any person who does not deal at arm's length with an advisor or promoter, for

(a) providing advice or an opinion with respect to the transaction or series;

(b) creating, developing, planning, organizing or implementing the transaction or series;

(c) promoting or selling an arrangement, plan or scheme that includes, or relates to, the transaction or series;

(d) preparing documents supporting the transaction or series, including tax returns or any information returns to be filed under the Act; or

(e) providing contractual protection.

Notes: For the meaning of "indirectly", see Notes to 17.1(1).

"person" includes a partnership.

"promoter", in respect of a transaction or series of transactions, means each person who

(a) promotes or sells (whether as principal or agent and whether directly or indirectly) an arrangement, plan or scheme (referred to in this definition as an "arrangement"), if it may reasonably be considered that the arrangement includes or relates to the transaction or series;

(b) makes a statement or representation (whether as principal or agent and whether directly or indirectly) that a tax benefit could result from an arrangement, if it may reasonably be considered that

(i) the statement or representation was made in furtherance of the promoting or selling of the arrangement, and

(ii) the arrangement includes or relates to the transaction or series; or

(c) accepts (whether as principal or agent and whether directly or indirectly) consideration in respect of an arrangement referred to in paragraph (a) or (b).

Related Provisions: 237.3(2)(c) — Promoter must file information return for reportable transaction; 237.3(8), (15) — Penalty for promoter not filing information return.

Notes: For the meaning of "indirectly", see Notes to 17.1(1).

"reportable transaction", at any time, means an avoidance transaction that is entered into by or for the benefit of a person, and each transaction that is part of a series of transactions that includes the avoidance transaction, if at the time any two of the following paragraphs apply in respect of the avoidance transaction or series:

(a) an advisor or a promoter, or any person who does not deal at arm's length with the advisor or promoter, has or had an entitlement, either immediately or in the future and either absolutely or contingently, to a fee that to any extent

(i) is based on the amount of a tax benefit that results, or would result but for section 245, from the avoidance transaction or series,

(ii) is contingent upon the obtaining of a tax benefit that results, or would result but for section 245, from the avoidance transaction or series, or may be refunded, recovered or reduced, in any manner whatever, based upon the failure of the person to obtain a tax benefit from the avoidance transaction or series, or

(iii) is attributable to the number of persons

(A) who participate in the avoidance transaction or series, or in a similar avoidance transaction or series, or

(B) who have been provided access to advice or an opinion given by the advisor or promoter regarding the tax consequences from the avoidance transaction or series, or from a similar avoidance transaction or series;

(b) an advisor or promoter in respect of the avoidance transaction or series, or any person who does not deal at arm's length with the advisor or promoter, obtains or obtained confidential protection in respect of the avoidance transaction or series,

(i) in the case of an advisor, from a person to whom the advisor has provided any assistance or advice with respect to the avoidance transaction or series under the terms of an engagement of the advisor by that person to provide such assistance or advice, or

(ii) in the case of a promoter, from a person

(A) to whom an arrangement, plan or scheme has been promoted or sold in the circumstances described in paragraph (a) of the definition "promoter",

(B) to whom a statement or representation described in paragraph (b) of the definition "promoter" has been made, or

(C) from whom consideration described in paragraph (c) of the definition "promoter" has been received; or

(c) either

(i) the person (in this subparagraph referred to as the "particular person"), another person who entered into the avoidance transaction for the benefit of the particular person or any other person who does not deal at arm's length with the particular person or with a person who entered into the avoidance transaction for the benefit of the particular person, has or had contractual protection in respect of the avoidance transaction or series, otherwise than as a result of a fee described in paragraph (a), or

(ii) an advisor or promoter in respect of the avoidance transaction or series, or any person who does not deal at arm's length with the advisor or promoter, has or had contractual protection in respect of the avoidance transaction or series, otherwise than as a result of a fee described in paragraph (a).

Proposed Amendments — 237.3(1)"reportable transaction"

Federal Budget, Supplementary Information, April 19, 2021: See at end of 237.3.

Related Provisions: 237.3(2) — Information return required; 237.3(14) — Reportable transaction does not include one where return filed as tax shelter or flow-through share; 237.3(17) — Exception for solicitor-client privilege.

Notes: Subparas. (b)(i) and (ii) were new in the Oct. 24, 2012 draft.

See Notes at end of 237.3.

Forms: RC312: Reportable transaction information return.

"solicitor-client privilege" has the meaning assigned by subsection 232(1).

Related Provisions: 237.3(17) — Privilege exception from requirement to report transaction.

Notes: This definition was first included on Oct. 24, 2012. Arguably, the exclusion of accounting records in 232(1)"solicitor-client privilege" might not apply to 237.3, since that exclusion applies only "for the purposes of this section [232]". Accounting records and lawyers' invoices may be privileged: see Notes to 232(2).

"tax benefit" has the meaning assigned by subsection 245(1).

Related Provisions: 237.3(2)(c) — Information return required for reportable transaction where tax benefit results.

"transaction" has the meaning assigned by subsection 245(1).

(2) Application [Information return required] — An information return in prescribed form and containing prescribed information in respect of a reportable transaction must be filed with the Minister by

(a) every person for whom a tax benefit results, or would result but for section 245, from the reportable transaction, from any other reportable transaction that is part of a series of transactions that includes the reportable transaction or from the series of transactions;

(b) every person who has entered into, for the benefit of a person described in paragraph (a), an avoidance transaction that is a reportable transaction;

(c) every advisor or promoter in respect of the reportable transaction, or in respect of any other transaction that is part of a series of transactions that includes the reportable transaction, who is or was entitled, either immediately or in the future and either absolutely or contingently, to a fee in respect of any of those transactions that is

(i) described in paragraph (a) of the definition "reportable transaction" in subsection (1), or

(ii) in respect of contractual protection provided in circumstances described in paragraph (c) of the definition "reportable transaction" in subsection (1); and

(d) every person who is not dealing at arm's length with an advisor or promoter in respect of the reportable transaction and who is or was entitled, either immediately or in the future and either absolutely or contingently, to a fee that is referred to in paragraph (c).

Related Provisions: 152(4)(b.1) — Extended reassessment deadline if information return not filed on time; 237.1(6), (7) — Information return required for tax shelter; 237.3(3) — Filing of return in respect of each transaction in series; 237.3(4) — Filing by one person constitutes filing by all; 237.3(5) — Filing deadline; 237.3(6) — Tax benefits disallowed if return not filed and penalty unpaid; 237.3(8), (15) — Penalty for not filing; 237.3(12) — Filing does not constitute admission that transaction is abusive; 237.3(14)(a) — No return required if tax shelter return filed under 237.1(7); 237.3(14)(b) — No return required for flow-through shares; 248(10) — Series of transactions.

Notes: See Notes at end of 237.3.

Forms: RC312: Reportable transaction information return.

(3) Clarification of reporting transactions in series — For greater certainty, and subject to subsection (11), if subsection (2) applies to a person in respect of each reportable transaction that is part of a series of transactions that includes an avoidance transaction, the filing of a prescribed form by the person that reports each transaction in the series is deemed to satisfy the obligation of the person under subsection (2) in respect of each transaction so reported.

(4) Application — For the purpose of subsection (2), if any person is required to file an information return in respect of a reportable transaction under that subsection, the filing by any such person of an information return with full and accurate disclosure in prescribed form in respect of the transaction is deemed to have been made by each person to whom subsection (2) applies in respect of the transaction.

(5) Time for filing return — An information return required by subsection (2) to be filed by a person for a reportable transaction is to be filed with the Minister on or before June 30 of the calendar year following the calendar year in which the transaction first became a reportable transaction in respect of the person.

Notes: Per 2002-2013 technical bill s. 356(3), if an information return under 237.3 would be due by July 2012, it is deemed on time if filed by Oct. 23, 2013. The CRA administratively extends the deadline for the 2012 return from June 30, 2013 to Oct. 23, 2013: tinyurl.com/237-3deadline.

(6) Tax benefits disallowed — Notwithstanding subsection 245(4), subsection 245(2) is deemed to apply at any time to any reportable transaction in respect of a person described in paragraph (2)(a) in relation to the reportable transaction if, at that time,

(a) the obligation under subsection (2) of the person in respect of the reportable transaction, or any other reportable transaction that is part of a series of transactions that includes the reportable transaction, has not been satisfied;

(b) a person is liable to a penalty under subsection (8) in respect of the reportable transaction or any other reportable transaction that is part of a series of transactions that includes the reportable transaction; and

(c) the penalty under subsection (8) or interest on the penalty has not been paid, or has been paid but an amount on account of the penalty or interest has been repaid under subsection 164(1.1) or applied under subsection 164(2).

Notes: See Notes at end of 237.3.

The references in paras. (a) and (b) to "any other reportable transaction that is part of a series of transactions that includes the reportable transaction", were added in the draft of Oct. 24, 2012.

(7) Assessments — Notwithstanding subsections 152(4) to (5), the Minister may make any assessments, determinations and redeterminations that are necessary to give effect to subsection (8).

Notes: This means that there is no time limit for assessing a penalty under 237.3(8).

(8) Penalty — Every person who fails to file an information return in respect of a reportable transaction as required under subsection (2) on or before the day required under subsection (5) is liable to a penalty equal to the total of each amount that is a fee to which an advisor or a promoter (or any person who does not deal at arm's length with the advisor or the promoter) in respect of the reportable transaction is or was entitled, either immediately or in the future and either absolutely or contingently, to receive in respect of the reportable transaction, any transaction that is part of the series of transactions that includes the reportable transaction or the series of transactions that includes the reportable transaction, if the fee is

(a) described in paragraph (a) of the definition "reportable transaction" in subsection (1); or

(b) in respect of contractual protection provided in circumstances described in paragraph (c) of the definition "reportable transaction" in subsection (1).

Related Provisions: 18(1)(t), 67.6 — Penalty is not deductible; 161(11)(b.1) — Interest on penalty; 163(2.9) — Where partnership is liable to penalty; 227(10)(b) — Assessment of penalty; 237.3(6) — Tax benefits disallowed if return not filed and penalty unpaid; 237.3(7) — No time limit for assessment of penalty; 237.3(9) — Joint and several liability for penalty; 237.3(10) — Limitation on liability of advisor or promoter; 237.3(11) — Due diligence defence to penalty; 237.3(15) — Limitation on penalty.

Notes: See Notes at end of 237.3.

(9) Joint and several liability — If more than one person is liable to a penalty under subsection (8) in respect of a reportable transaction, each of those persons are jointly and severally, or solidarily, liable to pay the penalty.

Related Provisions: 237.3(10) — Limitation on liability of advisor or promoter.

(10) Joint and several liability — special cases — Notwithstanding subsections (8) and (9), the liability of an advisor or a promoter, or a person with whom the advisor or promoter does not deal at arm's length, to a penalty under those subsections in respect of a reportable transaction shall not exceed the total of each amount that is a fee referred to in subsection (8) to which that advisor or promoter, or a person with whom the advisor or promoter does not deal at arm's length, is or was entitled, either immediately or in the future and either absolutely or contingently, to receive in respect of the reportable transaction.

(11) Due diligence — A person required to file an information return in respect of a reportable transaction is not liable for a penalty under subsection (8) if the person has exercised the degree of care, diligence and skill to prevent the failure to file that a reasonably prudent person would have exercised in comparable circumstances.

Notes: This is the same wording as is used for the due-diligence defence to a directors' liability assessment. See Notes to 227.1(3).

(12) Reporting not an admission — The filing of an information return under this section by a person in respect of a reportable transaction is not an admission by the person that

(a) section 245 applies in respect of any transaction; or

(b) any transaction is part of a series of transactions.

(13) Application of ss. 231 to 231.3 — Without restricting the generality of sections 231 to 231.3, even if a return of income has not been filed by a taxpayer under section 150 for the taxation year of the taxpayer in which a tax benefit results, or would result but for section 245, from a reportable transaction, sections 231 to 231.3 apply, with such modifications as the circumstances require, for the purpose of permitting the Minister to verify or ascertain any information in respect of that transaction.

(14) Tax shelters and flow-through shares — For the purpose of this section, a reportable transaction does not include a transaction that is, or is part of a series of transactions that includes,

(a) the acquisition of a tax shelter for which an information return has been filed with the Minister under subsection 237.1(7); or

(b) the issuance of a flow-through share for which an information return has been filed with the Minister under subsection 66(12.68).

Related Provisions: 237.3(16) — No application if shelter or flow-through share acquired to avoid 237.3.

(15) Tax shelters and flow-through shares — penalty — Notwithstanding subsection (8), the amount of the penalty, if any, that applies on a person under that subsection in respect of a reportable transaction shall not exceed the amount determined by the formula

$$A - B$$

where

A is the amount of the penalty imposed on the person under subsection (8), determined without reference to this subsection; and

B is

(a) if the reportable transaction is the acquisition of a tax shelter, the amount of the penalty, if any, that applies on the person under subsection 237.1(7.4) in respect of the tax shelter,

(b) if the reportable transaction is the issuance of a flow-through share, the amount of the penalty, if any, that applies on the person under subsection 66(12.74) in respect of the issuance of the flow-through share, and

(c) in any other case, nil.

Related Provisions: 257 — Formula cannot calculate to less than zero.

(16) Anti-avoidance — Subsection (14) does not apply to a reportable transaction if it is reasonable, having regard to all of the circumstances, to conclude that one of the main reasons for the acquisition of a tax shelter, or the issuance of a flow-through share, is to avoid the application of this section.

Notes: For the meaning of "one of the main reasons" see Notes to 83(2.1).

(17) Solicitor-client privilege — For greater certainty, for the purpose of this section, a lawyer who is an advisor in respect of a reportable transaction is not required to disclose in an information return in respect of the transaction any information in respect of which the lawyer, on reasonable grounds, believes that a client of the lawyer has solicitor-client privilege.

Notes: 237.3(17) does not provide as much protection as it appears to, due to the exclusions in 232(1)"solicitor-client privilege" (incorporated here by 237.3(1)). However, the Courts will likely apply the common law privilege and ignore the limitations in that definition: see Notes to 232(2).

237.3(17) was added in the draft of Oct. 24, 2012, in response to submissions from the Canadian Bar Association.

Proposed Amendments — 237.3

Federal Budget, Supplementary Information, April 19, 2021: *Mandatory Disclosure Rules*

The lack of timely, comprehensive and relevant information on aggressive tax planning strategies is one of the main challenges faced by tax authorities worldwide.

Early access to such information provides the opportunity to respond quickly to tax risks through informed risk assessments, audits and changes to legislation.

The *Income Tax Act* contains rules requiring that certain transactions be reported to the Canada Revenue Agency (CRA). However, the CRA's experience with these rules since their introduction indicates that they are not sufficiently robust to address these concerns.

The *Base Erosion and Profit Shifting Project, Action 12: Final Report* (BEPS Action 12 Report) of the Organisation for Economic Co-operation and Development and the Group of 20 [see Proposed Amendments at end of s. 95, under Action 12 — ed.] makes a number of recommendations relating to the enactment of mandatory disclosure rules. Many of the measures recommended in the BEPS Action 12 Report have been implemented in countries with comparable tax systems. In addition to measures recommended by the BEPS Action 12 Report, the United States and Australia both have reporting requirements for specified taxpayers that reflect uncertainty in relation to tax in their audited financial statements. The experience in these countries provides a useful model for developing similar rules in Canada.

The government is consulting on proposals to enhance Canada's mandatory disclosure rules. This consultation will address:

• changes to the *Income Tax Act*'s reportable transaction rules;

• a new requirement to report notifiable transactions;

• a new requirement for specified corporations to report uncertain tax treatments; and

• related rules providing for, in certain circumstances, the extension of the applicable reassessment period and the introduction of penalties.

It is proposed that, to the extent the proposed measure applies to taxation years, amendments made as a result of this consultation would apply to **taxation years that begin after 2021**. To the extent the proposed measure applies to transactions, the amendments would apply to **transactions entered into on or after January 1, 2022**. However, the penalties would not apply to transactions that occur before the date on which the enacting legislation receives Royal Assent.

Stakeholders are invited to provide comments on the proposals set out below, as well as on draft legislation and sample notifiable transactions which are expected to be released in the coming weeks as part of the consultation. Comments should be directed to the Department of Finance by September 3, 2021. Please send your comments to fin.taxdisclosure-divulgationfiscale.fin@canada.ca.

Reportable Transactions

The *Income Tax Act* contains rules that require that certain transactions entered into by, or for the benefit of, a taxpayer be reported to the CRA. In order for a transaction to be reportable under those rules [237.3(1)"reportable transaction" — ed.], it must be an "avoidance transaction", as that term is defined for the purposes of the general anti-avoidance rule in the *Income Tax Act*. As well, the transaction must bear at least two of the following three generic hallmarks:

• A promoter or tax advisor in respect of the transaction is entitled to fees, often referred to as "contingent fees", that are to any extent:

— attributable to the amount of the tax benefit from the transaction;

— contingent upon the obtaining of a tax benefit from the transaction; or

— attributable to the number of taxpayers who participate in the transaction or who have been provided access to advice given by the promoter or advisor regarding the tax consequences of the transaction.

• A promoter or tax advisor requires "confidential protection" with respect to the transaction.

• The taxpayer, or the person who entered into the transaction for the benefit of the taxpayer, obtains "contractual protection" in respect of the transaction (otherwise than as a result of a fee described in the first hallmark). For these purposes, contractual protection includes:

— any form of insurance (other than standard professional liability insurance) or other protection (including an indemnity, compensation or a guarantee) that, either immediately or in the future and either absolutely or contingently:

• protects a person against a failure to achieve any tax benefit from the transaction; or

    - pays for or reimburses any expense, fee, tax, interest, penalty or similar amount that may be incurred by a person in the course of a dispute in respect of a tax benefit from the transaction; and

- any form of undertaking provided by a promoter, or by any person who does not deal at arm's length with the promoter, that provides, either immediately or in the future and either absolutely or contingently, assistance, directly or indirectly in any manner whatever, to a person in the course of a dispute in respect of a tax benefit from the transaction.

A reportable transaction includes all the transactions in a series of transactions if at least one of the transactions in the series is an avoidance transaction [237.3(1)"reportable transaction" opening words — ed.]. If more than one party is required to report the transaction, a report by any of the parties can satisfy the requirement. A reportable transaction must be reported to the CRA on or before June 30 of the calendar year following the calendar year in which the transaction first became a reportable transaction.

While the current rules are intended to provide the CRA with the information it needs, they currently result in only limited reporting by taxpayers.

The BEPS Action 12 Report recommends that countries introducing mandatory disclosure regimes include a mixture of generic and specific hallmarks, with the existence of each of them resulting in a requirement for disclosure. Generic hallmarks target features that are common to promoted schemes, such as the requirement for confidentiality or the payment of a contingent fee. Specific hallmarks target particular areas of concern, such as trading in losses.

The BEPS Action 12 Report notes that the purpose of a mandatory disclosure regime is to provide the relevant tax administration with information on a wider range of tax policy and revenue risks than those raised by transactions that would be classified as avoidance under a general anti-avoidance rule. A "reportable scheme" for disclosure purposes should generally be broader than the definition of tax avoidance schemes covered by a general anti-avoidance rule and should also cover transactions that are perceived to be aggressive or high-risk from a tax planning perspective.

The BEPS Action 12 Report also notes that Canada's current June 30 reporting deadline renders it less able than other countries to react quickly to tax avoidance planning. It also concludes that the advantage of requiring both promoters and taxpayers to report is that this may have a stronger deterrent effect on both the supply (promoter) and demand (taxpayer) side of avoidance schemes. A dual reporting approach can also reduce the risk of inadequate disclosure because, for example, a taxpayer's disclosure can be checked against the promoter's disclosure to assess whether the information provided is accurate and complete.

To improve the effectiveness of Canada's mandatory disclosure rules and to bring them in line with international best practices, amendments to the reportable transaction rules are proposed. In particular, it is proposed that only one generic hallmark need be present in order for a transaction to be reportable. It is also proposed that the definition of "avoidance transaction" for these purposes be amended so that a transaction be considered an avoidance transaction if it can reasonably be concluded that one of the main purposes of entering into the transaction is to obtain a tax benefit.

It is proposed that a taxpayer who enters into a reportable transaction, or another person who enters into such a transaction in order to procure a tax benefit for the taxpayer, would be required to report the transaction to the CRA within 45 days of the earlier of:

- the day the taxpayer becomes contractually obligated to enter into the transaction or a person who entered into the transaction for the benefit of the taxpayer becomes contractually obligated to enter into the transaction; and
- the day the taxpayer enters into the transaction or a person who entered into the transaction for the benefit of the taxpayer enters into the transaction.

It is further proposed that reporting (as a reportable transaction) of a scheme that, if implemented, would be a reportable transaction be required to be made by a promoter or advisor (as well as by persons who do not deal at arm's length with the promoter or advisor and who are entitled to receive a fee with respect to the transaction) within the same time limits. In addition, it is proposed that an exception to the reporting requirement be available for advisors to the extent that solicitor-client privilege applies.

Notifiable Transactions

As noted above, the BEPS Action 12 Report recommends that an effective mandatory disclosure regime include a mixture of specific and generic hallmarks.

Specific hallmarks target particular areas of concern. The report recommends the timely disclosure of specific tax schemes to allow governments to quickly develop targeted and appropriate responses to them.

The United States has mandatory disclosure regimes relating to "listed transactions" and "transactions of interest", which are noted in the BEPS Action 12 Report. A U.S. listed transaction is a transaction that is the same as, or substantially similar to, one that the Internal Revenue Service (IRS) has determined to be a tax avoidance transaction and has identified by notice or other form of published guidance. A U.S. transaction of interest is a transaction that the IRS and the U.S. Treasury Department consider to be a transaction that has the potential for tax avoidance or evasion, but for which they lack sufficient information to make that determination.

Similar rules are also in force in the United Kingdom (disclosure of tax avoidance schemes or DOTAS), Australia (disclosed in the reportable tax position schedule, under category C), and the European Union. Quebec has also enacted a measure that requires taxpayers who have carried out certain transactions to file an information return with Revenu Québec.

To provide the CRA with pertinent information relating to tax avoidance transactions (including series of transactions) and other transactions of interest on a timely basis, it is proposed to introduce a category of specific hallmarks known as "notifiable transactions". Under this approach, the Minister of National Revenue would have the authority to designate, with the concurrence of the Minister of Finance, a transaction as a notifiable transaction.

Similar to the approach taken by the United States, notifiable transactions would include both transactions that the CRA has found to be abusive and transactions identified as transactions of interest. The description of a notifiable transaction would set out the fact patterns or outcomes that constitute that transaction in sufficient detail to enable taxpayers to comply with the disclosure rule. It would also include examples in appropriate circumstances. Sample descriptions of notifiable transactions will be issued as part of the consultation.

A taxpayer who enters into a notifiable transaction, or a transaction or series of transactions that is substantially similar to a notifiable transaction — or another person who enters into such a transaction or series in order to procure a tax benefit for the taxpayer — would be required to report the transaction or series in prescribed form to the CRA within 45 days of the earlier of:

- the day the taxpayer becomes contractually obligated to enter into the transaction or series or a person who entered into the transaction or series for the benefit of the taxpayer becomes contractually obligated to enter into the transaction or series; and
- the day the taxpayer enters into the transaction or series or a person who entered into the transaction or series for the benefit of the taxpayer enters into the transaction or series.

A promoter or advisor who offers a scheme that, if implemented, would be a notifiable transaction, or a transaction or series of transactions that is substantially similar to a notifiable transaction — as well as a person who does not deal at arm's length with the promoter or advisor and who is entitled to receive a fee in respect of the transaction — would be required to report within the same time limits. In addition, it is proposed that an exception to the reporting requirement be available for advisors to the extent that solicitor-client privilege applies.

These proposed amendments are intended to provide information to the CRA and would not change the tax treatment of a transaction.

For example, in a recent decision of the Tax Court of Canada (*Paletta v. The Queen* [2021 TCC 11, under appeal to FCA — ed.]) involving a taxpayer who entered into an aggressive series of transactions referred to as straddle planning, which was designed to defer indefinitely tax payable under the *Income Tax Act*, the CRA tried unsuccessfully to reassess the taxpayer for relevant taxation years outside the normal reassessment period. This series of transactions resulted in an immediate loss realization and an indefinite gain deferral for the taxpayer. Since the burden associated with the reassessment of a taxation year made after the normal reassessment period in a case such as *Paletta* requires the CRA to prove that the taxpayer made a misrepresentation on their tax return that was attributable to neglect, carelessness or wilful default, such a reassessment is challenging and time consuming for the CRA. If the transactions associated with this aggressive straddle planning had been designated as a notifiable transaction, the CRA would have been notified in time to be able to assess the taxpayer within the normal reassessment period. The proposed notifiable transaction regime would allow the CRA to challenge planning like this in a timely manner, based on their merits.

Uncertain Tax Treatments

An uncertain tax treatment is a tax treatment used, or planned to be used, in an entity's income tax filings for which there is uncertainty over whether the tax treatment will be accepted as being in accordance with tax law. At present, there is no requirement in Canada to disclose uncertain tax treatments. However, both the United States and Australia have reporting requirements related to uncertain tax treatments. In addition, the United Kingdom recently conducted a public consultation with respect to the introduction of uncertain tax treatment reporting requirements and has announced its intention to enact the required legislation. In this regard, it was noted that large corporations are already familiar with the Australian and the U.S. reporting regimes, and that this would facilitate transitioning taxpayers into a similar regime in the United Kingdom. The same can be said for the introduction of a similar regime in Canada.

Under the U.S. uncertain tax positions rule, a corporation meeting an asset threshold, and certain other conditions, must report (under Schedule UTP) when it has taken a tax position on a U.S. income tax return and either the corporation or a related party has recorded a reserve with respect to that tax position in its audited financial statements. Similarly, under the Australian rules, a corporation meeting a revenue threshold, and certain other conditions, must report (under category B: Tax uncertainty in financial statements) when it has taken a tax position on an Australian income tax return for a year and either the corporation or a related party has recognized or disclosed uncertainty with respect to that tax position in its audited financial statements.

It is proposed that a similar reporting regime be implemented in Canada. As such, specified corporate taxpayers would be required to report particular uncertain tax treatments to the CRA.

Introducing such requirement in Canada would:

- allow the CRA to more efficiently identify issues and allocate its resources for compliance activities; and
- ensure the CRA is able to conduct its audit activities with respect to transactions at issue in a timely manner.

Accounting Rules Regarding Uncertain Tax Treatments

If a corporation's financial statements, or those of its corporate parent, are prepared in accordance with Canadian generally accepted accounting principles (GAAP) and there is uncertainty regarding a tax position taken, or planned to be taken, in its tax return, the effect of that uncertainty might need to be reflected in those financial statements. Canadian GAAP provides that International Financial Reporting Standards (IFRS) are to be used by public corporations, and may be adopted by private corporations if they choose to do so. IFRS provide that an entity shall consider whether it is probable that a taxation authority will accept an uncertain tax treatment. "Taxation authority" in this context refers to the body or bodies that decide whether tax treatments are acceptable under tax law, and in the Canadian context ultimately means the courts. If an entity concludes it is probable that the taxation authority will accept an uncertain tax treatment, IFRS provide that the entity shall determine the taxable profit (tax loss), tax bases, unused tax losses, unused tax credits or tax rates consistently with the tax treatment used, or planned to be used, in its income tax filings.

However, if an entity concludes it is not probable that the taxation authority will accept a particular uncertain tax treatment (and thus, as described by the IFRS Interpretations Committee, it is probable that the entity will receive or pay amounts relating to the uncertain tax treatment), the entity shall reflect the effect of that uncertainty in determining the related taxable profit (tax loss), tax bases, unused tax losses, unused tax credits or tax rates by using either the most likely amount or the expected value, depending on which method the entity expects to better predict the resolution of the uncertainty.

As such, Canadian public corporations, and those Canadian private corporations that choose to use IFRS, have an existing requirement to identify uncertain tax treatments for financial statement purposes. When such a corporation determines that it is not probable that the taxation authority will accept an uncertain tax treatment (including an uncertain tax treatment relating to an entity controlled by the corporation), the effect of that uncertainty is reflected in the corporation's financial statements (which would be presented on a consolidated basis with those entities it controls).

Requirement to Report Uncertain Tax Treatments

It is proposed that specified corporate taxpayers be required to report particular uncertain tax treatments to the CRA. A reporting corporation would generally be required to report an uncertain tax treatment in respect of a taxation year where the following conditions are met:

- The corporation is required to file a Canadian return of income for the taxation year. That is, the corporation is a resident of Canada or is a non-resident corporation with a taxable presence in Canada.

- The corporation has at least $50 million in assets at the end of the financial year that coincides with the taxation year (or the last financial year that ends before the end of the taxation year). This threshold would apply to each individual corporation.

- The corporation, or a related corporation, has audited financial statements prepared in accordance with IFRS or other country-specific GAAP relevant for domestic public companies (e.g., U.S. GAAP).

- Uncertainty in respect of the corporation's Canadian income tax for the taxation year is reflected in those audited financial statements (i.e., the entity concluded it is not probable that the taxation authority will accept an uncertain tax treatment and thus, as described by the IFRS Interpretations Committee, it is probable that the entity will receive or pay amounts relating to the uncertain tax treatment).

The determination of whether a corporation has $50 million in assets would be made using the carrying value of the assets on the corporation's balance sheet at the end of the financial year. If the corporation did not prepare a balance sheet, or did not prepare a balance sheet in accordance with Canadian GAAP (or other country-specific GAAP relevant for domestic public companies), the amounts used would be those that would have been reflected in a balance sheet prepared in accordance with GAAP. Banks and insurance corporations that are regulated by the Superintendent of Financial Institutions, or a similar provincial authority, would use the amounts in the statements accepted by that authority for regulatory purposes.

As noted above, Canadian GAAP require that the audited financial statements of public corporations be prepared in accordance with IFRS. As a result, the requirement to report particular uncertain tax treatments would apply to Canadian public corporations, subject to the asset threshold. Since IFRS require that a public corporation's financial statements be prepared on a consolidated basis with those corporations that it controls, the requirement to report particular uncertain tax treatments would also apply, subject to the asset threshold, to those corporations that are controlled by a Canadian public corporation.

The requirement to report particular uncertain tax treatments would apply to a private corporation that meets the asset threshold if it, or a related corporation, has audited financial statements prepared in accordance with IFRS. While normally a private corporation would not have audited financial statements prepared in accordance with IFRS, where it does, those statements would be presented on a consolidated basis with those corporations it controls and would, when appropriate, reflect uncertainty pertaining to uncertain tax treatments relating to those corporations.

The requirement to report particular uncertain tax treatments would also apply to a corporation if it meets the asset threshold and it, or a related corporation, has audited financial statements prepared in accordance with another country-specific GAAP relevant for domestic public corporations (e.g., U.S. GAAP). For example, the requirement to report would apply, subject to the asset threshold, if a U.S.-resident corporation had taken a tax position on its Canadian income tax return for a year and recorded a reserve with respect to that tax position in its audited financial statements prepared in accordance with U.S. GAAP. This part of the proposal is meant to ensure that the requirement to report particular uncertain tax treatments would apply appropriately where a corporation is a Canadian corporation controlled by a non-resident corporation or is a non-resident corporation with a taxable presence in Canada (e.g., carrying on business in Canada through a permanent establishment).

For each reportable uncertain tax treatment of a corporation, the corporation would be required to provide prescribed information, such as the quantum of taxes at issue, a concise description of the relevant facts, the tax treatment taken (including the relevant sections of the *Income Tax Act*) and whether the uncertainty relates to a permanent or temporary difference in tax. It is expected that there would be a limited administrative burden for reporting corporations as the information to be reported would not be extensive and would be readily available given the need to analyze uncertain tax treatments as part of the preparation of financial statements.

It is proposed that uncertain tax treatments be required to be reported at the same time that the reporting corporation's Canadian income tax return is due. The introduction of a requirement to report particular uncertain tax treatments is intended to provide information to the CRA to allow it to more efficiently administer and enforce the *Income Tax Act*. It would not directly impact the income tax liabilities of corporate taxpayers.

Reassessment Period

When a taxpayer files an income tax return for a taxation year, the CRA is required to perform an initial examination of the return and to assess tax payable, if any, with all due dispatch. The CRA then normally has a fixed period, referred to as the "normal reassessment period", after its initial examination beyond which it is precluded from reassessing the taxpayer (i.e., reassessment of the taxation year becomes statute-barred). The normal reassessment period is generally three or four years, depending on the type of taxpayer.

In support of the new mandatory disclosure rules, it is proposed that, where a taxpayer has a reporting requirement in respect of a transaction relevant to the taxpayer's income tax return for a taxation year, the normal reassessment period would not commence in respect of the transaction until the taxpayer has complied with the reporting requirement. As a result, if a taxpayer does not comply with a mandatory disclosure reporting requirement for a taxation year in respect of a transaction, a reassessment of the year in respect of the transaction would not become statute-barred.

Penalties

The BEPS Action 12 Report recommends that countries introduce financial penalties that apply when disclosure rules are not complied with and that consideration be given to percentage-based penalties based upon transaction size or the extent of any tax savings.

Taxpayer Penalty

To support the proposed reporting requirements, it is proposed that, with respect to persons who enter into reportable or notifiable transactions, or for whom a tax benefit results from a reportable or notifiable transaction, a penalty of $500 per week apply for each failure to report a reportable transaction or a notifiable transaction,

- up to the greater of $25,000 and 25% of the tax benefit; or

- for corporations that have assets that have a total carrying value of $50 million or more, a penalty of $2,000 per week, up to the greater of $100,000 and 25% of the tax benefit.

Promoter Penalty

It is also proposed that, with respect to advisors and promoters of reportable or notifiable transactions, as well as with respect to persons who do not deal at arm's length with them and who are entitled to a fee with respect to the transactions, a penalty be imposed for each failure to report equal to the total of:

- 100% of the fees charged by that person to a person for whom a tax benefit results;

- $10,000; and

- $1,000 for each day during which the failure to report continues, up to a maximum of $100,000.

In order to avoid imposing two sets of penalties upon a person who both 1) enters into a reportable or notifiable transaction for the benefit of another person, and 2) is a person who does not deal at arm's length with an advisor or promoter in respect of the reportable or notifiable transaction and is entitled to a fee, it is proposed that such a person be subject only to the greater of the penalties discussed above.

Uncertain Tax Treatment Penalty

For corporations subject to the requirement to report uncertain tax treatments, it is proposed that the penalty for failure to report each particular uncertain tax treatment be $2,000 per week, up to a maximum of $100,000.

[See also Proposed Amendment under 160(1) — ed.]

Federal Budget, Chapter 10, April 19, 2021: *Mandatory Disclosure Rules*

It is important that the Canada Revenue Agency be able to obtain timely information on arrangements that involve aggressive tax planning. Canada has been an active participant in the Base Erosion and Profit Shifting (BEPS) Project — an initiative of the G20 and the Organisation for Economic Co-operation and Development. The BEPS Project is primarily devoted to tackling the problem of certain corporations and wealthy individuals inappropriately shifting profits offshore and using other international tax avoidance schemes. This project has shown that stronger rules are needed to strengthen the Canada Revenue Agency's ability to curtail tax evasion and aggressive tax avoidance in both the domestic and international context.

Budget 2021 launches public consultations on proposals to enhance Canada's income tax mandatory disclosure rules, building on the advice of the BEPS Project. This consultation will address changes to the *Income Tax Act*'s reportable transaction rules, a new requirement to report notifiable transactions, and a new requirement for specified corporations to report uncertain tax treatments.

Consultation document, Dept of Finance April 19, 2021: *Income Tax Mandatory Disclosure Rules Consultation*

Current Status: Open until September 3, 2021

Join In

A tax system in which everyone pays their fair share requires action on multiple fronts. This includes strengthening the Canada Revenue Agency's ability to curtail tax evasion and aggressive tax avoidance. In support of this goal, the government is consulting on proposals to enhance Canada's income tax mandatory disclosure rules. Details about this proposal are available in the Budget 2021 Annex entitled Tax Measures: Supplementary Information.

Specifically, this consultation will address changes proposed to the *Income Tax Act*'s reportable transaction rules, a new requirement to report notifiable transactions, and a new requirement for specified corporations to report uncertain tax treatments.

We also welcome any additional comments or feedback relevant to the scope of this consultation.

Who is the focus of this consultation?

Through this consultation, we want to hear from interested stakeholders including tax practitioners, civil society groups and members of the public. In submitting your comments, please include:

- Full name;
- Name of the organization;
- Telephone number, including area code; and
- Reply e-mail address.

Participate through email

Due to COVID-19 public health considerations, email submissions are preferred. Send us your comments at fin.taxdisclosure-divulgationfiscale.fin@canada.ca with "MDR Consultation" as the subject line.

Should you wish to provide comments by mail, please direct your submission to the attention of the Tax Policy Branch.

What's next?

Our conversation doesn't end here.

We'll be collecting your feedback and will consider your input alongside the analysis of departmental officials to help inform decisions on the proposed enhancement of Canada's income tax mandatory disclosure rules.

Information received through this comment process is subject to the *Access to Information Act* and the *Privacy Act*. Those providing comments are asked to indicate clearly the name of the individual or the organization that should be identified as having made the submission. In order to respect privacy and confidentiality, please advise when providing your comments whether you:

- consent to the disclosure of your comments in whole or in part;
- request that your identity and any personal identifiers be removed prior to release; or
- wish that any portions of your comments be kept confidential (if so, clearly identify the confidential portions).

Should you indicate that your comments, or any portions thereof, be considered confidential, the Department of Finance will make all reasonable efforts to protect this information.

Get in touch

fin.taxdisclosure-divulgationfiscale.fin@canada.ca

Notes [s. 237.3]: 237.3 requires reporting of a tax avoidance plan (on Form RC312) even if it is not a "tax shelter" under 237.1, if it has two of the three "hallmarks" in 237.3(1)"reportable transaction": (a) contingent fees for the promoter; (b) "confidential protection" (237.3(1)); and (c) "contractual protection" (237.3(1)) such as insurance or a promise to defend the scheme. Failure to file leads to: penalty under 237.3(8), (15); extended reassessment deadline under 152(4)(b.1); and denial of the tax savings by 237.3(6) until the RC312 is filed and all penalty and interest are paid.

237.3 does not apply if the tax-shelter reporting rules in 237.1 apply: 237.3(14)(a); VIEWS doc 2013-0486061E5.

For discussion see Oldewening, "Federal Proposals to Require Reporting of Tax Avoidance Transactions", 54 *McCarthy Tétrault on Tax Disputes* (CCH) 2-6 (July 2010); STEP Canada letters to Finance (step.ca > "Press Room"), July 6/10 and Sept. 27/10 (notes that 237.3 can make the client doubly liable for both the advisor's and the promoter's penalties); Carr & Nurmohamed, "Tax Avoidance Transaction Reporting Regime", VIII(1) *Resource Sector Taxation* (Federated Press) 550-54 (2010); Jang, "Aggressive Transaction Reporting Revisited", 1(3) *Canadian Tax Focus* (ctf.ca) 5-6 (Nov. 2011); Larin, "Some Thoughts on Disclosure Rules in Canada", 61(Supp.) *Cana-*

dian Tax Journal 209-20 (2013); Campbell, *Administration of Income Tax 2020* (Carswell), §3.7. Concerns about solicitor-client privilege have largely been resolved by 237.3(17).

Quebec brought in rules before 237.3, announcing provincial tax measures in Oct. 2009 to address "aggressive tax planning". The Quebec rules feature: (1) mandatory disclosure of arrangements resulting in a tax benefit if a confidentiality agreement applies or if the advisor is paid based on tax savings; (2) a three-year extension to the assessment limitation period if GAAR applies; (3) penalties on both taxpayers and promoters if GAAR applies. Disclosure is now done on Form TP-1079.DI. The penalty for non-disclosure is $10,000 plus $1,000 per day up to 90 days, so it is fixed at $100,000 after 90 days. See Lacelle, "Quebec's Measures to Combat Aggressive Tax Planning", 2009 Cdn Tax Foundation conference report, 34:1-24. Under *Morguard Investments v. De Savoye*, [1990] 3 S.C.R. 1077 (SCC), Quebec can perhaps enforce a penalty on a non-Quebec promoter, as the "revenue rule" (see 223(3) Notes) may not apply to provincial tax: see Pelletier, "Interprovincial Enforcement of Tax Judgments" (Uniform Law Conference of Canada, ulcc.ca, 2006). See also Finances Québec Information Bulletins 2010-4 (Feb. 26, 2010), and 2019-5 (May 17, 2019). Revenu Québec will not reveal how many disclosures have been made: 2011 conference report, CRA/RQ Round Table q.14 (p.4:10-11). Quebec Bill 42 (2019) adds a further rule (*Taxation Act* s. 1079.8.6.2) requiring disclosure of "specified transactions" similar to those publicly listed by Revenu Québec. The first "specified transactions" list was released on March 17, 2021: avoiding deemed disposal of trust property; payment to non-treaty country; multiplying the capital gains exemption; tax attribute trading. See E&Y *Tax Alert* 2021-14, "Quebec releases list of transactions for mandatory disclosure" (April 2021). See also Caillé & Barchichat, "Impact of Quebec's Required Planning Disclosure Reaches Beyond the Province", 11(2) *Canadian Tax Focus* (ctf.ca) 7-8 (May 2021). (See also end of Notes to 54"capital property" re Quebec requirement to disclose bare trust or nominee arrangements.)

Ontario incorporates 237.3 into a reporting requirement; *Taxation Act, 2007*, s. 110.1.

For similar rules in other countries see Wiebe et al., "Global Trends in Information Reporting", 2010 Cdn Tax Foundation conference report, 3:1-23; Tim Edgar review of 2011 publications, 59(4) *Canadian Tax Journal* 919-21 (2011); *The Global Forum on Transparency and Exchange of Information for Tax Purposes*, oecd.org/tax/transparency; OECD BEPS Action 12, under "Possible Future Amendments" at end of s. 95 [Barnicke & Huynh, "EU Mandatory Disclosure", 26(6) *Canadian Tax Highlights* (ctf.ca) 1-2 (June 2018); EU Directive 2018/822 (May 25, 2018), tinyurl.com/eu-2018-822].

237.3 added by 2002-2013 technical bill, for avoidance transactions that are entered into after 2010 or that are part of a series of transactions that began before 2011 and is completed after 2010, with limited grandfathering for a series that began before 2011.

See also Notes to 237.3(5) re extended deadline for a return required before July 2012.

Definitions [s. 237.3]: "advisor" — 237.3(1); "amount" — 248(1); "arm's length" — 251(1); "assessment" — 248(1); "avoidance transaction" — 237.3(1), 245(3); "calendar year" — *Interpretation Act* 37(1)(a); "confidential protection", "contractual protection", "fee" — 237.3(1); "flow-through share" — 66(15), 248(1); "lawyer" — 232(1), 248(1); "Minister" — 248(1); "partnership" — see 96(1) Notes; "person" — 237.3(1), 248(1); "prescribed" — 248(1); "promoter" — 237.3(1); "reportable transaction" — 237.3(1), (14); "series", "series of transactions" — 248(10); "solicitor-client privilege" — 232(1), 237.3(1); "tax benefit" — 237.3(1); "tax shelter" — 237.1(1), 248(1); "taxation year" — 249; "taxpayer" — 248(1); "transaction" — 237.3(1).

Offences and Punishment

238. (1) Offences and punishment — Every person who has failed to file or make a return as and when required by or under this Act or a regulation or who has failed to comply with subsection 116(3), 127(3.1) or (3.2), 147.1(7) or 153(1), any of sections 230 to 232, 244.7 and 267 or a regulation made under subsection 147.1(18) or with an order made under subsection (2) is guilty of an offence and, in addition to any penalty otherwise provided, is liable on summary conviction to

(a) a fine of not less than $1,000 and not more than $25,000; or

(b) both the fine described in paragraph (a) and imprisonment for a term not exceeding 12 months.

Related Provisions: 162, 163 — Penalties; 242 — Where corporation is guilty of offence; 243 — Minimum fine; 244(4) — Summary conviction charges must be laid within 8 years; *Interpretation Act* 34(1) — Indictable and summary conviction offences; *Interpretation Act* 34(2) — *Criminal Code* provisions apply.

Notes: See Notes to 239(1). CRA does not lay charges for failing to file a return unless a formal demand was made under 150(2) or 231.2(1)(a) and the person still did not comply, and the Courts in practice require a demand to have been made even though 238(1) does not. See also 2(1) Notes re OPCA (organized pseudo-legal commercial arguments). However, failing to file so as to evade tax can lead to conviction under 239(1)(d) even without a demand: *Balla*, 2010 BCSC 486.

For some convictions under 238(1) see *Sturby*, 2005 BCPC 583; *Blackburn*, 2006 BCPC 513; *Smith*, 2006 BCSC 1493 (leave to appeal denied 2007 BCCA 499); *McCul-*

lough, 2007 BCPC 87 (60 days in jail + $10,000 fine); *Maleki*, 2007 ONCJ 186 (blank return marked "N/A" throughout was not valid return); *McKinney*, 2008 BCCA 211; *Meikle*, 2008 BCPC 265 (leave to appeal denied 2010 BCCA 337) (trespass when serving demands to file was irrelevant); *Donaldson*, 2009 SKQB 251; *Brewer*, 2009 NBPC 37 (delays in filing returns after demand made); *Hanlon*, 2009 BCCA 598; *Burko*, 2011 ONSC 479 (failure to comply with Requirement for Information); *Skjonsby*, 2011 SKQB 341 (56 days of imprisonment ordered for non-payment of $16,500 in fines for non-filing); *Logan*, 2014 BCCA 240 (leave to appeal denied 2015 CarswellBC 75 (SCC)) (failure to comply with demand to file returns); *Nicol*, 2013 BCSC 1936 (hiring accountant shortly before the Requirement deadline was not due diligence); *O'Hara*, 2017 NSPC 31; *Steeves*, 2019 BCSC 1471 (trial was not unfair); *Merrill*, 2021 BCSC 1017 (OPCA: 90 days in jail + fine). See also tinyurl.com/cra-convict.

For acquittals see *Sarkis*, 2003 CarswellOnt 9276 (Ont. CJ) (demand to file 9 years' returns sought statements of assets, liabilities, income and expenses, which were not actually required, and S was unable to comply in time); *MacDonald*, 2005 BCPC 398 (Crown did not prove that 30 days to comply was reasonable); *Wells*, 2004 BCSC 1722 (due diligence defence); *Odishaw*, 2005 BCCA 363 (director charged with failing to file corporate returns but obligation was that of the corp); *Audiotrack GP*, 2006 ONCJ 375 (tax shelter promoters did everything possible to comply); *MacLean*, 2007 BCPC 269 (due diligence where M failed to file deceased mother's returns, as she relied on lawyer and bookkeeper who said returns were not ready). The Crown's appeal succeeded and a new trial was ordered in both *Packard*, 2006 BCSC 719 (demand to file returns was related directly to P's tax liability), and *Allard*, 2016 ONSC 7481 ("too hard to file T2s" was not valid due-diligence defence).

The reference to 244.7 imposes punishment for wilful failure to keep records of international electronic transfers. (Not filing the return for such transfers under 244.2 falls under "failed to file or make a return as an when required by or under this Act".)

The reference to 267 imposes punishment for wilful failure by a financial institution to keep records of US persons having interests in financial accounts. (Not filing the information return reporting such accounts under s. 266 falls under "failed to file or make a return as and when required...".) There is no punishment for a *taxpayer* who does not provide correct information, as ss. 263-269 do not obligate taxpayers to provide information.

238(1) opening words amended to add reference to 244.7 and 267 by 2014 budget bill #1, effective June 19, 2014.

Information Circulars: 00-1R4: Voluntary disclosures program.

Registered Plans Compliance Bulletins: 8 (requirements to provide information under s. 231.2).

CRA Audit Manual: 8.5.0: Non-compliance identification projects; 10.11.8: Referrals to enforcement and disclosure directorate; 15.5.0: Foreign-based information and documentation.

(2) Compliance orders

(2) Compliance orders — Where a person has been convicted by a court of an offence under subsection (1) for a failure to comply with a provision of this Act or a regulation, the court may make such order as it deems proper in order to enforce compliance with the provision.

Related Provisions: 231.7 — Compliance order for assistance with audit or demand.

Notes: See Notes to 231.7 for compliance orders relating to audits and Requirements for Information, and contempt proceedings on failing to comply.

In *Henneberry*, 2002 NSPC 20, 238(2) was used to order a bankrupt to pay the CRA the source deductions his corporation had withheld and not remitted, even though he had already been fined $12,000 and discharged from bankruptcy.

In *Tysowski*, 2008 SKCA 88, the provincial court was entitled to take notice of its own records to determine that it had issued a compliance order, so as to convict the taxpayer under 238(1).

In *Nelson*, 2013 ABPC 135, the Court reviewed numerous past cases and imposed a $2,000 fine (with imprisonment if not paid) for failing to comply with an order to file various returns.

A single information could be used to charge the accused with not filing multiple returns as ordered under 238(2): *Tardif*, 2017 BCPC 262.

Information Circulars: 73-10R3: Tax evasion.

(3) Saving

(3) Saving — Where a person has been convicted under this section of failing to comply with a provision of this Act or a regulation, the person is not liable to pay a penalty imposed under section 162 or 227 for the same failure unless the person was assessed for that penalty or that penalty was demanded from the person before the information or complaint giving rise to the conviction was laid or made.

Notes: See under 239(3), which provides a parallel rule for conviction under s. 239.

Definitions [s. 238]: "person", "regulation" — 248(1).

239. (1) Other offences and punishment

239. (1) Other offences and punishment — Every person who has

(a) made, or participated in, assented to or acquiesced in the making of, false or deceptive statements in a return, certificate, statement or answer filed or made as required by or under this Act or a regulation,

(b) to evade payment of a tax imposed by this Act, destroyed, altered, mutilated, secreted or otherwise disposed of the records or books of account of a taxpayer,

(c) made, or assented to or acquiesced in the making of, false or deceptive entries, or omitted, or assented to or acquiesced in the omission, to enter a material particular, in records or books of account of a taxpayer,

(d) wilfully, in any manner, evaded or attempted to evade compliance with this Act or payment of taxes imposed by this Act, or

(e) conspired with any person to commit an offence described by paragraphs (a) to (d),

is guilty of an offence and, in addition to any penalty otherwise provided, is liable on summary conviction to

(f) a fine of not less than 50%, and not more than 200%, of the amount of the tax that was sought to be evaded, or

(g) both the fine described in paragraph (f) and imprisonment for a term not exceeding 2 years.

Announced Administrative Change — More resources to combat tax evasion

Federal Budget, March 19, 2019, Chapter 4, Part 7: *Improving Tax Compliance*

The taxes we pay support government services that benefit all Canadians — from health care and education to affordable housing and public safety. By cracking down on tax evasion and aggressive tax avoidance, the Government is ensuring that it has the money needed to deliver the programs that Canadians depend on.

Significant investments have been made in recent years to strengthen the Canada Revenue Agency's (CRA's) ability to unravel complex tax schemes, increase collaboration with international partners, and ultimately bring offenders to justice.

These investments have already yielded positive results.

Starting in 2015, the CRA expanded the number of audit teams that focus on high net worth individuals and their associated corporate structures. As a result, there are now more than 1,100 offshore audits underway, resulting in more than 50 criminal investigations with links to offshore transactions.

To further combat tax evasion and aggressive tax avoidance, Budget 2019 proposes to invest an additional $150.8 million over five years, starting in 2019-20. This investment will allow the CRA to fund new initiatives and extend existing programs, including:

- Hiring additional auditors, conducting outreach and building technical expertise to target non-compliance associated with cryptocurrency transactions and the digital economy.

- Creating a new data quality examination team to ensure proper withholding, remitting and reporting of income earned by non-residents.

- Extending programs aimed at combatting offshore non-compliance.

Budget 2019 accounts for the expected revenue impact from these targeted compliance initiatives, of $369.0 million over five years. These amounts do not reflect the gain that will be realized by provinces and territories, whose tax revenues will also increase as a result of these initiatives.

To help the CRA stay ahead of non-compliance schemes driven by the use of new, advanced technologies, Budget 2019 also proposes to invest $65.8 million over five years to improve the CRA's information technology systems, including replacing legacy systems, so that the infrastructure used to fight tax evasion and aggressive tax avoidance continues to evolve.

Federal Economic Statement, Chapter 4, Nov. 30, 2020: *§4.8.2.3 Strengthening Tax Compliance*

Taxes help pay for the government services that benefit Canadians. They help pay for the medical care that keeps us healthy. They provide a social safety net so that in times of crisis, all Canadians have a lifeline. They create opportunities through investments in innovation and new infrastructure that can help the economy grow. They help ensure that Canada is a place where no one is left behind.

That is why, since Budget 2016, the government has committed $350 million per year on an ongoing basis for the Canada Revenue Agency (CRA) to crack down on tax evasion and combat aggressive tax avoidance. These investments target a range of complex tax schemes in areas such as offshore tax evasion and the underground economy. The government's efforts have yielded positive results.

Building on these investments, the government proposes an **additional $606 million over 5 years**, starting in 2021-22, to allow the CRA to fund new initiatives and extend existing programs targeting international tax evasion and aggressive tax avoidance. Specifically, the CRA will hire additional offshore-focused auditors to focus on individuals who avoid taxes by hiding income and assets offshore, enhance the audit function targeting higher-risk tax filings, including those of high-net worth individuals, and strengthen its ability to fight tax crimes such as money laundering and terrorist financing by upgrading tools and increasing international cooperation.

The government estimates that these measures to combat international tax evasion and aggressive tax avoidance will recover $1.4 billion in revenues over 5 years. These amounts do not reflect the gains that will be realized by provinces and territories, whose tax revenues will also increase as a result of these initiatives.

Federal Budget, Chapter 10, April 19, 2021: *Tackling Tax Avoidance and Evasion*

The government has made significant investments since 2015 to strengthen the Canada Revenue Agency's (CRA's) ability to crack down on complex tax schemes, increase collaboration with international partners, and ultimately bring offenders to justice. These investments have yielded positive results.

Budget 2021 builds on these previous investments with new measures to combat tax evasion and aggressive tax avoidance. Having the means to avoid paying one's fair share should not mean that one can.

Budget 2021 proposes an additional $304.1 million over five years, starting in 2021-22, to allow the CRA to fund new initiatives and extend existing programs, including:

- Increasing GST/HST audits of large businesses where risk assessment models have found the greatest risk of non-compliance.

- Modernizing the CRA's risk assessment process to prevent unwarranted and fraudulent GST/HST refund and rebate claims at the outset, and improve the ability to issue refunds for compliant businesses as quickly as possible.

- Enhancing capacity to identify tax evasion involving trusts and provide better service to executors and trustees.

Budget 2021 estimates that these measures to combat tax evasion and aggressive tax avoidance will recover $810 million in revenues over five years. Additional gains will be realized by provinces and territories, whose tax revenues will also increase as a result of these initiatives.

Related Provisions: 163(2) — Penalty — false statements; 239(1.1) — Offences re refunds and credits; 239(2) — Prosecution on indictment; 239.1 — Offences re zapper software; 242 — Where corporation is guilty of offence; 243 — Minimum fine; 244(4) — Summary conviction charges must be laid within 8 years; *Interpretation Act* 34(1) — Indictable and summary conviction offences; *Interpretation Act* 34(2) — *Criminal Code* provisions apply.

Notes: Assessment of a *penalty* under any of 162, 163, 163.1, 163.2, 163.3, 237.3(8) or 247(3) is CRA administrative action, and there is no *Charter of Rights* protection as there is for criminal law: *Martineau*, 2004 SCC 81; *Bisaillon*, 2005 TCC 17. See Notes to 162(1). However, *conviction* under 238 or 239 requires prosecution in provincial court and is criminal law: *Knox Contracting*, [1990] 2 C.T.C. 262 (SCC). For more on the distinction see *Guindon*, 2015 SCC 41, paras. 63-67. Failing to file (s. 238) is a "strict liability" offence requiring only proof of the act and no *mens rea* (*La Souveraine v. Autorité des marchés financiers*, 2013 SCC 63, para. 33), and has a "due diligence" defence (see Notes to 162(1)). For evasion (s. 239), which is a "true criminal offence" (*Klundert*, [2004] 5 C.T.C. 20 (Ont CA), para. 32; leave to appeal denied 2005 CarswellOnt 1118 (SCC)), there must be *mens rea* (guilty intent, or at least wilful blindness) and the accused must be found guilty beyond a reasonable doubt (see below). An incorrect belief that the Act is constitutionally invalid is no defence: see Notes to 2(1).

Due to *Interpretation Act* 34(2), the *Criminal Code* applies to proceedings under 238 and 239. See Notes to 239(3) re both penalties and criminal charges applying to the same actions. See 242 re charging both corporation and director/officer with the same offence. See also articles on penalties at end of Notes to 163(1). *Charter of Rights* issues: see Notes to 171(1).

There is no obligation in the ITA to correct a past error in a return (as there is for reporting on imports: *Customs Act* s. 32.2, and as Reg. 8401(6) requires for a T4 affected by a pension adjustment change, and as the UK now requires for offshore tax liabilities: tinyurl.com/uk-rtc, and as Tax Court Rule 98(1)(a) requires for errors in discovery answers), so failing to correct an error that comes to the taxpayer's attention, or to correct an incorrect information slip, is not a criminal offence and should not trigger any penalty that did not already apply to the error.

A judge can order that property be seized without a conviction as proceeds of crime, per *Criminal Code* s. 462.32 or provincial legislation such as the Ontario *Civil Remedies Act, 2001*: see CRA news releases, "Property seized as proceeds of crime in tax evasion case" (Nov. 22, 2018) (6 rental properties and car seized); "Money laundering scheme: enforcement measures taken" (Feb. 12, 2019) (restraint orders against 6 properties worth $15.8m).

See generally CRA *Criminal Investigations Manual* (CIM), on *TaxPartner* or *Taxnet Pro*. For a prosecution originating in Audit, CRA first refers the file to Investigations. If several levels of management then agree there is a good chance of conviction, the file is referred to the Public Prosecution Service of Canada (PPSC), which makes the final decision, lays charges and handles the prosecution. The Attorney General of Canada (and thus PPSC) has standing to prosecute, per *Criminal Code* ss. 2 and 785, since

the ITA is a federal Act: *Tyskerud*, 2011 BCPC 502. There is also "early resolution", whereby an accused pleads guilty quickly, before referral to PPSC: CIM §1.6.

CRA now fingerprints everyone charged with evasion: CBC, tinyurl.com/cra-fingerp.

"If at the preliminary investigation stage it is apparent that the subject's health is such that it impairs their ability to manage their affairs on a day-to-day basis or that they will be unable to withstand the emotional and public pressure of a full scale investigation and prosecution, the case should be closed": CIM §5.4(1).

"Reasonable doubt" was defined by the Supreme Court of Canada in *Lifchus*, [1997] 3 S.C.R. 320, para. 39 as: "not an imaginary or a frivolous doubt. It must not be based on sympathy or prejudice. Rather, it is based on reason and common sense. It is logically derived from the evidence or absence of evidence. Even if you believe the accused is probably guilty or likely guilty, that is not sufficient.... On the other hand you must remember that it is virtually impossible to prove anything to an absolute certainty and the Crown is not required to do so.... In short if, based on the evidence or lack of evidence you are sure that the accused committed the offence you should convict ..."

Where credibility is at issue, "the court must acquit the accused in three situations: a) if he is believed, or, b) even if he is not believed but the court is left with a reasonable doubt by his evidence, or c) even if not left in doubt by the evidence of the accused, whether on the basis of the evidence which is accepted, the evidence establishes proof of guilt beyond a reasonable doubt": *Samaroo*, 2011 BCPC 503.

Only if tax liability is "clear-cut, obvious, indisputable and unquestionable" can the taxpayer be convicted: *Redpath Industries*, [1984] C.T.C. 483 (Que. SC), para. 15; *Bromley*, 2004 BCPC 48, para. 165. However, this principle cannot be used to dismiss charges before trial, since the obviousness of the liability is determined after all evidence is led: *McCartie*, 2012 BCSC 928 and 2012 BCPC 510; *Anderson*, 2014 BCSC 2002, paras. 34-37. As to whether an accused can argue that optional deductions were available to reduce or eliminate the tax allegedly evaded, see Innes, *Tax Evasion* (*Taxnet Pro* Reference Centre), §6.8.

Where it was not certain beyond reasonable doubt that accused M, not his accountant, failed to report the income, M was acquitted: *McMahon*, 2013 ABPC 239.

On an investigator giving opinion evidence without being qualified as an expert, see *Ajise*, 2018 ONCA 494, aff'd 2018 SCC 51.

In 239(1)(b), "to evade payment" means "in order to evade payment".

In 239(1)(f), "tax that was sought to be *evaded*" does not refer only to "evade" in 239(1)(b) and (d), but to all of 239(1)(a)-(e): *Steinkey*, 2019 ABCA 259, paras. 11-12.

A fine under 239(1)(f) or 239(2)(a) is calculated on only the *federal* tax; charges would have to be laid under the parallel provincial provision (e.g., Ontario *Taxation Act, 2007* s. 144) for the fine to apply to the provincial tax evasion.

As an alternative to s. 239, the Crown increasingly lays charges of fraud under *Criminal Code* (CC) s. 380 in serious cases. (The exact amount of tax fraud need not be proven: *Khan*, 2015 ONSC 7283, paras. 606-621.) This may be due to higher sentences (max 14 years, and minimum 2 years if the fraud exceeds $1m, *per* 380(1.1), albeit no minimum fine): Andy Noroozi, "Les infractions fiscales: évasion selon les lois fiscales ou fraude selon le Code criminel?", 35(2) *Revue de planification fiscale et financière* (apff.org) 319-91 (2015). CC 380.1 lists aggravating circumstances the court must consider, such as the fraud exceeding $1 million.

See Notes to 231.2(1) re CRA not being permitted to use its audit powers for an investigation (the *Jarvis* principle). Criminal proceedings should not be used or threatened to collect tax debts: VIEWS doc 2010-0360191I7.

A *failure to file returns* for purposes of evading tax can be evasion under 239(1)(d). See *Nicolau*, 2011 ONSC 3809; *Andrus*, 2013 BCPC 160; *Wilm*, 2016 ONCJ 852. In *Taylor*, 2016 NLPC 113, late filing returns was not proven to have been for the purpose of evading tax.

The elements of tax evasion required for conviction are "jurisdiction, identification, the requisite conduct (*actus reus*) and the requisite mental element or intent (*mens rea*)": *Porisky*, 2012 BCSC 67, para. 10 (rev'd on other grounds 2014 BCCA 146). The exact amount of tax evaded is not an essential element of the offence, but is relevant to sentencing: para. 12. The conduct the Crown must prove is "that the accused voluntarily performed an act or engaged in a course of conduct that avoided or attempted to avoid payment of tax owing under the Act": para. 13. See also *Paveley*, [1976] C.T.C. 477 (Sask. CA, Bayda J.A.) on *actus reus* and *mens rea*.

An accused's argument that he could have claimed CCA to reduce unreported income to zero, so that no tax was evaded, was rejected as "completely without merit" in *Glubis*, 2015 SKPC 143, para. 153, because any CCA used would be unavailable in some other year.

Misleading CRA about a claim during the audit process was grounds for conviction even if the accused thought the claim was valid when it was first filed: *Global Enviro*, 2011 ABQB 32. (Note that 239(1)(a) applies to a "statement or answer" made.) In *Scholz*, 2020 BCPC 120, providing false and backdated documents to Audit led to conviction for evasion and using forged documents.

Withdrawing a guilty plea is not allowed if the accused was represented by competent counsel and made a voluntary decision to plead guilty: *Fawaz*, 2008 BCSC 656; *Chandra*, 2009 ABCA 298; *BT Céramiques*, 2018 QCCA 598; *Steinkey*, 2018 ABCA 361.

Sentencing: "The provisions of Part 23 of the *Criminal Code*, including specifically s. 718, which sets out the purpose and principles of sentencing, and s. 742, which allows for conditional sentences of imprisonment, apply to offences committed against the *Income Tax Act* or the *Excise Tax Act*": *Baudais*, 2014 BCSC 2161, para. 24. Among the longest sentences reported for tax fraud in Canada (sometimes combined with other offences) are: 11 years (*Cameron*, 2020 ABCA 405, leave to appeal denied 2021 CarswellAlta 651 (SCC): RRSP fraud on investors plus tax evasion); 10 years (*Tennina*, 2013 ONSC 4694); 10 years (*Bjellebo (Bellfield)*, 2003 CarswellOnt 3955 (Ont CA, leave to appeal denied 2004 CarswellOnt 1761 (SCC))); 9 years (*Wilder*, 2008 BCCA 370 (leave to appeal denied by SCC 2009 CarswellBC 572 (SCC))); 4+5 years if $1.2m fine not paid (*Dieckmann*, 2017 ONCA 575; leave to appeal denied 2018 CarswellOnt 4161 (SCC)). See also Ruby, *Sentencing* (LexisNexis, 10th ed., 2020, 1400pp); Robitaille & Winocur, *Sentencing: Principles and Practice* (emond.ca, 2020, 484pp); Innes, *Tax Evasion* (Carswell, looseleaf or *Taxnet Pro* Reference Centre), chap. 7, "Sentence" (includes table of sentences imposed); and Cases annotation to s. 327 in *Practitioner's Goods and Services Tax Annotated*. A joint sentencing submission (plea bargain) should normally be accepted by the judge; for exceptions see *Anthony-Cook*, 2016 SCC 43. A sentence can be varied on appeal only if the trial judge's decision is unreasonable: *Lacasse*, 2015 SCC 64, para. 78; *Mahmood*, 2016 ONCA 75, para. 18. In *Sharma*, 2018 ABCA 373, bail was revoked pending sentencing, due to delay by S checking himself into hospital to avoid being sent to prison.

Rowbotham applications: A state-funded lawyer was denied in tax evasion prosecutions or appeals in: *Schiel*, 2004 BCPC 436 and 2012 BCCA 1; *Bath*, 2013 BCCA 126; *Johnston*, [2014] G.S.T.C. 70 (Ont. SCJ); *Hennessey*, 2017 NLCA 23; *Mahmood*, 2015 ONCA 442; *Martin*, 2015 NSCA 82; *Lawson*, 2017 BCCA 288.

For discussion of evasion see Innes, *Tax Evasion* (Carswell, looseleaf or *Taxnet Pro* Reference Centre); Campbell, *Administration of Income Tax 2020* (Carswell), chap. 12; David Sherman's analysis of ETA s. 327 in the *Canada GST Service*, *GST Partner* or *Taxnet Pro*; Boddez & DelBigio, "Criminal Tax Evasion", 2012 Cdn Tax Foundation conference report, 38:1-28; Charbonneau, "Tax Evasion from the Government's Perspective", 2012 *Tax Dispute Resolution* conf. report (ctf.ca), 22:1-13; Sturrock & Meikle-Kahs, "Tax Evasion from the Government's Perspective", *ibid.*, 23:1-16; Cloutier, "Update on the CRA, Evasion and Avoidance", XX(3) *Tax Litigation* (Federated Press) 2-5 (2017); Roberge, "A Primer on Tax Evasion Charges and Convictions", 2501 *Tax Topics* (CCH) 1-8 (Feb. 13, 2020).

In 2017-18, the conviction rate was 91.7% (*Departmental Results Report*, tinyurl.com/cra-results, p. 20) (no data in 2018-19 or 2019-20 Reports).

Convictions: See generally canada.ca/cra-convictions and tinyurl.com/cra-trident. For convictions of "tax protesters" or "detaxers", see Notes to 2(1) and 248(1)"person". For shareholders not reporting appropriation of corporate property, see Notes to 15(1). For house and condo flippers, see Notes to 40(2)(b). For claiming false Child Tax Benefits, see Notes to 122.61(1).

eBay: See Notes to 231.2(1) re eBay being forced to disclose its vendor information. The first reported eBay conviction was Laurier Chabot of Nipawin, SK (fur coats), fined $68,000 (CRA news release, Aug. 27, 2010).

Net worth assessment convictions (see Notes to 152(7)) are possible: *Ross*, [1998] 3 C.T.C. 159 (NSSC); *Zuk*, 2005 ONCJ 428; *Zuk*, 2012 ONSC 2235; *Hunter*, 2008 ONCA 103; *Valovic*, 2011 ONCA 320 (leave to appeal denied [2011] G.S.T.C 152 (SCC)). In *Samaroo*, 2011 BCPC 503, the taxpayers were acquitted, sued for malicious prosecution, won at trial but lost on appeal: 2019 BCCA 113 (leave to appeal denied 2019 CarswellBC 2946 (SCC)).

Offshore accounts: Swiss and other foreign bank secrecy has disappeared, and taxpayers with unreported foreign bank accounts should assume CRA will find them. See Notes to: 281 (re 270-281: Common Reporting Standard automatic exchange of account information among 100 countries); 244.2(1) (re 244.1-244.7: international-transfer disclosure); 56(1)(z.4) (Offshore Informant Program); Zagaris, "Transparency and Disclosure", 2019 Cdn Tax Foundation conference report, 8:1-27; and issue 1(4) *Perspectives on Tax Law & Policy* (ctf.ca) 1-17 (Dec. 2020). Disclosure by the International Consortium of Investigative Journalists of the Panama Papers (2016), the Paradise Papers (2017) (both leaked from law firms) and others reveals a lot; see offshoreleaks.icij.org. The "Falciani List" of Swiss HSBC accounts as of 2007-08 was sold to the French government, which provided details on Canadians to CRA in 2010: *Stankovic*, 2018 FC 462, paras. 3, 23. See also *Report of the Standing Committee on Finance (House of Commons), The Canada Revenue Agency, Tax Avoidance and Tax Evasion: Recommended Actions* (Oct. 2016, 58pp.); CRA news releases, "Government of Canada participates in meeting of tax administrations to share findings on Panama Papers" (Jan. 20, 2017); "Government of Canada tables its response to the Standing Committee on Finance on efforts to crack down on tax cheats" (Feb. 23, 2017) (electronic transfers to and from Isle of Man, Guernsey and 2 other jurisdictions being audited); "Statement by the Canada Revenue Agency: Offshore Financial Structures" (Nov. 3, 2017); "Canada Revenue Agency conducts Panama Papers related searches in multiple locations" (Feb. 14, 2018); "Minister Lebouthillier strengthens international partnerships to fight offshore tax fraud, evasion and aggressive tax avoidance" (Feb. 21, 2018); "Tax Enforcement Authorities Unite to Combat International Tax Crime and Money Laundering" (July 3, 2018) (re "J5": Australia, Canada, Netherlands, UK and US); "Panama Papers: CRA executing search warrant in $77 million tax evasion case" (March 28, 2019); "Minister of National Revenue Welcomes the Offshore Compliance Advisory Committee's Recommendations and Observations on the Agency's Response to the Panama and Paradise Papers Leaks", June 11, 2019; letter from CRA Offshore Compliance Advisory Committee, "Re: OCAC Activities and the Processing and Analysis of Big Data", tinyurl.com/cra-ocac; "One Year In, J5 Making a Difference" (June 5, 2019); "Global Tax Chiefs Undertake Unprecedented Multi-Country Day of Action" (Jan. 23, 2020). See also Policy Forum articles, 65(3) *Canadian Tax Journal* 633-92 (2017); Chodikoff, "Fallout from the Panama Papers", 11(1) *Taxes & Wealth Management* (Carswell) 6-7 (March 2018) and "The Mauritius Leaks", 13(1) 4-5 (March 2020); US Dept. of Justice, "Four Defendants Charged in Panama Papers Investigation" (Dec. 4, 2018) and "U.S. Accountant Pleads Guilty in Panama Papers Investigation" (Feb 28, 2020); OECD, *Ending the Shell Game: Cracking down on the Professionals who enable Tax and White Collar Crimes* (Feb. 2021), 59pp (discusses strategies countries can take to deter and disrupt such activity); OECD, *Fighting Tax Crime* (2nd ed., June 2021) 78pp (strategies for tax authorities to use). On the "tax gap" (how much tax revenue is lost to non-compliance) see Parliamentary Budget Officer, *Preliminary Findings on International Taxation* (June 20, 2019), tinyurl.com/pbo-prelim; CRA, *Tax Gap and Compliance Results for the Federal Corporate Income Tax System*, June 2019.

RRSP strips: see Notes to 146(10) (taxpayers have their RRSPs invest in private companies that then send them the funds; often they are defrauded and lose the funds). RRSP promoters convicted include: Laurent Boulianne (CRA news release (NR) Jan. 21/08); Jacques Gagné (NR Oct. 6/10: 42 months for enabling 152 taxpayers to avoid reporting $3.3m of withdrawals, using "dummy" corporations 9056-2927 Québec Inc. (Servitek 2000), 9058-9557 Québec Inc. (Educamax), Énergie GYD Inc., Immeubles RV (1986) Inc. and 9063-3223 Québec Inc. (Services Financiers Mackenzie) [Gagné's appeal to Que. CA dismissed for delay: leave to appeal denied 2012 CarswellQue 2684 (SCC)]); Christopher Houston & Steven Kendall (5 years each: 2015 ABQB 177 and *Calgary Herald*, July 22/15: defrauded CRA of $11.7m and 500 investors of $48m using Capital Alternatives Inc., Institute for Financial Learning); Claude Lavigne (RQ NR, Feb. 17/15: 21 months for defrauding 178 investors); James Cameron (NR Sept 15/17: 11 years for diverting $2.5m of investors' funds [appeal dismissed 2020 ABCA 276; leave to appeal denied 2021 CarswellAlta 651 (SCC)]); *Gagné*, 2017 QCCA 788 (leave to appeal denied 2018 CarswellQue 3 (SCC)) (conviction).

"Zappers": Owning, making or using software that suppresses part of cash register sales is illegal: see 239.1.

In a complex prosecution, summaries prepared by an accountant who testifies can be allowed into evidence: *Porisky*, 2012 BCSC 67, para. 24 (rev'd on other grounds 2014 BCCA 146). (See also Notes to 169(1) under "Expert evidence".)

In *Goett*, 2010 ABQB 487, offsetting farm losses (determined after filing the false return) reduced the amount of evasion for purposes of setting the fine.

In *Tiffin*, 2013 SKPC 140, T was convicted of evasion for providing inaccurate "estimates" of his income on his returns each year, which he alleged he intended to go back and correct but never did.

See also cases under *Excise Tax Act* s. 327 (in David M. Sherman, *The Practitioner's Goods and Services Tax Annotated*), which provides a parallel offence of GST evasion.

Advisors and accountants: 239 can apply where the tax evaded is another person's: *Gagné*, 2017 QCCA 788 (leave to appeal denied 2018 CarswellQue 3 (SCC)) (RRSP scheme). In *Simons*, [1977] C.T.C. 371, the BC Prov. Court excoriated the Crown for prosecuting an accountant. In *Pinto*, 2010 QCCQ 8407, an accountant was convicted of preparing false information for a client's GST returns. In *Besler*, 2011 SKPC 134, a CA who under-reported a client's employees' income to steal $630,000 in payroll withholdings was sentenced to 3 years in prison. In *El-Akhal*, 2011 ONCJ 826, an advisor filing false citizenship applications, and false returns to make clients appear resident in Canada, was sentenced to 3 years. In *Witen*, aff'd 2014 ONCA 694 (extension of time to file leave to appeal denied by SCC Dec. 10/15, file 36533), a tax preparer who created false invoices to reduce clients' taxes was sentenced to 3 years, plus (by calling it forfeiture of proceeds of crime) a further 3 years if he does not pay a $450,000 fine. In *Dyck*, 2018 MBCA 33, the promoter of the One World United scheme of fictitious business losses for 325 taxpayers ($2.3m of tax) was sentenced to 3 years + 1 year if $2.3m fine not paid. See also Notes to 118.1(1)"total charitable gifts" for convictions of preparers for false donation claims; to 239(1.1); and Bruce Russell, "Avoiding Evasion: Tax Advisors' Professional Responsibilities", 2004 Cdn Tax Foundation conference report, 35:1-11. Advisors are also subject to administrative penalties under 163.2.

CRA may hold off on an objection while a prosecution is underway: see 165(3) Notes. See Notes to 220(3.1) re voluntary disclosure as a method of preventing both prosecution and penalties.

Delay: A criminal trial must be held within a reasonable time after charges are laid, or the charges will be stayed under *Charter* s. 11(b). Since 2016, the presumptive ceiling is 18 months for provincial court and 30 months for a superior court trial: *Jordan*, 2016 SCC 27; *Cody*, 2017 SCC 31; *Morris*, 2020 QCCQ 4200; *Wookey*, 2021 ONCA 68. Absence of prejudice to the accused is no longer relevant; nor is the seriousness of the offence. The calculation begins when the accused is arrested or served with a summons (i.e., aware of the charges), and ends at the end of trial with conviction: *Millar*, 2016 BCSC 1887, paras. 110-137, 199; *Métaux Kitco*, 2018 QCCQ 15754. Delay attributable to or waived by the accused is excluded (for tax evasion cases where the accused was responsible for the delay see *Kettle*, [2007] 1 C.T.C. 306 (Ont. SCJ); *Eddy*, 2016 ABQB 42, paras. 210, 217). Once the time limit is crossed, the onus is on the Crown to show the delay was reasonable based on exceptional circumstances, such as the case's complexity (for examples of complexity in tax evasion cases see *Dieckmann*, 2017 ONCA 575, paras. 20-25 (leave to appeal denied 2018 CarswellOnt 4161 (SCC)); *Tyskerud*, 2011 BCPC 492; *Witen*, above; *Millar*, 2016 BCSC 1887), or a "discrete event" (or, for charges laid before 2016, reasonable reliance on the pre-*Jordan* law: *Balogh*, 2020 BCCA 96; *Comparelli*, 2018 QCCQ 1767). *Pre-charge* delay of 7 years in a complex case was not grounds for stay without clear evidence it made the proceedings unfair: *Dolinski*, 2014 ONSC 681; and 2 years was acceptable in *Hennessey*, 2020 NLTD(G) 128, para. 141. *Post-verdict* sentencing delay must not exceed 5 months (at least in Ontario): *Charley*, 2019 ONCA 726; *Hartling*, 2020 ONCA 243; *Adu-Bekoe*,

2021 ONCA 136. In *Spears*, 2017 NSPC 17, the Court refused to hear a *Jordan* application until end of trial. The accused must apply for a stay before conviction: *Cameron*, 2017 ABQB 539.

Issue estoppel: Conviction of evasion should in theory be conclusive proof that the tax is owing for purposes of an appeal of the assessment, based on *Toronto v. CUPE Local 79*, 2003 SCC 63 and *SP v. AP*, 2020 ABCA 235 (leave to appeal denied 2021 CarswellAlta 534 (SCC)); but the effectiveness of this rule is mixed. It was applied to uphold assessments (or parts of assessments) in: *Van Rooy*, [1988] 2 C.T.C. 78 (FCA); *Boehm*, [1996] 2 C.T.C. 45 (FCTD); *DeCae*, [1998] 4 C.T.C. 2636 (TCC); *Golden*, 2008 TCC 173; *Kristensen*, 2010 TCC 178; *Mortenson*, 2010 TCC 164; *Cranston*, 2010 TCC 414 (extension of time to appeal denied 2010 FCA 327 and 2011 FCA 5); *Tyskerud*, 2019 TCC 84, para. 19. It would have applied in *Lee*, 2013 TCC 289 (FCA appeal discontinued A-349-13), para. 38, had the Crown not said the conviction was only *prima facie* proof. It does not apply when the conviction came from a guilty plea on a plea bargain, since there may be practical reasons to plead guilty such as legal costs: *Hagon*, [1999] 2 C.T.C. 2436 (TCC); *Harris*, 2005 TCC 501; *Pontarini*, 2009 TCC 395, para. 23. In both *Raposo*, 2013 TCC 265, para. 15, and *Harvey*, 2013 TCC 298, para. 25, conviction was *prima facie* proof, not conclusive proof, of gross negligence for 163(2); see also *Plate v. Atlas Copco*, 2019 ONCA 196 (non-tax case: judge's findings made in jury trial). In the following TCC cases conviction was *not* proof of liability: *Belfast Lime*, [1997] G.S.T.C. 108 (guilty plea to global amount did not cover identical period to the assessments); *Poulin*, [1998] G.S.T.C. 121 (appellant could seek to explain circumstances of signing confession leading to his conviction); *Choumann*, [2001] 3 C.T.C. 2045 (GST conviction was somewhat relevant to income tax assessment); *Morel*, 2008 FCA 53 (not clear the facts were identical); *Sterling-Ross*, 2009 TCC 525 (guilty plea to GST evasion apparently considered as evidence in denying input tax credits); *Mortenson*, 2010 TCC 164 and *Kristensen*, 2010 TCC 178 (facts were different so conviction was proof of only a small part of the liability). In *Dieckmann*, 2017 ONCA 575, para. 36 (leave to appeal denied 2018 CarswellOnt 4161 (SCC)), a consent judgment (settlement) on the civil assessment did not create issue estoppel requiring acquittal of evasion. See Notes to 169(2) for more on issue estoppel and *res judicata*.

Acquittal on evasion charges means nothing with respect to tax liability since the Crown's burden of proof is lower for an assessment: *Hirex Holdings*, [1997] 1 C.T.C. 103 (FCTD); *Lai*, [2001] G.S.T.C. 24 (TCC); *Wong*, 2010 TCC 171. Similarly, an Agreed Statement of Facts in a plea bargain did not bind CRA, so a reassessment could be for more tax than the evasion conviction: *McIntyre*, 2014 TCC 111. Similarly, CRA's allowing expenses for purposes of criminal charges does not mean they will be allowed by the TCC: *Elbadawi*, 2014 TCC 259, para. 41 (aff'd without discussing this point 2016 FCA 57). However, positive findings of fact by the court in an acquittal can create issue estoppel preventing the Crown from challenging those facts in a civil suit for malicious prosecution: *Samaroo*, 2016 BCSC 531, para. 124 (abuse of process can also apply; para. 134) [the suit succeeded but was reversed 2019 BCCA 113, leave to appeal denied 2019 CarswellBC 2947]. In *Samaroo*, 2016 TCC 290, the same findings could be introduced as evidence, but did not create estoppel.

Costs are rarely awarded to acquitted taxpayers: *R. v. M. (C.A.)*, [1996] 1 S.C.R. 500, para. 97; but may be if there is a "marked and unacceptable departure from the reasonable standards expected of the prosecution": *974649 Ontario Inc.*, 2001 SCC 81, para. 87; see also *Daley*, 2010 NBPC 6; *Tiffin*, 2008 ONCA 306. Costs cannot be awarded if the Crown stays a proceeding: *Martin*, 2016 ONCA 840, para. 36. In rare cases a lawsuit for malicious prosecution can succeed: see Notes to 171(1).

Where parties created false contracts to evade tax, access to the courts to enforce the contracts was denied: *Wojnarowski v. Bomar Alarms*, 2010 ONSC 273, para. 71; but in *St-Pierre v. Faubert*, 2016 QCCQ 2175, unjust enrichment applied to allow a claim against a kitchen supplier for defective work that was done with no invoice.

A lawyer who fails to inform the law society of being charged with an ITA offence may be committing professional misconduct: see LSUC "Invitations to Attend: for the information of the profession", *Ontario Reports*, Sept. 11, 2015, p. lxxxviii.

Disclosure of corporations' beneficial owners (anti-evasion rule): see Notes to 150(1)(a).

Interpretation Bulletins: IT-99R5: Legal and accounting fees.

Information Circulars: 73-10R3: Tax evasion; 78-10R5: Books and records retention/destruction; 00-1R4: Voluntary disclosures program; 05-1R1: Electronic record keeping.

Registered Charities Newsletters: 11 (audit of tax preparer lands registered charities and executive director in hot water).

CRA Audit Manual: 8.5.0: Non-compliance identification projects; 10.11.8: Referrals to enforcement and disclosure directorate; 28.14.0: Offences and penalties.

(1.1) Offences re refunds and credits — Every person who obtains or claims a refund or credit under this Act to which the person or any other person is not entitled or obtains or claims a refund or credit under this Act in an amount that is greater than the amount to which the person or other person is entitled

(a) by making, or participating in, assenting to or acquiescing in the making of, a false or deceptive statement in a return, certificate, statement or answer filed or made under this Act or a regulation,

(b) by destroying, altering, mutilating, hiding or otherwise disposing of a record or book of account of the person or other person,

(c) by making, or assenting to or acquiescing in the making of, a false or deceptive entry in a record or book of account of the person or other person,

(d) by omitting, or assenting to or acquiescing in an omission to enter a material particular in a record or book of account of the person or other person,

(e) wilfully in any manner, or

(f) by conspiring with any person to commit any offence under this subsection,

is guilty of an offence and, in addition to any penalty otherwise provided, is liable on summary conviction to

(g) a fine of not less than 50% and not more than 200% of the amount by which the amount of the refund or credit obtained or claimed exceeds the amount, if any, of the refund or credit to which the person or other person, as the case may be, is entitled, or

(h) both the fine described in paragraph (g) and imprisonment for a term not exceeding 2 years.

Related Provisions: 239(2) — Prosecution on indictment.

Notes: For convictions under 239(1.1), relating to overclaimed refunds and credits rather than underpayment of tax, see *Global Enviro*, 2011 ABQB 32 (SR&ED credits); *Rosie*, 2012 BCSC 1885 (sentencing 2013 BCSC 1039) (false claims for individual tax returns; 3.5 years in prison + $142,000 fine); *Hilcoff*, 2014 SKPC 28 (GST Credit claimed on income tax returns); *Kaba*, 2016 BCPC 62 (77 false returns with $1.1m of false claims: 1 year in jail); *Stancer*, 2016 BCSC 192 (200 returns with $9.9m of false refund claims: 33 months; *Mathur*, 2017 ONCA 403 (292 fraudulent returns claiming $343,000 of refunds for unsuspecting taxpayers: 12 months); *Éléments chauffants Tempora (Elhami)*, 2018 QCCA 1488, leave to appeal denied 2019 CarswellQue 1388 (SCC) (SR&ED credits); *Sharma*, 2020 ABCA 57 (tax preparer made $2.9 million in false claims; 6 years in prison + $290,000 restitution [2018 ABPC 288]); *Sharma*, 2019 ONCA 274 (tax preparer made false business loss claims for 37 clients with potential federal revenue loss of $488,000: conditional sentence of 2 years less a day); *Wallen*, 2020 ONCJ 652, sentencing 2021 ONCJ 64 (tax protestor claimed refunds of $1.7 million for his corps, alleging he set up an "international business corporation with a foreign trust": 24 months imprisonment, $500,000 fine). In *Michaud*, 2012 NBCA 77, a tax preparer's conviction on 134 counts of preparing false returns was overturned because there was no evidence he was involved in the fraud; the trial judge wrongly considered all the counts as similar-fact evidence without prior notice. (Per CRA news release July 5/11, previously convicted in the scheme were France Desjardins, Francine Laforest, Allain Maltais.)

Some recent CRA news releases on convictions for claiming false refunds: Tammy-Ann Deslongchamps (June 26/14: fine for claiming Child Tax Benefits for fictitious children); preparer Denis Wilson (Aug. 12/14: overstating losses from hobbies or non-existent businesses, causing 14 clients to evade federal tax of $83,000; fine and "conditional sentence" of 2 years less a day); preparer Ronald McKinnon (Aug. 26/14: 4 months for falsifying T4 information on returns, to claim refunds from source deductions); preparer Carmine Sorella (Sept. 17/14: 90 days (on weekends) for claiming $550,000 in false expenses on 77 returns); Maria Banhaw (Oct. 3/14: fine and 18-month conditional sentence for $390,000 in false RRSP claims on 96 returns); preparer Neil Smith (Oct. 6/14: fine and 18-month conditional sentence for claiming $540,000 of false refunds for 68 clients); Candiss Pettit (Oct. 9/14: 7 months for creating 13 false T4s for unemployed young persons who paid their refunds to her, totalling $20,000); Marian, Adam & Janina Dolinski (Oct. 20/14: 30 and 20 months in jail, and 6 months conditional sentence, for filing 299 false returns for new immigrants without their knowledge, obtaining $119,000 in refunds); Cemila Smikle-Kuznetzov (Feb. 2/15: fine and 30 days house arrest for claiming $48,000 for fictitious children); preparer Anthony McPhail (April 29/15: 18 months for claiming $3.8m in fictitious losses in 118 returns); Deanna LaValley (Nov. 12/15: $17,000 fine, 22 months house arrest for claiming $192m false losses on 224 client returns); David Gnanaratnam (Jan. 5/18: fine + 6 months conditional for false employment expenses on 24 client returns); Manoharan Thangarajah (Jan. 16/19: $150,000 fine for 30 false donation receipts); Omorogieva Woghiren (April 10/19: 1-year conditional sentence + fine for $231,000 in false child tax benefit claims for self and spouse); George Nnane (Feb. 7/20: 3 years for false loss and donation claims); Michael Hulme (May 12/20: 18 months conditional + fine for false Child Tax Benefit claims).

Charges laid: Raymond Mahoney, St. John's NL (April 21/17: alleged 25 false returns); Chun (Ted) Zhu, Calgary (July 17/20: alleged fake job postings to gather personal information used to file 317 returns claiming $760,000 in refunds).

See Notes to 118.1(1)"total charitable gifts" for convictions re false donations.

239(1.1) added by 1995-97 technical bill, effective June 18, 1998.

(2) Prosecution on indictment — Every person who is charged with an offence described in subsection (1) or (1.1) may, at the election of the Attorney General of Canada, be prosecuted on indictment and, if convicted, is, in addition to any penalty otherwise provided, liable to

    (a) a fine of not less than 100% and not more than 200% of

        (i) where the offence is described in subsection (1), the amount of the tax that was sought to be evaded, and

        (ii) where the offence is described in subsection (1.1), the amount by which the amount of the refund or credit obtained or claimed exceeds the amount, if any, of the refund or credit to which the person or other person, as the case may be, is entitled; and

    (b) imprisonment for a term not exceeding 5 years.

Related Provisions: 243 — Minimum fine; *Interpretation Act* 34(1) — Indictable and summary conviction offences; *Interpretation Act* 34(2) — *Criminal Code* provisions apply.

Notes: See Notes to 239(1). Quebec announced in its 2010-11 Budget that its tax legislation will be amended to increase the maximum sentence for major tax offences to 5 years less a day.

239(2) amended to refer to 239(1.1), and 239(2)(a)(ii) added, by 1995-97 technical bill, effective June 18, 1998.

Interpretation Bulletins: IT-99R5: Legal and accounting fees.

Information Circulars: 73-10R3: Tax evasion.

(2.1) Providing incorrect tax shelter identification number — Every person who wilfully provides another person with an incorrect identification number for a tax shelter is guilty of an offence and, in addition to any penalty otherwise provided, is liable on summary conviction to

    (a) a fine of not less than 100%, and not more than 200%, of the cost to the other person of that person's interest in the shelter;

    (b) imprisonment for a term not exceeding 2 years; or

    (c) both the fine described in paragraph (a) and the imprisonment described in paragraph (b).

Related Provisions: 237.1 — Tax shelters; 242 — Where corporation is guilty of offence; 243 — Minimum fine.

Notes: See Notes to 239(1).

Information Circulars: 89-4: Tax shelter reporting.

(2.2) Offence with respect to confidential information — Every person who

    (a) contravenes subsection 241(1), or

    (b) knowingly contravenes an order made under subsection 241(4.1)

is guilty of an offence and liable on summary conviction to a fine not exceeding $5,000 or to imprisonment for a term not exceeding 12 months, or to both.

Related Provisions: 239(2.21) — Offence with respect to confidential information; 239(2.22) — Definitions; 242 — Where corporation is guilty of offence; 244(4) — Summary conviction charges must be laid within 8 years.

Notes: CRA apparently has a policy of not prosecuting employees under 239(2.2): *Collins*, 2011 FCA 140. However, CRA takes strong disciplinary measures against even inadvertent disclosure: see *Lloyd*, 2016 FCA 115; 2021 FC 29 (under appeal by Crown to FCA).

239(2.2)(b) amended by 1992 technical bill, effective June 10, 1993.

(2.21) Idem — Every person

    (a) to whom taxpayer information has been provided for a particular purpose under paragraph 241(4)(b), (c), (e), (h), (k), (n), (o) or (p), or

    (b) who is an official to whom taxpayer information has been provided for a particular purpose under paragraph 241(4)(a), (d), (f), (f.1), (i), (j.1) or (j.2)

and who for any other purpose knowingly uses, provides to any person, allows the provision to any person of, or allows any person access to, that information is guilty of an offence and liable on summary conviction to a fine not exceeding $5,000 or to imprisonment for a term not exceeding 12 months, or to both.

Notes: 239(2.21)(b) amended to add reference to 241(4)(j.2) by 2013 budget bill #2, effective Dec. 12, 2013. Earlier amended by 2001 anti-terrorism bill, 2000, 1999 and 1998 budget bills. Added by 1992 technical bill.

(2.22) Definitions — In subsection (2.21), "official" and "taxpayer information" have the meanings assigned by subsection 241(10).

Notes: 239(2.22) added by 1992 technical bill, effective June 10, 1993.

(2.3) Offence with respect to an identification number — Every person to whom the business number of a taxpayer or partnership, to whom the Social Insurance Number of an individual or to whom the trust account number of a trust has been provided under this Act or the Regulations, and every officer, employee and agent of such a person, who without written consent of the individual, taxpayer, partnership or trust, as the case may be, knowingly uses, communicates or allows to be communicated the number (otherwise than as required or authorized by law, in the course of duties in connection with the administration or enforcement of this Act or for a purpose for which it was provided by the individual, taxpayer, partnership or trust, as the case may be) is guilty of an offence and liable on summary conviction to a fine not exceeding $5,000 or to imprisonment for a term not exceeding 12 months, or to both.

Related Provisions: 237(2)(b) — Social Insurance Number not to be used or communicated without individual's consent; 242 — Where corporation is guilty of offence.

Notes: See Notes to 239(1).

239(2.3) amended by 2018 budget bill #1, for 2018 and later tax years, to add reference to a trust account number and a trust.

Reference to the business number added by 1995-97 technical bill, effective June 18, 1998. However, this amendment is rather silly, since such numbers are disclosed for GST/HST purposes on all of a business's invoices and receipts. See Notes to 248(1)"business number".

239(2.3) amended by 1991 technical bill, effective for actions after Dec. 16, 1991.

Information Circulars: 82-2R2: SIN legislation that relates to the preparation of information slips.

(2.31) [Repealed]

Notes: 239(2.31) added by Private Member's Bill C-377, S.C. 2015, c. 41, for fiscal periods beginning after Dec. 30, 2015, and repealed by S.C. 2017, c. 12, effective June 19, 2017, without ever taking effect in practice. See Notes to repealed 149.01. It read:

    (2.31) Offence: s. 149.01 — Every labour organization or labour trust that contravenes section 149.01 is guilty of an offence and liable on summary conviction to a fine of $1,000 for each day that it fails to comply with that section, to a maximum of $25,000.

(3) Penalty on conviction — If a person is convicted under this section, the person is not liable to pay a penalty imposed under any of sections 162, 163, 163.2 and 163.3 for the same contravention unless the penalty is assessed before the information or complaint giving rise to the conviction was laid or made.

Notes: The reference to s. 163 in 239(3) overrules *Panko*, [1971] C.T.C. 467 (SCC). "Information or complaint" means the document initiating criminal proceedings before a court (see 244(3)): *Besner*, 2009 FCA 311.

239(3) does not offer much protection. The CRA need merely assess the penalty before a charge is laid. In *Lavers v. British Columbia*, [1990] 1 C.T.C. 265 (BCCA), the imposition of an administrative penalty plus a criminal fine was held not to offend para. 11(h) of the *Charter of Rights* by constituting double punishment for the same offence.

239(3) amended by 2013 budget bill #2, effective 2014, to change "section" to "any of sections" and add reference to 163.3.

239(3) amended by 1999 Budget (effective June 29, 2000) and 1995-97 technical bill.

(4) Stay of appeal — Where, in any appeal under this Act, substantially the same facts are at issue as those that are at issue in a prosecution under this section, the Minister may file a stay of proceedings with the Tax Court of Canada and thereupon the proceedings before that Court are stayed pending final determination of the outcome of the prosecution.

Notes: CRA will also hold an objection in abeyance while criminal charges are pursued; see 165(3) Notes. The Crown can proceed with criminal charges while tax liability is being disputed in the TCC: *McCartie*, 2012 BCSC 928.

(5) Offence and punishment without reference to subsec. 120(2.2) [aboriginals] — In determining whether an offence under this Act, for which a person may on summary conviction or indictment be liable for a fine or imprisonment, has been committed, and in determining the punishment for such an offence, this Act is to be read without reference to subsection 120(2.2).

Notes: 239(5) added by 2004 Budget bill, effective June 12, 2005. It provides that in determining whether a criminal offence has been committed, the fact that First Nations Tax is payable under a tax sharing agreement, rather than tax being payable under this Act, does not prevent an offence from having been committed. See Notes to 120(2.2).

Definitions [s. 239]: "business number" — 248(1); "contravene" — *Interpretation Act* 35(1); "individual", "Minister" — 248(1); "official" — 239(2.22), 241(10); "person", "record", "regulation", "taxpayer" — 248(1); "tax shelter" — 237.1(1), 248(1); "taxpayer information" — 239(2.22), 241(10); "trust account number" — 248(1).

239.1 [Zappers] — (1) Definitions — The definitions in subsection 163.3(1) apply in this section.

(2) Offences [zapper software or device] — Every person that, without lawful excuse, the proof of which lies on the person,

(a) uses an electronic suppression of sales device or a similar device or software in relation to records that are required to be kept by any person under section 230,

(b) acquires or possesses an electronic suppression of sales device, or a right in respect of an electronic suppression of sales device, that is, or is intended to be, capable of being used in relation to records that are required to be kept by any person under section 230,

(c) designs, develops, manufactures, possesses for sale, offers for sale, sells, transfers or otherwise makes available to another person an electronic suppression of sales device that is, or is intended to be, capable of being used in relation to records that are required to be kept by any person under section 230,

(d) supplies installation, upgrade or maintenance services for an electronic suppression of sales device that is, or is intended to be, capable of being used in relation to records that are required to be kept by any person under section 230, or

(e) participates in, assents to or acquiesces in the commission of, or conspires with any person to commit, an offence described in any of paragraphs (a) to (d),

is guilty of an offence and, in addition to any penalty otherwise provided, is liable on summary conviction to a fine of not less than $10,000 and not more than $500,000 or to imprisonment for a term not exceeding two years, or to both.

Related Provisions: 163.3 — Penalty for use, possession, manufacture or sale of zapper; 239.1(3) — Prosecution on indictment; 239.1(4) — Penalty valid only if assessed before charges laid; 243 — court has no power to impose less than the minimum fine; 244(4) — eight-year limitation on summary-conviction prosecution; *Interpretation Act* 34(1) — Indictable and summary conviction offences; *Interpretation Act* 34(2) — Criminal Code provisions apply to prosecution.

Notes: See Notes at end of 239.1.

(3) Prosecution on indictment — Every person that is charged with an offence described in subsection (2) may, at the election of the Attorney General of Canada, be prosecuted on indictment and, if convicted, is, in addition to any penalty otherwise provided, liable to a fine of not less than $50,000 and not more than $1,000,000 or to imprisonment for a term not exceeding five years, or to both.

Related Provisions: See under 239.1(2).

Notes: See Notes at end of 239.1.

(4) Penalty on conviction — A person that is convicted of an offence under this section is not liable to pay a penalty imposed under any of sections 162, 163, 163.2 and 163.3 for the same action unless a notice of assessment for that penalty was issued before the information or complaint giving rise to the conviction was laid or made.

Notes: This rule, requiring assessment of the penalty before being charged with the offence, is the same as under 239(3) for income tax evasion generally.

(5) Stay of appeal — If, in any appeal under this Act, substantially the same facts are at issue as those that are at issue in a prosecution under this section, the Minister may file a stay of proceedings with the Tax Court of Canada and, upon that filing, the proceedings before that Court are stayed pending final determination of the outcome of the prosecution.

Notes: This rule, permitting a stay of a Tax Court appeal pending resolution of the criminal charges, is the same as under 239(4) for income tax evasion charges.

Notes [s. 239.1]: 239.1(2) makes it a criminal offence to use, possess, manufacture or sell "zapper" software (or hardware) that suppresses a portion of cash register sales. The minimum punishment is a $10,000 fine on summary conviction (239.1(2)), or $50,000 if prosecution is by indictment (239.1(3)). (The fine cannot be reduced by the Court: s. 243.) The maximum punishment is a $1 million fine and 5 years' imprisonment (if prosecution is by indictment).

The person can also be assessed an administrative penalty under 163.3 (see Notes to 239(1) for the distinction).

Excise Tax Act s. 327.1, and some provinces' legislation, provides identical offences and punishment. However, the rules against double jeopardy and double punishment should prevent the minimum fine from being imposed twice for the same action: see *Kienapple*, [1975] 1 S.C.R. 729 (SCC), and s. 11(h) of the *Charter of Rights*.

The words "without lawful excuse, the proof of which lies on the person" in 239.1(2) put the onus on a person found using or possessing, or having programmed, zapper software to provide a "lawful excuse". This wording (re possession of house-breaking instruments) was held to be constitutional in *Holmes*, [1988] 1 S.C.R. 914 (SCC).

Before 239.1, a zapper vendor was acquitted of fraud, as "the law does not prohibit the making, possession, or sale of a zapper" and "selling a zapper is not a dishonest act" absent evidence that it was used to evade tax: *InfoSpec Systems*, 2013 CarswellBC 2145 (BCCA), paras. 21, 24.

Quebec has had similar sanctions since 2000. See ss. 34.1-34.2 of the *Tax Administration Act*, and David Sherman's *Canada GST Service* commentary to ETA s. 327 (also on *GST Partner* and *Taxnet Pro*), under the heading "Provincial Remedies and Zapper Software". Quebec announced on July 11, 2013 (Information Bulletin 2013-7) that it will modify its legislation to match the federal penalties and criminal sanctions.

To prevent zapper use, Quebec requires restaurants and bars to give every customer a receipt from an approved Sales Recording Module (SRM) that is supposedly zapper-proof, with severe penalties for non-compliance. See *Quebec Sales Tax Act* ss. 350.50-350.60; Information Bulletins IN-522-V, IN-575-V, IN-577-V, IN-582.1-V; Ainsworth & Hengartner, "Quebec's Sales Recording Module (SRM)", 57(4) *Canadian Tax Journal* 715-61 (2009); *9296-1846 Québec inc.*, 2018 QCCQ 7952. Ontario was considering similar action: *Preventing the Electronic Suppression of Sales in Ontario: A Discussion Paper*, Ministry of Finance, Oct. 2015. Revenu Québec announced on Sept. 25, 2015 revocation of approval to Xperio to install SRMs, as it was the continuation of a company (Logicaisse) convicted of installing zappers.

239.1 added by 2013 budget bill #2, effective 2014.

Definitions [s. 239.1]: "assessment" — 248(1); "electronic suppression of sales device" — 163.3(1), 239.1(1); "Minister", "person", "record" — 248(1); "service" — 163.3(1), 239.1(1).

240. (1) Definition of "taxable obligation" and "non-taxable obligation" — In this section, "taxable obligation" means any bond, debenture or similar obligation the interest on which would, if paid by the issuer to a non-resident person, be subject to the payment of tax under Part XIII by that non-resident person at the rate provided in subsection 212(1) (otherwise than by virtue of subsection 212(6)), and "non-taxable obligation" means any bond, debenture or similar obligation the interest on which would not, if paid by the issuer to a non-resident person, be subject to the payment of tax under Part XIII by that non-resident person.

(2) Interest coupon to be identified in prescribed manner — offence and punishment — Every person who, at any time after July 14, 1966, issues

(a) any taxable obligation, or

(b) any non-taxable obligation

the right to interest on which is evidenced by a coupon or other writing that does not form part of, or is capable of being detached from, the evidence of indebtedness under the obligation is, unless the coupon or other writing is marked or identified in prescribed manner by the letters "AX" in the case of a taxable obligation, and by the letter "F" in the case of a non-taxable obligation, on the face thereof, guilty of an offence and liable on summary conviction to a fine not exceeding $500.

Regulations [subsec. 240(2)]: 807 (prescribed manner of identifying obligation).

Notes [s. 240]: See Notes to 239(1).

Definitions [s. 240]: "non-resident", "person" — 248(1); "writing" — *Interpretation Act* 35(1).

241. (1) Provision of information — Except as authorized by this section, no official or other representative of a government entity shall

(a) knowingly provide, or knowingly allow to be provided, to any person any taxpayer information;

(b) knowingly allow any person to have access to any taxpayer information; or

(c) knowingly use any taxpayer information otherwise than in the course of the administration or enforcement of this Act, the *Canada Pension Plan*, the *Unemployment Insurance Act* or the *Employment Insurance Act* or for the purpose for which it was provided under this section.

Announced Administrative Change — More money to CRA for protecting information

Federal Budget, Chapter 10, April 19, 2021: *Protecting Taxpayer Information*

Cyber security is more important than ever and the government is committed to securing taxpayer information against any and all who would attempt to breach Canadians' private information. Millions of Canadians rely on the CRA's digital services to access financial lifelines like the CERB, wage subsidy, or rent subsidy. Since February 2020, registration for the CRA's secure digital services has increased by 36% and logins have increased by 170%. To further safeguard the electronic data stored by the CRA and protect Canadians' personal information from falling into the wrong hands:

Budget 2021 proposes to provide $330.6 million over five years, starting in 2021-22, with $1.6 million in remaining amortization, and $51.2 million ongoing, to the Canada Revenue Agency to invest in new technologies and tools that match the growing sophistication of cyber threats, and to ensure the CRA's workforce has the specialized skills to proactively monitor threats and better safeguard Canadian data.

Related Provisions: 149.1(15) — Charities — information can be communicated; 230.1(4) — Reports to chief electoral officer; 237(2)(b) — Communication of Social Insurance Number; 239(2.2) — Offence; 241(3) — Communication of information; 241(3.1) — Disclosure allowed in circumstances involving danger; 241(3.2) — Charities — additional information that may be communicated; 241(4) — Exceptions; 241(9.5) — Information may be provided about serious offences; 241(11) — Meaning of "this Act".

Notes: 241(1) prohibits a CRA or other government official from disclosing information to a third party, but a party in a lawsuit can be forced by the Court to obtain their own information from the CRA and disclose it to the other side, under threat of having their case dismissed, despite 241(1). See *McAvan Holdings v. BDO Dunwoody Ltd.*, [2003] 4 C.T.C. 90 (Ont. Master).

Of course, taxpayers' own information can be disclosed to them under 241(5)(a), and they can force CRA to release it under the *Privacy Act* (individuals) or *Access to Information Act* (corporations). A PA request is free. An AIA request costs $5 (AIA s. 11; charges for copying many pages and search time over 5 hours were eliminated in 2019). Use tinyurl.com/atip-req or Form RC378 to make a request. CRA's Access to Information and Privacy (ATIP) office number is 613-960-5393, fax 613-941-9395. There are exemptions/exclusions from disclosure (e.g., solicitor-client privilege, third-party information, Cabinet consultations, investigative techniques (which includes audits: *3412229 Canada*, 2020 FC 1156, para. 102), information from foreign governments), but they are to be construed narrowly: *Canadian Council of Christian Charities*, [1999] 3 C.T.C. 123 (FCTD), para. 15. If CRA refuses access or delays too much, a complaint can be made to the Information Commissioner (IC) (who since 2019 can order release of documents: AIA s. 36.1); but in *Coderre*, 2015 FC 776, an attempt to force the IC to disclose her findings was premature because the IC was still working on the file (though some requests were 14 months old by judgment date). After that, judicial review can be sought in Federal Court (see 171(1) Notes); but once CRA discloses the records under the ATIA, the FC loses jurisdiction: *3412229 Canada* (above), para. 91. Disclosure of documents CRA claimed were protected as part of a tax fraud investigation was ordered in *Palmerino*, 2013 FC 919 (FCA appeal settled A-319-13). In *Summers*, 2014 FC 880, third-party records allegedly needed for the taxpayer to pursue a TCC appeal were not ordered disclosed. In *John Doe*, 2014 SCC 36, Ontario Finance was not required to release drafts of papers with policy options for tax legislation, due to the "advice or recommendations" exclusion paralleling that in the federal ATIA ("advice" must be broader than "recommendations" and includes policy options: paras. 24, 47). In *Ludmer*, 2018 QCCS 3381, paras. 671-702; aff'd 2020 QCCA 697, paras. 18, 102, 117 (leave to appeal denied 2021 CarswellQue 2160 (SCC)), delaying ATIP disclosure for years was one reason damages were awarded against CRA (see 171(1) Notes at "Lawsuits in Quebec"). See also Notes to Canada-US Treaty Art. XXVI-A:1 for the author's dispute over getting data on treaty collection assistance. See generally McNairn & Woodbury, *Government Information: Access and Privacy* (Carswell, looseleaf); Drapeau & Racicot, *Federal Access to Information and Privacy Legislation Annotated 2017* (Carswell, 3000pp.); Power, *Halsbury's Laws of Canada — Access to Information and Privacy* (LexisNexis, 2020 Reissue, 750pp.); Grenon & Sandler, "The Use of Access to Information Processes in Tax Disputes", 2012 Cdn Tax Foundation conference report, 33:1-37; CRA publications RC4415, *Annual Report to Parliament — The Administration of the Access to Information Act*, and RC4415-1, *...of the Privacy Act*. CRA often fails to meet its legal obligations in ATIP timeliness: Taxpay-

ers' Ombudsman special report, *Acting on ATIP* (March 2012). Auditors and appeals officers should provide disclosure without a formal ATIP request, and ATIP officials may assist in this process: see Notes to 231.1(1). CRA delay in meeting an ATIP request may not justify an injunction to prohibit finalizing the audit: *Safe Workforce*, 2019 FC 645. If a TCC General Procedure appeal is filed (see Notes to 169(1)), information can also be obtained via discovery.

A breach of 241(1) does not entitle the taxpayer to have an assessment vacated: *St-Laurent [Simard]*, 2007 TCC 540, para. 386 (aff'd 2009 FCA 379). Disclosing FINTRAC information to Spanish officials investigating money-laundering was not a violation of the taxpayer's rights: *St-Laurent*, 2017 FC 776. A person whose privacy is violated by a CRA employee can sue CRA for "misfeasance in public office", but cannot force CRA to prosecute the employee: *Collins*, 2011 FCA 140.

The prohibition in 241(1) applies at the level of the individual "official" or "representative" rather than CRA or other department. This means that disclosure is not automatically permitted even within the CRA. See *Van Egmond*, [2002] G.S.T.C. 38 (BCCA) (income tax auditor was entitled to pass information on to GST auditors); *Gordon*, 2007 FC 253 (in lawsuit against CRA, court order obtained to allow CRA officials to release taxpayer information to counsel at the Department of Justice who were defending CRA).

The prohibition includes information that is in the public domain and can be found through other sources: *Investment Realty Services*, [2003] G.S.T.C. 96 (NBQB); *Scott Slipp Nissan Ltd. (No. 3)*, [2005] G.S.T.C. 170 (FC). It includes information about a defunct corporation: VIEWS doc 2012-0455781E5.

In *Murphy*, 2009 FC 1226, the Court criticized CRA officials for "cavalier" breaches of s. 241 in giving taxpayer information to police when obtaining "highly obtrusive" police assistance to serve Requirements for Information (which could have been sent by registered mail) on alleged gang members. (Costs of $214,000 were awarded: 2010 FC 448.)

In *9005-6342 Quebec*, 2011 FCA 196, a construction company was assessed to deny GST input tax credits after Revenu Québec and CRA audited its subcontractors. The company was entitled before discovery to copies of the audit reports on the subcontractors. It would also be entitled the last known coordinates of the subcontractors' shareholders, directors and employees if its directors showed that they could not otherwise get this information. (This disclosure was denied because only the company's lawyer had tried to get it through Internet searches, and the company's directors were presumed to have more information.)

When CRA says documents need to stay secret (whether in Access to Information, discovery, or the Federal Court Rules), CRA may have to disclose them to the Court for review, as "Untested ministerial claims of confidentiality can create an atmosphere that breeds suspicion and cynicism": *Chad*, 2018 FC 319, para. 18.

For general discussion of CRA's security and confidentiality measures see VIEWS doc 2005-0141241C6; and "Security of Taxpayer Information", tinyurl.com/cra-secur.

See also Alatopulos, Rios & Su, *Confidentiality of Taxpayer Information* newsletter (*Taxnet Pro*), Nov. 2014.

241(1) amended by 2008 budget bill #2 (effective March 12, 2009), 1995-97 technical bill, 1996 EI bill, 1992 technical bill.

Information Circulars: 94-4R: International transfer pricing — advance pricing arrangements (APAs); 94-4R-SR: APAs for small businesses.

I.T. Technical News: 8 (publication of advance tax rulings); 9 (electronic publication of severed rulings).

Application Policies: SR&ED 95-04: Conflict of interest.

Transfer Pricing Memoranda: TPM-04: Third-party information.

CRA Audit Manual: 3.4.0: Privacy and confidentiality; 9.8.4: Working papers as government information holdings; 10.11.0: Referrals and consultations.

Forms: T1013: Authorizing or cancelling a representative.

(2) Evidence relating to taxpayer information — Notwithstanding any other Act of Parliament or other law, no official or other representative of a government entity shall be required, in connection with any legal proceedings, to give or produce evidence relating to any taxpayer information.

Related Provisions: 149.1(15) — Charities — information may be communicated.

Notes: In *Gabriele*, [2009] 2 C.T.C. 126 (Ont. SCJ), CRA was *permitted* by 241(4)(k) to disclose third-party information (to assist a trustee in bankruptcy as authorized by *Bankruptcy and Insolvency Act* s. 164), but could not be *compelled* to disclose due to 241(2). In *Derakshan v. Narula*, 2017 ONSC 1415, a CRA official could not be subpoenaed to give evidence of tax filings in a family law trial.

241(2) amended by 2008 budget bill #2, effective March 12, 2009, to add "or other representative of a government entity".

241(2) amended by 1992 technical bill, effective June 10, 1993.

(3) Communication where proceedings have been commenced — Subsections (1) and (2) do not apply in respect of

(a) criminal proceedings, either by indictment or on summary conviction, that have been commenced by the laying of an information or the preferring of an indictment, under an Act of Parliament; or

(b) any legal proceedings relating to the administration or enforcement of this Act, the *Canada Pension Plan*, the *Unemployment Insurance Act* or the *Employment Insurance Act* or any other Act of Parliament or law of a province that provides for the imposition or collection of a tax or duty.

Related Provisions: 241(11) — Meaning of "this Act".

Notes: *241(3)(a)*: In *Nova Scotia Securities Commission*, 2007 NSSC 51, the commission could not "piggy-back" on a CRA criminal investigation to gain disclosure for its own investigation. In *Hanif's International Foods*, 2008 ABPC 238, the Crown could not use CRA information as evidence in sentencing under the federal *Meat Inspection Act*, as those proceedings were regulatory, not criminal. In *Dufour*, 2008 NBPC 41, CRA was required to disclose 3rd-party information to allow a person charged with evasion to defend himself. In *Barreiro*, 2008 FC 859, the Court allowed a *Charter* challenge to 241(3)(a) to proceed.

241(3)(b) is to be interpreted very broadly: *Slattery*, [1993] 2 C.T.C. 243 (SCC) (Revenue Canada could use taxpayer information in bankruptcy proceedings, to collect taxes owing by the bankrupt). A "legal proceeding" in 241(3)(b) can permit disclosure in: an objection (*Scott Slipp Nissan*, 2005 FC 1477; *Bradwick Property*, 2019 FC 289, para. 46 (aff'd on other grounds 2020 FCA 147)); a lawsuit arising out of a CRA investigation (*Daley*, 2016 FC 1154); defending a lawsuit against the Crown relating to handling of SR&ED claims [as long as notice was given beforehand to third parties whose information was to be disclosed] (*Gordon*, 2007 FC 253, varied 2008 FC 1031); a challenge of CRA refusal to recommend a remission order (*Fink*, 2017 FCA 87); a TCC appeal by a different person (*Scott*, 2017 TCC 224, para. 54), though notice should be given to the taxpayer (paras. 59, 64(c)); defending a lawsuit claiming abusive audit and collection action (*Restaurant Le Relais*, 2017 QCCS 5397, para. 325 (aff'd on other grounds 2020 QCCA 823; leave to appeal denied 2021 CarswellQue 5277 (SCC)).

In a tax appeal, information about whether other taxpayers in the same situation were assessed is arguably disclosable: *Fink*, [1999] 2 C.T.C. 2088 (TCC); *Toronto Transit Commission v. Ontario*, 2009 CarswellOnt 3203 (Ont. SCJ), para. 86. (But see Notes to 169(1) under "Inconsistent assessments".]

In *783783 Alberta [7837783 Alberta]*, 2010 ABCA 226, the ABQB had speculated that a claim CRA was not correctly dealing with a company's competitor might be "relating to the administration of this Act" and thus within 241(3)(b). The ABCA held that s. 241 did not resolve the appeal: para. 36.

241(3)(b) did not apply to court proceedings by the Commission de la Construction du Québec making claims on behalf of construction workers: *9033-6009 Québec*, 2013 QCCA 1754. In *Barreiro*, 2008 FC 850, the Court issued a limited confidentiality order overriding 241(3)(b).

241(3) does not permit disclosure of third-party information "if it is not relevant to nor was relied on by the Minister in reassessing": *Tor Can Waste*, 2015 TCC 157.

See also Bendin, "The Requirement of Confidentiality under the Income Tax Act and Its Effect on the Conduct of Appeals", 44(3) *Canadian Tax Journal* 680-722 (1996); Atkinson, "Release of Taxpayer Information", 1(3) *Canadian Tax Focus* (ctf.ca) 7-8 (Nov. 2011).

241(3) amended by 1995-97 technical bill (effective June 30, 1996), 1996 EI bill, 1992 technical bill.

Proposed 241(3)(c) in Dec. 21, 2000 draft legislation was enacted as 241(4)(p).

Information Circulars: 87-2R: International transfer pricing (archived).

(3.1) Circumstances involving danger — The Minister may provide to appropriate persons any taxpayer information relating to imminent danger of death or physical injury to any individual.

Related Provisions: 241(9.5) — Serious offences.

Notes: 241(3.1) added by 1992 technical bill, effective June 10, 1993.

(3.2) Certain qualified donees — An official may provide to any person the following taxpayer information relating to another person (in this subsection referred to as the "registrant") that was at any time a registered charity, registered Canadian amateur athletic association or registered journalism organization:

(a) a copy of the registrant's governing documents, including its statement of purpose, and function in the case of a Canadian amateur athletic association;

(b) any information provided in prescribed form to the Minister by the registrant on applying for registration under this Act;

(c) the names of the persons who at any time were the registrant's directors and the periods during which they were its directors;

(d) a copy of the notification of the registrant's registration, including any conditions and warnings;

(e) if the registration of the registrant has been revoked or annulled, a copy of the entirety of or any part of any letter sent by or on behalf of the Minister to the registrant relating to the grounds for the revocation or annulment;

(f) financial statements required to be filed with an information return referred to in subsection 149.1(14) or (14.1);

(g) a copy of the entirety of or any part of any letter or notice by the Minister to the registrant relating to a suspension under section 188.2 or an assessment of tax or penalty under this Act (other than the amount of a liability under subsection 188(1.1)); and

(h) in the case of a registrant that is a charity, an application by the registrant, and information filed in support of the application, for a designation, determination or decision by the Minister under any of subsections 149.1(5), (6.3), (7), (8) and (13).

Related Provisions: 149.1(6.4) — Rule applies to registered national arts service organizations; 149.1(15) — Disclosure permitted of information in public information return.

Notes: 241(3.2) amended by 2019 budget bill #1, effective 2020, to add "registered journalism organization" [defined in 248(1)] in opening words, and reference to 149.1(14.1) in para. (f),

241(3.2) amended by 2011 budget bill #2, effective 2012, so as to apply to RCAAAs (and referring in (a)-(h) to a "registrant" rather than "registered charity").

241(3.2) earlier amended by 2011 budget bill #2 (for documents sent by, filed with or required to be filed with the Minister after May 13, 2005), 2004 Budget, 2001 technical bill. Added by 1997 Budget.

Registered Charities Newsletters: 8 (increased transparency).

Charities Guidance: CG-008: Confidentiality — public information.

Forms: T1235: Directors/trustees and like officials worksheet.

(3.3) Information may be communicated [film productions] — The Minister of Canadian Heritage may communicate or otherwise make available to the public, in any manner that that Minister considers appropriate, the following taxpayer information in respect of a Canadian film or video production certificate (as defined under subsection 125.4(1)) that has been issued or revoked:

(a) the title of the production for which the Canadian film or video production certificate was issued;

(b) the name of the taxpayer to whom the Canadian film or video production certificate was issued;

(c) the names of the producers of the production;

(d) the names of the individuals in respect of whom and places in respect of which that Minister has allotted points in respect of the production in accordance with regulations made for the purpose of section 125.4;

(e) the total number of points so allotted; and

(f) any revocation of the Canadian film or video production certificate.

Notes: 241(3.3) added by 2014 budget bill #2, effective December 16, 2014. This amendment is identical to one proposed in 2007. See Notes to 125.4(1)"Canadian film or video production certificate".

(3.4) Information may be communicated [digital news credit] — The Minister may communicate or otherwise make available to the public, in any manner that the Minister considers appropriate, the following taxpayer information:

(a) the names of each organization in respect of which an individual can be entitled to a deduction under subsection 118.02(2);

(b) information relating to the eligibility, for the deduction under subsection 118.02(2), of subscriptions offered by organizations referred to in paragraph (a); and

(c) the start and, if applicable, end of the period in which paragraph (a) or (b) applies in respect of any particular organization or subscription.

Notes: 241(3.4) allows CRA to publish a list of news organizations whose digital subscriptions qualify for the 118.02 digital news credit; see 118.02(1)"qualifying subscription expense" Notes.

241(3.4)(a)-(b) replaced by (a)-(c) (essentially adding (b)) by 2021 budget bill #1, effective 2020. 241(3.4) added by 2019 budget bill #1, effective June 21, 2019.

(3.5) Information may be communicated [CEWS and CERS] — The Minister may communicate or otherwise make available to the public, in any manner that the Minister considers appropriate, the name of any person or partnership that makes an application under section 125.7.

Notes: Search at tinyurl.com/cews-registry. It lists names only, and only corporations. See also Neilson, "Tax Transparency: The CEWS", 1(4) *Perspectives on Tax Law & Policy* (ctf.ca) 12-14 (Dec. 2020).

241(3.5) added by 2020 COVID bill #2, effective April 11, 2020. See 125.7(2) Notes re the Canada Emergency Wage Subsidy.

(4) Where taxpayer information may be disclosed — An official may

(a) provide to any person taxpayer information that can reasonably be regarded as necessary for the purposes of the administration or enforcement of this Act, the *Canada Pension Plan*, the *Unemployment Insurance Act* or the *Employment Insurance Act*, solely for that purpose;

(b) provide to any person taxpayer information that can reasonably be regarded as necessary for the purposes of determining any tax, interest, penalty or other amount that is or may become payable by the person, or any refund or tax credit to which the person is or may become entitled, under this Act or any other amount that is relevant for the purposes of that determination;

(c) provide to the person who seeks a certification referred to in paragraph 147.1(10)(a) the certification or a refusal to make the certification, solely for the purposes of administering a registered pension plan;

(d) provide taxpayer information

(i) to an official of the Department of Finance solely for the purposes of the formulation or evaluation of fiscal policy,

(ii) to an official solely for the purposes of the initial implementation of a fiscal policy or for the purposes of the administration or enforcement of an Act of Parliament that provides for the imposition and collection of a tax or duty,

(iii) to an official solely for the purposes of the administration or enforcement of a law of a province that provides for the imposition or collection of a tax or duty,

(iv) to an official of the government of a province solely for the purposes of the formulation or evaluation of fiscal policy,

(v) to an official of the Department of Natural Resources or of the government of a province solely for the purposes of the administration or enforcement of a program of the Government of Canada or of the province relating to the exploration for or exploitation of Canadian petroleum and gas resources,

(vi) to an official of the government of a province that has received or is entitled to receive a payment referred to in this subparagraph, or to an official of the Department of Natural Resources, solely for the purposes of the provisions relating to payments to a province in respect of the taxable income of corporations earned in the offshore area with respect to the province under the *Canada–Nova Scotia Offshore Petroleum Resources Accord Implementation Act*, chapter 28 of the Statutes of Canada, 1988, the *Canada–Newfoundland and Labrador Atlantic Accord Implementation Act*, chapter 3 of the Statutes of Canada, 1987, or similar Acts relating to the exploration for or exploitation of offshore Canadian petroleum and gas resources,

foundland offshore area under the *Canada–Newfoundland and Labrador Atlantic Accord Implementation Act*, in the joint management area under the *Canada–Quebec Gulf of St. Lawrence Petroleum Resources Accord Implementation Act* or in similar areas under similar Acts relating to the exploration for or exploitation of offshore Canadian petroleum and gas resources,

(vi.1) to an official of the Department of Natural Resources solely for the purpose of determining whether property is prescribed energy conservation property or whether an outlay or expense is a Canadian renewable and conservation expense,

(vii) to an official solely for the purposes of the administration or enforcement of the *Pension Benefits Standards Act, 1985*, the *Pooled Registered Pension Plans Act* or a similar law of a province,

(vii.1) to an official solely for the purpose of the administration or enforcement of the *Canada Education Savings Act* or a designated provincial program as defined in subsection 146.1(1),

(vii.2) to an official solely for the purposes of the administration and enforcement of Part 1 of the *Energy Costs Assistance Measures Act*,

(vii.3) to an official solely for the purposes of the administration and enforcement of the *Children's Special Allowances Act* or the evaluation or formation of policy for that Act,

(vii.4) to an official solely for the purposes of the administration and enforcement of the *Universal Child Care Benefit Act* or the evaluation or formation of policy for that Act,

(vii.5) to an official solely for the purposes of the administration or enforcement of the *Canada Disability Savings Act* or a designated provincial program as defined in subsection 146.1(1),

(vii.6) to an official solely for the purposes of the administration and enforcement of the *Canada Emergency Response Benefit Act* or the evaluation or formulation of policy for that Act,

(vii.7) to an official solely for the purposes of the administration and enforcement of the *Canada Recovery Benefits Act* or the evaluation or formulation of policy for that Act,

(vii.8) to an official, if the taxpayer information is taxpayer information of an individual who has made an application under the *Canada Recovery Benefits Act*, solely for the purposes of the evaluation or formulation of policy for a program administered and enforced by

(A) the Minister of Employment and Social Development,

(B) the Minister of Labour, or

(C) the Canada Employment Insurance Commission,

(vii.9) to an official of a department or agency of the Government of Canada or of a provincial government (or to an individual who occupies a similar position in connection with an Aboriginal government) as to the name, Social Insurance Number, date of birth, address, telephone number, email address or occupation of an individual who has made an application under the *Canada Recovery Benefits Act*, solely for the purposes of

    (A) the administration and enforcement of employment benefits and supports and social assistance programs established by a department or agency of the Government of Canada, the government of a province or an Aboriginal government, or

    (B) the evaluation or formulation of policy of a program established by a department or agency of the Government of Canada, the government of a province or an Aboriginal government,

(vii.10) *[should have been numbered (vii.91) — ed.]* to an official of a department or agency of a provincial government solely for the purposes of the administration and enforcement, or evaluation or formulation of policy, of a program that provides financial assistance in respect of rent or interest payments in the context of the coronavirus disease 2019 (COVID-19) pandemic,

(viii) to an official of the Department of Veterans Affairs solely for the purposes of the administration of the *War Veterans Allowance Act*, the *Veterans Well-being Act* or Part XI of the *Civilian War-related Benefits Act*,

(ix) to an official of a department or agency of the Government of Canada or of a province as to the name, address, telephone number, occupation, size or type of business of a taxpayer, solely for the purpose of enabling that department or agency to obtain statistical data for research and analysis,

(x) to an official of the Canada Employment Insurance Commission or the Department of Employment and Social Development, solely for the purpose of the administration or enforcement of the *Employment Insurance Act*, an employment program of the Government of Canada (including, for greater certainty, any activity relating to a program for temporary foreign workers for which the administration or enforcement is the responsibility of the Minister of Employment and Social Development under the *Immigration and Refugee Protection Regulations*) or the evaluation or formation of policy for that Act or program,

(x.1) to an official of the Department of Employment and Social Development solely for the purpose of the administration or enforcement of a program established under the authority of the *Department of Employment and Social Development Act* in respect of children who are deceased or missing as a result of an offence, or a probable offence, under the *Criminal Code*,

(xi) to an official of the Department of Agriculture and Agri-Food or of the government of a province solely for the purposes of the administration or enforcement of a program of the Government of Canada or of the province established under an agreement entered into under the *Farm Income Protection Act*,

(xii) to a member of the Canadian Cultural Property Export Review Board or an official of the Administrative Tribunals Support Service of Canada solely for the purposes of administering sections 32 to 33.2 of the *Cultural Property Export and Import Act*,

(xiii) to an official solely for the purposes of setting off against any sum of money that may be due or payable by Her Majesty in right of Canada a debt due to

    (A) Her Majesty in right of Canada, or

    (B) Her Majesty in right of a province,

(xiv) to an official solely for the purposes of section 7.1 of the *Federal-Provincial Fiscal Arrangements Act*,

(xv) to an official of the Financial Transactions and Reports Analysis Centre of Canada *[FINTRAC — ed.]* solely for the purpose of enabling the Centre to evaluate the usefulness of information provided by the Centre to the Canada Revenue Agency under the *Proceeds of Crime (Money Laundering) and Terrorist Financing Act*,

(xvi) to a person employed or engaged in the service of an office or agency, of the Government of Canada or of a province, whose mandate includes the provision of assistance (as defined in subsection 125.4(1) or 125.5(1)) in respect of film or video productions or film or video production services, solely for the purpose of the administration or enforcement of the program under which the assistance is offered,

(xvi.1) to a person employed or engaged in the service of an office or agency, of the Government of Canada or of a province, whose mandate includes the provision of "assistance" (as defined in subsection 125.6(1)) in respect of qualified Canadian journalism organizations, solely for the purpose of the administration or enforcement of the program under which the assistance is offered,

(xvi.2) to a body referred to in paragraph (b) of the definition "qualified Canadian journalism organization" in subsection 248(1), solely for the purpose of determining eligibility for designation under that paragraph,

(xvii) to an official of the Canadian Radio-television and Telecommunications Commission, solely for the purpose of the administration or enforcement of a regulatory function of that Commission, or

(xviii) to an official of the Canada Revenue Agency solely for the purpose of the collection of amounts owing to Her Majesty in right of Canada or of a province under the *Government Employees Compensation Act*, the *Canada Labour Code*, the *Merchant Seamen Compensation Act*, the *Canada Student Loans Act*, the *Canada Student Financial Assistance Act*, the *Postal Services Continuation Act, 1997*, the *Wage Earner Protection Program Act*, the *Apprentice Loans Act* or a law of a province governing the granting of financial assistance to students at the post-secondary school level;

(e) provide taxpayer information, or allow the inspection of or access to taxpayer information, as the case may be, under, and solely for the purposes of,

(i) subsection 36(2) or section 46 of the *Access to Information Act*,

(ii) section 13 of the *Auditor General Act*,

(iii) section 92 of the *Canada Pension Plan*,

(iv) a warrant issued under subsection 21(3) of the *Canadian Security Intelligence Service Act*,

(v) an order made under subsection 462.48(3) of the *Criminal Code*,

(vi) section 26 of the *Cultural Property Export and Import Act*,

(vii) section 79 of the *Family Orders and Agreements Enforcement Assistance Act*,

(viii) paragraph 33.1(a) of the *Old Age Security Act*,

(ix) subsection 34(2) or section 45 of the *Privacy Act*,

(x) section 24 of the *Statistics Act*,

(xi) section 9 of the *Tax Rebate Discounting Act*,

(xii) a provision contained in a tax treaty with another country or in a listed international agreement, or

(xiii) an order made under the *Mutual Legal Assistance in Criminal Matters Act* to gather or send information, for the purposes of an investigation or prosecution relating to an act or omission that, if it had occurred in Canada, would constitute an offence for which an order could be obtained under subsection 462.48(3) of the *Criminal Code*, in response to a request made pursuant to

    (A) an administrative arrangement entered into under section 6 of the *Mutual Legal Assistance in Criminal Matters Act*, or

(B) a bilateral agreement for mutual legal assistance in criminal matters to which Canada is a party;

(f) provide taxpayer information solely for the purposes of sections 23 to 25 of the *Financial Administration Act*;

(f.1) provide taxpayer information to an official for the purposes of the administration and enforcement of the *Charities Registration (Security Information) Act*, and where an official has so received taxpayer information, the official may provide that information to another official as permitted by subsection (9.1);

(g) use taxpayer information to compile information in a form that does not directly or indirectly reveal the identity of the taxpayer to whom the information relates;

(h) use, or provide to any person, taxpayer information solely for a purpose relating to the supervision, evaluation or discipline of an authorized person by Her Majesty in right of Canada in respect of a period during which the authorized person was employed by or engaged by or on behalf of Her Majesty in right of Canada to assist in the administration or enforcement of this Act, the *Canada Pension Plan*, the *Unemployment Insurance Act* or the *Employment Insurance Act*, to the extent that the information is relevant for the purpose;

(h.1) use, or provide to an official of a department or agency of the Government of Canada, taxpayer information solely for a purpose relating to the administration or enforcement of a program to provide a one-time payment to persons with disabilities for reasons related to the coronavirus disease 2019 (COVID-19), to the extent that the information is relevant for the purpose;

(i) provide access to records of taxpayer information to the Librarian and Archivist of Canada or a person acting on behalf of or under the direction of the Librarian and Archivist, solely for the purposes of section 12 of the *Library and Archives of Canada Act*, and transfer such records to the care and control of such persons solely for the purposes of section 13 of that Act;

(j) use taxpayer information relating to a taxpayer to provide information to the taxpayer;

(j.1) provide taxpayer information to an official or a designated person solely for the purpose of permitting the making of an adjustment to a social assistance payment made on the basis of a means, needs or income test if the purpose of the adjustment is to take into account

(i) the amount determined in respect of a person for C in subsection 122.61(1), as it read before July 2018, in respect of a "base taxation year" (as defined in section 122.6) before 2017, or

(ii) an amount determined in respect of a person under subsection 122.61(1) or (1.1) in respect of a "base taxation year" (as defined in section 122.6) after 2014;

(j.2) provide information obtained under section 122.62 to an official of the government of a province solely for the purposes of the administration or enforcement of a prescribed law of the province;

(k) provide, or allow inspection of or access to, taxpayer information to or by any person otherwise legally entitled to it under an Act of Parliament solely for the purposes for which that person is entitled to the information;

(l) subject to subsection (9.2), provide to a representative of a government entity the business number of, the name of (including any trade name or other name used by), and any contact information, corporate information and registration information in respect of, the holder of a business number (other than an excluded individual), if the information is provided solely for the purposes of the administration or enforcement of

(i) an Act of Parliament or of a legislature of a province, or

(ii) a by-law of a municipality in Canada or a law of an aboriginal government;

(m) provide taxpayer information to an official of the government of a province solely for use in the management or adminis-

tration by that government of a program relating to payments under subsection 164(1.8);

(n) provide taxpayer information to any person, solely for the purposes of the administration or enforcement of a law of a province that provides for workers' compensation benefits;

(o) provide taxpayer information to any person solely for the purpose of enabling the Chief Statistician, within the meaning assigned by section 2 of the *Statistics Act*, to provide to a statistical agency of a province data concerning business activities carried on in the province, where the information is used by the agency solely for research and analysis and the agency is authorized under the law of the province to collect the same or similar information on its own behalf in respect of such activities;

(p) provide taxpayer information to a police officer (within the meaning assigned by subsection 462.48(17) of the *Criminal Code*) solely for the purpose of investigating whether an offence has been committed under the *Criminal Code*, or the laying of an information or the preferring of an indictment, where

(i) such information can reasonably be regarded as being necessary for the purpose of ascertaining the circumstances in which an offence under the *Criminal Code* may have been committed, or the identity of the person or persons who may have committed an offence, with respect to an official, or with respect to any person related to that official,

(ii) the official was or is engaged in the administration or enforcement of this Act, and

(iii) the offence can reasonably be considered to be related to that administration or enforcement;

(q) provide taxpayer information to an official of the government of a province solely for the use in the management or administration by that government of a program relating to earning supplementation or income support;

(r) provide taxpayer information to a person who has — under a program administered by the Canada Revenue Agency to obtain information relating to tax non-compliance — entered into a contract to provide information to the Canada Revenue Agency, to the extent necessary to inform the person of any amount they may be entitled to under the contract and of the status of their claim under the contract;

(s) provide taxpayer information, solely for the purpose of ensuring compliance with Part 1 of the *Proceeds of Crime (Money Laundering) and Terrorist Financing Act*, to an official of the Financial Transactions and Reports Analysis Centre of Canada, if the information

(i) can reasonably be considered to be relevant to a determination of whether a reporting entity (as defined in section 244.1) has complied with a duty or obligation under Part XV.1, and

(ii) does not directly or indirectly reveal the identity of a client (as defined in section 244.1); or

(t) provide taxpayer information to an official solely for the purpose of enabling the Chief Actuary of the Office of the Superintendent of Financial Institutions to conduct actuarial reviews of pension plans established under the *Old Age Security Act* as required by the *Public Pensions Reporting Act*.

Proposed Amendment — 241(4) — Social Insurance Number disclosure

Letter from Dept. of Finance, March 17, 1999:

Dear [xxx]

This is in reply to your letter of March 12, 1999 to Simon Thompson with respect to the transfer of Social Insurance Numbers and business numbers from [xxx] to a nominee.

We understand that [xxx] plans to put in place an arrangement under which legal ownership of shares will, in many cases, be with a nominee of the shareholders. The nominee will receive dividend payments on the shares for which it is the registered owner, and will then distribute each dividend to the beneficial owners of the shares. As a consequence, the nominee will have an independent tax-reporting obligation under subsection 201(2) of the *Income Tax Regulations*. Under the existing law and the proposed amendments to it that were released on December 15, 1998, we agree that it may not be technically possible for [xxx] to provide Social Insurance Numbers and business numbers of beneficial owners to the nominee.

Given the reasons for the creation of the nominee in these circumstances, and in the interests of ensuring timely and complete reporting with regard to Social Insurance Numbers and business numbers, we are prepared to recommend an amendment to the *Income Tax Act*. The amendment would, in the circumstance set out in your letter, allow the transfer of this information to the nominee for the purpose of allowing the nominee to comply with tax reporting requirements.

Thank you for writing.

Yours sincerely,

Brian Ernewein, Director, Tax Legislation Division, Tax Policy Branch

Notes: Finance has confirmed (June 2017) that this amendment is still pending.

Related Provisions: 37(3) — Consultation with other government departments to determine R&D claims; 146.1(14)(a) — Reference to *Canada Education Savings Act* in 241(4)(d)(vii.1) includes reference to earlier *DHRD Act*; 149.1(15) — Registered charity's information return may be communicated to public; 230.1(4) — Reports to chief electoral officer; 239(2.21) — Offence with respect to confidential information; 241(5) — Disclosure to taxpayer or with taxpayer's consent; 241(9.2) — No disclosure unless other government uses the Business Number; 241(11) — Meaning of "this Act"; Canada-U.S. Tax Treaty:Art. XXVII — Exchange of information with US government (for 241(4)(e)(xii)).

Notes: 241(4) provides exceptions to 241(1) but does not override common-law rules such as the implied undertaking not to use information obtained on discovery [discussed in Notes to 169(1)]: *Fio Corp.*, 2014 TCC 58, para. 58 (aff'd without discussing this issue 2015 FCA 236).

March 2007 Budget proposal "Sharing of RESP Information", shown as a Proposed Amendment under 241(4)(d)(vii.1) in the 32nd edition, was enacted as *Canada Education Savings Act* s. 12.1 (see Notes at end of 146.1).

In addition to 241(4), *Canada Revenue Agency Act* s. 63.1, enacted June 2021 (S.C. 2021, c. 12), allows CRA to collect and disclose to a province (or territory) information for an organ/tissue donor registry run by the province.

241(4)(a) and (e): Where an individual continues to cash his deceased father's OAS and CPP cheques and keeps the proceeds, CRA can disclose this information to other government departments for purposes of administering the CPP (241(4)(a)) and *Old Age Security Act* s. 33.1(a) (241(4)(e)(viii)): VIEWS doc 2009-0343291I7.

241(4)(b): CRA takes a strict interpretation: Information Circular 87-2R paras. 208-210 (though this IC was cancelled for other reasons); May 2001 ICAA Roundtable q. 2 (tinyurl.com/cra-abtax).

241(4)(d)(iii) applied in *SPE Valeur*, 2016 FC 56, so CRA could give Revenu Québec documents it had seized in a criminal investigation where no charges were laid.

241(4)(d)(vii.10) should have been numbered 241(4)(d)(vii.91), since both (vii.101) and (vii.11) would come between (vii.1) and (vii.2). Finance agrees.

241(4)(e)(xii) includes the InterGovernmental Agreement under FATCA (see Notes to 269), so disclosure under the IGA does not violate s. 241: *Hillis (Deegan)*, 2015 FC 1082 (FCA appeal discontinued A-407-15), paras. 51, 65.

241(4)(h.1) allows CRA to provide information on persons qualifying for the 118.3 Disability Tax Credit, for purpose of the one-time $600 COVID-19 payment.

241(4)(j.2) refers to Quebec; see Reg. 6500.

241(4)(k) justifies disclosure of a bankrupt taxpayer's information to the bankruptcy trustee "on an as-needs basis": docs 2009-035163I7, 2012-045113117. See also Notes to 241(2) re *Gabriele* case.

241(4))(l): see: 241(9.2); 241(9.3) and (9.4) (which generally permit disclosure of names and Business Numbers); and Notes to 248(1)"business number".

241(4)(n) reflects CRA's role in collecting workers' compensation premiums in Nova Scotia and possibly other provinces.

241(4)(r) applies to the Offshore Tax Informant Program: see Notes to 56(1)(z.4).

241(4)(s): "Part XV.1" is ss. 244.1-244.7, the rules requiring disclosure of international electronic transfers of $10,000 or more.

241(4)(t) was described in the March 2016 Budget, claiming it had been announced before. The 2014 Budget stated: "the Government proposes to take steps to ensure that the Office of the Chief Actuary can efficiently and effectively deliver its services to key clients, which include government departments, agencies and Crown corporations", but did not mention disclosure of taxpayer information.

History:

241(4)(d)(vii.10) added by 2020 COVID bill #5, effective Nov. 19, 2020.

241(4)(d)(vii.7)-(vii.9) added by 2020 COVID bill #4, effective Oct. 2, 2020.

241(4)(h.1) added by 2020 COVID bill #3, effective July 27, 2020.

241(4)(d)(vii.6) added by 2020 COVID bill #2, effective April 11, 2020.

241(4)(d)(xvi.1) and (xvi.2) added by 2019 budget bill #1, effective June 21, 2019.

241(4)(e)(xiii) added by 2018 budget bill #2, effective Dec. 13, 2018.

241(4)(j.1)(ii) added by 2018 budget bill #1, effective July 2018. Before then, read:

> (j.1) provide taxpayer information to an official or a designated person solely for the purpose of permitting the making of an adjustment to a social assistance payment made on the basis of a means, needs or income test if the purpose of the adjustment is to take into account the amount determined for C in subsection 122.61(1) in respect of a person for a taxation year;

241(4)(d)(viii) amended by 2017 budget bill #1, effective April 2018, to change "*Canadian Forces Members and Veterans Re-establishment and Compensation Act*" to "*Veterans Well-being Act*".

241(4)(d)(xviii) and 241(4)(t) added by 2016 budget bill #1, effective June 22, 2016.

241(4) earlier amended by *Offshore Health and Safety Act* (S.C. 2014 c. 13, effective Dec. 31, 2014), 2014 budget bills #1 and #2, 2013 budget bill #2, 2002-2013 technical bill, 2012 budget bills #1 and #2, S.C. 2012 c. 27, 2010 budget bill #1, 2008 budget bill #2, 2007 RDSPs bill, 2007 budget bill #2, 2006 budget bill #1, S.C. 2006 c. 12, S.C. 2005 cc. 21 and 34, 2004 RESPs bill, S.C. 2004 c. 11, 2001 anti-terrorism bill, 2001 technical bill, 2000 Budget, S.C. 1999 c. 10, 1999 and 1998 budget bills #1, 1995-97 technical bill, 1996 EI bill, 1996 Budget, 1995 *Dept. of Cdn Heritage Act*, 1995 cultural property bill, 1995 and 1994 Budgets, S.C. 1994 c. 38, 1992 technical bill.

Regulations: 6500 (prescribed laws of Quebec for 241(4)(j.2)); 8200.1 (prescribed energy conservation property for 241(4)(d)(vi.1)).

Transfer Pricing Memoranda: TPM-04: Third-party information.

CRA Audit Manual: 3.4.0: Privacy and confidentiality; 9.8.4: Working papers as government information holdings; 10.11.0: Referrals and consultations.

Forms: T1013: Authorizing or cancelling a representative.

(4.1) Measures to prevent unauthorized use or disclosure — The person who presides at a legal proceeding relating to the supervision, evaluation or discipline of an authorized person may order such measures as are necessary to ensure that taxpayer information is not used or provided to any person for any purpose not relating to that proceeding, including

(a) holding a hearing *in camera*;

(b) banning the publication of the information;

(c) concealing the identity of the taxpayer to whom the information relates; and

(d) sealing the records of the proceeding.

Related Provisions: 239(2.2) — Offence with respect to confidential information; 238(1) — Punishment for failing to comply.

Notes: 241(4.1) added by 1992 technical bill, effective June 10, 1993.

(5) Disclosure to taxpayer or on consent — An official or other representative of a government entity may provide taxpayer information relating to a taxpayer

(a) to the taxpayer; and

(b) with the consent of the taxpayer, to any other person.

Announced Temporary Administrative Change — Electronic signature to authorize online filing

Dept. of Finance Backgrounder, March 18, 2020: *Canada's COVID-19 Economic Response Plan: Support for Canadians and Businesses*

Flexibility for Taxpayers

. . .

In order to reduce the necessity for taxpayers and tax preparers to meet in person during this difficult time, and to reduce administrative burden, effective immediately the Canada Revenue Agency will recognize electronic signatures as having met the signature requirements of the *Income Tax Act*, as a temporary administrative measure. This provision applies to authorization forms T183 or T183CORP, which are forms that are signed in person by millions of Canadians every year to authorize tax preparers to file taxes.

CRA, EFILE news and program update, March 18, 2020: *Temporary measure immediately enabling electronic signatures for the T183, Information Return for Electronic Filing of an Individual's Income Tax and Benefit Return, and the T183CORP, Information Return for Corporations Filing Electronically*

If an individual or a corporate taxpayer wishes to file their income tax return through an electronic filer, they must authorize the electronic filer to do so by completing a T183, *Information Return for Electronic Filing of an Individual's Income Tax and Benefit Return*, or a T183CORP, *Information Return for Corporations Filing Electronically*.

The Canada Revenue Agency (CRA) is committed to improving and enhancing the services it offers to Canadians, including digital services, and is continuously striving to ease the burden imposed upon taxpayers and tax preparers when filing income tax returns. From March 18, 2020 to August 31, 2020, to meet the evolving expectations of taxpayers and electronic filers during this difficult time, and to reduce administrative burden, the CRA will recognize a Form T183 or T183CORP that contains an electronic signature as having met the signature requirements of the *Income Tax Act* as a temporary administrative measure.

An electronic signature would provide taxpayers and their representatives with further options to have these information returns signed. Electronic filers are already responsible for verifying the identity of the taxpayer, both to protect their own interests and the integrity of the tax system. This will not change.

In order for the CRA to accept an electronic signature from a taxpayer whose identity has been verified by the filer, the electronic signature will generally need to be provided in one of the following ways:

- It may be provided if the taxpayer sends the information return, including the electronic signature using the electronic address most recently provided by the taxpayer to the electronic filer;

- It may be provided in person by the taxpayer, in the presence of the electronic filer. e.g. using a stylus or finger on a tablet; or

- It may be provided through an access controlled, secured electronic location such as a secure website, that is accessible to the taxpayer only because the location of the secure website has been made known to the taxpayer and access has been granted by the filer.

The number of tax returns filed electronically by tax preparers continues to grow and industry stakeholders have been requesting this change, especially now with the recent rise in COVID 19 cases in Canada. The proposed change is expected to better meet the needs of this population, and will reduce an unintended burden that the current signature requirement imposes on some individuals. These provisions will be in place until August 31, 2020. The CRA will continue to pursue regulatory requirements to implement these measures permanently.

CRA, EFILE news and program update, Aug. 25, 2020: *Extended Temporary measure enabling electronic signatures for the T183, Information Return for Electronic Filing of an Individual's Income Tax and Benefit Return, and the T183CORP, Information Return for Corporations Filing Electronically*

If an individual or a corporate taxpayer wishes to file their income tax return through an electronic filer, they must authorize the electronic filer to do so by completing a T183, *Information Return for Electronic Filing of an Individual's Income Tax and Benefit Return*, or a T183CORP, *Information Return for Corporations Filing Electronically*.

Further to our message dated March 18, 2020, the Canada Revenue Agency (CRA) will continue to recognize a Form T183 or T183CORP that contains an electronic signature as having met the signature requirements of the *Income Tax Act* as a temporary administrative measure for the remainder of the filing season.

An electronic signature provides taxpayers and their representatives with further options to have these information returns signed. Electronic filers are already responsible for verifying the identity of the taxpayer, both to protect their own interests and the integrity of the tax system. This will not change.

In order for the CRA to continue to accept an electronic signature from a taxpayer whose identity has been verified by the filer, the electronic signature will generally need to be provided in one of the following ways:

- It may be provided if the taxpayer sends the information return, including the electronic signature using the electronic address most recently provided by the taxpayer to the electronic filer;

- It may be provided in person by the taxpayer, in the presence of the electronic filer. e.g. using a stylus or finger on a tablet; or

- It may be provided through an access controlled, secured electronic location such as a secure website, that is accessible to the taxpayer only because the location of the secure website has been made known to the taxpayer and access has been granted by the filer.

This measure is to better meet the needs of this population, and reduces an unintended burden that the signature requirement imposes on some individuals. These provisions will remain in place for the remainder of the current filing season. The CRA continues to pursue the regulatory requirements to implement these measures permanently.

CRA news release, January 19, 2021: *T183 / T183CORP Electronic Signatures — Extension of Temporary Measures*

Due to the global pandemic brought on by COVID-19, the Canada Revenue Agency (CRA) introduced temporary administrative measures to alleviate some of the difficulties Canadians were experiencing while trying to file their income tax return(s). In March 2020, the CRA announced that electronic signatures on the T183, *Information Return for Electronic Filing of an Individual's Income Tax and Benefit Return* and T183CORP, *Information Return for Corporations Filing Electronically* that meet specific criteria, would be accepted as having met the requirements of the *Income Tax Act*.

While the CRA is still pursuing the implementation of electronic signatures for the T183 and T183CORP as a permanent measure, the regulatory changes required to implement this change permanently will not be in place by the start of the upcoming tax filing season. As a result, further to our messages dated March 18, 2020, and August 25, 2020, the CRA will be extending the temporary administrative measures currently in place to allow electronic signatures on the T183 and T183CORP, as outlined below, for the 2021 tax filing season.

In order for the CRA to continue to accept an electronic signature from a taxpayer whose identity has been verified by the electronic filer, the electronic signature must be provided in one of the following ways:

- It may be provided if the taxpayer sends the information return, including the electronic signature using the electronic address most recently provided by the taxpayer to the electronic filer;

- It may be provided in person by the taxpayer, in the presence of the electronic filer (e.g., using a stylus or a finger on a tablet); or

- It may be provided through an access controlled, secured electronic location, such as a secure website, that is accessible to the taxpayer only because the location of the secure website has been made known to the taxpayer and access has been granted by the electronic filer.

In February 2020, the CRA held an online consultation requesting feedback from Canadians on a proposal that would enable the use of electronic signatures on the T183 and the T183CORP. The Consultation Summary Report can be found [at tinyurl.com/t183-report — ed.]. The CRA will continue to provide updates on a regular basis.

Related Provisions: 238(1) — Punishment for failing to comply; 241(4)(j) — Disclosure to taxpayer permitted.

Notes: 241(5) permits CRA to communicate with a person the taxpayer authorizes. Before Feb. 10, 2020, this was done on Form T1013 (personal income tax), RC59 (business account) or NR95 (non-resident). These are now all Form AUT-01, for phone and mail (not online) access: CRA, "We're changing how representatives are authorized" (Jan. 3, 2020); use AUT-01X to cancel an authorization. For online (as well as other) access, use Represent a Client (canada.ca/taxes-representatives) > "Authorization request", have the client sign the signature page, then scan and upload the signed page. (Using the AUT-01 for an existing client will result in losing online access.) Existing authorizations for individual tax accounts are no longer cancelled on death.

An authorization must choose Level 1 (CRA can disclose information), 2 (representative can also request changes), or 3 (rep can also make new authorizations). CRA will not accept a form signed more than 6 months back: May 2007 ICAA roundtable (tinyurl.com/cra-abtax), q.22 (though there is no legal basis for this). CRA requires evidence of who are a corporation's officers and directors, to accept authorization signed by one: May 2008 roundtable, q.41. CRA may return a form that does not include the rep's phone number: Rotenberg, "Please Give CRA Officials a Copy of the *Income Tax Act*", xxxi(9) *The Canadian Taxpayer* (Carswell) 72 (April 28, 2009).

CRA's target (tinyurl.com/cra-standards) is to process a paper authorization within 4 weeks (far too long in the author's view) and a digital one within 3 business days, 95% of the time; in 2019-20, it did 75% (paper) and 99% (digital).

Form RC321, "Delegation of Authority", allows a business to authorize a higher level than level 2, including changing the business's representatives, identification and banking information.

A non-resident representative (NRR) living in the U.S. who has no Social Insurance Number, Temporary Tax Number or Individual Tax Number can request a NRR Number on Form RC391 so as to be able to apply for Represent a Client.

Where representative R calls CRA to set up a non-resident account number for client C and provides all of C's information, CRA can set up the number but cannot provide it to R without C's written authorization: VIEWS doc 2013-0498811I7.

Individuals should be cautious about providing authorization, such as to a person who offers to obtain refunds or benefits for them. With Level 1 authorization, the representative can go online and see extensive details about the taxpayer's affairs. With Level 2, the representative can make changes to past years' returns, whether to the taxpayer's benefit or detriment. A list of all authorized representatives can be viewed on canada.ca/my-cra-account.

After an amalgamation, an authorized representative of *all* the predecessor companies will be considered authorized for the new company: VIEWS doc 2011-0404651I7. However, nothing in the Act appears to permit this, as 87(2) does not cover it. This has been pointed out to Finance.

241(5) permits CRA to disclose information about a bankrupt to the trustee in bankruptcy (as does 241(4)(k)): VIEWS doc 2012-0451131I7. CRA may provide an account statement to a discharged bankrupt even though the trustee was responsible for the period of bankruptcy: 2010-0385281I7.

See Notes to 241(1) re Privacy and Access requests to obtain information.

241(5) likely permits disclosure to a legal guardian who has power over a mentally incompetent person's property: VIEWS doc 2003-0022587.

241(5) opening words amended by 2008 budget bill #2, effective March 12, 2009, to add "or other representative of a government entity". 241(5) earlier amended by 1992 technical bill, effective June 10, 1993.

Transfer Pricing Memoranda: TPM-04: Third-party information.

Forms: AUT-01: Authorize a representative for access by phone and mail; AUT-01X: Cancel authorization for a representative; RC161: Authorization for parliamentarians; RC321: Delegation of Authority; RC391: Application for a Canada Revenue Agency non-resident representative number (NRNN).

(6) Appeal from order or direction — An order or direction that is made in the course of or in connection with any legal proceedings and that requires an official, other representative of a government entity or authorized person to give or produce evidence relating to any taxpayer information may, by notice served on all interested parties, be appealed forthwith by the Minister or by the person against whom the order or direction is made to

(a) the court of appeal of the province in which the order or direction is made, in the case of an order or direction made by a court or other tribunal established by or pursuant to the laws of the province, whether or not that court or tribunal is exercising a jurisdiction conferred by the laws of Canada; or

(b) the Federal Court of Appeal, in the case of an order or direction made by a court or other tribunal established by or pursuant to the laws of Canada.

Notes: 241(6) opening words amended by 2008 budget bill #2, effective March 12, 2009, to add "other representative of a government entity". 241(6) earlier amended by 1992 technical bill, effective June 10, 1993.

(7) Disposition of appeal — The court to which an appeal is taken pursuant to subsection (6) may allow the appeal and quash the order or direction appealed from or dismiss the appeal, and the rules of practice and procedure from time to time governing appeals to the courts shall apply, with such modifications as the circumstances require, to an appeal instituted pursuant to that subsection.

(8) Stay of order or direction — An appeal instituted pursuant to subsection (6) shall stay the operation of the order or direction appealed from until judgment is pronounced.

(9) Threats to security — An official may provide to the head of a recipient Government of Canada institution listed in Schedule 3 to the *Security of Canada Information Disclosure Act*, or to an official designated for the purposes of that Act by the head of that recipient institution,

(a) publicly accessible charity information;

(b) taxpayer information, if there are reasonable grounds to suspect that the information would be relevant to

(i) an investigation of whether the activity of any person may constitute threats to the security of Canada, as defined in section 2 of the *Canadian Security Intelligence Service Act*, or

(ii) an investigation of whether any of the following offences may have been committed:

(A) a terrorism offence as defined in section 2 of the *Criminal Code*, and

(B) an offence under section 462.31 of the *Criminal Code*, if that investigation is related to a terrorism offence as defined in section 2 of that Act; and

(c) information setting out the reasonable grounds referred to in paragraph (b), to the extent that any such grounds rely on information referred to in paragraph (a) or (b).

Related Provisions: 241(4)(f.1) — Provision of information permitted; 241(9.1) — Use of information by RCMP or CSIS.

Notes: 241(9) opening words amended by Bill C-59, *National Security Act, 2017* (S.C. 2019, c. 13), effective June 21, 2019. Before that date, read:

(9) An official may provide to the head, or their delegate, of a recipient Government of Canada institution listed in Schedule 3 to the *Security of Canada Information Sharing Act*

241(9) amended by Bill C-51, *Anti-terrorism Act, 2015* (S.C. 2015, c. 20), proclaimed in force Aug. 1, 2015 (P.C. 2015-1053).

241(9) added by S.C. 2006, c. 12 (amending the *Proceeds of Crime (Money Laundering) and Terrorist Financing Act*), in force Feb. 10, 2007 (P.C. 2007-142).

Former 241(9), repealed by 1988 tax reform, provided a fine or imprisonment for contravention of 241. See now 239(2.2).

Former proposed 241(9) (July 18, 2005 draft legislation), dealing with disclosure by the Minister of Canadian Heritage of information relating to a Canadian film or video production certificate, was renumbered 241(3.3) in former Bill C-10 (2007), but is not included in the 2002-2013 technical bill (C-48): see Notes to proposed 125.4(1)"Canadian film or video production certificate".

(9.1) Threats to security — Information — other than designated donor information — provided to an official of the Canadian Security Intelligence Service or the Royal Canadian Mounted Po-

lice, as permitted by paragraph (4)(f.1), may be used by such an official, or communicated by such an official to another official of the Canadian Security Intelligence Service or the Royal Canadian Mounted Police for use by that other official, for the purpose of

(a) investigating whether an offence may have been committed, ascertaining the identity of a person or persons who may have committed an offence, or prosecuting an offence, which offence is

(i) described in Part II.1 of the *Criminal Code*, or

(ii) described in section 462.31 of the *Criminal Code*, if that investigation, ascertainment or prosecution is related to an investigation, ascertainment or prosecution in respect of an offence described in Part II.1 of that Act; or

(b) investigating whether the activities of any person may constitute threats to the security of Canada, as defined in section 2 of the *Canadian Security Intelligence Service Act*.

Notes: 241(9.1) added by S.C. 2006, c. 12 (amending the *Proceeds of Crime (Money Laundering) and Terrorist Financing Act*), in force Feb. 10, 2007 (P.C. 2007-142).

(9.2) Restrictions on information sharing — No information may be provided to a representative of a government entity under paragraph (4)(l) in connection with a program, activity or service provided or undertaken by the government entity unless the government entity uses the business number as an identifier in connection with the program, activity or service.

Notes: Since the Business Number was introduced, the provinces have gradually begun to adopt it. 241(9.2) forces provinces to use it if they want to obtain information from the CRA about businesses.

241(9.2) added by 2008 budget bill #2, effective March 12, 2009.

(9.3) Public disclosure — The Minister may, in connection with a program, activity or service provided or undertaken by the Minister, make available to the public the business number of, and the name of (including any trade name or other name used by), the holder of a business number (other than an excluded individual).

Related Provisions: 241(9.4) — Disclosure by other government.

Notes: See Notes to 248(1)"business number". Preparing T5s is not a "program, activity or service undertaken by the Minister", so the CRA will not provide a payor with the Business Numbers of recipients of investment income: VIEWS doc 2013-048282117.

241(9.3) added by 2008 budget bill #2, effective March 12, 2009.

(9.4) Public disclosure by representative of government entity — A representative of a government entity may, in connection with a program, activity or service provided or undertaken by the government entity, make available to the public the business number of, and the name of (including any trade name or other name used by), the holder of a business number (other than an excluded individual), if

(a) a representative of the government entity was provided with that information pursuant to paragraph 4(l); and

(b) the government entity uses the business number as an identifier in connection with the program, activity or service.

Notes: 241(9.4) added by 2008 budget bill #2, effective March 12, 2009.

(9.5) Serious offences — An official may provide to a law enforcement officer of an appropriate police organization

(a) taxpayer information, if the official has reasonable grounds to believe that the information will afford evidence of an act or omission in or outside of Canada that, if committed in Canada, would be

(i) an offence under any of

(A) section 3 of the *Corruption of Foreign Public Officials Act*,

(B) sections 119 to 121 *[bribery, fraud on government — ed.]*, 123 to 125 *[municipal corruption, selling or purchasing an office, influencing appointments]* and 426 *[secret commissions]* of the *Criminal Code*,

(C) section 465 *[conspiracy]* of the *Criminal Code* as it relates to an offence described in clause (B), and

(D) sections 144 *[prison breach]*, 264 *[criminal harassment]*, 271 *[sexual assault]*, 279 *[kidnapping]*, 279.02 *[material benefit from trafficking in persons]*, 281 *[abduction of person under 14]* and 333.1 *[motor vehicle theft]*, paragraphs 334(a) *[theft over $5,000]* and 348(1)(e) *[breaking and entering a dwelling]* and sections 349 *[being unlawfully in a dwelling-house]*, 435 *[arson for fraudulent purpose]* and 462.31 *[laundering proceeds of crime]* of the *Criminal Code*,

(ii) a terrorism offence or a criminal organization offence, as those terms are defined in section 2 of the *Criminal Code*, for which the maximum term of imprisonment is 10 years or more, or

(iii) an offence

(A) that is punishable by a minimum term of imprisonment,

(B) for which the maximum term of imprisonment is 14 years or life, or

(C) for which the maximum term of imprisonment is 10 years and that

(I) resulted in bodily harm,

(II) involved the import, export, trafficking or production of drugs, or

(III) involved the use of a weapon; and

(b) information setting out the reasonable grounds referred to in paragraph (a), to the extent that any such grounds rely on information referred to in that paragraph.

Related Provisions: 241(3.1) — Disclosure allowed where imminent danger.

Notes: 241(9.5) (added by 2014 budget bill #1 effective June 19, 2014) permits disclosure of many offences to police. For possible *Charter* and other challenges see Alatopulos, *Confidentiality of Taxpayer Information*, *Taxnet Pro* Practical Insights, Jan. 2017, pp. 23-43; D'Aoust, "Release of Taxpayer Information to Police", 4(3) *Canadian Tax Focus* (ctf.ca) 8 (Aug. 2014).

Even without 241(9.5), disclosure to police may be allowed by 241(3), 241(4)(a) or (p) depending on the facts: *Accurso*, 2019 QCCQ 3705, paras. 164-200. (Breach of a CRA-RCMP Memorandum of Understanding is not unlawful: para. 214.)

For CRA policy see CRA Fact Sheet "Bill C-31: Serious crimes measures" (April 2, 2015, tinyurl.com/cra-serious). *Serious Crime Measures Operational Procedure* on *TaxPartner* and *Taxnet Pro*: "CRA will not provide information when police proactively request information and provide details in an attempt to convince a CRA official that a listed serious offence has taken place" (¶5.1). The Assistant Commissioner, Compliance Programs Branch must approve each release (5.8). Only the confidential information relevant to the listed serious offence will be released (5.12). The taxpayer will not be informed by CRA (5.13). There is "no expectation that CRA officials should proactively look for possible evidence of listed serious offences" (5.16).

(10) Definitions — In this section,

"aboriginal government" means an aboriginal government as defined in subsection 2(1) of the *Federal-Provincial Fiscal Arrangements Act*;

Related Provisions: Reg. 8901.1 — Aboriginal government corporations and partnerships prescribed as eligible employers for CEWS.

Notes: 241(10)"aboriginal government" added by 2008 budget bill #2, effective March 12, 2009.

"authorized person" means a person who is engaged or employed, or who was formerly engaged or employed, by or on behalf of Her Majesty in right of Canada to assist in carrying out the provisions of this Act, the *Canada Pension Plan*, the *Unemployment Insurance Act* or the *Employment Insurance Act*;

Related Provisions: 241(11) — Meaning of "this Act".

Notes: Definition "authorized person" amended by 1996 EI bill and 1995-97 technical bill (both effective June 30, 1996) and 1992 technical bill.

"business number" — [Repealed]

Notes: Definition "business number" added by 1995 Budget, and repealed by 1995-97 technical bill effective June 18, 1998. The definition now appears in 248(1).

"contact information", in respect of a holder of a business number, means the name, address, telephone number, facsimile number and preferred language of communication of the holder, or similar information as specified by the Minister in respect of the holder, and includes such information in respect of one or more

(a) trustees of the holder, if the holder is a trust,

(b) members of the holder, if the holder is a partnership,

(c) officers of the holder, if the holder is a corporation, or

(d) officers or members of the holder, if the holder is not described by any of paragraphs (a) to (c);

Notes: 241(10)"contact information" added by 2008 budget bill #2, effective March 12, 2009.

"corporate information", in respect of a holder of a business number that is a corporation, means the name (including the number assigned by the incorporating authority), date of incorporation, jurisdiction of incorporation and any information on the dissolution, reorganization, amalgamation, winding-up or revival of the corporation;

Notes: 241(10)"corporate information" added by 2008 budget bill #2, effective March 12, 2009.

"court of appeal" has the meaning assigned by the definition "court of appeal" in section 2 of the *Criminal Code*;

Notes: "Court of appeal" amended by 1992 technical bill, effective June 10, 1993.

"designated donor information" means information of a charity, or of a person who has at any time made an application for registration as a registered charity, that is directly attributable to a gift that has been made or proposed to be made to the charity or applicant and that is presented in any form that directly or indirectly reveals the identity of the donor or prospective donor, other than a donor or prospective donor who is not resident in Canada and is neither a citizen of Canada nor a person described in subsection 2(3);

Notes: "Designated donor information" added by S.C. 2006, c. 12 (amending the *Proceeds of Crime (Money Laundering) and Terrorist Financing Act*), proclaimed in force Feb. 10, 2007 (P.C. 2007-142).

"designated person" means any person who is employed in the service of, who occupies a position of responsibility in the service of, or who is engaged by or on behalf of,

(a) a municipality in Canada, or

(b) a public body performing a function of government in Canada,

or any person who was formerly so employed, who formerly occupied such a position or who was formerly so engaged;

Notes: For the meaning of "public body performing...", see Notes to 149(1)(c).

Definition added by 1998 budget bill #1, effective June 18, 1998.

"designated taxpayer information" — [Repealed]

Notes: "Designated taxpayer information" repealed by Bill C-51, *Anti-terrorism Act, 2015* (S.C. 2015, c. 20), proclaimed in force Aug. 1, 2015 (P.C. 2015-1053). It was used only in 241(9). See 241(10)"taxpayer information" now.

Definition added by S.C. 2006, c. 12 (amending the *Proceeds of Crime (Money Laundering) and Terrorist Financing Act*), in force Feb. 10, 2007 (P.C. 2007-142).

"excluded individual" means an individual who is a holder of a business number solely because the individual is required under this Act to deduct or withhold an amount from an amount paid or credited or deemed to be paid or credited;

Notes: An "excluded individual" is someone who has a payroll (RP) account for non-business reasons (and thus no "RT" GST/HST account), such as a person who employs a nanny. Under 241(4)(l), (9.2) and (9.3), the Business Number of an excluded individual cannot be disclosed.

Definition added by 2008 budget bill #2, effective March 12, 2009.

"government entity" means

(a) a department or agency of the government of Canada or of a province,

(b) a municipality in Canada,

(c) an aboriginal government,

(d) a corporation all of the shares (except directors' qualifying shares) of the capital stock of which are owned by one or more persons each of which is

(i) Her Majesty in right of Canada,

(ii) Her Majesty in right of a province,

(iii) a municipality in Canada, or

(iv) a corporation described in this paragraph, or

(e) a board or commission, established by Her Majesty in right of Canada or Her Majesty in right of a province, that performs an administrative or regulatory function of government, or by one or more municipalities in Canada, that performs an administrative or regulatory function of a municipality;

Notes: For para. (d), see Notes to 149(1)(d)-(d.4).

Definition added by 2008 budget bill #2, effective March 12, 2009.

"official" means any person who is employed in the service of, who occupies a position of responsibility in the service of, or who is engaged by or on behalf of,

(a) Her Majesty in right of Canada or a province, or

(b) an authority engaged in administering a law of a province similar to the *Pension Benefits Standards Act, 1985* or the *Pooled Registered Pension Plans Act*,

or any person who was formerly so employed, who formerly occupied such a position or who was formerly so engaged and, for the purposes of subsection 239(2.21), subsections (1) and (2), the portion of subsection (4) before paragraph (a), and subsections (5) and (6), includes a designated person;

Notes: Para. (b) amended by 2012 budget bill #2, effective Dec. 14, 2012, to add "or the *Pooled Registered Pension Plans Act*". Definition earlier amended by 1998 budget bill #1, 1992 technical bill.

Application Policies: SR&ED 95-04: Conflict of interest.

"publicly accessible charity information" means taxpayer information that is

(a) described in subsection (3.2), or that would be described in that subsection if the words "that was at any time a registered charity" were read as "that has at any time made an application for registration as a registered charity",

(b) information — other than designated donor information — submitted to the Minister with, or required to be contained in, any public information return filed or required to be filed under subsection 149.1(14), or

(c) information prepared from information referred to in paragraph (a) or (b);

Notes: "Publicly accessible charity information" added by S.C. 2006, c. 12 (amending the *Proceeds of Crime (Money Laundering) and Terrorist Financing Act*), proclaimed in force Feb. 10, 2007 (P.C. 2007-142).

"registration information", in respect of a holder of a business number, means

(a) any information pertaining to the legal form of the holder,

(b) the type of activities carried on or proposed to be carried on by the holder,

(c) each date on which

(i) the business number was issued to the holder,

(ii) the holder began activities,

(iii) the holder ceased or resumed activities, or

(iv) the business number assigned to the holder was changed, and

(d) the reasons for the cessation, resumption or change referred to in subparagraph (c)(iii) or (iv);

Notes: Definition added by 2008 budget bill #2, effective March 12, 2009.

"representative" of a government entity means a person who is employed in the service of, who occupies a position of responsibility in the service of, or who is engaged by or on behalf of, a government entity, and includes, for the purposes of subsections (1), (2),

(5) and (6), a person who was formerly so employed, who formerly occupied such a position or who formerly was so engaged;

Notes: Definition added by 2008 budget bill #2, effective March 12, 2009.

"taxpayer information" means information of any kind and in any form relating to one or more taxpayers that is

(a) obtained by or on behalf of the Minister for the purposes of this Act, or

(b) prepared from information referred to in paragraph (a),

but does not include information that does not directly or indirectly reveal the identity of the taxpayer to whom it relates and, for the purposes of applying subsections (2), (5) and (6) to a representative of a government entity that is not an official, taxpayer information includes only the information referred to in paragraph (4)(l);

Related Provisions: 241(11) — Meaning of "this Act".

Notes: Taxpayer information must be kept confidential by CRA officials even if it is available in the public domain. See Notes to 241(1).

241(10)"taxpayer information" closing words amended by 2008 budget bill #2, effective March 12, 2009, to add "and, for the purposes of..." to the end.

Definition added by 1992 technical bill, effective June 10, 1993.

(11) References to "this Act" — The references in subsections (1), (3), (4) and (10) to "this Act" shall be read as references to "this Act or the *Federal-Provincial Fiscal Arrangements Act*".

Proposed Amendment — 241(11)

(11) References to "this Act" — The references in subsections (1), (3), (4) and (10) to "this Act" are to be read as references to "this Act, the *Federal-Provincial Fiscal Arrangements Act* or Part 3 of the *Canada–Quebec Gulf of St. Lawrence Petroleum Resources Accord Implementation Act*".

Application: Bill C-74 (First Reading June 18, 2015; requires reintroduction in new Parliament), subsec. 253(2), will amend subsec. 241(11) to read as above, in force on Royal Assent.

Notes: 241(11) amended by 2002-2013 technical bill (Part 5 — technical), effective June 26, 2013, to change "*Petroleum and Gas Revenue Tax Act*" [which expired long ago] to "*Federal-Provincial Fiscal Arrangements Act*".

Definitions [s. 241]: "aboriginal government" — 241(10); "adjusted cost base" — 54, 248(1); "amount", "assessment" — 248(1); "assistance" — 125.6(1); "authorized person" — 241(10); "business", "business number" — 248(1); "Canada" — 255, *Interpretation Act* 35(1); "Canadian film or video production certificate" — 125.4(1); "contact information", "corporate information" — 241(10); "corporation" — 248(1), *Interpretation Act* 35(1); "court of appeal" — 241(10); "designated donor information", "designated person" — 241(10); "designated provincial program" — 146.1(1), 146.4(1); "designated taxpayer information" — 241(10); "employed", "employee", "employer" — 248(1); "Federal Court of Appeal" — *Federal Courts Act* s. 3; "government entity" — 241(10); "Her Majesty" — *Interpretation Act* 35(1); "individual", "listed international agreement", "Minister" — 248(1); "municipality" — 241(10); "Newfoundland offshore area", "non-resident", "office", "officer" — 248(1); "official" — 241(10); "Parliament" — *Interpretation Act* 35(1); "partnership" — see 96(1) Notes; "person", "prescribed" — 248(1); "prescribed energy conservation property" — Reg. 8200.1; "property" — 248(1); "province", "provincial" — *Interpretation Act* 35(1); "publicly accessible charity information" — 241(10); "qualified Canadian journalism organization" — 248(1); "qualifying share" — 192(6), 248(1) *[not intended to apply to this section]*; "record", "registered Canadian amateur athletic association", "registered charity", "registered journalism organization", "registered pension plan" — 248(1); "registrant" — 241(3.2); "registration information" — 241(10); "related" — 251(2)–(6); "reporting entity" — 244.1; "representative" — 241(10); "share", "tax treaty" — 248(1); "taxable income" — 2(2), 248(1); "taxation year" — 249; "taxpayer" — 248(1); "taxpayer information" — 241(10); "this Act" — 241(11); "trust" — 104(1), 248(1), (3); "writing" — *Interpretation Act* 35(1).

242. Officers, etc., of corporations — Where a corporation commits an offence under this Act, any officer, director or agent of the corporation who directed, authorized, assented to, acquiesced in or participated in the commission of the offence is a party to and guilty of the offence and is liable on conviction to the punishment provided for the offence whether or not the corporation has been prosecuted or convicted.

Related Provisions: 227.1 — Liability of directors; 236 — Corporate directors and officers entitled to execute documents; 239.1(2) — Offence of participating or acquiescing in the use of zapper software.

Notes: For 242 to apply, the Crown must prove beyond reasonable doubt that a director was a "principal or party", having *mens rea* ("the mental elements of s. 242 are that a person directed, authorized, assented to, acquiesced in, or participated in the commission of the offence"); but need not prove "intent" not to comply: *Bodnarchuk*, 2004 BCPC 235, paras. 17-18. For more examples of 242 applying see *Elless*, 2007 BCSC 737; *Lemieux*, 2007 SKPC 135; *Brewer*, 2009 NBPC 37; *O'Hara*, 2017 NSPC 31.

For a strict-liability offence (see 239(1) Notes), the Crown must prove the corporation's act and the officer's participation, but not the officer's intent to commit the offence: *Swendson*, [1987] 2 C.T.C. 199 (Alta. QB). Due diligence is the only defence: *Gibbs*, 2003 BCPC 526": *Samaroo*, 2018 BCSC 324, para. 104 (rev'd on other grounds 2019 BCCA 113; leave to appeal denied 2019 CarswellBC 2946 (SCC)).

Criminal Code s. 22.2 can make a corporation guilty of its officers' actions.

Definitions [s. 242]: "corporation" — 248(1), *Interpretation Act* 35(1); "officer" — 248(1)"office".

Information Circulars: 73-10R3: Tax evasion.

243. Power to decrease punishment — Notwithstanding the *Criminal Code* or any other statute or law in force on June 30, 1948, the court has, in any prosecution or proceeding under this Act, no power to impose less than the minimum fine or imprisonment fixed by this Act or to suspend sentence.

Notes: This rule has been sidestepped by making the minimum fine payable at $1 per month, with no jail time for default; or imposing a prison term on payment default that is concurrent with the rest of the sentence (*Terracina*, 1999 CarswellOnt 4718 (Ont. SCJ); *Hughes*, 1999 CarswellNfld 388 (Nfld. TD); *Cahoon*, 2003 CarswellOnt 9254 (Ont. CJ)). "Concurrent" fines (to avoid multiplying fines for multiple convictions) are allowed only if authorized by legislation: *Flex-N-Gate Canada*, 2014 ONCA 53.

Procedure and Evidence

244. (1) Information or complaint — An information or complaint under this Act may be laid or made by any officer of the Canada Revenue Agency, by a member of the Royal Canadian Mounted Police or by any person thereto authorized by the Minister and, where an information or complaint purports to have been laid or made under this Act, it shall be deemed to have been laid or made by a person thereto authorized by the Minister and shall not be called in question for lack of authority of the informant or complainant except by the Minister or by a person acting for the Minister or Her Majesty.

Notes: 244(1) amended by *CCRA Act*, effective Nov. 1, 1999, to change "Department of National Revenue" to "Canada Customs and Revenue Agency"; and by 2004 CRA/CBSA bill, effective Dec. 12, 2005, to change to "Canada Revenue Agency".

(2) Two or more offences — An information or complaint in respect of an offence under this Act may be for one or more offences and no information, complaint, warrant, conviction or other proceeding in a prosecution under this Act is objectionable or insufficient by reason of the fact that it relates to two or more offences.

(3) Venue — An information or complaint in respect of an offence under this Act may be heard, tried or determined by any court, judge or justice if the accused is resident, carrying on business, found or apprehended or is in custody within the territorial jurisdiction of the court, judge or justice, as the case may be, although the matter of the information or complaint did not arise within that jurisdiction.

Notes: See Notes to 239(3).

(4) Limitation period — An information or complaint under the provisions of the *Criminal Code* relating to summary convictions, in respect of an offence under this Act, may be laid or made at any time but not later than 8 years after the day on which the matter of the information or complaint arose.

Notes: See Notes to 239(1).

(5) Proof of service by mail — Where, by this Act or a regulation, provision is made for sending by mail a request for information, notice or demand, an affidavit of an officer of the Canada Revenue Agency, sworn before a commissioner or other person authorized to take affidavits, setting out that the officer has knowledge of the facts in the particular case, that such a request, notice or demand was sent by registered letter on a named day to the person to whom it was addressed (indicating the address) and that the officer identifies as exhibits attached to the affidavit the post office certificate of registration of the letter or a true copy of the relevant portion thereof and a true copy of the request, notice or demand, shall, in the absence of proof to the contrary, be received as evidence of the sending and of the request, notice or demand.

Related Provisions: 244(11) — Presumption that affidavit valid; 244(14) — Mailing date deemed to be date of notice; 248(7)(a) — Mail deemed received on day mailed; *Interpretation Act* 25(1) — Evidence is rebuttable.

Notes: 244(5) was used to justify registered mail being as good as regular mail for an objection confirmation in *Rossi*, 2015 FCA 267.

In *Luxury Home*, 2021 TCC 4, a CRA affidavit of mailing of a notice of confirmation by registered mail (following an objection) was inadequate, as it did not include the post office registration certificate.

See also Notes to 244(10) re proof of mailing.

244(5) amended by *CCRA Act*, effective Nov. 1, 1999, to change "Department of National Revenue" to "Canada Customs and Revenue Agency"; and by 2004 CRA/CBSA bill, effective Dec. 12, 2005, to "Canada Revenue Agency".

(6) Proof of personal service — Where, by this Act or a regulation, provision is made for personal service of a request for information, notice or demand, an affidavit of an officer of the Canada Revenue Agency sworn before a commissioner or other person authorized to take affidavits setting out that the officer has knowledge of the facts in the particular case, that such a request, notice or demand was served personally on a named day on the person to whom it was directed and that the officer identifies as an exhibit attached to the affidavit a true copy of the request, notice or demand, shall, in the absence of proof to the contrary, be received as evidence of the personal service and of the request, notice or demand.

Related Provisions: 244(11) — Presumption that affidavit valid; *Interpretation Act* 25(1) — Evidence is rebuttable.

Notes: 244(6) was applied in *Stevens*, 2006 BCSC 1585, and *Lemieux*, 2007 SKPC 135 to accept evidence of service of a demand to file on a person charged with failing to file tax returns.

244(6) amended by *CCRA Act*, effective Nov. 1, 1999, to change "Department of National Revenue" to "Canada Customs and Revenue Agency"; and by 2004 CRA/CBSA bill, effective Dec. 12, 2005, to "Canada Revenue Agency".

(6.1) Proof of electronic delivery — If, by this Act or a regulation, provision is made for sending a notice to a person electronically, an affidavit of an officer of the Canada Revenue Agency sworn before a commissioner or other person authorized to take affidavits, shall, in the absence of proof to the contrary, be received as evidence of the sending and of the notice if the affidavit sets out that

> (a) the officer has knowledge of the facts in the particular case;

> (b) the notice was sent electronically to the person on a named day; and

> (c) the officer identifies as exhibits attached to the affidavit copies of

>> (i) an electronic message confirming the notice has been sent to the person, and

>> (ii) the notice.

Related Provisions: 231.2(1.1), 231.6(3.1) — Electronic delivery of Requirement to bank or credit union.

Notes: 244(6.1) added by 2021 budget bill #1, effective June 29, 2021. It accommodates online delivery of notices via My Business Account or My Account. See also 231.2(1.1)(c).

(7) Proof of failure to comply — Where, by this Act or a regulation, a person is required to make a return, statement, answer or certificate, an affidavit of an officer of the Canada Revenue Agency, sworn before a commissioner or other person authorized to take affidavits, setting out that the officer has charge of the appropriate records and that after a careful examination and search of those records the officer has been unable to find in a given case that the return, statement, answer or certificate, as the case may be, has been made by that person, shall, in the absence of proof to the contrary, be received as evidence that in that case that person did not make the return, statement, answer or certificate, as the case may be.

Related Provisions: 244(11) — Presumption that affidavit valid; *Interpretation Act* 25(1) — Evidence is rebuttable.

Notes: 244(7) was used to prove that an accused had not filed returns in: *Maleki*, 2007 ONCJ 186; *Lemieux*, 2007 SKPC 135; *Tyskerud*, 2013 BCPC 27, para. 88. CRA tax centres apparently do not sign for registered mail, but see Notes to 244(10) and 248(7) re proving that a return or objection has been sent.

244(7) amended by *CCRA Act*, effective Nov. 1, 1999, to change "Department of National Revenue" to "Canada Customs and Revenue Agency"; and by 2004 CRA/CBSA bill, effective Dec. 12, 2005, to "Canada Revenue Agency".

(8) Proof of time of compliance

— Where, by this Act or a regulation, a person is required to make a return, statement, answer or certificate, an affidavit of an officer of the Canada Revenue Agency, sworn before a commissioner or other person authorized to take affidavits, setting out that the officer has charge of the appropriate records and that after careful examination of those records the officer has found that the return, statement, answer or certificate was filed or made on a particular day, shall, in the absence of proof to the contrary, be received as evidence that it was filed or made on that day and not prior thereto.

Related Provisions: 244(11) — Presumption that affidavit valid; *Interpretation Act* 25(1) — Evidence is rebuttable.

Notes: 244(8) amended by *CCRA Act*, effective Nov. 1, 1999, to change "Department of National Revenue" to "Canada Customs and Revenue Agency"; and by 2004 CRA/CBSA bill, effective Dec. 12, 2005, to "Canada Revenue Agency".

(9) Proof of documents

— An affidavit of an officer of the Canada Revenue Agency, sworn before a commissioner or other person authorized to take affidavits, setting out that the officer has charge of the appropriate records and that a document annexed to the affidavit is a document or true copy of a document, or a print-out of an electronic document, made by or on behalf of the Minister or a person exercising a power of the Minister or by or on behalf of a taxpayer, is evidence of the nature and contents of the document.

Related Provisions: 231.5(1) — Copy of document seized or examined may be used in court proceedings; 244(11) — Presumption that affidavit valid; *Interpretation Act* 25(1) — Evidence is rebuttable.

Notes: An affidavit under 244(9) "must comply strictly with the provisions", so one that did not set out that the officer had charge of the appropriate records was inadmissible: *Lemieux*, 2007 SKPC 135, para. 21. 244(9) was used by the Crown in *Tyskerud*, 2013 BCPC 27, para. 88.

In *Poulin*, 2013 TCC 104, para. 22, an affidavit as to the date an objection was received in the Burnaby-Fraser office did not determine that the objection had not been received earlier in the Surrey office. Furthermore, the affidavit should be by someone familiar with CRA mailroom practices: *Carcone*, 2011 TCC 550; *Poulin*, para. 29.

In *Leroux*, 2014 BCSC 720, para. 405, the Court had difficulty with CRA relying on 244(9) in a civil lawsuit, accepting the affidavits but stating this "should not be taken as a precedent for the use of such affidavits in civil cases in which CRA is a defendant".

Scott, 2017 TCC 224, paras. 36-64, discusses the use of CRA affidavits at trial without prior notice. In *Grenon*, 2021 TCC 30 (under appeal to FCA), paras. 115-124, such an affidavit was accepted as evidence that 35-40 children under 18 had (unlawfully) invested in income funds that G sought to create as mutual fund trusts.

244(9) amended by 2004 CRA/CBSA bill (effective Dec. 12, 2005), 1999 *CCRA Act*, 1995-97 technical bill.

(10) Proof of no [objection or] appeal

— An affidavit of an officer of the Canada Revenue Agency, sworn before a commissioner or other person authorized to take affidavits, setting out that the officer has charge of the appropriate records and has knowledge of the practice of the Agency and that an examination of those records shows that a notice of assessment for a particular taxation year or a notice of determination was mailed or otherwise communicated to a taxpayer on a particular day under this Act and that, after careful examination and search of those records, the officer has been unable to find that a notice of objection or of appeal from the assessment or determination or a request under subsection 245(6), as the case may be, was received within the time allowed, shall, in the absence of proof to the contrary, be received as evidence of the statements contained in it.

Related Provisions: 244(11) — Presumption that affidavit valid; *Interpretation Act* 25(1) — Evidence is rebuttable.

Notes: The affidavit should be sworn by someone familiar with CRA mailroom practices: *Carcone*, 2011 TCC 550; *Poulin*, 2013 TCC 104, para. 29. Notices of assessment were not proven mailed when the swearing officer did not have *personal* knowledge of the mailing or of the notice being included in a particular batch: *Central Springs*, 2006 TCC 524; *DaSilva*, 2018 TCC 74.

In *Poulin* (above), paras. 24-25, there was "evidence to the contrary", as an objection was apparently mailed to a different office on time.

244(10) amended by 2004 CRA/CBSA bill effective Dec. 12, 2005, and *CCRA Act* effective Nov. 1999.

(11) Presumption

— Where evidence is offered under this section by an affidavit from which it appears that the person making the affidavit is an officer of the Canada Revenue Agency, it is not necessary to prove the person's signature or that the person is such an officer nor is it necessary to prove the signature or official character of the person before whom the affidavit was sworn.

Notes: 244(11) amended by *CCRA Act*, effective Nov. 1, 1999, to change "Department of National Revenue" to "Canada Customs and Revenue Agency"; and by 2004 CRA/CBSA bill, effective Dec. 12, 2005, to "Canada Revenue Agency".

(12) Judicial notice

— Judicial notice shall be taken of all orders or regulations made under this Act without those orders or regulations being specially pleaded or proven.

(13) Proof of documents

— Every document purporting to have been executed under, or in the course of the administration or enforcement of, this Act over the name in writing of the Minister, the Deputy Minister of National Revenue, the Commissioner of Customs and Revenue, the Commissioner of Revenue or an officer authorized to exercise a power or perform a duty of the Minister under this Act is deemed to have been signed, made and issued by the Minister, the Deputy Minister, the Commissioner of Customs and Revenue, the Commissioner of Revenue or the officer unless it has been called in question by the Minister or by a person acting for the Minister or Her Majesty.

Notes: 244(13) prevents taxpayers from challenging the validity of CRA documents during court proceedings. The "person acting for the Minister or Her Majesty" would normally be Dept. of Justice tax litigation counsel, or a CRA officer appearing as a witness. See *Coulbeck v. Univ. of Toronto*, [2005] 5 C.T.C. 65 (Ont. SCJ); *Swyryda*, 1981 CarswellSask 214 (Sask. Q.B.) (requirement for information (RFI) did not have to be signed personally by Director); *Nagel*, 2008 SKPC 117 (RFI signed by person acting temporarily as Assistant Director Collections was valid). *Contra*, however, 244(13) must be read narrowly when considering an RFI ("a highly discretionary matter involving elements of government compulsion"), and the Court found invalid the stamp of an official authorized to issue RFIs, when the RFI had actually been issued by an officer not so authorized: *Murphy*, 2009 FC 1226.

244(13) amended by 2004 CRA/CBSA bill (effective Dec. 12, 2005), *CCRA Act* (Nov. 1, 1999) and 1995-97 technical bill.

(13.1) [Repealed]

Notes: 244(13.1) repealed by *Dept. of National Revenue Act* amending bill effective May 12, 1994. It allowed "Revenue Canada" in documents to mean the Dept. of National Revenue. It was replaced by s. 3.1 of the *Department of National Revenue Act*, which Act was later replaced Nov. 1999 by the *Canada Customs and Revenue Agency Act*, now the *Canada Revenue Agency Act*.

In *Besselt*, [2000] 4 C.T.C. 286 (FCTD), a writ of execution was rejected by the Court (Prothonotary) because the certificate was that of an official of the Department of National Revenue, but the debtor was alleged to be indebted to the CRA!

244(13.1) was originally enacted to override *Solway*, [1979] C.T.C. 154 and *Wel Holdings*, [1979] C.T.C. 116, where the Federal Court had held that documents issued under the name "Revenue Canada, Taxation" were a nullity.

See also s. 38 of the *Interpretation Act*.

(14) Mailing or sending date

— For the purposes of this Act, where any notice or notification described in subsection 149.1(6.3), 152(3.1), 165(3) or 166.1(5) or any notice of assessment or determination is mailed, or sent electronically, it shall be presumed to be mailed or sent, as the case may be, on the date of that notice or notification.

Related Provisions: 244(5) — Proof of service by mail; 244(14.1) — Date when electronic notice sent; 244(15) — Assessment deemed made on date of mailing; 248(7)(a) — Mail deemed received on day mailed; *Interpretation Act* 26 — Deadline on Sunday or holiday extended to next business day.

Notes: Because the word "presumed" is used, rather than "deemed", the presumption is rebuttable rather than conclusive. See *Hughes*, [1987] 2 C.T.C. 2360 (TCC). However, see 244(15), which uses the word "deemed".

CRA does not retain actual copies of many notices of assessment, and thus can only produce "reconstructed" versions from its computer system. This means that CRA often cannot prove when or whether the assessment was mailed, allowing an otherwise-late Notice of Objection to be considered filed on time: see Notes to 165(1). But where an assessment is found to have been mailed, time starts running even if it is never received by the taxpayer: *Schafer*, [2000] G.S.T.C. 82 (FCA).

In *Barrington Lane Developments*, 2010 TCC 388, CRA's evidence of its mailing procedures was sufficient evidence that a notice of assessment had been mailed by a particular date.

A CRA internal memo confirms that "it is necessary that the notice of assessment be mailed on the date printed" (VIEWS doc 2009-0331641I7), but if this is not done there is no legal remedy unless the taxpayer can prove it was mailed past a deadline.

See also Notes to 244(15).

244(14) amended by 2010 budget bill #2 (effective Dec. 15, 2010), 1995-97 and 1991 technical bills.

(14.1) Date when electronic notice sent — For the purposes of this Act, if a notice or other communication in respect of a person or partnership is made available in electronic format such that it can be read or perceived by a person or a computer system or other similar device, the notice or other communication is presumed to be sent to the person or partnership and received by the person or partnership on the date that an electronic message is sent, to the electronic address most recently provided before that date by the person or partnership to the Minister for the purposes of this subsection, informing the person or partnership that a notice or other communication requiring the person or partnership's immediate attention is available in the person or partnership's secure electronic account. A notice or other communication is considered to be made available if it is posted by the Minister in the person or partnership's secure electronic account and the person or partnership has authorized that notices or other communications may be made available in this manner and has not before that date revoked that authorization in a manner specified by the Minister.

Proposed Amendments — Electronic filing and communications

Federal Budget, Notice of Ways and Means Motion, April 19, 2021: *Electronic Filing and Certification of Tax and Information Returns*

15 The Act is modified to give effect to the proposals relating to Electronic Filing and Certification of Tax and Information Returns as described in the budget documents tabled by the Minister of Finance in the House of Commons on April 19, 2021.

Federal Budget, Supplementary Information, April 19, 2021: *Electronic Filing and Certification of Tax and Information Returns*

To improve the administration of, and compliance with, the tax system, Budget 2021 proposes various amendments to the *Income Tax Act*, *Income Tax Regulations*, *Excise Tax Act*, *Excise Act, 2001*, *Tax Rebate Discounting Act*, *Air Travellers Security Charge Act*, Part 1 of the *Greenhouse Gas Pollution Pricing Act*, and *Electronic Filing and Provision of Information (GST/HST) Regulations*. These proposed measures would improve the Canada Revenue Agency's (CRA) ability to operate digitally, resulting in faster, more convenient and accurate service, while also enhancing security.

Default Method of Correspondence

Notices of Assessment

Budget 2021 proposes to amend the *Income Tax Act* to provide the CRA with the ability to send certain notices of assessment [152(2), 244(14.1) — ed.] electronically without the taxpayer having to authorize the CRA to do so. This proposal would apply in respect of individuals who file their income tax return electronically and those who employ the services of a tax preparer that files their income tax return electronically. Taxpayers who continue to file their income tax returns with the CRA in paper format would continue to receive a paper notice of assessment from the CRA.

This measure would come into force on Royal Assent of the enacting legislation.

Correspondence with Businesses

Budget 2021 proposes to change the default method of correspondence for businesses that use the CRA's My Business Account portal to electronic only. However, businesses could still choose to also receive paper correspondence. This measure would apply in respect of the *Income Tax Act*, *Excise Tax Act*, *Excise Act, 2001*, *Air Travellers Security Charge Act* and Part 1 of the *Greenhouse Gas Pollution Pricing Act*.

This measure would come into force on Royal Assent of the enacting legislation.

[Presumably the "enacting legislation" will deem such a letter to have been received by the taxpayer. However, for Audit purposes this measure likely does not require legislative amendment, as Audit proposal letters are not governed by legislation and are technically just a courtesy provided by CRA. A reassessment is legally valid whether or not Audit advised ahead of time that it would be issued — ed.]

Information Returns

Budget 2021 proposes to amend the *Income Tax Regulations* to allow issuers of T4A (Statement of Pension, Retirement, Annuity and Other Income) and T5 (Statement of Investment Income) information returns [Reg. 201(1) — ed.] to provide them electronically without having to also issue a paper copy and without the taxpayer having to authorize the issuer to do so [see Reg. 209(3) for the current rule — ed.].

This measure would apply in respect of information returns sent after 2021.

Electronic Filing Thresholds

Tax Preparers

Budget 2021 proposes to amend the rule in the *Income Tax Act* [162(7.3) — ed.] that requires, subject to the exception below, professional preparers of income tax returns to file electronically where they prepare more than 10 income tax returns of corporations or 10 income tax returns of individuals (other than trusts) to apply instead where they file more than 5 of either type of return for a calendar year. Furthermore, the exception for trusts would be removed.

Budget 2021 also proposes to amend the exception in the *Income Tax Act* [150(2.3) — ed.] whereby a tax preparer is allowed to a file a maximum of 10 paper income tax returns of corporations and 10 paper income tax returns of individuals per calendar year to instead allow only a maximum of 5 paper returns of each type per calendar year.

These measures would apply in respect of calendar years after 2021.

Filer of Information Returns

Budget 2021 proposes that the threshold for mandatory electronic filing of income tax information returns for a calendar year under the *Income Tax Act* [Reg. 205.1(1) — ed.] be lowered from 50 to 5 returns, in respect of a particular type of information return. As such, persons or partnerships that file more than 5 information returns of a particular type for a calendar year would be required to file them electronically.

This measure would apply in respect of calendar years after 2021.

Corporations and GST/HST Registrants

Budget 2021 proposes to eliminate the mandatory electronic filing thresholds for returns of corporations under the *Income Tax Act* [Reg. 205.1(2) — ed.], and of Goods and Services Tax/Harmonized Sales Tax (GST/HST) registrants (other than for charities or Selected Listed Financial Institutions) under the *Excise Tax Act* [ETA 278.1(2.1) and *Electronic Filing and Provision of Information (GST/HST) Regulations* s. 2 — ed.]. As such, returns of most corporations and GST/HST registrants under these acts would be required to be filed electronically.

This measure would apply in respect of taxation years that begin after 2021 for the *Income Tax Act* amendments and in respect of reporting periods that begin after 2021 for the *Excise Tax Act*.

Electronic Payments

Budget 2021 proposes to clarify that payments required to be made at a financial institution under the *Income Tax Act*, the GST/HST portion of the *Excise Tax Act*, the *Excise Act, 2001*, the *Air Travellers Security Charge Act* and Part 1 of the *Greenhouse Gas Pollution Pricing Act*, include online payments made through such an institution. Budget 2021 also proposes that electronic payments be required for remittances over $10,000 under the *Income Tax Act* [153(1) closing words and Reg. 110 — ed.] and that the threshold for mandatory remittances to be made at a financial institution under the GST/HST portion of the *Excise Tax Act*, the *Excise Act, 2001*, the *Air Travellers Security Charge Act* and Part 1 of the *Greenhouse Gas Pollution Pricing Act* be lowered from $50,000 to $10,000.

This measure would apply to payments made on or after January 1, 2022.

Handwritten Signatures

Budget 2021 proposes to eliminate the requirement that signatures be in writing on certain prescribed forms, as follows:

- Forms prescribed under the *Income Tax Act*:
  - T183, Information Return for Electronic Filing of an Individual's Income Tax and Benefit Return [150.1 — ed.];
  - T183CORP, Information Return for Corporations Filing Electronically; and
  - T2200, Declaration of Conditions of Employment [8(10) — ed.].
- Forms prescribed under the *Tax Rebate Discounting Act*:
  - RC71, Statement of Discounting Transaction; and
  - RC72, Notice of the Actual Amount of the Refund of Tax.

This measure would come into force on Royal Assent of the enacting legislation.

Notes: 244(14.1) has two different rules. Once a notice (e.g. notice of assessment) is posted to the taxpayer's My Account or My Business Account, it is "considered" to be made available to the taxpayer; this is likely the same as "deemed", so that it is conclusive (see Notes to 244(15)).

Once the notice has been (deemed) "made available", it is "presumed" to be sent to the taxpayer when an email is sent to the taxpayer's email address on file with CRA. However, "presumed" (unlike "deemed") is rebuttable (see Notes to 244(14)), so if the taxpayer can convince CRA or a Court that they did not receive the email (e.g., due to a technical problem, or even because they changed their email address and didn't tell CRA), they can rebut the presumption and time will not start running (such as to object to the assessment). However, taxpayers who did not read email at the address they provided were not considered to have acted reasonably in missing CRA letters about TFSA over-contributions: see 207.06(1) Notes (*Rempel*, *Posmyk* cases).

CRA will likely apply this rule as it does 248(7) (and see 165(1) Notes), so that it will not accept a defence of "I changed my email address but didn't tell CRA".

For CRA answers to various questions about online mail see May 2016 Alberta CPA Roundtable (tinyurl.com/cra-abtax), q. 19.

244(14.1) added by 2010 budget bill #2, effective Dec. 15, 2010.

(15) Date when assessment made — If any notice of assessment or determination has been sent by the Minister as required by this Act, the assessment or determination is deemed to have been made on the day of sending of the notice of the assessment or determination.

Related Provisions: 244(5) — Proof of service by mail; 244(14) — Date of mailing presumed to be date of notice; 244(14.1) — Day of sending of electronic notice; *Interpretation Act* 26 — Deadline on Sunday or holiday extended to next business day.

Notes: 244(15) provides that once a notice's "day of sending" (mailing, or electronically under 244(14.1)) is known, the assessment or determination is deemed made on that date. The word "deemed" is conclusive: *Kushnir*, [1985] 1 C.T.C. 2301 (TCC); it creates a statutory fiction: *Verrette*, [1978] 2 S.C.R. 838 at 845; *La Survivance*, 2006 FCA 129; *Menzies*, 2016 TCC 73, para. 27; *Cheema*, 2018 FCA 45, para. 101, second bullet (leave to appeal to SCC requested). Thus, an assessment sent by mail is conclusively deemed received by 248(7)(a) even if it was never received: see Notes to 248(7). However, deeming might apply only if the deemed result does not factually apply: *Pellan*, 2016 QCCA 263 (leave to appeal denied 2016 CarswellQue 11690 (SCC)) (discussed in Notes to 250(1)). Deeming in a provincial statute might not apply to the ITA: *Fantini*, 1997 CarswellNat 2220 (TCC). See also Carr & Hass, "Deeming Provisions: How Far Do They Reach?", VIII(3) *Resource Sector Taxation* (Federated Press) 582-90 (2011); Kandev & Lennard, "Interpreting and Applying Deeming Provisions", 60(2) *Canadian Tax Journal* 275-303 (2012); *Vocalspruce Ltd.*, [2014] EWCA Civ 1302 (England) (extent to which deeming applies: para. 63).

The determination of the "day of sending" is done under 244(14): there is a (rebuttable) presumption that a notice was sent on the date that appears on it.

An assessment mailed to an incorrect address is considered not sent, but an assessment correctly mailed is deemed received even if not received. See Notes to 165(1).

An assessment can be made by having it picked up by courier by the deadline rather than putting it in the mail: *VIH Logging*, 2003 TCC 732 [aff'd on other grounds 2005 FCA 36].

244(15) amended by 2010 budget bill #2 (changing "mailing" to "sending" to accommodate electronic notices under 244(14.1)), 1995-97 technical bill.

(16) Forms prescribed or authorized — Every form purporting to be a form prescribed or authorized by the Minister shall be deemed to be a form authorized under this Act by the Minister unless called in question by the Minister or by a person acting for the Minister or Her Majesty.

Related Provisions: *Interpretation Act* 32 — Deviations from a prescribed form.

Notes: See Notes to 248(1)"prescribed". 244(16) amended by 1991 technical bill, effective December 17, 1991.

(17) Proof of return in prosecution for offence — In any prosecution for an offence under this Act, the production of a return, certificate, statement or answer required by or under this Act or a regulation, purporting to have been filed or delivered by or on behalf of the person charged with the offence or to have been made or signed by or on behalf of that person shall, in the absence of proof to the contrary, be received as evidence that the return, certificate, statement or answer was filed or delivered, or was made or signed, by or on behalf of that person.

Related Provisions: *Interpretation Act* 25(1) — Evidence is rebuttable.

(18) Idem, in proceedings under Division J of Part I — In any proceedings under Division J of Part I, the production of a return, certificate, statement or answer required by or under this Act or a regulation, purporting to have been filed or delivered, or to have been made or signed, by or on behalf of the taxpayer shall in the absence of proof to the contrary be received as evidence that the return, certificate, statement or answer was filed or delivered, or was made or signed, by or on behalf of the taxpayer.

Related Provisions: *Interpretation Act* 25(1) — Evidence is rebuttable.

(19) Proof of statement of non-receipt — In any prosecution for an offence under this Act, an affidavit of an officer of the Canada Revenue Agency, sworn before a commissioner or other person authorized to take affidavits, setting out that the officer has charge of the appropriate records and that an examination of the records shows that an amount required under this Act to be remitted to the Receiver General on account of tax for a year has not been received by the Receiver General, shall, in the absence of proof to the contrary, be received as evidence of the statements contained therein.

Related Provisions: 244(11) — Presumption that affidavit valid; *Interpretation Act* 25(1) — Evidence is rebuttable.

Notes: 244(19) amended by *CCRA Act*, effective Nov. 1, 1999, to change "Department of National Revenue" to "Canada Customs and Revenue Agency"; and by 2004 CRA/CBSA bill, effective Dec. 12, 2005, to "Canada Revenue Agency".

(20) Members of partnerships — For the purposes of this Act,

(a) a reference in any notice or other document to the firm name of a partnership shall be read as as a reference to all the members thereof; and

(b) any notice or other document shall be deemed to have been provided to each member of a partnership if the notice or other document is mailed to, served on or otherwise sent to the partnership

(i) at its latest known address or place of business, or

(ii) at the latest known address

(A) where it is a limited partnership, of any member thereof whose liability as a member is not limited, or

(B) in any other case, of any member thereof.

Related Provisions: 96(3) — Election by members; 152(1.4)–(1.8) — Binding determination of partnership income or loss; 224(6) — Service of garnishment notice on partnership.

Notes: In *Menzies*, 2016 TCC 73, a notice sent to a limited partnership was deemed to have been sent to the limited partners: "deemed" is conclusive (see 244(15) Notes) (see also VIEWS doc 2016-0640320I7 to the same effect). Similarly, in *Zeifmans LLP*, 2021 FC 363, paras. 72-73 (under appeal to FCA), a Requirement for Information about a CPA firm's clients was valid when sent to the firm without naming a specific partner.

244(20) added by 1991 technical bill, effective December 17, 1991.

(21) Proof of return filed — For the purposes of this Act, a document presented by the Minister purporting to be a print-out of the information in respect of a taxpayer received under section 150.1 by the Minister from a person shall be received as evidence and, in the absence of evidence to the contrary, is proof of the return filed by the person under that section.

Related Provisions: *Interpretation Act* 25(1) — Evidence is rebuttable.

Notes: 244(21) added by 1992 technical bill, effective 1992 and later taxation years.

(22) Filing of information returns — Where a person who is required by this Act or a regulation to file an information return in prescribed form with the Minister meets the criteria specified in writing by the Minister, the person may at any time file the information return with the Minister by way of electronic filing (within the meaning assigned by subsection 150.1(1)) and the person shall be deemed to have filed the information return with the Minister at that time, and a document presented by the Minister purporting to be a print-out of the information so received by the Minister shall be received as evidence and, in the absence of evidence to the contrary, is proof of the information return so deemed to have been filed.

Related Provisions: Reg. 205.1(1) — Forms of which more than 50 must be filed by Internet; *Interpretation Act* 25(1) — Evidence is rebuttable.

Notes: 244(22) added by 1992 technical bill, effective 1992.

Definitions [s. 244]: "assessment", "business" — 248(1); "Canada Revenue Agency" — *Canada Revenue Agency Act* s. 4(1); "Commissioner of Revenue" — *Canada Revenue Agency Act* s. 25; "day of sending" — 244(14), (14.1); "Her Majesty" — *Interpretation Act* 35(1); "Minister", "officer", "person", "prescribed", "record", "regulation" — 248(1); "taxation year" — 249; "taxpayer" — 248(1); "writing" — *Interpretation Act* 35(1).

PART XV.1 — REPORTING OF ELECTRONIC FUNDS TRANSFER

244.1 Definitions — The following definitions apply in this Part.

"cash" means coins referred to in section 7 of the *Currency Act*, notes issued by the Bank of Canada pursuant to the *Bank of Canada Act* that are intended for circulation in Canada or coins or bank notes of countries other than Canada.

"casino" means

(a) the government of a province that, in accordance with paragraph 207(1)(a) of the *Criminal Code*,

(i) in a permanent establishment that is held out to be a casino, conducts and manages a lottery scheme that includes games of roulette or card games, or

(ii) in any other permanent establishment, conducts and manages games that are operated on or through a slot machine, as defined in subsection 198(3) of that Act, or any other similar electronic gaming device, if there are more than 50 of those machines or other devices in the establishment;

(b) the government of a province that, in accordance with paragraph 207(1)(a) of the *Criminal Code*, conducts and manages a lottery scheme, other than bingo or the sale of lottery tickets, that is accessible to the public through the Internet or other digital network, except if the network is an internal network within an establishment referred to in subparagraph (a)(ii);

(c) an organization that, in accordance with paragraph 207(1)(b) of the *Criminal Code*, in a permanent establishment that is held out to be a casino, conducts and manages a lottery scheme that includes games of roulette or card games, unless the organization is a registered charity and the lottery scheme is conducted or managed for a period of not more than two consecutive days at a time; and

(d) the board of a fair or of an exhibition, or the operator of a concession leased by such a board, that, in accordance with paragraph 207(1)(c) of the *Criminal Code*, in a permanent establishment that is held out to be a casino, conducts and manages a lottery scheme that includes games of roulette or card games.

Notes: Definition "casino" enacted as per Notes to 244.7, and proclaimed in force effective June 29, 2017 by P.C. 2016-564.

Regulations: Nothing prescribed for "permanent establishment". This definition is copied from the *Proceeds of Crime (Money Laundering) and Terrorist Financing Regulations* s. 1(1), and "permanent establishment" is not defined in those Regulations.

"client" means a particular entity that engages in a financial transaction or activity with a reporting entity and includes an entity on whose behalf the particular entity is acting.

"credit union central" means a central cooperative credit society, as defined in section 2 of the *Cooperative Credit Associations Act*, or a credit union central or a federation of credit unions or caisses populaires that is regulated by a provincial Act other than one enacted by the legislature of Quebec.

Notes: S. 2 of the *Cooperative Credit Associations Act* provides:

"central cooperative credit society" means a cooperative credit society incorporated by or under an Act of the legislature of a province, one of whose principal purposes is to provide liquidity support to local cooperative credit societies, and

(a) whose membership consists wholly or primarily of local cooperative credit societies, or

(b) whose directors are wholly or primarily persons elected or appointed by local cooperative credit societies,

but does not include a deposit protection agency;

"electronic funds transfer" means the transmission — through any electronic, magnetic or optical device, telephone instrument or computer — of instructions for the transfer of funds, other than the transfer of funds within Canada. In the case of Society for Worldwide Interbank Financial Telecommunication messages, only SWIFT MT 103 messages are included.

"entity" means an individual, a body corporate, a partnership, a fund or an unincorporated association or organization.

Notes: This definition does not include a trust, but any action taken by a trust is actually taken by the trustee, who would be an "entity".

"funds" means cash, currency or securities, or negotiable instruments or other financial instruments, in any form, that indicate an entity's title or interest, or for civil law a right, in them.

"money services business" means an entity

(a) that has a place of business in Canada and that is engaged in the business of providing at least one of the following services:

(i) foreign exchange dealing,

(ii) remitting funds or transmitting funds by any means or through any entity or electronic funds transfer network,

(iii) issuing or redeeming money orders, traveller's cheques or other similar negotiable instruments except for cheques payable to a named entity,

(iv) dealing in virtual currencies, as defined by regulation, or

(v) a prescribed service; or

(b) that does not have a place of business in Canada, that is engaged in the business of providing at least one of the following services that is directed at entities in Canada, and that provides those services to their customers in Canada:

(i) foreign exchange dealing,

(ii) remitting funds or transmitting funds by any means or through any entity or electronic funds transfer network,

(iii) issuing or redeeming money orders, traveller's cheques or other similar negotiable instruments except for cheques payable to a named entity,

(iv) dealing in virtual currencies, as defined by regulation, or

(v) a prescribed service.

Notes: Definition added by 2014 budget bill #1, effective June 2020 (P.C. 2019-902).

"reporting entity" means an entity that is

(a) an authorized foreign bank within the meaning of section 2 of the *Bank Act* in respect of its business in Canada, or a bank to which that Act applies;

(b) a cooperative credit society, savings and credit union or caisse populaire regulated by a provincial Act;

(c) a financial services cooperative regulated by *An Act respecting financial services cooperatives*, R.S.Q., c. C-67.3, or *An Act respecting the Mouvement Desjardins*, S.Q. 2000, c. 77;

(d) an association regulated by the *Cooperative Credit Associations Act*;

(e) a company to which the *Trust and Loan Companies Act* applies;

(f) a trust company regulated by a provincial Act;

(g) a loan company regulated by a provincial Act;

(h) a money services business;

(i) a casino, including a casino owned or controlled by Her Majesty;

(j) a department or an agent of Her Majesty in right of Canada or of a province that is engaged in the business of accepting deposit liabilities in the course of providing financial services to the public; or

(k) a credit union central in respect of financial services it offers to an entity, other than an entity that is referred to in any of paragraphs (a) to (g) and (j) and is a member of that credit union central.

Related Provisions: 244.2(1) — Reporting entity required to report international electronic funds transfers over $10,000.

Notes: For "authorized foreign bank" in para. (a), see Notes to 248(1)"authorized foreign bank".

For para. (b), note that the definition of "credit union" in 137(6) does *not* apply (see 248(1)"credit union"), so the normal meaning applies.

Notes [s. 244.1]: See Notes at end of 244.7 for addition of 244.1-244.7.

Definitions [s. 244.1]: "authorized foreign bank", "bank", "business" — 248(1); "Canada" — 255, *Interpretation Act* 35(1); "cash", "casino", "credit union central", "electronic funds transfer", "entity", "funds" — 244.1; "Her Majesty" — *Interpretation Act* 35(1); "individual" — 248(1); "money services business" — 244.1; "partnership" — see 96(1) Notes; "province" — *Interpretation Act* 35(1); "provincial" — *Interpretation Act* 33(3), 35(1)"province"; "registered charity" — 248(1); "reporting entity" — 244.1; "trust" — 104(1), 248(1), (3).

244.2 (1) Electronic funds transfer — Every reporting entity shall file with the Minister an information return in prescribed form in respect of

(a) the sending out of Canada, at the request of a client, of an electronic funds transfer of $10,000 or more in the course of a single transaction; or

(b) the receipt from outside Canada of an electronic funds transfer, sent at the request of a client, of $10,000 or more in the course of a single transaction.

Related Provisions: 162(7) — Penalty for failure to comply; 238(1) — Offence of wilful failure to comply (failure to make or file a return); 244.2(2) — No application to transfer within Canada; 244.2(3) — Transfer through intermediary; 244.2(4) — Transfer conducted by agent; 244.3 — Temporary charity casino; 244.4(1) — Where multiple transfers under $10,000 deemed to be one transfer; 244.5 — Rate for conversion of transfer to C$; 244.6 — Deadline for return and manner of filing.

Notes: This section has little practical impact on financial institutions (FIs). A FI completes one form and sends it electronically once, and Shared Services Canada will forward it to both FINTRAC and the CRA. Finance advises that this legislation is needed because FINTRAC is administered under the *Proceeds of Crime (Money Laundering) and Terrorist Financing Act* and the CRA operates under the ITA, so "there are two reporting regimes". The only impact of 244.1-244.7, aside from providing CRA with authority to use this information (for GST/HST purposes as well: *Excise Tax Act* s. 273.3), will be that penalties and criminal punishment for non-compliance can be imposed under the ITA as well as under the PCMLTFA. CRA received 16.3 million EFT reports in 2018-19 (up from 14.9m in 2017-18): *Departmental Results Report* (tinyurl.com/cra-results), p. 23 (no data in 2019-20 Report).

CRA now sends letters to taxpayers who have had transfers to or from certain countries, inviting them to contact CRA if they have reported incorrectly. The letters do not say that Voluntary Disclosure (see Notes to 220(3.1)) is still permitted. See sample in *GST & HST Times* 329C (Carswell, April 2017).

See also Harry Chana, "International Electronic Funds Transfers", 22(3) *Canadian Tax Highlights* (ctf.ca) 10 (March 2014); Henry Chong, "EFT Reporting to the CRA", 22(7) *CTH* 7-9 (July 2014); Campbell, *Administration of Income Tax 2020* (Carswell), §7.10.

CRA news release "Ottawa dentist sentenced...", Jan. 17/19 (re Kin Tung Fong), acknowledges the "significant contribution of FINTRAC to this investigation" (re money transferred to Costa Rica).

See CRA news releases, "Harper Government cracks down on international tax evasion and aggressive tax avoidance with launch of Electronic Funds Transfer Initiative" (Jan. 7, 2015); "Government of Canada tables its response to the Standing Committee on Finance on efforts to crack down on tax cheats" (Feb, 23, 2017) (EFTs to and from Isle of Man, Guernsey and 2 other jurisdictions are currently being audited). The federal Budget Plan, Feb. 27, 2018, Chapter 1, states: "Over the last two fiscal years, the Government reviewed all large money transfers between Canada and eight countries of concern — a total of 187,000 transactions worth a total of over $177 billion that merited closer scrutiny. Working closely with partners in Canada and around the world, there are now over 1,000 offshore audits, and more than 40 criminal investigations with links to offshore transactions."

Information that the Minister obtains under 244.1-244.7 can be used for GST/HST audit and investigation purposes: *Excise Tax Act* s. 273.3.

Section 65.02 of the *Proceeds of Crime (Money Laundering) and Terrorist Financing Act*, also enacted by 2014 budget bill #1, provides that FINTRAC may disclose information to CRA for purpose of ensuring compliance with 244.1-244.7, but CRA may use the information only for that purpose.

Forms: RC438: International electronic funds transfer report.

(2) Transfer within Canada — For greater certainty and subject to subsection (3), subsection (1) does not apply to a reporting entity in respect of an electronic funds transfer if the entity

(a) sends the transfer to an entity in Canada, even if the final recipient is outside Canada; or

(b) receives the transfer from an entity in Canada, even if the initial sender is outside Canada.

Related Provisions: 241(4)(s) — Limited information can be disclosed to FINTRAC.

(3) Intermediary — Subsection (1) applies to a reporting entity in respect of an electronic funds transfer if the entity

(a) orders another reporting entity to send, at the request of a client, the transfer out of Canada, unless it provides the other reporting entity with the name and address of the client; or

(b) receives the transfer for a beneficiary in Canada from another reporting entity in circumstances where the initial sender is

outside Canada, unless the transfer contains the name and address of the beneficiary.

(4) Transfer conducted by agent — If a particular reporting entity is an agent of or is authorized to act on behalf of another reporting entity in respect of an electronic funds transfer, subsection (1) applies, in respect of the transfer, to the other reporting entity and not to the particular reporting entity.

(5) Entities outside Canada — Subsection (1) does not apply to an entity described in paragraph (b) of the definition "money services business" [in section 244.1 — ed.] in respect of the services it provides to entities outside Canada.

Notes: 244.2(5) added by 2014 budget bill #1, in force June 1, 2020 (P.C. 2019-902).

Notes [s. 244.2]: See Notes at end of 244.7 for addition of 244.1-244.7.

Definitions [s. 244.2]: "beneficiary" — 248(25) [Notes]; "Canada" — 255, *Interpretation Act* 35(1); "client", "electronic funds transfer", "entity", "funds" — 244.1; "Minister", "prescribed" — 248(1); "reporting entity" — 244.1.

244.3 Casino — An electronic funds transfer in respect of which subsection 244.2(1) applies that occurs in the course of a business, temporarily conducted for charitable purposes in the establishment of a casino by a registered charity carried on for not more than two consecutive days at a time under the supervision of the casino, shall be reported by the supervising casino.

Notes: See Notes at end of 244.7 for addition of 244.1-244.7.

Definitions [s. 244.3]: "business" — 248(1); "casino", "electronic funds transfer" — 244.1; "registered charity" — 248(1).

244.4 (1) Single transaction — For the purposes of this Part, two or more electronic funds transfers of less than $10,000 each that are made within 24 consecutive hours and that total $10,000 or more are considered to be made in the course of a single transaction of $10,000 or more if

(a) an individual, other than a trust, who is a reporting entity knows that the transfers are conducted by, or on behalf of, the same entity; and

(b) an employee of a reporting entity, other than an entity described in paragraph (a), knows that the transfers are conducted by, or on behalf of, the same entity.

Related Provisions: 244.2(2) — Exceptions.

(2) Exception — For greater certainty, subsection (1) does not apply in respect of an electronic funds transfer sent to two or more beneficiaries if the transfer is requested by

(a) an administrator of a pension fund that is regulated by or under an Act of Parliament or of the legislature of a province;

(b) a department or agent of Her Majesty in right of Canada or of a province;

(c) an incorporated city, town, village, metropolitan authority, township, district, county, rural municipality or other incorporated municipal body or an agent of any of them;

(d) an organization that operates a public hospital and that is designated by the Minister as a hospital authority under the *Excise Tax Act*, or an agent of such an organization; or

(e) a corporation that has minimum net assets of $75 million on its last audited balance sheet, whose shares are traded on a Canadian stock exchange or a designated stock exchange and that operates in a country that is a member of the Financial Action Task Force on Money Laundering established in 1989.

Notes [s. 244.4]: See Notes at end of 244.7 for addition of 244.1-244.7.

Definitions [s. 244.4]: "beneficiary" — 248(25) [Notes]; "corporation" — 248(1), *Interpretation Act* 35(1); "county" — *Interpretation Act* 35(1); "designated stock exchange" — 248(1), 262; "electronic funds transfer" — 244.1; "employee" — 248(1); "entity" — 244.1; "Her Majesty" — *Interpretation Act* 35(1); "individual", "Minister" — 248(1); "Parliament", "province" — *Interpretation Act* 35(1); "reporting entity" — 244.1; "share" — 248(1); "trust" — 104(1), 248(1), (3).

244.5 Foreign currency — If an electronic funds transfer is carried out by a reporting entity in a foreign currency, the amount of the transfer is to be converted into Canadian dollars using

(a) the official conversion rate of the Bank of Canada for the currency published in the Bank of Canada's *Daily Memorandum of Exchange Rates* that is in effect at the time of the transfer; or

(b) if no official conversion rate is set out in that publication for the currency, the conversion rate that the entity would use for the currency in the normal course of business at the time of the transfer.

Notes: See Notes at end of 244.7 for addition of 244.1-244.7.

Definitions [s. 244.5]: "amount", "business" — 248(1); "electronic funds transfer", "entity" — 244.1; "foreign currency" — 248(1); "reporting entity" — 244.1.

244.6 Filing of return — An information return in respect of an electronic funds transfer that is required to be filed by a reporting entity under this Part shall be filed

(a) not later than five working days after the day of the transfer; and

(b) using electronic media, in the manner specified by the Minister, if the entity has the technical capabilities to do so.

Notes: See Notes at end of 244.7 for addition of 244.1-244.7.

Definitions [s. 244.6]: "electronic funds transfer", "entity" — 244.1; "Minister" — 248(1); "reporting entity" — 244.1.

Forms: RC438: International electronic funds transfer report.

244.7 (1) Record keeping — Every reporting entity that is required to file an information return under this Part shall keep such records as will enable the Minister to determine whether the entity has complied with its duties and obligations under this Part.

Related Provisions: 238(1) — Offence — failure to comply.

(2) Form of records — A record that is required to be kept under this Part may be kept in machine-readable or electronic form if a paper copy can be readily produced from it.

(3) Retention of records — A reporting entity that is required to keep records under this Part in respect of an electronic funds transfer shall retain those records for a period of at least five years from the day of the transfer.

Related Provisions: 238(1) — Offence — failure to comply.

Notes [s. 244.7]: See Notes to 244.2(1). 244.1-244.7 (Part XV.1) added by 2014 budget bill #1, effective for electronic funds transfers made after 2014.

Definitions [s. 244.7]: "electronic funds transfer", "entity" — 244.1; "Minister", "record" — 248(1); "reporting entity" — 244.1.

PART XVI — TAX AVOIDANCE

245. [General Anti-Avoidance Rule — GAAR] — (1) Definitions — In this section,

Notes: Opening words of 245(1) amended to delete reference to 152(1.11) in RSC 1985 (5th Supp) consolidation. That rule of application is now in 152(1.111).

"tax benefit" means a reduction, avoidance or deferral of tax or other amount payable under this Act or an increase in a refund of tax or other amount under this Act, and includes a reduction, avoidance or deferral of tax or other amount that would be payable under this Act but for a tax treaty or an increase in a refund of tax or other amount under this Act as a result of a tax treaty;

Related Provisions: 237.3(1)"confidential protection" — Where disclosure is restricted of transaction that is a tax benefit; 237.3(1)"contractual protection" — Where financial protection is provided for transaction that is a tax benefit; 237.3(1)"tax benefit" — Definition applies to reportable-transaction rules.

Notes: Whether a tax benefit (**TB**) exists "is a factual determination ... The magnitude of the TB is not relevant at this stage of the analysis. If a deduction against taxable income is claimed, the existence of a TB is clear, since a deduction results in a reduction of tax. In some other instances, it may be that the existence of a TB can only be established by comparison with an alternative arrangement": *Canada Trustco*, 2005 SCC 54, paras. 19-20.

The burden is on the taxpayer to refute CRA's assumption of a tax benefit. If the Tax Court finds as a fact that there is a TB, an appeal court can overturn such finding only

if the taxpayer can show a palpable and overriding error: *Copthorne Holdings*, 2011 SCC 63, para. 34.

In *Triad Gestco*, 2012 FCA 258, a capital loss created a TB that arose from carrying back the loss to an earlier year (this was conceded by the taxpayer).

A TB "can be established by comparison of the taxpayer's situation with an alternative arrangement. If a comparison approach is used, the alternative arrangement must be one that might reasonably have been carried out but for the existence of the tax benefit": *Copthorne*, para. 35.

In *Univar*, 2005 TCC 723, paras. 34-35, the Court cited *McNichol*, [1997] 2 C.T.C. 2088 (TCC), stating: "Clearly a reduction or avoidance of tax does require the identification in any given set of circumstances of a norm or standard against which reduction is to be measured", and ruled that because the taxpayers' *intention* was to choose a method of extracting surplus that led to less tax, there was a "tax benefit". See also VIEWS doc 2006-0196051C6, re how CRA now views *McNichol* surplus stripping.

In *Grenon*, 2021 TCC 30 (under appeal to FCA), paras. 547-553, there was a TB in G enabling his RRSP to invest in his businesses without withdrawing the RRSP funds.

There was no TB in: saving foreign tax (*Alta Energy Luxembourg*, 2018 TCC 152, para. 75, footnote 14 (aff'd on other grounds 2020 FCA 43, SCC appeal heard March 19/21)); avoiding a cost base grind that would never have occurred (*Bank of Montreal*, 2020 FCA 82); avoiding 160(1) unexpectedly (*Damis Properties (Sabel Investments)* (under appeal to FCA as *Microbjo Properties*), 2021 TCC 24).

The words "other amount under this Act" are subject to "refund": *Rogers Enterprises*, 2020 TCC 92, paras. 28-37. Where capital dividends using a CDA increase had not yet been paid, there was no TB: paras. 46-49.

See also Buschke, "FCA Applying GAAR: Has a Tax Benefit Been Realized?", 8(3) *Canadian Tax Focus [CTFo]* (ctf.ca) 1-2 (Aug. 2018); Kroft, "Disputing the Existence of a Tax Benefit in GAAR Litigation", *Blakes on Cdn Tax Controversy* (*Taxnet Pro Tax Disputes Centre*), Aug. 2018, pp. 1-6; Nurmohamed, "Tax benefit for GAAR: The Defences", 11(1) *CTFo* 1-2 (Feb. 2021).

Definition "tax benefit" amended by 2004 Budget to add everything from "and includes...", effective with respect to transactions entered into after September 12, 1988.

Advance Tax Rulings: ATR-41: Convertible preferred shares; ATR-44: Utilization of deductions and credits within a related corporate group.

"tax consequences" to a person means the amount of income, taxable income, or taxable income earned in Canada of, tax or other amount payable by or refundable to the person under this Act, or any other amount that is relevant for the purposes of computing that amount;

"transaction" includes an arrangement or event.

Related Provisions: 94(1)"transaction" — Parallel definition for non-resident trust rules; 233.1(1)"transaction" — Parallel definition for reporting non-arm's length transactions with non-residents; 237.3(1)"transaction" — Definition applies to reportable-transaction rules; 247(1) — Parallel definition re transfer pricing.

Notes: The CRA states that filing an election constitutes a "transaction": VIEWS doc 2009-0329981C6.

Interpretation Bulletins: IT-233R: Lease-option agreements; sale-leaseback agreements (cancelled); IT-532: Part I.3 — tax on large corporations.

(2) General anti-avoidance provision [GAAR] — Where a transaction is an avoidance transaction, the tax consequences to a person shall be determined as is reasonable in the circumstances in order to deny a tax benefit that, but for this section, would result, directly or indirectly, from that transaction or from a series of transactions that includes that transaction.

Possible Future Amendment — GAAR expanded

Federal Economic Statement, Chapter 4, Nov. 30, 2020: *§4.8.2.4 Modernizing Anti-Avoidance Rules*

For too long, certain individuals and businesses have been able to create increasingly complex structures in order to artificially lower their tax obligations in a manner that does not serve an economic purpose, including by shifting profits offshore and creating artificial tax deductions. To address this, the government will launch consultations in the coming months on the modernization of Canada's anti-avoidance rules, in particular the General Anti-Avoidance Rule. It is essential to the integrity of the tax system that our anti-avoidance rules be updated so they are sufficiently robust for tax authorities and courts to address this sophisticated and aggressive tax planning.

Federal Budget, Chapter 10, April 19, 2021: *Protecting the Fairness and Integrity of Our Tax System*

. . .

The government will also take next steps to strengthen and modernize Canada's general anti-avoidance rule, as announced in the 2020 Fall Economic Statement.

[Full excerpt reproduced at 247(2), under "Possible Future Amendment — Transfer Pricing Rules (Consultation)" — ed.]

Related Provisions: 56(2) — Indirect payments; 237.3(2) — Reporting required of "reportable transactions"; 237.3(6) — GAAR deemed to apply if reportable transaction not reported and penalty is unpaid; 246 — Benefit conferred on a person; 247(2)(b)(ii) — GAAR test in transfer-pricing rules; 248(10) — Series of transactions; Reg. 5907(2.02) — Foreign affiliate surplus calculations — anti-avoidance rule; *Income Tax Conventions Interpretation Act* 4.1 — GAAR applies to tax treaty provisions; Canada-U.S. Tax Treaty:Art. XXIX-A: Limitations on using treaty benefits.

Notes: 245(2) is known as GAAR (General Anti-Avoidance Rule), to be used when specific anti-avoidance provisions do not suffice. The Supreme Court of Canada in *Canada Trustco*, 2005 SCC 54, set out the criteria for applying GAAR:

1. Three requirements must be established:

    (1) A tax benefit (see Notes to 245(1)"tax benefit") resulting from a transaction or part of a series of transactions (see 248(10)) [for the meaning of "indirectly", see Notes to 17.1(1)];

    (2) An "avoidance transaction" (see Notes to 245(3)) [this step cannot be skipped even if there is abuse: *Spruce Credit Union*, [2013] 1 C.T.C. 2096 (TCC), paras. 98, 105; aff'd 2014 CarswellNat 1736 (FCA)];

    (3) Abusive tax avoidance (245(4)): "it cannot be reasonably concluded that a tax benefit would be consistent with the object, spirit or purpose of the provisions relied upon by the taxpayer".

2. The onus is on the taxpayer to refute (1)-(2), and on the Minister to establish (3).

3. If the existence of abusive tax avoidance is unclear, the benefit of the doubt goes to the taxpayer.

4. The courts must conduct a unified "textual, contextual and purposive analysis" of the provisions giving rise to the tax benefit, to determine why they were put in place and why the benefit was conferred.

5. Whether the transactions were motivated by any economic, commercial, family or other non-tax purpose may form part of the factual context that the courts consider. Having only a tax purpose is insufficient by itself to establish abusive tax avoidance. The central issue is the proper interpretation of the provisions in light of their context and purpose.

6. "Abusive tax avoidance may be found where the relationships and transactions as expressed in the relevant documentation lack a proper basis relative to the object, spirit or purpose of the provisions that are purported to confer the tax benefit, or where they are wholly dissimilar to the relationships or transactions that are contemplated by the provisions."

7. Where the Tax Court judge has proceeded on a proper construction of the provisions of the Act and on findings supported by the evidence, appeal courts should not interfere, absent a palpable and overriding error.

The thresholds for "tax benefit" and "avoidance transaction" are both low, so in practice the dispute is usually about "misuse or abuse". It is an error for the trial court to skip directly to "abuse", but if this happens the appeal court can analyse the first two issues: *Husky Energy*, 2012 ABCA 231, para. 21 (Crown denied leave to appeal 2013 CarswellAlta 265 (SCC)). GAAR does not apply until the tax benefit is realized, not when a future benefit is created (e.g. increase to ACB, PUC or CDA): see "Benefit not yet realized" below.

See Schwartz, "Understanding what the Supreme Court of Canada Said in Canada Trustco", 2006 Cdn Tax Foundation conference report, 3:1-44; Thivierge, "GAAR Redux: After Canada Trustco", 4:1-23; Duff & Alarie, "Legislated Interpretation and Tax Avoidance" (April 2018, ssrn.com/abstract=3170711).

"Because of the potential to affect so many transactions, the court must approach a GAAR decision cautiously": *Copthorne Holdings*, 2011 SCC 63, para. 67.

Benefit not yet realized: GAAR does not apply. See *1245989 Alberta Ltd. (Wild)*, 2018 FCA 114; *Gladwin Realty*, 2020 FCA 142, para. 47; *Rogers Enterprises*, 2020 TCC 92, paras. 46-49.

Impact of later legislative amendment: see 245(4) Notes.

Discovery in a GAAR appeal: *Owen Holdings*, 1997 CarswellNat 1012 (FCA) (no access to unrelated rulings); *Superior Plus*, 2015 FCA 241 and 2016 TCC 217 (CRA and Finance policy documents); *Madison Pacific [MP Western]*, 2019 FCA 19 (leave to appeal denied 2019 CarswellNat 3243 (SCC)) (draft documents prepared during audit should be disclosed, as they "inform the Minister's mental process": para. 12; but no "fishing expedition" for correspondence between CRA and Finance on loss trading); *CHR Investment*, 2021 FCA 68 (CRA not required to produce letters to/from Finance re requested legislative changes, as discovery is for questions of fact and legislative purpose is question of law, and auditor did not consider letters); *Total Energy*, 2019 TCC 112 (FCA appeal discontinued A-180-19) (similar to *MP Western*: fishing expedition not allowed); Misutka, "Delineating the Crown's Obligations to Make Disclosure", XXII(2) *Tax Litigation* (Federated Press) 10-16 (2019); Virji & Haymour, "Pulling Back the Curtain on Policy", *Bennett Jones on Tax Disputes* (Taxnet Pro Tax Disputes Centre), May 2021, pp. 2-8.

See 245(4) Notes for more on what constitutes abuse under GAAR. See 245(7) Notes re interest running on a GAAR assessment from the original balance-due day.

GAAR was found to apply in the following cases:

Supreme Court of Canada

- *Mathew (Kaulius)*, 2005 SCC 55 (acquiring non-capital losses via partnership transfer)

- *Lipson*, 2009 SCC 1 (cycling home mortgage interest to make it deductible was OK [see 20(1)(c) Notes], but SCC ruled 4-3 that using 73(1) and 74.1(1) to attribute loss from wife to husband was misuse)

- *Copthorne Holdings*, 2011 SCC 63 (artificial increase in paid-up capital through double-counting via amalgamation that avoided exclusion in 87(3))

Federal Court of Appeal

[pre-Canada Trustco:]

- *OSFC Holdings*, 2001 FCA 260; leave to appeal denied 2002 CarswellNat 1388 (SCC) (acquiring non-capital losses via partnership transfer; same facts as *Mathew* above)

- *Water's Edge (Duncan)*, 2002 FCA 291; leave to appeal denied 2003 CarswellNat 707 (acquiring tax loss via partnership claiming terminal loss)

[post-Canada Trustco:]

- *MacKay*, 2008 FCA 105; leave to appeal denied 2009 CarswellNat 19 (acquisition of shopping centre structured to transfer losses to purchasers; primary purpose of certain transactions was tax avoidance)

- *Triad Gestco*, 2012 FCA 258 and *1207192 Ontario*, 2012 FCA 259; leave to appeal denied 2013 CarswellOnt 3394 ("value shift" transfer by company of subsidiary's shares to trust whose beneficiary was company's owner; artificial capital loss created with stock dividend of high-low pref shares)

- *Global Equity Fund*, 2012 FCA 272; leave to appeal denied 2013 CarswellNat 932 ("value shift": artificial income loss created with stock dividend of high-low pref shares had "no air of economic or business reality" [but GEF awarded costs because Crown changed its arguments at FCA])

[See Falk & Morand, "GAAR Trilogy — 'Value Shift' Planning", 2145 *Tax Topics* (CCH) 1-9 (April 18, 2013); Jolie, "Value Shifts", 21(10) *Canadian Tax Highlights* (ctf.ca) 3-4 (Oct. 2013).]

- *Gervais*, 2018 FCA 3 (half of capital gain transferred by G to let wife claim capital gains exemption [Korne & Elkeslassy comment, 66(2) *Canadian Tax Journal [CTJ]* 401-08 (2018)])

- *Oxford Properties*, 2018 FCA 30, paras. 111-116; leave to appeal denied 2018 CarswellNat 7871 (97(2) rollover, 88(1)(d) bump, 98(3) partnership windup and sale to tax-exempt entity after 69(11) 3-year limit frustrated object of 100(1)(b) [see 100(1) Notes])

- *Fiducie Financière Satoma*, 2018 FCA 74; leave to appeal denied 2019 CarswellNat 898 (deliberate use of 75(2) to move dividend to corp that paid no tax on it)

- *Pomerleau*, 2018 FCA 129 (surplus stripping that avoided 84.1)

- *594710 B.C.*, 2018 FCA 166; leave to appeal denied 2019 CarswellNat 434 (abuse of 96(1)(f) and 103(1) by selling shares of corporate partners to shift income to unrelated public corp with unused losses; abuse of 160(1) by triggering year-end so it would not apply [Morphy, "The Queen v. 594710", XXII(1) *Tax Litigation* (Federated Press) 2-10 (2019)])

- *2763478 Canada Inc.*, 2018 FCA 209 ("value shift" in estate freeze, despite double tax due to unrealized capital gain of related taxpayer who could have applied for relief under 245(6) (paras. 64-69); real capital gain should not be offset by theoretical loss (para. 56))

- *Birchcliff Energy*, 2019 FCA 151; leave to appeal denied 2019 CarswellNat 6298 (avoiding 256(7)(b)(ii) deemed change in control by having Lossco issue subscription receipts to trigger 256(7)(b)(iii)(B) before amalgamation; same result earlier at 2015 TCC 232 but decision nullified 2017 FCA 89 as issued by wrong judge)

- *Gladwin Realty*, 2020 FCA 142 (misuse of 40(3.12) and pre-2011 capital dividend account rules via partnership distribution to inflate CDA with offsetting gains and losses [Strawson & Bateman, "CDA Extraction", 19(3) *Tax for the Owner-Manager* (ctf.ca) 1-2 (July 2019)])

Federal Court — Trial Division

- *Michelin Tires*, [2000] G.S.T.C. 17 (sale of inventory to affiliated company to obtain refund of federal sales tax)

Tax Court of Canada

[pre-Canada Trustco:]

- *McNichol*, [1997] 2 C.T.C. 2088 (FCA appeal discontinued June 29/98) and *RMM Canadian Enterprises (Equilease)*, [1998] 1 C.T.C. 2300 (surplus stripping by selling shares of corp instead of paying dividend; both effectively overruled by *Canada Trustco* and *Evans*)

- *Nadeau*, [1999] 3 C.T.C. 2235 (paid-up capital increased)

- *Fredette*, [2001] 3 C.T.C. 2468 (two-year deferral via staggered partnership year-ends was abuse; one-year deferral was allowed) (see now 34.2)

[post-Canada Trustco:]

- *Desmarais*, 2006 TCC 44 (surplus stripping — dividends converted to capital gains)

- *Ceco Operations*, 2006 TCC 256 (FCA appeal discontinued A-312-06) (misuse of 97(2) partnership rollover)

- *Antle*, 2009 TCC 465 [aff'd on other grounds 2010 FCA 280; leave to appeal denied 2011 CarswellNat 1491; motion for SCC reconsideration dismissed 2012 CarswellNat 183] (capital property step-up using Barbados spousal trust, which defeated Canada's policy of taxing capital gains)

- *Pièces Automobiles Lecavalier*, 2013 TCC 310 (circumventing 80(2)(g) debt forgiveness and 80.01(6)-(8) debt parking rules, on sale of shares of Canco with underwater debt owed to its non-resident parent [Mailhot-Gamelin, "Two-Step Conversion of Debt into Shares Subject to GAAR", 2177 *Tax Topics* (CCH) 9-11 (Nov. 28, 2013); Morin, "Series of Transactions and GAAR", 4(1) *Canadian Tax Focus* (ctf.ca) 7 (Feb. 2014)])

- *Descarries*, 2014 TCC 75 (dividend strip, using capital loss to reduce deemed dividend, avoided 84.1(1) [Walker comment, 62(4) *CTJ* 1072-79 (2014)])

- *Barrasso*, 2014 TCC 156 (FCA appeal discontinued A-295-14) ("value shift" similar to *Triad Gestco* and *1207192 Ontario*; B's future real gain on death did not stop GAAR from applying)

- *Golini*, 2016 TCC 174 (FCA appeal discontinued A-349-16) ("RCA Optimizer Plan": $6m sent around in circles, including through offshore life insurance and limited-recourse loan, misused 84(1))

- *Grenon*, 2021 TCC 30, paras. 539-608 (under appeal to FCA) (G created mutual fund trusts to allow his RRSP to invest through them in his businesses)

Quebec Court of Appeal *(Quebec Taxation Act s. 1079.10 GAAR)*

- *OGT Holdings*, 2009 QCCA 1991; leave to appeal denied 2009 CarswellQue 8756 (Quebec shuffle [now stopped by Quebec *Taxation Act* s. 529.1], where rollover to Ontario corp done under Quebec legislation but not under the ITA; later amalgamation provided high ACB for Quebec tax)

- *9199-3899 Québec*, 2017 QCCA 1524 (interest-free loan to parent corp just before year-end, to reduce capital tax by claiming investment allowance, where loan was repaid soon after year-end so parent also did not pay capital tax on it)

- *Developpements Iberville*, 2018 QCCA 1886; leave to appeal denied 2019 CarswellQue 5376 (Quebec year-end shuffle, using corps with different federal and QC year-ends to avoid $728 million of QC tax on capital gain)

GAAR was found NOT to apply in the following cases:

Supreme Court of Canada

- *Canada Trustco*, 2005 SCC 54 (trailers bought from and circuitously leased back to the same company with guaranteed lease payments to create CCA; the CCA provisions require only "cost", not "economic risk")

Federal Court of Appeal

[pre-Canada Trustco:]

- *Canadian Pacific*, 2001 FCA 398 (weak-currency loans like *Shell Canada*; see now 20.3)

- *Donohue Forest Products*, 2020 FCA 422 (on reorganization, corp claimed loss while shareholder claimed ABIL on same loss)

- *Jabin Investments*, 2002 FCA 520 (pre-1994 debt parking)

- *Imperial Oil*, 2004 FCA 36 (loans structured to fall within "investment allowance" in 181.2(4)(b) to reduce Large Corporations Tax; this plan was foreseeable and the legislation could have addressed it)

- *CIT Financial*, 2004 FCA 201; leave to appeal denied 2004 CarswellNat 4370 (acquisition of software at inflated price for CCA was caught by s. 69, not GAAR)

- *Landrus*, 2009 FCA 113 (disposition from partnership to related partnership to trigger terminal loss early)

[post-Canada Trustco:]

- *MIL (Investments)*, 2007 FCA 236 (capital gain on Canadian public company shares avoided when corp reduced ownership to under 10% and transferred corporate residence to Luxembourg) [today this would be caught by the Multilateral Instrument (MLI)]

- *Remai*, 2009 FCA 340 (donation to R's private foundation of promissory notes issued by his corp, followed by sale of notes to his nephew's corp)

- *Lehigh Cement*, 2010 FCA 124; leave to appeal denied 2010 CarswellNat 4035 (restructuring of loan to access "5/25" withholding tax exemption under pre-2008 212(1)(b)) [Stikeman Elliott, "Lehigh Cement", 2010(11) *Tax Times* (Carswell) 1-2 (June 11, 2010)]

- *Collins & Aikman Products*, 2010 FCA 251 (reorganization followed by dividends to Canadian holdco and return of capital to non-resident shareholder — see now 212.3)

- *Garron (St. Michael Trust)*, 2010 FCA 309 (aff'd on other grounds as *Fundy Settlement*, 2012 SCC 14) (Barbados trust used to avoid tax on capital gains: "If the residence of the Trusts is Barbados for treaty purposes, the Trusts cannot misuse or abuse the Barbados Tax Treaty by claiming the exemption" (para. 90))

- *Spruce Credit Union*, 2014 FCA 14 (credit unions received dividends from deposit insurance corp as part of cycling funds to another DIC)

- *Univar Holdco*, 2017 FCA 207 (surplus stripping to non-resident: reorg to fit pre-2016 212.1(4) avoided 212.1 but arm's length sale would also have worked)

- *1245989 Alberta Ltd. (Wild)*, 2018 FCA 114 (surplus stripping: misuse of averaging in 89(1)"paid-up capital" to circumvent 84.1, but GAAR could not apply until corporate surplus was extracted)

- *Alta Energy Luxembourg*, 2020 FCA 43; SCC appeal heard March 19/21 (using Canada-Luxembourg treaty Art. 13(4) to have no capital gains tax paid in either country was not abuse; treaty shopping is not GAARable [pre-MLI])

- *Bank of Montreal*, 2020 FCA 82 (since 39(2) deemed loss on shares in a tower structure to be loss on currency, 112(3.1) did not apply to deny loss, so no "tax benefit")

Tax Court of Canada

[pre-Canada Trustco:]

- *Husky Oil*, [1999] 4 C.T.C. 2691 (sale of assets via partnership to transfer loss to purchaser)

- *Jabs Construction*, [1999] 3 C.T.C. 2556 (transfer of capital gain to charity via 110.1(3))

- *9000-6560 Québec (Chrysler St-Jovite)*, [2001] G.S.T.C. 16 (car dealer selling vehicles GST-free to status Indians, who then transferred the vehicles to a numbered company that sold them to an export company and failed to remit GST)

- *Ventes D'Auto Giordano*, [2001] G.S.T.C. 37 (export company on same facts as above; GAAR did not apply because there was a more specific remedy the Crown could have used)

- *Geransky*, [2001] 2 C.T.C. 2147 (sale of corporate assets achieved by dividending assets to holdco and crystallizing G's capital gains exemption; using ITA provisions in the course of a commercial transaction is not misuse or abuse) [CRA accepts this with qualifications: see 84(2) Notes]

- *Fredette*, [2001] 3 C.T.C. 2468 and *Rousseau-Houle*, 2001 CarswellNat 1126 (Crown's FCA appeal discontinued) (GAAR does not apply to misuse of the regulations, only the Act [now overridden by amendment to 245(4)]; also, putting rental property into partnership to circumvent CCA limits by deducting interest at partner level was not abuse; and deferral of income by 1 year was not abuse [now overridden by 34.2])

- *Hill*, [2003] 4 C.T.C. 2548 (payment of compound interest arrears was deductible even though identical advance of capital taken back)

- *Loyens*, 2003 TCC 214 (transfer of interest in real property inventory to existing partnership, and rollover of partnership interest to corp to offset capital losses)

- *Howe*, 2004 TCC 719 (limited partnerships were established to raise funds, so loss transactions were undertaken primarily for *bona fide* purposes other than to obtain tax benefit)

- *Brouillette*, 2005 TCC 203 (surplus stripping with arm's length party where tax avoidance was not primary motive)

[post-Canada Trustco:]

- *Univar Canada*, 2005 TCC 723 (using second-tier financing structure with Barbados corp to avoid 95(6)(b))

- *Evans*, 2005 TCC 684 (surplus strip via capital gains exemption)

- *Overs*, 2006 TCC 26 (transfer to spouse and reverse use of attribution rules — now wrong in light of *Lipson*)

- *McMullen*, 2007 TCC 16 (surplus stripping; primary purpose of transactions was severing business ties rather than to obtain tax benefits) [Anderson et al., "Breaking Up a Business or Surplus Stripping?", XV(1) *Tax Litigation* (Federated Press) 910-17 (2007)]

- *McClarty Family Trust*, 2012 TCC 80 (kiddie tax in 120.4 avoided through stock dividends and circular payments that converted dividend income to capital gains, but there was genuine creditor-proofing purpose) [CRA did not appeal, but considers everything after the conclusion there was no "avoidance transaction" to be *obiter*: Padina, "Canada Revenue Agency Clarifies Position in Deciding Not to Appeal", 67(5) *Tax Notes International* (taxnotes.com) 453-56 (July 30, 2012)]

- *MacDonald*, 2012 TCC 123 [rev'd on other grounds 2013 FCA 110] (capital gains on leaving Canada could have been offset by past genuine capital losses; surplus strip was used to extract funds to avoid future US tax)

- *Swirsky*, 2013 TCC 73 [aff'd on other grounds 2014 FCA 36] (attribution of losses incurred by wife on borrowed money when buying shares from S; tax reduction was not a main purpose of transactions (it was creditor-proofing))

- *Gwartz*, 2013 TCC 86 (dividends on high-low shares to family trust, generating capital gains to avoid kiddie tax before 120.4(4): there is no general policy against surplus stripping [see 84.1(1) Notes] or income splitting)

- *Loblaw Financial*, 2018 TCC 182 [rev'd on other grounds 2020 FCA 79; SCC appeal heard May 13/21] (despite misuse of FAPI exemption (para. 323), Barbados bank sub was not set up primarily for tax purposes: paras. 290-320)

- *Deans Knight*, 2019 TCC 76 (Crown's FCA appeal heard March 22/21) (loss trading: selling corp's unused losses and credits to third party taking 35% votes but 79% of equity, pre-256.1 [DiGregorio, "Deans Knight Wins Precedent-Setting 'Recap and Restart' Case" 2019(10) *Tax Times* (Carswell) 1-2 (May 24, 2019)])
- *MMV Capital*, 2020 TCC 82 (under appeal by Crown to FCA) (loss trading: as in *Deans Knight*, using non-capital losses with change in *de facto* (but not *de jure*) control did not abuse the loss restriction rules [Keey, "Recent Corporate Tax Developments", 2020(18) *Tax Times* (Carswell) 1-4 (Sept. 25, 2020)])
- *Rogers Enterprises*, 2020 TCC 92 (corp's capital dividend account addition from life insurance proceeds was not reduced by policy's adjusted cost basis to another corp, before 2016 amendment [Bhatia, "Rogers Enterprises", XXVI(1) *Insurance Planning* (Federated Press) 1-9 (2021)])
- *Damis Properties (Sabel Investments)* (under appeal to FCA as *Microbjo Properties*), 2021 TCC 24 (scheme did not avoid s. 160 as there was no "tax benefit")

British Columbia Court of Appeal *(BC Income Tax Act s. 68.1 GAAR)*

- *Veracity Capital*, 2017 BCCA 3; leave to appeal denied 2017 CarswellBC 1517 (Quebec Year-End Shuffle: using different fiscal year-ends in QC from BC to have 90% of capital gain taxed by no province was not abuse of any BC rule [Gilbert, "Veracity and the BC GAAR", 25(7) *Canadian Tax Highlights* (ctf.ca) 11-12 (July 2017)])

Alberta Court of Appeal *(Alberta Corporate Tax Act s. 72.1)*

- *Husky Energy*, 2012 ABCA 231; leave to appeal denied to Crown 2013 CarswellAlta 265 (circular refinancings to move interest expense from AB to ON were not abusive, even though due to legislative quirk certain income was not taxed by Ontario)
- *Canada Safeway*, 2012 ABCA 232; leave to appeal denied to Crown 2013 CarswellAlta 246 (Ontario shuffle was not abusive; the 112(1) intercorporate dividend deduction is not abused merely because the underlying stream of income was not taxable at the corporate level)

Ontario Court of Appeal *(Ontario, Corporations Tax Act s. 5)*

- *Inter-Leasing*, 2014 ONCA 575, para. 65; leave to appeal denied to Ontario 2015 CarswellOnt 2996 (refinancing arrangement that moved interest income to British Virgin Islands corp was not abusive because ON made clear choice not to tax non-resident corps on property income)

Ontario Superior Court of Justice *(Ontario, Corporations Tax Act s. 5)*

- *Safeway Ontario*, 2014 ONSC 5204 (same as *Inter-Leasing* above)

Quebec Court of Appeal *(Quebec Taxation Act s. 1079.10 GAAR)*

- *Custeau*, 2020 QCCA 1496 (leave to appeal denied 2021 CarswellQue 5283 (SCC)) (upward PUC averaging in 1998, due to regional development fund investments, was not done with any thought of tax savings realized in 2006)

Quebec Court *(Quebec Taxation Act s. 1079.10 GAAR)*

- *Panneaux Chambord*, 2003 CarswellQue 1157 (legitimate commercial investments at year-end reduced capital tax) [Bourgeois & Blanchette, "Quebec GAAR and Capital Tax", 11(5) *Canadian Tax Highlights* (ctf.ca) 8-9 (May 2013)]
- *Soucy*, 2018 QCCQ 4845 (transfer of car to ex-wife via daughter, where Quebec Sales Tax permitted tax-free transfer between related persons)

See also *Duha Printers*, [1998] 3 C.T.C. 303; *Continental Bank Leasing*, [1998] 4 C.T.C. 119; and *Shell Canada*, [1999] 4 C.T.C. 143, in all of which (plus others) the Supreme Court of Canada approved artificial tax avoidance in pre-GAAR transactions.

CRA applies specific anti-avoidance rules (SAARs) if it can (e.g., 55(2), 75(2), 84.1, 95(6), 103(1), 237.1, 247(2) — see Notes to those and Topical Index under "Anti-avoidance"). However in *Lipson*, 2009 SCC 1, the majority ruled that GAAR applied even though 74.5(11), a SAAR, might have applied. See also D'Avignon & Stewart, "The Interaction of Specific Anti-Avoidance Rules under GAAR", 2016 Cdn Tax Foundation conference report, 10:1-24; McCue, "An Update on Statutory Interpretation and Specific Anti-Avoidance Rules", 2017 conference report, 35:1-30; Dolson, Keung, & Kumar, "A Modern Overview of Specific Anti-Avoidance Rules", 2018 Cdn Tax Foundation conference report, 14:1-63.

Sham transactions can be ignored, where documents are deceptive: *Stubart*, [1984] C.T.C. 294 (SCC), paras. 50-51; *Dominion Bridge*, [1977] C.T.C. 554 (FCA); *Nunn*, 2006 FCA 403 ("the parties to a transaction together have deliberately set out to misrepresent the actual state of affairs to a third party (i.e. the Minister)": para. 19); *Faraggi*, 2008 FCA 398 (leave to appeal denied 2009 CarswellNat 1152 (SCC)); *Antle*, 2010 FCA 280 (leave to appeal denied 2011 CarswellNat 1491, reconsideration motion dismissed 2012 CarswellNat 183 (SCC)); *Dimane Enterprises*, 2014 TCC 334 (sham EPSP); *Mariano*, 2015 TCC 244, paras. 83-89; *Dingman*, 2017 TCC 206 (FCA appeal dismissed for delay A-336-17); *Paletta*, 2019 TCC 205 (under appeal to FCA), paras. 127-247 (film investment; Fox had pre-agreed to exercise option to repurchase film). "Sham is a serious allegation requiring convincing evidence to conclude that a Canadian taxpayer was deceitful": *Agracity*, 2020 TCC 91, para. 20. Confused books and records are not, on their own, evidence of sham: para. 78(xiv). **No sham was found in**: *Massey-Ferguson*, [1977] C.T.C. 6 (FCA); *J.R. Saint & Associates*, 2010 TCC 168; *McLarty*, 2014 TCC 30 (seismic data joint venture created real rights and obligations); *Birchcliff Energy*, 2017 TCC 234, paras. 95-103 (no deceit) (aff'd on other grounds 2019 FCA 151, leave to appeal denied 2019 CarswellNat 6298) [same result earlier at 2015 TCC 232, but decision nullified 2017 FCA 89 as issued by wrong judge]; *Golini*, 2016 TCC 174 (FCA appeal discontinued A-349-16) (circular structure was not sham due to one misrepresentation, but GAAR applied); *Cameco*, 2018 TCC 195, paras. 582-670 (selling uranium through offshore subsidiary) [aff'd 2020 FCA 112 (leave to appeal denied 2021 CarswellNat 377 (SCC)), but this issue not appealed: para. 15]; *Lee*, 2018 TCC 230 (Quebec trust set up by BC resident in "Quebec truffle" to avoid provincial tax [Wang & Tamm, "Reaffirming the Sham Doctrine", 9(2) *Canadian Tax Focus* (ctf.ca) 16-17 (May 2019)]); *Lee*, 2020 QCCQ 780, paras. 454-504 (Prospector Networks software shelter promissory notes); *Agracity*, 2020 TCC 91 (selling herbicide through Barbados corp); *Grenon*, 2021 TCC 30, paras. 350-382 (under appeal to FCA on other grounds) (failure to create valid mutual fund trusts did not involve deceit). Sham applies only when it is CRA that is deceived, not a taxpayer: *Coast Capital*, 2015 TCC 195 (aff'd with no firm ruling on this issue 2016 FCA 181, para. 21); *Mattacchione*, 2015 TCC 283, para. 72; *Paletta*, 2021 TCC 11 (under appeal by Crown to FCA), paras. 210-247 (foreign exchange trading straddles to defer tax for years: no evidence of fabricating documents). On the Crown amending its Reply to allege sham see *Pomeroy Acquireco*, 2020 TCC 107 (under appeal by Crown to FCA; procedural decision 2020 FCA 221). See also Loutzen, "Sham in the Canadian Courts", chap. 14 of Simpson & Stewart, *Sham Transactions* (Oxford University Press, 2013); Belley, "True Agreement and Sham", 2017 Cdn Tax Foundation conference report, 37:1-9; Crosbie, "Sham Under Review", XXIII(1) *Corporate Finance* (Federated Press) 2-7 (2020). For CRA policy on determining sham see Cdn Bar Assn Commodity Tax section meeting, Feb. 26, 2015 (cba.org > "Sections"), q. 6. The Quebec *Civil Code* equivalent is "simulation" or "counter letter" [which despite its name can be oral], e.g. *ZT22 Holding*, 2013 TCC 17, para. 18; *Abdulnour*, 2013 TCC 34, para. 22; *Laplante*, 2018 FCA 193 (leave to appeal denied 2019 CarswellNat 1522 (SCC)); *Caplan*, 2019 QCCQ 3269 (trust payments to children were really to the father); but in *Ludmer*, 2018 QCCS 3381, paras. 637, 777 (aff'd on other grounds 2020 QCCA 697; leave to appeal denied 2021 CarswellQue 2160 (SCC)), the Court used "sham". "Window dressing", unlike sham, is "a deception that is not about the legal validity of a transaction ...but about the taxpayer's intention for entering into the transaction": *Standard Life*, 2015 TCC 97, para. 158 (aff'd on other grounds as *SCDA (2015) Inc.*, 2017 FCA 177); and see *Paletta*, 2021 TCC 11 (under appeal by Crown to FCA), paras. 244-247, and *Grenon* (above), paras. 383-403 (no deception). Where a *trust* is a sham, see MacEachren, "Trusts and Mistaken Veils", 2018 STEP Canada conference, 59pp (contact member-services@step.ca). In Quebec, using a sham after May 16, 2019 triggers a penalty of 50% of the Quebec tax avoided, *minimum* $25,000 (and the Quebec reassessment deadline is extended by 3 years); and for advisors or promoters, 100% of fees charged: Information Bulletin 2019-5; Caillé & Barchichat, "Quebec: New Consequences Where GAAR or Sham Rule Applies", 10(1) *Canadian Tax Focus* (ctf.ca) 5 (Feb. 2020); RQ Round Table, 2019 Cdn Tax Foundation conference report at 4:7-13 (qq. 10-22).

"To the extent that it may not always be obvious whether the purpose of a provision is frustrated by an avoidance transaction, the GAAR may introduce a degree of uncertainty into tax planning, but such uncertainty is inherent in all situations in which the law must be applied to unique facts. The GAAR is neither a penal provision nor a hammer to pound taxpayers into submission. It is designed, in the complex context of the ITA, to restrain abusive tax avoidance and to make sure that the fairness of the tax system is preserved. A desire to avoid uncertainty cannot justify ignoring a provision of the ITA that is clearly intended to apply to transactions that would otherwise be valid on their face": Lebel J. in *Lipson*, 2009 SCC 1, para. 52.

GAAR can be used as a "shield" to justify another provision not being treated as a general anti-avoidance provision: *MacDonald*, [2012] 4 C.T.C. 2099, para. 83 (rev'd on other grounds, [2013] 4 C.T.C. 251 (FCA)).

For CRA policies on GAAR, see generally Information Circular 88-2 including Supplement, and *Income Tax Technical News* 22. The CRA will apply GAAR to a loss created by issuing shares with high redemption value and low PUC: VIEWS docs 2005-0113521I7, 2005-0113531I7, 2005-0113541I7. Where a scheme has already been found subject to GAAR by the SCC (*Lipson*), use of the same scheme could be subject to penalties under 163(2) and 163.2: 2009-0327071C6.

GAAR assessments (and ruling requests) must go to Headquarters for approval before they can be issued or formally proposed: IC88-2, para. 2. Before approving a GAAR assessment, Headquarters will refer it to the GAAR Committee, unless the issue is substantially similar to one previously considered by the Committee. (Where the tax benefit arises from a treaty, the Treaty Abuse Prevention (TAP) Committee will have responsibility instead: see Notes to MLI Art. 7:1, before the Canada-US treaty.)

The GAAR Committee is an *ad hoc* committee, so membership changes per meeting. As of fall 2020, the members are: Stéphane Prud'homme [Chair, 613-670-9065] (Director, Reorganizations Divn (RD), Income Tax Rulings Directorate (ITRD)); Jean Lafrenière and Henry Chong [Co-secretaries] (Manager and Industry Sector Specialists, RD); the other 3 directors of the ITRD divisions (Yves Moreno, Stéphane Charette, Louise Roy); Ted Cook (Finance); Shauna Pittman, Mélanie Sauriol, Ryan Gellings and Deen Olsen (Justice); Danny Gagnon (Legislative Policy Directorate); Intl & Large Business Directorate (some of Suzanne Saydeh, Len Lubbers, Jim Randall, Dominic Laroche, Patrick Bilodeau); and the rulings officer or auditor on the file.

The committee usually meets biweekly, but will not, as a committee, meet with taxpayers or representatives. It considers cases only if full taxpayer representations accompany the referral (*Income Tax Technical News* 22). As of March 2020 the committee had reviewed 1,608 cases (plus RRSP strips, Barbados spousal trust cases and provincial GAAR cases), and ruled GAAR applied in 1,292 (80%) of them (*Access to Information Act* disclosure). See also "The GAAR Committee", 2002 conference report, 10:1-20; VIEWS doc 2016-0672091C6 [2016 CTF q.7 (general information on the committee); 2016-0673001C6 [2016 TEI q.D4].

GAAR issues include: international financing arrangements used to create or import interest expense; avoidance of 85.1(4) on disposition of foreign affiliate shares; use of stock dividends to create losses to offset gains, create 164(6) loss carryback, or avoid 120.4 tax on split income; Barbados spousal trust arrangements; Canadian estate freezes with future growth shifted to offshore trusts with Canadian beneficiaries; treaty shopping; leveraged cash donation arrangement; RRSP strips; surplus stripping; retirement compensation arrangements. (*Income Tax Technical News* No. 34)

See Notes to 84.1(1) re the Act having no general policy against surplus stripping. In practice it seems that GAAR is likely to apply to surplus-stripping schemes that extract money with no tax, not those that convert dividends to lower-taxed capital gains.

GAAR applies to misuse of tax treaties, due to 245(4)(a)(iv) and *Income Tax Conventions Interpretation Act* s. 4.1 (reproduced before the Canada-US treaty); Meredith, "Treaty Interpretation and Assertions of Abuse", 2008 Cdn Tax Foundation conference report, 20:1-14. See however *MIL (Investments)*, 2007 FCA 236, and CRA's response in doc 2008-0278801C6 q. 11 [2008 STEP]. Treaty shopping was allowed in *Prévost Car*, 2009 FCA 57, when CRA did not apply GAAR (see Notes to 212(2)), and 2009-0343641R3. Effective 2020 or later, Multilateral Instrument (MLI) Art. 7 (reproduced before the Canada-US treaty) effectively amends most of Canada's treaties (but not Canada-US) to prevent treaty shopping by denying benefits that do not accord with the treaty's "object and purpose".

On form vs. substance in GAAR see McMechan, *Economic Substance and Tax Avoidance* (Carswell, 2013, 469pp.); McArthur, "Assessing the Fairness of Tax Avoidance", in *The Quest for Tax Reform Continues: The Royal Commission on Taxation Fifty Years Later* (Carswell, 2013), pp. 329-351; Elawny & Virji, "Form Still Matters...Right?!", 2167 *Tax Topics* (CCH) 1-4 (Sept. 19, 2013). Private Member's Bill C-621, introduced by NDP MP Murray Rankin June 16, 2014 based on McMechan's book, proposed that economic substance be considered a relevant factor for purposes of 245(3), with a presumption of misuse or abuse if an avoidance transaction does not have economic substance of value greater than the anticipated tax benefit.

Other GAARs: GST/HST: *Excise Tax Act* s. 274. Several provinces have a provincial income tax GAAR, to counter interprovincial planning schemes. See Notes to Reg. Part IV (before Reg. 400), and cases listed above. (Quebec also imposes a 50% penalty on a GAAR assessment; and *Tax Administration Act* s. 69.5.3 makes a business assessed this penalty ineligible for contracts with Quebec public bodies for 5 years [*Act respecting contracting by public bodies* ss. 21.1, 21.1.1].) Ontario *Land Transfer Tax Act*: s. 12.1. The UK has a General Anti-Abuse Rule: see tinyurl.com/uk-gaar. For tax avoidance rules in 38 countries, see Chodikoff (ed.), *Transfer Pricing (A Global Guide From Practical Law)* (Thomson Reuters UK, 2017, 670pp.). See also Huynh & Barnicke, "EU Anti-Tax-Avoidance Proposal", 24(2) *Canadian Tax Highlights* (ctf.ca) 4-5 (Feb. 2016) (re draft measures released Jan, 28, 2016).

See also Schwartz, *GAAR Interpreted* (Carswell, looseleaf or *Taxnet Pro* Reference Centre), including list of cases currently pending before the Tax Court; Bowman et al., "GAAR", 2009 Cdn Tax Foundation conference report, 2:1-23; Powrie, "GAAR", 2010 conference report, 8:1-32; Vidal & Prieur, "Criteria for Moral Judgment in Taxation", 2011 conference report, 36:1-27; Li & Hwong, "GAAR in Action", 61(2) *Canadian Tax Journal* 321-66 (2013); Pound, "GAAR at 25", 61(Supp.) *CTJ* 355-64 (2013); "Policy Forum: GAAR", 62(1) *CTJ* 111-164 (2014); Samtani & Kutyan, "GAAR Revisited", 62(2) *CTJ* 401-28 (2014); Goulard, "General Anti-Avoidance Rule Update", 2017 conference report, 36:1-8; Nanji & Biringer, "The General Anti-Avoidance Rule and its Application to the Loss Streaming Rules", XXII(2) *Corporate Finance* (Federated Press) 2-13 (2019); Duholke et al., "GAAR: 30 Years Later", 2018 conference report, 26:1-20; Carr, Finn & Wolfe, "GAAR: An Economic Test?", 68(1) *CTJ* 351-90; Krishna, "General Anti-Avoidance Rule" (*Practical Insights*, *Taxnet Pro* Tax Disputes Centre, Nov. 2020, 39pp.).

In *Taiga Building Products v Deloitte*, 2014 BCSC 1083, Deloitte recommended Taiga use a plan that was later assessed under GAAR. Taiga's lawsuit against Deloitte was dismissed, in part because Taiga settled with CRA without appealing its assessment. See Murray, "Contingency Fee Arrangements", 311 *Canadian GST/HST Monitor* (CCH) 1-5 (Aug. 2014). (See 237.1(1)"tax shelter" Notes for more on lawsuits against tax advisors.)

For the requirement to report transactions that may be subject to GAAR (and parallel Quebec rules), see Notes to 237.3.

Income Tax Folios: S4-F7-C1: Amalgamations of Canadian corporations [replaces IT-474R2]; S7-F1-C1: Split-receipting and deemed fair market value.

Interpretation Bulletins: IT-291R3: Transfer of property to a corporation under subsection 85(1); IT-489R: Non-arm's length sale of shares to a corporation.

Information Circulars: 88-2 and Supplement: General anti-avoidance rule — section 245 of the *Income Tax Act*.

I.T. Technical News: 3 (loss utilization within a corporate group); 9 (loss consolidation within a corporate group); 16 (*Neuman* case; *Duha Printers* case and GAAR statistics; *Continental Bank* case); 19 (Change in position in respect of GAAR — section 7); 22 (general anti-avoidance rule); 25 (refreshing losses); 30 (corporate loss utilization transactions; tax avoidance); 32 (update on GAAR reviews); 34 (income trust reorganizations: q.3; loss consolidation — unanimous shareholder agreements; sale of tax

losses; loss consolidation — provincial tax; creation of capital losses; general anti-avoidance rule and audit issues/concerns); 44 (update on committees).

Transfer Pricing Memoranda: TPM-02: Repatriation of funds by non-residents — Part XIII assessments.

CRA Audit Manual: 10.11.6: Tax avoidance and general anti-avoidance provision (GAAR).

Advance Tax Rulings: ATR-41: Convertible preferred shares; ATR-42: Transfer of shares; ATR-43: Utilization of a non-resident-owned investment corporation as a holding corporation; ATR-44: Utilization of deductions and credits within a related corporate group; ATR-47: Transfer of assets to Realtyco; ATR-50: Structured settlement; ATR-53: Purification of a small business corporation; ATR-54: Reduction of paid-up capital; ATR-55: Amalgamation followed by sale of shares; ATR-56: Purification of a family farm corporation; ATR-57: Transfer of property for estate planning purposes; ATR-58: Divisive reorganization; ATR-60: Joint exploration corporations; ATR-66: Non-arm's length transfer of debt followed by a winding-up and a sale of shares.

(3) Avoidance transaction — An avoidance transaction means any transaction

(a) that, but for this section, would result, directly or indirectly, in a tax benefit, unless the transaction may reasonably be considered to have been undertaken or arranged primarily for *bona fide* purposes other than to obtain the tax benefit; or

(b) that is part of a series of transactions, which series, but for this section, would result, directly or indirectly, in a tax benefit, unless the transaction may reasonably be considered to have been undertaken or arranged primarily for *bona fide* purposes other than to obtain the tax benefit.

Related Provisions: 237.3(1) — Definition applies to reportable-transaction rules; 248(10) — Series of transactions; Reg. 310"tax avoidance policy" — Where transaction re life insurance policy is avoidance transaction; Reg. 5907(2.02) — Foreign affiliate surplus calculations — avoidance transaction.

Notes: See Notes to 245(2), and see 237.3 re mandatory reporting of avoidance transactions.

The function of 245(3) is "to remove from the ambit of the GAAR transactions or series of transactions that may reasonably be considered to have been undertaken or arranged primarily for a non-tax purpose. The majority of tax benefits claimed by taxpayers on their annual returns will be immune from the GAAR as a result of s. 245(3). The GAAR was enacted as a provision of last resort in order to address abusive tax avoidance, it was not intended to introduce uncertainty in tax planning": *Canada Trustco*, 2005 SCC 54, para. 21.

"If there are both tax and non-tax purposes to a transaction, it must be determined whether it was reasonable to conclude that the non-tax purpose was primary. If so, the GAAR cannot be applied to deny the tax benefit": *Canada Trustco*, para. 27.

"The taxpayer cannot avoid the application of the GAAR by merely stating that the transaction was undertaken or arranged primarily for a non-tax purpose. The Tax Court judge must weigh the evidence to determine whether it is reasonable to conclude that the transaction was not undertaken or arranged primarily for a non-tax purpose. The determination invokes reasonableness, suggesting that the possibility of different interpretations of the events must be objectively considered": *Canada Trustco*, para. 29.

"The expression 'non-tax purpose' has a broader scope than the expression 'business purpose'. For example, transactions that may reasonably be considered to have been undertaken or arranged primarily for family or investment purposes would be immune from the GAAR under s. 245(3)... If at least one transaction in a series of transactions is an 'avoidance transaction', then the tax benefit that results from the series may be denied under the GAAR": *Canada Trustco*, paras. 33-34.

"Where ... the Minister assumes that the tax benefit resulted from a series of transactions rather than a single transaction, it is necessary to determine if there was a series, which transactions make up the series, and whether the tax benefit resulted from the series. If there is a series that results, directly or indirectly, in a tax benefit, it will be caught by s. 245(3) unless each transaction within the series could 'reasonably be considered to have been undertaken or arranged primarily for *bona fide* purposes other than to obtain [a] tax benefit'. If any transaction within the series is not undertaken primarily for a *bona fide* non-tax purpose that transaction will be an avoidance transaction": *Copthorne Holdings*, 2011 SCC 63, para. 40.

However, "Subsection 245(3) ... does not permit a transaction to be considered to be an avoidance transaction because some alternative transaction that might have achieved an equivalent result would have resulted in higher taxes." (Dept. of Finance Technical Notes, quoted in *Canada Trustco* para. 30; *Evans*, 2005 TCC 684, para. 22.)

For 245(3)(b), "a subset of transactions within a series of transactions is an avoidance transaction unless the *subset of transactions* may reasonably be considered to have been undertaken or arranged primarily for *bona fide* purposes other than to obtain the tax benefit. ... the conclusion that a series of transactions was undertaken primarily for *bona fide* non-tax purposes does not preclude a finding that the primary purpose of one or more steps within the series was to obtain a tax benefit": *MacKay*, 2008 FCA 105, para. 21, leave to appeal denied 2009 CarswellNat 19 (SCC).

In both *Triad Gestco*, 2012 FCA 258, and *Global Equity*, 2012 FCA 272 (leave to appeal denied 2013 CarswellNat 932 (SCC)), creation of a trust, payment of a nominal stock dividend by issuing high-low shares, and sale of common shares to the trust, to shift value from common to preferred shares and create a loss, were avoidance transactions (*Triad* para. 37, *Global* para. 10: TCC findings not challenged at the FCA).

In *1207192 Ontario*, 2012 FCA 259 (leave to appeal denied 2013 CarswellOnt 3394 (SCC)), the purpose of a series of transactions was creditor-proofing, but the TCC had found one step in the series to be an avoidance transaction. This was a "finding of mixed fact and law that must stand absent a palpable and overriding factual error or an extricable error of law" (para. 6). Each step had to be viewed objectively, rather than on the taxpayer's subjective motivation (para. 20).

"The act of choosing or deciding among alternative available transactions or structures to accomplish a non-tax purpose, based in whole or in part upon the differing tax result of each, is not a transaction" and thus not an avoidance transaction: *Spruce Credit Union*, 2012 TCC 357, para. 93; aff'd 2014 FCA 143, paras. 60-61 (the judge "was explaining correctly that the existence of an alternative transaction is but one factor to consider in assessing whether the requirements for an avoidance transaction are met", and "the Judge also did not err in stating that tax considerations may play a primary role in the choices a taxpayer makes without the chosen transaction being 'primarily' tax motivated").

There was an avoidance transaction in *Grenon*, 2021 TCC 30 (under appeal to FCA), paras. 554-569, in structuring income funds to be mutual fund trusts into which G's RRSP could invest to carry on his businesses.

There was no avoidance transaction in: *McClarty Family Trust*, 2012 TCC 80 (scheme avoided 120.4 and converted owner's dividends to family trust capital gains: genuine creditor-proofing purpose due to litigation threat); *Swirsky*, 2013 TCC 73 (aff'd on other grounds 2014 FCA 36) (primary purpose of S selling shares to his spouse was creditor-proofing; *Loblaw Financial*, 2018 TCC 182 (rev'd 2020 FCA 79 without discussing GAAR; SCC appeal heard May 13/21), paras. 290-320 (Barbados bank sub not set up primarily for tax purposes); *Custeau*, 2020 QCCA 1496 (upward PUC averaging in 1998, due to regional development fund investments, was done to save business from financial crisis, not with any thought of tax savings); *Damis Properties (Sabel Investments)* (under appeal to FCA as *Microbjo Properties*), 2021 TCC 24 (160(1) was unexpectedly avoided).

For CRA interpretation see VIEWS doc 2006-0195991C6.

See also Angelo Nikolakakis, "Policy Forum: Discerning an Avoidance Transaction", 57(2) *Canadian Tax Journal* 294-306 (2009); and end of Notes to 245(2).

Information Circulars: 88-2 and Supplement: General anti-avoidance rule — section 245 of the *Income Tax Act*.

Advance Tax Rulings: ATR-41: Convertible preferred shares; ATR-42: Transfer of shares; ATR-44: Utilization of deductions and credits within a related corporate group; ATR-54: Reduction of paid-up capital; ATR-55: Amalgamation followed by sale of shares; ATR-56: Purification of a family farm corporation; ATR-57: Transfer of property for estate planning purposes; ATR-58: Divisive reorganization.

(4) Application of subsec. (2) — Subsection (2) applies to a transaction only if it may reasonably be considered that the transaction

   (a) would, if this Act were read without reference to this section, result directly or indirectly in a misuse of the provisions of any one or more of

      (i) this Act,

      (ii) the *Income Tax Regulations*,

      (iii) the *Income Tax Application Rules*,

      (iv) a tax treaty, or

      (v) any other enactment that is relevant in computing tax or any other amount payable by or refundable to a person under this Act or in determining any amount that is relevant for the purposes of that computation; or

   (b) would result directly or indirectly in an abuse having regard to those provisions, other than this section, read as a whole.

Related Provisions: 237.3(6) — No misuse or abuse required if reportable transaction not reported and penalty is unpaid; ITCIA 4.1 — Application of GAAR to tax treaty interpretation.

Notes: See Notes to 245(2).

The Supreme Court of Canada explained 245(4) in *Canada Trustco*, 2005 SCC 54:

"In effect, the analysis of the misuse of the provisions and the analysis of the abuse having regard to the provisions of the Act read as a whole are inseparable" (para. 39).

"[There will be] a finding of abusive tax avoidance when a taxpayer relies on specific provisions ... to achieve an outcome that those provisions seek to prevent. As well, abusive tax avoidance will occur when a transaction defeats the underlying rationale of the provisions that are relied upon. An abuse may also result from an arrangement that circumvents the application of certain provisions, such as specific anti-avoidance rules, in a manner that frustrates or defeats [their] object, spirit or purpose" (para. 45).

"Unless the Minister can establish that the avoidance transaction frustrates or defeats the purpose for which the tax benefit was intended to be conferred, it is not abusive" (para. 52).

"...abusive tax avoidance may be found where the relationships and transactions as expressed in the relevant documentation lack a proper basis relative to the object, spirit or purpose of the provisions that are purported to confer the tax benefit, or where they are wholly dissimilar to the relationships or transactions that are contemplated by the provisions" (para. 60).

"... a finding of abuse is only warranted where the opposite conclusion — that the avoidance transaction was consistent with the object, spirit or purpose of the provisions of the Act that are relied on by the taxpayer — cannot be reasonably entertained. In other words, the abusive nature of the transaction must be clear" (para. 62).

Purpose or result? In *Lipson*, 2009 SCC 1, para. 34: "care should be taken not to shift the focus of the analysis to the 'overall purpose' of the transactions. Such an approach might incorrectly imply that the taxpayer's motivation or the purpose of the transaction is determinative.... it may be preferable to refer to the 'overall result', which more accurately reflects the wording of s. 245(4)." A transaction's purpose is irrelevant to finding misuse or abuse: *1245989 Alberta Ltd. (Wild)*, 2018 FCA 114, para. 45.

"The 'implied exclusion' [*expressio unius*] argument is that 'there is reason to believe that if the legislature had meant to include a particular thing within its legislation, it would have referred to that thing expressly' ... the implied exclusion argument is misplaced where it relies exclusively on the text of the ... provisions without regard to their underlying rationale. If such an approach were accepted, it would be a full response in all GAAR cases, because the actions of a taxpayer will always be permitted by the text of the Act": *Copthorne Holdings*, 2011 SCC 63, paras. 108-111. Circumvention of the PUC grind rules in 87(3) frustrated and defeated their purpose, and thus was an abuse.

Later legislative amendment does not mean using the pre-amendment rule was abuse, unless it "close[d] a blatant loophole": *Triad Gestco*, 2012 FCA 258, para. 56, citing *Water's Edge* (2002 FCA 291) as an example. In *Oxford Properties*, 2018 FCA 30, paras. 89-91 (leave to appeal denied 2018 CarswellNat 7871 (SCC)), the TCC had said the addition of 88(1)(d)(ii.1) meant 88(1)(d) had been abused, but the FCA said the purpose was already present and the amendment means simply that GAAR is no longer needed to get the right result. In *Univar*, 2017 FCA 207, paras. 27-28, a 2016 amendment did not make a 2007 transaction abusive. All of *Jabin*, *Landrus*, *Antle*, *120792 Ontario*, *Gwartz*, *Deans Knight* and *Rogers Enterprises* (TCC) denied that amendments indicate pre-amendment abuse. See also *Dynar*, 1997 CanLII 359 (SCC), para. 163 (dissenting opinion); David Nathanson, "Subsequent Amendments", 26(3) *Canadian Tax Highlights* (ctf.ca) 1-2 (March 2018).

Which transactions? In *Lipson*, 2009 SCC 1, para. 34, the majority (4:3) stated: "the misuse and abuse must be related to the specific transactions forming part of the series. However, the entire series of transactions should be considered in order to determine whether the individual transactions within the series abuse one or more provisions of the Act. Individual transactions must be viewed in the context of the series". The Crown must identify in its pleadings what provisions it claims were abused and how: *Birchcliff Energy*, [2013] 3 C.T.C. 2169 (TCC).

Alternative transactions that would not lead to tax are relevant in showing no abuse: *Univar* (above), para. 19 (so avoiding 212.1(1) with 212.1(4) was not abusive when it would not have applied to an arm's length sale).

Morality: The terms "misuse" and "abuse" do not imply moral opprobrium, as taxpayers are "entitled to select courses of action or enter into transactions that will minimize their tax liability": *Copthorne* (above), para. 65. GAAR applies only "when the abusive nature of the transaction is clear": para. 68.

Which schemes work? Attribution rules applying in reverse (74.1(1)) was abusive in *Lipson*, 2009 SCC 1. *Income splitting* is not inherently abusive: see 74.1(1) Notes. *Loss refreshing* via loss consolidation transactions is not abusive, provided 111(5) and similar loss-limitation rules are not circumvented: see 111(5) Notes. *Surplus stripping (dividend stripping)*: see 84.1(1) Notes. See also cases in 245(2) Notes.

Creating paper losses is abusive: "the capital gain system is generally understood to apply to real gains and real losses": *Triad Gestco*, 2012 FCA 258; "there must be an air of economic or business reality" to a business loss: *Global Equity Fund*, 2012 FCA 272, para. 63 (leave to appeal denied 2013 CarswellNat 932 (SCC)). However, the test is not that there be an "actual reduction in wealth" or "actual economic loss": *Global*, para. 60.

Taxpayers are not entitled to see drafts of policy options considered in developing legislation (under Ontario Freedom of Information legislation): *John Doe*, 2014 SCC 36 (see Notes to 241(1) for more on Access to Information issues). Determining policy for GAAR is a "question of law" for which current government documents may be irrelevant and inadmissible: *Madison Pacific [MP Western]*, 2019 FCA 19 (leave to appeal denied 2019 CarswellNat 3243 (SCC)), para. 28.

See also Darmo & Fournier, "Recent Developments Regarding the Application of Subsection 245(4)", 2011 Cdn Tax Foundation conference report, 37:1-33; Denis Lacroix, "GAAR: Observations on the Concept of Abuse", 61(Supp.) *Canadian Tax Journal* 182-94 (2013); Kristen Wang, "GAAR: The Search for Object, Spirit and Purpose", 18(3) *Tax for the Owner-Manager* (ctf.ca) 5-6 (July 2018); Awad, "Is Your Plan Astute or Abusive?", 15(5) *Tax Hyperion* (Carswell) 1-4 (Sept-Oct 2018).

245(4) amended by 2004 Budget, for transactions entered into after Sept. 12, 1988, to extend to misuse or abuse of the Regulations, ITARs, tax treaties and other legislation (e.g., *Indian Act* s. 87 — see Notes to 81(1)(a)). This addressed several pending treaty-shopping appeals, and overrules *Fredette*, [2001] 3 C.T.C. 2468 (TCC) and *Rousseau-*

Houle, 2001 CarswellNat 1126 (TCC) (Crown's FCA appeal discontinued), which held that GAAR did not apply to misuse of the Regulations. The massive retroactivity of this amendment was held valid in *MIL (Investments) S.A.*, 2007 FCA 236, paras. 27-28 (but the Tax Court found facts to prevent GAAR from applying). Such retroactivity is legal but undesirable: Thomas McDonnell, "Retroactivity: Policy and Practice", 2006 Cdn Tax Foundation conference report, 2:1-33. The retroactive amendment "cannot apply at ... appellate review, after the parties argued their cases and the Tax Court judge rendered his decision on the basis of the GAAR as it read prior to the amendment": *Canada Trustco*, 2005 SCC 54, para. 7.

I.T. Technical News: See under 245(2).

CRA Audit Manual: 15.11.3: Tax treaties — general anti-avoidance rule (GAAR).

Advance Tax Rulings: ATR-42: Transfer of shares; ATR-44: Utilization of deductions and credits within a related corporate group; ATR-54: Reduction of paid-up capital; ATR-55: Amalgamation followed by sale of shares; ATR-56: Purification of a family farm corporation; ATR-58: Divisive reorganization.

(5) Determination of tax consequences — Without restricting the generality of subsection (2), and notwithstanding any other enactment,

(a) any deduction, exemption or exclusion in computing income, taxable income, taxable income earned in Canada or tax payable or any part thereof may be allowed or disallowed in whole or in part,

(b) any such deduction, exemption or exclusion, any income, loss or other amount or part thereof may be allocated to any person,

(c) the nature of any payment or other amount may be recharacterized, and

(d) the tax effects that would otherwise result from the application of other provisions of this Act may be ignored,

in determining the tax consequences to a person as is reasonable in the circumstances in order to deny a tax benefit that would, but for this section, result, directly or indirectly, from an avoidance transaction.

Notes: In *Lipson*, 2009 SCC 1, the majority (4:3) stated (para. 51): "When considering the application of s. 245(5), a court must be satisfied that there is an avoidance transaction that satisfies the requirements of s. 245(4), that s. 245(5) provides for the tax consequences and that the tax benefits that would flow from the abusive transactions should accordingly be denied. The court must then determine whether these tax consequences are reasonable in the circumstances."

A penalty for failing to withhold could not apply when the withholding obligation arose only under GAAR: *Copthorne Holdings*, 2007 TCC 481, paras. 75-78 [aff'd on other grounds 2009 FCA 163, 2011 SCC 63].

In *Triad Gestco*, 2012 FCA 258, the FCA stated that on a "value shift" where value was transferred from common to preferred shares to create a capital loss on the common shares, and GAAR denied the loss, if there were a "credible scenario indicating that the preferred shares were to be sold" (para. 59), the taxpayer could have requested 245(5) be used to adjust the tax consequences on the sale of those shares.

In *Grenon*, 2021 TCC 30 (under appeal to FCA), paras. 609-631, where G structured income funds to be mutual fund trusts into which his RRSP could invest to carry on business, the appropriate tax consequences were to recharacterize the RRSP gains as income from non-qualified investments (NQIs), and to apply the 1% monthly Part X.1 tax on NQIs.

245(5)(a) and (b) amended by 2004 Budget to add "exemption or exclusion", for transactions entered into after Sept. 12, 1988.

(6) Request for adjustments — Where with respect to a transaction

(a) a notice of assessment, reassessment or additional assessment involving the application of subsection (2) with respect to the transaction has been sent to a person, or

(b) a notice of determination pursuant to subsection 152(1.11) has been sent to a person with respect to the transaction,

any person (other than a person referred to in paragraph (a) or (b)) shall be entitled, within 180 days after the day of sending of the notice, to request in writing that the Minister make an assessment, reassessment or additional assessment applying subsection (2) or make a determination applying subsection 152(1.11) with respect to that transaction.

Related Provisions: 166.1 — Extension of time by Minister; 244(10) — Proof that no notice of objection filed; 244(14), (14.1) — Date when notice sent; *Interpretation Act* 27(5) — Meaning of "within 180 days".

Notes: In *2763478 Canada Inc.*, 2018 FCA 209, para. 68, the Court noted that a related taxpayer could have applied for relief from double tax under 245(6), but did not.

245(6) closing words amended by 2010 budget bill #2, effective Dec. 15, 2010, to change "mailing" to "sending" (to accommodate electronic notices under 244(14.1)).

CRA Audit Manual: 11.5.10: Loss determination.

(7) Exception — Notwithstanding any other provision of this Act, the tax consequences to any person, following the application of this section, shall only be determined through a notice of assessment, reassessment, additional assessment or determination pursuant to subsection 152(1.11) involving the application of this section.

Notes: On its face, 245(7) seems to say that an Notice of Assessment must explicitly refer to GAAR, and that the CRA would not be able to apply GAAR when considering an objection if it was not applied at the assessment level. However, in *S.T.B. Holdings*, 2002 FCA 386; leave to appeal denied 2003 CarswellNat 754 (SCC), the Courts held that 245(7) must be read in the context of 245(6)–(8), and that "following" refers to a subsequent application of GAAR. No specific reference to GAAR is needed on a notice of reassessment.

Can or should a taxpayer self-assess GAAR? No, but even so, taxpayers must consider the risk of GAAR because interest runs on a GAAR assessment from the 248(1)"balance-due day" for the year: *Quinco Financial*, 2018 FCA 137. (Earlier cases on this question were *Copthorne Holdings*, 2007 TCC 481, para. 78 (aff'd on other grounds 2009 FCA 163, 2011 SCC 63); *J.K. Read Engineering*, 2014 TCC 309.)

(8) Duties of Minister — On receipt of a request by a person under subsection (6), the Minister shall, with all due dispatch, consider the request and, notwithstanding subsection 152(4), assess, reassess or make an additional assessment or determination pursuant to subsection 152(1.11) with respect to that person, except that an assessment, reassessment, additional assessment or determination may be made under this subsection only to the extent that it may reasonably be regarded as relating to the transaction referred to in subsection (6).

Related Provisions: 165(1.1) — Limitation of right to object to assessments or redetermination; 169(2)(a) — Limitation of right to appeal.

Notes [s. 245]: See Notes to 245(2).

Definitions [s. 245]: "amount", "assessment" — 248(1); "avoidance transaction" — 245(3); "day of sending" — 244(14), (14.1); "Minister", "person" — 248(1); "series of transactions" — 248(10); "tax benefit", "tax consequences" — 245(1); "taxable income" — 2(2), 248(1); "taxable income earned in Canada" — 115(1), 248(1); "tax treaty" — 248(1); "transaction" — 245(1); "writing" — *Interpretation Act* 35(1).

Information Circulars [s. 245]: 88-2 and Supplement: General anti-avoidance rule — section 245 of the *Income Tax Act*.

246. (1) Benefit conferred on a person — Where at any time a person confers a benefit, either directly or indirectly, by any means whatever, on a taxpayer, the amount of the benefit shall, to the extent that it is not otherwise included in the taxpayer's income or taxable income earned in Canada under Part I and would be included in the taxpayer's income if the amount of the benefit were a payment made directly by the person to the taxpayer and if the taxpayer were resident in Canada, be

(a) included in computing the taxpayer's income or taxable income earned in Canada under Part I for the taxation year that includes that time; or

(b) where the taxpayer is a non-resident person, deemed for the purposes of Part XIII to be a payment made at that time to the taxpayer in respect of property, services or otherwise, depending on the nature of the benefit.

Related Provisions: 56(2) — Inclusion in income of indirect payments; 142.7(4) — Deemed value of property on rollover from foreign bank subsidiary to branch; 247(15) — No application to transfer pricing amount deemed to be dividend for non-resident withholding tax.

Notes: 246(1) can be a standalone basis for assessment: *Massicotte (Consultants Pub Création)*, 2008 FCA 60 (leave to appeal denied 2008 CarswellNat 3438 (SCC)). It applied in *Massicotte* and in *Levert*, 2017 TCC 208 and *Grewal*, 2020 FC 356 (under appeal to FCA). In *Ludmer*, 2018 QCCS 3381, paras. 619-622 (aff'd on other grounds 2020 QCCA 697; leave to appeal denied 2021 CarswellQue 2160 (SCC)); it was reasonable for CRA to apply it. 246(1) was held not to apply in: *Pelletier*, 2002 CarswellNat 4855 (TCC); *943372 Ontario*, 2007 TCC 294; *Shahsavar*, 2005 TCC 184; *Osinski*, 2013 TCC 71.

CRA will not apply 246(1) where a father's company lends money interest-free to (or invests in retractable preferred shares of) his son's company (but 56(2) might apply): VIEWS doc 2005-0140961C6; or where a Cdn corp reimburses its non-resident parent for the value of stock options granted to its employees: 2010-0356401E5. For some rulings that 246(1) does not apply see 2007-0242871R3 (foreign divisive reorg); 2010-0369661R3 (reorg of incestuous shareholdings of Western Coal [Smit, "Recent Transactions of Interest", 2011 Cdn Tax Foundation conference report, 10:5-10]); 2012-0464841R3 (trust distribution); 2016-0630761R3 and 2017-0693751R3 (rollover of foreign-affiliate shares to another FA followed by transfer to related Cdn resident corp); 2018-0750471R3 (amalgamation of NPO and public foundation); 2018-0775221R3 (foreign investment with foreign government involvement). On application to a 15(1) indirect benefit to a non-resident, see 2019-0798821C6 [2019 IFA q.7]. On application to life insurance premiums paid by a corp for its shareholder see 2007-0257251E5, 2010-0359421C6. CRA prefers to use other provisions as the primary basis of assessment: 2009-0344991I7, but will use 246(1) if nothing else applies: 2009-0344251I7, 2010-0363361R3, 2014-0527842I7; and will apply it to tax paid by a US LLC for a Cdn-resident individual who indirectly holds an interest in the LLC through an Alberta ULC: 2011-0411491E5 [Lang, "Section 246 Catches Tax Payments Made by a US LLC", XVIII(1) *Corporate Finance* (Federated Press) 2084-85 (2012)]; May 2013 ICAA roundtable (tinyurl.com/cra-abtax), q. 22.

For the meaning of "indirectly" in the opening words, see Notes to 17.1(1).

Note that a 246(1) inclusion is not subject to income-splitting tax under 120.4, as is a shareholder appropriation under s. 15 (see 120.4(1)"split income"(a)(ii), (c)(ii)(B)).

See also Roth et al., *Canadian Taxation of Trusts* (ctf.ca, 2016), pp. 891-910; Smith & Pidborochynski, "Indirect Shareholder Benefits", 2009 Ontario Tax Conference (ctf.ca), 10:1-21; Stilwell, "Subsection 246(1)", 12(1) *Tax Hyperion* (Carswell) 5-6 (Jan. 2015).

Interpretation Bulletins: IT-432R2: Benefits conferred on shareholders.

CRA Audit Manual: 24.11.0: Indirect payments and benefits.

Transfer Pricing Memoranda: TPM-02R: Secondary transfer pricing adjustments, repatriation and Part XIII tax assessments.

(2) Arm's length — Where it is established that a transaction was entered into by persons dealing at arm's length, *bona fide* and not pursuant to, or as part of, any other transaction and not to effect payment, in whole or in part, of an existing or future obligation, no party thereto shall be regarded, for the purpose of this section, as having conferred a benefit on a party with whom the first-mentioned party was so dealing.

Interpretation Bulletins [subsec. 246(2)]: IT-432R2: Benefits conferred on shareholders.

Transfer Pricing Memoranda: TPM-03: Downward transfer pricing adjustments under subsec. 247(2).

Related Provisions [s. 246]: 56(2) — Indirect payments; 245(2) — General anti-avoidance rule.

Definitions [s. 246]: "amount" — 248(1); "arm's length" — 251(1); "Canada" — 255; "non-resident", "person", "property" — 248(1); "resident in Canada" — 250; "taxable income earned in Canada" — 115(1), 248(1); "taxation year" — 249; "taxpayer" — 248(1).

Abandoned Proposed Addition — 246.1

Notes: 246.1, proposed on July 18, 2017 and dropped on Oct. 19, 2017, would have applied to conversions of dividends into capital gains. See Abandoned Proposed Amendment under 84.1(1).

PART XVI.1 — TRANSFER PRICING

247. (1) Definitions — The definitions in this subsection apply in this section.

"arm's length allocation" means, in respect of a transaction, an allocation of profit or loss that would have occurred between the participants in the transaction if they had been dealing at arm's length with each other.

Related Provisions: 9(1) — Normal computation of profit.

Notes: Definitions in 247(1) added by 1995-97 technical bill, effective for taxation years and fiscal periods that begin after 1997.

"arm's length transfer price" means, in respect of a transaction, an amount that would have been a transfer price in respect of the transaction if the participants in the transaction had been dealing at arm's length with each other.

Notes: See under 247(1)"arm's length allocation".

Information Circulars: 87-2R: International transfer pricing (archived).

"documentation-due date" for a taxation year or fiscal period of a person or partnership means

(a) in the case of a person, the person's filing-due date for the year; or

(b) in the case of a partnership, the day on or before which a return is required by section 229 of the *Income Tax Regulations* to be filed in respect of the period or would be required to be so filed if that section applied to the partnership.

Transfer Pricing Memoranda: TPM-09: Reasonable efforts under section 247.

"qualifying cost contribution arrangement" means an arrangement under which reasonable efforts are made by the participants in the arrangement to establish a basis for contributing to, and to contribute on that basis to, the cost of producing, developing or acquiring any property, or acquiring or performing any services, in proportion to the benefits which each participant is reasonably expected to derive from the property or services, as the case may be, as a result of the arrangement.

Related Provisions: 247(4) — Contemporaneous documentation.

Notes: The word "derive" as used in this definition may be interpreted broadly: see Notes to 94(1)"resident portion".

See under 247(1)"arm's length allocation".

Transfer Pricing Memoranda: TPM-07: Referrals to the transfer pricing review committee.

"tax benefit" has the meaning assigned by subsection 245(1).

Notes: Definition "tax benefit" amended retroactive to its introduction (taxation years and fiscal periods that begin after 1997) by 2004 Budget bill, to use the new definition of the term in 245(1) in place of the old one.

"transaction" includes an arrangement or event.

Related Provisions: 152(4)(b)(iii)(A) — Definition applies to extension of reassessment period; 233.1(1)"transaction" — Parallel definition for reporting non-arm's length transactions with non-residents; 245(1) — Parallel definition for general anti-avoidance rule.

Transfer Pricing Memoranda: TPM-06: Bundled transactions.

"transfer price" means, in respect of a transaction, an amount paid or payable or an amount received or receivable, as the case may be, by a participant in the transaction as a price, a rental, a royalty, a premium or other payment for, or for the use, production or reproduction of, property or as consideration for services (including services provided as an employee and the insurance or reinsurance of risks) as part of the transaction.

Information Circulars: 87-2R: International transfer pricing (archived).

"transfer pricing capital adjustment" of a taxpayer for a taxation year means the total of

(a) all amounts each of which is

(i) $\frac{1}{2}$ of the amount, if any, by which the adjusted cost base to the taxpayer of a capital property (other than a depreciable property) is reduced in the year because of an adjustment made under subsection (2), or

(ii) [Repealed]

(iii) the amount, if any, by which the capital cost to the taxpayer of a depreciable property is reduced in the year because of an adjustment made under subsection (2); and

(b) all amounts each of which is that proportion of the total of

(i) $\frac{1}{2}$ of the amount, if any, by which the adjusted cost base to a partnership of a capital property (other than a depreciable property) is reduced in a fiscal period that ends in the year because of an adjustment made under subsection (2), and

(ii) [Repealed]

(iii) the amount, if any, by which the capital cost to a partnership of a depreciable property is reduced in the period because of an adjustment made under subsection (2),

that

(iv) the taxpayer's share of the income or loss of the partnership for the period

is of

> (v) the income or loss of the partnership for the period,

and where the income and loss of the partnership are nil for the period, the income of the partnership for the period is deemed to be $1,000,000 for the purpose of determining a taxpayer's share of the partnership's income for the purpose of this definition.

Notes: Subparas. (a)(ii) and (b)(ii) repealed by 2016 budget bill #2, effective 2017, as part of changing the eligible capital property rules to CCA Class 14.1 (see 20(1)(b) Notes). Before 2017, read:

[(a)](ii) ¾ of the amount, if any, by which the adjusted cost base to the taxpayer of an eligible capital expenditure of the taxpayer in respect of a business is reduced in the year because of an adjustment made under subsection (2), or

. . . . .

[(b)](ii) ¾ of the amount, if any, by which the adjusted cost base to a partnership of an eligible capital expenditure of the partnership in respect of a business is reduced in a fiscal period that ends in the year because of an adjustment made under subsection (2), and

247(1)"transfer pricing capital adjustment" amended by 2000 Budget, this version effective for taxation years that end after Oct. 17, 2000 (with transitional rules for years ending earlier in 2000).

Information Circulars: 87-2R: International transfer pricing (archived).

"transfer pricing capital setoff adjustment" of a taxpayer for a taxation year means the amount, if any, that would be the taxpayer's transfer pricing capital adjustment for the year if the references, in the definition "transfer pricing capital adjustment", to "reduced" were read as "increased".

"transfer pricing income adjustment" of a taxpayer for a taxation year means the total of all amounts each of which is the amount, if any, by which an adjustment made under subsection (2) (other than an adjustment included in determining a transfer pricing capital adjustment of the taxpayer for a taxation year) would result in an increase in the taxpayer's income for the year or a decrease in a loss of the taxpayer for the year from a source if that adjustment were the only adjustment made under subsection (2).

"transfer pricing income setoff adjustment" of a taxpayer for a taxation year means the total of all amounts each of which is the amount, if any, by which an adjustment made under subsection (2) (other than an adjustment included in determining a transfer pricing capital setoff adjustment of the taxpayer for a taxation year) would result in a decrease in the taxpayer's income for the year or an increase in a loss of the taxpayer for the year from a source if that adjustment were the only adjustment made under subsection (2).

Notes: See under 247(1)"arm's length allocation".

Proposed **247(1.1)** (March 19, 2019 Budget) has been replaced by 247(2.1).

(2) Transfer pricing adjustment — Where a taxpayer or a partnership and a non-resident person with whom the taxpayer or the partnership, or a member of the partnership, does not deal at arm's length (or a partnership of which the non-resident person is a member) are participants in a transaction or a series of transactions and

(a) the terms or conditions made or imposed, in respect of the transaction or series, between any of the participants in the transaction or series differ from those that would have been made between persons dealing at arm's length, or

(b) the transaction or series

> (i) would not have been entered into between persons dealing at arm's length, and

> (ii) can reasonably be considered not to have been entered into primarily for *bona fide* purposes other than to obtain a tax benefit,

any amounts (in subsection (2.1) referred to as the **"initial amounts"**) that would be determined for the purposes of this Act (if this Act were read without reference to this section and section 245) in respect of the taxpayer or the partnership for a taxation year or fiscal period shall be adjusted (in this section referred to as an **"adjustment"**) to the quantum or nature of the amounts (in subsection

(2.1) referred to as the **"adjusted amounts"**) that would have been determined if,

(c) where only paragraph (a) applies, the terms and conditions made or imposed, in respect of the transaction or series, between the participants in the transaction or series had been those that would have been made between persons dealing at arm's length, or

(d) where paragraph (b) applies, the transaction or series entered into between the participants had been the transaction or series that would have been entered into between persons dealing at arm's length, under terms and conditions that would have been made between persons dealing at arm's length.

Enacted Amendment — Corresponding adjustment in other country (MLI Art. 17)

Application: See the pages before the Canada-US Treaty for the Multilateral Instrument (MLI), which effectively amends most of Canada's tax treaties (but not Canada-US). MLI Article 17 provides that when a country makes a transfer-pricing adjustment, the other country "shall make an appropriate adjustment" to the tax on income in that country. However, see Notes to MLI Art. 17:2 and 17:3; Art. 17 might not actually have any impact in Canada.

Possible Future Amendment — Transfer Pricing Rules (Consultation)

Federal Budget, Chapter 10, April 19, 2021: *Protecting the Fairness and Integrity of Our Tax System*

The Federal Court of Appeal decision in *Her Majesty The Queen v Cameco Corporation* [2020 FCA 112, leave to appeal denied to Crown 2021 CarswellNat 377 (SCC) — ed.] has highlighted concerns with the application of Canada's domestic transfer pricing rules. Taking into account the court's reasoning, the government believes that, without reform, shortcomings in the current transfer pricing rules can encourage the inappropriate shifting of corporate income out of Canada, artificially reducing corporations' taxes owed in Canada. If not addressed, this poses a risk to the integrity of Canada's corporate income tax system. Furthermore, Canada must ensure that there is not a separate set of rules that large corporations can play by.

Budget 2021 announces the government's intention to consult on Canada's transfer pricing rules with a view to protecting the integrity of the tax system while preserving Canada's attractiveness as a destination for new investment and business activity.

In the coming months, the Department of Finance will release a consultation paper to provide stakeholders with an opportunity to comment on possible measures to improve Canada's transfer pricing rules. The government will also take next steps to strengthen and modernize Canada's general anti-avoidance rule [s. 245 — ed.], as announced in the 2020 Fall Economic Statement.

Related Provisions: 115.2(4) — Non-resident investment or pension fund deemed not to deal at arm's length with Canadian service provider; 142.7(4) — Deemed value of property on rollover from foreign bank subsidiary to branch; 152(4)(b)(iii), 152(4)(b.4) — Reassessment deadline extended by 3 years; 233.1 — Reporting transactions with related non-residents; 233.8 — Large multinationals — country-by-country reporting; 247(2.1) — Ordering — apply transfer pricing adjustments before other provisions; 247(3) — Penalty; 247(6) — Tiers of partnerships; 247(7) — Exclusion for loan to subsidiary; 247(7.1) — Exclusion for guarantee provided to subsidiary; 247(10) — Adjustment only if appropriate; 247(12)–(16) — Secondary adjustment — assessment of non-resident withholding tax; Canada-U.S. Tax Treaty:Art. IX — Adjustments on transactions between related persons; Canada-U.S. Tax Treaty:Art. XII:7 — Where royalties excessive due to special relationship.

Notes: 247(2) implements the rules for transfer pricing (**TP**). See the various CRA Transfer Pricing Memoranda.

Canada and over 100 other countries have signed the Multilateral Competent Authority Agreement, to implement OECD's TP documentation requirements and country-by-country reporting: tinyurl.com/mcaa-oecd. 233.8 now requires such reporting, for multinational groups with revenues over €750 million.

CRA follows OECD's TP guidelines (**TPG**): Information Circular 87-2R (cancelled because it does not reflect current TPG: CRA notice, Feb. 26, 2020). TPG are relevant but "not controlling as if they were a Canadian statute": *GlaxoSmithKline*, 2012 SCC 52, para. 20; *Cameco*, 2020 FCA 112, paras. 65-70 (leave to appeal denied 2021 CarswellNat 377 (SCC)). TPG do not require a transaction-by-transaction approach: *GlaxoSmithKline*, para. 40. Their core requirement is to follow the "arm's length principle" if possible: the transaction should be at the price that would apply between arm's length parties. (An interest-free loan to an active foreign sub is exempt: 247(7).) See Steeves, "Business Restructurings", 59(1) *Canadian Tax Journal* 151-66 (2011); review of the 2010 TPG at 59(1) *CTJ* 176-77; Vidal, *Introduction to International Tax in Canada* (Carswell, 8th ed., 2020), chap. 21. For CRA comment on the 2010 TPG see Transfer Pricing Memorandum TPM-14; docs 2011-0427311C6, 2012-0454201C6. OECD amended TPG in 2015; Canada announced in the 2016 Budget that CRA applies the revisions, "as they are consistent with current practices". See Nikolakakis & Halvorson, "The Future of International Tax and Transfer-Pricing Planning", 2015 Cdn Tax Foundation conference report, 23:1-78. OECD updated TPG again in 2017; CRA considers this clarifies the pre-existing rules so it applies TPG, and other OECD guidance, retroactively (but claims this is not retroactive): 2018-0779931C6 [2018 CTF q.4]; Milet & Horton, "CRA's Interpretation of the 2017 OECD Transfer Pricing Guidelines", 103 *International Tax* (CCH) 10-15 (Dec. 2018). However, in *Cameco*, the FCA in 2020 applied the 2010 TPG (paras. 67, 70) without mentioning the later amendments. See also Perez-Navarro, *Transfer pricing implications of the COVID-19 pandemic: New OECD guidance* (OECD, Dec. 2020).

A TP adjustment applies for all purposes of the Act including Part XIII withholding tax. It can apply in computing FAPI, except that CRA will not normally challenge TP accepted by a foreign tax authority if its guidelines use the arm's-length principle: VIEWS doc 2017-0691191C6 [2017 IFA q.2]. A TP adjustment applies before any other provision: 247(2.1). A corresponding foreign TP adjustment may require recalculating a foreign affiliate's FAPI "earnings" and "net earnings": VIEWS docs 2017-0729431R3, 2019-0798781C6 [2019 IFA q.10].

TP adjustments can also be done under the authority of a tax treaty. See Notes to Canada-US tax treaty Art. IX:1.

TP is a particular problem with intangible property, where businesses move ownership offshore to benefit from deductions in Canada and other high-tax jurisdictions. See Heather Kerr, "Update on Tax Issues Relateed to Intellectual Property", 2007 Cdn Tax Foundation conference report, 8:1-24, including discussion of the multi-billion dollar assessments of GlaxoSmithKline (IRS) and Merck (CRA).

The first major TP decision (albeit under former 69(2)) is *GlaxoSmithKline*, 2012 SCC 52, sending the matter back for a new decision from the TCC. The SCC ruled that the price paid for ranitidine (the active ingredient in ulcer drug Zantac), to be "reasonable in the circumstances", needed to take into account "economically relevant characteristics" such as related agreements entitling Glaxo to use the Zantac brand name. See Akin & Siegal, "GlaxoSmithKline", 2012 Cdn Tax Foundation conference report 24:1-22.

The second major decision is *General Electric Capital*, 2010 FCA 344, also under 69(2). A 1% guarantee fee paid to GECC's parent to guarantee GECC's debt were held not to exceed its value and so was deductible. The Tax Court accepted expert evidence that GECC's borrowing rate would have been 1.83% higher without the guarantees. See Ian Bradley & David Glicksman, "GE Capital Case", XVII(1) *Corporate Finance* (Federated Press) 1947-52 (2011). In *General Electric*, 2011 TCC 564 (under appeal to FCA), CRA was permitted to contest the same issue for related taxpayers and different taxation years, as *res judicata* did not apply.

The third major decision is *Alberta Printed Circuits*, [2011] 5 C.T.C. 2001 (TCC). Circuit board setup work had been moved to a Barbados company. The Court applied the OECD Guidelines and ruled the Comparable Uncontrolled Price (CUP) method was the best to use (using "internal CUP" based on the Canadian company's charges to its customers for the setup work), and that CRA should not have used the Transactional Net Margin Method. The company's appeal was mostly allowed, though $880,000 of CRA's $3.4m adjustment was upheld re additional charges for services. "The analysis is a strongly fact-driven one, carried out in the context of basic business principles, or the 'real business world' .... the test requires a consideration of all relevant factors that a reasonable business person in the Appellant's shoes would consider.... factors or circumstances that exist solely because of the non-arm's length relationship of the parties should not be ignored" (paras. 158-160).

The fourth major decision is *McKesson Canada*, 2013 TCC 404 (FCA appeal discontinued A-48-14), where a sale of MC's $460 million receivables to its Luxembourg parent, done to reduce MC's income, was held to be at too much of a discount; the Court's acceptance of CRA's reduction of the discount rate from 2.2% to 1.01% was not a "recharacterization of the transaction" (para. 127). See McMechan, "Transfer-Pricing Appeal", 22(2) *Canadian Tax Highlights* (ctf.ca) 3-4 (Feb. 2014); Hanna & Zioulas, "McKesson Canada", XIX(3) *International Tax Planning* (Federated Press) 1316-22 (2014). See also 2014 TCC 266, where Boyle J recused himself from the remaining issues (including costs) because he was offended by McKesson's FCA factum accusing him of being untruthful and deceitful in his reasons. McKesson's request to amend its Notice of Appeal was allowed: 2014 FCA 290. McKesson asked the FCA for a new trial, arguing the recusal reasons "tainted" the appeal. However, McKesson's SEC "10-K" filing reveals that the TP dispute was settled under an agreement in principle after its March 31, 2015 year-end, and that McKesson took a charge of $122 million.

The fifth major decision is *Marzen Artistic Aluminum*, 2016 FCA 34. Window manufacturer M paid fees to its Barbados affiliate Bco (an "empty shell" that provided no services of value), ostensibly to run M's US marketing operation (USco). The FCA upheld the TCC's denial of the deduction and application of the OECD Guidelines' CUP method; Bco and USco could not be combined for purposes of determining a reasonable payment to Bco.

The sixth major decision is *Cameco*, 2018 TCC 195; aff'd 2020 FCA 112 (criticizing the TCC for 197 pages of "factual data dump" in the TCC reasons: para. 5); leave to appeal denied 2021 CarswellNat 377 (SCC). Cameco's prices for sale of uranium to a Swiss sub, though tax motivated, were not a sham and did not trigger 247(2)(a), as they were within an "arm's length range": TCC para. 856; FCA paras. 90-94. Nor did 247(2)(b) and (d) apply, as discussed further below. CRA suggests that *Cameco* might be overturned by legislation: International Fiscal Assn CRA Q&A (Aug. 6, 2020), tinyurl.com/ifa-covid-qa, q. 17. See also Grigoriu, "Recharacterization: Cameco", XIV(3) *Resource Sector Taxation* (Federated Press) 8-16 (2020).

The seventh major decision is *Agracity*, 2020 TCC 91. Sales of herbicide to Canadian farmers through a Barbados corp were legitimate as direct sales in Canada were illegal,

and Agracity's service fees to that corp were within the arm's-length range (para. 112). See Huguet, "Echoes of Cameco", 69(1) *Canadian Tax Journal* 224-33 (2021) [Zhao, "Success for Taxpayer in Disputing Transfer Pricing Adjustment", 116 *International Tax* (CCH, Feb. 2021)].

In *1143132 Ontario*, 2009 TCC 477, 247(2) applied to sales to a Barbados subsidiary. Preliminary decisions: *Burlington Resources*, 2013 TCC 231, 2015 TCC 71 (FCA appeal discontinued A-173-15), 2017 TCC 144 and 2019 TCC 143 (guarantee fees) [but Crown dropped TP issues: 2020 TCC 32, paras. 4, 33, 105] (appeal conditionally settled at FCA A-72-20); *HSBC Canada*, 2010 TCC 462 (FCA appeal discontinued A-333-10) and 2011 TCC 37; *Suncor Energy*, 2016 CarswellNat 7053 (TCC); *Sundog Distributing*, 2010 TCC 392 (FCA appeal discontinued A-327-10) (limitation period in Canada-Barbados treaty did not prevent assessment); *Terasen International*, 2012 TCC 408 (Crown's FCA appeal discontinued A-439-12) (amendments to Reply); *Canadian Imperial Bank of Commerce*, 2018 TCC 248 (re number of expert witnesses allowed).

For a non-tax case on TP: *Nortel Networks*, 2014 ONSC 6973 (Ont. SCJ), paras. 130-57 (allocation of pension-related restructuring costs within group).

See also the Australian decisions in: *Chevron*, [2017] FCAFC 62 (interest borrowing rate was unreasonable [Kinsella, "*Chevron*", XXI(1) *Corporate Finance* (Federated Press) 38-45 (2018)]); *Glencore*, [2020] FCAFC 187 (allocation of copper prices was reasonable); and the US Tax Court decision in *Coca-Cola*, Nov. 18, 2020, tinyurl.com/coke-tax-case (under appeal to US Court of Appeals, 11th Circuit) (foreign manufacturing affiliate profits allocated to US) [Yau, "Coca-Cola Goes Flat", XXV(1) *International Tax Planning* (Federated Press) 1-7 (2021)].

247(2) may apply to non-commercial situations (e.g., an interest-free loan from a parent in Canada to a child living outside Canada). CRA was not generally expected to apply it in this way, but see Powrie, "Imputed Return on Capital", 5(10) *Canadian Tax Highlights* 75 (Oct. 1997); Bernstein, "Non-Business Transfer Pricing", 13(1) *CTH* 4-5 (Jan. 2005); "Non-Commercial Transfer Pricing", 13(6) *CTH* 5-6 (June 2005); Sambrook & Noble, "An Individual's Exposure to Transfer Pricing", 56(3) *Canadian Tax Journal* 753-70 (2008). In VIEWS doc 2014-0532051I7, below-market rent paid to a relative did not trigger 247(2); but 2020-0852221C6 [2020 APFF q.10] says 247(2) applies to a loan by an individual to a related foreign corp.

247(2)(b) and (d) apply an objective test based on hypothetical persons, not the particular taxpayer, and require that *no* arm's length persons would have entered into *that* transaction under any terms and conditions: *Cameco*, 2020 FCA 112, paras. 43-44, 82 (leave to appeal denied 2021 CarswellNat 377 (SCC)). One does not ask what only the Canadian taxpayer would have done: para. 55. Nor do (b) and (d) permit a court to ignore the corporate structure used and treat a Canadian corp as if it had bought and sold the goods its foreign sub did: para. 73. Nor do they allow CRA to reallocate a foreign sub's profits on the basis the Canadian corp would not have entered into transactions with the sub had they been at arm's length: para. 81.

The 247(2)(b)(ii) test is GAAR-like but without the 245(4) "no misuse or abuse" defence. CRA considers 247(2)(b) to be an anti-avoidance provision; on how CRA deals with related double tax competent authority requests, see 2020 IFA Roundtable q.3.

On recharacterization see also Bloom, "Paragraph 247(2)(b) Demystified", 1783 *Tax Topics* (CCH) 1-5 (May 11, 2006); Bloom & Vincent, "Canada's (Two) Transfer Pricing Rules", 2011 Cdn Tax Foundation conference report, 20:1-40; Rheault, "Recharacterization of Transactions", 2011 conference report, 21:1-16; Alty & Studniberg, "The Corporate Capital Structure: Thin Capitalization and the 'Recharacterization' Rules in 247(2)(b) and (d)", 62(4) *Canadian Tax Journal* 1159-1202 (2014); Montes & Goguen, "Recharacterization of Transactions Under Section 247", 2018 conference report, 21:1-25.

Texts on s. 247: Vincent & Ranger, *Transfer Pricing in Canada*, 2018 ed. (Carswell, 551pp+564pp appendix); Jamal Hejazi, *Transfer Pricing: The Basics* (LexisNexis Canada, 2009, 212pp.); Vidal, *Introduction to International Tax in Canada* (Carswell, 8th ed., 2020), chaps. 21-24; Li & Cockfield, *International Taxation in Canada*, 4th ed. (LexisNexis, 2018), chap. 4; Collier & Andrus, *Transfer Pricing and the Arm's Length Principle After BEPS* (Oxford Univ. Press, 2017, 336pp).

Articles on s. 247: 2002 Cdn Tax Foundation conference report, papers 16, 17, 22; 2003 conf report, papers 12, 13; 2004 conf report, paper 27; Maclagan, "Transfer Pricing Update", 2006 conf report, 17:1-18; John Oatway, "Current Issues in Transfer Pricing", 2007 conf report 22:1-24; Casas & Haslhofer, "Transfer Pricing and the Oil & Gas Industry", V(2) *Resource Sector Taxation* (Federated Press) 354-59 (2007); Purdy & Tang, "Transfer Pricing for Financial Services", 2009 conf report 23:1-38; Minard, "Limitation Period Considerations for Transfer Pricing Adjustments", 56 *McCarthy Tétrault on Tax Disputes* (CCH) 5-7; Oatway & Berthaudin, "Transfer Pricing Current Issues", 2010 conf report 22:1-18; Murray, "Transfer Pricing: Current Issues and Developments in Arbitration", 2010 conf report 23:1-17; Mustard et al., "Administrative and Competent Authority Issues in Transfer Pricing", 2012 Tax Dispute Resolution conf. report (ctf.ca), 13:1-13; Zorzi & Rizzuto, "The Rise and Dominance of Transfer Pricing in Canada", 61(Supp.) *CTJ* 415-35 (2013); Rogers & Tfaily, "An Overview of Transfer Pricing for Financial Instruments", 2014 conf report, 23:1-14; Ludwin, "Application of the Transactional Profit Split Method in Canada", 44(2) *Tax Management International Journal* (Bloomberg BNA) 98-102 (Feb. 13, 2015); Pichhadze, "The Arm's Length Comparable in Transfer Pricing", 7(3) *World Tax Journal* (2015); Robillard, "Is There a Sixth Comparability Factor in Canadian Transfer Pricing?", 63(2) *CTJ* 375-95 (2015); Hejazi & Kirkey, "Best Practices in Determining Arm's Length Interest Rates", XXI(1) *International Tax Planning* (Federated Press) 2-11 (2017); Rand et al, "Transfer Pricing and Dispute Resolution" (panel discussion), 2016 conf report, 17:1-15; Pichhadze, "The Role of Contract Interpretation in Transfer-Pricing Law", 65(4)

CTJ 849-92 (2017); Chodikoff & Loyer, "Transfer Pricing", *Practical Insights* (*Taxnet Pro* Tax Disputes Centre), Jan. 2018 (35pp); Tfaily, "Limit of Intercompany Debt Pricing", 26(8) *CTH* 7-8 (Aug. 2018); Tan, "The Emergence of the Profit-Split Method", 27(2) *CTH* 1-2 (Feb. 2019); Beswick, "Transfer Pricing and Transactions Between Foreign Entities", 67(1) *CTJ* 187-208 (2019); Tfaily, "Loan Comparables", 27(8) *CTH* 11-12 (Aug. 2019); Suarez, "Transfer Pricing in Canada", 96(9) *Tax Notes International* 781-813 (Dec. 2, 2019); Kobetsky, "The Transfer-Pricing Profit-Split Method After BEPS", 67(4) *CTJ* 1077-1105 (2019); Kohli, "Sharing COVID-19 Assistance with Foreign Entities", *COVID-19 and Canadian Tax* (ctf.ca) 5 (July 2020); Boidman, "Relationship Between *Cameco* and *Glencore*", 115 *International Tax* (CCH, Dec. 2020).

On attribution of profits to a permanent establishment, see Couzin and Vincent articles, Policy Forum, 53(2) *Canadian Tax Journal* 396-416 (2005). Annex B to the Fifth Protocol to the Canada-US Tax Treaty (reproduced after the treaty), para. 9, provides that OECD Transfer Pricing Guidelines principles apply in determining profits attributable to a PE under the treaty, and gives further details. See also the arbitration process in Art. XXVI:6, 7 (and Annex B to the Fifth Protocol) of the treaty; the process in Art. 23:6 of the Canada-UK treaty; and Multilateral Instrument (MLI) Art. 18-26 (reproduced before the Canada-US treaty).

For guarantee fees see Richard Tremblay & James Fuller, "Tax Consequences of Cross-Border Guarantee Fees", X(3) *International Tax Planning* (Federated Press) 716-22 (2001) (and the *General Electric* case above).

On calculating management fees that will withstand a TP audit, see Emma Purdy & Jeffrey Zanchelli, "Calculating and Supporting Management Fees", 44(1) *Canadian Tax Journal* 157-87 (1996).

Government assistance should not reduce cost when using a cost-based methodology: Transfer Pricing Memorandum TPM-17 [Mercier & Tfaily, "Does TPM-17 Solve or Create Issues?", 27(1) *Canadian Tax Highlights* (ctf.ca) 7-8 (Jan. 2019)]. CRA will apply TPM-17 to COVID-19 assistance: International Fiscal Assn CRA Q&A (Aug. 6, 2020), tinyurl.com/ifa-covid-qa, q.12; 2020 IFA Roundtable q.5 (example showing assistance does not reduce cost).

Using other ITA provisions: *15(9)* is more specific when it applies to a loan, so 247(2) will not be applied: VIEWS doc 2008-0280041R3. *18(1)(a)* and lack of evidence were used to deny management fees paid to a related company in Pakistan in *Celeste Resources*, 2017 TCC 200 (FCA appeal discontinued A-408-17). See Notes to *67* re unreasonable expenses. *69(1)*: see Vincent, "Subsection 247(2) Versus Subsection 69(1)", 13(3) *International Tax Planning* (Federated Press) 940-48 (2006). *94(2)(a) and (f)*: see 2018-0772971I7. See also 247(2.1): TP is applied before other rules.

Customs duties: A transfer price developed for 247(2) cannot be used for customs duty: Information Circular 06-1; however, if there is an agreement to adjust prices to match a TP assessment, customs duty paid on importation might be later reduced: CBSA Customs Memorandum D13-4-5 paras. 3, 23, 29. See also Werner Kreissl, "Customs valuation and transfer pricing: Closer to concordance?", 19(3) *Commodity Tax News* (CICA) 15-16 (March 2012); and *Tax Alert*, tinyurl.com/ey-alert-xfr.

The TP rules of the foreign country must also be considered, especially when doing business in the U.S (*Internal Revenue Code* §482). See David Chodikoff (ed.), *Transfer Pricing & Tax Avoidance* (Thomson Reuters UK, 2014, 591pp.) (discusses TP rules in 33 countries); Robert Misey, "A Primer on Transfer Pricing for Canadian Companies Conducting Business in the United States", IX(4) *International Tax Planning* (Federated Press), 664-68 (2000); Glicklich & Goldfarb, "US Transfer-Pricing Rules for Services Apply in 2007", 54(4) *Canadian Tax Journal* 1019-34 (2006); Willard Taylor, "Ninth Circuit Reverses Itself and Upholds the Supremacy of the Arm's Length Standard", XVI(3) *Corporate Finance* (Federated Press) 1875-78 (2010) (re *Xilinx*). See also MLI Art. 17, reproduced before the Canada-US treaty.

TP may have effects on GST/HST or another country's VAT: Matesanz, "Transfer Pricing Adjustments and VAT", 26(5) *International VAT Monitor* (ibfd.org) 295-99 (Sept./Oct. 2015) and 28(1) 6-10 (Jan/Feb 2018). Note that CRA GST/HST auditors may want to *increase* costs of acquiring intangibles and services from outside Canada (for *Excise Tax Act* ss. 217, 218.01), while income tax auditors want to *reduce* the same costs!

Assessments under 247(2) must be approved by the CRA Transfer Pricing Review Committee in the Intl Tax Division (ITD): tinyurl.com/xprc-cra; IC 87-2R paras. 46, 178; Transfer Pricing Memorandum TPM-13; VIEWS doc 2012-0444071C6. As of Sept. 2020 the members were: Venetia Putureanu [Chair, Venetia.Putureanu@cra.gc.ca, 343-291-4709] (Director); Blair Vokey, Mark Turnbull, Frederic Bourgeois, Jeffery Lapine, Chantal Tubie (Managers and Senior Advisers); Govindaray Nayak (Chief Economist); Elyse Goudie and Samantha Greenberg (Senior Technical Specialists); Shauna Pittman or Caroline Ebata or Ryan Hall (Legal Services Branch). For 247(2)(b) 2nd- or 3rd-stage recharacterization referrals, it also includes Len Lubbers and Suzanne Saydeh (Tax Avoidance Division), and Alexandra Diebel (Finance). As of Sept. 2020, the committee had considered 142 247(2)(b) recharacterizations (58 denied, 35 assessed, 49 ongoing); and 798 247(3) penalty referrals (336 recommended, 462 not). (*Access to Information Act* disclosure)

Objections to s. 247 assessments are mandatory referrals to CRA Headquarters Appeals if the federal tax in dispute exceeds $500,000: Ken Parkes, in "How To Deal with Transfer-Pricing Disputes", 2002 Cdn Tax Foundation conference report at 23:35. The threshold is now reportedly $1 million; this may be in *Appeals Manual* §4.5.4, but is blacked out from the copy publicly available.

CRA sometimes reassesses TP under 18(1)(a) rather than 247(2), leading to double tax because the other country's competent authority will not recognize this as a TP adjustment. See TEI submission to CRA, Dec. 4, 2012, q.11.

Non-resident withholding tax: Once a TP adjustment is determined, the excess paid to the non-resident may be a benefit subject to Part XIII tax. See 247(12).

Taxpayers may enter into Advance Pricing Arrangements with CRA and another jurisdiction's tax authority; since Feb 4, 2021, CRA no longer imposes "cost recovery charges" for an APA. Contact Competent Authority Services Division, map-apa.paaapp@cra.gc.ca. (For businesses with sales under $50 million or a TP transaction under $10m, see Information Circular 94-4R-SR Special Release, March 18, 2005.) See also: CRA annual *Advance Pricing Arrangement Program Report*; Transfer Pricing Memorandum TPM-10 on retroactive application (rollback) of an APA; VIEWS docs 2011-0427261C6 (reasons for reduced use of APAs); 2018-0748191C6 [2018 IFA q.6]; 2020-0862501C6 [2020 CTF q.12] (impact of COVID-19); *Checklist 10 — Advance Pricing Agreements*, *Taxnet Pro* Corporate Tax Centre (2021, 5pp); Markham, "Advance Pricing Arrangements: Are Australia's Recent Reforms Relevant to Canada?", 61(2) *Canadian Tax Journal* 387-409 (2013); Bernstein, "Transfer Pricing May Be EC State Aid", 23(12) *Canadian Tax Highlights [CTH]* (ctf.ca) 2-4 (Dec. 2015); Rheault & Tan, "Managing Transfer-Pricing Risk", 2019 Cdn Tax Foundation conference report, 31:1-21. CRA considers itself administratively bound by an APA, but it may not be legally enforceable: Clearwater, "A Note on the Enforceability of Advance Pricing Agreements", VII(2) *Tax Litigation* (Federated Press) 438-42 (1999). In the US, the IRS could not arbitrarily cancel an APA: *Eaton Corp*, TC Memo 2017-147 [Doobay, "Cancellation of Eaton's APAs", 25(9) *CTH* 9-10 (Sept. 2017)].

CRA frequently uses data from other businesses in the same industry in determining transfer prices. See Joel Nitikman, "Obtaining Disclosure of Secret Comparables in Canadian Transfer-Pricing Litigation", 50(1) *Canadian Tax Journal* 28-63 (2002).

See also VIEWS docs 2011-0427291C6 (non-coordination of TP audits with IRS); 2011-0427301C6 (Competent Authority conclusions will not apply to transactions with other countries; overbroad information requests; use of economists on audits); 2013-0474431E5 (where Canco seconds employees to a FA and charges a markup, 95(2)(b) will deem part of FA's income to be FAPI); 2013-0478621I7 (247(2) applies to arm's length sale of subsidiary as part of sale of US public corp [Stilwell, "Transfer Pricing Between Arm's Length Parties?", 11(5) *Tax Hyperion* (Carswell) 3-4 (May 2014)]); 2013-0490751I7 (impact on cumulative eligible capital balance and capital dividend account); 2014-0538201C6 [2014 APFF q.26] (arm's length standard takes precedence over FMV); 2016-0631631I7 (TP adjustment to ACB of property can be made even if that year is statute-barred); 2017-0694231I7 (upward TP adjustment does not reduce FA's exempt surplus, nor is it a contribution of capital that increases the shares' ACB [Barnicke & Huynh, "Transfer-Pricing Adjustments and CFAs", 26(4) *Canadian Tax Highlights* (ctf.ca) 8 (April 2018)]); CRA reply to TEI, Dec. 4, 2018, q. D.5 (TP audit procedures); "Notice to tax professionals" (July 5, 2019) (hybrid mismatch arrangement involving forward subscription agreement: 247(2) applied); Barnicke & Huynh, "CRA on Subsection 247(2) and FAs", 25(6) *Canadian Tax Highlights [CTH]* (ctf.ca) 8-9 (June 2017) (re 2017 IFA).

Text between (b) and (c) amended by 2021 budget bill #1, for tax years that begin after March 18, 2019 (see 247(2.1), added at the same time).

247(2) added by 1995-97 technical bill, effective for taxation years and fiscal periods that begin after 1997. For pre-1988 247(2), see Notes at end of 247.

Information Circulars: 87-2R: International transfer pricing (archived); 94-4R: International transfer pricing — advance pricing arrangements (APAs); 94-4R-SR: APAs for small businesses; 06-1: Income tax transfer pricing and customs valuation.

I.T. Technical News: 32 (application of penalties); 34 (update on transfer pricing); 41 (transfer pricing and dispute resolution); 44 (update on committees).

Transfer Pricing Memoranda: TPM-02: Repatriation of funds by non-residents — Part XIII assessments; TPM-03: Downward transfer pricing adjustments under subsec. 247(2); TPM-04: Third-party information; TPM-06: Bundled transactions; TPM-11: Advance pricing arrangement (APA) rollback; TPM-12: Accelerated Competent Authority Procedure (ACAP); TPM-13: Referrals to the transfer pricing review committee; TPM-14: 2010 update of the OECD transfer pricing guidelines; TPM-15: Intragroup services and section 247 of the ITA; TPM-16: Role of multiple year data in transfer pricing analyses; TPM-17: The impact of government assistance on transfer pricing.

CRA Audit Manual: 15.8.0: Non-arm's length transactions with non-residents; 15.9.0: Transfer pricing; 15.10.0: Tax havens.

Forms: T106: Information return of non-arm's length transactions with non-residents.

(2.1) Ordering — For the purpose of applying subsection (2) in the context of the other provisions of this Act, the following order is to be applied:

(a) first determine each of the initial amounts;

(b) then make the adjustments, if any, to each of the initial amounts; and

(c) then apply each of the provisions of this Act (other than subsection (2) and, for greater certainty, including section 245) using the adjusted amounts.

Notes: The March 19, 2019 Budget proposed a simpler 247(1.1): "For the purpose of applying the provisions of this Act, the adjustments under Part XVI.1 shall be made before any other provision of the Act is applied." This was criticized as confusing, and 247(2.1) (released July 2019) replaces it, but still may not work right, and may trigger double tax or double penalties. For criticism see CPA Canada/CBA Joint Committee letter, Nov. 5, 2019; Roy, "Proposed Transfer Pricing Ordering Rules", 109 *International Tax* (CCH, Dec. 2019); Smit, in "Recent Developments", 2019 Cdn Tax Foundation conference report at 1:9-11; Fournier-Gendron, "Amendments to the Act", 27(12) *Canadian Tax Highlights* (ctf.ca) 5-6 (Dec. 2019); Boidman & Kandev, "Evaluating Canada's Attempt to Reconcile General Transfer-Pricing Rules and Specific Antiabuse Provisions", 98(6) *Tax Notes International* (taxnotes.com) 699-708 (May 11, 2020); Fraser & Szeto, "Impact of Amendments to Transfer Pricing Rules on Outbound Lending", XXIV(3) *International Tax Planning* (Federated Press) 9-13 (2020).

247(2.1) added by 2021 budget bill #1, for tax years that begin after March 18, 2019 (along with amending 247(2) between (b) and (c) and repealing 247(8)).

(3) Penalty

— A taxpayer (other than a taxpayer all of whose taxable income for the year is exempt from tax under Part I) is liable to a penalty for a taxation year equal to 10% of the amount determined under paragraph (a) in respect of the taxpayer for the year, where

(a) the amount, if any, by which

(i) the total of

(A) the taxpayer's transfer pricing capital adjustment for the year, and

(B) the taxpayer's transfer pricing income adjustment for the year

exceeds the total of

(ii) the total of all amounts each of which is the portion of the taxpayer's transfer pricing capital adjustment or transfer pricing income adjustment for the year that can reasonably be considered to relate to a particular transaction, where

(A) the transaction is a qualifying cost contribution arrangement in which the taxpayer or a partnership of which the taxpayer is a member is a participant, or

(B) in any other case, the taxpayer or a partnership of which the taxpayer is a member made reasonable efforts to determine arm's length transfer prices or arm's length allocations in respect of the transaction, and to use those prices or allocations for the purposes of this Act, and

(iii) the total of all amounts, each of which is the portion of the taxpayer's transfer pricing capital setoff adjustment or transfer pricing income setoff adjustment for the year that can reasonably be considered to relate to a particular transaction, where

(A) the transaction is a qualifying cost contribution arrangement in which the taxpayer or a partnership of which the taxpayer is a member is a participant, or

(B) in any other case, the taxpayer or a partnership of which the taxpayer is a member made reasonable efforts to determine arm's length transfer prices or arm's length allocations in respect of the transaction, and to use those prices or allocations for the purposes of this Act,

is greater than

(b) the lesser of

(i) 10% of the amount that would be the taxpayer's gross revenue for the year if this Act were read without reference to subsection (2), subsections 69(1) and (1.2) and section 245, and

(ii) $5,000,000.

Related Provisions: 152(4)(b)(iii) — Reassessment deadline extended by 3 years; 247(4) — Requirement for contemporaneous documentation; 247(3) — Determination of partner's gross revenue; 247(9) — Anti-avoidance rule re increases in gross revenue; 247(11) — Payment and assessment of penalty.

Notes: See Notes to 239(1) and 247(2). Colborne & Barrett, "The Reasonable Efforts Standard", XX(4) *International Tax Planning* (Federated Press) 1424-27 (2015); Colborne et al., "Subsection 247(3)", 64(1) *Canadian Tax Journal* 229-43 (2016); Mustard et al. (panel discussion), "Transfer Pricing: What are Reasonable Efforts", 2015 Cdn Tax Foundation conference report, 32:1-33; Pandher, "Transfer-Pricing Penalties", 6(3) *Canadian Tax Focus* (ctf.ca) 8-9 (Aug. 2016).

The penalty applied in *Alberta Printed Circuits* and *Marzen Artistic Aluminum*, discussed in Notes to 247(2) (though in *Marzen*, paras. 4 and 216, the transfer-pricing adjustment was reduced to below $5 million so no penalty was actually payable).

CRA levied $192 million in transfer-pricing penalties in 2018-2019: *Departmental Results Report* (tinyurl.com/cra-results), p. 24 (no data in 2019-20 Report).

See also VIEWS doc 2016-0631631I7 (no time limit on 247(3) assessment as it is a Part XVI.1 assessment; penalty on acquisition of capital property applies to year of acquisition, not disposition).

247(3) added by 1995-97 technical bill, for 247(2) adjustments for tax years and fiscal periods that begin after 1998, except for transactions completed before Sept. 11, 1997.

Information Circulars: 87-2R: International transfer pricing (archived); 94-4R: International transfer pricing — advance pricing arrangements (APAs); 94-4R-SR: APAs for small businesses; 06-1: Income tax transfer pricing and customs valuation.

Transfer Pricing Memoranda: TPM-03: Downward transfer pricing adjustments under subsec. 247(2); TPM-06: Bundled transactions; TPM-07: Referrals to the transfer pricing review committee; TPM-09: Reasonable efforts under section 247; TPM-11: Advance pricing arrangement (APA) rollback.

CRA Audit Manual: 15.9.4: Transfer pricing penalties — reasonable effort; 28.9.0: Penalties under the transfer pricing provisions.

(4) Contemporaneous documentation

— For the purposes of subsection (3) and the definition "qualifying cost contribution arrangement" in subsection (1), a taxpayer or a partnership is deemed not to have made reasonable efforts to determine and use arm's length transfer prices or arm's length allocations in respect of a transaction or not to have participated in a transaction that is a qualifying cost contribution arrangement, unless the taxpayer or the partnership, as the case may be,

(a) makes or obtains, on or before the taxpayer's or partnership's documentation-due date for the taxation year or fiscal period, as the case may be, in which the transaction is entered into, records or documents that provide a description that is complete and accurate in all material respects of

(i) the property or services to which the transaction relates,

(ii) the terms and conditions of the transaction and their relationship, if any, to the terms and conditions of each other transaction entered into between the participants in the transaction,

(iii) the identity of the participants in the transaction and their relationship to each other at the time the transaction was entered into,

(iv) the functions performed, the property used or contributed and the risks assumed, in respect of the transaction, by the participants in the transaction,

(v) the data and methods considered and the analysis performed to determine the transfer prices or the allocations of profits or losses or contributions to costs, as the case may be, in respect of the transaction, and

(vi) the assumptions, strategies and policies, if any, that influenced the determination of the transfer prices or the allocations of profits or losses or contributions to costs, as the case may be, in respect of the transaction;

(b) for each subsequent taxation year or fiscal period, if any, in which the transaction continues, makes or obtains, on or before the taxpayer's or partnership's documentation-due date for that year or period, as the case may be, records or documents that completely and accurately describe each material change in the year or period to the matters referred to in any of subparagraphs (a)(i) to (vi) in respect of the transaction; and

(c) provides the records or documents described in paragraphs (a) and (b) to the Minister within 3 months after service, made personally or by registered or certified mail, of a written request therefor.

Related Provisions: 233.8 — Large multinationals — country-by-country reporting; 244(5) — Proof of service by mail or request under 247(4)(c); 247(1) — Documentation-due date; 248(7) — Mail sent under 247(4)(c) deemed received on day mailed; *Interpretation Act* 27(5) — Meaning of "within 3 months".

Notes: See Notes to 247(2), and Transfer Pricing Memorandum TPM-09.

In *Marzen Artistic Aluminum*, aff'd 2016 FCA 34, the TCC applied a 247(3) penalty because Marzen had not created adequate documentation to justify huge payments to its Barbados affiliate. The FCA upheld the decision without discussing the penalty.

247(4)(c) demands are often served at the beginning of a transfer-pricing audit, not just to non-compliant taxpayers. The documentation must be provided within 3 months, with no extensions allowed. See Transfer Pricing Memorandum TPM-05R; Albert Baker & Gary Zed, "Transfer Pricing: Admin", 11(9) *Canadian Tax Highlights* (ctf.ca) 2 (Sept. 2003), and "Contemporaneous Documentation", 13(1) 2 (Jan. 2005).

The term "records" as used in the opening words of 247(4)(a) includes information stored electronically: see 248(1)"record".

247(4) added by 1995-97 technical bill, effective with respect to adjustments made under 247(2) for tax years and fiscal periods that begin after 1998.

See also Notes to repealed 69(2).

Information Circulars: 87-2R: International transfer pricing (archived); 94-4R: International transfer pricing — advance pricing arrangements (APAs); 94-4R-SR: APAs for small businesses.

Transfer Pricing Memoranda: TPM-02: Repatriation of funds by non-residents — Part XIII assessments; TPM-05R: Requests for contemporaneous documentation; TPM-06: Bundled transactions; TPM-07: Referrals to the transfer pricing review committee; TPM-09: Reasonable efforts under section 247.

CRA Audit Manual: 15.5.0: Foreign-based information and documentation.

(5) Partner's gross revenue — For the purpose of subparagraph (3)(b)(i), where a taxpayer is a member of a partnership in a taxation year, the taxpayer's gross revenue for the year as a member of the partnership from any activities carried on by means of the partnership is deemed to be that proportion of the amount that would be the partnership's gross revenue from the activities if it were a taxpayer (to the extent that amount does not include amounts received or receivable from other partnerships of which the taxpayer is a member in the year), for a fiscal period of the partnership that ends in the year, that

(a) the taxpayer's share of the income or loss of the partnership from its activities for the period

is of

(b) the income or loss of the partnership from its activities for the period,

and where the income and loss of the partnership from its activities are nil for the period, the income of the partnership from its activities for the period is deemed to be $1,000,000 for the purpose of determining a taxpayer's share of the partnership's income from its activities for the purpose of this subsection.

Related Provisions: 247(6) — Tiers of partnerships; 248(1) — Definition of "gross revenue".

Notes: 247(5) added by 1995-97 technical bill, effective with respect to adjustments made under 247(2) for taxation years and fiscal periods that begin after 1998, but does not apply to transactions completed before Sept. 11, 1997.

(6) Deemed member of partnership — For the purposes of this section, where a person is a member of a partnership that is a member of another partnership,

(a) the person is deemed to be a member of the other partnership; and

(b) the person's share of the income or loss of the other partnership is deemed to be equal to the amount of that income or loss to which the person is directly or indirectly entitled.

Notes: This rule looks through tiers of partnerships.

247(6) added by 1995-97 technical bill, effective for taxation years and fiscal periods that begin after 1997.

(7) Exclusion for loans to certain controlled foreign affiliates — Where, in a taxation year of a corporation resident in Canada, a non-resident person owes an amount to the corporation, the non-resident person is a controlled foreign affiliate of the corporation for the purpose of section 17 throughout the period in the year during which the amount is owing and it is established that the amount owing is an amount owing described in paragraph 17(8)(a) or (b), subsection (2) does not apply to adjust the amount of interest paid, payable or accruing in the year on the amount owing.

Notes: 247(7) permits a corporation resident in Canada to make an interest-free loan to a controlled foreign affiliate (CFA) or to charge no interest on an amount owing by a

CFA without 247(2) applying to deem interest to be payable on the amount owing, provided the affiliate uses the money to earn active business income or the amount owing arose in the course of an active business carried on by the affiliate. Note that, although 247(2) will not apply to the interest payable, it could still apply to any other term of the transaction — e.g., to adjust the amount actually owing where the amount owing is the unpaid purchase price of goods sold to the non-resident and the purchase price is not one that persons dealing at arm's length would have agreed to.

For examples of 247(7) applying see VIEWS docs 2006-0195791E5, 2010-0386201R3. Where neither 17(1) nor 247(7) applies, 247(2) may still apply: doc 2003-0033891E5; but see 2007-0240241C6. For criticism of CRA's position see Brian Bloom, "A Policy of Disengagement: How Subsection 247(2) Relates to the Act's Income-Modifying Rules", 1957 *Tax Topics* (CCH) 1-4 (Sept. 10, 2009).

247(7) amended by 1998 Budget, effective for taxation years that begin after February 23, 1998. Added by 1995-97 technical bill.

(7.1) Exclusion — certain guarantees — Subsection (2) does not apply to adjust an amount of consideration paid, payable or accruing to a corporation resident in Canada (in this subsection referred to as the "parent") in a taxation year of the parent for the provision of a guarantee to a person or partnership (in this subsection referred to as the "lender") for the repayment, in whole or in part, of a particular amount owing to the lender by a non-resident person, if

(a) the non-resident person is a controlled foreign affiliate of the parent for the purposes of section 17 throughout the period in the year during which the particular amount is owing; and

(b) it is established that the particular amount would be an amount owing described in paragraph 17(8)(a) or (b) if it were owed to the parent.

Notes: See Geoffrey Turner, "Downstream Loan Guarantees and Subsec. 247(7.1) Transfer Pricing Relief", 2166 *Tax Topics* (CCH) 1-5 (Sept. 12, 2013).

247(7.1) added by 2013 budget bill #2, subsec. 88(1) (implementing March 11, 2003 and Jan. 24, 2005 Finance comfort letters), for tax years that begin after 1997, with an election for it not to apply to years that began before Dec. 22, 2012 (see VIEWS doc 2013-0515661E5).

(8) [Repealed]

Notes: 247(8) repealed by 2021 budget bill #1, for tax years that begin after March 18, 2019. It was replaced by 247(2.1). It read:

(8) Provisions not applicable — Where subsection (2) would, if this Act were read without reference to sections 67 and 68 and subsections 69(1) and (1.2), apply to adjust an amount under this Act, sections 67 and 68 and subsections 69(1) and (1.2) shall not apply to determine the amount if subsection (2) is applied to adjust the amount.

The old rule, added by 1995-97 technical bill, was essentially that 247(2) took precedence over 67, 68, 69(1) and 69(1.2).

(9) Anti-avoidance — For the purposes of determining a taxpayer's gross revenue under subparagraph (3)(b)(i) and subsection (5), a transaction or series of transactions is deemed not to have occurred, if one of the purposes of the transaction or series was to increase the taxpayer's gross revenue for the purpose of subsection (3).

Related Provisions: 248(10) — Series of transactions.

Notes: 247(9) added by 1995-97 technical bill, for 247(2) adjustments for tax years and fiscal periods that begin after 1998, except for transactions completed before Sept. 11, 1997.

(10) No adjustment unless appropriate — An adjustment (other than an adjustment that results in or increases a transfer pricing capital adjustment or a transfer pricing income adjustment of a taxpayer for a taxation year) shall not be made under subsection (2) unless, in the opinion of the Minister, the circumstances are such that it would be appropriate that the adjustment be made.

Notes: Downward adjustments are made in only limited circumstances: Transfer Pricing Memorandum TPM-03; Information Circulars 87-2R, 71-17R6; *Income Tax Technical News* 41 (2008 Cdn Tax Foundation conference report, 3:16-17); 115.1 Notes; Baker & Zed, "Transfer Pricing", 11(9) *Canadian Tax Highlights* (ctf.ca) 2-3 (Sept. 2003). CRA may choose not to adjust under 247(2) if the taxpayer is entitled to request, or has requested, relief from double tax under tax treaty mutual-agreement procedures. Contesting a denial: Sandler & Watzinger, "Disputing Denied Downward Transfer-Pricing Adjustments", 67(2) *Canadian Tax Journal* 281-308 (2019).

The Tax Court has jurisdiction to consider a CRA 247(10) decision, even though it involves CRA discretion: *Dow Chemical*, 2020 TCC 139 (under appeal by Crown to FCA).

247(10) added by 1995-97 technical bill, for tax years and fiscal periods that begin after 1997.

Information Circulars: 87-2R: International transfer pricing (archived).

I.T. Technical News: 41 (transfer pricing and dispute resolution).

Transfer Pricing Memoranda: TPM-03: Downward transfer pricing adjustments under subsec. 247(2); TPM-12: Accelerated Competent Authority Procedure (ACAP).

(11) Provisions applicable to Part — Sections 152, 158, 159, 162 to 167 and Division J of Part I apply to this Part, with such modifications as the circumstances require.

Related Provisions: 152(4)(b)(iii) — Reassessment deadline extended by 3 years.

Notes: 247(1)"transaction" does not apply to s. 152 as imported by 247(11): *Blackburn Radio*, 2009 TCC 155.

247(11) does not provide a right of appeal of a CRA decision under 247(10): *Dow Chemical*, 2020 TCC 139 (under appeal by Crown to FCA), para. 47 (detailed discussion at paras. 31-81).

247(11) added by 1995-97 technical bill, for tax years and fiscal periods beginning after 1997.

(12) Deemed dividends to non-residents [secondary adjustment] — For the purposes of Part XIII, if a particular corporation that is a resident of Canada for the purposes of Part XIII would have a transfer pricing capital adjustment or a transfer pricing income adjustment for a taxation year, if the particular corporation, or a partnership of which the particular corporation is a member, had undertaken no transactions or series of transactions other than those in which a particular non-resident person, or a partnership of which the particular non-resident person is a member, that does not deal at arm's length with the particular corporation (other than a corporation that was for the purposes of section 17 a controlled foreign affiliate of the particular corporation throughout the period during which the transaction or series of transactions occurred) was a participant,

(a) a dividend is deemed to have been paid by the particular corporation and received by the particular non-resident person immediately before the end of the taxation year; and

(b) the amount of the dividend is the amount, if any, by which

(i) the amount that would be the portion of the total of the particular corporation's transfer pricing capital adjustment and transfer pricing income adjustment for the taxation year that could reasonably be considered to relate to the particular non-resident person if

(A) the only transactions or series of transactions undertaken by the particular corporation were those in which the particular non-resident person was a participant, and

(B) the definition "transfer pricing capital adjustment" in subsection (1) were read without reference to the references therein to "¹/₂ of" and "³/₄ of"

exceeds

(ii) the amount that would be the portion of the total of the particular corporation's transfer pricing capital setoff adjustment, and transfer pricing income setoff adjustment, for the taxation year that could reasonably be considered to relate to the particular non-resident person if

(A) the only transactions or series of transactions undertaken by the particular corporation were those in which the particular non-resident person was a participant, and

(B) the definition "transfer pricing capital adjustment" in subsection (1) were read without reference to the references therein to "¹/₂ of" and "³/₄ of".

Related Provisions: 227(8.5) — No penalty for failing to withhold tax; 247(13) — Deemed dividend reduced where funds repatriated; 247(15) — No application of 15, 56(2) or 246 where 247(12)(a) applies.

Notes: 247(12) ensures that, once 247(2) applies, there can be a "secondary adjustment" of a deemed dividend for the benefit conferred on the non-resident parent, triggering 212(2), Part XIII non-resident withholding tax. (This applied anyway via 15(1), 15(9), 56(2), 246(1) and/or 214(3)(a) [most no longer apply, per 247(15)]; see *McKesson Canada*, 2013 TCC 404, paras. 359-396 (FCA appeal discontinued A-48-14); the Canada-Luxembourg treaty limitation period for transfer-pricing adjustments did not apply to the Part XIII tax.) See Nitikman, "Section 247 — Secondary Adjustments", XVIII(1) *International Tax Planning* (Federated Press) 1224-26 (2012); Zhu,

"Tax Due Diligence for Transfer-Pricing Secondary Adjustments", 10(2) *Canadian Tax Focus* (ctf.ca) 15-16 (May 2020).

The deemed dividend is eligible for treaty withholding tax rate reduction: VIEWS doc 2018-0753621I7. A notional guarantee fee imputed by 247(2) is exempt from Part XIII tax by Canada-US treaty Art. XXII:4: 2011-0416261E5. If 247(2) reduces the amount deductible by a Canadian branch on a payment to a related non-resident, 247(12) does not reduce the 212(13.2) withholding tax: 2014-0530911I7.

CRA will not defer the Part XIII assessment pending final resolution of the TP issue, and there are no collection restrictions on that assessment (though CRA will accept security): doc 2011-0427301C6. CRA may waive the Part XIII tax if NR repays the excess, subject to conditions: 247(13)-(14); Transfer Pricing Memorandum TPM-02R.

247(12) added by 2012 budget bill #2, for transactions after March 28, 2012.

Transfer Pricing Memoranda: TPM-02R: Secondary transfer pricing adjustments, repatriation and Part XIII tax assessments.

(13) Repatriation — If a dividend is deemed by subsection (12) to have been paid by a corporation and received by a non-resident person, and a particular amount has been paid with the concurrence of the Minister by the non-resident person to the corporation,

(a) the amount of the dividend may be reduced by the amount (in this subsection referred to as the "reduction") that the Minister considers appropriate, having regard to all the circumstances, and

(b) subsections 227(8.1) and (8.3) apply as if

(i) the amount of the dividend were not reduced, and

(ii) on the day on which the particular amount was paid, the corporation paid to the Receiver General an amount equal to the amount that would be required to be withheld and remitted under Part XIII in respect of the reduction.

Related Provisions: 53(2)(c)(xiii) — ACB reduction; 227(8.5) — No penalty for failing to withhold tax; 247(14) — Interest on withholding tax where deemed dividend repatriated.

Notes: See 247(12) Notes and Transfer Pricing Memorandum TPM-02R.

A CRA decision denying relief under 247(13) would be subject to judicial review by the Federal Court. See Notes to 220(3.1).

247(13) added by 2012 budget bill #2, for transactions after March 28, 2012.

Transfer Pricing Memoranda: TPM-02R: Secondary transfer pricing adjustments, repatriation and Part XIII tax assessments.

(14) Repatriation — interest — If the amount of a dividend is reduced under paragraph (13)(a), the amount of interest payable by a taxpayer because of paragraph (13)(b) may be reduced to the amount that the Minister considers appropriate, having regard to all the circumstances, including the provision of reciprocal treatment by the country in which the non-resident person referred to in subsection (13) is resident.

Related Provisions: 247(15) — Reduction of interest at CRA's discretion.

Notes: 247(14) added by 2012 budget bill #2, for transactions after March 28, 2012.

Transfer Pricing Memoranda: TPM-02R: Secondary transfer pricing adjustments, repatriation and Part XIII tax assessments.

(15) Non-application of provisions — Section 15, subsections 56(2) and 212.3(2) and section 246 do not apply in respect of an amount to the extent that a dividend is deemed by subsection (12) (determined without reference to subsection (13)) to have been paid in respect of the amount.

Notes: 247(15) added by 2012 budget bill #2, for transactions after March 28, 2012.

Notes [former 247]: Former 247(1) repealed by 1988 tax reform, but still in effect for any transactions, one of which was entered into before April 13, 1988, entered into by a taxpayer in the course of an arrangement and in respect of which the taxpayer received from Revenue Canada, before April 13, 1988, a confirmation or opinion in writing with respect to the tax consequences. (This parallels the introduction of GAAR in 245.) It provided a dividend-stripping rule. Dividend stripping (surplus stripping) is now covered by 84.1, 183.1, 212.1, 212.2 and 212.3 as well as GAAR. See also Information Circular 88-2 para. 25.

Former 247(2) and (3), repealed by 1988 tax reform (effective 1989–90), set out a rule dealing with corporations deemed associated (see now 256(2.1)).

Proposed **247.1** in the Sept. 11, 1997 draft legislation (transfer pricing penalties and interest) was replaced by 247(11), applying all the Part I administrative rules.

Definitions [s. 247]: "adjusted amounts" — 247(2); "adjusted cost base" — 54, 248(1); "adjustment" — 247(2); "amount" — 248(1); "arm's length" — 115.2(4), 251(1); "arm's length allocation", "arm's length transfer price" — 247(1); "business" — 248(1); "capital property" — 54, 248(1); "controlled foreign affiliate" —

17(15); "corporation" — 248(1), *Interpretation Act* 35(1); "depreciable property" — 13(21), 248(1); "dividend" — 248(1); "documentation-due date" — 247(1); "eligible capital expenditure" — 14(5), 248(1); "employee", "filing-due date" — 248(1); "fiscal period" — 249.1; "gross revenue" — 247(5), (9), 248(1); "initial amounts" — 247(2); "Minister", "non-resident" — 248(1); "partnership" — see 96(1) Notes; "person", "property" — 248(1); "qualifying cost contribution arrangement" — 247(1); "reasonable efforts" — 247(4); "record" — 248(1); "resident" — 250; "series", "series of transactions" — 248(10); "tax benefit" — 247(1); "taxation year" — 249; "taxpayer" — 248(1); "transaction", "transfer price", "transfer pricing capital adjustment", "transfer pricing capital setoff adjustment", "transfer pricing income adjustment", "transfer pricing income setoff adjustment" — 247(1); "written" — *Interpretation Act* 35(1) ["writing"].

PART XVII — INTERPRETATION

248. (1) Definitions — In this Act,

["10/8 policy"] — [See at end of subsec. 248(1).]

"active business", in relation to any business carried on by a taxpayer resident in Canada, means any business carried on by the taxpayer other than a specified investment business or a personal services business;

Related Provisions: 95(1) — Meaning of "active business" of a foreign affiliate for FAPI purposes; 125(1) — Small business deduction; 125(7)"active business" — Meaning of "active business" for purposes of the small business deduction; 248(1) — Small business corporation.

Notes: The business carried on need not actually be "active": *Ollenberger*, 2013 FCA 74.

Being constantly on the look-out for new markets or in negotiations for business can constitute carrying on active business even with no sales: *Harquail (Hudon)*, 2001 FCA 320.

In *Boulanger*, 2003 FCA 332, a company was found to have no active business where its only assets for years were vacant land and cash; it had no organizational structure or employees; had done no market research or cost benefit analysis; and "was unable to conduct any major transaction with respect to the type of business it was supposed to carry on".

Life insurance proceeds may be active business income in "very rare" cases: VIEWS doc 2014-0523341C6 [2014 CALU q.7], based on *Ensite Ltd.*, [1986] 2 C.T.C. 459 (SCC) and *Atlas Industries*, [1986] 2 C.T.C. 2392 (TCC).

See also VIEWS docs 2010-0387741E5 (leasing and maintaining 6 furnished trailers appears to be active business); 2018-0768871C6 [2018 APFF q.16] (apartment buildings: depends on the facts); François Auger, "Analysis of the Notion of Business", *The Harmonization of Federal Legislation with Quebec Civil Law: Collection of Studies in Tax Law* (APFF, 2002), at 4:23-28.

Interpretation Bulletins: IT-73R6: The small business deduction; IT-406R2: Tax payable by an *inter vivos* trust.

"additional voluntary contribution" to a registered pension plan means a contribution that is made by a member to the plan, that is used to provide benefits under a money purchase provision (within the meaning assigned by subsection 147.1(1)) of the plan and that is not required as a general condition of membership in the plan;

Related Provisions: 60.2 — Refund of undeducted past service AVCs; 147.2(4) — Amount of employee's pension contributions deductible.

Notes: 248(1)"additional voluntary contribution" added by 1990 pension bill, effective 1986.

Interpretation Bulletins: IT-167R6: Registered pension plans — employee's contributions.

Registered Pension Plans Technical Manual: §1.3 (additional voluntary contributions).

"adjusted cost base" has the meaning assigned by section 54;

"adjustment time" — [Repealed]

Notes: Definition repealed by 2016 budget bill #2, effective 2017, as part of changing the eligible capital property rules to CCA Class 14.1 (see Notes to 20(1)(b)). It read "has the meaning assigned by subsection 14(5)".

"advanced life deferred annuity" has the meaning assigned by subsection 146.5(1);

Notes: Definition added by 2021 budget bill #1, effective 2020. See 146.5.

"aggregate investment income" has the meaning assigned by subsection 129(4);

Notes: 248(1)"aggregate investment income" added by 2006 budget bill #2 (Part 2 — eligible dividends), effective for 2006 and later taxation years.

"allowable business investment loss" has the meaning assigned by section 38;

Related Provisions: 3(d) — Income for taxation year — application of allowable business investment losses; 111(1)(a), 111(8)"non-capital loss" — Carryforward of allowable business investment losses.

"allowable capital loss" has the meaning assigned by section 38;

Related Provisions: 3(b)(ii) — Income for taxation year — application of allowable capital losses.

"alter ego trust" means a trust to which paragraph 104(4)(a) would apply if that paragraph were read without reference to subparagraph 104(4)(a)(iii) and clauses 104(4)(a)(iv)(B) and (C);

Related Provisions: 54"principal residence"(c.1)(iii.1)(A) — Exemption for gain on principal residence owned by AET; 73(1.01)(c)(ii) — Rollover on transfer to AET; 104(5.8) — Transfers from AET to another trust; 104(6)(b)B(i) — Deduction from income of AET; 104(15)(a) — Preferred beneficiary election; 107(4)(a)(ii) — Distribution of property to person other than taxpayer; 248(1)"joint partner trust" — Parallel trust where spouse is also a beneficiary.

Notes: This means a trust described in 104(4)(a)(iv)(A): a trust settlor S creates at age 65 or older, with all income [as determined under trust law] payable to S and no income or capital payable to anyone else. Transfer to an *alter ego* trust (AET) is a rollover (triggering no capital gain): 73(1.01)(c)(ii), 73(1.02)(b)(i). A "self-benefit trust" (SBT, 73(1.02)(b)(ii)) is very similar, and is used by politicians whose assets are put in a "blind trust" to be insulated from the politician. 75(2) applies to AETs and SBTs, but with little practical effect since the income is payable to S anyway.

AETs and 248(1)"joint spousal or common-law partner trusts" (called "joint partner trusts" in the 2000 draft legislation) are used for estate planning, privacy and creditor-proofing and to avoid probate fees (estate administration tax, in Ontario). They effectively extend the spousal-trust rule in 73(1.01)(c)(i) (allowing transfer of property to the trust without triggering capital gains) to allow S to be a beneficiary as well. Possible advantages include: seamless transfer on death, avoiding probate fees and public disclosure of assets in probate court; no power of attorney needed if S becomes incapacitated; avoiding challenges to a Will; exemption of gain on home owned by trust (54"principal residence"(c.1)(iii.1)(A)). Possible disadvantages and costs include: trust must file annual T3 (150(1)(c)); gains on S's death are taxed at trust high tax rate (122(1)(a)); S's capital gains exemption and loss carryforwards cannot be used against the trust's capital gains (but gains can be flowed out to be used by S: 104(21.2)); no carryback of trust charitable donations on death to year before death; foreign tax credits lost because S pays the Canadian tax while trust pays the foreign tax; not having graduated rate estate's low tax rates (see 122(1)); losing access to 164(6) after death.

On S's death, the AET's accrued gains are taxed: 104(4)(a). To avoid double tax, the cost base of S's interest in the trust is bumped up: 108(1)"cost amount"(a.1).

An AET can be created by a person holding power of attorney: *Easingwood v. Cockroft*, 2013 BCCA 182; VIEWS doc 2014-0523331C6 [2014 CALU q.6].

For 2018 (most recent figures as of Dec. 2020), 3,970 AET T3 returns were assessed or reassessed, paying $54 million federal tax: tinyurl.com/stats-cra. (AETs paying no tax need not file a T3: 150(1.1).)

See Hoffstein, "Alter Ego Trusts/Joint Partner Trusts", 2004 Ontario Tax Conference (ctf.ca), 12A:1-47; Brown, "Alter Ego, Joint Conjugal and Self-Benefit Trusts", 53(1) *Canadian Tax Journal* 224-44 (2005); Louis & Prasad, "Alter Ego and Joint Partner Trusts", 152 & 153 *The Estate Planner* (CCH) 1-3 and 1-4 (Sept-Oct 2007); Newcombe, "Charitable Giving by Alter Ego and Joint Partner Trusts", 6(6) *Tax Hyperion [TH]* (Carswell, June 2009); Golombek, "Alter Ego Trust Planning" 11(2) *Tax for the Owner-Manager* (ctf.ca) 5-6 (April 2011) (combining AET with multiple-will strategy); Drache, "Alter Ego Trusts and Charitable Remainder Trusts", 19(9) *Canadian Not-for-Profit News* (Carswell) 69-70 (Sept. 2011); Main & McEachren, "Using Inter Vivos Trusts in Estate and Family Planning", 2013 Ontario Tax Conf. 9:1-29; Blucher, "Alter Ego and Joint Partner Trusts", 15(3) *TH* 1-4 (May-June 2018); Baxter, "Life Interest Trusts, 16(3) *TH* 1-5 (May-June 2019); Coles et al., "Considerations for Alter Ego Trusts", 2019 Atlantic Provinces Tax Conf 9:1-33; Berry & Cross, "The Use of Alter Ego Trusts", 2019 Cdn Tax Foundation conference report, 26:1-27.

For CRA interpretation see VIEWS docs 2001-0114045, 2008-0300401E5, 2018-0748341C6 [2018 STEP q.11] and 2018-0744161C6 [2018 STEP q.13] (application of 75(2)); 2003-0182905 and 2009-0350491R3 (whether AET can claim donation credit on distributing property to a charity); 2004-0066871E5 (AET can use principal residence exemption and can be an RRSP beneficiary); 2005-0132281C6 (effect of death); 2007-0221361R3 (ruling on various issues including donations, 104(4), 40(3.4) and death); 2007-0256521E5 (if legal and beneficial ownership are not separated, no trust is created); 2008-0285071C6 (sale of interest in an AET); 2008-0292121R3, 2009-0308611R3 and 2011-0423291E5 (application of 73(1) on transfer to AET); 2010-0359461C6 (using AET as charitable remainder trust); 2011-0394081E5 (no capital gains reserve if mortgage is transferred to an AET); 2012-0453111C6 (effect of taxpayer emigration); 2015-0607451E5 (after transfer of home to AET, beneficiary permitting spouse to live there with him does not taint AET); 2017-0717831E5 (deduction to trust in year beneficiary dies); 2018-0768841C6 [2018 APFF q.3] (if trust terms permit charitable gift before death, it does not qualify as AET even if no gift is made); 2019-0798491C6 [2019 STEP q.2] (whether transfer to charity after death qualifies as donation by AET); 2019-0799641E5 (AET donating capital property the year after the beneficiary dies); 2020-0861041C6 [2020 CTF q.7] (AET may lose its status if cottage it holds is used by settlor's children).

The B.C. *Fraudulent Conveyances Act* cannot invalidate a transfer of assets to an AET that defeats a spouse's claim under the province's *Wills Variation Act*, because such claim arises only on death: *Mawdsley v. Meshen*, 2012 BCCA 91.

Definition added by 2001 technical bill, for trusts created after 1999.

"amateur athlete trust" has the meaning assigned by subsection 143.1(1.2);

Notes: 248(1)"amateur athlete trust" amended by 2008 budget bill #2, effective for 2008 and later taxation years, to change "143.1(1)" to "143.1(1.2)".

Definition added by 1992 technical bill, effective 1988.

"amortized cost" of a loan or lending asset at any time to a taxpayer means the amount, if any, by which the total of

(a) in the case of a loan made by the taxpayer, the total of all amounts advanced in respect of the loan at or before that time,

(b) in the case of a loan or lending asset acquired by the taxpayer, the cost of the loan or lending asset to the taxpayer,

(c) in the case of a loan or lending asset acquired by the taxpayer, the part of the amount, if any, by which

(i) the principal amount of the loan or lending asset at the time it was so acquired

exceeds

(ii) the cost to the taxpayer of the loan or lending asset

that was included in computing the taxpayer's income for any taxation year ending at or before that time,

(c.1) the total of all amounts each of which is an amount in respect of the loan or lending asset that was included in computing the taxpayer's income for a taxation year that ended at or before that time in respect of changes in the value of the loan or lending asset attributable to the fluctuation in the value of a currency of a country other than Canada relative to Canadian currency,

(d) where the taxpayer is an insurer, any amount in respect of the loan or lending asset that was deemed by reason of paragraph 142(3)(a) of the *Income Tax Act*, chapter 148 of the Revised Statutes of Canada, 1952, as it read in its application to the 1977 taxation year, to be a gain for any taxation year ending at or before that time, and

(e) the total of all amounts each of which is an amount in respect of the loan or lending asset that was included under paragraph 12(1)(i) in computing the taxpayer's income for any taxation year ending at or before that time

exceeds the total of

(f) the part of the amount, if any, by which

(i) the amount referred to in subparagraph (c)(ii)

exceeds

(ii) the amount referred to in subparagraph (c)(i)

that was deducted in computing the taxpayer's income for any taxation year ending at or before that time,

(f.1) the total of all amounts each of which is an amount in respect of the loan or lending asset that was deducted in computing the taxpayer's income for a taxation year that ended at or before that time in respect of changes in the value of the loan or lending asset attributable to the fluctuation in the value of a currency of a country other than Canada relative to Canadian currency,

(g) the total of all amounts that, at or before that time, the taxpayer had received as or on account or in lieu of payment of or in satisfaction of the principal amount of the loan or lending asset,

(h) where the taxpayer is an insurer, any amount in respect of the loan or lending asset that was deemed by reason of paragraph 142(3)(b) of the *Income Tax Act*, chapter 148 of the Revised Statutes of Canada, 1952, as it read in its application to the 1977 taxation year, to be a loss for any taxation year ending at or before that time, and

(i) the total of all amounts each of which is an amount in respect of the loan or lending asset deducted under paragraph 20(1)(p) in computing the taxpayer's income for any taxation year ending at or before that time;

Related Provisions: 138(13) — Variation in amortized of certain insurers; 261(5)(f) — Functional currency reporting — meaning of "Canadian currency".

Notes: Paras (c.1) and (f.1) added by 1994 technical bill, retroactive to taxation years that begin after June 17, 1987 and end after 1987.

I.T. Application Rules: 69 (meaning of "chapter 148 of ...").

Interpretation Bulletins: IT-442R: Bad debts and reserves for doubtful debts.

"amount" means money, rights or things expressed in terms of the amount of money or the value in terms of money of the right or thing, except that,

(a) notwithstanding paragraph (b), in any case where subsection 112(2.1), (2.2) or (2.4), or section 187.2 or 187.3 or subsection 258(3) or (5) applies to a stock dividend, the "amount" of the stock dividend is the greater of

(i) the amount by which the paid-up capital of the corporation that paid the dividend is increased by reason of the payment of the dividend, and

(ii) the fair market value of the share or shares paid as a stock dividend at the time of payment,

(b) in any case where section 191.1 applies to a stock dividend, the "amount" of the stock dividend for the purposes of Part VI.1 is the greater of

(i) the amount by which the paid-up capital of the corporation that paid the dividend is increased by reason of the payment of the dividend, and

(ii) the fair market value of the share or shares paid as a stock dividend at the time of payment,

and for any other purpose the amount referred to in subparagraph (i), and

(b.1) [Repealed]

(c) in any other case, the "amount" of any stock dividend is the amount by which the paid-up capital of the corporation that paid the dividend is increased by reason of the payment of the dividend;

Related Provisions: 55(2.3) — Amount of stock dividend for purposes of 55(2); 95(7) — "Amount" of stock dividend paid by foreign affiliate; 257 — Amounts in formulas cannot calculate to less than zero.

Notes: For the "amount" of a stock dividend where "high/low" preferred shares are issued in payment of the dividend, see VIEWS doc 2001-0094305 and CRA May 2005 ICAA roundtable (tinyurl.com/cra-abtax), Supp. q. 6. See also docs 2007-0241561R3, 2008-0283681R3. See also Notes to 245(2) re *Triad Gestco, 1207192 Ontario Ltd.* and *Global Equity Fund* FCA decisions, and Notes to 248(1)"stock dividend"; and the deeming rules in 55(2.3) and 95(7).

Para. (b.1), which was in force for a period, provided an election for inclusion of at least the value of the shares issued on a stock dividend from a non-resident corp. CRA encouraged compliance with it pending enactment: VIEWS docs 2011-0420301M4, 2011-0414221M4. Para. (b.1) repealed by 2002-2013 technical bill, for taxation years that begin after 2012.

Para. (b.1) added by 2002-2013 technical bill, effective July 17, 2005.

Interpretation Bulletins: IT-88R2: Stock dividends.

Information Circulars: 88-2, para. 26: General anti-avoidance rule — section 245 of the *Income Tax Act*.

Charities Policies: CPS-009: Holding of property for charities.

"annuity" includes an amount payable on a periodic basis whether payable at intervals longer or shorter than a year and whether payable under a contract, will or trust or otherwise;

Related Provisions: 56(1)(d), 60(a), 212(1)(o) — Annuity payments taxable; 128.1(10)"excluded right or interest"(f) — Emigration — no deemed disposition of right under annuity contract; Canada-U.S. Tax Treaty:Art. XVIII:4 — Meaning of "annuities" for treaty purposes; *Income Tax Conventions Interpretation Act* 5 — Meaning of "annuity" for treaty purposes.

Notes: See Notes to 188.1(5) re meaning of "includes".

Income Tax Folios: S3-F9-C1: Lottery winnings, miscellaneous receipts, and income (and losses) from crime [replaces IT-185R, IT-213R, IT-256R, IT-334R2].

"appropriate percentage", for a taxation year, means the lowest percentage referred to in subsection 117(2) for the taxation year;

Notes: This means 15% since 2007. The effect of a credit at this rate (s. 118–118.7) is the same as a deduction at the lowest marginal rate: a deduction off the "bottom" of one's income instead of off the "top". This percentage is also used for the AMT in 127.51:A.

Definition amended by 2016 tax-rate bill, for 2016 and later tax years, to change "that is applicable in determining tax payable under Part I for the year" to "for the taxation year" (to make the wording consistent with 248(1)"highest individual percentage").

"assessment" includes a reassessment;

Related Provisions: 152 — Assessments; 244(14) — Assessment presumed mailed on date stated on notice; 244(15) — Assessment deemed made on date of mailing.

Notes: An assessment is an assessment, even if it is a "quick" assessment issued automatically upon filing a return. Thus, it can be objected to and appealed from, even though CRA may not yet have audited the return: *Imperial Oil (Inco)*, 2003 FCA 289.

"authorized foreign bank" has the meaning assigned by section 2 of the *Bank Act*;

Related Provisions: 20.2 — Interest deduction; 115(1)(a)(vii) — Taxable income earned in Canada; 116(6)(f) — No s. 116 certificate required on disposition of bank's Canadian banking property; 126(1.1) — Foreign tax credit; 142.7 — Conversion of foreign bank affiliate to branch; 190.13(d), 190.14(1)(c) — Capital tax; 212(13.3) — Application of non-resident withholding tax; 218.2 — Branch interest tax.

Notes: "Authorized foreign bank" (AFB) (added by 2001 technical bill, effective June 28, 1999) is a foreign bank that is authorized to operate branches in Canada. Before the *Bank Act* allowed this, foreign banks could operate only through a Canadian subsidiary. See 142.7 Notes for conversion of such a sub to a branch; 20.2 for the interest deduction allowed AFBs; and 218.2 for the special branch interest tax.

See Moysey & Maj, "New Canadian Branch Banking Rules for Foreign Banks" 48(6) *Canadian Tax Journal* 1869-1907 (2000); MacIntosh & Friedlander, "Treatment of Foreign Bank Branches", 2000 Cdn Tax Foundation conference report, 33:1-29.

Bank Act s. 2 (see CanLii.org) defines an AFB as a foreign bank that is the subject of a s. 524(1) order, which allows the Minister of Finance to make an order permitting a foreign bank to establish a branch in Canada and carry on business in Canada, subject to certain restrictions. Schedule III lists 32 AFBs.

"automobile" means

(a) a motor vehicle that is designed or adapted primarily to carry individuals on highways and streets and that has a seating capacity for not more than the driver and 8 passengers,

but does not include

(b) an ambulance,

(b.1) a clearly marked emergency-response vehicle that is used in connection with or in the course of an individual's office or employment with a fire department or the police,

(b.2) a clearly marked emergency medical response vehicle that is used, in connection with or in the course of an individual's office or employment with an emergency medical response or ambulance service, to carry emergency medical equipment together with one or more emergency medical attendants or paramedics,

(c) a motor vehicle acquired primarily for use as a taxi, a bus used in a business of transporting passengers or a hearse used in the course of a business of arranging or managing funerals,

(d) except for the purposes of section 6, a motor vehicle acquired to be sold, rented or leased in the course of carrying on a business of selling, renting or leasing motor vehicles or a motor vehicle used for the purpose of transporting passengers in the course of carrying on a business of arranging or managing funerals, and

(e) a motor vehicle

(i) of a type commonly called a van or pick-up truck, or a similar vehicle, that has a seating capacity for not more than the driver and two passengers and that, in the taxation year in which it is acquired or leased, is used primarily for the transportation of goods or equipment in the course of gaining or producing income,

(ii) of a type commonly called a van or pick-up truck, or a similar vehicle, the use of which, in the taxation year in which it is acquired or leased, is all or substantially all for the transportation of goods, equipment or passengers in the course of gaining or producing income, or

(iii) of a type commonly called a pick-up truck that is used in the taxation year in which it is acquired or leased primarily for the transportation of goods, equipment or passengers in the course of earning or producing income at one or more locations in Canada that are

(A) described, in respect of any of the occupants of the vehicle, in subparagraph 6(6)(a)(i) or (ii), and

(B) at least 30 kilometres outside the nearest point on the boundary of the nearest population centre, as defined by the last census dictionary published by Statistics Canada before the year, that has a population of at least 40,000 individuals as determined in the last census published by Statistics Canada before the year;

Related Provisions: 248(1) — "motor vehicle", "passenger vehicle".

Notes: An "automobile" (see also 248(1)"passenger vehicle") is subject to negative consequences, including: standby charge for using employer's automobile (6(2)); limit on capital cost for both CCA and GST/HST input tax credit (13(7)(g), *Excise Tax Act* 201); limit on interest deduction (67.2); limit on leasing cost (67.3, ETA 235); GST/HST on taxable benefits (ETA 173(1)); GST may require 90% business use for input tax credit (ETA 202(2)). A vehicle that is not an "automobile" can create a taxable benefit under 6(1)(a), but not the standby charge under 6(1)(e): VIEWS doc 2007-0225901E5.

When reading a VIEWS doc or article in French about this definition, note that the para. numbers differ in French from English!

In *para. (a)*, a pickup truck is arguably designed primarily to carry goods, not passengers: *Ruhl*, [1998] G.S.T.C. 4 (TCC), para. 14 (but this point was not argued). "Designed or adapted" is broader than "designed" and allows for adaptation by the owner: *Séguin*, 2003 CarswellNat 5401 (TCC).

For *para. (b)*, "ambulance" does not include an ambulance supervisor's emergency response vehicle, but it could fall within para. (e)(i) or (ii): VIEWS doc 2004-0073791E5.

For *para. (b.1)*, an unmarked police car or "ghost car" is not a "clearly-marked emergency response vehicle": CRA VIEWS 2003-0029355. A clearly marked fire emergency vehicle qualifies: 2010-0361991E5.

For *para. (d)*, a "business of ... leasing motor vehicles" does not include an individual who leased one or two cars to his own company, since such income is property income, not business income: *Jenner*, [2009] 1 C.T.C. 29 (FCA) (leave to appeal denied [2009] G.S.T.C. 3 (SCC)). Similarly, a parent corporation that buys a luxury car and leases it to its subsidiary would not succeed in avoiding the $30,000 Class 10.1 limit under 13(7)(g): VIEWS docs 2011-0399341E5, 2011-0395221E5.

Para. (e): "goods or equipment" can include tools: VIEWS doc 2004-0064541E5. The "use" test includes "dead head" trips back after carrying a load: 2004-0103311I7. For "used primarily" in (e)(i) see Notes to 73(3). For (e)(iii)(B), travel through urban areas does not disqualify travel between remote areas: *Myrdan Investments*, 2013 TCC 35, para. 48. To determine if place X is within 30 km of a population centre of at least 40,000 for (e)(iii)(B), see tinyurl.com/popu-centres and use maps.google.com to calculate normal road distance (see Notes to 248(1)"eligible relocation") from X.

For TCC cases ruling a truck or van was an automobile, see *Myshak*, [1997] G.S.T.C. 59 (farm pick-up with folded-down rear seats); *Bush Apes*, [2001] G.S.T.C. 72 (truck); *547931 Alberta*, 2003 TCC 170 (pick-up not used substantially all for transporting equipment); *Cohoon, Murphy*, 2006 TCC 376 (Court rejected testimony that rear seat was folded down and not used); *Distribution S.C.T.*, 2006 TCC 482 (van used partly for personal purposes); *Olson*, 2007 TCC 508 (purchase on Dec. 30 meant only Dec. 30-31 was tested for business use in (e)(ii), and O did not take possession of truck until January); *Gariépy*, 2007 TCC 513 (Chev Astro van was "designed" by manufacturer to carry individuals); *Gauthier*, 2007 TCC 573 (Chev Astro); *J. Raymond Couvreur Inc.*, 2008 TCC 587 (company did not prove trucks were used 90% in the business); *Martin*, 2009 TCC 3 (trucks not shown to fall under (e)(i) or (ii)); *Perron*, 2012 TCC 341 (Court did not believe P's evidence that he used the vehicle solely for business).

For TCC cases ruling a truck or van was *not* an automobile, see *Ruhl*, [1998] G.S.T.C. 4 (farm pick-up used substantially all for transporting goods); *McKay*, [2000] G.S.T.C. 93 (pick-up exclusively used in commercial activities, despite lying unused for extended periods); *Servais*, [2002] G.S.T.C. 59 (aff'd on other grounds 2003 FCA 329); *Ilott*, [2003] 1 C.T.C. 2384 (Court accepted that personal use of trucks never exceeded 5%; *Pronovost*, 2003 TCC 139 (pick-up used substantially all for transporting equipment); *Séguin*, 2003 CarswellNat 5401 (owner had adapted Jeep to carry tools and equipment and used it almost entirely for business); *764845 Alberta*, 2004 TCC 388 and *Kowalchuk*, 2005 TCC 757 (quad-cab trucks used 90% in business); *Muller*, 2004 TCC 562 (pick-up did not have proper rear seating even though there were rear seats); *Fournier*, 2004 TCC 786 (van used 93% for business); *BG Excel Plumbing*, 2006 TCC 252 (Hummer used substantially all for transporting goods); *Fraser*, 2006 TCC 427 (Court found F used truck 90% for transporting goods or equipment in business, despite imprecise evidence; truck was not "luxury" auto); *Betcher*, 2008 TCC 270 (B used pickup substantially all in business); *Amberhill Collection*, 2009 TCC 54 (Yukon

Denali had back seat permanently removed and middle seat always folded down; also was used 85% for business, which was "substantially all"); *Jorgensen*, 2009 TCC 37 (3/4 ton extended-cab truck had permanent adaptation reducing usable seating); *Cheema Cleaning*, 2009 TCC 145 (Chev Tahoe used substantially all in transportation of goods); *Myrdan Investments*, 2013 TCC 35 (GMC Sierra met tests in (e)(ii) and (iii)); *BH Parkway*, 2019 TCC 7 (Mercedes SUV used substantially all for transporting goods).

All-terrain vehicles (ATVs) were held not to be automobiles in *Fournier*, 2004 TCC 786, and *Cohoon, Murphy & Co.*, 2006 TCC 376.

CRA considers that "substantially all", used in (e)(ii), means 90% or more. See also VIEWS docs 9507975 (Hummer can be an automobile); 2004-0064901I7 (use of pick-up in business activity that is not a GST "commercial activity" does not prevent it from meeting the "transporting goods or equipment" test); 2007-0238631E5 (pick-up); 2011-040817117 (sport-utility vehicle (SUV) is "similar" to a van or pick-up truck, and a crossover utility vehicle (CUV) may be as well).

An "occupant" of the vehicle in (e)(iii)(A) need not be an employee of the taxpayer: VIEWS doc 2004-009125117.

The test for an "automobile" is applied the year the vehicle is acquired or leased, and its status does not change later even if it was acquired near year-end so the "use" test is skewed: *Olson*, 2007 TCC 508; VIEWS doc 2007-0251471E5. However, a change from personal use to a taxi will stop it being an "automobile", due to 13(7)(b): 2019-079622117.

A motor home is "automotive equipment" but is not an "automobile": VIEWS doc 2003-0045525.

See also Notes to 6(2); Marvin Zeavin, "The Taxation of Automobiles — Time for a Tuneup?", 4(4) *It's Personal* (Carswell) 5-8 (Nov. 2011).

Cl. (e)(iii)(B) amended by 2013 budget bill #2, effective for 2013 and later taxation years, to change "urban area" to "population centre".

Definition amended by 2005 Budget (effective 2005 and later taxation years), 2003 Budget and 1991 technical bill.

Interpretation Bulletins: IT-521R: Motor vehicle expenses claimed by self-employed individuals; IT-522R: Vehicle, travel and sales expenses of employees.

"balance-due day" of a taxpayer for a taxation year means,

(a) if the taxpayer is a trust,

(i) in the case where the time at which the taxation year ends is determined under paragraph 249(4)(a), the day that is

(A) in the case where that time occurs in a calendar year after the end of the trust's particular taxation year that ends on December 15 of that calendar year because of an election made under paragraph 132.11(1)(a), the balance-due day of the trust for the particular taxation year,

(B) in the case where clause (A) does not apply and the trust's particular taxation year that begins immediately after that time ends in the calendar year that includes that time, the balance-due day of the trust for the particular taxation year, and

(C) in any other case, 90 days after the end of the calendar year that includes that time, and

(ii) in any other case, the day that is 90 days after the end of the taxation year,

(b) where the taxpayer is an individual who died after October in the year and before May in the following taxation year, the day that is 6 months after the day of death,

(c) in any other case where the taxpayer is an individual, April 30 in the following taxation year, and

(d) where the taxpayer is a corporation,

(i) the day that is three months after the day on which the taxation year (in this subparagraph referred to as the "current year") ends, if

(A) an amount was deducted under section 125 in computing the corporation's tax payable under this Part for the current year or for its preceding taxation year,

(B) the corporation is, throughout the current year, a Canadian-controlled private corporation, and

(C) either

(I) in the case of a corporation that is not associated with another corporation in the current year, its taxable income for its preceding taxation year (determined

before taking into consideration the specified future tax consequences for that preceding taxation year) does not exceed its business limit for that preceding taxation year, or

(II) in the case of a corporation that is associated with one or more other corporations in the current year, the total of the taxable incomes of the corporation and of those other corporations for their last taxation years that ended in the last calendar year that ended before the end of the current year (determined before taking into consideration the specified future tax consequences for those last taxation years) does not exceed the total of the business limits of the corporation and of those other corporations for those last taxation years, and

(ii) the day that is two months after the day on which the taxation year ends, in any other case;

Related Provisions: 87(2)(oo.1) — Balance-due day of amalgamated corporation; 88(1)(e.9) — Balance-due day on windup of corporation; 104(13.4)(c)(i) — Death of beneficiary — spousal and similar trusts; 150(1) — Returns; 156.1(4) — Payment of balance — individuals who pay instalments; 157(1)(b) — Corporation to pay balance by balance-due day; 158 — Payment of balance on assessment; *Interpretation Act* 26 — Deadline on weekend or holiday extended to next business day; 251.2(7) — Trust subject to loss restriction event — short year-end ignored for certain purposes; 256 — Associated corporations.

Notes: The balance owing for the year must be paid by the balance-due day: see 156.1(4) (individuals and trusts) and 157(1)(b) (corporations).

A corporation's balance is normally due 2 months after year-end, even though the T2 return is not due until 6 months after year-end. Subpara. (d)(i) extends the balance-due day by one month for CCPCs that claim the small business deduction and that have taxable income (together with associated corporations) not over $500,000.

The balance-due day is the payment deadline for all corporate taxes: see 183.1(2), 186(1), 187.2, 187.3(1), 196(3), 204.86(1), 209(4)(b), 211.4, 219(1).

Due to COVID-19, payment deadlines March 18-Sept. 29, 2020 were extended to Sept. 30, 2020. See PITA 59th ed. at 150(1) opening words.

Subpara. (a)(i) added by 2016 budget bill #2, effective March 21, 2013. It extends both the balance-due day and the filing deadline (see 251.2(7)(c)) to the regular year's deadline, for a short year caused by a change in control.

Definition amended by 2001 Budget (for 2002 and later tax years), 1996 Budget. Added by 1991 technical bill.

Information Circulars: 98-1R5: Tax collection policies.

"bank" means a bank within the meaning assigned by section 2 of the *Bank Act* (other than a federal credit union) or an authorized foreign bank;

Notes: Under s. 2 of the *Bank Act*, "bank" means a bank listed in Schedule I or II to that Act. Schedule I banks are Canadian banks; see Notes to 95(2.43)"eligible Canadian bank". Schedule II banks are subsidiaries of foreign banks; see canlii.org for the list. See 248(1)"authorized foreign bank" for branches of foreign banks (Schedule III).

Exclusion of a "federal credit union" (see Notes to definition in 248(1)) added by 2010 budget bill #1, effective Dec. 19, 2012 (P.C. 2012-1623).

248(1)"bank" added by 2001 technical bill, effective June 28, 1999.

"bankrupt" has the meaning assigned by the *Bankruptcy and Insolvency Act*;

Related Provisions: 80(1)"forgiven amount"B(i) — Debt forgiveness rules do not apply when debtor is bankrupt; 128 — Rules on bankruptcy.

Notes: See Notes to 128(2). Definition "bankrupt" added by 1994 technical bill, effective for taxation years that end after February 21, 1994.

The *Bankruptcy and Insolvency Act*, R.S.C. 1985, c. B-3, s. 2 provides:

"bankrupt" means a person who has made an assignment or against whom a bankruptcy order has been made or the legal status of that person;

"assignment" means an assignment filed with the official receiver;

"benefit under a deferred profit sharing plan" received by a taxpayer in a taxation year means the total of all amounts each of which is an amount received by the taxpayer in the year from a trustee under the plan, minus any amounts deductible under subsections 147(11) and (12) in computing the income of the taxpayer for the year;

Related Provisions: 56(1)(i), 147(10) — DPSP benefits taxable.

"bituminous sands" means sands or other rock materials containing naturally occurring hydrocarbons (other than coal) which hydrocarbons have

(a) a viscosity, determined in a prescribed manner, equal to or greater than 10,000 centipoise, or

(b) a density, determined in a prescribed manner, equal to or less than 12 degrees API;

Notes: Definition "bituminous sands" added by 1996 Budget, effective March 7, 1996. References to "oil sands" throughout the Act were eliminated at the same time.

See Carr & Calverley, *Canadian Resource Taxation* (Carswell, looseleaf or *Taxnet Pro* Reference Centre), chap. 22; Bharat Patel, "Bituminous Sands — Tax Issues", 16 *Canadian Petroleum Tax Journal* (2003); Calverley, Carr & Haymour, "The Categorization of Expenses Incurred in Bituminous Sands Projects", IV(4) *Resource Sector Taxation* (Federated Press) 302-09 (2006).

Regulations: 1107 (prescribed manner for determining viscosity and density).

"borrowed money" includes the proceeds to a taxpayer from the sale of a post-dated bill drawn by the taxpayer on a bank;

Related Provisions: 15.1(4), 15.2(4) — Money borrowed for small business development bond or small business bond deemed used for purpose of earning income from business or property; 20(1)(c) — Interest on money borrowed for certain purposes is deductible; 20(2), (3) — Rules re borrowed money.

Income Tax Folios: S3-F6-C1: Interest deductibility [replaces IT-533].

Interpretation Bulletins: IT-121R3: Election to capitalize cost of borrowed money (cancelled).

"business" includes a profession, calling, trade, manufacture or undertaking of any kind whatever and, except for the purposes of paragraph 18(2)(c), section 54.2, subsection 95(1) and paragraph 110.6(14)(f), an adventure or concern in the nature of trade but does not include an office or employment;

Related Provisions: 253 — Extended meaning of "carrying on business" in Canada; 253.1 — Certain limited partners deemed not to carry on business for certain purposes.

Notes: "Adventure or concern in the nature of trade" includes the purchase of a single property (such as land) with the intention of reselling it: *Laramee (Casey)*, 2008 FCA 299. The gain on such property is business income rather than a half-taxed capital gain. See Notes to 54"capital property".

A business that is an "adventure or concern in the nature of trade" cannot write down inventory until it is sold. See 10(1.01). See Notes to 10(1.01) re the meaning of "adventure in the nature of trade".

See also Notes to 188.1(5) re meaning of "includes".

Where a taxpayer claims losses, CRA formerly denied the existence of a "business", and thus the losses, on the ground there was no reasonable expectation of profit. This was overturned by the Supreme Court of Canada in *Stewart*; see Notes to 9(2).

For the meaning of "business" in Quebec and common-law provinces, see François Auger, "Analysis of the Notion of Business", *The Harmonization of Federal Legislation with Quebec Civil Law: Collection of Studies in Tax Law* (APFF, 2002), 4:1-48; and Talbot, "A Business by Any Other Name", 2019 Atlantic Provinces Tax Conference (ctf.ca), 3A:1-30. See also Notes to 9(2).

CRA considers holding investments to be a "business" for 84(2): VIEWS doc 2012-0445341C6 [2012 Prairie Conf. q.14].

To determine where business is carried on, see *Cutlers Guild*, [1981] C.T.C. 115 (FCTD); VIEWS doc 2007-0224221I7; s. 253; and Notes to 2(3).

On business vs employment see 248(1)"employee". On business income vs property income see Notes to 9(1). On whether there is one business or separate businesses see Notes to Reg. 1101(1).

Reference to 95(1) added by 1994 technical bill, for tax years that end after 1994.

Interpretation Bulletins: IT-153R3: Land developers — subdivision and development costs and carrying charges on land; IT-206R: Separate businesses; IT-218R: Profit, capital gains and losses from the sale of real estate, including farmland and inherited land and conversion of real estate from capital property to inventory and vice versa; IT-371: Rental property — meaning of "principal business"; IT-459: Adventure or concern in the nature of trade.

I.T. Technical News: 41 (meaning of "business" — gambling).

Forms: RC4100: Employee or Self-Employed?.

"business limit" of a corporation for a taxation year means the amount determined under section 125 to be its business limit for the year;

Related Provisions: 125(2)–(5.1) — Determination of business limit.

Notes: The business limit is the amount of business income that can be earned at the low rate of tax for Canadian-controlled private corporations, in 125(1). The substantive rules defining the business limit are in 125(2)-(5.1). The business limit is $500,000

since 2009 but is shared among associated corporations and reduced for large corporations.

248(1)"business limit" added by 1996 Budget, retroactive to May 24, 1985.

"business number" means the number (other than a Social Insurance Number or trust account number) used by the Minister to identify

(a) a corporation or partnership, or

(b) any other association or taxpayer that carries on a business or is required by this Act to deduct or withhold an amount from an amount paid or credited or deemed to be paid or credited under this Act

and of which the Minister has notified the corporation, partnership, association or taxpayer;

Related Provisions: 241(4)(l), 241(9.2) — Disclosure of BN to third parties.

Notes: The Business Number (BN) takes the form "12345 6789 RC0001", where the "0001" represents multiple accounts of the same taxpayer and can be suppressed if there is only one account of a given type. "RC" is for corporate income tax; RD is excise duty; RE is excise tax; RG is the Air Travellers Security Charge; RI is used by the CRA where the account number would otherwise be the Social Insurance Number (e.g., s. 160 assessments); RM is for import/export (Customs); RN is excise insurance; RP is for payroll (source withholdings); RR is a charity registration; RT is GST/HST, including non-registrants; RZ is for Reg. 200-238 information returns (e.g., dividend payor, partnership return, RRSP or TFSA issuer, contract payments). (For a longer list see David Sherman's commentary to *Excise Tax Act* 241(1) in the *Canada GST Service* or on *Taxnet Pro*.)

The BN is also used for provincial programs such as Workers' Compensation and various provincial taxes in most provinces (for Alberta, under its *Common Business Number Act* since April 2015).

The April 21, 2015 federal Budget (ch. 3.2) "announces the Government's commitment to undertake the initial planning and preparation for federal adoption of the Business Number as a Common Business Identifier", so all business dealings with the federal government will use the BN. "This would make it simpler for businesses to interact with government, reducing red tape and enabling more efficient digital self-service."

While Social Insurance Numbers (see 237(1)) are private, BNs are not: 241(4)(l), (9.2) and (9.3) permit officials to disclose names and BNs in many cases. The BN appears on every GST-registered business's invoices and receipts as its registration number, so that business purchasers can claim an input tax credit to recover GST/HST paid. Individuals who carry on business and are GST-registered have a BN, but that number is not used for income tax purposes except for payroll withholding (para. (b)). For income tax returns, individuals use the SIN. A partnership is not a "person" for income tax purposes, but is a "person" for GST/HST purposes, and has a BN (see Notes to 96(1) and Reg. 229).

Amalgamating corporations can choose to keep the BN of the "dominant" company rather than getting a new BN (this can be helpful for GST/HST purposes, since the BN appears on invoices). See T4001, "Employer's Guide — Payroll Deductions", chap. 1 under "If your business amalgamates"; CRA Pacific Region meeting with Institute of CAs of BC, Jan. 22/13, q.14.

When federal incorporation (*Canada Business Corporations Act*) is approved by Industry Canada, the CRA assigns a BN automatically. The corporation can then apply for other accounts needed (GST, payroll, etc.).

Businesses can register and obtain a BN at businessregistration.gc.ca or on Form RC1. Businesses can register for any of GST/HST, payroll deductions, corporate income tax, import/export, and some provincial programs (NS, ON, BC: e.g., Ontario business name registration, Employer Health Tax and WSIB).

Charities with internal divisions were to receive new Business Numbers for each division starting fall 2017, but this was changed to getting a different 4-digit identifier at the end: tinyurl.com/charity-divisions.

Opening words amended by 2018 budget bill #1, for 2018 and later tax years, to add reference to a trust account number.

Definition "business number" added by 1995-97 technical bill, effective June 18, 1998. It was previously in 241(10), but without the closing words.

Registered Charities Newsletters: 14 (Business Number and donation receipts); 15 (registered charities as internal divisions of other charities).

Forms: RC2: The business number and your CRA accounts [guide].

"Canadian banking business" means the business carried on by an authorized foreign bank through a permanent establishment (as defined by regulation) in Canada, other than business conducted through a representative office registered or required to be registered under section 509 of the *Bank Act*;

Related Provisions: 116(6)(f) — No s. 116 certificate required on disposition of property of Canadian banking business.

Notes: 248(1)"Canadian banking business" added by 2001 technical bill, effective June 28, 1999. See Notes to 248(1)"authorized foreign bank".

For the text of s. 509 of the *Bank Act*, see canlii.org.

Regulations: Reg. 8201 (meaning of "permanent establishment").

"Canadian-controlled private corporation" has the meaning assigned by subsection 125(7);

Related Provisions: 248(1) — "Small business corporation".

I.T. Application Rules: 50(1) (status for 1972 taxation year).

Income Tax Folios: S4-F7-C1: Amalgamations of Canadian corporations [replaces IT-474R2].

Interpretation Bulletins: IT-458R2: Canadian-controlled private corporations.

"Canadian corporation" has the meaning assigned by subsection 89(1);

"Canadian development expense" has the meaning assigned by subsection 66.2(5);

"Canadian exploration and development expenses" has the meaning assigned by subsection 66(15);

"Canadian exploration expense" has the meaning assigned by subsection 66.1(6);

"Canadian field processing" means, except as otherwise prescribed,

(a) the processing in Canada of raw natural gas at a field separation and dehydration facility,

(b) the processing in Canada of raw natural gas at a natural gas processing plant to any stage that is not beyond the stage of natural gas that is acceptable to a common carrier of natural gas,

(c) the processing in Canada of hydrogen sulphide derived from raw natural gas to any stage that is not beyond the marketable sulphur stage,

(d) the processing in Canada of natural gas liquids, at a natural gas processing plant where the input is raw natural gas derived from a natural accumulation of natural gas, to any stage that is not beyond the marketable liquefied petroleum stage or its equivalent,

(e) the processing in Canada of crude oil (other than heavy crude oil recovered from an oil or gas well or a tar sands deposit) recovered from a natural accumulation of petroleum to any stage that is not beyond the crude oil stage or its equivalent, and

(f) prescribed activities

and, for the purposes of paragraphs (b) to (d),

(g) gas is not considered to cease to be raw natural gas solely because of its processing at a field separation and dehydration facility until it is received by a common carrier of natural gas, and

(h) where all or part of a natural gas processing plant is devoted primarily to the recovery of ethane, the plant, or the part of the plant, as the case may be, is considered not to be a natural gas processing plant;

Notes: Definition "Canadian field processing" added by 1996 Budget and amended by 1995-97 technical bill, effective 1997. See 125.1"manufacturing or processing"(k) and 127(9)"qualified property"(c)(ix). The term is also used in Reg. Parts XI and XII.

Income Tax Folios: S4-F15-C1: Manufacturing and processing [replaces IT-147R3].

Interpretation Bulletins: IT-476R: CCA — Equipment used in petroleum and natural gas activities.

"Canadian oil and gas property expense" has the meaning assigned by subsection 66.4(5);

"Canadian partnership" has the meaning assigned by section 102;

Related Provisions: 80(1) — "Eligible Canadian partnership".

Interpretation Bulletins: IT-123R6: Transactions involving eligible capital property.

"Canadian real, immovable or resource property" means

(a) a property that would, if this Act were read without reference to the definition "real or immovable property" in subsection 122.1(1), be a real or immovable property situated in Canada,

(b) a Canadian resource property,

(c) a timber resource property,

(d) a share of the capital stock of a corporation, an income or a capital interest in a trust or an interest in a partnership — other than a taxable Canadian corporation, a SIFT trust (determined without reference to subsection 122.1(2)), a SIFT partnership (determined without reference to subsection 197(8)) or a real estate investment trust (as defined in subsection 122.1(1)) — if more than 50% of the fair market value of the share or interest is derived directly or indirectly from one or any combination of properties described in paragraphs (a) to (c), or

(e) any right to or interest in — or, for civil law, any right to or in — any property described in any of paragraphs (a) to (d);

Notes: *Para. (d)*: For the meaning of "derived" see Notes to 18.1(12). For "indirectly" see Notes to 17.1(1).

Definition amended by 2002-2013 technical bill for 2011 and later tax years, or earlier by election. Added by 2007 budget bill #1 (see Backgrounder to Finance news release 2007-106 (Dec. 20, 2007).

"Canadian resident partnership" means a partnership that, at any time in respect of which the expression is relevant,

(a) is a Canadian partnership,

(b) would, if it were a corporation, be resident in Canada (including, for greater certainty, a partnership that has its central management and control in Canada), or

(c) was formed under the laws of a province;

Related Provisions: 249(1)(b) — Taxation year of Canadian resident partnership.

Notes: For the meaning of "central management and control", see Notes to 250(4).

Definition added by 2007 budget bill #1, effective Oct. 31, 2006.

"Canadian resource property" has the meaning assigned by subsection 66(15);

"capital dividend" has the meaning assigned by section 83;

"capital gain" for a taxation year from the disposition of any property has the meaning assigned by section 39;

"capital interest" of a taxpayer in a trust has the meaning assigned by subsection 108(1);

"capital loss" for a taxation year from the disposition of any property has the meaning assigned by section 39;

"capital property" has the meaning assigned by section 54;

"cash method" has the meaning assigned by subsection 28(1);

Notes: Definition "cash method" added to 248(1) by 1991 technical bill, effective 1989. The operative definition has been in 28(1) since 1972.

"cemetery care trust" has the meaning assigned by subsection 148.1(1);

Notes: "Cemetery care trust" added by 1995-97 technical bill, effective 1993.

Interpretation Bulletins: IT-531: Eligible funeral arrangements.

"common-law partner", with respect to a taxpayer at any time, means a person who cohabits at that time in a conjugal relationship with the taxpayer and

(a) has so cohabited throughout the 12-month period that ends at that time, or

(b) would be the parent of a child of whom the taxpayer is a parent, if this Act were read without reference to paragraphs 252(1)(c) and (e) and subparagraph 252(2)(a)(iii),

and, for the purpose of this definition, where at any time the taxpayer and the person cohabit in a conjugal relationship, they are, at any particular time after that time, deemed to be cohabiting in a conjugal relationship unless they were living separate and apart at the particular time for a period of at least 90 days that includes the particular time because of a breakdown of their conjugal relationship;

Notes: The leading definition of "cohabit in a conjugal relationship" was provided by the Supreme Court of Canada in *M v. H*, [1999] 2 S.C.R. 3 at p. 50:

Molodowich v. Penttinen [1980 CanLII 1537] (Ont. Dist. Ct.), sets out the generally accepted characteristics of a conjugal relationship. They include shared shelter, sexual and personal behaviour, services, social activities, economic support and children, as well as the societal perception of the couple. However, it was recognized that these elements may be present in varying degrees and not all are necessary for the relationship to be found to be conjugal....

Certainly an opposite-sex couple may, after many years together, be considered to be in a conjugal relationship although they have neither children nor sexual relations. Obviously the weight to be accorded the various elements or factors to be considered in determining whether an opposite-sex couple is in a conjugal relationship will vary widely and almost infinitely.... Courts have wisely determined that the approach to determining whether a relationship is conjugal must be flexible. This must be so, for the relationships of all couples will vary widely....

In *Molodowich v. Penttinen*, cited above, the Ontario District Court suggested the following questions as a guide (see also VIEWS doc 2006-0198341E5):

1. Shelter: (a) Did the parties live under the same roof? (b) What were the sleeping arrangements? (c) Did anyone else occupy or share the available accommodation?

2. Sexual and Personal Behaviour: (a) Did the parties have sexual relations? If not, why not? (b) Did they maintain an attitude of fidelity to each other? (c) What were their feelings toward each other? (d) Did they communicate on a personal level? (e) Did they eat their meals together? (f) What, if anything, did they do to assist each other with problems or during illness? (g) Did they buy gifts for each other on special occasions?

3. Services: What was the conduct and habit of the parties in relation to: (a) preparation of meals; (b) washing and mending clothes; (c) shopping; (d) household maintenance; and (e) any other domestic services?

4. Social: (a) Did they participate together or separately in neighbourhood and community activities? (b) What was the relationship and conduct of each of them toward members of their respective families and how did such families behave towards the parties?

5. Societal: What was the attitude and conduct of the community towards each of them and as a couple?

6. Support (economic): (a) what were the financial arrangements between the parties regarding the provision of or contribution toward the necessaries of life (food, clothing, shelter, recreation, etc.)? (b) What were the arrangements concerning the acquisition and ownership of property? (c) Was there any special financial arrangement between them which both agreed would be determinant of their overall relationship?

7. Children: What was the attitude and conduct of the parties concerning children?

In *Sanford*, [2001] 1 C.T.C. 2273 (TCC); aff'd 2002 FCA 381, a couple were held to be common-law partners (CLPs) even though they personally rejected the concept of marriage: "If a two-legged creature with feathers waddles like a duck, quacks like a duck, and looks like a duck, it must be a duck. By parallel reasoning, if a man and woman own and share the same dwelling; take their meals together; share housekeeping chores; live in physical intimacy; and bear and raise a child ... they cohabit in a conjugal relationship." (TCC; see also *Harrison*, 2008 TCC 314.)

Conjugal relationship was found (or not disproven) in: *Milot*, [1996] 1 C.T.C. 2247 (TCC); *Drysdelle*, 2007 TCC 390, *Leblanc*, 2008 TCC 7; *Verpaelst*, 2007 TCC 396; *Hendricken*, 2008 TCC 48; *Thibeault*, 2008 TCC 119; *Brunette*, 2009 TCC 584; *St-Pierre*, 2016 TCC 146; *McKay*, 2016 TCC 233; *Pierre*, 2019 QCCQ 2137; *Climans v. Latner*, 2019 ONSC 1311 (despite keeping separate homes); *AP*, 2020 FC 906 (gay man + straight woman who had a child together); *Climans v. Latner*, 2020 ONCA 554, paras. 58-62 (couple kept separate homes and finances, had no children together, but presented as a couple over 14 years); *Sookochoff*, 2020 TCC 131 (married couple could not live together as their respective children did not get along, but they were committed to the marriage); *Turner v. Stabeck*, 2020 BCSC 1553 (cohabitation was for 2 years (the provincial test), though the couple had separate homes for part of that). Relationships were held not to be conjugal in: *Savory*, 2008 TCC 69; *Robertson*, 2008 TCC 154; *DeRepentigny*, 2008 TCC 304. Two people still living under the same roof were found to have terminated their conjugal relationship in: *Bellavance*, 2004 TCC 5; *Aukstinaitis*, 2008 TCC 104; *Perron*, 2010 TCC 547; VIEWS doc 2016-0674821C6 [2017 CPA-QC q.1.3] (see also Notes to 56.1(4)"support amount" on this point).

Staying with a person 5 days a week before moving in could be conjugal: VIEWS doc 2007-0242611E5. Two people who maintain separate residences can be in a conjugal relationship: 2002-0161185, 2010-0365741M4, 2013-0501051E5. See also 2013-0490591E5, 2016-0668361E5 (general discussion).

For the (non-tax) case law to 1992 on "cohabit in a conjugal relationship", see David M. Sherman, "Till Tax Do Us Part: The New Definition of Spouse", 1992 Cdn Tax Foundation conference report, pp. 20:1-33. See also Jamie Golombek, "Sex and Taxes", 20(4) *Money & Family Law* (Carswell) 25-28 (April 2005); Paul Prendergast, "Social Policy and the *Income Tax Act* — Tax Planning in Light of the New Definition of 'Spouse' ", 2001 Prairie Provinces Tax Conference (ctf.ca), 10:1-B-5.

A person can have both a spouse and a CLP (fiscal bigamy) for tax purposes: VIEWS docs 2006-0189141E5, 2008-0299051M4; 2009-0330301C6 (states that some rules restrict a claim to only one spouse, but this may not be correct in the author's view); 2010-0373901I7 and 2014-0523091C6 [2014 STEP q.1] (70(6) can apply to both spouse and partner on different properties); 2010-0371961C6 (implications for TFSA

---

rollover on death). See also *Carrigan*, 2012 ONCA 736 (leave to appeal to SCC denied March 28/13), on which of the two should get a pension death benefit.

"A period of 90 days" in the closing words means a continuous period according to the CRA: VIEWS doc 2004-0069021E5. The 90-day rule does not apply to "living apart due to breakdown of a common-law partnership" in 74.5(3): 2012-0438021E5. CLPs who split up near year-end, and are filing returns after the 90 days have run, should indicate their status as "separated" on the return for the year; or if they file the return before the 90 days are up, they should later file an RC65 *Marital Status Change* to report the change to the CRA.

The term "common-law partner" has been added throughout the Act wherever "spouse" appears, to cover both common-law spouses and same-sex (homosexual/gay/lesbian) partners. This replaces former 252(4), which provided an extended meaning of (opposite-sex) "spouse" for all purposes. See also 149.1(6.21).

There are still cases where the Act treats CLPs different from married persons, who are still "related" after marriage breakdown until divorce. For example, CLPs cannot achieve a corporate split-up under 55(3)(a) (VIEWS doc 2011-0394001E5); a 70(6) rollover to a CLP will fail if the relationship has broken down; and a transfer by a tax debtor to a former CLP is not automatically subject to 160(1).

Para. (a) changed from "has so cohabited with the taxpayer for a continuous period of at least one year, or" by 2002-2013 technical bill (Part 5 — technical), for 2001 and later taxation years. The amendment does not apply for a taxation year for which an election under s. 144 of the 2000 same-sex partners bill applied before Feb. 27, 2004. However, after Feb. 27, 2004, no such election may be made to affect a current or subsequent taxation year.

Definition "common-law partner" added by 2000 same-sex partners bill, effective for 2001 and later taxation years, subject to an election to have it apply back to 1998.

Income Tax Folios: S1-F3-C1: Child care expense deduction [replaces IT-495R3]; S1-F5-C1: Related persons and dealing at arm's length [replaces IT-419R2].

Registered Pension Plans Technical Manual: §1.11 (common-law partner); §1.43 (spouse).

Registered Plans Frequently Asked Questions: RPFAQ-2 (RPPs), q. 6-8 (pension plans with survivor benefits to common-law partners).

Forms: RC65: Marital status change.

"common-law partnership" means the relationship between two persons who are common-law partners of each other;

Notes: Definition "common-law partnership" added by 2000 same-sex partners bill, effective on the same basis as "common-law partner".

"common share" means a share the holder of which is not precluded on the reduction or redemption of the capital stock from participating in the assets of the corporation beyond the amount paid up on that share plus a fixed premium and a defined rate of dividend;

Related Provisions: 248(1) — "Preferred share".

Notes: Shares designated as preferred shares can be common shares under the Act, depending on the rights the shareholders would have on redemption or reduction of the capital stock: *Terminal Dock*, 1959 CarswellNat 212 (TAB); VIEWS doc 2004-0088521E5.

Interpretation Bulletins: IT-116R3: Rights to buy additional shares.

"controlled foreign affiliate" has, except as expressly otherwise provided in this Act, the meaning assigned by subsection 95(1);

Related Provisions: See under 95(1)"controlled foreign affiliate".

Notes: Definition amended by 2002-2013 technical bill (Part 5 — technical), for taxation years that begin after 2006, to add "except as expressly otherwise provided in this Act".

Definition "controlled foreign affiliate" added by 1996 Budget, effective 1996.

"corporation" includes an incorporated company;

Proposed Amendments — Hybrid mismatch arrangements

Federal Budget, Supplementary Information, April 19, 2021: *Hybrid Mismatch Arrangements*

Hybrid mismatch arrangements are cross-border tax avoidance structures that exploit differences in the income tax treatment of business entities or financial instruments under the laws of two or more countries to produce mismatches in tax results.

The Action 2 report of the BEPS Action Plan [see Proposed Amendments at end of s. 95, under Action 2 — ed.] recommends detailed rules for countries to adopt in their domestic legislation to ensure that multinational enterprises cannot derive tax benefits from the use of hybrid mismatch arrangements. The two main forms of hybrid mismatch addressed by the Action 2 recommendations are:

- Deduction/non-inclusion mismatches: These arise where a country allows a deduction in respect of a cross-border payment, the receipt of which is not included within a reasonable period of time in ordinary income in the other country. For these purposes, "ordinary income" generally means income that is subject to income tax at the recipient's full tax rate and does not benefit from any exemption, exclusion, deduction, credit or comparable tax relief.

- Double deduction mismatches: These arise where a tax deduction is available in two or more countries in respect of a single economic expense.

The Action 2 recommendations also address a form of hybrid mismatch known as imported mismatches. These generally arise where a payment is deductible by an entity resident in one country and included in the ordinary income of a recipient entity resident in a second country, but that ordinary income is set off against a deduction under a hybrid mismatch arrangement between the second entity and an entity resident in a third country.

A supplement to the Action 2 report recommends additional rules to address branch mismatch arrangements, which generally produce mismatches similar to hybrid mismatch arrangements. These mismatches occur where the residence country of a taxpayer takes a different view from that of the country where the taxpayer's branch is located as to the allocation of income and expenditures between the two countries.

The Action 2 recommendations reflect a broad international consensus that hybrid mismatch and branch mismatch arrangements (collectively, hybrid arrangements) significantly erode the tax bases of affected countries. Hybrid arrangements may also have other adverse effects, such as distorting investment decisions and providing an unfair competitive advantage to multinational enterprises over domestic businesses.

The Action 2 report recognizes that coordinated international action is required in order to address the negative impacts of hybrid arrangements, without giving rise to double taxation or other unintended consequences. Accordingly, the Action 2 recommendations outline a common approach that is intended to ensure countries have consistent rules that operate in a coordinated manner. A number of countries (including the United States, the United Kingdom, Australia and the European Union member states) have already implemented, or committed to implement, rules consistent with the Action 2 recommendations.

There are existing Canadian income tax rules that the government can use to challenge certain hybrid arrangements. However, further specific legislative measures would provide certainty and, as noted above, there are significant advantages to adopting the common approach in the Action 2 report.

Budget 2021 proposes to implement rules consistent with the Action 2 recommendations, with appropriate adaptations to the Canadian income tax context.

In general terms, under the main proposed rules, payments made by Canadian residents under hybrid mismatch arrangements would not be deductible for Canadian income tax purposes to the extent that they give rise to a further deduction in another country or are not included in the ordinary income of a non-resident recipient. Conversely, to the extent that a payment made under such an arrangement by an entity that is not resident in Canada is deductible for foreign income tax purposes, no deduction in respect of the payment would be permitted against the income of a Canadian resident. Any amount of the payment received by a Canadian resident would also be included in income, and, if the payment is a dividend, it would not be eligible for the deduction otherwise available for certain dividends received from foreign affiliates. In effect, these rules would neutralize a mismatch by aligning the Canadian income tax treatment with the income tax treatment in the foreign country.

Rules implementing other Action 2 recommendations — such as those on branch mismatch arrangements, imported mismatch arrangements and reverse hybrids (i.e., entities that are fiscally transparent under the laws of the country where they are formed, but are treated as a separate entity under the laws of an investor's country) — would be introduced to the extent relevant and appropriate in the Canadian context.

Consistent with the Action 2 recommendations:

- The proposed rules would be mechanical in nature and would not be conditioned on a purpose test.
- With limited exceptions, the proposed rules would apply in respect of payments between related parties and payments under certain arrangements between unrelated parties that are designed to produce a mismatch.
- The ordering rules recommended by the report would also apply to ensure that the proposed rules are coordinated with similar rules in other countries.

The proposed rules to address hybrid arrangements would be implemented in two separate legislative packages. The first package would comprise rules implementing (with any modifications required for the Canadian income tax context) the recommendations in Chapters 1 and 2 of the Action 2 report. These would generally be intended to neutralize a deduction/non-inclusion mismatch arising from a payment in respect of a financial instrument.

The first legislative package would be released for stakeholder comment later in 2021, and those rules would apply as of July 1, 2022.

The second legislative package would be released for stakeholder comment after 2021, and those rules would apply no earlier than 2023. This package would comprise rules consistent with the Action 2 recommendations that were not addressed in the first package.

Federal Budget, Chapter 10, April 19, 2021: *Preventing Cross-border Tax Schemes*

Hybrid mismatch arrangements are cross-border tax schemes, used primarily by multinational enterprises, that exploit differences between Canadian and foreign income tax laws to avoid paying their fair share of tax. Under the current rules, a multinational company can exploit the different treatment of certain business entities and financial instruments in Canada and another country to earn income that is not taxed in any country. These schemes not only erode the tax base that supports programs and services for Canadians, but they also give an unfair advantage to multinational enterprises over Canadian businesses, particularly our small and medium-sized businesses.

Budget 2021 proposes to amend the *Income Tax Act* to eliminate the tax benefits of hybrid mismatch arrangements. These proposals would be implemented in stages starting July 1, 2022.

These proposals will level the playing field and help ensure everyone pays their fair share. It is estimated that this measure will increase federal revenues by $775 million over four years starting in 2022-23.

Notes: The MLI (Multilateral Instrument, reproduced before the Canada-US treaty), in its Art. 3, addresses hybrid mismatches, but Canada has not signed on to that Article.

Budget Table 1 projects that this measure will generate revenue for the federal government of $130 million in 2022-23, $205m in 2023-24, $215m in 2024-25 and $225m in 2025-26.

Related Provisions: 227.1 — Liability of directors; 236 — Execution of documents by corporations; 242 — Officers, directors and agents guilty of corporation's offences; *Interpretation Act* 21(1) — Powers vested in corporation; *Interpretation Act* 35(1) — Corporation does not include partnership that is separate legal entity.

Notes: The French version of this definition was amended in the R.S.C. 1985 statute revision process (now the *Legislative Revision and Consolidation Act*), not enacted by Parliament, and arguably without changing the previous meaning. See Lanthier, "Statute Revision", 23(5) *Canadian Tax Highlights* (ctf.ca) 1-2 (May 2015) and "The Perils of Statute Revision", 5(2) *The Newsletter* (Tax Executives Institute, Toronto Chapter) 2-4 (Dec. 2015).

Disclosure of corporations' beneficial owners: see Notes to 150(1)(a).

A corporation's branches are all part of the same legal entity, so Revenu Québec could serve on a Quebec branch of National Bank a demand for information from the bank's Calgary branch: *1068754 Alberta [Bitton Trust]*, 2019 SCC 37.

On corporations generally, see Sorensen, *Taxation of Private Corporations and their Shareholders* (ctf.ca, 5th ed., 2020), chap. 1. For how corps are taxed, see 123(1) Notes.

"It is a basic rule of company law that shareholders do not own the assets of the company", and this rule applies for tax purposes unless there are specific look-through rules such as 256(1.2): *Envision Credit Union*, 2013 SCC 48, para. 57. In rare cases the "corporate veil" will be pierced to make shareholders or affiliates liable, e.g. *9183-4507 Québec Inc.*, 2015 FC 901, paras. 37-43.

Provincial law applies to determine legal relationships to which the ITA applies (see Notes to 169(1) re rectification), so provincial legislation deeming an entity to be a corporation makes it a "corporation" for tax purposes.

In 2010, CRA said it would stop ruling on foreign entity status, as CRA officers are not experts in foreign law (VIEWS docs 2011-0415141E5, 2012-0434831E5); but said at the 2012 Ontario Tax Conference Roundtable (ctf.ca) Q6 (doc 2012-0463021C6) that Rulings "is again prepared to entertain ruling requests on entity classification". A request should include "a complete description of the characteristics of the entity, analysis as to its proper classification, and a translated copy of both the legislation under which the entity was created and its organizational documents." See also Crosbie, "Entity Classification", XVII(3) *Corporate Finance* (Federated Press) 2010-15 (2011).

"Corporation" is considered by CRA to include the foreign entities listed in IT-343R (e.g., Aktiengesellschaft, Aktieselskab, Anstalt [Liechtenstein], BV, Compania Anonima, GmbH, Kabushiki Kaisha, Sociedade anónima, Société anonyme, Società per Azioni); as well as Society with Restricted Liability (Barbados, VIEWS doc 2003-0007347); Limitada (Chile, doc 9415705); Kft (Hungary, 9829875); limited liability partnership (Kazakhstan, 9624595); joint stock company (Russia, doc 9625015); Dutch cooperative (2008-0264671R3, 2010-0373801R3, 2015-0571441R3, 2015-0581151I7); other foreign cooperative (2006-020691R3, 2006-0208571R3, 2007-0255241R3, 2007-0259921R3, 2007-0260861R3, 2008-0280791R3, 2009-0343991R3); foreign company (2006-0209631R3); foreign joint venture (2006-0202071R3); spółka z ograniczona odpowiedzialnoscia (sp z o.o.) (Poland, 2004-0087491E5). The CRA's position on Liechtenstein Anstalt might change in the future: 2008-030051I17; but was reconfirmed in 2010-038862117 (July 2011). A French société en nom collectif that has elected to be taxed as a corporation in France is treated as a corporation: 2001-0108715, 2003-0051301E5. A German "GmbH & CO KG" is likely a limited partnership: 9701825, 2004-0069741E5. The following are considered partnerships: French Société en nom collectif (SNC) (2005-0148311E5); Iceland Sameignarfélag (SF) (2006-0187681R3, 2015-059255117); Pakistan association of persons (2006-020318117, 2007-022126117).

A "Societas Europaea" (European public limited company, authorized since Oct. 2004) is a corporation: Marja De Best & Patrick Marley, "Implications of Recent EU Developments", XII(4) *International Tax Planning* (Federated Press) 895-900 (2005). French SLP (Société de Libre Partenariat): uncertain but not a partnership: 2018-0749481C6 [2018 IFA q.8].

The following are co-ownership arrangements, not corporations or trusts: Irish or other Common Contractual Fund (CCF) (VIEWS docs 2004-0106731R3, 2006-0199741R3, 2009-0341561R3, 2009-0343271R3, 2009-0345011R3, 2010-0353901R3, 2012-0432341R3, 2013-0496831R3, 2015-0606141R3); Luxembourg fonds commun de placement (FCP) (2007-0231581R3, 2009-0346131R3, 2015-0605161R3); Dutch closed FGR ("besloten Fonds voor Gemene Rekening": 2009-0335281R3, 2009-0347891R3, 2009-0347901R3 [see also tinyurl.com/cra-agreements under "Netherlands"]); arrangement of undisclosed country (2017-0738041R3).

See Notes to 104(1) for rulings that a German "fiduziarische Treuhand", a Liechtenstein "stiftung" (foundation) and various other entities are trusts.

See Gupta, "Characterization of Foreign Entities", IX(2) *Business Vehicles* (Federated Press) 438-47 (2003); Darmo, "Characterization of Foreign Business Associations", 53(2) *Canadian Tax Journal* 481-505 (2005); Owen, "Foreign Entity Classification", 2005 Cdn Tax Foundation conference report, 20:1-59; McLeod, "Entity Classification", 16(11) *Canadian Tax Highlights* (ctf.ca) 1-2 (Nov. 2000); Boidman & Kandev, "Foreign Entity Classification", 57(4) *CTJ* 880-904 (2009), and response by Couzin & Lanthier, "A Comment", 58(1) 223-27 (2010); Milet, "Hybrid Foreign Entities", 59(1) *CTJ* 25-57 (2011); Korovilas & Morier, "Non-Corporate Vehicles in the Foreign Affiliate Context", 2018 conference report, 20:1-114.

At the 2006 Cdn Tax Foundation annual conference roundtable (slides available), Wayne Adams stated that IT-343R will not be updated to reflect current CRA policy. The "two-step" approach used is based on Marc Darmo's paper above: (a) determine the entity's characteristics under foreign commercial law; (b) compare with the types of recognized categories under Cdn commercial law. Consider: (1) the nature of the rights in the entity's assets; (2) the right to participate in profits or receive distributions; (3) the right to vote or participate in decisions; (4) the right to share in distribution of assets on windup; (5) liabilities of the various parties. The CRA confirmed this at the 2007 conference (*Income Tax Technical News* 38) and in VIEWS docs 2008-0284241C6, 2011-0405261C6, 2012-0451261C6, 2015-0581511C6 [2015 IFA q.3].

A *limited-liability company (LLC)* created under US state law is considered a corporation for Canadian tax purposes, though it may be treated as a partnership for US tax purposes. Thus, US tax paid cannot be recovered as foreign tax credit (s. 126) by the Canadian "partner", who is actually a shareholder in the CRA's view; also, the FAPI regime may apply (see Notes to 91(1)) and the "partner" may need to file a Form T1134 (see 233.4). This applies to LLCs of (VIEWS doc 2001-0085845 except where noted) Arizona (2003-0004415), Delaware (except DRUPA; see below) (also 2008-0272141R3, 2010-0369311E5, 2015-0615041R3), Florida, Indiana, Kentucky, Michigan, Nevada (*Boliden Westmin v. BC*, 2007 BCSC 351; *Income Tax Technical News* 38), New Hampshire, New York, Ohio, Oregon, Tennessee, Texas, Wisconsin (2002-0120085) and Wyoming. See also *Income Tax Technical News* 25 and docs 2004-0064761R3, 2015-0588381I7 (even if shareholder is Quebec resident). (See Reg. 5907(11.2)(b) re the LLC being a foreign affiliate.)

Canada-US tax treaty Art. IV:6 effectively extends treaty relief to LLCs owned by US taxpayers. There was speculation that the CRA might not consider an LLC to be a corporation if it does not issue capital stock: Watson & Baum, "U.S. LLCs as Corporations — a New CRA Position?", XVI(4) *International Tax Planning* (Federated Press) 1136-41 (2011); Fabbro, "What is an LLC?", 2067 *Tax Topics* (CCH) 1-4 (Oct. 20, 2011), but this seems not to be the case. *Anson*, [2015] UKSC 44 (LLC was not a corp for UK foreign tax credit purposes) does not change the CRA's view that LLCs are corporations: 2015-0601781E5 [Kabouchi & Lang, "Timing Mismatches Affect Foreign Tax Credits Available on LLC Distributions", XX(4) *Corporate Finance* (Federated Press) 13-16 (2017)], 2015-0610611C6 [2015 CTF q.7], 2016-0634951C6 [2016 STEP q.8], 2016-0642051C6 [2016 IFA q.1].

A Delaware or Florida limited liability partnership (LLP) or limited liability limited partnership (LLLP) is now considered to be a corp: VIEWS doc 2015-056080117; but CRA will accept one formed before April 26, 2017 as being a partnership indefinitely (grandfathered), provided all members report consistent with that, there is no "significant change" in the membership, and it is not "being used to facilitate abusive tax avoidance": 2017-0691131C6 [2017 IFA q.3]; 2018-0749481C6 [2018 IFA q.8]; 2018-0768561E5 (grandfathered LLLP that wants to be treated as a corp *prospectively* does not qualify as a partnership at all). This replaces the earlier position that would have required the LLP or LLLP to convert to a "real" partnership before 2018: 2015-0587691I7, 2016-0634951C6 [2016 STEP q.8], 2016-0642051C6 [2016 IFA q.1]; 2016-0669751C6 [2016 CTF q.10]. CRA's view that these are corps may be legally wrong: Nitikman, "Is an LLP a Corporation?", 2313 *Tax Topics* (CCH) 1-7 (July 7, 2016); Discepola and Nearing, "A Reply to the CRA's Classification of Florida and Delaware LLLPs and LLPs", 2016 Cdn Tax Foundation conference report, 24:1-39. A UK LLP is normally a corp: 2020-0866671C6 [2020 CTF q.9] (see also Canada-UK tax treaty, 2014 Interpretative Protocol [before Art. 1], para. 1).

On the effects of converting from one form to another see Nikolakakis, "The Tax Treatment of Transformation Transactions", 2006 Cdn Tax Foundation conference report, 14:1-64; VIEWS docs 2002-0132163 and 2005-0109741R3 (converting French Société anonyme into Société par actions simplifiée); 2003-0049231E5 and 2004-0065921R3 (converting Delaware or California corporation to LLC); 2002-0166673 and 2002-0174703 (foreign affiliate reorganizations); 2017-0724091C6 [2017 CTF q.15] (converting US LP to LLC).

Where there is a "hybrid partnership" that the foreign country treats as a corporation, CRA is reviewing its position on whether to continue to give treaty benefits to partners resident in that country: VIEWS doc 2004-0102471C6 (Nov. 25, 2004).

The Multilateral Instrument (MLI — see before the Canada-US treaty), which effectively amends most tax treaties worldwide, specifically targets planning that uses hybrid mismatches to avoid tax. Canada has not signed on to this rule (MLI Art. 3). However, see the April 2021 Budget proposal above for Canada's proposed amendments.

See also Lanthier & Plutte, "International Hybrids", 1999 Cdn Tax Foundation conference report, 46:1-38, for discussion of hybrids created under various jurisdictions including the US, Barbados, China, France, Germany, Kazakhstan, the Netherlands and Russia; Tremblay & Milet, "Hybrid Entities and Dually-chartered Entities", XII(3) *International Tax Planning* (Federated Press) 864-68 (2004); Durrance, "Classification of Foreign Entities", XII(1) *Business Vehicles* (Federated Press) 618-22 (2008); Bernstein, "LLC and LLP Update", 24(1) *Canadian Tax Highlights* (ctf.ca) 9 (Jan. 2016).

For US tax issues re "domestic reverse hybrids" see Maiorano et al., "Final Regulations Under Section 894(c)", XI(1) *International Tax Planning* (Federated Press) 763-75 (2002).

A Nova Scotia unlimited liability corporation (NSULC) is a corporation for Canadian tax purposes but not in the US, per an IRS ruling. An NSULC with one US shareholder is effectively a branch for US tax purposes; with more shareholders it is effectively a partnership. See Gabrielle Richards, "Takeovers and Subsection 88(1) Hybrids; Update on LLCs/ULCs", 1996 Cdn Tax Foundation conference report, 6:13-27. Canada-US tax treaty Art. IV:7 effectively denies treaty benefits to NSULCs and other provinces' ULCs, resulting in 25% withholding tax under 212(1). See Barnicke & Roy, "New Protocol and Hybrids", 15(10) *CTH* 1-2 (Oct. 2007). For workarounds see Bernstein, "Planning for Existing ULCs", 15(11) *CTH* 3 (Nov. 2007); Peters, "Implications of Restructuring a Canadian ULC", 57(1) *Canadian Tax Journal* 171-92 (2009). See also Notes to Art. IV:7.

A Nova Scotia "limited by guarantee" company is considered a corporation: VIEWS doc 2000-0025855.

CRA considers a *Delaware Revised Uniform Partnership Act* (DRUPA) or *Delaware Revised Uniform Limited Partnership Act* (DRULPA) partnership to be a partnership for Canadian tax purposes, provided it carries on business for profit: VIEWS docs 2000-0056715, 2000-0057765, 2000-0062015, 2007-0247551E5; *Income Tax Technical News* 20, 25, 34.

For a ruling on converting a cooperative corporation into an ordinary corporation see VIEWS doc 2006-0176321R3.

Pre-incorporation expenses and contracts: Some expenses incurred before incorporation can be deducted: IT-454, VIEWS docs 2005-0159391E5, 2011-040067117. A pre-incorporation contract (PIC) is "one aspect of the objective circumstances which can be used to interpret the parties' post-incorporation conduct and from which the terms of a post-incorporation contract can be inferred": *Strata Plan LMS 3905 v. Crystal Square*, 2020 SCC 29, para. 33. Business corporations legislation may allow a corp to adopt, and thus be bound by, a PIC (e.g. Ontario *Business Corporations Act* s. 21(2); *Benedetto v. 2453912 Ontario*, 2019 ONCA 149).

Income Tax Folios: S4-F7-C1: Amalgamations of Canadian corporations [replaces IT-474R2].

Interpretation Bulletins: IT-343R: Meaning of the term "corporation" [for purposes of the definition of "foreign affiliate"]; IT-432R2: Benefits conferred on shareholders.

I.T. Technical News: 20 (*Delaware Revised Uniform Partnership Act*); 25 (partnership issues); 34 (*Delaware Revised Uniform Partnership Act*); 38 (foreign entity classification; limited liability company under the Protocol).

"corporation incorporated in Canada" includes a corporation incorporated in any part of Canada before or after it became part of Canada;

Related Provisions: 250(5.1) — Corporation continued outside Canada deemed incorporated in new jurisdiction.

Notes: If corporations are amalgamated in Canada, the Amalco is considered incorporated in Canada: *Deltona Corp.*, [1971] C.T.C. 297 (Exch. Ct); CRA, Cdn Bar Association Commodity Tax Section roundtable, Feb. 27, 2020, q.17.

248(1)"corporation incorporated in Canada" added in the RSC 1985 (5th Supp) consolidation, effective Dec. 1991. This definition was formerly under "corporation".

"cost amount" to a taxpayer of any property at any time means, except as expressly otherwise provided in this Act,

(a) where the property was depreciable property of the taxpayer of a prescribed class, the amount that would be that proportion of the undepreciated capital cost to the taxpayer of property of that class at that time that the capital cost to the taxpayer of the property is of the capital cost to the taxpayer of all property of that class that had not been disposed of by the taxpayer before that time if subsection 13(7) were read without reference to paragraph 13(7)(e) and if

(i) paragraph 13(7)(b) were read as follows:

"(b) where a taxpayer, having acquired property for some other purpose, has commenced at a later time to use it for the purpose of gaining or producing income, the taxpayer shall be deemed to have acquired it at that later time at a capital cost to the taxpayer equal to the fair market value of the property at that later time;", and

(ii) subparagraph 13(7)(d)(i) were read as follows:

"(i) if the use regularly made by the taxpayer of the property for the purpose of gaining or producing income has increased, the taxpayer shall be deemed to have acquired at that time depreciable property of that class at a capital cost equal to the proportion of its fair market value at that time that the amount of the increase in the use regularly made by the taxpayer of the property for that purpose is of the whole of the use regularly made of the property, and"

(b) where the property was capital property (other than depreciable property) of the taxpayer, its adjusted cost base to the taxpayer at that time,

(c) where the property was property described in an inventory of the taxpayer, its value at that time as determined for the purpose of computing the taxpayer's income,

(c.1) where the taxpayer was a financial institution in its taxation year that includes that time and the property was a mark-to-market property for the year, the cost to the taxpayer of the property,

(d) [Repealed]

(d.1) where the property was a loan or lending asset (other than a net income stabilization account or a property in respect of which paragraph (b), (c), (c.1) or (d.2) applies), the amortized cost of the property to the taxpayer at that time,

(d.2) where the taxpayer was a financial institution in its taxation year that includes that time and the property was a specified debt obligation (other than a mark-to-market property for the year), the tax basis of the property to the taxpayer at that time,

(e) where the property was a right of the taxpayer to receive an amount, other than property that is

(i) a debt the amount of which was deducted under paragraph 20(1)(p) in computing the taxpayer's income for a taxation year that ended before that time,

(ii) a net income stabilization account,

(iii) a right in respect of which paragraph (b), (c), (c.1), (d.1) or (d.2) applies, or

(iv) a right to receive production (as defined in subsection 18.1(1)) to which a matchable expenditure (as defined in subsection 18.1(1)) relates,

the amount the taxpayer has a right to receive,

(e.1) where the property was a policy loan (within the meaning assigned by subsection 138(12)) of an insurer, nil,

(e.2) where the property is an interest of a beneficiary under a qualifying environmental trust, nil, and

(f) in any other case, the cost to the taxpayer of the property as determined for the purpose of computing the taxpayer's income, except to the extent that that cost has been deducted in computing the taxpayer's income for any taxation year ending before that time;

and, for the purposes of this definition, "financial institution", "mark-to-market property" and "specified debt obligation" have the meanings assigned by subsection 142.2(1), and "tax basis" has the meaning assigned by subsection 142.4(1);

Related Provisions: 10(1) — Valuation of inventory for calculating income; 13(7) — Rule affecting capital cost of depreciable property; 13(33) — Consideration given for depreciable capital; 27.1(2) — Cost of emissions allowance; 52(3) — Cost of stock dividend; 53 — Adjusted cost base — adjustments; 70(14) — Order of disposal of depreciable property on death; 86.1(3) — Cost amount adjustments on foreign spin-off; 108(1) — Meaning of "cost amount" of capital interest in a trust; 112(11)–(13) — Cost reductions for partnership interest that is not capital property; 248(25.3) — Deemed cost of trust units; 261(7)(b) — Cost of property when functional currency election made.

Notes: For the meaning of "cost" see Notes to 54"adjusted cost base".

If an option is surrendered or sold to person X who issued it, there is no "cost" to X, as the option rights are extinguished due to the doctrine of merger: *Devon Canada*, 2018 TCC 170, paras. 118-126.

Para. (d) repealed by 2016 budget bill #2, effective 2017, as part of changing the eligible capital property rules to CCA Class 14.1 (see Notes to 20(1)(b)). Before 2017, read:

(d) where the property was eligible capital property of the taxpayer in respect of a business, ⁴∕₃ of the amount that would, but for subsection 14(3), be determined by the formula

$$A \times \frac{B}{C}$$

where

A   is the cumulative eligible capital of the taxpayer in respect of the business at that time,

B   is the fair market value at that time of the property, and

C   is the fair market value at that time of all the eligible capital property of the taxpayer in respect of the business,

"Cost amount" amended by 1995-97 technical bill (effective Nov. 18, 1996), 1994 technical bill, 1994 Budget, 1992 and 1991 technical bills.

I.T. Application Rules: 18 (property acquired before 1972).

Income Tax Folios: S3-F4-C1: General discussion of CCA [replaces IT-220R2]; S4-F7-C1: Amalgamations of Canadian corporations [replaces IT-474R2].

Interpretation Bulletins: IT-142R3: Settlement of debts on the winding-up of a corporation; IT-291R3: Transfer of property to a corporation under subsection 85(1); IT-457R: Election by professionals to exclude work in progress from income; IT-471R: Merger of partnerships; IT-488R2: Winding-up of 90%-owned taxable Canadian corporation (cancelled); IT-528: Transfers of funds between registered plans.

"credit union" has the meaning assigned by subsection 137(6), except for the purposes of Part XV.1;

Notes: Definition amended by 2014 budget bill #1, effective 2015, to add "except for the purposes of Part XV.1".

"cumulative eligible capital" — [Repealed]

Notes: Definition repealed by 2016 budget bill #2, effective 2017, as part of changing the eligible capital property rules to CCA Class 14.1 (see Notes to 20(1)(b)). It read "has the meaning assigned by subsection 14(5)".

"DRA share" *[dividend rental arrangement share — ed.]*, of a person or partnership, means a share

(a) that is owned by the person or partnership,

(b) in respect of which the person or partnership is deemed to have received a dividend under subsection 260(5.1) and is provided with all or substantially all of the risk of loss and opportunity for gain or profit under an agreement or arrangement,

(c) that is held by a trust under which the person or partnership is a beneficiary and in respect of which the person or partnership is deemed to have received a dividend as a result of a designation by the trust under subsection 104(19),

(d) in respect of which the person or partnership is deemed to have received a dividend under subsection 82(2), or

(e) in any other case, in respect of which the person or partnership is (or would be in the absence of subsection 112(2.3)) entitled to a deduction under subsection 112(1) in respect of dividends received on the share;

Notes: A share owned by the taxpayer can pay a dividend; this is the normal case. "DRA share" includes such shares, as well as other shares on which a dividend could be received or deemed received.

"DRA share" added by 2016 budget bill #1, effective April 22, 2015.

"death benefit" means the total of all amounts received by a taxpayer in a taxation year on or after the death of an employee in recognition of the employee's service in an office or employment minus

(a) where the taxpayer is the only person who has received such an amount and who is a surviving spouse or common-law partner of the employee (which person is, in this definition, referred to as the "surviving spouse or common-law partner"), the lesser of

(i) the total of all amounts so received by the taxpayer in the year, and

(ii) the amount, if any, by which $10,000[30] exceeds the total of all amounts received by the taxpayer in preceding taxation years on or after the death of the employee in recognition of the employee's service in an office or employment, or

(b) where the taxpayer is not the surviving spouse or common-law partner of the employee, the lesser of

(i) the total of all amounts so received by the taxpayer in the year, and

(ii) that proportion of

(A) the amount, if any, by which $10,000[30] exceeds the total of all amounts received by the surviving spouse or common-law partner of the employee at any time on or after the death of the employee in recognition of the employee's service in an office or employment

that

(B) the amount described in subparagraph (i)

is of

(C) the total of all amounts received by all taxpayers other than the surviving spouse or common-law partner of the employee at any time on or after the death of the employee in recognition of the employee's service in an office or employment;

Related Provisions: 56(1)(a)(iii) — Death benefit included in income; 104(28) — Death benefit flowed through trust; 128.1(10)"excluded right or interest"(h) — Emigration — no deemed disposition of right to death benefit.

Notes: A death benefit is taxable under 56(1)(a)(iii), but this definition excludes the first $10,000 (this figure unchanged since April 1959). For CRA interpretation see VIEWS docs 2006-0178501E5, 2008-0279241E5, 2008-0293131E5, 2009-0347131E5, 2010-0359171E5, 2011-0420391E5; 2012-0435591E5 (long time between end of employment and death does not disqualify payment); 2016-0656101E5 (sole shareholder who was paid salary, but only dividends in last 2 years, can qualify).

A death benefit paid under a pension or superannuation plan is pension income, not a "death benefit": *Woods*, 2011 FCA 90; doc 2014-0525681E5.

In *Scott*, 2017 TCC 224, paras. 135-142, a lump sum from the Nortel health & welfare trust, to compensate employees for losing death benefits when it shut down unfunded, was taxable.

Survivor benefits from a US employer under the Federal Employment Retirement System are likely pension benefits rather than death benefits: doc 2005-0140101E5.

248(1)"death benefit" amended by 2000 same-sex partners bill (last change effective 2001) and 1992 technical bill.

Interpretation Bulletins: IT-508R: Death benefits.

"deferred amount" at the end of a taxation year under a salary deferral arrangement in respect of a taxpayer means

(a) in the case of a trust governed by the arrangement, any amount that a person has a right under the arrangement at the end of the year to receive after the end of the year where the amount has been received, is receivable or may at any time become receivable by the trust as, on account or in lieu of salary or wages of the taxpayer for services rendered in the year or a preceding taxation year, and

(b) in any other case, any amount that a person has a right under the arrangement at the end of the year to receive after the end of the year,

and, for the purposes of this definition, a right under the arrangement shall include a right that is subject to one or more conditions unless there is a substantial risk that any one of those conditions will not be satisfied;

Notes: See VIEWS doc 2005-0151051R3 for a ruling interpreting this definition.

Definition "deferred amount" added by S.C. 1986, c. 55, effective Feb. 26, 1986, with certain exceptions for an agreement in writing made before that date. For interpretation of the transitional rule see doc 2008-0289341E5.

"deferred profit sharing plan" has the meaning assigned by subsection 147(1);

"depreciable property" has the meaning assigned by subsection 13(21);

Related Provisions: See under 13(21)"depreciable property".

I.T. Application Rules: 18, 20 (property acquired before 1972).

"derivative forward agreement", of a taxpayer, means an agreement entered into by the taxpayer to purchase or sell a capital property if

(a) the term of the agreement exceeds 180 days or the agreement is part of a series of agreements with a term that exceeds 180 days,

(b) in the case of a purchase agreement, the difference between the fair market value of the property delivered on settlement, including partial settlement, of the agreement and the amount paid for the property is attributable, in whole or in part, to an underlying interest (including a value, price, rate, variable, index, event, probability or thing) other than

(i) revenue, income or cashflow in respect of the property over the term of the agreement, changes in the fair market value of the property over the term of the agreement, or any similar criteria in respect of the property unless

(A) the property is

(I) a "Canadian security" (as defined in subsection 39(6)), or

(II) an interest in a partnership the fair market value of which is derived, in whole or in part, from a Canadian security,

(B) the agreement is an agreement to acquire property from

(I) a tax-indifferent investor, or

(II) a "financial institution" (as defined in subsection 142.2(1)), and

(C) it can reasonably be considered that one of the main purposes of the series of transactions or events, or any transaction or event in the series, of which the agreement is part is for all or any portion of the capital gain on a disposition (other than a disposition by the seller to the taxpayer under the agreement) of a Canadian security referred to in clause (A) — as part of the same series of transactions or events — to be attributable to amounts paid or payable on the Canadian security by the issuer of the Canadian security during the term of the agreement as

(I) interest,

(II) dividends, or

(III) income of a trust other than income paid out of the taxable capital gains of the trust,

(ii) if the purchase price is denominated in the currency of a country other than Canada, changes in the value of the Canadian currency relative to that other currency, or

(iii) an underlying interest that relates to a purchase of currency, if it can reasonably be considered that the purchase is agreed to by the taxpayer in order to reduce its risk of fluctuations in the value of the currency in which a purchase or sale by the taxpayer of a capital property is denominated, in which an obligation that is a capital property of the taxpayer is denominated or from which a capital property of the taxpayer derives its value, and

(c) in the case of a sale agreement,

(i) the difference between the sale price of the property and the fair market value of the property at the time the agreement is entered into by the taxpayer is attributable, in whole

---

[30] Not indexed for inflation.

or in part, to an underlying interest (including a value, price, rate, variable, index, event, probability or thing) other than

(A) revenue, income or cashflow in respect of the property over the term of the agreement, changes in the fair market value of the property over the term of the agreement, or any similar criteria in respect of the property,

(B) if the sale price is denominated in the currency of a country other than Canada, changes in the value of the Canadian currency relative to that other currency, or

(C) an underlying interest that relates to a sale of currency, if it can reasonably be considered that the sale is agreed to by the taxpayer in order to reduce its risk of fluctuations in the value of the currency in which a purchase or sale by the taxpayer of a capital property is denominated, in which an obligation that is a capital property of the taxpayer is denominated or from which a capital property of the taxpayer derives its value, and

(ii) the agreement is part of an arrangement that has the effect — or would have the effect if the agreements that are part of the arrangement and that were entered into by persons or partnerships not dealing at arm's length with the taxpayer were entered into by the taxpayer instead of non-arm's length persons or partnerships — of eliminating a majority of the taxpayer's risk of loss and opportunity for gain or profit in respect of the property for a period of more than 180 days;

Related Provisions: 12(1)(z.7) — Income inclusion; 20(1)(xx) — Deduction from income; 53(1)(s), (t), 53(2)(w), (x) — ACB adjustments.

Notes: The DFA rules were introduced by the 2013 Budget to catch "character conversion transactions" that artificially turn income into capital gains. A DFA is typically a forward agreement to buy or sell property on a future date, with payment linked to something other than the property's value (such as an interest component or dividends on a basket of stocks). 12(1)(z.7) includes the full gain into income rather than it being a capital gain under 39(1) (subject to certain grandfathering until March 2018 — see Notes to 12(1)(z.7)). This rule will affect mutual funds that make 39(4) elections.

The DFA definition can catch a currency forward contract, if the price includes an interest component.

In some cases the definition can be avoided by inserting terms into the security being bought or sold to cause its value to vary by the relevant criteria, so that (b)(i) or (c)(i)(A) applies.

The "amount paid for the property" in para. (b) is not the same wording as "cost", and thus appears not to include an amount paid for an *option* to acquire the property, which under 49(3) is part of cost.

Note that a DFA can also be a synthetic disposition arrangement (as defined in 248(1)).

For the possible impact of these rules on exchangeable share arrangements and on umbrella partnership real estate investment trusts, see Jack Bernstein, "Exchangeable Shares and UPREITs", 21(5) *Canadian Tax Highlights* (ctf.ca) 2-3 (May 2013).

For CRA interpretation see Cdn Tax Foundation 2014 conference roundtable q.1 (four questions) [VIEWS doc 2014-0546701C6].

See also Caines & Van Loan, "Character Conversion Transactions and Synthetic Dispositions", XVIII(4) *Corporate Finance* (Federated Press) 2161-67 and "...Updated", XIX(1) 2198-2200 (2013); Calvert & Mar, "Recent Transactions", 2013 Cdn Tax Foundation conference report at 7:5-9; Miller & Milet, "Derivative Forward Agreements and Synthetic Disposition Arrangements", *ibid.* at 10:1-19; Edgar, "Risk-Based Overrides of Share Ownership as Specific Anti-Avoidance Rules", 63(2) *Canadian Tax Journal* 397-465 (2015).

Subpara. (b)(i) amended by 2021 budget bill #1 to add "unless" and everything from cl (A); in force per s. 61(8)-(9) of the bill:

(8) Subsection (1) is deemed to have come into force on March 19, 2019. However, it does not apply before 2020 in respect of

(a) an agreement that is entered into after the final settlement of another derivative forward agreement (in this paragraph referred to as the "prior agreement") if

(i) having regard to the source of the funds used to purchase the property to be sold under the agreement, it is reasonable to conclude that the agreement is a continuation of the prior agreement,

(ii) the terms of the agreement and the prior agreement are substantially similar,

(iii) the final settlement date under the agreement is before 2020,

(iv) the amendment does not apply to the prior agreement, and

(v) the notional amount of the agreement is at all times less than or equal to the amount determined by the formula

$$(A + B + C + D + E) - (F + G)$$

where

A is the notional amount of the agreement when it is entered into,

B is the total of all amounts each of which is an increase in the notional amount of the agreement, at or before that time, that is attributable to the underlying interest,

C is the amount of the taxpayer's cash on hand immediately before March 19, 2019 that was committed, before March 19, 2019, to be invested under the agreement,

D is the total of all amounts each of which is an increase, at or before that time, in the notional amount of the agreement that is attributable to the final settlement of another derivative forward agreement if the amendment does not apply to the other agreement,

E is the lesser of

(A) either

(I) if the prior agreement was entered into before March 19, 2019, the amount, if any, by which the amount determined under subpara. (i) of the description of F in para. (b) for the prior agreement immediately before it was finally settled exceeds the total determined under subpara. (ii) of the description of F in para. (b) for the prior agreement immediately before it was finally settled, or

(II) in any other case, the amount, if any, by which the amount determined under this clause for the prior agreement immediately before it was finally settled exceeds the total determined under clause (B) for the prior agreement immediately before it was finally settled, and

(B) the total of all amounts each of which is an increase in the notional amount of the agreement before 2020 that is not otherwise described in this formula,

F is the total of all amounts each of which is a decrease in the notional amount of the agreement, at or before that time, that is attributable to the underlying interest, and

G is the total of all amounts each of which is the amount of a partial settlement of the agreement, at or before that time, to the extent that it is not reinvested in the agreement; or

(b) an agreement that is entered into before March 19, 2019, unless at any time on or after March 19, 2019, the notional amount of the agreement exceeds the amount determined by the formula

$$(A + B + C + D + E + F) - (G + H)$$

where

A is the notional amount of the agreement immediately before March 19, 2019,

B is the total of all amounts each of which is an increase in the notional amount of the agreement, on or after March 19, 2019 and at or before that time, that is attributable to the underlying interest,

C is the amount of the taxpayer's cash on hand immediately before March 19, 2019 that was committed, before March 19, 2019, to be invested under the agreement,

D is the amount, if any, of an increase, on or after March 19, 2019 and at or before that time, in the notional amount of the agreement as a consequence of the exercise of an over-allotment option granted before March 19, 2019,

E is the total of all amounts each of which is an increase, on or after March 19, 2019 and at or before that time, in the notional amount of the agreement that is attributable to the final settlement of another derivative forward agreement if the amendment does not apply to the other agreement,

F is the lesser of

(i) 5% of the notional amount of the agreement immediately before March 19, 2019, and

(ii) the total of all amounts each of which is an increase in the notional amount of the agreement on or after March 19, 2019 and before 2020 that is not otherwise described in this formula,

G is the total of all amounts each of which is a decrease in the notional amount of the agreement, on or after March 19, 2019 and at or before that time, that is attributable to the underlying interest, and

H is the total of all amounts each of which is the amount of a partial settlement of the agreement, on or after March 19, 2019 and at or before that time, to the extent that it is not reinvested in the agreement.

(9) For the purposes of subsection (8), the notional amount of a derivative forward agreement at any time is the fair market value at that time of the property that would be acquired under the agreement if the agreement were finally settled at that time.

Subpara. (b)(iii) and cl. (c)(i)(C) added by 2017 budget bill #2, retroactive to introduction of the definition (March 21, 2013).

Definition added by 2013 budget bill #2, effective March 21, 2013.

"designated insurance property" has the meaning assigned by subsection 138(12);

Notes: Definition "designated insurance property" added by 1996 Budget effective for 1997 and later taxation years.

"designated stock exchange" means a stock exchange, or that part of a stock exchange, for which a designation by the Minister of Finance under section 262 is in effect;

Related Provisions: See Related Provisions under 262(1).

Notes: See Notes to 262 for the list. This term has generally replaced "prescribed stock exchange" throughout the Act. (Three places use "recognized stock exchange" or simply "stock exchange": 116(6)(b), 260(1)"qualified security"(a), 260(1)"qualified trust unit".)

248(1)"designated stock exchange" added by 2007 budget bill #2, effective Dec. 14, 2007.

"designated surplus" — [Repealed under former Act]

Notes: The concept of "designated surplus" was eliminated effective April 1977.

"disposition" of any property, except as expressly otherwise provided, includes

(a) any transaction or event entitling a taxpayer to proceeds of disposition of the property,

(b) any transaction or event by which,

(i) where the property is a share, bond, debenture, note, certificate, mortgage, hypothecary claim, agreement of sale or similar property, or interest, or for civil law a right, in it, the property is in whole or in part redeemed, acquired or cancelled,

(ii) where the property is a debt or any other right to receive an amount, the debt or other right is settled or cancelled,

(iii) where the property is a share, the share is converted because of an amalgamation or merger,

(iv) where the property is an option to acquire or dispose of property, the option expires, and

(v) a trust, that can reasonably be considered to act as agent for all the beneficiaries under the trust with respect to all dealings with all of the trust's property (unless the trust is described in any of paragraphs (a) to (e.1) of the definition "trust" in subsection 108(1)), ceases to act as agent for a beneficiary under the trust with respect to any dealing with any of the trust's property,

(b.1) where the property is an interest in a life insurance policy, a disposition within the meaning of section 148,

(c) any transfer of the property to a trust or, where the property is property of a trust, any transfer of the property to any beneficiary under the trust, except as provided by paragraph (f) or (k), and

(d) where the property is, or is part of, a taxpayer's capital interest in a trust, except as provided by paragraph (h) or (i), a payment made after 1999 to the taxpayer from the trust that can reasonably be considered to have been made because of the taxpayer's capital interest in the trust,

but does not include

(e) any transfer of the property as a consequence of which there is no change in the beneficial ownership of the property, except where the transfer is

(i) from a person or a partnership to a trust for the benefit of the person or the partnership,

(ii) from a trust to a beneficiary under the trust, or

(iii) from one trust maintained for the benefit of one or more beneficiaries under the trust to another trust maintained for the benefit of the same beneficiaries,

(f) any transfer of the property as a consequence of which there is no change in the beneficial ownership of the property, where

(i) the transferor and the transferee are trusts that are, at the time of the transfer, resident in Canada,

(ii) [Repealed]

(iii) the transferee does not receive the property in satisfaction of the transferee's right as a beneficiary under the transferor trust,

(iv) the transferee held no property immediately before the transfer (other than property the cost of which is not included, for the purposes of this Act, in computing a balance of undeducted outlays, expenses or other amounts in respect of the transferee),

(v) the transferee does not file a written election with the Minister on or before the filing-due date for its taxation year in which the transfer is made (or on such later date as is acceptable to the Minister) that this paragraph not apply,

(vi) if the transferor is an amateur athlete trust, a cemetery care trust, an employee trust, a trust deemed by subsection 143(1) to exist in respect of a congregation that is a constituent part of a religious organization, a related segregated fund trust (in this paragraph having the meaning assigned by section 138.1), a trust described in paragraph 149(1)(o.4) or a trust governed by an eligible funeral arrangement, an employees profit sharing plan, a registered disability savings plan, a registered education savings plan, a registered supplementary unemployment benefit plan or a TFSA, the transferee is the same type of trust, and

(vii) the transfer results, or is part of a series of transactions or events that results, in the transferor ceasing to exist and, immediately before the time of the transfer or the beginning of that series, as the case may be, the transferee never held any property or held only property having a nominal value,

(g) [Repealed]

(h) where the property is part of a capital interest of a taxpayer in a trust (other than a personal trust or a trust prescribed for the purpose of subsection 107(2)) that is described by reference to units issued by the trust, a payment after 1999 from the trust in respect of the capital interest, where the number of units in the trust that are owned by the taxpayer is not reduced because of the payment,

(i) where the property is a taxpayer's capital interest in a trust, a payment to the taxpayer after 1999 in respect of the capital interest to the extent that the payment

(i) is out of the income of the trust (determined without reference to subsection 104(6)) for a taxation year or out of the capital gains of the trust for the year, if the payment was made in the year or the right to the payment was acquired by the taxpayer in the year, or

(ii) is in respect of an amount designated in respect of the taxpayer by the trust under subsection 104(20),

(j) any transfer of the property for the purpose only of securing a debt or a loan, or any transfer by a creditor for the purpose only of returning property that had been used as security for a debt or a loan,

(k) any transfer of the property to a trust as a consequence of which there is no change in the beneficial ownership of the property, where the main purpose of the transfer is

(i) to effect payment under a debt or loan,

(ii) to provide assurance that an absolute or contingent obligation of the transferor will be satisfied, or

(iii) to facilitate either the provision of compensation or the enforcement of a penalty, in the event that an absolute or contingent obligation of the transferor is not satisfied,

(l) any issue of a bond, debenture, note, certificate, mortgage or hypothecary claim,

(m) any issue by a corporation of a share of its capital stock, or any other transaction that, but for this paragraph, would be a disposition by a corporation of a share of its capital stock, and

(n) a redemption, an acquisition or a cancellation of a share or of a right to acquire a share (which share or which right, as the case may be, is referred to in this paragraph as the "security") of the capital stock of a corporation (referred to in this paragraph as the "issuing corporation") held by another corporation (referred to in this paragraph as the "disposing corporation") if

(i) the redemption, acquisition or cancellation occurs as part of a merger or combination of two or more corporations (including the issuing corporation and the disposing corporation) to form one corporate entity (referred to in this paragraph as the "new corporation"),

(ii) the merger or combination

(A) is an amalgamation (within the meaning assigned by subsection 87(1)) to which subsection 87(11) does not apply,

(B) is an amalgamation (within the meaning assigned by subsection 87(1)) to which subsection 87(11) applies, if the issuing corporation and the disposing corporation are described by subsection 87(11) as the parent and the subsidiary, respectively,

(C) is a foreign merger (within the meaning assigned by subsection 87(8.1)), or

(D) would be a foreign merger (within the meaning assigned by subsection 87(8.1)) if subparagraph 87(8.1)(c)(ii) were read without reference to the words "that was resident in a country other than Canada", and

(iii) either

(A) the disposing corporation receives no consideration for the security, or

(B) in the case where the merger or combination is described by clause (ii)(C) or (D), the disposing corporation receives no consideration for the security other than property that was, immediately before the merger or combination, owned by the issuing corporation and that, on the merger or combination, becomes property of the new corporation;

Related Provisions: 43(3) — No capital loss on capital interest of trust on payment out of trust's income or gains; 48.1(1) — Gain when small business corporation becomes public; 49(1) — Granting of option is a disposition; 49(5) — Extension or renewal of option; 49.1 — Satisfaction of obligation is not a disposition of property; 51(1)(c) — Conversion of convertible property deemed not to be a disposition; 69(1)(b)(iii) — Deemed proceeds on disposition to a trust where no change in beneficial ownership; 69(1)(c) — Deemed acquisition at fair market value where disposition with no change in beneficial interest; 70(5) — Deemed disposition on death; 80.03(2), (4) — Deemed capital gain on disposition of property following debt forgiveness; 80.6 — Deemed disposition on synthetic disposition arrangement; 84(9) — Cancellation or redemption of share is disposition by shareholder; 87(4) — Shares of predecessor corporation; 87(8.2) — Absorptive merger of foreign corporations; 94(4)(f) — Deeming non-resident trust to be resident in Canada does not apply to subpara. (f)(i); 104(1) — Reference to trust or estate; 104(5.8) — Transfer where para. (f) applies; 107(2), (2.1) — Effect of distribution of property by trust; 107.4 — Rollover on "qualifying disposition" to a trust; 128.1(1)(b) — Deemed disposition of property on becoming resident in Canada; 128.1(4) — Deemed disposition on emigration; 135.2(4)(h) — Para. (h) does not apply to eligible unit of Cdn Wheat Board Farmers' Trust; 148(9)"disposition" — Disposition of life insurance policy; 248(1.1) — Parallel rule to para. (n) before December 24, 1998; 248(10) — Series of transactions; 248(25.1) — Where para. (f) applies — continuation of trust; 248(25.2) — Where para. (j) applies — trust deemed to be agent.

Notes: Since the definition uses "includes" rather than "means", the ordinary meaning of "disposition" should apply as well (see Notes to 188.1(5)). See also the various deemed dispositions in the Topical Index under Disposition: deemed.

A disposition takes place when the taxpayer is entitled to proceeds of disposition (para. (a)): *Yellow Point*, 2020 FCA 195, para. 38. When securities are sold on the public market, disposition is on the settlement date: VIEWS doc 2012-0468931C6 (and see 40(1) Notes re 2-day settlement). In *Tibilla*, 2014 FCA 227, proceeds were received in 2007 so even if the purchaser challenged the price and this was not resolved until 2008, disposition took place in 2007. In *Hewlett Packard*, 2004 FCA 240, HP bought a new fleet of vehicles each year and sold back older vehicles one day after its year-end. Even though the arrangements for the sale were all in place before year-end, the FCA ruled

the disposition was after year-end, so HP could claim CCA for the year on the old fleet. On a contingent sale of property, disposition takes place when the parties intend ownership to pass, as evidenced by the terms of the contract, conduct of the parties and other circumstances: 2006-0171861E5. See also IT-170 and VIEWS doc 2012-0464131E5 (when disposition takes place may depend on legal relationships).

In *Royer*, 2019 QCCQ 4163, sale of a home while keeping the usufruct (right to use, under Quebec *Civil Code*) was a "disposition".

In *Leonard*, 2021 TCC 33 (under appeal to FCA), L acquired mortgage debt, then later bought the related land under foreclosure proceedings, but could not sell it. He had a "disposition" (and a loss) on the mortgage, because it was cancelled on the foreclosure and judicial sale: para. 86.

The following have been considered to cause a disposition: amending a corporation's articles to increase dividend rates for some classes of shares (VIEWS doc 2008-0263891R3); exchange of preferred shares for another class with same rights but a different dividend rate (2004-0092561E5 and 2009-0330161C6); conversion of Delaware LLC to limited partnership (2004-0104691E5 [Zimka, "New CRA Technical Interpretation", XII(2) *Business Vehicles* (Federated Press) 632-35 (2008)]); windup of corporation (2008-0275881R3, 2012-0456221R3); consolidation of publicly traded LP units (2005-0115771R3); distribution in satisfaction of a capital interest in a trust (para. (d) and 2006-0184741E5, 2009-0330291C6); settlement of a forward contract to buy or sell foreign currency ((b)(ii) and CRA May 2005 ICAA roundtable (tinyurl.com/cra-abtax), Supp. q. 8); transfer from sole ownership to joint tenancy (2004-0101971E5, 2006-0166551E5, 2008-0278801C6 q.5), but only if beneficial ownership changes (2004-0100201E5, 2005-0152011E5, 2006-0152011E5, 2009-035087117 [also discusses other consequences]) [and note that if it does not change, the original owner remains owner of the property, probate fees are not avoided on death, and the property remains part of the estate subject to capital gains tax on death]; entering into emphyteutic lease with purchase at end (2008-0287901R3, 2012-0472101E5 [this is no longer the CRA's position: 2013-0487791E5]); windup of non-profit association (see Notes to 149(1)(l)); transfer of property to defeat creditors (2010-0367961E5); transfer to *alter ego* trust (2011-0393401E5); redemption of gold bullion Exchange Traded Receipts for cash (2011-0426531E5); gift of French real estate via a usufruct under France's *Civil Code* (2012-0466081I87); varying trust terms to add a beneficiary (2012-0451791E5; existing beneficiaries have a disposition); assignment to a trust of a right to purchase a particular property (2015-0608211E5); share cancellation on vertical absorptive foreign merger (2017-0709331E5); windup of unincorporated labour union (2019-0779221R3: distributions are proceeds of disposition of membership rights). See also Notes to 39(2) re foreign exchange transactions.

There are also deemed dispositions: on death (70(5)), emigration (128.1(4)), gift (69(1)), synthetic disposition arrangement (80.6), share redemption (84(9)) and others (see Related Provisions above and "Disposition: deemed" in Topical Index).

The following *corporate conversions* have been held not to cause a disposition: continuance from one federal Act to another (2016-0643751R3 [2017-0703821R3], but the resulting share exchange is a disposition with 86(1) rollover); continuance in another jurisdiction (2005-0147131R3, 2012-0451421R3); cooperative corp to ordinary corp (2006-0176321R3); Delaware corp to LLC (2008-0272141R3, 2015-0615041R3); Georgia corp to Delaware LLC, if it is considered the same corp (2008-0298641E5); foreign "continuation type" amalgamation (2012-0457741E5); foreign divisive reorganization (2012-0463611R3); amalgamation of non-profit org and public foundation (2018-0750471R3); US corp stock split and reclassification (2019-0799981R3).

The following *mutual fund trust changes* have been held not to cause a disposition: conversion from closed-end to open-end fund (2007-0226101R3); creating and issuing new classes of units (2010-0361771R3 [RioCan REIT: Smit, "Recent Transactions of Interest", 2011 Cdn Tax Foundation conference report, 10:1-5]; 2010-0389921R3, 2014-0518521R3, 2015-0612931R3, 2017-0738021R3); conversion of class of units to another class (2017-0681471R3).

The following actions re *other trusts* have been held *not* to cause a disposition: extending term of a trust by Court order (2006-0187491R3); transfer from 5 commercial trusts to a master commercial trust (2006-0210271R3); variation of trust to modify powers, cancel transferability of units and give Manager right to redeem units (2006-0217321R3); administrative correction to change title to assets to reflect terms of a testamentary trust (2006-0218191E5); amendment to joint spousal trust to permit additional capital distribution to spouse (2007-0241581R3); transfer from spousal trust to new trust, or from family trust to new trust with extended division date or in which all interests have vested, due to para. (f) and 248(25.1) (2008-0288541E5, 2013-0492831R3 [Tollstam, "Trust-to-Trust Transfers", 22(9) *Canadian Tax Highlights* (ctf.ca) 8-9 (Sept. 2014)], 2014-0552321R3); variation of testamentary spousal trust to allow capital encroachment by spouse and disclaimer of beneficiary's capital interest (2010-0367401R3); variation of trust to extend distribution date (2011-0427511R3); trustee/beneficiary exercises power to add beneficiaries (2008-0281411I7; no disposition to trust, but yes to beneficiary); variation of trust to create and issue new class of preferred units (2011-0410181R3, 2011-0429611R3, 2015-0578051R3); amendment to 6801(d) plan to permit future value of deferred share units to be paid in common shares (2011-0418571R3); change of conditions for ceasing to be trustee (2017-0733441R3); amendment to permit replacement trustee and protector (2017-0722381R3); variation to clarify US-person beneficiary entitlements without changing beneficiaries (2018-0779201R3); variation to change division date (2019-0795761R3).

The following have also been considered *not* to cause a disposition: change from equal tenants in common to joint tenancy [see Notes to 70(5) re joint tenancy] (VIEWS doc 2004-0078771E5); bare trustee transfer of property back to settlor/beneficiary, since (b)(v) and (e) apply (2006-0174831E5); amendments to a will (2006-0201561R3); transfer of swap rights and obligations from one counterparty to another already involved in mirror-swap (2008-0269981R3, 2008-0276431R3); transfer of home from parent to child where parent always held it for child and child paid the expenses (2008-0281841E5, 2008-0282461E5, 2010-037971E5); transfer of legal title to shares from foundation back to corporation (2008-0294391R3); corporate share split (2010-0376681R3); transfer of partnership interest to another partnership with no change in beneficial ownership (2010-0380841R3); change in legal title with no change in beneficial ownership (2010-0383221E5, 2010-0385711E5, 2011-0430191E5, 2013-0411771E5); transfer from one employer's EPSP to another's for the same employee (2010-0385471E5); exchange of gold certificates or Exchange Traded Receipts for their underlying bullion (IT-387R2 para. 4, 2011-0426531E5); off-market swap of shares traded on TSX to same shares on NYSE (2012-0455431C6); exchange of shares for another class with same rights and conditions (2004-0092561E5, 2013-0495821C6); automatic renewal of foreign currency loan (2011-0422481R3, 2013-050766117); addition of exchange right to a note (2013-0514191R3, 2014-0547871R3); beneficiary's disclaimer of interest in testamentary trust (2015-0606771R3); converting (re-designating) limited partnership units to change management fee and retraction period (2017-0687061R3); LLC electing to be a corporation for US tax purposes (2018-0744121C6 [2018 STEP q.16]); change in financial instrument's benchmark rate from IBOR to Risk-Free-Rate, probably (2019-0828571C6). See also Notes to 54"capital property" re legal title without beneficial ownership.

Para. (a) applies to a bondholder if the issuer buys back its bonds on the market: VIEWS doc 2007-0241891C6.

In *Williams*, 2005 TCC 558, a transfer to a trust for W as sole beneficiary was held not to be a "disposition". Although the trust could apparently be amended with W's consent to allow for distributions to others, until this happened there was no change in beneficial ownership.

In *DMWSHNZ Ltd.*, [2015] EWCA Civ 2016 (England, Court of Appeal), para. 39, repaying a debt was not a disposition of the debt by the creditor to the debtor.

See also Wortsman, Nesbitt & Love, "Recent Transactions in Corporate Finance", 2008 Cdn Tax Foundation conference report, at 9:23-25.

For a taxpayer filing Quebec returns, an election under (f)(v) must be copied to Revenu Québec: *Taxation Act* ss. 248, 21.4.6.

The definition of "disposition" was formerly in s. 54 and applied only to capital gains and losses (a parallel definition in 13(21) applied to depreciable property). This definition now applies to the entire Act.

In the Dec. 17, 1999 draft legislation, para. (g) was not included; what are now paras. (h)–(l) were numbered (g)–(l).

Para. (n) implements an April 12, 2002 Finance comfort letter. (For the same rule before Dec. 24, 1998, see 248(1.1).)

A trust that Finance and the CRA call a "protective trust" may be a "blind trust", such as those set up by politicians to hold their interests and manage their affairs without their involvement. The term "protective trust" is used in some jurisdictions to mean a discretionary trust that effectively protects the beneficiary from creditors (see VIEWS doc 2012-0469331E5).

See also Notes to 104(1) re bare trusts.

See also Mike Hegedus, "Reserving a Royalty: A Disposition?!?", XI(2) *Resource Sector Taxation* (Federated Press) 11-23 (2017).

Subpara. (f)(vi) amended by 2014 budget bill #2, for 2016 and later taxation years, to change "an *inter vivos* trust" to "a trust" (no substantive change).

Definition earlier amended by 2002-2013 technical bill (last change effective for tax years that begin after 2006), 2008 budget bill #1 (for 2009 and later tax years), 2007 RDSPs bill, 2005 budget bill #1. Added by 2001 technical bill.

Income Tax Folios: S3-F4-C1: General discussion of CCA [replaces IT-220R2]; S3-F9-C1: Lottery winnings, miscellaneous receipts, and income (and losses) from crime [replaces IT-185R, IT-213R, IT-256R, IT-334R2]; S4-F7-C1: Amalgamations of Canadian corporations [replaces IT-474R2].

Interpretation Bulletins: IT-65: Stock splits and consolidations; IT-96R6: Options to acquire shares, bonds or debentures and by trusts to acquire trust units; IT-102R2: Conversion of property, other than real property, from or to inventory; IT-124R6: Contributions to registered retirement savings plans; IT-125R4: Dispositions of resource properties; IT-126R2: Meaning of "winding-up"; IT-133: Stock exchange transactions — date of disposition of shares; IT-146R4: Shares entitling shareholders to choose taxable or capital dividends; IT-170R: Sale of property — when included in income computation; IT-182: Compensation for loss of business income or property used in a business; IT-218R: Profit, capital gains and losses from the sale of real estate, including farmland and inherited land and conversion of real estate from capital property to inventory and vice versa; IT-444R: Corporations — involuntary dissolutions; IT-448: Dispositions — changes in terms of securities; IT-488R2: Winding-up of 90%-owned taxable Canadian corporations (cancelled); IT-505: Mortgage foreclosures and conditional sales repossessions (cancelled).

I.T. Technical News: 3 (loss utilization within a corporate group); 7 (revocable living trusts, protective trusts, bare trusts); 14 (changes in terms of debt obligations); 15 (tax consequences of the adoption of the "euro" currency); 39 (settlement of a shareholder class action suit).

CRA Audit Manual: 16.2.5: Bare trusts.

Advance Tax Rulings: ATR-1: Transfer of legal title in land to bare trustee corporation — mortgagee's requirements sole reason for transfer; ATR-54: Reduction of paid-up capital.

"dividend" includes a stock dividend (other than a stock dividend that is paid to a corporation or to a mutual fund trust by a non-resident corporation);

Related Provisions: 15(1)(b), 15(1.1) — No shareholder-benefit income inclusion unless stock dividend; 15(3), (4) — Interest or dividend on income bond or debenture; 52(3) — Cost of stock dividend; 55(2) — Capital gains stripping — Deemed dividend; 82(1) — Dividend from resident corporation — income inclusion; 84 — Deemed dividend; 90(1) — Dividend from non-resident corporation included in income; 90(2) — Deemed dividend from foreign affiliate; 90(5) — No amount is dividend from foreign affiliate unless deemed; 93(1) — Election re disposition of share in foreign affiliate; 96(1.11)(b) — SIFT partnership distribution deemed to be dividend; 104(16) — SIFT trust distribution deemed to be dividend; 120.4(1)"split income" — Certain capital gains deemed to be dividends; 120.4(4), (5) — Certain capital gains deemed to be taxable dividends for split-income rules; 128.1(1)(c.1), (c.2) — Deemed dividends on corporation becoming resident in Canada; 137(4.2) — Credit unions — deemed interest deemed not to be a dividend; 139.1(4)(f) — Deemed dividend on demutualization of insurance corporation; 139.2 — Deemed dividend on distribution by mutual holding corporation; 212.2 — Deemed dividend on surplus strip to non-resident insurer; 213.2(2)(a) — Foreign affiliate dumping — deemed dividend; 214(16) — Thin capitalization interest disallowance — deemed dividend for Part XIII tax; 247(12) — Deemed dividend for Part XIII purposes resulting from transfer pricing adjustment; 258 — Certain amounts deemed to be or not to be dividends.

Notes: Since this definition uses "includes" rather than "means", the ordinary meaning of "dividend" also applies (see Notes to 188.1(5)): "any distribution by a corporation of its income and capital gains made *pro rata* among shareholders": *Marshall*, 2011 TCC 497, para. 16. See also *Moose Jaw Flying Club*, [1949] C.T.C. 279 (Exch. Ct.), paras. 53-67; Ed Harris, "Words in Context: 'Contingent' and 'Dividend' ", 2002 Cdn Tax Foundation conference report, 38:19-37; John Owen, "Foreign Entity Classification and the Character of Foreign Distributions", 2005 conference report, 20:1-59. Distributions from most publicly traded partnerships and trusts (SIFTs) are deemed to be dividends: 96(1.11)(b), 104(16).

A dividend can be paid by way of promissory note: *Banner Pharmacaps*, 2003 FCA 367, paras. 6-7. A "dividend in kind" (of property, not cash) is in principle the same as any other dividend; and see 52(2); VIEWS doc 2017-0690331C6 [2017 CLHIA q.2].

Corporate legislation (e.g., Ontario *Business Corporations Act* s. 38(3)) prohibits dividends if the company is insolvent ("unable to pay its liabilities as they become due"). A dividend violating this rule may be void, depending on the province: *633746 Ontario Inc. v. Salvati* (1990), 73 O.R. (2d) 774 (Ont. SC). CRA could deny dividend-tax-credit treatment to such a dividend and consider it a 15(1) shareholder appropriation, though this does not appear to be CRA policy. (If it merely violates the rule *without* being void, see Notes to 9(1) under "Diverting income".) In *Kufsky*, 2019 TCC 254 (under appeal to FCA), a dividend was considered valid despite not being properly declared and the corp perhaps being insolvent.

A dividend cannot be undone by being repaid in the next year: VIEWS doc 2013-0488571E5. (See the discussion of rectification in Notes to 169(1).)

When is a distribution by a foreign entity a dividend? See VIEWS doc 2011-0427001C6. A redemption premium on Luxembourg mandatory redeemable pref shares is proceeds of disposition, not a dividend (unless a 93(1) election is made): 2014-0528361E5 (cancelling 2012-043974117). The "quota" of a Brazilian limitada is considered to be shares, so "interest on quotaholders' equity" is a dividend: 2007-025444117. Distribution of a share premium from a foreign corporation is a return of capital (2004-006013117), but could be taxed under 15(1): Paul Barnicke & Melanie Huynh, "CRA: May 2011 IFA Round Table", 19(6) *Canadian Tax Highlights* (ctf.ca) 2-3 (June 2011). Distributions from a US non-diversified closed-end management investment company (NCMIC) are considered dividends: 2010-0391621E5. Wayne Adams stated at the Toronto Centre TSO breakfast seminar, June 28/11 that 15(1) would be applied only to aggressive or unreasonable structures, not to impose double tax (see also 15(1)(b) and 15(1.1)). See also Notes to 86.1 on cases where shares received on foreign spinoffs were held to be or not to be dividends.

See Notes to 82(1), 112(1) and 121 for how a dividend is taxed.

"Dividend" amended by 1991 technical bill to add the parenthetical exclusion, effective for stock dividends paid to a corporation or to a mutual fund trust in 1991 or later (and, by election, for earlier stock dividends paid after March 23, 1985).

Interpretation Bulletins: IT-67R3: Taxable dividends from corporations resident in Canada; IT-88R2: Stock dividends; IT-243R4: Dividend refund to private corporations.

"dividend rental arrangement", of a person or a partnership (each of which is referred to in this definition as the "person"), means

(a) any arrangement entered into by the person where it can reasonably be considered that

(i) the main reason for the person entering into the arrangement was to enable the person to receive a dividend on a share of the capital stock of a corporation, other than a dividend on a prescribed share or on a share described in paragraph (e) of the definition "term preferred share" in this subsection or an amount deemed by subsection 15(3) to be received as a dividend on a share of the capital stock of a corporation, and

(ii) under the arrangement someone other than that person bears the risk of loss or enjoys the opportunity for gain or profit with respect to the share in any material respect,

(b) for greater certainty, any arrangement under which

(i) a corporation at any time receives on a particular share a taxable dividend that would, if this Act were read without reference to subsection 112(2.3), be deductible in computing its taxable income or taxable income earned in Canada for the taxation year that includes that time, and

(ii) the corporation or a partnership of which the corporation is a member is obligated to pay to another person or partnership an amount

(A) that is compensation for

(I) the dividend described in subparagraph (i),

(II) a dividend on a share that is identical to the particular share, or

(III) a dividend on a share that, during the term of the arrangement, can reasonably be expected to provide to a holder of the share the same or substantially the same proportionate risk of loss or opportunity for gain as the particular share, and

(B) that, if paid, would be deemed by subsection 260(5.1) to have been received by that other person or partnership, as the case may be, as a taxable dividend,

(c) any synthetic equity arrangement, in respect of a DRA share of the person, and

(d) one or more agreements or arrangements (other than agreements or arrangements described in paragraph (c)) entered into by the person, the connected person referred to in paragraph (a) of the definition "synthetic equity arrangement" or, for greater certainty, by any combination of the person and connected persons, if

(i) the agreements or arrangements have the effect, or would have the effect if each agreement or arrangement entered into by a connected person were entered into by the person, of eliminating all or substantially all of the person's risk of loss and opportunity for gain or profit in respect of a DRA share of the person,

(ii) as part of a series of transactions that includes these agreements or arrangements, a tax-indifferent investor, or a group of tax-indifferent investors each member of which is affiliated with every other member, obtains all or substantially all of the risk of loss and opportunity for gain or profit in respect of the DRA share or an "identical share" (as defined in subsection 112(10)), and

(iii) it is reasonable to conclude that one of the purposes of the series of transactions is to obtain the result described in subparagraph (ii);

Related Provisions: 82(1)(c) — Taxable dividends received; 112(2.3)–(2.34) — Intercorporate dividend deduction denied; 126(4.2) — No foreign tax credit on short-term securities acquisitions; 248(1)"DRA share" — Definition; 248(42) — Synthetic equity arrangement relating to multiple types of identical shares; 260(6.1) — Deductible amount under securities lending arrangement.

Notes: "Dividend rental arrangement" describes an arrangement whereby a corporation borrows a share for a period in order to receive an intercorporate dividend on it, which would normally be tax-free under 112(1). The lender under such an arrangement (e.g., an exempt pension fund) would be indifferent as to whether it received the dividend or an equivalent fee from the corporation for the "use" of the share. Under 112(2.3), the deduction for the intercorporate dividend is denied.

When reading a VIEWS doc or article in French about this definition, note that the para. numbers differ in French from English!

For criticism of paras. (c)-(d) see CBA/CPA Canada Joint Committee on Taxation letter to Finance, May 26, 2015. The subsequent July 31, 2015 draft made only minor changes from the April 21, 2015 version.

Definition amended, effectively to add paras. (c)-(d), by 2016 budget bill #1, effective on the same basis as the amendment to 112(2.3).

Definition amended by 2002-2013 technical bill, for arrangements made after Dec. 20, 2002 (earlier in certain cases); 1994 technical bill. Added by 1989 Budget.

Interpretation Bulletins: IT-67R3: Taxable dividends from corporations resident in Canada.

["DRA share"] — [See at beginning of 248(1)"d ..."]

"eligible capital amount" — [Repealed]

Notes: Definition repealed by 2016 budget bill #2, effective 2017, as part of changing the eligible capital property rules to CCA Class 14.1 (see 20(1)(b) Notes). It read "has the meaning assigned by subsection 14(1)".

"eligible capital expenditure" — [Repealed]

Notes: Definition repealed by 2016 budget bill #2, effective 2017, as part of changing the eligible capital property rules to CCA Class 14.1 (see 20(1)(b) Notes). It read "has the meaning assigned by subsection 14(5)".

"eligible capital property" — [Repealed]

Notes: Definition repealed by 2016 budget bill #2, effective 2017, as part of changing the ECP rules to CCA Class 14.1 (see 20(1)(b) Notes). It read "has the meaning assigned by section 54".

"eligible dividend" has the meaning assigned by subsection 89(1);

Notes: Definition added by 2006 budget bill #2, for 2006 and later tax years.

"eligible funeral arrangement" has the meaning assigned by subsection 148.1(1);

Related Provisions: 248(1)"disposition"(f)(vi) — Rollover from one trust to another.

Notes: Definition added by 1994 technical bill, effective 1993.

Interpretation Bulletins: IT-531: Eligible funeral arrangements.

"eligible relocation" means a relocation of a taxpayer in respect of which the following apply:

(a) the relocation occurs to enable the taxpayer

(i) to carry on a business or to be employed at a location (in section 62 and this definition referred to as "the new work location") that is, except if the taxpayer is absent from but resident in Canada, in Canada, or

(ii) to be a student in full-time attendance enrolled in a program at a post-secondary level at a location of a university, college or other educational institution (in section 62 and in this definition referred to as "the new work location"),

(b) the taxpayer ordinarily resided before the relocation at a residence (in section 62 and this definition referred to as "the old residence") and ordinarily resided after the relocation at a residence (in section 62 and this definition referred to as "the new residence"),

(c) except if the taxpayer is absent from but resident in Canada, both the old residence and the new residence are in Canada, and

(d) the distance between the old residence and the new work location is not less than 40 kilometres greater than the distance between the new residence and the new work location;

Related Provisions: 6(19)–(22) — Employer subsidy of housing loss; 6(23) — Employer-provided mortgage subsidy is taxable; 62 — Deduction for moving expenses.

Notes: This definition applies to the moving expenses deduction (s. 62), as well as 6(22) and 115(2)(f)(i).

40km requirement (para. (d)): A move that is not to a home at least 40 km closer to the new work location does not qualify, even if needed for the job: *Blais*, 2020 FCA 38, para. 4; VIEWS doc 2010-0353971E5. This is measured using road distance, not "as the crow flies": *Giannakopoulos*, [1995] 2 C.T.C. 316 (FCA); *Income Tax Technical News* 6. The road distance should be a "realistic, normal" route, not the shortest distance produced by mapping software where that was a "38 turn slalom": *Nagy*, 2007 TCC 394. It should be the *shortest* normal route, so Oakville to downtown Toronto via Highways 403-401-427 was invalid: *Lund*, 2010 TCC 252. Temporary construction does not justify ignoring a direct route that is "a normal route used by the travelling public": *Hauser*, 2014 TCC 328 (FCA appeal discontinued A-536-14). The measurement can be taken in either direction, if driving from point B to A is further than from A to B: 2014-0518791E5. Where CRA used Mapquest and no other data was available, the Court added 10% to each distance: *Podlesny*, 2008 TCC 591, paras. 55-57.

A move to become an apartment superintendent, even though required by the nature of the job, does not qualify if the 40 km test is not met: doc 2010-0353971E5.

"New work location" (NWL): the definition does not actually require either the job or the location to be "new": *Wunderlich*, 2011 TCC 539 (Webb J), para. 13 (*contra*, see *Zhao*, 2015 TCC 124 (Masse DJ), para. 15). In the author's view, Webb J (now on the FCA) is right: a word used in a defined term should never be considered for its actual meaning. Thus, a 63(3)"supporting person" need not actually support the child; a 122.6"shared-custody parent" is not based on the *Federal Child Support Guidelines* meaning of "shared custody"; a 125(7)"active business" need not be active; a 127(9)"taxable supplier" need not be taxable; a 248(1)"small business corporation" need not be small; and under the GST, the meaning of "substantial" is irrelevant in ETA 123(1)"substantial renovation" and a "university" as defined in ETA 123(1) need not really be a university: *Alexander College*, 2016 FCA 269. The NWL term should be interpreted broadly: *Dalisay*, 2004 TCC 126, VIEWS doc 2009-0308461E5. It can include an expanded sales territory: 2011-0394741E5, 2012-0440241E5. It can include a student moving home for a summer job: 2012-0440251E5. There is no NWL if there is no change in work location: *Broydell*, 2005 TCC 79; *Grill*, 2009 TCC 5 (move after marriage breakdown); *Moreland*, 2010 TCC 483 (moving down one floor); *Langelier*, 2013 TCC 322; *Dueck*, 2014 TCC 187; *Zhao* (above) (promotion in same department); docs 2006-0176061E5; 2014-0525511E5 (contract employee who becomes permanent employee). *Contra*, there was a NWL in *Gelinas*, 2009 TCC 111 (move from part-time to full-time at a different department in same hospital, where distance from old home was too much for daily commute), and *Wunderlich* (above) (promotion, no change in work location). CRA might still not accept *Gelinas* or *Wunderlich*: 2011-0423201E5.

Purpose: in *Lyn Kew*, 2015 TCC 193, LK had a "general plan to look for work" when he moved back to Canada, but he did not move "to enable" him to start a business at his mother's home, so he could not deduct moving expenses.

Home office move: For a person with a home office, moving to a new work location in the same location as the person's new residence qualifies: *Templeton*, [1998] 3 C.T.C. 207 (FCTD); doc 2005-0138461E5. However, the CRA now says there must be a causal link between the move and the new work location, so someone moving their home office might not qualify: 2012-0446601E5, 2012-0458801E5.

Ordinarily resided: In *Cavalier*, [2002] 1 C.T.C. 2001 (TCC), C moved to remote location X for a 1-year contract, then returned. Even though he did not give up his permanent home, he "ordinarily resided" at X during the contract and was allowed deduction for both moves. The same applied in *Persaud*, 2007 TCC 474, on a 3-month contract. *Contra*, in *Konecny*, 2014 TCC 114, a 1-month annual stay for a summer job did not qualify (tinyurl.com/cbc-konecny says K later moved in 2018 by canoe and "succeeded" in deducting the cost, but CBC misreported, as the mode of transport is irrelevant). See also VIEWS docs 2012-0471621E5, 2013-0497601E5 (move for temporary work does not qualify). Travel to different places to seek or take up employment did not qualify as changing where the taxpayer "ordinarily resided" in: *MacDonald*, 2007 TCC 250; *Drake*, 2007 TCC 582; *Sampson*, 2009 TCC 204; *Sears*, 2009 TCC 344; *Lapierre*, 2009 TCC 595.

"Taking her children and enrolling them in school in Calgary constitutes a change of residence for her entire family unit while she attended her course in Calgary. The furniture left in Lethbridge was merely an accoutrement left in storage. The children and the necessary things she took to Calgary are the essentials of living and residence": *McKenzie*, 2005 TCC 696, para. 6. Thus, the cost of the Lethbridge apartment was allowed as storage fees. *Contra*, in *Hasan*, 2005 FCA 114, rent on an apartment holding the taxpayer's personal effects was not allowed as storage fees.

Home not in Canada: per para. (c), an old or new home outside Canada qualifies if the person is "resident in Canada" (taxed on worldwide income) but "absent from Canada". (See Income Tax Folio S1-F3-C4 ¶4.12 for an example.) A move to Canada does not qualify if the taxpayer was non-resident: *Shao*, 2006 TCC 78; *Zhan*, 2006 TCC 312; *Ellaway*, 2019 TCC 118. Each home must meet the "ordinarily resided" test, so moving to a temporary job outside Canada while keeping a home (and spouse/children) in Canada will not qualify. Also, if the person ceases to be resident in Canada due to the move, the new home will not qualify.

Multiple moves: In *Jaschinski*, [2003] 1 C.T.C. 2571 (TCC), the taxpayer bought a temporary home when moving from Calgary to Toronto, because his wife was pregnant, and sold it and bought a permanent home 19 months later. Costs of both moves were allowed under 62(1) as being the same move. The same applied in *Dalisay*, [2004] 2 C.T.C. 2599 (TCC) (D moved from St. John's to Regina, took a new job, but transferred to Edmonton after 7 weeks; she was held never to have settled in Regina); and in *Myles*, [2010] 3 C.T.C. 2178 (TCC) (M and his wife took a temporary cramped apartment for 7 months while house-hunting in their new city). On the other hand, in *Calvano*, [2004] 2 C.T.C. 3004 (TCC), a house rented for 19 months until the family bought a permanent home was held to be where the taxpayer "ordinarily resided", so no deduction was allowed for the move to the permanent home (the CRA says the same in VIEWS doc 2011-0406871E5). A second move back near to the original home or to the original employer qualifies because each move is considered separately: docs 2009-0315101E5, 2010-0354531E5, 2010-0365151E5, 2013-0486911E5.

Moving earlier or later: There is no time limit on the move (even 5 or 10 years after job relocation), as long as the move was due to the change in work location: *Beyette*, [1990] 1 C.T.C. 2001 (TCC); *Simard*, [1998] 2 C.T.C. 2312 (TCC); *Beaudoin*, [2005] 1 C.T.C. 2821 (TCC); *Dierckens*, [2011] 3 C.T.C. 2328 (TCC); *Wunderlich*, 2011 CarswellNat 5079 (TCC). A move 16 months *before* finding new employment qualified in *Abrahamsen*, [2007] 3 C.T.C. 2001 (TCC). The CRA accepts this concept in some cases: VIEWS doc 2011-0394741E5. The new job can start in a later year than the expenses are incurred: *Evangélist*, 2013 CarswellNat 833 (TCC), para. 12.

For other cases allowing an "eligible relocation" see *Cusson*, 2006 TCC 121; *Graham*, 2006 TCC 92.

For the meaning of "post-secondary" in subpara. (a)(ii), see Notes to 118.5(1)(a).

See also Ryan Keey, "Moving expenses: Recent cases reject CRA's stringent interpretation of eligible relocations", 2012(6) *Tax Times* (Carswell) 1-3 (March 30, 2012).

Definition amended by 2002-2013 technical bill, for tax years that end after Oct. 2011. The Dept. of Finance Technical Notes state that the changes "clarify that, in order to claim these expenses, an individual who is absent from, but resident in, Canada must, like other individuals, ordinarily reside before the relocation at the old residence and after the relocation at the new residence". For discussion of this amendment see Eric Koh, "Moving In and Out of Canada", tinyurl.com/koh-reloc.

"Eligible relocation" added by 1998 Budget, effective for all taxation years. These conditions were formerly in 62(1).

Income Tax Folios: S1-F3-C4: Moving expenses [replaces IT-178R3].

I.T. Technical News: 6 (road distance to be used instead of "as the crow flies").

Forms: T1-M: Moving expenses deduction.

"emissions allowance" means an allowance, credit or similar instrument that represents a unit of emissions that can be used to satisfy a requirement under the laws of Canada or a province governing emissions of a regulated substance, such as greenhouse gas emissions;

Related Provisions: 27.1(2) — Tax treatment of emissions allowance; 248(1)"inventory"(b) — Emissions allowance excluded from definition of inventory.

Notes: See Notes to 27.1. Definition added by 2016 budget bill #2, effective 2017, but if a taxpayer elects as described in Notes to 27.1, it applies to EAs acquired in taxation years that end after 2012.

"emissions obligation" means an obligation to surrender an emissions allowance, or an obligation that can otherwise be satisfied through the use of an emissions allowance, under a law of Canada or a province governing emissions of a regulated substance;

Related Provisions: 27.1(3) — Restriction on deduction for emissions obligation.

Notes: Definition added by 2016 budget bill #2, effective on the same basis as 248(1)"emissions allowance".

"employed" means performing the duties of an office or employment;

"employee" includes officer;

Related Provisions: 248(1)"employment" — Further meaning of "employee".

Notes: The distinction between employee ("contract *of* service") and independent contractor (IC) ("contract *for* services") is not always obvious, and there is no one distinguishing factor. The leading cases are *Wiebe Door Services Ltd.*, [1986] 2 C.T.C. 200 (FCA); and *671122 Ontario Ltd. v. Sagaz Industries*, 2001 SCC 59. "The central question is whether the person who has been engaged to perform the services is performing them as a person in business on his own account. In making this determination, the level of control the employer has over the worker's activities will always be a factor. However, other factors to consider include whether the worker provides his or her own equipment, whether the worker hires his or her own helpers, the degree of financial risk taken by the worker, the degree of responsibility for investment and management held by the worker, and the worker's opportunity for profit in the performance of his or her tasks." (*Sagaz*, para. 47). However, see below re Quebec. A good way to measure "risk" is whether the worker has to fix mistakes on their own time.

In general, an employer controls (or has the right to control) the employee's hours and working conditions; the employee uses the employer's tools, equipment and facilities [for a truck driver, ownership of the truck is often especially significant] [can knowledge be a "tool"? *Asare-Quansah*, 2012 TCC 226, para. 20]; the employee does not share the employer's risk; the employee is an integral part of the business; and the employee may receive normal employee benefits. Where these factors are missing, the worker is likely an IC. Paying overtime rates suggests an employee relationship: *G & J Muirhead Holdings*, 2014 TCC 49, para. 31. In *Gagnon*, 2007 FCA 33, a drywaller was held to be an employee; it is the lack of *right* to control the worker that must be shown, not actual lack of control.

See Weisman, *The Worker's Status: Employee or Independent Contractor* (LexisNexis Canada, 2015, 205pp.); Keey, *Checklist 9 — Employed vs Self-Employed, Taxnet Pro* Corporate Tax Centre (2020, 8pp); Magee, "Whose Business Is It?" 45(3) *Canadian Tax Journal* 583-603 (1997) and "Personal Services Businesses", 55(1) *CTJ* 160 at 167-76 (2007); Friedlander, "... Distinguishing Between Employees and Independent Contractors", 51(4) *CTJ* 1467-1519 (2003); Clarke, "The Employee/Independent Contractor Conundrum", 2004 BC Tax Conference (ctf.ca), 10:1-33; Hutchinson & McLeod, "Hospital-Physician Relationship", 18(3) *Taxation of Executive Compensation & Retirement* (Federated Press) 740-44 (Oct. 2006); Wintermute, "A Worker's Status", 2007 Cdn Tax Foundation conf. report, 34:1-37. See also CRA pamphlet RC4110, *Employee or Self-Employed?*, for review of the factors and checklist of questions; CRA CPP/EI Appeals Manual (on Taxnet Pro); Income Tax Folio S4-F14-C1 ¶1.5-1.14 [replaces IT-525] for artists and writers; and tinyurl.com/cra-truck-drivers. Software that assists in the determination: *Worker Classification Classifier* at bluejlegal.com.

Note also that a person holding an "office" is included in the definition of "employee", and includes a director or board member. See Notes to 248(1)"office".

Consequences: An employee (as opposed to an IC) normally has tax withheld from pay at source (153(1)(a)); can deduct only specific permitted expenses (8(2)), but a commission employee is allowed broad expenses: 8(1)(f)); must file by April 30 instead of June 15 (150(1)(d)); does not collect and remit GST/HST on earnings; is eligible for Employment Insurance; has the employer pay a portion of EI premiums and CPP contributions; is taxed on income received rather than when earned (5(1)). In a few cases it is better to be an employee, e.g., when receiving stock option benefits (see 7(1), 110(1)(d)), or if claiming EI benefits. An employer who thinks employees are ICs and issues T4As instead of T4s is subject to penalty: see 162(7) Notes. For more on the tax consequences see Gaucher, "A Worker's Status as Employee or Independent Contractor", 1999 Cdn Tax Foundation conference report, 33:1-98; Melville et al., "Tax Considerations for the Newly Self-Employed", 59(4) *Canadian Tax Journal* 843-68 (2011).

Much of the case law comes from CPP/EI or GST appeals; the tests are the same as income tax. One thorough judicial discussion is in *Lang*, 2007 TCC 547 (Bowman CJ).

Rulings on employee-vs-IC status are CPP/EI rulings (see Form CPT1 to apply for one, which triggers an interview). Taxpayers' Ombudsman (oto-boc.gc.ca) report *Rights and Rulings* (March 2017) recommends that CRA, in rulings, advise taxpayers of the decision's effects, and how to obtain a copy of the Rulings Report. A ruling may trigger a payroll audit: VIEWS doc 2019-0798351C6 [2019 STEP q.15].

If the worker contracts through a corporation (and it is not a sham), the relationship must be IC: *TBT Personnel*, 2011 FCA 256, para. 30; *Butt*, 2013 TCC 284, para. 16 (but see 125(7)"personal services business").

Intention: some cases have said that if the parties choose an independent-contractor (IC) relationship, then in the absence of sham this choice must be respected: *Wolf*, 2002 FCA 96; *Royal Winnipeg Ballet*, 2006 FCA 87 (ballet dancers); *Order of St. John*, 2004 FCA 345 (St. John Ambulance first aid instructors); *Perrin*, 2007 TCC 138; *Guyard*, 2007 TCC 231 (retired consultant); *Viel*, 2007 TCC 299 (home care worker); *Pinfold*, 2007 TCC 304 (car salesman); *Starsky Enterprises*, 2008 TCC 194 (donation canvasser); *Panache Fine Cabinetry*, 2008 TCC 513 (cabinet maker); *Merchants of Green Coffee*, 2010 TCC 151 (part-time bookkeeper); *Trinity Innovations*, 2010 TCC 583 (workers building oil & gas flow controllers); *Smith*, 2011 TCC 20 (truck driver); *Accounting by Leandra Tang*, 2011 TCC 171 (bookkeeper); *Zoltan*, 2012 TCC 232. However, if other factors are determinative, intention need not be considered. Per *Connor Homes (1392644 Ontario)*, 2013 FCA 85, it is a 2-step inquiry: (1) what did the parties subjectively intend? (2) does objective reality sustain the subjective intent? The *Connor* approach was applied in *La Scala Conservatory*, 2013 TCC 122 (workers were pressured to sign contracts saying they were ICs); *Lippert Music Centre*, 2014 TCC 170; *Morris Meadows Country Holidays*, 2014 TCC 191; *3193099 Manitoba*, 2014 TCC 310 (nothing demonstrated that the services agreement did not generally reflect the objective reality of IC — i.e., onus of proof reversed); *Garfin*, 2014 TCC 331 (intention not confirmed by reality); *1065438 Alberta*, 2018 TCC 191; and others (it has now become standard). In *Symons*, 2015 TCC 270, para. 40, Hershfield J queried whether *Connor*'s step 1 means anything, and also noted *Connor* may not apply under Quebec law (see below); but in *Insurance Institute*, 2020 TCC 69, Graham J held step 1 is relevant: if the parties agreed on IC, step 2 has a "lesser standard" (para. 69). See also Chodikoff, "Employee vs Independent Contractor: An Unsatisfactory State of Law", 7(1) *Taxes & Wealth Management* (Carswell) 13-14 (Feb. 2014); Larre, "The Role of Intention in Distinguishing Employees from Independent Contractors", 62(4) *Canadian Tax Journal* 927-70 (2014) (suggests intention should not be relevant); *Weisman* (cited 6 paras. above), pp. 37-42.

For more cases rejecting IC intent because the facts showed employment, see *Maliyar*, 2006 TCC 671; *853998 Ontario*, 2008 TCC 196; *Gillespie*, 2009 TCC 26 (FCA appeal discontinued A-92-09); *Einarsson Law Corp.*, 2009 TCC 45 (legal secretary — parties cannot "opt out of the national schemes" for EI and CPP); *Ince-Mercer*, 2009 TCC 594 (litigation lawyer); *Kootenay Doukhobor*, 2010 TCC 256; *Wilford*, 2011 TCC 6; *Aquazition*, 2011 TCC 77; *1351678 Ontario*, 2011 TCC 252; *TBT Personnel*, 2011 FCA 256 (leave to appeal denied 2012 CarswellNat 983 (SCC)) (truck drivers); *Integranuity Marketing*, 2012 TCC 4 (relationship inconsistent with intention expressed in contract); *A-1 Lumpers*, 2012 TCC 243 (truck loader); *North Delta Real Hot Yoga*, 2012 TCC 369 (front desk worker). The intention does not create a presumption the Crown must rebut: *National Capital Outaouais Ski Team*, 2008 FCA 132.

Single client: In *Dynamic Industries*, 2005 FCA 211, the fact an individual had only one client for several years did not create an employment relationship when the business had previously existed with other clients.

Owner as IC: a company owner who is a director or officer can contract to provide the company additional services as IC, though "this would be unusual": *Pluri Vox*, 2012 FCA 295, para. 10 (leave to appeal denied 2013 CarswellNat 1436 (SCC)). An owner or officer was accepted as an IC in: *McDougall*, [1997] 3 C.T.C. 2927 (TCC: sole shareholder contracted with corp to provide services); *Criterion Capital*, [2001] 4 C.T.C. 2844 (TCC: President/CEO was IC re services he provided to corp outside the scope of those positions); *Zupet*, 2005 TCC 89; *765750 Alberta*, 2007 TCC 149; *Donald L. Mancell Personal Law Corp.*, 2008 TCC 521 (owners were independent as property managers); *Kewcorp Financial*, 2008 TCC 598 (president, sole shareholder of corp); *Quadra Planning*, 2009 TCC 144 (environmental consultant who was co-owner of corp); *Peter Cedar Products*, 2009 TCC 463 (3 directors of a company ceased being employees and their corps went into business as its sales representatives); *Bean*, 2010

TCC 292 and *Yetman*, 2010 TCC 437 (two consultants provided services to a company owned by their wives, formed solely for this purpose); *Humphries*, 2010 TCC 569 (H and his wife owned 78% of company and H was the sole worker); *Waziri*, 2011 TCC 115 (pizza store owner was independent of his company running the store); *AnMar Management*, 2012 TCC 15 (management consultant incorporated his business and was sole shareholder, director and president; he was not an "officer" or employee); *Lavin Associés*, 2012 TCC 87 (lawyers working for professional corp they owned, in Quebec); *Frenkel*, 2012 TCC 216 (company was essentially the owners' agent); *Murray*, 2013 TCC 253 (owner's compensation was not fixed and was based on companies' profit); *3193099 Manitoba*, 2014 TCC 310 (chief operating officer).

Contra, an owner or officer was an employee in: *MacMillan Properties*, 2005 TCC 654; *Lévesque*, 2007 TCC 426; *Pluri Vox* (above: sole shareholder and directing mind of corp, where there was no written agreement); *Sage*, 2011 TCC 249 (person who incorporated "cannot turn around ...and claim the activities he was carrying out on behalf of the company was really him carrying out his own business for the company": para. 20); *Pro-Style Stucco*, 2004 TCC 32 ("I find it difficult, but not necessarily impossible, to find that a corporation having one shareholder, who is also the sole director, can carry on business in the construction industry without any employees, even that sole director": para. 19). In *1148902 Ontario*, 2013 FC 703, CRA had told a company to treat its owner as an employee; when it ignored that advice and was assessed, CRA refused to waive penalties. See also Donohoe, "Owner-Manager", 21(1) *Canadian Tax Highlights* (ctf.ca) 1-2 (Jan. 2013).

Spouses were able to choose an independent-contractor relationship in *Gauthier*, 2007 TCC 563 and *Wyseman*, 2009 TCC 512.

Students paid for research work, and interns, may be employees or may be getting scholarship or grant income: see Notes to 5(1) and 56(1)(n). For post-doctoral fellows, see Notes to 56(3).

Uber drivers may be employees (for employment law purposes: see third-last para. of these Notes): *Heller v. Uber*, 2019 ONCA 1 (SCC appeal heard Nov. 6/19) (class action can proceed, overriding arbitration provision in contract); *Uber v. Aslam*, [2021] UKSC 5 (UK Supreme Court); *O'Connor v. Uber* (2018, US 9th Circuit Court of Appeals) (arbitration provision applies); *Uber*, tinyurl.com/uber-calif (California Court of Appeal, Oct. 2020). See also Doobay. "Uber Driver: Employee?", 24(1) *Canadian Tax Highlights* (ctf.ca) 3-4 (Jan. 2016).

Cases held to be employees include: administrative assistants (*Persuader Court Agents*, 2010 TCC 335; *Connor Financial*, 2017 TCC 242); apartment building superintendent (*Savoie*, 2008 TCC 660); apprentice electrician (*Isaac*, 2010 TCC 225); assistant rugby coach (*Follwell*, 2011 TCC 422); auditor (*Dempsey*, 2007 TCC 362); auto mechanic (*2068193 Ontario*, 2018 TCC 161); banquet server (*Johnson*, 2018 TCC 201; FCA appeal [as *The Butler Did It*] discontinued A-363-18); bartenders (*AE Hospitality*, 2020 FCA 207); bicycle courier (*Rapid Transit Systems*, 2011 TCC 219); bookkeepers (*Nightingale*, 2012 TCC 218; *Kilbride*, 2008 FCA 335; *Storrs*, 2019 TCC 38); caregivers (*Dean*, 2012 TCC 370); carpenter/framer (*Jolin*, 2008 TCC 275; *Twilley*, 2009 TCC 524; *Diamond D*, 2015 TCC 110); chefs (*AE Hospitality*, 2020 FCA 207); chief financial officer (*Logitek*, 2008 TCC 331); chiropractic and physiotherapy assistant (*Lyon*, 2018 TCC 89); cleaners (*Coloniale Maid*, 2010 TCC 115; *Priority One*, 2012 TCC 1; *Morris Meadows*, 2014 TCC 191; *Tagish Lake*, 2014 TCC 381 *SSR Maintenance*, 2018 TCC 216); concert set-up & take-down (*Hieneke*, 2011 TCC 475); construction estimator (*Perras*, 2016 TCC 242); construction project managers (*Hervieux*, 2007 TCC 729; *Guevara*, 2013 TCC 193); construction workers (*Copper Creek Homes*, 2011 TCC 570; *Murray*, 2013 TCC 220; *Drost*, 2015 TCC 291); controller (*Papp*, 2009 TCC 621); cooks (*Morris Meadows*, 2014 TCC 191; *Tagish Lake*, 2016 TCC 381); courier (*Dynamex*, 2010 TCC 17 (FCA appeal discontinued A-52-10)); delivery drivers (*Gutierrez*, 2012 TCC 234; *J.J. Smith Cartage*, 2015 TCC 108; *Karshan (Dominos Pizza)*, [2019] IEHC 894 (Ireland)); dental hygienist (*766743 Ontario Ltd.*, 2014 TCC 133); dietician (*OLTCPI Inc.*, 2010 FCA 74); drivers (*Van De's Accessible Transit*, 2009 TCC 297; *Kattous*, 2017 TCC 251); drywallers (*Gagnon*, 2007 FCA 33; *A.A.I. Contracting*, 2019 TCC 233); duct cleaner (*Titans Furnace*, 2011 TCC 496); electrician (*Settee*, 2014 TCC 173); farm workers (*Ferme Youanie*, 2007 TCC 391; *Dadwal*, 2008 TCC 34); film production assistants (*MWW*, 2019 TCC 127); fishing crew (*Limar Fishing*, 2007 TCC 639; *D.W. Thomas Holdings*, 2009 FCA 371); fitness instructors (*Quantum Fitness*, 2007 TCC 280; *The Girls Gym*, 2011 TCC 312); front desk worker (*North Delta Real Hot Yoga*, 2012 TCC 369); gas bar managers (*Canind International*, 2008 TCC 646); gas processing engineer (*Mathias*, 2019 TCC 271); hairdressers (*1546617 Ontario*, 2010 TCC 26); handymen (*Morris Meadows*, 2014 TCC 191); home care worker (*Gaudet*, 2008 TCC 542); house cleaners (*Thompson*, 2007 TCC 320; *4456735 Manitoba*, 2008 TCC 592); instructors retraining injured adults (*Robertson Human Asset*, 2014 TCC 23); insulation applicator (*Sadden*, 2011 TCC 450); insurance salesman (*6005021 Canada*, 2009 TCC 339); labourer (*Marcotte*, 2007 TCC 386); law clerk (*Wilford*, 2011 TCC 6); lawyer (*Ince-Mercer*, 2009 TCC 594); legal assistant (*Garfin*, 2014 TCC 331); limousine driver (*Hire Roller*, 2013 TCC 10); loggers (*Entreprises B. Smith*, 2007 TCC 456; *Sinclair*, 2009 TCC 495); lottery equipment repairman (*Powertrend Electric*, 2011 TCC 361); lumper [truck loader] (*A-1 Lumpers*, 2012 TCC 243); managers (*Duquet*, 2008 TCC 86; *1166787 Ontario*, 2008 TCC 93; *Critical Control*, 2008 TCC 412; *Canadian Bio Pellet*, 2011 TCC 406; *M.A.P.*, 2012 TCC 70; *Niagara Gorge Jet*, 2013 TCC 261 (Crown's FCA appeal discontinued A-335-13)); marketers/field agents (*Pareto Corp.*, 2015 TCC 47 (FCA appeal discontinued A-157-15)); medical diagnostic imaging technician (*Mehta*, 2011 TCC 558); museum curator (*Kootenay Doukhobor Historical*, 2010 TCC 256); music store salespersons (*La Scala Conservatory*, 2013 TCC 122); music teachers (*Lippert Music*, 2014 TCC 170; *Menoudakis*, 2015 TCC 248; *Sistema*

Toronto, 2016 TCC 193; *Cyr*, 2017 TCC 25; *Coathup*, 2017 TCC 54); nanny (*Graham*, 2011 TCC 565); newspaper handouters at subway stations (*9178-3472 Québec*, 2020 FCA 15); nurses placed temporarily (*617148 Ontario*, 2013 TCC 169); office workers (*Stawicki*, 2008 FCA 350; *Oldham Robinson*, 2010 TCC 596); oil & gas flow-controller builders (*Trinity Innovations*, 2010 TCC 583); oil well engineer who was also a director (*Hines*, 2015 TCC 317); operator in training (*Aquazition*, 2011 TCC 77); painter (*687352 BC*, 2012 TCC 127); personal care workers (*Loving Home Care*, 2015 FCA 68); pet groomers (*1536378 Ontario*, 2007 FCA 334); plant store worker (*Hausauer*, 2012 TCC 290 (FCA appeal dismissed for delay A-325-12)); plumber (*177398 Canada*, 2011 TCC 300, 2013 TCC 177); programmer for a festival (*Ollivierre*, 2009 TCC 490); property inspector (*9113-7307 Québec*, 2008 TCC 419); property maintenance worker (*Szeli*, 2014 TCC 203); property manager (*4453761 Manitoba*, 2014 TCC 321 (FCA appeal dismissed for delay A-524-14)); RCMP cadet in training (*Dhillon*, [2002] 4 C.T.C. 2648 (TCC)); real estate agent (*1351678 Ontario*, 2011 TCC 252); real estate sales administrators (*1770200 Ontario*, 2011 TCC 65); receptionist (*Body Boomers*, 2015 TCC 102); renovator and maintenance worker (*9020-8653 Québec*, 2007 TCC 604); researcher (*Sandberg*, 2013 TCC 301); roadside assistance providers (*SB Towing*, 2013 TCC 358); salespersons (*JFJ Agency*, 2008 TCC 83; *Nu-Tea Imports*, 2008 TCC 658; *Integranuity Marketing*, 2012 TCC 4; *875527 Ontario*, 2012 TCC 214; *Mallon*, 2014 TCC 14; *Monjazeb*, 2016 TCC 196); ship pilot (*MacIntyre*, 2010 TCC 27); stylist assistants and photography assistants (*1772887 Ontario*, 2011 TCC 204); taxi drivers (*Hayer*, 2012 TCC 392; *Badour*, 2014 TCC 279 [under *EI Regulations* para. 6(e) a taxi driver may be deemed an employee for EI purposes]; *Royal City*, 2019 TCC 105 (FCA appeal discontinued A-203-19)); teachers (*Sheppard*, 2009 TCC 97; *École de Langues ABCE*, 2012 TCC 410; *Apex Language*, 2016 TCC 109; *Canada Sun*, 2019 TCC 117); technical support agents (*Acanac Inc.*, 2014 FCA 248); therapist working with autistic child (*Hookham*, 2007 TCC 373); tile installers (*Young Tile*, 2012 TCC 383); tire store manager, installers and sorter (*A & A Tire*, 2009 TCC 640; *A&T Tire*, 2013 FCA 7); trainee at nails spa (*Canada Financial*, 2011 TCC 177); treasurer/chief admin. officer of municipality (*Free*, 2014 TCC 329); tree planter (*Lisovenko*, 2008 TCC 6); truck drivers (*Boulder Creek*, 2007 TCC 580; *Industrial Ready-Mix*, 2008 TCC 219; *Zazai Enterprises*, 2008 TCC 606; *Calder Enterprises*, 2010 TCC 341; *Traverse*, 2010 TCC 345; *TBT Personnel*, 2011 FCA 256 (leave to appeal denied 2012 CarswellNat 983 (SCC)); *Saindon*, 2014 TCC 172); tutor (*Choi*, 2010 TCC 461; *Marilake Education*, 2013 TCC 82); waiters (*LaChance*, 2009 TCC 561; *AE Hospitality*, 2020 FCA 207).

Cases finding ICs include: animation texture artist (*On Masse*, 2010 TCC 250); architecture ex-student (*Roecker*, 2010 TCC 230); babysitter (*Iarutina*, 2011 TCC 114); band player (*Mercier*, 2008 TCC 118); bicycle courier (*Velocity Express*, 2002 CarswellNat 594 (TCC)); bookkeepers (*Caluori*, 2007 TCC 490; *Suspended Power Lift*, 2007 TCC 519; *Merchants of Green Coffee*, 2010 TCC 151; *Accounting by Leandra Tang*, 2011 TCC 171; *Storrs*, 2019 TCC 38); carpenters (*Jolin*, 2008 TCC 275; *1772887 Ontario*, 2011 TCC 204; *Malleau*, 2013 TCC 47); carpet cleaner (*Alert Carpet*, 2011 TCC 321); catering hall workers (*Tréport Wedding*, 2015 TCC 203); chief operating officer (*3193099 Manitoba*, 2014 TCC 310); child and youth worker (*Quinte Children's Homes*, 2015 TCC 250); children of business owners (*Bosveld*, 2020 TCC 2); cleaners (*Vanderveld*, 2009 TCC 200; *Mediclean*, 2009 TCC 340; *Stanton*, 2012 TCC 169; *3142772 Nova Scotia*, 2013 TCC 129; *Morris Meadows*, 2014 TCC 191; *Victoria's Five Star*, 2019 TCC 73); clinical lead at long-term care home (*Porotti*, 2016 FCA 29); computer programmer and product development manager (*Avenza Systems*, 2007 TCC 507); construction workers (*Bishop*, 2007 TCC 541; *Nielsen*, 2010 TCC 77; *Wellbuilt General*, 2010 TCC 541; *Booker*, 2011 TCC 44; *Norman*, 2011 TCC 217; *Kowalchuk*, 2011 TCC 265); counsellor (*Fraser*, 2008 TCC 569); courier (*Aizenberg*, 2008 TCC 19; *Dynamex Canada*, 2008 TCC 71); dance instructor (*Lomness-Seely*, 2007 TCC 653); day-care worker (*Symons*, 2015 TCC 270); delivery drivers (*853998 Ontario*, 2008 TCC 196; *D & D Delivery*, 2011 TCC 266; *1065438 Alberta*, 2018 TCC 191); distiller (*Slow Pub*, 2019 TCC 247 [Z may have been co-owner but was not employee]); doctor (*Scarborough Centre*, 2011 TCC 45); driving instructors (*Bansal*, 2010 TCC 340; *Craigsmyle*, 2011 TCC 128); drywall installer (*McKenna*, 2010 TCC 601); duct cleaners (*Lang*, 2007 TCC 547); educational assessor (*Worldwide School*, 2012 TCC 137); environmental consultant (*Quadra Planning*, 2009 TCC 144); event planner (*Integrated Automotive*, 2011 TCC 468); exam monitors (*Ontario Real Estate Assn*, 2014 TCC 190); factory designer (*Royal Columbia*, 2015 TCC 12, appeal dismissed for procedural reasons as *Kraus*, A-58-15); farm workers (*Doan-Gillan*, 2009 TCC 157; *Johnson*, 2010 TCC 405; *Olson's Wild West*, 2011 TCC 56); fibre optic welders (*1663254 Ontario*, 2011 TCC 19); film production staff (*MWW*, 2019 TCC 127); fishers (*McDonald*, 2011 TCC 437 (Crown's FCA appeal discontinued A-388-11)); furniture fabric-protection technicians (*166020 Canada*, 2014 TCC 220); group home worker (*Woodcock Youth*, 2007 TCC 443; *Unison Treatment*, 2007 TCC 447); hair colour specialist (*Shonn's Makeovers*, 2010 TCC 542 — decision based on worker's Facebook page!); hotel managers (*Vegreville Hotel*, 2010 FCA 331); hunting guide (*Comeau*, 2007 TCC 595); insulation installers (*Derksen*, 2007 TCC 477); insurance adjuster (*Anderson*, 2021 TCC 28); insurance agent (*Giroux*, 2008 TCC 653 (FCA appeal dismissed for delay A-644-08)); land agent negotiating surface rights (*Cavalier Land*, 2011 TCC 490); language instructors (*Langmobile*, 2009 TCC 535); lawyer (*Watzke*, 2011 TCC 351 (FCA appeal dismissed for delay A-369-11)); mail carriers (*1483740 Ontario*, 2007 TCC 258; *Plant*, 2007 TCC 453); marketing consultant (*Ganpaul*, 2009 TCC 205); mechanical engineer & pipeline expert (*Carver PA Corp.*, 2013 TCC 125); music store salespersons (*La Scala Conservatory*, 2013 TCC 122); newspaper carrier (*Millard*, 2008 TCC 353); office administrator (*SIP Distribution*, 2011 TCC 423); orchard pruner (*Rai*, 2008 TCC 147); painters (*G.G. Painting*, 2008 TCC 607; *Abhar*, 2015 TCC 166); park manager (*Drader*, 2011 TCC 157); photographic studio stylists (*1772887 Ontario*, 2011 TCC 204); plant harvester (*Carey*, 2007 TCC 596); polysomnographic technologists (*York Region Sleep*, 2013 TCC 108); postal consultants (*Bean*, 2010 TCC 292; *Yetman*, 2010 TCC 437); product demonstrators (*Prue*, 2011 TCC 9; *Match Action*, 2018 TCC 171); professional education instructor (*Insurance Institute*, 2020 TCC 69); property managers (*Mancell Personal Law Corp.*, 2008 TCC 521); radiologist (*D'Ovidio*, 2007 TCC 282); roofer (*Model Roofing*, 2015 TCC 89 (FCA appeal dismissed for delay A-241-15)); sales manager (*O'Hara*, 2008 TCC 620); salespersons (*1268273 Ontario*, 2007 TCC 442; *Brigadier Security*, 2007 TCC 526; *Numa Technologies*, 2007 TCC 614; *Fleming*, 2010 TCC 212; *1423087 Ontario*, 2010 TCC 451; *Pro-Pharma Contract*, 2012 TCC 60); school manager (*Yun*, 2007 TCC 491); service technician (*1423087 Ontario*, 2010 TCC 451); swimming instructor (*Pavao*, 2013 TCC 305); taper (*Pytel*, 2009 TCC 615); taxi drivers (*Pemberton Taxi*, 2003 CarswellNat 3103 (TCC); *1022239 Ontario*, 2004 TCC 615; *Algoma Taxicab*, 2006 TCC 71; *City Cab*, 2009 TCC 218; *Labrash*, 2010 TCC 399; *2177936 Ontario*, 2013 TCC 317; *Beach Place*, 2019 TCC 24 (FCA appeal dismissed for delay A-128-19)); teacher at online school (*Kelowna Christian*, 2008 TCC 80); technical standards drafter (*Villeneuve*, 2014 TCC 224); telemarketers (*Greenshield Windows*, 2015 TCC 70; *Roberts*, 2015 TCC 142 (FCA appeal dismissed for delay A-383-15)); translator (*Marar*, 2018 TCC 259); truck drivers (*Landry*, 2005 TCC 347; *Preston*, 2007 TCC 511; *Cozart*, 2007 TCC 528; *Domart Energy*, 2007 TCC 585; *McMath*, 2008 TCC 152; *Ace-3 Transportation*, 2010 TCC 174; *Smith*, 2011 TCC 20; *5256951 Manitoba*, 2011 TCC 229; *Butt*, 2013 TCC 284; *Big Bird Trucking*, 2015 TCC 340 [even though BBT provided the trucks and insurance]; *Inowal Transport*, 2017 TCC 26); truck loader (*Samqo Transport*, 2012 TCC 132); tutor (*Preddie*, 2004 TCC 181); university lecturer who was a CA (*Asare-Quansah*, 2012 TCC 226); waiters and bartenders (*10tation Event*, 2008 TCC 562; *Ramos-Romo*, 2011 TCC 228); youth counsellor (*Peterborough Youth*, 2013 TCC 291).

In Quebec, the FCA first said *Wiebe Door* and *Sagaz* do not apply, and "control" is the only test under the *Civil Code*: *9041-6868 Québec Inc.*, 2005 FCA 334, approving a paper by TCC Justice Archambault, "Contract of Employment: Why *Wiebe Door Services Ltd.* Does Not Apply in Quebec", *The Harmonization of Federal Legislation with Quebec Civil Law: Second Collection* (2005, apff.org), 2:1-85; see also Auger, "Employee and Self-Employed Worker", *The Harmonization of Federal Legislation with Quebec Civil Law* (APFF, 2002), 3:1-82. However, *Combined Insurance*, 2007 FCA 60 (leave to appeal denied 2007 CarswellNat 3558 (SCC)), held that while the control test is of "special importance", the *Wiebe Door* factors must be considered as well. Further, *Grimard*, 2009 FCA 47, says the two tests are the same, because in considering "control" for the *Civil Code*, "a court does not err in taking into consideration as indicators of supervision the other criteria used under the common law, that is to say, the ownership of the tools, the chance of profit, the risk of loss, and integration into the business" (para. 43). See also *Fédération des caisses Desjardins (Payette)*, 2020 FCA 182 [leave to appeal to SCC requested] (no one factor is determinative; economic control is not legal control, and control of the results is not the same as control of the work); *Baribeau*, 2015 FC 615; lengthy discussion by Archambault J. in *Mazraani*, 2016 TCC 65 (but new trial ordered on procedural grounds 2018 SCC 50); *9267-2245 Québec*, 2020 TCC 10 (parties' intention does not override the facts); VIEWS doc 2010-0382441E5 (home child-care provider).

Thus, in Quebec under the *Civil Code* tests, the following were **employees**: accountants (*Martel*, 2017 TCC 238, aff'd as *Lalancette*, 2018 FCA 225); bar manager (*Laverdière*, 2008 FCA 293); cameraman and technical director (*Bernier*, 2011 TCC 99); caregiver or nanny (*Carola*, 2008 TCC 508; *Morin*, 2012 TCC 149 (FCA appeal discontinued A-305-12); *Cloutier*, 2012 TCC 164); Christmas decoration installers (*Plus Que Noël*, 2007 TCC 602); cleaners (*Bernier*, 2010 TCC 280; *Bernier*, 2011 TCC 156); day-care worker (*Hann*, 2013 TCC 359); excavator (*Blain*, 2015 TCC 162); executive assistant and media relations person (*Hendriks*, 2018 TCC 50); hockey players (*Demers (6094350 Canada)*, 2020 QCCA 681; leave to appeal denied 2021 CarswellQue 1 (SCC)); insurance agent with Industrial Alliance (*Mazraani*, 2016 TCC 65, but new trial ordered on procedural grounds 2018 SCC 50); janitor (*9079-2276 Québec*, 2014 TCC 106); mortgage representatives (*Payette*, 2019 TCC 235 — but rev'd 2020 FCA 182 as *Fédération des caisses Desjardins* and sent back to TCC for new decision; leave to appeal to SCC requested); nurses (*Agence Océanica*, 2015 TCC 168); owner-managers (*Lévesque*, 2007 TCC 426); pet groomer (*Kaviar International*, 2007 TCC 589); physical therapy instructor (*Rheaume*, 2007 TCC 591); salespersons (*3234339 Canada [Credico Marketing]*, 2006 FCA 308 (leave to appeal denied 2007 CarswellNat 616 (SCC)); *Propriétés Belcourt*, 2009 FCA 334; *Crédit Destination*, 2006 TCC 649; *Robillard*, 2008 TCC 326); shipping workers (*Ray-Mont*, 2020 FCA 113); snow shovelers (*Déneige-Toit*, 2019 TCC 257); store display workers (*Gagné*, 2009 TCC 549; *Meunier*, 2015 TCC 111; *7547978 Canada*, 2015 TCC 112 and 2021 TCC 7); telemarketer (*Desrobec Inc.*, 2007 TCC 459); travel agent (*Taupier Girard*, 2008 TCC 176); truck drivers (*9267-2245 Québec*, 2020 TCC 10); tutors (*NCJ Educational*, 2009 FCA 131 (leave to appeal denied 2009 CarswellNat 3673)); welder (*Beauport*, 2010 TCC 368).

In Quebec under the *Civil Code* tests, the following were **ICs**: acting CEO (*Vachon*, 2009 TCC 84, but FCA appeal allowed on consent A-107-09); architectural draftsman (*Beaucaire*, 2009 TCC 142); cabinetmaker (*Charbonneau*, 2013 TCC 55); caregiver (*Robert*, 2015 TCC 84); chef (*Talbot*, 2009 TCC 460; *Therrien*, 2013 TCC 116); Cirque du Soleil guest artist (*Dupuis*, 2006 FC 228); cleaners (*Barbeau*, 2015 TCC 131); day-care worker (*Symons*, 2015 TCC 270); driver (*Med Express*, 2021 TCC 8); estheticians (*Romanza Soins Capillaires*, 2015 TCC 328 [but the decision may be a nullity — see "Replacement by the Chief Justice" in 169(1) Notes]; *Venti*, 2019 TCC 142 (FCA appeal discontinued A-344-19)); garment maker (*Vertzagias*, 2013 TCC 219); human resources manager (*Gestion Maryse Benny*, 2014 TCC 89); insurance sales staff (*Compagnie d'Assurance Combined*, 2011 TCC 85; *Lamontagne*, 2018 TCC 153 (FCA appeal dismissed for delay 2019 FCA 162)); investment advisors (*Financière Banque Nationale*, 2008 FCA 624); language teachers (*Entreprises une affaire d'anglais*, 2009 FCA 372; *Enseignants de langue anglaise*, 2014 TCC 287); lawyers (*Lavin Associés*, 2012 TCC 87); maintenance workers (*Boucher*, 2007 TCC 467); parking enforcer (*Pichugin*, 2011 TCC 16); psychotherapist (*Maison Belfield*, 2009 TCC 129); salespersons (*Patisseries Jessica*, 2008 TCC 283; *Industries Kouper-FKS*, 2013 TCC 315); setting up trade show booths (*Borgia*, 2009 TCC 266); spouse, where no relationship of subordination (*Anctil*, 2013 TCC 131); tow truck driver (*Trudel*, 2008 TCC 488); travel agent (*3105822 Canada*, 2008 TCC 305); truckers (*Transports P.M. Levert*, 2008 TCC 570); waiter (*Ramos Romo I-L*, 2011 TCC 228).

In Quebec for employment law (non-tax) purposes, cleaners who were franchisees were held 2-1 to be employees in *Modern Concept*, 2017 QCCA 1237; leave has been granted to appeal to the SCC.

In Quebec, s. 6 of *An Act respecting the professional status and conditions of engagement of performing, recording and film artists* (RSQ, c. S-32.1) deems certain artists to "exercise an occupation on [their] own account", but this is only "For purposes of this Act" and does not override IT-525 [now Folio S4-F14-C1] in CRA's view: doc 2012-0451751E5.

Individuals doing work "analogous to a contract of service" through placement agencies (e.g., computer consultants) may be self-employed for tax purposes but subject to EI and CPP deductions by (and get a T4 from) the placement agency: *Canada Pension Plan Regulations* s. 34; VIEWS doc 9924815; RC4120 *Employers' Guide*, "Placement or employment agency workers" in Chap. 6; *Productions du Grand Bamboo*, 2017 TCC 161 (aff'd 2018 FCA 99); *European Staffing*, 2019 TCC 59 (workers were employees anyway); *B2C Intelligence*, 2012 TCC 203; *617148 Ontario Ltd.*, 2013 TCC 169; *Wholistic Child*, 2016 TCC 34; *AE Hospitality*, 2019 TCC 116. *Employment Insurance Regulations* para. 6(g) requires "employment", but for this purpose the term includes ICs: *Carver PA Corp.*, 2013 TCC 125, para. 11; *Wholistic Child*, para. 15. See also Gemmiti, "Placement Agencies: Insurable and Pensionable Employment", 22(3) *Canadian Tax Highlights* (ctf.ca) 10-11 (March 2014).

Film industry workers: In *Chao*, 2018 TCC 72, a payroll service provider that paid C was not her employer; each of the 5 companies for which she worked in the year was.

A contract of service (employment) can continue if the parties agree to continue it in a settlement agreement, even if the relationship has broken down and the employee is not working: *Verrault* (1986), 86 N.R. 389 (FCA); *Serafini*, [1989] 2 C.T.C. 2437 (TCC); *Sirois* (1999), 243 N.R. 212 (FCA); *Simone Sherman*, 2014 TCC 292; or if the employee is not working due to disability: *Goodwin*, 2014 CarswellNat 4951 (TCC). See also Notes to 248(1)"retiring allowance" re salary continuation.

A judge is technically not employed by anyone, but the government is the judge's "employer" for tax purposes: *St-Julien*, 2005 TCC 511.

Where a payor insists on treating a worker as an employee and withholding tax at source, the worker's services could instead be contracted for by a corporation, which clearly cannot be an employee. The corporation might be carrying on a personal services business (see Notes to 18(1)(p)), but no withholding applies.

The words "employment" and "employed" should have the corresponding meaning, due to *Interpretation Act* s. 33(3); but this may not apply to "employer".

In *Baribeau*, 2015 FC 615, B worked in Quebec for Environment Canada and was treated as an IC, but CRA ruled she was an employee. When she claimed past work as pensionable (employee) service, the government Pension Centre was wrong to refuse her without explaining its inconsistency with CRA and without applying Quebec law.

The tax criteria might not apply for employment law, when suing for unpaid wages (*Bagrianski v. Aero Surveys*, 2004 CanLII 24718 (Ont. SCJ); *Transport Vares v. Feng*, 2011 FC 1295) or bringing a union grievance (*Estwick*, 2007 FC 894); and see *Modern Cleaning*, 2019 SCC 28, *Azur Human Resources*, 2018 ONSC 5212 and *Dare Human Resources*, 2019 ONCA 549, para. 18; though they were considered the same for wrongful dismissal (*Engels v. Merit Insurance Brokers*, 2007 CanLII 6455 (Ont. SCJ)) and for accident income replacement benefits (*Ligocki v. Allianz Insurance*, 2010 ONSC 1166, where self-identification as IC on tax return did not trump other factors); and for an unpaid-wages claim: *Acanac*, 2018 SKQB 21. For wrongful-dismissal and labour-relations purposes there is an intermediate "dependent contractor" category: Ont. *Labour Relations Act* s. 1(1); *McKee v. Reid's Heritage*, 2009 ONCA 916; *Keenan v. Canac*, 2016 ONCA 79; *CUPW v. Foodora*, 2020 CanLII 16750 (Ont. LRB); *Med Express*, 2021 TCC 8, paras. 13-15.

Sagaz (SCC; see first para. of these Notes) dealt with an employer's vicarious liability. In *McCormick v. Fasken Martineau*, 2014 SCC 39, a partner at a large law firm was held not to be an employee for human-rights (discrimination) purposes, though this might be different for non-equity partners. In *Daniel v. Miller Canfield*, 2017 ONCA 697, a law firm "salaried international principal" was held to be a partner and not entitled to severance.

A person who changed his status from employee to subcontractor to escape source deductions was convicted of evasion: see McCaw conviction in 248(1)"person" Notes.

Interpretation Bulletins: IT-525R: Performing artists.

CRA Audit Manual: 27.11.0: Employed vs. self-employed; 40.13.8: Sector profiles — drywall contractors — employee vs. self-employed contractor.

Forms: CPT-1: Request for a ruling as to the status of a worker under the Canada Pension Plan or Employment Insurance Act; RC4100: Employee or Self-Employed?.

"employee benefit plan" means an arrangement under which contributions are made by an employer or by any person with whom the employer does not deal at arm's length to another person (in this Act referred to as the **"custodian"** of an employee benefit plan) and under which one or more payments are to be made to or for the benefit of employees or former employees of the employer or persons who do not deal at arm's length with any such employee or former employee (other than a payment that, if section 6 were read without reference to subparagraph 6(1)(a)(ii) and paragraph 6(1)(g), would not be required to be included in computing the income of the recipient or of an employee or former employee), but does not include any portion of the arrangement that is

(a) a fund, plan or trust referred to in subparagraph 6(1)(a)(i) or paragraph 6(1)(d) or (f),

(b) a trust described in paragraph 149(1)(y),

(c) an employee trust,

(c.1) a salary deferral arrangement, in respect of a taxpayer, under which deferred amounts are required to be included as benefits under paragraph 6(1)(a) in computing the taxpayer's income,

(c.2) a retirement compensation arrangement,

(d) an arrangement the sole purpose of which is to provide education or training for employees of the employer to improve their work or work-related skills and abilities, or

(e) a prescribed arrangement;

Abandoned Proposed Amendment — 248(1)"employee benefit plan"

Notes: The May 27, 2019 draft amendments for employee life and health trusts (144.1) included an amendment to this definition that would have caused a trust meeting certain conditions, but not the conditions for being an ELHT, to be an EBP. This proposal was dropped in the Nov. 27, 2020 draft legislation; the Finance Backgrounder of that date states: "If a Health and Welfare Trust does not convert to an Employee Life and Health Trust, or does not wind up, by the end of 2021, the CRA will apply the existing tax rules that apply to *inter vivos* trusts (and will not apply the rules for employee benefit plans to the Health and Welfare Trust)."

Related Provisions: 6(1)(g) — Amount received from EBP taxable; 12(11)"investment contract"(c) — Exemption from annual interest accrual rules; 32.1 — Deductions to employer re EBP; 75(3)(a) — Reversionary trust rules do not apply to EBP; 94(1)"exempt foreign trust"(f) — EBP excluded from non-resident trust rules; 104(6)(a.1) — Deduction in computing income of EBP; 104(13)(b) — Income inclusion to trust; 107.1(b) — Distribution of property by EBP deemed at cost amount; 108(1)"trust"(a) — "trust" does not include an EBP for certain purposes; 128.1(10)"excluded right or interest"(a)(v) — No deemed disposition of rights on emigration; 212(17) — No non-resident withholding tax on payments from EBP.

Notes: For discussion of EBPs see IT-502 and *McNeeley*, 2020 TCC 90 (under appeal to FCA). An EBP distribution is normally taxable: 6(1)(g). An EBP excludes plan payments that would not be taxable benefits under 6(1)(a). In *McNeeley*, EBP payments to B were taxable because B was an employee of the company, even though he was also the major shareholder.

See Hans, "Employee Benefit Plans", 13(3) *Taxation of Executive Compensation and Retirement* (Federated Press) 31-34 (Oct. 2001); Sweatman & Hodge, "Employee Benefit Plans", 16(9) *TECR* 539-47 (May 2005).

An employer's self-funded life insurance plan may be an EBP: VIEWS doc 2005-0129961E5. For rulings that a plan is an EBP see 2006-0206461R3, 2007-0220151R3, 2007-0251181R3. See also 2009-0308741E5 (training fund for laid-off workers may be EBP); 2004-0106481R3, 2008-0265651E5; 2009-0311181R3 (funding of group health insurance arrangement is not EBP); 2010-0373561C6 (EBP rules do not apply if s. 7 applies), 2012-0470801R3 (detailed amendments to EBP); 2018-0781941E5 (foreign retirement plan with no employer contributions is not EBP); 2018-0782381E5, 2019-0824281E5 (UK retirement plan can be EBP); 2020-0852671E5 (Isle of Man "provident fund" may be an EBP).

Opening words amended by 2002-2013 technical bill, effective Nov. 2011, to add "or of an employee or former employee" before the final closing parenthesis.

248(1)"employee benefit plan" amended by 2010 budget bill #2, effective 2010, to add "any portion of the arrangement that is" (end of opening words) and to change "fund or plan" to "fund, plan or trust" (para. (a)).

Para. (e) amended by 1993 technical bill, effective 1980.

Regulations: 6800 (prescribed plan, prescribed arrangement).

Income Tax Folios: S2-F1-C1: Health and welfare trusts [replaces IT-85R2].

Interpretation Bulletins: IT-502: Employee benefit plans and employee trusts.

Advance Tax Rulings: ATR-17: Employee benefit plan — purchase of company shares; ATR-21: Pension benefit from an unregistered pension plan.

"employee life and health trust" has the meaning assigned by subsection 144.1(2);

Notes: 248(1)"employee life and health trust" added by 2010 budget bill #2, effective 2010. See Notes at end of 144.1.

"employee trust" means an arrangement (other than an employees profit sharing plan, a deferred profit sharing plan or a plan referred to in subsection 147(15) as a "revoked plan") established after 1979

(a) under which payments are made by one or more employers to a trustee in trust solely to provide to employees or former employees of

(i) the employer, or

(ii) a person with whom the employer does not deal at arm's length,

benefits the right to which vests at the time of each such payment and the amount of which does not depend on the individual's position, performance or compensation as an employee,

(b) under which the trustee has, since the commencement of the arrangement, each year allocated to individuals who are beneficiaries thereunder, in such manner as is reasonable, the amount, if any, by which the total of all amounts each of which is

(i) an amount received under the arrangement by the trustee in the year from an employer or from a person with whom the employer does not deal at arm's length,

(ii) the amount that would, if this Act were read without reference to subsection 104(6), be the income of the trust for the year (other than a taxable capital gain from the disposition of property) from a property or other source other than a business, or

(iii) a capital gain of the trust for the year from the disposition of property

exceeds the total of all amounts each of which is

(iv) the loss of the trust for the year (other than an allowable capital loss from the disposition of property) from a property or other source other than a business, or

(v) a capital loss of the trust for the year from the disposition of property, and

(c) the trustee of which has elected to qualify the arrangement as an employee trust in its return of income filed within 90 days from the end of its first taxation year;

Related Provisions: 6(1)(h) — Amounts received from employee trust taxable; 12(1)(n) — Payments from trust to employer taxable; 104(6)(a) — Deduction in computing income of employee trust; 107.1(a) — Distribution of property by employee trust deemed at FMV; 108(1)"trust"(a) — "trust" does not include an employee trust for certain purposes; 128.1(10)"excluded right or interest"(e)(i) — No deemed disposition on emigration; 212(17) — No non-resident withholding tax on payments from employee trust; 248(1)"disposition"(f)(vi) — Rollover from one trust to another; *Interpretation Act* 27(5) — Meaning of "within 90 days".

Notes: If the trust is resident in Quebec, an election under para. (c) must be copied to Revenu Québec: *Taxation Act* ss. 47.7, 21.4.6.

Income Tax Folios: S2-F1-C1: Health and welfare trusts [replaces IT-85R2].

Interpretation Bulletins: IT-502: Employee benefit plans and employee trusts.

"employees profit sharing plan" has the meaning assigned by subsection 144(1);

"employer", in relation to an officer, means the person from whom the officer receives the officer's remuneration;

Related Provisions: 6(2) — Definition of "employer" for automobile standby charge; 6(17) — Extended definition for disability insurance top-up payments; 80.4(1)(b)(i) — Definition of "employer" for employee loans; 81(3)(c) — Definition of "employer" for municipal officer's expense allowance; 207.6(3)(a) — Definition of "employer" for incorporated employee/RCA rules; 252.1 — Application of pension rules where union is employer.

Notes: See Notes to 248(1)"employee".

"employment" means the position of an individual in the service of some other person (including Her Majesty or a foreign state or sov-

ereign) and **"servant"** or **"employee"** means a person holding such a position;

Notes: "Employee" is defined both here and above (in its alphabetical order). See Notes to "employee" above re the distinction from independent contractor.

Interpretation Bulletins: IT-525R: Performing artists.

Forms: CPT-1: Request for a ruling as to the status of a worker under the Canada Pension Plan or Employment Insurance Act.

"estate" has the meaning assigned by subsection 104(1) and includes, for civil law, a succession;

Notes: See Notes to *Interpretation Act* s. 8.1 re Quebec civil law. Definition amended by 2013 budget bill #2, effective Dec. 12, 2013, to add "and includes, for civil law, a succession". This amendment and that to 248(1)"trust" overrule the *Lipson* case discussed in the Notes to 104(1).

"estate of the bankrupt" has the same meaning as in the *Bankruptcy and Insolvency Act*;

Related Provisions: 128(1)(b) — Where corporation bankrupt; 128(2)(b) — Where individual bankrupt.

Notes: Definition "estate of the bankrupt" added by 1994 technical bill, effective for taxation years that end after February 21, 1994. This definition was previously in 128(3). The term "estate of the bankrupt" is not defined in the BIA.

"excessive eligible dividend designation" has the meaning assigned by subsection 89(1);

Notes: 248(1)"excessive eligible dividend designation" added by 2006 budget bill #2 (Part 2 — eligible dividends), effective for 2006 and later taxation years.

"exempt income" means property received or acquired by a person in such circumstances that it is, because of any provision of Part I, not included in computing the person's income, but does not include a dividend on a share or a support amount (as defined in subsection 56.1(4));

Related Provisions: 81 — Amounts not included in income; 149 — Exempt taxpayers.

Notes: Certain amounts such as workers' compensation payments and social assistance (welfare) are not "exempt income" because they are included in income and then subject to an offsetting deduction. (See 56(1)(u), (v) and 110(1)(f)(ii).)

Since support amounts are excluded, legal expenses of obtaining (even non-taxable) child support can be deducted: *Nadeau*, 2003 FCA 400. (See 18(1)(c) and Notes to 56(1)(b).)

Definition "exempt income" amended by 1996 Budget, effective 1997, to add the exclusion for a support amount and to delete a redundant reference to "money" (which is included in "property" as defined in 248(1)).

"farm loss" has the meaning assigned by subsection 111(8);

Related Provisions: 31(1), (1.1), 248(1) — Definition of "restricted farm loss"; 111(9) — Farm loss where taxpayer not resident in Canada.

Notes: A "farm loss" includes a fishing loss: 111(8)"farm loss"A(a)(i).

"farming" includes tillage of the soil, livestock raising or exhibiting, maintaining of horses for racing, raising of poultry, fur farming, dairy farming, fruit growing and the keeping of bees, but does not include an office or employment under a person engaged in the business of farming;

Related Provisions: 28–31 — Rules for computing income from farming; 110.6(2) — Capital gains exemption — qualified farm or fishing property; 248(29) — Property used in a combination of farming and fishing.

Notes: "Generally, farming is the raising and harvesting of animals or plants in a controlled environment." See Income Tax Folio S4-F11-C1 ¶1 and VIEWS doc 2004-0086271E5 for CRA views on farming and some of the case law: "the taxpayer must make an appreciable contribution to the growth and maturity of the crop and must be actively engaged in the management and/or day to day activities of the farming business". See also Notes to 31(1); and Notes to 188.1(5) re meaning of "includes". The definition is not exhaustive and includes the "ordinarily and generally accepted meaning" of farming: *Pollon*, para. 23. Income from an activity incidental to farming can be farming income if it is not "substantial" in relation to the farming revenue: 2010-0385151E5, and is not a separate business: IT-433R para. 7, 2014-0528251I7.

The following can be considered farming: beekeeping (definition); Christmas tree growing (Folio S4-F11-C1 ¶1.12, IT-373R2 para. 15); chick hatchery (S4-F11-C1 ¶1.5); dairy farming (definition); egg hatchery (*Pollon*, [1984] C.T.C. 131 (FCTD); VIEWS doc 2006-0198811E5); farm quota leasing, maybe (2007-0254211E5); feedlot operation (Guide T4003, IT-156R paras. 2-5); fish breeding or raising [aquaculture] (*Immeubles Dramis*, [1981] C.T.C. 2568 (TRB); S4-F11-C1 ¶1.9 [fishing is excluded: ¶1.14]; VIEWS doc 2014-0522091I7); fruit growing (definition); fur farming (definition); greenhouse growing (*Coop Belle-de-Jour*, 2019 QCCQ 6609); "Growing Forward"-funded programs (2011-0403761I7); hydroponics [cultivating crops in water]

(S4-F11-C1 ¶1.5, T4003); legume seed production, likely (2014-0523871E5); livestock raising or showing (definition, and see S4-F11-C1 ¶1.6); maple sugar bush operation (S4-F11-C1 ¶1.5); marijuana growing but not processing (S4-F11-C1 ¶1.5, 2011-0392741E5, 2013-0510711E5); peat harvesting (2004-0077321E5, 2011-040376117); poultry raising (definition, and S4-F11-C1 ¶1.8); nursery or greenhouse operation (S4-F11-C1 ¶1.5, 2007-0260271E5); racehorse ownership, whether or not the owners maintain the horses themselves (*Craig*, 2012 SCC 43; *Juster*, [1974] C.T.C. 681 (FCA); *Teelucksingh*, 2011 TCC 22 (limited partnership investors in Arabian horses); 2007-0229961E5); rodent raising for use as [human or animal] food, not as pets (2015-0564611E5); slaughtering and processing meat, if an integral part of a farming business (2015-0594721E5); soil tilling (definition); switchgrass pellet sales (2010-038126117); tobacco growing but not processing (S4-F11-C1 ¶1.5); wild-game reserve (T4003); winemaking and vineyard business (*Tinhorn Creek*, 2005 TCC 693); woodlot whose focus is planting, nurturing and harvesting trees rather than logging (S4-F11-C1 ¶1.11, IT-373R2); worm breeding to produce castings (2011-040376117, 2011-0405411E5).

The following are *not* considered farming: cheese aging, chicken plucking, bean cleaning, polishing and treating, and egg cleaning, sorting, grading and spraying (2013-0510351E5 — these are "processing"); agricultural monitoring (2013-0491141E5); electricity sales under solar-panel program, unless incidental to farming activities (2010-0360211E5, 2010-0371261E5, 2011-0424381E5); floral arranging (*Coop Belle-de-Jour*, 2019 QCCQ 6609); horse boarding and horse riding lessons (S4-F11-C1 ¶1.13, 2010-0390021E5); horse boarding, farmland rental and producing/selling wool products (2009-0333721E5); horse quarantine service and dressage training (2012-0438361E5); methane gas production from hog waste (S4-F11-C1 ¶1.13; 2010-038147117 was non-committal); pet breeding, e.g. dogs, parrots (*Sniderman*, [1989] 2 C.T.C. 2027 (TCC); *Partington*, [1991] 1 C.T.C. 2429 (TCC); S4-F11-C1 ¶1.13; 2015-0619501E5); ponies kept to power a children's carousel (*Crichton*, 2013 TCC 96, para. 8); sharecropping (2007-022924117); tending others' herds (2007-0259521E5); wild or exotic animal raising (S4-F11-C1 ¶1.13); wind farming, unless incidental to farming activities (2014-052825117); winemaking that is not incidental to grape growing (2013-0510351E5); zookeeping (S4-F11-C1 ¶1.13, 2014-0527651E5).

See Munro & Oelschlagel, *Taxation of Farmers and Fishermen* (Carswell, looseleaf or *Taxnet Pro* Reference Centre); *Checklist 45 — Tax Preparers of Cattle Ranching and Dairy Farmers* (*Taxnet Pro* Tax & Estate Planning Centre, 2020, 4pp); Fuller, *Agriculture Law in Canada* (LexisNexis, 2nd ed., 2019), chap. 11, "Taxation of farming"; Swanson, "The Difference a Farm Makes", 2004 Prairie Provinces Tax Conference (PPTC) (ctf.ca), 12:1-35; MacPhee & Power, "Issues Facing the Farming and Fishing Industries", 2010 Atlantic Provinces Tax Conf. 5A:1-19; Hanson and Yaskowich, "There is More to the Family Farm than Meets the Eye", 2014 PPTC, 5:1-28 (discusses other farm issues such as oil & gas rights, gravel, rentals, other revenue); Hornsby, "Income Tax and Farming", 15(3) *Tax Hyperion* (Carswell) 8-11 (May-June 2018).

Various tax credits are available for farmers including a Manitoba Odour Control Credit: Drache, "Does this Tax Credit Meet the Smell Test?", xxxiv(3) *The Canadian Taxpayer* (Carswell) 24 (Feb. 10, 2012).

See Income Tax Folio S4-F11-C1 ¶1.17-1.26, "What is a farming business?" A person employed by a farmer (see Notes to 248(1)"employee") is not "farming"; nor is a person providing consulting, landscaping or veterinary services to a farmer: ¶1.13.

Income Tax Folios: S4-F11-C1: Meaning of farming and farming business [replaces IT-433R].

Interpretation Bulletins: IT-156R: Feedlot operators (cancelled); IT-268R3: *Inter vivos* transfer of farm property to child.

CRA Audit Manual: 27.12.0: Farming and fishing income; 29.4.0: Farm losses and restricted farm losses.

Forms: RC602: Checklist for Tax Preparers — Cattle Ranching and Dairy Farming.

"federal credit union" has the meaning assigned by section 2 of the *Bank Act*;

Notes: The only federal credit unions are Caisse populaire acadienne ltée and Coast Capital Savings Federal Credit Union; see tinyurl.com/can-fedcu.

Bank Act (BA) s. 2(1) (see CanLii.org) provides that "federal credit union" means a bank that is organized and carried on business on a cooperative basis as per BA 12.1, which lists the conditions, including "a majority of its members are natural persons" and "it provides financial services primarily to its members".

"filing-due date" for a taxation year of a taxpayer means the day on or before which the taxpayer's return of income under Part I for the year is required to be filed or would be required to be filed if tax under that Part were payable by the taxpayer for the year;

Related Provisions: 150(1) — Due dates for filing returns; *Interpretation Act* 26 — Deadline on weekend or holiday extended to next business day.

Notes: An extension of time under 220(3) will extend the "filing-due date".

Definition "filing-due date" added by 1995 Budget, effective 1994.

Application Policies: SR&ED 2004-02R5: Filing requirements for claiming SR&ED.

"fiscal period" — [Repealed]

Notes: "Fiscal period" repealed by 1995 Budget, for fiscal periods that begin after 1994. See now 249.1(1) and (7).

"fishing" includes fishing for or catching shell fish, crustaceans and marine animals but does not include an office or employment under a person engaged in the business of fishing;

Related Provisions: 28 — Election to report fishing income on cash basis; 70(9)–(9.31), 73(3)–(4.1) — Intergenerational rollover of fishing property; 110.6(2) — Capital gains exemption — qualified farm or fishing property; 248(29) — Property used in a combination of farming and fishing.

Notes: In *Immeubles Dramis*, [1981] C.T.C. 2568 (TRB), fish breeding was considered farming.

See Silver, "Update on Issues Facing the Fishing Industry", 2010 Atlantic Provinces Tax Conference (ctf.ca), 5B:1-18; MacPhee & Power, "Issues Facing the Farming and Fishing Industries", *ibid.* 5A:1-19.

Income Tax Folios: S4-F11-C1: Meaning of farming and farming business [replaces IT-433R].

CRA Audit Manual: 27.12.0: Farming and fishing income.

"flow-through share" has the meaning assigned by subsection 66(15);

Notes: "Flow-through share" added by 1995-97 technical bill, effective Dec. 1994.

"foreign accrual property income" has the meaning assigned by section 95;

Related Provisions: 95(1)"foreign accrual property income", 95(2) — Definition.

Notes: Definition added by 2011 budget bill #2, for tax years that begin after 2006.

"foreign affiliate" has the meaning assigned by subsection 95(1);

Interpretation Bulletins: IT-343R: Meaning of the term "corporation"; IT-119R4: Debts of shareholders and certain persons connected with shareholders.

"foreign currency" means currency of a country other than Canada;

Related Provisions: 261(5)(g) — Functional currency reporting.

Notes: 248(1)"foreign currency" added by 2001 technical bill, effective June 28, 1999.

"foreign currency debt" has the meaning assigned by subsection 111(8);

Notes: 248(1)"foreign currency debt" added by 2008 budget bill #2, effective 2006. The term is used in 40(10)-(11) and 111(12), and is affected by 261(5)(f)(ii).

"foreign exploration and development expenses" has the meaning assigned by subsection 66(15);

"foreign resource expense" has the meaning assigned by subsection 66.21(1);

Notes: 248(1)"foreign resource expense" added by 2000 Budget, effective 2001.

"foreign resource pool expenses" of a taxpayer means the taxpayer's foreign resource expenses in respect of all countries and the taxpayer's foreign exploration and development expenses;

Notes: 248(1)"foreign resource pool expense" added by 2000 Budget, effective 2001.

"foreign resource property" has the meaning assigned by subsection 66(15), and a foreign resource property in respect of a country means a foreign resource property that is

(a) a right, licence or privilege to explore for, drill for or take petroleum, natural gas or related hydrocarbons in that country,

(b) a right, licence or privilege to

(i) store underground petroleum, natural gas or related hydrocarbons in that country, or

(ii) prospect, explore, drill or mine for minerals in a mineral resource in that country,

(c) an oil or gas well in that country or real or immovable property in that country the principal value of which depends on its petroleum or natural gas content (but not including depreciable property),

(d) any right to a rental or royalty computed by reference to the amount or value of production from an oil or gas well in that country, or from a natural accumulation of petroleum or natural gas in that country, if the payer of the rental or royalty has an interest in, or for civil law a right in, the well or accumulation, as the case may be, and 90% or more of the rental or royalty is payable out of, or from the proceeds of, the production from the well or accumulation,

(e) any right to a rental or royalty computed by reference to the amount or value of production from a mineral resource in that country, if the payer of the rental or royalty has an interest in, or for civil law a right in, the mineral resource and 90% or more of the rental or royalty is payable out of, or from the proceeds of, the production from the mineral resource,

(f) a real or immovable property in that country the principal value of which depends upon its mineral resource content (but not including depreciable property),

(g) a right to or an interest in — or for civil law a right to or in — any property described in any of paragraphs (a) to (e), other than a right or an interest that the taxpayer has because the taxpayer is a beneficiary under a trust or a member of a partnership, or

(h) an interest in real property described in paragraph (f) or a real right in an immovable described in that paragraph, other than an interest or a right that the taxpayer has because the taxpayer is a beneficiary under a trust or a member of a partnership;

Notes: For the meaning of "right, licence or privilege" in (a) and (b), see 66(15)"Canadian resource property" Notes.

Definition amended by 2002-2013 technical bill (last change effective June 26, 2013), 2000 Budget.

"foreign retirement arrangement" means a prescribed plan or arrangement;

Related Provisions: 12(11)"investment contract"(d) — Exemption from annual interest accrual rules; 56(12) — Deemed distribution from FRA included in income; 81(1)(r) — Exemption for income from FRA; 94(1)"exempt foreign trust"(e) — Arrangement excluded from non-resident trust rules; 108(1)"trust"(a) — "trust" does not include an FRA for certain purposes; 128.1(10)"excluded right or interest"(a)(x) — No deemed disposition on emigration.

Notes: A foreign retirement arrangement is a U.S. Individual Retirement Account (IRA); see Notes to Reg. 6803. The income earned within it is untaxed (81(1)(r)), while payments from it are taxed (56(1)(a)(i)(C.1)) but can be rolled into an RRSP (60.01). Note that such payments are taxed even when inherited on the death of another person: *Kaiser*, [1994] 2 C.T.C. 2385 (TCC). Note also that the US tax is eligible for foreign tax credit (FTC) even with an RRSP rollover: VIEWS docs 9634955, 2000-001463, 2000-0040241. If the FTC cannot be fully used, see 2003-0037301E5. For more on the rollover, see 2004-0065161E5, 2004-0084571E5, 2006-0197091C6; 2011-0398691E5 (conversion of traditional IRA to Roth IRA); 2011-0404071E5 (no election needed to defer tax); 2020-0846401E5 (Roth 401(k) is not a FRA). See also 56(12).

See generally Ball & Dietrich, "Canadian Taxation of Foreign Pensions", 48(6) *Canadian Tax Journal* 1908-32 (2000); Megoudis & Sinclair, "Canadian Taxation of US Compensation and Retirement Plans", 14(10) *Taxation of Executive Compensation and Retirement* (Federated Press) 291-98 (June 2003).

Definition added by 1991 technical bill, effective 1990.

Regulations: 6803 (prescribed plan or arrangement is U.S. IRA).

Income Tax Folios: S5-F3-C1: Taxation of a Roth IRA.

I.T. Technical News: 43 (taxation of Roth IRAs).

"former business property", in respect of a taxpayer, means a capital property of the taxpayer that was used by the taxpayer or a person related to the taxpayer primarily for the purpose of gaining or producing income from a business, and that was real or immovable property of the taxpayer, an interest of the taxpayer in real property, a right of the taxpayer in an immovable or a property that is the subject of an election under subsection 13(4.2), but does not include

(a) a rental property of the taxpayer,

(b) land subjacent to a rental property of the taxpayer,

(c) land contiguous to land referred to in paragraph (b) that is a parking area, driveway, yard or garden or that is otherwise necessary for the use of the rental property referred to therein, or

(d) a leasehold interest in any property described in paragraphs (a) to (c),

and, for the purpose of this definition, "rental property" of a taxpayer means real or immovable property owned by the taxpayer, whether jointly with another person or otherwise, and used by the taxpayer in the taxation year in respect of which the expression is

being applied principally for the purpose of gaining or producing gross revenue that is rent (other than property leased by the taxpayer to a person related to the taxpayer and used by that related person principally for any other purpose), but, for greater certainty, does not include a property leased by the taxpayer or the related person to a lessee, in the ordinary course of a business of the taxpayer or the related person of selling goods or rendering services, under an agreement by which the lessee undertakes to use the property to carry on the business of selling or promoting the sale of the goods or services of the taxpayer or the related person;

Related Provisions: 13(4), 44(1)(b), 44(6) — Rollovers of former business property replaced by new property; 87(2)(l.3) — Amalgamations — replacement property; 248(4) — Interest in real property.

Notes: See 44(1) and (6). A building situated on leased land can be a "former business property" (FBP), since it constitutes an interest in real property: VIEWS doc 2002-0173815. For the meaning of used "primarily" and "principally" in opening and closing words, see Notes to 73(3). In *Grove Acceptance*, [2003] 1 C.T.C. 2377 (TCC), a car dealership's property was held not to be FBP; qualitative factors were not sufficient to displace the principal "quantitative" test, that 60% of the property was leased to an unrelated party and thus not used in business. *Contra*, in *Gestions Calce*, 2019 QCCQ 7377 (on the parallel Quebec rule), a lease of less than 50% of a property to a related corp qualified as "principally", given the facts. In *St-Jean*, 2008 TCC 358, property merely acquired and not actually used before being sold did not qualify.

For a ruling approving an FBP, see doc 2014-0523551R3. Rental property cannot be FBP; see para. (a) and Notes to 44(1). The part of a building destroyed by fire can be FBP: 2014-0550761E5.

Closing words amended by 2002-2013 technical bill (Part 4 — bijuralism), effective June 26, 2013, to add "or immovable".

Opening words amended by 2002-2013 technical bill (Part 5 — technical), effective for dispositions and terminations that occur after Dec. 20, 2002, to add "in respect", "or immovable" and "a right of the taxpayer in an immovable or a property that is the subject of an election under subsection 13(4.2)". See Notes to 13(4.3).

"Former business property" amended by 1991 technical bill, effective for dispositions after July 13, 1990, to add references to a related person and to add the parenthetical exclusion in the middle of the closing words.

Interpretation Bulletins: IT-491: Former business property.

"fully collateralized arrangement" means a securities lending arrangement or a specified securities lending arrangement if, throughout the term of the arrangement, the borrower

(a) has provided the lender under the arrangement with money in an amount of, or securities described in paragraph (c) of the definition "qualified security" in subsection 260(1) that have a fair market value of, not less than 95% of the fair market value of the security that is transferred or lent under the arrangement, and

(b) is entitled to enjoy, directly or indirectly, the benefits of all or substantially all income derived from, and opportunity for gain in respect of, the money or securities provided;

Notes: For the meaning of "indirectly" in para. (b), see 17.1(1) Notes.

Definition added by 2021 budget bill #1, effective March 19, 2019.

"functional currency" — [Repealed]

Notes: 248(1)"functional currency" added by 2007 budget bill #2, effective in respect of taxation years that begin after Dec. 13, 2007; and repealed retroactive to its introduction by 2008 budget bill #2, as all references to the term are now in s. 261. It simply referred to the definition in 261.

"general rate income pool" has the meaning assigned by subsection 89(1);

Notes: 248(1)"general rate income pool" added by 2006 budget bill #2 (Part 2 — eligible dividends), effective for 2006 and later taxation years.

"goods and services tax" means the tax payable under Part IX of the *Excise Tax Act*;

Related Provisions: 248(15)–(18) — Rules with respect to GST.

Notes: Part IX of the ETA (ss. 122-363.2) imposes GST at 5% and the Harmonized Sales Tax (HST), instead of 5%, at 13% in ON and 15% in NB, NS, PEI and NL. This definition therefore includes the HST as well.

For the GST/HST legislation, see David M. Sherman, *Practitioner's Goods and Services Tax Annotated*, (Carswell, twice-yearly). It is also found, with detailed commentary, in David Sherman's Analysis in the *Canada GST Service* (Carswell, looseleaf), on *GST Partner* (CD-ROM) and *Taxnet Pro*, and with no commentary on canLii.org.

For GST interaction with the ITA, see Chiasson & Mitchener, "GST and Income Tax", *2000 Commodity Tax Symposium* (Canadian Institute of Chartered Accountants), file

"CROSS~12.PDF"; Roper & Rossiter, "Interaction Between GST and Income Tax", *2007 Commodity Tax Symposium.*

"Goods and services tax" added by 1990 GST, effective 1991.

"graduated rate estate", of an individual at any time, means the estate that arose on and as a consequence of the individual's death if

(a) that time is no more than 36 months after the death,

(b) the estate is at that time a testamentary trust,

(c) the individual's Social Insurance Number (or if the individual had not, before the death, been assigned a Social Insurance Number, such other information as is acceptable to the Minister) is provided in the estate's return of income under Part I for the taxation year that includes that time and for each of its earlier taxation years that ended after 2015,

(d) the estate designates itself as the graduated rate estate of the individual in its return of income under Part I for its first taxation year that ends after 2015, and

(e) no other estate designates itself as the graduated rate estate of the individual in a return of income under Part I for a taxation year that ends after 2015;

Related Provisions: 104(27), (27.1), (28) — Flow-out of pension, DPSP and death benefits to beneficiary; 117(2), 122(1) — Graduated tax brackets apply; 127(7) — Investment tax credits available to beneficiaries; 127.51:C — AMT $40,000 deduction available; 152(4.2), 164(1.5) — Late assessment allowed to reduce tax; 156.1(2)(c) — No instalments required; 165(1)(a) — Appeal deadline extended during first year after filing; 248(1)"personal trust"(a) — GRE treated as personal trust; 249(1)(b) — Taxation year may be non-calendar year; 249(4.1)(a)(ii) — Deemed year-end on ceasing to be GRE.

Notes: Since 2016, all special relief in the Act that applied to a testamentary trust (TT) applies only to a graduated rate estate (GRE, pronounced "gree" by some), e.g.: low marginal rates (122(1) [also available to a "qualified disability trust"]); flow-out of pension, DPSP and death benefits (104(27), (27.1), (28)); ITC flow-out to beneficiaries (127(7)); AMT $40,000 deduction (127.51:C(a)); no instalments required (156.1(2)(c)); late claims and refunds allowed (152(4.2), 164(1.5)); carryback of losses to deceased (164(6)); extended objection deadline (165(1))(a)); guaranteed personal trust status (248(1)"personal trust"(a)); non-calendar year (249(1)(b)).

Para. (a): if an estate cannot distribute assets within 36 months (e.g. because the will is contested, other estate litigation, or the executor is awaiting a clearance certificate under 159(2) or waiting for the limitation period for lawsuits against the estate to expire), then GRE status is still lost after 36 months, with a deemed year-end at that point: 249(4.1)(a)(ii). The CRA cannot extend the time, but is reviewing its procedures for issuing clearance certificates, and its existing procedures allow one permitting partial distribution: VIEWS doc 2016-0632641C6 [2016 CALU q.5]. An executor may wish to wait till almost 36 months to pay out bequests, to allow low-rate tax on income during that period (but a beneficiary who wants to be paid earlier can likely force payment with court action). Flow-out of pension, DPSP or death benefits to a beneficiary under 104(27)-(28) should be done before GRE status is lost. Para. (a) encourages an estate to remain open and earning income taxed at low rates for exactly 36 months. (By choosing a calendar year under 249(1)(b), the GRE can have 4 years of low marginal rates under 117(2).) After 36 months, up to 60 months the estate still qualifies to make charitable donations: see 118.1(1)"total charitable gifts"(c)(ii).

Para. (b): since a GRE must be a TT, a loan to the trust by a non-arm's length party can cause loss of GRE status: 108(1)"testamentary trust"(d). If the estate is the beneficiary of an insurance policy on the deceased held by a trust, receipt of the proceeds disqualifies the estate as a GRE: VIEWS doc 2016-0634891C6 [2016 STEP q.3].

Para. (c): note the requirement to provide the deceased's SIN. If there is no SIN (e.g., a US-resident deceased), a temporary tax number (TTN) or individual tax number (ITN) [see Notes to 237(1)] is "acceptable": VIEWS doc 2019-0809651C6 [2019 STEP q.10].

Para. (d): designation is done by entering Code 903 on the T3 return (CRA, T3 Guide). An estate that does not designate itself in its first return does not qualify, but no deadline is specified; see 104(13.1) Notes re *Lussier*. "In its return" is satisfied by designating in a late-filed return, and possibly even in an amended return; see Notes to 7(1.31). CRA may accept late designation with an explanation: May 2016 Alberta CPA Roundtable (tinyurl.com/cra-abtax), q. 18. A GRE is a GRE before it makes the designation, so it can make a charitable donation before filing its first return: 2017-0684481E5. An estate that becomes resident in Canada due to a trustee change can be a GRE, if it was not previously required to file a return: 2019-0798631C6 [2019 STEP q.9].

Para. (e): there can be only one GRE, but as noted in Finance Technical Notes (Oct. 30/14), an individual can have only one estate at law anyway (CRA agrees, and says the estate includes all worldwide property owned at death: VIEWS doc 2015-0572091C6 [2015 STEP q.2]). Para. (e) should therefore be considered as for greater certainty only. In practice, if there are multiple wills with different executors (even if one is offshore), they must cooperate to file only one estate return that will be a GRE: 2016-0634881C6 [2016 STEP q.2]. A TT created by will is not an "estate" and cannot be a GRE: 2014-0553181E5, 2016-0634871C6 [2016 STEP q.1].

See also Notes to 122(1).

A GRE whose beneficiary becomes disabled likely cannot become a 122(3)"qualified disability trust": VIEWS doc 2019-0805771C6 [2019 STEP q.11].

See also tinyurl.com/cra-gre; Blucher, "Graduated Rate Estates", 11(10) *Tax Hyperion* (Carswell) 1-3 (Oct. 2014); Ross, "New Tax Legislation Affects Trusts", XX(4) *Insurance Planning* (Federated Press) 1301-07 (2014); Frajman, "Graduated Rate Estate: Current Debt", 23(3) *Canadian Tax Highlights* (ctf.ca) 9-10 (March 2015); Woodbury, "Testamentary Trusts", 63(1) *Canadian Tax Journal* 269-89 (2015); Brayley & Thériault, "Death and Taxes", 2015 Cdn Tax Foundation conference report, 36:1-60.

Although numerous suggestions were made to amend these rules, the 2015 and 2016 Budgets announced no changes.

"grandfathered share" means

(a) a share of the capital stock of a corporation issued after 8:00 p.m. Eastern Daylight Saving Time, June 18, 1987 pursuant to an agreement in writing entered into before that time,

(b) a share of the capital stock of a corporation issued after 8:00 p.m. Eastern Daylight Saving Time, June 18, 1987 and before 1988 as part of a distribution to the public made in accordance with the terms of a prospectus, preliminary prospectus, registration statement, offering memorandum or notice filed before 8:00 p.m. Eastern Daylight Saving Time, June 18, 1987 with a public authority pursuant to and in accordance with the securities legislation of the jurisdiction in which the shares are distributed,

(c) a share (in this paragraph referred to as the "new share") of the capital stock of a corporation that is issued after 8:00 p.m. Eastern Daylight Saving Time, June 18, 1987 in exchange for

(i) a share of a corporation that was issued before 8:00 p.m. Eastern Daylight Saving Time, June 18, 1987 or is a grandfathered share, or

(ii) a debt obligation of a corporation that was

(A) issued before 8:00 p.m. Eastern Daylight Saving Time, June 18, 1987, or

(B) issued after 8:00 p.m. Eastern Daylight Saving Time, June 18, 1987 under an agreement in writing entered into before that time, or after that time and before 1988 as part of a distribution to the public made in accordance with the terms of a prospectus, preliminary prospectus, registration statement, offering memorandum or notice filed before that time with a public authority under and in accordance with the securities legislation of the jurisdiction in which the debt obligation is distributed,

where the right to the exchange and all or substantially all the terms and conditions of the new share were established in writing before that time, and

(d) a share of a class of the capital stock of a Canadian corporation listed on a designated stock exchange that is issued after 8:00 p.m. Eastern Daylight Saving Time, June 18, 1987 on the exercise of a right that

(i) was issued before that time, that was issued after that time under an agreement in writing entered into before that time or that was issued after that time and before 1988 as part of a distribution to the public made in accordance with the terms of a prospectus, preliminary prospectus, registration statement, offering memorandum or notice filed before that time with a public authority under and in accordance with the securities legislation of the jurisdiction in which the rights were distributed, and

(ii) was listed on a designated stock exchange,

where all or substantially all the terms and conditions of the right and the share were established in writing before that time,

except that a share that is deemed under the definition "short-term preferred share", "taxable preferred share" or "term preferred share" in this subsection or under subsection 112(2.22) to have been issued at any time is deemed after that time not to be a grandfathered share for the purposes of that provision;

Related Provisions: 87(4.2), (4.3) — Amalgamation.

Notes: CRA considers that "substantially all" means 90% or more.

Definition amended by 2007 budget bill #2 (effective Dec. 14, 2007), 2001 and 1991 technical bills.

"gross revenue" of a taxpayer for a taxation year means the total of

(a) all amounts received in the year or receivable in the year (depending on the method regularly followed by the taxpayer in computing the taxpayer's income) otherwise than as or on account of capital, and

(b) all amounts (other than amounts referred to in paragraph (a)) included in computing the taxpayer's income from a business or property for the year because of subsection 12(3) or (4) or section 12.2 of this Act or subsection 12(8) of the *Income Tax Act*, chapter 148 of the Revised Statutes of Canada, 1952.

Related Provisions: 149(9) — GR in determining non-profit R&D corporation status; 247(5), (9) — GR for transfer pricing rules; 250(6.01) — Partnership profit deemed GR for international shipping rules; Reg. 402(4)–(6) — GR for interprovincial allocation of corporate income; Reg. 1104(5.1) — GR from a mine.

Notes: See VIEWS doc 2003-0030597 on including interest rate swap receipts in "gross revenue".

"Gross revenue" under 248(1) may be different from that under Reg. 402(3): VIEWS doc 2013-0514921I7.

Para. (b) amended by 2003 resource bill, effective for taxation years that begin after 2006, to delete reference to 12(1)(o).

I.T. Application Rules: 69 (meaning of "chapter 148 of ...").

"group term life insurance policy" means a group life insurance policy under which the only amounts payable by the insurer are

(a) amounts payable on the death or disability of individuals whose lives are insured in respect of, in the course of or because of, their office or employment or former office or employment, and

(b) policy dividends or experience rating refunds;

Related Provisions: 6(1)(a)(i), 6(4) — Benefit from policy is taxable; 18(9.01) — Limitation on deduction for premiums paid; 138(15) — Meaning of "group term insurance policy"; 144.1(1)"designated employee benefit" — Employee life and health trust may pay benefit from policy; Reg. 1408(2) — Definition does not apply to regulations re policy reserves.

Notes: An administrative arrangement between an employer and an insurer, where the insurer pays an amount to an estate or beneficiary and is reimbursed by the employer, is likely not a "group term life insurance policy": VIEWS doc 2000-0010115.

For calculation of the taxable employee benefit on group term life insurance policy premiums, see 6(4) and Reg. 2700–2704.

Definition "group term life insurance policy" amended by 1994 Budget, effective for insurance provided in respect of periods after June 1994.

The phrase "subject to subsection 138(15)" added in the RSC 1985 (5th Supp) consolidation for tax years ending after Nov. 1991. See Notes to 138(15).

Income Tax Folios: S2-F1-C1: Health and welfare trusts [replaces IT-85R2].

Interpretation Bulletins: IT-529: Flexible employee benefit programs.

"highest individual percentage", for a taxation year, means the highest percentage referred to in subsection 117(2) for the taxation year;

Notes: Since 2016 this means 33% (see 117(2)(e)). The term is used for such things as the tax rate for trusts (122(1)(a)), the tax on split income (120.4(2)), and the charitable donation credit for high-income donors from top-rate income (118.1(3)C).

Definition added by 2016 tax-rate bill, for 2016 and later taxation years.

"home relocation loan" means a loan received by an individual or the individual's spouse or common-law partner in circumstances where the individual has commenced employment at a location in Canada (in this definition referred to as the "new work location") and by reason thereof has moved from the residence in Canada at which, before the move, the individual ordinarily resided (in this definition referred to as the "old residence") to a residence in Canada at which, after the move, the individual ordinarily resided (in this definition referred to as the "new residence") if

(a) the distance between the old residence and the new work location is at least 40 kilometres greater than the distance between the new residence and the new work location,

(b) the loan is used to acquire a dwelling, or a share of the capital stock of a cooperative housing corporation acquired for the sole purpose of acquiring the right to inhabit a dwelling owned by the corporation, where the dwelling is for the habitation of the individual and is the individual's new residence,

(c) the loan is received in the circumstances described in subsection 80.4(1), or would have been so received if subsection 80.4(1.1) had applied to the loan at the time it was received, and

(d) the loan is designated by the individual to be a home relocation loan, but in no case shall more than one loan in respect of a particular move, or more than one loan at any particular time, be designated as a home relocation loan by the individual;

Related Provisions: 6(23) — Employer-provided mortgage subsidy is taxable; 15(2.4)(b) — Housing loan to shareholder; 80.4(4) — Home purchase or relocation loan to employee.

Notes: The measurement of 40 km under para. (a) should be based on normal road distance. See 248(1)"eligible relocation" Notes.

Definition amended by 2000 same-sex partners bill (effective 2001), 1998 Budget and 1991 technical bill.

Interpretation Bulletins: IT-421R2: Benefits to individuals, corporations and shareholders from loans or debt.

"income-averaging annuity contract" of an individual means, except for the purposes of section 61, a contract

(a) that is an income-averaging annuity contract within the meaning assigned by subsection 61(4), and

(b) in respect of which the individual has made a deduction under section 61 in computing the individual's income for a taxation year;

Related Provisions: 128.1(10)"excluded right or interest"(f)(ii) — Emigration — no deemed disposition of right under IAAC.

"income bond" or **"income debenture"** of a corporation (in this definition referred to as the "issuing corporation") means a bond or debenture in respect of which interest or dividends are payable only to the extent that the issuing corporation has made a profit before taking into account the interest or dividend obligation and that was issued

(a) before November 17, 1978,

(b) after November 16, 1978 and before 1980 pursuant to an agreement in writing to do so made before November 17, 1978 (in this definition referred to as an "established agreement"), or

(c) by an issuing corporation resident in Canada for a term that may not, in any circumstances, exceed 5 years,

(i) as part of a proposal to or an arrangement with its creditors that had been approved by a court under the *Bankruptcy and Insolvency Act*,

(ii) at a time when all or substantially all of its assets were under the control of a receiver, receiver-manager, sequestrator or trustee in bankruptcy, or

(iii) at a time when, by reason of financial difficulty, the issuing corporation or another corporation resident in Canada with which it does not deal at arm's length was in default, or could reasonably be expected to default, on a debt obligation held by a person with whom the issuing corporation or the other corporation was dealing at arm's length and the bond or debenture was issued either wholly or in substantial part and either directly or indirectly in exchange or substitution for that obligation or a part thereof,

and, in the case of a bond or debenture issued after November 12, 1981, the proceeds from the issue may reasonably be regarded as having been used by the issuing corporation or a corporation with which it was not dealing at arm's length in the financing of its business carried on in Canada immediately before the bond or debenture was issued,

and, for the purposes of this definition,

(d) where the terms or conditions of an established agreement were amended after November 16, 1978, the agreement shall be deemed to have been made after that date, and

(e) where

(i) at any particular time the terms or conditions of a bond or debenture issued pursuant to an established agreement or of any agreement relating to such a bond or debenture have been changed,

(ii) under the terms or conditions of a bond or debenture acquired in the ordinary course of the business carried on by a specified financial institution or a partnership or trust (other than a testamentary trust) or under the terms or conditions of any agreement relating to any such bond or debenture (other than an agreement made before October 24, 1979 to which the issuing corporation or any person related thereto was not a party), the owner thereof could at any particular time after November 16, 1978 require, either alone or together with one or more taxpayers, the repayment, acquisition, cancellation or conversion of the bond or debenture otherwise than by reason of a failure or default under the terms or conditions of the bond or debenture or any agreement that related to, and was entered into at the time of, the issuance of the bond or debenture,

(iii) at any particular time after November 16, 1978, the maturity date of a bond or debenture was extended or the terms or conditions relating to the repayment of the principal amount thereof were changed,

(iv) at a particular time a specified financial institution (or a partnership or trust of which a specified financial institution or a person related to the institution is a member or beneficiary) acquires a bond or debenture that

(A) was issued before November 17, 1978 or under an established agreement,

(B) was issued to a person other than a corporation that was, at the time of issue,

(I) described in any of paragraphs (a) to (e) of the definition "specified financial institution", or

(II) a corporation that was controlled by one or more corporations described in subclause (I) and, for the purpose of this subclause, one corporation is controlled by another corporation if more than 50% of its issued share capital (having full voting rights under all circumstances) belongs to the other corporation, to persons with whom the other corporation does not deal at arm's length, or to the other corporation and persons with whom the other corporation does not deal at arm's length,

(C) was acquired from a person that was, at the time the person last acquired the bond or debenture and at the particular time, a person other than a corporation described in any of paragraphs (a) to (f) of that definition, and

(D) was acquired otherwise than under an agreement in writing made before October 24, 1979, or

(v) at a particular time after November 12, 1981, a specified financial institution (or a partnership or trust of which a specified financial institution or a person related to the institution is a member or beneficiary) acquires a bond or debenture that

(A) was not a bond or debenture referred to in paragraph (c),

(B) was acquired from a person that was, at the particular time, a corporation described in any of paragraphs (a) to (f) of the definition "specified financial institution", and

(C) was acquired subject to or conditional on a guarantee agreement (within the meaning that would be assigned by subsection 112(2.2) if the reference in that subsection to a "share" were read as a reference to an "income bond" or "income debenture") that was entered into after November 12, 1981,

the bond or debenture shall, for the purposes of determining at any time after the particular time whether it is an income bond or income debenture, be deemed to have been issued at the particular time otherwise than pursuant to an established agreement;

Related Provisions: 15(3), (4) — Payment on income bond deemed to be a dividend; 248(13) — Interests in trusts and partnerships; 256(6), (6.1) — Meaning of "controlled".

Notes: Subparas. (e)(iv) and (v) amended by 1998 Budget, for tax years that begin after 1998, with different reading (see up to 48th ed.) for a bond or debenture acquired from a corp that last acquired it in a tax year that began before 1999.

CRA considers that "substantially all", used in (c)(ii), means 90% or more.

Interpretation Bulletins: IT-52R4: Income bonds and income debentures (cancelled); IT-527: Distress preferred shares.

"income debenture" — [See under "income bond".]

"income interest" of a taxpayer in a trust has the meaning assigned by subsection 108(1);

"indexed debt obligation" means a debt obligation the terms or conditions of which provide for an adjustment to an amount payable in respect of the obligation for a period during which the obligation was outstanding that is determined by reference to a change in the purchasing power of money;

Related Provisions: 16(6) — Indexed debt obligations; 142.3(2) — Indexed debt obligation not subject to rules re income from specified debt obligations; 142.4(5)(a)(i) — Disposition of indexed debt obligation.

Notes: "indexed debt obligation" added by 1992 technical bill, effective for indexed debt obligations issued after October 16, 1991.

"indexed security", "indexed security investment plan" — [Repealed under former Act]

Notes: Indexed security investment plans existed from 1983-85, and were repealed by 1985 Budget with the introduction of the capital gains exemption in 110.6.

"individual" means a person other than a corporation;

Related Provisions: 104(2) — Trust deemed to be an individual.

Notes: The term "individual" includes both a human being and a trust (104(2)), as well as an exempt non-profit organization under 248(1)"person". However, for tax-treaty purposes it is considered not to include a trust: VIEWS doc 2001-0108517.

"Individual" did not include a non-resident seeking to claim a tuition credit (and carry it forward to when he became resident in Canada): *Marino*, 2020 TCC 50 (under appeal to FCA).

Interpretation Bulletins: IT-123R6, para. 11: Transactions involving eligible capital property.

"insurance corporation" means a corporation that carries on an insurance business;

Related Provisions: 138(1) — Corporation deemed to carry on insurance business; 148(10)(a) — Issuer of annuity contracts deemed to be insurer for certain purposes; 186.1(b) — Insurance corporation not liable for Part IV tax; 248(1)"insurer" — Same meaning; Reg. 205.1(2)(a) — Insurance corporation not required to file T2 electronically.

"insurance policy" includes a life insurance policy;

Notes: 248(1)"insurance policy" added by 1999 Budget, effective December 16, 1998.

"insurer" has the meaning assigned by this subsection to the expression "insurance corporation";

Related Provisions: See under "insurance corporation" above.

Notes: 248(1)"insurer" added in the RSC 1985 (5th Supp), effective Dec. 1, 1991. This was formerly included in the definition of "insurance corporation".

"inter vivos trust" has the meaning assigned by subsection 108(1);

"international shipping" means the operation of a ship owned or leased by a person or partnership (in this definition referred to as the "operator") that is used, either directly or as part of a pooling arrangement, primarily in transporting passengers or goods in international traffic — determined as if, except where paragraph (c) of the definition "international traffic" in this subsection applies, any port or other place on the Great Lakes or St. Lawrence River is in Canada — including the chartering of the ship, provided that one or more persons related to the operator (if the operator and each such person is a corporation), or persons or partnerships affiliated with the operator (in any other case), has complete possession, control and command of the ship, and any activity incident to or pertaining to the operation of the ship, but does not include

(a) the offshore storing or processing of goods,

(b) fishing,

(c) laying cable,

(d) salvaging,

(e) towing,

(f) tug-boating,

(g) offshore oil and gas activities (other than the transportation of oil and gas), including exploration and drilling activities,

(h) dredging, or

(i) leasing a ship by a lessor to a lessee that has complete possession, control and command of the ship, unless the lessor or a corporation, trust or partnership affiliated with the lessor has an eligible interest (as defined in subsection 250(6.04)) in the lessee;

Related Provisions: 81(1)(c) — Exemption for non-resident's income from international shipping; 250(6) — Foreign corporation with principal business as international shipping deemed non-resident; 250(6.02), (6.03) — Service provider deemed to have international shipping as principal business.

Notes: The 2013 amendment to 81(1)(c) introducing this definition only broadens, and does not restrict, the exemption: VIEWS doc 2014-0560831I7; so "lease" includes chartering arrangements, and "commercial management" of a ship is sufficient.

See also Notes to 81(1)(c) and 248(1)"international traffic"; Shields, "Taxation of International Shipping Companies", 88 *International Tax* (CCH) 1-5 (June 2016).

Definition added by 2014 budget bill #2, for tax years that begin after July 12, 2013.

"international traffic" means, in respect of a person or partnership carrying on the business of transporting passengers or goods, a voyage made in the course of that business if the principal purpose of the voyage is to transport passengers or goods

(a) from Canada to a place outside Canada,

(b) from a place outside Canada to Canada, or

(c) from a place outside Canada to another place outside Canada;

Related Provisions: 81(1)(c) — Exemption for non-resident's income from operating aircraft in international traffic; 250(6) — Residence of international shipping corporation; Canada-U.S. Tax Treaty:Art. III:1(h) — Meaning of "international traffic" for treaty purposes; Canada-U.S. Tax Treaty:Art. XV:3 — Exemption for US resident employee; Canada-U.S. Tax Treaty:Art. XXIII:3 — Capital tax on ship or aircraft employed in international traffic.

Notes: For interpretation of this definition see VIEWS doc 2013-0515431E5 (contracted non-resident airline qualifies).

Opening words amended by 2014 budget bill #2, for taxation years that begin after July 12, 2013, to change "non-resident person" to "person or partnership".

Interpretation Bulletins: IT-494: Hire of ships and aircraft from non-residents.

"inventory" means a description of property the cost or value of which is relevant in computing a taxpayer's income from a business for a taxation year or would have been so relevant if the income from the business had not been computed in accordance with the cash method and includes

(a) with respect to a farming business, all of the livestock held in the course of carrying on the business, and

(b) an emissions allowance;

Related Provisions: 10(1), (1.01) — Valuation of inventory property; 10(5) — Certain property deemed to be inventory; 27.1 — Treatment of emissions allowances; 66.3(1)(a)(ii) — Certain exploration and development shares deemed to be inventory; 142.5 — Mark-to-market rules for securities held by financial institutions; 142.6(3), (4) — Certain property of financial institution deemed not to be inventory; 231.1(1)(b) — Examination of inventory.

Notes: See Notes to 54"capital property" and 10(1).

Para. (b) (see Notes to 27.1) added by 2016 budget bill #2, effective 2017, except that it does not apply to emissions allowances (EAs) acquired in taxation years that begin before 2017. Also, if a taxpayer elects as described in Notes to 27.1, it applies to EAs acquired in taxation years that end after 2012. Before the amendment, read:

> "inventory" means a description of property the cost or value of which is relevant in computing a taxpayer's income from a business for a taxation year or would have been so relevant if the income from the business had not been computed in accordance with the cash method and, with respect to a farming business, includes all of the livestock held in the course of carrying on the business;

"Inventory" amended by 1991 technical bill, for fiscal periods beginning after 1988.

Interpretation Bulletins: IT-51R2: Supplies on hand at the end of a fiscal year; IT-218R: Profit, capital gains and losses from the sale of real estate, including farmland and inherited land and conversion of real estate from capital property to inventory and

---

vice versa; IT-427R: Livestock of farmers; IT-457R: Election by professionals to exclude work in progress from income; IT-473R: Inventory valuation.

"investment corporation" has the meaning assigned by subsection 130(3);

"investment tax credit" has the meaning assigned by subsection 127(9);

Notes: The Dec. 14, 1995 draft legislation proposed to add **"joint exploration corporation"** to 248(1) with a cross-reference to 66(15); however, the 1995-97 technical bill did not include this. The term is used in 53(2)(f) and (f.1) as well as in s. 66.

Proposed Addition — 248(1)"joint management area"

"joint management area" means the submarine areas within the limits described in Schedule 1 to the *Canada–Quebec Gulf of St. Lawrence Petroleum Resources Accord Implementation Act*;

Application: Bill C-74 (First Reading June 18, 2015; requires reintroduction in new Parliament), s. 254, will add the definition "joint management area" to subsec. 248(1), applicable to taxation years that begin after the day on which an administration agreement in respect of tax imposed under s. 235 of the *Canada–Quebec Gulf of St. Lawrence Petroleum Resources Accord Implementation Act* comes into effect.

Natural Resources Canada news release, June 11, 2015: *Government of Canada Moves Forward With Implementing Canada-Quebec Offshore Accord*

The Honourable Greg Rickford, Canada's Minister of Natural Resources, today delivered on Prime Minister Stephen Harper's commitment to implement the Canada-Quebec Offshore Accord.

The tabling of the Notice of Ways and Means Motion to introduce a bill to implement the Canada-Quebec Offshore Accord represents an important milestone for responsible resource development in the Gulf of St. Lawrence.

The proposed legislation would ensure that Quebec will benefit from revenues, including royalties and many taxes and fees, derived from the development of oil and gas resources. Pierre Arcand, Quebec's Minister of Energy and Natural Resources and Minister responsible for Plan Nord, introduced mirror provincial legislation in the National Assembly.

The Government is committed to protecting the safety of both Canadians and the environment while preserving, protecting and creating Canadian jobs. The bill is a central part of the Government's Responsible Resource Development Plan, through which it is taking action to create jobs, grow the economy and create long-term prosperity in Quebec and across Canada.

Quick Facts

- The Government of Canada estimates that the Gulf of St. Lawrence and surrounding areas have the potential for more than 39 trillion cubic feet of gas and 1.5 billion barrels of oil, based on preliminary geological studies of the area.

- Canada is committed to continuous improvements in its offshore system, and this legislation will incorporate the safety and environmental protections found in the Energy Safety and Security Act, which enshrines the "polluter pays" principle in law and raises the absolute liability limits to $1 billion.

- The 2011 Canada-Quebec Accord established two distinct phases of joint management. The bill covers the first or transitional phase in which the governments will establish a joint regulatory function. The second or permanent phase would be triggered by a commercial discovery of oil or natural gas resources and would see the creation of a joint independent offshore board.

Contacts

Media may contact: Alexandra Lemieux, Press Secretary, Office of Canada's Minister of Natural Resources and Minister for the Federal Economic Development Initiative for Northern Ontario, 613-996-2007; or Media Relations, Natural Resources Canada, Ottawa, 613-992-4447.

The general public may contact: Mon.-Fri. 8:30am-4:30pm EDT, 613-995-0947; questions@nrcan.gc.ca.

Related Provisions: 124(4)"province" — Joint management area deemed to be province for s. 124.

Notes: This is the area jointly managed by Canada and Quebec for oil and gas exploration in the Gulf of St. Lawrence.

"joint spousal or common-law partner trust" means a trust to which paragraph 104(4)(a) would apply if that paragraph were read without reference to subparagraph 104(4)(a)(iii) and clause 104(4)(a)(iv)(A);

Related Provisions: 54"principal residence"(c.1)(iii.1)(A) — Exemption for gain on principal residence owned by trust; 73(1.01)(c)(ii) — Rollover on transfer to joint partner trust; 104(5.8) — Transfers from joint partner trust to another trust; 104(6)(b)B(i) — Deduction from income of trust; 104(15)(a) — Preferred beneficiary election; 107(4)(a)(iii) — Distribution of property to person other than taxpayer or partner; 248(1)"*alter ego* trust" — Parallel trust where partner is not a beneficiary.

Notes: This means a trust described in 104(4)(a)(iv)(B) or (C). The settlor must be over 65 when creating the trust but the spouse/CLP need not be. *Alter ego* trusts and joint spousal or common-law partner trusts [JSCLPTs] (called joint spousal trust in the 1999 draft legislation and joint partner trust in the 2000 draft legislation) can be used as an estate planning tool to avoid probate fees or estate administration tax. They effectively extend the spousal-trust rule in 73(1.01) (former 73(1)(c)) to allow the settlor to be a beneficiary as well. For discussion see Notes to 248(1)"alter ego trust". A trust created by both spouses can qualify: VIEWS doc 2001-0099055. For a ruling that certain amendments to a trust declaration will not cause a resettlement or disposition, see 2007-0241581R3. A JSCLPT keeps its status after divorce: 2012-0473661E5. Payments received by an individual from an RPP or RRIF cannot be taxed in a JSCLPT: 2009-0327251E5. A trust providing all income to the taxpayer during life and to the surviving spouse after death will qualify: 2014-0523031C6. On the spouse's death, see Notes to 104(13.4).

For 2018 (most recent figures as of Dec. 2020), 2,880 JSCLPT T3 returns were assessed or reassessed, paying $55 million federal tax: tinyurl.com/stats-cra. (Trusts paying no tax need not file a T3: 150(1.1).)

248(1)"joint spousal or common-law partner trust" added by 2001 technical bill, effective for trusts created after 1999.

"LIA policy" *[leveraged insurance annuity policy — ed.]* means a life insurance policy (other than an annuity) where

(a) a particular person or partnership becomes obligated after March 20, 2013 to repay an amount to another person or partnership (in this definition referred to as the "lender") at a time determined by reference to the death of a particular individual whose life is insured under the policy, and

(b) the lender is assigned an interest in

(i) the policy, and

(ii) an annuity contract the terms of which provide that payments are to continue for a period that ends no earlier than the death of the particular individual;

Proposed Amendment — 248(1)"LIA policy" — Grandfathering

Letter from Dept. of Finance, June 17, 2019: Conference for Advanced Life Underwriting, Ottawa, ON

Dear [xxx]:

I am writing in response to your extended discussions with Department of Finance officials regarding grandfathering provisions related to the definition "LIA policy" that was added to subsection 248(1) of the *Income Tax Act* (the Act) in 2013.

One of the criteria to determine if a life insurance policy is a LIA policy is that a particular person or partnership becomes obligated after March 20, 2013 to repay an amount to another person or partnership at a time determined by reference to the death of a particular individual whose life is insured under the life insurance policy. You are concerned that refinancing after March 20, 2013 an obligation originally entered into before March 21, 2013 could result in a new obligation to repay an amount. In that context, you have requested amendments to the Act so that refinancing the obligation would not, in and of itself, cause an otherwise grandfathered policy to lose its grandfathered status and become an LIA policy.

We are prepared to recommend to the Minister of Finance that the Act be amended to clarify which insurance policies issued before March 21, 2013 are grandfathered policies and the conditions under which refinancing an obligation does not cause an otherwise grandfathered policy to become an LIA policy. Grandfathering will be limited to arrangements that existed on March 20, 2013 where each of the policy, the annuity and the obligation was issued on terms that, if each had been issued on a stand-alone basis, would have been reasonable and commercially available.

For such commercially reasonable arrangements, we are prepared to recommend that the Act be amended such that a "replacement obligation" does not cause an insurance policy to be an LIA policy, if the following conditions are met:

• The replacement obligation at a particular time replaces another obligation (the "preceding obligation") of the borrower in respect of the policy to repay an amount, on substantially similar terms.

• The lender for the replacement obligation and for the preceding obligation are both restricted financial institutions (as defined in subsection 248(1) of the Act) that are resident in Canada.

• The preceding obligation (i) was outstanding on March 20, 2013, or (ii) is a replacement obligation of the borrower in respect of the policy.

• The principal amount of the replacement obligation does not exceed the smallest amount of principal outstanding at any time, on or after March 21, 2013 and before the particular time, under any preceding obligation.

• An interest in the policy and the annuity contract in respect of the preceding obligation (i) is assigned to the tender of the replacement obligation, and (ii) was assigned, at all times at which an amount was outstanding under the preceding obligation, to the lender of the preceding obligation.

• The policy meets the following conditions:

— it is an exempt policy (as defined in the Act) that was issued before March 21, 2013 by a life insurance corporation that carries on a business in Canada;

— it was held at all times on or after March 21, 2013 and before the particular time by the borrower;

— the life (or lives) insured under the policy at the particular time and until the repayment of the obligation is the life (or lives) insured under the policy on March 20, 2013; and

— the total premiums and deposits paid into the policy on and after the date of this letter in respect of each policy year (or part of the policy year if it includes the date of this letter) shall not exceed the sum of the cost of insurance and administrative charges (as required under the terms of the policy) in respect of the policy year (or part of the policy year if it includes the date of this letter).

• The annuity contract (i) is a non-commutable annuity that was issued before March 21, 2013 by a life insurance corporation that carries on a business in Canada, (ii) was held at all times on or after March 21, 2013 and before the particular time by the borrower, and (iii) provides payments until the death of the life (or lives) insured under the policy.

We also intend to recommend that the proposed amendments apply in respect of taxation years that end after March 20, 2013.

While I cannot offer any assurance that the Minister will agree with our recommendations, I hope that this statement of our intention is helpful to you.

Thank you for writing to us on this matter.

Brian Ernewein, Assistant Deputy Minister — Legislation, Tax Policy Branch

Related Provisions: 20(1)(e.2) — No deduction for premium paid on LIA policy; 70(5.31) — Determination of FMV of annuity contract on death; 89(1)"capital dividend account"(d)(ii) — Limit on increase in CDA; Reg. 201(5.1) — Insurer required to file information return; Reg. 306(1) — Income accruing in LIA policy is not exempt.

Notes: The LIA (leveraged insured annuity) policy rules were introduced by the 2013 Budget (as were the "10/8 policy" rules), to deal with the following problem:

An LIA involves using borrowed funds together with a lifetime annuity and a life insurance policy, both issued on the life of an individual. Typically, the policy provides coverage for the individual's entire lifetime, the death benefit under the policy equals the amount invested in the annuity, and both policy and annuity are assigned to the lender of the borrowed funds. These arrangements are typically sold to a closely-held private corporation.

An LIA is an investment product acquired with borrowed funds and provides fixed and guaranteed income to an investor until the individual's death, at which time the capital invested in the annuity is returned as a tax-free death benefit. LIAs are integrated investment products and were marketed and sold as such. However, for tax purposes, each element of a LIA was treated separately. As a result, investors in LIAs obtained multiple tax benefits not available from comparable investment products.

Specifically, LIAs allowed part of the income earned on the capital invested to be tax-free (because the life insurance policy was an exempt policy under Reg. 306), while the interest on the borrowed funds was tax-deductible (20(1)(c)), and a deduction was also allowed on part of the capital invested (for the policy premium: 20(1)(e.2)). In addition, for closely-held private corporations and their owners, the arrangement eliminated tax on the corporation's retained earnings by avoiding tax on capital gains on the owner's death and, due to increase in the corporation's capital dividend account (CDA) (89(1)), on dividends paid after the owner's death (via 83(2)).

The 2013 Budget eliminated these unintended tax benefits by introducing rules for an "LIA policy", as defined here. Income accruing in an LIA policy is now subject to annual accrual-based taxation: Reg. 306(1) opening words. No deduction is allowed for any portion of a premium paid on the policy: 20(1)(e.2). A corporation's CDA is not increased by the death benefit received from the policy: 89(1)"capital dividend account"(d)(ii). For the deemed disposition on death, the value of an annuity contract assigned to the lender in connection with an LIA policy is deemed to be equal to the total of the premiums paid under the contract: 70(5.31).

For CRA views see "Watch out for offshore leveraged insured annuity schemes" (Aug. 26, 2020, tinyurl.com/cra-warn-LIA), docs 2014-0523261C6 [2014 CALU q.1] (impact of post-March 20/13 transactions on grandfathering); 2016-0632601C6 [2016 CALU q.1] (CRA concerned about products that technically escape the definition).

See also Peter Everett, "Life Insurance Planning after the 2013 Budget", 2013 Cdn Tax Foundation conference report at 32:2-6.

Definition added by 2013 budget bill #2, for tax years that end after March 20, 2013.

"lawyer" has the meaning assigned by subsection 232(1);

"legal representative" of a taxpayer means a trustee in bankruptcy, an assignee, a liquidator, a curator, a receiver of any kind, a trustee, an heir, an administrator, an executor, a liquidator of a succession, a committee, or any other like person, administering, winding up, controlling or otherwise dealing in a representative or fiduciary capacity with the property that belongs or belonged to, or that is or was held for the benefit of, the taxpayer or the taxpayer's estate;

Notes: A corporate director is not normally a legal representative (LR): *Groscki*, 2017 TCC 249, paras. 50-60.

A beneficiary of a Quebec deceased's estate was an "heir" under 248(1)"person" who could appeal the estate's assessment, but was not a LR liable under s. 159: *Straessle*, 2018 TCC 144.

A financial institution holding property for safekeeping is not considered a LR: VIEWS doc 2008-0264381E5. Where a corporation is the trustee of a trust, the corporation is the trust's LR: 2010-0373611C6. A parent corporation is considered the LR of its wound-up subsidiary: 2011-039919I17. A TFSA issuer is the TFSA trust's LR: 2011-0405531E5.

Definition amended by 2001 *Civil Code* harmonization bill (effective June 14, 2001) and 1995-97 technical bill.

"lending asset" means a bond, debenture, mortgage, hypothecary claim, note, agreement of sale or any other indebtedness or a prescribed share, but does not include a prescribed property;

Related Provisions: 95(1)"lending of money" closing words — Extended definition for FAPI purposes; 142.2(1) — Definition of "specified debt obligation".

Notes: Reference to "hypothecary claim" added by 2001 *Civil Code* harmonization bill, effective June 14, 2001 (non-substantive change; see *Interpretation Act* s. 8.2).

Definition "lending asset" amended by 1995-97 technical bill to change "prescribed security" to "prescribed property", effective for taxation years that end after September 1997 (or earlier by election) (see Notes to 20(1)(l)).

Regulations: 6209 (prescribed share, prescribed security, prescribed property).

Interpretation Bulletins: IT-442R: Bad debts and reserves for doubtful debts.

["LIA policy"] — [See at beginning of letter 'l' entries above.]

"licensed annuities provider" has the meaning assigned by subsection 147(1);

Notes: Definition added by 1995-97 technical bill, effective 1997.

"life insurance business" includes

(a) an annuities business, and

(b) the business of issuing contracts all or any part of the issuer's reserves for which vary in amount depending on the fair market value of a specified group of assets,

carried on by a life insurance corporation or a life insurer;

Related Provisions: 138(1)(b) — Corporation deemed carrying on (life) insurance business.

"life insurance capital dividend" has the meaning assigned by subsection 83(2.1);

Notes: The reference should be "subsection 83(2.1) of the *Income Tax Act*, chapter 148 of the Revised Statutes of Canada, 1952". The 83(2.1) that allowed a corporation to elect for a dividend to be a life insurance capital dividend was repealed for dividends paid after May 23, 1985, but still applies for limited transitional purposes. See 83(2.1) Notes.

"life insurance corporation" means a corporation that carries on a life insurance business that is not a business described in paragraph (a) or (b) of the definition "life insurance business" in this subsection, whether or not the corporation also carries on a business described in either of those paragraphs;

Related Provisions: 148(10)(a) — Issuer of annuity contracts deemed to be life insurer for certain purposes; 248(1)"life insurer" — Same meaning.

"life insurance policy" has the meaning assigned by subsection 138(12);

Related Provisions: 211(1) — Definitions.

"life insurance policy in Canada" has the meaning assigned by subsection 138(12);

"life insurer" has the meaning assigned by this subsection to the expression "life insurance corporation";

Notes: 248(1)"life insurer" added in the RSC 1985 (5th Supp) consolidation, effective December 1, 1991. This definition was formerly included in the definition of "life insurance corporation".

"limited partnership loss" has the meaning assigned by subsection 96(2.1);

Related Provisions: 111(9) — Limited partnership loss where taxpayer not resident in Canada.

"limited-recourse amount" means an amount that is a limited-recourse amount under section 143.2.

Notes: "Limited-recourse amount" added by 2003 Budget, effective Feb. 19, 2003. The term is used in 143.2(1) and 237.1(1)"gifting arrangement".

"listed international agreement" means

(a) the *Convention on Mutual Administrative Assistance in Tax Matters*, concluded at Strasbourg on January 25, 1988, as amended from time to time by a protocol, or other international instrument, as ratified by Canada, or

(b) a comprehensive tax information exchange agreement that Canada has entered into and that has effect, in respect of another country or jurisdiction;

Notes: For discussion of TIEAs (para. (b) of this definition), and the countries with which Canada has or is negotiating TIEAs, see Notes to 95(1)"non-qualifying country".

Canada signed the Convention on Mutual Administrative Assistance in Tax Matters (tinyurl.com/oecd-mutu) in 2004 and ratified it on Nov. 21, 2013. See Gray, "The Multilateral Convention", 2326 *Tax Topics* (CCH) 1-7 (Oct. 6, 2016); Detroyer, "New Developments in International Administrative Assistance in the Recovery of Taxes", *European Taxation* (ibfd.org), May 2018, pp. 179-85 (re EU). 19 countries with which Canada has no tax treaty have signed the convention, so exchange of information with them is possible: Brian Ernewein (Finance), Cdn Tax Foundation annual conference, Nov. 29, 2016.

248(1)"listed international agreement" added by 2002-2013 technical bill (Part 5 — technical), effective June 26, 2013.

"listed personal property" has the meaning assigned by section 54;

"low rate income pool" has the meaning assigned by subsection 89(1);

Notes: 248(1)"low rate income pool" added by 2006 budget bill #2, for 2006 and later tax years.

"majority-interest partner", of a particular partnership at any time, means a person or partnership (in this definition referred to as the "taxpayer")

(a) whose share of the particular partnership's income from all sources for the last fiscal period of the particular partnership that ended before that time (or, if the particular partnership's first fiscal period includes that time, for that period) would have exceeded 1/2 of the particular partnership's income from all sources for that period if the taxpayer had held throughout that period each interest in the partnership that the taxpayer or a person affiliated with the taxpayer held at that time, or

(b) whose share, if any, together with the shares of every person with whom the taxpayer is affiliated, of the total amount that would be paid to all members of the particular partnership (otherwise than as a share of any income of the partnership) if it were wound up at that time exceeds 1/2 of that amount;

Related Provisions: 251.1 — Affiliated persons.

Notes: Definition changed from "majority interest partner" to "majority-interest partner" (with a hyphen) by 2013 budget bill #2, effective Dec. 12, 2013. The term was changed throughout the Act.

Definition added by 1995-97 technical bill, effective April 27, 1995. This was formerly in 97(3.1), but was amended in two ways. First, it applies on the basis of a partner's entitlement to the partnership's income from all sources, rather than the partner's entitlement to income from each source. Second, it uses the concept of affiliated in 251.1.

"mineral" includes ammonite gemstone, bituminous sands, calcium chloride, coal, kaolin, oil shale and silica, but does not include petroleum, natural gas or a related hydrocarbon not expressly referred to in this definition;

Related Provisions: *Interpretation Act* 8(2.1), (2.2) — Application to exclusive economic zone and continental shelf.

Notes: Since the definition uses "includes" rather than "means", the ordinary meaning of "mineral" applies as well: see Notes to 188.1(5). In *Pacific Abrasives*, 2010 BCCA 369, slag was held to be a "mineral" under the BC *Mineral Tax Act*.

Definition "mineral" amended to delete "oil sands" and add "ammonite gemstone" by 1995-97 technical bill, for taxation years and fiscal periods that begin after 1996 (with transitional rules for 1997).

"Mineral" substituted for "minerals" by 1993 technical bill. Among other things, the change allows calcium chloride producers access to the income tax incentives for mining, including the resource allowance. (Finance news release, Dec. 2, 1992.) See also "mineral resource" below.

Interpretation Bulletins: IT-125R4: Dispositions of resource properties.

"mineral resource" means

(a) a base or precious metal deposit,

(b) a coal deposit,

(c) a bituminous sands deposit or oil shale deposit, or

(d) a mineral deposit in respect of which

    (i) the Minister of Natural Resources has certified that the principal mineral extracted is an industrial mineral contained in a non-bedded deposit,

    (ii) the principal mineral extracted is ammonite gemstone, calcium chloride, diamond, gypsum, halite, kaolin or sylvite, or

    (iii) the principal mineral extracted is silica that is extracted from sandstone or quartzite;

Related Provisions: *Interpretation Act* 8(2.1), (2.2) — Application to exclusive economic zone and continental shelf.

Notes: Mineral resource can include deposits of: diamond (VIEWS doc 9603015); graphite (2012-0449641E5, 2013-0474611E5, 2013-0488681E5, 2016-0669001E5, 2017-0682401E5); nephrite (jade) (2016-0674541E5, 2018-0785211E5, but see also next para.); serpentine or lizardite (2002-0173255); slate (2007-0227421E5); uranium (2003-0043505); unnamed mineral certified under (d)(i) (2011-0392781E5).

It does not include: gravel (2003-0048321E5); helium (2002-0141275); limestone (9315766, 2007-024239117, 2018-0755191E5); lithium, though a deposit could qualify under (d)(i) (2020-0858761E5); marble (2017-0682401E5); mining tailings (9414625); nephrite jade that is to be used as a construction material (2016-0673551E5) or that is *in-situ* in a claim covered by a previous certification (2016-0674541E5). See also IT-492 para. 3, IT-145R para. 9.

"Mineral resource" amended by 1995-97 technical bill (effective 1997-98), 1996 Budget [deleting "oil sands deposit": see now 248(1)"bituminous sands"], 1993 technical bill [adding "diamond", so exploration for diamond deposits can be financed by flow-through shares, as the costs are CEE: Finance news release, June 21, 1993].

Income Tax Folios: S3-F8-C1: Principal-business corporations in the resource industries [replaces IT-400]; S4-F15-C1: Manufacturing and processing [replaces IT-147R3].

Interpretation Bulletins: IT-125R4: Dispositions of resource properties; IT-492: CCA — Industrial mineral mines.

"minerals" — [Repealed]

Notes: See under "mineral" above.

"mining reclamation trust" — [Repealed]

Notes: Definition "mining reclamation trust" (MRT) repealed by 1997 Budget, effective 1998 and, if an election was made by a trust under 248(1)"qualifying environmental trust"(i), the trust is deemed to have never been a MRT. The broader QET term has replaced MRT throughout the Act. See Notes to 107.3(1), 211.6 and 248(1)"qualifying environmental trust".

Definition added by 1994 Budget, effective 1994. However, it did not apply to a trust the first contribution to which was made before Feb. 23, 1994, and which elected in writing, filed by the end of 1995, for the definition not to apply.

"Minister" means the Minister of National Revenue;

Related Provisions: 220 — Administration of the Act.

Notes: Recent Ministers of National Revenue have been: Otto Jelinek (1989-93); Garth Turner (1993); David Anderson (1993-96); Jane Stewart (1996-97); Herb Dhaliwal (1997-99); Martin Cauchon (1999-2002); Elinor Caplan (2002-03); Stan Keyes (2003-04); John McCallum (2004-06); Carol Skelton (2006-07); Gordon O'Connor (2007-08); Jean-Pierre Blackburn (2008-2010); Keith Ashfield (2010-2011); Gail Shea (2011-13); Kerry-Lynne Findlay (2013-15); Diane Lebouthillier (Nov. 4, 2015-present).

See 220(1) Notes re CRA. The *Canada Customs & Revenue Agency Act* changed Revenue Canada to the Canada Customs & Revenue Agency as of Nov. 1, 1999. The administrative split of the CCRA into the Canada Revenue Agency and the Canada Border Services Agency took effect Dec. 12, 2003. The 2004 CRA/CBSA bill legalized this change effective Dec. 12, 2005, and the *Canada Border Services Agency Act* makes the Minister of Public Safety and Emergency Preparedness responsible for the CBSA while the Minister of National Revenue remains in charge of CRA.

"money purchase limit" for a calendar year has the meaning assigned by subsection 147.1(1);

Notes: "Money purchase limit" added by 1990 pension bill, effective 1989.

"mortgage investment corporation" has the meaning assigned by subsection 130.1(6);

"motor vehicle" means an automotive vehicle designed or adapted to be used on highways and streets but does not include

(a) a trolley bus, or

(b) a vehicle designed or adapted to be operated exclusively on rails;

Related Provisions: 248(1) — "automobile", "passenger vehicle".

Interpretation Bulletins: IT-521R: Motor vehicle expenses claimed by self-employed individuals; IT-522R: Vehicle, travel and sales expenses of employees.

"mutual fund corporation" has the meaning assigned by subsection 131(8);

Related Provisions: 131(8.1) — Meaning of "mutual fund corporation".

"mutual fund trust" has the meaning assigned by subsection 132(6);

Related Provisions: 132(6.1), (6.2), (7), 132.2(3)(n) — Extensions and limitations to definition of mutual fund trust.

"NISA Fund No. 2" means the portion of a taxpayer's net income stabilization account

(a) that is described in paragraph 8(2)(b) of the *Farm Income Protection Act* or is a prescribed fund, and

(b) that can reasonably be considered to be attributable to a program that allows the funds in the account to accumulate;

Related Provisions: 12(10.4) — Fund deemed paid out on change in control of corporation; 248(1) — "net income stabilization account"; Reg. 9006(h) — NISA Fund No. 2 not reported to CRA for disclosure to foreign tax authorities.

Notes: Para. 8(2)(b) of the *Farm Income Protection Act* (FIPA) provides:

(2) Division of account into two funds — The account for each producer participating in a net income stabilization program shall be composed of

    (a) Fund No. 1, to which shall be credited all amounts paid by the producer in respect of the program; and

    (b) Fund No. 2, to which shall be credited all other amounts paid in respect of that producer by Canada or a province.

The AgriInvest program, designed to give farmers income stability, began in 2008. It is similar to the net income stabilization account program introduced in 1991 ("old NISA") under FIPA. Although deposits under old NISA ended at the end of 2003, funds in NISA Fund No. 2 could be withdrawn over a period of 5 years (at least 20% of the March 31, 2004 balance annually). They are taxable (see 12(10.2)) and deemed withdrawn on death (70(5.4)). See also guides RC4060 and RC4408.

A farmer's AgriInvest savings account is also a NISA under FIPA. Under AgriInvest, a participating farmer contributes to a savings account from farm revenues, with earnings from the fund taxable annually. This AgriInvest savings account is a NISA Fund No. 1. The government makes matching contributions to the farmer's NISA Fund No. 2, which accumulates on a tax-deferred basis (12(10.3)). The funds in both No. 1 and No. 2 can be invested by the farmer, with Fund No. 2 withdrawn first.

In *River Road Hutterian Brethren*, 2013 FC 857, Agriculture Canada combined two taxpayers (which had been reorganized and split from one) into one for purposes of AgriInvest so that they had a single Allowable Net Sales cap. The Court dismissed an application for judicial review.

For 2003-07, in place of old NISA was the Canadian Agricultural Income Stabilization (CAIS) program, which provided both income stabilization and disaster assistance. The farmer would make deposits, then withdraw the funds deposited and receive government contributions when experiencing production decline. See Reg. 234. CAIS is legislated under the authority of FIPA, but CAIS payments are not supposed to be tax-deferred. CAIS payments by Alberta Agriculture Financial Services Corp. are taxable: VIEWS doc 2005-0155851E5. CRA will not interfere with a finding by CAIS program staff that a person's income is not farming income and so does not qualify for CAIS: 2007-02292417. CAIS has been renamed AgriStability as of 2008. See agr.gc.ca, and Guides RC4060, RC4408.

Para. (a) amended by 2011 budget bill #2, for 2011 and later taxation years.

Para. (b) added by 2007 budget bill #2, for 2008 and later tax years. It limits the definition to the portion of the Fund No. 2 balance that can reasonably be considered to be attributable to a program that allows the funds in the account to accumulate. This is meant to distinguish a farmer's AgriInvest funds that may accumulate tax-free in the farmer's NISA Fund No. 2 from other government funds that may be paid to the farmer indirectly through the account (e.g., under CAIS). Unlike amounts contributed to, or earned by, a tax-deferred NISA Fund No. 2, farm receipts are generally taxable in the year paid by government as ordinary income from a farm business (s. 9 or 12(1)(x)). The amendment ensures that this applies to CAIS receipts. Related amendments were made to FIPA by Part 10 of 2007 budget bill #2.

"NISA Fund No. 2" added by 1992 technical bill, for 1991 and later taxation years.

Regulations: 5503(1) (prescribed fund).

Interpretation Bulletins: IT-291R3: Transfer of property to a corporation under subsection 85(1).

Forms: RC322: AgriInvest adjustment request; RC4060 (for PE, ON, AB): Farming income and the AgriStability and AgriInvest programs guide; RC4408 (for BC, SK, MB, NS, NL, YK): Farming income and the AgriStability and AgriInvest programs harmonized guide — joint forms and guide; T1163: Statement A — AgriStability and AgriInvest programs information and statement of farming activities for individuals; T1164: Statement B — AgriStability and AgriInvest programs information and statement of farming activities for additional farming operations; T1175: Farming — calculation of CCA and business-use-of-home expenses; T1273: Statement A — Harmonized AgriStability and AgriInvest programs information and statement of farming activities for individuals; T1274: Statement B — Harmonized AgriStability and AgriInvest programs information and statement of farming activities for additional farming operations; T1275: AgriStability and AgriInvest programs additional information and adjustment request form; T4003: Farming and fishing income [guide].

"net capital loss" has the meaning assigned by subsection 111(8), except as otherwise expressly provided;

Notes: 248(1)"net capital loss" amended by 2000 Budget, effective for taxation years that end after Feb. 27, 2000, to add "except as otherwise expressly provided" (since 104(21.5) defines the term for a specific purpose).

"net corporate income tax rate" in respect of a SIFT trust or SIFT partnership for a taxation year means the amount, expressed as a decimal fraction, by which

(a) the percentage rate of tax provided under paragraph 123(1)(a) for the taxation year

exceeds

(b) the total of

(i) the percentage that would, if the SIFT trust or SIFT partnership were a corporation, be its general rate reduction percentage, within the meaning assigned by subsection 123.4(1), for the taxation year, and

(ii) the percentage deduction from tax provided under subsection 124(1) for the taxation year;

Notes: The "net corporate income tax rate" (added by 2007 budget bill #1, effective Oct. 31, 2006) is 15% since 2012: see 123.4(1)"general rate reduction percentage" and 123.4(2). This is added to the 248(1)"provincial SIFT tax rate" for a combined tax on publicly-traded trusts and partnerships: 122(1)(b), 197(2). See 104(16) Notes.

"net income stabilization account" means an account of a taxpayer

(a) under the net income stabilization account program under the *Farm Income Protection Act*, or

(b) that is a prescribed account;

Related Provisions: 110.6(1.1) — NISA does not taint capital gains exemption; 248(1) — "NISA Fund No. 2"; Reg. 9006(h) — NISA not reported to CRA for disclosure to foreign tax authorities.

Notes: See Notes to 248(1)"NISA Fund No. 2".

Para. (b) added by 2011 budget bill #2, effective for 2011 and later taxation years. Definition added by 1992 technical bill, for 1991 and later taxation years.

Regulations: 5503(2) (prescribed account).

Forms: RC322: AgriInvest adjustment request; RC4060 (for PE, ON, AB): Farming income and the AgriStability and AgriInvest programs guide; RC4408 (for BC, SK, MB, NS, NL, YK): Farming income and the AgriStability and AgriInvest programs harmonized guide — joint forms and guide; T1163: Statement A — AgriStability and AgriInvest programs information and statement of farming activities for individuals; T1164: Statement B — AgriStability and AgriInvest programs information and statement of farming activities for additional farming operations; T1175: Farming — calculation of CCA and business-use-of-home expenses; T1273: Statement A — Harmonized AgriStability and AgriInvest programs information and statement of farming activities for individuals; T1274: Statement B — Harmonized AgriStability and AgriInvest programs information and statement of farming activities for additional farming operations; T1275: AgriStability and AgriInvest programs additional information and adjustment request form; T4003: Farming and fishing income [guide].

"Newfoundland offshore area" has the meaning assigned to the expression "offshore area" by the *Canada–Newfoundland and Labrador Atlantic Accord Implementation Act*, chapter 3 of the Statutes of Canada, 1987;

Notes: Definition amended by *Offshore Health and Safety Act* (S.C. 2014, c. 13), effective Dec. 31, 2014 (per P.C. 2014-1267), to change "*Canada-Newfoundland*" to "*Canada-Newfoundland and Labrador*".

"non-capital loss" has the meaning assigned by subsection 111(8);

Related Provisions: 111(1)(a) — Application of non-capital losses; 111(9) — Non-capital loss of person not resident in Canada.

Notes: The term **"non-discretionary trust"**, proposed in the Oct. 30, 2003 draft legislation, is no longer in 248(1). It is defined only in 17(15).

"non-portfolio property" has the same meaning as in subsection 122.1(1);

Notes: Definition added by 2007 budget bill #1, effective Oct. 31, 2006.

"non-resident" means not resident in Canada;

Related Provisions: 2(3) — Tax payable by non-resident persons; 94, 94.2 — Rules for non-resident trusts; 94(3)(a) — Certain trusts deemed resident in Canada; 138.1(1)(c)(iii) — Insurer deemed non-resident in respect of segregated fund property used outside Canada; 250 — Resident in Canada.

"non-resident-owned investment corporation" has the meaning assigned by subsection 133(8);

"Nova Scotia offshore area" has the meaning assigned to the expression "offshore area" by the *Canada-Nova Scotia Offshore Petroleum Resources Accord Implementation Act*, chapter 28 of the Statutes of Canada, 1988;

Related Provisions: 124(4)"province" — Taxable income earned in offshore area deemed earned in a province.

"OSFI risk-weighting guidelines" means the guidelines, issued by the Superintendent of Financial Institutions under the authority of section 600 of the *Bank Act*, requiring an authorized foreign bank to provide to the Superintendent on a periodic basis a return of the bank's risk-weighted on-balance sheet assets and off-balance sheet exposures, that apply as of August 8, 2000;

Notes: OSFI stands for Office of the Superintendent of Financial Institutions.

Definition added by 2001 technical bill, effective June 28, 1999.

"office" means the position of an individual entitling the individual to a fixed or ascertainable stipend or remuneration and includes a judicial office, the office of a minister of the Crown, the office of a member of the Senate or House of Commons of Canada, a member of a legislative assembly or a member of a legislative or executive council and any other office, the incumbent of which is elected by popular vote or is elected or appointed in a representative capacity and also includes the position of a corporation director, and **"officer"** means a person holding such an office;

Notes: For detailed discussion of the meaning of "office" see *9098-9005 Quebec*, 2012 TCC 324 (individual was "officer" of partnership of which he was member, and of estate he managed), and *Netten*, 2017 TCC 8 (vice-chair of Ontario Workplace Safety and Insurance Appeals Tribunal held an "office": para. 67).

For remuneration to be "ascertainable" it must be ascertainable in advance: *Merchant*, [1984] C.T.C. 253 (FCTD); the words "stipend" and "remuneration" mean gross income, not net of expenses: *Churchman*, 2004 TCC 191 (so unreimbursed expenses do not cause the per diem rate not to be fixed: VIEWS doc 2014-0549861I7). Where members of a committee are paid a per-hour or per-day rate but do not know in advance how many days they will work, they still hold an "office": *Ontario*, 2011 FCA 314; *Real Estate Council (Alberta)*, 2012 FCA 121 (leave to appeal denied 2012 CarswellNat 3750 (SCC)); *Nuclear Waste Management*, 2012 TCC 217 (Advisory Council members) (on this point, these overrule *Churchman* (above) and *Payette*, 2002 CarswellNat 4668 (TCC)).

In *Vachon [Conseil central des syndicats nationaux du Saguenay/Lac St-Jean]*, 2009 FCA 375 (leave to appeal denied 2010 CarswellNat 936 (SCC)), and *Sénéchal*, 2011 TCC 365, union members who worked on union business, were still paid by their employer and received expense allowances from the union, received a fixed or ascertainable stipend equal to their salary (because they were paid by their employers on behalf of the union) and thus held an "office".

CRA considers the following appointments an "office": Attendance Board under the Alberta *School Act* (VIEWS doc 2005-0142171E5); public hospital board (2015-0621571E5); unnamed Board (2012-0434491E5); unnamed Committee (2008-0273351E5).

Non-professional executors or liquidators who are compensated for their time earn income from an "office": *Messier*, 2008 TCC 349; *Boisvert*, 2011 TCC 290 (amount was compensation, not additional bequest); VIEWS doc 2005-0150881R3. See also Notes to 6(1)(c) re executors.

Expenses can be deducted against income from an "office", e.g. under 8(1)(h) or (i).

See also Pamela Rideout, "Painting With a Broad Brush: When Are Fees Received By Virtue of an Office or Employment?", 11(2) *Tax Hyperion* (Carswell) 3-4 (Feb. 2014).

Interpretation Bulletins: IT-377R: Director's, executor's or juror's fees (cancelled).

["officer"] — [See the final words of "office" above.]

"oil or gas well" means any well (other than an exploratory probe or a well drilled from below the surface of the earth) drilled for the purpose of producing petroleum or natural gas or of determining the existence, location, extent or quality of a natural accumulation of petroleum or natural gas, but, for the purpose of applying sections 13 and 20 and any regulations made for the purpose of paragraph 20(1)(a) in respect of property acquired after March 6, 1996, does not include a well for the extraction of material from a deposit of bituminous sands or oil shales;

Notes: The definition includes a shale natural gas well: VIEWS doc 2012-0459351E5.

Definition "oil or gas well" amended by 1996 Budget, effective March 7, 1996, to add everything from "but, for the purpose...".

Interpretation Bulletins: IT-125R4: Dispositions of resource properties.

"overseas Canadian Forces school staff" means personnel employed outside Canada whose services are acquired by the Minister of National Defence under a prescribed order relating to the provision of educational facilities outside Canada;

Related Provisions: 250(1)(d.1) — Optional deemed residence in Canada.

Regulations: 6600 (prescribed order).

["PRPP"] — [See "pooled registered pension plan" below.]

"paid-up capital" has the meaning assigned by subsection 89(1);

"paid-up capital deficiency" — [Repealed under former Act]

"Part VII refund" has the meaning assigned by subsection 192(2);

Notes: 248(1)"Part VII refund" added in the RSC 1985 (5th Supp) consolidation, effective December 1, 1991.

"Part VIII refund" has the meaning assigned by subsection 194(2);

Notes: 248(1)"Part VIII refund" added in the RSC 1985 (5th Supp) consolidation, effective December 1, 1991.

"participant" — [Repealed under former Act]

Notes: Repealed in 1985. This definition referred to a participant under an indexed security investment plan. The term as used in 67.1(3) (convention or seminar participant) is not defined; nor is the term as used in 247(1) and (3) (transfer pricing rules), or in 256(8.1)(b) (associated corporation rules).

"passenger vehicle" means an automobile

(a) acquired after June 17, 1987, other than an automobile that is acquired after that date pursuant to an obligation in writing entered into before June 18, 1987 or that is a zero-emission vehicle, or

(b) leased under a lease entered into, extended or renewed after June 17, 1987;

Notes: See 248(1)"automobile". The rules for automobiles introduced in 1988 tax reform (such as 13(7)(g), 67.2, 67.3) are worded in terms of "passenger vehicle" so as not to apply to vehicles acquired before those rules were announced.

See Notes to 248(1)"zero-emission vehicle", which is an electric, hydrogen or hybrid vehicle acquired after March 18, 2019.

Definition amended by 2019 budget bill #1, effective March 19, 2019, to add "or that is a zero-emission vehicle" (and to split the definition into paras. (a) and (b)). Before that date, read:

> "passenger vehicle" means an automobile acquired after June 17, 1987 (other than an automobile acquired after that date pursuant to an obligation in writing entered into before June 18, 1987) and an automobile leased under a lease entered into, extended or renewed after June 17, 1987;

Regulations: Sch. II:Cl. 10, Sch. II:Cl. 10.1, Sch. II:Cl. 16.

Interpretation Bulletins: IT-291R3: Transfer of property to a corporation under subsection 85(1); IT-521R: Motor vehicle expenses claimed by self-employed individuals; IT-522R: Vehicle, travel and sales expenses of employees.

"past service pension adjustment" of a taxpayer for a calendar year in respect of an employer has the meaning assigned by regulation;

Notes: See Notes to Reg. 8303(1).

"Past service pension adjustment" added by 1990 pension bill, effective 1989.

Regulations: 8303(1).

Interpretation Bulletins: IT-528: Transfers of funds between registered plans.

Registered Plans Compliance Bulletins: 1 (calculation of past service pension adjustment).

Forms: T215: Past service pension adjustment exempt from certification; T215 Segment; T215 Summ: Summary of past service pension adjustments exempt from certification; T1004: Applying for the certification of a provisional PSPA; T1006: Designating an RRSP, an PRPP or an SPP withdrawal as a qualifying withdrawal; T4104: Past service pension adjustment guide.

"pension adjustment" of a taxpayer for a calendar year in respect of an employer has the meaning assigned by regulation;

Related Provisions: 146(5.21) — Anti-avoidance.

Notes: See Guide T4084. In simple terms, the PA for a defined-benefit plan is normally the value of benefits earned times 9, minus $600. See Reg. 8301(6). See Willis Towers Watson, *Canadian Pensions and Retirement Income Planning*, 6th ed. (LexisNexis, 2017), chaps. 5-9; Millard & Théroux, "Private Health Services Plans and Pension Arbitrage", 2004 Cdn Tax Foundation conference report, at 12:25-46; Kutsenko, "Pension Plan Taxation in Canada", 38(4) *Estates, Trusts and Pensions Journal* 349 (2019) at 367-77. For a defined-contribution (money purchase) plan it is normally the amount of the contributions (Reg. 8301(4)).

The PA is reported on T4 slip Box 52, and reduces RRSP contribution room for the next year from the maximum dollar amount otherwise allowed. See 146(1)"RRSP deduction limit" Notes.

For case law on whether the PA must reduce the RRSP deduction, see 146(1)"RRSP deduction limit" Notes.

For the pension adjustment *reversal*, see 248(1)"total pension adjustment reversal".

"Pension adjustment" added by 1990 pension bill, effective 1989.

Regulations: 8301(1).

Registered Plans Compliance Bulletins: 1 (pension adjustments).

Forms: T1 General return, Line 20600 [former 206]; T4084: Pension adjustment guide.

"person", or any word or expression descriptive of a person, includes any corporation, and any entity exempt, because of subsection 149(1), from tax under Part I on all or part of the entity's taxable income and the heirs, executors, liquidators of a succession, administrators or other legal representatives of such a person, according to the law of that part of Canada to which the context extends;

Related Provisions: Canada-U.S. Tax Treaty:Art. III:1(e) — Meaning of "person" under the treaty. See also Related Provisions to 96(1) for provisions that deem "person" to include a partnership for specific purposes.

Notes: In most cases, the terms "person" and "taxpayer" are interchangeable. However, see Notes to 248(1)"taxpayer".

CRA considers a province to be a "person" for a 231.2 demand for information: doc 2012-0472761I7; but in *Brant*, [1998] G.S.T.C. 101 (FCTD), para. 45, the Ontario Minister of Finance was held not to be a "person" subject to a garnishment order.

A bare trustee is considered not to be a separate person; rather, the beneficial owner is considered to deal directly with the property to which the bare trustee holds legal title, subject to some legislated exceptions. See closing words of 104(1) and Notes to 104(1).

An Irish Common Contractual Fund and a Luxembourg fonds commun de placement are not "persons": see 248(1)"corporation" Notes.

In the definition, "legal representatives" (LR) does not take its meaning from the 248(1) definition of LR, due to the words "according to the law of that part of Canada...": *Straessle*, 2018 TCC 144, para. 40. Thus, a non-executor beneficiary of an estate was a "person" who could appeal the estate's assessment, but was not liable under s. 159 as a LR.

"Person" certainly includes a natural person (human being), despite spurious claims of "tax protesters" or "detaxers" that they are not subject to the Act: *Kennedy*, [2000] 4 C.T.C. 186 (Ont. SCJ); *Sargent*, 2004 ONCJ 356; *Ricci*, [2005] 1 C.T.C. 40 (Ont CA); *Lindsay*, 2005 BCCA 341 (leave to appeal denied 2008 CarswellNat 2862 (SCC)), 2006 BCCA 150 ["David-Kevin: Lindsay", who was very public in pushing these views, was sentenced to 30 days and fined $5,000: 2010 BCSC 831 (leave to appeal denied 2011 BCCA 99; leave to appeal denied 2011 CarswellBC 2525); he was also declared a vexatious litigant so he cannot bring more proceedings: 2009 CarswellBC 1022 (BCCA); and sentenced to 60 days for not filing returns: CRA news release Dec. 6/12]; *Sydel*, 2006 BCPC 346; *Hovey Ventures*, 2007 TCC 139 (FCA appeal dismissed for delay A-197-07); *McDougall*, 2008 TCC 383; *Klundert*, 2008 ONCA 767 (leave to appeal denied 2009 CarswellOnt 1883); *Loosdrecht*, 2008 BCPC 400, 2009 BCPC 196; *Stanchfield*, 2009 FC 99 (FCA appeal discontinued A-108-09) (person charged and person ordered to comply were same person); *Baudais*, 2009 TCC 199 (FCA appeal discontinued A-168-09); *Robert*, 2011 TCC 166 (bizarre purported distinctions between human being, natural person, fictitious corporation and "Animator"); *Turnnir*, 2011 TCC 495 ("sovereign person" argument invalid); *Bydeley*, 2012 TCC 142 (FCA appeal dismissed for delay A-154-12); *Morin*, 2012 QCCS 4564; *Janovsky*, 2013 TCC 140; *McLeod*, 2013 TCC 228; *Brown*, 2014 FCA 301 ("person" definition is not void for vagueness); *Girard*, 2014 TCC 107; *Mori*, 2016 CarswellOnt 6860 (Ont. CJ); *Na-*

deau, 2019 FCA 246; *Merrill*, 2020 BCPC 150. Gross-negligence penalties are normally upheld: see Notes to 163(2) under "Fiscal Arbitrators" and "Detaxers".

In *Porisky*, 2012 BCSC 67, the operator of the "Paradigm Education Group", which taught such ideas, was guilty of tax evasion and counselling others to commit evasion. His conviction was overturned (2014 BCCA 146) as he may not have understood he was giving up his right to a jury trial; but he was convicted in a new trial and sentenced to 5.5 years: 2016 BCSC 1757, aff'd 2019 BCCA 159. More Paradigm "educator" convictions: *Sigglekow*, 2014 ABCA 450 (bail refused while under appeal); *Blerot*, 2015 SKCA 69; *Millar*, 2016 BCSC 2039 and 2017 BCSC 323 (see also next para.); *Balogh*, 2020 BCCA 96; *Anderson*, 2021 BCCA 101. See *J.B.C. Securities*, 2003 NBCA 53, for more such cases; *Saran*, 2018 ONSC 6045 (bankruptcy of person using Paradigm tactics). See also 2(1) Notes including the *Meads* case; VIEWS doc 2007-0234531E5; tinyurl.com/cra-myths.

CRA announces convictions of "tax protesters" for evasion. Paradigm-related convictions (including for counselling evasion): Lee Williams, Tania Kovaluk (news release Nov. 22/12: 5 yrs and 2.4 yrs in prison; Oct. 19/16: +5 years for Kovaluk for not paying fine); Clarke & Mary Webster (Jan. 10/13: house arrest + fines); Jerry McCaw (April 25/13 and Aug. 12/13: 14 months + fine); Warren Fischer (Oct. 23/13: 6 months + fine); Carl Gustafson (Oct. 30/13: conditional sentence + fine); David Barrett (Oct. 4/13); Gerald Blerot (Jan. 14/14, 2014 SKQB 2); Edwin Sigglekow (Oct. 2/14: 15 months + fine); Donald Baudais (Sept. 16/14: 6 months + fine); Douglas Lewry (Nov. 16/15: 18 months conditional + fine); Cory Stanchfield (Nov. 26/15: 14 months conditional + fine); Keith Lawson (Nov. 2/16 and 2019 BCCA 109: 18 months + fine); Robert & Terry Steinkey (Jan. 5/17: 22 and 18 months conditional respectively + fines [aff'd 2019 ABCA 259]); Michael Millar (Feb. 28/17, 2017 BCSC 402: 2.5 years + fine); Debbie Anderson (2018 BCSC 651: 4.5 years + fine). ("Conditional" sentences are typically house arrest with conditions); Kin Tung Fong (Jan. 17/19: 2 years less a day conditional for failing to report $2m); Douglas Raymond (Nov. 27/19: 18 months conditional for accountant assisting Fong).

Other convictions: Doris Jung (news release Nov. 24/11); Rosalie Chobotar (Nov. 25/11); Christian Lachapelle (Dec. 12/12: 30 days for refusing to file; Nov. 27/15: 4 years for helping 93 individuals avoid $2m in tax by claiming "natural person"); *Tyskerud*, 2013 CarswellBC 362 (BC Prov. Ct); Deogracias Earl Gray (June 6/13: conditional sentence); Allan Curle, Bruce Johnson (June 16/14: 14 months, 10 months + fines); Dr. Gerald Vasilakos (Sept. 4/14: conditional sentence + fine); Jacques-Antoine Normandin (Dec. 12/14: 40 days + fines); Christine Bieri (May 27/16: facilitator for Lachapelle; 18 months conditional); William Mori (July 27/16: 12 months for failing to report $864,000 based on Paradigm); Timothée Bessette (Nov. 24/16: facilitator for Lachapelle: 18 months); Serge Fréchette and Jean-Pierre Ste-Marie (Feb. 9/18; 2 years less a day each for helping about 100 individuals evade about $1.5m); *Bekkerus*, 2018 ABPC 201 ($800,000 fine, 100 hours community service, $10,000 donation to United Way, letter of apology to CRA officials); Danièle Bérubé-Poulin (Aug. 7/18; 6 month conditional sentence for assisting Fréchette (above)); Marilyn Fleurent (Feb. 27/19: 200 hours community service for helping Fréchette); Sylvain Quirion (April 5/19: 9 month conditional sentence for enabling 50 people to evade $1m through Les Créditeurs); Pierre Cardin, Jean-Marc Paquin (March 11/21: 4 years for same scam).

Reference to liquidators of a succession added by 2001 *Civil Code* harmonization bill, effective June 14, 2001. The change is non-substantive; see *Interpretation Act* s. 8.2.

Definition of "person" amended by 1992 technical bill, effective May 5, 1993, to apply to entities exempt under 149(1), such as clubs and associations. The change allows such entities to be required to file information returns. See Notes to 149(12).

Interpretation Bulletins: IT-216: Corporation holds property as agent for shareholder (cancelled); IT-379R: Employees profit sharing plans — allocations to beneficiaries.

Information Circulars: 78-10R5: Books and records retention/destruction; 05-1R1: Electronic record keeping.

I.T. Technical News: 25 (partnership issues).

Advance Tax Rulings: ATR-1: Transfer of legal title in land to bare trustee.

"personal or living expenses" includes

(a) the expenses of properties maintained by any person for the use or benefit of the taxpayer or any person connected with the taxpayer by blood relationship, marriage or common-law partnership or adoption, and not maintained in connection with a business carried on for profit or with a reasonable expectation of profit,

(b) the expenses, premiums or other costs of a policy of insurance, annuity contract or other like contract if the proceeds of the policy or contract are payable to or for the benefit of the taxpayer or a person connected with the taxpayer by blood relationship, marriage or common-law partnership or adoption, and

(c) expenses of properties maintained by an estate or trust for the benefit of the taxpayer as one of the beneficiaries;

Related Provisions: 18(1)(h), 56(1)(o)(i) — No deduction for personal or living expenses.

Notes: See Notes to 18(1)(h), and Notes to 188.1(5) re meaning of "includes".

248(1)"personal or living expenses" amended by 2000 same-sex partners bill to refer to "common-law partnership", effective as per Notes to 248(1)"common-law partner".

"personal services business" has the meaning assigned by subsection 125(7);

"personal trust" means a trust (other than a trust that is, or was at any time after 1999, a unit trust) that is

(a) a graduated rate estate, or

(b) a trust in which no beneficial interest was acquired for consideration payable directly or indirectly to

(i) the trust, or

(ii) any person or partnership that has made a contribution to the trust by way of transfer, assignment or other disposition of property;

Related Provisions: 107.4(3)(i) — Trust deemed not to be personal trust (PT); 108(2) — Unit trust; 108(6) — Where terms of trust are varied; 108(7) — Meaning of "acquired for consideration"; 110.6(16) — Extension of definition for purposes of capital gains exemption; 128.1(10)"excluded right or interest"(j) — No deemed disposition on emigration of beneficiary; 135.2(4)(e)(i) — Cdn Wheat Board Farmers' Trust deemed not to be PT; 251(1)(b) — Trust deemed not at arm's length with beneficiary.

Notes: A trust that is not a personal trust (PT) is known informally as a "commercial trust" — a trust whose units or interests are bought and sold. See also "unit trust" (108(2)) and Notes to 104(1).

Where a trust's beneficiaries will contribute more capital to it in proportion to their interests, CRA would not confirm that it will remain a PT: VIEWS doc 2015-0596831E5. See also 2016-0635051R3 (assumption of debt by beneficiary on rollout does not cause trust to cease being PT).

For the meaning of "indirectly" in para. (b), see Notes to 17.1(1).

Para. (a), and (b) opening words, amended by 2014 budget bill #2, for 2016 and later taxation years, to change "testamentary trust" to "graduated rate estate" and "an *inter vivos* trust" to "a trust". (See Notes to 122(1).)

Definition earlier amended by 2008 budget bill #2 (effective July 15, 2008), 2001 and 1992 technical bills.

Income Tax Folios: S6-F2-C1: Disposition of an income interest in a trust [replaces IT-385R2]; S1-F5-C1: Related persons and dealing at arm's length [replaces IT-419R2].

Interpretation Bulletins: IT-342R: Trusts — Income payable to beneficiaries; IT-381R3: Trusts — capital gains and losses and the flow-through of taxable capital gains to beneficiaries.

"personal-use property" has the meaning assigned by section 54;

"pooled pension plan" has the same meaning as in subsection 147.5(1);

Notes: Definition added by 2012 budget bill #2, effective Dec. 14, 2012.

"pooled registered pension plan" or **"PRPP"** has the same meaning as in subsection 147.5(1);

Notes: See Notes to 147.5. Definition added by 2012 budget bill #2, effective Dec. 14, 2012.

"post-1971 spousal or common-law partner trust" means a trust that would be described in paragraph 104(4)(a) if that paragraph were read without reference to subparagraph 104(4)(a)(iv);

Related Provisions: 104(6)(b)B(i) — Deduction from income of trust; 104(15)(a) — Preferred beneficiary election; 107(4)(a)(i) — Distribution of property to person other than taxpayer or partner.

Notes: This term was "post-1971 spousal trust" in the 1999 draft legislation, and "post-1971 partner trust" in the 2000 draft legislation.

248(1)"post-1971 spousal or common-law partner trust" added by 2001 technical bill, effective for trusts created after 1971.

"preferred share" means a share other than a common share;

"prescribed" means

(a) in the case of a form, the information to be given on a form or the manner of filing a form, authorized by the Minister,

(a.1) in the case of the manner of making or filing an election, authorized by the Minister, and

(b) in any other case, prescribed by regulation or determined in accordance with rules prescribed by regulation;

Related Provisions: 147.1(18) — Regulation re pension plans; 220(3.21) — Certain designations in prescribed form deemed to be elections; 221 — Regulations generally; 244(16) — Forms prescribed or authorized; 248(1) — "Regulation"; *Interpretation Act* 32 — Deviations from prescribed form acceptable.

Notes: Despite para. (a), s. 32 of the *Interpretation Act* (reproduced near the end of this book) allows deviations from a prescribed form that do not affect the substance, provided they are not calculated to mislead.

The T1 is valid as the "prescribed form" (244(16)) required for personal income tax returns: *Watson*, 2006 BCCA 233; *Gibbs*, 2006 BCSC 481; *Smith*, 2007 BCCA 499; *Lemieux*, 2007 SKPC 135; VIEWS doc 2014-0547641E5. The information required on Form T661 for an SR&ED claim is "prescribed information": *Westsource Group*, 2017 TCC 9, para. 26.

"Prescribed" amended by 1991 technical bill, effective Dec. 17, 1991.

Regulations: Part I–XCII.

Application Policies: SR&ED 2004-02R5: Filing requirements for claiming SR&ED.

"principal amount", in relation to any obligation, means the amount that, under the terms of the obligation or any agreement relating thereto, is the maximum amount or maximum total amount, as the case may be, payable on account of the obligation by the issuer thereof, otherwise than as or on account of interest or as or on account of any premium payable by the issuer conditional on the exercise by the issuer of a right to redeem the obligation before the maturity thereof;

Related Provisions: 80.02(2)(a) — Principal amount of distress preferred share; 248(26) — Principal amount of debtor's liability.

Notes: This definition "does not expressly address whether or how foreign currency fluctuations are to be taken into account in determining the 'principal amount' of an obligation denominated in foreign currency ... the arguments based on the use of the phrase 'maximum amount' in the definition of 'principal amount' fail because there is no indication that foreign currency conversions were in Parliament's contemplation when that section was drafted": *Imperial Oil (Inco)*, 2006 SCC 46, para. 61.

I.T. Application Rules: 26(1.1) (where obligation outstanding on Jan. 1, 1972).

I.T. Technical News: 25 (foreign exchange losses).

"private corporation" has the meaning assigned by subsection 89(1);

"private foundation" has the meaning assigned by section 149.1;
Notes: Definition "private foundation" added by 1997 Budget, effective 1997.

"private health services plan" means

(a) a contract of insurance in respect of hospital expenses, medical expenses or any combination of such expenses, or

(b) a medical care insurance plan or hospital care insurance plan or any combination of such plans,

except any such contract or plan established by or pursuant to

(c) a law of a province that establishes a health care insurance plan as defined in section 2 of the *Canada Health Act*, or

(d) an Act of Parliament or a regulation made thereunder that authorizes the provision of a medical care insurance plan or hospital care insurance plan for employees of Canada and their dependants and for dependants of members of the Royal Canadian Mounted Police and the regular force where such employees or members were appointed in Canada and are serving outside Canada;

Related Provisions: 6(1)(a)(i) — Employer's contribution to PHSP not a taxable benefit; 20.01 — Deduction from business income for premiums paid to plan; 118.2(2)(q) — Medical expense credit for premiums paid to PHSP; 144.1(1)"designated employee benefit" — Employee life and health trust may pay benefit from PHSP.

Notes: See tinyurl.com/phsp-cra for CRA explanation. Neither employer contributions to a PSHP, nor benefits paid, are taxable as employment benefits: 6(1)(a)(i). This term includes extended health plans, drug plans and dental plans (see IT-339R2). It also includes a "Health Care Expense Account" or medical/dental spending account employment benefit (VIEWS docs 9629843, 2003-0051591R3, 2004-0091211R3, 2004-0105181E5), and a "trusteed plan" (2003-0024565). Amounts can be paid directly from the plan to health service providers: doc 2004-0098171E5. Premiums paid by self-employed persons may be deductible from business income: 20.01. For more discussion see VIEWS docs 2003-0012351E5, 2003-0030991E5, 2003-0031971E5, 2003-0045173, 2004-0058331E5, 2005-0120351E5, 2005-0126211E5, 2005-0139551E5, 2005-0139631R3, 2005-014121R3, 2005-0160671E5, 2005-0163771E5, 2006-0168351E5, 2006-0182821E5, 2006-0186741E5, 2006-0188061M4, 2006-0198221R3, 2006-0211191R3, 2006-0216751E5, 2007-0227881E5, 2007-0254811R3, 2007-0257631R3, 2008-0271211E5, 2008-0272241E5, 2008-0273771E5, 2008-0277981E5,

2008-0303211E5, 2008-0304591E5, 2009-0328741E5 ("cost-plus" plan), 2009-0351581E5, 2010-0355181E5, 2010-0366161E5, 2010-0372161M4, 2010-0373091E5, 2010-0380551E5, 2010-0385491E5 (Isolated Posts and Government Housing Directive), 2011-0406901E5, 2011-0417671E5, 2011-0422661E5, 2011-0427431E5, 2012-0436061E5 (self-administered health care spending account (HCSA)), 2012-0447041E5, 2012-0451901M4, 2012-0454051C6, 2013-0480711M4, 2013-0498001E5 (transfer of unused portion of HCSA to PSHP), 2013-0502031E5, 2014-0521301E5, 2014-0543891E5, 2016-0633741C6 [2016 CALU q.6] (PSHP valid with only one employee); 2016-0635351E5 (only employees are sole shareholder and spouse); 2016-0636871E5 (criteria for non-medical expenses to be covered); 2017-0703871C6 [2017 CPA Alberta q.9] (plan for sole shareholder does not qualify); 2017-0718661E5 (includes expenses outside Canada); 2018-0749261E5 (stabilization reserve is allowed); 2020-0846751E5, 2020-0847081E5 (HCSA credits unused due to COVID-19 can be carried forward up to 6 months); 2020-0857841E5 (extends COVID-19 relief to 12 months for credits expiring March 16/20 to March 15/21).

Since 2015, CRA accepts a PSHP if "substantially all" (normally 90% or more) of the premiums relate to medical expenses eligible under 118.2(2), so minor coverage of vitamins, fitness or weight loss programs, etc. will not put a plan offside: Nov. 25, 2015 news release; tinyurl.com/pshp-subst; docs 2015-0610751C6 [2015 CTF q.5], 2016-0643141E5, 2016-0651291E5. See Tollstam, "CRA on a PSHP 'All or Substantially All' Test", 27(4) *Canadian Tax Highlights* (ctf.ca) 5-6 (April 2019)). This overrules docs saying *all* expenses had to qualify (2010-0365801E5, 2010-0362941E5, 2010-0368231M4, 2010-0378121M4, 2010-0391961E5, 2011-0414301M4).

See also CRA news release "Warning: Buyer beware when it comes to Health Spending Accounts" (May 5, 2019), tinyurl.com/cra-beware-hsa: "Some insurance agents/brokers and financial planners are marketing HSAs to businesses operating as sole proprietorships that have no arm's-length employees. Participants are told that they will be onside with meeting the *Income Tax Act* rules for private health services plans if they purchase additional types of insurance."

See 144.1 and the 2021 amendments re employee life and health trusts. See also 6(1)(a) Notes under "Health and welfare trusts"; *Canadian Health Insurance Tax Guide: Private Health Services Plans* (Jan. 2017), tinyurl.com/sunlife-taxguides; Millard & Théroux, "Private Health Services Plans", 2004 Cdn Tax Foundation conference report, 12:1-24; Macnaughton, "Cosmetic Medical Services and PSHPs", 18(5) *Canadian Tax Highlights* (ctf.ca) 10-11 (May 2010); Cheng & Shah, "Private Health Services Plans for Small Businesses", 5(4) *Canadian Tax Focus* (ctf.ca) 52-3 (Nov. 2015); Dollar, "Health Insurance Strategies", 65(3) *Canadian Tax Journal* 747-74 (2017).

Para. (c): Section 2 of the *Canada Health Act* provides:

"health care insurance plan" means, in relation to a province, a plan or plans established by the law of the province to provide for insured health services;

Para. (d): "Regular force" is defined in the *National Defence Act* (via *Interpretation Act* s. 35(1)) in distinction to "reserve force":

2. (1) "regular force" means the component of the Canadian Forces that is referred to in subsection 15(1);

15. (1) There shall be a component of the Canadian Forces, called the regular force, that consists of officers and non-commissioned members who are enrolled for continuing, full-time military service.

Para. (c) amended by 1998 Budget, effective April 1996.

Income Tax Folios: S2-F1-C1: Health and welfare trusts [replaces IT-85R2].

Interpretation Bulletins: IT-339R2: Meaning of "private health services plan"; IT-529: Flexible employee benefit programs.

Advance Tax Rulings: ATR-8: Self-insured health and welfare trust fund; ATR-23: Private health services plan.

"professional corporation" means a corporation that carries on the professional practice of an accountant, dentist, lawyer, medical doctor, veterinarian or chiropractor;

Related Provisions: 249.1(1)(b) — Year-end of professional corporation.

Notes: Definition "professional corporation" added by 1995 Budget, effective 1995. See Notes to 125(1), 249.1(1). Note that 248(1)"lawyer" includes a Quebec notary.

"profit sharing plan" has the meaning assigned by subsection 147(1);

"property" means property of any kind whatever whether real or personal, immovable or movable, tangible or intangible, or corporeal or incorporeal and, without restricting the generality of the foregoing, includes

(a) a right of any kind whatever, a share or a chose in action,

(b) unless a contrary intention is evident, money,

(c) a timber resource property,

(d) the work in progress of a business that is a profession; and

(e) the goodwill of a business, as referred to in subsection 13(34);

Related Provisions: 13(34)–(42) — Rules for CCA for goodwill; Reg. 1100(1)(a)(xii.1), 1100(1)(c.1), Sch. II:Cl. 14.1 — CCA for goodwill.

Related Provisions: 9(1), 9(3) — Income from property; 79(1), 79.1(1) — Definition of property for purposes of rules re seizure of property by creditor; 248(5) — Meaning of substituted property.

Notes: In *Manrell*, 2003 FCA 128, signing a non-competition agreement was not a disposition of "property", since the taxpayer merely gave up a right shared with everyone to carry on business. The words "right of any kind whatever" in para. (a) do not cover such a right. (56.4 now taxes a payment for agreeing not to compete.)

A fishing license is "property" when surrendered to the government, even though the licensee has no right to continue to have the licence and cannot legally sell it: *Saulnier v. Royal Bank*, 2008 SCC 58; *Haché*, 2011 FCA 104; *Winsor*, 2007 TCC 692. See also Notes to 85(1.1) re fishing licences, and "(e) Is a License Property?", in Halpern & van Roosendaal, "2011 Property Potpourri", 26(10) *Money & Family Law* (Carswell) 74 (Oct. 2011) at 79-80.

The following were held to be property: woman's right to compensation for being underpaid relative to men, settled with a pay equity award (*Montgomery*, 2007 TCC 317); incomplete work on a TV series, which was inventory and could be written off as a loss once it was clearly not going to be paid for (*Gestion Raynald Lavoie*, 2008 TCC 204).

CRA considered the following to be property: a contract, for purposes of 160(1) (VIEWS doc 2010-0366821I7). Quebec maple syrup quota, if it is "goods" under the *Civil Code*: (2013-0503871E5).

The following were not [payment for] "property": deferred closing fees paid to broker following transfer of customer accounts, as they were payment for services (*Bergeron*, 2013 TCC 13; FCA appeal discontinued A-68-13); shareholder's non-exclusive "information, ideas, knowledge or know-how", allegedly transferred to his corp while he was non-resident (*Roth* (*Tri Pacific Gas*), 2007 FCA 38); written options (obligation of the writer): *Kruger Inc.*, 2016 FCA 186, para. 101; a right to invoice for legal services, by a lawyer who was an employee of his corporation (*Aitchison Prof Corp*, 2018 TCC 131). (*Highwood Congregation v. Wall*, 2018 SCC 26, para. 30, said a business person had no property right in his client base.)

Despite para. (b), CRA considered cash not to be "property" in applying 40(3.3) to a foreign exchange loss on disposition of cash: VIEWS doc 2008-028011117.

For legal title without beneficial ownership, see Notes to 54"capital property".

Para. (e) added by 2016 budget bill #2, effective 2017, as part of changing the eligible capital property rules to CCA Class 14.1 (see Notes to 20(1)(b)).

Opening words amended by 2002-2013 technical bill (Part 4 — bijuralism), effective June 26, 2013, to add "immovable or movable, tangible or intangible".

I.T. Application Rules: 26(6) (property disposed of and reacquired from June 19 to December 31, 1971).

Interpretation Bulletins: IT-432R2: Benefits conferred on shareholders; IT-457R: Election by professionals to exclude work in progress from income.

Application Policies: SR&ED 2000-04R2: Recapture of investment tax credit.

Advance Tax Rulings: ATR-60: Joint exploration corporations.

"province" — [Repealed under former Act]

Notes: This definition was repealed in 1981. Subsec. 35(1) of the *Interpretation Act* provides that "province" includes Yukon, Nunavut, and the NWT. See also the definition of "province" in 124(4), which applies for purposes of s. 124.

"provincial SIFT tax factor" — [Repealed]

Notes: Definition "provincial SIFT tax factor" (0.13) added by 2007 budget bill #1, effective Oct. 31, 2006, and repealed by 2008 budget bill #1, effective on the same basis as enactment of 248(1)"provincial SIFT tax rate".

"provincial SIFT tax rate" of a SIFT trust or a SIFT partnership for a taxation year means the prescribed amount determined in respect of the SIFT trust or SIFT partnership for the taxation year;

Related Provisions: 122(1)(b)A:D, 122(3)"taxable SIFT trust distributions"C, 197(2)C — Provincial SIFT tax rate used in calculation of tax payable.

Notes: SIFT tax under 122(1)(b) and 197(2) applies to distributions from SIFT trusts (122.1(1) — most income trusts) and SIFT partnerships (197(1)). See Notes to 104(16).

The SIFT tax rate is made up of two components: 248(1)"net corporate income tax rate" (see Notes thereto) and "provincial SIFT tax rate" (PSTR), which replaces "provincial SIFT tax factor" effective 2009 or earlier by election (see below).

The 2008 Budget states that the PSTR will be based on the general provincial corporate income tax rate in each province in which the SIFT has a permanent establishment. This will ensure that the SIFT tax rate is the same as the federal-provincial tax rate for large public corporations with the same activities.

To determine this rate for a SIFT, the taxable distributions of the SIFT will be notionally allocated to provinces according to the general corporate taxable income allocation formula. Specifically, the SIFT's taxable distributions will be allocated to provinces by taking half the total of:

- that proportion of the SIFT's taxable distributions for the year that the SIFT's wages and salaries in the province are of its total wages and salaries in Canada; and

- that proportion of the SIFT's taxable distributions for the year that the SIFT's gross revenues in the province are of its total gross revenues in Canada.

Applying the relevant provincial tax rates to these notionally allocated amounts will generate a dollar amount that, expressed as a proportion of the SIFT's total taxable distributions, will provide an average rate of provincial tax. This average rate will in turn be the provincial component of the SIFT tax rate of the SIFT for the taxation year.

Taxable distributions that are not allocated to any province will be subject to a 10% rate constituting the provincial component. The provincial tax rate applied to taxable distributions allocated to Quebec will be deemed to be nil to take into account the SIFT tax imposed by Quebec.

See also Janet Newcombe, "A Change to the Taxation of Specified Investment Flow-Throughs (SIFTs)", 5(6) *Tax Hyperion* (Carswell, June 2008).

248(1)"provincial SIFT tax rate" added by 2008 budget bill #1 (replacing "provincial SIFT tax factor"), for 2009 and later taxation years as well as earlier years by election.

Regulations: 414(3) (prescribed amount).

"public corporation" has the meaning assigned by subsection 89(1);

"public foundation" has the meaning assigned by section 149.1;

Notes: Definition "public foundation" added by 1997 Budget, effective 1997.

"public market" has the same meaning as in subsection 122.1(1);

Notes: Definition added by 2007 budget bill #1, effective Oct. 31, 2006.

"qualified Canadian journalism organization", at any time, means a corporation, partnership or trust that

(a) meets the following conditions:

  (i) in the case of a corporation,

    (A) it is incorporated under the laws of Canada or a province,

    (B) the chairperson or other presiding officer, and at least $3/4$ of the directors or other similar officers, are citizens of Canada, and

    (C) it is resident in Canada,

  (ii) in the case of a partnership,

    (A) it is formed under the laws of a province, and

    (B) individuals who are citizens of Canada or persons, or partnerships, described in any of subparagraphs (i) to (iii) hold interests in the partnership

      (I) representing in value at least 75% of the total value of the partnership property, and

      (II) that result in at least 75% of each income or loss of the partnership from any source being included in the determination of their incomes,

  (iii) in the case of a trust,

    (A) it is formed under the laws of a province,

    (B) it is resident in Canada, and

    (C) if interests as a beneficiary under the trust are held by one or more persons or partnerships, at least 75% of the fair market value of all interests as a beneficiary under the trust are held by

      (I) individuals who are citizens of Canada, or

      (II) persons or partnerships described in any of subparagraphs (i) to (iii),

  (iv) it operates in Canada, including that its content is edited, designed and, except in the case of digital content, published in Canada,

  (v) it is engaged in the production of original news content, which

    (A) must be primarily focused on matters of general interest and reports of current events, including coverage of democratic institutions and processes, and

    (B) must not be primarily focused on a particular topic such as industry-specific news, sports, recreation, arts, lifestyle or entertainment,

(vi) it regularly employs two or more journalists who deal at arm's length with the organization in the production of its content,

(vii) it is not significantly engaged in the production of content

(A) to promote the interests, or report on the activities, of an organization, an association or its members, or

(B) for a government, Crown corporation or government agency, and

(C) [Repealed]

(viii) it is not a Crown corporation, municipal corporation or government agency, and

(b) is designated at that time by the Minister and, for this purpose, the Minister shall take into account any recommendations of a body established for the purpose of this definition;

Related Provisions: 168.1(1) — Effective date of designation as QCJO; 168.1(2), (3) — Revocation of designation.

Notes: This term is distinct from "qualifying journalism organization", defined varyingly in 125.6(1) and 149.1(1). All these terms were introduced by the 2019 Budget as part of providing support for journalism in various forms. See 118.02 (credit for digital news subscriptions), 125.6 (labour credit for having newsroom employees) and 149.1(1)"qualified donee"(b.1) (charity status for registered journalism organization).

The word "employs" in (a)(vi) may require employees, so that an organization that hires journalists as independent contractors (see Notes to 248(1)"employee") will not qualify. (It is unclear whether *Interpretation Act* s. 33(3) will apply.)

The "body established" for para. (b) was announced by Canadian Heritage in "The Government of Canada Supports Canadian Journalism" (May 22, 2019: tinyurl.com/journ-panel); 8 associations were asked to submit candidates' names for an independent panel of experts. The panel issued its report on July 16, 2019: tinyurl.com/journ-report. See also 168.1. A media organization applies to CRA on Form T625, and a CRA Independent Advisory Board recommends on whether it meets the QCJO criteria: tinyurl.com/cra-qcjo; *Guidance on the income tax measures to support journalism* (tinyurl.com/cra-journalism), §2.

See also Frajman & Petraske, "Government Support of Journalism", xli(9) *The Canadian Taxpayer* (Carswell) 69-70 (May 3, 2019) and xli(10) 75-77 (May 17, 2019); Drache, "Supporting Non-Profit Journalism", 27(5) *Canadian Not-for-Profit News* (Carswell) 33-35 (May 2019).

Definition amended by 2021 budget bill #1, effective 2019, to change "primarily engaged" in (a)(v) to "engaged" and repeal (vii)(C), "to promote goods or services".

Definition added by 2019 budget bill #1, effective 2019. (Para. (b) was changed by Commons Finance Committee, before Third Reading, from "is designated at that time by a body prescribed for the purpose of this definition".)

Forms: T625: Application for qualified Canadian journalism organization designation.

"qualified donee" has the meaning assigned by subsection 149.1(1).

Related Provisions: 188.2(3)(a)(ii) — Effect of suspension of charity's receipting privileges.

Notes: "Qualified donee" added by 2001 technical bill, effective 1999.

"qualifying environmental trust" has the meaning assigned by subsection 211.6(1);

Related Provisions: 12(1)(z.1), (z.2) — Income from trust or from sale of interest; 20(1)(ss), (tt) — Deduction for contribution to trust or acquisition of interest; 75(3)(c) — Reversionary trust rules do not apply; 107.3(1), (2) — Rules applying to trust; 107.3(3) — Where trust ceases to be qualifying environmental trust; 127.41 — Tax credit to beneficiary of trust; 149(1)(z) — No Part I tax on trust; 211.6 — Part XII.4 tax on trust; 248(1)"cost amount"(e.2) — Cost amount of interest in trust is zero; 250(7) — Trust deemed resident in province where site is located [before 2012].

Notes: This term was "mining reclamation trust" before 1997 but was expanded to cover other reclamation. A taxpayer (beneficiary) can use a QET to fund future reclamation costs, and deduct the amounts put into the QET: 20(1)(ss). The QET is exempt from Part I tax (149(1)(z)) but taxed on investment income under 211.6 (Part XII.4) at the corporate tax rate. The beneficiary is taxed on its share of the income earned by the QET (107.3(1)) but receives a refundable credit under 127.41 for Part XII.4 tax paid by the QET, so the income from the fund is effectively taxed at the beneficiary's tax rate.

For detail see Carr & Calverley, *Canadian Resource Taxation* (Carswell, looseleaf or *Taxnet Pro* Reference Centre), chap. 15; Joseph Frankovic, "The Case for 'Reverse Depreciation' of Reclamation Costs", 52(1) *Canadian Tax Journal* 1 (2004) at 35-38; John Fuke, "Taxation of Newly Created Qualified Environmental Trusts", IV(3) *Business Vehicles* (Federated Press) 198-201 (1998); Brian Carr, "Qualifying Environmental Trusts", IV(3) *Resource Sector Taxation* (Federated Press) 296-300 (2006); TEI submission to Finance, Nov. 16, 2016, pp. 4-6.

See also VIEWS docs 2003-0048241E5 (deductibility of reclamation costs); 2003-0050303 (limited partnership deducts amount contributed to reclamation trust); 2007-0243271C6 (trust under Quebec *Environmental Quality Act* s. 56 qualifies); 2012-0463471R3 and 2012-0463871E3 (each ruling that a proposed Single Reclamation Trust is a QET); 2012-0463621R3 (mine site meets definition of "qualifying site" in 211.6(1)); 2014-0521951E5 (National Energy Board's Model Trust Agreement for pipeline QETs — "purpose" wording is acceptable); 2015-0572761R3, 2015-0573171R3, 2015-0573201R3, 2015-0573211R3, 2015-0573231R3, 2015-0573321R3, 2015-0574901R3, 2015-0619261R3, 2015-0619271R3, 2015-0619281R3, 2015-0619301R3 (QETs for pipelines, also ruling on 20(1)(ss) and 107.3(1)).

If the trust is resident in Quebec, an election under para. (i) must be copied to Revenu Québec: *Taxation Act* ss. 21.40, 21.4.6.

See Notes to 54"proceeds of disposition" re treatment of reforestation obligations and oil&gas reclamation obligations under *Daishowa-Marubeni*.

For a forestry revitalization trust, see the *British Columbia Forestry Revitalization Remission Order*.

Definition amended by 2011 budget bill #2, for 2012 and later tax years (substantive definition moved to 211.6(1)). Added by 1997 Budget, effective 1992.

"qualifying share" has the meaning assigned by subsection 192(6);

Notes: Added in RSC 1985 (5th Supp) consolidation, effective Dec. 1, 1991.

"qualifying trust annuity" has the meaning assigned by subsection 60.011(2);

Notes: Definition added by 2002-2013 technical bill (Part 5 — technical), effective 1989. See Notes to 60.011.

["RDSP"] — [See "registered disability savings plan" below.]

["RESP"] — [See "registered education savings plan" below.]

["RRIF"] — [See "registered retirement income fund" below.]

["RRSP"] — [See "registered retirement savings plan" below.]

"RRSP deduction limit" has the meaning assigned by subsection 146(1);

Notes: "RRSP deduction limit" added by 1990 pension bill, effective 1989.

"RRSP dollar limit" has the meaning assigned by subsection 146(1);

Notes: "RRSP dollar limit" added by 1990 pension bill, effective 1989.

"recognized derivatives exchange" means a person or partnership recognized or registered under the securities laws of a province to carry on the business of providing the facilities necessary for the trading of options, swaps, futures contracts or other financial contracts or instruments whose market price, value, delivery obligations, payment obligations or settlement obligations are derived from, referenced to or based on an underlying interest;

Notes: Definition added by 2016 budget bill #1, effective April 22, 2015.

"recognized stock exchange" means

(a) a designated stock exchange, and

(b) any other stock exchange, if that other stock exchange is located in Canada or in a country that is a member of the Organisation for Economic Co-operation and Development and that has a tax treaty with Canada;

Notes: 248(1)"recognized stock exchange" added by 2007 budget bill #2, effective Dec. 14, 2007. This term is used only in 116(6)(b). It includes NEX on the TSX Venture Exchange and the Alternative Investment Market of the London Stock Exchange: VIEWS docs 2012-045432117, 2012-0455741E5 (these also discuss the meaning of "stock exchange").

"record" includes an account, an agreement, a book, a chart or table, a diagram, a form, an image, an invoice, a letter, a map, a memorandum, a plan, a return, a statement, a telegram, a voucher, and any other thing containing information, whether in writing or in any other form;

Notes: See Notes to 230(1), and Notes to 188.1(5) re meaning of "includes".

Definition "record" added by 1995-97 technical bill, effective June 18, 1998.

Information Circulars: 78-10R5: Books and records retention/destruction.

Forms: RC4409: Keeping records [guide].

"refundable Part VII tax on hand" has the meaning assigned by subsection 192(3);

Notes: Added in RSC 1985 (5th Supp) consolidation, effective Dec. 1991.

"refundable Part VIII tax on hand" has the meaning assigned by subsection 194(3);

Notes: Added in RSC 1985 (5th Supp) consolidation, effective Dec. 1991.

"registered Canadian amateur athletic association" means a Canadian amateur athletic association within the meaning assigned by subsection 149.1(1) that has applied to the Minister in prescribed form for registration, that has been registered and whose registration has not been revoked;

Related Provisions: 143.1 — Amateur athletes' reserve funds; 149(1)(g) — RCAAA exempt from tax; 149.1(4.2) — Revocation of RCAAA registration; 149.1(14) — Annual information return; 149.1(15), 241(3.2) — Public disclosure of RCAAA information; Reg. 8901.1(e) — RCAAA qualifies for Canada Emergency Wage Subsidy.

Notes: An RCAAA is effectively treated the same as a registered charity, and donations to it qualify as charitable donations: 149.1(1)"qualified donee"(c). Use Form T1189 to apply for registration. For the list of current and revoked RCAAAs see tinyurl.com/cra-rcaaa.

An RCAAA must be "nation-wide" in scope, but may be restricted to adherents of one religion, and there is no "public benefit" requirement beyond the promotion of amateur athletics in Canada: *Maccabi Canada*, [1998] 4 C.T.C. 21 (FCA). Ongoing disputes over refusal to register: *Athletes 4 Athletes Foundation*, 2020 FCA 41; *Tomorrow's Champions Foundation*, 2020 FCA 42.

If an association promoting youth sports is not an RCAAA, it cannot be registered as a charity: *A.Y.S.A. Amateur Youth Soccer Association*, 2007 SCC 42. "The organization, in substance, must have as its main objective a purpose and activities that the common law will recognize as charitable. Examples of sporting activity that the government acknowledges would be charitable include therapeutic horseback riding for children with disabilities, or sports camps for children living in poverty" (para. 42).

RCAAAs that issue receipts for donation shelters risk having their status revoked. See Notes to 168(1). Since 2008, CRA has announced these revocations (news release date and CRA details in parentheses): Biathlon Canada (Oct. 29/10: issued $26m in receipts for an abusive tax shelter); Canadian Amateur Football Association (Sept. 3/08: no specifics given); Canadian Lacrosse Association (June 7/10: issued $60m in donation receipts for abusive tax shelters); Little League Baseball Canada (Jan. 12/09: issued $82 million in donation receipts for abusive transactions).

Since 2012, RCAAAs are subject to much more control by CRA. See 149.1(1)"qualified donee"(c), 149.1(4.2), (6.201), (14), (15), (22), 168(4), 188(1.4), 188.1, 188.2(1), 189(6.3) and 241(3.2) (and "Registered Canadian amateur athletic association" in Topical Index).

Definition amended by 2011 budget bill #2, effective 2012. (The substantive definition was moved to 149.1(1)"Canadian amateur athletic association".)

Interpretation Bulletins: IT-168R3: Athletes and players employed by football, hockey and similar clubs; IT-496R: Non-profit organizations.

Forms: T1189: Application to register a Canadian amateur athletic association under the ITA.

Registered Charities Newsletters: 2 (revised publications and forms).

Charities Policies: CPS-007: RCAAAs: Receipts — issuing policy; CPS-011: Registration of Canadian amateur athletic associations.

"registered charity" at any time means

    (a) a charitable organization, private foundation or public foundation, within the meanings assigned by subsection 149.1(1), that is resident in Canada and was either created or established in Canada, or

    (b) a branch, section, parish, congregation or other division of an organization or foundation described in paragraph (a), that is resident in Canada and was either created or established in Canada and that receives donations on its own behalf,

that has applied to the Minister in prescribed form for registration and that is at that time registered as a charitable organization, private foundation or public foundation;

Related Provisions: 149(1)(f) — No tax on registered charity; 149.1 — Rules for charities; 149.1(4.1)(c) — Revocation of registration if false statement made to obtain it; 149.1(6.3) — Designation as public foundation, etc; 149.1(6.4) — Registered national arts service organization treated as registered charity; 149.1(22) — Notice of refusal to register charity; 149.1(23) — Annulment of charity registration; 188.2(3)(a)(ii) — Effect of suspension of charity's receipting privileges; Canada-U.S. Tax Treaty:Art. XXI — Exempt organizations.

Notes: There are about 86,000 registered charities (RCs) in Canada; in 2017-18, CRA received 3,355 applications and registered (or re-registered) 1,585 charities (including internal divisions). Applications and approvals have dropped over the years: "Very surprising statistics", tinyurl.com/blumberg-char-stats. Information about every RC (including its information returns) is at charitydata.ca and tinyurl.com/list-cra-charities (the second link (CRA) shows only the past 5 years of data). Services and checklists for charities: tinyurl.com/charities-cra and tinyurl.com/cra-checklists. Charities Directorate Client Assistance: 1-800-267-2384 (see also CRA Directory in introductory pages).

For interesting statistics from the T3010 Registered Charity Information Return database (e.g., $284 billion total revenue; 551 employees paid $350,000 or more; $2.5b received from outside Canada) see *Blumbergs' Snapshot of the Canadian Charity Sector 2018* (Nov. 2020), tinyurl.com/char-snapshot-18. See also CRA, *Report on the Charities Program 2018 to 2020*, tinyurl.com/char-report; McRae, "A Shifting Charitable Marketplace", *The Philanthropist* (thephilanthropist.ca), April 30, 2018.

Rules governing charities: Charities are divided into three categories (see definitions in 149.1(1)): charitable organization, public foundation and private foundation (to request a change in designation use Form T2095). The rules for charities are mostly in 149.1 (conditions for revocation of registration including disbursement quota), 188.1 (penalties), 188.2 (suspension of receipting privileges), 168 and 172 (revocation procedures and appeals), 118.1 (donations by individuals — tax credit), 110.1 (donations by corporations — deduction) and Reg. 3500–3504 (receipts). Provincial legislation also governs charities, but is frequently not enforced, so CRA is the *de facto* charities regulator. See Wyatt, "It Should Have Been So Simple", chap. 4 of *Intersections and Innovations* (2021), muttart.org/intersections.

A charity is exempt from income tax: 149(1)(f). It can also obtain substantial Public Service Body rebates of GST/HST: *Excise Tax Act* s. 259 (David M. Sherman, *Practitioner's Goods and Services Tax Annotated* (Carswell)). It is also entitled a partial refund of federal excise tax on gasoline: CRA Form XE8. Most charities are eligible for the COVID-19 Canada Emergency Wage Subsidy: 125.7(1)"eligible entity"(c).

What qualifies as a charity: See Notes and Charities Policies annotations to 149.1(1)"charitable organization". Registering an unincorporated organization: see Drache, "Organizations as Charities", 19(4) *Canadian Not-for-Profit News* (Carswell) 25-26 (April 2011).

There are also statutorily deemed registered charities, which are less subject to CRA control because the CRA cannot revoke their registration. See Drache, "Deemed Charities Have Huge Advantages", 18(11) *Canadian Not-for-Profit News* 87 (Nov. 2010). A search in federal statutes (canlii.org) for "to be a registered charity" reveals about 10 such entities, including Asia-Pacific Foundation of Canada, Canadian Heritage Languages Institute and National Arts Centre. There may be others.

Under the 1976 legislation that introduced 149.1, an organization that was a registered Canadian charitable organization (as then defined) at the end of 1976 is deemed to be a registered charity unless and until its registration is revoked. See 1976-77, c. 4, s. 60(3)–(5) and ITAR 75.

Registering a new charity: Applications must be filed electronically under CHAMP (Charities IT Modernization Project); Form T2050 is no longer accepted. See tinyurl.com/apply-char; "Making sense of CRA's new online Canadian charity application system", tinyurl.com/cra-applic (Blumbergs, July 2019, 54pp); Tzannidakis, "CHAMP is Not a Winner", 22(11) *Canadian Not-for-Profit News [CNfpN]* (Carswell) 83-84 (Nov. 2019). Backdating the registration date: Arthur Drache, "CCRA Changes Timing on Charitable Registrations", 10(3) *CNfpN* (Carswell) 18-20 (March 2002). A charity registration uses the "RR" code: see Notes to 248(1)"business number". Carrying on activity before registration: Aptowitzer, "Charities in the Waiting Room", 27(12) *CNfpN* 92-93 (Dec. 2019). Mergers: Drache, "Mergers and Amalgamations of Charities", 25(3) *CNfpN* 17-19 (March 2017). Since July 2017, the CRA no longer reviews draft governing documents, but only certified ones (news release, June 29, 2017). Registration is normally retroactive to date of the application or beginning of the current fiscal year, whichever is later, but officials have discretion to use the earlier date: Policy CPS-017.

CRA's target (tinyurl.com/cra-standards) is to respond to "complete" applications within 6 months, 80% of the time; in 2019-20 it did 86.5%. See Drache, "Setting the Bar Low", 19(9) *CNfpN* 72 (Sept. 2011).

A charity issuing donation receipts to Quebec residents had to also be registered by Revenu Québec (RQ). This requirement, in *Regulation respecting the Taxation Act* s. 985.5R1(b), has been dropped.

Useful guides and checklists: Aptowitzer, *Starting and Maintaining a Charity in Canada* (charityinfo.ca, 2014, 160pp); Blumbergs *Canadian Charity Legal Checklist*, tinyurl.com/blumb-chklist; Carters *Legal Risk Management Checklist for Ontario-Based Charities*, tinyurl.com/carters-checklist; Blumbergs, "Top Canadian charity law compliance issues" (April 29, 2019), tinyurl.com/charity-compli.

Cases on CRA refusals to register: see Notes to 172(3). Cases on revocations: see Notes to 168(3).

More on charities: Kerr & Chan, "Charities and Charitable Donations", *Practical Insights*, *Taxnet Pro* Tax Disputes Centre (Dec. 2020, 85pp); Drache, Hayhoe and Stevens, *Charities Taxation, Policy and Practice* (Carswell, 10 vols. looseleaf or *Taxnet Pro* Reference Centre). See also Carter et al, *Charities Legislation and Commentary*, 2021 ed. (LexisNexis, 1266pp); back issues of Drache, *Canadian Not-for-Profit News* (Carswell, monthly); Innes & Boyle, *Charities, Non-Profits and Philanthropy under the Income Tax Act* (CCH, 2006, 244pp); Bourgeois, *The Law of Charitable and Not-for-Profit Organizations* (4th ed., LexisNexis, 2012, 640pp); Parks, "Registered Charities: A Primer", 17(4) *The Philanthropist [TPh]* (thephilanthropist.ca) 4-37 (2003); Mann & Carter, "A Comparison of the Three Categories of Registered Charities", 20(1) *TPh* 69-77 (2005). Non-tax issues: Seel, *Management of Nonprofit and Charita-*

ble *Organizations in Canada* (LexisNexis, 4th ed., 2018); Senate Special Committee, *A Roadmap to a Stronger Charitable Sector* (June 2019, 190pp), tinyurl.com/sen-charit.

The Charities Advisory Committee, which provided input to the CRA, was disbanded along with all other CRA advisory committees on Sept. 25, 2006, as part of a Conservative government cost-cutting measure.

For US charities see Notes to Canada-U.S. Treaty Art. XXI:1.

Interpretation Bulletins: IT-496R: Non-profit organizations.

Registered Charities Newsletters: 2 (revised publications and forms); 8 (changes in departmental policy on applications for re-registration); 10 (re-registration fee); 11 (renewal in the Charities Directorate; consultation on registering organizations that provide rental housing for low-income; facts about charities); 12 (promoting volunteerism: *Grand Forks Volunteer Society v. MNR*); 13 (from the Director General); 14 (registration process speeds up); 15 (facts and figures about charities and the CCRA; registered charities as internal divisions of other charities); 16 (issues: amalgamations, mergers, and consolidations); 18 (statistics on charities); 19 (new charity representative position created; facts and figures about charities and the CRA in 2003; what is the difference between a registered charity and a non-profit organization?); 20 (working outside Canada — board of directors); 21 (when is an amalgamation not an amalgamation?); 23 (facts and figures about charities and the CRA in 2004); 27, 28, 31 (facts and figures about charities and the CRA); 31 (Charities Directorate's priority for 08/09: reducing inventory); 32 (getting registered and staying registered: what we're doing to help; how to improve your application and avoid unnecessary delays); 33 (Guide RC4108 is no longer available); *Charities Connection* 4 (statistics on charities).

Charities Policies: CPS-017: Effective date of registration; CPS-028: Fundraising by registered charities. See under 149.1(1)"charitable organization" for Policies on what organizations will be registered.

Charities Guidance: See under 149.1(1)"charitable organization".

Forms: RC4106: Registered charities operating outside Canada [guide]; T2050: Application to register a charity under the ITA; T2095: Registered charities — application for re-designation; T4063: Registering a charity for income tax purposes [guide]; T4118: Auditing charities [booklet].

"registered disability savings plan" or **"RDSP"** has the same meaning as in subsection 146.4(1);

Notes: "RDSP" added by 2012 budget bill #2, effective Dec. 14, 2012. Definition added by 2007 RDSPs bill, for 2008 and later tax years.

"registered education savings plan" or **"RESP"** has the same meaning as in subsection 146.1(1);

Notes: "RESP" added by 2012 budget bill #2, effective Dec. 14, 2012.

"registered home ownership savings plan" — [Repealed under former Act]

Notes: See Notes to 146.2.

"registered investment" has the meaning assigned by subsection 204.4(1);

"registered journalism organization" means a "qualifying journalism organization" (as defined in subsection 149.1(1)) that has applied to the Minister in prescribed form for registration, that has been registered and whose registration has not been revoked;

Related Provisions: 149(1)(h) — RJO is exempt from tax; 149.1(1)"qualified donee"(b.1) — RJO qualifies for charitable donations; 149.1(14.1), (15) — Information return required and made public; 149.1(22) — Notice of refusal to register; 168(1)(c), (f) — Revocation of registration; Reg. 8901.1(e) — RJO qualifies for Canada Emergency Wage Subsidy.

Notes: Definition added by 2019 budget bill #1, effective 2020. For the list of RJOs see tinyurl.com/cra-rjos. See 149.1(1)"qualified donee" Notes re para. (b.1). For the other 2019 Budget measures supporting journalism see Notes to 248(1)"qualified Canadian journalism organization".

Forms: T624: Application to register a journalism organization under the ITA; T1000-1: Registered journalism organization information return.

"registered labour-sponsored venture capital corporation" means a corporation that was registered under subsection 204.81(1), the registration of which has not been revoked;

Notes: Definition added by 1996 Budget, effective 1996. This replaces the definition of the term in 204.8. See Notes to 127.4(5).

"registered national arts service organization", at any time, means a national arts service organization that has been registered by the Minister under subsection 149.1(6.4), which registration has not been revoked;

Notes: Definition added by 1991 technical bill, effective July 14, 1990.

"registered pension fund or plan" — [Repealed under former Act]

Notes: "Registered pension fund or plan" repealed by 1990 pension bill, effective 1986. The definition, which depended on administrative rules for registration, was replaced by "registered pension plan" (below), which is subject to the rules in 147.1.

"registered pension plan" means a pension plan (other than a pooled pension plan) that has been registered by the Minister for the purposes of this Act and whose registration has not been revoked;

Related Provisions: 56(1)(a) — Pension benefits taxable; 60.02(1)"eligible proceeds"(b) — Rollover of RPP payment to RDSP on death; 75(3)(a) — Reversionary trust rules do not apply to RPP; 108(1)"trust"(a) — "trust" does not include an RPP for certain purposes; 128.1(10)"excluded right or interest"(a)(viii) — No deemed disposition of pension rights on emigration; 147.1(2) — Registration of plan; 147.1(3) — Deemed registration; ITAR 17(8) — RPP includes approved superannuation or pension fund; Canada-U.S. Tax Treaty:Art. XVIII:7 — Deferral of US tax while income accrues in plan.

Notes: For discussion of RPPs see Notes to 147.1(2).

An employer's sale of RPP actuarial surplus is income under 56(1)(a)(i) in the CRA's view: doc 2007-025640117.

Definition amended by 2012 budget bill #2, effective Dec. 14, 2012, to exclude a PPP. "Registered pension plan" added by 1990 pension bill.

Interpretation Bulletins: IT-167R6: Registered pension plans — employee's contributions; IT-528: Transfers of funds between registered plans.

Registered Plans Frequently Asked Questions: RPFAQ-2 (RPPs), q. 22 (what is a complete application for registering a pension plan?).

Forms: T510: Application to register a pension plan.

"registered retirement income fund" or **"RRIF"** have the same meaning as "registered retirement income fund" in subsection 146.3(1);

Related Provisions: 248(1)"RRIF" — Same meaning.

Notes: Definition amended by 2011 budget bill #2, effective March 23, 2011, to apply to the term "RRIF". See 146.3 for RRIF rules.

"registered retirement savings plan" or **"RRSP"** have the same meaning as "registered retirement savings plan" in subsection 146(1);

Related Provisions: 248(1)"RRSP" — Same meaning.

Notes: Definition amended by 2011 budget bill #2, effective March 23, 2011, to apply to the term "RRSP". See Notes to 146(1)"registered retirement savings plan".

"registered securities dealer" means a person registered or licensed under the laws of a province to trade in securities, in the capacity of an agent or principal, without any restriction as to the types or kinds of securities in which that person may trade;

Related Provisions: 142.2(1)"investment dealer", 142.5 — Corporation subject to mark-to-market rules.

Notes: For interpretation of "without any restriction" see VIEWS doc 2001-0114667. Corporations registered as brokers, securities dealers or investment dealers normally fall into the definition: docs 2006-019431117, 2007-025693117.

Definition "registered securities dealer" added by 1994 technical bill, effective April 27, 1989.

"registered supplementary unemployment benefit plan" has the meaning assigned by subsection 145(1);

"regulation" means a regulation made by the Governor in Council under this Act;

Related Provisions: 65(2) — Regulations allowing resource allowances; 147.1(18) — Regulations re pension plans; 215(5) — Regulations reducing amount to be deducted or withheld; 221 — Regulations generally; 248(1) — "Prescribed".

Notes: This definition is redundant; see *Interpretation Act* 41(4). This definition does not appear in French; there is a definition "réglementaire", which is given the same meaning as "prescribed" (prescrit).

"relevant factor" means

(a) for taxation years that end before 2010, 3, and

(b) for taxation years that end after 2009, the amount determined by the formula

$$1/(A - B)$$

where

A   is the percentage set out in paragraph 123(1)(a), and

B   is the percentage that is the corporation's general rate reduction percentage (as defined by section 123.4) for the taxation year;

Notes: Since 2012, the relevant factor (see 123.4(1)) is: 1/(.38–.13) = 4.00, subject to changes in corporate tax rates. (See also 95(1)"relevant tax factor".)

Definition added by 2002-2013 technical bill, for 2003 and later tax years.

"restricted farm loss" has the meaning assigned by subsection 31(1.1);

Related Provisions: 111(1)(c) — Application of restricted farm losses; 111(9) — Restricted farm loss where taxpayer not resident in Canada.

Notes: Reference to 31(1) changed to 31(1.1) by 1994 technical bill, for tax years that end after Feb. 21, 1994.

"restricted financial institution" means

(a) a bank,

(b) a corporation licensed or otherwise authorized under the laws of Canada or a province to carry on in Canada the business of offering to the public its services as trustee,

(c) a credit union,

(d) an insurance corporation,

(e) a corporation whose principal business is the lending of money to persons with whom the corporation is dealing at arm's length or the purchasing of debt obligations issued by such persons or a combination thereof,

(e.1) a corporation described in paragraph (g) of the definition "financial institution" in subsection 181(1), or

(f) a corporation that is controlled by one or more corporations described in any of paragraphs (a) to (e.1);

Related Provisions: 131(10) — Mutual fund corporation or investment corporation — election not to be restricted financial institution; 142.2(1)"financial institution" — Definition for mark-to-market and related rules; 256(6), (6.1) — Meaning of "controlled".

Notes: The words "such persons" in para. (e) refer to "persons with whom the corporation is dealing at arm's length": VIEWS doc 2005-0131461I7. For the meaning of "principal business" in para. (e), see Notes to 20(1)(bb).

Para. (e.1) means that companies such as AVCO and GMAC, which have applied to be financial institutions for purpose of the large corporations tax (see the Schedule after s. 281), are stuck with all the negatives of being financial institutions as well.

Para. (e.1) added, and (f) amended to replace "(a) to (e)" with "(a) to (e.1)", by 1998 Budget, for tax years that begin after 1998.

I.T. Technical News: 25 (*Silicon Graphics* case — dispersed control is not control).

"retirement compensation arrangement" means a plan or arrangement under which contributions (other than payments made to acquire an interest in a life insurance policy) are made by an employer or former employer of a taxpayer, or by a person with whom the employer or former employer does not deal at arm's length, to another person or partnership (in this definition and in Part XI.3 referred to as the **"custodian"**) in connection with benefits that are to be or may be received or enjoyed by any person on, after or in contemplation of any substantial change in the services rendered by the taxpayer, the retirement of the taxpayer or the loss of an office or employment of the taxpayer, but does not include

(a) a registered pension plan,

(a.1) a pooled registered pension plan,

(b) a disability or income maintenance insurance plan under a policy with an insurance corporation,

(c) a deferred profit sharing plan,

(d) an employees profit sharing plan,

(e) a registered retirement savings plan,

(f) an employee trust,

(f.1) an employee life and health trust,

(g) a group sickness or accident insurance plan,

(h) a supplementary unemployment benefit plan,

(i) a vacation pay trust described in paragraph 149(1)(y),

(j) a plan or arrangement established for the purpose of deferring the salary or wages of a professional athlete for his[31] services as such with a team that participates in a league having regularly scheduled games (in this definition referred to as an "athlete's plan"), where

(i) the plan or arrangement would, but for paragraph (j) of the definition "salary deferral arrangement" in this subsection, be a salary deferral arrangement, and

(ii) in the case of a Canadian team, the custodian of the plan or arrangement carries on business through a fixed place of business in Canada and is licensed or otherwise authorized under the laws of Canada or a province to carry on in Canada the business of offering to the public its services as trustee,

(k) a salary deferral arrangement, whether or not deferred amounts thereunder are required to be included as benefits under paragraph 6(1)(a) in computing a taxpayer's income,

(l) a plan or arrangement (other than an athlete's plan) that is maintained primarily for the benefit of non-residents in respect of services rendered outside Canada,

(m) an insurance policy, or

(n) a prescribed plan or arrangement,

and, for the purposes of this definition, where a particular person holds property in trust under an arrangement that, if the property were held by another person, would be a retirement compensation arrangement, the arrangement shall be deemed to be a retirement compensation arrangement of which the particular person is the custodian;

Related Provisions: 8(1)(m.2) — Employee's contribution deductible; 12(11)"investment contract"(b) — Exemption from annual interest accrual rules; 20(1)(r) — Employer's contribution deductible; 75(3)(a) — Reversionary trust rules do not apply to RCA; 94(1)"exempt foreign trust"(e) — RCA excluded from non-resident trust rules; 118(8)(e), (f) — No pension income credit for income from RCA; 128.1(10)"excluded right or interest"(a)(ix) — No deemed disposition of right to RCA on emigration; 207.05(1) — Definitions of "advantage" and "prohibited investment" for RCA; 207.6(2) — Life insurance policies; 207.6(4) — Deemed contribution; 207.6(5) — Resident's arrangement; 207.61 — Tax on prohibited investment; 207.62 — Tax on "advantage" from RCA; 252.1(c), (d) — All branches of a union deemed to be a single employer.

Notes: Simplified, RCAs work as follows: Contributions to the plan bear a 50% refundable tax (207.7(1), 207.5(1)"refundable tax"(a)), which must be withheld at source (153(1)(p), Reg. 103(7)). They are not a taxable benefit to the employee: 6(1)(a)(ii). Income earned in the plan is also subject to 50% tax (207.5(1)"refundable tax"(b)); the custodian must file a return within 90 days of year-end (207.7(3)). Employer and employee contributions to the RCA are deductible (20(1)(r), 8(1)(m.2); VIEWS doc 2016-0627311E5). Employees include in income all receipts from the RCA (56(1)(x)–(z)), with tax withheld at source (153(1)(q), (r) and Reg. 106(1)). Payments to employees trigger a refund of the refundable tax to the RCA (207.7(2)).

For CRA interpretation of the definition see guide T4041 and VIEWS docs 9730067, 2002-0130701E5, 2002-0179771R3, 2004-0067871E5, 2004-0085591R3, 2004-0099631R3, 2005-0149161C6, 2005-0149261E5, 2005-0149321E5, 2005-0154911R3, 2006-0171171I7, 2006-0174121C6 q.11, 2006-0203271R3, 2007-0220151R3, 2007-0239881R3, 2007-0256141E5, 2008-0286071E5, 2009-0308771E5, 2009-0311181R3, 2009-0327021C6; 2010-0367831I7 (employer contributions to French pension funds); 2010-0388761R3; 2019-0803761R3 (supplemental plan).

A supplementary employee retirement plan (SERP — see Notes to 248(1)"salary deferral arrangement") that is funded is treated as an RCA: docs 2013-0501021E5, 2017-0720901R3.

For discussion of RCAs see Lurz, "A Practical Guide to Administering a Retirement Compensation Arrangement", 8(4) *Taxation of Executive Compensation and Retirement* (Federated Press) 211-15 (Nov. 1996); Willis Towers Watson, *Canadian Pensions and Retirement Income Planning*, 6th ed. (LexisNexis, 2017), chap. 23; Wark, "Retirement Compensation Arrangements", XXII(3) *Insurance Planning* (Federated Press) 8-13 (2017). On whether foreign plans are RCAs see Boyd, "Retirement Compensation Arrangement Rules and Foreign Pension Plans", 12(10) *TECR* 444-49 (June 2001); Rowbotham, "Canadian Tax Treatment of Foreign Pension Plan Participation", 12(4) *TECR* 351-55 (Nov. 2000); VIEWS doc 9800545.

For planning ideas with RCAs see Emes, "Tax Arbitrage and Asset Allocation Issues in RCAs", 13(2) *TECR* 15-23 (Sept. 2001); Askin & Butalia, "Leveraged RCAs", XI(4)

---

[31] Should be "the athlete's" — ed.

Insurance Planning [IP] (Federated Press) 726-30 (2005); Marino, "The New Dividend Rules and Leveraged RCAs", XIII(2) *IP* 826-29 (2007); Kahane et al, "A Fresh Look at RCAs", 61(2) *Canadian Tax Journal* 479-502 (2013); Antel, "An Owner-Manager Remuneration Perspective on IPPs and RCAs", 2018 Prairie Provinces Tax Conference (ctf.ca). In *Golini*, 2016 TCC 174 (FCA appeal discontinued A-349-16), an "RCA Optimizer Plan" that sent $6m around in circles, through offshore life insurance and a limited-recourse loan, was held not to work. (For another view of *Golini* despite G losing, see McNally, "Tax Court of Canada Upholds Offshore Insurance Structure", 9(3) *Taxes & Wealth Management* (Carswell) 14-17 (Oct. 2016).)

An RCA is not protected from seizure by creditors: see Notes to 146(4).

Para. (a.1) (added in 2012): see Bernstein, "Retirement Compensation Arrangements", 20(7) *Canadian Tax Highlights* (ctf.ca) 9-10 (July 2012).

CRA has audited RCAs extensively, challenging many as being SDAs (248(1)"salary deferral arrangement"): VIEWS doc 2011-0401941C6; Cuperfain, "Retirement Compensation Arrangements in the Cross-hairs", 17(9) *Taxation of Executive Compensation & Retirement* (Federated Press) 682-84 (May 2006); Bernstein, "RCAs Under Attack", 18(8) *Canadian Tax Highlights [CTH]* (ctf.ca) 7-8 (Aug. 2010); Chodikoff & Sharma, "RCAs and SDAs", XVII(4) *Insurance Planning* (Federated Press) 1106-09 (2011); Bernstein, "Retirement Compensation Arrangements", 209 *The Estate Planner* (CCH) 1-5 (June 2012); Nathanson, "Existing Retirement Compensation Arrangements Under Attack", 2108 *Tax Topics* (CCH) 1-3 (Aug. 2, 2012). See also Théroux, "CRA Pension Positions Change", 16(6) *CTH* 5 (June 2008) (re payment by bank under letter of credit).

Definition amended by 2012 budget bill #2 (effective Dec. 14, 2012), 2010 budget bill #2. Added in 1986, with grandfathering for a plan established before Oct. 9, 1986 or under an agreement entered into before that date.

Regulations: 6802 (prescribed plan or arrangement).

Interpretation Bulletins: IT-529: Flexible employee benefit programs.

I.T. Technical News: 34 (retirement compensation arrangements).

Advance Tax Rulings: ATR-45: Share appreciation rights plan.

Forms: T733: Application for an RCA account number; T4041: Retirement compensation arrangements guide.

"retirement income fund" has the meaning assigned by subsection 146.3(1);

"retirement savings plan" has the meaning assigned by subsection 146(1);

"retiring allowance" means an amount (other than a superannuation or pension benefit, an amount received as a consequence of the death of an employee or a benefit described in subparagraph 6(1)(a)(iv)) received

(a) on or after retirement of a taxpayer from an office or employment in recognition of the taxpayer's long service, or

(b) in respect of a loss of an office or employment of a taxpayer, whether or not received as, on account or in lieu of payment of, damages or pursuant to an order or judgment of a competent tribunal,

by the taxpayer or, after the taxpayer's death, by a dependant or a relation of the taxpayer or by the legal representative of the taxpayer;

Related Provisions: 56(1)(a)(ii) — Inclusion in income; 60(j.1) — Rollover of retiring allowance to RRSP; 60(o.1)(ii) — Deduction of legal expenses incurred to obtain retiring allowance; 128.1(10)"excluded right or interest"(d) — No deemed disposition of right to retiring allowance on emigration; 248(8) — Meaning of "consequence" of death.

Notes: See generally Income Tax Folio S2-F1-C2. A "retiring allowance" (RA) includes a wrongful dismissal award, severance pay and a termination payment, whether awarded by a court or settled privately, and even if paid by someone else: *Overin*, 1997 CarswellNat 2065 (TCC); *Putland*, 2009 TCC 349; *Naraine*, 2015 TCC 104, para. 11 (aff'd on other grounds 2016 FCA 6); VIEWS doc 2009-0348951E5 (payment by union to members). The test for an RA (per the case law and Folio S2-F1-C2 ¶2.8) is: (1) But for the loss of employment would the amount have been received? [no] *and* (2) Was the purpose of the payment to compensate a loss of employment? [yes].

However, continued payments of salary with the employee not working may be what CRA calls "salary continuation payments" (i.e., the employment contract continues) and taxed as employment income rather than RA: *Viau*, [1986] 1 C.T.C. 2570 (TCC); *Serafini*, [1989] 2 C.T.C. 2437 (TCC); *Whitecap Ltd.*, 2005 TCC 480; *Income Tax Technical News* 19; docs 2008-0285941E5, 2009-0340931I7, 2009-0350791E5; 2020-0848921E5 (shares issued as payment). (A non-resident receiving such payments is taxed under s. 115 only on days actually in Canada: *Nonis*, 2021 TCC 31.) If pension benefits continue to accrue, CRA considers that the payments are employment income (salary continuation): 2013-0475991I7; but not if salary stopped, a RA was paid, and then pension accrual somehow started again: 2015-0590411I7. A lump sum for lost wages paid to an employee ordered reinstated is taxable as employment income: 2011-

0407421E5. A RA can be paid many years after termination: 2003-0028025. A payment of accumulated sick time 5 months before retirement is not a RA: 2009-0349031E5.

Timing: A RA is taxable in the year(s) received: 56(1)(a)(ii), VIEWS doc 2019-0832241E5. If an advance is paid and thought to be a loan so that the RA is not taxable until later, CRA would likely apply the policy and case law that apply to an advance of wages: see 5(1) Notes at "*Received*:"

Withholding of tax: For a Canadian resident, RA is subject to lump sum source withholding (153(1)(c)) at 10-30% (30% once over $15,000) (21-35% in Quebec): Reg. 103(4), (6)(e)). The RA includes any non-cash benefits (e.g., use of company car); or shares issued: 2020-0848921E5, but if no cash is being paid no withholding is required: 2010-0385831E5. For a non-resident, 25% must be withheld by the payor (212(1)(j.1)); this is a tax, not a source deduction.

Reporting: A RA is reported by the employer (Reg. 200) on a T4 (boxes 66-67) rather than a T4A. It should be reported based on the province where the employee is resident: see Reg. 100(4) Notes.

Rolling into RRSP: to the extent the taxpayer has unused RRSP contribution room, part of the RA can be transferred to an RRSP, with a 146(5) deduction to offset the 56(1)(a)(ii) income inclusion. A further $2,000 per year (or part year) of employment before 1996 ($3,500 in some cases) can be transferred and deducted under 60(j.1).

If an amount is not a RA, it may be taxable as employment income under 5(1), 6(1)(a) or 6(3)(b). It may be non-taxable as damages for mental distress or harassment (though CRA in Income Tax Folio S2-F1-C2 ¶2.14-2.21 is restrictive) or to reimburse the taxpayer for losses: *Forest*, 2007 FCA 362 (amount exceeding ordinary severance was non-taxable); *Bédard*, [1991] 1 C.T.C. 2323 (TCC); *Mendes-Roux*, [1998] 2 C.T.C. 2274 (TCC); *Saardi*, [1999] 4 C.T.C. 2488 (TCC); *Fournier*, [1999] 4 C.T.C. 2247 (TCC); *Dunphy*, 2009 TCC 619 (Court allocated $11,000 of $45,000 settlement to human rights complaint); *Rae*, 2010 TCC 130 ($115,000 of $160,000 settlement was for claim under whistleblower protection legislation); *Abenaim*, 2017 TCC 223 (settlement included moral damages for A's humiliation on being fired twice from business he built, and CBCA oppression remedy). However, there must be clear intention that the payment is for personal injury, in the settlement agreement (*Fawkes*, 2004 TCC 653; *Guay*, 2006 TCC 84; *Grant*, 2008 TCC 163; *Tremblay*, 2009 TCC 437 [though in *Abenaim* there was not]) or Court judgment (*Tourigny*, 2006 TCC 28). CRA accepts that a human rights violation award is tax-free within limits (Folio S2-F1-C2 ¶2.18; VIEWS docs 2003-0014105, 2004-0067181I7, 2004-0079731E5, 2005-0126912E5, 2008-0292081R3, 2009-0311241E5, 2009-0345611E5, 2013-0477821I7), but says that aggravated damages for mental anguish caused by wrongful dismissal are a RA (2002-0172217, 2006-0204971I7), and that "only where an award of damages can be traced to events or actions unrelated to or separate from the loss of employment will damages be treated as non-taxable" (2006-0195221E5, 2007-025538I17, 2011-0398651E3, 2011-0403611E5, 2011-0423761E5, 2011-0428651E5, 2011-0431131E5); e.g., if the taxpayer "has suffered a personal injury before or after the loss of his job" (2010-0389701E5), or a "settlement for harassment received during employment" (2010-0391431E5). Thus, a payment under the *Canadian Human Rights Act* by a former employer for loss of salary is a RA: 2008-029962117. In 2008-0292081R3, pay equity payments to settle a human rights complaint were non-taxable. In 2018-0748731E5, damages under the *Labour Relations Act* for violating an employee's rights (unfair labour practices) were likely non-taxable.

Settlement of grievance: see VIEWS docs 2007-0249291E5 (payment from union to member as compensation for losing right to have grievance adjudicated: no RA); 2009-0322501E5 (settlement of grievance re life insurance benefits, to cover financial loss, may be non-taxable); 2011-0393351E5 (settlement to resolve grievances is RA); 2011-0406061E5 (compensation for waiving right to re-employment on a grievance is RA); 2014-0521901E5 (settlement of grievance is normally taxable, but where the parties agree the payment is for "moral damages" and unrelated to loss of employment, it is not); 2017-0685961E5 (settlement of grievance re cancellation of post-retirement benefits: likely partly taxable under 6(3) and partly tax-free).

Sick leave: see VIEWS doc 2009-0307791E5 (payout of unused sick time is employment income, not RA), but *contra* see 2013-0498251E5 (one-time payment for unused sick leave credits on retirement is RA), and 2017-0714931I7 (payment for sick leave credits on retirement is partly RA; only the portion over 20 days which would be paid out annually anyway is employment income).

CRA notes "In most cases, the parties to the settlement are in the best position to know what the settlement amount was for" (2013-0492281M4, 2014-0521901E5) or that the employer is in the best position to make the determination (2013-0487531M4, 2013-0479461E5), so the wording of a settlement agreement is often crucial to determining the status of the payment.

In *Newcombe*, 2013 FC 955, the Court ruled that a lump sum paid on termination "was not remuneration, but rather liquidated damages" and thus a T4 was "issued in error" (paras. 25-26), but the Court did not properly consider the definition of RA. (It denied a remedy anyway as the taxpayer should have appealed to the TCC.)

In *Ahmad*, [2002] 4 C.T.C. 2497 (TCC), damages, paid by the major customer of A's employer (AECL) for inducing AECL to demote A, were held not to be a RA and thus not taxable, since they were for the tort of inducing breach of contract.

Damages for breaching an employment contract before it begins are not taxable: *Schwartz*, [1996] 1 C.T.C. 303 (SCC); *Schewe*, 2010 TCC 47; *Robinson*, 2010 QCCQ 6481 (under similar but not identical Quebec rule); VIEWS docs 2005-0135831E5,

2011-042940I7. When the employee was fired after working for one day, the damages were a RA: *Girard*, 2017 QCCQ 3245 (under the Quebec rule).

In *Bouchard*, 2008 TCC 462, an attempt by investment advisers to report payments to them on retirement as capital gains was rejected, as these were RAs.

A retired accounting partner's 96(1.1) income could not be a RA since he had not been an employee: *Freitas*, 2017 TCC 46 (rev'd on other grounds 2018 FCA 110).

For more detail see David M. Sherman, "Tax Considerations", Chapter 8 of Harris, *Wrongful Dismissal* (Carswell, looseleaf); Julie Lee, "An Update on Retiring Allowances", 15(2) *Taxation of Executive Compensation* & Retirement (Federated Press) 322-25 (Sept. 2003); Pooja Samtani, "Surviving Severance: the Taxation of Retiring Allowances and Other Termination Payments", 19(5) *TECR* 923-34 (Dec./Jan. 2008); Phillip Peters, Don Sommerfeldt & Andrea Jarman, "Wrongful Dismissal and Tortious Damages", 21(8) *TECR* 1267-77 (April 2010).

See also VIEWS docs 2000-0041303, 2003-0028365, 2004-0065551E5 and 2006-0202791E5 (choosing lump sum vs. instalment option); 2003-0050451E5 (accruing pension benefits suggests payment is employment income, not RA); 2003-0051471R3; 2005-0135881E5, 2014-0565251E5 (arbitration award considered RA); 2005-0155577I7 (union's voluntary gift to terminated employee not RA); 2006-0196531E5 (portion of settlement for breach of contractual right to acquire employer's shares is RA); 2007-0238461E5 (payment to public servant under Executive Employment Transition Policy is RA); 2007-0246781R3 (phantom stock plan: no RA); 2009-0342381E5 (arranging to continue to work part-time will invalidate RA status); 2010-035678117 (compensation in lieu of notice under Quebec *Civil Code* art. 2091 is RA); 2010-0379831E5 (payment to terminated employee to obtain general release from future liability is RA); 2010-0362821E5 (rehiring employee does not invalidate RA if there was no arrangement or assurance the employee would be rehired — see *Income Tax Technical News* 7); 2010-0373341C6 (reimbursement of medical expenses in settlement is not exempt under 6(1)(a)(i) or (iv)); 2011-0421931E5 (payment for employee to relinquish right to reinstatement is RA); 2012-0468971E5 (court-ordered job search and job relocation fee paid to settle wrongful dismissal suit is RA); 2015-0599581E5 (proceeds of selling shares back to employer on termination could be RA); 2020-0850081R3 (periodic payments under employment agreement, following termination, are RA).

For SERPs, see Notes to 248(1)"salary deferral arrangement".

Damages for wrongful dismissal must take into account tax savings from employment being in a low-tax jurisdiction: *Schram v. Nunavut*, 2018 NBCA 41.

Reference to 6(1)(a)(iv) added by 1989 Budget, effective 1988.

Income Tax Folios: S2-F1-C2: Retiring allowances [replaces IT-337R4].

Interpretation Bulletins: IT-99R5: Legal and accounting fees; IT-365R2: Damages, settlements and similar receipts; IT-508R: Death benefits.

I.T. Technical News: 7 (retiring allowances); 19 (Retiring allowances — clarification to Interpretation Bulletin IT-337R3); 20 (retiring allowances — effect of re-employment or employment with affiliate).

Application Policies: SR&ED 2004-01: Retiring allowance.

Advance Tax Rulings: ATR-12: Retiring allowance.

"SIFT partnership" has the meaning assigned by section 197;

Related Provisions: 96(1.11) — Effect of SIFT partnership distributions on partners; 197 — Part IX.1 on distributions by SIFT partnership; 197(8) — Application of definition from 2006–2010; Reg. 229 — SIFT partnership required to file information return.

Notes: Definition added by 2007 budget bill #1, effective Oct. 31, 2006 (but see 197(8) for the actual effective dates). See Notes to 104(16).

"SIFT partnership balance-due day", in respect of a taxation year of a SIFT partnership, means the day on or before which the partnership is required to file a return for the taxation year under section 229 of the *Income Tax Regulations*;

Notes: Definition added by 2007 budget bill #1, effective Oct. 31, 2006.

"SIFT trust" has the meaning assigned by section 122.1;

Related Provisions: 104(16) — Treatment of SIFT trust distributions; 122.1(2) — Application of definition from 2006–2010.

Notes: Definition added by 2007 budget bill #1, effective Oct. 31, 2006 (but see 122.1(2) for the actual effective dates). See Notes to 104(16).

"SIFT trust wind-up event" means a distribution by a particular trust resident in Canada of property to a taxpayer in respect of which the following conditions are met:

(a) the distribution occurs before 2013,

(b) there is a resulting disposition of all of the taxpayer's interest as a beneficiary under the particular trust,

(c) the particular trust is

(i) a SIFT wind-up entity,

(ii) a trust whose only beneficiary throughout the period (referred to in this definition as the "qualifying period") that be-

gins on July 14, 2008 and that ends at the time of the distribution is another trust that throughout the qualifying period

(A) is resident in Canada, and

(B) is a SIFT wind-up entity or a trust described by this subparagraph, or

(iii) a trust whose only beneficiary at the time of distribution is another trust that throughout the qualifying period

(A) is resident in Canada,

(B) is a SIFT wind-up entity or a trust described by subparagraph (ii), and

(C) is a majority interest beneficiary (within the meaning that would be assigned by section 251.1 if the references in the definition "majority interest beneficiary" in subsection 251.1(3) to "50%" were read as references to "25%") of the particular trust,

(d) the particular trust ceases to exist immediately after the distribution or immediately after the last of a series of SIFT trust wind-up events (determined without reference to this paragraph) of the particular trust that includes the distribution, and

(e) the property was not acquired by the particular trust as a result of a transfer or an exchange

(i) that is

(A) a "qualifying exchange" as defined in subsection 132.2(1) or a "qualifying disposition" as defined in subsection 107.4(1),

(B) made after February 2, 2009, and

(C) from any person other than a SIFT wind-up entity, or

(ii) to which any of sections 51, 85, 85.1, 86, 87, 88, 107.4 or 132.2 applies, of another property acquired as a result of a transfer or an exchange described by subparagraph (i) or this subparagraph;

Related Provisions: 80.01(5.1) — Debt settlement on wind-up event; 107(2) — Exclusion from regular trust rollout; 107(3), (3.1) — Rollout of assets to beneficiaries; 256(7)(f) — Acquiring control of corporation.

Notes: See Notes to 85.1(8). 248(1)"SIFT trust wind-up event" added by 2008 budget bill #2, effective Dec. 20, 2007.

"SIFT wind-up corporation", in respect of a SIFT wind-up entity, means at any particular time a corporation

(a) that, at any time that is after July 13, 2008 and before the earlier of the particular time and January 1, 2013, owns all of the equity in the SIFT wind-up entity, or

(b) shares of the capital stock of which are at or before the particular time distributed on a SIFT trust wind-up event of the SIFT wind-up entity;

Related Provisions: 54"superficial loss"(j) — Deemed identical property for superficial-loss rule; 80.01(5.1) — Debt settlement on wind-up event; 87(2)(s.1) — Amalgamation — continuing corporation; 107(2) — Exclusion from regular trust rollout; 107(3), (3.1) — Rollout of assets to beneficiaries; 256(7)(f) — Acquiring control of corporation. See also under 248(1)"SIFT wind-up entity".

Notes: 248(1)"SIFT wind-up corporation" added by 2008 budget bill #2, effective Dec. 20, 2007. See Notes to 85.1(8).

"SIFT wind-up entity" means a trust or partnership that at any time in the period that began on October 31, 2006 and that ends on July 14, 2008 is

(a) a SIFT trust (determined without reference to subsection 122.1(2)),

(b) a SIFT partnership (determined without reference to subsection 197(8)), or

(c) a real estate investment trust (as defined in subsection 122.1(1));

Related Provisions: 7(1.4)(b)(vi) — Exchange of employee stock options; 54"superficial loss"(j) — Deemed identical property for superficial-loss rule; 80.01(5.1) — Deemed settlement of debt; 85.1(7), (8) — Rollover on exchange for shares before 2013; 88.1 — Wind-up into corporation before 2013; 107(3.1) — Rollout of assets to beneficiaries before 2013.

"SIFT wind-up entity equity", or equity in a SIFT wind-up entity, means

(a) if the SIFT wind-up entity is a trust, a capital interest (determined without reference to subsection (25)) in the trust, and

(b) if the SIFT wind-up entity is a partnership, an interest as a member of the partnership where, by operation of any law governing the arrangement in respect of the partnership, the liability of the member as a member of the partnership is limited,

except that if all of the interests described in paragraph (a) or (b), as the case may be, in the SIFT wind-up entity are described by reference to units, it means the part of the interest represented by such a unit;

Related Provisions: 116(6)(b)(ii)(B) — No section 116 certificate needed on disposition by non-resident. See also under 248(1)"SIFT wind-up entity".

Notes: 248(1)"SIFT wind-up entity equity" added by 2008 budget bill #2, effective Dec. 20, 2007. See Notes to 85.1(8).

"salary deferral arrangement", in respect of a taxpayer, means a

plan or arrangement, whether funded or not, under which any person has a right in a taxation year to receive an amount after the year where it is reasonable to consider that one of the main purposes for the creation or existence of the right is to postpone tax payable under this Act by the taxpayer in respect of an amount that is, or is on account or in lieu of, salary or wages of the taxpayer for services rendered by the taxpayer in the year or a preceding taxation year (including such a right that is subject to one or more conditions unless there is a substantial risk that any one of those conditions will not be satisfied), but does not include

(a) a registered pension plan,

(a.1) a pooled registered pension plan,

(b) a disability or income maintenance insurance plan under a policy with an insurance corporation,

(c) a deferred profit sharing plan,

(d) an employees profit sharing plan,

(e) an employee trust,

(e.1) an employee life and health trust,

(f) a group sickness or accident insurance plan,

(g) a supplementary unemployment benefit plan,

(h) a vacation pay trust described in paragraph 149(1)(y),

(i) a plan or arrangement the sole purpose of which is to provide education or training for employees of an employer to improve their work or work-related skills and abilities,

(j) a plan or arrangement established for the purpose of deferring the salary or wages of a professional athlete for the services of the athlete as such with a team that participates in a league having regularly scheduled games,

(k) a plan or arrangement under which a taxpayer has a right to receive a bonus or similar payment in respect of services rendered by the taxpayer in a taxation year to be paid within 3 years following the end of the year, or

(l) a prescribed plan or arrangement;

Related Provisions: 6(1)(i), 56(1)(w) — Income inclusion on payment from SDA; 6(11)–(14) — Income inclusion on having right to payment from SDA; 12(11) — Definitions — "investment contract"; 128.1(10)"excluded right or interest"(a)(vii), (b) — No deemed disposition of right to SDA on emigration.

Notes: A right to deferred income from an SDA is taxable currently under 6(11)-(14), and otherwise-untaxed payments from an SDA are taxable under 6(1)(i) and 56(1)(w). For discussion of SDAs see Murrill, "Taxation of Short-to-Medium-Term Cash Incentives in Canada", 9(7) *Taxation of Executive Compensation & Retirement [TECR]* (Federated Press) 103-115 (March 1998); Begun, "Employer Exposure for Unremitted Amounts", XXVI(3) *TECR* 2-4 (2018); Chodikoff & Sharma, "RCAs and SDAs", XVII(4) *Insurance Planning [IP]* (Federated Press) 1106-09 (2011); Fremont, "Supplemental Retirement Plans", XXVII(1) *IP* 4-8 (2019); Desroches & Vaillancourt, "Stock Options and Other Equity-Based Incentive Plans", 2019 Cdn Tax Foundation conference report at 15:22-37.

For "one of the main purposes" in the opening words, see Notes to 83(2.1).

For interpretation of para. (k), requiring a bonus to be actually paid within 3 years, see VIEWS docs 2003-0035115, 2003-0031811R3, 2004-0088601R3, 2004-0101501R3, 2005-0141651R3, 2005-0144541R3, 2005-0149261E5, 2005-0149321E5, 2007-026329117, 2008-029767117, 2010-0387161E5, 2016-0652801C6 [2016 APFF q.4]; 2020-086483117 (equity award RSU plan and recharge agreement). Rulings that an arrangement is not an SDA: 2004-0085591R3, 2004-0096311R3, 2005-0118901R3, 2005-0154911R3, 2006-0201541R3; 2010-0376531R3 (DSU under Reg. 6801(d) takes priority). However, since Nov. 2015 CRA no longer issues favourable rulings on conversion to a DSU plan, as they do not satisfy the conditions of para. (k) or Reg. 6801(d): 2015-0610801C6 [2015 CTF q.2]. Previous rulings will be revoked, but units in the plan prior to revocation will be allowed to be converted.

For para. (l), including sabbatical arrangements and deferred share unit plans, see Notes to Reg. 6801.

For SERPs (supplemental employee retirement plans) see VIEWS docs 9310640, 9716483, 9733923, 9922793, 2001-0072795, 2001-0096897, 2003-0042843, 2004-0075681R3, 2005-0149261E5, 2006-0203271R3, 2007-0229361C6 (factors considered in determining whether a SERP is an SDA), 2008-0270531C6 (2008 CALU q.5), 2008-0284481C6 ("unreasonable" superannuation or pension benefits), 2009-0306371E5 (determination of SERP benefits); 2013-0501021E5 (payments can qualify for 60.03 pension splitting); 2014-0547271E5 (lump sum from SERP can qualify for averaging under 110.2 and 120.31); 2016-0655071R3 (corp reorg involving transfer of SERP does not create an RCA); 2017-0692331C6 [CLHIA 2017 q.3] (post-retirement benefits paid directly by employer to retired employees under the plan); 2019-0817751R3 (proposed SERP will not be SDA or RCA); Lee, "Supplemental Executive Retirement Plans and the Risk of Salary Deferral Arrangement Treatment", 18(8) *Taxation of Executive Compensation & Retirement* (Federated Press) 815-21 (April 2007); Waldock, "Supplementary Executive Retirement Plans", 19(8) *TECR* 979-86 (April 2008) and 20(1) 1019-25 (July/Aug. 2008); Gascho, "Supplementary Employee Retirement Plans in a Troubled Economy", 20(3) *TECR* 1050-54 (Oct. 2008) and "Pension Standards Reform and SERPs", 22(3) 1337-39 (Oct. 2010); Winfield, "COVID-19 and Non-Equity Pension and Benefits Arrangements for Executives", XXVIII(1) *TECR* 2-7 (2020); and 8(1)(m.2) Notes.

See also docs 2007-025420117 (arrangement is SDA, not RA, and 6(12) applies); 2008-029784117 (employee asks employer to defer payment of bonus); 2009-0311941R3 (cash-out rights in employee stock option plan are not SDA); 2009-0352241R3 (arrangement is SDA); 2009-0311181R3 (funding of group health insurance arrangement is not SDA); 2012-0435221R3 and 2014-0546131R3 (Share Appreciation Rights (SAR) plans are not SDAs); 2014-0526941E5 (restricted stock unit plan — whether cash dividend equivalents cause a problem); 2015-0586831R3 (class action settlement with employees re pension plan funding is not SDA); 2017-0737571E5 (SAR plan providing for dividend equivalents); 2018-0740741E5 (accrued bonus and vacation pay converted to entitlements: plans are likely SDAs); 2020-084196117, 2020-085028117, 2020-0861061C6 [2020 CTF q.8], 2020-0864341C6 [2020 APFF Financial q.7] (formula-based incentive plans may be SDAs; various clarifications) [Campbell, "CRA Clarifies Position Relating to SARs", 17(5) *Tax Hyperion* (Carswell) 1-3 (Sept-Oct 2020); Firman, "Revenue Killed the Formula SAR", XXVIII(3) *TECR* 2-7 (2020)].

Definition amended by 2012 budget bill #2 (effective Dec. 14, 2012, adding (a.1)), 2010 budget bill #2 (adding (e.1)).

Regulations: 6801 (prescribed plan or arrangement).

Interpretation Bulletins: IT-109R2: Unpaid amounts; IT-168R3: Athletes and players employed by football, hockey and similar clubs; IT-529: Flexible employee benefit programs.

I.T. Technical News: 7 (salary deferral arrangement — paragraph (k)).

Advance Tax Rulings: ATR-39: Self-funded leave of absence; ATR-45: Share appreciation rights plan; ATR-64: Phantom stock award plan.

"salary or wages", except in sections 5 and 63 and the definition

"death benefit" in this subsection, means the income of a taxpayer from an office or employment as computed under Subdivision A of Division B of Part I and includes all fees received for services not rendered in the course of the taxpayer's business but does not include superannuation or pension benefits or retiring allowances;

Related Provisions: Reg. 2900(9) — Exclusions from "salary or wages" for SR&ED prescribed proxy amount.

Notes: "Subdivision a of Division B of Part I" is ss. 5-8 (employment income).

This definition applies to "salary, wages or other remuneration" in 153(1)(a), since that really means "salary *or* wages or...": *B. Boop Productions*, 2000 CarswellNat 2268 (TCC), para. 10; VIEWS doc 2017-0735481E5 (answering the author). CRA treats taxable employment benefits (ss. 6-7) as subject to withholding: tinyurl.com/cra-ben-whold; Guide T4001.

Lagace, 2019 TCC 249, para. 9, says this definition applies to "salary" in 8(1)(i)(ii). It is unclear whether this is correct, in the author's view.

Interpretation Bulletins: IT-99R5: Legal and accounting fees.

Application Policies: SR&ED 96-06: Directly undertaking, supervising or supporting v. "directly engaged" SR&ED salary and wages.

Provincial Income Allocation Newsletters: 4 (salaries and wages — inclusion of taxable benefits).

"scientific research and experimental development" means systematic investigation or search that is carried out in a field of science or technology by means of experiment or analysis and that is

(a) basic research, namely, work undertaken for the advancement of scientific knowledge without a specific practical application in view,

(b) applied research, namely, work undertaken for the advancement of scientific knowledge with a specific practical application in view, or

(c) experimental development, namely, work undertaken for the purpose of achieving technological advancement for the purpose of creating new, or improving existing, materials, devices, products or processes, including incremental improvements thereto,

and, in applying this definition in respect of a taxpayer, includes

(d) work undertaken by or on behalf of the taxpayer with respect to engineering, design, operations research, mathematical analysis, computer programming, data collection, testing or psychological research, where the work is commensurate with the needs, and directly in support, of work described in paragraph (a), (b), or (c) that is undertaken in Canada by or on behalf of the taxpayer,

but does not include work with respect to

(e) market research or sales promotion,

(f) quality control or routine testing of materials, devices, products or processes,

(g) research in the social sciences or the humanities,

(h) prospecting, exploring or drilling for, or producing, minerals, petroleum or natural gas,

(i) the commercial production of a new or improved material, device or product or the commercial use of a new or improved process,

(j) style changes, or

(k) routine data collection;

Related Provisions: 37(1) — SR&ED expenditures deductible; 37(3) — CRA may obtain advice from certain sources as to whether an activity is SR&ED; 37(8) — Amounts deemed not to be expenditures on SR&ED; 37(13) — Linked work deemed to be SR&ED; 127(9)"SR&ED qualified expenditure pool" — Investment tax credits.

Notes: For discussion of the tax incentives for SR&ED, see Notes to 127(9)"SR&ED qualified expenditure pool". For filing claims, see Notes to 37(11).

SR&ED includes not only lab research but also "shop floor" R&D. SR&ED can be for software developed for in-house use as well as for sale.

Para. (d): "engineering" need not be performed by professional engineers but can include other scientists: May 2009 ICAA roundtable (tinyurl.com/cra-abtax) q.21.

Para. (h) excludes mining expenses that qualify as Canadian exploration expenses, whether or not renounced to flow-through shareholders: VIEWS doc 2013-0512191E5.

Para. (i) was interpreted in *Feedlot Health*, 2015 TCC 32, paras. 79-80, to apply to commercial use by a third party as well as by the taxpayer.

An SR&ED claim requires "an accurate record of hours worked" (not an estimate): *Hypercube*, 2015 TCC 65, para. 48; *Concept Danat*, 2019 TCC 32, para. 53.

The criteria for determining whether an activity is SR&ED are in *Northwest Hydraulic*, [1998] 3 C.T.C. 2520 (TCC) and *C.W. Agencies*, 2001 FCA 393, para. 17: (1) Was there technological risk or uncertainty which could not be removed by routine engineering or standard procedures? (2) Did the person formulate hypotheses specifically aimed at reducing or eliminating that uncertainty? (3) Did the procedure adopted accord with the total discipline of the scientific method including formulation, testing and modification of hypotheses? (4) Did the process result in technological advancement? (5) Was a detailed record of the hypotheses tested and results kept as work progressed? Note that there cannot be technological *advancement* unless there is technological *uncertainty* (**"TU"**): *Abeilles Services*, 2014 TCC 313, para. 142.

For CRA policy see *Eligibility of Work for SR&ED Investment Tax Credits Policy* (Dec. 2014), which provides detail on the above 5 questions; and tinyurl.com/cra-sred-slides (Jan. 2017 webinar, 60 slides). See also IC 86-4R3 §2.10.2. *Murray Arlin Dentistry*, 2012 TCC 133 noted CRA's view that there was "insufficient evidence of systematic investigation because hypotheses were not determined prior to the data collection. This position is very narrow and I am reluctant to agree with it": para. 20. On claims by physicians and their corporations for medical research, see tinyurl.com/sred-med.

SR&ED can be proven by oral evidence: "the Act and the Regulations do not require that such written reports be produced in order for a taxpayer to qualify for the deduction of such expenditures": *116736 Canada*, [1998] 3 C.T.C. 2679 (TCC), para. 41;

ACSIS EHR, 2015 TCC 263, para. 39. See also MacDonald & Robinson, "Supporting SR & ED Claims", 6(4) *Tax for the Owner-Manager* (ctf.ca) 8-9 (Oct. 2006). *Joel Theatrical*, 2017 TCC 6, para. 12 implies that SR&ED evidence should come from "a scientist or an engineer", but presumably such person should not always need to testify if the evidence is reliable.

For cases **finding SR&ED** see *Rainbow Pipe Line*, [2000] 1 C.T.C. 2091 (TCC) (aff'd on other grounds 2002 FCA 259) (determining cause of pipeline "stress corrosion cracking"); *Hun-Medipharma*, [1999] 1 C.T.C. 2800 (TCC) (review of literature without doing clinical trials of drug was "systematic investigation"); *1726437 Ontario [AirMax]*, 2012 TCC 276 (improving HVAC system qualified); *Abeilles Services*, 2014 TCC 313 (technological advancement (TA) objective (including increased productivity in assembling dryers) was met even if advancement only partly achieved; there was TU; and project considered as a whole rather than each activity: para. 153); *6379249 Canada*, 2015 TCC 77 (too-early commercial release of printer with paper curling problems did not mean TU had been resolved; the evidence proved TU, systematic investigation and TA even if the improvement was "slight" (para. 100)); *ACSIS EHR* (above) (health information system for Belize where Internet was unreliable and TU solved with multi-write database; for a small company, "global overview" of software project rather than "minute dissecting" of the R&D work: para. 42); *Formadrain*, 2017 TCC 42 (improving process for repairing underground drains: engineers were systematic and there was TU); *A & D Precision*, 2019 TCC 48 (double wheel roll grinding machine; full spectrum versatile horizontal lathes); *CRL Engineering*, 2019 TCC 65 (Ph.Ds developing system to provide real-time on-board status for public transit buses); *Béton Mobile*, 2019 TCC 278 (concrete mixing projects: 6 of 14 projects had TU); *Allegro Wireless*, 2021 TCC 27 (software development for hand-held devices).

For cases **finding no SR&ED** see *Beaudry*, 2008 TCC 17, varied in *Romar*, 2009 FCA 48 (no real scientific project); *Jentel Manufacturing*, 2011 FCA 355 (work on "Multi-Bins" was routine engineering using well-known manufacturing processes, and there was no technological risk or TU); *R&D Pro-Innovation*, 2016 FCA 152 (chocolate spread "cold-tempering" was routine engineering: risk and TU unproven); *Kam-Press*, 2021 FCA 88 (memorial niche for funeral urns: trial and error, no TU); *Tacto Neuro Sensory*, 2004 TCC 341 (no TU); *Zeuter Development*, 2006 TCC 597 (TU not proven); *Logitek Technology*, 2008 TCC 145 (insufficient evidence re research done); *Advanced Agricultural Testing*, 2009 TCC 190 (testing effects of hormone implants in cattle growth was routine data collection); *Soneil International*, 2011 TCC 391 (insufficient evidence that work on battery chargers had TU or "required more than routine engineering or standard procedures"); *Murray Arlin Dentistry*, 2012 TCC 133 (insufficient evidence of research); *Hypercube*, 2015 TCC 65 (developing software to find defects in websites was done using standard techniques: TU unproven); *Highweb & Page*, 2015 TCC 137 (software development: no TU, and no clear hypothesis or technical investigations; insufficient record-keeping); *2037625 Ontario [ITC Invoice to Cash]*, 2015 TCC 269 (factoring and faxing software: no TU as solutions were "standard" and "routine"); *Emotion Picture Studios*, 2015 TCC 323 (identifying Google or Yahoo search algorithms was complicated but routine engineering: no TU); *Novalia*, 2016 TCC 81 (wind turbine work: none of the conditions are met); *Joel Theatrical*, 2017 TCC 6 (theatre curtain control work was routine engineering); *Life Choice*, 2017 TCC 21 (FCA appeal discontinued A-82-17) (natural health products: no systematic testing); *Robotx*, 2017 TCC 73 (safety devices: no TU); *Flavor Net*, 2017 TCC 179 (dissolving plant sterols and developing hot fill process for energy drinks: technical challenges but no TU); *Mac & Mac Hydrodemolition*, 2017 TCC 256 (removing lining from pipes transporting bitumen: testing notes were vague and did not allow experiments to be replicated); *Dock Edge*, 2019 TCC 11 (products for boat docks: no detailed records kept, and no expert or other evidence of TU); *Concept Danat*, 2019 TCC 32 (laser-printing clothing: no TU); *A & D Precision*, 2019 TCC 48 (full spectrum versatile horizontal lathes: first one qualified, but no TU in developing smaller versions); *Laforest Marketing*, 2019 TCC 45 (Spray Catcher water mist collector: no TU as techniques used were known to the industry); *Exxonmobil*, 2019 TCC 108 (purpose of drilling well was to find oil, not to validate methodology for reservoir connectivity); *Clevor Technologies*, 2019 TCC 166 (project management software: routine engineering, no TU); *Béton Mobile*, 2019 TCC 278 (concrete mixing projects: 8 of 14 projects had no TU); *National R&D*, 2020 TCC 47 (under appeal to FCA) (project tracking system to track SR&ED claims: TU but no "scientific method" or systematic testing); *Indusol*, 2020 TCC 103 (marine navigation information system: no systematic testing); *6398316 Canada*, 2021 TCC 17 (building energy-efficient house: no systematic testing, and reducing cost is not TU); *Logix Data*, 2021 TCC 36 (under appeal to FCA) (solar panels as roof shingles: no TU, no systematic testing); *WRD Borger Construction*, 2021 TCC 40 (blocking water flow in culvert: solved by trial-and-error, not scientific hypothesis).

Once the appellant has provided all facts, it need not specify at the discovery stage its precise position as to how it fits the criteria: *A & D Precision*, 2016 CarswellNat 2227 (TCC). Whether work is SR&ED if others have achieved the same advancement is a question requiring a trial, not a Rule 58 (see 174(1) Notes) hearing: *Lehigh Hanson*, 2017 TCC 205. It is a question of law; expert witnesses can assist the Court but are not determinative or necessary: *RIS-Christie*, 1998 CarswellNat 2485 (FCA), para. 12; *Kam-Press*, 2019 TCC 246, para. 25 (aff'd on other grounds 2021 FCA 88).

See also Hutson, "Finding SR&ED in the Unlikeliest of Places", 2004 Ontario Tax Conference (ctf.ca), 7:1-14; Brown & Thijs, "Experimental Production in Oil & Gas and Mining", VII(1) *Resource Sector Taxation* (Federated Press) 486-92 (2009); Machado, "Business Context in SR&ED", 19(5) *Canadian Tax Highlights* (ctf.ca) [*CTH*] 8-9 (May 2011); Hearn et al., "Jentel" [comment on TCC decision], 59(4) *Canadian Tax Journal* 816-21 (2011); Doobay, "SR & ED Technical Uncertainty", 20(3) *CTH* 8-9 (March 2012) and "The SR&ED Paradox", *Privately Held Companies and*

Taxes (*Taxnet Pro*), Dec. 2012, pp. 13-17; Fournier & McKindsey, "Recent Developments in SR&ED Tax Litigation", 2015 Cdn Tax Foundation conference report, 37:1-34; Adlington, "SR&ED — Proving Technological Risk", 15(1) *Tax Hyperion* (Carswell) 1-4 (Jan-Feb 2018); Katlai, "Documentation and Evidence Proving SR&ED", 27(7) *CTH* 9-10 (July 2019) and "Summary of Notable SR&ED cases by year — 1991 to 2019", *Taxnet Pro* Tax Disputes Centre (2020, 22pp). See also *SR&ED Activity Case Finder* at bluejlegal.com.

Some 8,000 taxpayers invested in the 1980s in Quebec partnerships that were found not to have done any SR&ED, so deductions were disallowed: *Brillon*, 2006 TCC 76; *Amar*, 2006 TCC 420; *Rouleau*, 2008 FCA 288; *Moledina*, 2007 TCC 354; *St-Laurent [Simard]*, 2009 FCA 379; *Konda*, 2007 TCC 648; *Beauregard*, 2008 TCC 224; *Foster*, 2007 TCC 659; *Cadorette*, 2008 TCC 233; *Income Tax Paid by Investors, Other than Promoters Remission Order*, P.C. 1996-1274.

Draft legislation of July 19 and Dec. 12, 1995 proposed this definition with an exclusion for information technology work done by or on behalf of certain financial institutions. This restriction was announced in the 1995 Budget in response to publicity about banks' claims for investment tax credits for software development. However, the restriction was dropped from the 1995 Budget bill before enactment.

In the U.S., SR&ED is called "research and experimentation" (R&E).

Definition "scientific research and experimental development" added by 1995 Budget (initially simply referring to the regulations) and amended retroactive to its introduction by 1995-97 technical bill, effective for work performed after February 27, 1995 except that, for the purposes of 149(1)(j) and (8)(b), the definition does not apply to work performed pursuant to an agreement in writing entered into before February 28, 1995. For earlier periods, see Reg. 2900.

Regulations: 2900 (meaning of "scientific research and experimental development" (no longer applicable now that the full definition is in the Act).

Information Circulars: 86-4R2 Supplement 1: Automotive industry application paper; 86-4R2 Supplement 2: Aerospace industry application paper; 86-4R3: Scientific research and experimental development; 94-1: Plastics industry application paper; 94-2: Machinery and equipment industry application paper; 97-1: Administrative guidelines for software development.

Application Policies: SR&ED 94-03: Testing activities on new substances required by the Canadian Environmental Protection Act (CEPA); SR&ED 95-01R: Linked activities — Reg. 2900(1)(d); SR&ED 95-02: Science eligibility guidelines for the oil and gas mining industries; SR&ED 95-03: Claims for ISO 9000 registration; SR&ED 95-04R: Conflict of interest with regard to outside consultants; SR&ED 96-02: Tests and studies required to meet requirements in regulated industries; SR&ED 96-08: Eligibility of the preparation of new drug submissions; SR&ED 96-09R: Eligibility of Clinical Research in the Pharmaceutical Industry; SR&ED 2001-02: Multinational clinical trials; SR&ED 2002-02R2: Experimental production and commercial production with experimental development work — allowable SR&ED expenditures; SR&ED 2004-03: Prototypes, Pilot Plants/Commercial Plants, Custom Products and Commercial Assets.

Forms: T2 Sched. 301: Newfoundland and Labrador research and development tax credit; T2 Sched. 340: Nova Scotia research and development tax credit; T2 Sched. 380: Manitoba research and development tax credit; T2 Sched. 403: Saskatchewan research and development tax credit; T661: SR&ED expenditures claim; T1263: Third-party payments for SR&ED; T4088: Claiming scientific research and experimental development expenditures — guide to form T661.

"scientific research and experimental development financing contract" has the meaning assigned by subsection 194(6);

Notes: Added in RSC 1985 (5th Supp) consolidation, effective Dec. 1, 1991.

"scientific research and experimental development tax credit" of a taxpayer for a taxation year has the meaning assigned by subsection 127.3(2);

Notes: Added in RSC 1985 (5th Supp) consolidation, effective Dec. 1, 1991.

"securities lending arrangement" has the meaning assigned by subsection 260(1);

Notes: "Securities lending arrangement" added by 1993 technical bill, effective for 1993 and later taxation years. It is needed outside s. 260 because of the rules in 212(1)(b)(xii) and 212(19) dealing with such arrangements.

"self-contained domestic establishment" means a dwelling-house, apartment or other similar place of residence in which place a person as a general rule sleeps and eats;

Notes: In *Neil Smith*, [2002] 1 C.T.C. 2837 (TCC), a husband who "separated" from his wife continued to live in the basement of the matrimonial home, while sharing the kitchen, bathroom, living room and television. The Court ruled that he resided in the home as his self-contained domestic establishment (SCDE).

In *Vaynshteyn*, 2004 TCC 573, V moved into her parents' apartment for three 2-month periods to help care for them, even though she continued to return to her home, where her husband and children lived and where her business was based. The Court held that she maintained a SCDE in the apartment.

In *Dupuis*, 2009 TCC 220, the taxpayer was held to have an SCDE in a remote area (Mistissini, QC) for purposes of 6(6). In *Spannier*, 2013 TCC 40, the taxpayer had an

SCDE in Kelowna while working near Fort McMurray, even though she paid no rent to the owner in Kelowna.

A hotel room can be an SCDE if the hotel is being operated as an apartment building: VIEWS doc 2005-0127641E5. See also 2008-0303131I7 (no SCDE for property of a 143(1) religious congregation); 2010-0363521E5 (general discussion); 2010-0367501E5 (house shared with landlord could be SCDE); 2013-0484781E5 and 2014-0527281E5 (to "maintain" an SCDE, an individual must be responsible for its upkeep).

See also Notes to 18(12) on bed-and-breakfast cases.

Interpretation Bulletins: IT-91R4: Employment at special work sites or remote work locations; IT-352R2: Employee's expenses, including work space in home expenses; IT-513R: Personal tax credits.

"separation agreement" includes an agreement by which a person agrees to make payments on a periodic basis for the maintenance of a former spouse or common-law partner, children of the marriage or common-law partnership or both the former spouse or common-law partner and children of the marriage or common-law partnership, after the marriage or common-law partnership has been dissolved whether the agreement was made before or after the marriage or common-law partnership was dissolved;

Notes: As this definition uses "includes" rather than "means", the ordinary meaning of "separation agreement" also applies: see Notes to 188.1(5). Such an agreement must address: support; property division; custody and support of any children: *Carrière*, 2006 TCC 289; *JB*, 2018 QCCQ 4200, para. 68; VIEWS doc 2011-042274117.

248(1)"separation agreement" amended by 2000 same-sex partners bill, effective as per Notes to 248(1)"common-law partner".

"servant" — [See under "employment".]

"share", except as the context otherwise requires, means a share or a fraction of a share of the capital stock of a corporation and, for greater certainty, a share of the capital stock of a corporation includes a share of the capital of a cooperative corporation (within the meaning assigned by subsection 136(2)), a share of the capital of an agricultural cooperative corporation (within the meaning assigned by subsection 135.1(1)) and a share of the capital of a credit union;

Related Provisions: 93.3(2) — Equity interests in non-resident corporation without share capital are deemed to be shares; 132.2(1)"share" — Definition for mutual fund corporation rollovers; 142.2(1)"mark-to-market property"(a), 142.5 — Mark-to-market rules for financial institutions; 143.3(2) — Issuing share is not expenditure of corporation.

Notes: The CBA-CICA Joint Committee has recommended that the definition of "share" be amended to include rights under a shareholders' rights plan that do not trade separately from the share: Sandra Jack & Siobhan Goguen, "Poison Pills to Boot?", 10(8) *Canadian Tax Highlights* (ctf.ca) 60-61 (Aug. 2002). A share does not include an option: VIEWS doc 2011-0416521E5.

The following have been considered "shares": membership units in Dutch cooperative (VIEWS doc 2010-0373801R3, per policy in IT-392 para. 3); foreign mandatory redeemable pref shares (2015-060449117). See also Notes to 248(1)"corporation" re various types of foreign entity, and to 79(1)"debt" on the meaning of "debt".

See also Notes to 56(2).

Definition amended by 2002-2013 technical bill (Part 5 — technical), for taxation years that begin after 2006, to add "except as the context otherwise requires" and reference to agricultural cooperative corp.

"Share" earlier amended by 1991 technical bill effective 1989.

Interpretation Bulletins: IT-116R3: Rights to buy additional shares; IT-392: Meaning of the term "share".

Advance Tax Rulings: ATR-26: Share exchange.

"shareholder" includes a member or other person entitled to receive payment of a dividend;

Notes: See Notes to 188.1(5) re meaning of "includes". A member of a non-share-capital corporation can be a "shareholder" in CRA's view: docs 2011-0415831E5, 2013-0473771E5; Burr, "Family Cottage Held in a Society", 20(2) *Canadian Tax Highlights* (ctf.ca) 8-9 (Feb. 2012); Adlington, "What is a Shareholder?", 9(3) *Tax Hyperion* (Carswell, March 2012); Drache, "The Member as Shareholder", xxxvi(15) *The Canadian Taxpayer* (Carswell) 119-20 (July 25, 2014) (CRA's view may be incorrect). A member of a mutual insurance company (but not a "factory mutual") is a shareholder: *Allendale Mutual*, [1973] C.T.C. 494 (FCTD). An "indirect" shareholder is not a shareholder: 2013-047862117.

Normand, 2020 QCCA 450 creates a "*de facto* shareholder" concept: Millette & Barchichat, "After De Facto Directors, We Now have De Facto Shareholders", 11(1) *Canadian Tax Focus* (ctf.ca) 12-13 (Feb. 2021).

Income Tax Folios: S3-F2-C1: Capital Dividends [replaces IT-66R6]; S4-F7-C1: Amalgamations of Canadian corporations [replaces IT-474R2].

Interpretation Bulletins: IT-116R3: Rights to buy additional shares; IT-432R2: Benefits conferred on shareholders.

"share-purchase tax credit" of a taxpayer for a taxation year has the meaning assigned by subsection 127.2(6);

Notes: Added in RSC 1985 (5th Supp) consolidation, effective Dec. 1, 1991.

"short-term preferred share" of a corporation at any particular time means a share, other than a grandfathered share, of the capital stock of the corporation issued after December 15, 1987 that at that particular time

(a) is a share where, under the terms and conditions of the share, any agreement relating to the share or any modification of those terms and conditions or that agreement, the corporation or a specified person in relation to the corporation is or may, at any time within 5 years after the date of its issue, be required to redeem, acquire or cancel, in whole or in part, the share (unless the requirement to redeem, acquire or cancel the share arises only in the event of the death of the shareholder or by reason only of a right to convert or exchange the share) or to reduce the paid-up capital of the share, and for the purposes of this paragraph

(i) an agreement in respect of a share of the capital stock of a corporation shall be read without reference to that part of the agreement under which a person agrees to acquire the share for an amount

(A) in the case of a share (other than a share that would, but for that part of the agreement, be a taxable preferred share) the agreement in respect of which provides that the share is to be acquired within 60 days after the day on which the agreement was entered into, that does not exceed the greater of the fair market value of the share at the time the agreement was entered into, determined without reference to the agreement, and the fair market value of the share at the time of the acquisition, determined without reference to the agreement, or

(B) that does not exceed the fair market value of the share at the time of the acquisition, determined without reference to the agreement, or for an amount determined by reference to the assets or earnings of the corporation where that determination may reasonably be considered to be used to determine an amount that does not exceed the fair market value of the share at the time of the acquisition, determined without reference to the agreement, and

(ii) "shareholder" includes a shareholder of a shareholder, or

(b) is a share that is convertible or exchangeable at any time within 5 years from the date of its issue, unless

(i) it is convertible into or exchangeable for

(A) another share of the corporation or a corporation related to the corporation that, if issued, would not be a short-term preferred share,

(B) a right or warrant that, if exercised, would allow the person exercising it to acquire only a share of the corporation or a corporation related to the corporation that, if issued, would not be a short-term preferred share, or

(C) both a share described in clause (A) and a right or warrant described in clause (B), and

(ii) all the consideration receivable for the share on the conversion or exchange is the share described in clause (i)(A) or the right or warrant described in clause (i)(B) or both, as the case may be, and for the purposes of this subparagraph, where a taxpayer may become entitled on the conversion or exchange of a share to receive any particular consideration (other than consideration described in any of clauses (i)(A) to (C)) in lieu of a fraction of a share, the particular consideration shall be deemed not to be consideration unless it may reasonably be considered that the particular consideration was receivable as part of a series of transactions or events

one of the main purposes of which was to avoid or limit the application of Part IV.1 or VI.1,

and, for the purposes of this definition,

(c) where at any particular time after December 15, 1987, otherwise than pursuant to a written arrangement to do so entered into before December 16, 1987, the terms or conditions of a share of the capital stock of a corporation that are relevant to any matter referred to in any of paragraphs (a), (b), (f) and (h) are established or modified, or any agreement in respect of any such matter to which the corporation or a specified person in relation to the corporation is a party, is changed or entered into, the share shall be deemed after that particular time to have been issued at that particular time,

(d) where at any particular time after December 15, 1987 a particular share of the capital stock of a corporation has been issued or its terms or conditions have been modified or an agreement in respect of the share is modified or entered into, and it may reasonably be considered, having regard to all the circumstances, including the rate of interest on any debt obligation or the dividend provided on any short-term preferred share, that

(i) but for the existence at any time of such a debt obligation or such a short-term preferred share, the particular share would not have been issued or its terms or conditions modified or the agreement in respect of the share would not have been modified or entered into, and

(ii) one of the main purposes for the issue of the particular share or the modification of its terms or conditions or the modification or entering into the agreement in respect of the share was to avoid or limit the tax payable under subsection 191.1(1),

the particular share shall be deemed after that particular time to have been issued at that particular time and to be a short-term preferred share of the corporation,

(e) where at any particular time after December 15, 1987, otherwise than pursuant to a written arrangement to do so entered into before December 16, 1987, the terms or conditions of a share of the capital stock of a corporation are modified or established or any agreement in respect of the share has been changed or entered into, and as a consequence thereof the corporation or a specified person in relation to the corporation may reasonably be expected to redeem, acquire or cancel (otherwise than by reason of the death of the shareholder or by reason only of a right to convert or exchange the share that would not cause the share to be a short-term preferred share by reason of paragraph (b)), in whole or in part, the share, or to reduce its paid-up capital, within 5 years from the particular time, the share shall be deemed to have been issued at that particular time and to be a short-term preferred share of the corporation after the particular time until the time that such reasonable expectation ceases to exist and, for the purposes of this paragraph,

(i) an agreement in respect of a share of the capital stock of a corporation shall be read without reference to that part of the agreement under which a person agrees to acquire the share for an amount

(A) in the case of a share (other than a share that would, but for that part of the agreement, be a taxable preferred share) the agreement in respect of which provides that the share is to be acquired within 60 days after the day on which the agreement was entered into, that does not exceed the greater of the fair market value of the share at the time the agreement was entered into, determined without reference to the agreement, and the fair market value of the share at the time of the acquisition, determined without reference to the agreement, or

(B) that does not exceed the fair market value of the share at the time of the acquisition, determined without reference to the agreement, or for an amount determined by reference to the assets or earnings of the corporation where that determination may reasonably be considered to be used to determine an amount that does not exceed the fair market value of the share at the time of the acquisition, determined without reference to the agreement, and

(ii) "shareholder" includes a shareholder of a shareholder,

(f) if a share of the capital stock of a corporation was issued after December 15, 1987 and at the time the share was issued the existence of the corporation was, or there was an arrangement under which it could be, limited to a period that was within five years from the date of its issue, the share is deemed to be a short-term preferred share of the corporation unless

(i) the share is a grandfathered share and the arrangement is a written arrangement entered into before December 16, 1987, or

(ii) the share is issued to an individual after April 14, 2005 under an agreement referred to in subsection 7(1), if when the individual last acquired a right under the agreement to acquire a share of the capital stock of the corporation, the existence of the corporation was not, and no arrangement was in effect under which it could be, limited to a period that was within five years from the date of that last acquisition,

(g) where a share of the capital stock of a corporation is acquired at any time after December 15, 1987 by the corporation or a specified person in relation to the corporation and the share is at any particular time after that time acquired by a person with whom the corporation or a specified person in relation to the corporation was dealing at arm's length if this Act were read without reference to paragraph 251(5)(b), from the corporation or a specified person in relation to the corporation, the share shall be deemed after that particular time to have been issued at that particular time,

(h) where at any particular time after December 15, 1987, otherwise than pursuant to a written arrangement to do so entered into before December 16, 1987, as a result of the terms or conditions of a share of the capital stock of a corporation or any agreement entered into by the corporation or a specified person in relation to the corporation, any person (other than the corporation or an individual other than a trust) was obligated, either absolutely or contingently and either immediately or in the future, to effect any undertaking within 5 years after the day on which the share was issued (in this paragraph referred to as a "guarantee agreement") including any guarantee, covenant or agreement to purchase or repurchase the share, and including the lending of funds or the placing of amounts on deposit with, or on behalf of the shareholder or a specified person in relation to the shareholder given

(i) to ensure that any loss that the shareholder or a specified person in relation to the shareholder may sustain, by reason of the ownership, holding or disposition of the share or any other property is limited in any respect, and

(ii) as part of a transaction or event or series of transactions or events that included the issuance of the share,

the share shall be deemed after that particular time to have been issued at the particular time and to be at and immediately after the particular time a short-term preferred share, and for the purposes of this paragraph, where a guarantee agreement in respect of a share is given at any particular time after December 15, 1987, otherwise than pursuant to a written arrangement to do so entered into before December 16, 1987, the share shall be deemed to have been issued at the particular time and the guarantee agreement shall be deemed to have been given as part of a series of transactions that included the issuance of the share,

(i) a share that is, at the time a dividend is paid thereon, a share described in paragraph (e) of the definition "term preferred share" in this subsection during the applicable time period referred to in that paragraph or a prescribed share shall, notwithstanding any other provision of this definition, be deemed not to be a short-term preferred share at that time, and

(j) "specified person" has the meaning assigned by paragraph (h) of the definition "taxable preferred share" in this subsection;

Related Provisions: 87(4.2) — Amalgamation; 248(10) — Series of transactions.

Notes: See Diep, "Preferred Share Rules", 2017 Prairie Provinces Tax Conf (ctf.ca).

Any minority discount must be considered in determining value for (a)(i)(B): VIEWS doc 2004-0108511E5. See also 2010-0354391I7 and 2011-0431481R3 (shares are not STPS due to subparas. (a)(i) and (e)(i)); 2012-0454171C6 (timing of when share becomes a STPS).

CRA considers that "convertible or exchangeable" in para. (b) applies to a share that is convertible or exchangeable at the option of either the shareholder or the corporation. (This may not have been the intention of the drafters of the legislation.) See Revenue Canada Round Table, 1993 Cdn Tax Foundation conference report, Q. 10.

For "one of the main purposes" in (b)(ii) and (d)(ii), see Notes to 83(2.1).

Subpara. (f)(ii) added by 2002-2013 technical bill (Part 5 — technical), for shares issued after April 14, 2005. It implements a May 11, 2005 Finance comfort letter.

"Short-term preferred share" amended by 1988 tax reform, effective for shares issued (or deemed to have been issued) after December 15, 1987.

Regulations: 6201(8) (prescribed shares).

Advance Tax Rulings: ATR-46: Financial difficulty.

"SIFT partnership", "SIFT trust" — [See at beginning of 's' entries above.]

"small business bond" has the meaning assigned by section 15.2;

"small business corporation", at any particular time, means, subject to subsection 110.6(15), a particular corporation that is a Canadian-controlled private corporation all or substantially all of the fair market value of the assets of which at that time is attributable to assets that are

(a) used principally in an active business carried on primarily in Canada by the particular corporation or by a corporation related to it,

(b) shares of the capital stock or indebtedness of one or more small business corporations that are at that time connected with the particular corporation (within the meaning of subsection 186(4) on the assumption that the small business corporation is at that time a "payer corporation" within the meaning of that subsection), or

(c) assets described in paragraphs (a) and (b),

including, for the purpose of paragraph 39(1)(c), a corporation that was at any time in the 12 months preceding that time a small business corporation, and, for the purpose of this definition, the fair market value of a net income stabilization account shall be deemed to be nil;

Related Provisions: 110.6(2.1) — Capital gains deduction — qualified small business corporation shares; 110.6(14)(b) — Interpretation rule for capital gains exemption purposes; 110.6(15) — Value of assets of corporation; 136(1) — Whether cooperative corporation can be a small business corporation; 137(7) — Whether credit union can be a small business corporation; 186(7) — Interpretation of "connected" for para. (b).

Notes: Note that a "small business corporation" (SBC) need not be small (see 248(1)"eligible relocation" Notes re "new work location"), and that "active business" is defined above in 248(1). A non-profit organization can be a SBC: VIEWS doc 2005-0122511I7. The "used principally" test generally means more than 50% and is applied on a property-by-property basis: 2009-0307931E5.

CRA considers that "substantially all" means 90% or more, though each case needs to be considered on its facts: VIEWS doc 2013-0495631C6.

A loan to an employee who is not a shareholder, or to an employee who is a shareholder on the same terms as loans to other employees, is an asset used in an active business and will not jeopardize SBC status: Revenue Canada Round Table, 1993 Cdn Tax Foundation conference report, Q. 45, pp. 58:27-28.

A partnership or limited partnership interest is used in an active business if the underlying assets are: May 2005 ICAA (tinyurl.com/cra-abtax), q. 10. A dividend refund receivable by paying out taxable dividends (see s. 129) can be an asset used in an active business, although the RDTOH account is not an asset: VIEWS doc 2006-0174131C6 [2006 CALU q. 6]. As to whether a pending income tax refund is "used in active business", see 2000-0015825F, 2002-0169565, 2008-0285301C6, 2008-0285291C6 and 12(1)(c) Notes. Funds held to satisfy employee bonuses or stock option requirements, or otherwise needed for the business, will qualify: 2009-0330071C6. A lease (as lessee) of an asset does not qualify: 2016-0652941C6 [2016 APFF q.11].

In *Belzile*, 2004 TCC 137, a company was held to be an SBC where its intention was to resell homes and it rented them out only because it could not sell them. However, in *Venneri*, 2006 FCA 165, a corp holding land for speculation was not engaged in "active business", so it was not an SBC.

Too much cash or securities in the corp will put it offside and the capital gains exemption (110.6(2.1)) will be lost, unless the cash is held "to fulfill a mandatory condition precedent to trade" or its withdrawal would "have a decidedly destabilizing effect on the corporate operations themselves": *Ensite Ltd.*, [1986] 2 C.T.C. 459 (SCC); *Skidmore*, [2000] 2 C.T.C. 325 (FCA); *Reilly Estate*, 2007 TCC 404; VIEWS doc 2006-0200791E5. See 110.6(1)"qualified small business corporation share" Notes re purifying the corp.

See also Notes to 39(1), 50(1) and 74.4(2).

Closing words of "small business corporation" amended by 1992 technical bill (effective for 1991 and later tax years) and 1991 technical bill.

Income Tax Folios: S4-F8-C1: Business investment losses [replaces IT-484R2].

Interpretation Bulletins: IT-268R3: *Inter vivos* transfer of farm property to child.

CRA Audit Manual: 29.3.0: Business investment losses.

Advance Tax Rulings: ATR-53: Purification of a small business corporation; ATR-55: Amalgamation followed by sale of shares.

"small business development bond" has the meaning assigned by section 15.1;

"specified employee" of a person means an employee of the person who is a specified shareholder of the person or who does not deal at arm's length with the person;

Related Provisions: 15(2.7) — Meaning of specified employee of a partnership for purpose of shareholder appropriations and loans; 144.1(1)"key employee" — Specified employee is "key employee" for employee life and health trust rules.

Notes: See VIEWS doc 2012-0439781E5 (whether shareholder of majority partner is "specified employee" for purposes of R&D limitations in 37(9.1)).

"Specified employee" added by 1992 Economic Statement, effective for taxation years ending after December 2, 1992.

"specified financial institution", at any time, means

(a) a bank,

(b) a corporation licensed or otherwise authorized under the laws of Canada or a province to carry on in Canada the business of offering to the public its services as trustee,

(c) a credit union,

(d) an insurance corporation,

(e) a corporation whose principal business is the lending of money to persons with whom the corporation is dealing at arm's length or the purchasing of debt obligations issued by such persons or a combination thereof,

(e.1) a corporation described in paragraph (g) of the definition "financial institution" in subsection 181(1),

(f) a corporation that is controlled by one or more corporations described in any of paragraphs (a) to (e.1) and, for the purpose of this paragraph, one corporation is controlled by another corporation if more than 50% of its issued share capital (having full voting rights under all circumstances) belongs to the other corporation, to persons with whom the other corporation does not deal at arm's length, or to the other corporation and persons with whom the other corporation does not deal at arm's length, or

(g) a corporation that is related to a particular corporation described in any of paragraphs (a) to (f), other than a particular corporation described in paragraph (e) or (e.1) the principal business of which is the factoring of trade accounts receivable that

(i) the particular corporation acquired from a related person,

(ii) arose in the course of an active business carried on by a person (in this paragraph referred to as the "business entity") related at that time to the particular corporation, and

(iii) at no particular time before that time were held by a person other than a person who was related to the business entity;

Related Provisions: 248(14) — Related corporations; 256(6), (6.1) — Meaning of "controlled".

Notes: For the meaning of "principal business" in (e) and (g), see Notes to 20(1)(bb).

Definition amended by 1998 Budget, effective for determining the status of a corporation as a specified financial institution, for all purposes of the Act, for taxation years of the corporation that begin after 1998.

"specified future tax consequence" for a taxation year means

(a) the consequence of the deduction or exclusion of an amount referred to in paragraph 161(7)(a),

(b) the consequence of a reduction under subsection 66(12.73) of a particular amount purported to be renounced by a corporation after the beginning of the year to a person or partnership under subsection 66(12.6) or (12.601) because of the application of subsection 66(12.66); determined as if the purported renunciation would, but for subsection 66(12.73), have been effective only where

(i) the purported renunciation occurred in January, February or March of a calendar year,

(ii) the effective date of the purported renunciation was the last day of the preceding calendar year,

(iii) the corporation agreed in that preceding calendar year to issue a flow-th[r]ough share to the person or partnership,

(iv) the particular amount does not exceed the amount, if any, by which the consideration for which the share is to be issued exceeds the total of all other amounts purported by the corporation to have been renounced under subsection 66(12.6) or (12.601) in respect of that consideration,

(v) paragraphs 66(12.66)(c) and (d) are satisfied with respect to the purported renunciation, and

(vi) the form prescribed for the purpose of subsection 66(12.7) in respect of the purported renunciation is filed with the Minister before May of the calendar year; and

(c) the consequence of an adjustment or a reduction described in subsection 161(6.1);

Related Provisions: 89(1)"general rate income pool"A, K — Specified future tax consequence (SFTC) ignored in determining eligible dividends for high dividend tax credit; 127(10.2)A — Effect of SFTC on investment tax credits; 156.1(1.1), (1.2), 157(2.1)(a), 161(4)(a), 161(4.01)(a), 161(4.1)(a) — Effect of SFTC on instalment obligations and instalment interest; 161(6.2) — Flow-through share renunciations and one-year look-back — effect of SFTC on interest; 162(11) — Effect of SFTC on penalties.

Notes: The term refers to adjustments from the carryback of losses or similar amounts or because of corrections of certain amounts renounced in connection with the issuance of flow-through shares. Note that there are no "specified future tax consequences" for previous taxation years unless they end after 1995.

Definition "specified future tax consequence" added by 1996 Budget, effective for 1996 and later taxation years; and, for greater certainty, for taxation years that ended before 1996, there are deemed to be no specified future tax consequences.

Para. (c) added by 1998 Budget, effective for 1998 and later taxation years.

"specified individual" has the meaning assigned by subsection 120.4(1);

Notes: 248(1)"specified individual" added by 1999 Budget, effective for 2000 and later taxation years.

"specified investment business" has the meaning assigned by subsection 125(7);

"specified member" of a partnership in a fiscal period or taxation year of the partnership, as the case may be, means

(a) any member of the partnership who is a limited partner (within the meaning assigned by subsection 96(2.4)) of the partnership at any time in the period or year, and

(b) any member of the partnership, other than a member who is

(i) actively engaged in those activities of the partnership business that are other than the financing of the partnership business, or

(ii) carrying on a similar business as that carried on by the partnership in its taxation year, otherwise than as a member of a partnership,

on a regular, continuous and substantial basis throughout that part of the period or year during which the business of the partnership is ordinarily carried on and during which the member is a member of the partnership;

Related Provisions: 40(3.131), 127.52(2.1) — Anti-avoidance.

Notes: For discussion of this definition see John Burghardt, "When is a Partner a 'Specified Member' of a Partnership?", I(4) *Resource Sector Taxation* (Federated Press) 62-65 (2003); VIEWS doc 2010-0391271R3.

Investors in R&D projects were "specified members", so various deductions and credits were denied, in: *Rouleau*, 2008 FCA 288; *St-Laurent [Simard]*, 2007 TCC 540, paras. 221-247, aff'd 2009 FCA 379; *Brillon*, 2006 TCC 76; *Raby*, 2006 TCC 406; *Lauger*, 2007 TCC 650 (despite extensive administrative work); *Foster (Atherton)*, 2007 TCC 659, paras. 38-39; *Ménard*, 2009 TCC 363.

"Actively engaged" in (b)(i) means more than financial contributions and sporadic completion of surveys, and requires a role in the decision-making process affecting the partnership's business: *Brillon*, 2006 TCC 76; *Lauger* (above). See also VIEWS doc 2010-0375341E5 (active partner must be directly involved in the company's management or daily operations, spending time, effort and energy on a regular, continuous and significant basis throughout the year).

A trust can be "actively engaged" in the partnership business if the trustee is: VIEWS doc 2009-0342081E5.

"specified mutual fund trust", at any time, means a mutual fund trust other than a mutual fund trust for which it can reasonably be considered, having regard to all the circumstances, including the terms and conditions of the units of the trust, that the total of all amounts each of which is the fair market value, at that time, of a unit issued by the trust and held by a person exempt from tax under section 149 is all or substantially all of the total of all amounts each of which is the fair market value, at that time, of a unit issued by the trust;

Notes: Definition added by 2016 budget bill #1, effective April 22, 2015.

"specified pension plan" means a prescribed arrangement;

Related Provisions: 146(21.1)–(21.3) — Specified pension plan (Saskatchewan Pension Plan) deemed to be RRSP for certain purposes.

Notes: The only specified pension plan is the Saskatchewan Pension Plan (SPP): Reg. 7800. The SPP "is a voluntary defined-contribution pension plan established by the Government of Saskatchewan. It offers an alternative for small businesses that do not offer their own pension plans, provides cost-effective professional investment management of retirement savings, and allows employees full portability of pension savings between employers" (Finance news release 2010-118, Dec. 7, 2010). SPP was created in 1986 and is the only pension plan in North America that does not require an employer-employee relationship [but see now PRPPs in 147.5]; more than 30,000 people participate either as contributors or pension recipients. Among defined contribution pension plans in Canada, SPP is the 26th largest, based on assets under management at end of 2009. Contributions are pooled for investment, and participants have the option to choose the Balanced Fund, Short-term Fund or both to deposit their contributions. See saskpension.com. (Sask. Ministry of Finance, Media Backgrounder, Dec. 7, 2010.)

Effective 2010, the annual SPP contribution limit is $2,500, and the SPP is treated as an RRSP and integrated with the RRSP rules for most purposes. See 146(21.1)–(21.3). The RRSP overcontribution rules do not apply to SPP contributions made in respect of taxation years before 2010 or to the first $600 of SPP contributions made for 2010.

For deduction for contributions before 2010 see former 60(v).

"Specified pension plan" added by 2011 budget bill #2, effective 2010.

Regulations: 7800 (Saskatchewan Pension Plan is prescribed arrangement).

"specified proportion", of a member of a partnership for a fiscal period of the partnership, means the proportion that the member's share of the total income or loss of the partnership for the partnership's fiscal period is of the partnership's total income or loss for that period and, for the purpose of this definition, where that income or loss for a period is nil, that proportion shall be computed as if the partnership had income for that period in the amount of $1,000,000;

Notes: Definition added by 2002-2013 technical bill (Part 5 — technical), effective Dec. 21, 2002.

"specified securities lending arrangement" has the same meaning as in subsection 260(1);

Notes: Definition added by 2021 budget bill #1, effective March 19, 2019.

"specified shareholder" of a corporation in a taxation year means a taxpayer who owns, directly or indirectly, at any time in the year, not less than 10% of the issued shares of any class of the capital stock of the corporation or of any other corporation that is related to the corporation and, for the purposes of this definition,

(a) a taxpayer shall be deemed to own each share of the capital stock of a corporation owned at that time by a person with whom the taxpayer does not deal at arm's length,

(b) each beneficiary of a trust shall be deemed to own that proportion of all such shares owned by the trust at that time that the fair market value at that time of the beneficial interest of the beneficiary in the trust is of the fair market value at that time of all beneficial interests in the trust,

(c) each member of a partnership shall be deemed to own that proportion of all the shares of any class of the capital stock of a corporation that are property of the partnership at that time that the fair market value at that time of the member's interest in the partnership is of the fair market value at that time of the interests of all members in the partnership,

(d) an individual who performs services on behalf of a corporation that would be carrying on a personal services business if the individual or any person related to the individual were at that time a specified shareholder of the corporation shall be deemed to be a specified shareholder of the corporation at that time if the individual, or any person or partnership with whom the individual does not deal at arm's length, is, or by virtue of any arrangement, may become, entitled, directly or indirectly, to not less than 10% of the assets or the shares of any class of the capital stock of the corporation or any corporation related thereto, and

(e) notwithstanding paragraph (b), where a beneficiary's share of the income or capital of the trust depends on the exercise by any person of, or the failure by any person to exercise, any discretionary power, the beneficiary shall be deemed to own each share of the capital stock of a corporation owned at that time by the trust;

Related Provisions: 18(5), (5.1) — Alternate definition for thin capitalization rules; 55(3.2)(a), 55(3.3) — Extended meanings for capital gains strip rules; 88(1)(c.2)(iii) — Restriction on definition for windups; 248(1)"specified unitholder" — Extension of definition to partnerships and trusts.

Notes: Para. (e) added by 1992 technical bill, effective January 1, 1992.

Income Tax Folios: S3-F10-C2: Prohibited investments — RRSPs, RRIFs and TFSAs.

Interpretation Bulletins: IT-73R6: The small business deduction; IT-88R2: Stock dividends; IT-153R3: Land developers — subdivision and development costs and carrying charges on land; IT-421R2: Benefits to individuals, corporations and shareholders from loans or debt; IT-432R2: Benefits conferred on shareholders.

Advance Tax Rulings: ATR-36: Estate freeze.

"specified synthetic equity arrangement", in respect of a DRA share of a person or partnership, means one or more agreements or other arrangements that

(a) have the effect of providing to a person or partnership all or any portion of the risk of loss or opportunity for gain or profit in respect of the DRA share and, for greater certainty, opportunity for gain or profit includes rights to, benefits from and distributions on a share, and

(b) can reasonably be considered to have been entered into in connection with a synthetic equity arrangement, in respect of the DRA share, or in connection with another specified synthetic equity arrangement, in respect of the DRA share;

Notes: Definition added by 2016 budget bill #1, effective April 22, 2015.

"specified unitholder", of a partnership or trust (referred to in this definition as the "entity"), the interests in which are described by reference to units, means a taxpayer who would be a specified shareholder of the entity if the entity were a corporation and each unit of the entity were a share of a class of the corporation having the same attributes as the unit;

Notes: Definition added by 2012 budget bill #2, effective Dec. 14, 2012.

"split income" has the meaning assigned by subsection 120.4(1);

Notes: 248(1)"split income" added by 1999 Budget, effective for 2000 and later taxation years. See Notes to 120.4.

"stock dividend" includes any dividend (determined without reference to the definition "dividend" in this subsection) paid by a corporation to the extent that it is paid by the issuance of shares of any class of the capital stock of the corporation;

Related Provisions: 15(1)(b), 15(1.1) — Whether stock dividend constitutes taxable benefit to shareholder; 52(3) — Cost of stock dividend; 95(7) — Stock dividend received from foreign affiliate; 248(1) — "Amount" (of stock dividend); 248(5)(b) — Stock dividend is deemed to be substituted property.

Notes: See Notes to 248(1)"amount", and Notes to 188.1(5) re meaning of "includes".

See VIEWS docs 2010-0374141R3 (distribution of stock dividend from share premium account of a controlled foreign affiliate); 2011-0410531I7 (stock dividend and stock split are different for shares held since before 1972); 2014-0538041C6 [2014 APFF q.19] (estate freeze using stock dividend).

See also Sanjaya Ranaginghe, "Tax Planning Through Stock Dividends", XV(1) *Business Vehicles* (Federated Press) 788-791 (2012).

"Stock dividend" amended by 1991 technical bill, effective Dec. 17, 1991, to add the parenthetical exclusion to avoid circularity.

Interpretation Bulletins: IT-67R3: Taxable dividends from corporations resident in Canada; IT-88R2: Stock dividends.

Information Circulars: 88-2 para. 26: General anti-avoidance rule — section 245 of the *Income Tax Act*.

"subsidiary controlled corporation" means a corporation more than 50% of the issued share capital of which (having full voting rights under all circumstances) belongs to the corporation to which it is subsidiary;

Notes: 248(1)"subsidiary controlled corporation" added in the RSC 1985 (5th Supp) consolidation, effective December 1991. It was formerly included in the definition of "subsidiary wholly-owned corporation".

"subsidiary wholly-owned corporation" means a corporation all the issued share capital of which (except directors' qualifying shares) belongs to the corporation to which it is subsidiary;

Related Provisions: 87(1.4) — Definition of "subsidiary wholly-owned corporation"; 87(2.11) — Losses, etc., on amalgamation with subsidiary wholly-owned corporation.

Notes: For "directors' qualifying shares", see Notes to 85(1.3).

An amendment to this definition proposed in a Nov. 5, 2004 Finance comfort letter was implemented by amending 138(11.94) to change a reference from "subsidiary wholly-owned corporation" to "qualified related corporation".

Interpretation Bulletins: IT-98R2: Investment corporations (cancelled).

"superannuation or pension benefit" includes any amount received out of or under a superannuation or pension fund or plan (including, except for the purposes of subparagraph 56(1)(a)(i), a pooled registered pension plan) and, without restricting the generality of the foregoing, includes any payment made to a beneficiary under the fund or plan or to an employer or former employer of the beneficiary under the fund or plan

(a) in accordance with the terms of the fund or plan,

(b) resulting from an amendment to or modification of the fund or plan, or

(c) resulting from the termination of the fund or plan;

Related Provisions: 6(1)(g) — Employee benefit plan benefits; 56(1)(a)(i) — Superannuation or pension benefit included in income.

Notes: This definition "casts a very wide net" and catches unregistered pension funds: *McKeating*, 2004 TCC 99. It requires employer contributions: VIEWS docs 2012-0439641E5, 2012-0468271E5. It can include: amount paid by a former employer rather than the plan (2006-0166891E5); receipt of actuarial surplus (2008-0294921I7); lump sum (2009-0321881R3); amount paid to beneficiary after retiree's death (2014-0525681E5); periodic government payment to aged, disabled or widowed persons (2015-0588521E5); remedial payment to an RPP (2013-0506291R3); payments replacing pension not paid to injured worker (2020-0849291E5). For foreign pensions, see 56(1)(a) Notes.

Definition amended by 2012 budget bill #2, effective Dec. 14, 2012, to exclude PRPPs.

Interpretation Bulletins: IT-499R: Superannuation or pension benefits; IT-508R: Death benefits.

"supplementary unemployment benefit plan" has the meaning assigned by subsection 145(1);

"synthetic disposition arrangement", in respect of a property owned by a taxpayer, means one or more agreements or other arrangements that

(a) are entered into by the taxpayer or by a person or partnership that does not deal at arm's length with the taxpayer,

(b) have the effect, or would have the effect if entered into by the taxpayer instead of the person or partnership, of eliminating all or substantially all the taxpayer's risk of loss and opportunity for gain or profit in respect of the property for a definite or indefinite period of time, and

(c) can, in respect of any agreement or arrangement entered into by a person or partnership that does not deal at arm's length with the taxpayer, reasonably be considered to have been entered into, in whole or in part, with the purpose of obtaining the effect described in paragraph (b);

Related Provisions: 80.6 — Deemed disposition of property on entering into synthetic disposition arrangement; 112(8), (9) — Effect on dividend stop-loss rules; 126(4.5), (4.6) — Effect on foreign tax credit.

Notes: An SDA is typically an arrangement to sell all the risk and profit in property without technically selling the property, so as to defer tax on the capital gain. 80.6 deems the property to have been disposed of at fair market value (subject to the exceptions in 80.6(2)). Note that there is no requirement that the property have been monetized for the deemed disposition to apply.

CRA interprets "substantially all", used in para. (b), as meaning 90% or more; but how does one measure 90% of a potentially infinite "opportunity for gain"?

An SDA can also be a derivative forward agreement (as defined in 248(1)).

The McCarthy Tétrault 2013 budget-day commentary noted: "The budget papers... [make] no mention of legitimate non-tax commercial reasons for taxpayers to enter into these types of transactions. For example, securities law or other commercial or contractual constraints may restrict an outright sale by a taxpayer of a large block of shares. It may also be important to an individual taxpayer to maintain voting rights over the shares, for example, in the case of a founder of a public company (or the family successors of the founder). An equity hedge transaction allows the taxpayer to reduce his or her exposure to a concentrated equity position, while at the same time retaining the rights associated with the beneficial ownership of the stock. The fact that the SDA definition implements an 'effects' test (as opposed to a 'purpose' test) may leave little room for transactions of this type to remain in effect for one year or more without triggering the application of the rules."

For CRA interpretation see VIEWS doc 2017-0727811E5 (reconsidering facts of doc 1999-0006705).

See also Panasiuk, "Synthetic Dispositions", 3(2) *Canadian Tax Focus* (ctf.ca) 10 (May 2013); Caines & Van Loan, "Character Conversion Transactions and Synthetic Dispositions", XVIII(4) *Corporate Finance* (Federated Press) 2161-67 and "...Updated", XIX(1) 2198-2200 (2013); Miller & Milet, "Derivative Forward Agreements and Synthetic Disposition Arrangements", 2013 Cdn Tax Foundation conference report at 10:19-50; Edgar, "Risk-Based Overrides of Share Ownership", 63(2) *Canadian Tax Journal* 397-465 (2015).

Definition added by 2013 budget bill #2, effective March 21, 2013.

"synthetic disposition period", of a synthetic disposition arrangement, means the definite or indefinite period of time during which the synthetic disposition arrangement has, or would have, the effect described in paragraph (b) of the definition "synthetic disposition arrangement" in this subsection;

Notes: Definition "synthetic disposition period" added by 2013 budget bill #2, effective March 21, 2013. See Notes to 248(1)"synthetic disposition arrangement".

"synthetic equity arrangement" in respect of a DRA share of a person or partnership (referred to in this definition as the "particular person"),

(a) means one or more agreements or other arrangements that

(i) are entered into by the particular person, by a person or partnership that does not deal at arm's length with, or is affiliated with, the particular person (referred to in this definition as a "connected person") or, for greater certainty, by any combination of the particular person and connected persons, with one or more persons or partnerships (referred to in this definition as a "counterparty" and in subsection 112(2.32) as a "counterparty" or an "affiliated counterparty" as appropriate),

(ii) have the effect, or would have the effect, if each agreement entered into by a connected person were entered into by the particular person, of providing all or substantially all of the risk of loss and opportunity for gain or profit in respect of the DRA share to a counterparty or a group of counterparties each member of which is affiliated with every other member and, for greater certainty, opportunity for gain or profit includes rights to, benefits from and distributions on a share, and

(iii) if entered into by a connected person, can reasonably be considered to have been entered into with the knowledge, or where there ought to have been the knowledge, that the effect described in subparagraph (ii) would result, and

(b) does not include

(i) an agreement that is traded on a recognized derivatives exchange unless it can reasonably be considered that, at the time the agreement is entered into,

(A) the particular person or the connected person, as the case may be, knows or ought to know that the agreement is part of a series of transactions that has the effect of providing all or substantially all of the risk of loss and opportunity for gain or profit in respect of the DRA share to a tax-indifferent investor, or a group of tax-indifferent investors each member of which is affiliated with every other member, or

(B) one of the main reasons for entering into the agreement is to obtain the benefit of a deduction in respect of a payment, or a reduction of an amount that would otherwise have been included in income, under the agreement, that corresponds to an expected or actual dividend in respect of a DRA share,

(ii) one or more agreements or other arrangements that, but for this subparagraph, would be a synthetic equity arrangement, in respect of a share owned by the particular person (in this subparagraph referred to as the "synthetic short position"), if

(A) the particular person has entered into one or more other agreements or other arrangements (other than, for greater certainty, an agreement under which the share is acquired or an agreement or arrangement under which the particular person receives a deemed dividend and is provided with all or substantially all of the risk of loss and opportunity for gain or profit in respect of the share) that have the effect of providing all or substantially all of the risk of loss and opportunity for gain or profit in respect of the share to the particular person (in this subparagraph referred to as the "synthetic long position"),

(B) the synthetic short position has the effect of offsetting all amounts included or deducted in computing the income of the particular person with respect to the synthetic long position, and

(C) the synthetic short position was entered into for the purpose of obtaining the effect referred to in clause (B), and

(iii) an agreement to purchase the shares of a corporation, or a purchase agreement that is part of a series of agreements to purchase the shares of a corporation, under which a counterparty or a group of counterparties each member of which is affiliated with every other member acquires control of the corporation that has issued the shares being purchased, unless the main reason for establishing, incorporating or operating the corporation is to have this subparagraph apply;

Related Provisions: 112(2.3)–(2.34) — Intercorporate dividend deduction denied; 248(1)"dividend rental arrangement"(c), (d) — SEA and other arrangement constitutes a DRA; 248(42) — SEA relating to multiple types of identical shares.

Notes: Definition added by 2016 budget bill #1, effective April 22, 2015. See 112(2.3) Notes, and Finance Technical Notes to this definition.

"synthetic equity arrangement chain", in respect of a share owned by a person or partnership, means a synthetic equity arrange-

ment — or a synthetic equity arrangement in combination with one or more specified synthetic equity arrangements — where

(a) no party to the synthetic equity arrangement or a specified synthetic equity arrangement, if any, is a tax-indifferent investor, and

(b) each other party to these agreements or arrangements is affiliated with the person or partnership;

Notes: Definition added by 2016 budget bill #1, effective April 22, 2015.

"TFSA", being a tax-free savings account, has the meaning assigned by subsection 146.2(5);

Notes: See Notes at end of 146.2. 248(1)"TFSA" added by 2008 budget bill #1, for 2009 and later taxation years; and amended retroactive to its introduction by 2008 budget bill #2 to change "146.2(3)" to "146.2(5)" (due to renumbering of 146.2).

"tar sands" means bituminous sands or oil shales extracted, otherwise than by a well, from a mineral resource, but, for the purpose of applying sections 13 and 20 and any regulations made for the purpose of paragraph 20(1)(a) in respect of property acquired after March 6, 1996, includes material extracted by a well from a deposit of bituminous sands or oil shales;

Notes: Definition "tar sands" amended by 1996 Budget, effective March 7, 1996. See Notes to 248(1)"bituminous sands".

["tax-free savings account"] — [See 248(1)"TFSA" above.]

"tax-indifferent investor", at any time, means a person or partnership that is at that time

(a) a person exempt from tax under section 149,

(b) a non-resident person, other than a person to which all amounts paid or credited under a derivative forward agreement, a synthetic equity arrangement or a specified synthetic equity arrangement, as the case may be, may reasonably be attributed to the business carried on by the person in Canada through a "permanent establishment" (as defined in section 8201 of the *Income Tax Regulations*) in Canada,

(c) a trust resident in Canada (other than a specified mutual fund trust) if any of the interests as a beneficiary under the trust is not a "fixed interest" (as defined in subsection 251.2(1)) in the trust (in this definition referred to as a "discretionary trust"),

(d) a partnership more than 10% of the fair market value of all interests in which can reasonably be considered to be held, directly or indirectly through one or more trusts or partnerships, by any combination of persons described in paragraphs (a) to (c), or

(e) a trust resident in Canada (other than a specified mutual fund trust or a discretionary trust) if more than 10% of the fair market value of all interests as beneficiaries under the trust can reasonably be considered to be held, directly or indirectly through one or more trusts or partnerships, by any combination of persons described in paragraph (a) or (c);

Notes: See 112(2.3) Notes. Para. (b) amended by 2021 budget bill #1, effective March 19, 2019, to add "derivative forward agreement" and to change "by regulation" to "in section 8201 of the *Income Tax Regulations*".

Definition added by 2016 budget bill #1, effective April 22, 2015.

Regulations: 8201 (permanent establishment, for para. (b)).

"tax-paid undistributed surplus on hand" — [Repealed under former Act]

Notes: See Notes to this definition (repealed) under 89(1).

"tax shelter" has the meaning assigned by subsection 237.1(1);

"tax treaty" with a country at any time means a comprehensive agreement or convention for the elimination of double taxation on income, between the Government of Canada and the government of the country, which has the force of law in Canada at that time;

Related Provisions: 81(1)(a) — Amount exempted by tax treaty (for corporation); 108(1)"exempt property" — Property exempted by treaty; 110(1)(d)(i) — Amount exempted by tax treaty for individual must be included and deducted; 231.2(1) — Requirement for Information for purposes of treaty; 241(4)(e)(xii) — Disclosure of taxpayer information for purposes of treaty.

Notes: For discussion of tax treaties and their interpretation, see Notes at the beginning of the *Income Tax Conventions Interpretation Act* (reproduced near the end of the book, before the Canada-US treaty); and Notes at beginning of the Canada-US treaty.

For the Multilateral Instrument (MLI), which effectively amends most worldwide treaties (but not those involving the US), seethe pages before the Canada-US treaty.

The treaty with Hong Kong (not a country) and the "arrangement" with Taiwan are both "tax treaties". See Notes to 219.2.

A Tax Information Exchange Agreement (TIEA) is not a "tax treaty" but a "listed international agreement". See Notes to 95(1)"non-qualifying country" for a list of Canada's TIEAs. See at end of the book, after the Canada-US and Canada-UK treaties, for a list of Canada's tax treaties.

Definition added by 1998 Budget, effective for 1998 and later taxation years. 2004 Budget bill, s. 52(4), provides that the definition is deemed to have come into force on Sept. 13, 1988 for purposes of s. 245 (GAAR).

"taxable Canadian corporation" has the meaning assigned by subsection 89(1);

"taxable Canadian property" of a taxpayer at any time in a taxation year means a property of the taxpayer that is

(a) real or immovable property situated in Canada,

(b) property used or held by the taxpayer in, property included in Class 14.1 of Schedule II to the *Income Tax Regulations* in respect of, or property described in an inventory of, a business carried on in Canada, other than

(i) property used in carrying on an insurance business, and

(ii) where the taxpayer is non-resident, ships and aircraft used principally in international traffic and personal or movable property pertaining to their operation if the country in which the taxpayer is resident does not impose tax on gains of persons resident in Canada from dispositions of such property,

(c) if the taxpayer is an insurer, its designated insurance property for the year,

(d) a share of the capital stock of a corporation (other than a mutual fund corporation) that is not listed on a designated stock exchange, an interest in a partnership or an interest in a trust (other than a unit of a mutual fund trust or an income interest in a trust resident in Canada), if, at any particular time during the 60-month period that ends at that time, more than 50% of the fair market value of the share or interest, as the case may be, was derived directly or indirectly (otherwise than through a corporation, partnership or trust the shares or interests in which were not themselves taxable Canadian property at the particular time) from one or any combination of

(i) real or immovable property situated in Canada,

(ii) Canadian resource properties,

(iii) timber resource properties, and

(iv) options in respect of, or interests in, or for civil law rights in, property described in any of subparagraphs (i) to (iii), whether or not the property exists,

(e) a share of the capital stock of a corporation that is listed on a designated stock exchange, a share of the capital stock of a mutual fund corporation or a unit of a mutual fund trust, if, at any particular time during the 60-month period that ends at that time,

(i) 25% or more of the issued shares of any class of the capital stock of the corporation, or 25% or more of the issued units of the trust, as the case may be, were owned by or belonged to one or any combination of

(A) the taxpayer,

(B) persons with whom the taxpayer did not deal at arm's length, and

(C) partnerships in which the taxpayer or a person referred to in clause (B) holds a membership interest directly or indirectly through one or more partnerships, and

(ii) more than 50% of the fair market value of the share or unit, as the case may be, was derived directly or indirectly

from one or any combination of properties described under subparagraphs (d)(i) to (iv), or

(f) an option in respect of, or an interest in, or for civil law a right in, a property described in any of paragraphs (a) to (e), whether or not the property exists,

and, for the purposes of section 2, subsection 107(2.001) and sections 128.1 and 150, and for the purpose of applying paragraphs 85(1)(i) and 97(2)(c) to a disposition by a non-resident person, includes

(g) a Canadian resource property,

(h) a timber resource property,

(i) an income interest in a trust resident in Canada,

(j) a right to a share of the income or loss under an agreement referred to in paragraph 96(1.1)(a), and

(k) a life insurance policy in Canada;

Related Provisions: 13(4.1)(c) — Replacement of depreciable TCP with new TCP; 44(5)(c) — Replacement of capital TCP with new TCP; 55(6) — Reorganization share deemed listed on designated stock exchange for purposes of this definition; 85(1)(i), 85.1(1)(a) — Shares received on rollover of TCP deemed to be TCP; 87(10) — New share issued on amalgamation of public corporation deemed listed; 107(2)(d.1) — TCP status retained on rollout of trust property to beneficiary; 115(1)(b) — Non-resident taxed on gain on disposition of TCP; 116 — Certificate required where non-resident disposes of TCP; 131(5.1), (5.2), 132(5.1), (5.2) — Mutual fund — distribution of gain on TCP; 141(5) — Demutualized life insurance corporation or holding corporation deemed not to be TCP; 219(1.1) — Restricted definition for branch tax purposes; 248(4), (4.1) — Interpretation of "interest" and "right" for para. (f); 248(25.1) — Deemed TCP retains status through trust-to-trust transfer. See also Related Provisions annotation to 115(1).

Notes: Capital gains on TCP are taxed when sold by a non-resident: see 115(1)(b) and Notes to 116(1). Art. 13 of each of Canada's tax treaties usually exempts TCP that is not real property (not always, e.g. Canada-Brazil treaty).

Before the March 2010 Budget, TCP included most private corporation shares, partnership units and trust units, but now they are only TCP if more than 50% of their value is derived from real property in Canada or certain other Canadian property (note that shares of a non-resident corporation can be TCP). There are some downsides to the change: 21-year trust deemed disposition with no 220(4.6) election [see Rudick article below]; deemed disposition on emigration under 128.1(4)(b), with no carryback under 128.1(8) [Valli article]. Also, it is unclear how widely "derived from real property" will be interpreted (mortgage broker income? derivatives? nursing home licence?) [Bowman paper at 32:16-24 and Notes to 116(1)]. (See also under "Para. (d)" below.)

Real property (in common-law provinces) includes "fixtures" attached to the land. See Notes to 248(4).

Note that under para. (f), an interest in or option on Canadian real property is TCP. See IT-176R2 and Notes to 116(1).

Estates: The Tax Court held in *Lipson*, 2012 TCC 20, that an estate was not a trust, so an heir's interest was not TCP, but the 2013 amendment to 248(1)"trust" overrides this (see Notes to 116(1)). However, a non-resident's interest in an estate that owns shares the deceased bought with proceeds from Canadian real property is not TCP, since the estate never held real property: VIEWS doc 2014-0542551E5.

See also the various Related Provisions above for property that is deemed to be TCP because TCP is exchanged for it or converted into it. This status now applies only for 60 months: see Notes to 44.1(2).

Subpara. (b)(ii): see Nitikman, "The Intricacies of the Reciprocation Exemption for Ships and Aircraft", XVI(3) *International Tax Planning* (Federated Press) 1120-23 (2011).

Para. (d) and subpara. (e)(ii): CRA interprets "value" as gross asset values, ignoring liabilities: VIEWS docs 2011-0425901C6 [2011 CTF q.23], 2012-0444091C6 [2012 IFA], 2015-062451117 (effect of intercompany debt) [before, see 2003-0029675]; but see also *Daishowa-Marubeni* (SCC), discussed in 54"proceeds of disposition" Notes. See also 2012-0453021C6 (corp owning mortgages does not derive its value from real property, due to 248(4)); 2012-0444431R3 (partnership interest in foreign partnership is TCP since it indirectly derives its value from Canadian real property); 18.1(12) Notes on the meaning of "derived"; and 17.1(1) Notes on "indirectly". See also Troup, "Purchasing Private Corporation Shares", 3(4) *Canadian Tax Focus* (ctf.ca) 4-5 (Nov. 2013); Mackey, "Canada Revenue Agency Views on Taxable Canadian Property Determinations Involving Subsidiaries", XX(4) *International Tax Planning* (Federated Press) 1416-21 (2015) and 2315 *Tax Topics* (CCH) 1-6 (July 21, 2016); Wen, "TCP and Intercompany Loans", 20(2) *Tax for the Owner-Manager* (ctf.ca) 9-10 (April 2020) (loans can be used to change to non-TCP status); Bowman & Kimiagar, "Restructuring Debt of a Resource Company", XIV(3) *Resource Sector Taxation* (Federated Press) 2-7 (2020) (conversion of debt to shares that are TCP).

Paras. (d), (e): The 60-month look-back, for shares whose value was previously attributable to real property, is reduced to zero by most of Canada's tax treaties, e.g. Canada-US treaty Art. XIII:3(b)(ii), Canada-UK treaty Art. 13:5(a). However, for many of these treaties (not Canada-US or Canada-UK), Article 9 of the Multilateral Instrument

(MLI — see before the Canada-US treaty) adds a 365-day look-back starting 2020 or later. This applies only if the other country has also signed on to MLI Article 9.

Para. (e): the 25% ownership and 50% asset tests must be met at the same time: 2011-0425931C6 [2011 CTF q.25, p.4:19-20]. An option to acquire 5% of the shares of a public corporation is not TCP where the holder already owns 20%, due to repeal of 115(3) (despite paras. (e) and (f)): VIEWS doc 2002-0151795; Stephanie Wong, "When Do Options Count for Listed Shares to Determine TCP?", XV(3) *Corporate Finance* (Federated Press) 1688-89 (2009). Para. (e) applies at the partner level for 2(3)(c) and 116 but at the partnership level for 115(1): 2010-0385931I7. Shares that temporarily replace listed shares as part of a corporate amalgamation are deemed listed: see 87(10). See also Lindsey et al, "US Investment in Canadian Resource Property", XVI(3) *International Tax Planning* (Federated Press) 1124-28 (2011).

Cl. (e)(i)(C) (added in 2014): For criticism see Bernstein & Gucciardo, "TCP Proposal Overshoots Objective?" 21(8) *Canadian Tax Highlights* (ctf.ca) 4-5 (Aug. 2013).

There are double-tax pitfalls for non-residents investing in Quebec rental property. See Ranger & Rudick, "Federal and Provincial Tax Considerations Relating to Non-Resident Investment", 2019 Cdn Tax Foundation conference report, 32:1-39.

2010 amendments: see Kennedy & Woo, "Narrowing of the Taxable Canadian Property Definition Welcomed by Foreign Vendors", XVI(3) *Corporate Finance* (Federated Press) 1847-50; Rudick, "New TCP Definition: 21-year Trust Rule", 18(7) *Canadian Tax Highlights [CTH]* (ctf.ca) 7-8 (July 2010); Valli, "New TCP Definition: Emigration Planning", 18(9) *CTH* 6 (Sept. 2010); Bowman, "Taxable Canadian Property", 2010 Cdn Tax Foundation conference report, 32:1-28; Ron Choudhury, "Impact of Changes to the Taxable Canadian Property Definition on Immigration and Emigration", III(3) *Personal Tax and Estate Planning* (Federated Press) 138-141 (2010).

History: Para. (b) opening words amended by 2016 budget bill #2, effective 2017, to change "eligible capital property" to Class 14.1 property (as part of replacing the ECP rules: see 20(1)(b) Notes).

248(1)"taxable Canadian property" earlier amended by 2014 budget bill #2 (for determining after July 11, 2013 whether property is TCP); 2002-2013 technical bill and 2010 budget bill #1, both for determining after March 4, 2010 whether property is TCP — see discussion above); 2007 budget bill #2, 2001 technical bill. The definition before Oct. 2, 1996 was in 115(1); it was amended by 1998 Budget, 1993 and 1991 technical bills.

Interpretation Bulletins: IT-176R2: Taxable Canadian property — Interests in and options on real property and shares; IT-420R3: Non-residents — income earned in Canada; IT-451R: Deemed disposition and acquisition on ceasing to be or becoming resident in Canada.

CRA Audit Manual: 12.13.0: Disposals of taxable Canadian property.

Forms: T2 Sched. 91: Information concerning claims for treaty-based exemptions.

"taxable capital gain" has the meaning assigned by section 38;

"taxable dividend" has the meaning assigned by subsection 89(1);

"taxable income" has the meaning assigned by subsection 2(2), except that in no case may a taxpayer's taxable income be less than nil;

"taxable income earned in Canada" means a taxpayer's taxable income earned in Canada determined in accordance with Division D of Part I, except that in no case may a taxpayer's taxable income earned in Canada be less than nil;

Related Provisions: 2(3) — Tax on TIEC; 115(1) — Non-resident's TIEC; 261(2) — Canadian currency used to determine TIEC.

Notes: Division D is ss. 115 to 116.

"taxable net gain" from dispositions of listed personal property has the meaning assigned by section 41;

"taxable preferred share" at any particular time means

(a) a share issued after December 15, 1987 that is a short-term preferred share at that particular time, or

(b) a share (other than a grandfathered share) of the capital stock of a corporation issued after 8:00 p.m. Eastern Daylight Saving Time, June 18, 1987 where, at that particular time by reason of the terms or conditions of the share or any agreement in respect of the share or its issue to which the corporation, or a specified person in relation to the corporation, is a party,

(i) it may reasonably be considered, having regard to all the circumstances, that the amount of the dividends that may be declared or paid on the share (in this definition referred to as the "dividend entitlement") is, by way of a formula or otherwise

(A) fixed,

(B) limited to a maximum, or

(C) established to be not less than a minimum (including any amount determined on a cumulative basis) and with respect to the dividend that may be declared or paid on the share there is a preference over any other dividend that may be declared or paid on any other share of the capital stock of the corporation,

(ii) it may reasonably be considered, having regard to all the circumstances, that the amount that the shareholder is entitled to receive in respect of the share on the dissolution, liquidation or winding-up of the corporation or on the redemption, acquisition or cancellation of the share (unless the requirement to redeem, acquire or cancel the share arises only in the event of the death of the shareholder or by reason only of a right to convert or exchange the share) or on a reduction of the paid-up capital of the share by the corporation or by a specified person in relation to the corporation (in this definition referred to as the "liquidation entitlement") is, by way of a formula or otherwise

(A) fixed,

(B) limited to a maximum, or

(C) established to be not less than a minimum,

and, for the purposes of this subparagraph, "shareholder" includes a shareholder of a shareholder,

(iii) the share is convertible or exchangeable at any time, unless

(A) it is convertible into or exchangeable for

(I) another share of the corporation or a corporation related to the corporation that, if issued, would not be a taxable preferred share,

(II) a right or warrant that, if exercised, would allow the person exercising it to acquire only a share of the corporation or a corporation related to the corporation that, if issued, would not be a taxable preferred share, or

(III) both a share described in subclause (I) and a right or warrant described in subclause (II), and

(B) all the consideration receivable for the share on the conversion or exchange is the share described in subclause (A)(I) or the right or warrant described in subclause (A)(II) or both, as the case may be, and, for the purposes of this clause, where a taxpayer may become entitled on the conversion or exchange of a share to receive any particular consideration (other than consideration described in any of subclauses (A)(I) to (III)) in lieu of a fraction of a share, the particular consideration shall be deemed not to be consideration unless it may reasonably be considered that the particular consideration was receivable as part of a series of transactions or events one of the main purposes of which was to avoid or limit the application of Part IV.1 or VI.1, or

(iv) any person (other than the corporation) was, at or immediately before that particular time, obligated, either absolutely or contingently, and either immediately or in the future, to effect any undertaking (in this subparagraph referred to as a "guarantee agreement"), including any guarantee, covenant or agreement to purchase or repurchase the share, and including the lending of funds to or the placing of amounts on deposit with, or on behalf of, the shareholder or any specified person in relation to the shareholder given

(A) to ensure that any loss that the shareholder or a specified person in relation to the shareholder may sustain by reason of the ownership, holding or disposition of the share or any other property is limited in any respect, or

(B) to ensure that the shareholder or a specified person in relation to the shareholder will derive earnings by reason of the ownership, holding or disposition of the share or any other property,

and the guarantee agreement was given as part of a transaction or event or a series of transactions or events that included the issuance of the share and, for the purposes of this paragraph, where a guarantee agreement in respect of a share is given at any particular time after 8:00 p.m. Eastern Daylight Saving Time, June 18, 1987, otherwise than pursuant to a written arrangement to do so entered into before 8:00 p.m. Eastern Daylight Saving Time, June 18, 1987, the share shall be deemed to have been issued at the particular time and the guarantee agreement shall be deemed to have been given as part of a series of transactions that included the issuance of the share,

but does not include a share that is at the particular time a prescribed share or a share described in paragraph (e) of the definition "term preferred share" in this subsection during the applicable time period referred to in that paragraph and, for the purposes of this definition,

(c) the dividend entitlement of a share of the capital stock of a corporation shall be deemed not to be fixed, limited to a maximum or established to be not less than a minimum where all dividends on the share are determined solely by reference to the dividend entitlement of another share of the capital stock of the corporation or of another corporation that controls the corporation that would not be a taxable preferred share if

(i) this definition were read without reference to paragraph (f),

(ii) the other share were issued after June 18, 1987, and

(iii) the other share were not a grandfathered share, a prescribed share or a share described in paragraph (e) of the definition "term preferred share" in this subsection,

(d) the liquidation entitlement of a share of the capital stock of a corporation shall be deemed not to be fixed, limited to a maximum or established to be not less than a minimum where all the liquidation entitlement is determinable solely by reference to the liquidation entitlement of another share of the capital stock of the corporation or of another corporation that controls the corporation that would not be a taxable preferred share if

(i) this definition were read without reference to paragraph (f),

(ii) the other share were issued after June 18, 1987, and

(iii) the other share were not a grandfathered share, a prescribed share or a share described in paragraph (e) of the definition "term preferred share" in this subsection,

(e) where at any particular time after 8:00 p.m. Eastern Daylight Saving Time, June 18, 1987, otherwise than pursuant to a written arrangement to do so entered into before 8:00 p.m. Eastern Daylight Saving Time, June 18, 1987, the terms or conditions of a share of the capital stock of a corporation that are relevant to any matter referred to in any of subparagraphs (b)(i) to (iv) are established or modified or any agreement in respect of any such matter, to which the corporation or a specified person in relation to the corporation is a party, is changed or entered into, the share shall, for the purpose of determining after the particular time whether it is a taxable preferred share, be deemed to have been issued at that particular time, unless

(i) the share is a share described in paragraph (b) of the definition "grandfathered share" in this subsection, and

(ii) the particular time is before December 16, 1987 and before the time at which the share is first issued,

(f) an agreement in respect of a share of the capital stock of a corporation shall be read without reference to that part of the agreement under which a person agrees to acquire the share for an amount

(i) in the case of a share the agreement in respect of which provides that the share is to be acquired within 60 days after

the day on which the agreement was entered into, that does not exceed the greater of the fair market value of the share at the time the agreement was entered into, determined without reference to the agreement, and the fair market value of the share at the time of the acquisition, determined without reference to the agreement, or

(ii) that does not exceed the fair market value of the share at the time of the acquisition, determined without reference to the agreement, or for an amount determined by reference to the assets or earnings of the corporation where that determination may reasonably be considered to be used to determine an amount that does not exceed the fair market value of the share at the time of the acquisition, determined without reference to the agreement,

(g) where

(i) it may reasonably be considered that the dividends that may be declared or paid to a shareholder at any time on a share (other than a prescribed share or a share described in paragraph (e) of the definition "term preferred share" in this subsection during the applicable time period referred to in that paragraph) of the capital stock of a corporation issued after December 15, 1987 or acquired after June 15, 1988 are derived primarily from dividends received on taxable preferred shares of the capital stock of another corporation, and

(ii) it may reasonably be considered that the share was issued or acquired as part of a transaction or event or series of transactions or events one of the main purposes of which was to avoid or limit the application of Part IV.1 or VI.1,

the share shall be deemed at that time to be a taxable preferred share, and

(h) "specified person", in relation to any particular person, means another person with whom the particular person does not deal at arm's length or any partnership or trust of which the particular person or the other person is a member or beneficiary, respectively;

Related Provisions: 87(4.2) — Amalgamation; 248(1) — "Grandfathered share"; 248(10) — Series of transactions; 248(13) — Interest in trust or partnerships.

Notes: Dividends on taxable preferred shares (TPS) are taxed to the recipient under Part IV.1 (see 187.2) and to the paying corp under Part VI.1 (see 191.1). See Downie & Martin, "The Preferred Share Rules", 2003 Cdn Tax Foundation conference report, at 52:16-28; Diep, "Preferred Share Rules", 2017 Prairie Provinces Tax Conference (ctf.ca); Fernando, "Planning Considerations for Taxable Preferred Shares", 14(6) *Tax Hyperion* (Carswell) 5-8 (2017); Joan Jung, "The Taxable Preferred Share Rules and the Private Corporation", 2017 Ontario Tax Conf.

A policy of paying dividends in the future does not establish a "minimum" under cl. (b)(i)(C) for Class B shares that have a preference over Class A shares such that the Class B shares become TPS: VIEWS doc 2003-0034073; Siobhan Monaghan, "Tax Planners' Notebook", VIII(4) *Corporate Structures & Groups* (Federated Press) at 444-46 (2003). A dividend of 75% of profit is considered "fixed": 2012-0443471E5.

Any minority discount must be considered in determining value for (f)(ii): VIEWS doc 2004-0108511E5. For a ruling that a "put" agreement does not cause shares to be TPS see 2005-0147881R3. Para. (f) applied so that shares were not TPS in 2010-0354391I7 and 2011-0431481R3. See also 2012-0454171C6 (timing of when share becomes a TPS).

For the meaning of "one of the main purposes" in (b)(iii)(B) and (g)(ii), see 83(2.1) Notes.

Regulations: 6201(7), (8) (prescribed shares).

I.T. Technical News: 7 (taxable preferred shares — stock dividend in lieu of cash dividend).

Advance Tax Rulings: ATR-46: Financial difficulty.

"taxable RFI share" at any particular time means a share of the capital stock of a corporation issued before 8:00 p.m. Eastern Daylight Saving Time, June 18, 1987 or a grandfathered share of the capital stock of a corporation, where at the particular time under the terms or conditions of the share or any agreement in respect of the share,

(a) it may reasonably be considered, having regard to all the circumstances, that the amount of the dividends that may be declared or paid on the share (in this definition referred to as the "dividend entitlement") is, by way of a formula or otherwise

(i) fixed,

(ii) limited to a maximum, or

(iii) established to be not less than a minimum, or

(b) it may reasonably be considered, having regard to all the circumstances, that the amount that the shareholder is entitled to receive in respect of the share on the dissolution, liquidation or winding-up of the corporation (in this definition referred to as the "liquidation entitlement") is, by way of formula or otherwise

(i) fixed,

(ii) limited to a maximum, or

(iii) established to be not less than a minimum,

but does not include a share that is at the particular time a prescribed share, a term preferred share, a share described in paragraph (e) of the definition "term preferred share" in this subsection during the applicable time period referred to in that paragraph or a taxable preferred share and, for the purposes of this definition,

(c) the dividend entitlement of a share of the capital stock of a corporation shall be deemed not to be fixed, limited to a maximum or established to be not less than a minimum where all dividends on the share are determined solely by reference to the dividend entitlement of another share of the capital stock of the corporation or of another corporation that controls the corporation that would not be a taxable preferred share if

(i) the definition "taxable preferred share" in this subsection were read without reference to paragraph (f) of that definition,

(ii) the other share were issued after June 18, 1987, and

(iii) the other share were not a grandfathered share, a prescribed share or a share described in paragraph (e) of the definition "term preferred share" in this subsection,

(d) the liquidation entitlement of a share of the capital stock of a corporation shall be deemed not to be fixed, limited to a maximum or established to be not less than a minimum where all the liquidation entitlement is determinable solely by reference to the liquidation entitlement of another share of the capital stock of the corporation or of another corporation that controls the corporation that would not be a taxable preferred share if

(i) the definition "taxable preferred share" in this subsection were read without reference to paragraph (f) of that definition,

(ii) the other share were issued after June 18, 1987, and

(iii) the other share were not a grandfathered share, a prescribed share or a share described in paragraph (e) of the definition "term preferred share" in this subsection, and

(e) where

(i) it may reasonably be considered that the dividends that may be declared or paid to a shareholder at any time on a share (other than a prescribed share or a share described in paragraph (e) of the definition "term preferred share" in this subsection during the applicable time period referred to in that paragraph) of the capital stock of a corporation issued after December 15, 1987 or acquired after June 15, 1988 are derived primarily from dividends received on taxable RFI shares of the capital stock of another corporation, and

(ii) it may reasonably be considered that the share was issued or acquired as part of a transaction or event or series of transactions or events one of the main purposes of which was to avoid or limit the application of Part IV.1,

the share shall be deemed at that time to be a taxable RFI share;

Related Provisions: 87(4.2) — Amalgamation; 187.3(1) — Tax on dividends on taxable RFI share; 248(10) — Series of transactions.

Notes: "RFI" stands for "restricted financial institution".

For the meaning of "one of the main purposes" in (e)(ii), see Notes to 83(2.1).

Regulations: 6201(4), (5.1), (9)–(11) (prescribed shares).

Advance Tax Rulings: ATR-46: Financial difficulty.

"taxpayer" includes any person whether or not liable to pay tax;

Related Provisions: See Related Provisions to 96(1) for provisions that deem "taxpayer" to include a partnership for specific purposes.

Notes: Generally, the terms "person" and "taxpayer" are interchangeable: *Bydeley*, 2012 TCC 142; *Pomerleau*, 2017 ABQB 123, paras. 61-63; *Kim*, 2017 TCC 246 (FCA appeal heard April 8/19), para. 31 (and see Notes to 248(1)"person"). However, in *Oceanspan Carriers*, [1987] 1 C.T.C. 210 (FCA), a non-resident (NR) corporation with no income from Canadian sources was not liable to pay tax under the Act on its foreign income and hence was held not to be contemplated by the definition of "taxpayer"; and in *Marino*, 2020 TCC 50 (under appeal to FCA), the same applied to a NR individual (who was denied tuition expenses carried forward to when he became resident), despite 250.1. Similarly, see *Cameco*, 2018 TCC 195, para. 801 (aff'd on other grounds 2020 FCA 112; leave to appeal denied 2021 CarswellNat 377 (SCC)). CRA says that based on *Oceanspan*, a non-resident is not a "taxpayer" eligible for the 118.3 disability credit, and so cannot transfer the credit to a resident spouse via 118.8: VIEWS doc 2019-083404117. See also Notes to 248(1)"person".

A bare trustee is not considered to be a separate person; rather, the beneficial owner is considered to deal directly with the property to which the bare trustee holds legal title, subject to some legislated exceptions. See Notes to 104(1) and 248(1)"disposition".

A partnership is considered a "taxpayer" for purposes of 51(1), 85.1(1) and 86(1): VIEWS doc 2005-0150411E5.

Interpretation Bulletins: IT-291R3: Transfer of property to a corporation under subsection 85(1).

"term preferred share" of a corporation (in this definition referred to as the "issuing corporation") means a share of a class of the capital stock of the issuing corporation if the share was issued or acquired after June 28, 1982 and, at the time the share was issued or acquired, the existence of the issuing corporation was, or there was an arrangement under which it could be, limited or, in the case of a share issued after November 16, 1978 if

(a) under the terms or conditions of the share, any agreement relating to the share or any modification of those terms or conditions or that agreement,

(i) the owner thereof may cause the share to be redeemed, acquired or cancelled (unless the owner of the share may cause the share to be redeemed, acquired or cancelled by reason only of a right to convert or exchange the share) or cause its paid-up capital to be reduced,

(ii) the issuing corporation or any other person or partnership is or may be required to redeem, acquire or cancel, in whole or in part, the share (unless the requirement to redeem, acquire or cancel the share arises by reason only of a right to convert or exchange the share) or to reduce its paid-up capital,

(iii) the issuing corporation or any other person or partnership provides or may be required to provide any form of guarantee, security or similar indemnity or covenant (including the lending of funds to or the placing of amounts on deposit with, or on behalf of, the holder thereof or any person related thereto) with respect to the share, or

(iv) the share is convertible or exchangeable unless

(A) it is convertible into or exchangeable for

(I) another share of the issuing corporation or a corporation related to the issuing corporation that, if issued, would not be a term preferred share,

(II) a right or warrant that, if exercised, would allow the person exercising it to acquire only a share of the issuing corporation or a corporation related to the issuing corporation that, if issued, would not be a term preferred share, or

(III) both a share described in subclause (I) and a right or warrant described in subclause (II), and

(B) all the consideration receivable for the share on the conversion or exchange is the share described in subclause (A)(I) or the right or warrant described in subclause (A)(II) or both, as the case may be, and, for the purposes of this clause, where a taxpayer may become entitled on the conversion or exchange of a share to receive any particular consideration (other than consideration described in any of subclauses (A)(I) to (III)) in lieu of a fraction of a share, the particular consideration shall be deemed not to be consideration unless it may reasonably be considered that the particular consideration was receivable as part of a series of transactions or events one of the main purposes of which was to avoid or limit the application of subsection 112(2.1) or 258(3), or

(b) the owner thereof acquired the share after October 23, 1979 and is

(i) a corporation described in any of paragraphs (a) to (e.1) of the definition "specified financial institution",

(ii) a corporation that is controlled by one or more corporations described in subparagraph (i),

(iii) a corporation that acquired the share after December 11, 1979 and is related to a corporation referred to in subparagraph (i) or (ii), or

(iv) a partnership or trust of which a corporation referred to in subparagraph (i) or (ii) or a person related thereto is a member or a beneficiary,

that (either alone or together with any of such corporations, partnerships or trusts) controls or has an absolute or contingent right to control or to acquire control of the issuing corporation,

but does not include a share of the capital stock of a corporation

(c) that was issued after November 16, 1978 and before 1980 pursuant to an agreement in writing to do so made before November 17, 1978 (in this definition referred to as an "established agreement"),

(d) that was issued as a stock dividend

(i) before April 22, 1980 on a share of the capital stock of a public corporation that was not a term preferred share, or

(ii) after April 21, 1980 on a share that was, at the time the stock dividend was paid, a share prescribed for the purposes of paragraph (f),

(d.1) that is listed on a designated stock exchange in Canada and was issued before April 22, 1980 by

(i) a corporation referred to in any of paragraphs (a) to (d) of the definition "specified financial institution" in this subsection,

(ii) a corporation whose principal business is the lending of money or the purchasing of debt obligations or a combination thereof, or

(iii) an issuing corporation associated with a corporation described in subparagraph (i) or (ii),

(e) for a period not exceeding ten years and, in the case of a share issued after November 12, 1981, for a period not exceeding five years, from the date of its issuance, which share was issued by a corporation resident in Canada,

(i) as part of a proposal to, or an arrangement with, its creditors that had been approved by a court under the *Bankruptcy and Insolvency Act*,

(ii) at a time when all or substantially all of its assets were under the control of a receiver, receiver-manager, sequestrator or trustee in bankruptcy, or

(iii) at a time when, by reason of financial difficulty, the issuing corporation or another corporation resident in Canada with which it does not deal at arm's length was in default, or could reasonably be expected to default, on a debt obligation held by a person with whom the issuing corporation or the other corporation was dealing at arm's length and the share was issued either wholly or in substantial part and either directly or indirectly in exchange or substitution for that obligation or a part thereof,

and, in the case of a share issued after November 12, 1981, the proceeds from the issue may reasonably be regarded as having been used by the issuing corporation or a corporation with which it was not dealing at arm's length in the financing of its business carried on in Canada immediately before the share was issued,

(f) that is a prescribed share, or

(f.1) that is a taxable preferred share held by a specified financial institution that acquired the share

(i) before December 16, 1987, or

(ii) before 1989 pursuant to an agreement in writing entered into before December 16, 1987,

other than a share deemed by paragraph (c) of the definition "short-term preferred share" in this subsection or by paragraph (i.2) to have been issued after December 15, 1987 or a share that would be deemed by paragraph (e) of the definition "taxable preferred share" in this subsection to have been issued after December 15, 1987 if the references therein to "8:00 p.m. Eastern Daylight Saving Time, June 18, 1987" were read as references to "December 15, 1987",

and, for the purposes of this definition,

(g) where the terms or conditions of an established agreement were amended after November 16, 1978, the agreement shall be deemed to have been made after that date,

(h) where

(i) at any particular time the terms or conditions of a share issued pursuant to an established agreement or of any agreement relating to such a share have been changed,

(ii) under the terms or conditions of

(A) a share of a class of the capital stock of the issuing corporation issued before November 17, 1978 (other than a share that was listed on November 16, 1978 on a prescribed stock exchange in Canada),

(B) a share issued pursuant to an established agreement,

(C) any agreement between the issuing corporation and the owner of a share described in clause (A) or (B), or

(D) any agreement relating to a share described in clause (A) or (B) made after October 23, 1979,

the owner thereof could at any particular time after November 16, 1978 require, either alone or together with one or more taxpayers, the redemption, acquisition, cancellation, conversion or reduction of the paid-up capital of the share otherwise than by reason of a failure or default under the terms or conditions of the share or any agreement that related to, and was entered into at the time of, the issuance of the share,

(iii) in respect of a share issued before November 17, 1978, at any particular time after November 16, 1978 the redemption date was extended or the terms or conditions relating to its redemption, acquisition, cancellation, conversion or reduction of its paid-up capital were changed,

(iv) at a particular time after October 23, 1979 and before November 13, 1981, a specified financial institution (or a partnership or trust of which a specified financial institution or a person related to the institution is a member or beneficiary) acquired a share that

(A) was issued before November 17, 1978 or under an established agreement,

(B) was issued to a person other than a corporation that was, at the time of issue,

(I) described in any of paragraphs (a) to (e) of the definition "specified financial institution", or

(II) a corporation that was controlled by one or more corporations described in subclause (I) and, for the purpose of this subclause, one corporation is controlled by another corporation if more than 50% of its issued share capital (having full voting rights under all circumstances) belongs to the other corporation, to persons with whom the other corporation does not deal at arm's length, or to the other corporation and persons with whom the other corporation does not deal at arm's length,

(C) was acquired from a person that was, at the particular time, a person other than a corporation described in subclause (B)(I) or (II), and

(D) was acquired otherwise than under an agreement in writing made before October 24, 1979,

(v) at any particular time after November 12, 1981

(A) in respect of

(I) a share (other than a share referred to in paragraph (e) or a share listed on November 13, 1981 on a prescribed stock exchange in Canada) issued after November 16, 1978 and before November 13, 1981, or

(II) a share issued after November 12, 1981 and before 1983 pursuant to an agreement in writing to do so made before November 13, 1981 (in this definition referred to as a "specified agreement")

the owner thereof could require, either alone or together with one or more taxpayers, the redemption, acquisition, cancellation, conversion or reduction of the paid-up capital of the share otherwise than by reason of a failure or default under the terms or conditions of the share or any agreement that related to, and was entered into at the time of, the issuance of the share, or

(B) the redemption date of

(I) a share issued after November 16, 1978 and before November 13, 1981 or

(II) a share issued pursuant to a specified agreement

was extended or the terms or conditions relating to its redemption, acquisition, cancellation, conversion or reduction of its paid-up capital were changed, or

(vi) at a particular time after November 12, 1981, a specified financial institution (or a partnership or trust of which a specified financial institution or a person related to the institution is a member or beneficiary) acquired a share (other than a share referred to in paragraph (e)) that

(A) was issued before November 13, 1981 or under a specified agreement,

(B) was acquired from a partnership or person, other than a person that was, at the particular time, a corporation described in any of paragraphs (a) to (f) of the definition "specified financial institution" in this subsection,

(C) was acquired in an acquisition that was not subject to nor conditional on a guarantee agreement, within the meaning assigned by subsection 112(2.2), entered into after November 12, 1981, and

(D) was acquired otherwise than under an agreement in writing made before October 24, 1979 or a specified agreement,

the share shall, for the purposes of determining at any time after the particular time whether it is a term preferred share, be deemed to have been issued at the particular time otherwise than pursuant to an established or specified agreement,

(i) where the terms or conditions of a share of the capital stock of the issuing corporation are modified or established after June 28, 1982 and as a consequence thereof the issuing corporation, any person related thereto or any partnership or trust of which the issuing corporation or a person related thereto is a member or a beneficiary may reasonably be expected at any time to redeem, acquire or cancel, in whole or in part, the share or to reduce its paid-up capital, the share shall be deemed as from the date of the modification or as from the date of the establishment, as the case may be, to be a share described in paragraph (a),

(i.1) where

(i) it may reasonably be considered that the dividends that may be declared or paid at any time on a share (other than a prescribed share or a share described in paragraph (e) during the applicable time period referred to in that paragraph) of the capital stock of a corporation issued after December 15, 1987 or acquired after June 15, 1988 are derived primarily from dividends received on term preferred shares of the capital stock of another corporation, and

(ii) it may reasonably be considered that the share was issued or acquired as part of a transaction or event or series of transactions or events one of the main purposes of which was to avoid or limit the application of subsection 112(2.1) or 138(6),

the share shall be deemed at that time to be a term preferred share acquired in the ordinary course of business,

(i.2) where at any particular time after December 15, 1987, otherwise than pursuant to a written arrangement to do so entered into before December 16, 1987, the terms or conditions of a taxable preferred share of the capital stock of a corporation relating to any matter referred to in subparagraphs (a)(i) to (iv) have been modified or established, or any agreement in respect of the share relating to any such matter has been changed or entered into by the corporation or a specified person (within the meaning assigned by paragraph (h) of the definition "taxable preferred share" in this subsection) in relation to the corporation, the share shall be deemed after that particular time to have been issued at that particular time, and,

(j) where a particular share of the capital stock of a corporation has been issued or its terms and conditions have been modified and it may reasonably be considered, having regard to all circumstances (including the rate of interest on any debt or the dividend provided on any term preferred share), that

(i) but for the existence at any time of the debt or the term preferred share, the particular share would not have been issued or its terms or conditions modified, and

(ii) one of the main purposes for the issue of the particular share or for the modification of its terms or conditions was to avoid a limitation provided by subsection 112(2.1) or 138(6) in respect of a deduction,

the particular share shall be deemed after December 31, 1982 to be a term preferred share of the corporation;

Related Provisions: 80(1) — Definition of "distress preferred share"; 87(4.1) — Amalgamations — exchanged shares; 112(2.1) — No deduction on intercorporate dividends; 112(2.6)"exempt share"(c) — Distress preferred shares excluded from restrictions on collateralized preferred shares; 248(10) — Series of transactions; 248(13) — Interests in trusts or partnerships; 256(1.6) — Fair market valuation; 256(6), (6.1) — Meaning of "controlled"; Canada-U.S. Tax Treaty:Art. XXIX-A:5(a) — Meaning of "debt substitute share".

Notes: Term preferred shares (TPS) result in no deduction under 112(2.1), so intercorporate dividends on such shares are taxable. For discussion see Elinore Richardson, "Term Preferred Shares Revisited", VIII(2) *Corporate Finance* (Federated Press) 726-30 (2000); David Downie & Tony Martin, "The Preferred Share Rules: An Introduction", 2003 Cdn Tax Foundation conference report, at 52:1-13; Elizabeth Johnson & James Wilson, "Financing Foreign Affiliates: The Term Preferred Share Rules and Tower Structures", 54(3) *Canadian Tax Journal* 726-61 (2006); Nancy Diep, "Preferred Share Rules", 2017 Prairie Provinces Tax Conference (ctf.ca).

In *Citibank Canada*, 2002 FCA 128, preferred shares with a conversion formula, drafted to avoid this definition, were held not to be TPS, as they were not debt.

For the meaning of "one of the main purposes" in (a)(iv)(B), (i.1)(ii) and (j)(ii), see Notes to 83(2.1).

For the meaning of "principal business" in (d.1)(ii), see Notes to 20(1)(bb).

The shares described in para. (e) are called "distress preferred" or "financial difficulty" shares. See Notes to 80.02(2).

CRA considers that "substantially all", used in (e)(ii), means 90% or more.

Para. (d.1) amended by 2007 budget bill #2, effective Dec. 14, 2007, to change "prescribed stock exchange" to "designated stock exchange".

Subpara. (h)(vi) amended by 1998 Budget, effective for taxation years that begin after 1998 except that, in application to a share acquired from a corporation that last acquired the share in a taxation year that began before 1999, read "described in any of paragraphs (a) to (f) of the definition "specified financial institution" in this subsection" as "described in subclause (iv)(B)(I) or (II)".

Definition also amended by 1998 Budget (effective for taxation years that begin after 1998) and 1995-97 technical bill.

"Term preferred share" amended extensively by 1988 tax reform. Some of the changes were effective June 19, 1987, others shares issued (or deemed issued) after 8pm EDST, June 18, 1987. The definition reads differently for shares issued before that time.

Regulations: 3200 (repealed — for "prescribed stock exchange in Canada" in (h)(ii)(A) and (h)(v)(A)(I)); 6201 (prescribed shares).

Interpretation Bulletins: IT-527: Distress preferred shares.

I.T. Technical News: 25 (*Silicon Graphics* case — dispersed control is not control).

Advance Tax Rulings: ATR-5: Preferred shares exchangeable for common shares; ATR-10: Issue of term preferred shares; ATR-18: Term preferred shares; ATR-46: Financial difficulty.

"termination payment" — [Repealed under former Act]

Notes: "Termination payment" repealed by 1981 Budget. Payments for termination of employment, including severance pay and wrongful dismissal awards, now fall under "retiring allowance", taxed under 56(1)(a)(ii). See Notes to 248(1)"retiring allowance".

"testamentary trust" has the meaning assigned by subsection 108(1);

["TFSA"] — [See "at beginning of 't' entries.]

"timber resource property" has the meaning assigned by subsection 13(21);

"total pension adjustment reversal" of a taxpayer for a calendar year has the meaning assigned by regulation;

Related Provisions: 147.1(18)(t) — Authorization for regulations for TPAR.

Notes: See Notes to Reg. 8304.1. Definition "total pension adjustment reversal" added by 1997 Budget, effective 1997.

Regulations: 8304.1 (pension adjustment reversal).

Forms: RC4137: Pension adjustment reversal guide; T4104: Past service pension adjustment guide.

"Treasury Board" means the Treasury Board established by section 5 of the *Financial Administration Act*;

Notes: Sections 5-13 of the *Financial Administration Act* create the Treasury Board and set out its powers.

"treaty-protected business" of a taxpayer at any time means a business in respect of which any income of the taxpayer for a period that includes that time would, because of a tax treaty with another country, be exempt from tax under Part I;

Notes: "Country" includes Hong Kong and Taiwan: see Notes to 219.2.

Definition "treaty-protected business" added by 1998 Budget, for 1998 and later taxation years. Note that a business can be a treaty-protected business even if it has generated no treaty-exempt income.

CRA Audit Manual: 15.2.10: Treaty-protected businesses.

"treaty-protected property" of a taxpayer at any time means property any income or gain from the disposition of which by the taxpayer at that time would, because of a tax treaty with another country, be exempt from tax under Part I;

Related Provisions: 13(4.1)(d) — Replacement of depreciable property that is not treaty-protected property; 44(5)(d) — Replacement of capital property that is not treaty-protected property; 116(5.01), (5.02), (6.1) — Acquisition of treaty-protected property from non-resident — notice requirement in place of s. 116 certificate.

Notes: See Notes to 116(1) and (5.01). It is not necessary, for this definition to apply, that there be income or gain from the disposition of the property, or that the property be disposed of. See VIEWS doc 2012-0444431R3 (partnership interest in foreign partnership is treaty-protected property).

"Country" includes Hong Kong and Taiwan: see Notes to 219.2.

Definition added by 1998 Budget, for 1998 and later taxation years.

"trust" has the meaning assigned by subsection 104(1) and, unless the context otherwise requires, includes an estate;

Related Provisions: 94(3)(a) — Trust deemed resident in Canada for certain purposes; 108(1) — Meaning of "trust" in ss. 104-108; 146.1(1) — RESPs — "Meaning of trust" in ss. 146.1 and 204.9-204.93; 149(5) — Exception re investment income of certain clubs; 207.6(1) — Definitions (re RCA tax); 233.2(4) — Reporting requirement re transfers to foreign trust; 233.6(1) — Reporting requirement re distributions from foreign trust; 248(3) — Deemed trusts in Quebec; 248(25.1) — Trust-to-trust transfers — deemed same trust.

Notes: Definition amended by 2013 budget bill #2, effective Dec. 12, 2013, to add "and, unless the context otherwise requires, includes an estate". This amendment and that to 248(1)"estate" overrule the *Homer* and *Lipson* cases in the Notes to 104(1).

"trust account number" means the number (other than a business number)

(a) used by the Minister to identify a trust, and

(b) of which the Minister has notified the trust;

Notes: "Trust account number" added by 2018 budget bill #1, for 2018 and later tax years, as part of amendments to increase reporting about trusts. See also Feb. 2018 Budget Supplementary Information and Backgrounder under 150(1.2).

"undepreciated capital cost" to a taxpayer of depreciable property of a prescribed class has the meaning assigned by subsection 13(21);

"unit trust" has the meaning assigned by subsection 108(2);

Related Provisions: 248(1)"personal trust" — Unit trust deemed not to be a personal trust.

Notes: A definition **"unrecognized gains balance"** was proposed in the draft trusts legislation of Dec. 23, 1998, but was not in the revised draft of Dec. 17, 1999 (which became the 2001 technical bill).

"unused RRSP deduction room" of a taxpayer at the end of a taxation year has the meaning assigned by subsection 146(1);

Notes: "Unused RRSP deduction room" added by 1990 pension bill, effective 1989.

"unused scientific research and experimental development tax credit" of a taxpayer for a taxation year has the meaning assigned by subsection 127.3(2);

Notes: "Unused scientific research and experimental development tax credit" added in RSC 1985 (5th Supp) consolidation, effective Dec. 1, 1991.

"unused share-purchase tax credit" of a taxpayer for a taxation year has the meaning assigned by subsection 127.2(6);

Notes: 248(1)"unused share-purchase tax credit" added in the RSC 1985 (5th Supp) consolidation, effective December 1, 1991.

"zero-emission passenger vehicle", of a taxpayer, means an automobile of the taxpayer that is included in Class 54 of Schedule II to the *Income Tax Regulations*;

Notes: ZEPV and "zero-emission vehicle" (ZEV) are definitions used for the incentives for electric, hydrogen and hybrid vehicles introduced in the 2019 Budget. They apply only to vehicles acquired after March 18, 2019. Only a Class 54 vehicle is a ZEPV; a taxi or rental car that is a ZEV goes into Class 55 and is not a ZEPV.

A ZEPV is limited for capital cost allowance purposes to a cost of $55,000: 13(7)(i), Reg. 7307(1.1). Subject to that limit (and the available-for-use rules in 13(26)-(32)), 100% can be deducted as CCA for Class 54 for the year of acquisition (if before 2024): Reg. 1100(2)A(e)(i). For Class 55, there is no cost cap and again 100% can be deducted: Reg. 1100(2)A(f)(i).

See also Notes to 248(1)"zero-emission vehicle", as well as 13(7)(i), 67.2, 20(4.11) and Reg. 1103(2j).

Definition added by 2019 budget bill #1, effective March 19, 2019.

"zero-emission vehicle", of a taxpayer, means a motor vehicle that

(a) is a plug-in hybrid that meets prescribed conditions or is fully

(i) electric, or

(ii) powered by hydrogen,

(b) is acquired, and becomes available for use, by the taxpayer after March 18, 2019 and before 2028,

(c) does not meet any of the following conditions:

(i) it is a vehicle in respect of which the taxpayer has, at any time, made an election under subsection 1103(2j) of the *Income Tax Regulations*,

(ii) it is a vehicle in respect of which assistance has been paid by the Government of Canada under a prescribed program, and

(iii) if the vehicle was acquired before March 2, 2020, either

(A) it has been used, or acquired for use, for any purpose before it was acquired by the taxpayer, or

(B) it is a vehicle in respect of which an amount has been deducted under paragraph 20(1)(a) or subsection 20(16) by another person or partnership, and

(d) would be accelerated investment incentive property of the taxpayer if subsection 1104(4) of the *Income Tax Regulations* were read without its exclusions for property included in Class 54 or Class 55 of Schedule II to those Regulations.

Related Provisions: Reg. Sch. II:Cl. 54, 55, 56 — CCA classes for ZEVs.

Notes: ZEV and "zero-emission passenger vehicle" (ZEPV) are definitions used for the incentives for electric, hydrogen and hybrid vehicles introduced in the 2019 Budget. They apply only to vehicles acquired after March 18, 2019.

Vehicles in respect of which assistance is paid under the new federal purchase incentive announced in Budget 2019 are ineligible: cl. (c)(ii)(B), Reg. 1102(26)(b). For para. (a), the prescribed condition is battery capacity of at least 7 kWh: Reg. 1102(26)(a).

See also Notes to 248(1)"zero-emission passenger vehicle".

Para. (c) amended and (d) added by 2021 budget bill #1, effective March 2, 2020. Before that date, read:

(c) is not a vehicle

(i) that has been used, or acquired for use, for any purpose before it was acquired by the taxpayer, or

(ii) in respect of which

(A) the taxpayer has, at any time, made an election under subsection 1103(2j) of the *Income Tax Regulations*,

(B) assistance has been paid by the Government of Canada under a prescribed program, or

(C) an amount has been deducted under paragraph 20(1)(a) or subsection 20(16) by another person or partnership.

Definition added by 2019 budget bill #1, effective March 19, 2019.

Regulations: 1102(26) (prescribed condition for para. (a) is battery capacity of at least 7 kWh; prescribed program for (c)(ii)(B) is 2019 Budget federal purchase incentive of up to $5,000 for electric battery or hydrogen fuel cell vehicles with a manufacturer.s suggested retail price of less than $45,000).

"10/8 policy" means a life insurance policy (other than an annuity) where

(a) an amount is or may become

(i) payable, under the terms of a borrowing, to a person or partnership that has been assigned an interest in the policy or in an investment account in respect of the policy, or

(ii) payable (within the meaning assigned by the definition "amount payable" in subsection 138(12)) under a policy loan (as defined in subsection 148(9)) made in accordance with the terms and conditions of the policy, and

(b) either

(i) the return credited to an investment account in respect of the policy

(A) is determined by reference to the rate of interest on the borrowing or policy loan, as the case may be, described in paragraph (a), and

(B) would not be credited to the account if the borrowing or policy loan, as the case may be, were not in existence, or

(ii) the maximum amount of an investment account in respect of the policy is determined by reference to the amount of the borrowing or policy loan, as the case may be, described in paragraph (a);

Related Provisions: 20(2.01) — No deduction for interest on money borrowed to acquire 10/8 policy; 20(1)(e.2)(ii) — No deduction for premiums on 10/8 policy; 89(1)"capital dividend account"(d)(iv) — Reduction in CDA increase on death.

Notes: The 10/8 policy rules were introduced by the 2013 Budget (along with the "LIA policy" rules). A 10/8 arrangement involves investing in a life insurance policy and borrowing against that investment to create a long-term annual interest-expense deduction (investing in other income-producing assets). If the policy is an exempt policy and yields 8% tax-free, paying deductible (20(1)(c)) interest of 10% would net a profit after tax (e.g., in a 50% bracket, the deductible interest really costs 5%). As well, there would be an annual deduction (20(1)(e.2)) for a portion of the premiums paid under the policy and an increase in the capital dividend account (CDA) of a private corporation that was a beneficiary under the policy.

Existing 10/8 arrangements are being challenged in the Courts, but the 2013 amendments now deny these benefits, by denying the 20(1)(c) deduction [see 20(2.01)], deductibility of the premium [see 20(1)(e.2)(ii)] and the CDA increase [see 89(1)"capital dividend account"(d)(iv)].

For discussion see Stone, "10/8 Arrangements", 2013 STEP Canada conference (contact memberservices@step.ca); Everett, "Life Insurance Planning after the 2013 Budget", 2013 Cdn Tax Foundation conference report at 32:6-15. CRA will monitor compliance with the 10/8 rules and communicate concerns to Finance: VIEWS doc 2016-0632611C6 [2016 CALU q.2].

For CRA attempts to get information on 10/8 policies before these proposals, see 231.2(3) Notes re the *RBC Life* case.

Definition added by 2013 budget bill #2, effective for taxation years that end after March 20, 2013.

Income Tax Folios: S3-F2-C1: Capital Dividends [replaces IT-66R6]; S3-F6-C1: Interest deductibility [replaces IT-533].

"1971 capital surplus on hand", "1971 undistributed income on hand" — [Repealed under former Act]

Notes: See Notes to repealed 89(1)"1971 capital surplus on hand".

(1.1) [No longer relevant]

Notes: This rule is now in 248(1)"disposition"(n), for a redemption, acquisition or cancellation after Dec. 23, 1998. 248(1.1), added by 2002-2013 technical bill, applies to an earlier redemption, acquisition or cancellation of a share or right.

(2) Tax payable — In this Act, the tax payable by a taxpayer under any Part of this Act by or under which provision is made for the assessment of tax means the tax payable by the taxpayer as fixed by assessment or reassessment subject to variation on objection or on appeal, if any, in accordance with the provisions of that Part.

Related Provisions: 117(1) — Meaning of "tax payable" for purposes of 117–127.4.

(3) Property subject to certain Quebec institutions and arrangements [deemed trusts] — For the purposes of this Act, if property is subject to an institution or arrangement that is described by this subsection and that is governed by the laws of the Province of Quebec, the following rules apply in respect of the property:

(a) if at any time property is subject to a usufruct, right of use or habitation, or substitution,

(i) the usufruct, right of use or habitation, or substitution, as the case may be, is deemed to be at that time

(A) a trust, and

(B) where the usufruct, right of use or habitation, or substitution, as the case may be, is created by will, a trust created by will,

(ii) the property is deemed

(A) where the usufruct, right of use or habitation, or substitution, as the case may be, arises on the death of a testator, to have been transferred to the trust on and as a consequence of the death of the testator, and not otherwise, and

(B) where the usufruct, right of use or habitation, or substitution, as the case may be, arises otherwise, to have been transferred (at the time it first became subject to the usufruct, right of use or habitation, or substitution, as the case may be) to the trust by the person that granted the usufruct, right of use or habitation, or substitution, and

(iii) the property is deemed to be, throughout the period in which it is subject to the usufruct, right of use or habitation, or substitution, as the case may be, held by the trust, and not otherwise;

(b) an arrangement (other than a partnership, a qualifying arrangement or an arrangement that is a trust determined without reference to this paragraph) is deemed to be a trust and property subject to rights and obligations under the arrangement is, if the arrangement is deemed by this paragraph to be a trust, deemed to be held in trust and not otherwise, where the arrangement

    (i) is established before October 31, 2003 by or under a written contract that

        (A) is governed by the laws of the Province of Quebec, and

        (B) provides that, for the purposes of this Act, the arrangement shall be considered to be a trust, and

    (ii) creates rights and obligations that are substantially similar to the rights and obligations under a trust (determined without reference to this subsection);

(c) if the arrangement is a qualifying arrangement,

    (i) the arrangement is deemed to be a trust,

    (ii) any property contributed at any time to the arrangement by an annuitant, a holder or a subscriber of the arrangement, as the case may be, is deemed to have been transferred, at that time, to the trust by the contributor, and

    (iii) property subject to rights and obligations under the arrangement is deemed to be held in trust and not otherwise;

(d) a person who has a right (whether immediate or future and whether absolute or contingent) to receive all or part of the income or capital in respect of property that is referred to in paragraph (a) or (b) is deemed to be beneficially interested in the trust; and

(e) notwithstanding that a property is at any time subject to a servitude, the property is deemed to be beneficially owned by a person at that time if, at that time, the person has in relation to the property

    (i) the right of ownership,

    (ii) a right as a lessee under an emphyteusis, or

    (iii) a right as a beneficiary in a trust.

Related Provisions: 248(3.1) — Gift of bare ownership of immovables; 248(3.2) — Qualifying arrangement; 248(8) — Meaning of "consequence" of death; 248(9.1) — Trust created by taxpayer's will; 248(25) — Beneficially interested; *Interpretation Act* 8.1, 8.2 — Common law and civil law equally authoritative.

Notes: 248(3) is needed because Quebec is governed by the *Civil Code*, which does not have the concept of "trust". The trust (see 104(1) Notes) was developed by the courts in common-law jurisdictions, including England and all other provinces. See *Interpretation Act* s. 8.1 Notes on the "bijuralism" project. See also Bruneau, "Problems in the Application of Tax Law to Civil Law Trusts", 51(1) *Canadian Tax Journal* 252-310 (2003); Brender, "Beneficial Ownership in Canadian Income Tax Law", 51(1) *CTJ* 311-54 (2003); Bergeron, "Principal Residence: When Civil Law Muddles Tax Law", 3(2) *Canadian Tax Focus* (ctf.ca) 8-9 (May 2013); Piccini Roy, "Demystifying the Quebec 'Fiducie' or Trust", 2013 STEP Canada conference (contact memberservices@step.ca).

The rules for usufruct are found in Quebec *Civil Code* art. 1120-1171. See VIEWS docs 2005-0133321E5, 2006-0214631E5, 2009-0310751I7, 2009-0314161E5, 2010-0367371E5, 2010-0389911R3, 2011-0421791E5, 2012-0449141E5, 2012-0451281C6, 2014-0519811E5, 2014-0522641E5; 2020-0852171C6 [2020 APFF q.5] (principal-residence exemption where deceased's will creates usufruct for spouse). On trusts/fiducies in Quebec, see also 2009-0317641E5; 2011-0422471E5; 2014-0527261E5 (X is both transferor and sole beneficiary of Quebec trust; 107.4(1)(a) applies); 2014-0537691E5 (Quebec administration of property created by will is not a trust). On a transfer of property in France via a usufruct under the French *Civil Code*, see 2012-0466081I7. On whether a usufruct can be a 70(6) spousal trust, see 2016-0672501E5.

Vallée, 2004 TCC 320, held that a Quebec "fiducie" should be treated like a trust and thus was ineligible for a GST new housing rebate.

In *Lee*, 2018 TCC 230, a Quebec trust set up by a BC resident to avoid provincial tax was held to be a valid Quebec trust and not a sham (this "Quebec truffle" failed anyway due to retroactive QC legislation).

248(3)(c) and 248(3.2) respond to *Bank of Nova Scotia v. Thibault*, 2004 SCC 29, which involved seizability of an arrangement that had been marketed as a self-directed trusteed RRSP. The SCC ruled that no trust was created under the *Civil Code*. This created uncertainty as to whether the arrangement (and similar ones) was an RRSP. The 248(3.2) conditions recognize that *Thibault* gives rise to concerns that the arrangement in that case (and similar ones seeking registered status) might not be able to satisfy the conditions for former 248(3)(d) (now (b)) to apply. [Finance Technical Notes]

Due to 248(3)(e)(ii), the income from an emphyteusis cannot be amortized over its duration: VIEWS doc 2013-0487791E5.

For comment on an earlier draft of the 2009 amendments see Jack Bernstein, "Usufructs, Foundations: NRTs", 11(12) *Canadian Tax Highlights* (ctf.ca) 5-6 (Dec. 2003).

Unless 248(3) applies, neither a usufructuary nor the bare owner could claim CCA on real property subject to a usufruct before the amendments: VIEWS doc 2003-0009697.

For the meaning of "beneficially owned" in common-law provinces, see *568864 B.C. Ltd.*, 2014 TCC 373 and the case law it cites; and Notes to 54"capital property".

248(3) amended by 2008 budget bill #2, this version effective for 2008 and later tax years.

248(3) earlier amended by 1991 technical bill.

Interpretation Bulletins: IT-305R4: Testamentary spouse trusts.

(3.1) Gift of bare ownership of immovables — Subsection (3) does not apply in respect of a usufruct or a right of use of an immovable in circumstances where a taxpayer disposes of the bare ownership of the immovable by way of a gift to a qualified donee and retains, for life, the usufruct or the right of use.

Notes: 248(3.1) amended by 2011 budget bill #2, effective 2012. Added by 2008 budget bill #2, for dispositions after July 18, 2005.

(3.2) Qualifying arrangement — For the purposes of paragraphs 248(3)(b) and (c), an arrangement is a qualifying arrangement if it is

(a) entered into with a corporation that is licensed or otherwise authorized under the laws of Canada or a province to carry on in Canada the business of offering to the public its services as trustee;

(b) established by or under a written contract that is governed by the laws of the Province of Quebec;

(c) presented as a declaration of trust or provides that, for the purposes of this Act, it shall be considered to be a trust; and

(d) presented as an arrangement in respect of which the corporation is to take action for the arrangement to become a registered disability savings plan, a registered education savings plan, a registered retirement income fund, a registered retirement savings plan or a TFSA.

Notes: See Notes to 248(3). 248(3.2) added by 2008 budget bill #2, this version effective for 2009 and later tax years.

(4) Interest in real property — In this Act, an interest in real property includes a leasehold interest in real property but does not include an interest as security only derived by virtue of a mortgage, agreement for sale or similar obligation.

Related Provisions: 43.1(1) — Life estates in real property; 248(4.1) — Real right in an immovable under Quebec civil law; *Interpretation Act* 8.1, 8.2 — Common law and civil law equally authoritative.

Notes: See 248(4.1) for the parallel rule under the Quebec *Civil Code*.

A mortgage or mortgage pool is not normally an interest in real property (RP): VIEWS docs 2011-0431891R3, 2012-0453021C6.

Fixtures attached to a building or land are RP at common law, depending on level of permanency, degree of affixation, and whether it improves the land: *Stack v. T. Eaton Co.* (1902), 4 O.L.R. 335 (Ont. Div Ct); *Royalite Oil* (1928), [1929] 4 D.L.R. 1070 (Alta. Dist. Ct) (oil tanks were RP); *British Columbia Forest Products*, [1971] C.T.C. 270 (SCC) (paper mill parts including tanks, supporting piers, steel uprights, trackage, mezzanine, stairs and platforms were part of building); *Metals and Alloys*, 1985 CanLII 2191 (Ont. CA) (special structure for machinery was RP); *Sulkers Ltd.*, 1985 CanLII 4268 (NSCA) (outdoor electrical signs, fixed conveyor system and courtesy desk/counter were RP; air compressors were personal property (PP)); *Boxrud*, 1996 CanLII 11754 (FC); *Ontario Hydro* (1996), 4 G.T.C. 6048 (Ont. Gen. Div.) (aff'd on other grounds 44 O.R. (3d) 1 (Ont. CA)) (microwave towers attached to building were PP); *Westshore Terminals*, 1999 CanLII 6069 (BCSC) ("shiploader" and "stacker-reclaimers" used in loading, handling and unloading of coal were RP); *Telus Communications*, 2003 BCCA 331 (printed circuit cards that were integral part of "large cabinet-like structures" firmly affixed to concrete floor of telephone exchange building were RP); *1518756 Ontario*, 2009 CanLII 11430 (Ont. Div. Ct) (ship berthed in harbour for 30 years and used as floating restaurant was RP); *Maple Leaf Foods*, 2008 MBCA 96 (evaporator and condenser unit at meat processing plant was RP); *Terasen Gas*, 2010 BCCA 255 (pipeline and related equipment were RP); *Zellstoff Celgar*, 2014 BCCA 279 (machinery and equipment in pulp mill were RP). See also VIEWS docs 2006-0175611E5 (TV monitors installed in railway stations are likely chattels); 2010-0376801R3 (solar panels are RP); Bocti & Mitchell, "Commodity Tax Administrative Issues", 1995 *Commodity Tax Symposium* (Canadian Institute of Chartered Accountants), at pp. 29-36, "Real property versus TPP"; Johnson & Novotny, "Cushion Gas — Chattel or Land", XII(3) *Resource Sector Taxation* 508 (2018).

An Ontario corporation that owns real property must record it on a register: *Business Corporations Act* ss. 140(4), 140.1.

For more on the meaning of real property see VIEWS doc 2020-0870041I7.

248(4) amended by 2002-2013 technical bill (Part 4 — bijuralism) (effective June 26, 2013), 2001 *Civil Code* harmonization bill.

(4.1) Real right in immovables — In this Act, a real right in an immovable includes a lease but does not include a security right derived by virtue of a hypothec, agreement for sale or similar obligation.

Related Provisions: 248(4) — Interest in real property under common law; *Interpretation Act* 8.1, 8.2 — Common law and civil law equally authoritative.

Notes: See 248(4) for the parallel rule under the common law. A right under a lease can qualify for the principal-residence exemption: VIEWS doc 2019-0812611C6 [2019 APFF q.2].

248(4.1) added by 2002-2013 technical bill (Part 4 — bijuralism), effective June 26, 2013.

(5) Substituted property — For the purposes of this Act, other than paragraph 98(1)(a),

(a) where a person has disposed of or exchanged a particular property and acquired other property in substitution therefor and subsequently, by one or more further transactions, has effected one or more further substitutions, the property acquired by any such transaction shall be deemed to have been substituted for the particular property; and

(b) any share received as a stock dividend on another share of the capital stock of a corporation shall be deemed to be property substituted for that other share.

Notes: See VIEWS docs 2009-0320211R3 (guarantee rights are not substituted property); 2012-046490117 and 2013-047631117 (loss on foreign affiliate — shares are not considered substituted shares for 93(2.01)B); 2015-0578551C6 [2015 STEP q.11] (cash cannot be "substituted" for shares, for 118.1(5.1)(b)).

248(5)(b), enacted in 1986, applies to exchanges of property made after November 21, 1985 and shares received as stock dividends after November 21, 1985 other than shares received as payment of a stock dividend declared on or before that date.

Interpretation Bulletins: IT-244R3: Gifts by individuals of life insurance policies as charitable donations; IT-369R: Attribution of trust income to settlor; IT-489R: Non-arm's length sale of shares to a corporation; IT-511R: Interspousal and certain other transfers and loans of property.

(6) "Class" of shares issued in series — In its application in relation to a corporation that has issued shares of a class of its capital stock in one or more series, a reference in this Act to the "class" shall be read, with such modifications as the circumstances require, as a reference to a "series of the class".

Notes: For an example see VIEWS doc 2020-0852191C6 [2020 APFF q.7].

Income Tax Folios: S3-F10-C2: Prohibited investments — RRSPs, RRIFs and TFSAs.

Interpretation Bulletins: IT-328R3: Losses on shares on which dividends have been received.

(7) [Deemed date of] Receipt of things mailed — For the purposes of this Act,

(a) anything (other than a remittance or payment described in paragraph (b)) sent by first class mail or its equivalent shall be deemed to have been received by the person to whom it was sent on the day it was mailed; and

(b) the remittance or payment of an amount

(i) deducted or withheld, or

(ii) payable by a corporation,

as required by this Act or a regulation shall be deemed to have been made on the day on which it is received by the Receiver General.

Related Provisions: 153(1) [closing words] — Certain remittances must be made directly to a financial institution; 204.81(8.2) — Rule in 248(7) does not apply to voluntary de-registration of LSVCC; 244(5) — Proof of service by mail; 244(14) — Mailing date presumed to be date of assessment or notice; Reg. 110 — Certain remittances must be made directly to a financial institution.

Notes: The "deemed" in 248(7)(a) is absolute, not rebuttable: *Schafer*, [2000] G.S.T.C. 82 (FCA); *Louisbourg SBC*, 2014 FCA 78; but CRA must still prove that a notice of assessment or confirmation was *sent* to the right address: see Notes to 165(1).

Administratively, CRA considers an item "received" 5 days before arrival in CRA's mailroom: 2019 Alberta CPA (tinyurl.com/cra-abtax), Plenary q.4. (Of course, if one can prove earlier mailing, 248(7) overrides this.)

This rule applies to what Canada Post now calls "letter mail": *Liao*, 2010 TCC 587, para. 9. CRA considers an item entrusted to a courier service for prompt delivery as equivalent to first-class mail: IT-433R para. 4. In *VIH Logging*, 2003 TCC 732, para. 24 [aff'd on other grounds 2005 FCA 36], the Court accepted courier pickup of a Notice of Assessment as constituting sending the notice. One can argue that sending by registered mail or courier is not "equivalent" to first-class mail if the mail carrier or courier will not leave the item without a signature because no-one is home. However, this argument was rejected for registered mail in *Rossi*, 2015 FCA 267, in light of 244(5).

In both *Erroca Enterprises*, [1986] 2 C.T.C. 2425 and *Skyway Developments*, 2007 TCC 616, the TCC accepted evidence of the appellant's or accountant's normal office procedures, and ruled that a corporate tax return was likely mailed (and thus deemed received) even though CRA had no record of it.

CRA has stated that 248(7)(a) does not apply to deem an employee to have received a paycheque "where the facts clearly show that the taxpayer, or someone else for the taxpayer's benefit, never received the amount": VIEWS doc 2003-0049497. CRA also thinks that 248(7)(a) does not apply to an RRSP contribution mailed to a financial institution: 2010-0363431E5. These views are wrong in light of *Schafer* (above), if the mail was sent. CRA agrees that instalments sent by an individual to CRA are deemed paid when put in the mail: 2013-048135117; and that interest and dividend payments are received when mailed: 2013-0474161E5.

Due to 248(7)(b), the date of an ATM receipt does not constitute the day of remittance of payroll deductions or payment by a corporation, as it can take several days for the funds to be sent by the bank to CRA. (See also the closing words of 153(1).)

Charities Policies: CPS-017: Effective date of registration.

(8) Occurrences as a consequence of death — For the purpose of this Act,

(a) a transfer, distribution or acquisition of property under or as a consequence of the terms of the will or other testamentary instrument of a taxpayer or the taxpayer's spouse or common-law partner or as a consequence of the law governing the intestacy of a taxpayer or the taxpayer's spouse or common-law partner shall be considered to be a transfer, distribution or acquisition of the property as a consequence of the death of the taxpayer or the taxpayer's spouse or common-law partner, as the case may be;

(b) a transfer, distribution or acquisition of property as a consequence of a disclaimer, release or surrender by a person who was a beneficiary under the will or other testamentary instrument or on the intestacy of a taxpayer or the taxpayer's spouse or common-law partner shall be considered to be a transfer, distribution or acquisition of the property as a consequence of the death of the taxpayer or the taxpayer's spouse or common-law partner, as the case may be; and

(c) a release or surrender by a beneficiary under the will or other testamentary instrument or on the intestacy of a taxpayer with respect to any property that was property of the taxpayer immediately before the taxpayer's death shall be considered not to be a disposition of the property by the beneficiary.

Related Provisions: 248(9) — Definitions; 248(9.1) — Whether trust created by taxpayer's will.

Notes: One use of 248(8) is where the taxpayer dies leaving property to children, which would result in capital gain under 70(5); if the children renounce their interest in favour of the surviving spouse, 70(6) defers the gain. See 207.01(1)"exempt contribution"(b) for another example.

In *Biderman*, [2000] 2 C.T.C. 35 (FCA), the Court discussed the effects of a disclaimer of an inheritance (and ruled that a valid disclaimer is not a transfer for purposes of 160(1)). See also 248(9). See also VIEWS doc 2019-0813451C6 [2019 APFF Financial q.6] (on disclaimer by other heir, property received by spouse is considered acquired in consequence of death).

If an *inter vivos* trust requires distribution of property on X's death, that is a distribution in consequence of death: 2019-0824401C6 [2019 CTF q.7]. An amount paid from a deceased's TFSA to a spousal trust in accordance with the Will is paid in consequence of death: 2020-0851601C6 [2020 APFF Financial q.5]. A right to acquire shares following a parent's death, when exercised, is not considered a transfer in consequence of death: VIEWS doc 2006-0197151C6 (it is uncertain whether CRA is correct on this). An agreement signed by the heirs of the deceased likely does not qualify: 2009-0328441E5. If there is no will and provincial law divides the estate among the heirs, allocating specific assets to specific heirs for tax purposes is allowed: 2011-0402291C6.

The common law also has *donatio mortis causa* (e.g. *Snitzler v. Snitzler*, 2015 ONSC 2539), which is a reversible gift made in contemplation of death, finalized on death.

248(8) amended by 2000 same-sex partners bill to refer to "common-law partner", effective as per Notes to 248(1)"common-law partner".

Income Tax Folios: S6-F2-C1: Disposition of an income interest in a trust [replaces IT-385R2].

Interpretation Bulletins: IT-305R4: Testamentary spouse trusts; IT-313R2: Eligible capital property — rules where a taxpayer has ceased carrying on a business or has died; IT-349R3: Intergenerational transfers of farm property on death; IT-449R: Meaning of "vested indefeasibly" (cancelled); IT-500R: RRSPs — death of an annuitant.

(9) Definitions — In subsection (8),

"disclaimer" includes a renunciation of a succession made under the laws of the Province of Quebec that is not made in favour of any person, but does not include any disclaimer made after the period ending 36 months after the death of the taxpayer unless written application therefor has been made to the Minister by the taxpayer's legal representative within that period and the disclaimer is made within such longer period as the Minister considers reasonable in the circumstances;

Notes: See Notes to 188.1(5) re meaning of "includes".

248(9)"disclaimer" amended by 1993 technical bill, effective June 15, 1994, to add everything from "but does not include" to the end. The circumstances described fall into the closing words of "release or surrender" below.

Interpretation Bulletins ["disclaimer"]: IT-305R4: Testamentary spouse trusts; IT-313R2: Eligible capital property — rules where a taxpayer has ceased carrying on a business or has died; IT-349R3: Intergenerational transfers of farm property on death.

"release or surrender" means

(a) a release or surrender made under the laws of a province (other than the Province of Quebec) that does not direct in any manner who is entitled to benefit therefrom, or

(b) a gift *inter vivos* made under the laws of the Province of Quebec of an interest in, or right to property of, a succession that is made to the person or persons who would have benefited if the donor had made a renunciation of the succession that was not made in favour of any person,

and that is made within the period ending 36 months after the death of the taxpayer or, where written application therefor has been made to the Minister by the taxpayer's legal representative within that period, within such longer period as the Minister considers reasonable in the circumstances.

Notes: It is uncertain whether "*inter vivos*" in para. (b) (literally, "between living persons") refers only to individuals: VIEWS doc 2013-0484321E5.

Interpretation Bulletins ["release or surrender"]: IT-305R4: Testamentary spouse trusts; IT-313R2: Eligible capital property — rules where a taxpayer has ceased carrying on a business or has died; IT-349R3: Intergenerational transfers of farm property on death.

(9.1) How trust created — For the purposes of this Act, a trust shall be considered to be created by a taxpayer's will if the trust is created

(a) under the terms of the taxpayer's will; or

(b) by an order of a court in relation to the taxpayer's estate made under any law of a province that provides for the relief or support of dependants.

Related Provisions: 108(1)"testamentary trust" — Trust created by taxpayer's will is a testamentary trust; 248(3) — Whether usufruct, right of use or habitation or substitution in Quebec deemed to be trust created by taxpayer's will.

Notes: 248(9.1) added by 1992 technical bill, for 1990 and later taxation years. This rule was formerly in 70(6.1), which applied only for certain specified purposes.

Interpretation Bulletins: IT-305R4: Testamentary spouse trusts.

(9.2) Vested indefeasibly — For the purposes of this Act, property shall be deemed not to have vested indefeasibly

(a) in a trust under which a taxpayer's spouse or common-law partner is a beneficiary, where the trust is created by the will of the taxpayer, unless the property vested indefeasibly in the trust before the death of the spouse or common-law partner; and

(b) in an individual (other than a trust), unless the property vested indefeasibly in the individual before the death of the individual.

Related Provisions: 248(9.1) — Whether trust created by taxpayer's will.

Notes: 248(9.2) ensures that a rollover on death to a qualifying individual or spousal trust is permitted only where appropriate gains will be recognized on the death of the

beneficiary spouse or the qualifying individual. 248(9.2) is not a complete definition; CRA's administrative definition in IT-449R is still relevant. That is "the unassailable right to ownership ... that, in consequence of death ... has been transferred or distributed ... to a spouse, spouse trust or child of the deceased ... property vests indefeasibly ... when such a person obtains a right to absolute ownership of that property in such a manner that such right cannot be defeated by any future event, even though that person may not be entitled to the immediate enjoyment of all the benefits arising from that right." See IT-449R and VIEWS docs 2002-0165635, 2006-0193111I7, 2007-0235171E5, 2007-0251591E5, 2010-0378451E5, 2011-0391911E5, 2018-0744111C6 [2018 STEP q.9] for examples.

For discussion of "vested indefeasibly" see *Boger Estate*, [1993] 2 C.T.C. 81 (FCA) (interest must not be subject to a condition subsequent or a determinable limitation set out in the grant); Diane Bruneau, "Problems in the Application of Tax Law to Civil Law Trusts", 51(1) *Canadian Tax Journal* 252 (2003) at 273-82; Véronique Denys, "Indefeasible Vesting", *The Harmonization of Federal Legislation with Quebec Civil Law: Second Collection of Studies in Tax Law* (2005, apff.org), 4:1-187 (very comprehensive); Catherine Brown, "Vested Indefeasibly: Its Importance for Tax Purposes", 54(4) *CTJ* 968-991 (2006).

See also Peter Megoudis & Lynne Lacoursière, "The Meanings and Uses of the Term 'Vesting' ", XXV(3) *Taxation of Executive Compensation & Retirement* (Federated Press) 11-20 (2018).

248(9.2) amended by 2000 same-sex partners bill to refer to "common-law partner", effective as per Notes to 248(1)"common-law partner". Added by 1992 technical bill.

Interpretation Bulletins: IT-305R4: Testamentary spouse trusts; IT-449R: Meaning of "vested indefeasibly" (cancelled).

CRA Audit Manual: 16.2.2: Estate of a deceased person — vested indefeasibly.

(10) Series of transactions — For the purposes of this Act, where there is a reference to a series of transactions or events, the series shall be deemed to include any related transactions or events completed in contemplation of the series.

Notes: The Supreme Court of Canada stated in *Canada Trustco*, 2005 SCC 54, paras. 25-26, that a series of transactions involves a number of transactions pre-ordained to produce a given result, with no practical likelihood that the pre-planned events would not take place in that order. (Thus, absent 248(10), transactions must be "pre-ordained" to constitute a series: *Toronto Dominion Bank*, 2011 FCA 221, para. 37.) 248(10)'s extended meaning of "series" occurs where the parties knew of the series, and considered it when deciding to complete the transaction. The SCC added that "in contemplation" does not mean actual knowledge but has the broader sense of "because of" or "in relation to" the series, and can apply to events before or after the 245(3) avoidance transaction. See also *2763478 Canada*, 2018 FCA 209: the fact a decision to engage in a given transaction is made later does not exclude it from 248(10).

The concept of "series of transactions" applies only to tax-driven transactions: *Eyeball Networks*, 2021 FCA 17, para. 46.

"Contemplation" applies both prospectively and retrospectively, so where an avoidance transaction takes place after a transaction that did not contemplate avoidance at the time, the two still form a series subject to GAAR: *Copthorne Holdings*, 2011 SCC 63, paras. 42-58. Similarly, in *3295036 Canada*, 2020 QCCA 1435 (leave to appeal denied 2021 CarswellQue 5311 (SCC)) (on the Quebec equivalent of 248(10)), a "Quebec shuffle" done in 1996, triggering capital losses in 2000 that were claimed in 2007-2008, was "in contemplation" of the series. However, in *Custeau*, 2020 QCCA 1496, "contemplation" did not apply looking backwards where upward PUC averaging in 1998, due to regional development fund investments, was done with no thought to later tax savings [Hamelin, "Quebec Court of Appeal Considers 'Series of Transactions' in GAAR Appeal", 21(2) *Tax for the Owner-Manager* (ctf.ca) 6-7 (April 2021)].

See also *OSFC Holdings*, 2001 FCA 260; leave to appeal denied 2002 CarswellNat 1388 (SCC). A preliminary transaction can be considered part of a series of later transactions, even if at the time the taxpayer had not determined all the important elements of the later transactions: *Granite Bay Charters*, [2001] 3 C.T.C. 2516 (TCC). See also Notes to 55(2) re the *Canutilities* case; *Loblaw Financial*, 2018 TCC 182 (rev'd 2020 FCA 79 without discussing 248(10); SCC appeal heard May 13/21), paras. 303-320; *Louie*, 2019 FCA 255, paras. 22-27 (leave to appeal denied 2020 CarswellNat 1258 (SCC)); *Morrison 2002 Maintenance Trust*, [2019] EWCA Civ 93 (England) (series was "pre-ordained").

In *Groupe Honco*, 2013 FCA 128, there was a "series of transactions" for purpose of 83(2.1) even though it took place over 7 years (this was a finding of fact by the TCC); similarly, see *3295036 Canada* (above).

For CRA interpretation see doc 2017-0670971R3 (repayments of upstream loans are not part of series of transactions); 2019 CPA Alberta (tinyurl.com/cra-abtax), income tax q.7.

See also Falk, "A 'Series' of Transactions", X(1) *Business Vehicles* (Federated Press) 487-94 (2004); Brender, "Series of Transactions", 55(1) *Canadian Tax Journal* 210-34 (2007); Carr & Milot, "Copthorne", 56(1) *CTJ* 243-68 (2008); Kandev et al., "The Meaning of 'Series of Transactions' ", 58(2) *CTJ* 277-330 (2010); Kepes et al., "The Meaning and Effect of the *Copthorne* Decision", 2012 Cdn Tax Foundation conference report, 12:1-37; Alarie & Lockhart, "The Importance of Family Resemblance", 61(1) *CTJ* 69-109 (2014).

Income Tax Folios: S7-F1-C1: Split-receipting and deemed fair market value.

Advance Tax Rulings: ATR-56: Purification of a family farm corporation; ATR-57: Transfer of property for estate planning purposes; ATR-58: Divisive reorganization.

I.T. Technical News: 22 (series of transactions).

(11) Compound interest — Interest computed at a prescribed rate under any of subsections 129(2.1) and (2.2), 131(3.1) and (3.2), 132(2.1) and (2.2), 133(7.01) and (7.02), 159(7), 160.1(1), 161(1), (2) and (11), 161.1(5), 164(3) to (4), 181.8(1) and (2) (as those two subsections read in their application to the 1991 and earlier taxation years), 185(2), 187(2) and 189(7), section 190.23 (as it read in its application to the 1991 and earlier taxation years) and subsections 193(3), 195(3), 202(5) and 227(8.3), (9.2) and (9.3) of this Act and subsection 182(2) of the *Income Tax Act*, chapter 148 of the Revised Statutes of Canada, 1952 (as that subsection read in its application to taxation years beginning before 1986) and subsection 191(2) of that Act (as that subsection read in its application to the 1984 and earlier taxation years) shall be compounded daily and, where interest is computed on an amount under any of those provisions and is unpaid or unapplied on the day it would, but for this subsection, have ceased to be computed under that provision, interest at the prescribed rate shall be computed and compounded daily on the unpaid or unapplied interest from that day to the day it is paid or applied and shall be paid or applied as would be the case if interest had continued to be computed under that provision after that day.

Related Provisions: 221.1 — Application of interest where legislation retroactive.

Notes: 248(11) amended by 1999 Budget to refer to 161.1(5), effective 2000. Earlier amended by 1992 technical bill (last change effective for tax years beginning after 1991), 1991 technical bill, 1989 Budget.

Regulations: 4301 (prescribed rate of interest).

I.T. Application Rules: 69 (meaning of "chapter 148 of ...").

(12) Identical properties — For the purposes of this Act, one bond, debenture, bill, note or similar obligation issued by a debtor is identical to another such obligation issued by that debtor if both are identical in respect of all rights (in equity or otherwise, either immediately or in the future and either absolutely or contingently) attaching thereto, except as regards the principal amount thereof.

Related Provisions: 18.1(12) — Identical properties for matchable-expenditure rules; 40(3.5) — Deemed identical properties for superficial loss/pregnant loss rules; 47 — Capital gains treatment of identical properties; 54"superficial loss"(i), (j) — Right to acquire property and SIFT wind-up share — deemed identical property for superficial-loss rule; 138(11.1) — Identical properties of life insurance corporation.

Notes: CRA considers index-based mutual funds from different financial institutions as identical if they track the same index (e.g., TSX 300): VIEWS doc 2001-0080385. "Two properties which are otherwise identical do not cease to be so merely because one is subject to a charge or other external condition which may affect its price and the other is not, provided the external condition does not change any of the constituent elements of the particular property (e.g., provincial retail sales tax, commission fees)": IT-387R2 (cancelled), para. 3. Partnership units in a Delaware LP are not identical to shares of a Delaware LLC: 2015-0588791I7.

Exchangeable shares are not identical to the shares they can be exchanged for: *10737 Newfoundland Ltd.*, 2011 TCC 346, para. 11.

I.T. Application Rules: 26(8)–(8.4) — Identical properties owned since before 1972.

Interpretation Bulletins: IT-387R2: Meaning of "identical properties".

(13) Interests in trusts and partnerships — Where after November 12, 1981 a person has an interest in a trust or partnership, whether directly or indirectly through an interest in any other trust or partnership or in any manner whatever, the person shall, for the purposes of the definitions "income bond", "income debenture" and "term preferred share" in subsection (1), paragraph (h) of the definition "taxable preferred share" in that subsection, subsections 84(4.2) and (4.3) and 112(2.6) and section 258, be deemed to be a beneficiary of the trust or a member of the partnership, as the case may be.

(14) Related corporations — For the purpose of paragraph (g) of the definition "specified financial institution" in subsection (1), where in the case of 2 or more corporations it can reasonably be considered, having regard to all the circumstances, that one of the main reasons for the separate existence of those corporations in a taxation year is to limit or avoid the application of subsection 112(2.1) or (2.2) or 138(6), the 2 or more corporations shall be deemed to be related to each other and to each other corporation to which any such corporation is related.

Notes: See Notes to 256(2.1), which provides a similar rule in determining associated corporations.

248(14) amended by 1991 technical bill, effective July 14, 1990.

(15) Goods and services tax — change of use — For the purposes of this Act, where a liability for the goods and services tax is incurred in respect of a change of use at any time of a property, the liability so incurred shall be deemed to have been incurred immediately after that time in respect of the acquisition of the property.

Notes: 248(15) added by 1990 GST, effective 1991.

(16) Goods and services tax — input tax credit and rebate — For the purposes of this Act, other than this subsection and subsection 6(8), an amount claimed by a taxpayer as an input tax credit or rebate with respect to the goods and services tax in respect of a property or service is deemed to be assistance from a government in respect of the property or service that is received by the taxpayer

(a) where the amount was claimed by the taxpayer as an input tax credit in a return under Part IX of the *Excise Tax Act* for a reporting period under that Act,

(i) at the particular time that is the earlier of the time that the goods and services tax in respect of the input tax credit was paid and the time that it became payable,

(A) if the particular time is in the reporting period, or

(B) if,

(I) the taxpayer's threshold amount, determined in accordance with subsection 249(1) of the *Excise Tax Act*, is greater than $500,000 for the taxpayer's fiscal year (within the meaning assigned by that Act) that includes the particular time, and

(II) the taxpayer claimed the input tax credit at least 120 days before the end of the normal reassessment period, as determined under subsection 152(3.1), for the taxpayer in respect of the taxation year that includes the particular time,

(ii) at the end of the reporting period, if

(A) subparagraph (i) does not apply, and

(B) the taxpayer's threshold amount, determined in accordance with subsection 249(1) of the *Excise Tax Act*, is $500,000 or less for the fiscal year (within the meaning assigned by that Act) of the taxpayer that includes the particular time, and

(iii) in any other case, on the last day of the taxpayer's earliest taxation year

(A) that begins after the taxation year that includes the particular time, and

(B) for which the normal reassessment period, as determined under subsection 152(3.1), for the taxpayer ends at least 120 days after the time that the input tax credit was claimed; or

(b) where the amount was claimed as a rebate with respect to the goods and services tax, at the time the amount was received or credited.

Related Provisions: 8(11) — GST/HST rebate deemed not to be reimbursement for employment expense purposes; 12(1)(x) — Inclusion in income; 12(2.2) — Deemed outlay or expense; 13(7.1) — Deemed capital cost of certain property; 37(1)(d) — Scientific research and experimental development; 53(2)(k) — Reduction in adjusted cost base; 66.1(6)"cumulative Canadian exploration expense"J — Assistance reduces CCEE; 66.2(5)"cumulative Canadian development expense"M — Assistance reduces CCDE; 66.4(5)"cumulative Canadian oil and gas property expense"I — Assistance reduces CCOGPE; 248(16.1) — Parallel rule for QST; 248(17) — Application of 248(16) to passenger vehicles and aircraft; 248(17.2) — Timing of deemed assistance where GST/HST assessed; 248(18) — GST/HST — repayment of input tax credit.

Notes: The references to GST include HST: see 248(1)"goods and services tax".

By being deemed to be government assistance, GST/HST input tax credits (ITCs) and rebates operate (depending on how they arose) to reduce the cost of depreciable property under 13(7.1), eligible capital expenditures under 14(10), the ACB of capital property under 53(2)(k), R&D expenditures under 37(1)(d) or resource pools under 66.1-66.4. Otherwise they are included in income under 12(1)(x). See VIEWS doc 2010-0390591E5. ITCs arise under *Excise Tax Act* s. 169(1); see David M. Sherman, *Practitioner's Goods and Services Tax Annotated*.

Where the taxpayer does not claim an ITC, the GST/HST forms part of the cost of property or part of a deductible expense: VIEWS docs 2004-0076561E5, 2009-030929117.

248(16) should not apply to a partnership that claims ITCs, since a partnership is not a "person" and thus not a "taxpayer" under the ITA (see annotations to 248(1)"person"). However, in *Blais*, 2010 TCC 195, the TCC applied 248(16) to a partnership without considering this point.

The rule in 248(16)(a) requiring earlier recognition of the assistance is a response to planning by large corporations that deferred claiming ITCs for several months before a year-end, so as to increase their expenses and thus reduce taxable income and income tax for that year. (ITCs can generally be claimed for 2-4 years after they are incurred: ETA 225(4).) For an example of this being done by The Brick, see *Quinco Financial*, 2014 FCA 108. See also Casuccio, "A Problem with Using Accounting Fiscal Periods for GST Reporting", 15(1) *Taxation Law* (Ontario Bar Assn, oba.org) 31-33 (Oct. 2004); Hull, "Government Proposes Change to ITA to Thwart Tax Planning", XVII(1) *GST & Commodity Tax* (Carswell) 6-8 (Jan/Feb 2003) and "How Will the Late Passage of Changes to Delayed ITCs Be Assessed?", XXVII(6) 47-48 (Oct. 2013). See also doc 2013-0503861E5 (application where ITC entitlement arises only on sale of property due to ETA s. 193).

248(16)(a) amended by 2002-2013 technical bill (Part 5 — technical), for ITCs that become eligible to be claimed in tax years that begin after Dec. 20, 2002.

248(16) added by 1990 GST, effective 1991.

Interpretation Bulletins: IT-273R2: Government assistance — general comments.

CRA Audit Manual: 27.20.0: Inducement payments.

(16.1) Quebec input tax refund and rebate — For the purpose of this Act, other than this subsection and subsection 6(8), an amount claimed by a taxpayer as an input tax refund or a rebate with respect to the Quebec sales tax in respect of a property or service is deemed to be assistance from a government in respect of the property or service that is received by the taxpayer

(a) where the amount was claimed by the taxpayer as an input tax refund in a return under *An Act respecting the Québec sales tax*, R.S.Q., c. T-0.1, for a reporting period under that Act,

(i) at the particular time that is the earlier of the time that the Quebec sales tax in respect of the input tax refund was paid and the time that it became payable,

(A) if the particular time is in the reporting period, or

(B) if,

(I) the taxpayer's threshold amount, determined in accordance with section 462 of that Act is greater than $500,000 for the taxpayer's fiscal year (within the meaning assigned by that Act) that includes the particular time, and

(II) the taxpayer claimed the input tax refund at least 120 days before the end of the normal reassessment period, as determined under subsection 152(3.1), for the taxpayer in respect of the taxation year that includes the particular time,

(ii) at the end of the reporting period, if

(A) subparagraph (i) does not apply, and

(B) the taxpayer's threshold amount, determined in accordance with section 462 of that Act is $500,000 or less for the fiscal year (within the meaning assigned by that Act) of the taxpayer that includes the particular time, and

(iii) in any other case, on the last day of the taxpayer's earliest taxation year

(A) that begins after the taxation year that includes the particular time, and

(B) for which the normal reassessment period, as determined under subsection 152(3.1), for the taxpayer ends at least 120 days after the time that the input tax refund was claimed; or

(b) where the amount was claimed as a rebate with respect to the Quebec sales tax, at the time the amount was received or credited.

Related Provisions: 12(1)(x) — Inclusion in income; 12(2.2) — Deemed outlay or expense; 13(7.1) — Deemed capital cost of certain property; 37(1)(d) — Scientific research and experimental development; 53(2)(k) — Reduction in adjusted cost base; 66.1(6)"cumulative Canadian exploration expense"J — Assistance reduces CCEE; 66.2(5)"cumulative Canadian development expense"M — Assistance reduces CCDE; 66.4(5)"cumulative Canadian oil and gas property expense"I — Assistance reduces CCOGPE; 248(16) — Parallel rule for GST/HST; 248(17.1) — Application of 248(16) to passenger vehicles and aircraft; 248(17.3) — Timing of deemed assistance where QST assessed; 248(18.1) — Repayment of input tax refund.

Notes: See Notes to 248(16). Input tax refunds (ITRs) are the Quebec Sales Tax (QST) equivalent of GST/HST input tax credits. The QST is generally synchronized with the GST/HST and follows the same rules, but it is not part of the Harmonized Sales Tax: non-Quebec entities that are not QST-registered do not collect QST (even on sales to Quebec customers) and cannot claim ITRs.

248(16.1) added by 2002-2013 technical bill, for ITRs and rebates that become eligible to be claimed in tax years that begin after Feb. 27, 2004.

(17) Application of subsec. (16) to certain vehicles and aircraft — If the input tax credit of a taxpayer under Part IX of the *Excise Tax Act* in respect of a passenger vehicle, zero-emission passenger vehicle or aircraft is determined with reference to subsection 202(4) of that Act, subparagraphs (16)(a)(i) to (iii) are to be read as they apply in respect of the vehicle or aircraft, as the case may be, as follows:

(i) at the beginning of the first taxation year or fiscal period of the taxpayer commencing after the end of the taxation year or fiscal period, as the case may be, in which the goods and services tax in respect of such property was considered for the purposes of determining the input tax credit to be payable, if the tax was considered for the purposes of determining the input tax credit to have become payable in the reporting period, or

(ii) if no such tax was considered for the purposes of determining the input tax credit to have become payable in the reporting period, at the end of the reporting period; or

Related Provisions: 248(17.1) — Parallel rule for QST.

Notes: 248(17) opening words amended by 2019 budget bill #1, effective March 19, 2019, to add "zero-emission passenger vehicle" (ZEPV) after "passenger vehicle". This does not change the rules; 248(1)"passenger vehicle" was amended to exclude a ZEPV, so 248(17) was amended to apply to one.

248(17) opening words amended by 2002-2013 technical bill (Part 5 — technical), effective for input tax credits that become eligible to be claimed in taxation years that begin after Dec. 20, 2002, to extend reference to 248(16)(a)(iii) and "the passenger vehicle or aircraft, as the case may be".

248(17) added by 1990 GST, effective 1991.

(17.1) Application of subsec. (16.1) to certain vehicles and aircraft — If the input tax refund of a taxpayer under *An Act respecting the Québec sales tax*, R.S.Q., c. T-0.1, in respect of a passenger vehicle, zero-emission passenger vehicle or aircraft is determined with reference to section 252 of that Act, subparagraphs (16.1)(a)(i) to (iii) are to be read as they apply in respect of the vehicle or aircraft, as the case may be, as follows:

(i) at the beginning of the first taxation year or fiscal period of the taxpayer that begins after the end of the taxation year or fiscal period, as the case may be, in which the Quebec sales tax in respect of such property was considered for the purposes of determining the input tax refund to be payable, if the tax was considered for the purposes of determining the input tax refund to have become payable in the reporting period, or

(ii) if no such tax was considered for the purposes of determining the input tax refund to have become payable in the reporting period, at the end of the reporting period; or

Related Provisions: 248(17) — Parallel rule for GST/HST.

Notes: 248(17.1) opening words amended by 2019 budget bill #1, effective March 19, 2019, to add "zero-emission passenger vehicle" (ZEPV) after "passenger vehicle". This does not change the rules; 248(1)"passenger vehicle" was amended to exclude a ZEPV, so 248(17.1) was amended to apply to one.

248(17.1) added by 2002-2013 technical bill, for input tax refunds and rebates that become eligible to be claimed in tax years that begin after Feb. 27, 2004.

(17.2) Input tax credit on assessment — An amount in respect of an input tax credit that is deemed by subsection 296(5) of the *Excise Tax Act* to have been claimed in a return or application filed under Part IX of that Act is deemed to have been so claimed for the reporting period under that Act that includes the time when the Minister makes the assessment referred to in that subsection.

Related Provisions: 248(17.3) — Parallel rule for QST.

Notes: 248(17.2) added by 2002-2013 technical bill, for input tax credits that become eligible to be claimed in tax years that begin after Dec. 20, 2002.

(17.3) Quebec input tax refund on assessment — An amount in respect of an input tax refund that is deemed by section 30.5 of the *Tax Administration Act*, R.S.Q., c. A-6.002, to have been claimed is deemed to have been so claimed for the reporting period under *An Act respecting the Québec sales tax*, R.S.Q., c. T-0.1, that includes the day on which an assessment is issued to the taxpayer indicating that the refund has been allocated under that section 30.5.

Related Provisions: 248(17.2) — Parallel rule for GST/HST.

Notes: 248(17.3) added by 2002-2013 technical bill (Part 5 — technical), effective for input tax refunds and rebates that become eligible to be claimed in taxation years that begin after Feb. 27, 2004, but before April 2011, read "the *Tax Administration Act*, R.S.Q., c. A-6.002" as "*An Act respecting the Ministère du Revenu*, R.S.Q., c. M-31".

(18) Goods and services tax — repayment of input tax credit — For the purposes of this Act, where an amount is added at a particular time in determining the net tax of a taxpayer under Part IX of the *Excise Tax Act* in respect of an input tax credit relating to property or a service that had been previously deducted in determining the net tax of the taxpayer, that amount shall be deemed to be assistance repaid at the particular time in respect of the property or service pursuant to a legal obligation to repay all or part of that assistance.

Related Provisions: 20(1)(hh) — Deduction for repayment of assistance; 39(13) — Capital loss on repayment of assistance; 53(1)(e)(ix)(B) — Adjusted cost base of partnership interest; 127(10.7) — Investment tax credit — repayment of assistance; 248(18.1) — Parallel rule for QST.

Notes: 248(18) added by 1990 GST, effective 1991. See Notes to 248(16). Amounts can be added to net tax in respect of previously claimed input tax credits for several reasons, including an audit assessment denying ITCs, a supplier refund of previously paid GST (credit note under *Excise Tax Act* s. 232(3)), and restrictions on meals and entertainment (ETA s. 236). If an assessment is appealed, it is unclear whether the "particular time" the "amount is added" is the date of the assessment, or the date of a final decision on the appeal (likely the former).

(18.1) Repayment of Quebec input tax refund — For the purposes of this Act, if an amount is added at a particular time in determining the net tax of a taxpayer under *An Act respecting the Québec sales tax*, R.S.Q., c. T-0.1, in respect of an input tax refund relating to property or service that had been previously deducted in determining the net tax of the taxpayer, that amount is deemed to be assistance repaid at the particular time in respect of the property or service under a legal obligation to repay all or part of that assistance.

Related Provisions: 20(1)(hh) — Deduction for repayment of assistance; 39(13) — Capital loss on repayment of assistance; 53(1)(e)(ix)(B) — Adjusted cost base of partnership interest; 127(10.7) — Investment tax credit — repayment of assistance; 248(18) — Parallel rule for GST/HST.

Notes: See Notes to 248(16.1). 248(18.1) added by 2002-2013 technical bill (Part 5 — technical), effective Feb. 28, 2004.

(19) When property available for use — Except as otherwise provided, property shall be considered to have become available for use for the purposes of this Act at the time at which it has, or would have if it were depreciable property, become available for use for the purpose of subsection 13(26).

Related Provisions: 13(27)–(31) — Meaning of "available for use"; 37(1.2) — R&D capital expenditures; 127(11.2) — Investment tax credit.

Notes: 248(19) added by 1991 technical bill, effective 1990.

(20) Partition of property — Subject to subsections (21) to (23), for the purposes of this Act, if at any time a property owned by two or more persons is the subject of a partition, the following rules apply, notwithstanding any retroactive or declaratory effect of the partition:

(a) each such person who had, immediately before that time, an interest in, or for civil law a right in, the property (which interest or right in the property is referred to in this subsection and subsection (21) as an "interest" or a "right", as the case may be) is deemed not to have disposed at that time of that proportion, not exceeding 100%, of the interest or right that the fair market value of that person's interest or right in the property immediately after that time is of the fair market value of that person's interest or right in the property immediately before that time,

(b) each such person who has an interest or a right in the property immediately after that time is deemed not to have acquired at that time that proportion of the interest or right that the fair market value of that person's interest or right in the property immediately before that time is of the fair market value of that person's interest or right in the property immediately after that time,

(c) each such person who had an interest or a right in the property immediately before that time is deemed to have had until that time, and to have disposed at that time of, that proportion of the person's interest or right to which paragraph (a) does not apply,

(d) each such person who has an interest or a right in the property immediately after that time is deemed not to have had before that time, and to have acquired at that time, that proportion of the person's interest or right to which paragraph (b) does not apply, and

(e) paragraphs (a) to (d) do not apply if the interest or right of the person is an interest or a right in fungible tangible property, or for civil law fungible corporeal property described in that person's inventory,

and, for the purposes of this subsection, if an interest or a right in the property is an undivided interest or right, the fair market value of the interest or right at any time is deemed to be equal to that proportion of the fair market value of the property at that time that the interest or right is of all the undivided interests or rights in the property.

Related Provisions: 248(21) — Subdivision of property; 248(22) — Matrimonial regimes.

Notes: Partition is normally used for real estate but can be used for other property such as shares. Partition can be ordered by a provincial superior court where property is owned in joint tenancy (explained in Notes to 70(5)) or as tenants in common (so that each person owns a fraction).

A conversion of a B.C. strata plan to a "bare land strata plan" may constitute a partition of property for purposes of 248(20) and (21): VIEWS doc 2003-0008655.

See also VIEWS doc 2014-0544381E5; and Notes to 248(21).

248(20) amended by 2002-2013 technical bill (effective June 26, 2013), 2001 *Civil Code* harmonization bill, 1991 technical bill.

(21) Subdivision of property — If a property that was owned by two or more persons is the subject of a partition among those persons and, as a consequence of it, each such person has, in the property, a new interest or right the fair market value of which immediately after the partition, expressed as a percentage of the fair market value of all the new interests or rights in the property immediately after the partition, is equal to the fair market value of that person's undivided interest or right immediately before the partition, expressed as a percentage of the fair market value of all the undivided interests or rights in the property immediately before the partition,

(a) subsection (20) does not apply to the property, and

(b) the new interest or right of each such person is deemed to be a continuation of that person's undivided interest or right in the property immediately before the partition,

and, for the purposes of this subsection,

(c) subdivisions of a building or of a parcel of land that are established in the course of, or in contemplation of, a partition and that are co-owned by the same persons who co-owned the building or the parcel of land, or by their assignee, shall be regarded as one property, and

(d) if an interest or a right in the property is or includes an undivided interest or right, the fair market value of the interest or right shall be determined without regard to any discount or premium that applies to a minority or majority interest or right in the property.

Related Provisions: 248(20) — Partition of property.

Notes: In CRA's view, if land with two buildings on it is partitioned so that each owner receives one, 248(21) does not apply to the buildings since each is a separate property: VIEWS doc 2005-0145251E5. For a ruling approving 248(21) where a corporation winds up and its shareholders acquired an undivided interest in its building, see 2005-0132221R3; on windup of a partnership, see 2003-0009513. For more interpretation see 9230665, 9730823, 2000-0038595, 2005-0141151C6, 2006-0205741E5, 2007-0225151R3, 2008-0297871E5, 2008-0287541E5, 2009-0338641E5, 2010-0383151E5, 2011-0408781R3, 2018-0787181R3.

248(21) amended by 2002-2013 technical bill (effective June 26, 2013), 2001 *Civil Code* harmonization bill. Added by 1991 technical bill.

(22) Matrimonial regimes — Where at any time property could, as the consequence of the dissolution of a matrimonial regime between 2 spouses or common-law partners, be the subject of a partition, for the purposes of this Act

(a) where that property was owned by one of the spouses or common-law partners immediately before it became subject to that regime and had not subsequently been disposed of before that time, it shall be deemed to be owned at that time by that spouse or common-law partner and not by the other spouse or common-law partner; and

(b) in any other case, the property shall be deemed to be owned by the spouse or common-law partner who has the administration of that property at that time and not by the other spouse or common-law partner.

Related Provisions: 248(20) — Partition of property; 248(21) — Subdivision of property; 248(23) — Dissolution of a matrimonial regime; 252(3) — Extended meaning of "spouse".

Notes: For an example of 248(22) see VIEWS doc 2006-0170851E5. For more interpretation see 2008-0297871E5, 2008-0287541E5. See also *Sokolowski Romar*, 2013 FCA 10 (leave to appeal denied 2013 CarswellNat 1634 (SCC)), where a change in the matrimonial regime was separate from the husband's transfer of half the family home to the wife, though the Courts did not discuss 248(22)-(23).

248(22) amended by 2000 same-sex partners bill to refer to "common-law partner", effective 2001 (or earlier).

248(22) added by 1991 technical bill, effective July 14, 1990.

Income Tax Folios: S1-F3-C2: Principal residence [replaces IT-120R6, IT-437R].

Interpretation Bulletins: IT-325R2: Property transfers after separation, divorce and annulment; IT-511R: Interspousal and certain other transfers and loans of property.

(23) Dissolution of a matrimonial regime — Where, immediately after the dissolution of a matrimonial regime (other than a dissolution occurring as a consequence of death), the owner of a property that was subject to that regime is not the person, or the estate of the person, who is deemed by subsection (22) to have been the owner of the property immediately before the dissolution, the person shall be deemed for the purposes of this Act to have transferred the property to the person's spouse or common-law partner immediately before the dissolution.

Related Provisions: 110.6(14)(g) — Related persons, etc.; 252(3) — Extended meaning of "spouse".

Notes: 248(23) amended by 2000 same-sex partners bill to refer to "common-law partner", effective as per Notes to 248(1)"common-law partner".

248(23) added by 1991 technical bill, effective July 14, 1990. Amended by 1993 technical bill, for dissolutions after Dec. 21, 1992.

Income Tax Folios: S1-F3-C2: Principal residence [replaces IT-120R6, IT-437R].

Interpretation Bulletins: IT-325R2: Property transfers after separation, divorce and annulment; IT-511R: Interspousal and certain other transfers and loans of property.

(23.1) Transfers after death — If, as a consequence of the laws of a province relating to spouses' or common-law partners' interests

or rights in respect of property as a result of marriage or common-law partnership, property is, after the death of a taxpayer,

(a) transferred or distributed to a person who was the taxpayer's spouse or common-law partner at the time of the death, or acquired by that person, the property shall be deemed to have been so transferred, distributed or acquired, as the case may be, as a consequence of the death; or

(b) transferred or distributed to the taxpayer's estate, or acquired by the taxpayer's estate, the property shall be deemed to have been so transferred, distributed or acquired, as the case may be, immediately before the time that is immediately before the death.

Notes: 248(23.1) deems property transferred under a *Family Law Act* election to be transferred as a consequence of death, so 70(6) can apply to the transfer even if there is no court order: VIEWS docs 2006-0202871E5, 2010-0371951C6; Barry Corbin, "Again With Rollovers?", 23(2) *Money & Family Law* 9-10 (Feb. 2008).

Since "common-law partner" is defined in 248(1), 248(23.1) will not apply to a person who is a common-law spouse under provincial law but does not meet that definition.

248(23.1) opening words amended by 2002-2013 technical bill (Part 4 — bijuralism), effective June 26, 2013, to add "or rights".

248(23.1) earlier amended by 2000 same-sex partners bill. Added by 1993 technical bill.

Interpretation Bulletins: IT-313R2: Eligible capital property — rules where a taxpayer has ceased carrying on a business or has died.

(24) Accounting methods — For greater certainty, it is hereby declared that, unless specifically required, neither the equity nor the consolidation method of accounting shall be used to determine any amount for the purposes of this Act.

Related Provisions: 61.3(1)(b)C(i) — Repetition of rule for purposes of debt forgiveness reserve calculation; 261 — Functional currency reporting.

Notes: 248(24) added by 1991 technical bill, effective July 14, 1990.

(25) Beneficially interested — For the purposes of this Act,

(a) a person or partnership beneficially interested in a particular trust includes any person or partnership that has any right (whether immediate or future, whether absolute or contingent or whether conditional on or subject to the exercise of any discretion by any person or partnership) as a beneficiary under a trust to receive any of the income or capital of the particular trust either directly from the particular trust or indirectly through one or more trusts or partnerships;

(b) except for the purpose of this paragraph, a particular person or partnership is deemed to be beneficially interested in a particular trust at a particular time where

(i) the particular person or partnership is not beneficially interested in the particular trust at the particular time,

(ii) because of the terms or conditions of the particular trust or any arrangement in respect of the particular trust at the particular time, the particular person or partnership might, because of the exercise of any discretion by any person or partnership, become beneficially interested in the particular trust at the particular time or at a later time, and

(iii) at or before the particular time, either

(A) the particular trust has acquired property, directly or indirectly in any manner whatever, from

(I) the particular person or partnership,

(II) another person with whom the particular person or partnership, or a member of the particular partnership, does not deal at arm's length,

(III) a person or partnership with whom the other person referred to in subclause (II) does not deal at arm's length,

(IV) a controlled foreign affiliate of the particular person or of another person with whom the particular person or partnership, or a member of the particular partnership, does not deal at arm's length, or

(V) a non-resident corporation that would, if the particular partnership were a corporation resident in Canada, be a controlled foreign affiliate of the particular partnership, or

(B) a person or partnership described in any of subclauses (A)(I) to (V) has given a guarantee on behalf of the particular trust or provided any other financial assistance whatever to the particular trust; and

(c) a member of a partnership that is beneficially interested in a trust is deemed to be beneficially interested in the trust.

Related Provisions: 94(1)"beneficiary" — Non-resident trust beneficiary; 104(1.1) — Restricted meaning of "beneficiary" of a trust; 108(1) — "Beneficiary"; 248(3) — Certain persons in Quebec deemed to be beneficially interested in trust.

Notes: The use of "includes" in para. (a) means that the normal meaning of "beneficially interested" applies as well (see Notes to 188.1(5)). For the meaning of "indirectly" in (a) and (b)(iii)(A), see Notes to 17.1(1).

The FCA stated in *Propep Inc.*, 2009 FCA 274 (leave to appeal denied 2010 CarswellNat 506 (SCC)) that 248(25) applies to the term "beneficiary" even when used outside ss. 104-108 (this is logically wrong, given that 108(1)"beneficiary" is limited to ss. 104-108). CRA agrees: VIEWS doc 2014-0538021C6 [2014 APFF q.3]. In *Lyrtech RD*, 2013 TCC 12, para. 56 (aff'd on other grounds 2014 FCA 267), the TCC held that 248(25) does not apply to 251(5)(b).

A newborn was a beneficiary retroactive to conception in *Pellerin*, 2015 TCC 130, due to Quebec civil law.

For a detailed discussion of "beneficial ownership", see Catherine Brown, "Beneficial Ownership and the Income Tax Act", 51(1) *Canadian Tax Journal* 401-53 (2003). On application in Quebec see VIEWS docs 2011-0417391E5; 2014-0538231C6 [2014 APFF q.4] and 2015-0565951E5 (legatee by particular). See also 2016-0653921E5 (whether a testamentary trust is beneficially interested in the estate).

A beneficiary of a discretionary trust who formally surrenders rights under the trust may cease to be a beneficiary, but CRA will not rule on this: doc 2015-0608781E5.

248(25) amended by 1995-97 technical bill (effective 1998), 1996 Budget, 1993 technical bill. Added by 1992 technical bill (the rule had been in 74.5(10) and 94(7), applying only for specific purposes).

A different draft 248(25), proposed in October 1991 to deal with indexed debt obligations, is now found in 16(6).

Income Tax Folios: S1-F5-C1: Related persons and dealing at arm's length [replaces IT-419R2]; S3-F10-C2: Prohibited investments — RRSPs, RRIFs and TFSAs.

Interpretation Bulletins: IT-394R2: Preferred beneficiary election; IT-511R: Interspousal and certain other transfers and loans of property.

(25.1) Trust-to-trust transfers

(25.1) Trust-to-trust transfers — If, at any time, a particular trust transfers property to another trust (other than a trust governed by a registered retirement savings plan or by a registered retirement income fund) in circumstances to which paragraph (f) of the definition "disposition" in subsection (1) applies, without affecting the personal liabilities under this Act of the trustees of either trust or the application of subsection 104(5.8),

(a) the other trust is deemed to be after that time the same trust as, and a continuation of, the particular trust; and

(b) for greater certainty, if, as a result of a transaction or event, the property was deemed to be taxable Canadian property of the particular trust by any of paragraphs 51(1)(f), 85(1)(i) and 85.1(1)(a), subsection 85.1(5), paragraph 85.1(8)(b), subsections 87(4) and (5) and paragraphs 97(2)(c) and 107(3.1)(d), the property is also deemed to be, at any time that is within 60 months after the transaction or event, taxable Canadian property of the other trust.

Related Provisions: 104(5.8) — Transfers between trusts; 108(1) — Definition of "capital interest"; 233.2(4) — Disclosure of transfer to CRA; 248(1)"disposition"(c) — Disposition incudes transfer to a trust.

Notes: 248(25.1) applies where there is a transfer of a property from a trust to a second trust (other than an RRSP or RRIF) in circumstances to which 248(1)"disposition"(f) applies. The result of para. (f) is that the transfer is not a disposition. 248(25.1) deems the second trust to be the same trust as, and a continuation of, the first trust. See VIEWS doc 2008-0288541E5.

248(25.1) can jeopardize a trust's status as a mutual fund trust. See Stephen Ruby, "Recent Transactions of Interest", 2007 Cdn Tax Foundation conference report at 3:25-26, discussing Dundee.

248(25.1) opening words amended by 2014 budget bill #2 to delete "and paragraph 122(2)(f)" from the end, for 2016 and later taxation years.

248(25.1) earlier amended by 2010 budget bill #1 (effective March 5, 2010, to add the 60-month rule), 2008 budget bill #2. Added by 2001 technical bill.

(25.2) Trusts to ensure obligations fulfilled

(25.2) Trusts to ensure obligations fulfilled — Except for the purpose of this subsection, where at any time property is transferred to a trust in circumstances to which paragraph (k) of the definition "disposition" in subsection (1) applies, the trust is deemed to deal with the property as agent for the transferor throughout the period that begins at the time of the transfer and ends at the time of the first change after that time in the beneficial ownership of the property.

Notes: See VIEWS doc 2004-0099081R3 for a ruling applying 248(25.2).

248(25.2) added by 2001 technical bill, for transfers after Dec. 23, 1998.

(25.3) Cost of trust interest

(25.3) Cost of trust interest — The cost to a taxpayer of a particular unit of a trust is deemed to be equal to the amount described in paragraph (a) where

(a) the trust issues the particular unit to the taxpayer directly in satisfaction of a right to enforce payment of an amount by the trust in respect of the taxpayer's capital interest in the trust;

(b) at the time that the particular unit is issued, the trust is neither a personal trust nor a trust prescribed for the purpose of subsection 107(2); and

(c) either

(i) the particular unit is capital property and the amount is not proceeds of disposition of a capital interest in the trust, or

(ii) the particular unit is not capital property and subparagraph 53(2)(h)(i.1) does not apply in respect of the amount described in paragraph (a) but would so apply if that subparagraph were read without reference to clauses 53(2)(h)(i.1)(A) and (B).

Notes: The cost of units acquired as determined under 248(25.3) is not included in box 42 of the T3 slip even though it forms part of the cost of the units: VIEWS doc 2006-0185621C6. See also doc 2007-025386117.

248(25.3)(c)(i) amended by 2002-2013 technical bill (Part 5 — technical), effective for units issued after Dec. 20, 2002.

248(25.3) added by 2001 technical bill, effective for 1999 and later taxation years.

(25.4) Where acquisition by another of right to enforce

(25.4) Where acquisition by another of right to enforce — If at a particular time a taxpayer's capital interest in a trust includes a right to enforce payment of an amount by the trust, the amount shall be added at the particular time to the cost otherwise determined to the taxpayer of the capital interest where

(a) immediately after the particular time there is a disposition by the taxpayer of the capital interest;

(b) as a consequence of the disposition, the right to enforce payment of the amount is acquired by another person or partnership; and

(c) if the right to enforce payment of the amount had been satisfied by a payment to the taxpayer by the trust, there would have been no disposition of that right for the purposes of this Act because of the application of paragraph (i) of the definition "disposition" in subsection (1).

Related Provisions: 107(1.1) — Cost of capital interest in a trust.

Notes: 248(25.4) provides relief from possible double taxation where a taxpayer disposes of a capital interest in a trust that includes a right to enforce payment of an amount by the trust. If, had the trust satisfied the right, there would have been no disposition of the right because of 248(1)"disposition"(i), the amount is added to the cost immediately before the disposition of the taxpayer's capital interest in the trust.

248(25.4) added by 2001 technical bill, for transfers after Dec. 23, 1998.

(26) Debt obligations

(26) Debt obligations — For greater certainty, where at any time a person or partnership (in this subsection referred to as the "debtor") becomes liable to repay money borrowed by the debtor or becomes liable to pay an amount (other than interest)

(a) as consideration for any property acquired by the debtor or services rendered to the debtor, or

(b) that is deductible in computing the debtor's income,

for the purposes of applying the provisions of this Act relating to the treatment of the debtor in respect of the liability, the liability shall be considered to be an obligation, issued at that time by the debtor, that has a principal amount at that time equal to the amount of the liability at that time.

Related Provisions: 43 — Partial disposition of capital property; 142.4(9) — Partial disposition of specified debt obligation by financial institution.

Notes: 248(26) was enacted to aid in applying the 1994 amendments to s. 80, re the tax consequences of discharge of a debt for less than its "principal amount". It does not compel a conclusion that the principal amount was necessarily the same at the times of issuance and redemption, because all it does is clarify s. 80: *Imperial Oil Ltd.*, [2005] 1 C.T.C. 65, para. 50 (FCA) [rev'd on other grounds [2007] 1 C.T.C. 41 (SCC)].

For CRA interpretation see VIEWS docs 2007-0259531R3, 2010-0371021E5.

248(26) added by 1994 technical bill, for tax years that end after Feb. 21, 1994.

(27) Parts of debt obligations — For greater certainty,

(a) unless the context requires otherwise, an obligation issued by a debtor includes any part of a larger obligation that was issued by the debtor;

(b) the principal amount of that part shall be considered to be the portion of the principal amount of that larger obligation that relates to that part; and

(c) the amount for which that part was issued shall be considered to be the portion of the amount for which that larger obligation was issued that relates to that part.

Related Provisions: 43 — Partial disposition of capital property; 142.4(9) — Partial disposition of specified debt obligation by financial institution.

Notes: 248(27) added by 1994 technical bill, for tax years that end after Feb. 21, 1994.

(28) Limitation respecting [double counting] inclusions, deductions and tax credits — Unless a contrary intention is evident, no provision of this Act shall be read or construed

(a) to require the inclusion or permit the deduction, either directly or indirectly, in computing a taxpayer's income, taxable income or taxable income earned in Canada, for a taxation year or in computing a taxpayer's income or loss for a taxation year from a particular source or from sources in a particular place, of any amount to the extent that the amount has already been directly or indirectly included or deducted, as the case may be, in computing such income, taxable income, taxable income earned in Canada or loss, for the year or any preceding taxation year;

(b) to permit the deduction, either directly or indirectly, in computing a taxpayer's tax payable under any Part of this Act for a taxation year of any amount to the extent that the amount has already been directly or indirectly deducted in computing such tax payable for the year or any preceding taxation year; or

(c) to consider an amount to have been paid on account of a taxpayer's tax payable under any Part of this Act for a taxation year to the extent that the amount has already been considered to have been paid on account of such tax payable for the year or any preceding taxation year.

Related Provisions: 118.041(4) — Home accessibility credit and medical expense credit can both be claimed for same expense; 181(4), 190(2) — Similar rules for Part I.3 and Part VI taxes.

Notes: 248(28), like its predecessor 4(4), "was enacted because Parliament recognized that, in a statute involving as many complex computations as the ITA, a transaction may fall literally within the scope of two separate provisions and so be counted twice as an income inclusion, a deduction or a tax credit ... 248(28) is intended to avoid such double counting unless the ITA clearly compels such a result": *Imperial Oil*, 2004 FCA 361, para. 68 [rev'd on other grounds 2006 SCC 46].

Although para. (a) refers only to deductions and (b) only to credits, 248(28)(b) appears to prevent both a deduction and a credit for the same expense (e.g., business expense and donation credit), since a deduction "indirectly" reduces tax payable. (See 17.1(1) Notes re "indirectly".) Note also that 12(1)(x) may tax a credit to bring it back into income (e.g., investment tax credit for 37(1) deductible expense is recaptured as "government assistance"). CRA and the Courts will normally disallow double-claiming (e.g., *Turcotte*, *Greene* and 2014-0562151E5 below). Double credit is explicitly permitted by 118.041(4).

Where two statutory provisions make the same adjustment on the same transaction, the fact they "have different objectives cannot, by itself, justify an inference that double taxation was intended": *Holder*, 2004 FCA 188. But see Notes to 207.03.

In *Turcotte*, 2015 QCCA 396 (leave to appeal denied 2015 CarswellQue 7382 (SCC)), a donation by will created a credit and could not also be a 104(6) deduction for the estate. In *Greene*, 2010 TCC 162, para. 11 (FCA appeal discontinued A-191-10), an amount rolled into an RRSP under 60(j.1) could not also be deducted as an RRSP contribution under 60(i) (the Court did not cite a source, but 146(5)(a)(ii) applied).

Where a bad debt deduction was mistakenly claimed twice in the same year (once as a capital loss, once as an income loss) and that year was statute-barred, 248(28) did not apply to a later recovery of the debt, which was a capital gain: *Barrington Lane Developments*, 2010 TCC 388.

In *Landry*, 2006 TCC 197 (aff'd 2007 FCA 344), an amount assessed on disposition of an insurance policy, which L argued had been included in a settlement of earlier years, was not being doubly taxed.

In *McKenzie*, 2017 TCC 56, taxing income from a US IRA following M's mother's death was not double tax because the mother, a non-resident, had not been subject to 70(5) on death.

Even without 248(28), double tax should be avoided: *Allfine Bowlerama*, [1972] C.T.C. 2603 (T.R.B.); *TechTouch Business Systems*, [1992] G.S.T.C. 12 (C.I.T.T.); *Bekins Leasing*, [1994] G.S.T.C. 80 (TCC); *Galon*, [1995] 2 C.T.C. 2521 (TCC), para. 7; *Royal Bank*, 2007 TCC 281, para. 68. However, double tax is only "where a single payment is taxed twice in the hands of the same taxpayer", not where "a single transaction generates income tax under different provisions in the hands of more than one taxpayer": *Ascot Enterprises*, [1996] 1 C.T.C. 384 (FCA), para. 16 (see also 15(1) Notes at "Double tax").

See also VIEWS docs 2008-0301241E5 (where both 75(2) and 104(13) apply), 2014-0562151E5 (psychotherapy allowed as business expense but not also as 118.2 credit); Barnicke & Huynh, "Upstream Loans: CRA Update", 21(12) *Canadian Tax Highlights* (ctf.ca) 3-4 (Dec. 2013); Éric Hamelin, "Trusts and Double Taxation", 17(3) *Tax for the Owner-Manager* (ctf.ca) 11-12 (July 2017).

248(28) added by 1995 Budget, for tax years that end after July 19, 1995. It replaces 4(4), and is somewhat more general.

A different 248(28), "Specified member of a partnership", in the draft legislation of April 26, 1995, was moved before enactment to 40(3.131) and 127.52(2.1). It no longer applies to 143.2(1)"tax shelter investment".

Registered Plans Compliance Bulletins: 3 (employer over-contributions to a registered pension plan: double taxation).

(29) Farming or fishing business [property used in both] — For the purposes of subsection 40(1.1) and sections 70, 73 and 110.6, if at any time a person or partnership carries on a farming business and a fishing business, a property used at that time principally in a combination of the activities of the farming business and the fishing business is deemed to be used at that time principally in the course of carrying on a farming or fishing business.

Related Provisions: 110.6(2) — Capital gains deduction — qualified farm or fishing property.

Notes: 248(29) added by 2014 budget bill #2, for property disposed of, or transferred, in the 2014 and later tax years. (The terms "farming business" and "fishing business" throughout the Act were changed to "farming or fishing business".)

Former 248(29) repealed by 2007 budget bill #2, effective Dec. 14, 2007, as the new definition "designated stock exchange" in 248(1) and 262 makes it unnecessary. It allowed a subdivision of a prescribed stock exchange. Former 248(29) added by 2001 technical bill, effective November 1999.

(30) Intention to give — The existence of an amount of an advantage in respect of a transfer of property does not in and by itself disqualify the transfer from being a gift to a qualified donee if

(a) the amount of the advantage does not exceed 80% of the fair market value of the transferred property; or

(b) the transferor of the property establishes to the satisfaction of the Minister that the transfer was made with the intention to make a gift.

Related Provisions: 248(40) — 248(30) does not apply to gift from registered charity.

Notes: See Notes to 248(32). See also *Cassan*, 2017 TCC 174 (FCA appeal settled A-304-17), paras. 319-338. 248(30) and (32) work together as a "cohesive whole" (para. 327); and only advantages that disqualify a transfer as a gift under the common law (or Quebec *Civil Code*) are considered in determining whether the 80% in 248(30)(a) is exceeded (para. 333) (it is not clear whether the latter point is correct).

248(30) added by 2002-2013 technical bill, for gifts and monetary contributions after Dec. 20, 2002.

Income Tax Folios: S7-F1-C1: Split-receipting and deemed fair market value.

Registered Charities Newsletters: 15 (new interim guidelines on gifts affect split-receipting); 17 (Q&A on split-receipting).

Charities Policies: CPC-025: Gift — expenses — volunteer; CPC-026: Fundraising — third-party fundraisers.

(31) Eligible amount of gift or monetary contribution [split receipting] — The eligible amount of a gift or monetary contribution is the amount by which the fair market value of the property that is the subject of the gift or monetary contribution exceeds the

amount of the advantage, if any, in respect of the gift or monetary contribution.

Related Provisions: 38.2 — Allocation of capital gain where advantage exists; 118.1(7)(d) [before 2016], 118.1(7.1)(b) [after 2015] — Determination of FMV of gift of art by artist; 127(4.1) — Monetary contribution (political); 248(30) — Existence of advantage does not negate gift; 248(32) — Determination of amount of advantage; 248(35)–(39) — Value of donation limited to cost if acquired within 3 years or as tax shelter; 248(41) — Donation value deemed nil if taxpayer does not inform donee of circumstances requiring reduction.

Notes: Although this rule is effective Dec. 21, 2002, it was not enacted until June 2013. See also Notes to 248(32) and 118.1(1)"total charitable gifts".

If the 248(32) "advantage" (A) exceeds 80% of the donation, no donation is allowed; if A is not more than $75 or 10% of the donation (whichever is less), the full donation is allowed: tinyurl.com/cra-split; Income Tax Folio S7-F1-C1.

See generally Drache, "Dealing with Donor Benefits", 24(2) *Canadian Not-for-Profit News [CNfpN]* (Carswell) 9-11 (Feb. 2016). On the effect of these rules on the purchase of annuities from charities, see Drache, "Collateral Damage", xxv(2) *The Canadian Taxpayer* (Carswell) 12-13 (Jan. 14-27, 2003). For fundraising tickets see Drache, "Receipting Fundraising Events", 15(2) *CNfpN* 14-15 (Feb. 2007); VIEWS doc 2010-0391511E5. For a participation fee paid by a sponsor in a fundraising event, see 2009-0321191I7.

For CRA comments on parents treating part of private school tuition as a gift, see doc 2003-0016297 (also Information Circular 75-23 re religious schools). See Notes to 248(32) re charitable gift annuities. For the eligible amount of a gift of life insurance see 2008-0267091E5, 2008-0270391C6, 2009-0312021E5, 2011-0398461C6. A right to purchase a cemetery plot at a discount (often provided by synagogues to members) would reduce the eligible amount of a membership donation: doc 2008-0284171E5; see Drache, "Benefits of Membership: Cemetery Plots", 17(2) *Canadian Not-for-Profit News* (Carswell) 16 (Feb. 2009). Congregation Adath Israel (Montreal) was penalized for issuing such receipts at full value; see 188.2 Notes.

See 69(1) Notes for meaning of "fair market value". For analysis of 248(30)-(33) see Loukidelis, "Comments on Certain Proposed Tax Rules Applicable to Charities", 18(4) *The Philanthropist [TPh]* 261-302 (2004) (thephilanthropist.ca); Boyle, "Gifts, Partial Gifts, Split Receipting", 20(3) *TPh* 205-241 (2006).

Even before 248(31), a sale for less than fair market value was a gift of the excess: *882885 Ontario*, 2007 TCC 131 and Quebec *Civil Code* art. 1810.

248(31) added by 2002-2013 technical bill, for gifts and monetary contributions made after Dec. 20, 2002.

Regulations: 2000(1)(i), (2)(j) (eligible amount to be disclosed in political contribution receipts); 3501(1)(h.2), (1.1)(h.2) (eligible amount to be disclosed in charitable donation receipts).

Income Tax Folios: S7-F1-C1: Split-receipting and deemed fair market value.

Registered Charities Newsletters: 15 (new interim guidelines on gifts affect split-receipting); 16 (important reminder for those selling annuities to donors); 17 (Q&A on split-receipting); 18 (can businesses receive receipts for donations made out of their inventory?); 23 (did you know? golf tournaments); 25 (split-receipting guidelines upheld); 31 (split receipting); *Charities Connection* 8 (golf tournaments).

Charities Policies: CPC-025: Gift — expenses — volunteer; CPC-026: Fundraising — third-party fundraisers.

(32) Amount of advantage

— The amount of the advantage in respect of a gift or monetary contribution by a taxpayer is the total of

(a) the total of all amounts, other than an amount referred to in paragraph (b), each of which is the value, at the time the gift or monetary contribution is made, of any property, service, compensation, use or other benefit that the taxpayer, or a person or partnership who does not deal at arm's length with the taxpayer, has received, obtained or enjoyed, or is entitled, either immediately or in the future and either absolutely or contingently, to receive, obtain, or enjoy

(i) that is consideration for the gift or monetary contribution,

(ii) that is in gratitude for the gift or monetary contribution, or

(iii) that is in any other way related to the gift or monetary contribution, and

(b) the limited-recourse debt, determined under subsection 143.2(6.1), in respect of the gift or monetary contribution at the time the gift or monetary contribution is made.

Related Provisions: 248(30) — Existence of advantage does not negate gift; 248(33) — Deemed cost of property acquired; 248(34) — Repayment of limited-recourse debt.

Notes: CRA policy on calculating the "advantage" is in Income Tax Folio S7-F1-C1; see VIEWS docs 2004-0103281E5 and 2005-0142431E5 for the calculation for a char-

ity golf or poker tournament. Where a fixed amount is paid to join a trip, a receipt can be issued for the eligible amount: 2008-0290311E5. Naming rights (e.g., "the John Doe Wing" or having one's name on a theatre seat with no right to occupy it) are not an "advantage" if there is no economic benefit: 2005-0110701R3, 2005-0130381R3, 2010-0375811E5; Drache, "When an Advantage is not an Advantage", 24(8) *Canadian Not-for-Profit News* (Carswell) 63-64 (Aug. 2016) (re engraving a message on a museum paving stone). A donation to a school with a general direction to use the money to buy books, where the donor's child attends the school, is not an "advantage": 2005-0159421E5; but a charity operating affordable housing for disabled persons, and which guarantees accommodation to donors' children, is providing an advantage: 2008-0271951E5 (and see Janet Newcombe, "Partial Charitable Giving", 6(10) *Tax Hyperion* (Carswell, Oct. 2009)). A church paying for children to attend a camp is an advantage if it benefits the donor or a person with whom the donor does not deal at arm's length: 2008-0289711E5.

Raffles: CRA (tinyurl.com/cra-fundrais) says no receipt can be issued for a standalone raffle because "the cost of the raffle tickets is not considered a gift". This may not be legally correct, if one can determine that purchasers pay more than a ticket's value and intend to donate the excess. (The problem can be avoided by setting a lower ticket price and requesting a voluntary donation with the purchase.) Where a raffle is included in a dinner or golf tournament, it is considered a door prize (tinyurl.com/cra-fundrais) and the "advantage" is the prizes' value divided by the number of tickets sold. See also VIEWS docs 2003-0008405, 2003-0008495, 2007-0244311E5 (similar interpretations).

For the amount of advantage of an annuity stream received by a donor on giving cash to a charity, see VIEWS docs 2003-0008195 and 2003-0009195. For the calculation on donating an item to a museum subject to a lifetime loan of the item back to the donor, see docs 2006-0170391R3, 2007-0229281R3. For structures where CRA ruled there was no "advantage" see docs 2006-0171421R3; 2006-0201411E5 (investment advisor's trailer fees on mutual funds acquired by charity); 2006-0218471R3; 2007-0247091R3 (transfer of ecologically sensitive land by corporate partnership to ensure its protection). See also Notes to 248(31).

A sale at a discount is a donation of the difference only if there is donative intent: VIEWS docs 2005-0125431E5, 2007-0227171R3, 2007-0248451E5.

Being cryogenically preserved after death is an "advantage": doc 2011-0408401E5. (This might not be correct since the supposed recipient of the advantage is dead, at least for the time being. See Chodorow article cited in 70(5) Notes at "Zombies".)

In *Richert v. Stewards' Charitable Foundation*, 2005 BCSC 211, the plaintiff donated $1,000 to support a cause; a luncheon and book were provided (his accountant attended the luncheon). His receipt (based on the "advantage") was for only $845, and he sued to get the $1,000 back based on mistake. He lost.

In *Duguay*, 2016 TCC 168, a tenant of a charity that operated low-income housing agreed to donate to the charity half of $20,000 it paid him to renovate his unit. The Court held that the "advantage" was $10,000, so he got no donation credit.

In *Cassan*, 2017 TCC 174 (FCA appeal settled A-304-17), paras. 361-362, the EquiGenesis shelter triggered both 248(32)(a) (below-market interest rate on loan) and 248(32)(b) (principal amount of loan, as it was a limited-recourse amount), wiping out the donation credit.

248(32) added by 2002-2013 technical bill (Part 5 — technical), this version effective for gifts and monetary contributions made after Dec. 5, 2003.

Regulations: 2000(1)(h), 2000(2)(i) (amount of advantage to be disclosed in political contribution receipts); 3501(1)(h.1), 3501(1.1)(h.1) (amount of advantage to be disclosed in charitable donation receipts).

Income Tax Folios: S7-F1-C1: Split-receipting and deemed fair market value.

Registered Charities Newsletters: 15 (new interim guidelines on gifts affect split-receipting); 17 (Q&A on split-receipting); 22 (advantages received by a donor: promotion, advertising, and sponsorship); 23 (did you know? golf tournaments); 24 (de minimis threshold); *Charities Connection* 8 (golf tournaments).

Charities Policies: CPC-025: Gift — expenses — volunteer; CPC-026: Fundraising — third-party fundraisers.

(33) Cost of property acquired by donor

— The cost to a taxpayer of a property, acquired by the taxpayer in circumstances where subsection (32) applies to include the value of the property in computing the amount of the advantage in respect of a gift or monetary contribution, is equal to the fair market value of the property at the time the gift or monetary contribution is made.

Notes: 248(33) added by 2002-2013 technical bill, for gifts and monetary contributions made after Dec. 20, 2002.

Income Tax Folios: S7-F1-C1: Split-receipting and deemed fair market value.

Registered Charities Newsletters: 17 (Q&A on split-receipting).

(34) Repayment of limited-recourse debt

— If at any time in a taxation year a taxpayer has paid an amount (in this subsection referred to as the "repaid amount") on account of the principal amount of an indebtedness which was, before that time, an unpaid principal amount that was a limited-recourse debt referred to in subsection 143.2(6.1) (in this subsection referred to as the "former limited-recourse debt") in respect of a gift or monetary contribution (in this subsection referred to as the "original gift" or "original monetary contribution", respectively, as the case may be) of the taxpayer (otherwise than by way of an assignment or transfer of a guarantee, security or similar indemnity or covenant, or by way of a payment in respect of which any taxpayer referred to in subsection 143.2(6.1) has incurred an indebtedness that would be a limited-recourse debt referred to in that subsection if that indebtedness were in respect of a gift or monetary contribution made at the time that that indebtedness was incurred, the following rules apply:

(a) if the former limited-recourse debt is in respect of the original gift, for the purposes of sections 110.1 and 118.1, the taxpayer is deemed to have made in the taxation year a gift to a qualified donee, the eligible amount of which deemed gift is the amount, if any, by which

(i) the amount that would have been the eligible amount of the original gift, if the total of all such repaid amounts paid at or before that time were paid immediately before the original gift was made,

exceeds

(ii) the total of

(A) the eligible amount of the original gift, and

(B) the eligible amount of all other gifts deemed by this paragraph to have been made before that time in respect of the original gift; and

(b) if the former limited-recourse debt is in respect of the original monetary contribution, for the purposes of subsection 127(3), the taxpayer is deemed to have made in the taxation year a monetary contribution referred to in that subsection, the eligible amount of which is the amount, if any, by which

(i) the amount that would have been the eligible amount of the original monetary contribution, if the total of all such repaid amounts paid at or before that time were paid immediately before the original monetary contribution was made,

exceeds

(ii) the total of

(A) the eligible amount of the original monetary contribution, and

(B) the eligible amount of all other monetary contributions deemed by this paragraph to have been made before that time in respect of the original monetary contribution.

Notes: 248(34) added by 2002-2013 technical bill (Part 5 — technical), effective for gifts and monetary contributions made after Feb. 18, 2003.

Income Tax Folios: S7-F1-C1: Split-receipting and deemed fair market value.

(35) Deemed fair market value [of donated property] — For the purposes of subsection (31), paragraph 69(1)(b) and subsections 110.1(2.1) and (3) and 118.1(5.4), (6) and (13.2), the fair market value of a property that is the subject of a gift made by a taxpayer to a qualified donee is deemed to be the lesser of the fair market value of the property otherwise determined and the cost or, in the case of capital property, the adjusted cost base or, in the case of a life insurance policy in respect of which the taxpayer is a policyholder, the adjusted cost basis (as defined in subsection 148(9)), of the property to the taxpayer immediately before the gift is made if

(a) the taxpayer acquired the property under a gifting arrangement that is a tax shelter as defined in subsection 237.1(1); or

(b) except where the gift is made as a consequence of the taxpayer's death,

(i) the taxpayer acquired the property less than three years before the day that the gift is made, or

(ii) the taxpayer acquired the property less than 10 years before the day that the gift is made and it is reasonable to conclude that, at the time the taxpayer acquired the property, one of the main reasons for the acquisition was to make a gift of the property to a qualified donee.

Related Provisions: 52(4) — Cost of property acquired as prize is its fair market value; 87(2)(m.2), 88(1)(e.2) — Amalgamation or windup — continuing corporation;

237.1(1) — Definitions of "gifting arrangement" and "tax shelter"; 248(36) — Non-arm's length acquisition by donor; 248(37) — Exceptions; 248(38) — Anti-avoidance rule — artificial transactions; 248(39) — Anti-avoidance — selling property and donating proceeds; 248(41) — Donation value deemed nil if taxpayer does not inform donee of circumstances requiring reduction.

Notes: This rule responds to "art flips" and other schemes involving "buy low donate high" valuations, which abused the fact that "fair market value" is the *highest* price an arm's-length purchaser will pay. Even before 248(35), if sale is soon after purchase, cost is likely a good indicator of FMV: *Nash (Tolley, Quinn)*, 2005 FCA 386, para. 29; *Miller*, 2019 TCC 204. See Notes to 118.1(1)"total charitable gifts". See also the additional rules and exceptions in 248(36)-(39).

For the meaning of "one of the main reasons" in (b)(ii), see Notes to 83(2.1).

Note that 248(35) applies for purposes of 69(1)(b)(ii), so there is no capital gain to the taxpayer on making the donation.

The application of 248(35) to 69(1)(b) is to the gift to a qualified donee. If the taxpayer *receives* a gift at arm's length (so 248(36) does not apply), 248(35) appears not to apply to that (first) gift, so that a (second) gift from the taxpayer to a charity can be receipted at fair market value!

For detailed discussion of this rule see Sandler & Edgar, "The Tax Expenditure Program for Charitable Giving", 51(6) *Canadian Tax Journal* 2193-2214 (2003). For the effect of 248(35) on donations of private corporation shares, see Provenzano & Mapa, "Private Corp Share Gifting", 12(2) *Canadian Tax Highlights* (ctf.ca) 5-6 (Feb. 2004).

Since the July 16/10 draft, 248(35) clearly applies to a donated life insurance policy; in earlier drafts it was unclear (VIEWS docs 2008-0284461C6, 2009-0316701C6, 2010-0359391C6). Where the policy is transferred to a corp at nil under 148(7), the donation value will be nil: 2010-0363091C6. See also Notes to 248(36).

The reference to 118.1(13.2) was first added in the Oct. 24, 2012 draft and is effective as of that date.

248(35) added by 2002-2013 technical bill for gifts after 6pm EST Dec. 5, 2003, and amended by same bill effective Oct. 24, 2012.

Income Tax Folios: S7-F1-C1: Split-receipting and deemed fair market value.

I.T. Technical News: 41 (donation of flow-through shares).

Registered Charities Newsletters: 18 (charitable donation tax shelter arrangements); 24 (determining fair market value).

(36) Non-arm's length transaction — If a taxpayer acquired a property, otherwise than by reason of the death of an individual, that is the subject of a gift to which subsection (35) applies because of subparagraph (35)(b)(i) or (ii) and the property was, at any time within the 3-year or 10-year period, respectively, that ends when the gift was made, acquired by a person or partnership with whom the taxpayer does not deal at arm's length, for the purpose of applying subsection (35) to the taxpayer, the cost, or in the case of capital property, the adjusted cost base, of the property to the taxpayer immediately before the gift is made is deemed to be equal to the lowest amount that is the cost, or in the case of capital property, the adjusted cost base, to the taxpayer or any of those persons or partnerships immediately before the property was disposed of by that person or partnership.

Related Provisions: 248(41) — Donation value deemed nil if taxpayer does not inform donee of circumstances requiring reduction.

Notes: An insurance policy's adjusted cost basis is a "reasonable proxy" for "cost": VIEWS doc 2017-0692361C6 [CLHIA 2017 q.4].

248(36) added by 2002-2013 technical bill (Part 5 — technical), for gifts and monetary contributions made after July 17, 2005.

Income Tax Folios: S7-F1-C1: Split-receipting and deemed fair market value.

(37) Non-application of subsec. (35) — Subsection (35) does not apply to a gift

(a) of inventory;

(b) of real property or an immovable situated in Canada;

(c) of an object referred to in subparagraph 39(1)(a)(i.1), other than an object acquired under a gifting arrangement (as defined in subsection 237.1(1)) that is a tax shelter;

(d) of property to which paragraph 38(a.1) or (a.2) applies;

(e) of a share of the capital stock of a corporation if

(i) the share was issued by the corporation to the donor,

(ii) immediately before the gift, the corporation was controlled by the donor, a person related to the donor or a group of persons each of whom is related to the donor, and

(iii) subsection (35) would not have applied in respect of the consideration for which the share was issued had that consideration been donated by the donor to the qualified donee when the share was so donated;

(f) by a corporation of property if

(i) the property was acquired by the corporation in circumstances to which subsection 85(1) or (2) applied,

(ii) immediately before the gift, the shareholder from whom the corporation acquired the property controlled the corporation or was related to a person or each member of a group of persons that controlled the corporation, and

(iii) subsection (35) would not have applied in respect of the property had the property not been transferred to the corporation and had the shareholder made the gift to the qualified donee when the corporation so made the gift; or

(g) of a property that was acquired in circumstances where subsection 70(6) or (9) or 73(1), (3) or (4) applied, unless subsection (36) would have applied if this subsection were read without reference to this paragraph.

Notes: On the effect of 248(37)(g) see VIEWS doc 2014-0538641C6 [2014 APFF q.10].

248(37)(c) amended by 2014 budget bill #1, for gifts made after Feb. 10, 2014.

248(37) added by 2002-2013 technical bill, on the same basis as 248(35).

Income Tax Folios: S7-F1-C1: Split-receipting and deemed fair market value.

(38) Artificial transactions — The eligible amount of a particular gift of property by a taxpayer is nil if it can reasonably be concluded that the particular gift relates to a transaction or series of transactions

(a) one of the purposes of which is to avoid the application of subsection (35) to a gift of any property; or

(b) that would, if this Act were read without reference to this paragraph, result in a tax benefit to which subsection 245(2) applies.

Related Provisions: 248(41) — Donation value deemed nil if taxpayer does not inform donee of circumstances requiring reduction.

Notes: 248(38) added by 2002-2013 technical bill (Part 5 — technical), effective on the same basis as 248(35).

Income Tax Folios: S7-F1-C1: Split-receipting and deemed fair market value.

(39) Substantive gift [selling property and donating proceeds] — If a taxpayer disposes of a property (in this subsection referred to as the "substantive gift") that is a capital property of the taxpayer, to a recipient that is a "registered party", a "registered association" or a "candidate", as those terms are defined in the *Canada Elections Act*, or that is a qualified donee, subsection (35) would have applied in respect of the substantive gift if it had been the subject of a gift by the taxpayer to a qualified donee, and all or a part of the proceeds of disposition of the substantive gift are (or are substituted, directly or indirectly in any manner whatever, for) property that is the subject of a gift or monetary contribution by the taxpayer to the recipient or any person dealing not at arm's length with the recipient, the following rules apply:

(a) for the purpose of subsection (31), the fair market value of the property that is the subject of the gift or monetary contribution made by the taxpayer is deemed to be that proportion of the lesser of the fair market value of the substantive gift and the cost, or if the substantive gift is capital property of the taxpayer, the adjusted cost base, of the substantive gift to the taxpayer immediately before the disposition to the recipient, that the fair market value otherwise determined of the property that is the subject of the gift or monetary contribution is of the proceeds of disposition of the substantive gift; and

(b) if the substantive gift is capital property of the taxpayer, for the purpose of the definitions "proceeds of disposition" of property in subsection 13(21) and section 54, the sale price of the substantive gift is to be reduced by the amount by which the fair market value of the property that is the subject of the gift (deter-

mined without reference to this section) exceeds the fair market value determined under paragraph (a);

(c) [Repealed]

Related Provisions: 248(41) — Donation value deemed nil if taxpayer does not inform donee of circumstances requiring reduction.

Notes: 248(39) opening words amended (to delete "or an eligible capital property" after "capital property"), and (c) repealed, by 2016 budget bill #2, effective 2017, as part of changing the ECP rules to CCA Class 14.1 (see Notes to 20(1)(b)). Para. (c) read:

(c) if the substantive gift is eligible capital property of the taxpayer, the amount determined under paragraph (a) in the description of E in the definition "cumulative eligible capital" in subsection 14(5) in respect of the substantive gift is to be reduced by the amount by which the fair market value of the property that is the subject of the gift (determined without reference to this section) exceeds the fair market value determined under paragraph (a).

248(39) added by 2002-2013 technical bill (Part 5 — technical), effective for gifts and monetary contributions made after Feb. 26, 2004.

Income Tax Folios: S7-F1-C1: Split-receipting and deemed fair market value.

(40) Inter-charity gifts — Subsection (30) does not apply in respect of a gift received by a qualified donee from a registered charity.

Related Provisions: 248(41) — Eligible amount deemed nil if information not provided.

Notes: This was not included in the July 18, 2005 draft legislation. That draft contained a 248(40) which proposed that charities be required to make inquiries with respect to any donation of $5,000 or more, before issuing a receipt, to ascertain compliance with 248(31)-(39). It was withdrawn following objections from the charity sector.

248(40) added by 2002-2013 technical bill (Part 5 — technical), effective for gifts and monetary contributions made after Nov. 8, 2006.

Income Tax Folios: S7-F1-C1: Split-receipting and deemed fair market value.

(41) Information not provided — Notwithstanding subsection (31), the eligible amount of a gift or monetary contribution made by a taxpayer is nil if the taxpayer does not — before a receipt referred to in subsection 110.1(2), 118.1(2) or 127(3), as the case may be, is issued in respect of the gift or monetary contribution — inform the qualified donee or the recipient, as the case may be, of any circumstances in respect of which subsection (31), (35), (36), (38) or (39) requires that the eligible amount of the gift or monetary contribution be less than the fair market value, determined without reference to subsections (35), 110.1(3) and 118.1(6), of the property that is the subject of the gift or monetary contribution.

Notes: 248(41) denies a credit for the "cash put in" to a donation scheme, such as was allowed in *Doubinin*, 2005 FCA 298.

248(41) added by 2002-2013 technical bill, for gifts and monetary contributions made after 2005.

Income Tax Folios: S7-F1-C1: Split-receipting and deemed fair market value.

(42) Synthetic equity arrangements — disaggregation — For the purposes of the definition "synthetic equity arrangement" in subsection (1), paragraphs (c) and (d) of the definition "dividend rental arrangement" in subsection (1) and subsections 112(2.31), (2.32) and (10), an arrangement that reflects the fair market value of more than one type of "identical share" (as defined in subsection 112(10)) is considered to be a separate arrangement with respect to each type of identical share the value of which the arrangement reflects.

Notes: 248(42) added by 2016 budget bill #1, effective April 22, 2015.

Definitions [s. 248]: "accelerated investment incentive property" — Reg. 1104(4); "acquired for consideration" — 108(7); "active business" — 248(1); "adjusted cost base" — 54, 248(1); "adjusted cost basis" — 148(9); "adoption" — 251(6)(c); "advantage" — 248(32); "adventure or concern in the nature of trade" — see 10(1.01) Notes; "affiliated" — 251.1; "agricultural cooperative corporation" — 135.1(1); "amateur athlete trust" — 143.1(1.2)(a), 248(1); "amount"; "annuity" — 248(1); "arm's length" — 251(1); "assessment" — 248(1); "associated" — 256; "authorized foreign bank", "automobile", "balance-due day" — 248(1); "bank" — 248(1), *Interpretation Act* 35(1); "beneficial ownership" — 248(3); "beneficially interested" — 248(25); "beneficially owned" — 248(3); "beneficiary" — 248(25) [Notes]; "bituminous sands" — 248(1); "blood relationship" — 251(6)(a); "business", "business limit" — 248(1); "calendar year" — *Interpretation Act* 37(1)(a); "Canada" — 255, *Interpretation Act* 35(1); "Canadian-controlled private corporation" — 125(7), 248(1); "Canadian currency" — 261(5)(f)(i); "Canadian partnership" — 102(1); "Canadian resource property" — 66(15), 248(1); "Canadian security" — 39(6); "capital gain" — 39(1)(a), 248(1); "capital interest" — 108(1), 248(1); "capital loss" — 39(1)(b), 248(1); "capital property" — 54, 248(1); "carrying on business" — 253; "cash method" — 28(1), 248(1); "cemetery care trust" — 148.1(1), 248(1); "child" — 252(1); "common-law partner", "common-law partnership", "common share" — 248(1); "connected" — 186(4), (7), 251(6); "consequence of the death", "consequence of the taxpayer's death" — 248(8); "consideration" — 108(7); "control", "controlled" — 256(6)–(9), 256.1(3); "controlled foreign affiliate" — 95(1), 248(1); "corporation" — 248(1), *Interpretation Act* 35(1); "corporeal property" — Quebec *Civil Code* art. 899, 906; "credit union" — 137(6), 248(1); "currency of a country other than Canada" — 261(5)(f)(ii); "custodian" — 248(1)"employee benefit plan", "retirement compensation arrangement", "DRA share", "deferred amount" — 248(1); "deferred profit sharing plan" — 147(1), 248(1); "depreciable property" — 13(21), 248(1); "derivative forward agreement" — 248(1); "designated insurance property" — 138(12), 248(1); "designated stock exchange" — 248(1), 262; "disclaimer" — 248(1); "disposition", "dividend" — 248(1); "eligible amount" — 248(31), (41), "eligible capital property" — 54, 248(1); "eligible funeral arrangement" — 148.1(1), 248(1); "emissions allowance", "employed", "employee", "employee benefit plan" — 248(1); "employee life and health trust" — 144.1(2), 248(1); "employee trust" — 248(1); "employees profit sharing plan" — 144(1), 248(1); "employer", "employment" — 248(1); "estate" — 104(1), 248(1); "fair market value" — 248(35) and see 69(1) Notes; "farming", "federal credit union" — 248(1); "filing-due date" — 150(1), 248(1); "financial institution" — 142.2(1); "fiscal period" — 249(2)(b), 249.1; "fishing" — 248(1); "foreign exploration and development expenses" — 66(15), 248(1); "foreign investment entity" — 248(1); "foreign merger" — 87(8.1); "foreign resource expense" — 66.21(1), 248(1); "general rate reduction percentage" — 123.4(1); "gifting arrangement" — 237.1(1); "goods and services tax" — 248(1); "goodwill" — 13(34); "graduated rate estate", "grandfathered share", "gross revenue" — 248(1); "Her Majesty" — *Interpretation Act* 35(1); "identical" — 248(12); "identical share" — 112(10); "immovable" — Quebec *Civil Code* art. 900–907; "income interest", "individual", "insurance policy", "insurer" — 248(1); "*inter vivos* trust" — 108(1), 248(1); "interest in", "interest in real property", "interest of the taxpayer in" — 248(4); "international traffic", "inventory" — 248(1); "land" — see 70(5.2) Notes; "lending asset" — 248(1); "life insurance policy", "life insurance policy in Canada" — 138(12), 248(1); "limited-recourse debt" — 143.2(6.1); "liquidation entitlement" — 248(1)"taxable preferred share"(b)(ii), "taxable RFI share"(b); "loss restriction event" — 251.2; "majority-interest beneficiary" — 251.1(3); "mark-to-market property" — 142.2(1); "mineral" — 248(1); "mineral resource", "Minister" — 248(1); "Minister of Finance" — *Financial Administration Act* 14; "Minister of Natural Resources" — *Department of Natural Resources Act* s. 3; "monetary contribution" — 127(4.1), *Canada Elections Act* s. 2(1); "month" — *Interpretation Act* 35(1); "motor vehicle" — 248(1); "movable" — Quebec *Civil Code* art. 900–907; "mutual fund corporation" — 131(8), 248(1); "mutual fund trust" — 132(6)–(7), 132.2(3)(n), 248(1); "net income stabilization account", "non-resident" — 248(1); "non-resident-owned investment corporation" — 133(8), 248(1); "office", "officer" — 248(1)"office"; "oil or gas well" — 248(1); "paid-up capital" — 89(1), 248(1); "parent" — 252(2)(a); "Parliament" — *Interpretation Act* 35(1); "partnership" — see 96(1) Notes; "passenger vehicle" — 248(1); "permanent establishment" — Reg. 8201; "person" — 248(1); "personal services business" — 125(7), 248(1); "personal trust" — 248(1); "policy loan" — 138(12), 148(9); "pooled pension plan", "pooled registered pension plan" — 147.5(1), 248(1); "prescribed" — 248(1); "prescribed plan or arrangement" — Reg. 6801, 6802, 6802.1, 6803; "prescribed rate" — Reg. 4301; "prescribed stock exchange in Canada" — Reg. 3200; "principal amount" — 248(1), (26); "property" — 248(1); "province" — *Interpretation Act* 35(1); "public corporation" — 89(1), 248(1); "qualified Canadian journalism organization" — 248(1); "qualified donee" — 149.1(1), 188.2(3)(a), 248(1); "qualifying arrangement" — 248(3.2); "qualifying disposition" — 107.4(1); "qualifying environmental trust" — 211.6(1), 248(1); "qualifying exchange" — 132.2(1); "qualifying journalism organization" — 149.1(1); "qualifying member" — 95(2)(o)–(r), 248(1); "qualifying period" — 248(1)"SIFT trust wind-up event"(c)(ii); "real estate investment trust" — 122.1(1); "real right" — 248(4.1); "recognized derivatives exchange", "registered charity" — 248(1); "registered disability savings plan" — 146.4(1), 248(1); "registered education savings plan" — 146.1(1), 248(1); "registered pension plan" — 248(1); "registered retirement income fund" — 146.3(1), 248(1); "registered retirement savings plan" — 146(1), 248(1); "registered securities dealer" — 248(1); "registered supplementary unemployment benefit plan" — 145(1), 248(1); "regular force" — *Interpretation Act* 35(1); "regulation" — 248(1); "related" — 248(1.4), 251; "related segregated fund trust" — 138.1(1)(a); "release or surrender" — 248(9); "resident" — 250; "resident in Canada" — 94(3)(a), 250; "restricted financial institution" — 248(1); "SIFT partnership" — 197(1), (8), 248(1); "SIFT trust" — 122.1(1), (2), 248(1); "SIFT trust wind-up event", "SIFT wind-up entity", "salary or wages" — 248(1); "security" — *Interpretation Act* 35(1); "series of transactions" — 248(10); "share", "shareholder", "short-term preferred share", "specified financial institution", "specified future tax consequence" — 248(1); "specified investment business" — 125(7), 248(1); "specified debt obligation" — 142.2(1); "specified mutual fund trust" — 248(1); "specified person" — 248(1)"short-term preferred share"(j), 248(1)"taxable preferred share"(h); "specified shareholder", "specified synthetic equity arrangement" — 248(1); "spouse" — 252(3); "stock dividend" — 248(1); "substituted" — 248(5); "supplementary unemployment benefit plan" — 145(1), 248(1); "synthetic disposition arrangement", "synthetic equity arrangement" — 248(1); "TFSA" — 146.2(5), 248(1); "tar sands" — 248(1); "tax basis" — 142.4(1); "tax shelter" — 237.1(1), 248(1); "tax treaty" — 248(1); "taxable Canadian corporation" — 89(1), 248(1); "taxable Canadian property" — 248(1); "taxable capital gain" — 38(a), 248(1); "taxable dividend" — 89(1), 248(1); "taxable income" — 2(2), 248(1); "taxable income earned in Canada", "taxable preferred share", "taxable RFI share" — 248(1); "taxation year" — 249; "taxpayer" — 248(1); "testamentary trust" — 108(1),

248(1); "timber resource property" — 13(21), 248(1); "trust" — 104(1), 248(1), (3); "trust account number" — 248(1); "unit trust" — 108(2), 248(1); "usufruct" — Quebec *Civil Code* art. 1120-1171; "writing", "written" — *Interpretation Act* 35(1)"writing"; "zero-emission passenger vehicle", "zero-emission vehicle" — 248(1).

249. (1) Definition of "taxation year" — In this Act, except as expressly otherwise provided, a "taxation year" is

(a) in the case of a corporation or Canadian resident partnership, a fiscal period;

(b) in the case of a graduated rate estate, the period for which the accounts of the estate are made up for purposes of assessment under this Act; and

(c) in any other case, a calendar year.

Related Provisions: 11(2) — Reference to "taxation year" of individual who carries on a business; 20(16.2) — Taxation year of individual — terminal loss rules; 87(2)(a) — Deemed year-end and new taxation year on amalgamation; 95(1)"taxation year" — Taxation year of foreign affiliate; 96(1)(b) — Taxation year of partnership; 104(23) — Testamentary trusts; 128(2)(d) — Deemed year-end where individual bankrupt; 128.1(1)(a) — Deemed year-end and new taxation year on becoming resident in Canada; 128.1(4)(a) — Deemed year-end and new taxation year on ceasing to be resident in Canada; 132.11 — Election for mutual fund trust to have December 15 year-end; 132.2(3)(b) — Deemed year-end and new taxation year on transfer of property between mutual funds; 144(11) — Deemed year-end on EPSP becoming DPSP; 149(10)(a) — Taxation year of corporation becoming or ceasing to be exempt; 149.1(1) — Taxation year of registered charity; 188(1) — Deemed year-end on notice of revocation of charity registration; 249(2), (3) — References to "taxation year" and "fiscal period"; 249(3.1) — Deemed year end on becoming or ceasing to be CCPC; 249(4) — Deemed year-end on change of control; 249(5), (6) — Rules for testamentary trust; 250.1(a) — Taxation year of non-resident person.

Notes: The winding-up of a Canadian branch of a US company does not trigger a taxation year-end: VIEWS doc 2003-0020715.

249(1)(b), (c) amended by 2014 budget bill #2, for 2016 and later taxation years. (See Notes to 122(1).) For previous years, read:

> (b) in the case of an individual (other than a testamentary trust), a calendar year; and

> (c) in the case of a testamentary trust, the period for which the accounts of the trust are made up for purposes of assessment under this Act.

249(1) amended by 2002-2013 technical bill (Part 5 — technical), effective Dec. 21, 2002, but read 249(1)(a) before Oct. 31, 2006 without "or Canadian resident partnership". The former closing words of 249(1) were moved to 249(1.1).

249(1)(a) amended by 2007 budget bill #1, effective Oct. 31, 2006, to add "or Canadian resident partnership".

Regulations: 1104(1) (taxation year of individual for capital cost allowance purposes).

Income Tax Folios: S4-F7-C1: Amalgamations of Canadian corporations [replaces IT-474R2]; S5-F2-C1: Foreign tax credit [replaces IT-270R3, IT-395R2, IT-520].

Interpretation Bulletins: IT-184R: Deferred cash purchase tickets issued by Canadian Wheat Board; IT-363R2: Deferred profit sharing plans — deductibility of employer contributions and taxation of amounts received by a beneficiary (cancelled).

(1.1) References to calendar year — When a taxation year is referred to by reference to a calendar year, the reference is to the taxation year or taxation years that coincide with, or that end in, that calendar year.

Notes: 249(1.1) added by 2002-2013 technical bill (Part 5 — technical), effective Dec. 21, 2002. This rule was formerly in the closing words of 249(1) and in 104(23)(b).

(2) References to certain taxation years and fiscal periods — For the purposes of this Act,

(a) a reference to a taxation year ending in another year includes a reference to a taxation year ending coincidentally with that other year; and

(b) a reference to a fiscal period ending in a taxation year includes a reference to a fiscal period ending coincidentally with that year.

Related Provisions: 249(1) — "Taxation year"; 250.1(a) — Taxation year of non-resident person.

Notes: 249(2)(b) amended by 1994 Budget, effective for fiscal periods that end after 1993 (formerly applied only to partnerships).

(3) Fiscal period exceeding 365 days — If a fiscal period of a corporation exceeds 365 days and for that reason the corporation

does not have a taxation year that ends in a particular calendar year, for the purposes of this Act,

(a) the corporation's first taxation year that would otherwise end in the immediately following calendar year is deemed to end on the last day of the particular calendar year and its next taxation year is deemed to commence on the first day of the immediately following calendar year; and

(b) the corporation's first fiscal period that would otherwise end in the immediately following calendar year is deemed to end on the last day of the particular calendar year and its next fiscal period is deemed to commence on the first day of the immediately following calendar year.

Notes: When 249(3) applies, the fiscal year is deemed to end on Dec. 31, so that year's version of the tax return should be used: VIEWS doc 2011-0410361I7. For interaction with 249.1(1) when 249(3) applies, see 9823456, 2005-0131701E5. (These interpretations were written before 249(3) was amended in 2013.) On the application of 249(3) to consecutive years, see 2014-0535561I7, 2014-0560131E5.

249(3) amended by 2002-2013 technical bill, for 2012 and later tax years.

(3.1) Year end on [CCPC] status change — If at any time a corporation becomes or ceases to be a Canadian-controlled private corporation, otherwise than because of an acquisition of control to which subsection (4) would, if this Act were read without reference to this subsection, apply,

(a) subject to paragraph (c), the corporation's taxation year that would, if this Act were read without reference to this subsection, include that time is deemed to end immediately before that time;

(b) a new taxation year of the corporation is deemed to begin at that time;

(c) notwithstanding subsections (1) and (3), the corporation's taxation year that would, if this Act were read without reference to this subsection, have been its last taxation year that ended before that time is deemed instead to end immediately before that time if

(i) were this Act read without reference to this paragraph, that taxation year would, otherwise than because of paragraph 128(1)(d), section 128.1 and paragraphs 142.6(1)(a) or 149(10)(a), have ended within the 7-day period that ended immediately before that time,

(ii) within that 7-day period no person or group of persons acquired control of the corporation, and the corporation did not become or cease to be a Canadian-controlled private corporation, and

(iii) the corporation elects, in its return of income under Part I for that taxation year to have this paragraph apply; and

(d) for the purpose of determining the corporation's fiscal period after that time, the corporation is deemed not to have established a fiscal period before that time.

Related Provisions: 89(4) — General rate income pool addition on becoming CCPC; 89(8) — Low rate income pool addition on ceasing to be CCPC; 125(7)"Canadian-controlled private corporation"(d) — Election not to be CCPC for purposes of 249(3.1).

Notes: See Notes to 249(4) for the effects of the deemed year-end. Loss of CCPC status can mean loss of the lifetime capital gains exemption on sale of the company's shares (110.6(2.1)), loss of ABIL treatment (see Notes to 39(1)), reduced entitlement to SR&ED investment tax credit (127(10.1), 127.1), and loss of the small business deduction (125(1)). LRIP is increased as per 89(8). On the positive side, the high-rate tax and refundable tax on investment income (see Notes to 123.3) will no longer apply.

For a corporation filing a Quebec return, a 249(3.1)(c)(iii) election must be copied to Revenu Québec: *Taxation Act* ss. 6.1.1, 21.4.6.

249(3.1) can be triggered on signing a purchase and sale agreement, due to 251(5)(b). See Duholke, "Deemed Year-End Trap", 15(2) *Canadian Tax Highlights* (ctf.ca) 9 (Feb. 2007); Blucher, "Share Purchase Agreements", 9(3) *Tax Hyperion* (Carswell, March 2012). This was confirmed by CRA, 2007 Cdn Tax Foundation conference report, 4:13; where the Act is clear, there will be no administrative relief.

249(3.1) did not prevent the capital gains exemption from being available in a specific situation: VIEWS doc 2006-0214691E5; Philip Friedlan, "Ceasing to be a CCPC: Impact on QSBC Status", 7(3) *Tax for the Owner-Manager* (ctf.ca) 2-3 (July 2007).

87(2)(a), 249(3.1) and 249(4) can trigger multiple year-ends from the same amalgamation; see 249(4) Notes (including using 89(11) to prevent 249(3.1) applying).

See also docs 2010-0377251E5 (interaction of 89(1)"public corporation"(c)(i) and 89(11)); 2010-0388101E5 (CCPC status); 2011-0424446E5 (change in control and CCPC status on same day [see Philip Friedlan, "Interaction of Subsections 249(3.1) and (4)", 12(2) *Tax for the Owner-Manager* (ctf.ca) 5-6 (April 2012)]); 2013-0504221E5 (new corp formed by amalgamation cannot elect under 249(3.1)); 2014-0523171E5 (249(3.1) does not apply when public corp becomes owner of corp that had elected under 89(11), since it was already not a CCPC); 2014-0524851E5 (249(3.1) does not apply where public corp has agreed to sell sub's shares to CCPC, until sale closes); 2014-0550191I7 (89(11) election and 89(12) revocation do not trigger 249(3.1) because they both apply from beginning of year).

249(3.1) added by 2006 budget bill #2 (Part 2 — eligible dividends), effective for 2006 and later taxation years.

(4) Loss restriction event [change in control] — year end — If at any time a taxpayer is subject to a loss restriction event (other than a foreign affiliate, of a taxpayer resident in Canada, that did not carry on a business in Canada at any time in its last taxation year that began before that time), then for the purposes of this Act,

(a) subject to paragraph (b), the taxpayer's taxation year that would, but for this paragraph, have included that time is deemed to end immediately before that time, a new taxation year of the taxpayer is deemed to begin at that time and, for the purpose of determining the taxpayer's fiscal period after that time, the taxpayer is deemed not to have established a fiscal period before that time; and

(b) subject to paragraph 128(1)(d), section 128.1 and paragraphs 142.6(1)(a) and 149(10)(a), and notwithstanding subsections (1) and (3), if the taxpayer is a corporation and the taxpayer's taxation year that would, but for this subsection, have been its last taxation year that ended before that time, would, but for this paragraph, have ended within the seven-day period that ended immediately before that time, that taxation year is, except if the taxpayer is subject to a loss restriction event within that period, deemed to end immediately before that time, provided that the taxpayer so elects in its return of income under Part I for that taxation year.

Related Provisions: 251.2(2) — Loss restriction event (LRE); 251.2(7) — Short year-end ignored for certain deadlines for trust subject to LRE.

Notes: The deemed year-end on change of control (of a corporation or trust: see 251.2(2)) has numerous effects (but for a trust, see filing- and payment-date exclusions in 251.2(7)). A return must be filed for the "short" year under 150(1)(a), and any elections required by X days after year-end must be filed. A loss carryforward or carryback year under 111(1)(a) can vanish due to the extra taxation year, as can other carryforward years such as for foreign tax credits (126(2)(a)), ITCs (127(9)"investment tax credit"(c)) and reserves (40(1)(a)(iii), 20(8)). A loan to a shareholder may have to be repaid sooner (15(2.6)). Amounts deducted but unpaid may have to be reincluded in income (78(1)). The due date for the current year's tax balance (157(1)(b)) is moved earlier. See also under "Short taxation year" in the Topical Index for prorating of various kinds. For a more detailed list see Ronit Florence, "Acquisition of Control of Canadian Resident Corporations: Checklist", V(4) *Business Vehicles* (Federated Press) 262-72 (1999); and Marc-André Bélanger, "Considerations Relating to a Short Taxation Year", 2327 *Tax Topics* (CCH) 1-4 (Oct. 13, 2016). See also Notes to 249(3.1).

Note that acquisition of control by a related person generally does not trigger these rules: 256(7)(a)(i)(B).

The last part of 249(4)(a) effectively overrides the rule in 249.1(7).

For examples of 249(4)(b) applying see VIEWS docs 2014-0528291R3, 2014-0539031R3.

For a corporation filing Quebec returns, an election under 249(4)(c) must be copied to Revenu Québec: *Taxation Act* ss. 6.2, 21.4.6.

It has been argued that "acquired" control under 249(4) is not the same as a "change" in control: Funt, "Acquisition or Change of Control: Is There a Difference?", V(2) *Business Vehicles* (Federated Press), 234-37 (1999); Notes to 111(5) and 256(7).

See also Notes to 256(9) re amalgamation on the same day as acquisition of control.

87(2)(a), 249(3.1) and 249(4) can trigger multiple year-ends from the same amalgamation: VIEWS docs 2004-0086741C6, 2007-0243341C6, 2014-0523251E5. Administratively, however, if an amalgamation takes place on the same day as an acquisition and no 256(9) election is filed, there is only 1 deemed year-end if the amalgamation certificate does not specify a time: Income Tax Folio S4-F7-C1 ¶1.19, 2002-0156725, 2004-0105481E5, 2010-0363081C6, 2010-0373201C6, 2010-0388081E5, 2014-0527231E5. See also Lindsey & Strawson, "Acquisition of Control and Amalgamation on the Same Day", 5(2) *Tax for the Owner-Manager* (ctf.ca) 4-5 (April 2005); Myroon, "Avoiding the Double Year-End", 11(1) *Canadian Tax Focus* (ctf.ca) 2-3 (Feb 2021) (using 89(11) to prevent 249(3.1) from applying).

See Notes to 249(3.1) re change in control and CCPC status on the same day.

An election under 249(4)(c) can result in a taxation year exceeding 53 weeks, despite 249.1(1)(a): VIEWS doc 2011-0416871E5.

If a corporation fails to recognize a change in control and files a return based on a non-existent taxation year, CRA's view is that an assessment of that period is invalid and thus the 152(4) reassessment clock never starts running: doc 2008-0285461C6.

249(4)(b) amended by 2016 budget bill #2, effective March 21, 2013, to add "the taxpayer is a corporation and". This amendment limiting 249(4)(b) to corporations was originally in the Jan. 15, 2016 draft legislation dealing with various trust matters.

249(4) amended by 2013 budget bill #2, effective March 21, 2013, to be based on "loss restriction event" instead of control of a corporation being acquired, so as to extend the rule to trusts (see Notes to 251.2(2)).

249(4) amended by 1994 technical bill (last change effective Feb. 23, 1994), 1993 and 1991 technical bills.

Remission Orders: *Blackberry Limited Remission Order*, P.C. 2013-1404 (Blackberry allowed to do a transaction that triggered an extra year-end without losing a carryback year).

Income Tax Folios: S4-F7-C1: Amalgamations of Canadian corporations [replaces IT-474R2]; S5-F2-C1: Foreign tax credit [replaces IT-270R3, IT-395R2, IT-520].

Interpretation Bulletins: IT-302R3: Losses of a corporation — the effect that acquisitions of control, amalgamations, and windings-up have on their deductibility.

I.T. Technical News: 7 (control by a group — 50/50 arrangement).

(4.1) Trust transition from graduated rate estate — For a particular trust that is a testamentary trust,

(a) its taxation year that otherwise includes a particular time is deemed to end immediately before the particular time if

(i) the particular trust is an estate and the particular time is the first time after 2015 at which the estate is not a graduated rate estate, or

(ii) the particular trust is not an estate and the particular time is immediately after 2015; and

(b) if the particular trust exists at the particular time,

(i) a new taxation year of the particular trust is deemed to begin at the particular time, and

(ii) for the purpose of determining the particular trust's fiscal period after the particular time, the particular trust is deemed not to have established a fiscal period before that time.

Notes: See VIEWS docs 2014-0556881E5 (no transitional rules where Dec. 31/15 year-end means more income is bunched into one year); 2015-0572131C6 [2015 STEP q.1] (graduated rate estate that chooses short first year will have 4 taxation years to use the low tax brackets until its 36 months run out).

249(4.1) added by 2014 budget bill #2, effective Dec. 31, 2015.

Proposed 249(4.1) in the June 29/06 draft legislation was enacted as 249(3.1).

(5) Graduated rate estate — The period for which the accounts of a graduated rate estate are made up for the purposes of an assessment under this Act may not exceed 12 months, and no change in the time when that period ends may be made for the purposes of this Act without the concurrence of the Minister.

Related Provisions: 249(4.1) — New calendar taxation year begins Jan. 1, 2016.

Notes: See VIEWS doc 2018-0744081C6 [2018 STEP q.3] (deadline for GRE's final T3 return is 90 days after windup).

249(5) amended by 2014 budget bill #2 for 2016 and later tax years, to change "testamentary trust" to "graduated rate estate". Added by 2002-2013 technical bill; this rule was previously in 104(23)(a).

(6) [Repealed]

Related Provisions: 249(4.1) — New calendar taxation year begins Jan. 1, 2016.

Notes: 249(6), "Loss of testamentary trust status", repealed by 2014 budget bill #2, for transactions and events that occur after 2015.

See Finance Technical Notes for a detailed explanation of this rule and examples. For CRA interpretation see VIEWS doc 2012-0456221R3.

249(6) added by 2002-2013 technical bill, effective July 19, 2005, or earlier by election.

Definitions [s. 249]: "acquired" — 256(7)–(9); "assessment" — 248(1); "business" — 248(1); "calendar year" — *Interpretation Act* 37(1)(a); "Canada" — 255; "Canadian resident partnership" — 248(1); "carry on a business in Canada", "carry on business in Canada" — 253; "consequence" — 248(8); "control" — 256(6)–(9), 256.1(3); "corporation" — 248(1), *Interpretation Act* 35(1); "estate" — 104(1), 248(1); "fiscal period" — 248(1), 249(2)(b), 249.1; "foreign affiliate" — 95(1), 248(1); "graduated rate estate", "individual" — 248(1); "loss restriction event" — 251.2; "Minister", "person" — 248(1); "month" — *Interpretation Act* 35(1); "property" — 248(1); "taxa-

tion year" — 249; "testamentary trust" — 108(1), 248(1); "trust" — 104(1), 248(1), (3).

249.1 (1) Definition of "fiscal period" — For the purposes of this Act, a "fiscal period" of a business or a property of a person or partnership means the period for which the person's or partnership's accounts in respect of the business or property are made up for purposes of assessment under this Act, but no fiscal period may end

(a) in the case of a corporation, more than 53 weeks after the period began,

(b) in the case of

(i) an individual (other than an individual to whom section 149 or 149.1 applies or a trust),

(i.1) a trust (other than a mutual fund trust if the fiscal period is one to which paragraph 132.11(1)(c) applies or a graduated rate estate),

(ii) a partnership of which

(A) an individual (other than an individual to whom section 149 or 149.1 applies or a graduated rate estate),

(B) a professional corporation, or

(C) a partnership to which this subparagraph applies,

would, if the fiscal period ended at the end of the calendar year in which the period began, be a member of the partnership in the period, or

(iii) a professional corporation that would, if the fiscal period ended at the end of the calendar year in which the period began, be in the period a member of a partnership to which subparagraph (ii) applies,

after the end of the calendar year in which the period began unless, in the case of a business, the business is not carried on in Canada,

(c) in the case of a partnership (other than a partnership to which subparagraph (b)(ii) or subsection (9) applies) that is a member of a partnership or has a member that is a partnership, after the end of the calendar year in which it began, if at the end of the calendar year

(i) a corporation has a significant interest, as defined in section 34.2, in the partnership,

(ii) the partnership is a member of another partnership in which a corporation has a significant interest as defined in section 34.2,

(iii) a membership interest in the partnership is held directly, or indirectly through one or more partnerships, by a partnership described in subparagraph (i) or (ii), or

(iv) the partnership holds directly, or indirectly through one or more partnerships, a membership interest in a partnership described in any of subparagraphs (i) to (iii), or

(d) in any other case, more than 12 months after the period began,

and, for the purpose of this subsection, the activities of a person to whom section 149 or 149.1 applies are deemed to be a business.

Related Provisions: 25(1) — Optional continuation of year-end after disposing of business; 34.1–34.3 — Partnership stub period income inclusion where partnership and partner year-ends do not match; 96(1.01) — Income allocation to former partner; 96(1.1) — Allocation of share of income to retiring partner; 99(2) — Optional continuation of original year-end of partnership that ceases to exist; 128.1(4)(a.1) — Deemed end of fiscal period (FP) on emigration; 249(2)(b) — Reference to FP ending in a taxation year; 249(3)(b) — Deemed end of FP where FP exceeds 365 days; 249.1(2), (3) — Interpretation; 249.1(4), (5) — Election for non-calendar year-end; 249.1(8)–(11) — Partnership — election to align fiscal period with corporate partner.

Notes: Subject to the 53-week limit, a corporation can choose any fiscal period it wishes for its first period: VIEWS doc 2006-0173701E5. Once selected, it cannot be changed without CRA's permission: 249.1(7). A non-resident corp can select a Canadian fiscal period that differs from what it uses to file in its home country.

An authorized foreign bank's first fiscal period begins no later than the date the Superintendent of Financial Institutions issues an order authorizing it to carry on business in Canada: VIEWS doc 2001-0086027.

Where a partnership has a different year-end than its partners, there may be an income inclusion for the "stub period" under 34.1 (individuals) or 34.2 (corporations). An election under 249.1(8)-(11) can be used to align a partnership's year-end with that of its corporate partners.

Joint venture (JV): CRA policy 1989-2011 allowed a JV to have a fiscal period, with income included in the venturer's taxation year in which the period ended. This allowed the same deferral as partnerships. This policy was "not in accordance with the Act": *Noran West*, 2012 TCC 434, para. 41 (settlement reached and FCA appeal discontinued A-552-12). With the 2011 introduction of 34.2 preventing partnership deferral, CRA's position is that for tax years ending after March 22, 2011, JVs can no longer select a fiscal period different from the participants' tax years. As with 34.2, "stub period" income that was deferred could be included in income over 5 years, if an election was made by the filing-due date for the first taxation year ending after Sept. 12, 2012; 2011 Cdn Tax Foundation conference report, p. 4:5-7; VIEWS docs 2011-0403081C6, 2011-0429581E5, 2011-0431141E5, 2011-0431271E5, 2011-0431461E5, 2012-0448091E5, 2012-0454811E5. See also CRA news release, "Joint Ventures — Elimination of Fiscal Period" (Dec. 22, 2011), reproduced here up to the 52nd ed. Doc 2012-0432111E5 provided further relief: CCA can be prorated over the entire period of incremental income inclusion, and estimated amounts (adjusted once actual amounts are known) are accepted for stub-period reporting.

See also doc 2014-0528001E5 (249.1(1)(c) does not apply to partnership whose wholly-owned corp becomes member of another partnership).

See also Form RC354; Hickey, "Joint Venture Deferral Deadline Extended", 20(3) *Canadian Tax Highlights* (ctf.ca) 3-4 (March 2012); and Notes to 34.2.

249.1(1)(b) through (b)(ii)(A) amended by 2014 budget bill #2, for 2016 and later tax years. (See Notes to 248(1)"graduated rate estate".)

249.1(1)(b) closing words amended by 2002-2013 technical bill (Part 5 — technical), for fiscal periods that begin after June 26, 2013.

249.1(1)(c) added (and former (c) renumbered (d)) by 2011 budget bill #2, for 2011 and later fiscal periods (see Notes to 249.1(8) re what this means).

249.1(1)(b) earlier amended by 2001 technical bill, 1998 Budget.

See also Notes at end of 249.1.

Income Tax Folios: S3-F4-C1: General discussion of CCA.

I.T. Technical News: 8 (bankrupt corporation — change of fiscal period).

CRA Audit Manual: 27.25.2: Individuals — business fiscal periods.

Forms: RC354: Election for transitional relief by a participant taxpayer of a joint venture.

(2) Not a member of a partnership

(2) Not a member of a partnership — For the purpose of subparagraph (1)(b)(ii) and subsection (4), a person or partnership that would not have a share of any income or loss of a partnership for a fiscal period of the partnership, if the period ended at the end of the calendar year in which the period began, is deemed not to be a member of the partnership in that fiscal period.

Related Provisions: 96(1.01) — Income allocation to former partner.

Notes: See Notes at end of 249.1. For interpretation of "share of any income ... of a partnership", see VIEWS doc 2011-0424191E5.

(3) Subsequent fiscal periods

(3) Subsequent fiscal periods — Where a fiscal period of a business or a property of a person or partnership ends at any time, the subsequent fiscal period, if any, of the business or property of the person or partnership is deemed to begin immediately after that time.

Notes: For a corporation filing Quebec returns, an election under 249.1(3)(c)(iii) must be copied to Revenu Québec: *Taxation Act* ss. 6.1.1, 21.4.6.

(4) Alternative method

(4) Alternative method — Paragraph (1)(b) does not apply to a fiscal period of a business carried on, throughout the period of time that began at the beginning of the fiscal period and ended at the end of the calendar year in which the fiscal period began,

(a) by an individual (otherwise than as a member of a partnership), or

(b) by an individual as a member of a partnership, where throughout that period

(i) each member of the partnership is an individual, and

(ii) the partnership is not a member of another partnership,

where

(c) in the case of an individual

(i) who is referred to in paragraph (a), or

(ii) who is a member of a partnership no member of which is a graduated rate estate,

an election in prescribed form to have paragraph (1)(b) not apply is filed with the Minister by the individual on or before the individual's filing-due date, and with the individual's return of income under Part I, for the taxation year that includes the first day of the first fiscal period of the business that begins after 1994, and

(d) in the case of an individual who is a member of a partnership a member of which is a graduated rate estate, an election in prescribed form to have paragraph (1)(b) not apply is filed with the Minister by the individual on or before the earliest of the filing-due dates of the members of the partnership for a taxation year that includes the first day of the first fiscal period of the business that begins after 1994.

Related Provisions: 34.1(1) — Additional income adjustment where election made; 96(1.01) — Income allocation to former partner; 96(1.1) — Allocation of share of income to retiring partner; 96(3) — Election by members of partnership; 249.1(5) — Alternative method not applicable to tax shelter; 249.1(6) — Revocation of election; Reg. 600(b.1) — Late filing of election by January 31, 1998.

Notes: See VIEWS doc 2014-0534341E5 re a partnership changing the fiscal period after making this election. See also Notes at end of 249.1 and to 249.1(1).

For a taxpayer filing Quebec returns, an election under 249.1(4) must be copied to Revenu Québec: *Taxation Act* ss. 7.0.3, 217.2, 21.4.6.

249.1(4)(c)(ii) and (d) amended by 2014 budget bill #2, for 2016 and later taxation years, to change "testamentary trust" to "graduated rate estate".

Income Tax Folios: S3-F4-C1: General discussion of CCA.

Forms: RC354: Election for transitional relief by a participant taxpayer of a joint venture.

(5) Alternative method not applicable to tax shelter investments

(5) Alternative method not applicable to tax shelter investments — Subsection (4) does not apply to a particular fiscal period of a business where, in a preceding fiscal period or throughout the period of time that began at the beginning of the particular period and ended at the end of the calendar year in which the particular period began, the expenditures made in the course of carrying on the business were primarily the cost or capital cost of tax shelter investments (as defined in subsection 143.2(1)).

Notes: 249.1(5) prevents tax shelters from electing a non-calendar year-end under 249.1(4). Of course, a tax shelter may have a non-calendar year-end if it is not otherwise subject to 249.1(1).

This rule covers tax shelters as defined in 237.1(1) as well as those under the broader definition in 143.2(1)"tax shelter investment"(b).

249.1(5) amended by 1995-97 technical bill, retroactive to its introduction (see Notes at end of 249.1).

(6) Revocation of election

(6) Revocation of election — Subsection (4) does not apply to fiscal periods of a business carried on by an individual that begin after the beginning of a particular taxation year of the individual where

(a) an election in prescribed form to revoke an election filed under subsection (4) in respect of the business is filed with the Minister; and

(b) the election to revoke is filed

(i) in the case of an individual

(A) who is not a member of a partnership, or

(B) who is a member of a partnership no member of which is a graduated rate estate,

by the individual on or before the individual's filing-due date, and with the individual's return of income under Part I, for the particular taxation year, and

(ii) in the case of an individual who is a member of a partnership a member of which is a graduated rate estate, by the individual on or before the earliest of the filing-due dates of the members of the partnership for a taxation year that includes the first day of the first fiscal period of the business that begins after the beginning of the particular year.

Related Provisions: 96(3) — Election by members of partnership.

Notes: See Notes at end of 249.1.

For a taxpayer filing Quebec returns, a 249.1(6) election must be copied to Revenu Québec: *Taxation Act* ss. 7.0.5, 21.4.6.

249.1(6)(b)(i)(B) and (b)(ii) amended by 2014 budget bill #2, for 2016 and later taxation years, to change "testamentary trust" to "graduated rate estate".

(7) Change of fiscal period

(7) Change of fiscal period — No change in the time when a fiscal period ends may be made for the purposes of this Act without the concurrence of the Minister.

Related Provisions: 87(2)(j.91), (qq) — Change in fiscal period after amalgamation; 149(10)(a) — Change in fiscal period on becoming or ceasing to be exempt; 249(4)(d) — Change in fiscal period allowed after change in control of corporation; 249.1(8)–(11) — Partnership can change fiscal period to align with corporate partner.

Notes: Once a fiscal period has been determined, it cannot be changed without CRA permission: *Bishay*, [1996] 1 C.T.C. 2286 (FCTD). However, after change in control of a corp, a new fiscal period may be chosen under 249(4)(d), and there is no time limit for choosing: *Sybron Canada*, [1999] 3 C.T.C. 2695 (TCC). The same applies after an amalgamation (87(2)(j.91)) and on becoming or ceasing to be exempt (149(10)(a)).

For CRA policy see IT-179R ("sound business reasons" required) [IT-179R was "cancelled": VIEWS doc 2019-0816111C6 [2019 CPTS], q.3, but the policy still seems to apply]. CRA will likely consent to a change in fiscal period to allow an incorporated proprietorship to match the individual's previous year-end (2002-0178485), or for ease of financial reporting (2009-0311061I7); but not to prevent a late-filing penalty: 2009-0334931I7; or where a partnership that includes an individual seeks an off-calendar year: 2010-0383261I7; or where a partner leaving a multi-tier partnership seeks to use a loss based on short fiscal period: 2014-0529311E5; or to change a past period already assessed: 2014-053940117. A change is no longer needed where partnership interests are disposed of in mid-fiscal period, due to 96(1.01): 2012-0433281E5. A corp with a Feb. 28 (as opposed to "last day of Feb.") year-end needs CRA consent to change it to Feb. 29 in a leap year: 2012-0438481E5. A partnership should write to its tax services office to request a change: Guide T4068.

Before 1995, the requirement for the Minister's consent to a year-end change was in 248(1)"fiscal period" closing words.

Income Tax Folios: S3-F4-C1: General discussion of CCA.

Interpretation Bulletins: IT-179R: Change of fiscal period.

Registered Charities Newsletters: 5 (how can you get the Department's permission to change your charity's fiscal period?).

(8) Single-tier fiscal period alignment

(8) Single-tier fiscal period alignment — The members of a partnership that has a fiscal period that begins before March 22, 2011 and that would, if this Act were read without reference to this subsection and subsection (10), end on a day after March 22, 2011, may elect to end that fiscal period on a particular day that is before the day on which the fiscal period would otherwise end (in this subsection and subsection (10) referred to as a **"single-tier alignment election"**) if

> (a) each member of the partnership is, on the particular day, a corporation that is not a professional corporation;

> (b) the partnership is not, on the particular day, a member of another partnership;

> (c) at least one member of the partnership is, on the particular day, a corporation that has a significant interest, as defined in section 34.2, in the partnership;

> (d) at least one member of the partnership referred to in paragraph (c) has a taxation year that ends on a day that differs from the day on which the fiscal period of the partnership would end if this Act were read without reference to this subsection and subsection (10);

> (e) the particular day is after March 22, 2011 and no later than the latest day that is the last day of the first taxation year that ends after March 22, 2011 of any corporation that has been a member of the partnership continuously since March 21, 2011; and

> (f) subsection (10) applies to the single-tier alignment election.

Related Provisions: 34.2(1)"single-tier alignment" — Alignment under 249.1(8); 249.1(10) — Conditions requirement for alignment.

Notes: See Notes to 34.2. 249.1(8)–(11) provide an election for a partnership to align its fiscal period with that of (one of) its corporate partners. 249.1(8) applies to a single-tier partnership. 249.1(9) applies to a multi-tier partnership (where at least one partner is itself a partnership).

For a partner filing a Quebec return, a 249.1(8) election must be copied to Revenu Québec: *Taxation Act* ss. 217.18, 21.4.6.

For CRA interpretation see VIEWS docs 2011-0421981E5 and 2011-0429481E5 (election cannot be made to end on a day later than when the fiscal period would otherwise have ended).

249.1(8) added by 2011 budget bill #2, for 2011 and later fiscal periods.

Income Tax Folios: S3-F4-C1: General discussion of CCA.

Forms: T2 Sched. 71: Income inclusion for corporations that are members of single-tier partnerships.

(9) Multi-tier fiscal period alignment — one-time election

(9) Multi-tier fiscal period alignment — one-time election — The members of a partnership to which paragraph (1)(c) would apply if it were read without reference to this subsection may elect (in this subsection and subsections (10) and (11) referred to as a **"multi-tier alignment election"**) to end a fiscal period of the partnership on a particular day if

> (a) as a consequence of the multi-tier alignment election, the fiscal period of the partnership, and of each other partnership described in relation to the partnership by any of subparagraphs (1)(c)(ii) to (iv), ends on the particular day;

> (b) the particular day is before March 22, 2012; and

> (c) subsection (10) applies to the multi-tier alignment election.

Related Provisions: 34.2(1)"multi-tier alignment" — Alignment under 249.1(9); 249.1(9.1) — When 249.1(9) ceases to apply; 249.1(10) — Conditions requirement for alignment; 249.1(11) — Deemed multi-tier alignment election for 2011.

Notes: See Notes to 249.1(8) and VIEWS docs 2012-0444451E5 (election allowed); 2012-0470921E5 (new partnership cannot be added: see Mitchell Sherman, "All Tiered Up", XIX(1) *Corporate Finance* (Federated Press) 2196-97 (2013)).

For a partner filing a Quebec return, a 249.1(9) election must be copied to Revenu Québec: *Taxation Act* ss. 217.18, 21.4.6.

In *Telus Communications*, 2015 ONSC 6245, a group's organizational structure was rectified to remove an overlooked partnership interest that should have been transferred out, to make the election valid. (See 169(1) Notes re rectification; due to *Fairmont Hotels* this would no longer be granted.)

249.1(9) added by 2011 budget bill #2, effective for 2011 and later fiscal periods.

(9.1) When subsec. (9) ceases to apply

(9.1) When subsec. (9) ceases to apply — If paragraph (1)(c) did not apply to end the fiscal period of a partnership on December 31 of a calendar year (in this subsection referred to as the "preceding year") because subsection (9) applies to the partnership, and to each other partnership described in relation to the partnership by any of subparagraphs (1)(c)(ii) to (iv), (in this subsection referred to collectively as the "aligned multi-tier partnerships" and each individually as an "aligned multi-tier partnership"),

> (a) subsection (9) ceases to apply — for the purpose of applying paragraph (1)(c) to each of the aligned multi-tier partnerships — in the calendar year following the preceding year (in this subsection referred to as the "current year") if another partnership (in this subsection referred to as the "new partnership") becomes in the current year a member of any of the aligned multi-tier partnerships, or any of the aligned multi-tier partnerships becomes in the current year a member of the new partnership, unless

>> (i) the fiscal period of the new partnership, and each other partnership described in relation to the new partnership by any of subparagraphs (1)(c)(ii) to (iv), ends in the current year on the same day as the fiscal period of each of the aligned multi-tier partnerships, and

>> (ii) each member (other than a partnership) of each aligned multi-tier partnership — or a subsidiary wholly-owned corporation of such a member — has been a member of the aligned multi-tier partnership from the end of the last fiscal period ending in the preceding year until the time at which the new partnership becomes a member of an aligned multi-tier partnership, or any of the aligned multi-tier partnerships becomes a member of the new partnership, as the case may be; and

> (b) if paragraph (a) does not apply because the conditions in subparagraphs (a)(i) and (ii) are met, the new partnership is deemed — for the purpose of applying paragraph (1)(c) to each of the aligned multi-tier partnerships and the new partnership in the current year and subsequent years — to have made the multi-tier alignment election referred to in subsection (9).

Notes: 249.1(1)(c) implements a June 10, 2014 Finance comfort letter. It generally provides that partnerships in a tiered-partnership structure must have a common fiscal period ending Dec. 31. However, this does not apply to a partnership for which a multi-tiered alignment election was made under 249.1(9) in 2011-2012.

249.1(9.1) allows partnerships in a tiered-partnership structure to which a 249.1(9) election applies to retain their common non-calendar fiscal period if certain conditions are met. Para. (a) provides that 249.1(9) ceases to apply for the purpose of 249(1)(c) if a new partnership joins the structure, or any of the aligned multi-tier partnerships becomes a member of a new partnership, unless conditions in (a)(i) and (ii) apply. These conditions generally require that the fiscal period of a new partnership to the structure end on the same day as the aligned multi-tiered partnerships and each partner of the structure that is not a partnership be a member of the aligned structure at the end of the preceding calendar year and immediately before the new partnership becomes part of the structure.

Para. (b) provides a continuity rule to ensure the original election remains operative despite the structure having a new partnership to which the exception in (a)(i) and (ii) applies. (Finance Technical Notes)

249.1(9.1) added by 2017 budget bill #2, for partnership fiscal periods that end after March 2014.

(10) Conditions to align a partnership fiscal period — This subsection applies to a single-tier alignment election or a multi-tier alignment election, as the case may be, for a partnership if

(a) the election is filed in writing and in prescribed form with the Minister

(i) in the case of a single-tier alignment election, by a corporation that is a member of the partnership on or before the day that is the earliest filing-due date of any corporation that is a member of the partnership for its first taxation year ending after March 22, 2011, and

(ii) in the case of a multi-tier alignment election,

(A) by a corporation that is a member of the partnership, or of a partnership described in relation to the partnership by any of subparagraphs (1)(c)(ii) to (iv), and

(B) on or before the day that is the earliest filing-due date of any corporation that is a member of a partnership referred to in clause (A) for the first taxation year of the corporation ending after March 22, 2011;

(b) as a consequence of the election, the fiscal period of each partnership to which the election applies is 12 months or less;

(c) the election was made by a corporation that has the authority to act for the members of the partnership and each member of any other partnership described in relation to the partnership in subparagraph (1)(c)(ii) to (iv); and

(d) no other election is filed with the Minister to end the fiscal period of the partnership, or of any other partnership described in relation to the partnership in subparagraph (1)(c)(ii) to (iv), on a day other than the particular day referred to in subsection (8) or (9), as the case may be.

Related Provisions: 249.1(8) — Single-tier fiscal period alignment; 249.1(9) — Multi-tier fiscal period alignment.

Notes: 249.1(10) added by 2011 budget bill #2, for 2011 and later fiscal periods. See Notes to 249.1(8). Per 2002-2013 technical bill s. 375, a 249.1(10) election is deemed filed on time if it is filed in writing with the Minister by Jan. 31, 2012.

(11) Deemed multi-tier alignment election — For the purposes of this Act, if paragraph (1)(c) applies to end the fiscal period of a partnership on December 31, 2011, a multi-tier alignment election under subsection (9) is deemed to have been made to end the fiscal period of the partnership on December 31, 2011.

Related Provisions: 34.2(1)"multi-tier alignment" — Alignment under 249.1(11).

Notes: 249.1(11) added by 2011 budget bill #2, effective for 2011 and later fiscal periods. See Notes to 249.1(8).

Definitions [s. 249.1]: "business" — 248(1); "calendar year" — *Interpretation Act* 37(1)(a); "Canada" — 255; "carried on in Canada" — 253; "corporation" — 248(1), *Interpretation Act* 35(1); "filing-due date" — 150(1), 248(1); "fiscal period" — 249.1; "graduated rate estate", "individual" — 248(1); "member" — of partnership — 249.1(2); "Minister" — 248(1); "month" — *Interpretation Act* 35(1); "multi-tier alignment election" — 249.1(9); "partnership" — see 96(1) Notes; "person", "prescribed", "professional corporation", "property" — 248(1); "single-tier alignment election" — 249.1(8); "subsidiary wholly-owned corporation" — 248(1); "taxation year" — 249; "writing" — *Interpretation Act* 35(1).

Income Tax Folios: S3-F4-C1: General discussion of CCA.

250. (1) Person deemed resident — For the purposes of this Act, a person shall, subject to subsection (2), be deemed to have been resident in Canada throughout a taxation year if the person

(a) sojourned in Canada in the year for a period of, or periods the total of which is, 183 days or more;

Announced Administrative Changes — 250(1)(a) — COVID-19

CRA notice (tinyurl.com/cra-internat, April 27, 2021): *International income tax issues*

This page has been updated with a new section VII. New section VII provides further guidance and administrative relief for Canadian-resident cross-border workers in respect of their 2020 income tax obligations. It also clarifies the CRA's views regarding the effect of the travel restrictions on the determination of a permanent establishment in Canada, and provides for an extension of the initial administrative relief in respect of individual Canadian income tax residence and employment income earned in Canada.

Examples and answers to frequently asked questions will be posted shortly. In the meantime, if you have questions about how this guidance will apply, or if you have a situation that is not addressed in the guidance, please contact PERESCOVIDG@cra-arc.gc.ca.

Guidance on international income tax issues raised by the COVID-19 crisis

The COVID-19 crisis has resulted in the imposition of safety measures by governments around the world, including the Canadian government, to protect the health of their citizens. Similarly, businesses have imposed safety measures to protect their employees. These measures include travel restrictions. The travel restrictions have resulted in certain taxpayers and their representatives expressing concerns about a number of potential Canadian income tax issues. This document describes each potential issue considered by the Canada Revenue Agency (the CRA) thus far, and outlines the agency's approach to address the issue.

[A non-mandatory government recommendation to return to Canada, and a mandatory quarantine period, may qualify as travel restrictions: International Fiscal Assn CRA Q&A (Aug. 6, 2020), tinyurl.com/ifa-covid-qa, qq. 1-2. Questions to CRA on "travel restrictions" can be sent to perescovidg@cra.gc.ca — ed.]

Some of these income tax issues will arise from the travel restrictions instituted by another country and not those of Canada. As well, in some situations, particular travel restrictions could have effect past the date on which the restrictions are officially lifted. Therefore, the CRA will consider whether a particular tax issue has arisen as the result of the travel restrictions, on a case by case basis. Except for subsection III. D. (sending international waivers, and notifications for certificates of compliance), the relief measures described in sections I-VI of this guidance are applicable from March 16 until September 30, 2020 (the initial relief period). The additional relief measures contained in the supplemental guidance in section VII apply for the periods described in that section.

The administrative approach taken by the CRA in addressing these issues is intended to help taxpayers during this time of crisis. The approach does not represent any interpretive position or intention to establish any broader policy by the CRA. Nor does it represent any change in Canada's ongoing commitment to fight international tax evasion and avoidance. Any taxpayer that engages in tax evasion or avoidance schemes that try to exploit the crisis or the temporary measures discussed below can expect the CRA to use all its compliance tools to protect the integrity of Canada's tax system.

I. Income tax residency

A. Individuals

In general, an individual's residence for Canadian tax purposes is a common-law factual determination based on the individual's residential ties to Canada [see Notes to 50(1) — ed.]. In addition, an individual who temporarily stays (is physically present) in Canada for a period of, or periods that total 183 days or more in a tax year will be deemed to be resident in Canada throughout the year [250(1)(a) — ed.].

Potential Issue

Individuals visiting Canada when the travel restrictions were imposed may not have been able to return to their country of tax residence as they intended and instead had to stay in Canada. Could this extended stay in Canada result in the individual being resident in Canada for Canadian tax purposes?

Agency position

If an individual stayed in Canada only because of the travel restrictions, that factor alone will not cause the CRA to consider the common-law factual test of residency to be met. Also, as an administrative matter and in light of the extraordinary circumstances, the CRA will not consider the days during which an individual is present in Canada and is unable to return to their country of residence solely as a result of the travel restrictions to count towards the 183-day limit for deemed residency. [The CRA's legal justification for this position might be that the person, though present in Canada, is not "sojourning" in Canada — ed.] This will be the CRA position where, among other things, the individual is usually a resident of another country and intends to return, and does in fact return, to their country of residence as soon as they are able to.

In this regard, in determining a taxpayer's eligibility for relief under this (or another) section of this guidance, we will generally view the Canadian government's recommendation to Canadians to return to Canada as a travel restriction. This would include a scenario where an individual would have been permitted under the laws of their country of residence to remain in (or return to) that country.

B. Corporations

Under the Canadian income tax system, corporations that have been established under foreign law are nevertheless considered resident in Canada if their central management and control is located in Canada [see Notes to 250(4) — ed.]. One of the key factors typically considered in applying this common-law concept is the jurisdiction in which the meetings of the board of directors take place.

Potential Issue

A corporation that, before the implementation of the travel restrictions, was tax resident in a foreign jurisdiction may have one or more directors present in Canada. The travel restrictions might have resulted in these directors being unable to travel to the foreign jurisdiction to attend board meetings. If directors of such a corporation participate in board meetings while physically present in Canada, will the CRA consider the corporation's central management and control to be in Canada, such that it is resident in Canada for Canadian tax purposes and therefore a dual resident (that is, a resident of Canada and a resident of the foreign jurisdiction)?

Agency Position

Some of Canada's income tax treaties will address the situation of the dual residency of a corporation by determining the corporation to be resident in the country under whose laws it was created. For example, if the corporation is an entity created under the laws of the United States as a C-corporation or S-corporation, the CRA expects that the corporate residency tiebreaker rule contained in Article IV of the Canada-United States income tax treaty [Art. IV:3 — ed.] will address this issue.

Other tax treaties contain a residency tiebreaker rule that looks to the corporation's place of effective management, among other factors [see Canada-UK treaty Art. 4:3 — ed.]. For corporations covered by such income tax treaties, in light of the extraordinary circumstances resulting from the travel restrictions, as an administrative matter, where a director of a corporation must participate in a board meeting from Canada because of the travel restrictions, the CRA will not consider the corporation to become resident in Canada solely for that reason.

Determinations of corporate residency involving potential dual residency with non-treaty countries will be determined on a case by case basis.

This administrative approach will also be followed in respect of other entities established in foreign jurisdictions that are considered corporations under Canadian income tax law, such as limited liability companies. In addition, where appropriate, the CRA will consider adopting a similar approach in determining the residency of a commercial trust. Finally, the CRA will also adopt a similar approach in determining the residence of a foreign affiliate of a Canadian corporation for surplus calculation purposes [113(1)(a) — ed.]. In other words, where a director of a foreign affiliate that, before the travel restrictions, was resident in a country with which Canada has an income tax treaty, is unable to participate in board meetings because of the travel restrictions, the CRA will not consider the corporation to cease being resident in that country for surplus calculation purposes [Reg. 5907(1)"exempt earnings"(d) opening words, for Reg. 5907(1)"exempt surplus"A(ii) — ed.] solely for that reason. Determinations of corporate residency involving foreign affiliates resident before the travel restrictions in non-treaty countries will be determined on a case by case basis.

It is important to note that, notwithstanding that our comments above concentrate on the location of board meetings, there is more to where central management and control of a corporation, or where place of effective management (for income tax treaty purposes) is located than the location of board meetings. The determination of the central management and control of a corporation is based on a number of factors, of which the location of board meetings is only one element. Similarly, the location of board meetings is also only one element in determining the location of a corporation's place of effective management. The CRA may still conclude that a corporation is resident in Canada where the actual management and control of the corporation takes place in Canada, even though the board meetings have taken place elsewhere.

II. Carrying on business in Canada/Permanent establishment

Under the Canadian income tax system, non-residents of Canada are liable to pay tax on their income from "carrying on business in Canada" [2(3)(b) and 115(1)(a)(ii) — ed.]. In general, where Canada has entered into an income tax treaty with another country, a resident of that country will only have to pay tax in Canada on that income if their activities in Canada meet the threshold of a "permanent establishment" under the relevant income tax treaty [normally Art. 7 — ed.].

Potential Issue

A non-resident entity may employ individuals to work outside of Canada. Due to the travel restrictions, the only way for some of these individuals to fulfil their employment duties might be by performing them in Canada. Will employees who regularly work outside of Canada but, due to the travel restrictions, exercise their employment duties in Canada result in the non-resident entity carrying on business in Canada or create a permanent establishment in Canada for the non-resident entity?

Agency Position

Non-resident entities that are resident in a jurisdiction with which Canada has an income tax treaty and that are carrying on business in Canada, but whose activities in Canada do not meet the threshold of permanent establishment, have to file a return for that year in order to claim an exemption from Canadian income tax. This filing obligation continues to apply for the tax years of non-resident entities that overlap with the period while the travel restrictions are in place. However, as an administrative matter and in light of the extraordinary circumstances resulting from the travel restrictions, the CRA **will not consider a non-resident entity to have a permanent establishment in Canada solely because its employees perform their employment duties in Canada solely as a result of the travel restrictions** being in force. Similarly, the CRA will not consider an "agency" permanent establishment to have been created for the non-resident entity solely due to a dependent agent concluding contracts in Canada on behalf of the non-resident entity, while the travel restrictions are in force, provided that such activities are limited to that period and would not have been performed in Canada but for the travel restrictions.

If Canada has not entered into an income tax treaty with the country in which the non-resident entity is resident, and if the non-resident entity carries on business in Canada, it is required to file a return for that year. If it can be demonstrated to the CRA that the non-resident entity has satisfied the Canadian income tax threshold of carrying on business in Canada only because of the travel restrictions, the CRA will consider whether administrative relief is appropriate on a case by case basis.

Finally, the CRA will exclude, in determining whether an individual meets the 183-day presence test in a "services-permanent-establishment" provision of Canada's tax treaties [such as article V(9)(a) of the Canada-United States income tax treaty], any days of physical presence in Canada due solely to the travel restrictions.

[These rules apply only to federal tax. See Kohli & Reid, "Travel Restrictions May Create Provincial PEs", 11(2) *Canadian Tax Focus* (ctf.ca) 3 (May 2021) — ed.]

III. Cross-border employment income

Many individuals residing on either side of the Canada-U.S. border may be employed and perform their employment duties in the other country.

A. US Resident Employees

Under the Canada-United States income tax treaty, Canada can tax salary, wages and other similar remuneration derived by a resident of the United States for employment services provided in Canada, if the employment is exercised in Canada. Notwithstanding the above rule, such remuneration is not taxable in Canada if either of the following apply [Art. XV:2 — ed.]:

- The remuneration is not greater than CAN$10,000
- The person is present in Canada for no more than 183 days in any 12-month period, starting or ending in the fiscal year concerned and the remuneration is not borne by either:
  - an employer who is a resident of Canada
  - a permanent establishment which the employer has in Canada

A reciprocal rule applies for residents of Canada working in the United States.

Potential Issue

Some U.S. residents who regularly exercise their employment in Canada and who are normally not present in Canada in excess of 183 days (and, for that reason alone, are not taxable in Canada on their employment income) may now be exercising their duties in Canada for an extended period of time, as a result of the travel restrictions. In these situations, will the employees' taxation in Canada be changed?

Agency Position

If such individuals are present in Canada, and are exercising their employment duties in Canada solely as a result of the travel restrictions, those days will not be counted toward the 183-day test in the Canada-United States income tax treaty. As such, these individuals will continue to benefit from the treaty relief provided under the Canada-United States income tax treaty.

B. Other resident employees

The CRA will also take this approach in applying the days-of-presence test in Canada's other tax treaties.

C. Canadian Resident Employees

Under Canadian rules [153(1) and Reg. 102(1) — ed.], a non-resident employer is required to deduct withholdings at source from the salary that it pays to an employee who is a resident of Canada, regardless where the services are rendered. Where appropriate, the Agency will issue a "letter of authority" to the employee authorizing the non-resident employer to reduce the Canadian deductions at source to take into account the foreign tax credit available to the employee in respect of their foreign tax liability.

Potential Issue

A non-resident entity may employ Canadian residents to work outside of Canada. As a result of the travel restrictions, the only way for some of these Canadian resident employees to fulfil their duties might be by performing them in Canada on an exceptional and temporary basis. Will the performance of employment duties from Canada affect the withholding obligations of the non-resident entity?

Agency Position

If a Canadian resident employee of a non-resident entity is forced to perform their employment duties in Canada on an exceptional and temporary basis as a result of the travel restrictions, and that employee has been issued a letter of authority applicable to the tax year including that period, the letter of authority will continue to apply and the withholding obligations of the non-resident entity will not change in Canada, as long as there are no changes to the withholding obligations of the non-resident entity in the other jurisdiction.

D. Non-resident employer withholdings with non-resident employee in Canada

The situation may arise where, due to the COVID-19 crisis, a non-resident employee of a non-resident employer travelled to Canada for personal reasons and, as a result of the travel restrictions, was unable to return to their country of residence when intended. Although it may not have been their intention, if the non-resident employee performs their duties of employment remotely while in Canada, and continues to receive remuneration for those duties, the non-resident employer would be subject to Canadian withholding, remitting, and reporting obligations, notwithstanding that the non-resident employee may ultimately be exempt from tax in Canada due to a tax treaty.

For the non-resident employer to be relieved of their obligation to withhold and remit the applicable taxes, the non-resident employee would have to apply for and receive a waiver of the tax required to be deducted [Reg. 102(1) — ed.]. Alternatively, the non-resident employer could apply for certification as a qualifying non-resident employer [153(6), (7) — ed.], and if the non-resident employee also qualifies, the non-resident employer would not have to withhold and remit tax on the payments they make to the non-resident employee. Both these remedies apply only where the non-resident employee is working in Canada for a limited time and is exempt from tax in Canada under a tax treaty. However, these remedies are only available in respect of a payment if granted prior to the date that the payment was made.

In light of the extraordinary circumstances caused by the COVID-19 crisis, it is plausible that a non-resident employee who customarily performed their duties of employment for the non-resident employer in their jurisdiction of residence travelled to Canada unexpectedly, in haste, or under personal distress, and commenced performing their duties of employment remotely while remaining in Canada due to the travel restrictions. The non-resident employer and the non-resident employee may not have had the time or knowledge necessary to obtain the available relief from Canadian withholdings, at that time.

Potential Issue

The non-resident employee would be subject to both Canadian payroll withholdings, and those of their jurisdiction of residence, and the resulting reduction in net pay could cause undue hardship.

Additionally, the non-resident employer, failing to withhold and remit the required Canadian amounts without authorization from the Agency, could be held liable for the whole amount with interest and penalties.

Agency Position

Note: The ending date referenced above for the application period of the guidance on this page, September 30, 2020, is not applicable to subsection III. D. Non-resident employer withholdings with non-resident employee in Canada. The ending date for this subsection is detailed below.

As an administrative matter and in light of these extraordinary circumstances, the Agency will not assess or penalize a non-resident employer for failing to withhold the required Canadian payroll deductions, in respect of remuneration paid to a non-resident employee performing duties of employment remotely in Canada, where the non-resident employer and the non-resident employee, as may be required, can reasonably demonstrate that:

- the non-resident employee is resident in a country with which Canada has a comprehensive tax treaty (treaty);

- the non-resident employee is not resident in Canada for tax purposes in accordance with the relevant treaty;

- the remuneration received by the non-resident employee for performing their duties of employment in Canada would otherwise be exempt from taxation in Canada in accordance with the relevant treaty;

- the non-resident employee regularly and customarily performs their duties of employment outside of Canada and has not previously performed duties of employment in Canada, as a non-resident of Canada, for any employer;

- there is no employer-employee relationship between the non-resident employee and any employer in Canada;

- there has been no significant change to: the non-resident employee's duties of employment (other than working remotely) while working in Canada; or the employer-employee relationship that existed between the non-resident employer and the non-resident employee at the time the non-resident employee travelled to Canada; and

- the non-resident employee travelled to Canada due to the COVID-19 crisis or for reasons not relating in any manner whatever to their employment, and could not return to their jurisdiction of residence solely due to COVID-19 travel restrictions.

The Agency will respect this position for the period beginning on the day the non-resident employee commenced exercising their duties of employment in Canada be-

cause they were unable to return to their jurisdiction of residence due to the COVID-19 travel restrictions, and ending on the date that is the earliest of:

- the day the non-resident employee returned or was able to return to their jurisdiction of residence;

- the day specified on a Regulation 102 waiver relieving the non-resident employee from the relevant Canadian withholdings;

- the day the non-resident employer was certified by the Minister as a qualifying non-resident employer and the non-resident employee was also a qualifying non-resident employee, or

- December 31, 2020.

IV. Waiver Requests – Payments to non-residents for services provided in Canada

Canadian income tax rules require that amounts must be deducted or withheld and remitted for:

- payments to non-residents for services rendered in Canada, other than those paid for an office or employment (regulation 105)

- remuneration paid to a non-resident officer or employee for an office, or employment services, provided in Canada (regulation 102)

In certain circumstances, an application to the CRA may be made for a waiver of the withholding requirement under regulation 105 or 102. Most often, this will be the case if a recipient is exempt from Canadian income tax for a payment because of an income tax treaty that Canada has with the recipient's country of residence.

Potential Issue

During the COVID-19 pandemic, processing times for international waivers may be longer than usual.

Agency Position

We are continuing to process international waivers. You can submit all waiver and non-resident employer certification applications by mail, fax or online using My Account for Individuals, Represent a Client, and My Business Account. The process for sending documents by email **was terminated effective March 31, 2021**.

For information on how to avoid processing delays, see *How to obtain international waivers and certificates of compliance during the COVID-19 crisis.*

In a situation where a waiver request for regulation 105 and/or 102 was sent to the CRA between March 1, 2020 and June 30, 2020 (the service interruption), and the CRA was unable to process the request within 30 days, the CRA will not assess a person who fails to deduct, withhold or remit any amount as required by regulations 102 and 105, for an amount paid to a non-resident person covered by the particular waiver request.

Relief will be applicable if the only reason a non-resident could not obtain a waiver of regulation 102 or 105 withholdings from the CRA was due to the delay caused by the service interruption, and the person paying the amount can demonstrate they took reasonable steps to ascertain that the non-resident was entitled to a reduction or elimination of Canadian withholding tax by virtue of an income tax treaty with Canada. Both the non-resident and the person paying the amount must otherwise have fulfilled their Canadian reporting and remitting obligations in respect of the waiver application.

Other situations may arise, during or after the period of service interruption provided above, where a waiver request could not be sent to the CRA due to the travel restrictions or other consequences of the COVID-19 crisis, and yet no amounts were withheld pursuant to regulations 102 and 105. The CRA will review these situations on a case-by-case basis to determine if the non-compliance can be solely and directly attributed to the effects of the COVID-19 crisis. In those cases, the CRA will not assess a person who fails to deduct, withhold or remit any amount as required by regulations 102 and 105, in respect of an amount paid to a non-resident person, and they can demonstrate they took reasonable steps to make sure that the non-resident person was entitled to a reduction or elimination of Canadian withholding tax by virtue of an income tax treaty with Canada. Both the non-resident and the person paying the amount must otherwise have fulfilled their Canadian reporting and remitting obligations in respect of the waiver application.

V. Disposition of taxable Canadian property by non-residents of Canada

Under Canadian income tax rules, a non-resident vendor who disposes of certain taxable Canadian property must notify the CRA about the disposition either before they dispose of the property or no later than 10 days after the disposition [116(3) — ed.]. Once the CRA has received either an amount to cover the tax on any gain the vendor may realize on the disposition of property, or appropriate security for the tax, the CRA will issue a certificate of compliance to the vendor (a section 116 certificate). A copy of the certificate is also sent to the purchaser.

If the purchaser does not receive a section 116 certificate within 30 days of the end of the month in which the property was acquired, they have to remit a specified amount to the Receiver General for Canada and is entitled to deduct that amount from the purchase price [116(5) — ed.]. Any payments or security provided by the vendor or purchaser will be credited to the vendor's account [116(5), words "on behalf of the non-resident person" — ed.]. A final settlement of tax will be made when the CRA assesses the vendor's income tax return for the year.

Potential Issue

During the COVID-19 pandemic, processing times of requests for section 116 certificates may be longer than usual.

Agency Position

If a vendor has submitted a request for a section 116 certificate, but the certificate has not been issued by the time a purchaser's remittance is due (that is, within 30 days of the end of the month in which the property was acquired), **the buyer or vendor may ask the CRA for a comfort letter.**

The comfort letter advises the purchaser/vendor/representative to retain the funds they have withheld (even though technically, the amounts are due) until the CRA's review is complete and the CRA asks the purchaser to remit the required tax. As long as the tax is remitted when requested, the CRA will not assess a penalty or interest on the amount [technically, CRA uses 220(3.1) to waive any penalty or interest — ed.].

A comfort letter can be requested directly from the CRA officer you are dealing with if one has been assigned, or may also be requested by contacting the CRA's individual tax enquiries line at 1-800-959-8281. Comfort letters can also be requested by fax at 1-833-329-1161 (Canada and U.S.) or 418-566-0324 (outside Canada and U.S.), or online through My Account, Represent a Client or My Business Account. Make sure to provide your name and case number (if available) on all requests.

The process for sending documents by email **was terminated effective March 31, 2021**.

VI. Non-resident employer certification

Non-resident employees providing employment services in Canada are subject to the same withholding, remitting, and reporting obligations as Canadian resident employees. Therefore, any employer, including a non-resident employer, has to withhold amounts on account of the income tax liability of an employee in Canada, even if the employee is likely to be exempt from tax in Canada because of a tax treaty. For the employer to be relieved of their obligation to withhold, the employee would have to apply for, and get, an income tax waiver from the CRA [as discussed in IV. Waiver requests–Payments to non-residents for services provided in Canada above].

However, there is an exception to the employer's withholding obligation for certain non-resident employers paying employment income to non-resident employees for performing the duties of an office or employment in Canada. These non-resident employers, who apply for and receive certification as a qualifying non-resident employer [153(6), (7) — ed.], will not have to withhold and remit tax on the payments they make to a qualifying non-resident employee who is working in Canada for a limited time and is exempt from tax in Canada under a tax treaty.

For more information, go to non-resident employer certification [tinyurl.com/cra-153-7 — ed.].

Potential Issue

An individual working in Canada as a qualifying non-resident employee when travel restrictions were imposed may not have been able to leave Canada as they had intended and instead had to stay in Canada. Could this extended stay in Canada result in the individual losing their status as a qualifying non-resident employee and obligate the qualifying non-resident employer to withhold and remit Canadian payroll deductions to the CRA on the employment income paid?

Agency Position

In light of the extraordinary circumstances, the CRA will not consider the days, during which a non-resident individual is working or present in Canada and cannot return to their country of residence due to the travel restrictions, to count towards the 45 days worked or the 90 days present in Canada for the definition of a qualifying non-resident employee. This will be the CRA position where it can reasonably be shown that the employer expected the employee to leave Canada before losing their status as a qualifying non-resident employee, and the employee returns to their country of residence as soon as they can.

To keep certification as a qualifying non-resident employer, the employer will track and document, among other things:

- the days during which the qualifying non-resident employee is working or present in Canada and cannot return to their country of residence, due to travel restrictions

  the employment income that corresponds to these days of work in Canada

VII. Supplemental guidance

The administrative relief provided under the guidance above generally applied in the initial relief period.

Despite this relief, the CRA is aware that certain individuals continue to have concerns about potential income tax issues because of the travel restrictions lasting past the initial relief period. Additionally, some individuals that were affected by the travel restrictions may be uncertain about how to satisfy their Canadian income tax obligations for 2020 and 2021.

This supplement provides additional guidance for individuals in these situations, by:

- extending the administrative relief in respect of individual income tax residence;
- clarifying some of the CRA's views regarding the effect of the travel restrictions on the determination of a permanent establishment in Canada; and
- providing an outline of the Canadian income tax and compliance requirements of certain cross-border employees and providing some relief in respect of these requirements.

As with the guidance initially provided, this supplemental guidance is intended to assist taxpayers during this time of crisis and does not represent any interpretive position or intention to establish any broader policy by the CRA. Accordingly, the supplemental guidance below is applicable only for the periods described in the specific section.

A. Individual income tax residency

For the initial relief period, the guidance provides that the CRA will not consider the common-law factual test of residency [see 250(1) Notes — ed.] to be met if an individual stayed in Canada only because of the travel restrictions. In such situations, an individual's days physically present in Canada will not count towards the 183-day limit for deemed residency [250(1)(a) — ed.].

This supplemental guidance extends the period to which this specific relief applies until the earlier of the date of the lifting of the travel restrictions and December 31, 2021. This extension of administrative relief applies solely in respect of individuals and does not extend to the determination of corporate residency.

With respect to the common-law test of residency, this relief continues to apply only in respect of the individual's physical presence in Canada. A determination that the individual is factually resident in Canada is still possible where other indicators of residence are present, such as having a permanent home in Canada or enrolling in government programs intended for Canadian residents.

B. Permanent establishment

For the initial relief period, the guidance above provides that, administratively, the CRA will not consider a non-resident entity to have a permanent establishment in Canada [for Art. 4 of treaties — ed.] solely because an employee performed their employment duties in Canada as a result of the travel restrictions being in force. The relief extends to the determination of an "agency" permanent establishment.

Some individuals, because of the travel restrictions, may have continued to exercise their employment duties in Canada after the initial relief period. For example, a Canadian resident who normally exercised their employment duties at the office of their United States employer may have begun working from their home in Canada during the pandemic and may continue to do so until the travel restrictions are lifted. Another example would be a Canadian citizen factually residing in the United States and working for a United States employer who followed the Canadian government's recommendation to Canadians to return to Canada and now continues to work remotely for their United States employer from Canada.

The administrative relief provided for the initial relief period is no longer applicable to determinations as to whether or not the non-resident employer has a fixed place of business in Canada. However, the CRA expects that the application of the relevant treaty provisions to their situation will generally not result in the finding of a permanent establishment for the employer. A location (for example, home office or other workspace) will constitute a permanent establishment if it is a fixed place of business through which a business is partly or wholly carried on. In order for there to be a fixed place of business in Canada, there must be a semblance of permanence to the site. As well, the site must be at the "disposal" of the employer. The fact, on its own, that an individual described in one of the examples above works remotely from their home or short term residence in Canada while the travel restrictions remain in place will generally not be sufficient to meet the thresholds of a permanent establishment.

This conclusion could change should the employee continue to exercise their employment duties in Canada after the lifting of the travel restrictions or if the individual and their employer take action to establish the workspace in Canada as an office of the employer which has a semblance of permanence and is at the disposal of the employer.

Similarly, in order to meet the requirements of an "agency" permanent establishment, an individual must not only have the right to conclude contracts on behalf of an enterprise, they must also habitually exercise that right. This habitual requirement would not be met where an individual described in one of the examples above has the right to conclude contracts on behalf of their employer and is doing so from Canada solely because of the travel restrictions.

As with the fixed place of business determination, this conclusion could change for both the period of time during which the travel restrictions are in place as well as afterwards if the employee remained in Canada past the lifting of the travel restrictions and continued to exercise the right to conclude contracts.

These conclusions would also be generally applicable in respect of employees that, before the COVID-19 crisis, were employed in a country other than the United States.

The Canada-United States income tax treaty also contains another type of permanent establishment, commonly referred to as a "services" permanent establishment. A services permanent establishment will be created where:

- services are performed in Canada by an individual who is present in Canada for a period or periods aggregating 183 days or more in any twelve-month period and, during that period or periods, more than 50 percent of the gross active business revenues of the enterprise consists of income derived from the services performed in Canada by that individual; or
- services are provided in Canada for an aggregate of 183 days or more in any twelve-month period with respect to the same or connected project for customers who are either residents of Canada or a permanent establishment in Canada.

Each affected individual will need to examine their personal situation to determine whether they meet either of these tests. However, most employees described in the examples above would not meet either of these thresholds if they are not working on projects for Canadian customers.

C. Cross-border employment income

(i) US Resident Employees

The guidance above provides that, in the initial relief period, if United States-resident individuals are present in Canada and exercising their employment duties in Canada solely as a result of the travel restrictions, those days will not be counted toward the 183-day test for employment income in the Canada-United States income tax treaty [Art. XV:2(b) — ed.].

In the absence of this relief, an affected individual would have become subject to Canadian income tax on a portion of their employment income. The Canadian income tax paid would be credited to the individual in determining their United States income tax. However, it would have created a more complicated 2020 income tax compliance burden on these individuals.

The administrative relief in the initial relief period in respect of the 183-day test in the employment article of the Canada-United States income tax treaty is being extended to December 31, 2020. An individual in this situation who has remained in Canada after December 31, 2020, must include each subsequent day present in Canada in calculating whether the 183-day test has been met.

As set out in section III. D. of the guidance above, an employer of an individual who continues to work remotely from Canada as of January 1, 2021, must, in accordance with Canadian legislation, either withhold and remit in respect of the employee or have the withholding requirement waived by the CRA. The CRA suggests that an affected individual in this situation refer their employer to the CRA webpage regarding employer withholding and remittance obligations, or contact the CRA's Liaison Officer service if further assistance is required.

As an administrative matter, where the conditions in subsection III.D. were met, a non-resident employer will not be required to submit a T4 slip for the 2020 taxation year in respect of the particular non-resident employee. However, the CRA expects the non-resident employer to track and document, among other things:

- the days during which the non-resident employee is working or present in Canada and cannot return to their country of residence, due to travel restrictions;

- the employment income that corresponds to these days of work in Canada.

(ii) Canadian Resident Employees

As a result of the travel restrictions, some Canadian resident individuals may have been forced to perform their employment duties from home in Canada instead of at the office of their United States employer. The CRA recognizes that there is uncertainty as to how affected individuals are to comply with their income tax obligations for 2020 and 2021. In order to reduce this uncertainty, this supplemental guidance provides information and relief in this regard.

The guidance in section III.C above provides that, for the initial relief period, where a letter of authority had been issued by the CRA in respect of withholdings, the letter would continue to apply. As a result, the withholding obligations of the non-resident employer would not change in Canada, as long as there are no changes to the withholding obligations of the non-resident employer in the other jurisdiction. However, notwithstanding that their employer's withholding obligations did not change, some individuals in this situation may now be subject to tax on a lower amount of income in the United States and, as a result, pay a greater amount of income tax in Canada. This is because of the rules in the Canada-United States income tax treaty.

For individuals in this situation, whose taxes continued to be withheld as if the income was earned in the United States, the CRA will provide an administrative concession in order to simplify the reporting obligations for those who so prefer. In such situations, the CRA will consider the employment income from the United States employer to be sourced from the United States for 2020. This means they can file their tax returns like they did in prior years and claim a foreign tax credit for amounts paid in the United States. Individuals who choose to file in this manner must maintain their records in case the CRA needs to confirm the amounts paid to the United States. Income that was not subject to withholding in the United States must be reported as if it was sourced in Canada. In addition, should any amounts paid to the United States be refunded at a later time, the employee must file an amended return adjusting the amount of the foreign tax credit claimed in Canada. Note this administrative concession applies only to individuals who, because of the travel restrictions, have been forced to perform their employment duties from their home in Canada instead of at the office of their United States employer.

Alternatively, these individuals may choose to file their 2020 Canadian income tax return in accordance with the income sourcing rules in the Canada-United States income tax treaty. In other words, they may choose to report their employment income as sourced from Canada since they performed their duties from Canada. Affected individuals whose 2020 income tax withholdings were changed to reflect the sourcing rules in the Canada-United States income tax treaty must file their Canadian income tax return using this method. The following outlines how an affected individual using this method should file their 2020 Canadian income tax return, and outlines how the CRA will treat specific amounts typically relevant to cross-border employees resident in Canada:

- If the individual has paid income tax to the United States, in respect of income that was taxable in the United States under the Canada-United States income tax treaty, the individual may claim a foreign tax credit in respect of that income tax.

- As in years for which the taxpayer was exercising their duties in the United States, if the individual has made valid contributions to the United States in 2020 under the United States Federal Insurance Contributions Act (FICA), the individual may claim a foreign tax credit in respect of those contributions. For the purpose of claiming the FICA contribution portion of the individual's foreign tax credit, administratively the entire amount of the individual's employment income on which the contributions were based may be included in the individual's 2020 foreign non-business income.

- If the individual has made contributions to a United States retirement plan in 2020, they may determine the amount deductible on form RC268 as if the individual had continued to exercise their employment duties in the United States throughout all of 2020.

- If the individual has paid state income tax in 2020, and the payee state has refused to give up its right to tax the individual, the individual may claim a foreign tax credit in respect of those taxes paid despite the income being earned in Canada. This is an administrative measure and is applicable only to the 2020 tax year of affected individuals. For the purpose of claiming the credit, the foreign non-business income of the individual would consist only of the portion of the employment income the individual would have earned in the state had they continued to commute to work in the United States in 2020. Should the state tax be refunded at a later time, the employee must file an amended return adjusting the amount of the foreign tax credit claimed in Canada.

Affected individuals who file their Canadian income tax return in accordance with the Canada-United States income tax treaty may have a higher Canadian tax liability. These individuals are expected to take whatever actions reasonably necessary to obtain any applicable refund of withholdings from the United States and to pay their Canadian income tax by the payment due date. However, some individuals may temporarily find it difficult to pay the full amount owing until after the payment due date when they receive a refund of their withholdings from the United States. In these circumstances, the CRA will cancel all or part of the interest or late-payment penalties that arise as a result until the time the individual receives their United States refund and pays it towards their amount owing within a reasonable time.

There may also be a number of affected individuals who, after filing their 2020 return, receive a notification that they must remit income tax instalments in 2021, as a result of the larger than usual Canadian income tax payable for 2020. In these circumstances, the CRA will also cancel instalment penalties and interest if charged.

Requests for relief of interest and penalties can be made online by selecting "Request relief of penalties and interest" in My Account at canada.ca/my-cra-account, or by filling out Form RC4288 Request for Taxpayer Relief - Cancel or Waive Penalties or Interest and submitting it along with all supporting documents online using the "Submit documents" service in My Account or by mail to one of the designated CRA offices listed at the end of the form. In making the request, the individual should provide a detailed description of their employment arrangement and provide a copy of their Form W-2, U.S. 1040 return, U.S. account transcript and any other document that confirms the receipt of the U.S. refund. For more information about the cancellation of penalties and interest and how to submit a request, go to canada.ca/penalty-interest-relief.

The CRA will provide additional guidance at a later date for impacts on affected individual's 2021 tax years. However, affected individuals should expect that the income sourcing rules in the Canada-United States income tax treaty will be applied should their working arrangements change to allow them to work permanently from Canada.

Example: Application of supplemental guidance to Canadian-resident cross border workers

My employer's office is in the United States. In previous years, I reported to work at my employer's office. Because of the travel restrictions imposed as the result of the COVID-19 crisis, I started working for my employer from my home in Canada in March and continued to do so for the rest of 2020. I understand that this may affect my 2020 Canadian income tax obligations and have some questions about this:

1. If I live in Canada but work for an employer in the United States, to which country do I pay my income tax, and how is that determined?

Under Canadian income tax law, residents of Canada are taxed on their worldwide income, including any employment income from working in the United States. Under the Canada-United States Income Tax Treaty (the "Treaty"), the United States also has the right to tax a Canadian resident working for an employer in the United States on their employment income if their employment duties were performed in the United States and they earned more than US$10,000 from employment in the United States. This creates a situation where both Canada and the United States have the right to tax the employment income of a Canadian resident. To address this situation, Canada will still impose tax but it will allow the individual to claim a foreign tax credit in respect of tax paid in the United States.

For previous years, because you reported to work at your employer's office in the United States, your employment income was taxed in the United States and you were granted a foreign tax credit when you filed your Canadian income tax return.

2. Although I have been working from my home in Canada, my employer continued to make and remit my payroll deductions (withholdings) in the United States. Can I just file as I have done in previous years and pay income tax on my employment income to the United States?

For the 2020 tax year of individuals in this situation, the CRA will provide an administrative concession in order to simplify the reporting obligations for those who so prefer.

In such situations, the CRA will consider the employment income from the United States employer to be sourced from the United States for 2020. This means individuals can file their tax returns like they did in prior years and claim a foreign tax credit for amounts paid in the United States. Alternatively, these individuals may choose to file their 2020 Canadian income tax return in accordance with the income sourcing rules in the Treaty.

3. My employer issued a revised W-2 to me and refunded the portion of my United States income tax withholdings taken on my income that would not be taxable in the United States under the Treaty. Can I also choose to file my 2020 Canadian income tax return as in I did in previous years?

Affected individuals whose 2020 income tax withholdings were changed to reflect the sourcing rules in the Treaty must file their Canadian income tax return using these sourcing rules. This means they can claim a foreign tax credit for the withholdings as per the revised W-2, but they must report the remainder of their employment income as taxable (sourced) solely in Canada.

4. I am filing my 2020 Canadian income tax return in accordance with the Treaty, but I participate in a United States retirement plan through my employer. In previous years I deducted my contributions to the plan on form RC268. Will I still be able to deduct these contributions? I also made contributions under the United States Federal Insurance Contributions Act (FICA) and paid state income tax to the state where my employer is located. Will I still be allowed to claim a foreign tax credit in Canada for these amounts?

If you have made contributions to a United States retirement plan in 2020, that would have been deductible on form RC268 if made in a previous year, you may deduct your 2020 contributions in the same manner as in previous years.

If you have made valid FICA contributions to the United States in 2020, you may claim a foreign tax credit in Canada in respect of those contributions.

If you have paid state income tax in 2020, and the payee state has refused to give up its right to tax, you may claim a foreign tax credit in respect of those taxes paid despite the income being earned in Canada. This is an administrative measure and is applicable only to the 2020 tax year. However, should the state tax be refunded at a later time, you must file an amended return adjusting the amount of the foreign tax credit claimed in Canada.

5. I am going to file my 2020 Canadian income tax in accordance with the Treaty. But I am unsure how to apply sourcing rules to determine the time I spent working in the United States and the time I spent working in Canada. Are there any resources that I can use to help me?

Income Tax Folio S5-F2-C1 — Foreign Tax Credit provides a comprehensive description of how to claim a foreign tax credit in Canada and includes guidance regarding how individuals should allocate their employment income.

6. My 2020 income tax withholdings were all remitted to the United States. I am going to file my 2020 Canadian income tax return in accordance with the Treaty, but I am concerned that I will not receive a refund of these withholdings in time to pay my Canadian tax liability. What should I do?

The CRA realizes that some individuals may temporarily find it difficult to pay the full amount owing until after the payment due date when they receive a refund of their withholdings from the United States. In these circumstances, the CRA will cancel all or part of the interest or late-payment penalties that arise as a result until the time the individual receives their United States refund and pays it towards their amount owing within a reasonable time. Similarly, there may also be a number of affected individuals who, after filing their 2020 return, receive a notification that they must remit income tax instalments in 2021, as a result of the larger than usual Canadian income tax payable for 2020. In these circumstances, the CRA will also cancel instalment penalties and interest if charged.

Instructions on how to apply for this relief are contained in subsection VII. C. of the guidance.

7. My employer told me that they are concerned my working from my home may cause it to be taxable in Canada (through the creation of a permanent establishment in Canada). Should they be concerned?

While the administrative relief in respect of permanent establishment did end on September 30, 2020, the CRA, in general, does not expect that a permanent establishment would be created in Canada because of an individual working from home solely because of the COVID-19 travel restrictions. For more detail, please refer to subsection VII. B. of the guidance.

Examples: Other issues

1. With respect to the section entitled "Persons entering Canada during the COVID-19 pandemic", can quarantine days be counted as workdays if I worked during those days? Or could those days be exempt from taxation? How does this relief apply in calculating Canadian source income in relation to services performed in Canada by non-resident individuals?

The relief in the guidance you have referenced is applicable only to the time in the quarantine period that an individual is in Canada but cannot work. It would not apply in respect of a person working during this period.

2. I am a Canadian citizen who returned to Canada due to COVID-19. In section VI. Non-resident employer certification, the Agency Position requires that "the employee returns to their country of residence as soon as they can", how is this defined?

The expectation for returning "as soon as they can" would generally be the same as that described for residency relief under section I.A. of the guidance.

3. How should I determine the "date of the lifting of the travel restrictions" in section VII.A? For example, if I returned to Canada during 2020 because of COVID-19 and remained in Canada for the year, would the CRA consider all days during this period to be as a result of a travel restriction, despite the fact that travel between Canada and the United States (US) remained possible for most of 2020?

Yes, in the example provided, we would consider all of the days in 2020 that you were present in Canada to be because of the travel restrictions, as long as the crisis and government travel recommendation were the sole reasons for returning to Canada.

The date of the lifting of the travel restrictions will be a question of fact. The CRA does not expect issues to arise from this approach, so long as any individual relying on the relief acts in good faith. If there is a specific concern it should be sent to the COVID mailbox at PERESCOVIDG@cra-arc.gc.ca.

4. In section VII.C there is no reference to employees who are resident of countries other than the US or Canada. Does the initial guidance provided to residents of other countries continue to apply until September 30, 2020?

The CRA will consider providing relief to an individual in this situation on a case-by-case basis.

5. I am a non-Canadian who chose to come to Canada during the pandemic period and worked in Canada (e.g. from a vacation property or while staying with family). Can my personal choice to avoid non-essential travel during the pandemic, or can my employer's instruction to avoid non-essential travel, be considered a "travel restriction" for purposes of the relief granted for the period of March 16 to September 30, 2020?

Relief for such situations is on a case-by-case basis, we would consider relief in such a situation but we would need to know the specifics.

6. In section VII.C(i), for the purposes of determining whether I met the 183-day test for 2020, I would exclude any 2020 days in Canada resulting from a travel restriction and would only consider the days in 2021. Does this also apply in determining whether the 183-day test was met in 2021, in other words, can 2020 days be excluded?

Yes. If you are eligible for the relief, no days in 2020 will be counted towards the 183-day test in respect of their 2020 or 2021 tax year.

7. Is the extended relief in section VII.C(ii) applicable to me if I am a Canadian resident employee who had to perform my employment duties from my home in Canada instead of at the office in a location other than the US? In the initial guidance, section III.C pertained to all Canadian resident employees, and not only to those working for a US employer?

The supplemental relief specifically addressed the situation of Canadian residents working for US employers because that was the largest group of individuals in this situation. The CRA will consider relief for those whose employers are in a country other than the US on a case-by-case basis.

8. Section VII.C(ii) provides relief from penalties and interest if an individual is waiting for a US refund to pay their Canadian balance due.

> *a. Am I required to pay the penalty and interest prior to submitting a request for cancellation of penalties and interest? Also, if I am waiting for either the US refund to pay the Canadian balance and/or the CRA to process the request to cancel penalties and interest, will the CRA automatically put a hold on any collections notices to me? If not, will there be a streamlined process for me to request a hold on any such collections notices?*

> The supplemental guidance does not require you to pay any assessed penalty or interest prior to submitting a request for relief. As the specific circumstances of individuals vary, there will be no automatic hold placed on collections notices. However, affected individuals who receive such a notice may contact the CRA's debt management call centre at 1-888-863-8657 to speak to an agent and inform them of their circumstances. Affected individuals should be prepared to provide any verification information requested.

> *b. Is it reasonable to assume that the cancellation of payment and interest will apply only to the amount of the US refund (and not the entire Canadian tax balance due)?*

> You may make a request for relief in excess of their US refund. However, whether relief is granted in respect of that portion of the interest and penalties would be determined on its own merits and separately from the US refund portion of the request.

9. I am a Canadian resident who works for a US employer, I would ordinarily work in the US, and I performed services in Canada for 2020 due to travel restrictions, therefore, the remuneration paid for my services performed in Canada may not be subject to the Federal Insurance Contribution Act (FICA). What would the CRA view as a "valid contribution" to FICA? What if I obtained a Certificate of Coverage to continue to contribute to FICA?

Generally, the intention is to allow an affected individual to claim a foreign tax credit in respect of amounts paid that are recognized as FICA contributions under that Act. Of particular concern would be an individual receiving a refund of their FICA contributions and attempting to claim a foreign tax credit in respect of those amounts. A Certificate of Coverage would generally be sufficient to show that an individual's contributions were validly made.

For further guidance on international income tax issues

If a taxpayer has questions about how this guidance will apply, or if they have a situation that is not addressed above, or if their situation persists past September 30th, please contact PERESCOVIDG@cra-arc.gc.ca.*

* Use of this mailbox is to allow the CRA to receive residency and permanent establishment questions related to COVID-19 travel restrictions, which may include information up to Protected B. Please include a contact phone number. The CRA will contact you at either the number you provided, if the request includes protected or personal information, or by the email address you provided, if your request is generic. The CRA will not respond to enquiries sent to this mailbox which are not about residency or permanent establishment matters affected by COVID-19 travel restrictions.

The CRA does not provide assurance about the protection, confidentiality, or security of unsecured email. Using this mailbox, you accept the risks of sending information by unsecured email and understand all such email messages may be considered as being accessed and disclosed to unknown third parties somewhere in the world. You agree not to hold the CRA or its employees liable for any damage or loss arising from the communication of personal information by this unsecured email.

How to obtain international waivers and certificates of compliance during the COVID-19 crisis

During the COVID-19 pandemic, the CRA is continuing to review international waivers (regulations 102 and 105, and Form RC473, Non-Resident Employer Certification) and requests for a certificate of compliance under section 116 (forms T2062 and T2062A, B, and C). However, processing times may be longer than usual. The following provides information about how to apply for international waivers and certificates of compliance during the COVID-19 crisis.

Persons entering Canada during the COVID-19 pandemic

The Government of Canada has made it mandatory for any person entering Canada to have a plan to quarantine for 14 days when they arrive in Canada. This plan is mandatory, even if the person has no symptoms.

When applying for a waiver, do not count the quarantine period as part of the days in Canada or the service period. This is consistent with the COVID-19 guidelines issued by the Organisation for Economic Co-operation and Development and the CRA.

Applying for an individual tax number

The CRA cannot process applications for an individual tax number (ITN) alongside a waiver application or request for certificate of compliance. Please apply for an ITN separately by completing Form T1261, Application for a Canada Revenue Agency Individual Tax Number (ITN) for Non-Residents and following the mailing instructions on the form. Make sure to tick the box indicating the reason you are asking for an ITN, because that will greatly speed up the process.

Submitting requests or submissions by mail after March 12, 2020

Due to restrictions on mail operations, and until operations resume in full, the CRA may experience delays accessing any documents sent by mail. You can still send your request and information by mail but there may be delays in processing.

If you have already sent your documents

The CRA is continuing to process requests, but there may be delays. If your situation is urgent, you may call the CRA's individual tax enquiries line at 1-800-959-8281, submit your documents electronically through the Agency's secured online portals , or send a fax to one of the numbers provided below.

New electronic submission of documents as of June 19, 2020

As of June 19, 2020, you or your representative can submit a request for an international waiver or a notification for a section 116 certificate of compliance online through My Account, Represent a Client or My Business Account. Make sure to provide your name and case number (if available) on all requests. For more information go to: international waivers or certificates of compliance under section 116.

You can also send it by fax to:

CRA Fax Numbers for International Waivers or Non-Resident Dispositions

	Canada and United States (toll-free number)	Outside Canada and United States
International Waivers	1-833-329-1160	418-566-0323
Non-resident Dispositions	1-833-329-1161	418-566-0324

Note: Applications that are not complete will delay processing.

History

This section identifies any amendments made to the guidance.

Original issue date — May 19, 2020.

Update — June 29, 2020

The application of the guidance was extended from March 16, 2020 - June 29, 2020 to March 16, 2020 - August 31, 2020.

Update — August 31, 2020

The application of the guidance was extended from March 16, 2020 - June 29, 2020 to March 16, 2020 - September 30, 2020.

Update — September 2, 2020

Section I.-B. has been updated to address a possible issue with corporate residency requirements as it relates to the surplus calculations of a foreign affiliate of a Canadian-resident corporation.

Section VI. has been added to address a possible issue for qualifying non-resident employers, as certified by the Minister, whose qualifying non-resident employees may have had to remain in Canada for an extended period as the result of the travel restrictions.

The guidance has been updated to make it more readable and consistent with existing government writing style. None of these changes indicate a change in policy or approach of the CRA in applying the guidance.

Update — October 15, 2020

Section I.-A has been updated to clarify that the CRA will generally view the Canadian government's recommendation to Canadians to return to Canada as a "travel restriction".

Section III.-D. has been added to address the situation that may arise if a non-resident employee of a non-resident employer travelled to Canada for personal reasons and, as a result of the travel restrictions, was unable to return to their country of residence. If the non-resident employee performs their duties of employment remotely while in Canada, the non-resident employer would be subject to Canadian withholding, remitting, and reporting obligations.

Update — April 1, 2021

Section IV. and V. have been updated to reflect current submission guidelines.

Section VII. has been added to provide further guidance on individual income tax residency, permanent establishment, and cross-border employment income.

Notes: For more CRA comments see International Fiscal Assn CRA Q&A (Aug. 6, 2020), tinyurl.com/ifa-covid-qa. See also Neil Gurmukh, "International Tax Issues Arising from the COVID-19 Pandemic", XXIV(3) *International Tax Planning* (Federated Press) 2-8 (2020); Chantal Baril, "COVID-19 and Travel Restrictions: Impacts on Foreign Workers", XXVIII(2) *Taxation of Executive Compensation & Retirement* (Federated Press) 2-8 (2020).

(b) was, at any time in the year, a member of the Canadian Forces;

(c) was, at any time in the year,

    (i) an ambassador, minister, high commissioner, officer or servant of Canada, or

    (ii) an agent-general, officer or servant of a province,

and was resident in Canada immediately prior to appointment or employment by Canada or the province or received representation allowances in respect of the year;

(d) performed services, at any time in the year, in a country other than Canada under a prescribed international development assistance program of the Government of Canada and was resident in Canada at any time in the 3 month period preceding the day on which those services commenced;

(d.1) was, at any time in the year, a member of the overseas Canadian Forces school staff who filed his or her return for the year on the basis that the person was resident in Canada throughout the period during which the person was such a member;

(e) [Repealed]

(f) was at any time in the year a child of, and dependent for support on, an individual to whom paragraph (b), (c), (d) or (d.1) applies and the person's income for the year did not exceed the amount determined for F in subsection 118(1.1) for the year; or

(g) was at any time in the year, under an agreement or a convention with one or more other countries that has the force of law in Canada, entitled to an exemption from an income tax otherwise payable in any of those countries in respect of income from any source (unless all or substantially all of the person's income from all sources was not so exempt), because at that time the person was related to or a member of the family of an individual (other than a trust) who was resident in Canada.

Related Provisions: 6(1)(b)(ii), (iii) — No tax on certain allowances to deemed residents; 64.1 — Application to deemed resident; 94(3)(a) — Non-resident trust deemed resident in Canada for certain purposes; 94(5), (5.1) — Trust deemed to cease being resident in Canada; 110.6(5) — Deemed residence in Canada for capital gains exemption; 115(2) — Certain persons deemed employed in Canada; 118.5(2) — Tuition credit — application to deemed residents; 120(1) — Federal surtax on non-resident's income not earned in a province; 128.1 — Effect of becoming or ceasing to be resident in Canada; 138.1(1)(c)(ii) — Insurer deemed resident in Canada in respect of segregated fund property used in Canada; 214(13)(a) — Regulations can deem person resident in Canada for purposes of Part XIII; 250(3) — "Resident" includes ordinarily resident; 250(6.1) — Deemed residence of trust that ceases to exist; Reg. 2600–2607 — Individual deemed resident in a province; Canada-U.S. Tax Treaty:Art. IV:5 — Residence of government employee working in the other country.

Notes: See Income Tax Folio S5-F1-C1 (which has replaced IT-221R3). 250(1) deems certain persons to be resident in Canada, but this can be overridden for dual residents by the "tie-breaker" rules in Canada's tax treaty with the other country. See 250(5); *Allchin*, 2004 FCA 206, redetermined 2005 TCC 711; *Trieste*, 2012 FCA 320; and Canada-US treaty Art. IV:2 Notes. CRA will issue a Certificate of Residency for treaty purposes to confirm that tax is being paid in Canada, or that a partnership is a 102(1) "Canadian partnership" and all partners are Canadian resident: tinyurl.com/cor-cra [but not for fiscally-transparent entities: tinyurl.com/cra-cor], doc 2014-0547501E5 (reverses 2013-0510851C6 [2013 TEI q.9] re partnership); TEI Dec. 4, 2018, q. B.4.

Where no treaty tie-breaker rule applies and none of the deeming provisions in 250(1) applies, an individual is resident in Canada if the individual is "ordinarily resident" in Canada (see 250(3)). The seminal case on determining residence of a person who has left Canada is *Thomson*, [1946] C.T.C. 51 (SCC). See Lefebvre, "Canada's Jurisdiction to Tax: Residency and the *Thomson* Decision 60 Years Later", 54(3) *Canadian Tax Journal* 762-80 (2006). (The term "domicile" is different from "residence" in some countries but is not generally used in Canada.)

Thomson says "it must be assumed that every person has at all times a residence". This is often thought to mean that everyone must be resident in some *country*, but does not say that. In theory one could move to a yacht or cruise ship and cease to be resident in Canada, though CRA may reject this position.

Immigration status not determinative: "The determination of a person's residence is a complex question which requires the judge to weigh many factors. It is clear that residence is not simply a matter of a person's status under the *Immigration Act*, though a person's status may be some evidence of residence": *Guo*, 2004 FCA 390, para. 2. In *Mahmood*, 2009 TCC 89, a Guyanese resident who came regularly to Canada but did not have permanent-resident status was held to be non-resident (though likely carrying on business in Canada).

Determining residence: The question is where the taxpayer, in his settled routine of life, regularly, normally or customarily lives. One must examine the degree to which the taxpayer in mind and fact settles into, maintains or centralizes his ordinary mode of living, with its accessories in social relations, interests and conveniences, at or in the place in question. Material factors include (a) past and present habits of life, (b) regularity and length of visits in the jurisdiction asserting residence, (c) ties within that jurisdiction, (d) ties elsewhere, and (e) permanence or otherwise of purposes of stay abroad: *Reeder*, [1975] C.T.C. 256 (FCTD); *Gaudreau*, 2005 FCA 388; *Cavalier*, [2002] 1 C.T.C. 2001 (TCC); *Persaud*, 2007 TCC 474; *Waring*, 2006 BCSC 2046; *Mandrusiak*, 2007 BCSC 1418; *Nedelcu*, 2010 FCA 156; *Minin*, 2008 TCC 429. (Note that taxpayers seeking to avoid Canadian tax on world income want to be *non-resident*, but those seeking Canada Child Benefits (122.61) and GST/HST Credit (122.5) want to be *resident*.)

The courts have held that a Canadian resident must generally cut his or her ties with Canada to become non-resident. CRA's former position was that the departing taxpayer must intend to remain outside Canada for at least 2 years: pre-2002 IT-221R2 para. 4. The 2-year rule had no basis in law; see, for example, *Peel*, [1995] 2 C.T.C. 2888 (TCC). Income Tax Folio S5-F1-C1 no longer includes this "rule". It considers the following ties as "significant": (a) dwelling place(s), (b) spouse or common-law partner, (c) dependants; and the following as secondary ties: (a) personal property in Canada (e.g., furniture, clothing, cars, RVs), (b) social ties (e.g., memberships in Canadian recreational and religious organizations), (c) economic ties with Canada (e.g., employment, business, bank accounts, RRSPs, credit cards, securities accounts), (d) Canadian permanent-resident status or work permits, (e) provincial health insurance coverage, (f) a Canadian driver's license, (g) a vehicle registered in Canada, (h) a cottage in Canada or a leased home, (i) Canadian passport, and (j) memberships in Canadian unions or professional organizations. Other residential ties, generally of "limited importance" except where combined with the others, include a Canadian mailing address, post office box, safety deposit box, business cards, telephone listings, and Canadian newspaper/magazine subscriptions.

Although the Courts hold that there is no precise calculation for determining when an individual has severed ties with Canada and that each case depends on its facts, CRA has developed an internal computer program, *Residency Determination Advisory*, that purports to provide an "automatic" answer. It lists 7 "primary ties" and 22 "secondary ties" to Canada, and uses calculations to determine residence (e.g., in certain cases, one primary tie or 6 secondary ties is sufficient to rule that a person is resident in Canada). See "Residency Determination Advisory" on davidsherman.ca/files for sample output. CRA stated at the May 13, 2002 IFA seminar (on ifacanada.org): "The electronic system is used by the CCRA to make all preliminary determinations of individual residence status ... In many cases, no other evaluation of the individual's residence status is pursued ... although further review is always possible and the result of the electronic resident status determination is not binding on the CCRA or the individual." Form NR73 can be used to ask CRA to provide a determination of residence status. CRA Rulings will not rule on residency, as it is determined by the International Tax Services Office: VIEWS docs 2011-0427451E5, 2012-0437691E5, 2012-0446361E5, 2013-

0508511E5; but did opine that the taxpayer was non-resident in 2012-0444821E5. For commercial software that assists in the determination see *Residency Classifier* at bluejlegal.com.

If ties have not been cut with Canada, it does not matter that the taxpayer is studying in another country even for 16 years: *Perlman*, 2010 TCC 658 (yeshiva student). CRA will not introduce a simplified method of determining residence for persons absent from Canada for many years: doc 2019-0812971C6 [2019 APFF Financial q.11].

For cases since 2004 finding taxpayers **resident** in Canada see: *Snow*, 2004 TCC 381 (ties not severed); *Hauser*, 2006 FCA 216 (Air Canada pilot did not sufficiently "divorce" from Canada when moving to the Bahamas); *Barton*, 2007 TCC 222 (B maintained family, social relations, interests and conveniences in Canada); *Johnson*, 2007 TCC 288 (taxpayers transferred for 3-year contract and retained ties to Canada including homes rented out, RRSPs, driver's license, credit cards and stocks); *Mullen*, 2008 TCC 294 (M kept home in Canada in son's name); *Filipek*, 2008 TCC 351 (Air Canada pilot's evidence not believed); *Bensouilah*, 2009 TCC 440 (dual citizen working in Saudi Arabia but his family stayed in Canada and he kept home in Canada); *Denisov*, 2010 TCC 101 (home, wife and personal property in Canada); *Fatima*, 2012 TCC 49 (F and family had established significant ties to Canada which temporary trip to Pakistan did not change); *Snow*, 2012 TCC 78 (wife still resident while with husband in NZ as he did his 2-year master's, but became non-resident once he began his doctorate); *Mullen*, 2013 FCA 101 (M, working in China and Thailand, had not cut sufficient ties with Canada, and reporting himself again as non-resident triggered gross-negligence penalty under 163(2)); *Edwards*, 2012 TCC 430 (E resident in Canada rather than UK); *Biya*, 2020 TCC 113 (B lived in Ethiopia but kept numerous financial and family ties to Canada). For provincial-residence cases using the same principles, see Reg. 2607 Notes.

For cases finding taxpayers **non-resident** see: *Revah*, 2004 TCC 312 (ties sufficiently cut); *Allchin*, 2004 FCA 206 (ties not severed but Canada-US treaty applied to deem A resident only in US); *Yoon*, 2005 TCC 366 (Y's ties were closer to Korea even though husband still resided in Canada); *Laurin*, 2008 FCA 58 (Air Canada pilot became resident in Turks & Caicos: "residual friendships and employment connections do not create residency" (para. 32)); *Song*, 2009 FCA 278 (leave to appeal denied 2010 CarswellNat 664 (SCC)) (settled routine of S's life was in Japan); *Hamel*, 2011 TCC 357 (H moved to Qatar on work permit, divorced spouse, kept two bank accounts in Canada); *Manotas*, 2011 TCC 408 (M married and moved to Italy 10 years earlier and cut ties with Canada); *Messar-Splinter*, 2012 TCC 72 (MS had cut most ties); *Vegh*, 2012 TCC 95 (V moved to China and cut ties with Canada); *Elliott (Dysert)*, 2013 TCC 57 (US cost engineers working at Syncrude and living in Edmonton for 4 years did not become "ordinarily resident"); *Goldstein*, 2014 FCA 27 and *Kaplan*, 2014 TCC 215 (settled routine of life of yeshiva or kollel student and wife was in US); *Bower*, 2013 TCC 183 (settled life was in Indonesia despite intention to eventually return to Canada); *Agrebi*, 2014 TCC 141 (A was more closely connected to Tunisia while under a removal order and not permitted to return to Canada); *Corkum*, 2015 TCC 38 (academic's wife lived in Egypt with him for 12 years, including after he got his Ph.D., and her life revolved around him).

Old Age Security entitlement requires certain periods of Canadian residence. The determination of being "resident" is the same as under the ITA: *Singh*, 2013 FC 437 (S did not meet test because he was resident in India part of the time); *Duncan*, 2013 FC 319 (OAS might be payable, but if so, D would be liable for Canadian tax on his income on certain years); *Saraffian*, 2013 FCA 232; *Gumboc*, 2014 FC 185.

If Air Canada pilots succeed in becoming non-resident (see mixed results above), they are still taxable on their income earned in Canada: see 115(3) (before 2013, see Notes to 115(1) re *Sutcliffe* and *Price* cases).

For a case of an "astronaut" taxpayer found not to be resident in Canada despite having many of the ties referred to in IT-221R2, see *Shih*, [2000] 2 C.T.C. 2921 (TCC).

To avoid having to "cut ties" when moving to a non-treaty country, consider moving first for 2-3 years to a treaty country that does not tax unremitted foreign income (e.g. Barbados, Hong Kong, Singapore, UK) or which has special rules for new immigrants (e.g. Israel).

For filing requirements after departure see tinyurl.com/cra-emigrants.

See also Vidal, *Introduction to International Tax in Canada* (Carswell, 8th ed., 2020), chap. 7; Auger, "Study of the Dissociation Between Federal Tax Legislation and Quebec Civil Law: Residence", *The Harmonization of Federal Legislation with Quebec Civil Law* (APFF, 2002), 5:1-38; H. Arnold Sherman, "Recent Jurisprudence Regarding Canadian Nonresidents", 40(4) *Tax Notes International* (taxnotes.com) 347-53 (Oct. 24, 2005), "Canada Revenue Agency Continues to Chase Departing Residents", 50(6) *TNI* 489-93 (May 12, 2008), "Canada Revenue Agency Continues Its Attack on 'Nonresidents' ", 58(13) *TNI* 1051-57 (June 28, 2010) and "The Canada Revenue Agency Pursues Individuals Who Claim Canadian Residence", XVIII(3) *International Tax Planning* (Federated Press) 1240-49 (2013); Atlas, "A Review of the Residence Rules", 2013 Ontario Tax Conf. (ctf.ca), 11:1-26; Kearl and Deeprose, "Leaving Canada's new High-Tax-Rate Regime", 2016 Cdn Tax Foundation conf report, 32:1-24; Montes, "Tax Residency", *YP Focus Virtual Conference* (ctf.ca, Sept. 2020), 3A:1-27.

See also Notes to 114 and 250(5). For corporations, see Notes to 250(4). See 128.1(1) on becoming resident in Canada, and 128.1(4) on becoming non-resident.

The word "sojourn" implies transient or short-term residence, so 250(1)(a) does not apply to a person who becomes or ceases to be resident in Canada during the year, and such a person is not resident in Canada "throughout" the year: *Sharma*, 2001 FCT 584 (FCTD); *Dixon*, 2001 FCA 216. See s. 114 instead for the "part-year" rule for such taxpayers. CRA considers stays in Canada exceeding 2-3 days per visit to be "sojourning" rather than commuting: VIEWS doc 2004-006124117. Commuting to Canada (arriving in the morning and leaving Canada that evening) is not "sojourning": 2010-0355531E5; *R&L Food Distributors*, [1977] C.T.C. 2579 (TRB). Living in Edmonton for 4 years was "sojourning": *Elliott (Dysert)*, 2013 TCC 57.

For an individual's residence in a province see Reg. 2600–2607, and Notes to Reg. 2601(1).

For international students in Canada, see VIEWS doc 2005-0139501E5.

For residence of a corporation, see Notes to 250(4).

A trust or estate, like a corporation, is resident based on "central management and control": *Garron* [also cited as *St. Michael Trust* and *Fundy Settlement*], 2012 SCC 14. This rule (introduced by the TCC in *Garron* and approved by the FCA and SCC) overrules the former view that a trust is resident where the trustee or executor is resident (VIEWS doc 2008-0264381E5). In *Garron*, since the foreign trustee followed directions and did not actively manage the trust assets, a Barbados trust was held resident in Canada. CRA accepts the SCC decision and "will consider any relevant factor": Income Tax Folio S6-F1-C1 (replacing former IT-447) ¶1.6, so there is no precise checklist taxpayers can use to get around this rule. Note also that a trust deed may restrict the trustee's powers the way a unanimous shareholder agreement can for a corporation (see Notes to 111(5)). CRA thinks a TFSA, RRSP, RRIF, RESP or DPSP is always resident in Canada, even if the owner manages it from outside Canada: 2018-0738201I7. See also Roth et al., *Canadian Taxation of Trusts* (ctf.ca, 2016), pp. 709-26; Taylor, "Trust Residency, a Comprehensive Review", 2010 Prairie Provinces Tax Conference (ctf.ca), 4:1-29; Bollefer, "Residency of Trusts, Particularly in the Context of Estates", 208 *The Estate Planner* (CCH) 2-5 (May 2012); Bella & Fowlis, "The Final Word on Trust Residence?", 2012 Cdn Tax Foundation conference report, 37:1-25 (includes best practices for ensuring a trust is resident in a given country); Dolson, "Trust Residence After Garron: Provincial Considerations", 62(3) *Canadian Tax Journal* 671-99 (2014); Trotta & Pandher, "Trust Residence Post-Fundy", 26(2) *Canadian Tax Highlights* (ctf.ca) 11-13 (Feb. 2018). For the meaning of "central management and control" see Notes to 250(4). See also 94(3)(a), which deems certain non-resident trusts to be resident in Canada for many purposes. For the province of residence of a trust (including the *Discovery Trust* and *Boettger* cases), see Notes to Reg. 2601(1). The BC and New Brunswick *Conflict of Laws Rules for Trusts Act*s each say that a trust's residence is "where the administration of a trust is carried out or is principally carried out", but it is unclear whether this affects residence for tax purposes.

Being resident in Canada for tax purposes made a person resident for purposes of filing an assignment in bankruptcy, *Maschek*, 2007 ABQB 325.

Deemed resident under 250(1)(a)-(g) applies only if the person is not already factually resident, so a Quebec rule applying to 250(1)(b) residents did not apply to a Canadian soldier abroad: *Pellan*, 2016 QCCA 263 (leave to appeal denied 2016 CarswellQue 11690 (SCC)).

250(1)(b) overrides *Beament*, [1952] C.T.C. 327 (SCC), by deeming Canadian military personnel to remain resident in Canada.

250(1)(c) did not apply to a taxpayer who had cut her ties with Canada years earlier, and would have been deemed resident under former 250(1)(e) had it not been repealed: *Messar-Splinter*, 2012 TCC 72 (meaning VIEWS doc 2011-042488117 is wrong). (The CRA does not accept *Messar-Splinter* even though it was a General Procedure decision: Padina, "Canada Revenue Agency Clarifies Position in Deciding Not to Appeal", 67(5) *Tax Notes International* (taxnotes.com) 453-56 (July 30, 2012).) In 250(1)(c), "immediately prior" means at the time the person is hired, not when they start work, according to CRA: VIEWS docs 2002-0118195, 2007-026154117.

A former Canadian resident working for a Canadian consulate outside Canada, if not deemed resident in Canada by 250(1)(c), will still be subject to Canadian tax on employment income due to 115(2)(b): VIEWS doc 2011-0415151E5.

A taxpayer working overseas on a CIDA program is deemed resident by 250(1)(d) and thus eligible for tax-free allowances under 6(1)(b)(iii), apparently even if the taxpayer is resident in Canada anyway: VIEWS doc 2010-0361561E5.

250(1)(g): "Countries" include Hong Kong and Taiwan: see Notes to 219.2.

Certain members of armed forces visiting Canada are deemed non-resident and exempt from Canadian income tax (see also 149(1)(a)). Section 22 of the *Visiting Forces Act*, R.S.C. 1985, c. V-2, provides:

> 22. (1) **Residence or domicile** — Where the liability for any form of taxation in Canada depends on residence or domicile, a period during which a member of a visiting force is in Canada by reason of his being a member of such visiting force shall, for the purpose of such taxation, be deemed not to be a period of residence in Canada and not to create a change of residence or domicile.
>
> (2) **Salaries** — A member of a visiting force is exempt from taxation in Canada on the salary and emoluments paid to the member as a member by a designated state and in respect of any tangible personal or corporeal movable property that is in Canada temporarily by reason of the member's presence in Canada as a member.
>
> (3) **Resident Canadian citizens excepted** — For the purposes of this section, the term "member of a visiting force" does not include a Canadian citizen resident or ordinarily resident in Canada.

250(1)(f) amended by 2021 budget bill #1, for 2020 and later tax years, to reflect the "basic personal amount" moving from 118(1)B(c) to 118(1.1)F.

250(1)(e) repealed by 1998 Budget, effective Feb. 24, 1998 except that, where

(a) any person would, but for 250(1)(e),

(i) have been non-resident at any time before Feb. 24, 1998 and

(ii) not have become resident in Canada after that time and before Feb. 24, 1998, and

(b) the person does not elect in writing filed with Revenue Canada with the person's Part I return for 1998 to have the repeal apply after February 23, 1998

the repeal does not apply in respect of the person before the first time after February 23, 1998 that the person would, but for 250(1)(e), cease to be resident in Canada. (See *Messar-Splinter*, 2012 TCC 72.)

Before the amendment, read:

(e) was resident in Canada in any previous year and was, at any time in the year, the spouse of a person described in paragraph 250(1) (b), (c), (d) or (d.1) living with that person;

(A human rights challenge to 250(1)(e), before its repeal, failed: *McFadyen*, 2009 FC 78 (FCA appeal discontinued A-136-09).)

250(1) also amended by 1999 and 1998 Budgets, 1993 technical bill, 1992 Child Benefit bill.

Regulations: 3400 (prescribed international development assistance program, for 250(1)(d)).

Remission Orders: *Income Earned in Quebec Income Tax Remission Order*, P.C. 1989-1204 (remission to certain individuals linked with Quebec but not resident in a province on the last day of the year).

Income Tax Folios: S1-F2-C2: Tuition tax credit [replaces IT-516R2]; S5-F1-C1: Determining an individual's residence status [replaces IT-221R3]; S6-F1-C1: Residence of a trust or estate [replaces IT-447].

Interpretation Bulletins: IT-91R4: Employment at special work sites or remote work locations; IT-106R3: Crown corporation employees abroad; IT-451R: Deemed disposition and acquisition on ceasing to be or becoming resident in Canada; IT-513R: Personal tax credits.

I.T. Technical News: 38 (control of corporation owned by income trust — impact of change in trustees).

CRA Audit Manual: 10.11.13: Consultation and referrals regarding non-residents; 15.4.0: Residency.

Forms: NR73: Determination of residency status (leaving Canada); NR74: Determination of residency status (entering Canada).

(2) Idem — Where at any time in a taxation year a person described in paragraph (1)(b), (c) or (d) ceases to be a person so described, or a person described in paragraph (1)(d.1) ceases to be a member of the overseas Canadian Forces school staff, that person shall be deemed to have been resident in Canada throughout the part of the year preceding that time and the spouse or common-law partner and child of that person who by reason of paragraph (1)(e) or (f) would, but for this subsection, be deemed to have been resident in Canada throughout the year shall be deemed to have been resident in Canada throughout that part of the year.

Notes: 250(2) amended by 2000 same-sex partners bill to refer to "common-law partner", for 2001 and later tax years, or earlier by election.

(3) Ordinarily resident — In this Act, a reference to a person resident in Canada includes a person who was at the relevant time ordinarily resident in Canada.

Notes: See Notes to 250(1), and Notes to 188.1(5) re meaning of "includes".

Income Tax Folios: S5-F1-C1: Determining an individual's residence status [replaces IT-221R3].

(4) Corporation deemed resident — For the purposes of this Act, a corporation shall be deemed to have been resident in Canada throughout a taxation year if

(a) in the case of a corporation incorporated after April 26, 1965, it was incorporated in Canada;

(b) in the case of a corporation that

(i) was incorporated before April 9, 1959,

(ii) was, on June 18, 1971, a foreign business corporation (within the meaning of section 71 of the *Income Tax Act*, chapter 148 of the Revised Statutes of Canada, 1952, as it read in its application to the 1971 taxation year) that was controlled by a corporation resident in Canada,

(iii) throughout the 10 year period ending on June 18, 1971, carried on business in any one particular country other than Canada, and

(iv) during the period referred to in subparagraph (iii), paid dividends to its shareholders resident in Canada on which its shareholders paid tax to the government of the country referred to in that subparagraph,

it was incorporated in Canada and, at any time in the taxation year or at any time in any preceding taxation year commencing after 1971, it was resident in Canada or carried on business in Canada; and

(c) in the case of a corporation incorporated before April 27, 1965 (other than a corporation to which subparagraphs (b)(i) to (iv) apply), it was incorporated in Canada and, at any time in the taxation year or at any time in any preceding taxation year of the corporation ending after April 26, 1965, it was resident in Canada or carried on business in Canada.

Announced Administrative Change — 250(4) — COVID-19

CRA notice (tinyurl.com/cra-internat, April 27, 2021): See under 250(1)(a), sections I.B "Income Tax Residency: Corporations" and VII.B "Permanent establishment".

Related Provisions: 126(1.1)(a) — Authorized foreign bank deemed resident in Canada for foreign tax credit purposes; 128.1 — Effect of becoming or ceasing to be resident in Canada; 128.2 — Predecessor corps take on residence status of amalgamated corp; 212(13.3) — Authorized foreign bank deemed resident in Canada for withholding tax purposes; 214(13)(a) — Regulations can deem person resident in Canada for purposes of Part XIII; 250(5) — Person deemed non-resident by treaty is non-resident; 250(5.1) — Continuance outside Canada; 256(6), (6.1) — Meaning of "controlled".

Notes: 250(4) applies to deem a corporation to be resident in Canada, most notably by being incorporated under Canadian (federal or provincial) law. Such a deemed-resident corporation can become non-resident only under 250(5) by having a treaty "tie-breaker" rule apply (see Notes to Canada-US tax treaty Art. IV:2); or under 250(5.1) by being "continued" in another jurisdiction. In either case, see 128.1(4) and 219.1(1) for the effect of this "emigration". See VIEWS doc 2008-0278431E5 for general discussion.

A corp can also be resident in Canada under the common-law test of having its "central management and control" (CM&C) (or "mind and management") in Canada. Normally this is "where its board of directors exercises its responsibilities", but "where the facts are that the central management and control is exercised by a shareholder who is resident and making decisions in another country, the corporation will be found to be resident where the shareholder resides": *Garron [St. Michael Trust Corp., Fundy Settlement]*, 2012 SCC 14, paras. 8-9. See also *De Beers*, [1906] A.C. 455 (HL); *Birmount Holdings*, [1978] C.T.C. 358 (FCA); *Gurd's Products*, [1985] 2 C.T.C. 85 (FCA); *Wood v. Holden*, [2006] EWCA Civ 26 (England & Wales Court of Appeal), leave to appeal to House of Lords denied June 14, 2006; *1143132 Ontario*, 2009 TCC 477; *Bywater Investments [Hua Wang Bank]*, [2016] HCA 45 (Australia); *Development Securities*, [2020] EWCA Civ 1705 (England, reversing UK Upper Tribunal) (Jersey directors were acting under UK parent's instructions [Wang & Tamm, "Parental Influence", 2567 *Tax Topics* (CCH) 1-4 (May 18, 2021)]); *Landbouwbedrijf Backx*, 2019 FCA 310, para. 10 (on this point upholding the TCC, which had noted the director merely "carried out clerical and administrative functions" for the shareholders) [Arrigo, "Landbouwbedrijf", XVI(1) *Corporate Structures and Groups* (Federated Press) 6-12 (2020)]. A corp seeking to remain non-resident, whose directors' meetings are held by phone, should ensure that a majority of directors attending each meeting are outside Canada. For software that assists in determining CM&C see *Central Management & Control Classifier* at bluejlegal.com.

See also Baker & Gamble, "Corporate Residence", 2010 Cdn Tax Foundation conference report, 24:1-23; Elawny, "*Mark Higgins Rallying v. HMRC* — A Guide to Management and Control", 2115 *Tax Topics* (CCH) 1-4 (Sept. 20, 2012); Nitikman, "Central Management and Control and the Rule in *Esquire Nominees*", XX(1) *International Tax Planning* (Federated Press) 1368-75 (2015), discussing cases overseas; Loomer, "The Disjunction Between Corporate Residence and Corporate Taxation", 63(1) *Canadian Tax Journal* 91-132 (2015); Aprile & Moussadji, "Corporate Residence", *Taxnet Pro* Tax Disputes Centre (Nov. 2017, 32pp); Heakes, "Corporate Residence: An Ongoing Dilemma", XXI(3) *International Tax Planning* (Federated Press) 2-6 (2017) (discusses *Development Securities* UK case).

If CM&C of a U.S. subsidiary's affairs is in Canada, the company must file a T2 return, and its income from active business will be taxable surplus rather than exempt surplus under 113(1): VIEWS doc 2000-0054455.

I.T. Application Rules: 69 (meaning of "chapter 148 of ...").

Interpretation Bulletins: IT-451R: Deemed disposition and acquisition on ceasing to be or becoming resident in Canada.

CRA Audit Manual: 15.4.0: Residency.

(5) Deemed non-resident [by treaty] — Notwithstanding any other provision of this Act (other than paragraph 126(1.1)(a)), a per-

son is deemed not to be resident in Canada at a time if, at that time, the person would, but for this subsection and any tax treaty, be resident in Canada for the purposes of this Act but is, under a tax treaty with another country, resident in the other country and not resident in Canada.

Related Provisions: 128.1(4) — Corporation becoming non-resident; 219.1(1) — Tax payable when corporation becomes non-resident; Canada-U.S. Tax Treaty:Art. IV:2, IV:3; Canada-U.K. Tax Treaty:Art. 4:2, 4:3 — Treaty tie-breaker rules.

Notes: 250(5) treats as non-resident a person who is resident in Canada (see Notes to 250(1)) but is deemed resident in another country by tax treaty "tie-breaker" rules (see Notes to Canada-US treaty Art. IV:2): e.g., *Davis*, 2018 TCC 110. This prevents taxpayers from arguing they are not subject to Part I tax as a resident of Canada (due to a treaty), but also not subject to Part XIII withholding tax because they are still resident in Canada under the Act. However, 250(5) does not apply to certain individuals, due to a transitional rule in the 1998 amendment below.

"Country" includes Hong Kong and Taiwan: see Notes to 219.2.

See Notes to Canada-U.S. Tax Treaty:Art. IV:2 for cases deeming a person non-resident due to 250(5).

CRA stated that "for purposes of this Act" need not mean "for all purposes of this Act": VIEWS doc 2001-0074395; 2005 STEP Conference Roundtable q. 10 (step.ca). However, in *Antle*, [2010] 4 C.T.C. 2327 (TCC) [aff'd on other grounds 2010 CarswellNat 3894 (FCA) and leave to appeal to SCC denied], paras. 124-126, the TCC (though quoting an old version of 250(5)) ruled that 250(5) does not apply to (pre-2008) 94(1)(c), since that applies only for purposes of Part I, not the Act.

In 2002, Conrad Black was "resident" in both Canada and the UK, but not subject to UK tax on Canadian-source income because he was not domiciled there. He was deemed resident in the UK under the Canada-UK treaty tiebreaker rule, but since 250(5) did not apply (due to the transitional rule below), Canada could tax him, avoiding "double non-taxation": *Black*, 2014 FCA 275 (leave to appeal denied 2015 CarswellNat 1274 (SCC)).

250(5) amended by 2001 technical bill to add "(other than paragraph 126(1.1)(a))", effective June 28, 1999 (and preserving the grandfathering below).

250(5) amended by 1998 Budget, effective after Feb. 24, 1998 except that (as per 2001 technical bill, Part 7), if on that day an individual who would, but for a tax treaty, be resident in Canada for the purposes of the Act is, under the treaty, resident in another country, the amendment does not apply to the individual until the first time after Feb. 24, 1998 at which the individual becomes, under a tax treaty, resident in a country other than Canada. Where the amendment does not apply (e.g., *Black* above), read:

> (5) Corporation deemed not resident — Notwithstanding subsection (4), for the purposes of this Act, a corporation, other than a prescribed corporation, shall be deemed to be not resident in Canada at any time if, by virtue of an agreement or convention between the Government of Canada and the government of another country that has the force of law in Canada, it would at that time, if it had income from a source outside Canada, not be subject to tax on that income under Part I.

Regulations: No prescribed corporations to date.

Interpretation Bulletins: IT-137R3: Additional tax on certain corporations carrying on business in Canada.

(5.1) Continued corporation — Where a corporation is at any time (in this subsection referred to as the "time of continuation") granted articles of continuance (or similar constitutional documents) in a particular jurisdiction, the corporation shall

(a) for the purposes of applying this Act (other than subsection (4)) in respect of all times from the time of continuation until the time, if any, of continuation in a different jurisdiction, be deemed to have been incorporated in the particular jurisdiction and not to have been incorporated in any other jurisdiction; and

(b) for the purpose of applying subsection (4) in respect of all times from the time of continuation until the time, if any, of continuation in a different jurisdiction, be deemed to have been incorporated in the particular jurisdiction at the time of continuation and not to have been incorporated in any other jurisdiction.

Related Provisions: 54"superficial loss"(c) — Non-application of superficial loss rule where corporation has elected for 250(5.1) to apply before 1993; 88.1 — Repeal of 88.1 before 1993 where corporation so elects; 128.1 — Effect of becoming or ceasing to be resident in Canada; 219.1(1) — Tax on corporate emigration; Canada-U.S. Tax Treaty:Art. IV:3 — Continuation in other jurisdictions.

Notes: 250(5.1) added by 1993 technical bill. The date on which a corporation is granted articles of continuation or similar constitutional documents is the corporation's "time of continuation". 250(5.1) applies as follows:

- If the time of continuation is July 1994 or later, 250(5.1) applies.
- If the time of continuation is January 1, 1993 through June 30, 1994, then 250(5.1) applies, unless arrangements evidenced in writing for obtaining the articles or other documents were substantially advanced before December 21, 1992, *and* the corpo-

ration elected by notifying Revenue Canada in writing by December 31, 1994 to have 250(5.1) not apply. (This election is under para. 111(4)(b) of the 1993 technical bill, S.C. 1994, c. 21.)

- If the time of continuation is before 1993, then 250(5.1) applies only if the corporation elected by notifying Revenue Canada in writing by December 31, 1994 to have it apply. (This election is under para. 111(4)(a) of the 1993 technical bill.) If this was done, then notwithstanding 152(4)-(5), such assessments and determinations in respect of any taxation year shall be made as are necessary to give effect to the election.

The basic principle of 250(5.1) is that the continued corporation is treated as having been incorporated in the jurisdiction into which it has continued. The corporation is not deemed to have disposed of its assets, nor are its shareholders deemed to have disposed of their shares: VIEWS doc 2005-0147131R3. A corporation incorporated in a third country but continued in a US jurisdiction is considered resident in the US for treaty purposes: doc 2002-0157355. See also 2010-0388741E5.

See also Jack Bernstein, "Corporate Continuance", 16(10) *Canadian Tax Highlights* (ctf.ca) 8-9 (Oct. 2008), re using continuance in tax planning.

Interpretation Bulletins: IT-137R3: Additional tax on certain corporations carrying on business in Canada.

(6) Residence of international shipping corporation — For the purposes of this Act, a corporation that was incorporated or otherwise formed under the laws of a country other than Canada or of a state, province or other political subdivision of such a country is deemed to be resident in that country throughout a taxation year and not to be resident in Canada at any time in the year, if

(a) the corporation

(i) has international shipping as its principal business in the year, or

(ii) holds eligible interests in one or more eligible entities throughout the year and at no time in the year is the total of the cost amounts to it of all those eligible interests and of all debts owing to it by an eligible entity in which an eligible interest is held by it, by a person related to it or by a partnership affiliated with it less than 50% of the total of the cost amounts to it of all its property;

(b) all or substantially all the corporation's gross revenue for the year consists of any one or more of

(i) gross revenue from international shipping,

(ii) gross revenue from an eligible interest held by it in an eligible entity, and

(iii) interest on a debt owing by an eligible entity in which an eligible interest is held by it, by a person related to it or by a partnership affiliated with it; and

(c) the corporation was not granted articles of continuance in Canada before the end of the year.

Related Provisions: 81(1)(c) — Amounts not included in income — ship or aircraft of non-resident; 250(6.01) — Partner's gross revenue; 250(6.02), (6.03) — Service provider deemed to have international shipping as principal business; 250(6.04) — Eligible interest and eligible entity; Canada-U.S. Tax Treaty:Art. VIII — International shipping.

Notes: See Notes to 81(1)(c) and 248(1)"international shipping". For the meaning of "principal business" in (a)(i), see 20(1)(bb) Notes. For "used primarily" in (a)(i) see 73(3) Notes. CRA considers that "substantially all", used in (b), means 90% or more.

250(6) before para. (c) amended by 2014 budget bill #2, for taxation years that begin after July 12, 2013.

250(6) amended by 1995-97 technical bill (effective for 1995 and later taxation years); added by 1991 technical bill.

(6.01) Partner's gross revenue [international shipping] — For the purposes of paragraph (6)(b), an amount of profit allocated from a partnership to a member of the partnership for a taxation year is deemed to be gross revenue of the member from [the] member's interest in the partnership for the year.

Notes: 250(6.01) added by 2014 budget bill #2, effective for taxation years that begin after July 12, 2013.

(6.02) Service providers — Subsection (6.03) applies to a corporation, trust or partnership (in this subsection and subsection (6.03) referred to as the "relevant entity") for a taxation year if

(a) the relevant entity does not satisfy the condition in subparagraph (6)(a)(i), determined without reference to subsection (6.03);

(b) all or substantially all the gross revenue of the relevant entity for the year consists of any one or more of

(i) gross revenue from the provision of services to one or more eligible entities, other than services described in any of paragraphs (a) to (h) of the definition "international shipping" in subsection 248(1),

(ii) gross revenue from international shipping,

(iii) gross revenue from an eligible interest held by it in an eligible entity, and

(iv) interest on a debt owing by an eligible entity in which an eligible interest is held by it or a person related to it;

(c) either the relevant entity is a subsidiary wholly-owned corporation (as defined in subsection 87(1.4)) of the eligible entity referred to in paragraph (b) or an eligible interest in each eligible entity referred to in paragraph (b) is held throughout the year by

(i) the relevant entity,

(ii) one or more persons related to the relevant entity (if the relevant entity and each such person is a corporation), or persons or partnerships affiliated with the relevant entity (in any other case), or

(iii) any combination of the relevant entity and persons or partnerships described in subparagraph (ii); and

(d) all or substantially all the shares of the capital stock of, or interests in, the relevant entity are held, directly or indirectly through one or more subsidiary wholly-owned corporations (as defined in subsection 87(1.4)), throughout the year by one or more corporations, trusts or partnerships that would be eligible entities if they did not own shares of, or interests in, the relevant entity.

Notes: 250(6.02)-(6.03) facilitate the use of single-purpose entities that provide services within the shipping group. They deem certain ancillary services provided by a member of an international shipping group in support of core shipping activities carried on by members of the group to qualify as international shipping activities: once the conditions in (6.02) are met, (6.03) applies so that such a service provider will be considered to have international shipping as its principal business, allowing it to potentially qualify for the deeming rule in 250(6). (Finance Technical Notes)

250(6.02) added by 2014 budget bill #2, for tax years that begin after July 12, 2013.

(6.03) Service providers — If this subsection applies for a taxation year, then for the purposes of subsection (6) and paragraph 81(1)(c),

(a) the relevant entity is deemed to have international shipping as its principal business in the year; and

(b) the gross revenue described in subparagraph (6.02)(b)(i) is deemed to be gross revenue from international shipping.

Related Provisions: 250(6.02) — Conditions for subsec. (6.03) to apply.

Notes: See Notes to 250(6.02). 250(6.03) added by 2014 budget bill #2, effective for taxation years that begin after July 12, 2013.

(6.04) Definitions — The following definitions apply in this subsection and subsections (6) to (6.03).

"**eligible entity**", for a taxation year, means

(a) a corporation that is deemed by subsection (6) to be resident in a country other than Canada for the year; or

(b) a partnership or trust, if

(i) it satisfies the conditions in subparagraph (6)(a)(i) or (ii), and

(ii) all or substantially all its gross revenue for the year consists of any combination of amounts described in any of subparagraphs (6)(b)(i) to (iii).

Notes: Definition added by 2014 budget bill #2, effective for taxation years that begin after July 12, 2013.

"eligible interest" means

(a) in respect of a corporation, shares of the capital stock of the corporation that

(i) give the holders of those shares not less than 25% of the votes that could be cast at an annual meeting of the shareholders of the corporation, and

(ii) have a fair market value that is not less than 25% of the fair market value of all the issued and outstanding shares of the capital stock of the corporation;

(b) in respect of a trust, an interest as a beneficiary (as defined in subsection 108(1)) under the trust with a fair market value that is not less than 25% of the fair market value of all the interests of all beneficiaries under the trust; and

(c) in respect of a partnership, an interest as a member of the partnership with a fair market value that is not less than 25% of the fair market value of all the membership interests in the partnership.

Related Provisions: 250(6.05) — Holdings by related and affiliated persons included.

Notes: Definition added by 2014 budget bill #2, effective for taxation years that begin after July 12, 2013.

(6.05) Holdings in eligible entities — For the purpose of determining whether a person or partnership (in this subsection referred to as the "holder") holds an eligible interest in an eligible entity in subsections (6) to (6.04), the holder is deemed to hold all of the shares or interests, as the case may be, in the eligible entity held by

(a) the holder;

(b) if the holder is a corporation,

(i) each corporation related to the holder, and

(ii) each person, other than a corporation, or partnership that is affiliated with the holder; and

(c) if the holder is not a corporation, each person or partnership affiliated with the holder.

Notes: 250(6.05) added by 2014 budget bill #2, for taxation years that begin after July 12, 2013.

(6.1) Residence of *inter vivos* trusts — For the purposes of provisions of this Act that apply to a trust for a taxation year only where the trust has been resident in Canada throughout the year, where a particular trust ceases at any time to exist and the particular trust was resident in Canada immediately before that time, the particular trust is deemed to be resident in Canada throughout the period that begins at that time and ends at the end of the year.

Related Provisions: 132(6.2) — Parallel rule for mutual fund trust that ceases to qualify as such.

Notes: 250(6.1) provides that a trust that ceases to exist at any time in a calendar year, and that was resident in Canada immediately before ceasing to exist, is deemed resident in Canada during the rest of the year. CRA takes the position that a trust's taxation year is generally not affected by the termination of the trust. 250(6.1) is meant to avoid unintended consequences of CRA's position that arise under provisions that require a trust to be resident in Canada throughout a taxation year (e.g., flow-through rules under 104). 250(6.1) is similar to 132(6.2).

250(6.1) added by 2001 technical bill, effective for 1990 and later taxation years.

Income Tax Folios: S6-F1-C1: Residence of a trust or estate [replaces IT-447].

(7) [Repealed]

Notes: 250(7) repealed by 2011 budget bill #2, for 2012 and later taxation years. Under amended 211.6, the requirement that a qualifying environmental trust be resident in the province in which the qualifying site is located has been dropped.

250(7) added by 1994 Budget effective 1994 and amended by 1997 Budget, effective 1996.

Definitions [s. 250]: "affiliated" — 251.1; "amount" — 248(1); "beneficiary" — 248(25) [Notes]; "business" — 248(1); "Canada" — 255, *Interpretation Act* 35(1); "carried on business in Canada" — 253; "child" — 252(1); "common-law partner" — 248(1); "controlled" — 256(6), (6.1); "corporation" — 248(1), *Interpretation Act* 35(1); "cost amount" — 248(1); "eligible entity", "eligible interest" — 250(6.04); "employment" — 248(1); "fair market value" — see 69(1) Notes; "gross revenue" — 248(1), 250(6.01); "incorporated in Canada" — 248(1)"corporation incorporated in

Canada"; "individual", "international shipping", "international traffic", "non-resident", "overseas Canadian Forces school staff" — 248(1); "partnership" — see 96(1) Notes; "person", "prescribed", "property" — 248(1); "province" — *Interpretation Act* 35(1); "qualifying environmental trust" — 248(1); "related" — 251(2)–(6); "relevant entity" — 250(6.02); "servant" — 248(1)"employment"; "share", "shareholder" — 248(1); "subsidiary wholly-owned corporation" — 87(1.4); "tax treaty" — 248(1); "taxation year" — 249; "trust" — 104(1), 248(1), (3).

250.1 Non-resident person's taxation year and income — For greater certainty, unless the context requires otherwise

(a) a taxation year of a non-resident person shall be determined, except as otherwise permitted by the Minister, in the same manner as the taxation year of a person resident in Canada; and

(b) a person for whom income for a taxation year is determined in accordance with this Act includes a non-resident person.

Related Provisions: 2(3) — Tax on taxable income earned in Canada of non-resident; 115(1) — Calculation of taxable income earned in Canada of non-resident.

Notes: 250.1(b) clarifies that a person for whom "income" for the year is determined under the Act includes a non-resident. It is a non-resident's "taxable income earned in Canada" that is relevant for Part I tax liability (see 115(1)). However, a non-resident does, in a few cases, have "income" for purposes of the Act. For example, there are references to a non-resident's "income" (rather than "taxable income earned in Canada") in 212(1)(c), 216(1)(b) and 217(3)(b)(ii). Also, the "income" of a non-resident person may affect the tax liability of a Canadian resident (e.g., 104(13)).

In *Marino*, 2020 TCC 50 (under appeal to FCA), 250.1 did not entitle a non-resident with no income in Canada to generate a tuition credit that could be carried forward and used when he was resident (paras. 37-40 explain what 250.1 is for).

250.1 does not cause 249(4) to apply to the acquisition of control of a foreign affiliate: VIEWS doc 2002-0174105. It does cause a capital gain to be only half-taxable to the beneficiary: 2012-0448021E5.

On a foreign affiliate's continuation into a new jurisdiction, a change in fiscal period will be allowed only if required by the new jurisdiction: VIEWS doc 2005-0165131E5.

250.1 added by 2001 technical bill, effective December 18, 1999.

Definitions [s. 250.1]: "Minister", "non-resident", "person" — 248(1); "resident in Canada" — 250; "taxation year" — 249.

251. (1) Arm's length — For the purposes of this Act,

(a) related persons shall be deemed not to deal with each other at arm's length;

(b) a taxpayer and a personal trust (other than a trust described in any of paragraphs (a) to (e.1) of the definition "trust" in subsection 108(1)) are deemed not to deal with each other at arm's length if the taxpayer, or any person not dealing at arm's length with the taxpayer, would be beneficially interested in the trust if subsection 248(25) were read without reference to subclauses 248(25)(b)(iii)(A)(II) to (IV); and

(c) in any other case, it is a question of fact whether persons not related to each other are, at a particular time, dealing with each other at arm's length.

Related Provisions

Determining whether persons deal at arm's length (AL) or not (NAL): 7(1.11) — Whether mutual fund trust AL with corporation for purposes of stock option rules; 55(4), 55(5)(e) — Rules for capital gains strips; 66(17) — Flow-through shares — partnership and corporation deemed NAL; 84.1(2)(b), (d), 212.1(3)(c) — Surplus stripping rules — deemed NAL; 95(2.1) — Taxpayer and FA deemed AL for certain FAPI purposes; 107.4(4) — Certain dispositions by trust deemed NAL; 143.2(14) — Parties deemed NAL for tax shelter cost calculation where information located outside Canada; 212.3(26) — Determining "related" and "control" for a trust for certain purposes; 248(25) — Meaning of "beneficially interested"; 251(2)–(6) — Related persons; 260(9.1) — Securities lending arrangement — deemed NAL for non-resident withholding tax; Reg. 1102(20) — Taxpayers deemed AL for certain purposes relating to depreciable property.

Effect of being NAL: 18(4), (5) — Thin capitalization rules — limitation on interest deduction; 69(1) — NAL transfer of property deemed at fair market value in at least one direction; 84.1(1), 212.1(1) — NAL sale of shares — surplus stripping; 186(2) — Corporation deemed controlled for Part IV tax purposes; 247 — Calculation of profit on NAL transactions with non-residents (transfer pricing).

Notes: See 251(2)-(6) on the meaning of "related", and Income Tax Folio S1-F5-C1 (replaces former IT-419R2); ¶1.20 presumes that 2-3 unrelated shareholders who together control a company act together to control it, absent evidence the decision-making process is "effectively deadlocked". For criticism of some interpretations in the Folio see CBA/CPA Canada Joint Committee on Taxation letter to CRA, June 16, 2014.

251(1)(c) applies "at a particular time", which is the relevant time for the rule in question, e.g. on property acquisition for 69(1)(a): *Keybrand Foods*, 2020 FCA 201, para. 35.

Despite 251(1)(c), the Tax Court stated that "whether, on the facts, there is in law an arm's-length relationship is necessarily a question of law... All that para. 251(1)[c] means is that in determining whether, as a matter of law, unrelated persons are at arm's length, the factual underpinning of the relationship must be ascertained." *RMM Canadian Enterprises (Equilease)*, 1997 CarswellNat 400, *per* Bowman J.

The tests used to determine non-arm's-length (NAL) are: (a) the existence of a common mind that directs the bargaining for both parties, (b) parties to a transaction acting in concert without separate interests, and (c) *de facto* control: *McLarty*, 2008 SCC 26, para. 62. In *Remai*, 2009 FCA 340, R and R's nephew's corp were found to deal at AL. In *Siracusa*, 2003 TCC 941, a 1/3 shareholder and director (widow of one of the company's 3 founders) was held to be at AL with the company. In *Alberta Printed Circuits*, 2011 TCC 232, Barbados company Bco set up to do part of Canadian company Cco's production work was held not to be at arm's length with Cco, as the two acted in concert, had a common mind, and 2/3 of BCo's profits went via offshore life insurance to Cco's owners (the Court held that the Bco shares owned through insurance policies were beneficially owned by the beneficiaries). See also VIEWS doc 2010-0373181C6 (overlapping boards may indicate common control).

Where parties act in concert to direct or dictate the conduct of another, the "mind" that directs may be that of the combination as a whole acting in concert, or of any of them in carrying out particular parts or functions of what the common object involves: *Swiss Bank*, [1972] C.T.C. 614 (SCC). (Note that parties having a common purpose to a *transaction* is not necessarily the same as a common mind.)

"Parties are not considered to be dealing with each other at arm's length if one person dictates the terms of the bargain on both sides of the transaction": *Brown*, 2003 FCA 192 (leave to appeal denied 2004 CarswellNat 84 (SCC)) (software shelter). In *McLarty* (SCC, above), the trial judge was entitled to find the parties were at arm's length even though the purchaser's involvement in determining the purchase price was minimal. In *Baxter*, 2006 TCC 230 (rev'd on other grounds 2007 FCA 172; leave to appeal denied 2007 CarswellNat 3625) (software shelter), B was found to deal at AL: "There was no control exercised by either party over the other. There was no common mind." There was no evidence leading to CRA's conclusion that because of a "lack of competing interests" the investor "acquiesced" to the vendor's terms. For more on AL see *Sheldon's Engineering*, [1955] C.T.C. 174 (SCC) ("controlling shareholder dictating the terms of the bargain": para. 15); *Robson Leather*, [1977] C.T.C. 132 (FCA) (directing mind "had *de facto* control of both sides of the transaction": para. 32); *Petro-Canada*, 2004 FCA 158 (leave to appeal denied 2004 CarswellNat 4108); *Aeronautic Development*, 2018 FCA 67 (leave to appeal denied 2019 CarswellNat 595); *Keybrand Foods*, 2020 FCA 201 (same as *Robson Leather*); *Merritt Estate*, [1969] C.T.C. 207 (Exch. Ct) ("same person was dictating the terms of the bargain on behalf of both parties": para. 60); *McCoy*, 2003 TCC 508; *Poulin*, 2016 TCC 154, paras. 58-84 (aff'd as *Turgeon*, 2017 FCA 103); *Boifor Equipment*, 2018 TCC 53, paras. 38-44, aff'd 2019 FCA 69 (where 2 shareholders each own 50% of Holdco that controls corp; CRA accepts *Boifor*: doc 2020-0852181C6 [2020 APFF q.6]); *Godcharles*, 2020 QCCQ 2219 (acting in concert); *Damis Properties (Sabel Investments)* (under appeal to FCA as *Microbjo Properties*), 2021 TCC 24, paras. 159-203.

It is an error of law for the Court not to make a finding of NAL before considering the value of property on a sale as being relevant under 69(1): *Downey*, 2006 FCA 353.

Note the extremely wide definition of "beneficially interested" in 248(25).

For more CRA interpretation see VIEWS docs 2009-0312791I7 (taxpayer is related to his RRSP); 2011-0428701E5 (limited partner with 98% interest in LP may be related to it); 2012-0465651E5 (non-resident corp owning 27% of Canco might not be at AL); 2014-0539791R3 (creditors reaching CCAA settlement with debtor trust were AL); 2015-0578561C6 [2015 STEP q.12] (estate deemed related to beneficiary due to 251(1)(b)).

See also Lamarre et al., *Taxation of Corporate Reorganizations* (Carswell, 3rd ed., 2019), §2.1; Moskowitz, "Dealing at Arm's Length", 1987 Cdn Tax Foundation conference report, 33:1-24; Eng, "The Arm's Length Rules", 1988 conference report, 13:1-31; Stack, "Arm's Length", 1997 conference report, 16:1-15; Mah & Meredith, "Factual Non-Arm's Length Relationships", 2014 conference report, 16:1-24.

251(1)(c) amended by 2002-2013 technical bill, effective Dec. 24, 1998, to change "where paragraph (b) does not apply" to "in any other case". Even without this amendment, 251(1)(c) already had the same meaning: *Remai*, 2009 FCA 340.

251(1)(b) renumbered (c) and new (b) added by 2001 technical bill, effective Dec. 24, 1998 except that, for the purpose of applying 248(1)"taxable Canadian property", the amendment does not apply in respect of property acquired before Dec. 24, 1998.

Income Tax Folios: S1-F5-C1: Related persons and dealing at arm's length [replaces IT-419R2]; S3-F10-C2: Prohibited investments — RRSPs, RRIFs and TFSAs.

Advance Tax Rulings: ATR-58: Divisive reorganization.

Forms: T2 Sched. 9: Related and associated corporations.

(2) Definition of "related persons" — For the purpose of this Act, "related persons", or persons related to each other, are

(a) individuals connected by blood relationship, marriage or common-law partnership or adoption;

(b) a corporation and

(i) a person who controls the corporation, if it is controlled by one person,

(ii) a person who is a member of a related group that controls the corporation, or

(iii) any person related to a person described in subparagraph (i) or (ii); and

(c) any two corporations

(i) if they are controlled by the same person or group of persons,

(ii) if each of the corporations is controlled by one person and the person who controls one of the corporations is related to the person who controls the other corporation,

(iii) if one of the corporations is controlled by one person and that person is related to any member of a related group that controls the other corporation,

(iv) if one of the corporations is controlled by one person and that person is related to each member of an unrelated group that controls the other corporation,

(v) if any member of a related group that controls one of the corporations is related to each member of an unrelated group that controls the other corporation, or

(vi) if each member of an unrelated group that controls one of the corporations is related to at least one member of an unrelated group that controls the other corporation.

Related Provisions: 55(4) — Anti-avoidance — persons deemed not related for purposes of s. 55; 55(5)(e) — Siblings deemed not related for purposes of s. 55; 80(2)(j) — Interpretation of "related" for debt forgiveness rules; 104(5.7)(b) — Designated contributor; 190.15(6) — Related financial institution; 248(14) — Corporations deemed related for certain purposes; 251(3) — Corporations related through a third corporation; 251(3.1), (3.2) — Amalgamated corporation deemed related to predecessors; 251(6) — Meaning of blood relationship, marriage and adoption; 256(6), (6.1) — Meaning of "controlled"; Canada-U.S. Tax Treaty:Art. IX:2 — Meaning of "related" for treaty purposes.

Notes: A key consequence of being "related" is being deemed not to deal at arm's length (251(1)(a)), triggering rules such as 69(1) and 160(1).

In *Gentile Holdings*, 2020 TCC 29, paras. 20-22, Mr. & Mrs. G owned all shares of Holdco, which owned all shares of Opco. The Court gave detailed reasons for finding Holdco and Opco related. It should have simply applied 251(2)(b)(i): Holdco controlled Opco.

For "connected" in 251(2)(a), see 251(6).

A person who controls a corporation is not part of a group that controls it: *Southside Car Market*, [1982] C.T.C. 214 (FCTD); VIEWS docs 2010-0363341E5, 2014-0547551E5; but for s. 256, see 256(1.2)(b)(i). See also Notes to 111(5), 251(6) and 256(6)-(7) on "control". See also May 2016 Alberta CPA Roundtable (tinyurl.com/cra-abtax), q. 20 (determining when a group acquires control).

See Income Tax Folio S1-F5-C1 ¶1.17-1.29; VIEWS docs 2003-0054211E5 (2 entities controlled by same provincial government are related, but municipality is not considered controlled by the province); 2007-0246721E5; 2009-031189117 (trust is considered related to beneficiary who is related to the trustee); 2010-0373141C6; 2012-0470931E5 (corp owned by spouses is related to corp owned by their children); 2016-066593117; 2018-0783741E5 (partnership agreement determines control of corp held through partnership); 2018-078756117 (corps are related where interest in one is held through a partnership).

A trust (or estate) is not related to any person (other than a corporation it controls): *Wright Estate*, 1996 CarswellNat 2886 (TCC), para. 27 (but see 251(1)(b)).

See also Diep & Micallef, "Associated, Affiliated and Related Transactions", 2005 Cdn Tax Foundation conference report, 38:1-14 and 39:1-15; Wen, "Partnership and the Meaning of Related", 19(4) *Tax for the Owner-Manager* (ctf.ca) 4-5 (Oct. 2019); Ideias, "Related, Affiliated and Associated Rules: What a Tax Planner Needs to Know" (*Taxnet Pro* Tax & Estate Planning Centre, 2021, 11pp).

251(2)(a) amended by 2000 same-sex partners bill, last change effective 2001.

Income Tax Folios: S1-F3-C1: Child care expense deduction [replaces IT-495R3]; S1-F5-C1: Related persons and dealing at arm's length [replaces IT-419R2]; S3-F10-C2: Prohibited investments — RRSPs, RRIFs and TFSAs.

Interpretation Bulletins: IT-363R2: Deferred profit sharing plans — deductibility of employer contributions and taxation of amounts received by a beneficiary (cancelled); IT-513R: Personal tax credits.

Forms: T2 Sched. 9: Related and associated corporations.

(3) Corporations related through a third corporation — Where two corporations are related to the same corporation within the meaning of subsection (2), they shall, for the purposes of subsections (1) and (2), be deemed to be related to each other.

Notes: See VIEWS doc 2014-0538071C6 [2014 APFF q.17] (CRA considers that where 251(3) applies, the parties form related group even though owners are not related).

(3.1) Relation where amalgamation or merger — Where there has been an amalgamation or merger of two or more corporations and the new corporation formed as a result of the amalgamation or merger and any predecessor corporation would have been related immediately before the amalgamation or merger if the new corporation were in existence at that time, and if the persons who were the shareholders of the new corporation immediately after the amalgamation or merger were the shareholders of the new corporation at that time, the new corporation and any such predecessor corporation shall be deemed to have been related persons.

Related Provisions: 251(3.2) — Further deeming on amalgamation of related corporations.

Notes: For an example of 251(3.1) applying see *Dow Chemical*, 2008 FCA 231.

Income Tax Folios: S1-F5-C1: Related persons and dealing at arm's length [replaces IT-419R2]; S4-F7-C1: Amalgamations of Canadian corporations [replaces IT-474R2].

(3.2) Amalgamation of related corporations — Where there has been an amalgamation or merger of 2 or more corporations each of which was related (otherwise than because of a right referred to in paragraph (5)(b)) to each other immediately before the amalgamation or merger, the new corporation formed as a result of the amalgamation or merger and each of the predecessor corporations is[32] deemed to have been related to each other.

Notes: For an example of 251(3.2) applying see *Dow Chemical*, 2008 FCA 231.

251(3.2) added by 1995-97 technical bill, for amalgamations and mergers after 1996.

Income Tax Folios: S4-F7-C1: Amalgamations of Canadian corporations [replaces IT-474R2].

(4) Definitions concerning groups — In this Act,

"related group" means a group of persons each member of which is related to every other member of the group;

Notes: 251(4)"related group" was 251(4)(a) before RSC 1985 (5th Supp) consolidation, effective December 1, 1991.

Income Tax Folios: S1-F5-C1: Related persons and dealing at arm's length [replaces IT-419R2].

"unrelated group" means a group of persons that is not a related group.

Income Tax Folios: S1-F5-C1: Related persons and dealing at arm's length [replaces IT-419R2].

Notes: 251(4)"related group" was 251(4)(a), and "unrelated group" was 251(4)(b), before RSC 1985 (5th Supp) consolidation, effective December 1, 1991.

(5) Control by related groups, options, etc. — For the purposes of subsection (2) and the definition "Canadian-controlled private corporation" in subsection 125(7),

(a) where a related group is in a position to control a corporation, it shall be deemed to be a related group that controls the corporation whether or not it is part of a larger group by which the corporation is in fact controlled;

(b) where at any time a person has a right under a contract, in equity or otherwise, either immediately or in the future and either absolutely or contingently,

(i) to, or to acquire, shares of the capital stock of a corporation or to control the voting rights of such shares, the person shall, except where the right is not exercisable at that time because the exercise thereof is contingent on the death, bankruptcy or permanent disability of an individual, be deemed to have the same position in relation to the control of the corporation as if the person owned the shares at that time,

(ii) to cause a corporation to redeem, acquire or cancel any shares of its capital stock owned by other shareholders of the corporation, the person shall, except where the right is not

exercisable at that time because the exercise thereof is contingent on the death, bankruptcy or permanent disability of an individual, be deemed to have the same position in relation to the control of the corporation as if the shares were so redeemed, acquired or cancelled by the corporation at that time,

(iii) to, or to acquire or control, voting rights in respect of shares of the capital stock of a corporation, the person is, except where the right is not exercisable at that time because its exercise is contingent on the death, bankruptcy or permanent disability of an individual, deemed to have the same position in relation to the control of the corporation as if the person could exercise the voting rights at that time, or

(iv) to cause the reduction of voting rights in respect of shares, owned by other shareholders, of the capital stock of a corporation, the person is, except where the right is not exercisable at that time because its exercise is contingent on the death, bankruptcy or permanent disability of an individual, deemed to have the same position in relation to the control of the corporation as if the voting rights were so reduced at that time; and

(c) where a person owns shares in two or more corporations, the person shall as shareholder of one of the corporations be deemed to be related to himself, herself or itself as shareholder of each of the other corporations.

Related Provisions: 17(11.1) — Limitation on 251(5)(b) re loans to non-residents; 110.6(14)(b) — Right under share purchase agreement does not trigger 251(5)(b) for purposes of capital gains exemption; 256(6), (6.1) — Meaning of "controlled"; 256(8) — Deemed acquisition of shares.

Notes: Under 251(5)(b), a right to purchase shares can create control and thus deem a corp not to be a Canadian-controlled private corporation; but it does not affect the capital gains exemption, due to 110.6(14)(b). See *Durocher*, 2015 TCC 297, para. 76 (aff'd 2016 FCA 299).

See Income Tax Folio S1-F5-C1 ¶1.22-1.29, and VIEWS doc 2017-0709171C6 [2017 APFF q.17]: CRA's view is that for 251(5)(b)(i), a separate determination of "control" must be made for each person that has a right. This contrasts with 256(1.4)(a), where "control" is determined taking into account all the shares that all persons with a right are deemed to own. See 2003-0048571C6, 2004-0086761C6; Hickey, "Control: All Rights Exercised?", 12(4) *Canadian Tax Highlights* (ctf.ca) 7 (April 2004). For application on bankruptcy or insolvency see doc 2006-0167361E5. See also 256(1.4).

When 251(5)(b) deems A to control B, that does not undo any existing control of B by another person: *Ekamant Canada*, 2009 TCC 408, para. 23; VIEWS doc 2014-0524851E5.

An option that is prohibited by provincial legislation still exists for purposes of 251(5)(b): *Durocher*, 2015 TCC 297 (aff'd on other grounds 2016 FCA 299) [see also Notes to 9(1) under "Diverting income"].

Lyrtech RD, 2013 TCC 12, para. 55 (aff'd on other grounds 2014 FCA 267), held that a trust's discretionary beneficiaries do not have a "right" to the trust property for purposes of 251(5)(b).

In *Sedona Networks*, 2007 FCA 169, 251(5)(b)(i) applied when counting disqualifying shareholders for 125(7)"Canadian-controlled private corporation"(b): "the legal fiction created by 251(5)(b) is directed at the concept of ownership, not control. Once it is determined that a person has a right that falls within the scope of 251(5)(b), it is necessary to assume that the right is exercised and the related shares are actually acquired by the holder of the right" (para. 28).

In *ARTV*, 2016 QCCQ 8757, a shareholder's right to sell shares did not give the other shareholder a 251(5)(b) right for purposes of Quebec payroll tax. Similarly, in *Deans Knight*, 2019 TCC 76 (Crown's FCA appeal heard March 22/21), paras. 49-62, a right to sell shares to Mco did not give Mco a right to buy those shares (and 256(8) did not apply).

An agreement under which a non-resident will acquire a CCPC owned by a SIFT, subject to unitholder approval, is a "contingent" right falling under 251(5)(b): *Income Tax Technical News* 38; 2007 Cdn Tax Foundation conference report at 4:13.

A letter of intent can trigger 251(5)(b) if it creates enforceable rights: VIEWS doc 2014-0552711E5 [Stillwell, "CRA View — LOI May Engage 251(5)(b)", 12(9) *Tax Hyperion* (Carswell) 5-7 (Sept. 2015)]. See also 2007-0243371C6 (interaction with 110.6(14)(b) and *Chartier*); 2007-0246721E5 (various fact situations); 2009-0329941C6 (various examples of "a right to, or to acquire..."); 2009-034333117 (application to fact situation); 2010-037935117 (251(5)(b) does not apply to a right of first refusal); 2010-0373131C6 (presumption of acting in concert); 2010-0373141C6 (251(5)(c)); 2010-0380571E5 (251(5)(b)(ii) and 256(1.4)(b)); 2015-0565741E5 (251(5)(b) applies, 256(6) does not); 2016-0652971C6 [2016 APFF q.7] (automatic re-

---

[32] *Sic*. Should be "are" — ed.

demption of shares under shareholder agreement does not trigger 251(5)(b)); 2016-0662381E5 (CRA views on various scenarios); 2019-0812701C6 [2019 APFF q.11] (application to convertible debenture).

See also Bernstein, "Buy-Sell Provisions and Their Effect on Canadian Control of Private Corporations", 277 *The Estate Planner* (CCH) 6-11 (Feb. 2018); Brown & Kind, "A Right under a Contract", IX(1) *Personal Tax & Estate Planning* (Federated Press) 1-10 (2020) (problems caused by having a power of attorney).

See also Notes to 249(3.1) re the change in control of a CCPC triggered on signing a share purchase agreement.

251(5)(b) amended by 1995-97 technical bill (effective Apr. 27, 1995), 1991 technical bill.

Income Tax Folios: S1-F5-C1: Related persons and dealing at arm's length [replaces IT-419R2]; S3-F8-C1: Principal-business corporations in the resource industries [replaces IT-400]; S3-F10-C2: Prohibited investments — RRSPs, RRIFs and TFSAs.

Interpretation Bulletins: IT-64R4: Corporations: association and control; IT-243R4: Dividend refund to private corporations; IT-302R3: Losses of a corporation — the effect that acquisitions of control, amalgamations, and windings-up have on their deductibility; IT-458R2: Canadian-controlled private corporation.

I.T. Technical News: 38 (CCPC determination — impact of the *Sedona* decision; para. 251(5)(b) — conditional agreements).

Advance Tax Rulings: ATR-13: Corporations not associated.

(6) Blood relationship, etc. — For the purposes of this Act, persons are connected by

(a) blood relationship if one is the child or other descendant of the other or one is the brother or sister of the other;

(b) marriage if one is married to the other or to a person who is so connected by blood relationship to the other;

(b.1) common-law partnership if one is in a common-law partnership with the other or with a person who is connected by blood relationship to the other; and

(c) adoption if one has been adopted, either legally or in fact, as the child of the other or as the child of a person who is so connected by blood relationship (otherwise than as a brother or sister) to the other.

Notes: *"Adoption in fact"*: for detailed review of the case law see *Leidal*, 2003 TCC 671 (one cannot have an "adopted brother"). For CRA's criteria see Income Tax Folio S1-F5-C1 ¶1.16. See also 252(1) re extended meaning of "child".

Death: for the effect on relationships see Notes to 252(2).

Half-brothers and half-sisters (1 common parent) are related by blood: *Huntley*, 2010 TCC 625, para. 17; *Diktakis*, 2016 TCC 262, para. 34 (FCA appeal dismissed for delay A-464-16); VIEWS doc 2018-0755471E5.

Married persons are deemed related by 251(6)(b) and thus non-arm's length even if they are separated and the relationship has broken down: *Mathieu*, 2014 TCC 207, paras. 37-46.

A *newborn* was "related" to its parent retroactive to conception in *Pellerin*, 2015 TCC 130, due to Quebec civil law.

Stepbrothers (common-law spouses' sons from previous relationships) are related: VIEWS docs 9429945, 2004-0074051R3, 2015-0584261E5.

Uncles/aunts and their nieces/nephews (as defined in 252(2)(e)-(g)) are not "related" (except for 94(1)"successor beneficiary" and 191(3)(d)(ii)), and thus can be at arm's length, though they may be *factually* non-arm's length under 251(1)(c). See VIEWS doc 2014-0525071E5; Income Tax Folio S1-F5-C1 ¶1.13. Curiously, however, an *adopted* child is technically related to their niece or nephew: if A is natural parent of B who is natural parent of C, and A adopted D, then D and C are related due to 251(6)(c), since D "has been adopted" by A, who is "connected by blood relationship" to C. This was doubtless not intended by the drafters and has been pointed out to Finance; this wording has not changed since 1952.

251(6)(b.1) added by 2000 same-sex partners bill, effective 2001 or earlier.

Income Tax Folios: S1-F3-C1: Child care expense deduction [replaces IT-495R3]; S1-F5-C1: Related persons and dealing at arm's length [replaces IT-419R2].

Interpretation Bulletins: IT-513R: Personal tax credits.

Definitions [s. 251]: "adoption" — 251(6)(c); "beneficially interested" — 248(25); "blood relationship" — 251(6)(a); "brother" — 252(2); "child" — 252(1); "common-law partnership" — 248(1); "connected" — 251(6); "control", "controlled" — 256(6), (6.1); "corporation", "individual" — 248(1); "person" — 248(1); "personal trust" — 251.1; "related" — 251(2); "related group" — 251(4); "share", "shareholder" — 248(1); "sister" — 252(2); "unrelated group" — 251(4).

Income Tax Folios [s. 251]: S4-F7-C1: Amalgamations of Canadian corporations [replaces IT-474R2].

251.1 (1) Definition of "affiliated persons" — For the purposes of this Act, "affiliated persons", or persons affiliated with each other, are

(a) an individual and a spouse or common-law partner of the individual;

(b) a corporation and

(i) a person by whom the corporation is controlled,

(ii) each member of an affiliated group of persons by which the corporation is controlled, and

(iii) a spouse or common-law partner of a person described in subparagraph (i) or (ii);

(c) two corporations, if

(i) each corporation is controlled by a person, and the person by whom one corporation is controlled is affiliated with the person by whom the other corporation is controlled,

(ii) one corporation is controlled by a person, the other corporation is controlled by a group of persons, and each member of that group is affiliated with that person, or

(iii) each corporation is controlled by a group of persons, and each member of each group is affiliated with at least one member of the other group;

(d) a corporation and a partnership, if the corporation is controlled by a particular group of persons each member of which is affiliated with at least one member of a majority-interest group of partners of the partnership, and each member of that majority-interest group is affiliated with at least one member of the particular group;

(e) a partnership and a majority-interest partner of the partnership;

(f) two partnerships, if

(i) the same person is a majority-interest partner of both partnerships,

(ii) a majority-interest partner of one partnership is affiliated with each member of a majority-interest group of partners of the other partnership, or

(iii) each member of a majority-interest group of partners of each partnership is affiliated with at least one member of a majority-interest group of partners of the other partnership;

(g) a person and a trust, if the person

(i) is a majority-interest beneficiary of the trust, or

(ii) would, if this subsection were read without reference to this paragraph, be affiliated with a majority-interest beneficiary of the trust; and

(h) two trusts, if a contributor to one of the trusts is affiliated with a contributor to the other trust and

(i) a majority-interest beneficiary of one of the trusts is affiliated with a majority-interest beneficiary of the other trust,

(ii) a majority-interest beneficiary of one of the trusts is affiliated with each member of a majority-interest group of beneficiaries of the other trust, or

(iii) each member of a majority-interest group of beneficiaries of each of the trusts is affiliated with at least one member of a majority-interest group of beneficiaries of the other trust.

Related Provisions: 125.7(11) — Extended meaning of "affiliated" for Canada Emergency Rent Subsidy; 251.1(3), (4) — Definitions and interpretation; 256(6), (6.1) — Meaning of "controlled".

Notes: See Notes at end of 251.1, and Notes to 111(5) on the meaning of "control". Before March 23, 2004, a trust and its beneficiary were not affiliated, but transfers were held to violate GAAR in *Triad Gestco*, 2012 FCA 258 and *1207192 Ontario*, 2012 FCA 259 (leave to appeal denied 2013 CarswellOnt 3394 (SCC)), so losses were denied. In *Triad*, the TCC took the 2004 Budget amendment as evidence that it was abusive to use a trust to bypass the affiliated-person rules, but the FCA (para. 56) rejected this argument.

Where a testamentary trust acquires shares of a corporation from a deceased's estate and the remaining shares are redeemed by the corporation, the estate and the corporation are not "affiliated" after the redemption, even though the estate and the trust have the same trustees: VIEWS doc 2002-0151025. A deceased person is not affiliated with the estate or with the surviving spouse: doc 2004-0105471E5. On whether X's spouse is affiliated with X's corporation see 2009-0330501E5. A corporation controlled by X is affiliated with a partnership of which X is majority-interest partner: 2013-0515651E5. An RRSP, RRIF, RESP or TFSA is affiliated with its beneficiary or holder: 2008-0299661E5, 2009-0343501M4, 2010-0352921E5. A RESP is normally affiliated with its subscriber: 2009-0348901E5. However, 2012-0453181C6 describes challenges in determining who is affiliated with a RESP or RDSP. See also Notes to 251.1(3)"contributor".

On how to determine the majority-interest beneficiary in an estate where the beneficiaries' interests have not yet been determined, see VIEWS doc 2006-0185581C6.

251.1(1)(e) amended by 2013 budget bill #2, effective Dec. 12, 2013, to change "majority interest partner" to "majority-interest partner" (with a hyphen).

251.1(1) earlier amended by 2004 Budget, 2000 same-sex partners bill.

Income Tax Folios: S4-F7-C1: Amalgamations of Canadian corporations [replaces IT-474R2].

Interpretation Bulletins: IT-291R3: Transfer of property to a corporation under subsection 85(1).

I.T. Technical News: 9 (loss consolidation within a corporate group — "affiliated" test to apply).

Forms: T5013 Sched. 9: List of partnerships.

(2) Affiliation where amalgamation or merger

Where at any time 2 or more corporations (in this subsection referred to as the "predecessors") amalgamate or merge to form a new corporation, the new corporation and any predecessor are deemed to have been affiliated with each other where they would have been affiliated with each other immediately before that time if

(a) the new corporation had existed immediately before that time; and

(b) the persons who were the shareholders of the new corporation immediately after that time had been the shareholders of the new corporation immediately before that time.

Notes: See Notes at end of 251.1.

(3) Definitions

The definitions in this subsection apply in this section.

"affiliated group of persons" means a group of persons each member of which is affiliated with every other member.

"beneficiary", under a trust, includes a person beneficially interested in the trust.

Related Provisions: 251.2(1)"beneficiary" — Definition applies to trust loss trading rules.

Notes: See Notes to 188.1(5) re meaning of "includes".

Definition "beneficiary" added by 2004 Budget, effective in determining whether persons are, at any time after March 22, 2004, affiliated.

"contributor", to a trust, means a person who has at any time made a loan or transfer of property, either directly or indirectly, in any manner whatever, to or for the benefit of the trust other than, if the person deals at arm's length with the trust at that time and is not immediately after that time a majority-interest beneficiary of the trust,

(a) a loan made at a reasonable rate of interest; or

(b) a transfer made for fair market value consideration.

Notes: A deceased person can be a "contributor": VIEWS docs 2014-0534851C6 [2014 APFF q.5], 2015-0571271E5 [this may be wrong in the author's view: this definition does not use the 94(1)"contributor" words that include a deceased person; but see *Kuchta*, 2015 TCC 289 (FCA appeal discontinued A-551-15), on whether death cancels a person's status].

Definition "contributor" added by 2004 Budget, effective in determining whether persons are, at any time after March 22, 2004, affiliated.

"controlled" means controlled, directly or indirectly in any manner whatever.

Related Provisions: 256(5.1), (6.2) — Controlled directly or indirectly.

"majority-interest beneficiary", of a trust at any time, means a person whose interest as a beneficiary, if any, at that time

(a) in the income of the trust has, together with the interests as a beneficiary in the income of the trust of all persons with whom

the person is affiliated, a fair market value that is greater than 50% of the fair market value of all the interests as a beneficiary in the income of the trust; or

(b) in the capital of the trust has, together with the interests as a beneficiary in the capital of the trust of all persons with whom the person is affiliated, a fair market value that is greater than 50% of the fair market value of all the interests as a beneficiary in the capital of the trust.

Related Provisions: 251.2(1)"majority-interest beneficiary" — Definition applies to trust loss trading rules; 251.2(2) — Person becoming MIB constitutes loss restriction event; 251.2(4) — Person deemed to become MIB.

Notes: On determining the MIB of an unadministered estate, see VIEWS doc 2004-0105471E5. A person need not be a beneficiary to be a MIB: 2014-0534841C6 [2014 APFF q.3]; but this will not apply to the loss-restriction rules in 251.2, per Finance comfort letter reproduced under 251.2(3). A contingent beneficial interest does not make one a MIB: 2019-0803691I7.

Definition added by 2004 Budget, effective in determining whether persons are, at any time after March 22, 2004, affiliated.

"majority-interest group of beneficiaries", of a trust at any time, means a group of persons each of whom is a beneficiary under the trust at that time such that

(a) if one person held the interests as a beneficiary of all of the members of the group, that person would be a majority-interest beneficiary of the trust; and

(b) if any member of the group were not a member, the test described in paragraph (a) would not be met.

Related Provisions: 251.2(1)"majority-interest group of beneficiaries" — Definition applies to trust loss trading rules; 251.2(2) — Group becoming MIGB constitutes loss restriction event; 251.2(4) — Person deemed to become member of MIGB.

Notes: Definition "majority-interest group of beneficiaries" added by 2004 Budget, for determining whether persons are, at any time after March 22, 2004, affiliated.

"majority-interest group of partners" of a partnership means a group of persons each of whom has an interest in the partnership such that

(a) if one person held the interests of all members of the group, that person would be a majority-interest partner of the partnership; and

(b) if any member of the group were not a member, the test described in paragraph (a) would not be met.

Related Provisions: 251.2(1)"majority-interest group of partners" — Definition applies to trust loss trading rules.

Notes: Para. (a) amended by 2013 budget bill #2, effective Dec. 12, 2013, to change "majority interest partner" to "majority-interest partner" (with a hyphen).

See Notes at end of 251.1.

(4) Interpretation

For the purposes of this section,

(a) persons are affiliated with themselves;

(b) a person includes a partnership;

(c) notwithstanding subsection 104(1), a reference to a trust does not include a reference to the trustee or other persons who own or control the trust property; and

(d) in determining whether a person is affiliated with a trust,

(i) if the amount of income or capital of the trust that a person may receive as a beneficiary under the trust depends on the exercise by any person of, or the failure by any person to exercise, a discretionary power, that person is deemed to have fully exercised, or to have failed to exercise, the power, as the case may be,

(ii) the interest of a person in a trust as a beneficiary is disregarded in determining whether the person deals at arm's length with the trust if the person would, in the absence of the interest as a beneficiary, be considered to deal at arm's length with the trust,

(iii) a trust is not a majority interest beneficiary of another trust unless the trust has an interest as a beneficiary in the income or capital, as the case may be, of the other trust, and

(iv) in determining whether a contributor to one trust is affiliated with a contributor to another trust, individuals connected by blood relationship, marriage, common-law partnership or adoption are deemed to be affiliated with one another.

Related Provisions: 251(6) — Connected by blood relationship, etc.

Notes: 251.1(4)(d)(i) did not apply in VIEWS doc 2019-0803691I7.

251.1(4) amended by 2013 budget bill #2 (changing "blood" to "blood relationship" effective Dec. 12, 2013), 2004 Budget.

Notes [s. 251.1]: 251.1 (added by 1995-97 technical bill effective April 27, 1995) was introduced as part of the "accrued loss" anti-avoidance rules. See Notes to 13(21.2) and 40(3.4). Many other stop-loss rules now refer to "affiliated" persons, while others still use "related" or "not at arm's length". Generally speaking, "affiliated" is much like "associated" (control-based) but includes *de facto* control and spouses.

See Carson & Watson, "Affiliated Person Rules", 2004 BC Tax Conference (ctf.ca), 13:1-41; Ireland, "The New Trust Affiliation Rule", 2005 Prairie Provinces Tax Conf. 8:1-15, and XI(3) *Insurance Planning* 713-16 (2005); Diep & Micallef, "Associated, Affiliated and Related Transactions", 2005 Cdn Tax Foundation conference report, 38:1-14, 39:1-15; Ideias, "Related, Affiliated and Associated Rules", Tax Planner Guide 16 (*Taxnet Pro*, 2019, 11pp); Love & Hauser, "How Various Aggregation Rules Apply to Trusts", 2018 conference report at 28:18-36.

Definitions [s. 251.1]: "adoption" — 251(6)(c); "affiliated" — 251.1(1); "affiliated group" — 251.1(3); "amount" — 248(1); "arm's length" — 251(1); "beneficiary" — 251.1(3); "blood relationship" — 251(6)(a); "common-law partner" — 248(1); "contributor" — 251.1(3); "control", "controlled" — 256(6), (6.1); "controlled directly or indirectly" — 256(5.1)-(6); "corporation" — 248(1), *Interpretation Act* 35(1); "fair market value" — see 69(1) Notes; "individual" — 248(1); "majority-interest beneficiary", "majority-interest group of beneficiaries" — 251.1(3); "majority-interest group of partners" — 251.1(3); "majority-interest partner" — 248(1); "partnership" — see 96(1) Notes; "person" — 248(1), 251.1(4)(b); "property" — 248(1); "trust" — 104(1), 248(1), (3).

251.2 [Loss restriction event] — (1) Definitions — The following definitions apply in this section.

"beneficiary" has the same meaning as in subsection 251.1(3).

"equity" has the same meaning as in subsection 122.1(1) read without reference to paragraph (e) of the definition "equity" in that subsection.

"equity value" has the same meaning as in subsection 122.1(1).

"fixed interest", at any time of a person in a trust, means an interest of the person as a beneficiary (in this definition, determined without reference to subsection 248(25)) under the trust provided that no amount of the income or capital of the trust to be distributed at any time in respect of any interest in the trust depends on the exercise by any person of, or the failure by any person to exercise, any discretionary power, other than a power in respect of which it is reasonable to conclude that

(a) the power is consistent with normal commercial practice;

(b) the power is consistent with terms that would be acceptable to the beneficiaries under the trust if the beneficiaries were dealing with each other at arm's length; and

(c) the exercise of, or failure to exercise, the power will not materially affect the value of an interest as a beneficiary under the trust relative to the value of other such interests under the trust.

Notes: Definition added by 2014 budget bill #2, effective March 21, 2013 (or Jan. 1, 2014 by election filed by the 2014 tax year filing date).

"investment fund", at any time, means a trust, if

(a) at all times throughout the period that begins at the later of March 21, 2013 and the end of the calendar year in which it is created and that ends at that time, the trust has a class of units outstanding that complies with the conditions prescribed for the purposes of paragraph 132(6)(c) determined without reference to paragraph 4801(b) of the *Income Tax Regulations*; and

(b) at all times throughout the period that begins at the later of March 21, 2013 and the time of its creation and that ends at that time, the trust

(i) is resident in Canada,

(ii) has no beneficiaries who may for any reason receive directly from the trust any of the income or capital of the trust, other than beneficiaries whose interests as beneficiaries

under the trust are fixed interests described by reference to units of the trust,

(iii) follows a reasonable policy of investment diversification,

(iv) limits its undertaking to the investing of its funds in property,

(v) does not alone, or as a member of a group of persons, control a corporation, and

(vi) does not hold

(A) property that the trust, or a person with which the trust does not deal at arm's length, uses in carrying on a business,

(B) real or immovable property, an interest in real property or an immovable, or a real right in an immovable,

(C) Canadian resource property, foreign resource property, or an interest or right in Canadian resource property or foreign resource property, or

(D) more than 20% of the securities of any class of securities of a person (other than an investment fund or a mutual fund corporation that would meet the conditions in this paragraph, other than in subparagraph (ii), if it were a trust), unless at that time

(I) the securities (other than liabilities) of the person held by the trust have a total fair market value that is no more than 10% of the equity value of the person, and

(II) the liabilities of the person held by the trust have a total fair market value that is no more than 10% of the fair market value of all of the liabilities of the person.

Related Provisions: 94(4)(b) — Rule in 94(3) deeming foreign trust resident in Canada does not apply to (b)(ii); 251.2(5)(c) — Anti-avoidance rule re (b)(v) and (b)(vi)(D); 253.1(1) — Limited partner not considered to carry on partnership business for certain purposes; 256(8) — Where share deemed to have been acquired.

Notes: Definition amended by 2016 budget bill #2, effective March 21, 2013 (or Jan. 1, 2014 or 2015 by election filed by the 2014 tax year filing date), except that, in applying amended para. (a) to a trust created before 2016, read "and the end of the calendar year" as "and 90 days after the end of the calendar year".

Definition added by 2014 budget bill #2, effective March 21, 2013 (or Jan. 1, 2014 by election filed by the 2014 tax year filing date).

"majority-interest beneficiary" has the same meaning as in subsection 251.1(3) read without reference to the expression ", if any," in the definition "majority-interest beneficiary" in that subsection.

Related Provisions: 251.2(2) — Person becoming MIB constitutes loss restriction event; 251.2(4) — Person deemed to become MIB.

Notes: Definition amended by 2016 budget bill #2, effective March 21, 2013 (or Jan. 1, 2014 or 2015 by election filed by the 2014 tax year filing date), to add everything after "251.1(3)".

"majority-interest group of beneficiaries" has the same meaning as in subsection 251.1(3).

Related Provisions: 251.2(2) — Group becoming MIGB constitutes loss restriction event; 251.2(4) — Person deemed to become member of MIGB.

"majority-interest group of partners" has the same meaning as in subsection 251.1(3).

"person" includes a partnership.

"portfolio investment fund" — [Repealed]

Notes: Definition repealed by 2016 budget bill #2, effective March 21, 2013 (or Jan. 1, 2014 or 2015 by election filed by the 2014 tax year filing date).

Definition added by 2014 budget bill #2, effective on the same basis as 251.2(7).

"specified right", held at any time by a person in respect of a trust, means a right under a contract, in equity or otherwise, to acquire, either immediately or in the future and either absolutely or contingently, equity of the trust, or to cause the trust to redeem or cancel equity of the trust, unless the right is not exercisable at that time because its exercise is contingent on the death, bankruptcy or permanent disability of an individual.

"subsidiary", of a particular person at any time, means a corporation, partnership or trust (in this definition referred to as the "subject entity") where

(a) the particular person holds at that time property

(i) that is equity of the subject entity, or

(ii) that derives all or part of its fair market value, directly or indirectly, from equity of the subject entity; and

(b) the total of the following amounts is at that time equal to more than 50% of the equity value of the subject entity:

(i) each amount that is the fair market value at that time of equity of the subject entity that is held at that time by the particular person or a person with whom the particular person is affiliated, and

(ii) each amount (other than an amount described in subparagraph (i)) that is the portion of the fair market value at that time — derived directly or indirectly from equity of the subject entity — of a property that is held at that time by the particular person or a person with whom the particular person is affiliated.

Notes: For the meaning of "derived" see Notes to 18.1(12). For "indirectly" see Notes to 17.1(1).

(2) Loss restriction event [defined] — For the purposes of this Act, a taxpayer is at any time subject to a loss restriction event if

(a) the taxpayer is a corporation and at that time control of the corporation is acquired by a person or group of persons; or

(b) the taxpayer is a trust and

(i) that time is after March 20, 2013 and after the time at which the trust is created, and

(ii) at that time a person becomes a majority-interest beneficiary, or a group of persons becomes a majority-interest group of beneficiaries, of the trust.

Related Provisions: 251.2(3) — Exceptions; 251.2(4) — Person deemed to become majority-interest beneficiary (MIB); 251.2(5)(b) — Rules in determining whether person becomes MIB or group becomes MIGB; 251.2(6) — When loss restriction event takes effect; 256(7), (8) — Whether control acquired; 256.1 — Deemed change in control if 75% FMV acquired.

Notes: A "loss restriction event" (LRE) is a change in control of a corporation (including acquisition of 75% fair market value (256.1), and see (256(7)-(8)), or a change in the "majority-interest beneficiary" of a trust. It triggers restrictions on carrying losses forward or back across the LRE, to prevent "loss trading" (buying entities to use their losses). See Notes to 111(5). For effects of an LRE, see Index under "Loss restriction event", and Keey, *Checklist 1 — Acquisition of Control*, *Taxnet Pro* Corporate Tax Centre (2020, 34pp). Note that although a year-end is triggered by 249(4)(a), a trust need not file its return and pay its balance for the short year until 90 days after its regular year-end: 251.2(7)(c), 248(1)"balance-due day".

See Burghardt & Chiu, "Loss is Just a Four Letter Word", 2013 Cdn Tax Foundation conference report, 14:1-43; Jiang, "Loss Restriction Events for the Family Trust", 23(1) *Canadian Tax Highlights* (ctf.ca) 6-7 (Jan. 2015); Barnay et al., "When Is a Loss a Loss", 2015 Prairie Provinces Tax Conf. (ctf.ca), 11:1-37; Keung, "The loss restriction event rules for trusts are broader than you think", tinyurl.com/keung-2015.

2013 Budget Table A2.1 forecast that 251.2 would save the federal government $65 million each year 2013-14 to 2015-16 and $70m in each of 2016-17, 2017-18.

See also 107(6) for an older anti-avoidance rule relevant to trust loss trading.

(3) Trusts — exceptions — For the purposes of paragraph (2)(b), a person is deemed not to become a majority-interest beneficiary, and a group of persons is deemed not to become a majority-interest group of beneficiaries, as the case may be, of a particular trust solely because of

(a) the acquisition of equity of the particular trust by

(i) a particular person from another person with whom the particular person was affiliated immediately before the acquisition,

(ii) a particular person who was affiliated with the particular trust immediately before the acquisition,

(iii) an estate from an individual, if the estate arose on and as a consequence of the death of the individual and the estate acquired the equity from the individual as a consequence of the death, or

(iv) a particular person from an estate that arose on and as a consequence of the death of an individual, if the estate acquired the equity from the individual as a consequence of the death and the individual was affiliated with the particular person immediately before the death;

(b) a variation in the terms of the particular trust, the satisfaction of, or failure to satisfy, a condition under the terms of the particular trust, the exercise by any person of, or the failure by any person to exercise, a power, or (without limiting the generality of the foregoing) the redemption, surrender or termination of equity of the particular trust at any time, if each majority-interest beneficiary, and each member of a majority-interest group of beneficiaries, of the particular trust immediately after that time was affiliated with the particular trust immediately before

(i) that time, or

(ii) in the case of the redemption or surrender of equity of the particular trust that was held, immediately before that time, by an estate and that was acquired by the estate from an individual as described in subparagraph (a)(iii), the individual's death;

(c) the transfer at any time of all the equity of the particular trust to a corporation, partnership or another trust (in this paragraph referred to as the "acquirer"), if

(i) the only consideration for the transfer is equity (determined without reference to paragraph (d) of the definition "equity" in subsection 122.1(1)) of the acquirer,

(ii) at all times before that time the acquirer held no property or held only property having a nominal value, and

(iii) immediately after that time the acquirer is neither

(A) a subsidiary of any person, nor

(B) a corporation controlled, directly or indirectly in any manner whatever, by a person or group of persons;

(d) the transfer at any time of equity of the particular trust to a corporation, partnership or another trust (in this paragraph referred to as the "acquirer"), if

(i) immediately before that time a person was a majority-interest beneficiary, or a group of persons was a majority-interest group of beneficiaries, of the particular trust,

(ii) immediately after that time the person, or group of persons, as the case may be, described in subparagraph (i) in respect of the particular trust, and no other person or group of persons, is

(A) if the acquirer is a corporation, a person by whom, or a group of persons by which, the corporation is controlled directly or indirectly in any manner whatever,

(B) if the acquirer is a partnership, a majority-interest partner, or a majority-interest group of partners, of the partnership, and

(C) if the acquirer is a trust, a majority-interest beneficiary, or a majority-interest group of beneficiaries, of the trust, and

(iii) at no time during a series of transactions or events that includes the transfer does the person or group of persons, as the case may be, described in subparagraph (i) in respect of the particular trust, cease to be a person or group of persons described in any of clauses (ii)(A) to (C) in respect of the acquirer;

(e) a transaction (other than a transaction one or more of the parties to which may be excused from completing as a result of changes to this Act) the parties to which are obligated to complete under the terms of an agreement in writing between the parties entered into before March 21, 2013; or

(f) the acquisition or disposition of equity of the particular trust at any time if

(i) the particular trust is an investment fund immediately before that time, and

(ii) the acquisition or disposition, as the case may be, is not part of a series of transactions or events that includes the particular trust ceasing to be an investment fund.

Related Provisions: 248(8) — Meaning of "consequence" of death; 248(10) — Series of transactions or events; 251.2(5)(a) — Changed meaning of "affiliated" for s. 251.2; 256(8) — Deemed exercise of right under 251(5)(b).

Notes: 251.2(3)(f) amended by 2016 budget bill #2 (implementing a Dec. 23, 2014 Finance comfort letter), effective March 21, 2013 (or Jan. 1, 2014 or 2015 by election filed by the 2014 tax year filing date).

See Notes to 251.2(2). 251.2(3)(f) added by 2014 budget bill #2, effective on the same basis as 251.2(7).

(4) Trusts — additional cases [deemed majority-interest beneficiary] — For the purposes of paragraph (2)(b) and subject to subsection (3), a person is deemed to become at a particular time a majority-interest beneficiary of a particular trust if

(a) a particular person is at and immediately before the particular time a majority-interest beneficiary, or a member of a majority-interest group of beneficiaries, of the particular trust, and the particular person is at the particular time, but is not immediately before the particular time, a subsidiary of another person (in this paragraph referred to as the "acquirer"), unless

(i) the acquirer is immediately before the particular time affiliated with the particular trust, or

(ii) this paragraph previously applied to deem a person to become a majority-interest beneficiary of the particular trust because the particular person became, as part of a series of transactions or events that includes the particular person becoming at the particular time a subsidiary of the acquirer, a subsidiary of another person that is at the particular time a subsidiary of the acquirer; or

(b) at the particular time, as part of a series of transactions or events, two or more persons acquire equity of the particular trust in exchange for or upon a redemption or surrender of equity of, or as a consequence of a distribution from, a corporation, partnership or another trust, unless

(i) a person affiliated with the corporation, partnership or other trust was immediately before the particular time a majority-interest beneficiary of the particular trust,

(ii) if all the equity of the particular trust that was acquired at or before the particular time as part of the series were acquired by one person, the person would not at the particular time be a majority-interest beneficiary of the particular trust, or

(iii) this paragraph previously applied to deem a person to become a majority-interest beneficiary of the particular trust because of an acquisition of equity of the particular trust that was part of the series.

Related Provisions: 251.2(5)(a) — Changed meaning of "affiliated" for s. 251.2.

(5) Trusts — special rules of application — For the purposes of this section,

(a) in determining whether persons are affiliated with each other

(i) except for the purposes of paragraph (b) of the definition "subsidiary" in subsection (1), section 251.1 is to be read without reference to the definition "controlled" in subsection 251.1(3),

(ii) in determining whether an individual (other than a trust) is affiliated with another individual (other than a trust), individuals connected by blood relationship, marriage or common-law partnership or adoption are deemed to be affiliated with one another, and

(iii) if, at any time as part of a series of transactions or events a person acquires equity of a corporation, partnership or trust, and it can reasonably be concluded that one of the reasons for the acquisition, or for making any agreement or undertaking in respect of the acquisition, is to cause a condition in paragraph (3)(a) or (b) or subparagraph (4)(a)(i) or (b)(i)

regarding affiliation to be satisfied at a particular time, the condition is deemed not to be satisfied at the particular time;

(b) in determining whether a particular person becomes at any time a majority-interest beneficiary, or a particular group of persons becomes at any time a majority-interest group of beneficiaries, of a trust, the fair market value of each person's equity of the trust is to be determined at and immediately before that time

(i) without reference to the portion of that fair market value that is attributable to property acquired if it can reasonably be concluded that one of the reasons for the acquisition is to cause paragraph (2)(b), or any provision that applies by reference to a trust being subject to a loss restriction event at any time, not to apply,

(ii) without reference to the portion of that fair market value that is attributable to a change in the fair market value of all or part of any equity of the trust if it can reasonably be concluded that one of the reasons for the change is to cause paragraph (2)(b), or any provision that applies by reference to a trust being subject to a loss restriction event at any time, not to apply, and

(iii) as if each specified right held immediately before that time by the particular person, or by a member of the particular group, in respect of the trust is at that time exercised if it can reasonably be concluded that one of the reasons for the acquisition of the right is to cause paragraph (2)(b), or any provision that applies by reference to a trust being subject to a loss restriction event at any time, not to apply; and

(c) if, at any time as part of a series of transactions or events a person acquires a "security" (as defined in subsection 122.1(1)) and it can reasonably be concluded that one of the reasons for the acquisition, or for making any agreement or undertaking in respect of the acquisition, is to cause a condition in subparagraph (b)(v) or clause (b)(vi)(D) of the definition "investment fund" in subsection (1) to be satisfied at a particular time in respect of a trust, the condition is deemed not to be satisfied at the particular time in respect of the trust.

Notes: 251.2(5)(c) added by 2016 budget bill #2, effective on the same basis as the amendment to 251.2(3)(f).

(6) Trusts — time of day [when loss restriction event takes effect] — For the purposes of this Act, if a trust is subject to a loss restriction event at a particular time during a day, the trust is deemed to be subject to the loss restriction event at the beginning of that day and not at the particular time unless the trust elects in its return of income under Part I filed for its taxation year that ends immediately before the loss restriction event to have this subsection not apply.

Related Provisions: 220(3.2), Reg. 600(b) — Late filing or revocation of election.

Notes: For a trust filing a Quebec return, a 251.2(6) election must be copied to Revenu Québec: *Taxation Act* ss. 21.0.10, 21.4.6.

(7) Filing and other deadlines [deemed year-end does not apply to trust's filing and payment obligations] — If at any time a trust is subject to a loss restriction event, in respect of the trust for its taxation year that ends immediately before that time,

(a) the reference in paragraph 132(2.1)(a) to "the day that is 90 days after the end of the year" is to be read as "the balance-due day of the trust for the year";

(b) the reference in subsection 132(6.1) to "before the 91st day after the end of" is to be read as "on or before the balance-due day of the trust for";

(c) the reference in paragraph 150(1)(c) to "within 90 days from the end of" is to be read as "on or before the balance-due day of the trust for";

(d) the reference in subsection 204.7(1) to "Within 90 days from the end of each taxation year commencing after 1980" is to be read as "On or before the balance-due day of the trust for each taxation year";

(e) the reference in subsection 210.2(5), and in subsection 221(2) of the *Income Tax Regulations*, to "within 90 days after the end of" is to be read as "on or before the balance-due day of the trust for"; and

(f) the references in subsections 202(8) and 204(2) of the *Income Tax Regulations* to "within 90 days from the end of" are to be read as "on or before the balance-due day of the trust for".

Notes [subsec. 251.2(7)]: 251.2(7) amended by 2016 budget bill #2 (implementing a Dec. 23, 2014 Finance comfort letter), retroactive to March 21, 2013.

251.2(7) added by 2014 budget bill #2, effective March 21, 2013 (or Jan. 1, 2014 by election filed by the 2014 tax year filing date). Along with 251.2(3)(f), and 251.2(1)"fixed interest", "investment fund" and "portfolio investment fund", this was added in the Oct. 20, 2014 Notice of Ways and Means Motion, as the only revision to the Oct. 10 NWMM before it became 2014 budget bill #2. The Oct. 20 Finance news release describes it as "a new measure that amends the trust loss restriction event rules to provide relief for investment trusts that meet specific conditions".

Notes [s. 251.2]: See Notes to 251.2(2). 251.2 added by 2013 budget bill #2, effective March 21, 2013.

Definitions [s. 251.2]: "adoption" — 251(6)(c); "affiliated" — 251.1; "amount" — 248(1); "arm's length" — 251(1); "bank" — 248(1); "beneficiary" — 251.1(3), 251.2(1); "blood relationship" — 251(6)(a); "business" — 248(1); "calendar year" — *Interpretation Act* 37(1)(a); "Canada" — 255, *Interpretation Act* 35(1); "Canadian resource property" — 66(15), 248(1); "common-law partnership" — 248(1); "connected" — 251(6); "consequence" — 248(8); "control" — 256(6)–(9), 256.1(3); "corporation" — 248(1), *Interpretation Act* 35(1); "credit union" — 137(6), 248(1); "equity" — 251.2(1); "equity value" — 122.1(1), 251.2(1); "estate" — 104(1), 248(1); "fair market value" — see 69(1) Notes; "immovable" — Quebec *Civil Code* art. 900-907; "individual" — 248(1); "interest in real property" — 248(4); "loss restriction event" — 251.2(2); "majority-interest beneficiary", "majority-interest group of beneficiaries", "majority-interest group of partners" — 251.1(3), 251.2(1); "majority-interest partner" — 248(1); "mutual fund trust" — 132(6)–(7), 132.2(3)(n), 248(1); "partnership" — see 96(1) Notes; "person" — 248(1), 251.2(1); "portfolio investment entity" — 122.2(1); "prescribed", "property" — 248(1); "real right" — 248(4.1); "resident in Canada" — 94(4)(b), 250; "series of transactions" — 248(10); "specified right", "subsidiary" — 251.2(1); "taxation year" — 249; "taxpayer" — 248(1); "trust" — 104(1), 248(1), (3); "writing" — *Interpretation Act* 35(1).

252. (1) Extended meaning of "child" — In this Act, words referring to a child of a taxpayer include

(a) a person of whom the taxpayer is the legal parent;

(b) a person who is wholly dependent on the taxpayer for support and of whom the taxpayer has, or immediately before the person attained the age of 19 years had, in law or in fact, the custody and control;

(c) a child of the taxpayer's spouse or common-law partner; and

(d) [Repealed]

(e) a spouse or common-law partner of a child of the taxpayer.

Related Provisions: 70(10), 75.1(2), 110.6(1) — Extended meaning of "child" for various purposes.

Notes: A child of a deceased spouse may or may not still be considered a child; see Notes to 252(2). See also the provisions extending the meaning of "child" to grandchild and great-grandchild: 70(10), 75.1(2), 110.6(1).

For the meaning of "wholly dependent" see Notes to 118(1)B(b). For "custody and control" see VIEWS doc 2011-0397251E5. In *Therrien*, 2019 QCCQ 28, T was held (for the parallel Quebec rule) to have custody and control of his ex-common-law spouse's adult child who moved in with him. A disabled adult living with X, receiving government support and paying rent to X is not "wholly dependent" on X: 2009-0352771E5. Nor is a foster child where the foster parent receives support payments from an agency responsible for the child's care: 2010-0382221E5, 2010-0382341E5. *De facto* adoption can qualify: 2012-0461521E5, IT-419R2 para. 10.

Before applying 252(1), the legal meaning of "child" depends on provincial law, which has changed in recent years; e.g. *MRR v. JM*, 2017 ONSC 2655 (in Ontario, pre-conception contract can cut biological relationship).

252(1) amended by 2005 same-sex marriage bill (effective July 20, 2005), 2000 same-sex partners bill.

I.T. Application Rules: 20(1.11) (extended meaning of "child" re disposition of depreciable property owned since before 1972); 26(20) (extended meaning of "child" re transfer of farmland owned since before 1972).

Income Tax Folios: S1-F2-C2: Tuition tax credit [replaces IT-516R2]; S1-F3-C1: Child care expense deduction [replaces IT-495R3].

Interpretation Bulletins: IT-268R4: *Inter vivos* transfer of farm property to child; IT-349R3: Intergenerational transfers of farm property on death; IT-394R2: Preferred beneficiary election.

(2) Relationships — In this Act, words referring to

(a) a parent of a taxpayer include a person

(i) whose child the taxpayer is,

(ii) whose child the taxpayer had previously been within the meaning of paragraph (1)(b), or

(iii) who is a parent of the taxpayer's spouse or common-law partner;

(b) a brother of a taxpayer include a person who is

(i) the brother of the taxpayer's spouse or common-law partner, or

(ii) the spouse or common-law partner of the taxpayer's sister;

(c) a sister of a taxpayer include a person who is

(i) the sister of the taxpayer's spouse or common-law partner, or

(ii) the spouse or common-law partner of the taxpayer's brother;

(d) a grandparent of a taxpayer include a person who is

(i) the grandfather or grandmother of the taxpayer's spouse or common-law partner, or

(ii) the spouse or common-law partner of the taxpayer's grandfather or grandmother;

(e) an aunt or uncle of a taxpayer include the spouse or common-law partner of the taxpayer's aunt or uncle, as the case may be;

(f) a great-aunt or great-uncle of a taxpayer include the spouse or common-law partner of the taxpayer's great-aunt or great-uncle, as the case may be; and

(g) a niece or nephew of a taxpayer include the niece or nephew, as the case may be, of the taxpayer's spouse or common-law partner.

Related Provisions: 252(1) — Extended meaning of "child".

Notes: See Notes to 252(1). For CRA interpretation see generally S1-F4-C2 ¶2.6-2.15.

Death: An "in-law" parent-child relationship terminates when the connecting person dies, in CRA's view: doc 2010-0389561E5. The case law is conflicting: *Crowthers*, [1978] 1 W.W.R. 262 (BCSC), and *Gale*, [1984] C.T.C. 3043 (TCC) say the relationship continues, while *Pembroke Ferry* (1952), 6 Tax A.B.C. 389, and *May Estate*, [1988] 1 C.T.C. 2303 (TCC) say it does not. 70(10)"child"(b.1) also implies it does not, as it deems the relationship to continue only for purposes of specific provisions, not generally. CRA does not consider the person a "child" for the capital gains exemption or farm/fishing property rollover (docs 9426215, 2002-0176465, 2008-0285271C6). (This is likely correct, given the use of "is" throughout 252(2).) For personal tax credits, CRA says the relationship continues: Income Tax Folio S1-F4-C2 ¶2.15 (also 2004-0063331E5, 2010-0389561E5). A step-parent is considered not related to their adult stepson after the other parent's death: 2005-0114721E5, 2019-0795291E5. Death does not break a biological parent-child relationship: *Dreger*, 2020 TCC 25.

See also Notes to 251(6) re adoption and half-siblings.

There is no such thing as adopting a brother or sister, unless a parent has adopted the person: *Leidal*, 2003 TCC 671; *O'Neill*, 2008 TCC 548.

A parent includes a grandparent or great-grandparent for some purposes, due to the extended definition of "child" in 70(10): VIEWS doc 2012-045470117.

252(2) amended by 2000 same-sex partners bill (effective 2001 or earlier), 1992 technical bill.

Income Tax Folios: S1-F2-C2: Tuition tax credit [replaces IT-516R2]; S1-F3-C1: Child care expense deduction [replaces IT-495R3].

Interpretation Bulletins: IT-349R3: Intergenerational transfers of farm property on death; IT-513R: Personal tax credits.

(3) Extended meaning of "spouse" and "former spouse" — For the purposes of paragraph 56(1)(b), section 56.1, paragraphs 60(b) and (j), section 60.1, subsections 70(6) and (6.1), 73(1) and (5) and 104(4) and (5.1), the definition "pre-1972 spousal trust" in subsection 108(1), subsection 146(16), the definition "survivor" in subsection 146.2(1), subparagraph 146.3(2)(f)(iv), subsection 146.3(14), section 146.5, subsections 147(19) and 147.3(5) and (7), section 147.5, subsections 148(8.1) and (8.2), the definition "qualifying transfer" in subsection 207.01(1), and subsections 210(1) and 248(22) and (23), **"spouse"** and **"former spouse"** of a

particular individual include another individual who is a party to a void or voidable marriage with the particular individual.

Related Provisions: 147.1(1) — RPP — Definition of spouse; Reg. 8500(5) — Rule in 252(3) applies to Regs. 8500–8520.

Notes: Same-sex marriages (and protection for those refusing to perform them for religious reasons) are authorized by the *Civil Marriage Act*, S.C. 2005, c. 33. For discussion of marriage see Pamela Rideout, "Tax Implications of Marriage", 10(8) *Tax Hyperion* (Carswell) 6-8 (Aug. 2013).

252(3) amended to add reference to 146.5 by 2021 budget bill #1, effective 2020.

252(3) amended by 2002-2013 technical bill (for 1996 and later tax years), 2012 budget bill #2 (effective Dec. 14, 2012), 2008 budget bill #1, 2005 same-sex marriage bill, 2003 and 1999 Budgets, 1992 and 1991 technical bills, 1990 pension bill.

Interpretation Bulletins: IT-305R4: Testamentary spouse trusts; IT-307R4: Spousal or common-law registered retirement savings plans; IT-325R2: Property transfers after separation, divorce and annulment.

Registered Pension Plans Technical Manual: §1.43 (spouse).

(4) [Repealed]

Notes: 252(4) repealed by 2000 same-sex partners bill (S.C. 2000, c. 12), effective for 2001 and later taxation years, or earlier by election (see Notes to 248(1)"common-law partner"). The bill also changed all instances of "spouse" throughout the Act to "spouse or common-law partner" (and "marriage" to "marriage or common-law partnership"). Thus, the extended meaning of "spouse" in 252(4), which covered common-law spouses, is no longer needed.

252(4) added by 1992 technical bill, effective 1993, to treat common-law couples (who met the definition) as spouses for all purposes. (This meant that a person could have more than one "spouse" at the same time.) This could be either good or bad for taxpayers, depending on circumstances. See David M. Sherman, "Till Tax Do Us Part: The New Definition of Spouse", 1992 Cdn Tax Foundation conference report, pp. 20:1–33.

252(4) amended by 1993 technical bill and 1995-97 technical bill, both retroactive to the introduction of 252(4).

252(4) was judicially amended by the Ontario Court of Appeal in *Rosenberg v. Canada* (1998), 38 O.R. (3d) 577, to change "of the opposite sex" to "of the opposite or the same sex", for purposes of pension registration. (This decision was not appealed to the Supreme Court of Canada.) Thus, the definition applied to same-sex couples for this purpose. This rule has been codified by the 2000 amendments adding 248(1)"common-law partner", generally effective 2001 but optionally back to 1998.

See also Notes to 248(1)"common-law partner".

Definitions [s. 252]: "aunt" — 252(2)(e); "brother" — 252(2)(b); "child" — 252(1); "common-law partner" — 248(1); "grandparent" — 252(2)(d); "great-aunt", "great-uncle" — 252(2)(f); "individual" — 248(1); "nephew", "niece" — 252(2)(g); "parent" — 252(2)(a); "person" — 248(1); "sister" — 252(2)(c); "taxpayer" — 248(1); "uncle" — 252(2)(e).

252.1 Union [as] employer

252.1 Union [as] employer — All the structural units of a trade union, including each local, branch, national and international unit, shall be deemed to be a single employer and a single entity for the purposes of the provisions of this Act and the regulations relating to

(a) pension adjustments and past service pension adjustments for years after 1994;

(b) the determination of whether a pension plan is, in a year after 1994, a multi-employer plan or a specified multi-employer plan (within the meanings assigned by subsection 147.1(1));

(c) the determination of whether a contribution made under a plan or arrangement is a resident's contribution (within the meaning assigned by subsection 207.6(5.1)); and

(d) the deduction or withholding and the remittance of any amount as required by subsection 153(1) in respect of a contribution made after 1991 under a retirement compensation arrangement.

Related Provisions: Reg. 6804(3) — Election by union re foreign pension plan.

Notes: Due to 252.1(d), all locals or branches are combined in determining "average monthly withholding amount" and thus payroll remittance timing under Reg. 108(1.1): VIEWS doc 2012-0441251E5.

252.1 added by 1993 technical bill, retroactive to October 9, 1986.

Definitions [s. 252.1]: "amount" — 248(1); "multi-employer plan" — 147.1(1), Reg. 8500(1), 8510(1); "past service pension adjustment" — 248(1), Reg. 8303(1); "pension adjustment" — 248(1), Reg. 8301(1); "retirement compensation arrangement" — 248(1); "specified multi-employer plan" — 147.1(1), Reg. 8510(2), (3).

253. Extended meaning of "carrying on business" [in Canada]

253. Extended meaning of "carrying on business" [in Canada] — For the purposes of this Act, where in a taxation year a person who is a non-resident person or a trust to which Part XII.2 applies

(a) produces, grows, mines, creates, manufactures, fabricates, improves, packs, preserves or constructs, in whole or in part, anything in Canada whether or not the person exports that thing without selling it before exportation,

(b) solicits orders or offers anything for sale in Canada through an agent or servant, whether the contract or transaction is to be completed inside or outside Canada or partly in and partly outside Canada, or

(c) disposes of

(i) Canadian resource property, except where an amount in respect of the disposition is included under paragraph 66.2(1)(a) or 66.4(1)(a),

(ii) property (other than depreciable property) that is a timber resource property, an option in respect of a timber resource property or an interest in, or for civil law a right in, a timber resource property, or

(iii) property (other than capital property) that is real or immovable property situated in Canada, including an option in respect of such property or an interest in, or for civil law a real right in, such property, whether or not the property is in existence,

the person shall be deemed, in respect of the activity or disposition, to have been carrying on business in Canada in the year.

Related Provisions: 115.2 — Non-resident investment or pension fund deemed not to be carrying on business in Canada for certain purposes; 248(4) — Meaning of "interest in real property"; 248(4.1) — Real right in immovable property.

Notes: Although 253 deems many non-residents to be carrying on business in Canada, such persons are often not required to pay Canadian tax because they do not have a permanent establishment in Canada, and are thus protected by tax treaty. See, e.g., Canada-US Tax Treaty:Art. VII. However, such a non-resident is still a "reporting person" under 233.1(1): see Notes to that definition.

A non-resident corporation carrying on business in Canada is generally required to file a Canadian corporate tax return: 150(1)(a)(i)(B).

For discussion of 253, see Kyres, "Carrying on Business in Canada", 43(5) *Canadian Tax Journal* 1629-71 (1995); Brown, "An Introduction to Carrying on Business in Canada", 2004 Cdn Tax Foundation conference report, 38:1-10; VIEWS docs 2010-0381951E5, 2012-0438691E5. For software that assists in the determination see *Carrying on Business Classifier* at bluejlegal.com.

Offering Costa Rican plantations for sale in Canada fell within 253(b) even though the contracts were concluded in Costa Rica: *Maya Forestales*, 2006 FCA 35. Offering Canadian shares for sale on a US stock exchange does not constitute offering for sale in Canada: *Zhu*, 2016 FCA 113, para. 12.

253 extends the meaning of "carrying on business in Canada" but the ordinary meaning applies also. For discussion of whether business is carried on in a country, see *Standard Life*, 2015 TCC 97, paras. 81-88 (FCA appeal heard March 6/17 as *SCDA (2015) Inc.*). For "carrying on business", see *United Geophysical*, [1961] C.T.C. 134 (Exch. Ct.); *Rubinstein*, 1962 CarswellNat 73 (TAB); *Sudden Valley*, [1976] C.T.C. 775 (FCA); *Backman*, 2001 SCC 10, para. 19; *AAi.FosterGrant*, 2004 FCA 259; *Google v. Equustek*, 2017 SCC 34; and Notes to 9(1), paras. under "Business income".

Leasing a storage facility is normally not carrying on business in Canada: VIEWS doc 2001-0116133. See also GST/HST Policy P-051R2 and Technical Information Bulletin B-090 (electronic commerce) for CRA interpretation of "carrying on business in Canada" in the GST/HST context.

253(c)(ii), (iii) amended by 2002-2013 technical bill, effective June 26, 2013.

253(c) and the closing words "in respect of such activity or disposition" added by 1991 technical bill, effective for the 1990 taxation year. However, ignore 253(c) for dispositions before February 21, 1990, as well as for later dispositions pursuant to agreements in writing entered into before February 21, 1990.

Definitions [s. 253]: "amount", "business" — 248(1); "Canada" — 255; "Canadian resource property" — 66(15), 248(1); "capital property" — 54, 248(1); "depreciable property" — 13(21), 248(1); "immovable" — Quebec *Civil Code* art. 900–907; "interest" — 248(4); "non-resident", "person", "property" — 248(1); "real right" — 248(4.1); "servant" — 248(1)"employment"; "taxation year" — 249; "timber resource property" — 13(21), 248(1).

Interpretation Bulletins [s. 253]: IT-420R3: Non-residents — income earned in Canada.

CRA Audit Manual [s. 253]: 15.2.7: Carrying on business "with" vs. "in" Canada; 15.2.8: Extended meaning of carrying on business in Canada; 15.2.9: Agent or servant vs. independent contractor.

253.1 (1) Investments in limited partnerships [deemed not carrying on business] — For the purposes of subparagraph 108(2)(b)(ii), paragraphs 130.1(6)(b), 131(8)(b), 132(6)(b) and 146.1(2.1)(c), subsection 146.2(6), paragraph 146.4(5)(b), subsection 147.5(8), paragraph 149(1)(o.2), the definition "private holding corporation" in subsection 191(1), the definition "investment fund" in subsection 251.2(1) and regulations made for the purposes of paragraphs 149(1)(o.3) and (o.4), if a trust or corporation holds an interest as a member of a partnership and, by operation of any law governing the arrangement in respect of the partnership, the liability of the member as a member of the partnership is limited, the member shall not, solely because of its acquisition and holding of that interest, be considered to carry on any business or other activity of the partnership.

Notes: 253.1(1) ensures that the mere acquiring and holding of a limited partnership interest by a trust, corporation or charity will not jeopardize its classification under provisions that require it to limit its undertakings to investing (for a charity, prohibitions against carrying on business). It responds to *Robinson*, [1998] 1 C.T.C. 272 (FCA), which held that limited partners carry on the partnership's business. See VIEWS docs 2004-0108821R3 and 2013-0487911R3 for rulings that mortgage investment corporations do not lose their status by acquiring a limited partnership interest; 2007-0226101R3 for a ruling that a mutual fund trust does not lose its status; and 2017-0723421E5 for a ruling on creation of a new MFT.

253.1(1) amended by 2016 budget bill #2 (effective March 21, 2013). 253.1 renumbered as 253.1(1) by 2016 budget bill #1, effective from when 253.1(2) added. Earlier amended by 2002-2013 technical bill, 2012 budget bill #2, 2008 budget bills #1 and #2, 2007 RDSPs bill. Added by 2001 technical bill.

(2) Investments in limited partnerships [by charities] — For the purposes of section 149.1 and subsections 188.1(1) and (2), if a registered charity, a registered Canadian amateur athletic association or a registered journalism organization holds an interest as a member of a partnership, the member shall not, solely because of its acquisition and holding of that interest, be considered to carry on any business of the partnership if

(a) by operation of any law governing the arrangement in respect of the partnership, the liability of the member as a member of the partnership is limited;

(b) the member deals at arm's length with each general partner of the partnership; and

(c) the member, or the member together with persons and partnerships with which it does not deal at arm's length, holds interests in the partnership that have a fair market value of not more than 20% of the fair market value of the interests of all members in the partnership.

Notes: 253.1(2) implements a 2015 Budget proposal to permit charities to invest in LPs without being considered to carry on a "business", violating 149.1(2)(a), (3)(a) or (4)(a). See Adam Aptowitzer, "Change in Limited Partnership Rule Presents New Opportunities", xxxvii(17) *The Canadian Taxpayer* (Carswell) 133-34 (Sept. 11, 2015) and 23(9) *Canadian Not-for-Profit News* (Carswell) 69 (Sept. 2015).

253.1(2) opening words amended by 2019 budget bill #1, effective 2020, to add "registered journalism organization" [defined in 248(1)].

253.1(2) added by 2016 budget bill #1, for investments in LPs made or acquired after April 20, 2015.

Definitions [s. 253.1]: "arm's length" — 251(1); "business" — 248(1); "corporation" — 248(1), *Interpretation Act* 35(1); "fair market value" — see 69(1) Notes; "partnership" — see 96(1) Notes; "person", "registered Canadian amateur athletic association", "registered charity", "registered journalism organization", "regulation" — 248(1); "trust" — 104(1), 248(1), (3).

254. [Pre-1998] Contract under pension plan — Where a document has been issued or a contract has been entered into before July 31, 1997 purporting to create, to establish, to extinguish or to be in substitution for, a taxpayer's right to an amount or amounts, immediately or in the future, out of or under a superannuation or pension fund or plan,

(a) if the rights provided for in the document or contract are rights provided for by the superannuation or pension plan or are rights to a payment or payments out of the superannuation or pension fund, and the taxpayer acquired an interest under the document or in the contract before that day, any payment under the document or contract is deemed to be a payment out of or

under the superannuation or pension fund or plan and the taxpayer is deemed not to have received, by the issuance of the document or entering into the contract, an amount out of or under the superannuation or pension fund or plan; and

(b) if the rights created or established by the document or contract are not rights provided for by the superannuation or pension plan or a right to payments out of the superannuation or pension fund, an amount equal to the value of the rights created or established by the document or contract shall be deemed to have been received by the taxpayer out of or under the superannuation or pension fund or plan when the document was issued or the contract was entered into.

Related Provisions: 147.3(10) — Taxation of amount transferred; 147.4(2) — Amendment to RPP annuity contract; 147.4(3) — Substitution of new RPP annuity contract.

Notes: 254 amended by 1995-97 technical bill, effective July 31, 1997.

Definitions [s. 254]: "amount", "taxpayer" — 248(1).

Interpretation Bulletins: IT-499R: Superannuation or pension benefits.

Information Circulars: 72-13R8: Employees' pension plans; 74-1R5: Form T2037 — Notice of purchase of annuity with "plan" funds.

Forms: T2037: Notice of purchase of annuity with "plan" funds.

255. "Canada" — For the purposes of this Act, "Canada" is hereby declared to include and to have always included

(a) the sea bed and subsoil of the submarine areas adjacent to the coasts of Canada in respect of which the Government of Canada or of a province grants a right, licence or privilege to explore for, drill for or take any minerals, petroleum, natural gas or any related hydrocarbons; and

(b) the seas and airspace above the submarine areas referred to in paragraph (a) in respect of any activities carried on in connection with the exploration for or exploitation of the minerals, petroleum, natural gas or hydrocarbons referred to in that paragraph.

Related Provisions: 37(1.3) — SR&ED within 200 nautical miles offshore is deemed done in Canada; 127(9)"qualified property" closing words — "Canada" includes prescribed offshore region for certain investment tax credit purposes; 248(1)"corporation incorporated in Canada" — "Canada" includes areas before they were part of Canada; 250 — Extended meaning of "resident in Canada"; 253 — Extended meaning of "carrying on business in Canada"; *Income Tax Conventions Interpretation Act* s. 5 — Meaning of "Canada" for treaty purposes; *Interpretation Act* 8(2.1), (2.2) — Application to exclusive economic zone and continental shelf; *Interpretation Act* 35(1) — "Canada" includes internal waters and territorial seas; Canada-U.S. Tax Treaty:Art. III:1(a) — Meaning of "Canada" for treaty purposes.

Notes: Income of a professional diver working in the area covered by s. 255 is taxable in Canada: VIEWS doc 2003-0003125. For interpretation of "exploration", "exploitation" and "in respect of" in 255(b) see doc 2006-0183921E5.

See also 37(1.3) and *Interpretation Act* 8(2.1) and (2.2) (near the end of this book), which extend the meaning of "Canada" to the exclusive economic zone and the continental shelf for certain purposes; and Daniel Lang & Lloyd Sparling, "Taxation of Satellites", 13(8) *Canadian Tax Highlights* (ctf.ca) 2 (Aug. 2005).

For the meaning of "right, licence or privilege" in para. (a), see Notes to 66(15)"Canadian resource property".

Definitions [s. 255]: "mineral" — 248(1); "province" — *Interpretation Act* 35(1).

Interpretation Bulletins: IT-494: Hire of ships and aircraft from non-residents.

256. (1) Associated corporations — For the purposes of this Act, one corporation is associated with another in a taxation year if, at any time in the year,

(a) one of the corporations controlled, directly or indirectly in any manner whatever, the other;

(b) both of the corporations were controlled, directly or indirectly in any manner whatever, by the same person or group of persons;

(c) each of the corporations was controlled, directly or indirectly in any manner whatever, by a person and the person who so controlled one of the corporations was related to the person who so controlled the other, and either of those persons owned, in respect of each corporation, not less than 25% of the issued shares of any class, other than a specified class, of the capital stock thereof;

(d) one of the corporations was controlled, directly or indirectly in any manner whatever, by a person and that person was related to each member of a group of persons that so controlled the other corporation, and that person owned, in respect of the other corporation, not less than 25% of the issued shares of any class, other than a specified class, of the capital stock thereof; or

(e) each of the corporations was controlled, directly or indirectly in any manner whatever, by a related group and each of the members of one of the related groups was related to all of the members of the other related group, and one or more persons who were members of both related groups, either alone or together, owned, in respect of each corporation, not less than 25% of the issued shares of any class, other than a specified class of the capital stock thereof.

Related Provisions: 18(2.2)–(2.4) — Associated corps (ACs) share $1,000,000 base level deduction; 37(9.5) — Extended meaning of "associated" for SR&ED specified-employee payment limitation; 125(2)–(4) — ACs share $500,000 income limit for small business deduction; 127(10.2)–(10.4) — ACs share $3m expenditure limit for investment tax credit; 127.1(2) — ACs share $500,000 taxable income limit to be qualifying corps for refundable investment tax credit; 128(1)(f) — Bankrupt corporation deemed not associated; 129(6) — Investment income from AC deemed active business income; 191.1(2)–(4) — ACs share dividend allowance for Part VI.1 tax; 256(1.1) — "Specified class" defined; 256(1.2) — Control, etc.; 256(1.5) — Person deemed related to self; 256(2) — Corporations associated through a third corp; 256(2.1) — Anti-avoidance rule; 256(5.1), (6.2) — Control in fact; 256(6.1) — Simultaneous control by different persons.

Notes: Associated corporations must share various limits, including the small business deduction limit of $500,000 of active business income (125(2)–(5)); see Related Provisions above for others. Note the additional rules in 256, especially 256(2) and (2.1).

Although a person who controls a corp is normally not part of a group that controls it (*Southside Car Market*, [1982] C.T.C. 214 (FCTD)), 256(1.2)(b)(i) provides otherwise for purposes of s. 256.

For discussion see Donnelly & Young, "The Associated Corporation Rules", 46(3) *Canadian Tax Journal* 589-625 (1998); Diep & Micallef, "Associated, Affiliated and Related", 2005 Cdn Tax Foundation conference report, 38:1-14 and 39:1-15; Marion, "Associated Corporations", 2008 Prairie Provinces Tax Conference (ctf.ca), 3:1-27; Blucher, "Association Rules", 10(11) *Tax Hyperion* (Carswell) 1-3 (Nov. 2013); Granelli, "Association and Control", 247 *The Estate Planner* (CCH) 1-4 (Aug. 2015) and 2260 *Tax Topics* 1-4 (July 2, 2015); Pisesky, "Trust Planning: Beware Association", 5(4) *Canadian Tax Focus* (ctf.ca) 5-6 (Nov. 2015); Ideias, "Related, Affiliated and Associated Rules", Tax Planner Guide 16 (*Taxnet Pro*, 2019, 11pp.); Arkin & McLeod, "It's Just Not Working Out! Disassociating Companies", 2019 Atlantic Provinces Tax Conf 7:1-48.

For an example of 256(1)(b) applying see VIEWS doc 2012-0467121E5. For examples of 256(1)(d) applying see 2008-0285021C6, 2009-0310821E5. Where a corporation is controlled by a trust, see 2009-0330271C6.

Interpretation Bulletins: IT-64R4: Corporations: association and control.

Advance Tax Rulings: ATR-13: Corporations not associated.

Forms: T2 Sched. 9: Related and associated corporations.

(1.1) Definition of "specified class"

For the purposes of subsection (1), "specified class" means a class of shares of the capital stock of a corporation where, under the terms or conditions of the shares or any agreement in respect thereof,

(a) the shares are not convertible or exchangeable;

(b) the shares are non-voting;

(c) the amount of each dividend payable on the shares is calculated as a fixed amount or by reference to a fixed percentage of an amount equal to the fair market value of the consideration for which the shares were issued;

(d) the annual rate of the dividend on the shares, expressed as a percentage of an amount equal to the fair market value of the consideration for which the shares were issued, cannot in any event exceed,

(i) where the shares were issued before 1984, the rate of interest prescribed for the purposes of subsection 161(1) at the time the shares were issued, and

(ii) where the shares were issued after 1983, the prescribed rate of interest at the time the shares were issued; and

(e) the amount that any holder of the shares is entitled to receive on the redemption, cancellation or acquisition of the shares by the corporation or by any person with whom the corporation does not deal at arm's length cannot exceed the total of an amount equal to the fair market value of the consideration for which the shares were issued and the amount of any unpaid dividends thereon.

Related Provisions: 256(1.2) — Control; 256(1.5) — Person deemed related to self.

Notes: Voting shares that are subject to a shareholders' agreement restricting the voting rights are still "voting" shares and cannot be a specified class: VIEWS doc 2003-0028075. A share that *might* be exchanged or converted, but only if the shareholder and corporation agree, falls within 256(1.1)(a): doc 2005-0114971E5.

For interpretation of 256(1.1)(d) see VIEWS doc 2009-0340591E5 (conditions must be met throughout the period the shares are issued and outstanding).

256(1.1)(d)(i) added by 1991 technical bill, effective 1989.

Regulations: 4301(c) (prescribed rate of interest).

Interpretation Bulletins: IT-64R4: Corporations: association and control.

(1.2) Control, etc.

For the purposes of this subsection and subsections (1), (1.1) and (1.3) to (5),

(a) a group of persons in respect of a corporation means any two or more persons each of whom owns shares of the capital stock of the corporation;

(b) for greater certainty,

(i) a corporation that is controlled by one or more members of a particular group of persons in respect of that corporation shall be considered to be controlled by that group of persons, and

(ii) a corporation may be controlled by a person or a particular group of persons notwithstanding that the corporation is also controlled or deemed to be controlled by another person or group of persons;

(c) a corporation shall be deemed to be controlled by another corporation, a person or a group of persons at any time where

(i) shares of the capital stock of the corporation having a fair market value of more than 50% of the fair market value of all the issued and outstanding shares of the capital stock of the corporation, or

(ii) common shares of the capital stock of the corporation having a fair market value of more than 50% of the fair market value of all the issued and outstanding common shares of the capital stock of the corporation

are owned at that time by the other corporation, the person or the group of persons, as the case may be;

(d) where shares of the capital stock of a corporation are owned, or deemed by this subsection to be owned, at any time by another corporation (in this paragraph referred to as the "holding corporation"), those shares shall be deemed to be owned at that time by any shareholder of the holding corporation in a proportion equal to the proportion of all those shares that

(i) the fair market value of the shares of the capital stock of the holding corporation owned at that time by the shareholder

is of

(ii) the fair market value of all the issued shares of the capital stock of the holding corporation outstanding at that time;

(e) where, at any time, shares of the capital stock of a corporation are property of a partnership, or are deemed by this subsection to be owned by the partnership, those shares shall be deemed to be owned at that time by each member of the partnership in a proportion equal to the proportion of all those shares that

(i) the member's share of the income or loss of the partnership for its fiscal period that includes that time

is of

(ii) the income or loss of the partnership for its fiscal period that includes that time and for this purpose, where the income and loss of the partnership for its fiscal period that includes that time are nil, that proportion shall be computed as if the partnership had had income for that period in the amount of $1,000,000;

(f) where shares of the capital stock of a corporation are owned, or deemed by this subsection to be owned, at any time by a trust,

(i) [Repealed]

(ii) where a beneficiary's share of the accumulating income or capital therefrom depends on the exercise by any person of, or the failure by any person to exercise, any discretionary power, those shares are deemed to be owned at that time by the beneficiary,

(iii) in any case where subparagraph (ii) does not apply, a beneficiary is deemed at that time to own the proportion of those shares that the fair market value of the beneficial interest in the trust of the beneficiary is of the fair market value of all beneficial interests in the trust, and

(iv) in the case of a trust referred to in subsection 75(2), the person referred to in that subsection from whom property of the trust or property for which it was substituted was directly or indirectly received shall be deemed to own those shares at that time; and

(g) in determining the fair market value of a share of the capital stock of a corporation, all issued and outstanding shares of the capital stock of the corporation shall be deemed to be non-voting.

Related Provisions: 127(10.22), (10.23), 127.1(2.2), (2.3) — Non-application of 256(1.2) to SR&ED credit in certain cases; 248(5) — Substituted property; 256(1.5) — Person deemed related to self; 256(1.6) — Exception; 256(6.1) — Simultaneous control by different persons.

Notes: 256(1.2)(b)(i) overrules *Southside Car Market*, [1982] C.T.C. 214 (FCTD) for purposes of s. 256.

256(1.2)(c) applied in *Kruger Wayagamack*, 2015 TCC 90, paras. 90-162; aff'd 2016 FCA 192 (control issues ignored for share valuation purposes due to para. (g)). 256(1.2)(c) does not take precedence over 256(9): VIEWS docs 9525315, 2009-0330131C6.

256(1.2)(f)(ii) applies to beneficiaries with a future conditional right under a discretionary trust: VIEWS doc 2005-0112511E5. For further broad CRA interpretations of (f)(ii) see 2005-0111731E5, 2006-0176801E5, 2006-0177781E5, 2006-0195971C6, 2008-0285041C6, 2015-0608671E5. In *Propep Inc.*, 2009 FCA 274 (leave to appeal denied 2010 CarswellNat 506 (SCC)), having an eventual right to a trust's capital if a corporation was dissolved (or after 100 years, per the Quebec *Civil Code*) made a person a beneficiary, so (f)(ii) applied. The FCA stated that 248(25) applies to the term "beneficiary" outside ss. 104-108 (this is logically wrong). A discretionary power limiting each beneficiary (B) to 24.99% of the trust's income and capital still led to (f)(ii) attributing 100% of shares held by the trust to the Bs: *Moules Industriels*, 2018 TCC 85 (under appeal to FCA) [Hamelin, "Discretionary Trusts and Associated Corporations", 18(3) *Tax for the Owner-Manager* (ctf.ca) 8-9 (July 2018)].

For the meaning of "indirectly" in (f)(iv), see Notes to 17.1(1).

See also Harris, "ITA 256(1.2)(f)(ii)", 2010 Atlantic Provinces Tax Conference (ctf.ca), 4C:1-8; Truster, "Trusts and the Associated-Corporation Rules", 11(4) *Tax for the Owner-Manager* (ctf.ca) 4 (Oct. 2011) (re 256(1.2)(f)(iii) and 256(1.3)).

256(1.2)(f)(i) repealed, and (f)(ii)-(iii) amended to delete references to it, by 2014 budget bill #2, for 2016 and later taxation years. There are no longer special rules for testamentary trusts, with the introduction of 248(1)"graduated rate estate".

Interpretation Bulletins: IT-64R4: Corporations: association and control.

(1.3) Parent deemed to own shares

— Where at any time shares of the capital stock of a corporation are owned by a child who is under 18 years of age, for the purpose of determining whether the corporation is associated at that time with any other corporation that is controlled, directly or indirectly in any manner whatever, by a parent of the child or by a group of persons of which the parent is a member, the shares shall be deemed to be owned at that time by the parent unless, having regard to all the circumstances, it can reasonably be considered that the child manages the business and affairs of the corporation and does so without a significant degree of influence by the parent.

Related Provisions: 256(1.2) — Control, etc.; 256(1.5) — Person deemed related to self; 256(5.1), (6.2) — Control in fact.

Notes: 256(1.3) applies even where the child turns 18 early in the year: VIEWS doc 2015-0610921E5. It applies together with 256(1.2)(f)(ii) to deem parents to own shares

owned by a discretionary trust for their children: 2015-0608781E5 (but shares are not double-counted for multiple children).

256(1.3) applied in *Propep Inc.*, 2009 FCA 274; leave to appeal denied 2010 CarswellNat 506 (SCC).

256(1.3) amended by 1991 technical bill, effective 1989-90.

Interpretation Bulletins: IT-64R4: Corporations: association and control.

(1.4) Options and rights

— For the purpose of determining whether a corporation is associated with another corporation with which it is not otherwise associated, where a person or any partnership in which the person has an interest has a right at any time under a contract, in equity or otherwise, either immediately or in the future and either absolutely or contingently,

(a) to, or to acquire, shares of the capital stock of a corporation, or to control the voting rights of shares of the capital stock of a corporation, the person or partnership shall, except where the right is not exercisable at that time because the exercise thereof is contingent on the death, bankruptcy or permanent disability of an individual, be deemed to own the shares at that time, and the shares shall be deemed to be issued and outstanding at that time; or

(b) to cause a corporation to redeem, acquire or cancel any shares of its capital stock owned by other shareholders of a corporation, the person or partnership shall, except where the right is not exercisable at that time because the exercise thereof is contingent on the death, bankruptcy or permanent disability of an individual, be deemed at that time to have the same position in relation to control of the corporation and ownership of shares of its capital stock as if the shares were redeemed, acquired or cancelled by the corporation.

Related Provisions: 256(1.2) — Control, etc.; 256(1.5) — Person deemed related to self; 256(1.6) — Exception; 256(5.1) — Control in fact.

Notes: For CRA application of 256(1.4) in specific situations see VIEWS docs 2002-0172315, 2004-0096991E5, 2006-0119901E5, 2006-0192291C6 (2006 ICAA Roundtable q. 14), 2006-0197841E5, 2007-0243211C6 (shotgun clauses), 2009-0329941C6 (various examples of "a right to, or to acquire..."), 2010-0380571E5 (interaction with 251(5)(b)(ii)); 2016-0652971C6 [2016 APFF q.7] (right to find prospective buyer, and automatic redemption of shares under shareholder agreement, do not trigger 256(1.4)). See also Notes to 251(5).

See also Bernstein, "Buy-Sell Provisions and Association", 24(11) *Canadian Tax Highlights* (ctf.ca) 9-10 (Nov. 2016); Carr, "An Expensive Power of Attorney", tinyurl.com/carr-expoa (July 2019).

256(1.4) amended by 1991 technical bill, retroactive to its introduction (1989-1990).

Interpretation Bulletins: IT-64R4: Corporations: association and control.

(1.5) Person related to himself, herself or itself

— For the purposes of subsections (1) to (1.4) and (1.6) to (5), where a person owns shares in two or more corporations, the person shall as shareholder of one of the corporations be deemed to be related to himself, herself or itself as shareholder of each of the other corporations.

Related Provisions: 256(1.2) — Control, etc.

Interpretation Bulletins: IT-64R4: Corporations: association and control.

(1.6) Exception

— For the purposes of subsection (1.2) and notwithstanding subsection (1.4), any share that is

(a) described in paragraph (e) of the definition "term preferred share" in subsection 248(1) during the applicable time referred to in that paragraph, or

(b) a share of a specified class within the meaning of subsection (1.1)

shall be deemed not to have been issued and outstanding and not to be owned by any shareholder and an amount equal to the greater of the paid-up capital of the share and the amount, if any, that any holder of the share is entitled to receive on the redemption, cancellation or acquisition of the share by the corporation shall be deemed to be a liability of the corporation.

Related Provisions: 256(1.2) — Control, etc.; 256(1.5) — Person deemed related to self.

(2) Corporations associated through a third corporation — For the purposes of

(a) this Act, subject to paragraph (b), two corporations are deemed to be associated with each other at a particular time if

(i) they would, but for this subsection, not be associated with each other at the particular time, and

(ii) each corporation is associated with, or is deemed by this subsection to be associated with, the same corporation (in this subsection referred to as the "third corporation") at the particular time; and

(b) section 125,

(i) if the third corporation is not a Canadian-controlled private corporation at the particular time, the two corporations are deemed not to be associated with each other at the particular time, and

(ii) if the third corporation is a Canadian-controlled private corporation that elects in prescribed form to apply this subparagraph in its taxation year that includes the particular time, the two corporations are deemed not to be associated with each other at the particular time and the business limit of the third corporation for its taxation year that includes the particular time is deemed to be nil.

Related Provisions: 125(1)(a)(i)(C) — When election made, exclusion of certain intercompany payments from small business deduction; 256(1.2) — Control, etc.; 256(1.5) — Person deemed related to self.

Notes: 256(2) provides a "transitivity" rule: if A and B are associated, and A and C are associated, then B and C are associated, unless A elects (on T2 Schedule 28) not to be associated with either — in which case A cannot claim any small business deduction (see 125(2)) but B and C can each claim the full amount. The election applies only for the small business deduction and not for 129(6) (VIEWS docs 2003-0030905, 2003-0037075, 2010-0387591E5) or for Large Corporations Tax business limit (2003-005170117) in CRA's view, even though 125(5.1) is used to determine that limit. For those other purposes, one might still get the same result from *Holiday Luggage*, [1987] 1 C.T.C. 23 (FCTD), if that case applies beyond s. 125.

256(2)(a) applied in *9181-4517 Québec*, 2021 QCCA 11 (parallel Quebec rule): XY&Z controlled A and B, X&Y controlled A and C, so B and C were associated.

Before 2016-17, the election could be used to de-associate all of A, B and C where A would have no small business deduction due to A's high taxable capital. This no longer works because the words "the third corporation [A] shall be deemed not to be associated with either of the other two corporations [B and C]" were changed to "the two corporations [B and C] are deemed not to be associated with each other", so C remains associated with A. See Notes to 125(5.1), and VIEWS doc 2017-0685121E5.

If there are more than 3 corporations, they can make multiple 256(2) elections: VIEWS docs 2003-0038235, 2004-0108311E5.

The election can affect when tax for the year is due: see 248(1)"balance-due day"(d).

For a corporation filing Quebec returns, a 256(2) election must be copied to Revenu Québec: *Taxation Act* ss. 771.2.1.3, 21.4.6.

For more discussion see Kirby, "Associated Corporations: Deemed Active Business Income", 6(2) *Tax for the Owner-Manager* (ctf.ca) 2-3 (Apr. 2006); VIEWS docs 2004-0065291E5, 2005-0163391E5, 2006-021633117, 2011-039447117.

256(2) amended by 2016 budget bill #2, effective for taxation years that begin after March 21, 2016. For earlier years, read:

(2) Where two corporations

(a) would, but for this subsection, not be associated with each other at any time, and

(b) are associated, or are deemed by this subsection to be associated, with the same corporation (in this subsection referred to as the "third corporation") at that time,

they shall, for the purposes of this Act, be deemed to be associated with each other at that time, except that, for the purposes of section 125, where the third corporation is not a Canadian-controlled private corporation at that time or elects, in prescribed form, for its taxation year that includes that time not to be associated with either of the other two corporations, the third corporation shall be deemed not to be associated with either of the other two corporations in that taxation year and its business limit for that taxation year shall be deemed to be nil.

Interpretation Bulletins: IT-64R4: Corporations: association and control; IT-243R4: Dividend refund to private corporations.

Advance Tax Rulings: ATR-13: Corporations not associated.

Forms: T2 Sched. 28: Election not to be associated through a third corporation (2016 and later tax years).

(2.1) Anti-avoidance — For the purposes of this Act, where, in the case of two or more corporations, it may reasonably be considered that one of the main reasons for the separate existence of those corporations in a taxation year is to reduce the amount of taxes that would otherwise be payable under this Act or to increase the amount of refundable investment tax credit under section 127.1, the two or more corporations shall be deemed to be associated with each other in the year.

Notes: This rule was in 247(2) before 1988. See also 256(5.1) for an alternative rule that may apply.

256(2.1) (or its predecessors) **applied** in: *Debruth Investments*, [1975] C.T.C. 55 (FCA) (land development corp owned by parents; 4 corps owned by trusts for their 4 minor children); *Decker Contracting*, 1978 CarswellNat 1155 (FCA) (non-tax reasons given for separate corp owned by owners' wives were not credible); *Levitt-Safety*, [1973] C.T.C. 483 (FCTD) (corps controlled by two brothers); *Covertite*, [1981] C.T.C. 464 (FCTD) (Ontario corp owned by wife, same business as Quebec corp owned by husband); *Maintenance Euréka*, 2011 TCC 307 (husband and wife each controlled 1 corp, and corps offered same services performed by same people, operated in same premises, used same telephone and fax numbers, and did not bid on same tenders); *Brownco*, 2008 TCC 58, para. 75 (tax reduction was a main reason for separate corps); *Jencal Holdings*, 2019 TCC 16 (insufficient evidence as to reasons for corps' separate existence); *Nicole L. Tiessen Interior Design*, 2021 TCC 29 (under appeal to FCA) (corp of architects and interior designers restructured into 15 pairs of corps to multiply the exemption) [Dolson, "Nicole L. Tiessen", XVI(2) *Corporate Structures & Groups* (Federated Press) 1-8 (2021)].

In practice, successful appeal on this issue requires showing that the reason for the existence of 2 corps is "asset protection, activity diversification, decentralization for greater profit, a spouse's intent to operate his or her own business, or estate planning", and witness credibility is crucial: *Maintenance Euréka*, para. 25.

256(2.1) **did not apply** in: *Bobbie Brooks*, [1973] C.T.C. 431 (FCTD) (business of 3 brothers selling dresses was separate from that of their wives, operated from different premises, selling sportswear); *Lenco Fibre*, [1979] C.T.C. 374 (FCTD) (spouses were unaware of different tax rates); *Hughes Homes*, 1997 CarswellNat 1513 (wife W's decorating business separate from H's construction business for asset protection and to allow W to have her own business); *LJP Sales*, 2003 TCC 851 (couple considering divorce reorganized into 2 corps to save their marriage); *Taber Solids*, 2009 TCC 527 (spouses would have reorganized even without doubling the small business deduction (SBD)); *Prairielane Holdings*, 2019 TCC 157 (corps were stacked to defer tax, not to access the SBD for 1 year).

For more on the meaning of "one of the main reasons" see Notes to 83(2.1).

For CRA interpretations that 256(2.1) may apply, see VIEWS docs 2008-0290721R3, 2008-029256117, 2008-0302121R3, 2011-039447117.

Interpretation Bulletins: IT-64R4: Corporations: association and control.

Advance Tax Rulings: ATR-13: Corporations not associated.

(3) Saving provision — Where one corporation (in this subsection referred to as the "controlled corporation") would, but for this subsection, be associated with another corporation in a taxation year by reason of being controlled, directly or indirectly in any manner whatever, by the other corporation or by reason of both of the corporations being controlled, directly or indirectly in any manner whatever, by the same person at a particular time in the year (which corporation or person so controlling the controlled corporation is in this subsection referred to as the "controller") and it is established to the satisfaction of the Minister that

(a) there was in effect at the particular time an agreement or arrangement enforceable according to the terms thereof, under which, on the satisfaction of a condition or the happening of an event that it is reasonable to expect will be satisfied or happen, the controlled corporation will

(i) cease to be controlled, directly or indirectly in any manner whatever, by the controller, and

(ii) be or become controlled, directly or indirectly in any manner whatever, by a person or group of persons, with whom or with each of the members of which, as the case may be, the controller was at the particular time dealing at arm's length, and

(b) the purpose for which the controlled corporation was at the particular time so controlled was the safeguarding of rights or interests of the controller in respect of

(i) any indebtedness owing to the controller the whole or any part of the principal amount of which was outstanding at the particular time, or

(ii) any shares of the capital stock of the controlled corporation that were owned by the controller at the particular time and that were, under the agreement or arrangement, to be redeemed by the controlled corporation or purchased by the person or group of persons referred to in subparagraph (a)(ii),

the controlled corporation and the other corporation with which it would otherwise be so associated in the year shall be deemed, for the purpose of this Act, not to be associated with each other in the year.

Related Provisions: 256(1.2) — Control, etc.; 256(1.5) — Person deemed related to self; 256(5.1), (6.2) — Controlled directly or indirectly; 256(6.1) — Simultaneous control by different persons.

Notes: For CRA interpretation see VIEWS doc 2010-0373161C6.

Interpretation Bulletins: IT-64R4: Corporations: association and control.

(4) Saving provision — Where one corporation would, but for this subsection, be associated with another corporation in a taxation year by reason of both of the corporations being controlled by the same executor, liquidator of a succession or trustee and it is established to the satisfaction of the Minister

(a) that the executor, liquidator or trustee did not acquire control of the corporations as a result of one or more estates or trusts created by the same individual or two or more individuals not dealing with each other at arm's length, and

(b) that the estate or trust under which the executor, liquidator or trustee acquired control of each of the corporations arose only on the death of the individual creating the estate or trust,

the two corporations are deemed, for the purposes of this Act, not to be associated with each other in the year.

Related Provisions: 256(1.2) — Control, etc.; 256(1.5) — Person deemed related to self; 256(6.1) — Simultaneous control by different persons.

Notes: References to "liquidator of a succession" added to 256(4) by 2001 *Civil Code* harmonization bill, effective June 14, 2001. The change is non-substantive; see *Interpretation Act* s. 8.2.

Interpretation Bulletins: IT-64R4: Corporations: association and control.

(5) Idem — Where one corporation would, but for this subsection, be associated with another corporation in a taxation year, by reason only that the other corporation is a trustee under a trust pursuant to which the corporation is controlled, the two corporations shall be deemed, for the purposes of this Act, not to be associated with each other in the year unless, at any time in the year, a settlor of the trust controlled or is a member of a related group that controlled the other corporation that is the trustee under the trust.

Related Provisions: 256(1.2) — Control, etc.; 256(1.5) — Person deemed related to self; 256(6.1) — Simultaneous control by different persons.

Interpretation Bulletins: IT-64R4: Corporations: association and control.

(5.1) Control in fact — For the purposes of this Act, where the expression "controlled, directly or indirectly in any manner whatever," is used, a corporation shall be considered to be so controlled by another corporation, person or group of persons (in this subsection referred to as the "controller") at any time where, at that time, the controller has any direct or indirect influence that, if exercised, would result in control in fact of the corporation, except that, where the corporation and the controller are dealing with each other at arm's length and the influence is derived from a franchise, licence, lease, distribution, supply or management agreement or other similar agreement or arrangement, the main purpose of which is to govern the relationship between the corporation and the controller regarding the manner in which a business carried on by the corporation is to be conducted, the corporation shall not be considered to be controlled, directly or indirectly in any manner whatever, by the controller by reason only of that agreement or arrangement.

Related Provisions: 256(5.11) — Factors to consider in determining direct or indirect influence; 256(6) — Idem; 256(6.2) — Simultaneous control — application of 256(6.1).

Notes: For *de facto* control (DFC), 256(5.11) now overrides *Silicon Graphics*, 2002 FCA 260, para. 67 and *McGillivray Restaurant*, 2016 FCA 99 (followed in *North American Lifestyles*, 2019 MBQB 29). See Notes to 256(5.11). Due to 256(5.11), the pre-*McGillivray* case law below is generally applicable.

DFC of Cco was found in: *Mimetix Pharmaceuticals*, 2003 FCA 106 (US company owned 50% of the shares, US director took or approved all key decisions for Cco and the US company was its "controlling mind"); *Plomberie J.C. Langlois*, 2006 FCA 113 (50% shareholder was the sole director and effectively ran Cco's administration and finances; the actual facts were more important than the written agreements); *Corpor-Air*, 2006 TCC 75 (wife's Cco was economically dependent on husband's company and she was not involved in day-to-day decisions, so he had DFC over it); *Avotus Corp.*, 2007 TCC 505 (chairman's (unused) power to cast deciding vote at directors' meetings gave him control); *Brownco Inc.*, 2008 TCC 58 (50% ownership plus casting vote on the board, per unanimous shareholders' agreement (UShA)); *Taber Solids*, 2009 TCC 527 (companies owned by spouses were "inextricably linked by family and by contract", and husband had influence over wife's company); *Lyrtech RD Inc.*, 2014 FCA 267 (leave to appeal denied 2015 CarswellNat 2528 (SCC)) (public corp exercised dominant economic influence over Cco); *Solutions MindReady*, 2015 TCC 17 (FCA appeal discontinued A-62-15) (same KPMG-designed structure as *Lyrtech*; company remained effective subsidiary of public corp after reorganization); *McGillivray Restaurant*, 2016 FCA 99 (wife owned 76% of shares of Cco, but oral agreement provided husband would be sole director); *Aeronautic Development*, 2018 FCA 67 (leave to appeal denied 2019 CarswellNat 595 (SCC)) (extreme economic dependence on non-resident customer meant they were not at arm's length); *CO2 Solution*, 2019 TCC 286 (aff'd 2021 FCA 115 as *Bresse Syndics*, on ground there was *de jure* control anyway) (public corp Pco created trust (with Pco's directors as trustees) to own R&Dco; Pco had right to control R&Dco through trust deed).

A lack of DFC was found in *Timco Holdings*, 2005 TCC 701 (50% shareholder did not have control); *Kruger Wayagamack*, 2015 TCC 90, paras. 72-89 (aff'd on other grounds 2016 FCA 192).

Franchises: Routine franchise arrangements do not create DFC by the franchisor: *Lenester Sales [Giant Tiger]*, 2004 FCA 217; note that 256(5.1) refers to control of the *corporation*, not control of the *business*. See Michele Anderson, "No De Facto Control in the Franchise Context?", XII(4) *Tax Litigation* (Federated Press) 787-91 (2005). On the other hand, in *9044-2807 Québec Inc. (Transport M.L. Couture)*, 2004 FCA 23, management contracts, economic dependence and family relationships were found to give 5 brothers DFC of their parents' company: "the evidence must show that the decision-making power of the corporation ... lies elsewhere than with those who have *de jure* control" (para. 24). CRA stated at the 2004 Cdn Tax Foundation annual conference (pp. 5A:4-5) that no policy change is required by *Lenester* and *9044-2807*, and that *Lenester* applies only to genuine franchises.

For more CRA interpretation see IT-64R4; VIEWS docs 2008-0285211C6, 2009-0343331I7, 2010-0359481E5 [Jeanne Chiang, "Partnerships of Corporations and the Small Business Deduction", 10(3) *Tax for the Owner-Manager* (ctf.ca) 1-2 (July 2010)], 2010-0382381E5, 2011-039447117; 2013-0495811C6 [2013 APFF q.13] (casting vote can give control, per *Avotus* and *Brownco*).

For more on 256(5.1) see Kroft, 2003 Cdn Tax Foundation conference report at 9:1-4; Prieur & Mayer, "Le fait et la théorie de l'influence", 53(1) *Canadian Tax Journal* 62-106 (2005); Couzin, "Some Reflections on Corporate Control", 53(2) *CTJ* 305-32 (2005); Christov, "De Facto Control", 1978 *Tax Topics [TT]* (CCH) 1-6 (Feb. 4, 2010); Friedlan, "De Facto Control", 2010 Ontario Tax Conference (ctf.ca), 4:1-21; Studniberg, "The Concept of De Facto Control", 54(1) *Canadian Business Law Journal* 17-37 (2013) (ssrn.com/abstract=2382190); Studniberg & Nitikman, "De Facto Control", 2244 *TT* (CCH) 1-7 (March 12, 2015) and 2245 1-6 (March 19, 2015); Fernando, "De Facto Control and CCPC Status", 15(3) *Tax Hyperion* (Carswell) 4-8 (May-June 2018) [re *McGillivray*, *Aeronautic* and 256(5.11)]; Goldberg, "Part 2 ... The Impact of Control", 2460 *TT* 1-5 (May 2, 2019) and "Part 3...", 2461 1-4 (May 16, 2019); Thompson & Katlai, "Venture Capital Financings", 21(2) *Tax for the Owner-Manager* (ctf.ca) 5-6 (April 2021).

Note that even if 256(5.1) does not apply, 256(2.1) can deem corps to be associated.

Interpretation Bulletins: IT-64R4: Corporations: association and control; IT-236R4: Reserves — disposition of capital property (cancelled); IT-313R2: Eligible capital property — rules where a taxpayer has ceased carrying on a business or has died; IT-291R2: Transfer of property to a corporation under subsection 85(1); IT-458R2: Canadian-controlled private corporation.

I.T. Technical News: 25 (*Silicon Graphics* case); 32 (control in fact: impact of recent jurisprudence).

(5.11) Factual control — Interpretation — For the purposes of the Act, the determination of whether a taxpayer has, in respect of a corporation, any direct or indirect influence that, if exercised, would result in control in fact of the corporation, shall

(a) take into consideration all factors that are relevant in the circumstances; and

(b) not be limited to, and the relevant factors need not include, whether the taxpayer has a legally enforceable right or ability to effect a change in the board of directors of the corporation, or its powers, or to exercise influence over the shareholder or shareholders who have that right or ability.

Notes: 256(5.11) overrules *McGillivray Restaurant*, 2016 FCA 99, which held that, for a factor to be considered in determining whether factual control exists (for 256(5.1)), it must include "a legally enforceable right and ability to effect a change to the board of directors or its powers, or to exercise influence over the shareholder or shareholders who have that right and ability".

For discussion see Peters, "Reversing the Flow on *De Facto* Control", XIV(1) *Corporate Structures & Groups* (Federated Press) 2-5 (2017); Manuel & Hausch, "CCPC and *De Facto* Control Rules: Proposed Subsection 256(5.11)", *SR&ED Newsletter, Taxnet Pro* Corporate Tax Centre (Sept. 2017, 3pp.); Adlington, "*De Facto* Control", 15(5) *Tax Hyperion* (Carswell) 7-9 (Sept-Oct 2018); Katlai, "*Buckerfield to McGillivray*", *Taxnet Pro* Tax Disputes Centre (Oct. 2018, 5pp) and "De Facto Control", 27(8) *Canadian Tax Highlights* (ctf.ca) 9-11 (Aug. 2019).

256(5.11) added by 2017 budget bill #2, for tax years that begin after March 21, 2017.

(6) Idem — For the purposes of this Act, where a corporation (in this subsection referred to as the "controlled corporation") would, but for this subsection, be regarded as having been controlled or controlled, directly or indirectly in any manner whatever, by a person or partnership (in this subsection referred to as the "controller") at a particular time and it is established that

(a) there was in effect at the particular time an agreement or arrangement enforceable according to the terms thereof, under which, on the satisfaction of a condition or the happening of an event that it is reasonable to expect will be satisfied or happen, the controlled corporation will

(i) cease to be controlled, or controlled, directly or indirectly in any manner whatever, as the case may be, by the controller, and

(ii) be or become controlled, or controlled, directly or indirectly in any manner whatever, as the case may be, by a person or group of persons, with whom or with each of the members of which, as the case may be, the controller was at the particular time dealing at arm's length, and

(b) the purpose for which the controlled corporation was at the particular time so controlled, or controlled, directly or indirectly in any manner whatever, as the case may be, was the safeguarding of rights or interests of the controller in respect of

(i) any indebtedness owing to the controller the whole or any part of the principal amount of which was outstanding at the particular time, or

(ii) any shares of the capital stock of the controlled corporation that were owned by the controller at the particular time and that were, under the agreement or arrangement, to be redeemed by the controlled corporation or purchased by the person or group of persons referred to in subparagraph (a)(ii),

the controlled corporation is deemed not to have been controlled by the controller at the particular time.

Related Provisions: 256(5.1), (6.2) — Controlled directly or indirectly; 256(6.1) — Simultaneous control by different persons.

Notes: See Notes to 111(5) on the meaning of "control". For CRA interpretation see VIEWS docs 2010-0373161C6, 2015-0565741E5.

256(6) amended by 1995-97 technical bill, for tax years that begin after 1988.

Interpretation Bulletins: IT-64R4: Corporations: association and control; IT-458R2: Canadian-controlled private corporation.

(6.1) Simultaneous control — For the purposes of this Act and for greater certainty,

(a) where a corporation (in this paragraph referred to as the "subsidiary") would be controlled by another corporation (in this paragraph referred to as the "parent") if the parent were not controlled by any person or group of persons, the subsidiary is controlled by

(i) the parent, and

(ii) any person or group of persons by whom the parent is controlled; and

(b) where a corporation (in this paragraph referred to as the "subject corporation") would be controlled by a group of persons (in this paragraph referred to as the "first-tier group") if no corporation that is a member of the first-tier group were controlled by any person or group of persons, the subject corporation is controlled by

(i) the first-tier group, and

(ii) any group of one or more persons comprised of, in respect of every member of the first-tier group, either the member, or a person or group of persons by whom the member is controlled.

Related Provisions: 256(6.2) — Application to 256(5.1).

Notes: 256(6.1) overrides *Parthenon Investments*, [1997] 3 C.T.C. 152 (FCA), where mid-tier control was ignored on the principle that "control cannot allow for two masters simultaneously". Under 256(6.1), a chain with a Canadian corporation at the bottom, U.S. corporation in the middle and a Canadian parent on top is considered "controlled" by a non-resident and will not be a Canadian-controlled private corporation. See also VIEWS doc 2010-0373241C6.

256(6.1) applied in *Lyrtech RD Inc.*, 2014 FCA 267, para. 38 (leave to appeal denied 2015 CarswellNat 2528 (SCC)): simultaneous *de jure* and *de facto* control are considered in determining CCPC status, and either one can put a corporation offside. It also applied in *Promutuel Réassurance*, 2020 TCC 13, where a group of mutual insurance corps controlled a Federation which controlled a corp.

256(6.1) added by 2001 technical bill, for tax years that begin after Nov. 1999.

(6.2) Application to control in fact — In its application to subsection (5.1), subsection (6.1) shall be read as if the references in subsection (6.1) to "controlled" were references to "controlled, directly or indirectly in any manner whatever,".

Notes: 256(6.2) added by 2001 technical bill, effective for taxation years that begin after November 1999 (changed from being effective December 1999 by Commons Finance Committee report, May 2001).

(7) Acquiring control — For the purposes of this subsection, of section 55, subsections 66(11), 66.5(3), 66.7(10) and (11), 85(1.2), 88(1.1) and (1.2), 110.1(1.2) and 111(5.4) and paragraph 251.2(2)(a) and of subsection 5905(5.2) of the *Income Tax Regulations*,

(a) control of a particular corporation shall be deemed not to have been acquired solely because of

(i) the acquisition at any time of shares of any corporation by

(A) a particular person who acquired the shares from a person to whom the particular person was related (otherwise than because of a right referred to in paragraph 251(5)(b)) immediately before that time,

(B) a particular person who was related to the particular corporation (otherwise than because of a right referred to in paragraph 251(5)(b)) immediately before that time,

(C) an estate that acquired the shares because of the death of a person,

(D) a particular person who acquired the shares from an estate that arose on and as a consequence of the death of an individual, if the estate acquired the shares from the individual as a consequence of the death and the individual was related to the particular person immediately before the death, [or]

(E) a corporation on a distribution (within the meaning assigned by subsection 55(1)) by a specified corporation (within the meaning assigned by that subsection) if a dividend, to which subsection 55(2) does not apply because of paragraph 55(3)(b), is received in the course of the reorganization in which the distribution occurs,

(ii) the redemption or cancellation at any particular time of, or a change at any particular time in the rights, privileges, restrictions or conditions attaching to, shares of the particular corporation or of a corporation controlling the particular corporation, where each person and each member of each group of persons that controls the particular corporation immediately after the particular time was related (otherwise than because of a right referred to in paragraph 251(5)(b)) to the corporation

(A) immediately before the particular time, or

(B) immediately before the death of a person, where the shares were held immediately before the particular time by an estate that acquired the shares because of the person's death, or

(iii) the acquisition at any time of shares of the particular corporation if

(A) the acquisition of those shares would otherwise result in the acquisition of control of the particular corporation at that time by a related group of persons, and

(B) each member of each group of persons that controls the particular corporation at that time was related (otherwise than because of a right referred to in paragraph 251(5)(b)) to the particular corporation immediately before that time;

(b) where at any time 2 or more corporations (each of which is referred to in this paragraph as a "predecessor corporation") have amalgamated to form one corporate entity (in this paragraph referred to as the "new corporation"),

(i) control of a corporation is deemed not to have been acquired by any person or group of persons solely because of the amalgamation unless it is deemed by subparagraph (ii) or (iii) to have been so acquired,

(ii) a person or group of persons that controls the new corporation immediately after the amalgamation and did not control a predecessor corporation immediately before the amalgamation is deemed to have acquired immediately before the amalgamation control of the predecessor corporation and of each corporation it controlled immediately before the amalgamation (unless the person or group of persons would not have acquired control of the predecessor corporation if the person or group of persons had acquired all the shares of the predecessor corporation immediately before the amalgamation), and

(iii) control of a predecessor corporation and of each corporation it controlled immediately before the amalgamation is deemed to have been acquired immediately before the amalgamation by a person or group of persons

(A) unless the predecessor corporation was related (otherwise than because of a right referred to in paragraph 251(5)(b)) immediately before the amalgamation to each other predecessor corporation,

(B) unless, if one person had immediately after the amalgamation acquired all the shares of the new corporation's capital stock that the shareholders of the predecessor corporation, or of another predecessor corporation that controlled the predecessor corporation, acquired on the amalgamation in consideration for their shares of the predecessor corporation or of the other predecessor corporation, as the case may be, the person would have acquired control of the new corporation as a result of the acquisition of those shares, or

(C) unless this subparagraph would, but for this clause, deem control of each predecessor corporation to have been acquired on the amalgamation where the amalgamation is an amalgamation of

(I) two corporations, or

(II) two corporations (in this subclause referred to as the "parents") and one or more other corporations (each of which is in this subclause referred to as a "subsidiary") that would, if all the shares of each subsidiary's capital stock that were held immediately before the amalgamation by the parents had been held by one person, have been controlled by that person;

(c) subject to paragraph (a), where 2 or more persons (in this paragraph referred to as the "transferors") dispose of shares of the capital stock of a particular corporation in exchange for shares of the capital stock of another corporation (in this paragraph referred to as the "acquiring corporation"), control of the acquiring corporation and of each corporation controlled by it immediately before the exchange is deemed to have been ac-

quired at the time of the exchange by a person or group of persons unless

(i) the particular corporation and the acquiring corporation were related (otherwise than because of a right referred to in paragraph 251(5)(b)) to each other immediately before the exchange, or

(ii) if all the shares of the acquiring corporation's capital stock that were acquired by the transferors on the exchange were acquired at the time of the exchange by one person, the person would not control the acquiring corporation;

(c.1) subject to paragraph (a), if, at any particular time, as part of a series of transactions or events, two or more persons acquire shares of a corporation (in this paragraph referred to as the "acquiring corporation") in exchange for or upon a redemption or surrender of interests in, or as a consequence of a distribution from, a SIFT trust (determined without reference to subsection 122.1(2)), SIFT partnership (determined without reference to subsection 197(8)) or real estate investment trust (as defined in subsection 122.1(1)), control of the acquiring corporation and of each corporation controlled by it immediately before the particular time is deemed to have been acquired by a person or group of persons at the particular time unless

(i) in respect of each of the corporations, a person (in this subparagraph referred to as a "relevant person") affiliated (within the meaning assigned by section 251.1 read without reference to the definition "controlled" in subsection 251.1(3)) with the SIFT trust, SIFT partnership or real estate investment trust owned shares of the particular corporation having a total fair market value of more than 50% of the fair market value of all the issued and outstanding shares of the particular corporation at all times during the period that

(A) begins on the latest of July 14, 2008, the date the particular corporation came into existence and the time of the last acquisition of control, if any, of the particular corporation by a relevant person, and

(B) ends immediately before the particular time,

(ii) if all the securities (in this subparagraph as defined in subsection 122.1(1)) of the acquiring corporation that were acquired as part of the series of transactions or events at or before the particular time were acquired by one person, the person would

(A) not at the particular time control the acquiring corporation, and

(B) have at the particular time acquired securities of the acquiring corporation having a fair market value of not more than 50% of the fair market value of all the issued and outstanding shares of the acquiring corporation, or

(iii) this paragraph previously applied to deem an acquisition of control of the acquiring corporation upon an acquisition of shares that was part of the same series of transactions or events;

(c.2) subject to paragraph (a), if, at any particular time, as part of a series of transactions or events, two or more persons acquire shares of a corporation (in this paragraph referred to as the "acquiring corporation") in exchange for or upon a redemption or surrender of interests in, or as a consequence of a distribution from, a partnership or trust, control of the acquiring corporation and of each corporation controlled by it immediately before the particular time is deemed to have been acquired by a person or group of persons at the particular time unless

(i) in respect of each of the corporations, a person affiliated with the partnership or trust owned immediately before the particular time shares of the particular corporation having a total fair market value of more than 50% of the fair market value of all the issued and outstanding shares of the particular corporation immediately before the particular time,

(ii) if all the "securities" (in this subparagraph as defined in subsection 122.1(1)) of the acquiring corporation that were acquired at or before the particular time as part of the series were acquired by one person, the person would

(A) not at the particular time control the acquiring corporation, and

(B) have at the particular time acquired securities of the acquiring corporation having a fair market value of not more than 50% of the fair market value of all the issued and outstanding shares of the acquiring corporation, or

(iii) paragraph (c.1) applies, or this paragraph or paragraph (c.1) previously applied, to deem an acquisition of control of the acquiring corporation upon an acquisition of shares that was part of the same series of transactions or events;

(d) where at any time shares of the capital stock of a particular corporation are disposed of to another corporation (in this paragraph referred to as the "acquiring corporation") for consideration that includes shares of the acquiring corporation's capital stock and, immediately after that time, the acquiring corporation and the particular corporation are controlled by a person or group of persons who

(i) controlled the particular corporation immediately before that time, and

(ii) did not, as part of the series of transactions or events that includes the disposition, cease to control the acquiring corporation,

control of the particular corporation and of each corporation controlled by it immediately before that time is deemed not to have been acquired by the acquiring corporation solely because of the disposition;

(e) control of a particular corporation and of each corporation controlled by it immediately before a particular time is deemed not to have been acquired at the particular time by a corporation (in this paragraph referred to as the "acquiring corporation") if at the particular time, the acquiring corporation acquires shares of the particular corporation's capital stock for consideration that consists solely of shares of the acquiring corporation's capital stock, and if

(i) immediately after the particular time

(A) the acquiring corporation owns all the shares of each class of the particular corporation's capital stock (determined without reference to shares of a specified class, within the meaning assigned by paragraph 88(1)(c.8)),

(B) the acquiring corporation is not controlled by any person or group of persons, and

(C) the fair market value of the shares of the particular corporation's capital stock that are owned by the acquiring corporation is not less than 95% of the fair market value of all of the assets of the acquiring corporation, or

(ii) any of clauses (i)(A) to (C) do not apply and the acquisition occurs as part of a plan of arrangement that, on completion, results in

(A) the acquiring corporation (or a new corporation that is formed on an amalgamation of the acquiring corporation and a subsidiary wholly-owned corporation of the acquiring corporation) owning all the shares of each class of the particular corporation's capital stock (determined without reference to shares of a specified class, within the meaning assigned by paragraph 88(1)(c.8)),

(B) the acquiring corporation (or the new corporation) not being controlled by any person or group of persons, and

(C) the fair market value of the shares of the particular corporation's capital stock that are owned by the acquiring corporation (or the new corporation) being not less than 95% of the fair market value of all of the assets of the acquiring corporation (or the new corporation);

(f) if a particular trust is the only beneficiary of another trust, the particular trust is described in paragraph (c) of the definition

"SIFT trust wind-up event", the particular trust would, in the absence of this paragraph, acquire control of a corporation solely because of a SIFT trust wind-up event that is a distribution of shares of the capital stock of the corporation by the other trust, and the other trust controlled the corporation immediately before the distribution, the particular trust is deemed not to acquire control of the corporation because of the distribution;

(g) a corporation (in this paragraph referred to as the "acquiring corporation") that acquires shares of another corporation on a distribution that is a SIFT trust wind-up event of a SIFT wind-up entity is deemed not to acquire control of the other corporation because of that acquisition if the following conditions are met:

(i) the SIFT wind-up entity is a trust whose only beneficiary immediately before the distribution is the acquiring corporation,

(ii) the SIFT wind-up entity controlled the other corporation immediately before the distribution,

(iii) as part of a series of transactions or events under which the acquiring corporation became the only beneficiary under the trust, two or more persons acquired shares in the acquiring corporation in exchange for their interests as beneficiaries under the trust, and

(iv) if all the shares described in subparagraph (iii) had been acquired by one person, the person would

(A) control the acquiring corporation, and

(B) have acquired shares of the acquiring corporation having a fair market value of more than 50% of the fair market value of all the issued and outstanding shares of the acquiring corporation;

(h) if at any time after September 12, 2013 a trust is subject to a loss restriction event and immediately before that time the trust, or a group of persons a member of which is the trust, controls a corporation, control of the corporation and of each corporation controlled by it immediately before that time is deemed to have been acquired at that time by a person or group of persons; and

(i) if at any time after September 12, 2013 a trust controls a corporation, control of the corporation is deemed not to be acquired solely because of a change in the trustee or legal representative having ownership or control of the trust's property if

(i) the change is not part of a series of transactions or events that includes a change in the beneficial ownership of the trust's property, and

(ii) no amount of income or capital of the trust to be distributed, at any time at or after the change, in respect of any interest in the trust depends upon the exercise by any person or partnership, or the failure of any person or partnership, to exercise any discretionary power.

Related Provisions: 139.1(18) — Control deemed not acquired on demutualization of insurer; 248(8) — Meaning of "consequence" of death; 251.2 — Loss restriction event; 256(8) — Where share deemed to have been acquired; 256(8.1) — Corporations without share capital; 256.1 — Deemed change in control if 75% FMV acquired.

Notes: See Notes to 111(5) and 251(2) on the meaning of "control". For discussion of 256(7) see Munoz, "Loss Utilization in Arm's-Length Business Combinations", 57(3) *Canadian Tax Journal* 660-98 (2009); Brown, "Estates, Trusts and the Acquisition of Control", IV(4) *Personal Tax and Estate Planning* (Federated Press) 198-203 (2013).

256(7) opening words formerly applied explicitly to 10(10), 13(21.2), 13(24), 14(12), 18(15), 18.1, 37, 40(3.4), 54"superficial loss", 66(11.4), 66(11.5), 80, 80.04(4)(h), 111, 127 and 249(4). These were all amended (as of March 21, 2013) to use "loss restriction event" instead of change of control (so as to expand to cover trusts), and 256(7) now applies to them via 251.2(2)(a).

256(7)(a)(i): see VIEWS docs 2007-0221361R3 ((i)(C) applies); 2010-0360921R3 ((i) applies on transfer of ownership of 1 of 3 corporate trustees to related person); 2013-0484031E5 ((i)(B)); 2013-0489771E5 ((i)(C), (D)); 2014-0540751E5 ((i)(A), (B)).

256(7)(b)(ii) was avoided and GAAR applied in *Birchcliff Energy*, 2019 FCA 151 (leave to appeal denied 2019 CarswellNat 6298) (same as earlier result at 2015 TCC 232, but decision nullified 2017 FCA 89 as issued by wrong judge). See Carr, "Birchcliff Energy", XII(1) *Resource Sector Taxation* (Federated Press) 2-11 (2018).

256(7)(c)-(c.2) are "reverse takeover" rules: Munoz paper (above), p. 671; Finance Technical Notes to (c.2).

256(7)(c.1) and (g) respond to 2008-09 income trust unwindings involving mergers with loss companies that avoided 111(5) (see 85.1(8) and 111(5) Notes). See McDougall & Lai, "Selected Aspects of Corporate Control", 2010 Cdn Tax Foundation conference report at 11:29-32; *Superior Plus*, 2015 TCC 132, para. 37; aff'd 2015 FCA 241 (discovery allowed of government policy relating to the change).

256(7)(d) applied in *Promutuel Réassurance*, 2020 TCC 13; 27 mutual insurance corps, acting together, were a "group" controlling a corp before its transfer to a non-share corp they controlled (under 256(8.1)) [Lee & Ross, "Promutuel", XVI(2) *Corporate Structures & Groups* (Federated Press) 6-11 (2020)]. See also doc 2010-0373241C6.

256(7)(f): see Notes to 85.1(8) re SIFT windups.

256(7)(g): see re 256(7)(c.1) above.

256(7)(i): Hickey, "Acquisition of Control: Change of Trustee". 21(11) *Canadian Tax Highlights* (ctf.ca) 6-7 (Nov. 2013); VIEWS doc 2019-0812781C6 [2019 APFF q.9].

History: 256(7)(c.2) added by 2017 budget bill #2, for transactions completed after Sept. 15, 2016, other than transactions the parties are obligated to complete pursuant to an agreement in writing entered into by that date. However, for this purpose, parties are considered not obligated if any of them may be excused from completing the transaction due to amendments to the Act.

256(7) amended by 2013 budget bill #2 (last change effective Sept. 13, 2013), 2002-2013 technical bill (last change for transactions after 4pm EST March 4, 2010, with grandfathering for agreements in place by then), 2008 budget bill #2, 2004 Budget, 1995-97 and 1994 technical bills, 1994 Budget, 1993 and 1991 technical bills.

Income Tax Folios: S4-F7-C1: Amalgamations of Canadian corporations [replaces IT-474R2].

Interpretation Bulletins: IT-64R4: Corporations: association and control; IT-302R3: Losses of a corporation — the effect that acquisitions of control, amalgamations, and windings-up have on their deductibility.

I.T. Technical News: 7 (control by a group — 50/50 arrangement); 16 (*Duha Printers* case); 34 (change in trustees and control).

Advance Tax Rulings: ATR-7: Amalgamation involving losses and control.

(8) Deemed exercise of right — Where at any time a taxpayer acquires a right referred to in paragraph 251(5)(b) in respect of a share and it can reasonably be concluded that one of the main purposes of the acquisition is

(a) to avoid any limitation on the deductibility of any non-capital loss, net capital loss, farm loss or any expense or other amount referred to in subsection 66(11), 66.5(3) or 66.7(10) or (11),

(b) to avoid the application of subsection 10(10) or 13(24), paragraph 37(1)(h) or subsection 55(2) or 66(11.4) or (11.5), paragraph 88(1)(c.3) or subsection 111(4), (5.1) or (5.3), 181.1(7), 190.1(6) or 251.2(2),

(c) to avoid the application of paragraph (j) or (k) of the definition "investment tax credit" in subsection 127(9),

(d) to avoid the application of section 251.1, or

(e) to affect the application of section 80,

the taxpayer is deemed to be in the same position in relation to the control of the corporation as if the right were immediate and absolute and as if the taxpayer had exercised the right at that time for the purpose of determining whether control of a corporation has been acquired for the purposes of subsections 10(10) and 13(24), section 37, subsections 55(2), 66(11), (11.4) and (11.5), 66.5(3), 66.7(10) and (11), section 80, paragraph 80.04(4)(h), subparagraph 88(1)(c)(vi), paragraph 88(1)(c.3), subsections 88(1.1) and (1.2), sections 111 and 127, subsections 181.1(7), 190.1(6) and 249(4) and paragraph 251.2(2)(a) and in determining for the purposes of section 251.1, paragraph (b) of the definition "investment fund" in subsection 251.2(1) and paragraphs 251.2(3)(c) and (d) and 256(7)(i) whether a corporation is controlled by any other person or group of persons.

Related Provisions: 256(8.1) — Corporations without share capital.

Notes: For the meaning of "one of the main purposes" see Notes to 83(2.1).

256(8) did not apply, and GAAR did not apply, in *Deans Knight*, 2019 TCC 76 (Crown's FCA appeal heard March 22/21), paras. 49-62: a right to sell shares to Mco did not give Mco a right to buy those shares.

256(8)(b) amended by 2016 budget bill #2 to delete reference to 111(5.2) effective 2017 (as part of changing the eligible capital property rules to CCA Class 14.1: see Notes to 20(1)(b)); and closing words amended to refer to 251.2(1)"investment fund"(b) and 256(7)(i), effective March 21, 2013.

256(8) earlier amended by 2013 budget bill #2 (effective March 21, 2013), 1995-97 and 1994 technical bills, 1994 Budget.

Interpretation Bulletins: IT-64R4: Corporations: association and control.

(8.1) Corporations without share capital — For the purposes of subsections (7) and (8),

(a) a corporation incorporated without share capital is deemed to have a capital stock of a single class;

(b) each member, policyholder and other participant in the corporation is deemed to be a shareholder of the corporation; and

(c) the membership, policy or other interest in the corporation of each of those participants is deemed to be the number of shares of the corporation's capital stock that the Minister considers reasonable in the circumstances, having regard to the total number of participants in the corporation and the nature of their participation.

Notes: 256(8.1) was interpreted in *Promutuel Réassurance*, 2020 TCC 13, para. 45, to mean that when mutual insurance corps that controlled a non-share corp transferred shares of Xco to it, they were deemed to have received shares from it.

256(8.1) added by 1995-97 technical bill, effective April 27, 1995.

(9) Date of acquisition of control — For the purposes of this Act, other than for the purposes of determining if a corporation is, at any time, a small business corporation or a Canadian-controlled private corporation, where control of a corporation is acquired by a person or group of persons at a particular time on a day, control of the corporation shall be deemed to have been acquired by the person or group of persons, as the case may be, at the beginning of that day and not at the particular time unless the corporation elects in its return of income under Part I filed for its taxation year that ends immediately before the acquisition of control not to have this subsection apply.

Related Provisions: 220(3.2), Reg. 600(b) — Late filing or revocation of election; 249(4) — Deemed year end where change of control occurs; Reg. 6204(4) — Subsec. 256(9) ignored for purposes of "specified person" in determining prescribed shares under 110(1)(d).

Notes: See Notes to 249(4) re events that trigger multiple year-ends on the same day.

In *La Survivance*, 2006 FCA 129, 256(9) was used by a public corp to create an ABIL (38(c), 39(1)(c)) when selling a subsidiary to a private corporation, even though the result was clearly counter to the legislative policy for ABILs. The 2009 amendment described below overrules *La Survivance*. Even before the Budget, CRA stated that it would continue to reassess to deny an ABIL in such cases: VIEWS doc 2006-0195961C6. (Before the amendment, the capital gains exemption could technically be lost due to *La Survivance*; see Notes to 110.6(2.1).) For a possible problem in the interaction of amended 256(9) with 249(3.1) and (4), see Nitikman & Moriartey, "Part-Time CCPCs Again", 17(5) *Canadian Tax Highlights* (ctf.ca) 6-7 (May 2009).

256(9) applied in *Damis Properties (Sabel Investments)* (under appeal to FCA as *Microbjo Properties*), 2021 TCC 24, to deem corps to be at arm's length with their subs at the time 160(1) would have applied.

256(9) takes precedence over 256(1.2)(c): VIEWS docs 9525315, 2009-0330131C6. On a sale of shares, 256(9) does not permit acquisition of control at a time different from when the purchaser acquires ownership: 2013-0495751C6.

256(9) amended by 2009 budget bill #1 to add "other than for the purposes of determining if a corporation is, at any time, a small business corporation or a Canadian-controlled private corporation" (and to change "commencement" to "beginning" and "ending" to "that ends"), effective in respect of an acquisition of control of a corporation that occurs after 2005, other than in respect of such an acquisition of control that occurs before Jan. 28, 2009 and in respect of which the taxpayer elects in writing, filed with the Minister of National Revenue by the "filing-due date" (see 248(1)) for the taxpayer's 2009 taxation year. Per 2009 budget bill #1 s. 78(5), a taxpayer is deemed to have made this election in respect of an acquisition of control that occurred before Jan. 28, 2009 if it can reasonably be considered, having regard to a return of income, notice of objection, or notice or appeal, filed or served by the taxpayer under the ITA before Jan. 28, 2009, that the taxpayer has interpreted and applied 256(9) for the purposes of determining if the corporation was a small business corporation or a Canadian-controlled private corporation at the time of the transfer of shares of the corporation that caused the acquisition of control to occur.

For a corporation filing Quebec returns, an election under 256(9) must be copied to Revenu Québec: *Taxation Act* ss. 21.4.2, 21.4.6.

Definitions [s. 256]: "affiliated" — 251.1; "amount" — 248(1); "arm's length" — 251(1); "associated" — 256; "beneficiary" — 248(25) [Notes]; "business", "business limit" — 248(1); "Canada" — 255; "Canadian-controlled private corporation" — 125(7), 248(1); "child" — 252(1); "class of shares" — 248(6); "common share" — 248(1); "consequence" — 248(8); "control", "controlled" — 256(6)–(9), 256.1(3); "corporation" — 248(1), *Interpretation Act* 35(1); "direct or indirect influence" — 256(5.11); "distribution date" — 256(1.2)(f)(i); "dividend" — 248(1); "estate" — 104(1), 248(1); "fair market value" — see 69(1) Notes; "farm loss" — 111(8), 248(1); "fiscal period" — 249(2)(b), 249.1; "group" — 256(1.2)(a); "individual" — 248(1);

"investment tax credit" — 127(9), 248(1); "legal representative" — 248(1); "loss restriction event" — 251.2; "Minister" — 248(1); "net capital loss", "non-capital loss" — 111(8), 248(1); "paid-up capital" — 89(1), 248(1); "parent" — 252(2)(a); "partnership" — see 96(1) Notes; "person", "prescribed" — 248(1); "prescribed rate" — Reg. 4301; "principal amount" — 248(1), (26); "property" — 248(1); "real estate investment trust" — 122.1(1); "related" — 251(2)–(6); "related group" — 251(4); "relevant person" — 256(7)(c.1)(i); "SIFT partnership" — 197(1), (8), 248(1); "SIFT trust" — 122.1(1), (2), 248(1); "SIFT trust wind-up event", "SIFT wind-up entity" — 248(1); "security" — 122.1(1); "series of transactions" — 248(10); "share", "shareholder", "small business corporation" — 248(1); "specified class" — 88(1)(c.8), 256(1.1); "subject corporation" — 256(6.1)(b); "subsidiary wholly-owned corporation" — 248(1); "substituted" — 248(5); "taxation year" — 249; "taxpayer" — 248(1); "trust" — 104(1), 248(1), (3).

Income Tax Folios [s. 256]: S4-F7-C1: Amalgamations of Canadian corporations [replaces IT-474R2].

256.1 [Acquisition of 75% FMV is control] — (1) Definitions — The following definitions apply in this section.

"attribute trading restriction" means a restriction on the use of a tax attribute arising on the application, either alone or in combination with other provisions, of any of this section, subsections 10(10) and 13(24), section 37, subsections 66(11.4) and (11.5), 66.7(10) and (11), 69(11) and 88(1.1) and (1.2), sections 111 and 127 and subsections 181.1(7), 190.1(6), 249(4) and 256(7).

Related Provisions: 256.1(6) — Application of attribute trading restrictions.

"person" includes a partnership.

"specified provision" means any of subsections 10(10) and 13(24), paragraph 37(1)(h), subsections 66(11.4) and (11.5), 66.7(10) and (11), 69(11) and 111(4), (5), (5.1) and (5.3), paragraphs (j) and (k) of the definition "investment tax credit" in subsection 127(9), subsections 181.1(7) and 190.1(6) and any provision of similar effect.

Related Provisions: 256.1(6) — Application of attribute trading restrictions.

Notes: Definition amended by 2016 budget bill #2, effective 2017, to delete reference to 111(5.2), as part of changing the eligible capital property rules to CCA Class 14.1 (see Notes to 20(1)(b)).

(2) Application of subsec. (3) — Subsection (3) applies at a particular time in respect of a corporation if

(a) shares of the capital stock of the corporation held by a person, or the total of all shares of the capital stock of the corporation held by members of a group of persons, as the case may be, have at the particular time a fair market value that exceeds 75% of the fair market value of all the shares of the capital stock of the corporation;

(b) shares, if any, of the capital stock of the corporation held by the person, or the total of all shares, if any, of the capital stock of the corporation held by members of the group, have immediately before the particular time a fair market value that does not exceed 75% of the fair market value of all the shares of the capital stock of the corporation;

(c) the person or group does not control the corporation at the particular time; and

(d) it is reasonable to conclude that one of the main reasons that the person or group does not control the corporation is to avoid the application of one or more specified provisions.

Related Provisions: 256.1(4) — Interpretation for para. (2)(a); 256.1(5) — Where FMV of shares is nil.

Notes: For the meaning of "one of the main reasons" in para. (d), see Notes to 83(2.1).

(3) Deemed acquisition of control [if 75% FMV acquired] — If this subsection applies at a particular time in respect of a corporation, then for the purposes of the attribute trading restrictions,

(a) the person or group referred to in subsection (2)

(i) is deemed to acquire control of the corporation, and each corporation controlled by the corporation, at the particular time, and

(ii) is not deemed to have control of the corporation, and each corporation controlled by the corporation, at any time

after the particular time solely because this paragraph applied at the particular time; and

(b) during the period that the condition in paragraph (2)(a) is satisfied, each corporation referred to in paragraph (a) — and any corporation incorporated or otherwise formed subsequent to that time and controlled by that corporation — is deemed not to be related to, or affiliated with, any person to which it was related to, or affiliated with, immediately before paragraph (a) applies.

Related Provisions: 256.1(2) — Conditions for subsec. (3) to apply; 256.1(5) — Where FMV of shares is nil.

Notes: For an example of a transaction that worked before 256.1 was introduced, see *Deans Knight*, 2019 TCC 76 (Crown's FCA appeal heard March 22/21): 35% votes, 79% equity was not "control" for purposes of 111(5) loss-trading restriction.

Table A2.1 forecast that this measure would save the federal government $5 million in 2013-14, $10m in 2014-15, $20m in 2015-16, $25m in 2016-17 and $35m in 2017-18.

See John Burghardt & Sarah Chiu, "Loss is Just a Four Letter Word", 2013 Cdn Tax Foundation conference report, 14:1-43.

(4) Special rules — For the purpose of applying paragraph (2)(a) in respect of a person or group of persons,

(a) if it is reasonable to conclude that one of the reasons that one or more transactions or events occur is to cause a person or group of persons not to hold shares having a fair market value that exceeds 75% of the fair market value of all the shares of the capital stock of a corporation, the paragraph is to be applied without reference to those transactions or events; and

(b) the person, or each member of the group, is deemed to have exercised each right that is held by the person or a member of the group and that is referred to in paragraph 251(5)(b) in respect of a share of the corporation referred to in paragraph (2)(a).

Related Provisions: 256.1(5) — Where FMV of shares is nil.

(5) Deeming rules — if share value nil — For the purposes of subsections (2) to (4), if the fair market value of the shares of the capital stock of a corporation is nil at any time, then for the purpose of determining the fair market value of those shares, the corporation is deemed, at that time, to have assets net of liabilities equal to $100,000 and to have $100,000 of income for the taxation year that includes that time.

(6) Deemed acquisition of control — If, at any time as part of a transaction or event or series of transactions or events, control of a particular corporation is acquired by a person or group of persons and it can reasonably be concluded that one of the main reasons for the acquisition of control is so that a specified provision does not apply to one or more corporations, the attribute trading restrictions are deemed to apply to each of those corporations as if control of each of those corporations were acquired at that time.

Notes: For the meaning of "one of the main reasons" see Notes to 83(2.1).

Notes [256.1]: See Notes to 256.1(3). 256.1 added by 2013 budget bill #2, effective March 21, 2013, with grandfathering for transactions or events before that date or contracted for before that date (see up to 56th ed. for details).

Definitions: "affiliated" — 251.1; "attribute trading restriction" — 256.1(1); "control" — 256(6)–(9); "corporation" — 248(1), *Interpretation Act* 35(1); "fair market value" — see 69(1) Notes; "partnership" — see 96(1) Notes; "person" — 248(1), 256.1(1); "related" — 251(2)–(6); "series of transactions" — 248(10); "share" — 248(1), 256.1(1); "specified provision" — 256.1(1); "taxation year" — 249.

257. Negative amounts — Except as specifically otherwise provided, where an amount or a number is required under this Act to be determined or calculated by or in accordance with an algebraic formula, if the amount or number when so determined or calculated would, but for this section, be a negative amount or number, it shall be deemed to be nil.

Related Provisions: 248(1)"taxable income" — Taxable income cannot be less than nil.

Notes: This rule overrides the principle that applies to calculations not expressed in algebraic or formula terms, but that use the word "minus". In such calculations, the word "minus" may be given its arithmetic or technical sense, so the result of a "minus" can be a negative number. See *Canterra Energy*, [1987] 1 C.T.C. 89 (FCA).

It is uncertain whether this rule applies to formulas in the *Income Tax Regulations*. Arguably, an amount in a formula in the Regulations is "required under this Act to be calculated", since the Act authorizes the Regulations. *Interpretation Act* s. 16 provides that "expressions" used in the Regulations have the same meanings as in the Act, but it is unclear whether a formula is an "expression" with a "meaning". Many formulas in the Regulations are evidently drafted on the assumption that s. 257 applies to them.

Definitions [s. 257]: "amount" — 248(1).

258. (1) [Repealed under former Act]

Notes: 258(1) repealed by 1988 tax reform. This rule, which provided for a deemed dividend on term preferred shares, was moved to 84(4.2).

(2) Deemed dividend on term preferred share — Notwithstanding subsection 15(3), an amount paid or payable after 1978 as interest on or as an amount in lieu of interest in respect of

(a) any interest or dividend payable after November 16, 1978 on an income bond or an income debenture issued before November 17, 1978 or pursuant to an agreement in writing made before that date, or

(b) a dividend that became payable or in arrears after November 16, 1978 on a share of the capital stock of a corporation that is not a term preferred share by reason of having been issued before November 17, 1978 or pursuant to an agreement in writing made before that date,

shall, for the purposes of subsections 112(2.1) and 138(6), be deemed to be a dividend received on a term preferred share.

Related Provisions: 248(13) — Interests in trusts and partnerships.

Interpretation Bulletins: IT-52R4: Income bonds and income debentures (cancelled).

(3) Deemed interest on preferred shares — Subject to subsection (4), for the purposes of paragraphs 12(1)(c) and (k) and sections 113 and 126, each amount that is a dividend received in a taxation year on

(a) a term preferred share by a specified financial institution resident in Canada from a corporation not resident in Canada, or

(b) any other share that

(i) is a grandfathered share, or

(ii) was issued before 8:00 p.m. Eastern Daylight Saving Time, June 18, 1987 and is not deemed by subsection 112(2.22) to have been issued after that time

by a corporation from a corporation not resident in Canada, if the dividend would have been a dividend in respect of which no deduction could have been made under subsection 112(1) or (2) or 138(6) because of subsection 112(2.2) of the *Income Tax Act*, chapter 148 of the Revised Statutes of Canada, 1952, as it read on June 17, 1987, if the corporation that paid the dividend were a taxable Canadian corporation

shall be deemed to be interest received in the year and not a dividend received on a share of the capital stock of a corporation.

Related Provisions: 248(1) — "amount" — stock dividend; 248(13) — Interests in trusts and partnerships; 258(4) — Exception.

Notes: 258(3) addresses the same issue as 112(2.1) where the share acquired by a specified financial institution is a share of a foreign affiliate. It deems a dividend to be interest. For rulings that 258(3) will not apply see VIEWS docs 2011-0400531R3, 2012-0452291R3.

258(3)(b)(ii) amended by 2001 technical bill to change reference from 112(2.2)(f) to 112(2.22), effective for dividends received after 1998.

258(3)(b) amended by 1992 technical bill, retroactive to dividends received or deemed to be received on shares acquired after 8:00 p.m. EDST, June 18, 1987.

I.T. Application Rules: 69 (meaning of "chapter 148 of ...").

Interpretation Bulletins: IT-88R2: Stock dividends.

(4) Exception — Subsection (3) does not apply to a dividend described in paragraph (3)(a)

(a) if the share on which the dividend was paid was not acquired in the ordinary course of the business carried on by the corporation; or

(b) to the extent that the dividend would be described by subparagraph 53(2)(b)(ii) if the corporation not resident in Canada were not a foreign affiliate of the corporation.

Notes: For an example of 258(4) applying see VIEWS doc 2010-0375111R3.

258(4)(b) added by 2002-2013 technical bill (Part 3 — FA reorganizations), effective for dividends paid after Aug. 19, 2011.

(5) Deemed interest on certain shares — For the purposes of paragraphs 12(1)(c) and (k) and sections 113 and 126, a dividend received after June 18, 1987 and in a taxation year from a corporation not resident in Canada, other than a corporation in which the recipient had or would have, if the corporation were a taxable Canadian corporation, a substantial interest (within the meaning assigned by section 191), on a share, if the dividend would have been a dividend in respect of which no deduction could have been made under subsection 112(1) or (2) or 138(6) by reason of subsection 112(2.2) or (2.4) if the corporation that paid the dividend were a taxable Canadian corporation, shall be deemed to be interest received in the year and not a dividend received on a share of the capital stock of the payer corporation.

Related Provisions: 191(2), (3) — Meaning of "substantial interest"; 248(1)"amount" — stock dividend; 248(13) — Interests in trusts and partnerships; 258(6) — Exception.

(6) Exception — Subsection (5) does not apply to a dividend described in that subsection to the extent that the dividend would be described by subparagraph 53(2)(b)(ii) if the corporation not resident in Canada were not a foreign affiliate of the recipient.

Notes: 258(6) added by 2002-2013 technical bill (Part 3 — FA reorganizations), effective for dividends paid after Aug. 19, 2011.

Definitions [s. 258]: "amount" — 248(1); "Canada" — 255; "corporation", "dividend", "income bond", "grandfathered share", "person" — 248(1); "resident in Canada" — 250; "share" — 248(1); "specified financial institution" — 248(1); "substantial interest" — 191(2), (3); "taxable Canadian corporation" — 89(1), 248(1); "taxation year" — 249; "term preferred share" — 248(1); "trust" — 248(1), (3); "writing" — *Interpretation Act* 35(1).

Interpretation Bulletins [s. 258]: IT-88R2: Stock dividends.

259. (1) Proportional holdings in trust property — For the purposes of designated provisions, if at any time a specified taxpayer acquires, holds or disposes of a particular unit in a qualified trust and the qualified trust elects for any period that includes that time to have this subsection apply,

(a) the taxpayer shall be deemed not to acquire, hold or dispose of at that time, as the case may be, the particular unit;

(b) where the taxpayer holds the particular unit at that time, the taxpayer shall be deemed to hold at that time that proportion (referred to in this subsection as the "specified portion") of each property (in this subsection referred to as a "relevant property") held by the trust at that time that one (or, where the particular unit is a fraction of a whole unit, that fraction) is of the number of units of the trust outstanding at that time;

(c) [Repealed]

(d) where that time is the later of

(i) the time the trust acquires the relevant property, and

(ii) the time the taxpayer acquires the particular unit,

the taxpayer shall be deemed to acquire the specified portion of a relevant property at that time;

(e) where that time is the time the specified portion of a relevant property is deemed by paragraph (d) to have been acquired, the fair market value of the specified portion of the relevant property at that time shall be deemed to be the specified portion of the fair market value of the relevant property at the time of its acquisition by the trust;

(f) where that time is the time immediately before the time the trust disposes of a particular relevant property, the taxpayer shall be deemed to dispose of, immediately after that time, the specified portion of the particular relevant property for proceeds equal to the specified portion of the proceeds of disposition to the trust of the particular relevant property;

(g) where that time is the time immediately before the time the taxpayer disposes of the particular unit, the taxpayer shall be deemed to dispose of, immediately after that time, the specified portion of each relevant property for proceeds equal to the specified portion of the fair market value of that relevant property at that time; and

(h) where the taxpayer is deemed because of this subsection

(i) to have acquired a portion of a relevant property as a consequence of the acquisition of the particular unit by the taxpayer and the acquisition of the relevant property by the trust, and

(ii) subsequently to have disposed of the specified portion of the relevant property,

the specified portion of the relevant property shall, for the purposes of determining the consequences under this Act of the disposition and without affecting the proceeds of disposition of the specified portion of the relevant property, be deemed to be the portion of the relevant property referred to in subparagraph (i).

Related Provisions: 250(5) — Person deemed non-resident by treaty is non-resident.

Notes: 259(1) provides a "look-through" rule when an RRSP, RPP or other tax-deferred plan (259(5)"specified taxpayer") acquires an interest in a 259(5)"qualified trust". If the trust elects, the plan is deemed to acquire, hold and dispose of proportionate percentages of the underlying trust property for purposes of the 259(5)"designated provisions" (rules re qualified investments).

259(1) amended by 2011 budget bill #2 (retroactive to 2000, overriding amendments by 2008 and 2005 budget bills #1). Added by 1993 technical bill.

(2) [Repealed]

Notes: 259(2) repealed by 2005 budget bill #1, for tax years that begin after 2004, due to the repeal of 205-207 (Part XI). Added by 1993 technical bill, for periods occurring after 1991.

(3) Election — An election by a qualified trust under subsection (1) shall be made by the qualified trust filing a prescribed form with the Minister and shall apply for the period

(a) that begins on the later of

(i) the day that is 15 months before the day on which the election is filed, and

(ii) the day, if any, that is designated by the qualified trust in the election; and

(b) that ends on the earlier of

(i) the day on which the qualified trust files with the Minister a notice of revocation of the election, and

(ii) the day, if any, that is designated by the qualified trust in the notice of revocation and that is not before the day that is 15 months before the day on which the notice of revocation is filed.

Notes: For a ruling that a pension corp can make the election, see VIEWS doc 2003-0052061R3.

An election by a qualifying trust can continue to be valid following a trust-to-trust transfer: VIEWS doc 2002-0147025.

259(3) amended by 2005 budget bill #1, effective for taxation years that begin after 2004, due to the repeal of Part XI (205-207), and to remove references to qualified corporations (see 259(5)).

259(3) added by 1993 technical bill, effective for periods occurring after 1985. See Notes at end of 259 for reference to former section.

Interpretation Bulletins: IT-412R2: Foreign property of registered plans.

Forms: T1024: Election to deem a proportional holding in qualified trust property.

(4) Requirement to provide information — Where a qualified trust elects under subsection (1),

(a) it shall provide notification of the election

(i) within 30 days after making the election, to each person who held a unit in the qualified trust at any time in the period before the election was made and during which the election is applicable, and

(ii) at the time of acquisition, to each person who acquires a unit in the qualified trust at any time in the period after the election was made and during which the election is applicable; and

(b) if a person who holds a unit in the qualified trust at any time in the period during which the election is applicable makes a written request to the qualified trust for information that is necessary for the purpose of determining the consequences under this Act of the election for that person, the qualified trust shall provide to the person that information within 30 days after receiving the request.

Related Provisions: *Interpretation Act* 27(5) — Meaning of "within 30 days".

Notes: 259(4) amended by 2005 budget bill #1, for tax years that begin after 2004, due to repeal of Part XI (205-207), and to remove references to qualified corporations (see 259(5)).

259(4) added by 1993 technical bill, for elections made after Dec. 21, 1992. See Notes at end of 259 for reference to former section.

(5) Definitions — In this section,

"designated provisions" means sections 146 and 146.1 to 146.4 and Parts X, XI.01 and XI.1, as they apply in respect of investments that are not qualified investments for a trust, and Part X.2;

Notes: Definition amended by 2017 budget bill #2, effective March 23, 2017, to change "Parts X and XI to XI.1" to "Parts X, XI.01 and XI.1". This deletes reference to Part XI (tax on RDSPs), which was repealed with Part XI.01 expanded to cover RDSPs and RESPs.

Definition added by 2011 budget bill #2, with various versions applying from 2000, last change effective for taxation years that end after March 22, 2011.

"qualified corporation" — [Repealed]

Notes: Definition "qualified corporation" repealed by 2005 budget bill #1, for tax years that begin after 2004. (Since none of the entities that are allowed to invest in these corps are subject to the qualified investment rules, the application of 259 to such corps was relevant only for the foreign property rules in Part XI.)

985c1s5 259(5)"qualified corporation" added by 1993 technical bill, effective for periods occurring after 1985. See Notes at end of 259 for reference to former section.

"qualified trust" at any time means a trust (other than a registered investment or a trust that is prescribed to be a small business investment trust) where

(a) each trustee of the trust at that time is a corporation that is licensed or otherwise authorized under the laws of Canada or a province to carry on in Canada the business of offering to the public its services as a trustee or a person who is a trustee of a trust governed by a registered pension plan,

(b) all the interests of the beneficiaries under the trust at that time are described by reference to units of the trust all of which are at that time identical to each other,

(c) it has never before that time borrowed money except where the borrowing was for a term not exceeding 90 days and the borrowing was not part of a series of loans or other transactions and repayments, and

(d) it has never before that time accepted deposits.

"specified taxpayer" means a taxpayer that is a registered investment or that is described in any of paragraphs 149(1)(r), (s), (u) to (u.2) and (x).

Notes: Definition added by 2011 budget bill #2, this version for tax years that begin after 2008.

A proposed amendment to refer to 149(1)(u.3) (pooled registered pension plans), in the Dec. 14/11 draft, was dropped when the PRPP legislation was introduced in 2012.

Related Provisions: 149(1)(o.4) — No tax payable by master trust; 248(10) — Series of transactions; 248(12) — Identical properties.

Notes: 259(5)"qualified trust" added by 1993 technical bill, effective for periods occurring after 1985. See Notes at end of 259 for reference to former section.

Regulations: 5103 (prescribed small business investment trust; needs to be amended to apply for 259(5) rather than 259(3)).

Notes [s. 259]: Former 259 replaced by the subsections of 259 as above, without a legislated repeal date for the former section as a whole, so the repeal is technically effective as of June 15, 1994, the date of Royal Assent to the 1993 technical bill. However, new 259(1), (3) and (5), which effectively replace all of the former 259, apply to periods after 1985 and so appear to supersede the old version.

Former 259 amended by 1992 technical bill, effective for borrowings after 1990.

Definitions [s. 259]: "business" — 248(1); "Canada" — 255; "corporation" — 248(1), *Interpretation Act* 35(1); "cost amount" — 248(1); "designated provisions" — 259(5); "fair market value" — see 69(1) Notes; "identical" — 248(12); "Minister" — 248(1); "month" — *Interpretation Act* 35(1); "person", "prescribed" — 248(1); "province" — *Interpretation Act* 35(1); "qualified trust" — 259(5); "registered investment" — 204.4(1), 248(1); "registered pension plan" — 248(1); "relevant property" — 259(1)(b); "series" — 248(10); "share" — 248(1); "small business investment trust" — Reg. 5103; "series" — 248(10); "specified portion" — 259(1)(b); "specified taxpayer" — 259(5); "taxpayer" — 248(1); "trust" — 104(1), 248(1), (3); "written" — *Interpretation Act* 35(1) ["writing"].

Regulations [s. 259]: 5103 (small business investment trust).

260. (1) Definitions — In this section,

"dealer compensation payment" means an amount received by a taxpayer as compensation, for an underlying payment,

(a) from a registered securities dealer resident in Canada who paid the amount in the ordinary course of a business of trading in securities, or

(b) in the ordinary course of the taxpayer's business of trading in securities, where the taxpayer is a registered securities dealer resident in Canada;

Notes: "Dealer compensation payment" added by 2002-2013 technical bill (Part 5 — technical), effective for arrangements made after 2001.

"qualified security" means

(a) a share of a class of the capital stock of a corporation that is listed on a stock exchange or of a class of the capital stock of a corporation that is a public corporation by reason of the designation of the class by the corporation in an election made under subparagraph (b)(i) of the definition "public corporation" in subsection 89(1) or by the Minister in a notice to the corporation under subparagraph (b)(ii) of that definition,

(b) a bond, debenture, note or similar obligation of a corporation described in paragraph (a) or of a corporation that is controlled by such a corporation,

(c) a bond, debenture, note or similar obligation of or guaranteed by the government of any country, province, state, municipality or other political subdivision, or a corporation, commission, agency or association controlled by any such person,

(d) a warrant, right, option or similar instrument with respect to a share described in paragraph (a), or

(e) a qualified trust unit;

Related Provisions: 212(1)(b)(xii), (xiii) — Exemption from withholding tax.

Notes: Para. (e) added by 2002-2013 technical bill (Part 5 — technical), effective for arrangements made after 2001.

260(1)"qualified security"(a) amended by 2007 budget bill #2, effective Dec. 14, 2007, to change "prescribed stock exchange" to "stock exchange". The Dept. of Finance Technical Notes state: "The term 'stock exchange', which is intended to include any stock exchange located anywhere in the world, including all designated stock exchanges and all recognized stock exchanges, is not defined — the generally accepted legal and commercial meaning of the term is intended to apply."

Definition "qualified security" added by 1989 Budget, effective for transfers, loans and payments made after April 26, 1989.

"qualified trust unit" means an interest, as a beneficiary under a trust, that is listed on a stock exchange;

Notes: Definition added by 2002-2013 technical bill (Part 5 — technical), for arrangements made after 2001, but in its application to arrangements made before Oct. 24, 2012, read as:

"qualified trust unit" means a unit of a mutual fund trust that is listed on a stock exchange;

and before Dec. 14, 2007, read "stock exchange" above as "prescribed stock exchange".

See also Notes to 260(1)"qualified security".

"SLA compensation payment" means an amount paid pursuant to

(a) a securities lending arrangement as compensation for an underlying payment; or

(b) a specified securities lending arrangement as compensation for an underlying payment, including, if the property transferred or lent is described in subparagraph (a)(ii) of the definition

"specified securities lending arrangement", as compensation for a taxable dividend paid on a share described in subparagraph (a)(i) of that definition;

Notes: An SLA compensation payment is commonly called a dividend compensation payment, but the definition also includes compensation for interest and for mutual fund trust distributions. See Notes to 260(1)"securities lending arrangement".

Para. (b) added by 2018 budget bill #2, effective on the same basis as 260(1)"specified securities lending arrangement".

"SLA compensation payment" added by 2002-2013 technical bill (Part 5 — technical), effective for arrangements made after 2001.

"securities lending arrangement" means an arrangement under which

(a) a person (in this section referred to as the **"lender"**) transfers or lends at any particular time a qualified security to another person (in this section referred to as the **"borrower"**),

(b) it may reasonably be expected, at the particular time, that the borrower will transfer or return after the particular time to the lender a security (in this section referred to as an **"identical security"**) that is identical to the security so transferred or lent,

(c) the borrower is obligated to pay to the lender amounts equal to and as compensation for all amounts, if any, paid on the security that would have been received by the borrower if the borrower had held the security throughout the period that begins after the particular time and that ends at the time an identical security is transferred or returned to the lender,

(d) the lender's risk of loss or opportunity for gain or profit with respect to the security is not changed in any material respect, and

(e) if the lender and the borrower do not deal with each other at arm's length, it is intended that neither the arrangement nor any series of securities lending arrangements, loans or other transactions of which the arrangement is a part be in effect for more than 270 days,

but does not include an arrangement one of the main purposes of which may reasonably be considered to be to avoid or defer the inclusion in income of any gain or profit with respect to the security.

Related Provisions: 112(2.3) — Dividend rental arrangements; 248(1)"securities lending arrangement" — Definition applies to entire Act; 248(12) — Identical properties; 256(6), (6.1) — Meaning of "controlled".

Notes: Securities lending arrangements (SLAs) include ordinary securities lending as well as many "repo" (securities repurchase) agreements. SLAs are used to facilitate the short-sale market. A person selling a share "short" may need or want to have the share in their account to cover the sale, and "borrows" the share for this purpose. Technically, the "borrowing" is a transfer with a commitment to later retransfer an identical share back to the counterparty. (This is done with other securities too, such as bonds and trust units.) 260 recognizes that such arrangements are not really transfers and should not trigger gains and losses. 260(2) provides that such a transfer or loan is deemed not to be a disposition (subject to 260(3) and (4)).

A dividend compensation payment (260(1)"SLA compensation payment") is paid by share borrower B to share lender L, to compensate for dividends received (260(1)"underlying payment") on the share while B is holding (and legally owns) the share. (Where the security is a bond, an interest compensation payment is also a 260(1)"SLA compensation payment". There can also be a trust distribution compensation payment.)

260(5.1) (see 260(5) for its conditions) preserves the underlying character of a dividend compensation payment in L's hands as a taxable dividend received, and, if the underlying dividend is an eligible dividend, as an "eligible dividend" (see 260(1.1)).

18(1)(w) prohibits a deduction for an amount deemed received by another person under 260(5.1), "except as expressly permitted", meaning only by 260(6) or (6.1). If B is a "registered securities dealer" (defined in 248(1)), 260(6)(a) normally allows B a 2/3 deduction for the compensation payment. (260(6)(b) allows a deduction in certain cases if the payment is not deemed received as taxable dividend (e.g., interest).)

B, if a corporation, may also claim the 112(1) intercorporate dividend deduction to offset the income inclusion for the actual dividend received. (260(6.1) allows B a full deduction for a dividend compensation payment, but only if the arrangement is a "dividend rental arrangement" (248(1)), in which case 112(2.3) prevents the 112(1) deduction.)

If B is an individual, dividend compensation payments B pays can be deducted under 82(1)(a.1)(ii) against "eligible dividend" income from any source (normally B will have eligible dividend income from the same corporation). If B does not have sufficient eligible dividends for the year, there is no other deduction or carryforward. (If the individual is a member of a partnership that borrowed the share, see 260(12).)

260(8) determines the non-resident withholding tax (s. 212) character of an SLA compensation payment paid to a non-resident. If the conditions in 260(8)(c) are satisfied, it is deemed to be a dividend and 212(2) imposes tax. Otherwise, it is usually deemed to be interest by 260(8)(a), and is not subject to withholding tax (since 212(1)(b) was amended in 2008 to eliminate most withholding tax on interest paid to non-residents).

Amendments to the SLA rules were proposed in 2002, amended several times and finally enacted by the 2002-2013 technical bill.

The most helpful discussion of s. 260 is Willson, "Securities Lending", 2009 Cdn Tax Foundation conference report, 9:1-36. See also Friedlander, *Taxation of Corporate Finance* (Carswell, looseleaf or *Taxnet Pro* Reference Centre), §7.3; Tamaki, "The Slow Expansion of the Securities Lending Rules", X(4) *Corporate Finance* (Federated Press) 993-96 (2003); Ruvinsky, "Securities Lending Arrangements — Recent Amendments", 13(4) *Taxation Law* (Ontario Bar Assn, oba.org) 10-13 (May 2003) and "Securities Lending Rules — Round '04", 14(3) 5-8 (May 2004); Kelly, "Recent Technical Amendments: Securities Lending Arrangements", 2003 conference report (updated to reflect Feb. 27/04 proposals), 26:1-25; Bernstein & Burns, "Securities Lending Arrangements", 14(12) *Canadian Tax Highlights* (ctf.ca) 8 (Dec. 2006).

A "repo" agreement (sale and repurchase of securities, for short-term financing) may be an SLA: VIEWS doc 2002-0152203. For para. (c) see 2004-0084891E5.

For the meaning of "one of the main purposes" in the closing words, see Notes to 83(2.1).

Definition amended by 2002-2013 technical bill (for arrangements made after 2002, or earlier), 1991 technical bill; added by 1989 Budget.

"security distribution" means an amount that is

(a) an underlying payment, or

(b) an SLA compensation payment, or a dealer compensation payment, that is deemed by subsection (5.1) to be an amount received as an amount described by any of paragraphs (5.1)(a) to (c);

Notes: "Security distribution" added by 2002-2013 technical bill (Part 5 — technical), for arrangements made after 2001.

"specified securities lending arrangement" means an arrangement, other than a securities lending arrangement, under which

(a) a particular person (referred to in this definition as a "transferor") transfers or lends at any particular time a property to another person (referred to in this definition as a "transferee") and the property is

(i) a particular share described in paragraph (a) of the definition "qualified security", or

(ii) a property in respect of which the following conditions are met:

(A) the property is

(I) an interest in a partnership, or

(II) an interest as a beneficiary under a trust, and

(B) all or any part of the fair market value of the property, immediately before the particular time, is derived, directly or indirectly, from a share described in subparagraph (i),

(b) it may reasonably be expected, at the particular time, that the transferee — or a person that does not deal at arm's length with, or is affiliated with, the transferee — will transfer or return after the particular time to the transferor — or a person that does not deal at arm's length with, or is affiliated with, the transferor (referred to in this definition as a "substitute transferor") — a property that is identical or substantially identical to the property so transferred or lent, and

(c) the transferor's (together with any substitute transferor's) risk of loss or opportunity for gain or profit with respect to the particular property is not changed in any material respect;

Related Provisions: 248(1)"specified securities lending arrangement" — Definition applies to entire Act.

Notes: This definition and amended 260(5), (6) and (6.1) are anti-avoidance rules introduced in the 2018 Budget. Some taxpayers sought a tax benefit by entering into securities lending or repurchase arrangements that were designed to fail the 260(1)"securities lending arrangement" definition (see Notes thereto). In such a case, dividend compensation payments (DCPs) made by the taxpayer were usually deductible, and the taxpayers took the position that the dividend rental arrangement rules did not apply and claimed a 112(1) deduction on the dividends received on the acquired Canadian share, resulting in tax-free dividend income, while also deducting the DCPs. See now 260(1)"SLA compensation payment"(b), 260(5) and 112(2.31).

Budget Table 1 predicts these changes will save the federal government $135 million in 2018-19, $245m in 2019-20, $265m in 2020-21, $275m in 2021-22 and $295m in 2022-23.

Cl. (a)(ii)(B): For the meaning of "derived" see Notes to 18.1(12). For "indirectly" see Notes to 17.1(1).

Definition added by 2018 budget bill #2, effective for amounts paid or payable, or received or receivable, as compensation for dividends after Feb. 26, 2018, except for those paid or payable, or received or receivable, after that date and before Oct. 2018 under a written arrangement entered into before Feb. 27, 2018.

"underlying payment" means an amount paid on a qualified security by the issuer of the security.

Notes: "Underlying payment" added by 2002-2013 technical bill (Part 5 — technical), effective for arrangements made after 2001.

(1.1) Eligible dividend — This subsection applies to an amount if the amount is received by a person who is resident in Canada, the amount is deemed under subsection (5.1) to be a taxable dividend, and the amount is either

(a) received as compensation for an eligible dividend, within the meaning assigned by subsection 89(1); or

(b) received as compensation for a taxable dividend (other than an eligible dividend) paid by a corporation to a non-resident shareholder in circumstances where it is reasonable to consider that the corporation would, if that shareholder were resident in Canada, have designated the dividend to be an eligible dividend under subsection 89(14).

Related Provisions: 260(5) — Dividend compensation payment deemed to be eligible dividend.

Notes: 260(1.1) amended to change "(5)" to "(5.1)" by 2002-2013 technical bill, for amounts received as compensation for dividends paid after 2005.

260(1.1) added by 2006 budget bill #2 (Part 2 — eligible dividends), effective for amounts received as compensation for dividends paid after 2005.

(1.2) References — borrower and lender — For the purposes of subsections (8), (8.1), (8.2), (8.3) and (9.1) and 212(2.1) and (3), in respect of a specified securities lending arrangement,

(a) a reference to a borrower includes a transferee; and

(b) a reference to a lender includes a transferor.

Notes: 260(1.2) added by 2021 budget bill #1, effective March 19, 2019.

(2) Non-disposition — Subject to subsections (3) and (4), for the purposes of this Act, any transfer or loan by a lender of a security under a securities lending arrangement shall be deemed not to be a disposition of the security and the security shall be deemed to continue to be property of the lender and, for the purposes of this subsection, a security shall be deemed to include an identical security that has been transferred or returned to the lender under the arrangement.

Related Provisions: 260(10), (11) — Application to partnerships.

Notes: 260(2) does not explicitly deem the borrower not to have acquired the security, though this can perhaps be inferred.

In many cases investors own "security entitlements" and do not own the shares they think they own. This could have implications for s. 260. See Notes to 233.3(1)"specified foreign property".

260(2) added by 1989 Budget, for transfers, loans and payments made after April 26, 1989.

(3) Disposition of right — Where, at any time, a lender receives property (other than an identical security or an amount deemed by subsection (4) to have been received as proceeds of disposition) in satisfaction of or in exchange for the lender's right under a securities lending arrangement to receive the transfer or return of an identical security, for the purposes of this Act the lender shall be deemed to have disposed at that time of the security that was transferred or lent for proceeds of disposition equal to the fair market value of the property received for the disposition of the right (other than any portion thereof that is deemed to have been received by the lender as a taxable dividend), except that section 51, 85.1, 86 or 87, as the case may be, shall apply in computing the income of the lender with respect to any such disposition as if the security transferred or lent had continued to be the lender's property and the lender had received the property directly.

Notes: 260(3) added by 1989 Budget, for transfers, loans and payments made after April 26, 1989.

(4) Idem — Where, at any time, it may reasonably be considered that a lender would have received proceeds of disposition for a security that was transferred or lent under a securities lending arrangement, if the security had not been transferred or lent, the lender shall be deemed to have disposed of the security at that time for those proceeds of disposition.

Notes: 260(4) added by 1989 Budget, for transfers, loans and payments made after April 26, 1989.

(5) Where subsec. (5.1) applies — Subsection (5.1) applies to a taxpayer for a taxation year in respect of a particular amount (other than an amount received as proceeds of disposition or an amount received by a person under an arrangement where it may reasonably be considered that one of the main reasons for the person entering into the arrangement was to enable the person to receive an SLA compensation payment pursuant to a securities lending arrangement, or a dealer compensation payment, that would be deductible in computing the taxable income, or not included in computing the income, for any taxation year of the person) received by the taxpayer in the taxation year

(a) as an SLA compensation payment,

(i) from a person resident in Canada, or

(ii) from a non-resident person who paid the particular amount in the course of carrying on business in Canada through a permanent establishment as defined by regulation; or

(b) as a dealer compensation payment.

Notes: See Notes to 260(1)"securities lending arrangement". For the meaning of "one of the main reasons" see Notes to 83(2.1).

260(5) opening words amended by 2018 budget bill #2 to add "pursuant to a securities lending arrangement", effective on the same basis as 260(1)"specified securities lending arrangement". See Notes to that definition.

260(5) earlier amended by 2002-2013 technical bill (for arrangements made after 2001), 2006 budget bill #2 (for amounts received as compensation for dividends paid after 2005), 1994 technical bill, 1989 Budget.

Regulations: 8201 (permanent establishment).

Interpretation Bulletins: IT-67R3: Taxable dividends from corporations resident in Canada.

(5.1) Deemed character of compensation payments — If this subsection applies in respect of a particular amount received by a taxpayer in a taxation year as an SLA compensation payment or as a dealer compensation payment, the particular amount is deemed, to the extent of the underlying payment to which the amount relates, to have been received by the taxpayer in the taxation year as,

(a) where the underlying payment is a taxable dividend paid on a share of the capital stock of a public corporation (other than an underlying payment to which paragraph (b) applies), a taxable dividend on the share and, if subsection (1.1) applies to the particular amount, an eligible dividend on the share;

(b) where the underlying payment is paid by a trust on a qualified trust unit issued by the trust,

(i) an amount of the trust's income that was, to the extent that subsection 104(13) applied to the underlying payment,

(A) paid by the trust to the taxpayer as a beneficiary under the trust, and

(B) designated by the trust in respect of the taxpayer to the extent of a valid designation, if any, by the trust under this Act in respect of the recipient of the underlying payment, and

(ii) to the extent that the underlying payment is a distribution of a property from the trust, a distribution of that property from the trust; or

(c) in any other case, interest.

Related Provisions: 82(1)(a.1)(ii) — Amount deemed received by another person excluded from taxable dividends of individual; 248(1)"dividend rental arrange-

ment"(b)(ii)(B) — DRA where 260(5.1) applies; 260(5) — Conditions for 260(5.1) to apply; 260(6) — Deductibility; 260(10)–(12) — Application to partnerships.

Notes: See Notes to 260(1)"securities lending arrangement". 260(5.1) added by 2002-2013 technical bill, for arrangements made after 2001, with transitional rules for payments before 2006.

(6) Deductibility — In computing the income of a taxpayer under Part I from a business or property for a taxation year, there may be deducted a particular amount, paid by the taxpayer in the year as an SLA compensation payment or as a dealer compensation payment, that is equal to

(a) if the taxpayer is a registered securities dealer and the particular amount is deemed by subsection (5.1) to have been received as a taxable dividend, no more than $\frac{2}{3}$ of the particular amount (unless, for greater certainty, the particular amount is an amount for which a deduction in computing income may be claimed under subsection (6.1) by the taxpayer); or

(b) if the particular amount is in respect of an amount other than an amount that is, or is deemed by subsection (5.1) to have been, received as a taxable dividend,

(i) where the taxpayer disposes of the borrowed security and includes the gain or loss, if any, from the disposition in computing its income from a business, the particular amount, or

(ii) in any other case, the lesser of

(A) the particular amount, and

(B) the amount, if any, in respect of the security distribution to which the SLA compensation payment or dealer compensation payment relates that is included in computing the income, and not deducted in computing the taxable income, for any taxation year of the taxpayer or of any person to whom the taxpayer is related.

Related Provisions: 18(1)(w) — No deduction allowed except as expressly permitted; 82(1)(a)(ii) — Deduction for individual; 260(6.1) — Deductible amount; 260(10), (11) — Application to partnerships.

Notes: See Notes to 260(1)"securities lending arrangement".

260(6)(a) amended by 2018 budget bill #2, to add the parenthesized words "(unless...)", effective on the same basis as 260(1)"specified securities lending arrangement". See Notes to that definition.

260(6) amended by 2002-2013 technical bill, for arrangements made after 2001. Added by 1989 Budget and amended retroactively by 1994 technical bill.

(6.1) Deductible amount — There may be deducted in computing a corporation's income under Part I from a business or property for a taxation year an amount equal to the lesser of

(a) the total of all amounts each of which is an amount that the corporation becomes obligated in the taxation year to pay to another person under an arrangement described in paragraph (b) of the definition "dividend rental arrangement" in subsection 248(1) that, if paid, would be deemed by subsection (5.1) to have been received by another person as a taxable dividend, and

(b) the amount of the dividends received by the corporation under the arrangement that were identified in its return of income under Part I for the year as an amount in respect of which no amount was deductible because of subsection 112(2.3) in computing the taxpayer's taxable income or taxable income earned in Canada.

Related Provisions: 18(1)(w) — No deduction allowed except as expressly permitted; 260(7)(b) — No dividend refund on amount deductible under 260(6.1); 260(10), (11) — Application to partnerships.

Notes: See Notes to 260(1)"securities lending arrangement".

260(6.1) opening words amended by 2018 budget bill #2 to delete "Notwithstanding subsection (6)", effective on the same basis as 260(1)"specified securities lending arrangement".

260(6.1) earlier amended by 2002-2013 technical bill (for arrangements made after Dec. 2002), 1994 technical bill.

(7) Dividend refund — For the purpose of section 129, if a corporation pays an amount for which no deduction in computing the corporation's income may be claimed under subsection (6.1) and subsection (5.1) deems the amount to have been received by another person as a taxable dividend,

(a) the corporation is deemed to have paid the amount as a taxable dividend, where the corporation is not a registered securities dealer; and

(b) the corporation is deemed to have paid ⅓ of the amount as a taxable dividend, where the corporation is a registered securities dealer.

Notes: 260(7) amended by 2002-2013 technical bill (Part 5 — technical), effective for arrangements made after 2001.

260(7) added by 1989 Budget, but amended retroactively by 1994 technical bill to add the rule in 260(7)(b), effective for payments made after June 1989.

Interpretation Bulletins: IT-243R4: Dividend refund to private corporations.

(8) Non-resident withholding tax — For the purpose of Part XIII, any amount paid or credited under a securities lending arrangement or a specified securities lending arrangement by or on behalf of the borrower to the lender

(a) as an SLA compensation payment in respect of a security that is not a qualified trust unit is, subject to paragraph (c), deemed

(i) to the extent of the amount of the interest paid in respect of the security, to be a payment made by the borrower to the lender of interest, and

(ii) to the extent of the amount of the dividend paid in respect of the security, to be a payment made by the borrower, as a corporation, to the lender of a dividend payable on the security;

(b) as an SLA compensation payment in respect of a security that is a qualified trust unit, is deemed, to the extent of the amount of the underlying payment to which the SLA compensation payment relates, to be an amount paid by the trust and having the same character and composition as the underlying payment;

(c) as an SLA compensation payment is deemed to be a payment of interest made by the borrower to the lender, if

(i) the security that is transferred or lent to the borrower under the arrangement is a share of a class of the capital stock of a non-resident corporation,

(ii) the borrower and the lender are not dealing at arm's length, and

(iii) the arrangement is not a fully collateralized arrangement; and

(d) as, on account of, in lieu of payment of or in satisfaction of, a fee for the use of the security is deemed to be a payment of interest made by the borrower to the lender.

Related Provisions: 212(1)(b)(xii), (xiii), 212(2.1) — Exemptions from non-resident withholding tax; 212(19) — Special tax on securities dealers re non-resident withholding tax exemption; 260(1.2) — Interpretation of "borrower" and "lender" for specified securities lending arrangement; 260(8.1) — Deemed fee for 260(8)(d); 260(8.2)–(8.4) — Effect for tax treaty purposes.

Notes: See Notes to 260(1)"securities lending arrangement".

CRA considers that "substantially all", used in 260(8)(a), means 90% or more.

260(8) amended by 2021 budget bill #1, for amounts paid or credited as SLA compensation payments after March 18, 2019, or after Sept. 30, 2019 if pursuant to a written arrangement entered into before March 19, 2019. It read:

(8) For the purpose of Part XIII, any amount paid or credited under a securities lending arrangement by or on behalf of the borrower to the lender

(a) as an SLA compensation payment is, subject to paragraph (b) or (c), deemed to be a payment of interest made by the borrower to the lender;

(b) as an SLA compensation payment in respect of a security that is a qualified trust unit, is deemed, to the extent of the amount of the underlying payment to which the SLA compensation payment relates, to be an amount paid by the trust and having the same character and composition as the underlying payment;

(c) as an SLA compensation payment, if the security is not a qualified trust unit and throughout the term of the securities lending arrangement, the borrower has provided the lender under the arrangement with money in an amount of, or securities described in paragraph (c) of the definition "qualified security" in subsection (1) that have a fair market value of, not less than

95% of the fair market value of the security and the borrower is entitled to enjoy, directly or indirectly, the benefits of all or substantially all income derived from, and opportunity for gain with respect of, the money or securities,

(i) is, to the extent of the amount of the interest or dividend paid in respect of the security, deemed to be a payment made by the borrower to the lender of interest or a dividend, as the case may be, payable on the security, and

(ii) is, to the extent of the amount of the interest, if any, paid in respect of the security, deemed to have been payable on a security described in paragraph (a) of the definition "fully exempt interest" in subsection 212(3) if the security is described in paragraph (c) of the definition "qualified security" in subsection (1); and

(d) as, on account of, in lieu of payment of or in satisfaction of, a fee for the use of the security is deemed to be a payment of interest made by the borrower to the lender.

See the Finance Technical Notes for explanation of the changes, The "fully collateralized" test in former 260(8)(c) was moved to 248(1)"fully collateralized arrangement". For discussion of the March 2019 draft of these amendments (which did not include what is now para. (c)), see Hughes et al., "Canada proposes changes to withholding tax on dividend equivalent payments", tinyurl.com/osler-260 or 2019(8) *Tax Times* (Carswell) 1-2 (April 26, 2019); Hughes & Smith, "2019 Budget's Impact on Canadian Withholding Tax on Dividend Compensation Payments in Cross-Border Stock Loans", 106 *International Tax* (CCH, June 2019).

260(8) earlier amended by 2002-2013 technical bill (last change effective 2008), 2007 budget bill #2, 1993 and 1991 technical bills, 1989 Budget.

(8.1) Deemed fee for borrowed security — For the purpose of paragraph (8)(d), if under a securities lending arrangement or a specified securities lending arrangement the borrower has at any time provided the lender with money, either as collateral or consideration for the security, and the borrower does not, under the arrangement, pay or credit a reasonable amount to the lender as, on account of, in lieu of payment of or in satisfaction of, a fee for the use of the security, the borrower is deemed to have, at the time that an identical or substantially identical security is or can reasonably be expected to be transferred or returned to the lender, paid to the lender under the arrangement an amount as a fee for the use of the security equal to the amount, if any, by which

(a) the interest on the money computed at the prescribed rates in effect during the term of the arrangement

exceeds

(b) the amount, if any, by which any amount that the lender pays or credits to the borrower under the arrangement exceeds the amount of the money.

Related Provisions: 260(1.2) — Interpretation of "borrower" and "lender" for specified securities lending arrangement.

Notes: 260(8.1) opening words amended by 2021 budget bill #1 to add "or a specified securities lending arrangement", for amounts paid or credited as SLA compensation payments after March 18, 2019, or after Sept. 30, 2019 if pursuant to a written arrangement entered into before March 19, 2019.

260(8.1) added by 2002-2013 technical bill, for arrangements made after 2001.

(8.2) Effect for tax treaties — interest — In applying subparagraph (8)(a)(i), if a securities lending arrangement or specified securities lending arrangement is a fully collateralized arrangement, any SLA compensation payment deemed to be a payment made by the borrower to the lender of interest is deemed for the purposes of any tax treaty to be payable on the security.

Related Provisions: 260(1.2) — Interpretation of "borrower" and "lender" for specified securities lending arrangement.

Notes: 260(8.2) amended by 2021 budget bill #1, for amounts paid or credited as SLA compensation payments after March 18, 2019, or after Sept. 30, 2019 if pursuant to a written arrangement entered into before March 19, 2019. Previously read:

(8.2) Effect for tax treaties — In applying subsection (8), any amount, paid or credited under a securities lending arrangement by or on behalf of the borrower to the lender, that is deemed by paragraph (8)(a), (b) or (d) to be a payment of interest, is deemed for the purposes of any tax treaty not to be payable on or in respect of the security.

260(8.2) added by 2002-2013 technical bill, for arrangements made after 2001.

(8.3) Effect for tax treaties — dividend — In applying subparagraph (8)(a)(ii), if the security is a share of a class of the capital stock of a corporation resident in Canada (in this subsection referred to as the "Canadian share"), for the purposes of determining the rate of tax that Canada may impose on a dividend because of the dividend article of a tax treaty,

(a) any SLA compensation payment deemed to be a payment made by the borrower to the lender of a dividend is deemed to be paid by the issuer of the Canadian share and not by the borrower;

(b) the lender is deemed to be the beneficial owner of the Canadian share; and

(c) the shares of the capital stock of the issuer owned by the lender are deemed to give it less than 10% of the votes that could be cast at an annual meeting of the shareholders of the issuer and have less than 10% of the fair market value of all of the issued and outstanding shares of the capital stock of the issuer, if

(i) the securities lending arrangement or the specified securities lending arrangement is not a fully collateralized arrangement, and

(ii) the borrower and the lender are not dealing at arm's length.

Related Provisions: 260(1.2) — Interpretation of "borrower" and "lender" for specified securities lending arrangement.

Notes: 260(8.3) added by 2021 budget bill #1, for amounts paid or credited as SLA compensation payments after March 18, 2019, or after Sept. 30, 2019 if pursuant to a written arrangement entered into before March 19, 2019.

Proposed **260(8.4)**, in the March 19, 2019 draft, contained a further rule for 260(8.3). It was dropped in the July 30, 2019 draft.

(9) Restricted financial institution — For the purposes of subsection 187.3(1), where at any time a dividend is received by a restricted financial institution on a share that was last acquired before that time pursuant to an obligation of a borrower to return or transfer a share under a securities lending arrangement, an acquisition of the share under the arrangement shall be deemed at and after that time not to be an acquisition of the share.

Notes: 260(9) added by 1989 Budget, effective for transfers, loans and payments made after April 26, 1989.

(9.1) Non-arm's length compensation payment — For the purpose of Part XIII, if the lender under a securities lending arrangement or a specified securities lending arrangement is not dealing at arm's length with either the borrower under the arrangement or the issuer of the security that is transferred or lent under the arrangement, or both, and subsection (8) deems an amount to be a payment of interest by a person to the lender, the lender is deemed, in respect of that payment, not to be dealing at arm's length with that person.

Related Provisions: 260(1.2) — Interpretation of "borrower" and "lender" for specified securities lending arrangement.

Notes: 260(9.1) amended by 2021 budget bill #1 to add "or a specified securities lending arrangement" and to delete "in respect of that security" after "to the lender", for amounts paid or credited as SLA compensation payments after March 18, 2019, or after Sept. 30, 2019 if pursuant to a written arrangement entered into before March 19, 2019.

260(10) renumbered as (9.1) by 2002-2013 technical bill, effective 2008. (260(10) had been added by 2007 budget bill #2, effective 2008.)

(10) Partnerships — For the purpose of this section,

(a) a person includes a partnership; and

(b) a partnership is deemed to be a registered securities dealer if each member of the partnership is a registered securities dealer.

Related Provisions: 260(11) — Corporate partners.

Notes: See Notes to 260(1)"securities lending arrangement". 260(10)-(12) added by 2002-2013 technical bill for arrangements made after Dec. 2002 (or earlier by election). For former 260(10) see Notes to 260(9.1).

(11) Corporate members of partnerships — A corporation that is, in a taxation year, a member of a partnership is deemed

(a) for the purpose of applying subsection (5) in respect of the taxation year,

(i) to receive its specified proportion, for each fiscal period of the partnership that ends in the taxation year, of each amount received by the partnership in that fiscal period, and

(ii) in respect of the receipt of its specified proportion of that amount, to be the same person as the partnership;

(b) for the purpose of applying paragraph (6.1)(a) in respect of the taxation year, to become obligated to pay its specified proportion, for each fiscal period of the partnership that ends in the taxation year, of the amount the partnership becomes, in that fiscal period, obligated to pay to another person under the arrangement described in that paragraph; and

(c) for the purpose of applying section 129 in respect of the taxation year, to have paid

(i) if the partnership is not a registered securities dealer, the corporation's specified proportion, for each fiscal period of the partnership that ends in the taxation year, of each amount paid by the partnership (other than an amount for which a deduction in computing income may be claimed under subsection (6.1) by the corporation), and

(ii) if the partnership is a registered securities dealer, $1/3$ of the corporation's specified proportion, for each fiscal period of the partnership that ends in the taxation year, of each amount paid by the partnership (other than an amount for which a deduction in computing income may be claimed under subsection (6.1) by the corporation).

Notes: For interpretation of 260(11)(c) see VIEWS doc 2013-0495461E5.

See Notes to 260(10) for in-force rule.

(12) Individual members of partnerships — An individual that is, in a taxation year, a member of a partnership is deemed

(a) for the purpose of applying subsection (5) in respect of the taxation year,

(i) to receive the individual's specified proportion, for each fiscal period of the partnership that ends in the taxation year, of each amount received by the partnership in that fiscal period, and

(ii) in respect of the receipt of the individual's specified proportion of that amount, to be the same person as the partnership; and

(b) for the purpose of subsection 82(1), to have paid the individual's specified proportion, for each fiscal period of the partnership that ends in the year, of each amount paid by the partnership in that fiscal period that is deemed by subsection (5.1) to have been received by another person as a taxable dividend.

Notes: See Notes to 260(10) for in-force rule.

Definitions [s. 260]: "affiliated" — 251.1; "amount" — 248(1); "arm's length" — 251(1); "beneficiary" — 248(25) [Notes]; "borrower" — 260(1)"securities lending arrangement"(a), 260(1.2)(a); "business" — 248(1); "Canada" — 255, *Interpretation Act* 35(1); "carrying on business in Canada" — 253; "corporation" — 248(1), *Interpretation Act* 35(1); "dealer compensation payment" — 260(1); "disposition", "dividend" — 248(1); "eligible dividend" — 89(1), 248(1), 260(5); "fair market value" — see 69(1) Notes; "fiscal period" — 249(2)(b), 249.1; "fully collateralized arrangement" — 248(1); "identical" — 248(12); "identical security" — 260(1)"securities lending arrangement"(b); "individual" — 248(1); "lender" — 260(1)"securities lending arrangement"(a), 260(1.2)(b); "non-resident" — 248(1); "partnership" — see 96(1) Notes; "permanent establishment" — Reg. 8201; "person", "prescribed", "property" — 248(1); "province" — *Interpretation Act* 35(1); "public corporation" — 89(1), 248(1); "qualified trust unit" — 260(1); "registered securities dealer", "regulation" — 248(1); "related" — 251(2)–(6); "resident in Canada" — 250; "SLA compensation payment" — 260(1); "securities lending arrangement" — 248(1), 260(1); "security distribution" — 260(1); "series" — 248(10); "share", "shareholder", "specified proportion" — 248(1); "specified securities lending arrangement" — 260(1); "tax treaty" — 248(1); "taxable dividend" — 89(1), 248(1); "taxable income" — 2(2), 248(1); "taxation year" — 249; "taxpayer" — 248(1); "trust" — 104(1), 248(1), (3); "underlying payment" — 260(1).

261. [Functional currency tax reporting] — (1) Definitions — The following definitions apply in this section.

"Canadian currency year" of a taxpayer means a taxation year that precedes the first functional currency year of the taxpayer.

Notes: See Notes at end of s. 261.

Income Tax Folios: S5-F4-C1: Income tax reporting currency.

"Canadian tax results" of a taxpayer for a taxation year means

(a) the amount of the income, taxable income or taxable income earned in Canada of the taxpayer for the taxation year;

(b) the amount (other than an amount payable on behalf of another person under subsection 153(1) or section 215) of tax or other amount payable under this Act by the taxpayer in respect of the taxation year;

(c) the amount (other than an amount refundable on behalf of another person in respect of amounts payable on behalf of that person under subsection 153(1) or section 215) of tax or other amount refundable under this Act to the taxpayer in respect of the taxation year; and

(d) any amount that is relevant in determining the amounts described in respect of the taxpayer under paragraphs (a) to (c).

Related Provisions: 93.3(3), (4)(a) — Special rule for certain Australian trusts; 261(2)(b) — Determination of Canadian tax results when no election filed; 261(5)(a), (c), 261(6), (6.1), (7)(h), (15)–(18) — Determination when election filed.

Income Tax Folios: S5-F4-C1: Income tax reporting currency.

"elected functional currency" of a taxpayer means the currency of a country other than Canada that was the functional currency of the taxpayer for its first taxation year in respect of which it made an election under paragraph (3)(b).

Income Tax Folios: S5-F4-C1: Income tax reporting currency.

"functional currency" of a taxpayer for a taxation year means the currency of a country other than Canada if that currency is, throughout the taxation year,

(a) a qualifying currency; and

(b) the primary currency in which the taxpayer maintains its records and books of account for financial reporting purposes.

Income Tax Folios: S5-F4-C1: Income tax reporting currency.

"functional currency year" of a taxpayer means a taxation year in respect of which subsection (5) applies to the taxpayer.

Income Tax Folios: S5-F4-C1: Income tax reporting currency.

"pre-reversion debt" of a taxpayer means a debt obligation of the taxpayer that was issued by the taxpayer before the beginning of the taxpayer's first reversionary year.

Related Provisions: 261(13) — Pre-reversion debt denominated in foreign currency; 261(14) — Deferred amount relating to pre-reversion debt.

Income Tax Folios: S5-F4-C1: Income tax reporting currency.

"pre-transition debt" of a taxpayer means a debt obligation of the taxpayer that was issued by the taxpayer before the beginning of the taxpayer's first functional currency year.

Related Provisions: 261(8)–(10), 261(12)(f) — Pre-transition debts.

Income Tax Folios: S5-F4-C1: Income tax reporting currency.

"qualifying currency" at any time means each of

(a) the currency of the United States of America;

(b) the currency of the European Monetary Union;

(c) the currency of the United Kingdom;

(d) the currency of Australia; and

(e) a prescribed currency.

Proposed Addition — 261(1)"qualifying currency" — Japanese yen

Letter from Dept. of Finance, July 29, 2019: Dear [xxx]:

Functional currency tax reporting — currency of Japan

I am writing in response to your correspondence and discussions with the Tax Legislation Division concerning a request to amend the functional currency tax reporting rules in section 261 of the *Income Tax Act* (the "Act") to allow a corporation resident in Canada to elect to compute its Canadian tax results using the currency of Japan (i.e., the yen). Specifically, you are asking for an expansion of the definition "qualifying currency" in subsection 261(1) of the Act such that it includes the Japanese yen.

You advise that your company has recently established operations in Japan and that financing for that operation is being raised in Japanese yen by a Canadian-resident corporation (Finco) that makes investments in Japanese-resident subsidiary corporations. You further advise that the books and records of Finco are maintained in Japanese yen and that your accountants have advised you that the accounting functional currency of Finco is the Japanese yen.

You note that, currently, the currencies of only the United States, the United Kingdom, the European Union and Australia are listed as "qualifying currencies" for the purposes of the functional currency tax reporting rules. You submit that, given the significance of the Japanese economy to Canada, it would be appropriate for Canadian corporations to have the ability to elect to determine their Canadian tax results in Japanese yen.

Our comments

We agree that it would be appropriate to permit taxpayers to elect to determine their Canadian tax results in Japanese yen, subject to the existing requirements of the functional currency tax reporting rules.

Accordingly, we will recommend to the Minister of Finance that the definition "qualifying currency" in subsection 261(1) of the Act be amended, effective for taxation years beginning after 2019, to include the currency of Japan.

While we cannot offer any assurance that either the Minister of Finance or Parliament will agree with our recommendation in respect of this matter, we hope that this statement of our intentions is helpful.

Yours sincerely,

Brian Ernewein, Assistant Deputy Minister — Legislation, Tax Policy Branch

Related Provisions: 261(1)"functional currency"(a) — Currency must be qualifying currency.

Income Tax Folios: S5-F4-C1: Income tax reporting currency.

"relevant spot rate", for a particular day, means, in respect of a conversion of an amount from a particular currency to another currency,

(a) if the particular currency or the other currency is Canadian currency, the rate quoted by the Bank of Canada on the particular day (or, if the Bank of Canada ordinarily quotes such a rate, but there is no such rate quoted for the particular day, the closest preceding day for which such a rate is quoted) for the exchange of the particular currency for the other currency, or, in applying paragraphs (2)(b) and (5)(c), another rate of exchange that is acceptable to the Minister; and

(b) if neither the particular currency nor the other currency is Canadian currency, the rate — calculated by reference to the rates quoted by the Bank of Canada on the particular day (or, if the Bank of Canada ordinarily quotes such rates, but either of such rates is not quoted for the particular day, the closest preceding day for which both such rates are quoted) for the exchange of Canadian currency for each of those currencies — for the exchange of the particular currency for the other currency, or, in applying paragraphs (2)(b) and (5)(c), another rate of exchange that is acceptable to the Minister.

Notes: *Korfage*, 2016 TCC 69, para. 22 held that "or, in applying paragraphs (2)(b) and (5)(c)" gives CRA discretion to choose a rate different from the taxpayer's. (This is wrong in the author's view. The choice is A *or* B; nothing says B overrides A.)

Exchange rate lookup: bankofcanada.ca/rates/exchange.

CRA always accepts the daily Bank of Canada (BoC) rate, and accepts other sources (e.g. Bloomberg, Thomson Reuters, OANDA) that are widely available, verifiable, published by an independent provider on an ongoing basis, recognized by the market, used in accordance with well-accepted business principles, used for preparation of the taxpayer's financial statements, and used consistently from year to year: VIEWS doc 2017-0684831I7 [Tollstam, "CRA Guidance on Foreign Exchange Rates", 25(7) *Canadian Tax Highlights* (ctf.ca) 9 (July 2017)]. (The BoC rate is still required for transitioning in or out of functional currency reporting.)

See also Max Thung & Clara Pham, "Issues for MNEs with the New Relevant Spot Rate", 7(2) *Canadian Tax Focus* (ctf.ca) 2-3 (May 2017).

Paras. (a) and (b) both amended by 2017 budget bill #2, effective March 2017, to change "for noon on the particular day" to "on the particular day" (since the BoC now publishes only one rate per day), and to add "if the Bank of Canada ordinarily quotes such [a] rate[s]".

Income Tax Folios: S5-F4-C1: Income tax reporting currency.

"reversionary year" of a taxpayer means a taxation year that begins after the last functional currency year of the taxpayer.

"tax reporting currency" of a taxpayer for a taxation year, and at any time in the taxation year, means the currency in which the taxpayer's Canadian tax results for the taxation year are to be determined.

(2) Canadian currency requirement — In determining the Canadian tax results of a taxpayer for a particular taxation year,

(a) subject to this section, other than this subsection, Canadian currency is to be used; and

(b) subject to this section, other than this subsection, subsections 20(14.2) and 79(7) and paragraphs 80(2)(k) and 142.7(8)(b), if a particular amount that is relevant in computing those Canadian tax results is expressed in a currency other than Canadian currency, the particular amount is to be converted to an amount expressed in Canadian currency using the relevant spot rate for the day on which the particular amount arose.

Related Provisions: 18(4) — Canadian currency used for thin-cap rules unless election made; 20(14.2)B — Sale of linked note — rule applies despite s. 261; 39(2) — Foreign exchange gains and losses; 76.1 — Debt of non-resident moved from (or assumed in) non-resident's Canadian business; 125.7(15) — Foreign currency — executive remuneration (for CEWS).

Notes: See Notes at end of 261 and to 39(2).

261(2)(b) amended to refer to 20(14.2) by 2016 budget bill #2, effective 2017.

(3) Application of subsec. (5) [election for functional currency reporting] — Subsection (5) applies to a taxpayer in respect of a particular taxation year if

(a) the taxpayer is, throughout the particular taxation year, a corporation (other than an investment corporation, a mortgage investment corporation or a mutual fund corporation) resident in Canada;

(b) the taxpayer has elected that subsection (5) apply to the taxpayer and has filed that election with the Minister in prescribed form and manner on or before the day that is 60 days after the first day of the particular taxation year;

(c) there is a functional currency of the taxpayer for the first taxation year of the taxpayer in respect of which subsection (5) would, if this subsection were read without reference to this paragraph, apply;

(d) the taxpayer has not filed another election under paragraph (b); and

(e) a revocation by the taxpayer under subsection (4) does not apply to the particular taxation year.

Related Provisions: 261(1)"elected functional currency" — Definition once election made; 261(2) — Rules where no election made; 261(4) — Revocation of election; 261(10), (10.1) — Pre-transition debts; 261(17.1) — Amalgamation — deemed application of 261(5); Reg. 205.1(2)(c) — Corporation electing functional currency not required to file T2 electronically.

Notes: See Notes at end of 261. For a taxpayer filing a Quebec return, a 261(3)(b) election must be copied to Revenu Québec: *Taxation Act* ss. 21.4.18, 21.4.6.

261(3)(b) amended by 2014 budget bill #2, for tax years that begin after July 12, 2013.

Forms: T1296: Election, or revocation of an election, to report in a functional currency.

(4) Revocation of election — A taxpayer may revoke its election under paragraph (3)(b) by filing, on a day that is in a functional currency year of the taxpayer (other than its first functional currency year), a notice of revocation in prescribed form and manner. The revocation applies to each taxation year of the taxpayer that begins on or after the day that is six months after that day.

Related Provisions: 261(14), (14.1) — Effect of revocation (reversion).

Forms: T1296: Election, or revocation of an election, to report in a functional currency.

(5) Functional currency tax reporting — If this subsection applies to a taxpayer in respect of a particular taxation year,

(a) **[elected currency to be used]** — the taxpayer's Canadian tax results for the particular taxation year are to be determined using the taxpayer's elected functional currency;

(b) **[dollar amounts]** — unless the context otherwise requires, each reference in this Act or the regulations to an amount (other than in respect of a penalty or fine) that is described as a particular number of Canadian dollars is to be read, in respect of the taxpayer and the particular taxation year, as a reference to that amount expressed in the taxpayer's elected functional currency using the relevant spot rate for the first day of the particular taxation year;

(c) **[conversion at date amount arose]** — subject to paragraph (9)(b), subsection (15), subsections 20(14.2) and 79(7) and paragraphs 80(2)(k) and 142.7(8)(b), if a particular amount that is relevant in computing the taxpayer's Canadian tax results for the particular taxation year is expressed in a currency other than the taxpayer's elected functional currency, the particular amount is to be converted to an amount expressed in the taxpayer's elected functional currency using the relevant spot rate for the day on which the particular amount arose;

(d) **[debt forgiveness]** — the definition "exchange rate" in subsection 111(8) is, in respect of the taxpayer and the particular taxation year, and with such modifications as the context requires, to be read as follows:

"exchange rate" at any time in respect of a particular currency other than the taxpayer's elected functional currency means the relevant spot rate, for the day that includes that time, in respect of the conversion of an amount from the particular currency to the taxpayer's elected functional currency, or a rate of exchange acceptable to the Minister;

(e) **[subsec. 39(2)]** — except in applying paragraph 95(2)(f.15) in respect of a taxation year, of a foreign affiliate of the taxpayer, that is a functional currency year of the foreign affiliate within the meaning of subsection (6.1), each reference in subsection 39(2) to "Canadian currency" is to be read, in respect of the taxpayer and the particular taxation year, and with such modifications as the context requires, as a reference to "the taxpayer's elected functional currency";

(f) **[loss carryovers]** — each reference in

(i) section 76.1, subsections 20(14.2) and 79(7), paragraph 80(2)(k), subsections 80.01(11), 80.1(8), 93(2.01) to (2.31), 142.4(1) and 142.7(8) and the definition "amortized cost" in subsection 248(1), and subparagraph 231(6)(a)(iv) of the *Income Tax Regulations*, to "Canadian currency" is, in respect of the taxpayer and the particular taxation year, and with such modifications as the context requires, to be read as "the taxpayer's elected functional currency", and

(ii) subparagraph 94.1(1)(b)(vii), the definition "foreign currency debt" in subsection 111(8), subsection 142.4(1), and the definition "amortized cost" in subsection 248(1) to "currency of a country other than Canada" is, in respect of the taxpayer and the particular taxation year, and with such modifications as the context requires, to be read as a reference to "currency other than the taxpayer's elected functional currency";

(g) **[definition "foreign currency"]** — the definition "foreign currency" in subsection 248(1) is, in respect of the taxpayer and the taxation year, and with such modifications as the context requires, to be read as follows:

"foreign currency" in respect of a taxpayer, at any time in a taxation year, means a currency other than the taxpayer's elected functional currency;

(h) **[FAPI rules]** — where a taxation year, of a foreign affiliate of the taxpayer, is a functional currency year of the foreign affiliate within the meaning of subsection (6.1),

(i) the references in section 95 (other than paragraph 95(2)(f.15)) and the references in regulations made for the purposes of section 95 or 113 to

(A) "Canadian currency" are to be read, in respect of the foreign affiliate and the taxation year, and with such modifications as the context requires, as references to "the taxpayer's elected functional currency", and

(B) "currency of a country other than Canada" are to be read, in respect of the foreign affiliate and the taxation year, and with such modifications as the context requires, as references to "currency other than the taxpayer's elected functional currency", and

(ii) the reference in paragraph 95(2)(f.13) to "the rate of exchange quoted by the Bank of Canada on" is to be read, in respect of the foreign affiliate and the taxation year, and with such modifications as the context requires, as a reference to "the relevant spot rate for".

Related Provisions: 76.1 — Debt of non-resident moved from (or assumed in) non-resident's Cdn business; 95(2)(f.12)–(f.15) — Currency calculations for foreign affiliates (FAPI); 125.7(15) — Foreign currency — executive remuneration (for CEWS); 261(1)"functional currency year" — Year to which 261(5) applies; 261(2) — Rules where no election made; 261(3) — Conditions for 261(5) to apply; 261(6) — Application to partnership; 261(7) — Converting Cdn currency amounts; 261(11) — Determination of amounts payable for administrative rules; 261(15) — Amounts carried back; 261(16)(a)(i), (b)(ii)(C) — Application on winding-up; 261(17.1) — Amalgamation — deemed application of 261(5); 261(18) — Anti-avoidance rule; Reg. 205.1(2)(c) — Corp electing functional currency not required to file T2 electronically.

Notes: 261(5)(h)(ii) amended by 2017 budget bill #2 to delete "at noon" after "Bank of Canada", effective March 2017 (BoC now publishes only 1 rate daily).

261(5)(c), (f)(i) amended by 2016 budget bill #2 to refer to 20(14.2), effective 2017.

261(5) earlier amended by 2002-2013 technical bill, last change effective for gains/losses in tax years that begin after Aug. 19, 2011.

Income Tax Folios: S5-F4-C1: Income tax reporting currency.

(6) Partnerships — For the purposes of computing the Canadian tax results of a particular taxpayer for each taxation year that is a functional currency year or a reversionary year of the particular taxpayer, this section is to be applied as if each partnership of which the particular taxpayer is a member at any time in the taxation year were a taxpayer that

(a) had as its first functional currency year its first fiscal period, if any, that

(i) is a fiscal period at any time during which the particular taxpayer is a member of the partnership,

(ii) begins after December 13, 2007, and

(iii) begins on or after the first day of the particular taxpayer's first functional currency year;

(b) had as its last Canadian currency year its last fiscal period, if any, that ends before its first functional currency year;

(c) had as its first reversionary year its first fiscal period, if any, that begins after the particular taxpayer's last functional currency year;

(d) is subject to subsection (5) for each of its fiscal periods that is, or begins after, its first functional currency year and that ends before its first reversionary year;

(e) had as its elected functional currency in respect of each fiscal period described in paragraph (d) the elected functional currency of the particular taxpayer; and

(f) had as its last functional currency year its last fiscal period, if any, that ends before its first reversionary year.

Related Provisions: 96(1) — Income determination for partnership; 261(22) — Partnership transactions — anti-avoidance rules.

Notes: For the treatment of partnership income where a partner elects to report in a functional currency, see VIEWS doc 2009-0324161C6. On reporting in the partnership information return, see 2012-0471831E5.

261(6)(a)(iii) changed from "ends at least six months after the day that is six months before the end of the particular taxpayer's first functional currency year" by 2014 budget bill #2, effective for taxation years that begin after July 12, 2013.

Income Tax Folios: S5-F4-C1: Income tax reporting currency.

(6.1) Foreign affiliates — For the purposes of computing the foreign accrual property income of a foreign affiliate of a particular taxpayer, in respect of the particular taxpayer, for each taxation year that is a functional currency year or a reversionary year of the particular taxpayer, this section is to be applied as if

(a) the foreign affiliate were a taxpayer that

(i) had, as its first functional currency year, its first taxation year that

(A) is a taxation year at any time during which the foreign affiliate is a foreign affiliate of the particular taxpayer,

(B) begins after December 13, 2007, and

(C) begins on or after the first day of the particular taxpayer's first functional currency year,

(ii) had as its last Canadian currency year its last taxation year, if any, that ends before its first functional currency year,

(iii) had as its first reversionary year its first taxation year, if any, that begins after the particular taxpayer's last functional currency year,

(iv) is subject to subsection (5) for each of its taxation years that is, or begins after, its first functional currency year and that ends before its first reversionary year,

(v) had as its elected functional currency in respect of each taxation year described in subparagraph (iv) the elected functional currency of the particular taxpayer, and

(vi) had as its last functional currency year its last taxation year, if any, that ends before its first reversionary year; and

(b) the Canadian tax results of the foreign affiliate for each taxation year that is a functional currency year or a reversionary year of the foreign affiliate, within the meaning of paragraph (a), were its foreign accrual property income, in respect of the particular taxpayer, for that taxation year and any amount that is relevant in determining such foreign accrual property income.

Related Provisions: 261(5)(h) — Where foreign affiliate's taxation year is functional currency year.

Notes: See Barnicke & Huynh, "Functional Currency and FAs", 17(4) *Canadian Tax Highlights* (ctf.ca) 7 (April 2009).

261(6.1)(a)(i)(C) changed from "ends at least six months after the day that is six months before the end of the particular taxpayer's first functional currency year" by 2014 budget bill #2, effective for taxation years that begin after July 12, 2013.

Income Tax Folios: S5-F4-C1: Income tax reporting currency.

(7) Converting Canadian currency amounts [— use last day of year] — In applying this Act to a taxpayer for a particular functional currency year of the taxpayer, the following amounts are to be converted from Canadian currency to the taxpayer's elected functional currency using the relevant spot rate for the last day of the taxpayer's last Canadian currency year:

(a) each particular amount that

(i) is, or is relevant to the determination of, an amount that may be deducted under subsection 37(1) or 66(4), variable F or F.1 in the definition "foreign accrual property income" in subsection 95(1), section 110.1 or 111 or subsection 126(2), 127(5), 129(1), 181.1(4) or 190.1(3), in the particular functional currency year, and

(ii) was determined for a Canadian currency year of the taxpayer;

(b) the cost to the taxpayer of a property that was acquired by the taxpayer in a Canadian currency year of the taxpayer;

(c) an amount that was required by section 53 to be added or deducted in computing, at any time in a Canadian currency year of the taxpayer, the adjusted cost base to the taxpayer of a capital property that was acquired by the taxpayer in such a year;

(d) an amount that

(i) is in respect of the taxpayer's undepreciated capital cost of depreciable property of a prescribed class, "cumulative Canadian exploration expense" (as defined in subsection 66.1(6)), "cumulative Canadian development expense" (as defined in subsection 66.2(5)), "cumulative foreign resource expense" in respect of a country other than Canada (as defined in subsection 66.21(1)) or "cumulative Canadian oil and gas property expense" (as defined in subsection 66.4(5)) (each of which is referred to in this paragraph as a "pool amount"), and

(ii) was added to or deducted from a pool amount of the taxpayer in respect of a Canadian currency year of the taxpayer;

(e) an amount that has been deducted or claimed as a reserve in computing the income of the taxpayer for its last Canadian currency year;

(f) an outlay or expense referred to in subsection 18(9) that was made or incurred by the taxpayer in respect of a Canadian currency year of the taxpayer, and any amount that was deducted in respect of the outlay or expense in computing the income of the taxpayer for such a year;

(g) an amount that was added or deducted in computing the taxpayer's paid-up capital in respect of a class of shares of its capital stock in a Canadian currency year of the taxpayer; and

(h) any amount (other than an amount referred to in any of paragraphs (a) to (g) or any of subsections (6), (6.1) and (8)) determined under the provisions of this Act in or in respect of a Canadian currency year of the taxpayer that is relevant in determining the Canadian tax results of the taxpayer for the particular functional currency year.

Related Provisions: 261(11) — Conversion rules for amounts of tax payable; 261(12) — Application to reversionary year.

Notes: 261(7) does not apply to the retained earnings (RE) balance, because RE is not relevant in computing income: VIEWS doc 2016-0633981E5.

261(7)(d)(i) amended by 2016 budget bill #2, effective 2017, to delete "cumulative eligible capital in respect of a business" (before "cumulative Canadian exploration expense"), as part of changing the eligible capital property rules to CCA Class 14.1 (see Notes to 20(1)(b)).

261(7)(a)(i) amended to add "or F.1" by 2002-2013 technical bill (Part 3 — FA reorganizations), effective Aug. 20, 2011.

Income Tax Folios: S5-F4-C1: Income tax reporting currency.

(8) Converting pre-transition debts — In determining, at any time in a particular functional currency year of a taxpayer, the amount for which a pre-transition debt of the taxpayer (other than a pre-transition debt denominated in the taxpayer's elected functional currency) was issued and its principal amount at the beginning of the taxpayer's first functional currency year,

(a) where the pre-transition debt is denominated in Canadian currency, those amounts are to be converted to the taxpayer's elected functional currency using the relevant spot rate for the last day of the taxpayer's last Canadian currency year; and

(b) where the pre-transition debt is denominated in a currency (referred to in this paragraph as the "debt currency") that is neither Canadian currency nor the taxpayer's elected functional currency, those amounts are to be converted from the debt currency to the taxpayer's elected functional currency using the relevant spot rate for the last day of the taxpayer's last Canadian currency year.

Related Provisions: 261(9) — Where denominated in other currency; 261(10) — Deferred amount relating to pre-transition debt; 261(12) — Application to reversionary year.

Income Tax Folios: S5-F4-C1: Income tax reporting currency.

(9) Pre-transition debts — A pre-transition debt of a taxpayer that is denominated in a currency other than the taxpayer's elected functional currency is deemed to have been issued immediately

before the taxpayer's first functional currency year for the purposes of

(a) determining the amount of the taxpayer's income, gain or loss, for a functional currency year of the taxpayer (other than an amount that subsection (10) deems to arise), that is attributable to a fluctuation in the value of a currency; and

(b) applying paragraph 80(2)(k) in respect of a functional currency year of the taxpayer.

Income Tax Folios: S5-F4-C1: Income tax reporting currency.

(10) Deferred amounts relating to pre-transition debts — If a taxpayer has, at any time in a taxation year that is a functional currency year or a reversionary year of the taxpayer, made a particular payment on account of the principal amount of a pre-transition debt of the taxpayer:

(a) where the taxpayer would have made a gain — or, if the pre-transition debt was not on account of capital, would have had income — (referred to in this paragraph as the "hypothetical gain or income") attributable to a fluctuation in the value of a currency if the pre-transition debt had been settled by the taxpayer's having paid, immediately before the end of its last Canadian currency year, an amount equal to the principal amount (expressed in the currency in which the pre-transition debt is denominated, which currency is referred to in this subsection as the "debt currency") at that time, the taxpayer is deemed to make a gain or to have income, as the case may be, for the taxation year equal to the amount determined by the formula

$$A \times B/C$$

where

A is

(i) if the taxation year is a functional currency year of the taxpayer, the amount of the hypothetical gain or income converted to the taxpayer's elected functional currency using the relevant spot rate for the last day of the taxpayer's last Canadian currency year, and

(ii) if the taxation year is a reversionary year of the taxpayer, the amount determined under subparagraph (i) converted to Canadian currency using the relevant spot rate for the last day of the taxpayer's last functional currency year,

B is the amount of the particular payment (expressed in the debt currency), and

C is the principal amount of the pre-transition debt at the beginning of the taxpayer's first functional currency year (expressed in the debt currency); and

(b) where the taxpayer would have sustained a loss — or, if the pre-transition debt was not on account of capital, would have had a loss — (referred to in this paragraph as the "hypothetical loss") attributable to a fluctuation in the value of a currency if the pre-transition debt had been settled by the taxpayer's having paid, immediately before the end of its last Canadian currency year, an amount equal to the principal amount (expressed in the debt currency) at that time, the taxpayer is deemed to sustain or to have a loss in respect of the particular payment for the taxation year equal to the amount that would be determined by the formula in paragraph (a) if the reference in the description of A in that paragraph to "hypothetical gain or income" were read as a reference to "hypothetical loss".

Related Provisions: 261(10.1) — Application to debt parking.

Notes: See at end of s. 261.

Income Tax Folios: S5-F4-C1: Income tax reporting currency.

(10.1) Debt parking — foreign exchange — For the purposes of determining a taxpayer's gain under subsection (10), if at a particular time a pre-transition debt of the taxpayer (referred to in this subsection as the "debtor") that is denominated in a currency other than Canadian currency becomes a parked obligation (within the meaning assigned by subsection 39(2.02)), the debtor is deemed to have made, at that time, a particular payment on account of the principal amount of the debt equal to

(a) if the debt has become a parked obligation at that particular time as a result of its acquisition by the holder of the debt, the portion of the amount paid by the holder to acquire the debt that can reasonably be considered to relate to the principal amount of the debt at the particular time; and

(b) in any other case, the portion of the fair market value of the debt that can reasonably be considered to relate to the principal amount of the debt at the particular time.

Notes: 261(10.1) added by 2016 budget bill #2, effective March 22, 2016. However, it does not apply to a debtor in respect of a debt owing by that debtor at the time the debt meets the conditions to become a parked obligation under 39(2.02), because of a written agreement entered into before March 22, 2016, if that time is before 2017.

(11) Determination of amounts payable [under the Act] — Notwithstanding subsections (5) and (7), for the purposes of applying this Act in respect of a functional currency year (referred to in this subsection as the "particular taxation year") of a taxpayer,

(a) for the purposes of determining the taxpayer's payment obligations under paragraph 157(1)(a) or (1.1)(a),

(i) the estimated amounts, each of which is described in subparagraph 157(1)(a)(i) or (1.1)(a)(i), that are payable by the taxpayer for the particular taxation year are to be determined by converting those amounts, as determined in the taxpayer's elected functional currency, to Canadian currency using the relevant spot rate for the day on which those amounts are due,

(ii) the taxpayer's first instalment base (within the meaning assigned by subsection 157(4)) for the particular taxation year is to be determined

(A) if the particular taxation year is the taxpayer's first functional currency year, without reference to this section, and

(B) in any other case, as if the taxes payable by the taxpayer for the taxpayer's functional currency year (referred to in this paragraph as the "first base year") immediately preceding the particular taxation year were the total of

(I) the total of the taxpayer's payment obligations under paragraph 157(1)(a) or (1.1)(a), as determined with reference to this subparagraph or subparagraph (i) or (iii), as the case may be, in respect of the first base year, and

(II) the amount, if any, of the remainder of the taxes payable by the taxpayer under paragraph 157(1)(b) or (1.1)(b), as determined under paragraph (b), in respect of the first base year, and

(iii) the taxpayer's second instalment base (within the meaning assigned by subsection 157(4)) for the particular taxation year is to be determined

(A) if the particular taxation year is the taxpayer's first functional currency year or its taxation year that immediately follows its first functional currency year, without reference to this section, and

(B) in any other case, as if the taxes payable by the taxpayer for the taxpayer's functional currency year (referred to in this subparagraph as the "second base year") immediately preceding the first base year were the total of

(I) the total of the taxpayer's payment obligations under paragraph 157(1)(a) or (1.1)(a), as determined with reference to this subparagraph or subparagraph (i) or (ii), as the case may be, in respect of the second base year, and

(II) the amount, if any, of the remainder of the taxes payable by the taxpayer under paragraph 157(1)(b) or (1.1)(b), as determined under paragraph (b), in respect of the second base year;

(b) the remainder of the taxes payable by the taxpayer under paragraph 157(1)(b) or (1.1)(b) for the particular taxation year is the amount, if any, determined by

(i) computing the amount, if any, by which

(A) the total of the taxes payable by the taxpayer under Parts I, VI, VI.1 and XIII.1 for the particular taxation year, as determined in the taxpayer's elected functional currency

exceeds

(B) the total of all amounts each of which is the amount determined by converting the amount of a payment obligation — determined by paragraph 157(1)(a) or (1.1)(a), as the case may be, with reference to subparagraph (a)(i), (ii) or (iii), as the case may be — of the taxpayer in respect of the particular taxation year to the taxpayer's elected functional currency using the relevant spot rate for the day on which the payment obligation was due, and

(ii) converting the amount, if any, determined by subparagraph (i) to Canadian currency using the relevant spot rate for the taxpayer's balance-due day for the particular taxation year;

(c) for the purposes of determining any amount (other than tax) that is payable by the taxpayer under Part I, VI, VI.1 or XIII.1 for the particular taxation year, the taxpayer's tax payable under the Part for the particular taxation year is deemed to be equal to the total of

(i) the total of the taxpayer's payment obligations under paragraph 157(1)(a) or (1.1)(a), in respect of the Part, as determined with reference to subparagraph (a)(i), (ii) or (iii), as the case may be, in respect of the particular taxation year, and

(ii) the amount, if any, of the remainder of the taxes payable by the taxpayer under paragraph 157(1)(b) or (1.1)(b), in respect of the Part, as determined under paragraph (b), in respect of the particular taxation year;

(d) amounts of tax that are payable under this Act (except under Parts I, VI, VI.1 and XIII.1) by the taxpayer for the particular taxation year are to be determined by converting those amounts, as determined in the taxpayer's elected functional currency, to Canadian currency using the relevant spot rate for the day on which those amounts are due;

(e) if a particular amount that is determined in the taxpayer's elected functional currency is deemed to be paid at any time on account of an amount payable by the taxpayer under this Act for the particular taxation year, the particular amount is to be converted to Canadian currency using the relevant spot rate for the day that includes that time;

(f) the following amounts are to be determined in the taxpayer's elected functional currency and converted to Canadian currency using the relevant spot rate for the taxpayer's balance-due day for the particular taxation year:

(i) amounts described in paragraph 163(1)(a) in respect of the particular taxation year, and

(ii) the amount of the taxpayer's taxable capital employed in Canada, for the purpose of applying section 235; and

(g) for greater certainty, all amounts payable by the taxpayer under this Act in respect of the particular taxation year are to be paid in Canadian currency.

Notes: See Notes at end of s. 261. The "balance-due day" (used in 261(11)(b)(ii) and (f)), defined in 248(1), is normally 3 months after year-end.

261(11)(b)(i)(A), (c) opening words and (d) amended by 2014 budget bill #2, for taxation years that begin after Dec. 13, 2007, to change "this Part and [or] Part VI" to "Part[s] I, VI".

Income Tax Folios: S5-F4-C1: Income tax reporting currency.

(12) Application of subsecs. (7) and (8) to reversionary years — In applying this Act to a reversionary year of a taxpayer, subsections (7) and (8) are to be read as if the references in those subsections to

(a) "Canadian currency" were references to "the taxpayer's elected functional currency";

(b) "Canadian currency year" were references to "functional currency year";

(c) "functional currency year" were references to "reversionary year";

(d) "first functional currency year" were references to "first reversionary year";

(e) "last Canadian currency year" were references to "last functional currency year";

(f) "pre-transition debt" were references to "pre-reversion debt"; and

(g) "the taxpayer's elected functional currency" were references to "Canadian currency".

Income Tax Folios: S5-F4-C1: Income tax reporting currency.

(13) Pre-reversion debts — A pre-reversion debt of a taxpayer that is denominated in a currency other than Canadian currency is deemed to have been issued immediately before the taxpayer's first reversionary year for the purposes of

(a) determining the amount of the taxpayer's income, gain or loss, for a reversionary year of the taxpayer (other than an amount that subsection (14) deems to arise), that is attributable to a fluctuation in the value of a currency; and

(b) applying paragraph 80(2)(k) in respect of a reversionary year of the taxpayer.

Income Tax Folios: S5-F4-C1: Income tax reporting currency.

(14) Deferred amounts relating to pre-reversion debts — If a taxpayer has, at any time in a reversionary year of the taxpayer, made a particular payment on account of the principal amount of a pre-reversion debt of the taxpayer:

(a) where the taxpayer would have made a gain — or, if the pre-reversion debt was not on account of capital, would have had income — (referred to in this paragraph as the "hypothetical gain or income") attributable to a fluctuation in the value of a currency if the pre-reversion debt had been settled by the taxpayer's having paid, immediately before the end of its last functional currency year, an amount equal to the principal amount (expressed in the currency in which the pre-reversion debt is denominated, which currency is referred to in this subsection as the "debt currency") at that time, the taxpayer is deemed to make a gain or to have income, as the case may be, for the reversionary year equal to the amount determined by the formula

$$A \times B / C$$

where

A is the amount of the hypothetical gain or income converted to Canadian currency using the relevant spot rate for the last day of the taxpayer's last functional currency year,

B is the amount of the particular payment (expressed in the debt currency), and

C is the principal amount of the pre-reversion debt at the beginning of the taxpayer's first reversionary year (expressed in the debt currency); and

(b) where the taxpayer would have sustained a loss — or, if the pre-reversion debt was not on account of capital, would have had a loss — (referred to in this paragraph as the "hypothetical loss") attributable to a fluctuation in the value of a currency if the pre-reversion debt had been settled by the taxpayer's having paid, immediately before the end of its last functional currency year, an amount equal to the principal amount (expressed in the debt currency) at that time, the taxpayer is deemed to sustain or to have a loss in respect of the particular payment for the rever-

sionary year equal to the amount that would be determined by the formula in paragraph (a) if the reference in the description of A in that paragraph to "hypothetical gain or income" were read as a reference to "hypothetical loss".

Related Provisions: 261(14.1) — Application to debt parking.

Income Tax Folios: S5-F4-C1: Income tax reporting currency.

(14.1) Debt parking — foreign exchange — For the purposes of determining a taxpayer's gain under subsection (14), if at a particular time a pre-reversion debt of the taxpayer (referred to in this subsection as the "debtor") that is denominated in a currency other than the taxpayer's elected functional currency becomes a parked obligation (within the meaning assigned by subsection 39(2.02)), the debtor is deemed to have made, at that time, a particular payment on account of the principal amount of the debt equal to

(a) if the debt has become a parked obligation at that particular time as a result of its acquisition by the holder of the debt, the portion of the amount paid by the holder to acquire the debt that can reasonably be considered to relate to the principal amount of the debt at the particular time; and

(b) in any other case, the portion of the fair market value of the debt that can reasonably be considered to relate to the principal amount of the debt at the particular time.

Notes: 261(14.1) added by 2016 budget bill #2, effective on the same basis as 261(10.1).

(15) Amounts carried back — For the purposes of determining the amount that may be deducted, in respect of a particular amount that arises in a taxation year (referred to in this subsection as the "later year") of a taxpayer, under section 111 or subsection 126(2), 127(5), 181.1(4) or 190.1(3) in computing the taxpayer's Canadian tax results for a taxation year (referred to in this subsection as the "current year") that ended before the later year, and for the purposes of determining the amount by which the amount included under subsection 91(1) for the current year is reduced because of a reduction referred to in paragraph 152(6.1)(b) in respect of the later year,

(a) if the later year is a functional currency year of the taxpayer and the current year is a Canadian currency year of the taxpayer, the following amounts (expressed in the taxpayer's elected functional currency) are to be converted to Canadian currency using the relevant spot rate for the last day of the taxpayer's last Canadian currency year:

(i) the particular amount, and

(ii) any amount so deducted in computing the taxpayer's Canadian tax results for another functional currency year of the taxpayer;

(b) if the later year is a reversionary year of the taxpayer and the current year is a functional currency year of the taxpayer,

(i) the following amounts (expressed in Canadian currency) are to be converted to the taxpayer's elected functional currency using the relevant spot rate for the last day of the taxpayer's last functional currency year:

(A) the particular amount, and

(B) any amount so deducted in computing the taxpayer's Canadian tax results for another reversionary year of the taxpayer, and

(ii) any amount (expressed in Canadian currency) so deducted in computing the taxpayer's Canadian tax results for a Canadian currency year of the taxpayer is to be converted to the taxpayer's elected functional currency using the relevant spot rate for the last day of the taxpayer's last Canadian currency year;

(c) if the later year is a reversionary year of the taxpayer and the current year is a Canadian currency year of the taxpayer, the following amounts (expressed in the taxpayer's elected functional currency) are to be converted to Canadian currency using the relevant spot rate for the last day of the taxpayer's last Canadian currency year:

(i) the amount that would be determined under clause (b)(i)(A) in respect of the particular amount if the current year were a functional currency year of the taxpayer, and

(ii) any amount so deducted in computing the taxpayer's Canadian tax results for a functional currency year of the taxpayer; and

(d) in any other case, this subsection does not apply.

Notes: 261(15) opening words amended by 2002-2013 technical bill (Part 2 — FA surplus rules) to add everything after "that ended before the later year", effective Dec. 14, 2007.

Income Tax Folios: S5-F4-C1: Income tax reporting currency.

(16) Windings-up — If a winding-up described in subsection 88(1) commences at any time (referred to in this subsection as the "commencement time") and the parent and the subsidiary referred to in that subsection would, in the absence of this subsection, have different tax reporting currencies at the commencement time, the following rules apply for the purposes of determining the subsidiary's Canadian tax results for its taxation years that end after the commencement time:

(a) where the subsidiary's tax reporting currency is Canadian currency,

(i) notwithstanding subsection (3), subsection (5) is deemed to apply to the subsidiary in respect of its taxation year that includes the commencement time and each of its subsequent taxation years, if any,

(ii) the subsidiary is deemed to have as its elected functional currency the parent's tax reporting currency, and

(iii) if the subsidiary's taxation year that includes the commencement time would, in the absence of this subsection, be a reversionary year of the subsidiary, this section is to be read with any modifications that the circumstances require; and

(b) where the subsidiary's tax reporting currency is not Canadian currency,

(i) the subsidiary is deemed to have filed, at the time that is six months and one day before the beginning of its taxation year that includes the commencement time, in prescribed form and manner, a notice of revocation described in subsection (4), and

(ii) if the parent's tax reporting currency is not Canadian currency,

(A) the subsidiary's first reversionary year is deemed to have ended at the particular time that is immediately after the time at which it began,

(B) a new taxation year of the subsidiary is deemed to have begun immediately after the particular time,

(C) notwithstanding subsection (3), subsection (5) is deemed to apply to the subsidiary in respect of its taxation year that includes the commencement time and each of its subsequent taxation years, if any, and

(D) the subsidiary is deemed to have as its elected functional currency the parent's tax reporting currency.

Related Provisions: 261(17) — Application to amalgamation; 261(18) — Anti-avoidance.

Income Tax Folios: S5-F4-C1: Income tax reporting currency.

(17) Amalgamations — If a predecessor corporation and the new corporation, in respect of an amalgamation within the meaning of subsection 87(1), have different tax reporting currencies for their last and first taxation years, respectively, paragraphs (16)(a) and (b) apply, for the purposes of determining the predecessor corporation's Canadian tax results for its last taxation year, as if the tax reporting currencies referred to in those paragraphs were the tax reporting currencies referred to in this subsection and as if the references in those paragraphs to

(a) "subsidiary" were references to "predecessor corporation";

(b) "parent" were references to "new corporation"; and

(c) "taxation year that includes the commencement time" were references to "last taxation year".

Related Provisions: 261(18) — Anti-avoidance.

Income Tax Folios: S5-F4-C1: Income tax reporting currency.

(17.1) Amalgamation — deemed application of subsec. (5) — Notwithstanding subsection (3), if each predecessor corporation in respect of an amalgamation (within the meaning assigned by subsection 87(1)) has the same elected functional currency for its last taxation year, then, unless a predecessor corporation has filed a notice of revocation under subsection (4) on or before the day that is six months before the end of its last taxation year,

(a) the new corporation formed as a result of the amalgamation is deemed to have made an election under paragraph (3)(b) and to have filed that election on the first day of its first taxation year; and

(b) that elected functional currency is deemed to be the new corporation's functional currency for its first taxation year.

Notes: 261(17.1) added by 2014 budget bill #2, effective for amalgamations that occur after July 12, 2013.

Income Tax Folios: S5-F4-C1: Income tax reporting currency.

(18) Anti-avoidance — The Canadian tax results of a corporation for any one or more taxation years shall be determined using a particular currency if

(a) at any time (referred to in this subsection as the "transfer time") one or more properties are directly or indirectly transferred

(i) by the corporation to another corporation (referred to in this subsection as the "transferor" and the "transferee", respectively), or

(ii) by another corporation to the corporation (referred to in this subsection as the "transferor" and the "transferee", respectively);

(b) the transferor and the transferee are related at the transfer time or become related in the course of a series of transactions or events that includes the transfer;

(c) the transfer time

(i) is, or would in the absence of subsections (16) and (17) be, in a functional currency year of the transferor and the transferor and the transferee have, or would in the absence of those subsections have, different tax reporting currencies at the transfer time, or

(ii) is, or would in the absence of those subsections be, in a reversionary year of the transferor and is not in a reversionary year of the transferee;

(d) it can reasonably be considered that one of the main purposes of the transfer or of any portion of a series of transactions or events that includes the transfer is to change, or to enable the changing of, the currency in which the Canadian tax results in respect of the property, or property substituted for it, for a taxation year would otherwise be determined; and

(e) the Minister directs that those Canadian tax results be determined in the particular currency.

Related Provisions: 261(19) — Mergers; 261(22) — Partnership transactions.

Notes: Although 261(18) is an anti-avoidance rule, CRA has used it to *help* taxpayers that were unable to make or revoke elections because deadlines were changed retroactively when s. 261 was amended. CRA used 261(18) to direct taxpayers to use the currency they wanted to use.

For the meaning of "indirectly" in para. (a), see 17.1(1) Notes. For "one of the main purposes" in para. (d), see 83(2.1) Notes.

For application of 261(18) in loss consolidations, see VIEWS docs 2010-0367251R3, 2010-0370671E5, 2019-0794891R3.

Income Tax Folios: S5-F4-C1: Income tax reporting currency.

(19) Mergers — For the purposes of subsection (18), if one corporate entity (referred to in this subsection as the "new corporation") is formed at a particular time by the amalgamation or other merger of two or more corporations (each of which is referred to in this subsection as a "predecessor corporation"),

(a) the predecessor corporation is deemed to have transferred to the new corporation at the time (referred to in this subsection as the "merger transfer time") that is immediately before the particular time each property that was held at the merger transfer time by the predecessor corporation and at the particular time by the new corporation;

(b) the new corporation is deemed to exist, and to be related to the predecessor corporation, at the merger transfer time; and

(c) the new corporation is deemed to have as its tax reporting currency at the merger transfer time its tax reporting currency at the particular time.

Related Provisions: 261(22) — Partnership transactions.

Income Tax Folios: S5-F4-C1: Income tax reporting currency.

(20) Application of subsec. (21) — Subsection (21) applies in determining a taxpayer's income, gain or loss for a taxation year in respect of a transaction (referred to in this subsection and subsection (21) as a "specified transaction") if

(a) the specified transaction was entered into, directly or indirectly, at any time by the taxpayer and a corporation (referred to in this subsection as the "related corporation") to which the taxpayer is at that time related;

(b) the taxpayer and the related corporation had different tax reporting currencies at any time during the period (referred to in this subsection as the "accrual period") in which the income, gain or loss accrued; and

(c) it would, in the absence of this subsection and subsection (21), be reasonable to consider that a fluctuation at any time in the accrual period in the value of the taxpayer's tax reporting currency relative to the value of the related corporation's tax reporting currency

(i) increased the taxpayer's loss in respect of the specified transaction,

(ii) reduced the taxpayer's income or gain in respect of the specified transaction, or

(iii) caused the taxpayer to have a loss, instead of income or a gain, in respect of the specified transaction.

Related Provisions: 261(22) — Partnership transactions.

Notes: For the meaning of "indirectly" in para. (a), see Notes to 17.1(1).

Income Tax Folios: S5-F4-C1: Income tax reporting currency.

(21) Income, gain or loss determinations — If this subsection applies, each fluctuation in value referred to in paragraph (20)(c) is, for the purposes of determining the taxpayer's income, gain or loss in respect of the specified transaction and notwithstanding any other provision of this Act, deemed not to have occurred.

Related Provisions: 261(20) — Conditions for 261(21) to apply; 261(22) — Partnership transactions.

Notes: For discussion of 261(21) see VIEWS docs 2011-0426981C6 [2011 TEI q.4]; 2015-061250117 (hedging arrangement); 2017-0691211C6 [2017 IFA q.4] (foreign exchange loss on settlement of loan from foreign affiliate of related Canadian corp [Wang & Zahary, "Functional Currency Election Issues", 7(3) *Canadian Tax Focus* (ctf.ca) 12-13 (Aug. 2017)]).

Income Tax Folios: S5-F4-C1: Income tax reporting currency.

(22) Partnership transactions — For the purposes of this subsection and subsections (18) to (21),

(a) if a property is directly or indirectly transferred to or by a partnership, the property is deemed to have been transferred to or by (as the case may be) each member of the partnership; and

(b) if a partnership is a party to a transaction, each member of the partnership is deemed to be that party to that transaction.

Notes: For the meaning of "indirectly" in para. (a), see Notes to 17.1(1).

Income Tax Folios: S5-F4-C1: Income tax reporting currency.

Related Provisions: See under 261(2).

Notes [s. 261]: See generally Income Tax Folio S5-F4-C1. 261(2) provides that income, taxable income and tax payable are to be determined in Canadian currency. However, 261(3) allows certain corporations to elect to use a "qualifying currency", as defined in 261(1), in which case 261(5)-(22) provide the rules that apply and the currency conversion dates to be used. For foreign-currency capital gains and losses, see Notes to 39(2).

261(2) was considered in: *Agnico-Eagle Mines*, 2016 FCA 130 (see Notes to 39(2)); *Ferlaino*, 2017 FCA 105 (US$ employee stock options taxed using FX rate on date options exercised); *9189-7397 Québec*, 2018 QCCQ 4692 (parallel Quebec rule required payments to US company to be calculated as the work was done, for QC film credit).

For discussion of 261 see Gamble, *Taxation of Canadian Mining* (Carswell, looseleaf or *Taxnet Pro* Reference Centre), chap. 18; Conway & Fitzgerald, "New Section 261: The Tax Calculating Currency Rules", 56(4) *Canadian Tax Journal* 957-89 (2008); CCH, "Functional Currency Reporting", 1951 *Tax Topics* 1-3 (July 30, 2009); Bretsen & Kerr, "Tax Planning for Foreign Currency", 2009 Cdn Tax Foundation conference report, 35:28-47; Keey, "Recent Developments in Accounting for Income Taxes", *General Corporate Tax Newsletter* (Carswell, Nov. 2009), pp. 14-28; O'Hagan et al., "Functional Currency Rules", XVI(1) *International Tax Planning [ITP]* (Federated Press) 1088-91 (2010); Alty, "The Interaction of the Functional Currency Election and the 88(1)(c) and (d) Bump Rules", XII(3) *Corporate Structures & Groups* (Federated Press) 680-85 (2010); Morreale, "Functional Currency Election Not Available to Branches", 6(1) *Canadian Tax Focus* (ctf.ca) 6-7 (Feb. 2016); Oldewening, "Duality of Paid-up Capital", XXI(2) *ITP* 7-19 (2017); Ancimer & Beswick, "Foreign Exchange Legislation", 2017 Cdn Tax Foundation conference report, 17:1-25.

For detailed recommendations for amendments see CBA/CICA Joint Committee letter to Finance, Jan. 19, 2012.

For CRA interpretation see *Income Tax Technical News* 41, 44 (Cdn Tax Foundation 2008 and 2009 conference roundtables [VIEWS doc 2009-0345361C6]); docs 2009-0332771E5, 2010-0370671E5, 2010-0373651C6, 2010-0385891C6 [2010 conf p.4:24-25, q.25], 2011-0421631R3, 2011-0426981C6, 2011-0430921E5, 2012-0453207117, 2012-047111117, 2012-0471261E5, 2014-0538181C6 [2014 APFF q.24]; 2014-0539951E5 (US dollar dividend designated as eligible dividend is converted when it is paid); 2014-054063117 (interaction with loss carryback and instalment requirements); 2014-0561001R3; 2015-0610601C6 [2014 CTF q.10] (application to 18(4)); 2016-0633981E5 (no loss allowed on making functional currency election); 2016-0642011E5 (where corporate partner has made 261(3) election, Reg. 229(1) partnership return must use the functional currency); 2016-0652781C6 [2016 APFF q.17] (functional currency and acquisition of control); 2016-0642111C6 (interaction with 84(3)-(4); see Notes to 84(3)); 2016-064963117 (FX gain on income tax refund is capital gain [Arrigo & Peters, "Tax Refunds for Functional Currency Reporters", XXIII(3) *Corporate Finance* (Federated Press) 43-49 (2020)]); 2018-0779911C6 [2018 CTF q.14] (application to 20(14)); 2019-0798811C6 [2019 IFA q.5] (currency fluctuation affecting CRA tax refund can trigger s. 39 gain or loss); 2019-0824381C6 [2019 CTF q.2] (use date of payment of foreign tax to determine rate for s. 126 foreign tax credit).

261 added by 2007 budget bill #2, and replaced by 2008 budget bill #2, both effective for tax years that begin after Dec. 13, 2007 (June 27, 2008 in some cases).

Definitions [s. 261]: "accrual period" — 261(20)(b); "adjusted cost base" — 54, 248(1); "amount", "balance-due day", "business" — 248(1); "Canada" — 255, *Interpretation Act* 35(1); "Canadian currency year" — 261(1); "Canadian development expense" — 66.2(5), 248(1); "Canadian exploration expense" — 66.1(6), 248(1); "Canadian oil and gas property expense" — 66.4(5), 248(1); "Canadian tax results" — 261(1); "capital property" — 54, 248(1); "class of shares" — 248(6); "commencement time" — 261(16); "corporation" — 248(1), *Interpretation Act* 35(1); "cumulative eligible capital" — 14(5), 248(1); "current year" — 261(15); "debt currency" — 261(10)(a); "depreciable property" — 13(21), 248(1); "elected functional currency" — 261(1); "fair market value" — see 69(1) Notes; "first base year" — 261(11)(a)(ii)(B); "fiscal period" — 249.1; "foreign affiliate" — 95(1), 248(1); "foreign resource expense" — 66.21(1), 248(1); "functional currency", "functional currency year" — 261(1); "hypothetical gain or income" — 261(10)(a), 261(14)(a); "hypothetical loss" — 261(10)(b), 261(14)(b); "investment corporation" — 130(3), 248(1); "later year" — 261(15); "merger transfer time" — 261(19)(a); "Minister" — 248(1); "month" — *Interpretation Act* 35(1); "mortgage investment corporation" — 130.1(6), 248(1); "mutual fund corporation" — 131(8), 248(1); "new corporation" — 261(19); "paid-up capital" — 89(1), 248(1); "partnership" — see 96(1) Notes; "person" — 248(1); "pool amount" — 261(7)(d); "pre-reversion debt", "pre-transition debt" — 261(1); "predecessor corporation" — 261(19); "prescribed" — 248(1); "principal amount" — 248(1), (26); "property" — 248(1); "qualifying currency" — 261(1); "record", "regulation" — 248(1); "related" — 251(2)–(6); "related corporation" — 261(20)(a); "relevant spot rate" — 261(1); "resident in Canada" — 250; "reversionary year" — 261(1); "second base year" — 261(11)(a)(iii)(B); "specified transaction" — 261(20); "substituted" — 248(5); "tax reporting currency" — 261(1); "taxable income", "taxable income earned in Canada" — 248(1); "taxation year" — 249; "taxpayer" — 248(1); "transfer time", "transferee", "transferor" — 261(18)(a); "undepreciated capital cost" — 13(21), 248(1); "United Kingdom", "United States" — *Interpretation Act* 35(1).

I.T. Technical News: 41 (functional currency tax reporting rules); 44 (foreign currency reporting).

262. (1) Authority to designate stock exchange — The Minister of Finance may designate a stock exchange, or a part of a stock exchange, for the purposes of this Act.

Related Provisions: 55(6) — Reorganization share deemed listed on designated stock exchange; 87(10) — Share deemed listed on designated stock exchange following amalgamation; 248(1)"designated stock exchange" — Definition applicable to entire Act; Canada-U.S. Tax Treaty:Art. XXIX-A:5(f)(ii) — Designated stock exchange is "recognized stock exchange" for treaty purposes.

Notes: See Notes at end of s. 262.

(2) Revocation of designation — The Minister of Finance may revoke the designation of a stock exchange, or a part of a stock exchange, designated under subsection (1).

(3) Timing — A designation under subsection (1) or a revocation under subsection (2) shall specify the time at and after which it is in effect, which time may, for greater certainty, precede the time at which the designation or revocation is made.

(4) Publication — The Minister of Finance shall cause to be published, by posting on the Internet website of the Department of Finance or by any other means that the Minister of Finance considers appropriate, the names of those stock exchanges, or parts of stock exchanges, as the case may be, that are or at any time were designated under subsection (1).

(5) Transition — The Minister of Finance is deemed to have designated under subsection (1) each stock exchange and each part of a stock exchange that was, immediately before the day on which this section came into force, a prescribed stock exchange, with effect on and after that day.

Regulations: 3200, 3201 (prescribed stock exchanges before Dec. 14, 2007).

Definitions [s. 262]: "prescribed" — 248(1); "Minister of Finance" — *Financial Administration Act* 14.

Notes [s. 262]: The term "designated stock exchange" has generally replaced "prescribed stock exchange". See 248(1)"designated stock exchange" Notes. For 262(5), the prescribed stock exchanges as of Dec. 13, 2007 (the day before s. 262 came into force) were in Reg. 3200 (Canada) and 3201 (outside Canada), as amended by 2007 Budget bill. As of June 2021, the designated exchanges (tinyurl.com/des-exch) are:

Canada: Aequitas NEO Exchange, Canadian National Stock Exchange (operating as the Canadian Securities Exchange); Montreal Exchange; TSX Venture Exchange (Tiers 1 and 2); Toronto Stock Exchange

Australia: Australian Securities Exchange

Austria: Vienna Stock Exchange

Belgium: Euronext Brussels

Bermuda: Bermuda Stock Exchange

Brazil: BM&F Bovespa Stock Exchange

Czech Republic: Prague Stock Exchange (Prime Market)

Denmark: Nasdaq Copenhagen

Finland: Nasdaq Helsinki

France: Euronext Paris

Germany: Frankfurt Stock Exchange; Boerse Stuttgart AG (Stuttgart Stock Exchange)

Hong Kong: The Hong Kong Stock Exchange

Ireland: Irish Stock Exchange

Israel: Tel Aviv Stock Exchange

Italy: Borsa Italiana S.p.A (Milan Stock Exchange)

Jamaica: Jamaica Stock Exchange (Senior Market)

Japan: Tokyo Stock Exchange

Korea: Korea Exchange (KOSPI and KOSDAQ)

Luxembourg: Luxembourg Stock Exchange

Mexico: Mexico City Stock Exchange

Netherlands: Euronext Amsterdam

New Zealand: New Zealand Stock Exchange

Norway: Oslo Stock Exchange

Poland: The main and parallel markets of the Warsaw Stock Exchange

Singapore: Singapore Stock Exchange

South Africa: Johannesburg Stock Exchange

Spain: Bolsa de Madrid (Madrid Stock Exchange)

Sweden: Nasdaq Stockholm

Switzerland: SWX Swiss Exchange

United Kingdom: London Stock Exchange

United States: BATS Exchange, Nasdaq BX; Chicago Board of Options; Chicago Board of Trade; Chicago Stock Exchange; Investors Exchange LLC; National Association of Securities Dealers Automated Quotation System (Nasdaq); National Stock Exchange; New York Stock Exchange; NYSE Arca; NYSE MKT; Nasdaq PHLX.

For past years, see past editions of PITA. The list has not changed much since 2008. Aequitas NEO and BATS Exchange were added in 2014-15. Investors Exchange LLC was added in 2019. For the Canadian National Stock Exchange (cnq.ca) Jan. 13/09 news release on becoming designated, see these Notes in the 37th-39th ed.

The American Stock Exchange changed its name to NYSE Alternext US, then NYSE Amex Equities, then NYSE MKT LLC, and is now NYSE American LLC. CRA suggests (doc 2012-0436031E5) that it is not listed until Finance adds the current name to the list; in the author's view it qualifies despite name changes: *Interpretation Act* s. 38.

The following do not qualify (though they may be a 248(1)"recognized stock exchange"): Alternative Investment Market of London Stock Exchange (VIEWS docs 2007-0253561E5, 2012-0455741E5); BATS (Better Alternative Trading System), before it was added (2014-0519461M4); NEX board on TSX Venture Exchange (2012-045432117); Open Market segment of Frankfurt Stock Exchange or similar unofficial exchange-regulated market operated by European stock exchange (2010-0359251E5, 2010-0387951M4).

For the guidelines to be designated as a stock exchange see Finance news release 2008-049 and Backgrounder, July 2, 2008 (on fin.gc.ca).

262 added, and Reg. 3200-3201 repealed, by 2007 budget bill #2, effective Dec. 14, 2007. Before that date, read:

> 3200. Stock exchanges in Canada — For the purposes of the Act, the following are prescribed stock exchanges in Canada:
>
> (a) Tiers 1 and 2 of the TSX Venture Exchange (also known as Tiers 1 and 2 of the Canadian Venture Exchange);
>
> (b) Montreal Stock Exchange; and
>
> (c) Toronto Stock Exchange.
>
> (d) [Repealed]
>
> (e) [Repealed]
>
> 3201. Stock exchanges outside Canada — For the purposes of the Act, the following are prescribed stock exchanges outside Canada:
>
> (a) in Australia, the Australian Securities Exchange;
>
> (b) in Belgium, Euronext Brussels;
>
> (c) in France, Euronext Paris;
>
> (d) in Germany, the Frankfurt Stock Exchange;
>
> (e) in Hong Kong, the Hong Kong Stock Exchange;
>
> (f) in Italy, the Milan Stock Exchange;
>
> (g) in Japan, the Tokyo Stock Exchange;
>
> (h) in Mexico, the Mexico City Stock Exchange;
>
> (i) in the Netherlands, Euronext Amsterdam;
>
> (j) in New Zealand, the New Zealand Stock Exchange;
>
> (k) in Singapore, the Singapore Stock Exchange;
>
> (l) in Spain, the Madrid Stock Exchange;
>
> (m) in Switzerland, the SWX Swiss Exchange;
>
> (n) in the United Kingdom, the London Stock Exchange;
>
> (o) in the United States,
>
>   (i) the American Stock Exchange,
>
>   (ii) the Boston Stock Exchange,
>
>   (iii) the Chicago Board of Options,
>
>   (iv) the Chicago Board of Trade,
>
>   (v) the National Stock Exchange,
>
>   (vi) [Repealed]
>
>   (vii) the Chicago Stock Exchange,
>
>   (viii) the National Association of Securities Dealers Automated Quotation System,
>
>   (ix) the New York Stock Exchange,
>
>   (x) NYSE Arca,
>
>   (xi) the Philadelphia Stock Exchange;
>
>   (xii) [Repealed]
>
> (p) in Ireland, the Irish Stock Exchange;
>
> (q) in Israel, the Tel Aviv Stock Exchange;
>
> (r) in Austria, the Vienna Stock Exchange;
>
> (s) in Denmark, the Copenhagen Stock Exchange;
>
> (t) in Finland, the Helsinki Stock Exchange;
>
> (u) in Norway, the Oslo Stock Exchange;
>
> (v) in South Africa, the Johannesburg Stock Exchange;
>
> (w) in Sweden, the Stockholm Stock Exchange;
>
> (x) in Luxembourg, the Luxembourg Stock Exchange; and
>
> (y) in Poland, the main and parallel markets of the Warsaw Stock Exchange.

Reg. 3200 amended by P.C. 2003-1919 (last effective Dec. 17, 2003), 2001-954.

Reg. 3201 amended by 2007 budget bill #2, effective Dec. 13, 2007 (various changes, so as to apply for 262(5)). Earlier amended by P.C. 2005-7 (effective June 24, 2003), 2001-954, 1997-1145, 1994-101, 1992-2334.

PART XVIII — ENHANCED INTERNATIONAL INFORMATION REPORTING [FOR U.S. FATCA]

263. (1) Definitions — The following definitions apply in this Part.

Notes: See Notes to 233.3(3). "This Part" is sections 263-269. The core obligation for a financial institution to file an information return is in 266(1).

"agreement" has the same meaning as in section 2 of the *Canada–United States Enhanced Tax Information Exchange Agreement Implementation Act.*

Notes: For the text of the agreement as set out in the schedule to the referenced *Implementation Act*, see after the Canada-US tax treaty.

"electronic filing" means using electronic media in a manner specified by the Minister.

"listed financial institution" means a financial institution that is

(a) an authorized foreign bank within the meaning of section 2 of the *Bank Act* in respect of its business in Canada, or a bank to which that Act applies;

(b) a cooperative credit society, a savings and credit union or a caisse populaire regulated by a provincial Act;

(c) an association regulated by the *Cooperative Credit Associations Act*;

(d) a central cooperative credit society, as defined in section 2 of the *Cooperative Credit Associations Act*, or a credit union central or a federation of credit unions or caisses populaires that is regulated by a provincial Act other than one enacted by the legislature of Quebec;

(e) a financial services cooperative regulated by *An Act respecting financial services cooperatives*, R.S.Q., c. C-67.3, or *An Act respecting the Mouvement Desjardins*, S.Q. 2000, c. 77;

(f) a life company or a foreign life company to which the *Insurance Companies Act* applies or a life insurance company regulated by a provincial Act;

(g) a company to which the *Trust and Loan Companies Act* applies;

(h) a trust company regulated by a provincial Act;

(i) a loan company regulated by a provincial Act;

(j) an entity authorized under provincial legislation to engage in the business of dealing in securities or any other financial instruments, or to provide portfolio management, investment advising, fund administration, or fund management, services;

(k) an entity that is represented or promoted to the public as a collective investment vehicle, mutual fund, exchange traded fund, private equity fund, hedge fund, venture capital fund, leveraged buyout fund or similar investment vehicle that is established to invest or trade in financial assets and that is managed by an entity referred to in paragraph (j);

(l) an entity that is a clearing house or clearing agency; or

(m) a department or an agent of Her Majesty in right of Canada or of a province that is engaged in the business of accepting deposit liabilities.

Related Provisions: 270(1)"Canadian financial institution"(b) — LFI is a CFI for reporting to other countries.

Notes: See Notes to s. 269.

"non-reporting Canadian financial institution" means any Canadian financial institution or other entity resident in Canada that

(a) is described in any of paragraphs C, D and G to J of section III of Annex II to the agreement;

(b) makes a reasonable determination that it is described in any of paragraphs A, B, E and F of section III of Annex II to the agreement;

(c) qualifies as an exempt beneficial owner under relevant U.S. Treasury Regulations in effect on the date of signature of the agreement; or

(d) makes a reasonable determination that it qualifies as a deemed-compliant FFI under relevant U.S. Treasury Regulations in effect on the date of signature of the agreement.

Related Provisions: 263(2) — Meaning of "Financial Institution" for purposes of this definition.

Notes: For the text of the agreement, see after the Canada-US tax treaty.

"U.S. reportable account" means a financial account that, under the agreement, is to be treated as a U.S. reportable account.

(2) Financial institution — For the purposes of this Part, "Canadian financial institution" and "reporting Canadian financial institution" each have the meaning that would be assigned by the agreement, and the definition "non-reporting Canadian financial institution" in subsection (1) has the meaning that would be assigned by that subsection, if the definition "Financial Institution" in subparagraph 1(g) of Article 1 of the agreement were read as follows:

g) The term "Financial Institution" means any Entity that is a Custodial Institution, a Depository Institution, an Investment Entity or a Specified Insurance Company, and that is a listed financial institution within the meaning of Part XVIII of the *Income Tax Act.*

Related Provisions: Agreement s. 1(l) — Definition of "Canadian Financial Institution"; Agreement s. 1(o) — Definition of "Reporting Canadian Financial Institution".

Notes: This definition has been criticized as too narrow relative to the Agreement, so that certain entities (including many trusts) are not required to comply with ss. 263-269 but could be subject to 30% US withholding on payments if they do not report directly to the IRS. See KPMG, "Canada's IGA Legislation Causes FATCA Concern for Some Trusts", *TaxNewsFlash* 2014-25 (April 4, 2014); Roy Berg & Paul Barba, "FATCA in Canada: The Restriction on the Class of Entities Subject to FATCA", 62(3) *Canadian Tax Journal* 587-633 (2014); Hasan Naqvi, "FATCA and its Application to Canadian Trusts", 12(2) *Tax Hyperion* (Carswell) 4-6 (Feb. 2015).

CRA *Guidance* (see Notes to 269), ¶3.27, Example C, confirms that a trust not represented or promoted to the public is not required to report to CRA. It is unclear whether such an entity could voluntarily opt into Canadian reporting to avoid FATCA reporting: Berg & Barba (above); Henry Chong, "Canada and FATCA", 43(9) *Tax Management International Journal* (Bloomberg BNA) 527-39 (Sept. 12, 2014). However, US Treasury official Brett York has stated that Treasury agrees with CRA's interpretation, apparently meaning that such entities need not report to the US: Alison Bennett, "Treasury OK with Canadian Stance on Listed Financial Institutions", 194 *Daily Tax Report* (Bloomberg BNA) p. G-4 (Oct. 7, 2014).

A money services business may be a financial institution: VIEWS doc 2015-0590061E5.

(3) Financial account — For the purposes of this Part, the agreement is to be read as if the definition "Financial Account" in subparagraph 1(s) of Article 1 of the agreement included the following subparagraph after subparagraph (1):

(1.1) an account that is a client name account maintained by a person or entity that is authorized under provincial legislation to engage in the business of dealing in securities or any other financial instruments, or to provide portfolio management or investment advising services.

(4) Identification number — For the purposes of this Part, a reference in the agreement to "Canadian TIN" or "taxpayer identification number" is to be read as including a reference to Social Insurance Number.

(5) Term defined in agreement — In this Part, any term has the meaning that is defined in, or assigned by, the agreement unless the term is defined in this Part.

Notes: For the text of the agreement, see after the Canada-US tax treaty.

(6) Amending instrument — No person shall be liable for a failure to comply with a duty or obligation imposed by this Act that results from an amendment to the agreement unless at the date of the alleged failure,

(a) the text of the instrument that effected the amendment had been published in the *Canada Gazette*; or

(b) reasonable steps had been taken to bring the purport of the amendment to the notice of those persons likely to be affected by it.

Notes [s. 263]: See Notes to 269.

Definitions [s. 263]: "agreement" — 263(1); "authorized foreign bank", "bank", "business" — 248(1); "Canada" — 263(5), ETIEA Art. 1:1(d); "Canadian financial institution" — 263(2); "credit union" — 137(6), 248(1); "entity" — 263(5), ETIEA Art. 1:1(gg); "listed financial institution" — 263(1); "Her Majesty" — *Interpretation Act* 35(1); "Minister", "person" — 248(1); "province" — *Interpretation Act* 35(1); "provincial" — *Interpretation Act* 33(3), 35(1)"province"; "reportable account" — 263(5), ETIEA Art. 1:1(aa); "resident in Canada" — 94(3)(a), 250; "trust" — 104(1), 248(1), (3).

264. (1) Designation of account — Subject to subsection (2), a reporting Canadian financial institution may designate a financial account to not be a U.S. reportable account for a calendar year if the account is

(a) a preexisting individual account described in paragraph A of section II of Annex I to the agreement;

(b) a new individual account described in paragraph A of section III of Annex I to the agreement;

(c) a preexisting entity account described in paragraph A of section IV of Annex I to the agreement; or

(d) a new entity account described in paragraph A of section V of Annex I to the agreement.

(2) U.S. reportable account — A reporting Canadian financial institution may not designate a financial account for a calendar year unless the account is part of a clearly identifiable group of accounts all of which are designated for the year.

(3) Applicable rules — The rules in paragraph C of section VI of Annex I to the agreement apply in determining whether a financial account is described in any of paragraphs (1)(a) to (d).

Notes [s. 264]: See Notes to 269. A New Individual Account that is a Depository Account over $50,000 cannot be designated under 264(1) in a later year if the balance drops below $50,000: VIEWS doc 2018-0759081E5.

Definitions [s. 264]: "agreement" — 263(1); "calendar year" — *Interpretation Act* 37(1); "entity" — 263(5), ETIEA Art. 1:1(gg); "individual" — 248(1); "new entity account" — ETIEA Annex I:V(A); "new individual account" — ETIEA Annex I:III(A); "preexisting entity account" — ETIEA Annex I:IV(A); "preexisting individual account" — ETIEA Annex I:II(A); "reportable account" — 263(5), ETIEA Art. 1:1(aa); "reporting Canadian financial institution" — 263(2).

265. (1) Identification obligation — financial accounts — Every reporting Canadian financial institution shall establish, maintain and document the due diligence procedures set out in subsections (2) and (3).

(2) Due diligence — general — Every reporting Canadian financial institution shall have the following due diligence procedures:

(a) for preexisting individual accounts that are lower value accounts, other than accounts described in paragraph A of section II of Annex I to the agreement, the procedures described in paragraphs B and C of that section, subject to paragraph F of that section;

(b) for preexisting individual accounts that are high value accounts, other than accounts described in paragraph A of section II of Annex I to the agreement, the procedures described in paragraphs D and E of that section, subject to paragraph F of that section;

(c) for new individual accounts, other than accounts described in paragraph A of section III of Annex I to the agreement, the procedures described in paragraph B of section III of Annex I to the agreement;

(d) for preexisting entity accounts, other than accounts described in paragraph A of section IV of Annex I to the agreement, the procedures described in paragraphs D and E of that section; and

(e) for new entity accounts, other than accounts described in paragraph A of section V of Annex I to the agreement, the procedures described in paragraphs B to E of that section.

Notes: 265(2)(c)(ii) repealed (and (c)(i), "the procedures...", folded into the para.) by 2016 budget bill #2, effective July 2017. From June 27, 2014 through June 2017, read:

or (c)(ii) in respect of a clearly identifiable group of accounts, the procedures that would be applicable if the accounts were preexisting individual accounts that were lower value accounts, with such modifications as the circumstances require, including procedures to review any documentary evidence obtained by the institution in connection with the opening of the accounts for the U.S. indicia described in subparagraph B(1) of section II of Annex I to the agreement;

Forms: RC518: Declaration of tax residence for individuals — Part XVIII and Part XIX of the *Income Tax Act*; RC519: Declaration of tax residence for entities — Part XVIII and Part XIX of the *Income Tax Act*.

(3) Due diligence — no designation — If a reporting Canadian financial institution does not designate a financial account under subsection 264(1) for a calendar year, the institution shall have the following due diligence procedures with respect to the account:

(a) if the account is a preexisting individual account described in paragraph A of section II of Annex I to the agreement, the procedures described in paragraphs B and C of that section, subject to paragraph F of that section;

(b) if the account is a new individual account described in paragraph A of section III of Annex I to the agreement, the procedures described in paragraph B of section III of Annex I to the agreement;

(c) if the account is a preexisting entity account described in paragraph A of section IV of Annex I to the agreement, the procedures described in paragraphs D and E of that section; and

(d) if the account is a new entity account described in paragraph A of section V of Annex I to the agreement, the procedures described in paragraphs B to E of that section.

Notes: 265(3)(b)(ii) repealed (and (b)(i), "the procedures...", folded into the para.) by 2016 budget bill #2, effective July 2017. From June 27, 2014 through June 2017, read:

or (b)(ii) in respect of an account that is part of a clearly identifiable group of accounts, the procedures that would be applicable if the account were a preexisting individual account that was a lower value account, with such modifications as the circumstances require, including procedures to review any documentary evidence obtained by the institution in connection with the opening of the account for the U.S. indicia described in subparagraph B(1) of section II of Annex I to the agreement;

Forms: RC518: Declaration of tax residence for individuals — Part XVIII and Part XIX of the *Income Tax Act*; RC519: Declaration of tax residence for entities — Part XVIII and Part XIX of the *Income Tax Act*.

(4) Rules and definitions — For the purposes of subsections (2) and (3), subparagraphs B(1) to (3) of section I, and section VI, of Annex I to the agreement apply except that

(a) in applying paragraph C of that section VI, an account balance that has a negative value is deemed to be nil; and

(b) the definition "NFFE" in subparagraph B(2) of that section VI is to be read as follows:

2. NFFE

An "NFFE" means any Non-U.S. Entity that is not an FFI as defined in relevant U.S. Treasury Regulations or is an Entity described in subparagraph B(4)(j) of this section, and also includes any Non-U.S. Entity

a) that is resident in Canada and is not a listed financial institution within the meaning of Part XVIII of the *Income Tax Act*; or

b) that is resident in a Partner Jurisdiction other than Canada and is not a Financial Institution.

Notes: For the text of the agreement, see after the Canada-US tax treaty.

(5) U.S. indicia — For the purposes of paragraphs (2)(a) and (b), subparagraph (2)(c)(ii), paragraph (3)(a) and subparagraph

(3)(b)(ii), subparagraph B(3) of section II of Annex I to the agreement is to be read as follows:

> 3. If any of the U.S indicia listed in subparagraph B(1) of this section are discovered in the electronic search, or if there is a change in circumstances that results in one or more U.S. indicia being associated with the account, then the Reporting Canadian Financial Institution must seek to obtain or review the information described in the portion of subparagraph B(4) of this section that is relevant in the circumstances and must treat the account as a U.S. Reportable Account unless one of the exceptions in subparagraph B(4) applies with respect to that account.

Notes: This provision was not in the Feb. 5, 2014 draft.

(6) Financial institution — For the purpose of applying the procedures referred to in paragraphs (2)(d) and (e) and (3)(c) and (d) to a financial account of an account holder that is resident in Canada, the definition "Financial Institution" in subparagraph 1(g) of Article 1 of the agreement is to be read as follows:

> g) The term "Financial Institution" means any Entity that is a Custodial Institution, a Depository Institution, an Investment Entity or a Specified Insurance Company, and that is a listed financial institution within the meaning of Part XVIII of the *Income Tax Act*.

Related Provisions: 263(1) — Definition of "listed financial institution".

Notes: This provision was not in the Feb. 5, 2014 draft.

(7) Dealer accounts — Subsection (8) applies to a reporting Canadian financial institution in respect of a client name account maintained by the institution if

> (a) property recorded in the account is also recorded in a financial account (in this subsection and subsection (8) referred to as the "related account") maintained by a financial institution (in this subsection and subsection (8) referred to as the "dealer") that is authorized under provincial legislation to engage in the business of dealing in securities or any other financial instrument, or to provide portfolio management or investment advising services; and

> (b) the dealer has advised the institution whether the related account is a U.S. reportable account.

However, subsection (8) does not apply if it can reasonably be concluded by the institution that the dealer has failed to comply with its obligations under this section.

Notes: This was 265(5) in the Feb. 5, 2014 draft.

(8) Dealer accounts — If this subsection applies to a reporting Canadian financial institution in respect of a client name account,

> (a) subsections (1) to (4) do not apply to the institution in respect of the account; and

> (b) the institution shall rely on the determination of the dealer in respect of the related account in determining whether the account is a U.S. reportable account.

Notes: This was 265(6) in the Feb. 5, 2014 draft.

Notes [s. 265]: See Notes to 269.

Definitions [s. 265]: "account holder" — 263(5), ETIEA Art. 1:1(dd); "agreement" — 263(1); "business" — 248(1); "calendar year" — *Interpretation Act* 37(1)(a); "Canada" — 263(5), ETIEA Art. 1:1(d); "dealer" — 265(5); "entity" — 263(5), ETIEA Art. 1:1(gg); "individual" — 248(1); "listed financial institution" — 263(1); "new entity account" — ETIEA Annex I:V(A); "new individual account" — ETIEA Annex I:III(A); "preexisting entity account" — ETIEA Annex I:IV(A); "preexisting individual account" — ETIEA Annex I:II(A); "property" — 248(1); "provincial" — *Interpretation Act* 33(3), 35(1)"province"; "related account" — 265(5); "reportable account" — 263(5), ETIEA Art. 1:1(aa); "reporting Canadian financial institution" — 263(2); "resident" — 250.

266. (1) Reporting — U.S. reportable accounts — Every reporting Canadian financial institution shall file with the Minister, before May 2 of each calendar year, an information return in prescribed form relating to each U.S. reportable account maintained by the institution at any time during the immediately preceding calendar year and after June 29, 2014.

Related Provisions: 162(6) — Penalty for US taxpayer failing to provide US federal taxpayer identifying number to financial institution; 238(1) — Offence of wilful failure to comply (failure to make or file a return); 268 — Anti-avoidance rule; 278 — Reporting of accounts to CRA for exchange with other tax authorities (non-US).

Notes: See Notes to 269. Due to COVID-19, the May 1, 2020 filing deadline was extended to Sept. 1, 2020; as well, no penalty applies for failure to obtain self-certification on financial accounts opened before 2021. See CRA information notice, April 20, 2020 (reproduced in PITA 59th ed.).

(2) Reporting — nonparticipating financial institutions [2016-2017] — Every reporting Canadian financial institution shall file with the Minister, before May 2 of each calendar year, an information return in prescribed form relating to payments, to a nonparticipating financial institution that is the holder of a financial account maintained by the reporting Canadian financial institution, during the immediately preceding calendar year if the immediately preceding year is 2015 or 2016.

Related Provisions: 238(1) — Offence of wilful failure to comply (failure to make or file a return).

(3) Filing of return — An information return required under subsection (1) or (2) shall be filed by way of electronic filing.

Definitions [s. 266]: "calendar year" — *Interpretation Act* 37(1)(a); "electronic filing" — 263(1); "Minister" — 248(1); "nonparticipating financial institution" — 263(5), ETIEA Art. 1:1(r); "prescribed" — 248(1); "reportable account" — 263(5), ETIEA Art. 1:1(aa); "reporting Canadian financial institution" — 263(2).

267. (1) Record keeping — Every reporting Canadian financial institution shall keep, at the institution's place of business or at such other place as may be designated by the Minister, records that the institution obtains or creates for the purpose of complying with this Part, including self-certifications and records of documentary evidence.

Related Provisions: 238(1) — Offence of failing to comply; 267(2) — Form of records kept electronically; 267(3) — Records to be kept for 6 years.

(2) Form of records — Every reporting Canadian financial institution required by this Part to keep records that does so electronically shall retain them in an electronically readable format for the retention period referred to in subsection (3).

Related Provisions: 238(1) — Offence of failing to comply.

(3) Retention of records — Every reporting Canadian financial institution that is required to keep, obtain, or create records under this Part shall retain those records for a period of at least six years following

> (a) in the case of a self-certification, the last day on which a related financial account is open; and

> (b) in any other case, the end of the last calendar year in respect of which the record is relevant.

Related Provisions: 238(1) — Offence of failing to comply; 230(4), Reg. 5800 — Time limit for keeping records for other purposes.

Notes [s. 267]: See Notes to 269.

Definitions [s. 267]: "business" — 248(1); "calendar year" — *Interpretation Act* 37(1)(a); "Minister", "record" — 248(1); "reporting Canadian financial institution" — 263(2).

268. Anti-avoidance — If a person enters into an arrangement or engages in a practice, the primary purpose of which can reasonably be considered to be to avoid an obligation under this Part, the person is subject to the obligation as if the person had not entered into the arrangement or engaged in the practice.

Related Provisions: 280 — Parallel rule for Common Reporting Standard.

Notes [s. 268]: See Notes to 269.

Definitions [s. 268]: "person" — 248(1).

269. Deemed-compliant FFI — If a Canadian financial institution makes a reasonable determination that it is to be treated as a deemed-compliant FFI under Annex II to the agreement, this Part applies to the institution, with such modifications as the circumstances require, to the extent that the agreement imposes due diligence and reporting obligations on the institution.

Notes [s. 269]: 263-269 implement the 2014 Canada-US Enhanced Tax Information Exchange Agreement (ETIEA), also called InterGovernmental Agreement (IGA), reproduced after the Canada-US tax treaty. This is done for FATCA, the US *Foreign Account Tax Compliance Act*. For detailed CRA interpretation see tinyurl.com/crsreport-cra and *Guidance on the Canada-U.S. Enhanced Tax Information Exchange Agreement* (July 10, 2020, 182pp), tinyurl.com/cra-etiea. (For similar "Common Reporting Standard" reporting whereby CRA reports to 100 other countries' governments, see 270-281.)

266 requires a "Canadian financial institution" (263(2)) to report to CRA any "U.S. reportable account" (263(1)), meaning (very simplified) a bank or investment account held or controlled by a US citizen, green-card holder, US resident or US corporation. *Accounts not exceeding $50,000 are not reportable*: ETIEA Annex I, II(A)(1), II(A)(4), III(A)(1). (Due diligence in collecting the data is required by 265, and record-keeping by 267.) CRA passes this information to the IRS. Exchange of information began fall 2015. For the filing procedures see tinyurl.com/cra-xviii.

CBC reports (tinyurl.com/cbc-fatca, March 2021) that CRA wrongly reported 600,000 under-$50,000 accounts to the IRS in 2019 (over 2/3 of those reported).

The ETIEA enacting legislation (reproduced before the ETIEA), s. 4, provides that it takes priority over all other legislation other than ITA 263-269 and the *Income Tax Conventions Interpretation Act*.

This system (and IGAs with other countries) allows the IRS to find US persons' non-US accounts and check they are reporting and paying US tax. See Notes to 128.1(1) re US citizens' US tax obligations and renouncing citizenship, and to 233.3(3) for US FBAR and other reporting requirements.

Had the IGA not been signed, FIs would have to report directly to the IRS, and those that did not would be subject to 30% FATCA withholding tax on US-source payments. The 30% withholding can still apply to a Canadian FI in significant and long-term non-compliance with its obligations under the agreement: IGA Art. 5:2. See Moodys Gartner, "FATCA in Canada: is the IGA a good deal?", tinyurl.com/iga-good-deal.

Non-reportable accounts include RRSPs, RRIFs, PRPPs, RPPs, TFSA, RDSPs, RESPs, DPSPs, AgriInvest accounts, eligible funeral arrangements and certain escrow accounts (IGA Annex II:IV); and credit unions with assets under US$175 million are exempt (Annex II:III(B)).

See also 263(2) Notes; Campbell, *Administration of Income Tax 2020* (Carswell), §7.11; papers by Johnston, Pearl-Weinberg+Snitman, and Nicolson, 2013 Cdn Tax Foundation conference report, 17:1-33, 18:1-12, 19:1-7; Turner, "Answers to Practical FATCA Questions for Canadian Financial Institutions", 43(8) *Tax Management International Journal* (Bloomberg BNA) 484-87 (Aug. 8, 2014); Berg & Barba, "FATCA in Canada", 62(3) *Canadian Tax Journal* at 587-612 (2014); Berg, "FATCA in Canada: The 'Cure' for a US Place of Birth", 2014 conference report, 33:1-38; Russell & Crawford, "FATCA for Non-Financial Institutions ...", *ibid*, 34:1-23; Lundenberg & Rezaeinia, "Exempt Market Dealers and FATCA", *Private Capital Markets* (pcma-canada.com), Fall 2014, pp. 48-49; Milet, "FATCA and Canadian Investment Entities", 26(3) *Journal of International Taxation* 29-37 (March 2015) (re hybrid FIs); Gray, "FATCA: Not Merely an Anti-Avoidance Law", 2308 *Tax Topics [TT]* (CCH) 1-5 (June 2, 2016) and "FATCA — A Progress Report", 2430 *TT* 1-6 (Oct. 4, 2018); "10 years Post FATCA", tinyurl.com/feigenbaum-fatca (Dec. 6, 2019); Ye, "Financial Institutions: Changes to FATCA and CRS Reporting", 10(3) *Canadian Tax Focus* (ctf.ca) 16 (Aug. 2020); "Newest developments on FATCA and CRS compliance" (Aug. 4, 2020), tinyurl.com/BLG-crs-fatca.

Nothing in 263-269 requires a person to provide information to an FI (though the ETIEA requires an FI to obtain "self-certification": see CRA *Guidance* §§7.13, 8.64-8.68, 9.23-9.28, 10.35-10.40); the sanction is that the FI will not let the person have an account. Providing false information to the FI does not appear to violate the ITA; *quaere* whether it violates the *Bank Act*, *Criminal Code* or some other statute. Failing to provide a US federal taxpayer number to a person who is required to make a return needing the number triggers a $100 penalty under 162(6). For information sharing with countries other than the US, 281(1) and (3) impose a $500 penalty for not disclosing one's Taxpayer Identification Number.

The late constitutional scholar Peter Hogg wrote to Finance in 2012 to say that requiring compliance in Canada based on US citizenship would violate the *Charter of Rights* by discriminating on the basis of national origin. *Hillis (Deegan)*, 2015 FC 1082 (FCA appeal discontinued A-407-15) sought to have 263–269 and the ETIEA declared unconstitutional as infringing on provincial jurisdiction, forfeiting Canada's sovereignty and violating the *Charter*, the Canada-US tax treaty and s. 241. The 2015 decision, on the non-constitutional and non-*Charter* issues only, found no violation of s. 241 or the treaty. Similarly, *Deegan (Highton)*, 2019 FC 960 (under appeal to FCA as *Highton*; appeal continuing though *Hillis* discontinued Dec. 2020), held the ETIEA does not violate the *Charter* as unreasonable seizure of financial information from US persons, or by discriminating on the basis of national origin. If *Highton* were to succeed, FATCA reporting to the IRS would be required from Canadian institutions, with 30% withholding on US payments if they do not comply. A US attempt to challenge the IGAs, *Crawford (Paul)*, was rejected by the Sixth Circuit in Aug. 2017 on the basis the plaintiffs had no standing: tinyurl.com/paul-fatca.

Bulk data exchange takes place every September since 2015. As of April 2019, CRA had sent 700,000 records to the IRS, which had not requested further info with respect to this data: VIEWS doc 2019-0798711C6 [2019 STEP q.17].

Under the IGA, the IRS also reports to CRA on Canadian residents' accounts at US FIs. For required reporting by Canadian residents of property outside Canada, see 233.3(3).

Non-FIs ("non-financial foreign entities" (NFFEs) under FATCA) are not affected by the IGA and must certify their "substantial United States owners" to FIs they deal with, or to the IRS (which makes them "Direct Reporting NFFEs") (or certify that they have none on Form W-8BEN-E) or will be subject to 30% withholding on payments from the US (*Internal Revenue Code* §1472(a)).

CRA "take[s] the position that the IRS cannot use such information to administer non-tax laws (such as the US *Bank Secrecy Act*) or in its dealings with federal entities (such as the Financial Crimes Enforcement Network of the US Treasury Department) who are involved in money laundering repression": *Hillis*, para. 55 (see *Internal Revenue Code* §6103). (How CRA could stop the IRS from doing so is unclear.)

263-269 (Part XVIII) added by 2014 budget bill #1, effective June 27, 2014 [in-force date of the IGA: Finance news release, July 2/14].

Definitions [s. 269]: "agreement" — 263(1); "Canadian financial institution" — 263(2).

PART XIX — COMMON REPORTING STANDARD

270. (1) Definitions — The following definitions apply in this Part.

Notes: See at end of s. 281.

["AML/KYC procedures"] — [See "anti-money laundering and know your customer procedures" below.]

"account holder" means

(a) the person listed or identified as the holder of a financial account by the financial institution that maintains the account, other than a person (other than a financial institution) holding a financial account for the benefit of, or on behalf of, another person as agent, custodian, nominee, signatory, investment advisor or intermediary; and

(b) in the case of a cash value insurance contract or an annuity contract,

(i) any person entitled to access the cash value or change the beneficiary,

(ii) if no person can access the cash value or change the beneficiary,

(A) any person named as the owner in the contract, and

(B) any person with a vested entitlement to payment under the terms of the contract, and

(iii) upon maturity of the cash value insurance contract or annuity contract, each person entitled to receive a payment under the contract.

"active NFE" means, at any time, a non-financial entity that meets any of the following criteria:

(a) less than 50% of the NFE's gross income for the preceding fiscal period is passive income and less than 50% of the assets held by the NFE during the preceding fiscal period are assets that produce or are held for the production of passive income;

(b) either

(i) interests in the NFE are regularly traded on an established securities market, or

(ii) the NFE is a related entity of an entity interests in which are regularly traded on an established securities market;

(c) the NFE is

(i) a governmental entity,

(ii) an international organization,

(iii) a central bank, or

(iv) an entity wholly owned by one or more entities described in subparagraphs (i) to (iii);

(d) both

(i) all or substantially all of the activities of the NFE consist of holding (in whole or in part) the outstanding stock of, or providing financing and services to, one or more of its subsidiaries that engage in trades or businesses other than the business of a financial institution, and

(ii) the NFE does not function as (and is not represented or promoted to the public as) an investment fund, including

(A) a private equity fund,

(B) a venture capital fund,

(C) a leveraged buyout fund, and

(D) an investment vehicle whose purpose is to acquire or fund companies and then hold interests in those companies as capital assets for investment purposes;

(e) the NFE

(i) is not yet operating a business,

(ii) has no prior operating history,

(iii) is investing capital into assets with the intent to operate a business other than that of a financial institution, and

(iv) was initially organized no more than 24 months prior to that time;

(f) the NFE has not been a financial institution in any of the past five years and is in the process of liquidating its assets or is reorganizing with the intent to continue or recommence operations in a business other than that of a financial institution;

(g) the NFE primarily engages in financing and hedging transactions with, or for, related entities that are not financial institutions, and does not provide financing or hedging services to any entity that is not a related entity, provided that the group of those related entities is primarily engaged in a business other than that of a financial institution; and

(h) the NFE meets all of the following requirements:

(i) it

(A) is established and operated in its jurisdiction of residence exclusively for religious, charitable, scientific, artistic, cultural, athletic or educational purposes, or

(B) is established and operated in its jurisdiction of residence and it is a professional organization, business league, chamber of commerce, labour organization, agricultural or horticultural organization, civic league or an organization operated exclusively for the promotion of social welfare,

(ii) it is exempt from income tax in its jurisdiction of residence,

(iii) it has no shareholders or members who have a proprietary or beneficial interest in its income or assets,

(iv) the applicable laws of the NFE's jurisdiction of residence or the NFE's formation documents do not permit any income or assets of the NFE to be distributed to, or applied for the benefit of, a private person or non-charitable entity other than pursuant to the conduct of the NFE's charitable activities, or as payment of reasonable compensation for services rendered, or as payment representing the fair market value of property which the NFE has purchased, and

(v) the applicable laws of the NFE's jurisdiction of residence or the NFE's formation documents require that, upon the NFE's liquidation or dissolution, all of its assets be distributed to a governmental entity or other non-profit organization, or escheat to the government of the NFE's jurisdiction of residence or any political subdivision thereof.

Notes: For the (Canadian) common-law meaning of "charitable activities" in (h)(iv), see Notes to 149.1(1)"charitable activities".

"annuity contract" means a contract under which the issuer agrees to make payments for a period of time determined in whole or in part by reference to the life expectancy of one or more individuals and includes a contract

(a) that is considered to be an annuity contract in accordance with the law, regulation or practice of the jurisdiction in which the contract was issued; and

(b) under which the issuer agrees to make payments for a term of years.

"anti-money laundering and know your customer procedures" or **"AML/KYC procedures"** means the record keeping, verification of identity, reporting of suspicious transactions and registration requirements required of a reporting financial institution under the *Proceeds of Crime (Money Laundering) and Terrorist Financing Act.*

Notes: These procedures include identifying and verifying the customer's identity (including its beneficial owners), understanding the nature and purpose of the account, and ongoing monitoring. (Finance Technical Notes)

"broad participation retirement fund" means a fund that is established to provide retirement, disability or death benefits to beneficiaries that are current or former employees (or persons designated by those employees) of one or more employers in consideration for services rendered, if the fund

(a) does not have a single beneficiary with a right to more than 5% of the fund's assets;

(b) is subject to government regulation and provides information reporting to the Minister; and

(c) satisfies at least one of the following requirements:

(i) the fund is generally exempt from tax on investment income, or taxation of investment income is deferred or taxed at a reduced rate, due to its status as a retirement or pension plan,

(ii) the fund receives at least 50% of its total contributions (other than transfers of assets from broad participation retirement funds, narrow participation retirement funds or from retirement and pension accounts described in paragraph (a) of the definition "excluded account") from the sponsoring employers,

(iii) distributions or withdrawals from the fund are

(A) allowed only upon the occurrence of specified events related to retirement, disability or death (except rollover distributions to broad participation retirement funds, narrow participation retirement funds and pension funds of a governmental entity, international organization or central bank or retirement and pension accounts described in paragraph (a) of the definition "excluded account"), or

(B) subject to penalties if they are made before such specified events, and

(iv) contributions (other than permitted make-up contributions) by an employee to the fund

(A) are limited by reference to the employee's remuneration, or

(B) must not exceed 50,000 USD annually, applying the rules set forth in subsection 277(3).

"Canadian financial institution" means a financial institution that is

(a) either

(i) resident in Canada, but excluding any branch of the financial institution that is located outside Canada, or

(ii) a branch of a financial institution that is not resident in Canada, if the branch is located in Canada; and

(b) a "listed financial institution" as defined in subsection 263(1).

Notes: The requirement that a FI be a "listed financial institution" under 263(1) is intended to restrict the types of FI that are subject to the reporting and due-diligence rules in 270-281.

"cash value", in respect of a contract held by a policyholder, means the greater of the amount that the policyholder is entitled to receive upon surrender or termination of the contract (determined without reduction for any surrender charge or policy loan) and the amount the policyholder can borrow under or with regard to the contract, but does not include an amount payable under an insurance contract

(a) solely by reason of the death of an individual insured under a life insurance contract;

(b) as a personal injury or sickness benefit, or other benefit, providing indemnification of an economic loss incurred upon the occurrence of an event insured against;

(c) as a refund of a previously paid premium (less any cost of insurance charges whether or not actually imposed) under an insurance contract (other than an investment-linked life insurance or annuity contract) due to the cancellation or termination of the contract, a decrease in risk exposure during the effective period of the contract or arising from the correction of a posting or similar error with regard to the premium for the contract;

(d) as a policyholder dividend (other than a termination dividend) if the dividend relates to an insurance contract under which the only benefits payable are described in paragraph (b); or

(e) as a return of an advance premium or premium deposit for an insurance contract for which the premium is payable at least annually, if the amount of the advance premium or premium deposit does not exceed the next annual premium that will be payable under the contract.

"cash value insurance contract" means an insurance contract (other than an indemnity reinsurance contract between two insurance companies) that has a cash value.

"central bank" means an institution that is, by law or government sanction, the principal authority, other than the government of the jurisdiction itself, issuing instruments intended to circulate as currency and may include an instrumentality that is separate from the government of the jurisdiction, whether or not owned in whole or in part by the jurisdiction.

"controlling persons", in respect of an entity, means the natural persons who exercise control over the entity (interpreted in a manner consistent with the *Financial Action Task Force Recommendations — International Standards on Combating Money Laundering and the Financing of Terrorism and Proliferation*, adopted in February 2012 and as amended from time to time) and includes

(a) in the case of a trust,

(i) its settlors,

(ii) its trustees,

(iii) its protectors (if any),

(iv) its beneficiaries (for this purpose, a discretionary beneficiary of a trust will only be considered a beneficiary of the trust in a calendar year if a distribution has been paid or made payable to the discretionary beneficiary in the calendar year), and

(v) any other natural persons exercising ultimate effective control over the trust; and

(b) in the case of a legal arrangement other than a trust, persons in equivalent or similar positions to those described in paragraph (a).

"custodial account" means an account (other than an insurance contract or annuity contract) that holds one or more financial assets for the benefit of another person.

"custodial institution" means an entity, if the entity's gross income attributable to the holding of financial assets for the account of others and related financial services equals or exceeds 20% of the entity's gross income during the shorter of

(a) the three-year period that ends at the end of the entity's last fiscal period, and

(b) the period during which the entity has been in existence.

"depository account" includes

(a) any commercial, chequing, savings, time or thrift account, or an account that is evidenced by a certificate of deposit, thrift certificate, investment certificate, certificate of indebtedness or other similar instrument maintained by a financial institution in the ordinary course of a banking or similar business; and

(b) an amount held by an insurance company under a guaranteed investment contract or similar agreement to pay or credit interest on the contract.

Notes: An account evidenced by a passbook is generally considered a depository account (DA). Negotiable debt instruments traded on a regulated or over-the counter market and distributed and held through financial institutions are not generally considered DAs. (Finance Technical Notes)

"depository institution" means any entity that accepts deposits in the ordinary course of a banking or similar business.

"documentary evidence" includes

(a) a certificate of residence issued by an authorized government body (such as a government or agency thereof, or a municipality) of the jurisdiction in which the payee claims to be a resident;

(b) with respect to an individual (other than a trust), any valid identification issued by an authorized government body that includes the individual's name and is typically used for identification purposes;

(c) with respect to an entity, any official documentation issued by an authorized government body that includes the name of the entity and either the address of its principal office in the jurisdiction in which it claims to be resident or the jurisdiction in which the entity was incorporated or organized; and

(d) any audited financial statement, third-party credit report, bankruptcy filing or securities regulator's report.

"entity" means a person (other than a natural person) or a legal arrangement, such as a corporation, partnership, trust or foundation.

Notes: This definition is meant to be broad and includes a unit, business or office of a financial institution (FI) that is treated as a branch under a jurisdiction's regulatory regime, or that is otherwise regulated under a jurisdiction's laws as separate from other offices, units or branches of the FI. For this purpose, all units, businesses or offices of a reporting FI in a jurisdiction are treated as one branch. (Finance Technical Notes)

"equity or debt interest" includes, in the case of a partnership that is a financial institution, either a capital or profits interest in the partnership.

Related Provisions: 270(4)(a) — Equity interest — deeming rule.

"established securities market" means an exchange that

(a) is officially recognized and supervised by a governmental authority in which the market is located; and

(b) has an annual value of shares traded on the exchange (or a predecessor exchange) exceeding one billion USD during each of the three calendar years immediately preceding the calendar year in which the determination is being made. For this purpose, if an exchange has more than one tier of market level on which stock may be separately listed or traded, each of those tiers must be treated as a separate exchange.

"excluded account" means

(a) a retirement or pension account that satisfies the following requirements:

(i) the account is

(A) subject to regulation as a personal retirement account, or

(B) part of a registered or regulated retirement or pension plan for the provision of retirement or pension benefits (including disability or death benefits),

(ii) the account is tax-favoured in that

(A) contributions to the account that would otherwise be subject to tax are deductible or excluded from the gross income of the account holder or taxed at a reduced rate, or

(B) taxation of investment income within the account is deferred or investment income within the account is taxed at a reduced rate,

(iii) information reporting to the Minister is required with respect to the account,

(iv) withdrawals are

(A) conditioned on reaching a specified retirement age, disability or death, or

(B) subject to penalties if made before the events specified in clause (A), and

(v) after applying the rules in subsection 277(3) to all similar accounts, annual contributions to the account are limited to 50,000 USD or less or there is a maximum lifetime contribution limit to the account of 1,000,000 USD or less (and an account that otherwise satisfies this requirement will not fail to satisfy this requirement solely because the account may receive assets or funds transferred from one or more accounts that meet the requirements of this paragraph or paragraph (b) or from one or more broad participation retirement funds, narrow participation retirement funds or pension funds of a governmental entity, international organization or central bank);

(b) an account that satisfies the following requirements:

(i) the account is

(A) both

(I) subject to regulation as an investment vehicle for purposes other than for retirement, and

(II) regularly traded on an established securities market, or

(B) subject to regulation as a savings vehicle for purposes other than for retirement,

(ii) the account is tax-favoured in that

(A) contributions to the account that would otherwise be subject to tax are deductible or excluded from the gross income of the account holder or taxed at a reduced rate, or

(B) taxation of investment income within the account is deferred or investment income within the account is taxed at a reduced rate,

(iii) withdrawals are

(A) conditioned on meeting specific criteria related to the purpose of the investment or savings account (including the provision of educational or medical benefits), or

(B) subject to penalties if made before the criteria in clause (A) are met, and

(iv) annual contributions are, after applying the rules in subsection 277(3) to all similar accounts, limited to 50,000 USD or less (and an account that otherwise satisfies this requirement will not fail to satisfy this requirement solely because the account may receive assets or funds transferred from one or more accounts that meet the requirements of paragraph (a) or this paragraph or from one or more broad participation retirement funds, narrow participation retirement funds or pension funds of a governmental entity, international organization or central bank);

(c) a life insurance contract with a coverage period that ends before the insured individual attains age 90, if the contract satisfies the following requirements:

(i) periodic premiums, which do not decrease over time, are payable at least annually until the earlier of

(A) the end of the period in which the contract is in existence, and

(B) the date that the insured attains age 90,

(ii) the contract has no contract value that any person can access (by withdrawal, loan or otherwise) without terminating the contract,

(iii) the amount (other than a death benefit) payable upon cancellation or termination of the contract must not exceed the amount determined by the formula

$$A - (B + C)$$

where

A   is the aggregate premiums paid for the contract,

B   is the total of all mortality, morbidity and expense charges (whether or not actually imposed) for the period or periods of the contract's existence, and

C   is the total of all amounts paid prior to the cancellation or termination of the contract, and

(iv) the contract has not been acquired by a transferee for value;

(d) an account held solely by an estate of a deceased individual, if the documentation for the account includes a copy of the will or death certificate of the individual;

(e) an account established in connection with any of the following:

(i) a court order or judgement,

(ii) a sale, exchange or lease of property, if the account satisfies the following requirements:

(A) the account is funded

(I) solely with a down payment, earnest money, deposit in an amount appropriate to secure an obligation directly related to the transaction or a similar payment, or

(II) with a financial asset that is deposited in the account in connection with the sale, exchange or lease of the property,

(B) the account is established and used solely to secure the obligation of

(I) the purchaser to pay the purchase price for the property,

(II) the seller to pay any contingent liability, or

(III) the lessor or lessee to pay for any damages relating to the leased property as agreed under the lease,

(C) the assets of the account, including the income earned on the account, will be paid or otherwise distributed for the benefit of the purchaser, seller, lessor or lessee (including to satisfy such person's obligation) when the property is sold, exchanged or surrendered or the lease terminates,

(D) the account is not a margin or similar account established in connection with a sale or exchange of a financial asset, and

(E) the account is not associated with an account described in paragraph (f),

(iii) an obligation of a financial institution servicing a loan secured by real or immovable property to set aside a portion of a payment solely to facilitate the payment of taxes or insurance related to the property at a later time, or

(iv) an obligation of a financial institution solely to facilitate the payment of taxes at a later time;

(f) a depository account that satisfies the following requirements:

(i) the account exists solely because a customer makes a payment in excess of a balance due with respect to a credit card or other revolving credit facility and the overpayment is not immediately returned to the customer, and

(ii) after June 2017, policies and procedures are in effect relating to overpayments (for this purpose, a customer overpayment does not include credit balances to the extent of disputed charges but does include credit balances resulting from merchandise returns) to either

(A) prevent a customer from making an overpayment in excess of 50,000 USD, or

(B) ensure that any customer overpayment in excess of 50,000 USD is refunded to the customer within 60 days; and

(g) a prescribed account.

Regulations: 9006 (prescribed accounts for para. (g)).

"exempt collective investment vehicle" means an investment entity that is regulated as a collective investment vehicle, provided that all of the interests in the collective investment vehicle are held by or through individuals or entities (other than a passive NFE with a controlling person who is a reportable person) that are not reportable persons.

Notes: "Collective investment vehicle" (not defined in the ITA) refers to funds that are widely-held, hold a diversified portfolio of securities and are subject to investor-protection regulation in the country in which they are established. The term includes "master" and "feeder" funds that are part of "funds of funds" structures where the master fund holds a diversified portfolio of investments. Private equity funds and hedge funds generally do not fall within the definition. (Finance Technical Notes)

"financial account" means an account maintained by a financial institution, and

(a) includes

(i) a depository account,

(ii) a custodial account,

(iii) in the case of an investment entity, any equity or debt interest in the financial institution, except that it does not include any equity or debt interest in an entity that is an investment entity solely because it,

(A) renders investment advice to, and acts on behalf of, a customer for the purpose of investing, managing or administering financial assets deposited in the name of the customer with a financial institution other than such entity, or

(B) manages portfolios for, and acts on behalf of, a customer for the purpose of investing, managing, or administering financial assets deposited in the name of the customer with a financial institution other than such entity,

(iv) any equity or debt interest in the financial institution if one of the purposes of establishing the class of interests was to avoid reporting in accordance with section 271, except that it does not include any equity or debt interest in an entity that is an investment entity solely because it meets the conditions described in clauses (iii)(A) or (B),

(v) any cash value insurance contract and any annuity contract issued or maintained by a financial institution, other than a non-investment-linked, non-transferable immediate life annuity that is issued to an individual and monetizes a pension or disability benefit provided under an account that is an excluded account, and

(vi) an account that is a client name account maintained by a person or entity that is authorized under provincial legislation to engage in the business of dealing in securities or any other financial instruments, or to provide portfolio management or investment advising services; and

(b) despite paragraph (a), does not include an excluded account.

Related Provisions: 270(4)(a) — Equity interest — deeming rule.

"financial asset"

(a) includes

(i) a security, such as

(A) a share of the capital stock of a corporation,

(B) an income or capital interest in a widely held or publicly traded trust, or

(C) a note, bond, debenture or other evidence of indebtedness,

(ii) a partnership interest,

(iii) a commodity,

(iv) a swap (such as interest rate swaps, currency swaps, basis swaps, interest rate caps, interest rate floors, commodity swaps, equity swaps, equity index swaps and similar agreements),

(v) an insurance contract or annuity contract, and

(vi) any interest (including a futures or forward contract or option) in a security, partnership interest, commodity, swap, insurance contract or annuity contract; and

(b) does not include a non-debt, direct interest in real or immovable property.

Notes: Negotiable debt instruments traded on a regulated market (or on an over-the-counter market and distributed and held through financial institutions), and shares or units in a real estate investment trust, are generally considered financial assets. (Finance Technical Notes)

"financial institution" means an entity, other than a passive NFE, that is a custodial institution, a depository institution, an investment entity or a specified insurance company.

"governmental entity" means the government of a jurisdiction, any political subdivision of a jurisdiction (which, for greater certainty, includes a state, province, county or municipality), a public body performing a function of government in a jurisdiction or any agency or instrumentality of a jurisdiction wholly owned by one or more of the foregoing, unless it is not an integral part or a controlled entity of a jurisdiction (or a political subdivision of a jurisdiction) and for these purposes

(a) an integral part of a jurisdiction means any person, organization, agency, bureau, fund, instrumentality or other body, however designated, that constitutes a governing authority of a jurisdiction and where the net earnings of the governing authority are credited to its own account or to other accounts of the jurisdiction, with no portion inuring to the benefit of any private person, except that an integral part does not include any individual who is a sovereign, official or administrator acting in a private or personal capacity;

(b) a controlled entity means an entity that is separate in form from the jurisdiction or that otherwise constitutes a separate juridical entity, provided that

(i) the entity is wholly owned and controlled by one or more governmental entities directly or indirectly through one or more controlled entities,

(ii) the entity's net earnings are credited to its own account or to the accounts of one or more governmental entities, with no portion of its income inuring to the benefit of any private person, and

(iii) the entity's assets vest in one or more governmental entities upon liquidation and dissolution; and

(c) for the purposes of paragraphs (a) and (b),

(i) income is deemed not to inure to the benefit of private persons if such persons are the intended beneficiaries of a governmental program and the program activities are performed for the general public with respect to the common welfare or relate to the administration of government, and

(ii) income is deemed to inure to the benefit of private persons if the income is derived from the use of a governmental entity to conduct a commercial business that provides financial services to private persons.

Notes: For the meaning of "public body performing…", see Notes to 149(1)(c).

"group annuity contract" means an annuity contract under which the obligees are individuals who are associated through an employer, trade association, labour union or other association or group.

"group cash value insurance contract" means a cash value insurance contract that

(a) provides coverage on individuals who are associated through an employer, trade association, labour union or other association or group; and

(b) charges a premium for each member of the group (or member of a class within the group) that is determined without regard to the individual health characteristics other than age, gender and smoking habits of the member (or class of members) of the group.

"high value account" means a preexisting individual account with an aggregate balance or value that exceeds 1 million USD on June 30, 2017 or on December 31 of any subsequent year.

Notes: Due to "any subsequent year", once an account becomes a HVA, it maintains this status until it is closed and can never be a "lower value account".

"insurance contract" means a contract (other than an annuity contract) under which the issuer agrees to pay an amount upon the occurrence of a specified contingency involving mortality, morbidity, accident, liability or property risk.

"international organization" means any intergovernmental organization (or wholly owned agency or instrumentality thereof), including a supranational organization

(a) that is comprised primarily of governments;

(b) that has in effect a headquarters or substantially similar agreement with a jurisdiction; and

(c) the income of which does not inure to the benefit of private persons.

"investment entity" means any entity (other than an entity that is an "active NFE" because of any of paragraphs (d) to (g) of that definition)

(a) that primarily carries on as a business one or more of the following activities or operations for or on behalf of a customer:

(i) trading in money market instruments (such as cheques, bills, certificates of deposit and derivatives), foreign exchange, transferable securities or commodity futures, exchange, interest rate and index instruments,

(ii) individual and collective portfolio management, or

(iii) otherwise investing, administering or managing financial assets or money on behalf of other persons; or

(b) the gross income of which is primarily attributable to investing, reinvesting or trading in financial assets, if the entity is managed by another entity that is a depository institution, a custodial institution, a specified insurance company or an investment entity described in paragraph (a).

Related Provisions: 270(3) — Interpretation — investment entity.

Notes: Generally, an "investment entity" is an entity whose business is primarily carrying on investment activities or operations on behalf of other persons. The definition is to be interpreted consistent with similar language in the definition of "financial institution" in the OECD Financial Action Task Force Recommendations, *International Standards on Combating Money Laundering and the Financing of Terrorism and Proliferation*. (Finance Technical Notes; see also 270(2) and (3))

"lower value account" means a preexisting individual account with an aggregate balance or value as of June 30, 2017 that does not exceed 1 million USD.

"narrow participation retirement fund" means a fund that is established to provide retirement, disability or death benefits to beneficiaries who are current or former employees (or persons designated by those employees) of one or more employers in consideration for services rendered, if

(a) the fund has fewer than 50 participants;

(b) the fund is sponsored by one or more employers that are not investment entities or passive NFEs;

(c) the employee and employer contributions to the fund (other than transfers of assets from retirement and pension accounts described in paragraph (a) of the definition "excluded account") are limited by reference to the employee's remuneration;

(d) participants that are not resident in Canada are not entitled to more than 20% of the fund's assets; and

(e) the fund is subject to government regulation and provides information reporting to the Minister.

["NFE"] — [See "non-financial entity" below.]

"natural person" means an individual other than a trust.

"new account" means a financial account maintained by a reporting financial institution opened after June 2017.

"new entity account" means a new account held by one or more entities.

"new individual account" means a new account held by one or more individuals (other than trusts).

"non-financial entity" or **"NFE"** means an entity if

(a) in the case of an entity that is resident in Canada, it is not a Canadian financial institution; and

(b) in the case of a non-resident entity, it is not a financial institution.

Notes: An NFE can be either an "active NFE" or a "passive NFE".

"non-reporting financial institution" means a Canadian financial institution that is

(a) the Bank of Canada;

(b) a governmental entity or international organization, other than with respect to a payment that is derived from an obligation held in connection with a commercial financial activity of a type engaged in by a specified insurance company, custodial institution or depository institution;

(c) a broad participation retirement fund, a narrow participation retirement fund, a pension fund of a governmental entity, international organization or central bank, or a qualified credit card issuer;

(d) an exempt collective investment vehicle;

(e) a trust if a trustee of the trust is a reporting financial institution and reports all information required to be reported under this Part with respect to all reportable accounts of the trust; or

(f) a prescribed entity.

Regulations: 9005 (prescribed entities for para. (f)).

"participating jurisdiction" means

(a) Canada; and

(b) each jurisdiction identified as a participating jurisdiction by the Minister on the Internet website of the Canada Revenue Agency or by any other means that the Minister considers appropriate.

Notes: This refers to jurisdictions that have an information agreement in place to share the information collected under the Common Reporting Standard. See Notes at end of 281.

"participating jurisdiction financial institution" means

(a) a financial institution that is resident in a participating jurisdiction, but excludes a branch of that financial institution that is located outside a participating jurisdiction; and

(b) a branch of a financial institution that is not resident in a participating jurisdiction, if that branch is located in a participating jurisdiction.

"passive NFE" means

(a) a non-financial entity that is not an active NFE; and

(b) an entity that is

(i) described in paragraph (b) of the definition "investment entity", and

(ii) not a participating jurisdiction financial institution.

"pension fund of a governmental entity, international organization or central bank" means a fund that is established by a governmental entity, international organization or central bank to provide retirement, disability or death benefits to beneficiaries or participants

(a) that are current or former employees (or persons designated by those employees); or

(b) that are not current or former employees, if the benefits provided to them are in consideration of personal services performed for the governmental entity, international organization or central bank.

"preexisting account" means

(a) a financial account maintained by a reporting financial institution on June 30, 2017; and

(b) a financial account of an account holder (other than a financial account described in paragraph (a)) maintained by a reporting financial institution if

(i) the account holder also holds with the reporting financial institution (or with a related entity within Canada) a financial account that is a preexisting account under paragraph (a),

(ii) the reporting financial institution (and, as applicable, the related entity within Canada) treats both of the aforementioned financial accounts, and any other financial accounts of the account holder that are preexisting accounts under this paragraph, as a single financial account for the purposes of

(A) satisfying the standards and knowledge requirements set forth under this Part, and

(B) determining the balance or value of any of the financial accounts, when applying any of the account thresholds,

(iii) with respect to a financial account that is subject to AML/KYC procedures, the reporting financial institution is permitted to satisfy those AML/KYC procedures for the financial account by relying upon the AML/KYC procedures performed for the preexisting account described in paragraph (a), and

(v) the opening of the financial account does not require the provision of new, additional or amended customer information by the account holder other than for purposes of this Part.

"preexisting entity account" means a preexisting account held by one or more entities.

"preexisting individual account" means a preexisting account held by one or more individuals (other than trusts).

"qualified credit card issuer" means a financial institution that satisfies the following requirements:

(a) the financial institution is a financial institution solely because it is an issuer of credit cards that accepts deposits only when a customer makes a payment in excess of a balance due with respect to the card and the overpayment is not immediately returned to the customer; and

(b) the financial institution has policies and procedures either to prevent a customer from making an overpayment in excess of 50,000 USD or to ensure that any customer overpayment in excess of 50,000 USD is refunded to the customer within 60 days, in each case applying the rules set forth in subsection 277(3) for account aggregation, and, for the purposes of this paragraph, a customer overpayment does not refer to credit balances to the extent of disputed charges but does include credit balances resulting from merchandise returns.

"related entity", in respect of an entity, means an entity if either entity controls the other entity or the two entities are controlled by the same entity or individual (and in the case of two entities that are investment entities described under paragraph (b) of the definition "investment entity", the two entities are under common management and such management fulfils the due diligence obligations of the investment entities). For this purpose, control includes direct or indirect ownership of

(a) in the case of a corporation, shares of the capital stock of a corporation that

(i) give their holders more than 50% of the votes that could be cast at the annual meeting of the shareholders of the corporation, and

(ii) have a fair market value of more than 50% of the fair market value of all the issued and outstanding shares of the capital stock of the corporation;

(b) in the case of a partnership, an interest as a member of the partnership that entitles the member to more than 50% of

(i) the income or loss of the partnership, or

(ii) the assets (net of liabilities) of the partnership if it were to cease to exist; and

(c) in the case of a trust, an interest as a beneficiary under the trust with a fair market value that is greater than 50% of the fair market value of all interests as a beneficiary under the trust.

"reportable account" means an account that

(a) is held by

(i) one or more reportable persons, or

(ii) by a passive NFE, if one or more controlling persons of the passive NFE is a reportable person; and

(b) has been identified as meeting the conditions in paragraph (a) in accordance with the due diligence procedures described in sections 272 to 277.

"reportable jurisdiction" means a jurisdiction other than Canada and the United States of America.

"reportable jurisdiction person" means a natural person or entity that is resident in a reportable jurisdiction under the tax laws of that jurisdiction, or an estate of an individual who was a resident of a reportable jurisdiction under the tax laws of that jurisdiction immediately before death. For this purpose, an entity that has no residence for tax purposes is deemed to be resident in the jurisdiction in which its place of effective management is situated.

"reportable person" means a reportable jurisdiction person other than

(a) a corporation the stock of which is regularly traded on one or more established securities markets;

b) any corporation that is a related entity of a corporation described in paragraph (a);

(c) a governmental entity;

(d) an international organization;

(e) a central bank; or

(f) a financial institution.

"reporting financial institution" means a Canadian financial institution that is not a non-reporting financial institution.

"specified insurance company" means any entity that is an insurance company (or the holding company of an insurance company) that issues, or is obligated to make payments with respect to, cash value insurance contracts or annuity contracts.

"TIN" *[taxpayer identification number — ed.]* means

(a) the number used by the Minister to identify an individual or entity, including

(i) a social insurance number,

(ii) a business number, and

(iii) an account number issued to a trust; and

(b) in respect of a jurisdiction other than Canada, a taxpayer identification number used in that jurisdiction to identify an individual or entity (or a functional equivalent in the absence of a taxpayer identification number).

Related Provisions: 281(3) — Penalty for failure to provide TIN to financial institution.

"USD" means dollars of the United States of America.

(2) Interpretation — This Part relates to the implementation of the *Common Reporting Standard* set out in the *Standard for Automatic Exchange of Financial Account Information in Tax Matters* approved by the Council of the Organisation for Economic Co-operation and Development and, unless the context otherwise requires, the provisions in this Part are to be interpreted consistently with the *Common Reporting Standard*, as amended from time to time.

(3) Interpretation — investment entity — For the purposes of the definition "investment entity" in subsection (1), an entity is considered to be primarily carrying on as a business one or more of the activities described in paragraph (a) of that definition, or an entity's gross income is primarily attributable to investing, reinvesting or trading in financial assets for the purposes of paragraph (b) of that definition, if the entity's gross income attributable to the relevant activities equals or exceeds 50% of the entity's gross income during the shorter of

(a) the three-year period that ends at the end of the entity's last fiscal period, and

(b) the period during which the entity has been in existence.

(4) Equity or debt interest — deeming rule — In the case of a trust that is a financial institution,

(a) an equity interest is deemed to be held by any person treated as a settlor or beneficiary of all or a portion of the trust or any other natural person exercising ultimate effective control over the trust, and

(b) a reportable person is treated as a beneficiary of a trust if the reportable person has the right to receive directly or indirectly (such as through a nominee) a mandatory distribution from the trust or may receive, directly or indirectly, a discretionary distribution from the trust.

Notes: For the meaning of "indirectly" in para. (b), see Notes to 17.1(1).

Notes: See Notes at end of 281.

Definitions [s. 270]: "AML/KYC procedures", "account holder", "active NFE" — 270(1); "amount", "annuity" — 248(1); "annuity contract", "anti-money laundering and know your customer procedures" — 270(1); "bank" — 248(1); "beneficiary" — 248(25) [Notes], 270(4)(b); "broad participation retirement fund" — 270(1); "business", "business number" — 248(1); "calendar year" — *Interpretation Act* 37(1)(a); "Canadian financial institution" — 270(1); "capital interest" — 108(1), 248(1); "cash value", "cash value insurance contract", "central bank", "controlling persons" — 270(1); "corporation" — 248(1), *Interpretation Act* 35(1); "county" — *Interpretation Act* 35(1); "custodial account", "custodial institution" — 270(1); "death benefit" — 248(1); "depository account", "depository institution" — 270(1); "dividend" — 248(1); "employee", "employer" — 248(1); "entity", "equity or debt interest", "established securities market" — 270(1); "estate" — 104(1), 248(1); "excluded account", "exempt collective investment vehicle" — 270(1); "fair market value" — see 69(1) Notes; "financial account", "financial asset", "financial institution" — 270(1); "fiscal period" — 249.1; "governmental entity" — 270(1); "immovable" — Quebec *Civil Code* art. 900-907; "individual" — 248(1); "insurance contract", "international organization", "investment entity" — 270(1); "Minister" — 248(1); "month" — *Interpretation Act* 35(1); "narrow participation retirement fund", "natural person", "new account", "NFE", "non-financial entity", "non-reporting financial institution" — 270(1); "non-resident" — 248(1); "participating jurisdiction", "participating jurisdiction financial institution" — 270(1); "partnership" — see 96(1) Notes; "passive NFE", "pension fund of a governmental entity, international organization or central bank" — 270(1); "person" — 248(1); "preexisting account", "preexisting entity account", "preexisting individual account" — 270(1); "prescribed", "property" — 248(1); "provincial" — *Interpretation Act* 33(3), 35(1) "province"; "qualified credit card issuer", "related entity", "reportable account", "reportable jurisdiction", "reportable jurisdiction person", "reportable person", "reporting financial institution" — 270(1); "resident" — 250; "resident in Can-

ada" — 94(3)(a), 250; "share", "shareholder", "taxpayer" — 248(1); "trust" — 104(1), 248(1), (3); "United States" — *Interpretation Act* 35(1); "USD" — 270(1).

271. (1) General reporting requirements — Subject to subsections (3) and (4), each reporting financial institution must report the following information to the Minister with respect to each of its reportable accounts:

(a) the name, address, jurisdiction of residence, TIN and date of birth (in the case of a natural person) of each reportable person that is an account holder of the account;

(b) in the case of any entity that is an account holder of the account and that, after applying the due diligence procedures in sections 275 to 277, is identified as having one or more controlling persons that is a reportable person,

(i) the name, address, jurisdiction of residence and TIN of the entity, and

(ii) the name, address, jurisdiction of residence, TIN and date of birth of each of those controlling persons;

(c) the account number (or functional equivalent in the absence of an account number) of the account;

(d) the name and identifying number (if any) of the reporting financial institution;

(e) the account balance or value (including, in the case of a cash value insurance contract or annuity contract, the cash value or surrender value)

(i) at the end of the relevant calendar year or other appropriate reporting period, or

(ii) if the account was closed during the relevant calendar year or period, on closure of the account;

(f) in the case of any custodial account,

(i) the total gross amount of interest, the total gross amount of dividends and the total gross amount of other income generated with respect to the assets held in the account, in each case paid or credited to the account (or with respect to the account) during the calendar year or other appropriate reporting period, and

(ii) the total gross proceeds from the sale or redemption of financial assets paid or credited to the account during the calendar year or other appropriate reporting period with respect to which the reporting financial institution acted as a custodian, broker, nominee or otherwise as an agent for the account holder;

(g) in the case of any depository account, the total gross amount of interest paid or credited to the account during the calendar year or other appropriate reporting period; and

(h) in the case of any account not described in paragraph (f) or (g), the total gross amount paid or credited to the account holder with respect to the account during the calendar year or other appropriate reporting period with respect to which the reporting financial institution is the obligor or debtor, including the aggregate amount of any redemption payments made to the account holder during the calendar year or other appropriate reporting period.

Related Provisions: 272-277 — Due diligence requirements; 278 — Obligation to file information return; 279 — Record-keeping requirements; 280 — Anti-avoidance; 281 — Taxpayer must provide TIN to financial institution.

Notes: See Notes at end of s. 281.

Forms: RC518: Declaration of tax residence for individuals — Part XVIII and Part XIX of the *Income Tax Act*; RC519: Declaration of tax residence for entities — Part XVIII and Part XIX; RC520: Declaration of tax residence for individuals — Part XIX; RC521: Declaration of tax residence for entities — Part XIX.

(2) Currency — The information reported must identify the currency in which each amount is denominated.

(3) TIN and date of birth [preexisting account — rules relaxed] — With respect to each reportable account that is a preexisting account,

(a) notwithstanding paragraphs (1)(a) and (b), the TIN or date of birth are not required to be reported if the TIN or the date of birth (as appropriate)

(i) are not in the records of the reporting financial institution, and

(ii) are not otherwise required to be collected by the reporting financial institution under the Act; and

(b) a reporting financial institution is required to use reasonable efforts to obtain the TIN and the date of birth with respect to a preexisting account by the end of the second calendar year following the year in which the preexisting account is identified as a reportable account.

(4) Exceptions [if other country does not use TINs] — Notwithstanding paragraphs (1)(a) and (b), a TIN of a reportable person is not required to be reported if

(a) the relevant reportable jurisdiction does not issue TINs; or

(b) the domestic law of the relevant reportable jurisdiction does not require the collection of the TIN issued by such reportable jurisdiction.

Notes: See Notes at end of s. 281.

Definitions [s. 271]: "account holder" — 270(1); "amount", "annuity" — 248(1); "annuity contract" — 270(1); "calendar year" — *Interpretation Act* 37(1)(a); "cash value", "cash value insurance contract", "controlling persons", "custodial account", "depository account" — 270(1); "dividend" — 248(1); "entity", "financial asset" — 270(1); "individual", "Minister", "person" — 248(1); "preexisting account" — 270(1); "record" — 248(1); "reportable account", "reportable jurisdiction", "reportable person", "reporting financial institution", "TIN" — 270(1).

272. (1) General due diligence rules — An account is treated as a reportable account as of the date it is identified as a reportable account under the due diligence procedures set out in this section and in sections 273 to 277.

(2) Timing — determination of balance or value — The balance or value of an account is determined on the last day of the calendar year or other appropriate reporting period.

(3) Determination — balance or value — For the purpose of determining whether the balance or value of an account exceeds a particular threshold on the last day of a calendar year, the balance or value must be determined on the last day of the last reporting period that ends on or before the end of the calendar year.

(4) Service provider — A reporting financial institution may use service providers to fulfil its reporting and due diligence obligations imposed, but these obligations shall remain the responsibility of the reporting financial institution.

(5) Optional due diligence procedures — A reporting financial institution may, either with respect to all preexisting accounts or, separately, with respect to any clearly identified group of those accounts, apply the due diligence procedures

(a) for new accounts to preexisting accounts (with the other rules for preexisting accounts continuing to apply); and

(b) for high value accounts to lower value accounts.

(6) Documentation of due diligence procedures — Every reporting financial institution shall establish, maintain and document the due diligence procedures set out in this section and sections 273 to 277.

Notes: See Notes at end of s. 281.

Definitions [s. 272]: "calendar year" — *Interpretation Act* 37(1)(a); "new account", "preexisting account", "reportable account", "reporting financial institution" — 270(1).

273. (1) Due diligence for preexisting individual accounts — A preexisting individual account that is a cash value insurance contract or an annuity contract is not required to be reviewed, identified or reported, if the reporting financial institution

is effectively prevented by law from selling those contracts to residents of a reportable jurisdiction.

(2) Lower value accounts — The following review procedures apply with respect to lower value accounts that are preexisting individual accounts:

(a) if the reporting financial institution has in its records the address of the individual account holder's current residence (in this section, their "current residence address") based on documentary evidence, the reporting financial institution may treat the individual account holder as being a resident for tax purposes of the jurisdiction in which the address is located for purposes of determining whether the individual account holder is a reportable person;

(b) if the reporting financial institution does not rely on a current residence address for the individual account holder based on documentary evidence as described in paragraph (a), the reporting financial institution must review electronically searchable data maintained by the reporting financial institution for any of the following indicia and apply paragraphs (c) to (f):

(i) identification of the account holder as a resident of a reportable jurisdiction,

(ii) current mailing or residence address (including post office box) in a reportable jurisdiction,

(iii) one or more telephone numbers in a reportable jurisdiction and no telephone number in the jurisdiction of the reporting financial institution,

(iv) standing instructions (other than with respect to a depository account) to transfer funds to an account maintained in a reportable jurisdiction,

(v) currently effective power of attorney or signatory authority granted to a person with an address in a reportable jurisdiction, and

(vi) a hold mail instruction or in-care-of address in a reportable jurisdiction if the reporting financial institution does not have any other address on file for the account holder;

(c) if none of the indicia listed in paragraph (b) are discovered in the electronic search, then no further review is required until the earlier of

(i) a change in circumstances that results in one or more of the indicia referred to in paragraph (b) being associated with the account, and

(ii) the account becoming a high value account;

(d) if any of the indicia listed in subparagraphs (b)(i) to (v) are discovered in the electronic search or if there is a change in circumstances that results in one or more of the indicia in paragraph (b) being associated with the account, then the reporting financial institution must treat the account holder as a resident for tax purposes of each reportable jurisdiction for which an indicium is identified, unless one of the exceptions in paragraph (f) applies with respect to that account;

(e) if a hold mail instruction or in-care-of address in a reportable jurisdiction is discovered in the electronic search and no other address and none of the other indicia listed in subparagraphs (b)(i) to (v) are identified for the account holder, then

(i) the reporting financial institution must do one (if the relevant information is obtained) or both (in the order most appropriate to the circumstances) of the following:

(A) apply the paper record search described in paragraph (3)(b), and

(B) seek to obtain from the account holder a self-certification or documentary evidence to establish the residence for tax purposes of the account holder, and

(ii) if the paper record search referred to in clause (i)(A) fails to establish an indicium and the attempt to obtain the self-certification or documentary evidence referred to in clause (i)(B) is not successful, then the reporting financial institution must report the account as an undocumented account; and

(f) notwithstanding the discovery of indicia under paragraph (b), a reporting financial institution is not required to treat an account holder as a resident of a reportable jurisdiction if

(i) both

(A) the account holder information contains

(I) a current mailing or residence address in the reportable jurisdiction,

(II) one or more telephone numbers in the reportable jurisdiction (and no telephone number in the jurisdiction of the reporting financial institution), or

(III) standing instructions (with respect to financial accounts other than depository accounts) to transfer funds to an account maintained in a reportable jurisdiction, and

(B) the reporting financial institution obtains, or has previously reviewed and currently maintains a record of,

(I) a self-certification from the account holder of the jurisdictions of residence of the account holder that does not include the reportable jurisdiction, and

(II) documentary evidence establishing the account holder's non-reportable status in relation to that jurisdiction, or

(ii) both

(A) the account holder information contains a currently effective power of attorney or signatory authority granted to a person with an address in the reportable jurisdiction, and

(B) the reporting financial institution obtains, or has previously reviewed and currently maintains a record of,

(I) a self-certification from the account holder of the jurisdictions of residence of the account holder that does not include the reportable jurisdiction, or

(II) documentary evidence establishing the account holder's non-reportable status in relation to that jurisdiction.

(3) Enhanced review procedure — high value accounts —
The following enhanced review procedures apply with respect to high value accounts that are preexisting individual accounts:

(a) the reporting financial institution must review electronically searchable data maintained by the reporting financial institution for any of the indicia described in paragraph (2)(b);

(b) subject to paragraph (c), the reporting financial institution must review for any of the indicia described in paragraph (2)(b)

(i) the current customer master file, and

(ii) the following documents associated with the account, and obtained by the reporting financial institution within the last five years, to the extent that they are not contained in the current customer master file:

(A) the most recent documentary evidence collected with respect to the account,

(B) the most recent account opening contract or documentation,

(C) the most recent documentation obtained by the reporting financial institution in accordance with AML/KYC procedures or for other regulatory purposes,

(D) any power of attorney or signature authority forms currently in effect, and

(E) any standing instructions (other than with respect to a depository account) to transfer funds currently in effect;

(c) a reporting financial institution is not required to perform the paper record search described in paragraph (b) to the extent that

the reporting financial institution's electronically searchable information includes the following:

(i) the account holder's residence status,

(ii) the account holder's residence address and mailing address currently on file with the reporting financial institution,

(iii) the account holder's telephone number currently on file, if any, with the reporting financial institution,

(iv) in the case of financial accounts other than depository accounts, whether there are standing instructions to transfer funds in the account to another account (including an account at another branch of the reporting financial institution or at another financial institution),

(v) whether there is a hold mail instruction or current in-care-of address for the account holder, and

(vi) whether there is any power of attorney or signatory authority for the account;

(d) in addition to the electronic and paper record searches described in paragraphs (a) to (c), the reporting financial institution must treat as a reportable account any high value account assigned to a relationship manager (including any financial accounts aggregated with that high value account under section 277) if the relationship manager has actual knowledge that the account holder is a reportable person;

(e) with respect to the enhanced review of high value accounts described in paragraphs (a) to (d),

(i) if none of the indicia listed in paragraph (2)(b) are discovered in the enhanced review and the account is not identified as being held by a reportable person in paragraph (d), then further action is not required until there is a change in circumstances that results in one or more indicia being associated with the account,

(ii) if any of the indicia listed in subparagraphs (2)(b)(i) through (v) are discovered in the enhanced review, or if there is a subsequent change in circumstances that results in one or more indicia being associated with the account, then the reporting financial institution must treat the account as a reportable account with respect to each reportable jurisdiction for which an indicium is identified unless one of the exceptions in paragraph (2)(f) applies with respect to that account, and

(iii) if a hold mail instruction or in-care-of address is discovered in the enhanced review and no other address or other indicia listed in subparagraphs (2)(b)(i) to (v) are identified for the account holder, then the reporting financial institution must

(A) obtain from the account holder a self-certification or documentary evidence to establish the residence for tax purposes of the account holder, and

(B) if the reporting financial institution cannot obtain a self-certification or documentary evidence, report the account as an undocumented account;

(f) if a preexisting individual account is not a high value account on June 30, 2017, but becomes a high value account as of the last day of a subsequent calendar year,

(i) the reporting financial institution must complete the enhanced review procedures described in this subsection with respect to the account within the calendar year following the year in which the account becomes a high value account, and

(ii) if the account is identified as a reportable account based on the review in subparagraph (i), the reporting financial institution must report the required information about the account with respect to the year in which it is identified as a reportable account (and subsequent years on an annual basis, unless the account holder ceases to be a reportable person);

(g) if a reporting financial institution applies the enhanced review procedures described in this subsection to a high value account in a year, then the reporting financial institution is not required to reapply those procedures — other than the relationship manager inquiry described in paragraph (d) — to the same high value account in any subsequent year unless the account is undocumented, in which case the reporting financial institution must re-apply them annually until the account ceases to be undocumented;

(h) if there is a change of circumstances with respect to a high value account that results in one or more indicia described in paragraph (2)(b) being associated with the account, then the reporting financial institution must treat the account as a reportable account with respect to each reportable jurisdiction for which an indicium is identified unless one of the exceptions in paragraph (2)(f) applies with respect to that account; and

(i) a reporting financial institution must implement procedures to ensure that a relationship manager identifies any change in circumstances of an account.

(4) Timing of review — Each preexisting individual account must be reviewed in accordance with subsection (2) or (3) before

(a) 2019, if the account is a high value account; or

(b) 2020, if the account is a lower value account.

(5) Reportable preexisting individual accounts — Any preexisting individual account that has been identified as a reportable account under this section must be treated as a reportable account in all subsequent years, unless the account holder ceases to be a reportable person.

Notes: See Notes at end of s. 281.

Definitions [s. 273]: "AML/KYC procedures", "account holder" — 270(1); "annuity" — 248(1); "annuity contract" — 270(1); "calendar year" — *Interpretation Act* 37(1)(a); "cash value insurance contract", "depository account", "documentary evidence", "financial account", "financial institution", "high value account" — 270(1); "individual" — 248(1); "lower value account" — 270(1); "person" — 248(1); "preexisting individual account" — 270(1); "record" — 248(1); "reportable account", "reportable jurisdiction", "reportable person", "reporting financial institution" — 270(1); "resident" — 250.

274. (1) Due diligence — new individual accounts — Upon opening a new individual account, the reporting financial institution must obtain a self-certification (which may be a part of the account opening documentation) that allows the reporting financial institution to

(a) determine the account holder's residence for tax purposes; and

(b) confirm the reasonableness of the self-certification taking into account information obtained by the reporting financial institution in connection with the opening of the account, including any documentation collected in accordance with the AML/KYC procedures.

Forms: RC518: Declaration of tax residence for individuals — Part XVIII and Part XIX of the *Income Tax Act*; RC520: Declaration of tax residence for individuals — Part XIX of the *Income Tax Act*.

(2) Determination of reportable account — If the self-certification for a new individual account establishes that the account holder is resident for tax purposes in a reportable jurisdiction, then

(a) the reporting financial institution must treat the account as a reportable account; and

(b) the self-certification must also include the account holder's TIN with respect to the reportable jurisdiction (subject to subsection 271(4)) and the account holder's date of birth.

(3) Requirement to obtain new self-certification — If there is a change in circumstances with respect to a new individual account that causes the reporting financial institution to know, or have reason to know, that the original self-certification is incorrect or unreliable, then the reporting financial institution

(a) cannot rely on the original self-certification; and

(b) must obtain a valid self-certification that establishes the residence for tax purposes of the account holder.

Notes: See Notes at end of s. 281.

Definitions [s. 274]: "AML/KYC procedures", "account holder", "new individual account", "reportable account", "reportable jurisdiction", "reporting financial institution" — 270(1); "resident" — 250; "TIN" — 270(1).

275. (1) Due diligence — preexisting entity accounts — Unless the reporting financial institution elects otherwise — either with respect to all preexisting entity accounts or, separately, with respect to any clearly identified group of those accounts — a preexisting entity account with an aggregate account balance or value that does not exceed 250,000 USD on June 30, 2017 is not required to be reviewed, identified or reported as a reportable account until the aggregate account balance or value exceeds 250,000 USD on the last day of any subsequent calendar year.

(2) Application of subsec. (4) — The review procedures set forth in subsection (4) apply to a preexisting entity account if it has an aggregate account balance or value that exceeds 250,000 USD on

(a) June 30, 2017; or

(b) the last day of any subsequent calendar year.

(3) Determination of reportable accounts — With respect to preexisting entity accounts described in subsection (2), the only accounts that shall be treated as reportable accounts are accounts that are held by

(a) one or more entities that are reportable persons; or

(b) passive NFEs with one or more controlling persons who are reportable persons.

(4) Review procedures — preexisting entity account — If this subsection applies to a preexisting entity account, a reporting financial institution must apply the following review procedures to determine whether the account is held by one or more reportable persons or by passive NFEs with one or more controlling persons who are reportable persons:

(a) review information maintained for regulatory or customer relationship purposes (including information collected in accordance with AML/KYC procedures) to determine whether the information indicates that the account holder is resident in a reportable jurisdiction and, if so, the reporting financial institution must treat the account as a reportable account unless it

(i) obtains a self-certification from the account holder to establish that the account holder is not a reportable person, or

(ii) reasonably determines, based on information in its possession or that is publicly available, that the account holder is not a reportable person; and

(b) with respect to an account holder of a preexisting account (including an entity that is a reportable person), the reporting financial institution must determine whether the account holder is a passive NFE with one or more controlling persons who are reportable persons and for the purposes of

(i) determining whether the account holder is a passive NFE, the reporting financial institution must obtain a self-certification from the account holder to establish its status, unless it has information in its possession or information is publicly available, based on which it can reasonably determine that the account holder is

(A) an active NFE, or

(B) a financial institution other than an entity described in paragraph (b) of the definition "investment entity" that is not a participating jurisdiction financial institution,

(ii) determining the controlling persons of an account holder, a reporting financial institution may rely on information collected and maintained in accordance with AML/KYC procedures, and

(iii) determining whether a controlling person of a passive NFE is a reportable person, a reporting financial institution may rely on

(A) information collected and maintained in accordance with AML/KYC procedures in the case of a preexisting entity account held by one or more NFEs with an aggregate account balance or value that does not exceed 1 million USD, or

(B) a self-certification from the account holder or the controlling person indicating the jurisdiction in which the controlling person is resident for tax purposes.

Forms: RC519: Declaration of tax residence for entities — Part XVIII and Part XIX of the *Income Tax Act*; RC521: Declaration of tax residence for entities — Part XIX of the *Income Tax Act*.

(5) Timing of review — Each preexisting entity account must be reviewed in accordance with subsection (4) before

(a) 2020, if the account has an aggregate account balance or value that exceeds 250,000 USD on June 30, 2017; or

(b) the end of the calendar year following the year in which the aggregate account balance or value exceeds 250,000 USD on December 31, if paragraph (a) does not apply.

(6) Change of circumstances — If there is a change of circumstances with respect to a preexisting entity account that causes the reporting financial institution to know, or have reason to know, that the self-certification or other documentation associated with the account is incorrect or unreliable, the reporting financial institution must redetermine the status of the account in accordance with subsection (4).

Notes: See Notes at end of s. 281.

Definitions [s. 275]: "AML/KYC procedures", "account holder", "active NFE" — 270(1); "calendar year" — *Interpretation Act* 37(1)(a); "controlling persons", "entity", "financial institution", "investment entity", "NFE", "participating jurisdiction financial institution", "passive NFE" — 270(1); "person" — 248(1); "preexisting account", "preexisting entity account", "reportable account", "reportable jurisdiction", "reportable person", "reporting financial institution" — 270(1); "resident" — 250; "USD" — 270(1).

276. Due diligence for new entity accounts — For new entity accounts, a reporting financial institution must apply the following review procedures to determine whether the account is held by one or more reportable persons or by passive NFEs with one or more controlling persons who are reportable persons:

(a) the reporting financial institution must

(i) obtain a self-certification (which may be part of the account opening documentation) that allows the reporting financial institution to determine the account holder's residence for tax purposes and confirm the reasonableness of the self-certification based on the information obtained by the reporting financial institution in connection with the opening of the account, including any documentation collected in accordance with AML/KYC procedures, and

(ii) if the self-certification referred to in subparagraph (i) indicates that the account holder is resident in a reportable jurisdiction, treat the account as a reportable account unless it reasonably determines, based on information in its possession or information that is publicly available, that the account holder is not a reportable person with respect to the reportable jurisdiction; and

(b) with respect to an account holder of a new entity account (including an entity that is a reportable person), the reporting financial institution must determine whether the account holder is a passive NFE with one or more controlling persons who are reportable persons and, if so, treat the account as a reportable account and, for the purposes of

(i) determining whether the account holder is a passive NFE, the reporting financial institution must obtain a self-certification from the account holder to establish its status, unless it has information in its possession or information is publicly

available, based on which it can reasonably determine that the account holder is

(A) an active NFE, or

(B) a financial institution other than an entity that

(I) is an "investment entity" because of paragraph (b) of that definition, and

(II) is not a participating jurisdiction financial institution,

(ii) determining the controlling persons of an account holder, a reporting financial institution may rely on information collected and maintained in accordance with AML/KYC procedures, and

(iii) determining whether a controlling person of a passive NFE is a reportable person, a reporting financial institution may rely on a self-certification from the account holder or the controlling person.

Notes: See Notes at end of s. 281.

Definitions [s. 276]: "AML/KYC procedures", "account holder", "active NFE" — 270(1); "controlling persons", "entity", "financial institution", "investment entity", "new entity account", "participating jurisdiction financial institution", "passive NFE" — 270(1); "person" — 248(1); "reportable account", "reportable jurisdiction", "reportable person", "reporting financial institution" — 270(1); "resident" — 250.

Forms: RC519: Declaration of tax residence for entities — Part XVIII and Part XIX of the *Income Tax Act*; RC521: Declaration of tax residence for entities — Part XIX of the *Income Tax Act*.

277. (1) Special due diligence rules — A reporting financial institution may not rely on a self-certification or documentary evidence if the reporting financial institution knows or has reason to know that the self-certification or documentary evidence is incorrect or unreliable.

(2) Exception — individual beneficiary receiving death benefit — A reporting financial institution may presume that an individual beneficiary (other than the owner) of a cash value insurance contract or an annuity contract receiving a death benefit is not a reportable person and may treat the financial account as other than a reportable account unless it has actual knowledge, or reason to know, that the beneficiary is a reportable person.

(3) Aggregation rules — For the purposes of

(a) determining the aggregate balance or value of financial accounts held by an individual or entity,

(i) a reporting financial institution is required to aggregate all financial accounts maintained by the reporting financial institution, or by a related entity, but only to the extent that the reporting financial institution's computerized systems

(A) link the financial accounts by reference to a data element such as a client number or TIN, and

(B) allow account balances or values to be aggregated, and

(ii) each holder of a jointly held financial account shall be attributed the entire balance or value of the jointly held financial account; and

(b) determining the aggregate balance or value of financial accounts held by an individual in order to determine whether a financial account is a high value account, a reporting financial institution is also required — in the case of any financial accounts that a relationship manager knows, or has reason to know, are directly or indirectly owned, controlled or established (other than in a fiduciary capacity) by the same individual — to aggregate all such accounts.

(4) Dealer accounts — Subsection (5)

(a) applies to a reporting financial institution in respect of a client name account maintained by the institution if

(i) property recorded in the account is also recorded in a financial account (in this subsection and subsection (5) referred to as the "related account") maintained by a financial institution (in this subsection and subsection (5) referred to as the "dealer") that is authorized under provincial legislation

(A) to engage in the business of dealing in securities or any other financial instrument, or

(B) to provide portfolio management or investment advising services, and

(ii) the dealer has advised the institution whether the related account is a reportable account; and

(b) does not apply, despite paragraph (a), if it can reasonably be concluded by the institution that the dealer has failed to comply with its obligations under this Part.

(5) Dealer accounts — If this subsection applies to a reporting financial institution in respect of a client name account,

(a) sections 272 to 276 do not apply to the institution in respect of the account; and

(b) the institution shall rely on the determination of the dealer in respect of the related account in determining whether the account is a reportable account.

(6) Group insurance and annuities — A reporting financial institution may treat a financial account that is a member's interest in a group cash value insurance contract or group annuity contract as a financial account that is not a reportable account until the day on which an amount becomes payable to the employee, certificate holder or beneficiary, if the financial account meets the following requirements:

(a) the group cash value insurance contract or group annuity contract is issued to an employer and covers 25 or more employees or certificate holders;

(b) the employees or certificate holders are entitled to

(i) receive any contract value related to their interest, and

(ii) name beneficiaries for the benefit payable upon the employee's or certificate holder's death; and

(c) the aggregate amount payable to any employee or certificate holder or beneficiary does not exceed 1 million USD.

Notes: See Notes at end of s. 281.

Definitions [s. 277]: "amount", "annuity" — 248(1); "annuity contract" — 270(1); "beneficiary" — 248(25) [Notes], 270(4)(b); "business" — 248(1); "cash value insurance contract" — 270(1); "death benefit" — 248(1); "documentary evidence" — 270(1); "employee", "employer" — 248(1); "entity", "financial account", "financial institution", "group annuity contract", "group cash value insurance contract", "high value account" — 270(1); "individual", "property" — 248(1); "provincial" — *Interpretation Act* 33(3), 35(1)"province"; "related account" — 277(4)(a)(i); "related entity", "reportable account", "reportable person", "reporting financial institution", "TIN", "USD" — 270(1).

278. (1) Reporting — Every reporting financial institution shall file with the Minister, before May 2 of each calendar year, an information return in prescribed form relating to each reportable account maintained by the institution at any time during the immediately preceding calendar year and after June 30, 2017.

Related Provisions: 266(1) — Reporting of US citizens' and residents' accounts (FATCA); 271(1) — Reporting requirements; 272–277 — Due diligence requirements.

Notes: See Notes at end of 281. Due to COVID-19, the May 1, 2020 filing deadline was extended to Sept. 1, 2020; as well, no penalty applies for failure to obtain self-certification on financial accounts opened before 2021. See CRA information notice, April 20, 2020 (reproduced in PITA 59th ed.).

(2) Electronic filing — The information return required under subsection (1) shall be filed by way of electronic filing.

Definitions [s. 278]: "calendar year" — *Interpretation Act* 37(1)(a); "Minister", "prescribed" — 248(1); "reportable account", "reporting financial institution" — 270(1).

279. (1) Record keeping — Every reporting financial institution shall keep, at the institution's place of business or at such other place as may be designated by the Minister, records that the institution obtains or creates for the purpose of complying with this Part, including self-certifications and records of documentary evidence.

(2) Form of records — Every reporting financial institution required by this Part to keep records that does so electronically shall retain them in an electronically readable format for the retention period referred to in subsection (3).

(3) Retention of records — Every reporting financial institution that is required to keep, obtain or create records under this Part shall retain those records for a period of at least six years following

(a) in the case of a self-certification, the last day on which a related financial account is open; and

(b) in any other case, the end of the last calendar year in respect of which the record is relevant.

Notes: See Notes at end of s. 281.

Definitions [s. 279]: "business" — 248(1); "calendar year" — *Interpretation Act* 37(1)(a); "documentary evidence", "financial account" — 270(1); "Minister", "record" — 248(1); "reporting financial institution" — 270(1).

280. Anti-avoidance — If a person enters into an arrangement or engages in a practice, the primary purpose of which can reasonably be considered to be to avoid an obligation under this Part, the person is subject to the obligation as if the person had not entered into the arrangement or engaged in the practice.

Related Provisions: 268 — Parallel rule for FATCA reporting.

Notes: See Notes at end of s. 281.

Definitions [s. 280]: "person" — 248(1).

281. (1) Production of TIN [Taxpayer Identification Number] — Every reportable person shall provide their TIN at the request of a reporting financial institution that is required under this Part to make an information return requiring the TIN.

Related Provisions: 281(2) — Confidentiality of TIN; 281(3) — Penalty for failing to provide TIN.

Notes: See 270(1)"TIN". A non-resident who has a Canadian Social Insurance Number (e.g., an ex-Canadian resident) can possibly satisfy their 281(1) obligation by providing the financial institution with that SIN and avoid providing their home country TIN to the CRA to be passed on to their home country's tax authority!

Forms: RC518: Declaration of tax residence for individuals — Part XVIII and Part XIX of the *Income Tax Act*; RC519: Declaration of tax residence for entities — Part XVIII and Part XIX of the *Income Tax Act*; RC520: Declaration of tax residence for individuals — Part XIX of the *Income Tax Act*; RC521: Declaration of tax residence for entities — Part XIX of the *Income Tax Act*.

(2) Confidentiality of TIN — A person required to make an information return referred to in subsection (1) shall not knowingly use, communicate or allow to be communicated, otherwise than as required or authorized under this Act or a regulation, the TIN without the written consent of the reportable person.

(3) Penalty for failure to provide TIN — Every reportable person who fails to provide on request their TIN to a reporting financial institution that is required under this Part to make an information return requiring the TIN is liable to a penalty of $500 for each such failure, unless

(a) an application for the assignment of the TIN is made to the relevant reportable jurisdiction not later than 90 days after the request was made and the TIN is provided to the reporting financial institution that requested it within 15 days after the reportable person received it; or

(b) the reportable person is not eligible to obtain a TIN from the relevant reportable jurisdiction (including because the relevant reportable jurisdiction does not issue TINs).

Related Provisions: 225.1(6)(a.1) — No restriction on collection of penalty pending appeal; 281(4) — Assessment of penalty.

Notes: See Notes to 239(1) on the difference between an administrative penalty (such as this one) and criminal prosecution for an offence. Unusually, however, this penalty can be collected even if it is being appealed: 225.1(6)(a.1).

(4) Assessment — The Minister may at any time assess any amount payable under subsection (3) by any person and, if the Minister sends a notice of assessment to the person, sections 150 to 163, subsections 164(1) and (1.4) to (7), sections 165 to 167 and Division J of Part I apply with such modifications as the circumstances require.

Related Provisions: 225.1(6)(a.1) — Amount assessed under s. 281 can be collected even if under appeal.

Notes: 270-281 (and Reg. 9005-9006) implement the "Common Reporting Standard" (CRS) developed by the Organisation for Economic Cooperation and Development (OECD) for automatic information exchange between countries to reduce tax evasion. See CRA *Guidance on the Common Reporting Standard* (July 10, 2020, 160pp); "How to complete and file a Part XVIII Information Return" (tinyurl.com/cra-crsfile).

Canadian banks, credit unions, brokerages and other financial institutions (FIs) must collect information about accounts owned by residents of other countries, using the "due diligence" procedures in 272-277, and must report this information to CRA under 271. (A person who fails to provide their Taxpayer Identification Number on request is subject to a $500 penalty: 281(3), but it is unclear whether any penalty applies to providing other false information to the FI since s. 281 imposes no obligation to provide any information other than the TIN.)

The federal Budget Plan, Feb. 27, 2018, Chapter 4, states: "To ensure that the information received [under the Common Reporting Standard] is properly leveraged to address the highest-risk population of tax evaders, the Government will provide $38.7 million over five years to the CRA. This will allow the CRA to expand its offshore compliance activities through the use of improved risk assessment systems and business intelligence, and will facilitate the hiring of additional auditors." See also CRA news release, "Better data and approaches help the Canada Revenue Agency identify Canadians trying to hide their assets overseas" (November 13, 2018) (first CRS exchanges completed in June 2018); 2019-0824511C6 [2019 CTF q.11] (64 jurisdictions activated for outgoing data, 90 for incoming data, which is "being incorporated into CRA systems and made available to those involved in the spectrum of compliance and collections efforts"); and Notes to 239(1) under "Offshore bank accounts".

For OECD guidance and direction on CRS see tinyurl.com/crs-oecd. For the 100+ countries implementing the CRS, and links to their legislation, see tinyurl.com/oecd-crs2018 (click on each year 2017, 2018, etc.). See also *Peer Review of the Automatic Exchange of Financial Account Information* (tinyurl.com/oecd-peer2020, Dec. 2020, 384pp), finding Canada has done most of CRS right but recommending changes to the "Investment Entity"definition and removing LSVCCs from the list of non-reporting FIs (Reg. 9005(a)).

For judicial comment on 270-281 (in a challenge to the US ETIEA rules in 263-269), see *Deegan (Highton)*, 2019 FC 960, paras. 330-337 (under appeal to FCA).

See Campbell, *Administration of Income Tax 2020* (Carswell), §7.9.2; Ideias, "The Common Reporting Standard in Canada", *Taxnet Pro* Tax Disputes Centre (Aug. 2017, 11pp); Koh, "What is the Common Reporting Standard", 2427 *Tax Topics [TT]* (CCH) 1-4 (Sept. 13, 2018); Tyyebi, "The OECD Releases CRS Anti-Avoidance Rules", 26(9) *Canadian Tax Highlights* (ctf.ca) 2-3 (Sept. 2018); Choudhury, "Common Reporting Standards", 2454 *TT* 1-3 (March 21, 2019); Zagaris, "Transparency and Disclosure", 2019 Cdn Tax Foundation conference report, 8:1-27; "Newest developments on FATCA and CRS compliance" (Aug. 4, 2020), tinyurl.com/BLG-crs-fatca; Ye, "Financial Institutions: Changes to FATCA and CRS Reporting", 10(3) *Canadian Tax Focus* (ctf.ca) 16 (Aug. 2020).

See also Notes to 248(1)"listed international agreement" re the Convention on Mutual Administrative Assistance in Tax Matters.

Part XIX (270-281) added by 2016 budget bill #2, effective July 2017. (281 was not in the draft of April 15, 2016.)

Definitions [s. 281]: "amount", "assessment", "Minister", "person", "regulation" — 248(1); "reportable jurisdiction", "reportable person", "reporting financial institution", "TIN" — 270(1); "written" — *Interpretation Act* 35(1)"writing".

SCHEDULE — LISTED CORPORATIONS

(181(1)"financial institution"(g))

Ally Credit Canada Limited/Ally Crédit Canada Limitée

AmeriCredit Financial Services of Canada Ltd.
AVCO Financial Services Quebec Limited
Bombardier Capital Ltd.
Canaccord Capital Credit Corporation/Corporation de crédit Canaccord capital
Canaccord Financial Holdings Inc./Corporation financière Canaccord Inc.
Canadian Cooperative Agricultural Financial Services
Canadian Home Income Plan Corporation
Citibank Canada Investment Funds Limited
Citicapital Commercial Corporation/Citicapital Corporation Commerciale
Citi Cards Canada Inc./Cartes Citi Canada Inc.
Citi Commerce Solutions of Canada Ltd.
CitiFinancial Canada East Corporation/CitiFinancière, corporation du Canada Est
CitiFinancial Canada, Inc./CitiFinancière Canada, Inc.
Citigroup Finance Canada Inc.
Crédit Industriel Desjardins
CU Credit Inc.
Ford Credit Canada Limited
GMAC Residential Funding of Canada, Limited
Household Commercial Canada Inc.
Household Finance Corporation Limited
Household Finance Corporation of Canada
Household Realty Corporation Limited
Hudson's Bay Company Acceptance Limited
John Deere Credit Inc./Crédit John Deere Inc.
Merchant Retail Services Limited
PACCAR Financial Ltd./Compagnie Financière Paccar Ltée
Paradigm Fund Inc./Le Fonds Paradigm Inc.
Prêts étudiants Atlantique Inc./Atlantic Student Loans Inc.
Principal Fund Incorporated
RT Mortgage-Backed Securities Limited
RT Mortgage-Backed Securities II Limited
State Farm Finance Corporation of Canada/Corporation de Crédit State Farm du Canada
Trans Canada Credit Corporation
Trans Canada Retail Services Company/Société de services de détails trans Canada
Wells Fargo Financial Canada Corporation

Notes: The Schedule was enacted to replace prescribed corps under Reg. 8604. Presumably, since the Act is amended regularly anyway, and amendments to the regulations now require a Regulatory Impact Analysis Statement and a lot of paperwork, it was considered simpler to put the list of corps into the Act.

Schedule added and amended by 2002-2013 technical bill, the last amendment effective 2004 other than Ally Credit Canada Ltd. having been General Motors Acceptance Corp. until Aug. 22, 2010.

DETAILED TABLE OF SECTIONS

INCOME TAX APPLICATION RULES

PART II — TRANSITIONAL CONCERNING THE 1985 STATUTE REVISION

Application of the 1971 Acts and the Revised Acts

Application of Certain Provisions

INCOME TAX APPLICATION RULES

REVISED STATUTES OF CANADA 1985, CHAPTER 2 (5TH SUPPLEMENT), AS AMENDED BY 1994, cc. 7, 21; 1995, cc. 3, 21; 1997, c. 25; 1998, c. 19; 2001, c. 17; 2005, c. 30; 2007, c. 35; 2016, c. 12.

Notes: The ITARs provide transitional rules for the Act introduced in 1972, except for ITAR 69-79, which relate to the RSC 1985 (5th Supp) consolidation in 1994 (see Introduction).

Sections 1 to 6 of 1970-71-72, c. 63 replaced the *Income Tax Act* and amended various other Acts. The *Income Tax Application Rules, 1971* began at section 7. With the consolidation of the Act as R.S.C. 1985, c. 1 (5th Supp.) as of March 1, 1994, the ITARs were re-enacted with the same numbering as before, as R.S.C. 1985, c. 2 (5th Supp.).

7. Short title — This Act may be cited as the *Income Tax Application Rules*.

PART I — INCOME TAX APPLICATION RULES, 1971

Interpretation

8. Definitions — In this Act,

"amended Act" means, according to the context in which that expression appears,

(a) the *Income Tax Act*, chapter 148 of the Revised Statutes of Canada, 1952, as amended by section 1 of chapter 63 of the Statutes of Canada, 1970-71-72, and by any subsequent Act, and

(b) the *Income Tax Act*, as amended from time to time;

"former Act" means the *Income Tax Act*, chapter 148 of the Revised Statutes of Canada, 1952, as it was before being amended by section 1 of chapter 63 of the Statutes of Canada, 1970-71-72.

Notes: ITAR 8"amended Act" was 8(a) and "former Act" was 8(b), before consolidation in RSC 1985 (5th Supp), effective for tax years ending after Nov. 1991.

Definitions [ITAR 8]: "Income Tax Act, chapter 148 of the Revised Statutes of Canada, 1952" — ITAR 69.

Application of 1970-71-72, c. 63, s. 1

9. Application of 1970-71-72, c. 63, s. 1 — Subject to the amended Act and this Act, section 1 of chapter 63 of the Statutes of Canada, 1970-71-72, applies to the 1972 and subsequent taxation years.

Related Provisions: ITAR 65.1 — Part XV of amended Act.

Notes: The referenced section repealed the pre-1972 version of the Act and enacted the version that was in force beginning Jan. 1, 1972.

Definitions [ITAR 9]: "amended Act" — ITAR 8; "taxation year" — ITA 249.

9.1 [Repealed under former Act]

Notes: ITAR 9.1, repealed in 1977, provided an application rule for the pre-1978 Part VIII of the Act.

Application of Part XIII of Amended Act

10. (1)–(3) [Repealed under former Act]

Notes: ITAR 10(1)–(3), repealed in 1985, provided application rules for the non-resident withholding tax for 1972-75.

(4) [No longer relevant]

Notes: See Notes to Reg. 1600.

(5) [Repealed]

Notes: ITAR 10(5) repealed by 2007 budget bill #2, effective 2008. It dealt with certificates of exemption for pre-2008 ITA 212(1)(b).

(6) Limitation on non-resident's tax rate — Notwithstanding any provision of the amended Act, where an agreement or conven-

tion between the Government of Canada and the government of any other country that has the force of law in Canada provides that where an amount is paid or credited, or deemed to be paid or credited, to a resident of that other country the rate of tax imposed thereon shall not exceed a specified rate,

(a) any reference in Part XIII of the amended Act to a rate in excess of the specified rate shall, in respect of such an amount, be read as a reference to the specified rate; and

(b) except where the amount can reasonably be attributed to a business carried on by that person in Canada, that person shall, for the purpose of the agreement or convention in respect of the amount, be deemed not to have a permanent establishment in Canada.

Notes: For "reasonably be attributed", see *729658 Alberta*, 2004 TCC 474.

Definitions [ITAR 10]: "amended Act" — ITAR 8; "amount", "business" — ITA 248(1); "Canada" — ITA 255, *Interpretation Act* 35(1); "former Act" — ITAR 8; "Minister", "non-resident", "person", "prescribed" — ITA 248(1); "resident", "resident in Canada" — ITA 250.

11. [Repealed under former Act]

Notes: ITAR 11 repealed in 1985. 11(1)–(3) reduced the 1972-75 branch tax under ITA Part XIV from 25% to 15%. 11(4) provided that tax treaty provisions reducing the withholding tax on dividends apply to the branch tax. This rule is now in ITA 219.2.

References and Continuation of Provisions

12. Definitions — In this section and sections 13 to 18,

"enactment" has the meaning assigned by section 2 of the *Interpretation Act*;

"new law" — [Not included in R.S.C. 1985]

"old law" means the *Income War Tax Act, The 1948 Income Tax Act*, and the *Income Tax Act*, chapter 148 of the Revised Statutes of Canada, 1952, as amended from time to time otherwise than by section 1 of chapter 63 of the Statutes of Canada, 1970-71-72, or any subsequent Act;

"The 1948 Income Tax Act"; means The *Income Tax Act*, chapter 52 of the Statutes of Canada, 1948, together with all Acts passed in amendment thereof.

Notes: ITAR 12"enactment" was 12(a), "new law" was 12(b), "old law" was 12(c), *The 1948 Income Tax Act* was 12(d), before consolidation in RSC 1985 (5th Supp), effective for tax years ending after Nov. 1991.

Definitions [ITAR 12]: "Canada" — ITA 255, *Interpretation Act* 35(1); "Income Tax Act, chapter 148 of the Revised Statutes of Canada, 1952" — ITAR 69.

13. (1) References relating to same subject-matter — Subject to this Act and unless the context otherwise requires, a reference in any enactment to a particular Part or provision of the amended Act shall be construed, as regards any transaction, matter or thing to which the old law applied, to include a reference to the Part or provision, if any, of the old law relating to, or that may reasonably be regarded as relating to, the same subject-matter.

Definitions [ITAR 13]: "amended Act" — ITAR 8; "enactment", "old law" — ITAR 12.

14. Part IV of former Act — Part IV of the former Act is continued in force but does not apply in respect of gifts made after 1971.

Definitions [ITAR 14]: "former Act" — ITAR 8.

15. Part VIII of former Act — Part VIII of the former Act is continued in force but as though the references in that Part that, according to the context in which they appear, are references to or to provisions of the *Income Tax Act* were read as references to or to provisions of the *Income Tax Act*, chapter 148 of the Revised Statutes of Canada, 1952, as amended from time to time otherwise than by section 1 of chapter 63 of the Statutes of Canada, 1970-71-72, or any subsequent Act.

I.T. Application Rules: 69 (meaning of "chapter 148 of ...").

Definitions [ITAR 15]: "former Act" — ITAR 8; "Income Tax Act, chapter 148 of the Revised Statutes of Canada, 1952" — ITAR 69.

16. Construction of certain references — In any enactment, a reference by number to any provision of the *Income Tax Act* that, according to the context in which the reference appears, is a reference to

(a) a provision of Part IV of the former Act,

(b) a provision of Part VIII of the former Act, or

(c) a provision of the amended Act having the same number as a provision described in paragraph (a) or (b),

shall, for greater certainty, be read as a reference to the provision described in paragraph (a), (b) or (c), as the case may be, and not to any other provision of the *Income Tax Act* or the *Income Tax Act*, chapter 148 of the Revised Statutes of Canada, 1952, having the same number.

Definitions [ITAR 16]: "amended Act" — ITAR 8; "enactment" — ITAR 12; "former Act" — ITAR 8; "Income Tax Act, chapter 148 of the Revised Statutes of Canada, 1952" — ITAR 69.

I.T. Application Rules: 69 (meaning of "chapter 148 of ...").

17. (1) *Income War Tax Act*, s. 8 — A taxpayer may deduct from the tax otherwise payable under Part I of the amended Act for a taxation year such amount as would, if the *Income War Tax Act* applied to the taxation year, be deductible from tax because of subsections 8(6), (7) and (7A) of the *Income War Tax Act*.

(2) S.C. 1947, c. 63, s. 16 — There may be deducted in computing income for a taxation year under Part I of the amended Act an amount that would be deductible under section 16 of chapter 63 of the Statutes of Canada, 1947, from income as defined by the *Income War Tax Act* if that Act applied to the taxation year.

(3) Idem — There may be deducted from the tax for a taxation year otherwise payable under Part I of the amended Act an amount that would be deductible under section 16 of chapter 63 of the Statutes of Canada, 1947, from the total of taxes payable under the *Income War Tax Act* and *The Excess Profits Tax Act, 1940*, if those Acts applied to the taxation year.

(4) Retrospection — Where there is a reference in the amended Act to any act, matter or thing done or existing before a taxation year, it shall be deemed to include a reference to the act, matter or thing, even though it was done or existing before the commencement of that Act.

(5) [Applies to income received before 1972 and taxable in a later year.]

(6) S.C. 1949 (2nd S.), c. 25, s. 53 — There may be deducted in computing income for a taxation year under Part I of the amended Act an amount that would be deductible under section 53 of chapter 25 of the Statutes of Canada, 1949 (Second Session), in computing income under *The 1948 Income Tax Act* if that Act applied to the taxation year.

(7) Idem — There may be deducted from the tax for a taxation year otherwise payable under Part I of the amended Act an amount that would be deductible under section 53 of chapter 25 of the Statutes of Canada, 1949 (Second Session) from the tax payable under Part I of *The 1948 Income Tax Act* if that Act applied to the taxation year.

(8) Registered pension plan — A reference in the amended Act to a registered pension plan shall, in respect of a period while the plan was an approved superannuation or pension fund or plan, be construed as a reference to that approved superannuation or pension fund or plan.

Definitions [ITAR 17]: "amended Act" — ITAR 8; "amount", "business" — ITA 248(1); "Canada" — ITA 255, *Interpretation Act* 35(1); "commencement" — *Interpretation Act* 35(1); "Income Tax Act, chapter 148 of the Revised Statutes of Canada, 1952" — ITAR 69; "property", "registered pension plan" — ITA 248(1); "taxation year" — ITA 249; "taxpayer" — ITA 248(1); "1948 Income Tax Act" — ITAR 12.

18. [CCA for depreciable property acquired before 1972.]

Special Transitional Rules

19. (1) Income maintenance payments — Notwithstanding section 9, paragraph 6(1)(f) of the amended Act does not apply in respect of amounts received by a taxpayer in a taxation year that were payable to the taxpayer in respect of the loss, in consequence of an event occurring before 1974, of all or any part of the taxpayer's income from an office or employment, under a plan, described in that paragraph, that was established before June 19, 1971.

(2) Effect of certain changes made in plan established before June 19, 1971 — For the purposes of this section, a plan described in paragraph 6(1)(f) of the amended Act that was in existence before June 19, 1971 does not cease to be a plan established before that date solely because of changes made therein on or after that date for the purpose of ensuring that the plan qualifies as one entitling the employer of persons covered under the plan to a reduction, as provided for by subsection 50(2) of the *Unemployment Insurance Act*, in the amount of the employer's premium payable under that Act in respect of insured persons covered under the plan.

Notes: Both disability and loss of employment must be before 1974 for ITAR 19 to apply: *Jastrebski*, [1994] 2 C.T.C. 136 (FCA); VIEWS doc 2006-0218401E5.

Interpretation Bulletins: IT-54: Wage loss replacement plans (archived); IT-428: Wage loss replacement plans.

Definitions [ITAR 19]: "amended Act" — ITAR 8; "amount", "employer", "employment", "office", "person" — ITA 248(1); "plan" — ITA 6(1)(f), ITAR 19(2); "taxation year" — ITA 249; "taxpayer" — ITA 248(1).

20. (1) Depreciable property — If the capital cost to a taxpayer of any depreciable property (other than a property that was, at any time, "eligible capital property" as defined in the amended Act at that time) acquired by the taxpayer before 1972 and owned by the taxpayer without interruption from December 31, 1971 until such time after 1971 as the taxpayer disposed of it is less than the fair market value of the property on valuation day and less than the proceeds of disposition thereof otherwise determined,

(a) for the purposes of section 13 of the amended Act, subdivision c of Division B of Part I of that Act and any regulations made under paragraph 20(1)(a) of that Act, the taxpayer's proceeds of disposition of the property shall be deemed to be an amount equal to the total of its capital cost to the taxpayer and the amount, if any, by which the proceeds of disposition thereof otherwise determined exceed the fair market value of the property on valuation day;

(b) where the property has, by one or more transactions or events (other than the death of a taxpayer to which subsection 70(5) of the amended Act applies) between persons not dealing at arm's length, become vested in another taxpayer

(i) for the purposes of the amended Act (other than, where paragraph 13(7)(e) of that Act applies in determining the capital cost to that other taxpayer of the property, for the purposes of paragraphs 8(1)(j) and (p) and sections 13 and 20 of that Act), that other taxpayer shall be deemed to have acquired the property at a capital cost equal to the proceeds deemed to have been received for the property by the person from whom that other taxpayer acquired the property, and

(ii) for the purposes of this subsection, that other taxpayer shall be deemed to have acquired the property before 1972 at a capital cost equal to the capital cost of the property to the taxpayer who actually owned the property at the end of 1971, and to have owned it without interruption from December 31, 1971 until such time after 1971 as that other taxpayer disposed of it; and

(c) where the disposition occurred because of an election under subsection 110.6(19) of the amended Act,

(i) for the purposes of that Act (other than paragraphs 8(1)(j) and (p) and sections 13 and 20 of that Act), the taxpayer is deemed to have reacquired the property at a capital cost equal to

(A) where the amount designated in respect of the property in the election did not exceed 110% of the fair market value of the property at the end of February 22, 1994, the taxpayer's proceeds of disposition determined under paragraph (a) in respect of the disposition of the property that immediately preceded the reacquisition minus the amount, if any, by which the amount designated in respect of the property in the election exceeded that fair market value, and

(B) in any other case, the amount otherwise determined under subsection 110.6(19) of that Act to be the cost to the taxpayer of the property immediately after the reacquisition referred to in that subsection minus the amount by which the fair market value of the property on valuation day exceeded the capital cost of the property at the time it was last acquired before 1972, and

(ii) for the purposes of this subsection, the taxpayer's capital cost of the property after the reacquisition shall be deemed to be equal to the taxpayer's capital cost of the property before the reacquisition and the taxpayer shall be considered to have owned the property without interruption from December 31, 1971 until such time after February 22, 1994 as the taxpayer disposes of it.

Related Provisions: ITAR 20(1.1) — Rollover to spouse, spouse trust or child; ITAR 20(1.2) — Other rollovers; ITA 257 — Formulas cannot calculate to less than zero [rule does not apply explicitly to the ITARs].

Notes: For CRA comments applying ITAR 20 to capital gains and recapture on disposition of property owned since before 1972, see docs 2003-0017065, 2005-0111911E5.

ITAR 20(1) opening words amended to add "(other than ...)" by 2016 budget bill #2, effective 2017, as part of changing the eligible capital property rules to CCA Class 14.1 (see Notes to ITA 20(1)(b)).

ITAR 20(1)(b)(i) amended by 1994 Budget, for property after May 22, 1985. ITAR 20(1)(c) added by 1994 Budget and amended by 1995-97 technical bill, both for 1994 and later tax years.

Income Tax Folios: S3-F4-C1: General discussion of CCA [replaces IT-220R2].

Interpretation Bulletins: IT-209R: *Inter vivos* gifts of capital property to individuals directly or through trusts; IT-217R: Depreciable property owned on December 31, 1971 (archived); IT-268R4: *Inter vivos* transfer of farm property to child; IT-432R2: Benefits conferred on shareholders; IT-488R2: Winding-up of 90%-owned taxable Canadian corporations (archived).

(1.1) Where depreciable property disposed of to spouse, common-law partner, trust or child — Subsection (1) does not apply in any case where

(a) subsection 70(6) or 73(1) of the amended Act applies in respect of the disposition by a taxpayer of any depreciable property of a prescribed class to the spouse, common-law partner, trust or transferee, as the case may be, referred to therein, and

(b) subsection 70(9) of the amended Act applies in respect of the disposition by a taxpayer of any depreciable property of a prescribed class to a child referred to therein,

except that where the spouse, common-law partner, trust, transferee or child, as the case may be, subsequently disposes of the property at any time, subsection (1) applies as if the spouse, common-law partner, trust, transferee or child, as the case may be, had acquired the property before 1972 and owned it without interruption from December 31, 1971 until that time.

Notes: ITAR 20(1.1) amended by 2000 same-sex partners bill to add references to "common-law partner", effective 2001 (or earlier).

Interpretation Bulletins: IT-209R: *Inter vivos* gifts of capital property to individuals directly or through trusts; IT-217R: Depreciable property owned on December 31, 1971 (archived).

(1.11) Extended meaning of "child" — For the purposes of subsection (1.1), "child" of a taxpayer includes

(a) a child of the taxpayer's child;

(b) a child of the taxpayer's child's child; and

(c) a person who, at any time before attaining the age of 21 years, was wholly dependent on the taxpayer for support and of whom the taxpayer had, at that time, in law or in fact, the custody and control.

Related Provisions: ITA 70(10) — Extended meaning of "child".

(1.2) Other transfers of depreciable property — Where, because of a transaction or an event in respect of which any of subsections 70(5), 85(1), (2) and (3), 87(2), section 88, subsections 97(2), 98(3) and (5) and 107(2) of the amended Act applies, a taxpayer has at any particular time after 1971 acquired any depreciable property of a prescribed class from a person who acquired the property before 1972 and owned it without interruption from December 31, 1971 until the particular time, for the purposes of subsection (1) the taxpayer shall be deemed to have acquired the property before 1972 and to have owned it without interruption from December 31, 1971 until such time after 1971 as the taxpayer disposed of it.

Interpretation Bulletins: IT-209R: *Inter vivos* gifts of capital property to individuals directly or through trusts; IT-217R: Depreciable property owned on December 31, 1971 (archived); IT-488R2: Winding-up of 90%-owned taxable Canadian corporation (archived).

(1.3) Transfers before 1972 not at arm's length — Without restricting the generality of section 18, if any depreciable property (other than a property that was, at any time, "eligible capital property" as defined in the amended Act at that time) has been transferred before 1972 in circumstances such that subsection 20(4) of the former Act would, if that provision applied to transfers of property made in the 1972 taxation year, apply, paragraph 69(1)(b) of the amended Act does not apply to the transfer and subsection 20(4) of the former Act applies thereto.

Notes: ITAR 20(1.3) amended to add "(other than ...)" by 2016 budget bill #2, effective 2017, as part of changing the eligible capital property rules to CCA Class 14.1 (see Notes to ITA 20(1)(b)).

(1.4) Depreciable property received as dividend in kind — The capital cost to a taxpayer, as of any particular time after 1971, of any depreciable property (other than depreciable property referred to in subsection (1.3) or deemed by subparagraph (1)(b)(ii) to have been acquired by the taxpayer before 1972 or a property that was, at any time, "eligible capital property" as defined in the amended Act at that time) acquired by the taxpayer before 1972 as, on account of, in lieu of payment of or in satisfaction of, a dividend payable in kind (other than a stock dividend) in respect of a share owned by the taxpayer of the capital stock of a corporation, is deemed to be the fair market value of that property at the time the property was so received.

Notes: ITAR 20(1.4) amended to add "or a property that was ... at that time" by 2016 budget bill #2, effective 2017, as part of changing the eligible capital property rules to CCA Class 14.1 (see Notes to ITA 20(1)(b)).

(2) Recapture of capital cost allowances — In determining a taxpayer's income for a taxation year from farming or fishing, subsection 13(1) of the amended Act does not apply in respect of the disposition by the taxpayer of property (other than a property that was, at any time, "eligible capital property" as defined in the amended Act at that time) acquired by the taxpayer before 1972 unless the taxpayer has elected to make a deduction for that or a preceding taxation year, in respect of the capital cost of property acquired by the taxpayer before 1972, under regulations made under paragraph 20(1)(a) of that Act other than a regulation providing solely for an allowance for computing income from farming or fishing.

Notes: ITAR 20(2) amended to add "(other than ...)" by 2016 budget bill #2, effective 2017, as part of changing the eligible capital property rules to CCA Class 14.1 (see Notes to ITA 20(1)(b)).

(3) Depreciable property of partnership of prescribed class — For the purposes of the amended Act, where a partnership had, on December 31, 1971, partnership property that was depreciable property of a prescribed class,

(a) the capital cost to the partnership of each property of that class shall be deemed to be an amount determined as follows:

(i) determine, for each person who, by reason of having been a member of the partnership on the later of June 18, 1971 and the day the partnership was created, and thereafter without interruption until December 31, 1971, can reasonably be regarded as having had an interest in the property of that class on December 31, 1971, the person's acquisition cost in respect of property of that class,

(ii) determine, for each such person, the amount that is that proportion of the person's acquisition cost in respect of property of that class that 100% is of the person's percentage in respect of property of that class,

(iii) select the amount determined under subparagraph (ii) for a person described therein that is not greater than any amount so determined for any other such person,

(iv) determine that proportion of the amount selected under subparagraph (iii) (in this subsection referred to as the "capital cost of that class") that the fair market value on December 31, 1971 of that property is of the fair market value on that day of all property of that class,

and the amount determined under subparagraph (iv) is the capital cost to the partnership of that property;

(b) for the purposes of sections 13 and 20 of the amended Act and any regulations made under paragraph 20(1)(a) of that Act, the undepreciated capital cost to the partnership of property of that class as of any time after 1971 shall be computed as though the amount, if any, by which the capital cost of that class to the partnership exceeds the undepreciated cost to the partnership of that class had been allowed to the partnership in respect of property of that class under regulations made under paragraph 20(1)(a) of the amended Act in computing income for taxation years before that time;

(c) in computing the income for the 1972 and subsequent taxation years of each person who was a member of the partnership on June 18, 1971 and thereafter without interruption until December 31, 1971, there may be deducted such amount as the person claims for the year, not exceeding the amount, if any, by which the total of

(i) the lesser of

(A) the amount, if any, by which the amount that was the capital cost to the person of all property of that class exceeds the percentage, equal to the person's percentage in respect of property of that class, of the capital cost of that class to the partnership, and

(B) the amount that was the undepreciated capital cost to the person of property of that class as of December 31, 1971, and

(ii) the amount, if any, by which

(A) the undepreciated capital cost to the person of property of that class as of December 31, 1971, less the amount, if any, determined under subparagraph (i) in respect of property of that class,

exceeds

(B) the percentage, equal to the person's percentage in respect of property of that class, of the undepreciated cost to the partnership of property of that class,

exceeds the total of all amounts deducted under this paragraph in computing the person's income for preceding taxation years;

and, for the purposes of section 3 of the amended Act, the amount so claimed shall be deemed to be a deduction permitted by subdivision e of Division B of Part I of that Act; and

(d) notwithstanding paragraph (c), a person who became a member of the partnership after June 18, 1971 and who was a member of the partnership thereafter without interruption until December 31, 1971 shall be deemed to be a person described in paragraph (c) and the amount that may be claimed thereunder as a deduction in computing the person's income for any taxation year shall not exceed 10% of the total of the amounts determined under subparagraphs (c)(i) and (ii).

(4) Definitions — In subsection (3),

"acquisition cost" of a person who was a member of a partnership on December 31, 1971 in respect of depreciable property of a prescribed class that was partnership property of the partnership on December 31, 1971 means the total of the undepreciated capital cost to that person of property of that class as of December 31, 1971 and the total depreciation allowed to the person before 1972 in respect of property of that class;

"percentage" of a member of a partnership in respect of any depreciable property of a prescribed class that was partnership property of the partnership on December 31, 1971 means the interest of the member of the partnership in property of that class, expressed as a percentage of the total of the interests of all members of the partnership in property of that class on that day;

"undepreciated cost to the partnership" of any class of depreciable property means an amount determined as follows:

(a) determine, for each person who, because of having been a member of the partnership on the later of June 18, 1971 and the day the partnership was created, and thereafter without interruption until December 31, 1971, can reasonably be regarded as having had an interest in property of that class on December 31, 1971, the amount, if any, by which the undepreciated capital cost to the person of property of that class as of December 31, 1971 exceeds the amount, if any, determined under subparagraph (3)(c)(i) for the person in respect of property of that class,

(b) determine, for each such person, the amount that is that proportion of the amount determined under paragraph (a) that 100% is of the person's percentage in respect of property of that class, and

(c) select the amount determined under paragraph (b) for a person described therein that is not greater than any amount so determined for any other such person,

and the amount selected under paragraph (c) is the undepreciated cost to the partnership of that class.

Notes: ITAR 20(4) "acquisition cost" was 20(4)(a), "percentage" was 20(4)(b), and "undepreciated cost to the partnership" was 20(4)(c), before consolidation in RSC 1985 (5th Supp), effective for tax years ending after Nov. 1991.

(5) Other depreciable property of partnership — For the purposes of the amended Act, where a partnership had, on December 31, 1971, any particular partnership property that was depreciable property other than depreciable property of a prescribed class,

(a) the cost to the partnership of the particular property shall be deemed to be the amount that would be determined under paragraph (3)(a) to be the capital cost thereof if

(i) the particular property constituted a prescribed class of property, and

(ii) the acquisition cost of each person described therein in respect of the particular property were its actual cost to the person or the amount at which the person was deemed by subsection 20(6) of the former Act to have acquired it, as the case may be;

(b) for the purposes of sections 13 and 20 of the amended Act and any regulations made under paragraph 20(1)(a) of that Act, the undepreciated capital cost of property of any class as of any particular time after 1971 shall be computed as if the amount, if any, by which

(i) the amount determined under paragraph (a) to have been the cost to the partnership of the particular property,

exceeds

(ii) the amount that would be determined under the definition "undepreciated cost to the partnership" in subsection (4) to be the undepreciated cost to the partnership of any class of depreciable property comprising the particular property if

(A) paragraph (a) of that definition were read without reference to the words "the later of June 18, 1971 and the day the partnership was created, and thereafter without interruption until",

(B) the amount determined under subparagraph (3)(c)(i) for any person in respect of that class were nil, and

(C) the undepreciated capital cost to each person described in the definition "acquisition cost" in subsection (4) of the particular property as of December 31, 1971 were the amount, if any, by which the amount assumed by subparagraph (a)(ii) to have been the acquisition cost of the person in respect of the property exceeds the total of all amounts allowed to the person in respect of the property under regulations made under paragraph 11(1)(a) of the former Act in computing income for taxation years ending before 1972,

had been allowed to the partnership in respect of the particular property under regulations made under paragraph 20(1)(a) of the amended Act in computing income for taxation years ending before the particular time; and

(c) in computing the income for the 1972 and subsequent taxation years of each person who was, on December 31, 1971, a member of the partnership, there may be deducted such amount as the person claims for the year, not exceeding the amount, if any, by which

(i) the amount by which

(A) the amount assumed by clause (b)(ii)(C) to have been the undepreciated capital cost to the person of the particular property as of December 31, 1971

exceeds

(B) a percentage of the amount determined under subparagraph (b)(ii) in respect of the particular property, equal to the percentage that would be the person's percentage (within the meaning assigned by subsection (4)) in respect of the particular property if that property constituted a prescribed class,

exceeds

(ii) the total of all amounts deducted under this paragraph in computing the person's income for preceding taxation years;

and for the purposes of section 3 of the amended Act the amount so claimed shall be deemed to be a deduction permitted by subdivision e of Division B of Part I of that Act.

Related Provisions: Reg. 1701(2) — Maximum CCA deduction from farming or fishing business where ITAR 20(5) applies.

Definitions [ITAR 20]: "acquired" — ITAR 20(1)(b)(ii), 20(1.2); "acquisition cost" — ITAR 20(4); "amended Act" — ITAR 8; "amount" — ITA 248(1); "arm's length" — ITA 251(1); "capital cost" — ITAR 20(1)(c)(ii), 20(1.4); "capital cost of that class" — ITAR 20(3)(a)(iv); "child" — ITAR 20(1.11); "common-law partner" — ITA 248(1); "corporation" — ITA 248(1), *Interpretation Act* 35(1); "depreciable property" — ITA 13(21), 248(1); "dividend" — ITA 248(1); "eligible capital property" — ITA 54 [repealed]; "fair market value" — see ITA 69(1) Notes; "farming", "fishing" — ITA 248(1); "former Act" — ITAR 8; "owned" — ITAR 20(1)(b)(ii), 20(1.2); "partnership" — see ITA 96(1) Notes; "percentage" — ITAR 20(4); "person", "prescribed", "property", "regulation", "share", "stock dividend" — ITA 248(1); "taxation year" — ITA 249; "taxpayer" — ITA 104(1), 248(1), (3); "trust" — ITA 104(1), 248(1); "undepreciated capital cost" — ITA 13(21), 248(1); "undepreciated cost to the partnership" — ITAR 20(4); "valuation day" — ITAR 24.

21. (1) Government right — If as a result of a disposition occurring after 1971 a taxpayer has or may become entitled to receive an amount (in this section referred to as the "actual amount") that may reasonably be considered to be consideration received by the taxpayer for the disposition of, or for allowing the expiration of, a government right, in respect of a business carried on by the taxpayer throughout the period beginning January 1, 1972 and ending immediately after the disposition occurred, for the purposes of the amended Act the amount that the taxpayer has or may become entitled to receive is deemed to be the amount, if any, by which the actual amount exceeds the greater of

(a) the total of all amounts each of which is an outlay or expenditure made or incurred by the taxpayer as a result of a transaction that occurred before 1972 for the purpose of acquiring the government right, or the taxpayer's original right in respect of the government right, to the extent that the outlay or expenditure was not otherwise deducted in computing the income of the taxpayer for any taxation year and would, if made or incurred by the taxpayer as a result of a transaction that occurred after 1971, be an eligible capital expenditure of the taxpayer; and

(b) the fair market value to the taxpayer on December 31, 1971 of the taxpayer's specified right in respect of the government right, if no outlay or expenditure was made or incurred by the taxpayer for the purpose of acquiring the right or, if an outlay or expenditure was made or incurred, if that outlay or expenditure would have been an eligible capital expenditure of the taxpayer if it had been made or incurred as a result of a transaction that occurred after 1971.

Related Provisions: ITA 14(1.02) — Election re property acquired with pre-1972 outlays.

Notes: ITAR 21(1) amended by 2016 budget bill #2, effective 2017, as part of changing the eligible capital property rules to CCA Class 14.1 (see Notes to ITA 20(1)(b)).

Opening words of ITAR 21(1) amended by 1988 tax reform, for dispositions after June 17, 1987 otherwise than pursuant to an obligation entered into in writing before that date.

Interpretation Bulletins: IT-268R4: *Inter vivos* transfer of farm property to child; IT-488R2: Winding-up of 90%-owned taxable Canadian corporations (archived). See also list at end of ITAR 21.

(2) Idem — Where the taxpayer and the person by whom the actual amount has become payable to the taxpayer were not dealing with each other at arm's length, for the purposes of computing the income of that person the portion of the actual amount in excess of the amount deemed by subsection (1) to be the amount that has become payable to the taxpayer shall be deemed not to have been an outlay, expense or cost, as the case may be, of that person.

Interpretation Bulletins: IT-268R4: *Inter vivos* transfer of farm property to child. See also list at end of ITAR 21.

(2.1) Idem — Where after 1971 a taxpayer has acquired a particular government right referred to in subsection (1)

(a) from a person with whom the taxpayer was not dealing at arm's length, or

(b) under an agreement with a person with whom the taxpayer was not dealing at arm's length, if under the terms of the agreement that person allowed the right to expire so that the taxpayer could acquire a substantially similar right from the authority that had issued the right to that person,

and an actual amount subsequently becomes payable to the taxpayer as consideration for the disposition by the taxpayer of, or for the taxpayer allowing the expiration of, the particular government right or any other government right acquired by the taxpayer for the purpose of effecting the continuation, without interruption, of rights that are substantially similar to the rights that the taxpayer had under the particular government right, for the purpose of the amended Act, the amount that has so become payable to the taxpayer shall be deemed to be the amount that would, if that person and the taxpayer had at all times been the same person, be determined under subsection (1) to be the amount that would have become so payable to the taxpayer.

Notes: ITAR 21(2.1) closing words amended by 2016 budget bill #2, effective 2017, to change "for the purpose of section 14 of the amended Act" to "for the purpose of the amended Act" (as part of changing the eligible capital property rules to CCA Class 14.1: see Notes to ITA 20(1)(b)).

Interpretation Bulletins: See list at end of ITAR 21.

(2.2) Amalgamations — For the purposes of this section, an amalgamation (within the meaning of section 87 of the amended Act) of two or more Canadian corporations shall be deemed to be a transaction between persons not dealing at arm's length.

(3) Definitions — In this section,

"government right" of a taxpayer means a right or licence

(a) that enables the taxpayer to carry on a business activity in accordance with a law of Canada or of a province or Canadian municipality, to an extent to which the taxpayer would otherwise be unable to carry it on in accordance therewith,

(b) that was granted or issued by Her Majesty in right of Canada or a province or a Canadian municipality, or by a department, board, agency or any other body authorized by or under a law of Canada, a province or a Canadian municipality to grant or issue such a right or licence, and

(c) that was acquired by the taxpayer

(i) as a result of a transaction that occurred before 1972, or

(ii) at a particular time for the purpose of effecting the continuation, without interruption, of rights that are substantially similar to the rights that the taxpayer had under a government right held by the taxpayer before the particular time;

"original right" of a taxpayer in respect of a government right means a right or licence

(a) described in the definition "government right" in this subsection, and

(b) acquired by the taxpayer as a result of a transaction that occurred before 1972 for a purpose other than the purpose described in subparagraph (c)(ii) of that definition,

if the government right was acquired by the taxpayer for the purpose of effecting the continuation, without interruption, of rights that are substantially similar to the rights that the taxpayer had under the right or licence;

"specified right" of a taxpayer in respect of a government right means a right owned by a taxpayer on December 31, 1971 that was

(a) an original right, or

(b) a government right that was acquired by the taxpayer in substitution for the original right or that was one of a series of government rights acquired by the taxpayer for the purpose of effecting the continuation, without interruption, of rights that are substantially similar to the rights that the taxpayer had under the original right.

Notes: ITAR 21(3)"government right" was 21(3)(a), "original right" was 21(3)(b), and "specified right" was 21(3)(c), before consolidation in RSC 1985 (5th Supp), effective for tax years ending after Nov. 1991.

Definitions [ITAR 21]: "actual amount" — ITAR 21(1); "amended Act" — ITAR 8; "amount" — ITA 248(1); "arm's length" — ITAR 21(2.2); "business" — ITA 248(1); "Canada" — ITA 255, *Interpretation Act* 35(1); "Canadian corporation" — ITA 89(1), 248(1); "eligible capital expenditure" — ITA 14(5), 248(1); "fair market value" — see ITA 69(1) Notes; "government right" — ITAR 21(3); "Her Majesty" — *Interpretation Act* 35(1); "original right" — ITAR 21(3); "person" — ITA 248(1); "province" — *Interpretation Act* 35(1); "specified right" — ITAR 21(3); "taxation year" — ITA 249; "taxpayer" — ITA 248(1).

Interpretation Bulletins [ITAR 21]: IT-123R6: Transactions involving eligible capital property; IT-313R2: Eligible capital property — rules where a taxpayer has ceased carrying on a business or has died.

22. [Repealed under former Act]

Notes: ITAR 22, repealed in 1985, dealt with the application of ITA 18(4) to 1972-73.

23. (1), (2) [Repealed under former Act]

Notes: ITAR 23(1) and (2), repealed in 1985, dealt with calculating professional income and work in progress for the 1972 taxation year.

(3) Rules applicable [to professional business] — For the purposes of computing the income of a taxpayer for a taxation year ending after 1971 from a business that is a profession,

(a) there may be deducted such amount as the taxpayer claims, not exceeding the lesser of

(i) the amount deducted under this paragraph in computing the taxpayer's income from the business for the preceding taxation year, and

(ii) the taxpayer's investment interest in the business at the end of the year;

(b) where the taxation year is the taxpayer's 1972 taxation year, the amount deducted under paragraph (a) in computing the taxpayer's income for the preceding taxation year from the business shall be deemed to be an amount equal to the taxpayer's 1971 receivables in respect of the business;

(c) there shall be included the amount deducted under paragraph (a) in computing the taxpayer's income for the preceding taxation year from the business; and

(d) there shall be included amounts received by the taxpayer in the year on account of debts in respect of the business that were established by the taxpayer to have become bad debts before the end of the 1971 fiscal period of the business.

Related Provisions: ITA 34 — Income from a professional business.

Interpretation Bulletins: IT-242R: Retired partners; IT-278R2: Death of a partner or of a retired partner. See also list at end of ITAR 23.

Forms: T2125: Statement of business or professional activities.

(4) Application of para. (3)(a) — Paragraph (3)(a) does not apply to allow a deduction in computing the income of a taxpayer from a business that is a profession

(a) for the taxation year in which the taxpayer died; or

(b) for any taxation year, if,

(i) in the case of a taxpayer who at no time in that year was resident in Canada, the taxpayer ceased to carry on the business, or

(ii) in the case of any other taxpayer, the taxpayer ceased to be resident in Canada and ceased to carry on the business

at any time in that year or the following year.

Interpretation Bulletins: IT-242R: Retired partners; IT-278R2: Death of a partner or of a retired partner. See also list at end of ITAR 23.

(4.1) Certain persons deemed to be carrying on business by means of partnership — For the purposes of paragraph (a) of the definition "investment interest" in subsection (5),

(a) where subsection 98(1) of the amended Act applies, the persons who are deemed not to have ceased to be members of a partnership because of that subsection shall be deemed to be carrying on business in Canada by means of that partnership; and

(b) a taxpayer who has a residual interest in a partnership (within the meaning assigned by section 98.1 of the amended Act) shall be deemed to be carrying on business in Canada by means of that partnership.

(5) Definitions — In this section,

"investment interest" in a business at the end of a taxation year means

(a) in the case of a taxpayer other than a corporation, the total of all amounts each of which is an amount in respect of a proprietorship or partnership by means of which the taxpayer carried on that business in Canada in the year, equal to,

(i) in respect of each such proprietorship, the amount, if any, by which

(A) the total of such of the amounts that were included in computing the taxpayer's income for that or a preceding taxation year as were receivable by the taxpayer at the end of the fiscal period of the proprietorship ending in the taxation year,

exceeds

(B) the amount claimed under paragraph 20(1)(l) of the amended Act as a reserve for doubtful debts in computing the taxpayer's income from the business for the fiscal period of the proprietorship ending in the year, and

(ii) in respect of each such partnership, the adjusted cost base to the taxpayer of the taxpayer's interest in the partnership immediately after the end of the fiscal period of the partnership ending in the year,

(b) in the case of a taxpayer that is a corporation, the lesser of

(i) the amount thereof that would be determined under paragraph (a) in respect of the corporation if that paragraph applied to a taxpayer that is a corporation, and

(ii) that proportion of its 1971 receivables in respect of the business that

(A) the amount, if any, by which 10 exceeds the number of its taxation years ending after 1971 and either before or coincidentally with the taxation year,

is of

(B) 10;

Notes: ITAR 23(5)"investment interest" was 23(5)(a), (b), before consolidation in RSC 1985 (5th Supp) for tax years ending after Nov. 1991.

Interpretation Bulletins: See list at end of ITAR 23.

"1971 receivables" in respect of a business of a taxpayer means the total of

(a) all amounts that became receivable by the taxpayer in respect of property sold or services rendered in the course of the business (within the meaning given that expression in section 34 of the amended Act) in taxation years ending before 1972 and that were not included in computing the taxpayer's income for any such taxation year, other than debts that were established by the taxpayer to have become bad debts before the end of the 1971 fiscal period of the business, and

(b) the total of all amounts each of which is an amount, in respect of each partnership by means of which the taxpayer carried on that business before 1972, equal to such portion of the total that would be determined under paragraph (a) in respect of the partnership, if the references in that paragraph to "the taxpayer" were read as references to "the partnership", as is designated by the taxpayer in the taxpayer's return of income under Part I of the amended Act for the year to be attributable to the taxpayer, except that where the total of the portions so designated by all members of the partnership is less than the total that would be so determined under paragraph (a) in respect of the partnership, the Minister may designate the portion of that total that is attributable to the taxpayer, in which case the portion so designated by the Minister in respect of the taxpayer shall be deemed to be the portion so designated by the taxpayer.

Notes: ITAR 23(5)"1971 receivables" was 23(5)(c), before consolidation in RSC 1985 (5th Supp), effective for taxation years ending after November 1991.

Definitions [ITAR 23]: "1971 receivables" — ITAR 23(5); "adjusted cost base" — ITA 54, 248(1); "amended Act" — ITAR 8; "amount", "business" — ITA 248(1); "Canada" — ITA 255, *Interpretation Act* 35(1); "carried on that business in Canada" — ITA 253, ITAR 23(4.1); "corporation" — ITA 248(1), *Interpretation Act* 35(1); "fiscal period" — ITA 249.1; "investment interest" — ITAR 23(5); "Minister" — ITA 248(1); "partnership" — see ITA 96(1) Notes; "person", "property" — ITA 248(1); "resident in Canada" — ITA 250; "taxation year" — ITA 249; "taxpayer" — ITA 248(1).

Interpretation Bulletins [ITAR 23]: IT-188R: Sale of accounts receivable; IT-189R: Corporations used by practising members of professions; IT-212R3: Income of deceased persons — rights or things.

24. Definition of "valuation day" for capital gains and losses — In this Act, "valuation day" means

(a) December 22, 1971, in relation to any property prescribed to be a publicly-traded share or security; and

(b) December 31, 1971, in relation to any other property.

Regulations: 4400 (prescribed property).

Definitions [ITAR 24]: "prescribed", "property", "share" — ITA 248(1).

25. [Not included in R.S.C. 1985]

Notes: ITAR 25 provided for proclamations of "valuation day" for ITAR 24. Those dates are now enacted directly in ITAR 24.

26. (1) Capital gains subject to tax — The provisions of subdivision c of Division B of Part I of the amended Act apply to dispositions of property made after 1971 and to transactions or events occurring after 1971 because of which any disposition of property was made or deemed to have been made in accordance with the provisions of that subdivision.

(1.1) Principal amount of certain obligations — For the purposes of subsection 39(3) and section 80 of the amended Act, the principal amount of any debt or other obligation of a taxpayer to pay an amount that was outstanding on January 1, 1972 (in this subsection referred to as an "obligation") shall be deemed to be the lesser of

(a) the principal amount, otherwise determined for the purposes of the amended Act, of the obligation, and

(b) the fair market value, on valuation day, of the obligation,

and in applying paragraph 39(3)(a) of the amended Act to an obligation, the reference in that paragraph to "the amount for which the obligation was issued" shall be read as a reference to "the lesser of the principal amount of the obligation and the amount for which the obligation was issued".

Related Provisions: ITAR 26(30) — Disposition by non-resident of taxable Canadian property.

Interpretation Bulletins: IT-293R: Debtor's gain on settlement of debt.

(2) [Repealed under former Act]

Notes: ITAR 26(2), repealed in 1985, applied to ITA s. 41 for 1972-76.

(3) Cost of acquisition of capital property owned on Dec. 31, 1971 — For the purpose of computing the adjusted cost base to a taxpayer of any capital property (other than depreciable property or an interest in a partnership) that was owned by the taxpayer on December 31, 1971 and thereafter without interruption until such time as the taxpayer disposed of it, its cost to the taxpayer shall be deemed to be the amount that is neither the greatest nor the least of the following three amounts, namely:

(a) its actual cost to the taxpayer or, if the property was an obligation, its amortized cost to the taxpayer on January 1, 1972,

(b) its fair market value on valuation day, and

(c) the amount, if any, by which the total of

(i) the taxpayer's proceeds of disposition of the property, determined without reference to subsection 13(21.1) of the amended Act,

(ii) all amounts required by subsection 53(2) of the amended Act to be deducted in computing its adjusted cost base to the taxpayer immediately before the disposition, and

(iii) all amounts described in clause (5)(c)(ii)(B) that are relevant in computing its adjusted cost base to the taxpayer immediately before the disposition,

exceeds the total of

(iv) all amounts required by subsection 53(1) of the amended Act (other than paragraphs 53(1)(f.1) to (f.2)) to be added in computing its adjusted cost base to the taxpayer immediately before the disposition, and

(v) all amounts described in clause (5)(c)(i)(B) that are relevant in computing its adjusted cost base to the taxpayer immediately before the disposition,

except that where two or more of the amounts determined under paragraphs (a) to (c) in respect of any property are the same amount, that amount shall be deemed to be its cost to the taxpayer.

Related Provisions: ITAR 26(7) — Election for cost to be V-day value; ITAR 26(29) — No tax-free zone following election to trigger capital gains exemption; ITAR

26(30) — Disposition by non-resident of taxable Canadian property; ITAR 35(1) — No application to disposition by foreign affiliate for purposes of FAPI.

Notes: ITAR 26(3) provides that the cost of capital property owned since before 1972 is the median value of the actual cost, the V-day value (fair market value at end of 1971 — see Notes to ITA 69(1) for meaning of FMV) and the proceeds of disposition. The effect is to allow any capital gain accruing to the end of 1971 to remain tax-free (capital gains were not taxed at all before 1972). The difference between the original cost and the value on December 31, 1971 is sometimes referred to as the "tax-free zone". See VIEWS docs 2009-031950117; 2011-041053117 (stock dividend is different from stock split for ITAR 26(3) purposes). Note also that the taxpayer can elect under ITAR 26(7) for the V-day value to be used as the deemed cost.

ITAR 26(3)(c)(iv) amended by 1994 technical bill, for tax years that end after Feb. 21, 1994.

Regulations: 4400, Sch. VII (V-day values for publicly-traded shares).

Interpretation Bulletins: IT-65: Stock splits and consolidations; IT-78: Capital property owned on December 31, 1971 — identical properties (archived); IT-84: Capital property owned on December 31, 1971 — median rule (tax-free zone) (archived); IT-93: Capital property owned on December 31, 1971 — meaning of actual cost and amortized cost (archived); IT-107: Costs of disposition of capital property affected by the median rule (archived); IT-130: Capital property owned on December 31, 1971 — actual cost of property owned by a testamentary trust; IT-209R: *Inter vivos* gifts of capital property to individuals directly or through trusts; IT-268R4: *Inter vivos* transfer of farm property to child; IT-319: Cost of obligations owned on December 31, 1971 (archived).

Information Circulars: 72-25R4: Business equity valuations.

Advance Tax Rulings: ATR-35: Partitioning of assets to get specific ownership — "butterfly".

Forms: T1105: Supplementary schedule for dispositions of capital property acquired before 1972.

(4) Determination of cost where property not disposed of — For the purpose of computing the adjusted cost base to a taxpayer of any capital property (other than depreciable property or an interest in a partnership) at any particular time before the taxpayer disposed of it, where the property was owned by the taxpayer on December 31, 1971 and thereafter without interruption until the particular time, its cost to the taxpayer shall be deemed to be the amount that would be determined under subsection (3) to be its cost to the taxpayer if the taxpayer had disposed of it at the particular time and the taxpayer's proceeds of disposition had been its fair market value at that time.

Related Provisions: ITAR 26(7) — Election for cost to be V-day value.

Forms: T1105: Supplementary schedule for dispositions of capital property acquired before 1972.

(5) Where property disposed of in transaction not at arm's length — Where any capital property (other than depreciable property or an interest in a partnership) that was owned by a taxpayer (in this subsection referred to as the "original owner") on June 18, 1971 has, by one or more transactions or events between persons not dealing at arm's length, become vested in another taxpayer (in this subsection referred to as the "subsequent owner") and the original owner has not elected under subsection (7) in respect of the property, notwithstanding the provisions of the amended Act, for the purposes of computing, at any particular time after 1971, the adjusted cost base of the property to the subsequent owner,

(a) the subsequent owner shall be deemed to have owned the property on June 18, 1971 and thereafter without interruption until the particular time;

(b) for the purposes of this section, the actual cost of the property to the subsequent owner or, if the property was an obligation, its amortized cost to him on January 1, 1972 shall be deemed to be the amount that was its actual cost or its amortized cost on January 1, 1972, as the case may be, to the original owner; and

(c) where the property became vested in the subsequent owner after 1971, there shall be added to the cost to the subsequent owner of the property (as determined under subsection (3)) the amount, if any, by which

(i) the total of all amounts each of which is

(A) a capital gain (other than any amount deemed by subsection 40(3) of the amended Act to be a capital gain) from the disposition after 1971 of the property by a per-

son who owned the property before it so became vested in the subsequent owner,

(B) an amount required by subsection 53(1) of the amended Act to be added in computing the adjusted cost base of the property to a person (other than the subsequent owner) described in clause (A),

(C) an amount determined under paragraph 88(1)(d) of the amended Act in computing the cost of the property to the subsequent owner or a person who owned the property before it became vested in the subsequent owner, or

(D) an amount by which a gain otherwise determined of a person who owned the property before it became so vested in the subsequent owner was reduced because of paragraph 40(2)(b) or (c) of the amended Act,

exceeds

(ii) the total of amounts each of which is

(A) a capital loss or an amount that would, but for paragraph 40(2)(e) and subsection 85(4) of the amended Act (as that Act read in its application to property disposed of on or before April 26, 1995) and paragraphs 40(2)(e.1) and (e.2) and subsection 40(3.3) of the amended Act, be a capital loss from the disposition to a corporation after 1971 of the property by a person who owned the property before it became vested in the subsequent owner, or

(B) an amount required by subsection 53(2) of the amended Act to be deducted in computing the adjusted cost base of the property to a person (other than the subsequent owner) described in clause (A),

and there shall be deducted from the cost to the subsequent owner of the property the amount, if any, by which the total determined under subparagraph (ii) exceeds the total determined under subparagraph (i).

Related Provisions: ITAR 26(30) — Disposition by non-resident of taxable Canadian property.

Notes: For interpretation on sale of a farm property see VIEWS doc 2006-0181771E5.

ITAR 26(5)(c)(ii)(A) amended by 1995-97 technical bill (for dispositions after April 26, 1995), 1994 technical bill.

Interpretation Bulletins: IT-132R2: Capital property owned on December 31, 1971 — non-arm's length transactions (archived); IT-199: Identical properties: acquired in non-arm's length transactions (archived); IT-209R: *Inter vivos* gifts of capital property to individuals directly or through trusts; IT-268R4: *Inter vivos* transfer of farm property to child; IT-370: Trusts — capital property owned on December 31, 1971 (archived); IT-432R2: Benefits conferred on shareholders; IT-488R2: Winding-up of 90%-owned taxable Canadian corporations (archived).

Advance Tax Rulings: ATR-35: Partitioning of assets to get specific ownership — "butterfly".

(5.1) Idem — For the purposes of subsection (5), an amalgamation (within the meaning assigned by section 87 of the amended Act) of two or more Canadian corporations shall be deemed to be a transaction between persons not dealing at arm's length.

(5.2) Transfer of capital property to a corporation — For the purposes of subsection (5), where a taxpayer has disposed of capital property after May 6, 1974 to a corporation in respect of which an election under section 85 of the amended Act was made, the disposition shall be deemed to be a transaction between persons not dealing at arm's length.

(6) Reacquired property — Where a taxpayer has, at any time after June 18, 1971 and before 1972, disposed of any property owned by the taxpayer on that day and has, within 30 days after that time, reacquired the same property or acquired a substantially identical property, for the purposes of this section

(a) the taxpayer shall be deemed to have owned the property so reacquired or the substantially identical property so acquired, as the case may be, on June 18, 1971 and thereafter without interruption until the time when the taxpayer so reacquired or acquired it, as the case may be;

(b) where the property was property so reacquired, its actual cost or its amortized cost on January 1, 1972, as the case may be, to the taxpayer shall be determined as if the taxpayer had not so disposed of and so reacquired it; and

(c) where the property was substantially identical property so acquired, its actual cost or its amortized cost on January 1, 1972, as the case may be, to the taxpayer shall be deemed to be the amount that was the actual cost or the amortized cost on January 1, 1972, as the case may be, to the taxpayer of the property so disposed of by the taxpayer.

(7) Election re cost — Where, but for this subsection, the cost to an individual of any property actually owned by the individual on December 31, 1971 would be determined under subsection (3) or (4) otherwise than because of subsection (5) and the individual has so elected, in prescribed manner and not later than the day on or before which the individual is required by Part I of the amended Act to file a return of income for the first taxation year in which the individual disposes of all or any part of the property, other than

(a) personal-use property of the individual that was not listed personal property or real property,

(b) listed personal property, if the individual's gain or loss, as the case may be, from the disposition thereof was, because of subsection 46(1) or (2) of the amended Act, nil,

(c) the individual's principal residence, if the individual's gain from the disposition thereof was, because of paragraph 40(2)(b) of the amended Act, nil,

(d) personal-use property of the individual that was real property (other than the individual's principal residence), if the individual's gain from the disposition thereof was, because of subsection 46(1) or (2) of the amended Act, nil, or

(e) any other property, the proceeds of disposition of which are equal to its fair market value on valuation day,

the cost to the individual of each capital property (other than depreciable property, an interest in a partnership or any property described in any of paragraphs (a) to (e) that was disposed of by the individual before that taxation year) actually owned by the individual on December 31, 1971 shall be deemed to be its fair market value on valuation day.

Regulations: 4700 (prescribed manner).

Interpretation Bulletins: IT-139R: Capital property owned on December 31, 1971 — fair market value (archived).

Forms: T1105: Supplementary schedule for dispositions of capital property acquired before 1972; T2076: Valuation Day value election for capital properties owned on December 31, 1971.

(8) Identical properties — For the purposes of computing, at any particular time after 1971, the adjusted cost base to a taxpayer of any capital property (other than depreciable property or an interest in a partnership) that was owned by the taxpayer on December 31, 1971 and thereafter without interruption until the particular time, if the property was one of a group of identical properties owned by the taxpayer on December 31, 1971,

(a) section 47 of the amended Act does not apply;

(b) where the property was an obligation,

(i) for the purpose of paragraph (3)(a), its amortized cost to the taxpayer on January 1, 1972 shall be deemed to be that proportion of the total of the amortized costs to the taxpayer on January 1, 1972 of all obligations of that group that the principal amount of the obligation is of the total of the principal amounts of all obligations of that group, and

(ii) for the purpose of paragraph (3)(b), its fair market value on valuation day shall be deemed to be that proportion of the fair market value on that day of all obligations of that group that the principal amount of the obligation is of the total of the principal amounts of all obligations of that group;

(c) where the property was not an obligation,

(i) for the purpose of paragraph (3)(a), its actual cost to the taxpayer shall be deemed to be the quotient obtained when the total of the actual costs to the taxpayer of all properties of that group is divided by the number of properties of that group, and

(ii) for the purpose of paragraph (3)(b), its fair market value on valuation day shall be deemed to be the quotient obtained when the fair market value on that day of all properties of that group is divided by the number of properties of that group;

(d) for the purpose of distinguishing any such property from an otherwise identical property acquired and disposed of by the taxpayer before 1972, properties acquired by the taxpayer at any time shall be deemed to have been disposed of by the taxpayer before properties acquired by the taxpayer after that time; and

(e) for the purposes of distinguishing any such property from an otherwise identical property acquired by the taxpayer after 1971, properties owned by the taxpayer on December 31, 1971 shall be deemed to have been disposed of by the taxpayer before properties acquired by the taxpayer at a later time.

Notes: See VIEWS doc 2011-0410531I7 (stock dividend is different from stock split for ITAR 26(8) purposes).

Interpretation Bulletins: IT-78: Capital property owned on December 31, 1971 — identical properties (archived); IT-115R2: Fractional interest in shares; IT-199: Identical properties acquired in non-arm's length transactions (archived); IT-387R2: Meaning of "identical properties".

(8.1) Idem — For the purposes of subsection (8), any property of a life insurance corporation that would, but for this subsection, be identical to any other property of the corporation shall be deemed not to be identical to that other property unless both properties are

(a) included in the same segregated fund of the corporation;

(b) non-segregated property used in the year in, or held in the course of, carrying on a life insurance business in Canada; or

(c) non-segregated property used in the year in, or held in the course of, carrying on an insurance business in Canada, other than a life insurance business.

Interpretation Bulletins: IT-387R2: Meaning of "identical properties".

(8.2) Idem — For the purposes of subsection (8), any bond, debenture, bill, note or other similar obligation issued by a debtor is identical to any other such obligation issued by that debtor if both are identical in respect of all rights (in equity or otherwise, either immediately or in the future and either absolutely or contingently) attaching thereto, except as regards the principal amount thereof.

Interpretation Bulletins: IT-387R2: Meaning of "identical properties".

(8.3) Idem — Where a corporation resident in Canada has, after 1971, received a stock dividend in respect of a share owned on June 18, 1971 and December 31, 1971 by it or by a corporation with which it did not deal at arm's length of the capital stock of a foreign affiliate of that corporation and the share or shares received as the stock dividend are identical to the share in respect of which the stock dividend was received, the share or shares received as the stock dividend may, at the option of the corporation, be deemed for the purposes of subsection (5) to be capital property owned by it on June 18, 1971 and for the purposes of this subsection, paragraph (3)(c) and subsection (8) to be capital property owned by it on June 18, 1971 and December 31, 1971 and not to be property acquired by the corporation after 1971 for the purposes of paragraph (8)(e).

(8.4) Idem — Where a corporation resident in Canada has, after 1971, received a stock dividend in respect of a share acquired by it after June 18, 1971 from a person with whom it was dealing at arm's length and owned by it on December 31, 1971 of the capital stock of a foreign affiliate of that corporation and the share or shares received as the stock dividend are identical to the share in respect of which the stock dividend was received, the share or shares received as the stock dividend may, at the option of the corporation, be deemed for the purposes of this subsection, paragraph

(3)(c) and subsection (8) to be capital property owned by it on December 31, 1971 and not to be property acquired by the corporation after 1971 for the purposes of paragraph (8)(e).

(8.5) Amalgamation — For the purposes of subsections (8.3) and (8.4), where there has been an amalgamation (within the meaning of section 87 of the amended Act), the new corporation shall be deemed to be the same corporation as, and a continuation of, each predecessor corporation.

(9) Cost of interest in partnership — For the purpose of computing, at any particular time after 1971, the adjusted cost base to a taxpayer of an interest in a partnership of which he was a member on December 31, 1971 and thereafter without interruption until the particular time, the cost to the taxpayer of the interest shall be deemed to be the amount that is neither the greatest nor the least of the following three amounts, namely:

(a) its actual cost to the taxpayer as of the particular time,

(b) the amount determined under subsection (9.1) in respect of the interest as of the particular time, and

(c) the amount, if any, by which the total of the fair market value of the interest at the particular time and all amounts required by subsection 53(2) of the amended Act to be deducted in computing its adjusted cost base to the taxpayer immediately before the particular time exceeds the total of all amounts required by subsection 53(1) of the amended Act to be added in computing its adjusted cost base to the taxpayer immediately before the particular time,

except that where two or more of the amounts determined under paragraphs (a) to (c) in respect of the interest are the same amount, that amount shall be deemed to be its cost to the taxpayer.

Forms: T4A-RCA Supp: Statement of distributions from an RCA; T2065: Determination of adjusted cost base of a partnership interest.

(9.1) Determination of amount for purposes of subsec. (9) — For the purposes of subsection (9), the amount determined under this subsection in respect of a taxpayer's interest in a partnership as of a particular time is the amount, if any, by which the total of

(a) the taxpayer's share, determined at the beginning of the first fiscal period of the partnership ending after 1971, of the tax equity of the partnership at the particular time,

(b) such part of any contribution of capital made by the taxpayer to the partnership (otherwise than by way of loan) before 1972 and after the beginning of the partnership's first fiscal period ending after 1971, as cannot reasonably be regarded as a gift made to, or for the benefit of, any other member of the partnership who was related to the taxpayer, and

(c) the amount of any consideration that became payable by the taxpayer after 1971 to any other person to acquire, after 1971, any right in respect of the partnership, the sole purpose of the acquisition of which was to increase the taxpayer's interest in the partnership,

exceeds the total of

(d) all amounts received by the taxpayer before 1972 and after the beginning of the partnership's first fiscal period ending after 1971 as, on account of, in lieu of payment of or in satisfaction of, a distribution of the taxpayer's share of the partnership profits or partnership capital, and

(e) all amounts each of which is an amount in respect of the disposition by the taxpayer after 1971 and before the particular time of a part of the taxpayer's interest in the partnership, equal to such portion of the adjusted cost base to the taxpayer of the interest immediately before the disposition as may reasonably be regarded as attributable to the part so disposed of.

(9.2) Where interest acquired before 1972 and after beginning of 1st fiscal period ending after 1971 — Where a taxpayer has, before 1972 and after the beginning of the first fiscal period of a partnership ending after 1971, acquired an interest in the partnership from another person, subsection (9.1) applies as if, for the purposes of paragraphs (a), (b) and (d) thereof, the taxpayer had had in respect of the interest, throughout the period beginning at the beginning of that fiscal period and ending at the time the taxpayer acquired the interest, the same position in relation to the partnership as the taxpayer would have had in relation thereto if, throughout that period, the taxpayer had been the owner of the interest.

(9.3) Amounts deemed to be required to be deducted in respect of interest in partnership — For the purpose of computing, at any particular time after 1971, the adjusted cost base to a taxpayer of an interest in a partnership of which the taxpayer was a member on December 31, 1971 and thereafter without interruption until the particular time, the lesser of

(a) the amount, if any, by which

(i) the total of all amounts in respect of the interest determined under paragraph (9.1)(d)

exceeds

(ii) the total of

(A) the taxpayer's share, determined at the beginning of the first fiscal period of the partnership ending after 1971, of the tax equity of the partnership at the particular time, and

(B) the amount in respect of the interest determined under paragraph (9.1)(b), and

(b) the amount, if any, by which

(i) the total of all amounts in respect of the interest determined as of the particular time under paragraphs (14)(e) to (g)

exceeds

(ii) the total of all amounts in respect of the interest determined as of the particular time under paragraphs (14)(a) to (d),

shall be deemed to be required by subsection 53(2) of the amended Act to be deducted.

(9.4) Application of section 53 of amended Act in respect of interest in partnership — For the purpose of computing, at any particular time after 1971, the adjusted cost base to a taxpayer of an interest in a partnership of which the taxpayer was a member on December 31, 1971 and thereafter without interruption until the particular time,

(a) the reference in clause 53(1)(e)(i)(B) of the amended Act to "relating to" shall be read as a reference to "relating to section 14 or to"; and

(b) clause 53(2)(c)(i)(B) of the amended Act shall be read as follows:

"(B) paragraphs 12(1)(o) and (z.5), 18(1)(m) and 20(1)(v.1), section 31, subsection 40(2), section 55 and subsections 69(6) and (7) of this Act, paragraphs 20(1)(gg) and 81(1)(r) and (s) of the *Income Tax Act*, chapter 148 of the Revised Statutes of Canada, 1952, and the provisions of the *Income Tax Application Rules* relating to section 14, and"

Notes: ITAR 26(9.4)(b) amended to add reference to ITA 12(1)(z.5) by 1996 Budget, for computing the adjusted cost base of property after 1996.

(10) Where paragraph 128.1(1)(b) applies — Where subsection 48(3) of the amended Act, as it read in its application before 1993, or paragraph 128.1(1)(b) of the amended Act applies for the purpose of determining the cost to a taxpayer of any property, this section does not apply for that purpose.

Notes: ITAR 26(10) amended by 1993 technical bill to add reference to ITA 128.1(1)(b), effective 1993. Where a corp continued before 1993 elects for ITA 250(5.1) to apply earlier (see Notes to ITA 250(5.1)), the amendment is effective from the corp's "time of continuation".

(11) Fair market value of publicly-traded securities — For the purposes of this section, the fair market value on valuation day of any property prescribed to be a publicly-traded share or security shall be deemed to be the greater of the amount, if any, prescribed in respect of that property and the fair market value of that property, otherwise determined, on valuation day.

Regulations: 4400 (prescribed property); Sch. VII (list of fair market values of publicly-traded securities).

Interpretation Bulletins: IT-84: Capital property owned on December 31, 1971 — Median rule (Tax-free zone) (archived).

Information Circulars: 72-25R4: Business equity valuations.

(11.1) Fair market value of share of foreign affiliate — For the purposes of computing the fair market value

(a) on December 31, 1971, or

(b) at any subsequent time for the purposes of subsection (4),

of any shares owned by a taxpayer resident in Canada of the capital stock of a foreign affiliate of the taxpayer, the fair market value at that time of any asset owned by the foreign affiliate at that time

(c) that was subsequently acquired by the taxpayer from the foreign affiliate

(i) as a dividend payable in kind,

(ii) as a benefit the amount of which was deemed by paragraph 80.1(4)(b) of the amended Act to have been received by the taxpayer as a dividend from the foreign affiliate, or

(iii) as consideration for the settlement or extinguishment of an obligation described in subsection 80.1(5) of the amended Act, and

(d) in respect of which subsection 80.1(4) or (5), as the case may be, of the amended Act applies because of an election described in that subsection made by the taxpayer,

shall be deemed to be the principal amount of that asset.

(11.2) Idem — For the purposes of computing the fair market value on December 31, 1971 of any shares owned by a taxpayer resident in Canada of the capital stock of a foreign affiliate of the taxpayer, the fair market value on that day of any asset owned by the foreign affiliate on that day

(a) that was subsequently acquired by the taxpayer from the foreign affiliate as described in paragraph 80.1(6)(a) or (b) of the amended Act, and

(b) in respect of which subsection 80.1(1) of the amended Act applies because of an election described in subsection 80.1(6) of that Act made by the taxpayer,

shall be deemed to be the principal amount of that asset.

(12) Definitions — In this section,

"amortized cost" to a taxpayer of any obligation on January 1, 1972 means

(a) the principal amount of the obligation, if its actual cost to the taxpayer was less than 100% but not less than 95% of that principal amount and the obligation was issued before November 8, 1969,

(b) the actual cost to the taxpayer of the obligation, if the actual cost to the taxpayer thereof was less than 105% but not less than 100% of the principal amount thereof, and

(c) in any other case, the actual cost to the taxpayer of the obligation, plus that proportion of the discount or minus that proportion of the premium, as the case may be, in respect thereof that

(i) the number of full months in the period commencing with the day the taxpayer last acquired the obligation and ending with valuation day,

is of

(ii) the number of full months in the period commencing with the day the taxpayer last acquired the obligation and ending with the date of its maturity;

Notes: ITAR 26(12)"amortized cost" was 26(12)(a) before consolidation in RSC 1985 (5th Supp), effective for taxation years ending after November 1991.

Interpretation Bulletins: IT-319: Cost of obligations owned on December 31, 1971 (archived).

"capital property" of a taxpayer means any depreciable property of the taxpayer, and any property (other than depreciable property) any gain or loss from the disposition of which would, if the property were disposed of after 1971, be a capital gain or a capital loss, as the case may be, of the taxpayer;

Notes: ITAR 26(12)"capital property" was 26(12)(b) before consolidation in RSC 1985 (5th Supp), effective for taxation years ending after November 1991.

"discount" in respect of any obligation owned by a taxpayer means the amount, if any, by which the principal amount thereof exceeds its actual cost to the taxpayer determined without reference to subsection (3);

Notes: ITAR 26(12)"discount" was 26(12)(c) before consolidation in RSC 1985 (5th Supp), effective for taxation years ending after November 1991.

"eligible capital property" of a taxpayer means any property, ½ of any amount payable to the taxpayer as consideration for the disposition of which would, if the property were disposed of after 1971, be an eligible capital amount in respect of a business within the meaning assigned by subsection 14(1) of the amended Act;

Notes: ITAR 26(12)"eligible capital property" was 26(12)(d) before consolidation in RSC 1985 (5th Supp) for tax years ending after Nov. 1991.

"obligation" means a bond, debenture, bill, note, mortgage, hypothecary claim or agreement of sale;

Notes: Reference to "hypothecary claim" added by 2001 *Civil Code* harmonization bill, effective June 14, 2001. The change is non-substantive; see *Interpretation Act* s. 8.2. See also Notes to ITA 20(1)(f).

ITAR 26(12)"obligation" was 26(12)(e) before consolidation in RSC 1985 (5th Supp) for taxation years ending after November 1991.

"premium" in respect of any obligation owned by a taxpayer means the amount, if any, by which its actual cost to the taxpayer determined without reference to subsection (3) exceeds the principal amount thereof;

Notes: ITAR 26(12)"premium" was 26(12)(f) before consolidation in RSC 1985 (5th Supp), effective for taxation years ending after November 1991.

"tax equity" of a partnership at any particular time means the amount, if any, by which the total of amounts each of which is

(a) the amount of any money of the partnership on hand at the beginning of its first fiscal period ending after 1971,

(b) the cost amount to the partnership, at the beginning of that fiscal period, of any partnership property other than capital property or eligible capital property,

(c) an amount in respect of any property (other than depreciable property) that was, at the beginning of that fiscal period, capital property of the partnership, equal to,

(i) where the property was disposed of before 1972, the proceeds of disposition thereof,

(ii) where the property was disposed of after 1971 and before the particular time, the amount determined under this section to be its cost to the partnership for the purposes of computing its adjusted cost base to the partnership immediately before it was disposed of, and

(iii) in any other case, the amount determined under this section to be its cost to the partnership for the purposes of computing its adjusted cost base to the partnership immediately before the particular time,

(d) an amount in respect of any prescribed class of depreciable property of the partnership, equal to the amount, if any, by which the total of the undepreciated capital cost to the partnership of property of that class as of January 1, 1972 exceeds the capital cost to the partnership of property of that class acquired by it after the beginning of that fiscal period and before 1972,

(e) an amount in respect of any other depreciable property of the partnership at the beginning of that fiscal period, equal to the amount by which

(i) the actual cost of the property to the partnership, or the amount at which the partnership was deemed to have acquired the property under subsection 20(6) of the Act as it read in its application to the 1971 taxation year, as the case may be,

exceeds

(ii) the total of all amounts in respect of the cost of the property that were allowed under paragraph 11(1)(a) of the Act as it read in computing the income from the partnership of the members thereof for taxation years ending before 1972,

(f) an amount in respect of any property that was, at the beginning of that fiscal period, partnership property that was depreciable property, equal to

(i) where the property was disposed of before 1972, the proceeds of disposition thereof minus the amount, if any, by which the lesser of

(A) the proceeds of disposition thereof, and

(B) the capital cost of the property,

exceeds

(C) in respect of depreciable property of a prescribed class, the undepreciated capital cost of all of the property of that class at the time of the disposition, or

(D) in respect of any other depreciable property, the amount that would be determined under paragraph (e) if the words "at the beginning of that fiscal period" were read as "at the time of the disposition",

(ii) where the property was disposed of after 1971 and before the particular time, the amount, if any, by which the lesser of

(A) the proceeds of disposition thereof, and

(B) the fair market value of the property on valuation day,

exceeds the capital cost to the partnership of the property, and

(iii) in any other case, the amount, if any, by which

(A) the lesser of the fair market value of the property on valuation day and its fair market value at the particular time

exceeds

(B) the capital cost to the partnership of the property, or

(g) an amount in respect of any business carried on by the partnership in its 1971 fiscal period and thereafter without interruption until the particular time, equal to the amount, if any, by which

(i) 2 times the eligible capital amounts (within the meaning assigned by section 14 of the amended Act) in respect of the business (computed without reference to section 21 of this Act) that would have become payable to the partnership

would exceed

(ii) the amount that would be deemed by subsection 21(1) to be the amount that had become payable to the partnership

if the partnership had disposed of the business at the particular time for an amount equal to its fair market value at that time,

exceeds the total of all amounts each of which is the amount of any debt owing by the partnership, or any other obligation of the partnership to pay an amount, that was outstanding at the beginning of the partnership's first fiscal period ending after 1971, minus such part, if any, thereof as would, if the amount had been paid by the partnership in that fiscal period, have been deductible in computing its income for that fiscal period.

Notes: ITAR 26(12)"tax equity" was 26(12)(g) before consolidation in RSC 1985 (5th Supp) for taxation years ending after November 1991.

(13) Meaning of "actual cost" — For the purposes of this section, the "actual cost" to a person of any property means, except as expressly otherwise provided in this section, the amount, if any, by which

(a) its cost to the person computed without regard to the provisions of this section

exceeds

(b) such part of that cost as was deductible in computing the person's income for any taxation year ending before 1972.

Interpretation Bulletins: IT-93: Capital property owned on December 31, 1971 — meaning of actual cost and amortized cost (archived).

(14) Idem — For the purposes of this section, the "actual cost" to a taxpayer, as of any particular time after 1971, of an interest in a partnership of which the taxpayer was a member on December 31, 1971 and thereafter without interruption until the particular time means the amount, if any, by which the total of

(a) the cost to the taxpayer of the interest, computed as of the particular time without regard to the provisions of this section,

(b) the total of all amounts each of which is an amount in respect of a fiscal period of the partnership that ended before 1972, equal to the total of

(i) the amount that the taxpayer's income from the partnership for the taxation year of the taxpayer in which the period ended would have been, if the former Act had been read without reference to subsection 83(5) of that Act, and

(ii) the taxpayer's share, determined at the end of the period, of all profits made from dispositions in the period of capital assets that were partnership property of the partnership, to the extent that those profits were not included in computing the income or loss, as the case may be, from the partnership, of any member thereof,

(c) where the taxpayer had, before 1972, made a contribution of capital to the partnership otherwise than by way of loan, such part of the contribution as cannot reasonably be regarded as a gift made to, or for the benefit of, any other member of the partnership who was related to the taxpayer, and

(d) where, by means of the partnership, the taxpayer carried on before 1972 a business that was a profession, the amount that the taxpayer's 1971 receivables (within the meaning assigned by subsection 23(5)) in respect of the business would have been if, before 1972, the taxpayer had carried on no businesses except by means of the partnership,

exceeds the total of

(e) all amounts each of which is an amount in respect of the disposition by the taxpayer before the particular time of a part of the taxpayer's interest in the partnership, equal to such portion of,

(i) where the disposition was made before 1972, the actual cost to the taxpayer of the interest, and

(ii) in any other case, the adjusted cost base to the taxpayer of the interest immediately before the disposition,

as can reasonably be regarded as attributable to the part so disposed of,

(f) all amounts each of which is an amount in respect of a fiscal period of the partnership that ended before 1972, equal to the total of

(i) the amount that would have been the taxpayer's loss from the partnership for the taxation year of the taxpayer in which the period ended if the former Act had been read without reference to subsection 83(5) of that Act,

(ii) the taxpayers' share, determined at the end of the period, of all losses sustained from dispositions in the period of capital assets that were partnership property of the partnership, to the extent that those losses were not included in computing the loss or income, as the case may be, from the partnership, of any member thereof, and

(iii) the taxpayer's share, determined at the end of the period, of such of the drilling and exploration expenses, including all general geological and geophysical expenses incurred by the partnership while the taxpayer was a member thereof, on or in respect of exploring or drilling for petroleum or natural gas in Canada as were incurred in the period and after 1948, to the extent that those expenses were not deducted in computing the taxpayer's income from the partnership for the taxpayer's 1971 or any preceding taxation year, and

(g) all amounts received by the taxpayer before 1972 as, on account of, in lieu of payment of or in satisfaction of, a distribution of the taxpayer's share of the partnership profits or partnership capital.

(15) Idem — For the purposes of this section and subsection 88(2.1) of the amended Act, the "actual cost" to a taxpayer, as of any particular time after 1971, of any shares (in this subsection referred to as "new shares") of any class of the capital stock of a new corporation formed as a result of an amalgamation of two or more corporations (within the meaning of section 85I of the former Act as it read in its application to the 1971 taxation year) that were

(a) owned by the taxpayer on December 31, 1971, and thereafter without interruption until the particular time, and

(b) acquired by the taxpayer by the conversion, because of the amalgamation, of shares of the capital stock of a predecessor corporation into shares of the capital stock of the new corporation,

means that proportion of the actual cost to the taxpayer of any shares owned by the taxpayer that were so converted because of the amalgamation that the fair market value, immediately after the amalgamation, of the new shares of that class so acquired by the taxpayer is of the fair market value, immediately after the amalgamation, of all of the shares of the capital stock of the new corporation so acquired by the taxpayer.

(16) Idem — For the purposes of this section, the "actual cost" to an individual, as of any particular time after 1971, of any share of the capital stock of a corporation that was

(a) owned by the individual on December 31, 1971 and thereafter without interruption until the particular time, and

(b) acquired by the individual in a taxation year before 1972 under an agreement referred to in subsection 85A(1) of the former Act as it read in its application to that taxation year,

means an amount equal to the greater of

(c) the actual cost to the individual of the share computed without regard to this subsection, and

(d) the fair market value of the share at the time the individual so acquired it.

(17) Idem — For the purposes of this section and subsection 88(2.1) of the amended Act, the "actual cost" to a taxpayer, as of any particular time after 1971, of any capital property received by the taxpayer before 1972 and owned by the taxpayer thereafter without interruption until the particular time means,

(a) where the property was so received as, on account of, in lieu of payment of or in satisfaction of, a dividend payable in kind (other than a stock dividend) in respect of a share owned by the taxpayer of the capital stock of a corporation, the fair market value of that property at the time the property was so received;

(b) where the property so received was a share of the capital stock of a corporation received by the taxpayer as a stock dividend, the amount that, because of the receipt of the share, was deemed by subsection 81(3) of the former Act to have been received by the taxpayer as a dividend; and

(c) where the property was so received from a pension fund or plan, an employees profit sharing plan, a retirement savings plan, a deferred profit sharing plan or a supplementary unemployment benefit plan, the fair market value of that property at the time the property was so received.

(17.1) Application — Where a taxpayer is deemed to have acquired a property because of subsection 138(11.3) of the amended Act, this section does not apply in respect of any subsequent disposition or deemed disposition of the property.

Interpretation Bulletins: IT-88R2: Stock dividends.

(18) Transfer of farm land by a farmer to [the farmer's] child at death — Where

(a) a taxpayer owned, on December 31, 1971 and thereafter without interruption until the taxpayer's death, any land referred to in subsection 70(9) of the amended Act,

(b) the land has, on or after the death of the taxpayer and as a consequence thereof, been transferred or distributed to a child of the taxpayer who was resident in Canada immediately before the death of the taxpayer, and

(c) it can be shown, within the period ending 36 months after the death of the taxpayer or, where written application therefor has been made to the Minister by the legal representative of the taxpayer within that period, within such longer period as the Minister considers reasonable in the circumstances, that the land has become vested indefeasibly in the child,

the following rules apply:

(d) paragraph 70(9)(b) of the amended Act does not apply for the purpose of determining the cost to the child of the land or part thereof, as the case may be, and

(e) subsection (5) applies in respect of the transfer or distribution of the land to the child as if the references in that subsection to "June 18, 1971" were references to "December 31, 1971".

Related Provisions: ITAR 26(20) — Extended meaning of "child".

Interpretation Bulletins: IT-349R3: Intergenerational transfers of farm property on death; IT-449R: Meaning of "vested indefeasibly" (archived).

(19) Inter vivos transfer of farm land by a farmer to child — Where a taxpayer owned, on December 31, 1971, and thereafter without interruption until a transfer thereof by the taxpayer to the taxpayer's child, in circumstances to which subsection 73(3) of the amended Act applies, land referred to in that subsection,

(a) paragraph 73(3)(d) of the amended Act does not apply for the purpose of determining the cost to the child of the land; and

(b) subsection (5) shall apply in respect of the transfer of the land to the child as if the references in that subsection to "June 18, 1971" were references to "December 31, 1971".

Related Provisions: ITAR 26(20) — Extended meaning of "child".

Interpretation Bulletins: IT-268R4: Inter vivos transfer of farm property to child.

(20) Extended meaning of "child" — For the purposes of subsections (18) and (19), "child" of a taxpayer includes

(a) a child of the taxpayer's child;

(b) a child of the taxpayer's child's child; and

(c) a person who, at any time before attaining the age of 21 years, was wholly dependent on the taxpayer for support and of whom the taxpayer had, at that time, in law or in fact, the custody and control.

Related Provisions: ITA 70(10) — Extended meaning of "child".

(21) Shares received on amalgamation — Where, after May 6, 1974, there has been an amalgamation (within the meaning assigned by section 87 of the amended Act) of two or more corporations (each of which is in this subsection referred to as a "predecessor corporation") to form one corporate entity (in this subsection referred to as the "new corporation"), and

(a) any shareholder (except any predecessor corporation) owned shares of the capital stock of a predecessor corporation on December 31, 1971 and thereafter without interruption until immediately before the amalgamation,

(b) any shares referred to in paragraph (a) were shares of one class of the capital stock of a predecessor corporation (in this subsection referred to as the "old shares"),

(c) no consideration was received by the shareholder for the disposition of the old shares on the amalgamation other than shares of one class of the capital stock of the new corporation (in this subsection referred to as the "new shares"), and

(c.1) the cost of the new shares received by the shareholder because of the amalgamation was determined otherwise than because of paragraph 87(4)(e) of the amended Act,

notwithstanding any other provision of this Act or of the amended Act, for the purposes of subsection 88(2.1) of the amended Act and of determining the cost to the taxpayer and the adjusted cost base to the taxpayer of the new shares,

(d) the property that was the old shares shall be deemed not to have been disposed of by the shareholder because of the amalgamation but to have been altered, in form only, because of the amalgamation and to have continued in existence in the form of the new shares, and

(e) the property that is the new shares shall be deemed not to have been acquired by the shareholder because of the amalgamation but to have been in existence prior thereto in the form of the old shares that were altered, in form only, because of the amalgamation.

Related Provisions: ITAR 26(30) — Disposition of TCP by non-resident.

(22) Options received on amalgamations — Where, after May 6, 1974, there has been an amalgamation (within the meaning assigned by section 87 of the amended Act) of two or more corporations (each of which is in this subsection referred to as a "predecessor corporation") to form one corporate entity (in this subsection referred to as the "new corporation") and a taxpayer has acquired an option to acquire capital property that was shares of the capital stock of the new corporation (in this subsection referred to as the "new option") as sole consideration for the disposition on the amalgamation of an option to acquire shares of the capital stock of a predecessor corporation (in this subsection referred to as the "old option") owned by the taxpayer on December 31, 1971 and thereafter without interruption until immediately before the amalgamation, notwithstanding any other provision of this Act or of the amended Act, for the purposes of subsection 88(2.1) of the amended Act and of determining the cost to the taxpayer and the adjusted cost base to the taxpayer of the new option,

(a) the property that was the old option shall be deemed not to have been disposed of by the taxpayer because of the amalgamation but to have been altered, in form only, because of the amalgamation and to have continued in existence in the form of the new option; and

(b) the property that is the new option shall be deemed not to have been acquired by the taxpayer because of the amalgamation but to have been in existence prior thereto in the form of the old option that was altered, in form only, because of the amalgamation.

(23) Obligations received on amalgamations — Where, after May 6, 1974, there has been an amalgamation (within the meaning assigned by section 87 of the amended Act) of two or more corporations (each of which is in this subsection referred to as a "predecessor corporation") to form one corporate entity (in this subsection referred to as the "new corporation") and a taxpayer has acquired a capital property that was a bond, debenture, note, mortgage, hypothecary claim or other similar obligation of the new corporation (in this subsection referred to as the "new obligation") as sole consideration for the disposition on the amalgamation of a bond, debenture, note, mortgage, hypothecary claim or other similar obligation respectively of a predecessor corporation (in this subsection referred to as the "old obligation") owned by the taxpayer on December 31, 1971 and thereafter without interruption until immediately before the amalgamation, notwithstanding any other provision of this Act or of the amended Act, for the purposes of subsection 88(2.1) of the amended Act and of determining the cost to the tax-

payer and the adjusted cost base to the taxpayer of the new obligation,

(a) the property that was the old obligation shall be deemed not to have been disposed of by the taxpayer because of the amalgamation but to have been altered, in form only, because of the amalgamation and to have continued in existence in the form of the new obligation; and

(b) the property that is the new obligation shall be deemed not to have been acquired by the taxpayer because of the amalgamation but to have been in existence prior thereto in the form of the old obligation that was altered, in form only, because of the amalgamation.

Notes: ITAR 26(23) opening words amended by 2001 *Civil Code* harmonization bill.

(24) Convertible properties — Where there has been an exchange to which subsection 51(1) of the amended Act applies on which a taxpayer has acquired shares of one class of the capital stock of a corporation (in this subsection referred to as the "new shares") in exchange for a share, bond, debenture or note of the corporation (in this subsection referred to as the "old property") owned by the taxpayer on December 31, 1971 and thereafter without interruption until immediately before the time of the exchange, notwithstanding any other provision of this Act or of the amended Act, for the purposes of subsection 88(2.1) of the amended Act and, where the exchange occurred after May 6, 1974, for the purposes of determining the cost to the taxpayer and the adjusted cost base to the taxpayer of the new shares,

(a) the property that was the old property shall be deemed not to have been disposed of by the taxpayer because of the exchange but to have been altered, in form only, because of the exchange and to have continued in existence in the form of the new shares; and

(b) the property that is the new shares shall be deemed not to have been acquired by the taxpayer because of the exchange but to have been in existence prior thereto in the form of the old property that was altered, in form only, because of the exchange.

Interpretation Bulletins: IT-146R3: Shares entitling shareholders to choose taxable or other kinds of dividends.

(25) Bond conversion — Where, after May 6, 1974, there has been an exchange to which section 51.1 of the amended Act applies on which a taxpayer has acquired a bond of a debtor (in this subsection referred to as the "new bond") in exchange for another bond of the same debtor (in this subsection referred to as the "old bond") owned by the taxpayer on December 31, 1971 and thereafter without interruption until immediately before the exchange, notwithstanding any other provision of this Act or of the amended Act, for the purposes of subsection 88(2.1) of the amended Act and of determining the cost to the taxpayer and the adjusted cost base to the taxpayer of the new bond,

(a) the property that was the old bond shall be deemed not to have been disposed of by the taxpayer because of the exchange but to have been altered, in form only, because of the exchange and to have continued in existence in the form of the new bond; and

(b) the property that is the new bond shall be deemed not to have been acquired by the taxpayer because of the exchange but to have been in existence prior thereto in the form of the old bond that was altered, in form only, because of the exchange.

Notes: ITAR 26(25) amended by 1995-97 technical bill, effective for exchanges after October 1994, to change reference from ITA 77 to ITA 51.1.

(26) Share for share exchange — Where, after May 6, 1974, there has been an exchange to which subsection 85.1(1) of the amended Act applies on which a taxpayer has acquired shares of any particular class of the capital stock of a corporation (in this subsection referred to as the "new shares") in exchange for shares of any particular class of the capital stock of another corporation (in this subsection referred to as the "old shares") owned by the taxpayer on December 31, 1971 and thereafter without interruption until immediately before the exchange, notwithstanding any other provision of this Act or of the amended Act, for the purposes of subsection 88(2.1) of the amended Act and of determining the cost to the taxpayer and the adjusted cost base to the taxpayer of the new shares,

(a) the property that was the old shares shall be deemed not to have been disposed of by the taxpayer because of the exchange but to have been altered, in form only, because of the exchange and to have continued in existence in the form of the new shares; and

(b) the property that is the new shares shall be deemed not to have been acquired by the taxpayer because of the exchange but to have been in existence prior thereto in the form of the old shares that were altered, in form only, because of the exchange.

Income Tax Folios: S4-F5-C1: Share for share exchange [replaces IT-450R].

(27) Reorganization of capital — Where, after May 6, 1974, there has been a reorganization of the capital of a corporation to which section 86 of the amended Act applies on which a taxpayer has acquired shares of a particular class of the capital stock of the corporation (in this subsection referred to as the "new shares") as the sole consideration for the disposition on the reorganization of shares of another class of the capital stock of the corporation (in this subsection referred to as the "old shares") owned by the taxpayer on December 31, 1971 and thereafter without interruption until immediately before the reorganization and the cost to the taxpayer of the new shares was determined otherwise than because of subsection 86(2) of the amended Act, notwithstanding any other provision of this Act or of the amended Act, for the purposes of subsection 88(2.1) of the amended Act and of determining the cost to the taxpayer and the adjusted cost base to the taxpayer of the new shares,

(a) the property that was the old shares shall be deemed not to have been disposed of by the taxpayer because of the reorganization but to have been altered, in form only, because of the reorganization and to have continued in existence in the form of the new shares; and

(b) the property that is the new shares shall be deemed not to have been acquired by the taxpayer by virtue of the reorganization but to have been in existence prior thereto in the form of the old shares that were altered, in form only, because of the reorganization.

Advance Tax Rulings: ATR-22R: Estate freeze using share exchange.

(28) Idem — Where a taxpayer acquired a property (in this subsection referred to as the "first property") in circumstances to which any of subsections (5) and (21) to (27) applied and subsequently acquires, in exchange for or in consideration for the disposition of the first property, another property in circumstances to which any of subsections (21) to (27) would apply if the taxpayer had owned the first property on December 31, 1971 and thereafter without interruption until the time of the subsequent acquisition, for the purposes of applying subsections (21) to (27) in respect of that subsequent acquisition, the taxpayer shall be deemed to have owned the first property on December 31, 1971 and thereafter without interruption until the time of the subsequent acquisition.

Notes: ITAR 26(28) added by 1991 technical bill, for acquisitions after July 13, 1990 (or earlier by election). It preserves the tax-free zone and pre-1972 capital surplus on hand on successive applications of ITAR 26(21)-(27) due to more than 1 reorganization.

Income Tax Folios: S4-F5-C1: Share for share exchange [replaces IT-450R].

(29) Effect of election under subsection 110.6(19) — Where subsection 110.6(19) of the amended Act applies to a particular property, for the purposes of determining the cost and the adjusted cost base to a taxpayer of any property at any time after February 22, 1994, the particular property shall be deemed not to have been owned by any taxpayer on December 31, 1971.

Notes: ITAR 26(29) added by 1994 Budget, effective March 26, 1995 (Royal Assent).

(30) Additions to taxable Canadian property — Subsections (1.1) to (29) do not apply to a disposition by a non-resident person of a property

(a) that the person last acquired before April 27, 1995;

(b) that would not be a taxable Canadian property immediately before the disposition if section 115 of the amended Act were read as it applied to dispositions that occurred on April 26, 1995; and

(c) that would be a taxable Canadian property immediately before the disposition if section 115 of the amended Act were read as it applied to dispositions that occurred on January 1, 1996.

Related Provisions: ITA 40(9) — Gains limited to those accruing after April 1995.

Notes: ITAR 26(30) provides that dispositions by non-residents of property that became TCP because of the ITA amendments that took effect in 1995 are not protected by ITAR 26(1.1)–(29), since ITA 40(9) ensures that a non-resident's gains are limited to those accruing after April 1995.

ITAR 26(30) amended by Part 4 of 2001 technical bill, for dispositions after Oct. 1, 1996. Added by 1995-97 technical bill, for dispositions after April 26, 1995.

Definitions [ITAR 26]: "actual cost" — ITAR 26(5)(b), (6)(b), (c), (8)(c)(i), 26(13)–(17); "adjusted cost base" — ITA 54, 248(1); "amended Act" — ITAR 8; "amortized cost" — ITAR 26(5)(b), (6)(b), (c), 26(12); "amount" — ITA 248(1); "arm's length" — ITA 26(5.1), (5.2); "business" — ITA 248(1); "Canada" — ITA 255, *Interpretation Act* 35(1); "Canadian corporation" — ITA 89(1), 248(1); "capital gain" — ITA 39(1), 248(1); "capital loss" — ITA 39(1)(b), 248(1); "capital property" — ITA 54, ITAR 26(8.3), (8.4), (12); "child" — ITAR 26(20); "consequence" — 248(8); "corporation" — ITA 248(1), ITAR 26(8.5); "cost amount" — ITA 248(1); "deferred profit sharing plan" — ITA 147(1), 248(1); "depreciable property" — ITA 13(21), 248(1); "discount" — ITAR 26(12); "dividend" — ITA 248(1); "eligible capital amount" — ITA 14(1); "eligible capital property" — ITAR 26(12); "employees profit sharing plan" — ITA 144(1), 248(1); "fair market value" — see ITA 69(1) Notes; "fair market value on valuation day" — ITAR 26(8)(b)(ii), (c)(ii), 26(11); "first property" — ITAR 26(28); "fiscal period" — ITA 249.1; "foreign affiliate" — ITA 95(1), 248(1); "former Act" — ITAR 8; "identical" — ITA 248(12), ITAR 26(8.1), (8.2); "Income Tax Act, chapter 148 of the Revised Statutes of Canada, 1952", "Income Tax Application Rules, 1971" — ITAR 69; "individual" — ITA 248(1); "land" — see ITA 70(5.2) Notes; "legal representative", "life insurance business", "life insurance corporation" — ITA 248(1); "listed personal property" — ITA 54, 248(1); "Minister" — ITA 248(1); "month" — *Interpretation Act* 35(1); "new bond" — ITAR 26(25); "new corporation" — ITAR 26(21)–(23); "new obligation" — ITAR 26(23); "new option" — ITAR 26(22); "new shares" — ITAR 26(21)(c), 26(24), (26), (27); "non-resident" — ITA 248(1); "obligation" — ITAR 26(1.1), (12); "old bond" — ITAR 26(25); "old obligation", "old option" — ITAR 26(22); "old property" — ITAR 26(24); "old shares" — ITAR 26(21)(b), 26(26), (27); "owned" — ITAR 26(5); "original owner" — ITAR 26(6)(a), 26(28); "partnership" — see ITA 96(1) Notes; "person" — ITA 248(1); "personal-use property" — ITA 54, 248(1); "predecessor corporation" — ITAR 26(21)–(23); "premium" — ITAR 26(12); "prescribed" ITA 248(1); "principal amount" — ITA 248(1), (26); "property" — ITA 248(1); "related" — ITA 251(2)–(6); "resident in Canada" — ITA 250; "retirement savings plan" — ITA 146(1), 248(1); "share", "shareholder", "stock dividend" — ITA 248(1); "subsequent owner" — ITAR 26(5); "supplementary unemployment benefit plan" — ITA 145(1), 248(1); "tax equity" — ITAR 26(12); "taxable Canadian property" — ITA 248(1); "taxation year" — ITA 249; "taxpayer" — ITA 248(1); "undepreciated capital cost" — ITA 13(21), 248(1); "valuation day" — ITAR 24; "writing" — *Interpretation Act* 35(1); "written" — *Interpretation Act* 35(1) "writing".

26.1 [No longer relevant]

Notes: ITAR 26.1 allowed an election in 1975-76 if X acquired a home (or co-op housing share) to inhabit and changed it to income-earning use before 1972. X is deemed to have made an ITA 45(2) election in 1972 for purposes of ITA 40(2)(b) and 54 "principal residence", and no CCA is allowed thereafter.

27, 28. [Repealed under former Act]

Notes: ITAR 27 and 28 repealed in 1985. 27 dealt with moving expenses paid before 1972, and 28 provided an exemption for mining income to the end of 1973.

29. [Pre-1972 exploration and drilling expenses] — [No longer relevant]

Notes: ITAR 29(1)-(5) and (9)-(15) and (21)-(34) allow deduction (or inclusion in Canadian exploration and development expenses, CEE or CDE) for oil & gas and mining expenses incurred before 1972. These rules still apply for any such expenses that have not yet been claimed. ITAR 29(16)-(20) provide rules for applying receipts from pre-1969 dispositions of exploration or drilling rights. ITAR 29(6)-(8), "Joint exploration corporation may renounce expenses", repealed by 1996 Budget, effective on the same basis as repeal of ITA 66(10)–(10.3).

30. (1), (2) [Repealed under former Act]

(3) Reference to this Act in amended Act — In subsection 66(14) of the amended Act, "any amount deductible under the *Income Tax Application Rules*" in respect of that subsection means any amount deductible under section 29 of this Act.

Definitions [ITAR 30]: "amended Act" — ITAR 8; "amount" — ITA 248(1).

31. Application of section 67 of amended Act — [No longer relevant]

Notes: ITAR 31 applies to pre-1972 expenses.

32. (1) Application of para. 69(1)(a) of amended Act — Paragraph 69(1)(a) of the amended Act does not apply to deem a taxpayer by whom anything was acquired at any time before 1972 to have acquired it at its fair market value at that time, unless, if subsection 17(1) of the former Act had continued to apply, that fair market value would have been deemed to have been paid or to be payable therefor for the purpose of computing the taxpayer's income from a business.

(2) Application of para. 69(1)(b) of amended Act — Paragraph 69(1)(b) of the amended Act does not apply to deem a taxpayer by whom anything was disposed of at any time before the 1972 taxation year to have received proceeds of disposition therefor equal to its fair market value at that time.

(3) Application of para. 69(1)(c) of amended Act — For greater certainty, paragraph 69(1)(c) of the amended Act applies to property acquired by a taxpayer before, at or after the end of 1971.

Definitions [ITAR 32]: "amended Act" — ITAR 8; "business" — ITA 248(1); "fair market value" — see ITA 69(1) Notes; "former Act" — ITAR 8; "property" — ITA 248(1); "taxation year" — ITA 249; "taxpayer" — ITA 248(1).

32.1 (1)–(3.2) [Repealed under former Act]

Notes: ITAR 32.1(1)–(3.2), repealed in 1978 and 1985, dealt with elections on dividends payable before 1975.

(4) Capital dividend account — Where a dividend became payable, or was paid if that time was earlier, by a corporation in a taxation year at a particular time that was before May 7, 1974, for the purpose of computing the corporation's capital dividend account immediately before the particular time, all amounts each of which is an amount in respect of a capital loss from the disposition of property in the taxation year and before the particular time shall be deemed to be nil.

(5), (6) [Repealed under former Act]

Notes: ITAR 32.1(5) and (6), repealed in 1985, allowed certain elections to be made late if they were filed by the end of June 1975.

Definitions [ITAR 32.1]: "amount" — ITA 248(1); "capital dividend" — ITA 83(2)–(2.4), 248(1); "capital loss" — ITA 39(1)(b), 248(1); "corporation" — ITA 248(1), *Interpretation Act* 35(1); "dividend", "property" — ITA 248(1); "taxation year" — ITA 249.

33. [Repealed under former Act]

Notes: ITAR 33, repealed in 1985, dealt with dividends deemed received as a result of pre-1972 transactions.

34. (1) Amalgamations — Notwithstanding section 9, subsections 85I(1) and (2) of the former Act continue to apply with such modifications as, in the circumstances, are necessary by virtue of this Act, in respect of any amalgamation of two or more corporations before 1972.

(2), (3) [Repealed under former Act]

Notes: ITAR 34(2)-(3) repealed in 1985. 34(2) dealt with taxation in 1972 of corporations that amalgamated in 1971. 34(3) provided for successor corporation rules in respect of pre-1972 resource expenses, now covered in ITAR 29(25) and 29(29).

(4) [No longer relevant — applies for purposes of ITAR 29(25)]

(5), (6) [Repealed under former Act]

Notes: ITAR 34(5) and (6), repealed in 1985, imposed a special tax on a new corporation formed as a result of an amalgamation in 1971.

(7) Definition of "amalgamation" — In this section, "amalgamation" has the meaning assigned by section 85I of the former Act.

(8) [Repealed under former Act]

Notes: ITAR 34(8), repealed in 1985, provided administrative rules for the special tax under ITAR 34(5) and (6).

Interpretation Bulletins [ITAR 34]: IT-60R2: 1971 undistributed income on hand.

Definitions [ITAR 34]: "amalgamation" — ITAR 34(7); "amended Act" — ITAR 8; "amount" — ITA 248(1); "Canada" — ITA 255, *Interpretation Act* 35(1); "corporation" — ITA 248(1), *Interpretation Act* 35(1); "former Act" — ITAR 8; "property" — ITA 248(1); "province" — *Interpretation Act* 35(1); "taxation year" — ITA 249.

35. (1) Foreign affiliates — Section 26 does not apply in determining for the purposes of section 91 of the amended Act the amount of any taxable capital gain or allowable capital loss of a foreign affiliate of a taxpayer.

(2) Idem — Any corporation that was a foreign affiliate of a taxpayer on January 1, 1972 shall be deemed, for the purposes of subdivision i of Division B of Part I of the amended Act, to have become a foreign affiliate of the taxpayer on that day.

(3) [Repealed under former Act]

Notes: ITAR 35(3), repealed in 1985, provided that the inclusion under 91(1) for the foreign accrual property income of a controlled foreign affiliate did not apply before the 1976 taxation year of the affiliate.

(4) Idem — Any corporation that was deemed to be a foreign affiliate of a taxpayer at any time prior to May 7, 1974 because of an election made by the taxpayer in accordance with subparagraph 95(1)(b)(iv) of the amended Act, as it read before being amended by chapter 26 of the Statutes of Canada, 1974-75-76, shall be deemed to have been a foreign affiliate of the taxpayer at that time.

Definitions [ITAR 35]: "allowable capital loss" — ITA 38(b), 248(1); "amended Act" — ITAR 8; "amount" — ITA 248(1); "Canada" — ITA 255, *Interpretation Act* 35(1); "corporation" — ITA 248(1), *Interpretation Act* 35(1); "foreign affiliate" — ITA 95(1), 248(1); "taxable capital gain" — ITA 38(a), 248(1); "taxpayer" — ITA 248(1).

35.1 [Repealed under former Act]

Notes: ITAR 35.1, repealed in 1985, provided that 94(1)(c)(i) and (ii) of the Act were only effective as of 1976.

36. Application of paras. 107(2)(b) to (d) of amended Act — In computing the income of a taxpayer for the taxpayer's 1972 or any subsequent taxation year, paragraphs 107(2)(b) to (d) of the amended Act do not apply in respect of any property of a trust distributed by the trust to the taxpayer at any time before the commencement of the taxpayer's 1972 taxation year.

Definitions [ITAR 36]: "amended Act" — ITAR 8; "property" — ITA 248(1); "taxation year" — ITA 249; "taxpayer" — ITA 248(1); "trust" — ITA 104(1), 248(1), (3).

37–39. [Repealed under former Act]

Notes: ITAR 37 to 39 repealed in 1985. 37 dealt with loss carryovers across the 1971-72 transition. 38 dealt with the transitional rules for general averaging for 1972-75. 39 provided transitional rules for specific income averaging provisions for 1972-75.

40. [No longer relevant]

Notes: ITAR 40 applies to pension income received in 1972-73.

41–48. [Repealed under former Act]

Notes: ITAR 41–48 repealed in 1985 (except 45.1, repealed in 1975). 41 dealt with two fiscal periods of an individual's business ending in the same pre-1974 year. 42 and 48 provided an election for averaging depreciation recapture for 1972-75. 43 provided an election for averaging an author's copyright income for 1972-73. 44 provided an election for averaging employee benefits before 1974. 45 and 46 provided an election before 1974 for averaging income from sale of inventory or accounts receivable on ceasing to carry on business. 45.1 was an application rule for interpreting certain provisions before 1975. 47 provided rules for averaging income on a death before 1976.

49. [No longer relevant.]

Notes: ITAR 49 provides rules for ITAR 40, and for applying ITA 120 in 1972.

50. (1) Status of certain corporations — For the purposes of the amended Act, a corporation that was, throughout that portion of its 1972 taxation year that is in 1972, a private corporation, a Canadian-controlled private corporation or a public corporation shall be deemed to have been throughout that taxation year a private corporation, a Canadian-controlled private corporation or a public corporation, as the case may be.

(2) Election to be public corporation — For the purposes of the definition "public corporation" in subsection 89(1) of the amended Act, where at any particular time before 1973 a corporation elected in the manner referred to in subparagraph (b)(i) of that definition to be a public corporation and at any time after 1971 and before the time of the election the corporation complied with the conditions referred to in that subparagraph, the corporation shall,

(a) at such time after 1971 and before the particular time as is specified in the election to be the effective date thereof, or

(b) where no time described in paragraph (a) is specified in the election to be the effective date thereof, at the particular time,

be deemed to have elected in the manner referred to in that subparagraph to be a public corporation and to have complied with the conditions referred to therein.

(3) Designation by Minister — For the purposes of the definition "public corporation" in subsection 89(1) of the amended Act, where at any particular time before March 22, 1972 the Minister, by notice in writing to a corporation, designated the corporation to be a public corporation or not to be a public corporation, as the case may be, and at the time of the designation the corporation complied with the conditions referred to in subparagraph (b)(i) or (c)(i) of that definition, as the case may be, the corporation shall, at such time as is specified by the Minister in the notice, be deemed

(a) to have been designated by the Minister, by notice in writing to the corporation, to be a public corporation or not to be a public corporation, as the case may be; and

(b) to have complied with the conditions referred to in subparagraph (b)(i) or (c)(i) of that definition, as the case may be.

Definitions [ITAR 50]: "amended Act" — ITAR 8; "Canadian-controlled private corporation" — ITA 125(7), 248(1); "corporation" — ITA 248(1), *Interpretation Act* 35(1); "Minister" — ITA 248(1); "private corporation", "public corporation" — ITA 89(1), 248(1); "taxation year" — ITA 249; "writing" — *Interpretation Act* 35(1).

51–56.1 [Repealed under former Act]

Notes: ITAR 51–56.1 repealed in 1985 (except for 53, repealed in 1975). 51 provided a transitional rule for determining corporate tax for the 1971-72 fiscal year. 52 and 54 provided transitional rules for non-calendar fiscal years from 1972-76. 53 provided a deduction from corporate tax for 1977. 55-56 provided transitional rules for the foreign-tax carryover and refundable dividend tax on hand for 1972. 56.01 provided transitional rules for capital gains dividends payable by a mutual fund corporation in 1973. 56.1 provided a rule relating to qualifying of a trust as a mutual fund trust in 1972.

57. (1)–(8) [Repealed under former Act]

Notes: ITAR 57(1)–(7), repealed in 1985, applied to "specified personal corporations" for 1972. 57(8), repealed in 1978, dealt with tax-paid undistributed surplus on hand.

(9) Capital dividend account — In computing a specified personal corporation's capital dividend account at any time after the end of its 1972 taxation year, there shall be added to the total of the amounts described in paragraphs (a) and (b) of the definition "capital dividend account" in subsection 89(1) of the amended Act the total of its net capital gains (within the meaning assigned by subsection 51(3) of the *Income Tax Application Rules, 1971*, Part III of Chapter 63 of the Statutes of Canada, 1970-71-72, as it read before October 29, 1985) for its 1972 taxation year and that proportion of the total of its incomes for that year, other than

(a) any taxable capital gains of the corporation for the year from dispositions of property, and

(b) any amounts that were, because of subsection 57(3) of the *Income Tax Application Rules, 1971*, Part III of chapter 63 of the Statutes of Canada, 1970-71-72, as it read before October 29, 1985 or under the provisions of subsection 67(1) of the former Act that applied because of subsection 57(12) of those Rules as it read before that date, required to be included in computing the income of the specified personal corporation for its 1972 taxation year,

that the number of days in that portion of the 1972 taxation year that is in 1972 is of the number of days in the whole year.

Related Provisions: ITAR 69 (meaning of "*Income Tax Application Rules, 1971*, Part III of chapter 63 of the Statutes of Canada, 1970-71-72").

(10) [Repealed under former Act]

Notes: ITAR 57(10), repealed in 1985, related to the rules in 57(1) regarding specified personal corporations.

(11) Meaning of "specified personal corporation" — For the purposes of this section, a corporation is a specified personal corporation if

(a) part of its 1972 taxation year was before and part thereof after the beginning of 1972; and

(b) during the whole of the period beginning on the earlier of June 18, 1971 and the beginning of its 1972 taxation year and ending at the end of its 1972 taxation year, it was a personal corporation within the meaning assigned by section 68 of the former Act.

(12) [Repealed under former Act]

Notes: ITAR 57(12), repealed in 1985, provided a transitional rule for 1972 for a personal corporation.

Definitions [ITAR 57]: "amended Act" — ITAR 8; "amount" — ITA 248(1); "Canada" — ITA 255, *Interpretation Act* 35(1); "capital dividend" — ITA 83(2)–(2.4), 248(1); "capital gain" — ITA 39(1), 248(1); "corporation" — ITA 248(1), *Interpretation Act* 35(1); "dividend" — ITA 248(1); "former Act" — ITAR 8; "Income Tax Application Rules, 1971" — ITAR 69; "property" — ITA 248(1); "specified personal corporation" — ITAR 57(11); "taxable capital gain" — ITA 38(a), 248(1); "taxation year" — ITA 249.

57.1 [Repealed under former Act]

Notes: ITAR 57.1 provided a transitional rule for 1972 for co-operative corporations.

58. [Credit union transitional rules for 1972]

Notes: Some of these rules still apply for determining balances for a credit union that has been in operation since before 1972. See up to PITA 59th ed.

59. (1) [Repealed under former Act]

Notes: ITAR 59(1), repealed in 1985, provided the tax rates for non-resident-owned investment corporations for 1972-75.

(2) Non-resident-owned investment corporation — [No longer relevant]

Notes: ITAR 59(2) applies to NROs, which no longer exist (see Notes to ITA 133).

60. [Repealed under former Act]

Notes: ITAR 60, repealed in 1985, provided rules for phasing out "foreign business corporations" from 1972-76.

60.1 Taxes payable by insurer under Part IA of former Act — For the purposes of the description of F in the definition "surplus funds derived from operations" in subsection 138(12) of the amended Act, the reference in that description to "this Part" shall be deemed to be a reference to "this Part and Part IA of the former Act".

Definitions [ITAR 60.1]: "amended Act" — ITAR 8.

61. (1) Registered retirement savings plans — For the purposes of the definition "non-qualified investment" in subsection 146(1) of the amended Act, property acquired after June 18, 1971 and before 1972 by a trust governed by a registered retirement savings plan shall, if owned or held by the trust on January 1, 1972, be deemed to have been acquired by the trust on January 1, 1972.

(2) [Not included in R.S.C. 1985]

Notes: ITAR 61(2) not included in RSC 1985 (5th Supp) consolidation. It dealt with refunds of RRSP premiums where the annuitant died before 1972.

Definitions [ITAR 61]: "amended Act" — ITAR 8; "property" — ITA 248(1); "registered retirement savings plan" — ITA 146(1), 248(1); "trust" — ITA 104(1), 248(1), (3).

62. (1) Assessments — Subsections 152(4) and (5) of the amended Act apply in respect of any assessment made after December 23, 1971, except that subsection 152(5) of that Act does not apply in respect of any such assessment made in consequence of a waiver filed with the Minister before December 23, 1971 in the form and within the time referred to in subsection 152(4) of that Act.

(2) Interest — Subsections 161(1) and (2), 164(3) and (4), 202(5) and 227(8) and (9) of the amended Act, subsection 183(2) of the *Income Tax Act*, chapter 148 of the Revised Statutes of Canada, 1952, and subsection 195(1) of that Act as it read in its application in respect of dividends paid or received before April 1, 1977, in so far as those subsections relate to the rate of interest payable thereunder, apply in respect of interest payable in respect of any period after December 23, 1971.

(3) [Repealed under former Act]

Notes: ITAR 62(3), repealed in 1988, provided for penalties under s. 163 of the Act to apply to pre-1972 returns that were due in 1972.

(4) Objections to assessment — Subsection 165(3) of the amended Act applies in respect of any notice of objection served on the Minister after December 23, 1971.

(5) Appeals — Division J of Part I of the amended Act applies in respect of any appeal or application instituted or made, as the case may be, after December 23, 1971.

(6) Appeals to Federal Court — Any appeal to the Federal Court instituted, within 2 years after December 23, 1971 and in accordance with Division J of Part I of the former Act and any rules made thereunder (as those rules read immediately before December 23, 1971), shall be deemed to have been instituted in the manner provided by the amended Act, and any document served on the Minister or a taxpayer in connection with an appeal so instituted in the manner provided in that Division and those rules shall be deemed to have been served in the manner provided by the amended Act.

Definitions [ITAR 62]: "amended Act" — ITAR 8; "assessment", "dividend" — ITA 248(1); "Federal Court" — *Federal Courts Act* s. 4; "former Act" — ITAR 8; "Income Tax Act, chapter 148 of the Revised Statutes of Canada, 1952" — ITAR 69; "Minister", "taxpayer" — ITA 248(1).

63–64.3 [Repealed under former Act]

Notes: ITAR 63 dealt with tax-paid undistributed surplus on hand in 1972. ITAR 64 provided a 1972 transitional rule for calculating the "preferred-rate amount" for purposes of the now-repealed Part VI tax. ITAR 64.1 dealt with a life insurance corp's control period earnings. ITAR 64.2 provided change-in-control rules for pre-1978 ITA Parts VII and VII. ITAR 64.3 provided for retroactive elections under the pre-1978 ITA Part IX.

65. [Repealed]

Notes: ITAR 65, rules for the "foreign investment limit" for RRSPs and other deferred income plans, repealed by 2005 budget bill #1, for tax years beginning after 2004, due to repeal of ITA Part XI. ITAR 65(5) amended by 1991 technical bill effective Nov. 1985.

65.1 Part XV of amended Act — For greater certainty,

(a) section 9 does not apply in respect of the repeal, by section 1 of chapter 63 of the Statutes of Canada, 1970-71-72, of Part V of the former Act and the substitution therefor, by that section, of Part XV of the amended Act, and

(b) [applies to offence committed before Dec. 23, 1971]

Definitions [ITAR 65.1]: "amended Act" — ITAR 8; "amount" — ITA 248(1); "Canada" — ITA 255, *Interpretation Act* 35(1); "former Act" — ITAR 8.

66. (1) Part II of former Act — For greater certainty, Part II of the former Act applies only in respect of elections made thereunder before 1972.

(2) [Repealed under former Act]

Notes: ITAR 66(2), repealed in 1977, dealt with the effect of a pre-1972 election on a corporation's "1971 undistributed income on hand".

Definitions [ITAR 66]: "former Act" — ITAR 8.

67. (1)–(4) [Not included in R.S.C. 1985]

Notes: ITAR 67(1)–(4) dealt with refunds under Part IID of the pre-1972 Act. They were not included in the RSC 1985 (5th Supp) consolidation.

(5) Prescription of unpaid amounts — Her Majesty in right of Canada is not liable, and no action shall be taken, for or in respect of any unrefunded instalment of tax paid under Part IID of the former Act or any interest thereon where

(a) a repayment date with respect to the instalment was prescribed by regulation and reasonable efforts were made thereafter to locate the corporation or trust entitled to the refund;

(b) at least 5 years have elapsed since publication in the *Canada Gazette* of the regulation referred to in paragraph (a); and

(c) no claim whatever has been received by or on behalf of Her Majesty from the corporation or trust entitled to the refund.

Definitions [ITAR 67]: "Canada" — ITA 255, *Interpretation Act* 35(1); "corporation" — ITA 248(1), *Interpretation Act* 35(1); "former Act" — ITAR 8; "Her Majesty" — *Interpretation Act* 35(1); "prescribed", "regulation" — ITA 248(1); "trust" — ITA 104(1), 248(1), (3).

68. [Not included in R.S.C. 1985]

Notes: ITAR 68 dealt with references in S.C. 1968-69, c. 44, s. 24(3), dealing with the predecessor to ITAR 33.

PART II — TRANSITIONAL CONCERNING THE 1985 STATUTE REVISION

Notes: Part II (ITAR 69–78) added in RSC 1985 (5th Supp) consolidation, to deal with the transition to the new Act that took effect on March 1, 1994.

69. Definitions — In this Act and the *Income Tax Act*, unless the context otherwise requires,

"*Income Tax Act*, chapter 148 of the Revised Statutes of Canada, 1952" means that Act as amended by section 1 of chapter 63 of the Statutes of Canada, 1970-71-72, and by any subsequent Act that received royal assent before December, 1991;

"*Income Tax Application Rules, 1971*, Part III of chapter 63 of the Statutes of Canada, 1970-71-72" means that Act as amended by any subsequent Act that received royal assent before December, 1991.

Definitions [ITAR 69]: "Canada" — ITA 255, *Interpretation Act* 35(1).

Application of the 1971 Acts and the Revised Acts

70. Application of *Income Tax Application Rules, 1971*, 1970-71-72, c. 63 — Subject to this Act and the *Income Tax Act* and unless the context otherwise requires,

(a) sections 7 to 9 and 12 to 68 of the *Income Tax Application Rules, 1971*, Part III of chapter 63 of the Statutes of Canada, 1970-71-72, apply with respect to taxation years that ended before December, 1991; and

(b) section 10 of the *Income Tax Application Rules, 1971*, Part III of chapter 63 of the Statutes of Canada, 1970-71-72, applies with respect to amounts paid or credited before December, 1991.

Definitions [ITAR 70]: "amount" — ITA 248(1); "Canada" — ITA 255, *Interpretation Act* 35(1); "Income Tax Application Rules, 1971" — ITAR 69; "taxation year" — ITA 249.

71. Application of this Act — Subject to this Act and the *Income Tax Act* and unless the context otherwise requires,

(a) sections 7 to 9 and 12 to 78 of this Act apply with respect to taxation years that end after November, 1991; and

(b) section 10 of this Act applies with respect to amounts paid or credited after November, 1991.

Definitions [ITAR 71]: "amount" — ITA 248(1); "taxation year" — ITA 249.

72. Application of *Income Tax Act*, R.S.C., 1952, c. 148 — Subject to this Act and the *Income Tax Act* and unless the context otherwise requires, the *Income Tax Act*, chapter 148 of the Revised Statutes of Canada, 1952, applies as follows:

(a) Parts I, I.1, I.2, I.3, II.1, IV, IV.1, V, VI, VI.1, VII, VIII, IX, XI.3, XII, XII.1, XII.2, XII.3 and XIV of that Act apply with respect to taxation years that ended before December 1991;

(b) Part III of that Act applies with respect to dividends that became payable before December, 1991;

(c) Parts X, X.1, X.2, XI, XI.1 and XI.2 of that Act apply with respect to calendar years that ended before December, 1991;

(d) Part XIII of that Act applies with respect to amounts paid or credited before December, 1991; and

(e) Parts XV, XVI and XVII of that Act apply before December, 1991.

Notes: Reference to Part XII.1 in ITAR 72(a) added by 1993 technical bill, deemed to have come into force on March 1, 1994 (i.e., retroactive to when RSC 1985 (5th Supp) came into force).

Definitions [ITAR 72]: "amount", "dividend" — ITA 248(1); "Income Tax Act, chapter 148 of the Revised Statutes of Canada, 1952" — ITAR 69; "taxation year" — ITA 249.

73. Application of *Income Tax Act* [R.S.C. 1985 (5th Supp.)] — Subject to this Act and the *Income Tax Act* and unless the context otherwise requires, the *Income Tax Act* applies as follows:

(a) Parts I, I.1, I.2, I.3, II.1, IV, IV.1, V, VI, VI.1, VII, VIII, IX, XI.3, XII, XII.1, XII.2, XII.3 and XIV of that Act apply with respect to taxation years that end after November 1991;

(b) Part III of that Act applies with respect to dividends that become payable after November, 1991;

(c) Parts X, X.1, X.2, XI, XI.1 and XI.2 of that Act apply with respect to calendar years that end after November, 1991;

(d) Part XIII of that Act applies with respect to amounts paid or credited after November, 1991; and

(e) Parts XV, XVI and XVII of that Act apply after November, 1991.

Notes: Reference to Part XII.1 in ITAR 73(a) added by 1993 technical bill, effective March 1, 1994.

Definitions [ITAR 73]: "amount", "dividend" — ITA 248(1); "taxation year" — ITA 249.

Application of Certain Provisions

74. Definition of "provision" — In sections 75 to 78, "provision" means the whole or part of a provision.

75. Continued effect of amending and application provisions — For greater certainty, where an enactment passed after 1971 in amendment of the *Income Tax Application Rules, 1971*, Part III of chapter 63 of the Statutes of Canada, 1970-71-72, or of the *Income Tax Act*, chapter 148 of the Revised Statutes of Canada, 1952, contains an amending, repeal, application or other provision that, immediately before the coming into force of the fifth supplement to the Revised Statutes of Canada, 1985, has any effect on, or in connection with, the application of either or both of those Acts, that provision has, on the coming into force of that supplement, the same effect on, or in connection with, the application of either this Act or the *Income Tax Act* or both.

Notes: See also the *Revised Statutes of Canada, 1985 Amendment Act*, S.C. 1987, c. 48, s. 4, which provides that the R.S.C. 1985 (Fifth Supplement) consolidation is not intended to change the law.

When certain sections were dropped from the official consolidations of Ontario legislation in the Revised Statutes of Ontario, those provisions remained in effect since the Revised Statutes were not intended to make a substantive change in the law: *SM v. Ontario*, 2003 CarswellOnt 3117 (Ont. CA).

See also Allan Lanthier, "Statute Revision", 23(5) *Canadian Tax Highlights* (ctf.ca) 1-2 (May 2015), for additional case law.

Definitions [ITAR 75]: "Canada" — ITA 255, *Interpretation Act* 35(1); "Income Tax Act, chapter 148 of the Revised Statutes of Canada, 1952", "Income Tax Application Rules, 1971" — ITAR 69; "provision" — ITAR 74.

76. Application of section 75 — Section 75 is applicable whether or not this Act or the *Income Tax Act*, as the case may be, contains, or contains the tenor of or any reference to,

(a) the amending, repeal, application or other provision referred to in that section; or

(b) any provision of the *Income Tax Application Rules, 1971*, Part III of chapter 63 of the Statutes of Canada, 1970-71-72, or the *Income Tax Act*, chapter 148 of the Revised Statutes of Canada, 1952, expressed or intended to be the subject of or otherwise affected by that amending, repeal, application or other provision.

Definitions [ITAR 76]: "Canada" — ITA 255, *Interpretation Act* 35(1); "Income Tax Act, chapter 148 of the Revised Statutes of Canada, 1952", "Income Tax Application Rules, 1971" — ITAR 69; "provision" — ITAR 74.

77. Continued effect of repealed provisions — For greater certainty, where a provision of the *Income Tax Application Rules, 1971*, Part III of chapter 63 of the Statutes of Canada, 1970-71-72, or the *Income Tax Act*, chapter 148 of the Revised Statutes of Canada, 1952, was repealed at any time after 1971 but, immediately before the coming into force of the fifth supplement to the Revised Statutes of Canada, 1985, continues to be applied to any extent or otherwise to have any effect on, or in connection with, the application of either or both of those Acts, the repealed provision, on the coming into force of that supplement, continues to be so applied or to have that effect on, or in connection with, the application of either this Act or the *Income Tax Act* or both.

Notes: See Notes to ITAR 75.

Definitions [ITAR 77]: "Canada" — ITA 255, *Interpretation Act* 35(1); "Income Tax Act, chapter 148 of the Revised Statutes of Canada, 1952", "Income Tax Application Rules, 1971" — ITAR 69; "provision" — ITAR 74.

78. Application of section 77 — Section 77 is applicable whether or not this Act or the *Income Tax Act*, as the case may be, contains any reference to the repealed provision referred to in that section or to the subject-matter of that provision.

Definitions [ITAR 78]: "provision" — ITAR 74.

79. (1) Effect of amendments on former ITA — Where a provision of an enactment amends the *Income Tax Act* or affects the application of the *Income Tax Act* and the provision applies to or with respect to a period, transaction or event to which the *Income Tax Act*, chapter 148 of the Revised Statutes of Canada, 1952, applies, the *Income Tax Act*, chapter 148 of the Revised Statutes of Canada, 1952, shall be read as if it had been amended or its application had been affected by the provision, with such modifications as the circumstances require, to the extent of the provision's application to or with respect to that period, transaction or event.

(2) Effect of amendments on former ITAR — Where a provision of an enactment amends this Act or affects the application of this Act and the provision applies to or with respect to a period, transaction or event to which the *Income Tax Application Rules, 1971*, Part III of chapter 63 of the Statutes of Canada, 1970-71-72, apply, the *Income Tax Application Rules, 1971*, Part III of chapter 63 of the Statutes of Canada, 1970-71-72, shall be read as if they had been amended or their application had been affected by the provision, with such modifications as the circumstances require, to the extent of the provision's application to or with respect to that period, transaction or event.

Notes: ITAR 79 added by 1993 technical bill, effective March 2, 1994.

Definitions [ITAR 79]: "Canada" — ITA 255, *Interpretation Act* 35(1); "Income Tax Act, chapter 148 of the Revised Statutes of Canada, 1952", "Income Tax Application Rules, 1971" — ITAR 69.

DETAILED TABLE OF SECTIONS

INCOME TAX REGULATIONS

PART III — [300–310] ANNUITIES AND LIFE INSURANCE POLICIES

DIVISION II — SEPARATE CLASSES

DIVISION III — PROPERTY RULES

DIVISION IV — INCLUSIONS IN AND TRANSFERS BETWEEN CLASSES

DIVISION V — INTERPRETATION

DIVISION VI — CLASSES PRESCRIBED

DIVISION VII — CERTIFICATES ISSUED BY THE MINISTER OF CANADIAN HERITAGE

Regulations

5905(5)   [Corporation transferring FA shares to related corporation]
5905(5.1)   [Amalgamation]
5905(5.11)–(5.13)   [Repealed]
5905(5.2)   [Change in control of parent]
5905(5.3)   [Ordering — interaction with ITA 111(4)]
5905(5.4)   [Prescribed amount for bump]
5905(5.5)   [Tax-free surplus balance]
5905(5.6)   [Tax-free surplus balance — interpretation]
5905(5.7)   [Amount for 5905(5.5)(a.1)]
5905(6)   [Repealed]
5905(7)   [Liquidation or dissolution of FA]
5905(7.1)   [Conditions for subsec. (7.2)]
5905(7.2)   [Blocking deficit — anti-avoidance]
5905(7.3)   [Conditions for subsec. (7.4)]
5905(7.4)   [Blocking deficit — limit on designation]
5905(7.5)   [Conditions for subsec. (7.6)]
5905(7.6)   [Increase to ACB of shares of lower-tier affiliates]
5905(7.7)   [Prescribed amount for ITA 93(3)(c)]
5905(8), (9)   [Repealed]
5905(10)   ["Surplus entitlement"]
5905(11)   [Interpretation for Reg. 5905(10)]
5905(12)   [Repealed]
5905(13)   ["Surplus entitlement percentage"]
5905(14)   ["Equity percentage"]
5906   Carrying on business in a country
5907   Interpretation
5907(1)   [Definitions]
5907(1.01) [Interpretation for ITA 113]
5907(1.02) [New FA deemed resident in treaty country throughout year]
5907(1.03) [Artificial foreign tax credit generators]
5907(1.04) [Specified owner]
5907(1.05) [Pertinent person or partnership]
5907(1.06) [Series of transactions]
5907(1.07) [Exception — hybrid entities]
5907(1.08) [Exception — partnerships]
5907(1.09) [Deemed ownership]
5907(1.091) [Conditions for Reg. 5907(1.092) to apply]
5907(1.092) [Where shareholder of fiscally transparent entity pays the foreign tax]
5907(1.1)   [Where FA is member of consolidated group]
5907(1.11) [Deemed FA for 5907(1.1)]
5907(1.12) [Conditions for (1.13) to apply]
5907(1.13) [Look-through of transparent affiliate]
5907(1.2)   [Where FA deducts loss of loss affiliate]
5907(1.21) [Conditions for (1.22) to apply]
5907(1.22) [Loss of transparent affiliate deemed loss of shareholder affiliate]
5907(1.3)   [Prescribed foreign accrual tax]
5907(1.4)   [Prescribed foreign accrual tax]
5907(1.5)   [Effect of (1.4)]
5907(1.6)   [Designated taxation year]
5907(1.7)   [Where amount under (1.3) is capital loss of other corporation]
5907(2)   [FA carrying on active business]
5907(2.01) [Packaging of assets for sale]
5907(2.011) [Corporate division under foreign law]
5907(2.02) [Avoidance transaction]
5907(2.03) [FA's earnings calculated on basis of maximum deductions]
5907(2.1)   [FA carrying on active business in Canada or treaty country]
5907(2.2), (2.3)   [Where election made under Reg. 5907(2.1)]
5907(2.4)   ["Subsequent corporation" for Reg. 5907(2.3)]
5907(2.5)   [Repealed]
5907(2.6)   [Corporations deemed to have elected under Reg. 5907(2.1)]
5907(2.7)   [Where ITA 95(2)(a)(i) or (ii) applies]
5907(2.8)   [Repealed]
5907(2.9)   [Where fresh start rules apply]
5907(3)   [Pre-1972 foreign affiliate]
5907(4)   ["Government of a country"]
5907(5)   [Capital gains and losses]
5907(5.01) [Rate of exchange for currency conversion]
5907(5.1)   [Where no gain or loss recognized by other country]
5907(6)   [Selection of currency]
5907(7)   [Stock dividend]
5907(7.1)   [Repealed]

PART LX — [6000] PRESCRIBED ACTIVITIES

PART LXI — [6100] RELATED SEGREGATED FUND TRUSTS

PART LXII — [6200–6210] PRESCRIBED SECURITIES, SHARES AND DEBT OBLIGATIONS

1729

Detailed Table of Sections

Regulations

INCOME TAX REGULATIONS

CONSOLIDATED REGULATIONS OF CANADA, CHAPTER 945

(CONSOLIDATED AS OF DECEMBER 31, 1977)

PROCLAIMED IN FORCE AUGUST 15, 1979, AS AMENDED TO JULY 5, 2021

Notes: Editorial annotations have been added in square brackets to update references to the ITA where the numbering of the provision has changed as a result of the R.S.C. 1985, c. 1 (5th Supp.) consolidation implemented in 1994. (See Reg. 700(1) and 2301 as examples.)

Regulations cannot override the Act, unless authorized by ITA 221: *G.H.C. Investment*, [1961] C.T.C. 187 (Exch. Ct.); *Phénix*, [1998] 1 C.T.C. 2379 (TCC), para. 72.

1. Short title — These Regulations may be cited as the *Income Tax Regulations*.

2. Interpretation — In these Regulations, "Act" means the *Income Tax Act*.

Notes re Definitions: Terms used in the regulations should be read with reference to ITA ss. 248–260. *Interpretation Act* s. 16 provides:

16. Words in Regulations — Where an enactment confers power to make regulations, expressions used in the regulations have the same respective meanings as in the enactment conferring the power.

Judicial notice is to be taken of the Regulations; see ITA 244(12).

PART I — [100–111] TAX DEDUCTIONS

Notes [Part I]: The CRA offers a free on-site consultative service to help employers with payroll deductions. Contact the local Tax Services Office.

100. Interpretation — **(1) [Definitions]** — In this Part and in Schedule I,

"employee" means any person receiving remuneration;

"employer" means any person paying remuneration;

Notes: The term "employer" means any person paying "remuneration" as defined below in Reg. 100(1). Thus, an RRSP trustee paying out a lump sum to the annuitant is an "employer" required to withhold under Reg. 103(4).

"estimated deductions" means, in respect of a taxation year, the total of the amounts estimated to be deductible by an employee for the year under any of paragraphs 8(1)(f), (h), (h.1), (i) and (j) of the Act and determined by the employee for the purpose of completing the form referred to in subsection 107(2);

Notes: Reference to ITA 8(1)(h.1) added by P.C. 1994-372, effective 1993.

"exemptions" — [Revoked]

Notes: Definition "exemptions" revoked effective 1988, when personal exemptions were eliminated from sections 109-110 of the Act. See "personal credits" now.

"pay period" includes

(a) a day,

(b) a week,

(c) a two week period,

(d) a semi-monthly period,

(e) a month,

(f) a four week period,

(g) one tenth of a calendar year, or

(h) one twenty-second of a calendar year;

Notes: See Notes to ITA 188.1(5) re meaning of "includes" in the opening words.

"personal credits" means, in respect of a particular taxation year, the greater of

(a) the amount referred to in paragraph 118(1)(c) of the Act, and

(b) the aggregate of the credits which the employee would be entitled to claim for the year under

(i) subsections 118(1), (2) and (3) of the Act if the description of A in those subsections were read as "is equal to one",

(ii) subsections 118.3(1) and (2) of the Act if the description of A in subsection 118.3(1) of the Act were read as "is equal to one" and if subsection 118.3(1) of the Act were read without reference to paragraph (c) thereof,

(iii) subsections 118.5(1) and 118.6(2) of the Act if subsection 118.5(1) of the Act were read without reference to "the product obtained when the appropriate percentage for the year is multiplied by" and the description of A in subsection 118.6(2) of the Act were read as "is equal to one", and after deducting from the aggregate of the amounts determined under those subsections the excess over $3,000 of the aggregate of amounts that the employee claims to expect to receive in the year on account of a scholarship, fellowship or bursary,

(iv) section 118.8 of the Act if the formula A + B - C in that section were read as

$$(A + B) / C$$

where

A is the value of A in that section,

B is the value of B in that section, and

C is the appropriate percentage for the year.

(v) section 118.9 of the Act if the formula A - B in section 118.81 of the Act were read as

$$A / B$$

where

A is the value of A set out in that section, and

B is the appropriate percentage for the year.

Notes: Reg. 100(1)"personal credits" amended by P.C. 1994-372, effective 1993, and by P.C. 2001-1115, effective for 2001 and later taxation years.

"remuneration" includes any payment that is

(a) in respect of

(i) salary or wages, or

(ii) commissions or other similar amounts fixed by reference to the volume of the sales made or the contracts negotiated (referred to as "commissions" in this Part),

paid to an officer or employee or former officer or employee,

(a.1) in respect of an employee's gratuities required under provincial legislation to be declared to the employee's employer,

(b) a superannuation or pension benefit (including an annuity payment made pursuant to or under a superannuation or pension fund or plan) other than a distribution

(i) that is made from a pooled registered pension plan and is not required to be included in computing a taxpayer's income under paragraph 56(1)(z.3) of the Act, or

(ii) that subsection 147.5(14) of the Act deems to have been made,

(b.1) an amount of a distribution out of or under a retirement compensation arrangement,

(c) a retiring allowance,

(d) a death benefit,

(e) a benefit under a supplementary unemployment benefit plan,

(f) a payment under a deferred profit sharing plan or a plan referred to in section 147 of the Act as a "revoked plan", reduced, if applicable, by amounts determined under subsections 147(10.1), (11) and (12) of the Act,

(g) a benefit under the *Employment Insurance Act*,

Possible Future Amendment — Reg. 100(1)"remuneration"(g)

Notes: It is expected that a paragraph similar to para. (g) will be added for benefits from the Quebec Parental Insurance Plan, which are subject to withholding parallel to that for Employment Insurance benefits. See ITA 56(1)(a)(vii) and 153(1)(d.1). Finance has confirmed (Oct. 2019) that this is still planned.

(g.1) an amount that is required by paragraph 56(1)(a.3) of the Act to be included in computing a taxpayer's income,

(h) an amount that is required by paragraph 56(1)(r) of the Act to be included in computing a taxpayer's income, except the portion of the amount that relates to child care expenses and tuition costs,

(i) a payment made during the lifetime of an annuitant referred to in the definition "annuitant" in subsection 146(1) of the Act out of or under a registered retirement savings plan of that annuitant, other than

(i) a periodic annuity payment, or

(ii) a payment made by a person who has reasonable grounds to believe that the payment may be deducted under subsection 146(8.2) of the Act in computing the income of any taxpayer,

(j) a payment out of or under a plan referred to in subsection 146(12) of the Act as an "amended plan" other than

(i) a periodic annuity payment, or

(ii) where paragraph 146(12)(a) of the Act applied to the plan after May 25, 1976, a payment made in a year subsequent to the year in which that paragraph applied to the plan, or

(j.1) a payment made during the lifetime of an annuitant referred to in the definition "annuitant" in subsection 146.3(1) of the Act under a registered retirement income fund of that annuitant, other than a particular payment to the extent that

(i) the particular payment is in respect of the minimum amount (in this paragraph having the meaning assigned by subsection 146.3(1) of the Act) under the fund for a year, or

(ii) where the fund governs a trust, the particular payment would be in respect of the minimum amount under the fund for a year if each amount that, at the beginning of the year, is scheduled to be paid after the time of the particular payment and in the year to the trust under an annuity contract that is held by the trust both at the beginning of the year and at the time of the particular payment, is paid to the trust in the year,

(k) a benefit described in section 5502,

(l) an amount as, on account or in lieu of payment of, or in satisfaction of, proceeds of the surrender, cancellation or redemption of an income-averaging annuity contract,

(m) in respect of an amount that can reasonably be regarded as having been received, in whole or in part, as consideration or partial consideration for entering into a contract of service, where the service is to be performed in Canada, or for an undertaking not to enter into such a contract with another party,

(n) a payment out of a registered education savings plan other than

(i) a refund of payments,

(ii) an educational assistance payment, or

(iii) an amount, up to $50,000, of an accumulated income payment that is made to a subscriber, as defined in subsection 204.94(1) of the Act, or if there is no subscriber at that

time, that is made to a person that has been a spouse or common-law partner of an individual who was a subscriber, if

(A) that amount is transferred to an RRSP in which the annuitant is either the recipient of the payment or the recipient's spouse, and

(B) it is reasonable for the person making the payment to believe that that amount is deductible for the year by the recipient of the payment within the limits provided for in subsection 146(5) or (5.1) of the Act,

(o) an amount of a disability assistance payment made under a registered disability savings plan that is required by paragraph 56(1)(q.1) of the Act to be included in computing a taxpayer's income, or

(p) an amount that is required by paragraph 56(1)(z.5) of the Act to be included in computing a taxpayer's income;

Related Provisions: Reg. 100(1)"employer" — Any person paying "remuneration" is an "employer".

Notes: See Notes to Reg. 103(4) re lump-sum payments including RRSP withdrawals. See Notes to ITA 188.1(5) re meaning of "includes" in the opening words.

"Salary or wages" in (a)(i) is defined in ITA 248(1) to include all employment income including benefits, so withholding is calculated on total pay and taxable benefits. A lump sum retroactive wage settlement is "remuneration" to which Reg. 103(4) applies: VIEWS doc 2002-0170207.

Para. (a.1) links to a rule allowing tips to qualify for EI where provincial legislation requires them to be declared to the employer (Quebec is the only province that does this). See Quebec news release of Nov. 26/97, and federal Finance news release of Dec. 23/97 (in *Dept. of Finance Technical Notes*).

Subpara. (j.1)(ii) provides exemption from withholding for RRIF distributions based on an estimate of the minimum amount. This is only relevant to RRIF trusts that hold annuity contracts, as permitted by ITA 146.3(1)"qualified investment"(b.1)–(b.2). In such cases, the minimum amount cannot be determined with certainty until the end of the year and an estimate is required to ensure the exemption applies.

Para. (p) (ALDA) added by 2021 budget bill #1, effective 2020.

Definition earlier amended by P.C. 2016-96 (adding para. (o) effective July 2015); 2012 budget bill #2; S.C. 2012, c. 27; P.C. 2001-957, 2000-184, 1998-2275, 1998-2270, 1998-654, 1995-1023, 1991-2540.

Income Tax Folios: S1-F2-C3: Scholarships, research grants and other education assistance [replaces IT-340R].

"**total remuneration**" means, in respect of a taxation year, the total of all amounts each of which is an amount referred to in paragraph (a) or (a.1) of the definition "remuneration".

Notes: Reference to para. (a.1) added by P.C. 1998-654, effective 1998.

(2) [Indexing] — Where the amount of any credit referred to in paragraph (a) or (b) of the definition "personal credits" in subsection (1) is subject to an annual adjustment under section 117.1 of the Act, such amount shall, in a particular taxation year, be subject to that annual adjustment.

Notes: Reg. 100(2) amended by P.C. 2001-1115 to change "subparagraph (a)(i) or (ii)" to "paragraph (a) or (b)", effective for 2001 and later taxation years.

(3) [Amounts excluded from base for withholding] — For the purposes of this Part, where an employer deducts or withholds from a payment of remuneration to an employee one or more amounts each of which is

(a) a contribution to or under a pooled registered pension plan, a registered pension plan or a specified pension plan, or

(b) dues described in subparagraph 8(1)(i)(iv), (v) or (vi) of the Act paid on account of the employee,

(b.1) a contribution by the employee under subparagraph 8(1)(m.2) of the Act,

(c) a premium under a registered retirement savings plan, to the extent that the employer believes on reasonable grounds that the premium is deductible under paragraph 60(j.1) or subsection 146(5) or (5.1) of the Act in computing the employee's income for the taxation year in which the payment of remuneration is made, or

(d) an amount that is deductible under paragraph 60(b) of the Act, the balance remaining after deducting or withholding this amount, as the case may be, shall be deemed to be the amount of that payment of remuneration.

Related Provisions: Reg. 100(3.1) — Northern Canada residents.

Notes: *Reg. 100(3)(a)* amended by 2012 budget bill #2, effective Dec. 14, 2012, to refer to a PRPP and a specified pension plan (i.e., the Saskatchewan Pension Plan).

Reg. 100(3)(b.1) added by P.C. 1997-1471, in force October 29, 1997.

Reg. 100(3)(c) allows an employer to pay an employee's RRSP contribution directly to the financial institution (such as for a group RRSP) without source withholdings. It also allows a "retiring allowance" (as defined in ITA 248(1), including severance or termination pay) to be paid to the RRSP without source withholdings to the extent deductible under ITA 60(j.1) (the retiring-allowance rollover) plus regular RRSP contribution room (ITA 146(5), (5.1)) — or to the extent the employer reasonably believes it to be deductible. See VIEWS doc 2006-0167501E5.

Reg. 100(3)(c) added by P.C. 1994-372, effective 1993, and amended by P.C. 2001-1053, effective June 20, 2001 (but administratively operated by the CRA with this amendment and the repeal of Reg. 100(3.2) since the beginning of 2001; *Employers' Guide*, RC4120).

Reg. 100(3)(d) added by P.C. 1994-372, effective 1993; amended by P.C. 1997-1471, effective May 1997; and amended by P.C. 2001-1053, effective June 20, 2001.

The stated reason for the 1997 change was that *child* support is now generally not deductible. However, as a result of this change, *spousal* support withheld by an employer, which is deductible to the payer, would not reduce source withholdings unless special application was made under ITA 153(1.1) (the "undue hardship" rule), or unless there was a Court garnishment issued before May 1997. The 2001 amendment restored the reduction.

Some provinces require spousal and child support payments to be withheld by the employer at source and paid to a central office (e.g., Ontario Family Support Plan), which pays them to the (ex-)spouse. Reg. 100(3)(d) acknowledges this by reducing the tax on which source withholdings are based to exclude such amounts, where they are deductible for income tax purposes under ITA 60(b).

Income Tax Folios: S1-F2-C3: Scholarships, research grants and other education assistance [replaces IT-340R].

I.T. Technical News: 19 (Retiring allowances — clarification to Interpretation Bulletin IT-337R3 — (d): Deductions at source).

(3.1) [Northern residents' deduction] — For the purposes of this Part, where an employee has claimed a deduction for a taxation year under paragraph 110.7(1)(b) of the Act as shown on the return most recently filed by the employee with the employee's employer pursuant to subsection 227(2) of the Act, the amount of remuneration otherwise determined, including the amount deemed by subsection (3) to be the amount of that payment of remuneration, paid to the employee for a pay period shall be reduced by an amount equal to the amount of the deduction divided by the maximum number of pay periods in the year in respect of the appropriate pay period.

Notes: Reg. 100(3.1) amended by P.C. 1994-372, effective 1993, to update reference from ITA 110.7(1)(e) to 110.7(1)(b).

(3.2) [Repealed]

Notes: Reg. 100(3.2) repealed by P.C. 2001-1053, effective June 20, 2001 (but administratively effective January 2001; see Notes to Reg. 100(3)(c)). The $10,000 threshold has been replaced with a deduction for any amount paid by the employer directly to the RRSP (see 100(3)(c)), up to the total of the retiring-allowance rollover plus RRSP contribution room.

Reg. 100(3.2) added by P.C. 1997-1471, in force October 29, 1997.

(4) [Establishment of the employer] — For the purposes of this Part, where an employee is not required to report for work at any establishment of the employer, he shall be deemed to report for work

(a) in respect of remuneration that is salary, wages or commissions, at the establishment of the employer from which the remuneration is paid; or

(b) in respect of remuneration other than salary, wages or commissions, at the establishment of the employer in the province where the employee resides at the time the remuneration is paid but, if the employer does not have an establishment in that province at that time, he shall, for the purposes of this paragraph, be deemed to have an establishment in that province.

Notes: CRA uses "permanent establishment" (see Reg. 400(2)) in determining where the employer has an "establishment": IC 73-21R8 para. 2; VIEWS doc 2004-0100071E5. An employee who lives in Quebec but reports to an Ontario office is considered employed in Ontario: 2010-0375251E5; but for remuneration that is not salary,

wages or commission, the employer would be deemed by Reg. 100(4)(b) to have an establishment in Quebec: 2011-0400121I7. A retiring allowance is reported based on where the employee is resident, since the employee is no longer reporting to work: Alan McEwen, "Determining province of employment when paying retiring allowance", *Canadian Payroll Reporter* (Carswell), Oct. 2012, pp. 2-3.

(5) [LSVCC share purchase] — For the purposes of this Part, where an employer deducts or withholds from a payment of remuneration to an employee an amount in respect of the acquisition by the employee of an approved share, as defined in subsection 127.4(1) of the Act, there shall be deducted from the amount determined under paragraph 102(1)(e) or (2)(e), as the case may be, in respect of that payment the lesser of

(a) $750, and

(b) 15% of the amount deducted or withheld in respect of the acquisition of an approved share.

Notes: Reg. 100(5) opening words amended by P.C. 2005-1133, effective for 2001 and later taxation years, to change "(2)(f)" to "(2)(e)".

Reg. 100(5)(a), (b) amended by P.C. 1998-2270, effective for 1998 and later taxation years. Reg. 100(5) added by P.C. 1994-372, effective 1993.

Definitions [Reg. 100]: "accumulated income payment" — ITA 146.1(1); "advanced life deferred annuity" — ITA 146.5(1), 248(1); "amount", "annuity", "appropriate percentage" — ITA 248(1); "calendar year" — *Interpretation Act* 37(1)(a); "Canada" — ITA 255, *Interpretation Act* 35(1); "commissions" — Reg. 100(1)"remuneration"(a)(ii); "common-law partner" — ITA 248(1); "death benefit" — ITA 248(1); "deferred profit sharing plan" — ITA 147(1), 248(1); "disability assistance payment" — ITA 146.4(1); "educational assistance payment" — ITA 146.1(1); "employee", "employer" — Reg. 100(1); "income-averaging annuity contract" — ITA 248(1); "minimum amount" — ITA 146.3(1); "month" — *Interpretation Act* 35(1); "officer" — ITA 248(1); "pay period" — Reg. 100(1); "person" — ITA 248(1); "personal credits" — Reg. 100(1); "personal or living expenses" — ITA 248(1); "pooled registered pension plan" — ITA 147.5(1), 248(1); "province" — *Interpretation Act* 35(1); "provincial" — *Interpretation Act* 33(3), 35(1)"province"; "refund of payments" — ITA 146.1(1); "registered disability savings plan" — ITA 146.4(1), 248(1); "registered education savings plan" — ITA 146.1(1), 248(1); "registered pension fund or plan" — ITA 248(1); "registered retirement income fund" — ITA 146.3(1), 248(1); "registered retirement savings plan" — ITA 146(1), 248(1); "remuneration" — Reg. 100(1); "retirement compensation arrangement", "retiring allowance" — ITA 248(1); "salary, wages" — ITA 248(1)"salary or wages"; "salary or wages", "share" — ITA 248(1); "subscriber" — ITA 146.1(1); "supplementary unemployment benefit plan" — ITA 145(1), 248(1); "taxation year" — ITA 249; "taxpayer" — ITA 248(1); "trust" — ITA 104(1), 248(1), (3).

101. Deductions and remittances — Every person who makes a payment described in subsection 153(1) of the Act in a taxation year shall deduct or withhold therefrom, and remit to the Receiver General, such amount, if any, as is determined in accordance with rules prescribed in this Part.

Related Provisions: ITA 227 — Obligations with respect to amounts withheld; Reg. Sch. I — Ranges of remuneration for Reg. 102(1)(c) and (d).

Definitions [Reg. 101]: "amount", "person", "prescribed" — ITA 248(1); "taxation year" — ITA 249.

102. Periodic payments — (1) [Amount to be withheld] — Except as otherwise provided in this Part, the amount to be deducted or withheld by an employer

(a) from any payment of remuneration (in this subsection referred to as the "payment") made to an employee in his taxation year where he reports for work at an establishment of the employer in a province, in Canada beyond the limits of any province or outside Canada, and

(b) for any pay period in which the payment is made by the employer

shall be determined for each payment in accordance with the following rules:

(c) an amount that is a notional remuneration for the year in respect of

(i) a payment to the employee, and

(ii) the amount, if any, of gratuities referred to in paragraph (a.1) of the definition "remuneration" in subsection 100(1)

is deemed to be the amount determined by the formula

$$A \times B$$

where

A   is the amount that is deemed for the purpose of this paragraph to be the mid-point of the applicable range of remuneration for the pay period, as provided in Schedule I, in which falls the total of

   (A) the payment referred to in subparagraph (i) made in the pay period, and

   (B) the amount of gratuities referred to in subparagraph (ii) declared by the employee for the pay period, and

B   is the maximum number of such pay periods in that year;

(d) if the employee is not resident in Canada at the time of the payment, no personal credits will be allowed for the purposes of this subsection and, if the employee is resident in Canada at the time of the payment, the employee's personal credits for the year are deemed to be the mid-point of the range of amounts of personal credits for a taxation year as provided for in section 2 of Schedule I;

(e) an amount (in this subsection referred to as the "notional tax for the year") shall be computed in respect of that employee by

   (i) calculating the amount of tax payable for the year, as if that amount were calculated under subsection 117(2) of the Act and adjusted annually pursuant to section 117.1 of the Act, on the amount determined in accordance with paragraph (c) as if that amount represented the employee's amount taxable for that year,

and deducting the aggregate of

   (ii) the amount determined in accordance with paragraph (d) multiplied by the appropriate percentage for the year,

   (iii) an amount equal to

   (A) the amount determined in accordance with paragraph (c) multiplied by the employee's premium rate for the year under the *Employment Insurance Act*, not exceeding the maximum amount of the premiums payable by the employee for the year under that Act,

   multiplied by

   (B) the appropriate percentage for the year, and

   (iv) an amount equal to

   (A) the product obtained when the difference between the amount determined in accordance with paragraph (c) and the amount determined under section 20 of the *Canada Pension Plan* for the year is multiplied by the employee's contribution rate for the year under the *Canada Pension Plan* or under a provincial pension plan as defined in subsection 3(1) of that Act, not exceeding the maximum amount of such contributions payable by the employee for the year under the plan,

   multiplied by

   (B) the appropriate percentage for the year;

(f) the amount determined in accordance with paragraph (e) shall be increased by, where applicable, the tax as determined under subsection 120(1) of the Act;

(g) where the amount of notional remuneration for the year is income earned in the Province of Quebec, the amount determined in accordance with paragraph (e) shall be reduced by an amount that is the aggregate of

   (i) the amount that is deemed to be paid under subsection 120(2) of the Act as if there were no other source of income or loss for the year, and

   (ii) the amount by which the amount referred to in subparagraph (i) is increased by virtue of section 27 of the *Federal-Provincial Fiscal Arrangements Act*; and

(h) [Revoked]

(i) the amount to be deducted or withheld shall be computed by

   (i) dividing the amount of the notional tax for the year by the maximum number of pay periods for the year in respect of the appropriate pay period, and

   (ii) rounding the amount determined under subparagraph (i) to the nearest multiple of five cents or, if such amount is equidistant from two such multiples, to the higher multiple.

Announced Administrative Change — COVID-19 — Email requests for Reg. 102(1) and 105(1) waivers, RC473 requests, section 116 certificates

CRA notice (tinyurl.com/cra-internat), April 27, 2021: See under ITA 250(1)(a), sections III and VII.C "Cross-border employment income"; IV "Waiver Requests — Payments to non-residents for services provided in Canada"; and at end, "How to obtain international waivers and certificates of compliance during the COVID-19 crisis" and "CRA Fax Numbers for International Waivers or Non-Resident Disposition".

Related Provisions: Reg. 100(4) — Where employee not required to report for work at an establishment of the employer; Reg. 102(5) — Commission employees — exception; Reg. 102(6) — Exception for high-risk Canadian Forces and police income; Reg. 104(2) — Limitation on withholding where employee not resident in Canada.

Notes: Any person paying "remuneration" as defined (very broadly) in Reg. 100(1) is a Reg. 100(1)"employer" and must withhold under Reg. 102. For the meaning of "reports for work" in Reg. 102(1)(a), see VIEWS doc 2015-0620821I7 ("recurring physical presence" normally required).

Paymentevolution.com offers free payroll reporting for a business with up to 5 employees, and a payroll calculator at tinyurl.com/payr-calc.

Reg. 102(1)(f) requires an addition for income *not* earned in a province, but otherwise leaves it to parallel provincial regs to calculate provincial withholding. (For non-periodic payments, see Notes to Reg. 103(4).)

Reg. 102(1) applies to salary continuation payments paid to a non-resident in respect of employment performed in Canada when the employee was resident in Canada: VIEWS doc 2007-0228561E5. For withholding for a teacher who receives pay over 12 months for 10 months' work, see 2009-0344691E5.

Non-residents: A non-resident employee working outside Canada is usually exempt from withholding: Reg. 104(2). A "qualifying non-resident employee" employed by a "qualifying non-resident employer" in Canada is also exempt: see ITA 153(1) Notes at "153(1)(a)(ii)". An employee working in Canada, but resident in a country having a tax treaty with Canada, can apply for withholding waiver: tinyurl.com/102-waiver, on Form R102-R. (Forms R102-J and R106, used by employers and in the film industry, are no longer used.)

Waiver may be denied if CRA believes the employer has a permanent establishment in Canada re the work the employee will be doing. In some cases CRA applies its administrative "240 days over 3 years" test from Reg. 105 to deny waiver: tinyurl.com/reg102-pwc.

Voluntary disclosure (see ITA 220(3.1) Notes) can eliminate penalties and reduce accrued interest if no waiver was obtained, but the funds still must be remitted by the payer (if they are treaty-protected they can be recovered only by cycling payment back through the employee, who gets the refund): Sorensen, 2015 Cdn Tax Foundation annual conference. See also VIEWS doc 2011-0403551E5 (re management services agreement); Hickey, "CRA: Regulations 102 and 105", 19(10) *Canadian Tax Highlights* (ctf.ca) 5-6 (Oct. 2011); Schermann, "Administrative Requirements of Reg. 105 and Reg. 102", 2012 Tax Dispute Resolution conf. report (ctf.ca), 24:1-9; Vincze & Fontaine, "Reg. 105 and Reg. 102", *ibid.*, 25:1-16; Miklaucic & Sinclair, "Regulations 102 and 105", 2013 conference report, 24:1-42; TEI letter to CRA, "Regulation 102 and Form RC473" March 17, 2016; Deeprose & Bertrand, "Non-Resident Employees: Withhold on Worldwide Income?" 9(2) *Canadian Tax Focus* (ctf.ca) 6 (May 2019).

Reg. 102(1) amended by P.C. 2001-1115 (for 2001 and later tax years), 1998-2270, 1998-654, 1994-372, 1992-2347, 1991-142.

Remission Orders: *Income Earned in Quebec Income Tax Remission Order*, P.C. 1989-1204 (reduction in withholdings for certain income related to Quebec).

Forms: R102-R: Regulation 102 waiver application; RC473: Application for non-resident employer certification; T4001: Employers' guide — payroll deductions and remittances [guide].

(2) [Commission employees] — Where an employee has elected pursuant to subsection 107(2) and has not revoked such election, the amount to be deducted or withheld by the employer from any payment of remuneration (in this subsection referred to as the "payment") that is

   (a) a payment in respect of commissions or is a combined payment of commissions and salary or wages, or

   (b) a payment in respect of salary or wages where that employee receives a combined payment of commissions and salary or wages, made to that employee in his taxation year where he reports for work at an establishment of the employer in a province, in Canada beyond the limits of any province or outside Canada, shall be determined for each payment in accordance with the following rules:

(c) an employee's "estimated annual taxable income" shall be determined by using the formula

$$A - B$$

where

A is the amount of that employee's total remuneration in respect of the year as recorded by the employee on the form referred to in subsection 107(2), and

B is the amount of that employee's expenses in respect of the year as recorded by that employee on that form;

(d) if the employee is not resident in Canada at the time of the payment, no personal credits will be allowed for the purposes of this subsection and if the employee is resident in Canada at the time of the payment, the employee's personal credits for the year shall be the total claim amount as recorded by that employee on the return for the year referred to in subsection 107(1);

(e) an amount (in this subsection referred to as the "notional tax for the year") shall be calculated in respect of that employee by using the formula

$$C - [(D + E + F) \times G] + H - I$$

where

C is the amount of tax payable for the year, calculated as if that amount of tax were computed under subsection 117(2) of the Act and adjusted annually pursuant to section 117.1 of the Act, on the amount determined under paragraph (c) as if that amount represented the employee's amount taxable for that year,

D is the amount determined in accordance with paragraph (d),

E is the amount determined in the description of A in paragraph (c) multiplied by the employee's premium rate for the year under the *Employment Insurance Act*, not exceeding the maximum amount of the premiums payable by the employee for the year under that Act,

F is the amount determined in the description of A in paragraph (c) less the amount for the year determined under section 20 of the *Canada Pension Plan* multiplied by the employee's contribution rate for the year under that Act or under a provincial pension plan as defined in section 3 of that Act, not exceeding the maximum amount of such contributions payable by the employee for the year under the plan,

G is the appropriate percentage for the year,

H is, where applicable, the tax as determined under subsection 120(1) of the Act,

I is, where the amount of total remuneration for the year is income earned in the Province of Quebec, an amount equal to the aggregate of

 (i) the amount that would be deemed to have been paid under subsection 120(2) of the Act with respect to the employee if the notional tax for the year for the employee were determined without reference to the elements H, I and J in this formula and if that tax were that employee's tax payable under Part I of the Act for that year, as if there were no other source of income or loss for the year, and

 (ii) the amount by which the amount referred to in subparagraph (i) is increased by virtue of section 27 of the *Federal-Provincial Fiscal Arrangements Act*;

(f) the employee's notional rate of tax for a year is calculated by dividing the amount determined under paragraph (e) by the amount referred to in the description of A in paragraph (c) in respect of that employee and expressed as a decimal fraction

rounded to the nearest hundredth, or where the third digit is equidistant from two consecutive one-thousandths, to the higher thereof;

(g) the amount to be deducted or withheld in respect of any payment made to that employee shall be determined by multiplying the payment by the appropriate decimal fraction determined pursuant to paragraph (f).

(h) [Repealed]

Related Provisions: ITA 257 — Negative amounts in formulas; Reg. 102(5) — Commission employees — exception; Reg. 104(2) — Limitation on withholding where employee not resident in Canada.

Notes: Reg. 102(2) amended by P.C. 2001-1115 (effective for 2001 and later taxation years), P.C. 1998-2270, 1994-1370, 1994-372, 1992-2347 and 1991-1643.

Remission Orders: *Income Earned in Quebec Income Tax Remission Order*, P.C. 1989-1204 (reduction in withholdings for certain income related to Quebec).

(3), (4) [Revoked]

(5) [Commission employees — exception] — Notwithstanding subsections (1) and (2), no amount shall be deducted or withheld in the year by an employer from a payment of remuneration to an employee in respect of commissions earned by the employee in the immediately preceding year where those commissions were previously reported by the employer as remuneration of the employee in respect of that year on an information return.

(6) [Certain international income — no withholding] — Despite subsection (1), no amount shall be deducted or withheld in the year by an employer from an amount determined in accordance with subparagraph 110(1)(f)(iii), (iv) or (v) of the Act.

Notes: Reg. 102(6) amended to refer to ITA 110(1)(f)(iii)–(iv) by 2014 budget bill #2, effective for amounts paid after July 11, 2013 [and see extended-reassessment rule in Notes to ITA 17(1)].

Reg. 102(6) added by P.C. 2005-1133, effective for 2004 and later taxation years.

Definitions [Reg. 102]: "amount" — ITA 248(1); "amount taxable" — ITA 117(2); "appropriate percentage" — ITA 248(1); "Canada" — ITA 255, *Interpretation Act* 35(1); "commissions", "employee", "employer" — Reg. 100(1); "employer" — Reg. 100(4); "estimated annual taxable income" — Reg. 102(2)(c); "estimated deductions" — Reg. 100(1); "form" — Reg. 102(2)(c); "notional net remuneration for the year" — Reg. 102(2)(e); "notional tax for the year" — Reg. 102(1)(e), 102(2)(f); "pay period" — Reg. 100(1); "payment" — Reg. 102(1)(a), 102(2); "personal credits" — Reg. 100(1); "province" — *Interpretation Act* 35(1); "provincial pension plan" — *Canada Pension Plan* s. 3; "remuneration"(a)(ii) — Reg. 100(1); "resident in Canada" — ITA 250; "salary or wages" — ITA 248(1); "taxation year" — ITA 249; "total remuneration" — Reg. 100(1).

103. Non-periodic payments — (1) Where a payment in respect of a bonus or retroactive increase in remuneration is made by an employer to an employee whose total remuneration from the employer (including the bonus or retroactive increase) may reasonably be expected not to exceed $5,000 in the taxation year of the employee in which the payment is made, the employer shall deduct or withhold, in the case of an employee who reports for work at an establishment of the employer

(a) in any province, 10 per cent, or

(b) in Canada beyond the limits of any province or outside Canada, 15 per cent,

(c)–(n) [Repealed]

of such payment in lieu of the amount determined under section 102.

Related Provisions: Reg. 104(2) — No withholding where recipient not resident in Canada [see ITA 212(1) instead].

Notes: The words "employer" and "employee" refer to *any* payer and payee, and "remuneration" is defined very broadly: see Reg. 100(1).

Reg. 103(1) amended by P.C. 2001-1115 (for 2001 and later taxation years), 2000-1334, 1999-2205, 1998-2271, 1997-1774, 1996-1557, 1996-500, 1994-1370, 1994-372, 1993-1552, 1992-2347, 1992-291, 1991-1643.

Remission Orders: *Income Earned in Quebec Income Tax Remission Order*, P.C. 1989-1204 (reduction in withholdings for certain income related to Quebec).

(2) [Bonus] — Where a payment in respect of a bonus is made by an employer to an employee whose total remuneration from the employer (including the bonus) may reasonably be expected to exceed

$5,000 in the taxation year of the employee in which the payment is made, the amount to be deducted or withheld therefrom by the employer is

(a) the amount determined under section 102 in respect of an assumed remuneration equal to the aggregate of

(i) the amount of regular remuneration paid by the employer to the employee in the pay period in which the remuneration is paid, and

(ii) an amount equal to the bonus payment divided by the number of pay periods in the taxation year of the employee in which the payment is made

minus

(b) the amount determined under section 102 in respect of the amount of regular remuneration paid by the employer to the employee in the pay period

multiplied by

(c) the number of pay periods in the taxation year of the employee in which the payment is made.

(3) [Retroactive pay increase] — Where a payment in respect of a retroactive increase in remuneration is made by an employer to an employee whose total remuneration from the employer (including the retroactive increase) may reasonably be expected to exceed $5,000 in the taxation year of the employee in which the payment is made, the amount to be deducted or withheld therefrom by the employer is

(a) the amount determined under section 102 in respect of the new rate of remuneration

minus

(b) the amount determined under section 102 in respect of the previous rate of remuneration

multiplied by

(c) the number of pay periods in respect of which the increase in remuneration is retroactive.

(4) [Lump sum payment] — Subject to subsections (4.1) and (5), where a lump sum payment is made by an employer to an employee who is a resident of Canada,

(a) if the payment does not exceed $5,000, the employer shall deduct or withhold therefrom, in the case of an employee who reports for work at an establishment of the employer

(i) in Quebec, 5 per cent,

(ii) in any other province, 7 per cent, or

(iii) in Canada beyond the limits of any province or outside Canada, 10 per cent,

(iv)–(xiv) [Repealed]

of such payment in lieu of the amount determined under section 102;

(b) if the payment exceeds $5,000 but does not exceed $15,000, the employer shall deduct or withhold therefrom, in the case of an employee who reports for work at an establishment of the employer

(i) in Quebec, 10 per cent,

(ii) in any other province, 13 per cent, or

(iii) in Canada beyond the limits of any province or outside Canada, 20 per cent,

(iv)–(xiv) [Repealed]

of such payment in lieu of the amount determined under section 102; and

(c) if the payment exceeds $15,000, the employer shall deduct or withhold therefrom, in the case of an employee who reports for work at an establishment of the employer

(i) in Quebec, 15 per cent,

(ii) in any other province, 20 per cent, or

(iii) in Canada beyond the limits of any province or outside Canada, 30 per cent,

(iv)–(xiv) [Repealed]

of such payment in lieu of the amount determined under section 102.

Related Provisions: Reg. 103(4.1) — Application to Canada Recovery Benefit; Reg. 104(2) — No withholding where recipient not resident in Canada [see ITA 212(1) instead].

Notes: See Notes to ITA 153(1). Except for the *Canada Recovery Benefits Act* payments (Reg. 103(4.1)), the rates in each subpara. (ii) (7%, 13%, 20%) are actually 10%, 20% and 30% due to a parallel 3%-7%-10% withholding obligation for provincial tax outside Quebec: B.C. Reg. 396/2000 s. 6(4); Alberta Reg. 34/2001 s. 4; Sask. *Income Tax Deduction Regulations* s. 9(5); Manitoba Reg. 31/2001 s. 4(2); Ont. Reg. 138/17 s. 2(2)4 [refers to CRA's guide RC4157, which has the withholding rates]; N.S. Reg. 11/73 s. 103(4); former N.B. Reg. 93-100 s. 5(4) [repealed; replacement *New Brunswick Income Tax Act* s. 124(3) does not have the correct rates]; PEI Reg. EC2001-505 s. 4(4); Nfld. Reg. 18/01 s. 5(4); NWT Reg. I-1 s. 4(4) [only up to 15% from $5,000]; Nunavut Reg. I-1 s. 4(4) [same]; Yukon Reg. O.I.C. 1980/13 s. 4(4). See also VIEWS doc 2010-0384102E5 and tinyurl.com/lumpsum-cra.

In Quebec, there is 5%/10%/15% federal withholding, plus provincial withholding (*Taxation Act* Reg. 1015R19; tinyurl.com/retiring-lump), of 15% up to $5,000 and 20% over $5,000 for a retiring allowance, DPSP and certain other lump sums; so the combined rates are 20/30/35% instead of 10/20/30% as in other provinces. For a lump sum from an RRSP or RRIF, it is 15%, so the combined rates are 20/25/30%: Reg. 1015R21; tinyurl.com/rrsp-lump.

These rates apply to RRSP withdrawals and payment of a "retiring allowance", including settlement of a wrongful dismissal claim. See Reg. 103(6)(c) and (e). Withdrawing private corporation shares from an RRSP requires withholding even if there is no cash in the plan: VIEWS doc 2005-0148831E5.

However, these rates do *not* apply to a non-resident, who is instead subject to a fixed withholding tax, e.g. under ITA 212(1)(j.1) for a retiring allowance and 212(1)(l) for an RRSP, possibly reduced by tax treaty.

RRSP periodic annuity payments and RRIF minimum amount payments are not subject to federal withholding: Reg. 100(1)"remuneration"(i), (j.1), 103(6)(d), (d.1).

If lump-sum payments are split into multiple payments (instalments), and each payment is made in fulfillment of a predetermined compensation, the CRA says the Reg. 103(4) rate for the total payment applies: docs 2005-0118351E5 (scheduled monthly RRIF payments above minimum amount); 2014-0531331I7 (retiring allowance — overrules 2002-0135807); tinyurl.com/multiwithdraw q.14; tinyurl.com/rrif-whold. On a lump-sum pension distributed to a beneficiary by an estate, see 2011-0420781C6.

A withdrawal from a RRIF in excess of twice the "minimum amount" for the year is not protected by tax treaty provisions that limit withholding tax on pension payments, due to s. 5"periodic pension payment"(c)(i) of the *Income Tax Conventions Interpretation Act* (reproduced before the Canada-US treaty). See Notes to Article XVIII(2) of the Canada-U.S. tax treaty.

In *Iskander v. BMO Nesbitt Burns*, 2014 ONCA 582, the trial court wrongly ordered that a requested withdrawal of private company shares from an RRSP be done with no withholding, because the Court failed to understand that BMO, as RRSP trustee, was an "employer" as defined in Reg. 100(1). The Ont. CA reversed this decision on the basis that this issue was not before the judge, and that BMO was right to refuse to withdraw the shares without an adequate valuation.

Where a forfeited amount is paid out of a DPSP and partly contributed back by the employer, withholding must still be based on the gross amount: VIEWS doc 2005-0130471E5. For withholding on refunds of excess RPP contributions and expense reimbursements, see 2002-0163535, 2004-0100601E5.

Exclusion of Reg. 103(4.1) added by 2020 COVID bill #4, effective Sept. 27, 2020.

Reg. 103(4) amended by P.C. 2001-1115 (for 2001 and later tax years), 2000-1334, 1999-2205, 1998-2271, 1997-1774, 1996-1557, 1996-500, 1994-1370, 1994-372, 1993-1552, 1992-2347, 1992-291, 1991-1643.

Remission Orders: *Income Earned in Quebec Income Tax Remission Order*, P.C. 1989-1204 (reduction in withholdings for certain income related to Quebec).

Forms: T1036: Home buyers' plan — request to withdraw funds from an RRSP; RC4157: Deducting income tax on pension and other income, and filing the T4A slip and summary [guide].

(4.1) [Canada Recovery Benefit] — For the purposes of a lump sum payment described in paragraph (6)(h), subsection (4) is to be read without reference to its paragraphs (b) and (c) and the portion of subsection (4) before subparagraph (a)(i) is to be read as follows:

"(4) Where a lump sum payment is made by an employer to an employee,

(a) the employer shall deduct or withhold therefrom, in the case of an employee who reports for work at an establishment of the employer"

Notes: This is for COVID-19 benefits under the *Canada Recovery Benefits Act*: Canada Recovery Benefit (CRB) (see ITA 60(v.2) Notes); Canada Recovery Sickness Benefit; Canada Recovery Caregiving Benefit (CRCB). These fall under ITA 56(1)(r) and Reg. 100(1)"remuneration"(h). Withholding is 10% even for a payment over $5,000 covering multiple weeks (including in Quebec: 5% federal + 5% QC). (Since CRBA 4(2) and 18(2) require application for CRB and CRCB to be made within 60 days of the end of the (2- or 1-week) period, the maximum CRB payment from an application is $6,000, and the maximum CRCB payment is $6,500.)

Reg. 103(4.1) added by 2020 COVID bill #4, effective Sept. 27, 2020.

(5) [Lump sum pension payment] — Where the payment referred to in subsection (4) would be pension income or qualified pension income of the employee in respect of which subsection 118(3) of the Act would apply if the definition "pension income" in subsection 118(7) of the Act were read without reference to subparagraphs (a)(ii) and (iii) thereof, the payment shall be deemed to be the amount of the payment minus

(a) where the payment does not exceed the amount taxable referred to in paragraph 117(2)(a) of the Act, as adjusted annually pursuant to section 117.1 of the Act, the lesser of $1,000 and the amount of the payment;

(b) where the payment exceeds the amount referred to in paragraph (a) but does not exceed $61,509, $727;

(c) where the payment exceeds $61,509 but does not exceed $100,000, $615; and

(d) where the payment exceeds $100,000, $552.

Notes: Reg. 103(5)(b)-(c) replaced with (b)-(d) by P.C. 2001-1115, effective for 2001 and later taxation years.

Reg. 103(5)(a)–(c) amended by P.C. 1992-2347, effective 1992.

(6) ["Lump sum payment"] — For the purposes of subsection (4), a "lump sum payment" means a payment that is

(a) a payment described in subparagraph 40(1)(a)(i) or (iii) or paragraph 40(1)(c) of the *Income Tax Application Rules*,

(b) a payment under a deferred profit sharing plan or a plan referred to in section 147 of the Act as a "revoked plan", except a payment referred to in subparagraph 147(2)(k)(v) of the Act,

(c) a payment made during the lifetime of an annuitant referred to in the definition "annuitant" in subsection 146(1) of the Act out of or under a registered retirement savings plan of that annuitant, other than

(i) a periodic annuity payment, or

(ii) a payment made by a person who has reasonable grounds to believe that the payment may be deducted under subsection 146(8.2) of the Act in computing the income of any taxpayer,

(d) a payment out of or under a plan referred to in subsection 146(12) of the Act as an "amended plan" other than

(i) a periodic annuity payment, or

(ii) where paragraph 146(12)(a) of the Act applied to the plan after May 25, 1976, a payment made in a year subsequent to the year in which that paragraph applied to the plan,

(d.1) a payment made during the lifetime of an annuitant referred to in the definition "annuitant" in subsection 146.3(1) of the Act under a registered retirement income fund of that annuitant, other than a payment to the extent that it is in respect of the minimum amount (within the meaning assigned by subsection 146.3(1) of the Act) under the fund for a year,

(e) a retiring allowance,

(f) a payment of an amount as, on account or in lieu of payment of, or in satisfaction of, proceeds of the surrender, cancellation or redemption of an income-averaging annuity contract,

(g) a payment described in paragraph (n) of the definition "remuneration" in subsection 100(1), or

(h) a payment made under the *Canada Recovery Benefits Act*.

Related Provisions: Reg. 100(3)(c) — No source withholding required where amount paid directly to employee's RRSP by employer.

Notes: Reg. 103(6)(h) added by 2020 COVID bill #4, effective Sept. 27, 2020. The withholding is a flat 10%: Reg. 103(4.1).

Reg. 103(6)(c)(ii) amended by P.C. 1991-2540, effective 1991.

Reg. 103(6)(g) added by P.C. 1998-2275, effective for 1998 and later taxation years. See Reg. 103(4) and (8) for withholding rates.

(7) [Retirement compensation arrangement] — For the purposes of subsection 153(1) of the Act, the amount to be deducted or withheld by a person shall be 50 per cent

(a) of the contribution made by the person under a retirement compensation arrangement, other than

(i) a contribution made by the person as an employee,

(ii) a contribution made to a plan or arrangement that is a prescribed plan or arrangement for the purposes of subsection 207.6(6) of the Act, or

(iii) a contribution made by way of a transfer from another retirement compensation arrangement under circumstances in which subsection 207.6(7) of the Act applies; or

(b) of the payment by the person to a resident of Canada of an amount on account of the purchase price of an interest in a retirement compensation arrangement.

Notes: Reg. 103(7)(a) amended, effectively to add subpara. (ii), by P.C. 1999-2211, retroactive to 1992 (but subpara. (iii) does not apply to contributions made before 1996).

Reg. 103(7)(a) amended by P.C. 1998-2770, for amounts transferred after 1995.

Forms: T4041: Retirement compensation arrangements guide.

(8) [RESP payment] — Every employer making a payment described in paragraph (n) of the definition "remuneration" in subsection 100(1) shall withhold — in addition to any other amount required to be withheld under Part I of these Regulations — on account of the tax payable under Part X.5 of the Act, an amount equal to

(a) where the amount is paid in the province of Quebec, 12 per cent of the payment, and

(b) in any other case, 20 per cent of the payment.

Notes: Reg. 103(8) applies only to certain payments out of a RESP; see Reg. 103(4) for regular withholding on "lump sum" amounts.

Reg. 103(8) added by P.C. 1998-2275, for 1998 and later taxation years; and amended by P.C. 1999-2205 effective June 17, 1999.

(9) [Tax Informant Program payment] — The amount to be deducted or withheld by a person from any payment of an amount described in paragraph 56(1)(z.4) of the Act is

(a) in the case of a payment to a resident of Quebec, 30% of the payment; or

(b) in the case of a payment to a resident of Canada who is not a resident of Quebec, 50% of the payment.

Notes: See Notes to ITA 56(1)(z.4). Revenu Québec will require further withholding in Quebec.

Reg. 103(9) added by 2014 budget bill #1, effective June 19, 2014.

Definitions [Reg. 103]: "amount" — ITA 248(1); "amount taxable" — ITA 117(2); "annuity" — ITA 248(1); "Canada" — ITA 255, *Interpretation Act* 35(1); "deferred profit sharing plan" — ITA 147(1), 248(1); "employee", "employer" — Reg. 100(1); "establishment of the employer" — Reg. 100(4); "income-averaging annuity contract" — ITA 248(1); "lump sum payment" — Reg. 103(6); "minimum amount" — ITA 146.3(1); "pay period" — Reg. 100(1); "person" — ITA 248(1); "province" — *Interpretation Act* 35(1); "registered retirement income fund" — ITA 146.3(1), 248(1); "registered retirement savings plan" — ITA 146(1), 248(1); "remuneration" — Reg. 100(1); "resident of Canada" — ITA 250; "retirement compensation arrangement", "retiring allowance" — ITA 248(1); "taxation year" — ITA 249; "taxpayer" — ITA 248(1); "total remuneration" — Reg. 100(1).

103.1 (1) ["Plan payment"] — For the purpose of the description of C in subsection (2), "plan payment" means

(a) in the case of a disability assistance payment that is a lifetime disability assistance payment, the total amount of all the lifetime disability assistance payments that have been made or that may reasonably be expected to be made to the employee under the plan in their taxation year and that the employer has reasonable grounds to believe are described in paragraph (o) of the definition "remuneration" in subsection 100(1); or

(b) in the case of a disability assistance payment that is other than a lifetime disability assistance payment, the amount of the payment that is made to the employee under the plan and that is described in paragraph (o) of the definition "remuneration" in subsection 100(1).

(2) [RDSP disability assistance payment — withholding amount] — If an employer makes a disability assistance payment under a registered disability savings plan to an employee who is a resident of Canada, the employer shall, in lieu of the amount determined under section 102, deduct or withhold from the payment an amount determined by the formula

$$(A - B) \times C$$

where

A is the amount of the disability assistance payment that is made to the employee and that is described in paragraph (o) of the definition "remuneration" in subsection 100(1);

B is

(a) if the beneficiary of the plan is deceased, nil, or

(b) the amount by which the total of the following amounts exceeds the total amount of all the disability assistance payments previously made to the employee in their taxation year and that are described in paragraph (o) of the definition "remuneration" in subsection 100(1):

(i) the amount determined for F in subsection 118(1.1) of the Act for the taxation year, and

(ii) the amount used under the description of B in subsection 118.3(1) of the Act for the taxation year; and

C is

(a) if the plan payment does not exceed $5,000 and the amount is paid

(i) in Quebec, 5 per cent,

(ii) in any other province, 7 per cent, or

(iii) in Canada beyond the limits of any province or outside Canada, 10 per cent,

(b) if the plan payment exceeds $5,000 but does not exceed $15,000 and the amount is paid

(i) in Quebec, 10 per cent,

(ii) in any other province, 13 per cent, or

(iii) in Canada beyond the limits of any province or outside Canada, 20 per cent, or

(c) if the plan payment exceeds $15,000 and the amount is paid

(i) in Quebec, 15 per cent,

(ii) in any other province, 20 per cent, or

(iii) in Canada beyond the limits of any province or outside Canada, 30 per cent.

Related Provisions: ITA 257 — Negative amounts in formulas; Reg. 100(1)"remuneration"(o) — Taxable amount of DAP is "remuneration"; Reg. 103.1(1) — "Plan payment"; Reg. 104(2) — No withholding where recipient not resident in Canada [see ITA 212(1)(r.1) instead].

Notes [Reg. 103.1]: As with Reg. 103(4), there is parallel provincial withholding so that the rates outside Quebec are 10%, 20% and 30%. Under Reg. 103.1(1), all "lifetime disability assistance payments" (see ITA 146.4(1)) in the year are totalled up to determine the total and thus the withholding rate under Reg. 103.1(2)C.

Reg. 103.1(2)B(b)(i) amended by 2021 budget bill #1, for 2020 and later tax years, to reflect the "basic personal amount" moving from ITA 118(1)B(c) to 118(1.1)F.

Reg. 103.1 added by P.C. 2016-96, effective July 2015.

Definitions [Reg. 103.1]: "amount" — ITA 248(1); "Canada" — ITA 255, *Interpretation Act* 35(1); "disability assistance payment" — ITA 146.4(1); "employee", "employer" — Reg. 100(1); "lifetime disability assistance payment" — ITA 146.4(1); "plan payment" — Reg. 103.1(1); "province" — *Interpretation Act* 35(1); "registered disability savings plan" — ITA 146.4(1), 248(1); "resident" — ITA 250; "taxation year" — ITA 249.

104. Deductions not required — (1) [Repealed]

Notes: Reg. 104(1) amended by P.C. 1992-2347 and 1994-372, and repealed by P.C. 2001-1115 effective for 2001 and later taxation years. It allowed deductions not to be withheld from an employee with sufficient credits on the TD1.

(2) [Employee not in Canada] — No amount shall be deducted or withheld from a payment in accordance with any of sections 102 to 103.1 in respect of an employee who was neither employed nor resident in Canada at the time of payment except in respect of

(a) remuneration described in subparagraph 115(2)(e)(i) of the Act that is paid to a non-resident person who has in the year, or had in any previous year, ceased to be resident in Canada; or

(b) remuneration reasonably attributable to the duties of any office or employment performed or to be performed in Canada by the non-resident person.

Notes: Due to Reg. 104(2), Reg. 103(4) does not apply to payment of a retiring allowance or other "lump sum payment" (see Reg. 103(6)) to a non-resident. Withholding may apply under ITA 212(1) instead, e.g. 212(1)(j.1) for a retiring allowance.

See VIEWS doc 2011-0397511E5 (no withholding required).

Reg. 104(2) amended to change "102 or 103" to "102 to 103.1" by P.C. 2016-96, effective July 1, 2015.

Reg. 104(2)(b) amended by P.C. 1997-1471, in force October 29, 1997, to change "*a* non-resident person" to "*the* non-resident person".

Interpretation Bulletins: IT-161R3: Non-residents — Exemption from tax deductions at source on employment income (archived).

(3) [Home Buyers' Plan] — No amount shall be deducted or withheld from a payment made by a person during the lifetime of an annuitant referred to in paragraph (a) of the definition "annuitant" in subsection 146(1) of the Act out of or under a registered retirement savings plan of the annuitant where, at the time of the payment, the annuitant has certified in prescribed form to the person that

(a) a written agreement has been entered into to acquire a home by either

(i) the annuitant, or

(ii) a disabled person who is related to the annuitant and who is entitled to the credit for mental or physical impairment under subsection 118.3 (1) of the Act;

(b) the annuitant intends that the home be used as a principal place of residence in Canada for the annuitant or the disabled person, as the case may be, within one year after its acquisition;

(c) the home has not been previously owned by the annuitant, the annuitant's spouse or common-law partner, the disabled person or the spouse or common-law partner of that person;

(d) the annuitant was resident in Canada;

(e) the total amount of the payment and all other such payments received by the annuitant in respect of the home at or before the time of the payment does not exceed the dollar amount specified in paragraph (h) of the definition "regular eligible amount" in subsection 146.01(1) of the Act;

(f) except where the annuitant certifies that he or she is a disabled person entitled to the credit for mental or physical impairment under subsection 118.3(1) of the Act or certifies that the payment is being withdrawn for the benefit of such a disabled person, the annuitant is a qualifying homebuyer at the time of the certification; and

(g) where the annuitant has withdrawn an eligible amount, within the meaning assigned by subsection 146.01(1) of the Act, before the calendar year of the certification, the total of all eligible amounts received by the annuitant before that calendar year does not exceed the total of all amounts previously designated under subsection 146.01(3) of the Act or included in computing the annuitant's income under subsection 146.01(4) or (5) of the Act.

Related Provisions: Reg. 104(3.01), (3.1), (4) — Interpretation.

Notes: Reg. 104(3) allows funds to be withdrawn from an RRSP under the Home Buyers' Plan (ITA 146.01) without the financial institution withholding at source.

Reg. 104(3) amended by 2002-2013 technical bill (effective Jan. 28, 2009), P.C. 2001-957, 1998-2272, 1994-438, 1993-271, 1992-480.

(3.01) ["Qualifying homebuyer"] — For the purpose of subsection (3), the annuitant is a qualifying homebuyer at a particular time unless

(a) the annuitant had an owner-occupied home in the period beginning on January 1 of the fourth calendar year preceding the particular time, and ending on the thirty-first day before the particular time; or

(b) the annuitant's spouse or common-law partner, in the period referred to in paragraph (a), had an owner-occupied home that was inhabited by the annuitant at any time during the annuitant's marriage to the spouse or the annuitant's common-law partnership with the common-law partner.

Notes: Reg. 104(3.01)(b) amended by P.C. 2001-957 to refer to common-law partner and common-law partnership, effective 2001 or earlier.

Reg. 104(3.01) added by P.C. 1998-2272, for payments made after 1998.

(3.1) ["Owner-occupied home"] — For the purpose of subsection (3.01), an individual shall be considered to have had an owner-occupied home at any time where the home was owned, whether jointly with another person or otherwise, by the individual at that time and inhabited by the individual as the individual's principal place of residence at that time.

Notes: Reg. 104(3.1) added by P.C. 1994-438, effective for payments made after March 1, 1994; and amended by P.C. 1998-2272, effective for payments made after 1998, to change reference to "(3)" to "(3.01)".

(4) ["Home"] — For the purposes of subsections (3), (3.01) and (3.1), "home" means

(a) a housing unit;

(b) a share of the capital stock of a cooperative housing corporation, where the holder of the share is entitled to possession of a housing unit; and

(c) where the context so requires, the housing unit to which a share described in paragraph (b) relates.

Notes: Reg. 104(4) added by P.C. 1992-480; reference to subsec. (3.1) added by P.C. 1994-438, effective for payments made after March 1, 1994; reference to subsec. (3.01) added by P.C. 1998-2772, for payments made after 1998.

Definitions [Reg. 104]: "amount" — ITA 248(1); "annuitant" — ITA 146.1(1); "calendar year" — *Interpretation Act* 37(1)(a); "Canada" — ITA 255, *Interpretation Act* 35(1); "common-law partner", "common-law partnership" — ITA 248(1); "corporation" — ITA 248(1), *Interpretation Act* 35(1); "eligible amount" — ITA 146.01(1); "employed", "employee", "employer" — Reg. 100(1); "employment" — ITA 248(1); "home" — Reg. 104(4); "individual" — ITA 248(1); "non-resident", "office" — ITA 248(1); "owner-occupied home" — Reg. 104(3.1); "person", "prescribed" — ITA 248(1); "qualifying homebuyer" — Reg. 104(3.01); "registered retirement savings plan" — ITA 146(1), 248(1); "remuneration" — Reg. 100(1); "resident in Canada" — ITA 250; "share" — ITA 248(1); "written" — *Interpretation Act* 35(1)"writing".

104.1 Lifelong Learning Plan — **(1)** No amount shall be deducted or withheld from a payment made by a person during the lifetime of an annuitant referred to in paragraph (a) of the definition "annuitant" in subsection 146(1) of the Act out of or under a registered retirement savings plan of the annuitant where, at the time of the payment, the annuitant has certified in prescribed form to the person that

(a) at the time of certification, the annuitant or the annuitant's spouse or common-law partner

(i) is a full-time student in a qualifying educational program,

(ii) is a part-time student in a qualifying educational program and is entitled to the credit for mental or physical impairment under subsection 118.3(1) of the Act, or

(iii) has received notification in writing of his or her entitlement, either absolutely or conditionally, to enrol before March of the year that follows the year of certification as

(A) a full-time student in a qualifying educational program, or

(B) a part-time student in a qualifying educational program where the annuitant or the annuitant's spouse or

common-law partner is entitled to the credit for mental or physical impairment under subsection 118.3(1) of the Act;

(b) the annuitant is resident in Canada;

(c) the total amount of the payment and all other such payments received by the annuitant for a year at or before that time does not exceed $10,000; and

(d) the total payments received by the annuitant do not exceed $20,000 throughout the period in which the annuitant participates in the Lifelong Learning Plan.

Related Provisions: Reg. 104.1(2) — Interpretation.

Notes: See at end of Reg. 104.1.

Forms: RC96: LLP — request to withdraw funds from an RRSP.

(2) ["Qualifying educational program"] — For the purpose of subsection (1), a "qualifying educational program" means a qualifying educational program at a designated educational institution (as those expressions are defined in subsection 118.6(1) of the Act), except that a reference to a "qualifying educational program" shall be read

(a) without reference to paragraphs (a) and (b) of that definition; and

(b) as if the reference to"3 consecutive weeks" in that definition were a reference to "3 consecutive months".

Notes [Reg. 104.1]: Reg. 104.1 allows funds to be withdrawn from an RRSP under the Lifelong Learning Plan (ITA 146.02) without the financial institution withholding funds at source.

Reg. 104.1 added by P.C. 1998-2272, for payments made after 1998.

Reg. 104.1(1)(a) amended by P.C. 2001-957 to add reference to "common-law partner", effective as per Notes to ITA 248(1)"common-law partner".

Definitions [Reg. 104.1]: "amount" — ITA 248(1); "annuitant" — ITA 146(1); "common-law partner" — ITA 248(1); "prescribed" — ITA 248(1); "qualifying educational program" — Reg. 104.1(2); "registered retirement savings plan" — ITA 146(1), 248(1); "resident in Canada" — ITA 250.

105. Non-residents — **(1)** Every person paying to a non-resident person a fee, commission or other amount in respect of services rendered in Canada, of any nature whatever, shall deduct or withhold 15 per cent of such payment.

(2) Subsection (1) does not apply to a payment

(a) described in the definition "remuneration" in subsection 100(1);

(b) made to a registered non-resident insurer (within the meaning assigned by section 804); or

(c) made to an authorized foreign bank in respect of its Canadian banking business.

Announced Administrative Change — Reg. 105 waivers — COVID-19

CRA notice (tinyurl.com/cra-internat), April 27, 2021: See under ITA 250(1)(a), sections III and VII.C "Cross-border employment income"; IV "Waiver Requests — Payments to non-residents for services provided in Canada"; and at end, "How to obtain international waivers and certificates of compliance during the COVID-19 crisis" and "CRA Fax Numbers for International Waivers or Non-Resident Disposition".

Related Provisions [Reg. 105]: ITA 153(1.1) — Waiver of withholding; ITA 164(1)(c)(i) — Late refund of amount overpaid due to assessment under Reg. 105; ITA 212(1)(a) — Withholding tax on fees for management services; ITA 244.2 — Banks, etc. required to report international transfers of $10,000 or more; Canada-U.S. Tax Treaty:Art. VII — Business profits.

Notes [Reg. 105]: If the service is rendered in Quebec, a further 9% must be withheld and remitted to Revenu Québec: Reg. 1015R18 under the Quebec *Taxation Act*, reproduced in *Provincial TaxPartner*, on *Taxnet Pro* and in *La Loi du Practicien — Loi sur les impôts de Québec* (Carswell, annual).

In *Ogden Palladium*, 2002 FCA 336, a US producer/promoter of the Elvis Stojko figure-skating show was held to be rendering "services", and the Canadian payers were subject to penalties for not withholding under Reg. 105.

Waiver: Even if the non-resident has no tax liability due to a treaty (e.g., Canada-US tax treaty Art. VII:1 or XV:1) or to not carrying on business in Canada, the withholding obligation applies unless CRA waives it (apply on Form R105). ITA 153(1.1) permits waiver: *Beggs*, 2016 TCC 11, para. 16. To obtain a refund, a payee must file a Part I return under s. 150 (for a corporation, a non-resident T2 with Schedules 91 and 97 claiming treaty exemption). Note that in some cases, Part I tax may exceed the withholding so further tax will be payable.

For guidelines for CRA waiver of withholding, see Information Circular 75-6R2 Appendixes A, B. The CRA target for processing waiver requests was 85% within 30 days: *Current-Year Service Standards 2009-2010* #27; but this no longer appears on tinyurl.com/cra-standards. CRA will not make a waiver retroactive to before the waiver letter date, so payers must withhold and remit the 15% until a waiver is issued: 2012 Ontario Tax Conference Roundtable (ctf.ca) Q7.

A CRA refusal to provide a waiver can be reviewed by the Federal Court: see Notes to 171(1). It cannot be appealed to the Tax Court: *Beggs*, 2016 TCC 11.

See also Baker & Meister, "Non-Residents Rendering Services in Canada", 47(5) *Canadian Tax Journal* 1321-41 (1999); Hallam, "Regulation 105 and Other Cross-Border Withholding Issues", 2004 B.C. Tax Conference (ctf.ca), 21:1-28; Horne, "Regulation 105 Source Deductions", II(2) *Resource Sector Taxation* (Federated Press) 110-15 (2004); Hickey, "Reg 105 Update", 10(4) *Canadian Tax Highlights [CTH]* (ctf.ca) 27-28 (April 2002) and "CRA: Regulations 102 and 105", 19(10) *CTH* 5-6 (Oct. 2011); Bernstein, "Professionals and Other Service Providers Beware", 1852 *Tax Topics* (CCH) 1-7 (Sept. 6, 2007) and "Refundable Withholding Tax Traps", 20(8) *CTH* 11-12 (Aug. 2012); Keey, "Regulation 105 and E-Commerce", 2013(8) *Tax Times* (Carswell) 1-3 (April 26, 2013); Schermann, "Administrative Requirements of Reg. 105 and Reg. 102", 2012 *Tax Dispute Resolution* conf. report (ctf.ca), 24:1-9; Vincze & Fontaine, "Reg. 105 and Reg. 102", *ibid.*, 25:1-16; Miklaucic & Sinclair, "Regulations 102 and 105 and Cross-Border Compliance Issues", 2013 Cdn Tax Foundation conference report, 24:1-42; Seto, "Update on International Secondments", 13(12) *Tax Hyperion* (Carswell) 3-5 (Dec. 2016); Aptowitzer, "Reporting Payments to Non-Residents", 25(9) *Canadian Not-for-Profit News* (Carswell) 71-72 (Sept. 2017); Baker & Dumalski, "Regulation 105", 26(8) *CTH* 1-2 (Aug. 2018) (re non-resident artists and athletes).

For CRA interpretation see Guide RC4445 (guidance on the T4A-NR form as well as deduction and remittance), Information Circular 75-6R2 and Guide T4001. Non-resident employees working outside Canada are exempt: Reg. 105(2), 104(2), VIEWS doc 2007-0245631E5. Non-resident directors' withholding is at regular rates under Reg. 102 rather than under Reg. 105: IC 75-6R2 paras. 76-79. For fees to non-resident trustees see 2005-0164831E5. Reg. 105 does not apply to a non-resident collecting fees from another non-resident as agent of Canadian resident X for services in Canada, because the fees belong to X: 2007-0260801R3. See also 2008-0271251R3 (certain mutual fund dealers' fees — no withholding); 2009-0325921E5, 2009-0331791E5, 2010-0355591E5 and 2010-0354791E5 (general comments); 2010-0377501R3 (no withholding required); 2011-0405561E5 (deposits paid to non-resident artist who will perform in Canada [note that waiver may be available due to Canada-US tax treaty Art. XVI:1]); 2011-0425041R3 (no withholding on racetrack paying purse winnings to racehorse owners); 2012-0444101C6 (each partner must apply for refund of withholdings from a partnership); 2012-0466671E5 (whether withholding required on payments to partnership formed in India); 2013-0505511E5 (withholding required on cancellation fees paid to US artist); 2011 Cdn Tax Foundation conference report, CRA/RQ Round Table q.5 (p.4:3-4); 2014-0526381I7, 2014-0531371I7 (federal government entity must withhold 15% of amount paid to non-resident contractor if no waiver, regardless of contract terms); 2015-0563611E5 (call centre outside Canada is not rendering services in Canada); 2016-063672117 (Reg. 105 applies to fees paid to lenders to assist in sale of a business, to the extent services performed in Canada).

ITA 153(1)(g) authorizes withholding only "for" services, not "in respect of" services. *Weyerhaeuser Co.*, 2007 TCC 65 rejected an argument that Reg. 105 is thus *ultra vires*, but ruled that withholding was required only for fees and commissions, not expense reimbursements, and that it applies only to work done in Canada and payment for time spent travelling within Canada (not *to* Canada). The purpose of Reg. 105 "is simply to provide security for tax that may later be assessed" to the non-resident (para. 7). CRA accepts this: VIEWS docs 2008-0297161E5, 2008-0300691E5; but in 2019-082364117 says Reg. 105 applies to reimbursements for subcontracted services. See also Boddez, "Regulation 105", 2007 BC Tax Conf (ctf.ca), 7:1-24.

Reg. 105 applied to fees paid by Petro Canada to a Swiss company in *FMC Technologies*, 2009 FCA 217; leave to appeal denied 2010 CarswellNat 33 (SCC); and to fees paid by a German corp to a Swedish company for work done for the German corp's Canadian affiliate, but not to the extent the Canadian affiliate had remitted tax: *Stora Enso*, 2009 TCC 282. See Hickey, "Non-Resident Withholding Tax", 17(8) *Canadian Tax Highlights* (ctf.ca) 2 (Aug. 2009); Mathison, "Regulation 105", 1953 *Tax Topics* (CCH) 1-3 (Aug. 13, 2009); Parks, "Unenforceability of Collection No Bar to Liability", XV(3) *International Tax Planning* (Federated Press) 1066-70 (2010).

Payments to international shipping companies, whose income is exempt under ITA 81(1)(c), have historically not been subject to withholding even without filing a Form R105, but this may be changing: *Valero Energy*, 2020 FCA 68.

No amount need be withheld from a non-resident on services rendered *outside* Canada, with some exceptions: Reg. 104(2), VIEWS docs 2010-0382921E5, 2011-0397511E5. For a Canadian resident employee working outside Canada, withholding is required under Reg. 102(1), even by non-resident employers: see Notes to ITA 153(1).

Consider also whether the non-resident needs to register for, and collect and remit, GST/HST. See ETA s. 240(1) in David M. Sherman, *Practitioner's Goods and Services Tax Annotated* (Carswell, twice-yearly).

Reg. 105(2)(b) and (c) added by P.C. 2009-1869, this version effective for payments made after Aug. 7, 2009. For payments made from June 28, 1999 through Aug. 7, 2009, read (b) as above and (c) as "made to an authorized foreign bank".

Information Circulars [Reg. 105]: 75-6R2: Required withholding from amounts paid to non-residents performing services in Canada.

Transfer Pricing Memoranda [Reg. 105]: TPM-06: Bundled transactions; TPM-08: The *Dudney* decision: effects on fixed base or permanent establishment audits and Reg. 105 treaty-based waiver guidelines.

CRA Audit Manual [Reg. 105]: 15.2.11: Withholding of Part I tax — income from carrying on a business in Canada; 15.2.14: Waivers of withholding tax.

Forms [Reg. 105]: NR302: Declaration of eligibility for benefits (reduced tax) under a tax treaty for a partnership with non-resident partners; NR303: Declaration of eligibility for benefits (reduced tax) under a tax treaty for a hybrid entity; R105: Regulation 105 waiver application; R105-S: Regulation 105 simplified waiver application for non-resident artists and athletes earning no more than CAN$15,000; T2 Sched. 97: Additional information on non-resident corporations in Canada; T4A-NR: Statement of fees (etc.) paid to non-residents for services rendered in Canada; T4A-NR Summ: Fees (etc.) paid to non-residents for services rendered in Canada.

Definitions [Reg. 105]: "amount", "authorized foreign bank" — ITA 248(1); "Canada" — ITA 255, *Interpretation Act* 35(1); "Canadian banking business" — ITA 248(1); "commission" — Reg. 100(1)"remuneration"(a)(ii); "non-resident", "person" — ITA 248(1); "registered non-resident insurer" — Reg. 804; "remuneration" — Reg. 100(1).

105.1 Fishermen's election — (1) Notwithstanding section 100, in this section,

"amount of remuneration" paid to a fisherman means

(a) where a boat crewed by one or more fishermen engaged in making a catch is owned, together with the gear, by a person, other than a member of the crew, to whom the catch is to be delivered for subsequent sale or other disposition, such portion of the proceeds from the disposition of the catch that is payable to the fisherman in accordance with an arrangement under which the proceeds of disposition of the catch are to be distributed (in this section referred to as a "share arrangement");

(b) where the boat or gear used in making a catch is owned or leased by a fisherman who alone or with another individual engaged under a contract of service makes the catch, such portion of the proceeds from the disposition of the catch that remains after deducting therefrom

(i) the amount in respect of any portion of the catch not caught by the fisherman or the other individual,

(ii) the amount payable to the other individual under the contract of service, and

(iii) the amount of such proportionate share of the catch as is attributable to the expenses of the operation of the boat or its gear pursuant to their share arrangement;

(c) where a crew includes the owner of the boat or gear (in this paragraph referred to as the "owner") and any other fisherman engaged in making a catch, such portion of the proceeds from the disposition of the catch that remains after deducting therefrom

(i) in the case of an owner,

(A) the amount in respect of that portion of the catch not caught by the crew or an owner,

(B) the aggregate of all amounts each of which is an amount payable to a crew member (other than the owner) pursuant to their share arrangement or to an individual engaged under a contract of service, and

(C) the amount of such proportionate share of the catch as is attributable to the expenses of the owner's operation of the boat or its gear pursuant to their share arrangement, or

(ii) in the case of any other crew member, such proceeds from the disposition of the catch as is payable to him in accordance with their share arrangement; or

(d) in any other case, the proceeds of disposition of the catch payable to the fisherman;

"catch" means a catch of shell fish, crustaceans, aquatic animals or marine plants caught or taken from any body of water;

"crew" means one or more fishermen engaged in making a catch;

"fisherman" means an individual engaged in making a catch other than under a contract of service.

(2) Every person paying at any time in a taxation year an amount of remuneration to a fisherman who, pursuant to paragraph 153(1)(n) of the Act, has elected for the year in prescribed form in respect of all amounts shall deduct or withhold 20% of each such amount paid to the fisherman while the election is in force.

Notes [Reg. 105.1(2)]: Where no prescribed form was signed, although fishermen expected source deductions to be taken, the company was not liable to deduct and withhold: *Billard Fisheries*, [1995] 2 C.T.C. 2505 (TCC).

Definitions [Reg. 105.1]: "amount" — ITA 248(1); "amount of remuneration" — Reg. 105.1(1); "catch", "crew" — Reg. 105.1(1)(d); "disposition" — ITA 248(1); "fisherman" — Reg. 105.1(1)(d); "individual" — ITA 248(1); "owner" — Reg. 105.1(1)(c); "person", "prescribed" — ITA 248(1); "remuneration" — Reg. 100(1); "share" — ITA 248(1); "share arrangement" — Reg. 105.1(1)(a); "taxation year" — ITA 249.

106. Variations in deductions — (1) Where an employer makes a payment of remuneration to an employee in his taxation year

(a) for a period for which no provision is made in Schedule I, or

(b) for a pay period referred to in Schedule I in an amount that is greater than any amount provided for therein,

(c), (d) [Repealed]

the amount to be deducted or withheld by the employer from any such payment is that proportion of the payment that the tax that may reasonably be expected to be payable under the Act by the employee with respect to the aggregate of all remuneration that may reasonably be expected to be paid by the employer to the employee in respect of that taxation year is of such aggregate.

Notes: Reg. 106(1) applies to certain distributions from a retirement compensation arrangement: VIEWS doc 2005-0119101E5. To calculate the withholding on payment to a partnership, see 2017-0711961I7.

Reg. 106(1)(c), (d) repealed by P.C. 2001-1115, for 2001 and later taxation years.

(2), (3) [Revoked]

Definitions [Reg. 106]: "amount", "employee", "employer", "estimated deductions", "pay period", "personal credits", "remuneration" — Reg. 100(1); "taxation year" — ITA 249; "total remuneration" — Reg. 100(1).

107. Employee's returns — (1) [Due date for TD1] — The return required to be filed by an employee under subsection 227(2) of the Act shall be filed by the employee with the employer when the employee commences employment with that employer and a new return shall be filed thereunder within 7 days of the date on which a change occurs that may reasonably be expected to result in a change in the employee's personal credits for the year.

Related Provisions: Reg. 104 — No deduction required where employee claims no tax payable; *Interpretation Act* 27(5) — Meaning of "within 7 days".

Forms: TD1: Personal tax credits return.

(2) [Commission employees] — Notwithstanding subsection (1), where, in a year, an employee receives payments in respect of commissions or in respect of commissions and salary or wages, and the employee elects to file a prescribed form for the year in addition to the return referred to in that subsection, that form shall be filed with the employee's continuing employer on or before January 31 of that year and, where applicable, within one month after the employee commences employment with a new employer or within one month after the date on which a change occurs that may reasonably be expected to result in a substantial change in the employee's estimated total remuneration for the year or estimated deductions for the year.

Related Provisions: Reg. 102(2) — Amount to be withheld; *Interpretation Act* 27(5) — Meaning of "within one month".

Notes: Reg 107(2) amended by P.C. 2001-1115, effectively to eliminate para. (a), effective for 2001 and later taxation years.

Forms: TD1X: Statement of commission income and expenses for payroll tax deductions.

(3) Where, in a taxation year, an employee has elected to file the prescribed form referred to in subsection (2) and has filed such

form with his employer, the employee may at any time thereafter in the year revoke that election and such revocation is effective from the date that he notifies his employer in writing of his intention.

Definitions [Reg. 107]: "commissions" — Reg. 100(1) "remuneration" "a"(a)(ii); "employee", "employer" — Reg. 100(1); "employment" — ITA 248(1); "estimated deductions" — Reg. 100(1); "month" — *Interpretation Act* 35(1); "personal credits" — Reg. 100(1); "prescribed", "salary or wages" — ITA 248(1); "taxation year" — ITA 249; "total remuneration" — Reg. 100(1); "writing" — *Interpretation Act* 35(1).

108. Remittances to Receiver General — (1) [Deadline] — Subject to subsections (1.1) to (1.13), amounts deducted or withheld in a month under subsection 153(1) of the Act shall be remitted to the Receiver General on or before the 15th day of the following month.

Notes: Payroll remittance deadlines are unchanged for COVID-19: tinyurl.com/covid-dates.

Reg. 108(1) amended by 2015 Budget bill to be subject to Reg. 108(1.13), effective for amounts deducted or withheld after 2015.

Reg. 108(1) amended to refer to 108(1.12) by P.C. 1997-1473, for amounts and contributions required to be remitted to the Receiver General after Oct. 1997.

Forms: RC4163: Employers' guide — remitting payroll deductions; T4001: Employers' guide — payroll deductions and remittances [guide]. See also under ITA 153(1).

(1.1) [Large employers] — Subject to subsection (1.11), where the average monthly withholding amount of an employer for the second calendar year preceding a particular calendar year is

(a) equal to or greater than $25,000 and less than $100,000, all amounts deducted or withheld from payments described in the definition "remuneration" in subsection 100(1) that are made in a month in the particular calendar year by the employer shall be remitted to the Receiver General

    (i) in respect of payments made before the 16th day of the month, on or before the 25th day of the month, and

    (ii) in respect of payments made after the 15th day of the month, on or before the 10th day of the following month; or

(b) equal to or greater than $100,000, all amounts deducted or withheld from payments described in the definition "remuneration" in subsection 100(1) that are made in a month in the particular calendar year by the employer shall be remitted to the Receiver General on or before the third day, not including a Saturday or holiday, after the end of the following periods in which the payments were made,

    (i) the period beginning on the first day and ending on the 7th day of the month,

    (ii) the period beginning on the 8th day and ending on the 14th day of the month,

    (iii) the period beginning on the 15th day and ending on the 21st day of the month, and

    (iv) the period beginning on the 22nd day and ending on the last day of the month.

Related Provisions: ITA 153(1) closing words — Large employers must make remittances through financial institution.

Notes: See Notes to *Interpretation Act* s. 26 for the meaning of "holiday", used in Reg. 108(1.1)(b).

Reg. 108(1.1) amended by 2014 budget bill #1, for amounts deducted or withheld after 2014, to change "$15,000" to "$25,000" and "$50,000" to "$100,000".

(1.11) [Option to use preceding year as base] — Where an employer referred to in paragraph (1.1)(a) or (b) would otherwise be required to remit in accordance with that paragraph the amounts withheld or deducted under subsection 153(1) of the Act in respect of a particular calendar year, the employer may elect to remit those amounts

(a) in accordance with subsection (1), if the average monthly withholding amount of the employer for the calendar year preceding the particular calendar year is less than $25,000 and the employer has advised the Minister that the employer has so elected; or

(b) if the average monthly withholding amount of the employer for the calendar year preceding the particular calendar year is equal to or greater than $25,000 and less than $100,000 and the employer has advised the Minister that the employer has so elected,

(i) in respect of payments made before the 16th day of a month in the particular calendar year, on or before the 25th day of the month, and

(ii) in respect of payments made after the 15th day of a month in [the] particular calendar year, on or before the 10th day of the following month.

Notes: Reg. 108(1.11) amended by 2014 budget bill #1, for amounts deducted or withheld after 2014, to change "$15,000" to "$25,000" and "$50,000" to "$100,000".

Reg. 108(1.11) added, and 108(1) and (1.1) amended to accommodate it, by P.C. 1993-321, effective March 11, 1993. 108(1.11) allows employers to use the previous year's base for determining instalment remittance deadlines, rather than the second preceding year, where that is to the employer's advantage. It was introduced in response to complaints from employers that had downsized during a recession.

(1.12) [Quarterly remittance] — If at any time

(a) the average monthly withholding amount in respect of an employer for either the first or the second calendar year before the particular calendar year that includes that time is less than $3,000,

(b) throughout the 12-month period before that time, the employer has remitted, on or before the day on or before which the amounts were required to be remitted, all amounts each of which was required to be remitted under subsection 153(1) of the Act, under subsection 21(1) of the *Canada Pension Plan*, under subsection 82(1) of the *Employment Insurance Act* or under Part IX of the *Excise Tax Act*, and

(c) throughout the 12-month period before that time, the employer has filed all returns each of which was required to be filed under this Act or Part IX of the *Excise Tax Act* on or before the day on or before which those returns were required to be filed under those Acts,

all amounts deducted or withheld from payments described in the definition "remuneration" in subsection 100(1) that are made by the employer in a month that ends after that time and that is in the particular calendar year may be remitted to the Receiver General

(d) in respect of such payments made in January, February and March of the particular calendar year, on or before the 15th day of April of the particular year,

(e) in respect of such payments made in April, May and June of the particular calendar year, on or before the 15th day of July of the particular year,

(f) in respect of such payments made in July, August and September of the particular calendar year, on or before the 15th day of October of the particular year, and

(g) in respect of such payments made in October, November and December of the particular calendar year, on or before the 15th day of January of the year following the particular year.

Notes: Reg. 108(1.12) gives effect to an announcement, in the February 1997 federal budget, that small employers would be allowed to remit source deductions quarterly instead of monthly. Employers must have a perfect compliance record (both filing and remitting) for source deductions and GST remittances over the past 12 months (Reg. 108(1.12)(b)), and average monthly withholding of less than $3,000 for either the first or second preceding year (Reg. 108(1.12)(a)) to qualify.

Reg. 108(1.12)(a) and (b) opening words amended by 2007 budget bill #2, effective in respect of amounts required to be deducted or withheld after 2007, to change $1,000 to $3,000 (para. (a)) and to redraft para. (b). The changes added reference to the CPP and EIA (no substantive change because CPP Reg. 8(1.12) and EI Reg. 4(3.1) already provided this rule, and note that "average monthly withholding amount" is defined in Reg. 108(1.2) to include CPP and EI), and changed "deducted or withheld" to "remitted" (re ITA 153(1)).

Reg. 108(1.12) added by P.C. 1997-1473, effective for amounts and contributions required to be remitted to the Receiver General after October 1997.

Forms: RC4163: Employers' guide — remitting payroll deductions. See also under ITA 153(1).

(1.13) [Quarterly remittance for new small employer] — If an employer is a new employer throughout a particular month in a

particular calendar year, all amounts deducted or withheld from payments described in the definition "remuneration" in subsection 100(1) that are made by the employer in the month may be remitted to the Receiver General

(a) in respect of such payments made in January, February and March of the particular calendar year, on or before the 15th day of April of the particular calendar year;

(b) in respect of such payments made in April, May and June of the particular calendar year, on or before the 15th day of July of the particular calendar year;

(c) in respect of such payments made in July, August and September of the particular calendar year, on or before the 15th day of October of the particular calendar year; and

(d) in respect of such payments made in October, November and December of the particular calendar year, on or before the 15th day of January of the year following the particular calendar year.

Related Provisions: Reg. 108(1.4) — Meaning of "new employer".

Notes: Reg. 108(1.13) (added by 2015 Budget bill for amounts deducted or withheld after 2015) was introduced to allow very small *new* employers to remit payroll only quarterly, at the "specified time" in Reg. 108(1.41). (Quarterly remitting normally requires average monthly withholdings under $3,000 and a perfect compliance record over the last 12 months: Reg. 108(1.12).) This applies to new employers with withholdings of under $1,000/month, which in effect means 1 employee at a salary of up to about $43,500. Such employers remain eligible for quarterly remitting provided their "monthly withholding amount" (Reg. 108(1.21)) remains under $1,000 (Reg. 108(1.4)).

(1.2) ["Average monthly withholding amount"] — For the purposes of this section, average monthly withholding amount, in respect of an employer for a particular calendar year, is the quotient obtained when

(a) the aggregate of all amounts each of which is an amount required to be remitted with respect to the particular year under

(i) subsection 153(1) of the Act and a similar provision of a law of a province which imposes a tax upon the income of individuals, where the province has entered into an agreement with the Minister of Finance for the collection of taxes payable to the province, in respect of payments described in the definition "remuneration" in subsection 100(1),

(ii) subsection 21(1) of the *Canada Pension Plan*, or

(iii) subsection 82(1) of the *Employment Insurance Act*,

by the employer or, where the employer is a corporation, by each corporation associated with the corporation in a taxation year of the employer ending in the second calendar year following the particular year

is divided by

(b) the number of months in the particular year, not exceeding twelve, for which such amounts were required to be remitted by the employer and, where the employer is a corporation, by each corporation associated with it in a taxation year of the employer ending in the second calendar year following the particular year.

Related Provisions: ITA 252.1 — All union locals and branches deemed to be one employer; Reg. 108(1.3) — Where business transferred.

Notes: The calculation is based on the number of months *for which withholdings apply*, so a once-a-year bonus with source deductions over $50,000, and no other source deductions all year, makes Reg. 108(1.1)(b) apply: *Manufax Holdings*, 2006 FCA 351.

Reg. 105 withholdings are not included in the calculation, but CRA may incorrectly do so: Manu Kakkar, "Reg 105", 12(1) *Tax for the Owner-Manager* (ctf.ca) 1 (Jan. 2012).

See also VIEWS doc 2012-0441251E5 (union branches are combined for Reg. 108(1.2)).

Reg. 108(1.2)(a)(iii) amended by 2014 budget bill #1, effective June 19, 2014, to delete "or subsection 53(1) of the *Unemployment Insurance Act*" from the end. The *UI Act* was replaced by the *EI Act* in 1996.

Reg. 108(1.2)(a)(iii) amended by P.C. 1998-2270, effective for 1998 and later taxation years, to add reference to 82(1) of the *Employment Insurance Act*.

(1.21) ["Monthly withholding amount"] — For the purposes of subsection (1.4), the monthly withholding amount, in respect of an employer for a month, is the total of all amounts each of which is an amount required to be remitted with respect to the month by the employer or, if the employer is a corporation, by each corporation associated with the corporation, under

(a) subsection 153(1) of the Act and a similar provision of a law of a province which imposes a tax upon the income of individuals, if the province has entered into an agreement with the Minister of Finance for the collection of taxes payable to the province, in respect of payments described in the definition "remuneration" in subsection 100(1);

(b) subsection 21(1) of the *Canada Pension Plan*; or

(c) subsection 82(1) of the *Employment Insurance Act*.

Notes: Reg. 108(1.21) added by 2015 Budget bill, for amounts deducted or withheld after 2015. See Notes to Reg. 108(1.13).

(1.3) [Where business transferred] — For the purposes of subsection (1.2), where a particular employer that is a corporation has acquired in a taxation year of the corporation ending in a particular calendar year all or substantially all of the property of another employer used by the other employer in a business

(a) in a transaction in respect of which an election was made under subsection 85(1) or (2) of the Act,

(b) by virtue of an amalgamation within the meaning assigned to that term by section 87 of the Act, or

(c) as the result of a winding-up in respect of which subsection 88(1) of the Act is applicable,

the other employer shall be deemed to be a corporation associated with the particular employer in the taxation year and each taxation year ending at any time in the next two following calendar years.

(1.4) ["New employer"] — For the purposes of subsection (1.13) an employer

(a) becomes a new employer at the beginning of any month after 2015 in which the employer first becomes an employer; and

(b) ceases to be a new employer at a specified time in a particular year, if in a particular month the employer does not meet any of the following conditions:

(i) the monthly withholding amount in respect of the employer for the particular month is less than $1,000,

(ii) throughout the 12-month period before that time, the employer has remitted, on or before the day on or before which the amounts were required to be remitted, all amounts each of which was required to be remitted under subsection 153(1) of the Act, subsection 21(1) of the *Canada Pension Plan*, subsection 82(1) of the *Employment Insurance Act* or Part IX of the *Excise Tax Act*, and

(iii) throughout the 12-month period before that time, the employer has filed all returns each of which was required to be filed under the Act or Part IX of the *Excise Tax Act* on or before the day on or before which those returns were required to be filed under those Acts.

Related Provisions: Reg. 108(1.21) — Monthly withholding amount; Reg. 108(1.41) — Specified time.

Notes: Reg. 108(1.4) added by 2015 Budget bill, for amounts deducted or withheld after 2015. See Notes to Reg. 108(1.13).

(1.41) ["Specified time"] — For the purposes of subsection (1.4), the specified time is the end of

(a) March of the particular year, if the particular month is January, February or March of that year;

(b) June of the particular year, if the particular month is April, May or June of that year;

(c) September of the particular year, if the particular month is July, August or September of that year; and

(d) December of the particular year, if the particular month is October, November or December of that year.

Notes: Reg. 108(1.41) added by 2015 Budget bill, for amounts deducted or withheld after 2015. See Notes to Reg. 108(1.13).

(2) [Ceasing to carry on business] — Where an employer has ceased to carry on business, any amount deducted or withheld under subsection 153(1) of the Act that has not been remitted to the Receiver General shall be paid within 7 days of the day when the employer ceased to carry on business.

Related Provisions: *Interpretation Act* 27(5) — Meaning of "within 7 days".

(3) [Return] — Remittances made to the Receiver General under subsection 153(1) of the Act shall be accompanied by a return in prescribed form.

(4) [Unclaimed dividends, interest on proceeds] — Amounts deducted or withheld under subsection 153(4) of the Act shall be remitted to the Receiver General within 60 days after the end of the taxation year subsequent to the 12-month period referred to in that subsection.

Related Provisions: *Interpretation Act* 27(5) — Meaning of "within 60 days".

Definitions [Reg. 108]: "amount" — ITA 248(1); "associated" — ITA 256, Reg. 108(1.3); "average monthly withholding amount" — Reg. 108(1.2); "business" — ITA 248(1); "calendar year" — *Interpretation Act* 37(1)(a); "Canada" — ITA 255, *Interpretation Act* 35(1); "corporation" — ITA 248(1), *Interpretation Act* 35(1); "employer" — Reg. 100(1); "holiday" — *Interpretation Act* 35(1); "individual", "Minister" — ITA 248(1); "Minister of Finance" — *Financial Administration Act* 14; "month" — *Interpretation Act* 35(1); "monthly withholding amount" — Reg. 108(1.21); "new employer" — Reg. 108(1.4); "prescribed", "property" — ITA 248(1); "province" — *Interpretation Act* 35(1); "remuneration" — Reg. 100(1); "specified time" — Reg. 108(1.41); "taxation year" — ITA 249.

109. Elections to increase deductions — (1) Any election under subsection 153(1.2) of the Act shall be made by filing with the person making the payment or class of payments referred to therein (in this section referred to as the "payer") the form prescribed by the Minister for that purpose.

(2) [Variation] — A taxpayer who has made an election in the manner prescribed by subsection (1) may require that the amount deducted or withheld pursuant to that election be varied by filing with the payer the form prescribed by the Minister for that purpose.

(3) [Time allowed to comply] — An election made in the manner prescribed by subsection (1) or a variation made pursuant to subsection (2) need not be taken into account by the payer in respect of the first payment to be made to the taxpayer after the election or variation, as the case may be, unless the election or variation, as the case may be, is made within such time, in advance of the payment, as may reasonably be required by the payer.

Definitions [Reg. 109]: "amount", "Minister" — ITA 248(1); "payer" — Reg. 109(1); "person", "prescribed", "taxpayer" — ITA 248(1).

110. Prescribed persons — (1) [Large employers] — The following are prescribed persons for the purposes of subsection 153(1) of the Act:

(a) an employer who is required, under subsection 153(1) of the Act and in accordance with paragraph 108(1.1)(b), to remit amounts deducted or withheld; and

(b) a person or partnership who, acting on behalf of one or more employers, remits the following amounts in a particular calendar year and whose average monthly remittance, in respect of those amounts, for the second calendar year preceding the particular calendar year, is equal to or greater than $50,000,

(i) amounts required to be remitted under subsection 153(1) of the Act and a similar provision of a law of a province that imposes a tax on the income of individuals, where the province has entered into an agreement with the Minister of Finance for the collection of taxes payable to the province, in respect of payments described in the definition "remuneration" in subsection 100(1),

(ii) amounts required to be remitted under subsection 21(1) of the *Canada Pension Plan*, and

(iii) amounts required to be remitted under subsection 82(1) of the *Employment Insurance Act* or subsection 53(1) of the *Unemployment Insurance Act*.

Notes: Reg. 110(1)(b)(iii) amended by P.C. 1998-2270, for 1998 and later tax years.

(2) [Average monthly remittance] — For the purposes of paragraph (1)(b), the average monthly remittance made by a person or partnership on behalf of all the employers for whom that person or partnership is acting, for the second calendar year preceding the particular calendar year, is the quotient obtained when the aggregate, for that preceding year, of all amounts referred to in subparagraphs (1)(b)(i) to (iii) remitted by the person or partnership on behalf of those employers is divided by the number of months, in that preceding year, for which the person or partnership remitted those amounts.

Notes [Reg. 110]: Reg. 110 added by P.C. 1993-1947, for remittances after 1992. See Notes to ITA 153(1).

ITA 229 and *Financial Administration Act* 159(2) require banks to accept tax payments.

Definitions [Reg. 110]: "amount" — ITA 248(1); "average monthly remittance" — Reg. 110(2); "calendar year" — *Interpretation Act* 37(1)(a); "Canada" — ITA 255, *Interpretation Act* 35(1); "employer" — Reg. 100(1); "individual" — ITA 248(1); "Minister" — ITA 248(1); "Minister of Finance" — *Financial Administration Act* 14; "month" — *Interpretation Act* 35(1); "partnership" — see ITA 96(1) Notes; "person", "prescribed" — ITA 248(1); "province" — *Interpretation Act* 35(1); "remuneration" — Reg. 100(1).

111. Deemed remittance — For the purpose of subsection 153(1.02) of the Act

(a) $25,000 is the amount prescribed for the purpose of the description of A in paragraph 153(1.02)(a) of the Act;

(b) 10%, or a lower percentage elected by the "eligible employer", as defined in subsection 153(1.03), is the percentage prescribed for the purpose of the description of C in paragraph 153(1.02)(b) of the Act; and

(c) $1,375 is the amount prescribed for the purpose of the description of E in paragraph 153(1.02)(c) of the Act.

Notes [Reg. 111]: Reg. 111 added by P.C. 2020-330, effective for an ITA 153(1.03)"eligible period".

Definitions [Reg. 111]: "amount" — ITA 248(1); "eligible employer" — ITA 153(1.3); "prescribed" — ITA 248(1).

PART II — [200–238] INFORMATION RETURNS

Notes [Part II]: Information returns under this Part use "RZ" accounts: see Notes to ITA 248(1)"business number".

Other requirements for information returns, not in Reg. Part II, include:

- notification of "non-qualified securities" for stock option benefit — ITA 110(1.9)(b)
- donation returned by charity to donor — ITA 110.1(16), 118.1(27)
- emigration from Canada: reporting the values of assets owned — ITA 128.1(9)
- Cdn Wheat Board Farmers' Trust annual form — ITA 135.2(15)
- RESP trustee annual return — ITA 146.1(13.1)
- non-profit R&D corporation: annual form — ITA 149(7)
- non-profit organization information return if assets over $200,000 or investment income over $10,000 — ITA 149(12)
- labour organization (union) or labour trust [repealed without taking effect], ITA 149.01
- registered charity or RCAAA information return — ITA 149.1(14)
- registered journalism organization information return — ITA 149.1(14.1)
- income tax return — ITA 150(1)
- non-arm's length transactions with non-residents, and holdings in foreign property or foreign trusts: information returns — ITA 233-233.7
- country-by-country reporting by multinational groups — ITA 233.8(3)
- tax shelter reporting — ITA 237.1(6), (7)
- reporting avoidance transactions — ITA 237.3(2)
- reporting of international electronic funds transfers of $10,000 or more by banks, casinos and other financial institutions — ITA 244.2(1), 244.6

- reporting by financial institutions of accounts owned by US persons (such as US citizens) to CRA for reporting to the US Internal Revenue Service — ITA 266
- "Common Reporting Standard" reporting by financial institutions of accounts to CRA for automatic exchange of information with other governments (other than US) — ITA 278
- pension adjustment, pension adjustment reversal and PSPA information returns — Reg. 8401-8402.01
- registered pension plan administrator: annual information return — Reg. 8409
- other pension-related information returns — Reg. 8400-8410
- securities dealers and others holding mutual fund and other "distributed investment plan" units: returns showing province of residence of beneficial owners for HST calculation purposes: *Selected Listed Financial Institution (GST/HST) Regulations* s. 53 (in David M. Sherman, *Practitioner's Goods and Services Tax Annotated* (Carswell)).

Information Circulars: 82-2R2: Social insurance number legislation that relates to the preparation of information slips.

200. Remuneration and benefits [T4 or T4A] — **(1)** Subject to subsection (1.1), every person who makes a payment described in subsection 153(1) of the Act (including an amount paid that is described in subparagraph 153(1)(a)(ii) of the Act) shall make an information return in prescribed form in respect of the payment unless an information return in respect of the payment has been made under sections 202, 214, 237 or 238.

Related Provisions: ITA 162(7.01) — Penalty for late filing; Reg. 200(1.1) — Exception — annuity payment or non-resident employee; Reg. 205 — Date return due; Reg. 205.1(1) — Forms of which more than 50 must be filed by Internet; Reg. 209 — Two copies to be sent (or one emailed) to taxpayer; Reg. 210 — Return on demand by Minister.

Notes: Employers must file a T4 for all individuals who received remuneration during the year if the employer deducted CPP, EI or income tax or if the remuneration exceeded $500: RC4120, *Employer's Guide: Filing the T4 Slip*, which includes detailed instructions. See also VIEWS doc 2010-0391131E5 (Box 26 — pensionable earnings).

See tinyurl.com/covid-empl-info for new T4 reporting codes during COVID-19.

Employers must T4 amounts paid to fishermen [replacing the T4F], placement agency workers, taxi drivers, hairdressers and barbers: RC4120.

A 248(1"retiring allowance" (includes a severance payment) is reported on a T4 rather than a T4A, to "reduce the burden of filing both a T4 slip and a T4A slip for many filers" ("What's new for payroll", CRA, Aug. 24, 2010).

A condominium corporation waiving its Treasurer's monthly fees in exchange for bookkeeping services should T4 the amount waived: VIEWS doc 2011-0393781E5.

Payments over $500 to self-employed persons for services (even lawyers and accountants) technically require a T4A even though no tax is withheld, but no penalty is assessed for non-compliance: RC4157 "Box 048"; VIEWS docs 2003-0048145, 2007-0223871E5, 2007-0262511E5, 2009-0330361C6. This was to continue until CRA completed consultations with "the business community and key stakeholders": CRA 2011 Budget news, q.5. 2016-0652761C6 [2016 APFF q.1B] says there is no change and T4As are required except for professional or business services provided to an individual in a personal capacity, or for repairs or maintenance to a principal residence; but the no-penalty policy in RC4157 apparently continues. Mysteriously, 2017-0709001C6 [2017 APFF q.2, Oct. 2017] claims the penalty "est applicable" even if an invoice with valid tax numbers has been issued, but RC4157, amended later, still says "The CRA is not assessing penalties for failures relating to the completion of box 048." Imposition of penalties could be coming: Grewal, "T4A", cadesky.tax/tt-19-05.

Where producer P pays incorporated artist A and also her artist-union dues, P must issue a T4A to the corp and the union must issue a T4 to A for the benefits: VIEWS doc 2016-067576117 (reversing 2013-050717117, which required P to issue both).

Rent does not require a T4A: VIEWS doc 2016-0675221E5. For T4A requirements of various payments by a CSSS (Quebec health and social service centre) see 2007-0255321E5. T4A amounts are pre-sales taxes, while T5018 amounts under Reg. 238 (payments to construction contractors) should include GST, HST and QST: 2010-0373691C6 (contrary statement in 2007-0230111E5 re T4A is presumably incorrect).

Correcting errors: An incorrect T4 or T4A (or any other slip) is not binding on the recipient; see Notes to ITA 5(1). CRA's view is that if a slip is wrong, the issuer has not complied with the Regulations and must amend it: docs 2013-0494441E5, 2019-0824301M4. However, this has no clear basis in the legislation: see Notes to ITA 239(1) under "There is no obligation". (Reg. 8401(6) requires an amended T4 only for a change in the pension adjustment.)

Many businesses can file T4 returns online; employers filing up to 100 slips can use T4 Web Forms. See tinyurl.com/t4-internet. Nil payroll returns can be filed by telephone; tinyurl.com/telereply.

For information about magnetic media filing of T4-related information slips, call CRA at 1-800-665-5164. For electronic filing generally, see ITA 150.1.

See Notes to ITA 231.1(1) re CRA's "matching" program, comparing information slips with taxpayers' returns.

Reg. 200(1) amended by 2016 budget bill #1, for payments made after 2015.

Reference to Reg. 237 and 238 added to Reg. 200(1) by P.C. 2002-2169, in force January 1, 2003.

I.T. Technical News: 11 (reporting of amounts paid out of an employee benefit plan).

Forms: See at end of Reg. 200.

(1.1) [Exception — annuity payment or non-resident employee] — Subsection (1) does not apply in respect of

(a) an annuity payment in respect of an interest in an annuity contract to which subsection 201(5) applies; or

(b) an amount paid by a qualifying non-resident employer to a qualifying non-resident employee that is exempted under subparagraph 153(1)(a)(ii) of the Act if the employer, after reasonable inquiry, has no reason to believe that the employee's total amount of taxable income earned in Canada under Part I of the Act during the calendar year that includes the time of this payment (including an amount described in paragraph 110(1)(f) of the Act) is more than $10,000.

Related Provisions: ITA 153(6) — Definitions of "qualifying non-resident employee", "qualifying non-resident employer".

Notes: Reg. 200(1.1) added by 2016 budget bill #1, for payments made after 2015.

(2) [Various payments — T4A] — Every person who makes a payment as or on account of, or who confers a benefit or allocates an amount that is,

(a) a scholarship, fellowship or bursary, or a prize for achievement in a field of endeavour ordinarily carried on by the recipient thereof (other than a prize prescribed by section 7700),

(b) a grant to enable the recipient thereof to carry on research or any similar work,

(b.1) an amount that is required by paragraph 56(1)(n.1) of the Act to be included in computing a taxpayer's income,

(c) an amount that is required by paragraph 56(1)(r) of the Act to be included in computing a taxpayer's income,

(d) a benefit under regulations made under an appropriation Act providing for a scheme of transitional assistance benefits to persons employed in the production of products to which the *Canada-United States Agreement on Automotive Products*, signed on January 16, 1965, applies,

(e) a benefit described in section 5502,

(f) an amount payable to a taxpayer on a periodic basis in respect of the loss of all or any part of his income from an office or employment, pursuant to

(i) a sickness or accident insurance plan,

(ii) a disability insurance plan, or

(iii) an income maintenance insurance plan,

to or under which his employer has made a contribution,

(g) an amount or benefit the value of which is required by paragraph 6(1)(a), (e) or (h) or subsection 6(9) of the Act to be included in computing a taxpayer's income from an office or employment, other than a payment referred to in subsection (1),

(h) a benefit the amount of which is required by virtue of subsection 15(5) of the Act to be included in computing a shareholder's income,

(i) a benefit deemed by subsection 15(9) of the Act to be a benefit conferred on a shareholder by a corporation, or

(j) a payment out of a registered education savings plan, other than a refund of payments,

shall make an information return in prescribed form in respect of such payment or benefit except where subsection (3) or (4) applies with respect to the payment or benefit.

Related Provisions: ITA 162(7.01) — Penalty for late filing; Reg. 205 — Date return due; Reg. 205.1(1) — Forms of which more than 50 must be filed by Internet; Reg. 209 — Two copies to be sent (or one emailed) to taxpayer.

Notes: CRA policy is that no T4A need be issued if total payments to an individual do not exceed $500 (except for group term life insurance taxable benefits to former employees) and no income tax was deducted from the payment: RC4157.

A T4A is required for a ITA 56(1)(n) scholarship or bursary even if the income is exempt under ITA 56(3): VIEWS docs 2008-0267551E5, 2010-0386261E5; 2011-0403931E5, 2015-0584221E5 (including primary and secondary school students), it is helpful for the school to provide letters to parents explaining why the income is exempt, to send in response to CRA audit inquiries). On the timing of the T4A for a bursary and who should issue it, see 2010-0360021I7, 2011-0397811E5.

Reg. 200(2)(f) requires a T4A for benefits under ITA 6(1)(f): doc 2011-0404951E5.

Reg. 200(2)(b.1) added by P.C. 2015-862, effective July 2015. Reg. 200(2) earlier amended by P.C. 1998-2270, 1998-2275, 1995-1023. In Reg. 200(2)(d), "*Appropriation Act*" corrected to "appropriation Act": laws.justice.gc.ca/eng/corrections.

Income Tax Folios: S1-F2-C3: Scholarships, research grants and other education assistance [replaces IT-340R].

Interpretation Bulletins: IT-421R2: Benefits to individuals, corporations and shareholders from loans or debt.

I.T. Technical News: 11 (reporting of amounts paid out of an employee benefit plan).

Forms: See at end of Reg. 200.

(3) [Automobile benefits — T4] — Where a benefit is included in computing a taxpayer's income from an office or employment pursuant to paragraph 6(1)(a) or (e) of the Act in respect of an automobile made available to the taxpayer or to a person related to the taxpayer by a person related to the taxpayer's employer, the employer shall make an information return in prescribed form in respect of the benefit.

Related Provisions: Reg. 205 — Date return due; Reg. 205.1(1) — Forms of which more than 50 must be filed by Internet; Reg. 209 — Two copies to be sent (or one emailed) to taxpayer.

Notes: Where a Canadian company's employee works at a U.S. affiliate and is given a company car to use, the Canadian company should report the standby-charge benefit on a T4 according to the CRA: VIEWS doc 2003-003506I17.

(4) [Automobile benefits — shareholder T4A] — Where a benefit is included in computing the income of a shareholder of a corporation by virtue of subsection 15(5) of the Act in respect of an automobile made available to the shareholder or to a person related to the shareholder by a person related to the corporation, the corporation shall make an information return in prescribed form in respect of the benefit.

Related Provisions: Reg. 205 — Date return due; Reg. 205.1(1) — Forms of which more than 50 must be filed by Internet; Reg. 209 — Two copies to be sent (or one emailed) to taxpayer.

Notes: This goes on a T4A slip, Box 28.

(5) [Employee stock option deferral] — Where a particular qualifying person (within the meaning assigned by subsection 7(7) of the Act) has agreed to sell or issue a security (within the meaning assigned by that subsection) of the particular qualifying person (or of a qualifying person with which it does not deal at arm's length) to a taxpayer who is an employee of the particular qualifying person (or of a qualifying person with which it does not deal at arm's length) and the taxpayer has acquired the security under the agreement in circumstances to which subsection 7(8) of the Act applied, each of the particular qualifying person, the qualifying person of which the security is acquired and the qualifying person which is the taxpayer's employer shall, for the particular taxation year in which the security is acquired, make an information return in the prescribed form in respect of the benefit from employment that the taxpayer would be deemed to have received in the particular taxation year in respect of the acquisition of the security if the Act were read without reference to subsection 7(8) and, for this purpose, an information return made by one of the qualifying persons in respect of the taxpayer's acquisition of the security is deemed to have been made by each of the qualifying persons.

Notes: See Chris D'Iorio paper cited in Notes to ITA 7(1).

Reg. 200(5) added by P.C. 2003-1497, for 2000 and later taxation years. It requires reporting of deferral of stock option benefits under (pre-March 4, 2010) ITA 7(8).

(6) [Universal Child Care Benefit] — Every person who makes a payment as or on account of an amount that is required by subsection 56(6) of the Act to be included in computing a taxpayer's in-

come shall make an information return in prescribed form in respect of that payment.

Notes: Reg. 200(6) added by P.C. 2015-862, effective July 2015.

Definitions [Reg. 200]: "amount", "annuity" — ITA 248(1); "arm's length" — ITA 251(1); "automobile" — ITA 248(1); "calendar year" — *Interpretation Act* 37(1)(a); "corporation" — ITA 248(1), *Interpretation Act* 35(1); "employed" — ITA 248(1); "employee", "employer", "employment", "office", "person", "personal or living expenses", "prescribed" — ITA 248(1); "qualifying non-resident employee", "qualifying non-resident employer" — ITA 153(6); "qualifying person" — ITA 7(7); "refund of payments" — ITA 146.1(1); "registered education savings plan" — ITA 146.1(1), 248(1); "related" — ITA 251(2)–(6); "shareholder", "taxable income earned in Canada" — ITA 248(1); "taxation year" — ITA 249; "taxpayer" — ITA 248(1).

Forms [Reg. 200]: RC4120: Employer's guide: Filing the T4 slip and summary form; RC4157: Deducting income tax on pension and other income, and filing the T4A slip and summary form [guide]; T2 Sched. 97: Additional information on non-resident corporations in Canada; T4: Statement of remuneration paid; T4 Segment; T4 Summ: Summary of remuneration paid; T4A: Statement of pension, retirement, annuity and other income; T4A Segment; T4A Summ: Summary of pension, retirement, annuity and other income; T4A-NR: Statement of fees (etc.) paid to non-residents for services rendered in Canada; T4A-RCA: Statement of distributions from an RCA; T4A-RCA Summ: Information return of distributions from an RCA; T737-RCA: Statement of contributions paid to a custodian of an RCA; T737-RCA Summary: Return of contributions paid to a custodian of an RCA; T4001: Employers' guide — payroll deductions and remittances [guide].

201. Investment income [T5 or T4A] — (1) Every person who makes a payment to a resident of Canada as or on account of

(a) a dividend or an amount deemed by the Act to be a dividend (other than a dividend deemed to have been paid to a person under any of subsections 84(1) to (4) of the Act where, pursuant to subsection 84(8) of the Act, those subsections do not apply to deem the dividend to have been received by the person),

(b) interest (other than the portion of the interest to which any of subsections (4) to (4.2) applies)

(i) on a fully registered bond or debenture,

(ii) in respect of

(A) money on loan to an association, corporation, institution, organization, partnership or trust,

(B) money on deposit with an association, corporation, institution, organization, partnership or trust, or

(C) property deposited or placed with an association, corporation, institution, organization, partnership or trust,

(iii) in respect of an account with an investment dealer or broker,

(iv) paid by an insurer in connection with an insurance policy or an annuity contract, or

(v) on an amount owing in respect of compensation for property expropriated,

(c) a royalty payment in respect of the use of a work or invention or a right to take natural resources,

(d) a payment referred to in subsection 16(1) of the Act that can reasonably be regarded as being in part a payment of interest or other payment of an income nature and in part a payment of a capital nature, where the payment is made by a corporation, association, organization or institution,

(e) an amount paid from a person's NISA Fund No. 2,

(f) an amount that is required by subsection 148.1(3) of the Act to be added in computing a person's income for a taxation year, or

(g) the portion of the price for which a debt obligation was assigned or otherwise transferred that is deemed by subsection 20(14.2) of the Act to be interest that accrued on the debt obligation to which the transferee has become entitled to for a period commencing before the time of the transfer and ending at that particular time that is not payable until after that particular time if the payment is made by a person that is a "financial company" (whether acting as principal or as agent for the transferee) for the purposes of section 211

shall make an information return in prescribed form in respect of the portion of such payment for which an information return has not previously been made under this section.

Proposed Amendment — Electronic T4A and T5 slips

Federal Budget, Supplementary Information, April 19, 2021: See under ITA 244(14.1), under heading "Information Returns".

Related Provisions: ITA 162(7.01) — Penalty for late filing; Reg. 201(4) — Reporting of annual accrued interest; Reg. 205 — Date return due; Reg. 205.1(1) — Forms of which more than 50 must be filed by Internet; Reg. 209 — Two copies to be sent (or one emailed) to taxpayer.

Notes: Although Reg. 201(1)(b) requires all interest and dividends to be reported, CRA administratively states that no T5 need be provided where the total for a recipient for the year is less than $50: T5 Guide (T4015), "When do you not have to prepare a T5 slip?". See ITA 12(1)(c) Notes for what constitutes "interest".

Correcting errors in information slips: see Notes to Reg. 200(1).

Interest accruing annually under ITA 12(4) (on an "investment contract") must be reported on a T5: VIEWS docs 2012-0449671E5, 2014-0519881E5.

Where a bank is used as paying agent for interest on debentures, see VIEWS doc 2014-0532941E5.

Where a hybrid security has had coupons removed, see VIEWS doc 2010-0371931E5 for the T5 reporting.

The fact a T5 is issued does not make the income taxable: see Notes to ITA 5(1).

No T5 is issued for capital gains: see Reg. 230(2) instead for Form T5008.

Where a child under 18 has expected annual income not over $2,500, the T5 need not show the Social Insurance Number: Information Circular 82-2R2 para. 2. The payer need not determine whether the attribution rules apply so as to show the parent's SIN: VIEWS doc 2007-0233801C6 (overruling doc 9812245).

See also docs 2000-0033735 (CRA considers "association" in Reg. 201(1)(b)(ii) to include a partnership); 2012-0436091E5 (trust paying interest to an individual must issue T5 if trustee is a corporation, association, organization or institution [this may not be correct, since the entity for Reg. 201(1)(b)(ii) is really the trust]); 2016-0653441E5 (US tax treatment of certain payments as dividend-equivalent payments under *Internal Revenue Code* 871(m) is irrelevant to Reg. 201(1) obligation).

Reg. 201(1)(b)(ii) amended by 2018 budget bill #1, for 2018 and later tax years, to add references to partnership and trust.

Reg. 201(1)(g) added by 2016 budget bill #2, effective 2017.

Reg. 201(1)(b) amended by P.C. 1996-1419, for debt obligations issued after Oct. 16, 1991, to add exclusion of Reg. 201(4.1) and (4.2). Reg. 201(1)(e) added by P.C. 1993-1939, effective 1994 for amounts paid after 1992. Reg. 201(1)(f) added by P.C. 1996-765, effective for payments made after 1995.

Interpretation Bulletins: IT-531: Eligible funeral arrangements.

Forms: RC4157: Deducting income tax on pension and other income, and filing the T4A slip and summary form [guide]; T3 Sched. 8: Investment income, carrying charges, and gross-up amount of dividends retained by the trust; T4A: Statement of pension, retirement, annuity and other income; T4A Segment; T4A Summ: Summary of pension, retirement, annuity and other income; T5: Statement of investment income; T5 Summ: Return of investment income; T619: Magnetic media transmittal; T4015: T5 guide — return of investment income; T4031: Computer specifications for data filed on Magnetic Media (T5, T5008, T4RSP, T4RIF, NR4, and T3) [guide]; T4126: How to file the T5 return of investment income [guide].

(2) [Nominees and agents] — Every person who receives as nominee or agent for a person resident in Canada a payment to which subsection (1) applies shall make an information return in prescribed form in respect of such payment.

Proposed Amendment — Reg. 201(2) — Social Insurance Number disclosure

Letter from Dept. of Finance, March 17, 1999: See under ITA 241(4).

Related Provisions: Reg. 205 — Date return due; Reg. 205.1(1) — Forms of which more than 50 must be filed by Internet; Reg. 209 — Two copies to be sent (or one emailed) to taxpayer.

I.T. Technical News: 11 (U.S. spin-offs (divestitures) — dividends in kind).

Forms: T5: Statement of investment income; T5 Summ: Return of investment income.

(3) [Bearer coupons, etc.] — Where a person negotiates a bearer coupon, warrant or cheque representing interest or dividends referred to in subsection 234(1) of the Act for another person resident in Canada and the name of the beneficial owner of the interest or dividends is not disclosed on an ownership certificate completed pursuant to that subsection, the person negotiating the coupon, warrant or cheque, as the case may be, shall make an information return in prescribed form in respect of the payment received.

Related Provisions: Reg. 205 — Date return due; Reg. 205.1(1) — Forms of which more than 50 must be filed by Internet; Reg. 209 — Two copies to be sent (or one emailed) to taxpayer.

(4) [Annual interest accrual] — A person or partnership that is indebted in a calendar year under a debt obligation in respect of which subsection 12(4) of the Act and paragraph (1)(b) apply with respect to a taxpayer shall make an information return in prescribed form in respect of the amount (other than an amount to which paragraph (1)(g) applies) that would, if the year were a taxation year of the taxpayer, be included as interest in respect of the debt obligation in computing the taxpayer's income for the year.

Related Provisions: Reg. 205 — Date return due; Reg. 205.1(1) — Forms of which more than 50 must be filed by Internet; Reg. 209 — Two copies to be sent (or one emailed) to taxpayer.

Notes: Reg. 201(4) amended by 2016 budget bill #2, effective 2017, to add exclusion for amount under Reg. 201(1)(g).

Reg. 201(4) amended by P.C. 1996-1419, for debt obligations issued after Oct. 16, 1991. For earlier investment contracts last acquired or materially altered after 1989, see up to the 56th ed.

Reg. 201(4) amended by P.C. 1991-172, effective for investment contracts acquired or materially altered after 1989 (Dept. of Finance officials have confirmed this should have been "last acquired after 1989", to be consistent with changes in 1991 technical bill). For investment contracts last acquired before 1990, see up to the 52nd ed.

(4.1) [Indexed debt obligation] — A person or partnership that is indebted in a calendar year under an indexed debt obligation in respect of which paragraph (1)(b) applies shall, for each taxpayer who holds an interest in the debt obligation at any time in the year, make an information return in prescribed form in respect of the amount that would, if the year were a taxation year of the taxpayer, be included as interest in respect of the debt obligation in computing the taxpayer's income for the year.

Related Provisions: Reg. 205 — Date return due; Reg. 205.1(1) — Forms of which more than 50 must be filed by Internet; Reg. 209 — Two copies to be sent (or one emailed) to the taxpayer.

Notes: Reg. 201(4.1) added by P.C. 1996-1419, for debt obligations issued after Oct. 16, 1991.

(4.2) [Nominee or agent — debt obligation] — Where, at any time in a calendar year, a person or partnership holds, as nominee or agent for a taxpayer resident in Canada, an interest in a debt obligation referred to in paragraph (1)(b) that is

(a) an obligation in respect of which subsection 12(4) of the Act applies with respect to the taxpayer, or

(b) an indexed debt obligation,

that person or partnership shall make an information return in prescribed form in respect of the amount that would, if the year were a taxation year of the taxpayer, be included as interest in respect of the debt obligation in computing the taxpayer's income for the year.

Related Provisions: Reg. 205 — Date return due; Reg. 205.1(1) — Forms of which more than 50 must be filed by Internet; Reg. 209 — Two copies to be sent (or one emailed) to the taxpayer.

Notes: Reg. 201(4.2) added by P.C. 1996-1419, for debt obligations issued after Oct. 16, 1991.

(5) [Insurers] — Every insurer, within the meaning assigned by paragraph 148(10)(a) of the Act, who is a party to a life insurance policy in respect of which an amount is to be included in computing a taxpayer's income under subsection 12.2(1) or (5) of the Act shall make an information return in prescribed form in respect of that amount.

Related Provisions: Reg. 201(5.1) — Application to leveraged insurance annuity policy; Reg. 205 — Date return due; Reg. 205.1(1) — Forms of which more than 50 must be filed by Internet; Reg. 209 — Two copies to be sent (or one emailed) to taxpayer.

Notes: Reg. 201(5) amended by P.C. 2010-548, for contracts last acquired after 1989 (no substantive changes).

Reg. 201(5) amended by P.C. 1991-172, for investment contracts acquired or materially altered after 1989 (Finance officials have confirmed this should be changed to "last acquired after 1989", to be consistent with changes in 1991 technical bill).

For investment contracts last acquired before 1990, add a reference to 12.2(4) of the Act along with 12.2(1), (3) and (5).

(5.1) [Insurer — leveraged insurance annuity policy] — Subsection (5) applies to an insurer in respect of an LIA policy in respect of a calendar year only if

(a) the insurer is notified in writing — before the end of the calendar year and by, or on behalf of, the policyholder — that the policy is an LIA policy; or

(b) it is reasonable to conclude that the insurer knew, or ought to have known, before the end of the calendar year, that the policy is an LIA policy.

Notes: Reg. 201(5.1) added by 2013 budget bill #2, for tax years that end after March 20, 2013. See Notes to ITA 248(1)"LIA policy".

(6) [Debt obligation in bearer form] — Every person who makes a payment to, or acts as a nominee or agent for, an individual resident in Canada in respect of the disposition or redemption of a debt obligation in bearer form shall make an information return in prescribed form in respect of the transaction indicating the proceeds of disposition or the redemption amount and such other information as may be required by the prescribed form.

Related Provisions: Reg. 205 — Date return due; Reg. 205.1(1) — Forms of which more than 50 must be filed by Internet; Reg. 209 — Two copies to be sent (or one emailed) to taxpayer.

Forms: RC257: Request for an information return program account (RZ); T4031: Computer specifications for data filed on Magnetic Media (T5, T5008, T4RSP, T4RIF, NR4, and T3) [guide]; T4091: T5008 guide — return of securities transactions; T5008: Statement of securities transactions; T5008 Segment; T5008 Summ: Return of securities transactions.

(7) ["Debt obligation in bearer form"] — For the purposes of subsection (6), "debt obligation in bearer form" means any debt obligation in bearer form other than

(a) a debt obligation that is redeemed for the amount for which the debt obligation was issued;

(b) a debt obligation described in paragraph 7000(1)(b); and

(c) a coupon, warrant or cheque referred to in subsection 207(1).

Definitions [Reg. 201]: "amount", "annuity" — ITA 248(1); "beneficial owner" — ITA 248(3); "calendar year" — *Interpretation Act* 37(1)(a); "Canada" — ITA 255, *Interpretation Act* 35(1); "corporation" — ITA 248(1), *Interpretation Act* 35(1); "debt obligation in bearer form" — Reg. 201(7); "disposition", "dividend", "indexed debt obligation", "individual", "insurance policy", "insurer", "LIA policy" — ITA 248(1); "life insurance policy" — ITA 138(12), 248(1); "NISA Fund No. 2" — ITA 248(1); "partnership" — see ITA 96(1) Notes; "person", "prescribed", "property" — ITA 248(1); "resident in Canada", "resident of Canada" — ITA 250; "taxation year" — ITA 249; "taxpayer" — ITA 248(1); "writing" — *Interpretation Act* 35(1).

202. Payments to non-residents [NR4] — (1) In addition to any other return required by the Act or these Regulations, every person resident in Canada shall make an information return in prescribed form in respect of any amount that the person pays or credits, or is deemed under Part I, XIII or XIII.2 of the Act to pay or credit, to a non-resident person as, on account or in lieu of payment of, or in satisfaction of,

(a) a management or administration fee or charge,

(b) interest,

(c) income of or from an estate or trust,

(d) rent, royalty or a similar payment referred to in paragraph 212(1)(d) of the Act, including any payment described in any of subparagraphs 212(1)(d)(i) to (viii) of the Act,

(e) a timber royalty as described in paragraph 212(1)(e) of the Act,

(f) an assessable distribution, as defined in subsection 218.3(1) of the Act;

(g) a dividend, including a patronage dividend as described in paragraph 212(1)(g) of the Act, or

(h) a payment for a right in or to the use of

(i) a motion picture film, or

(ii) a film or video tape for use in connection with television.

Related Provisions: Reg. 202(1.1), (2) — Other payments to non-residents; Reg. 202(6.1) — Deemed-resident trust deemed resident in Canada for purposes of Reg. 202(1); Reg. 202(7), (8) — Date return due; Reg. 205.1(1) — Forms of which more than 50 must be filed by Internet; Reg. 209 — Two copies to be sent (or one emailed) to taxpayer; Reg. 210 — Return on demand by Minister.

Notes: A cost reimbursement exempt under ITA 212(4)(b) still requires an NR4 as it falls within ITA 212(1)(a): VIEWS doc 2011-0402791E5.

Although Reg. 202(1)(b) requires an NR4 for any interest payment to a non-resident, Guide T4061 before 2015 appeared to say that one was required only if withholding tax applied, so that for most arm's-length interest (see ITA 212(1)(b)), no NR4 was required (CRA can waive a filing requirement: ITA 220(2.1)). This led to abuse as discussed in ITA 212(1)(b) Notes. Since 2015, this has changed, and every payment over $50 requires an NR4 even if there is no withholding; see VIEWS docs 2017-0691141C6 [2017 IFA q.8], 2017-0719491C6 [2017 APFF q.8]

Reg. 202(1)(c) requires all trust distributions to be reported on an NR4, since ITA 212(11) deems even capital distributions to be from the trust's income: VIEWS doc 2015-0608201E5.

Reg. 202(1) applies on a cash basis (paid or credited): VIEWS doc 2013-0493701C6 [2013 APFF q.6].

Reg. 202(1) opening words amended, closing words deleted and para. (f) added by P.C. 2011-936, effective Feb. 19, 2011, to modernize the wording and add reference to Part XIII.2 (certain mutual fund distributions to non-resident investors).

Reg. 202(1)(f) repealed by P.C. 2002-2169, effective 2003. It referred to alimony or support payments taxed before May 1997 under ITA 212(1)(f).

Forms: NR4: Statement of amounts paid or credited to non-residents of Canada; NR4 Segment; NR4 Summ: Return of amounts paid or credited to non-residents of Canada; NR4(OAS): Statement of OAS pension paid or credited to non-residents of Canada; T2 Sched. 19: Non-resident shareholder information; T1136: OAS return of income; T4031: Computer specifications for data filed on Magnetic Media (T5, T5008, T4RSP, T4RIF, NR4, and T3) [guide].

(1.1) [Payment to non-resident actor — NR4] — Every person who pays or credits an amount, or provides a benefit to or on behalf of a person who is either a non-resident individual who is an actor or that is a corporation related to such an individual, for the provision in Canada of acting services of the actor in a film or video production, shall, in addition to any other return required by the Act or these Regulations, make an information return in prescribed form in respect of such payment, credit or benefit.

Related Provisions: ITA 215(5.1)–(5.2) — Withholding tax; Reg. 202(7), (8) — Date return due; Reg. 209 — Two copies to be sent (or one emailed) to the taxpayer.

Notes: Reg. 202(1.1) is needed because ITA 153(1)(a) excludes amounts under ITA 212(5.1) from withholding, so Reg. 200 does not cover such payments.

Reg. 202(1.1) added by P.C. 2005-694, effective May 18, 2005.

(2) [Various payments to non-residents] — Every person resident in Canada who pays or credits, or is deemed by Part I or Part XIII of the Act to pay or credit, to a non-resident person an amount as, on account or in lieu of payment of, or in satisfaction of,

(a) a payment of a superannuation or pension benefit,

(b) a payment of any allowance or benefit described in any of subparagraphs 56(1)(a)(ii) to (vi) of the Act,

(c) a payment by a trustee under a registered supplementary unemployment benefit plan,

(d) a payment out of or under a registered retirement savings plan or a plan referred to in subsection 146(12) of the Act as an amended plan,

(e) a payment under a deferred profit sharing plan or a plan referred to in subsection 147(15) of the Act as a revoked plan,

(f) a payment under an income-averaging annuity contract, any proceeds of the surrender, cancellation, redemption, sale or other disposition of an income-averaging annuity contract, or any amount deemed by subsection 61.1(1) of the Act to have been received by the non-resident person as proceeds of the disposition of an income-averaging annuity contract,

(g) an annuity payment not described in any other paragraph of this subsection or subsection (1),

(h) a payment to which paragraph 212(1)(p) of the Act applies,

(i) a payment out of or under a registered retirement income fund,

(j) a payment that is or that would be, if paragraph 212(1)(r) of the Act were read without reference to subparagraph 212(1)(r)(ii), a payment described in that paragraph in respect of a registered education savings plan,

(k) a grant under a program prescribed for the purposes of paragraph 212(1)(s) of the Act,

(l) a payment described in paragraph 212(1)(j) of the Act in respect of a retirement compensation arrangement,

(m) a payment described in paragraph 212(1)(v) or (x) of the Act, or

(n) a payment described in paragraph 212(1)(r.1) of the Act,

shall, in addition to any other return required by the Act or these Regulations, make an information return in prescribed form in respect of such amount.

Related Provisions: Reg. 202(6.1) — Deemed-resident trust deemed resident in Canada for purposes of Reg. 202(2); Reg. 202(7), (8) — Date return due; Reg. 205.1(1) — Forms of which more than 50 must be filed by Internet; Reg. 209 — Two copies to be sent (or one emailed) to taxpayer.

Notes: Reg. 202(2)(n) added by P.C. 2016-96, effective July 2015.

Reg. 202(2)(m) amended by 2014 budget bill #1 to add reference to ITA 212(1)(x), effective June 19, 2014.

Reg. 202(2) earlier amended by 2008 budget bill #2 (for 2009 and later taxation years), P.C. 1999-2212 and 1998-2275.

Forms: NR4: Statement of amounts paid or credited to non-residents of Canada; NR4 Segment; NR4 Summ: Return of amounts paid or credited to non-residents of Canada; NR4A-RCA: Statement of amounts paid to non-residents of Canada to which para. 212(1)(j) applies.

(2.1) [NISA Fund No. 2] — Every person resident in Canada who pays an amount to a non-resident person from a NISA Fund No. 2 shall, in addition to any other return required by the Act or these Regulations, make an information return in prescribed form in respect of the amount.

Related Provisions: Reg. 202(7), (8) — Date return due; Reg. 205.1(1) — Forms of which more than 50 must be filed by Internet; Reg. 209 — Two copies to be sent (or one emailed) to taxpayer.

Notes: See Notes to ITA 248(1)"net income stabilization account". Reg. 202(2.1) added by P.C. 1993-1939, effective after 1993 in respect of amounts paid after 1992.

(3) [Nominee or agent] — Every person who is paid or credited with an amount referred to in subsection (1), (2) or (2.1) for or on behalf of a non-resident person shall make an information return in prescribed form in respect of the amount.

Related Provisions: Reg. 202(7), (8) — Date return due; Reg. 205.1(1) — Forms of which more than 50 must be filed by Internet; Reg. 209 — Two copies to be sent (or one emailed) to taxpayer.

Notes: Reference to Reg. 202(2.1) in Reg. 202(3) added by P.C. 1993-1939, effective after 1993 in respect of amounts paid after 1992.

(4) [Non-resident payer deemed resident in Canada] — A non-resident person who is deemed, under subsection 212(13) of the Act, to be a person resident in Canada for the purposes of section 212 of the Act shall be deemed, in the same circumstances, to be a person resident in Canada for the purposes of subsections (1) and (2).

(5) [Partnership payer deemed resident in Canada] — A partnership that is deemed, under paragraph 212(13.1)(a) of the Act, to be a person resident in Canada for the purposes of Part XIII of the Act shall be deemed, in the same circumstances, to be a person resident in Canada for the purposes of subsections (1) and (2).

(6) [Non-resident payer carrying on business in Canada] — A non-resident person who is deemed, under subsection 212(13.2) of the Act, to be a person resident in Canada for the purposes of Part XIII of the Act shall be deemed, in the same circumstances, to be a person resident in Canada for the purposes of subsections (1) and (2).

(6.1) [Non-resident trust deemed resident in Canada] — A trust that is deemed by subsection 94(3) of the Act to be resident in Canada for a taxation year for the purposes of computing its income, is deemed, in respect of amounts (other than an exempt amount as defined in subsection 94(1) of the Act) paid or credited by it, to be a person resident in Canada for the taxation year for the purposes of subsections (1) and (2).

Notes: Reg. 202(6.1) added by 2002-2013 technical bill (Part 1 — NRTs), effective for amounts paid or credited after Aug. 27, 2010.

(7) [Filing deadline] — Subject to subsection (8), an information return required under this section shall be filed on or before March 31 and shall be in respect of the preceding calendar year.

Related Provisions: ITA 162(7.01) — Penalty for late filing.

Notes: *COVID-19:* the deadlines for 2019 trust [Reg. 204(2)], partnership [Reg. 229(5)] and NR4 information returns [Reg. 202(7)] were all extended to May 1, 2020: CRA notice, March 26, 2020, reproduced here in PITA 59th ed.

(8) [Filing deadline — trust or estate] — Where an amount referred to in subsection (1) or (2) is income of or from an estate or trust, the information return required under this section in respect thereof shall be filed within 90 days from the end of the taxation year of the estate or trust in which the amount was paid or credited and shall be in respect of that taxation year.

Related Provisions: ITA 251.2(7)(f) — Deadline extended to regular year's deadline, for trust year deemed ended due to change in majority beneficiaries; *Interpretation Act* 27(5) — Meaning of "within 90 days".

Definitions [Reg. 202]: "amount" — ITA 248(1); "calendar year" — *Interpretation Act* 37(1)(a); "Canada" — ITA 255, *Interpretation Act* 35(1); "corporation" — ITA 248(1), *Interpretation Act* 35(1); "deferred profit sharing plan" — ITA 147(1), 248(1); "disposition", "dividend" — ITA 248(1); "estate" — ITA 104(1), 248(1); "income-averaging annuity contract", "individual", "NISA Fund No. 2", "non-resident", "person", "prescribed" — ITA 248(1); "registered education savings plan" — ITA 146.1(1), 248(1); "registered home ownership savings plan" — ITA 248(1); "registered retirement income fund" — ITA 146.3(1), 248(1); "registered retirement savings plan" — ITA 146(1), 248(1); "registered supplementary unemployment benefit plan" — ITA 145(1), 248(1); "related" — ITA 251(2)–(6); "resident" — ITA 250, Reg. 202(4), (5), (6); "retirement compensation arrangement", "superannuation or pension benefit" — ITA 248(1); "taxation year" — ITA 249; "trust" — ITA 104(1), 248(1), (3).

Forms [Reg. 202]: NR4: Statement of amounts paid or credited to non-residents of Canada; NR4 Segment; NR4 Summ: Return of amounts paid or credited to non-residents of Canada.

203. Requirement to file [by educational institution — T2202A, etc.]

— Every institution that is a "designated educational institution" (as defined in subsection 118.6(1) of the Act) because of paragraph (a) of that definition shall make an information return in prescribed form in respect of each individual enrolled at that institution who is a "qualifying student" (as defined in subsection 118.6(1)) for a month in a taxation year.

Related Provisions: ITA 162(7.01), (7.02) — Penalty for late or paper-filed forms; Reg. 205 — Date return due; Reg. 205.1(1) — Forms of which more than 50 must be filed by Internet; Reg. 209 — Two copies to be sent (or one emailed) to taxpayer.

Notes: Reg. 203 added by 2018 budget bill #2, for 2019 and later tax years. Its stated purpose is to facilitate provision of the Canada Workers Benefit (ITA 122.7) now that no separate application is made for it.

Former Reg. 203, repealed by P.C. 2002-2169 effective 2003, applied to a person in Canada receiving US-source income as agent of a person outside Canada.

Definitions [Reg. 203]: "designated educational institution" — ITA 118.6(1); "individual" — ITA 248(1); "month" — *Interpretation Act* 35(1); "prescribed" — ITA 248(1); "qualifying student" — ITA 118.6(1); "taxation year" — ITA 249.

Forms [Reg. 203]: T2202A: Tuition, education, and textbook amounts certificate; TL11A: Tuition, education, and textbook amounts certificate — university outside Canada; TL11B: Tuition fees certificate — flying school or club; TL11C: Tuition, education, and textbook amounts certificate — commuter to the United States.

204. Estates and trusts — (1) [Trustee to file return]

Every person having the control of, or receiving income, gains or profits in a fiduciary capacity, or in a capacity analogous to a fiduciary capacity, shall make a return in prescribed form in respect thereof.

Related Provisions: ITA 150(1)(c) — Trust tax return; Reg. 204(2) — Date return due; Reg. 204.1 — Early disclosure requirement for publicly-traded trusts; Reg. 205.1(1) — Forms of which more than 50 must be filed by Internet; Reg. 209 — Two copies to be sent (or one emailed) to taxpayer.

Notes: See Notes to ITA 150(1)(c). For discussion of the timing problems of T3 and T5 slips, see VIEWS doc 2007-0225871M4.

Reg. 204(1) includes both the T3 trust return (ITA 150(1)) and the trust's obligation to issue T3 slips to report trust income payments to beneficiaries (for non-residents, see Reg. 202(1)(c)). CRA can approve a customized or consolidated T3 slip for multiple funds: VIEWS doc 2006-0185621C6.

Interpretation Bulletins: IT-531: Eligible funeral arrangements.

Information Circulars: 78-5R3: Communal organizations; 78-14R4: Guidelines for trust companies and other persons responsible for filing T3GR, T3D, T3P, T3S, T3RI, and T3F returns.

Forms: T3: Statement of trust income allocations and designations; T3ATH-IND: Amateur athlete trust income tax return; T3D: Deferred profit sharing plan or revoked plan information return and income tax return; T3F: Investments prescribed to be qualified information return; T3GR: Group income tax and information return for RRSP, RRIF, RESP, or RDSP trusts (and worksheets); T3P: Employees' pension plan income tax return; T3RET: Trust income tax and information return; T3S: Supplementary unemployment benefit plan — income tax return; T4031: Computer specifications for data filed on Magnetic Media (T5, T5008, T4RSP, T4RIF, NR4, and T3) [guide].

(2) [Filing deadline] — The return required under this section shall be filed within 90 days from the end of the taxation year and shall be in respect of the taxation year.

Related Provisions: ITA 104(13.4)(c)(ii) — Death of beneficiary — spousal and similar trusts; ITA 162(7.01) — Penalty for late filing; ITA 251.2(7)(f) — Deadline extended to regular year's deadline, for trust year deemed ended due to change in majority beneficiaries; *Interpretation Act* 27(5) — Meaning of "within 90 days".

Notes: The deadline for 2019 was extended to May 1, 2020: see Reg. 202(7) Notes.

Interpretation Bulletins: IT-531: Eligible funeral arrangements.

(3) [Exceptions] — Subsection (1) does not require a trust to make a return for a taxation year at the end of which it is

  (a) governed by a deferred profit sharing plan or by a plan referred to in subsection 147(15) of the Act as a revoked plan;

  (b) governed by an employees profit sharing plan;

  (c) a registered charity;

  (d) governed by an eligible funeral arrangement;

  (d.1) a cemetery care trust;

  (e) governed by a registered education savings plan;

  (f) governed by a TFSA or by an arrangement that is deemed by paragraph 146.2(9)(a) of the Act to be a TFSA; or

  (g) governed by a registered disability savings plan, except if paragraph 146.4(5)(a) or (b) of the Act applies.

Related Provisions: ITA 148.1 — Eligible funeral arrangements; ITA 149.1(14) — Charity information return; Reg. 201(1)(f) — Eligible funeral arrangement information return; Reg. 212 — EPSP information return.

Notes: Reg. 204(3)(g) added by P.C. 2016-96, effective July 2015.

Opening words of Reg. 204(3) changed from "This section does not apply in respect of a trust that is", and para. (d) added, by P.C. 1996-765, effective 1993.

Para. (d.1) added by P.C. 1999-2212, effective for 1998 and later taxation years; (e) added by P.C. 1998-2275, effective for 1998 and later taxation years; (f) added by 2008 budget bill #2, effective for 2009 and later taxation years.

Interpretation Bulletins: IT-531: Eligible funeral arrangements.

Definitions [Reg. 204]: "cemetery care trust" — ITA 148.1(1), 248(1); "deferred profit sharing plan" — ITA 147(1), 248(1); "eligible funeral arrangement" — ITA 148.1(1), 248(1); "employees profit sharing plan" — ITA 144(1), 248(1); "person", "prescribed", "registered charity" — ITA 248(1); "registered disability savings plan" — ITA 146.4(1), 248(1); "registered education savings plan" — ITA 146.1(1), 248(1); "TFSA" — ITA 248(1); "taxation year" — ITA 249; "trust" — ITA 104(1), 248(1), (3).

204.1 (1) Interpretation — The following definitions apply in this section.

"public investment trust", at any time, means a public trust all or substantially all of the fair market value of the property of which is, at that time, attributable to the fair market value of property of the trust that is

  (a) units of public trusts;

  (b) partnership interests in public partnerships (as defined in subsection 229.1(1));

  (c) shares of the capital stock of public corporations; or

  (d) any combination of properties referred to in paragraphs (a) to (c).

"public trust", at any time, means a mutual fund trust the units of which are, at that time, listed on a designated stock exchange in Canada.

Notes: See Notes to Reg. 204.1(2) and at end of Reg. 204.1.

(2) Required information disclosure — A trust that is, at any time in a taxation year of the trust, a public trust shall, within the time required by subsection (3),

(a) make public, in prescribed form, information in respect of the trust for the taxation year by posting that prescribed form, in a manner that is accessible to the general public, on the Internet website of CDS Innovations Inc.; and

(b) notify the Minister in writing as to when the posting of the prescribed form, as required by paragraph (a), has been made.

Related Provisions: Reg. 229.1(2) — Parallel rule for public partnerships.

Notes: This measure and Reg. 229.1 are a response to ongoing requests from the Investment Dealers Association and others for an earlier disclosure deadline, to allow mutual fund trusts that invest in income trusts to prepare their T3 information slips by 90 days after year-end using this information. See VIEWS doc 2007-0233731C6.

To notify under para. (b), email pubtr-fo-g@cra.gc.ca: tinyurl.com/cra-pubtrust.

Authorization for this provision of the Regulations is in ITA 221(1)(d.2).

See Drache, "Investment Income Reporting Delays Addressed", xxix(17) *The Canadian Taxpayer* (Carswell) 133-34 (Aug. 28, 2007); Minicucci, "Proposals Seek to Ensure Investors Receive Information Slips on Time", 4(9) *Tax Hyperion [TH]* (Carswell, Sept. 2007) and "New Regulations Ineffective", 5(6) *TH* (June 2008); CRA May 2008 ICAA roundtable (tinyurl.com/cra-abtax), q. 42; May 2010 ICAA Roundtable, q. 23.

(3) Required disclosure time — The time required for a public trust to satisfy the requirements of subsection (2) in respect of the public trust for a taxation year of the public trust is

(a) subject to paragraph (b), on or before the day that is 60 days after the end of the taxation year; and

(b) where the public trust is, at any time in the taxation year, a public investment trust, on or before the day that is 67 days after the end of the calendar year in which the taxation year ends.

Notes [Reg. 204.1]: See Notes to Reg. 204.1(2) above. Reg. 204.1 added by 2007 budget bill #2, for information in respect of tax years that end after July 3, 2007.

Definitions [Reg. 204.1]: "calendar year" — *Interpretation Act* 37(1)(a); "fair market value" — see ITA 69(1) Notes; "Minister" — ITA 248(1); "mutual fund trust" — ITA 132(6)–(7), 132.2(3)(n), 248(1); "partnership" — see ITA 96(1) Notes; "prescribed", "property" — ITA 248(1); "public corporation" — ITA 89(1), 248(1); "public investment trust" — Reg. 204.1(1); "public partnership" — Reg. 229.1(1); "public trust" — Reg. 204.1(1); "share" — ITA 248(1); "taxation year" — ITA 249; "trust" — ITA 104(1), 248(1), (3); "writing" — *Interpretation Act* 35(1).

Proposed Addition — Reg. 204.2

204.2 Additional reporting [—] trusts — **(1)** For the purposes of subsection 150(1) of the Act, every person having the control of, or receiving income, gains or profits in a fiduciary capacity, or in a capacity analogous to a fiduciary capacity, shall provide information in respect of a trust, unless the trust is subject to one of the exceptions listed in paragraphs 150(1.2)(a) to (n) of the Act, that includes the name, address, date of birth (in the case of an individual other than a trust), jurisdiction of residence and "TIN" (as defined in subsection 270(1) of the Act) for each person who, in the year,

(a) is a trustee, beneficiary (subject to subsection (2)) or "settlor" (as defined in subsection 17(15) of the Act) of the trust; or

(b) has the ability (through the terms of the trust or a related agreement) to exert influence over trustee decisions regarding the appointment of income or capital of the trust.

(2) For the purposes of subsection (1), the requirement in paragraph (1)(a) to provide required information in respect of beneficiaries of a trust in a return is met if

(a) the required information is provided in respect of each beneficiary of the trust whose identity is known or ascertainable with reasonable effort by the person making the return at the time of filing the return; and

(b) in respect of beneficiaries not described in paragraph (a), the person making the return provides sufficiently detailed information to determine with certainty whether any particular person is a beneficiary of the trust.

Application: The July 27, 2018 draft legislation (Budget), s. 9, will add s. 204.2, applicable to taxation years that end after Dec. 30, 2021.

Technical Notes: New section 204.2 is introduced in order to provide for additional information reporting requirements for certain trusts.

New subsection 204.2(1) introduces a requirement for all trusts that are required to file a return of income to provide additional information (in the T3 form), except for those trusts specifically listed in paragraphs 150(1.2)(a) to (n) of the Act. This additional information includes the name, address, date of birth (in the case of an individual other than a trust), jurisdiction of residence and taxpayer identification number (or TIN, as defined in subsection 270(1) of the Act) for each person who, in the year,

- is a trustee, beneficiary or settlor (as defined in subsection 17(15) of the Act) of the trust; or

- has the ability (through the terms of the trust or a related agreement) to exert influence over trustee decisions regarding the appointment of income or capital of the trust. This would include, for example, a protector of the trust.

New subsection 204.2(2) provides that for the purposes of subsection (1), the requirement to provide information in respect of the beneficiaries of a trust is met if

- the required information is provided in respect of each beneficiary of the trust whose identity is known or ascertainable with reasonable effort by the person making the return at the time of filing the return; and

- for beneficiaries whose identity is not known or ascertainable with reasonable effort by the person making the return, the person making the return provides sufficiently detailed information to determine with certainty whether any particular person is a beneficiary of the trust.

For example, the beneficiary of a trust may not be known where the trust provides for a class of beneficiaries that includes the settlor's current children and grandchildren and any children or grandchildren that the settlor may have in the future. In these circumstances the reporting requirement will be met if the relevant information in respect of all of the settlor's current children and grandchildren are included as well as the details of the terms of the trust that extend the class of beneficiaries to any of the settlor's future children or grandchildren.

Federal Budget, Supplementary Information, Feb. 27, 2018 and Dept. of Finance news release, Dec. 11, 2017: See under ITA 150(1.2).

Notes: See Notes to ITA 150(1.2).

Definitions [Reg. 204.2]: "beneficiary" — ITA 248(25) [Notes]; "individual", "person" — ITA 248(1); "settlor" — ITA 17(15); "TIN" — ITA 270(1); "trust" — ITA 104(1), 248(1), (3).

205. Date returns to be filed — **(1)** All returns required under this Part shall be filed with the Minister without notice or demand and, unless otherwise specifically provided, on or before the last day of February in each year and shall be in respect of the preceding calendar year.

Related Provisions: ITA 162(7.01) — Penalty for late filing; Reg. 202(7), (8), 203(2), 204(2), 205(2) — Exceptions.

(2) [Where business discontinued] — Where a person who is required to make a return under this Part discontinues his business or activity, the return shall be filed within 30 days of the day of the discontinuance of the business or activity and shall be in respect of any calendar year or a portion thereof prior to the discontinuance of the business or activity for which a return has not previously been filed.

Related Provisions: *Interpretation Act* 27(5) — Meaning of "within 30 days".

(3) For the purpose of subsection 162(7.01) of the Act, the following types of information returns are prescribed:

Government Service Contract Payments	T1204
International Electronic Funds Transfer Report	[RC438]
International Exchange of Information on Financial Accounts Information Return (Part XVIII of the Act)	
Past Service Pension Adjustment (PSPA) Exempt from Certification	T215
Pension Adjustment Reversal (PAR)	T10
Pooled Registered Pension Plan (PRPP) Information Return	[RC368-CA]
Registered Retirement Savings Plan (RRSP) Contribution Information Return	
Statement of Amounts Paid or Credited to Non-residents of Canada	NR4

Statement of Benefits	T5007
Statement of Canada Pension Plan Benefits	T4A(P)
Statement of Contract Payments	T5018
Statement of Distributions from a Retirement Compensation Arrangement (RCA)	T4A-RCA
Statement of Employee Profit Sharing Plan Allocations and Payments	T4PS
Statement of Employment Insurance and Other Benefits	T4E
Statement of Farm-support Payments	AGR-1
Statement of Fees, Commissions, or Other Amounts Paid to Non-residents for Services Rendered in Canada	T4A-NR
Statement of Income from a Registered Retirement Income Fund	T4RIF
Statement of Investment Income	T5
Statement of Old Age Security	T4A(OAS)
Statement of Pension, Retirement, Annuity and Other Income	T4A
Statement of Registered Retirement Savings Plan (RRSP) Income	T4RSP
Statement of Remuneration Paid	T4
Statement of Securities Transactions	T5008
Statement of Trust Income Allocations and Designations	T3
Tax-free Savings Account (TFSA) Annual Information Return	
Tuition and Enrolment Certificate	[T2202]
Universal Child Care Benefit Statement	RC62

Notes: "Tuition and Enrolment Certificate" added by 2018 budget bill #2, effective 2019.

Reg. 205(3) amended by P.C. 2015-862, effective July 2015, to add "International Electronic Funds Transfer Report" and "International Exchange of Information on Financial Accounts Information Return (Part XVIII of the Act)". This was in advance of these forms being published, so no form numbers were shown.

Reg. 205(3) added by P.C. 2013-1152, effective 2012 (PRPP Information Return effective 2013). See Notes to ITA 162(7.01).

Definitions [Reg. 205]: "business" — ITA 248(1); "calendar year" — *Interpretation Act* 37(1)(a); "Minister", "person" — ITA 248(1).

205.1 (1) Electronic filing [required] — For the purpose of subsection 162(7.02) of the Act, the following types of information returns are prescribed and must be filed by Internet if more than 50 information returns of that type are required to be filed for a calendar year:

Government Service Contract Payments	T1204
International Electronic Funds Transfer Report	[RC438]
Part XVIII Information Return — International Exchange of Information on Financial Accounts	
Pooled Registered Pension Plan (PRPP) Information Return	[RC368-CA]
Registered Retirement Savings Plan (RRSP) Contribution Information Return	
Registered Retirement Savings Plans and Registered Retirement Income Funds Non-qualified Investments	
Statement of Amounts Paid or Credited to Non-residents of Canada	NR4
Statement of Benefits	T5007
Statement of Canada Pension Plan Benefits	T4A(P)
Statement of Contract Payments	T5018
Statement of Employment Insurance and Other Benefits	T4E

Statement of Farm-support Payments	AGR-1
Statement of Fees, Commissions, or Other Amounts Paid to Non-residents for Services Rendered in Canada	T4A-NR
Statement of Income from a Registered Retirement Income Fund (RIF)	T4RIF
Statement of Investment Income	T5
Statement of Old Age Security	T4A(OAS)
Statement of Partnership Income	T5013
Statement of Pension, Retirement, Annuity and Other Income	T4A
Statement of Remuneration Paid	T4
Statement of Registered Retirement Savings Plan (RRSP) Income	T4RSP
Statement of Securities Transactions	T5008
Statement of Trust Income Allocations and Designations	T3
Tax-free Savings Account (TFSA) Annual Information Return	
Tuition and Enrolment Certificate	[T2202]
Universal Child Care Benefit Statement	RC62

Proposed Amendment — 50-return threshold lowered to 5 returns

Federal Budget, Supplementary Information, April 19, 2021: See under ITA 244(14.1), under heading "Filer of Information Returns".

Related Provisions: ITA 162(7.02) — Penalty for failure to file electronically; ITA 244(22) — Electronic filing permitted.

Notes: "Tuition and Enrolment Certificate" added by 2018 budget bill #2, effective 2019.

Electronic filing must now be by Internet file transfer or through Web Forms: tinyurl.com/cra-info-efile. CRA no longer accepts CDs, DVDs, USB keys or diskettes.

Reg. 205.1(1) replaced by P.C. 2015-787, effective June 10, 2015. The previous version required electronic filing of more than 500 returns of any one type.

Reg. 205.1 previously amended by P.C. 2011-1531, for 2010 and later tax years. Added by P.C. 1998-2273.

(2) For purposes of subsection 150.1(2.1) of the Act, a "prescribed corporation" is any corporation whose gross revenue exceeds $1 million except

(a) an insurance corporation as defined in subsection 248(1) of the Act;

(b) a non-resident corporation;

(c) a corporation reporting in functional currency as defined in subsection 261(1) of the Act; or

(d) a corporation that is exempt under section 149 of the Act from tax payable.

Notes: Reg. 205.1(2) added by P.C. 2011-1531, for 2010 and later tax years.

Definitions [Reg. 205.1]: "calendar year" — *Interpretation Act* 37(1)(a); "corporation" — ITA 248(1), *Interpretation Act* 35(1); "gross revenue", "insurance corporation", "Minister", "non-resident", "person", "prescribed" — ITA 248(1).

206. Legal representatives and others — **(1)** Where a person, who is required to make a return under this Part, has died, such return shall be filed by his legal representative within 90 days of the date of death and shall be in respect of any calendar year or a portion thereof prior to the date of death for which a return has not previously been filed.

Related Provisions: *Interpretation Act* 27(5) — Meaning of "within 90 days".

(2) [Trustee in bankruptcy, etc.] — Every trustee in bankruptcy, assignee, liquidator, curator, receiver, trustee or committee and every agent or other person administering, managing, winding-up, controlling or otherwise dealing with the property, business, estate or income of a person who has not filed a return as required by this Part shall file such return.

Definitions [Reg. 206]: "calendar year" — *Interpretation Act* 37(1)(a); "legal representative", "person", "property" — ITA 248(1).

Regulations

207. Ownership certificates — (1) An ownership certificate completed pursuant to section 234 of the Act shall be delivered to the debtor or encashing agent at the time the coupon, warrant or cheque referred to in that section is negotiated.

(2) The debtor or encashing agent to whom an ownership certificate has been delivered pursuant to subsection (1) shall forward it to the Minister on or before the 15th day of the month following the month the coupon, warrant or cheque, as the case may be, was negotiated.

(3) The operation of section 234 of the Act is extended to a bearer coupon or warrant negotiated by or on behalf of a non-resident person who is subject to tax under Part XIII of the Act in respect of such a coupon or warrant.

Forms: T600, T600B: Ownership certificate; NR601: Non-resident ownership certificate (withholding tax); NR602: Non-resident ownership certificate (no withholding tax).

Definitions [Reg. 207]: "Minister" — ITA 248(1); "month" — *Interpretation Act* 35(1); "non-resident", "person" — ITA 248(1).

208. [Repealed]

Notes: Reg. 208 repealed by P.C. 2010-548, effective May 12, 2010. It required information returns for income-averaging annuity contracts (IAACs), under ITA s. 61. IAACs were discontinued in 1981.

209. Distribution of taxpayers' portions of returns — (1) A person who is required by section 200, 201, 202, 203, 204, 212, 214, 215, 217 or 218, subsection 223(2) or section 228, 229, 230, 232, 233 or 234 to make an information return shall forward to each taxpayer to whom the return relates two copies of the portion of the return that relates to that taxpayer.

Notes: Reg. 209(1) amended by 2018 budget bill #2, effective 2019, to refer to Reg. 203.

Reg. 209(1) earlier amended by P.C. 2010-548, effective May 12, 2010, P.C. 1993-1939 and 1992-1567.

(2) The copies referred to in subsection (1) shall be sent to the taxpayer at his last known address or delivered to him in person, on or before the date the return is required to be filed with the Minister.

Notes: If the last known address is known to be incorrect "and the issuer has taken reasonable efforts to obtain the taxpayer's correct address", the slip need not be sent: VIEWS doc 2013-0488891E5.

(3) A person may send a document, as required under subsection (1), in an electronic format if the person has received the express consent of the taxpayer, and in that case, the person shall send a single copy to the taxpayer, on or before the date on which the return referred to in subsection (1) is to be filed with the Minister.

Proposed Amendment — Electronic information slips

Federal Budget, Supplementary Information, April 19, 2021: See under ITA 244(14.1), under heading "Information Returns".

Notes: Reg. 209(3)-(4), added by P.C. 2002-2169, effective 2003, permit e-mailing or electronic downloading of a taxpayer's information slips (T4, T5, etc.) with the taxpayer's "express consent" [EC] (which can be given by email). In CRA's view, if X signs up for online access to a secure website to download tax slips, the EC requirement is met if X "is duly informed and acknowledges that they are consenting to receive their information slips electronically", and this consent can be granted on the website: VIEWS doc 2018-0768931E5.

EC (see Reg. 209(4)) does not include a letter telling employees they will get electronic T4s unless they opt out. An employer doing this could possibly be assessed a $2,500 penalty under ITA 162(7)(b) for *each* improperly-emailed T4. However, see now the option in Reg. 209(5).

CRA insists that even if an institution has issued a paper slip, it cannot provide an electronic copy to a client without express written consent: VIEWS doc 2017-0730761I7 and discussions with the author, Jan. 2019. This is wrong in the author's view: once a paper copy has been sent, a document sent electronically is not being provided "as required under subsection (1)" since Reg. 209(1) has already been satisfied, so Reg. 209(3) does not apply; and nothing prohibits making the document available electronically (e.g., by email to replace a lost paper copy).

(4) In subsection (3), **"express consent"** means consent given in writing or in an electronic format.

Notes: See Notes to Reg. 209(3).

(5) A person may provide a Statement of Remuneration Paid (T4) information return or a Tuition and Enrolment Certificate, as required under subsection (1), as a single document in an electronic format (instead of the two copies required under subsection (1)) to the taxpayer to whom the return relates, on or before the date on which the return is to be filed with the Minister, unless

(a) the specified criteria referred to in section 221.01 of the Act are not met;

(b) the taxpayer has requested that the information return be provided in paper format; or

(c) at the time the return is required to be issued,

(i) if the return is a T4, the taxpayer is on extended leave or is no longer an employee of the person, or

(ii) the taxpayer cannot reasonably be expected to have access to the information return in electronic format.

Notes: To issue an electronic T4 without the employee's consent, CRA requires a secure portal to access the T4, a secure site for printing it, and an option to receive paper copies: tinyurl.com/cra-t4-electr.

Reg. 209(5) amended by 2018 budget bill #2, effective 2019, to add "or a Tuition and Enrolment Certificate" to opening words and "if the return is a T4" to (c)(ii).

Reg. 209(5) added by 2017 budget bill #1, for information returns that are required to be filed after 2017.

Related Provisions [Reg. 209]: ITA 221.01 — Authorization for Minister to specify criteria.

Definitions [Reg. 209]: "employee" — ITA 248(1); "express consent" — Reg. 209(4); "Minister", "person", "taxpayer" — ITA 248(1).

Information Circulars: 72-22R9: Registered retirement savings plans, paras. 33-40.

210. Tax deduction information — Every person who makes a payment described in section 153 of the Act (including an amount paid that is described in subparagraph 153(1)(a)(ii) of the Act), or who pays or credits, or is deemed by any of Part I, XIII and XIII.2 of the Act to have paid or credited, an amount described in that section, Part XIII or XIII.2 of the Act, shall, on demand by registered letter from the Minister, make an information return in prescribed form containing the information required in the return and shall file the return with the Minister within such reasonable time as is stipulated in the registered letter.

Notes: Reg. 210 amended by 2016 budget bill #1, for payments made after 2015, to add "(including an amount paid that is described in subparagraph 153(1)(a)(ii) of the Act)". See Notes to ITA 153(1) under "153(1)(a)(ii)".

Reg. 210 amended by P.C. 2011-936, effective Feb. 19, 2011, to modernize the wording and add references to Part XIII.2.

Definitions [Reg. 210]: "amount", "Minister", "person", "prescribed" — ITA 248(1).

211. Accrued bond interest — (1) Every financial company making a payment in respect of accrued interest by virtue of redemption, assignment or other transfer of a bond, debenture or similar security (other than an income bond, an income debenture or an investment contract in respect of which subsection 201(4) applies), shall make an information return in prescribed form.

Related Provisions: Reg. 205.1(1) — Forms of which more than 50 must be filed by Internet.

Notes: Reg. 211(1) amended by P.C. 1991-172, for investment contracts acquired or materially altered after 1989 (Finance officials have confirmed this will be changed to "last acquired after 1989", to be consistent with changes in 1991 technical bill).

For investment contracts last acquired before 1990, ignore the words "or an investment contract in respect of which subsection 201(4) applies".

(2) The return referred to in subsection (1) shall be forwarded to the Minister on or before the 15th day of the month following the month in which the payment referred to in subsection (1) is made.

(3) For the purposes of this section, a financial company includes a bank, an investment dealer, a stockbroker, a trust company and an insurance company.

(4) The provisions of subsection (1) do not apply to a payment made by one financial company to another financial company.

Definitions [Reg. 211]: "bank" — ITA 248(1), *Interpretation Act* 35(1); "financial company" — Reg. 211(3); "income bond", "Minister" — ITA 248(1); "month" — *Interpretation Act* 35(1); "prescribed" — ITA 248(1); "trust" — ITA 104(1), 248(1), (3).

Forms: T600, T600B: Ownership certificate.

212. Employees profit sharing plans — (1) Every trustee of an employees profit sharing plan shall make an information return in prescribed form.

Related Provisions: Reg. 205 — Date return due; Reg. 209 — Two copies to be sent (or one emailed) to taxpayer.

(2) Notwithstanding subsection (1), the return required under this section may be filed by the employer instead of by the trustee.

Definitions [Reg. 212]: "employees profit sharing plan" — ITA 144(1), 248(1); "employer", "prescribed" — ITA 248(1).

Forms: T4PS: Statement of employee profit-sharing plan allocations and payments; T4PS Segment; T4PS Summ: Employee profit-sharing plan payments and allocations.

213. Pooled registered pension plans — An administrator of a PRPP must file with the Minister an information return for each calendar year in prescribed form in respect of the PRPP

(a) if an agreement concerning annual information returns has been entered into by the Minister and an authority responsible for the supervision of the PRPP under the *Pooled Registered Pension Plans Act* or a similar law of a province, on or before the day on which an information return required by that authority is to be filed for the calendar year; and

(b) in any other case, on or before May 1 of the following calendar year.

Notes: Reg. 213 added by 2012 budget bill #2, effective Dec. 14, 2012.

Former Reg. 213 repealed by P.C. 2010-548, effective for 2009 and later taxation years. It required information returns from corporations engaged in distribution of electrical energy, gas or steam.

Definitions [Reg. 213]: "administrator" — ITA 147.5(1); "calendar year" — *Interpretation Act* 37(1)(a); "Minister", "prescribed" — ITA 248(1); "PRPP" — ITA 248(1)"pooled registered pension plan"; "province" — *Interpretation Act* 35(1).

Forms: T3PRP: T3 Pooled registered pension plan tax return; RC368, RC368-CA: Pooled registered pension plan annual information return.

214. Registered retirement savings plans [T4RSP] — (1) Every person who pays any of the following amounts shall make an information return in prescribed form:

(a) an amount that is required by subsection 146(8) of the Act to be included in computing the income of a taxpayer for a taxation year;

(b) an amount that is an eligible amount, within the meaning of subsection 146.01(1) of the Act; or

(c) an amount that is an eligible amount, within the meaning of subsection 146.02(1) of the Act.

Related Provisions: Reg. 205 — Date return due; Reg. 205.1(1) — Forms of which more than 50 must be filed by Internet; Reg. 209 — Two copies to be sent (or one emailed) to taxpayer.

Notes: Reg. 214(1) amended to add para. (b) for payments made after 2001, and para. (c) for payments made after 1998, by P.C. 2002-2169, effective upon the repeal of ITA 146.01(8) on June 26, 2013.

Forms: See at end of Reg. 214.

(2) If, in a taxation year, subsection 146(7), (9) or (10) of the Act or, in relation to a non-qualified investment, subsection 207.04(1) or (4) of the Act applies in respect of a trust governed by a registered retirement savings plan, the trustee of the plan shall make an information return in prescribed form.

Related Provisions: Reg. 205 — Date return due; Reg. 205.1(1) — Forms of which more than 50 must be filed by Internet; Reg. 209 — Two copies to be sent (or one emailed) to taxpayer.

Notes: Reg. 214(2) amended by 2011 budget bill #2, effective in respect of investments acquired after March 22, 2011, essentially to extend the rule to ITA 207.04.

Forms: See at end of Reg. 214.

(3) Where, in respect of an amended plan referred to in subsection 146(12) of the Act, an amount is required to be included in computing the income of a taxpayer for a taxation year, the issuer of the plan shall make an information return in prescribed form.

Related Provisions: Reg. 205 — Date return due; Reg. 205.1(1) — Forms of which more than 50 must be filed by Internet; Reg. 209 — Two copies to be sent (or one emailed) to taxpayer.

Forms: See at end of Reg. 214.

(4) Where subsection 146(8.8) of the Act deems an amount to be received by an annuitant as a benefit out of or under a registered retirement savings plan and such amount is required by subsection 146(8) of the Act to be included in computing the income of that annuitant for a taxation year, the issuer of the plan shall make an information return in prescribed form.

Related Provisions: Reg. 205 — Date return due; Reg. 205.1(1) — Forms of which more than 50 must be filed by Internet; Reg. 209 — Two copies to be sent (or one emailed) to taxpayer.

Notes: The T4RSP is issued in the surviving spouse's name if the RRSP is transferred to the spouse and conditions are met: Guide T4079; VIEWS doc 2016-0668991E5.

Forms: See at end of Reg. 214.

(5) If a payment or transfer of property to which paragraph 146(16)(b) of the Act applies is made from a plan, the issuer of the plan shall make an information return in prescribed form in respect of the payment or transfer.

Related Provisions: Reg. 205 — Date return due; Reg. 205.1(1) — Forms of which more than 50 must be filed by Internet; Reg. 209 — Two copies to be sent (or one emailed) to taxpayer.

Notes: Reg. 214(5) amended by P.C. 2002-2169 and amended retroactively by P.C. 2005-1508 to correct a cross-reference, effective 2003. This eliminates the requirement for RRSP annuitants to file information returns of payments or transfers. Only the issuer must file.

Reg. 214(5) amended by P.C. 2001-957, effective as per Notes to ITA 248(1)"common-law partner".

Forms: See at end of Reg. 214.

(6) Where an amount may be deducted under subsection 146(8.92) of the Act in computing the income of a deceased annuitant under a registered retirement savings plan, the issuer of the plan shall make an information return in prescribed form in respect of the amount.

Notes: Reg. 214(6) added by 2009 budget bill #1, effective 2009.

Former Reg. 214(6) repealed by P.C. 2002-2169, effective 2003, so as to let Reg. 205 apply, thus changing the filing deadline from 30 days after payment to the end of February.

(7) In this section, **"annuitant"** and **"issuer"** have the meanings assigned by subsection 146(1) of the Act.

Notes: Reg. 214(7) updated by P.C. 2002-2169 to correct ITA references (formerly 146(1)(a) and (c.1)).

Reg. 214(7)"spouse" repealed by P.C. 2001-957, effective as per Notes to ITA 248(1)"common-law partner". It referred to these definitions in former ITA 146(1.1).

Definitions [Reg. 214]: "amount" — ITA 248(1); "annuitant" — ITA 146(1), Reg. 214(7); "common-law partner" — ITA 248(1); "individual" — ITA 248(1); "issuer" — ITA 146(1), Reg. 214(7); "person", "prescribed" — ITA 248(1); "registered retirement savings plan" — ITA 146(1), 248(1); "spouse" — ITA 146(1.1), Reg. 214(7); "taxation year" — ITA 249; "taxpayer" — ITA 248(1); "trust" — ITA 104(1), 248(1), (3).

Forms [Reg. 214]: T4RSP: Statement of registered retirement savings plan income; T4RSP Summ: Return of registered retirement savings plan income; T4031: Computer specifications for data filed on Magnetic Media (T5, T5008, T4RSP, T4RIF, NR4, and T3) [guide]; T4079: T4RSP and T4RIF guide.

214.1 [RRSP contributions — annual return] — (1) The issuer of a registered retirement savings plan shall make an information return in prescribed form in respect of the amounts that have been paid by the annuitant, or by the spouse or common-law partner of the annuitant, under the plan in a contribution year

(a) as consideration for any contract referred to in paragraph (a) of the definition "retirement savings plan" in subsection 146(1) of the Act to pay a retirement income; or

(b) as a contribution or deposit referred to in paragraph (b) of that definition for the purpose stated in that paragraph.

(2) For greater certainty and for the purposes of subsection (1), amounts that have been paid do not include amounts that have been paid or transferred under the plan in accordance with subsection

146(16) of the Act, or those that have been transferred under the plan in accordance with any of subsections 146(21), 146.3(14), 147(19) or 147.3(1), (4) or (5) to (7) of the Act.

(3) The return shall be filed with the Minister on or before the 1st day of May of the year in which the contribution year ends and shall be in respect of the contribution year.

(4) The following definitions apply in this section.

"contribution year" means the period beginning on 61st day of one year and ending on the 60th day of the following year.

"issuer" has the same meaning as in subsection 146(1) of the Act, with any modifications that the circumstances require.

Related Provisions [Reg. 214.1]: ITA146(21.1) — Contribution to Saskatchewan Pension Plan deemed to be RRSP premium for purposes of Reg. 214.1.

Notes: Reg. 214.1 added by P.C. 2005-694, for payments or transfers received after March 1, 2004 by RRSP issuers.

Definitions [Reg. 214.1]: "amount" — ITA 248(1); "contribution year", "issuer" — Reg. 214.1(3); "Minister", "prescribed" — ITA 248(1); "registered retirement savings plan" — ITA 146(1), 248(1).

215. Registered retirement income funds [T4RIF] — (1) In this section, "annuitant" and "carrier" have the meanings assigned by subsection 146.3(1) of the Act.

Notes: Reg. 215(1) updated by P.C. 2002-2169 to correct ITA references (formerly 146.3(1)(a) and (b)).

(2) Every carrier of a registered retirement income fund who pays out of or under it an amount any portion of which is required under subsection 146.3(5) of the Act to be included in computing the income of a taxpayer shall make an information return in prescribed form in respect of the amount.

Related Provisions: Reg. 205 — Date return due; Reg. 205.1(1) — Forms of which more than 50 must be filed by Internet; Reg. 209 — Two copies to be sent (or one emailed) to taxpayer.

Forms: T4RIF: Statement of income from a registered retirement income fund; T4RIF Summary; T4031: Computer specifications for data filed on Magnetic Media (T5, T5008, T4RSP, T4RIF, NR4, and T3) [guide]; T4079: T4RSP and T4RIF guide.

(3) If subsection 146.3(4), (7) or (10) of the Act or, in relation to a non-qualified investment, subsection 207.04(1) or (4) of the Act applies in respect of any transaction or event with respect to property of a registered retirement income fund, the carrier of the fund shall make an information return in prescribed form in respect of the transaction or event.

Related Provisions: Reg. 205 — Date return due; Reg. 205.1(1) — Forms of which more than 50 must be filed by Internet; Reg. 209 — Two copies to be sent (or one emailed) to taxpayer.

Notes: Reg. 215(3) amended by 2011 budget bill #2, effective in respect of investments acquired after March 22, 2011, essentially to extend the rule to ITA 207.04.

Forms: T4RIF: Statement of income from a registered retirement income fund; T4RIF Summary; T4031: Computer specifications for data filed on Magnetic Media (T5, T5008, T4RSP, T4RIF, NR4, and T3) [guide]; T4079: T4RSP and T4RIF guide.

(4) Where an amount is deemed under subsection 146.3(6) or (12) of the Act to be received by an annuitant out of or under a registered retirement income fund, the carrier of the fund shall make an information return in prescribed form in respect of the amount.

Related Provisions: Reg. 205 — Date return due; Reg. 205.1(1) — Forms of which more than 50 must be filed by Internet; Reg. 209 — Two copies to be sent (or one emailed) to taxpayer.

Forms: T4RIF: Statement of income from a registered retirement income fund; T4RIF Summary; T4031: Computer specifications for data filed on Magnetic Media (T5, T5008, T4RSP, T4RIF, NR4, and T3) [guide]; T4079: T4RSP and T4RIF guide.

(5) If a transfer of an amount to which subsection 146.3(14) of the Act applies is made from a fund, the carrier of the fund shall make an information return in prescribed form in respect of the transfer.

Related Provisions: Reg. 205 — Date return due; Reg. 205.1(1) — Forms of which more than 50 must be filed by Internet; Reg. 209 — Two copies to be sent (or one emailed) to taxpayer.

Notes: Reg. 215(5) requires the RRIF carrier from which a transfer is made to a spouse's RRSP or RRIF to file an information return.

Notes: Reg. 215(5) amended, effectively to change reference from ITA 146.3(14)(b) to 146.3(14), by P.C. 2005-1508, effective 2004.

Notes: Reg. 215(5) added by P.C. 2002-2169, effective for transfers made after 2001.

(6) Where an amount may be deducted under subsection 146.3(6.3) of the Act in computing the income of a deceased annuitant under a registered retirement income fund, the carrier of the fund shall make an information return in prescribed form in respect of the amount.

Notes: Reg. 215(6) added by 2009 budget bill #1, effective 2009.

Definitions [Reg. 215]: "amount" — ITA 248(1); "annuitant" — ITA 146.3(1), Reg. 215(1); "carrier" — ITA 146.3(1), Reg. 215(1); "prescribed", "property" — ITA 248(1); "registered retirement income fund" — ITA 146.3(1), 248(1); "taxpayer" — ITA 248(1).

216. Advanced life deferred annuity — (1) In this section, "designated entity" means

    (a) an administrator of a registered pension plan;

    (b) an administrator of a pooled registered pension plan;

    (c) an issuer of a registered retirement savings plan;

    (d) a carrier of a registered retirement income fund; and

    (e) a trustee of a deferred profit sharing plan.

(2) A designated entity that transfers an amount to acquire an advanced life deferred annuity for an individual shall make an information return in prescribed form in respect of the year in which the transfer was made.

(3) A licensed annuities provider shall make an information return in prescribed form in respect of a year in which

    (a) a payment is made that is required by section 146.5 of the Act to be included in computing the income of a taxpayer; or

    (b) a refund described in paragraph (g) of the definition "advanced life deferred annuity" in subsection 146.5(1) of the Act was received by a taxpayer.

Notes: Reg. 216 added by 2021 budget bill #1, effective 2020. See ITA 146.5.

Former Reg. 216 repealed by 2011 budget bill #2, for fiscal periods of a registered Canadian amateur athletic association that begin after 2011. RCAAAs are now required to file information returns by ITA 149.1(14) instead of Reg. 216.

Definitions [Reg. 216]: "advanced life deferred annuity" — ITA 146.5(1), 248(1); "amount" — ITA 248(1); "deferred profit sharing plan" — ITA 147(1), 248(1); "designated entity" — Reg. 216(1); "individual" — ITA 248(1); "licensed annuities provider" — ITA 147(1), 248(1); "pooled registered pension plan" — ITA 147.5(1), 248(1); "prescribed", "registered pension plan" — ITA 248(1); "registered retirement income fund" — ITA 146.3(1), 248(1); "registered retirement savings plan" — ITA 146(1), 248(1); "taxpayer" — ITA 248(1).

217. Disposition of interest in annuities and life insurance policies — (1) In this section,

"disposition" has the meaning assigned by subsection 148(9) of the Act and includes anything deemed to be a disposition of a life insurance policy under subsection 148(2) of the Act;

"insurer" has the meaning assigned by paragraph 148(10)(a) of the Act;

"life insurance policy" — [Repealed]

Notes: Definition "life insurance policy" (cross-referencing to ITA 138(12)) repealed by P.C. 2011-936, effective Feb. 19, 2011 (it is now in ITA 248(1)). Definitions "disposition" and "life insurance policy" earlier updated by P.C. 2002-2169 to correct ITA references (formerly 148(9)(c) and 138(12)(f)).

(2) Where by reason of a disposition of an interest in a life insurance policy an amount is required, pursuant to paragraph 56(1)(j) of the Act, to be included in computing the income of a taxpayer and the insurer that is the issuer of the policy is a party to, or is notified in writing of, the disposition, the insurer shall make an information return in prescribed form in respect of the amount.

Proposed Amendment — Reg. 217(2)

Federal Budget, Supplementary Information, March 22, 2016: *Life Insurance Policies — Distributions Involving Life Insurance Proceeds*

Although the Government is challenging a number of these structures under the existing tax rules, Budget 2016 proposes to amend the *Income Tax Act* to ensure that the capital dividend account rules for private corporations, and the adjusted cost base rules for partnership interests, apply as intended. This measure will provide that the insurance benefit limit applies regardless of whether the corporation or partnership that receives the policy benefit is a policyholder of the policy. To that end, the measure will also introduce information-reporting requirements that will apply where a corporation or partnership is not a policyholder but is entitled to receive a policy benefit.

Federal Budget, Supplementary Information, March 22, 2017: *Previously Announced Measures*

Budget 2017 confirms the Government's intention to proceed with the following previously announced tax and related measures, as modified to take into account consultations and deliberations since their release: . . .

* The measure announced in Budget 2016 on information-reporting requirements for certain dispositions of an interest in a life insurance policy; . . .

Federal Budget, Supplementary Information, Feb. 27, 2018: *Previously Announced Measures*

Budget 2018 confirms the Government's intention to proceed with the following previously announced tax and related measures, as modified to take into account consultations and deliberations since their release: . . .

* The income tax measure announced in Budget 2016 on information-reporting requirements for certain dispositions of an interest in a life insurance policy; . . .

Federal Budget, Supplementary Information, March 19, 2019: *Previously Announced Measures*

Budget 2019 confirms the Government's intention to proceed with the following previously announced tax and related measures, as modified to take into account consultations and deliberations since their release: ...

* The income tax measures announced in Budget 2016 on information-reporting requirements for certain dispositions of an interest in a life insurance policy.

Related Provisions: Reg. 205 — Date return due; Reg. 205.1(1) — Forms of which more than 50 must be filed by Internet; Reg. 209 — Two copies to be sent (or one emailed) to taxpayer.

Definitions [Reg. 217]: "amount" — ITA 248(1); "disposition" — ITA 248(1), Reg. 217(1); "insurer" — ITA 148(10)(a), Reg. 217(1); "life insurance policy", "prescribed", "taxpayer" — ITA 248(1); "writing" — *Interpretation Act* 35(1).

Forms: T5: Statement of investment income; T5 Summ: Return of investment income.

218. Patronage payments — (1)
Every person who, within the meaning of section 135 of the Act, makes payments to residents of Canada pursuant to an allocation in proportion to patronage shall make an information return in prescribed form in respect of payments so made.

Related Provisions: Reg. 205.1(1) — Forms of which more than 50 must be filed by Internet; Reg. 209 — Two copies to be sent (or one emailed) to taxpayer.

(2) Every person who receives a payment referred to in subsection (1) as nominee or agent for another person resident in Canada shall make an information return in prescribed form in respect of the payment so received.

Related Provisions: Reg. 205 — Date return due; Reg. 205.1(1) — Forms of which more than 50 must be filed by Internet; Reg. 209 — Two copies to be sent (or one emailed) to taxpayer.

Definitions [Reg. 218]: "Canada" — ITA 255, *Interpretation Act* 35(1); "person", "prescribed" — ITA 248(1); "resident", "resident in Canada" — ITA 250.

Forms [Reg. 218]: RC4157: Deducting income tax on pension and other income, and filing the T4A slip and summary form [guide]; T4A: Statement of pension, retirement, annuity and other income; T4A Segment; T4A Summ: Summary of pension, retirement, annuity and other income.

219. [Repealed]

Notes: Reg. 219 repealed by P.C. 2002-2169, effective 2003. Family allowances, taxable under ITA 56(5), were discontinued after 1992. Canada Child Benefit payments to low-income families (ITA 122.61) are now non-taxable.

220. Cash bonus payments on Canada Savings Bonds —
(1) Every person authorized to redeem Canada Savings Bonds (in this section referred to as the "redemption agent") who pays an amount in respect of a Canada Savings Bond as a cash bonus that the Government of Canada has undertaken to pay (other than any amount of interest, bonus or principal agreed to be paid at the time of the issue of the bond under the terms of the bond) shall make an information return in prescribed form in respect of such payment.

Related Provisions: Reg. 205.1(1) — Forms of which more than 50 must be filed by Internet.

(2) Every redemption agent required by subsection (1) to make an information return shall

(a) issue to the payee, at the time the cash bonus is paid, two copies of the portion of the return relating to him; and

(b) file the return with the Minister on or before the 15th day of the month following the month in which the cash bonus was paid.

Notes: See ITA 12.1.

Definitions [Reg. 220]: "amount" — ITA 248(1); "Canada" — ITA 255, *Interpretation Act* 35(1); "Minister" — ITA 248(1); "month" — *Interpretation Act* 35(1); "person", "prescribed" — ITA 248(1); "redemption agent" — Reg. 220(1).

221. Qualified investments [T3F] — (1)
In this section, **"reporting person"** means

(a) a mutual fund corporation;

(b) an investment corporation;

(c) a mutual fund trust;

(d) [Repealed]

(e) [Repealed]

(f) a trust that would be a mutual fund trust if Part XLVIII were read without reference to paragraph 4801(b); or

(g) [Repealed]

(h) a small business investment trust (within the meaning assigned by subsection 5103(1)).

(i) [Repealed]

Notes: Reg. 221(1) amended by P.C. 2010-548 to move "or" from end of para. (h) to end of para. (f), effective May 12, 2010.

Reg. 221(1)(d), (e), (g) and (i) repealed by P.C. 2005-1508, effective June 29, 2005, and title changed from "Qualified investments and foreign property", due to repeal of ITA Part XI (foreign property limit).

(2) Where in any taxation year a reporting person (other than a registered investment) claims that a share of its capital stock issued by it, or an interest as a beneficiary under it, is a qualified investment under section 146, 146.1, 146.3, 146.4, 204 or 207.01 of the Act, the reporting person shall, in respect of the year and within 90 days after the end of the year, make an information return in prescribed form.

Related Provisions: *Interpretation Act* 27(5) — Meaning of "within 90 days".

Notes: Reg. 221(2) amended by 2017 budget bill #2, effective March 23, 2017, to delete reference to ITA 205 (now repealed) and add reference to 146.4 (since "qualified investment" has been added to 146.4(1) for RDSPs).

Earlier amended by 2008 budget bill #2 (for 2009 and later tax years), 2007 RDSPs bill, P.C. 2001-1106.

(3) [Repealed]

Notes: Reg. 221(3) repealed by P.C. 2005-1508, effective June 29, 2005, due to repeal of ITA Part XI (foreign property limit).

Notes [Reg. 221]: Reg. 221 amended and 222 repealed by P.C. 2000-183, effective for taxation years that begin after 1995. The amendment consolidates the two into one section and narrows their scope to conform with CRA administrative practice.

Definitions [Reg. 221]: "business" — ITA 248(1); "investment corporation" — ITA 130(3), 248(1); "mutual fund corporation" — ITA 131(8), 248(1); "mutual fund trust" — ITA 132(6)–(7), 132.2(3)(n), 248(1); "person", "prescribed" — ITA 248(1); "registered investment" — ITA 204.4(1), 248(1); "reporting person" — Reg. 221(1); "share" — ITA 248(1); "taxation year" — ITA 249; "trust" — ITA 104(1), 248(1), (3).

Information Circulars: 78-14R4: Guidelines for trust companies and other persons responsible for filing T3GR, T3D, T3P, T3S, T3RI, and T3F returns.

Forms: T3F: Investments prescribed to be qualified information return.

222. [RDSP or RESP — non-qualified investment] —
The issuer of a RDSP, or the promoter of a RESP, that governs a trust shall notify the holders of the RDSP, or subscribers of the RESP, in prescribed form and manner before March of a calendar year if, at any time during the preceding calendar year,

(a) the trust acquires or disposes of property that is a not a qualified investment for the trust; or

(b) property held by the trust becomes or ceases to be a qualified investment for the trust.

Notes: See Notes to Reg. 221. Reg. 222 added by 2017 budget bill #2, effective March 23, 2017.

Definitions [Reg. 222]: "calendar year" — *Interpretation Act* 37(1)(a); "prescribed", "property" — ITA 248(1); "RDSP" — ITA 248(1)"registered disability savings plan"; "RESP" — ITA 248(1)"registered education savings plan"; "trust" — ITA 104(1), 248(1), (3).

223. TFSAs — (1) An issuer of a TFSA shall make an information return for each calendar year in prescribed form in respect of the TFSA.

Related Provisions: Reg. 205 — Date return due.

Notes: In *Marquest Asset v. Stone Investment*, 2021 ONSC 1476, MA sold an investment business to SI, representing that all TFSA returns had been filed. As it turned out they had not been, MA fixed the problem and paid the late filing fees. SI claimed damages but could not explain why. The Court awarded a nominal $100: para. 86.

(2) An issuer of a TFSA who makes a payment of an amount that is required because of paragraph 146.2(9)(b) of the Act to be included in computing the income of a taxpayer for a taxation year shall make an information return in prescribed form.

Related Provisions: Reg. 205 — Date return due; Reg. 209 — Two copies to be sent (or one emailed) to taxpayer.

(3) An issuer of a TFSA that governs a trust shall notify the holder of the TFSA in prescribed form and manner before March of a calendar year if, at any time during the preceding calendar year,

(a) the trust acquires or disposes of property that is a non-qualified investment for the trust; or

(b) property held by the trust becomes or ceases to be a non-qualified investment for the trust.

Notes: Reg. 223 replaced by 2008 budget bill #2, for 2009 and later tax years. The previous version, dealing with registered home ownership savings plans (see Notes to ITA 146.2), had not been relevant since the 1980s.

Definitions [Reg. 223]: "amount" — ITA 248(1); "calendar year" — *Interpretation Act* 37(1)(a); "holder", "issuer" — ITA 146.2(1); "prescribed", "property" — ITA 248(1); "taxation year" — ITA 249; "TFSA", "taxpayer" — ITA 248(1); "trust" — ITA 104(1), 248(1), (3).

224. Canadian home insulation program and Canada oil substitution program — Where an amount has been paid to a person pursuant to a program prescribed for the purposes of paragraph 12(1)(u), 56(1)(s) and 212(1)(s) of the Act, the payor shall

(a) make an information return in prescribed form in respect of such payment; and

(b) forward to the person at his latest known address on or before the date the return is required to be filed with the Minister two copies of the portion of the return relating to that person.

Related Provisions: Reg. 205 — Date return due; Reg. 205.1(1) — Forms of which more than 50 must be filed by Internet.

Definitions [Reg. 224]: "amount", "Minister", "person", "prescribed" — ITA 248(1).

225. Certified films and video tapes — (1) Where principal photography or taping of a film or tape (within the meanings assigned by subsection 1100(21)) has occurred during a year or has been completed within 60 days after the end of the year, the producer of the film or tape or production company that produced the film or tape, or an agent of the producer or production company, shall

(a) make an information return in prescribed form in respect of any person who owns an interest in the film or tape at the end of the year; and

(b) forward to the person referred to in paragraph (a) at his latest known address on or before the date the return is required to be filed with the Minister two copies of the portion of the return relating to that person.

Related Provisions: Reg. 205.1(1) — Forms of which more than 50 must be filed by Internet.

(2) The return required under this section shall be filed on or before March 31 and shall be in respect of the preceding calendar year.

Definitions [Reg. 225]: "calendar year" — *Interpretation Act* 37(1)(a); "film or tape" — Reg. 1100(21); "Minister", "person", "prescribed" — ITA 248(1).

Forms: T1-CP Summ: Summary of certified productions.

226. Scientific research tax credits — [No longer relevant]

Notes: SRTCs were eliminated in 1985. See Notes to ITA 127.3.

227. Share purchase tax credits — [No longer relevant]

Notes: SPTCs were eliminated in 1986. See Notes to ITA 127.2.

228. Resource flow-through shares — (1) Each corporation that has renounced an amount under subsection 66(12.6), (12.601), (12.62) or (12.64) of the Act to a person shall make an information return in prescribed form in respect of the amount renounced.

(2) The return required under subsection (1) shall be filed with the Minister together with the prescribed form required to be filed under subsection 66(12.7) of the Act in respect of the amount renounced.

Related Provisions [Reg. 228]: Reg. 209 — Two copies to be sent (or one emailed) to taxpayer.

Notes: Reference to ITA 66(12.601) added to Reg. 228(1) by P.C. 1996-494, effective December 3, 1992.

Definitions [Reg. 228]: "amount" — ITA 248(1); "corporation" — ITA 248(1), *Interpretation Act* 35(1); "Minister", "person", "prescribed" — ITA 248(1).

Forms: T2 Sched. 12: Resource-related deductions; T101: Statement of resource expense; T101A: Claim for renouncing CEEs and CDEs; T101B: Adjustments to CEEs and CDEs previously renounced; T101C: Part XII.6 tax return; T101D: Summary of assistance; T1229: Statement of resource expenses and depletion allowance; T5013 Sched. 9: List of partnerships; T5013A: Statement of partnership income for tax shelters and renounced resource expenses.

229. Partnership return [T5013] — (1) Every member, of a partnership that carries on a business in Canada at any time in a fiscal period of the partnership (other than a member that is, because of subsection 115.2(2) of the Act, not considered to be carrying on business in Canada at that time), or of a partnership that is at any time in a fiscal period of the partnership, a Canadian partnership or a SIFT partnership, shall make for that period an information return in prescribed form containing the following information:

(a) the income or loss of the partnership for the fiscal period;

(b) in respect of each member of the partnership who is entitled to a share referred to in paragraph (c) or (d) for the fiscal period, the member's

(i) name,

(ii) address, and

(iii) business number, Social Insurance Number or trust account number, as the case may be;

(c) the share of each member of the income or loss of the partnership for the fiscal period;

(d) the share of each member for the fiscal period of each deduction, credit or other amount in respect of the partnership that is relevant in determining the member's income, taxable income, tax payable or other amount under the Act;

(e) the prescribed information contained in the form prescribed for the purposes of subsection 37(1) of the Act, where the partnership has made an expenditure in respect of scientific research and experimental development in the fiscal period; and

(f) such other information as may be required by the prescribed form.

Related Provisions: ITA 96(1) — Taxation of partnership income; ITA 152(1.4) — Determination by CRA of income or loss of partnership; ITA 197(4) — Part IX.1 return required for publicly traded partnership's distributions; ITA 233.1(3) — Information return for partnership re non-arm's length transactions with non-residents; ITA 233.3 — Requirement to file information return re foreign property; ITA 248(1)"SIFT partnership balance-due day" — Information return due date is balance-due day; Reg. 205.1(1) — Forms of which more than 50 must be filed by Internet; Reg. 209 — Two copies to be sent (or one emailed) to taxpayer; Reg. 229(2) — Only one partner need file; Reg. 229(5) — Filing deadline; Reg. 229.1 — Early disclosure requirement for publicly-traded partnerships; Reg. 236 — Partners to provide information.

Notes: The information return (financial return) is the T5013-FIN (T5013 before 2020), which can be filed electronically: tinyurl.com/t5013-electr. See Reg. 229(5) for the filing deadline.

See Notes to ITA 96(1) re taxation of partnership income. Under CRA administrative policy (tinyurl.com/cra-partners), certain partnerships need not file; this is a waiver under ITA 220(2.1). A partnership that carries on a business in Canada, or a Canadian partnership with Canadian or foreign operations or investments, must file a T5013 for each fiscal period of the partnership:

- If, at the end of the fiscal period,
  - the partnership has an absolute value of revenues plus an absolute value of expenses of more than $2 million, or has more than $5 million in assets; or
- If, at anytime during the fiscal period
  - the partnership is a tiered partnership (has another partnership as a partner or is itself a partner in another partnership);
  - the partnership has a corporation or a trust as a partner;
  - the partnership invested in flow-through shares of a principal-business corporation that incurred Canadian resource expenses and renounced those expenses to the partnership; or
  - the Minister of National Revenue requests one in writing.

(Absolute value is the numerical value of a positive or negative amount. If revenues are $1.5 million and expenses are $1m, the total is $2.5m so a T5013 must be filed.) The revenues and expenses details come from the financial statement amounts. "Revenues" refers to revenues that have not been netted. Expenses include both current costs and capital costs (e.g. depreciation). Revenues from all sources (revenues that have not been netted) are added to the total of all expenses (expenses are expressed as a positive number), and the total is used to determine whether or not the criterion has been met. To determine whether the partnership has more than $5m of assets, the cost figure of both tangible and intangible assets should be used without factoring in depreciation.

However, farm partnerships (even above the threshold) whose partners are all individuals other than trusts need not file through the 2020 fiscal year (rule for 2021 will be announced at tinyurl.com/cra-partners early in 2022).

Where no return is required, it is still advisable for partnerships to file, to start time running under ITA 152(1.4)(b). Otherwise the partners may be open for reassessment indefinitely: ITA 152(1.7)(b), VIEWS docs 9726115, 2000-0010935; Strawson, "Should Partnership Information Returns Be Filed as a Matter of Course?", 9(4) *Tax for the Owner-Manager* (ctf.ca) 3-4 (Oct. 2009). A late-filed return that was not required is not subject to penalty: 2014-0538211C6 [2014 APFF q.27].

The T5013 Summary and T5013 information slips are prescribed information returns for Reg. 229(1): VIEWS doc 2010-0383701I7. The filing deadline is in Reg. 229(5).

CRA will not issue a paper notification acknowledging the T5013 has been filed, but allows it to be seen on My Business Account: VIEWS doc 2011-0427231C6, q. (c).

Only one partner need file the return: see Reg. 229(2).

A publicly-traded partnership (SIFT partnership) must file a Part IX.1 return to report and pay tax on distributions to partners: ITA 197.

CRA's view is that a partnership return cannot be amended after the statute-barred date: doc 2014-0562271I7.

Where a corporate partner has made a functional currency election under ITA s. 261, see VIEWS docs 2012-0471831E5, 2016-0642011E5.

Reg. 229(1)(b) amended by 2018 budget bill #1, for 2018 and later tax years, effectively to add references to business number and trust account number. For earlier years, read:

(b) the name, address and, in the case of an individual, the social insurance number of each member of the partnership who is entitled to a share referred to in paragraph (c) or (d) for the fiscal period;

Reg. 229(1) opening words amended by 2002-2013 technical bill, for fiscal periods that end after 2007.

Reg. 229(1) amended by 2007 budget bill #1 to add "or a SIFT partnership", effective Oct. 31, 2006 (but see ITA 197(8) for the actual effective date).

Information Circulars: 82-2R2: SIN legislation that relates to the preparation of information slips; 89-5R: Partnership information return.

I.T. Technical News: 38 (filing requirements for T5013).

Forms: RC257: Request for an information return program account (RZ); T1229: Statement of resource expenses and depletion allowance; T4068: Guide for the partnership information return; T4068-1: 2007 Supplement to the 2006 T4068 — Guide for the T5013 partnership information return; T5011: Application for a partnership's filer identification number; T5013: Statement of partnership income; T5013 FIN: Partnership financial return; T5013-Inst: Statement of partnership income — instructions for recipient; T5013 Sched. 1: Partnership's net income (loss) for income tax purposes; T5013 Sched. 2: Charitable donations, gifts, and political contributions; T5013 Sched. 6: Summary of dispositions of capital property; T5013 Sched. 8: Capital cost allowance; T5013 Sched. 10: Calculations relating to cumulative eligible capital; T5013 Sched. 12: Resource-related deductions; T5013 Sched. 19: Non-resident member infor-

mation; T5013 Sched. 25: Investment in foreign affiliates; T5013 Sched. 50: Partner's ownership and account activity; T5013 Sched. 52: Summary information for partnerships that allocated renounced resource expenses to their members; T5013 Sched. 100: Partnership's balance sheet information; T5013 Sched. 125: Partnership's income statement information; T5013 Sched. 141: Partnership's financial statement notes checklist; T5013 Summ: Summary of partnership income; T5013-1: Part IX.1 income tax calculation — SIFT partnership; T5013A: Statement of partnership income for tax shelters and renounced resource expenses; T5015: Reconciliation of partner's capital account.

(2) For the purposes of subsection (1), an information return made by any member of a partnership shall be deemed to have been made by each member of the partnership.

(3) Every person who holds an interest in a partnership as nominee or agent for another person shall make an information return in prescribed form in respect of that interest.

Related Provisions: Reg. 205.1(1) — Forms of which more than 50 must be filed by Internet; Reg. 209 — Two copies to be sent (or one emailed) to taxpayer.

(4) [Revoked]

Notes: Reg. 229(4) repealed by P.C. 1993-1691, effective Sept. 8, 1993. It allowed the Minister to exempt the members of a partnership or class of partnerships from Reg. 229. ITA 220(2.1) now provides authority for the CRA to waive documentary requirements in general.

(5) Subject to subsection (6), a return required by this section shall be filed with the Minister without notice or demand

(a) in the case of a fiscal period of a partnership all the members of which are corporations throughout the fiscal period, within five months after the end of the fiscal period;

(b) in the case of a fiscal period of a partnership all the members of which are individuals throughout the fiscal period, on or before the last day of March in the calendar year immediately following the calendar year in which the fiscal period ended or with which the fiscal period ended coincidentally; and

(c) in the case of any other fiscal period of a partnership, on or before the earlier of

(i) the day that is five months after the end of the fiscal period, and

(ii) the last day of March in the calendar year immediately following the calendar year in which the fiscal period ended or with which the fiscal period ended coincidentally.

Related Provisions: *Interpretation Act* 27(5) — Meaning of "within five months".

Notes: These deadlines ensure the partnership information is available 1 month before the partner must file under ITA 150(1). See also VIEWS doc 2012-0440151E5 (5-month deadline applies to partnership of professional corporations); 2012-0466951E5 (para. (c) applies where one end member of tiered partnership is a First Nations band).

The deadline for the 2019 return was extended to May 1, 2020: see Reg. 202(7) Notes, VIEWS doc 2020-0848401M4.

Forms: See under Reg. 229(1).

(6) Where a partnership discontinues its business or activity, the return required under this section shall be filed, in respect of any fiscal period or portion thereof prior to the discontinuance of the business or activity for which a return has not previously been filed under this section, on or before the earlier of

(a) the day that is 90 days after the discontinuance of the business or activity, and

(b) the day the return is required to be filed under subsection (5).

Definitions [Reg. 229]: "amount", "business" — ITA 248(1); "calendar year" — *Interpretation Act* 37(1)(a); "Canada" — ITA 255, *Interpretation Act* 35(1); "carries on a business in Canada" — ITA 253; "corporation" — ITA 248(1), *Interpretation Act* 35(1); "fiscal period" — ITA 249.1; "individual", "Minister" — ITA 248(1); "month" — *Interpretation Act* 35(1); "partnership" — see ITA 96(1) Notes; "person", "prescribed", "scientific research and experimental development", "share" — ITA 248(1); "SIFT partnership" — ITA 197(1), (8), 248(1); "taxable income", "trust account number" — ITA 248(1).

229.1 [Public partnership early disclosure] — (1) Definitions — The definitions in this subsection apply in this section.

"public investment partnership", at any time, means a public partnership all or substantially all of the fair market value of the property of which is, at that time, attributable to the fair market value of property of the partnership that is

(a) units of public trusts (as defined in subsection 204.1(1));

(b) partnership interests in public partnerships;

(c) shares of the capital stock of public corporations; or

(d) any combination of properties referred to in paragraphs (a) to (c).

"public partnership", at any time, means a partnership the partnership interests in which are, at that time, listed on a designated stock exchange in Canada if, at that time, the partnership carries on a business in Canada or is a Canadian partnership.

Notes: See Notes to Reg. 204.1(2) and at end of Reg. 229.1.

(2) Required information disclosure — Every member of a partnership that is, at any time in a fiscal period of the partnership, a public partnership shall, within the time required by subsection (3),

(a) make public, in prescribed form, information in respect of the public partnership for the fiscal period by posting the prescribed form, in a manner that is accessible to the general public, on the Internet website of CDS Innovations Inc.; and

(b) notify the Minister in writing as to when the posting of the prescribed form, as required by paragraph (a), has been made.

Related Provisions: Reg. 204.1(2) — Parallel rule for public trusts; Reg. 229.1(4) — Any one partner can fulfill obligation.

Notes: See Notes to Reg. 204.1(2).

Authorization for this provision of the Regulations is in ITA 221(1)(d.2).

(3) Required disclosure time — The time required for the members of a public partnership to satisfy the requirements of subsection (2) in respect of the public partnership for a fiscal period of the public partnership is

(a) subject to paragraph (b), on or before the day that is the earlier of

(i) 60 days after the end of the calendar year in which the fiscal period ends, and

(ii) four months after the end of the fiscal period; and

(b) where the public partnership is, at any time in the fiscal period, a public investment partnership, on or before the day that is 67 days after the end of the calendar year in which the fiscal period ends.

(4) Obligation fulfilled by one partner deemed fulfilled by all — Every member of a partnership that is required to satisfy the requirements of subsection (2) in respect of the partnership for a fiscal period of the partnership will be deemed to have satisfied those requirements if a particular member of the partnership, who has authority to act for the partnership, has satisfied those requirements in respect of the partnership for the fiscal period.

Related Provisions: ITA 96(3) — Parallel rule for partnership elections and agreements.

Notes [Reg. 229.1]: Reg. 229.1 added by 2007 budget bill #2, effective in respect of fiscal periods that end after July 3, 2007. See Notes to Reg. 204.1(2).

Definitions [Reg. 229.1]: "business" — ITA 248(1); "calendar year" — *Interpretation Act* 37(1)(a); "Canada" — ITA 255, *Interpretation Act* 35(1); "Canadian partnership" — ITA 102(1), 248(1); "fair market value" — see ITA 69(1) Notes; "fiscal period" — ITA 249(2)(b), 249.1; "Minister" — ITA 248(1); "partnership" — see ITA 96(1) Notes; "prescribed" — ITA 248(1); "property" — ITA 248(1); "public corporation" — ITA 89(1), 248(1); "public investment partnership", "public partnership" — Reg. 229.1(1); "public trust" — Reg. 204.1(1); "share" — ITA 248(1); "trust" — ITA 104(1), 248(1), (3); "writing" — *Interpretation Act* 35(1).

230. Security transactions — **(1)** In this section,

"publicly traded" means, with respect to any security,

(a) a security that is listed or posted for trading on a stock exchange, commodity exchange, futures exchange or any other exchange, or

(b) a security in respect of the sale and distribution of which a prospectus, registration statement or similar document has been filed with a public authority;

"sale" includes the granting of an option and a short sale;

Notes: See Notes to ITA 188.1(5) re meaning of "includes".

"security" means

(a) a publicly traded share of the capital stock of a corporation,

(b) a publicly traded debt obligation,

(c) a debt obligation of or guaranteed by

(i) the Government of Canada,

(ii) the government of a province or an agent thereof,

(iii) a municipality in Canada,

(iv) a municipal or public body performing a function of government in Canada, or

(v) the government of a foreign country or of a political subdivision of a foreign country or a local authority of such a government,

(c.1) a debt obligation that is, at any time, described in paragraph 7000(1)(d);

(d) a publicly traded interest in a trust,

(e) a publicly traded interest in a partnership,

(f) an option or contract in respect of any property described in any of paragraphs (a) to (e), or

(g) a publicly traded option or contract in respect of any property including any commodity, financial futures, foreign currency or precious metal or in respect of any index relating to any property;

Notes: For the meaning of "municipal or public body..." in (c)(iv), see Notes to ITA 149(1)(c).

Para. (c.1) added by 2016 budget bill #2, effective 2017.

"trader or dealer in securities" means

(a) a person who is registered or licensed under the laws of a province to trade in securities, or

(b) a person who in the ordinary course of business makes sales of securities as agent on behalf of others.

(2) [Information return on trading — T5008] — Every trader or dealer in securities who, in a calendar year, purchases a security as principal or sells a security as agent for any vendor shall make an information return for the year in prescribed form in respect of the purchase or sale.

Related Provisions: Reg. 205 — Date return due; Reg. 205.1(1) — Forms of which more than 50 must be filed by Internet; Reg. 209 — Two copies to be sent (or one emailed) to taxpayer; Reg. 230(7) — Exceptions.

Notes: For CRA guidance on filing the T5008 see guide RC4268. A money market fund is not reported on a T5008 (the interest is reported on a T3 or T5); but this is for a C$ fund only: VIEWS doc 2016-0676961E5. Where mutual fund securities are held in nominee form through an IIROC dealer, only the dealer need file, to avoid duplication: VIEWS doc 2016-0673361E5. A dealer need not file when X transfers publicly-traded shares to X's TFSA, as this is not a "sale": 2019-0822161E5 [note this is still a disposition at FMV under ITA 69(1)].

T5008 Box 20, "Cost or book value", is left blank by many brokers, despite CRA's guide saying it should be filled in (doc 2014-0559281E5 explains what to do for options and short sales); instead the broker sends the client a T5008 Summary with cost data. In *Chen v. TD Waterhouse*, 2020 ONSC 1477, leaving Box 20 blank (which CRA permits: para. 45) did not make a broker liable to C for CRA arbitrarily assessing C. (Non-enforcement of Box 20 seems to be CRA's response after reviewing the concern that the broker often cannot determine cost: 2008-0284491C6.) If Box 20 is blank and no gain/loss is reported, CRA's "matching program" (see ITA 231.1(1) Notes) may assess all the proceeds as being gain, e.g. *Strachan*, 2020 TCC 37, paras. 34-35 (under appeal to FCA).

No Form T5008 is needed for clients who are exempt under ITA 149, due to Reg. 230(7)(d): VIEWS doc 2004-0077561E5. For futures contracts, see 2009-0319211E5.

Forms: RC257: Request for an information return program account (RZ); RC4268: Handbook on securities transactions — A summary of the reporting requirements under the ITR [guide]; T5008: Statement of securities transactions; T5008 Summ: Return of securities transactions.

(3) [Information return on redeeming securities] — Every person (other than an individual who is not a trust) who in a calendar year redeems, acquires or cancels in any manner whatever any securities issued by that person shall make an information return for the year in prescribed form in respect of each such transaction, other than a transaction to which section 51, 51.1, 86 (if there is no consideration receivable other than new shares) or 87 or subsection 98(3) or (6) of the Act applies.

Related Provisions: Reg. 209 — Two copies to be sent (or one emailed) to taxpayer; Reg. 230(4) — Application.

Notes: Reference to ITA 51.1 added to Reg. 230(3) by P.C. 2002-2169, in force January 1, 2003.

(4) [Application of subsec. (3)] — Subsection (3) applies to

(a) Her Majesty in right of Canada or a province;

(b) a municipal or public body performing a function of government in Canada; and

(c) an agent of a person referred to in paragraph (a) or (b).

Notes: For the meaning of "municipal or public body...", see Notes to ITA 149(1)(c).

(5) [Gold and silver — T5008] — Every person who, in the ordinary course of a business of buying and selling precious metals in the form of certificates, bullion or coins, makes a payment in a calendar year to another person in respect of a sale by that other person of any such property shall make an information return for that year in prescribed form in respect of each such sale.

Related Provisions: Reg. 205.1(1) — Forms of which more than 50 must be filed by Internet; Reg. 209 — Two copies to be sent (or one emailed) to taxpayer.

(6) [Nominee or agent] — Every person who, while acting as nominee or agent for another person in respect of a sale or other transaction to which subsection (2), (3) or (5) applies, receives the proceeds of the sale or other transaction shall, where the transaction is carried out in the name of the nominee or agent, make an information return in prescribed form in respect of the sale or other transaction.

Related Provisions: Reg. 205.1(1) — Forms of which more than 50 must be filed by Internet; Reg. 209 — Two copies to be sent (or one emailed) to taxpayer; Reg. 230(7) — Exceptions.

Notes: See VIEWS doc 2010-0366781E5 (general comments).

(7) [Exceptions] — This section does not apply in respect of

(a) a purchase of a security by a trader or dealer in securities from another trader or dealer in securities other than a non-resident trader or dealer in securities;

(b) a sale of currencies or precious metals in the form of jewellery, works of art or numismatic coins;

(c) a sale of precious metals by a person who, in the ordinary course of business, produces or sells precious metals in bulk or in commercial quantities;

(d) a sale of securities by a trader or dealer in securities on behalf of a person who is exempt from tax under Part I of the Act; or

(e) a redemption by the issuer or an agent of the issuer of a debt obligation where

(i) the debt obligation was issued for its principal amount,

(ii) the redemption satisfies all of the issuer's obligations in respect of the debt obligation,

(iii) each person with an interest in the debt obligation is entitled in respect thereof to a proportion of all payments of principal equal to the proportion to which the person is entitled of all payments other than principal, and

(iv) an information return is required under another section of this Part to be made as a result of the redemption in respect of each person with an interest in the debt obligation.

Related Provisions: Reg. 205 — Date return due.

Notes: Reg. 230 added by P.C. 1989-2156, effective 1991.

Definitions [Reg. 230]: "business" — ITA 248(1); "calendar year" — *Interpretation Act* 37(1)(a); "Canada" — ITA 255, *Interpretation Act* 35(1); "corporation" — ITA 248(1), *Interpretation Act* 35(1); "foreign currency" — ITA 248(1); "Her Majesty" — *Interpretation Act* 35(1); "individual", "non-resident" — ITA 248(1); "partnership" — see ITA 96(1) Notes; "person", "prescribed", "principal amount", "property" — ITA 248(1); "province" — *Interpretation Act* 35(1); "publicly traded", "sale", "security" — Reg. 230(1); "share" — ITA 248(1); "trader or dealer in securities" — Reg. 230(1); "trust" — ITA 104(1), 248(1), (3).

231. [Repealed]

Notes: Reg. 231, prescribing information required for tax shelters, repealed by P.C. 2011-936, effective Feb. 19, 2003. These rules were moved to Reg. 3100–3101. In *Paletta*, 2019 TCC 205 (under appeal to FCA), paras. 260-271, Reg. 231(6) was held to be satisfied so an investment was a "tax shelter" for ITA 237.1(6); but although Reg. 231 was in force when the transactions took place in 2006-07, it was replaced in 2011 retroactive to 2003, so Reg. 3100(1) should have been applied instead.

232. Workers' compensation — (1) [Information return — payment] — Every person who pays an amount in respect of compensation described in subparagraph 110(1)(f)(ii) of the Act shall make an information return in prescribed form in respect of that payment.

Related Provisions: Reg. 205.1(1) — Forms of which more than 50 must be filed by Internet; Reg. 209 — Two copies to be sent (or one emailed) to taxpayer; Reg. 232(3) — Date return due; Reg. 232(4) — Exceptions.

Forms: RC257: Request for an information return program account (RZ); T4115: T5007 guide — return of benefits; T5007: Statement of benefits; T5007 Summ: Summary of benefits.

(2) [Information return — award] — Where a workers' compensation board, or a similar body, adjudicates a claim for compensation described in subparagraph 110(1)(f)(ii) of the Act and stipulates the amount of the award, that board or body shall make an information return in prescribed form in respect of the amount of the award.

Related Provisions: Reg. 205.1(1) — Forms of which more than 50 must be filed by Internet; Reg. 209 — Two copies to be sent (or one emailed) to taxpayer; Reg. 232(4) — Exceptions.

(3) [Deadline] — A return required under this section must be filed on or before the last day of February of each year and shall be in respect of

(a) the preceding calendar year, if the return is required under subsection (1); and

(b) the amount of the award that pertains to the preceding calendar year, if the return is required under subsection (2).

(4) [Exceptions] — Subsections (1) and (2) are not applicable in respect of a payment or an award in respect of

(a) medical expenses incurred by or on behalf of the employee;

(b) funeral expenses in respect of the employee;

(c) legal expenses in respect of the employee;

(d) job training or counselling of the employee; or

(e) the death of the employee, other than periodic payments made after the death of the employee.

Notes: See Notes to ITA 56(1)(v) for what workers' compensation payments are subject to Reg. 232.

Lump sum WCB payments on death need not be reported on a T5007 due to Reg. 232(4)(e); the fact a lump sum is received in 3-4 instalments does not make the payments periodic: VIEWS doc 2004-0065271E5.

Reg. 232 added by P.C. 1992-1567, effective 1991.

Definitions [Reg. 232]: "amount" — ITA 248(1); "calendar year" — *Interpretation Act* 37(1)(a); "employee", "person", "prescribed" — ITA 248(1).

233. Social assistance — (1) [Information return] — Every person who makes a payment described in paragraph 56(1)(u) of the Act shall make an information return in prescribed form in respect of the payment.

Related Provisions: Reg. 205 — Date return due; Reg. 205.1(1) — Forms of which more than 50 must be filed by Internet; Reg. 209 — Two copies to be sent (or one emailed) to taxpayer; Reg. 233(2) — Exceptions.

CRA Audit Manual: 27.34.5: Social assistance payments — reporting of payments.

Forms: RC257: Request for an information return program account (RZ); T4115: T5007 guide — return of benefits; T5007: Statement of benefits; T5007 Summ: Summary of benefits.

(2) [Exceptions] — Subsection (1) is not applicable in respect of a payment that

(a) is in respect of medical expenses incurred by or on behalf of the payee;

(b) is in respect of child care expenses, as defined in subsection 63(3) of the Act, incurred by or on behalf of the payee or a person related to the payee;

(c) is in respect of funeral expenses in respect of a person related to the payee;

(d) is in respect of legal expenses incurred by or on behalf of the payee or a person related to the payee;

(e) is in respect of job training or counselling of the payee or a person related to the payee;

(f) is paid in a particular year as a part of a series of payments, the total of which in the particular year does not exceed $500; or

(g) is not a part of a series of payments.

Related Provisions: ITA 248(10) — Series of transactions; Reg. 205 — Date return due.

Notes: Where amounts are excluded from reporting by Reg. 233(2), CRA's policy is not to require them to be included in the recipient's net income, so as not to affect the calculation of income-tested benefits such as the GST Credit and Canada Child Benefit: VIEWS docs 2003-0053511E5, 2018-0764761E5.

CRA interprets "medical expenses" in Reg. 233(2)(a) as in IT-519R2 [now Folio S1-F1-C1] (i.e., based on 118.2(2)): VIEWS doc 2003-0004725. The term does not include medication dispensers or personal alert assistance devices: 2013-050671117.

Reg. 233(2)(b) amended by P.C. 2010-548, effective May 12, 2010, to change "63(3)(a)" to "63(3)". Reg. 233 added by P.C. 1992-1567, effective 1991.

Definitions [Reg. 233]: "child" — ITA 252(1); "person", "prescribed" — ITA 248(1); "related" — ITA 251(2)–(6); "series" — ITA 248(10).

234. Farm support payments — **(1)** Every government, municipality or municipal or other public body (in sections 235 and 236 referred to as the "government payer") or producer organization or association that makes a payment of an amount that is a farm support payment (other than an amount paid out of a net income stabilization account) to a person or partnership shall make an information return in prescribed form in respect of the amount.

Related Provisions: Reg. 205 — Date return due; Reg. 205.1(1) — Forms of which more than 50 must be filed by Internet; Reg. 209 — Two copies to be sent (or one emailed) to taxpayer; Reg. 235, 236 — Identification of recipients.

Notes: See Notes at end of Reg. 234.

Forms: AGR-1SUM: Return of farm support payments.

(2) For the purposes of subsection (1) **"farm support payment"** includes

(a) a payment that is computed with respect to an area of farm land;

(b) a payment that is made in respect of a unit of farm commodity grown or disposed of or a farm animal raised or disposed of; and

(c) a rebate of, or compensation for, all or a portion of

(i) a cost or capital cost incurred in respect of farming, or

(ii) unsowed or unplanted land or crops, or destroyed crops, farm animals or other farm output.

Notes [Reg. 234]: See Notes to ITA 248(1)"NISA Fund No. 2". VIEWS doc 9636065 doubted that Farm Credit Corporation was an entity described in Reg. 234(1), and opined that payments made by FCC as an adjustment to the purchase price of land, in accordance with a purchase and sale agreement under the Western Grain Transition Payments Program, were not "farm support payments". See Notes to ITA 12(1)(x). See also Notes to ITA 188.1(5) re meaning of "includes" in Reg. 234(2) opening words.

Payments should be reported on an AGR-1 slip if under: Cdn Agricultural Income Stabilization, by Alberta Agriculture Financial Services Corp. (VIEWS doc 2005-0155851E5); PEI Agri-Food Market Development Program (2008-029515I7 — but not the Agri-Food Promotion Program); PEI Alternative Land Use Services Program (2008-0299151I7); most Canada-PEI Business Development Programs (2010-0355841E5); Saskatchewan Gopher Control Rebate Program (apparently) (2011-0398601E5).

Reg. 234 added by P.C. 1993-1939, effective 1994 in respect of amounts paid after 1992. The payments described may be taxable under ITA 12(1)(p) or 12(1)(x).

Definitions [Reg. 234]: "amount" — ITA 248(1); "disposed" — ITA 248(1)"disposition"; "farm support payment" — Reg. 234(2); "farming", "net income stabilization account" — ITA 248(1); "partnership" — see ITA 96(1) Notes; "prescribed" — ITA 248(1).

235. Identifier information — Every corporation or trust for which an information return is required to be made under these Regulations by a government payer or by a producer organization or association shall provide its legal name, address and income tax identification number to the government payer or the producer organization or association, as the case may be.

Notes: Reg. 235 added by P.C. 1993-1939, effective after 1993 in respect of amounts paid after 1992.

Definitions [Reg. 235]: "corporation" — ITA 248(1), *Interpretation Act* 35(1); "government payer" — Reg. 234(1); "trust" — ITA 104(1), 248(1), (3).

236. [Partnership receiving farm support payments] — Every person who is a member of a partnership for which an information return is required to be made under these Regulations by a government payer or by a producer organization or association shall provide the government payer or the producer organization or association, as the case may be, with the following information:

(a) the person's legal name, address and Social Insurance Number, or, where the person is a trust or is not an individual, the person's income tax identification number; and

(b) the partnership's name and business address.

Related Provisions: Reg. 229 — Partnership information return.

Notes: Reg. 236 added by P.C. 1993-1939, effective after 1993 in respect of amounts paid after 1992. See also Notes at beginning of Part II.

Definitions [Reg. 236]: "business" — ITA 248(1); "government payer" — Reg. 234(1); "individual" — ITA 248(1); "partnership" — see ITA 96(1) Notes; "person" — ITA 248(1); "trust" — ITA 104(1), 248(1), (3).

Information Circulars: 82-2R2: SIN legislation that relates to the preparation of information slips.

237. Contract for goods and services [for federal government] — **(1)** The definitions in this subsection apply in this section.

"federal body" means a department or a Crown corporation, within the meaning of section 2 of the *Financial Administration Act*.

Notes: *Financial Administration Act* s. 2 provides:

"Crown corporation" has the meaning assigned by subsection 83(1); ... 83.(1) *"Crown corporation"* means a parent Crown corporation or a wholly-owned subsidiary; ... *"parent Crown corporation"* means a corporation that is wholly owned directly by the Crown, but does not include a departmental corporation; ... *"wholly-owned subsidiary"* means a corporation that is wholly owned by one or more parent Crown corporations directly or indirectly through any number of subsidiaries each of which is wholly owned directly or indirectly by one or more parent Crown corporations.

"department" means

(a) any of the departments named in Schedule I,

(a.1) any of the divisions or branches of the federal public administration set out in column I of Schedule I.1,

(b) a commission under the *Inquiries Act* that is designated by order of the Governor in Council as a department for the purposes of this Act,

(c) the staffs of the Senate, House of Commons, Library of Parliament, office of the Senate Ethics Officer, office of the Conflict of Interest and Ethics Commissioner, Parliamentary Protective Service and office of the Parliamentary Budget Officer, and

(d) any departmental corporation;

"departmental corporation" means a corporation named in Schedule II;

Schedule I lists the federal Departments, such as Finance, Industry, Justice, etc., and the Treasury Board. Schedule I.1 lists divisions of government branches, such as Atlantic Canada Opportunities Agency, Canadian Human Rights Commission, Canadian Transportation Agency, Immigration and Refugee Board, National Film Board, Office of the Auditor General, Public Service Commission, RCMP and Statistics Canada. Schedule II lists: Canada Border Services Agency; Canada Emission Reduction Incentives Agency; Canada Employment Insurance Commission; Canada Revenue Agency; Canada School of Public Service; Canadian Accessibility Standards Development Organization; Canadian Centre for Occupational Health and Safety; Canadian Energy Regulator; Canadian Food Inspection Agency; Canadian High Arctic Research Station; Canadian Institutes of Health Research; Canadian Nuclear Safety Commission; Canadian Transportation Accident Investigation and Safety Board; Invest in Canada Hub; Law Commission of Canada; The National Battlefields Commission; National Research Council of Canada; Natural Sciences and Engineering Research Council; Parks Canada Agency; Social Sciences and Humanities Research Council. (See CanLII.org.)

Definition "federal body" added by P.C. 1998-2274, this version effective for amounts paid or credited after 1998.

"payee" means a person or partnership to whom an amount is paid or credited in respect of goods for sale or lease, or services rendered, by or on behalf of the person or the partnership.

Notes: See at end of Reg. 237.

(2) [Information return] — A federal body that pays or credits an amount to a payee shall file an information return in prescribed form in respect of the amount on or before March 31 in each year in respect of the preceding calendar year.

Related Provisions: Reg. 205 — Date return due; Reg. 205.1(1) — Forms of which more than 50 must be filed by Internet; Reg. 237(3) — Exceptions.

Notes: See at end of Reg. 237.

Forms: T1204 and T1204 Summ: Government service contract payments; T4026: Government service contract payments [guide]; T4027: Statement of contract payments [guide]; T5011: Application for a partnership's filer identification number.

(3) [Exceptions] — Subsection (2) does not apply in respect of an amount

(a) all or substantially all of which is paid or credited in the year in respect of goods for sale or lease by the payee;

(b) to which section 212 of the Act applies;

(c) that is not required to be included in computing the income of the payee, if the payee is an employee of the federal body;

(d) that is paid or credited in respect of services rendered outside Canada by a payee who was not resident in Canada during the period in which the services were rendered; or

(e) that is paid or credited in respect of a program administered under the *Witness Protection Program Act* or any other similar program.

Notes [Reg. 237]: Reg. 237 effectively ensures that entities receiving federal government contract payments will report the income earned and GST/HST collected. GL accounts of a federal body are subject to Reg. 237 only where they show payment for "goods" (merchandise or wares) or "services" (work of the hand or brain, not in themselves articles of trade or commerce): VIEWS doc 2012-044182I17.

Where Reg. 237 does not apply because the payor is not a "federal body", a T4A is still required: doc 2005-0154801E5. Contracts with Quebec public authorities require a Revenu Québec "attestation" that the supplier is compliant: tinyurl.com/qc-attestation.

Reg. 237 does not apply to a reimbursement or allowance where there is no "remuneration for services": VIEWS docs 2007-0222981E5 (guest expert), 2007-0229201E5 (volunteer reimbursement), 2008-0278971E5 (advisory committees: non-contractual relationship); 2009-0320681M4 (honoraria for voluntary services; changes to Form T1204 may be considered). It does apply to travel expense reimbursements to a consultant who has a contractual relationship with the federal body: 2013-049761117.

Reg. 237(3)(b) amended to change "section 153 or 212" to "section 212", by P.C. 2002-2169, in force Jan. 1, 2003. Finance stated that this eliminates an unintended consequence of removing the filing requirements for all the payments named in ITA 153.

Reg. 237 added by P.C. 1998-2274, effective for amounts paid or credited after 1997.

Proposed Reg. 237 in draft regulations of Oct. 21, 1994, which would have imposed a requirement for an information return with respect to eligible funeral arrangements, was moved to Reg. 201(1)(f).

Definitions [Reg. 237]: "calendar year" — *Interpretation Act* 35(1); "Canada" — ITA 255, *Interpretation Act* 35(1); "employee" — ITA 248(1); "federal body" — Reg. 237(1); "partnership" — see ITA 96(1) Notes; "payee" — Reg. 237(1); "person", "prescribed" — ITA 248(1); "resident in Canada" — ITA 250.

238. Reporting of payments in respect of construction activities — (1) ["Construction activities"] — In this section, "construction activities" includes the erection, excavation, installation, alteration, modification, repair, improvement, demolition, destruction, dismantling or removal of all or any part of a building, structure, surface or sub-surface construction, or any similar property.

Notes: See IT-411R. Construction activities are considered to include cable network construction and installation (VIEWS doc 2007-023746117), installation (but not maintenance) of refrigeration units for commercial kitchens, and of heating and air conditioning (2007-0226871E5), manufacturing prefabricated homes (2012-0458651E5), providing heavy equipment with an operator (2011-0425281E5), well drilling (2010-0360581E5), and landscaping in most cases (2012-0465591E5); and to exclude landfill site excavation (2000-0013055) and manufacture of portable oil tanks and pressure vehicles (2007-0226971E5). See also CRA's list at tinyurl.com/t5018 under "Examples", and Notes at end of Reg. 238; and Notes to ITA 188.1(5) re meaning of "includes".

Interpretation Bulletins: IT-411R: Meaning of "Construction".

Forms: RC257: Request for an information return program account (RZ); T5018: Statement of contract payments; T5018 Summ: Summary of contract payments.

(2) [Information return] — Every person or partnership that pays or credits, in a reporting period, an amount in respect of goods or services rendered on their behalf in the course of construction activities shall make an information return in the prescribed form in respect of that amount, if the person's or partnership's business income for that reporting period is derived primarily from those activities.

Related Provisions: ITA 162(7) — Penalty for failure to file; Reg. 205.1(1) — Forms of which more than 50 must be filed by Internet; Reg. 238(4) — Date return due; Reg. 238(5) — Exceptions.

Notes: See at end of Reg. 238.

Forms: RC257: Request for an information return program account (RZ); T4027: Statement of contract payments [guide]; T5018: Statement of contract payments; T5018 Summ: Summary of contract payments; RC4406: Will you do it for cash? [pamphlet].

(3) [Reporting period] — The reporting period may be either on a calendar year basis or a fiscal period basis. Once a period is chosen, it cannot be changed for subsequent years, unless the Minister authorizes it.

(4) [Deadline] — The return shall be filed within six months after the end of the reporting period to which it pertains.

Related Provisions: *Interpretation Act* 27(5) — Meaning of "within six months".

(5) [Exceptions] — Subsection (2) does not apply in respect of an amount

(a) all of which is paid or credited in the reporting period in respect of goods for sale or lease by the person or partnership;

(b) to which section 212 of the Act applies; or

(c) that is paid or credited in respect of services rendered outside Canada by a person or partnership who was not resident in Canada during the period in which the services were rendered.

Notes [Reg. 238]: Reg. 238 (Contract Payment Reporting System) targets the underground economy by requiring construction contractors to report payments to subcontractors (of at least $500 services per year per subcontractor) along with the subcontractor's Business Number or Social Insurance Number, either on Form T5018 slips (given to subcontractors) or line-by-line on a summary. It applies to payments made as agent of a third party: VIEWS doc 2004-008137117. See Drache, "CRA Targets Construction Industry", xxviii(3) *The Canadian Taxpayer* (Carswell) 24 (Jan. 31, 2006). See also tinyurl.com/cra-cprs; CRA May 2005 ICAA roundtable (tinyurl.com/cra-abtax), q. 21. See also news release, Oct. 6/10, "Mission resident fined $5,000 for not filing returns" ($1,000 fine for not filing T5108 Summ.). For an example of Reg. 238 working see CRA news release, Sept. 14, 2010, "Home renovator fined $16,098 for making false statements on his tax returns" (re Ron Vondrasek). See also Notes to Reg. 238(1), and VIEWS doc 2017-0691361E5 (general discussion).

Where a contractor fails to identify subcontractors as required by Reg. 238, an ITA 162(7) penalty applies, but the subcontractor expenses cannot be disallowed under ITA s. 67: VIEWS doc 2006-018165117.

For "derived primarily from [construction] activities" in Reg. 238(2), see tinyurl.com/t5018; and Notes to ITA 94(1)"resident portion". Because of these words, Reg. 238 applies to a developer who hires a contractor to construct buildings and then rents or sells them, if more than 50% of the developer's business income is derived from such rentals or sales: VIEWS docs 2006-020297117, 2009-0315211E5. In *Apex City Homes*, 2018 TCC 247, a partnership that hired a general contractor to build homes was thus liable for penalties for not filing a T5018.

A joint venture (JV) is not a "person", so each venturer is required to file a separate form for payments by the JV: VIEWS doc 2000-0016205. TEI (submission, Dec. 4, 2012, q.8) has asked CRA for a policy permitting the JV to file.

T5018 amounts should include GST, HST and QST, while amounts on a T4A should be pre-sales taxes: doc 2010-0373691C6.

In *Bouchard*, 2016 FC 983, a lawsuit claiming B had been entitled to ignore the filing requirement (due to privacy concerns) was struck out.

Note that in Quebec, construction contracts for $25,000 or more, or building service contracts for $10,000 or more or of unspecified duration, require a Revenu Québec "attestation" that the supplier is compliant: tinyurl.com/qc-attestation, tinyurl.com/qc-attest-2021.

Reg. 238 amended by P.C. 2002-2169, effective 2003. Added by P.C. 1999-2204, for reporting periods beginning after 1998; the first return was required by June 30, 2000.

For other information returns not in Reg. Part II, see Notes at beginning of Part II.

Definitions [Reg. 238]: "business" — ITA 248(1); "calendar year" — *Interpretation Act* 37(1)(a); "Canada" — ITA 255; "construction activities" — Reg. 238(1); "month" — *Interpretation Act* 35(1); "partnership" — See ITA 96(1) Notes; "person", "prescribed", "property" — ITA 248(1); "reporting period" — Reg. 238(3); "resident in Canada" — ITA 250.

PART III — [300–310] ANNUITIES AND LIFE INSURANCE POLICIES

300. Capital element of annuity payments — (1) [Capital element] — For the purposes of paragraphs 32.1(3)(b) and 60(a) of the Act, where an annuity is paid under a contract (other than an income-averaging annuity contract or an annuity contract purchased pursuant to a deferred profit sharing plan or pursuant to a plan referred to in subsection 147(15) of the Act as a "revoked plan") at a particular time, that part of the annuity payment determined in prescribed manner to be a return of capital is that proportion of a taxpayer's interest in the annuity payment that the adjusted purchase price of the taxpayer's interest in the contract at that particular time is of his interest, immediately before the commencement under the contract of payments to which paragraph 56(1)(d) of the Act applies, in the total of the payments

(a) to be made under the contract, in the case of a contract for a term of years certain; or

(b) expected to be made under the contract, in the case of a contract under which the continuation of the payments depends in whole or in part on the survival of an individual.

(1.1) For the purposes of subsections (1) and (2), "annuity payment" does not include any portion of a payment under a contract the amount of which cannot be reasonably determined immediately before the commencement of payments under the contract except where the payment of such portion cannot be so determined because the continuation of the annuity payments under the contract depends in whole or in part on the survival of an individual.

Notes: Reg. 300(1.1) added by P.C. 1982-1421, effective for annuity contracts under which annuity payments commence after 1981.

(2) [Where continuance depends on survival] — For the purposes of this section, if the continuance of the annuity payments under a contract depends in whole or in part on the survival of an individual,

(a) the total of the payments expected to be made under the contract is

(i) in the case of a contract that provides for equal payments and does not provide for a guaranteed period of payment, to be equal to the product obtained by multiplying the total of the annuity payments expected to be received throughout a year under the contract by the complete expectations of life determined

(A) using the table of mortality known as the *1971 Individual Annuity Mortality Table* as published in Volume XXIII of the *Transactions of the Society of Actuaries*, if the annuity rates in respect of the contract were fixed and determined before 2017, and

(I) annuity payments under the contract commenced before 2017, or

(II) on December 31, 2016, the contract would be a prescribed annuity contract if paragraph 304(1)(c) were read without reference to its subparagraph (i) and the contract cannot be terminated other than on the death of an individual on whose life payments under the contract are contingent, and

(B) in any other case, using the table of mortality known as the *Annuity 2000 Basic Table* as published in the *Transactions of Society of Actuaries, 1995-96 Reports*, and

(ii) in any other case, to be calculated in accordance with subparagraph (i) with such modifications as the circumstances may require;

(b) the age of the individual on any particular date as of which a calculation is being made is

(i) if the life insured was determined by the insurer that issued the contract to be a substandard life at the time the contract was issued and the *Annuity 2000 Basic Table* as published in the *Transactions of Society of Actuaries, 1995-96 Reports* applies to determine the total of the payments expected to be made under the contract, the age that is equal to the total of the age used for the purpose of determining the annuity rate under the policy at the date of issue of the contract and the number determined by subtracting the calendar year in which the contract was issued from the calendar year in which the particular date occurs, and

(ii) in any other case, determined by subtracting the calendar year of the individual's birth from the calendar year in which the particular date occurs; and

(c) if, in the event of the death of the individual before the annual payments total a stated sum, the contract provides that the unpaid balance of the stated sum is to be paid in a lump sum or instalments, then for the purpose of determining the expected term of the contract, the contract is deemed to provide for the continuance of the payments under the contract for a minimum term certain equal to the nearest whole number of years required to complete the payment of the stated sum.

Notes: Reg. 300(2) amended by 2014 budget bill #2 (effective Dec. 16, 2014), P.C. 2011-936 (for annuity contracts and life insurance policies last acquired after 1989), 2011-936.

(3) [Adjusted purchase price] — Where

(a) an annuity contract is a life annuity contract entered into before November 17, 1978 under which the annuity payments commence on the death of an individual,

(a.1) [Revoked]

(b) an annuity contract (other than an annuity contract described in paragraph (a)) is

(i) a life annuity contract entered into before October 23, 1968, or

(ii) any other annuity contract entered into before January 4, 1968,

under which the annuity payments commence

(iii) on the expiration of a term of years, and

(iv) before the later of January 1, 1970 or the tax anniversary date of the annuity contract,

the adjusted purchase price of a taxpayer's interest in the annuity contract shall be

(c) the lump sum, if any, that the person entitled to the annuity payments might have accepted in lieu thereof, at the date the annuity payments commence;

(d) if no lump sum described in paragraph (c) is provided for in the contract, the sum ascertainable from the contract as the present value of the annuity at the date the annuity payments commence; and

(e) if no lump sum described in paragraph (c) is provided for in the contract and no sum is ascertainable under paragraph (d),

(i) in the case of a contract issued under the *Government Annuities Act*, the premiums paid, accumulated with interest at the rate of four per cent per annum to the date the annuity payments commence, and

(ii) in the case of any other contract, the present value of the annuity payments at the date on which payments under the contract commence, computed by applying

(A) a rate of interest of four per cent per annum where the payments commence before 1972 and 5½ per cent per annum where the payments commence after 1971, and

(B) the provisions of subsection (2) where the payments depend on the survival of a person.

Related Provisions: Reg. 300(4), 310 — Adjusted purchase price.

(4) [Adjusted purchase price] — Where an annuity contract would be described in paragraph (3)(b) if the reference in subparagraph (iv) thereof to "before the later of" were read as a reference to "on or after the later of", the adjusted purchase price of a taxpayer's interest in the annuity contract at a particular time shall be the greater of

(a) the aggregate of

(i) the amount that would be determined in respect of that interest under paragraph (3)(c), (d) or (e), as the case may be, if the date referred to therein was the tax anniversary date of the contract and not the date the annuity payments commence, and

(ii) the adjusted purchase price that would be determined in respect of that interest if the expression "before that time" in the descriptions of A, B, C, D and H in the definition "adjusted cost basis" in subsection 148(9) of the Act were read as "before that time and after the tax anniversary date"; and

(b) the amount determined under paragraph (2)(b) in respect of that interest.

Related Provisions: Reg. 300(3), 310 — Adjusted purchase price.

Notes: Reg. 300(4)(a)(ii) amended non-substantively by P.C. 2011-936, effective March 1994.

Reg. 300(4) added by P.C. 1982-1421, effective for annuity contracts under which annuity payments commence after 1981.

Definitions [Reg. 300]: "adjusted purchase price" — Reg. 300(3), (4), 310; "amount", "annuity" — ITA 248(1); "annuity payment" — Reg. 300(1.1); "calendar year" — *Interpretation Act* 37(1)(a); "commencement" — *Interpretation Act* 35(1); "deferred profit sharing plan" — ITA 147(1), 248(1); "income-averaging annuity contract", "individual", "insurer" — ITA 248(1); "life annuity contract" — Reg. 301(1), (2); "person", "prescribed" — ITA 248(1); "tax anniversary date" — Reg. 310; "taxpayer" — ITA 248(1); "total of the payments" — Reg. 300(2)(a).

Income Tax Folios: S3-F9-C1: Lottery winnings, miscellaneous receipts, and income (and losses) from crime [replaces IT-185R, IT-213R, IT-256R, IT-334R2].

301. Life annuity contracts — (1) For the purposes of this Part and section 148 of the Act, "life annuity contract" means a contract under which a person authorized under the laws of Canada or of a province to carry on in Canada an annuities business agrees to make annuity payments to one person or partnership (in this section referred to as "the annuitant") or jointly to two or more annuitants, which annuity payments are, under the terms of the contract,

(a) to be paid annually or at more frequent periodic intervals;

(b) to commence on a specified day; and

(c) to continue throughout the lifetime of one or more individuals (each of whom is referred to in this section as "the identified individual").

Related Provisions: Reg. 301(2) — Interpretation.

Notes: Where an annuity is payable for an individual's lifetime but that individual is not the recipient of the payments (e.g. the person's corporation is the purchaser and owner of the annuity contract and the recipient of the annuity payments), the contract is not a "life annuity contract" under Reg. 301 because the payments are not made to the individual: CRA, 2002 CALU q.4 (VIEWS doc 2002-0127495).

Reg. 301(1) amended by P.C. 2011-936, as proposed in a Sept. 12/02 Finance comfort letter, to expand para. (c) to apply to any individual rather than only an annuitant (and to modernize the wording). The amendment applies to 1997 and later taxation years, and for those taxation years the adjusted costs basis of a policyholder's interest in a life insurance policy is to be determined as if the amendments to Reg. 301 also applied to taxation years that begin after 1980.

Reg. 301(1) amended by P.C. 1982-1421, for annuity contracts under which annuity payments commence after 1981.

(2) [Interpretation] — For the purposes of subsection (1), a contract shall not fail to be a life annuity contract by reason that

(a) the contract provides that the annuity payments may be assigned by the annuitant or owner;

(b) the contract provides for annuity payments to be made for a period ending on the death of the identified individual or for a specified period of not less than 10 years, whichever is the lesser;

(c) the contract provides for annuity payments to be made for a specified period or throughout the lifetime of the identified individual, whichever is longer, to the annuitant and, if the specified period is longer, to a specified person after that period;

(d) the contract provides, in addition to the annuity payments to be made throughout the lifetime of the identified individual, for a payment to be made on the death of the identified individual;

(e) the contract provides that the date

(i) on which the annuity payments commence, or

(ii) on which the contract holder becomes entitled to proceeds of the disposition,

may be changed with respect to the whole contract or any portion thereof at the option of the annuitant or owner; or

(f) the contract provides that all or a portion of the proceeds payable at any particular time under the contract may be received in the form of an annuity contract other than a life annuity contract.

Notes: Reg. 301(2)(b)-(d) amended by P.C. 2011-936 to change "annuitant" to "identified individual", effective on the same basis as the amendment to Reg. 301(1).

Reg. 301(2) amended by P.C. 1982-1421, for annuity contracts under which annuity payments commence after 1981.

Definitions [Reg. 301]: "annuitant" — Reg. 301(1); "annuity", "business" — ITA 248(1); "Canada" — ITA 255, *Interpretation Act* 35(1); "identified individual" — Reg. 301(1)(c); "individual" — ITA 248(1); "life annuity contract" — Reg. 301(1), (2); "partnership" — see ITA 96(1) Notes; "person" — ITA 248(1); "proceeds of the disposition" — ITA 148(9), Reg. 310; "province" — *Interpretation Act* 35(1).

302. [Revoked]

303. (1) Where in a taxation year the rights of a holder under an annuity contract cease upon termination or cancellation of the contract and

(a) the aggregate of all amounts, each of which is an amount in respect of the contract that was included in computing the income of the holder for the year or any previous taxation year by virtue of subsection 12(3) of the Act

exceeds the aggregate of

(b) such proportion of the amount determined under paragraph (a) that the annuity payments made under the contract before the rights of the holder have ceased is of the total of the payments expected to be made under the contract, and

(c) the aggregate of all amounts, each of which is an amount in respect of the contract that was deductible in computing the income of the holder for the year or any previous year by virtue of subsection (2),

the amount of such excess may be deducted by the holder under subsection 20(19) of the Act in computing his income for the year.

(2) For the purposes of subsection 20(19) of the Act, where an annuity contract was acquired after December 19, 1980 and annuity payments under the contract commenced before 1982, the amount that may be deducted by a holder under that subsection in respect of an annuity contract for a taxation year is that proportion of

(a) the aggregate of all amounts, each of which is an amount that was included in computing the income of the holder for any previous taxation year by virtue of subsection 12(3) of the Act in respect of the contract

that

(b) the aggregate of all annuity payments received by the holder in the year in respect of the contract

is of

(c) the total of the payments determined under paragraph 300(1)(a) or (b) in respect of the holder's interest in the contract.

Definitions [Reg. 303]: "amount", "annuity" — ITA 248(1); "taxation year" — ITA 249.

304. Prescribed annuity contracts — (1) For the purposes of this Part and of subsections 12.2(1) and 20(20) and paragraph 148(2)(b) of the Act, "prescribed annuity contract", for a taxation year, means

(a) an annuity contract that is, or is issued pursuant to, an arrangement described in any of paragraphs 148(1)(a) to (b.3) and (d) of the Act;

(b) an annuity contract described in paragraph 148(1)(c) or (e) of the Act; and

(c) an annuity contract

(i) under which annuity payments have commenced in the taxation year or a preceding taxation year,

(ii) issued by any one of the following (referred to in this section as the "issuer"):

(A) a life insurance corporation,

(B) a registered charity,

(C) a corporation referred to in any of paragraphs (a) to (c) of the definition "specified financial institution" in subsection 248(1) of the Act,

(D) a corporation referred to in subparagraph (b)(ii) of the definition "retirement savings plan" in subsection 146(1) of the Act, and

(E) a corporation (other than a mutual fund corporation or a mortgage investment corporation) the principal business of which is the making of loans,

(iii) each holder of which

(A) is

(I) an individual other than a trust,

(II) a trust described in paragraph 104(4)(a) of the Act (in this paragraph referred to as a "specified trust"),

(III) a trust that is a qualified disability trust (as defined in subsection 122(3) of the Act) for the taxation year in which the annuity is issued, or

(IV) if the annuity is issued before 2016, a trust that is a testamentary trust at the time the annuity is issued,

(B) is an annuitant under the contract, and

(C) throughout the taxation year, dealt at arm's length with the issuer,

(iv) the terms and conditions of which require that, from the time the contract meets the requirements of this paragraph,

(A) all payments made out of the contract be equal annuity payments made at regular intervals but not less frequently than annually, subject to the holder's right to vary the frequency and quantum of payments to be made out of the contract in any taxation year without altering the present value at the beginning of the year of the total payments to be made in that year out of the contract,

(B) the annuity payments thereunder continue for a fixed term or

(I) if the holder is an individual (other than a trust), for the life of the first holder or until the day of the later of the death of the first holder and the death of any of the spouse, common-law partner, former spouse, former common-law partner, brothers and sisters (in this subparagraph referred to as "the survivor") of the first holder, or

(II) if the holder is a trust

1. in the case of a specified trust, for the life of an individual referred to in paragraph 104(4)(a) of the Act who is entitled to receive all of the income of the trust that arose before the individual's death, or, in the case of a joint spousal or common-law partner trust, until the day of the later of the death of the individual and the death of the beneficiary under the trust who is the individual's spouse or common-law partner,

2. in the case of a qualified disability trust, for the life of an individual who is an electing beneficiary (as defined in subsection 122(3) of the Act) of the trust for the taxation year in which the annuity is issued,

3. in the case of a trust (other than a qualified disability trust or specified trust) where the annuity is issued before October 24, 2012, for the life of an individual who is entitled to receive income from the trust, and

4. in the case of a trust (other than a qualified disability trust or specified trust) where the annuity is issued after October 23, 2012, for the life of an individual who was entitled when the contract was first held to receive all of the trust's income that is from an amount received by the trust on or before the individual's death as a payment under the annuity,

(C) if the annuity payments are to be made over a term that is guaranteed or fixed, the guaranteed or fixed term not exceed 91 years minus the age, when the contract was first held, in whole years of the following individual:

(I) if the holder is not a trust, the individual who is

1. in the case of a joint and last survivor annuity, the younger of the first holder and the survivor,

2. in the case of a contract that is held jointly, the younger of the first holders, and

3. in any other case, the first holder,

(II) if the holder is a specified trust, the individual who is

1. in the case of a joint and last survivor annuity held by a joint spousal or common-law partner trust, the younger of the individuals referred to in paragraph 104(4)(a) of the Act who are in combination entitled to receive all of the income of the trust that arose before the later of their deaths, and

2. in the case of an annuity that is not a joint and last survivor annuity, the individual referred to in paragraph 104(4)(a) of the Act who is entitled to receive all of the income of the trust that arose before the individual's death,

(III) if the holder is a qualified disability trust, an individual who is an electing beneficiary of the trust for the taxation year in which the annuity is issued, and

(IV) if the holder is a trust (other than a qualified disability trust or specified trust) and the annuity is issued before 2016, the individual who was the youngest beneficiary under the trust when the contract was first held,

(D) no loans exist under the contract,

(E) the holder's rights under the contract not be disposed of otherwise than

(I) if the holder is an individual, on the holder's death,

(II) if the holder is a specified trust (other than a joint spousal or common-law partner trust), on the death of the individual referred to in paragraph 104(4)(a) of the

Act who is entitled to receive all of the income of the trust that arose before the individual's death,

(III) if the holder is a specified trust that is a joint spousal or common-law partner trust, on the later of the deaths of the individuals referred to in paragraph 104(4)(a) of the Act who are in combination entitled to receive all of the income of the trust that arose before the later of their deaths, and

(IV) if the holder is a trust, other than a specified trust, and the contract is first held after October 2011, on the earlier of

1. the time at which the trust ceases to be a testamentary trust, and

2. the death of the individual referred to in subclause (B)(II) or (C)(III) or (IV), as the case may be, in respect of the trust, and

(F) no payments be made out of the contract other than as permitted by this section,

(v) none of the terms and conditions of which provide for any recourse against the issuer for failure to make any payment under the contract, and

(vi) where annuity payments under the contract have commenced

(A) before 1987, in respect of which a holder thereof has notified the issuer in writing, before the end of the taxation year, that the contract is to be treated as a prescribed annuity contract,

(B) after 1986, in respect of which a holder thereof has not notified the issuer in writing, before the end of the taxation year in which the annuity payments under the contract commenced, that the contract is not to be treated as a prescribed annuity contract, or

(C) after 1986, in respect of which a holder thereof has notified the issuer in writing, before the end of the taxation year in which the annuity payments under the contract commenced, that the contract is not to be treated as a prescribed annuity contract and a holder thereof has rescinded the notification by so notifying the issuer in writing before the end of the taxation year.

(2) Notwithstanding subsection (1), an annuity contract shall not fail to be a prescribed annuity contract by reason that

(a) where the contract provides for a joint and last survivor annuity or is held jointly, the terms and conditions thereof provide that there will be a decrease in the amount of the annuity payments to be made under the contract from the time of death of one of the annuitants thereunder;

(b) the terms and conditions thereof provide that where the holder thereof dies at or before the time he attains the age of 91 years, the contract will terminate and an amount will be paid out of the contract not exceeding the amount, if any, by which the total premiums paid under the contract exceeds the total annuity payments made under the contract;

(c) where the annuity payments are to be made over a term that is guaranteed or fixed, the terms and conditions thereof provide that as a consequence of the death of the holder thereof during the guaranteed or fixed term any payments that, but for the death of the holder, would be made during the term may be commuted into a single payment; or

(d) the terms and conditions thereof, as they read on December 1, 1982 and at all subsequent times, provide that the holder participates in the investment earnings of the issuer and that the amount of such participation is to be paid within 60 days after the end of the year in respect of which it is determined.

(3) For the purposes of this section, the annuitant under an annuity contract is deemed to be the holder of the contract where

(a) the contract is held by another person in trust for the annuitant; or

(b) the contract was acquired by the annuitant under a group term life insurance policy under which life insurance was effected on the life of another person in respect of, in the course of, or by virtue of the office or employment or former office or employment of that other person.

(4) In this section, "annuitant" under an annuity contract, at any time, means a person who, at that time, is entitled to receive annuity payments under the contract.

(5) For the purpose of this section, "spouse" and "former spouse" of a particular individual include another individual who is a party to a void or voidable marriage with the particular individual.

Notes [Reg. 304]: A foreign currency contract can be a prescribed annuity contract: VIEWS doc 2005-0116611C6.

A "movable hypothec" charge (Quebec *Civil Code* art. 2696-2714) against a prescribed annuity contract will not violate Reg. 304(1)(c)(iv)(D): VIEWS doc 2006-0197041C6. Nor will a collateral assignment of an annuity contract for a loan, provided the assignee cannot force a disposition of the policy by the holder and has only a right to the annuity payments: 2008-0270471C6. See also 2011-0398471C6 (timing of annuity payment).

For the meaning of "principal business" in Reg. 304(1)(c)(ii)(E), see Notes to ITA 20(1)(bb).

For interpretation of Reg. 304(2)(b) see VIEWS doc 2013-0481391C6.

See also Lea Koiv, "Changes to the Taxation of Prescribed Annuities", XX(4) *Insurance Planning* (Federated Press) 1308-10 (2014); Tina Tehranchian, "Consider Prescribed Annuities Before Tax Changes in 2017", 9(2) *Taxes & Wealth Management* (Carswell) 6-7 (May 2016).

Reg. 304(1)(c)(iii)(A), (c)(iv)(B)(II)2-4, (c)(iv)(C)(III)-(IV), (c)(iv)(E)(IV) amended by 2014 budget bill #2, for 2016 and later taxation years. For 2000-2015, read:

> (A) is an individual, other than a trust that is neither a trust described in paragraph 104(4)(a) of the Act (in this paragraph referred to as a "specified trust") nor a testamentary trust,
>
> . . . . .
>
> 2. in the case of a testamentary trust (other than a specified trust) where the annuity is issued before October 24, 2012, for the life of an individual who is entitled to receive income from the trust, and
>
> 3. in the case of any other testamentary trust other than a specified trust, for the life of an individual who was entitled when the contract was first held to receive all of the income of the trust that arose before the individual's death,
>
> . . . . .
>
> (III) if the holder is a testamentary trust other than a specified trust, the individual who was the youngest beneficiary under the trust when the contract was first held,
>
> . . . . .
>
> (IV) if the holder is a testamentary trust, other than a specified trust, and the contract was first held after October 2011, on the earlier of
>
> 1. the time at which the trust ceases to be a testamentary trust, and
>
> 2. the death of the individual referred to in subclause (B)(II) or (C)(III), as the case may be, in respect of the trust, and

Reg. 304(1)(c)(iv)(B)(II) amended, (c)(iv)(C)-(E) amended and (F) added by 2002-2013 technical bill (Part 5 — technical), for 2000 and later taxation years, except that with regard to a contract held by a trust created by a taxpayer at a particular time in 2000 for the benefit of another individual, ignore the words "or common-law partner" in (c)(iv)(B)(II) and (C)(II) unless because of an election under s. 144 of the 2000 same-sex partners bill, ITA 248(1)"common-law partner" applies to the taxpayer and the other individual.

Reg. 304(1)(a) extended to apply to ITA 148(1)(b.3) by 2012 budget bill #2, effective Dec. 14, 2012.

Reg. 304(1) opening words amended by P.C. 2011-936 to add reference to ITA 20(20) effective Feb. 19, 2011, and to delete reference to ITA 12.2(3) and (4) effective for life insurance policies last acquired after 1989.

Reg. 304(1)(c)(ii) amended by P.C. 2009-1212 effective Feb. 23, 1994, consequential on terminology changes in ITA 39(5).

Reg. 304(1)(a) amended by 2008 budget bill #2, effective for annuity contracts issued after 2008, effectively to extend the exclusion to TFSAs and RRIFs.

Reg. 304 earlier amended by P.C. 2007-849 (effective June 13, 2007), 2001-957, 1994-940, 1988-1115, 1988-390, 1986-1048, 1983-3530. Added by P.C. 1982-1421.

Definitions [Reg. 304]: "amount" — ITA 248(1); "annuitant" — Reg. 304(4); "annuity" — ITA 248(1); "Canada" — ITA 255, *Interpretation Act* 35(1); "common-law partner" — ITA 248(1); "consequence of the death" — ITA 248(8); "corporation" — ITA 248(1), *Interpretation Act* 35(1); "deferred profit sharing plan" — ITA 147(1), 248(1); "disposed" — ITA 248(1)"disposition"; "employment" — ITA 248(1); "former spouse" — Reg. 304(5); "group term life insurance policy" — ITA 248(1); "holder" — Reg. 304(3); "individual" — ITA 248(1); "issuer" — Reg. 304(1)(c)(ii); "life insurance corporation" — ITA 248(1); "mortgage investment corporation" — ITA 130.1(6), 248(1); "mutual fund corporation" — ITA 131(8), 248(1); "office", "person", "prescribed" — ITA 248(1); "prescribed annuity contract" — Reg. 304(1), (2); "qualified disability trust" — ITA 122(3); "registered pension plan" — ITA 248(1); "specified trust" — Reg. 304(1)(c)(iii)(A); "spouse" — Reg. 304(5); "survivor" — Reg. 304(1)(c)(iv)(B)(I); "taxation year" — ITA 249; "testamentary trust" — ITA 108(1), 248(1); "trust" — ITA 104(1), 248(1), (3); "writing" — *Interpretation Act* 35(1).

Income Tax Folios: S3-F9-C1: Lottery winnings, miscellaneous receipts, and income (and losses) from crime [replaces IT-185R, IT-213R, IT-256R, IT-334R2].

Interpretation Bulletins: IT-87R2: Policyholders' income from life insurance policies.

305. [Repealed]

Notes [Reg. 305]: Reg. 305 repealed by P.C. 2011-936, for annuity contracts and life insurance policies last acquired after 1989. It read:

305. Unallocated income accrued before 1982 — (1) For the purposes of section 12.2 and paragraph 56(1)(d.1) of the Act, the amount at any time of "unallocated income accrued in respect of the interest before 1982, as determined in prescribed manner", in respect of a taxpayer's interest in an annuity contract (other than an interest last acquired after December 1, 1982) or in a life insurance policy referred to in subsection (3), means the amount, if any, by which

(a) the accumulating fund at December 31, 1981 in respect of the interest

exceeds the aggregate of

(b) his adjusted cost basis (within the meaning assigned by paragraph 148(9)(a) [148(9)"adjusted cost basis"] of the Act) at December 31, 1981 in respect of the interest; and

(c) that proportion of the amount, if any, by which the amount determined under paragraph (a) exceeds the amount determined under paragraph (b) that

(i) the aggregate of all amounts each of which is the amount of an annuity payment received before that time in respect of the interest

is of

(ii) the taxpayer's interest, immediately before the commencement of payments under the contract, in the total of the annuity payments

(A) to be made under the contract, in the case of a contract for a term of years certain, or

(B) expected to be made under the contract, in the case of a contract under which the continuation of the payments depends in whole or in part on the survival of an individual.

(2) For the purposes of paragraph (1)(c), "annuity payment" does not include any portion of a payment under a contract the amount of which cannot be reasonably determined immediately before the commencement of payments under the contract except where such portion cannot be so determined because the continuation of the annuity payments under the contract depends in whole or in part on the survival of an individual.

(3) For the purposes of this section, an interest in an annuity contract to which subsection 12.2(9) of the Act applies shall be deemed to be a continuation of the interest in the life insurance policy in respect of which it was issued.

Definitions [former Reg. 305]: "accumulating fund" — Reg. 307; "amount", "annuity" — ITA 248(1); "annuity payment" — Reg. 305(2); "commencement" — *Interpretation Act* 35(1); "continuation" — Reg. 305(3); "individual" — ITA 248(1); "life insurance policy" — ITA 138(12), 248(1); "prescribed", "taxpayer" — ITA 248(1); "total of the payments" — Reg. 300(2)(a).

Interpretation Bulletins [former Reg. 305]: IT-87R2: Policyholders' income from life insurance policies.

306. Exempt policies — (1) [Exempt policy] — For the purposes of this Part and subsection 12.2(11) of the Act, "exempt policy" at any time means a life insurance policy (other than an annuity contract, LIA policy or a deposit administration fund policy) in respect of which the following conditions are met at that time:

(a) if that time is a policy anniversary of the policy, the accumulating fund of the policy at that time (determined without regard to any policy loan) does not exceed the total of the accumulating funds at that time of the exemption test policies issued at or before that time in respect of the policy;

(b) assuming that the terms and conditions of the policy do not change from those in effect on the last policy anniversary of the policy at or before that time and, where necessary, making rea-

sonable assumptions about all other factors (including, in the case of a participating life insurance policy within the meaning assigned by subsection 138(12) of the Act, the assumption that the amounts of dividends paid will be as shown in the dividend scale),

(i) if the policy is issued before 2017, it is reasonable to expect that the condition in paragraph (a) will be met on each policy anniversary of the policy on which the policy could remain in force after that time and before the endowment date of the exemption test policies issued in respect of the policy, and

(ii) if the policy is issued after 2016, it is reasonable to expect — without reference to any automatic adjustments under the policy that may be made after that time to ensure that the policy is an exempt policy and, where applicable, making projections using the most recent values that are used to calculate the accumulating fund in respect of the policy or in respect of each exemption test policy issued in respect of a coverage under the policy, as the case may be — that the condition in paragraph (a) will be met on the policy's next policy anniversary;

(c) the condition in paragraph (a) was met on all policy anniversaries of the policy before that time; and

(d) the condition in paragraph (b) was met at all times on and after the first policy anniversary of the policy and before that time.

Related Provisions: ITA 20(1)(e.2) — No deduction for premiums on "10/8" policy or LIA policy; ITA 20(2.01) — No deduction for interest relating to "10/8" policy; ITA 89(1)"capital dividend account"(d)(ii), (iv) — no increase in CDA for death benefit on 10/8 policy or LIA policy; ITA 148(11), Reg. 306(10) — Loss of pre-2017 grandfathering; Reg. 306(4) — Rule for determining whether condition in Reg. 306(1)(a) is met.

Notes: For explanation of exempt policies and the taxation of policyholders see Kevin Wark, "Policyholder Taxation Rules Revisited", XIX(1) *Insurance Planning [IP]* (Federated Press) 1193-96 (2012) and XIX(2) 1198-1202 (2013), "New Policyholder Tax Rules", XXI(1) 1314-28 (2015), and "The Next Phase of Life Insurance Policyholder Taxation", 64(4) *Canadian Tax Journal* 705-50 (2016); Steve Krupicz, "Exempt Test Changes — The Impact on Insurance Products", XXII(1) *IP* 8-13 (2017) and "CDA Planning Under the G3 Tax Rules", XXIII(1) 6-13 (2018). See also Finance Technical Notes to Reg. 306(1).

For discussion of the Aug. 2013 proposals (enacted by 2014 budget bill #2), see Peter Everett, "Life Insurance Planning after the 2013 Budget", 2013 Cdn Tax Foundation conference report at 32:15-20; Kevin Wark, "Policyholder Taxation Rules — Part III", XIX(3) *Insurance Planning* (Federated Press) 1214-26 (2013). A proposed amendment in those proposals to the opening words of Reg. 306(1) has been dropped.

On whether a life insurer must continue to ensure that a policy remains exempt, see VIEWS doc 2013-0497901E5.

For the meaning of "issued before 2017" in Reg. 306(1)(b)(i), see Notes to ITA 148(11).

In determining whether a foreign currency policy is an exempt policy, Canadian currency should be used: VIEWS doc 2004-0065391C6. On policies issued on non-resident lives see 2019-0799101C6 [CLHIA 2019 q.6].

A US Individual Flexible Premium Variable Annuity is not an exempt policy: VIEWS doc 2010-0371161E5.

Reg. 306(1)(b)(ii) added, and (b)(i) amended to add "if the policy is issued before 2017" and to change "the date determined under subparagraph (3)(d)(ii) with respect to" to "the endowment date of", by 2014 budget bill #2, effective Dec. 16, 2014. (Before the amendment, (b)(i) was in the body of the para.)

Reg. 306(1) opening words amended to add "LIA policy" by 2013 budget bill #2, for tax years that end after March 20, 2013. See Notes to ITA 248(1)"LIA policy".

Reg. 306(1) amended by P.C. 1994-940 (see Notes to Reg. 307(4)), effective

(a) for life insurance policies issued after March 26, 1992, other than a policy for which written application was made by that date, and

(b) for life insurance policies amended at any time after March 26, 1992 to increase the amount of the benefit on death.

For policies to which the new version does not apply, read:

306. (1) For the purposes of this Part and paragraph 12.2(11)(a) of the Act, "exempt policy" at any time means a life insurance policy (other than an annuity contract or a deposit administration fund policy)

(a) in respect of which

(i) on the policy anniversary thereof, if any, occurring at that time, and

(ii) assuming that the terms and conditions of the policy do not change from those in effect on the last policy anniversary at or before that time and, where necessary, making reasonable assumptions about all other factors (including, in the case of a participating life insurance policy within the meaning assigned by paragraph 138(12)(k) [138(12)"participating life insurance policy"] of the Act, the assumption that the amounts of dividends paid will be shown in the dividend scale), on each policy anniversary after that time on which the policy could remain in force and before the date determined under subparagraph (3)(d)(ii) with respect to any exemption test policy issued in respect of the policy,

the accumulating fund (determined without regard to any policy loan) does not exceed (or, in the case of subparagraph (ii), would not exceed) the aggregate of the accumulating funds of the exemption test policies in respect of the life insurance policy at the time; and

(b) that has met the requirements of paragraph (a) on and after the date of its first policy anniversary.

Interpretation Bulletins: IT-87R2: Policyholders' income from life insurance policies.

(2) [Exempt on first policy anniversary] — For the purposes of subsection (1), a life insurance policy that is an exempt policy on its first policy anniversary shall be deemed to have been an exempt policy from the time of its issue until that anniversary.

Notes: Reg. 306(2) amended by P.C. 1994-940, effective on the same basis as the amendments to Reg. 306(1) above. For policies to which the new version does not apply, read:

(2) For the purposes of subsection (1), any life insurance policy that meets the requirements of paragraph (1)(a) on its first policy anniversary shall be deemed to have been an exempt policy from the time of its issue until that anniversary.

(3) [Deemed separate exemption test policy] — For the purposes of this section and section 307,

(a) in the case of a life insurance policy issued before 2017, a separate exemption test policy is deemed, subject to subsection (7), to be issued in respect of the life insurance policy

(i) on the date of issue of the life insurance policy, and

(ii) on each policy anniversary of the life insurance policy on which

(A) the amount of the benefit on death under the life insurance policy

exceeds

(B) 108% of the amount of the benefit on death under the life insurance policy on the later of the life insurance policy's date of issue and the date of the life insurance policy's preceding policy anniversary, if any; and

(b) in the case of a life insurance policy issued after 2016, a separate exemption test policy is deemed, subject to subsection (7), to be issued in respect of each coverage under the life insurance policy

(i) on the date of

(A) issue of the life insurance policy, if the coverage is issued before the first policy anniversary of the life insurance policy,

(B) issue of the coverage, if the coverage is issued on a policy anniversary of the life insurance policy, or

(C) the life insurance policy's preceding policy anniversary, if the coverage is issued on any date that is after the policy's first policy anniversary and that is not a policy anniversary,

(ii) on each policy anniversary of the life insurance policy on which

(A) the amount of the benefit on death under the coverage on that policy anniversary

exceeds

(B) 108% of the amount of the benefit on death under the coverage, on the later of the coverage's date of issue and the date of the life insurance policy's preceding policy anniversary (or, if there is no preceding policy anniversary, the coverage's date of issue), and

(iii) on each policy anniversary of the life insurance policy — except to the extent that another exemption test policy has been issued on that date under this subparagraph in respect of a coverage under the life insurance policy — on which

(A) the amount by which the fund value benefit under the life insurance policy on that policy anniversary exceeds the fund value benefit under the life insurance policy on the life insurance policy's preceding policy anniversary (or, if there is no preceding policy anniversary, the date of issue of the policy)

exceeds

(B) the amount by which

(I) 8% of the amount of the benefit on death under the life insurance policy on the life insurance policy's preceding policy anniversary (or, if there is no preceding policy anniversary, the date of issue of the policy)

exceeds

(II) the total of all amounts each of which is, in respect of a coverage under the policy, the lesser of

1. the amount by which the amount of the benefit on death under the coverage on that policy anniversary exceeds the amount of the benefit on death under the coverage on the later of the coverage's date of issue and the date of the life insurance policy's preceding policy anniversary (or, if there is no preceding policy anniversary, the coverage's date of issue), and

2. 8% of the amount of the benefit on death under the coverage on the later of the coverage's date of issue and the date of the life insurance policy's preceding policy anniversary (or, if there is no preceding policy anniversary, the coverage's date of issue).

Related Provisions: ITA 148(11), Reg. 306(10) — Loss of pre-2017 grandfathering.

Notes: See Kevin Wark, "Review of Proposed Changes to the Exempt Test Legislation", 2013 Ontario Tax Conf. (ctf.ca), 13A:1-16. Note also the 2013 budget bill #2 amendments, which catch 10/8 plans and leveraged insured annuities: see ITA 248(1)"10/8 policy", 248(1)"LIA policy", 20(2.01), 20(1)(e.2) and 89(1)"capital dividend account"(d)(ii), (iv).

For the meaning of "issued before 2017" in Reg. 306(3)(a), (4)(b)(i)(A), (5)(a) and (6)(c)(i)(A), see Notes to ITA 148(11).

Reg. 306(3) amended by 2017 budget bill #2, effective Dec. 14, 2017. The amendments removed special rules that applied when ITA 148(11) has applied to treat a life insurance policy as having been issued at a particular time (these rules are now in Reg. 306(10)). Before that date, read:

(3) For the purposes of this section and section 307,

(a) in the case of a life insurance policy issued before 2017 or at a particular time determined under subsection 148(11) of the Act, a separate exemption test policy is deemed, subject to subsection (7), to be issued in respect of the life insurance policy

(i) on the date of issue of the life insurance policy, and

(ii) on each policy anniversary (that ends before the particular time, if any, determined under subsection 148(11) of the Act in respect of the policy) of the life insurance policy on which

(A) the amount of the benefit on death under the life insurance policy

exceeds

(B) 108% of the amount of the benefit on death under the life insurance policy on the later of the life insurance policy's date of issue and the date of the life insurance policy's preceding policy anniversary, if any; and

(b) in the case of a life insurance policy issued after 2016 (including, for greater certainty, at a particular time determined under subsection 148(11) of the Act in respect of the policy), a separate exemption test policy is deemed, subject to subsection (7), to be issued in respect of each coverage under the life insurance policy

(i) unless the particular time when the policy is issued is determined under subsection 148(11) of the Act and the coverage was issued before the particular time, on the date of

(A) issue of the life insurance policy, if the coverage is issued before the first policy anniversary of the life insurance policy,

(B) issue of the coverage, if the coverage is issued on a policy anniversary of the life insurance policy, or

(C) the life insurance policy's preceding policy anniversary, if the coverage is issued on any date that is after the policy's first policy anniversary and that is not a policy anniversary,

(ii) on each policy anniversary of the life insurance policy (except that, if a particular time when the policy is issued has been determined under subsection 148(11) of the Act, only on a policy anniversary that ends at or after the particular time) on which

(A) the amount of the benefit on death under the coverage on that policy anniversary

exceeds

(B) 108% of the amount of the benefit on death under the coverage, on the later of the coverage's date of issue and the date of the life insurance policy's preceding policy anniversary (or, if there is no preceding policy anniversary, the coverage's date of issue), and

(iii) on each policy anniversary of the life insurance policy (except that, if a particular time when the policy is issued has been determined under subsection 148(11) of the Act, only on a policy anniversary that ends at or after the particular time) — except to the extent that another exemption test policy has been issued on that date under this subparagraph in respect of a coverage under the life insurance policy — on which

(A) the amount by which the fund value benefit under the life insurance policy on that policy anniversary exceeds the fund value benefit under the life insurance policy on the life insurance policy's preceding policy anniversary (or, if there is no preceding policy anniversary, the date of issue of the policy)

exceeds

(B) the amount by which

(I) 8% of the amount of the benefit on death under the life insurance policy on the life insurance policy's preceding policy anniversary (or, if there is no preceding policy anniversary, the date of issue of the policy)

exceeds

(II) the total of all amounts each of which is, in respect of a coverage under the policy, the lesser of

1. the amount by which the amount of the benefit on death under the coverage on that policy anniversary exceeds the amount of the benefit on death under the coverage on the later of the coverage's date of issue and the date of the life insurance policy's preceding policy anniversary (or, if there is no preceding policy anniversary, the coverage's date of issue), and

2. 8% of the amount of the benefit on death under the coverage on the later of the coverage's date of issue and the date of the life insurance policy's preceding policy anniversary (or, if there is no preceding policy anniversary, the coverage's date of issue).

Reg. 306(3) amended by 2014 budget bill #2, effective Dec. 16, 2014.

Reg. 306(3) amended by P.C. 1994-940, effective on the same basis as the amendments to Reg. 306(1) above.

(4) [Condition in Reg. 306(1)(a)] — For the purpose of determining whether the condition in paragraph (1)(a) is met on a policy anniversary of a life insurance policy, each exemption test policy issued in respect of the life insurance policy, or in respect of a coverage under the life insurance policy, is deemed

(a) to have a benefit on death that is uniform throughout the term of the exemption test policy and that, subject to subsection (5), is equal to

(i) if the date on which the exemption test policy is issued is determined by subparagraph (3)(a)(i), the amount by which the amount on that policy anniversary of the benefit on death under the life insurance policy exceeds the total of all amounts each of which is the amount, if any, on that policy anniversary of the benefit on death under another exemption

test policy issued on or before that policy anniversary in respect of the life insurance policy,

(ii) if the date on which the exemption test policy is issued is determined by subparagraph (3)(a)(ii), the amount of the excess referred to in that subparagraph on that date in respect of the life insurance policy,

(iii) if the date on which the exemption test policy is issued is determined by subparagraph (3)(b)(i), the amount determined by the formula

$$A + B - C$$

where

A is the amount on that policy anniversary of the benefit on death under the coverage,

B is

(A) if the benefit on death under the life insurance policy includes a fund value benefit on that policy anniversary, the portion of the fund value benefit on that policy anniversary that is equal to the lesser of

(I) the maximum amount of the fund value benefit that could be payable on that policy anniversary if no other coverage were offered under the life insurance policy and the life insurance policy were an exempt policy, and

(II) the amount by which the fund value benefit on that policy anniversary exceeds the total of all amounts each of which is the portion of the fund value benefit allocated to other coverages under the life insurance policy, and

(B) in any other case, nil, and

C is the total of all amounts each of which is the amount, if any, on that policy anniversary of the benefit on death under another exemption test policy issued on or before that policy anniversary in respect of the coverage,

(iv) if the date on which the exemption test policy is issued is determined by subparagraph (3)(b)(ii), the amount of the excess referred to in that subparagraph on that date in respect of the coverage, and

(v) if the date on which the exemption test policy is issued is determined by subparagraph (3)(b)(iii), the lesser of

(A) the amount by which the amount determined under clause (3)(b)(iii)(A) exceeds the amount determined under clause (3)(b)(iii)(B) on that date in respect of the coverage, and

(B) the amount determined in respect of the coverage under subclause (A)(I) of the description of B in subparagraph (iii) on that date; and

(b) to pay the amount of its benefit on death on the earlier of

(i) if the life insurance policy

(A) is issued before 2017, the date of death of the individual whose life is insured under the life insurance policy, or

(B) is issued after 2016,

(I) if two or more lives are jointly insured under the coverage, the date at which the benefit would be payable as a result of the death of any of the lives, and

(II) in any other case, the date of death of the individual whose life is insured under the coverage, and

(ii) the exemption test policy's endowment date.

Related Provisions: ITA 148(2)(e) — Where benefit on death paid and fund value benefit exceeds amount under Reg. 306(4)(a)(iii)B(A); ITA 257 — Whether formula can calculate to less than zero; Reg. 309(1) — Prescribed premium.

Notes: Reg. 306(4) opening words amended by 2017 budget bill #2, effective Dec. 14, 2017, to delete "Subject to subsection (10)" from the beginning.

See Notes to Reg. 306(3). Reg. 306(4) amended by 2014 budget bill #2, effective Dec. 16, 2014.

(5) [Benefit on death under exemption test policy] — For the purpose of determining the amount of a benefit on death under an exemption test policy,

(a) if the exemption test policy is issued in respect of a life insurance policy issued before 2017 and at any time the amount of a benefit on death under the life insurance policy is reduced, a particular amount that is equal to the reduction is to be applied at that time to reduce the amount of the benefit on death under each exemption test policy issued before that time in respect of the life insurance policy (other than the exemption test policy the date of issue of which is determined under subparagraph (3)(a)(i)) in the order in which the dates of their issuance are proximate to that time, by an amount equal to the lesser of

(i) the portion, if any, of the particular amount not applied to reduce the benefit on death under one or more other such exemption test policies, and

(ii) the amount, immediately before that time, of the benefit on death under the relevant exemption test policy; and

(b) if the exemption test policy is issued in respect of a coverage under a life insurance policy issued after 2016 and at any time there is a particular reduction in the amount of a benefit on death under the coverage, or the portion, if any, of the fund value benefit referred to in clause (A) of the description of B in subparagraph (4)(a)(iii) in respect of the coverage, the amount of the benefit on death under each exemption test policy issued before that time in respect of the coverage (other than the exemption test policy the date of issue of which is determined under subparagraph (3)(b)(i)) is reduced at that time by an amount equal to the least of

(i) the particular reduction,

(ii) the amount, immediately before that time, of the benefit on death under the relevant exemption test policy, and

(iii) the portion, if any, of the particular reduction not applied to reduce the benefit on death under one or more other such exemption test policies issued on or after the date of issue of the relevant exemption test policy.

Related Provisions: ITA 148(11), Reg. 306(10) — Loss of pre-2017 grandfathering.

Notes: See Notes to Reg. 306(3). Reg. 306(5) added by 2014 budget bill #2, effective Dec. 16, 2014.

Reg. 306(5) opening words amended by 2017 budget bill #2, effective Dec. 14, 2017, to delete "Subject to subsection (10)" from the beginning.

(6) [Conditions for Reg. 306(7)] — Subsection (7) applies at any time in respect of a life insurance policy if

(a) that time is on its tenth or a later policy anniversary;

(b) the accumulating fund (computed without regard to any amount payable in respect of a policy loan) in respect of the policy at that time exceeds 250% of

(i) in the case where the particular time at which the policy is issued is determined under subsection 148(11) of the Act and the policy's third preceding policy anniversary is before the particular time, the accumulating fund (computed without regard to any amount payable in respect of a policy loan and as though the policy were issued after 2016) in respect of the policy on that third preceding policy anniversary, and

(ii) in any other case, the accumulating fund (computed without regard to any amount payable in respect of a policy loan) in respect of the policy on its third preceding policy anniversary; and

(c) where that time is after 2016,

(i) the accumulating fund (computed without regard to any amount payable in respect of a policy loan) in respect of the policy at that time exceeds the total of all amounts each of which is

(A) if the policy is issued before 2017, $3/20$ of the accumulating fund, at that time, in respect of an exemption test policy issued in respect of the policy, and

(B) if the policy is issued after 2016, $3/8$ of the accumulating fund, at that time, in respect of an exemption test policy issued in respect of a coverage under the policy, and

(ii) subsection (7) did not apply on any of the policy's six preceding policy anniversaries.

Related Provisions: ITA 148(11), Reg. 306(10) — Loss of pre-2017 grandfathering.

Notes: See Notes to Reg. 306(3). Reg. 306(6) added by 2014 budget bill #2, effective Dec. 16, 2014; and amended by 2017 budget bill #2, effective Dec. 14, 2017, effectively to add (b)(i). (What is now (b)(ii) was previously in the body of para. (b) without "in any other case".)

(7) [Deemed issue date of exemption test policy] — If this subsection applies at any time in respect of a life insurance policy, each exemption test policy issued before that time in respect of the life insurance policy is at and after that time deemed to be issued (except for purposes of this subsection, paragraph (4)(a) and subsection (5))

(a) on the later of

(i) the date of the third preceding policy anniversary described in paragraph (6)(b) in respect of the policy, and

(ii) the date on which it was deemed by subsection (3) or (10), as the case may be, to be issued (determined immediately before that time); and

(b) not at any other time.

Related Provisions: ITA 148(11), Reg. 306(10) — Loss of pre-2017 grandfathering; Reg. 306(6) — Conditions for Reg. 306(7) to apply.

Notes: See Notes to Reg. 306(3). Reg. 306(7) added by 2014 budget bill #2, effective Dec. 16, 2014; and amended by 2017 budget bill #2, effective Dec. 14, 2017, to add "or (10), as the case may be".

(8) [Where policy would cease to be exempt policy] — A life insurance policy that would, in the absence of this subsection, cease (other than by reason of its conversion into an annuity contract) on a policy anniversary of the policy to be an exempt policy is deemed to be an exempt policy on that policy anniversary if

(a) had that policy anniversary occurred on the particular day that is 60 days after that policy anniversary, the policy would have been an exempt policy on the particular day; or

(b) the person whose life is insured under the policy dies on that policy anniversary or within 60 days after that policy anniversary.

Related Provisions: ITA 148(11) — Loss of pre-2017 grandfathering.

Notes: See Notes to Reg. 306(3). Reg. 306(8) added by 2014 budget bill #2, effective Dec. 16, 2014.

(9) [Deemed exempt policy] — A life insurance policy (other than an annuity contract or deposit administration fund policy) issued before December 2, 1982 is deemed to be an exempt policy at all times from the date of its issue until the first time after December 1, 1982 at which

(a) a prescribed premium is paid by a taxpayer in respect of an interest, last acquired before December 2, 1982, in the policy; or

(b) an interest in the policy is acquired by a taxpayer from the person who held the interest continuously since December 1, 1982.

Notes: See Notes to Reg. 306(3). Reg. 306(9) added by 2014 budget bill #2, effective Dec. 16, 2014.

(10) [Where ITA 148(11) applies] — Notwithstanding subsections (3) and (4), if a life insurance policy is issued for any purpose at a particular time determined under subsection 148(11) of the Act, then for the purposes of applying this section (other than this subsection and subsection (9)) and section 307 in respect of the life insurance policy at and after the particular time,

(a) in respect of each coverage issued before the particular time under the life insurance policy, a separate exemption test policy is deemed to be issued in respect of a coverage under the life insurance policy

(i) on the date of issue of the life insurance policy, and

(ii) on each policy anniversary that ends before the particular time of the life insurance policy on which

(A) the amount of the benefit on death under the life insurance policy

exceeds

(B) 108% of the amount of the benefit on death under the life insurance policy on the later of the life insurance policy's date of issue and the date of the life insurance policy's preceding policy anniversary, if any;

(b) in respect of each coverage issued before the particular time under the life insurance policy, subsection (3) does not apply to deem an exemption test policy to be issued in respect of the policy, or in respect of a coverage under the policy, at any time before the particular time;

(c) in respect of each exemption test policy the date of issuance of which is determined under subparagraph (a)(i), the references in subparagraph (4)(a)(iii) and paragraph (5)(b) to "subparagraph (3)(b)(i)" are to be read as references to "subparagraph (10)(a)(i)";

(d) in respect of each exemption test policy the date of issuance of which is determined under subparagraph (a)(ii), subparagraph (4)(a)(iv) is to be read as follows:

(iv) if the date on which the exemption test policy is issued is determined by subparagraph (10)(a)(ii) at a time before a particular time, the portion of the amount — that amount being the amount that would be determined, at the time immediately before the particular time, under subparagraph (a)(ii), if the exemption test policy were issued in respect of the policy on the same date as the date determined for it under subparagraph (10)(a)(ii) — that can be reasonably allocated to the coverage in the circumstances (and for these purposes, an allocation is considered not to be reasonable if the total of the amounts determined for A and B in subparagraph (a)(iii) is less than the amount determined for C in that subparagraph in respect of the exemption test policy the date of issuance of which is determined under subparagraph (10)(a)(i) in respect of the coverage), and

and

(e) in applying paragraph (5)(b), the reference in that paragraph to "any time" is to be read as "any time at or after the particular time referred to in subsection (10) in respect of the life insurance policy".

Notes: Reg. 306(10) replaced by 2017 budget bill #2, effective Dec. 14, 2017. The previous Reg. 306(10) (added by 2014 budget bill #2, effective Dec. 16, 2014) read:

(10) If a particular time when a life insurance policy is issued has been determined under subsection 148(11) of the Act, in applying subsections (4) and (5) at or after the particular time to an exemption test policy issued before the particular time in respect of the policy,

(a) subparagraphs (4)(a)(iii) and (iv), and not subparagraph (4)(a)(i) or (ii), apply to the exemption test policy; and

(b) for greater certainty, paragraph (5)(b), and not paragraph (5)(a), applies to the exemption test policy.

That provision was new with the Oct. 10, 2014 Notice of Ways and Means Motion. An earlier proposed Reg. 306(10) in the Aug. 23, 2013 draft legislation was dropped.

Definitions [Reg. 306]: "accumulating fund" — Reg. 307(1); "amount" — ITA 248(1); "amount payable" — ITA 138(12), Reg. 310; "annuity" — ITA 248(1); "benefit on death" — Reg. 310, 1401(3); "Canada" — ITA 255, *Interpretation Act* 35(1); "coverage" — Reg. 310; "dividend" — ITA 248(1); "endowment date" — Reg. 310; "exempt policy" — Reg. 306(1), (2), 306(4)(d); "exemption test policy" — Reg. 306(3); "fund value benefit" — Reg. 310, 1401(3); "individual", "insurer", "LIA policy", "life insurance business" — ITA 248(1); "life insurance policy", "life insurance policy in Canada" — ITA 138(12), 248(1); "life insurer" — ITA 248(1); "participating life insurance policy" — ITA 138(12); "person" — ITA 248(1); "policy anniversary" — Reg. 310; "policy loan" — ITA 148(9), Reg. 310; "prescribed" — ITA 248(1); "prescribed premium" — Reg. 309(1); "reduction" — Reg. 306(4)(a); "tax avoidance policy" — Reg. 310; "taxpayer" — ITA 248(1).

307. Accumulating funds — (1) [Meaning of "accumulating fund"] — For the purposes of this Part and sections 12.2 and 148 of the Act, "accumulating fund", at any particular time, means

(a) in respect of a taxpayer's interest in an annuity contract (other than a contract issued by a life insurer), the amount that is the greater of

(i) the amount, if any, by which the cash surrender value of the taxpayer's interest at that time exceeds the amount payable, if any, in respect of a loan outstanding at that time made under the contract in respect of the interest, and

(ii) the amount, if any, by which

(A) the present value at that time of future payments to be made out of the contract in respect of the taxpayer's interest

exceeds

(B) the total of

(I) the present value at that time of future premiums to be paid under the contract in respect of the taxpayer's interest, and

(II) the amount payable, if any, in respect of a loan outstanding at that time, made under the contract in respect of the taxpayer's interest;

(b) in respect of a taxpayer's interest in a life insurance policy (other than an exemption test policy or an annuity contract to which paragraph (1)(a) applies), the product obtained when,

(i) where the policy is not a deposit administration fund policy and the particular time is immediately after the death of any person on whose life the life insurance policy is issued or effected, the aggregate of the maximum amounts that could be determined by the life insurer immediately before the death in respect of the policy under paragraph 1401(1)(c) and subparagraph 1401(1)(d)(i) if the mortality rates used were adjusted to reflect the assumption that the death would occur at the time and in the manner that it did occur, and

(ii) in any other case, the maximum amount that could be determined at that particular time by the life insurer under paragraph 1401(1)(a), computed as though there were only one deposit administration fund policy, or under paragraph 1401(1)(c), as the case may be, in respect of the policy

is multiplied by

(iii) the taxpayer's proportionate interest in the policy; and

(c) in respect of an exemption test policy,

(i) if the particular time is during the exemption test policy's pay period, the amount determined by the formula

$$A \times B/C$$

where

A is the amount that would be determined under subparagraph (ii) in respect of the exemption test policy

(A) if the exemption test policy's pay period is determined by subparagraph (b)(i) or (ii) of the definition "pay period" in section 310, on the first policy anniversary that is on or after the day on which the individual whose life is insured would, if the individual survived, attain the age of 105 years, as defined under the terms of the policy, and

(B) in any other case, on the exemption test policy's policy anniversary represented by the adjectival form of the number of years in its pay period,

B is the number of years since the exemption test policy was issued, and

C is the number of years in the exemption test policy's pay period,

(ii) if the particular time is after the exemption test policy's pay period and before its endowment date, the amount that is the present value at the particular time of the future benefit on death under the exemption test policy, and

(iii) if the particular time is on or after the exemption test policy's endowment date and the relevant life insurance policy is issued after 2016, the amount that is the benefit on death under the exemption test policy at the particular time.

Related Provisions: ITA 148(11) — Loss of pre-2016 grandfathering; Reg. 1401(4) — Application rules for life insurance policy issued after 2016.

Notes: Reg. 307(1)(a)(ii) and (c) amended, and (b) closing words repealed, by 2014 budget bill #2, effective Dec. 16, 2014.

Reg. 307(1) opening words amended by P.C. 2011-936 to delete reference to ITA 56(1)(d.1), effective with respect to annuity contracts and life insurance policies last acquired after 1989.

See also Notes to Reg. 306(1) and 307(4).

(2) [Rules for computing accumulating fund] — For the purposes of subsection (1), when computing the accumulating fund in respect of

(a) an interest described in paragraph (1)(a), the amounts determined under clauses (1)(a)(ii)(A) and (B) are to be computed using,

(i) where an interest rate for a period used by the issuer when the contract was issued in determining the terms of the contract was less than any rate so used for a subsequent period, the single rate that would, if it applied for each period, have produced the same terms, and

(ii) in any other case, the rates used by the issuer when the contract was issued in determining the terms of the contract;

(b) an interest described in paragraph (1)(b) in respect of a life insurance policy issued before 2017 or an annuity contract, if an interest rate used for a period by a life insurer in computing the relevant amounts in paragraph 1403(1)(a) or (b) is determined under paragraph 1403(1)(c), (d) or (e), as the case may be, and that rate is less than an interest rate so determined for a subsequent period, the single rate that could, if it applied for each period, have been used in determining the premiums for the policy is to be used;

(c) an exemption test policy issued in respect of a life insurance policy issued before 2017,

(i) the rates of interest and mortality used and the age of the person whose life is insured shall be the same as those used in computing the amounts described in paragraph 1403(1)(a) or (b) in respect of the life insurance policy in respect of which the exemption test policy was issued except that

(A) where the life insurance policy is one to which paragraph 1403(1)(e) applies and the amount determined under subparagraph 1401(1)(c)(i) in respect of that policy is greater than the amount determined under subparagraph 1401(1)(c)(ii) in respect thereof, the rates of interest and mortality used may be those used in computing the cash surrender values of that policy, and

(B) where an interest rate for a period otherwise determined under this subparagraph in respect of that interest is less than an interest rate so determined for a subsequent period, the single rate that could, if it applied for each period, have been used in determining the premiums for the life insurance policy shall be used, and

(ii) notwithstanding subparagraph (i),

(A) where the rates referred to in subparagraph (i) do not exist, the minimum guaranteed rates of interest used under the life insurance policy to determine cash surrender values and the rates of mortality under the *Commissioners 1958 Standard Ordinary Mortality Table*, as published in Volume X of the *Transactions of the Society of Actuaries*, relevant to the person whose life is insured under the life insurance policy shall be used, or

(B) where, in respect of the life insurance policy, the particular period over which the amount determined under

clause (B) of the description of A in subparagraph 1401(1)(c)(ii) does not extend to the exemption test policy's endowment date, the weighted arithmetic mean of the interest rates used to determine the amount is to be used for the period that is after the particular period and before that date,

(iii) notwithstanding subparagraphs (i) and (ii), no rate of interest used for the purpose of determining the accumulating fund in respect of an exemption test policy issued in respect of the life insurance policy is to be less than

(A) if the life insurance policy is issued after April 1985, 4% per annum, and

(B) if the life insurance policy is issued before May 1985, 3% per annum, and

(iv) each amount of a benefit on death is to be determined net of any portion in respect of the benefit on death of the exemption test policy related to a segregated fund; and

(d) an exemption test policy issued in respect of a coverage under a life insurance policy issued after 2016,

(i) the rates of interest and mortality used and the age of the individual whose life is insured under the coverage are to be the same as those used in computing amounts under paragraph 1401(1)(c) in respect of the policy, and

(ii) each amount of a benefit on death is to be determined net of any portion in respect of the benefit on death of the exemption test policy related to a segregated fund.

Notes: For the meaning of "issued before 2017" in Reg. 307(2)(b) and (c), see Notes to ITA 148(11).

Reg. 307(2) amended by 2014 budget bill #2, effective Dec. 16, 2014.

(3), (4) [Repealed]

Notes: Reg. 307(3), (4) repealed by 2014 budget bill #2, effective Dec. 16, 2014.

(5) [References to Reg. 1401] — In this section, any amount determined by reference to section 1401 shall be determined

(a) without regard to section 1402; and

(b) as if each reference to "policy loan" in section 1401 were read as a reference to "policy loan, as defined in subsection 148(9) of the Act,".

(c) [Repealed]

Notes: Reg. 307(5)(c) repealed by 2014 budget bill #2, effective Dec. 16, 2014.

Reg. 307(5) amended to update ITA reference due to R.S.C. 1985 renumbering, by P.C. 2011-936, effective March 1994.

Definitions [Reg. 307]: "accumulating fund" — Reg. 307(1); "amount" — ITA 248(1); "amount payable" — ITA 138(12), Reg. 310; "annuity" — ITA 248(1); "benefit on death" — Reg. 310, 1401(3); "Canada" — ITA 255, *Interpretation Act* 35(1); "cash surrender value" — ITA 148(9), Reg. 310; "coverage", "endowment date" — Reg. 310; "exemption test policy" — Reg. 306(3); "individual", "insurer", "life insurance business" — ITA 248(1); "life insurance policy", "life insurance policy in Canada" — ITA 138(12), 248(1); "life insurer" — ITA 248(1); "pay period" — Reg. 310; "person" — ITA 248(1); "policy anniversary" — Reg. 310; "policy loan" — ITA 148(9), Reg. 310; "taxation year" — ITA 249; "taxpayer" — ITA 248(1).

Interpretation Bulletins: IT-87R2: Policyholders' income from life insurance policies.

308. Net cost of pure insurance and mortality gains and losses — (1) [Meaning of "net cost of pure insurance"] —
For the purposes of subparagraph 20(1)(e.2)(ii) and paragraph (a) of the description of L in the definition "adjusted cost basis" in subsection 148(9) of the Act, the net cost of pure insurance for a year in respect of a taxpayer's interest in a life insurance policy is

(a) if, determined at the end of the year, the policy was issued before 2017, the amount determined by the formula

$$A \times (B - C)$$

where

A is the probability, computed on the basis of the rates of mortality under the 1969–75 mortality tables of the Canadian Institute of Actuaries published in Volume XVI of the *Pro-*

ceedings of the Canadian Institute of Actuaries, or on the basis described in subsection (1.1), that an individual who has the same relevant characteristics as the individual whose life is insured will die in the year,

B is the benefit on death in respect of the interest at the end of the year, and

C is the accumulating fund (determined without regard to any amount payable in respect of the policy loan) in respect of the interest at the end of the year or the interest's cash surrender value at the end of the year, depending on the method regularly followed by the life insurer in computing amounts under this subsection; and

(b) if, determined at the end of the year, the policy was issued after 2016, the total of all amounts each of which is an amount determined in respect of a coverage in respect of the interest by the formula

$$A \times (B - C)$$

where

A is the probability, computed on the basis of the rates of mortality determined in accordance with paragraph 1401(4)(b), or on the basis described in subsection (1.2), that an individual whose life is insured under the coverage will die in the year,

B is the benefit on death under the coverage in respect of the interest at the end of the year, and

C is the amount determined by the formula

$$D + E$$

where

D is the portion, in respect of the coverage in respect of the interest, of the amount that would be the present value, determined for the purposes of section 307, on the last policy anniversary that is on or before the last day of the year, of the fund value of the coverage if the fund value of the coverage were equal to the fund value of the coverage at the end of the year, and

E is the portion, in respect of the coverage in respect of the interest, of the amount that would be determined, on that policy anniversary, for paragraph (a) of the description of C in the definition "net premium reserve" in subsection 1401(3) in respect of the coverage, if the benefit on death under the coverage, and the fund value of the coverage, on that policy anniversary were equal to the benefit on death under the coverage and the fund value of the coverage, respectively, at the end of the year.

Related Provisions: ITA 148(11) — Loss of pre-2016 grandfathering; ITA 257 — Whether formula can calculate to less than zero.

Notes: See Kevin Wark, "Net Cost of Pure Insurance", XI(4) *Insurance Planning* (Federated Press) 738-40 (2005). Where a case is not covered by the tables, the insurer's actuary will need to extrapolate: VIEWS doc 2005-0114801E5. The formula denies a deduction for premiums paid by a taxpayer who dies later in the year: 2012-0435671C6.

For the meaning of "issued before 2017" in Reg. 308(1)(a), see Notes to ITA 148(11).

For a case where Reg. 308(1) applied see *Brousseau*, 2006 TCC 646.

Reg. 308(1) amended by 2014 budget bill #2, effective Dec. 16, 2014.

Opening words of Reg. 308(1) amended by P.C. 1994-940, for years ending after 1989.

Interpretation Bulletins: IT-87R2: Policyholders' income from life insurance policies; IT-309R2: Premiums on life insurance used as collateral.

(1.1) [Use of mortality rates] — If premiums for a life insurance policy do not depend directly on smoking or sex classification, the probability referred to in paragraph (1)(a) may be determined using rates of mortality otherwise determined, provided that for each age for the policy, the expected value of the aggregate net cost of pure insurance, calculated using those rates of mortality, is equal to the expected value of the aggregate net cost of pure insurance, calculated using the rates of mortality under the 1969–75 mortality tables

of the Canadian Institute of Actuaries published in Volume XVI of the *Proceedings of the Canadian Institute of Actuaries*.

Notes: Reg. 308(1.1) amended by 2014 budget bill #2, effective Dec. 16, 2014.

(1.2) [Use of mortality rates] — If premiums or costs of insurance charges for a coverage under a life insurance policy do not depend directly on smoking or sex classification, the probability referred to in paragraph (1)(b) may be determined using rates of mortality otherwise determined, provided that for each age for the coverage, the expected value of the aggregate net cost of pure insurance, calculated using those rates of mortality, is equal to the expected value of the aggregate net cost of pure insurance, calculated using the rates of mortality that would be calculated under paragraph (1)(b) in respect of the coverage using the mortality tables described in paragraph 1401(4)(b).

Notes: Reg. 308(1.2) added by 2014 budget bill #2, effective Dec. 16, 2014.

(2) [Meaning of "mortality gain"] — Subject to subsection (4), for the purposes of this section and of the description of G in the definition "adjusted cost basis" in subsection 148(9) of the Act, a "mortality gain" immediately before the end of any calendar year after 1982 in respect of a taxpayer's interest in a life annuity contract means such reasonable amount in respect of the taxpayer's interest in the life annuity contract at that time that the life insurer determines to be the increase to the accumulating fund in respect of the interest that occurred during that year as a consequence of the survival to the end of the year of one or more of the annuitants under the life annuity contract.

Notes: Reg. 308(2) amended by P.C. 2011-936 to modernize the wording and update ITA references due to R.S.C. 1985 renumbering, effective March 1994.

(3) [Meaning of "mortality loss"] — Subject to subsection (4), for the purposes of this section and of paragraph (c) of the description of L in the definition "adjusted cost basis" in subsection 148(9) of the Act, a "mortality loss" immediately before a particular time after 1982 in respect of an interest in a life annuity contract disposed of immediately after that particular time as a consequence of the death of an annuitant under the life annuity contract means such reasonable amount that the life insurer determines to be the decrease, as a consequence of the death, in the accumulating fund in respect of the interest assuming that, in determining such decrease, the accumulating fund immediately after the death is determined in the manner described in subparagraph 307(1)(b)(i).

Notes: Reg. 308(3) amended by P.C. 2011-936 to modernize the wording and update ITA references due to R.S.C. 1985 renumbering, effective March 1994.

(4) In determining an amount for a year in respect of an interest in a life annuity contract under subsection (2) or (3), the expected value of the mortality gains in respect of the interest for the year shall be equal to the expected value of the mortality losses in respect of the interest for the year and the mortality rates for the year used in computing those expected values shall be those that would be relevant to the interest and that are specified under such of paragraphs 1403(1)(c), (d) and (e) as are applicable.

Definitions [Reg. 308]: "accumulating fund" — Reg. 307(1); "amount", "annuity" — ITA 248(1); "benefit on death" — Reg. 310; "cash surrender value" — ITA 148(9), Reg. 310; "consequence of the death" — ITA 248(8); "coverage" — Reg. 310; "disposed" — ITA 248(1)"disposition"; "fund value of the coverage" — Reg. 310; "individual", "insurer" — ITA 248(1); "life annuity contract" — Reg. 301(1), (2); "life insurance policy" — ITA 138(12), 248(1); "life insurer" — ITA 248(1); "mortality gain" — Reg. 308(2); "mortality loss" — Reg. 308(3); "person" — ITA 248(1); "policy loan" — ITA 148(9), Reg. 310; "probability" — Reg. 308(1.1); "taxation year" — ITA 249; "taxpayer" — ITA 248(1).

309. Prescribed premiums and prescribed increases — (1)

For the purposes of this section and section 306, and of subsection 89(2) of the Act, a premium at any time under a life insurance policy is a **"prescribed premium"** if the total amount of one or more premiums paid at that time under the policy exceeds the amount of premium that, under the policy, was scheduled to be paid at that time and that was fixed and determined on or before December 1,

1982, adjusted for such of the following transactions and events that have occurred after that date in respect of the policy:

(a) a change in underwriting class;

(b) a change in premium due to a change in frequency of premium payments within a year that does not alter the present value, at the beginning of the year, of the total premiums to be paid under the policy in the year;

(c) an addition or deletion of accidental death or guaranteed purchase option benefits or disability benefits that provide for annuity payments or waiver of premiums;

(d) a premium adjustment as a result of interest, mortality or expense considerations, or of a change in the benefit on death under the policy relating to an increase in the Consumer Price Index (as published by Statistics Canada under the authority of the *Statistics Act*) where such adjustment

(i) is made by the life insurer on a class basis pursuant to the policy's terms as they read on December 1, 1982, and

(ii) is not made as a result of the exercise of a conversion privilege under the policy;

(e) a change arising from the provision of an additional benefit on death under a participating life insurance policy, as defined in subsection 138(12) of the Act, as, on account or in lieu of payment of, or in satisfaction of

(i) policy dividends or other distributions of the life insurer's income from its participating life insurance business, or

(ii) interest earned on policy dividends that are held on deposit by the life insurer;

(f) redating lapsed policies, if the policy was reinstated not later than 60 days after the end of the calendar year in which the lapse occurred, or redating for policy loan indebtedness;

(g) a change in premium due to a correction of erroneous information contained in the application for the policy;

(h) payment of a premium after its due date, or payment of a premium no more than 30 days before its due date, as established on or before December 1, 1982; and

(i) the payment of interest described in paragraph (a) of the definition "premium" in subsection 148(9) of the Act.

Related Provisions: Reg. 309.1 — Income from participating life insurance businesses.

Notes: Reg. 309(1)(e)(i) amended by 2002-2013 technical bill (Part 5 — technical), for taxation years that begin after Oct. 2011, to change "participating life insurance business as determined under section 2402" to "participating life insurance business". (See now Reg. 309.1.)

Reg. 309(1) opening words amended by P.C. 2011-936 to delete reference to ITA 12.2(9), for annuity contracts and life insurance policies last acquired after 1989. Reg. 309(1)(e), (f) and (i) amended by P.C. 2011-936 to update ITA references due to R.S.C. 1985 renumbering, effective March 1994.

(2) For the purposes of subsections 12.2(9) and 89(2) of the Act, a **"prescribed increase"** in a benefit on death under a life insurance policy has occurred at any time where the amount of the benefit on death under the policy at that time exceeds the amount of the benefit on death at that time under the policy that was fixed and determined on or before December 1, 1982, adjusted for such of the following transactions and events that have occurred after that date in respect of the policy:

(a) an increase resulting from a change described in paragraph (1)(e);

(b) a change as a result of interest, mortality or expense considerations, or an increase in the Consumer Price Index (as published by Statistics Canada under the authority of the *Statistics Act*) where such change is made by the life insurer on a class basis pursuant to the policy's terms as they read on December 1, 1982;

(c) an increase in consequence of the prepayment of premiums (other than prescribed premiums) under the policy where such increase does not exceed the aggregate of the premiums that would otherwise have been paid;

(d) an increase in respect of a policy for which

(i) the benefit on death was, at December 1, 1982, a specific mathematical function of the policy's cash surrender value or factors including the policy's cash surrender value, and

(ii) that function has not changed since that date,

unless any part of such increase is attributable to a prescribed premium paid in respect of a policy or to income earned on such a premium; and

(e) an increase that is granted by the life insurer on a class basis without consideration and not pursuant to any term of the contract.

(3) For the purposes of subsections (1) and (2), a life insurance policy that is issued as a result of the exercise of a renewal privilege provided under the terms of another policy as they read on December 1, 1982 shall be deemed to be a continuation of that other policy.

(4) For the purposes of subsection (2), a life insurance policy that is issued as a result of the exercise of a conversion privilege provided under the terms of another policy as they read on December 1, 1982 shall be deemed to be a continuation of that other policy except that any portion of the policy relating to the portion of the benefit on death, immediately before the conversion, that arose as a consequence of an event occurring after December 1, 1982 and described in paragraph (1)(e) shall be deemed to be a separate life insurance policy issued at the time of the conversion.

Definitions [Reg. 309]: "amount", "annuity" — ITA 248(1); "benefit on death" — Reg. 310; "Canada" — ITA 255, *Interpretation Act* 35(1); "cash surrender value" — ITA 148(9), Reg. 310; "continuation" — Reg. 309(3), (4); "dividend" — ITA 248(1); "income from its participating life insurance business" — Reg. 309.1; "insurer", "life insurance business" — ITA 248(1); "life insurance policy" — ITA 138(12), 248(1); "life insurer" — ITA 248(1); "policy loan" — ITA 148(9), Reg. 310; "prescribed" — ITA 248(1); "prescribed increase" — Reg. 309(2); "prescribed premium" — Reg. 309(1).

Interpretation Bulletins: IT-87R2: Policyholders' income from life insurance policies.

309.1 Income from participating life insurance businesses — For the purpose of subparagraph 309(1)(e)(i), in computing a life insurer's income for a taxation year from its participating life insurance business carried on in Canada,

(a) there shall be included the amount determined by the formula

$$A \times B/C$$

where

A is the insurer's gross Canadian life investment income (in this section as defined in subsection 2400(1)) for the year,

B is the total of

(i) the insurer's mean maximum tax actuarial reserve (in this section as defined in subsection 2400(1)) for the year in respect of participating life insurance policies in Canada, and

(ii) ½ of the total of

(A) all amounts on deposit with the insurer as at the end of the year in respect of policies described in subparagraph (i), and

(B) all amounts on deposit with the insurer as at the end of the immediately preceding taxation year in respect of policies described in subparagraph (i), and

C the total of all amounts, each of which is

(i) the insurer's mean maximum tax actuarial reserve for the year in respect of a class of life insurance policies in Canada, or

(ii) ½ of the total of

(A) all amounts on deposit with the insurer as at the end of the year in respect of a class of policies described in subparagraph (i), and

(B) all amounts on deposit with the insurer as at the end of the immediately preceding taxation year in respect of a class of policies described in subparagraph (i);

(b) there shall be included

(i) the insurer's maximum tax actuarial reserve for the immediately preceding taxation year in respect of participating life insurance policies in Canada, and

(ii) the maximum amount deductible by the insurer under subparagraph 138(3)(a)(ii) of the Act in computing its income for the immediately preceding taxation year in respect of participating life insurance policies in Canada;

(c) there shall not be included any amount in respect of the insurer's participating life insurance policies in Canada that was deducted under subparagraph 138(3)(a)(i) or (ii) of the Act in computing its income for the immediately preceding taxation year;

(d) subject to paragraph (a),

(i) there shall not be included any amount

(A) as a reserve that was deducted under paragraph 20(1)(l) of the Act in computing the insurer's income for the immediately preceding taxation year, or

(B) that was included in determining the insurer's gross Canadian life investment income for the year, and

(ii) no deduction shall be made in respect of any amount

(A) taken into account in determining the insurer's gross Canadian life investment income for the year, or

(B) deductible under paragraph 20(1)(l) of the Act in computing the insurer's income for the year;

(e) there shall be deducted

(i) the insurer's maximum tax actuarial reserve for the year in respect of participating life insurance policies in Canada, and

(ii) the maximum amount deductible by the insurer under subparagraph 138(3)(a)(ii) of the Act in computing its income for the year in respect of participating life insurance policies in Canada;

(f) no deduction shall be made in respect of any amount deductible under subparagraph 138(3)(a)(iii) of the Act in computing the insurer's income for the year;

(g) except as otherwise provided in paragraph (e), no deduction shall be made in respect of a reserve deductible under subparagraph 138(3)(a)(i) or (ii) of the Act in computing the insurer's income for the year; and

(h) except as otherwise provided in this section, the provisions of the Act relating to the computation of income from a source shall apply.

Notes: Reg. 309.1 added by 2002-2013 technical bill (Part 5 — technical), for taxation years that begin after Oct. 2011, except that if a taxpayer has deducted an amount under ITA 138(3)(a)(iv) as it applied to the taxpayer's last taxation year that began before Nov. 1, 2011, then for the taxpayer's first taxation year that begins after Oct, 31, 2011 read Reg. 309.1(b) differently.

Definitions [Reg. 309.1]: "amount" — ITA 248(1); "Canada" — ITA 255, *Interpretation Act* 35(1); "gross Canadian life investment income" — Reg. 2400(1); "insurer", "life insurance business" — ITA 248(1); "life insurance policy" — ITA 138(12), 248(1); "life insurer" — ITA 248(1); "mean maximum tax actuarial reserve" — Reg. 2400(1); "participating life insurance policy" — ITA 138(12); "taxation year" — ITA 249; "taxpayer" — ITA 248(1).

310. Interpretation — The following definitions apply for the purposes of this section and sections 300, 301 and 304 to 309.

"adjusted purchase price", of a taxpayer's interest in an annuity contract at any time, means, subject to subsections 300(3) and (4), the amount that would be determined at that time in respect of the interest under the definition "adjusted cost basis" in subsection 148(9) of the Act if the formula in that definition were read without reference to K.

Notes: Definition added by 2014 budget bill #2, effective Dec. 16, 2014.

"amount payable" has the same meaning as in subsection 138(12) of the Act.

"benefit on death" has the same meaning as in subsection 1401(3).

Notes: Definition amended by 2014 budget bill #2, effective Dec. 16, 2014.

"cash surrender value" has the same meaning as in subsection 148(9) of the Act.

"coverage", under a life insurance policy,

(a) for the purposes of section 306, means all life insurance (other than a fund value benefit) under the policy in respect of a specific life, or two or more specific lives jointly insured; and

(b) for the purposes of sections 307 and 308, has the same meaning as in subsection 1401(3).

Notes: Definition added by 2014 budget bill #2, effective Dec. 16, 2014.

"endowment date", of an exemption test policy, means

(a) where the exemption test policy is issued in respect of a life insurance policy issued before 2017, the later of

(i) 10 years after the date of issue of the life insurance policy, and

(ii) the first policy anniversary that is on or after the day on which the individual whose life is insured under the life insurance policy would, if the individual survived, attain the age of 85 years, as defined under the terms of the policy; and

(b) where the exemption test policy is issued in respect of a coverage under a life insurance policy issued after 2016,

(i) if two or more lives are jointly insured under the coverage, the date that would be determined under subparagraph (ii) using the equivalent single age, determined on the coverage's date of issue and in accordance with accepted actuarial principles and practices, that reasonably approximates the mortality rates of those lives, and

(ii) in any other case, the later of

(A) the earlier of

(I) 15 years after the date of issue of the exemption test policy, and

(II) the first policy anniversary that is on or after the day on which the individual whose life is insured under the coverage would, if the individual survived, attain the age of 105 years, as defined under the terms of the policy, and

(B) the first policy anniversary that is on or after the day on which the individual whose life is insured under the coverage would, if the individual survived, attain the age of 90 years, as defined under the terms of the policy.

Notes: For the meaning of "issued before 2017" in para. (a), see Notes to ITA 148(11).

Definition added by 2014 budget bill #2, effective Dec. 16, 2014.

"fund value benefit" has the same meaning as in subsection 1401(3).

Notes: Definition added by 2014 budget bill #2, effective Dec. 16, 2014.

"fund value of a coverage" has the same meaning as in subsection 1401(3).

Notes: Definition added by 2014 budget bill #2, effective Dec. 16, 2014.

"pay period", of an exemption test policy, means

(a) where the exemption test policy is issued in respect of a life insurance policy issued before 2017,

(i) if on the date of issue of the exemption test policy, the individual whose life is insured has attained the age of 66 years, as defined under the terms of the policy, but not the age of 75 years, as defined under the terms of the policy, the period that starts on that date and that ends after the number of years obtained when the number of years by which the age of the individual exceeds 65 years, as defined under the terms of the policy, is subtracted from 20,

(ii) if on the date of issue of the exemption test policy, the individual whose life is insured has attained the age of 75 years, as defined under the terms of the policy, the 10-year period that starts on that date, and

(iii) in any other case, the 20-year period that starts on the date of issue of the exemption test policy; and

(b) where the exemption test policy is issued in respect of a coverage under a life insurance policy issued after 2016,

(i) subject to subparagraph (ii), if the individual whose life is insured under the coverage would, if the individual survived, attain the age of 105 years, as defined under the terms of the policy, within the eight-year period that starts on the date of issue of the exemption test policy, the period that starts on that date and that ends on the first policy anniversary that is on or after the day on which the individual would, if the individual survived, attain the age of 105 years, as defined under the terms of the policy,

(ii) if two or more lives are jointly insured under the coverage and an individual of an age equal to the equivalent single age on the date of the issue of the coverage would, if the individual survived, attain the age of 105 years, as defined under the terms of the policy, within the eight-year period that starts on the date of issue of the exemption test policy, the period that starts on that date and that ends on the first policy anniversary that is on or after the day on which the individual would, if the individual survived, attain the age of 105 years, as defined under the terms of the policy, and

(iii) in any other case, the eight-year period that starts on the date of issue of the exemption test policy.

Notes: For the meaning of "issued before 2017" in para. (a), see Notes to ITA 148(11).

Definition added by 2014 budget bill #2, effective Dec. 16, 2014.

"policy anniversary" includes, in the case of a life insurance policy that is in existence throughout a calendar year and that would not otherwise have a policy anniversary for the calendar year, the end of the calendar year.

Related Provisions: Reg. 1401(3)"policy anniversary" — Definition applies to Reg. 1401.

"policy loan" has the same meaning as in subsection 148(9) of the Act.

"proceeds of the disposition" has the same meaning as in subsection 148(9) of the Act.

"tax anniversary date", in relation to an annuity contract, means the second anniversary date of the contract to occur after October 22, 1968.

Notes [Reg. 310]: The Aug. 23, 2013 draft regulations proposed to also add a definition of "tax avoidance policy", which has been dropped.

Definitions in Reg. 310 amended to update ITA references (due to R.S.C. 1985 renumbering) by P.C. 2011-936, effective March 1994 ("life insurance policy" and "life insurance policy in Canada" deleted, as these terms are now in ITA 248(1)).

Definitions [Reg. 310]: "amount" — ITA 248(1); "amount payable" — ITA 138(12), Reg. 310; "annuity" — ITA 248(1); "calendar year" — *Interpretation Act* 37(1)(a); "coverage" — Reg. 310; "dividend", "individual", "insurer" — ITA 248(1); "life insurance policy" — ITA 138(12), 248(1); "Minister" — ITA 248(1); "policy anniversary" — Reg. 310; "taxpayer" — ITA 248(1); "writing" — *Interpretation Act* 35(1).

PART IV — [400–415] TAXABLE INCOME EARNED IN A PROVINCE BY A CORPORATION

Notes: Part IV allocates a corporation's income among provinces. For the equivalent rules for individuals (including trusts), see Part XXVI (Reg. 2600–2607).

See Horner & Haber, *Taxation of Private Corporations and their Shareholders* (ctf.ca, 5th ed., 2020), chap. 18; "Interprovincial Tax Planning by Corporate Groups", in *Tax Expenditures and Evaluations 2014* (Dept. of Finance), pp. 71-96; Auger & Bélanger,

"Interprovincial Allocation of Income", 1999 Cdn Tax Foundation conference report, 10:1-43; Boehmer & Landau, "Update on Capital Tax and Interprovincial Tax Planning", 2002 conference report, 24:13-21; Matthews, "Water Runs Downhill: Interprovincial Tax Planning", 2004 conference report, 25:1-50; Provenzano & Mapa, "Provincial Income Allocation", 13(12) *Canadian Tax Highlights [CTH]* (ctf.ca) 1 (Dec. 2005); Forget, "Strategies and Issues Relating to the Transfer of Businesses or Assets Within a Corporate Group", 2007 conference report at 7:13-21; Chan & Taylor, "Provincial General Anti-Avoidance Rules", 2008 conference report, 7:1-42; Pantry, "The Role of the Provincial General Anti-avoidance Rules", 2013 conference report, 36:1-25; Robson, "Provincial Income Allocation", 24(8) *CTH* 2-3 (Aug. 2016).

CRA targets plans that shift income to low-tax provinces such as Alberta: *Income Tax Technical News* 38; 2007 conference report at 4:2-3. At the 2008 conference (*Technical News* 41; conference report p. 3:18), CRA stated that before issuing a loss consolidation ruling (see Notes to ITA 111(5)), Rulings will "recommend that practitioners obtain comfort from provincial tax authorities to minimize the risk of double taxation". CRA can rule that provincial GAAR (other than Quebec or Alberta) is not violated, e.g. VIEWS doc 2013-0504301R3 (loss consolidation).

CRA and various provinces have entered into Memoranda of Understanding to avoid double tax by resolving disputes between jurisdictions. A province proposing to adjust a taxpayer's provincial allocation of taxable income or taxable capital will provide other affected provinces with information to review the merits of the proposed adjustments, which are not processed without all involved provinces' concurrence. See also VIEWS docs 2002-0156735, 2020-0852241C6 [2020 APFF q.12] (explains the arbitration process; taxpayer can make submissions).

The Allocation Review Committee (ARC) reviews these issues. As of 2020 its members are: Gord Parr, Jason Beaulac, John Parker, Cornelis (Kees) Rystenbil (all CRA), and officials from the provinces. The agenda and minutes of the meetings were almost entirely suppressed from disclosure under the *Access to Information Act*. There is also a CRA-Finance Coordinating Committee on Income Allocation (CCIA), which includes members from each province and territory, and has replaced the Provincial Income Allocation Task Force. As of fall 2020, its federal members are Tracy Annett (Director, Legislative Amendments Division, 613-670-9568) and Michelle Adkins (Finance). Its minutes were also almost entirely suppressed. See also the Provincial Income Allocation Newsletters.

I.T. Technical News: 38 (interprovincial tax planning arrangements); 41 (loss consolidation and provincial GAAR; provincial income allocation).

CRA Audit Manual: 12.14.0: Multiple jurisdictions and allocation of income.

400. Interpretation — (1) ["Taxable income..."] — In applying the definition "taxable income earned in the year in a province" in subsection 124(4) of the Act for a corporation's taxation year

(a) the prescribed rules referred to in that definition are the rules in this Part; and

(b) the amount determined under those prescribed rules means the total of all amounts each of which is the taxable income of the corporation earned in the taxation year in a particular province as determined under this Part.

Notes: Reg. 400(1) amended by 2008 budget bill #2, for 2009 and later tax years.

CRA Audit Manual: 12.14.2: Multiple jurisdictions — definitions.

(1.1) [Repealed]

Notes: Reg. 400(1.1) repealed by 2013 budget bill #1, for taxation years that begin after March 20, 2013 (definition of "taxable income" in para. (a) moved to Reg. 413(1)(b), and para. (b) repealed consequential on elimination of international banking centres in ITA 33.1).

Reg. 400(1.1) added by 2008 budget bill #2, for 2009 and later taxation years. Para. (b) and Reg. 413.1 implemented §4.1(b) of the *Canada-Ontario Memorandum of Agreement Concerning a Single Administration of Ontario Corporate Tax* (Oct. 2006) (reproduced here in the 35th ed.).

(2) [Permanent establishment] — For the purposes of this Part, "permanent establishment" in respect of a corporation means a fixed place of business of the corporation, including an office, a branch, a mine, an oil well, a farm, a timberland, a factory, a workshop or a warehouse, and

(a) where the corporation does not have any fixed place of business it means the principal place in which the corporation's business is conducted;

(b) where a corporation carries on business through an employee or agent, established in a particular place, who has general authority to contract for his employer or principal or who has a stock of merchandise owned by his employer or principal from which he regularly fills orders which he receives, the corporation shall be deemed to have a permanent establishment in that place;

(c) an insurance corporation is deemed to have a permanent establishment in each province and country in which the corporation is registered or licensed to do business;

(d) where a corporation, otherwise having a permanent establishment in Canada, owns land in a province, such land shall be deemed to be a permanent establishment;

(e) where a corporation uses substantial machinery or equipment in a particular place at any time in a taxation year it shall be deemed to have a permanent establishment in that place;

(e.1) if, but for this paragraph, a corporation would not have a permanent establishment, the corporation is deemed to have a permanent establishment at the place designated in its incorporating documents or bylaws as its head office or registered office;

(f) the fact that a corporation has business dealings through a commission agent, broker or other independent agent or maintains an office solely for the purchase of merchandise shall not of itself be held to mean that the corporation has a permanent establishment; and

(g) the fact that a corporation has a subsidiary controlled corporation in a place or a subsidiary controlled corporation engaged in trade or business in a place shall not of itself be held to mean that the corporation is operating a permanent establishment in that place.

Related Provisions: Reg. 5906 — Carrying on business in a country.

Notes: See Notes to Canada-U.S. Tax Treaty:Art. V:2 for case law on the meaning of "permanent establishment" (PE). A non-resident corp with no PE in Ontario is no longer subject to Ontario corporate tax: VIEWS doc 2011-0414821E5.

For analysis of particular cases see VIEWS docs 9832857, 2010-0370221E5, 2012-0460191E5. A server could be a PE: 2012-0435401E5. Employee X's home office is normally not a PE unless X has general authority to contract for the employer: 2010-0378421I7, 2015-062082117.

A placement agency placing employees at a location is normally not a PE: VIEWS doc 2011-039533117.

CRA argued in *Inwest Investments*, 2015 BCSC 1375, para. 136, that a place of "business" in Reg. 400(2)(a) includes earning income from property and capital gains. The Court did not have to resolve the issue beyond finding Inwest's position reasonable, but suggested (para. 181) that CRA was wrong.

"Agent" in Reg. 400(2)(b) was interpreted broadly (IT-177R), but in light of *Merchant Law Group*, 2010 FCA 206, the CRA now uses the *legal* meaning of agent, which requires the ability to contract on behalf of the principal, for taxation years ending after 2011: VIEWS doc 2011-0426561C6 [2011 CTF conf. q.13, p.4:9-10].

"Land" in Reg. 400(2)(b) includes buildings: see ITA 70(5.2) Notes.

"Uses substantial machinery or equipment" (Reg. 400(2)(e)) does not require the corp to *own* the equipment: IT-177R2 para. 6; *No. 630* (1959), 22 Tax A.B.C. 91. The Supreme Court of Canada stated in *Sunbeam Corp.*, [1962] C.T.C. 657: " 'substantial' is intended to mean substantial in size and the subsection was intended only to apply to machinery and equipment such as is used by contractors or builders in the course of their operations . . . to come within the subsection, the machinery or equipment would have to be used by the taxpayer for the purpose for which it was created". Equipment brought by a sports team to a visitors' locker room is not "substantial": *Toronto Blue Jays*, 2005 CarswellOnt 504 (Ont CA). CRA *Income Tax Technical News* 41 and *Provincial Income Allocation Newsletter* 2 state that 400(2)(e) applies only after 30 continuous days (one contract or project) or 90 total days (all contracts or projects) in a 12-month period. See also VIEWS doc 2010-036260117; GST/HST ruling 133588r (test for Reg. 400(2)(e) is 30 continuous days or 90 days in a 12-month period).

Reg. 400(2)(e.1) added by 2008 budget bill #2, for 2009 and later tax years. It implements §4.1(a)(ii) of the *Canada-Ontario Memorandum of Agreement Concerning a Single Administration of Ontario Corporate Tax* (Oct. 2006) (reproduced here in the 35th ed.). This amendment "significantly alters the interaction between the federal and provincial tax systems": see Nathan Boidman & Michael Kandev, "Reg 400 Surprise", 17(3) *Canadian Tax Highlights* (ctf.ca) 2 (March 2009).

Reg. 400(2) amended by P.C. 1994-139, effective 10pm EDST, April 26, 1989, to no longer apply for purposes of ITA 112(2). "Permanent establishment" for purposes of that provision is now defined in Reg. 8201.

Interpretation Bulletins: IT-177R2: Permanent establishment of a corporation in a province; IT-393R2: Election re tax on rents and timber royalties — non-residents.

I.T. Technical News: 2 (permanent establishment in province through an agent); 33 (permanent establishment — the *Dudney* case update); 41 (provincial income allocation).

Provincial Income Allocation Newsletters: 2 (interpretation of "at any time in a taxation year" for Reg. 400(2)(e)).

CRA Audit Manual: 12.14.3: Permanent establishment; 15.2.15: Tax calculations; 15.6.0: Permanent establishment.

Definitions [Reg. 400]: "amount", "business" — ITA 248(1); "Canada" — ITA 255, *Interpretation Act* 35(1); "corporation" — ITA 248(1), *Interpretation Act* 35(1); "employee", "employer", "insurance corporation" — ITA 248(1); "land" — see ITA 70(5.2) Notes; "office" — ITA 248(1); "permanent establishment" — Reg. 400(2); "prescribed" — ITA 248(1); "province" — *Interpretation Act* 35(1); "subsidiary controlled corporation" — ITA 248(1); "taxable income" — Reg. 413(1)(b); "taxable income earned in Canada" — ITA 248(1); "taxation year" — ITA 249.

Forms: T2 Sched. 366: New Brunswick corporation tax calculation; T2 Sched. 383: Manitoba corporation tax calculation; T2 Sched. 443: Yukon corporation tax calculation; T2 Sched. 500: Ontario corporation tax calculation.

401. Computation of taxable income — This Part applies to determine the amount of taxable income of a corporation earned in a taxation year in a particular province.

Notes: Reg. 401 amended by 2008 budget bill #2, effective for 2009 and later taxation years. (The changes were non-substantive.)

Definitions [Reg. 401]: "amount" — ITA 248(1); "corporation" — ITA 248(1), *Interpretation Act* 35(1); "province" — *Interpretation Act* 35(1); "taxable income" — Reg. 413(1)(b); "taxation year" — ITA 249.

Forms: T2 Sched. 346: Nova Scotia corporation tax calculation; T2 Sched. 383: Manitoba corporation tax calculation; T2 Sched. 384: Manitoba co-operative education tax credit; T2 Sched. 385: Manitoba odour control tax credit; T2 Sched. 411: Saskatchewan corporation tax calculation; T2 Sched. 427: B.C. corporation tax calculation.

402. General rules — (1) Where, in a taxation year, a corporation had a permanent establishment in a particular province and had no permanent establishment outside that province, the whole of its taxable income for the year shall be deemed to have been earned therein.

(2) Where, in a taxation year, a corporation had no permanent establishment in a particular province, no part of its taxable income for the year shall be deemed to have been earned therein.

(3) Except as otherwise provided, where, in a taxation year, a corporation had a permanent establishment in a province and a permanent establishment outside that province, the amount of its taxable income that shall be deemed to have been earned in the year in the province is

(a) in any case other than a case specified in paragraph (b) or (c), $\frac{1}{2}$ the aggregate of

(i) that proportion of its taxable income for the year that the gross revenue for the year reasonably attributable to the permanent establishment in the province is of its total gross revenue for the year, and

(ii) that proportion of its taxable income for the year that the aggregate of the salaries and wages paid in the year by the corporation to employees of the permanent establishment in the province is of the aggregate of all salaries and wages paid in the year by the corporation;

(b) in any case where the gross revenue for the year of the corporation is nil, that proportion of its taxable income for the year that the aggregate of the salaries and wages paid in the year by the corporation to employees of the permanent establishment in the province is of the aggregate of all salaries and wages paid in the year by the corporation; and

(c) in any case where the aggregate of the salaries and wages paid in the year by the corporation is nil, that proportion of its taxable income for the year that the gross revenue for the year reasonably attributable to the permanent establishment in the province is of its total gross revenue for the year.

Related Provisions: Reg. 402(4)–(8) — Interpretation; Reg. 413(2) — "Total gross revenue" for non-resident corp.

Notes [Reg. 402(3)]: See Notes at beginning of Reg. Part IV. "Salaries and wages" are considered to include all taxable benefits including stock option benefits (even though they are reduced by ITA 110(1)(d)): *Provincial Income Allocation Newsletter* 4.

"Gross revenue" is different from financial-statement gross revenue, and does not include amounts in respect of expenditures such as volume rebates or government financial assistance (this is a change from 2010-038216117): VIEWS doc 2013-051492117. CRA will adjust it to reflect transfer-pricing revenue adjustments: 2013-050738117.

CRA's view is that "salaries and wages" include non-resident employees' salary at PEs outside Canada, and that ITA s. 8 expenses are not deducted despite ITA 248(1)"salary or wages": VIEWS doc 2013-0506801I7 [Hickey, "Provincial Income Allocation", 22(7) *Canadian Tax Highlights* (ctf.ca) 11 (July 2014)].

A corp in a joint venture should include in the Reg. 402(3)(a)(ii) calculation its share of the JV employee salaries and wages it pays directly: 2005-0115041I7, but only if it is contributing employees and is legally responsible for paying them: 2013-0508121I7. A corporate partner should include its share of the gross revenue and salaries and wages of the partnership (2011-0394091I7), including for a SIFT partnership (2012-0460511E5). Where a franchisor takes over one of its franchisees, see 2012-0455731E5.

CRA's view is that the assessment deadline for reallocating income is extended by ITA 152(4)(b)(iii) if it relates to a transaction with a related non-resident: 2016-0651411I7.

Interpretation Bulletins: IT-177R2: Permanent establishment of a corporation in a province.

Provincial Income Allocation Newsletters: 3 (allocation of leasing revenue); 4 (salaries and wages — inclusion of taxable benefits).

Forms: T2S-TC: Tax calculation supplementary — corporations.

(4) [Attribution to permanent establishment] — For the purpose of determining the gross revenue for the year reasonably attributable to a permanent establishment in a province or country other than Canada, within the meaning of subsection (3), the following rules shall apply:

(a) where the destination of a shipment of merchandise to a customer to whom the merchandise is sold is in the particular province or country, the gross revenue derived therefrom shall be attributable to the permanent establishment in the province or country;

(b) except as provided in paragraph (c), where the destination of a shipment of merchandise to a customer to whom the merchandise is sold is in a province or country other than Canada in which the taxpayer has no permanent establishment, if the person negotiating the sale may reasonably be regarded as being attached to the permanent establishment in the particular province or country, the gross revenue derived therefrom shall be attributable to that permanent establishment;

(c) where the destination of a shipment of merchandise to a customer to whom the merchandise is sold is in a country other than Canada in which the taxpayer has no permanent establishment,

(i) if the merchandise was produced or manufactured or produced and manufactured, entirely in the particular province by the taxpayer, the gross revenue derived therefrom shall be attributable to the permanent establishment in the province, or

(ii) if the merchandise was produced or manufactured, or produced and manufactured, partly in the particular province and partly in another place by the taxpayer, the gross revenue derived therefrom attributable to the permanent establishment in the province shall be that proportion thereof that the salaries and wages paid in the year to employees of the permanent establishment in the province where the merchandise was partly produced or manufactured (or partly produced and manufactured) is of the aggregate of the salaries and wages paid in the year to employees of the permanent establishments where the merchandise was produced or manufactured (or produced and manufactured);

(d) where a customer to whom merchandise is sold instructs that shipment be made to some other person and the customer's office with which the sale was negotiated is located in the particular province or country, the gross revenue derived therefrom shall be attributable to the permanent establishment in the province or country;

(e) except as provided in paragraph (f), where a customer to whom merchandise is sold instructs that shipment be made to some other person and the customer's office with which the sale was negotiated is located in a province or country other than Canada in which the taxpayer has no permanent establishment, if the person negotiating the sale may reasonably be regarded as being attached to the permanent establishment in the particular province or country, the gross revenue derived therefrom shall be attributable to that permanent establishment;

(f) where a customer to whom merchandise is sold instructs that shipment be made to some other person and the customer's office with which the sale was negotiated is located in a country other than Canada in which the taxpayer has no permanent establishment,

(i) if the merchandise was produced or manufactured, or produced and manufactured, entirely in the particular province by the taxpayer, the gross revenue derived therefrom shall be attributable to the permanent establishment in the province, or

(ii) if the merchandise was produced or manufactured, or produced and manufactured, partly in the particular province and partly in another place by the taxpayer, the gross revenue derived therefrom attributable to the permanent establishment in the province shall be that proportion thereof that the salaries and wages paid in the year to employees of the permanent establishment in the province where the merchandise was partly produced or manufactured (or partly produced and manufactured) is of the aggregate of the salaries and wages paid in the year to employees of the permanent establishments where the merchandise was produced or manufactured (or produced and manufactured);

(g) where gross revenue is derived from services rendered in the particular province or country, the gross revenue shall be attributable to the permanent establishment in the province or country;

(h) where gross revenue is derived from services rendered in a province or country other than Canada in which the taxpayer has no permanent establishment, if the person negotiating the contract may reasonably be regarded as being attached to the permanent establishment of the taxpayer in the particular province or country, the gross revenue shall be attributable to that permanent establishment;

(i) where standing timber or the right to cut standing timber is sold and the timber limit on which the timber is standing is in the particular province or country, the gross revenue from such sale shall be attributable to the permanent establishment of the taxpayer in the province or country; and

(j) gross revenue which arises from leasing land owned by the taxpayer in a province and which is included in computing its income under Part I of the Act shall be attributable to the permanent establishment, if any, of the taxpayer in the province where the land is situated.

Notes: See Notes at beginning of Reg. Part IV. For interpretation see VIEWS docs 2004-0106031E5 (para. (j)), 2011-0430811E5 (para. (c)). For the meaning of "derived" see Notes to ITA 18.1(12). "Land" in Reg. 402(4)(j) includes buildings: see ITA 70(5.2) Notes.

Interpretation Bulletins: IT-177R2: Permanent establishment of a corporation in a province.

Provincial Income Allocation Newsletters: 3 (allocation of leasing revenue); 4 (salaries and wages — inclusion of taxable benefits).

(4.1) For the purposes of subsections (3) and (4), where, in a taxation year,

(a) the destination of a shipment of merchandise to a customer to whom the merchandise is sold by a corporation is in a country other than Canada or the customer to whom merchandise is sold by a corporation instructs that the shipment of merchandise be made by the corporation to another person and the customer's office with which the sale was negotiated is located in a country other than Canada,

(b) the corporation has a permanent establishment in the other country, and

(c) the corporation is not subject to taxation on its income under the laws of the other country, or its gross revenue derived from the sale is not included in computing the income or profit or other base for income or profits taxation by the other country, because of

(i) the provisions of any taxing statute of the other country, or

(ii) the operation of any tax treaty or convention between Canada and the other country,

the following rules apply:

(d) with respect to the gross revenue derived from the sale,

(i) paragraphs 4(a) and (d) do not apply,

(ii) that portion of paragraph 4(c) preceding subparagraph (i) thereof shall be read as follows:

"(c) where the destination of a shipment of merchandise to a customer to whom the merchandise is sold is in a country other than Canada," and

(iii) that portion of paragraph 4(f) preceding subparagraph (i) thereof shall be read as follows:

"(f) where a customer to whom the merchandise is sold instructs that shipment be made to some other person and the customer's office with which the sale was negotiated is located in a country other than Canada,"; and

(e) for the purposes of subparagraph (3)(a)(ii), paragraph (3)(b) and subparagraphs (4)(c)(ii) and (f)(ii), salaries and wages paid in the year to employees of any permanent establishment of the corporation located in that other country shall be deemed to be nil.

Notes: Reg. 402(4.1) added by P.C. 1994-662, for tax years that begin in 1993 or later (or 1992 by election). It alleviates the problem resulting from Reg. 402(4) where goods are shipped to a foreign destination, the foreign jurisdiction does not impose tax, and the provincial taxing statutes treat the income as having been earned in the province, leading to double taxation. Reg. 402(4.1) ensures that the income neither escapes provincial taxation nor is double-taxed.

For interpretation of Reg. 402(4.1) see VIEWS docs 2005-0112891E5, 2012-0470361I7. For the meaning of "derived" in (c) and (d), see Notes to ITA 18.1(12).

Provincial Income Allocation Newsletters: 4 (salaries and wages — inclusion of taxable benefits).

(5) For the purposes of subsection (3), "gross revenue" does not include interest on bonds, debentures or mortgages, dividends on shares of capital stock, or rentals or royalties from property that is not used in connection with the principal business operations of the corporation.

Notes: For interpretation of Reg. 402(5) see VIEWS doc 2004-0106031E5 and Provincial Income Allocation Newsletter # 1.

I.T. Technical News: 41 (provincial income allocation).

Provincial Income Allocation Newsletters: 1 (exclusion of interest should be interpreted broadly).

(6) For the purposes of subsection (3), where part of the corporation's operations were conducted in partnership with one or more other persons

(a) the corporation's gross revenue for the year, and

(b) the salaries and wages paid in the year by the corporation,

shall include, in respect of those operations, only that proportion of

(c) the total gross revenue of the partnership for its fiscal period ending in or coinciding with the year, and

(d) the total salaries and wages paid by the partnership in its fiscal period ending in or coinciding with the year,

respectively, that

(e) the corporation's share of the income or loss of the partnership for the fiscal period ending in or coinciding with the year,

is of

(f) the total income or loss of the partnership for the fiscal period ending in or coinciding with the year.

Notes: For interpretation of Reg. 402(6) see VIEWS doc 2005-0112891E5.

Provincial Income Allocation Newsletters: 4 (salaries and wages — inclusion of taxable benefits).

(7) Where a corporation pays a fee to another person under an agreement pursuant to which that other person or employees of that other person perform services for the corporation that would normally be performed by employees of the corporation, the fee so paid shall be deemed to be salary paid in the year by the corporation and that part of the fee that may reasonably be regarded as payment in respect of services rendered at a particular permanent establishment of the corporation shall be deemed to be salary paid to an employee of that permanent establishment.

Notes: For interpretation of Reg. 402(7) see VIEWS doc 2013-0477571E5.

Income Tax Folios: S4-F15-C1: Manufacturing and processing [replaces IT-147R3].

(8) For the purposes of subsection (7), a fee does not include a commission paid to a person who is not an employee of the corporation.

Definitions [Reg. 402]: "amount", "business" — ITA 248(1); "Canada" — ITA 255, *Interpretation Act* 35(1); "corporation" — ITA 248(1), *Interpretation Act* 35(1); "dividend", "employee" — ITA 248(1); "fee" — Reg. 402(8); "fiscal period" — ITA 249.1; "gross revenue" — Reg. 402(4), (5), (6); "land" — see ITA 70(5.2) Notes; "office" — ITA 248(1); "partnership" — see ITA 96(1) Notes; "permanent establishment" — Reg. 400(2); "person", "property" — ITA 248(1); "province" — *Interpretation Act* 35(1); "salaries and wages paid in the year" — Reg. 413(1)(a); "share", "tax treaty" — ITA 248(1); "taxable income" — Reg. 413(1)(b); "taxation year" — ITA 249; "taxpayer" — ITA 248(1); "total gross revenue for the year" — Reg. 413(2).

Interpretation Bulletins [Reg. 402]: IT-177R2: Permanent establishment of a corporation in a province.

CRA Audit Manual [Reg. 402]: 12.14.4: Gross revenue, salaries and wages paid.

402.1 Central paymaster — **(1)** In this Part, if an individual (referred to in this section as the "employee") is employed by a person (referred to in this section as the "employer") and performs a service in a particular province for the benefit of or on behalf of a corporation that is not the employer, an amount that may reasonably be regarded as equal to the amount of salary or wages earned by the employee for the service (referred to in this section as the "particular salary") is deemed to be salary paid by the corporation to an employee of the corporation in the corporation's taxation year in which the particular salary is paid if

(a) at the time the service is performed,

(i) the corporation and the employer do not deal at arm's length, and

(ii) the corporation has a permanent establishment in the particular province;

(b) the service

(i) is performed by the employee in the normal course of the employee's employment by the employer,

(ii) is performed for the benefit of or on behalf of the corporation in the ordinary course of a business carried on by the corporation, and

(iii) is of a type that could reasonably be expected to be performed by employees of the corporation in the ordinary course of the business referred to in subparagraph (ii); and

(c) the amount is not otherwise included in the aggregate, determined for the purposes of this Part, of the salaries and wages paid by the corporation.

(2) In this Part, an amount deemed under subsection (1) to be salary paid by a corporation to an employee of the corporation for a service performed in a particular province is deemed to have been paid,

(a) if the service was performed at one or more permanent establishments of the corporation in the particular province, to an employee of the permanent establishment or establishments; or

(b) if paragraph (a) does not apply, to an employee of any other permanent establishment (as is reasonably determined in the circumstances) of the corporation in the particular province.

(3) In determining under this Part the amount of salaries and wages paid in a year by an employer, there shall be deducted the total of all amounts each of which is a particular salary paid by the employer in the year.

(4) Despite subparagraph (1)(a)(i), this section applies to a corporation and an employer that deal at arm's length if the Minister determines that the corporation and the employer have entered into an arrangement the purpose of which is to reduce, through the provision of services as described in subsection (1), the total amount of income tax payable by the corporation under a law of the particular province referred to in subsection (1).

(5) For the purposes of this section, a partnership is deemed to be a corporation and the corporation's taxation year is deemed to be the partnership's fiscal period.

Notes: Reg. 402.1 replaced by 2008 budget bill #2, for 2009 and later tax years. It implements §4.1(a)(i) of the *Canada-Ontario Memorandum of Agreement Concerning a Single Administration of Ontario Corporate Tax* (Oct. 2006) (reproduced here in the 35th ed.). The previous Reg. 402.1 applied only to taxable income earned in 1978 in the Northwest Territories. See also Robson article in Notes at beginning of Part IV.

Where the employer is a partnership, see VIEWS doc 2017-0728331I7.

Definitions [Reg. 402.1]: "amount" — ITA 248(1); "arm's length" — ITA 251(1); "business" — ITA 248(1); "Canada" — ITA 255, *Interpretation Act* 35(1); "corporation" — Reg. 402.1(5), ITA 248(1), *Interpretation Act* 35(1); "employed" — ITA 248(1); "employee", "employer" — Reg. 402.1(1); "employment" — ITA 248(1); "fiscal period" — Reg. 402.1(5), ITA 249.1; "individual", "insurance corporation", "Minister" — ITA 248(1); "particular salary" — Reg. 402.1(1); "partnership" — see ITA 96(1) Notes; "permanent establishment" — Reg. 400(2); "person", "property" — ITA 248(1); "province" — *Interpretation Act* 35(1); "resident" — ITA 250; "salary or wages" — ITA 248(1); "taxation year" — ITA 249.

I.T. Technical News: 44 (central paymaster rules).

Provincial Income Allocation Newsletters: 4 (salaries and wages — inclusion of taxable benefits).

402.2 [Repealed]

Notes: Reg. 402.2 repealed by 2008 budget bill #2, effective for 2009 and later taxation years. It applied only to taxable income earned in 1980 in the Yukon.

403. Insurance corporations — (1)

Notwithstanding subsections 402(3) and (4), the amount of taxable income that shall be deemed to have been earned in a taxation year in a particular province by an insurance corporation is that proportion of its taxable income for the year that the aggregate of

(a) its net premiums for the year in respect of insurance on property situated in the province, and

(b) its net premiums for the year in respect of insurance, other than on property, from contracts with persons resident in the province,

is of the total of such of its net premiums for the year as are included in computing its income for the purposes of Part I of the Act.

Notes: For application to partnerships see VIEWS doc 2018-0744881I7.

(2) In this section, **"net premiums"** of a corporation for a taxation year means the aggregate of the gross premiums received by the corporation in the year (other than consideration received for annuities), minus the aggregate for the year of

(a) premiums paid for reinsurance,

(b) dividends or rebates paid or credited to policyholders, and

(c) rebates or returned premiums paid in respect of the cancellation of policies,

by the corporation.

(3) For the purposes of subsection (1), where an insurance corporation had no permanent establishment in a taxation year in a particular province,

(a) each net premium for that year in respect of insurance on property situated in the particular province shall be deemed to be a net premium in respect of insurance on property situated in the province in which the permanent establishment of the corporation to which the net premium is reasonably attributable is situated; and

(b) each net premium for that year in respect of insurance, other than on property, from contracts with persons resident in the particular province shall be deemed to be a net premium in respect of insurance, other than on property, from contracts with

persons resident in the province in which the permanent establishment of the corporation to which the net premium is reasonably attributable is situated.

(4) For the purposes of subsection (1), if in a taxation year an insurance corporation has no permanent establishment in a particular country other than Canada, but provides insurance on property in the particular country or has a contract for insurance, other than on property, with a person resident in the particular country, each net premium for the taxation year in respect of the insurance is deemed to be a net premium in respect of insurance on property situated in, or from contracts with persons resident in, as the case may be, the province in Canada or country other than Canada in which is situated the permanent establishment of the corporation to which the net premium is reasonably attributable in the circumstances.

Notes: Reg. 403(4) added by 2008 budget bill #2, for 2009 and later tax years. It implements §4.1(a)(iii) of the *Canada-Ontario Memorandum of Agreement Concerning a Single Administration of Ontario Corporate Tax* (Oct. 2006) (reproduced here in the 35th ed.). See VIEWS doc 2018-0741041I7 (premiums allocated to PE to which they are reasonably attributable).

Definitions [Reg. 403]: "amount", "annuity" — ITA 248(1); "Canada" — ITA 255, *Interpretation Act* 35(1); "corporation" — ITA 248(1), *Interpretation Act* 35(1); "dividend", "insurance corporation" — ITA 248(1); "net premiums" — Reg. 403(2), (3); "permanent establishment" — Reg. 400(2); "person", "property" — ITA 248(1); "province" — *Interpretation Act* 35(1); "resident" — ITA 250; "taxable income" — Reg. 413(1)(b); "taxation year" — ITA 249.

404. Banks — (1)

Notwithstanding subsections 402(3) and (4), the amount of taxable income that is deemed to have been earned by a bank in a taxation year in a province in which it had a permanent establishment is $\frac{1}{3}$ of the total of

(a) the proportion of its taxable income for the year that the total of the salaries and wages paid in the year by the bank to employees of its permanent establishment in the province is of the total of all salaries and wages paid in the year by the bank; and

(b) twice the proportion of its taxable income for the year that the total amount of loans and deposits of its permanent establishment in the province for the year is of the total amount of all loans and deposits of the bank for the year.

Related Provisions: Reg. 413(3) — Application to authorized foreign bank.

Notes: On the meaning of "loan" for Reg. 404, see VIEWS docs 2008-0275951E5, 2012-0439931I7.

Reg. 404(1)(a) and (b) amended by 2017 budget bill #2, effective Sept. 16, 2016, to change "that proportion" to "the proportion" (2x) and "aggregate" to "total" (4x).

Reg. 404(1) opening words amended by P.C. 2009-1869, effective June 28, 1999, to change "chartered bank" to "bank" (so as to include an authorized foreign bank).

Provincial Income Allocation Newsletters: 4 (salaries and wages — inclusion of taxable benefits).

(2) For the purposes of subsection (1), the amount of loans for a taxation year is $\frac{1}{12}$ of the total of the amounts outstanding, on the loans made by the bank, at the close of business on the last day of each month in the year.

Notes: Reg. 404(2) amended by 2017 budget bill #2, effective Sept. 16, 2016, to change "aggregate" to "total".

(3) For the purposes of subsection (1), the amount of deposits for a taxation year is $\frac{1}{12}$ of the total of the amounts on deposit with the bank at the close of business on the last day of each month in the year.

Notes: Reg. 404(3) amended by 2017 budget bill #2, effective Sept. 16, 2016, to change "aggregate" to "total".

(4) For the purposes of subsections (2) and (3), loans and deposits do not include bonds, stocks, debentures, items in transit and deposits in favour of Her Majesty in right of Canada.

Definitions [Reg. 404]: "all loans and deposits of the bank for the year" — Reg. 413(3); "amount" — ITA 248(1); "bank" — ITA 248(1), *Interpretation Act* 35(1); "business" — ITA 248(1); "Canada" — ITA 255, *Interpretation Act* 35(1); "deposits" — Reg. 404(3), (4); "employee" — ITA 248(1); "Her Majesty" — *Interpretation Act* 35(1); "loans" — Reg. 404(2), (4); "month" — *Interpretation Act* 35(1); "permanent establishment" — Reg. 400(2); "province" — *Interpretation Act* 35(1); "salaries and wages paid in the year" — Reg. 413(1)(a); "taxable income" — Reg. 413(1)(b); "taxation year" — ITA 249.

404.1 [Federal credit unions] — **(1)** Notwithstanding subsections 402(3) and (4), the amount of taxable income that is deemed to have been earned by a federal credit union in a taxation year in a province in which it had a permanent establishment is $1/3$ of the total of

(a) the proportion of its taxable income for the year that the total of the salaries and wages paid in the year by the federal credit union to employees of its permanent establishment in the province is of the total of all salaries and wages paid in the year by the federal credit union, and

(b) twice the proportion of its taxable income for the year that the total amount of loans and deposits of its permanent establishment in the province for the year is of the total amount of all loans and deposits of the federal credit union for the year.

(2) For the purposes of subsection (1), the amount of loans for a taxation year is $1/12$ of the total of the amounts outstanding, on the loans made by the federal credit union, at the close of business on the last day of each month in the year.

(3) For the purposes of subsection (1), the amount of deposits for a taxation year is $1/12$ of the total of the amounts on deposit with the federal credit union at the close of business on the last day of each month in the year.

(4) For the purposes of subsections (2) and (3), loans and deposits do not include bonds, stocks, debentures, items in transit and deposits in favour of Her Majesty in right of Canada.

Notes: Reg. 404.1 added by 2017 budget bill #2, effective Sept. 16, 2016.

Definitions [Reg. 404.1]: "amount", "business", "employee", "federal credit union" — ITA 248(1); "Her Majesty", "month" — *Interpretation Act* 35(1); "permanent establishment" — Reg. 400(2); "province" — *Interpretation Act* 35(1); "salaries and wages paid in the year" — Reg. 413(1)(a); "taxable income" — Reg. 413(1)(b); "taxation year" — ITA 249.

405. Trust and loan corporations — **(1)** Notwithstanding subsections 402(3) and (4), the amount of taxable income that shall be deemed to have been earned in a taxation year by a trust and loan corporation, trust corporation or loan corporation in a province in which it had a permanent establishment is that proportion of its taxable income for the year that the gross revenue for the year of its permanent establishment in the province is of the total gross revenue for the year of the corporation.

(2) In subsection (1), **"gross revenue for the year of its permanent establishment in the province"** means the aggregate of the gross revenue of the corporation for the year arising from

(a) loans secured by lands situated in the province;

(b) loans, not secured by land, to persons residing in the province;

(c) loans

(i) to persons residing in a province or country other than Canada in which the corporation has no permanent establishment, and

(ii) administered by a permanent establishment in the province,

except loans secured by land situated in a province or country other than Canada in which the corporation has a permanent establishment; and

(d) business conducted at the permanent establishment in the province, other than revenue in respect of loans.

Notes: For CRA interpretation see VIEWS docs 2001-0066667, 2010-0386421I7.

Definitions [Reg. 405]: "amount", "business" — ITA 248(1); "Canada" — ITA 255, *Interpretation Act* 35(1); "corporation" — ITA 248(1), *Interpretation Act* 35(1); "gross revenue" — ITA 248(1); "gross revenue for the year of its permanent establishment in the province" — Reg. 405(2); "permanent establishment" — Reg. 400(2); "person" — ITA 248(1); "province" — *Interpretation Act* 35(1); "taxable income" — Reg. 413(1)(b); "taxation year" — ITA 249; "trust" — ITA 104(1), 248(1), (3).

406. Railway corporations — **(1)** Notwithstanding subsections 402(3) and (4), the amount of taxable income that shall be deemed to have been earned by a railway corporation in a taxation year in a province in which it had a permanent establishment is, unless subsection (2) applies, $1/2$ the aggregate of

(a) that proportion of the taxable income of the corporation for the year that the equated track miles of the corporation in the province is of the equated track miles of the corporation in Canada; and

(b) that proportion of the taxable income of the corporation for the year that the gross ton miles of the corporation for the year in the province is of the gross ton miles of the corporation for the year in Canada.

(2) Where a corporation to which subsection (1) would apply, if this subsection did not apply thereto, operates an airline service, ships or hotels or receives substantial revenues that are petroleum or natural gas royalties, or does a combination of two or more of those things, the amount of its taxable income that shall be deemed to have been earned in a taxation year in a province in which it had a permanent establishment is the aggregate of the amounts computed

(a) by applying the provisions of section 407 to that part of its taxable income for the year that may reasonably be considered to have arisen from the operation of the airline service;

(b) by applying the provisions of section 410 to that part of its taxable income for the year that may reasonably be considered to have arisen from the operation of the ships;

(c) by applying the provisions of section 402 to that part of its taxable income for the year that may reasonably be considered to have arisen from the operation of the hotels;

(d) by applying the provisions of section 402 to that part of its taxable income for the year that may reasonably be considered to have arisen from the ownership by the taxpayer of petroleum or natural gas rights or any interest therein; and

(e) by applying the provisions of subsection (1) to the remaining portion of its taxable income for the year.

(3) In this section, **"equated track miles"** in a specified place means the aggregate of

(a) the number of miles of first main track,

(b) 80 per cent of the number of miles of other main tracks, and

(c) 50 per cent of the number of miles of yard tracks and sidings,

in that place.

(4) For the purpose of making an allocation under paragraph (2)(b), a reference in section 410 to "salaries and wages paid in the year by the corporation to employees" shall be read as a reference to salaries and wages paid by the corporation to employees employed in the operation of permanent establishments (other than ships) maintained for the shipping business.

(5) For the purpose of making an allocation under paragraph (2)(c),

(a) a reference in section 402 to "gross revenue for the year reasonably attributable to the permanent establishment in the province" shall be read as a reference to the gross revenue of the taxpayer from operating hotels therein;

(b) a reference in section 402 to "total gross revenue for the year" shall be read as a reference to the total gross revenue of the taxpayer for the year from operating hotels; and

(c) a reference in section 402 to "salaries and wages paid in the year by the corporation to employees" shall be read as a reference to salaries and wages paid to employees engaged in the operations of its hotels.

(6) Notwithstanding subsection 402(5), for the purpose of making an allocation under paragraph (2)(d),

(a) a reference in section 402 to "gross revenue for the year reasonably attributable to the permanent establishment in the province" shall be read as a reference to the gross revenue of the taxpayer from the ownership by the taxpayer of petroleum and natural gas rights in lands in the province and any interest therein;

(b) a reference in section 402 to "total gross revenue for the year" shall be read as a reference to the total gross revenue of the taxpayer from ownership by the taxpayer of petroleum and natural gas rights and any interest therein; and

(c) a reference in section 402 to "salaries and wages paid in the year by the corporation to employees" shall be read as a reference to salaries and wages paid to employees employed in connection with the corporation's petroleum and natural gas rights and interests therein.

Definitions [Reg. 406]: "amount", "business" — ITA 248(1); "Canada" — ITA 255, *Interpretation Act* 35(1); "corporation" — ITA 248(1), *Interpretation Act* 35(1); "employed", "employee" — ITA 248(1); "equated track miles" — Reg. 406(3); "gross revenue" — ITA 248(1); "permanent establishment" — Reg. 400(2); "province" — *Interpretation Act* 35(1); "taxable income" — Reg. 413(1)(b); "taxation year" — ITA 249; "taxpayer" — ITA 248(1).

407. Airline corporations — (1) Notwithstanding subsections 402(3) and (4), the amount of taxable income that shall be deemed to have been earned in a taxation year by an airline corporation in a province in which it had a permanent establishment is the amount that is equal to ¼ of the aggregate of

(a) that proportion of its taxable income for the year that the capital cost of all the corporation's fixed assets, except aircraft, in the province at the end of the year is of the capital cost of all its fixed assets, except aircraft, in Canada at the end of the year; and

(b) that proportion of its taxable income for the year that three times the number of revenue plane miles flown by its aircraft during the year in the province is of the total of all amounts, each of which is the total number of revenue plane miles flown by its aircraft during the year in a province in which the corporation had a permanent establishment.

Notes: For the meaning of "aircraft" see Notes to ITA 8(1)(j).

Reg. 407(1)(b) amended by 2002-2013 technical bill, for tax years that end after Oct. 24, 2012. The Finance Technical Notes describe the change as "to exclude miles flown over the territorial waters of Canada from the computation of total number of revenue plane miles flown. As a result, only revenue plane miles flown in the provinces in which an airline corporation has a PE are considered for allocation purposes."

Reg. 407(1)(b) amended by P.C. 1994-662, for taxation years that begin after 1992.

(2) For the purposes of this section, **"revenue plane miles flown"** shall be weighted according to take-off weight of the aircraft operated.

(3) For the purposes of this section, **"take-off weight"** of an aircraft means

(a) for an aircraft in respect of which an application form for a Certificate of Airworthiness has been submitted to and accepted by the Department of Transport, the maximum permissible take-off weight, in pounds, shown on the form; and

(b) for any other aircraft, the weight, in pounds, that may reasonably be considered to be the equivalent of the weight referred to in paragraph (a).

Definitions [Reg. 407]: "amount" — ITA 248(1); "Canada" — ITA 255, *Interpretation Act* 35(1); "corporation" — ITA 248(1), *Interpretation Act* 35(1); "permanent establishment" — Reg. 400(2); "province" — *Interpretation Act* 35(1); "revenue plane miles flown" — Reg. 407(2); "take-off weight" — Reg. 407(3); "taxable income" — Reg. 413(1)(b); "taxation year" — ITA 249.

408. Grain elevator operators — Notwithstanding subsections 402(3) and (4), the amount of taxable income of a corporation whose chief business is the operation of grain elevators that shall be deemed to have been earned by that corporation in a taxation year in a province in which it had a permanent establishment is ½ of the aggregate of

(a) that proportion of its taxable income for the year that the number of bushels of grain received in the year in the elevators operated by the corporation in the province is of the total number of bushels of grain received in the year in all the elevators operated by the corporation; and

(b) that proportion of its taxable income for the year that the aggregate of salaries and wages paid in the year by the corporation to employees of its permanent establishment in the province is of the aggregate of all salaries and wages paid in the year by the corporation.

Definitions [Reg. 408]: "amount", "business" — ITA 248(1); "corporation" — ITA 248(1), *Interpretation Act* 35(1); "employee" — ITA 248(1); "permanent establishment" — Reg. 400(2); "province" — *Interpretation Act* 35(1); "salaries and wages paid in the year" — Reg. 413(1)(a); "taxable income" — Reg. 413(1)(b); "taxation year" — ITA 249.

409. Bus and truck operators — Notwithstanding subsections 402(3) and (4), the amount of taxable income of a corporation whose chief business is the transportation of goods or passengers (other than by the operation of a railway, ship or airline service) that shall be deemed to have been earned by that corporation in a taxation year in a province in which it had a permanent establishment is ½ of the aggregate of

(a) that proportion of its taxable income for the year that the number of kilometres driven by the corporation's vehicles, whether owned or leased, on roads in the province in the year is of the total number of kilometres driven by those vehicles in the year on roads other than roads in provinces or countries in which the corporation had no permanent establishment; and

(b) that proportion of its taxable income for the year that the aggregate of salaries and wages paid in the year by the corporation to employees of its permanent establishment in the province is of the aggregate of all salaries and wages paid in the year by the corporation.

Definitions [Reg. 409]: "amount", "business" — ITA 248(1); "corporation" — ITA 248(1), *Interpretation Act* 35(1); "permanent establishment" — Reg. 400(2); "province" — *Interpretation Act* 35(1); "salaries and wages paid in the year" — Reg. 413(1)(a); "taxable income" — Reg. 413(1)(b); "taxation year" — ITA 249.

410. Ship operators — (1) Notwithstanding subsections 402(3) and (4), the amount of taxable income of a corporation whose chief business is the operation of ships that shall be deemed to have been earned by the corporation in a taxation year in a province in which it had a permanent establishment is the aggregate of,

(a) that portion of its allocable income for the year that its port-call-tonnage in the province is of its total port-call-tonnage in all the provinces in which it had a permanent establishment; and

(b) if its taxable income for the year exceeds its allocable income for the year, that proportion of the excess that the aggregate of the salaries and wages paid in the year by the corporation to employees of the permanent establishment (other than a ship) in the province is of the aggregate of salaries and wages paid in the year by the corporation to employees of its permanent establishments (other than ships) in Canada.

(2) In this section,

(a) **"allocable income for the year"** means that proportion of the taxable income of the corporation for the year that its total port-call-tonnage in Canada is of its total port-call-tonnage in all countries; and

(b) **"port-call-tonnage"** in a province or country means the aggregate of the products obtained by multiplying, for each ship operated by the corporation, the number of calls made in the year by that ship at ports in that province or country by the number of tons of the registered net tonnage of that ship.

Definitions [Reg. 410]: "allocable income for the year" — Reg. 410(2)(a); "amount", "business" — ITA 248(1); "Canada" — ITA 255, *Interpretation Act* 35(1); "corporation" — ITA 248(1), *Interpretation Act* 35(1); "employee" — ITA 248(1); "permanent establishment" — Reg. 400(2); "port-call tonnage" — Reg. 410(2)(b); "province" — *Interpretation Act* 35(1); "salaries and wages paid in the year" — Reg. 413(1)(a); "taxable income" — Reg. 413(1)(b); "taxation year" — ITA 249.

Provincial Income Allocation Newsletters: 4 (salaries and wages — inclusion of taxable benefits).

Regulations

411. Pipeline operators

411. Pipeline operators — Notwithstanding subsections 402(3) and (4), the amount of taxable income of a corporation whose chief business is the operation of a pipeline that shall be deemed to have been earned by that corporation in a taxation year in a province in which it had a permanent establishment is ½ of the aggregate of

(a) that proportion of its taxable income for the year that the number of miles of pipeline of the corporation in the province is of the number of miles of pipeline of the corporation in all the provinces in which it had a permanent establishment; and

(b) that proportion of its taxable income for the year that the aggregate of the salaries and wages paid in the year by the corporation to employees of its permanent establishment in the province is of the aggregate of salaries and wages paid in the year by the corporation to employees of its permanent establishments in Canada.

Notes: For the CRA's administrative definition of "pipeline", see IT-482R.

Definitions [Reg. 411]: "amount", "business" — ITA 248(1); "Canada" — ITA 255, *Interpretation Act* 35(1); "corporation" — ITA 248(1), *Interpretation Act* 35(1); "employee" — ITA 248(1); "permanent establishment" — Reg. 400(2); "province" — *Interpretation Act* 35(1); "salaries and wages paid in the year" — Reg. 413(1)(a); "taxable income" — Reg. 413(1)(b); "taxation year" — ITA 249.

Provincial Income Allocation Newsletters: 4 (salaries and wages — inclusion of taxable benefits).

412. Divided businesses

412. Divided businesses — If part of the business of a corporation for a taxation year, other than a corporation described in any of sections 403, 404, 404.1, 405, 406, 407, 408, 409, 410 and 411, consisted of operations normally conducted by a corporation described in one of those sections, the corporation and the Minister may agree to determine the amount of taxable income deemed to have been earned in the year in a particular province to be the total of the amounts computed

(a) by applying the provisions of such of those sections as would have been applicable if it had been a corporation described therein to the portion of its taxable income for the year that might reasonably be considered to have arisen from that part of the business; and

(b) by applying the provisions of section 402 to the remaining portion of its taxable income for the year.

Notes: Reg. 412 amended by 2017 budget bill #2, effective Sept. 16, 2016, to add reference to 404.1 and change "aggregate" to "total".

Definitions [Reg. 412]: "amount", "business" — ITA 248(1); "corporation" — ITA 248(1), *Interpretation Act* 35(1); "Minister" — ITA 248(1); "province" — *Interpretation Act* 35(1); "taxable income" — Reg. 413(1)(b); "taxation year" — ITA 249.

413. [Non-resident corporation]

413. [Non-resident corporation] — **(1)** In this Part, if a corporation is not resident in Canada

(a) **"salaries and wages paid in the year"** by the corporation does not include salaries and wages paid to employees of a permanent establishment outside Canada; and

(b) **"taxable income"** of the corporation is deemed to refer to the corporation's taxable income earned in Canada.

Notes: Reg. 413(1)(b) added by 2013 budget bill #1, for taxation years that begin after March 20, 2013. This rule was previously in Reg. 400(1.1)(a). It had earlier been moved there from here by 2008 budget bill #2, for 2009 and later taxation years.

Provincial Income Allocation Newsletters: 4 (salaries and wages — inclusion of taxable benefits).

CRA Audit Manual: 15.2.15: Tax calculations.

(2) For the purposes of paragraph 402(3)(a), where a corporation is not resident in Canada, "total gross revenue for the year" of the corporation does not include gross revenue reasonably attributable to a permanent establishment outside Canada.

(3) For the purpose of paragraph 404(1)(b), in the case of an authorized foreign bank, "all loans and deposits of the bank for the year" is to be read as a reference to "all loans and deposits of the bank for the year in respect of its Canadian banking business".

Notes: Reg. 413(3) added by P.C. 2009-1869, effective June 28, 1999.

Definitions [Reg. 413]: "Canada" — ITA 255, *Interpretation Act* 35(1); "corporation" — ITA 248(1), *Interpretation Act* 35(1); "employee" — ITA 248(1); "permanent establishment" — Reg. 400(2); "resident in Canada" — ITA 250; "taxable income earned in Canada" — Reg. 400(1.1).

413.1 [Repealed]

413.1 [Repealed]

Notes: Reg. 413.1 repealed by 2013 budget bill #1, for taxation years that begin after March 20, 2013. For earlier years since 2009, it provided an exception for an international banking centre under ITA 33.1. Added by 2008 budget bill #2.

414. Provincial SIFT tax rate

414. Provincial SIFT tax rate — **(1) [Definitions]** — The following definitions apply in this section.

"general corporate income tax rate", in a province for a taxation year, means

(a) for Quebec, 0%;

(b) for the Newfoundland offshore area, the highest percentage rate of tax imposed under the laws of Newfoundland and Labrador on the taxable income of a public corporation earned in the taxation year in Newfoundland and Labrador;

(c) for the Nova Scotia offshore area, the highest percentage rate of tax imposed under the laws of Nova Scotia on the taxable income of a public corporation earned in the taxation year in Nova Scotia; and

(d) for each other province, the highest percentage rate of tax imposed under the laws of the province on the taxable income of a public corporation earned in the taxation year in the province.

Related Provisions: Reg. 414(4) — Limitation on application of para. (a).

"province" includes the Newfoundland offshore area and the Nova Scotia offshore area.

Related Provisions: ITA 124(4) — Same definition applies to corporations.

"taxable SIFT distributions", for a taxation year, means

(a) in the case of a SIFT trust, its non-deductible distributions amount for the taxation year; and

(b) in the case of a SIFT partnership, its taxable non-portfolio earnings for the taxation year.

Related Provisions: ITA 104(16), 122(3) — Non-deductible distributions amount; ITA 197(1) — Taxable non-portfolio earnings.

(2) [Application to SIFT] — In determining the amount of a SIFT trust's or SIFT partnership's taxable SIFT distributions for a taxation year earned in a province

(a) except as provided in paragraph (b), this Part applies in respect of the SIFT trust or SIFT partnership as though

(i) each reference to "corporation" (other than in the expression "subsidiary controlled corporation") were read as a reference to "SIFT trust" or "SIFT partnership", as the case may be,

(ii) each reference to "taxable income" were read as a reference to "taxable SIFT distributions",

(iii) each reference to "its incorporating documents or by-laws" were read as a reference to "the agreement governing the SIFT trust" or "the agreement governing the SIFT partnership", as the case may be, and

(iv) "subsidiary controlled corporation" in respect of a SIFT trust or a SIFT partnership meant a corporation more than 50% of the issued share capital of which (having full voting rights under all circumstances) belongs to the SIFT trust or SIFT partnership, as the case may be; and

(b) subsection 400(1), section 401, subsections 402(1) and (2) and sections 403 to 413 do not apply.

Notes: See Notes at end of Reg. 414.

(3) Subject to subsection (4), in applying the definition "provincial SIFT tax rate" in subsection 248(1) of the Act in respect of a SIFT trust or SIFT partnership for a taxation year, the prescribed amount determined in respect of the SIFT trust or SIFT partnership for the taxation year is

(a) if the SIFT trust or SIFT partnership has no permanent establishment in a province in the taxation year, 0.10;

(b) if the SIFT trust or SIFT partnership has a permanent establishment in a province in the taxation year and has no permanent establishment outside that province in the taxation year, the decimal fraction equivalent of the general corporate income tax rate in the province for the taxation year; and

(c) if the SIFT trust or SIFT partnership has a permanent establishment in the taxation year in a province, and has a permanent establishment outside that province in the taxation year, the amount, expressed as a decimal fraction, determined by the formula

$$A + B$$

where

A is the total of all amounts, if any, each of which is in respect of a province in which the SIFT trust or SIFT partnership has a permanent establishment in the taxation year and is determined by the formula

$$C/D \times E$$

where

C is its taxable SIFT distributions for the taxation year earned in the province,

D is its total taxable SIFT distributions for the taxation year, and

E is the decimal fraction equivalent of the general corporate income tax rate in the province for the taxation year, and

B is the amount determined by the formula

$$(1 - F/D) \times 0.1$$

where

F is the total of all amounts each of which is an amount determined under the description of C in the description of A in respect of a province in which the SIFT trust or SIFT partnership has a permanent establishment in the taxation year.

(4) If a SIFT trust or a SIFT partnership has a permanent establishment in Quebec in a taxation year, paragraph (a) of the definition "general corporate income tax rate" in subsection (1) does not apply in determining the prescribed amount under subsection (3) in respect of the SIFT trust or the SIFT partnership for the taxation year for the purposes of applying the definition "provincial SIFT tax rate" in determining:

(a) in the case of the SIFT partnership, the amount of a dividend deemed by paragraph 96(1.11)(b) of the Act to have been received by it in the taxation year; and

(b) in the case of the SIFT trust, the amount of its taxable SIFT trust distributions for the taxation year.

Notes: Reg. 414 replaced by 2008 budget bill #2, for 2007 and later tax years, except that para. (4)(b) does not apply for taxation years of a SIFT trust that ended before Feb. 3, 2009. The previous Reg. 414 prescribed an amount for ITA 123(2), repealed in 1989.

Definitions [Reg. 414]: "amount" — ITA 248(1); "corporation" — ITA 248(1), *Interpretation Act* 35(1); "dividend" — ITA 248(1); "general corporate income tax rate" — Reg. 414(1); "Newfoundland offshore area" — ITA 248(1); "non-deductible distributions amount" — 104(16), 122(3); "Nova Scotia offshore area" — ITA 248(1); "permanent establishment" — Reg. 400(2); "prescribed" — ITA 248(1); "province" — Reg. 414(1), *Interpretation Act* 35(1); "public corporation" — ITA 89(1), 248(1); "share" — ITA 248(1); "SIFT partnership" — ITA 197.1, 248(1); "SIFT trust" — ITA 122.1, 248(1); "taxable income" — Reg. 413(1)(b); "taxable non-portfolio earnings" — ITA 197(1); "taxable SIFT distributions" — Reg. 414(1), (2); "taxation year" — ITA 249.

415. [Repealed]

Notes: Reg. 415 repealed by 2008 budget bill #2, for 2007 and later taxation years. It prescribed the "Nova Scotia offshore area" for ITA 123(2), repealed in 1989.

PART V — [500–503] NON-RESIDENT-OWNED INVESTMENT CORPORATIONS

500-502. [No longer relevant]

Notes: Reg. 500-502 are for electing NRO status before 2001. See Notes to ITA 133.

503. [Revoked]

PART VI — [600] ELECTIONS

600. [Prescribed provisions for late elections] — For the purposes of paragraphs 220(3.2)(a) and (b) of the Act, the following are prescribed provisions:

(a) section 21 of the Act;

(b) subsections 13(4), (7.4) and (29), 20(24), 44(1) and (6), 45(2) and (3), 50(1), 53(2.1), 56.4(13), 70(6.2), (9.01), (9.11), (9.21) and (9.31), 72(2), 73(1), 80.1(1), 82(3), 83(2), 91(1.4), 104(14), 107(2.001), 143(2), 146.01(7), 146.02(7), 164(6) and (6.1), 184(3), 251.2(6) and 256(9) of the Act;

(c) paragraphs 12(2.2)(b), 66.7(7)(c), (d) and (e) and (8)(c), (d) and (e), 80.01(4)(c), 86.1(2)(f) and 128.1(4)(d), (6)(a) and (c), (7)(d) and (g) and (8)(c) of the Act;

(d) subsections 1103(1), (2) and (2d) and 5907(2.1) of these Regulations.

Notes: Reg. 600 prescribes the elections that may be made, amended or revoked late under ITA 220(3.2). (Note that para. (a) lists sections, para. (b) subsections and para. (c) paragraphs of the ITA.) CRA likely will not accept late-filed election forms that are not listed; see Notes to ITA 220(3.2).

Reg. 600(b) amended by 2017 budget bill #2, effective July 12, 2013, to add reference to ITA 91(1.4).

Reg. 600(b) amended by 2016 budget bill #2, effective 2017, to delete reference to ITA 14(6) (as part of changing the eligible capital property rules to CCA Class 14.1: see Notes to ITA 20(1)(b)).

Reg. 600(b) amended by 2013 budget bill #2, effective March 21, 2013, to add ITA 251.2(6).

Reg. 600 earlier amended by 2002-2013 technical bill (to add 56.4(13) effective May 13, 2010, and delete 7(10) and 104(5.3) effective Nov. 2011), P.C. 2010-551, 2006-815, 2005-1133, 2005-694, 2002-531, 2001-1106, 1998-2270, 1997-1472, 1996-214, 1995-1210, 1993-1942. Reg. 600 added by P.C. 1992-914, effective Dec. 17, 1991.

The Finance Technical Notes describe the provisions added in 1991 as follows:

ITA 13(4), 14(6) and 44(1) allow a taxpayer or partnership to elect to defer an income inclusion or the recognition of a capital gain where a replacement property is acquired for a property that was stolen, expropriated or destroyed or for a former business property that was sold.

ITA 21 allows a taxpayer or partnership to elect to treat interest as a capital cost instead of an expense.

ITA 66.7(7)(c), (d) and (e) and (8)(c), (d) and (e) allow a predecessor corporation and a successor corporation to elect to transfer the unused pools of resource expenses from the predecessor to the successor.

ITA 70(6.2) allows a taxpayer's legal representative to elect to have the rollover rules under ITA 70(6) not apply, thus causing the assets transferred to a taxpayer's spouse on the death of the taxpayer to be considered to be transferred at fair market value for tax purposes.

ITA 70(9) allows a taxpayer's legal representative to elect an amount, within limits, as proceeds of disposition for farm [or fishing — ed.] property transferred to a child on the taxpayer's death.

ITA 70(9.1) allows a spousal trust to elect an amount, within limits, as proceeds of disposition for farm [or fishing — ed.] property transferred from the trust to a child on the spouse's death.

ITA 70(9.2) allows a taxpayer's legal representative to elect an amount, within limits, as proceeds of disposition for a share in a family farm corporation or an interest in a family farm partnership transferred to a child on the taxpayer's death.

ITA 70(9.3) allows a spousal trust to elect an amount, within limits, as proceeds of disposition for a share in a family farm corporation or an interest in a family farm partnership transferred from the trust to a child on the spouse's death.

ITA 72(2) permits a legal representative of a deceased taxpayer to elect to claim a deduction for certain reserves provided that the amount so deducted is subsequently included in the income of the taxpayer's spouse or a spousal trust.

ITA 73(1) allows a taxpayer to elect to have the rollover provisions in respect of an inter-vivos transfer of assets to a spouse or spousal trust not apply, thus causing the assets to be considered to be transferred at fair market value for tax purposes.

ITA 104(14) allows a trust and its preferred beneficiaries to elect to have the income of the trust included in the income of the preferred beneficiaries instead of being taxes as income of the trust.

Reg. 1103(1) allows a taxpayer or partnership to elect, for capital cost allowance purposes, to include in Class 1 all properties included in Classes 2 to 12.

Reg. 1103(2) allows a taxpayer or partnership to elect, for capital cost allowance purposes, to include in Class 2, 4 or 17 all properties included in any other classes where Class 2, 4 or 17 are the classes in which the chief depreciable properties of the taxpayer or partnership are included.

Reg. 1103(2d) allows a taxpayer or partnership to elect to defer a capital cost allowance recapture by transferring the property disposed of to a new class of which the taxpayer or partnership has property where the property disposed of would have been a property of the new class if it had been acquired when the property of the new class was acquired.

Definitions [Reg. 600]: "Canada" — ITA 255, *Interpretation Act* 35(1); "Minister" — ITA 248(1); "month" — *Interpretation Act* 35(1); "prescribed" — ITA 248(1).

Information Circulars: 07-1R1: Taxpayer relief provisionss.

PART VII — [700–701] LOGGING TAXES ON INCOME

700. Logging — **(1)** Except as provided in subsection (2), for the purposes of paragraph 127(2)(a) [127(2)"income for the year from logging operations in the province"] of the Act "income for the year from logging operations in the province" means the aggregate of

(a) where standing timber is cut in the province by the taxpayer or logs cut from standing timber in the province are acquired by the taxpayer and the logs so obtained are sold by the taxpayer in the province before or on delivery to a sawmill, pulp or paper plant or other place for processing logs, the taxpayer's income for the year from the sale, other than any portion thereof that was included in computing the taxpayer's income from logging operations in the province for a previous year;

(b) where standing timber in the province or the right to cut standing timber in the province is sold by the taxpayer, the taxpayer's income for the year from the sale, other than any portion thereof that was included in computing the taxpayer's income from logging operations in the province for a previous year;

(c) where standing timber is cut in the province by the taxpayer or logs cut from standing timber in the province are acquired by the taxpayer, if the logs so obtained are

(i) exported from the province and are sold by him prior to or on delivery to a sawmill, pulp or paper plant or other place for processing logs, or

(ii) exported from Canada,

the amount computed by deducting from the value, as determined by the province, of the logs so exported in the year, the aggregate of the costs of acquiring, cutting, transporting and selling the logs; and

(d) where standing timber is cut in the province by the taxpayer or logs cut from standing timber in the province are acquired by the taxpayer, if the logs are processed by the taxpayer or by a person on his behalf in a sawmill, pulp or paper plant or other place for processing logs in Canada, the income of the taxpayer for the year from all sources minus the aggregate of

(i) his income from sources other than logging operations carried on in Canada and other than the processing in Canada by him or on his behalf and sale by him of logs, timber and products produced therefrom,

(ii) each amount included in the aggregate determined under this subsection by virtue of paragraph (a), (b) or (c), and

(iii) an amount equal to eight per cent of the original cost to him of properties described in Schedule II used by him in the year in the processing of logs or products derived therefrom or, if the amount so determined is greater than 65 per cent of

the income remaining after making the deductions under subparagraphs (i) and (ii), 65 per cent of the income so remaining or, if the amount so determined is less than 35 per cent of the income so remaining, 35 per cent of the income so remaining.

Notes: In *Weyerhaeuser Co.*, 2012 TCC 106, gain from sale of an integrated forest product company's surplus logging assets (saw mills and real estate) were not part of its logging income under Reg. 700(1)(d), even though the gain was subject to logging tax as "income derived from logging operations" under the BC *Logging Tax Act.* (BC intervened in the case and appeared willing to change its interpretation of the *Logging Tax Act* based on the TCC decision.)

For the meaning of "derived" see also Notes to ITA 18.1(12).

Reg. 700(1)(a)-(b) amended by P.C. 1992-1862 for taxation years beginning after 1990.

(2) Where the taxpayer cuts standing timber or acquires logs cut from standing timber in more than one province, for the purposes of paragraph 127(2)(a) [127(2)"income for the year from logging operations in the province"] of the Act "income for the year from logging operations in the province" means the aggregate of

(a) the amounts determined in respect of that province in accordance with paragraphs (1)(a), (b) and (c); and

(b) where the logs are processed by the taxpayer or by a person on his behalf in a sawmill, pulp or paper plant or other place for processing logs in Canada, an amount equal to the proportion of the income of the taxpayer for the year from all sources minus the aggregate of

(i) his income from sources other than logging operations carried on in Canada and other than the processing in Canada by him or on his behalf and sale by him of logs, timber and products produced therefrom,

(ii) the aggregate of amounts determined in respect of each province in accordance with paragraphs (1)(a), (b) and (c), and

(iii) an amount equal to eight per cent of the original cost to him of properties described in Schedule II used by him in the year in the processing of logs or products derived therefrom or, if the amount so determined is greater than 65 per cent of the income remaining after making the deductions under subparagraphs (i) and (ii), 65 per cent of the income so remaining or, if the amount so determined is less than 35 per cent of the income so remaining, 35 per cent of the income so remaining,

that

(iv) the quantity of standing timber cut in the province in the year by the taxpayer and logs cut from standing timber in the province acquired by the taxpayer in the year,

is of

(v) the total quantity of standing timber cut and logs acquired in the year by the taxpayer.

Notes: For the meaning of "derived" in (b)(iii) see Notes to ITA 18.1(12).

Forms: T2 Sched. 21: Federal foreign income tax credits and logging tax credit.

(3) For the purpose of the definition "logging tax" in subsection 127(2) of the Act, each of the following is declared to be a tax of general application on income from logging operations:

(a) the tax imposed by the Province of British Columbia under the *Logging Tax Act*, R.S.B.C. 1996, c. 277; and

(b) the tax imposed by the Province of Quebec under Part VII of the *Taxation Act*, R.S.Q., c. I-3.

Notes: Reg. 700(3) amended by P.C. 2010-548, effective May 12, 2010 (no substantive change).

Definitions [Reg. 700]: "amount" — ITA 248(1); "Canada" — ITA 255, *Interpretation Act* 35(1); "legislature" — *Interpretation Act* 35(1)"legislative assembly"; "person" — ITA 248(1); "province" — *Interpretation Act* 35(1); "taxpayer" — ITA 248(1).

701. [Revoked]

PART VIII — [800–810] NON-RESIDENT TAXES

800. Registered non-resident insurers
— Subsections 215(1), (2) and (3) of the Act do not apply to amounts paid or credited to a registered non-resident insurer.

Related Provisions: Reg. 803.1 — Application to authorized foreign bank before Aug. 8/09.

Notes: The Feb. 13, 2003 draft of Reg. 800-803 included references to an authorized foreign bank (AFB). These were moved to Reg. 803.1 and repealed effective Aug. 8, 2009, after which the ordinary withholding and remittance regime applies to an AFB.

Reg. 800 amended by P.C. 2009-1869, for tax years that end after June 27, 1999.

Definitions [Reg. 800]: "amount" — ITA 248(1); "registered non-resident insurer" — Reg. 804.

801. Filing of returns by registered non-resident insurers
— A taxpayer that is a registered non-resident insurer in a taxation year shall file a return for the taxation year in prescribed form with the Minister on or before its filing-due date for the taxation year.

Related Provisions: Reg. 803.1 — Application to authorized foreign bank before Aug. 8/09.

Notes: Reg. 801 amended by P.C. 2009-1869, for tax years that end after June 27, 1999.

Definitions [Reg. 801]: "Minister" — ITA 248(1); "prescribed" — ITA 248(1); "registered non-resident insurer" — Reg. 804; "taxation year" — ITA 249; "taxpayer" — ITA 248(1).

Forms: T2016: Part XIII tax return — tax on income from Canada of approved non-resident insurers.

802. Amounts taxable
— The amounts that are taxable under Part XIII of the Act in a taxation year of a taxpayer that is a registered non-resident insurer in the taxation year are amounts paid or credited to the taxpayer in the taxation year other than amounts included under Part I of the Act in computing the taxpayer's income from a business carried on by it in Canada.

Related Provisions: Reg. 803.1 — Application to authorized foreign bank before Aug. 8/09.

Notes: Reg. 802 amended by P.C. 2009-1869, for tax years that end after June 27, 1999.

Definitions [Reg. 802]: "amount", "business" — ITA 248(1); "Canada" — ITA 255, *Interpretation Act* 35(1); "registered non-resident insurer" — Reg. 804; "taxation year" — ITA 249; "taxpayer" — ITA 248(1).

803. Payment of tax by registered non-resident insurers
— A taxpayer that is a registered non-resident insurer in a taxation year shall pay to the Receiver General, on or before its filing-due date for the taxation year, the tax payable by it under Part XIII of the Act in the taxation year.

Related Provisions: Reg. 803.1 — Application to authorized foreign bank before Aug. 8/09.

Notes: Reg. 803 amended by P.C. 2009-1869, for taxation years that end after June 27, 1999, and (per P.C. 2009-1869 s. 14) an amount required to be paid by an authorized foreign bank under Reg. 803 is deemed paid on time if paid by June 9, 2010.

Definitions [Reg. 803]: "amount" — ITA 248(1); "registered non-resident insurer" — Reg. 804; "taxation year" — ITA 249; "taxpayer" — ITA 248(1).

803.1 [Repealed]

Notes: Reg. 803.1, for authorized foreign banks, added and repealed by P.C. 2009-1869. It applied only to amounts paid or credited before Aug. 8, 2009.

804. Interpretation
— In this Part, "registered non-resident insurer" means a non-resident corporation approved to carry on business in Canada under the *Insurance Companies Act*.

Notes: Reg. 804 amended by P.C. 2000-1714, retroactive to June 1992, to replace references to older legislation with the *Insurance Companies Act*.

Definitions [Reg. 804]: "business" — ITA 248(1); "Canada" — ITA 255, *Interpretation Act* 35(1); "corporation" — ITA 248(1), *Interpretation Act* 35(1); "non-resident" — ITA 248(1).

805. Other non-resident persons
— Subject to section 802, every non-resident person who carries on business in Canada is taxable under Part XIII of the Act on all amounts otherwise taxable under that Part except those amounts that

(a) may reasonably be attributed to the business carried on by the person through a permanent establishment (within the meaning assigned by section 8201) in Canada; or

(b) are required by subparagraph 115(1)(a)(iii.3) of the Act to be included in computing the person's taxable income earned in Canada for the year.

Related Provisions: Reg. 805.1 — Certificate confirming application of Reg. 805(a) or (b).

Notes: This rule applies even if the non-resident is a non-taxable non-profit organization: VIEWS doc 2007-0225861R3. A waiver [now a Reg. 805.1 certificate] is required even if the amount is attributable to a permanent establishment in Canada: 2002-0132815. For an example of how Reg. 805 might apply see 2013-0509771E5.

For "reasonably be attributed" in para. (a), see *729658 Alberta*, 2004 TCC 474.

Reg. 805(1)-(3) replaced with 805 by P.C. 2009-1869, this version for tax years that begin after Aug. 7, 2009. (Former Reg. 805(2) was effectively moved to Reg. 805.1.)

Definitions [Reg. 805]: "amount", "business" — ITA 248(1); "Canada" — ITA 255, *Interpretation Act* 35(1); "carries on business in Canada" — ITA 253; "corporation" — ITA 248(1), *Interpretation Act* 35(1); "non-resident" — ITA 248(1); "permanent establishment" — Reg. 8201; "person", "taxable income" — ITA 248(1).

Interpretation Bulletins [Reg. 805]: IT-420R3: Non-residents — income earned in Canada; IT-438R2: Crown charges — resource properties in Canada.

805.1 Payee certificate
— If a person (in this section referred to as the **"payee"**) files an application under this section with the Minister in respect of the anticipated payment or crediting of an amount to the payee, and the Minister determines that the amount is an amount described in paragraph 805(a) or (b), the Minister shall issue to the payee a certificate that records that determination.

Notes: Reg. 805.1 added by P.C. 2009-1869, effective Aug 9, 2009. It replaces former Reg. 805(2). See Notes to Reg. 805.

Definitions [Reg. 805.1]: "amount", "Minister", "person" — ITA 248(1).

806. [International organizations and agencies]
— For the purposes of paragraph (c) of the definition "fully exempt interest" in subsection 212(3) of the Act, the Bank for International Settlements and the European Bank for Reconstruction and Development are prescribed.

Notes: Reg. 806 replaced by 2017 budget bill #2, effective 2008. The former version listed international organizations and agencies for pre-2008 ITA 212(1)(b)(ii)(B).

806.1 [Repealed]

Notes: Reg. 806.1 repealed by 2017 budget bill #2, effective 2008. It listed international organizations and agencies for pre-2008 ITA 212(1)(b)(x).

806.2 Prescribed obligation
— For the purposes of the definition "participating debt interest" in subsection 212(3) of the Act, an obligation is a prescribed obligation if it is an indexed debt obligation and no amount payable in respect of it is

(a) contingent or dependent upon the use of, or production from, property in Canada; or

(b) computed by reference to

(i) revenue, profit, cash flow, commodity price or any other similar criterion, other than a change in the purchasing power of money, or

(ii) dividends paid or payable to shareholders of any class of shares.

Notes: Reg. 806.2 opening words amended by 2013 budget bill #2, effective 2008, to change application from ITA 212(1)(b) to 212(3)"participating debt interest".

Reg. 806.2 added by P.C. 1993-1331 and amended retroactively by P.C. 1996-1419, effective for debt obligations issued after October 16, 1991. The 1996 amendment effectively restricts the exception for a change in the purchasing power of money to subpara. (b)(i), rather than applying to the entire provision.

Definitions [Reg. 806.2]: "amount" — ITA 248(1); "Canada" — ITA 255, *Interpretation Act* 35(1); "class of shares" — ITA 248(6); "dividend", "indexed debt obligation", "prescribed", "property", "share", "shareholder" — ITA 248(1).

Interpretation Bulletins: IT-361R3: Exemption from Part XIII tax on interest payments to non-residents.

807. Identification of obligations — For the purposes of subsection 240(2) of the Act, the letters "AX" or the letter "F" as the case may be, shall be clearly and indelibly printed in gothic or similar style capital letters of seven point or larger size either as a prefix to the coupon number or on the lower right hand corner of each coupon or other writing issued in evidence of a right to interest on an obligation referred to in that subsection.

Definitions [Reg. 807]: "writing" — *Interpretation Act* 35(1).

808. Allowances in respect of investment in property in Canada — (1) [Allowance] — For the purposes of paragraph 219(1)(j) of the Act, the allowance of a corporation (other than an authorized foreign bank) for a taxation year in respect of its investment in property in Canada is prescribed to be the amount, if any, by which

(a) the corporation's qualified investment in property in Canada at the end of the year,

exceeds

(b) the amount determined under this paragraph for the immediately preceding taxation year.

Related Provisions: Reg. 808(1.1) — Where corporation becomes resident in Canada.

Notes: Reg. 808(1)(b) amended by P.C. 2010-548, for 2009 and later tax years.

Reg. 808(1) opening words amended by P.C. 2009-1869, this version effective for tax years that end after June 27, 1999.

Interpretation Bulletins: IT-137R3: Additional tax on certain corporations carrying on business in Canada.

(1.1) [Where corporation becomes resident] — Notwithstanding subsections (1) and (8), for the purpose of paragraph 219(1)(j) of the Act, the allowance of a corporation that becomes resident in Canada at any time is, in respect of its investment in property in Canada for its last taxation year that ends before that time, prescribed to be nil.

Notes: See Notes to ITA 128.1(1) re 128.1(1)(c.1). ITA 219 imposes branch tax, which is a proxy for Part XIII withholding tax on dividends if the non-resident corporation earned the income through a Canadian corporation. Reg. 808(1) specifies the allowance of a non-resident corporation in respect of its investment in property in Canada, for purposes of the branch tax. Reg. 808(1.1) overrides 808(1) and 808(8) when a non-resident corporation becomes resident in Canada. The corporation's investment allowance for the taxation year deemed to end immediately before immigration is nil. Thus, the corporation cannot claim an investment allowance for that year and is liable for branch tax on any unremitted profits of a Canadian branch arising in that year, or deferred from previous years. This treatment of unremitted profits from a Canadian branch on the parent's immigration to Canada is analogous to the treatment that would result under the migration rules in ITA 128.1(1)(c.1) if the Canadian branch of the immigrating corporation were instead a Canadian corporation it owned.

Reg. 808(1.1) added by P.C. 2009-1869, this version effective June 28, 1999.

(2) ["Qualified investment in property ..."] — For the purposes of subsection (1), where, at the end of a taxation year, a corporation is not a member of a partnership that was carrying on business in Canada at any time in the year, the corporation's "qualified investment in property in Canada at the end of the year" is the amount, if any, by which the aggregate of

(a) the cost amount to the corporation, at the end of the year, of land in Canada owned by it at that time for the purpose of gaining or producing income from a business carried on by it in Canada, other than land that is

(i) described in the corporation's inventory,

(ii) depreciable property,

(iii) a Canadian resource property, or

(iv) land the cost of which is or was deductible in computing the corporation's income,

(b) an amount equal to the aggregate of the cost amount to the corporation, immediately after the end of the year, of each depreciable property in Canada owned by it for the purpose of gaining or producing income from a business carried on by it in Canada,

(c) [Repealed]

(d) where the corporation is not a principal-business corporation, within the meaning assigned by subsection 66(15) of the Act, an amount equal to the total of the corporation's

(i) Canadian exploration and development expenses incurred by the corporation before the end of the year, except to the extent that those expenses were deducted in computing the corporation's income for the year or for a previous taxation year, and

(ii) cumulative Canadian exploration expense, within the meaning assigned by subsection 66.1(6) of the Act, at the end of the year minus any deduction under subsection 66.1(3) of the Act in computing the corporation's income for the year,

(d.1) an amount equal to the corporation's cumulative Canadian development expense, within the meaning assigned by subsection 66.2(5) of the Act, at the end of the year minus any deduction under subsection 66.2(2) of the Act in computing the corporation's income for the year,

(d.2) an amount equal to the corporation's cumulative Canadian oil and gas property expense, within the meaning assigned by subsection 66.4(5) of the Act, at the end of the year minus any deduction under subsection 66.4(2) of the Act in computing the corporation's income for the year,

(e) an amount equal to the aggregate of the cost amount to the corporation at the end of the year of each debt owing to it, or any other right of the corporation to receive an amount, that was outstanding as a result of the disposition by it of property in respect of which an amount would be included, by virtue of paragraph (a), (b) or (h), in its qualified investment in property in Canada at the end of the year if the property had not been disposed of by it before the end of that year,

(f) an amount equal to the aggregate of the cost amount to the corporation at the end of the year of each property, other than a Canadian resource property, that was described in the corporation's inventory in respect of a business carried on by it in Canada,

(g) an amount equal to the aggregate of the cost amount to the corporation at the end of the year of each debt (other than a debt referred to in paragraph (e) or a debt the amount of which was deducted under paragraph 20(1)(p) of the Act in computing the corporation's income for the year) owing to it

(i) in respect of any transaction by virtue of which an amount has been included in computing its income for the year or for a previous year from a business carried on by it in Canada, or

(ii) where any part of its ordinary business carried on in Canada was the lending of money, in respect of a loan made by the corporation in the ordinary course of that part of its business, and

(h) [Repealed]

(i) an amount equal to the allowable liquid assets of the corporation at the end of the year,

exceeds the aggregate of

(j) an amount equal to the total of all amounts each of which is an amount deducted under paragraph 20(1)(l), (l.1) or (n) of the Act in computing the corporation's income for the year from a business carried on by the corporation in Canada,

(k) an amount equal to the aggregate of all amounts each of which is an amount deducted by the corporation in the year under subparagraph 40(1)(a)(iii) or 44(1)(e)(iii) of the Act in respect of a debt referred to in paragraph (e);

(l) an amount equal to the aggregate of each amount owing by the corporation at the end of the year on account of

(i) the purchase price of property that is referred to in paragraph (a), (b) or (f) or that would be so referred to but for the fact that it has been disposed of before the end of the year,

(ii) Canadian exploration and development expenses, Canadian exploration expense, Canadian development expense or Canadian oil and gas property expense, or

(iii) [Repealed]

(iv) any other outlay or expense made or incurred by the corporation to the extent that it was deducted in computing its income for the year or for a previous taxation year from a business carried on by it in Canada;

(m) an amount equal to the aggregate of all amounts each of which is an amount equal to that proportion of the amount owing (other than an amount owing on account of an outlay or expense referred to in paragraph (l)) by the corporation at the end of the year on account of an obligation outstanding at any time in the year in respect of which interest is stipulated to be payable by it that

(i) the interest paid or payable on the obligation by the corporation in respect of the year that is deductible, or would be deductible but for subsection 18(2), (3.1) or (4) or section 21 of the Act, in computing its income for the year from a business carried on by it in Canada,

is of

(ii) the interest paid or payable on the obligation by the corporation in respect of the year;

(n) the amount, if any, by which

(i) the amount (referred to in this paragraph as "Part I liability"), if any, by which the tax payable for the year by the corporation under Part I of the Act exceeds the amount, if any, paid by the corporation before the end of the year on account thereof,

exceeds

(ii) that proportion of the Part I liability that the amount, if any, in respect of the corporation for the year that is the lesser of

(A) the amount, if any, by which the total of all amounts each of which is a taxable capital gain of the corporation for the year from a disposition of a taxable Canadian property that was not used or held by it in the year in the course of carrying on business in Canada exceeds the total of all amounts each of which is an allowable capital loss of the corporation for the year from a disposition of such a property, and

(B) the amount that would be determined under clause (A) for the year if it were read without reference to the expression "that was not used or held by it in the year in the course of carrying on business in Canada",

is of the corporation's taxable income earned in Canada for the year; and

(iii) [Repealed]

(o) the amount, if any, by which

(i) the amount (referred to in this paragraph as "provincial tax liability"), if any, by which any income taxes payable for the year by the corporation to the government of a province (to the extent that such taxes were not deductible under Part I of the Act in computing the corporation's income for the year from a business carried on by it in Canada) exceeds the amount, if any, paid by the corporation before the end of the year on account thereof,

exceeds

(ii) that proportion of the provincial tax liability that the amount, if any, in respect of the corporation for the year that is the lesser of

(A) the amount, if any, by which the total of all amounts each of which is a taxable capital gain of the corporation for the year from a disposition of a taxable Canadian property that was not used or held by it in the year in the course of carrying on business in Canada exceeds the total of all amounts each of which is an allowable capital loss of the corporation for the year from a disposition of such a property, and

(B) the amount that would be determined under clause (A) for the year if it were read without reference to the expression "that was not used or held by it in the year in the course of carrying on business in Canada",

is of the corporation's taxable income earned in Canada for the year.

(iii) [Repealed]

(p) [Repealed]

Notes: "Land" in (2)(a) includes buildings: see ITA 70(5.2) Notes. For "part of its ordinary business... was the lending of money" in (g)(ii), see ITA 15(2.3) Notes.

Reg. 808(2)(c) and (l)(iii) repealed, and (e) amended to delete reference to (c), by 2016 budget bill #2, effective 2017, as part of changing the eligible capital property rules to CCA Class 14.1 (see Notes to ITA 20(1)(b)). Before the amendment, read:

(c) an amount equal to ⁴/₃ of the cumulative eligible capital of the corporation immediately after the end of the year in respect of each business carried on by it in Canada,

. . . . .

(l)(iii) an eligible capital expenditure made or incurred by the corporation before the end of the year in respect of a business carried on by it in Canada, or

Reg. 808(2) amended by P.C. 2010-548 (for dispositions after Nov. 12, 1981 unless grandfathered), 2009-1869 (last change effective Nov. 19, 2009), 1994-1817.

(3) ["Allowable liquid assets ..."] — For the purposes of paragraph (2)(i), the "allowable liquid assets of the corporation at the end of the year" is an amount equal to the lesser of

(a) the aggregate of

(i) the amount of Canadian currency owned by the corporation at the end of that year,

(ii) the balance standing to the credit of the corporation at the end of that year as or on account of amounts deposited with a branch or other office in Canada of

(A) a bank,

(B) a corporation licensed or otherwise authorized under the laws of Canada or a province to carry on in Canada the business of offering to the public its services as trustee, or

(C) a credit union, and

(iii) an amount equal to the aggregate of the cost amount to the corporation at the end of that year of each bond, debenture, bill, note, mortgage or similar obligation that was not described in the corporation's inventory in respect of a business carried on by it in Canada (other than a debt referred to in paragraph (2)(e) or (g) or a debt the amount of which was deducted under paragraph 20(1)(p) of the Act in computing the corporation's income for the year), that was issued by a person resident in Canada with whom the corporation was dealing at arm's length and that matures within one year after the date on which it was acquired by the corporation,

to the extent that such amounts are attributable to the profits of the corporation from carrying on a business in Canada, or are used or held by the corporation in the year in the course of carrying on a business in Canada; and

(b) an amount equal to ⁴/₃ of the quotient obtained by dividing

(i) the aggregate of all amounts that would otherwise be determined under subparagraphs (a)(i), (ii) and (iii) if the references therein to "at the end of that year" were read as references to "at the end of each month in that year",

by

(ii) the number of months in that year.

Notes: CRA states that a pending refund of Reg. 105 withholdings is not an allowable liquid asset until the return is filed to claim it: VIEWS doc 2007-0257621I7.

Closing words of Reg. 808(3)(a) added by P.C. 1993-1548, for tax years ending after Aug. 11, 1993, to clarify that allowable liquid assets of a corporation do not include amounts that were not either generated by the Canadian branch operation or intended for the use of the Canadian branch.

(4) ["Qualified investment in property ..."] — For the purposes of subsection (1), where, at the end of a taxation year, a corporation is a member of a partnership that was carrying on business in Canada at any time in that year, the corporation's qualified investment in property in Canada at the end of the year is an amount equal to the aggregate of

(a) the amount, if any, that would be determined under subsection (2) if the corporation were not, at the end of the year, a member of a partnership that was carrying on business in Canada at any time in the year; and

(b) an amount equal to the portion of the amount of the partnership's qualified investment in property in Canada at the end of the last fiscal period of the partnership ending in the taxation year of the corporation that may reasonably be attributed to the corporation, having regard to all the circumstances including the rights the corporation would have, if the partnership ceased to exist, to share in the distribution of the property owned by the partnership for the purpose of gaining or producing income from a business carried on by it in Canada.

Notes: For interpretation of "reasonably be attributed" in para. (b), see *729658 Alberta*, 2004 TCC 474.

A corporate partner can look through an upper-tier partnership to pick up properties owned by a lower-tier partnership for Reg. 808(4): VIEWS doc 2016-0632881E5.

(5) ["Qualified investment ..." of partnership] — For the purposes of subsection (4), a partnership's "qualified investment in property in Canada" at the end of a fiscal period is the amount, if any, by which the aggregate of

(a) the cost amount to the partnership, at the end of the fiscal period, of land in Canada owned by it at that time for the purpose of gaining or producing income from a business carried on by it in Canada, other than land that is

(i) described in the inventory of the partnership,

(ii) depreciable property,

(iii) a Canadian resource property, or

(iv) land the cost of which is or was deductible in computing the income of the partnership or the income of a member of the partnership,

(b) an amount equal to the aggregate of the cost amount to the partnership immediately after the end of the fiscal period, of each depreciable property in Canada owned by it for the purpose of gaining or producing income from a business carried on by it in Canada,

(c) an amount equal to 4/3 of the cumulative eligible capital of the partnership immediately after the end of the fiscal period in respect of each business carried on by it in Canada,

(d) an amount equal to the aggregate of the cost amount to the partnership at the end of the fiscal period of each debt owing to it, or any other right of the partnership to receive an amount, that was outstanding as a result of the disposition by it of property in respect of which an amount would be included, by virtue of paragraph (a), (b) or (c), in its qualified investment in property in Canada at the end of the fiscal period if the property had not been disposed of by it before the end of that fiscal period,

(e) an amount equal to the aggregate of the cost amount to the partnership at the end of the fiscal period of each property, other than a Canadian resource property, that was described in the

partnership's inventory in respect of a business carried on by it in Canada,

(f) an amount equal to the aggregate of the cost amount to the partnership at the end of the fiscal period of each debt (other than a debt referred to in paragraph (d) or a debt the amount of which was deducted under paragraph 20(1)(p) of the Act in computing the partnership's income for the fiscal period) owing to it

(i) in respect of any transaction by virtue of which an amount has been included in computing its income for the fiscal period or for a previous fiscal period or in computing the income of a member of the partnership for a previous taxation year from a business carried on in Canada by the partnership, or

(ii) where any part of its ordinary business carried on in Canada was the lending of money, in respect of a loan made by the partnership in the ordinary course of that part of its business, and

(g) an amount equal to the allowable liquid assets of the partnership at the end of the fiscal period,

exceeds the aggregate of

(h) an amount equal to the total of all amounts each of which is an amount deducted under paragraph 20(1)(l), (l.1) or (n) of the Act in computing the partnership's income for the fiscal period from a business carried on by the partnership in Canada;

(i) an amount equal to the aggregate of all amounts each of which is an amount deducted by the partnership in the fiscal period under subparagraph 40(1)(a)(iii) or 44(1)(e)(iii) of the Act in respect of a debt referred to in paragraph (d);

(j) an amount equal to the aggregate of each amount owing by the partnership at the end of the fiscal period on account of

(i) the purchase price of property that is referred to in paragraph (a), (b) or (e) or that would be so referred to but for the fact that it has been disposed of before the end of the fiscal period,

(ii) Canadian exploration and development expenses, Canadian exploration expense, Canadian development expense or Canadian oil and gas property expense,

(iii) an eligible capital expenditure made or incurred by the partnership before the end of the fiscal period in respect of a business carried on by it in Canada, or

(iv) any other outlay or expense made or incurred by the partnership to the extent that it was deducted in computing its income for the fiscal period or for a previous fiscal period, or in computing the income of a member of the partnership for a previous taxation year, from a business carried on in Canada by the partnership; and

(k) an amount equal to the aggregate of all amounts each of which is an amount equal to that proportion of the amount owing (other than an amount owing on account of an outlay or expense referred to in paragraph (j)) by the partnership at the end of the fiscal period on account of an obligation outstanding at any time in the period in respect of which interest is stipulated to be payable by it that

(i) the interest paid or payable on the obligation by the partnership in respect of the fiscal period that is deductible, or would be deductible but for subsection 18(2) or (3.1) or section 21 of the Act, in computing its income for the fiscal period from a business carried on by it in Canada,

is of

(ii) the interest paid or payable on the obligation by the partnership in respect of the fiscal period.

Notes: "Land" in (5)(a) can include buildings: see ITA 70(5.2) Notes. For "part of its ordinary business ... was the lending of money" in (f)(ii), see ITA 15(2.3) Notes.

Reg. 808(5)(h) amended by P.C. 2010-548 (for dispositions after Nov. 12, 1981 unless grandfathered), 2009-1869 (effective Nov. 19, 2009).

(6) ["Allowable liquid assets ..." of partnership] — For the purposes of paragraph (5)(g), the "allowable liquid assets of the partnership at the end of the fiscal period" is an amount equal to the lesser of

(a) the total of the following amounts (to the extent that those amounts are attributable to the profits of the partnership from carrying on a business in Canada, or are used or held by the partnership in the year in the course of carrying on a business in Canada):

(i) the amount of Canadian currency owned by the partnership at the end of that fiscal period,

(ii) the balance standing to the credit of the partnership at the end of that fiscal period as or on account of amounts deposited with a branch or other office in Canada of

(A) a bank,

(B) a corporation licensed or otherwise authorized under the laws of Canada or a province to carry on in Canada the business of offering to the public its services as trustee, or

(C) a credit union, and

(iii) an amount equal to the aggregate of the cost amount to the partnership at the end of that fiscal period of each bond, debenture, bill, note, mortgage, hypothec or similar obligation that was not described in the partnership's inventory in respect of a business carried on by it in Canada (other than a debt referred to in paragraph (5)(d) or (f) or a debt the amount of which was deducted under paragraph 20(1)(p) of the Act in computing the partnership's income for the fiscal period), that was issued by a person resident in Canada with whom all the members of the partnership were dealing at arm's length and that matures within one year after the date on which it was acquired by the partnership; and

(b) an amount equal to ⁴/₃ of the quotient obtained by dividing

(i) the aggregate of all amounts that would otherwise be determined under subparagraphs (a)(i), (ii) and (iii) if the references therein to "at the end of that fiscal period" were read as references to "at the end of each month in that fiscal period",

by

(ii) the number of months in that fiscal period.

Notes: Reg. 808(6)(a) opening words changed from simply "the aggregate of" by P.C. 2009-1869, effective Aug. 8, 2000. The amendment clarifies that a partnership's allowable liquid assets do not include amounts that were not either generated by, or intended for the use of, its business carried on in Canada.

(7) [Partnerships] — Subsections (4) to (6) shall be read and construed as if each of the assumptions in paragraphs 96(1)(a) to (g) of the Act were made.

(8) [Allowance of authorized foreign bank] — For the purpose of paragraph 219(1)(j) of the Act, the allowance of an authorized foreign bank for a taxation year in respect of its investment in property in Canada is prescribed to be the amount, if any, by which

(a) the average of all amounts, each of which is the amount for a calculation period (within the meaning assigned by subsection 20.2(1) of the Act) of the bank for the year that is the greater of

(i) the amount determined by the formula

$$0.05 \times A$$

where

A is the amount of the element A in the formulae in subsection 20.2(3) of the Act for the period, and

(ii) the amount by which

(A) the total of the cost amount to the bank, at the end of the period (or, in the case of depreciable property or eligible capital property, immediately after the end of the year), of each asset in respect of the bank's Canadian banking business that is an asset recorded in the books of account of the business in a manner consistent with the

manner in which it is required to be treated for the purpose of the branch financial statements (within the meaning assigned by subsection 20.2(1) of the Act) for the year

exceeds

(B) the amount equal to the total of

(I) the amount determined by the formula

$$L + BA$$

where

L is the amount of the element L in the formulae in subsection 20.2(3) of the Act for the period, and

BA is the amount of the element BA in the formulae in subsection 20.2(3) of the Act for the period, and

(II) the amount claimed by the bank under clause 20.2(3)(b)(ii)(A) of the Act

exceeds

(b) the total of all amounts each of which is an amount that would be determined under paragraph (2)(j), (k), (n) or (o) if that provision applied to the bank for the year, except to the extent that the amount reflects a liability of the bank that has been included in the element L in the formulae in subsection 20.2(3) of the Act for the bank's last calculation period for the year.

Notes: Reg. 808(8) determines the allowance for investment in property in Canada by an authorized foreign bank (AFB). This is an exception to the general rule in Reg. 808(1). It recognizes that AFBs are required to have a minimum capital amount in Canada, and allows them to take that minimum into account in calculating the investment allowance for branch tax purposes.

Reg. 808(8) added by P.C. 2009-1869, effective June 28, 1999.

Definitions [Reg. 808]: "allowable capital loss" — ITA 38(b), 248(1); "allowable liquid assets of the corporation at the end of the year" — Reg. 808(3); "allowable liquid assets of the partnership at the end of the fiscal period" — Reg. 808(6); "amount" — ITA 248(1); "amount taxable" — ITA 123(1); "arm's length" — ITA 251(1); "authorized foreign bank" — ITA 248(1); "bank" — ITA 248(1), *Interpretation Act* 35(1); "branch financial statements" — ITA 20.2(1); "business" — ITA 248(1); "calculation period" — ITA 20.2(1); "Canada" — ITA 255, *Interpretation Act* 35(1); "Canadian banking business" — ITA 248(1); "Canadian development expense" — ITA 66.2(5), 248(1); "Canadian exploration and development expenses" — ITA 66(15), 248(1); "Canadian exploration expense" — ITA 66.1(6), 248(1); "Canadian oil and gas property expense" — ITA 66.4(5), 248(1); "carrying on a business in Canada", "carrying on business in Canada" — ITA 253; "corporation" — ITA 248(1), *Interpretation Act* 35(1); "cost amount" — ITA 248(1); "credit union" — ITA 137(6), 248(1); "cumulative eligible capital" — ITA 14(5), 248(1); "depreciable property" — ITA 13(21), 248(1); "disposed" — ITA 248(1)"disposition"; "disposition" — ITA 248(1); "eligible capital expenditure" — ITA 14(5), 248(1); "eligible capital property" — ITA 54 [repealed]; "fiscal period" — ITA 249.1; "inventory" — ITA 248(1); "land" — see ITA 70(5.2) Notes; "month" — *Interpretation Act* 35(1); "office" — ITA 248(1); "Part I liability" — Reg. 808(2)(n)(i); "partnership" — see ITA 96(1) Notes; "person", "prescribed" — ITA 248(1); "principal-business corporation" — ITA 66(15); "property" — ITA 248(1); "province" — *Interpretation Act* 35(1); "provincial tax liability" — Reg. 808(2)(o)(i); "qualified investment in property in Canada at the end of the fiscal period" — Reg. 808(5); "qualified investment in property in Canada at the end of the year" — Reg. 808(2), (4); "resident in Canada" — ITA 250; "share", "taxable Canadian property" — ITA 248(1); "taxable capital gain" — ITA 38(a), 248(1); "taxable income earned in Canada" — ITA 248(1); "taxation year" — ITA 249.

Interpretation Bulletins [Reg. 808]: IT-137R3: Additional tax on certain corporations carrying on business in Canada.

809. Reduction of certain amounts to be deducted or withheld — (1) Subject to subsection (2), where a non-resident person (in this section referred to as the **"payee"**) has filed with the Minister the payee's required statement for the year, the amount otherwise required by subsections 215(1) to (3) of the Act to be deducted or withheld from any qualifying payment paid or credited by a person resident in Canada (in this section referred to as the **"payer"**) to the payee in the year and after the required statement for the year was so filed is hereby reduced by the amount determined in accordance with the following rules:

(a) determine the amount by which

(i) the amount that would, if the payee does not make an election in respect of the year under section 217 of the Act, be the tax payable by the payee under Part XIII of the Act on the aggregate of the amounts estimated by him in his required statement for the year pursuant to paragraph (a) of the definition "required statement" in subsection (4),

exceeds

(ii) the amount that would, if the payee makes the election referred to in subparagraph (i), be the tax payable (on the assumption that no portion of the payee's income for the year was income earned in the year in a province) by the payee under Part I of the Act on his estimated taxable income calculated by him in his required statement for the year pursuant to paragraph (b) of the definition "required statement" in subsection (4),

(b) determine the percentage that the amount determined under paragraph (a) is of the aggregate of the amounts estimated by him in his required statement for the year pursuant to paragraph (a) of the definition "required statement" in subsection (4),

(c) where the determination of a percentage under paragraph (b) results in a fraction, disregard the fraction for the purposes of paragraph (d),

(d) multiply the percentage determined under paragraph (b) by the amount of the qualifying payment,

and the product obtained under paragraph (d) is the amount by which the amount required to be deducted or withheld is reduced.

Forms: NR5: Application by a non-resident of Canada for a reduction in the amount of non-resident tax required to be withheld; NR7-R: Application for refund of non-resident tax withheld; NR304: Direct deposit request for non-resident account holders and NR7-R refund applicants.

(2) Subsection (1) does not apply to reduce the amount to be deducted or withheld from a qualifying payment if, after the qualifying payment has been paid or credited by the payer, the aggregate of all qualifying payments that the payer has paid or credited to the payee in the year would exceed the amount estimated, in respect of that payer, by the payee in his required statement for the year pursuant to paragraph (a) of the definition "required statement" in subsection (4).

(3) Where a payee has filed with the Minister a written notice indicating that certain information or estimates in the payee's required statement for the year are incorrect and setting out the correct information or estimates that should be substituted therefor or where the Minister is satisfied that certain information or estimates in a payee's required statement for the year are incorrect and that the Minister has the correct information or estimates that should be substituted therefor, for the purposes of making the calculations in subsection (1) with respect to any qualifying payment paid or credited to the payee after the time when he has filed that notice or after the time when the Minister is so satisfied, as the case may be, the incorrect information or estimates shall be disregarded and the required statement for the year shall be deemed to contain only the correct information or estimates.

(4) In this section,

"qualifying payment" in relation to a non-resident person means any amount

(a) paid or credited, or to be paid or credited, to him as, on account or in lieu of payment of, or in satisfaction of, any amount described in paragraph 212(1)(f) or (h) or in any of paragraphs 212(1)(j), (k), (l), (m) or (q) of the Act, and

(b) on which tax under Part XIII of the Act is, or would be, but for an election by him under section 217 of the Act, payable by him;

"required statement" of a payee for a taxation year means a written statement signed by him that contains, in respect of the payee,

(a) the name and address of each payer of a qualifying payment in the year and, in respect of each such payer, an estimate by the payee of the aggregate of such qualifying payments, and

(b) a calculation by him of his estimated taxable income earned in Canada for the year, on the assumption that he makes the

election in respect of the year under section 217 of the Act, and such information as may be necessary for the purpose of estimating such income.

Definitions [Reg. 809]: "amount", "Minister", "non-resident" — ITA 248(1); "payee", "payer" — Reg. 809(1); "person" — ITA 248(1); "province" — *Interpretation Act* 35(1); "qualifying payment", "required statement" — Reg. 809(4); "resident in Canada" — ITA 250; "taxable income" — ITA 248(1); "taxable income earned in Canada" — ITA 248(1); "taxation year" — ITA 249; "written" — *Interpretation Act* 35(1)"writing".

810. [Repealed]

Notes: Reg. 810 repealed by P.C. 2009-1869, effective June 28, 1999. Its substance was moved to ITA 116(6)(e).

PART IX — [900] [REPEALED]

900. [Repealed.]

Notes: Reg. 900 repealed by P.C. 2002-2169, effective 2003. It provided for delegation of the Minister's powers to specific officials. See Notes to ITA 220(2.01), which now permits delegation by the Minister without regulations.

PART X — [1000–1001] ELECTION IN RESPECT OF DECEASED TAXPAYERS

1000. Property dispositions — **(1)** Any election under subsection 164(6) of the Act shall be made by the legal representative of a deceased taxpayer by filing with the Minister the following documents:

(a) a letter from the legal representative specifying

(i) the part of the one or more capital losses from the disposition of properties, if any, under paragraph 164(6)(c) of the Act, and

(ii) the part of the amount, if any, under paragraph 164(6)(d) of the Act

in respect of which the election is made;

(b) where an amount is specified under subparagraph (a)(i), a schedule of the capital losses and capital gains referred to in paragraph 164(6)(a) of the Act;

(c) where an amount is specified under subparagraph (a)(ii),

(i) a schedule of the amounts of undepreciated capital cost described in paragraph 164(6)(b) of the Act,

(ii) a statement of the amount that, but for subsection 164(6) of the Act, would be the non-capital loss of the estate for its first taxation year, and

(iii) a statement of the amount that, but for subsection 164(6) of the Act, would be the farm loss of the estate for its first taxation year.

(2) The documents referred to in subsection (1) shall be filed not later than the day that is the later of

(a) the last day provided by the Act for the filing of a return that the legal representative of a deceased taxpayer is required or has elected to file under the Act in respect of the income of that deceased taxpayer for the taxation year in which he died; and

(b) the day the return of the income for the first taxation year of the deceased taxpayer's estate is required to be filed under paragraph 150(1)(c) of the Act.

Definitions [Reg. 1000]: "amount" — ITA 248(1); "capital gain" — ITA 39(1), 248(1); "disposition" — ITA 248(1); "estate" — ITA 104(1), 248(1); "farm loss" — ITA 111(8), 248(1); "legal representative", "Minister" — ITA 248(1); "non-capital loss" — ITA 111(8), 248(1); "taxation year" — ITA 249; "taxpayer" — ITA 248(1); "undepreciated capital cost" — ITA 13(21), 248(1).

1000.1 Realization of [deceased employee's] options — **(1)** An election under subsection 164(6.1) of the Act shall be made by the legal representative of a deceased taxpayer by filing with the

Minister a letter from the legal representative setting out the following:

(a) the amount of the benefit referred to in subparagraph 164(6.1)(a)(i) of the Act;

(b) the value of the right, and the amount paid for the right, referred to in subparagraph 164(6.1)(a)(ii) of the Act;

(c) the deducted amount, referred to in subparagraph 164(6.1)(a)(iii) of the Act; and

(d) the amount of the loss referred to in paragraph 164(6.1)(b) of the Act.

(2) The letter shall be filed not later than the day that is the later of

(a) the last day provided by the Act for the filing of a return that the legal representative of a deceased taxpayer is required or has elected to file under the Act in respect of the income of that deceased taxpayer for the taxation year in which he or she died, and

(b) the day the return of the income for the first taxation year of the deceased taxpayer's estate is required to be filed under paragraph 150(1)(c) of the Act.

Notes: Reg. 1000.1 added by P.C. 2005-694, effective for deaths occurring after July 13, 1990; the letter referred to in Reg. 1000.1(2) could be filed by Nov. 14, 2005.

Definitions [Reg. 1000.1]: "amount" — ITA 248(1); "estate" — ITA 104(1), 248(1); "legal representative", "Minister" — ITA 248(1); "taxation year" — ITA 249; "taxpayer" — ITA 248(1).

1001. Annual instalments — Any election by a deceased taxpayer's legal representative under subsection 159(5) of the Act shall be made by filing with the Minister the prescribed form on or before the day on or before which payment of the first of the "equal consecutive annual instalments" referred to in that subsection is required to be made.

Definitions [Reg. 1001]: "legal representative", "Minister", "prescribed", "taxpayer" — ITA 248(1).

Forms: T2075: Election to defer payment of income tax, under subsection 159(5) by a deceased taxpayer's legal representative or trustee.

PART XI — [1100–1107] CAPITAL COST ALLOWANCES

Related Provisions [Part XI]: ITA 20(1.1) — Definitions in ITA 13(21) apply to regulations.

Forms [Part XI]: See under ITA 20(1)(a).

DIVISION I — DEDUCTIONS ALLOWED

1100. (1) For the purposes of paragraphs 8(1)(j) and (p) and 20(1)(a) of the Act, the following deductions are allowed in computing a taxpayer's income for each taxation year:

(a) **rates** — subject to subsection (2), such amount as the taxpayer may claim in respect of property of each of the following classes in Schedule II not exceeding in respect of property

Proposed Amendment — $1.5m immediate expensing for CCPCs

Federal Budget, Supplementary Information, April 19, 2021: *Immediate Expensing*

The capital cost allowance (CCA) system determines the deductions that a business may claim each year for income tax purposes in respect of the capital cost of its depreciable property. With some exceptions, depreciable property is divided into CCA classes and a CCA rate for each class of property is prescribed in the *Income Tax Regulations* [Reg. 1100(1)(a) — ed.].

Prior to November 21, 2018, the CCA allowed in the first year that a property was available for use was generally limited to half the amount that would otherwise be available (the "half-year" rule) [Reg. 1100(2) — ed.]. On November 21, 2018, the government announced a temporary enhanced first-year allowance, referred to as the Accelerated Investment Incentive, equal to up to three times the previously applicable first-year allowance [amended Reg. 1100(2) — ed.]. In addition, the government announced immediate expensing for investments in machinery and equipment used in manufacturing or processing, as well as for specified clean energy generation equipment.

Budget 2021 proposes to provide temporary immediate expensing in respect of certain property acquired by a Canadian-Controlled Private Corporation (CCPC). This immediate expensing would be available for "eligible property" acquired by a CCPC on or after April 19, 2021 and that becomes available for use before January 1, 2024, up to a maximum amount of $1.5 million per taxation year. The immediate expensing would only be available for the year in which the property becomes available for use. The $1.5 million limit would be shared among associated members of a group of CCPCs [ITA 256 — ed.]. The limit would be prorated for taxation years that are shorter than 365 days [Reg. 1100(3) — ed.]. The half-year rule [Reg. 1100(2), " — 0.5(C)" — ed.] would be suspended for property for which this measure is used. For those CCPCs with less than $1.5 million of eligible capital costs, no carry-forward of excess capacity would be allowed.

Eligible Property

Eligible property under this new measure would be capital property that is subject to the CCA rules, other than property included in CCA classes 1 to 6, 14.1, 17, 47, 49 and 51, which are generally long lived assets.

Interactions of the Immediate Expensing with Other Provisions

CCPCs with capital costs of eligible property in a taxation year that exceed $1.5 million would be allowed to decide to which CCA class the immediate expensing would be attributed and any excess capital cost would be subject to the normal CCA rules. The availability of other enhanced deductions under existing rules — such as the full expensing for manufacturing and processing machinery and equipment and for clean energy equipment, introduced in the 2018 Fall Economic Statement — would not reduce the maximum amount available under this new measure. In other words, a CCPC may expense up to $1.5 million in addition to all other CCA claims under existing provisions of the *Income Tax Act*, provided the total CCA deduction does not exceed the capital cost of the property.

Immediate expensing under this new rule would not change the total amount that can be deducted over the life of a property — the larger deduction taken in the first year in respect of a property would eventually be offset by a smaller deduction, if any, in respect of the property in future years.

Example of Benefits of Immediate Expensing of $1.5 million

A CCPC invests $2,000,000 in equal amounts for two properties, one falling under CCA Class 7, and the other under Class 10. Under this scenario, the CCPC would be allowed a total first-year deduction of up to $1,725,000 versus $675,000 under the existing rules, as illustrated in the table below. This would represent an additional deduction of $1,050,000 in the first year.

CCA Class (rate)	Cost of Acquisitions	Immediate Expensing	1st Year Allowance on Remainder of Class*	Total 1st Year Allowance	Current 1st Year Allowance*
Class 7 (15%)	1,000,000	1,000,000	0	1,000,000	225,000
Class 10 (30%)	1,000,000	500,000	225,000	725,000	450,000
Total	2,000,000	1,500,000	225,000	1,725,00	675,000

* Assuming eligible for the triple first-year allowance under the Accelerated Investment Incentive

Restrictions

The *Income Tax Act* and the Income Tax Regulations include a series of rules designed to protect the integrity of the CCA regime and the tax system more broadly. These include rules related to limited partners [ITA 96(2.1)–(2.7) — ed.], specified leasing properties [Reg. 1100(15)–(20) — ed.], specified energy properties [Reg. 1100(24)–(25) — ed.] and rental properties [Reg. 1100(11)–(14.2) — ed.]. In certain circumstances, these rules can restrict a CCA deduction, or a loss in respect of such a deduction, that would otherwise be available. These integrity rules would continue to apply.

Certain additional restrictions would be placed on property eligible for this new measure. Property that has been used, or acquired for use, for any purpose before it was acquired by the taxpayer would be eligible for the immediate expensing only if both of the following conditions are met:

• neither the taxpayer nor a non-arm's length person previously owned the property; and

• the property has not been transferred to the taxpayer on a tax-deferred "rollover" basis.

Coming Into Force

This measure would apply for eligible property that is acquired on or after April 19, 2021 and that becomes available for use before 2024.

Strategic Environmental Assessment Statement

This temporary measure is expected to encourage capital investments across all sectors of the economy and in a variety of assets. It is unclear whether it would result in net positive or negative environmental effects.

The consumption, transportation and fabrication of capital assets can lead to various negative environmental effects. These effects would be unequal across sectors and

Regulations

types of investments. For example, investment in certain capital intensive industries is associated with higher greenhouse gas and air pollutant emissions, water and soil pollution, and faster depletion of natural resources. These activities are subject to applicable federal and provincial environmental regulations. There may be positive offsetting environmental impacts if the measure causes businesses to upgrade to the latest technology, as newer technologies are generally more efficient and greener than older technologies.

Overall, the measure could have both positive and negative impacts on the achievement of some of the Federal Sustainable Development Strategy goals, in particular those of Effective Action on Climate Change, Clean Growth, Pristine Lakes and Rivers, Sustainably Managed Lands and Forests, and Safe and Healthy Communities. Based on available data, it is not possible to assess whether the net environmental impact would be positive or negative in the short run. In the long run, the net environmental impact is not expected to be significant, given that the measure would be temporary.

Notes: Budget Table 1 projects that this measure will cost the federal government $615 million in 2021-22, $1,055m in 2022-23, $985m in 2023-24, and will generate $145m of revenue [i.e., later CCA that will not be claimed] in 2024-25 and $265m in 2025-26.

   (i) of Class 1, 4 per cent,

Related Provisions: Reg. 1100(1)(a.1), (a.2) — Additional allowances for non-residential buildings; Reg. 1100(1)(a.3) — Additional 6% for LNG liquefaction building; Reg. 1100(1)(zc) — Additional allowance — railway property.

   (ii) of Class 2, 6 per cent,

Related Provisions: Reg. 1101(5i) — Separate class.

   (iii) of Class 3, 5 per cent,

Related Provisions: Reg. 1100(1)(sb), (zc).

   (iv) of Class 4, 6 per cent,

   (v) of Class 5, 10 per cent,

   (vi) of Class 6, 10 per cent,

Related Provisions: Reg. 1100(1)(sb), (zc).

   (vii) of Class 7, 15 per cent,

   (viii) of Class 8, 20 per cent,

Related Provisions: Reg. 1100(1)(sb), (zc).

   (ix) of Class 9, 25 per cent,

   (x) of Class 10, 30 per cent,

Related Provisions: Reg. 1100(1)(m) — Additional allowance — Canadian film or video production; Reg. 1100(1)(zc) — Additional allowance — railway property; Reg. 1100(21) — Certified films and video tapes — CCA limitation; Reg. 1100(21.1) — Non-certified films and video tapes — CCA limitation; Reg. 1101(5a), (5k), (5k.1) — Separate classes for telecommunications spacecraft, certified productions and Canadian film or video productions.

   (x.1) of Class 10.1, 30 per cent,

Related Provisions: Reg. 1101(1af) — Separate class.

   (xi) of Class 11, 35 per cent,

   (xii) of Class 12, 100 per cent,

Related Provisions: Reg. 1100(1)(l) — Additional allowance — certified production; 1100(21), (21.1), (22) — Films and videotapes.

   (xii.1) of Class 14.1, 5 per cent,

Related Provisions: Reg. 1100(1)(c.1) — Additional allowance until 2027 — pre-2017 eligible capital property.

   (xiii) of Class 16, 40 per cent,

   (xiv) of Class 17, 8 per cent,

   (xv) of Class 18, 60 per cent,

   (xvi) of Class 22, 50 per cent,

   (xvii) of Class 23, 100 per cent,

   (xviii) of Class 25, 100 per cent,

   (xix) of Class 26, 5 per cent,

   (xx) of Class 28, 30 per cent,

Related Provisions: Reg. 1100(1)(w), 1100(1)(zc)(i)(H).

   (xxi) of Class 30, 40 per cent,

Related Provisions: Reg. 1101(5a) — Separate class.

   (xxii) of Class 31, 5 per cent,

Related Provisions: Reg. 1101(5b) — Separate class.

   (xxiii) of Class 32, 10 per cent,

Related Provisions: Reg. 1101(5b) — Separate class.

   (xxiv) of Class 33, 15 per cent,

   (xxv) of Class 35, 7 per cent,

Related Provisions: Reg. 1100(1)(zc).

   (xxvi) of Class 37, 15 per cent,

   (xxvii) of Class 41, 25 per cent,

Related Provisions: Reg. 1100(1)(y), (ya).

   (xxvii.1) of Class 41.1, 25 per cent,

Related Provisions: Reg. 1100(1)(y.1), (ya.1) — Additional allowances.

   (xxvii.2) of Class 41.2, 25 per cent,

Related Provisions: Reg. 1100(1)(y.2), (ya.2) — Additional allowances.

   (xxviii) of Class 42, 12 per cent,

   (xxix) of Class 43, 30 per cent,

   (xxix.1) of Class 43.1, 30 per cent,

Related Provisions: Reg. 1100(2)A(b) — Accelerated incentive for year of acquisition.

   (xxix.2) of Class 43.2, 50 per cent,

Related Provisions: Reg. 1100(2)A(c) — Accelerated incentive for year of acquisition.

   (xxx) of Class 44, 25 per cent,

   (xxxi) of Class 45, 45 per cent,

   (xxxii) of Class 46, 30 per cent,

   (xxxiii) of Class 47, 8 per cent,

   (xxxiv) of Class 48, 15 per cent,

   (xxxv) of Class 49, 8 per cent,

   (xxxvi) of Class 50, 55 per cent,

Related Provisions: Reg. 1100(20.1), (20.2) — Limitation on claiming computer tax shelter property.

   (xxxvii) of Class 51, 6 per cent,

   (xxxviii) of Class 52, 100 per cent,

Related Provisions: Reg. 1100(20.1), (20.2) — Limitation on claiming computer tax shelter property.

   (xxxix) of Class 53, 50 per cent,

Related Provisions: Reg. 1100(2)A(d) — Accelerated incentive for year of acquisition.

   (xl) of Class 54, 30 per cent,

Related Provisions: Reg. 1100(2)A(e)(i) — 100% deduction for year of acquisition pre-2024.

   (xli) of Class 55, 40 per cent, and

Related Provisions: Reg. 1100(2)A(f)(i) — 100% deduction for year of acquisition pre-2024.

   (xlii) of Class 56, 30 per cent,

Related Provisions: Reg. 1100(2)A(e)(i) — 100% deduction for year of acquisition pre-2024.

of the undepreciated capital cost to the taxpayer as of the end of the taxation year (before making any deduction under this subsection for the taxation year) of property of the class;

Related Provisions [Reg. 1100(1)(a)]: Reg. 1100(2) — Half-year rule; Reg. 1100(3) — Short taxation year. See also list at end of Reg. 1100(1).

Notes [Reg. 1100(1)(a)]: For the year property is acquired, see the special rule in Reg. 1100(2).

Reg. 1100(1)(a)(xlii) added by 2021 budget bill #1, effective March 2, 2020.

Reg. 1100(1)(a)(xii.1) added by 2016 budget bill #2, effective 2017.

Reg. 1100(1)(a)(xxvii.2), for mining property, added by 2013 budget bill #2, effective for taxation years that end after March 20, 2013.

Reg. 1100(1)(a)(xxvii.1), for oil sands property, added by P.C. 2011-44, effective for taxation years ending after March 18, 2007.

Reg. 1100(1)(a)(xxviii), for fibre optic cable, added by P.C. 1994-139, effective for property acquired after Dec. 23, 1991, other than acquired pursuant to an agreement in writing entered into by the taxpayer by that date. However, if the taxpayer elected in a letter filed with Revenue Canada by Aug. 8, 1994 or filed with the taxpayer's return for the first taxation year ending after Dec. 23, 1991, then it, new Classes 3(j) and (l) and Class 42 apply to property acquired after the beginning of that taxation year.

Reg. 1100(1)(a)(xxix), for property in manufacturing and processing, added by P.C. 1994-230, effective for property acquired after February 25, 1992.

Reg. 1100(1)(a)(xxix.1), for energy conservation equipment, added by P.C. 1997-1033, effective February 22, 1994.

Reg. 1100(1)(a)(xxx), for patents or rights to use patented information, added by P.C. 1994-231, effective for property acquired after April 26, 1993.

Reg. 1100(1)(a)(xxxi) and (xxxii), for computers and data network equipment, added by P.C. 2005-2286, effective March 23, 2004.

Reg. 1100(1)(a)(xxix.2) and (xxxiii)-(xxxv), for high-energy and renewable energy generation equipment, transmission equipment, combustion turbines and transmission pipeline, added by P.C. 2006-439, effective Feb. 23, 2005.

Reg. 1100(1)(a)(xxxvi)-(xxxvii) added by P.C. 2009-581, effective March 19, 2007.

Reg. 1100(1)(a)(xxxviii), temporary incentive for computers and software, added by P.C. 2009-660, effective for property acquired after Jan. 27, 2009.

Reg. 1100(1)(a)(xxxix) added by 2015 Budget bill, effective June 23, 2015. See Notes to Reg. Sch. II:Cl. 53.

Reg. 1100(1)(a)(xl) and (xli) added by 2019 budget bill #1, effective June 21, 2019.

Income Tax Folios [Reg. 1100(1)(a)]: S3-F4-C1: General discussion of CCA [replaces IT-285R2].

Interpretation Bulletins [Reg. 1100(1)(a)]: IT-521R: Motor vehicle expenses claimed by self-employed individuals; IT-522R: Vehicle, travel and sales expenses of employees.

Information Circulars [Reg. 1100(1)(a)]: 84-1: Revision of capital cost allowance claims and other permissive deductions.

(a.1) Class 1 [M&P building] — where a separate class is prescribed by subsection 1101(5b.1) for a property of a taxpayer that is a building and at least 90 per cent of the floor space of the building is used at the end of the taxation year for the manufacturing or processing in Canada of goods for sale or lease, such amount as the taxpayer may claim not exceeding six per cent of the undepreciated capital cost to the taxpayer of the property of that class as of the end of the taxation year (before making any deduction under this subsection for the taxation year);

Related Provisions: Reg. 1100(1)(a.2) — Other non-residential buildings; Reg. 1102(23), (24) — Additions and alterations to buildings; Reg. 1102(25) — Building under construction on March 19, 2007; Reg. 1104(2)"eligible non-residential building" — Definition; Reg. 1104(9) — Meaning of "manufacturing or processing".

Notes [Reg. 1100(1)(a.1)]: This 6% allowance is in addition to the 4% allowed by Class 1. It applies only if an election is made with the return for the year of acquisition: Reg. 1101(5b.1). The building must be an "eligible non-residential building" as defined in Reg. 1104(2): VIEWS doc 2013-0515361E5. For interpretation see 2009-0332581E5 (evidence needed to show no use before March 19/07; effect of transfer of property to non-arm's length party); 2009-0342571I7; 2012-0469441E5 (bathroom, cafeteria and office can be counted towards the 90% if they are used by M&P staff); 2014-0530631E5 (SR&ED can be part of M&P). The first-year rule in Reg. 1100(2) applies to this allowance. See also Reg. 1104(9), and ITA 125.1(3)"manufacturing or processing" Notes, re that term.

Reg. 1100(1)(a.1) added by P.C. 2009-581, for property acquired after March 18, 2007.

Income Tax Folios: S4-F15-C1: Manufacturing and processing [replaces IT-147R3].

(a.2) [Class 1 — non-residential property] — where a separate class is prescribed by subsection 1101(5b.1) for a property of a taxpayer that is a building, at least 90 per cent of the floor space of the building is used at the end of the taxation year for a non-residential use in Canada and an additional allowance is not allowed for the year under paragraph (a.1) in respect of the property, such amount as the taxpayer may claim not exceeding two per cent of the undepreciated capital cost to the taxpayer of the property of that class as of the end of the taxation year (before making any deduction under this subsection for the taxation year);

Related Provisions: Reg. 1100(1)(a.3) — Additional allowance for LNG liquefaction building; Reg. 1102(23), (24) — Additions and alterations to buildings; Reg. 1102(25) — Building under construction on March 19, 2007; Reg. 1104(2)"eligible non-residential building" — Definition.

Notes [Reg. 1100(1)(a.2)]: This 2% allowance is in addition to the 4% allowed by Class 1, but it applies only if the 6% additional allowance for a building used in M&P (Reg. 1100(1)(a.1)) does not apply, and only if an election is made with the return for the year of acquisition: Reg. 1101(5b.1) (see Notes thereto). The building must be an "eligible non-residential building" as defined in Reg. 1104(2): VIEWS doc 2013-0515361E5. The first-year rule in Reg. 1100(2) applies to this allowance.

For interpretation of "non-residential" see VIEWS doc 2010-0361081E5 (test is objective *intended* use for sleeping and eating). A seniors' building is clearly not "non-residential use": 2009-0318441E5.

Reg. 1100(1)(a.2) added by P.C. 2009-581, for property acquired after March 18, 2007.

(a.3) [LNG liquefaction building acquired before 2025] — any additional amount that the taxpayer may claim in respect of property that is used as part of an eligible liquefaction facility for which a separate class is prescribed by subsection 1101(5b.2), not exceeding the lesser of

(i) the income for the taxation year from the taxpayer's eligible liquefaction activities in respect of the eligible liquefaction facility (taking into consideration any deduction under paragraph (yb) and before making any deduction under this paragraph), and

(ii) 6% of the undepreciated capital cost to the taxpayer of property of that separate class as of the end of the taxation year (before making any deduction under this subsection for the taxation year);

> ### Proposed Non-Amendment — Reg. 1100(1)(a.3), 1100(1)(yb)
>
> **Federal Budget, Chapter 8, March 22, 2016:** *Accelerated Capital Cost Allowance for Liquified Natural Gas Facilities*
>
> An accelerated capital cost allowance (CCA) is currently available for certain liquefied natural gas (LNG) facilities. For assets acquired before 2025 [Reg. 1104(2)"eligible liquefaction building", "eligible liquefaction equipment"(a) — ed.], an effective CCA rate of 30% is available for eligible liquefaction equipment [Reg. 1100(1)(a)(xxxiii), (yb)(ii) — ed.] and 10% for related buildings [Reg. 1100(1)(a)(i), (a.3)(ii) — ed.]. This treatment serves as an incentive to invest in new facilities that supply LNG to new markets.
>
> Consistent with Canada's G20 commitment to eliminate fossil fuel subsidies over the medium term, the Government intends to maintain this tax preference as currently legislated and allow it to expire as scheduled.

Related Provisions: Reg. 1100(1)(a)(i) — Initial 4% allowance (+6=10); Reg. 1100(1)(yb) — Additional CCA for LNG facility *equipment* acquired before 2025; Reg 1104(18) — Income from eligible liquefaction activities.

Notes: See Reg. 1101(5b.2) and 1104(2)"eligible liquefaction building". This 6% allowance (for property acquired before 2025) is in addition to the 4% allowed for Class 1 by Reg. 1100(1)(a)(i). The 2% usually allowed by Reg. 1100(1)(a.2) does not apply because Reg. 1101(5b.1) now excludes an eligible liquefaction building.

Reg. 1100(1)(a.3) added by P.C. 2015-629, effective Feb. 19, 2015 (date of the draft LNG regulations).

(b) Class 13 — such amount as the taxpayer may claim in respect of the capital cost to the taxpayer of property of Class 13 in Schedule II, not exceeding

(i) if the capital cost of the property was incurred in the taxation year and after November 12, 1981,

(A) if the property is an accelerated investment incentive property and the capital cost of the property was incurred before 2024, the lesser of

(I) 150 per cent of the amount for the year calculated in accordance with Schedule III, and

(II) the amount determined for paragraph 1(b) of Schedule III, and

(B) if the property is not an accelerated investment incentive property and is not described in any of subparagraphs (b)(iii) to (v) of the description of F in subsection (2), 50 per cent of the amount for the year calculated in accordance with Schedule III, and

(ii) in any other case, the amount for the year calculated in accordance with Schedule III,

and, for the purposes of this paragraph and Schedule III, the capital cost to a taxpayer of a property shall be deemed to have been incurred at the time at which the property became available for use by the taxpayer;

Related Provisions: Reg. 1102(4), (5) — Improvements or alterations to leased properties; Reg. 1104(4) — Accelerated investment incentive property.

Notes: Reg. 1100(1)(b)(i) amended by 2019 budget bill #1, effective June 21, 2019. Before that date, read:

> (i) where the capital cost of the property, other than property described in subparagraph (2)(a)(v), (vi) or (vii), was incurred in the taxation year and after November 12, 1981, 50 per cent of the amount for the year calculated in accordance with Schedule III, and

Regulations

Reference to Reg. 1100(2)(a)(vii) and closing words of Reg. 1100(1)(b) added by P.C. 1994-139, for property acquired after 1989. Reference to Reg. 1100(2)(a)(v) and (vi) added by P.C. 1991-465, for taxation years ending after April 26, 1989.

Interpretation Bulletins: IT-324: CCA — Emphyteutic lease (archived); IT-464R: CCA — Leasehold interests.

(c) **Class 14** — such amount as he may claim in respect of property of Class 14 in Schedule II not exceeding the lesser of

(i) the total of

(A) the aggregate of the amounts for the year obtained by apportioning the capital cost to the taxpayer of each property over the life of the property remaining at the time the cost was incurred, and

(B) if the property is accelerated investment incentive property, the portion of the amount determined under clause (A) that is in respect of the property multiplied by

(I) 0.5, if the property becomes available for use in the year and before 2024, and

(II) 0.25, if the property becomes available for use in the year and after 2023, and

(ii) the undepreciated capital cost to him as of the end of the taxation year (before making any deduction under this subsection for the taxation year) of property of the class;

Related Provisions: Reg. 1100(1)(a)(xxx) — 25% CCA rate for certain patents; Reg. 1100(3) — Short taxation year rule does not apply to Reg. 1100(1)(c); Reg. 1100(9) — Patents; Reg. 1104(4) — Accelerated investment incentive property.

Notes: See Notes to Reg. Schedule II, Class 14.

Reg. 1100(1)(c)(i)(B) added by 2019 budget bill #1, effective June 21, 2019.

Interpretation Bulletins: IT-143R3: Meaning of eligible capital expenditure; IT-477: CCA — Patents, franchises, concessions and licences.

(c.1) **additional allowances — Class 14.1** — for a taxation year that ends before 2027, such additional amount as the taxpayer may claim in respect of property of Class 14.1 of Schedule II not exceeding

(i) 2% of the particular amount by which the undepreciated capital cost of the class at the beginning of 2017 exceeds the total of all amounts each of which is

(A) the amount of a deduction taken under paragraph 20(1)(a) of the Act in respect of the class for a preceding taxation year, and

(B) equal to three times the amount of the capital cost of a property deemed by subsection 13(39) of the Act to be acquired by the taxpayer in the year or a preceding year, and

(ii) the amount determined by the formula

$$A - B$$

where

A is the lesser of

(A) $500, and

(B) the undepreciated capital cost of the class to the taxpayer as of the end of the year (before making any deduction under paragraph 20(1)(a) of the Act in respect of the class for the year), and

B is the total of all amounts deductible for the year under paragraph 20(1)(a) of the Act in respect of the class because of subparagraph (i) or (a)(xii.1);

Related Provisions: ITA 257 — Negative amounts in formulas.

Notes: See Notes to ITA 20(1)(b). The words "not exceeding" before subpara. (i) are intended to mean "not exceeding either of" (not "...the total of").

Subpara. (i) allows an extra 2%, over the 5% under Reg. 1100(1)(a)(xii.1), for pre-2017 eligible capital property (goodwill, etc.).

Subpara. (ii) allows the subpara. (i) amount to be topped up to $500 to the extent there is UCC still available in the class, to clear out small pre-2017 balances.

Reg. 1100(1)(c.1) added by 2016 budget bill #2, effective 2017, as part of changing the eligible capital property rules to Class 14.1.

(d) **in lieu of double depreciation** — such additional amount as he may claim not exceeding in the case of property described in each of the classes in Schedule II, the lesser of

(i) one-half the amount that would have been allowed to him in respect of property of that class under subparagraph 6(n)(ii) of the *Income War Tax Act* if that Act were applicable to the taxation year, and

(ii) the undepreciated capital cost to him as of the end of the taxation year (before making any deduction under this paragraph for the taxation year) of property of the class;

(e) **timber limits and cutting rights** — such amount as he may claim not exceeding the amount calculated in accordance with Schedule VI in respect of the capital cost to him of a property, other than a timber resource property, that is a timber limit or a right to cut timber from a limit;

Related Provisions: Reg. 1100(3) — Short taxation year rule does not apply to Reg. 1100(1)(e); Reg. 1101(3) — Separate class; Reg. 5202"cost of capital"(a), 5204"cost of capital"(a) — Manufacturing and processing credit.

Notes: For CRA interpretation see VIEWS doc 2014-0528021E5. For the meaning of "timber limit" see Notes to ITA 13(21)"timber resource property".

Interpretation Bulletins: IT-481: Timber resource property and timber limits.

(f) **Class 15** — such amount as he may claim not exceeding the amount calculated in accordance with Schedule IV, in respect of the capital cost to him of property of Class 15 in Schedule II;

Related Provisions: Reg. 1100(3) — Short taxation year rule does not apply to Reg. 1100(1)(f); Reg. 1102(7) — River improvements; Reg. 1102(17) — Recreational property; Reg. 5202"cost of capital"(a), 5204"cost of capital"(a) — Manufacturing and processing credit.

Notes: For CRA interpretation see VIEWS doc 2014-0528021E5.

(g) **industrial mineral mines** — such amount as he may claim not exceeding the amount calculated in accordance with Schedule V in respect of the capital cost to him of a property that is an industrial mineral mine or a right to remove industrial minerals from an industrial mineral mine;

Related Provisions: Reg. 1100(3) — Short taxation year rule does not apply to Reg. 1100(1)(g); Reg. 1101(4) — Separate class; Reg. 1104(3) — "Industrial mineral mine"; Reg. 3900 — Deduction for mining taxes; Reg. 5202"cost of capital"(a), 5204"cost of capital"(a) — Manufacturing and processing credit.

Notes: For the meaning of "industrial minerals" see ITA 125.3(1)"manufacturing or processing" Notes. CCA is claimed under Sch. V, not under any Class: VIEWS docs 2010-0385461E5, 2020-0850001E5. See also Reg. 1104(3)"industrial mineral mine" Notes.

Interpretation Bulletins: IT-423: Sale of sand, gravel or top soil (archived); IT-492: Industrial mineral mines.

(h) [Revoked]

(i) **additional allowances — fishing vessels** — such additional amount as he may claim in the case of property of a separate class prescribed by subsection 1101(2) not exceeding the lesser of

(i) the amount by which the depreciation that could have been taken on the property, if the Orders in Council referred to in that subsection were applicable to the taxation year, exceeds the amount allowed under paragraph (a) in respect of the property, and

(ii) the undepreciated capital cost to him as of the end of the taxation year (before making any deduction under this paragraph for the taxation year) of property of the class;

Interpretation Bulletins: IT-267R2: CCA — vessels.

(j), (k) [Repealed]

Notes: Reg. 1100(1)(j)-(k) repealed by P.C. 1995-775, effective May 31, 1995. They provided an additional allowance for property for which a certificate was issued by the Minister of Supply and Services under former Reg. 1106. Such certificates were introduced during the Korean War in 1951 and have not been used for many years.

(l) **additional allowances — certified productions** — [No longer relevant]

Notes: This rule applies only to Reg. 1101(5k) property, which is a "certified production" (Reg. 1104(2)) acquired before March 1996 (Class 10(w)).

(m) additional allowance — Canadian film or video production — such additional amount as the taxpayer claims in respect of property for which a separate class is prescribed by subsection 1101(5k.1) not exceeding the lesser of

(i) the taxpayer's income for the year from the property, determined before making any deduction under this paragraph, and

(ii) the undepreciated capital cost to the taxpayer of the property of that separate class at the end of the year (before making any deduction under this paragraph for the year and computed without reference to subsection (2));

Notes: For CRA interpretation see VIEWS doc 2008-0267041I7.

Reg. 1100(1)(m) added by P.C. 2005-698, for 1995 and later tax years. It implements a 1995 Budget proposal to replace the exclusion from the at-risk rules for film productions (ITA 96(2.2)(d)(ii)) with a new credit (ITA 125.4) and eligibility for additional CCA. (An earlier Reg. 1100(1)(m) was revoked in 1978.)

(n) [Applies only to obsolete Class 19]

(o) [Applies only to obsolete Class 19]

(p) **Class 20** — [Applies only to obsolete Class 20]

(q) **Class 21** — [Applies only to obsolete Class 21]

(r), (s), (sa) [Revoked]

(sb) additional allowances — grain storage facilities — such additional amount as he may claim in respect of property included in Class 3, 6 or 8 in Schedule II

(i) that is

(A) a grain elevator situated in that part of Canada that is defined in section 2 of the *Canada Grain Act* as the "Eastern Division" the principal use of which

(I) is the receiving of grain directly from producers for storage or forwarding or both,

(II) is the receiving and storing of grain for direct manufacture or processing into other products, or

(III) has been certified by the Minister of Agriculture to be the receiving of grain that has not been officially inspected or weighed,

(B) an addition to a grain elevator described in clause (A),

(C) fixed machinery installed in a grain elevator in respect of which, or in respect of an addition to which, an additional amount has been or may be claimed under this paragraph,

(D) fixed machinery, designed for the purpose of drying grain, installed in a grain elevator described in clause (A),

(E) machinery designed for the purpose of drying grain on a farm, or

(F) a building or other structure designed for the purpose of storing grain on a farm,

(ii) that was acquired by the taxpayer in the taxation year or in one of the three immediately preceding taxation years, at a time that was after April 1, 1972 but before August 1, 1974, and

(iii) that was not used for any purpose whatever before it was acquired by the taxpayer,

not exceeding the lesser of

(iv) where the property is included in Class 3, 22 per cent of the capital cost thereof, where the property is included in Class 6, 20 per cent of the capital cost thereof or where the property is included in Class 8,

(A) 14 per cent of the capital cost thereof in the case of property referred to in clause (i)(C), (D) or (F), and

(B) 14 per cent of the lesser of $15,000 and the capital cost thereof in the case of property described in clause (i)(E), and

(v) the undepreciated capital cost to him as of the end of the taxation year (before making any deduction under this paragraph for the taxation year) of property of the class;

(t) Classes 24, 27, 29 and 34 — [applies only to the taxation year that includes Nov. 12, 1981]

Related Provisions: Reg. 1100(24) — Specified energy property.

(ta) [Classes 24, 27, 29 and 34] — for taxation years commencing after November 12, 1981, such amount as he may claim in respect of property of each of Classes 24, 27, 29 and 34 in Schedule II not exceeding the aggregate of

(i) the aggregate of

(A) the lesser of

(I) 50 per cent of the capital cost to him of all designated property of the class acquired by him in the year, and

(II) the undepreciated capital cost to him of property of the class as of the end of the year (before making any deduction under this paragraph for the year and, where any of the property referred to in subclause (I) was acquired by virtue of a specified transaction, computed as if no amount were included in respect of property, other than designated property of the class acquired by him in the year), and

(B) 25 per cent of the lesser of

(I) the undepreciated capital cost to him of property of the class as of the end of the year (computed as if no amount were included in respect of designated property of the class acquired by him in the year and before making any deduction under this paragraph for the year), and

(II) the capital cost to him of all property, other than designated property, of the class acquired by him in the year, and

(ii) the lesser of

(A) the amount, if any, by which

(I) the undepreciated capital cost to him of property of the class as of the end of the year (before making any deduction under this paragraph for the year)

exceeds

(II) the capital cost to him of all property of the class acquired by him in the year, and

(B) an amount equal to the aggregate of

(I) 50 per cent of the capital cost to him of all property of the class acquired by him in the immediately preceding taxation year, other than designated property of the class acquired in a specified transaction, and

(II) the amount, if any, by which the amount determined under clause (A) for the year with respect to the class exceeds the aggregate of 75 per cent of the capital cost to him of all property, other than designated property, of the class acquired by him in the immediately preceding taxation year and 50 per cent of the capital cost to him of designated property of the class acquired by him in the immediately preceding taxation year, other than designated property of the class acquired in a specified transaction,

and for the purposes of this paragraph and paragraph (t), "designated property" of a class means

(iii) property of the class acquired by him before November 13, 1981,

(iv) property deemed to be designated property of the class by virtue of paragraph (2.1)(g) or (2.2)(j), and

(v) property described in any of subparagraphs (b)(iii) to (v) of the description of F in subsection (2),

1797

and, for the purposes of this paragraph,

(vi) "specified transaction" means a transaction to which subsection 85(5), 87(1), 88(1), 97(4) or 98(3) or (5) of the Act applies, and

(vii) subject to paragraph (2.2)(j), a property shall be deemed to have been acquired by a taxpayer at the time at which the property became available for use by the taxpayer;

Related Provisions: Reg. 1100(2.2)(j); Reg. 1100(24) — Specified energy property.

Notes: Reg. 1100(1)(ta) allows 25%, 50%, 25% straight-line over 3 years: tinyurl.com/class29-cra. For year 1 (Y1), (ta)(i)(B) allows 25%; for Y2, (ta)(ii)(B)(I) allows 50%; for Y3, (ta)(ii)(A)(I) allows the final 25%. However, for property acquired after Nov. 20, 2018, the Accelerated Investment Incentive in Reg. 1100(2) doubles the first-year claim to 50%. Where Cl. 29 property is transferred not at arm's length, see VIEWS doc 2018-0785371E5.

Reg. 1100(1)(ta)(v) amended by 2019 budget bill #1, effective June 21, 2019, to change "in subparagraph (2)(a)(v), (vi) or (vii)" to "in any of subparagraphs (b)(iii) to (v) of the description of F in subsection (2)" (due to renumbering of Reg. 1100(2)).

Reg. 1100(1)(ta)(vii) and reference to 1100(2)(a)(vii) in Reg. 1100(1)(ta)(v) added by P.C. 1994-139, for property acquired after 1989. Reg. 1100(1)(ta)(v) added by P.C. 1991-465, for tax years ending after April 26, 1989.

Income Tax Folios: S4-F15-C1: Manufacturing and processing [replaces IT-147R3].

Interpretation Bulletins: IT-336R: CCA — Pollution control property (archived).

(u) [Revoked]

(v) **Canadian vessels** — such amount as the taxpayer may claim in respect of property that is

(i) a vessel described in subsection 1101(2a),

(ii) included in a separate prescribed class because of subsection 13(14) of the Act, or

(iii) a property that has been constituted a prescribed class by subsection 24(2) of Chapter 91 of the Statutes of Canada, 1966-67,

not exceeding the lesser of

(iv) the capital cost of the property to the taxpayer multiplied by

(A) 50 per cent, in the case of an accelerated investment incentive property acquired in the year and before 2024,

(B) 16 ⅔ per cent, in the case of property acquired in the year, other than

(I) accelerated investment incentive property, and

(II) property described in any of subparagraphs (b)(iii) to (v) of the description of F in subsection (2), and

(C) 33 ⅓ per cent, in any other case, and

(v) the undepreciated capital cost to the taxpayer as of the end of the taxation year (before making any deduction under this paragraph for the taxation year) of property of the class,

and, for the purposes of subparagraph (iv), a property shall be deemed to have been acquired by a taxpayer at the time at which the property became available for use by the taxpayer for the purposes of the Act;

Related Provisions: Reg. 1104(4) — Accelerated investment incentive property.

Notes: Reg. 1100(1)(v)(iv) amended by 2019 budget bill #1, effective June 21, 2019, effectively to add cl. (A). Before that date, read:

(iv) where the property, other than property described in subparagraph (2)(a)(v), (vi) or (vii), was acquired in the taxation year and after November 12, 1981, 16 ⅔ per cent of the capital cost thereof to the taxpayer and, in any other case, 33 ⅓ per cent of the capital cost thereof to the taxpayer, and

Reg. 1100(1)(v)(i) and (ii) amended, reference to Reg. 1100(2)(a)(vii) in Reg. 1100(1)(v)(iv) added, and closing words of Reg. 1100(1)(v) added by P.C. 1994-139, this version for property acquired after July 13, 1990. Accelerated CCA for vessels and conversion costs is now verified by CRA as part of the normal audit process.

Parenthetical exclusion in Reg. 1100(1)(v)(iv) added by P.C. 1991-465, effective for taxation years ending after April 26, 1989.

Interpretation Bulletins: IT-267R2: CCA — Vessels.

Advance Tax Rulings: ATR-52: Accelerated rate of CCA for vessels.

(va) **additional allowances — offshore drilling vessels** — such additional amount as he may claim in respect of property for which a separate class is prescribed by subsection

1101(2b) not exceeding 15 per cent of the undepreciated capital cost to him of property of that class as of the end of the taxation year (before making any deduction under this subsection for the taxation year);

Interpretation Bulletins: IT-267R2: CCA — vessels.

(w) **additional allowances — Class 28** — subject to section 1100A, such additional amount as he may claim in respect of property described in Class 28 acquired for the purpose of gaining or producing income from a mine or in respect of property acquired for the purpose of gaining or producing income from a mine and for which a separate class is prescribed by subsection 1101(4a), not exceeding the lesser of

(i) the taxpayer's income for the taxation year from the mine, before making any deduction under this paragraph, paragraph (x), (y), (y.1), (y.2), (ya), (ya.1) or (ya.2), section 65, 66, 66.1, 66.2 or 66.7 of the Act or section 29 of the *Income Tax Application Rules*, and

(ii) the undepreciated capital cost to him of property of that class as of the end of the taxation year (before making any deduction under this paragraph for the taxation year);

Related Provisions: Reg. 1100(3) — Short taxation year rule does not apply to Reg. 1100(1)(w); Reg. 1104(5) — Income from a mine; Reg. 1104(7) — Meaning of "mine".

Notes: Reg. 1100(1)(w)(i) amended by 2013 budget bill #2, for tax years that end after March 20, 2013, to change "year" to "taxation year" and add reference to paras. (y.2) and (ya.2).

Reg. 1100(1)(w)(i) amended to add reference to paras. (y.1) and (ya.1) by P.C. 2011-44, effective for taxation years ending after March 18, 2007.

Reg. 1100(1)(w)(i) amended by P.C. 2007-114, for taxation years that begin after 2006, to delete references to ITA 12(1)(z.5) and 20(1)(v.1).

Reg. 1100(1)(w)(i) amended by P.C. 1999-629, for taxation years that begin after 1996, to add reference to ITA 12(1)(z.5).

(x) subject to section 1100A, such additional amount as he may claim in respect of property acquired for the purpose of gaining or producing income from more than one mine and for which a separate class is prescribed by subsection 1101(4b), not exceeding the lesser of

(i) the taxpayer's income for the taxation year from the mines, before making any deduction under this paragraph, paragraph (ya), (ya.1) or (ya.2), section 65, 66, 66.1, 66.2 or 66.7 of the Act or section 29 of the *Income Tax Application Rules*, and

(ii) the undepreciated capital cost to him of property of that class as of the end of the taxation year (before making any deduction under this paragraph for the taxation year);

Related Provisions: Reg. 1100(3) — Short taxation year rule does not apply to Reg. 1100(1)(x); Reg. 1104(5) — Income from a mine; Reg. 1104(7) — Meaning of "mine".

Notes: Reg. 1100(1)(x)(i) amended by 2013 budget bill #2, for taxation years that end after March 20, 2013, to change "year" to "taxation year" and add reference to paras. (y.2) and (ya.2).

Reg. 1100(1)(x)(i) amended to add reference to para. (ya.1) by P.C. 2011-44, effective for taxation years ending after March 18, 2007.

Reg. 1100(1)(x)(i) amended by P.C. 2007-114, for taxation years that begin after 2006, to delete references to ITA 12(1)(z.5) and 20(1)(v.1).

Reg. 1100(1)(x)(i) amended by P.C. 1999-629, for taxation years that begin after 1996, to add reference to ITA 12(1)(z.5).

(y) **additional allowances — Class 41** — such additional amount as the taxpayer may claim in respect of property acquired for the purpose of gaining or producing income from a mine and for which a separate class is prescribed by subsection 1101(4c), not exceeding the lesser of

(i) the taxpayer's income for the taxation year from the mine, before making any deduction under this paragraph, paragraph (x), (ya), (ya.1) or (ya.2), section 65, 66, 66.1, 66.2 or 66.7 of the Act or section 29 of the *Income Tax Application Rules*, and

(ii) the undepreciated capital cost to the taxpayer of property of that class as of the end of the taxation year (computed without reference to subsection (2) and before making any deduction under this paragraph for the taxation year);

Related Provisions: Reg. 1100(3) — Short taxation year rule does not apply to Reg. 1100(1)(y); Reg. 1104(5) — Income from a mine; Reg. 1104(7) — Meaning of "mine".

Notes: For a CRA ruling see VIEWS doc 2007-02222741R3.

Reg. 1100(1)(y)(i) amended by 2013 budget bill #2, for tax years that end after March 20, 2013, to change "year" to "taxation year" and add reference to para. (ya.2).

Reg. 1100(1)(y)(i) amended to add reference to para. (ya.1) by P.C. 2011-44, effective for taxation years ending after March 18, 2007.

Reg. 1100(1)(y)(i) amended by P.C. 2007-114, effective for taxation years that begin after 2006, to delete references to ITA 12(1)(z.5) and 20(1)(v.1).

Reg. 1100(1)(y)(i) amended by P.C. 1999-629, effective for taxation years that begin after 1996, to add reference to ITA 12(1)(z.5).

Reg. 1100(1)(y)(ii) amended by P.C. 1992-2335, to correct "end of a taxation year" to "end of the taxation year", effective 1988.

Interpretation Bulletins: IT-476R: CCA — Equipment used in petroleum and natural gas activities.

(y.1) additional allowances — Class 41.1 — such additional amount as the taxpayer may claim in respect of property acquired for the purpose of gaining or producing income from a mine and for which a separate class is prescribed by subsection 1101(4e), not exceeding the amount determined by the formula

$$A \times B$$

where

A is the lesser of

(i) the taxpayer's income for the taxation year from the mine, before making any deduction under this paragraph, paragraph (x), (y), (y.2), (ya), (ya.1) or (ya.2), section 65, 66, 66.1, 66.2 or 66.7 of the Act or section 29 of the *Income Tax Application Rules*, and

(ii) the undepreciated capital cost to the taxpayer of property of that class as of the end of the taxation year computed

(A) without reference to subsection (2),

(B) after making any deduction under paragraph (a) for the taxation year, and

(C) before making any deduction under this paragraph; and

B is the percentage that is the total of

(i) that proportion of 100% that the number of days in the taxation year that are before 2011 is of the number of days in the taxation year,

(ii) that proportion of 90% that the number of days in the taxation year that are in 2011 is of the number of days in the taxation year,

(iii) that proportion of 80% that the number of days in the taxation year that are in 2012 is of the number of days in the taxation year,

(iv) that proportion of 60% that the number of days in the taxation year that are in 2013 is of the number of days in the taxation year,

(v) that proportion of 30% that the number of days in the taxation year that are in 2014 is of the number of days in the taxation year, and

(vi) 0%, if one or more days in the year are after 2014;

Related Provisions: Reg. 1100(1)(ya.1) — Additional allowances — multiple mine properties; Reg. 1104(5) — Income from a mine; Reg. 1104(7) — Meaning of "mine".

Notes: For rulings applying (y.1) see docs 2009-0307841R3, 2009-0314541R3.

Reg. 1100(1)(y.1)A(i) amended by 2013 budget bill #2, for tax years that end after March 20, 2013, to change "year" to "taxation year" and add reference to paras. (y.2) and (ya.2).

Reg. 1100(1)(y.1)B(vi) added by 2013 budget bill #2, for taxation years that end after March 20, 2013.

Reg. 1100(1)(y.1) added by P.C. 2011-44, effective for tax years ending after March 18, 2007. It and 1100(1)(ya.1) are part of the 2007 Budget changes phasing out accelerated CCA for oil sands projects from 2010-15.

(y.2) additional allowances — Class 41.2 — single mine properties — such additional amount as the taxpayer may claim in respect of property acquired for the purpose of gaining or producing income from a mine and for which a separate class is prescribed by subsection 1101(4g), not exceeding the amount determined by the formula

$$A \times B$$

where

A is the lesser of

(i) the taxpayer's income for the taxation year from the mine, before making any deduction under this paragraph, paragraph (x), (y), (ya), (ya.1) or (ya.2), section 65, 66, 66.1, 66.2 or 66.7 of the Act or section 29 of the *Income Tax Application Rules*, and

(ii) the undepreciated capital cost to the taxpayer of property of that class as of the end of the year computed

(A) without reference to subsection (2),

(B) after making any deduction under paragraph (a) for the year, and

(C) before making any deduction under this paragraph, and

B is the percentage that is the total of

(i) that proportion of 100% that the number of days in the year that are before 2017 is of the number of days in the year,

(ii) that proportion of 90% that the number of days in the year that are in 2017 is of the number of days in the year,

(iii) that proportion of 80% that the number of days in the year that are in 2018 is of the number of days in the year,

(iv) that proportion of 60% that the number of days in the year that are in 2019 is of the number of days in the year,

(v) that proportion of 30% that the number of days in the year that are in 2020 is of the number of days in the year, and

(vi) 0%, if one or more days in the year are after 2020;

Related Provisions: Reg. 1100(1)(a)(xxvii.2) — Base CCA of 25%; Reg. 1100(1)(ya.2) — Multiple mine properties; Reg. 1104(5) — Income from a mine.

Notes: Reg. 1100(1)(y.2) and (ya.2) phase out the additional allowance for mining properties. Both added by 2013 budget bill #2, effective for taxation years that end after March 20, 2013. Table A2.1 in the Budget papers forecast that these measures would save the federal government $10 million in 2017-18.

Proposed **Reg. 1100(1)(y.3)** of the Feb. 19, 2015 draft regulations is now Reg. 1100(1)(yb).

(ya) [property for more than one mine] — such additional amount as the taxpayer may claim in respect of property acquired for the purpose of gaining or producing income from more than one mine and for which a separate class is prescribed by subsection 1101(4d), not exceeding the lesser of

(i) the taxpayer's income for the year from the mines, before making any deduction under this paragraph, section 65, 66, 66.1, 66.2 or 66.7 of the Act or section 29 of the *Income Tax Application Rules*, and

(ii) the undepreciated capital cost to the taxpayer of property of that class as of the end of the taxation year (computed without reference to subsection (2) and before making any deduction under this paragraph for the taxation year);

Related Provisions: Reg. 1100(3) — Short taxation year rule does not apply to Reg. 1100(1)(ya); Reg. 1104(5) — Income from a mine; Reg. 1104(7) — Meaning of "mine".

Notes: Reg. 1100(1)(ya)(i) amended by P.C. 2007-114, for tax years that begin after 2006, to delete references to ITA 12(1)(z.5) and 20(1)(v.1).

Reg. 1100(1)(ya)(i) amended by P.C. 1999-629, effective for taxation years that begin after 1996, to add reference to ITA 12(1)(z.5).

Interpretation Bulletins: IT-476R: CCA — Equipment used in petroleum and natural gas activities.

(ya.1) additional allowances — Class 41.1 — multiple mine properties — such additional amount as the taxpayer may claim in respect of property acquired for the purpose of gaining or producing income from more than one mine and for which a separate class is prescribed by subsection 1101(4f), not exceeding the amount determined by the formula

$$A \times B$$

where

A is the lesser of

(i) the taxpayer's income for the taxation year from the mines, before making any deduction under this paragraph, paragraph (ya) or (ya.2), section 65, 66, 66.1, 66.2 or 66.7 of the Act or section 29 of the *Income Tax Application Rules*, and

(ii) the undepreciated capital cost to the taxpayer of property of that class as of the end of the taxation year computed

(A) without reference to subsection (2),

(B) after making any deduction under paragraph (a) for the taxation year, and

(C) before making any deduction under this paragraph; and

B is the percentage that is the total of

(i) that proportion of 100% that the number of days in the taxation year that are before 2011 is of the number of days in the taxation year,

(ii) that proportion of 90% that the number of days in the taxation year that are in 2011 is of the number of days in the taxation year,

(iii) that proportion of 80% that the number of days in the taxation year that are in 2012 is of the number of days in the taxation year,

(iv) that proportion of 60% that the number of days in the taxation year that are in 2013 is of the number of days in the taxation year,

(v) that proportion of 30% that the number of days in the taxation year that are in 2014 is of the number of days in the taxation year, and

(vi) 0%, if one or more days in the year are after 2014;

Related Provisions: Reg. 1100(1)(y.1) — Additional allowances — single mine properties; Reg. 1104(5) — Income from a mine; Reg. 1104(7) — Meaning of "mine".

Notes: Reg. 1100(1)(ya.1)A(i) amended by 2013 budget bill #2, for tax years that end after March 20, 2013, to change "year" to "taxation year" and add reference to (ya.2).

Reg. 1100(1)(ya.1)B(vi) added by 2013 budget bill #2, for taxation years that end after March 20, 2013.

Reg. 1100(1)(ya.1) added by P.C. 2011-44, effective for taxation years ending after March 18, 2007. See Notes to Reg. 1100(1)(y.1).

(ya.2) additional allowances Class 41.2 — multiple mine properties — such additional amount as the taxpayer may claim in respect of a property acquired for the purpose of gaining or producing income from more than one mine and for which a separate class is prescribed by subsection 1101(4h), not exceeding the amount determined by the formula

$$A \times B$$

where

A is the lesser of

(i) the taxpayer's income for the taxation year from the mines, before making any deduction under this paragraph, paragraph (ya), section 65, 66, 66.1, 66.2 or 66.7 of the Act or section 29 of the *Income Tax Application Rules*, and

(ii) the undepreciated capital cost to the taxpayer of property of that class as of the end of the year computed

(A) without reference to subsection (2),

(B) after making any deduction under paragraph (a) for the year, and

(C) before making any deduction under this paragraph, and

B is the percentage that is the total of

(i) that proportion of 100% that the number of days in the year that are before 2017 is of the number of days in the year,

(ii) that proportion of 90% that the number of days in the year that are in 2017 is of the number of days in the year,

(iii) that proportion of 80% that the number of days in the year that are in 2018 is of the number of days in the year,

(iv) that proportion of 60% that the number of days in the year that are in 2019 is of the number of days in the year,

(v) that proportion of 30% that the number of days in the year that are in 2020 is of the number of days in the year, and

(vi) 0%, if one or more days in the year are after 2020;

Related Provisions: Reg. 1100(1)(a)(xxvii.2) — Base CCA of 25%; Reg. 1100(1)(y.2) — Single mine properties; Reg. 1104(5) — Income from a mine; Reg. 1104(7) — Meaning of "mine".

Notes: See Notes to Reg. 1100(1)(y.2).

(yb) additional allowance — Class 47 [LNG liquefaction facility equipment] — any additional amount as the taxpayer may claim in respect of property used as part of an eligible liquefaction facility for which a separate class is prescribed by subsection 1101(4i), not exceeding the lesser of

(i) the income for the taxation year from the taxpayer's eligible liquefaction activities in respect of the eligible liquefaction facility (taking into consideration any deduction under paragraph (a.3) and before making any deduction under this paragraph), and

(ii) 22% of the undepreciated capital cost to the taxpayer of property of that separate class as of the end of the taxation year (before making any deduction under this subsection for the taxation year);

Proposed Non-Amendment — Reg. 1100(1)(yb)

Federal Budget, Chapter 8, March 22, 2016: See under Reg. 1100(1)(a.3).

Related Provisions: Reg. 1100(1)(a)(xxxiii) — Initial 8% allowance (+22=30); Reg. 1100(1)(a.3) — Additional allowance for LNG liquefaction building acquired before 2025; Reg 1104(18) — Income from eligible liquefaction activities.

Notes: See Reg. 1101(4i) and 1104(2)"eligible liquefaction equipment". This 22% allowance (for property acquired before 2025) is in addition to the 8% allowed for Class 47 by Reg. 1100(1)(a)(xxxiii), so the total allowed is 30%. See PMO and Finance news releases, Feb. 19, 2015.

Reg. 1100(1)(yb) added by P.C. 2015-629, effective Feb. 19, 2015. This was proposed 1100(1)(y.3) in the Feb. 19, 2015 draft regulations.

(z) additional allowances — railway cars — such additional amount as the taxpayer may claim in respect of property for which a separate class is prescribed by paragraph 1101(5d)(c) not exceeding eight per cent of the undepreciated capital cost to the taxpayer of property of that class as of the end of the taxation year (before making any deduction under this subsection for the taxation year);

Notes: Reg. 1100(1)(z) amended by P.C. 1991-465, effective April 27, 1989, to refer to Reg. 1101(5d)(c) rather than Reg. 1101(5d).

(z.1a) [additional allowance — railway cars] — such additional amount as the taxpayer may claim in respect of property for which a separate class is prescribed by paragraph 1101(5d)(d), (e) or (f), not exceeding six per cent of the undepreciated capital cost to the taxpayer of property of that class as of the end of the taxation year (before making any deduction under this subsection for the taxation year);

Related Provisions: Reg. 1103(2i) — Election to include Class 7(h) property in Class 35.

Notes: Reg. 1100(1)(z.1a) added by P.C. 1991-465, for property acquired after April 26, 1989 or Feb. 2, 1990 (for details see up to the 55th ed.).

(z.1b) **[railway property]** — where throughout the taxation year the taxpayer was a common carrier that owned and operated a railway, such additional amount as the taxpayer may claim in respect of property for which a separate class is prescribed by subsection 1101(5d.1), not exceeding three per cent of the undepreciated capital cost to the taxpayer of property of that class as of the end of the year (before making any deduction under this subsection for the year);

Notes: Reg. 1100(1)(z.1b) added by P.C. 1994-139, for property acquired after Dec. 6, 1991.

(z.1c) **[railway property]** — where throughout the taxation year the taxpayer was a common carrier that owned and operated a railway, such additional amount as the taxpayer may claim in respect of property for which a separate class is prescribed by subsection 1101(5d.2), not exceeding six percent of the undepreciated capital cost to the taxpayer of property of that class as of the end of the year (before making any deduction under this subsection for the year);

Related Provisions: Reg. 1103(2i) — Election to include Class 7(h) property in Class 35.

Notes: Reg. 1100(1)(z.1c) added by P.C. 2005-2186, for property acquired after Feb. 27, 2000. It provides an extra 6% CCA for railway property included in a separate Class 35 (7% CCA) due to Reg. 1101(5d.2). See Notes to Reg. 1103(2i).

(za) **additional allowances — railway track and related property** — such additional amount as he may claim in respect of property for which a separate class is prescribed by subsection 1101(5e) not exceeding four per cent of the undepreciated capital cost to him of property of that class as of the end of the taxation year (before making any deduction under this subsection for the taxation year);

(za.1) **[railway track and related property]** — where throughout the taxation year the taxpayer was a common carrier that owned and operated a railway, such additional amount as the taxpayer may claim in respect of property for which a separate class is prescribed by subsection 1101(5e.1), not exceeding six per cent of the undepreciated capital cost to the taxpayer of property of that class as of the end of the year (before making any deduction under this subsection for the year);

Notes: Reg. 1100(1)(za.1) added by P.C. 1994-139, for property acquired after Dec. 6, 1991.

(za.2) **[trestles]** — where throughout the taxation year the taxpayer was a common carrier that owned and operated a railway, such additional amount as the taxpayer may claim in respect of property for which a separate class is prescribed by subsection 1101(5e.2), not exceeding five per cent of the undepreciated capital cost to the taxpayer of property of that class as of the end of the year (before making any deduction under this subsection for the year);

Notes: Reg. 1100(1)(za.2) added by P.C. 1994-139, for property acquired after Dec. 6, 1991.

(zb) **[trestles]** — such additional amount as he may claim in respect of property for which a separate class is prescribed by subsection 1101(5f) not exceeding three per cent of the undepreciated capital cost to him of property of that class as of the end of the taxation year (before making any deduction under this subsection for the taxation year);

(zc) **additional allowances — railway expansion and modernization property** — where the taxpayer owns and operates a railway as a common carrier, such additional amount as he may claim in respect of property of a class in Schedule II (in this paragraph referred to as "designated property" of the class)

(i) that is

(A) included in Class 1 in Schedule II by virtue of paragraph (h) or (i) of that Class,

(B) a bridge, culvert, subway or tunnel included in Class 1 in Schedule II that is ancillary to railway track and grading,

(C) a trestle included in Class 3 in Schedule II that is ancillary to railway track and grading,

(D) included in Class 6 in Schedule II by virtue of paragraph (j) of that Class,

(E) machinery or equipment included in Class 8 in Schedule II that is ancillary to

(I) railway track and grading, or

(II) railway traffic control or signalling equipment, including switching, block signalling, interlocking, crossing protection, detection, speed control or retarding equipment, but not including property that is principally electronic equipment or systems software therefor,

(F) machinery or equipment included in Class 8 in Schedule II that

(I) was acquired principally for the purpose of maintaining or servicing, or

(II) is ancillary to and used as part of,

a railway locomotive or railway car,

(G) included in Class 10 in Schedule II by virtue of subparagraph (m)(i), (ii) or (iii) of that Class,

(H) included in Class 28 in Schedule II by virtue of subparagraph (d)(ii) of that Class (other than property referred to in subparagraph (m)(iv) of Class 10), or

(I) included in Class 35 in Schedule II,

(ii) that was acquired by him principally for use in or is situated in Canada,

(iii) that was acquired by him in respect of the railway in the taxation year or in one of the four immediately preceding taxation years, at a time that was after April 10, 1978 but before 1988, and

(iv) that was not used for any purpose whatever before it was acquired by him,

not exceeding the lesser of

(v) six per cent of the aggregate of the capital cost to him of the designated property of the class, and

(vi) the undepreciated capital cost to him as of the end of the taxation year (after making all deductions claimed by him under other provisions of this subsection for the taxation year but before making any deduction under this paragraph for the taxation year) of property of the class;

(zd) **Class 38** — such amount as the taxpayer may claim in respect of property of Class 38 in Schedule II not exceeding that percentage which is the aggregate of

(i) that proportion of 40 per cent that the number of days in the taxation year that are in 1988 is of the number of days in the taxation year that are after 1987,

(ii) that proportion of 35 per cent that the number of days in the taxation year that are in 1989 is of the number of days in the taxation year, and

(iii) that proportion of 30 per cent that the number of days in the taxation year that are after 1989 is of the number of days in the taxation year

of the undepreciated capital cost to the taxpayer of property of that class as of the end of the taxation year (before making any deduction under this paragraph for the taxation year);

(ze) [Applies only to obsolete Class 39]

(zf) [Applies only to obsolete Class 40]

(zg) **additional allowance — year 2000 computer hardware and systems software** — [No longer relevant.]

Notes: Reg. 1100(1)(zg) added by P.C. 2000-1000, for 1998 and later tax years. It and (zh) allowed accelerated CCA to small- and medium-sized businesses for an immediate full writeoff of computer equipment and software acquired by Oct. 31, 1999 to replace systems that were not Y2K compliant.

(zh) additional allowance — year 2000 computer software — [No longer relevant.]

Notes: Reg. 1100(1)(zh) added by P.C. 2000-1000, effective for 1998 and later taxation years. See Notes to Reg. 1100(1)(zg).

Former proposed Reg. **1100(1)(zi)** in the Feb. 26/08 draft regulations (2008 Budget), which would have provided an additional allowance for certain Class 43 property acquired in 2010-11, has been superseded by the 2009 Budget regulations which place such property acquired before 2012 in Class 29.

Related Provisions [Reg. 1100(1)]: Reg. 1100(1.1) — Specified leasing property; Reg. 1100(3) — Taxation year less than 12 months; Reg. 1100(11) — Rental properties; Reg. 1100(15) — Leasing properties; ITA 20(1.1) — Definitions in ITA 13(21) apply to regulations.

Interpretation Bulletins [Reg. 1100(1)]: See at start of Reg. Part XI.

Forms [Reg. 1100(1)]: See at start of Reg. Part XI.

(1.1) [Specified leasing property — limitation] — Notwithstanding subsections (1) and (3), the amount deductible by a taxpayer for a taxation year in respect of a property that is a specified leasing property at the end of the year is the lesser of

(a) the amount, if any, by which the aggregate of

(i) all amounts that would be considered to be repayments in the year or a preceding year on account of the principal amount of a loan made by the taxpayer if

(A) the taxpayer had made the loan at the time that the property last became a specified leasing property and in a principal amount equal to the fair market value of the property at that time,

(B) interest had been charged on the principal amount of the loan outstanding from time to time at the rate, determined in accordance with section 4302, in effect at the earlier of

(I) the time, if any, before the time referred to in subclause (II), at which the taxpayer last entered into an agreement to lease the property, and

(II) the time that the property last became a specified leasing property

(or, where a particular lease provides that the amount paid or payable by the lessee of the property for the use of, or the right to use, the property varies according to prevailing interest rates in effect from time to time, and the taxpayer so elects, in respect of all of the property that is the subject of the particular lease, in the taxpayer's return of income under Part I of the Act for the taxation year of the taxpayer in which the particular lease was entered into, the rate determined in accordance with section 4302 that is in effect at the beginning of the period for which the interest is being calculated), compounded semi-annually not in advance, and

(C) the amounts that were received or receivable by the taxpayer before the end of the year for the use of, or the right to use, the property before the end of the year and after the time it last became a specified leasing property were blended payments of principal and interest, calculated in accordance with clause (B), on the loan applied firstly on account of interest on principal, secondly on account of interest on unpaid interest, and thirdly on account of principal, and

(ii) the amount that would have been deductible under this section for the taxation year (in this subparagraph referred to as the "particular year") that includes the time (in this subparagraph referred to as the "particular time") at which the property last became a specified leasing property of the taxpayer, if

(A) the property had been transferred to a separate prescribed class at the later of

(I) the beginning of the particular year, and

(II) the time at which the property was acquired by the taxpayer,

(B) the particular year had ended immediately before the particular time, and

(C) where the property was not a specified leasing property immediately before the particular time, subsection (3) had applied,

exceeds

(iii) the aggregate of all amounts deducted by the taxpayer in respect of the property by reason of this subsection before the commencement of the year and after the time at which it last became a specified leasing property; and

(b) the amount, if any, by which,

(i) the aggregate of all amounts that would have been deducted by the taxpayer under this Part in respect of the property under paragraph 20(1)(a) of the Act in computing the income of the taxpayer for the year and all preceding taxation years had this subsection and subsections (11) and (15) not applied, and had the taxpayer, in each such year deducted under paragraph 20(1)(a) of the Act the maximum amount allowed under this Part, read without reference to this subsection and subsection (11) and (15), in respect of the property,

exceeds

(ii) the total depreciation allowed to the taxpayer before the commencement of the year in respect of the property.

Related Provisions: ITA 16.1 — Election to treat lease as a sale; Reg. 1100(1.11) — Meaning of "specified leasing property"; Reg. 1100(1.12); Reg. 4302 — Prescribed rate of interest.

Notes: The prescribed interest rate for Reg. 1100(1.1)(a)(i)(B) is set in Reg. 4302, unlike the general prescribed rate in Reg. 4301.

An election "in the taxpayer's return" (Reg. 1100(1.1)(a)(i)(B)) is valid even if the return is filed late. See Notes to ITA 7(1.31).

See also Notes to Reg. 1100(1.3).

I.T. Technical News: 21 (cancellation of Interpretation Bulletin IT-233R).

(1.11) ["Specified leasing property"] — In this section and subsection 1101(5n), "specified leasing property" of a taxpayer at any time means depreciable property (other than exempt property) that is

(a) used at that time by the taxpayer or a person with whom the taxpayer does not deal at arm's length principally for the purpose of gaining or producing gross revenue that is rent or leasing revenue,

(b) the subject of a lease at that time to a person with whom the taxpayer deals at arm's length and that, at the time the lease was entered into, was a lease for a term of more than one year, and

(c) the subject of a lease of property where the tangible property, other than exempt property, that was the subject of the lease had, at the time the lease was entered into, an aggregate fair market value in excess of $25,000,

but, for greater certainty, does not include intangible property, or for civil law incorporeal property, (including systems software and property referred to in paragraph (w) of Class 10 or paragraph (n) or (o) of Class 12 in Schedule II).

Related Provisions: Reg. 1100(1.12)–(1.3), (17.2) — Interpretation; Reg. 1101(5n) — Separate class.

Notes: For CRA interpretation see VIEWS doc 2013-0382821I (solar photovoltaic generating equipment would be non-exempt specified leasing property). SLP of a principal-business leasing corporation is excluded from the half-year rule by Reg. 1100(2)(a)(v) [proposed Reg. 1100(2)I:R(b)(iii)]. See 2010-0384021E5.

Reg. 1100(1.11) closing words amended by P.C. 2010-548, effective May 12, 2010, to add "or for civil law incorporeal property".

(1.12) [Specified leasing property — new property] — Notwithstanding subsections (1) and (1.1), where, in a taxation year, a taxpayer has acquired a property that was not used by the taxpayer for any purpose in that year and the first use of the property by the taxpayer is a lease of the property in respect of which subsection (1.1) applies, the amount allowed to the taxpayer under subsection (1) in respect of the property for the year shall be deemed to be nil.

(1.13) [Specified leasing property — interpretation] — For the purposes of this section,

(a) **"exempt property"** means

(i) general purpose office furniture or office equipment included in Class 8 in Schedule II (including, for greater certainty, mobile office equipment such as cellular telephones and pagers) or general purpose electronic data processing equipment and ancillary data processing equipment, included in paragraph (f) of Class 10 in Schedule II, other than any individual piece thereof having a capital cost to the taxpayer in excess of $1,000,000,

(i.1) general-purpose electronic data processing equipment and ancillary data processing equipment, included in Class 45, 50 or 52 in Schedule II, other than any individual item of that type of equipment having a capital cost to the taxpayer in excess of $1,000,000,

(ii) furniture, appliances, television receivers, radio receivers, telephones, furnaces, hot-water heaters and other similar properties, designed for residential use,

(iii) a property that is a motor vehicle that is designed or adapted primarily to carry individuals on highways and streets and that has a seating capacity for not more than the driver and eight passengers, or a motor vehicle of a type commonly called a van or pick-up truck, or a similar vehicle,

(iv) a truck or tractor that is designed for hauling freight on highways,

(v) a trailer that is designed for hauling freight and to be hauled under normal operating conditions by a truck or tractor described in subparagraph (iv),

(vi) a building or part thereof included in Class 1, 3, 6, 20, 31 or 32 in Schedule II (including component parts such as electric wiring, plumbing, sprinkler systems, air-conditioning equipment, heating equipment, lighting fixtures, elevators and escalators) other than a building or part thereof leased primarily to a lessee that is

(A) a person who is exempt from tax by reason of section 149 of the Act,

(B) a person who uses the building in the course of carrying on a business the income from which is exempt from tax under Part I of the Act by reason of any provision of the Act, or

(C) a Canadian government, municipality or other Canadian public authority,

who owned the building or part thereof at any time before the commencement of the lease (other than at any time during a period ending not later than one year after the later of the date the construction of the building or part thereof was completed and the date the building or part thereof was acquired by the lessee),

(vii) vessel mooring space, and

(viii) property that is included in Class 35 in Schedule II,

and for the purposes of subparagraph (i), where a property is owned by two or more persons or partnerships, or any combination thereof, the capital cost of the property to each such person or partnership shall be deemed to be the total of all amounts each of which is the capital cost of the property to such a person or partnership;

(a.1) notwithstanding paragraph (a), **"exempt property"** does not include property that is the subject of a lease if that property

had, at the time the lease was entered into, an aggregate fair market value in excess of $1,000,000 and the lessee of the property is

(i) a person who is exempt from tax by reason of section 149 of the Act,

(ii) a person who uses the property in the course of carrying on a business, the income from which is exempt from tax under Part I of the Act by reason of any provision of the Act,

(iii) a Canadian government, or

(iv) a person not resident in Canada, except if the person uses the property primarily in the course of carrying on a business in Canada that is not a treaty-protected business;

(a.2) for the purposes of paragraph (a.1), if it is reasonable, having regard to all the circumstances, to conclude that one of the main reasons for the existence of two or more leases was to avoid the application of paragraph (a.1) by reason of each such lease being a lease of property where the property that was the subject of the lease had an aggregate fair market value, at the time the lease was entered into, not in excess of $1,000,000, each such lease shall be deemed to be a lease of property that had, at the time the lease was entered into, an aggregate fair market value in excess of $1,000,000;

(b) property shall be deemed to be the subject of a lease for a term of more than one year at any time where, at that time

(i) the property had been leased by the lessee thereunder, a person with whom the lessee does not deal at arm's length, or any combination thereof, for a period of more than one year ending at that time, or

(ii) it is reasonable, having regard to all the circumstances, to conclude that the lessor thereunder knew or ought to have known that the lessee thereunder, a person with whom the lessee does not deal at arm's length, or any combination thereof, would lease the property for more than one year; and

(c) for the purposes of paragraph (1.11)(c), where it is reasonable, having regard to all the circumstances, to conclude that one of the main reasons for the existence of two or more leases was to avoid the application of subsection (1.1) by reason of each such lease being a lease of property where the tangible property, other than exempt property, that was the subject of the lease had an aggregate fair market value, at the time the lease was entered into, not in excess of $25,000, each such lease shall be deemed to be a lease of tangible property that had, at the time the lease was entered into, an aggregate fair market value in excess of $25,000.

Related Provisions: Reg. 1100(1.14); Reg. 8200 — Prescribed property for leasing rules.

Notes: A Ground Source Heat Pump System designed for residential use falls within (a)(ii) and (vi): VIEWS doc 2008-0284691E5.

Reg. 1100(1.13)(a.1) and (a.2) implement a March 2010 Budget proposal to extend the Specified Leasing Property rules to otherwise exempt property that is the subject of a lease to a government or other tax-exempt entity. See Monica Biringer, "Budget Proposal Regarding Specified Leasing Rules", XVI(3) *Corporate Finance* (Federated Press) 1855-57 (2010).

For "one of the main reasons" in paras. (a.2) and (c), see ITA 83(2.1) Notes.

Reg. 1100(1.13)(a.1) and (a.2) added by 2002-2013 technical bill, for property that is the subject of a lease entered into after 4pm EST, March 4, 2010.

Reg. 1100(1.13)(a)(i.1) amended by P.C. 2009-581, for property acquired after March 18, 2007, to refer to Class 50; and by P.C. 2009-660, for property acquired after Jan. 27, 2009, to refer to Class 52.

P.C. 2001-1378 provides that notwithstanding P.C. 1991-465 and 1994-139, Reg. 1100(1.13)(a)(iii) is deemed to apply in respect of leases entered into after 10pm EDT, April 26, 1989, other than leases entered into pursuant to an agreement in writing entered into before that time under which the lessee thereunder has the right to require the lease of the property, and for these purposes a lease in respect of which a material change has been agreed to by the parties to it effective at any particular time that is after 10pm EDT, April 26, 1989, is deemed entered into at that particular time.

Reg. 1100(1.13)(a)(i.1) added by P.C. 2005-2286, effective March 23, 2004.

Reg. 1100(1.13)(a)(iii) amended by P.C. 1994-139, for tax years and fiscal periods that start after June 17, 1987 and end after 1987.

Reg. 1100(1.13)(a)(viii) amended by P.C. 1994-139, for property acquired after December 23, 1991, with certain grandfathering for property acquired before 1993.

For earlier acquisitions, read (viii) "a railway car".

See also Reg. 1100(1.3) Notes.

(1.14) [Specified leasing property — election] — For the purposes of subsection (1.11) and notwithstanding subsection (1.13), where a taxpayer referred to in subsection (16) so elects in the taxpayer's return of income under Part I of the Act for a taxation year in respect of the year and all subsequent taxation years, all of the property of the taxpayer that is the subject of leases entered into in those years shall be deemed not to be exempt property for those years and the aggregate fair market value of all of the tangible property that is the subject of each such lease shall be deemed to have been, at the time the lease was entered into, in excess of $25,000.

Notes: An election "in the taxpayer's return" is valid even if the return is filed late. See Notes to ITA 7(1.31).

(1.15) [Specified leasing property — term of more than one year] — Subject to subsection (1.16) and for the purposes of subsection (1.11), where at any time a taxpayer acquires property that is the subject of a lease with a remaining term at that time of more than one year from a person with whom the taxpayer was dealing at arm's length, the taxpayer shall be deemed to have entered into a lease of the property at that time for a term of more than one year.

(1.16) [Specified leasing property — amalgamation] — Where, at any time, a taxpayer acquires from a person with whom the taxpayer is not dealing at arm's length, or by virtue of an amalgamation (within the meaning assigned by subsection 87(1) of the Act), property that was specified leasing property of the person from whom the taxpayer acquired it, the taxpayer shall, for the purposes of paragraph (1.1)(a) and for the purpose of computing the income of the taxpayer in respect of the lease for any period after the particular time, be deemed to be the same person as, and a continuation of, that person.

(1.17) [Specified leasing property — replacement property] — For the purposes of subsections (1.1) and (1.11), where at any particular time a property (in this subsection referred to as a "replacement property") is provided by a taxpayer to a lessee for the remaining term of a lease as a replacement for a similar property of the taxpayer (in this subsection referred to as the "original property") that was leased by the taxpayer to the lessee, and the amount payable by the lessee for the use of, or the right to use, the replacement property is the same as the amount that was so payable in respect of the original property, the following rules apply:

(a) the replacement property shall be deemed to have been leased by the taxpayer to the lessee at the same time and for the same term as the original property;

(b) the amount of the loan referred to in clause (1.1) (a) (i) (A) shall be deemed to be equal to the amount of that loan determined in respect of the original property;

(c) the amount determined under subparagraph (1.1)(a)(ii) in respect of the replacement property shall be deemed to be equal to the amount so determined in respect of the original property;

(d) all amounts received or receivable by the taxpayer for the use of, or the right to use, the original property before the particular time shall be deemed to have been received or receivable, as the case may be, by the taxpayer for the use of, or the right to use, the replacement property; and

(e) the original property shall be deemed to have ceased to be subject to the lease at the particular time.

(1.18) [Specified leasing property — breakdown of property] — For the purposes of subsection (1.1), where for any period of time any amount that would have been received or receivable by a taxpayer during that period in respect of the use of, or the right to use, a property of the taxpayer during that period is not received or receivable by the taxpayer as a consequence of a breakdown of the property during that period and before the lease of that property is terminated, that amount shall be deemed to have been received or receivable, as the case may be, by the taxpayer.

(1.19) [Specified leasing property — addition or alteration] — For the purposes of subsections (1.1) and (1.11), where at any particular time

(a) an addition or alteration (in this subsection referred to as "additional property") is made by a taxpayer to a property (in this subsection referred to as the "original property") of the taxpayer that is a specified leasing property at the particular time, and

(b) as a consequence of the addition or alteration, the aggregate amount receivable by the taxpayer after the particular time for the use of, or the right to use, the original property and the additional property exceeds the amount so receivable in respect of the original property,

the following rules apply:

(c) the taxpayer shall be deemed to have leased the additional property to the lessee at the particular time,

(d) the term of the lease of the additional property shall be deemed to be greater than one year,

(e) the prescribed rate in effect at the particular time in respect of the additional property shall be deemed to be equal to the prescribed rate in effect in respect of the lease of the original property at the particular time,

(f) subsection (1.11) shall be read without reference to paragraph (c) thereof in respect of the additional property, and

(g) the excess described in paragraph (b) shall be deemed to be an amount receivable by the taxpayer for the use of, or the right to use, the additional property.

(1.2) [Specified leasing property — renegotiation of lease] — For the purposes of subsections (1.1) and (1.11), where at any time

(a) a lease (in this subsection referred to as the "original lease") of property is in the course of a *bona fide* renegotiation, and

(b) as a result of the renegotiation, the amount paid or payable by the lessee of the property for the use of, or the right to use, the property is altered in respect of a period after that time (otherwise than by reason of an addition or alteration to which subsection (1.19) applies),

the following rules apply:

(c) the original lease shall be deemed to have expired and the renegotiated lease shall be deemed to be a new lease of the property entered into at that time, and

(d) paragraph (1.13)(b) shall not apply in respect of any period before that time during which the property was leased by the lessee or a person with whom the lessee did not deal at arm's length.

(1.3) [Specified leasing property — lease of building] — For the purposes of subsections (1.1) and (1.11), where a taxpayer leases to another person a building or part thereof that is not exempt property, the references to "one year" in paragraphs (1.11)(b) and (1.13)(b), subsection (1.15) and paragraph (1.19)(d) shall in respect of that building or part thereof be read as references to "three years".

Related Provisions: Reg. 1100(1.13) — Meaning of "exempt property".

Notes: Reg. 1100(1.1)-(1.3) added by P.C. 1991-465, effective (but see also Notes to Reg. 1100(1.13)) for leases entered into after 10pm EDST, April 26, 1989, with grandfathering for leases entered into before March 15, 1991 (reproduced here up to the 44th edition).

Reg. 1100(1.17)(b) amended by P.C. 1992-2335, to delete the word "so" before "determined", effective on the same basis as the introduction of Reg. 1100(1.1) to (1.3).

(2) Property acquired in the year [First-year rule] — The amount that a taxpayer may deduct for a taxation year under subsection (1) in respect of property of a class in Schedule II is to be determined as if the undepreciated capital cost to the taxpayer at the end of the taxation year (before making any deduction under subsection (1) for the taxation year) of property of the class were adjusted by adding the positive or negative amount determined by the formula

$$A(B) - 0.5(C)$$

where

A is, in respect of property of the class that became available for use by the taxpayer in the taxation year and that is accelerated investment incentive property or property included in any of Classes 54 to 56,

(a) if the property is not included in paragraph (1)(v) or in any of Classes 12, 13, 14, 15, 43.1, 43.2, 53, 54, 55 and 56 or in Class 43 in the circumstances described in paragraph (d),

(i) ½, for property that became available for use by the taxpayer before 2024, and

(ii) nil, for property that became available for use by the taxpayer after 2023,

(b) if the class is Class 43.1,

(i) 2 ⅓, for property that became available for use by the taxpayer before 2024,

(ii) 1 ½, for property that became available for use by the taxpayer in 2024 or 2025, and

(iii) ⅚, for property that became available for use by the taxpayer after 2025,

(c) if the class is Class 43.2,

(i) 1, for property that became available for use by the taxpayer before 2024,

(ii) ½, for property that became available for use by the taxpayer in 2024 or 2025, and

(iii) ⅒, for property that became available for use by the taxpayer after 2025,

(d) if the property is included in Class 53 or — for property acquired after 2025 — is included in Class 43 and would have been included in Class 53 if it had been acquired in 2025,

(i) 1, for property that became available for use by the taxpayer before 2024,

(ii) ½, for property that became available for use by the taxpayer in 2024 or 2025,

(iii) ⅚, for property included in Class 43 that became available for use by the taxpayer after 2025, and

(iv) ⅒, for property included in Class 53 that became available for use by the taxpayer after 2025,

(e) if the class is Class 54 or Class 56,

(i) 2 ⅓, for property that became available for use by the taxpayer before 2024,

(ii) 1 ½, for property that became available for use by the taxpayer in 2024 or 2025, and

(iii) ⅚, for property that became available for use by the taxpayer after 2025,

(f) if the class is Class 55,

(i) 1 ½, for property that became available for use by the taxpayer before 2024,

(ii) ⅞, for property that became available for use by the taxpayer in 2024 or 2025, and

(iii) ⅜, for property that became available for use by the taxpayer after 2025, and

(g) in any other case, nil;

B is the amount determined, in respect of the class, by the formula

$$D - E$$

where

D is the total of all amounts, if any, each of which is an amount included in the description of A in the definition "un-

depreciated capital cost" in subsection 13(21) of the Act in respect of property of the class that became available for use by the taxpayer in the taxation year and that is accelerated investment incentive property or property included in any of Classes 54 to 56, and

E is the amount, if any, by which the amount determined for G exceeds the amount determined for F in the description of C; and

C is the amount determined, in respect of the class, by the formula

$$F - G$$

where

F is the total of all amounts each of which

(a) is an amount added to the undepreciated capital cost to the taxpayer of property of the class

(i) because of element A in the definition "undepreciated capital cost" in subsection 13(21) of the Act in respect of property (other than accelerated investment incentive property) that was acquired, or became available for use, by the taxpayer in the taxation year, or

(ii) because of element C or D in the definition "undepreciated capital cost" in subsection 13(21) of the Act in respect of an amount that was repaid in the taxation year, and

(b) is not in respect of

(i) property included in paragraph (1)(v), in paragraph (w) of Class 10 or in any of paragraphs (a) to (c), (e) to (i), (k), (l) and (p) to (s) of Class 12,

(ii) property included in any of Classes 13, 14, 15, 23, 24, 27, 29, 34, 52 and 54 to 56,

(iii) where the taxpayer was a corporation described in subsection (16) throughout the taxation year, property that was specified leasing property of the taxpayer at that time,

(iv) property that was deemed to have been acquired by the taxpayer in a preceding taxation year by reason of the application of paragraph 16.1(1)(b) of the Act in respect of a lease to which the property was subject immediately before the time at which the taxpayer last acquired the property, or

(v) property considered to have become available for use by the taxpayer in the taxation year by reason of paragraph 13(27)(b) or (28)(c) of the Act, and

G is the total of all amounts each of which is an amount deducted from the undepreciated capital cost to the taxpayer of property of the class

(a) because of element F or G in the definition "undepreciated capital cost" in subsection 13(21) of the Act in respect of property disposed of in the taxation year, or

(b) because of element J in the definition "undepreciated capital cost" in subsection 13(21) of the Act in respect of an amount the taxpayer received or was entitled to receive in the taxation year.

Proposed Amendment — 100% deduction for any property, for CCPC (up to $1.5 million)

Federal Budget, Supplementary Information, April 19, 2021: See under Reg. 1100(1)(a) opening words.

Related Provisions: Reg. 1100(1)(ta)(v) — Class 29 property; Reg. 1100(2.01) — Application to non-calendar taxation years in 2023-2026; Reg. 1100(2.02) — Application when Reg. 1104(4)(b)(i) applies; Reg. 1100(2.2), (2.3) — Half-year rule does not apply to acquisition on butterfly or from related person who owned it for a year; Reg. 1100(2.21) — Effect of deemed disposition and reacquisition; Reg. 1104(4) — Accelerated investment incentive property.

Notes: *New rules effective Nov. 21, 2018 and March 19, 2019*

Reg. 1100(2), which applies to the first year property is acquired (or the first year it is "available for use" per ITA 13(26)-(32)), implements both the "Accelerated Investment

Incentive" announced in the Nov. 2018 Economic Statement, and the March 2019 Budget proposals for zero-emission vehicles. It also maintains the previous "half year rule".

"Accelerated investment incentive property" (AIIP) is defined in Reg. 1104(4), generally as unused property acquired after Nov. 20, 2018 (other than Class 54 or 55) that becomes available for use before 2028.

Generally, Reg. 1100(2) maintains the pre-2019 "half year rule" discussed below by *deducting* "0.5C" from the undepreciated capital cost (UCC) of a class, where element C is the new purchases during the year (but as per C:F(a)(i), this does not include AIIP). For AIIP, it *adds* A(B), the rate in A varying depending on the class of property. For AIIP outside any class listed in A(a) (i.e., not 12-15, 43-43.2, 53-55), available for use before 2024, the deduction is increased by 50%: A(a) (as well as the half-year rule not applying). Thus, for example, for a $1,000 computer (Class 50, 55%), the first-year claim is $550 × 1.5 = $825.

Element B is common to all AIIP and zero-emission vehicles and, generally, computes the net capital cost additions to the class, expressed as the formula D – E.

D is generally the amount added to the UCC of the class in respect of AIIP or zero-emission vehicles that become available for use in the year.

E is computed as G minus F. Along with F – G in the description of C (the half-year rule), E generally provides that where the UCC of a class is increased in a year by both the cost of AII property and non-AII property and an amount (e.g., a disposition) reduces the UCC of that class, the reduction first offsets non-AII property before reducing the amount available for the enhanced CCA deduction. For Classes 54 and 55 (zero-emission vehicles), the amount determined for F will always be nil as those properties are never subject to the half-year rule.

For a "zero-emission vehicle" (defined in 248(1)) in Class 54 or 55 (bought after March 18, 2019) that is "available for use" (see ITA 13(26)-(32)) before 2024, first-year CCA is 100%, calculated as follows. Class 54: 30% under Reg. 1100(1)(a)(xl), plus 2.3333 times 30% (i.e., another 70%) under Reg. 1100(2)A(e)(i). Class 55: 40% under Reg. 1100(1)(a)(xli), plus 1.5 times 40% (i.e., another 60%) under Reg. 1100(2)A(f)(i).

For a vehicle available for use in 2024 or 2025, first-year CCA is 75%, calculated as follows. Class 54: 30% under Reg. 1100(1)(a)(xl), plus 1.5 times 30% (i.e., another 45%) under Reg. 1100(2)A(e)(ii). Class 55: 40% under Reg. 1100(1)(a)(xli), plus 7/8 times 40% (i.e., another 35%) under Reg. 1100(2)A(f)(ii). If the taxation year is not a calendar year, use Reg. 1100(2.01) instead.

For a vehicle available for use in 2026 or 2027 (after 2027 it is excluded by ITA 248(1)"zero-emission vehicle"(b)), first-year CCA is 55%, calculated as follows. Class 54: 30% under Reg. 1100(1)(a)(xl), plus 5/6 times 30% (i.e., another 25%) under Reg. 1100(2)A(e)(iii). Class 55: 40% under Reg. 1100(1)(a)(xli), plus 3/8 times 40% (i.e., another 15%) under Reg. 1100(2)A(f)(iii). If the taxation year is not a calendar year, use Reg. 1100(2.01) instead.

Similar calculations apply to the other classes listed in Reg. 1100(2)A(a)-(d).

A business that has a loss in the year it acquires an asset for which 100% writeoff is available should still claim 100% and carry forward the business loss, as otherwise the 100% is not available the next year.

There is a further reduction for a short taxation year; see Reg. 1100(3).

Economic Statement p. 86 estimates that the cost to the federal government of the CCA accelerations will be $485 million in 2018-19, $4,885m in 2019-20, $3,795m in 2020-21, $1,905m in 2021-22, $1,595m in 2022-23 and $1,375m in 2023-24.

See also Cameron Mancell, "Accelerated CCA and Other Measures from the 2018 Fall Economic Statement", 2439 *Tax Topics* (CCH) 1-5 (Dec. 6, 2018); Kim Moody, "Proposed CCA Amendments Provide Limited Incentives", 19(1) *Tax for the Owner-Manager* (ctf.ca) 8-9 (Jan. 2019); Yip & LaBuik, "Canada Introduces New Accelerated Capital Cost Allowance Incentives", tinyurl.com/fasken-aii.

Reg. 1100(2) amended by 2021 budget bill #1, to add all references to Class 56 effective March 2, 2020; and for property acquired after Nov. 20, 2018, to change (c)(ii)-(iii) from 1/2 in 2024 and nil after 2024 to 1/2 in 2024-2025 and 1/10 after 2025, to limit (d)(iii) (5/6 after 2025) to Class 43, and to add (d)(iv) with 1/10 after 2025 for Class 53.

Pre-2019 half-year rule

Reg. 1100(2) amended by 2019 budget bill #1, effective June 21, 2019. Before that date, read:

> (2) The amount that a taxpayer may deduct for a taxation year under subsection (1) in respect of property of a class in Schedule II is to be determined as if the undepreciated capital cost to the taxpayer at the end of the taxation year (before making any deduction under subsection (1) for the taxation year) of property of the class were reduced by an amount equal to 50 per cent of the amount, if any, by which
>
> > (a) the total of all amounts, each of which is an amount added
> >
> > > (i) because of element A in the definition "undepreciated capital cost" in subsection 13(21) of the Act in respect of property that was acquired in the year or that became available for use by the taxpayer in the year, or
> > >
> > > (ii) because of element C or D in the definition "undepreciated capital cost" in subsection 13(21) of the Act in respect of an amount that was repaid in the year,

to the undepreciated capital cost to the taxpayer of property of a class in Schedule II, other than

> (iii) property included in paragraph (1)(v), in paragraph (w) of Class 10 or in any of paragraphs (a) to (c), (e) to (i), (k), (l) and (p) to (s) of Class 12,
>
> (iv) property included in any of Classes 13, 14, 15, 23, 24, 27, 29, 34 and 52,
>
> (v) where the taxpayer was a corporation described in subsection (16) throughout the year, property that was specified leasing property of the taxpayer at that time,
>
> (vi) property that was deemed to have been acquired by the taxpayer in a preceding taxation year by reason of the application of paragraph 16.1(1)(b) of the Act in respect of a lease to which the property was subject immediately before the time at which the taxpayer last acquired the property, and
>
> (vii) property considered to have become available for use by the taxpayer in the year by reason of paragraph 13(27)(b) or (28)(c) of the Act

exceeds

> (b) the total of all amounts, each of which is an amount deducted from the undepreciated capital cost to the taxpayer of property of the class
>
> > (i) because of element F or G in the definition "undepreciated capital cost" in subsection 13(21) of the Act in respect of property disposed of in the year, or
> >
> > (ii) because of element J in the definition "undepreciated capital cost" in subsection 13(21) of the Act in respect of an amount the taxpayer received or was entitled to receive in the year.

For property acquired before Nov. 21, 2018 (i.e., before the 2019 amendment), Reg. 1100(2) is informally called the "half-year rule". The CCA allowed for the first year in which an asset is acquired (or becomes "available for use" under ITA 13(26)-(32)) is normally 1/2 of the amount otherwise allowable. Exceptions were in Reg. 1100(2)(a)(iii)-(vii) [now 1100(2)C:F(b)(i)-(v)], but Class 29 (Reg. 1100(2)(a)(iv) [now C:F(b)(ii)]) effectively has the half-year rule applied by Reg. 1100(1)(ta). There is a further reduction for a short tax year; see Reg. 1100(3). See also Income Tax Folio S3-F4-C1 ¶1.38-1.41.

Property acquired from a related person is excluded (Reg. 1100(2.2)), but this may be overlooked if tax preparation software classifies such property as "Additions", triggering the half-year rule.

On the exception in Reg. 1100(2)(a)(v) [now C:F(b)(iii)], see VIEWS doc 2010-0384021E5.

For "disposed of" in Reg. 1100(2)(b)(i), see ITA 248(1)"disposition" due to *Interpretation Act* 33(3) (and the French version uses "disposition").

Reg. 1100(2) applied in *Erickson*, 2012 TCC 398.

See also Sarah Chiu, "Half-Year Rule and Amalgamations", IX(2) *Resource Sector Taxation* (Federated Press) 638-42 (2013).

Reg. 1100(2) amended by P.C. 2009-660, for property acquired after Jan. 27, 2009, to modernize the wording and add reference to Class 52.

Reg. 1100(2)(a)(iii) amended by P.C. 2005-698, for property acquired after Dec. 12, 1995, to change "(p), (q) and (s)" to "(p) to (s)". This extended exclusion of the half-year rule to Class 12(r), allowing rental videotapes and DVDs to be fully written off in the year acquired.

The words "or that became available for use by the taxpayer in the year" added to Reg. 1100(2)(a)(i), and Reg. 1100(2)(a)(vii) added, by P.C. 1994-139, effective for property acquired after 1989.

Reg. 1100(2)(a) amended by P.C. 1991-465, for tax years ending after April 26, 1989.

Interpretation Bulletins: IT-283R2: CCA — Videotapes, videotape cassettes, films, computer software and master recording media (archived); IT-469R: CCA — Earth-moving equipment; IT-521R: Motor vehicle expenses claimed by self-employed individuals; IT-522R: Vehicle, travel and sales expenses of employees; IT-525R: Performing artists.

Advance Tax Rulings: ATR-11: "50% rule" on non-arm's length transactions.

Forms: T2 Sched. 8: Capital cost allowance.

(2.01) Straddle years [2023-2026] — For the purposes of subsection (2),

(a) if a taxation year begins in 2023 and ends in 2024, the factor determined for A in subsection (2) is to be replaced by the factor determined by the formula

$$(A(B) + C(D))/(B + D)$$

where

A is the factor otherwise determined for A in subsection (2) for 2023,

B is the amount that would be determined for D in subsection (2) if the only property that became available for use by the taxpayer in the taxation year were property that became available for use by the taxpayer in 2023,

C is the factor otherwise determined for A in subsection (2) for 2024, and

D is the amount that would be determined for D in subsection (2) if the only property that became available for use by the taxpayer in the taxation were property that became available for use by the taxpayer in 2024; and

(b) if a taxation year begins in 2025 and ends in 2026, the factor determined for A in subsection (2) is to be replaced by the factor determined by the formula

$$(A(B) + C(D))/(B + D)$$

where

A is the factor otherwise determined for A in subsection (2) for 2025,

B is the amount that would be determined for D in subsection (2) if the only property that became available for use by the taxpayer in the taxation year were property that became available for use by the taxpayer in 2025,

C is the factor otherwise determined for A in subsection (2) for 2026, and

D is the amount that would be determined for D in subsection (2) if the only property that became available for use by the taxpayer in the taxation year were property that became available for use by the taxpayer in 2026.

Notes: See Notes to Reg. 1100(2). 1100(2.01) added by 2019 budget bill #1, effective June 21, 2019.

(2.02) Expenditures excluded from element D — For the purposes of subsection (2), in respect of property of a class in Schedule II that is accelerated investment incentive property of a taxpayer solely because of subparagraph 1104(4)(b)(i),

(a) amounts incurred by any person or partnership in respect of the property are not to be included in determining the amount for D in subsection (2) in respect of the class

(i) if the amounts are incurred before November 21, 2018, unless

(A) the property was acquired after November 20, 2018 by a person or partnership from another person or partnership (referred to in this subparagraph as the "transferee" and the "transferor", respectively),

(B) the transferee was either

(I) the taxpayer, or

(II) a person or partnership that does not deal at arm's length with the taxpayer, and

(C) the transferor

(I) dealt at arm's length with the transferee, and

(II) held the property as inventory, and

(ii) if the amounts are incurred after November 20, 2018 and amounts are deemed to have been deducted under paragraph 20(1)(a) or subsection 20(16), in respect of those amounts incurred, under paragraph 1104(4.1)(b); and

(b) any amount excluded from the amount determined for D in subsection (2) in respect of the class because of paragraph (a) is to be included in determining the amount for F in subsection (2) in respect of the class, unless no amount in respect of the property would be so included if the property were not accelerated investment incentive property of the taxpayer.

Related Provisions: Reg. 1102(20.1) — Anti-avoidance.

Notes: See Notes to Reg. 1100(2). 1100(2.02) added by 2019 budget bill #1, effective June 21, 2019, and amended by 2021 budget bill #1, for property acquired after Nov. 20, 2018. Before the 2021 amendment, paras. (a)-(b) read:

(a) no amount is to be included in respect of the property in determining the amount for D in subsection (2) in respect of the class to the extent that the

amount includes expenditures incurred by any person or partnership before November 21, 2018, unless the person or partnership from which the taxpayer acquired the property dealt at arm's length with the taxpayer and held the property as inventory; and

(b) any amount excluded from the amount determined for D in subsection (2) in respect of the class because of paragraph (a) is to be included in determining the amount for F in subsection (2) in respect of the class, unless no amount in respect of the property would be so included if the property were not accelerated investment incentive property of the taxpayer.

(2.1) [Grandfathering — acquisition before 1983] — [No longer relevant.]

(2.2) [Exception to half-year rule] — Where a property of a class in Schedule II is acquired by a taxpayer

(a) in the course of a reorganization in respect of which, if a dividend were received by a corporation in the course of the reorganization, subsection 55(2) of the Act would not be applicable to the dividend by reason of the application of paragraph 55(3)(b) of the Act, or

(b), (c), (d) [Revoked]

(e) from a person with whom the taxpayer was not dealing at arm's length (otherwise than by virtue of a right referred to in paragraph 251(5)(b) of the Act) at the time the property was acquired,

and where

(f) the property was depreciable property of the person from whom it was acquired and was owned continuously by that person for the period from

(i) a day that was at least 364 days before the end of the taxation year of the taxpayer during which he acquired the property, or

(ii) November 12, 1981

to the day it was acquired by the taxpayer, or

(g) the rules provided in subsection (2.1) or this subsection applied in respect of the property for the purpose of determining the allowance under subsection (1) to which the person from whom the taxpayer acquired the property was entitled,

the following rules apply:

(h) no amount shall be included in determining an amount for F in subsection (2) in respect of the property;

(i) where the property is a property to which paragraph (1)(b) applies, that paragraph shall be read, in respect of the property, as "such amount, not exceeding the amount for the year calculated in accordance with Schedule III, as he may claim in respect of the capital cost to him of property of Class 13 in Schedule II";

(j) where the property is a property of a class to which paragraph (1)(ta) applies,

(i) the property shall be deemed to be designated property of the class,

(ii) for the purposes of computing the amount determined under paragraph (1)(ta) for any taxation year of the taxpayer ending after the time the property was actually acquired by the taxpayer, the property shall be deemed, other than for the purposes of paragraph (f), to have been acquired by the taxpayer immediately after the commencement of the taxpayer's first taxation year that commenced after the time that is the earlier of

(A) the time the property was last acquired by the transferor of the property, and

(B) where the property was transferred in a series of transfers to which this subsection applies, the time the property was last acquired by the first transferor in that series,

unless

(C) where clause (A) applies, the property was acquired by the taxpayer before the end of the taxation year of the transferor of the property that includes the time at which that transferor acquired the property, or

(D) where clause (B) applies, the property was acquired by the taxpayer before the end of the taxation year of the first transferor that includes the time at which that transferor acquired the property;

(iii) where the taxpayer is a corporation that was incorporated or otherwise formed after the end of the transferor's, or where applicable, the first transferor's, taxation year in which the transferor last acquired the property, the taxpayer shall be deemed, for the purposes of subparagraph (ii),

(A) to have been in existence throughout the period commencing immediately before the end of that year and ending immediately after the taxpayer was incorporated or otherwise formed, and

(B) to have had, throughout the period referred to in clause (A), fiscal periods ending on the day of the year on which the taxpayer's first fiscal period ended; and

(iv) the property shall be deemed to have become available for use by the taxpayer at the earlier of

(A) the time it became available for use by the taxpayer, and

(B) if applicable,

(I) the time it became available for use by the person from whom the taxpayer acquired the property, determined without reference to paragraphs 13(27)(c) and (28)(d) of the Act, or

(II) the time it became available for use by the first transferor in a series of transfers of the same property to which this subsection applies, determined without reference to paragraphs 13(27)(c) and (28)(d) of the Act; and

(k) if the property is a property described in paragraph (1)(v), its subparagraph (iv) shall be read, in respect of the property, as "33 1/3 per cent of the capital cost of the property to the taxpayer, and".

Related Provisions: ITA 248(10) — Series of transfers; Reg. 1100(2.21) — Effect of deemed disposition and reacquisition; Reg. 1100(2.3) — No inclusion under Reg. 1100(2)G; Reg. 1102(20) — Non-arm's length exception.

Notes: This exception does not apply to property held by a non-resident outside Canada, because such property is not depreciable property (Reg. 1102(3)): VIEWS doc 2004-0080201I7. Nor does it apply to a deemed acquisition under ITA 96(8): 2011-0401381E5. For some rulings applying Reg. 1100(2.2) on butterflies see 2011-0425441R3, 2012-0439381R3, 2014-0530961R3, 2015-0582421R3.

Reg. 1100(2.2) amended by 2019 budget bill #1, effective June 21, 2019, to change (in para. (h)) "under paragraph (2)(a)" to "in determining an amount for F in subsection (2)" (due to renumbering of Reg. 1100(2)), and to modernize the wording of para. (k).

Reg. 1100(2.2)(j) amended by P.C. 1994-139, for property acquired after 1987. Reg. 1100(2.2)(j)(iv) added by P.C. 1995-775, for property acquired after 1989.

Income Tax Folios [Reg. 1100(2.1), (2.2)]: S3-F4-C1: General discussion of CCA.

Interpretation Bulletins [Reg. 1100(2.1), (2.2)]: IT-302R3: Losses of a corporation — the effect that acquisitions of control, amalgamations, and windings-up have on their deductibility; IT-464R: CCA — Leasehold interests.

Advance Tax Rulings: ATR-11: "50% rule" on non-arm's length transactions.

Interpretation Bulletins: IT-476R: CCA — Equipment used in petroleum and natural gas activities.

(2.21) [Half-year rule — effect of deemed disposition] —
Where a taxpayer is deemed by a provision of the Act to have disposed of and acquired or reacquired a property,

(a) for the purposes of paragraph (2.2)(e) and subsections (19), 1101(1ad) and 1102(14) and (14.1), the acquisition or reacquisition shall be deemed to have been from a person with whom the taxpayer was not dealing at arm's length at the time of the acquisition or reacquisition; and

(b) for the purposes of paragraphs (2.2)(f) and (g), the taxpayer shall be deemed to be the person from whom the taxpayer acquired or reacquired the property.

Notes: The CRA considers that Reg. 1100(2.21) does not apply to a deemed acquisition under ITA 96(8): VIEWS doc 2011-0401381E5.

(2.3) [Disposition of property excluded from half-year rule] — If a taxpayer has disposed of a property and, because of paragraph (2.2)(h), no amount is required to be included in determining an amount for F in subsection (2) in respect of the property by the person that acquired the property, no amount shall be included by the taxpayer in determining an amount for G in subsection (2) in respect of the disposition of the property.

Notes: Reg. 1100(2.3) amended by 2019 budget bill #1, effective June 21, 2019, to reflect the renumbering of Reg. 1100(2) and modernize the wording. Before then, read:

(2.3) Where a taxpayer has disposed of a property and, by virtue of paragraph (2.2)(h), no amount is required to be included under paragraph (2)(a) in respect of the property by the person that acquired the property, no amount shall be included by the taxpayer under paragraph (2)(b) in respect of the disposition of the property.

Advance Tax Rulings: ATR-11: "50% rule" on non-arm's length transactions.

(2.4) [Disposition of short-term rental vehicle acquired before 1982] — [No longer relevant.]

(2.5) [Disposition of luxury automobile] — Where in a particular taxation year a taxpayer disposes of a property included in Class 10.1 in Schedule II that was owned by the taxpayer at the end of the immediately preceding taxation year,

(a) the deduction allowed under subsection (1) in respect of the property in computing the taxpayer's income for the year shall be determined as if the property had not been disposed of in the particular year and the number of days in the particular year were one-half of the number of days in the particular year otherwise determined; and

(b) no amount shall be deducted under subsection (1) in respect of the property in computing the taxpayer's income for any subsequent taxation year.

Notes: Reg. 1100(2.5) added by P.C. 1994-103, effective for taxation years that start after June 18, 1987 and end after 1987. Since ITA 20(16.1) prevents a terminal loss from being claimed in the year of disposition of an automobile in Class 10.1, this provision was introduced to allow a claim in the year of disposition of 1/2 of the CCA that would have been allowed. The "1/2" effect is provided by Reg. 1100(3), which prorates the CCA for a short taxation year.

Interpretation Bulletins: IT-521R: Motor vehicle expenses claimed by self-employed individuals; IT-522R: Vehicle, travel and sales expenses of employees.

(3) [Taxation year less than 12 months] — Where a taxation year is less than 12 months, the amount allowed as a deduction under this section, other than under any of paragraphs (1)(c), (e), (f), (g), (l), (m), (w), (x), (y), (ya), (zg) and (zh), shall not exceed that proportion of the maximum amount otherwise allowable that the number of days in the taxation year is of 365.

Related Provisions: Reg. 1100(1.1) — Specified leasing property; Reg. 1104(1) — "taxation year".

Notes: CRA takes the position that the "short taxation year" rule does not apply to an individual's income from property, since the taxation year for such purposes is the calendar year: IT-172R para. 2. Tax shelters involving the co-ownership of depreciable assets (such as computer software) were often based on this reasoning before the introduction of the CSTSP restrictions in Reg. 1100(20.1), (20.2). *Quaere* whether the same technique can be used by a shareholder borrowing funds to lend to a corporation at no interest, where the corporation invests in a rental property and claims CCA while the individual deducts the interest on the borrowed money under ITA 20(1)(c).

Reg. 1100(3) amended by P.C. 2005-698 (for 1995 and later taxation years), 2000-1000 (for 1998 and later taxation years), 1994-139.

Income Tax Folios: S3-F4-C1: General discussion of CCA.

Interpretation Bulletins: IT-434R: Rental of real property by individual; IT-441: Certified feature productions and certified short productions (archived).

(4)–(7) [Revoked]

(8) Railway sidings — Where a taxpayer, other than an operator of a railway system, has made a capital expenditure pursuant to a contract or arrangement with an operator of a railway system under which a railway siding that does not become the taxpayer's property is constructed to provide service to the taxpayer's place of business or to a property acquired by the taxpayer for the purpose of gaining or producing income, there is hereby allowed to the taxpayer, in

computing income for the taxation year from the business or property, as the case may be, a deduction equal to such amount as he may claim not exceeding four per cent of the amount remaining, if any, after deducting from the capital expenditure the aggregate of all amounts previously allowed as deductions in respect of the expenditure.

(9) Patents — Where a part or all of the cost of a patent is determined by reference to the use of the patent, in lieu of the deduction allowed under paragraph (1)(c), a taxpayer, in computing his income for a taxation year from a business or property, as the case may be, may deduct such amount as he may claim in respect of property of Class 14 in Schedule II not exceeding the lesser of

(a) the aggregate of

(i) that part of the capital cost determined by reference to the use of the patent in the year, and

(ii) the amount that would be computed under subparagraph (1)(c)(i) if the capital cost of the patent did not include the amounts determined by reference to the use of the patent in that year and previous years; and

(b) the undepreciated capital cost to him as of the end of the taxation year (before making any deduction under this subsection for the taxation year) of property of the class.

Interpretation Bulletins: IT-477: CCA — Patents, franchises, concessions and licences.

(9.1) [Class 44] — Where a part or all of the capital cost to a taxpayer of property that is a patent, or a right to use patented information, is determined by reference to the use of the property and that property is included in Class 44 in Schedule II, in lieu of the deduction allowed under paragraph (1)(a), there may be deducted in computing the taxpayer's income for a taxation year from a business or property such amount as the taxpayer may claim in respect of property of the class not exceeding the lesser of

(a) the total of

(i) that part of the capital cost that is determined by reference to the use of the property in the year, and

(ii) the amount that would be deductible for the year by reason of paragraph (1)(a) in respect of property of the class if the capital cost of the property of the class did not include the amounts determined under subparagraph (i) for the year and preceding taxation years; and

(b) the undepreciated capital cost to the taxpayer as of the end of the taxation year (before making any deduction under this subsection for the taxation year) of property of the class.

Related Provisions: Reg. 1100(1)(a)(xxx) — Alternative 25% write-off for patents.

Notes: Reg. 1100(9.1) added by P.C. 1994-231, effective for property acquired after April 26, 1993.

(10) [Revoked]

(11) Rental properties — Notwithstanding subsection (1), in no case shall the aggregate of deductions, each of which is a deduction in respect of property of a prescribed class owned by a taxpayer that includes rental property owned by him, otherwise allowed to the taxpayer by virtue of subsection (1) in computing his income for a taxation year, exceed the amount, if any, by which

(a) the aggregate of amounts each of which is

(i) his income for the year from renting or leasing a rental property owned by him, computed without regard to paragraph 20(1)(a) of the Act, or

(ii) the income of a partnership for the year from renting or leasing a rental property of the partnership, to the extent of the taxpayer's share of such income,

exceeds

(b) the aggregate of amounts each of which is

(i) his loss for the year from renting or leasing a rental property owned by him, computed without regard to paragraph 20(1)(a) of the Act, or

(ii) the loss of a partnership for the year from renting or leasing a rental property of the partnership, to the extent of the taxpayer's share of such loss.

Related Provisions: ITA 127.52(3)"rental or leasing property" — Minimum tax; Reg. 1100(12) — Exceptions; Reg. 1100(14) — Meaning of "rental property".

Notes: Reg. 1100(11) and (15) are almost identical, and limit CCA to income from the property, for both "rental property" (building or leasehold interest: Reg. 1100(14)) and "leasing property" (Reg. 1100(17)) .

Reg. 1100(11) prohibits CCA on rental property from creating or increasing a loss: *Ruest*, 2007 TCC 331. However, in *Fredette*, [2001] 3 C.T.C. 2468 (TCC) and *Rousseau-Houle*, 2001 CarswellNat 1126 (TCC) (Crown's FCA appeal discontinued), the Court held that placing rental property in a partnership to circumvent Reg. 1100(11) by deducting interest at the partner level avoided this rule and that GAAR (ITA 245(2)) did not apply.

Reg. 1100(11) applied in *Sivasubramnian*, 2008 TCC 261 (taxpayer argued he acquired condominiums for resale purposes), and *McInnes*, 2014 TCC 247 (cottage rentals were property income, not business). It did not apply in *LeCaine*, 2009 TCC 382, para. 96 (taxpayer was personally active in the business).

A terminal loss under ITA 20(16) can be claimed on rental property when it is disposed of: VIEWS docs 2002-0177677, 2002-0177695.

On interaction with ITA 13(21.2) see VIEWS doc 9831627F. Income attributed under 75(2) is not included in Reg. 1100(11)(a)(i) because the rental property is not "owned" by the taxpayer: docs 2006-0216491E5, 2008-0278801C6 q.4. Where rental property is transferred to a revocable trust, see doc 2007-0239951E5.

Interpretation Bulletins: IT-195R4: Rental property — CCA restrictions; IT-274R: Rental properties — Capital cost of $50,000 or more; IT-304R2: Condominiums; IT-367R3: Capital cost allowance — multiple-unit residential buildings (archived); IT-434R: Rental of real property by individual.

Forms: T776: Statement of real estate rentals.

(12) [Rental properties — exceptions] — Subject to subsection (13), subsection (11) does not apply in respect of a taxation year of a taxpayer that was, throughout the year,

(a) a life insurance corporation, or a corporation whose principal business was the leasing, rental, development or sale, or any combination thereof, of real property owned by it; or

(b) a partnership each member of which was

(i) a corporation described in paragraph (a), or

(ii) another partnership described in this paragraph.

Related Provisions: Reg. 1100(13) — Exception.

Notes: For "principal business" in para. (a), see IT-371 and ITA 20(1)(bb) Notes.

Reg. 1100(12)(b)(ii) added by 2013 budget bill #2, for fiscal periods that end after Oct. 2010 (consistent with amendment to Reg. 1100(26)(b)).

Interpretation Bulletins: IT-195R4: Rental property — CCA restrictions; IT-371: Meaning of "principal business".

(13) [Rental properties — leasehold interest] — For the purposes of subsection (11), where a taxpayer or partnership has a leasehold interest in a property that is property of Class 1, 3 or 6 in Schedule II by virtue of subsection 1102(5) and the property is leased by the taxpayer or partnership to a person who owns the land, an interest therein or an option in respect thereof, on which the property is situated, this section shall be read without reference to subsection (12) with respect to that property.

Related Provisions: Reg. 1101(5h) — Separate classes.

Interpretation Bulletins: IT-195R4: Rental property — CCA restrictions.

(14) ["Rental property"] — In this section and section 1101, "rental property" of a taxpayer or a partnership means

(a) a building owned by the taxpayer or the partnership, whether owned jointly with another person or otherwise, or

(b) a leasehold interest in real property, if the leasehold interest is property of Class 1, 3, 6 or 13 in Schedule II and is owned by the taxpayer or the partnership,

if, in the taxation year in respect of which the expression is being applied, the property was used by the taxpayer or the partnership principally for the purpose of gaining or producing gross revenue that is rent, but, for greater certainty, does not include a property leased by the taxpayer or the partnership to a lessee, in the ordinary course of the taxpayer's or partnership's business of selling goods or rendering services, under an agreement by which the lessee undertakes to use the property to carry on the business of selling, or promoting the sale of, the taxpayer's or partnership's goods or services.

Related Provisions: ITA 127.52(3)"rental or leasing property" — Minimum tax; Reg. 1100(11) — Limitation on CCA for rental property; Reg. 1100(14.1) — Interpretation; Reg. 1101(1ac), (1ae) — Separate classes; Reg. 1104(13) — Definitions; Reg. 2411(4)B(e) — Insurers.

Notes: *Suncor Energy*, 2015 TCC 210, was an appeal on whether Reg. 1100(14) applies to an entire office complex or only the taxpayer's percentage interest in it. The appeal was withdrawn in May 2016.

Reg. 1100(14)(a) amended by P.C. 1989-2464 for 1994 and later taxation years. For a ruling applying it on a butterfly see 2011-0425441R3.

Interpretation Bulletins: IT-195R4: Rental property — CCA restrictions; IT-274R: Rental properties — Capital cost of $50,000 or more; IT-304R2: Condominiums; IT-367R3: Capital cost allowance — multiple-unit residential buildings (archived).

(14.1) ["Gross revenue"] — For the purposes of subsection (14), gross revenue derived in a taxation year from

(a) the right of a person or partnership, other than the owner of a property, to use or occupy the property or a part thereof, and

(b) services offered to a person or partnership that are ancillary to the use or occupation by the person or partnership of the property or the part thereof

shall be considered to be rent derived in that year from the property.

Related Provisions: Reg. 1100(14.2) — Exception; Reg. 1104(13) — Definitions.

Interpretation Bulletins: IT-195R4: Rental property — CCA restrictions.

(14.2) ["Gross revenue" — exception] — Subsection (14.1) does not apply in any particular taxation year to property owned by

(a) a corporation, where the property is used in a business carried on in the year by the corporation;

(b) an individual, where the property is used in a business carried on in the year by the individual in which he is personally active on a continuous basis throughout that portion of the year during which the business is ordinarily carried on; or

(c) a partnership, where the property is used in a business carried on in the year by the partnership if at least ⅔ of the income or loss, as the case may be, of the partnership for the year is included in the determination of the income of

(i) members of the partnership who are individuals that are personally active in the business of the partnership on a continuous basis throughout that portion of the year during which the business is ordinarily carried on, and

(ii) members of the partnership that are corporations.

Related Provisions: Reg. 1104(13) — Definitions.

Interpretation Bulletins: IT-195R4: Rental property — CCA restrictions.

(15) Leasing properties — Notwithstanding subsection (1), in no case shall the aggregate of deductions, each of which is a deduction in respect of property of a prescribed class that is leasing property owned by a taxpayer, otherwise allowed to the taxpayer under subsection (1) in computing his income for a taxation year, exceed the amount, if any, by which

(a) the aggregate of amounts each of which is

(i) his income for the year from renting, leasing, or earning royalties from, a leasing property or a property that would be a leasing property but for subsection (18), (19) or (20) where such property is owned by him, computed without regard to paragraph 20(1)(a) of the Act, or

(ii) the income of a partnership for the year from renting, leasing or earning royalties from, a leasing property or a property that would be a leasing property but for subsection (18), (19) or (20) where such property is owned by the partnership, to the extent of the taxpayer's share of such income,

exceeds

(b) the aggregate of amounts each of which is

(i) his loss for the year from renting, leasing or earning royalties from, a property referred to in subparagraph (a)(i), computed without regard to paragraph 20(1)(a) of the Act, or

(ii) the loss of a partnership for the year from renting, leasing or earning royalties from, a property referred to in subparagraph (a)(ii), to the extent of the taxpayer's share of such loss.

Related Provisions: Reg. 1100(16) — Exception; Reg. 1100(17)–(20) — Meaning of "leasing property"; Reg. 1104(13) — Definitions.

Notes: See Notes to Reg. 1100(11). For CRA description of the leasing property rules, see VIEWS docs 2004-0090591E5, 2005-0141551E5.

In *Canada Trustco*, 2005 SCC 54, trailers bought from and circuitously leased back to the same company successfully created CCA despite the "leasing property" rules. GAAR did not apply.

Reg. 1100(15) applied in *Oke*, 2010 FCA 350, and *Thibeault*, 2015 TCC 271: see Reg. 1100(17.3) Notes. The parallel Quebec rule did not apply in *J.D. Irving Ltd.*, 2020 QCCQ 2423, where equipment was transferred from Xco to Yco in the same corporate group (to use up losses) but Xco continued to operate it under an agency agreement.

Interpretation Bulletins: IT-195R4: Rental property — CCA restrictions; IT-283R2: CCA — Video tapes, videotape cassettes, films, computer software and master recording media (archived); IT-434R: Rental of real property by individual; IT-443: Leasing property — CCA restrictions.

(16) [Leasing property — exception] — Subsection (15) does not apply in respect of a taxation year of a taxpayer that was, throughout the year,

(a) a corporation whose principal business was

(i) renting or leasing of leasing property or property that would be leasing property but for subsection (18), (19) or (20), or

(ii) renting or leasing of property referred to in subparagraph (i) combined with selling and servicing of property of the same general type and description,

if the gross revenue of the corporation for the year from such principal business was not less than 90 per cent of the gross revenue of the corporation for the year from all sources; or

(b) a partnership each member of which was

(i) a corporation described in paragraph (a), or

(ii) another partnership described in this paragraph.

Related Provisions: Reg. 1100(1.14) — Election; Reg. 1100(2):F(b)(iii) — Year of acquisition — no half-year rule for specified leasing property; Reg. 1104(13) — Definitions.

Notes: Interest rate swap payments are considered not to be included in calculating gross revenue from renting of leasing: VIEWS doc 2003-0030597; Stephen Bowman, "Recent Canada Revenue Agency Comments on Swaps", XII(1) *Corporate Finance* (Federated Press) 1164-66 (2004).

For the meaning of "principal business" in para. (a), see Notes to ITA 20(1)(bb). For CRA interpretations of Reg. 1100(16) see VIEWS docs 2002-0156515 (re subpara. (a)(ii)) and 2003-0030597 (net payments or receipts from interest rate swaps are excluded from gross revenue in the numerator).

Reg. 1100(16)(b)(ii) added by 2013 budget bill #2, effective for fiscal periods that end after Oct. 2010 (consistent with amendment to Reg. 1100(26)(b)).

Interpretation Bulletins: IT-267R2: CCA — vessels.

(17) ["Leasing property"] — Subject to subsection (18), in this section and section 1101, "leasing property" of a taxpayer or a partnership means depreciable property other than

(a) rental property,

(b) computer tax shelter property, or

(c) property referred to in paragraph (w) of Class 10 or in paragraph (n) of Class 12 in Schedule II,

where such property is owned by the taxpayer or the partnership, whether jointly with another person or otherwise, if, in the taxation year in respect of which the expression is being applied, the property was used by the taxpayer or the partnership principally for the purpose of gaining or producing gross revenue that is rent, royalty or leasing revenue, but for greater certainty, does not include a property leased by the taxpayer or the partnership to a lessee, in the ordinary course of the taxpayer's or partnership's business of selling goods or rendering services, under an agreement by which the lessee undertakes to use the property to carry on the business of selling, or promoting the sale of, the taxpayer's or partnership's goods or services.

Related Provisions: Reg. 1100(14) — Meaning of "rental property"; Reg. 1100(17.1), (17.2), (18), (19), (20) — Interpretation; Reg. 1100(20.1) — Limitation on CCA claims for computer tax shelter property; Reg. 1100(20.2) — Meaning of "computer tax shelter property"; Reg. 1101(5c) — Separate class; Reg. 1104(13) — Definitions; Reg. 2411(4)B(e) — Insurers.

Notes: Leasing property restrictions are in Reg. 1100(15). A film distribution licence was not leasing property in doc 2010-0374221R3.

Reg. 1100(17) amended by P.C. 2009-581 (for property acquired after March 18, 2007), 2000-1000, 1989-2464.

Interpretation Bulletins: IT-195R4: Rental property — CCA restrictions; IT-283R2: CCA — Videotapes, videotape cassettes, films, computer software and master recording media (archived).

(17.1) [Deemed use of property] — For the purposes of subsection (17), where, in a taxation year, a taxpayer or a partnership has acquired a property

(a) that was not used for any purpose in that year, and

(b) the first use of the property by the taxpayer or the partnership was principally for the purpose of gaining or producing gross revenue that is rent, royalty or leasing revenue,

the property shall be deemed to have been used in the taxation year in which it was acquired principally for the purpose of gaining or producing gross revenue that is rent, royalty or leasing revenue.

(17.2) [Deemed rent] — For the purposes of subsections (1.11) and (17), gross revenue derived in a taxation year from

(a) the right of a person or partnership, other than the owner of a property, to use or occupy the property or a part thereof, and

(b) services offered to a person or partnership that are ancillary to the use or occupation by the person or partnership of the property or the part thereof

shall be considered to be rent derived in the year from the property.

Related Provisions: Reg. 1100(17.3) — Exception.

Notes: Reg. 1100(17.2) amended by P.C. 1991-465, effective for leases entered into after 10pm EDST, April 26, 1989, with certain grandfathering for earlier leases.

(17.3) [Deemed rent — exception] — Subsection (17.2) does not apply in any particular taxation year to property owned by

(a) a corporation, where the property is used in a business carried on in the year by the corporation;

(b) an individual, where the property is used in a business carried on in the year by the individual in which he is personally active on a continuous basis throughout that portion of the year during which the business is ordinarily carried on;

(c) a partnership, where the property is used in a business carried on in the year by the partnership if at least $2/3$ of the income or loss, as the case may be, of the partnership for the year is included in the determination of the income of

(i) members of the partnership who are individuals that are personally active in the business of the partnership on a continuous basis throughout that portion of the year during which the business is ordinarily carried on, and

(ii) members of the partnership that are corporations.

Notes: Reg. 1100(17.3)(b) was held not to apply in both *Oke*, 2010 FCA 350 (business of leasing RV was that of another company), and *Thibeault*, 2015 TCC 271 (leasing one vessel was insufficient activity).

(18) [Leasing property — exclusions] — Leasing property of a taxpayer or a partnership referred to in subsection (17) does not include

(a) property that the taxpayer or the partnership acquired before May 26, 1976 or was obligated to acquire under the terms of an agreement in writing entered into before May 26, 1976;

(b) property the construction, manufacture or production of which was commenced by the taxpayer or the partnership before May 26, 1976 or was commenced under an agreement in writing entered into by the taxpayer or the partnership before May 26, 1976; or

(c) property that the taxpayer or the partnership acquired on or before December 31, 1976 or was obligated to acquire under the

terms of an agreement in writing entered into on or before December 31, 1976, if

(i) arrangements, evidenced by writing, respecting the acquisition, construction, manufacture or production of the property had been substantially advanced before May 26, 1976, and

(ii) the taxpayer or the partnership had before May 26, 1976 demonstrated a *bona fide* intention to acquire the property for the purpose of gaining or producing gross revenue that is rent, royalty or leasing revenue.

(19) [Leasing property — exclusions] — Notwithstanding subsection (17), a property acquired by a taxpayer

(a) in the course of a reorganization in respect of which, if a dividend were received by a corporation in the course of the reorganization, subsection 55(2) of the Act would not be applicable to the dividend by reason of the application of paragraph 55(3)(b) of the Act, or

(b) from a person with whom the taxpayer was not dealing at arm's length (otherwise than by virtue of a right referred to in paragraph 251(5)(b) of the Act) at the time the property was acquired,

that would otherwise be leasing property of the taxpayer, shall be deemed not to be leasing property of the taxpayer if immediately before it was so acquired by the taxpayer, it was, by virtue of subsection (18) or (20) or this subsection, not a leasing property of the person from whom the property was so acquired.

Related Provisions: Reg. 1100(2.21)(a); Reg. 1100(17), (18) — Meaning of "leasing property"; Reg. 1102(20) — Non-arm's length exception.

Interpretation Bulletins: IT-443: Leasing property — CCA restrictions.

(20) [Leasing property — replacement property] — Notwithstanding subsection (17), a property acquired by a taxpayer or partnership that is a replacement property (within the meaning assigned by subsection 13(4) of the Act), that would otherwise be a leasing property of the taxpayer or partnership, shall be deemed not to be a leasing property of the taxpayer or partnership if the property replaced, referred to in paragraph 13(4)(a) or (b) of the Act, was, by reason of subsection (18) or (19) or this subsection, not a leasing property of the taxpayer or partnership immediately before it was disposed of by the taxpayer or partnership.

Related Provisions: Reg. 1100(17), (18) — Meaning of "leasing property".

Notes: The words "or this subsection" added to Reg. 1100(20) by P.C. 1994-139, retroactive to 1986, so as to allow a second or subsequent replacement property to qualify as not a leasing property.

(20.1) Computer tax shelter property — The total of all amounts each of which is a deduction in respect of computer tax shelter property allowed to the taxpayer under subsection (1) in computing a taxpayer's income for a taxation year shall not exceed the amount, if any, by which

(a) the total of all amounts each of which is

(i) the taxpayer's income for the year from a business in which computer tax shelter property owned by the taxpayer is used, computed without reference to any deduction under subsection (1) in respect of such property, or

(ii) the income of a partnership from a business in which computer tax shelter property of the partnership is used, to the extent of the share of such income that is included in computing the taxpayer's income for the year,

exceeds

(b) the total of all amounts each of which is

(i) a loss of the taxpayer from a business in which computer tax shelter property owned by the taxpayer is used, computed without reference to any deduction under subsection (1) in respect of such property, or

(ii) a loss of a partnership from a business in which computer tax shelter property of the partnership is used, to the extent of the share of such loss that is included in computing the taxpayer's income for the year.

Related Provisions: Reg. 1100(20.2) — Definition of "computer tax shelter property"; Reg. 1101(5r) — Separate class for all computer tax shelter property.

Notes: See Notes to Class 12 (in Reg. Schedule II) re software tax shelters. The parallel Quebec rule applied in *Lee*, 2020 QCCQ 780, paras. 432, 451 (Prospector Networks shelter).

Reg. 1100(20.1) amended by P.C. 2009-581, for property acquired after March 18, 2007, to change "computer software tax shelter property" to "computer tax shelter property" throughout [amended definition in Reg. 1100(20.2)].

Reg. 1100(20.1) added by P.C. 2000-1000, for tax years and fiscal periods that end after Aug. 5, 1997, with grandfathering for 1997-1998.

(20.2) ["Computer tax shelter property"] — For the purpose of this Part, computer tax shelter property of a person or partnership is depreciable property of a prescribed class in Schedule II that is computer software or property described in Class 50 or 52 where

(a) the person's or partnership's interest in the property is a tax shelter investment (as defined by subsection 143.2(1) of the Act) determined without reference to subsection (20.1); or

(b) an interest in the person or partnership is a tax shelter investment (as defined by subsection 143.2(1) of the Act) determined without reference to subsection (20.1).

Related Provisions: Reg. 1100(20.1) — Limitation on CCA claim; Reg. 1101(5r) — Separate class for all computer tax shelter property; Reg. 1104(2) "computer software" — Definition.

Notes: Reg. 1100(20.2) opening words amended by P.C. 2009-581, effective for property acquired after March 18, 2007, to change "computer software tax shelter property" to "computer tax shelter property" and to refer to Class 50; and by P.C. 2009-660, for property acquired after Jan. 27, 2009, to refer to Class 52.

Reg. 1100(20.2) added by P.C. 2000-1000, effective on the same basis as Reg. 1100(20.1).

(21) Certified films and video tapes — [No longer relevant]

Notes: Reg. 1100(21) reduces the depreciable cost of a taxpayer's interest in a "certified production" (eliminated in 1995) or "certified feature film" (eliminated in 1976). These terms are defined in Reg. 1104(2). Amended by P.C. 2005-698.

(21.1) [Film or videotape — deemed cost reduction] — Notwithstanding subsection (1), where a taxpayer has acquired property described in paragraph (s) of Class 10 in Schedule II, or in paragraph (m) of Class 12 of Schedule II, the deduction in respect of the property otherwise allowed to the taxpayer under subsection (1) in computing the taxpayer's income for a taxation year shall not exceed the amount that it would be if the capital cost to the taxpayer of the property were reduced by the portion of any debt obligation of the taxpayer outstanding at the end of the year that is convertible into an interest in the property or in the taxpayer.

Proposed Amendment — Reg. 1100(21.1)

(21.1) [Film or videotape — deemed cost reduction] — Notwithstanding subsection (1), where a taxpayer has acquired property described in paragraph (s) of Class 10, or in paragraph (m) of Class 12, in Schedule II, the deduction in respect of the property otherwise allowed to the taxpayer under subsection (1) in computing the taxpayer's income for a taxation year shall not exceed the amount that it would be if the capital cost to the taxpayer of the property were reduced by the portion of any debt obligation of the taxpayer outstanding at the end of the year that is convertible into an interest (or, for civil law, a right) in the property or an interest in the taxpayer.

Application: The July 16, 2010 draft regulations (Part 1 — technical), s. 163, will amend subsec. 1100(21.1) to read as above, in force on Royal Assent.

Technical Notes (July 2010): Subsection 1100(21.1) is amended as part of the harmonization initiative of the federal government, related to bijuralism, to reflect the concepts and terminology of the common law and the civil law in both official languages. In particular, the words "interest in the property" are replaced by "interest (or, for civil law, a right) in the property". This amendment is not intended to change the current application of the amended provision.

Notes: This amendment was not included in the bijuralism amendments enacted by the 2002-2013 technical bill (Part 4 — bijuralism). Finance advises (Sept. 2020) that it is still pending and will be done "in the near future".

Notes: Reg. 1100(21.1) added by P.C. 2005-698, effective on the same basis as Reg. 1100(21)(e).

(22) [Film or tape acquired before 1979] — [No longer relevant.]

(23) [Film or tape acquired in 1987 or 1988] — [No longer relevant.]

(24) Specified energy property — Notwithstanding subsection (1), in no case shall the total of deductions, each of which is a deduction in respect of property of Class 34, 43.1, 43.2, 47 or 48 in Schedule II that is specified energy property owned by a taxpayer, otherwise allowed to the taxpayer under subsection (1) in computing the taxpayer's income for a taxation year, exceed the amount, if any, by which

(a) the total of all amounts each of which is

(i) the total of

(A) the amount that would be the income of the taxpayer for the year from property described in Class 34, 43.1, 43.2, 47 or 48 in Schedule II (other than specified energy property), or from the business of selling the product of that property, if that income were calculated after deducting the maximum amount allowable in respect of the property for the year under paragraph 20(1)(a) of the Act, and

(B) the taxpayer's income for the year from specified energy property or from the business of selling the product of that property, computed without regard to paragraph 20(1)(a) of the Act, or

(ii) the total of

(A) the taxpayer's share of the amount that would be the income of a partnership for the year from property described in Class 34, 43.1, 43.2, 47 or 48 in Schedule II (other than specified energy property), or from the business of selling the product of that property, if that income were calculated after deducting the maximum amount allowable in respect of the property for the year under paragraph 20(1)(a) of the Act, and

(B) the income of a partnership for the year from specified energy property or from the business of selling the product of that property of the partnership, to the extent of the taxpayer's share of that income,

exceeds

(b) the total of all amounts each of which is

(i) the taxpayer's loss for the year from specified energy property or from the business of selling the product of that property, computed without regard to paragraph 20(1)(a) of the Act, or

(ii) the loss of a partnership for the year from specified energy property or from the business of selling the product of that property of the partnership, to the extent of the taxpayer's share of that loss.

Related Provisions: ITA 127.52(1)(e) — Alternative Minimum Tax; Reg. 1100(25) — Meaning of "specified energy property"; Reg. 1100(26) — Exception.

Notes: CCA on specified energy property cannot be used to create a loss. See Notes to Reg. 1100(25).

Reg. 1100(24) amended by P.C. 2006-439, effective Feb. 23, 2005, to add references to Cls. 43.2, 47 and 48; and by P.C. 1997-1033, effective Feb. 22, 1994, to add Cl. 43.1.

(25) ["Specified energy property"] — Subject to subsections (27) to (29), in this section and section 1101, "specified energy property" of a taxpayer or partnership (in this subsection referred to as "the owner") for a taxation year means property of Class 34 in Schedule II acquired by the owner after February 9, 1988 and property of Class 43.1, 43.2, 47 or 48 in Schedule II, other than a particular property

(a) acquired to be used by the owner primarily for the purpose of gaining or producing income from a business carried on in Canada (other than the business of selling the product of the particular property) or from another property situated in Canada, or

(b) leased in the year, in the ordinary course of carrying on a business of the owner in Canada, to

(i) a person who can reasonably be expected to use the property primarily for the purpose of gaining or producing income from a business carried on in Canada (other than the business of selling the product of the particular property) or from another property situated in Canada, or

(ii) a corporation or partnership described in subsection (26),

where the owner was

(iii) a corporation whose principal business was, throughout the year,

(A) the renting or leasing of leasing property or property that would be leasing property but for subsection (18), (19) or (20),

(B) the renting or leasing of property referred to in clause (A) combined with the selling and servicing of property of the same general type and description, or

(C) the manufacturing of property described in Class 34, 43.1, 43.2, 47 or 48 in Schedule II that it sells or leases,

and the gross revenue of the corporation for the year from that principal business was not less than 90 per cent of the gross revenue of the corporation for the year from all sources, or

(iv) a partnership each member of which was

(A) a corporation described in subparagraph (iii) or paragraph (26)(a), or

(B) another partnership described in this subparagraph.

Related Provisions: Reg. 1101(5m) — Separate class.

Notes: For CRA interpretation see Income Tax Folio S3-F8-C2 ¶2.18-2.21.

Taxpayers cannot classify equipment as Cl. 8 instead of 43.1 to avoid the specified energy property rules, due to the wording of Cl. 43.1: VIEWS doc 2008-0265011E5.

CRA will apply Reg. 1100(25) to a homeowner with a rooftop solar panel feeding electricity into the grid: docs 2008-0275351E5, 2008-0287671E5, 2009-0341721E5, 2009-0342121E5, 2009-0343551E5, 2009-0343881E5, 2010-0353421E5, 2010-0361131E5, 2011-0396841E5, 2013-0480951E5, 2016-0670661E5; but not if more than 50% of the energy will be used in earning income from another business or property: 2012-0435151E5, 2012-0458201E5. It will apply to a wind energy conversion system: 2010-0373951E5.

For the meaning of "principal business" in (b)(iii), see Notes to ITA 20(1)(bb).

Reg. 1100(25)(b)(iv)(B) added by 2013 budget bill #2, effective for fiscal periods that end after Oct. 2010 (consistent with amendment to Reg. 1100(26)(b)).

Reg. 1100(25) amended by P.C. 2006-439, effective Feb. 23, 2005, to add references to Cls. 43.2, 47 and 48; and by P.C. 1997-1033, effective Feb. 22, 1994, to add Cl. 43.1.

(26) [Specified energy property — exception] — Subsection (24) does not apply to a taxation year of a taxpayer that was, throughout the year,

(a) a corporation whose principal business throughout the year was

(i) manufacturing or processing,

(ii) mining operations, or

(iii) the sale, distribution or production of electricity, natural gas, oil, steam, heat or any other form of energy or potential energy; or

(b) a partnership each member of which was

(i) a corporation described in paragraph (a), or

(ii) another partnership described in this paragraph.

Related Provisions: Reg. 1104(9) — Meaning of "manufacturing and processing".

Notes: For the meaning of "principal business" in para. (a), see Notes to ITA 20(1)(bb). For M&P see Reg. 1104(9), and ITA 125.1(3)"manufacturing or processing" Notes. "Distribution" of electricity in (a)(iii) includes transmission: IT-476R para. 23; VIEWS doc 2012-0465501E5.

Reg. 1100(26)(b)(ii) added by 2013 budget bill #2, for fiscal periods that end after Oct. 2010 (implementing an Oct. 28, 2010 Finance comfort letter).

Reg. 1100(26)(a)(i) and (ii) added by P.C. 1997-1033, for tax years ending after March 6, 1996.

Income Tax Folios: S4-F15-C1: Manufacturing and processing [replaces IT-147R3].

(27) [Specified energy property — acquisition before 1990] — [No longer relevant.]

(28) [Specified energy property — exclusion] — A property acquired by a taxpayer

(a) in the course of a reorganization in respect of which, if a dividend were received by a corporation in the course of the reorganization, subsection 55(2) of the Act would not be applicable to the dividend by reason of the application of paragraph 55(3)(b) of the Act, or

(b) from a person with whom the taxpayer was not dealing at arm's length (otherwise than by virtue of a right referred to in paragraph 251(5)(b) of the Act) at the time the property was acquired

that would otherwise be specified energy property of the taxpayer shall be deemed not to be specified energy property of the taxpayer if, immediately before it was so acquired by the taxpayer, it was not, by virtue of subsection (27), this subsection or subsection (29), specified energy property of the person from whom the property was so acquired.

(29) [Specified energy property — replacement property] — A property acquired by a taxpayer or partnership that is a replacement property (within the meaning assigned by subsection 13(4) of the Act), that would otherwise be specified energy property of the taxpayer or partnership, shall be deemed not to be specified energy property of the taxpayer or partnership if the property replaced, referred to in paragraph 13(4)(a) or (b) of the Act, was, by virtue of subsection (27), (28) or this subsection, not specified energy property of the taxpayer or partnership immediately before it was disposed of by the taxpayer or partnership.

Definitions [Reg. 1100]: "accelerated investment incentive property" — Reg. 1104(4), (4.1); "additional property" — Reg. 1100(1.19)(a); "amount" — ITA 248(1); "arm's length" — ITA 251(1), Reg. 1102(20); "associated" — ITA 256; "broadcasting" — *Interpretation Act* 35(1); "business" — ITA 248(1); "calendar year" — *Interpretation Act* 37(1)(a); "Canada" — ITA 255, *Interpretation Act* 35(1); "Canadian" — Reg. 1104(10)(a), (c.2); "capital cost" — Reg. 1100(1)(b), 1100(1.13), 1102(4), (7); "certified feature film", "certified production" — Reg. 1104(2); "class" — Reg. 1101(6), 1102(1)–(3), (14), (14.1); "commencement" — *Interpretation Act* 35(1); "computer software" — Reg. 1104(2); "computer tax shelter property" — Reg. 1100(20.2); "corporation" — ITA 248(1), *Interpretation Act* 35(1); "depreciable property" — ITA 13(21), 248(1); "designated property" — Reg. 1100(1)(ta), (zc); "disposed" — ITA 248(1)"disposition"; "disposes" — ITA 248(1)"disposition"; "disposition" — ITA 248(1); "dividend" — ITA 248(1); "eligible liquefaction activities" — Reg. 1100(18); "eligible liquefaction facility" — Reg. 1100(18); "end of the taxation year" — Reg. 1104(1); "exempt property" — Reg. 1100(1.13)(a), (a.1); "fair market value" — see ITA 69(1) Notes; "film or tape" — Reg. 1100(21); "fiscal period" — ITA 249.1; "general-purpose electronic data processing equipment" — Reg. 1104(2); "gross revenue" — ITA 248(1); "guarantor" — Reg. 1100(21)(c)(ii); "income from a mine" — Reg. 1104(5); "individual" — ITA 248(1); "industrial mineral mine" — Reg. 1104(3); "inventory" — ITA 248(1); "investor" — Reg. 1100(21); "leasing property" — Reg. 1100(17)–(20); "life insurance corporation" — ITA 248(1); "manufacturing or processing" — Reg. 1104(9); "mine" — Reg. 1104(7)(a); "mineral", "mining" — Reg. 1104(3); "Minister" — ITA 248(1); "month" — *Interpretation Act* 35(1); "motor vehicle", "office" — ITA 248(1); "original lease" — Reg. 1100(1.2)(a); "original property" — Reg. 1100(1.17), (1.19)(a); "owner" — Reg. 1100(25); "Parliament" — *Interpretation Act* 35(1); "particular time", "particular year" — Reg. 1100(1.1)(a)(ii); "partnership" — see ITA 96(1) Notes; "person" — ITA 248(1), Reg. 1100(1.16); "prescribed" — ITA 248(1); "prescribed rate" — Reg. 4301, 4302; "principal amount", "property" — ITA 248(1); "province" — *Interpretation Act* 35(1); "radio" — *Interpretation Act* 35(1); "railway system" — Reg. 1104(2); "received or receivable" — Reg. 1100(1.18); "related" — ITA 251(2)–(6); "remuneration" — Reg. 1104(10)(c); "rent" — Reg. 1100(14.1), (17.2); "rental property" — Reg. 1100(14); "replacement property" — Reg. 1100(1.17); "resident in Canada" — ITA 250; "revenue guarantee" — Reg. 1104(10)(c.1); "series" — ITA 248(10); "share" — ITA 248(1); "specified energy property" — Reg. 1100(25), (27)–(29); "specified leasing property" — Reg. 1100(1.11); "specified transaction" — Reg. 1100(1)(ta); "systems software" — Reg. 1104(2); "tax shelter" — ITA 237.1(1), 248(1); "taxation year" — ITA 249, Reg. 1104(1); "taxpayer" — ITA 248(1); "treaty-protected business" — ITA 248(1); "undepreciated capital cost" — ITA 13(21), 248(1); "unit of production" — Reg. 1104(10)(d); "vendor" — Reg. 1100(21)(c)(ii); "within 60 days after the end of the year" — Reg. 1100(23)(a), (b); "writing", "written" — *Interpretation Act* 35(1)"writing".

Interpretation Bulletins [Reg. 1100]: IT-474R2: Amalgamations of Canadian corporations.

1100A. Exempt mining income — (1) [Revoked]

(2) Any election under subparagraph 13(21)(f)(vi) [13(21)"undepreciated capital cost"H] of the Act in respect of property of a prescribed class acquired by a corporation for the purpose of gaining or producing income from a mine shall be made by filing with the Minister, not later than the day on or before which the corporation is required to file a return of income pursuant to section 150 of the Act for its taxation year in which the exempt period in respect of the mine ended, one of the following documents in duplicate:

(a) where the directors of the corporation are legally entitled to administer the affairs of the corporation, a certified copy of their resolution authorizing the election to be made in respect of that class; and

(b) where the directors of the corporation are not legally entitled to administer the affairs of the corporation, a certified copy of the authorization of the making of the election in respect of that class by the person or persons legally entitled to administer the affairs of the corporation.

Related Provisions: Reg. 1100(1)(w), (x).

Definitions [Reg. 1100A]: "class" — Reg. 1101(6), 1102(1)–(3), (14), (14.1); "corporation" — ITA 248(1), *Interpretation Act* 35(1); "Minister", "person", "prescribed", "property" — ITA 248(1); "taxation year" — ITA 249, Reg. 1104(1).

Income Tax Folios: S3-F4-C1: General discussion of CCA.

DIVISION II — SEPARATE CLASSES

Notes: Reg. 1101 prescribes property to be in a "separate class", not pooled with other property that would otherwise be in the same Schedule II class. The principal effect is that on disposition of such property, recapture of depreciation (under ITA 13(1)) or a terminal loss (under ITA 20(16)) is available without regard to other properties of the same class that the taxpayer owns. See also ITA 37(6) re R&D expenditures.

Separate classes are also deemed into existence under ITA 13(5)(b)(ii), 13(5.2)(c), 13(14) and 37(6).

1101. (1) Businesses and properties — Where more than one property of a taxpayer is described in the same class in Schedule II and where

(a) one of the properties was acquired for the purpose of gaining or producing income from a business, and

(b) one of the properties was acquired for the purpose of gaining or producing income from another business or from the property,

a separate class is hereby prescribed for the properties that

(c) were acquired for the purpose of gaining or producing income from each business, and

(d) would otherwise be included in the class.

Related Provisions: Reg. 1101(1a) — Insurance businesses.

Notes: *Same business*: In *Dupont Canada*, 2001 FCA 114, Reg. 1101(1) did not apply to require recapture on sale of business assets, as Du Pont's explosives manufacturing was not a "separate business" from chemical and paint manufacturing. See also *Blanchard*, [2001] G.S.T.C. 94 (TCC), para. 18 (commissions and income tax return preparation fees were part of same interconnected business); *Arbeau*, 2010 TCC 307 (electronics repair and safety inspector businesses were separate); *S.T.B. Holdings*, 2011 TCC 144 (land speculation and land development were same business); *CAE Inc.*, 2011 TCC 354, para. 71 (rev'd on other grounds 2013 FCA 92) (CAE had a "single civil aviation simulator business", with no "distinct simulator leasing or training business"); *Coop Belle-de-Jour*, 2019 QCCQ 6609 (floral arranging was not part of same business as greenhouse flower growing); *Atlantic Packaging*, 2018 TCC 183, para. 9; aff'd 2020 FCA 75; leave to appeal denied 2020 CarswellNat 4337 (SCC) (treating operations as one business might preclude a division being separate business for ITA 54.2); *Ferme Lunick*, 2020 QCCQ 1703 (potato farming and washing/bagging in separate corporate divisions were one vertically-integrated business). See also IT-206R; Income Tax Folio S4-F11-C1 ¶1.22-1.26 (for farming business); VIEWS docs 2009-0348571I7 (whether interest rate swaps are a separate source of income from resource business); 2011-0424381E5 (whether microFIT solar panels are separate from farming business); 2017-0695131C6 [2017 CPTS q.5] (oil and gas industry).

Income Tax Folios: S3-F4-C1: General discussion of CCA.

Interpretation Bulletins: IT-206R: Separate businesses; IT-218R: Profit, capital gains and losses from the sale of real estate, including farmland and inherited land and conversion of real estate from capital property to inventory and vice versa.

(1a) [Life insurance business deemed corporate business] — For the purposes of subsection (1),

(a) a life insurance business, and

(b) an insurance business other than a life insurance business,

shall each be regarded as a separate business.

(1ab) [Partnership property separate] — Where, at the end of 1971, more than one property of a taxpayer who was a member of a partnership at that time is described in the same class in Schedule II and where

(a) one of the properties can reasonably be regarded to be the interest of the taxpayer in a depreciable property that is partnership property of the partnership, and

(b) one of the properties is property other than property referred to in paragraph (a),

a separate class is hereby prescribed for all properties each of which

(c) is a property referred to in paragraph (a); and

(d) would otherwise be included in the class.

(1ac) [Rental property over $50,000] — Subject to subsection (5h), where more than one property of a taxpayer is described in the same class in Schedule II, and one or more of the properties is a rental property of the taxpayer the capital cost of which to the taxpayer was not less than $50,000[1], a separate class is hereby prescribed for each such rental property of the taxpayer that would otherwise be included in the same class, other than a rental property that was acquired by the taxpayer before 1972 or that is

(a) a building or an interest therein, or

(b) a leasehold interest acquired by the taxpayer by reason of the fact that the taxpayer erected a building on leased land,

erection of which building was commenced by the taxpayer before 1972 or pursuant to an agreement in writing entered into by the taxpayer before 1972.

Related Provisions: Reg. 1100(14) — Meaning of "rental property"; Reg. 1101(1ad) — Exceptions; Reg. 1101(1ae) — Rental property separate.

Notes: See Notes to Reg. 1103(1).

Interpretation Bulletins: IT-274R: Rental property — Capital cost of $50,000 or more; IT-304R2: Condominiums.

(1ad) [Rental property over $50,000 — exception] — Notwithstanding subsection (1ac), a rental property acquired by a taxpayer

(a) in the course of a reorganization in respect of which, if a dividend were received by a corporation in the course of the reorganization, subsection 55(2) of the Act would not be applicable to the dividend by reason of the application of paragraph 55(3)(b) of the Act, or

(b) from a person with whom the taxpayer was not dealing at arm's length (otherwise than by virtue of a right referred to in paragraph 251(5)(b) of the Act) at the time the property was acquired,

that would otherwise be rental property of the taxpayer of a separate class prescribed under subsection (1ac), shall be deemed not to be property of a separate class prescribed under that subsection if, immediately before it was so acquired by the taxpayer, it was a rental property of the person from whom the property was so acquired of a prescribed class other than a separate class prescribed under that subsection.

Related Provisions: Reg. 1100(2.21)(a); Reg. 1100(14) — Meaning of "rental property"; Reg. 1102(20) — Non-arm's length exception.

Interpretation Bulletins: IT-274R: Rental properties — Capital cost of $50,000 or more.

---

[1] Not indexed for inflation — ed.

(1ae) [Rental property separate] — Except in the case of a corporation or partnership described in subsection 1100(12), where more than one property of a taxpayer is described in the same class in Schedule II and where

(a) one of the properties is a rental property other than a property of a separate class prescribed under subsection (1ac), and

(b) one of the properties is a property other than rental property,

a separate class is hereby prescribed for properties that

(c) are described in paragraph (a); and

(d) would otherwise be included in the class.

Related Provisions: Reg. 1100(14) — Meaning of "rental property".

Interpretation Bulletins: IT-195R4: Rental property — CCA restrictions; IT-304R2: Condominiums.

(1af) [Expensive automobiles] — A separate class is hereby prescribed for each property included in Class 10.1 in Schedule II.

Notes: See Notes to ITA 13(7)(g).

Income Tax Folios: S3-F4-C1: General discussion of CCA.

Interpretation Bulletins: IT-521R: Motor vehicle expenses claimed by self-employed individuals; IT-522R: Vehicle, travel and sales expenses of employees.

(1ag) [Franchise, concession or license] — If more than one property of a taxpayer is described in the same class in Schedule II, and one or more of the properties is a property in respect of which the taxpayer is a transferee that has elected under subsection 13(4.2) of the Act (each of which is referred to in this subsection as an "elected property"), a separate class is prescribed for each elected property of the taxpayer that would otherwise be included in the same class.

Notes: Reg. 1101(1ag) added by 2002-2013 technical bill (Part 5 — technical), effective Dec. 21, 2002.

(2) Fishing vessels — Where a property of a taxpayer that would otherwise be included in Class 7 in Schedule II is a property in respect of which a depreciation allowance could have been taken under Order in Council

(a) P.C. 2798 of April 10, 1942,

(b) P.C. 7580 of August 26, 1942, as amended by P.C. 3297 of April 22, 1943, or

(c) P.C. 3979 of June 1, 1944,

if those Orders in Council were applicable to the taxation year, a separate class is hereby prescribed for each property, including the furniture, fittings and equipment attached thereto.

Related Provisions: Reg. 1100(1)(i).

(2a) Canadian vessels — A separate class is hereby prescribed for each vessel of a taxpayer, including the furniture, fittings, radiocommunication equipment and other equipment attached thereto, that

(a) was constructed in Canada;

(b) is registered in Canada; and

(c) had not been used for any purpose whatever before it was acquired by the taxpayer.

Related Provisions: Reg. 1100(1)(v) — additional allowance; Reg. 1101(2c) — No application if structured financing facility in place.

Notes: Reg. 1101(2a) amended by P.C. 1994-139, effective July 14, 1990.

Interpretation Bulletins: IT-267R2: CCA — vessels.

Advance Tax Rulings: ATR-52: Accelerated rate of CCA for vessels.

(2b) Offshore drilling vessels — A separate class is hereby prescribed for all vessels described in Class 7 in Schedule II, including the furniture, fittings, radiocommunication equipment and other equipment attached thereto, acquired by a taxpayer

(a) after May 25, 1976 and designed principally for the purpose of

(i) determining the existence, location, extent or quality of accumulations of petroleum or natural gas (other than mineral resources); or

(ii) drilling oil or gas wells; or

(b) after May 22, 1979 and designed principally for the purpose of determining the existence, location, extent or quality of mineral resources.

Related Provisions: Reg. 1100(1)(va) — Additional allowance; Reg. 1101(2c) — No application if structured financing facility in place.

Interpretation Bulletins: IT-267R2: CCA — Vessels; IT-317R: Radio and television equipment (archived).

(2c) Vessels and a structured financing facility — Subsections (2a) and (2b) do not apply to a vessel, nor to the furniture, fittings, radio communications equipment and other equipment attached to the vessel, if a structured financing facility relating to any such property has been agreed to by the Minister of Industry under the *Department of Industry Act*.

Related Provisions: Reg. Sch. II:Cl. 41(b) — Exclusion from Class 41.

Notes: Reg. 1101(2c) added by P.C. 2005-2186, effective Nov. 7, 2001.

(3) Timber limits and cutting rights — For the purposes of this Part and Schedules IV and VI, each property of a taxpayer that is

(a) a timber limit other than a timber resource property, or

(b) a right to cut timber from a limit other than a right that is a timber resource property,

is hereby prescribed to be a separate class of property.

Related Provisions: Reg. 1100(1)(e) — Capital cost allowance.

Notes: For the meaning of "timber limit" see Notes to ITA 13(21)"timber resource property".

Interpretation Bulletins: IT-469R: CCA — Earth-moving equipment; IT-481: Timber resource property and timber limits.

(4) Industrial mineral mines — For the purposes of this Part and Schedule V, where a taxpayer has

(a) more than one industrial mineral mine in respect of which he may claim an allowance under paragraph 1100(1)(g),

(b) more than one right to remove industrial minerals from an industrial mineral mine in respect of which he may claim an allowance under that paragraph, or

(c) both such a mine and a right,

each such industrial mineral mine and each such right to remove industrial minerals from an industrial mineral mine is hereby prescribed to be a separate class of property.

Related Provisions: Reg. 1104(3) — Meaning of "industrial mineral mine".

Notes: For the meaning of "industrial minerals" see Notes to ITA 125.1(3)"manufacturing or processing".

(4a) Class 28 — Single mine properties — If one or more properties of a taxpayer are described in Class 28 of Schedule II and some or all of the properties were acquired for the purpose of gaining or producing income from one mine and not from any other mine (which properties are referred to as "single mine properties" in this subsection), a separate class is prescribed for the single mine properties that

(a) were acquired for the purpose of gaining or producing income from that mine;

(b) would otherwise be included in Class 28; and

(c) are not included in a separate class by reason of subsection (4b).

Related Provisions: Reg. 1100(1)(w), 1104(5), 1104(7); Reg. 1104(5), (6.1) — Income from a mine; Reg. 1104(7) — Interpretation.

Notes: Reg. 1101(4a) amended by P.C. 2011-44, for tax years ending after March 18, 2007.

(4b) Class 28 — Multiple mine properties — If more than one property of a taxpayer is described in Class 28 in Schedule II and some or all of the properties were acquired for the purpose of gaining or producing income from particular mines and not from any other mine (which properties are referred to as "multiple mine properties" in this subsection), a separate class is prescribed for the multiple mine properties that

(a) were acquired for the purpose of gaining or producing income from the particular mines; and

(b) would otherwise be included in Class 28.

Related Provisions: Reg. 1100(1)(x), 1104(5), 1104(7); Reg. 1104(5), (6.1) — Income from a mine; Reg. 1104(7) — Interpretation.

Notes: Reg. 1101(4b) amended by P.C. 2011-44, for tax years ending after March 18, 2007.

(4c) Class 41 — Single mine properties — If one or more properties of a taxpayer are described in paragraph (a), (a.1) or (a.2) of Class 41 of Schedule II and some or all of the properties were acquired for the purpose of gaining or producing income from one mine and not from any other mine (which properties are referred to as "single mine properties" in this subsection), a separate class is prescribed for the single mine properties that

(a) were acquired for the purpose of gaining or producing income from that mine;

(b) would otherwise be included in Class 41; and

(c) are not included in a separate class by reason of subsection (4d).

Related Provisions: Reg. 1100(1)(y), 1104(5), 1104(7); Reg. 1104(5), (6.1) — Income from a mine; Reg. 1104(7) — Interpretation.

Notes: For a ruling that all the wells for extraction of material from a bituminous sands deposit are one project, see VIEWS doc 2004-0105021R3.

Reg. 1101(4c) amended by P.C. 2011-44, for tax years ending after March 18, 2007.

Reference to Cl. 41(a.1) and (a.2) added by P.C. 1998-49, effective March 7, 1996.

Interpretation Bulletins: IT-476R: CCA — Equipment used in petroleum and natural gas activities.

(4d) Class 41 — Multiple mine properties — If more than one property of a taxpayer is described in paragraph (a), (a.1) or (a.2) of Class 41 in Schedule II and some or all of the properties were acquired for the purpose of gaining or producing income from particular mines and not from any other mine (which properties are referred to as "multiple mine properties" in this subsection), a separate class is prescribed for the multiple mine properties that

(a) were acquired for the purpose of gaining or producing income from the particular mines; and

(b) would otherwise be included in Class 41.

Related Provisions: Reg. 1100(1)(ya), 1104(5), 1104(7); Reg. 1104(5), (6.1) — Income from a mine; Reg. 1104(7) — Interpretation.

Notes: See Notes to Reg. 1101(4c).

Reg. 1101(4d) amended by P.C. 2011-44, for tax years ending after March 18, 2007.

Reference to Cl. 41(a.1) and (a.2) added by P.C. 1998-49, effective March 7, 1996.

Interpretation Bulletins: IT-476R: CCA — Equipment used in petroleum and natural gas activities.

(4e) Class 41.1 — Single mine properties — If one or more properties of a taxpayer are described in paragraph (a) of Class 41.1 of Schedule II and some or all of the properties were acquired for the purpose of gaining or producing income from one mine and not from any other mine (which properties are referred to as "single mine properties" in this subsection), a separate class is prescribed for the single mine properties that

(a) were acquired for the purpose of gaining or producing income from that mine;

(b) would otherwise be included in Class 41.1, because of paragraph (a) of that class; and

(c) are not included in a separate class by reason of subsection (4f).

Related Provisions: Reg. 1100(1)(y.1) — Additional allowance.

Notes: Reg. 1101(4e) added by P.C. 2011-44, for tax years ending after March 18, 2007.

(4f) Class 41.1 — Multiple mine properties — If more than one property of a taxpayer is described in paragraph (a) of Class 41.1 in Schedule II and some or all of the properties were acquired

for the purpose of gaining or producing income from particular mines and not from any other mine (which properties are referred to as "multiple mine properties" in this subsection), a separate class is prescribed for the multiple mine properties that

(a) were acquired for the purpose of gaining or producing income from the particular mines; and

(b) would otherwise be included in Class 41.1 because of paragraph (a) of that class.

Related Provisions: Reg. 1100(1)(ya.1) — Additional allowance.

Notes: Reg. 1101(4f) added by P.C. 2011-44, for tax years ending after March 18, 2007.

(4g) Class 41.2 — single mine properties — If one or more properties of a taxpayer are described in paragraph (a) of Class 41.2 of Schedule II and some or all of the properties were acquired for the purpose of gaining or producing income from one mine and not from any other mine (in this subsection referred to as "single mine properties"), a separate class is prescribed for the single mine properties that

(a) were acquired for the purpose of gaining or producing income from that mine;

(b) would otherwise be included in Class 41.2 because of paragraph (a) of that class; and

(c) are not included in a separate class because of subsection (4h).

Related Provisions: Reg. 1100(1)(a)(xxvii.2) — Base CCA of 25%; Reg. 1100(1)(y.2) — Additional CCA until 2020; Reg. 1101(4h) — Multiple mine property.

Notes: Reg. 1101(4g) added by 2013 budget bill #2, for tax years that end after March 20, 2013.

(4h) Class 41.2 — multiple mine properties — If more than one property of a taxpayer is described in paragraph (a) of Class 41.2 in Schedule II and some or all of the properties were acquired for the purpose of gaining or producing income from particular mines and not from any other mine (in this subsection referred to as "multiple mine properties"), a separate class is prescribed for the multiple mine properties that

(a) were acquired for the purpose of gaining or producing income from the particular mines; and

(b) would otherwise be included in Class 41.2 because of paragraph (a) of that class.

Related Provisions: Reg. 1100(1)(a)(xxvii.2) — Base CCA of 25%; Reg. 1100(1)(ya.2) — Additional CCA until 2020; Reg. 1101(4g) — Single mine property.

Notes: Reg. 1101(4h) added by 2013 budget bill #2, effective for taxation years that end after March 20, 2013.

(4i) Class 47 — Liquefaction equipment — If a taxpayer acquires property that is eligible liquefaction equipment to be used as part of an eligible liquefaction facility of the taxpayer, a separate class is prescribed for those properties that were acquired for the purpose of gaining or producing income from that eligible liquefaction facility.

Related Provisions: Reg. 1100(1)(yb) — Additional CCA.

Notes: Reg. 1101(4i) added by P.C. 2015-629, effective Feb. 19, 2015 (date of the draft LNG regulations).

(5) Lease option agreements — Where, by virtue of an agreement, contract or arrangement entered into on or after May 31, 1954, a taxpayer is deemed by section 18 of the *Income Tax Act*, as enacted by the Statutes of Canada, 1958, Chapter 32, subsection 8(1), to have acquired a property, a separate class is hereby prescribed for each such property and if the taxpayer subsequently actually acquires the property it shall be included in the same class.

(5a) Telecommunication spacecraft — For the purposes of this Part, each property of a taxpayer that is an unmanned telecommunication spacecraft described in paragraph (f.2) of Class 10 or in Class 30 in Schedule II is hereby prescribed to be a separate class of property.

(5b) Multiple-unit residential buildings — For the purposes of this Part, when any property of a taxpayer is a property of Class 31 or 32 in Schedule II and the capital cost of that property to the taxpayer was not less than $50,000, a separate class is hereby prescribed for each such property of the taxpayer that would otherwise be included in the same class.

Interpretation Bulletins: IT-274R: Rental properties — Capital cost of $50,000 or more; IT-367R3: Capital cost allowance — multiple-unit residential buildings (archived).

(5b.1) Eligible non-residential building — For the purposes of this Part, a separate class is prescribed for each eligible non-residential building (other than an eligible liquefaction building) of a taxpayer in respect of which the taxpayer has (by letter attached to the return of income of the taxpayer filed with the Minister in accordance with section 150 of the Act for the taxation year in which the building is acquired) elected that this subsection apply.

Related Provisions: Reg. 1100(1)(a.1), (a.2) — Additional allowances for property in separate class; Reg. 1101(5b.2) — Eligible liquefaction building; Reg. 1102(23), (24) — Additions and alterations to buildings; Reg. 1102(25) — Building under construction on March 19, 2007; Reg. 1104(2)"eligible non-residential building" — Definition.

Notes: On whether the election is valid in a return filed late, see Notes to ITA 7(1.31). For how to elect in a return filed electronically, see Notes to ITA 150.1.

For CRA interpretation see docs 2008-0271891E5, 2009-0348411E5; 2010-0381311E5 (election cannot be made by simply claiming right CCA amount); 2011-0411811C6; 2013-0489101E5 (election can be made on an addition to a building [Hickey, "Building Additions Attract 6% CCA", 21(9) *Canadian Tax Highlights* (ctf.ca) 14-15 (Sept. 2013)]); 2016-0626641E5 (where addition is split over 2 taxation years or 2 additions are made over 2 years). A partnership can make the election: 2010-0379751E5.

Reg. 1101(5b.1) amended by P.C. 2015-629, effective Feb. 19, 2015, to add "(other than an eligible liquefaction building)" (see (5b.2) below).

Reg. 1101(5b.1) added by P.C. 2009-581, for property acquired after March 18, 2007.

(5b.2) Liquefaction buildings — If a taxpayer acquires property that is an eligible liquefaction building to be used as part of an eligible liquefaction facility of the taxpayer, a separate class is prescribed for those properties that were acquired for the purpose of gaining or producing income from that eligible liquefaction facility.

Related Provisions: Reg. 1100(1)(a.3) — Additional allowance for property in separate class; Reg. 1101(5b.1) — Other building.

Notes: Reg. 1101(5b.2) added by P.C. 2015-629, effective Feb. 19, 2015.

(5c) Leasing properties — For the purposes of this Part, except in the case of a corporation or partnership described in subsection 1100(16), where more than one property of a taxpayer is described in the same class in Schedule II and where

(a) one of the properties is a leasing property, and

(b) one of the properties is a property other than a leasing property,

a separate class is hereby prescribed for properties that

(c) are described in paragraph (a); and

(d) would otherwise be included in the class.

Related Provisions: Reg. 1100(17), (18) — Meaning of "leasing property".

Interpretation Bulletins: IT-443: Leasing property — CCA restrictions.

(5d) Railway cars — Where more than one property of a taxpayer is a railway car included in Class 35 in Schedule II that was rented, leased or used by the taxpayer in Canada in the taxation year, other than a railway car owned by a corporation, or a partnership any member of which is a corporation, that

(a) was at any time in that taxation year a common carrier that owned or operated a railway, or

(b) rented or leased the railway cars at any time in that taxation year, by one or more transactions between persons not dealing at arm's length, to an associated corporation that was, at that time, a common carrier that owned or operated a railway,

a separate class is prescribed

(c) for all such properties acquired by the taxpayer before February 3, 1990 (other than such properties acquired for rent or lease to another person),

(d) for all such properties acquired by the taxpayer after February 2, 1990 (other than such properties acquired for rent or lease to another person),

(e) for all such properties acquired by the taxpayer before April 27, 1989 for rent or lease to another person, and

(f) for all such properties acquired by the taxpayer after April 26, 1989 for rent or lease to another person.

Related Provisions: Reg. 1100(1)(z), (z.1a); Reg. 1103(2i) — Election to include Class 7(h) property in Class 35.

Notes: There is no requirement that the lessee use the railway cars in Canada or be resident in Canada: VIEWS doc 2003-0009767.

Reg. 1101(5d) substituted by P.C. 1991-465, effective April 27, 1989, with grandfathering.

(5d.1) [Railway property] — A separate class is hereby prescribed for all property included in Class 35 in Schedule II acquired at a time after December 6, 1991 and before February 28, 2000 by a taxpayer that was at that time a common carrier that owned and operated a railway.

Related Provisions: Reg. 1100(1)(z.1b) — Additional allowance.

Notes: Reg. 1101(5d.1) added by P.C. 1994-139, for property acquired after Dec. 6, 1991, and amended by P.C. 2005-2186, effective for property acquired after Feb. 27, 2000, to add "and before February 28, 2000". See now Reg. 1101(5d.2).

(5d.2) [Railway property] — A separate class is hereby prescribed for all property included in Class 35 in Schedule II acquired at a time after February 27, 2000 by a taxpayer that was at that time a common carrier that owned and operated a railway.

Related Provisions: Reg. 1100(1)(z.1c) — Additional 6% CCA for property in this class; Reg. 1103(2i) — Election to include Class 7(h) property in Class 35.

Notes: Reg. 1101(5d.2) added by P.C. 2005-2186, for property acquired after Feb. 27, 2000 (before, see Reg. 1101(5d.1)). See Notes to Reg. 1103(2i).

(5e) Railway track and related property — A separate class is hereby prescribed for all property included in Class 1 in Schedule II acquired by a taxpayer after March 31, 1977 and before 1988 that is

(a) railway track and grading, including components such as rails, ballast, ties and other track material;

(b) railway traffic control or signalling equipment, including switching, block signalling, interlocking, crossing protection, detection, speed control or retarding equipment, but not including property that is principally electronic equipment or systems software therefor; or

(c) a bridge, culvert, subway or tunnel that is ancillary to railway track and grading.

Related Provisions: Reg. 1100(1)(za), (za.1) — Additional allowance.

(5e.1) [Railway property] — A separate class is hereby prescribed for all property included in Class 1 in Schedule II acquired at a time after December 6, 1991 by a taxpayer that was at that time a common carrier that owned and operated a railway, where the property is

(a) railway track and grading, including components such as rails, ballast, ties and other track material;

(b) railway traffic control or signalling equipment, including switching, block signalling, interlocking, crossing protection, detection, speed control or retarding equipment, but not including property that is principally electronic equipment or systems software therefor; or

(c) a bridge, culvert, subway or tunnel that is ancillary to railway track and grading.

Related Provisions: Reg. 1100(1)(za.1) — Additional allowance.

Notes: Reg. 1101(5e.1) added by P.C. 1994-139, effective for property acquired after December 6, 1991.

(5e.2) [Trestles] — A separate class is hereby prescribed for all trestles included in Class 3 in Schedule II acquired at a time after December 6, 1991 by a taxpayer that was at that time a common carrier that owned and operated a railway, where the trestles are ancillary to railway track and grading.

Related Provisions: Reg. 1100(1)(za.2) — Additional allowance.

Notes: Reg. 1101(5e.2) added by P.C. 1994-139, effective for property acquired after December 6, 1991.

(5f) [Trestles] — A separate class is hereby prescribed for all trestles included in Class 3 in Schedule II acquired by a taxpayer after March 31, 1977 and before 1988 that are ancillary to railway track and grading.

Related Provisions: Reg. 1100(1)(zb).

(5g) Deemed depreciable property — A separate class is hereby prescribed for each property of a taxpayer described in Class 36 in Schedule II.

(5h) Leasehold interest in real properties — For the purposes of this Part, where more than one property of a taxpayer is described in the same class in Schedule II and where

(a) one of the properties is a leasehold interest in real property described in subsection 1100(13), and

(b) one of the properties is a property other than a leasehold interest in real property described in subsection 1100(13),

a separate class is hereby prescribed for properties that

(c) are described in paragraph (a); and

(d) would otherwise be included in the class.

(5i) Pipelines — A separate class is hereby prescribed for each property of a taxpayer described in Class 2 in Schedule II that is

(a) a pipeline the construction of which was commenced after 1984 and completed after September 1, 1985 and the capital cost of which to the taxpayer is not less than $10,000,000,

(b) a pipeline that has been extended or converted where the extension or conversion was completed after September 1, 1985 and the capital cost to the taxpayer of the extension or the cost to him of the conversion, as the case may be, is not less than $10,000,000, or

(c) a pipeline that has been extended and converted as part of a single program of extension and conversion of the pipeline where the program was completed after September 1, 1985 and the aggregate of the capital cost to the taxpayer of the extension and the cost to him of the conversion is not less than $10,000,000,

and in respect of which the taxpayer has, by letter attached to the return of his income filed with the Minister in accordance with section 150 of the Act for the taxation year in which the construction, extension, conversion or program, as the case may be, was completed, elected that this subsection apply.

Related Provisions: Reg. 1101(5j) — Effect of election.

Notes: See Notes to Reg. 1101(5b.1) re "letter attached to the return".

(5j) [Election effective forever] — An election under subsection (5i), (5l) or (5o) shall be effective from the first day of the taxation year in respect of which the election is made and shall continue to be effective for all subsequent taxation years.

Notes: Reg. 1101(5j) amended by P.C. 1991-465, effective for taxation years ending after April 26, 1989.

(5k) Certified productions — A separate class is hereby prescribed for all property of a taxpayer included in Class 10 in Schedule II by reason of paragraph (w) thereof.

Related Provisions: Reg. 1100(1)(l).

Interpretation Bulletins: IT-283R2: CCA — Videotapes, videotape cassettes, films, computer software and master recording media (archived).

(5k.1) Canadian film or video production — A separate class is hereby prescribed for all property of a corporation included in Class 10 in Schedule II because of paragraph (x) of that Class that is property

(a) in respect of which the corporation is deemed under subsection 125.4(3) of the Act to have paid an amount on account of its tax payable under Part I of the Act for a taxation year; or

(b) acquired by the corporation from another corporation where

(i) the other corporation is deemed under subsection 125.4(3) of the Act to have paid an amount on account of its tax payable under Part I of the Act for a taxation year in respect of the property, and

(ii) the corporations were related to each other throughout the period that began when the other corporation first incurred a qualified labour expenditure (as defined in subsection 125.4(1) of the Act) in respect of the property and ended when the other corporation disposed of the property to the corporation.

Related Provisions: Reg. 1100(1)(m) — Additional allowance.

Notes: For CRA interpretation see VIEWS doc 2008-0267041I7.

Reg. 1101(5k.1) added by P.C. 2005-698, for 1995 and later tax years.

(5l) Class 38 property and outdoor advertising signs — A separate class is hereby prescribed for each property of a taxpayer described in Class 38 in Schedule II or in paragraph (l) of Class 8 in Schedule II in respect of which the taxpayer has, by letter attached to the return of income of the taxpayer filed with the Minister in accordance with section 150 of the Act for the taxation year in which the property was acquired, elected that this subsection apply.

Related Provisions: Reg. 1101(5j) — Effect of election.

Notes: See Notes to Reg. 1101(5b.1) re "letter attached to the return".

Interpretation Bulletins: IT-469R: CCA — Earth-moving equipment.

(5m) Specified energy property — Where, for any taxation year, a property of a taxpayer or partnership is a specified energy property, a separate class is prescribed in respect of that property for that and subsequent taxation years.

Related Provisions: Reg. 1100(25) — Meaning of "specified energy property".

(5n) [Specified leasing property] — Notwithstanding subsection (5c), where at the end of any taxation year a property of a taxpayer is specified leasing property, a separate class is prescribed in respect of that property (including any additions or alterations to that property included in the same class in Schedule II) for that year and all subsequent taxation years.

Related Provisions: Reg. 1100(1.1), (1.11) — Specified leasing property.

Notes: Reg. 1101(5n) added by P.C. 1991-465, for tax years ending after April 26, 1989.

(5o) [Exempt leasing properties] — A separate class is prescribed for one or more properties of a class in Schedule II that are exempt properties, as defined in paragraph 1100(1.13)(a), of a taxpayer referred to in subsection 1100(16) in respect of which the taxpayer has, by letter attached to the return of income of the taxpayer filed with the Minister in accordance with section 150 of the Act for the taxation year in which the property or properties were acquired, elected that this subsection apply.

Related Provisions: Reg. 1101(5j) — Effect of election.

Notes: See Notes to Reg. 1101(5b.1) re "letter attached to the return".

Reg. 1101(5o) added by P.C. 1991-465, effective for property acquired after April 26, 1989; an election is valid if made by September 23, 1991.

(5p) Rapidly depreciating electronic equipment [optional] — Subject to subsection (5q), a separate class is prescribed for one or more properties of a taxpayer acquired in a taxation year and included in the year in Class 8 in Schedule II, where each of the properties has a capital cost to the taxpayer of at least $1,000 and is

(a) computer software;

(b) a photocopier; or

(c) office equipment that is electronic communications equipment, such as a facsimile transmission device or telephone equipment.

Related Provisions: Reg. 1101(5q) — Election required for Reg. 1101(5p) to apply; Reg. 1103(2g) — Property transferred back to pool if still owned after 5 years.

Notes: Reg. 1101(5p) allows a terminal loss for certain equipment that can depreciate rapidly, at the taxpayer's election made in the return for the year the property is acquired (see Reg. 1101(5q)). If the equipment is not disposed of after 5 years, it returns to the pool rather than being treated as a separate item. See Reg. 1103(2g).

Reg. 1101(5p) amended by P.C. 2005-2286, for property acquired after 2004, to delete reference to Class 10 property and to delete para. (a) referring to computers, which are now in Class 45 instead (paras. (b)-(d) were renumbered (a)-(c)).

Reg. 1101(5p) added by P.C. 1994-231, for property acquired after April 26, 1993.

(5q) [Election required] — Each of subsections (5p) and (5s) apply to a property or properties of a taxpayer only if the taxpayer has (by letter attached to the taxpayer's return of income filed with the Minister in accordance with section 150 of the Act for the taxation year in which the property or properties were acquired) elected that the subsection apply to the property or properties, as the case may be.

Related Provisions: Reg. 1101(5t) — Similar election permitted for combustion turbines.

Notes: See Notes to Reg. 1101(5b.1) re "letter attached to the return".

Reg. 1101(5q) amended by P.C. 2005-2186, for property acquired after Feb. 27, 2000, to add reference to Reg. 1101(5s).

Reg. 1101(5q) added by P.C. 1994-231, effective for property acquired after April 26, 1993. Any election under Reg. 1101(5q) was on time if filed by August 31, 1994.

(5r) Computer tax shelter property — For the purpose of this Part, where

(a) more than one property of a taxpayer is described in the same class in Schedule II,

(b) one of the properties is a computer tax shelter property, and

(c) one of the properties is not a computer tax shelter property,

for properties that are described in paragraph (b) and that would otherwise be included in the class, a separate class is prescribed.

Related Provisions: Reg. 1100(20.1) — Limitation on CCA claim; Reg. 1100(20.2) — Definition of "computer tax shelter property".

Notes: Reg. 1101(5r) amended by P.C. 2009-581, for property acquired after March 18, 2007.

Reg. 1101(5r) added by P.C. 2000-1000, on the same basis as Reg. 1100(20.1).

(5s) Manufacturing or processing property [optional] — Subject to subsection (5q), a separate class is prescribed for one or more properties of a taxpayer

(a) that were acquired in a taxation year and included in the year in Class 43 in Schedule II because of paragraph (a) of that Class; and

(b) that had a capital cost to the taxpayer of at least $1,000.

Related Provisions: Reg. 1101(5q) — Election required for Reg. 1101(5s) to apply; Reg. 1103(2g) — Property transferred back to pool if still owned after 5 years.

Notes: Reg. 1101(5s) added by P.C. 2005-2186, for property acquired after Feb. 27, 2000.

Former proposed Reg. 1101(5s.1)–(5s.5) in the draft regulations would have provided a separate class for certain Class 43 property acquired in 2010-11 (and an additional allowance under 2008 Budget-proposed Reg. 1100(1)(zi)). They were superseded by 2009 Budget regulations which place such property acquired before 2012 in Class 29.

(5t) [Repealed]

Notes: Reg. 1101(5t) repealed by P.C. 2006-439, effective for property acquired after 2005. Combustion turbines are now in Class 48 and there is no separate-class election.

Reg. 1101(5t) added by P.C. 2005-2186, for property acquired after Feb. 27, 2000.

(5u) Equipment related to transmission pipelines — A separate class is prescribed for one or more properties of a taxpayer that is property included in Class 7 in Schedule II because of paragraph (j) or (k) of that Class if the taxpayer has (by letter attached to the taxpayer's return of income filed with the Minister in accordance with section 150 of the Act for the taxation year in which the property or properties were acquired) elected that this subsection apply to the property or properties.

Notes: "In accordance with section 150" suggests that if the return is filed even one day late, the election is invalid unless the CRA extends time under ITA 220(2.1) or (3). See Notes to Reg. 1101(5b.1) re "letter attached to the return".

Reg. 1101(5u) amended by P.C. 2009-660 to add reference to Cl. 7(k), effective for property acquired after Feb. 25, 2008.

Reg. 1101(5u) and (5v) added by P.C. 2006-439, effective Feb. 23, 2005.

Interpretation Bulletins: IT-476R: CCA — Equipment used in petroleum and natural gas activities.

(5v) Transmission pipelines — A separate class is prescribed for one or more properties of a taxpayer that is property included in Class 49 in Schedule II if the taxpayer has (by letter attached to the taxpayer's return of income filed with the Minister in accordance with section 150 of the Act for the taxation year in which the property or properties were acquired) elected that this subsection apply to the property or properties.

Notes: See Notes to Reg. 1101(5u).

Interpretation Bulletins: IT-476R: CCA — Equipment used in petroleum and natural gas activities.

(6) Reference — A reference in this Part to a class in Schedule II includes a reference to the corresponding separate classes prescribed by this section.

Notes [Reg. 1101]: See at beginning of Reg. 1101.

Definitions [Reg. 1101]: "amount" — ITA 248(1); "arm's length" — ITA 251(1), Reg. 1102(20); "business" — Reg. 1101(1a); "Canada" — ITA 255, *Interpretation Act* 35(1); "class" — Reg. 1101(5), 1102(1)–(3), (14), (14.1); "computer software" — Reg. 1104(2); "computer software tax shelter property" — Reg. 1100(20.2); "corporation" — ITA 248(1), *Interpretation Act* 35(1); "depreciable property" — ITA 13(21), 248(1); "disposed" — ITA 248(1)"disposition"; "dividend" — ITA 248(1); "eligible liquefaction building", "eligible liquefaction equipment", "eligible liquefaction facility" — Reg. 1104(2); "eligible non-residential building", "general-purpose electronic data processing equipment" — Reg. 1104(2); "income from a mine" — Reg. 1104(5); "industrial mineral mine" — Reg. 1104(3); "leasing property" — Reg. 1100(17-20); "life insurance business" — ITA 248(1); "mine" — Reg. 1104(7)(a); "mineral" — Reg. 1104(3); "mineral resource", "Minister", "office" — ITA 248(1); "partnership" — see ITA 96(1) Notes; "person" — ITA 248(1); "pipeline" — Reg. 1104(2); "prescribed", "property" — ITA 248(1); "related" — ITA 251(2)–(6); "rental property" — Reg. 1100(14); "specified energy property" — Reg. 1100(25), (27)–(29); "specified leasing property" — Reg. 1100(1.11); "systems software" — Reg. 1104(2); "tax shelter" — ITA 237.1(1), 248(1); "taxation year" — ITA 249, Reg. 1104(1); "taxpayer" — ITA 248(1); "timber resource property" — ITA 13(21), 248(1); "writing" — *Interpretation Act* 35(1).

DIVISION III — PROPERTY RULES

1102. (1) Property not included — The classes of property described in this Part and in Schedule II shall be deemed not to include property

(a) **[otherwise deductible]** — the cost of which would be deductible in computing the taxpayer's income if the Act were read without reference to sections 66 to 66.4 of the Act;

Notes: Depreciable property is excluded from CEE and CDE under 66.1(6)"Canadian exploration expense"(l) and 66.2(5)"Canadian development expense"(j).

Reg. 1102(1)(a) amended by P.C. 1999-629, for tax years that end after December 5, 1996 (see ITA 13(34) for 1988–96).

I.T. Technical News: IT-476R: CCA — Equipment used in petroleum and natural gas activities.

(a.1) **[CRCE]** — the cost of which is included in the taxpayer's Canadian renewable and conservation expense (within the meaning assigned by section 1219);

Notes: Reg. 1102(1)(a.1) added by P.C. 2000-1331, effective for expenses incurred after December 5, 1996. CRCE is fully deductible under ITA 66.1(1)"Canadian exploration expense"(g.1), and so is excluded from CCA pools.

(b) **[inventory]** — that is described in the taxpayer's inventory;

Notes: Property held for sale is not eligible for CCA, "even if it is used in the meantime to earn income": *CAE Inc.*, 2013 FCA 92, para. 104. See also Notes to ITA 10(1), 13(21)"depreciable property" and 54"capital property".

(c) **[no income purpose]** — that was not acquired by the taxpayer for the purpose of gaining or producing income;

Notes: The "income" required by Reg. 1102(1)(c) is gross income, not net income or profit after expenses and CCA: *Peter Brown*, [2002] 1 C.T.C. 2451 (TCC) [aff'd on other grounds 2003 FCA 192, leave to appeal denied 2004 CarswellNat 84], based on the 2001 SCC decision in *Ludco*, where this interpretation was applied to interest deductibility (see Notes to 20(1)(c)).

In *Hickman Motors*, [1998] 1 C.T.C. 213 at 222 (SCC), the Supreme Court stated that the fact a taxpayer may have intended to obtain a tax saving by acquiring the asset is does not bring it within Reg. 1102(1)(c). "A transaction may be effectual and not in any sense a sham but may have no business purpose other than the tax purpose". However, in *Sherman*, 2008 TCC 186, para. 77 (aff'd 2009 FCA 9), the TCC ruled this principle applies "only if an income-earning purpose has already been established", so no CCA was allowed on software that the TCC held was acquired solely for tax savings. In *568864 B.C.*, 2014 TCC 373, patents held as loan security and seized when the loan went bad, by a company in the same industry, were depreciable property despite Reg. 1102(1)(c).

In *Jolly Farmer*, 2008 TCC 409, an employer that acquired property for its share-holder-employees to live in did so for business purposes, so Reg. 1102(1)(c) did not apply.

Where property is acquired on an 88(1) windup and is not used to produce income, no CCA can be claimed but a terminal loss can arise on disposition: VIEWS doc 2014-0553731I7.

I.T. Technical News: 3 (loss utilization within a corporate group; use of a partner's assets by a partnership.

(d) **[R&D expense]** — that was acquired by an expenditure in respect of which the taxpayer is allowed a deduction in computing income under section 37 of the Act;

Related Provisions: Reg. 5202"cost of capital"(a), 5204"cost of capital"(a) — Manufacturing and processing credit.

(e) **[non-Canadian art and antiques]** — that was acquired by the taxpayer after November 12, 1981, other than property acquired from a person with whom the taxpayer was not dealing at arm's length (otherwise than by virtue of a right referred to in paragraph 251(5)(b) of the Act) at the time the property was acquired if the property was acquired in the circumstances where subsection (14) applies, and is

(i) a print, etching, drawing, painting, sculpture, or other similar work of art, the cost of which to the taxpayer was not less than $200,

(ii) a hand-woven tapestry or carpet or a handmade appliqué, the cost of which to the taxpayer was not less than $215 per square metre,

(iii) an engraving, etching, lithograph, woodcut, map or chart, made before 1900, or

(iv) antique furniture, or any other antique object, produced more than 100 years before the date it was acquired, the cost of which to the taxpayer was not less than $1,000,

other than any property described in subparagraph (i) or (ii) where the individual who created the property was a Canadian (within the meaning assigned by paragraph 1104(10)(a)) at the time the property was created;

Notes: In *Roger Dubois Inc.*, 2015 FCA 235, Reg. 1102(1)(e) applied to disallow CCA on several antique violins and bows; "antique" meant nothing beyond "more than 100 years old" (para. 33).

For CRA interpretation see VIEWS docs 2010-0373311C6, 2015-0580391E5. For more on CCA for art see Joel Secter, "Corporate Art Collections", xxxvi(7) *The Canadian Taxpayer* (Carswell) 54-55 (April 4, 2014).

(f) **[yacht, camp, lodge, golf course facility]** — that is property referred to in paragraph 18(1)(l) of the Act acquired after December 31, 1974, an outlay or expense for the use or maintenance of which is not deductible by virtue of that paragraph;

Related Provisions: Reg. 1102(17) — Grandfathering to November 13, 1974.

(g) **[pre-1972 farming/fishing property]** — in respect of which an allowance is claimed and permitted under Part XVII;

Notes: See Notes to Reg. 1700–1705.

(h) **[pre-1966 automobile]** — that is a passenger automobile acquired after June 13, 1963 and before January 1, 1966, the cost to the taxpayer of which, minus the initial transportation charges and retail sales tax in respect thereof, exceeded $5,000, unless the automobile was acquired by a person before June 14, 1963 and has by one or more transactions between persons not dealing at arm's length become vested in the taxpayer;

Related Provisions: Reg. 1102(11)–(13) — Interpretation.

(i) **[pre-1963 property]** — that was deemed by section 18 of the *Income Tax Act*, as enacted by the Statutes of Canada, 1958, Chapter 32, subsection 8(1), to have been acquired by the taxpayer and that did not vest in the taxpayer before the 1963 taxation year;

(j) **[life insurer]** — of a life insurer, that is property used by it in, or held by it in the course of, carrying on an insurance business outside Canada; or

(k) **[linefill]** — that is linefill in a pipeline.

Notes: A proposed definition of "pipeline" in Reg. 1104(2), released Dec. 23, 1991, has been abandoned. See Interpretation Bulletin IT-482R para. 1 for the CRA's administrative definition.

Reg. 1102(1)(k) added by P.C. 1994-139, effective for property acquired after December 23, 1991, with grandfathering for certain property acquired before 1993.

Interpretation Bulletins [Reg. 1102(1)(k)]: IT-482R: Pipelines.

Income Tax Folios [Reg. 1102(1)]: S3-F4-C1: General discussion of CCA [replaces IT-220R2 and IT-478R].

Interpretation Bulletins [Reg. 1102(1)]: IT-148R3: Recreational properties and club dues; IT-218R: Profit, capital gains and losses from the sale of real estate, including farmland and inherited land and conversion of real estate from capital property to inventory and vice versa; IT-350R: Investigation of site.

(1a) Partnership property — Where the taxpayer is a member of a partnership, the classes of property described in this Part and in Schedule II shall be deemed not to include any property that is an interest of the taxpayer in depreciable property that is partnership property of the partnership.

Income Tax Folios: S3-F4-C1: General discussion of CCA.

(2) Land — The classes of property described in Schedule II shall be deemed not to include the land upon which a property described therein was constructed or is situated.

(3) Non-residents — Where the taxpayer is a non-resident person, the classes of property described in this Part and in Schedule II shall, except for the purpose of determining the foreign accrual property income of the taxpayer for the purposes of subdivision i of Division B of Part I of the Act, be deemed not to include property that is situated outside Canada.

(4) Improvements or alterations to leased properties — Subject to subsection (5), "capital cost" for the purposes of paragraph 1100(1)(b) includes any amount expended by a taxpayer for or in respect of an improvement or alteration to a leased property.

(5) Buildings on leased properties — Where the taxpayer has a leasehold interest in a property, a reference in Schedule II to a property that is a building or other structure shall include a reference to that leasehold interest to the extent that that interest

(a) was acquired by reason of the fact that the taxpayer

(i) erected a building or structure on leased land,

(ii) made an addition to a leased building or structure, or

(iii) made alterations to a leased building or structure that substantially changed the nature of the property; or

(b) was acquired after 1975 or, in the case of any property of Class 31 or 32, after November 18, 1974, from a former lessee who had acquired it by reason of the fact that he or a lessee before him

(i) erected a building or structure on leased land,

(ii) made an addition to a leased building or structure, or

(iii) made alterations to a leased building or structure that substantially changed the nature of the property.

Related Provisions: Reg. 1102(4) — Improvements or alterations to leased property; Reg. 1102(5.1) — References to "building".

Notes: Reg. 1102(5) deems a tenant's leasehold improvements to be a building for CCA purposes (e.g., Class 1). It applied in docs 2012-0455081I7, 2014-0552291R3.

Income Tax Folios: S3-F4-C1: General discussion of CCA.

Interpretation Bulletins: IT-79R3: CCA — Buildings or other structures; IT-195R4: Rental property — CCA restrictions; IT-324: CCA — Emphyteutic lease (archived); IT-367R3: Capital cost allowance — multiple-unit residential buildings (archived); IT-464R: Leasehold interests.

(5.1) [Buildings on leased properties] — Where a taxpayer has acquired a property that would, if the property had been acquired by a person with whom the taxpayer was not dealing at arm's length at the time the property was acquired by the taxpayer, be described in paragraph (5)(a) or (b) in respect of that person, a reference in Schedule II to a property that is a building or other structure shall, in respect of the taxpayer, include a reference to that property.

Notes: Reg. 1102(5.1) added by P.C. 1994-139, effective for property acquired after Dec. 23, 1991, with grandfathering for certain property acquired before 1993.

(6) Leasehold interests acquired before 1949 — [No longer relevant.]

(7) River improvements — For the purposes of paragraph 1100(1)(f), capital cost includes an amount expended on river improvements by the taxpayer for the purpose of facilitating the removal of timber from a timber limit.

Notes: For the meaning of "timber limit" see Notes to ITA 13(21) "timber resource property".

(8) Electrical plant used for mining — Where the generating or distributing equipment and plant (including structures) of a producer or distributor of electrical energy were acquired for the purpose of providing power to a consumer for use by the consumer in the operation in Canada of a mine, ore mill, smelter, metal refinery or any combination thereof and at least 80 per cent of the producer's or distributor's output of electrical energy

    (a) for his 1948 and 1949 taxation years, or

    (b) for his first two taxation years in which he sold power,

whichever period is later, was sold to the consumer for that purpose, the property shall be included in

    (c) Class 10 in Schedule II if it is property acquired

        (i) before 1988, or

        (ii) before 1990

            (A) pursuant to an obligation in writing entered into by the taxpayer before June 18, 1987,

            (B) that was under construction by or on behalf of the taxpayer on June 18, 1987, or

            (C) that is machinery or equipment that is a fixed and integral part of the building, structure, plant facility or other property that was under construction by or on behalf of the taxpayer on June 18, 1987, or

    (d) Class 41, 41.1 or 41.2 in Schedule II in any other case, unless the property would otherwise be included in Class 43.1 or 43.2 in Schedule II and the taxpayer has, by a letter filed with the taxpayer's return of income filed with the Minister in accordance with section 150 of the Act for the taxation year in which the property was acquired, elected to include the property in Class 43.1 or 43.2, as the case may be.

Related Provisions: Reg. 1102(9.1) — Acquisition before November 8, 1969; Reg. 1102(9.2) — Acquisition not at arm's length; Reg. 1103(4) — When election under para. (d) effective; Reg. 1104(7) — Meaning of "mine".

Notes: Generally, Reg. 1102(8) provides that, where 80% or more of the power generated by electrical generating equipment of a taxpayer is used to provide power to a consumer at a mine, ore mill, smelter, or metal refinery operated in Canada by the consumer, the taxpayer's generating and distribution equipment and plant (including structures) acquired after 1987 is to be included in Class 41, 41.1 or 41.2. Where it would otherwise be included in Class 43.1 or 43.2, the taxpayer may elect to include the property in that Class.

Reg. 1102(8)(d) amended by 2013 budget bill #2, to add reference to Class 41.2 (and change "except where" to "unless"), for property acquired after March 20, 2013. An election referred to in amended Reg. 1102(8)(d) or (9)(d), made by a taxpayer in respect of a property, is deemed filed in the manner described in those paras. for the taxation year in which the property was acquired if

    (a) the election is filed with the Minister in writing by June 10, 2014, and

    (b) the property is

        (i) an eligible mine development property as defined in amended Reg. 1104(2), or

        (ii) described in Class 41.2.

Reg. 1102(8)(d) amended by P.C. 2011-44 to add reference to Class 41.1, effective for property acquired after March 18, 2007, except that for property acquired before May 3, 2010, read "the taxation year in which the property was acquired" as "the taxation year that includes May 3, 2010".

Reg. 1102(8)(d) amended by P.C. 2006-439 to add references to Class 43.2, effective Feb. 23, 2005; for property acquired from Feb. 24, 2005 through June 13, 2006, the election to include property in Class 43.2 can also be made by notifying the Minister in writing by the end of 2006.

Reg. 1102(8) amended by P.C. 1997-1033, effective for property acquired after Feb. 21, 1994 (if acquired before Aug. 21, 1997, the election under para. (d) could be filed until Feb. 28/98).

For property acquired from 1988-Feb. 21, 1994, read "customer" instead of "consumer" between paras. (b) and (c) (this drafting error should have been corrected retroactive to 1988), and read Reg. 1102(8)(d) as simply "Class 41 in Schedule II in any other case".

(9) [Generating or distributing equipment] — Where a taxpayer has acquired generating or distributing equipment and plant (including structures) for the purpose of providing power for his own consumption in operating a mine, ore mill, smelter, metal refinery or any combination thereof and at least 80 per cent of the output of electrical energy was so used

    (a) in his 1948 and 1949 taxation years, or

    (b) in the first two taxation years in which he so produced power,

whichever period is the later, the property shall be included in

    (c) Class 10 in Schedule II if it is property acquired

        (i) before 1988, or

        (ii) before 1990

            (A) pursuant to an obligation in writing entered into by the taxpayer before June 18, 1987,

            (B) that was under construction by or on behalf of the taxpayer on June 18, 1987, or

            (C) that is machinery or equipment that is a fixed and integral part of a building, structure, plant facility or other property that was under construction by or on behalf of the taxpayer on June 18, 1987, or

    (d) Class 41, 41.1 or 41.2 in Schedule II in any other case, unless the property would otherwise be included in Class 43.1 or 43.2 in Schedule II and the taxpayer has, by a letter filed with the taxpayer's return of income filed with the Minister in accordance with section 150 of the Act for the taxation year in which the property was acquired, elected to include the property in Class 43.1 or 43.2, as the case may be.

Related Provisions: Reg. 1102(9.2) — Acquisition not at arm's length; Reg. 1103(4) — When election under para. (d) effective; Reg. 1104(7) — Meaning of "mine".

Notes: Reg. 1102(9)(d) amended by 2013 budget bill #2, effective on the same basis as the amendment to Reg. 1102(8), to add reference to Class 41.2 and to change "except where" to "unless".

Reg. 1102(9)(d) amended by P.C. 2011-44 to add reference to Class 41.1, for property acquired after March 18, 2007, except that for property acquired before May 3, 2010, read "the taxation year in which the property was acquired" as "the taxation year that includes May 3, 2010".

Reg. 1102(9)(d) amended by P.C. 2006-439 to add references to Class 43.2, effective Feb. 23, 2005; for property acquired from Feb. 24, 2005 through June 13, 2006, the election to include property in Class 43.2 can also be made by notifying the Minister in writing by the end of 2006.

Reg. 1102(9)(d) amended by P.C. 1997-1033, for property acquired after Feb. 21, 1994 (if acquired before Aug. 21, 1997, the election under para. (d) could be filed until Feb. 28/98).

For property acquired from 1988-Feb. 21, 1994, read Reg. 1102(9)(d) as simply "Class 41 in Schedule II in any other case".

(9.1) [pre-1970 acquisition] — In their application to generating or distributing equipment and plant (including structures) that were acquired by the taxpayer before November 8, 1969, subsections (8) and (9) shall be read without reference to a "metal refinery".

(9.2) [Property under Reg. 1102(8) or (9)] — Where a taxpayer acquires property after November 7, 1969 from a person with whom he was not dealing at arm's length that is property referred to in subsection (8) or (9), notwithstanding those subsections, that property shall not be included in Class 10 in Schedule II by the taxpayer unless the property had been included in that class by the person from whom it was acquired, by virtue of subsection (8) or (9) as it read in its application before November 8, 1969.

(10) [Repealed]

Notes: Reg. 1102(10), "Railway companies", repealed by 2013 budget bill #2, for expenditures incurred in tax years that begin after Dec. 21, 2012 (due to repeal of ITA s. 36).

(11) Passenger automobiles — In paragraph (1)(h),

"cost to the taxpayer" of an automobile means, except as provided in subsections (12) and (13),

(a) except in any case coming under paragraph (b) or (c), the capital cost to the taxpayer of the automobile,

(b) except in any case coming under paragraph (c), where the automobile was acquired by a person (in this section referred to as the "original owner") after June 13, 1963, and has, by one or more transactions between persons not dealing at arm's length, become vested in the taxpayer, the greater of

(i) the actual cost to the taxpayer, and

(ii) the actual cost to the original owner, and

(c) where the automobile was acquired by the taxpayer outside Canada for use in connection with a permanent establishment, as defined for the purposes of Part IV or Part XXVI, outside Canada, the lesser of

(i) the actual cost to the taxpayer, and

(ii) the amount that such an automobile would ordinarily cost the taxpayer if he purchased it from a dealer in automobiles in Canada for use in Canada;

"initial transportation charges" in respect of an automobile means the costs incurred by a dealer in automobiles for transporting the automobile (before it had been used for any purpose whatever) from,

(a) in the case of an automobile manufactured in Canada, the manufacturer's plant, and

(b) in any other case, to the place in Canada, if any, at which the automobile was received or stored by a wholesale distributor,

to the dealer's place of business;

"passenger automobile" means a vehicle, other than an ambulance or hearse, that was designed to carry not more than nine persons, and that is

(a) an automobile designed primarily for carrying persons on highways and streets except an automobile that

(i) is designed to accommodate and is equipped with auxiliary folding seats installed between the front and the rear seats,

(ii) was acquired by a person carrying on the business of operating a taxi or automobile rental service, or arranging and managing funerals, for use in such business, and

(iii) is not a vehicle described in paragraph (b), or

(b) a station wagon or substantially similar vehicle;

"retail sales tax" in respect of an automobile means the aggregate of municipal and provincial retail sales taxes payable in respect of the purchase of the automobile by the taxpayer.

(12) [Pre-1966 automobile] — For the purposes of paragraph (1)(h), where an automobile is owned by two or more persons or by partners, a reference to "cost to the taxpayer" shall be deemed to be a reference to the aggregate of the cost, as defined in subsection (11), to each such person or partner.

(13) [Pre-1966 automobile] — In determining cost to a taxpayer for the purposes of paragraph (1)(h), subsection 13(7) of the Act shall not apply unless the automobile was acquired by gift.

(14) Property acquired by transfer, amalgamation or winding-up — Subject to subsections (14.11) to (14.13), for the purposes of this Part and Schedule II, if a property is acquired by a taxpayer

(a) in the course of a reorganization in respect of which, if a dividend were received by a corporation in the course of the reorganization, subsection 55(2) of the Act would not be applica-

ble to the dividend by reason of the application of paragraph 55(3)(b) of the Act, or

(b), (c) [Revoked]

(d) from a person with whom the taxpayer was not dealing at arm's length (otherwise than by virtue of a right referred to in paragraph 251(5)(b) of the Act) at the time the property was acquired, and

(e) [Revoked]

the property, immediately before it was so acquired by the taxpayer, was property of a prescribed class or a separate prescribed class of the person from whom it was so acquired, the property shall be deemed to be property of that same prescribed class or separate prescribed class, as the case may be, of the taxpayer.

Related Provisions: Reg. 1100(2.21)(a); Reg. 1102(20) — Non-arm's length exception.

Notes: See Notes to Reg. 1103(2d). Reg. 1102(14) applies to the distribution of depreciable property to partners on dissolution of a partnership: VIEWS doc 2007-021811R3. It applied on a capital loss consolidation in 2018-0772921R3. The rule does not result in automatic entitlement to "extra" CCA such as under Reg. 1100(1)(a.1)–(a.2): 2009-0332581E5.

Reg. 1102(14) opening words amended by 2019 budget bill #1, effective March 19, 2019, to make it subject to Reg. 1102(14.13).

Reg. 1102(14) opening words amended to add reference to subsec. (14.12) by 2013 budget bill #2, for property acquired after March 20, 2013.

Reg. 1102(14) opening words amended by P.C. 2011-44, for property acquired after March 18, 2007, to add "Subject to subsection (14.11)".

Income Tax Folios: S3-F4-C1: General discussion of CCA.

Interpretation Bulletins: IT-267R2: CCA — vessels; IT-476R: CCA — Equipment used in petroleum and natural gas activities; IT-481: Timber resource property and timber limits; IT-488R2: Winding-up of 90%-owned taxable Canadian corporations (archived).

(14.1) [Change in class] — For the purposes of this Part and Schedule II, if a taxpayer has acquired, after May 25, 1976, property of a class in Schedule II (in this subsection referred to as the "present class"), that had been previously owned before May 26, 1976 by the taxpayer or by a person with whom the taxpayer was not dealing at arm's length (otherwise than by virtue of a right referred to in paragraph 251(5)(b) of the Act) at the time the property was acquired, and at the time the property was previously so owned it was a property of a different class (other than Class 28 or 41) in Schedule II (in this subsection referred to as the "former class"), the property is deemed to be property of the former class and not to be property of the present class.

Related Provisions: Reg. 1100(2.21)(a).

Notes: Reg. 1102(14.1) amended by P.C. 2011-44, for property acquired after March 18, 2007.

Interpretation Bulletins: IT-267R2: CCA — vessels.

(14.11) [Oil sands property on reorganization] — If, after March 18, 2007, a taxpayer acquires an oil sands property in circumstances to which subsection (14) applies and the property was depreciable property that was included in Class 41, because of paragraph (a), (a.1) or (a.2) of that Class, by the person or partnership from whom the taxpayer acquired the property, the following rules apply:

(a) there may be included in Class 41 of the taxpayer only that portion of the property the capital cost of which portion to the taxpayer is the lesser of the undepreciated capital cost of Class 41 of that person or partnership immediately before the disposition of the property by the person or partnership and the amount, if any, by which that undepreciated capital cost is reduced as a result of that disposition; and

(b) there shall be included in Class 41.1 of the taxpayer that portion, if any, of the property that is not the portion included in Class 41 of the taxpayer under paragraph (a).

Notes: Reg. 1102(14.11) added by P.C. 2011-44, for property acquired after March 18, 2007.

(14.12) [Rules for Reg. 1102(14) — Classes 41, 41.2] — If, after March 20, 2013, a taxpayer acquires a property (other than an

oil sands property) in circumstances to which subsection (14) applies and the property was depreciable property that was included in Class 41, because of paragraph (a) or (a.1) of that Class, by the person or partnership from whom the taxpayer acquired the property, the following rules apply:

(a) there may be included in Class 41 of the taxpayer only that portion of the property the capital cost of which portion to the taxpayer is the lesser of the undepreciated capital cost of Class 41 of that person or partnership immediately before the disposition of the property by the person or partnership and the amount, if any, by which that undepreciated capital cost is reduced as a result of that disposition; and

(b) there shall be included in Class 41.2 of the taxpayer that portion, if any, of the property that is not the portion included in Class 41 of the taxpayer under paragraph (a).

Notes: Reg. 1102(14.12) (added by 2013 budget bill #2, for property acquired after March 20, 2013) ensures that the UCC pool of a mining property (other than an oil sands property) included in Class 41 is preserved, to allow additional CCA, if Reg. 1102(14) applies.

(14.13) [Class 54-56 status not preserved] — Subsection (14) does not apply to an acquisition of property by a taxpayer from a person in respect of which the property was included in any of Classes 54 to 56.

Notes: Reg. 1102(14) ensures that, subject to certain exceptions, property acquired in certain transactions remains in the same class as it was for the vendor. Reg. 1102(14.13) provides that this rule does not apply to a 248(1)"zero-emission vehicle" (ZEV) (Class 54 or 55) or off-road ZEV (Class 56). This ensures that the enhanced CCA for those classes (Reg. 1100(2) Notes) applies only to new vehicles.

Reg. 1102(14.13) added by 2019 budget bill #1 effective March 19, 2019, and amended by 2021 budget bill #1 to apply to Class 56, effective March 2, 2020.

(14.2) Townsite costs — For the purpose of paragraph 13(7.5)(a) of the Act, a property is prescribed in respect of a taxpayer where the property would, if it had been acquired by the taxpayer, be property included in Class 10 in Schedule II because of paragraph (l) of that Class.

Notes: Reg. 1102(14.2) added by P.C. 1999-629, effective March 7, 1996. These "townsite costs" under Class 10(l) were previously eligible under Reg. 1102(18) for depreciable property treatment.

Interpretation Bulletins: IT-476R: CCA — Equipment used in petroleum and natural gas activities.

(14.3) Surface construction and bridges — For the purpose of paragraph 13(7.5)(b) of the Act, prescribed property is any of

(a) a road (other than a specified temporary access road), sidewalk, airplane runway, parking area, storage area or similar surface construction;

(b) a bridge; and

(c) a property that is ancillary to any property described in paragraph (a) or (b).

Related Provisions: Reg. 1104(2) — Definition of "specified temporary access road".

Notes: For the meaning of "similar surface construction" in para. (a), see Notes to Reg. Sch. II:Class 17.

Reg. 1102(14.3) added by P.C. 1999-629, effective March 7, 1996.

Income Tax Folios: S3-F4-C1: General discussion of CCA.

Interpretation Bulletins: IT-476R: CCA — Equipment used in petroleum and natural gas activities.

(15) Manufacturing and processing enterprises — For the purposes of subsection 13(10) of the Act,

(a) property is hereby prescribed that is

(i) a building included in Class 3 or 6 in Schedule II, or

(ii) machinery or equipment included in Class 8 in Schedule II,

except

(iii) property that may reasonably be regarded as having been acquired for the purpose of producing coal from a coal mine or oil, gas, metals or industrial minerals from a resource re-

ferred to in section 1201 as it read immediately before it was repealed by section 2 of Order in Council P.C. 1975-1323 of June 12, 1975, or

(iv) property acquired for use outside Canada; and

(b) a business carried on by the taxpayer is hereby prescribed as a manufacturing or processing business if,

(i) for the fiscal period in which the property was acquired, or

(ii) for the fiscal period in which a reasonable volume of business was first carried on,

whichever was later, the revenue received by the taxpayer, in the course of carrying on the business from

(iii) the sale of goods processed or manufactured by the taxpayer in Canada,

(iv) the leasing or renting of goods that were processed or manufactured by the taxpayer in Canada,

(v) advertisements in a newspaper or magazine that was produced by the taxpayer in Canada, and

(vi) construction carried on by the taxpayer in Canada,

was not less than ⅔ of the revenue of the business for the period.

Related Provisions: Reg. 1102(16) — Meaning of "revenue".

(16) ["Revenue"] — For the purposes of paragraph (15)(b), "revenue" means gross revenue minus the aggregate of

(a) amounts that were paid or credited in the period, to customers of the business, in relation to such revenue as a bonus, rebate or discount or for returned or damaged goods; and

(b) amounts included therein by virtue of section 13 or subsection 23(1) of the Act.

(16.1) Election for certain manufacturing or processing equipments — A taxpayer who acquires a property after March 18, 2007 and before 2016 that is manufacturing or processing machinery or equipment may (by letter attached to the return of income of the taxpayer filed with the Minister in accordance with section 150 of the Act for the taxation year in which the property is acquired) elect to include the property in Class 29 in Schedule II if

(a) Class 43.1 or 43.2 in Schedule II would otherwise apply to the property; and

(b) Class 29 in Schedule II would apply to the property if that schedule were read without reference to Classes 43.1 and 43.2.

Notes: See Notes to Reg. 1101(5b.1) re "letter attached to the return" and "filed . . . in accordance with section 150".

Reg. 1102(16.1) amended by 2013 budget bill #1 to change "2012" to "2016", effective 2012.

Reg. 1102(16.1) opening words amended by P.C. 2009-660, effective for property acquired after Feb. 25, 2008, to add "of the taxpayer filed with the Minister in accordance with section 150 of the Act" and to change "before 2009" to "before 2012".

Reg. 1102(16.1) added by P.C. 2009-581, effective March 19, 2007. An 1102(16.1) election in writing is deemed filed in the manner and by the time required if it is received by the Minister of National Revenue by August 11, 2009.

Income Tax Folios: S3-F4-C1: General discussion of CCA.

(17) Recreational property — Property referred to in paragraph (1)(f) does not include

(a) any property that the taxpayer was obligated to acquire under the terms of an agreement in writing entered into before November 13, 1974; or

(b) any property the construction of which was

(i) commenced by the taxpayer before November 13, 1974 or commenced under an agreement in writing entered into by the taxpayer before November 13, 1974, and

(ii) completed substantially according to plans and specifications agreed to by the taxpayer before November 13, 1974.

Interpretation Bulletins: IT-148R3: Recreational properties and club dues.

(18) [Repealed]

Notes: Reg. 1102(18) repealed by P.C. 1999-629, for payments required to be made under the terms of contracts made after March 6, 1996. See now ITA 13(7.5)(a) and Reg. 1102(14.2). For payments under earlier contracts, see up to PITA 49th ed.

(19) Additions and alterations — For the purposes of this Part and Schedule II, where

(a) a taxpayer acquired a property that is included in a class in Schedule II (in this subsection referred to as the "actual class"),

(b) the taxpayer acquires property that is an addition or alteration to the property referred to in paragraph (a),

(c) the property that is the addition or alteration referred to in paragraph (b) would have been property of the actual class if it had been acquired by the taxpayer at the time he acquired the property referred to in paragraph (a), and

(d) the property referred to in paragraph (a) would have been property of a class in Schedule II (in this subsection referred to as the "present class") that is different from the actual class if it had been acquired by the taxpayer at the time he acquired the addition or alteration referred to in paragraph (b),

the addition or alteration referred to in paragraph (b) shall, except as otherwise provided in this Part or in Schedule II, be deemed to be an acquisition by the taxpayer of property of the present class.

Income Tax Folios: S3-F4-C1: General discussion of CCA.

Interpretation Bulletins: IT-79R3: CCA — Buildings or other structures.

(19.1) For the purposes of this Part and Schedule II, if subsection (19.2) applies to the refurbishment or reconditioning of a railway locomotive of a taxpayer, any property acquired by the taxpayer after February 25, 2008 that is incorporated into the locomotive in the course of the refurbishment or reconditioning is, except as otherwise provided in this Part or in Schedule II, deemed to be included in paragraph (y) of Class 10 in Schedule II.

Notes: Reg. 1102(19.1) added by P.C. 2009-660, for property acquired after Feb. 25, 2008.

(19.2) This subsection applies to the refurbishment or reconditioning of a railway locomotive, of a taxpayer, that

(a) is included in a class in Schedule II other than Class 10; and

(b) would be included in Class 10 in Schedule II if it had not been used or acquired for use for any purpose by any taxpayer before February 26, 2008.

Related Provisions: Reg. 1102(19.1) — Effect of Reg. 1102(19.2) applying.

Notes: Reg. 1102(19.2) added by P.C. 2009-660 for property acquired after Feb. 25, 2008.

(20) Non-arm's length exception — For the purposes of subsections 1100(2.2) and (19), 1101(1ad) and 1102(14) (in this subsection referred to as the "relevant subsections"), where, but for this subsection, a taxpayer would be considered to be dealing not at arm's length with another person as a result of a transaction or series of transactions the principal purpose of which may reasonably be considered to have been to cause one or more of the relevant subsections to apply in respect of the acquisition of a property, the taxpayer shall be considered to be dealing at arm's length with the other person in respect of the acquisition of that property.

Related Provisions: ITA 248(10) — Series of transactions.

Notes: For a ruling that Reg. 1102(20) does not apply see doc 2018-0772921R3.

Income Tax Folios: S4-F7-C1: Amalgamations of Canadian corporations [replaces IT-474R2].

Interpretation Bulletins: IT-267R2: CCA — vessels; IT-488R2: Winding-up of 90%-owned taxable Canadian corporations (archived).

(20.1) [Anti-avoidance] — For the purposes of subsections 1100(2.02) and 1104(4), a particular person or partnership and another person or partnership shall be considered not to be dealing at arm's length with each other in respect of the acquisition or ownership of a property if, in the absence of this subsection, they would be considered to be dealing at arm's length with each other and it

may reasonably be considered that the principal purpose of any transaction or event, or a series of transactions or events, is to cause

(a) the property to qualify as accelerated investment incentive property; or

(b) the particular person or partnership and the other person or partnership to satisfy the condition in subclause 1100(2.02)(a)(i)(C)(I).

Notes: Reg. 1102(20.1) is intended to prevent taxpayers from contriving arm's length relationships in order to obtain favourable treatment available to accelerated investment incentive property (see Notes to Reg. 1100(2)), by creating an arm's length transfer for Reg. 1104(4)(b)(ii)(B). (Such schemes would likely fall under GAAR in 245(2) anyway.)

Reg. 1102(20.1) amended by 2021 budget bill #1, for property acquired after July 30, 2019. For property acquired earlier, read:

(20.1) For the purposes of subsection 1104(4), if, in the absence of this subsection, a taxpayer would be considered to be dealing at arm's length with another person or partnership as a result of a transaction or series of transactions the principal purpose of which may reasonably be considered to have been to cause one or more properties of the taxpayer to qualify as accelerated investment incentive property, the taxpayer shall be considered not to be dealing at arm's length with the other person or partnership in respect of the acquisition of those properties.

Reg. 1102(20.1) added by 2019 budget bill #1, effective June 21, 2019.

(21) [Class 43.1 property] — Where a taxpayer has acquired a property described in Class 43.1 of Schedule II in circumstances in which clauses (b)(iii)(A) and (B) or (e)(iii)(A) and (B) of that class apply,

(a) the portion of the property, determined by reference to capital cost, that is equal to or less than the capital cost of the property to the person from whom the property was acquired, is included in that class; and

(b) the portion of the property, if any, determined by reference to capital cost, that is in excess of the capital cost of the property to the person from whom it was acquired, shall not be included in that class.

Notes: Reg. 1102(21) added by P.C. 2000-1331, for property acquired after June 26, 1996.

(22) [Class 43.2 property] — Where a taxpayer has acquired a property that is described in Class 43.2 in Schedule II in circumstances in which clauses (b)(iii)(A) and (B) or (e)(iii)(A) and (B) of Class 43.1 in Schedule II apply and the property was included in Class 43.2 in Schedule II of the person from whom the taxpayer acquired the property,

(a) the portion of the property, determined by reference to capital cost, that is equal to or less than the capital cost of the property to the person from whom the property was acquired is included in Class 43.2 in Schedule II; and

(b) the portion of the property, if any, determined by reference to capital cost, that is in excess of the capital cost of the property to the person from whom it was acquired shall not be included in Class 43.1 or 43.2 in Schedule II.

Notes: Reg. 1102(22) added by P.C. 2006-439, effective June 14, 2006.

(23) Rules for additions to and alterations of certain buildings — For the purposes of applying paragraphs 1100(1)(a.1) and (a.2) and subsection 1101(5b.1), the capital cost of an addition to or an alteration of a taxpayer's building is deemed to be the capital cost to the taxpayer of a separate building if the building to which the addition or alteration was made is not included in a separate class under subsection 1101(5b.1).

Related Provisions: Reg. 1104(2)"eligible non-residential building" — Definition.

Notes: For CRA interpretation see VIEWS doc 2009-0348411E5.

Reg. 1102(23) added by P.C. 2009-581 for additions/alterations made after March 18, 2007.

(24) If an addition or an alteration is deemed to be a separate building under subsection (23), the references in paragraphs 1100(1)(a.1) and (a.2) to "the floor space of the building" are to be read as references to "the total floor space of the separate building and the building to which the addition or alteration was made".

Related Provisions: Reg. 1104(2)"eligible non-residential building" — Definition.

Notes: For CRA interpretation see VIEWS doc 2009-0348411E5.

Reg. 1102(24) added by P.C. 2009-581 for additions/alterations made after March 18, 2007.

(25) Acquisition costs of certain buildings — For the purposes of this Part and Schedule II, if an eligible non-residential building of a taxpayer was under construction on March 19, 2007, the portion, if any, of the capital cost of the building that was incurred by the taxpayer before March 19, 2007 is deemed to have been incurred by the taxpayer on March 19, 2007 unless the taxpayer elects (by letter attached to the taxpayer's return of income filed with the Minister in accordance with section 150 of the Act for the taxation year in which the building was acquired) that this subsection not apply to that cost.

Related Provisions: Reg. 1104(2)"eligible non-residential building" — Definition.

Notes: Reg. 1102(25) added by P.C. 2009-581 for additions/alterations made after March 18, 2007.

(26) [Rules for zero-emission vehicles] — For the purpose of the definition "zero-emission vehicle" in subsection 248(1) of the Act,

(a) it is a prescribed condition that the motor vehicle has a battery capacity of at least 7 kWh; and

(b) the federal purchase incentive announced on March 19, 2019 is a prescribed program.

Notes: Para. (a): the required battery capacity was to be 15 kWh as announced in the Budget, and per 2019 budget bill #1 as introduced. It was changed to 7 kWh by the Commons Finance Committee before Third Reading.

Para. (b): The federal purchase incentive is described in the 2019 Budget Chapter 2: "To encourage more Canadians to buy zero-emission vehicles, Budget 2019 proposes to provide $300 million over three years, starting in 2019-20, to Transport Canada to introduce a new federal purchase incentive of up to $5,000 for electric battery or hydrogen fuel cell vehicles with a manufacturer's suggested retail price of less than $45,000. Program details to follow." For details on the incentive see tinyurl.com/zev-incentive, on the Transport Canada website.

Reg. 1102(26) added by 2019 budget bill #1, effective March 19, 2019.

Definitions [Reg. 1102]: "accelerated investment incentive property" — Reg. 1104(4), (4.1); "actual class" — Reg. 1102(19)(a); "amount" — ITA 248(1); "arm's length" — ITA 251(1), Reg. 1102(20); "automobile", "business" — ITA 248(1); "Canada" — ITA 255, *Interpretation Act* 35(1); "class" — Reg. 1101(6), 1102(1)–(3), (14), (14.1); "commencement" — *Interpretation Act* 35(1); "corporation" — ITA 248(1), *Interpretation Act* 35(1); "cost to the taxpayer" — Reg. 1102(11), (12); "depreciable property" — ITA 13(21), 248(1); "disposed" — ITA 248(1)"disposition"; "disposition", "dividend" — ITA 248(1); "eligible non-residential building" — Reg. 1104(2); "fiscal period" — ITA 249.1; "foreign accrual property income" — ITA 95(1), (2), 248(1); "former class" — Reg. 1102(14.1); "gross revenue" — ITA 248(1); "Her Majesty" — *Interpretation Act* 35(1); "individual" — ITA 248(1); "initial transportation charges" — Reg. 1102(11); "inventory" — ITA 248(1); "mine" — Reg. 1104(7)(a); "mineral" — Reg. 1104(3); "Minister", "non-resident" — ITA 248(1); "oil sands property", "ore" — Reg. 1104(2); "original owner" — Reg. 1102(11)"cost to the taxpayer"(b); "partnership" — see ITA 96(1) Notes; "passenger automobile" — Reg. 1102(11); "person" — ITA 248(1); "pipeline" — Reg. 1104(2); "prescribed" — ITA 248(1); "present class" — Reg. 1102(14.1), (19)(d); "property" — ITA 248(1); "provincial" — *Interpretation Act* 33(3), 35(1)"province"; "relevant subsections" — Reg. 1102(20); "retail sales tax" — Reg. 1102(11); "revenue" — Reg. 1102(16); "series" — ITA 248(10); "specified temporary access road" — Reg. 1104(2); "taxation year" — ITA 249, Reg. 1104(1); "taxpayer" — ITA 248(1); "undepreciated capital cost" — ITA 13(21), 248(1); "writing" — *Interpretation Act* 35(1); "zero-emission vehicle" — ITA 248(1).

DIVISION IV — INCLUSIONS IN AND TRANSFERS BETWEEN CLASSES

1103. (1) Elections to include properties in Class 1 — In respect of properties otherwise included in any of Classes 2 to 10, 11 and 12 in Schedule II, a taxpayer may elect to include in Class 1 in Schedule II all such properties acquired for the purpose of gaining or producing income from the same business.

Related Provisions: ITA 13(5) — Effect of transfer; ITA 220(3.2), Reg. 600(d) — Late filing or revocation of election; Reg. 1103(3)–(5) — How election made and when effective.

Notes: See Income Tax Folio S3-F4-C1 ¶1.132 and CRA reply to TEI, Dec. 4, 2018, q. E.1: the election does not affect properties acquired after year-end. When this election is made (see Reg. 1103(3) and (5) for timing and filing requirement), *all* assets in

classes 2-12 (other than 10.1) are moved to Class 1. Assets acquired in years after the year to which the election applies stay in their class unless a new election is made: VIEWS doc 2018-0782341C6 [2018 TEI q. E.1].

Grouping assets together can be useful to avoid recapture on disposing of an asset in one class when UCC is still available in other classes. *G.H.C. Investment*, [1961] C.T.C. 187 (Exch. Ct.) held that, unless the election was filed *before* selling the assets, the Regulations could not override recapture required by the ITA so Reg. 1103(1) was ineffective. This was fixed by a 1960 amendment to Reg. 1103(4) and the current wording of ITA 13(1); CRA now accepts the election as valid: Folio S3-F4-C1 ¶1.132.

Reg. 1103(1) might be used when disposing of land, building, machinery and equipment, to combine all the assets in Class 1 so as to reduce the impact of ITA 13(21.1): VIEWS doc 2004-0072411E5.

When assets are transferred to a new class (by any provision of Reg. 1103), ITA 13(5) transfers over the cost, UCC and CCA claimed to date.

Reg. 1103(1) applies only to assets used in the same business, as assets in different businesses are in separate classes (see Reg. 1101(1) Notes): docs 2000-0033755, 2006-0171111E5. The election can be used for a specified investment business (rental properties): 2000-0009515; but does not override Reg. 1101(1ac), which deems each rental property to be a separate class: doc 9301685.

Interpretation Bulletins: IT-274R: Rental properties — capital cost of $50,000 or more.

Information Circulars: 07-1R1: Taxpayer relief provisions.

(2) Elections to include properties in Class 2, 4 or 17 — Where the chief depreciable properties of a taxpayer are included in Class 2, 4 or 17 in Schedule II, the taxpayer may elect to include in Class 2, 4 or 17 in Schedule II, as the case may be, a property that would otherwise be included in another class in Schedule II and that was acquired by him before May 26, 1976 for the purpose of gaining or producing income from the same business as that for which those properties otherwise included in the said Class 2, 4 or 17 were acquired.

Related Provisions: ITA 220(3.2), Reg. 600(d) — Late filing or revocation of election; Reg. 1103(3)–(5) — How election made and when effective.

Notes: See Notes to Reg. 1103(1).

Information Circulars: 07-1R1: Taxpayer relief provisions.

(2a) Elections to include properties in Class 8 — [Applies only to obsolete Classes 19 and 21]

(2b) Elections to include properties in Class 37 — In respect of properties that would have been included in Class 37 in Schedule II had they been acquired after the date on which Class 37 became effective, a taxpayer may, by letter attached to the return of his income for a taxation year filed with the Minister in accordance with section 150 of the Act, elect to include in Class 37 all such properties acquired by the taxpayer before that date.

Related Provisions: Reg. 1103(3)–(5) — How election made and when effective.

Notes: See Notes to Reg. 1101(5b.1) re "letter attached to the return".

(2c) Elections to make certain transfers — [Applies only to property started or committed to before May 26, 1976]

(2d) [Deferral of recapture] — Where a taxpayer has

(a) disposed of a property (in this subsection referred to as the "former property") of a class in Schedule II (in this subsection referred to as the "former class"), and

(b) before the end of the taxation year in which the former property was disposed of, acquired property (in this subsection referred to as the "new property") of a class in Schedule II (in this subsection referred to as the "present class") and the present class is neither

(i) the former class, nor

(ii) a separate class described in section 1101, other than subsection 1101(5d),

such that

(c) if the former property had been acquired at the time that the new property was acquired and from the person from whom the new property was acquired, the former property would have been included in the present class, and

(d) if the new property had been acquired at the time that the former property was acquired and from the person from whom the former property was acquired, the new property would have been included in the former class,

the taxpayer may, by letter attached to the return of income of the taxpayer filed with the Minister in accordance with section 150 of the Act in respect of the taxation year in which the former property was disposed of, elect to transfer the former property from the former class to the present class in the year of its disposition and, for greater certainty, the transfer shall be considered to have been made before the disposition of the property.

Related Provisions: ITA 13(5) — Effect of transfer; ITA 220(3.2), Reg. 600(d) — Late filing or revocation of election; Reg. 1103(3)–(5) — How election made and when effective.

Notes: Reg. 1103(2d) allows a taxpayer to elect to defer recapture under ITA 13(1) by transferring the property disposed of to a new class of which the taxpayer has other property, where the property disposed of would have been in the new class had it been acquired when the property of the new class was acquired.

For a ruling allowing a Reg. 1103(2d) election on property acquired in a transaction under Reg. 1102(14), see VIEWS doc 2002-0136163.

See Notes to Reg. 1101(5b.1) re "letter attached to the return".

Reg. 1103(2d)(b)(ii) amended by P.C. 1991-465, effective April 27, 1989, to add the reference to Reg. 1101(5d).

Interpretation Bulletins: IT-469R: CCA — Earth-moving equipment; IT-476R: CCA — Equipment used in petroleum and natural gas activities.

Information Circulars: 07-1R1: Taxpayer relief provisions.

(2e) Transfers from Class 40 to Class 10 — [Applies only to property acquired before 1990]

(2f) Elections to include properties in Class 1, 3 or 6 — In respect of properties otherwise included in Class 20 in Schedule II, a taxpayer may, by letter attached to the return of income of the taxpayer for a taxation year filed with the Minister in accordance with section 150 of the Act, elect to include in Class 1, 3 or 6 in Schedule II, as specified in the letter, all properties of Class 20 in Schedule II owned by the taxpayer at the commencement of the year.

Related Provisions: Reg. 1103(3)–(5) — How election made and when effective.

Notes: See Notes to Reg. 1101(5b.1) re "letter attached to the return".

(2g) Transfers to Class 8, Class 10 or Class 43 — For the purposes of this Part and Schedule II, where one or more properties of a taxpayer are included in a separate class pursuant to an election filed by the taxpayer in accordance with subsection 1101(5q), all the properties included in that class immediately after the beginning of the taxpayer's fifth taxation year beginning after the end of the first taxation year in which a property of the class became available for use by the taxpayer for the purposes of subsection 13(26) of the Act shall be transferred immediately after the beginning of that fifth taxation year from the separate class to the class in which the property would, but for the election, have been included.

Related Provisions: ITA 13(5) — Effect of transfer; Reg. 1103(3)–(5) — How election made and when effective.

Notes: See Notes to Reg. 1103(1).

P.C. 2005-2186, s. 14 provides that for the purpose of Reg. 1103(2g), an election under Reg. 1101(5s) that is made under P.C. 2005-2186 s. 13(1) (see Notes to Reg. 1101(5t)) is deemed to have been made in accordance with Reg. 1101(5q).

Reg. 1103(2g) added by P.C. 1994-231, for property acquired after April 26, 1993.

Former proposed Reg. 1103(2g.1)–(2g.2) in the Feb. 26/08 draft regulations (2008 Budget), which would have applied to certain Class 43 property acquired in 2010-11, were superseded by the 2009 Budget regulations which place such property acquired before 2012 in Class 29.

(2h) Elections not to include properties in Class 44 — A taxpayer may, by letter attached to the taxpayer's return of income filed with the Minister in accordance with section 150 of the Act for the taxation year in which a property was acquired, elect not to include the property in Class 44 in Schedule II.

Related Provisions: Reg. 1103(3)–(5) — How election made and when effective.

Notes: When this election is made, the property will normally go into Class 14.

See Notes to Reg. 1101(5b.1) re "letter attached to the return".

Reg. 1103(2h) added by P.C. 1994-231, effective for property acquired after April 26, 1993 (the election could be filed by August 31, 1994).

(2i) Election to include properties in Class 35 — In respect of any property otherwise included in Class 7 in Schedule II because of paragraph (h) of that Class and to which paragraph 1100(1)(z.1a) and subsection 1101(5d), or paragraph 1100(1)(z.1c) and subsection 1101(5d.2), would apply if Class 35 of that Schedule applied to the property, the taxpayer may (by letter attached to the taxpayer's return of income filed with the Minister in accordance with section 150 of the Act for the taxation year in which the property was acquired) elect to include the property in Class 35 rather than in Class 7.

Related Provisions: Reg. 1103(3)–(5) — How election made and when effective.

Notes: Reg. 1103(2i) provides an election to include certain railway assets in Cl. 35 (7% CCA) rather than Cl. 7(h) (15%). A further 6% is allowed by Reg. 1100(1)(z.1a) or (z.1c), and 1101(5d) or (5d.2). While the total CCA rate is 13% rather than 15%, the property is "exempt property" for the specified leasing property rules (see Reg. 1100(1.13)(a)(viii)).

See Notes to Reg. 1101(5b.1) re "letter attached to the return". See also Notes to Reg. 1103(1).

Reg. 1103(2i) added by P.C. 2005-2186, for property acquired after Feb. 27, 2000.

(2j) [Election out of Class 54, 55 or 56] — A taxpayer may, in its return of income filed with the Minister on or before its filing-due date for the taxation year in which a property is acquired, elect not to include the property in any of Classes 54 to 56 in Schedule II, as the case may be.

Related Provisions: Reg. 1103(3)–(5) — How election made and when effective.

Notes: Reg. 1103(2j) provides that taxpayer T may elect *not* to include in new Class 54 or 55 a vehicle that would otherwise be a 248(1)"zero-emission vehicle" (see cl. (c)(ii)(A) of that definition, which excludes a vehicle for which the election is made). The vehicle then goes into its usual class, generally Class 10, 10.1 or 16. T must file the election with the CRA "in" (see Notes to ITA 7(1.31)) its return for the taxation year in which the vehicle is acquired. There is no provision for late-filed or amended elections. See also Notes to ITA 13(7)(i).

Reg. 1103(2j) amended by 2021 budget bill #1, effective March 2, 2020, to apply to Class 56.

Reg. 1103(2j) added by 2019 budget bill #1, effective March 19, 2019.

(3) Election rules — To be effective in respect of a taxation year, an election under this section must be made not later than the last day on which the taxpayer may file a return of his income for the taxation year in accordance with section 150 of the Act.

Notes: A late election is not possible: *Terminal Norco*, [2006] 4 C.T.C. 2329 (TCC).

(4) [Timing of election] — An election under paragraph 1102(8)(d) or (9)(d) or this section shall be effective from the first day of the taxation year in respect of which the election is made and shall continue to be effective for all subsequent taxation years.

Notes: References to Reg. 1102(8)(d) and (9)(d) added to Reg. 1103(4) by P.C. 1997-1033, effective February 22, 1994.

(5) [How election made] — An election under subsection (1) or (2) shall be made by sending a letter to that effect by registered mail to the Tax Centre at which the taxpayer customarily files the returns required by section 150 of the Act.

Notes: Reg. 1103(5) amended by P.C. 2007-849, effective June 13, 2007.

Definitions [Reg. 1103]: "business" — ITA 248(1); "class" — Reg. 1101(6), 1102(1)–(3), (14), (14.1); "commencement" — *Interpretation Act* 35(1); "disposed" — ITA 248(1)"disposition"; "disposition" — ITA 248(1); "end of the taxation year" — Reg. 1104(1); "former class" — Reg. 1103(2c), (2d)(a); "former property" — Reg. 1103(2d)(a); "Minister" — ITA 248(1); "new property" — Reg. 1103(2d)(b); "person" — ITA 248(1); "present class" — Reg. 1103(2c), (2d)(b); "property" — ITA 248(1); "taxation year" — ITA 249, Reg. 1104(1); "taxpayer" — ITA 248(1); "writing" — *Interpretation Act* 35(1).

Income Tax Folios: S3-F4-C1: General discussion of CCA [replaces IT-190R2 and IT-478R2].

Interpretation Bulletins [Reg. 1103]: IT-327: Elections under Regulation 1103 (archived).

DIVISION V — INTERPRETATION

1104. (1) Definitions — Where the taxpayer is an individual and his income for the taxation year includes income from a business the fiscal period of which does not coincide with the calendar year, in respect of the depreciable properties acquired for the purpose of gaining or producing income from the business, a reference in this Part to

"end of the taxation year" shall be deemed to be a reference to the end of the fiscal period of the business; and

"taxation year" shall be deemed to be a reference to the fiscal period of the business.

Related Provisions: ITA 34.1 — Income inclusion where fiscal year is not calendar year.

(2) In this Part and Schedule II,

"bitumen development phase" of a taxpayer's oil sands project means a development phase that expands the oil sands project's capacity to extract and initially process tar sands to produce bitumen or a similar product;

Notes: Definition "bitumen development phase" added by P.C. 2011-44, effective March 19, 2007.

"certified feature film" — [Film whose photography or art work commenced before May 26, 1976 — no longer relevant]

"certified production" — [No longer relevant]

Notes: Certified productions acquired after Feb. 1996 are no longer eligible for Class 10 (see Class 10(w)), and the government has not certified productions since 1995. See now the Canadian film/video production credit in ITA 125.4.

"certified short production" — [Revoked]

Notes: This definition was revoked in 1986.

"completion" of a specified development phase of a taxpayer's oil sands project means the first attainment of a level of average output, attributable to the specified development phase and measured over a sixty day period, equal to at least 60% of the planned level of average daily output (as determined in paragraph (b) of the definition "specified development phase") in respect of that phase;

Notes: Definition "completion" added by P.C. 2011-44, effective March 19, 2007.

"computer software" includes systems software and a right or licence to use computer software;

Related Provisions: Reg. 1100(20.1) — Limitation on CCA claim for computer tax shelter property; Reg. 1100(20.2) — Computer tax shelter property deemed to be computer software.

Notes: See Notes to Class 12 (in Reg. Schedule II). See also Notes to ITA 188.1(5) re meaning of "includes".

Interpretation Bulletins: IT-283R2; CCA — Videotapes, videotape cassettes, films, computer software and master recording media (archived).

"data network infrastructure equipment" means network infrastructure equipment that controls, transfers, modulates or directs data, and that operates in support of telecommunications applications such as e-mail, instant messaging, audio- and video-over-Internet Protocol or Web browsing, Web searching and Web hosting, including data switches, multiplexers, routers, remote access servers, hubs, domain name servers, and modems, but does not include

(a) network equipment (other than radio network equipment) that operates in support of telecommunications applications, if the bandwidth made available by that equipment to a single end-user of the network is 64 kilobits per second or less in either direction,

(b) radio network equipment that operates in support of wireless telecommunications applications unless the equipment supports digital transmission on a radio channel,

(c) network equipment that operates in support of broadcast telecommunications applications and that is unidirectional,

(d) network equipment that is end-user equipment, including telephone sets, personal digital assistants and facsimile transmission devices,

(e) equipment that is described in paragraph (f.2) or (v) of Class 10, or in any of Classes 45, 50 and 52, in Schedule II,

(f) wires or cables, or similar property, and

(g) structures;

Related Provisions: Reg. Sch. II:Cl. 46 — 30% CCA rate.

Notes: An IP telephone and related hardware are excluded from this definition by paras. (a) and (e) in the CRA's view: VIEWS doc 2010-0362061E5.

Para. (e) amended by P.C. 2009-581, effective March 19, 2007, to refer to Cl. 50, and by P.C. 2009-660, for property acquired after Jan. 27, 2009, to refer to Cl. 52.

Definition "data network infrastructure equipment" added by P.C. 2005-2286, effective March 23, 2004.

"designated asset" in respect of a development phase of a taxpayer's oil sands project, means a property that is a building, a structure, machinery or equipment and is, or is an integral and substantial part of,

(a) in the case of a bitumen development phase,

(i) a crusher,

(ii) a froth treatment plant,

(iii) a primary separation unit,

(iv) a steam generation plant,

(v) a cogeneration plant, or

(vi) a water treatment plant, or

(b) in the case of an upgrading development phase,

(i) a gasifier unit,

(ii) a vacuum distillation unit,

(iii) a hydrocracker unit,

(iv) a hydrotreater unit,

(v) a hydroprocessor unit, or

(vi) a coker;

Notes: Definition "designated asset" added by P.C. 2011-44, effective March 19, 2007.

"designated overburden removal cost" of a taxpayer means any cost incurred by him in respect of clearing or removing overburden from a mine in Canada owned or operated by him where the cost

(a) was incurred after November 16, 1978 and before 1988,

(b) was incurred after the mine came into production in reasonable commercial quantities,

(c) as of the end of the taxation year in which the cost was incurred, has not been deducted by the taxpayer in computing his income, and

(d) is not deductible, in whole or in part, by the taxpayer in computing his income for a taxation year subsequent to the taxation year in which the cost was incurred, other than by virtue of paragraph 20(1)(a) of the Act;

"designated underground storage cost" of a taxpayer means any cost incurred by him after December 11, 1979 in respect of developing a well, mine or other similar underground property for the storage in Canada of petroleum, natural gas or other related hydrocarbons;

Notes: See Mike Hegedus, "Designated Underground Storage Cost", XII(2) *Resource Sector Taxation* (Federated Press) 2-9 (2018).

Interpretation Bulletins: IT-476R: CCA — Equipment used in petroleum and natural gas activities.

"development phase" of a taxpayer's oil sands project means the acquisition, construction, fabrication or installation of a group of assets, by or on behalf of the taxpayer, that may reasonably be considered to constitute a discrete expansion in the capacity of the oil sands project when complete (including, for greater certainty, the initiation of a new oil sands project);

Notes: "Development phase" added by P.C. 2011-44, effective March 19, 2007.

"eligible liquefaction building" of a taxpayer, in respect of an eligible liquefaction facility of the taxpayer, means property (other than property that has been used or acquired for use for any purpose before it was acquired by the taxpayer or a residential building) acquired by the taxpayer after February 19, 2015 and before 2025 that is included in Class 1 in Schedule II because of paragraph (q) of that Class and that is used as part of the eligible liquefaction facility;

Related Provisions: Reg. 1100(1)(a.3) — Additional 6% allowance (total 10%).

Notes: Definition "eligible liquefaction building" added by P.C. 2015-629, effective Feb. 19, 2015.

"eligible liquefaction equipment" in respect of an eligible liquefaction facility of a taxpayer, means property of the taxpayer that is used in connection with the liquefaction of natural gas and that

(a) is acquired by the taxpayer after February 19, 2015 and before 2025,

(b) is included in Class 47 in Schedule II because of paragraph (b) of that Class,

(c) has not been used or acquired for use for any purpose before it was acquired by the taxpayer,

(d) is not excluded equipment, and

(e) is used as part of the eligible liquefaction facility;

Related Provisions: Reg. 1100(1)(yb) — Additional 22% allowance (total 30%).

Notes: Definition "eligible liquefaction equipment" added by P.C. 2015-629, effective Feb. 19, 2015 (date of the draft LNG regulations).

"eligible liquefaction facility" of a taxpayer means a self-contained system located in Canada — including buildings, structures and equipment — that is used or intended to be used by the taxpayer for the purpose of liquefying natural gas;

Related Provisions: Reg. 1100(1)(a.3), (yb) — Additional allowances; Reg. 1104(18) — Income from eligible liquefaction activities.

Notes: Definition "eligible liquefaction facility" added by P.C. 2015-629, effective Feb. 19, 2015 (date of the draft LNG regulations).

"eligible mine development property" means a property acquired by a taxpayer after March 20, 2013 and before 2018 for the purpose of gaining or producing income

(a) from a new mine or an expansion of a mine, if the property was acquired under a written agreement entered into by the taxpayer before March 21, 2013,

(b) from a new mine, if

(i) the construction of the new mine was started by, or on behalf of, the taxpayer before March 21, 2013 (and for this purpose construction does not include obtaining permits or regulatory approvals, conducting environmental assessments, community consultations or impact benefit studies, and similar activities), or

(ii) the engineering and design work for the construction of the new mine, as evidenced in writing, was started by, or on behalf of, the taxpayer before March 21, 2013 (and for this purpose engineering and design work does not include obtaining permits or regulatory approvals, conducting environmental assessments, community consultations or impact benefit studies, and similar activities), or

(c) from an expansion of a mine, if

(i) the construction for the expansion of the mine was started by, or on behalf of, the taxpayer before March 21, 2013 (and for this purpose construction does not include obtaining permits or regulatory approvals, conducting environmental assessments, community consultations or impact benefit studies, and similar activities), or

(ii) the engineering and design work for the construction of the expansion of the mine, as evidenced in writing, was started by, or on behalf of, the taxpayer before March 21, 2013 (and for this purpose engineering and design work does not include obtaining permits or regulatory approvals, conducting environmental assessments, community consultations or impact benefit studies, and similar activities);

Related Provisions: Reg. Sch. II:Cl. 41.2 — Eligible mine development property excluded from Class 41.2.

Notes: "Eligible mine development property" (added by 2013 budget bill #2 effective March 21, 2013) is relevant for the phase-out of accelerated CCA for property used in mining projects (other than oil sands projects) and the consequential introduction of Class 41.2. EMDP can be included in Class 41 rather than in the new Class 41.2 (i.e., accelerated CCA continues to be available, without any phase-out, for EMDP acquired after March 20, 2013 and before 2018). (See opening words of Class 41.2.)

This phase-out of accelerated CCA does not apply to property used in an oil sands project; that accelerated CCA is phased out based on the schedule set out in the 2007 Budget amendments to Reg. 1104(2).

"eligible non-residential building" means a taxpayer's building (other than a building that was used, or acquired for use, by any person or partnership before March 19, 2007) that is located in Canada, that is included in Class 1 in Schedule II and that is acquired by the taxpayer on or after March 19, 2007 to be used by the taxpayer, or a lessee of the taxpayer, for a non-residential use;

Related Provisions: Reg. 1100(1)(a.1). (a.2) — Additional allowance for building; Reg. 1101(5b.1) — Separate class for each non-residential building; Reg. 1102(23), (24) — Addition or alteration to building; Reg. 1102(25) — Building under construction on March 19, 2007.

Notes: For CRA interpretation see doc 2008-0271891E5; May 2011 ICAA roundtable (tinyurl.com/cra-abtax), q. 6. The "for use" test is an objective intention test: 2013-0515361E5.

Reg. 1104(2)"eligible non-residential building" added by P.C. 2009-581, effective March 19, 2007.

A proposed definition **"excluded building"** in the Feb. 19, 2015 draft regulations was not enacted, as that exclusion was built into "eligible liquefaction building".

"excluded equipment" means

(a) pipelines (other than pipelines used to move natural gas, or its components that are extracted, within an eligible liquefaction facility during the liquefaction process or used to move liquefied natural gas),

(b) equipment used exclusively to regasify liquefied natural gas, and

(c) electrical generation equipment;

Notes: The only use of this term is in Reg. 1104(2)"eligible liquefaction equipment".

Definition "excluded equipment" added by P.C. 2015-629, effective Feb. 19, 2015.

"gas or oil well equipment" includes

(a) equipment, structures and pipelines, other than a well casing, acquired to be used in a gas or oil field in the production therefrom of natural gas or crude oil, and

(b) a pipeline acquired to be used solely for transmitting gas to a natural gas processing plant,

but does not include

(c) equipment or structures acquired for the refining of oil or the processing of natural gas including the separation therefrom of liquid hydrocarbons, sulphur or other joint products or by-products, or

(d) a pipeline for removal or for collection for immediate removal of natural gas or crude oil from a gas or oil field except a pipeline referred to in paragraph (b);

Notes: See Notes to ITA 188.1(5) re meaning of "includes" in the opening words.

Interpretation Bulletins: IT-476R: CCA — Equipment used in petroleum and natural gas activities.

"general-purpose electronic data processing equipment" means electronic equipment that, in its operation, requires an internally stored computer program that

(a) is executed by the equipment,

(b) can be altered by the user of the equipment,

(c) instructs the equipment to read and select, alter or store data from an external medium such as a card, disk or tape, and

(d) depends upon the characteristics of the data being processed to determine the sequence of its execution;

Related Provisions: Reg. 1100(20.1), (20.2) — Limitation on CCA claim for computer tax shelter property; Reg. Sch. II:Cl. 50 — CCA rate 55%.

Notes: Property meeting this definition is given fast-writeoff CCA under Cl. 52 or 50 (earlier, Cl. 45).

This definition includes electronic video games: *Funtronix Amusements*, [1989] 2 C.T.C. 2296 (TCC). CRA considers that the following qualify: iPhone (VIEWS doc 2009-0344551I7); laptop (2009-0315881M4); personal digital assistant (PDA) (2009-0347471E5); office desktop and ancillary printer (2010-0375011M4); point-of-sale system including computer, monitor, cash drawer, receipt printer and software (maybe) (2009-0311501E5).

CRA considers that the following do not qualify: Avaya computerized phone system (2010-0362061E5); GPS equipment used in construction and surveying (2011-0425111E5); golf simulator computer (2010-0376141E5: it is used primarily to monitor golf swings); laser cutting machine (2010-0386381E5); MRI machine (2012-0434821E5); MultiDAT Datalogger used in forestry operations, and FM300 Communicator used for truck fleets (2009-0331861E5); Pulstar MIT (Multiple Impulse Therapy) used by chiropractors (2009-0340861E5: there is no indication the user can change the programming). See also 2009-0322841M4, 2009-0322861M4, 2009-0322881M4, 2009-0322891M4, 2009-0322921M4, 2009-0325861M4 (general discussion).

"oil sands project" of a taxpayer means an undertaking by the taxpayer for the extraction of tar sands from a mineral resource owned by the taxpayer, which undertaking may include the processing of the tar sands to a stage that is not beyond the crude oil stage or its equivalent;

Notes: Definition added by P.C. 2011-44, effective March 19, 2007.

"oil sands property" of a taxpayer means property acquired by the taxpayer for the purpose of earning income from an oil sands project of the taxpayer;

Related Provisions: Reg. 1100(1)(a)(xxvii.1), 1100(1)(y.1), 1100(1)(ya.1) — capital cost allowance; Reg. 1101(4e), (4f) — separate class; Reg. 1102(14.11) — effect of transfer due to reorganization; Reg. Sch. II:Cl. 41, 41.1 — CCA class.

Notes: Definition added by P.C. 2011-44, effective March 19, 2007.

"ore" includes ore from a mineral resource that has been processed to any stage that is prior to the prime metal stage or its equivalent;

Notes: For "includes" see ITA 188.1(5) Notes. For "prime metal stage or its equivalent", see Reg. 1104(5) Notes.

"preliminary work activity" means activity that is preliminary to the acquisition, construction, fabrication or installation by or on behalf of a taxpayer of designated assets in respect of the taxpayer's oil sands project including, without limiting the generality of the foregoing, the following activities:

(a) obtaining permits or regulatory approvals,

(b) performing design or engineering work,

(c) conducting feasibility studies,

(d) conducting environmental assessments,

(e) clearing or excavating land,

(f) building roads, and

(g) entering into contracts;

Notes: Definition added by P.C. 2011-44, effective March 19, 2007.

"railway system" includes a railway owned or operated by a common carrier, together with all buildings, rolling stock, equipment and other properties pertaining thereto, but does not include a tramway;

Notes: See Notes to ITA 188.1(5) re meaning of "includes".

"specified development phase" of a taxpayer's oil sands project means a bitumen development phase or an upgrading development phase of the oil sands project which can reasonably be expected to result in a planned level of average daily output (where that output is bitumen or a similar product in the case of a bitumen development phase, or synthetic crude oil or a similar product in the case of an upgrading development phase), and in respect of which phase,

(a) not including any preliminary work activity, one or more designated assets was, before March 19, 2007,

(i) acquired by the taxpayer, or

(ii) in the process of being constructed, fabricated or installed, by or on behalf of the taxpayer, and

(b) the planned level of average daily output is the lesser of,

(i) the level that was the demonstrated intention of the taxpayer as of March 19, 2007 to produce from the specified development phase, and

(ii) the maximum level of output associated with the design capacity, as of March 19, 2007, of the designated asset referred to in paragraph (a);

Notes: Definition added by P.C. 2011-44, effective March 19, 2007.

"specified oil sands property" of a taxpayer means oil sands property, acquired by the taxpayer before 2012, the taxpayer's use of which is reasonably required

(a) for a specified development phase of an oil sands project of the taxpayer to reach completion; or

(b) as part of a bitumen development phase of an oil sands project of the taxpayer,

(i) to the extent that the output from the bitumen development phase is required for an upgrading development phase that is a specified development phase of the oil sands project to reach completion, and it is reasonable to conclude that all or substantially all of the output from the bitumen development phase will be so used; and

(ii) where it was the demonstrated intention of the taxpayer as of March 19, 2007 to produce, from a mineral resource owned by the taxpayer, the bitumen feedstock required for the upgrading development phase to reach completion;

Notes: Definition added by P.C. 2011-44, effective March 19, 2007.

"specified temporary access road" means

(a) a temporary access road to an oil or gas well in Canada, and

(b) a temporary access road the cost of which would, if the definition "Canadian exploration expense" in subsection 66.1(6) of the Act were read without reference to paragraphs (k.1) and (l) of that definition, be a Canadian exploration expense because of paragraph (f) or (g) of that definition;

Related Provisions: Reg. 1102(14.3)(a) — Exclusion from prescribed property; Reg. Sch. II:Cl. 8(i)(vi), 17(c) — Specified temporary access road excluded from other classes.

Notes: Para. (b) amended to add (k.1) by P.C. 2011-44, effective March 6, 1996.

Definition "specified temporary access road" added by P.C. 1999-629, effective March 7, 1997. The intent of the special rule for such roads is to not preclude the costs of temporary access roads in the oil and gas and mining sectors from qualifying as CEE or CDE. (Depreciable property is excluded from CEE and CDE under 66.1(6)"Canadian exploration expense"(l), 66.2(5)"Canadian development expense"(j).)

Interpretation Bulletins: IT-476R: CCA — Equipment used in petroleum and natural gas activities.

"systems software" means a combination of computer programs and associated procedures, related technical documentation and data that

(a) performs compilation, assembly, mapping, management or processing of other programs,

(b) facilitates the functioning of a computer system by other programs,

(c) provides service or utility functions such as media conversion, sorting, merging, system accounting, performance measurement, system diagnostics or programming aids,

(d) provides general support functions such as data management, report generation or security control, or

(e) provides general capability to meet wide-spread categories of problem solving or processing requirements where the specific attributes of the work to be performed are introduced mainly in the form of parameters, constants or descriptors rather than in program logic,

and includes a right or licence to use such a combination of computer programs and associated procedures, related technical documentation and data;

Interpretation Bulletins: IT-283R2: CCA — Video tapes, videotape cassettes, films, computer software and master recording tapes (archived).

"tar sands ore" means ore extracted from a deposit of bituminous sands or oil shales;

Notes: Definition amended by P.C. 1998-49, effective March 7, 1996. The amendment was consequential on the 1996 budget proposal that all oil sands projects, whether surface mining or *in-situ*, be treated as mines for CCA purposes.

"telegraph system" includes the buildings, structures, general plant and communication and other equipment pertaining thereto;

Notes: See also the definition of "telegraph" in *Interpretation Act* s. 36.

"telephone system" includes the buildings, structures, general plant and communication and other equipment pertaining thereto;

"television commercial message" means a commercial message as defined in the *Television Broadcasting Regulations, 1987* made under the *Broadcasting Act*;

Notes: Definition "television commercial message" amended by P.C. 1995-775, retro-active to January 9, 1987, to correct the reference to the relevant regulations.

"tramway or trolley bus system" includes the buildings, struc-tures, rolling stock, general plant and equipment pertaining thereto and where buses other than trolley buses are operated in connection therewith includes the properties pertaining to those bus operations.

"upgrading development phase" of a taxpayer's oil sands project means a development phase that expands the oil sands project's ca-pacity to process bitumen or a similar feedstock (all or substantially all of which is from a mineral resource owned by the taxpayer) to the crude oil stage or its equivalent.

Notes: Definition added by P.C. 2011-44, effective March 19, 2007.

(3) Except as otherwise provided in subsection (6), in this Part and Schedules II and V,

"industrial mineral mine" includes a peat bog or deposit of peat but does not include a mineral resource;

Notes: Since the definition uses "includes" rather than "means", the ordinary meaning of "industrial mineral mine" (IMM) applies as well (see Notes to ITA 188.1(5)): "a portion of the earth containing mineral deposits": *Avril Holdings*, [1970] C.T.C. 572 (SCC). In *Boulet*, [1967] Tax A.B.C. 1100, a sod farm was held not to be an IMM. See also IT-145R; IT-492; VIEWS docs 2014-0520941E5 (treatments of stone quarry ex-penses), 2013-0506641E5 (mineral claims and mining leases); Carr & Calverley, *Ca-nadian Resource Taxation* (Carswell, looseleaf or *Taxnet Pro* Reference Centre), chap. 16 on IMMs.

"mineral" includes peat;

"mining" includes the harvesting of peat.

(4) **["Accelerated investment incentive property"]** — For the purposes of this Part and Schedules II to VI, "accelerated invest-ment incentive property" means property of a taxpayer (other than property included in any of Classes 54 to 56) that

(a) is acquired by the taxpayer after November 20, 2018 and be-comes available for use before 2028; and

(b) meets either of the following conditions:

(i) the property is not a property in respect of which an amount has been deducted under paragraph 20(1)(a) or sub-section 20(16) of the Act by any person or partnership for a taxation year ending before the time the property was ac-quired by the taxpayer, or

(ii) the property was not

(A) acquired in circumstances where

(I) the taxpayer was deemed to have been allowed or deducted an amount under paragraph 20(1)(a) of the Act in respect of the property in computing income for previous taxation years, or

(II) the undepreciated capital cost of depreciable pro-perty of a prescribed class of the taxpayer was reduced by an amount determined by reference to the amount by which the capital cost of the property to the tax-payer exceeds its cost amount, or

(B) previously owned or acquired by the taxpayer or by a person or partnership with which the taxpayer did not deal at arm's length at any time when the property was owned or acquired by the person or partnership.

Related Provisions: Reg. 1100(2.02) — Application to first-year rule when Reg. 1104(4)(b)(i) applies; Reg. 1102(20.1) — Anti-avoidance; Reg. 1104(4.1) — Deemed separate properties where cost includes amounts incurred at different times.

Notes: Reg. 1104(4) defines "accelerated investment incentive property" (AIIP), which is generally unused property purchased starting Nov. 21, 2018, the date of the Economic Statement announcing this incentive (in response to US corporate tax reduc-tions). See Reg. 1100(2) for how CCA is claimed on AIIP in the year of acquisition.

Class 54, 55 and 56, for zero-emission vehicles (electric cars etc., plus off-road vehi-cles), are excluded because Reg. 1100(2)A(e) and (f) provide specific acceleration rules, including a 100% writeoff in the year of purchase through 2023. See Reg. 1100(2) Notes.

Note the anti-avoidance rule in Reg. 1102(20.1), to counter schemes to create arms-length transactions for Reg. 1104(4)(b)(ii)(B).

Opening words amended by 2021 budget bill #1, effective March 2, 2020, to exclude Class 56. Subpara. (b)(i) amended by same bill, for property acquired after Nov. 20, 2018, to delete "(A) has not been used for any purpose before it was acquired by the taxpayer, and" [what is now just subpara. (i) was "the property / (A) ... / (B) is not a property..."].

Reg. 1104(4) added by 2019 budget bill #1, effective June 21, 2019.

(4.1) Deemed separate properties — For the purpose of sub-paragraph (4)(b)(i), if the capital cost to a taxpayer of a depreciable property (referred to in this subsection as the "single property") in-cludes amounts incurred at different times, then amounts deducted under paragraph 20(1)(a) or subsection 20(16) of the Act in respect of the single property are deemed to have been deducted in respect of a separate property that is not part of the single property to the extent the deducted amounts can reasonably be considered to be in respect of amounts

(a) incurred before November 21, 2018; or

(b) incurred after November 20, 2018, if any portion of the sin-gle property is considered to have become available for use before the time the single property is first used for the purpose of earning income.

Notes: Reg. 1104(4.1) applies for the AIIP definition in Reg. 1104(4), to ensure ap-propriate results where property constructed over multiple years is transferred between non-arm's length parties before it is put in use. It is relevant only for property that does not qualify as AIIP under Reg. 1104(4)(b)(ii).

Reg. 1104(4)(b)(i) allows property acquired from a non-arm's length party to qualify as AIIP if no prior CCA claims have been made for it. The capital cost of a single pro-perty can include several expenditures incurred over multiple years. Under ITA 13(27) and (29), some of these expenditures can be eligible for CCA claims before the pro-perty is completed and ready for use. Where a taxpayer avails itself of these claims, this could preclude any expenditures in respect of the property from qualifying as AIIP in the event of later non-arm's length transfer of the property.

Reg. 1104(4.1) ensures that any portions of a single property for which CCA claims are made do not taint expenditures for which CCA claims are not made. It deems such portions of the single property to be separate properties so that the "other" expenditures can satisfy the Reg. 1104(4)(b)(i) condition and be eligible for the enhanced CCA for AIIP. However, to preclude multiple taxpayers in a non-arm's length group from bene-fitting from the AII incentive more than once from the same expenditures, Reg. 1100(2.02) ensures that any amounts deemed to be separate properties under Reg. 1104(4.1) cannot be included in determining enhanced CCA under Reg. 1100(2)D.

Reg. 1104(4.1) added by 2021 budget bill #1, for property acquired after Nov. 20, 2018.

(5) Mining [— "income from a mine"] — For the purposes of paragraphs 1100(1)(w) to (ya.2), subsections 1101(4a) to (4h) and Classes 10, 28 and 41 to 41.2 of Schedule II, a taxpayer's "income from a mine", or any expression referring to a taxpayer's income from a mine, includes income reasonably attributable to

(a) the processing by the taxpayer of

(i) ore (other than iron ore or tar sands ore) all or substan-tially all of which is from a mineral resource owned by the taxpayer to any stage that is not beyond the prime metal stage or its equivalent,

(ii) iron ore all or substantially all of which is from a mineral resource owned by the taxpayer to any stage that is not be-yond the pellet stage or its equivalent,

(iii) tar sands ore all or substantially all of which is from a mineral resource owned by the taxpayer to any stage that is not beyond the crude oil stage or its equivalent, or

(iv) material extracted by a well, all or substantially all of which is from a deposit of bituminous sands or oil shales owned by the taxpayer, to any stage that is not beyond the crude oil stage or its equivalent;

(b) the production by the taxpayer of material from a deposit of bituminous sands or oil shales; and

(c) the transportation by the taxpayer of

(i) output, other than iron ore or tar sands ore, from a mineral resource owned by the taxpayer that has been processed by him to any stage that is not beyond the prime metal stage or its equivalent,

(ii) iron ore from a mineral resource owned by the taxpayer that has been processed by him to any stage that is not beyond the pellet stage or its equivalent, or

(iii) tar sands ore from a mineral resource owned by the taxpayer that has been processed by him to any stage that is not beyond the crude oil stage or its equivalent,

to the extent that such transportation is effected through the use of property of the taxpayer that is included in Class 10 in Schedule II because of paragraph (m) thereof or that would be so included if that paragraph were read without reference to subparagraph (v) thereof and if Class 41 in Schedule II were read without the reference therein to that paragraph.

Related Provisions: Reg. 1104(2) — "Ore"; Reg. 1104(3) — "Mineral", "mining"; Reg. 1104(6) — Income from a mine for Class 10 purposes.

Notes: "Prime metal stage or its equivalent" (PMSE) ((a)(i) and (c)(i)) is, for potash: generally marketable potash meeting grain size specifications, with at least 60% K_2O (potassium oxide) equivalent, treated with anticaking anime and dedusting oil and ready for shipment to customers: VIEWS doc 2006-0197591E5. For coal: at pulverization stage, sub-bituminous coal was not beyond PMSE for Reg. 1204(1)(b)(ii)(A): *ATCO Electric*, 2008 FCA 188. The determination of PMSE "requires an examination of the facts of the actual production and processing operation for each specific taxpayer" (paras. 32-33). For coal, see also 2012-0462361I7 and the cases it cites.

See also Notes to Reg. 1104(6).

CRA considers that "substantially all", used in para. (a), means 90% or more.

Reg. 1104(5) amended by P.C. 2011-44 (effective March 19, 2007), P.C. 1998-49, 1994-230.

Interpretation Bulletins: IT-469R: CCA — Earth-moving equipment; IT-476R: CCA — Equipment used in petroleum and natural gas activities; IT-492: CCA — Industrial mineral mines.

(5.1) ["Gross revenue from a mine"] — For the purposes of Classes 41 to 41.2 of Schedule II, a taxpayer's "gross revenue from a mine" includes

(a) revenue reasonably attributable to the processing by the taxpayer of

(i) ore (other than iron ore or tar sands ore) from a mineral resource owned by the taxpayer to any stage that is not beyond the prime metal stage or its equivalent,

(ii) iron ore from a mineral resource owned by the taxpayer to any stage that is not beyond the pellet stage or its equivalent,

(iii) tar sands ore from a mineral resource owned by the taxpayer to any stage that is not beyond the crude oil stage or its equivalent, and

(iv) material extracted by a well from a mineral resource owned by the taxpayer that is a deposit of bituminous sands or oil shales to any stage that is not beyond the crude oil stage or its equivalent;

(b) the amount, if any, by which any revenue reasonably attributable to the processing by the taxpayer of

(i) ore (other than iron ore or tar sands ore) from a mineral resource not owned by the taxpayer, to any stage that is not beyond the prime metal stage or its equivalent,

(ii) iron ore from a mineral resource not owned by the taxpayer to any stage that is not beyond the pellet stage or its equivalent,

(iii) tar sands ore from a mineral resource not owned by the taxpayer to any stage that is not beyond the crude oil stage or its equivalent, and

(iv) material extracted by a well from a mineral resource not owned by the taxpayer that is a deposit of bituminous sands or oil shales to any stage that is not beyond the crude oil stage or its equivalent

exceeds the cost to the taxpayer of the ore or material processed; and

(c) revenue reasonably attributable to the production by the taxpayer of material from a deposit of bituminous sands or oil shales.

Related Provisions: Reg. 1104(5.2) — Interpretation.

Notes: Reg. 1104(5.1) includes revenue from custom processing (less the cost of the ore or material processed) in the "gross revenue from a mine", a concept introduced by the 1996 budget for accelerated CCA for Class 41 property.

For the meaning of "includes", see Notes to ITA 188.1(5). For "prime metal stage or its equivalent", see Notes to Reg. 1104(5).

Reg. 1104(5.1) amended by by 2013 budget bill #2 (for tax years ending after March 20, 2013), P.C. 2011-44. Added by P.C. 1998-49.

(5.2) ["Gross revenue from a mine"] — For the purpose of subsection (5.1), "gross revenue from a mine" does not include revenue reasonably attributable to the addition of diluent, for the purpose of transportation, to material extracted from a deposit of bituminous sands or oil shales.

Notes: Reg. 1104(5.2) added by P.C. 1998-49, effective March 7, 1996.

(6) For the purposes of Class 10 in Schedule II,

(a) **["income from a mine"]** — "income from a mine" includes income reasonably attributable to the processing of

(i) ore, other than iron ore or tar sands ore, from a mineral resource not owned by the taxpayer to any stage that is not beyond the prime metal stage or its equivalent,

(ii) iron ore from a mineral resource not owned by the taxpayer to any stage that is not beyond the pellet stage or its equivalent, or

(iii) tar sands ore from a mineral resource not owned by the taxpayer to any stage that is not beyond the crude oil stage or its equivalent; and

(iv) material extracted by a well from a mineral resource not owned by the taxpayer that is a deposit of bituminous sands or oil shales to any stage that is not beyond the crude oil stage or its equivalent; and

(b) **["mine"]** — "mine" includes a well for the extraction of material from a deposit of bituminous sands or oil shales or from a deposit of calcium chloride, halite or sylvite.

Related Provisions: Reg. 1104(6.1) — Income from a mine excludes income from services.

Notes: Income from custom processing is included in "income from a mine" only if it comprises less than 10% of all the ore processed by the taxpayer: VIEWS docs 2001-0112757 and 2003-0022535.

For the meaning of "includes", see Notes to ITA 188.1(5). For "prime metal stage or its equivalent" in (a)(i), see Notes to Reg. 1104(5).

Reg. 1104(6) amended by P.C. 1998-49 (effective March 7, 1996), 1996-495, 1994-340.

Interpretation Bulletins: IT-469R: CCA — Earth-moving equipment; IT-476R: CCA — Equipment used in petroleum and natural gas activities.

(6.1) [Repealed]

Notes: Reg. 1104(6.1), defining "income from a mine", added by P.C. 1996-1488 and then repealed retroactive to its introduction by P.C. 1999-629.

(7) ["Mine"] — For the purposes of paragraphs 1100(1)(w) to (ya.2), subsections 1101(4a) to (4h) and 1102(8) and (9), section 1107 and Classes 12, 28 and 41 to 41.2 of Schedule II,

(a) "mine" includes

(i) a well for the extraction of material from a deposit of bituminous sands or oil shales or from a deposit of calcium chloride, halite or sylvite, and

(ii) a pit for the extraction of kaolin or tar sands ore,

but does not include

(iii) an oil or gas well, or

(iv) a sand pit, gravel pit, clay pit, shale pit, peat bog, deposit of peat or a stone quarry (other than a kaolin pit or a deposit of bituminous sands or oil shales);

(b) all wells of a taxpayer for the extraction of material from one or more deposits of calcium chloride, halite or sylvite, the material produced from which is sent to the same plant for processing, are deemed to be one mine of the taxpayer; and

(c) all wells of a taxpayer for the extraction of material from a deposit of bituminous sands or oil shales that the Minister, in consultation with the Minister of Natural Resources, determines constitute one project, are deemed to be one mine of the taxpayer.

Related Provisions: Reg. 1104(8) — "Stone quarry".

Notes: Since para. (a) uses "includes" rather than "means", the ordinary meaning of "mine" applies as well (see Notes to ITA 188.1(5)). See *Bethlehem Copper*, [1974] C.T.C. 707 (SCC) ("body of ore together with workings, equipment and machinery"); *Nomad Sand*, 1990 CarswellNat 504 (FCA), para. 29 (meaning is not fixed and depends on context); *Pelton v. Black Hawk* (1903), 40 NSR 35 (NSTD) ("an excavation in the earth which yields minerals"); *Bloom Lake v. Fermont*, 2019 QCCQ 7326 (upheld tribunal decision limiting "mine" to openings and excavations for extraction, so property tax relief for mining equipment and access roads did not apply to processing).

For rulings that all of a bituminous sands deposit is one "mine", see docs 2004-0105021R3, 2004-0106281R3, 2006-0188921R3, 2007-0222741R3, 2007-0251451R3. For well pairings on oil sands projects: 2009-0307841R3, 2009-0314541R3.

Reg. 1104(7) opening words extended to apply to 1100(1)(ya.2), 1101(4g)-(4h) and Cl. 41.2 by 2013 budget bill #2, for taxation years that end after March 20, 2013.

Reg. 1104(7) opening words extended to apply to 1100(1)(ya.1), 1101(4e)-(4f) and Cl. 41.1 by P.C. 2011-44, effective March 19, 2007.

Reg. 1104(7) amended by P.C. 1998-49, effective March 7, 1996. Earlier amended by P.C. 1994-230 (effective 1988) and P.C. 1996-495 (effective 1985).

Interpretation Bulletins: IT-476R: CCA — Equipment used in petroleum and natural gas activities.

(8) ["Stone quarry"] — For the purposes of subsection (7), "stone quarry" includes a mine producing dimension stone or crushed rock for use as aggregates or for other construction purposes.

Notes: See Notes to ITA 188.1(5) re meaning of "includes".

(8.1) ["Production"] — For greater certainty, for the purposes of paragraphs (c) and (e) of Class 28 and paragraph (a) of Classes 41 to 41.2 in Schedule II, "production" means production in reasonable commercial quantities.

Notes: Reg. 1104(8.1) amended to add reference to Class 41.1 by P.C. 2011-44, effective March 19, 2007; and to Class 41.2 by 2013 budget bill #2, for tax years that end after March 20, 2013.

Reg. 1104(8.1) added by P.C. 2007-114, effective for property acquired after 1987, to ensure consistency with "reasonable commercial quantities" in Class 28(b).

(9) Manufacturing or processing — For the purposes of paragraph 1100(1)(a.1), subsection 1100(26) and Class 29 in Schedule II, "manufacturing or processing" does not include

(a) farming or fishing;

(b) logging;

(c) construction;

(d) operating an oil or gas well or extracting petroleum or natural gas from a natural accumulation thereof;

(e) extracting minerals from a mineral resource;

(f) processing of

(i) ore, other than iron ore or tar sands ore, from a mineral resource to any stage that is not beyond the prime metal stage or its equivalent,

(ii) iron ore from a mineral resource to any stage that is not beyond the pellet stage or its equivalent, or

(iii) tar sands ore from a mineral resource to any stage that is not beyond the crude oil stage or its equivalent;

(g) producing industrial minerals;

(h) producing or processing electrical energy or steam, for sale;

(i) processing natural gas as part of the business of selling or distributing gas in the course of operating a public utility;

(j) processing heavy crude oil recovered from a natural reservoir in Canada to a stage that is not beyond the crude oil stage or its equivalent; or

(k) Canadian field processing.

Related Provisions: ITA 125.1(2)(a) — Credit for generating electrical energy for sale; ITA 125.1(3) — Definition of M or P for M&P credit purposes.

Notes: For the meaning of "prime metal stage or its equivalent" in (f)(i), see Notes to Reg. 1104(5). For "producing industrial minerals" in (g) see Notes to ITA 125.1(3)"manufacturing or processing".

Reg. 1104(9) amended to refer to Reg. 1100(1)(a.1) by P.C. 2009-581, effective March 19, 2007. Earlier amended by P.C. 1999-629 (for taxation years that begin after 1996), 1997-1033 and 1994-230.

Income Tax Folios: S4-F15-C1: Manufacturing and processing [replaces IT-147R3].

Interpretation Bulletins: IT-411R: Meaning of "construction".

(10) Certified films and video tapes — [No longer relevant]

Notes: Reg. 1104(10) provides interpretation rules for Reg. 1100(21) and 1104(2)"certified feature film" and "certified production".

(11) Certified Class 34 properties — For the purposes of paragraph (h) of Class 34 in Schedule II, a certificate issued under

(a) subparagraph (d)(i) of that class may be revoked by the Minister of Industry, Trade and Commerce, or

(b) subparagraph (d)(ii) or paragraph (g) of that class, as the case may be, may be revoked by the Minister of Energy, Mines and Resources

where

(c) an incorrect statement was made in the furnishing of information for the purpose of obtaining the certificate, or

(d) the taxpayer does not conform to the plan described in subparagraph (d)(i) or (d)(ii) of that class, as the case may be,

and a certificate that has been so revoked shall be void from the time of its issue.

(12) Amusement parks — For the purposes of Class 37 in Schedule II, "amusement park" means a park open to the public where amusements, rides and audio-visual attractions are permanently situated.

(13) Classes 43.1 and 43.2 — energy conservation property — The definitions in this subsection apply for the purposes of this subsection, subsections (14) to (17) and Classes 43.1 and 43.2 in Schedule II.

Notes: Reg. 1104(13) opening words extended to apply to Reg. 1100(17) by 2012 budget bill #2, effective March 29, 2012.

Opening words amended by P.C. 2006-439, effective Feb. 23, 2005, to extend to Reg. 1104(15), (16) and Class 43.2.

"basic oxygen furnace gas" means the gas that is produced intermittently in a basic oxygen furnace of a steel mill by the chemical reaction of carbon in molten steel and pure oxygen.

Notes: "Basic oxygen furnace gas" added by P.C. 2005-2287, for property acquired after 2000.

"biogas" means the gas produced by the anaerobic digestion of organic waste that is food and animal waste, manure, plant residue, pulp and paper by-product, separated organics, wood waste or sludge from an eligible sewage treatment facility.

Related Provisions: Reg. Sch. II:Cl. 43.1(d)(xiii) — Biogas used to produce electricity.

Notes: See VIEWS doc 2010-0385231E5 (digester producing biogas from sludge).

Definition amended by 2013 budget bill #2, for property acquired after March 20, 2013 that has not been used or acquired for use before March 21, 2013, to add "pulp and paper by-product" and "separated organics" and reorder the definition.

Reg. 1104(13)"biogas" amended by 2010 budget bill #2, for property acquired after Feb. 25, 2008.

Reg. 1104(13)"biogas" added by P.C. 2009-581, for property acquired after March 18, 2007.

"bio-oil" means liquid fuel that is created from wood waste or plant residues using a thermo-chemical conversion process that takes place in the absence of oxygen.

Related Provisions: Reg. 1104(13)"eligible waste fuel" — Inclusion of bio-oil.

Notes: "Bio-oil" added by P.C. 2005-2287, for property acquired after Feb. 18, 2003.

"blast furnace gas" means the gas produced in a blast furnace of a steel mill, by the chemical reaction of carbon (in the form of coke, coal or natural gas), the oxygen in air and iron ore.

Notes: "Blast furnace gas" added by P.C. 2005-2287, effective for property acquired after 2000.

"digester gas" means a mixture of gases that are produced from the decomposition of organic waste in a digester and that are extracted from an eligible sewage treatment facility for that organic waste.

Related Provisions: Reg. 1104(13)"eligible waste fuel" — Inclusion of digester gas.

Notes: See VIEWS doc 2010-0385231E5 (digester producing biogas from sludge).

"distribution equipment" means equipment (other than transmission equipment) used to distribute electrical energy generated by electrical generating equipment.

"district energy equipment" means property that is part of a district energy system and that consists of pipes or pumps used to collect and distribute an energy transfer medium, meters, control equipment, chillers and heat exchangers that are attached to the main distribution line of a district energy system, but does not include

(a) property used to distribute water that is for consumption, disposal or treatment; or

(b) property that is part of the internal heating or cooling system of a building.

Notes: "District energy equipment" added by P.C. 2006-439, effective Feb. 23, 2005.

"district energy system" means a system that is used primarily to provide heating or cooling by continuously circulating, from a central generation unit to one or more buildings through a system of interconnected pipes, an energy transfer medium that is heated or cooled using thermal energy.

Related Provisions: Reg. 1104(16) — Conditions for Class 43.1/43.2 treatment.

Notes: For the meaning of "used primarily", see Notes to ITA 73(3).

Definition amended by 2010 budget bill #2, for property acquired after March 3, 2010, to delete the final words "that is primarily produced by electrical cogeneration equipment that meets the requirements of paragraphs (a) to (c) of Class 43.1, or paragraph (a) of Class 43.2, in Schedule II".

"District energy system" added by P.C. 2006-439, effective Feb. 23, 2005.

"eligible landfill site" means a landfill site that is situated in Canada, or a former landfill site that is situated in Canada, and, if a permit or license in respect of the site is or was required under any law of Canada or of a province, for which the permit or license has been issued.

"eligible sewage treatment facility" means a sewage treatment facility that is situated in Canada and for which a permit or license is issued under any law of Canada or of a province.

"eligible waste fuel" means biogas, bio-oil, digester gas, landfill gas, municipal waste, plant residue, pulp and paper waste and wood waste.

Related Provisions: Reg. Sch. II:Cl. 43.1(c)(a)(i)(A) — Eligible waste fuel used in energy generation system.

Notes: See VIEWS docs 2010-0385231E5 (digester producing biogas from sludge); 2012-0444401E5 (wood pellets manufactured from wood waste are EWF); 2012-0468301E5 (cooking oil waste is not EWF, but is "food and animal waste").

Definition amended by 2012 budget bill #2, effective March 29, 2012, to add "plant residue".

Definition amended by 2010 budget bill #2, for property acquired after Feb. 25, 2008, to add "biogas".

Reg. 1104(13)"eligible waste fuel" added by P.C. 2009-581, effective for property acquired after March 18, 2007.

"eligible waste management facility" means a waste management facility that is situated in Canada and for which a permit or license is issued under any law of Canada or of a province.

"enhanced combined cycle system" means an electrical generating system in which thermal waste from one or more natural gas compressor systems is recovered and used to contribute at least 20

per cent of the energy input of a combined cycle process in order to enhance the generation of electricity, but does not include the natural gas compressor systems.

"food and animal waste" means organic waste that is disposed of in accordance with the laws of Canada or a province and that is

(a) generated during the preparation or processing of food or beverage for human or animal consumption;

(b) food or beverage that is no longer fit for human or animal consumption; or

(c) animal remains.

Notes: See VIEWS doc 2012-0468301E5 (cooking oil waste is FAW).

Paras. (a) and (b) amended to add "or beverage" by 2013 budget bill #2, for property acquired after March 20, 2013 that has not been used or acquired for use by that date.

Reg. 1104(13)"food and animal waste" added by 2010 budget bill #2, effective for property acquired after Feb. 25, 2008. (For property acquired earlier, see "food waste".)

"food waste" — [Repealed]

Notes: Reg. 1104(13)"food waste" repealed by 2010 budget bill #2, effective for property acquired after Feb. 25, 2008 (see now "food and animal waste"). Added by P.C. 2009-581, effective for property acquired after March 18, 2007.

"fossil fuel" means a fuel that is petroleum, natural gas or related hydrocarbons, basic oxygen furnace gas, blast furnace gas, coal, coal gas, coke, coke oven gas, lignite or peat.

Notes: "Fossil fuel" amended by P.C. 2005-2287 to include basic oxygen furnace gas, blast furnace gas and coke oven gas, effective for property acquired after 2000.

"landfill gas" means a mixture of gases that are produced from the decomposition of organic waste and that are extracted from an eligible landfill site.

Related Provisions: Reg. 1104(13)"eligible waste fuel" — Inclusion of landfill gas.

"municipal waste" means the combustible portion of waste material (other than waste material that is considered to be toxic or hazardous waste pursuant to any law of Canada or of a province) that is generated in Canada and that is accepted at an eligible landfill site or an eligible waste management facility and that, when burned to generate energy, emits only those fluids or other emissions that are in compliance with the law of Canada or of a province.

Related Provisions: Reg. 1104(13)"eligible waste fuel" — Inclusion of municipal waste.

"plant residue" means residue of plants (not including wood waste and waste that no longer has the chemical properties of the plants of which it is a residue) that would otherwise be waste material and that is used

(a) in a system that converts biomass into bio-oil or biogas; or

(b) as an eligible waste fuel.

Notes: Straw can be "plant residue", so equipment used in a co-gen system that uses straw as feedstock will qualify for Cl. 43.1: VIEWS doc 2011-0398851M4.

Definition amended by 2012 budget bill #2, effective March 29, 2012.

Reg. 1104(13)"plant residue" amended by P.C. 2009-581, effective for property acquired after March 18, 2007, to add reference to biogas.

"Plant residue" added by P.C. 2005-2287, effective for property acquired after February 18, 2003.

"producer gas" means fuel the composition of which, excluding its water content, is all or substantially all non-condensable gases that is generated primarily from eligible waste fuel using a thermo-chemical conversion process and that is not generated using any fuels other than eligible waste fuel or fossil fuel.

Notes: Definition added by 2014 budget bill #2, effective Feb. 11, 2014.

"pulp and paper by-product" means tall oil soaps and crude tall oil that are produced as by-products of the processing of wood into pulp or paper and the by-product of a pulp or paper plant's effluent treatment or its de-inking processes.

Notes: Definition added by 2013 budget bill #2, effective Dec. 12, 2013.

"pulp and paper waste" means

(a) tall oil soaps, crude tall oil and turpentine that are produced as by-products of the processing of wood into pulp or paper; and

(b) the by-product of a pulp or paper plant's effluent treatment, or its de-inking processes, if that by-product has a solid content of at least 40 per cent before combustion.

Related Provisions: Reg. 1104(13)"eligible waste fuel" — Inclusion of pulp and paper waste.

Notes: Reg. 1104(13)"pulp and paper waste" added by P.C. 2009-581, effective for property acquired after March 18, 2007.

"separated organics" means organic waste (other than waste that is considered to be toxic or hazardous waste under any law of Canada or a province) that could, but for its use in a system that converts biomass into biogas, be disposed of in an eligible waste management facility or eligible landfill site.

Notes: Definition added by 2013 budget bill #2, effective Dec. 12, 2013.

"solution gas" means a fossil fuel that is gas that would otherwise be flared and has been extracted from a solution of gas and produced oil.

Notes: Definition "solution gas" added by P.C. 2000-1331, effective Feb. 17, 1999.

"spent pulping liquor" means the by-product of a chemical process of transforming wood into pulp, consisting of wood residue and pulping agents.

Notes: Spent pulping liquor has been added to the list of fuels for cogeneration systems listed in Classes 43.1 and 43.2.

Definition "spent pulping liquor" added by P.C. 2006-1103, effective Nov. 14, 2005.

"thermal waste" means waste heat energy extracted from a distinct point of rejection in an industrial process that would otherwise

(a) be vented to the atmosphere or transferred to a liquid; and

(b) not be used for a useful purpose.

Notes: Definition changed from "means heat energy extracted from a distinct point of rejection in an industrial process" by 2011 budget bill #2, effective in respect of property acquired after March 21, 2011.

"transmission equipment" means equipment used to transmit more than 75 per cent of the annual electrical energy generated by electrical generating equipment, but does not include a building.

"wood waste" includes scrap wood, sawdust, wood chips, bark, limbs, saw-ends and hog fuel, but does not include spent pulping liquor and any waste that no longer has the physical or chemical properties of wood.

Related Provisions: Reg. 1104(13)"eligible waste fuel" — Inclusion of wood waste.

Notes: See Notes to ITA 188.1(5) re meaning of "includes".

"Wood waste" is a byproduct of forestry activities, not plants grown for combustion: VIEWS doc 2012-0444401E5.

Definition "wood waste" amended by P.C. 2006-1103, effective November 14, 2005, to change "residuals (known as 'black liquor') from wood pulp operations" to "spent pulping liquor" (now defined above in Reg. 1104(13)).

Notes [Reg. 1104(13)]: Reg. 1104(13) added by P.C. 1997-1033, effective Feb. 22, 1994.

(14) [Class 43.1(c)/43.2(a) compliance] — Where property of a taxpayer is not operating in the manner required by paragraph (c) of Class 43.1, or paragraph (a) of Class 43.2, in Schedule II solely because of a deficiency, failing or shutdown that is beyond the control of the taxpayer of the system of which it is a part and that previously operated in the manner required by that paragraph, as the case may be, that property is deemed, for the purpose of that paragraph, to be operating in the manner required under that paragraph during the period of the deficiency, failing or shutdown, if the taxpayer makes all reasonable efforts to rectify the circumstances within a reasonable time.

Related Provisions: Reg. 1104(13) — Definitions; Reg. 1104(15) — Interpretation of "system"; Reg. 1104(16) — District energy system.

Notes: Reg. 1104(14) amended by P.C. 2006-439, effective Feb. 23, 2005, to add reference to Class 43.2(a).

Reg. 1104(14) added by P.C. 1997-1033, effective February 22, 1994.

(15) [Interpretation of "system" for subsec. (14)] — For the purpose of subsection (14), a taxpayer's system referred to in that subsection that has at any particular time operated in the manner required by paragraph (c) of Class 43.1, or paragraph (a) of Class 43.2, in Schedule II includes at any time after the particular time a property of another person or partnership if

(a) the property would reasonably be considered to be part of the taxpayer's system were the property owned by the taxpayer;

(b) the property utilizes steam obtained from the taxpayer's system primarily in an industrial process (other than the generation of electrical energy);

(c) the operation of the property is necessary for the taxpayer's system to operate in the manner required by paragraph (c) of Class 43.1, or paragraph (a) of Class 43.2, in Schedule II, as the case may be; and

(d) at the time that the taxpayer's system first became operational, the deficiency, failing or shutdown in the operation of the property could not reasonably have been anticipated by the taxpayer to occur within five years after that time.

Related Provisions: Reg. 1104(13) — Definitions.

Notes: Reg. 1104(15) amended by P.C. 2006-439, effective Feb. 23, 2005, to add references to Class 43.2(a).

Reg. 1104(15) added by P.C. 2005-2186, for property acquired after Feb. 21, 1994.

(16) [District energy system] — For the purpose of subsection (14), a district energy system is deemed to satisfy the requirements of paragraph (c) of Class 43.1, or paragraph (a) of Class 43.2, in Schedule II, as the case may be, if the electrical cogeneration equipment that produces the thermal energy used by the system is deemed by subsection (14) to meet the requirements of paragraph (c) of Class 43.1, or paragraph (a) of Class 43.2, in Schedule II, as the case may be.

Related Provisions: Reg. 1104(13) — Definitions.

Notes: Reg. 1104(16) added by P.C. 2006-439, effective Feb. 23, 2005.

(17) [Compliance with environmental laws] — A property that would otherwise be eligible for inclusion in Class 43.1 or Class 43.2 in Schedule II by a taxpayer is deemed not to be eligible for inclusion in either of those classes if

(a) the property is

(i) included in Class 43.1 because of its subparagraph (c)(i), or

(ii) described in

(A) any of subparagraphs (d)(vii) to (ix), (xi), (xiii), (xiv), (xvi) and (xvii) of Class 43.1, or

(B) paragraph (a) of Class 43.2; and

(b) at the time the property becomes available for use by the taxpayer, the taxpayer has not satisfied the requirements of all environmental laws, by-laws and regulations

(i) of Canada, a province or a municipality in Canada, or

(ii) of a municipal or public body performing a function of government in Canada

applicable in respect of the property.

Related Provisions: Reg. 1219(5) — Same rule for CRCE.

Notes: For "municipal or public body..." in (b)(ii), see Notes to ITA 149(1)(c).

Reg. 1104(17)(a) amended by 2019 budget bill #1, to split it into subparas. (i) and (ii) and add reference to Cl. 43.1(d)(xvii) for property acquired after March 21, 2016 that has not been used or acquired for use by that date.

Reg. 1104(17)(a) amended by 2017 budget bill #2 to add reference to Cl. 43.1(d)(vii) for property acquired for use after March 21, 2017 that has not been used or acquired for use by that date.

Reg. 1104(17)(a) amended by 2014 budget bill #2 to add reference to Cl. 43.1(d)(xiv) and (xvi), effective for property acquired after Feb 10, 2014.

Reg. 1104(17) added by 2012 budget bill #2, effective March 29, 2012.

(18) Classes 1 and 47 — Liquefaction property — For the purposes of paragraphs 1100(1)(a.3) and (yb), a taxpayer's income for a taxation year from eligible liquefaction activities in respect of an eligible liquefaction facility of the taxpayer is determined as if

(a) the taxpayer carried on a separate business

(i) the only income of which is any combination of:

(A) in the case of natural gas that is owned by the taxpayer at the time it enters the taxpayer's eligible liquefaction facility, income from the sale by the taxpayer of the natural gas that has been liquefied, whether sold as liquefied natural gas or regasified natural gas, and

(B) in any other case, income reasonably attributable to the liquefaction of natural gas at the taxpayer's eligible liquefaction facility, and

(ii) in respect of which the only permitted deductions in computing the separate business' income are those deductions that are attributable to income described in subparagraph (i) and, in the case of income described in clause (i)(A), that are reasonably attributable to income derived after the natural gas enters the eligible liquefaction facility; and

(b) in the case of income described in clause (a)(i)(A), the taxpayer acquired the natural gas that has been liquefied at a cost equal to the fair market value of the natural gas at the time it entered the eligible liquefaction facility.

Notes: For the meaning of "separate business" in para. (a), see Notes to Reg. 1101(1). For the meaning of "derived" in (a)(ii), see Notes to ITA 18.1(12).

Reg. 1104(18) added by P.C. 2015-629, effective Feb. 19, 2015. The draft regulations of that date had proposed adding a special rule for a peak shaving facility (reproduced here up to the 58th ed.), but it was left out of the final regulation. Finance advises that it was withdrawn because it had no substantive effect, and comments received suggested that it provided no useful clarity.

Related Provisions [Reg. 1104]: ITA 20(1.1) — Definitions in ITA 13(21) apply.

Definitions [Reg. 1104]: "amount" — ITA 248(1); "arm's length" — ITA 251(1); "assessment" — ITA 248(1); "associated" — ITA 256; "basic oxygen furnace gas" — Reg. 1104(13); "beneficially owned" — ITA 248(3); "biogas", "bio-oil" — Reg. 1104(13); "bitumen development phase" — Reg. 1104(2); "bituminous sands" — ITA 248(1); "blast furnace gas" — Reg. 1104(13); "business" — ITA 248(1); "calendar year" — *Interpretation Act* 37(1)(a); "Canada" — ITA 255, *Interpretation Act* 35(1); "Canadian" — Reg. 1104(10)(a), (c.2); "Canadian exploration expense" — ITA 66.1(6), 248(1); "Canadian field processing" — ITA 248(1); "certified production" — Reg. 1104(2); "class" — Reg. 1101(6), 1102(1)–(3), (14), (14.1); "coal mine operator", "completion", "computer software" — Reg. 1104(2); "corporation" — ITA 248(1), *Interpretation Act* 35(1); "depreciable property" — ITA 13(21), 248(1); "designated asset", "development phase" — Reg. 1104(2); "digester gas", "distribution equipment", "district energy system", "eligible landfill site" — Reg. 1104(13); "eligible liquefaction activities" — Reg. 1104(18); "eligible liquefaction facility" — Reg. 1104(2); "eligible sewage treatment facility", "eligible waste fuel", "eligible waste management facility" — Reg. 1104(13); "end of the taxation year" — Reg. 1104(1); "enhanced combined cycle system" — Reg. 1104(13); "excluded equipment" — Reg. 1104(2); "fair market value" — see ITA 69(1) Notes; "farming" — ITA 248(1); "fiscal period" — ITA 249.1; "fishing" — ITA 248(1); "food and animal waste", "fossil fuel" — Reg. 1104(13); "individual" — ITA 248(1); "landfill gas" — Reg. 1104(13); "mineral" — Reg. 1104(3); "mineral resource", "Minister" — ITA 248(1); "Minister of Natural Resources" — *Department of Natural Resources Act* s. 3; "month" — *Interpretation Act* 35(1); "municipal waste" — Reg. 1104(13); "non-resident", "oil or gas well" — ITA 248(1); "oil sands project", "oil sands property", "ore" — Reg. 1104(2); "Parliament" — *Interpretation Act* 35(1); "partnership" — see ITA 96(1) Notes; "person" — ITA 248(1); "pipeline" — Reg. 1104(2); "plant residue" — Reg. 1104(13); "preliminary work activity" — Reg. 1104(2); "prescribed", "property" — ITA 248(1); "province" — *Interpretation Act* 35(1); "pulp and paper byproduct", "pulp and paper waste" — Reg. 1104(13); "radio" — *Interpretation Act* 35(1); "related" — ITA 251(2)–(6); "remuneration" — Reg. 1104(10)(c); "resident" — ITA 250; "revenue guarantee" — Reg. 1104(10)(c.1); "security" — *Interpretation Act* 35(1); "separated organics" — Reg. 1104(13); "specified development phase" — Reg. 1104(2); "spent pulping liquor" — Reg. 1104(13); "stone quarry" — Reg. 1104(8); "system" — Reg. 1104(15); "systems software" — Reg. 1104(2); "tar sands" — ITA 248(1); "tar sands ore" — Reg. 1104(2); "taxation year" — ITA 249, Reg. 1104(1); "taxpayer" — ITA 248(1); "telecommunications" — *Interpretation Act* 35(1); "thermal waste", "transmission equipment" — Reg. 1104(13); "undepreciated capital cost" — ITA 13(21), 248(1); "unit of production" — Reg. 1104(10)(d); "upgrading development phase" — Reg. 1104(2); "wood waste" — Reg. 1104(13); "written" — *Interpretation Act* 35(1)"writing".

DIVISION VI — CLASSES PRESCRIBED

1105. The classes of property provided in this Part and in Schedule II are hereby prescribed for the purposes of the Act.

Notes: Reg. 1105 amended by P.C. 1996-571, for tax years that end after February 21, 1994, to apply for all the Act instead of just ITA 13, 20(1)(a) and 59(3.3). This ensures it applies for ITA 80.

Definitions [Reg. 1105]: "class" — Reg. 1101(6), 1102(1)–(3), (14), (14.1); "prescribed", "property" — ITA 248(1).

DIVISION VII — CERTIFICATES ISSUED BY THE MINISTER OF CANADIAN HERITAGE

1106. (1) Interpretation — The following definitions apply in this Division and in paragraph (x) of Class 10 in Schedule II.

"application for a certificate of completion", in respect of a film or video production, means an application by a prescribed taxable Canadian corporation in respect of the production, filed with the Minister of Canadian Heritage before the day (in this Division referred to as "the production's application deadline") that is the later of

(a) the day that is 24 months after the end of the corporation's taxation year in which the production's principal photography began, or

(b) the day that is 18 months after the day referred to in paragraph (a), if the corporation has filed, with the Canada Revenue Agency, and provided to the Minister of Canadian Heritage a copy of, a waiver described in subparagraph 152(4)(a)(ii) of the Act, within the normal reassessment period for the corporation in respect of the first and second taxation years ending after the production's principal photography began.

Proposed Amendments — Film and Video Credits

Federal Budget, Supplementary Information, April 19, 2021: *Film or Video Production Tax Credits*

In recognition of the disruptions caused by the COVID-19 pandemic on film and video productions, Budget 2021 proposes to temporarily extend certain timelines for the Canadian Film or Video Production Tax Credit (CPTC) and the Film or Video Production Services Tax Credit (PSTC).

The CPTC [ITA 125.4 — ed.] provides a 25% refundable tax credit on qualified labour expenditures and is available to productions certified to be Canadian film or video productions. The PSTC [ITA 125.5 — ed.] provides a 16% refundable credit on qualified Canadian labour expenditures and is available to foreign films and videos produced in Canada.

Extending Timelines for the CPTC

Budget 2021 proposes to extend by 12 months the following timelines with respect to the CPTC:

- The 24-month period to incur qualifying expenditures before the date that principal photography begins [Reg. 1106(1)"application for a certificate of completion"(a) — ed.].

- The timeline to submit a certificate of completion to the Canadian Audiovisual Certification Office within 24 months of the end of the tax year in which principal photography began. This new 12-month extension would apply in addition to the existing 18-month extension that is available in this respect [Reg. 1106(1)"application for a certificate of completion"(b) — ed.].

- The requirement that there be a written agreement with a Canadian distributor or with a broadcaster licensed by the Canadian Radio-television and Telecommunications Commission to show the production in Canada within 24 months of its completion [Reg. 1106(1)"excluded production"(a)(iv) — ed].

Extending Timelines for the PSTC

Budget 2021 also proposes to extend by 12 months the 24-month timelines in respect of when aggregate expenditure thresholds must be met for film or video productions for the purposes of the PSTC [Reg. 9300(1) — ed.].

In respect of both the CPTC and the PSTC, taxpayers would be required to file a waiver with the Canada Revenue Agency [ITA 152(4)(c) — ed.] and the Canadian Audiovisual Certification Office [presumably a copy of the CRA waiver — ed.] in order to extend the assessment limitation period in respect of the relevant years to take into account this 12-month extension.

These measures would be available in respect of productions for which eligible expenditures were incurred by taxpayers in their taxation years ending in 2020 or 2021.

Notes: Budget Table 1 projects that these measures will cost the federal government $20 million in 2022-23, $25m in 2023-24, $15m in 2024-25 and $5m in 2025-26.

Related Provisions: Reg. 1106(2) — Prescribed taxable Canadian corporation.

Notes: Definition "application for..." amended by P.C. 2010-551, effective May 12, 2010, to change "Canada Customs and Revenue Agency" to "Canada Revenue Agency". See also Notes at end of Reg. 1106.

"Canadian" means a person that is

(a) an individual who is

(i) a citizen, as defined in subsection 2(1) of the *Citizenship Act*, of Canada, or

(ii) a permanent resident, as defined in subsection 2(1) of the *Immigration and Refugee Protection Act*, or

(b) a corporation that is a Canadian-controlled entity, as determined under sections 26 to 28 of the *Investment Canada Act*.

Related Provisions: Reg. 1106(8)(c) — Principal screenwriter deemed not Canadian.

Notes: See Notes at end of Reg. 1106.

"Canadian government film agency" means a federal or provincial government agency whose mandate is related to the provision of assistance to film productions in Canada.

Related Provisions: ITA 241(4)(d)(xv) — Disclosure of information to government agency providing assistance.

"certificate of completion", in respect of a film or video production of a corporation, means a certificate certifying that the production has been completed, issued by the Minister of Canadian Heritage before the day (in this Division referred to as "the production's certification deadline") that is six months after the production's application deadline.

Notes: See Notes at end of Reg. 1106.

"copyright owner", of a film or video production, at any time means

(a) the maker, as defined in section 2 of the *Copyright Act*, who at that time owns copyright, in relation to the production, within the meaning of section 3 of that Act; or

(b) a person to whom that copyright has been assigned, under an assignment described in section 13 of the *Copyright Act*, either wholly or partially, by the maker or by another owner to whom this paragraph applied before the assignment.

Related Provisions: Reg. 1106(1)"excluded production"(a)(iii)(A) — Effect of being copyright owner; Reg. 1106(12) — Limitations on meaning of "copyright owner".

Notes: *Copyright Act* ss. 2"maker", 3(1) and 13(4) provide:

2. "maker" means

(a) in relation to a cinematographic work, the person by whom the arrangements necessary for the making of the work are undertaken, or

(b) in relation to a sound recording, the person by whom the arrangements necessary for the first fixation of the sounds are undertaken;

3. (1) Copyright in works — For the purposes of this Act, "copyright", in relation to a work, means the sole right to produce or reproduce the work or any substantial part thereof in any material form whatever, to perform the work or any substantial part thereof in public or, if the work is unpublished, to publish the work or any substantial part thereof, and includes the sole right

(a) to produce, reproduce, perform or publish any translation of the work,

(b) in the case of a dramatic work, to convert it into a novel or other non-dramatic work,

(c) in the case of a novel or other non-dramatic work, or of an artistic work, to convert it into a dramatic work, by way of performance in public or otherwise,

(d) in the case of a literary, dramatic or musical work, to make any sound recording, cinematograph film or other contrivance by means of which the work may be mechanically reproduced or performed,

(e) in the case of any literary, dramatic, musical or artistic work, to reproduce, adapt and publicly present the work as a cinematographic work,

(f) in the case of any literary, dramatic, musical or artistic work, to communicate the work to the public by telecommunication,

(g) to present at a public exhibition, for a purpose other than sale or hire, an artistic work created after June 7, 1988, other than a map, chart or plan,

(h) in the case of a computer program that can be reproduced in the ordinary course of its use, other than by a reproduction during its execution in conjunction with a machine, device or computer, to rent out the computer program,

(i) in the case of a musical work, to rent out a sound recording in which the work is embodied, and

(j) in the case of a work that is in the form of a tangible object, to sell or otherwise transfer ownership of the tangible object, as long as that owner-

ship has never previously been transferred in or outside Canada with the authorization of the copyright owner,

and to authorize any such acts.

13. (4) Assignments and licences — The owner of the copyright in any work may assign the right, either wholly or partially, and either generally or subject to limitations relating to territory, medium or sector of the market or other limitations relating to the scope of the assignment, and either for the whole term of the copyright or for any other part thereof, and may grant any interest in the right by licence, but no assignment or grant is valid unless it is in writing signed by the owner of the right in respect of which the assignment or grant is made, or by the owner's duly authorized agent.

"Copyright owner" added by P.C. 2015-307, effective Nov. 13, 2014, but it does not apply in respect of a prescribed taxable Canadian corporation's film or video production if before that day

(a) the Minister of Canadian Heritage has revoked a certificate or refused to issue a certificate of completion in respect of the production; or

(b) the Minister of National Revenue has assessed a return of income of the corporation on the basis that the production is not a Canadian film or video production and that assessment's basis is not vacated or varied on or after that particular day.

"excluded production" means a film or video production, of a particular corporation that is a prescribed taxable Canadian corporation,

(a) in respect of which

(i) the particular corporation has not filed an application for a certificate of completion before the production's application deadline,

(ii) a certificate of completion has not been issued before the production's certification deadline,

(iii) if the production is not a treaty co-production, a person (other than the particular corporation or a prescribed person)

(A) is a copyright owner of the production for any commercial exploitation purposes at any time during the 25-year period that begins at the earliest time after the production was completed that it is commercially exploitable, or

(B) controls the initial licensing of commercial exploitation,

(iv) there is not an agreement in writing, for consideration at fair market value, to have the production shown in Canada within the 2-year period that begins at the earliest time after the production was completed that it is commercially exploitable,

(A) with a corporation that is a Canadian and is a distributor of film or video productions, or

(B) with a corporation that holds a broadcasting license issued by the Canadian Radio-television and Telecommunications Commission for television markets, or

Proposed Amendment — Reg. 1106(1)"excluded production"(a)(iv)

Federal Budget, Supplementary Information, April 19, 2021: See under Reg. 1106(1)"application for a certificate of completion".

(v) distribution is made in Canada within the 2-year period that begins at the earliest time after the production was completed that it is commercially exploitable by a person that is not a Canadian, or

(b) that is

(i) news, current events or public affairs programming, or a programme that includes weather or market reports,

(ii) [Repealed]

(iii) a production in respect of a game, questionnaire or contest (other than a production directed primarily at minors),

(iv) a sports event or activity,

(v) a gala presentation or an awards show,

(vi) a production that solicits funds,

(vii) reality television,

(viii) pornography,

(ix) advertising,

(x) a production produced primarily for industrial, corporate or institutional purposes, or

(xi) a production, other than a documentary, all or substantially all of which consists of stock footage.

Related Provisions: Reg. 1106(2) — Prescribed taxable Canadian corporation; Reg. 1106(10) — Prescribed person.

Notes: CRA/CAVCO decisions under (b)(iii), that productions with a game show component were ineligible, were held reasonable in: *Zone3-XXXVI*, 2016 FCA 242 (CRA applied unpublished "decision tree"); *Productions GFP (III)*, 2019 FC 1613 (FCA appeal dismissed for delay A-19-20) (CAVCO provided preliminary approval, then changed its mind on seeing final production).

In *Serdy Vidéo*, 2018 FC 413, it was reasonable for the Minister of Canadian Heritage to revoke a certificate, as the production (showing luxurious Caribbean villas available for rent) was "advertising" ((b)(ix)).

For CRA interpretation see VIEWS docs 2008-0296351E5 (25-year requirement in (a)(iii)(A)); 2010-0390131I7 (various questions); 2012-0449101E5 (effect of amalgamation or windup on 25-year rule); 2012-0463231R3 (ruling that granting of option by production company to related distributor, and exercise of option, do not cause production to become excluded production); 2013-0513991R3 (effect of production company granting option to related company).

CRA considers that "substantially all", used in (b)(xi), means 90% or more.

Subpara. (b)(ii), "a talk show", repealed by P.C. 2016-855, for film or video productions for which principal photography begins after Feb. 16, 2016. Thus, a talk show can now qualify for the credit. CAVCO had put out a request for comments (tinyurl.com/cavco-16-01) on Feb. 18, 2016, but this change was not announced until it was done, and the reasons for it are unclear. The amendment's Regulatory Impact Analysis Statement states that talk shows were originally ineligible because they were largely produced in-house by broadcasters, but "some talk shows are produced by independent production corporations and given that talk shows are of cultural value to Canadians", they are now eligible. One of the talk shows rescued by this change is *BazzoTV* in Quebec. See CBC report at tinyurl.com/talk-credit. This change was expected to cost the government $33 million per year.

Subpara. (a)(iii) before (B) amended by P.C. 2015-307, effective on the same basis as Reg. 1106(1)"copyright owner". Before the amendment, read:

(iii) where the production is not a treaty co-production, neither the particular corporation nor another prescribed taxable Canadian corporation related to the particular corporation

(A) is, except to the extent of an interest in the production held by a prescribed taxable Canadian corporation as a co-producer of the production or by a prescribed person, the exclusive worldwide copyright owner in the production for all commercial exploitation purposes for the 25-year period that begins at the earliest time after the production was completed that it is commercially exploitable, and

"producer" means a producer of a film or video production, except that it does not include a person unless the person is the individual who

(a) controls and is the central decision maker in respect of the production;

(b) is directly responsible for the acquisition of the production story or screenplay and the development, creative and financial control and exploitation of the production; and

(c) is identified in the production as being the producer of the production.

"remuneration" means remuneration other than an amount determined by reference to profits or revenues.

"twinning arrangement" means the pairing of two distinct film or video productions, one of which is a Canadian film or video production and the other of which is a foreign film or video production.

(2) Prescribed taxable Canadian corporation — For the purposes of section 125.4 of the Act and this Division, "prescribed taxable Canadian corporation" means a taxable Canadian corporation that is a Canadian, other than a corporation that is

(a) controlled directly or indirectly in any manner whatever by one or more persons all or part of whose taxable income is exempt from tax under Part I of the Act; or

(b) a prescribed labour-sponsored venture capital corporation, as defined in section 6701.

Related Provisions: ITA 256(5.1), (6.2) — Meaning of "controlled directly or indirectly"; Reg. 6701 — Prescribed labour-sponsored venture capital corporation.

Notes: See Notes at end of Reg. 1106.

CRA's view is that a corporation controlled by status Indians is still a prescribed taxable Canadian corporation, because an Indian's income is exempt under the *Indian Act* and ITA 81(1)(a), while para. (a) refers to exemptions under ITA 149: VIEWS doc 2009-0350931E5.

The rule in ITA 256(1.2) does not apply for purposes of this determination, although ITA 256(5.1) does: VIEWS doc 2006-0218101E5.

(3) Treaty co-production — For the purpose of this Division, "treaty co-production" means a film or video production whose production is contemplated under any of the following instruments, and to which the instrument applies:

(a) a co-production treaty entered into between Canada and another State;

(b) the Memorandum of Understanding between the Government of Canada and the Government of the Hong Kong Special Administrative Region of the People's Republic of China on Film and Television Co-Production;

(c) the Common Statement of Policy on Film, Television and Video Co-Productions between Japan and Canada;

(d) the Memorandum of Understanding between the Government of Canada and the Government of the Republic of Korea on Television Co-Production;

(e) the Memorandum of Understanding between the Government of Canada and the Government of the Republic of Malta on Audio-Visual Relations; and

(f) the Memorandum of Understanding between the Government of Canada and the Respective Governments of the Flemish, French and German-Speaking Communities of the Kingdom of Belgium concerning Audiovisual Coproduction.

Notes: See VIEWS docs 2002-0143563 and 2002-012195A for rulings on UK treaty co-production arrangements. See also Notes to ITA 125.4.

See Notes to ITA 125.4(6) re certificates revoked where a co-producer in France went into receivership.

Reg. 1106(3)(f) added by 2019 budget bill #1, effective March 12, 2018. This allows joint projects of producers from Canada and Belgium to qualify for the Canadian film/video production tax credit.

The draft legislation of April 8/14 proposed to amend this definition to apply to ITA 125.4(1)"Canadian film or video production certificate", but that was not necessary because references there to "treaty co-production" explicitly refer to Reg. 1106(3).

(4) Canadian film or video production — Subject to subsections (6) to (9), for the purposes of section 125.4 of the Act, this Part and Schedule II, "Canadian film or video production" means a film or video production, other than an excluded production, of a prescribed taxable Canadian corporation in respect of which the Minister of Canadian Heritage has issued a certificate (other than a certificate that has been revoked under subsection 125.4(6) of the Act) and that is

(a) a treaty co-production; or

(b) a film or video production

(i) whose producer is a Canadian at all times during its production,

(ii) in respect of which the Minister of Canadian Heritage has allotted not less than six points in accordance with subsection (5),

(iii) in respect of which not less than 75% of the total of all costs for services provided in respect of producing the production (other than excluded costs) was payable in respect of services provided to or by individuals who are Canadians, and for the purpose of this subparagraph, excluded costs are

(A) costs determined by reference to the amount of income from the production,

(B) remuneration payable to, or in respect of, the producer or individuals described in any of subparagraphs (5)(a)(i) to (viii) and (b)(i) to (vi) and paragraph (5)(c) (including any individuals that would be described in paragraph (5)(c) if they were Canadians),

(C) amounts payable in respect of insurance, financing, brokerage, legal and accounting fees, and similar amounts, and

(D) costs described in subparagraph (iv), and

(iv) in respect of which not less than 75% of the total of all costs incurred for the post-production of the production, including laboratory work, sound re-recording, sound editing and picture editing, (other than costs that are determined by reference to the amount of income from the production and remuneration that is payable to, or in respect of, the producer or individuals described in any of subparagraphs (5)(a)(i) to (viii) and (b)(i) to (vi) and paragraph (5)(c), including any individuals that would be described in paragraph (5)(c) if they were Canadians) was incurred in respect of services provided in Canada.

Related Provisions: ITA 241(3.3) — Disclosure to public of information on production certificate; Reg. 1101(5k.1) — Separate class for certain property under Class 10(x); Reg. 1106(1) — Definitions; Reg. 1106(2) — Prescribed taxable Canadian corporation; Reg. 1106(5) — Points for creative services; Reg. Sch. II:Cl. 10(x) — CCA class for Canadian film or video production.

Notes: See Notes to 1106(1)"excluded production".

(5) [Creative services] — For the purposes of this Division, the Minister of Canadian Heritage shall allot, in respect of a film or video production

(a) that is not an animation production, in respect of each of the following persons if that person is an individual who is a Canadian,

(i) for the director, two points,

(ii) for the screenwriter, two points,

(iii) for the lead performer for whose services the highest remuneration was payable, one point,

(iv) for the lead performer for whose services the second highest remuneration was payable, one point,

(v) for the art director, one point,

(vi) for the director of photography, one point,

(vii) for the music composer, one point, and

(viii) for the picture editor, one point;

(b) that is an animation production, in respect of each of the following persons if that person is an individual who is a Canadian,

(i) for the director, one point,

(ii) for the lead voice for which the highest or second highest remuneration was payable, one point,

(iii) for the design supervisor, one point,

(iv) for the camera operator where the camera operation is done in Canada, one point,

(v) for the music composer, one point, and

(vi) for the picture editor, one point;

(c) that is an animation production, one point if both the principal screenwriter and the storyboard supervisor are individuals who are Canadians; and

(d) that is an animation production, in respect of each of the following places if that place is in Canada,

(i) for the place where the layout and background work is done, one point,

(ii) for the place where the key animation is done, one point, and

(iii) for the place where the assistant animation and in-betweening is done, one point.

Related Provisions: Reg. 1106(1) — Definitions; Reg. 1106(6) — Specific points required; Reg. 1106(7) — Special rule for animation production; Reg. 1106(8) — Lead performer/screenwriter; Reg. 1106(9) — Special rule for documentary production.

(6) [Specific points required] — A production (other than a production that is an animation production or a treaty co-production) is a Canadian film or video production only if there is allotted

in respect of the production two points under subparagraph (5)(a)(i) or (ii) and one point under subparagraph (5)(a)(iii) or (iv).

Notes: In *Tricon Television*29, 2011 FC 435, the "docu-soap" *Beautiful People* was found to be a reality show rather than a documentary, and as the two "lead performers" (the hosts) were non-Canadian, it did not qualify for the credit.

(7) [Specific points required] — An animation production (other than a production that is a treaty co-production) is a Canadian film or video production only if there is allotted, in respect of the production,

(a) one point under subparagraph (5)(b)(i) or paragraph (5)(c);

(b) one point under subparagraph (5)(b)(ii); and

(c) one point under subparagraph (5)(d)(ii).

(8) Lead performer/screenwriter — For the purposes of this Division,

(a) a lead performer in respect of a production is an actor or actress who has a leading role in the production having regard to the performer's remuneration, billing and time on screen;

(b) a lead voice in respect of an animation production is the voice of the individual who has a leading role in the production having regard to the length of time that the individual's voice is heard in the production and the individual's remuneration; and

(c) where a person who is not a Canadian participates in the writing and preparation of the screenplay for a production, the screenwriter is not a Canadian unless the principal screenwriter is an individual who is otherwise a Canadian, the screenplay for the production is based upon a work authored by a Canadian, and the work is published in Canada.

(9) Documentary production — A documentary production that is not an excluded production, and that is allotted less than six points because one or more of the positions referred to in paragraph (5)(a) is unoccupied, is a Canadian film or video production if all of the positions described in that paragraph that are occupied in respect of the production are occupied by individuals who are Canadians.

(10) Prescribed person — For the purpose of section 125.4 of the Act and this Division, "prescribed person" means any of the following:

(a) a corporation that holds a television, speciality or pay-television broadcasting licence issued by the Canadian Radio-television and Telecommunications Commission;

(b) a corporation that holds a broadcast undertaking licence and that provides production funding as a result of a "significant benefits" commitment given to the Canadian Radio-television and Telecommunications Commission;

(c) a person to which paragraph 149(1)(l) of the Act applies and that has a fund that is used to finance Canadian film or video productions;

(d) a Canadian government film agency;

(e) in respect of a film or video production, a non-resident person that does not carry on a business in Canada through a permanent establishment in Canada and whose interest (or, for civil law, right) in the production is acquired to comply with the certification requirements of a treaty co-production twinning arrangement;

(f) a person

(i) to which paragraph 149(1)(f) of the Act applies,

(ii) that has a fund that is used to finance Canadian film or video productions, all or substantially all of which financing is provided by way of a direct ownership interest (or, for civil law, right) in those productions, and

(iii) that, after 1996, has received donations only from persons described in any of paragraphs (a) to (e);

(g) a prescribed taxable Canadian corporation;

(h) an individual who is a Canadian; and

1838

(i) a partnership, each member of which is described in any of paragraphs (a) to (h).

Related Provisions: ITA 253 — Extended meaning of "carry on business in Canada"; Reg. 1106(2) — Prescribed taxable Canadian corporation (for para. (g)).

Notes: This definition applies only to Reg. 1106(1)"excluded production"(a)(iii). It previously applied to ITA 125.4(1)"investor" as well, until that definition was repealed in 2014.

Paras. (e)-(f) changed to (e)-(i) by P.C. 2015-307, effective on the same basis as Reg. 1106(1)"copyright owner". Before the amendment, read:

> (e) in respect of a film or video production, a non-resident person that does not carry on a business in Canada through a permanent establishment in Canada where the person's interest in the production is acquired to comply with the certification requirements of a treaty co-production twinning arrangement; and

> (f) a person

>> (i) to which paragraph 149(1)(f) of the Act applies,

>> (ii) that has a fund that is used to finance Canadian film or video productions, all or substantially all of which financing is provided by way of a direct ownership interest in those productions, and

>> (iii) that, after 1996, has received donations only from persons described in paragraphs (a) to (e).

Regulations: 1106(2) (prescribed taxable Canadian corporation); 8201 ("permanent establishment": applies to ITA 125.4(1) and thus to 125.4(1)"Canadian film or video production", thence Reg. 1106(4) and Reg. 1106(1)"excluded production", which refers to a "prescribed person" under Reg. 1106(10)).

(11) Prescribed amount — For the purpose of the definition "assistance" in subsection 125.4(1) of the Act, "prescribed amount" means an amount paid or payable to a taxpayer under the License Fee Program of the Canadian Television Fund or as a licence-fee top-up contribution from the Canada Media Fund.

Notes: Reg. 1106(11) amended by P.C. 2015-307, retroactive to April 2010, to change "License Fee Program of the Canada Media Fund" to "License Fee Program of the Canadian Television Fund or as a licence-fee top-up contribution from the Canada Media Fund".

Reg. 1106(11) amended by 2002-2013 technical bill (Part 5 — technical), effective April 2010, to change "Canada Television and Cable Production Fund or the Canada Television Fund/Fonds canadien de télévision" to "Canada Media Fund".

(12) Copyright owner — For the purpose of the definition "copyright owner" in subsection (1),

(a) the right of a person to share in the revenues from or proceeds of disposition of an interest or, for civil law, a right, in a film or video production is not, in and by itself, an interest or right as a copyright owner of the production; and

(b) for greater certainty, a grant of an exclusive licence, within the meaning assigned by the *Copyright Act*, is not an assignment of a copyright.

Notes: Reg. 1106(12) added by P.C. 2015-307, effective on the same basis as Reg. 1106(1)"copyright owner".

Notes [Reg. 1106]: Reg. 1106 (Division VII) added by P.C. 2005-698, effective for the 1995 and subsequent taxation years, with various grandfathering rules for productions begun before 2004 (see up to PITA 49th ed.).

Former Reg. 1106 (Division VII of Part XI) repealed by P.C. 1995-775, effective for property acquired after May 30, 1995. It allowed the Minister of Supply and Services to issue a certificate in respect of property that would then be entitled to an additional allowance under Reg. 1100(1)(j) or (k). Such certificates were introduced during the Korean War in 1951 and have not been used for many years.

Definitions [Reg. 1106]: "amount" — ITA 248(1); "animation production" — Reg. 1106(6); "application deadline" — Reg. 1106(1)"application for a certificate of completion"; "application for a certificate of completion" — Reg. 1106(1); "broadcasting" — *Interpretation Act* 35(1); "business" — ITA 248(1); "Canada" — ITA 255, *Interpretation Act* 35(1); "Canadian" — Reg. 1106(1); "Canadian film or video production" — Reg. 1106(4); "Canadian government film agency" — Reg. 1106(1); "carry on a business in Canada" — ITA 253; "certificate of completion" — Reg. 1106(1); "controlled directly or indirectly" — ITA 256(5.1)-(6); "copyright owner" — Reg. 1106(1); "corporation" — ITA 248(1), *Interpretation Act* 35(1); "disposition" — ITA 248(1); "excluded production" — Reg. 1106(1); "fair market value" — see ITA 69(1) Notes; "individual" — ITA 248(1); "lead performer" — Reg. 1106(8)(a); "lead voice" — Reg. 1106(8)(b); "Minister" — ITA 248(1); "month" — *Interpretation Act* 35(1); "non-resident" — ITA 248(1); "partnership" — see ITA 96(1) Notes; "permanent establishment" — Reg. 8201 (applies to ITA 125.4(1)); "person", "prescribed" — ITA 248(1); "prescribed labour-sponsored venture capital corporation" — Reg. 6701; "prescribed person" — Reg. 1106(10); "prescribed taxable Canadian corporation" — Reg. 1106(2); "producer" — Reg. 1106(1); "provincial" — *Interpretation Act* 33(3), 35(1)"province"; "related" — ITA 251(2)-(6); "remuneration" — Reg. 1106(1); "resi-

dent" — ITA 250; "taxable Canadian corporation" — ITA 89(1), 248(1); "taxable income" — ITA 248(1); "taxation year" — ITA 249, Reg. 1104(1); "taxpayer" — ITA 248(1); "the production's application deadline" — Reg. 1106(1)"application for a certificate of completion"; "the production's certification deadline" — Reg. 1106(1)"certificate of completion"; "treaty co-production" — Reg. 1106(3); "twinning arrangement" — Reg. 1106(1); "writing" — *Interpretation Act* 35(1).

DIVISION VIII — DETERMINATION OF VISCOSITY AND DENSITY

1107. For the purpose of the definition "bituminous sands" in subsection 248(1) of the Act, viscosity or density of hydrocarbons shall be determined using a number of individual samples (constituting a representative sampling of that deposit or those deposits, as the case may be, from which the taxpayer is committed to produce by means of one mine) tested

(a) at atmospheric pressure;

(b) at a temperature of 15.6 degrees Celsius; and

(c) free of solution gas.

Notes: Reg. 1107 added by P.C. 1998-49, effective March 7, 1996.

Definitions [Reg. 1107]: "individual" — ITA 248(1); "solution gas" — Reg. 1104(13); "taxpayer" — ITA 248(1).

PART XII — [1200–1219] RESOURCE AND PROCESSING ALLOWANCES

1200. For the purposes of section 65 of the Act, there may be deducted in computing the income of a taxpayer for a taxation year such of the amounts determined in accordance with sections 1201 to 1209 and 1212 as are applicable.

Definitions [Reg. 1200]: "amount" — ITA 248(1); "taxation year" — ITA 249; "taxpayer" — ITA 248(1).

1201. Earned depletion allowances — [No longer relevant]

Notes: Reg. 1201 allows a deduction for "earned depletion allowance", based on the "earned depletion base" (EDB) under Reg. 1205. It is still in force, but since no amounts can be added to EDB after 1989, in practice all such expenses have now been claimed. For the text, see up to PITA 46th ed.

1202. [Rules] — [No longer relevant]

Notes: Reg. 1202 provides rules relevant to "earned depletion allowance" in Reg. 1201 and 1205, including successor-corp rules. For the text, see up to PITA 46th ed.

1203. Mining exploration depletion — [No longer relevant]

Notes: Reg. 1203 allows a deduction of a portion of the "mining exploration depletion base", which is based on mining expenses incurred before 1990 (Reg. 1203(2)(a)(i), 1206(1)"stated percentage"). It is still in force, but in practice all such expenses have now been claimed. For the text, see up to PITA 46th ed.

1204. Resource profits — (1) ["Gross resource profits"] — For the purposes of this Part, "gross resource profits" of a taxpayer for a taxation year means the amount, if any, by which the total of

(a) the amount, if any, by which the aggregate of

(i) the aggregate of amounts, if any, that would be included in computing the taxpayer's income for the year by virtue of subsection 59(2) and paragraphs 59(3.2)(b) and 59.1(b) of the Act if subsection 59(2) were read without reference to subsection 64(1) therein, and

(i.1) the amount, if any, by which the amount included in computing his income for the year by virtue of paragraph 59(3.2)(c) of the Act exceeds the proceeds of disposition of property described in clause 66(15)(c)(ii)(A) [66(15)"Canadian resource property"(b)(i)] of the Act that became receivable in the year or a preceding taxation year and after December 31, 1982 to the extent that such proceeds have not been deducted in determining the amount under this subparagraph for a preceding taxation year

exceeds

(ii) the aggregate of amounts, if any, deducted in computing his income for the year by virtue of paragraph 59.1(a) and subsections 64(1.1) and (1.2) of the Act,

(b) the amount, if any, of the aggregate of his incomes for the year from

(i) the production of petroleum, natural gas, related hydrocarbons or sulphur from

(A) oil or gas wells in Canada operated by the taxpayer, or

(B) natural accumulations (other than mineral resources) of petroleum or natural gas in Canada operated by the taxpayer,

(ii) the production and processing in Canada of

(A) ore, other than iron ore or tar sands ore, from mineral resources in Canada operated by him to any stage that is not beyond the prime metal stage or its equivalent,

(B) iron ore from mineral resources in Canada operated by him to any stage that is not beyond the pellet stage or its equivalent, and

(C) tar sands ore from mineral resources in Canada operated by him to any stage that is not beyond the crude oil stage or its equivalent,

(iii) the processing in Canada of

(A) ore, other than iron ore or tar sands ore, from mineral resources in Canada not operated by him to any stage that is not beyond the prime metal stage or its equivalent,

(B) iron ore from mineral resources in Canada not operated by him to any stage that is not beyond the pellet stage or its equivalent, and

(C) tar sands ore from mineral resources in Canada not operated by him to any stage that is not beyond the crude oil stage or its equivalent,

(iv) the processing in Canada of

(A) ore, other than iron ore or tar sands ore, from mineral resources outside Canada to any stage that is not beyond the prime metal stage or its equivalent,

(B) iron ore from mineral resources outside Canada to any stage that is not beyond the pellet stage or its equivalent, and

(C) tar sands ore from mineral resources outside Canada to any stage that is not beyond the crude oil stage or its equivalent,

(v) the processing in Canada of heavy crude oil recovered from an oil or gas well in Canada to any stage that is not beyond the crude oil stage or its equivalent, and

(vi) Canadian field processing,

(b.1) the total of all amounts (other than an amount included because of paragraph (b) in computing the taxpayer's gross resource profits for the year) each of which is an amount included in computing the taxpayer's income for the year as a rental or royalty computed by reference to the amount or value of production from a natural accumulation of petroleum or natural gas in Canada, an oil or gas well in Canada or a mineral resource in Canada, and

(c) if the taxpayer owns all the issued and outstanding shares of the capital stock of a railway company throughout the year, the amount that may reasonably be considered to be the railway company's income for its taxation year ending in the year from the transportation of such of the taxpayer's ore as is described in clause (b)(ii)(A), (B) or (C),

exceeds the aggregate of the taxpayer's losses for the year from the sources described in paragraph (b), where the taxpayer's incomes and losses are computed in accordance with the Act on the assumption that the taxpayer had during the year no incomes or losses ex-

cept from those sources and was allowed no deductions in computing the taxpayer's income for the year other than

(d) amounts deductible under section 66 of the Act (other than amounts in respect of foreign exploration and development expenses) or subsection 17(2) or (6) or section 29 of the *Income Tax Application Rules*, for the year;

(e) the amounts deductible or deducted, as the case may be, under section 66.1, 66.2 (other than an amount that is in respect of a property described in clause 66(15)(c)(ii)(A) [66(15)"Canadian resource property"(b)(i)] of the Act), 66.4, 66.5 or 66.7 (other than subsection (2) thereof) of the Act for the year; and

(f) any other deductions for the year that can reasonably be regarded as applicable to the sources of income described in paragraph (b) or (b.1), other than a deduction under paragraph 20(1)(ss) or (tt) of the Act or section 1201 or subsection 1202(2), 1203(1), 1207(1) or 1212(1).

Notes: Reg. 1204 is now effectively obsolete: see Carr & Calverley, *Canadian Resource Taxation* (Carswell, looseleaf or *Taxnet Pro* Reference Centre), chap. 5. See also Notes to ITA 248(1)"mineral resource".

For the meaning of "prime metal stage or its equivalent", see Notes to Reg. 1104(5).

Refund interest from tax overpayments was income from "production" for Reg. 1204(1)(b) in *3850625 Canada*, 2011 FCA 117, consistent with *Irving Oil* and *Munich Reinsurance* (see Notes to ITA 12(1)(c)), and overruling VIEWS doc 2003-000323A. See also *Cameco*, 2018 TCC 195, paras. 866-887 (aff'd 2020 FCA 112 without mentioning Reg. 1204; leave to appeal denied 2021 CarswellNat 377 (SCC)).

Only a portion of a hedging gain was to be included in gross resource profits, in VIEWS doc 2003-0003777. Income from crushing nickel ore on surface qualified under (b)(iii)(A): doc 2005-0121291E5. Limestone quarry profits do not qualify: doc 2007-024239I17.

Reg. 1204(1) amended by P.C. 1999-629 (for tax years that begin after 1996), 1996-1488.

(1.1) ["Resource profits"] — For the purposes of this Part, "resource profits" of a taxpayer for a taxation year means the amount, if any, by which the taxpayer's gross resource profits for the year exceeds the total of

(a) all amounts deducted in computing the taxpayer's income for the year other than

(i) an amount deducted in computing the taxpayer's gross resource profits for the year,

(ii) an amount deducted under any of section 8, paragraphs 20(1)(ss) and (tt), sections 60 to 64 and subsections 66(4), 66.7(2) and 104(6) and (12) of the Act and section 1201 and subsections 1202(2), 1203(1), 1207(1) and 1212(1) in computing the taxpayer's income for the year,

(iii) an amount deducted under section 66.2 of the Act in computing the taxpayer's income for the year, to the extent that it is attributable to any right, licence or privilege to store underground petroleum, natural gas or related hydrocarbons in Canada,

(iv) an amount deducted in computing the taxpayer's income for the year from a business, or other source, that does not include any resource activity of the taxpayer, and

(v) an amount deducted in computing the taxpayer's income for the year, to the extent that the amount

(A) relates to an activity

(I) that is not a resource activity of the taxpayer, and

(II) that is

1. the production, processing, manufacturing, distribution, marketing, transportation or sale of any property,

2. carried out for the purpose of earning income from property, or

3. the rendering of a service by the taxpayer to another person for the purpose of earning income of the taxpayer, and

(B) does not relate to a resource activity of the taxpayer,

(b) all amounts each of which is the amount, if any, by which

(i) the amount that would have been charged to the taxpayer by a person or partnership with whom the taxpayer was not dealing at arm's length if the taxpayer and that person or partnership had been dealing at arm's length

(A) for the use after March 6, 1996 and in the year of a property (other than money) owned by that person or partnership, or

(B) for the provision after March 6, 1996 and in the year by that person or partnership of a service to the taxpayer

exceeds the total of

(ii) the amount charged to the taxpayer for the use of that property or the provision of that service in that period, and

(iii) the portion of the amount described in subparagraph (i) that, if it had been charged, would not have been deductible in computing the taxpayer's resource profits, and

(c) where the year ends after February 21, 1994, all amounts added under subsection 80(13) of the Act in computing the taxpayer's gross resource profits for the year.

Related Provisions: Reg. 1204(1.2) — Interpretation.

Notes: Losses on foreign exchange forward contracts or interest rate swaps reduce resource profits if they are integral to the taxpayer's resource business and not a separate source of income: VIEWS docs 2005-0117751I7, 2009-0348571I7. See also Notes to Reg. 1101(1) re "separate business"; and *Cameco*, 2018 TCC 195, paras. 867-887 (aff'd 2020 FCA 112 without mentioning Reg. 1204; leave to appeal denied 2021 CarswellNat 377 (SCC)).

Reg. 1204(1.1) added by P.C. 1996-1488, this version effective for taxation years that begin after July 23, 1992. New Reg. 1204(1.1), and the change in 1204(1) from defining "resource profits" to "gross resource profits", are in response to *Gulf Canada*, [1992] 1 C.T.C. 183 (FCA). See also amendments to Reg. 1210.

(1.2) [Interpretation for (1.1)] — For the purposes of paragraph (1.1)(b) and this subsection,

(a) a taxpayer is considered not to deal at arm's length with a partnership where the taxpayer does not deal at arm's length with any member of the partnership;

(b) a partnership is considered not to deal at arm's length with another partnership where any member of the first partnership does not deal at arm's length with any member of the second partnership;

(c) where a taxpayer is a member, or is deemed by this paragraph to be a member, of a partnership that is a member of another partnership, the taxpayer is deemed to be a member of the other partnership; and

(d) the provision of a service to a taxpayer does not include the provision of a service by an individual in the individual's capacity as an employee of the taxpayer.

Notes: Reg. 1204(1.2) added by P.C. 1996-1488, effective for taxation years that end after March 6, 1996. (That is the date of the 1996 federal budget, when this amendment was first released. This amendment was originally proposed as effective for taxation years ending after Dec. 20, 1991, along with amendments to Reg. 1204(1) and introduction of Reg. 1204(1.1).)

(2) [Income of a trust] — For greater certainty, for the purposes of this section, in computing the income or loss of a trust for a taxation year from the sources described in paragraphs (1)(b) and (b.1), no deduction shall be made in respect of amounts deductible by the trust pursuant to subsection 104(6) or (12) of the Act.

(3) [Exclusions] — A taxpayer's income or loss from a source described in paragraph (1)(b) does not include

(a) any income or loss derived from transporting, transmitting or processing (other than processing described in clause (1)(b)(ii)(C), (iii)(C) or (iv)(C) or subparagraph (1)(b)(v) or (vi)) petroleum, natural gas or related hydrocarbons or sulphur from a natural accumulation of petroleum or natural gas;

(b) any income or loss arising because of the application of paragraph 12(1)(z.1) or (z.2) or section 107.3 of the Act; and

(c) any income or loss that can reasonably be attributable to a service rendered by the taxpayer (other than processing described in subparagraph (1)(b)(iii), (iv), (v) or (vi) or activities carried out by the taxpayer as a coal mine operator).

Notes: See Notes to ITA 20(1)(v.1) re *Exxonmobil* case. Reg. 1204(3)(b) amended by P.C. 2007-114, effective for taxation years that begin after 2006, to delete reference to ITA 12(1)(z.5). Reg. 1204(3) earlier amended by P.C. 1999-629 and P.C. 1996-1488.

(4)–(6) [Repealed]

Notes: Reg. 1204(4), (5) repealed by P.C. 2007-114, effective for taxation years that begin after 2003, due to expiry of the *Syncrude Remission Order* (reproduced under "Remission Orders" following the Regulations) on Dec. 31, 2003. They excluded from resource profits any royalties subject to remission under the remission order.

Reg. 1204(6) repealed by P.C. 1996-1488, retroactive to taxation years that begin after 1990. Along with Reg. 1204(1)(b.1), it provided an exclusion relating to tax-exempt persons that no longer applies. However, tax-exempt persons are subject to a penalty tax under ITA 208 re certain interests in resource property in which taxable and tax-exempt persons each have an interest. This amendment is consequential upon the expiration of transitional relief under ITA 208 effective 1990.

Definitions [Reg. 1204]: "amount" — ITA 248(1); "arm's length" — ITA 251(1), Reg. 1204(1.2)(a), (b); "business" — ITA 248(1); "Canada" — ITA 255, *Interpretation Act* 35(1); "Canadian development expense" — ITA 66.2(5), 248(1), Reg. 1206(4)(b); "Canadian exploration and development expenses" — ITA 66(15), 248(1), Reg. 1206(4)(b); "Canadian exploration expense" — ITA 66.1(6), 248(1), Reg. 1206(4)(b); "Canadian field processing" — ITA 248(1); "coal mine operator" — Reg. 1206(1); "disposition", "employee" — ITA 248(1); "foreign exploration and development expenses" — ITA 66(15), 248(1); "gross resource profits" — Reg. 1204(1.1); "individual" — ITA 248(1); "member" — Reg. 1204(1.2)(c); "mineral resource", "oil or gas well" — ITA 248(1); "ore" — Reg. 1206(1); "partnership" — see ITA 96(1) Notes; "person" — ITA 248(1); "proceeds of disposition" — Reg. 1206(1); "production" — ITA 66(15), Reg. 1206(2); "property" — ITA 248(1); "provision of a service" — Reg. 1204(1.2)(d); "resource" — ITA 251(2)–(6); "resource activity" — Reg. 1206(1); "resource profits" — Reg. 1204(1.1); "share" — ITA 248(1); "tar sands ore" — Reg. 1206(1); "taxation year" — ITA 249; "taxpayer" — ITA 248(1); "trust" — ITA 104(1), 248(1), (3).

1205. Earned depletion base — [No longer relevant]

Notes: Reg. 1205 determines the "earned depletion base" (EDB) for Reg. 1201. It is still in force, but no amounts can be added to EDB after 1989, due to dates in Reg. 1205(1) and 1206(1)"stated percentage", and in practice all such expenses have now been claimed. For the text, see up to PITA 46th ed.

1206. Interpretation — (1) In this Part,

"bituminous sands equipment" means property of a taxpayer that

(a) is included in Class 28 or in paragraph (a) of Class 41 in Schedule II, other than property so included

(i) by virtue of the first reference in Class 28 to paragraph (l) of Class 10 in Schedule II, where the property was acquired by the taxpayer before November 17, 1978, or

(ii) by virtue of the reference in Class 28 to paragraph (m) of Class 10 in Schedule II, and

(b) was acquired by the taxpayer after April 10, 1978 principally for the purpose of gaining or producing income from one or more mines, each of which is a location in a bituminous sands deposit, oil sands deposit or oil shale deposit from which material is extracted;

"Canadian exploration and development overhead expense" of a taxpayer means a Canadian exploration expense or a Canadian development expense of the taxpayer made or incurred after 1980 that is not a Canadian renewable and conservation expense (in this definition having the meaning assigned by subsection 66.1(6) of the Act) nor a taxpayer's share of a Canadian renewable and conservation expense incurred by a partnership and

(a) that was in respect of the administration, management or financing of the taxpayer,

(b) that was in respect of the salary, wages or other remuneration or related benefits paid in respect of a person employed by the taxpayer whose duties were not all or substantially all directed towards exploration or development activities,

(c) that was in respect of the upkeep or maintenance of, taxes or insurance in respect of, or rental or leasing of, property other than property all or substantially all of the use of which by the taxpayer was for the purposes of exploration or development activities, or

(d) that may reasonably be regarded as having been in respect of

(i) the use of or the right to use any property in which any person who was connected with the taxpayer had an interest,

(ii) compensation for the performance of a service for the benefit of the taxpayer by any person who was connected with the taxpayer, or

(iii) the acquisition of any materials, parts or supplies from any person who was connected with the taxpayer

to the extent that the expense exceeds the least of amounts, each of which was the aggregate of the costs incurred by a person who was connected with the taxpayer

(iv) in respect of the property,

(v) in respect of the performance of the service, or

(vi) in respect of the materials, parts or supplies;

Related Provisions: Reg. 1206(4.2) — Prescribed CEDOE; Reg. 1206(5) — Meaning of "connected" and "costs incurred by a person".

Notes: CEDOE cannot be renounced to flow-through shareholders even if is CEE: Reg. 1206(4.2), ITA 66(12.6)(b), VIEWS doc 2007-0246921E5.

See Stephen Doyle, "Selected Revenue Canada Assessing Issues", 12 *Canadian Petroleum Tax Journal* (1999) §2; Zul Ladak, "Legislation Dealing with CEE, CDE and COGPE & Proposed Policy on CEDOE", 16 *CPTJ* (2003). For CRA interpretation of this definition see VIEWS doc 2004-0102041E5.

In *Forsberg*, 2005 TCC 591, CEE expenses were held to be CEDOE because they were paid to a "connected person".

CRA considers that "substantially all", used in paras. (b) and (c), means 90% or more.

Opening words of definition amended by P.C. 2000-1331, for expenses incurred after Dec. 5, 1996.

"Canadian oil and gas exploration expense", of a taxpayer, means an outlay or expense that is made or incurred after 1980 and that would be a Canadian exploration expense, as defined in subsection 66.1(6) of the Act, of the taxpayer (other than an outlay or expense in respect of a qualified tertiary oil recovery project that is a Canadian exploration expense of the taxpayer because of subparagraph (c)(ii) or (d)(ii) of that definition) if

(a) that definition were read without reference to its paragraphs (f) to (g.4),

(b) the reference in paragraph (h) of that definition to "any of paragraphs (a) to (d) and (f) to (g.4)" were read as "any of paragraphs (a) to (e)", and

(c) the reference in paragraph (i) of that definition to "any of paragraphs (a) to (g)" were read as "any of paragraphs (a) to (e)";

Notes: Definition amended by P.C. 2016-933, this version effective March 21, 2011.

"coal mine operator" means a person who undertakes all or substantially all of the activities involved in the production of coal from a resource;

Related Provisions: Reg. 1104(2)"coal mine operator" — Same definition for capital cost allowance.

Notes: CRA considers that "substantially all" means 90% or more.

"Coal mine operator" added by P.C. 1999-629, effective March 7, 1996.

"conventional lands" means lands situated in Canada other than non-conventional lands;

"disposition of property" has the meaning assigned by paragraph 13(21)(c) [13(21)"disposition of property"] of the Act;

"enhanced recovery equipment" means property of a taxpayer that

(a) is included in Class 10 in Schedule II by virtue of paragraph (j) of the description of that Class, and

(b) was acquired by the taxpayer after April 10, 1978 and before 1981 for use in the production of oil, from a reservoir or a deposit of bituminous sand, oil sand or oil shale in Canada operated by the taxpayer, that is incremental to oil that would be recovered using primary recovery techniques alone,

other than property

(c) used by the taxpayer as part of a primary recovery process prior to the use described in paragraph (b),

(d) that had, before it was acquired by the taxpayer, been used for any purpose whatever by any person with whom the taxpayer was not dealing at arm's length, or

(e) that has been used by any person before April 11, 1978 in the production of oil, from a reservoir in Canada, that is incremental to oil that would be recovered using primary recovery techniques alone;

"exempt partnership" — [Repealed]

Notes: Reg. 1206(1)"exempt partnership" repealed by P.C. 2007-114, for taxation years that begin after 2006, due to repeal of Reg. 1210 and 1206(1)"production royalty". Added by P.C. 1996-1488.

"exporting resource" — [No longer relevant]

Notes: This term is used only in Reg. 1205.

"mine" means any location where material is extracted from a resource but does not include a well for the extraction of material from a deposit of bituminous sand, oil sand or oil shale;

"non-conventional lands" means lands that belong to Her Majesty in right of Canada, or in respect of which Her Majesty in right of Canada has the right to dispose of or exploit the natural resources, situated in

(a) the Yukon Territory, the Northwest Territories, or Sable Island, or

(b) those submarine areas, not within a province, adjacent to the coast of Canada and extending throughout the natural prolongation of the land territory of Canada to the outer edge of the continental margin or to a distance of two hundred nautical miles from the baselines from which the breadth of the territorial sea of Canada is measured, whichever is the greater;

Notes: Para. (a) should be amended to refer to Nunavut, effective April 1999.

"ore" includes ore from a mineral resource that has been processed to any stage that is prior to the prime metal stage or its equivalent;

Notes: For the meaning of "prime metal stage or its equivalent", see Reg. 1104(5) Notes.

"original owner" — [No longer relevant]

Notes: This term is used only in Reg. 1202, 1205, and 1206(1)"predecessor owner".

"predecessor owner" — [No longer relevant]

Notes: This term is used only in Reg. 1202 and 1205.

"primary recovery" means the recovery of oil from a reservoir as a result of utilizing the natural energy of the reservoir to move the oil toward a producing well;

"proceeds of disposition" of property has the meaning assigned by paragraph 13(21)(d) [13(21)"proceeds of disposition"] of the Act;

"processing property" means property

(a) that is included in Class 10 of Schedule II because of paragraph (g) of the description of that Class or would be so included if that paragraph were read without reference to subparagraph (ii) of that paragraph and Schedule II were read without reference to Class 41, or

(b) that is included in Class 10 in Schedule II because of paragraph (k) of the description of that Class or would be so included if that paragraph were read without reference to the words following subparagraph (ii) of that paragraph and Schedule II were read without reference to Class 41,

other than property that had, before it was acquired by a taxpayer, been used for any purpose whatever by any person with whom the taxpayer was not dealing at arm's length;

Notes: "Processing property" amended by P.C. 1996-1488 to add reference to Class 41, effective for taxation years that end after 1987.

"production royalty" — [Repealed]

Notes: Reg. 1206(1)"production royalty" repealed by P.C. 2007-114, effective for taxation years that begin after 2006, due to repeal of Reg. 1210. Earlier amended by P.C. 1996-1488 and P.C. 1992-2335.

"qualified resource" — [No longer relevant]

Notes: This term is used only in Reg. 1205.

"qualified tertiary oil recovery project" in respect of an expense incurred in a taxation year means a project that uses a method (including a method that uses carbon dioxide miscible, hydrocarbon miscible, thermal or chemical processes but not including a secondary recovery method) that is designed to recover oil from an oil well in Canada that is incremental to oil that would be recovered therefrom by primary recovery and a secondary recovery method, if

(a) a specified royalty provision applies in the year or in the immediately following taxation year in respect of the production, if any, or any portion thereof from the project or in respect of the ownership of property to which such production relates,

(b) the project is on a reserve within the meaning of the *Indian Act*, or

(c) the project is located in the Province of Ontario;

Related Provisions: Reg. 1206(8) — Specified royalty provision; Reg. 1206(8.1) — Timing for para. (a).

"resource" means any mineral resource in Canada;

"resource activity" of a taxpayer means

(a) the production by the taxpayer of petroleum, natural gas or related hydrocarbons or sulphur from

(i) an oil or gas well in Canada, or

(ii) a natural accumulation (other than a mineral resource) of petroleum or natural gas in Canada,

(b) the production and processing in Canada by the taxpayer or the processing in Canada by the taxpayer of

(i) ore (other than iron ore or tar sands ore) from a mineral resource in Canada to any stage that is not beyond the prime metal stage or its equivalent,

(ii) iron ore from a mineral resource in Canada to any stage that is not beyond the pellet stage or its equivalent, and

(iii) tar sands ore from a mineral resource in Canada to any stage that is not beyond the crude oil stage or its equivalent,

(c) the processing in Canada by the taxpayer of heavy crude oil recovered from an oil or gas well in Canada to any stage that is not beyond the crude oil stage or its equivalent,

(c.1) Canadian field processing carried on by the taxpayer,

(d) the processing in Canada by the taxpayer of

(i) ore (other than iron ore or tar sands ore) from a mineral resource outside Canada to any stage that is not beyond the prime metal stage or its equivalent,

(ii) iron ore from a mineral resource outside Canada to any stage that is not beyond the pellet stage or its equivalent, and

(iii) tar sands ore from a mineral resource outside Canada to any stage that is not beyond the crude oil stage or its equivalent, or

(e) the ownership by the taxpayer of a right to a rental or royalty computed by reference to the amount or value of production from a natural accumulation of petroleum or natural gas in Canada, an oil or gas well in Canada or a mineral resource in Canada,

and, for the purposes of this definition,

(f) the production of a substance by a taxpayer includes exploration and development activities of the taxpayer with respect to the substance, whether or not extraction of the substance has begun or will ever begin,

(g) the production or the processing, or the production and processing, of a substance by a taxpayer includes activities performed by the taxpayer that are ancillary to, or in support of, the production or the processing, or the production and processing, of that substance by the taxpayer,

(h) the production or processing of a substance by a taxpayer includes an activity (including the ownership of property) that is undertaken before the extraction of the substance and that is undertaken for the purpose of extracting or processing the substance,

(i) the production or the processing, or the production and processing, of a substance by a taxpayer includes activities that the taxpayer undertakes as a consequence of the production or the processing, or the production and processing, of that substance, whether or not the production, the processing or the production and processing of the substance has ceased, and

(j) notwithstanding paragraphs (a) to (i), the production, the processing or the production and processing of a substance does not include any activity of a taxpayer that is part of a source described in paragraph 1204(1)(b), where

(i) the activity

(A) is the transporting, transmitting or processing (other than processing described in subparagraph 1206(1)"resource activity"(b) (iii), paragraph 1206(1)"resource activity"(c) or (c.1) or subparagraph 1206(1)"resource activity"(d) (iii)) of petroleum, natural gas or related hydrocarbons or of sulphur, or

(B) can reasonably be attributed to a service rendered by the taxpayer, and

(ii) revenues derived from the activity are not taken into account in computing the taxpayer's gross resource profits;

Notes: For the meaning of "prime metal stage or its equivalent" in (b)(i) and (d)(i), see Reg. 1104(5) Notes. For "reasonably be attributed" in (j)(i)(B), see *729658 Alberta*, 2004 TCC 474.

"Resource activity" amended by P.C. 1999-629, for tax years that begin after 1996. Added by P.C. 1996-1488.

"secondary recovery method" means a method to recover from a reservoir oil that is incremental to oil that would be recovered therefrom by primary recovery, by supplying energy to supplement or replace the natural energy of the reservoir through the use of technically proven methods, including waterflooding;

"specified development well" — [Revoked]

"specified percentage" — [No longer relevant]

Notes: This term is used only in Reg. 1205.

"specified property" of a person means all or substantially all of the property used by the person in carrying on in Canada such of the businesses described in subparagraphs 66(15)(h)(i) to (vii) [66(15)"principal-business corporation"(a) to (g)] of the Act as were carried on by the person;

Notes: CRA considers that "substantially all" means 90% or more.

"specified royalty" — [Repealed]

Notes: Reg. 1206(1)"specified royalty" repealed by P.C. 2007-114, for taxation years that begin after 2006, due to repeal of Reg. 1210 and 1206(1)"production royalty". Added by P.C. 1999-629, effective March 7, 1996, with grandfathering where an election was filed before July 1998.

"stated percentage" — [No longer relevant]

Notes: This term is used only in Reg. 1203 and 1205.

"tar sands ore" means ore extracted, other than through a well, from a mineral resource that is a deposit of bituminous sand, oil sand or oil shale;

"tertiary recovery equipment" — [No longer relevant]

Notes: This term is used only in Reg. 1205.

(2) In this Part, **"joint exploration corporation"**, **"principal-business corporation"**, **"production"** from a Canadian resource property, **"reserve amount"** and **"shareholder corporation"** have the meanings assigned by subsection 66(15) of the Act.

Regulations

(3) For the purposes of sections 1201 to 1209 and 1212, where at the end of a fiscal period of a partnership, a taxpayer was a member thereof

(a) the resource profits of the partnership for the fiscal period, to the extent of the taxpayer's share thereof, shall be included in computing his resource profits for his taxation year in which the fiscal period ended;

(b) any property acquired or disposed of by the partnership shall be deemed to have been acquired or disposed of by the taxpayer to the extent of his share thereof;

(c) any property deemed by paragraph (b) to have been acquired or disposed of by the taxpayer shall be deemed to have been acquired or disposed of by him on the day the property was acquired or disposed of by the partnership;

(d) any amount that has become receivable by the partnership and in respect of which the consideration given by the partnership therefor was property (other than property referred to in paragraph 59(2)(a), (c) or (d) of the Act or a share or interest therein or right thereto) or services, all or part of the original cost of which to the partnership may reasonably be regarded primarily as an exploration or development expense of the taxpayer, shall be deemed to be an amount receivable by the taxpayer to the extent of his share thereof, and the consideration so given by the partnership shall, to the extent of the taxpayer's share thereof, be deemed to have been given by the taxpayer for the amount deemed to be receivable by him;

(e) any expenditure incurred or deemed to have been incurred by the partnership shall be deemed to have been incurred by the taxpayer to the extent of the taxpayer's share thereof; and

(f) any amount or expenditure deemed by paragraph (d) or (e) to have been receivable or incurred, as the case may be, by the taxpayer shall be deemed to have become receivable or been incurred, as the case may be, by the taxpayer on the day the amount became receivable or the expenditure was incurred or deemed to have been incurred by the partnership.

(3.1) [No longer relevant]

Notes: This rule applies only for purposes of Reg. 1201–1203, 1205 and 1217–1218.

(4), (4.1) [Renounced expenses incurred 1969-72] — [No longer relevant.]

(4.2) For the purposes of paragraphs 66(12.6)(b), (12.601)(d) and (12.62)(b) of the Act, a prescribed Canadian exploration and development overhead expense of a corporation is

(a) a Canadian exploration and development overhead expense of the corporation;

(b) an expense that would be a Canadian exploration and development overhead expense of the corporation if the references to "connected with the taxpayer" in paragraph (d) of the definition "Canadian exploration and development overhead expense" in subsection (1) were read as "connected with the person to whom the expense is renounced under subsection 66(12.6), (12.601) or (12.62) of the Act"; and

(c) an expense that would be a Canadian exploration and development overhead expense of the corporation if the references to "person who was connected with the taxpayer" in paragraph (d) of the definition "Canadian exploration and development overhead expense" in subsection (1) were read as "person to whom the expense is renounced under subsection 66(12.6), (12.601) or (12.62) of the Act".

Notes: All references to ITA (12.601) added to Reg. 1206(4.2) by P.C. 1996-494, effective for expenses incurred after December 2, 1992.

Reg. 1206(4.2) added by P.C. 1990-2256, effective for expenditures or expenses incurred after February 1986.

(4.3) For the purposes of subsections (4.2) and (5), a partnership shall be deemed to be a person and its taxation year shall be deemed to be its fiscal period.

Notes: Reg. 1206(4.3) added by P.C. 1990-2256, effective for expenditures or expenses incurred after February 1986.

(5) For the purposes of subsection (6) and the definition "Canadian exploration and development overhead expense" in subsection (1),

(a) a person and a particular corporation are connected with each other if

(i) the person and the particular corporation are not dealing at arm's length,

(ii) the person has an equity percentage in the particular corporation that is not less than 10 per cent, or

(iii) the person is a corporation in which another person has an equity percentage that is not less than 10 per cent and the other person has an equity percentage in the particular corporation that is not less than 10 per cent;

(a.1) a person and another person that is not a corporation are connected with each other if they are not dealing at arm's length; and

(b) **"costs incurred by a person"** shall not include

(i) an outlay or expense described in any of paragraphs (a) to (c) of that definition made or incurred by the person if the references in those paragraphs to "taxpayer" were read as references to "person",

(ii) an outlay or expense made or incurred by the person to the extent that it is not reasonably attributable to the use of a property by, the performance of a service for, or any materials, parts, or supplies acquired by, the taxpayer referred to in that definition, and

(iii) an amount in respect of the capital cost to the person of a property, other than, where the property is a depreciable property of the person, that proportion of the capital allowance of the person for his taxation year in respect of the property that may reasonably be considered attributable to the use of the property by, or in the performance of a service for, the taxpayer referred to in that definition.

Related Provisions: Reg. 1206(7) — Equity percentage.

Notes: Reg. 1206(5)(a.1) added by P.C. 1990-2256, effective for expenditures or expenses incurred after February 1986.

(6) For the purpose of subparagraph (5)(b)(iii), the "capital allowance" of a person (in this subsection referred to as the "owner") for his taxation year in respect of a property owned by him means that proportion of an amount not exceeding 20 per cent of the amount that is

(a) in the case of a property owned by the owner on December 31, 1980, the lesser of

(i) the capital cost of the property to the owner computed as if no amount had been included therein that is a cost of borrowing capital, including any cost incurred prior to the commencement of carrying on a business, and

(ii) the fair market value of the property on December 31, 1980,

(b) in the case of a property acquired by the owner after December 31, 1980 that was previously owned by a person connected with the owner, the lesser of

(i) the capital cost of the property, computed as if no amount had been included therein that is a cost of borrowing capital, including any cost incurred prior to the commencement of carrying on a business, to the person, who was connected with the owner, who was the first person to acquire the property from a person with whom the owner was not connected, and

(ii) the fair market value of the property at the time it was acquired by the owner, and

(c) in any other case, the capital cost of the property to the owner computed as if no amount had been included therein that is a cost of borrowing capital, including any cost incurred prior to the commencement of carrying on a business,

that the number of days in the taxation year during which the property was owned by the owner is of 365.

(7) For the purposes of paragraph (5)(a), "equity percentage" has the meaning assigned by paragraph 95(4)(b) [95(4)"equity percentage"] of the Act.

(8) For the purposes of the definition "qualified tertiary oil recovery project" in subsection (1), a "specified royalty provision" means:

(a) the *Experimental Project Petroleum Royalty Regulation* of Alberta (Alta. Reg. 36/79);

(b) *The Experimental Oil Sands Royalty Regulations* of Alberta (Alta. Reg. 287/77);

(c) section 4.2 of the *Petroleum Royalty Regulations* of Alberta (Alta. Reg. 93/74);

(d) section 58A of the *Petroleum and Natural Gas Regulations, 1969* of Saskatchewan (Saskatchewan Regulation 8/69);

(e) section 204 of *The Freehold Oil and Gas Production Tax Regulations, 1983* of Saskatchewan (Saskatchewan Regulation 11/83);

(f) item 9 of section 2 of the *Petroleum and Natural Gas Royalty Regulations* of British Columbia (B.C. Reg. 549/78);

(g) the *Freehold Mineral Taxation Act* of Alberta;

(h) the *Freehold Mineral Rights Tax Act* of Alberta;

(i) Order in Council 427/84 pursuant to section 9(a) of the *Mines and Minerals Act* of Alberta;

(j) Order in Council 966/84 pursuant to section 9 of the *Mines and Minerals Act* of Alberta; or

(k) Order in Council 870/84 pursuant to section 9 of the *Mines and Minerals Act* of Alberta.

(8.1) For the purpose of paragraph (a) of the definition "qualified tertiary oil recovery project" in subsection (1), a specified royalty provision is deemed to apply as of a particular time if, at the particular time, unconditional approval for the specified royalty provision to apply at a time after the particular time is given by

(a) Her Majesty in right of Canada or of a province;

(b) an agent of her Majesty in right of Canada or of a province; or

(c) a corporation, a commission or an association that is controlled by Her Majesty in right of Canada or of a province or by an agent of Her Majesty in right of Canada or of a province.

Notes: Reg. 1206(8.1) amended by P.C. 2007-114, effective Dec. 20, 2002, due to amendments to ITA 18(1)(m).

(9) [Repealed]

Notes: Reg. 1206(9) repealed by P.C. 2007-114, for tax years that begin after 2006, due to repeal of Reg. 1210 and 1206(1)"production royalty".

Closing words of Reg. 1206(9) amended by P.C. 1996-1488, effective February 1990.

Definitions [Reg. 1206]: "amount" — ITA 248(1); "arm's length" — ITA 251(1); "bituminous sands", "business" — ITA 248(1); "calendar year" — *Interpretation Act* 37(1)(a); "Canada" — ITA 255, *Interpretation Act* 35(1); "Canadian development expense" — ITA 66.2(5), 248(1); "Canadian exploration and development overhead expense" — Reg. 1206(1), (4.1); "Canadian exploration expense" — ITA 66.1(6), 248(1); "Canadian field processing" — ITA 248(1); "Canadian oil and gas exploration expense" — Reg. 1206(1); "Canadian resource property" — ITA 66(15), 248(1); "capital allowance" — Reg. 1206(6); "commencement" — *Interpretation Act* 35(1); "connected" — Reg. 1206(5); "conventional lands" — Reg. 1206(1); "corporation" — ITA 248(1), *Interpretation Act* 35(1); "costs incurred by a person" — Reg. 1206(5)(b); "depreciable property" — ITA 13(21), 248(1); "disposed", "disposes" — ITA 248(1)"disposition"; "disposition", "employed" — ITA 248(1); "equity percentage" — ITA 95(4), Reg. 1206(7); "fair market value" — see ITA 69(1) Notes; "fiscal period" — ITA 249.1; "gross resource profits" — Reg. 1204(1); "Her Majesty" — *Interpretation Act* 35(1); "individual" — ITA 248(1); "joint exploration corporation" — ITA 66(15), Reg. 1206(2); "mine" — Reg. 1206(1); "mineral", "mineral resource" — ITA 248(1); "non-conventional lands" — Reg. 1206(1); "oil or gas well" — ITA 248(1); "ore", "original owner" — Reg. 1206(1); "owner" — Reg. 1206(5); "partnership" — see ITA 96(1) Notes; "person" — ITA 248(1), Reg. 1206(4.3); "prescribed" — ITA 248(1); "primary recovery" — Reg. 1206(1); "principal-business corporation" — ITA 66(15), Reg. 1206(2); "proceeds of disposition" — Reg. 1206(1); "processing property" — Reg. 1206(1); "production" — ITA 66(15), Reg. 1206(2); "property" — ITA 248(1); "province" — *Interpretation Act* 35(1); "qualified tertiary oil recovery project" — Reg.

1206(1); "related" — ITA 251(2)–(6); "reserve amount" — ITA 66(15), Reg. 1206(2); "resource" — Reg. 1206(1); "resource profits" — Reg. 1204(1.1); "salary, wages", "salary or wages" — ITA 248(1)"salary or wages"; "secondary recovery method" — Reg. 1206(1); "series" — ITA 248(10); "share" — ITA 248(1); "shareholder corporation" — Reg. 1206(2); "specified royalty provision" — Reg. 1206(8), (8.1); "tar sands ore" — Reg. 1206(1); "taxation year" — ITA 249; "taxpayer" — ITA 248(1); "territorial sea" — *Interpretation Act* 35(1); "trust" — ITA 104(1), 248(1), (3); "writing" — *Interpretation Act* 35(1).

1207. Frontier exploration allowances — [No longer relevant]

Notes: Reg. 1207 allows a deduction of a portion of the "frontier exploration base", based on oil and gas well expenses incurred before 1980. It is still in force, but in practice all such expenses have now been claimed. For the text, see up to PITA 46th ed.

1208. Additional allowances in respect of certain oil or gas wells — [No longer relevant]

Notes: Reg. 1208 allows a current deduction for certain oil and gas well drilling costs, up to the income from the well, but only for costs incurred before 1972 (wells outside Canada) or before April 11, 1962 (wells in Canada). Unused costs can be carried forward. Reg. 1208 is still in force, but in practice all such costs have now been claimed or else the wells did not generate enough income. For the text, see up to PITA 46th ed.

1209. Additional allowances in respect of certain mines — [No longer relevant]

Notes: Reg. 1209 allows a deduction for certain mining costs incurred before 1972. Unused costs can be carried forward. Reg. 1209 is still in force, but in practice all such costs have now been claimed. For the text, see up to PITA 46th ed.

1210–1211. [Repealed]

Notes [Reg. 1210–1211]: Reg. 1210 (Resource allowance), 1210.1 (Prescribed resource loss) and 1211 (Prescribed amounts) repealed by P.C. 2007-114, for tax years that begin after 2006, due to repeal of ITA 20(1)(v.1). Earlier amended by P.C. 2007-114, 1999-629, 1996-1448 and 1993-415.

1212. Supplementary depletion allowances — [No longer relevant]

Notes: Reg. 1212 allows a deduction for a portion of the "supplementary depletion base", which is based on certain costs incurred before 1981. Unused costs can be carried forward. Reg. 1212 is still in force, but in practice all such costs have now been claimed. For the text, see up to PITA 46th ed.

1213. Prescribed deductions — For the purposes of subparagraph 66.1(2)(a)(ii) of the Act, "prescribed deduction" in respect of a corporation for a taxation year means an amount deducted under subsection 1202(2) by the corporation in computing its income for the year.

Definitions [Reg. 1213]: "amount" — ITA 248(1); "corporation" — ITA 248(1), *Interpretation Act* 35(1); "taxation year" — ITA 249.

1214. Amalgamations and windings-up — (1) Where a particular corporation amalgamates with another corporation to form a new corporation, or the assets of a subsidiary are transferred to its parent corporation on the winding-up of the subsidiary, and subsection 87(1.2) or 88(1.5) of the Act is applicable to the new corporation or the parent corporation, as the case may be, the new corporation or the parent corporation, as the case may be, shall be deemed to be the same corporation as, and a continuation of, the particular corporation or the subsidiary, as the case may be, for the purposes of

(a) computing the mining exploration depletion base (within the meaning assigned by subsection 1203(2)), the earned depletion base, the frontier exploration base (within the meaning assigned by subsection 1207(2)) and the supplementary depletion base (within the meaning assigned by subsection 1212(3)) of the new corporation or the parent corporation, as the case may be; and

(b) determining the amounts, if any, that may be deducted under subsection 1202(2) in computing the income of the new corporation or the parent corporation, as the case may be, for a particular taxation year.

(2) Where there has been an amalgamation (within the meaning assigned by subsection 87(1) of the Act) of two or more particular corporations to form one corporate entity, that entity shall be deemed to be the same corporation as, and a continuation of, each of the particular corporations for the purposes of subsection 1202(9).

(3) Where a taxable Canadian corporation (in this subsection referred to as the "subsidiary") has been wound up in circumstances in which subsection 88(1) of the Act applies in respect of the subsidiary and another taxable Canadian corporation (in this subsection referred to as the "parent"), the parent shall be deemed to be the same corporation as, and a continuation of, the subsidiary for the purposes of subsection 1202(9).

Definitions [Reg. 1214]: "amount" — ITA 248(1); "corporation" — ITA 248(1), *Interpretation Act* 35(1); "earned depletion base" — Reg. 1202(1), 1205(1); "parent", "subsidiary" — Reg. 1214(3); "supplementary depletion base" — Reg. 1212(2)–(4); "taxable Canadian corporation" — ITA 89(1), 248(1); "taxation year" — ITA 249.

1215. [Revoked]

1216, 1217, 1218. [No longer relevant.]

Notes: Reg. 1216 prescribes persons for ITA 208(1), which was repealed for tax years that begin after 2006. Reg. 1217 and 1218 prescribe "prescribed Canadian exploration expense" and "prescribed Canadian development expense" for ITA 66(14.1) and (14.2), which allowed non-taxable corporations to use CEE and CDE incurred before Oct. 1986 to obtain relief from petroleum and gas revenue tax liability.

1219. Canadian renewable and conservation expense —
(1) [Definition] — Subject to subsections (2) to (4), for the purpose of subsection 66.1(6) of the Act, "Canadian renewable and conservation expense" means an expense incurred by a taxpayer, and payable to a person or partnership with whom the taxpayer is dealing at arm's length, in respect of the development of a project for which it is reasonable to expect that at least 50% of the capital cost of the depreciable property to be used in the project would be the capital cost of any property that is included in Class 43.1 or 43.2 in Schedule II, or that would be so included if this Part were read without reference to this section, and includes such an expense incurred by the taxpayer

(a) for the purpose of making a service connection to the project for the transmission of electricity to a purchaser of the electricity, to the extent that the expense so incurred was not incurred to acquire property of the taxpayer;

(b) for the construction of a temporary access road to the project site;

(c) for a right of access to the project site before the earliest time at which a property described in Class 43.1 or 43.2 in Schedule II is used in the project for the purpose of earning income;

(d) for clearing land to the extent necessary to complete the project;

(e) for process engineering for the project, including

(i) collection and analysis of site data,

(ii) calculation of energy, mass, water, or air balances,

(iii) simulation and analysis of the performance and cost of process design options, and

(iv) selection of the optimum process design;

(f) for the drilling or completion of a well for the project, other than

(i) a well that is, or can reasonably be expected to be, used for the installation of underground piping that is included in paragraph (d) of Class 43.1 or paragraph (b) of Class 43.2 in Schedule II, or

(ii) a well referred to in paragraph (h);

(g) for a test wind turbine that is part of a wind farm project of the taxpayer; or

(h) if at least 50% of the depreciable property to be used in the project, determined by reference to its capital cost, is described in subparagraph (d)(vii) of Class 43.1,

(i) for the drilling of a well, or

(ii) solely for the purpose of determining the extent and quality of a geothermal resource.

Related Provisions: Reg. 1219(4) — Whether CRCE for wind energy conversion system; Reg. 1219(5) — Compliance required with environmental law for 1219(1)(h).

Notes: See Notes to ITA 66.1(6)"Canadian renewable and conservation expense" for the binding Technical Guide available from Natural Resources Canada.

For general comments see VIEWS docs 2005-0113771E5; 2016-0635031E5 (geothermal energy); 2018-0747311E5 (geothermal energy — various expenses). CRA considered that a wide-area wind resource exploration program to develop a wind energy production capability database was a "project" under Reg. 1219(1): VIEWS doc 2002-0119355. A feasibility study, pre-feasibility study, negotiation and site approval costs, and certain site preparation costs not directly related to installing equipment can all qualify: docs 2003-002382A, 2003-0042215, 2006-0180041E5. The taxpayer must own the property used in the project: doc 2003-0039525. Where the project does not proceed, see doc 2005-0110371E5. See also docs 2005-0122351E5 (equipment to make interconnection to high-voltage transmission line), 2005-0143071E5 and 2006-0168291E5 (small-scale hydro-electric installations), 2008-0296181E5 (tidal energy), 2011-0427561E5 (amended 1219(1)(f) — geothermal well drilling and completion costs); 2015-0587981E5 (ground-source heat pump — Technical Guide now determines qualification).

See also Notes to Reg. 1219(3) and at end of Reg. 1219.

Reg. 1219(1)(f)(ii) and (h) added by 2017 budget bill #2, for expenses incurred after March 21, 2017.

Reg. 1219(1) earlier amended by 2010 budget bill #2 (for expenses incurred after May 2, 2010), P.C. 2006-439, 2005-1510.

(2) [Exclusions] — A Canadian renewable and conservation expense does not include any expense that

(a) is described in paragraphs 20(1)(c), (d), (e) or (e.1) of the Act; or

(b) is incurred by a taxpayer directly or indirectly and is

(i) for the acquisition of, or the use of or the right to use, land, except as provided by paragraph (1)(b), (c) or (d),

(ii) for grading or levelling land or for landscaping, except as provided by paragraph (1)(b),

(iii) payable to a non-resident person or a partnership other than a Canadian partnership (other than an expense described in paragraph (1)(g)),

(iv) included in the capital cost of property that, but for this section, would be depreciable property (other than property that would be included in Class 14.1 of Schedule II), except as provided by paragraph (1)(b), (d), (e), (f), (g) or (h),

(v) included in the capital cost of property that, but for this section, would be property included in Class 14.1 of Schedule II, except as provided by any of paragraphs (1)(a) to (e) or subparagraph (h)(ii),

(vi) included in the cost of inventory of the taxpayer,

(vii) an expenditure on or in respect of scientific research and experimental development,

(viii) a Canadian development expense or a Canadian oil and gas property expense,

(ix) incurred, for a project, in respect of any time at or after the earliest time at which a property described in Class 43.1 or 43.2 in Schedule II was used in the project for the purpose of earning income,

(x) incurred in respect of the administration or management of a business of the taxpayer, or

(xi) a cost attributable to the period of the construction, renovation or alteration of depreciable property, other than property described in Class 43.1 or 43.2 in Schedule II, that relates to

(A) the construction, renovation or alteration of the property, except as provided by paragraph (1)(b), (f), (g) or (h), or

(B) the ownership of land during the period, except as provided by paragraph (1)(b), (c) or (d).

Notes: For examples of the exclusions in Reg. 1219(2), see VIEWS doc 2007-0250131E5.

For the meaning of "indirectly" in (b) opening words, see Notes to 17.1(1). "Land" in (b)(i) includes buildings: see ITA 70(5.2) Notes.

Reg. 1219(2)(b)(iv), (v) and (b)(xi)(A) amended by 2017 budget bill #2 to add references to 1219(1)(h), for expenses incurred after March 21, 2017.

Reg. 1219(2)(b)(iv), (v) amended by 2016 budget bill #2, effective 2017, as part of changing the eligible capital property rules to CCA Class 14.1 (see Notes to ITA 20(1)(b)). Before 2017, read:

> (iv) included in the capital cost of property that, but for this section, would be depreciable property, except as provided by paragraph (1)(b), (d), (e), (f) or (g),

> (v) an expenditure that, but for this section, would be an eligible capital expenditure, except as provided by any of paragraphs (1)(a) to (e),

Reg. 1219(2)(b)(ix) and (xi) amended by P.C. 2006-329, effective Feb. 23, 2005, to add reference to Class 43.2.

(3) ["Test wind turbine"]

(3) ["Test wind turbine"] — For the purpose of paragraph (1)(g), "test wind turbine" means a fixed location device that is a wind energy conversion system that would, if this Part were read without reference to this section, be property included in Class 43.1 in Schedule II because of subparagraph (d)(v) of that Class, or in Class 43.2 in Schedule II because of paragraph (b) of that Class, in respect of which the Minister, in consultation with the Minister of Natural Resources, determines that

(a) the device is installed as part of a wind farm project of the taxpayer at which the electrical energy produced from wind by the device, and by all other test wind turbines that are part of the project, does not exceed

(i) one third of the project's planned nameplate capacity if

(A) the Minister of Natural Resources determines that the project's planned nameplate capacity is limited from an engineering or scientific perspective, and

(B) the project's planned nameplate capacity does not exceed six megawatts, or

(ii) 20% of the project's planned nameplate capacity, in any other case;

(b) the project does not share with any other project a point of interconnection to an electrical energy transmission or distribution system;

(c) if the project does not have a point of interconnection to an electrical energy transmission or distribution system, the project has a point of interconnection to an electrical system

(i) of the taxpayer

(A) which system is more than 10 kilometres from any transmission system and from any distribution system, and

(B) from which system at least 90% of the electrical energy produced by the project is used in a business carried on by the taxpayer, or

(ii) of another person or partnership that deals at arm's length with the taxpayer

(A) which system is more than 10 kilometres from any transmission system and from any distribution system, and

(B) from which system at least 90% of the electrical energy produced by the project is used in a business carried on by the other person or partnership;

(d) the primary purpose for installing the device is to test the level of electrical energy produced by the device from wind at the place of installation;

(e) no other test wind turbine is installed within 1500 metres of the device; and

(f) no other wind energy conversion system is installed within 1500 metres of the device until the level of electrical energy produced from wind by the device has been tested for at least 120 calendar days.

Notes: Taxpayers wishing to determine in advance whether a proposed installation would be a "test wind turbine" should contact CRA Income Tax Rulings Directorate, Place de Ville, Tower A, 320 Queen St., Ottawa K1A 0L5, telephone (613) 957-8953.

See Income Tax Folio S3-F8-C2 ¶2.38-2.41. For examples of CRA approving test wind turbines under Reg. 1219(3), see VIEWS docs 2003-0034773, 2003-0045825, 2004-0057841E5, 2004-0068581E5, 2004-0098901E5, 2004-0099421E5, 2004-0099571E5, 2004-0101621E5, 2004-0103081E5, 2004-0108461E5, 2005-0124801E5, 2005-0149411E5, 2005-0149421E5, 2005-0152451E5, 2005-0161391E5, 2005-0140751E5, 2005-0163751E5, 2006-0170971E5 (wind turbines did not qualify), 2006-0171351E5, 2006-0179851E5, 2006-0183861E5, 2006-0201271E5, 2006-0201272E5, 2006-0208831E5, 2006-0209621E5, 2006-0212171E5, 2007-0242891E5, 2007-0254591E5, 2007-0259461E5, 2009-0307501E5, 2009-0324631E5, 2009-0351571E5, 2010-0379651E5, 2012-0439171E5, 2012-0473301E5, 2013-0490631E5, 2015-0592441E5, 2017-0695101E5. See also 2004-0103601E5 interpreting Reg. 1219(3)(d) and (f); 2005-0114331E5 re manufacturer warranties endangering the flow-through share status of shares issued to fund the acquisition of the turbines; 2010-0373951E5 and 2011-0423451E5 (general description of CCA on wind turbines). (Wind turbines do not qualify for investment tax credits: 2011-0409111E5.)

The "nameplate capacity" in Reg. 1219(3)(a) can include leased wind turbines: VIEWS doc 2004-0109141E5.

Reg. 1219(3)(a)(i)(A) amended by P.C. 2007-849, effective June 13, 2007.

Opening words of Reg. 1219(3) amended by P.C. 2006-329, effective Feb. 23, 2005.

Reg. 1219(3)(a), (b) replaced with (a)-(f) by P.C. 2005-1510, effective for expenses incurred after July 25, 2002, or earlier by election. See Finance news release of July 26, 2002 for description of the amendments.

(4) [Wind energy conversion system]

(4) [Wind energy conversion system] — For greater certainty, a Canadian Renewable and Conservation Expense includes an expense incurred by a taxpayer to acquire a fixed location device that is a wind energy conversion system only if the device is described in paragraph (1)(g).

Notes: Reg. 1219(4) added by P.C. 2005-1510, effective for expenses incurred after April 8, 2005.

(5) [Compliance with environmental law]

(5) [Compliance with environmental law] — A Canadian renewable and conservation expense does not include an expense incurred by a taxpayer at any time that is in respect of a geothermal project

(a) that at that time is described in paragraph (1)(h); and

(b) in respect of which the taxpayer is not at that time in compliance with the requirements of all environmental laws, by-laws and regulations of

(i) Canada,

(ii) a province or a municipality in Canada, or

(iii) a municipal or public body performing a function of government in Canada.

Related Provisions: Reg. 1104(17) — Same rule for clean-energy CCA.

Notes: For the meaning of "municipal or public body..." in (b)(iii), see Notes to ITA 149(1)(c).

Reg. 1219(5) added by 2017 budget bill #2, for expenses incurred after March 21, 2017.

Related Provisions [Reg. 1219]: Reg. 1102(1)(a.1) — CRCE ineligible for capital cost allowance.

Notes [Reg. 1219]: Reg. 1219 added by P.C. 2000-1331, for expenses incurred after December 5, 1996. CRCE is deductible by being included in CEE: see 66.1(6)"Canadian exploration expense"(g.1).

See Notes to ITA 66.1(6)"Canadian renewable and conservation expense".

Definitions [Reg. 1219]: "arm's length" — ITA 251(1); "business" — ITA 248(1); "Canadian development expense" — ITA 66.2(5), 248(1); "Canadian oil and gas property expense" — ITA 66.4(5), 248(1); "Canadian partnership" — ITA 102(1), 248(1); "depreciable property" — ITA 13(21), 248(1); "eligible capital expenditure" — ITA 14(5), 248(1); "inventory" — ITA 248(1); "land" — see ITA 70(5.2) Notes; "Minister" — ITA 248(1); "Minister of Natural Resources" — *Department of Natural Resources Act* s. 3; "non-resident" — ITA 248(1); "partnership" — see ITA 96(1) Notes; "person", "property" — ITA 248(1); "province" — *Interpretation Act* 35(1); "regulation" — ITA 248(1); "resource" — Reg. 1206(1); "scientific research and experimental development", "taxpayer" — ITA 248(1); "test wind turbine" — Reg. 1219(3).

Income Tax Folios [Reg. 1219]: S3-F8-C1: Principal-business corporations in the resource industries [replaces IT-400].

PART XIII — [1300–1302] ELECTIONS IN RESPECT OF TAXPAYERS CEASING TO BE RESIDENT IN CANADA

1300. Elections to defer capital gains — **(1)** Any election by an individual under paragraph 48(1)(c) of the Act shall be made by filing with the Minister the prescribed form on or before the day on or before which the return of income for the year in which the taxpayer ceased to be resident in Canada is required to be filed under section 150 of the Act.

(2) Any election by a Canadian corporation under paragraph 48(1)(c) of the Act shall be made by filing with the Minister, on or before the day on or before which the return of income for the year in which the corporation ceased to be resident in Canada is required to be filed under section 150 of the Act, the following documents in duplicate:

(a) the form prescribed by the Minister;

(b) where the directors of the corporation are legally entitled to administer the affairs of the corporation, a certified copy of their resolution authorizing the election to be made; and

(c) where the directors of the corporation are not legally entitled to administer the affairs of the corporation, a certified copy of the authorization of the making of the election by the person or persons legally entitled to administer the affairs of the corporation.

Notes: Reg. 1300(1) and (2) are expected to be amended to refer to ITA 128.1(4)(b)(iv), which was enacted by the 1993 technical bill in place of ITA 48(1)(c).

Definitions [Reg. 1300]: "Canadian corporation" — ITA 89(1), 248(1); "corporation" — ITA 248(1), *Interpretation Act* 35(1); "individual", "Minister", "person", "prescribed" — ITA 248(1); "resident in Canada" — ITA 250; "taxpayer" — ITA 248(1).

Interpretation Bulletins: IT-434R: Rental of real property by individual; IT-451R: Deemed disposition and acquisition on ceasing to be or becoming resident in Canada.

Forms: T1244: Election, under subsec. 220(4.5) of the *ITA*, to defer the payment of tax on income re deemed disposition of property.

1301. Elections to defer payment of taxes — **(1)** Any election by an individual under subsection 159(4) of the Act shall be made by filing with the Minister the prescribed form on or before the day on or before which the return of income for the year in which the taxpayer ceased to be resident in Canada is required to be filed under section 150 of the Act.

(2) Any election by a Canadian corporation under subsection 159(4) of the Act shall be made by filing with the Minister, on or before the day on or before which the return of income for the year in which the corporation ceased to be resident in Canada is required to be filed under section 150 of the Act, the following documents in duplicate:

(a) the form prescribed by the Minister;

(b) where the directors of the corporation are legally entitled to administer the affairs of the corporation, a certified copy of their resolution authorizing the election to be made; and

(c) where the directors of the corporation are not legally entitled to administer the affairs of the corporation, a certified copy of the authorization of the making of the election by the person or persons legally entitled to administer the affairs of the corporation.

Definitions [Reg. 1301]: "Canadian corporation" — ITA 89(1), 248(1); "corporation" — ITA 248(1), *Interpretation Act* 35(1); "individual", "Minister", "person", "prescribed" — ITA 248(1); "resident in Canada" — ITA 250; "taxpayer" — ITA 248(1).

1302. Elections to realize capital gains — Any election by an individual under paragraph 48(1)(a) of the Act shall be made by filing with the Minister the prescribed form on or before the day on or before which the return of income for the year in which the taxpayer ceased to be resident in Canada is required to be filed under section 150 of the Act.

Notes: Finance has confirmed (June 2020) that Reg. 1302 is to be amended to refer to ITA 128.1(4)(d) enacted by the 1993 technical bill, in place of ITA 48(1)(a).

Definitions [Reg. 1302]: "individual", "Minister", "prescribed" — ITA 248(1); "resident in Canada" — ITA 250; "taxpayer" — ITA 248(1).

PART XIV — [1400–1408] INSURANCE BUSINESS POLICY RESERVES

DIVISION 1 — POLICY RESERVES

1400. Non-life insurance business — **(1)** **[Policy reserve]** — For the purpose of paragraph 20(7)(c) of the Act, the amount prescribed in respect of an insurer for a taxation year is

(a) the amount determined under subsection (3) in respect of the insurer for the year, where that amount is greater than nil, and

(b) nil, in any other case.

(2) **[Negative reserves]** — For the purpose of paragraph 12(1)(e.1) of the Act, the amount prescribed in respect of an insurer for a taxation year is

(a) the absolute value of the amount determined under subsection (3) in respect of the insurer for the year, where that amount is less than nil, and

(b) nil, in any other case.

Related Provisions: Reg. 1402.1 — Negative amounts.

(3) **[Amount of reserve]** — For the purposes of paragraphs (1)(a) and (2)(a), the amount determined under this subsection in respect of an insurer for a taxation year is the amount, which may be positive or negative, determined by the formula

$$A + B + C + D + E + F + G$$
$$+ H + I + J + K + L$$

where

A is the total of all amounts each of which is the unearned portion at the end of the year of the premium paid by the policyholder for a policy, (other than a policy that insures a risk in respect of

(a) a financial loss of a lender on a loan made on the security of real property,

(b) a home warranty,

(c) a lease guarantee, or

(d) an extended motor vehicle warranty),

which is determined by apportioning the premium equally over the period to which that premium relates;

B is the total of all amounts each of which is an amount determined in respect of a policy referred to in paragraph (a), (b), (c) or (d) of the description of A equal to the lesser of

(a) the amount of the reported reserve of the insurer at the end of the year in respect of the unearned portion at the end of the year of the premium paid by the policyholder for the policy, and

(b) a reasonable amount as a reserve determined as at the end of the year in respect of the unearned portion at the end of the year of the premium paid by the policyholder for the policy;

C is the total of all amounts each of which is the amount in respect of a policy, where all or a portion of a risk under the policy was reinsured, equal to the unearned portion at the end of the year of a reinsurance commission in respect of the policy determined by apportioning the reinsurance commission equally over the period to which it relates;

D is the amount, in respect of policies (other than policies in respect of which an amount can be determined under the description of E) under which

(a) a claim that was incurred before the end of the year has been reported to the insurer before the end of the year and in respect of which the insurer is, or may be, required to make a payment or incur an expense after the year, or

(b) there may be a claim incurred before the end of the year that has not been reported to the insurer before the end of the year,

equal to 95% of the lesser of

(c) the total of the reported reserves of the insurer at the end of the year in respect of such claims or possible claims, and

(d) the total of the claim liabilities of the insurer at the end of the year in respect of such claims or possible claims;

E   is the amount, in respect of policies under which

(a) a claim that was incurred before the end of the year has been reported to the insurer before the end of the year,

(b) the claim is in respect of damages for personal injury or death, and

(c) the insurer has agreed to a structured settlement of the claim,

equal to the lesser of

(d) the total of the reported reserves of the insurer at the end of the year in respect of such claims, and

(e) the total of the claim liabilities of the insurer at the end of the year in respect of such claims;

F   is an additional amount, in respect of policies that insure a fidelity risk, a surety risk, a nuclear risk, or a risk related to a financial loss of a lender on a loan made on the security of real property, equal to the lesser of

(a) the total of the reported reserves of the insurer at the end of the year in respect of such risks (other than an amount included in determining the value of A, B, C, D, E, G, H, I, J, K or L), and

(b) a reasonable amount as a reserve determined as at the end of the year in respect of such risks (other than an amount included in determining the value of A, B, C, D, E, G, H, I, J, K or L);

G   is the amount of a guarantee fund at the end of the year provided for under an agreement in writing between the insurer and Her Majesty in right of Canada under which Her Majesty has agreed to guarantee the obligations of the insurer under a policy that insures a risk related to a financial loss of a lender on a loan made on the security of real property;

H   is the amount in respect of risks under pre-1996 non-cancellable or guaranteed renewable accident and sickness policies equal to

(a) where the amounts determined under subparagraphs (i) and (ii) are greater than nil, the lesser of

(i) the total of the reported reserves of the insurer at the end of the year in respect of such risks (other than an amount included in determining the value of A, B, C, D, E, F, G, I, J, K or L), and

(ii) a reasonable amount as a reserve determined as at the end of the year in respect of such risks (other than an amount included in determining the value of A, B, C, D, E, F, G, I, J, K or L), and

(b) nil, in any other case;

I   is the amount in respect of risks under post-1995 non-cancellable or guaranteed renewable accident and sickness policies equal to the lesser of

(a) the total of the reported reserves of the insurer at the end of the year in respect of such risks (other than an amount included in determining the value of A, B, C, D, E, F, G, H, J, K or L), and

(b) the total of the policy liabilities of the insurer at the end of the year in respect of such risks (other than an amount included in determining the value of A, B, C, D, E, F, G, H, J, K or L);

J   is the total of all amounts (other than an amount deductible under subsection 140(1) of the Act) each of which is the amount, which is the least of P, Q and R, in respect of a dividend, refund of premiums or refund of premium deposits provided for under the terms of a group accident and sickness insurance policy that will be

(a) used by the insurer to reduce or eliminate a future adverse claims experience under the policy,

(b) paid or unconditionally credited to the policyholder by the insurer, or

(c) applied in discharge, in whole or in part, of a liability of the policyholder to pay premiums to the insurer under the policy,

where

P   is a reasonable amount as a reserve determined as at the end of the year in respect of the dividend, refund of premiums or refund of premium deposits,

Q   is 25% of the amount of the premium payable under the terms of the policy for the 12-month period ending

(i) if the policy is terminated in the year, on the day the policy is terminated, and

(ii) in any other case, at the end of the year, and

R   is the reported reserve of the insurer at the end of the year in respect of the dividend, refund of premiums or refund of premium deposits; and

K   is the total of all amounts each of which is the amount, in respect of a policy under which a portion of the particular amount paid or payable by the policyholder for the policy before the end of the year is deducted under paragraph 1408(4)(b), equal to the portion of that particular amount that the insurer has determined will, after the end of the year, be returned to, or credited to the account of the policyholder on the termination of the policy; and

L   is an amount in respect of policies that insure earthquake risks in Canada equal to the lesser of

(a) the portion of the reported reserve of the insurer at the end of the year in respect of those risks that is attributable to accumulations from premiums in respect of those risks (other than an amount included in determining the value of A, B, C, D, E, F, G, H, I, J, or K), and

(b) a reasonable amount as a reserve determined as at the end of the year in respect of those risks (other than an amount included in determining the value of A, B, C, D, E, F, G, H, I, J, or K).

Related Provisions: Reg. 1400(4) — Where actuarial principles not required for element D or E; Reg. 1402 — All amounts to be net of reinsurance ceded; Reg. 1402.1 — Amounts in Reg. 1400 may be less than zero.

Notes: For interpretation of D see VIEWS doc 2006-0169571I7. For E (structured settlement), see ITA 56(1)(d) Notes. L allows earthquake reserves, as proposed in the 1998 federal budget.

Reg. 1400(3) amended by P.C. 2002-346, for tax years that begin after 1999.

(4) [Elements D and E] — Where the relevant authority does not require an insurer (other than an insurer that is required by law to report to the Superintendent of Financial Institutions) to determine its liabilities in respect of claims referred to in the description of D or E in subsection (3) in accordance with actuarial principles,

(a) the value of D is deemed to be 95% of the amount determined under paragraph (c) of the description of D; and

(b) the value of E is deemed to be the amount determined under paragraph (d) of the description of E.

Related Provisions: ITA 95(2)(j.2)(ii) — Operator deemed to be required by law to report to regulatory authority.

(5) [Transitional — Before 2001] — [Repealed]

Notes: Reg. 1400(5) repealed by P.C. 2002-346, for taxation years that end after 2000.

Notes [Reg. 1400]: Reg. 1400 replaced with Reg. 1400(1)–(5) by P.C. 1999-1154, last change effective for 1998 and later taxation years. Previously amended by P.C. 1996-1452.

Regulations

Definitions [Reg. 1400]: "amount" — ITA 248(1), Reg. 1402.1; "claim liability" — Reg. 1408(1); "dividend" — ITA 248(1); "extended motor vehicle warranty" — Reg. 1408(1); "Her Majesty" — *Interpretation Act* 35(1); "insurance policy", "insurer", "life insurer" — ITA 248(1); "month" — *Interpretation Act* 35(1); "net premium" — Reg. 1408(1); "non-cancellable or guaranteed renewable accident and sickness policy" — Reg. 1408(1), (6); "policy liability", "post-1995 non-cancellable or guaranteed renewable" — Reg. 1408(1); "pre-1996 non-cancellable or guaranteed renewable" — Reg. 1408(1), (7); "premium paid by the policyholder" — Reg. 1408(4); "prescribed" — ITA 248(1); "reinsurance commission", "relevant authority" — Reg. 1408(1); "reported" — Reg. 1408(8); "reported reserve" — Reg. 1408(1); "security" — *Interpretation Act* 35(1); "taxation year" — ITA 249; "writing" — *Interpretation Act* 35(1).

DIVISION 2 — AMOUNTS DETERMINED

1401. (1) [Policy reserves] — For the purposes of applying section 307 and subsection 211.1(3) of the Act at any time, the amounts determined under this subsection are,

(a) in respect of a deposit administration fund policy, the total of the insurer's liabilities under the policy calculated in the manner that

(i) if the insurer is required to file an annual report with its relevant authority for a period that includes that time, is required to be used in preparing that report, and

(ii) in any other case, is required to be used in preparing its annual financial statements for the period that includes that time;

(b) in respect of a group term life insurance policy that provides insurance for a period not exceeding 12 months, the unearned portion of the premium paid by the policyholder for the policy at that time determined by apportioning the premium paid by the policyholder equally over the period to which that premium pertains;

(c) in respect of a life insurance policy, other than a policy referred to in paragraph (a) or (b), the greater of

(i) the amount determined by the formula

$$A - B$$

where

A is

(A) if the policy is issued after 2016 and is not an annuity contract, the cash surrender value of the policy at that time determined without reference to surrender charges, and

(B) in any other case, the cash surrender value of the policy at that time, and

B is the total of all amounts each of which is an amount payable at that time in respect of a policy loan in respect of the policy, and

(ii) the amount determined by the formula

$$A - (B + C)$$

where

A is

(A) if the policy is issued after 2016 and is not an annuity contract, the net premium reserve in respect of the policy at that time, and

(B) in any other case, the present value at that time of the future benefits provided by the policy,

B is

(A) if the policy is issued after 2016 and is not an annuity contract, nil, and

(B) in any other case, the present value at that time of any future modified net premiums in respect of the policy, and

C is the total of all amounts each of which is an amount payable at that time in respect of a policy loan in respect of the policy;

(c.1) in respect of a group life insurance policy, the amount (other than an amount in respect of which a deduction may be claimed by the insurer under subsection 140(1) of the Act because of subparagraph 138(3)(a)(v) of the Act in computing the insurer's income for its taxation year that includes that time) in respect of a dividend, refund of premiums or refund of premium deposits provided for under the terms of the policy that will be used by the insurer to reduce or eliminate a future adverse claims experience under the policy or that will be paid or unconditionally credited to the policyholder by the insurer or applied in discharge, in whole or in part, of a liability of the policyholder to pay premiums to the insurer, which is the least of

(i) a reasonable amount in respect of such a dividend, refund of premiums or refund of premium deposits,

(ii) 25% of the amount of the premium payable under the terms of the policy for the 12-month period ending at that time, and

(iii) the amount of the reserve or liability in respect of such a dividend, refund of premiums or refund of premium deposits that

(A) if the insurer is required to file an annual report with its relevant authority for a period that includes that time, is used in preparing that report, and

(B) in any other case, is used in preparing its annual financial statements for the period that includes that time; and

(d) in respect of a policy, other than a policy referred to in paragraph (a), in respect of a benefit, risk or guarantee that is

(i) an accidental death benefit,

(ii) a disability benefit,

(iii) an additional risk as a result of insuring a substandard life,

(iv) an additional risk in respect of the conversion of a term policy or the conversion of the benefits under a group policy into another policy after that time,

(v) an additional risk under a settlement option,

(vi) an additional risk under a guaranteed insurability benefit,

(vii) a guarantee in respect of a segregated fund policy, or

(viii) any other benefit that is ancillary to the policy, subject to the prior approval of the Minister on the advice of the Superintendent of Insurance for Canada,

but is not

(ix) a benefit, risk or guarantee in respect of which an amount has been claimed under any other paragraph of this subsection by the insurer as a deduction in computing its income for its taxation year that includes that time,

equal to the lesser of

(x) a reasonable amount in respect of the benefit, risk or guarantee, and

(xi) the reserve in respect of the benefit, risk or guarantee that

(A) if the insurer is required to file an annual report with its relevant authority for a period that includes that time, is used in preparing that report, and

(B) in any other case, is used in preparing its annual financial statements for the period that includes that time.

(d.1), (d.2), (e) [Repealed]

Related Provisions: ITA 95(2)(j.2)(ii)(A) — Operator deemed subject to regulatory authority for FAPI purposes; ITA 148(11) — Loss of pre-2016 grandfathering; ITA 211.1(3) — Effect of Reg. 1401(1) on Part XII.3 tax; ITA 257 — Whether formula can calculate to less than zero; Reg. 1401(4) — Rules for applying para. (1)(c) for Reg. 307; Reg. 1401(5) — Rules for applying para. (1)(c) for ITA 211.1(3); Reg. 1402 — All amounts to be net of reinsurance ceded; Reg. 1403(1) — Rules for computation; Reg. 1408 — Definitions.

Notes: For interpretation of Reg. 1401(1)(c) see VIEWS doc 2005-0145821E5.

Reg. 1401(1) amended by 2014 budget bill #2 (effective Dec. 16, 2014), P.C. 2002-346, 1999-1154, P.C. 1994-940.

(1.1) [Repealed]

Notes: Reg. 1401(1.1), which limited deductions to pre-1996 policies, repealed by 2008 budget bill #2, for taxation years that began after Sept. 2006.

Reg. 1401(1.1) added by P.C. 1999-1154, effective for 1996 and later taxation years. Policy reserves for post-1995 policies are now covered in Reg. 1404.

(2) [Segregated funds] — For the purposes of subsection (1), (except in respect of subparagraph (d)(vii) thereof), any amount claimed by an insurer for the year shall not include an amount in respect of a liability of a segregated fund (within the meaning assigned "segregated fund" by section 138.1 of the Act).

(3) [Definitions] — The following definitions apply in this section.

"benefit on death" includes the amount of an endowment benefit but does not include

(a) any additional amount payable as a result of accidental death; and

(b) where interest, if any, on an amount held on deposit by an insurer is included in computing the income of a policyholder for a taxation year, the amount held on deposit and interest on the deposit.

Related Provisions: Reg. 310"benefit on death" — Definition applies to Reg. 300–310.

Notes: See Notes at end of Reg. 1401(3).

"coverage", under a life insurance policy, means each life insurance (other than a fund value benefit) under the policy in respect of a specific life, or two or more specific lives jointly insured, and in respect of which a particular schedule of premium or cost of insurance rates applies. For greater certainty, each such insurance is a separate coverage.

"fund value benefit", under a life insurance policy at any time, means a benefit under the policy the amount of which is the amount by which the fund value of the policy at that time exceeds the total of all amounts each of which is a fund value of a coverage under the policy at that time.

"fund value of a coverage", under a life insurance policy at any time, means the total of all amounts each of which is the amount at that time of an investment account in respect of the policy that reduces the net amount at risk as determined for the purpose of calculating the cost of insurance charges for the coverage during the period over which those charges are incurred or would be incurred if they were to apply until the termination of the coverage.

"fund value of a policy", at any time, means the total of all amounts each of which is the amount at that time of an investment account in respect of the policy and, for greater certainty,

(a) includes, where interest, if any, on an amount held on deposit by an insurer is not included in computing the income of a policyholder for a taxation year, the amount held on deposit and interest on the deposit; and

(b) excludes, where interest, if any, on an amount held on deposit by an insurer is included in computing the income of a policyholder for a taxation year, the amount held on deposit and interest on the deposit.

Notes: In the Aug. 23/13 draft, this was "fund value of a life insurance policy".

"future benefits to be provided", in respect of a coverage under a life insurance policy at any time, means

(a) if there is a fund value of the coverage at that time, each benefit on death that would be payable under the coverage at a particular time after that time determined as if the amount of the benefit were equal to the amount by which the benefit on death at that time exceeds the fund value of the coverage at that time; and

(b) in any other case, each benefit on death payable under the coverage at a particular time after that time.

"future net premiums or cost of insurance charges", in respect of a coverage at any time, means

(a) for the purposes of paragraph (a) of the description of C in the definition "net premium reserve" in this subsection, each amount determined by the formula

$$A \times B/C$$

where

A   is future premiums or cost of insurance charges in respect of the coverage at that time,

B   is the present value at the date of issue of the coverage of future benefits to be provided in respect of the coverage on that date, and

C   is the present value at the date of issue of the coverage of future premiums or cost of insurance charges in respect of the coverage on that date; and

(b) for the purposes of paragraph (b) of the description of C in the definition "net premium reserve" in this subsection,

(i) each amount determined by the formula

$$A \times (B + C)/(D + E)$$

where

A   is future premiums or cost of insurance charges in respect of the coverage at that time,

B   is the present value at the date of issue of the coverage of future benefits to be provided in respect of the coverage on the particular day that is one year after that date and, if the coverage has a fund value on that date, determined as if the fund value of the coverage were nil on that date,

C   is the present value at the date of issue of the coverage of future benefits to be provided in respect of the coverage on the particular day that is two years after that date and, if the coverage has a fund value on that date, determined as if the fund value of the coverage were nil on that date,

D   is the present value at the date of issue of the coverage of future premiums or cost of insurance charges in respect of the coverage on the particular day that is one year after that date and, if the coverage has a fund value on that date, determined as if the fund value of the coverage were nil on that date, and

E   is the present value at the date of issue of the coverage of future premiums or cost of insurance charges in respect of the coverage on the particular day that is two years after that date and, if the coverage has a fund value on that date, determined as if the fund value of the coverage were nil on that date, and

(ii) notwithstanding subparagraph (i), in respect of the second year of the coverage, the amount determined by the formula

$$(A + B)/2$$

where

A   is the amount determined under subparagraph (i), and

B   is the amount of a one-year term insurance premium or cost of insurance charge that would be payable in respect of the coverage if the benefit on death were equal to the amount by which the benefit on death at the end of the first year of the coverage exceeds the fund value of the coverage, if any, at the end of the first year of the coverage.

"future premiums or cost of insurance charges", in respect of a coverage at any time, means

(a) if there is a fund value of the coverage at that time, each cost of insurance charge in respect of the coverage that would be in-

Regulations

curred at a particular time after that time determined as if the net amount at risk under the coverage after that time were equal to the amount by which the benefit on death under the coverage at that time exceeds the fund value of the coverage at that time; and

(b) in any other case, each premium in respect of the coverage that is fixed and determined on the date of issue of the coverage that will become payable, or each cost of insurance charge in respect of the coverage that will be incurred, as the case may be, at a particular time after that time.

"interpolation time", of a coverage, means the time that is the earlier of

(a) the time that is eight years after the date of issue of the coverage; and

(b) the first time at which no premiums are payable or cost of insurance charges are incurred, as the case may be, in respect of the coverage.

"net premium reserve", in respect of a life insurance policy at any time, means the amount determined by the formula

$$A + B + C$$

where

A is the total of all amounts, if any, each of which is the present value at that time of the fund value of a coverage under the policy at that time;

B is the amount, if any, of the fund value benefit under the policy at that time; and

C is

(a) in applying paragraph (1)(c) for the purposes of section 307, the total of all amounts each of which is, in respect of a coverage under the policy,

(i) if that time is at or after the interpolation time of the coverage, the amount determined by the formula

$$D - E$$

where

D is the present value at that time of future benefits to be provided in respect of the coverage at that time, and

E is the present value at that time of future net premiums or cost of insurance charges in respect of the coverage at that time, and

(ii) if that time is before the interpolation time of the coverage, the amount determined by the formula

$$F/G \times (H - I)$$

where

F is the number of years that the coverage has been in effect as of that time,

G is the number of years that the coverage would have been in effect if that time were the interpolation time,

H is the present value at the interpolation time of future benefits to be provided in respect of the coverage at the interpolation time and, if the coverage has a fund value at that time, determined as if the amount of the benefit on death under the coverage at the interpolation time were equal to the amount by which the benefit on death at that time exceeds the fund value of the coverage at that time, and

I is the present value at the interpolation time of future net premiums or cost of insurance charges in respect of the coverage at the interpolation time and, if the coverage has a fund value at that time, determined as if the net amount at risk under the coverage after the interpolation time were equal to the amount by which the benefit on death at that time exceeds the fund value of the coverage at that time, and

(b) in applying paragraph (1)(c) for the purposes of subsection 211.1(3) of the Act, the total of all amounts each of which is, in respect of a coverage under the policy, the amount determined by the formula

$$J - K$$

where

J is the present value at that time of future benefits to be provided in respect of the coverage at that time, and

K is the present value at that time of future net premiums or cost of insurance charges in respect of the coverage at that time.

Related Provisions: ITA 257 — Whether formula can calculate to less than zero.

"policy anniversary" has the same meaning as in section 310.

Notes: Reg. 1401(3) added by 2014 budget bill #2, effective December 16, 2014.

Former Reg. 1401(3), (4), on group life insurance policies and unpaid claims reserves, repealed by 2008 budget bill #2, for taxation years that begin after Sept. 2006.

(4) [Application to Reg. 307] — In applying paragraph (1)(c) for the purposes of section 307 in respect of a life insurance policy (other than an annuity contract) issued after 2016, the following rules apply:

(a) in computing present values

(i) an annual interest rate of 3.5% is to be used, and

(ii) mortality rates are to be used;

(b) in determining the mortality rates that apply to a life insured under a coverage under the policy,

(i) if a single life is insured under the coverage,

(A) the age that is to be used is the age of the life insured at the time at which the coverage was issued, or that which is attained on the birthday of the life insured nearest to the time at which the coverage was issued, depending on the method used by the insurer that issued the policy in determining the premium or cost of insurance rates in respect of the life insured,

(B) if the life insured was determined by the insurer that issued the policy to be a standard life at the time the coverage was issued, the *Proposed CIA Mortality Tables, 1986–1992* included in the *May 17, 1995 Canadian Institute of Actuaries Memorandum*, extended to include select mortality rates from age 81 to age 90 developed using the methodology used by the Canadian Institute of Actuaries to derive select mortality rates from age 71 to age 80, applicable for an individual who has the same relevant characteristics as the life insured, are to be used, and

(C) if the life insured was determined by the insurer that issued the policy to be a substandard life at the time the coverage was issued, the mortality rates that apply are to be equal to, depending on the method used by the insurer for the purpose of determining the premium or cost of insurance rates in respect of the coverage,

(I) the lesser of one and the product of the rating attributed to the life by the insurer and the mortality rates that would be determined under clause (B) if the life were not a substandard life, or

(II) the mortality rates that would have been determined under clause (B) had the life insured been a standard life and the age of the life insured been the age used by the life insurer for the purpose of determining the premium or cost of insurance rates in respect of the coverage, and

(ii) if two or more lives are jointly insured under the coverage, the mortality rates to be used are those determined by applying the methodology used by the insurer that issued the policy to estimate the mortality rates of the lives jointly insured for the purpose of determining the premium or cost of insurance rates in respect of the coverage to the *Proposed*

CIA Mortality Tables, 1986–1992 included in the *May 17, 1995 Canadian Institute of Actuaries Memorandum*, extended to include select mortality rates from age 81 to age 90 developed using the methodology used by the Canadian Institute of Actuaries to derive select mortality rates from age 71 to age 80; and

(c) in determining the net premium reserve in respect of the policy, the present value of future net premiums or cost of insurance charges is to be calculated as if a premium or cost of insurance charge payable or incurred on a policy anniversary were payable or incurred, as the case may be, one day after the policy anniversary.

Notes: Reg. 1401(4) added by 2014 budget bill #2, effective Dec. 16, 2014. See also Notes to Reg. 1401(3).

(5) [Application to ITA 211.1(3)] — In applying paragraph (1)(c) for the purposes of subsection 211.1(3) of the Act in respect of a life insurance policy (other than an annuity contract)

(a) if the policy is issued after 2016,

(i) the rates of interest, mortality and lapses described in subsection 1403(1) are to be used in computing present values, determined as if

(A) subsections 1403(2) to (8) did not apply, and

(B) the reference to "premiums for the policy" in paragraph 1403(1)(e) were read as a reference to "premiums or cost of insurance charges in respect of a coverage under the policy",

(ii) subparagraph (1)(c)(i) is to be read without reference to "determined without reference to surrender charges", and

(iii) in determining the net premium reserve in respect of the policy, the present value of future net premiums or cost of insurance charges is to be calculated as if a premium or cost of insurance charge payable or incurred on a policy anniversary were payable or incurred, as the case may be, one day after the policy anniversary; and

(b) if the policy is issued before 2017 and at a particular time after 2016 life insurance — in respect of a life, or two or more lives jointly insured, and in respect of which a particular schedule of premium or cost of insurance rates applies — is added to the policy or is term insurance that is converted into permanent life insurance within the policy, then that insurance is deemed to be a separate life insurance policy issued at the particular time unless

(i) the insurance is part of a rider deemed by subsection 211(2) of the Act to be a separate life insurance policy issued at the particular time, or

(ii) in the case of insurance added to the policy,

(A) the insurance is medically underwritten

(I) to obtain a reduction in the premium or cost of insurance rates under the policy, or

(II) before 2017, or

(B) the insurance is paid for with policy dividends or is reinstated.

Notes: For the meaning of "issued before 2017", see Notes to ITA 148(11).

Reg. 1401(5)(b) opening words amended by 2017 budget bill #2, effective Dec. 14, 2017. Before that date, read:

(b) if the policy is issued before 2017 and at a particular time after 2016 life insurance — in respect of a life, or two or more lives jointly insured, and in respect of which a particular schedule of premium or cost of insurance rates applies — is converted (other than only because of a change in premium or cost of insurance rates) into another type of life insurance under the policy or is added to the policy, then that insurance is deemed to be a separate life insurance policy issued at the particular time unless

Reg. 1401(5) added by 2014 budget bill #2, effective Dec. 16, 2014.

Definitions [Reg. 1401]: "amount" — ITA 248(1); "amount payable" — ITA 138(12), Reg. 1408(1); "annuity" — ITA 248(1); "benefit" — Reg. 1408(1); "benefit on death" — Reg. 1401(3); "Canada" — ITA 255, *Interpretation Act* 35(1); "cash surrender value" — ITA 148(9), Reg. 1408(1); "coverage" — Reg. 1401(3); "dividend" — ITA 248(1); "fund value benefit", "fund value of a coverage", "fund value of

a policy", "future benefits to be provided", "future net premiums or cost of insurance charges", "future premiums or cost of insurance charges" — Reg. 1401(3); "group term life insurance policy" — Reg. 1408(2); "individual", "insurance policy", "insurer" — ITA 248(1); "interest" — ITA 138(12), Reg. 1408(1); "interpolation time" — Reg. 1401(3); "life insurance business" — ITA 248(1); "life insurance policy", "life insurance policy in Canada" — ITA 138(12), Reg. 1408(1), (5); "life insurer", "Minister" — ITA 248(1); "modified net premium" — Reg. 1408(1), (3); "month" — *Interpretation Act* 35(1); "net premium" — Reg. 1408(1); "net premium reserve" — Reg. 1401(3); "policy anniversary" — Reg. 310, 1401(3); "policy loan" — ITA 138(12), Reg. 1408(1); "pre-1996 life insurance policy" — Reg. 1408(1), (7); "premium paid by the policyholder" — Reg. 1408(4); "qualified annuity", "relevant authority" — Reg. 1408(1); "reported" — Reg. 1408(8); "segregated fund" — ITA 138.1(1), Reg. 1408(1); "segregated fund policy" — ITA 138.1(1)(a), Reg. 1408(1); "taxable income" — ITA 248(1); "taxation year" — ITA 249.

Interpretation Bulletins: IT-87R2: Policyholders' income from life insurance policies.

DIVISION 3 — SPECIAL RULES

1402. Non-life and life insurance businesses — Any amount determined under section 1400 or 1401 shall be determined

(a) net of relevant reinsurance recoverable amounts; and

(b) without reference to any amount in respect of a deposit accounting insurance policy.

Notes: Reg. 1402 amended by 2010 budget bill #2 (for tax years that begin after 2010), P.C. 1999-1154, 1997-1670.

Definitions [Reg. 1402]: "amount" — ITA 248(1); "deposit accounting insurance policy" — ITA 138(12); "reinsurance recoverable amount" — Reg. 1408(1).

1402.1 [Negative amounts] — For greater certainty, any amount referred to or determined under section 1400 may be equal to, or less than, nil.

Notes: Reg. 1402.1 added by P.C. 1999-1154, for 1996 and later tax years. It overrides ITA 257 for each individual element of the formula in Reg. 1400(3).

Definitions [Reg. 1402.1]: "amount" — ITA 248(1).

1403. (1) Subject to subsections (2) and (3), for the purposes of applying paragraph 1401(1)(c) in respect of a life insurance policy issued before 2017 or an annuity contract, a modified net premium and an amount determined by paragraph 1401(1)(c) are to be computed

(a) in the case of a lapse-supported policy effected after 1990, based on rates of interest, mortality and policy lapse only, and

(b) in any other case, based on rates of interest and mortality only,

using

(c) in respect of the modified net premiums and benefits (other than a benefit described in paragraph (d)) of a participating life insurance policy (other than an annuity contract) under the terms of which the policyholder is entitled to receive a specified amount in respect of the policy's cash surrender value, the rates used by the insurer when the policy was issued in computing the cash surrender values of the policy;

(d) in respect of any benefit provided

(i) in lieu of a cash settlement on the termination or maturity of a policy, or

(ii) in satisfaction of a dividend on a policy,

the rates used by the insurer in determining the amount of such benefit; and

(e) in respect of all or part of any other policy, the rates used by the insurer in determining the premiums for the policy.

Related Provisions: ITA 148(11) — Loss of pre-2016 grandfathering.

Notes: For the meaning of "issued before 2017", see Notes to ITA 148(11).

Reg. 1403(1) opening words amended by 2014 budget bill #2, effective Dec. 16, 2014.

Reg. 1403(1) amended by P.C. 1994-940, for tax years beginning after 1990 (or earlier, with amendments, by election).

(2) For the purposes of subsection (1), where a rate of mortality or other probability used by an insurer in determining the premium for a policy is not reasonable in the circumstances, the Minister on the advice of the Superintendent of Insurance for Canada may make such revision to the rate as is reasonable in the circumstances and the revised rate shall be deemed to have been used by the insurer in determining the premium.

(3) For the purposes of subsection (1), where the present value of the premiums for a policy as at the date of issue of the policy is less than the aggregate of

(a) the present value, at that date, of the benefits provided for by the policy, and

(b) the present value, at that date, of all outlays and expenses made or incurred by the insurer or outlays and expenses that the insurer reasonably estimates it will make or incur in respect of the policy (except outlays and expenses to maintain the policy after all premiums under the policy have been paid and for which explicit provision has not been made in calculating the premiums) and such part of any other outlays and expenses made or incurred by the insurer that may reasonably be regarded as applicable thereto,

an increased rate of interest shall be determined by multiplying the rate of interest used in determining the premiums by a constant factor so that when the increased rate of interest is used,

(c) the present value of the premiums at the date of issue of the policy

shall equal

(d) the aggregate of the present values of the benefits, outlays and expenses referred to in paragraphs (a) and (b),

and the increased rate of interest shall be deemed to have been used by the insurer in determining the premiums for the policy.

Related Provisions: Reg. 1403(4) — Computation of present value.

(4) For the purposes of subsection (3), a "present value" referred to in that subsection shall be computed by using the rates of mortality and other probabilities used by the insurer in determining its premiums, after making any revision required by subsection (2).

(5) For the purposes of subsection (1), where a record of the rate of interest or mortality used by an insurer in determining the premiums for a policy is not available,

(a) the insurer may, if the policy was issued before 1978, make a reasonable estimate of the rate; and

(b) the Minister, on the advice of the Superintendent of Insurance for Canada, may

(i) if the policy was issued before 1978 and the insurer has not made the estimate referred to in paragraph (a), or

(ii) if the policy was issued after 1977,

make a reasonable estimate of the rate.

(6) Notwithstanding paragraph 1401(1)(c), a life insurer in computing its income for a taxation year may, in respect of any class of life insurance policies issued before its 1988 taxation year, other than policies referred to in paragraph 1401(1)(a) or (b), use a method of approximation to convert the reserve in respect of such policies reported by the insurer in its annual report to the relevant authority for the year to an amount that is a reasonable estimate of the amount that would otherwise be determined for such policies under paragraph 1401(1)(c), provided that that method of approximation is acceptable to the Minister on the advice of the relevant authority.

(7) For the purposes of subsection (1) and notwithstanding any other provision of this section, where

(a) an individual annuity contract was issued prior to 1969 by a life insurer, or

(b) a benefit was purchased prior to 1969 under a group annuity contract issued by a life insurer, and

the contract

(c) is a policy in respect of which the provisions of paragraph 1401(1)(c) as it read in its application to the insurer's 1977 taxation year applied,

the rates of interest and mortality used by the insurer in computing its reserve for the policy under that paragraph for its 1977 taxation year shall be used by the insurer in respect of that policy.

(8) Subsections (9) and (10) apply to an insurer if

(a) in a taxation year of the insurer, there has been a disposition to the insurer by another person with whom the insurer was dealing at arm's length in respect of which subsection 138(11.92) of the Act applied;

(b) as a result of the disposition, the insurer assumed obligations under life insurance policies (in this subsection and subsections (9) and (10) referred to as the "transferred policies") in respect of which an amount may be claimed by the insurer as a reserve under paragraph 1401(1)(c) for the taxation year;

(c) the amount (referred to in this subsection and subsections (9) and (10) as the "reserve deficiency") determined by the following formula is a positive amount:

$$(A - B) - C$$

where

A is the total of all amounts received or receivable by the insurer from the other person in respect of the transferred policies,

B is the total of all amounts paid or payable by the insurer to the other person in respect of commissions in respect of the amounts referred to in the description of A, and

C is the total of the maximum amounts that may be claimed by the insurer as a reserve under 1401(1)(c) (determined without reference to this subsection) in respect of the transferred policies for the taxation year; and

(d) the reserve deficiency can reasonably be attributed to the fact that the rates of interest, mortality or policy lapse used by the issuer of the transferred policies in determining the cash surrender values or premiums under the transferred policies are no longer reasonable in the circumstances.

Related Provisions: ITA 257 — Negative amounts in formulas.

Notes: For interpretation of "reasonably be attributed" in para. (d), see *729658 Alberta*, 2004 TCC 474.

Reg. 1403(8) amended by 2002-2013 technical bill (Part 5 — technical), effective for dispositions after Nov. 1999.

(9) If this subsection applies to an insurer in respect of transferred policies for which there was a reserve deficiency, then, for the purposes of subsection (1) and subject to subsection (10),

(a) the insurer may make such revisions to the rates of interest, mortality or policy lapse used by the issuer of the transferred policies to eliminate all or any part of the reserve deficiency; and

(b) the revised rates are deemed to have been used by the issuer of the transferred policies in determining the cash surrender value or premiums under the policies.

Related Provisions: Reg. 1403(8) — Conditions for Reg. 1403(9) to apply.

Notes: Reg. 1403(9) added by 2002-2013 technical bill (Part 5 — technical), effective for dispositions after Nov. 1999.

(10) If, under subsection (9), an insurer has revised the rates of interest, mortality or policy lapse used by the issuer of transferred policies, the Minister may, for the purposes of subsection (1) and paragraph (9)(b), make further revisions to the revised rates to the extent that the insurer's revisions to those rates are not reasonable in the circumstances.

Notes: Reg. 1403(10) added by 2002-2013 technical bill (Part 5 — technical), effective for dispositions after Nov. 1999.

Definitions [Reg. 1403]: "amount", "annuity" — ITA 248(1); "arm's length" — ITA 251(1); "benefit" — Reg. 1408(1); "cash surrender value" — ITA 148(9), Reg.

1408(1); "disposition", "dividend", "insurer" — ITA 248(1); "lapse-supported policy" — Reg. 1408(1); "life insurance policy" — ITA 138(12), 248(1), Reg. 1408(5); "life insurer", "Minister" — ITA 248(1); "modified net premium" — Reg. 1408(1), (3); "participating life insurance policy" — ITA 138(12), Reg. 1404(1); "person" — ITA 248(1); "present value" — Reg. 1403(4); "record" — ITA 248(1); "relevant authority" — Reg. 1408(1); "reported" — Reg. 1408(8); "reserve deficiency" — Reg. 1403(8)(c); "taxation year" — ITA 249; "transferred policies" — Reg. 1403(8)(b).

DIVISION 4 — LIFE INSURANCE POLICY RESERVES

1404. (1) For the purpose of subparagraph 138(3)(a)(i) of the Act, there may be deducted, in computing a life insurer's income from carrying on its life insurance business in Canada for a taxation year in respect of its life insurance policies in Canada, the amount the insurer claims, not exceeding

(a) the amount determined under subsection (3) in respect of the insurer for the year, where that amount is greater than nil; and

(b) nil, in any other case.

(2) For the purpose of paragraph 138(4)(b) of the Act, the amount prescribed in respect of an insurer for a taxation year, in respect of its life insurance policies in Canada, is

(a) the absolute value of the amount determined under subsection (3) in respect of the insurer for the year, where that amount is less than nil; and

(b) nil, in any other case.

(3) For the purposes of paragraphs (1)(a) and (2)(a), the amount determined under this subsection in respect of an insurer for a taxation year, in respect of its life insurance policies in Canada, is the amount, which may be positive or negative, determined by the formula

$$A + B + C + D - M$$

where

A is the amount (except to the extent the amount is determined in respect of a claim, premium, dividend or refund in respect of which an amount is included in determining the value of B, C or D), in respect of the insurer's life insurance policies in Canada, equal to the lesser of

(a) the total of the reported reserves of the insurer at the end of the year in respect of those policies, and

(b) the total of the policy liabilities of the insurer at the end of the year in respect of those policies;

B is the amount, in respect of the insurer's life insurance policies in Canada under which there may be claims incurred before the end of the year that have not been reported to the insurer before the end of the year, equal to 95% of the lesser of

(a) the total of the reported reserves of the insurer at the end of the year in respect of the possibility that there are such claims, and

(b) the total of the policy liabilities of the insurer at the end of the year in respect of the possibility that there are such claims;

C is the total of all amounts each of which is the unearned portion at the end of the year of the premium paid by the policyholder for the policy, determined by apportioning the premium paid by the policyholder equally over the period to which that premium relates, where the policy is a group term life insurance policy that

(a) provides coverage for a period that does not exceed 12 months, and

(b) is a life insurance policy in Canada;

D is the total of all amounts (other than an amount deductible under subparagraph 138(3)(a)(v) of the Act) each of which is the amount, which is the least of P, Q and R, in respect of a dividend, refund of premiums or refund of premium deposits provided for under the terms of a group life insurance policy that is a life insurance policy in Canada that will be

(a) used by the insurer to reduce or eliminate a future adverse claims experience under the policy,

(b) paid or unconditionally credited to the policyholder by the insurer, or

(c) applied in discharge, in whole or in part, of a liability of the policyholder to pay premiums to the insurer under the policy,

where

P is a reasonable amount as a reserve determined as at the end of the year in respect of the dividend, refund of premiums or refund of premium deposits provided for under the terms of the policy,

Q is 25% of the amount of the premium under the terms of the policy for the 12-month period ending

(a) on the day the policy is terminated, if the policy is terminated in the year, and

(b) at the end of the year, in any other case, and

R is the amount of the reported reserve of the insurer at the end of the year in respect of the dividend, refund of premiums or refund of premium deposits provided for under the terms of the policy; and

M is the total of all amounts determined in respect of a life insurance policy in Canada each of which is

(a) an amount payable in respect of a policy loan under the policy, or

(b) interest that has accrued to the insurer to the end of the year in respect of a policy loan under the policy.

Notes: In *National Life Assurance*, 2008 FCA 14, an insurance reserve under ITA 138(3)(a)(i) was adjusted under Reg. 1406(b) to remove a negative reserve amount; that decision has been overruled by amendments to Reg. 1406(b). The Court discussed Reg. 1404(3) in some detail.

Reg. 1404(3)C amended by P.C. 2002-346 to change "net premium" to "premium paid by the policyholder", effective for taxation years that begin after 1999 (or that end after 1997, for a taxpayer that elects as per Notes to ITA 18(9.02)).

Notes [Reg. 1404]: Reg. 1404 amended by 2008 budget bill #2 (for tax years that begin after Sept. 2006), P.C. 2002-346, 1999-1154, 1996-1452, 1994-940, 1993-2025. (The definitions in Reg. 1404 before 1996 are now in Reg. 1408(1).)

Definitions [Reg. 1404]: "amount" — ITA 248(1), Reg. 1406, 1407; "amount payable" — ITA 138(12), Reg. 1408(1); "business" — ITA 248(1); "Canada" — ITA 255, *Interpretation Act* 35(1); "dividend" — ITA 248(1); "group term life insurance policy" — Reg. 1408(2); "insurance policy", "insurer" — ITA 248(1); "interest" — ITA 138(12), Reg. 1408(1); "life insurance business" — ITA 248(1); "life insurance policy", "life insurance policy in Canada" — ITA 138(12), Reg. 1408(1), (5); "life insurer" — ITA 248(1); "month" — *Interpretation Act* 35(1); "net premium for the policy" — Reg. 1408(1), (6); "non-cancellable or guaranteed renewable accident and sickness policy" — Reg. 1408(1); "policy liability" — Reg. 1408(1); "policy loan" — ITA 138(12), Reg. 1408(1); "post-1995 non-cancellable or guaranteed renewable accident and sickness policy" — Reg. 1408(1); "premium paid by the policyholder" — Reg. 1408(4); "prescribed" — ITA 248(1); "reported" — Reg. 1408(8); "reported reserve" — Reg. 1408(1); "taxation year" — ITA 249.

1405. [Unpaid claims reserve] — For the purpose of subparagraph 138(3)(a)(ii) of the Act, there may be deducted, in computing a life insurer's income for a taxation year, the amount it claims as a reserve in respect of an unpaid claim received by the insurer before the end of the year under a life insurance policy in Canada, not exceeding the lesser of

(a) the reported reserve of the insurer at the end of the year in respect of the claim, and

(b) the policy liability of the insurer at the end of the year in respect of the claim.

Related Provisions [Reg. 1405]: ITA 20(26) — Deduction for unpaid claims reserve adjustment; Reg. 1406 — All amounts to be net of reinsurance ceded and ignoring seg funds; Reg. 1407 — Amounts in Reg. 1405 may be less than zero.

Notes: Reg. 1405 opening words amended by 2008 budget bill #2, for tax years that begin after Sept. 2006.

Reg. 1405 replaced by P.C. 1999-1154, for 1996 and later tax years. (For unpaid claims in respect of pre-1996 policies, see Reg. 1401(4).)

Definitions [Reg. 1405]: "amount" — ITA 248(1), Reg. 1406, 1407; "insurer" — ITA 248(1); "life insurance policy" — ITA 138(12), 248(1), Reg. 1408(5); "life insurance policy in Canada" — ITA 138(12), Reg. 1408(1); "life insurer" — ITA 248(1); "policy liability", "post-1995 life insurance policy", "reported reserve" — Reg. 1408(1); "taxation year" — ITA 249.

1406. [Interpretation] — Any amount determined under section 1404 or 1405 shall be determined

(a) net of relevant reinsurance recoverable amounts;

(b) by excluding any obligation to pay a benefit under a segregated fund policy if

(i) the amount of the benefit varies with the fair market value of the segregated fund at the time the benefit becomes, or may become, payable, and

(ii) the benefit is not in respect of a guarantee given by the insurer under a segregated fund policy; and

(c) without reference to any amount in respect of a deposit accounting insurance policy.

Related Provisions: ITA 138(26) — Policy reserve transition — application rules.

Notes: *National Life Assurance*, 2008 FCA 14, held that Reg. 1406(b) permitted the policy reserves under Reg. 1404 and 1405 to be computed without reference to any liabilities of an insurer in respect of a segregated fund other than liabilities in respect of an obligation on the part of a life insurer to make a guarantee payment. The 2013 amendment to Reg. 1406(b), with new ITA 138(26), ensures "that the acquisition expenses associated with an insurer's segregated fund policies are amortized appropriately over the term of the policies" (Finance Technical Notes). Amounts determined under Reg. 1404 and 1405 continue to include liabilities in respect of guarantees in respect of the insurer's segregated fund policies. As a result of these changes, they also include amounts in respect of the insurer's segregated fund policies that are not amounts payable by the insurer as a benefit.

Reg. 1406 amended by 2002-2013 technical bill (for 2012 and later tax years), 2010 budget bill #2, P.C. 1999-1154.

Definitions [Reg. 1406]: "amount" — ITA 248(1); "deposit accounting insurance policy" — ITA 138(12), Reg. 1408(1); "reinsurance recoverable amount" — Reg. 1408(1); "segregated fund" — ITA 138.1(1), Reg. 1408(1); "segregated fund policy" — ITA 138.1(1)(a), Reg. 1408(1).

1407. [Negative amounts] — For greater certainty, any amount referred to in or determined under section 1404 or 1405 may be equal to, or less than, nil.

Notes: Reg. 1407 added by P.C. 1999-1154, for 1996 and later tax years. It overrides ITA 257 for each individual element of the calculations in Reg. 1404 and 1405.

Definitions [Reg. 1407]: "amount" — ITA 248(1).

DIVISION 5 — INTERPRETATION

1408. Insurance businesses — **(1)** The definitions in this subsection apply in this Part.

"acquisition costs" — [Repealed]

Notes: Definition "acquisition costs" repealed by P.C. 2002-346, effective for taxation years that begin after 1999 (or that end after 1997, for a taxpayer that elects as per Notes to ITA 18(9.02)). The change addresses the insurance industry's concern that amounts deemed incurred as acquisition costs (generally 20% of premiums) under the old definition no longer reflect the real acquisition costs being incurred by insurers.

See Notes at end of Reg. 1408 and Reg. 1404.

"amount payable", in respect of a policy loan at a particular time, means the amount of the policy loan and the interest that is outstanding on the policy loan at that time.

"benefit", in respect of a policy, includes

(a) a policy dividend (other than a policy dividend in respect of a policy described in paragraph 1403(1)(c)) in respect of the policy to the extent that the dividend was specifically treated as a benefit by the insurer in determining a premium for the policy, and

(b) an expense of maintaining the policy after all premiums in respect of the policy have been paid to the extent that the ex-

pense was specifically provided for by the insurer in determining a premium for the policy,

but does not include

(c) a policy loan,

(d) interest on funds left on deposit with the insurer under the terms of the policy, and

(e) any other amount under the policy that was not specifically provided for by the insurer in determining a premium for the policy.

Notes: For interpretation see VIEWS doc 2005-0164721C6. See also Notes to ITA 188.1(5) re meaning of "includes" in the opening words.

"capital tax" means a tax imposed under Part I.3 or VI of the Act or a similar tax imposed under an Act of the legislature of a province.

"cash surrender value" has the meaning assigned by subsection 148(9) of the Act.

"claim liability" of an insurer at the end of a taxation year means

(a) in respect of a claim reported to the insurer before that time under an insurance policy, the amount, if any, by which

(i) the present value at that time, computed using a rate of interest that is reasonable in the circumstances, of a reasonable estimate, determined in accordance with accepted actuarial practice, of the insurer's future payments and claim adjustment expenses in respect of the claim

exceeds

(ii) the present value at that time, computed using a rate of interest that is reasonable in the circumstances, of a reasonable estimate, determined in accordance with accepted actuarial practice, of the amounts that the insurer will recover after that time in respect of the claim because of salvage, subrogation or any other reason; and

(b) in respect of the possibility that there are claims under an insurance policy incurred before that time that have not been reported to the insurer before that time, the amount, if any, by which

(i) the present value at that time, computed using a rate of interest that is reasonable in the circumstances, of a reasonable estimate, determined in accordance with accepted actuarial practice, of the insurer's payments and claim adjustment expenses in respect of those claims

exceeds

(ii) the present value at that time, computed using a rate of interest that is reasonable in the circumstances, of a reasonable estimate, determined in accordance with accepted actuarial practice, of the amounts that the insurer will recover in respect of those claims because of salvage, subrogation or any other reason.

"deposit accounting insurance policy" has the meaning assigned by subsection 138(12) of the Act.

Notes: Reg. 1408(1)"deposit accounting insurance policy" added by 2010 budget bill #2, effective for taxation years that begin after 2010.

"extended motor vehicle warranty" means an agreement under which a person agrees to provide goods or render services in respect of the repair or maintenance of a motor vehicle manufactured by the person or a corporation related to the person where

(a) the agreement is in addition to a basic or limited warranty in respect of the vehicle;

(b) the basic or limited warranty has a term of 3 or more years, although it may expire before the end of such term on the vehicle's odometer registering a specified number of kilometres or miles;

(c) more than 50% of the expenses to be incurred under the agreement are reasonably expected to be incurred after the expiry of the basic or limited warranty; and

(d) the person's risk under the agreement is insured by an insurer that is subject to the supervision of a relevant authority.

Related Provisions: ITA 95(2)(j.2)(ii) — Operator deemed to be under supervision of regulatory authority.

"general amending provision", of an insurance policy, means a provision of the policy that allows it to be amended with the consent of the policyholder.

"interest", in relation to a policy loan, has the meaning assigned by subsection 138(12) of the Act.

"lapse-supported policy" means a life insurance policy that would require materially higher premiums if premiums were determined using policy lapse rates that are zero after the fifth policy year.

"life insurance policy" has the same meaning as defined in subsection 138(12) of the Act.

Notes: Reg. 1408(1)"life insurance policy" added by 2008 budget bill #2, effective for taxation years that begin after Nov. 7, 2007.

"life insurance policy in Canada" has the same meaning as defined in subsection 138(12) of the Act.

Related Provisions: ITA 95(2)(j.2)(ii)(B) — Deemed life insurance policies in Canada for FAPI purposes.

Notes: Reg. 1408(1)"life insurance policy in Canada" amended by 2008 budget bill #2, effective for taxation years that begin after Nov. 7, 2007. See Notes at end of Reg. 1408.

"modified net premium", in respect of a premium under a policy (other than a prepaid premium under a policy that cannot be refunded except on termination of the policy), means

(a) where all benefits (other than policy dividends) and premiums (other than the frequency of payment of premiums) in respect of the policy are determined at the date of issue of the policy, the amount determined by the formula

$$A \times [(B + C)/(D + E)]$$

where

A is the amount of the premium,

B is the present value, at the date of the issue of the policy, of the benefits to be provided under the terms of the policy after the day that is one year after the date of the issue of the policy,

C is the present value, at the date of the issue of the policy, of the benefits to be provided under the terms of the policy after the day that is two years after the date of the issue of the policy,

D is the present value, at the date of the issue of the policy, of the premiums payable under the terms of the policy on or after the day that is one year after the date of the issue of the policy, and

E is the present value, at the date of the issue of the policy, of the premiums payable under the terms of the policy on or after the day that is two years after the date of the issue of the policy,

except that the amount determined by the formula in respect of the premium for the second year of a policy is deemed to be the amount that is 50% of the total of

(i) the amount that would otherwise be determined under the formula, and

(ii) the amount of a one-year term insurance premium (determined without regard to the frequency of payment of the premium) that would be payable under the policy; and

(b) in any other case, the amount that would be determined under paragraph (a) if that paragraph applied and the amount were adjusted in a manner that is reasonable in the circumstances.

Related Provisions: Reg. 1408(3) — Interpretation.

"net premium for the policy" — [Repealed]

Notes: Definition "net premium for the policy" repealed by P.C. 2002-346, for tax years that begin after 1999 (or earlier by election). Part XIV no longer determines any amount on the basis of the unearned portion of a net premium for a policy. See Notes at end of Reg. 1408. This definition was in Reg. 1404(2) before 1996.

"non-cancellable or guaranteed renewable accident and sickness policy" includes a non-cancellable or guaranteed renewable accident and sickness benefit under a group policy.

Related Provisions: Reg. 1408(6) — Riders.

"participating life insurance policy" has the meaning assigned by subsection 138(12) of the Act.

Notes: See Notes at end of Reg. 1408. For the pre-1996 version of this definition, see former Reg. 1404(1) in Notes to Reg. 1404.

"policy liability" of an insurer at the end of the taxation year in respect of an insurance policy or a claim, possible claim or risk under an insurance policy means the positive or negative amount of the insurer's reserve in respect of its potential liability in respect of the policy, claim, possible claim or risk at the end of the year determined in accordance with accepted actuarial practice, but without reference to projected income and capital taxes (other than the tax payable under Part XII.3 of the Act).

"policy loan" has the meaning assigned by subsection 138(12) of the Act.

"post-1995 life insurance policy" means a life insurance policy that is not a pre-1996 life insurance policy.

"post-1995 non-cancellable or guaranteed renewable accident and sickness policy" means a non-cancellable or guaranteed renewable accident and sickness policy that is not a pre-1996 non-cancellable or guaranteed renewable accident and sickness policy.

"pre-1996 life insurance policy", at any time, means a life insurance policy where

(a) the policy was issued before 1996; and

(b) before that time and after 1995 there has been no change, except in accordance with the provisions (other than a general amending provision) of the policy as they existed on December 31, 1995, to

(i) the amount of any benefit under the policy,

(ii) the amount of any premium or other amount payable under the policy, or

(iii) the number of premium or other payments under the policy.

Related Provisions: Reg. 1408(7) — Interpretation.

"pre-1996 non-cancellable or guaranteed renewable accident and sickness policy", at any time, means a non-cancellable or guaranteed renewable accident and sickness policy where

(a) the policy was issued before 1996; and

(b) before that time and after 1995 there has been no change, except in accordance with the provisions (other than a general amending provision) of the policy as they existed on December 31, 1995, to

(i) the amount of any benefit under the policy,

(ii) the amount of any premium or other amount payable under the policy, or

(iii) the number of premium or other payments under the policy.

Related Provisions: Reg. 1408(7) — Interpretation.

"qualified annuity" means an annuity contract issued before 1982, other than a deposit administration fund policy or a policy referred to in paragraph 1403(7)(c),

(a) in respect of which regular periodic annuity payments have commenced;

(b) in respect of which a contract or certificate has been issued that provides for regular periodic annuity payments to commence within one year after the date of issue of the contract or certificate;

(c) that is not issued as or under a registered retirement savings plan, registered pension plan or deferred profit sharing plan and that

(i) does not provide for a guaranteed cash surrender value at any time, and

(ii) provides for regular periodic annuity payments to commence not later than the attainment of age 71 by the annuitant; or

(d) that is issued as or under a registered retirement savings plan, registered pension plan or deferred profit sharing plan, if the interest rate is guaranteed for at least 10 years and the plan does not provide for any participation in profits, directly or indirectly.

"reinsurance commission", in respect of a policy, means

(a) where the risk under the policy is fully reinsured, the amount, if any, by which

(i) the premium paid by the policyholder for the policy

exceeds

(ii) the consideration payable by the insurer in respect of the reinsurance of the risk; and

(b) where the risk under the policy is not fully reinsured, the amount, if any, by which

(i) the portion of the premium paid by the policyholder for the policy that may reasonably be considered to be in respect of the portion of the risk that is reinsured with a particular reinsurer

exceeds

(ii) the consideration payable by the insurer to the particular reinsurer in respect of the risk assumed by the reinsurer.

Notes: Definition amended by P.C. 2002-346 to change "net premium" to "premium paid by the policyholder", for tax years that begin after 1999 (earlier by election).

"reinsurance recoverable amount" of an insurer means an amount reported as a reinsurance asset of the insurer as at the end of a taxation year in respect of an amount recoverable from a reinsurer.

Related Provisions: Reg. 1408(8) — Reference to amount reported as asset.

Notes: Reg. 1408(1) "reinsurance recoverable amount" added by 2010 budget bill #2, for tax years that begin after 2010.

"relevant authority" of an insurer means

(a) the Superintendent of Financial Institutions, if the insurer is required by law to report to the Superintendent of Financial Institutions; and

(b) in any other case, the Superintendent of Insurance or other similar officer or authority of the province under whose laws the insurer is incorporated.

Related Provisions: ITA 95(2)(j.2)(ii) — Operator deemed to be required by law to report to regulatory authority.

"reported reserve" of an insurer at the end of a taxation year in respect of an insurance policy or a claim, possible claim, risk, dividend, refund of premiums or refund of premium deposits under an insurance policy means the amount equal to

(a) where the insurer is required to file an annual report with its relevant authority for a period ending coincidentally with the year, the positive or negative amount of the reserve that would be reported in that report in respect of the insurer's potential liability under the policy if the reserve were determined without reference to projected income and capital taxes (other than the tax payable under Part XII.3 of the Act);

(b) where the insurer is, throughout the year, subject to the supervision of its relevant authority and paragraph (a) does not apply, the positive or negative amount of the reserve that would be

reported in its financial statements for the year in respect of the insurer's potential liability under the policy if

(i) those statements were prepared in accordance with generally accepted accounting principles, and

(ii) the reserve were determined without reference to projected income and capital taxes (other than the tax payable under Part XII.3 of the Act);

(c) where the insurer is the Canada Mortgage and Housing Corporation or a foreign affiliate of a taxpayer resident in Canada, the positive or negative amount of the reserve that would be reported in its financial statements for the year in respect of the insurer's potential liability under the policy if

(i) those statements were prepared in accordance with generally accepted accounting principles, and

(ii) the reserve were determined without reference to projected income and capital taxes (other than the tax payable under Part XII.3 of the Act); and

(d) in any other case, nil.

Related Provisions: ITA 95(2)(j.2)(ii)(A) — Operator deemed subject to regulatory authority for FAPI purposes.

"segregated fund" has the meaning assigned by subsection 138.1(1).

"segregated fund policy" has the meaning assigned by subsection 138.1(1).

Notes: See Notes at end of Reg. 1408.

(2) ["Group term life insurance policy"] — The definition "group term life insurance policy" in subsection 248(1) of the Act does not apply to this Part.

(3) [Interpretation — modified net premium] — For the purpose of the formula referred to in the definition "modified net premium" in subsection (1), it may be assumed that premiums are payable annually in advance.

(4) ["Premium paid by the policyholder"] — For the purposes of this Part,

(a) a reference to a "premium paid by the policyholder" shall, depending on the method regularly followed by the insurer in computing its income, be read as a reference to a "premium paid or payable by the policyholder"; and

(b) in determining the premium paid by a policyholder for a policy, there may be deducted by the insurer the portion, if any, of the premium that

(i) can reasonably be considered, at the time the policy is issued, to be a deposit that, pursuant to the terms of the policy or the by-laws of the insurer, will be returned to the policyholder, or credited to the account of the policyholder, by the insurer on the termination of the policy, and

(ii) was not otherwise deducted under section 140 of the Act.

(5) [Riders] — For the purposes of this Part, any rider that is attached to a life insurance policy and that provides for additional life insurance or for an annuity is a separate life insurance policy.

(6) [Riders] — For the purposes of this Part, any rider that is attached to a policy and that provides for additional non-cancellable or guaranteed renewable accident and sickness insurance, as the case may be, is a separate non-cancellable or guaranteed renewable accident and sickness policy.

(7) [No change in amount] — For the purposes of the definitions "pre-1996 life insurance policy" and "pre-1996 non-cancellable or guaranteed renewable accident and sickness policy" in subsection (1), a change in the amount of any benefit or in the amount or number of any premiums or other amounts payable under a policy is deemed not to have occurred where the change results from

(a) a change in underwriting class;

(b) a change in frequency of premium payments within a year that does not alter the present value, at the beginning of the year, of the total premiums to be paid under the policy in the year;

(c) the deletion of a rider;

(d) the correction of erroneous information;

(e) the reinstatement of the policy after its lapse, if the reinstatement occurs not later than 60 days after the end of the calendar year in which the lapse occurred;

(f) the redating of the policy for policy loan indebtedness; or

(g) a change in the amount of a benefit under the policy that is granted by the insurer on a class basis, where

(i) no consideration was payable by the policyholder or any other person for the change, and

(ii) the change was not made because of the terms or conditions of the policy or any other policy or contract to which the insurer is a party.

(8) A reference in this Part to an amount or item reported as an asset or a liability of an insurer as at the end of a taxation year means

(a) if reporting by the insurer to the insurer's relevant authority is required at the end of the year, an amount or item that is reported, as at the end of the year, as an asset or a liability in the insurer's non-consolidated balance sheet accepted by the insurer's relevant authority; and

(b) in any other case, an amount or item that is reported as an asset or a liability in a non-consolidated balance sheet that is prepared in a manner consistent with the requirements that would have applied had reporting to the insurer's relevant authority been required at the end of the year.

Notes: Reg. 1408(8) added by 2010 budget bill #2, effective for taxation years that begin after 2010.

Notes [Reg. 1408]: Reg. 1408 added by P.C. 1999-1154, effective for 1996 and later taxation years. The definitions had been in Reg. 1404.

Definitions [Reg. 1408]: "acquisition costs" — Reg. 1408(1); "amount" — ITA 248(1); "amount payable" — ITA 138(12), Reg. 1408(1); "annuity" — ITA 248(1); "arm's length" — ITA 251(1); "benefit" — Reg. 1408(1); "business" — ITA 248(1); "calendar year" — *Interpretation Act* 37(1)(a); "capital tax" — Reg. 1408(1); "cash surrender value" — ITA 148(9), Reg. 1408(1); "corporation" — ITA 248(1), *Interpretation Act* 35(1); "deferred profit sharing plan" — ITA 147(1), 248(1); "dividend" — ITA 248(1); "foreign affiliate" — ITA 95(1), 248(1); "general amending provision" — Reg. 1408(1); "insurance policy", "insurer" — ITA 248(1); "interest" — ITA 138(12), Reg. 1408(1); "legislature" — *Interpretation Act* 35(1)"legislative assembly"; "life insurance policy" — ITA 138(12), 248(1), Reg. 1408(5); "motor vehicle" — ITA 248(1); "net premium for the policy" — Reg. 1408(1); "non-cancellable or guaranteed renewable accident and sickness policy" — Reg. 1408(1), (6); "officer", "person" — ITA 248(1); "policy loan" — ITA 138(12), Reg. 1408(1); "pre-1996 life insurance policy", "pre-1996 non-cancellable or guaranteed renewable accident and sickness policy" — Reg. 1408(1), (7); "property" — ITA 248(1); "province" — *Interpretation Act* 35(1); "premium paid by the policyholder" — Reg. 1408(4); "registered pension plan" — ITA 248(1); "registered retirement savings plan" — ITA 146(1), 248(1); "related" — ITA 251(2)–(6); "relevant authority" — Reg. 1408(1); "reported" — Reg. 1408(8); "resident in Canada" — ITA 250; "security" — *Interpretation Act* 35(1); "taxation year" — ITA 249; "taxpayer" — ITA 248(1).

PART XV — [1500–1503] PROFIT SHARING PLANS

DIVISION I — EMPLOYEES PROFIT SHARING PLANS

1500. (1) An election under subsection 144(4.1) of the Act by the trustee of a trust governed by an employees profit sharing plan shall be made by filing with the Minister the prescribed form in duplicate.

(2) An election under subsection 144(4.2) of the Act by the trustee of a trust governed by an employees profit sharing plan shall be made by filing with the Minister the prescribed form in duplicate on or before the last day of a taxation year of the trust in respect of any capital property deemed to have been disposed of in that taxation year by virtue of the election.

(3) An election under subsection 144(10) of the Act shall be made by sending the following documents by registered mail to the Commissioner of Revenue at Ottawa:

(a) a letter from the employer stating that he elects to have the arrangement qualify as an employees profit sharing plan;

(b) if the employer is a corporation,

(i) where the directors of the corporation are legally entitled to administer the affairs of the corporation, a certified copy of their resolution authorizing the election to be made, and

(ii) where the directors of the corporation are not legally entitled to administer the affairs of the corporation, a certified copy of the authorization of the making of the election by the person or persons legally entitled to administer the affairs of the corporation; and

(c) a copy of the agreement and any supplementary agreement setting out the plan.

Notes: Reg. 1500(3) amended by P.C. 2007-849, effective June 13, 2007.

Definitions [Reg. 1500]: "capital property" — ITA 54, 248(1); "corporation" — ITA 248(1), *Interpretation Act* 35(1); "disposed" — ITA 248(1)"disposition"; "employees profit sharing plan" — ITA 144(1), 248(1); "employer", "Minister", "person", "prescribed" — ITA 248(1); "taxation year" — ITA 249; "trust" — ITA 104(1), 248(1), (3).

Interpretation Bulletins: IT-280R: Employees profit sharing plans — payments computed by reference to profits.

Forms: T3009: Election from deemed disposition and reacquisition of any capital property of an employees profit sharing plan under subsection 144(4.2).

DIVISION II — DEFERRED PROFIT SHARING PLANS

1501. Registration of plans — For the purpose of the definition "deferred profit sharing plan" in subsection 147(1) of the Act, an application for registration of a plan shall be made by sending the following documents by registered mail to the Commissioner of Revenue at Ottawa:

(a) a letter from the trustee and the employer whereby the trustee and the employer apply for the registration of the plan as a deferred profit sharing plan;

(b) if the employer is a corporation, a certified copy of a resolution of the directors authorizing the application to be made; and

(c) a copy of the agreement and any supplementary agreement setting out the plan.

Notes: Reg. 1501 amended by P.C. 2007-849, effective June 13, 2007.

Definitions [Reg. 1501]: "corporation" — ITA 248(1), *Interpretation Act* 35(1); "deferred profit sharing plan" — ITA 147(1), 248(1); "employer", "Minister" — ITA 248(1).

Information Circulars: 77-1R4: Deferred profit sharing plans.

Forms: T2214: Application for registration as a deferred profit sharing plan.

1502. [Revoked]

Notes: Reg. 1502, revoked in 1981, prescribed qualified investments for deferred profit sharing plans and revoked plans. See now Reg. 4900.

DIVISION III — ELECTIONS IN RESPECT OF CERTAIN SINGLE PAYMENTS

1503. Any election by a beneficiary under subsection 147(10.1) of the Act shall be made by filing the prescribed form in duplicate as follows:

(a) one form shall be filed by the beneficiary with the trustee of the deferred profit sharing plan not later than 60 days after the end of the taxation year in which the beneficiary received the payment referred to in subsection 147(10.1) of the Act; and

(b) the other form shall be filed by the beneficiary with the Minister on or before the day on which the beneficiary is required to file a return of income pursuant to section 150 of the Act for the taxation year in which the beneficiary received the payment referred to in subsection 147(10.1) of the Act.

Definitions [Reg. 1503]: "deferred profit sharing plan" — ITA 147(1), 248(1); "Minister", "prescribed" — ITA 248(1); "taxation year" — ITA 249.

Interpretation Bulletins: IT-281R2: Elections on single payments from a deferred profit sharing plan (archived).

Forms: T2078: Election under subsec. 147(10.1) for a single payment received from a deferred profit sharing plan.

PART XVI — [1600] PRESCRIBED COUNTRIES

1600. [No longer relevant]

Notes: Reg. 1600 lists 16 countries whose residents pay only 15% rather than 25% withholding tax on interest on pre-1976 arm's length debt: ITAR 10(4). No withholding tax generally applies on arm's length interest since 2008: ITA 212(1)(b).

PART XVII — [1700–1704] CAPITAL COST ALLOWANCES, FARMING AND FISHING

Notes: The CCA rates in this Part apply only to farming and fishing property owned continuously since before 1972: Reg. 1702(1)(k). (CRA does not know whether anyone is still using these rules: *Access to Information Act* disclosure to the author, Oct. 6, 2006.) For property acquired since 1972, see Part XI and Schedule II classes.

Interpretation Bulletins [Part XVII]: IT-268R4: *Inter vivos* transfer of farm property to child; IT-349R3: Intergenerational transfers of farm property on death.

DIVISION I — DEDUCTIONS ALLOWED

1700. [No longer relevant]

DIVISION II — MAXIMUM DEDUCTIONS

1701. [No longer relevant]

DIVISION III — PROPERTY NOT INCLUDED

1702. [No longer relevant]

DIVISION IV — INTERPRETATION

1703. [No longer relevant]

DIVISION V — APPLICATION OF THIS PART

1704. [No longer relevant]

PART XVIII — [1800–1802] INVENTORIES

1800. Manner of keeping inventories — For the purposes of section 230 of the Act, an inventory shall show quantities and nature of the properties that should be included therein in such a manner and in sufficient detail that the property may be valued in accordance with this Part or section 10 of the Act.

Definitions [Reg. 1800]: "inventory", "property" — ITA 248(1).

1801. Valuation — Except as provided by section 1802, for the purpose of computing the income of a taxpayer from a business, all the property described in all the inventories of the business may be valued at its fair market value.

Related Provisions: ITA 10(1), (1.01) — Rules for valuing inventory.

Notes: Reg. 1801 was applied to foreign exchange option contracts in *Kruger Inc.*, 2015 TCC 119; rev'd 2016 FCA 186 on the basis the contracts were not inventory (but mark-to-market method could be applied, before 10.1 was introduced).

Definitions [Reg. 1801]: "business" — ITA 248(1); "fair market value" — see ITA 69(1) Notes; "inventory", "property", "taxpayer" — ITA 248(1).

Interpretation Bulletins: IT-98R2: Investment corporations (archived); IT-473R: Inventory valuation; IT-504R2: Visual artists and writers.

CRA Audit Manual: 20.0: Valuation of inventory.

1802. Valuation of animals — **(1)** Except as provided in subsection (2), a taxpayer who is carrying on a business that includes the breeding and raising of animals may elect in prescribed form for a taxation year and subsequent taxation years to value each animal of a particular species (except a registered animal, an animal purchased for feedlot or similar operations, or an animal purchased by a drover or like person for resale) included in his inventory in respect of the business at a unit price determined in accordance with this section.

Forms: T2034: Election to establish inventory unit prices for animals.

(2) An election made in accordance with subsection (1) may be revoked in writing by the taxpayer, but where a taxpayer has made a revocation in accordance with this subsection a further election may not be made under subsection (1) except with the concurrence of the Minister.

(3) The unit price with respect to an animal of a particular class of animal shall be determined in accordance with the following rules:

(a) where animals of a particular class of animal were included in the inventory of a taxpayer at the end of the taxation year immediately preceding the first year in respect of which the taxpayer elected under subsection (1), the unit price of an animal of that class shall be computed by dividing the total value of all animals of the class in the inventory of the preceding year by the number of animals of the class described in that inventory, and

(b) in any other case, the unit price of an animal of a class shall be determined by the Minister, having regard, among other things, to the unit prices of animals of a comparable class of animal used in valuing the inventories of other taxpayers in the district.

(4) Notwithstanding subsection (1), where the aggregate value of the animals of a particular class determined in accordance with that subsection exceeds the market value of those animals, the animals of that class may be valued at fair market value.

(5) In this section

"class of animal" means a group of animals of a particular species segregated on the basis of age, breed or other recognized division, as determined by the taxpayer at the time of election under this section;

"district" means the territory served by a Tax Centre of the Canada Revenue Agency;

Notes: Definition "district" amended by P.C. 2007-849, effective June 13, 2007, to change "District Office of the Taxation Division of the Department of National Revenue" to "Tax Centre of the Canada Revenue Agency".

"registered animal" means an animal for which a certificate of registration has been issued by the registrar of the breed to which the animal belongs or by the registrar of the Canadian National Livestock Records;

a reference to **"taxation year"** shall be deemed to be a reference to the fiscal period of a business.

Definitions [Reg. 1802]: "business" — ITA 248(1); "class of animal", "district" — Reg. 1802(5); "fair market value" — see ITA 69(1) Notes; "fiscal period" — ITA 249.1; "inventory", "Minister", "person", "prescribed" — ITA 248(1); "registered animal", "taxation year" — Reg. 1802(5); "taxpayer" — ITA 248(1); "territory" — *Interpretation Act* 35(1); "unit price" — Reg. 1802(3); "writing" — *Interpretation Act* 35(1).

PART XIX — [1900] INVESTMENT INCOME TAX

1900. [No longer relevant]

Notes: Reg. 1900 added by P.C. 1994-619, for tax years that begin after June 17, 1987 but before 1990 and that end after 1987. It prescribes amounts for ITA 211.1(3). It no longer applies because ITA 211.1(3) has been revised.

PART XX — [2000–2002] POLITICAL CONTRIBUTIONS

2000. Contents of receipts — **(1)** Every official receipt issued by a particular person who is a registered agent of a registered party or an electoral district agent of a registered association, to an individual who makes a monetary contribution to the registered party or registered association, as the case may be, shall contain a statement that it is an official receipt for income tax purposes and shall, in a manner that cannot readily be altered, show clearly

(a) the name of the registered party or registered association, as the case may be;

(b) the serial number of the receipt;

(c) the name of the particular person, as recorded in the registry maintained by the Chief Electoral Officer under section 374 or 403.08 of the *Canada Elections Act*;

(d) the date on which the receipt is issued;

(e) the date on which the monetary contribution is received;

(f) the individual's name and address;

(g) the amount of the monetary contribution;

(h) a description of the advantage, if any, in respect of the monetary contribution and the amount of that advantage; and

(i) the eligible amount of the monetary contribution.

Notes: The terms "eligible contribution" and "advantage", defined in ITA 248(31)-(32), apply to political donations as well as charitable contributions.

Reg. 2000(1) amended by 2002-2013 technical bill (Part 5 — technical), effective for receipts issued after June 26, 2013.

(2) Subject to subsection (3), every official receipt issued by an official agent of a candidate to an individual who makes a monetary contribution to the candidate shall contain a statement that it is an official receipt for income tax purposes and shall, in a manner that cannot readily be altered, show clearly

(a) the name of the candidate, as it appears in the candidate's nomination papers;

(b) the serial number of the receipt;

(c) the name of the official agent;

(d) the date on which the receipt is issued;

(e) the date on which the monetary contribution is received;

(f) the polling day;

(g) the individual's name and address;

(h) the amount of the monetary contribution;

(i) a description of the advantage, if any, in respect of the monetary contribution and the amount of that advantage; and

(j) the eligible amount of the monetary contribution.

Notes: Reg. 2000(2) amended by 2002-2013 technical bill (Part 5 — technical), effective for receipts issued after June 26, 2013.

(3) The information required by paragraph (2)(f) may be shown by use of a code on an official receipt form issued by the Chief Electoral Officer, provided that the Minister is advised of the meaning of the code used.

(4) For the purposes of subsections (1) and (2), an official receipt issued to replace an official receipt previously issued shall show clearly that it replaces the original receipt and, in addition to its own serial number, shall show the serial number of the receipt originally issued.

(5) A spoiled official receipt form shall be marked "cancelled" and, together with its duplicate, shall be filed by the electoral district agent, the official agent or the registered agent, as the case may be, together with the information return required to be filed with the Minister under subsection 230.1(2) of the Act.

Notes: Reg. 2000(5) amended by 2002-2013 technical bill (Part 5 — technical), effective for receipts issued after June 26, 2013.

(6) An official receipt form on which any of the following is incorrectly or illegibly entered is to be regarded as spoiled:

(a) the date on which the monetary contribution is received;

(b) the amount of the monetary contribution;

(c) a description of the advantage, if any, in respect of the monetary contribution and the amount of that advantage; and

(d) the eligible amount of the monetary contribution.

Notes: Reg. 2000(6) amended by 2002-2013 technical bill (Part 5 — technical), effective for receipts issued after June 26, 2013.

Definitions [Reg. 2000]: "advantage" — ITA 248(32); "amount" — ITA 248(1); "calendar year" — *Interpretation Act* 37(1)(a); "Canada" — ITA 255, *Interpretation Act* 35(1); "Chief Electoral Officer" — Reg. 2002(1); "contribution" — ITA 127(4.1), Reg. 2002(1); "eligible amount" — ITA 248(31); "individual", "Minister" — ITA 248(1); "nomination paper" — Reg. 2002(1); "official agent" — Reg. 2002(2); "official receipt" — Reg. 2002(1); "official receipt form" — Reg. 2002(1); "person" — ITA 248(1); "polling day", "registered agent" — Reg. 2002(2); "registered party" — Reg. 2002(1).

2001. [Repealed]

Notes: Reg. 2001 repealed by 2002-2013 technical bill (Part 5 — technical), effective 2004. The filing deadline is now in ITA 230.1(2).

2002. [Definitions] — **(1)** The following definitions apply in this Part.

"Chief Electoral Officer" means the person named as chief electoral officer or substitute chief electoral officer under section 13 or 14 of the *Canada Elections Act*.

"nomination paper" means, in respect of a candidate, a nomination paper filed in respect of the candidate under the *Canada Elections Act*, with the corrections, if any, made under that Act to the nomination paper after its filing.

"official receipt" means a receipt issued for the purposes of subsection 127(3) of the Act containing the information that is required under that subsection.

"official receipt form" means

(a) in the case of an official receipt issued by an electoral district agent or a registered agent under subsection 2000(1), any printed form that an electoral district agent or a registered agent, as the case may be, has that is capable of being completed, or that originally was intended to be completed, as an official receipt of the electoral district agent or registered agent; and

(b) in the case of an official receipt issued by an official agent under subsection 2000(2), the official form prescribed under section 477 of the *Canada Elections Act*.

(2) In this Part, **"official agent"**, **"polling day"** and **"registered agent"** have the meanings assigned to them by the *Canada Elections Act*.

Notes: Reg. 2002 amended by 2002-2013 technical bill (Part 5 — technical), effective June 26, 2013.

Definitions [Reg. 2002]: "amount" — ITA 248(1); "Canada" — ITA 255, *Interpretation Act* 35(1); "official agent" — Reg. 2002(2); "official receipt" — Reg. 2002(1); "person" — ITA 248(1); "registered agent" — Reg. 2002(1).

PART XXI — [2100–2107] ELECTIONS IN RESPECT OF SURPLUSES

2100. Reduction of tax-paid undistributed surplus on hand or 1971 capital surplus on hand — [No longer relevant]

Notes: Reg. 2100 provides rules for an election under ITA 83(1) in respect of a dividend payable before 1979.

2101. Capital dividends and life insurance capital dividends payable by private corporations — Any election under subsection 83(2) of the Act in respect of a dividend payable by a private corporation shall be made by filing with the Minister the following documents:

(a) the form prescribed by the Minister;

(b) where the directors of the corporation are legally entitled to administer the affairs of the corporation, a certified copy of their resolution authorizing the election to be made;

(c) where the directors of the corporation are not legally entitled to administer the affairs of the corporation, a certified copy of the authorization of the making of the election by the person or persons legally entitled to administer the affairs of the corporation;

(d) where the election has been made under subsection 83(2) of the Act and paragraph (e) is not applicable, schedules showing the computation of the amount, immediately before the election, of the corporation's

(i) capital dividend account, and

(ii) 1971 undistributed income on hand, if any, if the dividend was payable on or prior to March 31, 1977; and

(e) where the election has been made under subsection 83(2) of the Act and subsection 83(3) of the Act is applicable, schedules showing the computation of the amount, immediately before the dividend became payable, of the corporation's

(i) capital dividend account, and

(ii) 1971 undistributed income on hand, if any, if the dividend was payable on or prior to March 31, 1977.

Notes: See Notes to ITA 83(2) and 184(3).

Income Tax Folios: S3-F2-C1: Capital Dividends [replaces IT-66R6].

Forms: T2054: Election for a capital dividend under subsec. 83(2).

2102. Tax on 1971 undistributed income on hand — (1) [Revoked]

(2) [No longer relevant]

Notes: Reg. 2102(2) provides rules for making a retroactive election under ITA 196(1.1) (now repealed) for a dividend payable before 1979.

2103. [Revoked]

2104. Capital gains dividends payable by mutual fund corporations and investment corporations — Any election under subsection 131(1) of the Act in respect of a dividend payable by a mutual fund corporation or an investment corporation shall be made by filing with the Minister the following documents:

(a) the form prescribed by the Minister;

(b) where the directors of the corporation are legally entitled to administer the affairs of the corporation, a certified copy of their resolution authorizing the election to be made;

(c) where the directors of the corporation are not legally entitled to administer the affairs of the corporation, a certified copy of the authorization of the making of the election by the person or persons legally entitled to administer the affairs of the corporation;

(d) where paragraph (f) is not applicable, a schedule showing the computation of the amount, immediately before the election, of the corporation's capital gains dividend account; and

(e) [Revoked]

(f) where subsection 131(1.1) of the Act is applicable, a schedule showing the computation of the amount, immediately before the earlier of

(i) the date the dividend became payable, and

(ii) the first day on which any part of the dividend was paid,

of the corporation's capital gains dividend account.

Definitions [Reg. 2104]: "amount" — ITA 248(1); "capital gain" — ITA 39(1), 248(1); "corporation" — ITA 248(1), *Interpretation Act* 35(1); "dividend" — ITA 248(1); "investment corporation" — ITA 130(3), 248(1); "Minister" — ITA 248(1);

"mutual fund corporation" — ITA 131(8), 248(1); "person", "prescribed" — ITA 248(1).

Forms: T2055: Election in respect of a capital gains dividend under subsection 131(1).

2104.1 [Capital gains dividends payable by mortgage investment corporations] — Any election under subsection 130.1(4) of the Act in respect of a dividend payable by a mortgage investment corporation shall be made by filing with the Minister the following documents:

(a) the documents referred to in paragraphs 2104(a) to (c); and

(b) a schedule showing the computation of the capital gains dividend in accordance with paragraph 130.1(4)(a) of the Act.

Definitions [Reg. 2104.1]: "capital gain" — ITA 39(1), 248(1); "dividend", "Minister" — ITA 248(1); "mortgage investment corporation" — ITA 130.1(6), 248(1).

Forms: T2012: Election in respect of a capital gains dividend under subsection 130.1(4); T2143: Election not to be a restricted financial institution.

2105. Capital gains dividends payable by non-resident-owned investment corporations — [No longer relevant.]

Notes: NROs have been eliminated. See ITA 133.

2106. Alternative to additional tax on excessive elections [for capital dividends] — Any election under subsection 184(3) of the Act in respect of a dividend that was paid or payable by a corporation shall be made by

(a) filing with the Minister the following documents:

(i) a letter stating that the corporation elects under subsection 184(3) of the Act in respect of the said dividend,

(ii) where the directors of the corporation are legally entitled to administer the affairs of the corporation, a certified copy of

(A) their resolution authorizing the election to be made, and

(B) their declaration that the election is made with the concurrence of all shareholders who received or were entitled to receive all or any portion of the said dividend and whose addresses were known to the corporation,

(iii) where the directors of the corporation are not legally entitled to administer the affairs of the corporation, a certified copy of

(A) the authorization of the making of the election, and

(B) the declaration that the election is made with the concurrence of all shareholders who received or were entitled to receive all or any portion of the said dividend and whose addresses were known to the corporation,

by the person or persons legally entitled to administer the affairs of the corporation,

(iv) a schedule showing the following information:

(A) the date of the notice of assessment of the tax that would, but for the election, have been payable under Part III of the Act,

(B) the full amount of the said dividend,

(C) the date the said dividend became payable, or the first day on which any part of the said dividend was paid if that day is earlier,

(D) the portion, if any, of the said dividend described in paragraph 184(3)(a) of the Act,

(E) the portion, if any, of the said dividend that the corporation is claiming for the purposes of an election in respect thereof under subsection 83(1) or (2), 130.1(4) or 131(1) of the Act pursuant to paragraph 184(3)(b) of the Act, and

(F) the portion, if any, of the said dividend that is deemed by paragraph 184(3)(c) of the Act to be a separate dividend that is a taxable dividend; and

(b) making an election in prescribed manner and prescribed form in respect of any amount claimed under paragraph 184(3)(b) of the Act.

Notes: See Notes to ITA 184(3) for the Short Cut Method, which avoids the need to comply with Reg. 2106.

Definitions [Reg. 2106]: "amount", "assessment" — ITA 248(1); "corporation" — ITA 248(1), *Interpretation Act* 35(1); "dividend", "Minister", "person", "prescribed", "shareholder" — ITA 248(1); "taxable dividend" — ITA 89(1), 248(1).

Income Tax Folios: S3-F2-C1: Capital Dividends [replaces IT-66R6].

2107. [No longer relevant]

Notes: Reg. 2107 lists shares on which a "qualifying dividend" paid before 1991 was tax-free under ITA 83(1).

PART XXII — [2200–2201] SECURITY INTERESTS

2200. [Discharge of security] — Where under subsection 220(4) of the Act the Minister has accepted, as security for payment of taxes, a mortgage or other security or guarantee, he may, by a document in writing, discharge such mortgage or other security or guarantee.

Notes: Reg. 2200 amended to change "mortgage, hypothec" to "mortgage" by P.C. 1994-1817, effective Nov. 30, 1994. The change was intended to be non-substantive.

Definitions [Reg. 2200]: "Minister" — ITA 248(1); "security", "writing" — *Interpretation Act* 35(1).

2201. (1) For the purpose of subsection 227(4.2) of the Act, "prescribed security interest", in relation to an amount deemed by subsection 227(4) of the Act to be held in trust by a person, means that part of a mortgage securing the performance of an obligation of the person, that encumbers land or a building, where the mortgage is registered pursuant to the appropriate land registration system before the time the amount is deemed to be held in trust by the person.

(2) For the purpose of subsection (1), where, at any time after 1999, the person referred to in subsection (1) fails to pay an amount deemed by subsection 227(4) of the Act to be held in trust by the person, as required under the Act, the amount of the prescribed security interest referred to in subsection (1) is deemed not to exceed the amount by which the amount, at that time, of the obligation outstanding secured by the mortgage exceeds the total of

(a) all amounts each of which is the value determined at the time of the failure, having regard to all the circumstances including the existence of any deemed trust for the benefit of Her Majesty pursuant to subsection 227(4) of the Act, of all the rights of the secured creditor securing the obligation, whether granted by the person or not, including guarantees or rights of set-off but not including the mortgage referred to in subsection (1), and

(b) all amounts applied after the time of the failure on account of the obligation,

so long as any amount deemed under any enactment administered by the Minister, other than the *Excise Tax Act*, to be held in trust by the person, remains unpaid.

(3) For greater certainty, a prescribed security interest includes the amount of insurance or expropriation proceeds relating to land or a building that is the subject of a registered mortgage interest, adjusted after 1999 in accordance with subsection (2), but does not include a lien, a priority or any other security interest created by statute, an assignment or hypothec of rents or leases, or a mortgage interest in any equipment or fixtures that a mortgagee or any other person has the right absolutely or conditionally to remove or dispose of separately from the land or building.

Notes: See Notes to ITA 227(4). Parallel rules for GST/HST are in the *Security Interest (GST/HST) Regulations*, P.C. 2011-262.

For detailed CRA discussion of Reg. 2201, see VIEWS doc 2013-0506991E5. In *Caisse Desjardins de Limoilou*, 2020 QCCA 1612 (leave to appeal denied 2021 Car-

swellQue 7085 (SCC)), a prescribed security interest was reduced by a guarantee provided by the borrower's shareholders.

Reg. 2201 added by P.C. 1999-1341, effective June 15, 1994.

Definitions [Reg. 2201]: "amount" — ITA 248(1); "Her Majesty" — *Interpretation Act* 35(1); "Minister", "person", "prescribed" — ITA 248(1); "trust" — ITA 104(1), 248(1), (3).

PART XXIII — [2300–2301] PRINCIPAL RESIDENCES

2300. Any election by a taxpayer under subparagraph 40(2)(c)(ii) of the Act shall be made by attaching to the return of income required by section 150 of the Act to be filed by him for his taxation year in which the disposition of the land, including the property that was his principal residence, occurred, a letter signed by the taxpayer

(a) stating that he is electing under that subparagraph;

(b) stating the number of taxation years ending after the acquisition date (within the meaning assigned by paragraph 40(2)(b) of the Act) for which the property was his principal residence and during which he was resident in Canada; and

(c) giving a description of the property sufficient to identify it with the property designated as his principal residence.

Notes: See Notes to ITA 150.1 re how to "attach" a "letter" to an electronic return.

Definitions [Reg. 2300]: "disposition", "property" — ITA 248(1); "resident in Canada" — ITA 250; "taxation year" — ITA 249; "taxpayer" — ITA 248(1).

2301. Any designation by a taxpayer under subparagraph 54(g)(iii) [54"principal residence"(c)] of the Act shall be made in the return of income required by section 150 of the Act to be filed by him for any taxation year of the taxpayer in which

(a) he has disposed of a property that is to be designated as his principal residence; or

(b) he has granted an option to acquire such property.

Related Provisions: ITA 220(3.21)(a.1) — Late filing, amendment or revocation of designation.

Notes: See Notes to ITA 150.1 re how to make an election in an e-filed return.

Reg. 2301 is technically invalid, since ITA 54"principal residence"(c) says "designated by the taxpayer in prescribed form and manner", and ITA 248(1)"prescribed"(a) says this means "authorized by the Minister" rather than by regulations. However, CRA authorizes the same manner of filing in Income Tax Folio S1-F3-C2 ¶2.15. (ITA 220(3.21)(a.1) allows CRA to accept a late designation.) See also ITA 40(2)(b) Notes.

Definitions [Reg. 2301]: "disposed" — ITA 248(1)"disposition"; "property" — ITA 248(1); "taxation year" — ITA 249; "taxpayer" — ITA 248(1).

Income Tax Folios: S1-F3-C2: Principal residence [replaces IT-120R6, IT-437R].

Forms: T1079: Designation of a property as a principal residence by a personal trust; T1079-WS: Principal residence worksheet; T1255: Designation of a property as a principal residence by the legal representative of a deceased individual; T2091(IND): Designation of a property as a principal residence by an individual (other than a personal trust); T2091(IND)-WS: Principal residence worksheet.

PART XXIV — [2400–2412] INSURERS

2400. (1) Definitions — The definitions in this subsection apply in this Part.

"attributed surplus" of a non-resident insurer for a taxation year is the total of

(a) the insurer's property and casualty surplus for the year, and

(b) either,

(i) if the insurer elects for the year in prescribed form and manner, 50% of the total of

(A) the amount that would have been determined at the end of the year in respect of the insurer under subparagraph (a)(ii) of the definition "Canadian investment fund", and

(B) the amount that would have been determined at the end of the preceding taxation year in respect of the insurer under subparagraph (a)(ii) of the definition "Canadian investment fund",

each amount being calculated as if throughout the year and the preceding taxation year the insurer had been a life insurer resident in Canada and had not carried on any insurance business other than a life insurance business or an accident and sickness insurance business, or

(ii) if the insurer does not elect under subparagraph (i) for the year, 120% of the total of all amounts each of which is 50% of the amount determined in accordance with regulations or guidelines made under Part XIII of the *Insurance Companies Act* to be the margin of assets in Canada over liabilities in Canada required to be maintained by the insurer as at the end of the year or as at the end of the preceding taxation year in respect of an insurance business carried on in Canada (other than a property and casualty insurance business).

Notes: For interpretation see VIEWS doc 2007-0250111I7.

"Canadian business property" of an insurer for a taxation year in respect of an insurance business means

(a) if the insurer was resident in Canada throughout the year and did not carry on an insurance business outside Canada in the year, property used or held by it in the year in the course of carrying on the business in Canada; and

(b) in any other case, designated insurance property of the insurer for the year in respect of the business.

"Canadian equity property" of a person or partnership (in this definition referred to as the "taxpayer") at any time means property of the taxpayer that is

(a) a share of the capital stock of, or an income bond, income debenture, small business development bond or small business bond issued by, a person (other than a corporation affiliated with the taxpayer) resident in Canada or a Canadian partnership; or

(b) that proportion of property that is shares of the capital stock of an entity that is a corporation affiliated with the taxpayer or an interest in an entity that is a partnership or trust that

(i) the total value for the taxation year or fiscal period of the entity that includes that time of Canadian equity property of the entity,

is of

(ii) the total value for the year or period of all property of the entity.

Related Provisions: Reg. 2400(7) — No double counting.

"Canadian investment fund" of an insurer at the end of a taxation year means

(a) in the case of a life insurer resident in Canada, the total of

(i) the amount determined by the formula

$$A - B$$

where

A is the amount of the insurer's Canadian reserve liabilities as at the end of the year (to the extent that the amount exceeds the amount of surplus appropriations included in that amount), and

B is the amount of the insurer's Canadian outstanding premiums and policy loans as at the end of the year (to the extent that the amount of the premiums and loans are in respect of policies referred to in paragraphs (a) to (c) of the description of A in the definition "Canadian reserve liabilities" and were not otherwise deducted in computing the amount of the insurer's Canadian reserve liabilities as at the end of the year), and

(ii) the greater of

(A) the amount determined by the formula

$$C + ((D - E + F) \times (G/H))$$

where

C is 8% of the amount determined under subparagraph (i),

D is the total of all amounts each of which is the amount of a deferred realized net gain or an amount expressed as a negative number of a deferred realized net loss of the insurer as at the end of the year,

E is the total of all amounts each of which is the amount of an item reported as an asset that is owned by the insurer at the end of the year and is a share of the capital stock of, or a debt owing to the insurer by, a financial institution affiliated with the insurer,

F is the total of all amounts each of which is the amount as at the end of the year of a debt assumed or incurred by the insurer in respect of the acquisition of an asset described in E (or another property for which an asset described in E is a substituted property),

G is the amount of the insurer's weighted Canadian liabilities as at the end of the year, and

H is the amount of the insurer's weighted total liabilities as at the end of the year, and

(B) the amount determined by the formula

$$(I - J + K + L) \times (M/N)$$

where

I is the total of all amounts each of which is the amount of an item reported as an asset of the insurer as at the end of the year (other than an item that at no time in the year was used or held by the insurer in the course of carrying on an insurance business),

J is the total of all amounts each of which is the amount of an item reported as a liability of the insurer (other than a liability that was at any time in the year connected with an asset that was not used or held by the insurer in the course of carrying on an insurance business at any time in the year) as at the end of the year in respect of an insurance business carried on by the insurer in the year,

K is the total of all amounts each of which is an amount of an item reported by the insurer as at the end of the year as a general provision or allowance for impairment in respect of investment property of the insurer for the year,

L is the total of all amounts each of which is an amount of a deferred realized net gain or an amount expressed as a negative number of a deferred realized net loss of the insurer as at the end of the year,

M is the amount of the insurer's weighted Canadian liabilities as at the end of the year, and

N is the amount of the insurer's weighted total liabilities as at the end of the year; and

(b) in the case of a non-resident insurer, the total of

(i) the amount, if any, by which the amount of the insurer's Canadian reserve liabilities as at the end of the year exceeds the total of

(A) the amount of the insurer's Canadian outstanding premiums and policy loans (to the extent that the amount of the premiums or loans are in respect of policies referred to in paragraphs (a) to (c) of the description of A in the definition "Canadian reserve liabilities" and were not otherwise deducted in computing the amount of the insurer's Canadian reserve liabilities as at the end of the year), and

(B) the amount of the insurer's deferred acquisition expenses as at the end of the year in respect of its property and casualty insurance business carried on in Canada, and

(ii) the greatest of

(A) the total of

(I) 8% of the amount determined under subparagraph (i), and

(II) the total of all amounts each of which is an amount of a deferred realized net gain or an amount expressed as a negative number of a deferred realized net loss of the insurer as at the end of the year in respect of an insurance business carried on by the insurer in Canada,

(B) the amount, if any, by which the total of

(I) the amount of the insurer's surplus funds derived from operations as at the end of its preceding taxation year,

(II) the total determined under subclause (A)(II) to the extent not included in subclause (I), and

(III) the total of all amounts in respect of which the insurer made an election under subsection 219(4) or (5.2) of the Act, each of which is an amount included in the total determined in respect of the insurer under subparagraph 219(4)(a)(i.1) of the Act as at the end of its preceding taxation year

exceeds

(IV) the total of amounts determined in respect of the insurer under subparagraphs 219(4)(a)(ii), (iii), (iv) and (v) of the Act, as at the end of the year, and

(C) the total of

(I) the amount of the insurer's attributed surplus for the year, and

(II) if the amount under subclause (I) was determined without the taxpayer electing under subparagraph (b)(i) of the definition "attributed surplus", the amount determined under subclause (A)(II).

Related Provisions: Reg. 2400(6) — Interpretation for cl. (a)(ii)(B).

Notes: 2010 budget bill #2 added "the description of A in" to (a)(i)B and amended (b)(i)(A), effective for taxation years that begin after 2010.

"Canadian investment property" of an insurer for a taxation year means an investment property of the insurer for the year (other than, if the insurer is non-resident, property established by the insurer as not being effectively connected with its insurance businesses carried on in Canada in the year) that is, at any time in the year

(a) real property situated in Canada;

(b) depreciable property situated in Canada or leased to a person resident in Canada for use inside and outside of Canada;

(c) a mortgage, a hypothec, an agreement of sale or any other form of indebtedness in respect of property described in paragraph (a) or (b);

(d) a Canadian equity property;

(e) a Canadian resource property;

(f) a deposit balance of the insurer that is in Canadian currency;

(g) a bond, debenture or other form of indebtedness, in Canadian currency, issued by

(i) a person resident in Canada or a Canadian partnership, or

(ii) the government of Canada, a province or any of their political subdivisions; or

(h) a property that is

(i) a share of the capital stock of a corporation resident in Canada that is affiliated with the insurer, if at least 75% of the total value for the year of all property of the corporation is attributable to property that would be Canadian investment property if it were owned by an insurer, or

(ii) an interest in a Canadian partnership, or a trust resident in Canada, if at least 75% of the total value for the year of all property of the partnership or trust, as the case may be, is

attributable to property that would be Canadian investment property if it were owned by an insurer; or

(i) an amount due or an amount accrued to the insurer on account of income that

(i) is from designated insurance property for the year that is Canadian investment property of the insurer for the year because of any of paragraphs (a) to (h), and

(ii) was assumed in computing the insurer's Canadian reserve liabilities for the year.

Notes: For interpretation of (i)(ii) see VIEWS doc 2002-0167477. For "real property" in para. (a), see Notes to ITA 248(4).

"Canadian outstanding premiums" of an insurer at any time means the total of all amounts each of which is the amount of an outstanding premium of the insurer with respect to an insurance policy at that time, to the extent that the amount of the premium has been assumed to have been paid in computing the insurer's Canadian reserve liabilities as at that time.

"Canadian reserve liabilities" of an insurer as at the end of a taxation year means the amount determined by the formula

$$A - B$$

where

A is the total of the insurer's liabilities and reserves (other than liabilities and reserves in respect of a segregated fund) as at the end of the year in respect of

(a) life insurance policies in Canada,

(b) fire insurance policies issued or effected in respect of property situated in Canada, and

(c) insurance policies of any other class covering risks ordinarily within Canada at the time the policy was issued or effected; and

B is the total of the reinsurance recoverable reported as a reinsurance asset by the insurer as at the end of the year relating to its liabilities and reserves in A.

Related Provisions: ITA 257 — Negative amounts in formulas.

Notes: An insurer's "Reserves for reinsurance ceded to unregistered insurers" and "Due to reinsurer" may both be included in CRL: VIEWS doc 2004-008257117. CRL is based on the balance sheet as accepted by the Superintendent of Financial Institutions: 2007-0240221C6.

Reg. 2400(1)"Canadian reserve liabilities" amended by 2010 budget bill #2, for tax years that begin after 2010.

"deposit balance" of an insurer means an amount standing to the insurer's credit as or on account of amounts deposited with a corporation authorized to accept deposits or to carry on the business of offering to the public its services as a trustee.

"equity limit" of an insurer for a taxation year means

(a) in respect of a life insurer resident in Canada, that proportion of the total of all amounts each of which is the value for the year of an equity property of the insurer that

(i) the insurer's weighted Canadian liabilities as at the end of the year

is of

(ii) the insurer's weighted total liabilities as at the end of the year;

(b) in respect of a non-resident insurer (other than a life insurer), 25% of the total of

(i) the amount, if any, by which the insurer's mean Canadian reserve liabilities for the year exceeds 50% of the total of its premiums receivable and deferred acquisition expenses as at the end of the year and its premiums receivable and deferred acquisition expenses as at the end of its preceding taxation year to the extent that those amounts were included in the insurer's Canadian reserve liabilities for the year or the preceding taxation year, as the case may be, in respect of the insurer's business in Canada, and

(ii) the insurer's property and casualty surplus for the year; and

(c) in respect of a non-resident life insurer, the total of

(i) either,

(A) if the insurer makes an election referred to in subparagraph (b)(i) of the definition "attributed surplus" for the year, the greater of

(I) that proportion of the total of all amounts each of which is the value for the year of an equity property of the insurer that

1. the insurer's weighted Canadian liabilities as at the end of the year

is of

2. the insurer's weighted total liabilities as at the end of year, and

(II) 8% of the insurer's mean Canadian investment fund for the year, or

(B) if the insurer does not make this election for the year, 8% of the insurer's mean Canadian investment fund for the year,

(ii) 25% of the amount, if any, by which

(A) the insurer's mean Canadian reserve liabilities for the year (determined on the assumption that the insurer's property and casualty insurance business carried on in Canada during the year was its only insurance business carried on in Canada that year)

exceeds

(B) 50% of the total of its premiums receivable and deferred acquisition expenses as at the end of the year and its premiums receivable and deferred acquisition expenses as at the end of its preceding taxation year, to the extent that those amounts were included in the insurer's Canadian reserve liabilities as at the end of the year or the preceding taxation year, as the case may be, (determined on the assumption that the insurer's property and casualty insurance business carried on in Canada during the year was its only insurance business carried on in Canada that year), and

(iii) 25% of the insurer's property and casualty surplus for the year.

Notes: Reg. 2400(1)"equity limit"(b)(i) amended by 2010 budget bill #2, effective for taxation years that begin after 2010.

"equity property" of a person or partnership (in this definition referred to as the "taxpayer") at any time means property of the taxpayer that is

(a) a share of the capital stock of, or an income bond, income debenture, small business development bond or small business bond issued by, another person (other than a corporation affiliated with the taxpayer) or partnership; or

(b) that proportion of property that is shares of the capital stock of a corporation affiliated with the taxpayer or an interest in a partnership or trust that

(i) the total value for the taxation year or fiscal period of the corporation, partnership or trust that includes that time of equity property of the corporation, partnership or trust, as the case may be,

is of

(ii) the total value for the year or period of all property of the corporation, partnership or trust, as the case may be.

Related Provisions: Reg. 2400(7) — No double counting.

"financial institution" means a corporation that is

(a) a corporation described in any of paragraphs (a) to (e) of the definition "restricted financial institution" in subsection 248(1) of the Act; or

(b) a particular corporation all or substantially all of the value of the assets of which is attributable to shares or indebtedness of one or more corporations described in paragraph (a) to which the particular corporation is affiliated.

Notes: CRA considers that "substantially all" means 90% or more.

"foreign policy loan" means an amount advanced by an insurer to a policyholder in accordance with the terms and conditions of a life insurance policy, other than a life insurance policy in Canada.

"gross Canadian life investment income" of a life insurer for a taxation year means the amount, if any, by which

(a) the total of all amounts each of which is

(i) the insurer's gross investment revenue for the year, to the extent that the revenue is from Canadian business property of the insurer for the year in respect of the insurer's life insurance business,

(ii) the amount included in computing the insurer's income for the year under paragraph 138(9)(b) of the Act,

(iii) the portion of the amount deducted under paragraph 20(1)(l) of the Act in computing the insurer's income for its preceding taxation year that was in respect of Canadian business property of the insurer for that year in respect of the insurer's life insurance business,

(iv) the amount included under section 142.4 of the Act in computing the insurer's income for the year in respect of property disposed of by the insurer that was, in the taxation year of disposition, Canadian business property of the insurer for that year in respect of the insurer's life insurance business,

(v) the insurer's gain for the year from the disposition of a Canadian business property of the insurer for the year in respect of the insurer's life insurance business, other than a capital property or a property in respect of the disposition of which section 142.4 of the Act applies, or

(vi) the insurer's taxable capital gain for the year from the disposition of a Canadian business property of the insurer for the year in respect of the insurer's life insurance business

exceeds

(b) the total of all amounts each of which is

(i) the portion of the amount deducted under paragraph 20(1)(l) of the Act in computing the insurer's income for the year that is in respect of Canadian business property of the insurer for the year in respect of the insurer's life insurance business,

(ii) the amount deductible under section 142.4 of the Act in computing the insurer's income for the year in respect of a property disposed of by the insurer that was, in the taxation year of disposition, a Canadian business property of the insurer for that year in respect of the insurer's life insurance business,

(iii) the insurer's loss for the year from the disposition of a Canadian business property of the insurer for the year in respect of the insurer's life insurance business, other than a capital property or a property in respect of the disposition of which section 142.4 of the Act applies, or

(iv) the insurer's allowable capital loss for the year from the disposition of a Canadian business property of the insurer for the year in respect of the insurer's life insurance business.

"investment property" of an insurer for a taxation year means non-segregated property owned by the insurer, other than a policy loan payable to the insurer, at any time in the year that is

(a) property acquired by the insurer for the purpose of earning gross investment revenue in the year, other than property that is

(i) property, a proportion of which is investment property of the insurer for the year because of paragraph (b),

(ii) a share of the capital stock of, or a debt owing to the insurer by, a corporation affiliated with the insurer, or

(iii) an interest in a partnership or trust;

(b) that proportion, if any, of property of the insurer that is land, depreciable property or property that would have been depreciable property if it had been situated in Canada and used or held by the insurer in the year in the course of carrying on an insurance business in Canada that

(i) the use made of the property by the insurer in the year for the purpose of earning gross investment revenue in the year

is of

(ii) the whole use made of the property by the insurer in the year;

(c) if the insurer is a life insurer, property described in any of paragraphs 138(4.4)(a) to (d) of the Act;

(d) either

(i) a share of the capital stock of, or a debt owing to the insurer by, a corporation (other than a corporation that is a financial institution) affiliated with the insurer, if the total value for the year of all investment property of the corporation for the year is not less than 75% of the total value for the year of all its property, or

(ii) an interest in a partnership or trust, if the total value for the year of all investment property of the partnership or trust, as the case may be, for the year is not less than 75% of the total value for the year of all its property,

and for the purpose of this paragraph (other than for the purpose of determining whether a corporation is a financial institution) every corporation, partnership and trust is deemed to be an insurer; or

(e) an amount due or an amount accrued to the insurer on account of income that

(i) is from designated insurance property for the year that is investment property of the insurer for the year because of any of paragraphs (a) to (d), and

(ii) was assumed in computing the insurer's Canadian reserve liabilities for the year.

Notes: For interpretation of (e)(ii) see VIEWS doc 2002-0167477.

"mean Canadian outstanding premiums" of an insurer for a taxation year means 50% of the total of

(a) its Canadian outstanding premiums as at the end of the year, and

(b) its Canadian outstanding premiums as at the end of its preceding taxation year.

"mean Canadian reserve liabilities" of an insurer for a taxation year means 50% of the total of

(a) its Canadian reserve liabilities as at the end of the year, and

(b) its Canadian reserve liabilities as at the end of its preceding taxation year.

"mean maximum tax actuarial reserve" in respect of a particular class of life insurance policies of an insurer for a taxation year means 50% of the total of

(a) its maximum tax actuarial reserve for that class of policies for the year, and

(b) its maximum tax actuarial reserve for that class of policies for its preceding taxation year.

"mean policy loans" of an insurer for a taxation year means 50% of the total of

(a) its policy loans as at the end of the year, and

(b) its policy loans as at the end of its preceding taxation year.

"outstanding premiums" of an insurer with respect to an insurance policy at any time means premiums due to the insurer under the policy at that time but unpaid.

"property and casualty surplus" of an insurer for a taxation year means the total of

(a) 7.5% of the total of

(i) its unearned premium reserve as at the end of the year (net of reinsurance recoverables in respect of the reserve) in respect of its property and casualty insurance business,

(ii) its unearned premium reserve as at the end of its preceding taxation year (net of reinsurance recoverables in respect of the reserve) in respect of its property and casualty insurance business,

(iii) its provision for unpaid claims and adjustment expenses as at the end of the year (net of reinsurance recoverables in respect of the provision) in respect of its property and casualty insurance business, and

(iv) its provision for unpaid claims and adjustment expenses as at the end of its preceding taxation year (net of reinsurance recoverables in respect of the provision) in respect of its property and casualty insurance business,

and

(b) 50% of the total of

(i) its investment valuation reserve as at the end of the year in respect of its property and casualty insurance business, and

(ii) its investment valuation reserve as at the end of its preceding taxation year in respect of its property and casualty insurance business.

"reinsurance recoverable" of an insurer means the total of all amounts each of which is an amount reported as a reinsurance asset of the insurer as at the end of a taxation year in respect of an amount recoverable from a reinsurer.

Related Provisions: Reg. 8600"total reserve liabilities" — Reinsurance recoverable deducted from total reserve liabilities.

Notes: Reg. 2400(1)"reinsurance recoverable" amended by 2010 budget bill #2, effective for taxation years that begin after 2010.

"value" for a taxation year of a property of a person or partnership (in this definition referred to as the "owner") means

(a) in the case of a property that is a mortgage, hypothec, an agreement of sale or an investment property that is a deposit balance, the amount, if any, by which

(i) the amount obtained when the gross investment revenue of the owner for the year from the property is divided by the average rate of interest earned by the owner (expressed as an annual rate) on the amortized cost of the property during the year

exceeds

(ii) the amount obtained when the interest payable by the owner, for the period in the year during which the property was held by the owner, on debt assumed or incurred by the owner in respect of the acquisition of the property (or another property for which the property is a substituted property) is divided by the average rate of interest payable by the owner (expressed as an annual rate) on the debt for the year;

(b) in the case of a property that is an amount due or an amount accrued to the owner, the total of the amounts due or accrued at the end of each day in the year divided by the number of days in the year;

(c) in the case of a property (other than a property referred to in paragraph (a) or (b)) that was not owned by the owner throughout the year, the amount, if any, by which

(i) that proportion of

(A) the carrying value of the property as at the end of the preceding taxation year, if the property was owned by the owner at that time,

(B) the carrying value of the property as at the end of the year, if the property was owned by the owner at that time and not at the end of the preceding taxation year, and

(C) in any other case, the cost of the property to the owner when it was acquired,

that the number of days that are in the year and at the end of which the owner owned the property is of the number of days in the year,

exceeds

(ii) the amount obtained when the interest payable by the owner, for the period in the year during which the property was held by the owner, on debt assumed or incurred by the owner in respect of the acquisition of the property (or another property for which the property is a substituted property) is divided by the average rate of interest payable by the owner (expressed as an annual rate) on the debt for the year; and

(d) in the case of any other property, the amount, if any, by which

(i) 50% of the total of

(A) the carrying value of the property as at the end of the year, and

(B) the carrying value of the property as at the end of the preceding taxation year

exceeds

(ii) the amount obtained when the interest payable by the owner, for the period in the year during which the property was held by the owner, on debt assumed or incurred by the owner in respect of the acquisition of the property (or another property for which the property is a substituted property) is divided by the average rate of interest payable by the owner (expressed as an annual rate) on the debt for the year.

Notes: For the "value" of investment property where the asset is funded with non-interest-bearing debt see VIEWS doc 2005-0164701C6.

"weighted Canadian liabilities" of an insurer as at the end of a taxation year means the total of

(a) 300% of the amount, if any, by which

(i) the total of all amounts each of which is an amount that is in respect of an insurance business carried on by the insurer in Canada and that is reported as a liability (other than a liability in respect of an amount payable out of a segregated fund) of the insurer in respect of a life insurance policy in Canada (other than an annuity) or an accident and sickness insurance policy as at the end of the year

exceeds

(ii) the total of

(A) the insurer's policy loans (other than policy loans in respect of annuities) as at the end of the year, and

(B) the reinsurance recoverable reported by the insurer as at the end of the year relating to its liabilities described in subparagraph (i), and

(b) the amount, if any, by which

(i) the total of all amounts each of which is an amount in respect of an insurance business carried on by the insurer in Canada that is reported as a liability of the insurer as at the end of the year, except to the extent that the amount is

(A) in respect of an insurance policy (other than an annuity) described in subparagraph (a)(i),

(B) a liability in respect of an amount payable out of a segregated fund, or

(C) a debt incurred or assumed by the insurer to acquire a property of the insurer,

exceeds

(ii) the total of

(A) the insurer's policy loans in respect of annuities as at the end of the year, and

(B) the reinsurance recoverable reported by the insurer as at the end of the year relating to its liabilities described in subparagraph (i).

Notes: Cls. (a)(ii)(B) and (b)(ii)(B) added by 2010 budget bill #2, effective for taxation years that begin after 2010.

"weighted total liabilities" of an insurer as at the end of a taxation year means the total of

(a) 300% of the amount, if any, by which

(i) the total of all amounts each of which is an amount that is in respect of an insurance business carried on by the insurer and that is reported as a liability (other than a liability in respect of an amount payable out of a segregated fund) of the insurer in respect of a life insurance policy (other than an annuity) or an accident and sickness insurance policy

exceeds

(ii) the total of

(A) the insurer's policy loans and foreign policy loans (other than policy loans and foreign policy loans in respect of annuities) as at the end of the year, and

(B) the reinsurance recoverable reported by the insurer as at the end of the year relating to its liabilities described in subparagraph (i), and

(b) the amount, if any, by which

(i) the total of all amounts each of which is an amount that is in respect of an insurance business carried on by the insurer and that is reported as a liability of the insurer as at the end of the year, except to the extent that the amount is

(A) in respect of an insurance policy (other than an annuity) described in subparagraph (a)(i),

(B) a liability in respect of an amount payable out of a segregated fund, or

(C) a debt incurred or assumed by the insurer to acquire a property of the insurer,

exceeds

(ii) the total of

(A) the insurer's policy loans and foreign policy loans in respect of annuities as at the end of the year, and

(B) the reinsurance recoverable reported by the insurer as at the end of the year relating to its liabilities described in subparagraph (i).

Notes: Subparas. (a)(ii)(B) and (b)(ii)(B) amended by 2010 budget bill #2, effective for taxation years that begin after 2010.

(2) Carrying value — For the purposes of this Part, the carrying value of a taxpayer's property for a taxation year, except as otherwise provided in this Part, means

(a) if the taxpayer is an insurer, the amounts reflected in the taxpayer's non-consolidated balance sheet as at the end of the taxation year accepted (or, if that non-consolidated balance sheet was not prepared, the taxpayer's non-consolidated balance sheet as at the end of the year that would have been accepted) by the Superintendent of Financial Institutions, in the case of an insurer that is required under the *Insurance Companies Act* to report to that Superintendent, or by the superintendent of insurance or other similar officer or authority of the province under the laws of which the insurer is incorporated or otherwise formed, in the case of an insurer that is required by law to report to that officer or authority; and

(b) in any other case, the amounts that would be reflected in the taxpayer's non-consolidated balance sheet as at the end of the taxation year if that balance sheet were prepared in accordance with generally accepted accounting principles.

(3) Amount or item reported — A reference in this Part to an amount or item reported as an asset or a liability of a taxpayer as at the end of a taxation year means an amount or item that is reported as an asset or a liability in the taxpayer's non-consolidated balance sheet as at the end of the year accepted (or, if that non-consolidated balance sheet was not prepared, the taxpayer's non-consolidated balance sheet as at the end of the year that would have been accepted) by the Superintendent of Financial Institutions, in the case of an insurer that is required under the *Insurance Companies Act* to report to that Superintendent, or by the superintendent of insurance or other similar officer or authority of the province under the laws of which the insurer is incorporated or otherwise formed, in the case of an insurer that is required by law to report to that officer or authority.

Notes: Reference to ITA 51.1 added to Reg. 2400(3)(a) by P.C. 2000-1714, effective for transactions occurring after October 1994.

(4) Application of certain definitions — For the purposes

(a) of subsection 138(14) of the Act, the expressions "Canadian investment fund for a taxation year", "specified Canadian assets" and "value for the taxation year" have the meanings prescribed for them by subsection 2404(1) as it read in its application to the 1977 taxation year; and

(b) of subsection 219(7) of the Act, the expressions "attributed surplus" and "Canadian investment fund" have the meaning prescribed for them by subsection (1).

(5) Deeming rules for certain assets — For the purposes of this Part, other than subsection 2401(6), an asset of an insurer is deemed not to have been used or held by the insurer in a taxation year in the course of carrying on an insurance business if the asset

(a) is owned by the insurer at the end of the year; and

(b) is a share of the capital stock of, or a debt owing to the insurer by, a financial institution affiliated with the insurer during each of the days in the year during which the insurer owned the asset.

(6) [Deeming rules for certain assets] — For the purposes of clause (a)(ii)(B) of the definition "Canadian investment fund" in subsection (1), an asset of an insurer is deemed not to have been used or held by the insurer in a taxation year in the course of carrying on an insurance business if the asset

(a) is owned by the insurer at the end of the year; and

(b) is

(i) goodwill, or

(ii) real property (or the portion of real property) owned by the insurer and occupied by the insurer for the purposes of carrying on an insurance business.

Notes: For interpretation of "goodwill" in (b)(i) see VIEWS doc 2009-0307911I7.

Reg. 2400(6) amended by P.C. 2011-936 (for tax years beginning after Oct, 12, 2011, or earlier by election), 1994-1817.

(7) No double counting — For greater certainty, a particular property or a particular proportion of a property shall not, directly or indirectly, be used or included more than once in determining, for a particular taxation year, the Canadian equity property or the equity property of a person or partnership.

(8) Transition year — A computation that is required to be made under this Part in respect of an insurer's taxation year that included September 30, 2006 and that is relevant to a computation (in this subsection referred to as the "transition year computation") that is required to be made under this Part in respect of the insurer's first taxation year that begins after that date shall, for the purposes only of the transition year computation, be made using the same definitions, rules and methodologies that are used in the transition year computation.

Notes: Reg. 2400(8) added by 2008 budget bill #2, effective for taxation years that begin after September 2006.

(9) A computation that is required to be made under this Part in respect of an insurer's taxation year that included December 31, 2010 and that is relevant to a computation (in this subsection referred to as the "transition year computation") that is required to be made under this Part in respect of the insurer's first taxation year

that begins after that date shall, for the purposes only of the transition year computation, be made using the same definitions, rules and methodologies that are used in the transition year computation.

Notes: Reg. 2400(9) added by 2010 budget bill #2, effective for taxation years that begin after 2010.

Notes [Reg. 2400]: Reg. 2400 replaced by P.C. 2000-1714, effective for 1999 and later taxation years.

Definitions [Reg. 2400]: "affiliated" — ITA 251.1; "allowable capital loss" — ITA 38(b), 248(1); "amortized cost", "amount" — ITA 248(1); "amount payable" — ITA 138(12); "annuity" — ITA 248(1); "arm's length" — ITA 251(1); "attributed surplus" — Reg. 2400(1); "business" — ITA 248(1); "Canada" — ITA 255, *Interpretation Act* 35(1); "Canadian business property", "Canadian equity property", "Canadian investment property", "Canadian outstanding premiums" — Reg. 2400(1); "Canadian partnership" — ITA 102(1), 248(1); "Canadian reserve liabilities" — Reg. 2400(1); "Canadian resource property" — ITA 66(15), 248(1); "capital property" — ITA 54, 248(1); "corporation" — ITA 248(1), *Interpretation Act* 35(1); "deposit balance" — Reg. 2400(1); "depreciable property" — ITA 13(21), 248(1); "designated insurance property" — ITA 138(12), 248(1); "disposition" — ITA 248(1); "equity property", "financial institution" — Reg. 2400(1); "fiscal period" — ITA 249.1; "foreign policy loan" — Reg. 2400(1); "gross investment revenue" — ITA 138(12); "income bond", "income debenture", "insurance policy", "insurer" — ITA 248(1); "investment property" — Reg. 2400(1); "land" — see ITA 70(5.2) Notes; "life insurance business" — ITA 248(1); "life insurance policies in Canada", "life insurance policy", "life insurance policy in Canada" — ITA 138(12); "life insurer" — ITA 248(1); "maximum tax actuarial reserve" — ITA 138(12); "mean Canadian investment fund" — Reg. 2412(1); "mean Canadian reserve liabilities" — Reg. 2400(1); "non-resident" — ITA 248(1); "non-segregated property" — ITA 138(12); "officer" — ITA 248(1); "partnership" — see ITA 96(1) Notes; "person" — ITA 248(1); "policy loan" — ITA 138(12); "prescribed", "property" — ITA 248(1); "property and casualty surplus" — Reg. 2400(1); "province" — *Interpretation Act* 35(1); "regulation" — ITA 248(1); "reinsurance recoverable" — Reg. 2400(1); "resident in Canada" — ITA 250; "segregated fund" — ITA 138.1(1), Reg. 2400(1); "share" — ITA 248(1); "small business bond" — ITA 15.2(3), 248(1); "small business development bond" — ITA 15.1(3), 248(1); "substituted" — ITA 248(5); "surplus funds derived from operations" — ITA 138(12); "taxable capital gain" — ITA 38(a), 248(1); "taxation year" — ITA 249; "taxpayer" — ITA 248(1); "trust" — ITA 104(1), 248(1), (3); "value", "weighted Canadian liabilities", "weighted total liabilities" — Reg. 2400(1).

2401. (1) For the purposes of the definition "designated insurance property" in subsection 138(12) of the Act, "designated insurance property" of an insurer for a taxation year means property that is designated in accordance with subsections (2) to (7) for the year

(a) by the insurer in its return of income under Part I of the Act for the year; or

(b) if the Minister determines that the insurer has not made a designation that is in accordance with the prescribed rules found in this section, by the Minister.

(2) Designation rules — For the purposes of subsection (1), an insurer, or the Minister if paragraph (1)(b) applies,

(a) shall designate for a taxation year investment property of the insurer for the year with a total value for the year equal to the amount, if any, by which the insurer's mean Canadian reserve liabilities for the year in respect of its life insurance business in Canada exceeds the total of the insurer's mean Canadian outstanding premiums and mean policy loans for the year in respect of that business (to the extent that the amount of the mean policy loans was not otherwise deducted in computing the insurer's mean Canadian reserve liabilities for the year);

(b) shall designate for a taxation year investment property of the insurer for the year with a total value for the year equal to the amount, if any, by which the insurer's mean Canadian reserve liabilities for the year in respect of its accident and sickness insurance business in Canada exceeds the insurer's mean Canadian outstanding premiums for the year in respect of that business;

(c) shall designate for a taxation year in respect of the insurer's insurance business in Canada (other than a life insurance business or an accident and sickness insurance business) investment property of the insurer for the year with a total value for the year equal to the amount, if any, by which the insurer's mean Canadian reserve liabilities for the year in respect of that business exceeds 50% of the total of all amounts each of which is the amount, as at the end of the year or as at the end of its preceding taxation year, of a premium receivable or a deferred acquisition expense (to the extent that it is included in the insurer's Canadian reserve liabilities as at the end of the year or preceding taxation year, as the case may be) of the insurer in respect of that business;

(d) if

(i) the insurer's mean Canadian investment fund for a taxation year

exceeds

(ii) the total value for the year of all property required to be designated under paragraph (a), (b) or (c) for the year,

shall designate for the year, in respect of a particular insurance business that the insurer carries on in Canada, investment property of the insurer for the year with a total value for the year equal to that excess;

(e) for greater certainty, under each of paragraphs (a), (b), (c) and (d), shall designate for the taxation year investment property with a total value for the year equal to the amount, if any, determined under each of those paragraphs, and no investment property, or portion of investment property, designated for the year under any of paragraphs (a) to (d) may be designated for the year under any other paragraph; and

(f) may designate for a taxation year a portion of a particular investment property if the designation of the entire property would result in a designation of property with a total value for the year exceeding that required to be designated under paragraphs (a) to (d) for the year.

Notes: Reg. 2401(2)(b) and (c) amended by 2010 budget bill #2, effective for taxation years that begin after 2010, effectively to delete subpara. (ii) from each.

(3) Order of designation of properties — For the purpose of subsection (2), investment property of an insurer for a taxation year shall be designated for the year in respect of the insurer's insurance businesses carried on by it in Canada in the following order:

(a) Canadian investment property of the insurer for the year owned by the insurer at the beginning of the year that was designated insurance property of the insurer for its preceding taxation year, except that such property shall be designated in the following order:

(i) real and depreciable property,

(ii) mortgages, hypothecs, agreements of sale and other forms of indebtedness in respect of real property situated in Canada or depreciable property situated in Canada or depreciable property leased to a person resident in Canada for use inside and outside of Canada, and

(iii) other property;

(b) investment property (other than Canadian investment property of the insurer for the year) owned by the insurer at the beginning of the year that was designated insurance property of the insurer for its preceding taxation year;

(c) Canadian investment property of the insurer for the year (other than property included in paragraph (a)) in the order set out in subparagraphs (a)(i) to (iii); and

(d) other investment property.

(4) Equity limit for the year — Notwithstanding subsections (2) and (3),

(a) the total value for the year of Canadian equity property of an insurer that may be designated in respect of the insurer's insurance businesses for a taxation year shall not exceed the insurer's equity limit for the year; and

(b) for a taxation year a portion of a particular Canadian equity property of an insurer may be designated if the designation of the entire property would result in a designation of Canadian equity property of the insurer for the year with a total value for the year exceeding the insurer's equity limit for the year.

(5) Exchanged property — For the purposes of subsection (3), property acquired by an insurer in a particular taxation year is deemed to be designated insurance property of the insurer in respect of a particular business of the insurer for its preceding taxation year and to have been owned by the insurer at the beginning of the particular taxation year if the property was acquired

(a) by reason of

(i) a transaction to which any of sections 51, 51.1, 85.1 and 86 of the Act applies,

(ii) a transaction in respect of which an election is made under subsection 85(1) or (2) of the Act,

(iii) an amalgamation (within the meaning assigned by subsection 87(1) of the Act), or

(iv) a winding-up of a corporation to which subsection 88(1) of the Act applies, and

(b) as consideration for or in exchange for property of the insurer that was designated insurance property of the insurer in respect of the particular insurance business for its preceding taxation year.

(6) Non-investment property — Non-segregated property owned by an insurer at any time in a taxation year (other than investment property of the insurer for the year) that is used or held by the insurer in the year in the course of carrying on an insurance business in Canada is deemed to be designated insurance property of the insurer for the year in respect of the business.

(7) Policy loan excluded from designated property — Notwithstanding any other provision in this Part, a policy loan payable to an insurer is not designated insurance property of the insurer.

Notes [Reg. 2401]: Reg. 2401 replaced by P.C. 2000-1714, effective for 1999 and later taxation years.

Definitions [Reg. 2401]: "amount", "business" — ITA 248(1); "Canada" — ITA 255, *Interpretation Act* 35(1); "Canadian equity property", "Canadian investment property", "Canadian reserve liabilities" — Reg. 2400(1); "corporation" — ITA 248(1), *Interpretation Act* 35(1); "depreciable property" — ITA 13(21), 248(1); "designated insurance property" — ITA 138(12), 248(1); "equity limit" — Reg. 2400(1); "insurer" — ITA 248(1); "investment property" — Reg. 2400(1); "life insurance business" — ITA 248(1); "mean Canadian investment fund" — Reg. 2412(1); "mean Canadian outstanding premiums", "mean Canadian reserve liabilities", "mean policy loans" — Reg. 2400(1); "Minister", "person" — ITA 248(1); "policy loan" — ITA 138(12); "prescribed", "property" — ITA 248(1); "reinsurance recoverable" — Reg. 2400(1); "resident in Canada" — ITA 250; "segregated fund" — ITA 138.1(1); "taxation year" — ITA 249; "value" — Reg. 2400(1).

2402. [Repealed]

Notes [Reg. 2402]: Reg. 2402 repealed by 2002-2013 technical bill (Part 5 — technical), for taxation years that begin after Oct. 2011. See now Reg. 309.1, which has replaced it. Earlier amended by P.C. 2009-1212.

Definitions [Reg. 2402]: "allowable capital loss" — ITA 38(b), 248(1); "amount" — ITA 248(1); "Canada" — ITA 255, *Interpretation Act* 35(1); "disposition" — ITA 248(1); "financial institution", "gross Canadian life investment income" — Reg. 2400(1); "insurer", "life insurance business" — ITA 248(1); "life insurance policies in Canada" — ITA 138(12); "life insurer" — ITA 248(1); "maximum tax actuarial reserve" — ITA 138(12); "mean maximum tax actuarial reserve" — Reg. 2400(1); "participating life insurance policy" — ITA 138(12); "property" — ITA 248(1); "taxable capital gain" — ITA 38(a), 248(1); "taxation year" — ITA 249.

2403. Branch tax elections — (1) An election referred to in subsection 219(4) of the Act shall be made by a non-resident insurer in respect of a taxation year by filing, with its return of income required by subsection 150(1) of the Act to be filed for the year, a letter in duplicate stating

(a) the insurer elects under subsection 219(4) of the Act; and

(b) the amount the insurer elects to deduct under subsection 219(4) of the Act.

(2) Where a joint election referred to in subsection 219(5.2) of the Act is made by a non-resident insurer and a qualified related corporation (within the meaning assigned by subsection 219(8) of the Act) of the non-resident insurer in respect of a taxation year of the non-resident insurer, it shall be made by filing, with the non-resident insurer's return of income required by subsection 150(1) of the Act to be filed for the year in which the event to which the election relates occurred, a letter in duplicate signed by an authorized officer of the non-resident insurer and an authorized officer of the qualified related corporation stating

(a) whether paragraphs 219(5.2)(a) and (b) of the Act apply; and

(b) the amount elected under subsection 219(5.2) of the Act.

Notes: Reg. 2403(2)(a) amended by P.C. 2000-1714, effective for 1999 and later taxation years, to change "(a) *or* (b)... is applicable" to "(a) *and* (b)... apply".

Definitions [Reg. 2403]: "amount" — ITA 248(1); "corporation" — ITA 248(1), *Interpretation Act* 35(1); "insurer", "non-resident", "officer" — ITA 248(1); "related" — ITA 251(2)–(6); "taxation year" — ITA 249.

2404–2409. [Repealed]

Notes: Reg. 2404-2409 repealed by 2002-2013 technical bill (Part 5 — technical), for taxation years that begin after Oct. 2011. Reg. 2404-2405 did not apply to 1999 and later taxation years (per Reg. 2406). Reg. 2407 and 2408 prescribed the amount of a life insurer's "1977 excess policy dividend" and "1977 carryforward deduction". Reg. 2409 provided transitional rules for 1977-78 and 1987.

2410. Prescribed amount — For the purpose of subsection 138(4.4) of the Act, the amount prescribed in respect of an insurer's cost or capital cost, as the case may be, of a property for a period in a taxation year is the amount determined by the formula

$$[(A \times B) \times C/365] - D$$

where

A is the average annual rate of interest determined by reference to rates of interest prescribed in section 4301 for the months or portion thereof in the period;

B is the amount, if any, by which, the average cost or average capital cost, as the case may be, of the property for the period exceeds the average amount of debt relating to the acquisition of the property outstanding during the period that bears a fair market interest rate and, for this purpose,

(a) the average cost or average capital cost, as the case may be, of a property is the total of

(i) the aggregate of all amounts each of which is the cost or capital cost, as the case may be, if any, immediately before the beginning of the period in respect of the property, and

(ii) the aggregate of all amounts each of which is the proportion of any expenditure incurred on any day in the period in respect of the cost or capital cost, as the case may be, of the property that

(A) the number of days from that day to the end of the period

is of

(B) the number of days in the period, and

(b) the average amount of debt relating to the acquisition of a property is the amount, if any, by which the total of

(i) the aggregate of all amounts each of which is an indebtedness relating to the acquisition that was outstanding at the beginning of the period, and

(ii) the aggregate of all amounts each of which is the proportion of an indebtedness relating to the acquisition that was incurred on any day in the period that

(A) the number of days from that day to the end of the period

is of

(B) the number of days in the period,

exceeds

(iii) the aggregate of all amounts each of which is the proportion of an amount that was paid in respect of any indebtedness referred to in subparagraph (i) or (ii) on any

day in the period (other than a payment of interest in respect thereof) that

(A) the number of days from that day to the end of the period

is of

(B) the number of days in the period;

C is the number of days in the period; and

D is the income derived from the property in the period by the person or partnership that owned the property.

Related Provisions: ITA 257 — Negative amounts in formulas.

Notes: For the meaning of "derived" in D, see Notes to ITA 18.1(12).

Reg. 2410(1) amended (and renumbered 2410), and Reg. 2410(2) repealed, by P.C. 2000-1714, effective for 1999 and later taxation years.

Definitions [Reg. 2410]: "amount", "insurer" — ITA 248(1); "month" — *Interpretation Act* 35(1); "partnership" — see ITA 96(1) Notes; "person", "prescribed", "property" — ITA 248(1); "taxation year" — ITA 249.

2411. (1) Subject to subsection (2), the amount prescribed in respect of an insurer for a taxation year for the purposes of paragraph 138(9)(b) of the Act shall be the amount determined by the formula

$$A - (B + B.1 + C)$$

where

A is the positive or negative amount, as the case may be, determined in respect of the insurer for the year under subsection (3);

B is the positive or negative amount, as the case may be, determined in respect of the insurer for the year under subsection (4) in respect of the insurer's investment property for the year that is designated insurance property of the insurer for the year;

B.1 is the positive or negative amount, as the case may be, determined in respect of the insurer for the year under subsection (4.1) in respect of property disposed of by the insurer in a taxation year for which it was designated insurance property of the insurer; and

C is the amount claimed by the insurer for the year in respect of any balance of its cumulative excess account at the end of the year.

Related Provisions: ITA 257 — Negative amounts in formulas.

Notes: Formula element B amended and B.1 added by P.C. 2000-1714, last change effective for 1999 and later tax years.

(2) Where an amount computed under subsection (1) in respect of an insurer is a negative amount, that amount shall be deemed to be nil.

(3) The positive or negative amount, as the case may be, determined under this subsection in respect of an insurer for a taxation year shall be

(a) if the value for the year of the insurer's foreign investment property that is designated insurance property for the year is not greater than 5% of the amount of the insurer's mean Canadian investment fund for the year and the insurer so elects in its return of income under Part I of the Act for the year, the amount determined by the formula

$$\{ [((A + A.1) / B) \times (C + J)] + [(D \times F) / E] \}$$

or

(b) in any other case, the amount determined by the formula

$$\{ [((A + A.1) / B) \times C] + [(D \times F) / E] + [((G + G.1) / H) \times J] \}$$

where

A is the positive or negative amount, as the case may be, determined in respect of the insurer for the year under subsection (4) in respect of Canadian investment property (other than Canadian equity property) owned by the insurer at any time in the year;

A.1 is the positive or negative amount, as the case may be, determined in respect of the insurer for the year under subsection (4.1) in respect of Canadian investment property (other than Canadian equity property) disposed of by the insurer in the year or a preceding taxation year;

B is the total value for the year of Canadian investment property (other than Canadian equity property and any property described in paragraph (i) of the definition "Canadian investment property" in subsection 2400(1)) owned by the insurer at any time in the year;

C is the total value for the year of the insurer's Canadian investment property for the year (other than Canadian equity property and any property described in paragraph (i) of the definition "Canadian investment property" in subsection 2400(1)) that is designated insurance property of the insurer for the year;

D is the positive or negative amount, as the case may be, determined in respect of the insurer for the year under subsection (4) in respect of Canadian investment property that is Canadian equity property owned by the insurer at any time in the year;

E is the total value for the year of Canadian investment property that is Canadian equity property (other than any property described in paragraph (i) of the definition "Canadian investment property" in subsection 2400(1)) owned by the insurer at any time in the year;

F is the total value for the year of the insurer's Canadian investment property (other than any property described in paragraph (i) of the definition "Canadian investment property" in subsection 2400(1)) for the year that is Canadian equity property that is designated insurance property of the insurer for the year;

G is the positive or negative amount, as the case may be, determined in respect of the insurer for the year under subsection (4) in respect of foreign investment property owned by the insurer at any time in the year;

G.1 is the positive or negative amount, as the case may be, determined in respect of the insurer for the year under subsection (4.1) in respect of foreign investment property disposed of by the insurer in the year or a preceding taxation year;

H is the total value for the year of foreign investment property (other than any property described in paragraph (e) of the definition "investment property" in subsection 2400(1)) owned by the insurer at any time in the year; and

J is the total value for the year of the insurer's foreign investment property (other than any property described in paragraph (e) of the definition "investment property" in subsection 2400(1)) that is designated insurance property of the insurer for the year.

Notes: The Reg. 2411(3)(a) election cannot be filed late: VIEWS doc 2015-0573861C6 [2015 CLHIA q.3].

Reg. 2411(3) amended by P.C. 2009-1212 (for 1995 and later tax years), 2005-2215 (for tax years ending after Feb. 27, 2004), 2000-1714.

(4) The positive or negative amount, as the case may be, determined under this subsection in respect of an insurer for a taxation year in respect of property shall be the amount determined by the formula

$$A - B$$

where

A is the total of the following amounts determined in respect of the property for the year, or that would be determined in respect of the property for the year if the property were designated insurance property of the insurer in respect of an insurance business in Canada for each taxation year in which the property was held by the insurer:

    (a) the insurer's gross investment revenue for the year (other than taxable dividends that were or would be deductible in computing the insurer's taxable income for the year under section 112 or subsection 138(6) of the Act) derived from the property,

    (b) [Repealed]

    (c) all amounts that were or would be included in computing the insurer's taxable capital gains for the year from the disposition of the property,

    (c.1) all amounts that were or would be included under paragraph 142.4(5)(e) of the Act in respect of the property in computing the insurer's income for the year,

    (d) all amounts that were or would be included in computing the insurer's income for the year as gains from the disposition of such of the property as is not capital property or a specified debt obligation (as defined in subsection 142.2(1) of the Act),

    (e) all amounts that were or would be included in computing the insurer's income for the year under subsection 13(1) of the Act in respect of the property,

    (f) all amounts that were or would be included in computing the insurer's income for the year under paragraph 12(1)(d), (d.1) or (i) of the Act in respect of the property,

    (g) all amounts that were or would be included in computing the insurer's income for the year under subsection 59(3.2) or (3.3) of the Act in respect of the property, and

    (h) [Repealed]

    (i) all other amounts that were or would be included in computing the insurer's income for the year in respect of the property otherwise than because of subsection 142.4(4) of the Act; and

B is the total of the following amounts determined in respect of the property for the year, or that would be determined in respect of the property for the year if the property were designated insurance property of the insurer in respect of an insurance business in Canada for each taxation year in which the property was held by the insurer:

    (a) all amounts that were or would be included in computing the insurer's allowable capital losses for the year from the disposition of the property,

    (a.1) all amounts that were or would be deductible under paragraph 142.4(5)(f) of the Act in respect of the property in computing the insurer's income for the year,

    (b) all amounts that were or would be deductible in computing the insurer's income for the year as losses from the disposition of such of the property as is not capital property or a specified debt obligation (as defined in subsection 142.2(1) of the Act),

    (c) [Repealed]

    (d) all amounts that were or would be deductible in computing the insurer's income for the year under paragraph 20(1)(a) of the Act in respect of the capital cost of the property or under paragraphs 20(1)(c) and (d) of the Act in respect of interest paid or payable on borrowed money used to acquire the property,

    (e) where any such property is rental property or leasing property (within the meaning assigned by subsections 1100(14) and (17), respectively), all amounts that were or would be deductible in computing the insurer's income for the year in respect of expenses directly related to the earning of rental income derived from the property,

    (f) all amounts that were or would be deductible by the insurer in computing the insurer's income for the year under paragraph 20(1)(l), (l.1) or (p) of the Act as reserve or bad debt in respect of the property,

    (g) all amounts that were deducted or would be deductible in computing the insurer's income for the year under section 66, 66.1, 66.2 or 66.4 of the Act in respect of the property, and

    (h) [Repealed]

    (i) all amounts that were or would be deductible in computing the insurer's income for the year in respect of other expenses directly related to the earning of gross investment revenue derived from the property.

Related Provisions: ITA 257 — Negative amounts in formulas.

Notes: For the meaning of "derived", see Notes to ITA 18.1(12).

Reg. 2411(4)A(h) and B(h) repealed by 2016 budget bill #2, effective 2017, as part of changing the eligible capital property rules to CCA Class 14.1 (see Notes to ITA 20(1)(b)).

Reg. 2411(4) amended by P.C. 2009-1212 (for 1999 and later tax years), 2005-2215 (for tax years ending after 2001), 2000-1714.

(4.1) The positive or negative amount, as the case may be, determined under this subsection in respect of an insurer for a taxation year in respect of property disposed of by the insurer in the year or a preceding taxation year is the amount determined by the formula

$$A - B$$

where

A   is the total of the amounts included under paragraphs 142.4(4)(a) and (c) of the Act in the insurer's income for the year in respect of the property, or that would be so included if the property were designated insurance property of the insurer in respect of an insurance business in Canada for each taxation year in which it was held by the insurer; and

B   is the total of the amounts deductible under paragraphs 142.4(4)(b) and (d) of the Act in respect of the property in computing the insurer's income for the year, or that would be so deductible if the property were designated insurance property of the insurer in respect of an insurance business in Canada for each taxation year in which it was held by the insurer.

Related Provisions: ITA 257 — Negative amounts in formulas.

Notes: Reg. 2411(4.1) added by P.C. 2000-1714, for 1999 and later taxation years.

(5) [Repealed]

(6) For the purposes of subsection (1), the balance of an insurer's cumulative excess account at the end of a taxation year shall be determined as the amount, if any, by which

(a) the aggregate of all amounts each of which is a positive amount, if any, determined in respect of each of such of its seven immediately preceding taxation years that began after June 17, 1987 and ended after 1987 by the formula

$$B - A$$

where A and B are the amounts determined under subsection (1) in respect of the insurer for such immediately preceding taxation year,

exceeds

(b) the aggregate of all amounts each of which is an amount claimed by the insurer under subsection (1) in respect of its cumulative excess account for a preceding taxation year that can be attributed to a positive amount determined under paragraph (a) for that year and, for the purpose of this paragraph, a positive amount determined in respect of a taxation year shall be deemed to have been claimed before a positive amount determined in respect of any subsequent taxation year.

Related Provisions: ITA 257 — Negative amounts in formulas.

(7) [Repealed]

Notes: Reg. 2411(7) repealed by P.C. 2000-1714, for 1999 and later taxation years.

(8) For the purposes of this section, "foreign investment property" of an insurer means investment property of the insurer (unless the insurer is a non-resident insurer and it is established by the insurer that the investment property is not effectively connected with its Canadian insurance businesses) that is not Canadian investment property of the insurer.

Definitions [Reg. 2411]: "allowable capital loss" — ITA 38(b), 248(1); "amount", "borrowed money", "business" — ITA 248(1); "Canada" — ITA 255, *Interpretation Act* 35(1); "Canadian equity property", "Canadian investment property" — Reg. 2400(1); "capital property" — ITA 54, 248(1); "designated insurance property" — ITA 138(12), 248(1); "disposition" — ITA 248(1); "gross investment revenue" — ITA 138(12); "insurer" — ITA 248(1); "investment property" — Reg. 2400(1); "mean Canadian investment fund" — Reg. 2412(1); "non-resident", "prescribed", "property" — ITA 248(1); "taxable capital gain" — ITA 38(a), 248(1); "taxable dividend" — ITA 89(1), 248(1); "taxable income" — ITA 248(1); "taxation year" — ITA 249; "value" — Reg. 2400(1).

2412. (1) Mean Canadian investment fund — For the purposes of this Part, the mean Canadian investment fund of an insurer for a particular taxation year is the total of

(a) 50% of the total of

(i) its Canadian investment fund at the end of the particular year, and

(ii) either,

(A) if the insurer is resident in Canada, its Canadian investment fund at the end of its preceding taxation year, or

(B) if the insurer is non-resident, its Canadian investment fund at the end of its preceding taxation year determined as if its attributed surplus for that preceding taxation year were its attributed surplus for the particular year, and

(b) the insurer's cash-flow adjustment for the particular year.

(2) Cash-flow adjustment — An insurer's cash-flow adjustment for a taxation year is the amount equal to

(a) if the year ended two months or more after it began, the positive or negative amount determined by the formula

$$50\% \times (A - B/C)$$

where

A   is the total of all amounts each of which is the amount determined under subsection (3) in respect of a full month in the year (or in respect of the part of the month that ends after the last full month in the year, if that part is greater than 15 days),

B   is the total of all amounts each of which is the amount determined in respect of a full month in the year (or in respect of the part of the month that ends after the last full month in the year, if that part is greater than 15 days) by the formula

$$D \times (1 + 2E)$$

where

D   is the amount determined under subsection (3) in respect of the month or part of the month, and

E   is the number of months in the year that ended before the beginning of the month or part of the month, and

C   is the number of full months in the year (plus 1, if the year ends more than 15 days after the end of the last full month in the year); and

(b) if the year ended less than two months after it began, nil.

Related Provisions: ITA 257 — Negative amounts in formulas.

(3) Amounts paid and received — The amount determined in respect of an insurer for a particular month or part of a month (in this subsection referred to as a "month") in a taxation year is the positive or negative amount determined by the formula

$$G - H$$

where

G   is the total of all amounts each of which is

(a) the amount of a premium or consideration received by the insurer in the month in respect of a contract of insurance (including a settlement annuity) entered into in the course of carrying on its insurance businesses in Canada,

(b) an amount received by the insurer in the month in respect of interest on or a repayment in respect of a policy loan made under a life insurance policy in Canada, or

(c) an amount received by the insurer in the month in respect of reinsurance (other than reinsurance undertaken to effect a transfer of a business in respect of which subsection 138(11.5), (11.92) or (11.94) of the Act applies) arising in the course of carrying on its insurance businesses in Canada; and

H is the total of all amounts each of which is

(a) the amount of a claim or benefit (including a payment under an annuity or settlement annuity, a payment of a policy dividend and an amount paid on a lapsed or terminated policy), a refund of premiums, a premium or a commission paid by the insurer in the month under a contract of insurance in the course of carrying on its insurance businesses in Canada,

(b) the amount of a policy loan made by the insurer in the month under a life insurance policy in Canada, or

(c) an amount paid by the insurer in the month in respect of reinsurance (other than reinsurance undertaken to effect a transfer of a business in respect of which subsection 138(11.5), (11.92) or (11.94) of the Act applies) in the course of carrying on its insurance businesses in Canada.

Related Provisions: ITA 257 — Negative amounts in formulas.

(4) [Meaning of "month"] — A reference to a "month" in this section means

(a) if an insurer's taxation year does not begin on the first day of a calendar month and the insurer elects to have this paragraph apply for the year, the period beginning on the day in a calendar month that has the same calendar number as the particular day on which the taxation year began and ending

(i) on the day immediately before the day in the next calendar month that has the same calendar number as the particular day, or

(ii) if the next calendar month does not have a day that has the same calendar number as the particular day, the last day of that next calendar month; and

(b) in any other case, a calendar month.

Related Provisions: ITA 257 — Negative amounts in formulas.

Notes [Reg. 2412]: Reg. 2412 amended by P.C. 2000-1714, effective for 1999 and later taxation years.

Definitions [Reg. 2412]: "amount", "annuity" — ITA 248(1); "attributed surplus" — Reg. 2400(1); "business" — ITA 248(1); "Canada" — ITA 255, *Interpretation Act* 35(1); "Canadian investment fund" — Reg. 2400(1); "cash-flow adjustment" — Reg. 2412(2); "dividend", "insurer" — ITA 248(1); "life insurance policy in Canada" — ITA 138(12); "mean Canadian investment fund" — Reg. 2400(1); "month" — Reg. 2412(4); "non-resident" — ITA 248(1); "policy loan" — ITA 138(12); "resident in Canada" — ITA 250; "taxation year" — ITA 249.

PART XXV — [2500–2501] SPECIAL T1 TAX TABLE FOR INDIVIDUALS

2500, 2501. [No longer relevant]

Notes: Reg. 2500 provides specifics for "tax tables", authorized by former ITA 117(6). These were printed with the T1 General tax return guide, to allow most individuals to look up their tax payable (based on taxable income rounded to the nearest $2). With widespread use of software and calculators, the tables were eliminated to save costs (Revenue Canada news release, Nov. 22, 1995.)

PART XXVI — [2600–2608] INCOME EARNED IN PROVINCE BY AN INDIVIDUAL

Notes [Part XXVI]: Part XXVI allocates an individual's (including a trust's) income among the provinces. For the equivalent rules for corporations, see Reg. 400–413.

2600. Interpretation — **(1)** In applying the definition **"income earned in the year in a province"** in subsection 120(4) of the Act for an individual's taxation year

(a) the prescribed rules referred to in that definition are the rules in this Part; and

(b) the amount determined under those prescribed rules means the total of all amounts each of which is the individual's income earned in the taxation year in a particular province as determined under this Part.

Notes: Reg. 2600(1) amended by 2008 budget bill #2, for 2009 and later tax years.

(2) In this Part, **"permanent establishment"** means a fixed place of business of the individual including an office, a branch, a mine, an oil well, a farm, a timberland, a factory, a workshop or a warehouse, and

(a) where an individual carries on business through an employee or agent, established in a particular place, who has general authority to contract for his employer or principal or who has a stock of merchandise owned by his employer or principal from which he regularly fills orders which he receives, the individual shall be deemed to have a permanent establishment in that place;

(b) where an individual uses substantial machinery or equipment in a particular place at any time in a taxation year he shall be deemed to have a permanent establishment in that place; and

(c) the fact that an individual has business dealings through a commission agent, broker, or other independent agent or maintains an office solely for the purchase of merchandise, shall not of itself be held to mean that the individual has a permanent establishment.

Notes: See Notes to Canada-U.S. Tax Treaty:Art. V:2 for case law on the meaning of "permanent establishment". See Notes to Reg. 400(2) for the meaning of "agent" and of "substantial machinery or equipment". See also Notes to Reg. 2601(1).

Interpretation Bulletins: IT-242R: Retired partners.

I.T. Technical News: 33 (permanent establishment — the *Dudney* case update).

CRA Audit Manual: 15.6.0: Permanent establishment.

(3) [Revoked]

Definitions [Reg. 2600]: "amount", "business", "employee", "employer", "individual", "office" — ITA 248(1); "permanent establishment" — Reg. 2600(2); "prescribed" — ITA 248(1); "province" — *Interpretation Act* 35(1); "taxation year" — ITA 249.

2601. Residents of Canada — **(1)** If an individual resides in a particular province on the last day of a taxation year and has no income for the taxation year from a business with a permanent establishment outside the province, the individual's income earned in the taxation year in the particular province is the individual's income for the taxation year.

Related Provisions: Reg. 2607 — When person is resident in two provinces, principal place of residence applies.

Notes: Provincial taxation depends on the province of residence as of Dec. 31, even for capital gains on sale of property: VIEWS doc 2011-0395821E5. The CRA applies the same criteria as for residence in Canada (see Notes to ITA 250(1)) to determine provincial residence: Income Tax Folio S5-F1-C1 ¶1.2-1.4; docs 2002-0139005, 2004-0057301E5, 2004-0054681I7; 2014-0519481M4 (provincial health care eligibility rules are irrelevant).

See also Rule & Kakkar, "Deemed Residence Issue", 2(4) *Tax for the Owner-Manager* (ctf.ca) 29-30 (Oct. 2002); Matthews, "Water Runs Downhill: Interprovincial Tax Planning", 2004 Cdn Tax Foundation conference report, at 25:13-19; Grower, "Current Interprovincial Issues", 2006 conference report, at 24:1-11; Gartner, "Residence of Individuals", 2013 Prairie Provinces Tax Conference (ctf.ca), 4B:1-23.

The disparity in provincial rates creates an incentive to misreport the province of residence. "The CRA catches and fines people who attempt to evade taxes by filing a tax return claiming to live in one province but who actually reside in another" (news release, March 27/07).

For the residency of a trust (central management and control (CM&C)), see ITA 250(1) Notes; Dolson, "Provincial Residency — Trusts", 2013 Prairie Provinces Tax Conference (ctf.ca), 4A:1-17; VIEWS doc 2019-0800551E5 (TFSA trust: trustee or investment firm's office, not holder's residence). In *Discovery Trust*, 2015 NLTD(G) 86, a trust for Nfld. beneficiaries was held to have successfully moved its CM&C to Alberta; obtaining beneficiaries' consent did not mean the trustee was delegating power (paras. 41, 57). Absent GAAR, CRA was wrong to consider a tax-avoidance motive as relevant [Poon, "Interprovincial Tax Planning Using Trusts Upheld", 5(3) *Canadian Tax Focus* (ctf.ca) 6-7 (Aug. 2015)]. *Contra*, trusts did not successfully become Alberta resident in: *Boettger*, 2017 QCCA 1670 (passive AB trustee); *Herman Grad 2000 Family Trust*, 2016 ONSC 2402 (AB trustees took direction from Ontario beneficiary); *895410 Alberta [Haifa Trust]*, 2018 QCCQ 2581 (only AB connection was corporate trustee, whose sole shareholder was Quebec resident whose family were the trust beneficiaries). These cases do not change CRA's view; family trusts are examined to determine where is the "high-level strategic decision making and governance": 2015-0610791C6 [2015 CTF q.3]. CRA cannot assess a trust as resident in AB and then say it never assessed Ontario tax so that time has not started running to assess it: *Aubrey Dan Family Trust*, 2016 ONSC 3801, para. 17 (aff'd on other grounds 2017 ONCA 875: the assessment was valid since a 152(4) waiver had been filed).

An appeal on the basis the taxpayer is not resident in a province cannot go to the Tax Court, but must be taken to the court of that province. See Notes to ITA 169(1). There is no specific mechanism for the provinces to settle a question on the residence of a trust under the "central management and control" test (see Notes to 250(1)): VIEWS doc 2011-0412221C6.

CRA will apply Reg. 2601(1) to a Quebec partnership with non-business income from outside the province: VIEWS doc 2011-0411911C6.

Reg. 2601(1) amended by P.C. 2010-548, effective May 12, 2010 (non-substantive wording cleanup).

(2) If an individual resides in a particular province on the last day of a taxation year and has income for the taxation year from a business with a permanent establishment outside the particular province, the individual's income earned in the taxation year in the particular province is the amount, if any, by which

(a) the individual's income for the taxation year

exceeds

(b) the total of all amounts each of which is the individual's income for the taxation year from carrying on a business that is earned in a province other than the particular province or in a country other than Canada, determined in accordance with this Part.

Notes: Reg. 2601(2) amended by P.C. 2010-548, effective May 12, 2010.

(3) If an individual, who resides in Canada on the last day of a taxation year and who has carried on business in a particular province at any time in the taxation year, does not reside in the particular province on the last day of the taxation year, the individual's income earned in the taxation year in the particular province is the individual's income for the taxation year from carrying on business earned in the particular province, determined in accordance with this Part.

Notes: Reg. 2601(3) amended by P.C. 2010-548, effective May 12, 2010.

(4) If an individual resides in Canada on the last day of a taxation year and carried on business in another country at any time in the taxation year, the individual's income earned in the taxation year in that other country is the individual's income for the taxation year from carrying on business earned in the other country, determined in accordance with this Part.

Notes: Reg. 2601(4) amended by P.C. 2010-548, effective May 12, 2010.

(5) In this section, a reference to the **"last day of a taxation year"** is deemed to be a reference to

(a) the "last day in the year on which the individual resided in Canada", in the case of an individual who resided in Canada at any time in the year but ceased to reside in Canada before the end of the year; and

(b) the "day in the year on which the individual would have ceased to reside in Canada, if the Act were read without reference to paragraphs 250(1)(d.1) and (f) of the Act,", in the case of a particular individual described in paragraph 250(1)(d.1) of the Act, or of another individual who is a spouse, common-law partner or child of the particular individual, who

(i) was resident in Canada at any time in the year,

(ii) would have ceased to be resident in Canada before the end of the year, if the Act were read without reference to paragraphs 250(1)(d.1) and (f) of the Act, and

(iii) is, pursuant to paragraph 250(1)(d.1) or (f) of the Act, deemed to have been resident in Canada throughout the year.

Notes [Reg. 2601(5)]: Reg. 2601(5) amended by P.C. 2007-849 (effective June 13, 2007), 2001-957.

Definitions [Reg. 2601]: "amount", "business" — ITA 248(1); "Canada" — ITA 255, *Interpretation Act* 35(1); "child" — ITA 252(1); "individual" — ITA 248(1); "last day of a taxation year" — Reg. 2601(5); "permanent establishment" — Reg. 2600(2); "province" — *Interpretation Act* 35(1); "resident in Canada", "resident of Canada" — ITA 250; "taxation year" — ITA 249.

Remission Orders [Reg. 2601]: *Income Earned in Quebec Income Tax Remission Order*, P.C. 1989-1204, as amended by P.C. 1991-1661 and P.C. 1992-2593 (special interpretation of Reg. 2601(1) and (2) for residents of Quebec).

Income Tax Folios: S5-F1-C1: Determining an individual's residence status [replaces IT-221R3].

Forms [Reg. 2601]: T3 Sched. 12: Minimum tax; T3 Sched. 12A Chart 2: Ontario minimum tax carryover; T1219: Provincial alternative minimum tax; T1219-ON: Ontario minimum tax carryover; T1256: Manitoba community enterprise development tax credit; T1256-1: Manitoba small business venture capital tax credit (individuals); T2203: Provincial and territorial taxes — multiple jurisdictions.

2602. Non-residents — **(1)** Subject to subsection (2), if an individual does not reside in Canada at any time in a taxation year, the individual's income earned in the taxation year in a province is the total of

(a) the portion of the taxpayer's income from an office or employment that is included in the taxpayer's taxable income earned in Canada for the taxation year under subparagraph 115(1)(a)(i) of the Act and that is reasonably attributable to the duties performed by the taxpayer [in] the province; and

(b) the taxpayer's income for the taxation year from carrying on business earned in the province, determined in accordance with this Part.

Notes: A non-resident NHL hockey player should allocate income to each province in which he plays games, according to VIEWS doc 2012-0440381E5.

Reg. 2602(1) amended by P.C. 2010-548, effective May 12, 2010.

Remission Orders: *Income Earned in Quebec Income Tax Remission Order*, P.C. 1989-1204, as amended by P.C. 1991-1661 and P.C. 1992-2593 (special interpretation of Reg. 2602(1) for Quebec).

Interpretation Bulletins: IT-393R2: Election re tax on rents and timber royalties — non-residents; IT-434R: Rental of real property by individual.

(2) Where the aggregate of the amounts of an individual's income as determined under subsection (1) for all provinces for a taxation year exceeds the aggregate of the amounts of his income described in subparagraphs 115(1)(a)(i) and (ii) of the Act, the amount of his income earned in the taxation year in a particular province shall be that proportion of his income so described that the amount of his income earned in the taxation year in the province as determined under subsection (1) is of the aggregate of all such amounts.

Definitions [Reg. 2602]: "amount", "business" — ITA 248(1); "Canada" — ITA 255, *Interpretation Act* 35(1); "employment", "individual", "office" — ITA 248(1); "province" — *Interpretation Act* 35(1); "taxable income earned in Canada" — ITA 248(1); "taxation year" — ITA 249.

2603. Income from business — **(1)** Where, in a taxation year, an individual had a permanent establishment in a particular province or a country other than Canada and had no permanent establishment outside that province or country, the whole of his income from carrying on business for the year shall be deemed to have been earned therein.

(2) Where, in a taxation year, an individual had no permanent establishment in a particular province or country other than Canada, no part of his income for the year from carrying on business shall be deemed to have been earned therein.

(3) Except as otherwise provided, where, in a taxation year, an individual had a permanent establishment in a particular province or in a particular country other than Canada and had a permanent establishment outside that particular province or particular country, the amount of the individual's income for the taxation year from carrying on business that is deemed to have been earned in the particular province or particular country is half of the total of

(a) that proportion of the individual's income for the year from carrying on business that the gross revenue for the fiscal period that ends in the taxation year that is reasonably attributable to the permanent establishment in the particular province or particular country is of the individual's total gross revenue for that period from the business; and

(b) that proportion of the individual's income for the taxation year from carrying on business that the total of all amounts that are salaries and wages paid in the fiscal period that ends in the taxation year to employees of the permanent establishment in the particular province or particular country is of the total of all amounts that are salaries and wages paid in that period to employees of the business.

(4) For the purpose of determining the gross revenue for the year reasonably attributable to the permanent establishment in a particular province or country other than Canada within the meaning of paragraph (3)(a), the following rules shall apply:

(a) where the destination of a shipment of merchandise to a customer to whom the merchandise is sold is in the particular province or country, the gross revenue derived therefrom shall be attributable to the permanent establishment in the province or country;

(b) except as provided in paragraph (c), where the destination of a shipment of merchandise to a customer to whom the merchandise is sold is in a province or country other than Canada in which the taxpayer has no permanent establishment, if the person negotiating the sale may reasonably be regarded as being attached to the permanent establishment in the particular province or country, the gross revenue derived therefrom shall be attributable to that permanent establishment;

(c) where the destination of a shipment of merchandise to a customer to whom the merchandise is sold is in a country other than Canada in which the taxpayer has no permanent establishment,

(i) if the merchandise was produced or manufactured, or produced and manufactured, entirely in the particular province by the taxpayer, the gross revenue derived therefrom shall be attributable to the permanent establishment in the province, or

(ii) if the merchandise was produced or manufactured, or produced and manufactured, partly in the particular province and partly in another place by the taxpayer, the gross revenue derived therefrom attributable to the permanent establishment in the province shall be that proportion thereof that the salaries and wages paid in the year to employees of the permanent establishment in the province where the merchandise was partly produced or manufactured (or partly produced and manufactured) is of the aggregate of the salaries and wages paid in the year to employees of the permanent establishments where the merchandise was produced or manufactured (or produced and manufactured);

(d) where a customer to whom merchandise is sold instructs that shipment be made to some other person and the customer's office with which the sale was negotiated is located in the particular province or country, the gross revenue derived therefrom shall be attributable to the permanent establishment in the province or country;

(e) except as provided in paragraph (f), where a customer to whom merchandise is sold instructs that shipment be made to some other person and the customer's office with which the sale was negotiated is located in a province or country other than Canada in which the taxpayer has no permanent establishment, if the person negotiating the sale may reasonably be regarded as being attached to the permanent establishment in the particular province or country, the gross revenue derived therefrom shall be attributable to that permanent establishment;

(f) where a customer to whom merchandise is sold instructs that shipment be made to some other person and the customer's office with which the sale was negotiated is located in a country other than Canada in which the taxpayer has no permanent establishment,

(i) if the merchandise was produced or manufactured, or produced and manufactured, entirely in the particular province by the taxpayer, the gross revenue derived therefrom shall be attributable to the permanent establishment in the province, or

(ii) if the merchandise was produced or manufactured, or produced and manufactured, partly in the particular province and partly in another place by the taxpayer, the gross revenue derived therefrom attributable to the permanent establishment in the province shall be that proportion thereof that the salaries and wages paid in the year to employees of the per-

manent establishment in the province where the merchandise was partly produced or manufactured (or partly produced and manufactured) is of the aggregate of the salaries and wages paid in the year to employees of the permanent establishments where the merchandise was produced or manufactured (or produced and manufactured);

(g) where gross revenue is derived from services rendered in the particular province or country, the gross revenue shall be attributable to the permanent establishment in the province or country;

(h) where gross revenue is derived from services rendered in a province or country other than Canada in which the taxpayer has no permanent establishment, if the person negotiating the contract may reasonably be regarded as being attached to the permanent establishment of the taxpayer in the particular province or country, the gross revenue shall be attributable to that permanent establishment;

(i) where standing timber or the right to cut standing timber is sold and the timber limit on which the timber is standing is in the particular province or country, the gross revenue from such sale shall be attributable to the permanent establishment of the taxpayer in the province or country; and

(j) where land is a permanent establishment of the taxpayer in the particular province, the gross revenue which arises from leasing the land shall be attributable to that permanent establishment.

(5) Where an individual pays a fee to another person under an agreement pursuant to which that other person or employees of that other person perform services for the individual that would normally be performed by employees of the individual, the fee so paid shall be deemed to be salary paid by the individual and that part of the fee that may reasonably be regarded as payment in respect of services rendered at a particular permanent establishment of the individual shall be deemed to be salary paid to an employee of that permanent establishment.

(6) For the purposes of subsection (5), a fee does not include a commission paid to a person who is not an employee of the individual.

Notes [Reg. 2603]: A limited partner's income is allocated based on where the partnership earned the income: VIEWS doc 2010-0367621E5.

For the meaning of "derived" in Reg. 2603(4), see Notes to ITA 18.1(12). "Land" in (4)(j) includes buildings: see ITA 70(5.2) Notes.

Reg. 2603(3) amended by P.C. 2011-951, effective Oct. 12, 2011.

Definitions [Reg. 2603]: "amount" — ITA 248(1); "business" — Reg. 2606(3)(a); "Canada" — ITA 255, *Interpretation Act* 35(1); "employee" — ITA 248(1); "fee" — Reg. 2603(6); "fiscal period" — ITA 249.1; "gross revenue" — ITA 248(1); "income for the year from carrying on business" — Reg. 2606(1), 2606(3)(b); "individual" — ITA 248(1); "land" — see ITA 70(5.2) Notes; "office" — ITA 248(1); "permanent establishment" — Reg. 2600(2); "person" — ITA 248(1); "province" — *Interpretation Act* 35(1); "salaries and wages paid in the year" — Reg. 2606(3)(c); "taxation year" — ITA 249; "taxpayer" — ITA 248(1); "total gross revenue for the year" — Reg. 2606(3)(d).

Provincial Income Allocation Newsletters: 4 (salaries and wages — inclusion of taxable benefits).

2604. Bus and truck operators — Notwithstanding subsections 2603(3) and (4), the amount of income that shall be deemed to have been earned in a particular province or country other than Canada by an individual from carrying on the business of transportation of goods or passengers (other than by the operation of a railway, ships or an airline service) is $\frac{1}{2}$ of the aggregate of

(a) that proportion of his income therefrom for the year that the number of miles travelled by his vehicles in the province or country in the fiscal period ending in the year is of the total number of miles travelled by his vehicles in that period; and

(b) that proportion of his income therefrom for the year that the aggregate of salaries and wages paid in the fiscal period ending in the year to employees of the permanent establishment in the province or country is of the aggregate of all salaries and wages paid in that period to employees of the business.

Definitions [Reg. 2604]: "amount" — ITA 248(1); "business" — Reg. 2606(3)(a); "Canada" — ITA 255, *Interpretation Act* 35(1); "employee" — ITA 248(1); "fiscal period" — ITA 249.1; "income for the year from carrying on business" — Reg. 2606(1), 2606(3)(b); "individual" — ITA 248(1); "permanent establishment" — Reg. 2600(2); "province" — *Interpretation Act* 35(1); "salaries and wages paid in the year" — Reg. 2606(3); "total gross revenue for the year" — Reg. 2606(3)(d).

Provincial Income Allocation Newsletters: 4 (salaries and wages — inclusion of taxable benefits).

2605. More than one business — Where an individual operates more than one business, the provisions of sections 2603 and 2604 shall be applied in respect of each business and the amount of income for the year from carrying on business earned in a particular province or country in the year is the aggregate of the amounts so determined.

Notes [Reg. 2605]: For CRA interpretation see VIEWS doc 2004-0073371E5.

Definitions [Reg. 2605]: "amount" — ITA 248(1); "business" — Reg. 2606(3)(a); "income for the year from carrying on business" — Reg. 2606(1), 2606(3)(b); "individual" — ITA 248(1); "province" — *Interpretation Act* 35(1); "salaries and wages" — Reg. 2606(3)(c); "total gross revenue for the year" — Reg. 2606(3)(d).

Interpretation Bulletins: IT-206R: Separate businesses.

2606. Limitations of business income — (1) [Limitations of business income] — If, in the case of an individual to whom section 2601 applies, the total of the amounts otherwise determined to be the individual's income for a taxation year from carrying on business that is earned in all provinces and countries other than Canada is greater than the individual's income for the year, the individual's income for the year from carrying on business earned in a particular province or country other than Canada is deemed to be that proportion of the individual's income for the year that

(a) the individual's income for the year from carrying on business in the particular province or country as otherwise determined

is of

(b) that total.

Notes: Reg. 2606(1) amended by P.C. 2009-1869, for 1998 and later taxation years.

(2) [Part-year residents] — If section 114 of the Act applies in respect of an individual for a taxation year, the following rules apply:

(a) the portion of subsection (1) before paragraph (a) is to be read as follows in respect of the individual for the year:

2606. (1) If, in the case of an individual to whom section 2601 applies, the total of the amounts otherwise determined to be the individual's income for a taxation year from carrying on business that is earned in all provinces and countries other than Canada is greater than the individual's taxable income for the year, the individual's income for the year from carrying on business earned in a particular province or country other than Canada is deemed to be that proportion of the individual's taxable income for the year that

(b) for the purpose of this Part, the individual's income for the year from carrying on a business in any place shall be computed by reference only to the income from that business that is included in computing the individual's taxable income for the year.

Notes: Reg. 2606(2) amended by P.C. 2009-1869, for 1998 and later taxation years.

(3) For the purposes of sections 2603 to 2605, where an individual's taxable income for the taxation year is computed in accordance with section 115 of the Act

(a) a reference to a "business" shall be deemed to refer only to a business that was wholly or partly carried on in Canada;

(b) a reference to "income for the year from carrying on business" shall be deemed to refer only to income for the year from carrying on a business in Canada as determined for the purposes of section 115 of the Act;

(c) a reference to "salaries and wages paid in the year" shall be deemed to be a reference to salaries and wages paid to employees of his permanent establishments in Canada; and

(d) a reference to "total gross revenue for the year" from the business shall be deemed to be a reference to total gross revenue reasonably attributable to his permanent establishments in Canada.

Provincial Income Allocation Newsletters: 4 (salaries and wages — inclusion of taxable benefits).

Definitions [Reg. 2606]: "amount", "business" — ITA 248(1); "Canada" — ITA 255, *Interpretation Act* 35(1); "employee", "gross revenue" — ITA 248(1); "his income for the taxation year" — Reg. 2606(2); "individual" — ITA 248(1); "permanent establishment" — Reg. 2600(2); "province" — *Interpretation Act* 35(1); "taxable income" — ITA 248(1); "taxation year" — ITA 249.

2607. Dual residence — Where an individual was resident in more than one province on the last day of the taxation year, for the purposes of this Part, he shall be deemed to have resided on that day only in that province which may reasonably be regarded as his principal place of residence.

Notes: For discussion of how CRA is involved in auditing individuals' provincial residence on behalf of the provinces, see May 2009 ICAA roundtable (tinyurl.com/cra-abtax) q.17. An appeal of only province of residence cannot be brought in the Tax Court: *Nagel*, 2018 TCC 32 (under appeal to FCA), and see ITA 169(1) Notes.

CRA administrative policy on "residence in Canada", in Income Tax Folio S5-F1-C1, applies to residence in a province: ¶1.2-1.4, and Reg. 2607 provides the tie-breaker rule for a dual resident: ¶1.2, VIEWS doc 2004-0054681I7. See also Notes to Reg. 2601(1).

Taxpayers were found to be ordinarily resident in Alberta in *Waring*, 2006 BCSC 2046; *Mandrusiak*, 2007 BCSC 1418 (resident in both AB and BC but slightly more ties and roots in AB); *Owens*, 2007 NSSC 341 (WestJet pilot moved his base from NS to AB); *Persaud*, 2007 TCC 474 (moving expenses to take 3-month job allowed); *Smolensky*, 2008 BCSC 1509 (resident in both AB and BC but more ties to AB); *Smale*, 2009 SKQB 114 (taxpayer had relinquished SK residency and taken up residency in AB).

Taxpayers were found not to have become resident in Alberta in: *Sears*, 2009 TCC 344 (despite working there for over two years); *Sampson*, 2018 BCSC 1503 (S had small condo for work in AB and his wife had large home in BC, and ties to BC were much deeper so primary residence was BC); *Rousseau*, 2018 QCCQ 7340 (aff'd on other grounds 2020 QCCA 1308; leave to appeal denied 2021 CarswellQue 3905 (SCC)) (working in Fort McMurray but family stayed in QC; no penalty for not filing in QC, as R relied on accountant's advice); *Baril*, 2020 QCCQ 1466 (B had Calgary apartment for work but was more tied to husband and children at their QC home).

In *Stubbs*, 2009 BCPC 247, taxpayers who filed returns as AB residents using their daughter's address were acquitted of charges of making false statements. For the mother, there was uncertainty as to where she was resident. For the father, there was a false statement but no fraudulent intent, only extreme carelessness. CRA announced on Oct. 17/12 the conviction and $24,750 fine of Air Canada pilot Robert Parnell for reporting as resident in AB when he lived in MB.

In *Fono*, 2018 QCCQ 10534, F moved to ON but was held still resident in QC, due to his family and numerous "secondary" ties staying there. In *Adou*, 2020 QCCQ 131, A moved from QC to ON for 3 years but kept certain ties in QC; he was held not resident in QC for those years. In *Sanctuary*, 2020 QCCQ 1903, a Montreal university professor's ties to (and time spent in) QC were much closer than to ON.

Where a trust is reassessed as resident in a higher-tax jurisdiction, the provincial tax already paid will be credited to the account: 2012 Ontario Tax Conf. Roundtable (ctf.ca) Q9.

Definitions: "individual" — ITA 248(1); "province" — *Interpretation Act* 35(1); "resident" — ITA 250; "taxation year" — ITA 249.

Income Tax Folios: S5-F1-C1: Determining an individual's residence status [replaces IT-221R3].

2608. SIFT trusts — For the purposes of this Part, if the individual is a SIFT trust, a reference to income earned in a taxation year shall be read as a reference to the amount that would, if this Part were read without reference to this section, be the amount, if any, by which its income for the taxation year exceeds its taxable SIFT trust distributions for the taxation year.

Notes: See Notes to ITA 104(16). Taxable SIFT trust distributions are kept in the trust's income to calculate the income trust distributions tax: ITA 104(6)(b)(iv), 104(16) and 122(1)(b). However, they have been distributed to beneficiaries, so they are not really part of the trust's income. Thus, Reg. 2608 excludes them, so the SIFT tax will not cause a trust to change province of residence.

Reg. 2608 added by 2007 budget bill #1, effective Oct. 31, 2006 (but see ITA 122.1(2) for the actual effective date).

Regulations

Definitions [Reg. 2608]: "amount", "individual" — ITA 248(1); "SIFT trust" — ITA 122.1(1), (2), 248(1); "taxable SIFT trust distributions" — ITA 122(3); "taxation year" — ITA 249; "trust" — ITA 104(1), 248(1), (3).

PART XXVII — [2700–2705] GROUP TERM LIFE INSURANCE BENEFITS

2700. Interpretation — (1) Definitions — The definitions in this subsection apply in this Part.

"lump-sum premium" in relation to a group term life insurance policy means a premium for insurance under the policy on the life of an individual where all or part of the premium is for insurance that is (or would be if the individual survived) in respect of a period that ends more than 13 months after the earlier of the day on which the premium becomes payable and the day on which it is paid.

"paid-up premium" in relation to a group term life insurance policy means a premium for insurance under the policy on the life of an individual where the insurance is for the remainder of the lifetime of the individual and no further premiums will be payable for the insurance.

"premium category" in relation to term insurance provided under a group term life insurance policy means,

(a) where the premium rate applicable in respect of term insurance on the life of an individual depends on the group to which the individual belongs, any of the groups for which a premium rate is established, and

(b) in any other case, all individuals on whose lives term insurance is in effect under the policy,

and, for the purpose of this definition, a single premium rate is deemed to apply for all term insurance under a policy in respect of periods in 1994, and where individuals are divided into separate groups solely on the basis of their age, sex, or both, the groups are deemed to be a single group for which a premium rate is established.

"term insurance" in relation to an individual and a group term life insurance policy means insurance under the policy on the life of the individual, other than insurance in respect of which a lump-sum premium has become payable or been paid.

(2) Accidental death insurance — For greater certainty, a premium for insurance on the life of an individual does not include an amount for accidental death insurance.

Notes [Reg. 2700]: Reg. 2700 added by P.C. 1997-1623, for 1994 and later tax years.

Definitions [Reg. 2700]: "amount", "group term life insurance policy", "individual" — ITA 248(1); "lump-sum premium" — Reg. 2700(1); "month" — Interpretation Act 35(1); "term insurance" — Reg. 2700(1).

Income Tax Folios: S2-F1-C1: Health and welfare trusts [replaces IT-85R2].

2701. Prescribed benefit — (1) Subject to subsection (2), for the purpose of subsection 6(4) of the Act, the amount prescribed for a taxation year in respect of insurance under a group term life insurance policy on the life of a taxpayer is the total of

(a) the taxpayer's term insurance benefit under the policy for the calendar year in which the taxation year ends,

(b) the taxpayer's prepaid insurance benefit under the policy for that calendar year, and

(c) the total of all sales and excise taxes payable in respect of premiums paid under the policy in that calendar year for insurance on the life of the taxpayer, other than

(i) taxes paid, directly or by way of reimbursement, by the taxpayer, and

(ii) taxes in respect of premiums for term insurance that, if the taxpayer were to die, would be paid otherwise than

(A) to the taxpayer,

(B) for the benefit of the taxpayer,

(C) as a benefit that the taxpayer desired to have conferred on any person.

Related Provisions: ITA 139.1(15) — Effect of demutualization of insurance corporation.

Notes: See Notes to ITA 6(4).

(2) Bankrupt individual — Where a taxpayer who has become a bankrupt has two taxation years ending in a calendar year, for the purpose of subsection 6(4) of the Act, the amount prescribed for the first taxation year in respect of insurance under a group term life insurance policy on the life of the taxpayer is nil.

Notes [Reg. 2701]: Reg. 2701 added by P.C. 1997-1623, effective for insurance provided for periods after June 1994, with a transitional rule for 1994.

Definitions [Reg. 2701]: "amount", "bankrupt" — ITA 248(1); "calendar year" — Interpretation Act 37(1)(a); "group term life insurance policy", "person" — ITA 248(1); "prepaid insurance benefit" — Reg. 2703(1); "prescribed" — ITA 248(1); "taxation year" — ITA 249; "taxpayer" — ITA 248(1); "term insurance" — Reg. 2700(1); "term insurance benefit" — Reg. 2702(1).

Income Tax Folios: S2-F1-C1: Health and welfare trusts [replaces IT-85R2].

2702. Term insurance benefit — (1) Amount of benefit — Subject to section 2704, for the purpose of paragraph 2701(1)(a), a taxpayer's term insurance benefit under a group term life insurance policy for a calendar year is

(a) where

(i) the policyholder elects to determine, under this paragraph, the term insurance benefit for the year of each individual whose life is insured under the policy,

(ii) no premium rate that applies for term insurance provided under the policy on the life of an individual in respect of the year depends on the age or sex of the individual,

(iii) no amounts are payable under the policy for term insurance on the lives of individuals in respect of the year other than premiums payable on a regular basis that are based on the amount of term insurance in force in the year for each individual, and

(iv) the year is after 1995,

the amount determined by the formula

$$A - B$$

where

A is the total of the premiums payable for term insurance provided under the policy on the taxpayer's life in respect of periods in the year, to the extent that each such premium is in respect of term insurance that, if the taxpayer died in the year, would be paid to or for the benefit of the taxpayer or as a benefit that the taxpayer desired to have conferred on any person, and

B is the total amount paid by the taxpayer in respect of term insurance under the policy on the taxpayer's life in respect of the year; and

(b) in any other case, the amount, if any, by which

(i) the total of all amounts each of which is, for a day in the year on which term insurance is in effect under the policy on the taxpayer's life, the amount determined by the formula

$$A \times B$$

where

A is the amount of term insurance in effect on that day under the policy on the taxpayer's life, except the portion, if any, of the amount that, if the taxpayer were to die on that day, would be paid otherwise than

(A) to the taxpayer,

(B) to benefit of the taxpayer, or

(C) as a benefit that the taxpayer desired to have conferred on any person, and

B is the average daily cost of insurance for the year for the premium category in which the taxpayer is included on that day

exceeds

(ii) the total amount paid by the taxpayer in respect of term insurance under the policy on the taxpayer's life in respect of the year.

Related Provisions: ITA 144.1(10) — Employee contributions to employee life and health trust deemed to be payment of group life insurance premiums if so identified; ITA 257 — Negative amounts in formulas.

(2) Average daily cost of insurance — The average daily cost of insurance under a group term life insurance policy for a calendar year for a premium category is

(a) subject to paragraph (b), the amount determined by the formula

$$\frac{(A + B - C)}{D}$$

where

A is the total of the premiums payable for term insurance provided under the policy on the lives of individuals in respect of periods in the year while they are in the premium category,

B is the total of the amounts paid in the year under the policy for term insurance in respect of periods in preceding years (other than amounts that have otherwise been taken into account for the purpose of subsection 6(4) of the Act), to the extent that the total can reasonably be considered to relate to term insurance provided on the lives of individuals in the premium category,

C is the total amount of policy dividends and experience rating refunds paid in the year under the policy and not distributed to individuals whose lives are insured under the policy, to the extent that the total can reasonably be considered to relate to term insurance provided on the lives of individuals in the premium category, and

D is the total of all amounts each of which is the amount of term insurance in force on a day in the year on the lives of individuals in the premium category on that day; or

(b) the amount that the policyholder determines using a reasonable method that is substantially similar to the method set out in paragraph (a).

Related Provisions: ITA 257 — Negative amounts in formulas.

Notes: For interpretation see VIEWS doc 2015-0618191E5.

(3) Survivor income benefits — For the purposes of this section, where the proceeds of term insurance on the life of an individual are payable in the form of periodic payments, and the periodic payments are not an optional form of settlement of a lump-sum amount, the amount of term insurance in effect on the individual's life on any day is the present value, on that day, of the periodic payments that would be made if the individual were to die on that day.

(4) Determination of present value — For the purpose of subsection (3), the present value on a day in a calendar year

(a) shall be determined using assumptions that are reasonable at some time in the year; and

(b) may be determined assuming that an individual on whose life the present value depends is the same age on that day as on another day in the year.

Notes [Reg. 2702]: Reg. 2702 added by P.C. 1997-1623, this version effective with respect to insurance provided in respect of periods after 1994.

Definitions [Reg. 2702]: "amount" — ITA 248(1); "amount of term insurance" — Reg. 2702(3); "calendar year" — *Interpretation Act* 37(1)(a); "dividend", "group term life insurance policy", "individual", "person" — ITA 248(1); "premium category" — Reg. 2700(1); "present value" — Reg. 2702(4); "taxpayer" — ITA 248(1); "term insurance" — Reg. 2700(1).

Income Tax Folios: S2-F1-C1: Health and welfare trusts [replaces IT-85R2].

2703. Prepaid insurance benefit — **(1) Amount of benefit** — Subject to section 2704, for the purpose of paragraph 2701(1)(b), a taxpayer's prepaid insurance benefit under a group term life insurance policy for a calendar year is

(a) where the taxpayer is alive at the end of the year, the total of all amounts each of which is

(i) a lump-sum premium (other than the taxpayer portion) paid in the year and after February 1994 in respect of insurance under the policy on the life of the taxpayer, other than a paid-up premium paid before 1997, or

(ii) $\frac{1}{3}$ of a paid-up premium (other than the taxpayer portion) in respect of insurance under the policy on the life of the taxpayer that was paid

(A) after February 1994 and before 1997, and

(B) in the year or one of the two preceding years; and

(b) where the taxpayer died after June 1994 and in the year, the amount, if any, by which

(i) the total of all amounts each of which is a lump-sum premium (other than the taxpayer portion) paid under the policy after February 1994 in respect of insurance on the life of the taxpayer

exceeds

(ii) the portion of that total that was included in computing the taxpayer's prepaid insurance benefit under the policy for preceding years.

Related Provisions: ITA 18(9.01) — Matching deduction for employer.

(2) Taxpayer portion of premiums — For the purpose of subsection (1), the taxpayer portion of a premium is the portion, if any, of the premium that the taxpayer paid, either directly or by way of reimbursement.

Related Provisions: ITA 144.1(10) — Employee contributions to employee life and health trust deemed to be payment of group life insurance premiums if so identified.

Notes [Reg. 2703]: Reg. 2703 added by P.C. 1997-1623, effective with respect to insurance provided in respect of periods after June 1994.

Definitions [Reg. 2703]: "amount" — ITA 248(1); "calendar year" — *Interpretation Act* 37(1)(a); "group term life insurance policy" — ITA 248(1); "lump-sum premium", "paid-up premium" — Reg. 2700(1); "portion" — Reg. 2703(2); "taxpayer" — ITA 248(1).

Income Tax Folios: S2-F1-C1: Health and welfare trusts [replaces IT-85R2].

2704. Employee-paid insurance — **(1)** For the purpose of subsection 2701(1), where the full cost of insurance under a group term life insurance policy in a calendar year is borne by the individuals whose lives are insured under the policy, each individual's term insurance benefit and prepaid insurance benefit under the policy for the year is deemed to be nil.

Related Provisions: ITA 144.1(10) — Employee contributions to employee life and health trust deemed to be payment of group life insurance premiums if so identified.

(2) Where the premiums for part of the life insurance (in this subsection referred to as the "additional insurance") under a group term life insurance policy are determined separately from the premiums for the rest of the life insurance under the policy, and it is reasonable to consider that the individuals on whose lives the additional insurance is provided bear the full cost of the additional insurance, the additional insurance, the premiums, policy dividends and experience rating refunds in respect of that insurance, and the amounts paid in respect of that insurance by the individuals whose lives are insured, shall not be taken into account for the purposes of this Part.

Notes [Reg. 2704]: Reg. 2704 added by P.C. 1997-1623, for insurance provided in respect of periods after June 1994.

Definitions [Reg. 2704]: "additional insurance" — Reg. 2704(2); "amount" — ITA 248(1); "calendar year" — *Interpretation Act* 37(1)(a); "dividend", "group term life insurance policy", "individual" — ITA 248(1); "term insurance" — Reg. 2700(1).

Income Tax Folios: S2-F1-C1: Health and welfare trusts [replaces IT-85R2].

2705. Prescribed premium and insurance — [Applies to pre-July 1994 insurance periods only]

Notes [Reg. 2705]: Reg. 2705 added by P.C. 1997-1623, effective with respect to insurance provided in respect of periods that are in 1994 and before July 1994.

Notes [Part XXVII]: Part XXVII added by P.C. 1997-1623. See Notes to ITA 6(4). Former Part XXVII, "Employer Contributions to Registered Pension Plans", revoked by P.C. 1991-2540, effective for taxation years that begin after 1990. The limits for employer contributions to pension plans are now determined under ITA 147.2(1).

PART XXVIII — [2800] ELECTION IN RESPECT OF ACCUMULATING INCOME OF TRUSTS

2800. [Preferred beneficiary election] — (1) Any election under subsection 104(14) of the Act in respect of a taxation year shall be made by filing with the Minister a written statement

(a) in which the election in respect of the year is made;

(b) in which is designated the part of the accumulating income in respect of which the election is being made; and

(c) that is signed by the preferred beneficiary and a trustee having the authority to make the election.

(2) The statement shall be filed within 90 days after the end of the trust's taxation year in respect of which the election referred to in subsection (1) is made.

Related Provisions [Reg. 2800]: *Interpretation Act* 27(5) — Meaning of "within 90 days".

Notes: ITA 220(3.2) and Reg. 600(b) permit the election to be filed late, if CRA accepts it. CRA officials will not accept a late preferred beneficiary election if it appears the taxpayer is doing retroactive tax planning: Information Circular 07-1R1 para. 57(a).

Reg. 2800 amended by P.C. 2007-849 (effective June 13, 2007), 2001-806.

Definitions [Reg. 2800]: "amount", "individual", "Minister", "property", "share" — ITA 248(1); "taxation year" — ITA 249; "trust" — ITA 104(1), 248(1), (3).

Interpretation Bulletins: IT-394R2: Preferred beneficiary election.

PART XXIX — [2900–2903] SCIENTIFIC RESEARCH AND EXPERIMENTAL DEVELOPMENT

2900. (1) [Repealed]

Notes: Reg. 2900(1) repealed by P.C. 2000-1095, for work performed after Feb. 27, 1995, with grandfathering for work under an earlier contract. The definition was moved to ITA 248(1)"scientific research and experimental development".

Reg. 2900(1) earlier amended by P.C. 1995-16.

(2) For the purposes of clause 37(8)(a)(i)(B) and subclause 37(8)(a)(ii)(A)(II) of the Act, the following expenditures are directly attributable to the prosecution of scientific research and experimental development:

(a) the cost of materials consumed or transformed in such prosecution;

(b) where an employee directly undertakes, supervises or supports such prosecution, the portion of the amount incurred for salary or wages of the employee that can reasonably be considered to be in respect of such prosecution; and

(c) other expenditures, or those portions of other expenditures, that are directly related to such prosecution and that would not have been incurred if such prosecution had not occurred.

Related Provisions: ITA 127(27) — ITC recapture.

Notes: Note that on a subsequent disposition of any materials described in Reg. 2900(2)(a), there may be recapture under ITA 127(27).

Reg. 2900(2) amended by P.C. 2000-1095 (for costs incurred after Feb. 23, 1998), 1995-16.

Information Circulars: See at end of Reg. 2900.

Application Policies: SR&ED 96-06: Directly undertaking, supervising or supporting "directly engaged" SR&ED salary and wages; SR&ED 2000-01: Cost of materials; SR&ED 2002-01: Expenditures incurred for administrative salaries or wages — "directly related" test; SR&ED 2002-02R2: Experimental production and commercial production with experimental development work — allowable SR&ED expenditures; SR&ED 2004-03: Filing requirements for claiming SR&ED carried out in Canada.

(3) For the purposes of subclause 37(8)(a)(ii)(A)(II) of the Act, the following expenditures are directly attributable to the provision of premises, facilities or equipment for the prosecution of scientific research and experimental development:

(a) the cost of the maintenance and upkeep of such premises, facilities or equipment; and

(b) other expenditures, or those portions of other expenditures, that are directly related to that provision and that would not have been incurred if those premises or facilities or that equipment had not existed.

Notes: Opening words of Reg. 2900(3) amended by P.C. 1995-16, for tax years ending after Dec. 2, 1992.

Reg. 2900(3)(b) amended by P.C. 1995-16, for 1990 and later tax years.

(4) For the purposes of the definition "qualified expenditure" in subsection 127(9) of the Act, the prescribed proxy amount of a taxpayer for a taxation year, in respect of a business, in respect of which the taxpayer elects under clause 37(8)(a)(ii)(B) of the Act is 55% of the total of all amounts each of which is that portion of the amount incurred in the year by the taxpayer in respect of salary or wages of an employee of the taxpayer who is directly engaged in scientific research and experimental development carried on in Canada that can reasonably be considered to relate to the scientific research and experimental development having regard to the time spent by the employee on the scientific research and experimental development.

Related Provisions: ITA 37(1.3) — SR&ED within 200 nautical miles offshore is deemed done in Canada; Reg. 2900(5)–(7) — Additional rules re prescribed proxy amount; Reg. 2900(9) — Benefits and bonuses excluded from wages.

Notes: The "proxy method" (elected under ITA 37(8)(a)(ii)(B), on Form T661 Line 160, and claimed in T661 Part 5) allows a gross-up of labour costs (excluding benefits and bonuses: Reg. 2900(9)) by 55% to cover overhead, but capped at total expenses minus certain deductions (Reg. 2900(6) — see scitax.com/proxy for examples). Key employee salaries are capped by Reg. 2900(7) for this calculation. The prescribed amount goes into ITA 127(9)"qualified expenditure"(b) and thence to 127(9)"SR&ED qualified expenditure pool" and 127(9)"investment tax credit"(a.1). For an example see *Allegro Wireless*, 2021 TCC 27, paras. 211, 225.

Once under the election, only "directly undertaken" SR&ED qualifies: ITA 37(8)(a)(ii)(B)(II). The salary of the direct supervisor of the person doing the research can qualify, including for planning work: *Béton Mobile*, 2019 TCC 278, para. 70.

See CRA SR&ED policies: *Prescribed Proxy Amount Policy* (Dec. 2014); *Traditional & Proxy Methods Policy* (Dec. 2014).

Reg. 2900(4) amended to change "65%" to "55%" by 2012 budget bill #2, for tax years that end after 2012, effectively with a rate of 65% for days in the year before 2013, 60% starting 2013 and 55% starting 2014. Earlier amended by P.C. 1995-16.

Application Policies: SR&ED 96-06: Directly undertaking, supervising or supporting "directly engaged" SR&ED salary and wages.

Forms: RC4613: Election to use the SR&ED proxy to report the recapture of input tax credits; T661: Scientific research and experimental development (SR&ED) expenditures claim, Line 160 and Part 5.

(5) Subject to subsections (6) to (8), where in subsection (4) the portion of an expenditure is all or substantially all of the expenditure, that portion shall be replaced by the amount of the expenditure.

Notes: See under Reg. 2900(4). CRA considers that "substantially all" means 90% or more.

Application Policies: SR&ED 96-06: Directly undertaking, supervising or supporting "directly engaged" SR&ED salary and wages.

(6) The amount determined under subsection (4) as the prescribed proxy amount of a taxpayer for a taxation year in respect of a business shall not exceed the amount, if any, by which

(a) the total of all amounts deducted in computing the taxpayer's income for the year from the business,

exceeds the total of all amounts each of which is

(b) an amount deducted in computing the income of the taxpayer for the year from the business under any of sections 20, 24, 26, 30, 32, 37, 66 to 66.8 and 104 of the Act, or

(c) an amount incurred by the taxpayer in the year in respect of any outlay or expense made or incurred for the use of, or the right to use, a building other than a special-purpose building.

Notes: See under Reg. 2900(4).

(7) In determining the prescribed proxy amount of a taxpayer for a taxation year, the portion of the amount incurred in the year by the taxpayer in respect of salary or wages of a specified employee of the taxpayer that is included in computing the total described in subsection (4) shall not exceed the lesser of

(a) 75% of the amount incurred by the taxpayer in the year in respect of salary or wages of the employee, and

(b) the amount determined by the formula

$$2.5 \times A \times B / 365$$

where

A is the Year's Maximum Pensionable Earnings (as determined under section 18 of the *Canada Pension Plan*) for the calendar year in which the taxation year ends, and

B is the number of days in the taxation year in which the employee is an employee of the taxpayer.

Related Provisions: Reg. 2900(9) — Benefits and bonuses excluded from wages.

Notes: See under Reg. 2900(4).

The YMPE for 2020 is $58,700 and for 2021 is $61,600, so the maximum in the formula is $146,750 for 2020 and $154,000 for 2021. See Table I-8 for other years.

(8) Where

(a) a taxpayer is a corporation,

(b) the taxpayer employs in a taxation year ending in a calendar year an individual who is a specified employee of the taxpayer,

(c) the taxpayer is associated with another corporation (referred to as the "associated corporation") in a taxation year of the associated corporation ending in the calendar year, and

(d) the individual is an employee of the associated corporation in the taxation year of the associated corporation ending in the calendar year,

the total of all amounts that may be included in computing the total described in subsection (4) in respect of salaries or wages of the individual by the taxpayer in its taxation year ending in the calendar year and by all associated corporations in their taxation years ending in the calendar year shall not exceed the amount that is 2.5 times the Year's Maximum Pensionable Earnings (as determined under section 18 of the *Canada Pension Plan*) for the calendar year.

Notes: See Notes to Reg. 2900(4) and (7).

(9) For the purposes of subsections (4) and (7), an amount incurred in respect of **salary or wages** of an employee in a taxation year does not include

(a) an amount described in section 6 or 7 of the Act;

(b) an amount deemed under subsection 78(4) of the Act to have been incurred;

(c) bonuses; or

(d) remuneration based on profits.

Notes: In *Oldcastle Building*, 2016 TCC 183, a research centre manager's bonus based on sales, high enough to displace base salary, was held not to be a "bonus" or "remuneration based on profits" (Reg. 2900(9)(c), (d)) but "variable salary"; CRA confused the nature of the amount paid with the method of calculating it (para. 30).

Application Policies: SR&ED 96-06: Directly undertaking, supervising or supporting "directly engaged" SR&ED salary and wages.

(10) For the purpose of subsection (8),

(a) an individual related to a particular corporation, and

(b) a partnership any member of which is an individual related to a particular corporation or is a corporation associated with a particular corporation,

shall be deemed to be a corporation associated with the particular corporation.

Notes: See under Reg. 2900(4).

(11) The depreciable property of a taxpayer that is prescribed for the purposes of the definition "first term shared-use-equipment" in subsection 127(9) of the Act is

(a) a building of the taxpayer;

(b) a leasehold interest of the taxpayer in a building;

(c) a property of the taxpayer if, at the time it was acquired by the taxpayer, the taxpayer or a person related to the taxpayer intended that it would be used in the prosecution of scientific research and experimental development during the assembly, construction or commissioning of a facility, plant or line for commercial manufacturing, commercial processing or other commercial purposes (other than scientific research and experimental development) and intended

(i) that it would be used during its operating time in its expected useful life primarily for purposes other than scientific research and experimental development, or

(ii) that its value would be consumed primarily in activities other than scientific research and experimental development; and

(d) part of a property of the taxpayer if, at the time the part was acquired by the taxpayer, the taxpayer or a person related to the taxpayer intended that the part would be used in the prosecution of scientific research and experimental development during the assembly, construction or commissioning of a facility, plant or line for commercial manufacturing, commercial processing or other commercial purposes (other than scientific research and experimental development), and intended

(i) that it would be used during its operating time in its expected useful life primarily for purposes other than scientific research and experimental development, or

(ii) that its value would be consumed primarily in activities other than scientific research and experimental development.

Notes: For CRA interpretation see VIEWS doc 2009-0316561E5.

Reg. 2900(11) added by P.C. 1995-16, for property acquired after December 2, 1992.

Application Policies: SR&ED 96-07: Prototypes, custom products/commercial assets, pilot plants and experimental production; SR&ED 2004-03: Filing requirements for claiming SR&ED carried out in Canada; SR&ED 2005-01: Shared-used equipment.

Definitions [Reg. 2900]: "amount" — ITA 248(1); "amount incurred" — Reg. 2900(9); "associated" — Reg. 2900(10)(b); "associated corporation" — Reg. 2900(8)(c); "business" — ITA 248(1); "calendar year" — *Interpretation Act* 37(1)(a); "Canada" — ITA 37(1.3), 255, *Interpretation Act* 35(1); "corporation" — ITA 248(1), *Interpretation Act* 35(1); "depreciable property" — ITA 13(21), 248(1); "employee", "individual", "mineral" — ITA 248(1); "partnership" — see ITA 96(1) Notes; "person", "prescribed", "property" — ITA 248(1); "related" — ITA 251(2)–(6); "salary or wages" — ITA 248(1), Reg. 2900(9); "scientific research and experimental development" — Reg. 2900(1); "specified employee" — ITA 248(1); "taxation year" — ITA 249; "taxpayer" — ITA 248(1); "total of all amounts" — Reg. 2900(8).

Information Circulars [Reg. 2900]: 86-4R3: Scientific research and experimental development; 94-2: Machinery and equipment industry application paper; 97-1: SR&ED — Administrative guidelines for software development.

2901. Prescribed expenditures — [No longer relevant]

Notes: Reg. 2901 prescribes expenditures for pre-1989 ITA 37.1(5).

2902. For the purposes of the definition "qualified expenditure" in subsection 127(9) of the Act, a prescribed expenditure is

(a) an expenditure of a current nature incurred by a taxpayer in respect of

(i) the general administration or management of a business, including

(A) administrative salary or wages and related benefits in respect of a person whose duties are not all or substantially all directed to the prosecution of scientific research and experimental development, except to the extent that such expenditure is described in subsection 2900(2) or (3),

(B) a legal or accounting fee,

(C) an amount described in any of paragraphs 20(1)(c) to (g) of the Act,

(D) an entertainment expense,

(E) an advertising or selling expense,

(F) a conference or convention expense,

(G) a due or fee in respect of membership in a scientific or technical society or organization, and

(H) a fine or penalty, or

(ii) the maintenance and upkeep of premises, facilities or equipment to the extent that such expenditure is not attributable to the prosecution of scientific research and experimental development;

(b) an expenditure incurred by a taxpayer in respect of

(i) the acquisition of property that is qualified property or qualified resource property within the meaning assigned by subsection 127(9) of the Act, or

(ii) the acquisition of property that has been used, or acquired for use or lease, for any purpose whatever before it was acquired by the taxpayer;

(c) an expenditure made to acquire rights in, or arising out of, scientific research and experimental development; or

(d) an expenditure on scientific research and experimental development in respect of which an amount is deductible under section 110.1 or section 118.1 of the Act; or

(e) an expenditure of a taxpayer, to the extent that the taxpayer has received or is entitled to receive a reimbursement in respect of it from

(i) a person resident in Canada, other than

(A) Her Majesty in right of Canada or a province,

(B) an agent of Her Majesty in right of Canada or a province,

(C) a corporation, commission or association that is controlled, directly or indirectly in any manner whatever, by Her Majesty in right of Canada or a province or by an agent of Her Majesty in right of Canada or a province, or

(D) a municipality in Canada or a municipal or public body performing a function of government in Canada, or

(ii) a person not resident in Canada to the extent that the said reimbursement is deductible by the person in computing his taxable income earned in Canada for any taxation year.

Related Provisions: ITA 37(1.3) — SR&ED within 200 nautical miles offshore is deemed done in Canada; ITA 256(5.1), (6.2) — Meaning of "controlled directly or indirectly".

Notes: In *Mimetix Pharmaceuticals*, 2003 FCA 106, property had been leased by MP for a year before MP bought it. The property was held to fall within Reg. 2902(b)(iii) and so it could not be a "qualified expenditure".

In *Armada Equipment*, 2007 TCC 260, a fee paid to AE's accounting firm to prepare the R&D claim was disallowed as a qualified expenditure because it was a "legal or accounting fee" under Reg. 2902(a)(i)(B).

For "municipal or public body..." in (e)(i)(D), see ITA 149(1)(c) Notes.

CRA considers that "substantially all", used in (a)(i)(A), means 90% or more.

Reg. 2902 amended by 2012 budget bill #2 (for expenditures incurred after 2013, due to repeal of ITA 37(1)(b) allowing capital expenditures; adding "or qualified resource property" for expenditures incurred after March 28, 2012); P.C. 1995-16, 1994-139.

Definitions [Reg. 2902]: "amount", "business" — ITA 248(1); "Canada" — ITA 37(1.3), 255, *Interpretation Act* 35(1); "controlled directly or indirectly" — ITA 256(5.1)–(6); "corporation" — ITA 248(1), *Interpretation Act* 35(1); "Her Majesty" — *Interpretation Act* 35(1); "person", "prescribed", "property" — ITA 248(1); "province" — *Interpretation Act* 35(1); "qualified property", "qualified resource property" — ITA 127(9); "related" — ITA 251(2)–(6); "resident in Canada" — ITA 250; "salary or wages" — ITA 248(1); "scientific research and experimental development" — Reg. 2900(1); "taxable income earned in Canada" — ITA 248(1); "taxation year" — ITA 249; "taxpayer" — ITA 248(1).

Interpretation Bulletins: IT-104R2: Deductibility of fines or penalties.

Application Policies: SR&ED 2002-01: Expenditures incurred for administrative salaries or wages — "directly related" test; SR&ED 2003-01: Capital property intended to be used all or substantially all for SR&ED.

2903. [Repealed]

Notes: Reg. 2903, "Special-purpose buildings", repealed by 2012 budget bill #2, effective 2014 (due to repeal of ITA 37(1)(b), which allowed deduction for capital expenditures).

PART XXX — [3000–3004] [REPEALED]

3000–3004. [Repealed]

Notes: Part XXX (Reg. 3003-3004) repealed by 2013 budget bill #2, effective Dec. 12, 2013. It prescribed Quebec legislation for ITA 122.64(2)(a). Earlier amended by P.C. 2002-2169, 1997-1688, 1994-1658, 1994-560, 1993-1943, 1993-538, 1992-2653.

PART XXXI — [3100–3101] TAX SHELTER

3100. Prescribed benefits — **(1)** For the purposes of paragraph (b) of the definition "tax shelter" in subsection 237.1(1) of the Act, "prescribed benefit", in respect of an interest in a property, means any amount that may reasonably be expected, having regard to statements or representations made in respect of the interest, to be received or enjoyed by a person (in this subsection referred to as "the purchaser") who acquires the interest, or a person with whom the purchaser does not deal at arm's length, which receipt or enjoyment would have the effect of reducing the impact of any loss that the purchaser may sustain in respect of the interest, and includes such an amount

(a) that is, either immediately or in the future, owed to any other person by the purchaser or a person with whom the purchaser does not deal at arm's length, to the extent that

(i) liability to pay that amount is contingent,

(ii) payment of that amount is or will be guaranteed by, security is or will be provided by, or an agreement to indemnify the other person to whom the amount is owed is or will be entered into by

(A) a promoter in respect of the interest,

(B) a person with whom the promoter does not deal at arm's length, or

(C) a person who is to receive a payment (other than a payment made by the purchaser) in respect of the guarantee, security or agreement to indemnify,

(iii) the rights of that other person against the purchaser, or against a person with whom the purchaser does not deal at arm's length, in respect of the collection of all or part of the purchase price are limited to a maximum amount, are enforceable only against certain property, or are otherwise limited by agreement, or

(iv) payment of that amount is to be made in a foreign currency or is to be determined by reference to its value in a foreign currency and it may reasonably be considered, having regard to the history of the exchange rate between the foreign currency and Canadian currency, that the total of all such payments, when converted to Canadian currency at the exchange rate expected to prevail at the date on which each such payment would be required to be made, will be substantially less than that total would be if each such payment was converted to Canadian currency at the time that each such payment became owing;

(b) that the purchaser or a person with whom the purchaser does not deal at arm's length is entitled at any time to, directly or indirectly, receive or have available

(i) as a form of assistance from a government, municipality or other public authority, whether as a grant, a subsidy, a forgivable loan, a deduction from tax (other than an amount described in clause (b)(i)(B) of the definition "tax shelter" in subsection 237.1(1) of the Act) or an investment allowance, or as any other form of assistance, or

(ii) by reason of a revenue guarantee or other agreement in respect of which revenue may be earned by the purchaser or a person with whom the purchaser does not deal at arm's length, to the extent that the revenue guarantee or other agreement may reasonably be considered to ensure that the purchaser or person will receive a return of all or a portion of the purchaser's outlays in respect of the interest;

(c) that is the proceeds of disposition to which the purchaser may be entitled by way of an agreement or other arrangement under which the purchaser has a right, either absolutely or contingently, to dispose of the interest (otherwise than as a consequence of the purchaser's death), including the fair market value of any property that the agreement or arrangement provides for the acquisition of in exchange for all or any part of the interest; and

(d) that is owed to a promoter, or a person with whom the promoter does not deal at arm's length, by the purchaser or a person with whom the purchaser does not deal at arm's length in respect of the interest.

Related Provisions: Reg. 3101(2) — Prescribed benefit excludes profits; Reg. 3101(3) — Prescribed benefit includes certain limited-recourse amounts.

Notes: In *Paletta*, 2019 TCC 205 (under appeal to FCA), paras. 260-271, Reg. 231(6) was held to be satisfied so an investment in 2006-07 was a "tax shelter" under ITA 237.1(6). However, Reg. 231 was replaced in 2011 retroactive to 2003, so Reg. 3100(1) should have been applied instead, to the same effect.

In *Lee*, 2020 QCCQ 780, para. 369, certain agreements were held to be prescribed benefits for purposes of the parallel Quebec rule.

For "indirectly" in (b) opening words, see ITA 17.1(1) Notes. For interpretation of (b)(i) see ITA 12(1)(x) Notes.

(2) Notwithstanding subsection (1), for the purpose of paragraph (b) of the definition "tax shelter" in subsection 237.1(1) of the Act, "prescribed benefit", in respect of an interest in a property, does not, except as otherwise provided in subparagraph (1)(b)(ii), include profits earned in respect of the interest.

(3) For the purpose of paragraph (b) of the definition "tax shelter" in subsection 237.1(1) of the Act, "prescribed benefit", in respect of an interest in a property, includes an amount that is a limited-recourse amount because of subsection 143.2(1), (7) or (13) of the Act, but does not include an amount of indebtedness that is a limited-recourse amount

(a) solely because it is not required to be repaid within 10 years from the time the indebtedness arose where the debtor would, if the interest were acquired by the debtor immediately after that time, be

(i) a partnership

(A) at least 90% of the fair market value of the property of which is attributable to the partnership's tangible capital property located in Canada, and

(B) at least 90% of the value of all interests in which are held by limited partners (within the meaning assigned by subsection 96(2.4) of the Act) of the partnership,

except where it is reasonable to conclude that one of the main reasons for the acquisition of one or more properties by the partnership, or for the acquisition of one or more interests in the partnership by limited partners, is to avoid the application of this subsection, or

(ii) a member of a partnership having fewer than six members, except where

(A) the partnership is a member of another partnership,

(B) there is a limited partner (within the meaning assigned by subsection 96(2.4) of the Act) of the partnership,

(C) less than 90% of the fair market value of the partnership's property is attributable to the partnership's tangible capital property located in Canada, or

(D) it is reasonable to conclude that one of the main reasons for the existence of one of two or more partnerships, one of which is the partnership, or the acquisition of one

or more properties by the partnership, is to avoid the application of this section to the member's indebtedness,

(b) of a partnership

(i) where

(A) the indebtedness is secured by and used to acquire the partnership's tangible capital property located in Canada (other than rental property, within the meaning assigned by subsection 1100(14), leasing property, within the meaning assigned by subsection 1100(17), or specified energy property, within the meaning assigned by subsection 1100(25)), and

(B) the person to whom the indebtedness is repayable is a member of the Canadian Payments Association, and

(ii) throughout the period during which any amount is outstanding in respect of the indebtedness,

(A) at least 90% of the fair market value of the property of which is attributable to tangible capital property located in Canada of the partnership,

(B) at least 90% of the value of all interests in which are held by limited partners (within the meaning assigned by subsection 96(2.4) of the Act) that are corporations, and

(C) the principal business of each such limited partner is related to the principal business of the partnership,

except where it is reasonable to conclude that one of the main reasons for the acquisition of one or more properties by the partnership, or for the acquisition of one or more interests in the partnership by limited partners, is to avoid the application of this subsection, or

(c) of a corporation where the amount is a *bona fide* business loan made to the corporation for the purpose of financing a business that the corporation operates and the loan is made under a loan program of the Government of Canada or of a province the purpose of which is to extend financing to small- and medium-sized Canadian businesses.

Notes: For the meaning of "one of the main reasons" in (a)(i), (a)(ii)(D) and (b)(ii), see ITA 83(2.1) Notes. For "principal business" in (3)(b)(ii)(C), see ITA 20(1)(bb) Notes.

Reg. 3100 added by P.C. 2011-936, effective Feb. 19, 2003. It replaced Reg. 231.

Definitions [Reg. 3100]: "amount" — ITA 248(1); "arm's length" — ITA 251(1); "business" — ITA 248(1); "Canada" — ITA 255, *Interpretation Act* 35(1); "capital property" — ITA 54, 248(1); "consequence" — ITA 248(8); "corporation" — ITA 248(1), *Interpretation Act* 35(1); "disposition" — ITA 248(1); "foreign currency" — ITA 248(1); "limited partner" — ITA 96(2.4); "limited-recourse amount" — ITA 143.2(1), 248(1); "person" — ITA 237.1(1), 248(1); "promoter" — ITA 237.1(1); "property" — ITA 248(1); "province" — *Interpretation Act* 35(1); "purchaser" — Reg. 3100(1); "security" — *Interpretation Act* 35(1).

3101. Prescribed property — For the purpose of paragraph (b) of the definition "tax shelter" in subsection 237.1(1) of the Act, "prescribed property", in relation to a tax shelter, means property that is a registered pension plan, a registered retirement savings plan, a deferred profit sharing plan, a registered retirement income fund, a registered education savings plan or a property in respect of which paragraph 40(2)(i) of the Act applies.

Notes: Reg. 3101 added by P.C. 2011-936, effective Feb. 19, 2003.

Definitions [Reg. 3101]: "deferred profit sharing plan" — ITA 147(1), 248(1); "property" — ITA 248(1); "registered education savings plan" — ITA 146.1(1), 248(1); "registered pension plan" — ITA 248(1); "registered retirement income fund" — ITA 146.3(1), 248(1); "registered retirement savings plan" — ITA 146(1), 248(1); "tax shelter" — ITA 237.1(1), 248(1).

Notes: Former Part XXXI, revoked in 1984, set out rules for establishing a "degree of Canadian ownership" under former ITA 257. Where a corporation was more than 25% Canadian-owned, the withholding tax on dividends was reduced. Reduction of withholding tax on dividends is provided in Canada's tax treaties. See Notes to ITA 212(2).

PART XXXII — [3200–3202] [REPEALED]

3200–3202. [Repealed]

Notes: Reg. 3200 (Part XXXII, replacing former Part XXXII described below) added and repealed by P.C. 2011-936. It applied to tax that ended after March 22, 2003 and began before Oct. 29, 2008. It prescribed certain payments for ITA 135(1.1).

Former Reg. 3200-3201 (prescribed stock exchanges) repealed by 2007 budget bill #2, effective Dec. 14, 2007. See Notes to ITA 262 for their wording before repeal.

Former Reg. 3202 repealed by P.C. 2011-936, for tax years that end after March 22, 2003. It prescribed a fund for ITA 47.1, repealed in 1985.

PART XXXIII — [3300] TAX TRANSFER PAYMENTS

3300. For the purposes of subsection 154(2) of the Act, a rate of 45% is prescribed.

Notes: Rate changed from 45% to 40% by P.C. 1998-2270 effective 1999, and back to 45% by P.C. 2005-2315 for 2005 and later tax years.

Definitions [Reg. 3300]: "prescribed" — ITA 248(1).

PART XXXIV — [3400] INTERNATIONAL DEVELOPMENT ASSISTANCE PROGRAMS

3400. For the purposes of paragraphs 122.3(1)(a) and 250(1)(d) of the Act, each international development assistance program of the Canadian International Development Agency that is financed with funds (other than loan assistance funds) provided under External Affairs Vote 30a, *Appropriation Act No. 3, 1977-78*, or another vote providing for such financing, is hereby prescribed as an international development assistance program of the Government of Canada.

Notes: *Bell*, [1996] 2 C.T.C. 2191 (TCC), held that the Crown had the onus of proving a particular project was CIDA-funded, since CRA had better access to this information. Without such evidence, B was allowed the overseas employment tax credit.

Definitions [Reg. 3400]: "Canada" — ITA 255, *Interpretation Act* 35(1); "prescribed" — ITA 248(1).

Interpretation Bulletins: IT-497R4: Overseas employment tax credit.

PART XXXV — [3500–3505] GIFTS [RECEIPTS]

Notes [Part XXXV]: Heading changed from "Receipts for Donations and Gifts" by 2011 budget bill #2, effective March 23, 2011.

3500. Interpretation — In this Part,

"employees' charity trust" means a registered charity that is organized for the purpose of remitting, to other registered charities, donations that are collected from employees by an employer;

Notes: Definition "employees' charity trust" amended by P.C. 1994-139, retroactive to 1986, to delete a requirement that donations collected by the employer be "by means of payroll deductions".

"official receipt" means a receipt for the purposes of paragraph 110.1(2)(a) or 118.1(2)(a) of the Act, containing information required by section 3501 or 3502;

Notes: Definition amended by 2017 budget bill #2, effective Dec. 14, 2017, to change "subsection 110.1(2) or (3) or 118.1(2), (6) or (7)" to "paragraph 110.1(2)(a) or 118.1(2)(a)". Earlier amended by P.C. 1994-139.

"official receipt form" means any printed form that a registered organization or other recipient of a gift has that is capable of being completed, or that originally was intended to be completed, as an official receipt by it;

"other recipient of a gift" means a person, to whom a gift is made by a taxpayer, referred to in any of paragraph 110.1(1)(c), subparagraph 110.1(2.1)(a)(ii) and paragraphs (a) and (d) of the definition "qualified donee" in subsection 149.1(1) of the Act;

Notes: See Notes to ITA 149.1(1)"qualified donee". Definition amended by 2017 budget bill #2, effective Dec. 14, 2017. Before that date, read:

> "other recipient of a gift" means a person, to whom a gift is made by a taxpayer, referred to in any of paragraphs (a) and (d) of the definition "qualified donee" in subsection 149.1(1), paragraph 110.1(1)(c) and subparagraph 110.1(3)(a)(ii) of the Act;

Earlier amended by 2011 budget bill #2, effective 2012.

"registered organization" means a registered charity, a registered Canadian amateur athletic association, registered journalism organization or a registered national arts service organization.

Notes: Definition amended by 2019 budget bill #1, effective 2020, to add "registered journalism organization" [defined in ITA 248(1)].

Reference to registered national arts service organization added to definition by P.C. 1994-139, effective July 14, 1990.

Definitions [Reg. 3500]: "employee", "employer" — ITA 248(1); "official receipt", "other recipient of a gift" — Reg. 3500; "person" — ITA 248(1); "qualified donee" — ITA 149.1(1); "registered Canadian amateur athletic association", "registered charity", "registered journalism organization", "registered national arts service organization" — ITA 248(1); "registered organization" — Reg. 3500; "taxpayer" — ITA 248(1).

3501. Contents of [donation] receipts — **(1)** Every official receipt issued by a registered organization shall contain a statement that it is an official receipt for income tax purposes, and shall show clearly, in such a manner that it cannot readily be altered,

(a) the name and address in Canada of the organization as recorded with the Minister;

(b) the registration number assigned by the Minister to the organization;

(c) the serial number of the receipt;

(d) the place or locality where the receipt was issued;

(e) where the gift is a cash gift, the date on which or the year during which the gift was received;

(e.1) where the gift is of property other than cash

(i) the day on which the gift was received,

(ii) a brief description of the property, and

(iii) the name and address of the appraiser of the property if an appraisal is done;

(f) the date on which the receipt was issued;

(g) the name and address of the donor including, in the case of an individual, the individual's first name and initial;

(h) the amount that is

(i) the amount of a cash gift, or

(ii) if the gift is of property other than cash, the amount that is the fair market value of the property at the time that the gift is made;

(h.1) a description of the advantage, if any, in respect of the gift and the amount of that advantage;

(h.2) the eligible amount of the gift;

(i) the signature, as provided in subsection (2) or (3), of a responsible individual who has been authorized by the organization to acknowledge gifts; and

(j) the name and Internet website of the Canada Revenue Agency.

Related Provisions: ITA 168(1)(d) — Revocation of registration for issuing incorrect receipt; ITA 188.1(7)–(8) — Penalties for incorrect receipts; ITA 188.1(9)–(10) — Penalties for false information relating to receipts; ITA 188.2(3)(a)(iii) — Effect of suspension of charity's receipting privileges; ITA 248(35)–(37) — Value of gift limited to cost if acquired within 3 years or as tax shelter; ITA 248(41) — Donation value deemed nil if taxpayer does not inform donee of circumstances requiring reduction; Reg. 3501.1 — Information return required where donation returned.

Notes: Charities may issue and email electronic receipts for donations made via the Internet. See Charities Policy CPS-014.

For para. (j), use canada.ca/charities-giving. Charities had until March 31, 2019 to change from the old cra.gc.ca/charities (CRA announcement March 1, 2018).

The terms "eligible amount" and "advantage", used in Reg. 3501(1)(h.1) and (h.2), are defined in ITA 248(31)–(32).

Lack of technical compliance with Reg. 3501(1) is fatal to a donation claim, due in part to Reg. 3501(6): *Castro*, 2015 FCA 225 (leave to appeal denied 2016 CarswellNat 1067 (SCC)), paras. 77-85. This includes not showing the **first name and middle initial** of the donor on the receipt: *Kueviakoe*, 2021 FCA 64, para. 11; and the "place or locality where the receipt was issued": para. 14. However, minor spelling errors "in normal circumstances, might be overlooked": *Perry*, 2016 TCC 210, para. 17 (the errors there were more serious). Donations were disallowed due to imperfect receipts in: *Trottier*, 2004 TCC 526; *Chinyelugo*, 2009 TCC 355; *Oloya*, 2011 TCC 308; *Afovia*,

2012 TCC 391; *Sklodowski*, 2013 TCC 37; *Lapointe*, 2014 TCC 356; *Mapish*, 2015 TCC 12; *Okeke*, 2015 TCC 301 (aff'd on other grounds 2016 FCA 293); *Iqbal*, 2015 TCC 324; *Nazih*, 2016 TCC 70 (taxpayer's children's names on receipts from language school meant that receipts were for services, not donations); *Shahbazi*, 2016 TCC 129 (receipt failed to describe donated property); *Guobadia*, 2016 TCC 182; *Purba*, 2016 TCC 218; *Madamidola*, 2017 TCC 245 (gift in kind did not show date, and address of charity "as recorded with the Minister" not shown); *Okafor*, 2018 TCC 31, para. 22 (receipts were missing "place or locality where the receipt was issued"); *Ruremesha*, 2018 TCC 57, para. 20 (charity's address on receipts was not the one "recorded with the Minister"). See also Drache, "Contents of Charitable Receipts", 21(2) *Canadian Not-for-Profit News* (Carswell) 9-11 (Feb. 2013); and ITA 118.1(1)"total charitable gifts" Notes.

There is no time limit on a charity issuing receipts, though the donor can normally only use a receipt within 5 years of the donation: VIEWS doc 2003-0181975.

CRA allows anonymous donation if the donor formally appoints an agent to hold funds in trust and donate them, and the receipt is issued to the agent "in trust": Charities Summary Policy CSP-G03.

A charity should not issue a donation receipt for gifts from other registered charities: tinyurl.com/cra-chargift.

Where an ITA 118.1(6) designation is made to value a donation of property at less than FMV to reduce the capital gain, the receipt should still show the actual donation value: VIEWS doc 2015-0593921E5.

Now that almost all professionally prepared returns are E-filed (ITA 150.1(2.3)), compliance with post-assessing reviews takes up a lot of time. CRA now allows documents to be submitted electronically, and is exploring ways to allow donation receipts to be submitted at time of filing: VIEWS doc 2012-0465931C6.

For comprehensive instructions on issuing receipts see *Blumbergs' Receipting Kit 2018* (207pp), tinyurl.com/receipt-kit18. See also Drache et al., *Charities Taxation, Policy and Practice — Taxation* (Carswell, looseleaf or *Taxnet Pro* Reference Centre), chap. 19, "Issuing Receipts" (35pp); Dawe, "Charitable Donation Receipts", 12(4) *Tax Hyperion* (Carswell) 5-8 (April 2015).

Reg. 3501(1)(e) to (i) amended (adding (h.1) and (h.2)) by 2002-2013 technical bill, for gifts made after Dec. 20, 2002, but (h.1) read differently for receipts issued before 2013.

Reg. 3501(1)(j) added by P.C. 2007-553, for receipts issued after 2005.

Income Tax Folios: S7-F1-C1: Split-receipting and deemed fair market value [replaces IT-110R3].

Interpretation Bulletins: IT-171R2: Non-resident individuals — computation of taxable income earned in Canada and non-refundable tax credits (archived); IT-226R: Gift to a charity of a residual interest in real property or an equitable interest in a trust; IT-288R2: Gifts of tangible capital properties to a charity and others; IT-504R2: Visual artists and writers.

Registered Charities Newsletters: 10 (can charities issue electronic official donation receipts by email or on the Internet? can an organization that is applying for registration borrow a charity's BN/Registration number for tax-receipt purposes? gift certificates); 11 (audit of tax preparer lands registered charities and executive director in hot water); 13 (about auditing charities); 14 (Business Number and donation receipts); 18 (how should charitable gifts in kind be valued?; can businesses receive receipts for donations made out of their inventory?; can shares or stock options be gifts?; can a charity issue a charitable receipt for a court-ordered payment made to it?); 27 (receipts — who is the donor?); 33 (improper receipting); *Charities Connection* 10 (things to remember when issuing official donation receipts).

Charities Policies: CPC-006: Gift-in-kind; CPC-009: Official donation receipt — Newly registered charity; CPC-010: Official donation receipt — Names; CPC-015: Official donation receipt — Registered charity's address; CPC-017: Official donation receipts — Gifts of services; CPC-018: Official donation receipts — Gifts out of inventory; CPC-019: Official donation receipts — Payment for participation in a youth band or choir; CPC-026: Fundraising — Third-party fundraisers; CPS-014: Computer-generated official donation receipts.

(1.1) Every official receipt issued by another recipient of a gift shall contain a statement that it is an official receipt for income tax purposes and shall show clearly in such a manner that it cannot readily be altered,

(a) the name and address of the other recipient of the gift;

(b) the serial number of the receipt;

(c) the place or locality where the receipt was issued;

(d) where the gift is a cash gift, the date on which the gift was received;

(e) where the gift is of property other than cash

(i) the date on which the gift was received,

(ii) a brief description of the property, and

(iii) the name and address of the appraiser of the property if an appraisal is done;

(f) the date on which the receipt was issued;

(g) the name and address of the donor including, in the case of an individual, the individual's first name and initial;

(h) the amount that is

(i) the amount of a cash gift, or

(ii) if the gift is of property other than cash, the amount that is the fair market value of the property at the time that the gift was made;

(h.1) a description of the advantage, if any, in respect of the gift and the amount of that advantage;

(h.2) the eligible amount of the gift;

(i) the signature, as provided in subsection (2) or (3.1), of a responsible individual who has been authorized by the other recipient of the gift to acknowledge donations; and

(j) the name and Internet website of the Canada Revenue Agency.

Related Provisions: Reg. 3501.1 — Information return required where donation returned.

Notes: Reg. 3501(1.1) amended by 2002-2013 technical bill (for gifts made after Dec. 20, 2002, but (h.1) read differently for receipts issued before 2013), P.C. 2007-553.

Information Circulars: 84-3R6: Gifts to certain charitable organizations outside Canada.

Registered Charities Newsletters: 27 (receipts — who is the donor?).

(2) Except as provided in subsection (3) or (3.1), every official receipt shall be signed personally by an individual referred to in paragraph (1)(i) or (1.1)(i).

(3) Where all official receipt forms of a registered organization are

(a) distinctively imprinted with the name, address in Canada and registration number of the organization,

(b) serially numbered by a printing press or numbering machine, and

(c) kept at the place referred to in subsection 230(2) of the Act until completed as an official receipt,

the official receipts may bear a facsimile signature.

Charities Policies: CPS-014: Computer-generated official donation receipts.

(3.1) Where all official receipt forms of another recipient of the gift are

(a) distinctively imprinted with the name and address of the other recipient of the gift,

(b) serially numbered by a printing press or numbering machine,

(c) if applicable, kept at a place referred to in subsection 230(1) of the Act until completed as an official receipt,

the official receipts may bear a facsimile signature.

Charities Policies: CPS-014: Computer-generated official donation receipts.

(4) An official receipt issued to replace an official receipt previously issued shall show clearly that it replaces the original receipt and, in addition to its own serial number, shall show the serial number of the receipt originally issued.

Related Provisions: Reg. 3501.1 — Information return required where donation returned.

(5) A spoiled official receipt form shall be marked "cancelled" and such form, together with the duplicate thereof, shall be retained by the registered organization or the other recipient of a gift as part of its records.

(6) Every official receipt form on which any of the following is incorrectly or illegibly entered is deemed to be spoiled:

(a) the date on which the gift is received;

(b) the amount of the gift, in the case of a cash gift;

(c) a description of the advantage, if any, in respect of the gift and the amount of that advantage; and

(d) the eligible amount of the gift.

Notes: Reg. 3501(6) denies *any* credit if the receipt amount does not match the donated amount: *Castro*, 2015 FCA 225, para. 83 (leave to appeal denied 2016 CarswellNat 1067 (SCC)). See also Notes to Reg. 3501(1).

Reg. 3501(6) amended by 2002-2013 technical bill (Part 5 — technical), for gifts made after Dec. 20, 2002, but for receipts issued before 2013, read 3501(6)(c) as "the amount of the advantage, if any, in respect of the gift; and".

Definitions [Reg. 3501]: "advantage" — ITA 248(32); "amount" — ITA 248(1); "Canada" — ITA 255, *Interpretation Act* 35(1); "eligible amount" — ITA 248(31); "fair market value" — see ITA 69(1) Notes; "individual", "Minister" — ITA 248(1); "official receipt", "official receipt form", "other recipient of a gift" — Reg. 3500; "property", "record" — ITA 248(1); "registered organization" — Reg. 3500.

3501.1 Contents of information returns [— returned property] — Every information return required to be filed under subsection 110.1(16) or 118.1(27) of the Act in respect of a transfer of property must contain

(a) a description of the transferred property;

(b) the fair market value of the transferred property at the time of the transfer;

(c) the date on which the property was transferred;

(d) the name and address of the transferee of the property including, in the case of an individual, their first name and initial; and

(e) if the transferor of the property, or a person not dealing at arm's length with the transferor, issued the receipt referred to in subsection 110.1(14) or 118.1(25) of the Act, the information contained in that receipt.

Notes: See Notes to ITA 118.1(26). Reg. 3501.1 added by 2011 budget bill #2, effective March 23, 2011.

Definitions [Reg. 3501.1]: "arm's length" — ITA 251(1); "fair market value" — see ITA 69(1) Notes; "individual", "person", "property" — ITA 248(1).

Charities Guidance: CG-016: Qualified donees — Consequences of returning donated property.

3502. Employees' charity trusts — Where

(a) a registered organization

(i) is an employees' charity trust, or

(ii) has appointed an employer as agent for the purpose of remitting, to that registered organization, donations that are collected by the employer from the employer's employees, and

(b) each copy of the return required by section 200 to be filed for a year by an employer of employees who donated to the registered organization in that year shows

(i) the amount of each employee's donations to the registered organization for the year collected by the employer, and

(ii) the registration number assigned by the Minister to the registered organization,

section 3501 shall not apply and the copy of the portion of the return, relating to each employee who made a donation to the registered organization in that year, that is required by section 209 to be distributed to the employee for filing with the employee's income tax return shall be an official receipt.

Notes: Reg. 3502 amended by P.C. 1994-139, retroactive to 1986, to allow for direct collection and distribution by employers of employees' donations without going through an employees' charity trust.

Definitions [Reg. 3502]: "amount", "employee" — ITA 248(1); "employees' charity trust" — Reg. 3500; "employer", "Minister" — ITA 248(1); "official receipt", "registered organization" — Reg. 3500.

3503. [Repealed]

Notes: Reg. 3503 repealed by 2018 budget bill #1, effective Feb. 27, 2018. The list of universities that qualify for charitable donations as though they were Canadian charities is now maintained by CRA rather than prescribed in Sch. VIII. See ITA 149.1(1)"qualified donee"(a)(iv), and tinyurl.com/univs-cra. Before Feb. 27, 2018, read:

> 3503. Universities outside Canada — For the purposes of subparagraph (a)(iv) of the definition "qualified donee" in subsection 149.1(1) of the Act, the universities outside Canada named in Schedule VIII are prescribed to be universities the student body of which ordinarily includes students from Canada.

Even before repeal of Reg. 3503, since 2012, a university must also be "registered by the Minister" (ITA 149.1(1)"qualified donee"(a)) for donations to qualify.

Reg. 3503 earlier amended by 2011 budget bill #2, effective 2012.

3504. Prescribed donees — For the purposes of subparagraphs 110.1(2.1)(a)(ii) and 118.1(5.4)(a)(ii) of the Act, the following are prescribed donees:

(a) Friends of the Nature Conservancy of Canada, Inc., a charity established in the United States;

(b) The Nature Conservancy, a charity established in the United States; and

(c) American Friends of Canadian Land Trusts.

Notes: Reg. 3504 opening words amended by 2002-2013 technical bill (Part 5 — technical), effective May 2, 2007, to change 110.1(3)(a)(ii) to 110.1(2.1)(a)(ii), and 118.1(6)(b) to 118.1(5.4)(a)(ii).

Reg. 3504(c) added by P.C. 2010-1112, effective for 2010 and later taxation years. Finance news release 2010-102 (Oct. 29/10) and Backgrounder explains that this is to encourage US residents to donate Canadian real property (such as nature reserves) for use in the Canadian public interest.

Reg. 3504(a) added by P.C. 2007-533, effective for donations made after May 2, 2007. Reg. 3504 amended by P.C. 1994-139, effective 1988, to change reference from former ITA 110(2.2)(a)(ii) to the provisions that now deal with gifts.

Definitions [Reg. 3504]: "prescribed" — ITA 248(1); "United States" — *Interpretation Act* 35(1).

Interpretation Bulletins: Regs. 3500–3504 — See at beginning of Part XXXV.

3505. [Repealed]

Notes [Reg. 3505]: Reg. 3505 repealed by 2017 budget bill #1, for gifts made after March 21, 2017, due to repeal of the extra deduction for donations of pharmaceuticals in ITA 110.1(1)(a.1). It read:

> 3505. Conditions — (1) The following conditions are prescribed in respect of a donee for the purposes of paragraph 110.1(8)(e) of the Act:
>
> (a) the donee has applied to the Minister for International Cooperation (or, if there is no such Minister, the Minister responsible for the Canadian International Development Agency) for a determination that the conditions described in this section have been met;
>
> (b) medicines received by the donee for use in charitable activities outside Canada are
>
> (i) delivered outside Canada by the donee for use in its charitable activities, or
>
> (ii) transferred to another registered charity that would meet the conditions contained in this section if that registered charity were a donee described in subsection 110.1(8) of the Act;
>
> (c) in the course of delivering medicines outside Canada for use in its charitable activities, the donee acts in a manner consistent with the principles and objectives of the inter-agency *Guidelines for Drug Donations* issued by the World Health Organization, as amended from time to time, (referred to in this section as "the WHO Guidelines");
>
> (d) the donee has sufficient expertise in delivering medicines for use in charitable activities carried on outside Canada;
>
> (e) the donee carries on a program that includes delivering medicines for use in charitable activities carried on outside Canada and that is
>
> (i) an international development assistance program, or
>
> (ii) an international humanitarian assistance program, responding to situations of international humanitarian crisis (resulting from either natural disaster or complex emergency); and
>
> (f) the donee has sufficient expertise to design, implement and monitor each program described in subparagraph (e)(i) or (ii) that it carries on, unless the donee has declared that it will not deliver medicines in that program.
>
> (2) Without limiting the application of the WHO Guidelines, for the purposes of paragraph (1)(c), a donee does not act in a manner consistent with the principles and objectives of those guidelines if the donee's directors, trustees, officers or like officials have not
>
> (a) approved a policy and procedural framework, under which the donee is required to act in a manner consistent with the WHO Guidelines; and
>
> (b) declared that the donee acts in compliance with that policy and procedural framework.
>
> (3) A donee is considered not to have sufficient expertise for the purpose of a program to which paragraph (1)(d) or (e) applies if
>
> (a) the program does not address the specific and differentiated needs, interests and vulnerabilities of affected women and men, girls and boys;

(b) the program does not incorporate, in the design of projects under the program, consideration for environmental effects of those projects; or

(c) the donee does not have policies and practices for the design, implementation and monitoring of the program.

(4) The Minister referred to in subsection (1) may

(a) rely on any information or evidence in making a determination under subsection (1); and

(b) require the donee to provide any other information or evidence that the Minister considers relevant and sufficient for the purpose of this section.

Reg. 3505 added by 2008 budget bill #2, for determinations re gifts made after June 2008.

PART XXXVI — [3600] RESERVES FOR SURVEYS

3600. **(1)** For the purpose of paragraph 20(1)(o) of the Act, the amount hereby prescribed is

(a) for the third taxation year preceding the taxation year during which a survey is scheduled to occur, the amount that is $1/4$ of the estimate of the expenses of the survey;

(b) for the second taxation year preceding the taxation year during which a survey is scheduled to occur, the amount that is $1/2$ of the estimate of the expenses of the survey;

(c) for the first taxation year preceding the taxation year during which a survey is scheduled to occur, the amount that is $3/4$ of the estimate of the expenses of the survey; and

(d) for the taxation year during which a survey is scheduled to occur, if the quadrennial or other special surveys have not, at the end of the year, been completed to the extent that the vessel is permitted to proceed on a voyage, the amount remaining after deducting from the estimate of the expenses of the survey the amount of expenses actually incurred in the year in carrying out the survey.

(2) In this section,

"classification society" means a society or association for the classification and registry of shipping approved by the Minister of Transport under the *Canada Shipping Act*.

"estimate of the expenses of survey" means a fair and reasonable estimate, made by a taxpayer at the time of filing his return of income for the third taxation year preceding the taxation year in which a quadrennial survey is scheduled to occur, of the costs, charges and expenses which might be expected to be necessarily incurred by him by reason of that survey and in respect of which he does not have or possess nor is he likely to have or possess any right of reimbursement, recoupment, recovery or indemnification from any other person or source;

"inspector" means a steamship inspector appointed under Part VIII of the *Canada Shipping Act*.

"quadrennial survey" means a periodical survey, not being an annual survey nor a survey coinciding as to time with the construction of a vessel, in accordance with the rules of a classification society or, an extended inspection, not being an annual inspection nor an inspection coinciding as to time with the construction of a vessel, pursuant to the provisions of the *Canada Shipping Act*, and the regulations thereunder;

"survey" means the drydocking of a vessel, the examination and inspection of its hull, boilers, machinery, engines and equipment by an inspector or a surveyor and everything done to such vessel, its hull, boilers, machinery, engines and equipment pursuant to an order, requirement or recommendation given or made by the inspector or surveyor as the result of the examination and inspection so that a safety and inspection certificate might be issued in respect of the vessel pursuant to the provisions of the *Canada Shipping Act*, and the regulations thereunder or, as the case may be, so that the vessel might be entitled to retain the character assigned to it in the registry book of a classification society;

"surveyor" means a surveyor to a classification society.

Definitions [Reg. 3600]: "amount" — ITA 248(1); "Canada" — ITA 255, *Interpretation Act* 35(1); "classification society", "estimate of the expenses of survey", "inspector" — Reg. 3600(2); "Minister", "person", "prescribed" — ITA 248(1); "quadrennial survey", "survey" — Reg. 3600(2); "surveyor" — Reg. 3600(2); "taxation year" — ITA 249; "taxpayer" — ITA 248(1).

PART XXXVII — [3700–3702] REGISTERED CHARITIES

Notes: Heading changed from "Charitable Foundations" by 2010 budget bill #2, effective for taxation years that end after March 3, 2010.

3700. [Repealed]

Notes: Reg. 3700 repealed by 2010 budget bill #2, for tax years that end after March 3, 2010. Since Reg. 3701-3702 apply for purposes of ITA 149.1, the terms "charitable foundation" and "non-qualified investment" do not need to be defined here, and "limited-dividend housing company" was moved to Reg. 3702(1)(c).

"Prescribed stock exchange" repealed by 2007 budget bill #2, effective Dec. 14, 2007. Reg. 3702(1) now uses "designated stock exchange".

3701. Disbursement quota — **(1)** For the purposes of the description of B in the definition "disbursement quota" in subsection 149.1(1) of the Act, the prescribed amount for a taxation year of a registered charity is determined as follows:

(a) choose a number, not less than two and not more than eight, of equal and consecutive periods that total twenty-four months and that end immediately before the beginning of the year;

(b) aggregate for each period chosen under paragraph (a) all amounts, each of which is the value, determined in accordance with section 3702, of a property, or a portion of a property, owned by the registered charity, and not used directly in charitable activities or administration, on the last day of the period;

(c) aggregate all amounts, each of which is the aggregate of values determined for each period under paragraph (b); and

(d) divide the aggregate amount determined under paragraph (c) by the number of periods chosen under paragraph (a).

Notes: For the meaning of "charitable activities" in para. (b), see Notes to ITA 149.1(1)"charitable activities".

Reg. 3701(1) opening words and (b) amended by 2010 budget bill #2, effective for taxation years that end after March 3, 2010.

(2) For the purposes of subsection (1) and subject to subsection (3),

(a) the number of periods chosen by a registered charity under paragraph (1)(a) shall, unless otherwise authorized by the Minister, be used for the taxation year and for all subsequent taxation years; and

(b) a registered charity is deemed to have existed on the last day of each of the periods chosen by it.

Notes: Reg. 3701(2)(a) and (b) amended by 2010 budget bill #2, for taxation years that end after March 3, 2010.

(3) The number of periods chosen under paragraph (1)(a) may be changed by the registered charity for its first taxation year commencing after 1986 and the new number shall, unless otherwise authorized by the Minister, be used for that taxation year and all subsequent taxation years.

Notes: Reg. 3701(3) amended by 2010 budget bill #2, effective for taxation years that end after March 3, 2010.

Definitions [Reg. 3701]: "amount" — ITA 248(1); "charitable foundation" — ITA 149.1(1); "Minister" — ITA 248(1); "month" — *Interpretation Act* 35(1); "prescribed", "property", "registered charity" — ITA 248(1); "taxation year" — ITA 149.1(1); "value" — Reg. 3702(1).

3702. Determination of value — **(1)** For the purposes of subsection 3701(1), the value of a property, or a portion of a property, owned by a registered charity, and not used directly in charitable activities or administration, on the last day of a period is determined as of that day to be

(a) in the case of a non-qualified investment of a private foundation, the greater of its fair market value on that day and its cost amount to the private foundation;

(b) subject to paragraph (c), in the case of property other than a non-qualified investment that is

(i) a share of a corporation that is listed on a designated stock exchange, the closing price or the average of the bid and asked prices of that share on that day or, if there is no closing price or bid and asked prices on that day, on the last preceding day for which there was a closing price or bid and asked prices,

(ii) a share of a corporation that is not listed on a designated stock exchange, the fair market value of that share on that day,

(iii) an interest in real property or a real right in an immovable, the fair market value on that day of the interest or right less the amount of any debt of the registered charity incurred in respect of the acquisition of the interest or right and secured by the interest or right, where the debt bears a reasonable rate of interest,

(iv) a contribution that is the subject of a pledge, nil,

(v) an interest, or for civil law a right, in property where the registered charity does not have the present use or enjoyment of the interest or right, nil,

(vi) a life insurance policy, other than an annuity contract, that has not matured, nil, and

(vii) a property not described in any of subparagraphs (i) to (vi), the fair market value of the property on that day; and

(c) in the case of any property described in paragraph (b) that is owned in connection with the charitable activities of the registered charity and is a share of a limited-dividend housing company referred to in paragraph 149(1)(n) of the Act or a loan, that has ceased to be used for charitable purposes and is being held pending disposition or for use in charitable activities, or that has been acquired for use in charitable activities, the lesser of the fair market value of the property on that day and an amount determined by the formula:

$$(A / 0.035) \times (12 / B)$$

where

A is the income earned on the property in the period, and

B is the number of months in the period.

Notes: For meaning of "charitable activities" see Notes to ITA 149.1(1)"charitable activities".

Reg. 3702(1) amended by 2010 budget bill #2, for taxation years that end after March 3, 2010. Earlier amended by 2007 budget bill #2, effective Dec. 14, 2007.

Registered Charities Newsletters: 27 (debts incurred by charitable foundations).

(2) For the purposes of subsection (1), a method that the Minister may accept for the determination of the fair market value of property or a portion thereof on the last day of a period is an independent appraisal made

(a) in the case of property described in subparagraph (1)(b)(ii) or (iii), not more than three years before that day; and

(b) in the case of property described in paragraph (1)(a), subparagraph (1)(b)(vii) or paragraph (1)(c), not more than one year before that day.

Definitions [Reg. 3702]: "amount", "annuity" — ITA 248(1); "charitable foundation" — ITA 149.1(1); "corporation" — ITA 248(1), *Interpretation Act* 35(1); "cost amount" — ITA 248(1); "designated stock exchange" — ITA 248(1), 262; "disposition" — ITA 248(1); "fair market value" — see ITA 69(1) Notes; "interest in real property" — ITA 248(4); "life insurance policy" — ITA 138(12), 248(1); "limited-dividend housing company" — ITA 149(1)(n); "Minister" — ITA 248(1); "month" — *Interpretation Act* 35(1); "non-qualified investment" — ITA 149.1(1); "private foundation" — ITA 149.1(1), 248(1); "property" — ITA 248(1); "real right" — ITA 248(4.1); "registered charity", "share" — ITA 248(1).

PART XXXVIII — [3800] SOCIAL INSURANCE NUMBER APPLICATIONS

3800. Every individual who is required by subsection 237(1) of the Act to apply to the Minister of Human Resources Development for assignment to him of a Social Insurance Number shall do so by delivering or mailing to the local office of the Canada Employment Insurance Commission nearest to the individual's residence, a completed application in the form prescribed by the Minister for that purpose.

Notes: The Minister is now the Minister of Families, Children and Social Development: see edsc.gc.ca. For the application mechanism, see now servicecanada.ca.

Reg. 3800 amended by S.C. 1996, c. 11, effective July 12, 1996.

Definitions [Reg. 3800]: "individual", "Minister", "office", "prescribed" — ITA 248(1).

Information Circulars: 82-2R2: SIN legislation that relates to the preparation of information slips.

PART XXXIX — [3900] MINING TAXES

3900. (1) [Definitions] — The following definitions apply in this section.

"income" of a taxpayer for a taxation year from mining operations in a province means the income, for the taxation year, that is derived from mining operations in the province as computed under the laws of the province that impose an eligible tax described in subsection (3).

Related Provisions: Reg. 3900(3) — Eligible tax.

Notes: See Notes at end of Reg. 3900.

"Derived" may be interpreted broadly: see Notes to ITA 94(1)"resident portion".

"mine" includes any work or undertaking in which a mineral ore is extracted or produced and includes a quarry.

Notes: See Notes to ITA 188.1(5) re meaning of "includes".

"mineral ore" includes an unprocessed mineral or mineral-bearing substance.

Notes: See Notes at end of Reg. 3900. Former Reg. 3900(2) contained a restrictive definition of "minerals", repealed for taxation years ending after 2002, so the broader definition in ITA 248(1)"mineral" applies. This relieving amendment is consistent with the phase-out and repeal of ITA 18(1)(m). See Rowe, "Deductibility of Crown Charges Under Bill C-48", II(1) *Resource Sector Taxation* (Federated Press) 91 at 94-95 (2003); Carr & Milot, "Mining Taxes: An Old Problem Revisited", *ibid*. 98-104. See also VIEWS doc 2003-0046481E5.

"mining operations" means

(a) the extraction or production of mineral ore from or in a mine;

(b) the transportation of mineral ore to the point of egress from the mine; and

(c) the processing of

(i) mineral ore (other than iron ore) to the prime metal stage or its equivalent, and

(ii) iron ore to a stage that is not beyond the pellet stage or its equivalent.

Notes: For the meaning of "prime metal stage or its equivalent" in (c)(i), see Notes to Reg. 1104(5).

"non-Crown royalty" means a royalty contingent on production of a mine or computed by reference to the amount or value of production from mining operations in a province but does not include a royalty that is payable to the Crown in right of Canada or a province.

"processing" includes all forms of beneficiation, smelting and refining.

Notes: See Notes to ITA 188.1(5) re meaning of "includes".

(2) [Mining tax deduction] — For the purpose of paragraph 20(1)(v) of the Act, the amount allowed in respect of taxes on income from mining operations of a taxpayer for a taxation year is the total of all amounts each of which is an eligible tax paid or payable by the taxpayer

(a) on the income of the taxpayer for the taxation year from mining operations; or

(b) on a non-Crown royalty included in computing the income of the taxpayer for the taxation year.

Proposed Addition — Deduction of mining taxes paid for statute-barred years

Letter from Dept. of Finance, Sept. 3, 2019: See under ITA 20(1)(v).

Notes: See Notes at end of Reg. 3900. Saskatchewan potash production tax included in profits from the sale of purchased and resold processed potash by a producer does not qualify as an eligible tax: VIEWS doc 2006-0197591E5.

(3) ["Eligible tax"] — An eligible tax referred to in subsection (2) is

(a) a tax, on the income of a taxpayer for a taxation year from mining operations in a province, that is

(i) levied under a law of the province,

(ii) imposed only on persons engaged in mining operations in the province, and

(iii) paid or payable to

(A) the province,

(B) an agent of Her Majesty in right of the province, or

(C) a municipality in the province, in lieu of taxes on property or on any interest, or for civil law any right, in property (other than in lieu of taxes on residential property or on any interest, or for civil law any right, in residential property); and

(b) a tax, on an amount received or receivable by a person as a non-Crown royalty, that is

(i) levied under a law of a province,

(ii) imposed specifically on persons who hold a non-crown royalty on mining operations in the province, and

(iii) paid or payable to the province or to an agent of Her Majesty in right of the province.

Notes: For discussion of new Reg. 3900 see Brian Carr, "Draft Regulation 3900 — Is it Perfect?", III(3) *Resource Sector Taxation* (Federated Press) 219-22 (2005).

The 2006 amendments extended Reg. 3900 by removing a prorating formula that reduced the deduction for mining taxes to the extent mining income determined for federal income tax purposes was less than mining income determined for provincial mining tax purposes. The formula, which limited the extent of the federal deduction based on the relative scope of the provincial mining tax base and the federal income tax base, did "not serve a current federal policy objective. Nonetheless, the federal government will continue to monitor provincial mining tax regimes and will be attentive to any situation where provincial income tax rates on resource income are reduced below the level of tax applied to other sectors if those reductions are undertaken as part of a strategy to replace non- deductible taxes on resource income with deductible resource-based charges." (Regulatory Impact Analysis Statement, P.C. 2006-999)

The amendments also expanded the deduction for mining taxes to include a deduction for provincial taxes on certain non-Crown mining royalties, limited royalties that are contingent on production or computed by reference to the value of production from mining operations in the province.

Detailed discussion of the rationale for these changes is in *Improving the Income Taxation of the Resource Sector in Canada*, Dept. of Finance, March 3, 2003 (fin.gc.ca under "Publications").

Reg. 3900(3) amended by P.C. 2007-1443 to change "imposed *only* on persons who hold a non-Crown royalty" to "imposed *specifically* on persons who hold a non-crown royalty", retroactive to taxes paid or payable in taxation years that end after 2002. (Thus, a tax imposed under a provincial mining tax statute on persons who receive amounts under a non-Crown royalty, but also imposed on persons who dispose of certain rights in a mining property, can be deductible under ITA 20(1)(v).)

Reg. 3900 amended by P.C. 2006-999, for tax years that end after 2002 with a phaseout for tax years beginning before 2007.

Definitions [Reg. 3900]: "amount" — ITA 248(1); "Canada" — ITA 255, *Interpretation Act* 35(1); "eligible tax" — Reg. 3900(3); "income", "mine" — Reg. 3900(1); "mineral" — ITA 248(1); "mineral ore", "mining operations", "non-Crown royalty" — Reg. 3900(1); "processing" — ITA 248(1); "province" — *Interpretation Act* 35(1); "taxation year" — ITA 249; "taxpayer" — ITA 248(1).

PART XL — [4000–4001] BORROWED MONEY COSTS

4000. [Revoked]

Notes: Reg. 4000, revoked effective 1979-80, provided a prescribed manner (no longer needed) for making an election under ITA s. 21.

4001. Interest on insurance policy loans — For the purposes of subsection 20(2.1) of the Act, the amount of interest to be verified by the insurer in respect of a taxpayer shall be verified in prescribed form no later than the last day on which the taxpayer is required to file his return of income under section 150 of the Act for the taxation year in respect of which the interest was paid.

Definitions [Reg. 4001]: "amount", "insurer", "prescribed" — ITA 248(1); "taxation year" — ITA 249; "taxpayer" — ITA 248(1).

Income Tax Folios: S3-F6-C1: Interest deductibility [replaces IT-533].

Forms: T2210: Verification of policy loan interest by the insurer.

PART XLI — [4100] REPRESENTATION EXPENSES

4100. For the purposes of subsection 20(9) of the Act, an election shall be made by filing with the Minister the following documents in duplicate:

(a) a letter from the taxpayer specifying the amount in respect of which the election is being made; and

(b) where the taxpayer is a corporation, a certified copy of the resolution of the directors authorizing the election to be made.

Definitions [Reg. 4100]: "amount" — ITA 248(1); "corporation" — ITA 248(1), *Interpretation Act* 35(1); "Minister", "taxpayer" — ITA 248(1).

PART XLII — [4200] VALUATION OF ANNUITIES AND OTHER INTERESTS

4200. [No longer relevant]

Notes: Reg. 4200 prescribes rules for subpara. 115E(f)(i) of the pre-1972 Act.

PART XLIII — [4300–4302] INTEREST RATES

4300. Interpretation — For the purposes of this Part, "quarter" means any of the following periods in a calendar year:

(a) the period beginning on January 1 and ending on March 31;

(b) the period beginning on April 1 and ending on June 30;

(c) the period beginning on July 1 and ending on September 30; and

(d) the period beginning on October 1 and ending on December 31.

Interpretation Bulletins: IT-421R2: Benefits to individuals, corporations and shareholders from loans or debt.

Definitions [Reg. 4300]: "calendar year" — *Interpretation Act* 37(1)(a).

4301. Prescribed rate of interest — Subject to section 4302, for the purposes of

(a) every provision of the Act that requires interest at a prescribed rate to be paid to the Receiver General, the prescribed rate in effect during any particular quarter is the total of

(i) the rate that is the simple arithmetic mean, expressed as a percentage per year and rounded to the next higher whole percentage where the mean is not a whole percentage, of all amounts each of which is the average equivalent yield, expressed as a percentage per year, of Government of Canada Treasury Bills that mature approximately three months after their date of issue and that are sold at auctions of Government of Canada Treasury Bills during the first month of the quarter preceding the particular quarter, and

(ii) 4 per cent;

(b) every provision of the Act that requires interest at a prescribed rate to be paid or applied on an amount payable by the Minister to a taxpayer, the prescribed rate in effect during any particular quarter is the total of

(i) the rate determined under subparagraph (a)(i) in respect of the particular quarter, and

(ii) if the taxpayer is a corporation, zero per cent, and in any other case, 2 per cent;

(b.1) subsection 17.1(1) of the Act, the prescribed rate in effect during any particular quarter is the rate that would be determined under paragraph (a) in respect of the particular quarter if the reference in subparagraph (a)(i) to "the next higher whole percentage where the mean is not a whole percentage" were read as "two decimal points"; and

(c) every other provision of the Act in which reference is made to a prescribed rate of interest or to interest at a prescribed rate, the prescribed rate in effect during any particular quarter is the rate determined under subparagraph (a)(i) in respect of the particular quarter.

Notes: There are four rates:

(a) applies for interest payable by a taxpayer to CRA (i.e., *late payments of tax*), and to "offset interest" credited to a taxpayer for early payments of instalments. Examples: ITA 129(2.2), 161(1), (2), (2.2). Interest is compounded daily: ITA 248(11). This rate also applies to late CPP contributions and EI premiums, and to late remittances of GST/HST since April 2007 (*Interest Rates (Excise Tax Act) Regulations*: see in David M. Sherman, *The Practitioner's Goods and Services Tax Annotated*).

(b) applies for interest payable by CRA to a taxpayer (i.e., *late refunds*). Examples: ITA 129(2.1), 164(3), (3.2). Interest is compounded daily: ITA 248(11). This rate also applies to late GST refunds since April 2007. However, for corporations since July 2010 the rate is 2 percentage points lower (same rate as (c)).

(b.1) applies to determine the minimum interest inclusion under ITA 17.1(1) for the "pertinent loan of indebtedness" election for the shareholder loan (15(2)) and foreign affiliate dumping (212.3) rules.

(c) applies for provisions that require a prescribed rate of interest to be paid by one party to another in order for there not to be a *deemed benefit*, or that use a prescribed rate as a measure of a fair return on capital. Examples: ITA 17(1), 18(2.2), 18(9.7), 56(4.2), 74.4(2)(d), 74.5(1), 74.5(2), 80.4(1), 80.4(2), 94.1(1)(f)(ii), 120.4(1)"safe harbour capital return"A, 143.2(7)(b).

For the leasing rules in ITA 16.1, Reg. 4302 applies instead of Reg. 4301.

Reg. 4301(b.1) added by 2012 budget bill #2, effective March 29, 2012. See ITA 17.1(1) Notes.

Reg. 4301(b)(ii) changed from "2 per cent" by 2010 budget bill #1, effective July 1, 2010. The reduced refund rate for corporations, announced in the March 2010 Budget, responds to the Auditor General spring 2009 report, ch. 4 (oag-bvg.gc.ca) that corporations were parking billions of dollars with the CRA to earn relatively high refund interest. Table A5.1 in the Budget papers projected that this measure would generate revenue for the federal government of $45 million in 2010-11, $100m in 2011-12, $140m in 2012-13, $170m in 2013-14 and $190m in 2014-15.

Reg. 4301 amended by P.C. 1989-1792, for interest in respect of periods after Sept. 1989, to increase the rate by 2% for amounts owing *to* and *by* the government; and amended by P.C. 1995-926, effective for interest in respect of periods after June 1995, to increase the rate by a further 2% for amounts owing *to* the government. (This change was announced in the 1995 federal budget.)

Reg. 4301(a)(i) amended effective Dec. 31, 1997 to change "weekly average" to "average", and "a weekly auction" to "auctions", to reflect change in the cycle of treasury bill auctions that took effect Sept. 18, 1997 (Finance news release 97-67, Aug. 5/97).

Prescribed Interest Rates Per Annum

Year	Quarter	Reg. 4301(c) Benefits %	Reg. 4301(b) Refunds %	Reg. 4301(a) Late Tax %
1984	1st, 2nd	10	10	10
	3rd	11	11	11
	4th	13	13	13
1985	1st	12	12	12
	2nd, 3rd, 4th	10	10	10
1986	1st	9	9	9
	2nd	11	11	11

Year	Quarter	Reg. 4301(c) Benefits %	Reg. 4301(b) Refunds %	Reg. 4301(a) Late Tax %
	3rd	10	10	10
	4th	9	9	9
[Compounding under 248(11) applies since Jan. 1/87]				
1987	1st	9	9	9
	2nd, 3rd	8	8	8
	4th	9	9	9
1988	1st, 2nd, 3rd	9	9	9
	4th	10	10	10
1989	1st	11	11	11
	2nd	12	12	12
	3rd	13	13	13
	4th	13	15	15
1990	1st, 2nd	13	15	15
	3rd, 4th	14	16	16
1991	1st	13	15	15
	2nd	11	13	13
	3rd	10	12	12
	4th	9	11	11
1992	1st	9	11	11
	2nd	8	10	10
	3rd	7	9	9
	4th	6	8	8
1993	1st	8	10	10
	2nd	7	9	9
	3rd	6	8	8
	4th	5	7	7
1994	1st	5	7	7
	2nd	4	6	6
	3rd	4	6	6
	4th	7	9	9
1995	1st	6	8	8
	2nd	8	10	10
	3rd	9	11	13
	4th	7	9	11
1996	1st	7	9	11
	2nd	6	8	10
	3rd, 4th	5	7	9
1997	1st	4	6	8
	2nd	3	5	7
	3rd, 4th	4	6	8
1998	1st	4	6	8
	2nd, 3rd, 4th	5	7	9
1999	1st–4th	5	7	9
2000	1st	5	7	9
	2nd, 3rd, 4th	6	8	10
2001	1st, 2nd	8	8	10
	3rd, 4th	5	7	9
2002	1st	3	5	7
	2nd	2	4	6
	3rd, 4th	3	5	7
2003	1st, 2nd	3	5	7
	3rd	4	6	8
	4th	3	5	7
2004	1st, 2nd	3	5	7
	3rd	2	4	6
	4th	3	5	7
2005	1st–4th	3	5	7
2006	1st	3	5	7
	2nd, 3rd	4	6	8
	4th	5	7	9
2007	1st–4th	5	7	9
2008	1st, 2nd	4	6	8
	3rd, 4th	3	5	7
2009	1st	2	4	6
	2nd–4th	1	3	5

Year	Quarter	Reg. 4301(c) Benefits %	Reg. 4301(b) Refunds %	Reg. 4301(a) Late Tax %
2010	1st, 2nd	1	3	5

		Reg. 4301(c)	Reg. 4301(b) Refunds		Reg. 4301(a)
Year	Quarter	Benefits %	Corporate %	Other %	Late Tax %
2010	3rd, 4th	1	1	3	5
2011	1st–4th	1	1	3	5
2012	1st–4th	1	1	3	5
2013	1st–3rd	1	1	3	5
2013	4th	2	2	4	6
2014	1st–4th	1	1	3	5
2015	1st–4th	1	1	3	5
2016	1st–4th	1	1	3	5
2017	1st–4th	1	1	3	5
2018	1st	1	1	3	5
2018	2nd–4th	2	2	4	6
2019	1st–4th	2	2	4	6
2020	1st, 2nd	2	2	4	6
2020	3rd, 4th	1	1	3	5
2021	1st–3rd	1	1	3	5

(Rates at tinyurl.com/cra-intrates.)

Interpretation Bulletins: IT-153R3: Land developers — Subdivision and development costs and carrying charges on land; IT-243R4: Dividend refund to private corporations; IT-421R2: Benefits to individuals, corporations and shareholders from loans or debt.

Definitions [Reg. 4301]: "amount" — ITA 248(1); "Canada" — ITA 255, *Interpretation Act* 35(1); "corporation" — ITA 248(1), *Interpretation Act* 35(1); "Minister" — ITA 248(1); "month" — *Interpretation Act* 35(1); "prescribed" — ITA 248(1); "quarter" — Reg. 4300; "taxpayer" — ITA 248(1).

4302. Notwithstanding section 4301, for the purposes of paragraph 16.1(1)(d) of the Act and subsection 1100(1.1), the interest rate in effect during any month is the rate that is one percentage point greater than the rate that was, during the month before the immediately preceding month, the average yield, expressed as a percentage per year rounded to two decimal points, prevailing on all outstanding domestic Canadian-dollar Government of Canada bonds on the last Wednesday of that month with a remaining term to maturity of over 10 years, as first published by the Bank of Canada.

Notes: Reg. 4302 added by P.C. 1991-465, effective for leases entered into after 10pm EDST, April 26, 1989, other than leases entered into pursuant to an agreement in writing entered into before that time under which the lessee thereunder has the right to require the lease of the property (and for these purposes a lease in respect of which a material change has been agreed to by the parties thereto effective at any particular time that is after 10pm EDST, April 26, 1989 is deemed to have been entered into at that particular time).

Prescribed Interest Rates for Leasing Rules

For leases entered into before July 1989, the prescribed rate is 11.2%. The rates for leases entered into after that date are:

	1989	1990	1991	1992	1993	1994
Jan.	—	10.80	11.70	10.18	9.66	8.45
Feb.	—	10.69	11.51	9.97	9.54	8.12
March	—	11.04	11.22	9.92	9.67	7.86
April	11.20	11.64	10.89	9.97	9.19	8.33
May	11.20	11.91	10.88	10.28	9.27	9.25
June	11.20	12.54	10.91	10.51	9.27	9.18
July	10.85	11.86	10.91	10.17	9.12	9.55
Aug.	10.60	11.72	11.36	9.87	8.96	10.29
Sept.	10.62	11.78	11.17	9.21	8.79	10.50
Oct.	10.62	11.83	10.97	9.19	8.40	9.89
Nov.	10.91	12.54	10.59	9.53	8.55	10.04
Dec.	10.54	12.15	10.12	9.33	8.35	10.29

	1995	1996	1997	1998	1999	2000
Jan.	10.24	8.44	7.42	6.78	6.35	7.12
Feb.	10.16	8.43	7.77	6.84	6.08	7.25
March	10.41	8.35	8.07	6.63	6.08	7.36
April	9.86	8.84	7.78	6.64	6.37	6.98
May	9.70	8.94	7.97	6.54	6.23	6.96
June	9.44	9.07	7.97	6.64	6.34	7.03
July	9.11	8.92	7.95	6.49	6.54	6.94
Aug.	9.02	8.98	7.49	6.45	6.63	6.90
Sept.	9.50	8.86	7.11	6.56	6.74	6.83
Oct.	9.24	8.60	7.38	6.78	6.69	6.79
Nov.	9.11	8.48	6.99	6.15	6.92	6.83
Dec.	9.11	7.81	6.80	6.27	7.38	6.79

	2001	2002	2003	2004	2005	2006
Jan.	6.63	6.66	6.55	6.24	5.87	5.20
Feb.	6.59	6.75	6.37	6.14	5.86	5.04
March	6.71	6.72	6.45	6.15	5.69	5.22
April	6.63	6.68	6.39	5.98	5.71	5.17
May	6.74	7.00	6.52	5.94	5.75	5.26
June	6.94	6.89	6.34	6.23	5.55	5.59
July	7.08	6.76	6.01	6.23	5.41	5.51
Aug.	6.97	6.73	5.98	6.30	5.27	5.69
Sept.	7.01	6.70	6.35	6.29	5.31	5.46
Oct.	6.72	6.55	6.40	6.14	5.11	5.22
Nov.	6.86	6.38	6.19	6.02	5.21	5.08
Dec.	6.32	6.61	6.33	5.96	5.38	5.25

	2007	2008	2009	2010	2011	2012
Jan.	5.03	5.22	5.00	4.84	4.60	3.61
Feb.	5.11	5.18	4.45	5.08	4.51	3.42
March	5.23	5.17	4.74	4.92	4.71	3.55
April	5.10	5.14	4.70	4.98	4.69	3.48
May	5.21	4.91	4.63	4.99	4.66	3.56
June	5.21	5.02	4.72	4.99	4.67	3.55
July	5.43	5.07	5.11	4.58	4.41	3.20
Aug.	5.59	5.07	4.96	4.59	4.47	3.24
Sept.	5.52	5.18	5.10	4.71	4.28	3.14
Oct.	5.44	5.02	4.96	4.39	4.00	3.28
Nov.	5.50	5.14	4.87	4.25	3.74	3.24
Dec.	5.39	5.31	4.98	4.38	3.91	3.27

	2013	2014	2015	2016	2017	2018
Jan.	3.20	4.01	3.36	3.17	3.06	3.16
Feb.	3.27	4.09	3.22	3.04	3.24	3.15
March	3.47	3.80	2.75	2.90	3.34	3.35
April	3.39	3.80	2.76	2.78	3.29	3.35
May	3.34	3.82	2.79	2.86	3.14	3.22
June	3.19	3.76	3.01	2.94	3.01	3.45
July	3.48	3.60	3.08	2.87	2.87	3.28
Aug.	3.90	3.72	3.29	2.67	2.99	3.15
Sept.	3.88	3.59	3.09	2.60	3.29	3.31
Oct.	4.00	3.44	3.08	2.53	3.19	3.33
Nov.	4.00	3.61	3.09	2.52	3.42	3.43
Dec.	3.87	3.46	3.13	2.68	3.32	3.52

	2019	2020	2021
Jan.	3.39	2.57	2.06
Feb.	3.12	2.67	2.13
March	3.11	2.42	2.32
April	3.10	2.32	2.77
May	2.76	2.25	2.90
June	2.90	1.99	2.96
July	2.75	1.92	2.91
Aug.	2.70	1.95	2.77
Sept.	2.67	1.86	
Oct.	2.34	2.01	
Nov.	2.54	1.99	
Dec.	2.60	2.01	

(Rate calculation method provided at tinyurl.com/reg-4302.)

Definitions [Reg. 4302]: "Canada" — ITA 255, *Interpretation Act* 35(1); "month" — *Interpretation Act* 35(1).

Regulations

PART XLIV — [4400] PUBLICLY-TRADED SHARES OR SECURITIES

4400. (1) For the purpose of section 24 and subsection 26(11) of the *Income Tax Application Rules*,

(a) a share or security named in Schedule VII is hereby prescribed to be a publicly-traded share or security; and

(b) for each such share or security, the amount set out in Column II of Schedule VII opposite that share or security is hereby prescribed as the amount, if any, prescribed in respect of that property.

(2) In Schedule VII, the abbreviation

(a) "Cl" means "Class";

(b) "Com" means "Common";

(c) "Cv" means "Convertible";

(d) "Cu" means "Cumulative";

(e) "Pc" means "Per Cent";

(f) "Pr" means "Preferred" or "Preference" as the case may be;

(g) "Pt" means "Participating";

(h) "Rt" means "Right"; and

(i) "Wt" means "Warrant".

Notes: Schedule VII, which lists the December 23, 1971 share values of all publicly listed shares, is not reproduced. See *TaxPartner* or canlii.org.

Definitions [Reg. 4400]: "amount", "prescribed", "property" — ITA 248(1); "share" — ITA 248(1).

PART XLV — [4500] ELECTIONS IN RESPECT OF EXPROPRIATION ASSETS

4500. Any election by a taxpayer under subsection 80.1(1), (2), (4), (5), (6) or (9) of the Act shall be made on or before the day on or before which the return of income is required to be filed pursuant to section 150 of the Act for the taxation year in which the assets referred to in the particular election were acquired by him.

Definitions [Reg. 4500]: "taxation year" — ITA 249; "taxpayer" — ITA 248(1).

Forms: T2079: Election re expropriation assets acquired as compensation for or a consideration for sale of foreign property taken by or sold to foreign issuer.

PART XLVI — [4600–4610] INVESTMENT TAX CREDIT

Forms: T2038 (Ind.): Investment tax credit (Individuals); T2038 (Corp): Investment tax credit (Corporations).

4600. Qualified property — **(1)** Property is a prescribed building for the purposes of the definitions "qualified property" and "qualified resource property" in subsection 127(9) of the Act if it is depreciable property of the taxpayer that is a building or grain elevator and it is erected on land owned or leased by the taxpayer,

(a) that is included in Class 1, 3, 6, 20, 24 or 27 or paragraph (c), (d) or (e) of Class 8 in Schedule II; or

(b) that is included or would, but for Class 28, 41, 41.1 or 41.2 in Schedule II, be included in paragraph (g) of Class 10 in Schedule II.

Notes: Reg. 4600(1)(b) amended by 2013 budget bill #2 (to refer to Class 41.2, for property acquired after March 20, 2013), 2012 budget bill #2, P.C. 2011-44.

(2) Property is prescribed machinery and equipment for the purposes of the definitions "qualified property" and "qualified resource property" in subsection 127(9) of the Act if it is depreciable property of the taxpayer (other than property referred to in subsection (1)) that is

(a) a property included in paragraph (k) of Class 1 or paragraph (a) of Class 2 in Schedule II;

(b) an oil or water storage tank;

(c) a property included in Class 8 in Schedule II (other than railway rolling stock);

(d) a vessel, including the furniture, fittings and equipment attached thereto;

(e) a property included in paragraph (a) of Class 10 or Class 22 or 38 in Schedule II (other than a car or truck designed for use on highways or streets);

(f) notwithstanding paragraph (e), a logging truck acquired after March 31, 1977 to be used in the activity of logging and having a weight, including the weight of property the capital cost of which is included in the capital cost of the truck at the time of its acquisition (but for greater certainty not including the weight of fuel), in excess of 16,000 pounds;

(g) a property included in any of paragraphs (b) to (f), (h), (j), (k), (o), (r), (t) or (u) of Class 10 in Schedule II, or property included in paragraph (b) of Class 41 in Schedule II and that would otherwise be included in paragraph (j), (k), (r), (t) or (u) of Class 10 in Schedule II;

(h) a property included in paragraph (n) of Class 10, or Class 15, in Schedule II (other than a roadway);

(i) a property included in any of paragraphs (a) to (f) of Class 9 in Schedule II;

(j) a property included in Class 28, in paragraph (a), (a.1), (a.2) or (a.3) of Class 41 or in Class 41.1 or 41.2 in Schedule II that would, but for Class 28, 41, 41.1 or 41.2, as the case may be, be included in paragraph (k) or (r) of Class 10 of Schedule II;

(k) a property included in Class 21, 24, 27, 29, 34, 39, 40, 43, 45, 46, 50, 52 or 53 in Schedule II;

(l) a property included in paragraph (c) or (d) of Class 41 in Schedule II;

(m) property included in Class 43.1 in Schedule II because of paragraph (c) of that Class; or

(n) a property included in Class 43.2 in Schedule II because of paragraph (a) of that Class.

Notes: Property listed here is "qualified property" under ITA 127(9), eligible for ITC under 127(9)"investment tax credit"(a).

In *Good Equipment*, 2008 TCC 28, equipment held as inventory and leased out was converted to capital property on entering into a financing lease, so it qualified as "depreciable property" under Reg. 4600(2).

In *H.B. Barton Trucking*, 2009 TCC 376, tractors and chip trailers used to transport wood chips qualified under para. (f), and did not fall within ITA 127(11)(b)(i). While logging is "essentially for the production of raw or resource material, a certain degree of processing is inevitable": (para. 28). Building logging roads can be part of "logging": *Lor-Wes Contracting*, [1985] 2 C.T.C. 79 (FCA).

The following can qualify: building for storing fishing vessel and lobster traps (VIEWS doc 2007-0238901E5); logging truck for transporting logs (2005-0130101I7); potato farmers' foreign material detection equipment (2015-0601661E5); soft drink "post-mix" dispensing equipment (2002-0143485).

Wind turbines did not qualify (docs 2010-0390971I7, 2011-0394051E5, 2011-0409111E5), but do since March 29, 2012: Reg. 4600(3).

Para. (k) amended to refer to Class 53 by 2015 Budget bill, effective June 23, 2015.

Para. (j) amended to add references to Class 41.2 by 2013 budget bill #2, for property acquired after March 20, 2013.

Reg. 4600(2) earlier amended by 2002-2013 technical bill (last change effective for property acquired after Jan. 27, 2009), 2012 budget bill #2 (effective March 29, 2012), P.C. 2011-44, 2006-329, 2005-2286, 2005-2186, 1999-629, 1998-49, 1994-230.

Interpretation Bulletins: IT-411R: Meaning of "construction".

(3) Property is prescribed energy generation and conservation property for the purposes of the definition "qualified property" in subsection 127(9) of the Act if it is depreciable property of the taxpayer (other than property referred to in subsection (1) or (2)) that is a property included in any of subparagraph (a.1)(i) of Class 17 and Classes 43.1, 43.2 and 48 in Schedule II.

Notes: A wind turbine can qualify under Reg. 4600(3): VIEWS doc 2017-0726891E5.

Reg. 4600(3) added by 2012 budget bill #2, effective March 29, 2012.

Definitions [Reg. 4600]: "depreciable property" — ITA 13(21), 248(1); "prescribed", "property" — ITA 248(1); "qualified property", "qualified resource property" — ITA 127(9); "taxpayer" — ITA 248(1).

Income Tax Folios: S4-F15-C1: Manufacturing and processing [replaces IT-147R3].

4601. Qualified transportation equipment — [No longer relevant]

Notes: Reg. 4601 prescribes property for pre-1989 ITA 127(9)"qualified transportation equipment". Amended by P.C. 1995-775.

4602. Certified property — [No longer relevant]

Notes: Certified property is ineligible for investment tax credit since 1996, unless acquired under an agreement entered into before (or already under construction by) Feb. 22, 1994. See ITA 127(9)"certified property".

4603. Qualified construction equipment — [No longer relevant]

Notes: Reg. 4603 prescribes property for pre-1991 ITA 127(9)"qualified construction equipment".

4604. Approved project property — [No longer relevant]

Notes: Reg. 4604 prescribes property for repealed ITA 127(9)"approved project property".

4605. Prescribed activities — [No longer relevant]

Notes: Reg. 4605 prescribes activities for ITA 127(9)"approved project property", now repealed.

4606. Prescribed amount — For the purposes of paragraph (b) of the definition "contract payment" in subsection 127(9) of the Act, a prescribed amount is an amount received from the Canadian Commercial Corporation in respect of an amount received by that Corporation from a government, municipality or other public authority other than the government of Canada or of a province, a Canadian municipality or other Canadian public authority.

Definitions [Reg. 4606]: "amount" — ITA 248(1); "Canada" — ITA 255, *Interpretation Act* 35(1); "prescribed" — ITA 248(1); "province" — *Interpretation Act* 35(1).

4607. Prescribed designated regions — For the purposes of the definition "specified percentage" in subsection 127(9) of the Act, "prescribed designated region" means a region of Canada, other than the Gaspé peninsula and the provinces of Nova Scotia, New Brunswick, Prince Edward Island, and Newfoundland, including Labrador, that was a designated region on December 31, 1984, under the *Regional Development Incentives Designated Region Order, 1974*.

Definitions [Reg. 4607]: "Canada" — ITA 255, *Interpretation Act* 35(1); "province" — *Interpretation Act* 35(1).

4608. Prescribed expenditure for qualified Canadian exploration expenditure — [No longer relevant]

Notes: Reg. 4608 prescribes expenditures for ITA 127(9)"qualified Canadian exploration expenditure", now repealed.

4609. Prescribed offshore region — For the purposes of the definition "specified percentage" in subsection 127(9) of the Act, the following region is a prescribed offshore region:

(a) that submarine area, not within a province, adjacent to the coast of Canada and extending throughout the natural prolongation of that portion of the land territory of Canada comprising the Gaspé Peninsula and the provinces of Newfoundland, Prince Edward Island, Nova Scotia and New Brunswick to the outer edge of the continental margin or to a distance of two hundred nautical miles from the baselines from which the territorial sea of Canada is measured, whichever is the greater; and

(b) the waters above the submarine area referred to in paragraph (a).

Notes: A fishing vessel used in the prescribed offshore region qualifies for the Atlantic Investment Tax Credit: VIEWS doc 2015-0576511E5.

Definitions [Reg. 4609]: "Canada" — ITA 255, *Interpretation Act* 35(1); "prescribed" — ITA 248(1); "province", "territorial sea" — *Interpretation Act* 35(1).

4610. Prescribed area — For the purpose of paragraph (c.1) of the definition "qualified property" in subsection 127(9) of the Act, the area prescribed is the area comprising the Provinces of Nova Scotia, New Brunswick, Prince Edward Island and Newfoundland and the Gaspé Peninsula.

Notes: Reg. 4610 added by P.C. 1995-775, effective for property acquired after 1991.

Definitions [Reg. 4610]: "prescribed" — ITA 248(1).

PART XLVII — [4700] ELECTION IN RESPECT OF CERTAIN PROPERTY OWNED ON DECEMBER 31, 1971

4700. Any election by an individual under subsection 26(7) of the *Income Tax Application Rules* shall be made by filing with the Minister the form prescribed.

Definitions [Reg. 4700]: "individual", "Minister", "prescribed" — ITA 248(1).

Interpretation Bulletins: IT-139R: Capital property owned on December 31, 1971 — Fair market value (archived).

Forms: T1105: Supplementary schedule for dispositions of capital property acquired before 1972; T2076: Valuation day value election for capital properties owned on December 31, 1971.

PART XLVIII — [4800–4803] STATUS OF CORPORATIONS AND TRUSTS

4800. (1) [Public corporation — prescribed conditions] — For the purposes of subparagraph (b)(i) of the definition "public corporation" in subsection 89(1) of the Act, the following conditions are prescribed in respect of a corporation other than a cooperative corporation (within the meaning assigned by section 136 of the Act) or a credit union:

(a) a class of shares of the capital stock of the corporation designated by the corporation in its election or by the Minister in his notice to the corporation, as the case may be, shall be qualified for distribution to the public;

(b) there shall be no fewer than

(i) where the shares of that class are equity shares, 150, and

(ii) in any other case, 300

persons, other than insiders of the corporation, each of whom holds

(iii) not less than one block of shares of that class, and

(iv) shares of that class having an aggregate fair market value of not less than $500; and

(c) insiders of the corporation shall not hold more than 80 per cent of the issued and outstanding shares of that class.

Forms: T2073: Election to be a public corporation.

(2) [Public corporation — prescribed conditions] — For the purposes of subparagraph (c)(i) of the definition "public corporation" in subsection 89(1) of the Act, the following conditions are prescribed in respect of a corporation:

(a) insiders of the corporation shall hold more than 90 per cent of the issued and outstanding shares of each class of shares of the capital stock of the corporation that

(i) was, at any time after the corporation last became a public corporation, listed on a designated stock exchange in Canada, or

(ii) was a class, designated as described in paragraph (1)(a), by virtue of which the corporation last became a public corporation;

(b) in respect of each class of shares described in subparagraph (a)(i) or (ii), there shall be fewer than

(i) where the shares of that class are equity shares, 50, and

(ii) in any other case, 100

persons, other than insiders of the corporation, each of whom holds

(iii) not less than one block of shares of that class, and

(iv) shares of that class having an aggregate fair market value of not less than $500; and

(c) there shall be no class of shares of the capital stock of the corporation that is qualified for distribution to the public and complies with the conditions described in paragraphs (1)(b) and (c).

Notes: See Notes to ITA 89(1)"public corporation".

Reg. 4800(2)(a)(i) amended by 2007 budget bill #2, effective Dec. 14, 2007, to change "stock exchange in Canada prescribed for the purposes of section 89 of the Act" to "designated stock exchange in Canada".

Forms: T2067: Election not to be a public corporation.

(3) [Public corporation — amalgamation] — Where, by virtue of an amalgamation (within the meaning assigned by section 87 of the Act) of predecessor corporations any one or more of which was, immediately before the amalgamation, a public corporation, shares of any class of the capital stock of any such public corporation that was

(a) at any time after the corporation last became a public corporation, listed on a designated stock exchange in Canada, or

(b) the class, designated as described in paragraph (1)(a), by virtue of which the corporation last became a public corporation,

are converted into shares of any class (in this subsection referred to as the "new class") of the capital stock of the new corporation, the new class shall, for the purposes of subsection (2), be deemed to be a class, designated as described in paragraph (1)(a), by virtue of which the new corporation last became a public corporation.

Notes: Reg. 4800(3)(a) amended by 2007 budget bill #2, effective Dec. 14, 2007, to change "stock exchange in Canada prescribed for the purposes of section 89 of the Act" to "designated stock exchange in Canada".

(4) [Public corporation — election requirements] — Any election under subparagraphs (b)(i) or (c)(i) of the definition "public corporation" in subsection 89(1) of the Act shall be made by filing with the Minister the following documents:

(a) the form prescribed by the Minister;

(b) where the directors of the corporation are legally entitled to administer the affairs of the corporation, a certified copy of their resolution authorizing the election to be made;

(c) where the directors of the corporation are not legally entitled to administer the affairs of the corporation, a certified copy of the authorization of the making of the election by the person or persons legally entitled to administer the affairs of the corporation; and

(d) a statutory declaration made by a director of the corporation stating that, after reasonable inquiry for the purpose of informing himself in that regard, to the best of his knowledge the corporation complies with all the prescribed conditions that must be complied with at the time the election is made.

Definitions [Reg. 4800]: "block of shares" — Reg. 4803(1); "Canada" — ITA 255, *Interpretation Act* 35(1); "class" — ITA 248(6); "class of shares" — Reg. 4803(2); "corporation" — ITA 248(1), *Interpretation Act* 35(1); "credit union" — ITA 137(6), 248(1); "designated stock exchange" — ITA 248(1), 262; "equity share" — ITA 204, Reg. 4803(1); "fair market value" — see ITA 69(1) Notes; "Minister" — ITA 248(1); "new class" — Reg. 4800(3); "person" — ITA 248(1), Reg. 4803(3); "prescribed" — ITA 248(1); "public corporation" — ITA 89(1), 248(1); "share" — ITA 248(1); "statutory declaration" — *Interpretation Act* 35(1).

Interpretation Bulletins: IT-391R: Status of corporations.

Forms: T2067: Election not to be a public corporation; T2073: Election to be a public corporation.

4800.1 [Prescribed trusts] — For the purposes of paragraph 107(1)(a) and subsections 107(1.1), (2) and (4.1) of the Act, the following are prescribed trusts:

(a) a trust maintained primarily for the benefit of employees of a corporation or two or more corporations which do not deal at arm's length with each other, where one of the main purposes of

the trust is to hold interests in shares of the capital stock of the corporation or corporations, as the case may be, or any corporation not dealing at arm's length therewith;

(b) a trust established exclusively for the benefit of one or more persons each of whom was, at the time the trust was created, either a person from whom the trust received property or a creditor of that person, where one of the main purposes of the trust is to secure the payments required to be made by or on behalf of that person to such creditor; and

(c) a trust all or substantially all of the properties of which consist of shares of the capital stock of a corporation, where the trust was established pursuant to an agreement between two or more shareholders of the corporation and one of the main purposes of the trust is to provide for the exercise of voting rights in respect of those shares pursuant to that agreement.

Related Provisions: ITA 107.4(3)(i) — Trust deemed not to be prescribed trust; ITA 135.2(4)(e)(iii) — Cdn Wheat Board Farmers' Trust deemed not to be prescribed trust.

Notes: In CRA's view, a trust would not be established for the benefit of employees if they are not beneficiaries, even if they realize a tax benefit through the trust arrangement: 2005 STEP Conference Roundtable q.5 (www.step.ca).

For the meaning of "one of the main purposes" see ITA 83(2.1) Notes. CRA considers that "substantially all", used in para. (c), means 90% or more.

On this rule's application and interaction with ITA 108(1)"trust", see *McNeeley*, 2020 TCC 90 (under appeal to FCA), paras. 25-41 (employee benefit plan cannot be a prescribed trust).

Reg. 4800.1 amended by 2002-2013 technical bill (effective 2000), P.C. 1992-2338.

Definitions [Reg. 4800.1]: "arm's length" — ITA 251(1); "corporation" — ITA 248(1), *Interpretation Act* 35(1); "employee", "person", "prescribed", "property", "share", "shareholder" — ITA 248(1); "trust" — ITA 104(1), 248(1), (3).

4801. [Mutual fund trust — prescribed conditions] — In applying at any time paragraph 132(6)(c) of the Act, the following are prescribed conditions in respect of a trust:

(a) either

(i) the following conditions are met:

(A) there has been at or before that time a lawful distribution in a province to the public of units of the trust and a prospectus, registration statement or similar document was not, under the laws of the province, required to be filed in respect of the distribution, and

(B) the trust

(I) was created after 1999 and on or before that time, or

(II) satisfies, at that time, the conditions prescribed in section 4801.001, or

(ii) a class of the units of the trust is, at that time, qualified for distribution to the public; and

(b) in respect of a class of the trust's units that meets at that time the conditions described in paragraph (a), there are at that time no fewer than 150 beneficiaries of the trust, each of whom holds

(i) not less than one block of units of the class, and

(ii) units of the class having an aggregate fair market value of not less than $500.

Related Provisions: Reg. 221(1)(f) — Reporting requirements.

Notes: See Notes to ITA 132(6). The "150" can include X, X's TFSA, X's RRSP and X's spouse's RRSP as 4 beneficiaries (subject to GAAR): VIEWS doc 2019-0822901E5. (On "counting" persons, see also ITA 130.1(6) Notes re 130.1(6)(d).)

"Distribution to the public" can include to RRIFs of retired employees under a securities commission exemption: VIEWS docs 2007-0234421R3, 2008-0292761R3.

In *Grenon*, 2021 TCC 30 (under appeal to FCA), G created a trust with 171 small investors (so his RRSP could invest through them in LPs carrying on his businesses). The Court held (paras. 192-337) that the "lawful distribution" condition in (a)(i)(A) was not met, because many investors were minors or did not pay for their units.

Reg. 4801 amended by 2002-2013 technical bill (last change effective for 2004 and later tax years), P.C. 2001-1106.

Definitions [Reg. 4801]: "block of units" — Reg. 4803(1); "class of units" — Reg. 4803(2); "fair market value" — see ITA 69(1) Notes; "person" — Reg. 4803(3); "prescribed" — ITA 248(1); "province" — *Interpretation Act* 35(1); "trust" — ITA 104(1), 248(1), (3).

4801.001 [Mutual fund trust — prescribed conditions] — For the purpose of applying at any particular time subclause 4801(a)(i)(B)(II), the following are the prescribed conditions:

(a) the trust was created before 2000;

(b) the trust was a unit trust on July 18, 2005;

(c) the particular time is after 2003; and

(d) the trusts elects by notifying the Minister, in writing before the trust's filing-due date for its 2012 taxation year, that this section applies to it.

Notes: Reg. 4801.001 added by 2002-2013 technical bill (Part 5 — technical), for 2004 and later taxation years.

Definitions [Reg. 4801.001]: "filing-due date", "Minister", "prescribed" — ITA 248(1); "taxation year" — ITA 249; "trust" — ITA 104(1), 248(1), (3); "unit trust" — ITA 108(2), 248(1); "writing" — *Interpretation Act* 35(1).

4801.01 [Mutual fund trust — exclusion from December 15 year-end] — For the purpose of subsection 132.11(1) of the Act, a trust that is a money market fund as defined in *National Instrument 81-102 Mutual Funds,* as amended from time to time, of the Canadian Securities Administrators is a prescribed trust.

Notes: Reg. 4801.01 added by P.C. 2001-1106, effective for any filing, after March 10, 1999, for an election under ITA 132.11(1).

Definitions [Reg. 4801.01]: "prescribed" — ITA 248(1); "trust" — ITA 104(1), 248(1), (3).

4801.02 [LSVCC — prescribed corporation] — For the purposes of the definition "eligible business entity" in subsection 204.8(1), clause 204.82(2.2)(d)(i)(B) and paragraph 204.82(6)(a) of the Act, a corporation registered under Part III.1 of the *Community Small Business Investment Funds Act*, chapter 18 of the Statutes of Ontario, 1992, is a prescribed corporation.

Notes: Reg. 4801.02 added by P.C. 2001-1106, for 1999 and later taxation years.

Definitions [Reg. 4801.02]: "corporation" — ITA 248(1), *Interpretation Act* 35(1); "prescribed" — ITA 248(1).

4801.1 [Foreign trust reporting exemption] — For the purpose of paragraph (c) of the definition "exempt trust" in subsection 233.2(1) of the Act, the following conditions are hereby prescribed in respect of a trust:

(a) at least 150 beneficiaries of the trust are beneficiaries in respect of the same class of units of the trust; and

(b) at least 150 of the beneficiaries in respect of that class each hold

(i) at least one block of units of that class, and

(ii) units of that class having a total fair market value of at least $500.

Notes: Reg. 4801.1 added by P.C. 1998-1573, for taxation years that begin after 1995.

4802. (1) [Pension investment corporation — prescribed investors] — For the purposes of clause 149(1)(o.2)(iv)(D) of the Act, the following are prescribed persons:

(a) a trust all the beneficiaries of which are trusts described in clause 149(1)(o.2)(iv)(B) of the Act;

(b) a corporation incorporated before November 17, 1978 solely in connection with, or for the administration of, a registered pension plan;

(c) a trust or corporation established by or arising by virtue of an act of a province the principal activities of which are to administer, manage or invest the monies of a pension fund or plan that is established pursuant to an act of the province or an order or regulation made thereunder;

(c.1) the Canada Pension Plan Investment Board;

(c.2) the Public Sector Pension Investment Board;

(c.3) a pooled registered pension plan;

(d) a trust or corporation established by or arising by virtue of an act of a province in connection with a scheme or program for the compensation of workers injured in an accident arising out of or in the course of their employment;

(e) Her Majesty in right of a province;

(f) a trust all of the beneficiaries of which are any combination of

(i) registered pension plans,

(ii) trusts described in clause 149(1)(o.2)(iv)(B) or (C) of the Act, and

(iii) persons described in this subsection; and

(g) a corporation all of the shares of the capital stock of which are owned by one or more of the following:

(i) registered pension plans,

(ii) trusts described in clause 149(1)(o.2)(iv)(B) or (C) of the Act, and

(iii) persons described in this subsection.

Related Provisions: Reg. 8502(b)(vii) — Permissible pension contributions by person described in para. (d).

Notes: A provincial Crown corp (or its subsidiary) qualifies under (e) (or (g)) if its enabling legislation deems its property to be owned by the Crown: VIEWS doc 2019-0829811E5.

Reg. 4802(1) amended by 2012 budget bill #2 (effective Dec. 14, 2012), P.C. 2011-936, P.C. 2003-1497, P.C. 1996-569, P.C. 1992-2338.

(1.1) [Master trust] — For the purposes of subparagraph 127.55(f)(iii) and paragraph 149(1)(o.4) of the Act, a trust is prescribed at any particular time if, at all times after its creation and before the particular time,

Proposed Amendment — Reg. 4802(1.1) opening words

(1.1) Master trust — For the purposes of subparagraph 127.55(f)(iii) and paragraphs 149(1)(o.4) and 150(1.2)(h) of the Act, a trust is prescribed at any particular time if, at all times after its creation and before the particular time,

Application: The July 27, 2018 draft legislation (Budget), s. 10, will amend the opening words of subsec. 4802(1.1) to read as above, applicable to taxation years that end after Dec. 30, 2021.

Technical Notes: Subsection 4802(1.1) sets out the conditions to prescribe a trust as a "master trust" for the purposes of paragraph 149(1)(o.4) of the Act. Among other things, a master trust holds investments exclusively for beneficiaries that are registered pension plans or deferred profit sharing plans.

Subsection 4802(1.1) is amended so that the conditions for prescribing a trust as a master trust apply for the purposes of new paragraph 150(1.2)(h) of the Act. For more information, see the commentary on subsection 150(1.2).

(a) it was resident in Canada;

(b) its only undertaking was the investing of its funds;

(c) it never borrowed money except where the borrowing was for a term not exceeding 90 days and it is established that the borrowing was not part of a series of loans or other transactions and repayments;

(d) it never accepted deposits; and

(e) each of the beneficiaries of the trust was a trust governed by a deferred profit sharing plan, a pooled registered pension plan or a registered pension plan.

Related Provisions: ITA 248(10) — Series of transactions; ITA 253.1 — Limited partner not considered to carry on partnership business.

Notes: Reg. 4802(1.1)(e) amended by 2012 budget bill #2, effective Dec. 14, 2012, to add reference to a PRPP.

Reference to 127.55(f)(iii) added to opening words by P.C. 2011-936, effective June 29, 2005. Opening words of Reg. 4802(1.1) modernized by P.C. 2011-936, effective for 1992 and later tax years.

Reg. 4802(1.1) added by P.C. 2005-1508, effective June 29, 2005. It was moved from Reg. 5001 due to repeal of ITA Part XI (foreign property limit).

(2) [Repealed]

Notes: Reg. 4802(2) repealed by 2017 budget bill #1, for tax years that begin after 2018, due to repeal of ITA 149(1)(t). It prescribed insurers for that rule: Union Québécoise, Les Clairvoyants and Laurentian Farm. Added by P.C. 1994-785, for 1989 and later tax years.

Regulations

Definitions [Reg. 4802]: "borrowed money" — ITA 248(1); "corporation" — ITA 248(1), *Interpretation Act* 35(1); "deferred profit sharing plan" — ITA 147(1), 248(1); "employment" — ITA 248(1); "Her Majesty" — *Interpretation Act* 35(1); "insurer", "person" — ITA 248(1); "pooled registered pension plan" — ITA 147.5(1), 248(1); "prescribed" — ITA 248(1); "province" — *Interpretation Act* 35(1); "registered pension plan" — ITA 248(1); "resident in Canada" — ITA 250; "share" — ITA 248(1); "trust" — ITA 104(1), 248(1), (3).

4803. (1) In this Part,

"block of shares" means, with respect to any class of the capital stock of a corporation,

(a) 100 shares, if the fair market value of one share of the class is less than $25,

(b) 25 shares, if the fair market value of one share of the class is $25 or more but less than $100, and

(c) 10 shares, if the fair market value of one share of the class is $100 or more;

"block of units" means, with respect to any class of units of a trust,

(a) 100 units, if the fair market value of one unit of the class is less than $25,

(b) 25 units, if the fair market value of one unit of the class is $25 or more but less than $100, and

(c) 10 units, if the fair market value of one unit of the class is $100 or more;

"equity share" has the meaning assigned by section 204 of the Act;

"insider of a corporation" has the meaning that would be assigned by section 100 of the *Canada Corporations Act*, as it read on June 22, 2009, if the references in that section to "insider of a company", "public company" and "equity shares" were read as references to "insider of a corporation", "corporation" and "shares" respectively, and includes a person who is an employee of the corporation, or of a person who does not deal at arm's length with the corporation, and whose right to sell or transfer any share of the capital stock of the corporation, or to exercise the voting rights, if any, attaching to the share, is restricted by

(a) the terms and conditions attaching to the share, or

(b) any obligation of the person, under a contract, in equity or otherwise, to the corporation or to any person with whom the corporation does not deal at arm's length.

Notes: Before being repealed by 2009, c. 23, s. 313, the definition in CCA s. 100 read:

"insider" or "insider of a company" means

(a) any director or officer of a public company,

(b) any person who beneficially owns, directly or indirectly, equity shares of a public company carrying more than ten per cent of the voting rights attached to all equity shares of the company for the time being outstanding, but in computing the percentage of voting rights attached to equity shares owned by an underwriter there shall be excluded any equity shares that have been acquired by him as underwriter in the course of distribution to the public of such shares, but such exclusion ceases to have effect on completion or cessation of the distribution to the public by him, or

(c) any person who exercises control or direction over the equity shares of a public company carrying more than ten per cent of the voting rights attached to all equity shares of the public company for the time being outstanding;

Wording modernized, and "as it read on June 22, 2009" added, by P.C. 2011-936, effective Feb. 19, 2011.

(2) [Meaning of "qualified for distribution to the public"] — For the purposes of this Part, a class of shares of the capital stock of a corporation or a class of units of a trust is qualified for distribution to the public only if

(a) a prospectus, registration statement or similar document has been filed with, and, where required by law, accepted for filing by, a public authority in Canada pursuant to and in accordance with the law of Canada or of any province and there has been a lawful distribution to the public of shares or units of that class in accordance with that document;

(b) the class is a class of shares, any of which were issued by the corporation at any time after 1971 while it was a public corpora-

tion in exchange for shares of any other class of the capital stock of the corporation that was, immediately before the exchange, qualified for distribution to the public;

(c) in the case of any class of shares, any of which were issued and outstanding on January 1, 1972, the class complied on that date with the conditions described in paragraphs 4800(1)(b) and (c); or

(d) in the case of any class of units, any of which were issued and outstanding on January 1, 1972, the class complied on that date with the condition described in paragraph 4801(b).

Notes: For "similar document" in Reg. 4803(2)(a), see VIEWS docs 5-7577, 9409416, 9529225, 2011-0413861E5 (offering memorandum is similar to prospectus).

(3) [Group holdings] — For the purposes of paragraphs 4800(1)(b), 4800(2)(b) and 4801(b), where a group of persons holds

(a) not less than one block of shares of any class of shares of the capital stock of a corporation or one block of units of any class of a trust, as the case may be, and

(b) shares or units, as the case may be, of that class having an aggregate fair market value of not less than $500,

that group shall, subject to subsection (4), be deemed to be one person for the purposes of determining the number of persons who hold shares or units, as the case may be, of that class.

(4) [Determination of group] — In determining under subsection (3) the persons who belong to a group for the purposes of determining the number of persons who hold shares or units, as the case may be, of a particular class, the following rules apply:

(a) no person shall be included in more than one group;

(b) no person shall be included in a group if he holds

(i) not less than one block of shares or one block of units, as the case may be, of that class, and

(ii) shares or units, as the case may be, of that class having an aggregate fair market value of not less than $500; and

(c) the membership of each group shall be determined in the manner that results in the greatest possible number of groups.

Interpretation Bulletins: IT-391R: Status of corporations.

Definitions [Reg. 4803]: "arm's length" — ITA 251(1); "block of shares", "block of units" — Reg. 4803(1); "Canada" — ITA 255, *Interpretation Act* 35(1); "class of shares", "class of units" — Reg. 4803(2); "corporation" — ITA 248(1), *Interpretation Act* 35(1); "employee" — ITA 248(1); "fair market value" — see ITA 69(1) Notes; "group" — Reg. 4803(4); "person" — ITA 248(1); "province" — *Interpretation Act* 35(1); "public corporation" — ITA 89(1), 248(1); "share" — ITA 248(1); "trust" — ITA 104(1), 248(1), (3).

PART XLIX — [4900–4901] REGISTERED PLANS — INVESTMENTS

Notes: Part XLIX heading changed from "Deferred Income Plans, Qualified Investments" by 2013 budget bill #2, effective March 23, 2011.

4900. (1) [Qualified investment for RRSP, RESP, RRIF, DPSP, RDSP, TFSA] — For the purposes of paragraph (d) of the definition "qualified investment" in subsection 146(1) of the Act, paragraph (e) of the definition "qualified investment" in subsection 146.1(1) of the Act, paragraph (c) of the definition "qualified investment" in subsection 146.3(1) of the Act, paragraph (d) of the definition "qualified investment" in subsection 146.4(1) of the Act, paragraph (h) of the definition "qualified investment" in section 204 of the Act and paragraph (c) of the definition "qualified investment" in subsection 207.01 (1) of the Act, each of the following investments is prescribed as a qualified investment for a plan trust at a particular time if at that time it is

(a) **[registered investment]** — an interest in a trust or a share of the capital stock of a corporation that was a registered investment for the plan trust during the calendar year in which the particular time occurs or the immediately preceding year;

(b) **[share of public corporation]** — a share of the capital stock of a public corporation other than a mortgage investment corporation;

(c) **[share of mortgage investment corporation]** — a share of the capital stock of a mortgage investment corporation that does not hold as part of its property at any time during the calendar year in which the particular time occurs any indebtedness, whether by way of mortgage or otherwise, of a person who is a connected person under the governing plan of the plan trust;

(c.1) **[bond of public corporation]** — a bond, debenture, note or similar obligation of a public corporation other than a mortgage investment corporation;

(d) **[unit of mutual fund trust]** — a unit of a mutual fund trust;

(d.1) [Repealed]

(d.2) **[unit of a trust]** — a unit of a trust if

(i) the trust would be a mutual fund trust if Part XLVIII were read without reference to paragraph 4801(a), and

(ii) there has been a lawful distribution in a province to the public of units of the trust and a prospectus, registration statement or similar document was not required under the laws of the province to be filed in respect of the distribution;

(e) **[warrant or option]** — an option, a warrant or a similar right (each of which is, in this paragraph, referred to as the "security") issued by a person or partnership (in this paragraph referred to as the "issuer") that gives the holder the right to acquire, either immediately or in the future, property all of which is a qualified investment for the plan trust or to receive a cash settlement in lieu of delivery of that property, where

(i) the property is

(A) a share of the capital stock of, a unit of, or a debt issued by, the issuer or another person or partnership that does not, when the security is issued, deal at arm's length with the issuer, or

(B) a warrant issued by the issuer or another person or partnership that does not, when the security is issued, deal at arm's length with the issuer, that gives the holder the right to acquire a share or unit described in clause (A), and

(ii) the issuer is not a connected person under the governing plan of the plan trust;

(e.01) [Repealed]

(e.1) **[société d'entraide économique]** — a share of, or deposit with, a société d'entraide économique;

(f) **[share of credit union]** — a share of, or similar interest in a credit union;

(g) **[bond of credit union]** — a bond, debenture, note or similar obligation (in this paragraph referred to as the "obligation") issued by, or a deposit with, a credit union that has not at any time during the calendar year in which the particular time occurs granted any benefit or privilege to a person who is a connected person under the governing plan of the plan trust, as a result of the ownership by

(i) the plan trust of a share or obligation of, or a deposit with, the credit union, or

(ii) a registered investment of a share or obligation of, or a deposit with, the credit union if the plan trust has invested in that registered investment,

and a credit union shall be deemed to have granted a benefit or privilege to a person in a year if at any time in that year that person continues to enjoy a benefit or privilege that was granted in a prior year;

(h) **[bond of cooperative corporation]** — a bond, debenture, note or similar obligation (in this paragraph referred to as the "obligation") issued by a cooperative corporation (within the meaning assigned by subsection 136(2) of the Act)

(i) that throughout the taxation year of the cooperative corporation immediately preceding the year in which the obligation was acquired by the plan trust had not less than 100 shareholders or, if all its shareholders were corporations, not less than 50 shareholders,

(ii) whose obligations were, at the end of each month of

(A) the last taxation year, if any, of the cooperative corporation prior to the date of acquisition of the obligation by the plan trust, or

(B) the period commencing three months after the date an obligation was first acquired by any plan trust and ending on the last day of the taxation year of the cooperative corporation in which that period commenced,

whichever of the periods referred to in clause (A) or (B) commences later, held by plan trusts the average number of which is not less than 100 computed on the basis that no two plan trusts shall have the same individual as an annuitant or a beneficiary, as the case may be, and

(iii) that, except where the plan trust is governed by a registered education savings plan, has not at any time during the calendar year in which the particular time occurs granted any benefit or privilege to a person who is a connected person under the governing plan of the plan trust, as a result of the ownership by

(A) the plan trust of a share or obligation of the cooperative corporation, or

(B) a registered investment of a share or obligation of the cooperative corporation if the plan trust has invested in that registered investment,

and a cooperative corporation shall be deemed to have granted a benefit or privilege to a person in a year if at any time in that year that person continues to enjoy a benefit or privilege that was granted in a prior year;

(i) **[bonds of certain corporations]** — a bond, debenture, note or similar obligation (in this paragraph referred to as the "obligation") of a Canadian corporation

(i) if payment of the principal amount of the obligation and the interest on the principal amount is guaranteed by a corporation or a mutual fund trust whose shares or units, as the case may be, are listed on a designated stock exchange in Canada,

(ii) if the corporation is controlled directly or indirectly by

(A) one or more corporations,

(B) one or more mutual fund trusts, or

(C) one or more corporations and mutual fund trusts

whose shares or units, as the case may be, are listed on a designated stock exchange in Canada, or

(iii) if, at the time the obligation is acquired by the plan trust, the corporation that issued the obligation is

(A) a corporation that, in respect of its capital stock, has issued and outstanding share capital carried in its books at not less than $25 million, or

(B) a corporation that is controlled by a corporation described in clause (A),

and has issued and outstanding bonds, debentures, notes or similar obligations having in the aggregate a principal amount of at least $10 million that are held by at least 300 different persons and were issued by the corporation by means of one or more offerings, provided that in respect of each such offering a prospectus, registration statement or similar document was filed with and, where required by law, accepted for filing by a public authority in Canada pursuant to and in accordance with the laws of Canada or a province and there was a lawful distribution to the public of those bonds, debentures, notes or similar obligations in accordance with that document;

(i.1) [community bond guaranteed by province] — a security of a Canadian corporation

(i) that was issued pursuant to *The Community Bonds Act*, chapter C-16.1 of the Statutes of Saskatchewan, 1990, *The Rural Development Bonds Act*, chapter 47 of the Statutes of Manitoba, 1991-92, the *Community Economic Development Act, 1993*, chapter 26 of the Statutes of Ontario, 1993, or the New Brunswick Community Development Bond Program through which financial assistance is provided under the *Economic Development Act*, chapter E-1.11 of the Acts of New Brunswick, 1975, and

(ii) the payment of the principal amount of which is guaranteed by Her Majesty in right of a province;

(i.11) [Nova Scotia *Equity Tax Credit Act*] — a share of the capital stock of a Canadian corporation that is registered under section 11 of the *Equity Tax Credit Act*, chapter 3 of the Statutes of Nova Scotia, 1993, the registration of which has not been revoked under that Act;

(i.12) [NWT risk capital investment] — a share of the capital stock of a Canadian corporation that is registered under section 39 of the *Risk Capital Investment Tax Credits Act*, chapter 22 of the Statutes of the Northwest Territories, 1998, the registration of which has not been revoked under that Act;

(i.13) [PEI *Community Development Equity Tax Credit Act*] — a share of the capital stock of a Canadian corporation that is registered under section 2 of the *Community Development Equity Tax Credit Act*, chapter C-13.01 of the Revised Statutes of Prince Edward Island, 1988, the registration of which has not been revoked under that Act;

(i.2) [banker's acceptance] — indebtedness of a Canadian corporation (other than a corporation that is a connected person under the governing plan of the plan trust) represented by a bankers' acceptance;

(i.3) [Repealed]

(j) [mortgage] — a debt obligation of a debtor, or an interest, or for civil law a right, in that debt obligation, where

(i) the debt obligation is fully secured by a mortgage, charge, hypothec or similar instrument in respect of real or immovable property situated in Canada, or would be fully secured were it not for a decline in the fair market value of the property after the debt obligation was issued, and

(ii) the debtor (and any partnership that does not deal at arm's length with the debtor) is not a connected person under the governing plan of the plan trust;

(j.1) [insured mortgage] — a debt obligation secured by a mortgage, charge, hypothec or similar instrument in respect of real or immovable property situated in Canada, or an interest, or for civil law a right, in that debt obligation, where the debt obligation is

(i) administered by an approved lender under the *National Housing Act*, and

(ii) insured

(A) under the *National Housing Act*, or

(B) by a corporation that offers its services to the public in Canada as an insurer of mortgages or hypothecary claims and that is approved as a private insurer of mortgages or hypothecary claims by the Superintendent of Financial Institutions under subsection 6(1) of the *Office of the Superintendent of Financial Institutions Act*;

(j.2) [mortgage certificate] — a certificate evidencing an undivided interest, or for civil law an undivided right, in one or more properties, where

(i) all or substantially all of the fair market value of the certificate is attributable to property that is, or is incidental to, a debt obligation secured by

(A) a mortgage, charge, hypothec or similar instrument in respect of real or immovable property situated in Canada, or

(B) property described in paragraph (a) or (b) of the definition "qualified investment" in section 204 of the Act that was substituted for the security referred to in clause (A) under the terms of the debt obligation,

(ii) the certificate has, at the time of acquisition by the plan trust, an investment grade rating with a credit rating agency referred to in subsection (2), and

(iii) the certificate is issued as part of an issue of certificates by the issuer for a total amount of at least $25 million;

(k)–(p.1) [Repealed]

(q) [debt of privatized Crown corporation] — a debt issued by a Canadian corporation (other than a corporation with share capital or a corporation that is a connected person under the governing plan of the plan trust) where

(i) the taxable income of the corporation is exempt from tax under Part I of the Act because of paragraph 149(1)(l) of the Act, and

(ii) either

(A) before the particular time and after 1995, the corporation

(I) acquired, for a total consideration of not less than $25 million, property from Her Majesty in right of Canada or a province, and

(II) put that property to a use that is the same as or similar to the use to which the property was put before the acquisition described in subclause (I), or

(B) at the time of the acquisition of the debt by the plan trust, it was reasonable to expect that clause (A) would apply in respect of the debt no later than one year after the time of the acquisition;

(r) [debt of large non-profit organization] — a debt issued by a Canadian corporation (other than a corporation with share capital or a corporation that is a connected person under the governing plan of the plan trust) if

(i) the taxable income of the corporation is exempt from tax under Part I of the Act because of paragraph 149(1)(l) of the Act, and

(ii) either

(A) the debt is issued by the corporation as part of an issue of debt by the corporation for an amount of at least $25 million,

or

(B) at the time of the acquisition of the debt by the plan trust, the corporation had issued debt as part of a single issue for an amount of at least $25 million;

(s) [Repealed]

(t) [gold or silver coin] — a gold or silver legal tender bullion coin

(i) that is of a minimum fineness of 995 parts per 1000 in the case of gold and 999 parts per 1000 in the case of silver,

(ii) that was produced by the Royal Canadian Mint,

(iii) that has a fair market value at the particular time not exceeding 110 per cent of the fair market value of the coin's gold or silver content, and

(iv) that is acquired by the plan trust directly from the Royal Canadian Mint or from a corporation (in paragraphs (u) and (v) referred to as a "specified corporation")

(A) that is a bank, a trust company, a credit union, an insurance corporation or a registered securities dealer,

(B) that is resident in Canada, and

(C) that is a corporation whose business activities are subject by law to the supervision of a regulating authority that is the Superintendent of Financial Institutions or a similar authority of a province;

(u) **[gold or silver]** — a gold or silver bullion bar, ingot or wafer

(i) that is of a minimum fineness of 995 parts per 1000 in the case of gold and 999 parts per 1000 in the case of silver,

(ii) that was produced by a metal refiner included in the London Bullion Market Association's good delivery list of acceptable refiners for gold or silver, as the case may be,

(iii) that bears the hallmark of the metal refiner that produced it and a stamp indicating its fineness and its weight, and

(iv) that is acquired by the plan trust either directly from the metal refiner that produced it or from a specified corporation;

(v) **[gold or silver certificate]** — a certificate issued by a specified corporation or the Royal Canadian Mint representing a claim of the holder of the certificate to property held by the issuer of the certificate, where

(i) the property would be property described in paragraph (t) or (u) if those paragraphs were read without reference to subparagraphs (t)(iv) and (u)(iv), respectively, and

(ii) the certificate is acquired by the plan trust directly from the issuer of the certificate or from a specified corporation; or

(w) **[American Depositary Receipt]** — an American Depositary Receipt where the property represented by the receipt is listed on a designated stock exchange.

Related Provisions [Reg. 4900(1)]: ITA 207.01(1)"excluded property"(a) — Property in Reg. 4900(1)(j.1) is not prohibited investment for RRSP etc.; ITA 248(5) — Substituted property (for Reg. 4900(1)(j.2)(i)(B)); Reg. 221 — Information return where entity claims that its shares or units are qualified investments.

Notes: A qualified investment **(QI)** may be in ITA 204"qualified investment", or in "qualified investment" in ITA 146(1), 146.1(1), 146.3(1) and 207.01(1), rather than in Reg. 4900. See also Income Tax Folio S3-F10-C1. CRA does not maintain lists of QIs and non-QIs: doc 2005-0110451M4. Certain foreign exchange contracts are not QIs, and active currency trading could be a "business" whose income is taxed in a TFSA: 2009-0318671E5, 2010-0356811E5. Re option investing and option writing, see 2010-0364811E5. Purchasing solar panels for a home's roof under Ontario's microFIT program does not qualify: 2013-0506351E5.

A proposal to add annuity contracts to Reg. 4900(1), in a Finance news release of Dec. 19, 1996, was enacted instead in ITA 146(1)"qualified investment"(c.1), (c.2) and 146.3(1)"qualified investment"(b.1), (b.2).

A life insurance policy may effectively be treated as a QI. See Notes to ITA 198(6).

A share subject to an escrow agreement can be a QI if identical shares not subject to escrow are: Income Tax Folio S3-F10-C1 ¶1.68; VIEWS doc 2012-0433811M4.

Money is a QI if its value is as legal tender. Bitcoin is not: Folio S3-F10-C1 ¶1.12.

An RRSP, RRIF or DPSP can write a covered call option, since that results only in cash being received in the plan: VIEWS doc 0056251E5.

Reg. 4900(1) opening words amended by 2017 budget bill #2, effective March 23, 2017, to refer to 146.4(1)"qualified investment"(d).

Reg. 4900(1) opening words amended by 2008 budget bill #2, effective for 2009 and later taxation years, to change 204(1) to 204 and to add reference to 207.01(1)"qualified investment"(c).

Reg. 4900(1) opening words amended by 2007 RDSPs bill, effective for 2008 and later taxation years, to add reference to ITA 205.

Reg. 4900(1) opening words amended by 2007 budget bill #1, effective in determining whether a property is, at any time after March 18, 2007, a QI, to change the reference from 204"qualified investment"(i) to (h).

Reg. 4900(1) opening words and 4900(1)(c), (g), (h)(iii), (i.2), (j) and (q) amended by P.C. 2001-1106, for property acquired after October 27, 1998, to add references to ITA 146.1, RESPs and a RESP "subscriber".

Reg. 4900(1)(b) can cover de-listed shares, since such corporations normally continue to be "public corporations": VIEWS docs 2002-0168645, 2003-0033581E5. For NASDAQ over-the-counter shares see below re Reg. 4900(1)(s), and doc 2008-0310431E5.

Reg. 4900(1)(b) amended by P.C. 1994-1074, effective 1993, to change "other than a share of a mortgage investment corporation that is not listed on a prescribed stock exchange in Canada" to "other than a mortage investment corporation". The change is non-substantive, since a mortgage investment corporation that is listed on a Canadian stock exchange is covered under 204"qualified investment"(d) anyway.

Reg. 4900(1)(c), (e)(ii), (g), (h)(iii), (i.2), (j)(ii), (q) and (r) amended by 2007 RDSPs bill, effective for 2008 and later taxation years, to change "an annuitant, a beneficiary, an employer or a subscriber" (or a subset of those words) to "a connected person" (see definition in Reg. 4901(2)). (These amendments were non-substantive.)

For Reg. 4900(1)(c), the RRSP annuitant's sibling is a "connected person" under Reg. 4901(2): VIEWS doc 2014-0528311E5.

Reg. 4900(1)(c.1) added by P.C. 1994-1074, effective 1993.

Reg. 4900(1)(d): an income trust and royalty trust is usually, but not always, a mutual fund trust (MFT): VIEWS doc 2004-0056271E5. 2006-0217441R3 is a ruling approving a trust as a MFT and thus as a QI. In *Grenon*, 2021 TCC 30 (under appeal to FCA), G created income funds with 171 small investors, so his RRSP could invest through them in LPs carrying on his businesses. The Court held that a condition in Reg. 4801 was not met, so the funds were not MFTs and not QIs.

Reg. 4900(1)(d.1) (bond of mutual fund trust) added by P.C. 1998-629, effective for property acquired after 1996, and repealed by 2007 budget bill #1, effective in determining whether a property is, at any time after March 18, 2007, a QI (due to the broadening of the definition in ITA 204). (For bonds of mutual fund corporations, see 4900(1)(c.1).)

Reg. 4900(1)(d.2) added by P.C. 2001-1106, for property acquired after 1993. It allows a widely-held unit trust that makes a lawful distribution in a province of its units to qualify as a mutual fund trust without filing a prospectus where it was not required to be filed. MFT units are qualified investments under Reg. 4900(1)(d), for trusts established after 1999; 4900(1)(d.2) extends such status to trust units acquired after 1993. In *Grenon* (see under Reg. 4900(1)(d) above), paras. 338-345, para. (d.2) could not be used to get around non-compliance with para. (d).

Reg. 4900(1)(e) amended by P.C. 2005-1508, for property acquired after Feb. 27, 2004. Before the amendment, read:

(e) a warrant or right giving the owner thereof the right to acquire either immediately or in the future property all of which is a qualified investment for the plan trust;

Reg. 4900(1)(e) amended by P.C. 1994-1074, effective 1993, to remove a requirement that the warrant or right be listed on an exchange. The change allows RRSPs, RRIFs and DPSPs to acquire shares that are qualified investments together with warrants with respect to such shares.

For Reg. 4900(1)(e), employee stock options and warrants can qualify: VIEWS doc 2009-0307821E5. Subscription receipts (entitling the holder to shares once they are listed) do not qualify until the underlying stock is listed: 2009-0345001E5. For the value of warrants contributed to a TFSA see 2008-0303791E5, 2009-0305431E5.

Reg. 4900(1)(e.01) added by P.C. 2005-1508, for property acquired after Feb. 27, 2004, and repealed by 2007 budget bill #1, effective in determining whether a property is, at any time after March 18, 2007, a QI (due to the broadening of the definition in ITA 204). It applied to publicly-listed put options and cash-settled index options, in addition to call options and warrants (which were already qualified investments under former Reg. 4900(1)(e)): VIEWS doc 2005-0158531E5. It could also apply to subscription receipts: 2007-0227591E5, 2007-0247291E5.

Reg. 4900(1)(e.1): "A société d'entraide économique is a company dealing in financing of undertakings or persons, whose role is to promote regional economic development. The object of a société d'entraide économique is to grant loans, receive deposits and promote economic awareness": *Act respecting the sociétés d'entraide économique*, R.S.Q., c. S-25.1, s. 47.

Reg. 4900(1)(g) opening words amended by 2017 budget bill #2 to delete "except where the plan trust is governed by a registered education savings plan" after "credit union", effective for any investment acquired after March 22, 2017 and one acquired earlier that ceases to be a 146.1(1)"qualified investment" after March 22, 2017.

Reg. 4900(1)(h)(i): to count shareholders, see ITA 130.1(6) Notes re 130.1(6)(d).

Reg. 4900(1)(i) can apply to notes issued by a partnership of corporations where all of the corporations' notes would qualify: VIEWS doc 2006-0213241R3.

Reg. 4900(1)(i)(i) and (i)(ii) amended by 2007 budget bill #2, effective Dec. 14, 2007, to change "stock exchange referred to in section 3200" to "designated stock exchange in Canada".

Reg. 4900(1)(i.1) added by P.C. 1992-2334, effective for property acquired after June 1991, applying to a "bond, debenture, note or similar obligation of a Canadian corporation" issued under the Saskatchewan or Manitoba statutes. Amended to add reference to the Ontario and New Brunswick statutes, and the opening words changed to "a security of a Canadian corporation", by P.C. 1994-1075, effective for property acquired after August 1993.

Reg. 4900(1)(i.11) added by P.C. 1996-1487, effective for property acquired after 1995. It refers to Community Economic Development Corporations under Nova Scotia's *Equity Tax Credit Act*.

Reg. 4900(1)(i.12) added by P.C. 1999-249, effective for property acquired Aug. 1998.

Reg. 4900(1)(i.13) added by P.C. 2012-1629, effective Sept. 2011 (an Oct. 28/11 Finance comfort letter to the PEI Minister of Finance and Municipal Affairs had said it would apply to "investments acquired after August 2011").

Reg. 4900(1)(i.2) added by P.C. 1994-1074, effective 1993.

Reg. 4900(1)(i.3) added by P.C. 2005-1508, effective Feb. 28, 2004, and repealed by 2008 budget bill #2, effective for property acquired after March 12, 2009, as it is not needed (204"qualified investment"(c.1) covers it). It applied to asset-backed securities, backed by cash flows from pools of loans, leases and other receivables. See Kevin Kelly & David Glicksman, "Asset-backed and Mortgage-backed Securities: Qualified Investments" XIII(1) *Corporate Finance* (Federated Press) 1282-85 (2005).

Reg. 4900(1)(j) amended by P.C. 2005-1508, effective Feb. 28, 2004 for property acquired after Feb. 27, 2004 and effective 2007 for property acquired earlier. Insured mortgage obligations are now dealt with under (j.1). A mortgage obligation now qualifies under (j) only if it is fully secured by the real property (but if it ceases to be fully secured after issuance, it will not lose its status if this is due to a drop in value of the property). See Jonathan Wilson, "MBS Certificates and Proposed Paragraph 4900(1)(j)", XII(2) *Corporate Finance* (Federated Press) 1191-93 (2004); Shayne Saskiw, "Raising Capital for Real Estate — The Use of a Secured Mortgage for RRSP Purposes", XII(2) *Business Vehicles* (Federated Press) 636-38 (2008).

Reg. 4900(1)(j) amended by P.C. 2001-1106, for property acquired after Oct. 27, 1998, except that the amendment does not apply to property acquired by a DPSP before March 31, 2001. This consolidates the rules for mortgages (Reg. 4900(1)(j), 4900(4)) in one place.

For the administrative rules that apply for mortgages in addition to the Regulations, see Wayland Chau, "Financing the Executive Home with RRSPs", 8(7) *Taxation of Executive Compensation and Retirement* (Federated Press) 265-270 (March 1997). See also VIEWS docs 2003-0027811E5 (mortgage insured by a life insurance policy), 2004-0083491R3 (investment in a debenture secured by a mortgage), 2006-0201031M4 (debt obligation secured by a mortgage); 2017-0712611M4 (general discussion).

Reg. 4900(1)(j.1) added by P.C. 2005-1508, effective February 28, 2004. This rule was formerly in Reg. 4900(1)(j)(ii). See VIEWS doc 2015-0601211E5 (mortgage loan used to lend money to taxpayer's corporation: RRSP-eligible but *could* trigger ITA 207.01(1)"advantage" and "prohibited investment").

Reg. 4900(1)(j.2)(i)(B) added by P.C. 2007-1443, effective 2006, so that a mortgage certificate keeps its status if a mortgage registered in connection with it is released in exchange for other high quality substitute security (as promised in a Finance comfort letter, Aug. 30, 2006).

Reg. 4900(1)(j.2)(ii) amended by 2008 budget bill #2, effective for property acquired after March 12, 2009, to change "bond rating agency that rates debt in the ordinary course of its business" to "credit rating agency referred to in subsection (2)".

Reg. 4900(1)(j.2) added by P.C. 2005-1508, effective 2001. Mortgage certificates formerly qualified under Reg. 4900(1)(j), but in some cases a substitution of security could make them cease to qualify. See article referenced under 4900(1)(i.3) above.

Reg. 4900(1)(k) repealed by 2008 budget bill #2, for property acquired after March 12, 2009. It referred to property acquired before 1981 that was a QI under pre-1981 rules.

Reg. 4900(1)(l) repealed by 2008 budget bill #2, for property acquired after March 12, 2009, as it is not needed (204"qualified investment"(c.1) covers it). It listed bonds of 7 international organizations. Earlier amended by P.C. 1999-133 (effective 1997), 1994-1075 and 1994-1074.

Reg. 4900(1)(m)-(n.1) (listed royalty unit, listed limited partnership unit or debt, foreign stock exchange index unit) repealed by 2007 budget bill #1, effective in determining whether a property is, at any time after March 18, 2007, a QI (due to the broadening of the definition in ITA 204).

Reg. 4900(1)(m) added by P.C. 1992-2334, effective for property acquired after July 16, 1992. Reg. 4900(1)(n) added by P.C. 1994-1074, effective 1993. Reg. 4900(1)(n.01) added by P.C. 2005-1508, effective February 28, 2004. Reg. 4900(1)(n.1) added by P.C. 2001-1106, effective for property acquired after 1993. (It applied to foreign stock exchange index units, as announced by Finance news release, December 18, 1998. Qualifying units included Standard & Poor 500 Depositary Receipts (SPDRs), units valued on the basis of the Dow Jones Industrial Average (DIAMONDs) and units for a particular country (WEBs) valued on the basis of the Morgan Stanley Capital Investment Index.) See now Reg. 4900(2) as well.

Reg. 4900(1)(o) added by P.C. 1994-1075, for property acquired after June 21, 1993, and repealed by 2008 budget bill #2, for property acquired after March 12, 2009, as it is not needed (204"qualified investment"(c.1) covers it). It permitted RRSPs and other deferred plans to hold Israel Bonds as well as debts of certain other countries.

Reg. 4900(1)(p), (p.1) (debt of corporation listed outside Canada, listed depository receipt) repealed by 2007 budget bill #1, effective in determining whether a property is, at any time after March 18, 2007, a QI (due to the broadening of the definition in ITA 204).

Reg. 4900(1)(p) added by P.C. 1994-1075, for property acquired after June 21, 1993. Reg. 4900(1)(p.1) added by P.C. 1998-629, effective for 1997 and later taxation years.

Reg. 4900(1)(q) added by P.C. 1996-1487, effective for property acquired after 1995. It is designed to accommodate certain situations where provincial or federal Crown assets are privatized, so that Crown corporations are issuing debt to the public. The specific case contemplated was that of Nav Canada (air traffic control operations).

Reg. 4900(1)(r) added by P.C. 1999-133, effective March 1998.

Reg. 4900(1)(s) added by P.C. 2001-1106, effective for property acquired before September 2000, and repealed by 2008 budget bill #2, effective for property acquired after March 12, 2009, since it applied to property acquired in the past. Its purpose was to provide relief until the end of 2001 for non-qualifying securities inadvertently acquired by RRSPs, RRIFs and DPSPs. See now Reg. 4900(1)(b); and VIEWS docs 2003-0043564, 2008-0301431E5.

Reg. 4900(1)(t)–(v) added by P.C. 2005-1508, effective Feb. 23, 2005, as proposed in the 2005 Budget, to cover gold and silver coins, bars, ingots, wafers and certificates. See VIEWS doc 2005-0157491E5.

Reg. 4900(1)(w) added by 2008 budget bill #2, effective in determining whether a property is, at any time after 2005, a QI; but before Dec. 14, 2007, read as "an American Depositary Receipt where the property represented by the receipt is listed on a stock exchange referred to in section 3200 or 3201".

Income Tax Folios: S3-F10-C1: Qualified investments — RRSPs, RESPs, RRIFs, RDSPs and TFSAs [replaces IT-320R3].

(2) [Prescribed credit rating agency] — For the purposes of paragraph (c.1) of the definition "qualified investment" in section 204 of the Act, each of the following is a prescribed credit rating agency:

    (a) A.M. Best Company, Inc.;

    (b) DBRS Limited;

    (c) Fitch, Inc.;

    (d) Moody's Investors Service, Inc.; and

    (e) Standard & Poor's Financial Services LLC.

Related Provisions: Reg. 4900(1)(j.2)(ii) — Mortgage certificate that has investment grade rating from agency.

Notes: Reg. 4900(2)(b) and (e) changed from "Dominion Bond Rating Service Limited" and "the Standard and Poor's Division of the McGraw-Hill Companies, Inc." by P.C. 2011-936, effective Feb. 20, 2011.

Reg. 4900(2) replaced by 2007 budget bill #1, effective in determining whether a property is, at any time after March 18, 2007, a qualified investment (due to changes to the definition in ITA 204). The previous version provided that an employer's bonds were not qualified investments for a DPSP for its employees. Reg. 4900(2) previously amended by P.C. 1994-1074, effective 1993.

(3) [Annuity contract] — For the purpose of paragraph (h) of the definition "qualified investment" in section 204 of the Act, a contract with a licensed annuities provider for an annuity payable to an employee who is a beneficiary under a deferred profit sharing plan beginning not later than the end of the year in which the employee attains 71 years of age, the guaranteed term of which, if any, does not exceed 15 years, is prescribed as a qualified investment for a trust governed by such a plan or revoked plan.

Notes: Reg. 4900(3) amended by 2007 budget bill #1, to change reference from 204"qualified investment"(i) to (h) effective March 19, 2007, and "69" to "71" effective 2007 (in conjunction with increase in the RRSP age limit to 71: see ITA 146(2)(b.4)).

Reg. 4900(3) amended by P.C. 1998-2256, for annuity contracts acquired after 1996, except where the annuitant turned 70 before 1997; and in applying it to a contract where the annuitant turned 69 in 1996, read "69" as "70".

For contracts acquired earlier, read:

    (3) For the purposes of subparagraph 204(e)(x) [204"qualified investment"(i)] of the Act, a contract with a person licensed or otherwise authorized under the laws of Canada or a province to carry on in Canada an annuities business for an annuity payable to an employee or other beneficiary under a deferred profit sharing plan commencing not later than a day 71 years after the day of his birth, the guaranteed term of which, if any, does not exceed 15 years is a qualified investment for a trust governed by such a plan or revoked plan.

This is consistent with the 1996 Budget amendment to ITA 147(2)(k).

(4) [Repealed]

Notes: Reg. 4900(4) repealed by P.C. 2001-1106, for property acquired after Oct. 27, 1998. See Reg. 4900(1)(j), consolidating the rules for mortgages into one place.

(5) [Qualified investment for RESP, RDSP or TFSA] — For the purposes of paragraph (e) of the definition "qualified investment" in subsection 146.1(1) of the Act, paragraph (d) of the definition "qualified investment" in subsection 146.4(1) of the Act and paragraph (c) of the definition "qualified investment" in subsection 207.01(1) of the Act, a property is prescribed as a qualified investment for a trust governed by a registered disability savings plan, a registered education savings plan or a TFSA at any time if at that time the property is an interest in a trust or a share of the capital stock of a corporation that was a registered investment for a trust governed by a registered retirement savings plan during the calendar year in which that time occurs or during the preceding year.

Related Provisions: ITA 204.4(1) — Definition of registered investment; ITA 204.5 — List of registered investments.

Notes: Reg. 4900(5) amended by 2017 budget bill #2, effective March 23, 2017, to change reference from 205(1) to 146.4(1) (as Part XI was repealed and "qualified investment" is now defined in 146.4(1) for RDSPs).

Reg. 4900(5) earlier amended by 2008 budget bill #2 (for 2009 and later taxation years), 2007 RDSPs bill, P.C. 2001-1106.

(6) [Small business investment] — Subject to subsection (9), for the purposes of paragraph (d) of the definition "qualified investment" in subsection 146(1) of the Act, paragraph (e) of the definition "qualified investment" in subsection 146.1(1) of the Act and paragraph (c) of the definition "qualified investment" in subsection 146.3(1) of the Act, a property is prescribed as a qualified investment for a trust governed by a registered retirement savings plan, a registered education savings plan and a registered retirement income fund at any time if at that time the property is not a prohibited investment for the trust and is

(a) a share of the capital stock of an "eligible corporation" (as defined in subsection 5100(1));

(b) an interest of a limited partner in a small business investment limited partnership; or

(c) an interest in a small business investment trust.

Related Provisions: Reg. 4900(12), (14) — Alternative definitions of qualified investment.

Notes: Reg. 4900(6) and (14) (4900(12) before 2012) provide overlapping mechanisms for RRSPs, RRIFs, RESPs and TFSAs to invest in small businesses. It used to be preferable to qualify under Reg. 4900(12) [now moved to 4900(14) for RRSPs] because it was a one-time test measured when the property was acquired; but new Reg. 4900(15) [formerly Reg. 5001] now requires the conditions be met on an ongoing basis. For the pre-2011 rules see William Holmes, "Qualifying Investments in Private Corporations", III(4) *RRSP Planning* (Federated Press) 206-12 (1996); VIEWS docs 2005-0141081C6, 2005-0154551E5.

The new rules may require removing private company shares from an RRSP. See Shane Brown, "Unwind RRSP SBC Investments?", 19(7) *Canadian Tax Highlights* (ctf.ca) 3-4 (July 2011).

A small business investment can be transferred from one RRSP to another under ITA 146(16), but must qualify under Reg. 4900(6) or (12) [now (14)] for the transferee RRSP: VIEWS doc 2009-0321921E5.

Some promoters market schemes that purport to allow investors to put their RRSP funds into a small business corp and then extract 70-80% of the funds. These "RRSP strips" usually do not work. See 146(10) Notes for some of the case law. Since March 23, 2011, 207.01(1)"RRSP strip" and 207.05(2)(c) are aimed at these schemes.

In *Chiasson*, 2017 FCA 239, a company (Landmark) whose assets were primarily a Barbados company did not qualify.

Reg. 4900(6) amended by 2017 budget bill #2, effective on the same basis as the amendment to 4900(1)(g), to change "Subject to subsections (8) and (9)" to "Subject to subsection (9)" and to delete "unless, in the case of a registered education savings plan, a beneficiary or subscriber under the plan is a designated shareholder of the corporation" at the end of para. (a).

Reg. 4900(6) amended by 2011 budget bill #2, for investments acquired after March 22, 2011, to add "is not a prohibited investment for the trust and" to the opening words and to amend para. (a), which previously read:

(a) a share of the capital stock of an eligible corporation (within the meaning assigned by subsection 5100(1)), unless a person who is an annuitant, a beneficiary or a subscriber under the plan or fund is a designated shareholder of the corporation;

Reg. 4900(6) amended by P.C. 2001-1106, effective for property acquired after Oct. 27, 1998, to apply to RESPs.

(7) [Small business investment for DPSP] — Subject to subsection (11), for the purposes of paragraph (h) of the definition "qualified investment" in section 204 of the Act, a property is prescribed as a qualified investment for a trust governed by a deferred profit sharing plan or revoked plan at any time if at that time the property is an interest

(a) of a limited partner in a small business investment limited partnership; or

(b) in a small business investment trust.

Notes: Reg. 4900(7) opening words amended by 2007 budget bill #1, effective in determining whether a property is, at any time after March 18, 2007, a qualified investment, to change the reference from 204"qualified investment"(i) to (h).

(8) [Repealed]

Notes: Reg. 4900(8) repealed by 2017 budget bill #2, effective on the same basis as the amendment to 4900(1)(g). It read:

(8) [Small business investment — payment for services] — For the purposes of subsection (6), a property that is held by a trust governed by a registered education savings plan ceases to be a qualified investment for the trust immediately before an amount is received if

(a) the property is a share referred to in paragraph (6)(a), an interest in a small business investment limited partnership that holds a small business security, or an interest in a small business investment trust that holds a small business security;

(b) a person who is a beneficiary or subscriber under the plan provides services to or for the issuer of the share or small business security, or to or for a person related to that issuer;

(c) the amount is received in respect of the share or small business security; and

(d) it can reasonably be considered, having regard to all the circumstances (including the terms and conditions of the share or small business security or of any related agreement, and the rate of interest or the dividend provided on the share or small business security), that the amount is on account, in lieu or in satisfaction of payment for the services.

Reg. 4900(8) amended by 2011 budget bill #2, effective in respect of investments acquired after March 22, 2011. For those acquired earlier, read:

(8) For the purposes of subsection (6), where

(a) a trust governed by a registered retirement savings plan, a registered education savings plan or a registered retirement income fund holds

(i) a share of the capital stock of an eligible corporation (within the meaning assigned by subsection 5100(1)),

(ii) an interest in a small business investment limited partnership that holds a small business security, or

(iii) an interest in a small business investment trust that holds a small business security, and

(b) a person who is an annuitant, a beneficiary or a subscriber under the plan or fund provides services to or for the issuer of the share or small business security, or to or for a person related to that issuer, and it can reasonably be considered, having regard to all the circumstances (including the terms and conditions of the share or small business security or of any related agreement, and the rate of interest or the dividend provided on the share or small business security), that any amount received in respect of the share or small business security is on account, in lieu or in satisfaction of payment for the services,

the property referred to in subparagraph (a)(i), (ii) or (iii) held by the plan or fund shall, immediately before that amount is received, cease to be and shall not thereafter be a qualified investment for the trust governed by the plan or fund.

Reg. 4900(8) amended by P.C. 2001-1106, effective for property acquired after October 27, 1998, to add references to RESPs and to a "beneficiary" or "subscriber".

(9) [Small business investment — conditions] — For the purposes of subsection (6), where

(a) a trust governed by a registered retirement savings plan, a registered education savings plan or a registered retirement income fund holds

(i) an interest in a small business investment limited partnership, or

(ii) an interest in a small business investment trust

that holds a small business security (referred to in this subsection as the **"designated security"**) of a corporation, and

(b) a person who is an annuitant, a beneficiary or a subscriber under the plan or fund is a designated shareholder of the corporation,

the interest shall not be a qualified investment for the trust governed by the plan or fund unless

(c) the designated security is a share of the capital stock of an eligible corporation,

(d) the partnership or trust, as the case may be, has no right to set off, assign or otherwise apply, directly or indirectly, the designated security against the interest,

(e) no person is obligated in any way, either absolutely or contingently, under any undertaking the intent or effect of which is

(i) to limit any loss that the plan or fund may sustain by virtue of the ownership, holding or disposition of the interest, or

(ii) to ensure that the plan or fund will derive earnings by virtue of the ownership, holding or disposition of the interest,

(f) in the case of the partnership, there are more than 10 limited partners and no limited partner or group of limited partners who do not deal with each other at arm's length holds more than 10 per cent of the units of the partnership, and

(g) in the case of the trust, there are more than 10 beneficiaries and no beneficiary or group of beneficiaries who do not deal with each other at arm's length holds more than 10 per cent of the units of the trust.

Notes: For meaning of "indirectly" in (d), see Notes to ITA 17.1(1).

Reg. 4900(9) amended by P.C. 2001-1106, for property acquired after Oct. 27, 1998.

(10) [Repealed]

Notes: Reg. 4900(10) repealed by 2011 budget bill #2, effective Dec. 15, 2011. It deemed plans for persons not at arm's length (NAL) to be NAL for purposes of (9)(f)-(g). Earlier amended by P.C. 2001-1106.

(11) [Small business investment for DPSP] — For the purposes of subsection (7), where

(a) a trust governed by a deferred profit sharing plan or revoked plan holds

(i) an interest in a small business investment limited partnership, or

(ii) an interest in a small business investment trust

that holds a small business security of a corporation,

(b) payments have been made in trust to a trustee under the deferred profit sharing plan or revoked plan for the benefit of beneficiaries thereunder by the corporation or a corporation related thereto, and

(c) the small business security is not an equity share described in paragraph (e) of the definition "qualified investment" in section 204 of the Act,

the interest referred to in subparagraphs (a)(i) and (ii) shall not be a qualified investment for the trust referred to in paragraph (a).

(12) [Repealed]

Notes: Reg. 4900(12) repealed by 2017 budget bill #2, effective on the same basis as the amendment to 4900(1)(g). It read:

(12) [Small business corporation] — For the purposes of paragraph (e) of the definition "qualified investment" in subsection 146.1(1) of the Act, a property is prescribed as a qualified investment for a trust governed by a registered education savings plan at any time if

(a) at the time the property was acquired by the trust,

(i) the property was a share of the capital stock of a specified small business corporation,

(ii) the property was a share of the capital stock of a venture capital corporation described in any of sections 6700 to 6700.2, or

(iii) the property was a qualifying share in respect of a specified cooperative corporation and the plan; and

(b) immediately after the time the property was acquired by the trust, each person who is a beneficiary or a subscriber under the plan was not a connected shareholder of the corporation.

See Notes to Reg. 4900(6). The application to RRSPs was moved from here to Reg. 4900(14) for investments acquired after March 22, 2011.

For CRA interpretation before the 2011 amendment see VIEWS docs 2008-0294531E5, 2009-0324331E5, 2009-0325101E5, 2009-0347981E5. After the amendment see 2011-0426041E5, 2012-0438701E5.

In *Beaulieu*, 2012 FCA 186, an RRSP strip scheme did not work because the taxpayer was found to be a "connected shareholder" of the company his RRSP invested in.

Reg. 4900(12) amended by 2011 budget bill #2, effective in respect of investments acquired after March 22, 2011. For those acquired earlier, read:

(12) For the purposes of paragraph (d) of the definition "qualified investment" in subsection 146(1) of the Act, paragraph (e) of the definition "qualified investment" in subsection 146.1(1) of the Act and paragraph (c) of the definition "qualified investment" in subsection 146.3(1) of the Act, a property is prescribed

as a qualified investment for a trust governed by a registered retirement savings plan, a registered education savings plan or a registered retirement income fund at any time if, at the time the property was acquired by the trust,

(a) the property was a share of the capital stock of a specified small business corporation,

(b) the property was a share of the capital stock of a venture capital corporation described in any of sections 6700, 6700.1 or 6700.2, or

(c) the property was a qualifying share in respect of a specified cooperative corporation and the plan or fund

and, immediately after the time the property was acquired by the trust, each person who is an annuitant, a beneficiary or a subscriber under the plan or fund at that time was not a connected shareholder of the corporation.

Reg. 4900(12) earlier amended by 2008 budget bill #2 (for 2009 and later taxation years); P.C. 2001-1360, 2001-1106, 1999-249, 1995-1820. Added by P.C. 1994-1074.

(13) [Repealed]

Notes: Reg. 4900(13) repealed by 2017 budget bill #2, effective on the same basis as the amendment to 4900(1)(g). It read:

(13) Notwithstanding subsection (12), where

(a) a share that is otherwise a qualified investment for the purposes of paragraph (e) of the definition "qualified investment" in subsection 146.1(1) of the Act solely because of subsection (12) is held by a trust governed by a registered education savings plan,

(b) an individual

(i) provides services to or for,

(ii) acquires goods from, or

(iii) is provided services by

the issuer of the share or a person related to that issuer,

(c) an amount is received in respect of the share by the trust, and

(d) the amount can reasonably be considered, having regard to all the circumstances, including the terms and conditions of the share, or any agreement relating thereto and any dividend provided on the share to be

(i) on account of, or in lieu or in satisfaction of, payment for the services to or for the issuer or the person related to the issuer, or

(ii) in respect of the acquisition of the goods from, or the services provided by, the issuer or the person related to the issuer,

the share shall, immediately before the amount is received, cease to be and shall not thereafter be a qualified investment for the trust.

Reg. 4900(13) ensured that amounts received in respect of shares qualifying under Reg. 4900(12) are in the nature of a return from an investment.

Reg. 4900(13)(a) amended by 2011 budget bill #2, effective in respect of investments acquired after March 22, 2011, so that it no longer applies to RRSPs and RRIFs. For investments acquired earlier, read:

(a) a share that is otherwise a qualified investment for the purposes of paragraph (d) of the definition "qualified investment" in subsection 146(1) of the Act, paragraph (e) of the definition "qualified investment" in subsection 146.1(1) of the Act and paragraph (c) of the definition "qualified investment" in subsection 146.3(1) of the Act solely because of subsection (12) is held by a trust governed by a registered retirement savings plan, registered education savings plan or registered retirement income fund,

Reg. 4900(13)(a) amended by P.C. 2001-1106 to add reference to ITA 146.1 and a RESP, effective for property acquired after October 27, 1998.

Reg. 4900(13) added by P.C. 1994-1074, effective December 3, 1992.

(14) For the purposes of paragraph (d) of the definition "qualified investment" in subsection 146(1) of the Act, paragraph (e) of the definition "qualified investment" in subsection 146.1(1) of the Act, paragraph (c) of the definition "qualified investment" in subsection 146.3(1) of the Act and paragraph (c) of the definition "qualified investment" in subsection 207.01(1) of the Act, a property is prescribed as a qualified investment for a trust governed by a RESP, RRIF, RRSP or TFSA at any time if, at the time the property was acquired by the trust, the property

(a) was

(i) a share of the capital stock of a specified small business corporation,

(ii) a share of the capital stock of a venture capital corporation described in any of sections 6700 to 6700.2, or

(iii) a qualifying share in respect of a specified cooperative corporation and the RESP, RRIF, RRSP or TFSA; and

(b) was not a prohibited investment for the trust.

Related Provisions: Reg. 4900(15) — Conditions must be met on ongoing basis for prohibited-investment rules.

Notes: For RRSP investments acquired before March 23, 2011, Reg. 4900(12) applies. See Notes to Reg. 4900(6) and (12). See also VIEWS doc 2009-0305501E5 (general discussion in application to TFSAs).

For CRA interpretation since the 2011 amendment see VIEWS docs 2011-0426041E5, 2012-0441781E5, 2012-0457011E5.

The wording "at the time the property was acquired by the trust" looks like a one-time test, but new Reg. 4900(15) [formerly Reg. 5001] effectively requires that the conditions be met on an ongoing basis for purposes of the prohibited-investment rules.

Shares of a corp that ceases to be a specified small business corporation do not become a prohibited investment until the beginning of its next taxation year: VIEWS doc 2015-0579671E5 [Gosselin, "Reversing Prohibited Status of Small Business Shares in RRSPs", 15(4) *Tax for the Owner-Manager* (ctf.ca) 2-3 (Oct. 2015)].

Reg. 4900(14) amended by 2017 budget bill #2, effective on the same basis as the amendment to 4900(1)(g), to add reference to 146.1(1)"qualified investment"(e) in opening words, and "RESP" in both opening words and (a)(iii).

Reg. 4900(14) opening words and (a)(iii) amended by 2011 budget bill #2, effective in respect of investments acquired after March 22, 2011, to add "RRIF, RRSP or" in (a)(iii). For investments acquired earlier, the opening words read:

> (14) For the purposes of paragraph (c) of the definition "qualified investment" in subsection 207.01(1) of the Act, a property is prescribed as a qualified investment for a trust governed by a TFSA at any time if, at the time the property was acquired by the trust, the property

Reg. 4900(14) added by 2008 budget bill #2, for 2009 and later taxation years.

Income Tax Folios: S3-F10-C2: Prohibited investments — RRSPs, RRIFs and TFSAs.

(15) For the purposes of the definition "prohibited investment" in subsection 207.01(1) of the Act, property that is a qualified investment for a trust governed by a RESP, RRIF, RRSP or TFSA solely because of subsection (14) is prescribed property for the trust at any time if, at that time, the property is not described in any of subparagraphs (14)(a)(i) to (iii).

Notes: See Notes to Reg. 4900(14).

Reg. 4900(15) amended by 2017 budget bill #2, effective on the same basis as amendment to 4900(1)(g), to add "RESP".

Reg. 4900(15) added by 2013 budget bill #2, effective March 23, 2011. It replaced former Reg. 5001.

Income Tax Folios: S3-F10-C2: Prohibited investments — RRSPs, RRIFs and TFSAs.

Definitions [Reg. 4900]: "amount", "annuity" — ITA 248(1); "arm's length" — ITA 251(1); "bank", "business" — ITA 248(1); "calendar year" — *Interpretation Act* 37(1)(a); "Canada" — ITA 255, *Interpretation Act* 35(1); "Canadian corporation" — ITA 89(1), 248(1); "Canadian resource property" — ITA 66(15), 248(1); "connected person" — Reg. 4901(2); "connected shareholder" — Reg. 4901(2), (2.1), (2.2); "controlled" — ITA 256(6), (6.1); "controlled directly or indirectly" — ITA 256(5.1)–(6); "corporation" — ITA 248(1), *Interpretation Act* 35(1); "cost amount" — ITA 248(1); "credit union" — ITA 137(6), 248(1); "deferred profit sharing plan" — ITA 147(1), 248(1); "designated shareholder" — Reg. 4901(2), (2.3); "designated stock exchange" — ITA 248(1), 262; "disposition", "dividend" — ITA 248(1); "eligible corporation" — Reg. 5100(1); "employee", "employer" — ITA 248(1); "fair market value" — see ITA 69(1) Notes; "governing plan" — Reg. 4901(2); "Her Majesty" — *Interpretation Act* 35(1); "immovable" — Quebec *Civil Code* art. 900-907; "individual", "insurance corporation", "insurer" — ITA 248(1); "issuer" — ITA 146.2(1), 207.01(1); "licensed annuities provider" — ITA 147(1), 248(1); "month" — *Interpretation Act* 35(1); "mortgage" — Reg. 4901(3)(a); "mortgage investment corporation" — ITA 130.1(6), 248(1); "mutual fund trust" — ITA 132(6)–(7), 132.2(3)(n), 248(1); "non-resident" — ITA 248(1); "obligation" — Reg. 4900(1)(g), (h), (i); "partnership" — see ITA 96(1) Notes; "person" — ITA 248(1); "plan trust" — Reg. 4901(2); "prescribed" — ITA 248(1); "prescribed venture capital corporation" — Reg. 6700; "principal amount" — ITA 248(1); "prohibited investment" — ITA 207.01(1); "property" — ITA 248(1); "province" — *Interpretation Act* 35(1); "public corporation" — ITA 89(1), 248(1); "qualified investment" — ITA 146(1), 146.1(1), 146.3(1), 146.4(1), 207.01(1); "qualifying share" — Reg. 4901(2); "RESP" — ITA 248(1)"registered education savings plan"; "RRIF" — ITA 248(1)"registered retirement income fund"; "RRSP" — ITA 248(1)"registered retirement savings plan"; "registered disability savings plan" — ITA 146.4(1), 248(1); "registered education savings plan" — ITA 146.1(1), 248(1); "registered home ownership savings plan" — ITA 248(1); "registered investment" — ITA 204.4(1), 248(1); "registered retirement income fund" — ITA 146.3(1), 248(1); "registered retirement savings plan" — ITA 146(1), 248(1); "registered securities dealer" — ITA 248(1); "related" — ITA 251(2)–(6); "resident in Canada" — ITA 250; "revoked plan" — ITA 204, Reg. 4901(2); "share", "shareholder", "small business corporation" — ITA 248(1); "small business investment limited partnership" — Reg. 4901(2), 5102(1); "small business investment trust" — Reg. 4901(2), 5103(1); "small business security" — Reg. 4901(2), 5100(2); "specified cooperative corporation" — ITA 136(2), Reg. 4901(2); "specified corporation" — Reg. 4900(1)(t)(iv); "specified small business corporation" — Reg. 4901(2); "substi-

tuted" — ITA 248(5); "TFSA", "taxable income" — ITA 248(1); "taxation year" — ITA 249; "taxpayer" — ITA 248(1); "trust" — ITA 104(1), 146.1(1), 207.01(1), 248(1), (3).

4901. Interpretation — (1) For the purposes of paragraphs 204.4(2)(b), (d) and (f) and of subsection 204.6(1) of the Act, a property is a prescribed investment for a corporation or trust, as the case may be, if it is a qualified investment for a plan or fund described in paragraphs 204.4(1)(a) to (d) of the Act in respect of which the corporation or trust is seeking registration or has been registered, as the case may be.

(1.1) [Revoked]

Notes: Reg. 4901(1.1) revoked by P.C. 1994-1074, retroactive to its introduction (Nov. 1985). It prescribed property for purposes of ITA 207.1(5), also repealed retroactively, which imposed a penalty tax on excessive holdings of small business properties by an RRSP or RRIF.

(2) In this Part,

"allocation in proportion to patronage" has the meaning assigned by subsection 135(4) of the Act;

Notes: Definition "allocation in proportion to patronage" added by P.C. 1995-1820, effective December 3, 1992.

"connected person" under a governing plan of a plan trust means a person who is an annuitant, a beneficiary, an employer or a subscriber under, or a holder of, the governing plan and any person who does not deal at arm's length with that person;

Notes: Reg. 4901(2)"connected person" amended by 2008 budget bill #2, for 2009 and later tax years. Added by 2007 RDSPs bill, for 2008 and later tax years.

"connected shareholder" of a corporation at any time is a person (other than an exempt person in respect of the corporation) who owns, directly or indirectly, at that time, not less than 10% of the issued shares of any class of the capital stock of the corporation or of any other corporation that is related to the corporation and, for the purposes of this definition,

(a) paragraphs (a) to (e) of the definition "specified shareholder" in subsection 248(1) of the Act apply, and

(b) an exempt person in respect of a corporation is a person who deals at arm's length with the corporation where the total of all amounts, each of which is the cost amount of any share of the capital stock of the corporation, or of any other corporation that is related to it, that the person owns or is deemed to own for the purposes of the definition "specified shareholder" in subsection 248(1) of the Act, is less than $25,000;

Related Provisions: Reg. 4901(2.1), (2.2) — Additional rules.

Notes: See Reg. 4900(12). In *Beaulieu*, 2012 FCA 186, a taxpayer was found to be a "connected shareholder" of the company his RRSP invested in. See also VIEWS doc 2014-0528311E5.

Definition "connected shareholder" added by P.C. 1994-1074 and amended by P.C. 1995-1820, effective December 3, 1992. However, where

- a property was acquired by a trust governed by an RRSP or RRIF before November 30, 1994, and
- the annuitant under the RRSP or RRIF would, if this version of the definition and Reg. 4901(2.1)-(2.3) applied, be a connected shareholder of the corporation immediately after that time,

read the definition differently (see up to 51st ed. for the text).

"consumer goods or services" has the meaning assigned by subsection 135(4) of the Act;

Notes: Definition added by P.C. 1995-1820, effective December 3, 1992.

"designated shareholder" of a corporation at any time means a taxpayer who at that time

(a) is, or is related to, a person (other than an exempt person) who owns, directly or indirectly, not less than 10% of the issued shares of any class of the capital stock of the corporation or of any other corporation that is related to the corporation and, for the purposes of this definition,

(i) paragraphs (a) to (e) of the definition "specified shareholder" in subsection 248(1) of the Act apply, and

(ii) an exempt person in respect of a corporation is a person who deals at arm's length with the corporation where the total of all amounts, each of which is the cost amount of any share of the capital stock of the corporation, or of any other corporation that is related to it, that the person owns or is deemed to own for the purposes of the definition "specified shareholder" in subsection 248(1) of the Act, is less than $25,000;

(b) is or is related to a member of a partnership that controls the corporation,

(c) is or is related to a beneficiary under a trust that controls the corporation,

(d) is or is related to an employee of the corporation or a corporation related thereto, where any group of employees of the corporation or of the corporation related thereto, as the case may be, controls the corporation, except where the group of employees includes a person or a related group that controls the corporation, or

(e) does not deal at arm's length with the corporation;

Related Provisions: Reg. 4901(2.3) — Deemed designated shareholder.

Notes: Para. (a) of "designated shareholder" amended by P.C. 1995-1820, effective for property acquired after Nov. 29, 1994. For property acquired earlier, see up to 51st ed. for the text.

"governing plan" means a deferred profit sharing plan or a revoked plan, a registered disability savings plan, a registered education savings plan, a registered retirement income fund, a registered retirement savings plan or a TFSA;

Notes: Reg. 4901(2)"governing plan" amended by 2007 RDSPs bill, for 2008 and later tax years, to refer to an RDSP; and by 2008 budget bill #2, for 2009 and later tax years, to refer to a TFSA.

Amended by P.C. 2001-1106, for property acquired after Oct. 27, 1998, to refer to a RESP.

"plan trust" means a trust governed by a governing plan;

"qualifying share", in respect of a specified cooperative corporation and a governing plan, means a share of the capital or capital stock of the corporation where

(a) ownership of the share or a share identical to the share is not a condition of membership in the corporation, or

(b) a connected person under the governing plan

(i) has not received a payment from the corporation pursuant to an allocation in proportion to patronage in respect of consumer goods or services, and

(ii) can reasonably be expected not to receive a payment, after the acquisition of the share by the plan trust, from the corporation pursuant to an allocation in proportion to patronage in respect of consumer goods or services;

Notes: For interpretation see VIEWS docs 2007-0252081E5, 2008-0294531E5, 2009-0324331E5, 2009-0325101E5.

Reg. 4901(2)"qualifying share" amended by 2008 budget bill #2, for 2009 and later tax years (no substantive change).

Reg. 4901(2)"qualifying share" amended by P.C. 2001-1106 to add reference to a RESP and to a "beneficiary" or a [RESP] "subscriber", effective for property acquired after October 27, 1998.

Definition "qualifying share" added by P.C. 1995-1820, effective Dec. 3, 1992. However, for property acquired before Nov. 30, 1994, read para. (a) as: "the share is not required to be purchased as a condition of membership in the corporation, or".

"revoked plan" has the meaning assigned by section 204 of the Act;

"small business investment limited partnership" has the meaning assigned by subsection 5102(1);

"small business investment trust" has the meaning assigned by subsection 5103(1); and

"small business security" has the meaning assigned by subsection 5100(2).

"specified cooperative corporation" means

(a) a cooperative corporation within the meaning assigned by subsection 136(2) of the Act, or

(b) a corporation that would be a cooperative corporation within the meaning assigned by subsection 136(2) of the Act if the purpose described in that subsection were the purpose of providing employment to the corporation's members or customers.

Notes: Definition "specified cooperative corporation" added by P.C. 1994-1074, effective December 3, 1992 (see Reg. 4900(12)).

"specified small business corporation", at any time, means a corporation (other than a cooperative corporation) that would, at that time or at the end of the last taxation year of the corporation that ended before that time, be a small business corporation if the expression "Canadian-controlled private corporation" in the definition "small business corporation" in subsection 248(1) of the Act were read as "Canadian corporation (other than a corporation controlled at that time, directly or indirectly in any manner whatever, by one or more non-resident persons)".

Notes: For CRA interpretation see VIEWS doc 2017-0717561E5 (general discussion).

Reg. 4901(2)"specified small business corporation" added by 2008 budget bill #2, effective for 2009 and later taxation years. See Notes to Reg. 4900(12).

(2.1) For the purposes of the definition "connected shareholder" in subsection (2) and of subsection (2.2), each share of the capital of a specified cooperative corporation and all other shares of the capital of the corporation that have attributes identical to the attributes of that share shall be deemed to be shares of a class of the capital stock of the corporation.

Notes: Reg. 4901(2.1) added by P.C. 1995-1820, effective December 3, 1992. However, it does not apply where a property was acquired by a trust governed by an RRSP or RRIF before November 30, 1994, and the annuitant under the RRSP or RRIF would, if Reg. 4901(2.1)–(2.3) and the amended version of 4901(2)"connected shareholder" applied, be a connected shareholder of the corporation immediately after that time.

(2.2) For the purpose of this Part, a person is deemed to be a connected shareholder of a corporation at any time where the person would be a connected shareholder of the corporation at that time if, at that time,

(a) the person had each right that the person would be deemed to own at that time for the purposes of the definition "specified shareholder" in subsection 248(1) of the Act if that right were a share of the capital stock of a corporation;

(b) the person owned each share of a class of the capital stock of a corporation that the person had a right at that time under a contract, in equity or otherwise, either immediately or in the future and either absolutely or contingently, to acquire; and

(c) the cost amount to the person of a share referred to in paragraph (b) were the cost amount to the person of the right to which the share relates.

Notes: Reg. 4901(2.2) added by P.C. 1995-1820, effective on the same basis as Reg. 4901(2.1) (see Notes thereto).

(2.3) For the purpose of this Part, a person is deemed to be a designated shareholder of a corporation at any time if the person would be a designated shareholder of the corporation at that time if, at that time, paragraphs (2.2)(a) to (c) applied in respect of that person.

Notes: Reg. 4901(2.3) added by P.C. 1995-1820, effective for property acquired after November 29, 1994.

(3) [Repealed]

Notes: Reg. 4901(3) repealed by P.C. 2005-1508, effective Sept. 21, 2005. This rule is now incorporated into Reg. 4900(1)(j)–(j.2).

Definitions [Reg. 4901]: "allocation in proportion to patronage" — ITA 135(4), Reg. 4901(2); "amount" — ITA 248(1); "arm's length" — ITA 251(1); "connected person" — Reg. 4901(2); "connected shareholder" — Reg. 4901(2), (2.1), (2.2); "consumer goods or services" — ITA 135(4), Reg. 4901(2); "controlled" — ITA 256(5.1)–(6); "corporation" — ITA 248(1), *Interpretation Act* 35(1); "cost amount" — ITA 248(1); "deferred profit sharing plan" — ITA 147(1), 248(1); "designated shareholder" — Reg. 4901(2), (2.3); "employee", "employer", "employment" — ITA 248(1); "exempt person" — Reg. 4901(2)"connected shareholder"(b), "designated shareholder"(a)(ii); "governing plan" — Reg. 4901(2); "identical" — ITA 248(12); "partnership" — see ITA 96(1) Notes; "person" — ITA 248(1); "plan trust" — Reg. 4901(2); "property" — ITA 248(1); "registered disability savings plan" — ITA

146.4(1), 248(1); "registered education savings plan" — ITA 146.1(1), 248(1); "registered home ownership savings plan" — ITA 248(1); "registered retirement income fund" — ITA 146.3(1), 248(1); "registered retirement savings plan" — ITA 146(1), 248(1); "related" — ITA 251(2)–(6); "revoked plan" — ITA 204, Reg. 4901(2); "share" — ITA 248(1), Reg. 4901(2.1); "small business corporation" — ITA 248(1); "specified cooperative corporation" — ITA 136(2), Reg. 4901(2); "specified shareholder", "TFSA" — ITA 248(1); "taxation year" — ITA 249; "taxpayer" — ITA 248(1); "trust" — ITA 104(1), 248(1), (3).

PART L — [5000, 5001] [REPEALED]

5000, 5001. [Repealed]

Notes: Reg. 5000-5001 (Part L) repealed by 2013 budget bill #2, retroactive to March 23, 2011. Reg. 5000, which defined "prescribed excluded property" for the past version of ITA 207.01(1)"prohibited investment", was replaced by ITA 207.01(1)"excluded property". Reg. 5001 was moved to Reg. 4900(15).

For CRA interpretation before the repeal, see VIEWS doc 2011-0426041E5.

Reg. 5000-5001 earlier amended by 2011 budget bill #2, effective March 23, 2011. Part L added by 2008 budget bill #2, for 2009 and later tax years.

Earlier Part L (Reg. 5000-5002) repealed by P.C. 2005-1508 effective June 29, 2005, due to repeal of ITA Part XI (foreign property limit). For the text, see up to the 36th ed.

PART LI — [5100–5104] DEFERRED INCOME PLANS, INVESTMENTS IN SMALL BUSINESS

5100. (1) In this Part,

"designated rate", at any time, means 150 per cent of the highest of the prime rates generally quoted at that time by the banks to which Schedule A to the *Bank Act* applies;

"eligible corporation", at any time, means

(a) a particular corporation that is a taxable Canadian corporation all or substantially all of the property of which is at that time

(i) used in a qualifying active business carried on by the particular corporation or by a corporation controlled by it,

(ii) shares of the capital stock of one or more eligible corporations that are related to the particular corporation, or debt obligations issued by those eligible corporations,

(iii) any combination of the properties described in subparagraph (i) and (ii),

(a.1) a specified holding corporation, or

(b) a venture capital corporation described in section 6700,

but does not include

(c) a corporation (other than a mutual fund corporation) that is

(i) a trader or dealer in securities,

(ii) a bank,

(iii) a corporation licensed or otherwise authorized under the laws of Canada or a province to carry on in Canada the business of offering to the public its services as a trustee,

(iv) a credit union,

(v) an insurance corporation, or

(vi) a corporation the principal business of which is the lending of money or the purchasing of debt obligations or a combination of them,

(d) a corporation controlled by one or more non-resident persons,

(e) a venture capital corporation, other than a venture capital corporation described in section 6700, or

(f) a corporation that has made an election in respect of a particular taxation year under subparagraph (iv) of the description of B in paragraph 204.82(2.2)(c.1) of the Act, if that time is in the 12-month period that begins on the day that is six months after the day on which the particular taxation year ends;

Related Provisions: ITA 256(6), (6.1) — Meaning of "controlled".

Notes: CRA considers that "substantially all", used in para. (a), means 90% or more. For the meaning of "principal business" in (c)(vi), see Notes to ITA 20(1)(bb).

Para. (f) excludes from the definition an LSVCC that has made an election under ITA 204.82(2.2)(c.1), which typically has the effect of reducing the amount an LSVCC is required to invest in small- and medium-sized businesses.

Definition amended by P.C. 2001-1370 (last change effective June 10, 2001), 1999-249.

I.T. Technical News: 25 (*Silicon Graphics* case — dispersed control is not control).

"qualifying active business", at any time, means any business carried on primarily in Canada by a corporation, but does not include

(a) a business (other than a business of leasing property other than real property) the principal purpose of which is to derive income from property (including interest, dividends, rent and royalties), or

(b) a business of deriving gains from the disposition of property (other than property in the inventory of the business),

and, for the purposes of this definition, a business carried on primarily in Canada by a corporation, at any time, includes a business carried on by the corporation if, at that time,

(c) at least 50 per cent of the full time employees of the corporation and all corporations related thereto employed in respect of the business are employed in Canada, or

(d) at least 50 per cent of the salaries and wages paid to employees of the corporation and all corporations related thereto employed in respect of the business are reasonably attributable to services rendered in Canada;

"qualifying obligation", at any time, means a bond, debenture, mortgage, note or other similar obligation of a corporation described in paragraph 149(1)(o.2) or (o.3) of the Act, if

(a) the obligation was issued by the corporation after October 31, 1985,

(b) the corporation used all or substantially all of the proceeds of the issue of the obligation within 90 days after the receipt thereof to acquire

(i) small business securities,

(ii) interests of a limited partner in small business investment limited partnerships,

(iii) interests in small business investment trusts, or

(iv) any combination of the properties described in subparagraphs (i) to (iii)

and, except as provided in subsection 5104(1), the corporation was the first person (other than a broker or dealer in securities) to have acquired the properties and the corporation has owned the properties continuously since they were so acquired,

(c) the corporation does not hold, and no group of persons who do not deal with each other at arm's length and of which it is a member holds, more than 30 per cent of the outstanding shares of any class of voting stock of another corporation, except where all or any part of those shares were acquired in specified circumstances, within the meaning of subsection 5104(2),

(d) the recourse of the holder of the obligation against the corporation with respect to the obligation is limited to the properties acquired with the proceeds of the issue of the obligation and any properties substituted therefor, and

(e) the properties acquired with the proceeds of the issue of the obligation have not been disposed of, unless the disposition occurred within the 90 day period immediately preceding that time;

Notes: CRA considers that "substantially all", used in para. (b), means 90% or more.

Opening words of definition amended to change "mortgage, hypothec" to "mortgage" by P.C. 1994-1817, effective Nov. 30, 1994.

"specified holding corporation", at any time, means a taxable Canadian corporation where

(a) all or substantially all of the collective property of the corporation and of all other corporations controlled by it (each of which other corporations is referred to in this definition as a "controlled corporation"), other than shares in the capital stock of the corporation or of a corporation related to it and debt obligations issued by it or by a corporation related to it, is at that time used in a qualifying active business carried on by the corporation, and

(b) all or substantially all of the property of the corporation is at that time

(i) property used in a qualifying active business carried on by the corporation or a controlled corporation,

(ii) shares of the capital stock of one or more controlled corporations or eligible corporations related to the corporation,

(iii) debt obligations issued by one or more controlled corporations or eligible corporations related to the corporation, or

(iv) any combination of the properties described in subparagraphs (i), (ii) and (iii),

and in a determination of whether property is used in a qualifying active business for the purposes of paragraph (a),

(c) where a business is carried on by a controlled corporation,

(i) the business shall be deemed to be a business carried on only by the corporation, and

(ii) the controlled corporation shall be deemed to be the corporation in the application of paragraphs (c) and (d) of the definition "qualifying active business", and

(d) if a business of the corporation is substantially similar to one or more other businesses of the corporation, all those businesses shall be deemed collectively to be one business of the corporation.

Related Provisions: ITA 256(6), (6.1) — Meaning of "controlled".

Notes: CRA considers that "substantially all", used in para. (b), means 90% or more.

"specified property" means property described in any of (a), (b), (c), (f) and (g) of the definition "qualified investment" in section 204 of the Act.

Notes: "Specified property" amended by P.C. 2005-1508, effective June 29, 2005, to update references from ITA 204(e)(i)–(iii) and (vii)–(viii).

(2) [Small business security] — For the purposes of this Part and clause (b)(iii)(A) of the definition "eligible investment" in subsection 204.8(1) of the Act, a small business security of a person, at any time, is property of that person that is, at that time,

(a) a share of the capital stock of an eligible corporation,

(b) a debt obligation of an eligible corporation (other than a venture capital corporation described in section 6700) that does not by its terms or any agreement related to the obligation restrict the corporation from incurring other debts and that is

(i) secured solely by a floating charge on the assets of the corporation and that by its terms or any agreement related thereto is subordinate to all other debt obligations of the corporation (other than a small business security issued by the corporation, or a debt obligation that is owing by the corporation to a shareholder of the corporation or a person related to a shareholder of the corporation and that is not secured in any manner whatever), or

(ii) not secured in any manner whatever,

other than a debt obligation that

(iii) where the debt obligation specifies an invariant rate of interest, has an effective annual rate of return that exceeds the designated rate for the day on which the obligation was issued, and

(iv) in any other case, may have an effective annual rate of return at a particular time that exceeds the designated rate at the particular time,

(c) an option or right granted by an eligible corporation in conjunction with the issue of a share or debt obligation that qualifies as a small business security to acquire a share of the capital stock of the corporation, or

(d) an option or right granted for no consideration by an eligible corporation to a holder of a share that qualifies as a small business securities to acquire a share of the capital stock of the corporation

if, immediately after the time of acquisition thereof,

(e) the aggregate of the cost amounts to the person of all shares, options, rights and debt obligations of the eligible corporation and all corporations associated therewith held by the person does not exceed $10,000,000, and

(f) the total assets (determined in accordance with generally accepted accounting principles, on a consolidated or combined basis, where applicable) of the eligible corporation and all corporations associated with it do not exceed $50,000,000

and includes

(g) property of the person that is, at that time,

(i) a qualifying obligation, or

(ii) [Repealed]

(iii) a security (in this subparagraph referred to as the "new security") described in any of paragraphs (a) to (d), where the new security was issued at a particular time

(A) in exchange for, on the conversion of, or in respect of rights pertaining to a security (in this paragraph referred to as the "former security") that would, if this subsection were read without reference to this subparagraph and paragraph (h), be a small business security of the person immediately before the particular time, and

(B) pursuant to an agreement entered into before the particular time and at or before the time that the former security was last acquired by the person, or

(h) where the person is a small business investment corporation, small business investment limited partnership or small business investment trust, property of the person that is, at that time, a security (in this paragraph referred to as the "new security") described in any of paragraphs (a) to (d), where the new security was issued at a particular time not more than 5 years before that time in exchange for, on the conversion of, or in respect of rights pertaining to a security that would, if this subsection were read without reference to this paragraph, be a small business security of the person immediately before the particular time.

Related Provisions: ITA 204.8(1)"eligible investment"(f).

Notes: *Opening words* of Reg. 5100(2) amended by P.C. 2005-1508, effective for taxation years that begin after 2004, due to repeal of ITA Part XI (foreign property limit).

Opening words of Reg. 5100(2)(b) amended by P.C. 2001-1370 to change "prescribed venture capital corporation" to "venture capital corporation", effective June 10, 2001.

Reg. 5100(2)(b) amended by P.C. 1998-782 to add the parenthesized exclusion and to change "thereto" to "to the obligation", effective for debt obligations issued after December 5, 1996, other than debt obligations that were required to be issued pursuant to agreements in writing made on or before that date.

Reg. 5100(2)(b) amended by P.C. 1990-1837, effective for debt obligations issued after September 12, 1990 other than debt obligations that were required to be issued pursuant to agreements in writing entered into on or before that date.

Reg. 5100(2)(f) amended by P.C. 1994-1074, effective 1992, to change the limit from $35 million to $50 million. This is consistent with ITA 204.8(1)"eligible investment"(f).

Reg. 5100(2)(g)(ii) repealed by P.C. 2005-1508, effective June 29, 2005.

Reg. 5100(2)(g)(iii) and (h) added by P.C. 1992-258, for property acquired after 1989.

(2.1) [Prescribed venture capital corporation] — Where all or part of the property of a person consists of the shares of the capital stock of a venture capital corporation described in section 6700, options or rights granted by the corporation, or debt obligations of the corporation,

(a) the aggregate of the cost amounts to the person of all such property shall be deemed for the purposes of paragraph (2)(e) not to exceed $10,000,000; and

(b) the total assets (determined in accordance with generally accepted accounting principles, on a consolidated or combined basis, where applicable) of the corporation and all corporations associated with it shall be deemed for the purposes of paragraph (2)(f) not to exceed $50,000,000.

Notes: Reg. 5100(2.1) amended by P.C. 2001-1370 to change "prescribed venture capital corporation within the meaning assigned by" to "venture capital corporation described in", effective June 10, 2001.

Reg. 5100(2.1)(b) amended by P.C. 1994-1074, effective 1992, to change $35 million to $50 million. See Notes to Reg. 5100(2)(f).

(3) [Interpretation for subsec. (2)] — For the purposes of subsection (2),

(a) in determining the effective annual rate of return in respect of a debt obligation of an eligible corporation, the value of any right to convert the debt obligation or any part thereof into, or to exchange the debt obligation or any part thereof for, shares of the capital stock of the corporation or an option or right to acquire such shares shall not be considered; and

(b) a corporation shall be deemed not to be associated with another at any time where the corporation would not be associated with the other if

(i) the references to "controlled, directly or indirectly, in any manner whatever" in section 256 of the Act (other than subsection (5.1) thereof) were read as references to "controlled", and

(ii) such rights described in subsection 256(1.4) of the Act and shares, as were held at that time by a small business investment corporation, small business investment limited partnership or small business investment trust, were disregarded.

(4) [Repealed]

Notes: Reg. 5100(4) repealed by P.C. 2005-1508, effective June 29, 2005, due to repeal of ITA Part XI (foreign property limit).

Reg. 5100(4)(d) and (e) added by P.C. 1990-1837, effective 1990.

Definitions [Reg. 5100]: "arm's length" — ITA 251(1); "associated" — Reg. 5100(3)(b); "bank" — ITA 248(1), *Interpretation Act* 35(1); "business" — ITA 248(1); "Canada" — ITA 255, *Interpretation Act* 35(1); "controlled" — ITA 256(6), (6.1); "corporation" — ITA 248(1), *Interpretation Act* 35(1); "cost amount" — ITA 248(1); "credit union" — ITA 137(6), 248(1); "designated rate" — Reg. 5100(1); "disposed" — ITA 248(1)"disposition"; "disposition", "dividend" — ITA 248(1); "eligible corporation" — Reg. 5100(1); "employed", "employee" — ITA 248(1); "former security" — Reg. 5100(2)(g)(iii)(A); "insurance corporation", "inventory" — ITA 248(1); "new security" — Reg. 5100(2)(g)(iii), 5100(2)(h); "non-resident" — ITA 248(1); "partnership" — see ITA 96(1) Notes; "person" — ITA 248(1), Reg. 5104(6); "prescribed" — ITA 248(1); "prescribed venture capital corporation" — Reg. 6700; "property" — ITA 248(1); "province" — *Interpretation Act* 35(1); "qualifying active business" — Reg. 5100(1); "qualifying obligation" — ITA 149(1)(o.2), (o.3), Reg. 5100(1); "related" — ITA 251(2)–(6); "share", "shareholder" — ITA 248(1); "small business investment corporation" — Reg. 5101(1); "small business investment limited partnership" — Reg. 5102(1); "small business security" — Reg. 5100(2), 5104(3), (5); "specified circumstances" — Reg. 5104(2); "specified holding corporation" — Reg. 5100(1); "substituted" — ITA 248(5); "taxable Canadian corporation" — ITA 89(1), 248(1); "taxpayer" — ITA 248(1); "trust" — ITA 104(1), 248(1), (3).

5101. [Small business investment corporation] — **(1)** Subject to subsection (4), for the purposes of this Part and paragraph 149(1)(o.3) and paragraph (b) of the definition "small business property" in subsection 206(1) of the Act, a corporation is a small business investment corporation at any time if it is a Canadian corporation incorporated after May 22, 1985 and at all times after it was incorporated and before that time

(a) all of the shares, and rights to acquire shares, of the capital stock of the corporation were owned by

(i) one or more registered pension plans,

(ii) one or more trusts all the beneficiaries of which were registered pension plans,

(iii) one or more related segregated fund trusts (within the meaning assigned by paragraph 138.1(1)(a) of the Act) all the beneficiaries of which were registered pension plans, or

(iv) one or more persons prescribed by section 4802 for the purposes of clause 149(1)(o.2)(iv)(D) of the Act;

(b) its only undertaking was the investing of its funds and its investments consisted solely of

(i) small business securities,

(ii) interests of a limited partner in small business investment limited partnerships,

(iii) interests in small business investment trusts,

(iv) property (other than a small business security) that is

(A) a share of the capital stock of a corporation (other than a share that is issued to the corporation and that is either a share described in section 66.3 of the Act or a share in respect of which an amount has been designated under subsection 192(4) of the Act), or

(B) a put, call, warrant or other right to acquire or sell a share described by clause (A),

(v) specified properties, or

(vi) any combination of properties described in any of subparagraphs (i) to (v)

and, except as provided in subsection 5104(1), with respect to properties referred to in any of subparagraphs (i) to (iii), the corporation was the first person (other than a broker or dealer in securities) to have acquired the properties and the corporation has owned the properties continuously since they were so acquired;

(c) it has complied with subsection (2);

(d) it did not hold, and no group of persons who did not deal with each other at arm's length and of which it was a member held, more than 30 per cent of the outstanding shares of any class of voting stock of a corporation, except where

(i) all or any part of those shares were acquired in specified circumstances within the meaning of subsection 5104(2), or

(ii) those shares were of any class of voting stock of a venture capital corporation described in section 6700;

(e) it has not borrowed money except from its shareholders; and

(f) it has not accepted deposits.

Related Provisions: ITA 253.1(1) — Limited partner not considered to carry on partnership business.

Notes: Reg. 5101(1)(b)(iv) amended by P.C. 2005-1508, effective June 29, 2005, due to repeal of Reg. 5000 (no substantive change).

Reg. 5101(1)(d)(ii) amended by P.C. 2001-1370 to change "prescribed venture capital corporation within the meaning assigned by" to "venture capital corporation described in", effective June 10, 2001.

Reg. 5101(1)(b)(iv) added by P.C. 1994-1074, effective 1991. (Subparas. (v) and (vi) were previously numbered (iv) and (v).)

(2) Every small business investment corporation shall at all times hold properties referred to in subparagraphs (1)(b)(i) to (iii), the aggregate of the cost amounts of which is not less than 75 per cent of the amount, if any, by which

(a) the aggregate of all amounts each of which is the amount of consideration for the issue of shares of its capital stock or debt to its shareholders or the amount of a contribution of capital by its shareholders received by it more than 90 days before that time

exceeds

(b) the aggregate of

(i) all amounts paid by it before that time to its shareholders as a return of capital or a repayment of debt, and

(ii) the amount, if any, by which the aggregate of its losses from the disposition of properties disposed of before that time exceeds the aggregate of its gains from the disposition of properties disposed of before that time.

(3) For the purposes of subsection (2), where a small business investment corporation disposes of a property referred to in subparagraphs (1)(b)(i) to (iii), it shall be deemed to continue to hold the investment for a period of 90 days following the date of the disposition.

(4) For the purposes of paragraph 149(1)(o.3) of the Act, where a small business investment corporation holds an interest in a partnership or trust that qualified as a small business investment limited partnership or small business investment trust, as the case may be, when the interest was acquired and that, but for this subsection, would cease at a subsequent time to so qualify, the interest in the partnership or trust shall be deemed to be an interest in a small business investment limited partnership or small business investment trust, as the case may be, for the 24 months immediately following the subsequent time.

Definitions [Reg. 5101]: "amount" — ITA 248(1); "arm's length" — ITA 251(1); "borrowed money", "business" — ITA 248(1); "Canadian corporation" — ITA 89(1), 248(1); "corporation" — ITA 248(1), *Interpretation Act* 35(1); "cost amount" — ITA 248(1); "disposed", "disposes" — ITA 248(1) "disposition", "disposition" — ITA 248(1); "month" — *Interpretation Act* 35(1); "partnership" — see ITA 96(1) Notes; "person" — ITA 248(1), Reg. 5104(6); "prescribed" — ITA 248(1); "prescribed venture capital corporation" — Reg. 6700; "property", "registered pension plan" — ITA 248(1); "related" — ITA 251(2)–(6); "share", "shareholder" — ITA 248(1); "small business investment corporation" — Reg. 5101(1); "small business investment limited partnership" — Reg. 5102(1); "small business security" — Reg. 5100(2), 5104(3), (5); "specified circumstances" — Reg. 5104(2); "specified property" — ITA 204 "qualified investment"(a), (b), (c), (f), (g), Reg. 5100(1); "trust" — ITA 104(1), 248(1), (3).

5102. [Small business investment limited partnership] —

(1) For the purpose of this Part, a partnership is a small business investment limited partnership at any particular time if at all times after it was formed and before the particular time

(a) it had only one general partner,

(b) the share of the general partner, as general partner, in any income of the partnership from any source in any place, for any period, was the same as his share, as general partner, in

(i) the income of the partnership from that source in any other place,

(ii) the income of the partnership from any other source,

(iii) the loss of the partnership from any source,

(iv) any capital gain of the partnership, and

(v) any capital loss of the partnership

for that period, except that the share of the general partner, as general partner, in the income or loss of the partnership from specified properties may differ from his share, as general partner, in the income or loss of the partnership from other sources,

(c) the share of the general partner, as general partner, in any income or loss of the partnership for any period was not less than his share, as general partner, in the income or loss of the partnership for any preceding period;

(d) the interests of the limited partners were described by reference to units of the partnership that were identical in all respects,

(e) no limited partner or group of limited partners who did not deal with each other at arm's length held more than 30 per cent of the units of the partnership and, for the purposes of this paragraph,

(i) a small business investment corporation that has not borrowed money and in which no shareholder or group of shareholders who did not deal with each other at arm's length held more than 30 per cent of the outstanding shares of any class of voting stock shall be deemed not to be a limited partner, and

(ii) the general partner shall be deemed not to hold any unit of the partnership as a limited partner, and

(f) its only undertaking was the investing of its funds and its investments consisted solely of

(i) small business securities where, except as provided in subsection 5104(1), the partnership was the first person (other than a broker or dealer in securities) to have acquired the securities and it has owned the securities continuously since they were so acquired,

(ii) property (other than a small business security) that is

(A) a share of the capital stock of a corporation (other than a share that is issued to the partnership and that is either a share described in section 66.3 of the Act or a share in respect of which an amount has been designated under subsection 192(4) of the Act), or

(B) a put, call, warrant or other right to acquire or sell a share described by clause (A),

(iii) specified properties, or

(iv) any combination of properties described in any of subparagraphs (i) to (iii),

(g) it has complied with subsection (2),

(h) it has not borrowed money except for the purpose of earning income from its investments and the amount of any such borrowings at any time did not exceed 20 per cent of the partnership capital at that time, and

(i) it has not accepted deposits.

Notes: Reg. 5102(1) opening words and (f)(ii) amended by P.C. 2005-1508, effective June 29, 2005, due to repeal of ITA Part XI (foreign property limit) and Reg. 5000.

Reg. 5102(1)(f)(ii) added by P.C. 1994-1074, effective 1991.

(2) The aggregate of the cost amounts to a small business investment limited partnership of small business securities held by it at any time shall not be less than the amount, if any, by which the aggregate of

(a) 25 per cent of the amount, if any, by which

(i) the aggregate of all amounts received by it more than 12 months before that time and not more than 24 months before that time as consideration for the issue of its units or in respect of its units

exceeds

(ii) the aggregate of all amounts paid by it before that time to its members and designated by the partnership as a return of the consideration referred to in subparagraph (i),

(b) 50 per cent of the amount, if any, by which

(i) the aggregate of all amounts received by it more than 24 months before that time and not more than 36 months before that time as consideration for the issue of its units or in respect of its units

exceeds

(ii) the aggregate of all amounts paid by it before that time to its members and designated by the partnership as a return of the consideration referred to in subparagraph (i), and

(c) 75 per cent of the amount, if any, by which

(i) the aggregate of all amounts received by it more than 36 months before that time as consideration for the issue of its units or in respect of its units

exceeds

(ii) the aggregate of all amounts paid by it before that time to its members and designated by the partnership as a return of the consideration referred to in subparagraph (i),

exceeds 75 per cent of the amount, if any, by which the aggregate of its losses from the disposition of properties disposed of before that time exceeds the aggregate of its gains from the disposition of properties disposed of before that time.

(3) For the purposes of subsection (2), where a small business investment limited partnership disposes of a small business security it shall be deemed to continue to hold the investment for a period of 90 days following the date of the disposition.

Definitions [Reg. 5102]: "amount" — ITA 248(1); "arm's length" — ITA 251(1); "borrowed money", "business" — ITA 248(1); "capital gain" — ITA 39(1), 248(1); "capital loss" — ITA 39(1)(b), 248(1); "corporation" — ITA 248(1), *Interpretation Act* 35(1); "cost amount" — ITA 248(1); "disposed", "disposes" — ITA 248(1) "disposition", "disposition" — ITA 248(1); "month" — *Interpretation Act* 35(1); "partnership" — see ITA 96(1) Notes; "person" — ITA 248(1), Reg. 5104(6); "property" — ITA 248(1); "share", "shareholder" — ITA 248(1); "small business investment corporation" — Reg. 5101(1); "small business investment limited partnership" — Reg. 5102(1); "small business security" — Reg. 5100(2), 5104(3), (5); "specified property" — ITA 204"qualified investment"(a), (b), (c), (f), (g), Reg. 5100(1).

5103. [Small business investment trust] — (1) For the purposes of this Part and subsection 259(5) of the Act, a trust is a small business investment trust at any particular time if at all times after it was created and before the particular time

(a) it was resident in Canada;

(b) the interests of the beneficiaries under the trust were described by reference to units of the trust that were identical in all respects; and

(c) no beneficiary or group of beneficiaries who did not deal with each other at arm's length held more than 30% of the units of the trust and, for the purposes of this paragraph, a small business investment corporation that has not borrowed money and in which no shareholder or group of shareholders who did not deal with each other at arm's length held more than 30 per cent of the outstanding shares of any class of voting stock shall be deemed not to be a beneficiary;

(d) its only undertaking was the investing of its funds and its investments consisted solely of

(i) small business securities where, except as provided in subsection 5104(1), the trust was the first person (other than a broker or dealer in securities) to have acquired the securities and it has owned the securities continuously since they were so acquired,

(ii) property (other than a small business security) that is

(A) a share of the capital stock of a corporation (other than a share that is issued to the trust and that is either a share described in section 66.3 of the Act or a share in respect of which an amount has been designated under subsection 192(4) of the Act), or

(B) a put, call, warrant or other right to acquire or sell a share described by clause (A),

(iii) specified properties, or

(iv) any combination of properties described in subparagraphs (i) to (iii);

(e) it has complied with subsection (2);

(f) it has not borrowed money except for the purpose of earning income from its investments and the amount of any such borrowings at any time did not exceed 20 per cent of the trust capital at that time; and

(g) it has not accepted deposits.

Notes: Reg. 5103(1) opening words and (d)(ii) amended by P.C. 2005-1508, effective June 29, 2005, due to repeal of ITA Part XI (foreign property limit) and Reg. 5000.

Reg. 5103(1)(d)(ii) added by P.C. 1994-1074, effective 1991.

(2) The aggregate of the cost amounts to a small business investment trust of small business securities held by it at any time shall not be less than the amount, if any, by which the aggregate of

(a) 25 per cent of the amount, if any, by which

(i) the aggregate of all amounts received by it more than 12 months before that time and not more than 24 months before that time as consideration for the issue of its units or in respect of its units

exceeds

(ii) the aggregate of all amounts paid by it before that time to its beneficiaries and designated by the trust as a return of the consideration referred to in subparagraph (i),

(b) 50 per cent of the amount, if any, by which

(i) the aggregate of all amounts received by it more than 24 months before that time and not more than 36 months before that time as consideration for the issue of its units or in respect of its units

exceeds

(ii) the aggregate of all amounts paid by it before that time to its beneficiaries and designated by the trust as a return of the consideration referred to in subparagraph (i), and

(c) 75 per cent of the amount, if any, by which

(i) the aggregate of all amounts received by it more than 36 months before that time as consideration for the issue of its units or in respect of its units

exceeds

(ii) the aggregate of all amounts paid by it before that time to its beneficiaries and designated by the trust as a return of the consideration referred to in subparagraph (i)

exceeds 75 per cent of the amount, if any, by which the aggregate of its losses from the disposition of properties disposed of before that time exceeds the aggregate of its gains from the disposition of properties disposed of before that time.

(3) For the purposes of subsection (2), where a small business investment trust disposes of a small business security it shall be deemed to continue to hold the investment for a period of 90 days following the date of disposition.

Definitions [Reg. 5103]: "amount" — ITA 248(1); "arm's length" — ITA 251(1); "borrowed money", "business" — ITA 248(1); "corporation" — ITA 248(1), *Interpretation Act* 35(1); "cost amount" — ITA 248(1); "disposed", "disposes" — ITA 248(1)"disposition"; "disposition" — ITA 248(1); "month" — *Interpretation Act* 35(1); "person" — ITA 248(1), Reg. 5104(6); "property" — ITA 248(1); "resident in Canada" — ITA 250; "share", "shareholder" — ITA 248(1); "small business investment corporation" — Reg. 5101(1); "small business security" — Reg. 5100(2), 5104(3), (5); "specified property" — ITA 204"qualified investment"(a), (b), (c), (f), (g), Reg. 5100(1); "trust" — ITA 104(1), 248(1), (3).

5104. (1) Notwithstanding paragraph (b) of the definition "qualifying obligation" in subsection 5100(1) and paragraphs 5101(1)(b), 5102(1)(f) and 5103(1)(d), the corporation, partnership or trust, as the case may be, may acquire a small business security that another person (other than a broker or dealer in securities) had previously acquired if

(a) the small business security is a share of the capital stock of an eligible corporation having full voting rights under all circumstances; and

(b) except where the share was acquired in specified circumstances within the meaning of subsection (2), the share was acquired from an officer or employee of the eligible corporation or a person related to the officer or employee.

(2) For the purposes of this Part,

(a) where a person acquires a share of a corporation

(i) as part of a proposal to, or an arrangement with, the corporation's creditors that has been approved by a court under the *Bankruptcy and Insolvency Act* or the *Companies' Creditors Arrangement Act*,

(ii) at a time when all or substantially all of the corporation's assets were under the control of a receiver, receiver-manager, sequestrator or trustee in bankruptcy, or

(iii) at a time when, by reason of financial difficulty, the corporation was in default, or could reasonably be expected to default, on a debt obligation held by a person with whom the corporation was dealing at arm's length,

the person shall be deemed, at any time within 36 months after he acquired the share, to have acquired it in specified circumstances;

(b) where a person acquires a share of a corporation for the purposes of facilitating the disposition of the entire investment of the person in the corporation, the person shall be deemed, at any time within 12 months after he acquired the share, to have acquired it in specified circumstances; and

(c) a qualified trust (within the meaning assigned by subsection 259(3) of the Act) is deemed not to hold any property for any period in respect of which subsection 259(1) of the Act is applicable.

Notes: CRA considers that "substantially all", used in Reg. 5104(2)(a)(ii), means 90% or more.

(3) Where the purchaser of a property that, but for this subsection, would at the time of its acquisition be a small business security (or, where the purchaser is a partnership, a member thereof) knew at the time of acquisition that the issuer of the security would, within the immediately following 12 months, cease to qualify as an eligible corporation, the property shall be deemed never to have been a small business security of the purchaser.

(4) Where a person who holds a share of or an interest in a corporation, partnership or trust that, but for this subsection, would be a small business investment corporation, small business investment limited partnership or small business investment trust knew at the time of issue of the share or interest, as the case may be, or at the time of making any contribution in respect of the share or interest, that

(a) a substantial portion of

(i) the consideration for the issue of the share or interest, or

(ii) the contribution in respect of the share or interest

would not be invested by the corporation, partnership or trust, as the case may be, directly or indirectly in small business securities, and

(b) all or substantially all of

(i) the consideration for the issue of the share or interest, or

(ii) the contribution in respect of the share or interest

would be returned to the purchaser within the immediately following 24 months,

the corporation, partnership or trust shall be deemed to have ceased at that time to be a small business investment corporation, small business investment limited partnership or small business investment trust.

Notes: CRA considers that "substantially all", used in para. (b), means 90% or more.

(5) Where, but for this subsection, a property that qualified as a small business security when it was acquired would cease at a subsequent time to so qualify, the property shall be deemed to be a small business security for the 24 months immediately following the subsequent time.

(6) For the purposes of this Part, a partnership shall be deemed to be a person.

Definitions [Reg. 5104]: "arm's length" — ITA 251(1); "business" — ITA 248(1); "corporation" — ITA 248(1), *Interpretation Act* 35(1); "disposition" — ITA 248(1); "eligible corporation" — Reg. 5100(1); "employee" — ITA 248(1); "month" — *Interpretation Act* 35(1); "officer" — ITA 248(1); "partnership" — see ITA 96(1) Notes; "person" — ITA 248(1), Reg. 5104(6); "property" — ITA 248(1); "related" — ITA 251(2)–(6); "share" — ITA 248(1); "small business investment corporation" — Reg. 5101(1); "small business investment limited partnership" — Reg. 5102(1); "small business security" — Reg. 5100(2), 5104(3), (5); "specified circumstances" — Reg. 5104(2), (2)(b); "trust" — ITA 104(1), 248(1), (3).

PART LII — [5200–5204] CANADIAN MANUFACTURING AND PROCESSING PROFITS

5200. Basic formula — Subject to section 5201, for the purposes of paragraph 125.1(3)(a) [125.1(3)"Canadian manufacturing and processing profits"] of the Act, "Canadian manufacturing and processing profits" of a corporation for a taxation year are hereby prescribed to be that proportion of the corporation's adjusted business income for the year that

(a) the aggregate of its cost of manufacturing and processing capital for the year and its cost of manufacturing and processing labour for the year,

is of

(b) the aggregate of its cost of capital for the year and its cost of labour for the year.

Definitions [Reg. 5200]: "adjusted business income" — Reg. 5202, 5203(1); "corporation" — ITA 248(1), *Interpretation Act* 35(1); "cost of capital", "cost of labour" — Reg. 5202, 5203(1), 5204; "cost of manufacturing and processing capital", "cost of manufacturing and processing labour" — Reg. 5202, 5204; "prescribed" — ITA 248(1); "taxation year" — ITA 249.

Income Tax Folios: S4-F15-C1: Manufacturing and processing [replaces IT-147R3].

Interpretation Bulletins: IT-145R: Canadian manufacturing and processing profits — reduced rate of corporate tax.

5201. Small manufacturers' rule — For the purposes of paragraph 125.1(3)(a) [125.1(3)"Canadian manufacturing and processing profits"] of the Act, "Canadian manufacturing and processing profits" of a corporation for a taxation year are hereby prescribed to be equal to the corporation's adjusted business income for the year where

(a) the activities of the corporation during the year were primarily manufacturing or processing in Canada of goods for sale or lease;

(b) the aggregate of

(i) the aggregate of all amounts each of which is the income of the corporation for the year from an active business minus the aggregate of all amounts each of which is the loss of the corporation for the year from an active business, and

(ii) if the corporation is associated in the year with a Canadian corporation, the aggregate of all amounts each of which is the income of the latter corporation from an active business for its taxation year coinciding with or ending in the year,

did not exceed $200,000;

(c) the corporation was not engaged in any of the activities listed in subparagraphs 125.1(3)(b)(i) to (ix) [125.1(3)"manufacturing or processing"(a) to (k)] of the Act at any time during the year;

(c.1) the corporation was not engaged in the processing of ore (other than iron ore or tar sands) from a mineral resource located outside Canada to any stage that is not beyond the prime metal stage or its equivalent;

(c.2) the corporation was not engaged in the processing of iron ore from a mineral resource located outside Canada to any stage that is not beyond the pellet stage or its equivalent;

(c.3) the corporation was not engaged in the processing of tar sands located outside Canada to any stage that is not beyond the crude oil stage or its equivalent; and

(d) the corporation did not carry on any active business outside Canada at any time during the year.

Notes: For the meaning of "prime metal stage or its equivalent" in (c.1), see Notes to Reg. 1104(5). For M&P see ITA 125.1(3)"manufacturing or processing" Notes.

Reg. 5201(c.1) to (c.3) added by P.C. 1994-230, for 1990 and later taxation years.

Definitions [Reg. 5201]: "active business" — ITA 248(1); "adjusted business income" — Reg. 5202, 5203(1); "amount" — ITA 248(1); "associated" — ITA 256; "Canada" — ITA 255, *Interpretation Act* 35(1); "Canadian corporation" — ITA 89(1), 248(1); "corporation" — ITA 248(1), *Interpretation Act* 35(1); "mineral resource", "prescribed", "tar sands" — ITA 248(1); "taxation year" — ITA 249.

Income Tax Folios: S4-F15-C1: Manufacturing and processing [replaces IT-147R3].

5202. Interpretation — In this Part, except as otherwise provided in section 5203 or 5204,

"adjusted business income" of a corporation for a taxation year means the amount, if any, by which

(a) the aggregate of all amounts each of which is the income of the corporation for the year from an active business carried on in Canada

exceeds

(b) the aggregate of all amounts each of which is the loss of the corporation for the year from an active business carried on in Canada;

"Canadian resource profits" has the meaning that would be assigned to the expression "resource profits" by section 1204 if

(a) section 1204 were read without reference to subparagraph 1204(1)(b)(iv), and

(b) the definition "resource activity" in subsection 1206(1) were read without reference to paragraph (d) of that definition;

Notes: Definition "Canadian resource profits" added by P.C. 1994-230, for 1990 and later tax years. Amended by P.C. 1996-1488 to refer to "section 1204" rather than "subsection 1204(1)", for tax years that begin after Dec. 20, 1991.

"cost of capital" of a corporation for a taxation year means an amount equal to the aggregate of

(a) 10 per cent of the aggregate of all amounts each of which is the gross cost to the corporation of a property referred to in paragraph 1100(1)(e), (f), (g) or (h), paragraph 1102(1)(d) or (g) or Schedule II that

(i) was owned by the corporation at the end of the year, and

(ii) was used by the corporation at any time during the year, and

(b) the aggregate of all amounts each of which is the rental cost incurred by the corporation during the year for the use of any property a portion of the gross cost of which would be included by virtue of paragraph (a) if the property were owned by the corporation at the end of the year,

but for the purposes of this definition, the gross cost of a property or rental cost for the use of any property does not include that portion of those costs that reflects the extent to which the property was used by the corporation during the year

(c) in an active business carried on outside Canada, or

(d) to earn Canadian investment income or foreign investment income as defined in subsection 129(4) of the Act;

"cost of labour" of a corporation for a taxation year means an amount equal to the aggregate of

(a) the salaries and wages paid or payable during the year to all employees of the corporation for services performed during the year, and

(b) all other amounts each of which is an amount paid or payable during the year for the performance during the year, by any person other than an employee of the corporation, of functions relating to

(i) the management or administration of the corporation,

(ii) scientific research and experimental development, or

(iii) a service or function that would normally be performed by an employee of the corporation,

but for the purposes of this definition, the salaries and wages referred to in paragraph (a) or other amounts referred to in paragraph (b) do not include that portion of those amounts that

(c) was included in the gross cost to the corporation of a property (other than a property that was manufactured by the corporation and leased during the year by the corporation to another person) that was included in computing the cost of capital of the corporation for the year, or

(d) was related to an active business carried on outside Canada by the corporation;

Notes: Functions performed by a "person" include those performed by a corporation: *Quali-T-Tube ULC*, 2005 TCC 373.

"Cost of labour"(b)(ii) amended by P.C. 2000-1095, for costs incurred after Feb. 27, 1995, to refer to SR&ED instead of "scientific research as defined in section 2900". The definition of SR&ED was moved from Reg. 2900(1) to ITA 248(1).

"cost of manufacturing and processing capital" of a corporation for a taxation year means 100/85 of that portion of the cost of capi-

tal of the corporation for that year that reflects the extent to which each property included in the calculation thereof was used directly in qualified activities of the corporation during the year, but the amount so calculated shall not exceed the cost of capital of the corporation for the year;

"cost of manufacturing and processing labour" of a corporation for a taxation year means 100/75 of that portion of the cost of labour of the corporation for that year that reflects the extent to which

(a) the salaries and wages included in the calculation thereof were paid or payable to persons for the portion of their time that they were directly engaged in qualified activities of the corporation during the year, and

(b) the other amounts included in the calculation thereof were paid or payable to persons for the performance of functions that would be directly related to qualified activities of the corporation during the year if those persons were employees of the corporation,

but the amount so calculated shall not exceed the cost of labour of the corporation for the year;

"gross cost" to a particular person of a property at any time means, in respect of property that has become available for use by the particular person for the purposes of subsection 13(26) of the Act, the capital cost to the particular person of the property computed without reference to subsections 13(7.1), (7.4) and (10), sections 21 and 80 and paragraph 111(4)(e) of the Act and, in respect of any other property, nil, and where the particular person acquired the property

(a) in the course of a reorganization in respect of which, if a dividend were received by the particular person in the course of the reorganization, subsection 55(2) of the Act would not apply to the dividend by reason of the application of paragraph 55(3)(b) of the Act, or

(b) from another person with whom the particular person was not dealing at arm's length (otherwise than by reason of a right referred to in paragraph 251(5)(b) of the Act) immediately after the property was acquired,

the capital cost to the particular person of the property for the purposes of this definition shall be computed as if the property had been acquired at a capital cost equal to the gross cost of the property to the person from whom the property was acquired by the particular person;

Notes: Definition "gross cost" amended by P.C. 1994-139, for 1985 and later taxation years, but with certain transitional rules if the taxpayer elected by notifying Revenue Canada by the return due date for the first taxation year that ended after Feb. 9, 1994.

"qualified activities" means

(a) any of the following activities, when they are performed in Canada in connection with manufacturing or processing (not including the activities listed in subparagraphs 125.1(3)(b)(i) to (ix) [125.1(3)"manufacturing or processing"(a) to (k)] of the Act) in Canada of goods for sale or lease:

(i) engineering design of products and production facilities,

(ii) receiving and storing of raw materials,

(iii) producing, assembling and handling of goods in process,

(iv) inspecting and packaging of finished goods,

(v) line supervision,

(vi) production support activities including security, cleaning, heating and factory maintenance,

(vii) quality and production control,

(viii) repair of production facilities, and

(ix) pollution control,

(b) all other activities that are performed in Canada directly in connection with manufacturing or processing (not including the activities listed in subparagraphs 125.1(3)(b)(i) to (ix) [125.1(3)"manufacturing or processing"(a) to (k)] of the Act) in Canada of goods for sale or lease, and

(c) scientific research and experimental development, as defined in section 2900, carried on in Canada,

but does not include any of

(d) storing, shipping, selling and leasing of finished goods,

(e) purchasing of raw materials,

(f) administration, including clerical and personnel activities,

(g) purchase and resale operations,

(h) data processing, and

(i) providing facilities for employees, including cafeterias, clinics and recreational facilities;

Notes: See ITA 125.1(3)"manufacturing or processing" Notes re that term.

The definition of SR&ED in Reg. 2900(1) has been repealed. Finance is expected to change para. (c) so that it uses the definition in ITA 248(1).

Definition "qualified activities" amended by P.C. 1994-139, to add "and experimental development" and "carried on in Canada", effective for SR&ED done or carried on after Dec. 23, 1991, other than SR&ED done or carried on by or on behalf of a taxpayer pursuant to an agreement in writing entered into by the taxpayer by that date.

"rental cost" of a property means the rents incurred for the use of that property;

"resource profits" has the meaning assigned by section 1204;

Notes: Definition "resource profits" added by P.C. 1994-230, for 1990 and later taxation years. Amended by P.C. 1996-1488 for taxation years that begin after Dec. 20, 1991.

"salaries and wages" means salaries, wages and commissions, but does not include any other type of remuneration, any superannuation or pension benefits, any retiring allowances or any amount referred to in section 6 or 7 of the Act;

"specified percentage" for a taxation year means

(a) where the year commences after 1998, 100%, and

(b) [No longer relevant.]

Notes: Definition "specified percentage" added by P.C. 1994-230, for 1990 and later tax years.

Definitions [Reg. 5202]: "active business", "amount" — ITA 248(1); "arm's length" — ITA 251(1); "Canada" — ITA 255, *Interpretation Act* 35(1); "corporation" — ITA 248(1), *Interpretation Act* 35(1); "cost of capital", "cost of labour" — Reg. 5202, 5203(1), 5204; "dividend", "employee" — ITA 248(1); "gross cost" — Reg. 5202, 5204; "person", "property" — ITA 248(1); "qualified activities" — Reg. 5202; "related" — ITA 251(2)–(6); "rental cost" — Reg. 5202; "retiring allowance" — ITA 248(1); "salaries and wages" — ITA 248(1), Reg. 5202; "scientific research and experimental development" — ITA 248(1); "superannuation or pension benefit" — ITA 248(1); "taxation year" — ITA 249.

Income Tax Folios: S4-F15-C1: Manufacturing and processing [replaces IT-147R3].

5203. Resource income — **(1)** Where a corporation has resource activities for a taxation year the following rules apply, except as otherwise provided in section 5204

"adjusted business income" of the corporation for the year means the amount, if any, by which

(a) the amount otherwise determined under section 5202 to be the adjusted business income of the corporation for the year

exceeds the total of

(b) the total, if any, by which the corporation's net resource income for the year exceeds the corporation's net resource adjustment for the year, and

(c) all amounts each of which is an amount in respect of refund interest included in computing the taxpayer's income for the year, to the extent that the amount is included in the amount otherwise determined to be the adjusted business income, within the meaning of section 5202, of the corporation for the year;

(d) [Repealed]

Related Provisions: Reg. 5203(3.1) — Net resource adjustment.

Notes: Definition amended by P.C. 2007-114 (for tax years that begin after 2006), 1999-629, 1996-1488.

"cost of capital" of the corporation for the year means the amount, if any, by which

(a) the amount otherwise determined under section 5202 to be the cost of capital of the corporation for the year

exceeds

(b) that portion of the gross cost of property or rental cost for the use of property included in computing the cost of capital of the corporation for the year that reflects the extent to which the property was used by the corporation during the year,

(i) in activities engaged in for the purpose of earning Canadian resource profits of the corporation, or

(ii) in activities referred to in subparagraph 66(15)(b)(i), (ii) or (v) [66(15)"Canadian exploration and development expenses"(a), (b) or (e)], subparagraph 66(15)(e)(i) or (ii) [66(15)"foreign exploration and development expenses"(a) or (b)], subparagraph 66.1(6)(a)(i), (ii), (iii) or (v) [66.1(6)"Canadian exploration expense"(a), (c), (f) or (i)] or subparagraph 66.2(5)(a)(i), (ii) or (v) [66.2(5)"Canadian development expense"(a), (c) or (g)] of the Act;

Notes: Subpara. (b)(i) amended by P.C. 1994-230, for 1990 and later taxation years.

"cost of labour" of the corporation for the year means the amount, if any, by which

(a) the amount otherwise determined under section 5202 to be the cost of labour of the corporation for the year

exceeds

(b) that portion of the salaries and wages and other amounts included in computing the cost of labour of the corporation for the year that,

(i) was related to the activities engaged in for the purpose of earning Canadian resource profits of the corporation, or

(ii) was included in the Canadian exploration and development expenses, foreign exploration and development expenses, Canadian exploration expense or Canadian development expense, within the meanings assigned by paragraphs 66(15)(b) and (e) [66(15)"Canadian exploration and development expenses" and "foreign exploration and development expenses"], paragraph 66.1(6)(a) [66.1(6)"Canadian exploration expense"] and 66.2(5)(a) [66.2(5)"Canadian development expense"] of the Act respectively, of the corporation.

Notes: Subpara. (b)(i) amended by P.C. 1994-230, for 1990 and later taxation years.

(2) ["Resource activities"] — For the purposes of subsection (1), a corporation has "resource activities" for a taxation year if

(a) in computing its income for the year, an amount is deductible pursuant to any of sections 65 to 66.2 of the Act;

(b) the corporation was at any time during the year engaged in activities for the purpose of earning resource profits of the corporation; or

(c) in computing the corporation's income for the year, an amount was included pursuant to section 59 of the Act.

Notes: Reg. 5203(2) amended by P.C. 2007-114 (for tax years that begin after 2006), 1994-230.

(3) ["Net resource income"] — In subsection (1), "net resource income" of a corporation for a taxation year means the amount, if any, by which the total of

(a) the resource profits of the corporation for the year, and

(b) the amount, if any, by which

(i) the total of amounts included in computing the income of the corporation for the year, from an active business carried on in Canada, pursuant to section 59 of the Act (other than amounts that may reasonably be regarded as having been included in computing the resource profits of the corporation for the year),

exceeds

(ii) the total of amounts deducted in computing the income of the corporation for the year under section 64 of the Act, as that section applies with respect to dispositions occurring before November 13, 1981 and to dispositions occurring after November 12, 1981 pursuant to the terms in existence on that date of an offer or agreement in writing made or entered into on or before that date, except those amounts that may reasonably be regarded as having been deducted in computing the resource profits of the corporation for the year,

exceeds the total of

(c) the total of amounts deducted in computing the income of the corporation for the year under section 65 of the Act (other than amounts that may reasonably be regarded as having been deducted in computing the resource profits of the corporation for the year), and

(d) the specified percentage for the year of the amount, if any, by which

(i) the corporation's resource profits for the year

exceeds the total of

(ii) the corporation's Canadian resource profits for the year, and

(iii) the earned depletion base (within the meaning assigned by subsection 1205(1)) of the corporation at the beginning of its immediately following taxation year.

Notes: Reg. 5203(3) amended by P.C. 1994-230, for 1990 and later taxation years.

(3.1) ["Net resource adjustment"] — In subsection (1), the net resource adjustment of a corporation for a taxation year is the amount determined by the formula

$$A - B$$

where

A is the amount of Canadian resource profits of the corporation for the year, and

B is the amount that would be the Canadian resource profits of the corporation for the year if

(a) subsections 1204(1) and (1.1) provided for the computation of negative amounts where the amounts subtracted in computing gross resource profits (as defined by subsection 1204(1)) and resource profits exceed the amounts added in computing those amounts, and

(b) paragraph 1206(3)(a) applied so that a negative amount of resource profits of a partnership for a fiscal period that ended in the year were, to the extent of the corporation's share thereof, deducted in computing the corporation's resource profits for the year.

Related Provisions: ITA 257 — Negative amounts in formulas.

Notes: Reg. 5203(3.1) added by P.C. 1999-629, for taxation years that begin after Dec. 20, 1991.

(4) ["Refund interest"] — For the purpose of subsection (1), "refund interest" means an amount that is received, or that becomes receivable, after March 6, 1996 from an authority (including a government or municipality) situated in Canada as a consequence of the overpayment of a tax that was not deductible under the Act in computing any taxpayer's income and that was imposed by an Act of Canada or a province or a bylaw of a municipality.

Notes: Reg. 5203(4) amended, effectively to repeal paras. (b) and (c), by P.C. 2007-114, effective for taxation years that begin after 2006.

Reg. 5203(4) added by P.C. 1996-1488, for taxation years that end after March 6, 1996.

Definitions [Reg. 5203]: "active business" — ITA 248(1); "adjusted business income" — Reg. 5202, 5203(1); "amount" — ITA 248(1); "Canada" — ITA 255, *Interpretation Act* 35(1); "Canadian development expense" — ITA 66.2(5), 248(1); "Canadian exploration and development expenses" — ITA 66(15), 248(1); "Canadian exploration expense" — ITA 66.1(6), 248(1); "Canadian resource profits" — Reg. 5202; "corporation" — ITA 248(1), *Interpretation Act* 35(1); "cost of capital", "cost of labour" — Reg. 5202, 5203(1), 5204; "disposition" — ITA 248(1); "foreign exploration and development expenses" — ITA 66(15), 248(1); "gross cost" — Reg. 5202,

5204; "net resource adjustment" — Reg. 5203(3.1); "net resource income — Reg. 5203(3); "person", "property" — ITA 248(1); "province" — *Interpretation Act* 35(1); "refund interest" — Reg. 5203(4); "related" — ITA 251(2)–(6); "rental cost" — Reg. 5202; "resource activities — Reg. 5203(2); "resource profits" — Reg. 5202; "salaries and wages" — ITA 248(1), Reg. 5202; "specified percentage" — Reg. 5202; "taxation year" — ITA 249; "taxpayer" — ITA 248(1); "writing" — *Interpretation Act* 35(1).

Income Tax Folios: S4-F15-C1: Manufacturing and processing [replaces IT-147R3].

5204. Partnerships — Where a corporation is a member of a partnership at any time in a taxation year of the corporation, the following rules apply:

"cost of capital" of the corporation for the year means an amount equal to the aggregate of

(a) 10 per cent of the aggregate of all amounts each of which is the gross cost to the corporation of a property referred to in paragraph 1100(1)(e), (f), (g) or (h), paragraph 1102(1)(d) or (g) or Schedule II that

(i) was owned by the corporation at the end of the year, and

(ii) was used by the corporation at any time during the year,

(b) the aggregate of all amounts each of which is the rental cost incurred by the corporation during the year for the use of any property a portion of the gross cost of which would be included by virtue of paragraph (a) if the property were owned by the corporation at the end of the year, and

(c) that proportion of the aggregate of the amounts that would be determined under paragraphs (a) and (b) in respect of the partnership for its fiscal period coinciding with or ending in the taxation year of the corporation if the references in those paragraphs to "the corporation" were read as references to "the partnership" and the references in those paragraphs to "the year" were read as references to "the fiscal period of the partnership coinciding with or ending in the year", that

(i) the corporation's share of the income or loss of the partnership for that fiscal period

is of

(ii) the income or loss of the partnership for that fiscal period, as the case may be,

but for the purposes of this definition, the gross cost of a property or rental cost for the use of any property does not include that portion of those costs that reflects the extent to which the property was used by the corporation during the year or by the partnership during its fiscal period coinciding with or ending in the year

(d) in an active business carried on outside Canada,

(e) to earn Canadian investment income or foreign investment income as defined in subsection 129(4) of the Act on the assumption that subsection 129(4) of the Act applied to a partnership as well as to a corporation,

(f) in activities engaged in for the purpose of earning Canadian resource profits of the corporation or the partnership, as the case may be, or

(g) in activities referred to in subparagraph 66(15)(b)(i), (ii) or (v) [66(15)"Canadian exploration and development expenses"(a), (b) or (e)], subparagraph 66(15)(e)(i) or (ii) [66(15)"foreign exploration and development expenses"(a) or (b)], subparagraph 66.1(6)(a)(i), (ii), (iii) or (v) [66.1(6)"Canadian exploration expense"(a), (c), (f) or (i)] or subparagraph 66.2(5)(a)(i), (ii) or (v) [66.2(5)"Canadian development expense"(a), (c) or (g)] of the Act;

Notes: Para. (f) amended by P.C. 1994-230, for 1990 and later taxation years.

"cost of labour" of the corporation for the year means an amount equal to the aggregate of

(a) the salaries and wages paid or payable during the year to all employees of the corporation for services performed during the year,

(b) all other amounts each of which is an amount paid or payable during the year for the performance during the year, by any person other than an employee of the corporation, of functions relating to

(i) the management or administration of the corporation,

(ii) scientific research as defined in section 2900, or

(iii) a service or function that would normally be performed by an employee of the corporation, and

(c) that proportion of the aggregate of the amounts that would be determined under paragraphs (a) and (b) in respect of the partnership for its fiscal period coinciding with or ending in the taxation year of the corporation if the references in those paragraphs to the "corporation" were read as references to "the partnership" and the references in those paragraphs to "the year" were read as references to "the fiscal period of the partnership coinciding with or ending in the year", that

(i) the corporation's share of the income or loss of the partnership for that fiscal period

is of

(ii) the income or loss of the partnership for that fiscal period, as the case may be,

but for the purposes of this definition, the salaries and wages referred to in paragraph (a) or other amounts referred to in paragraph (b), of the corporation or the partnership, as the case may be, do not include that portion of those amounts that

(d) was included in the gross cost to the corporation or partnership of a property (other than a property that was manufactured by the corporation or partnership and leased during the year by the corporation or the partnership to another person) that was included in computing the cost of capital of the corporation for the year,

(e) was related to an active business carried on outside Canada by the corporation or the partnership,

(f) was related to the activities engaged in for the purpose of earning Canadian resource profits of the corporation or the partnership, as the case may be, or

(g) was included in the Canadian exploration and development expenses, foreign exploration and development expenses, Canadian exploration expense or Canadian development expense, within the meanings assigned by paragraphs 66(15)(b) and (e) [66(15)"Canadian exploration and development expenses" and "foreign exploration and development expenses"], 66.1(6)(a) [66.1(6)"Canadian exploration expense"] and 66.2(5)(a) [66.2(5)"Canadian development expense"] of the Act respectively, of the corporation;

Notes: Para. (f) amended by P.C. 1994-230, for 1990 and later taxation years.

"cost of manufacturing and processing capital" of the corporation for the year means 100/85 of that portion of the cost of capital of the corporation for that year that reflects the extent to which each property included in the calculation thereof was used directly in qualified activities

(a) of the corporation during the year, or

(b) of the partnership during its fiscal period coinciding with or ending in the year, as the case may be,

but the amount so calculated shall not exceed the cost of capital of the corporation for the year;

"cost of manufacturing and processing labour" of the corporation for the year means 100/75 of that portion of the cost of labour of the corporation for that year that reflects the extent to which

(a) the salaries and wages included in the calculation thereof were paid or payable to persons for the portion of their time that they were directly engaged in qualified activities

(i) of the corporation during the year, or

(ii) of the partnership during its fiscal period coinciding with or ending in the year, and

(b) the other amounts included in the calculation thereof were paid or payable to persons for the performance of functions that would be directly related to qualified activities

(i) of the corporation during the year, or

(ii) of the partnership during its fiscal period coinciding with or ending in the year,

if those persons were employees of the corporation or the partnership, as the case may be,

but the amount so calculated shall not exceed the cost of labour of the corporation for the year;

"gross cost" of a property at any time means

(a) in respect of a property that has become available for use by the partnership for the purposes of subsection 13(26) of the Act, the capital cost to the partnership of the property computed without reference to subsections 13(7.1), (7.4) and (10) and sections 21 and 80 of the Act, and

(b) in respect of any other property of the partnership, nil

and, for the purposes of paragraph (a), if the partnership acquired the property from a person who was a majority-interest partner of the partnership immediately after the property was acquired, the capital cost to the partnership of the property is to be computed as if the property had been acquired at a capital cost equal to the gross cost to the person of the property, except that if the property was partnership property on December 31, 1971, its gross cost is its capital cost to the partnership as determined under subsection 20(3) or (5) of the *Income Tax Application Rules*.

Notes: Definition amended by 2013 budget bill #2, effective Dec. 12, 2013, to change "majority interest partner of the partnership (within the meaning assigned by subsection 97(3.1) of the Act)" to "majority-interest partner" (with a hyphen).

Definition "gross cost" amended by P.C. 1994-139, last change effective for taxation years ending before Feb. 9, 1994.

Definitions [Reg. 5204]: "active business", "amount" — ITA 248(1); "Canada" — ITA 255, *Interpretation Act* 35(1); "Canadian development expense" — ITA 66.2(5), 248(1); "Canadian exploration and development expenses" — ITA 66(15), 248(1); "Canadian exploration expense" — ITA 66.1(6), 248(1); "Canadian resource profits" — Reg. 5202; "corporation" — ITA 248(1), *Interpretation Act* 35(1); "cost of capital", "cost of labour" — Reg. 5202, 5203(1), 5204; "employee" — ITA 248(1); "fiscal period" — ITA 249.1; "foreign exploration and development expenses" — ITA 66(15), 248(1); "gross cost" — Reg. 5202, 5204; "majority-interest partner" — ITA 248(1); "partnership" — see ITA 96(1) Notes; "person", "property" — ITA 248(1); "qualified activities" — Reg. 5202; "related" — ITA 251(2)–(6); "rental cost" — Reg. 5202; "salaries and wages" — ITA 248(1), Reg. 5202; "share" — ITA 248(1); "taxation year" — ITA 249.

PART LIII — [5300–5301] INSTALMENT BASE

5300. [Individuals] — For the purposes of subsections 155(2), 156(3) and 161(9) of the Act, the instalment base of an individual for a taxation year is the amount by which

(a) the individual's tax payable under Part I of the Act for the year, determined before taking into consideration the specified future tax consequences for the year

exceeds

(b) the amount deemed by subsection 120(2) of the Act to have been paid on account of the individual's tax under Part I of the Act for the year, determined before taking into consideration the specified future tax consequences for the year.

Related Provisions: ITA 248(1) — Definition of "specified future tax consequence".

Notes: Reg. 5300 amended by P.C. 1999-196, effective for computing instalments for 1997 and later taxation years.

Definitions [Reg. 5300]: "amount", "individual", "prescribed", "specified future tax consequence" — ITA 248(1); "taxation year" — ITA 249.

5301. Corporations under Part I of the Act — (1) Subject to subsections 5301 (6) and (8), for the purposes of subsections 157(4) and 161(9) of the Act, the first instalment base of a corporation for a particular taxation year means the product obtained when the aggregate of

(a) the tax payable under Part I of the Act by the corporation for its taxation year preceding the particular year, and

(b) the total of the taxes payable by the corporation under Parts VI, VI.1 and XIII.1 of the Act for its taxation year preceding the particular year

is multiplied by the ratio that 365 is of the number of days in that preceding year.

Related Provisions: ITA 261(11)(a)(ii) — Functional currency reporting; Reg. 5301(10) — Tax payable under Part I.

Notes: The "first instalment base" is not reduced by the prior year's dividend refund under ITA 129: VIEWS doc 2003-0017995. (The dividend refund does not actually reduce Part I tax, and ITA 157(3)(b) provides an instalment adjustment for it.)

See Notes to ITA 191.3(3) re inclusion of Part VI.1 tax liability.

Reg. 5301(1) amended by P.C. 2009-1869 (last change effective for tax years that begin after 2007), 1999-196, 1994-556.

(2) Subject to subsections (6) and (8), for the purposes of subsections 157(4) and 161(9) of the Act, the "second instalment base" of a corporation for a particular taxation year means the amount of the first instalment base of the corporation for the taxation year immediately preceding the particular year.

Related Provisions: ITA 261(11)(a)(iii) — Effect of functional currency election.

(3) For the purposes of subsection (1), where the number of days in the taxation year of a corporation immediately preceding the particular taxation year referred to therein is less than 183, the amount determined for the corporation under that subsection shall be the greater of

(a) the amount otherwise determined for it under subsection (1); and

(b) the amount that would be determined for it under subsection (1) if the reference in that subsection to "its taxation year preceding the particular year" were read as a reference to "its last taxation year, preceding the particular year, in which the number of days exceeds 182".

Notes: Reg. 5301(3)(b) amended by P.C. 1999-196, retroactive to 1989.

(4) Notwithstanding subsections (1) and (2), for the purposes of subsections 157(4) and 161(9) of the Act,

(a) where a particular taxation year of a new corporation that was formed as a result of an amalgamation (within the meaning assigned by section 87 of the Act) is its first taxation year,

(i) its "first instalment base" for the particular year means the total of all amounts each of which is equal to the product obtained when the total of

(A) the tax payable under Part I of the Act, and

(B) the total of the taxes payable under Parts VI, VI.1 and XIII.1 of the Act

by a predecessor corporation (as defined in section 87 of the Act) for its last taxation year is multiplied by the ratio that 365 is of the number of days in that year, and

(ii) its "second instalment base" for the particular year means the aggregate of all amounts each of which is an amount equal to the amount of the first instalment base of a predecessor corporation for its last taxation year; and

(b) where a particular taxation year of a new corporation referred to in paragraph (a) is its second taxation year,

(i) its "first instalment base" for the particular year means

(A) where the number of days in its first taxation year is greater than 182, the amount that would, but for this subsection, be determined under subsection (1) for the year, and

(B) in any other case, the greater of the amount that would, but for this subsection, be determined under subsection (1) for the year and its first instalment base for its first taxation year, and

(ii) its "second instalment base" for the particular year means the amount of the first instalment base of the new corporation for its first taxation year.

Related Provisions: ITA 261(11)(a)(ii), (iii) — Effect of functional currency election.

Notes: Reg. 5301(4) amended by P.C. 2009-1869 (last change effective for tax years that begin after 2007), 1999-196, 1994-556.

(5) For the purposes of subsection (4), where the number of days in the last taxation year of a predecessor corporation is less than 183, the amount determined under subparagraph (4)(a)(i) in respect of the predecessor corporation shall be the greater of

(a) the amount otherwise determined under subparagraph (4)(a)(i) in respect of the predecessor corporation; and

(b) the amount of the first instalment base of the predecessor corporation for its last taxation year.

(6) Subject to subsection (7), where a subsidiary within the meaning of subsection 88(1) of the Act is winding up, and, at a particular time in the course of the winding up, all or substantially all of the property of the subsidiary has been distributed to a parent within the meaning of subsection 88(1) of the Act, the following rules apply:

(a) there shall be added to the amount of the parent's first instalment base for its taxation year that includes the particular time the amount of the subsidiary's first instalment base for its taxation year that includes the particular time;

(b) there shall be added to the amount of the parent's second instalment base for its taxation year that includes the particular time the amount of the subsidiary's second instalment base for its taxation year that includes the particular time;

(c) there shall be added to the amount of the parent's first instalment base for its taxation year immediately following its taxation year referred to in paragraph (a) the amount that is the proportion of the subsidiary's first instalment base for its taxation year referred to in paragraph (a) that

(i) the number of complete months that ended at or before the particular time in the taxation year of the parent that includes the particular time

is of

(ii) 12; and

(d) there shall be added to the amount of the parent's second instalment base for its taxation year immediately following its taxation year referred to in paragraph (a) the amount of the subsidiary's first instalment base for its taxation year that includes the particular time.

Notes: CRA considers that "substantially all" means 90% or more.

(7) The amount of an instalment of tax for the taxation year referred to in paragraphs (6)(a) and (b) that a parent is deemed under subsection 161(4.1) of the Act to have been liable to pay before the particular time referred to in subsection (6) shall be determined as if subsection (6) were not applicable in respect of a distribution of property described in that subsection occurring after the day on or before which the instalment was required to be paid.

(8) Subject to subsection (9), if at a particular time a corporation (in this subsection referred as the "transferor") has disposed of all or substantially all of its property to another corporation with which it was not dealing at arm's length (in this subsection and subsection (9) referred to as the "transferee") and subsection 85(1), (2) or 142.7(3) of the Act applied in respect of the disposition of any of the property, the following rules apply:

(a) there shall be added to the amount of the transferee's first instalment base for its taxation year that includes the particular time the amount of the transferor's first instalment base for its taxation year that includes the particular time;

(b) there shall be added to the amount of the transferee's second instalment base for its taxation year that includes the particular time the amount of the transferor's second instalment base for its taxation year that includes the particular time;

(c) there shall be added to the amount of the transferee's first instalment base for its taxation year immediately following its taxation year referred to in paragraph (a) the amount that is the proportion of the transferor's first instalment base for its taxation year referred to in paragraph (a) that

(i) the number of complete months that ended at or before the particular time in the taxation year of the transferee that includes the particular time

is of

(ii) 12; and

(d) there shall be added to the amount of the transferee's second instalment base for its taxation year immediately following its taxation year referred to in paragraph (a) the amount of the transferor's first instalment base for its taxation year that includes the particular time.

Notes: CRA considers that "substantially all" means 90% or more.

Reg. 5301(8) opening words amended to add reference to ITA 142.7(3) by P.C. 2009-1869, effective June 28, 1999.

(9) The amount of an instalment of tax for the taxation year referred to in paragraphs (8)(a) and (b) that a transferee is deemed under subsection 161(4.1) of the Act to have been liable to pay before the particular time referred to in subsection (8) shall be determined as if subsection (8) were not applicable in respect of a disposition of property described in that subsection occurring after the day on or before which the instalment was required to be paid.

(10) For the purpose of this section, tax payable under Part I, VI or XIII.1 of the Act by a corporation for a taxation year means the corporation's tax payable for the year under the relevant Part, determined before taking into consideration the specified future tax consequences for the year.

Related Provisions: ITA 248(1) — Definition of "specified future tax consequence".

Notes: See VIEWS doc 2011-0411121I7 (general explanation).

Reg. 5301(10) amended by P.C. 2009-1869 (for tax years that begin after 2007), 1999-196. Added by P.C. 1994-556.

Definitions [Reg. 5301]: "amount" — ITA 248(1); "arm's length" — ITA 251(1); "corporation" — ITA 248(1), *Interpretation Act* 35(1); "disposed" — ITA 248(1)"disposition"; "disposition" — ITA 248(1); "first instalment base" — Reg. 5301(4)(a)(i); "month" — *Interpretation Act* 35(1); "property" — ITA 248(1); "second instalment base" — Reg. 5301(4)(a)(ii); "specified future tax consequence" — ITA 248(1); "taxation year" — ITA 249; "transferee", "transferor" — Reg. 5301(8).

PART LIV — [5400–5401] [REPEALED]

5400–5401. [Repealed]

Notes: Reg. 5400-5401 repealed by P.C. 2011-936, effective for any obligation settled or extinguished in taxation years that end after Feb. 21, 1994 [corrected from 1984 by 2017 budget bill #2 s. 105], except where the new version of ITA 80 does not apply (see Notes at end of ITA 80). These regs applied for the pre-1994 debt forgiveness rules (which still apply to an obligation settled or extinguished under an agreement in writing entered into by Feb. 21, 1994).

PART LV — [5500–5503] PRESCRIBED PROGRAMS AND BENEFITS

5500. Canadian Home Insulation Program — For the purposes of paragraphs 12(1)(u), 56(1)(s) and 212(1)(s) of the Act, the Canadian Home Insulation Program, as authorized and described in Vote 11a of *Appropriation Act No. 3, 1977–78*, as amended, Energy, Mines and Resources Vote 35, Main Estimates, 1981-82 as authorized by *Appropriation Act No. 1, 1981–82*, as amended, or the *Canadian Home Insulation Program Act*, is hereby prescribed to be a program of the Government of Canada relating to home insulation.

Definitions [Reg. 5500]: "Canada" — ITA 255, *Interpretation Act* 35(1); "prescribed" — ITA 248(1).

5501. Canada Oil Substitution Program — For the purposes of paragraphs 12(1)(u), 56(1)(s) and 212(1)(s) of the Act, the Canada Oil Substitution Program, as authorized and described in paragraph (a) or (b) of Energy, Mines and Resources Vote 45, Main Estimates, 1981–82 as authorized by *Appropriation Act No. 1, 1981–82*, as amended, or the *Oil Substitution and Conservation Act* is hereby prescribed to be a program of the Government of Canada relating to energy conversion.

Definitions [Reg. 5501]: "Canada" — ITA 255, *Interpretation Act* 35(1); "prescribed" — ITA 248(1).

5502. Benefits under government assistance programs — For the purposes of subparagraph 56(1)(a)(vi) and paragraph 153(1)(m) of the Act, the following benefits are prescribed:

(a) benefits under the *Labour Adjustment Benefits Act*;

(b) benefits under programs to provide income assistance payments, established pursuant to agreements under section 5 of the *Department of Labour Act*; and

(c) benefits under programs to provide income assistance payments, administered pursuant to agreements under section 5 of the *Department of Fisheries and Oceans Act*.

Notes: Reg. 5502 added by P.C. 1995-1023, June 23, 1995, effective for benefits received after Oct. 1991 (for ITA 56(1)(a)(vi)), and for benefits paid after Oct. 1991 (for ITA 153(1)(m)). The referenced programs include the Program for Older Worker Adjustment, the Plant Worker Adjustment Program, the Northern Cod Adjustment and Recovery Program, the Atlantic Groundfish Adjustment Program and the Atlantic Groundfish Strategy.

In *Layton*, [1995] 2 C.T.C. 2408 and *Law*, [1996] 1 C.T.C. 2252 (both decided March 14, 1995 before Reg. 5502 was passed), the TCC ruled that payments received in 1993 were not taxable because they were not (yet) prescribed.

Definitions [Reg. 5502]: "prescribed" — ITA 248(1).

5503. Stabilization of farm income — **(1)** For the purposes of the definition "NISA Fund No. 2" in subsection 248(1) of the Act, a prescribed fund is Fonds 2 as defined under the Agri-Québec program established by La Financière agricole du Québec.

(2) For the purposes of the definition "net income stabilization account" in subsection 248(1) of the Act, a prescribed account is an account created under the Agri-Québec program established by La Financière agricole du Québec.

Notes: Reg. 5503 added by 2011 budget bill #2, for 2011 and later taxation years.

Definitions [Reg. 5503]: "NISA Fund No. 2", "prescribed" — ITA 248(1).

PART LVI — [5600] PRESCRIBED DISTRIBUTIONS

5600. For the purpose of section 86.1 of the Act, the following distributions of shares are prescribed:

(a) the distribution by Active Biotech AB, on May 10, 1999, of shares of Wilhelm Sonesson AB;

(b) the distribution by Orckit Communications Ltd., on June 30, 2000, of shares of Tioga Technologies Ltd.;

(c) the distribution by Electrolux AB, on June 12, 2006, of shares of Husqvarna AB;

(d) the distribution by Fiat S.p.A., on January 1, 2011 to its common shareholders, of common shares of Fiat Industrial S.p.A;

(e) the distribution by Foster's Group Limited, on May 9, 2011 to its common shareholders, of common shares of Treasury Wine Estates Limited;

(f) the distribution by Telecom Corporation of New Zealand Limited, on November 30, 2011 to its common shareholders, of common shares of Chorus Limited;

(g) the distribution by Tyco International Ltd. of Switzerland, on September 28, 2012 to its common shareholders, of common shares of Pentair Ltd. of Switzerland;

(h) the distribution by Siemens AG, on July 5, 2013 to its common shareholders, of common shares of OSRAM Licht AG;

(i) the distribution by Brambles Limited, on December 18, 2013 to its common shareholders, of common shares of Recall Holdings Limited; and

(j) the distribution by BHP Billiton Limited, on May 24, 2015 to its common shareholders, of common shares of South32 Limited.

Proposed Addition — Reg. 5600

Letter from Dept. of Finance, April 30, 2018: Mr. Todd Thornton, PricewaterhouseCoopers LLP, Oakville, ON

Dear Mr. Thornton:

Re: Svenska Cellulosa Aktiebolaget SCA (pupl) — Spin-off of Common Shares of Essity Aktiebolag (pupl)

I am replying to your submission of December 11, 2017 to the Canada Revenue Agency (the "CRA") concerning your request on behalf of Svenska Cellulosa Aktiebolaget SCA (pupl) ("SCA") and the follow-up emails of February 16 and 26, 2018 by you and Mary Thompson of PwC to Kerry Harnish of the Department of Finance. You ask that SCA's distribution of common shares of Essity Aktiebolag (publ) ("Essity") to SCA's common shareholders be "prescribed" for the purpose of the foreign spin-off tax-deferral rules in section 86.1 of the *Income Tax Act*.

The CRA has confirmed to the Department of Finance that SCA's *pro rata* distribution of Class A and Class B common shares of Essity to SCA's Class A and Class B common shareholders, respectively, satisfies the technical requirements of the foreign spin-off rules in section 86.1 of the *Income Tax Act*.

The Department of Finance understands that SCA's common shares were widely held and actively traded on the NASDAQ Stockholm Exchange at the time of the distribution, that SCA distributed all of its shares of Essity immediately before the distribution, and that SCA's distribution of common shares of Essity occurred on June 15, 2017. We note that the Swedish Tax Agency Notice indicates that the distribution is not taxable under Swedish law.

Based on our understanding of the information referred to above, we are prepared to recommend to the Minister of Finance that SCA's *pro rata* distribution to its shareholders of the common shares of Essity on June 15, 2017 be a prescribed distribution for the purpose of section 86.1 of the *Income Tax Act*. While we cannot offer any assurance that our recommendation will be accepted, we trust that this information is of assistance.

As per the separate written authorizations we received from SCA and Essity on March 21, 2018, the Government of Canada intends to release this letter under the *Access to Information Act* without redacting the names of the parties given that Canadian shareholders who held common shares of SCA at the time of the distribution may be interested in knowing the content of this letter.

Yours sincerely,

Brian Ernewein, General Director, Legislation, Tax Policy Branch

c.c.: Ian Carpentier, International Tax Auditor, International and Large Business Directorate, Eastern Quebec Tax Services Office, Canada Revenue Agency, Québec, QC

Notes: See Notes at end of ITA 86.1.

Reg. 5600(j) added by 2017 budget bill #2, effective Dec. 14, 2017. 5600(g)-(i) added by P.C. 2015-862, effective July 2015 (implementing Finance comfort letters of May 28, 2013, Feb. 26, 2015 and March 18, 2015). 5600(d)-(f) added by 2013 budget bill #2, effective 2011 (two Finance comfort letters of Dec. 23, 2011 and one of Sept. 25, 2012). 5600(c) added by P.C. 2011-936 (Sept. 11/07 Finance comfort letter), effective June 12, 2006. Reg. 5600 added by P.C. 2004-425, effective 1998, replacing former Reg. 5600, which provided a deadline for ITAR 61(2) (refund of RRSP premiums where the annuitant died before 1972).

Definitions [Reg. 5600]: "prescribed", "share" — ITA 248(1).

PART LVII — [5700–5701] MEDICAL EXPENSE TAX CREDIT

5700. For the purposes of paragraph 118.2(2)(m) of the Act, a device or equipment is prescribed if it is a

(a) wig made to order for individuals who have suffered abnormal hair loss owing to disease, medical treatment or accident;

(b) needle or syringe designed to be used for the purpose of giving an injection;

(c) device or equipment, including a replacement part, designed exclusively for use by an individual suffering from a severe chronic respiratory ailment or a severe chronic immune system disregulation, but not including an air conditioner, humidifier, dehumidifier, heat pump or heat or air exchanger;

(c.1) air or water filter or purifier for use by an individual who is suffering from a severe chronic respiratory ailment or a severe chronic immune system disregulation to cope with or overcome that ailment or disregulation;

(c.2) electric or sealed combustion furnace acquired to replace a furnace that is neither an electric furnace nor a sealed combustion furnace, where the replacement is necessary solely because of a severe chronic respiratory ailment or a severe chronic immune system disregulation;

(c.3) air conditioner acquired for use by an individual to cope with the individual's severe chronic ailment, disease or disorder, to the extent of the lesser of $1,000 and 50% of the amount paid for the air conditioner;

(d) device or equipment designed to pace or monitor the heart of an individual who suffers from heart disease;

(e) orthopaedic shoe or boot and an insert for a shoe or boot made to order for an individual in accordance with a prescription to overcome a physical disability of the individual;

(f) power-operated guided chair installation, for an individual, that is designed to be used solely in a stairway;

(g) mechanical device or equipment designed to be used to assist an individual to enter or leave a bathtub or shower or to get on or off a toilet;

(h) hospital bed including such attachments thereto as may have been included in a prescription therefor;

(i) device that is exclusively designed to assist an individual in walking where the individual has a mobility impairment;

(j) external breast prosthesis that is required because of a mastectomy;

(k) teletypewriter or similar device, including a telephone ringing indicator, that enables a deaf or mute individual to make and receive telephone calls;

(l) optical scanner or similar device designed to be used by a blind individual to enable him to read print;

(l.1) device or software designed to be used by a blind individual, or an individual with a severe learning disability, to enable the individual to read print;

(m) power-operated lift or transportation equipment designed exclusively for use by, or for, a disabled individual to allow the individual access to different areas of a building or to assist the individual to gain access to a vehicle or to place the individual's wheelchair in or on a vehicle;

(n) device designed exclusively to enable an individual with a mobility impairment to operate a vehicle;

(o) device or equipment, including a synthetic speech system, braille printer and large print-on-screen device, designed exclusively to be used by a blind individual in the operation of a computer;

(p) electronic speech synthesizer that enables a mute individual to communicate by use of a portable keyboard;

(q) device to decode special television signals to permit the script of a program to be visually displayed;

(q.1) a visual or vibratory signalling device, including a visual fire alarm indicator, for an individual with a hearing impairment;

(r) device designed to be attached to infants diagnosed as being prone to sudden infant death syndrome in order to sound an alarm if the infant ceases to breathe;

(s) infusion pump, including disposable peripherals, used in the treatment of diabetes or a device designed to enable a diabetic to measure the diabetic's blood sugar level;

(s.1) blood coagulation monitor, including disposable peripherals, for use by an individual who requires anti-coagulation therapy;

(t) electronic or computerized environmental control system designed exclusively for the use of an individual with a severe and prolonged mobility restriction;

(u) extremity pump or elastic support hose designed exclusively to relieve swelling caused by chronic lymphedema;

(v) inductive coupling osteogenesis stimulator for treating non-union of fractures or aiding in bone fusion;

(w) talking textbook for use by an individual with a perceptual disability in connection with the individual's enrolment at an educational institution in Canada, or a designated educational institution;

(x) Bliss symbol board, or similar device, designed to be used to help an individual who has a speech impairment communicate by selecting the symbols or spelling out words;

(y) Braille note-taker designed to be used by a blind individual to allow them to take notes (that can be read back to them or printed or displayed in Braille) with the help of a keyboard;

(z) page turner, designed to be used by an individual who has a severe and prolonged impairment that markedly restricts their ability to use their arms or hands to turn the pages of a book or other bound document;

(z.1) altered auditory feedback device designed to be used by an individual who has a speech impairment;

(z.2) electrotherapy device designed to be used by an individual with a medical condition or by an individual who has a severe mobility impairment;

(z.3) standing device designed to be used by an individual who has a severe mobility impairment to undertake standing therapy; and

(z.4) pressure pulse therapy device designed to be used by an individual who has a balance disorder.

Related Provisions: ITA 64 — Disability supports deduction for various expenses.

Notes: See Notes to ITA 118.2(2). Devices in Reg. 5700 qualify only if prescribed by a medical practitioner: 118.2(2)(m)(ii).

The last word of para. (z.3) should be "or", not "and". This has been pointed out to Finance.

Some of the devices in Reg. 5700 also qualify as deductible business expenses even though they would normally be capital purchases. See ITA 20(1)(qq) and (rr).

5700(b) can cover a syringe used for a feeding tube (G-tube), if the cost can be identified and isolated: VIEWS doc 2007-0220531E5. It also covers an insulin pen, both disposable and reusable: 2015-0621231I7.

5700(c) does not cover a MEDIC medical marijuana vaporization system in the CRA's view, because it "was also designed for use by individuals currently suffering from non-respiratory ailments": doc 2012-0432791E5. A dental device custom-made for a person with sleep apnea will qualify only if that is a "severe chronic respiratory ailment": 2011-0429541E5.

For *5700(c.1)*, the fact a device acts as an air exchanger, in addition to its function as an air purifier, will not generally preclude it from qualifying, unless the exchanger is a separate unit that can be purchased separately: VIEWS doc 2002-0140205. A water softener qualifies as a "water filter or purifier": 2007-0255191E5. An air purifier qualifies when needed for asthma and a compromised immune system: 2010-0379331E5.

For *5700(c.3)*, a central air conditioner appeared to qualify in VIEWS doc 2009-0314751E5. The cost of electricity to operate an air conditioner does not qualify: 2007-0251291I7 (electricity for a dialysis machine does, because ITA 118.2(2)(i) uses the broader words "for or in respect of").

For *5700(g)*, a "raised toilet seat, superpole and extender" appear to qualify, and a commode may qualify: VIEWS doc 2009-0332141E5.

For *5700(h)*, a Slumberland adjustable bed was a hospital bed: *Crockart*, [1999] 2 C.T.C. 2409 (TCC), as was a Sleep Country adjustable bed with a remote and a vibrating system: *Young*, 2009 CarswellNat 4364 (TCC); but a "Ceragem massager bed" (not really a bed) was not: *Reid*, 2008 TCC 382. Rebuilding a bed to make it like a hospital bed qualified: *Vucurevich*, [2000] 1 C.T.C. 3044 (TCC). A RIK Fluid Overlay mattress does not qualify in CRA's view: doc 2009-0318231E5. Nor does a massage chair: 2009-0341601E5; or an orthopedic mattress: 2011-0397731E5. "If the bed is of the type usually found in hospitals, the bed, rails and mattress" fall under 5700(h): 2009-0332141E5. Non-allergenic mattresses and mattress covers did not qualify in *Henschel*, 2010 TCC 344, para. 8.

5700(i), before being changed from "designed" to "exclusively designed" in 2007 (effective for property acquired after Feb. 22, 2005), applied to an air conditioner needed by a person with multiple sclerosis: *Nigel Brown*, [1995] 1 C.T.C. 208 (FCTD) (Crown's appeal to FCA discontinued) (see now Reg. 5700(c.3)); and to an exercise bike, which was "designed to assist an individual in walking" by helping blood circula-

tion and improving flexibility: *Urdang*, 2007 TCC 479. The "exclusively" amendment likely prevents these interpretations. To qualify, a device must "provide actual support in the action of walking": VIEWS doc 2009-0351441E5; and a "Theracycle" stationary bike does not qualify: 2012-0440931E5. Nor does a Segway (for 5700(i) or (m)), as it is not designed exclusively for a person with mobility impairment: 2015-059631117.

Exercise equipment for a victim of spinal cord damage was allowed where it was prescribed by a Swiss neuro-physiotherapist (*T. Preugschas*, 2005 TCC 657), but not where it was not prescribed by a medical practitioner (*W. Preugschas*, 2005 TCC 567). General-purpose exercise equipment does not qualify: doc 2010-0385911E5.

5700(j) does not cover undergarments to hold a breast prosthesis in place after a mastectomy: doc 2012-0436991E5.

5700(l.1) may apply to WiViK software used by a disabled student to take notes, and to "Read and Write Gold" software: doc 2011-0431291E5.

5700(m) and (n) can be used when purchasing a van for a disabled person, beyond the $5,000 allowed under ITA 118.2(2)(l.7), to claim the cost of the power-operated lift and hand control modifications: doc 2011-0420021E5. (This seems technically wrong, given the "single supply" concept in the GST case law: the taxpayer is acquiring a van, not its component parts.) They cannot be used for the cost of a bicycle or tricycle that will be modified after purchase (though a bicycle or tricycle is a "vehicle" for (n)): 2016-0645021C6 [2016 CPA Alberta q.16]. They can be used for devices designed exclusively to enable a Segway or other vehicle to be used by a disabled person; 2016 Alberta CPA (tinyurl.com/cra-abtax), q. 16(b)).

5700(q) applies to the closed-caption decoder chip in a TV but not the TV: 2004-006865117 (but see above re "single supply").

5700(s) does not cover a mobile app that monitors (but does not measure) a diabetic's blood sugar and advises what to do, in CRA's view: doc 2019-0804001E5.

Before *5700(s.1)* was added effective 2012, a coagulation meter did not qualify: VIEWS doc 2010-0370651M4.

5700(v), in CRA's view (doc 2019-0798981E5), covers a Seqex electro-medical device for magnetotherapy only if it is "used" as per the 5700(v) wording; it is "implied that the Device must be prescribed by a medical practitioner for that specific use" (see ITA 118.2(2)(m)(ii)).

5700(x): a digital camera that parents used to make Bliss symbol boards did not qualify: *Henschel*, 2010 TCC 344. An Apple iPad does not qualify: VIEWS doc 2010-0383021E5, but Proloquo2Go software for it likely does: 2017-0719651E5.

5700(z.2) covers an iontophoresis device prescribed for hyperhidrosis: doc 2011-0391861E5; and an Electrical Muscle Stimulation (EMS) device: 2011-0428191E5. It does not cover a pulsed electromagnetic field (PEMF) therapy device in CRA's view, as "electrotherapy" does not include electromagnetic therapy: 2019-0798981E5, 2019-0812161E5.

5700(z.3) covers a whole body vibration (WBV) unit: VIEWS doc 2010-0358821E5. It does not cover a Segway: 2015-059631117.

Reg. 5700(s.1) added by 2012 budget bill #1, for expenses incurred after 2011. Reg. 5700(z.1)-(z.4) added by 2008 budget bill #2, for 2008 and later tax years. Reg. 5700 earlier amended by P.C. 2007-1443, 2000-1770, 1999-1767, 1994-271.

Definitions [Reg. 5700]: "Canada" — ITA 255, *Interpretation Act* 35(1); "designated educational institution" — 118.6(1); "individual" — ITA 248(1); "medical practitioner" — ITA 118.4(2); "prescribed" — ITA 248(1).

Interpretation Bulletins: IT-519R2: Medical expense and disability tax credits.

5701. For the purpose of subparagraph 118.2(2)(n)(ii) of the Act, a drug, medicament or other preparation or substance is prescribed if it

(a) is manufactured, sold or represented for use in the diagnosis, treatment or prevention of a disease, disorder or abnormal physical state, or its symptoms, or in restoring, correcting or modifying an organic function;

(b) is prescribed for a patient by a medical practitioner; and

(c) may, in the jurisdiction in which it is acquired, be lawfully acquired for use by the patient only with the intervention of a medical practitioner.

Notes: "It is a question of fact whether a particular drug may lawfully be acquired only by prescription (or only with the intervention of a medical practitioner). Therefore, it would be necessary to examine the applicable federal and provincial/territorial legislation and regulations in order to make that determination for a particular drug": VIEWS doc 2011-0426031E5.

Reg. 5701 added by 2008 budget bill #2, effective Feb. 27, 2008.

Definitions [Reg. 5701]: "medical practitioner" — ITA 118.4(2); "patient" — ITA 118.2(2)(a); "prescribed" — ITA 248(1); "province" — *Interpretation Act* 35(1).

Interpretation Bulletins: IT-519R2: Medical expense and disability tax credits.

PART LVIII — [5800] RETENTION OF BOOKS AND RECORDS

5800. (1) For the purposes of paragraph 230(4)(a) of the Act, the required retention periods for records and books of account of a person are prescribed as follows:

(a) in respect of

(i) any record of the minutes of meetings of the directors of a corporation,

(ii) any record of the minutes of meetings of the shareholders of a corporation,

(iii) any record of a corporation containing details with respect to the ownership of the shares of the capital stock of the corporation and any transfers thereof,

(iv) the general ledger or other book of final entry containing the summaries of the year-to-year transactions of a corporation, and

(v) any special contracts or agreements necessary to an understanding of the entries in the general ledger or other book of final entry referred to in subparagraph (iv),

the period ending on the day that is two years after the day that the corporation is dissolved;

(b) in respect of all records and books of account that are not described in paragraph (a) of a corporation that is dissolved and in respect of the vouchers and accounts necessary to verify the information in such records and books of account, the period ending on the day that is two years after the day that the corporation is dissolved;

(c) in respect of

(i) the general ledger or other book of final entry containing the summaries of the year-to-year transactions of a business of a person (other than a corporation), and

(ii) any special contracts or agreements necessary to an understanding of the entries in the general ledger or other book of final entry referred to in subparagraph (i),

the period ending on the day that is six years after the last day of the taxation year of the person in which the business ceased;

(d) in respect of

(i) any record of the minutes of meetings of the executive of a registered charity, registered Canadian amateur athletic association or registered journalism organization,

(ii) any record of the minutes of meetings of the members of a registered charity, registered Canadian amateur athletic association or registered journalism organization, and

(iii) all documents and by-laws governing a registered charity, registered Canadian amateur athletic association or registered journalism organization,

the period ending on the day that is two years after the date on which the registration of the registered charity, the registered Canadian amateur athletic association or the registered journalism organization under the Act is revoked;

(e) in respect of all records and books of account that are not described in paragraph (d) and that relate to a registered charity, registered Canadian amateur athletic association or registered journalism organization whose registration under the Act is revoked, and in respect of the vouchers and accounts necessary to verify the information in such records and books of account, the period ending on the day that is two years after the date on which the registration of the registered charity, the registered Canadian amateur athletic association or the registered journalism organization under the Act is revoked;

(f) in respect of duplicates of receipts for gifts that are received by a qualified donee to which subsection 230(2) of the Act applies, the period ending on the day that is two years after the end of the last calendar year to which the receipts relate; and

(g) notwithstanding paragraphs (c) to (f), in respect of all records, books of account, vouchers and accounts of a deceased taxpayer or a trust in respect of which a clearance certificate is issued pursuant to subsection 159(2) of the Act with respect to the distribution of all the property of such deceased taxpayer or trust, the period ending on the day that the clearance certificate is issued.

Notes: Reg. 5800(1)(d), (e) amended by 2019 budget bill #1, effective 2020, to add "registered journalism organization" [defined in ITA 248(1)].

Reg. 5800(1)(d)(iv) repealed and (f) amended by 2011 budget bill #2, effective 2012. (See Notes to ITA 149.1(1)"qualified donee".)

(2) For the purposes of subsection 230.1(3) of the Act, with respect to the application of paragraph 230(4)(a) of the Act, the required retention period for records and books of account that are required to be kept pursuant to section 230.1 of the Act is prescribed to be the period ending on the day that is two years after the end of the last calendar year to which the records or books of account relate.

Definitions [Reg. 5800]: "business" — ITA 248(1); "calendar year" — *Interpretation Act* 37(1)(a); "corporation" — ITA 248(1), *Interpretation Act* 35(1); "person", "prescribed", "property" — ITA 248(1); "qualified donee" — ITA 149.1(1), 188.2(3)(a), 248(1); "record", "registered Canadian amateur athletic association", "registered charity", "registered journalism organization", "share", "shareholder" — ITA 248(1); "taxation year" — ITA 249; "taxpayer" — ITA 248(1); "trust" — ITA 104(1), 248(1), (3).

Information Circulars [Reg. 5800]: 75-2R8: Contributions to a registered party, a registered association or to a candidate at a federal election; 78-10R5: Books and records retention/destruction; 05-1R1: Electronic record keeping.

PART LIX — [5900–5911] FOREIGN AFFILIATES

5900. Dividends out of exempt, taxable and pre-acquisition surplus — (1) Where at any time a corporation resident in Canada or a foreign affiliate of the corporation receives a dividend on a share of any class of the capital stock of a foreign affiliate of the corporation,

(a) for the purposes of this Part and paragraph 113(1)(a) of the Act, the portion of the dividend paid out of the exempt surplus of the affiliate is prescribed to be that proportion of the dividend received that

(i) such portion of the whole dividend paid by the affiliate on the shares of that class at that time as was deemed by section 5901 to have been paid out of the affiliate's exempt surplus in respect of the corporation

is of

(ii) the whole dividend paid by the affiliate on the shares of that class at that time;

(a.1) for the purposes of this Part and paragraph 113(1)(a.1) of the Act, the portion of the dividend paid out of the hybrid surplus of the affiliate is prescribed to be that proportion of the dividend received that

(i) the portion of the whole dividend paid by the affiliate on the shares of that class at that time that was deemed by section 5901 to have been paid out of the affiliate's hybrid surplus in respect of the corporation

is of

(ii) the whole dividend paid by the affiliate on the shares of that class at that time;

(b) for the purposes of this Part and subsection 91(5) and paragraphs 113(1)(b) and (c) of the Act, the portion of the dividend paid out of the taxable surplus of the affiliate is prescribed to be that portion of the dividend received that

(i) such portion of the whole dividend paid by the affiliate on the shares of that class at that time as was deemed by section 5901 to have been paid out of the affiliate's taxable surplus in respect of the corporation

is of

 (ii) the whole dividend paid by the affiliate on the shares of that class at that time;

(c) for the purposes of this Part and paragraph 113(1)(d) of the Act, the portion of the dividend paid out of the pre-acquisition surplus of the affiliate is prescribed to be that proportion of the dividend received that

 (i) such portion of the whole dividend paid by the affiliate on the shares of that class at that time as was deemed by section 5901 to have been paid out of the affiliate's pre-acquisition surplus in respect of the corporation

is of

 (ii) the whole dividend paid by the affiliate on the shares of that class at that time;

(c.1) for the purposes of this Part and paragraph 113(1)(a.1) of the Act, the foreign tax applicable to the portion of the dividend prescribed to have been paid out of the hybrid surplus of the affiliate is prescribed to be that proportion of the hybrid underlying tax applicable, in respect of the corporation, to the whole dividend paid by the affiliate on the shares of that class at that time that

 (i) the amount of the dividend received by the corporation or the affiliate, as the case may be, on that share at that time

is of

 (ii) the whole dividend paid by the affiliate on the shares of that class at that time; and

(d) for the purposes of this Part and paragraph 113(1)(b) of the Act, the foreign tax applicable to the portion of the dividend prescribed to have been paid out of the taxable surplus of the affiliate is prescribed to be that proportion of the underlying foreign tax applicable, in respect of the corporation, to the whole dividend paid by the affiliate on the shares of that class at that time that

 (i) the amount of the dividend received by the corporation or the affiliate, as the case may be, on that share at that time

is of

 (ii) the whole dividend paid by the affiliate on the shares of that class at that time.

Related Provisions: Reg. 5902(1) — Rules for calculating surplus accounts on elected dividend; Reg. 5907(2.02) — Anti-avoidance rule.

Notes: See Notes to ITA 113(1). For an example of a 5900(1)(c) and 5901(1)(c) dividend from pre-acquisition surplus, see VIEWS doc 2008-0290351E5.

Reg. 5900(1)(a.1), (c.1) added by 2002-2013 technical bill, for dividends received after Aug. 19, 2011.

(2) Notwithstanding paragraphs (1)(a) and (b), where at any time a foreign affiliate of a corporation resident in Canada pays a dividend on a share of a class of its capital stock (other than a share in respect of which an election is made under subsection 93(1) of the Act) to the corporation, the corporation may, in its return of income under Part I of the Act for its taxation year in which the dividend was received by it, designate an amount not exceeding the portion of the dividend received that would, but for this subsection, be prescribed to have been paid out of the affiliate's exempt surplus in respect of the corporation and that amount

(a) is prescribed to have been paid out of the affiliate's taxable surplus in respect of the corporation and not to have been paid out of that exempt surplus; and

(b) for the purposes of paragraph (1)(d) and the definitions "underlying foreign tax" and "underlying foreign tax applicable" in subsection 5907(1) is deemed to have been paid by the affiliate to the corporation as a separate whole dividend on the shares of that class of the capital stock immediately after that time, and that whole dividend is deemed to have been paid out of the affiliate's taxable surplus in respect of the corporation.

Related Provisions: Reg. 5908(8)(a) — Reference to ITA 93(1) includes 93(1.2).

Notes: Reg. 5900(2)(a), (b) amended by P.C. 1997-1670, for foreign affiliates' tax years that end after 1994.

A March 16, 2001 proposed amendment to Reg. 5900(2), adding reference to ITA 93(1.2), is no longer needed due to Reg. 5908(8)(a).

(3) For the purposes of subsection 91(5) of the Act, if a person resident in Canada (other than a corporation) receives a dividend on a share of any class of the capital stock of a foreign affiliate of the person, the dividend is prescribed to have been paid out of the affiliate's taxable surplus.

Notes: For application of Reg. 5900(3) see VIEWS docs 2007-0247551E5, 2016-0658171I7.

Reg. 5900(3) amended by 2002-2013 technical bill, for dividends received after Nov. 1999.

Definitions [Reg. 5900]: "amount" — ITA 248(1), Reg. 5907(7); "corporation" — ITA 248(1), *Interpretation Act* 35(1); "dividend" — ITA 248(1); "exempt surplus" — Reg. 5902(1)–(2), (7), 5905(7)(d), 5907(1); "foreign affiliate" — ITA 95(1), 248(1), Reg. 5907(3); "foreign tax applicable" — Reg. 5900(1)(d); "hybrid surplus", "hybrid underlying tax applicable" — Reg. 5907(1); "individual", "person", "prescribed" — ITA 248(1); "pre-acquisition surplus" — Reg. 5900(1)(c); "resident in Canada" — ITA 250; "share" — ITA 248(1); "taxable surplus" — Reg. 5902(1)–(2), (7), 5905(7)(e), 5907(1); "taxation year" — ITA 249; "underlying foreign tax applicable", "whole dividend" — Reg. 5907(1).

Interpretation Bulletins: IT-392: Meaning of term "share".

5901. Order of surplus distributions — (1) Subject to subsection (1.1), if at any time in its taxation year a foreign affiliate of a corporation resident in Canada has paid a whole dividend on the shares of any class of its capital stock, for the purposes of this Part

(a) the portion of the whole dividend deemed to have been paid out of the affiliate's exempt surplus in respect of the corporation at that time is an amount equal to the lesser of

 (i) the amount of the whole dividend, and

 (ii) the amount, if any, by which the exempt surplus exceeds the total of

  (A) the affiliate's hybrid deficit, if any, in respect of the corporation at that time, and

  (B) the affiliate's taxable deficit, if any, in respect of the corporation at that time;

(a.1) the portion of the whole dividend deemed to have been paid out of the affiliate's hybrid surplus in respect of the corporation at that time is an amount equal to the lesser of

 (i) the amount, if any, by which the amount of the whole dividend exceeds the portion determined under paragraph (a), and

 (ii) the amount, if any, by which the hybrid surplus exceeds

  (A) if the affiliate has an exempt deficit and a taxable deficit, in respect of the corporation at that time, the total of the exempt deficit and the taxable deficit,

  (B) if the affiliate has an exempt deficit and no taxable deficit, in respect of the corporation at that time, the amount of the exempt deficit, and

  (C) if the affiliate has a taxable deficit and no exempt deficit, in respect of the corporation at that time, the amount, if any, by which the taxable deficit exceeds the affiliate's exempt surplus in respect of the corporation at that time;

(b) the portion of the whole dividend deemed to have been paid out of the affiliate's taxable surplus in respect of the corporation at that time is an amount equal to the lesser of

 (i) the amount, if any, by which the amount of the whole dividend exceeds the total of the portions determined under paragraphs (a) and (a.1), and

 (ii) the amount, if any, by which the taxable surplus exceeds

  (A) if the affiliate has an exempt deficit and a hybrid deficit, in respect of the corporation at that time, the total of the exempt deficit and the hybrid deficit,

  (B) if the affiliate has an exempt deficit and no hybrid deficit, in respect of the corporation at that time, the amount, if any, by which the exempt deficit exceeds the affiliate's hybrid surplus in respect of the corporation at that time, and

(C) if the affiliate has a hybrid deficit and no exempt deficit, in respect of the corporation at that time, the amount, if any, by which the hybrid deficit exceeds the affiliate's exempt surplus in respect of the corporation at that time; and

(c) the portion of the whole dividend deemed to have been paid out of the affiliate's pre-acquisition surplus in respect of the corporation at that time is the amount, if any, by which the whole dividend exceeds the total of the portions determined under paragraphs (a) to (b).

Related Provisions: Reg. 5901(1.1) — Election for dividend to come out of taxable surplus before hybrid surplus; Reg. 5901(2)(b) — Election for dividend (return of capital) to come out of pre-acquisition surplus; Reg. 5902(1) — Rules for calculating surplus accounts on elected dividend.

Notes: See Notes to Reg. 5900(1).

Reg. 5901(1) amended by 2002-2013 technical bill for dividends paid after Aug. 19, 2011, to accommodate the "hybrid surplus" concept.

(1.1) If the corporation resident in Canada that is referred to in subsection (1) elects in writing under this subsection in respect of the whole dividend referred to in subsection (1) and files the election with the Minister on or before the corporation's filing-due date for its taxation year that includes the day the whole dividend was paid, subsection (1) applies in respect of the whole dividend as if its paragraphs (a.1) and (b) read as follows:

(a.1) the portion of the whole dividend deemed to have been paid out of the affiliate's taxable surplus in respect of the corporation at that time is an amount equal to the lesser of

(i) the amount, if any, by which the amount of the whole dividend exceeds the portion determined under paragraph (a), and

(ii) the amount, if any, by which the taxable surplus exceeds

(A) if the affiliate has an exempt deficit and a hybrid deficit, in respect of the corporation at that time, the total of the exempt deficit and the hybrid deficit,

(B) if the affiliate has an exempt deficit and no hybrid deficit, in respect of the corporation at that time, the amount of the exempt deficit, and

(C) if the affiliate has a hybrid deficit and no exempt deficit, in respect of the corporation at that time, the amount, if any, by which the hybrid deficit exceeds the affiliate's exempt surplus in respect of the corporation at that time;

(b) the portion of the whole dividend deemed to have been paid out of the affiliate's hybrid surplus in respect of the corporation at that time is an amount equal to the lesser of

(i) the amount, if any, by which the amount of the whole dividend exceeds the total of the portions determined under paragraphs (a) and (a.1),

(ii) the amount, if any, by which the hybrid surplus exceeds

(A) if the affiliate has an exempt deficit and a taxable deficit, in respect of the corporation at that time, the total of the exempt deficit and the taxable deficit,

(B) if the affiliate has an exempt deficit and no taxable deficit, in respect of the corporation at that time, the amount, if any, by which the exempt deficit exceeds the affiliate's taxable surplus in respect of the corporation at that time, and

(C) if the affiliate has a taxable deficit and no exempt deficit, in respect of the corporation at that time, the amount, if any, by which the taxable deficit exceeds the affiliate's exempt surplus in respect of the corporation at that time; and

Notes: Reg. 5901(1.1) added by 2002-2013 technical bill, for dividends paid after Aug. 19, 2011.

(2) Notwithstanding subsection (1),

(a) if a foreign affiliate of a corporation resident in Canada pays a whole dividend (other than a whole dividend referred to in subsection 5902(1)) at any particular time in its taxation year that is more than 90 days after the commencement of that year or at any particular time in its 1972 taxation year that is before January 1, 1972, the portion of the whole dividend that would, in the absence of this paragraph, be deemed to have been paid out of the affiliate's pre-acquisition surplus in respect of the corporation (otherwise than because of an election under paragraph (b)) is instead deemed to have been paid out of the exempt surplus, hybrid surplus and taxable surplus of the affiliate in respect of the corporation to the extent that it would have been deemed to have been so paid if, immediately after the end of that year, that portion were paid as a separate whole dividend before any whole dividend paid after the particular time and after any whole dividend paid before the particular time by the affiliate, and for the purposes of determining the exempt deficit, exempt surplus, hybrid deficit, hybrid surplus, hybrid underlying tax, taxable deficit, taxable surplus and underlying foreign tax of the affiliate in respect of the corporation at any time, that portion is deemed to have been paid as a separate whole dividend immediately following the end of the year and not to have been paid at the particular time; and

(b) a whole dividend referred to in subsection (1) that is paid at any time by a foreign affiliate of a corporation resident in Canada and that would, in the absence of this paragraph, be deemed under subsection (1) to have been, in whole or in part, paid out of the exempt surplus, hybrid surplus or taxable surplus of the affiliate in respect of the corporation is instead deemed to have been paid out of the pre-acquisition surplus of the affiliate in respect of the corporation if

(i) the corporation, and each other corporation, if any, of which the affiliate would, at that time, be a foreign affiliate if paragraph (b) of the definition "equity percentage" in subsection 95(4) were read as if the reference in that paragraph to "any corporation" were a reference to "any corporation other than a corporation resident in Canada" and that is, at that time, related to the corporation,

(A) where there is no such other corporation, elects in writing under this subparagraph and files the election with the Minister on or before the filing-due date for its taxation year in which the whole dividend is paid, and

(B) in any other case, jointly elect in writing under this subparagraph and file the election with the Minister on or before the earliest of the filing-due dates for their taxation years in which the whole dividend is paid,

(ii) no shareholder of the affiliate is, at that time, a partnership a member of which is

(A) a corporation that would, in the absence of this subparagraph, be eligible to elect under subparagraph (i), or

(B) a foreign affiliate of such a corporation, and

(iii) no particular person or particular partnership — in respect of which the affiliate would, at that time, be a foreign affiliate if paragraph (b) of the definition "equity percentage" in subsection 95(4) of the Act were read in the manner required by subparagraph (i) — has elected under subsection 90(3) of the Act in respect of the distribution that is the whole dividend where

(A) in the case of a particular person, the particular person is, or is at that time related to, the corporation, or

(B) in the case of a particular partnership, a member of the particular partnership is, or is at that time related to, the corporation.

Related Provisions: ITA 90(2) — Any distribution deemed to be dividend; ITA 93(1.11)(b) — Application of 93(1.1) when election under Reg. 5901(2)(b)(i) triggers gain under ITA 40(3); Reg. 5901(2.1), (2.2) — Late election; *Interpretation Act* 27(5) — Meaning of "within 365 days".

Notes: *Reg. 5901(2)(a)* applies to an ITA 90(9)(a) notional dividend: VIEWS doc 2013-0488881E5.

Reg. 5901(2)(b)(i)(A): the election allows tax-free return of capital by electing for a dividend to be out of pre-acquisition surplus, non-taxable due to ITA 113(1)(d). This allows access to the ACB of a FA's shares as a surrogate for the FA's capital (in place of former proposals for "foreign paid-up capital"). See 2020 IFA Roundtable q.7. For a late election see Reg. 5901(2.1)-(2.2), VIEWS doc 2014-056081117.

See also Turner, "Upending the Surplus Ordering Rules", 2079 *Tax Topics* (CCH) 1-5 (Jan. 12, 2012) (interaction with ITA 90(2)); Pham, "Paying FA Dividends when Surplus Balances are Unclear", 7(1) *Canadian Tax Focus* (ctf.ca) 2 (Feb. 2017); Mckilligan, "The 90-Day Rule and Mergers or Liquidations of Foreign Affiliates", 96 *International Tax* (CCH) 10-11 (Oct. 2017); TEI submissions to Finance, Nov. 16, 2016, pp. 14-17 (concern about 90-day rule in (2)(a)), and Dec. 6, 2017 q. B1 with Finance reply.

Reg. 5901(2) amended by 2002-2013 technical bill (for dividends paid after Aug. 19, 2011, or earlier by election); P.C. 1997-1670.

(2.1) [Conditions for late election] — Subsection (2.2) applies if, in respect of a whole dividend paid by a foreign affiliate of a corporation resident in Canada,

(a) the corporation determined not to make an election under subparagraph (2)(b)(i) in respect of the whole dividend before the filing-due date specified in the relevant clause of that subparagraph;

(b) the corporation demonstrates that the determination was made using reasonable efforts; and

(c) the corporation, whether jointly with one or more other corporations or otherwise, files such an election on or before the day that is 10 years after that filing-due date.

Notes: If a corp fails to make detailed calculations of its surplus accounts, hoping it can make a late election if needed, CRA will disallow the election: VIEWS doc 2019-0798761C6 [2019 IFA q.9], 2019-0821311C6 [2019 APFF q.8].

Reg. 5901(2.1), (2.2) added by 2002-2013 technical bill, for dividends paid after Aug. 19, 2011 (or earlier by election).

(2.2) [Late election permitted] — If this subsection applies and, in the opinion of the Minister, the circumstances are such that it would be just and equitable to permit an election referred to in subsection (2.1) to be filed after the filing-due date specified in the relevant clause of subparagraph (2)(b)(i), that election is deemed to have been filed on that filing-due date.

Related Provisions: Reg. 5901(2.1) — Conditions for subsec. (2.2) to apply.

Notes: See Notes to Reg. 5901(2.1). For "just and equitable", see Notes to ITA 85(7.1).

(3) Notwithstanding subsections (1) and (2), for the purposes of the definitions "exempt deficit", "exempt surplus", "taxable deficit" and "taxable surplus" in subsection 5907(1), any amount designated pursuant to subsection 5900(2) in respect of a dividend paid by a foreign affiliate of a corporation resident in Canada increases the portion of the whole dividend deemed to have been paid out of the affiliate's taxable surplus in respect of the corporation and decrease the portion of the whole dividend deemed to have been paid out of the affiliate's exempt surplus in respect of the corporation.

Notes: Reg. 5901(3) amended by P.C. 1997-1670, last effective for foreign affiliates' tax years ending after 1994.

Definitions [Reg. 5901]: "amount" — ITA 248(1), Reg. 5907(7); "commencement" — *Interpretation Act* 35(1); "corporation" — ITA 248(1), *Interpretation Act* 35(1); "dividend" — ITA 248(1); "exempt deficit" — Reg. 5902(1)–(2), (7), 5905(7)(b), 5907(1); "exempt surplus" — Reg. 5902(1)–(2), (7), 5905(7)(c), 5907(1); "filing-due date" — ITA 248(1); "foreign affiliate" — ITA 95(1), 248(1), Reg. 5907(3); "hybrid deficit", "hybrid surplus", "hybrid underlying tax" — Reg. 5907(1); "Minister" — ITA 248(1); "partnership" — see ITA 96(1) Notes; "pre-acquisition surplus" — Reg. 5900(1)(c); "related" — ITA 251(2)–(6); "resident in Canada" — ITA 250; "share", "shareholder" — ITA 248(1); "taxable deficit" — Reg. 5902(1)–(2), (7), 5905(7)(c), 5907(1); "taxable surplus" — Reg. 5902(1)–(2), (7), 5905(7)(e), 5907(1); "taxation year" — ITA 249; "underlying foreign tax" — Reg. 5902(1)–(2), (7), 5907(1); "whole dividend" — Reg. 5907(1); "writing" — *Interpretation Act* 35(1).

5902. Election in respect of capital gains — (1) [Rules for surplus accounts on elected dividend] — If at any time a dividend (such time and each such dividend, respectively, referred to in this subsection and subsection (2) as the "dividend time" and an "elected dividend") is, by virtue of an election made under subsection 93(1) of the Act by a corporation in respect of a disposition,

deemed to have been received on a share (each such share referred to in this subsection as an "elected share") of a class of the capital stock of a particular foreign affiliate of the corporation, the following rules apply:

(a) for the purposes of subsection 5900(1), in applying the provisions of subsection 5901(1),

(i) the particular affiliate's exempt surplus or exempt deficit, hybrid surplus or hybrid deficit, hybrid underlying tax, taxable surplus or taxable deficit, underlying foreign tax and net surplus, in respect of the corporation at the dividend time, are deemed to be those amounts that would otherwise be determined immediately before the dividend time if

(A) each other foreign affiliate of the corporation in which the affiliate had an equity percentage (within the meaning assigned by subsection 95(4) of the Act) at the dividend time had, immediately before the time that is immediately before the dividend time, paid a dividend equal to its net surplus in respect of the corporation, determined immediately before the time the dividend was paid, and

(B) any dividend referred to in clause (A) that any other foreign affiliate would have received had been received by it immediately before any such dividend that it would have paid, and

(ii) the particular affiliate is deemed to have paid a whole dividend at the dividend time on the shares of that class of its capital stock in an amount determined by the formula

$$A \times B$$

where

A is the total of all amounts each of which is the amount of an elected dividend, and

B is the greater of

(A) one, and

(B) the quotient determined by the formula

$$C/D$$

where

C is the amount of the particular affiliate's net surplus determined under subparagraph (a)(i), and

D is the greater of

(I) one unit of the currency in which the amount determined for C is expressed, and

(II) the amount that would have been received on the elected shares if the particular affiliate had at the dividend time paid dividends, on all shares of its capital stock, the total of which was equal to the amount of its net surplus referred to in subparagraph (a)(i); and

(b) subject to paragraph 5905(5)(c), there is to be included, at the dividend time,

(i) under subparagraph (v) of the description of B in the definition "exempt surplus" in subsection 5907(1) in computing the particular affiliate's exempt surplus or exempt deficit, as the case may be, in respect of the corporation an amount equal to the product obtained when the specified adjustment factor in respect of the disposition is multiplied by the total of all amounts each of which is the portion of any elected dividend that is prescribed by paragraph 5900(1)(a) to have been paid out of the exempt surplus of the particular affiliate,

(i.1) under subparagraph (vi) of the description of B in the definition "hybrid surplus" in subsection 5907(1) in computing the particular affiliate's hybrid surplus or hybrid deficit, as the case may be, in respect of the corporation an amount equal to the product obtained when the specified adjustment factor in respect of the disposition is multiplied by the total of all amounts each of which is the portion of any elected dividend that is prescribed by paragraph 5900(1)(a.1) to have been paid out of the hybrid surplus of the particular affiliate,

(i.2) under subparagraph (iii) of the description of B in the definition "hybrid underlying tax" in subsection 5907(1) in computing the particular affiliate's hybrid underlying tax in respect of the corporation an amount equal to the product obtained when the specified adjustment factor in respect of the disposition is multiplied by the total of all amounts each of which is the amount prescribed by paragraph 5900(1)(c.1) to be the foreign tax applicable to the portion of any elected dividend that is prescribed by paragraph 5900(1)(a.1) to have been paid out of the hybrid surplus of the particular affiliate,

(ii) under subparagraph (v) of the description of B in the definition "taxable surplus" in subsection 5907(1) in computing the particular affiliate's taxable surplus or taxable deficit, as the case may be, in respect of the corporation an amount equal to the product obtained when the specified adjustment factor in respect of the disposition is multiplied by the total of all amounts each of which is the portion of any elected dividend that is prescribed by paragraph 5900(1)(b) to have been paid out of the taxable surplus of the particular affiliate, and

(iii) under subparagraph (iii) of the description of B in the definition "underlying foreign tax" in subsection 5907(1) in computing the particular affiliate's underlying foreign tax in respect of the corporation an amount equal to the product obtained when the specified adjustment factor in respect of the disposition is multiplied by the total of all amounts each of which is the amount prescribed by paragraph 5900(1)(d) to be the foreign tax applicable to such portion of any elected dividend as is prescribed by paragraph 5900(1)(b) to have been paid out of the taxable surplus of the particular affiliate.

Related Provisions: Reg. 5902(2) — Interpretation; Reg. 5908(8)(a) — Reference to ITA 93(1) includes 93(1.2).

Notes: Reg. 5902(1) amended by 2002-2013 technical bill, last effective for elections in respect of dispositions after Aug. 19, 2011. The bill included an election to use the Consolidated Net Surplus regime, proposed in 2004 and dropped in 2010 (see Notes to ITA 92(1.2)), for a disposition of FA shares Dec. 21, 2002-Dec. 18, 2009. See up to PITA 47th ed. Earlier amended by P.C. 1997-1670.

For discussion before the amendments see Colborne & McLaren, "Section 93 Elections", 55(4) *Canadian Tax Journal* 856 at 866-70 (2007), and 58(2) 357-91 (2010).

Forms: T2107: Election for a share disposition in a foreign affiliate.

(2) [Rules for 5902(1)] — In this section,

(a) for the purpose of paragraph (1)(a),

(i) if a particular foreign affiliate of a corporation has an equity percentage (within the meaning assigned by subsection 95(4) of the Act) in another foreign affiliate of the corporation that has an equity percentage in the particular affiliate, the exempt surplus or exempt deficit, hybrid surplus or hybrid deficit, hybrid underlying tax, taxable surplus or taxable deficit, underlying foreign tax and net surplus of, and the amount of a dividend paid or received by, the particular affiliate are to be determined in a manner that is

(A) reasonable in the circumstances, and

(B) consistent with the results that would be obtained if a series of actual dividends had been paid and received by the foreign affiliates of the corporation that are relevant to the determination, and

(ii) if any foreign affiliate of a corporation resident in Canada has issued shares of more than one class of its capital stock, the amount that would be paid as a dividend on the shares of any class is the portion of its net surplus that, in the circumstances, it might reasonably be expected to have paid on all the shares of the class, and

(b) the specified adjustment factor in respect of a disposition is the percentage determined by the formula

$$A/B$$

where

A is

(i) if the elected dividend is received by the corporation, 100 per cent, and

(ii) if the elected dividend is received by another foreign affiliate of the corporation, the surplus entitlement percentage of the corporation in respect of the other affiliate immediately before the dividend time, and

B is the surplus entitlement percentage of the corporation in respect of the particular affiliate immediately before the dividend time.

Related Provisions: Reg. 5908(1) — Where FA owned by partnership.

Notes: Reg. 5902(2)(a)(i) and (ii) amended by 2002-2013 technical bill, last effective for elections in respect of dispositions after Aug. 19, 2011.

See also Notes to Reg. 5902(1) re Consolidated Net Surplus election.

(3) [Repealed]

Notes: Reg. 5902(3) repealed by 2002-2013 technical bill, for elections in respect of dispositions after Dec. 18, 2009. See also Reg. 5902(1) Notes re Consolidated Net Surplus election.

(4) [Revoked]

(5) Any election under subsection 93(1) of the Act by a corporation resident in Canada in respect of any share of the capital stock of a foreign affiliate of the corporation disposed of by it or by another foreign affiliate of the corporation shall be made by filing the prescribed form with the Minister on or before the day that is the later of

(a) December 31, 1989; and

(b) where the election is made

(i) in respect of a share disposed of by the corporation, the day on or before which the corporation's return of income for its taxation year in which the disposition was made is required to be filed pursuant to subsection 150(1) of the Act, or

(ii) in respect of a share disposed of by another foreign affiliate of the corporation, the day on or before which the corporation's return of income for its taxation year, in which the taxation year of the foreign affiliate in which the disposition was made ends, is required to be filed pursuant to subsection 150(1) of the Act,

as the case may be.

Related Provisions: Reg. 5908(8)(a) — Reference to ITA 93(1) does not include 93(1.2).

Notes: A March 16, 2001 proposed amendment to Reg. 5902(5), adding reference to ITA 93(1.2), is no longer needed due to Reg. 5908(8)(a).

Forms: T2107: Election for a share disposition in a foreign affiliate.

(6) If at any time a corporation resident in Canada is deemed under subsection 93(1.11) of the Act to have made an election under subsection 93(1) of the Act in respect of a disposition of a share of the capital stock of a particular foreign affiliate of the corporation, the prescribed amount is the lesser of

(a) the capital gain, if any, otherwise determined in respect of the disposition of the share; and

(b) the amount that would reasonably be expected to have been received in respect of the share if the particular affiliate had at that time paid dividends, on all shares of its capital stock, the total of which was equal to the amount determined under subparagraph (1)(a)(i) to be its net surplus in respect of the corporation for the purposes of the election.

Related Provisions: Reg. 5908(8)(a) — Reference to ITA 93(1) does not include 93(1.2).

Notes: For a ruling on Reg. 5902(6) see VIEWS doc 2008-0290361R3.

Reg. 5902(6) amended by 2002-2013 technical bill, last effective for elections in respect of dispositions after Aug. 19, 2011.

Proposed **Reg. 5902(7)** in the Feb. 27/04 draft regulations, prescribing an amount for ITA 93(1.2), is now Reg. 5908(8)(c).

Definitions [Reg. 5902]: "amount" — ITA 248(1), Reg. 5907(7); "arm's length" — ITA 251(1); "capital gain" — ITA 39(1), 248(1); "corporation" — ITA 248(1), *Inter-*

Regulations

pretation Act 35(1); "direct equity percentage" — ITA 95(4); "disposed", "disposition" — ITA 248(1)"disposition"; "dividend" — ITA 248(1); "dividend time" — Reg. 5902(1); "elected dividend", "elected share" — Reg. 5902(1); "equity percentage" — ITA 95(4); "exempt deficit" — Reg. 5902(1)–(2), (7), 5905(7)(b), 5907(1); "exempt surplus" — Reg. 5902(1)–(2), (7), 5905(7)(c), 5907(1); "foreign affiliate" — ITA 95(1), 248(1), Reg. 5907(3); "foreign tax applicable" — Reg. 5900(1)(d); "hybrid deficit", "hybrid surplus", "hybrid underlying tax" — Reg. 5907(1); "Minister" — ITA 248(1); "net surplus" — Reg. 5902(1)–(2), 5907(1); "prescribed" — ITA 248(1); "resident in Canada" — ITA 250; "share", "shareholder" — ITA 248(1); "specified adjustment factor" — Reg. 5902(2)(b); "surplus entitlement percentage" — Reg. 5905(13); "taxable capital gain" — ITA 38(a), 248(1); "taxable deficit" — Reg. 5902(1)–(2), (7), 5905(7)(c), 5907(1); "taxable surplus" — Reg. 5902(1)–(2), (7), 5905(7)(e), 5907(1); "taxation year" — ITA 249; "taxpayer" — ITA 248(1); "underlying foreign tax" — Reg. 5902(1)–(2), (7), 5907(1); "underlying foreign tax applicable", "whole dividend" — Reg. 5907(1).

5903. (1) [Application of foreign accrual property loss] —

For the purposes of the description of F in the definition "foreign accrual property income" in subsection 95(1) of the Act, subject to subsection (2), the prescribed amount for the year (referred to in this subsection and subsection (2) as the "particular year") is the total of all amounts each of which is a portion designated for the particular year by the taxpayer of the foreign accrual property loss of the affiliate for a taxation year of the affiliate that is

(a) one of the 20 taxation years of the affiliate that immediately precede the particular year; or

(b) one of the three taxation years of the affiliate that immediately follow the particular year.

Related Provisions: ITA 152(6.1) — Reassessment to apply FAPL carryback; ITA 161(7)(a)(xii), 161(7)(b)(iii), 164(5)(h.4), (k) — Interest calculation on carryback of FAPL; Reg. 5903(2)–(7) — Interpretation.

Notes: Reg. 5903 replaced by 2002-2013 technical bill, last effective for foreign affiliates' (FA) tax years that begin after Dec. 18, 2009. For a ruling (before the amendment) where a FA incurred losses in previous years and its shares were transferred to a new Canadian sub, see VIEWS doc 2005-0121481R3.

Earlier amended by P.C. 1997-1670, to ensure losses would be included in an FA's deductible loss only where the FA is a controlled FA during the year the loss was incurred. As well, the amendments provided that active business losses do not form part of an FA's deductible loss and so are unavailable to reduce FAPI.

(2) [FAPL restrictions] — For the purposes of this subsection and subsection (1),

(a) a portion of a foreign accrual property loss of the affiliate for any taxation year of the affiliate may be designated for the particular year only to the extent that the foreign accrual property loss exceeds the total of all amounts each of which is a portion, of the foreign accrual property loss, designated by the taxpayer for a taxation year of the affiliate that precedes the particular year;

(b) no portion of the affiliate's foreign accrual property loss for a taxation year of the affiliate is to be designated for the particular year until the affiliate's foreign accrual property losses for the preceding taxation years referred to in paragraph (1)(a) have been fully designated; and

(c) if any person or partnership that was, at the end of a taxation year (referred to in this paragraph as the "relevant loss year") of the affiliate, a relevant person or partnership in respect of the taxpayer designates for a taxation year (referred to in this paragraph as the "relevant claim year") of the affiliate a particular portion of the affiliate's foreign accrual property loss for the relevant loss year, there is deemed to have been designated for the relevant claim year by the taxpayer the portion of that loss that is the greater of

(i) the particular portion, and

(ii) the greatest of the portions of that loss that are so designated by any other relevant persons or partnerships in respect of the taxpayer.

Notes: See Notes to Reg. 5903(1).

Interpretation Bulletins: IT-95R: Foreign exchange gains and losses.

Information Circulars: 77-9R: Books, records and other requirements for taxpayers having foreign affiliates.

(3) ["Foreign accrual property loss"] — For the purposes of

this section, and subject to subsection (4), "foreign accrual property loss" of the affiliate for a taxation year of the affiliate means

(a) where, at the end of the year, the affiliate is a controlled foreign affiliate of a person or partnership that is, at the end of the year, a relevant person or partnership in respect of the taxpayer, the amount, if any, determined by the formula

$$J - (K + L + M + N)$$

where

J is the amount determined for D in the formula in the definition "foreign accrual property income" in subsection 95(1) of the Act in respect of the affiliate for the year,

K is the amount, if any, by which

(i) the amount determined for A in that formula in respect of the affiliate for the year

exceeds

(ii) the amount determined for H in that formula in respect of the affiliate for the year,

L is the amount, if any, by which

(i) the amount determined for B in that formula in respect of the affiliate for the year

exceeds

(ii) the total of

(A) the amount determined for E in that formula in respect of the affiliate for the year, and

(B) the amount determined for F.1 in that formula in respect of the affiliate for the year,

M is the amount determined for C in that formula in respect of the affiliate for the year, and

N is the amount, if any, by which

(i) the total of

(A) the amount determined for A.1 in that formula in respect of the affiliate for the year, and

(B) the amount determined for A.2 in that formula in respect of the affiliate for the year

exceeds

(ii) the amount determined for G in that formula in respect of the affiliate for the year; and

(b) in any other case, nil.

Related Provisions: ITA 152(6.1) — Reassessment to apply FAPL carryback; ITA 257 — Negative amounts in formulas; Reg. 5907(1.4) — Where loss is in respect of another corporation's loss.

Notes: See VIEWS doc 2003-0025091E5 for CRA interpretation of the March 16, 2001 draft of Reg. 5903(3)(b).

Reg. 5903(3)(a) amended by 2002-2013 technical bill, last change effective for FAs' capital losses incurred in FA tax years ending after Aug. 19, 2011.

(4) [Certain losses deemed nil] — In computing under subsec-

tion (3) the foreign accrual property loss of the affiliate for a taxation year, if the affiliate or another corporation receives a payment described in subsection 5907(1.3) from a non-resident corporation that is, at the time of the payment, a foreign affiliate of a relevant person or partnership in respect of the taxpayer and any portion of the payment can reasonably be considered to relate to a loss or portion of a loss of the affiliate for the year described in the description of D in the definition "foreign accrual property income" in subsection 95(1) of the Act, the amount of the loss or portion of the loss is deemed to be nil.

Notes: Reg. 5903(4) amended by 2002-2013 technical bill, for foreign affiliates' capital losses incurred in tax years that end after Aug. 19, 2011.

(5) [Mergers and windups] — For the purposes of this section

and section 5903.1,

(a) if paragraph 95(2)(d.1) of the Act applies to a foreign merger, the new foreign corporation referred to in that paragraph is, except in the determination of the foreign accrual property income of a foreign affiliate predecessor referred to in that paragraph, deemed to be the same corporation as, and a continuation of, each foreign affiliate predecessor; and

(b) if paragraph 95(2)(e) of the Act applies to a liquidation and dissolution, of a disposing affiliate referred to in that paragraph, that is a designated liquidation and dissolution of the disposing affiliate, the shareholder affiliate referred to in that paragraph is, except in the determination of the foreign accrual property income of the disposing affiliate, deemed to be the same corporation as, and a continuation of, the disposing affiliate.

Related Provisions: ITA 87(8.2) — Absorptive mergers.

Notes: For CRA interpretation see VIEWS doc 2015-0592551I7.

Reg. 5903(5) amended by 2002-2013 technical bill, last change effective for FAs' capital losses incurred in FA tax years ending after Aug. 19, 2011.

(6) ["Relevant person or partnership"] — In this section and section 5903.1, a **"relevant person or partnership"**, in respect of the taxpayer at any time, means the taxpayer or a person (other than a designated acquired corporation of the taxpayer), or a partnership, that is at that time

(a) a person (other than a partnership) that is resident in Canada and does not, at that time, deal at arm's length (otherwise than because of a right referred to in paragraph 251(5)(b) of the Act) with the taxpayer;

(b) an antecedent corporation of a relevant person or partnership in respect of the taxpayer;

(c) a partnership a member of which is at that time a relevant person or partnership in respect of the taxpayer under this subsection; or

(d) where paragraph (1)(b) is being applied, a corporation of which the taxpayer is an antecedent corporation.

Related Provisions: Reg. 5903(7) — Interpretation.

Notes: Reg. 5903(6) amended by 2002-2013 technical bill, for foreign affiliates' (FA) capital losses incurred in FA tax years ending after Aug. 19, 2011.

(7) [Non-arm's length dealings] — For the purposes of paragraphs (6)(a) to (d),

(a) if a person or partnership (referred to in this subsection as the "relevant person") is not dealing at arm's length (otherwise than because of a right referred to in paragraph 251(5)(b) of the Act) with another person or partnership (referred to in this paragraph as the "particular person") at a particular time, the relevant person is deemed to have existed and not to have dealt at arm's length with the particular person, nor with each antecedent corporation (other than a designated acquired corporation of the particular person) of the particular person, throughout the period that began when the particular person or the antecedent corporation, as the case may be, came into existence and that ends at the particular time; and

(b) where paragraph (1)(b) is being applied, if a corporation of which a particular person (other than a designated acquired corporation of the corporation) is an antecedent corporation is not dealing at arm's length (otherwise than because of a right referred to in paragraph 251(5)(b) of the Act) with another person or partnership at any time, the particular person is deemed to exist and not to be dealing at arm's length with the other person or the partnership, as the case may be, at that time.

Definitions: "amount" — ITA 248(1), Reg. 5907(7); "antecedent corporation" — ITA 95(1); "arm's length" — ITA 251(1); "controlled foreign affiliate" — ITA 94.1(2)(h), 95(1), 248(1), Reg. 5907(1); "corporation" — ITA 248(1), *Interpretation Act* 35(1); "designated acquired corporation", "designated liquidation and dissolution", "entity" — ITA 95(1); "foreign accrual property income" — ITA 95(1), (2), 248(1); "foreign accrual property loss" — Reg. 5903(3), (4); "foreign affiliate" — ITA 95(1), 248(1), Reg. 5907(3); "loss" — Reg. 5907(1); "non-resident" — ITA 248(1); "partnership" — see ITA 96(1) Notes; "person", "prescribed", "property" — ITA 248(1); "relevant person" — Reg. 5903(7); "relevant person or partnership" — Reg. 5903(6); "resident in Canada" — ITA 250; "shareholder" — ITA 248(1); "surplus entitlement percentage" — ITA 95(1), Reg. 5905(13); "taxation year" — ITA 249; "taxpayer" — ITA 248(1).

5903.1 [Prescribed amount for FAPI F.1 — FACL] — (1) For the purposes of the description of F.1 in the definition "foreign accrual property income" in subsection 95(1) of the Act, subject to subsection (2), the prescribed amount for the year (referred to in this subsection and subsection (2) as the "particular year") is the total of all amounts each of which is a portion designated for the particular year by the taxpayer of the foreign accrual capital loss of the affiliate for a taxation year of the affiliate that is

(a) one of the twenty taxation years of the affiliate that immediately precede the particular year; or

(b) one of the three taxation years of the affiliate that immediately follow the particular year.

Related Provisions: Reg. 5903(5) — Effect of merger or liquidation-and-dissolution.

(2) For the purposes of this subsection and subsection (1),

(a) a portion of a foreign accrual capital loss of the affiliate for any taxation year of the affiliate may be designated for the particular year only to the extent that the foreign accrual capital loss exceeds the total of all amounts each of which is a portion, of the foreign accrual capital loss, designated by the taxpayer for a taxation year of the affiliate that precedes the particular year;

(b) no portion of the foreign accrual capital loss of the affiliate for a taxation year of the affiliate is to be designated for the particular year until the foreign accrual capital losses of the affiliate for the preceding taxation years referred to in paragraph (1)(a) have been fully designated; and

(c) if any person or partnership that was, at the end of a taxation year (referred to in this paragraph as the "relevant loss year") of the affiliate, a relevant person or partnership in respect of the taxpayer designates for a taxation year (referred to in this paragraph as the "relevant claim year") of the affiliate a particular portion of the foreign accrual capital loss of the affiliate for the relevant loss year, there is deemed to have been designated for the relevant claim year by the taxpayer the portion of that loss that is the greater of

(i) the particular portion, and

(ii) the greatest of the portions of that loss that are so designated by any other relevant persons or partnerships in respect of the taxpayer.

(3) For the purposes of this section, and subject to subsection (4), **"foreign accrual capital loss"** of the affiliate for a taxation year of the affiliate means

(a) where, at the end of the year, the affiliate is a controlled foreign affiliate of a person or partnership that is, at the end of the year, a relevant person or partnership in respect of the taxpayer, the amount, if any, by which

(i) the amount determined under paragraph (a) of the description of E in the formula in the definition "foreign accrual property income" in subsection 95(1) of the Act in respect of the affiliate for the year

exceeds

(ii) the amount determined for E in that formula in respect of the affiliate for the year; and

(b) in any other case, nil.

Related Provisions: ITA 152(6.1)(b)(ii)(A) — Reassessment to apply FACL carryback; Reg. 5907(1.4) — Where loss is in respect of another corporation's loss.

(4) In computing under subsection (3) the foreign accrual capital loss of the affiliate for a taxation year, if the affiliate or another corporation receives a payment described in subsection 5907(1.3) from a non-resident corporation that is, at the time of the payment, a foreign affiliate of a relevant person or partnership in respect of the taxpayer and any portion of the payment can reasonably be considered to relate to an allowable capital loss or a portion of an allowable capital loss of the affiliate for the year described in the description of E in the definition "foreign accrual property income" in subsection 95(1) of the Act, the amount of the loss or portion of the loss is deemed to be nil.

Notes: Reg. 5903.1 added by 2002-2013 technical bill, for foreign affiliates' (FA) capital losses incurred in FAs' tax years that end after Aug. 19, 2011. On carrying back a foreign accrual capital loss across that date, see VIEWS doc 2014-056081I17.

Definitions [Reg. 5903.1]: "allowable capital loss" — ITA 38(b), 248(1); "amount" — ITA 248(1), Reg. 5907(7); "capital loss" — ITA 39(1)(b), 248(1); "controlled foreign affiliate" — ITA 94.1(2)(h), 95(1), 248(1), Reg. 5907(1); "corporation" — ITA 248(1), *Interpretation Act* 35(1); "foreign accrual capital loss" — Reg. 5903.1(3), (4); "foreign affiliate" — ITA 95(1), 248(1), Reg. 5907(3); "loss" — Reg. 5907(1); "non-resident" — ITA 248(1); "particular year" — Reg. 5903.1(1); "partnership" — see ITA 96(1) Notes; "person", "prescribed", "property" — ITA 248(1); "relevant person or partnership" — Reg. 5903(6); "taxation year" — ITA 249; "taxpayer" — ITA 248(1).

5904. Participating percentage — (1) For the purpose of subparagraph (b)(ii) of the definition "participating percentage" in subsection 95(1) of the Act, the participating percentage of a particular share owned by a taxpayer of the capital stock of a corporation in respect of any foreign affiliate of the taxpayer that was, at the end of its taxation year, a controlled foreign affiliate of the taxpayer is prescribed to be the percentage that would be the taxpayer's equity percentage in the affiliate at that time on the assumption that

(a) the taxpayer owned no shares other than the particular share;

(b) the direct equity percentage of a person in any foreign affiliate of the taxpayer, for which the total of the distribution entitlements of all the shares of all classes of the capital stock of the affiliate was greater than nil, was determined by the following rules and not by the rules contained in the definition "direct equity percentage" in subsection 95(4) of the Act:

(i) for each class of the capital stock of the affiliate, determine that amount that is the proportion of the distribution entitlement of all the shares of that class that the number of shares of that class owned by that person is of all the issued shares of that class, and

(ii) determine the proportion that

(A) the aggregate of the amounts determined under subparagraph 5904(1)(b)(i) for each class of the capital stock of the affiliate

is of

(B) the aggregate of the distribution entitlements of all the issued shares of all classes of the capital stock of the affiliate

and the proportion determined under subparagraph 5904(1)(b)(ii) when expressed as a percentage is that person's direct equity percentage in the affiliate; and

(c) the direct equity percentage of a person in any foreign affiliate of the taxpayer, for which the total of the distribution entitlements of all the shares of all classes of the capital stock of the affiliate would not, in the absence of this paragraph, be greater than nil, was determined on the assumption that the amount determined under subparagraph (2)(b)(i) were the greater of

(i) the amount of the affiliate's retained earnings, if any, determined at the end of the taxation year under accounting principles that are relevant to the affiliate for the taxation year, and

(ii) the amount determined by the formula

$$A \times B$$

where

A is the amount of the affiliate's total assets determined at the end of the taxation year under accounting principles that are relevant to the affiliate for the taxation year, and

B is 25%.

Related Provisions: Reg. 5904(2) — Distribution entitlement.

Notes: Reg. 5904(1) amended by 2002-2013 technical bill (for foreign affiliates' tax years that begin after Aug. 19, 2011); P.C. 1997-1670.

(2) For the purposes of this section, the distribution entitlement of all the shares of a class of the capital stock of a foreign affiliate of the taxpayer at the end of its taxation year is the aggregate of

(a) the distributions made during the year by the affiliate to holders of shares of that class; and

(b) the amount that the affiliate might reasonably be expected to distribute to holders of shares of that class immediately after the end of the year if at that time it had distributed to its shareholders an amount equal to the aggregate of

(i) the amount, if any, by which the net surplus of the affiliate in respect of the taxpayer at the end of the year, computed as though any adjustments resulting from the provisions of sections 5902 and 5905 and subsections 5907(2.1) and (2.2) and any references thereto during the year were ignored, exceeds the net surplus of the affiliate in respect of the taxpayer at the end of its immediately preceding taxation year, and

(ii) the amount that the affiliate would receive if at that time each controlled foreign affiliate of the taxpayer in which the affiliate had an equity percentage had distributed to its shareholders an amount equal to the aggregate of

(A) the amount that would be determined under subparagraph 5904(2)(b)(i) for the controlled foreign affiliate if the controlled foreign affiliate were the foreign affiliate referred to in subparagraph 5904(2)(b)(i), for each of the taxation years of the controlled foreign affiliate ending in the taxation year of the affiliate, and

(B) each such amount that the controlled foreign affiliate would receive from any other controlled foreign affiliate of the taxpayer in which it had an equity percentage.

Related Provisions: ITA 94.2(3)(b) — Relief from double tax where non-resident trust deemed to be corporation; Reg. 5904(3) — Interpretation.

(3) For the purposes of subsection 5904(2),

(a) the net surplus of a foreign affiliate of a person resident in Canada is, in respect of that person, to be computed as if that person were a corporation resident in Canada;

(b) if a particular foreign affiliate of a corporation has an equity percentage (within the meaning assigned by subsection 95(4) of the Act) in another foreign affiliate of the corporation that has an equity percentage in the particular affiliate, the net surplus of, or the amount of a distribution received by, the particular affiliate is to be determined in a manner that is

(i) reasonable in the circumstances, and

(ii) consistent with the results that would be obtained if a series of actual distributions had been made and received by the foreign affiliates of the corporation that are relevant to the determination;

(c) if any controlled foreign affiliate of a taxpayer resident in Canada has issued shares of more than one class of its capital stock, the amount that would be distributed to the holders of shares of any class is such portion of the amount determined under subparagraph 5904(2)(b)(ii) as, in the circumstances, it might reasonably be expected to distribute to the holders of those shares; and

(d) in determining the distribution entitlement

(i) of a class of shares of the capital stock of a foreign affiliate that is entitled to cumulative dividends, the amount of any distribution referred to in paragraph (2)(a) shall be deemed not to include any distribution in respect of such class that is, or would, if it were made, be referable to profits of a preceding taxation year, and

(ii) of any other class of shares of the capital stock of the affiliate, the net surplus of the affiliate at the end of the year referred to in subparagraph (2)(b)(i) shall be deemed not to have been reduced by any distribution described in subparagraph (i) with respect to a class of shares that is entitled to cumulative dividends to the extent that the distribution was referable to profits of a preceding taxation year.

Notes: Reg. 5904(3) amended by 2002-2013 technical bill, last change effective for foreign affiliates' tax years that begin after Aug. 19, 2011.

Definitions [Reg. 5904]: "amount" — ITA 248(1), Reg. 5907(7); "class" — ITA 248(6); "controlled foreign affiliate" — ITA 95(1), 248(1), Reg. 5907(1); "corporation" — ITA 248(1), *Interpretation Act* 35(1); "direct equity percentage" — Reg. 5904(1)(b); "distribution entitlement" — Reg. 5904(2); "dividend" — ITA 248(1); "earnings" — Reg. 5907(1); "equity percentage" — ITA 95(4); "foreign affiliate" — ITA 95(1), 248(1), Reg. 5907(3); "individual" — ITA 248(1); "net surplus" — Reg. 5902(1)–(2), 5904(3)(a), 5907(1); "person", "prescribed" — ITA 248(1); "resident in Canada" — ITA 250; "share", "shareholder" — ITA 248(1); "taxation year" — ITA 249; "taxpayer" — ITA 248(1).

5905. Special rules — (1) [Corporation or FA acquiring shares of FA]

— If, at any time, there is an acquisition or a disposition of shares of the capital stock of a particular foreign affiliate of a corporation resident in Canada and the surplus entitlement percentage of the corporation in respect of the particular foreign affiliate or any other foreign affiliate (the particular affiliate and those other affiliates each being referred to in this subsection as a "relevant affiliate") of the corporation in which the particular affiliate has an equity percentage (within the meaning assigned by subsection 95(4) of the Act) changes, for the purposes of the definitions "exempt surplus", "hybrid surplus", "hybrid underlying tax", "taxable surplus", and "underlying foreign tax" in subsection 5907(1), each of the opening exempt surplus or opening exempt deficit, opening hybrid surplus or opening hybrid deficit, opening hybrid underlying tax, opening taxable surplus or opening taxable deficit, and opening underlying foreign tax, as the case may be, of the relevant affiliate in respect of the corporation is, except where the acquisition or disposition occurs in a transaction to which paragraph (3)(a) or subsection (5) or (5.1) applies, the amount determined at that time by the formula

$$A \times B/C$$

where

A is the amount of that surplus, deficit or tax, as the case may be, as otherwise determined at that time;

B is the corporation's surplus entitlement percentage immediately before that time in respect of the relevant affiliate; and

C is the corporation's surplus entitlement percentage immediately after that time in respect of the relevant affiliate.

Related Provisions: Reg. 5908(2) — Deemed disposition on change in FA shares owned through partnership.

Notes: For discussion of the 2013 amendments to Reg. 5905 see Woolford & Favre, "The Latest Foreign Affiliate Proposals", 58(4) *Canadian Tax Journal* at 837-42 (2010).

Reg. 5905(1) amended by 2002-2013 technical bill, last effective for acquisitions and dispositions after Aug. 19, 2011. (The bill included an election to use the Consolidated Net Surplus regime, proposed in 2004 and dropped in 2010; see Notes to ITA 92(1.2) and these Notes up to the 47th ed.) Earlier amended by P.C. 1997-1670.

(2) [Repealed]

Notes: Reg. 5905(2) repealed by 2002-2013 technical bill, for redemptions, acquisitions and cancellations after Dec. 18, 2009. For discussion before its repeal see Colborne & McLaren, "Section 93 Elections", 55(4) *Canadian Tax Journal* 856 at 872-77 (2007), and 58(2) *CTJ* 357-91 (2010). Earlier amended by P.C. 1997-1670.

(3) [FA formed by foreign merger]

— If at any time (referred to in this subsection as the "merger time") a foreign affiliate (referred to in this subsection as the "merged affiliate") of a corporation resident in Canada has been formed as a result of a foreign merger (within the meaning assigned by subsection 87(8.1) of the Act) of two or more corporations (referred to individually in this subsection as a "predecessor corporation"), the following rules apply:

(a) for the purposes of the definitions "exempt surplus", "hybrid surplus", "hybrid underlying tax", "taxable surplus" and "underlying foreign tax" in subsection 5907(1), as they apply in respect of the merged affiliate,

(i) the merged affiliate's opening exempt surplus, in respect of the corporation, shall be the amount, if any, by which the total of all amounts each of which is the exempt surplus of a predecessor corporation, in respect of the corporation, immediately before the merger time exceeds the total of all amounts each of which is the exempt deficit of a predecessor corporation, in respect of the corporation, immediately before the merger time,

(ii) the merged affiliate's opening exempt deficit, in respect of the corporation, shall be the amount, if any, by which the total of all amounts each of which is the exempt deficit of a predecessor corporation, in respect of the corporation, immediately before the merger time exceeds the total of all amounts each of which is the exempt surplus of a predecessor corporation, in respect of the corporation, immediately before the merger time,

(ii.1) the merged affiliate's opening hybrid surplus, in respect of the corporation, shall be the amount, if any, by which the total of all amounts each of which is the hybrid surplus of a predecessor corporation, in respect of the corporation, immediately before the merger time exceeds the total of all amounts each of which is the hybrid deficit of a predecessor corporation, in respect of the corporation, immediately before the merger time,

(ii.2) the merged affiliate's opening hybrid deficit, in respect of the corporation, shall be the amount, if any, by which the total of all amounts each of which is the hybrid deficit of a predecessor corporation, in respect of the corporation, immediately before the merger time exceeds the total of all amounts each of which is the hybrid surplus of a predecessor corporation, in respect of the corporation, immediately before the merger time,

(ii.3) the merged affiliate's opening hybrid underlying tax in respect of the corporation shall be the total of all amounts each of which is the hybrid underlying tax of a predecessor corporation, in respect of the corporation, immediately before the merger time,

(iii) the merged affiliate's opening taxable surplus, in respect of the corporation, shall be the amount, if any, by which the total of all amounts each of which is the taxable surplus of a predecessor corporation, in respect of the corporation, immediately before the merger time exceeds the total of all amounts each of which is the taxable deficit of a predecessor corporation, in respect of the corporation, immediately before the merger time,

(iv) the merged affiliate's opening taxable deficit, in respect of the corporation, shall be the amount, if any, by which the total of all amounts each of which is the taxable deficit of a predecessor corporation, in respect of the corporation, immediately before the merger time exceeds the total of all amounts each of which is the taxable surplus of a predecessor corporation, in respect of the corporation, immediately before the merger time, and

(v) the merged affiliate's opening underlying foreign tax in respect of the corporation shall be the total of all amounts each of which is the underlying foreign tax of a predecessor corporation, in respect of the corporation, immediately before the merger time;

(b) for the purposes of paragraph (a),

(i) each of the exempt surplus or exempt deficit, hybrid surplus or hybrid deficit, hybrid underlying tax, taxable surplus or taxable deficit and underlying foreign tax, in respect of the corporation, of each predecessor corporation immediately before the merger time is deemed to be the amount determined by the formula

$$A \times B/C$$

where

A is the amount of that surplus, deficit or tax, as the case may be, as otherwise determined,

B is the surplus entitlement percentage of the corporation immediately before the merger time in respect of the predecessor corporation, and

C is the percentage that would be the surplus entitlement percentage of the corporation immediately after the merger time in respect of the merged affiliate if the merged affiliate's net surplus were the total of all amounts each of which is the net surplus of a predecessor corporation immediately before the merger time, but

(ii) the values for A, B and C in the formula in subparagraph (i) shall take into account the application of paragraph 5902(1)(b) and subsection 5907(8) in respect of the merger; and

(c) in respect of any foreign affiliate (other than a predecessor corporation) of the corporation in which a predecessor corporation had an equity percentage (within the meaning assigned by subsection 95(4) of the Act) immediately before the merger time, for the purposes of subsection (1), there is deemed to be an acquisition or a disposition of shares of the capital stock of that affiliate at the merger time.

Related Provisions: ITA 87(8), 95(2)(d) — Further effects of foreign merger; ITA 87(8.2) — Absorptive mergers.

Notes: Where a FA ceases to exist in an absorptive merger, Reg. 5905(3) and (7.2) do not allow its exempt deficit to count twice in CRA's view: doc 2015-0581611C6 [2015 IFA q.7].

Reg. 5905(3) amended by 2002-2013 technical bill (last effective Aug. 20, 2011); P.C. 1997-1670.

(4) [Repealed]

Notes: Reg. 5905(4) repealed by 2002-2013 technical bill, for mergers or combinations after Dec. 18, 2009.

(5) [Corporation transferring FA shares to related corporation] — If there is, at any time, a disposition by a corporation (referred to in this subsection as the "disposing corporation") resident in Canada of any of the shares (referred to in this subsection as the "disposed shares") of the capital stock of a particular foreign affiliate of the disposing corporation to a taxable Canadian corporation (referred to in this subsection as the "acquiring corporation") with which the disposing corporation is not dealing at arm's length,

(a) each of the opening exempt surplus or opening exempt deficit, opening hybrid surplus or opening hybrid deficit, opening hybrid underlying tax, opening taxable surplus or opening taxable deficit, and opening underlying foreign tax, in respect of the acquiring corporation, of the particular affiliate and of each foreign affiliate of the disposing corporation in which the particular affiliate has, immediately before that time, an equity percentage (within the meaning assigned by subsection 95(4) of the Act) is deemed to be the amount, if any,

(i) in the case of its opening exempt surplus, by which the total of its exempt surplus in respect of each of the disposing corporation and the acquiring corporation, determined immediately before that time, exceeds the total of its exempt deficit in respect of each of the disposing corporation and the acquiring corporation, determined immediately before that time,

(ii) in the case of its opening exempt deficit, by which the total of its exempt deficit in respect of each of the disposing corporation and the acquiring corporation, determined immediately before that time, exceeds the total of its exempt surplus in respect of each of the disposing corporation and the acquiring corporation, determined immediately before that time,

(ii.1) in the case of its opening hybrid surplus, by which the total of its hybrid surplus in respect of each of the disposing corporation and the acquiring corporation, determined immediately before that time, exceeds the total of its hybrid deficit in respect of each of the disposing corporation and the acquiring corporation, determined immediately before that time,

(ii.2) in the case of its opening hybrid deficit, by which the total of its hybrid deficit in respect of each of the disposing corporation and the acquiring corporation, determined immediately before that time, exceeds the total of its hybrid surplus in respect of each of the disposing corporation and the acquiring corporation, determined immediately before that time,

(ii.3) in the case of its opening hybrid underlying tax, that is the total of its hybrid underlying tax in respect of each of the disposing corporation and the acquiring corporation, determined immediately before that time,

(iii) in the case of its opening taxable surplus, by which the total of its taxable surplus in respect of each of the disposing corporation and the acquiring corporation, determined immediately before that time, exceeds the total of its taxable deficit in respect of each of the disposing corporation and the acquiring corporation, determined immediately before that time,

(iv) in the case of its opening taxable deficit, by which the total of its taxable deficit in respect of each of the disposing corporation and the acquiring corporation, determined immediately before that time, exceeds the total of its taxable surplus in respect of each of the disposing corporation and the acquiring corporation, determined immediately before that time, and

(v) in the case of its opening underlying foreign tax, that is the total of its underlying foreign tax in respect of each of the disposing corporation and the acquiring corporation, determined immediately before that time;

(b) for the purposes of paragraph (a), each of the exempt surplus or exempt deficit, hybrid surplus or hybrid deficit, hybrid underlying tax, taxable surplus or taxable deficit, and underlying foreign tax of an affiliate in respect of the disposing corporation and the acquiring corporation, determined immediately before that time, is deemed to be the amount determined by the formula

$$A \times B/C$$

where

A is the amount of that surplus, deficit or tax, as the case may be, as determined without reference to this subsection but taking into account the application of subparagraph (c)(i), if applicable,

B is the surplus entitlement percentage immediately before that time of the disposing corporation or the acquiring corporation, as the case may be, in respect of the affiliate, determined as if the disposed shares were the only shares owned by the disposing corporation immediately before that time, and

C is the surplus entitlement percentage immediately after that time of the acquiring corporation in respect of the affiliate;

(c) if the disposing corporation makes an election under subsection 93(1) of the Act in respect of the disposed shares,

(i) for the purposes of paragraph (b), the exempt surplus or exempt deficit, hybrid surplus or hybrid deficit, hybrid underlying tax, taxable surplus or taxable deficit, and underlying foreign tax of an affiliate in respect of the disposing corporation, as determined without reference to this subsection, immediately before that time, shall be adjusted in accordance with paragraph 5902(1)(b) as if the disposing corporation's surplus entitlement percentage that is referred to in the description of B in paragraph 5902(2)(b) were determined as if the disposed shares were the only shares owned by the disposing corporation immediately before that time, and

(ii) no adjustment shall be made to the amount of the exempt surplus or exempt deficit, hybrid surplus or hybrid deficit, hybrid underlying tax, taxable surplus or taxable deficit, or underlying foreign tax of an affiliate in respect of the disposing corporation under paragraph 5902(1)(b) other than for the purpose of paragraph (b); and

(d) for greater certainty, no adjustment shall be made under subsection (1) to the exempt surplus or exempt deficit, hybrid surplus or hybrid deficit, hybrid underlying tax, taxable surplus or taxable deficit, or underlying foreign tax of an affiliate in respect of the disposing corporation.

Related Provisions: Reg. 5908(2) — Deemed disposition on change in FA shares owned through partnership; Reg. 5908(4) — Disposition of FA shares by corporation to related corporation; Reg. 5908(8)(a) — Reference to ITA 93(1) includes 93(1.2).

Notes: Reg. 5905(5) amended by 2002-2013 technical bill, last effective Aug. 20, 2011.

(5.1) [Amalgamation] — If there is, at any time, an amalgamation within the meaning of subsection 87(1) of the Act and, as a result of the amalgamation, shares of the capital stock of a particular foreign affiliate of a predecessor corporation become property of the new corporation,

(a) each of the opening exempt surplus or opening exempt deficit, opening hybrid surplus or opening hybrid deficit, opening hybrid underlying tax, opening taxable surplus or opening taxable deficit, and opening underlying foreign tax, in respect of the new corporation, of the particular affiliate and of each foreign affiliate of the predecessor corporation in which the particular affiliate has, immediately before that time, an equity percentage (within the meaning assigned by subsection 95(4) of the Act) is deemed to be the amount, if any,

(i) in the case of its opening exempt surplus, by which the total of its exempt surplus in respect of each predecessor corporation, determined immediately before that time, exceeds the total of its exempt deficit in respect of each predecessor corporation, determined immediately before that time,

(ii) in the case of its opening exempt deficit, by which the total of its exempt deficit in respect of each predecessor corporation, determined immediately before that time, exceeds the total of its exempt surplus in respect of each predecessor corporation, determined immediately before that time,

(ii.1) in the case of its opening hybrid surplus, by which the total of its hybrid surplus in respect of each predecessor corporation, determined immediately before that time, exceeds the total of its hybrid deficit in respect of each predecessor corporation, determined immediately before that time,

(ii.2) in the case of its opening hybrid deficit, by which the total of its hybrid deficit in respect of each predecessor corporation, determined immediately before that time, exceeds the total of its hybrid surplus in respect of each predecessor corporation, determined immediately before that time,

(ii.3) in the case of its opening hybrid underlying tax, that is the total of its hybrid underlying tax in respect of each predecessor corporation, determined immediately before that time,

(iii) in the case of its opening taxable surplus, by which the total of its taxable surplus in respect of each predecessor corporation, determined immediately before that time, exceeds the total of its taxable deficit in respect of each predecessor corporation, determined immediately before that time,

(iv) in the case of its opening taxable deficit, by which the total of its taxable deficit in respect of each predecessor corporation, determined immediately before that time, exceeds the total of its taxable surplus in respect of each predecessor corporation, determined immediately before that time, and

(v) in the case of its opening underlying foreign tax, that is the total of its underlying foreign tax in respect of each predecessor corporation, determined immediately before that time; and

(b) for the purpose of paragraph (a), each of the exempt surplus or exempt deficit, hybrid surplus or hybrid deficit, hybrid underlying tax, taxable surplus or taxable deficit, and underlying foreign tax of an affiliate in respect of a predecessor corporation,

determined immediately before that time, is deemed to be the amount determined by the formula

$$A \times B/C$$

where

A is the amount of that surplus, deficit or tax, as the case may be, as determined without reference to this subsection,

B is the predecessor corporation's surplus entitlement percentage immediately before that time in respect of the affiliate, and

C is the new corporation's surplus entitlement percentage immediately after that time in respect of the affiliate.

Related Provisions: ITA 87(2)(u) — Further effects of amalgamation; Reg. 5908(5) — Where predecessor owned FA shares through partnership.

Notes: Reg. 5905(5.1) added and amended by 2002-2013 technical bill, last change effective Aug. 20, 2011.

(5.11)–(5.13) [Repealed]

Notes: Reg. 5905(5.11)–(5.13) added by 2002-2013 technical bill, for amalgamations that occur, or windups that begin, after Feb. 27, 2004; then repealed by the same bill for acquisitions of control after Dec. 18, 2009, except those resulting from an acquisition of shares under an agreement in writing entered into before that date.

(5.2) [Change in control of parent] — If, at a particular time, control of a corporation resident in Canada has been acquired by a person or a group of persons and, at the particular time, the corporation owns shares of the capital stock of a foreign affiliate of the corporation, there shall be included — under subparagraph (v) of the description of B in the definition "exempt surplus" in subsection 5907(1) in computing the affiliate's exempt surplus or exempt deficit, as the case may be, in respect of the corporation at the time that is immediately before the particular time — the amount, if any, determined by the formula

$$(A + B - C)/D$$

where

A is the amount determined by the formula

$$E \times F$$

where

E is the affiliate's tax-free surplus balance in respect of the corporation, determined at the time (referred to in this subsection as the "relevant time") that is immediately before the time that is immediately before the particular time, and

F is the corporation's surplus entitlement percentage in respect of the affiliate determined at the relevant time;

B is the total of all amounts each of which is the corporation's cost amount, determined at the particular time, of a share of the capital stock of the affiliate that is owned by the corporation at the particular time;

C is the total of

(a) the fair market value, determined at the particular time, of all of the shares of the capital stock of the affiliate that are owned by the corporation at the particular time, and

(b) the amount, if any, determined under paragraph 5908(6)(b); and

D is the corporation's surplus entitlement percentage in respect of the affiliate determined at the relevant time.

Related Provisions: ITA 256(7) — Where control deemed not to be acquired; ITA 257 — Negative amounts in formulas; Reg. 5905(5.3) — Interaction with ITA 111(4); Reg. 5905(5.5) — Tax-free surplus balance; Reg. 5908(6) — Where corporation owns FA shares through partnership.

Notes: For discussion of Reg. 5905(5.2)-(5.6) see Heale, "Recent Proposed Amendments", XII(1) *Corporate Structures & Groups* (Federated Press) 655-68 (2010) (re Dec. 18/09 draft, substantively the same as what was enacted); Turner, "The Acquisition of Control Surplus/ACB Trade-Off", 2026 *Tax Topics* (CCH) 1-6 (Jan. 6, 2011) (re Aug. 27/10 draft).

Reg. 5905(5.2) added by 2002-2013 technical bill, for acquisitions of control after Dec. 18, 2009, except those resulting from an acquisition of shares under an agreement in writing entered into before that date.

(5.3) [Ordering — interaction with ITA 111(4)] — The cost amount of a share that is referred to in the description of B in subsection (5.2) shall be determined after taking into account the application of subsection 111(4) of the Act.

Notes: Reg. 5905(5.3) added by 2002-2013 technical bill, effective on the same basis as Reg. 5905(5.2).

(5.4) [Prescribed amount for bump] — For the purposes of clause (B) *[now formula element C — ed.]* of subparagraph 88(1)(d)(ii) of the Act, the prescribed amount is

(a) if the property described in that subparagraph is a share of the capital stock of a foreign affiliate of the subsidiary, the amount determined by the formula

$$A \times B$$

where

A is the affiliate's tax-free surplus balance, in respect of the subsidiary, determined at the time at which the parent last acquired control of the subsidiary, and

B is the percentage that would be the subsidiary's surplus entitlement percentage, determined at that time, in respect of the affiliate if at that time the subsidiary had owned no shares of the affiliate's capital stock other than the share;

(b) if the property described in that subparagraph is an interest in a partnership, the amount determined by subsection 5908(7); and

(c) in any other case, nil.

Related Provisions: Reg. 5905(5.5) — Tax-free surplus balance; Reg. 5908(7) — Calculation where corporation owns FA shares through partnership.

Notes: Reg. 5905(5.4) added by 2002-2013 technical bill, effective on the same basis as Reg. 5905(5.2).

(5.5) [Tax-free surplus balance] — For the purposes of subsections (5.2), (5.4), (7.2) and (7.3), the "tax-free surplus balance" of a foreign affiliate of a corporation resident in Canada, in respect of the corporation, at any time, is the total of

(a) the amount, if any, by which the affiliate's exempt surplus in respect of the corporation at that time exceeds the total of

(i) the affiliate's hybrid deficit, if any, in respect of the corporation at that time, and

(ii) the affiliate's taxable deficit, if any, in respect of the corporation at that time;

(a.1) the amount, if any, by which the amount of the affiliate's hybrid surplus in respect of the corporation at that time exceeds the amount determined under subsection (5.7) in respect of the corporation at that time if, at that time, the amount of that hybrid surplus is less than or equal to the amount determined by the formula

$$[A \times (B - 0.5)] + (C \times 0.5)$$

where

A is the affiliate's hybrid underlying tax in respect of the corporation at that time,

B is the corporation's relevant tax factor (within the meaning assigned by subsection 95(1) of the Act) for the corporation's taxation year that includes that time, and

C is the affiliate's hybrid surplus in respect of the corporation at that time; and

(b) the lesser of

(i) the amount, if any, determined by the formula

$$A \times B$$

where

A is the affiliate's underlying foreign tax in respect of the corporation at that time, and

B is the amount by which the corporation's relevant tax factor (within the meaning assigned by subsection 95(1) of

the Act), for the corporation's taxation year that includes that time, exceeds one, and

(ii) the amount, if any, by which the affiliate's taxable surplus in respect of the corporation at that time exceeds

(A) if the affiliate has an exempt deficit and a hybrid deficit, in respect of the corporation at that time, the total of the exempt deficit and the hybrid deficit,

(B) if the affiliate has an exempt deficit and no hybrid deficit, in respect of the corporation at that time, the amount, if any, by which the exempt deficit exceeds the affiliate's hybrid surplus in respect of the corporation at that time, and

(C) if the affiliate has a hybrid deficit and no exempt deficit, in respect of the corporation at that time, the amount, if any, by which the hybrid deficit exceeds the affiliate's exempt surplus in respect of the corporation at that time.

Related Provisions: ITA 88(1.8), (1.9) — Amended designation re tax-free surplus balance; Reg. 5905(5.6) — Interpretation; Reg. 5905(5.7) — Amount determined for para. (a.1).

Notes: Reg. 5905(5.5) added and amended by 2002-2013 technical bill, last effective Aug. 20, 2011.

(5.6) [Tax-free surplus balance — interpretation] — For the purposes of subsection (5.5), the amounts of exempt surplus or exempt deficit, hybrid surplus or hybrid deficit, hybrid underlying tax, taxable surplus or taxable deficit, and underlying foreign tax, of a foreign affiliate of corporation resident in Canada, in respect of the corporation, at a particular time are those amounts that would be determined, at the particular time, under subparagraph 5902(1)(a)(i) if that subparagraph were applicable at the particular time and the references in that subparagraph to "the dividend time" were references to the particular time.

Related Provisions: ITA 55(5)(d)(i) — Reg. 5905(5.6) to be ignored in safe-income determination.

Notes: Reg. 5905(5.6) added and amended by 2002-2013 technical bill, last effective Aug. 20, 2011.

(5.7) [Amount for 5905(5.5)(a.1)] — For the purposes of paragraph (5.5)(a.1), the amount determined under this subsection in respect of the corporation at any time is

(a) if the affiliate has an exempt deficit and a taxable deficit, in respect of the corporation at that time, the total of the exempt deficit and the taxable deficit;

(b) if the affiliate has an exempt deficit and no taxable deficit, in respect of the corporation at that time, the amount of the exempt deficit; and

(c) if the affiliate has a taxable deficit and no exempt deficit, in respect of the corporation at that time, the amount, if any, by which the taxable deficit exceeds the affiliate's exempt surplus in respect of the corporation at that time.

Notes: Reg. 5905(5.7) added by 2002-2013 technical bill, effective Aug. 20, 2011.

(6) [Repealed]

Notes: Reg. 5905(6) repealed by 2002-2013 technical bill, for dispositions and amalgamations that occur, and windups that begin, after Dec. 18, 2009. Earlier amended by P.C. 1997-1670.

(7) [Liquidation or dissolution of FA] — If at any time there has been a liquidation and dissolution of a foreign affiliate (referred to in this subsection as the **"dissolved affiliate"**) of a corporation resident in Canada that is a designated liquidation and dissolution (within the meaning assigned by subsection 95(1) of the Act) of the dissolved affiliate, each other foreign affiliate of the corporation that had a direct equity percentage (within the meaning assigned by subsection 95(4) of the Act) in the dissolved affiliate immediately before that time is, for the purposes of computing its exempt surplus or exempt deficit, hybrid surplus or hybrid deficit, hybrid underlying tax, taxable surplus or taxable deficit, and underlying foreign tax, in respect of the corporation, deemed to have received dividends immediately before that time the total of which is equal to the amount it might reasonably have expected to receive if the dissolved affiliate had, immediately before that time, paid dividends on all shares of its capital stock the total of which was equal to the amount of its net surplus in respect of the corporation immediately before that time, determined on the assumption that the taxation year of the dissolved affiliate that otherwise would have included that time had ended immediately before that time.

Notes: Reg. 5905(7) amended by 2002-2013 technical bill, for liquidations and dissolutions of foreign affiliates that begin after Aug. 19, 2011 (or earlier by election).

Former proposed Reg. 5905(7)-(7.4) contained "deficit levitation" proposals, first released Feb. 27, 2004 and reproduced in the 26th-36th ed. Finance was expected to reintroduce these [Barnicke & Ong, "Foreign Affiliate Deficits", 18(2) *Canadian Tax Highlights* (ctf.ca) 5-6 (Feb. 2010)], but they were not in the 2002-2013 technical bill, and are no longer expected.

(7.1) [Conditions for subsec. (7.2)] — Subsection (7.2) applies if

(a) a foreign affiliate (referred to in this subsection and subsections (7.2) to (7.6) as the **"deficit affiliate"**) of a corporation resident in Canada has an exempt deficit, in respect of the corporation, at a particular time; and

(b) at the time (referred to in this paragraph and subsections (7.2) to (7.6) as the **"acquisition time"**) that is immediately after the particular time, shares of the capital stock of a foreign affiliate (referred to in this subsection and subsections (7.2) to (7.6) as an **"acquired affiliate"**) of the corporation in which the deficit affiliate has, at the particular time, an equity percentage (within the meaning assigned by subsection 95(4) of the Act) are acquired by, or otherwise become property of,

(i) the corporation, or

(ii) another foreign affiliate of the corporation, in the case where the percentage that would, if the deficit affiliate were resident in Canada, be the deficit affiliate's surplus entitlement percentage in respect of the acquired affiliate immediately after the acquisition time is less than the percentage that would, if the deficit affiliate were so resident, be its surplus entitlement percentage in respect of the acquired affiliate at the particular time.

Related Provisions: Reg. 5908(2) — Deemed disposition on change in FA shares owned through partnership.

Notes: Reg. 5905(7.1) added by 2002-2013 technical bill, effective where a share of the capital stock of a corporation's foreign affiliate is acquired by, or otherwise becomes property of, a person after Dec. 18, 2009.

(7.2) [Blocking deficit — anti-avoidance] — If this subsection applies, there is to be included,

(a) at the time (referred to in this subsection and subsections (7.6) and (7.7) and 5908(11) and (12) as the "adjustment time") that is immediately before the time that is immediately before the time that is immediately before the acquisition time, under subparagraph (v) of the description of B in the definition "exempt surplus" in subsection 5907(1) in computing an acquired affiliate's exempt surplus or exempt deficit in respect of the corporation, the amount, if any, equal to the lesser of

(i) the amount determined by the formula

$$A/B$$

where

A is the deficit affiliate's exempt deficit in respect of the corporation immediately before the acquisition time, and

B is the percentage that would, if the deficit affiliate were resident in Canada, be the deficit affiliate's surplus entitlement percentage in respect of the acquired affiliate immediately before the acquisition time, and

(ii) the lesser of

(A) the acquired affiliate's tax-free surplus balance in respect of the corporation immediately before the adjustment time, and

(B) either

(I) if there is more than one acquired affiliate, the amount designated by the corporation, in its return of income for the taxation year in which the taxation year of the acquired affiliate that includes the acquisition time ends, in respect of the acquired affiliate, or

(II) in any other case, the amount determined under clause (A);

(b) at the time that is immediately after the acquisition time, under subparagraph (vi.1) of the description of A in the definition "exempt surplus" in subsection 5907(1) in computing the deficit affiliate's exempt deficit in respect of the corporation, the total of all amounts each of which is the amount determined in respect of an acquired affiliate by the formula

$$C \times D$$

where

C is the amount determined under paragraph (a) in respect of the acquired affiliate, and

D is the percentage that would, if the deficit affiliate were resident in Canada, be the deficit affiliate's surplus entitlement percentage immediately before the acquisition time in respect of the acquired affiliate; and

(c) at the time that is immediately after the acquisition time, under subparagraph (vi.1) of the description of A in the definition "exempt surplus" in subsection 5907(1) in computing the exempt surplus or exempt deficit of any other foreign affiliate (referred to in this paragraph and paragraph (7.6)(b) as a **"subordinate affiliate"**) of the corporation, in respect of the corporation, that has immediately before the acquisition time a direct equity percentage (within the meaning assigned by subsection 95(4) of the Act) in the acquired affiliate and in which, immediately before the acquisition time, the deficit affiliate does not have an equity percentage (within the meaning assigned by subsection 95(4) of the Act), the amount determined by the formula

$$E \times F$$

where

E is the amount determined under paragraph (a) in respect of the acquired affiliate, and

F is the percentage that would, if the subordinate affiliate were resident in Canada, be the subordinate affiliate's surplus entitlement percentage immediately before the acquisition time in respect of the acquired affiliate if the subordinate affiliate owned no shares of the capital stock of any corporation other than its shares of the capital stock of the acquired affiliate.

Related Provisions: Reg. 5905(5.5) — Tax-free surplus balance; Reg. 5905(7.1) — Conditions for subsec. (7.2) to apply; Reg. 5905(7.4) — Amount deemed designated for (a)(ii)(B)(I); Reg. 5908(11) — Adjustments.

Notes: See Woolford & Favre, "The Latest Foreign Affiliate Proposals", 58(4) *Canadian Tax Journal* 791 at 810-17 (2010); and Notes to Reg. 5905(3) on overlap with that provision.

Reg. 5905(7.2) added by 2002-2013 technical bill, effective on the same basis as Reg. 5905(7.1).

(7.3) [Conditions for subsec. (7.4)] — Subsection (7.4) applies if

(a) the lesser of

(i) the deficit affiliate's exempt deficit in respect of the corporation immediately before the acquisition time, and

(ii) the total of all amounts each of which is the amount, if any, that is the product obtained by multiplying

(A) the tax-free surplus balance immediately before the acquisition time in respect of the corporation of an acquired affiliate, and

(B) the surplus entitlement percentage of the corporation in respect of that acquired affiliate immediately before the acquisition time

exceeds

(b) the total of all amounts each of which is the amount, if any, that is the product obtained by multiplying

(i) the amount, if any, actually designated under subclause (7.2)(a)(ii)(B)(I) in respect of an acquired affiliate, and

(ii) the surplus entitlement percentage of the corporation in respect of that acquired affiliate immediately before the acquisition time.

Related Provisions: Reg. 5905(5.5) — Tax-free surplus balance.

Notes: Reg. 5905(7.3) added by 2002-2013 technical bill, effective on the same basis as Reg. 5905(7.1).

(7.4) [Blocking deficit — limit on designation] — If this subsection applies, the amount designated by the corporation in respect of a particular acquired affiliate is deemed, for the purposes of subclause (7.2)(a)(ii)(B)(I),

(a) to be the amount determined by the Minister in respect of the particular acquired affiliate; and

(b) not to be the amount, if any, actually designated under subclause (7.2)(a)(ii)(B)(I).

Related Provisions: Reg. 5905(7.3) — Conditions for subsec. (7.4) to apply.

Notes: Reg. 5905(7.4) added by 2002-2013 technical bill, effective on the same basis as Reg. 5905(7.1).

(7.5) [Conditions for subsec. (7.6)] — Subsection (7.6) applies if

(a) subsection (7.2) applies;

(b) the deficit affiliate, or any other foreign affiliate of the corporation in which the deficit affiliate has, immediately before the acquisition time, an equity percentage (which percentage has, for the purposes of this subsection, the meaning assigned by subsection 95(4) of the Act and which deficit affiliate or other affiliate is referred to in subsection (7.6) as the "direct holder"), has, immediately before the acquisition time, a direct equity percentage (within the meaning assigned by that subsection 95(4)) in any other foreign affiliate (referred to in paragraph (c) and subsection (7.6) as the "subject affiliate") of the corporation; and

(c) the subject affiliate is the acquired affiliate or has, immediately before the acquisition time, an equity percentage in the acquired affiliate.

Notes: Reg. 5905(7.5) added by 2002-2013 technical bill, effective on the same basis as Reg. 5905(7.1).

(7.6) [Increase to ACB of shares of lower-tier affiliates] — Subject to paragraph 5908(11)(c), for the purposes of paragraph 92(1.1)(a) of the Act, if this subsection applies, there shall be added, in computing on and after the adjustment time

(a) the direct holder's adjusted cost base of a share of the capital stock of the subject affiliate, the amount determined by the formula

$$A \times B$$

where

A is the amount determined under paragraph (7.2)(a) in respect of the acquired affiliate, and

B is the percentage that would, if the direct holder were resident in Canada, be the direct holder's surplus entitlement percentage in respect of the acquired affiliate immediately before the acquisition time if the direct holder owned only the share; and

(b) the subordinate affiliate's adjusted cost base of a share of the capital stock of the acquired affiliate, the amount determined by the formula

$$C \times D$$

where

C is the amount determined under paragraph (7.2)(a) in respect of the acquired affiliate, and

D is the percentage that would, if the subordinate affiliate were resident in Canada, be the subordinate affiliate's surplus entitlement percentage in respect of the acquired affiliate immediately before the acquisition time if the subordinate affiliate owned only the share.

Related Provisions: Reg. 5905(7.5) — Conditions for subsec. (7.6) to apply.

Notes: Reg. 5905(7.6) added by 2002-2013 technical bill, effective on the same basis as Reg. 5905(7.1).

(7.7) [Prescribed amount for ITA 93(3)(c)] — For the purposes of paragraph 93(3)(c) of the Act, if an amount (referred to in this subsection and subsection 5908(12) as the "adjustment amount") is required by subsection 92(1.1) of the Act to be added in computing, on or after the adjustment time, the adjusted cost base of a share of the capital stock of a foreign affiliate of a corporation resident in Canada,

(a) where paragraph 92(1.1)(a) of the Act applies, the prescribed amount is the adjustment amount; and

(b) where paragraph 92(1.1)(b) of the Act applies, the prescribed amount is the amount determined under subsection 5908(12).

Notes: Reg. 5905(7.7) added by 2002-2013 technical bill, effective on the same basis as Reg. 5905(7.1).

See Notes to Reg. 5905(7) re former proposed (7)-(7.4).

(8), (9) [Repealed]

Notes: Reg. 5905(8)–(9) repealed by 2002-2013 technical bill, for dispositions after Dec. 18, 2009. Earlier amended by P.C. 1997-1670.

(10) ["Surplus entitlement"] — For the purposes of this section, the surplus entitlement at any time of a share owned by a corporation resident in Canada of the capital stock of a foreign affiliate of the corporation in respect of a particular foreign affiliate of the corporation is the portion of

(a) the amount that would have been received on the share if the foreign affiliate had at that time paid dividends the aggregate of which on all shares of its capital stock was equal to the amount that would be its net surplus in respect of the corporation at that time assuming that

(i) each other foreign affiliate of the corporation in which the foreign affiliate had an equity percentage had immediately before that time paid a dividend equal to its net surplus in respect of the corporation immediately before the dividend was paid, and

(ii) any dividend referred to in subparagraph (i) that would be received by another foreign affiliate was received by such other foreign affiliate immediately before any such dividend that it would have paid,

that may reasonably be considered to relate to

(b) the amount that would be the net surplus of the particular affiliate in respect of the corporation at that time assuming that

(i) each other foreign affiliate of the corporation in which the particular affiliate had an equity percentage had immediately before that time paid a dividend equal to its net surplus in respect of the corporation immediately before the dividend was paid, and

(ii) any dividend referred to in subparagraph (i) that would be received by another foreign affiliate was received by such other foreign affiliate immediately before any such dividend that it would have paid.

Related Provisions: Reg. 5905(11) — Interpretation.

(11) [Interpretation for Reg. 5905(10)] — For the purposes of subsection (10),

(a) if a particular foreign affiliate of a corporation has an equity percentage in another foreign affiliate of the corporation that has an equity percentage in the particular affiliate, the amount that would be the net surplus of, or the amount that would be a dividend received by, the particular affiliate is to be determined in a manner that is

(i) reasonable in the circumstances, and

(ii) consistent with the results that would be obtained if a series of actual dividends had been paid and received by the foreign affiliates of the corporation that are relevant to the determination;

(b) if any foreign affiliate of a corporation resident in Canada has issued shares of more than one class of its capital stock, the amount that would be paid as a dividend on the shares of any class is the portion of its net surplus that, in the circumstances, it might reasonably be expected to have paid on all the shares of that class; and

(c) if the particular affiliate's net surplus as determined for the purposes of subsection (10) would, in the absence of this paragraph, be nil the particular affiliate's net surplus for the purposes of that subsection is deemed to be the greater of

(i) the amount of the particular affiliate's retained earnings, if any, determined at the end of its last taxation year ending before the time referred to in that subsection under accounting principles that are relevant to the particular affiliate for that year, and

(ii) the amount determined by the formula

$$A \times B$$

where

A is the amount of the particular affiliate's total assets determined at the end of that year under accounting principles that are relevant to the particular affiliate for that year, and

B is 25%.

Notes: Reg. 5905(11) amended by 2002-2013 technical bill, effective Aug. 20, 2011.

(12) [Repealed]

Notes: Reg. 5905(12) repealed by 2002-2013 technical bill, effective Dec. 19, 2009.

(13) ["Surplus entitlement percentage"] — For the purposes of the definition "surplus entitlement percentage" in subsection 95(1) of the Act and of this Part, the surplus entitlement percentage at any time of a corporation resident in Canada in respect of a particular foreign affiliate of the corporation is,

(a) the percentage that is the corporation's equity percentage in the particular affiliate at that time if

(i) the particular affiliate and each corporation that is relevant to the determination of the corporation's equity percentage in the particular affiliate have, at that time, only one class of issued shares, and

(ii) no foreign affiliate (referred to in this subparagraph as the "upper-tier affiliate") of the corporation that is relevant to the determination of the corporation's equity percentage in the particular affiliate has, at that time, an equity percentage in a foreign affiliate (including, for greater certainty, the particular affiliate) of the corporation that has an equity percentage in the upper-tier affiliate; and

(b) in any other case, the proportion of 100 that

(i) the aggregate of all amounts, each of which is the surplus entitlement at that time of a share owned by the corporation of the capital stock of a foreign affiliate of the corporation in respect of the particular foreign affiliate of the corporation

is of

(ii) the amount determined under paragraph (10)(b) to be the net surplus of the particular affiliate in respect of the corporation at that time.

Related Provisions: ITA 91(1.1)–(1.5) — Deemed year-end to trigger FAPI when SEP reduced.

Notes: Reg. 5905(13)(a) amended by 2002-2013 technical bill (effective Aug. 20, 2011); P.C. 1997-1670.

(14) ["Equity percentage"] — For the purposes of subsections (10), (11) and (13), "equity percentage" has the meaning that would be assigned by subsection 95(4) of the Act if the reference in paragraph (b) of the definition "equity percentage" in that subsection to "any corporation" were read as a reference to "any corporation other than a corporation resident in Canada".

Notes: Reg. 5905(14) added by 2002-2013 technical bill, effective Aug. 20, 2011. This definition was previously in Reg. 5905(13) closing words.

Former proposed Reg. 5905(14)-(15) in the March 16, 2001 draft regs were replaced by Reg. 5908.

For transitional Reg. **5905(16)-(23)** and **Reg. 5905.1**, part of the Consolidated Net Surplus regime for acquisitions/dispositions before Dec. 19, 2009, see up to the 47th ed.

Definitions [Reg. 5905]: "acquired affiliate", "acquisition time" — Reg. 5905(7.1)(b); "adjusted cost base" — ITA 54, 248(1); "adjustment time" — 5905(7.2)(a); "amount" — ITA 248(1), Reg. 5907(7); "arm's length" — ITA 251(1); "corporation" — ITA 248(1), *Interpretation Act* 35(1); "cost amount" — ITA 248(1), Reg. 5905(5.3); "deficit affiliate" — Reg. 5905(7.1)(a); "direct holder" — Reg. 5905(7.5)(b); "designated liquidation and dissolution" — ITA 95(1); "disposition", "dividend" — ITA 248(1); "earnings" — Reg. 5907(1); "equity percentage" — Reg. 5905(14); "exempt deficit" — Reg. 5902(1)–(2), (7), 5905(7)(b), 5907(1); "exempt surplus" — Reg. 5902(1)–(2), (7), 5905(7)(c), 5907(1); "fair market value" — see ITA 69(1) Notes; "foreign affiliate" — ITA 95(1), 248(1), Reg. 5907(3); "foreign merger" — ITA 87(8.1); "hybrid deficit", "hybrid surplus", "hybrid underlying tax" — Reg. 5907(1); "merged affiliate", "merger time" — Reg. 5905(3); "net surplus" — Reg. 5902(1)–(2), 5907(1); "opening exempt deficit" — Reg. 5905(1), 5905(5)(a)(i), 5905.1; "opening exempt surplus" — Reg. 5905(5)(a)(ii), 5905.1; "opening taxable deficit" — Reg. 5905(1), 5905(5)(a)(iii), 5905.1; "opening taxable surplus" — Reg. 5905(5)(a)(iv), 5905.1; "opening underlying foreign tax" — Reg. 5905(5)(a)(v), 5905(5.1); "partnership" — see ITA 96(1) Notes; "person", "prescribed", "property" — ITA 248(1); "relevant tax factor" — ITA 95(1); "resident", "resident in Canada" — ITA 250; "share" — ITA 248(1); "subject affiliate" — Reg. 5905(7.5)(b); "subordinate affiliate" — Reg. 5905(7.2)(c); "substituted" — ITA 248(5); "surplus entitlement percentage" — ITA 95(1), Reg. 5905(13); "surplus entitlement percentage" — Reg. 5905(13); "tax-free surplus balance" — Reg. 5905(5.5); "taxable Canadian corporation" — ITA 89(1), 248(1); "taxable deficit" — Reg. 5902(1)–(2), (7), 5905(7)(c), 5907(1); "taxable income" — ITA 248(1); "taxable surplus" — Reg. 5902(1)–(2), (7), 5905(7)(e), 5907(1); "taxation year" — ITA 249; "underlying foreign tax" — Reg. 5902(1)–(2), (7), 5907(1); "upper-tier affiliate" — Reg. 5905(13)(a)(ii).

5906. Carrying on business in a country — **(1)** For the purposes of this Part, where a foreign affiliate of a corporation resident in Canada carries on an active business, it shall be deemed to carry on that business

(a) in a country other than Canada only to the extent that such business is carried on through a permanent establishment situated therein; and

(b) in Canada only to the extent that its income therefrom is subject to tax under Part I of the Act.

Related Provisions: Reg. 5906(2) — Meaning of "permanent establishment".

(2) The expression **"permanent establishment"** means

(a) for the purposes of paragraph (1)(a) and the definition "earnings" in subsection 5907(1) (which paragraph or definition is referred to in this paragraph as a "provision"),

(i) if the expression is given a particular meaning in a tax treaty with a country, a permanent establishment within the meaning assigned by that tax treaty with respect to the business carried on in that country by the foreign affiliate referred to in the provision, and

(ii) in any other case, a fixed place of business of the affiliate, including an office, a branch, a mine, an oil well, a farm, a timberland, a factory, a workshop or a warehouse, or if the affiliate does not have any fixed place of business, the principal place at which the affiliate's business is conducted; and

(b) for the purposes of subdivision i of Division B of Part I of the Act [ITA ss. 90–95 — ed.],

(i) if the expression is given a particular meaning in a tax treaty with a country, a permanent establishment within the meaning assigned by that tax treaty if the person or partnership referred to in the relevant portion of that subdivision (which person or partnership is referred to in this paragraph and subsection (3) as the "person") is a resident of that country for the purpose of that tax treaty, and

(ii) in any other case, a fixed place of business of the person, including an office, a branch, a mine, an oil well, a farm, a timberland, a factory, a workshop or a warehouse, or if the person does not have any fixed place of business, the principal place at which the person's business is conducted.

Related Provisions: Reg. 5906(3) — Interpretation.

Notes: Reg. 5906(2) amended by 2002-2013 technical bill (last change effective for foreign affiliates' tax years ending after Dec. 18, 2009), 2008 budget bill #2.

(3) For the purposes of subparagraphs (2)(a)(ii) and (b)(ii),

(a) if the affiliate or the person, as the case may be, carries on business through an employee or agent, established in a particular place, who has general authority to contract for the affiliate or the person or who has a stock of merchandise owned by the affiliate or the person from which the employee or agent regularly fills orders, the affiliate or the person is deemed to have a fixed place of business at that place;

(b) if the affiliate or the person, as the case may be, is an insurance corporation, the affiliate or the person is deemed to have a fixed place of business in each country in which the affiliate or the person is registered or licensed to do business;

(c) if the affiliate or the person, as the case may be, uses substantial machinery or equipment at a particular place at any time in a taxation year, the affiliate or the person is deemed to have a fixed place of business at that place;

(d) the fact that the affiliate or the person, as the case may be, has business dealings through a commission agent, broker or other independent agent or maintains an office solely for the purchase of merchandise at a particular place does not of itself mean that the affiliate or the person has a fixed place of business at that place; and

(e) the fact that the affiliate or the person, as the case may be, has a subsidiary controlled corporation at a place or a subsidiary controlled corporation engaged in trade or business at a place does not of itself mean that the affiliate or person has a fixed place of business at that place.

Notes: For the meaning of "substantial machinery or equipment" in Reg. 5906(3)(c), see Notes to Reg. 400(2).

Reg. 5906(3) added by 2002-2013 technical bill, for foreign affiliates' tax years that end after 1999.

Definitions [Reg. 5906]: "active business" — ITA 95(1), Reg. 5907(1); "business" — ITA 248(1); "Canada" — ITA 255, *Interpretation Act* 35(1); "corporation" — ITA 248(1), *Interpretation Act* 35(1); "foreign affiliate" — ITA 95(1), 248(1), Reg. 5907(3); "permanent establishment" — ITA 95(1), Reg. 5906(2); "resident in Canada" — ITA 250; "tax treaty" — ITA 248(1).

5907. Interpretation — (1) [Definitions] — For the purposes of this Part,

"active business" has the meaning assigned by subsection 95(1) of the Act;

Notes: Definition added by P.C. 1997-1670, last effective for foreign affiliates' tax years that end after 1994.

"controlled foreign affiliate" has the meaning assigned by subsection 95(1) of the Act;

Notes: Definition added by P.C. 1997-1670, last effective for foreign affiliates' tax years that end after 1994.

"designated person or partnership", in respect of a taxpayer at any time, means

(a) the taxpayer,

(b) a person or partnership that is at that time

(i) a person (other than a partnership) that does not, at that time, deal at arm's length with the taxpayer, or

(ii) a partnership a member of which is, at that time, a designated person or partnership in respect of the taxpayer under this definition, and

(c) if a foreign affiliate of the taxpayer is an original corporation that undergoes a division in respect of which subsection 15(1.5) of the Act applies, a new corporation in respect of the division;

Notes: Definition amended by 2018 budget bill #2, effective July 27, 2018, effectively to add para. (c) ["the taxpayer" in opening words is now para. (a); (a) is now (b); and (b) is now (b)(i), (ii)]. Before that date, read:

"designated person or partnership", in respect of a taxpayer at any time, means the taxpayer or a person or partnership that is at that time

(a) a person (other than a partnership) that does not, at that time, deal at arm's length with the taxpayer, or

(b) a partnership a member of which is, at that time, a designated person or partnership in respect of the taxpayer under this definition;

Definition added by 2002-2013 technical bill, effective Aug. 20, 2011.

"earnings" of a foreign affiliate of a taxpayer resident in Canada for a taxation year of the affiliate from an active business means

(a) in the case of an active business carried on by it in a country,

(i) the income or profit from the active business for the year computed in accordance with the income tax law of the country in which the affiliate is resident, in any case where the affiliate is required by that law to compute that income or profit,

(ii) the income or profit from the active business for the year computed in accordance with the income tax law of the country in which the business is carried on, in any case not described in subparagraph (i) where the affiliate is required by that law to compute that income or profit, and

(iii) in any other case, the amount that would be the income from the active business for the year under Part I of the Act if the business were carried on in Canada, the affiliate were resident in Canada and the Act were read without reference to subsections 18(4), 80(3) to (12), (15) and (17) and 80.01(5) to (11) and sections 80.02 to 80.04,

adjusted in each case in accordance with subsections (2), (2.1), (2.2) and (2.9) and, for the purposes of this Part, to the extent that the earnings of an affiliate from an active business carried on by it cannot be attributed to a permanent establishment in any particular country, they shall be attributed to the permanent establishment in the country in which the affiliate is resident and, if the affiliate is resident in more than one country, to the permanent establishment in the country that may reasonably be regarded as the affiliate's principal place of residence, and

(b) in any other case, the total of all amounts each of which is an amount of income that would be required under paragraph 95(2)(a) or subsection 95(2.44) of the Act to be included in computing the affiliate's income or loss from an active business for the year if that income were computed taking into account the rules in subsection (2.03);

Related Provisions: Reg. 5906(2)(a) — Meaning of "permanent establishment"; Reg. 5907(2.03) — Earnings determined on basis that foreign affiliate claimed maximum deductions; Reg. 5907(2.9)(a)(i) — Fresh-start rule — addition to earnings.

Notes: *Disregarded LLCs*: CRA's 2009 position was that such an LLC carrying on an active business should compute earnings under (a)(i): VIEWS doc 2011-0404501C6 [2011 IFA q.9]. Its 2016 position is that the LLC should use (a)(iii): 2016-0669761C6 [2016 CTF q.11]; Barnicke & Huynh, "Earnings of Disregarded US LLC", 25(2) *Canadian Tax Highlights* (ctf.ca) 5-6 (Feb. 2017). Grandfathering in 2017-0691201C6 [IFA 2017 q.9]: for tax years that end after Aug. 19, 2011 and begin before Nov. 29, 2016, taxpayer X can choose to compute the LLC's earnings either way, provided X and all taxpayers related to X consistently use either the 2009 or the 2016 position to calculate earnings of all FAs that are disregarded US LLCs for all years. For tax years ending after Nov. 29, 2016, all must use the 2016 position.

For more CRA interpretation see docs 2008-0287701R3; 2011-0431031E5 (FA carrying on business in Guatemala); 2014-0523341C6 [2014 CALU q.7] (treatment of life insurance proceeds received by FA); 2015-0592921E5 (methodology for computing earnings of Singapore company with foreign branch); 2017-0729431R3 (foreign transfer pricing adjustment requires recomputation of earnings).

"Earnings" amended by 2014 budget bill #2 (implementing Finance comfort letters of May 16 and Aug. 17, 2005 to Charles Webster, last change effective for FAs' tax years that begin after July 12, 2013), 2002-2013 technical bill. Added by P.C. 1997-1670.

"exempt deficit" of a foreign affiliate of a corporation in respect of the corporation at any time means the amount, if any, by which

(a) the total of all amounts each of which is an amount determined at that time under any of subparagraphs (i) to (vi) of the description of B in the definition "exempt surplus" in this subsection

exceeds

(b) the total of all amounts each of which is an amount determined at that time under any of subparagraphs (i) to (vii) of the description of A in that definition;

Related Provisions: ITA 13(21.2)(e)(iii)(E), 18(15)(b)(iv)(A), 40(3.4)(b)(v) — Calculation of exempt deficit on transfer of loss property within affiliated group; ITA 34.2(8)(b) — Whether corporate partner stub-period accrual applies.

Notes: Definition added by P.C. 1997-1670, last change effective for foreign affiliates' tax years that end after 1994; it was formerly at the end of Reg. 5907(1)(d).

"exempt earnings", of a particular foreign affiliate of a particular corporation for a taxation year of the particular affiliate, means, subject to subsection (2.02), the total of all amounts each of which is

(a) the amount by which the capital gains of the particular affiliate for the year (other than capital gains included in computing the amount, at any time in the year, of the particular affiliate's hybrid surplus, or hybrid deficit, in respect of the particular corporation) exceed the total of

(i) the amount of the taxable capital gains for the year referred to in the description of B in the definition "foreign accrual property income" in subsection 95(1) of the Act,

(ii) the amount of the taxable capital gains for the year referred to in subparagraphs (c)(i), (e)(i) and (f)(iv) of the definition "net earnings", and

(iii) the portion of any income or profits tax paid to the government of a country for the year by the particular affiliate that can reasonably be regarded as tax in respect of the amount by which the capital gains of the particular affiliate for the year exceed the total of the amounts referred to in subparagraphs (i) and (ii),

[Closing words repealed]

(a.1) the amount determined by the formula

$$A - B$$

where

A is the total of all amounts each of which is a particular amount that would be included, in respect of a particular business of the particular affiliate, by paragraph (c), (c.1) or (c.2) of the definition "capital dividend account" in subsection 89(1) of the Act in determining the particular affiliate's capital dividend account at the end of the year if

(i) the particular affiliate were the corporation referred to in that definition,

(ii) the references in paragraphs (c.1) and (c.2) of that definition, and in paragraph (c) of that definition as that paragraph (c) read in its application to taxation years that ended before February 28, 2000, to "a business" were read as references to a business that

(A) is not an active business (as defined in subsection 95(1) of the Act), or

(B) is an active business (as defined in that subsection 95(1)) the particular affiliate's earnings from which for the year are determined under subparagraph (a)(iii) of the definition "earnings", and

(iii) the particular amount did not include any amount that can reasonably be considered to have accrued while no person or partnership that carried on the particular business was a specified person or partnership (within the meaning of section 95 of the Act) in respect of the particular corporation, and

B is the amount determined for A at the end of the particular affiliate's taxation year that immediately precedes the year,

(b) where the year is the 1975 or any preceding taxation year of the particular affiliate, the total of all amounts each of which is the particular affiliate's net earnings for the year,

(c) where the year is the 1975 or any preceding taxation year of the particular affiliate, the earnings as determined in paragraph (b) of the definition "earnings" in this subsection to the extent that those earnings have not been included because of paragraph (b) or deducted in determining an amount included in subparagraph (b)(i) of the definition "exempt loss" in this subsection,

(d) where the year is the 1976 or any subsequent taxation year of the particular affiliate and the particular affiliate is, throughout the year, resident in a designated treaty country,

(i) the particular affiliate's net earnings for the year from an active business carried on by it in Canada or a designated treaty country, or

(ii) the particular affiliate's earnings for the year from an active business to the extent that they derive from

(A) income that is required to be included in computing the particular affiliate's income or loss from an active business for the year under subparagraph 95(2)(a)(i) of the Act and that would

(I) if earned by the other foreign affiliate referred to in subclause 95(2)(a)(i)(A)(I) or (IV) of the Act, be included in computing the exempt earnings or exempt loss of the other foreign affiliate for a taxation year,

(II) if earned by the life insurance corporation referred to in subclause 95(2)(a)(i)(A)(II) of the Act and based on the assumptions contained in subclause 95(2)(a)(i)(B)(II) of the Act, be included in computing the exempt earnings or exempt loss, of the life insurance corporation for a taxation year, or

(III) if earned from the active business activities carried on by the particular affiliate, or the partnership referred to in subclause 95(2)(a)(i)(A)(III) of the Act, be included in computing the exempt earnings or exempt loss of the particular affiliate for a taxation year,

(B) income that is required to be included in computing the particular affiliate's income or loss from an active business for the year under clause 95(2)(a)(ii)(A) of the Act where the income is derived from amounts that are paid or payable by the life insurance corporation referred to in that clause and are for expenditures that would, if that life insurance corporation were a foreign affiliate of the particular corporation, be deductible in computing its exempt earnings or exempt loss for a taxation year,

(C) income that is required to be included in computing the particular affiliate's income or loss from an active business for the year under clause 95(2)(a)(ii)(B) of the Act to the extent that the amounts paid or payable referred to in that clause are for expenditures that are deductible in computing the exempt earnings or exempt loss, for a taxation year, of the other foreign affiliate referred to in that clause,

(D) income that is required to be included in computing the particular affiliate's income or loss from an active business for the year under clause 95(2)(a)(ii)(C) of the Act to the extent that the amounts paid or payable referred to in that clause are for expenditures that are deductible in computing its exempt earnings or exempt loss for a taxation year,

(E) income that is required to be included in computing the particular affiliate's income or loss from an active business for the year under clause 95(2)(a)(ii)(D) of the Act if

(I) the second and third affiliates referred to in subclause 95(2)(a)(ii)(D)(IV) of the Act are each resident in a designated treaty country throughout their relevant taxation years (within the meaning assigned by that subclause), and

(II) that income would be required to be so included if

1. paragraph (a) of the definition "excluded property" in subsection 95(1) of the Act were read as follows:

(a) used or held by the foreign affiliate principally for the purpose of gaining or producing income from an active business carried on by it in a designated treaty country (within the meaning assigned by subsection 5907(11) of the *Income Tax Regulations*),

2. paragraph (c) of that definition "excluded property" were read as follows:

(c) property all or substantially all of the income from which is, or would be, if there were income from the property, income from an active business (which, for this purpose, includes income that would be deemed to be income from an active business by paragraph (2)(a) if that paragraph were read without reference to subparagraph (v)) that is included in computing the foreign affiliate's exempt earnings, or exempt loss, as defined in subsection 5907(1) of the *Income Tax Regulations*, for a taxation year,

(F) income that is required to be included in computing the particular affiliate's income or loss from an active business for the year under subparagraph 95(2)(a)(iii) of the Act to the extent that the trade accounts receivable referred to in that subparagraph arose in the course of an active business carried on by the other foreign affiliate referred to in that subparagraph the income or loss from which is included in computing its exempt earnings or exempt loss for a taxation year,

(G) income that is required to be included in computing the particular affiliate's income or loss from an active business for the year under subparagraph 95(2)(a)(iv) of the Act to the extent that the loans or lending assets referred to in that subparagraph arose in the course of an active business carried on by the other foreign affiliate referred to in that subparagraph the income or loss from which is included in computing its exempt earnings or exempt loss for a taxation year,

(H) income that is required to be included in computing the particular affiliate's income or loss from an active business for the year under subparagraph 95(2)(a)(v) of the Act, where all or substantially all of its income, from the property described in that subparagraph, is, or would be if there were income from the property, income from an active business (which, for this purpose, includes income that would be deemed to be income from an active business by paragraph 95(2)(a) of the Act if that paragraph were read without reference to its subparagraph (v) and, for greater certainty, excludes income arising as a result of the disposition of the property) that is included in computing its exempt earnings or exempt loss for a taxation year,

(I) income that is required to be included in computing the particular affiliate's income or loss from an active business for the year under subparagraph 95(2)(a)(vi) of

the Act, where the agreement for the purchase, sale or exchange of currency referred to in that subparagraph can reasonably be considered to have been made by the particular affiliate to reduce its risk with respect to an amount of income or loss that is included in computing its exempt earnings or exempt loss for a taxation year, or

(J) an amount that is required to be included in computing the particular affiliate's income from an active business for the year under subsection 95(2.44) of the Act if the amount is in respect of income that would, in the absence of paragraph 95(2)(a.3) of the Act, be income from an active business carried on by the particular affiliate in a designated treaty country, or

(e) where the year is the 1976 or any subsequent taxation year of the particular affiliate, each amount that is included in the particular affiliate's exempt earnings for the year because of subsection (10),

minus the portion of any income or profits tax paid to the government of a country for the year by the particular affiliate that can reasonably be regarded as tax in respect of the earnings referred to in paragraph (c) or in subparagraph (d)(ii);

Related Provisions: ITA 95(2)(n) — Deemed FA and deemed qualifying interest for para. (d); ITA 257 — Negative amounts in formulas; Reg. 5906(2)(a) — Meaning of "permanent establishment"; Reg. 5907(1.02) — New FA deemed resident in designated treaty country throughout year; Reg. 5907(2.02) — Anti-avoidance rule; Reg. 5910(1) — FA carrying on foreign oil & gas business deemed to have paid income or profits tax.

Notes: See VIEWS docs 2003-0016811R3 (designated treaty country residence requirement in para. (d) is satisfied); 2009-0316641C4 (where FA is resident in country A and has a branch in B, Canada would have to have a treaty or TIEA with both countries, but not if the FA is only incorporated (and not resident) in A); 2009-0347271R3 (opinion on amendment to (d)(ii)(E) enacted in 2013); 2015-0573141R3 (ruling applying (d)(ii)(A)(I)); 2015-0592921E5 (earnings from branch in non-treaty country are not included in exempt earnings).

For the meaning of "income or profits tax" in (a)(iii) and the closing words, see Notes to ITA 126(4). For "derived" in (d)(ii)(B), see Notes to ITA 18.1(12). CRA considers that "substantially all", used in (d)(ii)(E)(II)2 and (d)(ii)(H), means 90% or more.

Definition amended by 2014 budget bill #2 (last effective for foreign affiliates' tax years that end after July 12, 2013), 2002-2013 technical bill. Added by P.C. 1997-1670; it was formerly Reg. 5907(1)(b).

"exempt loss", of a foreign affiliate of a corporation for a taxation year of the affiliate, means, subject to subsection (2.02), the total of all amounts each of which is

(a) the amount by which the capital losses of the affiliate for the year (other than capital losses included in computing the amount, at any time in the year, of the particular affiliate's hybrid surplus, or hybrid deficit, in respect of the particular corporation) exceed the total of

(i) the amount of the allowable capital losses for the year referred to in the description of E in the definition "foreign accrual property income" in subsection 95(1) of the Act,

(ii) the amount of the allowable capital losses for the year referred to in subparagraphs (c)(i), (e)(i) and (f)(iv) of the definition "net loss", and

(iii) the portion of any income or profits tax refunded by the government of a country for the year to the affiliate that can reasonably be regarded as tax refunded in respect of the amount by which the capital losses of the affiliate for the year exceed the total of the amounts referred to in subparagraphs (i) and (ii),

(a.1) the total of all amounts each of which is the portion of an eligible capital expenditure of the affiliate, in respect of a business of the affiliate, that was not included at any time in the affiliate's cumulative eligible capital in respect of the business, if

(i) the business

(A) is not an active business (as defined in subsection 95(1) of the Act), or

(B) is an active business (as defined in subsection 95(1) of the Act) the affiliate's earnings from which for the year are determined under subparagraph (a)(iii) of the definition "earnings", and

(ii) in computing its income for the year, the affiliate has deducted an amount described in paragraph 24(1)(a) of the Act for the year in respect of the business,

(b) where the year is the 1975 or any preceding taxation year of the affiliate, the total of all amounts each of which is

(i) the affiliate's net loss for the year from an active business carried on by it in a country, or

(ii) the amount, if any, for the year by which

(A) the amount determined under the description of D in the definition "foreign accrual property income" in subsection 95(1) of the Act for the year

exceeds

(B) the amount determined under the description of A in the definition "foreign accrual property income" in subsection 95(1) of the Act for the year,

(c) where the year is the 1976 or any subsequent taxation year of the affiliate and the affiliate is, throughout the year, resident in a designated treaty country,

(i) the affiliate's net loss for the year from an active business carried on by it in Canada or a designated treaty country, or

(ii) the amount by which

(A) the affiliate's loss for the year from an active business to the extent determined under subparagraph (d)(ii) of the definition "exempt earnings" in respect of the year with any modifications that the circumstances require

exceeds

(B) the portion of any income or profits tax refunded by the government of a country for the year to the affiliate that can reasonably be regarded as tax that was refunded in respect of the amount determined under clause (A), or

(d) where the year is the 1976 or any subsequent taxation year of the affiliate, each amount that is included in the affiliate's exempt loss for the year because of subsection (10);

Related Provisions: ITA 95(2)(n) — Deemed FA and deemed qualifying interest for para. (c); Reg. 5907(1.02) — New FA deemed resident in designated treaty country throughout year; Reg. 5907(2.02) — Anti-avoidance rule; Reg. 5910(1) — FA carrying on foreign oil & gas business deemed to have paid income or profits tax.

Notes: For the meaning of "income or profits tax" in (a)(iii) and (c)(ii)(B), see Notes to ITA 126(4).

Definition amended by 2002-2013 technical bill, last change effective for foreign affiliates' tax years that begin after 2012.

"exempt surplus", of a foreign affiliate (in this definition referred to as the "subject affiliate") of a corporation in respect of the corporation, at any particular time, means the amount determined by the following formula in respect of the period that begins with the latest of the following times and that ends with the particular time:

(a) the first day of the taxation year of the subject affiliate in which it last became a foreign affiliate of the corporation,

(b) the last time for which the opening exempt surplus of the subject affiliate in respect of the corporation was required to be determined under section 5905, and

(c) the last time for which the opening exempt deficit of the subject affiliate in respect of the corporation was required to be determined under section 5905

$$A - B$$

where

A is the total of all amounts, in respect of the period, each of which is

(i) the opening exempt surplus, if any, of the subject affiliate in respect of the corporation as determined under section 5905, at the time established in paragraph (b),

(ii) the exempt earnings of the subject affiliate for any of its taxation years ending in the period,

(iii) the portion of any dividend received in the period and before the particular time by the subject affiliate from another foreign affiliate of the corporation (including, for greater certainty, any dividend deemed by subsection 5905(7) to have been received by the subject affiliate) that was prescribed by paragraph 5900(1)(a) to have been paid out of the payer affiliate's exempt surplus in respect of the corporation,

(iv) the portion of any income or profits tax refunded by or the amount of a tax credit paid by the government of a country to the subject affiliate that can reasonably be regarded as having been refunded or paid in respect of any amount referred to in subparagraph (iii) and that was not deducted in determining any amount referred to in subparagraph (iii) of the description of B,

(v) the portion of any taxable dividend received in the period and before the particular time by the subject affiliate that would, if the dividend were received by the corporation, be deductible by it under section 112 of the Act,

(vi) an amount added to the exempt surplus of the subject affiliate or deducted from its exempt deficit in the period and before the particular time under subsection (1.092), (1.1) or (1.2),

(vi.1) each amount that is required, under section 5905, to be included under this subparagraph in the period and before the particular time, or

(vii) an amount added, in the period and before the particular time, to the exempt surplus of the subject affiliate under paragraph (7.1)(d) (as that paragraph applied to dividends paid on or before August 19, 2011), and

B is the total of those of the following amounts that apply in respect of the period:

(i) the opening exempt deficit, if any, of the subject affiliate in respect of the corporation as determined under section 5905, at the time established in paragraph (c),

(ii) the exempt loss of the subject affiliate for any of its taxation years ending in the period,

(iii) the portion of any income or profits tax paid to the government of a country by the subject affiliate that may reasonably be regarded as having been paid in respect of any amount referred to in subparagraph (iii), (iv) or (v) of the description of A,

(iv) the portion of any whole dividend paid by the subject affiliate in the period and before the particular time deemed by paragraph 5901(1)(a) to have been paid out of the subject affiliate's exempt surplus in respect of the corporation,

(v) each amount that is required under section 5902 or 5905 to be included under this subparagraph, or subparagraph (1)(d)(xii) as it applies to taxation years that end before February 22, 1994, in the period and before the particular time, or

(vi) an amount, in the period and before the particular time, deducted from the exempt surplus of the subject affiliate or added to its exempt deficit under subsection (1.092), (1.1) or (1.2);

Related Provisions: ITA 13(21.2)(e)(iii)(E), 18(15)(b)(iv)(A), 40(3.4)(b)(v) — Calculation of exempt surplus on transfer of loss property within affiliated group; ITA 34.2(8)(b) — Whether corporate partner stub-period accrual applies; ITA 257 — Negative amounts in formulas; Reg. 5905(1) — Acquisition or disposition of foreign affiliate; Reg. 5905(3) — Effect of foreign merger; Reg. 5905(5.1) — Exempt surplus after amalgamation or windup of corporation holding FA; Reg. 5905(7.2) — Blocking deficit — inclusions in A(vi.1) and B(v); Reg. 5907(1)"exempt deficit" — Where A–B is negative; Reg. 5907(11) — Designated treaty country; Reg. 5910(1) — FA carrying on foreign oil & gas business deemed to have paid income or profits tax.

Notes: See Notes to ITA 113(1); Talakshi & Samuel, "Foreign Affiliate Surplus" 18 *Canadian Petroleum Tax Journal* §4 (2005); Edwards & Buttenham, "TIEAs: Not All

For "income or profits tax" in A(iv) and B(iii), see Notes to ITA 126(4).

Definition amended by 2014 budget bill #2 (last change effective for foreign affiliates' tax years that end after July 11, 2013), 2002-2013 technical bill. Added by P.C. 1997-1670; it was formerly Reg. 5907(1)(d).

"hybrid deficit", of a foreign affiliate of a corporation in respect of the corporation at any time, means the amount, if any, by which

(a) the total of all amounts each of which is an amount determined at that time under any of subparagraphs (i) to (vii) of the description of B in the definition "hybrid surplus"

exceeds

(b) the total of all amounts each of which is an amount determined at that time under any of subparagraphs (i) to (v) of the description of A in that definition;

Related Provisions: ITA 40(3.4)(b)(v) — Calculation of hybrid deficit on transfer of loss property within affiliated group; ITA 257 — Negative amounts in formulas; Reg. 5905 — Computation of amounts affecting hybrid surplus; Reg. 5907(1)"hybrid deficit" — Where A–B is negative; Reg. 5907(5.01) — Where amount in B(iii) is not in Canadian currency.

Notes: See Notes to Reg. 5907(1)"hybrid surplus". Definition added by 2002-2013 technical bill, effective Aug. 20, 2011.

"hybrid surplus", of a foreign affiliate (in this definition referred to as the "subject affiliate") of a corporation in respect of the corporation, at any particular time, means the amount determined by the following formula in respect of the period that begins with the latest of the following times and that ends with the particular time:

(a) the first day of the taxation year of the subject affiliate in which it last became a foreign affiliate of the corporation,

(b) the last time for which the opening hybrid surplus of the subject affiliate in respect of the corporation was required to be determined under section 5905, and

(c) the last time for which the opening hybrid deficit of the subject affiliate in respect of the corporation was required to be determined under section 5905

$$A - B$$

where

A is the total of all amounts, in respect of the period, each of which is

(i) the opening hybrid surplus, if any, of the subject affiliate in respect of the corporation as determined under section 5905, at the time established in paragraph (b),

(ii) the amount of a capital gain (except to the extent that the taxable portion of the capital gain is included under the description of B in the definition "foreign accrual property income" in subsection 95(1) of the Act in respect of the subject affiliate), for a taxation year, of the subject affiliate, or of a partnership of which the subject affiliate is a member (to the extent that the capital gain is reasonably attributable to the subject affiliate), in respect of a disposition, at any time in the period, of

(A) a share of the capital stock of another foreign affiliate of the corporation,

(B) a partnership interest, or

(C) a property, that is an excluded property of the subject affiliate because of paragraph (c.1) of the definition "excluded property" in subsection 95(1) of the Act, that related to

(I) an amount that was receivable under an agreement that relates to the sale of a property that is referred to in clause (A) or (B) the capital gain or capital loss from the sale of which is included under this subparagraph or subparagraph (ii) of the description of B, as the case may be, or

(II) an amount payable, or an amount of indebtedness, described in clause (c.1)(ii)(B) of that defini-

tion "excluded property" arising in respect of the acquisition of an excluded property of the affiliate that is referred to in clause (A) or (B) any capital gain or capital loss from the disposition of which would, if that excluded property were disposed of, be included under this subparagraph or subparagraph (ii) of the description of B, as the case may be,

(iii) the portion of any income or profits tax refunded by the government of a country to the subject affiliate that can reasonably be regarded as having been refunded in respect of an amount referred to in subparagraph (ii) or (iii) of the description of B,

(iv) the portion of any dividend received in the period and before the particular time by the subject affiliate from another foreign affiliate of the corporation (including, for greater certainty, any dividend deemed under subsection 5905(7) to have been received by the subject affiliate) that was prescribed under paragraph 5900(1)(a.1) to have been paid out of the payer affiliate's hybrid surplus in respect of the corporation, or

(v) an amount added to the hybrid surplus of the subject affiliate or deducted from its hybrid deficit in the period and before the particular time under subsection (1.092), (1.1) or (1.2), and

B is the total of those of the following amounts that apply in respect of the period:

(i) the opening hybrid deficit, if any, of the subject affiliate in respect of the corporation as determined under section 5905, at the time established in paragraph (c),

(ii) the amount of a capital loss (except to the extent that the allowable portion of the capital loss is included under paragraph (a) of the description of E in the definition "foreign accrual property income" in subsection 95(1) of the Act in respect of the subject affiliate), for a taxation year, of the subject affiliate, or of a partnership of which the subject affiliate is a member (to the extent that the capital loss is reasonably attributable to the subject affiliate), in respect of a disposition, at any time in the period, of

(A) a share of the capital stock of another foreign affiliate of the corporation,

(B) a partnership interest, or

(C) a property, that is an excluded property of the subject affiliate because of paragraph (c.1) of the definition "excluded property" in subsection 95(1) of the Act, that related to

(I) an amount that was receivable under an agreement that relates to the sale of a property that is referred to in clause (A) or (B) the capital gain or capital loss from the sale of which is included under subparagraph (ii) of the description of A or this subparagraph, as the case may be, or

(II) an amount payable, or an amount of indebtedness, described in clause (c.1)(ii)(B) of that definition "excluded property" arising in respect of the acquisition of an excluded property of the affiliate that is referred to in clause (A) or (B) any capital gain or capital loss from the disposition of which would, if that excluded property were disposed of, be included under subparagraph (ii) of the description of A or this subparagraph, as the case may be,

(iii) the amount of a capital loss for a taxation year of the subject affiliate that would arise in respect of a disposition, at any time in the period, of a share of the capital stock of another foreign affiliate of the corporation in the course of the liquidation and dissolution of that other affiliate if subclause 95(2)(e)(iv)(A)(II) of the Act were read without reference to its sub-subclause 1 and section 93 of the Act were read without reference to its subsection (4),

(iv) the portion of any income or profits tax paid to the government of a country by the subject affiliate that can reasonably be regarded as having been paid in respect of an amount referred to in subparagraph (ii) or (iv) of the description of A,

(v) the portion of any whole dividend paid by the subject affiliate in the period and before the particular time deemed under paragraph 5901(1)(a.1) or, if subsection 5901(1.1) applied to the whole dividend, paragraph 5901(1)(b) to have been paid out of the subject affiliate's hybrid surplus in respect of the corporation,

(vi) each amount that is required under section 5902 to be included under this subparagraph in the period and before the particular time, or

(vii) an amount deducted from the hybrid surplus of the subject affiliate or added to its hybrid deficit in the period and before the particular time under subsection (1.092), (1.1) or (1.2);

Related Provisions: ITA 40(3.4)(b)(v) — Calculation of hybrid surplus on transfer of loss property within affiliated group; ITA 257 — Negative amounts in formulas; Reg. 5905 — Computation of amounts affecting hybrid surplus; Reg. 5907(1)"hybrid deficit" — Where A–B is negative; Reg. 5907(5.01) — Where amount in B(iii) is not in Canadian currency.

Notes: See Notes to ITA 113(1). Simplified, hybrid surplus (HS) is capital gains on the sale of partnership interests and of other foreign affiliates. Half of HS paid to the Canadian parent is deductible against the dividend, like exempt surplus (113(1)(a.1)(i)); the other half is deductible based on grossed-up underlying foreign tax, like taxable surplus (113(1)(a.1)(ii)). The Reg. 5901(1.1) election allows taxable surplus to be extracted before HS if that is more beneficial.

For "income or profits tax" in (c)A(iii) and (c)B(iv), see ITA 126(4) Notes.

Definition amended by 2014 budget bill #2 (last effective for foreign affiliates' tax years that end after July 11, 2013), 2002-2013 technical bill.

"hybrid underlying tax", of a foreign affiliate (in this definition referred to as the "subject affiliate") of a corporation in respect of the corporation, at any particular time, means the amount determined by the following formula in respect of the period that begins with the later of the following times and that ends with the particular time:

(a) the first day of the taxation year of the subject affiliate in which it last became a foreign affiliate of the corporation, and

(b) the last time for which the opening hybrid underlying tax of the subject affiliate in respect of the corporation was required to be determined under section 5905

$$A - B$$

where

A is the total of all amounts, in respect of the period, each of which is

(i) the opening hybrid underlying tax, if any, of the subject affiliate in respect of the corporation as determined under section 5905, at the time established in paragraph (b),

(ii) the portion of any income or profits tax paid to the government of a country by the subject affiliate that can reasonably be regarded as having been paid in respect of any amount referred to in subparagraph (ii) or (iv) of the description of A in the definition "hybrid surplus",

(iii) each amount that was prescribed by paragraph 5900(1)(c.1) to have been the foreign tax applicable to the portion of any dividend received in the period and before the particular time by the subject affiliate from another foreign affiliate of the corporation (including, for greater certainty, any dividend deemed under subsection 5905(7) to have been received by the subject affiliate) that was

prescribed by paragraph 5900(1)(a.1) to have been paid out of the payer affiliate's hybrid surplus in respect of the corporation, or

(iv) the amount by which the subject affiliate's hybrid underlying tax is required to be increased in the period and before the particular time under subsection (1.092), (1.1) or (1.2),

B is the total of those of the following amounts that apply in respect of the period:

(i) the portion of any income or profits tax refunded by the government of a country to the subject affiliate that can reasonably be regarded as having been refunded in respect of an amount referred to in subparagraph (ii) or (iii) of the description of B in the definition "hybrid surplus",

(ii) the hybrid underlying tax applicable to any whole dividend paid by the subject affiliate in the period and before the particular time deemed under paragraph 5901(1)(a.1) or, if subsection 5901(1.1) applied to the whole dividend, paragraph 5901(1)(b) to have been paid out of the subject affiliate's hybrid surplus in respect of the corporation before that time,

(iii) each amount that is required under section 5902 to be included under this subparagraph in the period and before the particular time, or

(iv) the amount by which the subject affiliate's hybrid underlying tax is required to be decreased in the period and before the particular time under subsection (1.092), (1.1) or (1.2);

Related Provisions: ITA 257 — Negative amounts in formulas.

Notes: For "income or profits tax" in (b)A(ii) and (b)B(i), see Notes to ITA 126(4).

Definition amended by 2014 budget bill #2, last effective for foreign affiliates' tax years that end after July 11, 2013. Added by 2002-2013 technical bill.

"hybrid underlying tax applicable", in respect of a corporation to a whole dividend paid at any time on the shares of any class of the capital stock of a foreign affiliate of the corporation by the affiliate, means the proportion of the hybrid underlying tax of the affiliate at that time in respect of the corporation that

(a) the portion of the whole dividend deemed to have been paid out of the affiliate's hybrid surplus in respect of the corporation

is of

(b) the affiliate's hybrid surplus at that time in respect of the corporation;

Notes: Definition added by 2002-2013 technical bill, effective Aug. 20, 2011.

"loss", of a foreign affiliate of a taxpayer resident in Canada for a taxation year of the affiliate from an active business, means

(a) in the case of an active business carried on by it in a country, the amount of its loss for the year from the active business carried on in the country computed by applying the provisions of paragraph (a) of the definition "earnings" respecting the computation of earnings from that active business carried on in that country, with any modifications that the circumstances require, and

(b) in any other case, the total of all amounts each of which is an amount of a loss that would be required under paragraph 95(2)(a) of the Act to be included in computing the affiliate's income or loss from an active business for the year if that loss were computed taking into account the rules in subsection (2.03);

Related Provisions: Reg. 5907(2.03) — Loss determined on basis that foreign affiliate claimed maximum deductions; Reg. 5907(2.9)(a)(ii) — Fresh-start rule — addition to loss.

Notes: Definition amended by 2002-2013 technical bill, last change effective for foreign affiliates' tax years that end after Aug. 19, 2011. Added by P.C. 1997-1670; it was formerly Reg. 5907(1)(e).

"net earnings" of a foreign affiliate of a corporation for a taxation year of the affiliate

(a) from an active business carried on by it in a country is the amount of its earnings for the year from that active business carried on in that country minus the portion of any income or profits tax paid to the government of a country for the year by the affiliate that can reasonably be regarded as tax in respect of those earnings,

(b) in respect of foreign accrual property income is the amount that would be its foreign accrual property income for the year, if the formula in the definition "foreign accrual property income" in subsection 95(1) of the Act were read without reference to F and F.1 in that formula and the amount determined for E in that formula were the amount determined under paragraph (a) of the description of E in that formula, minus the portion of any income or profits tax paid to the government of a country for the year by the affiliate that can reasonably be regarded as tax in respect of that income,

(c) from dispositions of property used or held by it principally for the purpose of gaining or producing income from an active business carried on by it in a country that is not a designated treaty country (other than Canada) is the amount, if any, by which

(i) the portion of the affiliate's taxable capital gains for the year from those dispositions that can reasonably be considered to have accrued after November 12, 1981

exceeds

(ii) the portion of any income or profits tax paid to the government of a country for the year by the affiliate that can reasonably be regarded as tax in respect of the amount determined under subparagraph (i),

(d) [Repealed]

(e) from the disposition of a property that is an excluded property of the affiliate that is described in paragraph (c) of the definition "excluded property" in subsection 95(1) of the Act but that would not be an excluded property of the affiliate if that paragraph were read in the manner described in sub-subclause (d)(ii)(E)(II)2 of the definition "exempt earnings" is the amount, if any, by which

(i) the portion of the affiliate's taxable capital gain for the year from the disposition of the property that accrued after its 1975 taxation year

exceeds

(ii) the portion of any income or profits tax paid to the government of a country for the year by the affiliate that can reasonably be regarded as tax that was paid in respect of the amount determined under subparagraph (i), and

(f) from a particular disposition of a property, that is an excluded property of the affiliate because of paragraph (c.1) of the definition "excluded property" in subsection 95(1) of the Act, that related to

(i) an amount that was receivable under an agreement that relates to the sale of a particular property the taxable capital gain or allowable capital loss from the sale of which is included under any of paragraphs (c) to (e) of this definition or of the definition "net loss", as the case may be,

(ii) an amount that was receivable and was a property that was described in paragraph (c) of that definition "excluded property" but that would not have been an excluded property of the affiliate if that paragraph were read in the manner described in sub-subclause (d)(ii)(E)(II)2 of the definition "exempt earnings", or

(iii) an amount payable, or an amount of indebtedness, described in clause (c.1)(ii)(B) of that definition "excluded property" arising in respect of the acquisition of an excluded property of the affiliate any taxable capital gain or allowable capital loss from the disposition of which would, if that ex-

cluded property were disposed of, be included under any of paragraphs (c) to (e) of this definition or of the definition "net loss", as the case may be,

is the amount, if any, by which

(iv) the portion of the affiliate's taxable capital gain for the year from the particular disposition that accrued after its 1975 taxation year

exceeds

(v) the portion of any income or profits tax paid to the government of a country for the year by the affiliate that can reasonably be regarded as tax that was paid for the year in respect of the amount determined under subparagraph (iv);

Related Provisions: Reg. 5910(1) — FA carrying on foreign oil & gas business deemed to have paid income or profits tax.

Notes: For the meaning of "income or profits tax", see Notes to ITA 126(4).

Definition amended by 2002-2013 technical bill, last change effective for FAs' tax years that begin after 2012. Added by P.C. 1997-1670; it was formerly Reg. 5907(1)(f).

"net loss" of a foreign affiliate of a corporation for a taxation year of the affiliate

(a) from an active business carried on by it in a country is the amount of its loss for the year from that active business carried on in that country minus the portion of any income or profits tax refunded by the government of a country for the year to the affiliate that can reasonably be regarded as tax refunded in respect of that loss,

(b) in respect of foreign accrual property income is the amount, if any, by which

(i) the amount, if any, by which

(A) the total of

(I) the amount determined for D in the formula in the definition "foreign accrual property income" in subsection 95(1) of the Act for the year,

(II) the amount determined under paragraph (a) of the description of E in that formula for the year,

(III) the amount determined for G in that formula for the year, and

(IV) the amount determined for H in that formula for the year

exceeds

(B) the total of the amounts determined under the descriptions of A, A.1, A.2, B and C in the definition "foreign accrual property income" in subsection 95(1) of the Act for the year

exceeds

(ii) the portion of any income or profits tax refunded by the government of a country for the year to the affiliate that can reasonably be regarded as tax refunded in respect of the amount determined under subparagraph (i),

(c) from dispositions of property used or held by it principally for the purpose of gaining or producing income from an active business carried on by it in a country that is not a designated treaty country (other than Canada) is the amount, if any, by which

(i) the portion of the affiliate's allowable capital losses for the year from those dispositions that can reasonably be considered to have accrued after November 12, 1981

exceeds

(ii) the portion of any income or profits tax refunded by the government of a country for the year to the affiliate that can reasonably be regarded as tax refunded in respect of the amount determined under subparagraph (i),

(d) [Repealed]

(e) from the disposition of a property, that is an excluded property of the affiliate that is described in paragraph (c) of the definition "excluded property" in subsection 95(1) of the Act but that would not be an excluded property of the affiliate if that paragraph were read in the manner described in sub-subclause (d)(ii)(E)(II)2 of the definition "exempt earnings" is the amount, if any, by which

(i) the portion of the affiliate's allowable capital loss for the year from the disposition of the property that accrued after its 1975 taxation year

exceeds

(ii) the portion of any income or profits tax refunded by the government of a country for the year to the affiliate that can reasonably be regarded as tax that was refunded in respect of the amount determined under subparagraph (i), and

(f) from a particular disposition of a property, that is an excluded property of the affiliate because of paragraph (c.1) of the definition "excluded property" in subsection 95(1) of the Act, that related to

(i) an amount that was receivable under an agreement that relates to the sale of a particular property the taxable capital gain or allowable capital loss from the sale of which is included under any of paragraphs (c) to (e) of this definition or of the definition "net earnings", as the case may be,

(ii) an amount that was receivable and was a property that was described in paragraph (c) of that definition "excluded property" but that would not have been an excluded property of the affiliate if that paragraph were read in the manner described in sub-subclause (d)(ii)(E)(II)2 of the definition "exempt earnings", or

(iii) an amount payable, or an amount of indebtedness, described in clause (c.1)(ii)(B) of that definition "excluded property" arising in respect of the acquisition of an excluded property of the affiliate any taxable capital gain or allowable capital loss from the disposition of which would, if that excluded property were disposed of, be included under any of paragraphs (c) to (e) of this definition or of the definition "net earnings", as the case may be,

is the amount, if any, by which

(iv) the portion of the affiliate's allowable capital loss for the year from the particular disposition that accrued after its 1975 taxation year

exceeds

(v) the portion of any income or profits tax refunded by the government of a country for the year to the affiliate that can reasonably be regarded as tax that was refunded in respect of the amount determined under subparagraph (iv);

Related Provisions: Reg. 5910(1) — FA carrying on foreign oil & gas business deemed to have paid income or profits tax.

Notes: For the meaning of "income or profits tax", see Notes to ITA 126(4).

Definition amended by 2002-2013 technical bill, last change effective for foreign affiliates' tax years that begin after 2012. Added by P.C. 1997-1670; it was formerly Reg. 5907(1)(g).

"net surplus" of a foreign affiliate of a corporation resident in Canada in respect of the corporation is, at any particular time,

(a) if the affiliate has no exempt deficit, no hybrid deficit and no taxable deficit, the amount that is the total of its exempt surplus, hybrid surplus and taxable surplus in respect of the corporation,

(b) if the affiliate has no exempt deficit but has a hybrid deficit and a taxable deficit, the amount, if any, by which its exempt surplus exceeds the total of its hybrid deficit and taxable deficit in respect of the corporation,

(c) if the affiliate has no exempt deficit and no hybrid deficit but has a taxable deficit, the amount, if any, by which the total of its exempt surplus and hybrid surplus exceeds its taxable deficit in respect of the corporation,

(d) if the affiliate has no exempt deficit and no taxable deficit but has a hybrid deficit, the amount, if any, by which the total of

its exempt surplus and taxable surplus exceeds its hybrid deficit in respect of the corporation,

(e) if the affiliate has an exempt deficit but no hybrid deficit or taxable deficit, the amount, if any, by which the total of its hybrid surplus and taxable surplus exceeds its exempt deficit in respect of the corporation,

(f) if the affiliate has an exempt deficit and a hybrid deficit but no taxable deficit, the amount, if any, by which its taxable surplus exceeds the total of its exempt deficit and hybrid deficit in respect of the corporation, or

(g) if the affiliate has an exempt deficit and a taxable deficit but no hybrid deficit, the amount, if any, by which its hybrid surplus exceeds the total of its exempt deficit and taxable deficit in respect of the corporation,

as the case may be, at that time;

Notes: Definition amended by 2002-2013 technical bill, effective Aug. 20, 2011. Added by P.C. 1997-1670; it was formerly Reg. 5907(1)(h).

"taxable deficit" of a foreign affiliate of a corporation in respect of the corporation at any time is the amount, if any, by which

(a) the total of all amounts each of which is an amount determined at that time under any of subparagraphs (i) to (vi) of the description of B in the definition "taxable surplus" in this subsection

exceeds

(b) the total of all amounts each of which is an amount determined at that time under any of subparagraphs (i) to (v) of the description of A in that definition;

Related Provisions: ITA 13(21.2)(e)(iii)(E), 18(15)(b)(iv)(A), 40(3.4)(b)(v) — Calculation of taxable deficit on transfer of loss property within affiliated group; ITA 34.2(8)(b) — Whether corporate partner stub-period accrual applies; Reg. 5905(5.1) — Taxable deficit after amalgamation of corporation holding foreign affiliate; Reg. 5905(5.2) — Taxable deficit after windup of corporation holding foreign affiliate.

Notes: Definition added by P.C. 1997-1670, last change effective for foreign affiliates' tax years ending after 1994; it was formerly the end of Reg. 5907(1)(k).

"taxable earnings" of a foreign affiliate of a corporation for a taxation year of the affiliate is

(a) where the year is the 1975 or any preceding taxation year of the affiliate, nil, and

(b) in any other case, the total of all amounts each of which is

(i) the affiliate's net earnings for the year from an active business carried on by it in a country,

(ii) the affiliate's net earnings for the year in respect of its foreign accrual property income,

(iii) the affiliate's earnings for the year as determined under paragraph (b) of the definition "earnings" minus the portion of any income or profits tax paid to the government of a country for a year by the affiliate that can reasonably be regarded as tax in respect of those earnings,

(iv) to the extent not included under subparagraph (ii), the affiliate's net earnings for the year determined under paragraphs (c) to (f) of the definition "net earnings", or

(iv.1) the amount, if any, by which

(A) the total of all amounts each of which is an amount required by paragraph (2.02)(a) to be included under this definition for the year

exceeds

(B) the total of all amounts each of which is an amount required by paragraph (2.02)(b) to be deducted under this definition for the year,

(v) [Repealed]

but does not include any amount included in the affiliate's exempt earnings for the year;

Related Provisions: Reg. 5910(1) — FA carrying on foreign oil & gas business deemed to have paid income or profits tax.

Notes: See VIEWS doc 2008-0287701R3 (amount included in taxable earnings).

For "income or profits tax" in (b)(iii), see Notes to ITA 126(4).

Definition amended by 2002-2013 technical bill, last effective for foreign affiliates' tax years that end after Aug. 19, 2011. Added by P.C. 1997-1670; it was formerly Reg. 5907(1)(i).

"taxable loss" of a foreign affiliate of a corporation for a taxation year of the affiliate is

(a) where the year is the 1975 or any preceding taxation year of the affiliate, nil, and

(b) in any other case, the total of all amounts each of which is

(i) the affiliate's net loss for the year from an active business carried on by it in a country,

(ii) the affiliate's net loss for the year in respect of foreign accrual property income,

(iii) the affiliate's loss for the year as determined under paragraph (b) of the definition "loss" minus the portion of any income or profits tax refunded by the government of a country for a year to the affiliate that can reasonably be regarded as tax refunded in respect of that loss, or

(iv) to the extent not included under subparagraph (ii), the affiliate's net loss for the year determined under paragraphs (c) to (f) of the definition "net loss",

but does not include any amount included in the affiliate's exempt loss for the year;

Notes: For the meaning of "income or profits tax" in (b)(iii), see Notes to ITA 126(4).

Definition amended by 2002-2013 technical bill, last change effective for dispositions after Dec. 18, 2009. Added by P.C. 1997-1670; it was formerly Reg. 5907(1)(j).

"taxable surplus", of a foreign affiliate (in this definition referred to as the "subject affiliate") of a corporation in respect of the corporation, at any particular time, means the amount determined by the following formula in respect of the period that begins with the latest of the following times and that ends with the particular time:

(a) the first day of the taxation year of the affiliate in which it last became a foreign affiliate of the corporation,

(b) the last time for which the opening taxable surplus of the subject affiliate in respect of the corporation was required to be determined under section 5905, and

(c) the last time for which the opening taxable deficit of the subject affiliate in respect of the corporation was required to be determined under section 5905

$$A - B$$

where

A is the total of all amounts, in respect of the period, each of which is

(i) the opening taxable surplus, if any, of the subject affiliate in respect of the corporation as determined under section 5905, at the time established in paragraph (b),

(ii) the taxable earnings of the subject affiliate for any of its taxation years ending in the period,

(iii) the portion of any dividend received in the period and before the particular time by the subject affiliate from another foreign affiliate of the corporation (including, for greater certainty, any dividend deemed by subsection 5905(7) to have been received by the subject affiliate) that was prescribed by paragraph 5900(1)(b) to have been paid out of the payer affiliate's taxable surplus in respect of the corporation,

(iv) an amount added to the taxable surplus of the subject affiliate or deducted from its taxable deficit in the period and before the particular time under subsection (1.092), (1.1) or (1.2),

(iv.1) each amount that is required under section 5905 to be included under this subparagraph in the period and before the particular time, or

(v) an amount added, in the period and before the particular time, to the subject affiliate's taxable surplus under paragraph (7.1)(e) (as that paragraph applied to dividends paid on or before August 19, 2011), and

B is the total of those of the following amounts that apply in respect of the period:

(i) the opening taxable deficit, if any, of the subject affiliate in respect of the corporation as determined under section 5905, at the time established in paragraph (c),

(ii) the taxable loss of the subject affiliate for any of its taxation years ending in the period,

(iii) the portion of any income or profits tax paid to the government of a country by the subject affiliate that can reasonably be regarded as having been paid in respect of that portion of a dividend referred to in subparagraph (iii) of the description of A,

(iv) the portion of any whole dividend paid by the subject affiliate in the period and before the particular time deemed under paragraph 5901(1)(b) or, if subsection 5901(1.1) applied to the whole dividend, paragraph 5901(1)(a.1) to have been paid out of the subject affiliate's taxable surplus in respect of the corporation,

(v) each amount that is required under section 5902 or 5905 to be included under this subparagraph, or subparagraph (1)(k)(xi) as it applies to taxation years that end before February 22, 1994, in the period and before the particular time, or

(vi) an amount, in the period and before the particular time, deducted from the taxable surplus of the subject affiliate or added to its taxable deficit under subsection (1.092), (1.1) or (1.2);

Related Provisions: ITA 13(21.2)(e)(iii)(E), 18(15)(b)(iv)(A), 40(3.4)(b)(v) — Calculation of taxable surplus on transfer of loss property within affiliated group; ITA 34.2(8)(b) — Whether corporate partner stub-period accrual applies; ITA 257 — Negative amounts in formulas; Reg. 5905(1) — Acquisition or disposition of foreign affiliate; Reg. 5905(3) — Effect of foreign merger; Reg. 5905(5.1) — Taxable surplus after amalgamation of corporation holding foreign affiliate; Reg. 5905(5.2) — Taxable surplus after windup of corporation holding foreign affiliate\; Reg. 5907(1)"taxable deficit" — Where A–B is negative; Reg. 5910(1) — FA carrying on foreign oil & gas business deemed to have paid income or profits tax.

Notes: For the meaning of "income or profits tax" in B(iii), see ITA 126(4) Notes.

Definition amended to by 2014 budget bill #2 (last change effective for foreign affiliates' tax years that end after July 11, 2013), 2002-2013 technical bill. Added by P.C. 1997-1670; it was formerly Reg. 5907(1)(k).

"underlying foreign tax", of a foreign affiliate (in this definition referred to as the "subject affiliate") of a corporation in respect of the corporation, at any particular time, means the amount determined by the following formula in respect of the period that begins with the later of the following times and that ends with the particular time:

(a) the first day of the taxation year of the subject affiliate in which it last became a foreign affiliate of the corporation, and

(b) the last time for which the opening underlying foreign tax of the subject affiliate in respect of the corporation was required to be determined under section 5905

(c) [Repealed]

$$A - B$$

where

A is, subject to subsection (1.03), the total of all amounts, in respect of the period, each of which is

(i) the opening underlying foreign tax, if any, of the subject affiliate in respect of the corporation as determined under section 5905, at the time established in paragraph (b),

(ii) the portion of any income or profits tax paid to the government of a country by the subject affiliate that can reasonably be regarded as having been paid in respect of the taxable earnings, including for greater certainty any amounts included because of paragraph (2.02)(a) in computing the taxable earnings, of the affiliate for a taxation year ending in the period,

(iii) the portion of any income or profits tax referred to in subparagraph (iii) of the description of B in the definition "taxable surplus" in this subsection paid by the subject affiliate in respect of a dividend received from any other foreign affiliate of the corporation,

(iv) each amount that was prescribed by paragraph 5900(1)(d) to have been the foreign tax applicable to the portion of any dividend received in the period and before the particular time by the subject affiliate from another foreign affiliate of the corporation (including, for greater certainty, any dividend deemed by subsection 5905(7) to have been received by the subject affiliate) that was prescribed by paragraph 5900(1)(b) to have been paid out of the payer affiliate's taxable surplus in respect of the corporation, or

(v) the amount by which the subject affiliate's underlying foreign tax is required to be increased in the period and before the particular time under subsection (1.092), (1.1) or (1.2),

B is the total of those of the following amounts that apply in respect of the period:

(i) the portion of any income or profits tax refunded by the government of a country to the affiliate that can reasonably be regarded as having been refunded in respect of the taxable loss of the subject affiliate for a taxation year ending in the period,

(ii) the underlying foreign tax applicable to any whole dividend paid by the subject affiliate in the period and before the particular time deemed under paragraph 5901(1)(b) or, if subsection 5901(1.1) applied to the whole dividend, paragraph 5901(1)(a.1) to have been paid out of the subject affiliate's taxable surplus in respect of the corporation before that time,

(iii) each amount that is required under section 5902 or 5905 to be included under this subparagraph, or subparagraph (1)(l)(x) as it applies to taxation years that end before February 22, 1994, in the period and before the particular time, or

(iv) the amount by which the subject affiliate's underlying foreign tax is required to be decreased in the period and before the particular time under subsection (1.092), (1.1) or (1.2);

Related Provisions: ITA 257 — Negative amounts in formulas; Reg. 5905(1) — Acquisition or disposition of foreign affiliate; Reg. 5905(3) — Effect of foreign merger; Reg. 5905(5.1) — UFT after amalgamation of corporation holding foreign affiliate; Reg. 5905(5.2) — UFT after windup of corporation holding foreign affiliate; Reg. 5907(1.03) — Exclusion of artificially generated amounts; Reg. 5910(1) — FA carrying on foreign oil & gas business deemed to have paid income or profits tax.

Notes: For the meaning of "income or profits tax" in A(ii)-(iii) and B(i), see Notes to ITA 126(4), and see Reg. 5907(1.03) for A(ii)-(iii).

Definition amended by 2014 budget bill #2 (last change effective for foreign affiliates' tax years that end after July 11, 2013), 2002-2013 technical bill. Added by P.C. 1997-1670; it was formerly Reg. 5907(1)(l).

"underlying foreign tax applicable" in respect of a corporation to a whole dividend paid at any time on the shares of any class of the capital stock of a foreign affiliate of the corporation by the affiliate is the total of

(a) the proportion of the underlying foreign tax of the affiliate at that time in respect of the corporation that

(i) the portion of the whole dividend deemed to have been paid out of the affiliate's taxable surplus in respect of the corporation

is of

(ii) the affiliate's taxable surplus at that time in respect of the corporation, and

(b) any additional amount in respect of the whole dividend that the corporation claims in its return of income under Part I of the Act in respect of the whole dividend, not exceeding the amount that is the lesser of

(i) the amount by which the portion of the whole dividend deemed to have been paid out of the affiliate's taxable surplus in respect of the corporation exceeds the amount determined under paragraph (a), and

(ii) the amount by which the affiliate's underlying foreign tax in respect of the corporation immediately before the whole dividend was paid exceeds the amount determined under paragraph (a);

Notes: See VIEWS doc 2012-0460671E5 (disproportionate para. (b) election).

Definition amended by 2002-2013 technical bill, for dividends paid after Dec. 18, 2009. Added by P.C. 1997-1670; it was formerly Reg. 5907(1)(m).

"whole dividend" paid at any time on the shares of a class of the capital stock of a foreign affiliate of a taxpayer resident in Canada is the total of all amounts each of which is the dividend paid at that time on a share of that class except that

(a) where a dividend is paid at the same time on shares of more than one class of the capital stock of an affiliate, for the purpose only of section 5900, the whole dividend referred to in section 5901 paid at that time on the shares of a class of the capital stock of the affiliate is deemed to be the total of all amounts each of which is the dividend paid at that time on a share of the capital stock of the affiliate,

(b) where a whole dividend is deemed by subparagraph 5902(1)(a)(ii) to have been paid at the same time on shares of more than one class of an affiliate's capital stock, for the purpose only of that subparagraph, the whole dividend deemed to have been paid at that time on the shares of a class of the affiliate's capital stock is deemed to be the total of all amounts each of which is a whole dividend deemed to have been paid at that time on the shares of a class of the affiliate's capital stock, and

(c) where more than one whole dividend is deemed by paragraph 5900(2)(b) to have been paid at the same time on shares of a class of the capital stock of an affiliate, for the purposes only of paragraph 5900(1)(d) and the definitions "underlying foreign tax" and "underlying foreign tax applicable" in this subsection, the whole dividend deemed to have been paid at that time on the shares of a class of the capital stock of the affiliate is deemed to be the total of all amounts each of which is a whole dividend deemed to have been paid at that time on the shares of a class of the capital stock of the affiliate and all of that whole dividend shall be deemed to have been paid out of the affiliate's taxable surplus in respect of the corporation.

Notes: Definition amended by 2002-2013 technical bill, for elections in respect of dispositions after Dec. 18, 2009. Added by P.C. 1997-1670; it was formerly Reg. 5907(1)(n).

Notes [Reg. 5907(1)]: Reg. 5907(1) amended by P.C. 1997-1670, for foreign affiliates' tax years ending after 1994, to change all paragraph definitions to subsection-level (to be in alphabetical order in both English and French). See Notes to the definitions above. The application to ITA 113, formerly in Reg. 5901(1) opening words, is now in 5907(1.01). Earlier amended by P.C. 1996-571, 1994-1129.

(1.01) [Interpretation for ITA 113] — For the purposes of section 113 of the Act, **"exempt surplus"**, **"hybrid surplus"** and **"taxable surplus"** have the meanings assigned by subsection (1).

Notes: Reg. 5907(1.01) amended by 2002-2013 technical bill, effective Aug. 20, 2011. Added by P.C. 1997-1670. (Reg. 5907(1), by its opening words, previously applied for purposes of ITA s. 113.)

(1.02) [New FA deemed resident in treaty country throughout year] — For the purposes of paragraph (d) of the definition "exempt earnings" and paragraph (c) of the definition "exempt loss" in subsection (1), if a foreign affiliate of a corporation becomes a foreign affiliate of the corporation in a taxation year of the affiliate, otherwise than as a result of a transaction between persons that do not deal with each other at arm's length, and the affiliate is resident in a designated treaty country at the end of the year, the affiliate is deemed to be so resident throughout the year.

Notes: Reg. 5907(1.02) added by 2002-2013 technical bill, for foreign affiliates' tax years that begin after Dec. 18, 2009.

Former 5907(1.02), setting out rules for determining a "qualifying interest" and whether corporations were "related", repealed by 2002-2013 technical bill, for foreign affiliates' tax years that begin after 2008. Added by P.C. 1997-1670. It was 5907(1.01) in the Jan. 23, 1995 draft regs.

(1.03) [Artificial foreign tax credit generators] — For the purposes of the description of A in the definition "underlying foreign tax" in subsection (1), income or profits tax paid in respect of the taxable earnings of a particular foreign affiliate of a particular corporation or in respect of a dividend received by the particular affiliate from another foreign affiliate of the particular corporation, and amounts by which the underlying foreign tax of the particular affiliate or any other foreign affiliate of the particular corporation is required under any of subsections (1.092), (1.1) and (1.2) to be increased, is not to include any income or profits tax paid, or amounts by which the underlying foreign tax would otherwise be so required to be increased, as the case may be, in respect of the foreign accrual property income of the particular affiliate for a taxation year of the particular affiliate if, at any time in the year, a specified owner in respect of the particular corporation is considered,

(a) under the income tax laws (referred to in subsection (1.07) as the "relevant foreign tax law") of any country other than Canada under the laws of which any income of another corporation — that is, at any time in the year, a pertinent person or partnership in respect of the particular affiliate — is subject to income taxation, to own less than all of the shares of the capital stock of the other corporation that are considered to be owned by the specified owner for the purposes of the Act; or

(b) under the income tax laws (referred to in subsection (1.08) as the "relevant foreign tax law") of any country other than Canada under the laws of which any income of a particular partnership — that is, at any time in the year, a pertinent person or partnership in respect of the particular affiliate — is subject to income taxation, to have a lesser direct or indirect share of the income of the particular partnership than the specified owner is considered to have for the purposes of the Act.

Related Provisions: ITA 91(4.1), 126(4.11) — Parallel rules to Reg. 5907(1.03); Reg. 5907(1.04) — Specified owner; Reg. 5907(1.05) — Pertinent person or partnership; Reg. 5907(1.07) — Exception — hybrid entities; Reg. 5907(1.08) — Exception — partnerships; Reg. 5907(1.09) — Deemed ownership.

Notes: Reg. 5907(1.03)–(1.09) are part of the "foreign tax credit generator" rules, along with ITA 91(4.1)–(4.7) and 126(4.11)–(4.13). See Notes to ITA 126(4.11).

Reg. 5907(1.03) amended by 2014 budget bill #2, last change effective for foreign affiliates' tax years that end after July 11, 2013. Added by 2002-2013 technical bill.

(1.04) [Specified owner] — For the purposes of subsections (1.03) and (1.07), a "specified owner", at any time, in respect of a corporation means the corporation or a person or partnership that is, at that time,

(a) a partnership of which the corporation is a member;

(b) a foreign affiliate of the corporation;

(c) a partnership a member of which is a foreign affiliate of the corporation; or

(d) a person or partnership referred to in any of subparagraphs (1.06)(a)(i) to (iii).

Related Provisions: ITA 91(4.2) — Parallel rule; Reg. 5907(1.06) — Interpretation.

Notes: See Notes to Reg. 5907(1.03).

(1.05) [Pertinent person or partnership] — For the purposes of this subsection and subsection (1.03), a "pertinent person or partnership", at any time, in respect of a particular foreign affiliate of a corporation means the particular affiliate or a person or partnership that is, at that time,

(a) another foreign affiliate of the corporation

(i) in which the particular affiliate has an equity percentage, or

(ii) that has an equity percentage in the particular affiliate;

(b) a partnership a member of which is at that time a pertinent person or partnership in respect of the particular affiliate under this subsection; or

(c) a person or partnership referred to in any of subparagraphs (1.06)(b)(i) to (iii).

Related Provisions: ITA 91(4.3) — Parallel rule; Reg. 5907(1.06) — Interpretation.

Notes: See Notes to Reg. 5907(1.03).

(1.06) [Series of transactions] — For the purposes of subsections (1.04) and (1.05), if, as part of a series of transactions or events that includes the earning of the foreign accrual property income referred to in subsection (1.03), a foreign affiliate (referred to in this subsection as the "funding affiliate") of the corporation or of a person (referred to in this subsection as the "related person") resident in Canada that is related to the corporation, or a partnership (referred to in this subsection as the "funding partnership") of which such an affiliate is a member, directly or indirectly provided funding to the particular affiliate, or a partnership of which the particular affiliate is a member, otherwise than by way of loans or other indebtedness that are subject to terms or conditions made or imposed, in respect of the loans or other indebtedness, that do not differ from those that would be made or imposed between persons dealing at arm's length or by way of an acquisition of shares of the capital stock of any corporation, then

(a) if the funding affiliate is, or the funding partnership has a member that is, a foreign affiliate of the related person, the following persons and partnerships are deemed, at all times during which the foreign accrual property income is earned by the particular affiliate, to be specified owners in respect of the corporation:

(i) the related person,

(ii) each foreign affiliate of the related person, and

(iii) each partnership a member of which is referred to in subparagraph (i) or (ii); and

(b) the following persons and partnerships are deemed, at all times during which the foreign accrual property income is earned by the particular affiliate, to be pertinent persons or partnerships in respect of the particular affiliate:

(i) the funding affiliate or the funding partnership,

(ii) a non-resident corporation

(A) in which the funding affiliate has an equity percentage, or

(B) that has an equity percentage in the funding affiliate, and

(iii) a partnership a member of which is a person or partnership referred to in subparagraph (i) or (ii).

Related Provisions: ITA 91(4.4) — Parallel rule.

Notes: For the meaning of "indirectly" in opening words, see Notes to ITA 17.1(1).

(1.07) [Exception — hybrid entities] — For the purposes of paragraph (1.03)(a), a specified owner in respect of the particular corporation is not to be considered, under the relevant foreign tax law, to own less than all of the shares of the capital stock of another corporation that are considered to be owned for the purposes of the Act solely because the specified owner or the other corporation is not treated as a corporation under the relevant foreign tax law.

Related Provisions: ITA 91(4.5) — Parallel rule; Reg. 5907(1.04) — Specified owner.

Notes: See Notes to Reg. 5907(1.03).

Reg. 5907(1.07) amended by 2017 budget bill #2 (implementing a March 1, 2016 Finance comfort letter), for foreign affiliates' tax years that end in the corporation's tax years that end after Oct. 24, 2012.

(1.08) [Exception — partnerships] — For the purposes of paragraph (1.03)(b), a member of a partnership is not to be considered to have a lesser direct or indirect share of the income of the partnership under the relevant foreign tax law than for the purposes of the Act solely because of one or more of the following:

(a) a difference between the relevant foreign tax law and the Act in the manner of

(i) computing the income of the partnership, or

(ii) allocating the income of the partnership because of the admission to, or withdrawal from, the partnership of any of its members;

(b) the treatment of the partnership as a corporation under the relevant foreign tax law; or

(c) the fact that the member is not treated as a corporation under the relevant foreign tax law.

Related Provisions: ITA 91(4.6), 126(4.12) — Parallel rule.

Notes: See Notes to Reg. 5907(1.03).

(1.09) [Deemed ownership] — For the purposes of subsection (1.03), if a specified owner owns, for the purposes of the Act, shares of the capital stock of a corporation and the dividends, or similar amounts, in respect of those shares are treated under the income tax laws of any country other than Canada under the laws of which any income of the corporation is subject to income taxation as interest or another form of deductible payment, the specified owner is deemed to be considered, under those tax laws, to own less than all of the shares of the capital stock of the corporation that are considered to be owned by the specified owner for the purposes of the Act.

Related Provisions: ITA 91(4.7) — Parallel rule.

Notes: See Notes to Reg. 5907(1.03).

(1.091) [Conditions for Reg. 5907(1.092) to apply] — Subsection (1.092) applies in respect of income or profits tax paid by, or refunded to, a foreign affiliate (in this subsection and subsection (1.092) referred to as the "shareholder affiliate") of a taxpayer for a taxation year of the shareholder affiliate in respect of its income or profits, or loss, as the case may be, and the income or profits, or loss, as the case may be, of another foreign affiliate (in this subsection and subsection (1.092) referred to as the "transparent affiliate") of the taxpayer if

(a) the shareholder affiliate has an equity percentage in the transparent affiliate;

(b) the income or profits tax is paid to, or refunded by, a government of a country other than Canada; and

(c) under the income tax laws of the country referred to in paragraph (b), the shareholder affiliate, and not the transparent affiliate, is liable for that tax payable to, or entitled to that refund from, a government of that country for that year (otherwise than solely because the shareholder affiliate is part of a group of corporations that determines its liabilities for income or profits tax payable to the government of that country on a consolidated or combined basis).

Notes: For the meaning of "income or profits tax", see Notes to ITA 126(4).

Reg. 5907(1.091) added by 2014 budget bill #2, last effective for foreign affiliates' tax years that end after July 11, 2013.

(1.092) [Where shareholder of fiscally transparent entity pays the foreign tax] — If this subsection applies in respect of income or profits tax paid by, or refunded to, a shareholder affiliate for a taxation year

(a) in respect of the shareholder affiliate,

(i) any such income or profits tax paid by the shareholder affiliate for the year is deemed not to have been paid and any such refund to the shareholder affiliate of income or profits tax otherwise payable by it for the year is deemed not to have been made,

(ii) any such income or profits tax that would have been payable by the shareholder affiliate for the year if the shareholder affiliate had no other taxation year and had not been liable for income or profits tax in respect of income or profits of the transparent affiliate is deemed to have been paid for the year,

(iii) to the extent that

(A) any such income or profits tax that would otherwise have been payable by the shareholder affiliate for the year on behalf of the shareholder affiliate and the transparent

affiliate is reduced because of any loss of the shareholder affiliate for the year or any previous taxation year, the amount of such reduction is deemed to have been received by the shareholder affiliate as a refund for the year of the loss of income or profits tax in respect of the loss, and

(B) the shareholder affiliate receives, in respect of a loss of the shareholder affiliate for the year or a subsequent taxation year, a refund of income or profits tax otherwise payable for the year by the shareholder affiliate on behalf of the shareholder affiliate and the transparent affiliate, the amount of such refund is deemed to have been received by the shareholder affiliate as a refund for the year of the loss of income or profits tax in respect of the loss,

(iv) any such income or profits tax that would have been payable by the transparent affiliate for the year if the transparent affiliate had no other taxation year, had no income or profits other than those that are included in computing the income or profits of the shareholder affiliate under the income tax laws referred to in paragraph (1.091)(c) and had been liable, and no other person had been liable, for income or profits tax in respect of income or profits of the transparent affiliate is, at the end of the year,

(A) to the extent that such income or profits tax would otherwise have reduced the net earnings included in the exempt earnings of the transparent affiliate, to be deducted from the exempt surplus or added to the exempt deficit, as the case may be, of the shareholder affiliate,

(B) to the extent that such income or profits tax would otherwise have reduced the hybrid surplus or increased the hybrid deficit of the transparent affiliate,

(I) to be deducted from the hybrid surplus or added to the hybrid deficit, as the case may be, of the shareholder affiliate, and

(II) to be added to the hybrid underlying tax of the shareholder affiliate, and

(C) to the extent that such income or profits tax would otherwise have reduced the net earnings included in the taxable earnings of the transparent affiliate,

(I) to be deducted from the taxable surplus or added to the taxable deficit, as the case may be, of the shareholder affiliate, and

(II) to be added to the underlying foreign tax of the shareholder affiliate, and

(v) to the extent that the income or profits tax that would otherwise have been payable by the shareholder affiliate for the year on behalf of the shareholder affiliate and the transparent affiliate is reduced because of a loss of the transparent affiliate for the year or a previous taxation year, or to the extent that the shareholder affiliate receives, in respect of a loss of the transparent affiliate for the year or a subsequent taxation year, a refund of income or profits tax otherwise payable for the year by the shareholder affiliate on behalf of the shareholder affiliate and the transparent affiliate, the amount of such reduction or refund, as the case may be, is, at the end of the year of the loss,

(A) to the extent that such loss reduces the exempt surplus or increases the exempt deficit of the transparent affiliate, to be added to the exempt surplus or deducted from the exempt deficit, as the case may be, of the shareholder affiliate,

(B) to the extent that such loss reduces the hybrid surplus or increases the hybrid deficit of the transparent affiliate,

(I) to be added to the hybrid surplus or deducted from the hybrid deficit, as the case may be, of the shareholder affiliate, and

(II) to be deducted from the hybrid underlying tax of the shareholder affiliate, and

(C) to the extent that such loss reduces the taxable surplus or increases the taxable deficit of the transparent affiliate,

(I) to be added to the taxable surplus or deducted from the taxable deficit, as the case may be, of the shareholder affiliate, and

(II) to be deducted from the underlying foreign tax of the shareholder affiliate;

(b) where, because of the shareholder affiliate being responsible for paying, or claiming a refund of, income or profits tax for the year on behalf of the shareholder affiliate and the transparent affiliate,

(i) an amount is paid to the shareholder affiliate by the transparent affiliate in respect of the income or profits tax that would have been payable by the transparent affiliate for the year had it been liable, and no other person had been liable, for income or profits tax in respect of income or profits of the transparent affiliate,

(A) in respect of the transparent affiliate, the amount so paid is deemed to be a payment of such income or profits tax for the year, and

(B) in respect of the shareholder affiliate,

(I) such portion of the amount so paid as may reasonably be regarded as relating to an amount included in the exempt surplus or deducted from the exempt deficit of the transparent affiliate is, at the end of the year, to be added to the exempt surplus or deducted from the exempt deficit, as the case may be, of the shareholder affiliate,

(II) such portion of the amount so paid as may reasonably be regarded as relating to an amount included in the hybrid surplus or deducted from the hybrid deficit of the transparent affiliate is, at the end of the year, to be added to the hybrid surplus or deducted from the hybrid deficit, as the case may be, of the shareholder affiliate and deducted from the hybrid underlying tax of the shareholder affiliate, and

(III) such portion of the amount so paid as may reasonably be regarded as relating to an amount included in the taxable surplus or deducted from the taxable deficit of the transparent affiliate is, at the end of the year, to be added to the taxable surplus or deducted from the taxable deficit, as the case may be, of the shareholder affiliate and be deducted from the underlying foreign tax of the shareholder affiliate, or

(ii) an amount is paid by the shareholder affiliate to the transparent affiliate in respect of a reduction or refund, because of a loss or a tax credit of the transparent affiliate for a taxation year, of the income or profits tax that would otherwise have been payable by the shareholder affiliate for the year on behalf of the shareholder affiliate and the transparent affiliate,

(A) in respect of the shareholder affiliate,

(I) the portion of the amount so paid that can reasonably be regarded as relating to an amount deducted from the exempt surplus or included in the exempt deficit of the transparent affiliate is, at the end of the year to which the loss or the tax credit relates, to be deducted from the exempt surplus or added to the exempt deficit, as the case may be, of the shareholder affiliate,

(II) the portion of the amount so paid that can reasonably be regarded as relating to an amount deducted from the hybrid surplus or included in the hybrid deficit of the transparent affiliate is, at the end of the year of the loss, to be deducted from the hybrid surplus or added to the hybrid deficit, as the case may be, of the

shareholder affiliate and added to the hybrid underlying tax of the shareholder affiliate, and

(III) the portion of the amount so paid that can reasonably be regarded as relating to an amount deducted from the taxable surplus or included in the taxable deficit of the transparent affiliate is, at the end of the year to which the loss or the tax credit relates, to be deducted from the taxable surplus or added to the taxable deficit, as the case may be, of the shareholder affiliate and be added to the underlying foreign tax of the shareholder affiliate, and

(B) in respect of the transparent affiliate, the amount is deemed to be a refund to the transparent affiliate, for the year to which the loss or the tax credit relates, of income or profits tax in respect of the loss or the tax credit; and

(c) for the purposes of paragraph (b), any amount paid by a particular transparent affiliate in respect of the shareholder affiliate to another transparent affiliate in respect of the shareholder affiliate in respect of any income or profits tax that would have been payable by the particular transparent affiliate for the year had it been liable, and no other person had been liable, for income or profits tax in respect of income or profits of the transparent affiliate is deemed to have been paid in respect of such tax by the particular transparent affiliate to the shareholder affiliate and to have been paid in respect of such tax by the shareholder affiliate to the other transparent affiliate.

Related Provisions: Reg. 5907(1)"exempt surplus"A(vi), B(vi) — Effect on exempt surplus; Reg. 5907(1)"hybrid surplus"A(v), B(vii) — Effect on hybrid surplus; Reg. 5907(1)"hybrid underlying tax"A(iv), B(iv) — Effect on hybrid underlying tax; Reg. 5907(1)"taxable surplus"A(iv), B(vi) — Effect on taxable surplus; Reg. 5907(1)"underlying foreign tax"A(v), B(v) — Effect on underlying foreign tax; Reg. 5907(1.03) — Artificial FTC generators; Reg. 5907(1.091) — Conditions for subsec. 5907(1.092).

Notes: Reg. 5907(1.092) ensures that appropriate surplus adjustments are made where, under foreign tax law, the shareholder of a fiscally transparent entity (FTE) that is a foreign affiliate, and not the FTE itself, is liable for and pays foreign tax on income of the FTE. This situation is also addressed by the 2014 amendments to ITA 95(1)"foreign accrual tax".

Reg. 5907(1.092) added by 2014 budget bill #2, last change effective for foreign affiliates' tax years that end after July 11, 2013.

(1.1) [Where FA is member of consolidated group] — For the purposes of this Part, if, under, the income tax laws of a country other than Canada, a group (in this subsection referred to as the "consolidated group") of two or more foreign affiliates of a corporation resident in Canada determine their liabilities for income or profits tax payable to the government of that country for a taxation year on a consolidated or combined basis and one of the affiliates (in this subsection referred to as the "primary affiliate") is responsible for paying, or claiming a refund of, such tax on behalf of itself and the other affiliates (in this subsection referred to as the "secondary affiliates") that are members of the consolidated group, the following rules apply:

(a) in respect of the primary affiliate,

(i) any such income or profits tax paid by the primary affiliate for the year shall be deemed not to have been paid and any refund to the primary affiliate of income or profits tax otherwise payable by it for the year shall be deemed not to have been made,

(ii) any such income or profits tax that would have been payable by the primary affiliate for the year if the primary affiliate had no other taxation year and had not been a member of the consolidated group shall be deemed to have been paid for the year,

(iii) to the extent that

(A) the income or profits tax that would otherwise have been payable by the primary affiliate for the year on behalf of the consolidated group is reduced by virtue of any loss of the primary affiliate for the year or any previous taxation year, or

(B) the primary affiliate receives, in respect of a loss of the primary affiliate for the year or a subsequent taxation year, a refund of income or profits tax otherwise payable for the year by the primary affiliate on behalf of the consolidated group,

the amount of such reduction or refund, as the case may be, shall be deemed to have been received by the primary affiliate as a refund for the year of the loss of income or profits tax in respect of the loss,

(iv) any such income or profits tax that would have been payable by a secondary affiliate for the year if the secondary affiliate had no other taxation year and had not been a member of the consolidated group shall at the end of the year,

(A) to the extent that such income or profits tax would otherwise have reduced the net earnings included in the exempt earnings of the secondary affiliate, be deducted from the exempt surplus or added to the exempt deficit, as the case may be, of the primary affiliate,

(A.1) to the extent that such income or profits tax would otherwise have reduced the hybrid surplus or increased the hybrid deficit of the secondary affiliate,

(I) be deducted from the hybrid surplus or added to the hybrid deficit, as the case may be, of the primary affiliate, and

(II) be added to the hybrid underlying tax of the primary affiliate, and

(B) to the extent that such income or profits tax would otherwise have reduced the net earnings included in the taxable earnings of the secondary affiliate,

(I) be deducted from the taxable surplus or added to the taxable deficit, as the case may be, of the primary affiliate, and

(II) be added to the underlying foreign tax of the primary affiliate,

(v) to the extent that

(A) the income or profits tax that would otherwise have been payable by the primary affiliate for the year on behalf of the consolidated group is reduced by virtue of a loss of a secondary affiliate for the year or a previous taxation year, or

(B) the primary affiliate receives, in respect of a loss of a secondary affiliate for the year or a subsequent taxation year, a refund of income or profits tax otherwise payable for the year by the primary affiliate on behalf of the consolidated group,

the amount of such reduction or refund, as the case may be, shall at the end of the year of the loss,

(C) where such loss reduces the exempt surplus or increases the exempt deficit, as the case may be, of the secondary affiliate, be added to the exempt surplus or deducted from the exempt deficit, as the case may be, of the primary affiliate,

(C.1) where such loss reduces the hybrid surplus or increases the hybrid deficit, as the case may be, of the secondary affiliate,

(I) be added to the hybrid surplus or deducted from the hybrid deficit, as the case may be, of the primary affiliate, and

(II) be deducted from the hybrid underlying tax of the primary affiliate, and

(D) where such loss reduces the taxable surplus or increases the taxable deficit, as the case may be, of the secondary affiliate,

(I) be added to the taxable surplus or deducted from the taxable deficit, as the case may be, of the primary affiliate, and

(II) be deducted from the underlying foreign tax of the primary affiliate; and

(b) where by virtue of the primary affiliate being responsible for paying, or claiming a refund of, income or profits tax for the year on behalf of the consolidated group,

(i) an amount is paid to the primary affiliate by a secondary affiliate in respect of the income or profits tax that would have been payable by the secondary affiliate for the year had it not been a member of the group,

(A) in respect of the secondary affiliate, the amount so paid shall be deemed to be a payment of such income or profits tax for the year, and

(B) in respect of the primary affiliate,

(I) such portion of the amount so paid as may reasonably be regarded as relating to an amount included in the exempt surplus or deducted from the exempt deficit, as the case may be, of the secondary affiliate shall at the end of the year be added to the exempt surplus or deducted from the exempt deficit, as the case may be, of the primary affiliate,

(I.1) such portion of the amount so paid as may reasonably be regarded as relating to an amount included in the hybrid surplus or deducted from the hybrid deficit, as the case may be, of the secondary affiliate is, at the end of the year, to be added to the hybrid surplus or deducted from the hybrid deficit, as the case may be, of the primary affiliate and deducted from the hybrid underlying tax of the primary affiliate, and

(II) such portion of the amount so paid as may reasonably be regarded as relating to an amount included in the taxable surplus or deducted from the taxable deficit, as the case may be, of the secondary affiliate shall at the end of the year be added to the taxable surplus or deducted from the taxable deficit, as the case may be, of the primary affiliate and be deducted from the underlying foreign tax of the primary affiliate, or

(ii) an amount is paid by the primary affiliate to a secondary affiliate in respect of a reduction or refund, because of a loss or a tax credit of the secondary affiliate for a taxation year, of the income or profits tax that would otherwise have been payable by the primary affiliate for the year on behalf of the consolidated group

(A) in respect of the primary affiliate,

(I) the portion of the amount so paid that can reasonably be regarded as relating to an amount deducted from the exempt surplus or included in the exempt deficit, as the case may be, of the secondary affiliate shall, at the end of the year to which the loss or the tax credit relates, be deducted from the exempt surplus or added to the exempt deficit, as the case may be, of the primary affiliate,

(I.1) such portion of the amount so paid as may reasonably be regarded as relating to an amount deducted from the hybrid surplus or included in the hybrid deficit, as the case may be, of the secondary affiliate is, at the end of the year of the loss, to be deducted from the hybrid surplus or added to the hybrid deficit, as the case may be, of the primary affiliate and added to the hybrid underlying tax of the primary affiliate, and

(II) the portion of the amount so paid that can reasonably be regarded as relating to an amount deducted from the taxable surplus or included in the taxable deficit, as the case may be, of the secondary affiliate shall, at the end of the year to which the loss or the tax credit relates, be deducted from the taxable surplus or added to the taxable deficit, as the case may be, of the primary affiliate and be added to the underlying foreign tax of the primary affiliate, and

(B) in respect of the secondary affiliate, the amount is deemed to be a refund to the secondary affiliate, for the year to which the loss or the tax credit relates, of income or profits tax in respect of the loss or the tax credit,

and, for the purposes of this paragraph, any amount paid by a particular secondary affiliate to another secondary affiliate in respect of any income or profits tax that would have been payable by the particular secondary affiliate for the year had it not been a member of the consolidated group shall be deemed to have been paid in respect of such tax by the particular secondary affiliate to the primary affiliate and to have been paid in respect of such tax by the primary affiliate to the other secondary affiliate.

Related Provisions: Reg. 5907(1)"exempt surplus"A(vi), B(vi) — Effect on exempt surplus; Reg. 5907(1)"hybrid surplus"A(v), B(vii) — Effect on hybrid surplus; Reg. 5907(1)"hybrid underlying tax"A(iv), B(iv) — Effect on hybrid underlying tax; Reg. 5907(1)"taxable surplus"A(iv), B(vi) — Effect on taxable surplus; Reg. 5907(1)"underlying foreign tax"A(v), B(iv) — Effect on underlying foreign tax; Reg. 5907(1.03) — Artificial FTC generators; Reg. 5907(1.11) — Interpretation — deemed foreign affiliate.

Notes: A refund of foreign taxes received by a foreign corp after it ceased to be an FA does not fall within Reg. 5907(1.1)(a)(v)(B): VIEWS doc 2004-0087081I7.

For the meaning of "income or profits tax", see Notes to ITA 126(4).

Reg. 5907(1.1) amended, and 5907(1.11) added by 2014 budget bill #2 (implementing a June 9, 2006 Finance comfort letter to Allan Lanthier), for foreign affiliates' tax years ending after 2003. Earlier amended by 2002-2013 technical bill.

(1.11) [Deemed FA for 5907(1.1)] — For the purposes of subsection (1.1), a non-resident corporation is deemed to be, at any time, a foreign affiliate of a particular corporation resident in Canada if at that time the non-resident corporation is a foreign affiliate of another corporation that is resident in Canada and is related (otherwise than because of a right referred to in paragraph 251(5)(b) of the Act) to the particular corporation.

Notes: See Notes to Reg. 5907(1.1) for 2014 enactment.

(1.12) [Conditions for (1.13) to apply] — Subsection (1.13) applies in respect of a particular foreign affiliate of a corporation resident in Canada that is a secondary affiliate (within the meaning assigned by subsection (1.1)) and in respect of a foreign affiliate of the corporation that is the primary affiliate (within the meaning assigned by subsection (1.1)) in respect of the particular affiliate if

(a) the particular affiliate has an equity percentage in another foreign affiliate (in this subsection and subsection (1.13) referred to as the "transparent affiliate");

(b) under the income tax laws of the country referred to in subsection (1.1), if the particular affiliate were not a member of a consolidated group, the particular affiliate, and not the transparent affiliate, would be liable for any tax payable to, or entitled to any refund from, a government of that country for that year in respect of the income or profits, or loss, as the case may be, for the year of the transparent affiliate; and

(c) the primary affiliate pays income or profits tax, or receives a refund, in respect of the income or profits, or loss, as the case may be, for the year of the transparent affiliate.

Notes: Reg. 5907(1.12) added by 2014 budget bill #2, last change effective for foreign affiliates' tax years that end after July 11, 2013.

(1.13) [Look-through of transparent affiliate] — If this subsection applies, then in respect of the particular foreign affiliate and the primary affiliate referred to in subsection (1.12)

(a) for the purposes of applying subparagraphs (1.1)(a)(iv) and (1.1)(b)(i), where any income or profits tax that would otherwise be payable by the particular affiliate for the year, if the particular affiliate had no other taxation year and were not a member of the consolidated group referred to in subsection (1.1), is increased

because of income or profits of the transparent affiliate referred to in paragraph (1.12)(a),

(i) to the extent that the income or profits increases the net earnings included in the exempt earnings of the transparent affiliate,

(A) the amount of any such increase is deemed to have been included in the exempt surplus, or deducted from the exempt deficit, as the case may be, of the particular affiliate, and

(B) any such income or profits tax that would have been payable by the particular affiliate in respect of the income or profits is deemed to be income or profits tax that would otherwise have reduced the net earnings that are included in the exempt earnings of the particular affiliate,

(ii) to the extent that the income or profits increases the hybrid surplus or reduces the hybrid deficit of the transparent affiliate,

(A) the amount of the increase or reduction is deemed to have been included in the hybrid surplus, or deducted from the hybrid deficit, as the case may be, of the particular affiliate, and

(B) any such income or profits tax that would have been payable by the particular affiliate in respect of the income or profits is deemed to be income or profits tax that would otherwise have reduced the hybrid surplus or increased the hybrid deficit, as the case may be, of the particular affiliate, and

(iii) to the extent that the income or profits increases the net earnings included in the taxable earnings of the transparent affiliate,

(A) the amount of any such increase is deemed to have been included in the taxable surplus, or deducted from the taxable deficit, as the case may be, of the particular affiliate, and

(B) any such income or profits tax that would have been payable by the particular affiliate in respect of the income or profits is deemed to be income or profits tax that would otherwise have reduced the net earnings that are included in the taxable earnings of the particular affiliate; and

(b) for the purpose of applying subparagraphs (1.1)(a)(v) and (1.1)(b)(ii), to the extent that the income or profits tax that would otherwise have been payable by the primary affiliate for the year on behalf of the consolidated group is reduced because of a loss, for the year or a previous taxation year, of the transparent affiliate referred to in paragraph (1.12)(a), or to the extent that the primary affiliate receives, in respect of a loss of the transparent affiliate for the year or a subsequent taxation year, a refund of income or profits tax otherwise payable for the year by the primary affiliate on behalf of the consolidated group,

(i) such loss is deemed to be a loss of the particular affiliate,

(ii) to the extent that such loss reduces the exempt surplus or increases the exempt deficit of the transparent affiliate, such loss is deemed to reduce the exempt surplus or increase the exempt deficit, as the case may be, of the particular affiliate,

(iii) to the extent that such loss reduces the hybrid surplus or increases the hybrid deficit of the transparent affiliate, such loss is deemed to reduce the hybrid surplus or increase the hybrid deficit, as the case may be, of the particular affiliate, and

(iv) to the extent that such loss reduces the taxable surplus or increases the taxable deficit of the transparent affiliate, such loss is deemed to reduce the taxable surplus or increase the taxable deficit, as the case may be, of the particular affiliate.

Related Provisions: Reg. 5907(1.12) — Conditions for (1.13) to apply.

Notes: Reg. 5907(1.13) added by 2014 budget bill #2, last change effective for foreign affiliates' tax years that end after July 11, 2013.

(1.2) [Where FA deducts loss of loss affiliate] — For the purposes of this Part, where, pursuant to the income tax law of a country other than Canada, a corporation resident in that country that is a foreign affiliate of a corporation resident in Canada (in this subsection referred to as the "taxpaying affiliate") deducts, in computing its income or profits tax payable for a taxation year to a government of that country, a loss of another corporation resident in that country that is a foreign affiliate of the corporation resident in Canada (in this subsection referred to as the "loss affiliate"), the following rules apply:

(a) any such income or profits tax paid by the taxpaying affiliate for the year shall be deemed not to have been paid;

(b) any such income or profits tax that would have been payable by the taxpaying affiliate for the year if the taxpaying affiliate had not been allowed to deduct such loss shall be deemed to have been paid for the year;

(c) to the extent that the income or profits tax that would otherwise have been payable by the taxpaying affiliate for the year is reduced by virtue of such loss, the amount of such reduction shall at the end of the year,

(i) where such loss reduces the exempt surplus or increases the exempt deficit, as the case may be, of the loss affiliate, be added to the exempt surplus or deducted from the exempt deficit, as the case may be, of the taxpaying affiliate,

(i.1) where such loss reduces the hybrid surplus or increases the hybrid deficit, as the case may be, of the loss affiliate,

(A) be added to the hybrid surplus or deducted from the hybrid deficit, as the case may be, of the taxpaying affiliate, and

(B) be deducted from the hybrid underlying tax of the taxpaying affiliate, and

(ii) where such loss reduces the taxable surplus or increases the taxable deficit, as the case may be, of the loss affiliate,

(A) be added to the taxable surplus or deducted from the taxable deficit, as the case may be, of the taxpaying affiliate, and

(B) be deducted from the underlying foreign tax of the taxpaying affiliate; and

(d) where an amount is paid by the taxpaying affiliate to the loss affiliate in respect of the reduction, by virtue of such loss, of the income or profits tax that would otherwise have been payable by the taxpaying affiliate for the year,

(i) in respect of the taxpaying affiliate,

(A) such portion of the amount as may reasonably be regarded as relating to an amount deducted from the exempt surplus or included in the exempt deficit, as the case may be, of the loss affiliate shall at the end of the year be deducted from the exempt surplus or added to the exempt deficit, as the case may be, of the taxpaying affiliate,

(A.1) such portion of the amount as may reasonably be regarded as relating to an amount deducted from the hybrid surplus or included in the hybrid deficit, as the case may be, of the loss affiliate is, at the end of the year, to be deducted from the hybrid surplus or added to the hybrid deficit, as the case may be, of the taxpaying affiliate and added to the hybrid underlying tax of the taxpaying affiliate, and

(B) such portion of the amount as may reasonably be regarded as relating to an amount deducted from the taxable surplus or included in the taxable deficit, as the case may be, of the loss affiliate shall at the end of the year be deducted from the taxable surplus or added to the taxable deficit, as the case may be, of the taxpaying affiliate and be added to the underlying foreign tax of the taxpaying affiliate, and

(ii) in respect of the loss affiliate, the amount shall be deemed to be a refund to the loss affiliate of income or profits tax in respect of the loss for the taxation year of the loss.

Related Provisions: Reg. 5907(1)"exempt surplus"A(vi), B(vi) — Effect on exempt surplus; Reg. 5907(1)"hybrid surplus"A(v), B(vii) — Effect on hybrid surplus; Reg. 5907(1)"hybrid underlying tax"A(iv), B(iv) — Effect on hybrid underlying tax; Reg. 5907(1)"taxable surplus"A(iv), B(vi) — Effect on taxable surplus; Reg. 5907(1)"underlying foreign tax"A(v), B(iv) — Effect on underlying foreign tax; Reg. 5907(1.03) — Artificial FTC generators.

Notes: For the meaning of "income or profits tax", see Notes to ITA 126(4).

Reg. 5907(1.2) amended by 2002-2013 technical bill, for foreign affiliates' tax years that end after Aug. 19, 2011.

(1.21) [Conditions for (1.22) to apply] — Subsection (1.22) applies if

(a) a foreign affiliate of the taxpayer (in this subsection and subsection (1.22) referred to as the "shareholder affiliate") has an equity percentage in another foreign affiliate (in this subsection and subsection (1.22) referred to as the "transparent affiliate"); and

(b) under the income tax laws of the country in which the shareholder affiliate is resident, the shareholder affiliate, and not the transparent affiliate, is liable for any tax payable to, or entitled to any refund from, a government of that country for that year in respect of the income or profits, or loss, as the case may be, for the year of the transparent affiliate.

Notes: Reg. 5907(1.21) added by 2014 budget bill #2, last effective for foreign affiliates' tax years that end after July 11, 2013.

(1.22) [Loss of transparent affiliate deemed loss of shareholder affiliate] — If this subsection applies, for the purpose of applying subsection (1.2), any loss of the transparent affiliate, to the extent that the loss is deducted in computing the income, profits or loss of the shareholder affiliate under an income tax law referred to in paragraph (1.21)(b),

(a) is deemed to be a loss of the shareholder affiliate; and

(b) is deemed to

(i) reduce the exempt surplus, or increase the exempt deficit, as the case may be, of the shareholder affiliate to the extent that it reduces the exempt surplus or increases the exempt deficit of the transparent affiliate,

(ii) reduce the hybrid surplus or increase the hybrid deficit, as the case may be, of the shareholder affiliate to the extent that it reduces the hybrid surplus or increases the hybrid deficit of the transparent affiliate, and

(iii) reduce the taxable surplus or increase the taxable deficit, as the case may be, of the shareholder affiliate to the extent that it reduces the taxable surplus or increases the taxable deficit of the transparent affiliate.

Related Provisions: Reg. 5907(1.21) — Conditions for (1.22) to apply.

Notes: Reg. 5907(1.22) added by 2014 budget bill #2, last change effective for FAs' tax years that end after July 11, 2013.

(1.3) [Prescribed foreign accrual tax] — For the purpose of paragraph (b) of the definition "foreign accrual tax" in subsection 95(1) of the Act and subject to subsection (1.4),

(a) if under the income tax laws of the country in which the particular affiliate or a shareholder affiliate of the particular affiliate, as the case may be, referred to in that paragraph is resident, the particular affiliate, or shareholder affiliate, and one or more other corporations, each of which is resident in that country, determine their liabilities for income or profits tax payable to the government of that country for a taxation year on a consolidated or combined basis, then any amount paid by the particular affiliate, or shareholder affiliate, to any of those other corporations to the extent that the amount paid may reasonably be regarded as being in respect of income or profits tax that would otherwise have been payable by the particular affiliate, or shareholder affiliate, in respect of a particular amount that is included under subsection 91(1) of the Act in computing the taxpayer's income for a taxation year of the taxpayer in respect of the particular affiliate, if the tax liability of the particular affiliate, or shareholder affiliate, and those other corporations had not been determined on a consolidated or combined basis, is prescribed to be foreign accrual tax applicable to the particular amount; and

(b) if, under the income tax laws of the country in which the particular affiliate or a shareholder affiliate of the particular affiliate, as the case may be, referred to in that paragraph is resident, the particular affiliate, or shareholder affiliate, deducts, in computing its income or profits subject to tax in that country for a taxation year, an amount in respect of a loss of another corporation (referred to in this paragraph and paragraph (1.6)(a) as the "loss transferor") resident in that country (referred to in this paragraph and paragraph (1.6)(a) as the "transferred loss"), then any amount paid by the particular affiliate, or shareholder affiliate, to the loss transferor to the extent that the amount paid may reasonably be regarded as being in respect of income or profits tax that would otherwise have been payable by the particular affiliate, or shareholder affiliate, in respect of a particular amount that is included under subsection 91(1) of the Act in computing the taxpayer's income for a taxation year of the taxpayer in respect of the particular affiliate, if the tax liability of the particular affiliate, or shareholder affiliate, had been determined without deducting the transferred loss, is prescribed to be foreign accrual tax applicable to the particular amount.

Related Provisions: Reg. 5903(4) — Effect of payment on foreign accrual property loss; Reg. 5903.1(4) — Effect of payment on foreign accrual capital loss; Reg. 5907(1.4) — Where amount prescribed is in respect of loss of other corporation; Reg. 5907(1.7) — Where amount prescribed is in respect of capital loss of other corporation.

Notes: For CRA interpretation of Reg. 5907(1.3)-(1.6) see docs 2003-0037291I7 (compensatory payment made by FA that is a US LLC); 2014-0542281E5 (timing of 5907(1.4) determination and (1.5) FAT reinstatement [Cepparo, "FAPI: Prescribed FAT Reduction", 23(7) *Canadian Tax Highlights* (ctf.ca) 9 (July 2015)]).

See also Adam Freiheit, "Reinstated Foreign Accrual Tax and the Multi-Period Perspective", 63(2) *Canadian Tax Journal* 521-42 (2015).

For the meaning of "income or profits tax", see Notes to ITA 126(4).

Reg. 5907(1.3) amended by 2014 budget bill #2 (last change effective for FAs' tax years that end after July 11, 2013), 2002-2013 technical bill; P.C. 1997-1670.

(1.4) [Prescribed foreign accrual tax] — If the amount prescribed under paragraph (1.3)(a) or (b), or any portion of the amount, can reasonably be considered to be in respect of a particular loss (other than a capital loss) or a capital loss of another corporation for a taxation year of the other corporation, then the amount so prescribed is to be reduced to the extent that it can reasonably be considered to be in respect of the portion of the particular loss or capital loss, as the case may be, that would, if sections 5903 and 5903.1 were read without reference to their subsection (4), not be a foreign accrual property loss (within the meaning assigned by subsection 5903(3)), or a foreign accrual capital loss (within the meaning assigned by subsection 5903.1(3)), as the case may be, of a controlled foreign affiliate of a person or partnership that is, at the end of that taxation year, a relevant person or partnership (within the meaning assigned by subsection 5903(6)) in respect of the taxpayer.

Related Provisions: Reg. 5907(1.5) — Effect of subsec. (1.4); Reg. 5907(1.7) — Parallel rule for capital losses.

Notes: Reg. 5907(1.4) added and amended by 2002-2013 technical bill, last change effective for foreign affiliates' tax years that end after Aug. 19, 2011.

(1.5) [Effect of (1.4)] — If subsection (1.4) applied to reduce an amount that would, in the absence of subsection (1.4), be prescribed by subsection (1.3) to be foreign accrual tax applicable to an amount (referred to in this subsection as the "FAPI amount") included under subsection 91(1) of the Act in computing the taxpayer's income for a taxation year (referred to in subsection (1.6) as the "FAPI year") of the taxpayer in respect of the particular affiliate referred to in paragraph (1.3)(a) or (b), then an amount equal to that reduction is, for the purposes of paragraph (b) of the definition "foreign accrual tax" in subsection 95(1) of the Act, prescribed to be foreign accrual tax applicable to the FAPI amount in the taxpayer's taxation year that includes the last day of the designated taxation year, if any, of the particular affiliate or the shareholder affiliate referred to in paragraph (1.3)(a) or (b), as the case may be.

Related Provisions: Reg. 5907(1.6) — Designated taxation year.

Notes: Reg. 5907(1.5) amended by 2014 budget bill #2, last change effective for FAs' tax years that end after July 11, 2013. Added by 2002-2013 technical bill.

(1.6) [Designated taxation year] — For the purposes of subsection (1.5), the designated taxation year of the particular affiliate or the shareholder affiliate, as the case may be, is a particular taxation year of the particular affiliate, or the shareholder affiliate, if

(a) in the particular year, or in the taxation year of the particular affiliate or shareholder affiliate (referred to in this paragraph as the "PATY") ending in the FAPI year and one or more taxation years of the particular affiliate (or shareholder affiliate) each of which follows the PATY and the latest of which is the particular year, all losses of the particular affiliate (or shareholder affiliate) and the other corporations referred to in paragraph (1.3)(a) — or of the particular affiliate, the loss transferor and each corporation that would have been permitted to deduct the transferred loss against its income under the income tax laws referred to in paragraph (1.3)(b) if the transferred loss had not been deducted by the particular affiliate and if the corporation had taxable income for its taxation years ending in the FAPI year in excess of the transferred loss — for their taxation years ending in the FAPI year would, on the assumption that the particular affiliate (or shareholder affiliate) and each of those other corporations had no foreign accrual property income for any taxation year, reasonably be considered to have been fully deducted (under the tax laws referred to in paragraph (1.3)(a) or (b)) against income (as determined under those tax laws) of the particular affiliate (or shareholder affiliate) or those other corporations;

(b) the taxpayer demonstrates that no other losses of the particular affiliate (or shareholder affiliate) or those other corporations for any taxation year were, or could reasonably have been, deducted under those tax laws against that income; and

(c) the last day of the particular year occurs in one of the five taxation years of the taxpayer that immediately follow the FAPI year.

Related Provisions: Reg. 5907(1.5) — Meaning of "FAPI year".

Notes: Reg. 5907(1.6) amended by 2014 budget bill #2 (implementing an Oct. 15, 2010 Finance comfort letter to Heather Kerr), last change effective for FAs' tax years that end after July 11, 2013. Added by 2002-2013 technical bill.

(1.7) [Where amount under (1.3) is capital loss of other corporation] — If the amount prescribed under paragraph (1.3)(a) or (b), or any portion of the amount, can reasonably be considered to be in respect of a capital loss of another corporation for a taxation year of the other corporation, then the amount so prescribed, as reduced by subsection (1.4), if applicable, shall be reduced to the extent that it can reasonably be considered to be in respect of the portion of that capital loss that would not be deductible by the particular affiliate in computing its foreign accrual property income for the year if the capital loss had been incurred by the particular affiliate.

Notes: Reg. 5907(1.7) added by 2002-2013 technical bill, for foreign affiliates' tax years that end after Aug. 19, 2011.

(2) [FA carrying on active business] — In computing the earnings of a foreign affiliate of a taxpayer resident in Canada for a taxation year of the affiliate from an active business carried on by it in a country, there shall be added to the amount thereof determined under subparagraph (a)(i) or (ii) of the definition "earnings" in subsection (1) (in this subsection referred to as the "earnings amount") such portion of the following amounts as was deducted or was not included, as the case may be, in computing the earnings amount,

(a) any income or profits tax paid to the government of a country by the affiliate so deducted,

(b) if established by the taxpayer, the amount by which any amount so deducted in respect of an expenditure made by the affiliate exceeds the amount, if any, by which

(i) the amount of the expenditure

exceeds

(ii) the aggregate of all other deductions in respect of that expenditure made by the affiliate in computing the earnings amounts for preceding taxation years,

(c) any loss of the affiliate referred to in the description of D in the definition "foreign accrual property income" in subsection 95(1) of the Act so deducted,

(d) any capital loss of the affiliate in respect of the disposition of capital property so deducted (for greater certainty, capital property of the affiliate for the purposes of this paragraph includes all the property of the affiliate other than property referred to in subparagraph 39(1)(b)(i) or (ii) of the Act on the assumption for this purpose that the affiliate is a corporation resident in Canada),

(e) any loss of the affiliate for a preceding or a subsequent taxation year so deducted,

(f) any revenue, income or profit (other than an amount referred to in paragraph (f.1), (h) or (i)) of the affiliate derived in the year from such business carried on in that country to the extent that such revenue, income or profit

(i) is not otherwise required to be included in computing the earnings amount of the affiliate for any taxation year by the income tax law that is relevant in computing that amount, and

(ii) subject to subsections (2.01) and (2.011), does not arise with respect to a disposition (other than a disposition to which subsection (9) applies), of property by the affiliate,

(A) to a person or partnership that was, at the time of the disposition, a designated person or partnership in respect of the taxpayer, and

(B) to which a tax deferral, rollover or similar tax postponement provision of the income tax laws that are relevant in computing the earnings amount of the affiliate applied, and

(f.1) any assistance from a government, municipality or other public authority (other than any such assistance that reduced the amount of an expenditure for purposes of computing the earnings amount for any taxation year) that the affiliate received or became entitled to receive in the year in connection with such business carried on in that country that is not otherwise required to be included in computing the earnings amount for the year or for any other taxation year,

and there shall be deducted such portion of the following amounts as were included or were not deducted, as the case may be, in computing the earnings amount,

(g) any income or profits tax refunded by the government of a country to the affiliate so included;

(h) any capital gain of the affiliate in respect of the disposition of capital property so included (for greater certainty, capital property of the affiliate for the purposes of this paragraph includes all the property of the affiliate other than property referred to in any of subparagraphs 39(1)(a)(i) to (iv) of the Act on the assumption for this purpose that the affiliate is a corporation resident in Canada);

(i) any amount that is included in the foreign accrual property income of the affiliate so included;

(j) any loss, outlay or expense made or incurred in the year by the affiliate for the purpose of gaining or producing such earnings amount to the extent that

(i) such loss, outlay or expense is not otherwise permitted to be deducted in computing the earnings amount of the affiliate for any taxation year by the income tax law that is relevant in computing that amount, or

(ii) such outlay or expense can reasonably be regarded as applicable to any revenue added to the earnings amount of the affiliate under paragraph (f),

where such loss, outlay or expense

(iii) subject to subsections (2.01) and (2.011), does not arise with respect to a disposition (other than a disposition to which subsection (9) applies), of property by the affiliate,

(A) to a person or partnership that was, at the time of the disposition, a designated person or partnership in respect of the taxpayer, and

(B) to which a loss deferral or similar loss postponement provision of the income tax laws that are relevant in computing the earnings amount of the affiliate applied, and

(iv) is not

(A) a loss referred to in paragraph (c) or (d),

(B) a capital expenditure other than interest, or

(C) income or profits tax paid to the government of a country;

(k) any outlay made in the year in repayment of an amount referred to in paragraph (f.1); and

(l) if any property of the affiliate that was acquired from a person or partnership that was, at the time of the acquisition, a designated person or partnership in respect of the taxpayer has been disposed of, the amount in respect of that property that may reasonably be considered as having been included under paragraph (f) in computing the earnings amount of any foreign affiliate of the taxpayer or of a person or partnership that was, at the time of the disposition, a designated person or partnership in respect of the taxpayer.

Related Provisions: ITA 245(2) — General anti-avoidance rule; Reg. 5907(2.01)–(2.03) — Subparas. (f)(ii) and (j)(iii) do not apply where assets packaged for sale; Reg. 5907(2.011) — Foreign divisive reorganization — Reg. 5907(2)(f)(ii) and (j)(iii) do not apply.

Notes: See Talakshi & Samuel, "Foreign Affiliate Surplus", 2008 Cdn Tax Foundation conference report, 28:1-34.

For a case applying Reg. 5907(2)(b) see VIEWS doc 2013-0499141I7 (safe income and US *Internal Revenue Code* §338(h)(10) election). 5907(2)(f) did not apply in 2018-0762581R3.

For "income or profits tax" in (a), (g) and (j)(iv)(C), see Notes to ITA 126(4). For "derived" in (2)(f), see Notes to ITA 18.1(12).

Reg. 5907(2)(f)(ii) and (j)(iii) amended by 2018 budget bill #2, for dispositions after Oct. 23, 2012, to refer to Reg. 5907(2.011). Reg. 5907(2) earlier amended by 2002-2013 technical bill (for dispositions after Aug. 19, 2011, or earlier by election); P.C. 1997-1670.

(2.01) [Packaging of assets for sale] — Subparagraphs (2)(f)(ii) and (j)(iii) and subsection (5.1) do not apply to a particular disposition of property (referred to in this subsection as the "affiliate property") by a particular foreign affiliate of a taxpayer if

(a) the only consideration received in respect of the particular disposition is shares of the capital stock of another foreign affiliate of the taxpayer;

(b) all of the shares of the capital stock of the other affiliate that are, immediately after the particular disposition, owned by the particular affiliate are disposed of, at a particular time that is within 90 days of the day that includes the time of the particular disposition, to a person or partnership that at the particular time is not a designated person or partnership in respect of the taxpayer; and

(c) the affiliate property is not disposed of by the other affiliate as part of a series of transactions or events that includes the particular disposition.

Notes: Assumption of liabilities constitutes "consideration received" for para. (a): VIEWS doc 2014-0550451E5. See also Barnicke & Huynh, "Packaging Rule in Reg. 5907(2.01) Deficient", 23(10) *Canadian Tax Highlights [CTH]* (ctf.ca) 6-7 (Oct. 2015), and "Exempt Earnings Anti-Avoidance", 23(12) *CTH* 5 (Dec. 2015).

This 5907(2.01) is unrelated to the Feb. 27/04 proposed 5907(2.01), which would have determined earnings of a foreign affiliate when one of various provisions had applied to a disposition. Most of the referenced provisions were withdrawn; what remains of that rule was enacted as Reg. 5907(9.1).

Reg. 5907(2.01) added by 2002-2013 technical bill, for dispositions after Aug. 19, 2011 (or earlier by election).

Regulations

(2.011) [Corporate division under foreign law] — Subparagraphs (2)(f)(ii) and (j)(iii) and subsection (5.1) do not apply to a particular disposition of property (referred to in this subsection as the "affiliate property") by a particular foreign affiliate of a taxpayer to another foreign affiliate of the taxpayer if

(a) the particular disposition is a disposition referred to in subparagraph 15(1.5)(c)(i) of the Act;

(b) all of the shares of the capital stock of the other affiliate are owned, at a particular time that is within 180 days after the day that includes the time of the particular disposition, by a person or partnership that at the particular time is not a designated person or partnership in respect of the taxpayer; and

(c) the affiliate property is not disposed of by the other affiliate as part of a series of transactions or events that includes the particular disposition.

Notes: See ITA 15(1.5), which applies to a Mexico *escisión* and similar corporate divisions. Reg. 5907(2.011) added by 2018 budget bill #2, for dispositions after Oct. 23, 2012.

(2.02) [Avoidance transaction] — If an amount or a portion of an amount would, in the absence of this subsection, be included in computing the exempt earnings, or deducted in computing the exempt loss, of a foreign affiliate of a corporation in respect of the corporation for a taxation year of the affiliate and the amount or portion arises from a disposition of property (other than money), at any time, to a person or partnership that was, at that time, a designated person or partnership in respect of the corporation where that disposition is a transaction (within the meaning of subsection 245(1) of the Act) that is, or would be (if the amount or portion were a tax benefit for the purposes of section 245 of the Act), an avoidance transaction (within the meaning of subsection 245(3) of the Act), the following rules apply:

(a) the amount or portion is instead to be included in the affiliate's taxable earnings for the year in respect of the corporation; and

(b) any income or profits tax relating to the transaction that would otherwise be deducted in computing the exempt earnings, or included in computing the exempt loss, of the affiliate for the year in respect of the corporation, is instead to be deducted from the affiliate's taxable earnings for the year in respect of the corporation.

Related Provisions: ITA 245(2) — General anti-avoidance rule; Reg. 5907(2.01)–(2.03) — Subparas. (f)(ii) and (j)(iii) do not apply where assets packaged for sale.

Notes: See Notes to ITA 245(1)"tax benefit" and 245(3) for interpretation. Note that this rule has no "misuse or abuse" test as GAAR has in ITA 245(4) (though it does depend on 245(3), which has a "non-tax purpose" test). This was criticized by Tax Executives Institute (letter to Finance, Oct. 19, 2011, p. 8).

For the meaning of "income or profits tax" in para. (b), see Notes to ITA 126(4).

See also Gwendolyn Watson, "The Foreign Affiliate Surplus Reclassification Rule", 67(4) *Canadian Tax Journal* 1233-66 (2019).

Reg. 5907(2.02) added by 2002-2013 technical bill, for transactions entered into after Aug. 19, 2011.

(2.03) [FA's earnings calculated on basis of maximum deductions] — The determination — under subparagraph (a)(iii) and paragraph (b) of the definition "earnings", and paragraph (b) of the definition "loss", in subsection (1) — of the earnings or loss of a foreign affiliate of a taxpayer resident in Canada for a particular taxation year from an active business is to be made as if the affiliate

(a) had, in computing its income or loss from the business for each taxation year (referred to in this paragraph as an "earnings or loss year") that is the particular year or is any preceding taxation year that ends after August 19, 2011,

(i) claimed all deductions that it could have claimed under the Act, up to the maximum amount deductible in computing the income or loss from the business for that earnings or loss year, and

(ii) made all claims and elections and taken all steps under applicable provisions of the Act, or of enactments imple-

menting amendments to the Act or its regulations, to maximize the amount of any deduction referred to subparagraph (i); and

(b) had, in computing its income or loss from the business for any preceding taxation year that ended on or before August 19, 2011, claimed all deductions, if any, that it actually claimed under the Act, up to the maximum amount deductible, and made all claims and elections, if any, and taken all steps, if any, under applicable provisions of the Act, or of enactments implementing amendments to the Act or its regulations, that it actually made.

Related Provisions: Reg. 5907(1)"earnings"(b) — Application of subsec. (2.03) to definition; Reg. 5907(1)"loss"(b) — Application of subsec. (2.03) to definition.

Notes: Reg. 5907(2.03) provides that where an FA's income is calculated using Canadian tax rules, this must be done on the basis that it claimed maximum deductions, to prevent artificial inflation of surplus (see Notes to ITA 113(1)). See Colborne, "Regulation 5907(2.03) and Offshore Metal Streams", IX(2) *Resource Sector Taxation* (Federated Press) 647-48 (2013); Colborne & Paton, "2013 Mining Update", 2013 Cdn Tax Foundation conference report at 9:15-17; VIEWS docs 2012-0460121E5, 2016-0669761C6 [2016 CTF q.11].

Reg. 5907(2.03) added by 2002-2013 technical bill, for foreign affiliates' tax years that end after Aug. 19, 2011.

(2.1) [FA carrying on active business in Canada or treaty country] — In computing the earnings of a foreign affiliate of a corporation resident in Canada for a taxation year of the affiliate from an active business carried on by it in Canada or in a designated treaty country, where the affiliate is resident in a designated treaty country and the corporation, together with all other corporations resident in Canada with which the corporation does not deal at arm's length and in respect of which the affiliate is a foreign affiliate, have so elected in respect of the business for the taxation year or any preceding taxation year of the affiliate, the following rules apply:

(a) there shall be added to the amount determined under subparagraph (a)(i) of the definition "earnings" in subsection (1) after adjustment in accordance with the provisions of subsection (2) (in this subsection and in subsection (2.2) referred to as the "adjusted earnings amount") the total of all amounts each of which is the amount, if any, by which

(i) the amount that can reasonably be regarded as having been deducted in respect of the cost of a capital property or foreign resource property of the affiliate in computing the adjusted earnings amount

exceeds

(ii) the amount that may reasonably be regarded as having been deducted in respect of the cost of that capital property or foreign resource property in computing income or profit of the affiliate for the year from that business in its financial statements prepared in accordance with the laws of the country in which the affiliate is resident;

(b) there shall be deducted from the adjusted earnings amount the aggregate of all amounts each of which is the amount, if any, by which

(i) the amount determined under subparagraph (a)(ii) in respect of that capital property or foreign resource property

exceeds

(ii) the amount determined under subparagraph (a)(i) in respect of that capital property or foreign resource property;

(c) where any capital property or foreign resource property of the affiliate has been disposed of in the taxation year,

(i) there shall be added to the adjusted earnings amount the aggregate of the amounts deducted pursuant to paragraphs (b) and (2.2)(b) for preceding taxation years of the affiliate in respect of that capital property or foreign resource property, and

(ii) there shall be deducted from the adjusted earnings amount the aggregate of the amounts added pursuant to paragraphs (a) and (2.2)(a) for the preceding taxation years of the affiliate in respect of that capital property or foreign resource property; and

(d) for the purposes of paragraph (c), where the affiliate has merged with one or more corporations to form a new corporation, any capital property or foreign resource property of the affiliate that becomes a property of the new corporation shall be deemed to have been disposed of by the affiliate in its last taxation year before the merger.

Related Provisions: ITA 220(3.2), Reg. 600(d) — Late filing or revocation of election; Reg. 5907(2.2), (2.4) — Application rules; Reg. 5907(2.6) — Corporation deemed to have elected.

Notes: See Talakshi & Samuel, "Foreign Affiliate Surplus", 2008 Cdn Tax Foundation conference report, 28:1-34; Baker & Bunn, "FAs and the Repeal of the ECP Regime", 24(9) *Canadian Tax Highlights* (ctf.ca) 4 (Sept. 2016). The affiliate's financial statements for (b)(ii) can be prepared using IFRS if permitted by the affiliate's country of residence: VIEWS docs 2010-0373661C6, 2018-0762581R3.

Reg. 5907(2.1) amended by P.C. 1997-1670, for foreign affiliates' tax years that begin after 1995 (or earlier by election).

Information Circulars: 77-9R: Books, records and other requirements for taxpayers having foreign affiliates.

(2.2) [Where election made under Reg. 5907(2.1)] — Where the taxation year of a foreign affiliate of a particular corporation resident in Canada for which the particular corporation has made an election under subsection (2.1) in respect of an active business carried on by the affiliate is not the first taxation year of the affiliate in which it carried on the business and in which it was a foreign affiliate of the particular corporation or of another corporation resident in Canada with which the particular corporation was not dealing at arm's length at any time (hereinafter referred to as the "non-arm's length corporation"), in computing the earnings of the affiliate from the business for the taxation year for which the election is made, the following rules, in addition to those set out in subsection (2.1), apply:

(a) there shall be added to the adjusted earnings amount the aggregate of all amounts each of which is an amount that would have been determined under paragraph (2.1)(a) or subparagraph (2.1)(c)(i)

(i) for any preceding taxation year of the affiliate in which it was a foreign affiliate of the particular corporation if the particular corporation had made an election under subsection (2.1) for the first taxation year of the affiliate in which it was a foreign affiliate of the particular corporation and carried on the business, and

(ii) for any preceding taxation year of the affiliate (other than a taxation year referred to in subparagraph (i)) in which it was a foreign affiliate of the non-arm's length corporation if the non-arm's length corporation had made an election under subsection (2.1) for the first taxation year of the affiliate in which it was a foreign affiliate of the non-arm's length corporation and carried on the business; and

(b) there shall be deducted from the adjusted earnings amount the aggregate of all amounts each of which is an amount that would have been determined under paragraph (2.1)(b) or subparagraph (2.1)(c)(ii)

(i) for any preceding taxation year of the affiliate in which it was a foreign affiliate of the particular corporation if the particular corporation had made an election under subsection (2.1) for the first taxation year of the affiliate in which it was a foreign affiliate of the particular corporation and carried on the business, and

(ii) for any preceding taxation year of the affiliate (other than a taxation year referred to in subparagraph (i)) in which it was a foreign affiliate of the non-arm's length corporation if the non-arm's length corporation had made an election under subsection (2.1) for the first taxation year of the affiliate in which it was a foreign affiliate of the non-arm's length corporation and carried on the business.

(2.3) [Where election made under Reg. 5907(2.1)] — For the purposes of this subsection and subsections (2.1) and (2.2), where an election under subsection (2.1) has been made by a corporation resident in Canada (in this subsection and in subsection (2.4) referred to as the "electing corporation") in respect of an active business of a foreign affiliate of the electing corporation and the affiliate subsequently becomes a foreign affiliate of another corporation resident in Canada (in this subsection and in subsection (2.4) referred to as the "subsequent corporation") that does not deal at arm's length with the electing corporation, in computing the earnings of the affiliate from such business in respect of the subsequent corporation for any taxation year of the affiliate ending after the affiliate so became a foreign affiliate of the subsequent corporation, the subsequent corporation shall be deemed to have made an election under subsection (2.1) in respect of the business of the affiliate for the first such taxation year and for the purposes of paragraph (2.1)(d), the earnings of the affiliate for all of the preceding taxation years shall be deemed to have been adjusted in accordance with subsections (2.1) and (2.2) in the same manner as if the subsequent corporation had been the electing corporation.

Notes: Reg. 5907(2.3) amended by P.C. 1997-1670, last change effective for foreign affiliates' tax years that end after 1994.

(2.4) ["Subsequent corporation" for Reg. 5907(2.3)] — For the purposes of subsection (2.3)

(a) a corporation formed as a result of a merger, to which section 87 of the Act applies, of the electing corporation and one or more other corporations, or

(b) a corporation that has acquired shares of the capital stock of a foreign affiliate, in respect of which an election under subsection (2.1) has been made, from the electing corporation in a transaction in respect of which an election under section 85 of the Act was made

shall be deemed to be a subsequent corporation that does not deal at arm's length with the electing corporation.

(2.5) [Repealed]

Notes: Reg. 5907(2.5) repealed by P.C. 1997-1670, last change effective for foreign affiliates' tax years that end after 1994.

(2.6) [Corporations deemed to have elected under Reg. 5907(2.1)] — A corporation resident in Canada, and all other corporations resident in Canada with which the corporation does not deal at arm's length, shall each be considered to have elected under subsection (2.1) in respect of an active business carried on by a non-resident corporation that is a foreign affiliate of each such corporation for a taxation year if there is filed with the Minister on or before the day that is the later of

(a) June 30, 1986, and

(b) the earliest of the days on or before which any one of the said corporations is required to file a return of income pursuant to section 150 of the Act for its taxation year following the taxation year in which the taxation year of the affiliate in respect of which the election is made ends,

the following information:

(c) a description of the active business sufficient to identify the business, and

(d) a statement on behalf of each such corporation, signed by an authorized official of the corporation on behalf of which the statement is made, that the corporation is electing under subsection (2.1) in respect of the business.

(2.7) [Where ITA 95(2)(a)(i) or (ii) applies] — Notwithstanding any other provision of this Part, if an amount (referred to in this subsection as the "inclusion amount") is included in computing the income or loss from an active business of a foreign affiliate of a taxpayer for a taxation year under subparagraph 95(2)(a)(i) or (ii) of

Regulations

the Act and the inclusion amount is in respect of a particular amount paid or payable,

(a) if clause 95(2)(a)(ii)(D) of the Act is applicable, by the second affiliate referred to in that clause,

(i) the particular amount is to be deducted in computing the second affiliate's income or loss from an active business carried on by it in the country in which it is resident for its earliest taxation year in which that amount was paid or payable,

(ii) the second affiliate is deemed to have carried on an active business in that country for that earliest taxation year, and

(iii) in computing the second affiliate's income or loss for a taxation year from any source, no amount is to be deducted in respect of the particular amount except as required under subparagraph (i); and

(b) in any other case, by the other foreign affiliate referred to in subparagraph 95(2)(a)(i) or (ii) of the Act, as the case may be, or by a partnership of which the other foreign affiliate is a member, the particular amount is, except where it has been deducted under paragraph (2)(j) in computing the other foreign affiliate's earnings or loss from an active business,

(i) to be deducted in computing the earnings or loss of the other foreign affiliate or the partnership, as the case may be, from the active business for its earliest taxation year in which the particular amount was paid or payable, and

(ii) not to be deducted in computing its earnings or loss from the active business for any other taxation year.

Related Provisions: Reg. 5908(9) — Tiered partnerships — look-through rule.

Notes: For an opinion on Reg. 5907(2.7) see VIEWS doc 2009-0347271R3.

Reg. 5907(2.7) amended (combining former (2.7) and (2.8)) by 2002-2013 technical bill, for foreign affiliates' tax years that begin after 2008. Added by P.C. 1997-1670.

(2.8) [Repealed]

Notes: Reg. 5907(2.8) repealed by 2002-2013 technical bill, for FAs' tax years that begin after 2008 (it was combined with (2.7) above). Added by P.C. 1997-1670.

Proposed **Reg. 5907(2.8)–(2.83)** in the Feb. 27, 2004 draft, the "interest push-down rules", will not be enacted: Finance Technical Notes to Reg. 5900-5919 (Sept. 10, 2010), #6.

(2.9) [Where fresh start rules apply] — If paragraph 95(2)(k.1) of the Act applies in respect of a particular taxation year of a foreign affiliate of a taxpayer or in respect of a particular fiscal period of a partnership (which foreign affiliate or partnership is referred to in this subsection as the "operator" and which particular taxation year or particular fiscal period is referred to in this subsection as the "specified taxation year") a member of which is, at the end of the period, a foreign affiliate of a taxpayer,

(a) in computing the affiliate's earnings or loss from the foreign business referred to in that paragraph for the affiliate's taxation year (referred to in subparagraphs (i) and (ii) as the "preceding taxation year") that includes the day that is immediately before the beginning of the specified taxation year,

(i) there is to be added to the amount determined under paragraph (a) of the definition "earnings" in subsection (1), after adjustment in accordance with subsections (2) to (2.2),

(A) where the operator is the affiliate, the total of

(I) the amount, if any, by which the total determined under sub-subclause (ii)(A)(I)2 in respect of the operator for the preceding taxation year exceeds the total determined under sub-subclause (ii)(A)(I)1 in respect of the operator for that year, and

(II) if the operator was deemed under paragraph 95(2)(k.1) of the Act to have, at the end of the preceding taxation year, disposed of property owned by it that was used or held by it in the course of carrying on the foreign business in that year, the amount that is the total of all amounts each of which is determined by the formula

$$(A - B) - C$$

where

A is the fair market value, immediately before the end of that year, of a property deemed because of that paragraph to have been disposed of,

B is the amount determined under paragraph (a) of the definition "relevant cost base" in subsection 95(4) of the Act in respect of the property, in respect of the taxpayer, immediately before the time of the disposition, and

C is the amount, if any, of the capital gain determined in respect of the disposition of the property at that time, and

(B) where the operator is the partnership, the amount determined under subsection 5908(13); and

(ii) there is to be added to the amount determined under paragraph (a) of the definition "loss" in subsection (1),

(A) where the operator is the affiliate, the total of

(I) the amount, if any, by which

1. the total of all amounts each of which is an amount deemed under paragraph 95(2)(k.1) of the Act to have been claimed under any of paragraphs 20(1)(l), (l.1) and (7)(c), and subparagraphs 138(3)(a)(i), (ii) and (iv), of the Act (each of which provisions is referred to in this subparagraph as a "reserve provision") in computing the income from the foreign business for the preceding taxation year

exceeds

2. the total of all amounts each of which is an amount actually claimed by the operator as a reserve in computing its income from the foreign business for that year that can reasonably be considered to be in respect of amounts in respect of which a reserve could have been claimed under a reserve provision on the assumption that the operator could have claimed amounts in respect of the reserve provisions for that year, and

(II) the total of all amounts each of which is the amount, if any, by which the amount determined under the description of B in the formula in subclause (i)(A)(II) in respect of a property described in that subclause exceeds the amount determined under the description of A in the formula in that clause in respect of the property, and

(B) where the operator is the partnership, the amount determined under subsection 5908(13); and

(b) any property of the operator that is, under that paragraph, deemed to have been disposed of and reacquired by the operator is, for the purposes of this section, deemed to have been disposed of and reacquired by the operator in the same manner and for the same amounts as if that paragraph applied for the purposes of this section.

Related Provisions: ITA 257 — Negative amounts in formulas; Reg. 5907.1 — Transitional rule.

Notes: Reg. 5907(2.9) amended by 2002-2013 technical bill, for FAs' tax years that begin after Dec. 20, 2002 (or earlier by election). Added by P.C. 1997-1670.

(3) [Pre-1972 foreign affiliate] — For the purposes of this Part, any corporation that was, on January 1, 1972, a foreign affiliate of a taxpayer shall be deemed to have become a foreign affiliate of the taxpayer on that day.

(4) ["Government of a country"] — For the purposes of this Part, "government of a country" includes the government of a state, province or other political subdivision of that country.

(5) [Capital gains and losses] — For the purposes of this section, each capital gain, capital loss, taxable capital gain or allowable capital loss of a foreign affiliate of a taxpayer from the disposition

of property is to be computed in accordance with the rules set out in subsection 95(2) of the Act.

Related Provisions: ITA 261 — Functional currency election; Reg. 5907(5.01) — Rate of exchange for currency conversion.

Notes: FAPI can be offset with losses from year-end exchange rate fluctuations on mark-to-market properties: VIEWS doc 2010-035442117.

Reg. 5907(5) amended by 2002-2013 technical bill, last effective Aug. 20, 2011.

(5.01) [Rate of exchange for currency conversion] — For the purposes of subsection (6), if any capital gain, capital loss, taxable capital gain or allowable capital loss referred to in subsection (5), or any capital loss referred to in subparagraph (iii) of the description of B in the definition "hybrid surplus" in subsection (1), of a foreign affiliate of a corporation is required to be computed in Canadian currency and the currency referred to in subsection (6) is not Canadian currency, the amount of the gain or loss is to be converted from Canadian currency into the currency referred to in subsection (6) at the rate of exchange prevailing on the date of disposition of the property.

Notes: Reg. 5907(5.01) added by 2002-2013 technical bill, effective Aug. 20, 2011.

(5.1) [Where no gain or loss recognized by other country] — Notwithstanding subsection (5), if, under the income tax laws of a country other than Canada that are relevant in computing the earnings of a foreign affiliate of a taxpayer resident in Canada from an active business carried on by it in a country, no gain or loss is recognized in respect of a disposition (other than a disposition to which subsection (9) applies) by the affiliate of a capital property used or held principally for the purpose of gaining or producing income from an active business to a person or partnership (in this subsection referred to as the "transferee") that was, at the time of the disposition, a designated person or partnership in respect of the taxpayer, for the purposes of this section,

(a) the affiliate's proceeds of disposition of the property shall be deemed to be an amount equal to the aggregate of the adjusted cost base to the affiliate of the property immediately before the disposition and any outlays and expenses to the extent they were made or incurred by the affiliate for the purpose of making the disposition;

(b) the cost to the transferee of the property acquired from the affiliate shall be deemed to be an amount equal to the affiliate's proceeds of disposition, as determined under paragraph (a); and

(c) the transferee shall be deemed to have acquired the property on the date that it was acquired by the affiliate.

Related Provisions: Reg. 5907(2.01)–(2.03) — Exclusion where assets packaged for sale; Reg. 5907(2.011) — Foreign divisive reorganization — Reg. 5907(5.1) does not apply.

Notes: For rulings on Reg. 5907(5.1) see VIEWS docs 2008-0290081R3, 2008-0290361R3.

Reg. 5907(5.1) amended by 2002-2013 technical bill, for dispositions after Aug. 19, 2011.

(6) [Selection of currency] — All amounts referred to in subsections (1) and (2) shall be maintained on a consistent basis from year to year in the currency of the country in which the foreign affiliate of the corporation resident in Canada is resident or any currency that the corporation resident in Canada demonstrates to be reasonable in the circumstances.

Related Provisions: ITA 261 — Functional currency election; Reg. 5907(5.01) — Rate of exchange for currency conversion; Reg. 5907(5.1) — Exception.

Notes: For what CRA considers reasonable see Darling, "Revenue Canada Perspectives", 1992 Corporate Management Tax Conference (ctf.ca), q.7 at p. 5:13 (still current: CRA Rulings Nov. 6/14, Toronto Centre Tax Professionals breakfast, repeating answer given at APFF); VIEWS doc 2014-0538181C6 [2014 APFF q.24]. See also Kotecha, "Practical Issues and Problems Involved in Selecting a Calculating Currency", X(4) *International Tax Planning* (Federated Press) 737-42 (2002).

Conversion of a foreign affiliate's surplus accounts to a functional currency for tax return purposes is not a taxable event: VIEWS doc 2004-0072851C6.

Reg. 5907(6) amended by 2002-2013 technical bill, for foreign affiliates' tax years that begin after Dec. 18, 2009.

Information Circulars: 77-9R: Books, records and other requirements for taxpayers having foreign affiliates.

(7) [Stock dividend] — For the purposes of this Part, the amount of any stock dividend paid by a foreign affiliate of a corporation resident in Canada on a share of a class of its capital stock shall be deemed to be nil.

(7.1) [Repealed]

Notes: Reg. 5907(7.1), applying where a foreign affiliate paid a dividend that triggered a foreign tax credit in another country, repealed by 2002-2013 technical bill, effective Aug. 20, 2011. It is no longer needed because the UK advance corporation tax, for which it was designed, was abolished in 1999.

(8) [Deemed new taxation year on merger] — For the purposes of computing the various amounts referred to in this section,

(a) the first taxation year of a foreign affiliate, of a corporation resident in Canada, that is formed as a result of a "foreign merger" (within the meaning assigned by subsection 87(8.1) of the Act) is deemed to have commenced at the time of the merger, and a taxation year of a "predecessor corporation" (within the meaning assigned by subsection 5905(3)) that would otherwise have ended after that time is deemed to have ended immediately before that time; and

(b) if subsection 91(1.2) of the Act applies at any particular time in respect of a foreign affiliate of a corporation, the various amounts are to be computed, in respect of attributed amounts for the stub period in respect of the particular time, as if

(i) the affiliate's taxation year that would have included the particular time ended at the stub-period end time in respect of the particular time, and

(ii) all transactions or events, giving rise to attributed amounts, that occurred at the particular time, occurred at the stub-period end time in respect of the particular time.

Related Provisions: ITA 87(8.2) — Absorptive mergers; Reg. 5907(8.1) — Definitions.

Notes: Reg. 5907(8)(b) added by 2017 budget bill #2, effective July 12, 2013, except that if at any time from that day through Sept. 7, 2017, ITA 91(1.2) applies in respect of taxpayer T, and T and all corporations that are connected persons (under ITA 91(1.3)"connected person"(a)) to T at the time file with the Minister an election in prescribed manner by the earliest of the filing-due date of T and those corps for their tax year that includes Dec. 14, 2017, then for T and those corps, para. (b) is effective Sept. 8, 2017.

Reg. 5907(8) earlier amended by 2002-2013 technical bill, for FA mergers or combinations after Aug. 19, 2011.

(8.1) [Definitions] — The following definitions apply in paragraph 5907(8)(b).

"attributed amounts", for a stub period, in respect of a particular time referred to in paragraph (8)(b), of a foreign affiliate of a corporation, means

(a) the amounts of any income, gain or loss of the affiliate for the stub period that are relevant in determining amounts that are to be included or may be deducted under section 91 of the Act in respect of the affiliate for the particular stub period, in computing the income of the corporation;

(b) any portion of the affiliate's capital gain or capital loss — from a disposition, in the stub period or at the particular time referred to in paragraph (8)(b), of a property that is not an excluded property — that is not described in paragraph (a); and

(c) any income or profits tax paid to the government of a country, in respect of amounts described in paragraph (a) or (b).

"stub period", in respect of a particular time at which subsection 91(1.2) of the Act applies in respect of a foreign affiliate of a corporation, means a period that ends at the stub-period end time in respect of the particular time and begins immediately after the later of

(a) the last time, if any, before the particular time that subsection 91(1.2) applied in respect of the affiliate, and

(b) the end of the affiliate's last taxation year before the particular time.

"stub-period end time", in respect of a particular time at which subsection 91(1.2) of the Act applies in respect of a foreign affiliate

Regulations

of a corporation, means the time that is immediately before the particular time.

Notes: Reg. 5907(8.1) added by 2017 budget bill #2, effective on the same basis as Reg. 5907(8)(b).

(9) [Where FA dissolved] — If a foreign affiliate of a taxpayer has been liquidated and dissolved (otherwise than as a result of a foreign merger within the meaning assigned by subsection 87(8.1) of the Act), for the purposes of computing the various amounts referred to in this section, the following rules apply:

(a) where, at a particular time, property having a fair market value equal to or greater than 90 percent of the fair market value of all of the property that was owned by the affiliate immediately before the commencement of the liquidation and dissolution has been disposed of by the affiliate in the course of the liquidation and dissolution, the taxation year of the affiliate that otherwise would have included the particular time is deemed to have ended immediately before that time; and

(b) each property of the affiliate that was disposed of by the affiliate in the course of the liquidation and dissolution is deemed to have been

(i) disposed of by the affiliate, at the time that is the earlier of the time it was actually disposed of and the time that is immediately before the time that is immediately before the particular time, for proceeds of disposition equal to

(A) if the liquidation and dissolution is one to which subsection 88(3) of the Act applies in respect of the disposition, the amount that would, in the absence of subsection 88(3.3) of the Act, be determined under paragraph 88(3)(a) or (b) of the Act, as the case may be,

(B) if the liquidation and dissolution is one to which paragraph 95(2)(e) of the Act applies in respect of the disposition, the amount determined under subparagraph 95(2)(e)(i) or (ii) of the Act, as the case may be, and

(C) in any other case, the fair market value of the property at the time it was actually disposed of, and

(ii) acquired by the person or partnership to which the affiliate disposed of the property, at the time it was actually acquired, at a cost equal to the affiliate's proceeds of disposition of the property.

Related Provisions: ITA 87(8.2) — Absorptive mergers.

Notes: Reg. 5907(9) amended by 2002-2013 technical bill, last change effective for foreign affiliate liquidations and dissolutions that begin after Aug. 19, 2011.

(9.1) Notwithstanding any other provision of this Part, in determining the earnings or loss of a foreign affiliate of a taxpayer resident in Canada, for a taxation year of the affiliate from an active business carried on by it in a country,

(a) from a disposition of property to which paragraph 95(2)(d.1) of the Act applies, those earnings or that loss are to be determined using the rules in that paragraph; and

(b) from a disposition of property acquired in a transaction to which paragraph 95(2)(d.1) of the Act applies, the cost to the affiliate of the property is to be determined using the rules in that paragraph.

Notes: Reg. 5907(9.1) added by 2002-2013 technical bill, for mergers or combinations after Aug. 19, 2011 (or earlier by election). It is a pared-down version of Reg. 5907(2.01) from the Feb. 27, 2004 draft.

(10) [Tax sparing] — Where

(a) the net earnings or net loss for a taxation year of a foreign affiliate of a corporation resident in Canada from an active business carried on in a country other than Canada would otherwise be included in the affiliate's taxable earnings or taxable loss, as the case may be, for the year,

(b) the rate of the income or profits tax to which any earnings of that active business of the affiliate are subjected by the government of that country is, by virtue of a special exemption from or reduction of tax (other than an export incentive) that is provided

under a law of such country to promote investments or projects in pursuance of a program of economic development, less than the rate of such tax that would, but for such exemption or reduction, be paid by the affiliate, and

(c) the affiliate qualified for such exemption from or reduction of tax in respect of an investment made by it in that country before January 1, 1976 or in respect of an investment made by it or a project undertaken by it in that country pursuant to an agreement in writing entered into before January 1, 1976,

for the purposes of this Part, such net earnings or net loss shall be included in the affiliate's exempt earnings or exempt loss, as the case may be, for the year and not in the affiliate's taxable earnings or taxable loss, as the case may be, for the year.

Notes: Reg. 5907(10)(b) refers to "tax sparing", where the host country exempts or reduces tax on income from an investment for incentive purposes. See Toaze, "Tax Sparing", 49(4) *Canadian Tax Journal* 879-924 (2001); Brooks, "Tax Sparing", 34(2) *Queen's Law Journal* (Spring 2009), reviewed at 57(2) *CTJ* 411-12 (2009). However, such protection from "taxable surplus" treatment applies only for pre-1976 investments (see para. (c)), preserving such treatment from the days when dividends from foreign affiliates were not taxed at all.

There is no need for tax sparing for dividends received by Canadian corporations from countries listed or designated under Reg. 5907(11), since the dividends are not taxed. Tax sparing of Canadian tax on income earned abroad directly (such as through a branch or joint venture), or as dividends received by Canadian resident individuals, is provided in some of Canada's tax treaties with developing countries.

In *Société Générale Valeurs*, 2017 FCA 3, a tax sparing provision in the Canada-Brazil treaty was held to be "intended to avoid neutralizing any tax incentive offered by Brazil" rather than "maximally encouraging the lending of funds by Canadian enterprises in Brazil". See 103 *The Arnold Report* (ctf.ca, Oct. 28, 2016) on the TCC decision. Canada-Brazil tax sparing does not apply to Ontario tax: VIEWS doc 2016-0632711I7.

See also Notes to ITA 126(7)"non-business-income tax" re tax sparing that deems foreign tax to have been paid for purpose of the foreign tax credit.

For the meaning of "income or profits tax" in para. (b), see Notes to ITA 126(4).

(11) ["Designated treaty country"] — For the purposes of this Part, a sovereign state or other jurisdiction is a "designated treaty country" for a taxation year of a foreign affiliate of a corporation if Canada has entered into a comprehensive agreement or convention for the elimination of double taxation on income, or a comprehensive tax information exchange agreement, in respect of that sovereign state or jurisdiction, that has entered into force and has effect for that taxation year, but any territory, possession, department, dependency or area of that sovereign state or jurisdiction to which that agreement or convention does not apply is not considered to be part of that sovereign state or jurisdiction for the purpose of determining whether it is a designated treaty country.

Related Provisions: Reg. 5907(1.02) — New FA deemed resident in designated treaty country throughout year; Reg. 5907(11.1) — Effective date of treaty; Reg. 5907(11.11) — When tax information exchange agreement in force; Reg. 5907(11.2) — Whether FA resident in treaty country.

Notes: Under Reg. 5907(11), only for countries with which Canada has a tax treaty or TIEA are dividends paid out of earnings effectively exempt from tax in the hands of Canadian corporate shareholders.

For a list of countries with which Canada has or is negotiating tax treaties, see at the end of this book, after the Canada-UK treaty. For countries with which Canada has or is negotiating a TIEA, see Notes to ITA 95(1)"non-qualifying country".

For CRA interpretation see VIEWS docs 2009-0316641C6 [2009 CHLIA q.4] (corp incorporated in country A but resident in country B); 2017-0710641E5 (Interest Charge Domestic International Sales Corp is considered resident in US).

See also Barnicke & Huynh, "Exempt Surplus and TIEAs", 16(2) *Canadian Tax Highlights* (ctf.ca) 2 (Feb. 2008).

Reg. 5907(11) amended by 2008 budget bill #2 (effective 2008); P.C. 1997-1670.

(11.1) [Effective date of treaty for Reg. 5907(11)] — For the purpose of subsection (11), where a comprehensive agreement or convention between Canada and another country for the elimination of double taxation on income has entered into force, that convention or agreement is deemed to have entered into force and have effect in respect of a taxation year of a foreign affiliate of a corporation any day of which is in the period that begins on the day on which the agreement or convention was signed and that ends on the last day of the last taxation year of the affiliate for which the agreement or convention is effective.

Notes: Reg. 5907(11.1) added by P.C. 1997-1670.

(11.11) [When TIEA deemed in force] — For the purpose of applying subsection (11) in respect of a foreign affiliate of a corporation, where a comprehensive tax information exchange agreement enters into force on a particular day, the agreement is deemed to enter into force and to come into effect on the first day of the foreign affiliate's taxation year that includes the particular day.

Notes: See Edwards & Buttenham, "TIEAs: Not All Exempt Surplus Is Created Equal", XV(2) *International Tax Planning* (Federated Press) 1036-41 (2009).

Reg. 5907(11.11) added by 2008 budget bill #2, effective 2008.

(11.2) [Whether FA resident in treaty country] — For the purposes of this Part, a foreign affiliate of a corporation is, at any time, deemed not to be resident in a country with which Canada has entered into a comprehensive agreement or convention for the elimination of double taxation on income unless

(a) the affiliate is, at that time, a resident of that country for the purpose of the agreement or convention;

(b) the affiliate would, at that time, be a resident of that country for the purpose of the agreement or convention if the affiliate were treated, for the purpose of income taxation in that country, as a body corporate;

(c) where the agreement or convention entered into force before 1995, the affiliate would, at that time, be a resident of that country for the purpose of the agreement or convention but for a provision in the agreement or convention that has not been amended after 1994 and that provides that the agreement or convention does not apply to the affiliate; or

(d) the affiliate would, at that time, be a resident of that country, as provided by paragraph (a), (b) or (c) if the agreement or convention had entered into force.

Notes: See VIEWS docs 2005-0149771E5, 2009-0341441E5 (Barbados qualifying insurance co); 2008-0267821R3, 2008-0287701R3, 2008-0300351R3; 2007-0261551I7, 2009-0316631C6 (Barbados exempt insurance co) [Haag, "Exempt Earnings for Barbados Insurers", 18(2) *Canadian Tax Highlights* (ctf.ca) 1-2 (Dec. 2010)]; 2017-0710641E5 (Interest Charge DISC). See also *Antle*, 2009 TCC 465, para. 109 (Reg. 5907(11.2) does not "extend to annihilating Canada's capital gains policy"), and *Sundog Distributing*, 2010 TCC 392, paras. 27-29 (para. (c) applied to Barbados IBC).

Reg. 5907(11.2) added by P.C. 1997-1670, for foreign affiliates' tax years that begin after 1995 (or earlier by election).

I.T. Technical News: 16 (U.S. S-Corps and LLCs).

(12) [Repealed]

Notes: Reg. 5907(12) repealed by 2002-2013 technical bill, effective Dec. 19, 2009. It was moved to Reg. 5908(10) when consolidating the partnership rules in Reg. 5908.

For a case applying Reg. 5907(12)(a)(ii) see VIEWS doc 2007-0247551E5; for (b)(iv) see 2006-0187681R3.

Reg. 5907(12) amended by P.C. 1997-1670, last effective for foreign affiliates' tax years that end after 1994.

(13) [Where foreign affiliate becomes resident in Canada] — For the purposes of subparagraph (ii) of paragraph 128.1(1)(d) of the Act, the prescribed amount is the amount determined by the formula

$$X + Y$$

where

X is the amount, if any, by which

(a) the amount, if any, determined by the formula

$$A - B - (C - D) + (E - F)$$

where

A is the taxable surplus of the foreign affiliate of the other taxpayer referred to in that paragraph, in respect of the other taxpayer, at the end of the year referred to in that subparagraph,

B is the affiliate's net earnings for the year in respect of the affiliate's foreign accrual property income for the year to the extent those net earnings have been included in the amount referred to in the description of A,

C is the total of all amounts each of which is the amount by which the affiliate's underlying foreign tax in respect of the other taxpayer at the end of the year would have increased because of the gain or income of the affiliate that would have arisen if a disposition, deemed under paragraph 128.1(1)(b) of the Act, of a property by the affiliate had been an actual disposition of the property by the affiliate,

D is the total of all amounts each of which is the amount otherwise added in computing the affiliate's underlying foreign tax in respect of the other taxpayer at the end of the year in respect of income or profits taxes paid to the government of a country in respect of all or a portion of a gain or an income of the affiliate referred to in the description of C,

E is the total of all amounts each of which is the amount by which the affiliate's underlying foreign tax in respect of the other taxpayer at the end of the year would have decreased because of the loss of the affiliate that would have arisen if a disposition, deemed under paragraph 128.1(1)(b) of the Act, of a property by the affiliate had been an actual disposition of the property by the affiliate, and

F is the total of all amounts each of which is the amount otherwise deducted in computing the affiliate's underlying foreign tax in respect of the other taxpayer at the end of the year in respect of income or profits taxes refunded by the government of a country in respect of all or a portion of a loss of the affiliate referred to in the description of E

exceeds

(b) the amount, if any, determined by the formula

$$[(G - H) \times (J - 1)] + K$$

where

G is the amount determined by the formula

$$L + M - N$$

where

L is the underlying foreign tax of the affiliate in respect of the other taxpayer at the end of the year,

M is the amount, if any, by which the amount determined under the description of C in paragraph (a) exceeds the amount determined under the description of D in that paragraph, and

N is the amount, if any, by which the amount determined under the description of E in paragraph (a) exceeds the amount determined under the description of F in that paragraph,

H is the portion of the value of L that can reasonably be considered to relate to the affiliate's net earnings for the year in respect of the affiliate's foreign accrual property income,

J is the other taxpayer's relevant tax factor (within the meaning assigned by subsection 95(1) of the Act) for its taxation year that includes the time that is immediately before the particular time, and

K is the amount, if any, by which

(i) the total of all amounts required by paragraph 92(1)(a) of the Act to be added at any time in a preceding taxation year in computing the adjusted cost base to the other taxpayer of the shares of the affiliate owned by the other taxpayer at the end of the year

exceeds

(ii) the total of all amounts required by paragraph 92(1)(b) of the Act to be deducted at any time in a preceding taxation year in computing the adjusted cost base to the other taxpayer of the shares of the affiliate owned by the other taxpayer at the end of the year, and

Y is the amount, if any, by which

(a) the amount, if any, determined by the formula

$$P - (Q - R) + (S - T)$$

where

P is the affiliate's hybrid surplus in respect of the other taxpayer at the end of the year,

Q is the total of all amounts each of which is the amount by which the affiliate's hybrid underlying tax in respect of the other taxpayer at the end of the year would have increased because of the capital gain of the affiliate that would have arisen if a disposition, deemed under paragraph 128.1(1)(b) of the Act, of a property by the affiliate had been an actual disposition of the property by the affiliate,

R is the total of all amounts each of which is the amount otherwise added in computing the affiliate's hybrid underlying tax in respect of the other taxpayer at the end of the year in respect of income or profits taxes paid to the government of a country in respect of all or a portion of a capital gain of the affiliate referred to in the description of Q,

S is the total of all amounts each of which is the amount by which the affiliate's hybrid underlying tax in respect of the other taxpayer at the end of the year would have decreased because of the capital loss of the affiliate that would have arisen if a disposition, deemed under paragraph 128.1(1)(b) of the Act, of a property by the affiliate had been an actual disposition of the property by the affiliate, and

T is the total of all amounts each of which is the amount otherwise deducted in computing the affiliate's hybrid underlying tax in respect of the other taxpayer at the end of the year in respect of income or profits taxes refunded by the government of a country in respect of all or a portion of a capital loss of the affiliate referred to in the description of S;

exceeds

(b) the amount, if any, determined by the formula

$$[U \times (V - 0.5)] + (W \times 0.5)$$

where

U is the amount determined by the formula

$$U.1 + U.2 - U.3$$

where

U.1 is the hybrid underlying tax of the affiliate in respect of the other taxpayer at the end of the year,

U.2 is the amount, if any, by which the amount determined under the description of Q in paragraph (a) exceeds the amount determined under the description of R in that paragraph, and

U.3 is the amount, if any, by which the amount determined under the description of S in paragraph (a) exceeds the amount determined under the description of T in that paragraph,

V is the other taxpayer's relevant tax factor (within the meaning assigned by subsection 95(1) of the Act) for its taxation year that includes the time that is immediately before the particular time, and

W is the amount determined under paragraph (a).

Related Provisions: ITA 257 — Negative amounts in formulas; Reg. 5907(14), (15) — Interpretation.

Notes: Reg. 5907(13), (14) amended by 2002-2013 technical bill, last change effective for dispositions after Aug. 19, 2011. However, if the foreign affiliate (FA) elected

under 1993 technical bill para. 111(4)(a) [see Notes to ITA 250(5.1)], the amendments apply to the FA only from its "time of continuation" (as defined in that para.). Reg. 5707(13) earlier amended by P.C. 1997-1670, subject to the same election.

Interpretation Bulletins: IT-451R: Deemed disposition and acquisition on ceasing to be or become a registrant in Canada.

(14) [Interpretation for subsec. (13)] — For the purposes of the description of C in paragraph (a) of the description of X in subsection (13) and the description of Q in paragraph (a) of the description of Y in subsection (13), the amount by which the underlying foreign tax or the hybrid underlying tax, as the case may be, of the affiliate in respect of the other taxpayer at the end of the year would have increased if a disposition (referred to in this subsection as the "notional actual disposition") deemed under paragraph 128.1(1)(b) of the Act of any property by the affiliate had been an actual disposition of the property by the affiliate is the total of all amounts each of which is the amount, if any, by which

(a) the amount (determined on the assumption that the notional actual disposition occurred at the time of the deemed disposition) that can reasonably be considered to be the amount of income or profits tax that the affiliate would, because of the notional actual disposition, have had to pay to the government of a particular country (other than Canada), in addition to any other income or profits tax otherwise payable to that government, in relation to the gain or income of the affiliate from the notional actual disposition

exceeds

(b) the amount that can reasonably be considered to be the portion of the notional income or profits tax payable by the affiliate to the government of the particular country in relation to the gain or income of the affiliate from the notional actual disposition (determined on the assumptions that the notional actual disposition occurred immediately after the time that is immediately after the time of the deemed disposition and that the notional income or profits tax payable by the affiliate to the government of the particular country in relation to the notional actual disposition is equal to the amount determined under paragraph (a)) that, because of a comprehensive agreement or convention for the elimination of double taxation on income between the government of the particular country and the government of any other country, would not have been payable to the government of the particular country.

Notes: See Notes to Reg. 5907(13). For the meaning of "income or profits tax" see Notes to ITA 126(4).

(15) [Interpretation for subsec. (13)] — For the purposes of the description of E in paragraph (a) of the description of X in subsection (13) and the description of S in paragraph (a) of the description of Y in subsection (13), the amount by which the underlying foreign tax or the hybrid underlying tax, as the case may be, of the affiliate in respect of the other taxpayer at the end of the year would have decreased if a disposition (referred to in this subsection as the "notional actual disposition") deemed under paragraph 128.1(1)(b) of the Act of any property by the affiliate had been an actual disposition of the property by the affiliate is the total of all amounts each of which the amount, if any, by which

(a) the amount (determined on the assumption that the notional actual disposition occurred at the time of the deemed disposition) that can reasonably be considered to be the amount of income or profits tax that the affiliate would, because of the notional actual disposition, have had refunded to it by the government of a particular country (other than Canada), in addition to any other income or profits tax otherwise refundable by that government, in relation to the loss or capital loss, as the case may be, of the affiliate from the notional actual disposition

exceeds

(b) the amount that can reasonably be considered to be the portion of the notional income or profits tax refundable to the affiliate by the government of the particular country in relation to the loss or capital loss, as the case may be, of the affiliate from the notional actual disposition (determined on the assumptions that the notional actual disposition occurred immediately after the time that is immediately after the time of the deemed disposition and that the notional income or profits tax refundable to the affiliate by the government of the particular country in relation to the notional actual disposition is equal to the amount determined by paragraph (a)) that, because of a comprehensive agreement or convention for the elimination of double taxation on income between the government of the particular country and the government of any other country, would not have been refundable by the government of the particular country.

Notes: For the meaning of "income or profits tax", see Notes to ITA 126(4).

Reg. 5907(15) added by 2002-2013 technical bill, for dispositions after Aug. 19, 2011.

Definitions [Reg. 5907]: "active business" — ITA 95(1), Reg. 5907(1); "adjusted cost base" — ITA 54, 248(1); "adjusted earnings amount" — Reg. 5907(2.1)(a); "allowable capital loss" — ITA 38(b), 248(1); "amount" — ITA 248(1), Reg. 5907(7); "arm's length" — ITA 251(1); "attributed amounts" — Reg. 5907(8.1); "avoidance transaction" — ITA 245(3); "borrowed money", "business" — ITA 248(1); "Canada" — ITA 255, *Interpretation Act* 35(1); "Canadian currency" — ITA 261(5)(h)(i)(A); "capital dividend" — ITA 83(2)–(2.4), 248(1); "capital dividend account" — ITA 89(1); "capital gain" — ITA 39(1)(a), 248(1); "capital loss" — ITA 39(1)(b), 248(1); "capital property" — ITA 54, 248(1); "class of shares" — ITA 248(6); "consolidated group" — Reg. 5907(1.1); "controlled foreign affiliate" — ITA 94.1(2)(h), 95(1), 248(1), Reg. 5907(1); "corporation" — ITA 248(1), *Interpretation Act* 35(1); "cost amount" — ITA 248(1); "cumulative eligible capital" — ITA 14(5), 248(1); "designated person or partnership" — Reg. 5907(1); "designated taxation year" — Reg. 5907(1.6); "designated treaty country" — Reg. 5907(11); "disposed", "disposition" — ITA 248(1)"disposition"; "dividend" — ITA 248(1); "earnings" — Reg. 5907(1); "eligible capital expenditure" — ITA 14(5), 248(1); "eligible capital property" — ITA 54, 248(1); "equity percentage" — ITA 95(4); "excluded property" — ITA 95(1); "exempt deficit" — Reg. 5902(1)–(2), (7), 5905(7)(b), 5907(1); "exempt earnings", "exempt loss" — Reg. 5907(1), (10); "exempt surplus" — Reg. 5902(1)–(2), (7), 5905(7)(c), 5907(1); "fair market value" — see ITA 69(1) Notes; "fiscal period" — ITA 249.1; "foreign accrual capital loss" — Reg. 5903.1(3); "foreign accrual property income" — ITA 95(1), (2), 248(1); "foreign accrual property loss" — Reg. 5903(3); "foreign accrual tax" — ITA 95(1); "foreign affiliate" — ITA 95(1), 248(1), Reg. 5907(3); "foreign merger" — ITA 87(8.1); "foreign resource property" — ITA 66(15), 248(1); "foreign tax applicable" — Reg. 5900(1)(d); "government of a country" — Reg. 5907(4); "hybrid deficit", "hybrid surplus", "hybrid underlying tax", "hybrid underlying tax applicable" — Reg. 5907(1); "income from an active business", "income from property" — ITA 95(1); "income or profits tax" — ITA 126(4.1); "insurer", "lending asset", "life insurance business", "life insurance corporation" — ITA 248(1); "loss" — Reg. 5907(1); "Minister" — ITA 248(1); "net earnings", "net loss" — Reg. 5907(1); "net surplus" — Reg. 5902(1)–(2), 5907(1); "non-resident" — ITA 248(1); "notional actual disposition" — Reg. 5907(15); "opening exempt deficit" — Reg. 5905(5)(a), 5905(5.1); "opening exempt surplus" — Reg. 5905(5)(a), 5905(5.1); "opening taxable deficit" — Reg. 5905(5)(a), 5905(5.1); "opening taxable surplus" — Reg. 5905(5)(a), 5905(5.1); "opening underlying foreign tax" — Reg. 5905(5)(a)(v), 5905(5.1); "partnership" — see ITA 96(1) Notes; "permanent establishment" — Reg. 5906(2)(a); "person" — ITA 248(1); "pertinent person or partnership" — Reg. 5907(1.05); "prescribed", "property" — ITA 248(1); "province" — *Interpretation Act* 35(1); "qualifying member" — ITA 95(2)(o)–(r), 248(1); "regulation" — ITA 248(1); "related" — ITA 251(2)–(6); "relevant foreign tax law" — Reg. 5907(1.03)(a), (b); "relevant person or partnership" — Reg. 5903(6); "relevant tax factor" — ITA 95(1); "resident" — ITA 250, Reg. 5907(11.2); "resident in Canada" — ITA 250; "share", "shareholder" — ITA 248(1); "shareholder affiliate" — Reg. 5907(1.091); "specified member" — ITA 248(1); "specified owner" — Reg. 5907(1.04); "specified person or partnership" — ITA 95(1); "stock dividend" — ITA 248(1); "stub period", "stub-period end time" — Reg. 5907(8.1); "subsequent corporation" — Reg. 5907(2.3), (2.4); "surplus entitlement percentage" — Reg. 5905(13); "taxable capital gain" — ITA 38(a), 248(1); "taxable deficit" — Reg. 5902(1)–(2), (7), 5905(7)(c), 5907(1); "taxable dividend" — ITA 89(1), 248(1); "taxable earnings", "taxable loss" — Reg. 5907(1), (10); "taxable surplus" — Reg. 5902(1)–(2), (7), 5905(7)(e), 5907(1); "taxation year" — ITA 249; "taxpayer" — ITA 248(1); "territory" — *Interpretation Act* 35(1); "transparent affiliate" — Reg. 5907(1.091), (1.12), (1.21); "trust" — ITA 104(1), 248(1), (3); "underlying foreign tax" — Reg. 5902(1)–(2), (7), 5907(1); "underlying foreign tax applicable", "whole dividend" — Reg. 5907(1); "writing" — *Interpretation Act* 35(1).

5908. (1) [FA owned by partnership — look-through rule] — For the purposes of this subsection, subsections (2) to (7), paragraph 5902(2)(b) and section 5905, if at any time shares of a class of the capital stock of a foreign affiliate of a corporation resident in Canada are, based on the assumptions contained in paragraph 96(1)(c) of the Act, owned by a partnership, or are deemed under this subsection to be owned by a partnership, each member of the partnership is deemed to own at that time the number of shares of that class that is determined by the formula

$$A \times B/C$$

where

A is the number of shares of that class that are so owned or so deemed owned by the partnership;

B is the fair market value of the member's interest in the partnership at that time; and

C is the fair market value of all members' interests in the partnership at that time.

Related Provisions: Reg. 5908(9) — Tiered partnerships — look-through rule.

Notes: Reg. 5908(1) added by 2002-2013 technical bill, this version for acquisitions, dispositions, redemptions, cancellations, foreign mergers, amalgamations and issuances that occur, and windups that begin, after Dec. 18, 2009.

(2) [Change in FA shares owned through partnership] — For the purposes of subsections (4) and 5905(1), (5) and (7.1), if a person is deemed by subsection (1) to own at a particular time a different number of shares of a class of the capital stock of a foreign affiliate of a corporation resident in Canada (which shares so deemed owned are referred to in this subsection as "affiliate shares") than the person was deemed by that subsection to have owned immediately before the particular time, the number of affiliate shares equal to that difference is deemed to be

(a) disposed of, at the particular time, by the person, when that person is deemed to own fewer affiliate shares at the particular time than immediately before it; and

(b) acquired by, at the particular time, the person, when that person is deemed to own more affiliate shares at the particular time than immediately before it.

Related Provisions: Reg. 5908(1) — Look-through rule for shares owned by partnership; Reg. 5908(3) — Interpretation; Reg. 5908(9) — Tiered partnerships — look-through rule.

Notes: Reg. 5908(2) added by 2002-2013 technical bill, on the same basis as Reg. 5908(1).

(3) [Interpretation for subsec. (2)] — For the purposes of subsection (2),

(a) if a partnership of which a person is a member at any time does not own, and (but for this subsection) is not deemed by subsection (1) to own, any shares of a class of the capital stock of the foreign affiliate at that time, subsection (1) is deemed to have applied in respect of the person and to have deemed the person to own, because of subsection (1) in respect of the partnership, no shares of that class at that time; and

(b) if a corporation resident in Canada or a foreign affiliate of such a corporation disposes of or acquires its entire interest in a partnership that, based on the assumptions contained in paragraph 96(1)(c) of the Act, owns shares of a class of the capital stock of a nonresident corporation, the corporation resident in Canada or the foreign affiliate, as the case may be, is deemed at the time that is immediately after the disposition or immediately before the acquisition, as the case may be, to own, because of subsection (1) in respect of the partnership, no shares of that class.

Related Provisions: Reg. 5908(1) — Look-through rule for shares owned by partnership.

Notes: Reg. 5908(3) added by 2002-2013 technical bill, for foreign affiliates' tax years that begin after Dec. 18, 2009.

(4) [Disposition of FA shares by corporation to related corporation] — For the purposes of subsection 5905(5), if at any time a corporation resident in Canada (referred to in this subsection as the "disposing corporation") disposes of shares of a class of the capital stock of a foreign affiliate of the disposing corporation and, as a consequence of the same transaction or event (other than one to which neither paragraph (2)(a) nor paragraph (2)(b) applies) that caused the disposition, a taxable Canadian corporation with which the disposing corporation is not, at that time, dealing at arm's length acquires shares of that class, the disposing corporation is, at that time, deemed to have disposed of, to the taxable Canadian corporation, the number of the shares of that class that is determined by the formula

$$A \times B$$

where

A is the number of shares of that class disposed of by the disposing corporation; and

B is

(a) if the taxable Canadian corporation acquires, because of paragraph (2)(b), shares of that class, the fraction determined by the formula

$$C/D$$

where

C is the number of shares of that class that is deemed by that paragraph to be acquired by the taxable Canadian corporation as a result of the transaction or event, and

D is the total of all amounts each of which is the number of shares of that class that is deemed by that paragraph to be acquired by a person as a result of the transaction or event, and

(b) in any other case, one.

Related Provisions: Reg. 5908(1) — Look-through rule for shares owned by partnership; Reg. 5908(2) — Deemed disposition on change in FA shares owned through partnership.

Notes: For a case applying Reg. 5908(4) see VIEWS doc 2012-0435881E5.

Reg. 5908(4) added by 2002-2013 technical bill, for foreign affiliates' tax years that begin after Dec. 18, 2009.

(5) [Amalgamation of corporation owning FA shares through partnership] — For the purposes of subsection 5905(5.1), if a predecessor corporation described in that subsection is, at the time that is immediately before the amalgamation described in that subsection, a member of a particular partnership that, based on the assumptions contained in paragraph 96(1)(c) of the Act, owns, at that time, shares of the capital stock of a foreign affiliate of the predecessor corporation and the predecessor corporation's interest in the particular partnership, or in another partnership that is a member of the particular partnership, becomes, upon the amalgamation, property of the new corporation described in that subsection, the shares of the capital stock of the affiliate that are deemed under subsection (1) to be owned by the predecessor corporation at that time are deemed to become property of the new corporation upon the amalgamation.

Related Provisions: Reg. 5908(1) — Look-through rule for shares owned by partnership.

Notes: Reg. 5908(5) added by 2002-2013 technical bill, for foreign affiliates' tax years that begin after Dec. 18, 2009.

(6) [Surplus adjustment rule — where corporation owns FA shares through partnership] — In applying subsection 5905(5.2), if the corporation is a member of a partnership that, based on the assumptions contained in paragraph 96(1)(c) of the Act, owns shares (referred to individually in paragraph (a) as a "relevant share") of the affiliate's capital stock at the particular time,

(a) for the purposes of the description of B in subsection 5905(5.2), the corporation's cost amount of each relevant share at the particular time is to be determined by the formula

$$P \times Q/R$$

where

P is the partnership's cost amount of that relevant share at the particular time,

Q is the number of shares of the capital stock of the affiliate that are deemed by subsection (1), in respect of the partnership, to be owned by the corporation at the particular time, and

R is the total number of relevant shares at the particular time; and

(b) for the purposes of paragraph (b) of the description of C in subsection 5905(5.2), the amount determined under this paragraph is the total of all amounts each of which is the amount that

would be the corporation's portion of a gain that would be deemed under subsection 92(5) of the Act to be a gain of the member of the partnership from the disposition of a share of the capital stock of the affiliate by the partnership if that share were disposed of immediately before the particular time.

Related Provisions: Reg. 5908(1) — Look-through rule for shares owned by partnership.

Notes: Reg. 5908(6) added by 2002-2013 technical bill, for an acquisition of control after Dec. 18, 2009, unless it results from an acquisition of shares under an agreement in writing entered into before that date.

(7) [Bump limitation rule — where corporation owns FA shares through partnership] — For the purposes of paragraph 5905(5.4)(b), the amount determined by this subsection is the amount determined by the following formula for shares of the capital stock of a foreign affiliate of the subsidiary that were deemed by subsection (1), in respect of the partnership, to be owned by the subsidiary at the time at which the parent last acquired control of the subsidiary:

$$A \times B$$

where

A is the tax-free surplus balance of the affiliate, in respect of the subsidiary, at that time; and

B is the percentage that would be the subsidiary's surplus entitlement percentage in respect of the affiliate at that time if the only shares of that capital stock that were owned at that time by the subsidiary were the shares of that capital stock that were deemed by subsection (1), in respect of the partnership, to be owned by the subsidiary at the time at which the parent last acquired control of the subsidiary.

Related Provisions: Reg. 5908(1) — Look-through rule for shares owned by partnership.

Notes: Reg. 5908(7) added by 2002-2013 technical bill, for an acquisition of control after Dec. 18, 2009, unless it results from an acquisition of shares under an agreement in writing entered into before that date.

(8) [Application of ITA s. 93] — If a particular corporation resident in Canada or a particular foreign affiliate of a particular corporation resident in Canada is a member of a particular partnership, the particular partnership owns (based on the assumptions contained in paragraph 96(1)(c) of the Act) shares of a class of the capital stock of a foreign affiliate of the particular corporation and the particular partnership disposes of any of those shares,

(a) any reference in this Part (other than subsections 5902(5) and (6)) to subsection 93(1) of the Act is deemed to include a reference to subsection 93(1.2) of the Act;

(b) an election under subsection 93(1.2) of the Act by the particular corporation is to be made by filing the prescribed form with the Minister on or before

(i) where the particular corporation is the disposing corporation referred to in that subsection, the particular corporation's filing-due date for its taxation year that includes the last day of the particular partnership's fiscal period in which the disposition was made, and

(ii) where the particular affiliate is the disposing corporation referred to in that subsection, the particular corporation's filing-due date for its taxation year that includes the last day of the particular affiliate's taxation year that includes the last day of the disposing partnership's fiscal period in which the disposition was made; and

(c) the prescribed amount for the purposes of subparagraph 93(1.2)(a)(ii) of the Act is the lesser of

(i) the taxable capital gain, if any, of the particular affiliate otherwise determined in respect of the disposition, and

(ii) the amount determined by the formula

$$A \times B \times C/D$$

where

A   is the fraction referred to in paragraph 38(a) of the Act that applies to the particular affiliate's taxation year that includes the last day of the particular partnership's fiscal period that includes the time of the disposition,

B   is the amount that could reasonably be expected to have been received in respect of all the shares of that class if the second foreign affiliate referred to in subsection 93(1.2) of the Act had, immediately before that time, paid dividends, on all shares of its capital stock, the total of which was equal to the amount determined under subparagraph 5902(1)(a)(i) to be its net surplus in respect of the particular corporation,

C   is the number of shares of that class that is determined under subsection 93(1.3) of the Act, and

D   is the total number of issued shares of that class immediately before that time.

Notes: Reg. 5908(8) added by 2002-2013 technical bill, effective for ITA 93(1.2) elections in respect of dispositions after Nov. 1999.

(9) [Tiered partnerships — look-through rule] — For the purposes of this Part, except to the extent that the context otherwise requires, if a person or partnership is (or is deemed by this subsection to be) a member of a particular partnership that is a member of another partnership, the person or partnership is deemed to be a member of the other partnership.

Notes: Reg. 5908(9) added by 2002-2013 technical bill, this version effective for foreign affiliates' tax years that end after Aug. 27, 2010.

(10) [Prescribed amount for ITA 95(2)(j)] — For the purposes of paragraph 95(2)(j) of the Act, the adjusted cost base to a foreign affiliate of a taxpayer of an interest in a partnership at any time is prescribed to be the cost to the affiliate of the interest as otherwise determined at that time, and for those purposes

(a) there shall be added to that cost such of the following amounts as are applicable:

(i) any amount included in the affiliate's earnings for a taxation year ending after 1971 and before that time that may reasonably be considered to relate to profits of the partnership,

(ii) the affiliate's incomes as described by the description of A in the definition "foreign accrual property income" in subsection 95(1) of the Act for a taxation year ending after 1971 and before that time that can reasonably be considered to relate to profits of the partnership,

(iii) any amount included in computing the exempt earnings or taxable earnings, as the case may be, of the affiliate for a taxation year ending after 1971 and before that time that may reasonably be considered to relate to a capital gain of the partnership,

(iii.1) any amount included in computing the hybrid surplus or hybrid deficit of the affiliate before that time that may reasonably be considered to relate to a capital gain of the partnership,

(iv) where the affiliate has, at any time before that time and in a taxation year ending after 1971, made a contribution of capital to the partnership otherwise than by way of a loan, such part of the amount of the contribution as cannot reasonably be regarded as a gift made to or for the benefit of any other member of the partnership who was related to the affiliate,

(v) such portion of any income or profits tax refunded before that time by the government of a country to the partnership as may reasonably be regarded as tax refunded in respect of an amount described in any of subparagraphs (b)(i) to (iii), and

(vi) the amount, if any, determined under paragraph (11)(b);

(b) there shall be deducted from that cost such of the following amounts as are applicable:

(i) any amount included in the affiliate's loss for a taxation year ending after 1971 that may reasonably be considered to relate to a loss of the partnership,

(ii) the affiliate's losses as described by the description of D in the definition "foreign accrual property income" in subsection 95(1) of the Act for a taxation year ending after 1971 and before that time that can reasonably be considered to relate to the losses of the partnership,

(iii) any amount included in computing the exempt loss or taxable loss, as the case may be, of the affiliate for a taxation year ending after 1971 and before that time that may reasonably be considered to relate to a capital loss of the partnership,

(iii.1) any amount included in computing the hybrid surplus or hybrid deficit of the affiliate before that time that may reasonably be considered to relate to a capital loss of the partnership,

(iv) any amount received by the affiliate before that time and in a taxation year ending after 1971 as, on account or in lieu of payment of, or in satisfaction of, a distribution of the affiliate's share of the partnership profits or partnership capital, and

(v) such portion of any income or profits tax paid before that time to the government of a country by the partnership as may reasonably be regarded as tax paid in respect of an amount described in any of subparagraphs (a)(i) to (iii); and

(c) for greater certainty, where any interest of a foreign affiliate in a partnership was reacquired by the affiliate after having been previously disposed of, no adjustment that was required to be made under this subsection before such reacquisition shall be made under this subsection to the cost to the affiliate of the interest as reacquired property of the affiliate.

Notes: For CRA interpretation see VIEWS doc 2015-0592551I7. For the meaning of "income or profits tax" in (b)(v), see Notes to ITA 126(4).

Reg. 5908(10) is the former Reg. 5907(12), renumbered by 2002-2013 technical bill, effective Dec. 19, 2009. See VIEWS docs 2007-0247551E5 (example of subpara. (a)(ii) applying); 2006-0187681R3 (subpara. (b)(iv)).

Reg. 5908(10)(a)(iii.1), (b)(iii.1) added by 2002-2013 technical bill, effective Aug. 20, 2011.

(11) [FA owning FA shares through partnership] — If at any time a partnership owns, based on the assumptions contained in paragraph 96(1)(c) of the Act, a share of the capital stock of a particular foreign affiliate of a corporation resident in Canada and one or more members of the partnership is at that time a direct holder referred to in paragraph 5905(7.6)(a) or a subordinate affiliate referred to in paragraph 5905(7.6)(b), the following rules apply:

(a) for the purposes of paragraph 92(1.1)(b) of the Act, there is to be added, in computing at or after that time the partnership's adjusted cost base of the share, the total of all amounts each of which is the amount determined, in respect of an acquired affiliate referred to in subsection 5905(7.6), by the formula

$$A \times B$$

where

A   is the amount, if any, determined under paragraph 5905(7.2)(a) in respect of the acquired affiliate, and

B   is the percentage that would, if the partnership were a corporation resident in Canada, be the partnership's surplus entitlement percentage in respect of the acquired affiliate, at the adjustment time, if the partnership owned only the share;

(b) for the purposes of subparagraph (10)(a)(vi), the amount determined under this paragraph, in respect of the interest in the partnership of the direct holder or the subordinate affiliate, is the amount determined by the formula

$$A \times B/C$$

where

A is the total of all amounts each of which is the amount, if any, determined under paragraph (a) in respect of a share of the capital stock of the particular affiliate,

B is the fair market value, at the adjustment time, of the interest in the partnership of the direct holder or the subordinate affiliate, as the case may be, and

C is the fair market value, at the adjustment time, of all members' interests in the partnership; and

(c) no amount is to be added under subsection 5905(7.6) to the direct holder's or the subordinate affiliate's adjusted cost base of the share.

Related Provisions: Reg. 5905(7.2)(a) — Meaning of "adjustment time".

Notes: Reg. 5908(11) and (12) added by 2002-2013 technical bill, effective where a share of the capital stock of a corporation's foreign affiliate is acquired by, or otherwise becomes property of, a person after Dec. 18, 2009.

(12) [Amount for Reg. 5905(7.7)(b)] — For the purposes of paragraph 5905(7.7)(b), the amount determined under this subsection is the amount determined by the formula

$$A \times B/C$$

where

A is the adjustment amount;

B is the fair market value, at the adjustment time, of the interest in the partnership that is referred to in paragraph 92(1.1)(b) of the Act of the particular foreign affiliate that is referred to in paragraph 93(3)(c) of the Act; and

C is the fair market value, at the adjustment time, of all members' interests in the partnership.

Related Provisions: Reg. 5905(7.2)(a) — Meaning of "adjustment time"; Reg. 5905(7.5)(b) — Meaning of "direct holder" and "subject affiliate"; Reg. 5905(7.7) — Meaning of "adjustment amount".

Notes: See Notes to Reg. 5908(11).

(13) [Amount for 5907(2.9)(a)(i)(B), (ii)(B)] — For the purposes of clauses 5907(2.9)(a)(i)(B) and (ii)(B), the amount determined under this subsection is, subject to subsection (14), the amount determined by the formula

$$A \times B/C$$

where

A is

(a) if clause 5907(2.9)(a)(i)(B) applies, the amount determined under clause 5907(2.9)(a)(i)(A), and

(b) if clause 5907(2.9)(a)(ii)(B) applies, the amount determined under clause 5907(2.9)(a)(ii)(A),

B is the affiliate's direct or indirect share of the partnership's income or loss for the preceding taxation year, and

C is the partnership's income or loss for the preceding taxation year.

Related Provisions: Reg. 5908(14) — Where both income and loss of partnership are nil.

Notes: Reg. 5908(13), (14) added by 2002-2013 technical bill, effective for foreign affiliates' tax years that begin after Dec. 20, 2002 (or earlier by election).

(14) [Interpretation of subsec. (13)] — For the purposes of subsection (13), if both the income and loss of the partnership for the preceding taxation year are nil, the descriptions of B and C in the formula in that subsection are to be applied as if the partnership had income for that year in the amount of $1,000,000.

Notes: See Notes to Reg. 5908(13).

Notes [Reg. 5908]: Former Reg. 5908 repealed by P.C. 1997-1670, effective Dec. 10, 1997. It contained elections to have different rules apply for foreign affiliates' 1976-80 tax years.

Definitions [Reg. 5908]: "adjusted cost base" — ITA 54, 248(1); "adjustment amount" — Reg. 5905(7.7); "adjustment time" — ITA 14(5), 248(1), Reg. 5905(7.2)(a); "amount" — ITA 248(1), Reg. 5907(7); "arm's length" — ITA 251(1); "capital gain" — ITA 39(1)(a), 248(1); "capital loss" — ITA 39(1)(b), 248(1); "corporation" — ITA 248(1), *Interpretation Act* 35(1); "cost amount" — ITA 248(1); "direct holder" — Reg. 5905(7.5)(b); "disposition", "dividend" — ITA 248(1); "earnings" —

Reg. 5907(1); "equity percentage" — ITA 95(4); "exempt earnings", "exempt loss" — Reg. 5907(1), (10); "fair market value" — see ITA 69(1) Notes; "filing-due date" — ITA 248(1); "fiscal period" — ITA 249.1; "foreign affiliate" — ITA 95(1), 248(1), Reg. 5907(3); "government of a country" — Reg. 5907(4); "hybrid deficit", "hybrid surplus" — Reg. 5907(1); "loss" — Reg. 5907(1); "Minister" — ITA 248(1); "net surplus" — Reg. 5902(1)–(2), 5907(1); "partnership" — see ITA 96(1) Notes; "person", "prescribed", "property" — ITA 248(1); "related" — ITA 251(2)–(6); "resident in Canada" — ITA 250; "share" — ITA 248(1); "subject affiliate" — Reg. 5905(7.5)(b); "surplus entitlement percentage" — Reg. 5905(13); "taxable Canadian corporation" — ITA 89(1), 248(1); "taxable capital gain" — ITA 38(a), 248(1); "taxable earnings", "taxable loss" — Reg. 5907(1), (10); "taxation year" — ITA 249; "taxpayer" — ITA 248(1).

5909. [Repealed]

Notes: Reg. 5909, "Prescribed circumstances" for former ITA 94(1)(b)(i), repealed by 2002-2013 technical bill, for trust tax years that end after 2006.

5910. [Foreign oil and gas business of FA — foreign tax deemed paid] — **(1)** If a foreign affiliate of a corporation resident in Canada carries on in a particular taxation year an active business that is a foreign oil and gas business in a taxing country, the affiliate is deemed for the purposes of this Part to have paid for the particular year, as an income or profits tax to the government of the taxing country in respect of its earnings from the business for the particular year, an amount equal to the lesser of

(a) the amount, if any, determined by the formula

$$(A \times B) - C$$

where

A is the percentage determined under subsection (2) for the particular year,

B is the affiliate's earnings from the business for the particular year, and

C is the total of all amounts each of which is an amount that would, but for this subsection, be an income or profits tax paid to the government of the taxing country by the affiliate for the particular year in respect of its earnings from the business for the particular year; and

(b) the affiliate's production tax amount for the business in the taxing country for the particular year.

Related Provisions: ITA 257 — Negative amounts in formulas; Reg. 5910(4) — Meaning of "foreign oil and gas business", "production tax amount", "taxing country".

Notes: For the meaning of "income or profits tax", see Notes to ITA 126(4).

Reg. 5910(1)(a)B amended by 2002-2013 technical bill, for foreign affiliates' tax years that end after Aug. 19, 2011.

(2) [Percentage for A] — The percentage determined under this subsection for the particular year is the percentage determined by the formula

$$P - Q$$

where

P is the percentage set out in paragraph 123(1)(a) of the Act for the corporation's taxation year that includes the last day of the particular year; and

Q is the corporation's general rate reduction percentage (within the meaning assigned by subsection 123.4(1) of the Act) for that taxation year of the corporation.

Related Provisions: Reg. 5910(1)A — Application of percentage.

Notes: This percentage does not include the 10% reduction in 124(1), so it is 25% since 2012. See Notes to ITA 123.4(2).

(3) [Repealed]

Notes: Reg. 5910(3) repealed by 2002-2013 technical bill, for foreign affiliates' tax years that end after Aug. 19, 2011.

(4) [Definitions] — In this section, **"foreign oil and gas business"**, **"production tax amount"** and **"taxing country"** have the meanings assigned by subsection 126(7) of the Act.

Notes: Reg. 5910 added by 2002-2013 technical bill, last change effective for foreign affiliates' tax years that begin after Dec. 18, 2009.

Definitions [Reg. 5910]: "active business" — ITA 95(1), Reg. 5907(1); "amount" — ITA 248(1), Reg. 5907(7); "business" — ITA 248(1); "corporation" — ITA 248(1), *Interpretation Act* 35(1); "earnings" — Reg. 5907(1); "filing-due date" — ITA 248(1); "foreign affiliate" — ITA 95(1), 248(1), Reg. 5907(3); "foreign oil and gas business" — ITA 126(7), Reg. 5910(4); "general rate reduction percentage" — ITA 123.4(1); "Minister" — ITA 248(1); "production tax amount" — ITA 126(7), Reg. 5910(4); "regulation" — ITA 248(1); "resident in Canada" — ITA 250; "taxation year" — ITA 249; "taxing country" — ITA 126(7), Reg. 5910(4); "taxpayer" — ITA 248(1); "writing" — *Interpretation Act* 35(1).

5911. (1) [How listed election to be made] — A listed election is to be made by the taxpayer and, if applicable, the disposing affiliate by so notifying the Minister in writing on or before

(a) if the taxpayer is a partnership, the earliest of the filing-due dates of any member of the partnership for the member's taxation year that includes the last day of the partnership's fiscal period that includes the last day of the foreign affiliate's taxation year that includes the time of distribution of a distributed property; and

(b) in any other case, the taxpayer's filing-due date for its taxation year that includes the last day of the foreign affiliate's taxation year that includes the time of distribution of a distributed property.

Related Provisions: Reg. 5911(2) — Listed elections.

(2) [Meaning of "listed election"] — For the purposes of subsection (1), a listed election is any of the following:

(a) an election by the taxpayer under subsection 88(3.1) of the Act in respect of a liquidation and dissolution of a disposing affiliate;

(b) an election by the taxpayer under subsection 88(3.3) of the Act in respect of a distribution of distributed property; and

(c) a joint election by the taxpayer and a disposing affiliate under subsection 88(3.5) of the Act in respect of a distribution of distributed property.

Related Provisions: Reg. 5911(3), (4) — Late election.

(3) [Conditions for late election] — Subsection (4) applies if

(a) a taxpayer has made an election (referred to in this subsection and subsection (4) as the "initial election") under subsection 88(3.3) of the Act in respect of a distribution of distributed property on or before the filing-due date specified in subsection (1);

(b) the taxpayer made reasonable efforts to determine all amounts, in respect of the disposing affiliate, that may reasonably be considered to be relevant in making the claim under the initial election; and

(c) the taxpayer amends the initial election on or before the day that is 10 years after the filing-due date referred to in paragraph (a).

Notes: See VIEWS doc 2009-0331321E5 (when election can be filed).

(4) [Late election permitted] — If this subsection applies and, in the opinion of the Minister, the circumstances are such that it would be just and equitable to permit the initial election to be amended, the amended election under paragraph (3)(c) is deemed to have been made on the day on which the initial election was made and the initial election is deemed not to have been made.

Related Provisions: Reg. 5911(3) — Conditions for subsec. (4) to apply.

Notes: For the meaning of "just and equitable", see Notes to ITA 85(7.1).

(5) An election under the definition "relevant cost base" in subsection 95(4) of the Act in respect of a property of a foreign affiliate of a taxpayer, in respect of the taxpayer, is to be made by the taxpayer by so notifying the Minister in writing on or before

(a) if the taxpayer is a partnership, the earliest of the filing-due dates of any member of the partnership for the member's taxation year that includes the last day of the partnership's fiscal period that includes the last day of the foreign affiliate's taxation year in which the determination of the relevant cost base of the property, in respect of the taxpayer, is relevant; and

(b) in any other case, the taxpayer's filing-due date for its taxation year that includes the last day of the foreign affiliate's taxation year in which the determination of the relevant cost base of the property, in respect of the taxpayer, is relevant.

Notes: This was Reg. 5911(3) in the Aug. 19/11 draft.

(6) An election, or joint election, as the case may be, under subsection 90(3) of the Act in respect of a distribution made by a foreign affiliate of a taxpayer is to be made by the taxpayer, or by the taxpayer and each connected person or partnership referred to in that subsection, as the case may be, by so notifying the Minister in writing on or before

(a) in the case of an election by the taxpayer,

(i) if the taxpayer is a partnership, the earliest of the filing-due dates of any member of the partnership for the member's taxation year that includes the last day of the partnership's fiscal period in which the distribution was made, and

(ii) in any other case, the taxpayer's filing-due date for its taxation year that includes the last day of the foreign affiliate's taxation year in which the distribution was made; and

(b) in the case of a joint election, the earliest of the filing-due dates that would be determined under paragraph (a) for each taxpayer that is required to make the joint election if there were no connected persons or partnerships in respect of the taxpayer.

Notes: Reg. 5911 added by 2002-2013 technical bill: (1)-(4) effective for foreign affiliate liquidations and dissolutions that begin after Feb. 27, 2004; (5)-(6) last effective for determinations and distributions after Aug. 19, 2011.

Proposed **Reg. 5912-5918**, in the Feb. 27, 2004 draft legislation, were withdrawn. They would have provided rules for various proposed ITA provisions that were withdrawn.

Definitions [Reg. 5911]: "amount" — ITA 248(1); "connected person or partnership" — ITA 90(4); "filing-due date" — ITA 248(1); "fiscal period" — ITA 249.1; "foreign affiliate" — ITA 95(1), 248(1), Reg. 5907(3); "listed election" — Reg. 5911(2); "Minister" — ITA 248(1); "partnership" — see ITA 96(1) Notes; "property" — ITA 248(1); "taxation year" — ITA 249; "taxpayer" — ITA 248(1); "writing" — *Interpretation Act* 35(1).

PART LX — [6000] PRESCRIBED ACTIVITIES

6000. For the purpose of clause 122.3(1)(b)(i)(C) of the Act, a prescribed activity is an activity performed under contract with the United Nations.

Notes: If there is no contract between the Government of Canada and the UN, but only an arrangement whereby Canada participates in a mission under a UN Security Council resolution, it does not qualify in CRA's view: VIEWS doc 2009-0343221E5. A NATO International Security Assistance Force (ISAF) operation does not qualify, because it is not a UN operation: 2013-0492491E5.

Reg. 6000 added by P.C. 1995-1723 effective 1994. Former Reg. 6000, rules for the employment tax credit under ITA 127(16), repealed by 1988 tax reform effective 1989.

Definitions [Reg. 6000]: "prescribed" — ITA 248(1).

Interpretation Bulletins: IT-497R4: Overseas employment tax credit.

PART LXI — [6100] RELATED SEGREGATED FUND TRUSTS

6100. An election under subsection 138.1(4) of the Act by the trustee of a related segregated fund trust shall be made by filing with the Minister the prescribed form within 90 days from the end of the taxation year of the trust in respect of any capital property deemed to have been disposed of in that taxation year by virtue of the election.

Related Provisions: *Interpretation Act* 27(5) — Meaning of "within 90 days".

Definitions [Reg. 6100]: "capital property" — ITA 54, 248(1); "disposed" — ITA 248(1) "disposition"; "Minister", "prescribed" — ITA 248(1); "related segregated fund trust" — ITA 138.1(1)(a); "taxation year" — ITA 249; "trust" — ITA 104(1), 248(1), (3).

Forms: T3018: Election for deemed disposition and reacquisition of capital property of a life insurance segregated fund under subsection 138.1(4).

PART LXII — [6200–6210] PRESCRIBED SECURITIES, SHARES AND DEBT OBLIGATIONS

6200. Prescribed securities [for election re Canadian securities] — For the purposes of subsection 39(6) of the Act, a prescribed security is, with respect to the taxpayer referred to in subsection 39(4) of the Act,

(a) a share of the capital stock of a corporation, other than a public corporation, the value of which is, at the time it is disposed of by that taxpayer, a value that is or may reasonably be considered to be wholly or primarily attributable to

(i) real property, an interest therein or an option in respect thereof,

(ii) Canadian resource property or a property that would have been a Canadian resource property if it had been acquired after 1971,

(iii) foreign resource property or a property that would have been a foreign resource property if it had been acquired after 1971, or

(iv) any combination of properties described in subparagraphs (i) to (iii)

owned by

(v) the corporation,

(vi) a person other than the corporation, or

(vii) a partnership;

(b) a bond, debenture, bill, note, mortgage or similar obligation, issued by a corporation, other than a public corporation, if at any time before that taxpayer disposes of the security he does not deal at arm's length with the corporation;

(c) a security that is

(i) a share, or

(ii) a bond, debenture, bill, note, mortgage or similar obligation

that was acquired by the taxpayer from a person with whom the taxpayer does not deal at arm's length (other than from a person subject to subsection 39(4) of the Act for the person's taxation year that includes the time of the acquisition);

(c.1) a security described in subparagraph (c)(i) or (ii) that was acquired by the taxpayer from a person (other than from a person subject to subsection 39(4) of the Act for the person's taxation year that includes the time of the acquisition) in circumstances to which subsection 85(1) or (2) of the Act applied;

(d) a share acquired by that taxpayer under circumstances referred to in section 66.3 of the Act; or

(e) a security described in subparagraph (c)(i) or (ii) that was acquired by the taxpayer

(i) as proceeds of disposition for a security of the taxpayer to which paragraph (a), (b), (c) or (d) applied in respect of the taxpayer, or

(ii) as a result of one or more transactions that can reasonably be considered to have been an exchange or substitution of a security of the taxpayer to which paragraph (a), (b), (c) or (d) applied in respect of the taxpayer.

Notes: See ITA 39(6) Notes. On the meaning of "real property" see ITA 248(4) Notes.

Reg. 6200 amended by P.C. 1998-1449 (for 1993 and later tax years), 1994-1817.

Definitions [Reg. 6200]: "arm's length" — ITA 251(1); "Canadian resource property" — ITA 66(15), 248(1); "corporation" — ITA 248(1), *Interpretation Act* 35(1); "disposed", "disposes" — ITA 248(1)"disposition"; "foreign resource property" — ITA 66(15), 248(1); "interest therein" — ITA 248(4); "partnership" — see ITA 96(1) Notes; "person", "prescribed", "property" — ITA 248(1); "public corporation" — ITA 89(1), 248(1); "share" — ITA 248(1); "substitution" — ITA 248(5); "taxpayer" — ITA 248(1).

Interpretation Bulletins: IT-479R: Transactions in securities.

6201. Prescribed shares — (1) [Term preferred share] — For the purposes of paragraph (f) of the definition "term preferred share" in subsection 248(1) of the Act, a share last acquired before June 29, 1982 and of a class of the capital stock of a corporation that is listed on a designated stock exchange in Canada is a prescribed share unless more than 10 per cent of the issued and outstanding shares of that class are owned by

(a) the owner of that share; or

(b) the owner of that share and persons related to him.

Notes: Reg. 6201(1) opening words amended by 2007 budget bill #2, effective Dec. 14, 2007.

(2) [Term preferred share] — For the purposes of paragraph (f) of the definition "term preferred share" in subsection 248(1) of the Act, a share acquired after June 28, 1982 and of a class of the capital stock of a corporation that is listed on a designated stock exchange in Canada is a prescribed share at any particular time with respect to another corporation that receives a dividend at the particular time in respect of the share unless

(a) where the other corporation is a restricted financial institution,

(i) the share is not a taxable preferred share,

(ii) dividends (other than dividends received on shares prescribed under subsection (5)) are received at the particular time by the other corporation or by the other corporation and restricted financial institutions with which the other corporation does not deal at arm's length, in respect of more than 5 per cent of the issued and outstanding shares of that class, and

(iii) a dividend is received at the particular time by the other corporation or a restricted financial institution with which the other corporation does not deal at arm's length, in respect of a share (other than a share prescribed under subsection (5)) of that class acquired after December 15, 1987 and before the particular time;

(b) where the other corporation is a restricted financial institution, the share

(i) is not a taxable preferred share,

(ii) was acquired after December 15, 1987 and before the particular time, and

(iii) was, by reason of subparagraph (h)(i), (ii), (iii) or (v) of the definition "term preferred share" in subsection 248(1) of the Act, deemed to have been issued after December 15, 1987 and before the particular time; or

(c) in any case, dividends (other than dividends received on shares prescribed under subsection (5)) are received at the particular time by the other corporation or by the other corporation and persons with whom the other corporation does not deal at arm's length in respect of more than 10 per cent of the issued and outstanding shares of that class.

Notes: A deemed dividend under ITA 84(3) on redemption of shares is technically deemed to be on shares of a separate class, which would put the dividend offside of Reg. 6201(2) for publicly listed shares held by a specified financial institution. However, in VIEWS doc 2000-0039035, CRA states that "shares of that class" in Reg. 6201(2)(c) is not a reference to the deemed separate class.

Reg. 6201(2) opening words amended by 2007 budget bill #2, effective Dec. 14, 2007.

(3) [Term preferred share] — For the purposes of paragraph 112(2.2)(g) of the Act and paragraph (f) of the definition "term preferred share" in subsection 248(1) of the Act, a share of any of the following series of preferred shares of the capital stock of Massey-Ferguson Limited issued after July 15, 1981 and before March 23, 1982 is a prescribed share:

(a) $25 Cumulative Redeemable Retractable Convertible Preferred Shares, Series C;

(b) $25 Cumulative Redeemable Retractable Preferred Shares, Series D; or

(c) $25 Cumulative Redeemable Retractable Convertible Preferred Shares, Series E.

(4) [Taxable RFI share] — For the purposes of the definition "taxable RFI share" in subsection 248(1) of the Act, a share of a class of the capital stock of a corporation that is listed on a designated stock exchange in Canada is a prescribed share at any particular time with respect to another corporation that is a restricted financial institution that receives a dividend at the particular time in respect of the share unless dividends (other than dividends received on shares prescribed under subsection (5.1)) are received at that time by the other corporation, or by the other corporation and restricted financial institutions with which the other corporation does not deal at arm's length, in respect of more than

(a) 10 per cent of the shares of that class that were issued and outstanding at the last time, before the particular time, at which the other corporation or a restricted financial institution with which the other corporation does not deal at arm's length acquired a share of that class, where no dividend is received at the particular time by any such corporation in respect of a share (other than a share prescribed under subsection (5.1)) of that class acquired after December 15, 1987 and before the particular time; or

(b) 5 per cent of the shares of that class that were issued and outstanding at the last time, before the particular time, at which the other corporation or a restricted financial institution with which the other corporation does not deal at arm's length acquired a share of that class, where a dividend is received at the particular time by any such corporation in respect of a share (other than a share prescribed under subsection (5.1)) of that class acquired after December 15, 1987 and before the particular time.

Notes: Reg. 6201(4) opening words amended by 2007 budget bill #2, effective Dec. 14, 2007, to change "stock exchange referred to in section 3200" to "designated stock exchange in Canada".

Reg. 6201(4) amended by P.C. 1995-1198, for dividends received after Dec. 20, 1991, essentially to measure a financial institution's percentage holding of a class of shares as relative to the shares outstanding when the shares were last acquired by the institution (or another member of the same corporate group), rather than by measuring percentage ownership on the date a dividend is received. (The former rule could lead to problems where other persons' shares had been redeemed in the interim.)

(5) [Term preferred share] — For the purpose of paragraph (f) of the definition "term preferred share" in subsection 248(1) of the Act, a share of a class of the capital stock of a corporation that is listed on a designated stock exchange in Canada is a prescribed share at any particular time with respect to another corporation that is registered or licensed under the laws of a province to trade in securities and that holds the share for the purpose of sale in the course of the business ordinarily carried on by it unless

(a) it may reasonably be considered that the share was acquired as part of a series of transactions or events one of the main purposes of which was to avoid or limit the application of subsection 112(2.1) of the Act; or

(b) the share was not acquired by the other corporation in the course of an underwriting of shares of that class to be distributed to the public and

(i) dividends are received at the particular time by the other corporation or by the other corporation and corporations controlled by the other corporation in respect of more than 10 per cent of the issued and outstanding shares of that class,

(ii) the other corporation is a restricted financial institution and

(A) the share is not a taxable preferred share,

(B) dividends are received at the particular time by the other corporation or by the other corporation and corporations controlled by the other corporation in respect of more than 5 per cent of the issued and outstanding shares of that class, and

(C) a dividend is received at the particular time by the other corporation or a corporation controlled by the other corporation in respect of a share of that class acquired after December 15, 1987 and before the particular time, or

(iii) the other corporation is a restricted financial institution and the share

(A) is not a taxable preferred share,

(B) was acquired after December 15, 1987 and before the particular time, and

(C) was, by reason of subparagraph (h)(i), (ii), (iii) or (v) of the definition "term preferred share" in subsection 248(1) of the Act, deemed to have been issued after December 15, 1987 and before the particular time.

Related Provisions: ITA 248(10) — Series of transactions; ITA 256(6), (6.1) — Meaning of "controlled".

Notes: For "one of the main purposes" in para. (a), see Notes to ITA 83(2.1).

Reg. 6201(5) amended by 2007 budget bill #2, last change effective Dec. 14, 2007. Earlier amended by P.C. 1995-1198.

(5.1) [Taxable RFI share — prescribed share] — For the purpose of the definition "taxable RFI share" in subsection 248(1) of the Act, a share of a class of the capital stock of a corporation that is listed on a designated stock exchange in Canada is a prescribed share at any particular time with respect to another corporation that is registered or licensed under the laws of a province to trade in securities and that holds the share for the purpose of sale in the course of the business ordinarily carried on by it unless

(a) it may reasonably be considered that the share was acquired as part of a series of transactions or events one of the main purposes of which was to avoid or limit the application of section 187.3 of the Act; or

(b) the share was not acquired by the other corporation in the course of an underwriting of shares of that class to be distributed to the public and

(i) dividends are received at the particular time by the other corporation, or by the other corporation and corporations controlled by the other corporation, in respect of more than 10 per cent of the shares of that class issued and outstanding at the last time before the particular time at which any such corporation acquired a share of that class,

(ii) the other corporation is a restricted financial institution and

(A) dividends are received at the particular time by the other corporation, or by the other corporation and corporations controlled by the other corporation, in respect of more than 5 per cent of the shares of that class issued and outstanding at the last time before the particular time at which any such corporation acquired a share of that class, and

(B) a dividend is received at the particular time by the other corporation, or a corporation controlled by the other corporation, in respect of a share of that class acquired after December 15, 1987 and before the particular time, or

(iii) the other corporation is a restricted financial institution and the share

(A) was acquired after December 15, 1987 and before the particular time, and

(B) was, because of subparagraph (h)(i), (ii), (iii) or (v) of the definition "term preferred share" in subsection 248(1) of the Act, deemed to have been issued after December 15, 1987 and before the particular time.

Related Provisions: ITA 248(10) — Series of transactions; ITA 256(6), (6.1) — Meaning of "controlled".

Notes: For "one of the main purposes" in para. (a), see Notes to ITA 83(2.1).

Reg. 6201(5.1) amended by 2007 budget bill #2, last change effective Dec. 14, 2007.

(6) [Term preferred share — prescribed share] — For the purposes of paragraph (f) of the definition "term preferred share" in subsection 248(1) of the Act, a share of the capital stock of a corporation that is a member institution of a deposit insurance corporation, within the meaning assigned by section 137.1 of the Act, is a prescribed share with respect to the deposit insurance corporation and any subsidiary wholly-owned corporation of the deposit insurance corporation deemed by subsection 137.1(5.1) of the Act to be a deposit insurance corporation.

(7) [Taxable preferred share — prescribed share] — For the purposes of the definition "taxable preferred share" in subsection 248(1) of the Act, the following shares are prescribed shares at any particular time:

(a) the 8.5 per cent Cumulative Redeemable Convertible Class A Preferred Shares of St. Marys Paper Inc. issued on July 7, 1987, where such shares are not deemed, by reason of paragraph (e) of the definition "taxable preferred share" in subsection 248(1) of the Act, to have been issued after that date and before the particular time; and

(b) the Cumulative Redeemable Preferred Shares of CanUtilities Holdings Ltd. issued before July 1, 1991, unless the amount of the consideration for which all such shares were issued exceeds $300,000,000 or the particular time is after July 1, 2001.

(8) [Canada Cement Lafarge] — For the purposes of paragraph 112(2.2)(d) of the Act, paragraph (i) of the definition "short-term preferred share", the definition "taxable preferred share" and paragraph (f) of the definition "term preferred share" in subsection 248(1) of the Act, the Exchangeable Preference Shares of Canada Cement Lafarge Ltd. (in this subsection referred to as the "subject shares"), the Exchangeable Preference Shares of Lafarge Canada Inc. and the shares of any corporation formed as a result of an amalgamation or merger of Lafarge Canada Inc. with one or more other corporations are prescribed shares at any particular time where the terms and conditions of such shares at the particular time are the same as, or substantially the same as, the terms and conditions of the subject shares as of June 18, 1987 and, for the purposes of this subsection, the amalgamation or merger of one or more corporations with another corporation formed as a result of an amalgamation or merger of Lafarge Canada Inc. with one or more other corporations shall be deemed to be an amalgamation of Lafarge Canada Inc. with another corporation.

(9) [Time when share acquired] — For the purposes of determining under subsections (2), (4), (5) and (5.1) the time at which a share of a class of the capital stock of a corporation was acquired by a taxpayer, shares of that class acquired by the taxpayer at any particular time before a disposition by the taxpayer of shares of that class shall be deemed to have been disposed of before shares of that class acquired by the taxpayer before that particular time.

Notes: Reference to Reg. 6201(5.1) added to Reg. 6201(9) by P.C. 1995-1198, effective for dividends received after December 20, 1991.

(10) [Trusts and partnerships] — For the purposes of subsections (2), (4), (5) and (5.1) and this subsection,

(a) where a taxpayer is a beneficiary of a trust and an amount in respect of the beneficiary has been designated by the trust in a taxation year pursuant to subsection 104(19) of the Act, the taxpayer shall be deemed to have received the amount so designated at the time it was received by the trust; and

(b) where a taxpayer is a member of a partnership and a dividend has been received by the partnership, the taxpayer's share of the dividend shall be deemed to have been received by the taxpayer at the time the dividend was received by the partnership.

Notes: Reference to Reg. 6201(5.1) added to opening words of Reg. 6201(10) by P.C. 1995-1198, effective for dividends received after December 20, 1991.

(11) [Grandfathering] — For the purposes of subsections (2), (4), (5) and (5.1),

(a) a share of the capital stock of a corporation acquired by a person after December 15, 1987 pursuant to an agreement in writing entered into before December 16, 1987 shall be deemed to have been acquired by that person before December 16, 1987;

(b) a share of the capital stock of a corporation acquired by a person after December 15, 1987 and before July, 1988 as part of a distribution to the public made in accordance with the terms of a prospectus, preliminary prospectus, registration statement, offering memorandum or notice filed before December 16, 1987 with a public authority pursuant to and in accordance with the securities legislation of the jurisdiction in which the shares were distributed shall be deemed to have been acquired by that person before December 16, 1987;

(c) where a share that was owned by a particular restricted financial institution on December 15, 1987 has, by one or more transactions between related restricted financial institutions, been transferred to another restricted financial institution, the share shall be deemed to have been acquired by the other restricted financial institution before that date and after June 28, 1982 unless at any particular time after December 15, 1987 and before the share was transferred to the other restricted financial institution the share was owned by a shareholder who, at that particular time, was a person other than a restricted financial institution related to the other restricted financial institution; and

(d) where at any particular time there has been an amalgamation (within the meaning assigned by section 87 of the Act) and

(i) each of the predecessor corporations (within the meaning assigned by section 87 of the Act) was a restricted financial institution throughout the period beginning December 16, 1987 and ending at the particular time and the predecessor corporations were related to each other throughout that period, or

(ii) each of the predecessor corporations and the new corporation (within the meaning assigned by section 87 of the Act) is a corporation described in any of paragraphs (a) to (d) of the definition "restricted financial institution" in subsection 248(1) of the Act,

a share acquired by the new corporation from a predecessor corporation on the amalgamation shall be deemed to have been acquired by the new corporation at the time it was acquired by the predecessor corporation.

Notes: Reference to Reg. 6201(5.1) added to opening words of Reg. 6201(11) by P.C. 1995-1198, effective for dividends received after December 20, 1991.

Definitions [Reg. 6201]: "amount" — ITA 248(1); "arm's length" — ITA 251(1); "business" — ITA 248(1); "Canada" — ITA 255, *Interpretation Act* 35(1); "controlled" — ITA 256(6), (6.1); "corporation" — ITA 248(1), *Interpretation Act* 35(1); "deposit insurance corporation" — ITA 137.1(5); "designated stock exchange" — ITA 248(1), 262; "disposed" — ITA 248(1)"disposition"; "disposition" — ITA 248(1); "dividend", "inventory" — ITA 248(1); "partnership" — see ITA 96(1) Notes; "person", "preferred share", "prescribed" — ITA 248(1); "province" — *Interpretation Act* 35(1); "related" — ITA 251(2)–(6); "restricted financial institution" — ITA 248(1); "series" — ITA 248(10); "share", "shareholder", "subsidiary wholly-owned corporation", "taxable preferred share" — ITA 248(1); "taxation year" — ITA 249; "taxpayer" — ITA 248(1); "trust" — ITA 104(1), 248(1), (3); "writing" — *Interpretation Act* 35(1).

6202. [Resource expenditures — prescribed share] — **(1)** For the purposes of paragraph 66(15)(d.1) [66(15)"flow-through share"] and subparagraphs 66.1(6)(a)(v) [66.1(6)"Canadian exploration expense"(i)], 66.2(5)(a)(v) [66.2(5)"Canadian development expense"(g)] and 66.4(5)(a)(iii) [66.4(5)"Canadian oil and gas property expense"(c)] of the Act, a share of a class of the capital stock of a corporation (in this section referred to as the **"issuing corporation"**) is a prescribed share if it was issued after December 31, 1982 and

(a) the issuing corporation, any person related to the issuing corporation or of whom the issuing corporation has effective management or control or any partnership or trust of which the issuing corporation or a person related thereto is a member or beneficiary (each of which is referred to in this section as a "member of the related issuing group") is or may be required to redeem, acquire or cancel, in whole or in part, the share or to reduce its paid-up capital at any time within five years from the date of its issue,

(b) a member of the related issuing group provides or may be required to provide any form of guarantee, security or similar indemnity with respect to the share (other than a guarantee, security or similar indemnity with respect to any amount of assistance or benefit from a government, municipality or other public authority in Canada or with respect to eligibility for such assistance or benefit) that could take effect within five years from the date of its issue,

(c) the share (referred to in this section as the "convertible share") is convertible under its terms or conditions at any time within five years from the date of its issue directly or indirectly into debt, or into a share (referred to in this section as the "acquired share") that is, or if issued would be, a prescribed share,

(d) immediately after the share was issued, the person to whom the share was issued or a person related to the person to whom the share was issued (either alone or together with a related person, a related group of persons of which he is a member or a partnership or trust of which he is a member or beneficiary) controls directly or indirectly, or has an absolute or contingent right to control directly or indirectly or to acquire direct or indirect control of, the issuing corporation and the issuing corporation has the right under the terms and conditions in respect of which the share was issued to redeem, purchase or otherwise acquire the share within five years from the date of its issue,

(e) at the time the share was issued, the existence of the issuing corporation was, or there was an arrangement (other than an amalgamation within the meaning assigned by subsection 87(1) of the Act) under which the existence of the issuing corporation could be, limited to a period that ends within five years from the date of its issue, or

(f) the terms or conditions of the share (referred to in this paragraph as the "first share") or of an agreement in existence at the time of its issue provide that a share (referred to in this section as the "substituted share") that is, or if issued would be, a prescribed share may be substituted or exchanged for the first share within five years from the date of issue of the first share,

but does not include a share of the capital stock of a corporation

(g) that was issued after December 31, 1982 pursuant to an agreement or offering in writing made on or before December 31, 1982 or in accordance with a prospectus, registration statement or similar document that was filed with and, where required by law, accepted for filing by, a public authority in Canada pursuant to and in accordance with the laws of Canada or of any province on or before December 31, 1982,

(h) that would be a prescribed share solely by virtue of one or more of the terms or conditions of an agreement if such terms or conditions are not effective or exercisable until the death, disability or bankruptcy of the person to whom the share is issued,

(i) that is

(i) convertible under its terms into one or more shares of a class of the capital stock of the corporation for no consideration other than the share or shares,

(ii) described in paragraph (a) solely because

(A) it is to be cancelled on the conversion within five years from the date of its issue,

(B) its paid-up capital is to be reduced on the conversion within five years from the date of its issue, or

(C) both clauses (A) and (B) apply, and

(iii) not described in paragraph (c), or

(j) that

(i) may have a share substituted or exchanged for it pursuant to its terms or the terms or conditions of an agreement in existence at the time of its issue and no consideration is to be received or receivable for it in respect of the substitution or exchange other than the share substituted or exchanged for it,

(ii) is described in paragraph (a) solely because it is to be redeemed, acquired or cancelled on the substitution or exchange within five years from the date of its issue, and

(iii) is not a share to which paragraph (f) applies,

and for the purposes of this section,

(k) where a person has an interest in a trust, whether directly or indirectly, through an interest in any other trust or in any other manner whatever, the person shall be deemed to be a beneficiary of the trust;

(l) in determining whether an acquired share would be a prescribed share if issued,

(i) the references in paragraphs (a), (b), (d) and (e) to "date of its issue" shall be read as "date of the issue of the convertible share",

(ii) the reference in paragraph (f) to "issue of the first share" shall be read as "issue of the convertible share", and

(iii) this section shall be read without reference to paragraph (g) and to the words "after December 31, 1982";

(m) in determining whether a substituted share would be a prescribed share if issued,

(i) the references in paragraphs (a) to (e) to "date of its issue" shall be read as "date of the issue of the first share", and

(ii) this section shall be read without reference to paragraph (g) and to the words "after December 31, 1982";

(m.1) an excluded obligation in relation to a share of a class of the capital stock of the issuing corporation and an obligation that would be an excluded obligation in relation to the share if the share had been issued after June 17, 1987, shall be deemed not to be a guarantee, security or similar indemnity with respect to the share for the purposes of paragraph (b);

(n) a guarantee, security or similar indemnity referred to in paragraph (b) shall, for greater certainty, not be considered to take effect within five years from the date of issue of a share if the effect of the guarantee, security or indemnity is to provide that a member of the related issuing group will be able to redeem, acquire or cancel the share at a time that is not within five years from the date of issue of the share; and

(o) where an expense is incurred partly in consideration for shares (referred to in this section as **"first corporation shares"**) of the capital stock of one corporation and partly in consideration for an interest in, or right to, shares (referred to in this paragraph as "second corporation shares") of the capital stock of another corporation, in determining whether the second corporation shares are prescribed shares, the references in paragraphs (a), (d) and (e) to "date of its issue" shall be read as "date of the issue of the first corporation shares".

Related Provisions: *Interpretation Act* 27(5) — Meaning of "within five years".

(2) For the purposes of paragraph 66(15)(d.1) [66(15)"flow-through share"] of the Act, subsection (1) does not apply in respect of a share of the capital stock of an issuing corporation that is a new share.

Definitions [Reg. 6202]: "amount" — ITA 248(1); "Canada" — ITA 255, *Interpretation Act* 35(1); "control" — ITA 256(5.1)–(6); "corporation" — ITA 248(1), *Interpretation Act* 35(1); "excluded obligation" — Reg. 6202.1(5); "issuing corporation" — Reg. 6202(1); "new share" — Reg. 6202.1(5); "paid-up capital" — ITA 89(1), 248(1); "partnership" — see ITA 96(1) Notes; "person", "prescribed", "property" — ITA 248(1); "province" — *Interpretation Act* 35(1); "related" — ITA 251(2)–(6); "security" — *Interpretation Act* 35(1); "share" — ITA 248(1); "specified person" — Reg. 6202.1(5); "substituted", "substitution" — ITA 248(5); "trust" — ITA 104(1), 248(1), (3); "writing" — *Interpretation Act* 35(1).

6202.1 (1) [Flow-through shares — prescribed share] — For the purposes of the definition "flow-through share" in subsection 66(15) of the Act, a new share of the capital stock of a corporation is a prescribed share if, at the time it is issued,

(a) under the terms or conditions of the share or any agreement in respect of the share or its issue,

(i) the amount of the dividends that may be declared or paid on the share (in this section referred to as the **"dividend entitlement"**) may reasonably be considered to be, by way of a formula or otherwise,

(A) fixed,

(B) limited to a maximum, or

(C) established to be not less than a minimum (including any amount determined on a cumulative basis), where with respect to the dividends that may be declared or paid on the share there is a preference over any other dividends that may be declared or paid on any other share of the capital stock of the corporation,

(ii) the amount that the holder of the share is entitled to receive in respect of the share on the dissolution, liquidation or winding-up of the corporation, on a reduction of the paid-up capital of the share or on the redemption, acquisition or cancellation of the share by the corporation or by specified persons in relation to the corporation (in this section referred to as the **"liquidation entitlement"**) may reasonably be considered to be, by way of a formula or otherwise, fixed, limited to a maximum or established to be not less than a minimum,

(iii) the share is convertible or exchangeable into another security issued by the corporation unless

(A) it is convertible or exchangeable only into

(I) another share of the corporation that, if issued, would not be a prescribed share,

(II) a right (including a right conferred by a warrant) that

1. if it were issued, would not be a prescribed right, and

2. if it were exercised, would allow the person exercising it to acquire only a share of the corporation that, if the share were issued, would not be a prescribed share, or

(III) both a share described in subclause (I) and a right described in subclause (II), and

(B) all the consideration receivable by the holder on the conversion or exchange of the share is the share described in subclause (A)(I) or the right described in subclause (A)(II), or both, as the case may be, or

(iv) the corporation has, either absolutely or contingently, an obligation to reduce, or any person or partnership has, either absolutely or contingently, an obligation to cause the corporation to reduce, the paid-up capital in respect of the share (other than pursuant to a conversion or exchange of the share, where the right to so convert or exchange does not cause the share to be a prescribed share under subparagraph (iii));

(b) any person or partnership has, either absolutely or contingently, an obligation (other than an excluded obligation in relation to the share)

(i) to provide assistance,

(ii) to make a loan or payment,

(iii) to transfer property, or

(iv) otherwise to confer a benefit by any means whatever, including the payment of a dividend,

either immediately or in the future, that may reasonably be considered to be, directly or indirectly, a repayment or return by the corporation or a specified person in relation to the corporation of all or part of the consideration for which the share was issued or for which a partnership interest was issued in a partnership that acquires the share;

(c) any person or partnership has, either absolutely or contingently, an obligation (other than an excluded obligation in relation to the share) to effect any undertaking, either immediately or in the future, with respect to the share or the agreement under which the share is issued (including any guarantee, security, indemnity, covenant or agreement and including the lending of funds to or the placing of amounts on deposit with, or on behalf of, the holder of the share or, where the holder is a partnership, the members thereof or specified persons in relation to the holder or the members of the partnership, as the case may be) that may reasonably be considered to have been given to ensure, directly or indirectly, that

(i) any loss that the holder of the share and, where the holder is a partnership, the members thereof or specified persons in relation to the holder or the members of the partnership, as the case may be, may sustain by reason of the holding, ownership or disposition of the share or any other property is limited in any respect, or

(ii) the holder of the share and, where the holder is a partnership, the members thereof or specified persons in relation to the holder or the members of the partnership, as the case may be, will derive earnings, by reason of the holding, ownership or disposition of the share or any other property;

(d) the corporation or a specified person in relation to the corporation may reasonably be expected

(i) to acquire or cancel the share in whole or in part otherwise than on a conversion or exchange of the share that meets the conditions set out in clauses (a)(iii)(A) and (B),

(ii) to reduce the paid-up capital of the corporation in respect of the share otherwise than on a conversion or exchange of the share that meets the conditions set out in clauses (a)(iii)(A) and (B), or

(iii) to make a payment, transfer or other provision (otherwise than pursuant to an excluded obligation in relation to the share), directly or indirectly, by way of a dividend, loan, purchase of shares, financial assistance to any purchaser of the share or, where the purchaser is a partnership, the members thereof or in any other manner whatever, that may reasonably be considered to be a repayment or return of all or part of the consideration for which the share was issued or for which a partnership interest was issued in a partnership that acquires the share,

within 5 years after the date the share is issued, otherwise than as a consequence of an amalgamation of a subsidiary wholly-owned corporation, a winding-up of a subsidiary wholly-owned corporation to which subsection 88(1) of the Act applies or the payment of a dividend by a subsidiary wholly-owned corporation to its parent;

(e) any person or partnership can reasonably be expected to effect, within 5 years after the date the share is issued, any undertaking which, if it were in effect at the time the share was issued, would result in the share being a prescribed share by reason of paragraph (c); or

(f) it may reasonably be expected that, within 5 years after the date the share is issued,

(i) any of the terms or conditions of the share or any existing agreement relating to the share or its issue will thereafter be modified, or

(ii) any new agreement relating to the share or its issue will be entered into,

in such a manner that the share would be a prescribed share if it had been issued at the time of the modification or at the time when the new agreement is entered into.

Related Provisions: Reg. 6202.1(1.1), (2.1) — Prescribed right; Reg. 6202.1(3) — Dividend entitlement and liquidation entitlement; Reg. 6202.1(4) — Agreement deemed not to be undertaking; *Interpretation Act* 27(5) — Meaning of "within five years".

Notes: In *JES Investments*, 2007 FCA 337, shares were held to be prescribed shares under Reg. 6202.1(1)(c)(i), due to an indemnity given by the corporation to the taxpayer. The phrase "may reasonably be considered to have been given" required an objective determination of the indemnity: para. 11.

For the meaning of "indirectly" in (b), (c) and (d)(iii), see Notes to ITA 17.1(1).

VIEWS docs on Reg. 6202.1(1)(c): 2005-0114331E5, 2008-0269711I7.

Reg. 6202.1(1)(a)(iii)(A)(II)1 added (and "right or warrant" in (iii)(B) changed to "right") by 2002-2013 technical bill, effective for shares and rights issued under an agreement made after Dec. 20, 2002.

(1.1) [Flow-through shares — prescribed right] — For the purpose of the definition "flow-through share" in subsection 66(15) of the Act, a new right to acquire a share of the capital stock of a corporation is a prescribed right if, at the time the right is issued,

(a) the amount that the holder of the right is entitled to receive in respect of the right on the dissolution, liquidation or winding-up of the corporation or on the redemption, acquisition or cancellation of the right by the corporation or by specified persons in relation to the corporation (referred to in this section as the **"liquidation entitlement"** of the right) can reasonably be considered to be, by way of a formula or otherwise, fixed, limited to a maximum or established to be not less than a minimum;

(b) the right is convertible or exchangeable into another security issued by the corporation unless

(i) the right is convertible or exchangeable only into

(A) a share of the corporation that, if issued, would not be a prescribed share,

(B) another right (including a right conferred by a warrant) that

(I) if it were issued, would not be a prescribed right, and

(II) if it were exercised, would allow the person exercising it to acquire only a share of the corporation that, if the share were issued, would not be a prescribed share, or

(C) both a share described in clause (A) and a right described in clause (B), and

(ii) all the consideration receivable by the holder on the conversion or exchange of the right is the share described in clause (A) or the right described in clause (B), or both, as the case may be;

(c) any person or partnership has, either absolutely or contingently, an obligation (other than an excluded obligation in relation to the right)

(i) to provide assistance,

(ii) to make a loan or payment,

(iii) to transfer property, or

(iv) to otherwise confer a benefit by any means whatever, including the payment of a dividend,

either immediately or in the future, that can reasonably be considered to be, directly or indirectly, a repayment or return by the corporation or a specified person in relation to the corporation of all or part of the consideration for which the right was issued or for which a partnership interest was issued in a partnership that acquires the right;

(d) any person or partnership has, either absolutely or contingently, an obligation (other than an excluded obligation in relation to the right) to effect any undertaking, either immediately or in the future, with respect to the right or the agreement under which the right is issued (including any guarantee, security, indemnity, covenant or agreement and including the lending of funds to or the placing of amounts on deposit with, or on behalf of, the holder of the right or where the holder is a partnership, the members of the partnership or specified persons in relation to the holder or the members of the partnership, as the case may

be) that can reasonably be considered to have been given to ensure, directly or indirectly, that

(i) any loss that the holder of the right and, where the holder is a partnership, the members of the partnership or specified persons in relation to the holder or the members of the partnership, as the case may be, may sustain because of the holding, ownership or disposition of the right or any other property is limited in any respect, or

(ii) the holder of the right and, where the holder is a partnership, the members of the partnership or specified persons in relation to the holder or the members of the partnership, as the case may be, will derive earnings, because of the holding, ownership or disposition of the right or any other property;

(e) the corporation or a specified person in relation to the corporation can reasonably be expected

(i) to acquire or cancel the right in whole or in part otherwise than on a conversion or exchange of the right that meets the conditions set out in subparagraphs (b)(i) and (ii), or

(ii) to make a payment, transfer or other provision (otherwise than pursuant to an excluded obligation in relation to the right), directly or indirectly, by way of a dividend, loan, purchase of rights, financial assistance to any purchaser of the right or, where the purchaser is a partnership, the members of the partnership or in any other manner whatever, that can reasonably be considered to be a repayment or return of all or part of the consideration for which the right was issued or for which a partnership interest was issued in a partnership that acquires the right,

within five years after the date the right is issued, otherwise than as a consequence of an amalgamation of a subsidiary wholly-owned corporation, a winding-up of a subsidiary wholly-owned corporation to which subsection 88(1) of the Act applies or the payment of a dividend by a subsidiary wholly-owned corporation to its parent;

(f) any person or partnership can reasonably be expected to effect, within five years after the day the right is issued, any undertaking which, if it were in effect at the time the right was issued, would result in the right being a prescribed right because of paragraph (d);

(g) it can reasonably be expected that, within five years after the date the right is issued,

(i) any of the terms or conditions of the right or any existing agreement relating to the right or its issue will be modified in such a manner that the right would be a prescribed right if it had been issued at the time of the modification, or

(ii) any new agreement relating to the right or its issue will be entered into in such a manner that the right would be a prescribed right if it had been issued at the time the new agreement is entered into; or

(h) it can reasonably be expected that the right, if exercised, would allow the person exercising the right to acquire a share in a corporation that, if that share were issued, would be a prescribed share within five years after the day the right was issued.

Related Provisions: Reg. 6202.1(3) — Dividend entitlement and liquidation entitlement; Reg. 6202.1(4) — Agreement deemed not to be undertaking; *Interpretation Act* 27(5) — Meaning of "within five years".

Notes: For the meaning of "indirectly" in (c), (d) and (e)(ii), see Notes to ITA 17.1(1).

Reg. 6202.1(1.1) added by 2002-2013 technical bill (Part 5 — technical), effective for shares and rights issued under an agreement made after Dec. 20, 2002.

(2) [Flow-through shares — prescribed share] — For the purposes of the definition "flow-through share" in subsection 66(15) of the Act, a new share of the capital stock of a corporation is a prescribed share if

(a) the consideration for which the share is to be issued is to be determined more than 60 days after entering into the agreement pursuant to which the share is to be issued;

(b) the corporation or a specified person in relation to the corporation, directly or indirectly,

(i) provided assistance,

(ii) made or arranged for a loan or payment,

(iii) transferred property, or

(iv) otherwise conferred a benefit by any means whatever, including the payment of a dividend,

for the purpose of assisting any person or partnership in acquiring the share or any person or partnership in acquiring an interest in a partnership acquiring the share (otherwise than by reason of an excluded obligation in relation to the share); or

(c) the holder of the share or, where the holder is a partnership, a member thereof, has a right under any agreement or arrangement entered into under circumstances where it is reasonable to consider that the agreement or arrangement was contemplated at or before the time when the agreement to issue the share was entered into,

(i) to dispose of the share, and

(ii) through a transaction or event or a series of transactions or events contemplated by the agreement or arrangement, to acquire a share (referred to in this paragraph as the "acquired share") of the capital stock of another corporation that would be a prescribed share under subsection (1) if the acquired share were issued at the time the share was issued, other than a share that would not be a prescribed share if subsection (1) were read without reference to subparagraphs (a)(iv) and (d)(i) and (ii) thereof where the acquired share is a share

(A) of a mutual fund corporation, or

(B) of a corporation that becomes a mutual fund corporation within 90 days after the acquisition of the acquired share.

Related Provisions: ITA 248(10) — Series of transactions.

Notes: The definition of "prescribed share" does not include every benefit offered to the investor, but only those that may "reasonably be considered" to be a return of part of the consideration provided for the shares. This objective standard does not include benefits of very little intrinsic economic value or those that are in fact unlikely ever to be provided: *Furukawa*, [2001] 1 C.T.C. 39 (FCA).

For the meaning of "indirectly" in (b) opening words, see Notes to ITA 17.1(1).

A share acquired through an employee stock option plan is considered a prescribed share due to subpara. (b)(iv): VIEWS doc 2013-0497641E5. Fair market value fees paid by an issuer to an arm's length promoter for finding investors do not cause shares to be prescribed shares: 2020-0852321E5.

Reg. 6202.1(2)(a) and (b) added by P.C. 1990-51, for shares issued after Dec. 15, 1987, with grandfathering for arrangements in place by that date.

(2.1) [Prescribed right] — For the purpose of the definition "flow-through share" in subsection 66(15) of the Act, a new right is a prescribed right if

(a) the consideration for which the new right is to be issued is to be determined more than 60 days after entering into the agreement pursuant to which the new right is to be issued;

(b) the corporation or a specified person in relation to the corporation, directly or indirectly, for the purpose of assisting any person or partnership to acquire the new right or any person or partnership to acquire an interest in a partnership acquiring the new right (otherwise than because of an excluded obligation in relation to the new right),

(i) provided assistance,

(ii) made or arranged for a loan or payment,

(iii) transferred property, or

(iv) otherwise conferred a benefit by any means whatever, including the payment of a dividend; or

(c) the holder of the new right or, where the holder is a partnership, a member of the partnership, has a right under any agreement or arrangement entered into under circumstances where it is reasonable to consider that the agreement or arrangement was

contemplated at or before the time the agreement to issue the new right was entered into,

(i) to dispose of the new right, and

(ii) through a transaction or event or a series of transactions or events contemplated by the agreement or arrangement, to acquire

(A) a share (referred to in this paragraph as the "acquired share") of the capital stock of another corporation that would be a prescribed share under subsection (1) if the acquired share were issued at the time the new right was issued, other than a share that would not be a prescribed share if subsection (1) were read without reference to subparagraphs (1)(a)(iv) and (1)(d)(i) and (ii) where the acquired share is a share

(I) of a mutual fund corporation, or

(II) of a corporation that becomes a mutual fund corporation within 90 days after the acquisition of the acquired share, or

(B) a right (referred to in this paragraph as the "acquired right") to acquire a share of the capital stock of another corporation that would, if it were issued at the time the new right was issued, be a prescribed right, other than a right that would not be a prescribed right if subsection (1.1) were read without reference to subparagraph (1.1)(e)(i) where the acquired right is a right to acquire a share of the capital stock

(I) of a mutual fund corporation, or

(II) of a corporation that becomes a mutual fund corporation within 90 days after the acquisition of the acquired right.

Related Provisions: ITA 248(10) — Series of transactions.

Notes: For the meaning of "indirectly" in (b) opening words, see ITA 17.1(1) Notes.

Reg. 6202.1(2.1) added by 2002-2013 technical bill, for shares and rights issued under an agreement made after Dec. 20, 2002.

(3) [Dividend entitlement and liquidation entitlement] — For the purposes of subsections (1) and (1.1),

(a) the dividend entitlement of a share of the capital stock of a corporation is deemed not to be fixed, limited to a maximum or established to be not less than a minimum where all dividends on the share are determined solely by reference to a multiple or fraction of the dividend entitlement of another share of the capital stock of the corporation, or of another corporation that controls the corporation, where the dividend entitlement of that other share is not described in subparagraph (1)(a)(i); and

(b) the liquidation entitlement of a share of the capital stock of a corporation, or of a right to acquire a share of the capital stock of the corporation, as the case may be, is deemed not to be fixed, limited to a maximum or established to be not less than a minimum where

(i) all the liquidation entitlement is determinable solely by reference to

(A) the liquidation entitlement of another share of the capital stock of the corporation (or a share of the capital stock of another corporation that controls the corporation), or

(B) the liquidation entitlement of a right to acquire the capital stock of the corporation (or another corporation that controls the corporation),

(ii) the liquidation entitlement described in clause (i)(A), if any, is not described in subparagraph (1)(a)(ii), and

(iii) the liquidation entitlement described in clause (i)(B), if any, is not described in paragraph (1.1)(a).

Notes: Reg. 6202.1(3) amended by 2002-2013 technical bill, for shares and rights issued under an agreement made after Dec. 20, 2002. For earlier ones, see up to the 58th ed.

(4) [Agreement deemed not to be undertaking] — For the purposes of paragraphs (1)(c) and (e) and (1.1)(d) and (f), an agreement entered into between the first holder of a share or right and another person or partnership for the sale of the share or right to that other person or partnership for its fair market value at the time the share or right is acquired by the other person or partnership (determined without regard to the agreement) is deemed not to be an undertaking with respect to the share or right, as the case may be.

Notes: Reg. 6202.1(4) amended by 2002-2013 technical bill (Part 5 — technical), effective for shares and rights issued under an agreement made after Dec. 20, 2002. For earlier ones, see up to the 58th ed.

(5) [Definitions] — For the purposes of section 6202 and this section,

"excluded obligation", in relation to a share or new right issued by a corporation, means

(a) an obligation of the corporation

(i) with respect to eligibility for, or the amount of, any assistance under the *Canadian Exploration and Development Incentive Program Act*, the *Canadian Exploration Incentive Program Act*, the *Ontario Mineral Exploration Program Act*, R.S.O., c. O.27, or *The Mineral Exploration Incentive Program Act*, S.M. 1991-92, c. 45, or

(ii) with respect to the making of an election respecting such assistance and the flowing out of such assistance to the holder of the share or the new right in accordance with any of those Acts,

(b) an obligation of the corporation, in respect of the share or the new right, to distribute an amount that represents a payment out of assistance to which the corporation is entitled

(i) as a consequence of the corporation making expenditures funded by consideration received for shares or new rights issued by the corporation in respect of which the corporation purports to renounce an amount under subsection 66(12.6) of the Act, and

(ii) under section 25.1 of the *Income Tax Act*, R.S.B.C., 1996, c. 215, or

(c) an obligation of any person or partnership to effect an undertaking to indemnify a holder of the share or the new right or, where the holder is a partnership, a member of the partnership, for an amount not exceeding the amount of any tax payable under the Act or the laws of a province by the holder or the member of the partnership, as the case may be, as a consequence of

(i) the failure of the corporation to renounce an amount to the holder in respect of the share or the new right, or

(ii) a reduction, under subsection 66(12.73) of the Act, of an amount purported to be renounced to the holder in respect of the share or the new right;

Notes: Para. (b) accommodates a program under which a corporation performing mining exploration can qualify for a BC mining exploration tax credit.

Definition amended by 2002-2013 technical bill, for shares and rights issued under an agreement made after Dec. 20, 2002. The changes add references to a "right", consequential on the definition "new right" (below). For earlier ones, see up to the 58th ed.

Definition earlier amended by P.C. 1999-196, 1994-618, 1991-2475.

"new right" means a right that is issued after December 20, 2002 to acquire a share of the capital stock of a corporation, other than a right that is issued at a particular time before 2003

(a) pursuant to an agreement in writing made on or before December 20, 2002,

(b) as part of a distribution of rights to the public made in accordance with the terms of a prospectus, preliminary prospectus, registration statement, offering memorandum or notice, required by law to be filed before distribution of the rights begins, filed on or before December 20, 2002 with a public authority in Canada in accordance with the securities legislation of the province in which the rights are distributed, or

(c) to a partnership interests in which were issued as part of a distribution to the public made in accordance with the terms of a prospectus, preliminary prospectus, registration statement, offering memorandum or notice, required by law to be filed before distribution of the interests begins, filed on or before December 20, 2002 with a public authority in Canada in accordance with the securities legislation of the province in which the interests are distributed, where all interests in the partnership issued at or before the particular time were issued

(i) as part of the distribution, or

(ii) before the beginning of the distribution;

Notes: Definition added by 2002-2013 technical bill (Part 5 — technical), effective for shares and rights issued under an agreement made after Dec. 20, 2002.

"new share" means a share of the capital stock of a corporation issued after June 17, 1987, other than a share issued at a particular time before 1989

(a) pursuant to an agreement in writing entered into before June 18, 1987,

(b) as part of a distribution of shares to the public made in accordance with the terms of a prospectus, preliminary prospectus, registration statement, offering memorandum or notice, required by law to be filed before distribution of the shares begins, filed before June 18, 1987 with a public authority in Canada in accordance with the securities legislation of the province in which the shares were distributed, or

(c) to a partnership in which interests were issued as part of a distribution to the public made in accordance with the terms of a prospectus, preliminary prospectus, registration statement, offering memorandum or notice, required by law to be filed before distribution of the interests begins, filed before June 18, 1987 with a public authority in Canada in accordance with the securities legislation of the province in which the interests were distributed, where all interests in the partnership issued at or before the particular time were issued as part of the distribution or prior to the beginning of the distribution;

"specified person", in relation to any particular person, means another person with whom the particular person does not deal at arm's length or any partnership or trust of which the particular person or the other person is a member or beneficiary, respectively.

Related Provisions: ITA 96(2.2)(d)(vii) — Exclusion from limited partnership at-risk rules; ITA 143.2(3)(b)(iv) — Exclusion from tax shelter at-risk adjustments.

Notes: Reg. 6202.1 added by P.C. 1990-51, effective (other than (2)(a) and (b) — see Notes thereto) for shares issued after June 17, 1987.

Definitions [Reg. 6202.1]: "amount" — ITA 248(1); "arm's length" — ITA 251(1); "Canada" — ITA 255, *Interpretation Act* 35(1); "corporation" — ITA 248(1), *Interpretation Act* 35(1); "disposition", "dividend" — ITA 248(1); "dividend entitlement" — Reg. 6202.1(1)(a)(i); "excluded obligation" — Reg. 6202.1(5); "fair market value" — see ITA 69(1) Notes; "liquidation entitlement" — Reg. 6202.1(1)(a)(ii), (1.1)(a), (3)(b); "mutual fund corporation" — ITA 131(8), 248(1); "new right", "new share" — Reg. 6202.1(5); "paid-up capital" — ITA 89(1), 248(1); "partnership" — see ITA 96(1) Notes; "person", "prescribed" — ITA 248(1); "prescribed right" — Reg. 6202.1(1.1), (2.1); "property" — ITA 248(1); "province", "security" — *Interpretation Act* 35(1); "series" — ITA 248(10); "share" — ITA 248(1); "specified person" — Reg. 6202.1(5); "subsidiary wholly-owned corporation" — ITA 248(1); "trust" — ITA 104(1), 248(1), (3); "undertaking" — Reg. 6202.1(4); "writing" — *Interpretation Act* 35(1).

Interpretation Bulletins: IT-503: Exploration and development shares (archived).

6203. (1) [Share-purchase tax credit] — For the purposes of subsection 192(6) of the Act, a prescribed share of the capital stock of a taxable Canadian corporation is a share (other than a share acquired by a taxpayer under circumstances referred to in section 66.3 of the Act, a share acquired as consideration for a disposition of property in respect of which an election was made under subsection 85(1) or (2) of the Act and a share that can be considered to have been issued, directly or indirectly, for consideration that includes

Regulations

other shares of the capital stock of the corporation) where, at the time it is issued,

(a) under the terms or conditions of the share or any agreement in respect of the share or its issue,

(i) the amount of the dividends (in this section referred to as the **"dividend entitlement"**) that the corporation may declare or pay on the share is not limited to a maximum amount or fixed at a minimum amount at that time or any time thereafter by way of a formula or otherwise,

(ii) the amount (in this section referred to as the **"liquidation entitlement"**) that the holder of the share is entitled to receive on the share on the dissolution, liquidation or winding-up of the corporation is not limited to a maximum amount or fixed at a minimum amount by way of a formula or otherwise,

(iii) the share cannot be converted into any other security, other than into another security of the corporation that would, if it were issued for consideration that does not include other shares of the capital stock of the corporation, be a prescribed share,

(iv) the holder of the share cannot at that time or at any time thereafter cause the share to be redeemed, acquired or cancelled by the corporation or any specified person in relation to the corporation, except where the redemption, acquisition or cancellation is required pursuant to a conversion that is not prohibited by subparagraph (iii),

(v) no person or partnership has, either absolutely or contingently, an obligation to reduce, or to cause the corporation to reduce, at that time or at any time thereafter, the paid-up capital in respect of the share, except where the reduction is required pursuant to a conversion that is not prohibited by subparagraph (iii),

(vi) no person or partnership has, either absolutely or contingently, an obligation at that time or at any time thereafter to

(A) provide assistance to acquire the share,

(B) make a loan or payment,

(C) transfer property, or

(D) otherwise confer a benefit by any means whatever, including the payment of a dividend,

that may reasonably be considered to be, directly or indirectly, a repayment or return by the corporation or a specified person in relation to the corporation of all or part of the consideration for which the share was issued,

(vii) neither the corporation nor any specified person in relation to the corporation has, either absolutely or contingently, the right or obligation to redeem, acquire or cancel, at that time or at any time thereafter, the share in whole or in part other than for an amount that approximates the fair market value of the share (determined without reference to any such right or obligation), and

(viii) no person or partnership has, either absolutely or contingently, an obligation to provide, at that time or at any time thereafter, any form of undertaking with respect to the share (including any guarantee, security, indemnity, covenant or agreement and including the lending of funds to or the placing of amounts on deposit with, or on behalf of, the holder of the share or any specified person in relation to holder) that may reasonably be considered to have been given to ensure that

(A) any loss that the holder of the share may sustain by virtue of the holding, ownership or disposition of the share is limited in any respect, or

(B) the holder of the share will derive earnings by virtue of the holding, ownership or disposition of the share;

(b) the corporation or a specified person in relation to the corporation cannot reasonably be expected to, within two years after the time the share is issued,

(i) acquire or cancel the share in whole or in part,

(ii) reduce the paid-up capital of the corporation in respect of the share, or

(iii) make a payment, transfer or other provision, directly or indirectly, by way of a dividend, loan, purchase of shares, financial assistance to any purchaser of the share or in any other manner whatever, that may reasonably be considered to be a repayment or return of all or part of the consideration for which the share was issued

otherwise than as a consequence of the payment of a dividend paid by a subsidiary wholly-owned corporation to its parent, of an amalgamation of a subsidiary wholly-owned corporation or of a winding-up to which subsection 88(1) of the Act applies;

(c) no person or partnership can reasonably be expected to provide, within two years after the time the share is issued, any form of undertaking with respect to the share (including any guarantee, security, indemnity, covenant or agreement and including the lending of funds to, or the placing of amounts on deposit with, or on behalf of, the holder of the share or any specified person in relation to the holder); and

(d) it cannot reasonably be expected that any of the terms or conditions of the share or any existing agreement in respect of the share or its issue will thereafter be modified or amended, or that any new agreement in respect of the share or its issue will be entered into, within two years after the time the share is issued, in such a manner that the share would not be a prescribed share if it had been issued at the time of such modification or amendment or at the time the new agreement is entered into.

(2) **[Interpretation]** — For the purposes of subsection (1),

(a) the dividend entitlement of a share of the capital stock of a corporation shall be deemed not to be limited to a maximum amount or fixed at a minimum amount where it may reasonably be considered that all or substantially all of the dividend entitlement is determinable by reference to the dividend entitlement of another share of the capital stock of the corporation that meets the requirements of subparagraph (1)(a)(i);

(b) the liquidation entitlement of a share of the capital stock of a corporation shall be deemed not to be limited to a maximum amount or fixed at a minimum amount where it may reasonably be considered that all or substantially all of the liquidation entitlement is determinable by reference to the liquidation entitlement of another share of the capital stock of the corporation that meets the requirements of subparagraph (1)(a)(ii);

(c) where a corporation has merged or amalgamated with one or more other corporations, the corporation formed as a result of the merger or amalgamation shall be deemed to be the same corporation as, and a continuation of, each of its predecessor corporations and a share issued on the merger or amalgamation as consideration for another share shall be deemed to be the same share as the share for which it was issued but this paragraph does not apply if the share issued on the merger or amalgamation is not a prescribed share at the time of its issue; and

(d) an agreement entered into between the first purchaser of a share and another person or partnership, other than a specified person in relation to the corporation issuing the share, for the sale of the share to that other person or partnership shall be deemed not to be an undertaking with respect to the share.

(3) **["Specified person"]** — For the purposes of subsections (1) and (2), "specified person", in relation to a corporation or a holder of a share, as the case may be (in this subsection referred to as the "taxpayer"), means any person or partnership with whom the taxpayer does not deal at arm's length or any partnership or trust of which the taxpayer (or a person or partnership with whom the tax-

payer does not deal at arm's length) is a member or beneficiary, respectively.

Notes: Reg. 6203 prescribes shares for purposes of ITA 192(6), the share-purchase tax credit, which applied before 1987. It is still needed for 149.1(1)"non-qualified investment"(b), which refers to qualifying shares under 192(6) before 1987.

Definitions [Reg. 6203]: "amount" — ITA 248(1); "arm's length" — ITA 251(1); "corporation" — ITA 248(1), *Interpretation Act* 35(1); "disposition" — ITA 248(1); "dividend" — ITA 248(1); "dividend entitlement" — Reg. 6203(1)(a)(i), 6203(2)(a); "fair market value" — see ITA 69(1) Notes; "liquidation entitlement" — Reg. 6203(1)(a)(ii), 6203(2)(b); "paid-up capital" — ITA 89(1), 248(1); "partnership" — see ITA 96(1) Notes; "person", "prescribed", "property" — ITA 248(1); "security" — *Interpretation Act* 35(1); "share" — ITA 248(1); "specified person" — Reg. 6203(3); "subsidiary wholly-owned corporation" — ITA 248(1); "taxable Canadian corporation" — ITA 89(1), 248(1); "taxpayer" — ITA 248(1); "trust" — ITA 104(1), 248(1), (3).

6204. (1) [Employee stock option deduction — prescribed share] — For the purposes of subparagraph 110(1)(d)(i.1) of the Act, a share is a prescribed share of the capital stock of a corporation at the time of its sale or issue, as the case may be, if, at that time,

(a) under the terms or conditions of the share or any agreement in respect of the share or its issue,

(i) the amount of the dividends (in this section referred to as the **"dividend entitlement"**) that the corporation may declare or pay on the share is not limited to a maximum amount or fixed at a minimum amount at that time or at any time thereafter by way of a formula or otherwise,

(ii) the amount (in this section referred to as the **"liquidation entitlement"**) that the holder of the share is entitled to receive on the share on the dissolution, liquidation or winding-up of the corporation is not limited to a maximum amount or fixed at a minimum amount by way of a formula or otherwise,

(iii) the share cannot be converted into any other security, other than into another security of the corporation or of another corporation with which it does not deal at arm's length that is, or would be at the date of conversion, a prescribed share,

(iv) the holder of the share cannot at that time or at any time thereafter cause the share to be redeemed, acquired or cancelled by the corporation or any specified person in relation to the corporation, except where the redemption, acquisition or cancellation is required pursuant to a conversion that is not prohibited by subparagraph (iii),

(v) no person or partnership has, either absolutely or contingently, an obligation to reduce, or to cause the corporation to reduce, at that time or at any time thereafter, the paid-up capital in respect of the share, except where the reduction is required pursuant to a conversion that is not prohibited by subparagraph (iii), and

(vi) neither the corporation nor any specified person in relation to the corporation has, either absolutely or contingently, the right or obligation to redeem, acquire or cancel, at that time or any later time, the share in whole or in part other than for an amount that approximates the fair market value of the share (determined without reference to any such right or obligation) or a lesser amount;

(b) the corporation or a specified person in relation to the corporation cannot reasonably be expected to, within two years after the time the share is sold or issued, as the case may be, redeem, acquire or cancel the share in whole or in part, or reduce the paid-up capital of the corporation in respect of the share, otherwise than as a consequence of

(i) an amalgamation of a subsidiary wholly-owned corporation,

(ii) a winding-up to which subsection 88(1) of the Act applies, or

(iii) a distribution or appropriation to which subsection 84(2) of the Act applies; and

Proposed Addition — Reg. 6204(1)(b)(iv)

(iv) an exchange to which subsection 51(1) of the Act applies or a disposition to which subsection 86(1) of the Act applies, if no consideration is provided by the corporation for the share other than shares of the capital stock of the corporation that are prescribed shares; and

Application: The Sept. 16, 2016 draft technical legislation, subsec. 58(2), will add subpara. 6204(1)(b)(iv), applicable to 2012 *et seq.*

Technical Notes: Second, paragraph 6204(1)(b) is amended [as per Nov. 28, 2012 comfort letter below — ed.] to expand the listed exceptions to the requirement that the corporation or a specified person (within the meaning assigned by subsection 6204(3)) in relation to the corporation cannot reasonably be expected to, within two years after the time the share is sold or issued, redeem, acquire or cancel the share in whole or in part, or reduce the paid-up capital of the corporation in respect of the share. Specifically, new subparagraph 6204(1)(b)(iv) provides that a share is not precluded from being a prescribed share where the redemption, acquisition or cancellation of the share of the corporation, or the reduction in the paid-up capital of the corporation in respect of the share, arises a consequence of an exchange to which subsection 51(1) of the Act applies or a disposition to which subsection 86(1) of the Act applies, if the corporation provides no consideration for the share other than shares of the capital stock of the corporation that are prescribed shares.

Notes: This amendment was not included in 2017 budget bill #2, as was the rest of the Sept. 16, 2016 draft legislation, because it is under further consideration in light of *Montminy* (FCA; see Notes to ITA 110(1)(d)).

Letter from Dept. of Finance, Nov. 29, 2012:

Mr. Ian Gamble, Vancouver, BC

Dear Mr. Gamble:

I am writing in response to your letter of October 30, 2012, outlining a technical issue that you and your clients are encountering with paragraph 6204(1)(b) of the *Income Tax Regulations* (the "Regulations").

TELUS Corporation (the Corporation) has had both non-voting shares as well as common shares. Shareholders of each class of shares of the Corporation have voted to approve a Plan of Arrangement to convert the non-voting shares into common shares by way of a share-for-share exchange. The Corporation also has outstanding employee stock options of the non-voting shares. Some employee stock options have expiry dates after the execution of the Plan of Arrangement, and they will be in a position to exchange their options for new options on the voting shares.

The issue that has arisen relates to employees whose options on the non-voting shares will expire before the share-for-share exchange occurs. They must exercise before the expiry date but, under the current wording of paragraph 6204(1)(b), the acquired shares would not at the time of exercise satisfy all of the requirements to be "prescribed shares" for the purposes of the stock option deduction in paragraph 110(1)(d) of the *Income Tax Act*. Specifically, the non-voting shares, which until now have been "prescribed shares", are expected to be acquired by the Corporation very soon, as part of the Plan of Arrangement, in exchange for the new common shares, which will also be "prescribed shares" when issued. Because the acquisition is clearly anticipated, paragraph (b), which requires that the Corporation "cannot reasonably be expected to...redeem, acquire or cancel" the shares (except by way of certain listed re-organization transactions, none of which apply in the circumstances) cannot be satisfied.

We agree that in policy terms, the plan to convert the non-voting shares to voting shares should not affect the availability of the employee stock option deduction in paragraph 110(1)(d) for those employees who must exercise their options before the relevant expiry dates. We are therefore prepared to recommend to the Minister of Finance that paragraph 6204(1)(b) of the Regulations be amended to add a new exception to the list of existing exceptions in paragraph (b)(i) to (iii). This new exception would describe exchanges of shares in circumstances to which subsection 51(1) or subsection 86(1) of the *Income Tax Act* applies, provided that the new shares issued on the exchange are, or will be, themselves prescribed shares under regulation 6204 and that no consideration other than the new shares is payable to the shareholders for the old shares on the exchange.

We would also recommend that this proposed amendment apply to the 2012 and subsequent taxation years.

While I cannot offer any assurance that the Minister or the Governor in Council will agree with our recommendations, I hope that this statement of intention is helpful to you.

Yours sincerely,

Brian Ernewein, Tax Policy Branch — Legislation

(c) it cannot reasonably be expected that any of the terms or conditions of the share or any existing agreement in respect of the share or its sale or issue will be modified or amended, or that any new agreement in respect of the share, its sale or issue will be entered into, within two years after the time the share is sold or issued, in such a manner that the share would not be a prescribed share if it had been sold or issued at the time of such modification or amendment or at the time the new agreement is entered into.

Related Provisions: Reg. 6204(2) — Rules.

Notes: To qualify for ITA 110(1)(d), Reg. 6204 shares must be "plain vanilla common shares" with no retraction rights or other gimmicks, so the taxpayer carries the risk of them losing value. For discussion see Funt, "The Prescribed Share Rules for Stock Options", VII(1) *Business Vehicles* (Federated Press) 322-24 (2001); Pantry, "Paragraph 110(1)(d)", 17(1) *Taxation of Executive Compensation & Retirement* (Federated Press) 563-66 (July/Aug. 2005); Krasa, "Private Company Employee Stock Options", 17(3) *TECR* 600-03 (Oct. 2005); Nijhawan, "Stock Option Deduction Under Paragraph 110(1)(d): Unexpected Issues Arising in the Context of Corporate Acquisitions", 17(10) *TECR* 687-92 (June 2006); Geddes, "Dealing with Stock Options in Corporate Acquisitions", 21(9) *TECR* 1283-87 (May 2010) and 21(10) 1295-98 (June 2010); Mc-Clure & Kearl, "Stock Options in Spinout Transactions", 24(7) *Canadian Tax Highlights* (ctf.ca) 7 (July 2016).

See also VIEWS docs 2005-012811E5, 2005-014984117 (reload stock options); 2005-0151001R3 (corporation will not be "specified person"; 2005-0157381E5 (effect of covenant not to declare dividends); 2007-0241931C6 (general comments); 2007-0251101E5, 2011-0411951C6 (redemption right disqualifies share).

Reg. 6204(1) opening words amended by 2017 budget bill #2 to change reference from ITA 110(1)(d)(i) to 110(1)(d)(i.1), for acquisitions of securities and transfers or dispositions of rights after 4:00 pm EST, March 4, 2010.

The March 16, 2001 draft regulations had proposed to amend the opening words to apply to ITA 44.1. This was dropped because 44.1(1)"common share" already refers to a share "prescribed for the purpose of paragraph 110(1)(d)".

Reg. 6204(1) opening words amended by P.C. 2010-548, effective May 12, 2010, to change 110(1)(d) to 110(1)(d)(i).

Reg. 6204(1)(a)(vi) amended by P.C. 1997-1146, for shares issued or sold after 1994, to add "or a lesser amount". Reg. 6204(1) also amended by P.C. 2003-1497 (for options exercised after 1998), 1997-1146 and 1994-618.

(2) [Rules] — For the purposes of subsection (1),

(a) the dividend entitlement of a share of the capital stock of a corporation shall be deemed not to be limited to a maximum amount or fixed at a minimum amount where it may reasonably be considered that all or substantially all of the dividend entitlement is determinable by reference to the dividend entitlement of another share of the capital stock of the corporation that meets the requirements of subparagraph (1)(a)(i);

(b) the liquidation entitlement of a share of the capital stock of a corporation shall be deemed not to be limited to a maximum amount or fixed at a minimum amount where it may reasonably be considered that all or substantially all of the liquidation entitlement is determinable by reference to the liquidation entitlement of another share of the capital stock of the corporation that meets the requirements of subparagraph (1)(a)(ii); and

(c) the determination of whether a share of the capital stock of a particular corporation is a prescribed share shall be made without reference to a right or obligation to redeem, acquire or cancel the share, or to cause the share to be redeemed, acquired or cancelled, where

(i) the person (in this paragraph referred to as the "holder") to whom the share is sold or issued is, at the time the share is sold or issued, dealing at arm's length with the particular corporation and with each corporation with which the particular corporation is not dealing at arm's length,

(ii) the right or obligation is provided for in the terms or conditions of the share or in an agreement in respect of the share or its issue and, having regard to all the circumstances, it can reasonably be considered that

(A) the principal purpose of providing for the right or obligation is to protect the holder against any loss in respect of the share, and the amount payable on the redemption, acquisition or cancellation (in this subparagraph and in subparagraph (iii) referred to as the "acquisition") of the share will not exceed the adjusted cost base of the share to the holder immediately before the acquisition, or

(B) the principal purpose of providing for the right or obligation is to provide the holder with a market for the

share, and the amount payable on the acquisition of the share will not exceed the fair market value of the share immediately before the acquisition, and

(iii) having regard to all the circumstances, it can reasonably be considered that no portion of the amount payable on the acquisition of the share is directly determinable by reference to the profits of the particular corporation, or of another corporation with which the particular corporation does not deal at arm's length, for all or any part of the period during which the holder owns the share or has a right to acquire the share, unless the reference to the profits of the particular corporation or the other corporation is only for the purpose of determining the fair market value of the share pursuant to a formula set out in the terms or conditions of the share or the agreement in respect of the share or its issue, as the case may be.

Notes: See Notes to ITA 110(1)(d) re *Montminy* case.

CRA considers that "substantially all" means 90% or more.

Reg. 6204(2)(c) amended by P.C. 2007-1443, for shares sold or issued, and rights to acquire shares disposed of, after 2003. The amendment (implementing a Finance comfort letter, March 30, 2005) allows the right or obligation to be provided for in any agreement in respect of the share or its issue, or in the terms or conditions of the share. (This accommodates share liquidity rights provided for in a shareholders' agreement, rather than in the employee share purchase agreement.) Before the amendment, read:

(c) the determination of whether a share of the capital stock of a corporation is a prescribed share shall be made without reference to a right or obligation to redeem, acquire or cancel the share or to cause the share to be redeemed, acquired or cancelled where

(i) the share was issued or sold pursuant to an employee share purchase agreement (in this paragraph referred to as "the agreement") to an employee (in this paragraph referred to as "the holder") of the corporation or of another corporation with which the corporation was not dealing at arm's length,

(ii) the holder was dealing at arm's length with each corporation referred to in subparagraph (i) at the time the share was issued or sold, and

(iii) having regard to all the circumstances, including the terms of the agreement, it can reasonably be considered that

(A) the amount payable on the redemption, acquisition or cancellation (in this clause and in clause (B) referred to as the "acquisition") of the share will not exceed

(I) the adjusted cost base to the holder of the share immediately before the acquisition, where the acquisition was provided for in the agreement and the principal purpose for its provision was to protect the holder against any loss in respect of the share, or

(II) the fair market value of the share immediately before the acquisition, where the acquisition was provided for in the agreement and the principal purpose for its provision was to provide the holder with a market for the share, and

(B) no portion of the amount payable on the acquisition of the share is directly determinable by reference to the profits of the corporation, or of another corporation with which the corporation does not deal at arm's length, for all or any part of the period during which the holder owned the share or had a right to acquire the share, unless the reference to the profits of the corporation or the other corporation is only for the purpose of determining the fair market value of the share pursuant to a formula set out in the agreement.

Reg. 6204(2)(c) added by P.C. 1994-618 and amended by P.C. 1997-1146, both retroactive to 1985 and later taxation years.

(3) ["Specified person"] — For the purposes of subsection (1), "specified person", in relation to a corporation, means

(a) any person or partnership with whom the corporation does not deal at arm's length otherwise than because of a right referred to in paragraph 251(5)(b) of the Act that arises as a result of an offer by the person or partnership to acquire all or substantially all of the shares of the capital stock of the corporation, or

(b) any partnership or trust of which the corporation (or a person or partnership with whom the corporation does not deal at arm's length) is a member or beneficiary, respectively.

Related Provisions: Reg. 6204(4) — Interpretation.

Notes: CRA considers that "substantially all" means 90% or more.

Reg. 6204(3) amended by P.C. 1994-618, for 1985 and later tax years. Amended non-substantively by P.C. 1997-1146, for 1996 and later tax years.

(4) [Interpretation] — For the purposes of subsection (3), the Act shall be read without reference to subsection 256(9) of the Act.

Notes: Reg. 6204(4) added by P.C. 1997-1146, for 1996 and later taxation years.

Definitions [Reg. 6204]: "adjusted cost base" — ITA 54, 248(1); "amount" — ITA 248(1); "arm's length" — ITA 251(1); "corporation" — ITA 248(1), *Interpretation Act* 35(1); "disposition", "dividend" — ITA 248(1); "dividend entitlement" — Reg. 6204(1)(a)(i), 6204(2)(a); "employee" — ITA 248(1); "fair market value" — see ITA 69(1) Notes; "liquidation entitlement" — Reg. 6204(1)(a)(ii), 6204(2)(b); "paid-up capital" — ITA 89(1), 248(1); "partnership" — see ITA 96(1) Notes; "person", "prescribed" — ITA 248(1); "share", "subsidiary wholly-owned corporation" — ITA 248(1); "trust" — ITA 104(1), 248(1), (3).

Interpretation Bulletins: IT-113R4: Benefits to employees — stock options; IT-171R2: Non-resident individuals — computation of taxable income earned in Canada and non-refundable tax credits (archived).

6205. (1) [Capital gains deduction — prescribed share] — For the purposes of subsections 110.6(8) and (9) of the Act and subject to subsection (3), a prescribed share is a share of the capital stock of a corporation where

(a) under the terms or conditions of the share or any agreement in respect of the share or its issue,

(i) at the time the share is issued,

(A) the amount of the dividends (in this section referred to as the **"dividend entitlement"**) that the corporation may declare or pay on the share is not limited to a maximum amount or fixed at a minimum amount at that time or at any time thereafter by way of a formula or otherwise,

(B) the amount (in this section referred to as the **"liquidation entitlement"**) that the holder of the share is entitled to receive on the share on the dissolution, liquidation or winding-up of the corporation is not limited to a maximum amount or fixed at a minimum amount by way of a formula or otherwise,

(C) the share cannot be converted into any other security, other than into another security of the corporation that is, or would be at the date of conversion, a prescribed share,

(D) the holder of the share does not, at that time or at any time thereafter, have the right or obligation to cause the share to be redeemed, acquired or cancelled by the corporation or a specified person in relation to the corporation, except where the redemption, acquisition or cancellation is required pursuant to a conversion that is not prohibited by clause (C),

(E) no person or partnership has, either absolutely or contingently, an obligation to reduce, or to cause the corporation to reduce, at that time or at any time thereafter, the paid-up capital in respect of the share, otherwise than by way of a redemption, acquisition or cancellation of the share that is not prohibited by this section,

(F) no person or partnership has, either absolutely or contingently, an obligation (other than an excluded obligation in relation to the share, as defined in subsection 6202.1(5)) at that time or any time thereafter to

(I) provide assistance to acquire the share,

(II) make a loan or payment,

(III) transfer property, or

(IV) otherwise confer a benefit by any means whatever, including the payment of a dividend,

that may reasonably be considered to be, directly or indirectly, a repayment or return by the corporation or a specified person in relation to the corporation of all or part of the consideration for which the share was issued, and

(G) neither the corporation nor any specified person in relation to the corporation has, either absolutely or contingently, the right or obligation to redeem, acquire or cancel, at that time or at any time thereafter, the share in whole or in part, except where the redemption, acquisition

or cancellation is required pursuant to a conversion that is not prohibited by clause (C),

(ii) no person or partnership has, either absolutely or contingently, an obligation (other than an excluded obligation in relation to the share, as defined in subsection 6202.1(5)) to provide, at any time, any form of undertaking with respect to the share (including any guarantee, security, indemnity, covenant or agreement and including the lending of funds to or the placing of amounts on deposit with, or on behalf of, the holder of the share or any specified person in relation to that holder) that may reasonably be considered to have been given to ensure that

(A) any loss that the holder of the share may sustain by virtue of the holding, ownership or disposition of the share is limited in any respect, or

(B) the holder of the share will derive earnings by virtue of the holding, ownership or disposition of the share; and

(b) at the time the share is issued, it cannot reasonably be expected, having regard to all the circumstances, that any of the terms or conditions of the share or any existing agreement in respect of the share or its issue will thereafter be modified or amended or that any new agreement in respect of the share or its issue will be entered into, in such a manner that the share would not be a prescribed share if it had been issued at the time of such modification or amendment or at the time the new agreement is entered into.

Related Provisions: Reg. 6205(4) — Interpretation.

Notes: For meaning of "indirectly" in (a)(i)(F), see Notes to ITA 17.1(1).

(2) [Capital gains deduction — prescribed share] — For the purposes of subsections 110.6(8) and (9) of the Act and subject to subsection (3), a prescribed share is a share of the capital stock of a particular corporation where

(a) it is a particular share that is owned by a person and that was issued by the particular corporation as part of an arrangement to that person, to a spouse, common-law partner or parent of that person or, if the person is a trust described in paragraph 104(4)(a) of the Act, to the person who created the trust or by whose will the trust was created or, if the person is a corporation, to another person owning all of the issued and out-standing shares of the capital stock of the corporation or to a spouse, common-law partner or parent of that other person, and

(i) the main purpose of the arrangement was to permit any increase in the value of the property of the particular corporation to accrue to other shares that would, at the time of their issue, be prescribed shares if this section were read without reference to this subsection, and

(ii) at the time of the issue of the particular share or at the end of the arrangement,

(A) the other shares were owned by

(I) the person to whom the particular share was issued (in this paragraph referred to as the "original holder"),

(II) a person who did not deal at arm's length with the original holder,

(III) a trust none of the beneficiaries of which were persons other than the original holder or a person who did not deal at arm's length with the original holder, or

(IV) any combination of persons described in subclause (I), (II) or (III),

(B) the other shares were owned by employees of the particular corporation or of a corporation controlled by the particular corporation, or

(C) the other shares were owned by any combination of persons each of whom is described in clause (A) or (B); or

(b) it is a share that was issued by a mutual fund corporation.

Related Provisions: ITA 256(6), (6.1) — Meaning of "controlled"; Reg. 6205(4) — Interpretation.

Notes: See VIEWS docs 2012-0454021C6 (meaning of "arrangement" and when it ends); 2013-0496511C6 (multiple shareholders doing estate freezes); 2014-0538041C6 [2014 APFF q.19] (meaning of "arrangement" in estate-freeze context).

Reg. 6205(2)(a) amended by P.C. 2001-957 to add references to "common-law spouse", effective as per Notes to ITA 248(1) "common-law partner".

(3) [Capital gains deduction — prescribed share] — For the purposes of subsections 110.6(8) and (9) of the Act, a prescribed share does not include a share of the capital stock issued by a mutual fund corporation (other than an investment corporation) the value of which can reasonably be considered to be, directly or indirectly, derived primarily from investments made by the mutual fund corporation in one or more corporations (in this subsection referred to as an "investee corporation") connected with it (within the meaning of subsection 186(4) of the Act on the assumption that the references in that subsection to "payer corporation" and "particular corporation" were read as references to "investee corporation" and "mutual fund corporation", respectively).

Related Provisions: ITA 186(7) — Interpretation of "connected".

Notes: For the meaning of "derived", see Notes to ITA 18.1(12). For "indirectly" see Notes to ITA 17.1(1).

(4) [Rules] — For the purposes of this section,

(a) the dividend entitlement of a share of the capital stock of a corporation shall be deemed not to be limited to a maximum amount or fixed at a minimum amount where it may reasonably be considered that

(i) all or substantially all of the dividend entitlement is determinable by reference to the dividend entitlement of another share of the capital stock of the corporation that meets the requirements of clause (1)(a)(i)(A), or

(ii) the dividend entitlement cannot be such as to impair the ability of the corporation to redeem another share of the capital stock of the corporation that meets the requirements of paragraph (2)(a);

(b) the liquidation entitlement of a share of the capital stock of a corporation shall be deemed not to be limited to a maximum amount or fixed at a minimum amount where it may reasonably be considered that all or substantially all of the liquidation entitlement is determinable by reference to the liquidation entitlement of another share of the capital stock of the corporation that meets the requirements of clause (1)(a)(i)(B);

(c) where two or more corporations (each of which is referred to in this paragraph as a "predecessor corporation") have merged or amalgamated, the corporation formed as a result of the merger or amalgamation (in this paragraph referred to as the "new corporation") shall be deemed to be the same corporation as, and a continuation of, each of the predecessor corporations and a share of the capital stock of the new corporation issued on the merger or amalgamation as consideration for a share of the capital stock of a predecessor corporation shall be deemed to be the same share as the share of the predecessor corporation for which it was issued, but this paragraph does not apply if the share issued on the merger or amalgamation is not a prescribed share at the time of its issue and either

(i) the terms and conditions of that share are not identical to those of the share of the predecessor corporation for which it was issued, or

(ii) at the time of its issue the fair market value of that share is not the same as that of the share of the predecessor corporation for which it was issued;

(d) a reference in clauses (1)(a)(i)(D) and (G) and subparagraph (1)(a)(ii) to a right or obligation of the corporation or a person or partnership does not include a right or obligation provided in a written agreement among shareholders of a private corporation owning more than 50% of its issued and outstanding share capital having full voting rights under all circumstances to which the corporation, person or partnership is a party unless it may rea-

sonably be considered, having regard to all the circumstances, including the terms of the agreement and the number and relationship of the shareholders, that one of the main reasons for the existence of the agreement is to avoid or limit the application of subsection 110.6(8) or (9) of the Act;

(e) where at any particular time after November 21, 1985, the terms or conditions of a share are changed or any existing agreement in respect thereof is changed or a new agreement in respect of the share is entered into, the share shall, for the purpose of determining whether it is a prescribed share, be deemed to have been issued at that particular time; and

(f) the determination of whether a share of the capital stock of a corporation is a prescribed share for the purposes of subsection (1) shall be made without reference to a right or obligation to redeem, acquire or cancel the share or to cause the share to be redeemed, acquired or cancelled where

(i) the share was issued pursuant to an employee share purchase agreement (in this paragraph referred to as "the agreement") to an employee (in this paragraph referred to as "the holder") of the corporation or of a corporation with which it did not deal at arm's length,

(ii) the holder was dealing at arm's length with each corporation referred to in subparagraph (i) at the time the share was issued, and

(iii) having regard to all the circumstances including the terms of the agreement, it may reasonably be considered that

(A) the amount payable on the redemption, acquisition or cancellation (in this clause and in clause (B) referred to as the "acquisition") of the share will not exceed

(I) the adjusted cost base of the share to the holder immediately before the acquisition, where the acquisition was provided for in the agreement and the principal purpose for its provision was to protect the holder against any loss in respect of the share, or

(II) the fair market value of the share immediately before the acquisition, where the acquisition was provided for in the agreement and the principal purpose for its provision was to provide the holder with a market for the share, and

(B) no portion of the amount payable on the acquisition of the share is directly determinable by reference to the profits of the corporation, or of another corporation with which it does not deal at arm's length, for all or any part of the period during which the holder owned the share or had a right to acquire the share, unless the reference to the profits of the corporation or the other corporation is only for the purpose of determining the fair market value of the share pursuant to a formula set out in the agreement.

Notes: CRA considers that "substantially all" means 90% or more. For the meaning of "one of the main reasons" in para. (d), see Notes to ITA 83(2.1).

Reg. 6205(4)(c) amended by P.C. 1994-618, retroactive to mergers and amalgamations occurring after 1984.

(5) ["Specified person"] — For the purposes of this section, "specified person", in relation to a corporation or a holder of a share, as the case may be (in this subsection referred to as the "taxpayer"), means any person or partnership with whom the taxpayer does not deal at arm's length or any partnership or trust of which the taxpayer (or a person or partnership with whom the taxpayer does not deal at arm's length) is a member or beneficiary, respectively.

Definitions [Reg. 6205]: "adjusted cost base" — ITA 54, 248(1); "amount" — ITA 248(1); "arm's length" — ITA 251(1); "connected" — ITA 186(4), (7); "controlled" — ITA 256(6), (6.1); "corporation" — ITA 248(1), *Interpretation Act* 35(1); "disposition" — ITA 248(1); "dividend" — ITA 248(1); "dividend entitlement" — Reg. 6205(1)(a)(i)(A), 6205(4)(a); "employee" — ITA 248(1); "excluded obligation" — Reg. 6202.1(5); "fair market value" — see ITA 69(1) Notes; "investment corporation" — ITA 130(3), 248(1); "liquidation entitlement" — Reg. 6205(1)(a)(i)(B), 6205(4)(b); "mutual fund corporation" — ITA 131(8), 248(1); "paid-up capital" — ITA 89(1), 248(1); "partnership" — see ITA 96(1) Notes; "person", "prescribed" —

ITA 248(1); "private corporation" — ITA 89(1), 248(1); "property" — ITA 248(1); "security" — *Interpretation Act* 35(1); "share", "shareholder" — ITA 248(1); "specified person" — Reg. 6205(5); "taxpayer" — ITA 248(1); "trust" — ITA 104(1), 248(1), (3); "written" — *Interpretation Act* 35(1)"writing".

6206. [Prescribed share for ITA 84(8)] — The Class I Special Shares of Reed Stenhouse Companies Limited, issued before January 1, 1986, are prescribed for the purposes of subsection 84(8) of the Act.

6207. [No longer relevant]

Notes: Reg. 6207 defines a prescribed share for ITA 183.1(4)(c), an anti-avoidance rule that was repealed with the introduction of the general anti-avoidance rule in ITA 245(2), effective Sept. 13, 1988 (with certain grandfathering to the end of 1988).

6208. (1) [Non-resident withholding tax — prescribed security] — For the purposes of [pre-2008 — ed.] clause 212(1)(b)(vii)(E) of the Act, a prescribed security with respect to an obligation of a corporation is

(a) a share of the capital stock of the corporation unless

(i) under the terms and conditions of the share, any agreement relating to the share or any modification of such terms, conditions or agreement, the corporation or a specified person in relation to the corporation is or may, at any time within 5 years after the date of the issue of the obligation, be required to redeem, acquire or cancel, in whole or in part, the share (unless the share is or may be required to be redeemed, acquired or cancelled by reason only of a right to convert the share into, or exchange the share for, another share of the corporation that, if issued, would be a prescribed security) or to reduce its paid-up capital,

(ii) as a result of the modification or establishment of the terms or conditions of the share or the changing or entering into of any agreement in respect of the share, the corporation or a specified person in relation to the corporation may, within 5 years after the date of the issue of the obligation, reasonably be expected to redeem, acquire or cancel, in whole or in part, the share (unless the share is or may be required to be redeemed, acquired or cancelled by reason only of a right to convert the share into, or exchange the share for, another share of the corporation that, if issued, would be a prescribed security) or to reduce its paid-up capital, or

(iii) as a result of the terms or conditions of the share or any agreement entered into by the corporation or a specified person in relation to the corporation or any modification of such terms, conditions or agreement, any person is required, either absolutely or contingently, within 5 years after the date of the issue of the obligation, to effect any undertaking, including any guarantee, covenant or agreement to purchase or repurchase the share, and including a loan of funds to or the placing of amounts on deposit with, or on behalf of, the shareholder or a specified person in relation to the shareholder given

(A) to ensure that any loss that the shareholder or a specified person in relation to the shareholder may sustain, by reason of the ownership, holding or disposition of the share or any other property, is limited in any respect, and

(B) as part of a transaction or event or series of transactions or events that included the issuance or acquisition of the obligation,

and for the purposes of this subparagraph, where such an undertaking in respect of a share is given at any particular time after the date of the issue of the obligation, the obligation shall be deemed to have been issued at the particular time and the undertaking shall be deemed to have been given as part of a series of transactions that included the issuance or acquisition of the obligation, and

(b) a right or warrant to acquire a share of the capital stock of the corporation that would, if issued, be a prescribed security with respect to the obligation,

where all the consideration receivable upon a conversion or exchange of the obligation or the prescribed security, as the case may be, is a share of the capital stock of the corporation described in paragraph (a) or a right or warrant described in paragraph (b), or both, as the case may be.

Related Provisions: ITA 248(10) — Series of transactions; Reg. 6208(2) — Consideration for fractional share; *Interpretation Act* 27(5) — Meaning of "within 5 years".

Interpretation Bulletins: IT-361R3: Exemption from Part XIII tax on interest payments to non-residents.

(2) [Consideration for fraction of a share] — For the purposes of this section, where a taxpayer may become entitled upon the conversion or exchange of an obligation or a prescribed security to receive consideration in lieu of a fraction of a share, that consideration shall be deemed not to be consideration unless it may reasonably be considered to be receivable as part of a series of transactions or events one of the main purposes of which is to avoid or limit the application of Part XIII of the Act.

Related Provisions: ITA 248(10) — Series of transactions.

Notes: For the meaning of "one of the main purposes" see Notes to ITA 83(2.1).

(3) ["Specified person"] — In this section, "specified person", in relation to a corporation or a shareholder, means any person with whom the corporation or the shareholder, as the case may be, does not deal at arm's length or any partnership or trust of which the corporation or the shareholder, as the case may be, or the person is a member or beneficiary, respectively.

Definitions [Reg. 6208]: "amount" — ITA 248(1); "arm's length" — ITA 251(1); "corporation" — ITA 248(1), *Interpretation Act* 35(1); "disposition" — ITA 248(1); "paid-up capital" — ITA 89(1), 248(1); "partnership" — see ITA 96(1) Notes; "person", "prescribed", "property" — ITA 248(1); "series" — ITA 248(10); "share", "shareholder" — ITA 248(1); "specified person" — Reg. 6208(3); "taxpayer" — ITA 248(1); "trust" — ITA 104(1), 248(1), (3).

6209. [Lending assets — prescribed shares and property] — For the purposes of the definition "lending asset" in subsection 248(1) of the Act,

(a) a share owned by a bank is a prescribed share for a taxation year where it is a preferred share of the capital stock of a corporation that is dealing at arm's length with the bank that may reasonably be considered to be, and is reported as, a substitute or alternative for a loan to the corporation, or another corporation with whom the corporation does not deal at arm's length, in the bank's annual report for the year to the relevant authority or, where the bank was throughout the year subject to the supervision of the relevant authority but was not required to file an annual report for the year with the relevant authority, in its financial statements for the year; and

(b) a property is a prescribed property for a taxation year where

(i) the security is a mark-to-market property (as defined in subsection 142.2(1) of the Act) for the year of a financial institution (as defined in subsection 142.2(1) of the Act),

(ii) the security is at any time in the year a property described in an inventory of a taxpayer, or

(iii) the property is a direct financing lease, or is any other financing arrangement, of a taxpayer that is reported as a loan in the taxpayer's financial statement for the year prepared in accordance with generally accepted accounting principles and an amount is deductible under paragraph 20(1)(a) of the Act in respect of the property that is the subject of the lease or arrangement in computing the taxpayer's income for the year.

Notes: Reg. 6209(b)(i) and (ii) amended by P.C. 2009-1212, for tax years that end after Feb. 22, 1994. Due to this amendment, a specified debt obligation (defined in ITA 142.2(1)) held by a bank in its trading account will be treated as a lending asset if it is not a mark-to-market property. This applies to the debt obligations of a country designated by the Office of the Superintendent of Financial Institutions, and to the United Mexican States Collateralized Par or Discount Bonds Due 2019 (Brady bonds).

Regulations

Reg. 6209 earlier amended by P.C. 1999-195.

Definitions [Reg. 6209]: "amount" — ITA 248(1); "arm's length" — ITA 251(1); "bank" — ITA 248(1), *Interpretation Act* 35(1); "corporation" — ITA 248(1), *Interpretation Act* 35(1); "inventory" — ITA 248(1); "mark-to-market property" — ITA 142.2(1); "preferred share", "prescribed", "property" — ITA 248(1); "share" — ITA 248(1); "taxation year" — ITA 249; "taxpayer" — ITA 248(1).

6210. [Prescribed debt obligation — donation of listed shares] — For the purposes of paragraph 38(a.1) of the Act, a prescribed debt obligation is a bond, debenture, note, mortgage or similar obligation

(a) of or guaranteed by the Government of Canada; or

(b) of the government of a province or an agent of that government.

Notes: Reg. 6210 added by P.C. 2001-954, effective February 19, 1997.

PART LXIII — [6300–6302] CHILD TAX BENEFITS

6300. Interpretation — In this Part, "qualified dependant" has the meaning assigned by section 122.6 of the Act.

6301. Non-application of [mother] presumption — (1) For the purposes of paragraph (g) of the definition "eligible individual" in section 122.6 of the Act, the presumption referred to in paragraph (f) of that definition does not apply in the circumstances where

(a) subject to paragraph (c), the female parent of the qualified dependant declares in writing to the Minister that she resides with the other parent of that qualified dependant and that that other parent primarily fulfils the responsibility for the care and upbringing of each of the qualified dependants with whom both parents reside;

(b) the female parent is a qualified dependant of an eligible individual and each of them files a notice with the Minister under subsection 122.62 (1) of the Act in respect of the same qualified dependant;

(c) there is more than one female parent of the qualified dependant who resides with the qualified dependant and each female parent files a notice with the Minister under subsection 122.62 (1) of the Act in respect of the qualified dependant; or

(d) more than one notice is filed with the Minister under subsection 122.62 (1) of the Act in respect of the same qualified dependant who resides with each of the persons filing the notices if such persons live at different locations.

Notes: The mother's waiver under Reg. 6301(1)(a) can be made even if the mother is non-resident and could not be an eligible individual: *Vegh*, 2012 TCC 95, para. 3.

Reg. 6301(1)(a) amended by P.C. 2021-304, effective July 1, 2021, to accommodate the "other parent" not being male (responding in part to the Auditor General's 2021 Report 4 on the Canada Child Benefit, tinyurl.com/ccb-audit, §4.65-4.77). Before then, read:

(a) the female parent of the qualified dependant declares in writing to the Minister that the male parent, with whom she resides, is the parent of the qualified dependant who primarily fulfils the responsibility for the care and upbringing of each of the qualified dependants who reside with both parents;

Reg. 6301(1)(a)-(d) amended by P.C. 1998-2770 and S.C. 1996, c. 11.

(2) For greater certainty, a person who files a notice referred to in paragraph (1)(b), (c) or (d) includes a person who is not required under subsection 122.62(3) of the Act to file such a notice.

Notes: Reg. 6301(2) amended by by P.C. 1998-2770, effective August 28, 1995, to delete words permitting waiver of the filing requirement. ITA 220(2.1) gives a general discretion to CRA to waive filing requirements.

Definitions [Reg. 6301]: "eligible individual" — ITA 122.6; "individual", "Minister" — ITA 248(1); "parent" — ITA 252(2)(a); "person" — ITA 248(1); "qualified dependant" — Reg. 6300; "writing" — *Interpretation Act* 35(1).

6302. Factors — For the purposes of paragraph (h) of the definition "eligible individual" in section 122.6 of the Act, the following factors are to be considered in determining what constitutes care and upbringing of a qualified dependant:

(a) the supervision of the daily activities and needs of the qualified dependant;

(b) the maintenance of a secure environment in which the qualified dependant resides;

(c) the arrangement of, and transportation to, medical care at regular intervals and as required for the qualified dependant;

(d) the arrangement of, participation in, and transportation to, educational, recreational, athletic or similar activities in respect of the qualified dependant;

(e) the attendance to the needs of the qualified dependant when the qualified dependant is ill or otherwise in need of the attendance of another person;

(f) the attendance to the hygienic needs of the qualified dependant on a regular basis;

(g) the provision, generally, of guidance and companionship to the qualified dependant; and

(h) the existence of a court order in respect of the qualified dependant that is valid in the jurisdiction in which the qualified dependant resides.

Notes: See Notes to ITA 122.6"eligible individual". Cases finding the **mother** (M), not father (F), was primary caregiver (PCG): *Schreiner*, 2004 TCC 314 (girl became more connected with M on turning 15); *Morin*, 2005 TCC 572 (son resided more regularly and had more secure environment with M); *Roy*, 2007 TCC 496; *Rose*, 2007 TCC 572; *Grimard*, 2008 TCC 98 (even though children spent more time with F for a period); *Scott*, 2008 TCC 150; *Lafontaine*, 2008 TCC 191; *Fouillard*, 2008 TCC 597 (because child's siblings lived with M); *CD*, 2009 TCC 578 (violent common-law on-off relationship); *Penney*, 2009 TCC 596; *Heubach*, 2010 TCC 409 (M was "more responsible" for children's medical appointments, activities and clothing); *Murphy*, 2010 TCC 411; *Couillard*, 2010 TCC 470; *Ross*, 2011 TCC 515 *Desjardins*, 2011 TCC 556; *Ethier*, 2012 TCC 241 (even when son lived with F part-time); *Hrushka*, 2013 TCC 335; *Guerrero*, 2013 TCC 342; *Karim*, 2016 TCC 91, para. 34-35 (no clear answer, but assumption that M was PCG not rebutted); *Rubinov-Liberman*, 2016 TCC 188; *Frobb*, 2018 TCC 121.

Cases finding the **father** was PCG: *Piorkowski*, [2000] 2 C.T.C. 2308 (TCC); *Priest*, 2005 TCC 30 (slight advantage to F); *Bouchard*, 2006 TCC 539 (girl lived primarily with F, who had legal custody); *Perry*, 2007 TCC 40; *Walsh*, 2007 TCC 263 (court order giving custody to F was determinative); *Streitenberger*, 2007 TCC 430; *Cantin*, 2007 TCC 633; *Delage*, 2009 TCC 119 (daughter did not actually reside with M despite F's agreement that she would); *White*, 2010 TCC 394; *Desmarais*, 2013 TCC 83; *Armstrong*, 2013 TCC 238; *Fortin*, 2014 TCC 209; *Mageau*, 2016 TCC 142; *Wachal*, 2020 TCC 78.

Other [note that ITA 252(1)(b) and 252(2)(a) extend the definition of "parent"]: *Penner*, 2006 TCC 413 (grandmother, even though child boarded with another family for school); *Judge*, 2006 TCC 408 (different PCGs for different periods); *Poulin*, 2006 TCC 495 (stepmother did not qualify); *Dufour*, 2007 TCC 701 (stepmother was PCG rather than M); *Deblois*, 2007 TCC 700 (child resided with M and F for different periods); *Gervais*, 2008 TCC 190 (grandmother); *McLaughlin*, 2009 TCC 300 (each parent was PCG during different periods); *Pearson*, 2011 TCC 455 (each M was PCG part of the time); *B.*, 2012 TCC 126 (M was PCG of one child; other child was shared equally); *Brady*, 2011 TCC 240 (parents shared custody nearly equally); *Peixoto DaFonseca*, 2014 TCC 88 (M, not grandmother, was PCG); *Reynolds*, 2015 TCC 109 (M, not stepmother, was PCG).

In *Bourret*, 2008 TCC 108 and *Fraser*, 2010 TCC 23, where both parents were approximately equal caregivers, the court honoured an agreement that benefits would go to M. In *Barceloux*, 2011 TCC 324, the parents' caregiving was equal, so in the absence of agreement between them to split the benefit, neither qualified. See however Notes to 122.61(1) for case law saying parties cannot agree as to who will get the CTB.

In *Furlan*, 2018 TCC 25, the Reg. 6302 criteria were used to find that F had primary custody of his son D during the days D was living with him, so F was a 122.6"shared-custody parent".

Definitions [Reg. 6302]: "eligible individual" — ITA 122.6; "person" — ITA 248(1); "qualified dependant" — Reg. 6300.

Notes [Part LXIII]: Part LXIII added by P.C. 1992-2714, effective 1993.

PART LXIV — [6400–6401] PRESCRIBED DATES

6400. Child tax credits — [No longer relevant]

Notes: Reg. 6400 prescribed dates for ITA 122.2, the pre-1993 child tax credit.

6401. Quebec tax abatement — For the purposes of subsection 120(2) of the Act, the prescribed date for each of the 1980 and subsequent taxation years is December 31 of that year.

Definitions [Reg. 6401]: "prescribed" — ITA 248(1); "taxation year" — ITA 249.

PART LXV — [6500–6503] PRESCRIBED LAWS

6500. For the purposes of paragraph 241(4)(j.2) of the Act, the following are prescribed laws of the Province of Quebec:

(a) *An Act respecting the Québec Pension Plan*, R.S.Q., c. R-9; and

(b) *Individual and Family Assistance Act*, R.S.Q., c. A-13.1.1, as it relates to the additional amounts for dependent children.

Notes: Reg. 6500 added by 2013 budget bill #2, effective Dec. 12, 2013. It replaces former Reg. 3003, as ITA 122.64 was repealed.

Former Reg. 6500 repealed by P.C. 2007-849, effective June 13, 2007. It prescribed provincial family law provisions for ITA 73(1)(d) for transfers of property up to July 13, 1990, and for ITA 148(8)(a)(iii) for transfers before 1990.

Definitions [Reg. 6500]: "prescribed" — ITA 248(1).

Interpretation Bulletins: IT-325R2: Property transfers after separation, divorce and annulment.

6501. [Prescribed provisions — non-taxable indemnities] — For the purposes of paragraph 81(1)(q) of the Act, "prescribed provision of the law of a province" means

(a) in respect of the Province of Alberta

(i) subsections 7(1) and 14(1) of *The Criminal Injuries Compensation Act*, R.S.A. 1970, c. 75, and

(ii) subsections 8(3), 10(2) and 13(8) of *The Motor Vehicle Accident Claims Act*, R.S.A. 1970, c. 243;

(b) in respect of the Province of British Columbia

(i) paragraphs 3(1)(a) and (b) and section 9 of the *Criminal Injury Compensation Act*, R.S.B.C. 1979, c. 83, and

(ii) subsection 106(1) of the *Motor-vehicle Act*, R.S.B.C. 1960, c. 253, as amended by S.B.C. 1965, c. 27;

(c) in respect of the Province of Manitoba

(i) subsection 6(1) of *The Criminal Injuries Compensation Act*, S.M. 1970, c. 56, and

(ii) subsections 7(9) and 12(11) of *The Unsatisfied Judgement Fund Act*, R.S.M. 1970, c. U70;

(d) in respect of the Province of New Brunswick

(i) subsections 3(1) and (2) of the *Compensation for Victims of Crime Act*, R.S.N.B. 1973, c. C-14, and

(ii) subsections 319(3), (10) and 321(1) of the *Motor Vehicle Act*, R.S.N.B. 1973, c. M-17;

(e) in respect of the Province of Newfoundland

(i) subsection 27(1) of the *Criminal Injuries Compensation Act*, R.S.N. 1970, c. 68, and

(ii) subsection 106(2) of *The Highway Traffic Act*, R.S.N. 1970, c. 152;

(f) in respect of the Northwest Territories, subsections 3(1) and 5(2) and section 13 of the *Criminal Injuries Compensation Ordinance*, R.O.N.W.T. 1974, c. C-23;

(g) in respect of the Province of Nova Scotia, subsections 190(5) and 191(2) of the *Motor Vehicle Act*, R.S.N.S. 1967, c. 191;

(h) in respect of the Province of Ontario

(i) section 5, subsection 7(2) and section 14 of *The Compensation for Victims of Crime Act, 1971*, S.O. 1971, c. 51, and

(ii) subsections 5(3) and 6(1) and section 18 of *The Motor Vehicle Accident Claims Act*, R.S.O. 1970, c. 281;

(i) in respect of the Province of Prince Edward Island, subsection 351(3) of the *Highway Traffic Act*, R.S.P.E.I. 1974, c. H-6;

(j) in respect of the Province of Quebec

(i) sections 5, 5b and 14 of the *Crime Victims Compensation Act*, S.Q. 1971, c. 18, and

(ii) sections 13 and 26, subsection 37(1) and sections 44 and 54 of the *Automobile Insurance Act*, S.Q. 1977, c. 68;

(k) in respect of the Province of Saskatchewan

(i) subsection 10(1) of *The Criminal Injuries Compensation Act*, R.S.S. 1978, c. C-47, and

(ii) subsections 23(1) to (4) and (7), 24(2) to (7) and (9), 25(1), 26(1), 27(1) and (2), 27(5), 51(8) and (9), 54(3) and 55(1) of *The Automobile Accident Insurance Act*, R.S.S. 1978, c. A-35; and

(l) in respect of the Yukon Territory, subsection 3(1) of the *Compensation for the Victims of Crime Ordinance*, O.Y.T. 1975 (1st), c. 2 as amended by O.Y.T. 1976 (1st), c. 5.

Notes: See Notes to ITA 81(1)(q).

6502. [Prescribed provisions — Ontario family law] — For the purposes of paragraph 56(1)(c.1), section 56.1, paragraph 60(c.1) and section 60.1 of the Act, the class of individuals

(a) who were parties, whether in a personal capacity or by representation, to proceedings giving rise to an order made in accordance with the laws of the Province of Ontario, and

(b) who, at the time the application for the order was made, were persons described in subclause 14(b)(i) of the *Family Law Reform Act*, Revised Statutes of Ontario 1980, c. 152,

is prescribed as a class of persons described in the laws of a province.

Definitions [Reg. 6502]: "individual", "person", "prescribed" — ITA 248(1); "province" — *Interpretation Act* 35(1).

6503. [Prescribed provisions — pensions] — For the purposes of paragraphs 60(j.02) to (j.04) of the Act, subsection 41(5) of the *Canadian Forces Superannuation Act*, subsections 39(7) and 42(8) of the *Public Service Superannuation Act* and subsection 24(6) of the *Royal Canadian Mounted Police Superannuation Act* are prescribed.

Notes: Reg. 6503 amended by 2017 budget bill #2, for repayments made after March 2007, to add "subsection 41(5) of the *Canadian Forces Superannuation Act*".

Reg. 6503 added by P.C. 1994-738, for 1990 and later tax years (for ITA 60(j.02) and (j.04)) and 1991 and later tax years (for ITA 60(j.03)). Finance's Technical Notes released with the draft regulations had indicated that similar provisions in the *Members of Parliament Retiring Allowances Act* and the *Canadian Forces Superannuation Act* would be prescribed. However, the former is covered by regulations under the *Public Service Superannuation Act*, and the latter is not needed because no one was expected to move from the public service to the Canadian Forces reserves late in their career. (Evidently, by 2016 it was determined that the last statement above is incorrect; hence the 2017 amendment.)

Definitions [Reg. 6503]: "prescribed" — ITA 248(1).

PART LXVI — [6600] PRESCRIBED ORDER

6600. For the purpose of the definition "overseas Canadian Forces school staff" in subsection 248(1) of the Act, the *Canadian Forces Overseas Schools Regulations* is prescribed.

Notes [Reg. 6600]: Reg. 6600 amended by P.C. 2010-548, effective May 12, 2010.

Definitions [Reg. 6600]: "prescribed" — ITA 248(1).

Part LXVII — [6700–6709] Prescribed Venture Capital Corporations, Labour-Sponsored Venture Capital Corporations, Investment Contract Corporations, Qualifying Corporations and Prescribed Stock Savings Plan

Interpretation Bulletins [Part LXVII]: IT-73R6: The small business deduction; IT-269R4: Part IV tax on taxable dividends received by a private corporation or a subject corporation.

6700. [Prescribed venture capital corporation] — For the purposes of paragraph 40(2)(i), clause 53(2)(k)(i)(C), the definition "private corporation" in subsection 89(1), subsection 125(6.2), the definition "Canadian-controlled private corporation" in subsection 125(7), section 186.2 and the definition "financial intermediary corporation" in subsection 191(1) of the Act, the following are prescribed venture capital corporations:

(a) a corporation that is registered under the provisions of

(i) *An Act Respecting Corporations for the Development of Quebec Business Firms*, Statutes of Quebec 1976, c. 33,

(ii) the *Small Business Development Corporations Act, 1979*, Statutes of Ontario 1979, c. 22,

(iii) *Manitoba Regulation 194/84*, being a regulation made under *The Loans Act, 1983(2)*, Statutes of Manitoba 1982-83-84, c. 36,

(iv) *The Venture Capital Tax Credit Act*, Statutes of Saskatchewan 1983-84, c. V-4.1,

(v) the *Small Business Equity Corporations Act*, Statutes of Alberta 1984, c. S-13.5,

(vi) the *Small Business Venture Capital Act*, Statutes of British Columbia 1985, c. 56,

(vii) *An Act respecting Quebec business investment companies*, Statutes of Quebec 1985, c. 9,

(viii) *The Venture Capital Act*, Statutes of Newfoundland 1988, c. 15,

(ix) *The Labour-sponsored Venture Capital Corporations Act*, Statutes of Saskatchewan 1986, c. L-0.2,

(x) Part 2 of the *Employee Investment Act*, Revised Statutes of British Columbia, 1996, c. 112,

(xi) Part III of the *Community Small Business Investment Funds Act*, chapter 18 of the Statutes of Ontario, 1992,

(xii) *The Labour-Sponsored Venture Capital Corporations Act*, Continuing Consolidation of the Statutes of Manitoba c. L12;

(xiii) Part II of the *Risk Capital Investment Tax Credits Act*, chapter 22 of the Statutes of the Northwest Territories, 1998; or

(xiv) section 11 or Part II of the *Equity Tax Credit Act*, Statutes of Nova Scotia, 1993, c. 3;

Proposed Amendment — Reg. 6700(a) — PEI

Letter from Dept. of Finance, Apr. 20, 2014:

The Honourable Wesley J. Sheridan, Minister of Finance, Energy and Municipal Affairs, Government of Prince Edward Island

Dear Minister Sheridan:

Thank you for your correspondence of January 20, 2014 to my predecessor regarding a potential amendment to the *Income Tax Regulations* to allow corporations (including incorporated cooperative associations) registered under the *Community Economic Development Equity Tax Credit Act* of Prince Edward Island to be prescribed venture capital corporations. Please excuse the delay in replying.

A review of your request has confirmed that the *Community Economic Development Equity Tax Credit Act* creates a program that is similar to an existing program in Nova Scotia under its *Equity Tax Credit Act*. Since corporations registered under that program are prescribed venture capital corporations, prescribing corporations registered

under PEI's new program will help ensure consistent treatment of programs and taxpayers in different provinces. On that basis, I am prepared to recommend to the Governor in Council that the list of prescribed venture capital corporations under section 6700 of the *Income Tax Regulations* be expanded to include corporations (including incorporated cooperative associations) registered under section 2 of the *Community Economic Development Equity Tax Credit Act*. I would also recommend that the amendment apply effective from August 2011, when PEI's program commenced.

While I cannot offer any assurance that the Treasury Board will agree with my recommendation. I trust that this statement of intention is helpful to you.

Yours sincerely,

Joe Oliver [Minister of Finance]

(b) the corporation established by *An Act to Establish the Fonds de solidarité des travailleurs du Québec (F.T.Q.)*, Revised Statutes of Quebec, F-3.2.1;

(c) a corporation that is registered with the Department of Economic Development and Tourism of the Government of the Northwest Territories pursuant to the Venture Capital Policy and Directive issued by the Government of the Northwest Territories on June 27, 1985;

(d) a corporation that is a registered labour-sponsored venture capital corporation;

(e) the corporation established by *The Manitoba Employee Ownership Fund Corporation Act*, Continuing Consolidation of the Statutes of Manitoba, c. E95;

(e.1) the corporation established by *An Act constituting Capital régional et coopératif Desjardins*, R.S.Q., c. C-6.1; or

(f) the corporation established by *An Act to establish Fondaction, le Fonds de développement de la Confédération des syndicats nationaux pour la coopération et l'emploi*, Statutes of Québec 1995, c. 48;

(g) [Repealed]

Notes [Reg. 6700]: Reg. 6700(e.1) added by P.C. 2011-936, effective for 2001 and later taxation years.

Reg. 6700 earlier amended by P.C. 2001-1370 (last change effective June 10, 2001), 1999-249, 1998-782, 1997-1943, 1997-1669, 1996-436, 1993-1549, 1992-1307, 1992-1306.

Definitions [Reg. 6700]: "business" — ITA 248(1); "corporation" — ITA 248(1), *Interpretation Act* 35(1); "registered labour-sponsored venture capital corporation" — ITA 248(1).

Interpretation Bulletins: IT-458R2: Canadian-controlled private corporation.

6700.1 [Prescribed venture capital corporation] — For the purposes of paragraph 40(2)(i) and clause 53(2)(k)(i)(C) of the Act, a corporation that has an employee share ownership plan registered under Part 1 of the *Employee Investment Act*, R.S.B.C. 1996, c. 112, is also a prescribed venture capital corporation.

Notes: Reg. 6700.1 amended by P.C. 2001-1370, effective June 10, 2001. Added by P.C. 1992-1036, effective for taxation years ending after Sept. 26, 1989.

Definitions [Reg. 6700.1]: "corporation" — ITA 248(1), *Interpretation Act* 35(1).

6700.2 [Prescribed venture capital corporation] — For the purposes of paragraph 40(2)(i) and clause 53(2)(k)(i)(C) of the Act, "prescribed venture capital corporation" at any time includes a corporation that at that time is a corporation registered under the provisions of Part II of the *Community Small Business Investment Funds Act*, chapter 18 of the Statutes of Ontario, 1992, or of Part II of the *Risk Capital Investment Tax Credits Act*, chapter 22 of the Statutes of the Northwest Territories, 1998.

Notes: Reg. 6700.2 added by P.C. 1993-1549, effective for 1991 and later taxation years. Amended by P.C. 1999-249, last change effective for the 1998 and later taxation years.

Definitions [Reg. 6700.2]: "corporation" — ITA 248(1), *Interpretation Act* 35(1).

6701. [Prescribed labour-sponsored venture capital corporation] — For the purposes of paragraph 40(2)(i), clause 53(2)(k)(i)(C), the definition "public corporation" in subsection 89(1), the definition "specified investment business" in subsection 125(7), the definition "approved share" in subsection 127.4(1), subsections 131(8) and (11), section 186.1, the definition "financial intermediary corporation" in subsection 191(1), the definition "eligible investment" in subsection 204.8(1) and subsection 204.81(8.3) of the Act, "prescribed labour-sponsored venture capital corporation" means, at any particular time,

(a) the corporation established by the *Act to establish the Fonds de solidarité des travailleurs du Québec 1983*, c. 58,

(b) a corporation that is registered under the provisions of *The Labour-sponsored Venture Capital Corporations Act*, Statutes of Saskatchewan 1986, c. L-0.2,

(c) a corporation that is registered under Part 2 of the *Employee Investment Act*, Revised Statutes of British Columbia, 1996, c. 112;

(d) a registered labour-sponsored venture capital corporation,

(e) a corporation that is registered under Part III of the *Community Small Business Investment Funds Act*, chapter 18 of the Statutes of Ontario, 1992;

(f) the corporation established by *The Manitoba Employee Ownership Fund Corporation Act*, Continuing Consolidation of the Statutes of Manitoba, c. E95,

(f.1) a corporation that is registered under *The Labour-Sponsored Venture Capital Corporations Act*, Continuing Consolidation of the Statutes of Manitoba c. L12, or

(g) the corporation established by *An Act to establish Fondaction, le Fonds de développement de la Confédération des syndicats nationaux pour la coopération et l'emploi*, Statutes of Québec 1995, c. 48,

(h) a corporation that is registered under Part II of the *Equity Tax Credit Act*, Statutes of Nova Scotia 1993, c. 3, or

(i) a corporation that is registered under Part II of the *Risk Capital Investment Tax Credits Act*, chapter 22 of the Statutes of Northwest Territories, 1998.

Notes: Reg. 6701 opening words amended to add reference to 204.81(8.3) by 2002-2013 technical bill (Part 5 — technical), effective Oct. 24, 2012.

Reg. 6701 earlier amended by P.C. 2005-698 (for 1995 and later tax years), P.C. 2001-1370 (last change effective June 10, 2001), and P.C. 1999-249, 1998-782, 1997-1943, 1997-1669, 1996-436, 1993-1549, 1992-1307, 1992-1306.

Definitions [Reg. 6701]: "corporation" — ITA 248(1), *Interpretation Act* 35(1); "registered labour-sponsored venture capital corporation" — ITA 248(1).

Interpretation Bulletins: IT-73R6: The small business deduction.

6701.1 [Repealed]

Notes: Reg. 6701.1 added by 2013 budget bill #2 effective March 21, 2013, and repealed by 2016 budget bill #1 effective March 22, 2016. It prescribed, for certain purposes, that corporations established or registered under certain provincial statutes, or registered under ITA 204.81, would be considered prescribed LSVCCs. It was added, with the phase-out of the labour-sponsored funds tax credit, to prevent a corporation that had not submitted its application for registration under one of the provincial statutes in Reg. 6701 by March 20, 2013 from qualifying as a prescribed LSVCC. It was repealed because the federal credit continues to be available for provincially-registered LSVCCs (see Notes to ITA 127.4(5)).

Definitions [Reg. 6701.1]: "corporation" — ITA 248(1), *Interpretation Act* 35(1); "provincial" — *Interpretation Act* 33(3), 35(1)"province".

6702. [Prescribed assistance] — For the purposes of subparagraph 40(2)(i)(ii) and clause 53(2)(k)(i)(C) of the Act, each of the following is prescribed assistance:

(a) the assistance received from a province that has been provided in respect of, or for the acquisition of, a share of the capital stock of a venture capital corporation described in section 6700;

(a.1) the assistance provided under the *Employee Investment Act*, R.S.B.C. 1996, c. 112, in respect of, or for the acquisition of, a share of the capital stock of a venture capital corporation described in section 6700.1;

(a.2) the assistance provided under the *Community Small Business Investment Funds Act*, S.O. 1992, c. 18, the *Risk Capital Investment Tax Credits Act*, S.N.W.T. 1998, c. 22, or the *Risk Capital Investment Tax Credits Act*, S.N.W.T. 1998, c. 22, as

duplicated for Nunavut, in respect of, or for the acquisition of, a share of the capital stock of a venture capital corporation described in section 6700.2;

(b) a tax credit provided in respect of, or for the acquisition of, a share of a labour-sponsored venture capital corporation described in section 6701; and

(c) a tax credit provided by a province in respect of, or for the acquisition of, a share of the capital stock of a taxable Canadian corporation (other than a share of the capital stock of a corporation in respect of which an amount has been renounced by the corporation under subsection 66(12.6), (12.601), (12.62) or (12.64) of the Act) that is held in a stock savings plan described in section 6705.

Related Provisions: Reg. 7300(b) — Prescribed assistance under Reg. 6702 is a prescribed amount for ITA 12(1)(x).

Notes: Reg. 6702 amended by P.C. 2001-1370, effective June 10, 2001.

Reg. 6702(a.1) added by P.C. 1992-1306, for tax years ending after Sept. 26, 1989. 6702(a.2) added by P.C. 1993-1549, for 1991 and later tax years. 6702(a.2) amended by P.C. 1999-249, effective May 8, 1997 for the 1997 and later tax years, to change reference from *Labour-Sponsored Venture Capital Corporations Act, 1992* to the CSBIF Act, and effective for the 1998 and later tax years to add reference to the *Risk Capital Investment Tax Credits Act*.

Reference to ITA 66(12.601) added to Reg. 6702(c) by P.C. 1996-494 effective December 3, 1992.

Definitions [Reg. 6702]: "amount" — ITA 248(1); "corporation" — ITA 248(1), *Interpretation Act* 35(1); "prescribed labour-sponsored venture capital corporation" — Reg. 6701; "prescribed stock savings plan" — Reg. 6705; "prescribed venture capital corporation" — Reg. 6700; "province" — *Interpretation Act* 35(1); "share" — ITA 248(1); "taxable Canadian corporation" — ITA 89(1), 248(1).

6703. [Prescribed investment contract corporation] — For the purposes of section 186.1 of the Act, a "prescribed investment contract corporation" means a corporation described in clause 146(1)(j)(ii)(B) [146(1)"retirement savings plan"(b)(ii)] of the Act.

Definitions [Reg. 6703]: "corporation" — ITA 248(1), *Interpretation Act* 35(1).

6704. [Prescribed qualifying corporation] — For the purposes of section 186.2 of the Act, a corporation is a prescribed qualifying corporation in respect of dividends received by a shareholder on shares of its capital stock if, when the shares were acquired by the shareholder, they constituted

(a) an investment described in sections 33 and 34 of the Act referred to in subparagraph 6700(a)(i);

(b) an eligible investment under the provisions of an Act referred to in subparagraph 6700(a)(ii), (iv), (v), (vi) or (viii) or the regulation referred to in subparagraph 6700(a)(iii);

(c) a qualified investment under the provisions of the Act referred to in subparagraph 6700(a)(vii);

(d) an investment in an eligible business under the Venture Capital Policy and Directive referred to in paragraph 6700(c); or

(e) an investment in an eligible entity described in sections 17 and 18 of *An Act constituting Capital régional et coopératif Desjardins*, R.S.Q., c. C-6.1.

Notes: Reg. 6704(e) added by P.C. 2011-936, for 2001 and later tax years.

Reg. 6704(b), (d) amended, (e) revoked by P.C. 1993-1549, effective for dividends received after Feb. 18, 1987 (para. (b)) and after Sept. 26, 1989 (para. (d)).

Definitions [Reg. 6704]: "business" — ITA 248(1); "corporation" — ITA 248(1), *Interpretation Act* 35(1); "dividend", "prescribed", "share", "shareholder" — ITA 248(1).

6705. [Prescribed stock savings plan] — For the purposes of paragraph 40(2)(i) and clause 53(2)(k)(i)(C) of the Act, a stock savings plan governed by any of the following is a prescribed stock savings plan:

(a) the *Alberta Stock Savings Plan Act*, Statutes of Alberta 1986, c. A-37.7;

(b) *The Stock Savings Tax Credit Act*, Statutes of Saskatchewan 1986, c. S-59.1;

(c) the *Stock Savings Plan Act*, Revised Statutes of Nova Scotia, 1989, c. 445;

(d) the *Stock Savings Tax Credit Act*, Revised Statutes of Newfoundland, 1990, c. S-28; or

(e) section 11.6 of the *Income Tax Act*, Continuing Consolidation of the Statutes of Manitoba c. I10.

Notes: Reg. 6705 amended by P.C. 2001-1370, for 1999 and later tax years.

6706. [Prescribed condition]

— For the purpose of clause 204.81(1)(c)(v)(F) of the Act, a prescribed condition is that, in respect of a redemption of a Class A share of a corporation's capital stock, the shareholder requires the corporation to withhold an amount in respect of the redemption in accordance with Part XII.5 of the Act.

Related Provisions: ITA 204.81 — Conditions for registration; ITA 211.7 — Recovery of credit from provincial LSVCCs; ITA 211.8(1) — Disposition of approved share.

Notes: See ITA 211.7. Reg. 6706 amended by P.C. 1998-782 (for redemptions after 1997), 1996-437. Added by P.C. 1992-1307.

Definitions [Reg. 6706]: "amount" — ITA 248(1); "corporation" — ITA 248(1), *Interpretation Act* 35(1); "prescribed", "share", "shareholder" — ITA 248(1).

Forms: T1149: Remittance form for labour-sponsored funds tax credits withheld on redeemed shares; T2152: Part X.3 tax return for a labour-sponsored venture capital corporation; T5006: Statement of registered labour-sponsored venture capital corporation Class A shares; T5006 Summ: Summary of registered LSVCC Class A shares.

6707. [Provincially registered LSVCCs]

— For the purpose of subsection 204.82(5) of the Act, a "prescribed provision of a law of a province" means section 25.1 of the *Community Small Business Investment Funds Act*, chapter 18 of the Statutes of Ontario, 1992.

Notes: Reg. 6707 added by P.C. 1999-249, effective May 8, 1997.

6708. [Provincial wind-up rules for LSVCCs — Ontario]

— For the purposes of paragraph 204.8(2)(b), section 27.2 of the *Community Small Business Investment Funds Act, 1992*, S.O. 1992, c. 18, is a prescribed wind-up rule.

Notes: Reg. 6708 amended by 2014 budget bill #1 to delete application to ITA 204.81(8.3), effective Nov. 27, 2013.

Reg. 6708 added by 2002-2013 technical bill, effective Oct. 24, 2012.

Definitions [Reg. 6708]: "prescribed" — ITA 248(1).

6709. [Penalty for failing to reacquire LSVCC shares — Quebec]

— For the purposes of section 211.81 of the Act, sections 1086.14 and 1086.20 of the *Taxation Act*, R.S.Q., c. I-3, are prescribed provisions of a provincial law.

Notes: Reg. 6709 added by 2002-2013 technical bill (Part 5 — technical), effective Oct. 24, 2012.

Definitions [Reg. 6709]: "prescribed" — ITA 248(1); "provincial" — *Interpretation Act* 33(3), 35(1)"province".

PART LXVIII — [6800–6804] PRESCRIBED PLANS, ARRANGEMENTS AND CONTRIBUTIONS

6800. [Prescribed arrangement — employee benefit plan]

— For the purpose of paragraph (e) of the definition "employee benefit plan" in subsection 248(1) of the Act, each of the following is a prescribed arrangement:

(a) the Major League Baseball Players Benefit Plan;

(b) an arrangement under which all contributions are made pursuant to a law of Canada or a province, where one of the main purposes of the law is to enforce minimum standards with respect to wages, vacation entitlement or severance pay; and

(c) an arrangement under which all contributions are made in connection with a dispute regarding the entitlement of one or more persons to benefits to be received or enjoyed by the person or persons.

Notes: Reg. 6800(b) and (c) added by P.C. 1996-911, effective 1980.

Definitions [Reg. 6800]: "Canada" — ITA 255, *Interpretation Act* 35(1); "person", "prescribed" — ITA 248(1); "province" — *Interpretation Act* 35(1).

6801. [Prescribed plan or arrangement — salary deferral arrangement]

— For the purposes of paragraph (l) of the definition "salary deferral arrangement" in subsection 248(1) of the Act, a prescribed plan or arrangement is an arrangement in writing

(a) between an employer and an employee that is established on or after July 28, 1986 where

(i) it is reasonable to conclude, having regard to all the circumstances, including the terms and conditions of the arrangement and any agreement relating thereto, that the arrangement is not established to provide benefits to the employee on or after retirement but is established for the main purpose of permitting the employee to fund, through salary or wage deferrals, a leave of absence from the employee's employment of not less than

(A) where the leave of absence is to be taken by the employee for the purpose of permitting the full-time attendance of the employee at a designated educational institution (within the meaning assigned by subsection 118.6(1) of the Act, three consecutive months, or

(B) in any other case, six consecutive months

that is to commence immediately after a period (in this section referred to as the "deferral period") not exceeding six years after the date on which the deferrals for the leave of absence commence,

(ii) the amount of salary or wages deferred by the employee under all such arrangements for the services rendered by the employee to the employer in a taxation year does not exceed $33\frac{1}{3}$ per cent of the amount of the salary or wages that the employee would, but for the arrangements, reasonably be expected to have received in the year in respect of the services,

(iii) the arrangement provides that throughout the period of the leave of absence the employee does not receive any salary or wages from the employer, or from any other person or partnership with whom the employer does not deal at arm's length, other than

(A) the amount by which the employee's salary or wages under the arrangement was deferred or is to be reduced or, amounts that are based on a percentage of the salary or wage scale of employees of the employer, which percentage is fixed in respect of the employee for the deferral period and the leave of absence, and

(B) the reasonable fringe benefits that the employer usually pays to or on behalf of employees,

(iv) the arrangement provides that the amounts deferred in respect of the employee under the arrangement

(A) are held by or for the account of a trust governed by a plan or arrangement that is an employee benefit plan within the meaning of the definition thereof in subsection 248(1) of the Act, and provides that the amount that may reasonably be considered to be the income of the trust for a taxation year that has been earned by it for the benefit of the employee shall be paid in the year to the employee, or

(B) are held by or for the account of any person other than a trust referred to in clause (A), and provides that the amount in respect of interest or other additional amounts that may reasonably be considered to have accrued to or for the benefit of the employee to the end of a taxation year shall be paid in the year to the employee,

(v) the arrangement provides that the employee is to return to his regular employment with the employer or an employer that participates in the same or a similar arrangement after the leave of absence for a period that is not less than the period of the leave of absence, and

(vi) subject to subparagraph (iv), the arrangement provides that all amounts held for the employee's benefit under the arrangement shall be paid to the employee out of or under the arrangement no later than the end of the first taxation year that commences after the end of the deferral period;

(b) between an employer and an employee that is established before July 28, 1986 where it is reasonable to conclude, having regard to all the circumstances, including the terms and conditions of the arrangement and any agreement relating thereto, that the arrangement is not established to provide benefits on or after retirement but is established for the main purpose of permitting the employee to fund, through salary or wage deferrals, a leave of absence from the employment and under which the deferrals in respect of the leave of absence commenced before 1987;

(c) that is established for the purpose of deferring the salary or wages of a professional on-ice official for his services as such with the National Hockey League if, in the case of an official resident in Canada, the trust or other person who has custody and control of any funds, investments or other property under the arrangement is resident in Canada; or

(d) between a corporation and an employee of the corporation or a corporation related thereto under which the employee (or, after the employee's death, a dependant or relation of the employee or the legal representative of the employee) may or shall receive an amount that may reasonably be attributable to duties of an office or employment performed by the employee on behalf of the corporation or a corporation related thereto where

(i) all amounts that may be received under the arrangement shall be received after the time of the employee's death or retirement from, or loss of, the office or employment and no later than the end of the first calendar year commencing thereafter, and

(ii) the aggregate of all amounts each of which may be received under the arrangement depends on the fair market value of shares of the capital stock of the corporation or a corporation related thereto at a time within the period that commences one year before the time of the employee's death or retirement from, or loss of, the office or employment and ends at the time the amount is received,

unless, by reason of the arrangement or a series of transactions that includes the arrangement, the employee or a person with whom the employee does not deal at arm's length is entitled, either immediately or in the future, either absolutely or contingently, to receive or obtain any amount or benefit granted or to be granted for the purpose of reducing the impact, in whole or in part, of any reduction in the fair market value of the shares of the corporation or a corporation related thereto.

Related Provisions: ITA 81(1)(s) — Exemption for recontributed amount received from leave-of-absence plan; ITA 248(10) — Series of transactions; Reg. 6801.1 — COVID-19 relief for 2020-22; Reg. 8508 — Effect of salary deferral leave plan on registered pension plan.

Notes: The arrangement described in Reg. 6801(a) is commonly called a "sabbatical" or "deferred salary leave plan", often used by teachers and professors. See Brown, "Executive Sabbaticals and the Deferred Salary Leave Program", 9(2) *Taxation of Executive Compensation and Retirement* (Federated Press) 24–32 (1997); VIEWS docs 2004-0091411E5, 2005-0122901E5, 2005-0149671E5, 2005-0154431E5, 2006-0169391R3, 2006-0195811E5, 2006-0211401117, 2006-0214641E5; 2007-0226571E5 (salary deferral can be temporarily suspended for up to 6 years); 2007-0250811R3, 2008-0268831M4; 2008-0268241E5 (deferral under 2 plans at once), 2008-0292771E5; 2008-029826117 (gross negligence penalty if parties knew conditions not met), 2009-0350851E5; 2010-0383461E5 (terminating and creating a new plan), 2010-035410117 (receipt of additional salary violates 6801(a)(iii)); 2012-0451771R3; 2013-0488501E5 (fringe benefits during leave of absence); 2013-0515721E5 (return to part-time employment does not meet condition in (a)(v); leave of absence can be taken during the plan), 2014-0520851E5 (interpretation of (a)(iv)(B); effect of annual withdrawal fees); 2015-0577801E5 (interaction with maternity leave); 2016-0643191E5 (numerous interpretations and conditions); 2017-0728851E5 (plan must require employee to return to work for at least as long as the leave period); 2018-0758461R3 (self-funded sabbatical qualifies); 2020-0848511E5, 2020-0848641E5, 2020-0849681E5, 2020-0849841E5 (minimum absence and maximum deferral periods in (a)(i) cannot be varied by CRA, but Finance is reviewing these due to COVID-19, and CRA will not require employers

to terminate a DSLP in the interim); 2020-0869961E5 (DLSP cannot be used immediately before retirement; a paid leave is not a "return to regular employment").

If the employee does not intend to return to work when a 6801(a) arrangement is made, amounts deferred under the plan are taxed under ITA 6(11) since the plan is not a prescribed plan: VIEWS docs 2004-0069211E5, 2007-0238961E5. (If employee advances are actually a loan, it will create deemed interest under 80.4(1), taxed under 6(9): 2006-0203131E5.) If however an employee decides not to return to work (or becomes disabled or pregnant and so will not return immediately), once this is determined any deferred amounts not previously paid out should be paid to the employee and included in income at that time: 2002-0154615, 2003-0003705, 2006-0211891E5, 2008-0288661E5, 2008-0295261E5. An employee cannot teach a course and be paid by the employer for teaching while on leave under a 6801(a) plan: 2003-0016045.

Reg. 6801(d) describes a "deferred share unit" plan; see rulings in VIEWS docs 9922093, 2003-0006071, 2003-0051111R3, 2004-0067521R3, 2004-0088331R3, 2005-0118261R3, 2006-0168861R3, 2006-0185501R3, 2006-0194461R3, 2006-0210171R3, 2007-0223531R3, 2007-0237501R3, 2007-0246431R3, 2008-0265631R3, 2008-0268921R3, 2008-0271191R3, 2008-0287641R3, 2009-030697117, 2009-0329411R3, 2010-0353121R3, 2010-0376531R3; 2011-0418571R3 (plan amendment to permit DSUs to be paid in common shares); 2012-0457101R3 (plan amendment to allow DSUs that track LP interests' tracking shares). A consolidation of 6801(d) plans of related corporations can be allowed: 2002-0123153. A signing bonus can be deferred: 2007-0259371R3. The election to defer salary must be made before the employee has the right to receive it or constructively receive it: 2014-0535951E5 [Pereira, "The Doctrine of Constructive Receipt", 24(6) *Taxation of Executive Compensation & Retirement [TECR]* (Federated Press) 1636-39 (2015)]. A DSU plan cannot be terminated and converted to an employee stock option plan on a tax-deferred basis: 2006-0178881E5. An amendment giving participants the option to be paid the value of their awards in instalments over 6 years after retirement would cause the plan to cease to qualify: 2015-0565181E5. See also Bullock, "Recent Administrative Positions of the CRA Regarding Deferred Share Unit Arrangements", 22(6) *TECR* 1373-76 (Feb. 2011); Nijhawan, "Canada-US Cross-border DSU Plans — Trips and Traps", 24(1) *TECR* 1559-61 (July/Aug. 2012); Boyd, "DSUs — Permissible Payment Events and Extraordinary Circumstances", XXV(2) *TECR* 2-5 (2017). A US plan under *Internal Revenue Code* §409A does not qualify, but a sub-plan for Canadian residents could be designed to meet Reg. 6801: 2015-0610801C6 [2015 CTF q.2]; but see also 2016-064196117 (plan does not qualify) [Tollstam, "Grandfathering Denied for DSU Plan", 25(10) *Canadian Tax Highlights* (ctf.ca) 5-6 (Oct. 2017)]. See also Notes to ITA 248(1) "salary deferral arrangement" re conversion of a "para. (k)" plan to a DSU.

Definitions [Reg. 6801]: "amount" — ITA 248(1); "arm's length" — ITA 251(1); "calendar year" — *Interpretation Act* 37(1)(a); "corporation" — ITA 248(1), *Interpretation Act* 35(1); "deferral period" — Reg. 6801(a)(i); "employee", "employee benefit plan", "employer", "employment" — ITA 248(1); "fair market value" — see ITA 69(1) Notes; "legal representative" — ITA 248(1); "month" — *Interpretation Act* 35(1); "office" — ITA 248(1); "partnership" — see ITA 96(1) Notes; "person", "prescribed", "property" — ITA 248(1); "related" — ITA 251(2)–(6); "resident in Canada" — ITA 250; "salary or wages" — ITA 248(1); "series" — ITA 248(10); "share" — ITA 248(1); "taxation year" — ITA 249; "trust" — ITA 104(1), 248(1), (3); "writing" — *Interpretation Act* 35(1).

I.T. Technical News: 11 (reporting of amounts paid out of an employee benefit plan.

Advance Tax Rulings: ATR-39: Self-funded leave of absence.

6801.1 COVID-19 — Deferred salary leave plan — (1) [Leave ending up to April 2022] — For the purposes of paragraph 6801(a), if an employee's leave of absence is suspended on or after March 15, 2020 (referred to in this subsection as the "first period") and the leave of absence resumes on or before April 30, 2022 (referred to in this subsection as the "second period"),

(a) the employee's first period and second period are deemed to be one continuous leave of absence; and

(b) amounts held for the employee's benefit under the arrangement shall be paid to the employee out of or under the arrangement no later than the end of the first taxation year that commences after the start of the second period.

(2) [Deferral up to 8 years] — If the six-year period referred to in subparagraph 6801(a)(i) in respect of an arrangement would end during the period beginning on March 15, 2020 and ending on April 30, 2022, the reference in that subparagraph to "six years" is to be read as a reference to "eight years".

Notes: Reg. 6801.1, added by P.C. 2021-522 effective June 10, 2021, is part of a package that included Reg. 8308(4.1), (5.1)-(5.3), 8500(1.3), 8502(i.1). See Finance news release + Backgrounder "Government extends relief for Registered Pension Plans and deferred salary leave plans" (May 20, 2021): "Extended temporary relief would continue to ensure that employees who participate in DSLPs who postponed their leave of absence because of COVID-19 do not face adverse tax consequences for staying on the job during the pandemic. It would also ensure RPP sponsors and their beneficiaries

Regulations

have the flexibility they need to administer their plans and support employees through the pandemic-related disruptions."

The amendments: (1) add temporary "stop-the-clock" rules to DSLPs from March 15/20 to April 30/22 [Reg. 6801.1]; (2) remove restrictions that prohibited RPP administrators from borrowing money [Reg. 8502(i.1)]; (3) extend the deadline for decisions to retroactively credit pensionable service under a defined benefit plan or to make catch-up contributions to money purchase accounts [Reg. 8308(4.1), (5.1)]; (4) permit RPP catch-up contributions by April 2022, towards remaining required contributions that were not made in 2020-21 [Reg. 8308(5.2)-(5.3)]; (5) waive the requirement that an employee have at least 36 months employment to qualify for an "eligible period of reduced pay", so new employees receive unreduced pension coverage [Reg. 8500(1.3)(a)]; (6) in cases of wage rollback periods, allow employers to provide pension contributions at 100% of pre-rollback wages [Reg. 8500(1.3)(c)].

Definitions [Reg. 6801.1]: "amount", "employee", "Minister" — ITA 248(1); "taxation year" — ITA 249.

6802. [Prescribed plan or arrangement — retirement compensation arrangement] — For the purposes of paragraph (n) of the definition "retirement compensation arrangement" in subsection 248(1) of the Act, a prescribed plan or arrangement is

(a) the plan instituted by the *Canada Pension Plan*;

(b) a provincial pension plan as defined in section 3 of the *Canada Pension Plan*;

(c) a plan instituted by the *Unemployment Insurance Act*;

(d) a plan pursuant to an agreement in writing that is established for the purpose of deferring the salary or wages of a professional on-ice official for the official's services as such with the National Hockey League if, in the case of an official resident in Canada, the trust or other person who has custody and control of any funds, investments or other property under the plan is resident in Canada;

(e) an arrangement under which all contributions are made pursuant to a law of Canada or a province, where one of the main purposes of the law is to enforce minimum standards with respect to wages, vacation entitlement or severance pay;

(f) an arrangement under which all contributions are made in connection with a dispute regarding the entitlement of one or more persons to benefits to be received or enjoyed by the person or persons;

(g) a plan or arrangement instituted by the social security legislation of a country other than Canada or of a state, province or other political subdivision of such a country; or

(h) a trust established

(i) to hold shares of Air Canada, pursuant to the June 2009 memorandum of understanding between Air Canada and certain trade unions who represent employees of Air Canada, if

(A) the shares are held by the trust for the benefit of the trade unions, and

(B) each of the trade unions may direct the trustee to contribute, from time to time, amounts received or receivable by the trust in respect of the shares, whether as dividends, proceeds of disposition or otherwise, to one or more registered pension plans under which Air Canada is a participating employer, or

(ii) in relation to the wind-up of a registered pension plan sponsored by Fraser Papers Inc., if

(A) shares are held by the trust for the benefit of the registered pension plan, and

(B) the trustee will contribute amounts received or receivable by the trust in respect of the shares, whether as dividends, proceeds of disposition or otherwise, to the registered pension plan, not later than December 31, 2018.

Proposed Amendment — Reg. 6802

Letter from Dept. of Finance, June 19, 2017: Dear [xxx]:

I am writing in response to your letter of February 15, 2017 and further discussions in which you outline proposed transactions and identify certain technical issues with the income tax rules that would apply to the transactions.

You advise that your client, [xxx] (the "Employer"), [xxx] as purchaser (the "Purchaser") [xxx]. As part of the [xxx]

- [xxx] (the "Trust") will be established for the benefit of [xxx] registered pension plans ("RPPs") sponsored by the Employer [xxx].

- A partnership (the "Partnership") will be established to hold certain [xxx] assets sold to it at fair market value by the Employer in exchange for a promissory note.

- The Trust will be a limited partner receiving 50% of the common units of the Partnership. The other limited partners of the Partnership will receive (in aggregate) 50% of the common units and will be employee life and health trusts ("ELHTs") established to provide non-pension benefits to retirees (and their survivors) of the Employer.

- The Employer will make cash contributions to the RPPs and ELHTs equal to the face amount of the promissory note, 50% to the RPPs ("RPP Contributions") and 50% to the ELHTs ("ELHT Contributions"). The RPPs and ELHTs will use the cash to subscribe for special units of the Partnership. The Partnership will use the proceeds to repay the promissory note.

- It is expected that the Partnership [xxx] will make priority distributions on the special units of the Partnership to the RPPs not exceeding the RPP Contributions and to the ELHTs not exceeding the ELHT Contributions.

- Pursuant to the agreement establishing the Trust, the Trust will receive a 50% share of the "balance of the Partnership's income and distributable cash-flow", after the priority distributions made on the special units of the Partnership. The Trust will also receive a portion of dividends and profits that the Purchaser will derive from the ownership or disposition of shares of the Employer.

- The Trust will make cash contributions to the RPPs based on an allocation formula to be determined by provincial regulation.

You note that the RPPs have large solvency deficits and that one of the purposes of the [xxx] is to provide additional funding to reduce those deficits.

In this context, you have requested that we recommend amendments to the Income Tax Regulations (the "Regulations") which would:

- ensure that the Trust and the Partnership are not considered to be retirement compensation arrangements as defined in the *Income Tax Act*; and

- permit contributions from the Trust to the RPPs without jeopardizing the registration of those plans.

We agree that the requested changes would not raise income tax policy concerns. We are prepared to recommend to the Minister of Finance that he recommend to the Governor General in Council that section 6802 of the Regulations be amended to add the Trust and the Partnership to the list of prescribed arrangements that are excluded from the definition "retirement compensation arrangement" and therefore also from the retirement compensation arrangement rules.

We would also recommend that these proposed amendments apply in respect of a trust and partnership established, and pension contributions made, after May 2017.

While I cannot offer any assurance that the Minister of Finance or the Governor General in Council will agree with our recommendations, I hope that this statement of our intention is helpful to you.

Thank you for writing to us on this matter.

Yours sincerely,

Brian Ernewein, General Director, Legislation, Tax Policy Branch

Related Provisions: ITA 207.6(6) — Rules applicable to a prescribed plan or arrangement; Reg. 8502(b)(v.1) — Air Canada or Fraser Papers pension trust.

Notes: Reg. 6802(c) needs to be amended to refer to the *Employment Insurance Act*.

Reg. 6802(h) added by 2002-2013 technical bill, effective 2009. It implements proposals in Finance comfort letters of Oct. 23, 2009 and Dec. 23, 2010.

Reg. 6802(e) replaced and (f) and (g) added by P.C. 1996-911, effective October 9, 1996. The rules formerly under Reg. 6802(e) have been incorporated in new Reg. 6804.

Definitions [Reg. 6802]: "amount" — ITA 248(1); "Canada" — ITA 255, *Interpretation Act* 35(1); "disposition", "dividend", "employee", "employer" — ITA 248(1); "person", "prescribed", "property" — ITA 248(1); "province" — *Interpretation Act* 35(1); "provincial pension plan" — *Canada Pension Plan* s. 3; "registered pension plan" — ITA 248(1); "resident in Canada" — ITA 250; "salary or wages", "share" — ITA 248(1); "trust" — ITA 104(1), 248(1), (3); "writing" — *Interpretation Act* 35(1).

6802.1 [Prescribed pension plan] — (1) For the purpose of paragraph 8(1)(m.2) of the Act, each of the following is a prescribed plan:

(a) the pension plan established as a consequence of the establishment, by section 27 of the *Members of Parliament Retiring Allowances Act*, of the Members of Parliament Retirement Compensation Arrangements Account; and

(b) the pension plan established by the *Retirement Compensation Arrangements Regulations, No. 1*.

(2) For the purpose of subsection 207.6(6) of the Act, each of the following is a prescribed plan or arrangement:

(a) the pension plan established as a consequence of the establishment, by section 27 of the *Members of Parliament Retiring Allowances Act*, of the Members of Parliament Retirement Compensation Arrangements Account;

(b) the pension plan established by the *Retirement Compensation Arrangements Regulations, No. 1*; and

(c) the pension plan established by the *Retirement Compensation Arrangements Regulations, No. 2*.

Notes [Reg. 6802.1]: Reg. 6802.1 added by P.C. 1999-2211, paras. (1)(a) and (2)(a) effective 1992; paras. (1)(b) and (2)(b) effective December 15, 1994; and para. (2)(c) effective April 1995.

Definitions [Reg. 6802.1]: "Parliament" — *Interpretation Act* 35(1); "prescribed" — ITA 248(1).

6803. [Prescribed plan or arrangement — foreign retirement arrangement]

— For the purposes of the definition "foreign retirement arrangement" in subsection 248(1) of the Act, a prescribed plan or arrangement is a plan or arrangement to which subsection 408(a), (b) or (h) of the United States' *Internal Revenue Code of 1986*, as amended from time to time, applies.

Notes: IRC §408(a) defines "individual retirement account" (IRA) as a trust that meets certain conditions. §408(b) defines "individual retirement annuity", which is similar but is an annuity or endowment contract issued by an insurer. §408(h) defines a "custodial account" as an account held by a bank or other person that meets all of the other conditions for an IRA, and which is treated as a trust and therefore effectively deemed to be an IRA. An IRA is a "foreign retirement arrangement" (FRA) even if it is a custodial account: *McKenzie*, 2017 TCC 56.

A UK or Swiss pension is not a FRA: VIEWS docs 2005-0156471E5, 2008-0274271E5. Nor is a 408(p) SIMPLE IRA, 408(k) SEP IRA, 401(a), 401(k), 403(b) or 457(b) plan, or a Roth IRA: Income Tax Folio S5-F3-C1 ¶1.26.

See also Notes to ITA 248(1)"foreign retirement arrangement" and 56(12).

Reg. 6803 added by P.C. 1992-2416, effective 1990; amended by P.C. 2007-849 effective June 13, 2007.

Definitions [Reg. 6803]: "prescribed" — ITA 248(1); "United States" — *Interpretation Act* 35(1).

Income Tax Folios: S5-F3-C1: Taxation of a Roth IRA.

I.T. Technical News: 43 (taxation of Roth IRAs).

6804. Contributions to foreign plans — (1) Definitions
— The definitions in this subsection apply in this section.

"foreign non-profit organization" means,

(a) at any time before 1995, an organization

(i) that at that time meets the conditions in subparagraphs (b)(i) to (iii), or

(ii) that at that time is not operated for the purpose of profit, and whose assets are situated primarily outside Canada throughout the calendar year that includes that time, and

(b) at any time after 1994, an organization that at that time

(i) is not operated for the purpose of profit,

(ii) has its main place of management outside Canada, and

(iii) carries on its activities primarily outside Canada.

"foreign plan" means a plan or arrangement (determined without regard to subsection 207.6(5) of the Act) that would, but for paragraph (l) of the definition "retirement compensation arrangement" in subsection 248(1) of the Act, be a retirement compensation arrangement.

"qualifying entity" means a non-resident entity that holds all or part of the assets of a foreign plan where the following conditions are satisfied:

(a) the entity is resident in a country under the laws of which an income tax is imposed, and

(b) where those laws provide an exemption from tax, a reduced rate of tax or other favourable tax treatment for entities that hold assets of pension or other retirement plans, the entity qualifies for the favourable treatment.

(2) Electing employer — For the purposes of this section, an employer is an electing employer for a calendar year with respect to a foreign plan where

(a) the employer has sent or delivered to the Minister a letter stating that the employer elects to have this section apply with respect to contributions to the foreign plan, and

(b) the letter was sent or delivered on or before

(i) the last day of February in the year following the first calendar year after 1991 in which a contribution that is or would be if subsection 207.6(5.1) of the Act were read without reference to paragraph (a) of that subsection, a resident's contribution (as defined in that subsection) was made under the foreign plan in respect of services rendered by an individual to the employer, or

(ii) any later date that is acceptable to the Minister,

except that an employer is not an electing employer for a year with respect to a foreign plan if the Minister has granted written permission for the employer to revoke, for the year or a preceding calendar year, the election made under paragraph (a) in respect of the foreign plan.

(3) Election by union — Except as otherwise permitted in writing by the Minister, an election made by a trade union for the purpose of subsection (2) is valid only if it is made by the highest-level structural unit of the union.

(4) Contributions made before 1992 — For the purpose of paragraph 207.6(5.1)(a) of the Act, a contribution made under a foreign plan by a person or body of persons in a calendar year before 1992 is a prescribed contribution where

(a) the contribution is paid to a qualifying entity;

(b) each employer (in this subsection referred to as a "contributor") that makes a contribution under the foreign plan in the year is

(i) a non-resident corporation throughout the year,

(ii) a partnership that makes contributions under the foreign plan primarily in respect of services rendered outside Canada to the partnership by non-resident employees, or

(iii) a foreign non-profit organization throughout the year;

(c) if a corporation or partnership (other than a corporation or partnership that is a foreign non-profit organization throughout the year) is a contributor, no individual who is entitled (either absolutely or contingently) to benefits under the foreign plan is a member of a registered pension plan, or a beneficiary under a deferred profit sharing plan, to which a contributor, or a person or body of persons not dealing at arm's length with a contributor, makes, or is required to make, contributions in relation to the year;

(d) contributions made in the year under the foreign plan for the benefit of individuals resident in Canada are reasonable in relation to contributions made under the plan for the benefit of non-resident individuals; and

(e) the foreign plan is not a pension plan the registration of which under the Act has been revoked.

(5) Contributions made in 1992, 1993 or 1994 — For the purpose of paragraph 207.6(5.1)(a) of the Act, a contribution made under a foreign plan by a person or body of persons at any time in 1992, 1993 or 1994 in respect of services rendered by an individual to an employer is a prescribed contribution where

(a) the contribution is paid to a qualifying entity;

(b) the employer is an electing employer for the year with respect to the foreign plan;

(c) if the employer is not at that time a foreign non-profit organization, the individual is not a member of a registered pension plan (other than a specified multi-employer plan, as defined in subsection 147.1(1) of the Act), or a deferred profit sharing plan, in which the employer, or a person or body of persons that does not deal at arm's length with the employer, participates; and

(d) either

(i) the employer is

(A) a corporation that is not resident in Canada at that time,

(B) a partnership that makes contributions under the foreign plan primarily in respect of services rendered outside Canada to the partnership by non-resident employees, or

(C) a foreign non-profit organization at that time, or

(ii) the individual was non-resident at any time before the contribution is made and became a member of the foreign plan before the end of the month after the month in which the individual became resident in Canada.

(6) Contributions made after 1994 — For the purposes of paragraph 207.6(5.1)(a) of the Act, a contribution made under a foreign plan by a person or body of persons at any time in a calendar year after 1994 in respect of services rendered by an individual to an employer is a prescribed contribution where

(a) the contribution is paid to a qualifying entity;

(b) the employer is an electing employer for the year with respect to the foreign plan;

(c) if the employer is at that time a foreign non-profit organization,

(i) the amount that, if subsection 8301(1) were read without reference to paragraph (b) of that subsection, would be the individual's pension adjustment for the year in respect of the employer is nil, or

(ii) the amount that would be the individual's pension adjustment for the year in respect of the employer if

(A) all contributions made under the foreign plan in the year in respect of the individual were prescribed by this subsection,

(B) where the year is 1996, section 8308.1 were read without reference to subsection (4.1), and

(C) where the year is 1997, subparagraph 8308.1(2)(b)(v) were read as:

"(v) the amount, if any, by which 18% of the individual's resident compensation from the employer for the year exceeds $1,000, and"

does not exceed the lesser of

(D) the money purchase limit for the year, and

(E) 18% of the individual's compensation (as defined in subsection 147.1(1) of the Act) for the year from the employer;

(d) if

(i) the employer is at that time a foreign non-profit organization, and

(ii) a period in the year throughout which the individual rendered services to the employer would be, under paragraph 8507(3)(a), a qualifying period of the individual with respect to another employer if that paragraph were read without reference to subparagraph (iv) of that paragraph,

subsection 8308(7) applies with respect to the determination of the individual's pension adjustment for the year with respect to each employer; and

(e) if the employer is not at that time a foreign non-profit organization,

(i) the individual was non-resident at any time before the contribution is made,

(ii) the individual became a member of the foreign plan before the end of the month after the month in which the individual became resident in Canada, and

(iii) the individual is not a member of a registered pension plan, or a deferred profit sharing plan, in which the employer, or a person or body of persons that does not deal at arm's length with the employer, participates.

Notes: Reg. 6804(6)(c)(ii) amended by P.C. 1998-2256, effective 1996 (thus overriding its enactment; see Notes at end of Reg. 6804). The amendment effectively added cls. (B) and (C).

(7) Replacement plan — For the purposes of subparagraphs (5)(d)(ii) and (6)(e)(ii), where benefits provided to an individual under a particular plan or arrangement are replaced by benefits under another plan or arrangement, the other plan or arrangement is deemed, in respect of the individual, to be the same plan or arrangement as the particular plan or arrangement.

Notes [Reg. 6804]: Reg. 6804 added by P.C. 1996-911, effective Oct. 9, 1996. (To some extent these rules were formerly in Reg. 6802(e).) Prescribed contributions under Reg. 6804(4)–(6) are excluded from the definition of "resident's contributions" in ITA 207.6(5.1). They are thus exempted from the rules in ITA 207.6(5) which treat certain contributions to foreign pension plans as RCA contributions.

Definitions [Reg. 6804]: "amount" — ITA 248(1); "arm's length" — ITA 251(1); "calendar year" — *Interpretation Act* 37(1)(a); "Canada" — ITA 255, *Interpretation Act* 35(1); "contributor" — Reg. 6804(4); "corporation" — ITA 248(1), *Interpretation Act* 35(1); "deferred profit sharing plan" — ITA 147(1), 248(1); "electing employer" — Reg. 6804(2); "employee", "employer" — ITA 248(1); "foreign non-profit organization", "foreign plan" — Reg. 6804(1); "individual", "Minister" — ITA 248(1); "money purchase limit" — ITA 147.1(1), 248(1); "month" — *Interpretation Act* 35(1); "non-resident" — ITA 248(1); "partnership" — see ITA 96(1) Notes; "pension adjustment", "person", "prescribed" — ITA 248(1); "qualifying entity" — Reg. 6804(1); "registered pension plan" — ITA 248(1); "resident in Canada" — ITA 250; "retirement compensation arrangement" — ITA 248(1); "specified multi-employer plan" — ITA 147.1(1), Reg. 8510(2), (3); "written" — *Interpretation Act* 35(1)"writing".

PART LXIX — [6900] PRESCRIBED OFFSHORE INVESTMENT FUND PROPERTIES

Notes: Added in 1986. An earlier Part LXIX, "Aviation Turbine Fuel", applied from Feb. 1982 to April 1983 for purposes of (now-repealed) ITA 234.1.

6900. [Prescribed offshore investment fund property] — For the purpose of paragraph 94.1(2)(a) [94.1(2)"designated cost"] of the Act, an offshore investment fund property (within the meaning assigned by subsection 94.1(1) of the Act) of a taxpayer that

(a) was acquired by him by way of bequest or inheritance from a deceased person who, throughout the five years immediately preceding his death, was not resident in Canada,

(b) had not been acquired by the deceased from a person resident in Canada, and

(c) is not property substituted for property acquired by the deceased from a person resident in Canada

is a prescribed offshore investment fund property of the taxpayer.

Notes [Reg. 6900]: Where a non-resident who owns Reg. 6900 property immigrates to Canada, ITA 128.1(1) does not cause the property to cease to be prescribed: VIEWS doc 2014-0555081E5.

Definitions [Reg. 6900]: "person", "prescribed", "property" — ITA 248(1); "resident in Canada" — ITA 250; "substituted" — ITA 248(5); "taxpayer" — ITA 248(1).

PART LXX — [7000–7001] ACCRUED INTEREST ON DEBT OBLIGATIONS

7000. (1) Prescribed debt obligations — For the purpose of subsection 12(9) of the Act, each of the following debt obligations (other than a debt obligation that is an indexed debt obligation) in respect of which a taxpayer has at any time acquired an interest is a prescribed debt obligation:

(a) a particular debt obligation in respect of which no interest is stipulated to be payable in respect of its principal amount;

(b) a particular debt obligation in respect of which the proportion of the payments of principal to which the taxpayer is entitled is not equal to the proportion of the payments of interest to which he is entitled;

(c) a particular debt obligation, other than one described in paragraph (a) or (b), in respect of which it can be determined, at the time the taxpayer acquired the interest therein, that the maximum amount of interest payable thereon in a year ending after that time is less than the maximum amount of interest payable thereon in a subsequent year; and

(d) a particular debt obligation, other than one described in paragraph (a), (b) or (c), in respect of which the amount of interest to be paid in respect of any taxation year is, under the terms and conditions of the obligation, dependent on a contingency existing after the year,

and, for the purposes of this subsection, a debt obligation includes, for greater certainty, all of the issuer's obligations to pay principal and interest under that obligation.

Related Provisions: ITA 18.1(14) — Right to receive production deemed to be debt obligation; ITA 20(14.2) — Sale of linked note — deemed interest; Reg. 230(1)"security"(c.1) — Information return required.

Notes: In *Goulet*, 2011 FCA 164 (leave to appeal denied 2011 CarswellNat 5307 (SCC)), non-interest-bearing debt was held to be a prescribed debt obligation (PDO).

For detailed discussion of the purpose and operation of Reg. 7000(1)-(2) see *Cassan*, 2017 TCC 174 (FCA appeal settled A-304-17), paras. 389-410. Loans in the EquiGenesis donation shelters were held not to be PDO, as there was no determinable return for 19 years.

CRA practice from 1992, per numerous VIEWS docs, was not to tax equity-linked notes under Reg. 7000(1)-(2) annually, but only on maturity, or when the return was locked in, or when the note was sold: *Ludmer*, 2018 QCCS 3381, paras. 250-265 and footnotes; aff'd 2020 QCCA 697; leave to appeal denied 2021 CarswellQue 2160 (SCC). (CRA was liable for proposing to apply Reg. 7000 because it did not take the same position with other taxpayers even though its view was otherwise reasonable: QCCS paras. 386-440, QCCA para. 67.) CRA also issued 6 technical interpretations that were never released as VIEWS docs so as not to alert the public to its position: QCCS paras. 107, 293, 459-465. See also QCCS paras. 518-539 on applying Reg. 7000. Reg. 7000 requires conversion to C$ before calculating deemed annual interest: QCCS paras. 522-531, QCCA para. 88.

For more CRA interpretation see VIEWS docs 2003-0006645 (callable step-up bonds fall under para. (c)), 2005-0137041C6 (banker's acceptance is a PDO), 2007-0225141R3 (pool of mortgages not PDO), 2007-0237351R3 (stock-linked note is PDO but cannot be calculated until maturity; see also Martin Sorensen, "Canada Revenue Agency Reviews Index-linked Notes", XV(4) *Corporate Finance* (Federated Press) 1715 (2009)); 2011-0407301R3 and 2011-0431891R3 (mortgage pool is not PDO).

Opening words of Reg. 7000(1) amended by P.C. 1996-1419, effective for debt obligations issued after October 16, 1991, to add the exclusion for indexed debt obligations.

Advance Tax Rulings: ATR-61: Interest accrual rules.

(2) [Deemed interest on prescribed debt obligation] — For the purposes of subsection 12(9) of the Act, the amount determined in prescribed manner that is deemed to accrue to a taxpayer as interest on a prescribed debt obligation in each taxation year during which he holds an interest in the obligation is,

(a) in the case of a prescribed debt obligation described in paragraph (1)(a), the amount of interest that would be determined in respect thereof if interest thereon for that year were computed on a compound interest basis using the maximum of all rates each of which is a rate computed

(i) in respect of each possible circumstance under which an interest of the taxpayer in the obligation could mature or be surrendered or retracted, and

(ii) using assumptions concerning the interest rate and compounding period that will result in a present value, at the date of purchase of the interest, of all the maximum payments thereunder, equal to the cost thereof to the taxpayer;

(b) in the case of a prescribed debt obligation described in paragraph (1)(b), the aggregate of all amounts each of which is the amount of interest that would be determined in respect of his interest in a payment under the obligation if interest thereon for that year were computed on a compound interest basis using the specified cost of his interest therein and the specified interest rate in respect of his total interest in the obligation, and for the purposes of this paragraph,

(i) the **"specified cost"** of his interest in a payment under the obligation is its present value at the date of purchase computed using the specified interest rate, and

(ii) the **"specified interest rate"** is the maximum of all rates each of which is a rate computed

(A) in respect of each possible circumstance under which an interest of the taxpayer in the obligation could mature or be surrendered or retracted, and

(B) using assumptions concerning the interest rate and compounding period that will result in a present value, at the date of purchase of the interest, of all the maximum payments to the taxpayer in respect of his total interest in the obligation, equal to the cost of that interest to the taxpayer;

(c) in the case of a prescribed debt obligation described in paragraph (1)(c), other than an obligation in respect of which paragraph (c.1) applies, the greater of

(i) the maximum amount of interest thereon in respect of the year, and

(ii) the maximum amount of interest that would be determined in respect thereof if interest thereon for that year were computed on a compound interest basis using the maximum of all rates each of which is a rate computed

(A) in respect of each possible circumstance under which an interest of the taxpayer in the obligation could mature or be surrendered or retracted, and

(B) using assumptions concerning the interest rate and compounding period that will result in a present value, at the date of issue of the obligation, of all the maximum payments thereunder, equal to its principal amount;

(c.1) in the case of a prescribed debt obligation described in paragraph (1)(c) for which

(i) the rate of interest stipulated to be payable in respect of each period throughout which the obligation is outstanding is fixed at the date of issue of the obligation, and

(ii) the stipulated rate of interest applicable at each time is not less than each stipulated rate of interest applicable before that time,

the amount of interest that would be determined in respect of the year if interest on the obligation for that year were computed on a compound interest basis using the maximum of all rates each of which is the compound interest rate that, for a particular assumption with respect to when the taxpayer's interest in the obligation will mature or be surrendered or retracted, results in a present value (at the date the taxpayer acquires the interest in the obligation) of all payments under the obligation after the acquisition by the taxpayer of the taxpayer's interest in the obligation equal to the principal amount of the obligation at the date of acquisition; and

(d) in the case of a prescribed debt obligation described in paragraph (1)(d), the maximum amount of interest thereon that could be payable thereunder in respect of that year.

Related Provisions: ITA 18.1(14) — Right to receive production deemed to be debt obligation.

Notes: See Reg. 7000(1) Notes. For interpretation of paras. (c) and (c.1) see VIEWS doc 2004-0102421E5. See also Wortsman, Nesbitt et al., "Recent Transactions in Corporate Finance", 2008 Cdn Tax Foundation conference report, at 9:37-49.

Reg. 7000(2)(c.1) added, and (c) amended to refer to it, by P.C. 1996-570, effective for 1993 and later taxation years.

Advance Tax Rulings: ATR-61: Interest accrual rules.

(3) [Bonus or premium] — For the purpose of this section, any bonus or premium payable under a debt obligation is considered to be an amount of interest payable under the obligation.

Notes: Reg. 7000(3) amended by P.C. 1996-1419, for debt obligations issued after Oct. 16, 1991, to apply for purposes of s. 7000 rather than for all of Part LII.

Advance Tax Rulings: ATR-61: Interest accrual rules.

Regulations

(4) [Conversion privilege or option to extend] — For the purposes of this section, where

(a) a taxpayer has an interest in a debt obligation (in this subsection referred to as the "first interest") under which there is a conversion privilege or an option to extend its term upon maturity, and

(b) at the time the obligation was issued (or, if later, at the time the conversion privilege or option was added or modified), circumstances could reasonably be foreseen under which the holder of the obligation would, by exercising the conversion privilege or option, acquire an interest in a debt obligation with a principal amount less than its fair market value at the time of acquisition,

the subsequent interest in any debt obligation acquired by the taxpayer by exercising the conversion privilege or option shall be considered to be a continuation of the first interest.

Notes: Reg. 7000(4)(b) added by P.C. 1996-570, for debt obligations acquired by reason of the exercise after Aug. 11, 1993 of a conversion privilege or an option to extend the term of another debt obligation.

(5) [Interest computations] — For the purposes of making the computations referred to in paragraphs (2)(a), (b), (c) and (c.1), the compounding period shall not exceed one year and any interest rate used shall be constant from the date of acquisition or issue, as the case may be, until the time of maturity, surrender or retraction.

Notes: Reg. 7000(5) amended by P.C. 1996-570, for 1993 and later tax years, to add reference to Reg. 7000(2)(c.1) and to change "date" to "time" (two places).

(6) [Prescribed contract] — For the purpose of the definition "investment contract" in subsection 12(11) of the Act, a registered retirement savings plan or a registered retirement income fund, other than a plan or fund to which a trust is a party, is a prescribed contract throughout a calendar year where an annuitant (as defined in subsection 146(1) or 146.3(1) of the Act, as the case may be) under the plan or fund is alive at any time in the year or was alive at any time in the preceding calendar year.

Related Provisions: ITA 142.3(1)(c) — No income accrual from specified debt obligation.

Notes: Reg. 7000(6) amended by P.C. 1996-568, for 1993 and later tax years. The effect of the amendment is to extend the exemption from the accrual rules, where an RRSP or RRIF annuitant has died, to after the end of the first calendar year beginning after the death. (This is consistent with amendments to ITA 146(4) and 146.3(3.1) made by 1993 technical bill.)

Definitions [Reg. 7000]: "amount" — ITA 248(1); "calendar year" — *Interpretation Act* 37(1)(a); "debt obligation" — Reg. 7000(1); "fair market value" — see ITA 69(1) Notes; "first interest" — Reg. 7000(4)(a); "indexed debt obligation", "prescribed", "principal amount" — ITA 248(1); "registered retirement income fund" — ITA 146.3(1), 248(1); "registered retirement savings plan" — ITA 146(1), 248(1); "specified cost" — Reg. 7000(2)(b)(i); "specified interest rate" — Reg. 7000(2)(b)(ii); "taxation year" — ITA 249; "taxpayer" — ITA 248(1); "trust" — ITA 104(1), 248(1), (3).

7001. Indexed debt obligations — **(1)** For the purpose of subparagraph 16(6)(a)(i) of the Act, where at any time in a taxation year a taxpayer holds an interest in an indexed debt obligation, there is prescribed as interest receivable and received by the taxpayer in the year in respect of the obligation the total of

(a) the amount, if any, by which

(i) the total of all amounts each of which is the amount by which the amount payable in respect of the taxpayer's interest in an indexed payment under the obligation (other than a payment that is an excluded payment with respect to the taxpayer for the year) has, because of a change in the purchasing power of money, increased over an inflation adjustment period of the obligation that ends in the year

exceeds the total of

(ii) that portion of the total, if any, determined under subparagraph (i) that is required, otherwise than by subsection 16(6) of the Act, to be included in computing the taxpayer's income for the year or a preceding taxation year, and

(iii) the total of all amounts each of which is the amount by which the amount payable in respect of the taxpayer's interest in an indexed payment under the obligation (other than a

payment that is an excluded payment with respect to the taxpayer for the year) has, by reason of a change in the purchasing power of money, decreased over an inflation adjustment period of the obligation that ends in the year, and

(b) where the non-indexed debt obligation associated with the indexed debt obligation is an obligation that is described in any of paragraphs 7000(1)(a) to (d), the amount of interest that would be determined under subsection 7000(2) to accrue to the taxpayer in respect of the non-indexed debt obligation in the particular period that

(i) begins at the beginning of the first inflation adjustment period of the indexed debt obligation in respect of the taxpayer that ends in the year, and

(ii) ends at the end of the last inflation adjustment period of the indexed debt obligation in respect of the taxpayer that ends in the year

if the particular period were a taxation year of the taxpayer and the taxpayer's interest in the indexed debt obligation were an interest in the non-indexed debt obligation.

(2) For the purposes of subparagraph 16(6)(a)(ii) of the Act, where at any time in a taxation year a taxpayer holds an interest in an indexed debt obligation, there is prescribed as interest payable and paid by the taxpayer in the year in respect of the obligation the amount, if any, by which

(a) the total of the amounts, if any, determined under subparagraphs (1)(a)(ii) and (iii) for the year in respect of the taxpayer's interest in the obligation

exceeds

(b) the amount, if any, determined under subparagraph (1)(a)(i) for the year in respect of the taxpayer's interest in the obligation.

(3) For the purposes of subparagraph 16(6)(b)(i) of the Act, where at any time in a taxation year an indexed debt obligation is an obligation of a taxpayer, there is prescribed as interest payable in respect of the year by the taxpayer in respect of the obligation the amount, if any, that would be determined under paragraph (1)(a) in respect of the taxpayer for the year if, at each time at which the obligation is an obligation of the taxpayer, the taxpayer were the holder of the obligation and not the debtor under the obligation.

(4) For the purposes of subparagraph 16(6)(b)(ii) of the Act, where at any time in a taxation year an indexed debt obligation is an obligation of a taxpayer, there is prescribed as interest receivable and received by the taxpayer in the year in respect of the obligation the amount, if any, that would be determined under subsection (2) in respect of the taxpayer for the year if, at each time at which the obligation is an obligation of the taxpayer, the taxpayer were the holder of the obligation and not the debtor under the obligation.

(5) For the purpose of determining the amount by which an indexed payment under an indexed debt obligation has increased or decreased over a period because of a change in the purchasing power of money, the amount of the indexed payment at any time shall be determined using the method for computing the amount of the payment at the time it is to be made, adjusted in a reasonable manner to take into account the earlier date of computation.

(6) For the purposes of this section, the non-indexed debt obligation associated with an indexed debt obligation is the debt obligation that would result if the indexed debt obligation were amended to eliminate all adjustments determined by reference to changes in the purchasing power of money.

(7) In this section,

"excluded payment" with respect to a taxpayer for a taxation year means an indexed payment under an indexed debt obligation where

(a) the non-indexed debt obligation associated with the indexed debt obligation provides for the payment, at least annually, of interest at a single fixed rate, and

(b) the indexed payment corresponds to one of the interest payments referred to in paragraph (a),

but does not include payments under an indexed debt obligation where, at any time in the year, the taxpayer's proportionate interest in a payment to be made under the obligation after that time differs from the taxpayer's proportionate interest in any other payment to be made under the obligation after that time;

"indexed payment" means, in relation to an indexed debt obligation, an amount payable under the obligation that is determined by reference to the purchasing power of money;

"inflation adjustment period" of an indexed debt obligation means, in relation to a taxpayer,

(a) where the taxpayer acquires and disposes of the taxpayer's interest in the obligation in the same regular adjustment period of the obligation, the period that begins when the taxpayer acquires the interest in the obligation and ends when the taxpayer disposes of the interest, and

(b) in any other case, each of the following consecutive periods:

(i) the period that begins when the taxpayer acquires the taxpayer's interest in the obligation and ends at the end of the regular adjustment period of the obligation in which the taxpayer acquires the interest in the obligation,

(ii) each succeeding regular adjustment period of the obligation throughout which the taxpayer holds the interest in the obligation, and

(iii) where the taxpayer does not dispose of the interest in the obligation at the end of a regular adjustment period of the obligation, the period that begins immediately after the last period referred to in subparagraphs (i) and (ii) and that ends when the taxpayer disposes of the interest in the obligation;

"regular adjustment period" of an indexed debt obligation means

(a) where the terms or conditions of the obligation provide that, while the obligation is outstanding, indexed payments are to be made at regular intervals not exceeding 12 months in length, each of the following periods:

(i) the period that begins when the obligation is issued and ends when the first indexed payment is required to be made, and

(ii) each succeeding period beginning when an indexed payment is required to be made and ending when the next indexed payment is required to be made,

(b) where paragraph (a) does not apply and the obligation is outstanding for less than 12 months, the period that begins when the obligation is issued and ends when the obligation ceases to be outstanding, and

(c) in any other case, each of the following periods:

(i) the 12-month period that begins when the obligation is issued,

(ii) each succeeding 12-month period throughout which the obligation is outstanding, and

(iii) where the obligation ceases to be outstanding at a time other than the end of a 12-month period referred to in subparagraph (i) or (ii), the period that commences immediately after the last period referred to in those subparagraphs and that ends when the obligation ceases to be outstanding.

Notes: Reg. 7001 added by P.C. 1996-1419, for debt obligations issued after Oct. 16, 1991.

Definitions [Reg. 7001]: "amount" — ITA 248(1); "associated" — ITA 256; "debt obligation" — Reg. 7001(6); "disposes" — ITA 248(1)"disposition"; "excluded payment" — Reg. 7001(7); "indexed debt obligation" — ITA 248(1); "indexed payment", "inflation adjustment period" — Reg. 7001(7); "month" — *Interpretation Act* 35(1); "prescribed" — ITA 248(1); "regular adjustment period" — Reg. 7001(7); "taxation year" — ITA 249; "taxpayer" — ITA 248(1).

PART LXXI — [7100] PRESCRIBED FEDERAL CROWN CORPORATIONS

7100. For the purposes of subsections 27(2) and (3), the definition "private corporation" in subsection 89(1) and subsection 124(3) of the Act, the following are prescribed federal Crown corporations:

(a) Canada Deposit Insurance Corporation;

(b) Canada Hibernia Holding Corporation;

(c) Canada Lands Company Limited;

(d) Canada Mortgage and Housing Corporation;

(e) Canada Post Corporation;

(f) Canadian Broadcasting Corporation;

(g) Cape Breton Development Corporation;

(h) Freshwater Fish Marketing Corporation;

(i) Royal Canadian Mint;

(j) VIA Rail Canada Inc.; and

(k) Project Deliver II Ltd.

Notes: See Notes to ITA 27(2).

Project Deliver II Ltd. (Crown corp that bought Kinder Morgan pipeline) added by P.C. 2018-989, effective July 25, 2018.

Reg. 7100 amended to apply to ITA 89(1)"private corporation" by P.C. 2003-1921, effective July 14, 1990. This had been proposed in the May 1991 Dept. of Finance Technical Notes to then ITA 89(1)(f).

Reg. 7100 amended by P.C. 2003-1921 to change from a simple list to paras. (a)–(j), effective for taxation years that begin after Dec. 10, 2001. The effect was to remove Farm Credit Canada (see below), Petro Canada (no longer a Crown corporation), the St. Lawrence Seaway Authority (dissolved on Dec. 1, 1998) and Teleglobe Canada (the federal government sold its interest in Teleglobe on July 29, 1993).

Air Canada deleted by P.C. 1996-1927, effective November 1, 1995.

Canada Development Investment Corp (CDIC) deleted by P.C. 2003-1921, effective Jan. 3, 1995. CDIC has not competed with private sector entities since that date.

Canada Hibernia Holding Corp added by P.C. 2003-1921, effective January 3, 1995. This was a subsidiary of CDIC; the amendment causes it to keep its tax status when CDIC was deleted.

Canada Lands Company Ltd. added by P.C. 1996-1927, effective Nov. 1, 1996.

Canada Post Corp. added by P.C. 1994-930, effective March 27, 1994.

Farm Credit Corp. changed to Farm Credit Canada by S.C. 2001, c. 22 (*Farm Credit Corporation Act*), effective June 14, 2001, and removed from the list for tax years that begin after Dec. 10, 2001. This puts FCC on the same footing for tax purposes as Export Development Corp. and Business Development Bank, both of which are not prescribed.

National Railways (as defined in the pre-1966 *CN-CP Act*) deleted by P.C. 1996-1927, effective 1996.

Theratronics International Corp. added and deleted by P.C. 2003-1921, effective from Jan. 3, 1995 (the date CDIC was removed) to May 20, 1998 (the date it was privatized).

Definitions [Reg. 7100]: "prescribed" — ITA 248(1).

Interpretation Bulletins: IT-347R2: Crown corporations (archived).

PART LXXII — [7200] [REPEALED]

Notes: Reg. 7200 repealed by P.C. 2001-1378, effective Aug. 15, 2001. It set out the prescribed addition and reduction for a corporation's cumulative deduction account. The CDA, which limited a corporation's lifetime retained earnings eligible for the small business deduction to a fixed dollar amount, was repealed in 1984 as part of simplification of the small business rules in ITA 125. Large corporations are now prevented from using the small business deduction by ITA 125(5.1)(a).

PART LXXIII — [7300–7310] PRESCRIBED AMOUNTS AND AREAS [AND PENALTIES]

7300. [Prescribed amounts] — For the purposes of paragraph 12(1)(x) of the Act, "prescribed amount" means

(a) any amount paid to a corporation by the Native Economic Development Board created under Order in Council P.C. 1983-3394 of October 31, 1983 pursuant to the Native Economic Development Program or paid to a corporation under the Aboriginal Capital Corporation Program of the Canadian Aboriginal Ec-

Regulations

onomic Development Strategy, where all of the shares of the capital stock of the corporation are

(i) owned by aboriginal individuals,

(ii) held in trust for the exclusive benefit of aboriginal individuals,

(iii) owned by a corporation, all the shares of which are owned by aboriginal individuals, or

(iv) owned or held in a combination of ownership structures described in subparagraph (i), (ii) or (iii)

and the purpose of the corporation is to provide loans, loan guarantees, bridge financing, venture capital, lease financing, surety bonding or other similar financing services to aboriginal enterprises;

(b) prescribed assistance within the meaning assigned by section 6702;

(c) an amount that is the portion of a student loan forgiven under section 9.2 of the *Canada Student Financial Assistance Act* or under section 11.1 of the *Canada Student Loans Act*;

(c.1) an amount that is the portion of a student loan forgiven under a provincial program that would be a prescribed amount because of paragraph (c) if section 11.1 of the *Canada Student Loans Act* or 9.2 of the *Canada Student Financial Assistance Act* applied to loans under that program; or

(d) an emissions allowance issued to the taxpayer under the laws of Canada or a province.

Related Provisions: ITA 80(1)"excluded obligation"(a)(i) — Debt forgiveness rules do not apply to prescribed amount.

Notes: Reg. 7300(c) applies to loans forgiven to physicians and nurses working in rural or remote communities. It was added by 2011 budget bill #2 along with *CSFAA* s. 9.2 and *CSLA* 11.1 (all effective 2013: P.C. 2012-1591), both of which provide:

(1) Portion of loan forgiven — The Minister may forgive an amount in respect of a *["guaranteed" — CSLA]* student loan to a borrower who begins to work in an under-served rural or remote community as a family physician, nurse or nurse practitioner, if the borrower meets the prescribed conditions.

(2) Effective date of forgiveness — The forgiveness takes effect on the prescribed day.

(3) Agreement — For the purposes of subsection (1), the Minister may enter into an agreement with a lender for the purchase of a *["guaranteed" — CSLA]* student loan made by the lender.

Reg. 7300(c.1) added by 2017 budget bill #2, effective 2013. It was 7300(d) in the Sept. 16, 2016 draft legislation. It implements a Nov. 18, 2013 Finance comfort letter to the Saskatchewan government.

Reg. 7300(d) added by 2016 budget bill #2, for emissions allowances [EAs: see Notes to ITA 27.1] acquired in taxation years that begin after 2016. However, if a taxpayer elects as described in Notes to ITA 27.1, it applies to EAs acquired by the taxpayer in taxation years that end after 2012.

Reg. 7300(a)(ii) to (iv) added by P.C. 1991-729, effective May 8, 1991.

Definitions [Reg. 7300]: "amount" — ITA 248(1); "corporation" — ITA 248(1); *Interpretation Act* 35(1); "emissions allowance", "individual", "prescribed" — ITA 248(1); "province" — *Interpretation Act* 35(1); "share" — ITA 248(1); "taxation year" — ITA 249; "taxpayer" — ITA 248(1); "trust" — ITA 104(1), 248(1), (3).

Forms: T2125: Statement of business or professional activities.

7301. [Repealed]

Notes: Reg. 7301 repealed by P.C. 2001-1378, effective Aug. 15, 2001. It prescribed a 1987 amount for prepayment of the Child Tax Credit under ITA 164.1. For 1988-92, the prepayment was specified in the Act. This credit was discontinued as of 1993; the Canada Child Benefit is now provided by ITA 122.6–122.63.

7302, 7303. [Repealed]

Notes: Reg. 7302 and 7303 repealed by P.C. 1993-1688, effective for 1993 and later taxation years. They set out prescribed areas for ITA 110.7 as it applied before 1993.

7303.1 (1) [Prescribed northern zone] — An area is a prescribed northern zone for a taxation year for the purposes of section 110.7 of the Act where it is

(a) the Yukon Territory, the Northwest Territories or Nunavut;

(b) those parts of British Columbia, Alberta and Saskatchewan that lie north of 57°30'N latitude;

(c) that part of Manitoba that lies

(i) north of 56°20'N latitude, or

(ii) north of 52°30'N latitude and east of 95°25'W longitude;

(d) that part of Ontario that lies

(i) north of 52°30'N latitude, or

(ii) north of 51°05'N latitude and east of 89°10'W longitude;

(e) that part of Quebec that lies

(i) north of 51°05'N latitude, or

(ii) north of the Gulf of St. Lawrence and east of 63°00'W longitude; or

(f) Labrador, including Belle Isle.

Notes: See Notes at end of Reg. 7303.1.

(2) [Prescribed intermediate zone] — An area is a prescribed intermediate zone for a taxation year for the purposes of section 110.7 of the Act where it is the Queen Charlotte Islands, Anticosti Island, the Magdalen Islands or Sable Island, or where it is not part of a prescribed northern zone referred to in subsection (1) for the year and is

(a) that part of British Columbia that lies

(i) north of 55°35'N latitude,

(ii) north of 55°00'N latitude and east of 122°00'W longitude, or

(iii) north of 55°13'N latitude and east of 123°16'W longitude;

(b) that part of Alberta that lies north of 55°00'N latitude;

(c) that part of Saskatchewan that lies

(i) north of 55°00'N latitude,

(ii) north of 54°15'N latitude and east of 107°00'W longitude, or

(iii) north of 53°20'N latitude and east of 103°00'W longitude;

(d) that part of Manitoba that lies

(i) north of 53°20'N latitude,

(ii) north of 52°10'N latitude and east of 97°40'W longitude, or

(iii) north of 51°30'N latitude and east of 96°00'W longitude;

(e) that part of Ontario that lies north of 50°35'N latitude; or

(f) that part of Quebec that lies

(i) north of 50°35'N latitude and west of 79°00'W longitude,

(ii) north of 49°00'N latitude, east of 79°00'W longitude and west of 74°00'W longitude,

(iii) north of 50°00'N latitude, east of 74°00'W longitude and west of 70°00'W longitude,

(iv) north of 50°45'N latitude, east of 70°00'W longitude and west of 65°30'W longitude, or

(v) north of the Gulf of St. Lawrence, east of 65°30'W longitude and west of 63°00'W longitude.

Notes: A complete list of places in the prescribed northern and intermediate zones appears in CRA publication T4039.

In *Dupuis*, 2009 TCC 220, Mistissini, QC was held to be in the prescribed intermediate zone. Loon Straits, MB is not in a prescribed zone: VIEWS doc 2013-0481841M4. Nor is Northern Cape Breton: 2013-0483321M4. The Magdalen Islands (Îles de la Madeleine) are in the prescribed intermediate zone: 2016-0659041E5.

Reg. 7303.1 amended by 2007 Budget bill (last change effective 2007). Added by P.C. 1993-1688, effective 1988.

Definitions [Reg. 7303.1]: "prescribed" — ITA 248(1); "taxation year" — ITA 249.

Remission Orders [Reg. 7303.1]: *Prescribed Areas Forward Averaging Remission Order*, P.C. 1994-109 (remission for certain residents of prescribed areas who filed forward averaging elections for 1987).

Interpretation Bulletins [Reg. 7303.1]: IT-91R4: Employment at special work sites or remote work locations.

Forms [Reg. 7303.1]: T4039: Northern residents deductions — places in prescribed zones [guide].

7304. (1) In this section,

"member of the taxpayer's household" includes the taxpayer;

"designated city" means St. John's, Halifax, Moncton, Quebec City, Montreal, Ottawa, Toronto, North Bay, Winnipeg, Saskatoon, Calgary, Edmonton and Vancouver.

(2) [Trip cost] — For the purposes of this section, the trip cost to a taxpayer in respect of a trip made by an individual who, at the time the trip was made, was a member of the taxpayer's household is the least of

(a) the aggregate of

(i) the value of travel assistance, if any, provided by the taxpayer's employer in respect of travelling expenses for the trip, and

(ii) the amount, if any, received by the taxpayer from his employer in respect of travelling expenses for the trip,

(b) the aggregate of

(i) the value of travel assistance, if any, provided by the taxpayer's employer in respect of travelling expenses for the trip, and

(ii) travelling expenses incurred by the taxpayer for the trip, and

(c) the lowest return airfare ordinarily available, at the time the trip was made, to the individual for flights between the place in which the individual resided immediately before the trip, or the airport nearest thereto, and the designated city that is nearest to that place.

Proposed Amendments — Reg. 7304(2)

Federal Budget, Supplementary Information, April 19, 2021: *Northern Residents Deductions*

Individuals who live in prescribed northern areas of Canada for at least six consecutive months beginning or ending in a taxation year may claim the Northern Residents Deductions in computing their taxable income for that year. These include both a residency component and a travel component.

The travel component allows a taxpayer receiving employer-provided travel benefits to deduct, in respect of a trip taken by the taxpayer or a member of the taxpayer's household, up to the least of:

* the amount of the employer-provided travel benefit received in respect of the trip;
* the total travel expenses paid for the trip; and
* the cost of the lowest return airfare to the nearest city designated in the *Income Tax Regulations*.

A taxpayer may deduct amounts in respect of travel for any number of trips made to obtain medical services not available locally and up to two trips per person per year for non-medical personal reasons. Residents of the prescribed Northern Zone may claim 100% of the amounts described above, while residents of the prescribed Intermediate Zone may claim 50%.

Budget 2021 proposes to expand access to the travel component of the Northern Residents Deductions. Under the new approach, subject to the other restrictions noted above, a taxpayer would have the option to claim, in respect of each of the taxpayer and each "eligible family member", up to:

* the amount of employer-provided travel benefits the taxpayer received in respect of travel by that individual; or
* a $1,200 standard amount that may be allocated across eligible trips taken by that individual.

After application of the 50% factor for residents of the Intermediate Zone, the second limit effectively becomes a $600 standard amount.

For these purposes, an eligible family member would be an individual living in the taxpayer's household who is:

* the spouse or common-law partner of the taxpayer;
* a child of the taxpayer (including a child of the taxpayer's spouse or common-law partner) under the age of 18; or
* another individual who is related to the taxpayer and who is wholly dependent on the taxpayer (and/or on the taxpayer's spouse or common-law partner) for support, and who is, except in the case of a parent or grandparent of the taxpayer, so dependent by reason of mental or physical infirmity.

If any taxpayer claims a deduction in respect of an employer-provided benefit for travel by the taxpayer or an eligible family member of the taxpayer in a year, no other taxpayer would be allowed to also claim all or part of the $1,200 standard amount in respect of travel by that first mentioned taxpayer or that eligible family member in that year. If any taxpayer claims all or part of the $1,200 standard amount in respect of travel by an individual, the maximum total amount that could be claimed in respect of that individual by all taxpayers would be $1,200.

Budget 2021 proposes that across all taxpayers in a given individual's household, a maximum of two trips taken by that individual would be allowed to be claimed in total for non-medical personal travel in a year. A taxpayer would continue to be able to claim any number of trips for medical purposes.

In light of the proposed changes described above, claims for a given trip would be limited to the least of:

* the amount of the employer-provided travel benefit received in respect of the trip or the amount allocated to that particular trip by the taxpayer out of the $1,200 standard amount;
* the total travel expenses paid for that trip; and
* the cost of the lowest return airfare to the nearest designated city.

Example:

* Kim and her husband Ryan live in Whitehorse and have a 10-year-old child. Kim has higher income than her husband and claims all travel expenses for the household.
* Kim receives a travel benefit of $1,500 from her employer in respect of each of two non-medical trips she took herself. She also receives a benefit of $1,000 in respect of a non-medical trip that Ryan took. Kim, Ryan, and their child also take one non-medical trip together, but do not receive any travel benefit for this trip.
* Kim may claim up to two trips for non-medical reasons. She decides to claim the two trips for which she received a travel benefit, as the amount of her travel benefit is greater than the $1,200 standard amount. Kim is eligible to claim up to the amount of her travel benefit of $1,500, subject to a limit of her actual expenses and the lowest return airfare, in respect of each trip.
* Kim decides not to claim the amount of the travel benefit she received for Ryan's travel, as the amount she received is less than the $1,200 standard amount. Instead, she allocates the $1,200 standard amount across the two trips that Ryan took, and is eligible to deduct the amount allocated to each trip, subject to the actual expenses and the lowest return airfare for each trip.
* Kim allocates the full $1,200 standard amount to the one trip her child took, and is eligible to deduct up to $1,200 for her child's travel, subject to the actual expenses and the lowest return airfare in respect of that trip.

This measure would apply to the 2021 and subsequent taxation years.

Strategic Environmental Assessment Statement

The proposal would effectively expand access to a rebate on the cost of travel, including carbon-intensive air travel. This may encourage additional travel among northern residents and result in associated greenhouse gas emissions. However, the rules of the deduction allow only two trips to be claimed in respect of any individual for non-medical personal reasons, and further limit the amount that may be claimed in respect of any trip. These rules constrain the circumstances in which an individual may receive a rebate in respect of additional travel taken in response to the proposal. Accordingly, any negative environmental impacts are expected to be negligible.

Federal Budget, Chapter 5, April 19, 2021: *Extending the Northern Residents Deduction*

The remote nature of many northern communities makes travel, even essential travel for school or medical care, unaffordable for many. The Northern Residents Deduction only provides tax relief to those who already receive travel benefits through work. To reduce travel costs for northerners:

Budget 2021 proposes to expand access to the travel component of the Northern Residents Deduction.

Northerners without employer-provided travel benefits would be allowed to claim up to $1,200 in eligible travel expenses. This measure would take effect starting with the 2021 tax year.

The Minister of Northern Affairs will work with the Minister of Innovation, Science and Industry, who is the Minister responsible for the Competition Bureau, to ensure that these savings are for the benefit of citizens in the North rather than transportation providers.

It is estimated that this measure will reduce federal revenues by $125 million over five years starting in 2021-22.

CRA news release, March 18, 2019: *Making it easier for northern residents to claim lowest return airfare*

The Canada Revenue Agency (CRA) is responding to the challenges northern residents face in meeting their tax obligations. We are making it easier for northern residents to report the lowest return airfare element of the northern residents deductions and we want to hear from Canadians on what we're proposing.

Northern residents have told us the difficulty they have in determining and documenting the lowest return airfare in relation to a trip. This information is currently required to claim the travel benefits deduction portion of the northern residents deductions.

In response to these concerns, the CRA is proposing to simplify the lowest return airfare requirement. Under the proposed simplified requirement, individuals would have to determine and document the cost of return economy airfare in relation to their

Regulations

trip. This documentation can be dated within a reasonable amount of time of when the trip is made, but has to be for the date travelled.

For example, a claimant could get the airfare amount for the day of travel from a travel website in the days leading up to a trip. This change would eliminate both the need to get a quote on the day of travel and to ensure that it is the lowest available.

It is anticipated this additional flexibility will reduce the administrative burden for northern residents claiming the travel benefits deduction, while maintaining fairness by ensuring that the amount claimed for each trip is not excessive.

This change, which is detailed in a consultation document, would require amendments to the federal *Income Tax Regulations*.

Canadians are invited to provide comments on this proposed regulatory amendment by April 17, 2019. Comments can be sent by email at Regulations-Reglements@cra-arc.gc.ca or by mail to: Northern Residents Deductions Consultations, Legislative Amendments Division, Legislative Policy and Regulatory Affairs Branch, Canada Revenue Agency, 320 Queen Street, Ottawa, Ontario K1A 0L5.

Consultation on the lowest return airfare requirement for the northern residents deductions

Northerners have told the Canada Revenue Agency (CRA) that they experience difficulty determining the lowest return airfare for claiming the travel benefits portion of the northern residents deductions. Determining the lowest return airfare ordinarily available at the time a trip is made is currently a required element for claiming the travel benefits deduction.

What are the northern residents deductions

[Description of how ITA 110.7 works, omitted — ed.]

Employee travel benefits

If an employer pays or reimburses an employee for non-work related travel expenses (or pays the employee an allowance), such amounts are generally considered a taxable benefit. The value of any such benefit is included in income on the employee's T4, Statement of Remuneration Paid or T4A, Statement of Pension, Retirement, Annuity, and Other Income issued by the employer for the year in which the amount was paid. The individual is required to pay tax on the amount of these benefits in the same way as if the amounts were provided as salary. Individuals residing in the prescribed zones who received taxable travel benefits from their arm's length employer and incurred expenses for personal travel (including for medical purposes) in that year, are eligible for the travel benefits deduction. The travel benefits deduction may offset all or part of the taxable benefit and the resulting increased amount of taxes that the individual would ordinarily be required to pay on these benefits.

The travel benefits deduction can be claimed for trips taken by the individual, or members of their household living with them at the time of the trip, for vacation, family or medical reasons (maximum of two non-medical trips per person). While the trip must start from a prescribed zone, it does not have to include travel outside of the prescribed northern or intermediate zones to claim the travel benefits deduction. Currently, the maximum deduction for each eligible trip is the lowest of the following three amounts:

- the value of the taxable travel benefit received from the employer;
- the actual cost of the trip (supported by receipts); and
- the lowest return airfare ordinarily available at the time of the trip between the airport closest to the taxpayer's residence and the nearest designated city to that airport.

These maximum deduction rules, including the list of designated cities, are contained in Section 7304 of the *Income Tax Regulations*.

Considerations for simplifying the lowest return airfare requirement

The purpose of the lowest return airfare element in the calculation of the travel benefits deduction is to ensure that the amount claimed for each trip is not excessive. As such, the lowest return airfare determination is required for all trips regardless of whether the actual trip involves air travel. This requirement serves a purpose in ensuring fairness in terms of the treatment of taxpayers living in the prescribed zones by putting a cap on the maximum amount that can be claimed.

The lowest return airfare is a rigid target that can change. The current wording of the *Income Tax Regulations* requires the determination of not only the airfare on the day of the trip, but also that it be the lowest fare available. The CRA recognizes that this can be difficult to identify and that airfare pricing has increased in complexity since the northern residents deductions were introduced in 1987. While it may be easier than ever to determine an airfare amount, the difficulty is in determining if it is the lowest cost airfare available during the day of travel.

Using an airfare amount to the nearest designated city outside the prescribed zones to determine the maximum amount of the travel benefits deduction is a reasonable proxy to reflect the higher costs of travel from the North because the cost of airfare would normally increase for individuals living in more remote regions.

Proposed amendment

The CRA is proposing that the lowest return airfare requirement be simplified. Taxpayers would be required instead to document a reasonable amount in respect of return economy airfare. The proposed amendment would require that a reasonable amount in respect of return airfare be obtained for the date of travel within a reasonable amount of time of when the trip is made. The CRA is seeking feedback from Canadians on this proposed amendment.

This change would require an amendment to the federal *Income Tax Regulations*.

Current wording of the relevant portion of the regulations

Paragraph 7304(2)(c) of the *Income Tax Regulations* currently reads:

(c) the lowest return airfare ordinarily available, at the time the trip was made, to the individual for flights between the place in which the individual resided immediately before the trip, or the airport nearest thereto, and the designated city that is nearest to that place.

Proposed new wording of the relevant portion of the regulations

(c) a reasonable amount in respect of return economy airfare for the date of travel that was ordinarily available, within a reasonable amount of time of when the trip was made, for flights between the place in which the individual resided immediately before the trip, or the airport nearest thereto, and the designated city that is nearest to that place.

The proposed regulatory amendment would eliminate both the need to make the determination of the airfare on the actual day of travel and to ensure that it is the lowest available. Instead the taxpayer would be required to determine a reasonable amount in respect of return economy airfare ordinarily available for the date of travel. For example, a claimant can obtain a reasonable airfare amount for the day of travel from a travel website in the days leading up to a trip.

It is anticipated that the additional flexibility provided by the proposed regulatory amendment would reduce the administrative burden for taxpayers claiming the travel benefits deduction, while at the same time maintaining fairness by ensuring that the amount claimed for each trip is not excessive.

It should be noted that no changes are being proposed with regard to what expenses would be considered eligible for the travel benefits deduction. Travel expenses for medical or personal trips that were acceptable to the CRA in the past would continue to be acceptable. All that would change is how the limit on the expenses would be determined and documented.

The reasonable return economy airfare would include mandatory taxes, fees and charges such as sales taxes, airport improvement fees and the Air Travellers Security Charge. The airfare would not include non-mandatory fees such as baggage fees, flight cancellation insurance, or pre-paid meals as is currently the case.

Consultation questions

1. Would it be preferable for the proposed amendment to specify what is intended by a "reasonable amount of time"? For example, should the regulation specify a number of days? Would the addition of this clarification be at the expense of reduced flexibility for individuals claiming the travel benefits deduction?

2. Is the term "a reasonable amount in respect of return economy airfare" easy to understand?

3. Would the proposed new requirement simplify the claiming of the travel benefits deduction?

Comments

Canadians are invited to provide comments on this proposed regulatory amendment by April 17, 2019. Comments can be sent to Regulations-Reglements@cra-arc.gc.ca. Alternatively, comments can be sent to: Northern Residents Deductions Consultations, Legislative Amendments Division, Legislative Policy and Regulatory Affairs Branch, Canada Revenue Agency, 320 Queen Street, Ottawa, Ontario K1A 0L5.

Once received by the CRA, all submissions will be subject to the *Access to Information Act* and may be disclosed in accordance with its provisions. Should you express an intention that your submission be considered confidential, the CRA will make all efforts to protect this information within the requirements of the law.

Notes: Budget Table 1 projects that these measures will cost the federal government $26 million in each of 2021-22 through 2025-26.

Notes: For interpretation of "lowest return airfare" see VIEWS docs 2005-0136061E5, 2011-0403981I7. For "designated city that is nearest" see 2007-0239191E5.

Reg. 7304(2)(c) amended by P.C. 1993-1688, for 1988 and later taxation years.

(3) [Period travel cost] — For the purposes of subsection (4), the "period travel cost" to a taxpayer for a period in a taxation year, in respect of an individual who was a member of the taxpayer's household at any time during the period, is the total of the trip costs to the taxpayer in respect of all trips that were made by the individual at a time when the individual was a member of the taxpayer's household where the trips may reasonably be considered to relate to the period.

(4) [Travel assistance — prescribed amount] — For the purposes of clause 110.7(1)(a)(i)(A) of the Act, the prescribed amount in respect of a taxpayer for a period in a taxation year is the lesser of

(a) the total of

(i) the value of travel assistance, if any, provided in the period by the taxpayer's employer in respect of travelling expenses for trips, each of which was made by an individual who, at the time the trip was made, was a member of the taxpayer's household, where the trips may reasonably be considered to relate to the period, and

(ii) the amount, if any, received in the period by the taxpayer from the taxpayer's employer in respect of travelling expenses for trips, each of which was made by an individual who, at the time the trip was made, was a member of the taxpayer's household, where the trips may reasonably be considered to relate to the period; and

(b) the total of all the period travel costs to the taxpayer for the period in respect of all individuals who were members of the taxpayer's household at any time in the period.

Notes: Reg. 7304(3), (4) amended by P.C. 1993-1688, for 1988 and later tax years.

Definitions [Reg. 7304]: "amount" — ITA 248(1); "designated city" — Reg. 7304(1); "employer", "individual" — ITA 248(1); "member of the taxpayer's household" — Reg. 7304(1); "period travel cost" — Reg. 7304(3); "prescribed" — ITA 248(1); "taxation year" — ITA 249; "taxpayer" — ITA 248(1); "trip cost" — Reg. 7304(2).

7305. [Prescribed drought regions] — [To 2012 only — no longer relevant]

Notes: Reg. 7305 lists prescribed drought regions for ITA 80.4(4) for 1997-2012. For later years (there were none for 2013) see Reg. 7305.01, which covers both drought regions and regions with flooding or excessive moisture.

Reg. 7305 renumbered 7305(1) effective March 3, 2011, and paras. (n)-(o) added to prescribe regions for 2010, 2012, by P.C. 2013-1253. Earlier amended by P.C. 2011-205, 2007-1444, 2005-1656, 2004-1386, 2004-246, 2002-1412, 2001-1369, 2000-1769. No regions were prescribed for 2005 or 2011. Reg. 7305(2), re surrounded areas, added effective March 3, 2011 (this rule was in Reg. 7305.01 before), by P.C. 2013-1253.

7305.01 (1) [Prescribed drought regions — after 2012] —

For the purposes of subsections 80.3(4) and (4.1) of the Act, the following regions are prescribed drought regions or prescribed regions of flood or excessive moisture:

(a)-(c) [Apply to 2014, 2015 and 2016.]

(d) in respect of the 2017 calendar year, the Consolidated Census Subdivisions, based on the 2016 Statistics Canada Census, of

(i) in Quebec, Albertville, Amqui, Auclair, Baie-des-Sables, Biencourt, Cacouna, Causapscal, Dégelis, Esprit-Saint, Kamouraska, La Malbaie, Lac-à-la-Croix, Lac-Alfred, Lac-des-Aigles, Lac-des-Eaux-Mortes, Lac-Huron, Lac-Matapédia, Lejeune, Les Bergeronnes, L'Isle-Verte, Notre-Dame-des-Neiges, Pohénégamook, Rimouski, Rivière-du-Loup, Routhierville, Ruisseau-Ferguson, Sacré-Cœur, Saint-Alexandre-de-Kamouraska, Saint-André, Saint-Antonin, Saint-Arsène, Saint-Bruno-de-Kamouraska, Saint-Clément, Saint-Cléophas, Saint-Cyprien, Sainte-Angèle-de-Mérici, Sainte-Flavie, Sainte-Jeanne-d'Arc, Saint-Éloi, Sainte-Luce, Saint-Elzéar-de-Témiscouata, Saint-Épiphane, Saint-Eusèbe, Saint-Fabien, Saint-Gabriel-de-Rimouski, Saint-Germain, Saint-Guy, Saint-Hubert-de-Rivière-du-Loup, Saint-Jean-de-Dieu, Saint-Léon-le-Grand, Saint-Mathieu-de-Rioux, Saint-Octave-de-Métis, Saint-Pascal, Saint-Simon, Saint-Ulric, Sayabec, Témiscouata-sur-le-Lac and Val-Brillant,

(ii) in British Columbia, Alberni-Clayoquot A, B, D and F, Cariboo A to L, Central Kootenay A to E, G, H, J and K, Central Okanagan, Central Okanagan J, Columbia-Shuswap A and C to F, Comox Valley A, Comox Valley C (Puntledge-Black Creek), East Kootenay A to C and E to G, Fraser Valley B and D to G, Fraser-Fort George C to E, Kootenay Boundary B/Lower Columbia-Old-Glory, Kootenay Boundary D/Rural Grand Forks, Kootenay Boundary E/West Boundary, North Okanagan B and D to F, Okanagan-Similkameen A to H, Spallumcheen, Squamish-Lillooet B and C, Strathcona D (Oyster Bay-Buttle Lake), Thompson-Nicola A (Wells Gray Country), Thompson-Nicola B (Thompson Headwaters), Thompson-Nicola E (Bonaparte Plateau), Thompson-Nicola I (Blue Sky Country), Thompson-Nicola J (Copper Desert Country), Thompson-Nicola L (Grasslands), Thompson-Nicola M (Beautiful Nicola Valley-North), Thompson-Nicola N (Beautiful Nicola Valley-South), Thompson-Nicola O (Lower North Thompson) and Thompson-Nicola P (Rivers and the Peaks),

(iii) in Saskatchewan, Aberdeen No. 373, Abernethy No. 186, Antelope Park No. 322, Arlington No. 79, Arm River No. 252, Auvergne No. 76, Baildon No. 131, Bayne No. 371, Bengough No. 40, Benson No. 35, Big Arm No. 251, Big Quill No. 308, Big Stick No. 141, Birch Hills No. 460, Blucher No. 343, Bone Creek No. 108, Bratt's Lake No. 129, Brock No. 64, Brokenshell No. 68, Browning No. 34, Buckland No. 491, Caledonia No. 99, Cambria No. 6, Canaan No. 225, Carmichael No. 109, Caron No. 162, Chaplin No. 164, Chester No. 125, Chesterfield No. 261, Clinworth No. 230, Coalfields No. 4, Colonsay No. 342, Connaught No. 457, Corman Park No. 344, Coteau No. 255, Coulee No. 136, Craik No. 222, Cupar No. 218, Cymri No. 36, Deer Forks No. 232, Dufferin No. 190, Dundurn No. 314, Edenwold No. 158, Elcapo No. 154, Elfros No. 307, Elmsthorpe No. 100, Emerald No. 277, Enfield No. 194, Enterprise No. 142, Estevan No. 5, Excel No. 71, Excelsior No. 166, Eyebrow No. 193, Fertile Valley No. 285, Fillmore No. 96, Fish Creek No. 402, Flett's Springs No. 429, Foam Lake No. 276, Fox Valley No. 171, Francis No. 127, Frontier No. 19, Garden River No. 490, Garry No. 245, Glen Bain No. 105, Glen McPherson No. 46, Golden West No. 95, Grant No. 372, Grassy Creek No. 78, Gravelbourg No. 104, Griffin No. 66, Gull Lake No. 139, Happy Valley No. 10, Happyland No. 231, Harris No. 316, Hart Butte No. 11, Hazelwood No. 94, Hillsborough No. 132, Hoodoo No. 401, Humboldt No. 370, Huron No. 223, Indian Head No. 156, Insinger No. 275, Invergordon No. 430, Ituna Bon Accord No. 246, Kellross No. 247, Key West No. 70, Kindersley No. 290, King George No. 256, Kingsley No. 124, Kinistino No. 459, Lac Pelletier No. 107, Lacadena No. 228, Lajord No. 128, Lake Alma No. 8, Lake Johnston No. 102, Lake Lenore No. 399, Lake of the Rivers No. 72, Lakeside No. 338, Lakeview No. 337, Last Mountain Valley No. 250, Laurier No. 38, Lawtonia No. 135, Leroy No. 339, Lipton No. 217, Lomond No. 37, Lone Tree No. 18, Longlaketon No. 219, Loreburn No. 254, Lost River No. 313, Lumsden No. 189, Mankota No. 45, Maple Bush No. 224, Maple Creek No. 111, Marquis No. 191, Marriott No. 317, McCraney No. 282, McKillop No. 220, McLeod No. 185, Milden No. 286, Milton No. 292, Miry Creek No. 229, Monet No. 257, Montmartre No. 126, Montrose No. 315, Moose Jaw No. 161, Morris No. 312, Morse No. 165, Mount Hope No. 279, Mountain View No. 318, Newcombe No. 260, Nipawin No. 487, North Qu'Appelle No. 187, Norton No. 69, Oakdale No. 320, Old Post No. 43, Paddockwood No. 520, Pense No. 160, Perdue No. 346, Piapot No. 110, Pinto Creek No. 75, Pittville No. 169, Pleasant Valley No. 288, Pleasantdale No. 398, Poplar Valley No. 12, Prairie Rose No. 309, Prairiedale No. 321, Prince Albert No. 461, Redburn No. 130, Reno No. 51, Riverside No. 168, Rodgers No. 133, Rosedale No. 283, Rudy No. 284, Sarnia No. 221, Saskatchewan Landing No. 167, Saskatoon, Scott No. 98, Shamrock No. 134, Sherwood No. 159, Snipe Lake No. 259, Souris Valley No. 7, South Qu'Appelle No. 157, Spalding No. 368, St. Andrews No. 287, St. Louis No. 431, St. Peter No. 369, Stanley No. 215, Star City No. 428, Stonehenge No. 73, Surprise Valley No. 9, Sutton No. 103, Swift Current No. 137, Tecumseh No. 65, Terrell No. 101, The Gap No. 39, Three Lakes No. 400, Torch River No. 488, Touchwood No. 248, Tullymet No. 216, Usborne No. 310, Val Marie No. 17, Vanscoy No. 345, Victory No. 226, Viscount No. 341, Waverley No. 44, Webb No. 138, Wellington No. 97, Weyburn No. 67, Wheatlands No. 163, Whiska Creek No. 106, White Valley No. 49, Willner No. 253, Willow Bunch No. 42, Willow Creek No. 458, Winslow No. 319, Wise Creek No. 77, Wolseley No. 155, Wolverine No. 340, Wood Creek No. 281, Wood River No. 74 and Wreford No. 280, and

Regulations

(iv) in Alberta, the City of Calgary, the Counties of Cardston, Clearwater, Cypress, Kneehill, Lacombe, Lethbridge, Mountain View, Newell, Red Deer, Rocky View, Starland, Vulcan and Wheatlands, Forty Mile County No. 8, Paintearth County No. 18, Stettler County No. 6, Warner County No. 5, the Municipal Districts of Bighorn No. 8, Foothills No. 31, Pincher Creek No. 9, Ranchland No. 66, Taber and Willow Creek No. 26 and Special Areas No. 2, 3 and 4.

Proposed Addition — Reg. 7305.01(1) — BC, Alberta, Sask., Manitoba, Ontario, Quebec, NB (2018)

Agriculture and Agri-Food Canada news release, Sept. 14, 2018: *Livestock Producers Receive Tax Relief for 2018*

Extreme weather conditions have caused feed shortfalls in several provinces, which has led to designated regions in British Columbia, Alberta, Saskatchewan, Manitoba, and Quebec being eligible for livestock tax deferral provision.

Our Government today released an initial list of these designated regions where livestock tax deferral has been authorized for 2018 due to drought or excess moisture conditions.

The livestock tax deferral provisions allow livestock producers in prescribed drought, flood or excess moisture regions to defer a portion of their 2018 sale proceeds of breeding livestock until 2019 to help replenish the herd. The cost of replacing the animals in 2019 will offset the deferred income, thereby reducing the tax burden associated with the original sale.

Eligibility for the tax deferral is limited to those producers located inside the designated prescribed areas. Producers in those regions can request the tax deferral when filing their 2018 income tax returns.

Quick facts

- Low moisture levels resulted in significant forage shortages for livestock producers in British Columbia, Alberta, Saskatchewan, Manitoba and Quebec in 2018. One option for producers is to reduce their breeding herd in order to manage feed supplies.

- In addition to the livestock tax deferral provision, producers have access to assistance through existing Canadian Agricultural Partnership Business Risk Management programs, which include AgriInsurance, AgriStability and AgriInvest.

Contacts: Katie Hawkins, Director of Communications, Office of the Honourable Lawrence MacAulay, 613-773-1059, Katie.hawkins@agr.gc.ca; Media Relations, Agriculture and Agri-Food Canada, Ottawa, Ontario, 613-773-7972, 1-866-345-7972.

2018 Initial List of Designated Regions

[Superseded by list in Jan. 30, 2019 news release below — ed.]

Agriculture and Agri-Food Canada news release, Oct. 31, 2018: *Livestock Producers Receive Tax Relief for 2018*

New Regions Added under the Livestock Tax Deferral Provision

The Government of Canada today released a list of additional regions in Alberta, Saskatchewan, Manitoba, Quebec and New Brunswick where livestock tax deferral has been authorized for 2018 due to drought.

On September 14th, 2018, the Government announced the initial list of prescribed regions in British Columbia, Alberta, Saskatchewan, Manitoba, and Quebec for livestock tax deferral purposes.

The livestock tax deferral provision allows producers in prescribed drought or excess moisture regions to defer a portion of their 2018 sale proceeds of breeding livestock until 2019 to help replenish the herd. The cost of replacing the animals in 2019 will offset the deferred income, thereby reducing the tax burden associated with the original sale.

Eligibility for the tax deferral is limited to those producers located inside the prescribed areas. Producers in those regions can request the tax deferral when filing their 2018 income tax returns.

Quick facts

- Low moisture levels resulted in significant forage shortages for livestock producers in British Columbia, Alberta, Saskatchewan, Manitoba, Quebec and New Brunswick in 2018. One option for producers is to reduce their breeding herd in order to manage feed supplies.

- In addition to the livestock tax deferral provision, producers have access to assistance through existing Canadian Agricultural Partnership Business Risk Management programs, which include AgriInsurance, AgriStability and AgriInvest.

Contacts: Katie Hawkins, Director of Communications, Office of the Honourable Lawrence MacAulay, 613-773-1059, katie.hawkins@canada.ca; Media Relations, Agriculture and Agri-Food Canada, Ottawa, Ontario, 613-773-7972, 1-866-345-7972, aafc.mediarelations-relationsmedias.aac@canada.ca.

2018 List of Designated Regions

[Superseded by list in Jan. 30, 2019 news release below — ed.]

Agriculture and Agri-Food Canada news release, Jan. 30, 2019: *Livestock Producers Receive Tax Relief for 2018*

Final List of Designated Regions under the Livestock Tax Deferral Provision Released

The Government of Canada today released the final list of designated regions where livestock tax deferral has been authorized for 2018 due to drought conditions in British Columbia, Alberta, Saskatchewan, Manitoba, Ontario, Quebec and New Brunswick.

On September 14th, 2018, the Government announced the initial list of prescribed regions in British Columbia, Alberta, Saskatchewan, Manitoba, and Quebec eligible for livestock tax deferral. A second designation of eligible regions was made on October 31st, 2018. Ongoing analysis of drought conditions has indicated the need to expand the list of designated regions for 2018, with new regions identified for Alberta, Saskatchewan, Manitoba, and Ontario.

The livestock tax deferral provision allows producers in prescribed drought or excess moisture regions to defer a portion of their 2018 sale proceeds of breeding livestock until 2019 to help replenish the herd. The cost of replacing the animals in 2019 will offset the deferred income, thereby reducing the tax burden associated with the original sale.

Eligibility for the tax deferral is limited to those producers located inside the prescribed areas. Producers in those regions can request the tax deferral when filing their 2018 income tax returns.

Quick facts

- Low moisture levels resulted in significant forage shortages for livestock producers in British Columbia, Alberta, Saskatchewan, Manitoba, Quebec and New Brunswick in 2018. One option for producers is to reduce their breeding herd in order to manage feed supplies.

- In addition to the livestock tax deferral provision, producers have access to assistance through existing Canadian Agricultural Partnership Business Risk Management programs, which include AgriInsurance, AgriStability and AgriInvest.

Contacts: Katie Hawkins, Director of Communications, Office of the Honourable Lawrence MacAulay, 613-773-1059, katie.hawkins@canada.ca; Media Relations, Agriculture and Agri-Food Canada, Ottawa, Ontario, 613-773-7972, 1-866-345-7972, aafc.mediarelations-relationsmedias.aac@canada.ca.

2018 List of Designated Regions

[Map not reproduced; see agr.gc.ca/drought > Livestock Tax Deferral — ed.]

British Columbia — 2018 Livestock Tax Deferral

Consolidated Census Subdivisions

Based on the 2016 Statistics Canada Census

Abbotsford	Fraser-Fort George D
Alberni-Clayoquot A	Fraser-Fort George E
Alberni-Clayoquot B	Fraser-Fort George F
Alberni-Clayoquot D	Fraser Valley D
Alberni-Clayoquot F	Fraser Valley E
Bulkley-Nechako A	Fraser Valley F
Bulkley-Nechako B	Fraser Valley G
Bulkley-Nechako C	Greater Vancouver A
Bulkley-Nechako D	Juan de Fuca (Part 2)
Bulkley-Nechako E	Kitimat-Stikine B
Bulkley-Nechako F	Kitimat-Stikine C (Part 1)
Bulkley-Nechako G	Kootenay Boundary B / Lower Columbia-Old-Glory
Burnaby	Kootenay Boundary D / Rural Grand Forks
Cariboo A	Langley
Cariboo B	Maple Ridge
Cariboo C	Mount Waddington C
Cariboo I	Nanaimo
Central Coast A	Nanaimo C
Central Kootenay A	Nanaimo E
Central Kootenay B	Nanaimo F
Central Kootenay C	Nanaimo G
Central Kootenay D	Nanaimo H
Central Kootenay E	North Cowichan
Central Kootenay G	Pitt Meadows
Central Kootenay H	Powell River A
Central Kootenay J	Powell River C
Central Kootenay K	Powell River E
Comox Valley A	Richmond
Comox Valley B (Lazo North)	Saltspring Island
Comox Valley C (Puntledge - Black Creek)	Skeena-Queen Charlotte C
Cowichan Valley B	Skeena-Queen Charlotte D
Cowichan Valley F	Skeena-Queen Charlotte E
Cowichan Valley G	Southern Gulf Islands
Delta	Squamish-Lillooet C
East Kootenay A	Strathcona C

East Kootenay B	Strathcona D (Oyster Bay - Buttle Lake)
East Kootenay C	Sunshine Coast A
East Kootenay E	Surrey
Fraser-Fort George A	Vancouver
Fraser-Fort George C	

Alberta — 2018 Livestock Tax Deferral

Municipalities–Consolidated Census Subdivisions

Based on the 2016 Statistics Canada Census

Beaver County	Newell County
Bighorn No. 8*	Paintearth County No.18**
Brazeau County**	Parkland County**
City of Calgary	Pincher Creek No. 9
Camrose County	Ponoka County
Cardston County	Ranchland No. 66*
Clearwater County*	Red Deer County
Cypress County	Rocky View County
Flagstaff County*	Special Area No. 2**
Foothills No. 31*	Special Area No. 3**
Forty Mile County No. 8	Starland County*
Kneehill County	Stettler County No. 6*
Lacombe County	Municipal District of Taber
Lac Ste. Anne County**	Vulcan County
Lamont County*	Warner County No. 5
Leduc County**	Wetaskiwin County No. 10
Lethbridge County	Wheatland County
Mackenzie County*	Willow Creek No. 26
Minburn County No. 27*	Yellowhead County**
Mountain View County	

*Second Designation

**Third Designation

Saskatchewan — 2018 Livestock Tax Deferral

Municipalities–Consolidated Census Subdivisions

Based on the 2016 Statistics Canada Census

Aberdeen No. 373*	Leroy No. 339*
Abernethy No. 186	Lipton No. 217
Antler No. 61*	Lomond No. 37
Argyle No. 1	Lone Tree No. 18
Arlington No. 79	Longlaketon No. 219
Arm River No. 252	Loreburn No. 254
Auvergne No. 76	Lost River No. 313
Baildon No. 131	Lumsden No. 189
Bayne No. 371*	Mankota No. 45
Bengough No. 40	Maple Bush No. 224
Benson No. 35*	Maple Creek No. 111
Big Arm No. 251	Marquis No. 191
Big Quill No. 308	Marriott No. 317
Big Stick No. 141	Martin No. 122*
Biggar No. 347	Mayfield No. 406**
Birch Hills No. 460*	Maryfield No. 91*
Blaine Lake No. 434**	McCraney No. 282
Blucher No. 343*	McKillop No. 220
Bone Creek No. 108	McLeod No. 185
Bratt's Lake No. 129	Milden No. 286
Brock No. 64*	Miry Creek No. 229
Brokenshell No. 68	Milton No. 292**
Browning No. 34*	Monet No. 257
Buckland No. 491*	Montmartre No. 126
Caledonia No. 99	Montrose No. 315
Cambria No. 6	Moose Creek No. 33*
Canaan No. 225	Moose Jaw No. 161
Carmichael No. 109	Moose Mountain No. 63*
Caron No. 162	Moosomin No. 121*
Chaplin No. 164	Morris No. 312
Chester No. 125	Morse No. 165
Chesterfield No. 261**	Mount Hope No. 279
Clinworth No. 230*	Mount Pleasant No. 2*
Coalfields No. 4*	Mountain View No. 318
Colonsay No. 342*	Newcombe No. 260**
Corman Park No. 344	Nipawin No. 487*
Coteau No. 255	North Qu'Appelle No. 187
Coulee No. 136	Norton No. 69
Craik No. 222	Old Post No. 43
Cupar No. 218	Paddockwood No. 520*

Cymri No. 36	Pense No. 160
Deer Forks No. 232*	Perdue No. 346
Duck Lake No. 463**	Piapot No. 110
Dufferin No. 190	Pinto Creek No. 75
Dundurn No. 314	Pittville No. 169
Eagle Creek No. 376*	Pleasant Valley No. 288
Edenwold No. 158	Poplar Valley No. 12
Elcapo No. 154	Prairie Rose No. 309
Elfros No. 307	Prince Albert No. 461*
Elmsthorpe No. 100	Reciprocity No. 32*
Emerald No. 277	Redberry No. 435**
Enfield No. 194	Redburn No. 130
Enniskillen No. 3*	Reno No. 51
Enterprise No. 142	Riverside No. 168
Estevan No. 5*	Rocanville No. 151*
Excel No. 71	Rodgers No. 133
Excelsior No. 166	Rosedale No. 283
Eyebrow No. 193	Rosthern No. 403**
Fertile Belt No. 183*	Rudy No. 284
Fertile Valley No. 285	Sarnia No. 221
Fillmore No. 96	Saskatchewan Landing No. 167
Fish Creek No. 402*	Scott No. 98
Flett's Springs No. 429*	Shamrock No. 134
Foam Lake No. 276	Shellbrook No. 493**
Fox Valley No. 171	Sherwood No. 159
Francis No. 127	Silverwood No. 123*
Frontier No. 19	Snipe Lake No. 259*
Garden River No. 490*	Souris Valley No. 7
Glen Bain No. 105	South Qu'Appelle No. 157
Glen McPherson No. 46	St. Andrews No. 287
Glenside No. 377*	St. Louis No. 431*
Golden West No. 95	St. Peter No. 369*
Grandview No. 349**	Stanley No. 215
Grant No. 372*	Star City No. 428*
Grassy Creek No. 78	Stonehenge No. 73
Gravelbourg No. 104	Storthoaks No. 31*
Grayson No. 184	Surprise Valley No. 9
Great Bend No. 405**	Sutton No. 103
Griffin No. 66	Swift Current No. 137
Gull Lake No. 139	Tecumseh No. 65
Happy Valley No. 10	Terrell No. 101
Happyland No. 231*	The Gap No. 39
Harris No. 316	Three Lakes No. 400*
Hart Butte No. 11	Torch River No. 488*
Hazelwood No. 94*	Touchwood No. 248
Hillsborough No. 132	Tullymet No. 216
Hoodoo No. 401*	Usborne No. 310*
Humboldt No. 370*	Val Marie No. 17
Huron No. 223	Vanscoy No. 345
Indian Head No. 156	Victory No. 226
Invergordon No. 430*	Viscount No. 341*
Ituna Bon Accord No. 246	Walpole No. 92*
Kellross No. 247	Waverley No. 44
Key West No. 70	Wawken No. 93*
Kindersley No. 290**	Webb No. 138
King George No. 256	Wellington No. 97
Kingsley No. 124	Weyburn No. 67
Kinistino No. 459*	Wheatlands No. 163
Lac Pelletier No. 107	Whiska Creek No. 106
Lacadena No. 228	White Valley No. 49
Laird No. 404**	Willner No. 253
Lajord No. 128	Willow Bunch No. 42
Lake Alma No. 8	Willow Creek No. 458*
Lake Johnston No. 102	Willowdale No. 153*
Lake Lenore No. 399*	Winslow No. 319*
Lake of the Rivers No. 72	Wise Creek No. 77
Lakeside No. 338*	Wolseley No. 155
Last Mountain Valley No. 250	Wolverine No. 340*
Laurier No. 38	Wood Creek No. 281
Lawtonia No. 135	Wood River No. 74
Leask No. 464**	Wreford No. 280

*Second Designation

**Third Designation

Manitoba — 2018 Livestock Tax Deferral

Regulations

Municipalities–Consolidated Census Subdivisions

Based on the 2016 Statistics Canada Census

Alexander	North Cypress-Langford
Alonsa*	North Norfolk
Argyle	Oakland-Wawanesa
Armstrong	Oakview*
Bifrost-Riverton	Pembina
Boissevain-Morton	Piney
Brenda-Waskada	Pipestone*
Brokenhead	Portage la Prairie
Cartier	Prairie Lakes
Cartwright-Roblin	Prairie View*
Clanwilliam-Erickson*	Rhineland
Coldwell	Ritchot
De Salaberry	Riverdale*
Deloraine-Winchester	Rockwood
Division No. 18, Unorganized, East Part	Roland
Dufferin	Rosedale*
Ellice-Archie*	Rosser
Elton	Sifton*
Emerson-Franklin	Souris-Glenwood
Fisher	Springfield
Gimli	St. Andrews
Glenboro-South Cypress	St. Clements
Glenella-Lansdowne*	St. François Xavier
Grahamdale	St. Laurent
Grassland	Stanley
Grey	Ste. Anne
Hamiota*	Ste. Rose*
Hanover	Stuartburn
Harrison Park*	Taché
Headingley	Thompson
Killarney - Turtle Mountain	Two Borders
La Broquerie	Victoria
Lakeshore**	Wallace-Woodworth*
Lorne	West Interlake
Louise	West St. Paul
Macdonald	WestLake-Gladstone
McCreary*	Whitehead
Minto-Odanah*	City of Winnipeg
Montcalm	Woodlands
Morris	Yellowhead*
Norfolk-Treherne	

*Second Designation

**Third Designation

Ontario — 2018 Livestock Tax Deferral

Consolidated Census Subdivisions

Based on the 2016 Statistics Canada Census

Arran-Elderslie**	Meaford**
Brockton**	Northeastern Manitoulin and the Islands**
Chatsworth**	Northern Bruce Peninsula**
Georgian Bluffs**	Saugeen Shores**
Gordon/Barrie Island**	South Bruce Peninsula**
Grey Highlands**	The Blue Mountains**
Kincardine**	West Grey**

**Third Designation

Quebec — 2018 Livestock Tax Deferral

Consolidated Census Subdivisions

Based on the 2016 Statistics Canada Census

Albertville	Rivière-Bonjour
Amqui	Rivière-Nouvelle*
Baie-des-Sables*	Routhierville*
Bonaventure*	Ruisseau-des-Mineurs
Cap-Chat	Ruisseau-Ferguson*
Caplan*	Saint-Cléophas
Carleton-sur-Mer*	Saint-François-d'Assise*
Causapscal	Saint-Gabriel-de-Rimouski*
Collines-du-Basque	Saint-Léon-le-Grand (Census Division - La Matapédia)
Gaspé	Saint-Octave-de-Métis*
Grosses-Roches	Saint-Ulric
Lac-à-la-Croix*	Sainte-Angèle-de-Mérici*
Lac-Alfred	Sainte-Félicité (Census Division - Matane)

Lac-des-Eaux-Mortes*	Sainte-Flavie*
Lac-Matapédia	Sainte-Jeanne-d'Arc*
Matane	Sainte-Luce*
Mont-Alexandre*	Sayabec
New Richmond*	Shigawake
Percé*	Val-Brillant
Rivière-Bonaventure*	

*Second Designation

New Brunswick — 2018 Livestock Tax Deferral

Consolidated Census Subdivisions

Based on the 2016 Statistics Canada Census

Durham*	Caraquet*
Dalhousie*	Beresford*
Tracadie*	Shippagan*
New Bandon*	Paquetville*

*Second Designation

Proposed Addition — Reg. 7305.01(1) — BC, Alberta, Sask., Manitoba, Ontario, Quebec (2019)

Agriculture and Agri-Food Canada news release, July 22, 2019: *Livestock Producers Receive Tax Relief for 2019*

List of Designated Regions for 2019 under the Livestock Tax Deferral Provision

The Government of Canada today released an initial list of designated regions in British Columbia, Alberta, Saskatchewan, Manitoba and Quebec where livestock tax deferral has been authorized for 2019 due to extreme weather conditions.

Preliminary analysis indicates that livestock producers in Western Canada and Quebec are experiencing significant forage shortages due to drought conditions, supporting an early designation under the livestock tax deferral provision. Ongoing analysis and consultations will continue to determine if additional regions will be added to the designated list.

The livestock tax deferral provision allows livestock producers in prescribed drought, flood or excess moisture regions to defer a portion of their 2019 sale proceeds of breeding livestock until 2020 to help replenish the herd. The cost of replacing the animals in 2020 will offset the deferred income, thereby reducing the tax burden associated with the original sale.

The criteria for identifying regions for livestock tax deferral is forage shortfalls of 50 percent or more caused by drought or excess moisture. Eligible regions are identified based on weather, climate, and production data, in consultation with industry and provinces.

Eligibility for the tax deferral is limited to those producers located inside the designated prescribed areas. Producers in those regions can request the tax deferral when filing their 2019 income tax returns.

2019 Livestock Tax Deferral — Initial Prescribed Regions

[Superseded by list below — ed.]

Agriculture and Agri-Food Canada news release, Feb. 18, 2020: *Livestock Producers Receive Tax Relief for 2019*

New regions added under the Livestock Tax Deferral Provision for 2019

The Government of Canada today released the final list of designated regions where livestock tax deferral has been authorized for 2019 due to extreme weather conditions.

The livestock tax deferral provision allows livestock producers in prescribed drought, flood or excess moisture regions to defer a portion of their 2019 sale proceeds of breeding livestock until 2020 to help replenish the herd. The cost of replacing the animals in 2020 will offset the deferred income, thereby reducing the tax burden associated with the original sale.

On July 22, 2019, the Government announced the initial list of prescribed regions in British Columbia, Alberta, Saskatchewan, Manitoba and Quebec for livestock tax deferral purposes. Ongoing analysis of drought conditions and excess moisture has indicated the need to expand the list of designated regions for 2019, with new regions identified for British Columbia, Alberta, Saskatchewan, Manitoba, Ontario, and Quebec.

The criteria for identifying regions for livestock tax deferral is forage shortfalls of 50 percent or more caused by drought or excess moisture. Eligible regions are identified based on weather, climate, and production data, in consultation with industry and provinces (See attached Map for designated regions).

Eligibility for the tax deferral is limited to those producers located inside the designated prescribed areas. Producers in those regions can request the tax deferral when filing their 2019 income tax returns.

Quick facts

- Low moisture levels resulted in significant forage shortages for livestock producers in British Columbia, Alberta, Saskatchewan, Manitoba, Ontario and Quebec in 2019. One option for producers is to reduce their breeding herd in order to manage feed supplies.

- In addition to the livestock tax deferral provision, producers have access to assistance through existing Canadian Agricultural Partnership Business Risk Management programs, which include AgriInsurance, AgriStability and AgriInvest.

Contacts: Oliver Anderson, Director of Communications, Office of the Minister of Agriculture and Agri-Food, oliver.anderson@canada.ca, 613-462-4327; Media Relations, Agriculture and Agri-Food Canada, Ottawa, Ontario, 613-773-7972, 1-866-345-7972, aafc.mediarelations-relationsmedias.aac@canada.ca.

2019 List of Prescribed Regions

Designated Regions

Alberta–2019 Livestock Tax Deferral

Municipalities–Consolidated Census Subdivisions

Based on the 2016 Statistics Canada Census

Athabasca County	Paintearth County No. 18
Barrhead County No. 11*	Parkland County*
Beaver County*	Peace No. 135
Big Lakes County	Ponoka County*
Birch Hills County	Provost No. 52
Bonnyville No. 87*	Red Deer County*
Brazeau County*	Saddle Hills County
Camrose County*	Smoky Lake County*
Cardston County	Smoky River No. 130
Clear Hills	Special Area No. 2
Clearwater County*	Special Area No. 3
Cypress County	Special Area No. 4
Edmonton*	Spirit River No. 133
Fairview No. 136	St. Paul County No. 19*
Flagstaff County*	Starland County*
Forty Mile County No. 8	Stettler County No. 6*
Grande Prairie County No. 1	Strathcona County*
Greenview No. 16*	Sturgeon County*
Kneehill County*	Taber
Lac la Biche County*	Thorhild County*
Lac Ste. Anne County*	Two Hills County No. 21*
Lacombe County*	Vermilion River County*
Lamont County*	Vulcan County
Leduc County*	Wainwright No. 61
Lesser Slave River No.124	Warner County No. 5
Lethbridge County	Westlock County*
Mackenzie County	Wetaskiwin County No. 10*
Minburn County No. 27*	Wheatland County
Newell County	Willow Creek No. 26
Northern Lights County	Woodlands County*
Northern Sunrise County	Yellowhead County*

*Second designation

British Columbia — 2019 Livestock Tax Deferral

Consolidated Census Subdivisions

Based on the 2016 Statistics Canada Census

Alberni-Clayoquot A	Fraser-Fort George C
Alberni-Clayoquot B	Fraser-Fort George D
Alberni-Clayoquot D	Fraser-Fort George E
Alberni-Clayoquot F	Fraser-Fort George F
Bulkley-Nechako A	Juan de Fuca (Part 2)
Bulkley-Nechako B	Kitimat-Stikine C (Part 1)
Bulkley-Nechako C	Nanaimo (City)
Bulkley-Nechako D	Nanaimo C
Bulkley-Nechako F	Nanaimo E
Bulkley-Nechako G	Nanaimo F
Cariboo A	Nanaimo G
Cariboo B	Nanaimo H
Cariboo C	North Cowichan
Cariboo D*	North Saanich
Cariboo E*	Peace River B
Cariboo I	Peace River C
Cariboo J*	Peace River D
Cariboo K*	Peace River E
Central Saanich	Powell River E
Comox Valley A	Saanich
Comox Valley B (Lazo North)	Saltspring Island
Comox Valley C (Puntledge - Black Creek)	Skeena-Queen Charlotte C
Cowichan Valley B	Skeena-Queen Charlotte D
Cowichan Valley F	Skeena-Queen Charlotte E
Cowichan Valley G	Southern Gulf Islands
Fraser-Fort George A	Strathcona D (Oyster Bay - Buttle Lake)

*Second designation

Manitoba — 2019 Livestock Tax Deferral

Municipalities–Consolidated Census Subdivisions

Based on the 2016 Statistics Canada Census

Alexander	Morris
Alonsa	Mossey River
Argyle	Mountain (North)*
Armstrong	Mountain (South)
Bifrost-Riverton	Norfolk-Treherne
Boissevain-Morton	North Cypress-Langford
Brenda-Waskada	North Norfolk
Brokenhead	Oakland-Wawanesa
Cartier	Oakview
Cartwright-Roblin	Pembina
Clanwilliam-Erickson	Piney*
Coldwell	Pipestone
Dauphin	Portage la Prairie
De Salaberry	Prairie Lakes
Deloraine-Winchester	Prairie View
Division No. 1, Unorganized*	Reynolds
Division No. 17, Unorganized	Rhineland
Division No. 18, Unorganized, East Part*	Riding Mountain West
Division No. 18, Unorganized, West Part	Ritchot
Division No. 19, Unorganized*	Riverdale
Division No. 20, Unorganized, South Part	Rockwood
Dufferin	Roland
Ellice-Archie	Rosedale
Elton	Rossburn
Emerson-Franklin	Rosser
Ethelbert	Russell-Binscarth
Fisher	Sifton
Gilbert Plains	Souris-Glenwood
Gimli	Springfield
Glenboro-South Cypress	St. Andrews
Glenella-Lansdowne	St. Clements
Grahamdale	St. François Xavier
Grandview	St. Laurent
Grassland	Stanley
Grey	Ste. Anne
Hamiota	Ste. Rose
Hanover	Stuartburn*
Harrison Park	Swan Valley West
Headingley	Taché
Hillsburg-Roblin-Shell River	Thompson
Killarney - Turtle Mountain	Two Borders
La Broquerie	Victoria
Lac du Bonnet	Wallace-Woodworth
Lakeshore	West Interlake
Lorne	West St. Paul
Louise	WestLake-Gladstone
Macdonald	Whitehead
McCreary	Whitemouth
Minitonas-Bowsman	Winnipeg
Minto-Odanah	Woodlands
Montcalm	Yellowhead

*Second designation

Ontario — 2019 Livestock Tax Deferral

Consolidated Census Subdivisions

Based on the 2016 Statistics Canada Census

Alberton*	La Vallee*
Chapple*	Lake of the Woods*
Dawson*	Morley*
Emo*	Rainy River, Unorganized*

*Second designation

Quebec — 2019 Livestock Tax Deferral

Consolidated Census Subdivisions

Based on the 2016 Statistics Canada Census

Albertville	Rivière-Bonjour
Amqui	Ruisseau-des-Mineurs
Cap-Chat	Saint-Cléophas

Regulations

Causapscal	Sainte-Félicité* (Census Division - Matane)
Collines-du-Basque	Saint-Léon-le-Grand (Census Division - La Matapédia)
Grosses-Roches*	Saint-Ulric*
Lac-Matapédia	Sayabec*
Matane*	Val-Brillant

*Second designation

Saskatchewan — 2019 Livestock Tax Deferral

Municipalities–Consolidated Census Subdivisions

Based on the 2016 Statistics Canada Census

Aberdeen No. 373	Leroy No. 339	Estevan No. 5	Rosedale No. 283
Abernethy No. 186	Lipton No. 217	Excel No. 71	Rosemount No. 378
Antelope Park No. 322	Livingston No. 331	Excelsior No. 166	Rosthern No. 403
Antler No. 61	Lomond No. 37	Eye Hill No. 382	Round Valley No. 410
Argyle No. 1	Lone Tree No. 18	Eyebrow No. 193	Rudy No. 284
Arlington No. 79	Longlaketon No. 219	Fertile Belt No. 183	Saltcoats No. 213
Arm River No. 252	Loon Lake No. 561*	Fertile Valley No. 285	Sarnia No. 221
Auvergne No. 76	Loreburn No. 254	Fillmore No. 96	Saskatchewan Landing No. 167
Baildon No. 131	Lost River No. 313	Foam Lake No. 276	Saskatoon
Battle River No. 438	Lumsden No. 189	Fox Valley No. 171	Sasman No. 336
Bayne No. 371	Manitou Lake No. 442	Francis No. 127	Scott No. 98
Beaver River No. 622*	Mankota No. 45	Frenchman Butte No. 501*	Senlac No. 411
Bengough No. 40	Maple Bush No. 224	Frontier No. 19	Shamrock No. 134
Benson No. 35	Maple Creek No. 111	Garry No. 245	Sherwood No. 159
Big Arm No. 251	Mariposa No. 350	Glen Bain No. 105	Silverwood No. 123
Big Quill No. 308	Marquis No. 191	Glen McPherson No. 46	Sliding Hills No. 273
Big Stick No. 141	Marriott No. 317	Glenside No. 377	Snipe Lake No. 259
Biggar No. 347	Martin No. 122	Golden West No. 95	Souris Valley No. 7
Blucher No. 343	Maryfield No. 91	Good Lake No. 274	South Qu'Appelle No. 157
Bone Creek No. 108	Mayfield No. 406	Grandview No. 349	Spalding No. 368
Bratt's Lake No. 129	McCraney No. 282	Grant No. 372	Spy Hill No. 152
Britannia No. 502*	McKillop No. 220	Grass Lake No. 381	St. Andrews No. 287
Brock No. 64	McLeod No. 185	Grassy Creek No. 78	St. Peter No. 369
Brokenshell No. 68	Meadow Lake No. 588*	Gravelbourg No. 104	St. Philips No. 301
Browning No. 34	Milden No. 286	Grayson No. 184	Stanley No. 215
Buchanan No. 304	Milton No. 292	Great Bend No. 405	Stonehenge No. 73
Buffalo No. 409	Miry Creek No. 229	Griffin No. 66	Storthoaks No. 31
Calder No. 241	Monet No. 257	Gull Lake No. 139	Surprise Valley No. 9
Caledonia No. 99	Montmartre No. 126	Happy Valley No. 10	Sutton No. 103
Cambria No. 6	Montrose No. 315	Happyland No. 231	Swift Current No. 137
Cana No. 214	Moose Creek No. 33	Harris No. 316	Tecumseh No. 65
Canaan No. 225	Moose Jaw No. 161	Hart Butte No. 11	Terrell No. 101
Carmichael No. 109	Moose Mountain No. 63	Hazel Dell No. 335	The Gap No. 39
Caron No. 162	Moosomin No. 121	Hazelwood No. 94	Three Lakes No. 400
Chaplin No. 164	Morris No. 312	Heart's Hill No. 352	Touchwood No. 248
Chester No. 125	Morse No. 165	Hillsborough No. 132	Tramping Lake No. 380
Chesterfield No. 261	Mount Hope No. 279	Hillsdale No. 440	Tullymet No. 216
Churchbridge No. 211	Mount Pleasant No. 2	Humboldt No. 370	Usborne No. 310
Clayton No. 333	Mountain View No. 318	Huron No. 223	Val Marie No. 17
Clinworth No. 230	Newcombe No. 260	Indian Head No. 156	Vanscoy No. 345
Coalfields No. 4	North Battleford No. 437	Insinger No. 275	Victory No. 226
Colonsay No. 342	North Qu'Appelle No. 187	Invermay No. 305	Viscount No. 341
Corman Park No. 344	Norton No. 69	Ituna Bon Accord No. 246	Wallace No. 243
Cote No. 271	Oakdale No. 320	Kellross No. 247	Walpole No. 92
Coteau No. 255	Old Post No. 43	Key West No. 70	Waverley No. 44
Coulee No. 136	Orkney No. 244	Keys No. 303	Wawken No. 93
Craik No. 222	Pense No. 160	Kindersley No. 290	Webb No. 138
Cupar No. 218	Perdue No. 346	King George No. 256	Wellington No. 97
Cut Knife No. 439	Piapot No. 110	Kingsley No. 124	Weyburn No. 67
Cymri No. 36	Pinto Creek No. 75	Lac Pelletier No. 107	Wheatlands No. 163
Deer Forks No. 232	Pittville No. 169	Lacadena No. 228	Whiska Creek No. 106
Douglas No. 436	Pleasant Valley No. 288	Laird No. 404	White Valley No. 49
Dufferin No. 190	Poplar Valley No. 12	Lajord No. 128	Willner No. 253
Dundurn No. 314	Prairie Rose No. 309	Lake Alma No. 8	Willow Bunch No. 42
Eagle Creek No. 376	Prairiedale No. 321	Lake Johnston No. 102	Willowdale No. 153
Edenwold No. 158	Preeceville No. 334	Lake Lenore No. 399	Wilton No. 472*
Elcapo No. 154	Progress No. 351	Lake of the Rivers No. 72	Winslow No. 319
Eldon No. 471*	Reciprocity No. 32	Lakeside No. 338	Wise Creek No. 77
Elfros No. 307	Redburn No. 130	Lakeview No. 337	Wolseley No. 155
Elmsthorpe No. 100	Reford No. 379	Langenburg No. 181	Wolverine No. 340
Emerald No. 277	Reno No. 51	Last Mountain Valley No. 250	Wood Creek No. 281
Enfield No. 194	Riverside No. 168	Laurier No. 38	Wood River No. 74
Enniskillen No. 3	Rocanville No. 151	Lawtonia No. 135	Wreford No. 280
Enterprise No. 142	Rodgers No. 133		

*Second designation

Proposed Addition — Reg. 7305.01(1) — Quebec, New Brunswick, PEI, Nova Scotia (2020)

Agriculture and Agri-Food Canada news release, May 10, 2021: *Livestock producers in Gaspésie, New Brunswick, Prince Edward Island and Northwestern Nova Scotia eligible to receive tax relief for 2020*

The Government of Canada today released a list of prescribed drought regions in Nova Scotia, New Brunswick, Prince Edward Island and Quebec where livestock tax deferral has been authorized for the 2020 tax year.

The Livestock Tax Deferral provision will allow livestock producers in these prescribed regions who reduced their breeding herds by at least 15% to defer a portion of their 2020 income from sales until the 2021 tax year when the income may be at least partially offset by the cost of reacquiring breeding animals, thus reducing the potential tax burden.

The criteria for identifying regions for livestock tax deferral is forage yields of less than 50% of the long-term average as a result of drought or flooding in a particular year. Eligible regions are identified based on weather, climate and production data, in consultation with industry and provinces. See attached map for designated regions.

Quotes

"Extreme weather conditions this past year have caused many challenges for Canadian producers. The Government of Canada is committed to providing support that will help livestock producers manage the impacts of drought and focus on rebuilding their herds and businesses."

— The Honourable Marie-Claude Bibeau, Minister of Agriculture and Agri-Food

Quick facts

- Low moisture levels resulted in significant forage shortages for livestock producers in Nova Scotia, New Brunswick, Prince Edward Island and Quebec in 2020. One option for producers was to reduce their breeding herd in order to manage feed supplies.

- In addition to the Livestock Tax Deferral provision, producers have access to a suite of business risk management programs to help them manage significant risks that threaten the viability of their farm and are beyond their capacity to manage.

Contacts: Jean-Sébastien Comeau, Press Secretary, Office of the Minister of Agriculture and Agri-Food, jean-sebastien.comeau@canada.ca, 343-549-2326; Media Relations, Agriculture and Agri-Food Canada, Ottawa, Ontario, 613-773-7972, 1-866-345-7972, aafc.mediarelations-relationsmedias.aac@canada.ca.

2020 List of Prescribed Regions

Drought

Quebec–2020 Livestock Tax Deferral

Consolidated Census Subdivisions

Based on the 2016 Statistics Canada Census

Albertville	Ruisseau-Ferguson
Amqui	Saint-Alexandre-de-Kamouraska
Auclair	Saint-André
Baie-des-Sables	Saint-Antonin
Biencourt	Saint-Arsène
Bonaventure	Saint-Bruno-de-Kamouraska
Cacouna	Saint-Clément
Cap-Chat	Saint-Cléophas
Caplan	Saint-Cyprien (Census Division - Rivière-du-Loup)
Carleton-sur-Mer	Saint-Denis-De La Bouteillerie
Causapscal	Sainte-Angèle-de-Mérici
Collines-du-Basque	Sainte-Anne-de-la-Pocatière
Dégelis	Sainte-Félicité (Census Division–Matane)
Esprit-Saint	Sainte-Flavie
Gaspé	Sainte-Jeanne-d'Arc (Census Division–La Mitis)
Grosses-Roches	Saint-Éloi
Kamouraska	Sainte-Luce
Lac-à-la-Croix	Saint-Elzéar-de-Témiscouata
Lac-Alfred	Saint-Épiphane
Lac-des-Aigles	Saint-Eusèbe
Lac-des-Eaux-Mortes	Saint-Fabien
Lac-Huron	Saint-François-d'Assise
Lac-Matapédia	Saint-Gabriel-de-Rimouski
Lejeune	Saint-Germain
L'Isle-Verte	Saint-Guy
Matane	Saint-Hubert-de-Rivière-du-Loup
Mont-Alexandre	Saint-Jean-de-Dieu
Mont-Carmel	Saint-Jean-de-la-Lande
New Richmond	Saint-Léon-le-Grand (Census Division–La Matapédia)
Notre-Dame-des-Neiges	Saint-Mathieu-de-Rioux
Percé	Saint-Octave-de-Métis
Petit-Lac-Sainte-Anne	Saint-Onésime-d'Ixworth
Pohénégamook	Saint-Pacôme
Rimouski	Saint-Pascal
Rivière-Bonaventure	Saint-Philippe-de-Néri
Rivière-Bonjour	Saint-Simon (Census Division–Les Basques)
Rivière-du-Loup	Saint-Ulric
Rivière-Nouvelle	Sayabec
Rivière-Ouelle	Shigawake
Routhierville	Témiscouata-sur-le-Lac
Ruisseau-des-Mineurs	Val-Brillant

New Brunswick–2020 Livestock Tax Deferral

Consolidated Census Subdivisions

Based on the 2016 Statistics Canada Census

Entire Province

Nova Scotia–2020 Livestock Tax Deferral

Consolidated Census Subdivisions

Based on the 2016 Statistics Canada Census

- Colchester, Subd. A
- Cumberland, Subd. A
- Cumberland, Subd. B
- Cumberland, Subd. C
- Cumberland, Subd. D

Prince Edward Island–2020 Livestock Tax Deferral

Consolidated Census Subdivisions

Based on the 2016 Statistics Canada Census

Entire Province

Notes: A decision on the regions for each year is usually announced during the year by Agriculture and Agri-Food Canada news release. See tinyurl.com/agr-deferral.

Para. (d) added by P.C. 2019-911, for 2017 and later tax years.

Reg. 7305.01 covers both prescribed drought regions (in Reg. 7305 before 2014) and prescribed regions of flooding or excessive moisture (in Reg. 7305.02 before 2014). Added by P.C. 2018-52, for 2014 and later taxation years.

Former Reg. 7305.01, added by P.C. 2000-1769 effective 1988 and repealed for 2014 and later years, provided the "surrounded areas" rule now in 7305.01(3), for purposes of (then) Reg. 7305.

(2) [Meaning of "reserve"] — For the purpose of this section, reserve has the same meaning as assigned by the *Indian Act*.

Notes: The *Indian Act*, s. 2(1), provides:

"**reserve**"

(a) means a tract of land, the legal title to which is vested in Her Majesty, that has been set apart by Her Majesty for the use and benefit of a band, and

(b) except in subsection 18(2), sections 20 to 25, 28, 37, 38, 42, 44, 46, 48 to 51 and 58 to 60 and the regulations made under any of those provisions, includes designated lands;

"**band**" means a body of Indians

(a) for whose use and benefit in common, lands, the legal title to which is vested in Her Majesty, have been set apart before, on or after September 4, 1951,

(b) for whose use and benefit in common, moneys are held by Her Majesty, or

(c) declared by the Governor in Council to be a band for the purposes of this Act;

"**designated lands**" means a tract of land or any interest therein the legal title to which remains vested in Her Majesty and in which the band for whose use and benefit it was set apart as a reserve has, otherwise than absolutely, released or surrendered its rights or interests, whether before or after the coming into force of this definition;

(3) [Surrounded areas] — For the purpose of this section, if a portion of territory is surrounded by the territory of a census division, census subdivision, municipal entity or other geographic designation listed in subsection (1) in respect of a year, that portion of territory is deemed to be listed under that subsection in respect of that year.

Definitions [Reg. 7305.01]: "calendar year" — *Interpretation Act* 37(1)(a); "prescribed" — ITA 248(1); "reserve" — Reg. 7305.01(2).

7305.02 [Prescribed flood/moisture regions] — [To 2011 only — no longer relevant]

Notes: Reg. 7305.02 lists prescribed regions of flood or excessive moisture for ITA 80.4(4) for 2008-2011. For later years (there were none for 2012 or 2013) see Reg. 7305.01, which covers both prescribed drought regions and those with flooding or excessive moisture.

7305.1 [Automobile operating expenses] — For the purpose of subparagraph (v) of the description of A in paragraph 6(1)(k) of the Act, the amount prescribed for a taxation year is

(a) if a taxpayer is employed in a taxation year by a particular person principally in selling or leasing automobiles and an automobile is made available in the year to the taxpayer or a person related to the taxpayer by the particular person or a person related to the particular person, 22 cents; and

(b) in any other case, 25 cents.

Proposed Amendment — Reg. 7305.1

Department of Finance news release, Dec. 27, 2018: *Government Announces the 2019 Automobile Deduction Limits and Expense Benefit Rates for Business*

2. The general prescribed rate that is used to determine the taxable benefit of employees relating to the personal portion of automobile operating expenses paid by their employers will be increased by 2 cents to 28 cents per kilometre [for 2019 — ed.]. For taxpayers who are employed principally in selling or leasing automobiles, the prescribed rate used to determine the employee's taxable benefit will be increased by 2 cents to 25 cents per kilometre.

The amount of this benefit is intended to reflect the costs of operating an automobile. The additional benefit of having an employer-provided vehicle available for personal use (i.e., the automobile standby charge) is calculated separately based on capital costs and is also included in the employee's income.

[Other portions of this news release are reproduced under Reg. 7306–7307 — ed.]

Department of Finance news release, Dec. 19, 2019: *Government Announces the 2020 Automobile Deduction Limits and Expense Benefit Rates for Business*

. . . The following limits from 2019 will remain in place for 2020:

* The general prescribed rate that is used to determine the taxable benefit of employees relating to the personal portion of automobile operating expenses paid by their employers will remain at 28 cents per kilometre. For taxpayers who are employed principally in selling or leasing automobiles, the prescribed rate used to determine the employee's taxable benefit will remain at 25 cents per kilometre.

[Other portions of this news release are reproduced under Reg. 7306–7307 — ed.]

Department of Finance news release, Dec. 21, 2020: *Government Announces the 2021 Automobile Deduction Limits and Expense Benefit Rates for Businesses and Temporary Adjustments to the Automobile Standby Charge due to COVID-19*

Today, the Department of Finance Canada announced the automobile income tax deduction limits and expense benefit rates that will apply in 2021.

Most of the limits and rates that applied in 2020 will continue to apply in 2021, with one change taking effect as of January 1, 2021:

* The general prescribed rate used to determine the taxable benefit of employees relating to the personal portion of automobile expenses paid by their employers will be **decreased by one cent to 27 cents per kilometre**. For people who are employed principally in selling or leasing automobiles, the rate used to determine the employee's taxable benefit will be decreased by one cent to 24 cents per kilometre.

[Other portions of this news release are reproduced under Reg. 7306–7307 — ed.]

Notes: The Department of Finance announces changes to the "automobile numbers" in Reg. 7305.1, 7306 and 7307 each December for the following year. The operating cost employee benefit per personal-use kilometre under Reg. 7305.1 is:

Taxation year	Regular employee	Auto Salesperson
2008–11	24¢	21¢
2012	26¢	23¢
2013-15	27¢	24¢
2016	26¢	23¢
2017	25¢	22¢
2018	26¢	23¢
2019–2020	28¢	25¢
2021	27¢	24¢

Reg. 7305.1 amended to reflect the figures in the above table to 2017, by P.C. 2018-335 (for 2017), 2016-984 (for 2016); P.C. 2014-573 (for 2012-15); 2008 budget bill #2 (for 2008-11); P.C. 2006-1104, 2005-1509, 2003-1110, 2001-1235, 2000-1330, 1999-1056. Added by P.C. 1995-775.

Definitions [Reg. 7305.1]: "amount", "automobile", "employed", "person", "prescribed" — ITA 248(1); "related" — ITA 251(2)–(6); "taxation year" — ITA 249; "taxpayer" — ITA 248(1).

I.T. Technical News: 10 (1997 deduction limits and benefit rates for automobiles); 12 (1998 deduction limits and benefit rates for automobiles).

7306. [Tax-free car allowances] — For the purposes of paragraph 18(1)(r) of the Act, the amount in respect of the use of one or more automobiles in a taxation year by an individual for kilometres driven in the year for the purpose of earning income of the individual is the total of

(a) the product of 48 cents multiplied by the number of those kilometres;

(b) the product of 6 cents multiplied by the lesser of 5,000 and the number of those kilometres; and

(c) the product of 4 cents multiplied by the number of those kilometres driven in the Yukon Territory, the Northwest Territories or Nunavut.

Proposed Amendment — Reg. 7306

Department of Finance news release, Dec. 22, 2017: *Government Announces the 2018 Automobile Deduction Limits and Expense Benefit Rates for Business*

1. The limit on the deduction of tax-exempt allowances that are paid by employers to employees who use their personal vehicle for business purposes for 2018 will be increased by 1 cent to 55 cents per kilometre for the first 5,000 kilometres driven, and to 49 cents per kilometre for each additional kilometre to reflect that, since the last change to this limit, the per kilometre costs associated with owning and operating an automobile have increased by roughly 1 cent. For the Northwest Territories, Nunavut and Yukon, the tax-exempt allowance is 4 cents higher, and will be increased to 59 cents per kilometre for the first 5,000 kilometres driven, and 53 cents per kilometre for each additional kilometre. These allowances are intended to reflect the main costs of owning and operating an automobile, such as depreciation, financing, insurance, maintenance and fuel.

[Other portions of this news release are reproduced under Reg. 7305.1 — ed.]

Department of Finance news release, Dec. 27, 2018: *Government Announces the 2019 Automobile Deduction Limits and Expense Benefit Rates for Business*

1. The limit on the deduction of tax-exempt allowances that are paid by employers to employees who use their personal vehicle for business purposes for 2019 will be increased by 3 cents to 58 cents per kilometre for the first 5,000 kilometres driven, and to 52 cents per kilometre for each additional kilometre. For the Northwest Territories, Nunavut and Yukon, the tax-exempt allowance is 4 cents higher, and will be increased to 62 cents per kilometre for the first 5,000 kilometres driven, and 56 cents per kilometre for each additional kilometre. These allowances are intended to reflect the main costs of owning and operating an automobile, such as depreciation, financing, insurance, maintenance, and fuel.

[Other portions of this news release are reproduced under Reg. 7305.1 and 7307 — ed.]

Department of Finance news release, Dec. 19, 2019: *Government Announces the 2020 Automobile Deduction Limits and Expense Benefit Rates for Business. . .*

* The limit on the deduction of tax-exempt allowances that are paid by employers to employees who use their personal vehicle for business purposes for 2020 will be increased by one cent to 59 cents per kilometre for the first 5,000 kilometres driven, and to 53 cents per kilometre for each additional kilometre. For the Northwest Territories, Nunavut and Yukon, the tax-exempt allowance is four cents higher, and will be increased to 63 cents per kilometre for the first 5,000 kilometres driven, and 57 cents per kilometre for each additional kilometre. These allowances are intended to reflect the main costs of owning and operating an automobile, such as depreciation, financing, insurance, maintenance, and fuel.

[Other portions of this news release are reproduced under Reg. 7305.1 and 7307 — ed.]

Department of Finance news release, Dec. 21, 2020: *Government Announces the 2021 Automobile Deduction Limits and Expense Benefit Rates for Businesses and Temporary Adjustments to the Automobile Standby Charge due to COVID-19*

. . .The following limits from 2020 will remain in place for 2021:

* The limit on the deduction of tax-exempt allowances paid by employers to employees who use their personal vehicle for business purposes will remain at 59 cents per kilometre for the first 5,000 kilometres driven, and 53 cents per kilometre for each additional kilometre. For the Northwest Territories, Nunavut and Yukon the allowance is 4 cents higher, and will remain at 63 cents per kilometre for the first 5,000 kilometres driven, and 57 cents per kilometre for each additional kilometre.

[Other portions of this news release are reproduced under Reg. 7305.1 and 7307 — ed.]

Notes: The Department of Finance announces changes to the "automobile numbers" in Reg. 7305.1, 7306 and 7307 each December for the following year. The per-kilometre tax-free allowance limits under Reg. 7306 are:

When driven	All Provinces		Yukon/NWT/Nunavut	
	First 5,000 km	Over 5,000 km	First 5,000 km	Over 5,000 km
2012	53¢	47¢	57¢	51¢
2013-14	54¢	48¢	58¢	52¢
2015	55¢	49¢	59¢	53¢
2016-17	54¢	48¢	58¢	52¢
2018	55¢	49¢	59¢	53¢
2019	58¢	52¢	62¢	56¢
2020-21	59¢	53¢	63¢	57¢

The reference to "taxation year" in Reg. 7306 is to the individual's taxation year (the calendar year), not the employer's: VIEWS doc 2005-0114011I7.

Reg. 7306(a) amended to reflect the second column in the above table, by P.C. 2016-984 (effective 2016), 2015-634, 2014-573; 2008 budget bill #2; P.C. 2006-1104, 2005-1509, 2003-1110, 2001-1235, 2000-1330.

For the per-km rates allowed for certain travel expense purposes including moving and medical expenses, see ITA 62(1) Notes.

Definitions [Reg. 7306]: "amount", "automobile", "individual" — ITA 248(1); "taxation year" — ITA 249.

I.T. Technical News: 10 (1997 deduction limits and benefit rates for automobiles); 12 (1998 deduction limits and benefit rates for automobiles).

7307. (1) [Automobiles — CCA cost limit] — For the purposes of subsection 13(2), paragraph 13(7)(g), subparagraph 13(7)(h)(iii), subsections 20(4) and (16.1), the description of B in paragraph 67.3(d) and subparagraph 85(1)(e.4)(i) of the Act, the amount prescribed is

(a) with respect to an automobile acquired, or leased under a lease entered into, after August 1989 and before 1991, $24,000; and

(b) with respect to an automobile acquired, or leased under a lease entered into, after 1990, the amount determined by the formula

$$A + B$$

where

A is, with respect to an automobile acquired, or leased under a lease entered into,

(i) before 1997, $24,000,

(ii) in 1997, $25,000,

(iii) in 1998 or 1999, $26,000,

(iv) in 2000, $27,000, or

(v) after 2000, $30,000, and

B is the sum that would have been payable in respect of federal and provincial sales taxes on the acquisition of the automobile if it had been acquired, at a cost equal to A before the application of the federal and provincial sales taxes, if the automobile

(i) was acquired, at the time of the acquisition, or

(ii) was leased, at the time the lease was entered into.

Proposed Non-Amendment — Reg. 7307(1)

Department of Finance news release, Dec. 27, 2018: *Government Announces the 2019 Automobile Deduction Limits and Expense Benefit Rates for Business*

The following limits from 2018 will remain in place for 2019:

- The ceiling on the capital cost of passenger vehicles for capital cost allowance (CCA) purposes will remain at $30,000 (plus applicable federal and provincial-territorial sales taxes) for purchases after 2018. This ceiling restricts the cost of a vehicle on which CCA may be claimed for business purposes.

[Other portions of this news release are reproduced under Reg. 7305.1, 7306, 7307(2), 7307(3) — ed.]

Department of Finance news release, Dec. 19, 2019: *Government Announces the 2020 Automobile Deduction Limits and Expense Benefit Rates for Business*

. . . The following limits from 2019 will remain in place for 2020: . . .

- For purchases after 2019, the ceiling on the capital cost of passenger vehicles for capital cost allowance (CCA) purposes will remain at $30,000 (plus applicable federal and provincial-territorial sales taxes) for non zero-emission passenger vehicles, and at $55,000 (plus applicable federal and provincial-territorial sales taxes) for eligible zero-emission passenger vehicles. Eligible zero-emission passenger vehicles include plug-in hybrids with a battery capacity of at least 7 kWh and vehicles that are fully electric or fully powered by hydrogen. These ceilings restrict the cost of a vehicle on which CCA may be claimed for business purposes.

[Other portions of this news release are reproduced under Reg. 7305.1, 7306, 7307(2), 7307(3) — ed.]

Department of Finance news release, Dec. 21, 2020: *Government Announces the 2021 Automobile Deduction Limits and Expense Benefit Rates for Businesses and Temporary Adjustments to the Automobile Standby Charge due to COVID-19*

. . .The following limits from 2020 will remain in place for 2021:. . .

- The ceiling for capital cost allowances (CCA) for passenger vehicles [ITA 13(7)(g) — ed.] will remain at $30,000, before tax, for non zero-emission passenger vehicles, and at $55,000, before tax, for eligible zero-emission passenger vehicles [ITA 13(7)(i) — ed.]. These ceilings restrict the cost of a vehicle on which CCA may be claimed for business purposes.

[Other portions of this news release are reproduced under Reg. 7305.1, 7306, 7307(2), 7307(3) — ed.]

Related Provisions: Reg. 1100(2.5) — 50% CCA in year of disposition; Reg. Sch. II:Cl. 10.1.

Notes: The Department of Finance announces changes to the "automobile numbers" in Reg. 7305.1, 7306 and 7307 each December for the following year. The capital cost limit for an automobile has been unchanged, at $30,000 plus GST/HST and PST, for acquisitions since 2001 ($55,000 for zero-emission vehicles since March 19, 2019: see Reg. 7307(1.1)).

The allowable amount is $30,000 plus the sales tax *payable* even if not paid. In *McKay*, 2009 TCC 612, the taxpayer's status-Indian wife paid for the vehicle without sales taxes, but since he owned it the Court found that he was liable to pay the sales taxes and could include them in the cost!

Reg. 7307(1)(b)A(iv) amended and (v) added by P.C. 2001-1235, effective 2001. Reg. 7307(1)(b)A(iii) amended and (iv) added by P.C. 2000-1330, effective 2000.

Reference to ITA 85(1)(e.4)(i) in opening words of Reg. 7307(1) added by P.C. 1994-103, effective for automobiles acquired or leased under leases entered into after August 31, 1989 (i.e., retroactive to the original effective date of Reg. 7307(1)).

Reference to ITA 20(4) added to opening words of Reg. 7307(1) by P.C. 1995-775, also retroactive to the original effective date.

Income Tax Folios: S3-F4-C1: General discussion of CCA [replaces IT-478R2].

Interpretation Bulletins: IT-291R3: Transfer of property to a corporation under subsection 85(1); IT-522R: Vehicle, travel and sales expenses of employees.

I.T. Technical News: 10 (1997 deduction limits and benefit rates for automobiles); 12 (1998 deduction limits and benefit rates for automobiles).

(1.1) [Zero-emission automobile — CCA cost limit] — For the purposes of paragraph 13(7)(i) of the Act, the amount prescribed in respect of a zero-emission passenger vehicle of a taxpayer is the amount determined by the formula

$$A + B$$

where

A is $55,000; and

B is the sum that would have been payable in respect of federal and provincial sales taxes on the acquisition of the vehicle if it had been acquired by the taxpayer at a cost equal to A, before the application of the federal and provincial sales taxes.

Proposed Non-Amendment — Reg. 7307(1.1)

Department of Finance news release, Dec. 19, 2019 and Dec. 21, 2020: See under Reg. 7307(1) above.

Notes: This means $55,000 plus sales taxes, for 2019-2021. Reg. 7307(1.1) added by 2019 budget bill #1, effective March 19, 2019. See ITA 13(7)(i) Notes.

(2) [Automobiles — interest expense limit] — For the purpose of the description of A in section 67.2 of the Act, the amount prescribed in respect of an automobile that is acquired either after August 1989 and before 1997 or after 2000 is $300.

Proposed Non-Amendment — Reg. 7307(2)

Department of Finance news release, Dec. 27, 2018: *Government Announces the 2019 Automobile Deduction Limits and Expense Benefit Rates for Business*

The following limits from 2018 will remain in place for 2019:

- The maximum allowable interest deduction for amounts borrowed to purchase an automobile will remain at $300 per month for loans related to vehicles acquired after 2018.

Department of Finance news release, Dec. 19, 2019: *Government Announces the 2020 Automobile Deduction Limits and Expense Benefit Rates for Business*

. . . The following limits from 2019 will remain in place for 2020: . . .

- The maximum allowable interest deduction for amounts borrowed to purchase an automobile will remain at $300 per month for loans related to vehicles acquired after 2019.

Department of Finance news release, Dec. 21, 2020: *Government Announces the 2021 Automobile Deduction Limits and Expense Benefit Rates for Businesses and Temporary Adjustments to the Automobile Standby Charge due to COVID-19*

. . .The following limits from 2020 will remain in place for 2021:. . .

- The maximum allowable interest deduction for new automobile loans will remain at $300 per month.

Notes: See Notes to Reg. 7307(1). The interest expense deduction limit for money borrowed to purchase an automobile has been unchanged at $300 per 30 days since 2001.

Reg. 7307(2) added by P.C. 2001-1235, effective 2001.

Former Reg. 7307(2) repealed by P.C. 1999-1056, for automobiles acquired after 1996. The effect was to reduce the rate from $300 to the $250 that appears in ITA 67.2:A.

I.T. Technical News: 10 (1997 deduction limits and benefit rates for automobiles); 12 (1998 deduction limits and benefit rates for automobiles).

(3) [Automobiles — leasing limit] — For the purpose of the description of A in paragraph 67.3(c) of the Act, the amount prescribed in respect of a taxation year of a lessee is, with respect to an automobile leased under a lease entered into

(a) after August 1989 and before 1991, $650; and

(b) after 1990, the amount determined by the formula

$$A + B$$

where

A is

(i) for leases entered into after 1990 but before 1997, $650,

(ii) for leases entered into in 1997, $550,

(iii) for leases entered into in 1998 or 1999, $650,

(iv) for leases entered into in 2000, $700, and

(v) for leases entered into after 2000, $800, and

B is the sum of the federal and provincial sales taxes that would have been payable on a monthly payment under the lease in the taxation year of the lessee if, before those taxes, the lease had required monthly payments equal to A.

Proposed Non-Amendment — Reg. 7307(3)

Department of Finance news release, Dec. 27, 2018: *Government Announces the 2019 Automobile Deduction Limits and Expense Benefit Rates for Business*

The following limits from 2018 will remain in place for 2019:

- The limit on deductible leasing costs will remain at $800 per month (plus applicable federal and provincial-territorial sales taxes) for leases entered into after 2018. This limit is one of two restrictions on the deduction of automobile lease payments. A separate restriction prorates deductible lease costs where the value of the vehicle exceeds the capital cost ceiling.

Department of Finance news release, Dec. 19, 2019: *Government Announces the 2020 Automobile Deduction Limits and Expense Benefit Rates for Business*

. . . The following limits from 2019 will remain in place for 2020: . . .

- The limit on deductible leasing costs will remain at $800 per month (plus applicable federal and provincial-territorial sales taxes) for leases entered into after 2019. This limit is one of two restrictions on the deduction of automobile lease payments. A separate restriction prorates deductible lease costs where the value of the vehicle exceeds the capital cost ceiling of $30,000.

Department of Finance news release, Dec. 21, 2020: *Government Announces the 2021 Automobile Deduction Limits and Expense Benefit Rates for Businesses and Temporary Adjustments to the Automobile Standby Charge due to COVID-19*

. . . The following limits from 2020 will remain in place for 2021: . . .

- The limit on deductible leasing costs will remain at $800 per month, before tax for new leases entered into. For automobiles valued over $30,000, a separate restriction [ITA 67.3(d), Reg. 7307(4) — ed.] will continue to prorate deductible lease costs.

Notes: See Notes to Reg. 7307(1). The deductible lease cost for an automobile has been unchanged at $800 per 30-day period since 2001. (Note the alternative limit in ITA 67.3(d), however.)

Reg. 7307(3)(b) amended by P.C. 2001-1235 (effective 2001), P.C. 2000-1330 (effective 2000) and P.C. 1999-1056 (effective 1997).

I.T. Technical News: 10 (1997 deduction limits and benefit rates for automobiles); 12 (1998 deduction limits and benefit rates for automobiles).

(4) For the purpose of the description of C in paragraph 67.3(d) of the Act, the amount prescribed in respect of an automobile leased under a lease entered into after August 1989 is the amount equal to 100/85 of the amount determined in accordance with subsection (1) in respect of the automobile.

Notes: Under this rule, the figure is $35,294 (100/85 of $30,000) for 2001-2021.

Definitions [Reg. 7307]: "amount", "automobile", "prescribed" — ITA 248(1); "provincial" — *Interpretation Act* 33(3), 35(1)"province"; "taxation year" — ITA 249; "taxpayer", "zero-emission passenger vehicle" — ITA 248(1).

Interpretation Bulletins: IT-521R: Motor vehicle expenses claimed by self-employed individuals.

7308. (1) ["Carrier"] — In this section, "carrier" has the meaning assigned by subsection 146.3(1) of the Act.

(2) ["Qualifying retirement income fund"] — For the purposes of this section, a retirement income fund is a qualifying retirement income fund at a particular time if

(a) the fund was entered into before 1993 and the carrier has not accepted any property as consideration under the fund after 1992 and at or before the particular time, or

(b) the carrier has not accepted any property as consideration under the fund after 1992 and at or before the particular time, other than property transferred from a retirement income fund that, immediately before the time of the transfer, was a qualifying retirement income fund.

(3) [Minimum amount for pre-1993 RRIF] — For the purposes of the definition "minimum amount" in subsection 146.3(1) of the Act, the prescribed factor in respect of an individual for a year in connection with a retirement income fund that was a qualifying retirement income fund at the beginning of the year is the factor, determined pursuant to the following table, that corresponds to the age in whole years (in the table referred to as "X") attained by the individual at the beginning of that year or that would have been so attained by the individual if the individual had been alive at the beginning of that year.

X	Factor
Under 72	1/(90 - X)
72	0.0540
73	0.0553
74	0.0567
75	0.0582
76	0.0598
77	0.0617
78	0.0636
79	0.0658
80	0.0682
81	0.0708
82	0.0738
83	0.0771
84	0.0808
85	0.0851
86	0.0899
87	0.0955
88	0.1021
89	0.1099
90	0.1192
91	0.1306
92	0.1449
93	0.1634
94	0.1879
95 or older	0.2000

Related Provisions: ITA 146.3(1.3) — Minimum amount for 2015 for certain purposes.

Notes: Reg. 7308(3) applies only to a RRIF set up before 1993 (see Reg. 7308(2)), and someone setting up a RRIF at age 71 in 1992 is 99 in 2020, so in practice only the last two lines of the table are relevant to almost all pre-1993 RRIFs.

Table amended by 2015 Budget bill, for 2015 and later tax years. Earlier amended by P.C. 2000-184, for 1998 and later tax years.

(4) [Minimum amount for current RRIF] — For the purposes of the definition "minimum amount" in subsection 146.3(1) of the Act and subsection 8506(5), the prescribed factor in respect of an individual for a year in connection with a retirement income fund (other than a fund that was a qualifying retirement income fund at the beginning of the year) or the designated factor in respect of an individual for a year in connection with an account under a money purchase provision of a registered pension plan, as the case may be, is the factor, determined in accordance with the following table, that corresponds to the age in whole years (in the table referred to as "Y") attained by the individual at the beginning of the year or that would have been so attained by the individual if the individual was alive at the beginning of the year.

Y	Factor
under 71	1/(90 - Y)
71	0.0528
72	0.0540
73	0.0553
74	0.0567
75	0.0582
76	0.0598
77	0.0617
78	0.0636
79	0.0658
80	0.0682
81	0.0708
82	0.0738
83	0.0771
84	0.0808
85	0.0851
86	0.0899
87	0.0955
88	0.1021
89	0.1099
90	0.1192
91	0.1306
92	0.1449
93	0.1634
94	0.1879
95 or older	0.2000

Related Provisions: ITA 60.022 — Recontribution of over-withdrawal for 2015; ITA 146.3(1.3) — Minimum amount for 2015 for certain purposes; Reg. 8506(4)–(6) — Minimum amount for RPP.

Notes: See Notes to ITA 146.3(1)"minimum amount". See Reg. 7308(3) for a RRIF set up before 1993.

Table amended by 2015 Budget bill, for 2015 and later tax years. Reg. 7308(4) earlier amended by P.C. 2005-1508 (effective 2004) and 2000-184.

Reg. 7308 added by P.C. 1994-102, for 1992 and later tax years.

Registered Pension Plans Technical Manual: §14.6 (minimum amount).

Definitions [Reg. 7308]: "amount" — ITA 248(1); "carrier" — ITA 146.3(1), Reg. 7308(1); "individual" — ITA 248(1); "minimum amount" — ITA 146.3(1); "money purchase provision" — ITA 147.1(1); "prescribed", "property" — ITA 248(1); "qualifying retirement income fund" — Reg. 7308(2); "registered pension plan" — ITA 248(1); "retirement income fund" — ITA 146.3(1), 248(1).

7309. [Prescribed deductible penalties] — For the purpose of section 67.6 of the Act, penalties imposed under paragraph 110.1(1)(a) of the *Excise Act* are prescribed.

Notes [Reg. 7309]: *Excise Tax Act* s. 280 imposes a penalty at an annual rate of 6% compounded daily for periods before April 2007, in lieu of a high interest rate, on late remittances of GST/HST. This penalty still applies on assessments of pre-April 2007 periods, after which a higher rate of interest applies, in sync with Reg. 4301 for income tax purposes. (That interest is non-deductible for tax years that begin after March 2007: ITA 18(1)(t).)

GST/HST late remittance penalty for pre-April 2007 reporting periods remains deductible if claimed in later years, and can be deducted for either the year to which it relates or the year it is assessed: VIEWS docs 2007-0236641I7, 2011-0423601E5; CRA roundtable, Cdn Bar Association Commodity Tax section, Feb. 26, 2008 (cba.org > "Sections"), Q21. However, it was not enacted that way. Reg. 7309 was added and amended by P.C. 2011-935. Effective for penalties imposed after March 22, 2004, it provided:

> 7309. For the purpose of section 67.6 of the Act, penalties imposed under any of the following provisions are prescribed:
>
> (a) paragraph 110.1(1)(a) of the *Excise Act*;
>
> (b) paragraphs 280(1)(a), (1.1)(a) and (2)(a) of the *Excise Tax Act*; and
>
> (c) subsection 53(1) of the *Air Travellers Security Charge Act*, as it read before April 2007.

The amendment to introduce the current version (effectively repealing Reg. 7309(b)-(c)) was made by P.C. 2011-935 subsec. 1(2); and subsec. 3(2) states: "Subsection 1(2) applies to taxation years that begin after March 2007."

Thus, a penalty under ETA s. 280, for late remittance of GST or HST for periods before April 2007, is technically non-deductible in a later year if imposed in that later year. (Finance is aware that it drafted an in-force rule that conflicts with CRA's administrative position, but did so anyway, apparently because it would be inconsistent with the non-deductibility of interest under 18(1)(t).) However, CRA stated to the author in December 2011 (doc 2011-0423601E5) that "for the ease of administration", such penalty is "deductible in the year in which it was paid or became payable even if the penalty is imposed in a taxation year that began after April 1, 2007".

Other GST/HST penalties under the ETA, such as the gross-negligence penalty (s. 285), failing to file information (s. 284) and third-party civil penalty (s. 285.1) are non-deductible since March 23, 2004, as are other penalties (280.1, 280.11, 284.01, 284.1) introduced since 2007. Penalties for late payment under the Quebec Sales Tax are not prescribed and so are also not deductible. The same applies to provincial retail sales tax penalties for non-collection of tax, even though they are merely a constitutionally valid way of assessing uncollected tax (see Notes to ITA 67.6).

The *Excise Act* has been replaced by the *Excise Act, 2001* for most purposes except for duties on beer. *EA* 110.1(1)(a) imposes a penalty of 0.5% per month on late payment of a duty or penalty.

The *Air Travellers Security Charge Act* imposes a tax on air travel to pay for security upgrades since Sept. 11, 2001. Subsec. 53(1) imposes a penalty at an annual rate of 6% compounded daily on late payments of amounts owing under that Act. Like the GST penalty, this was changed to a higher, non-deductible interest rate effective April 2007.

Definitions [Reg. 7309]: "amount", "prescribed" — ITA 248(1).

7310. [Prescribed trade] — For the purpose of the definition "eligible apprentice" in subsection 127(9) of the Act, a prescribed trade in respect of a province means, at all times in a taxation year, a trade that is, at any time in that taxation year, a Red Seal trade for the province under the Interprovincial Standards Red Seal Program.

Notes [Reg. 7310]: There are 56 Red Seal trades (red-seal.ca; not all are designated in all provinces): agricultural equipment technician, appliance service technician, auto body and collision technician (formerly: motor vehicle body repairer (metal and paint)), automotive refinishing technician (formerly: automotive painter), automotive service technician, baker, boilermaker, bricklayer, cabinetmaker, carpenter, concrete finisher, construction craft worker, construction electrician, cook, drywall finisher/plasterer, electric motor system technician, floorcovering installer, gasfitter Classes A and B, glazier, hairstylist, heavy duty equipment technician, heavy equipment operator [HEO] (dozer), HEO (excavator), HEO (tractor-loader-backhoe), industrial electrician, industrial mechanic (millwright), instrumentation & control technician, insulator (heat & frost), ironworker [IW] (generalist), IW (reinforcing), IW (structural/ornamental), landscape horticulturalist, lather (interior systems mechanic), machinist, metal fabricator (fitter), mobile crane operator, motorcycle technician (formerly motorcycle mechanic), oil heat system technician, painter & decorator, parts technician (formerly partsperson), plumber, powerline technician, recreation vehicle service technician, refrigeration & air conditioning mechanic, rig technician, roofer, sheet metal worker, sprinkler fitter, steamfitter/pipefitter, tilesetter, tool & die maker, tower crane operator, transport trailer technician, truck & transport mechanic, welder.

Aircraft maintenance engineer and aircraft structural technician do not qualify: VIEWS docs 2009-0307391I7, 2013-0474471M4.

Reg. 7310 added by 2007 budget bill #2, this version effective for taxation years ending after Sept. 2007. For taxation years ending from May 2, 2006 through Oct. 2007, read "at any time in that taxation year" as "on September 30, 2007".

Definitions [Reg. 7310]: "prescribed" — ITA 248(1); "province" — *Interpretation Act* 35(1); "taxation year" — ITA 249.

PART LXXIV — [7400] PRESCRIBED FOREST MANAGEMENT PLANS FOR WOODLOTS

7400. (1) For the purposes of subsections 70(9), (9.3) and (10) and 73(3) of the Act, a prescribed forest management plan in respect of a woodlot of a taxpayer is a written plan for the management and development of the woodlot that

(a) describes the composition of the woodlot, provides for the attention necessary for the growth, health and quality of the trees on the woodlot and is approved in accordance with the requirements of a provincial program established for the sustainable management and conservation of forests; or

(b) has been certified in writing by a recognized forestry professional to be a plan that describes the composition of the woodlot, provides for the attention necessary for the growth, health and quality of the trees on the woodlot and includes

(i) a description of, or a map indicating, the location of the woodlot,

(ii) a description of the characteristics of the woodlot, including a map of the woodlot site that shows those characteristics,

(iii) a description of the development of the woodlot, including the activities carried out on the woodlot, since the taxpayer acquired it,

(iv) information acceptable to the recognized forestry professional estimating

(A) the ages and heights of the trees on the woodlot, and their species,

(B) the quantity of wood on the woodlot,

(C) the quality and composition of the soil underlying the woodlot, and

(D) the quantity of wood that the woodlot could yield as a result of the implementation of the plan,

(v) a description of, and the timing for, the activities proposed to be carried out on the woodlot under the plan, including any of those activities that deal with

(A) harvesting,

(B) renewal and regeneration,

(C) the application of silviculture techniques, and

(D) responsible stewardship and the protection of the environment, and

(vi) a description of the objectives and strategies for the management and development of the woodlot over a period of at least five years.

Related Provisions: Reg. 7400(2) — Meaning of "recognized forestry professional"; Reg. 7400(3) — Scope of forestry professional's opinion.

(2) A recognized forestry professional referred to in subsection (1) is a forestry professional who has a degree, diploma or certificate recognized by the Canadian Forestry Accreditation Board, the Canadian Institute of Forestry or the Canadian Council of Technicians and Technologists.

(3) A recognized forestry professional referred to in subsection (1) is not required to express an opinion as to the completeness or correctness of a description of past activities referred to in subparagraph (1)(b)(iii) or of information referred to in subparagraph (1)(b)(iv) if the information was not prepared by that recognized forestry professional.

Definitions [Reg. 7400]: "prescribed" — ITA 248(1); "provincial" — *Interpretation Act* 33(3), 35(1)"province"; "recognized forestry professional" — Reg. 7400(2); taxpayer — ITA 248(1); "written" — *Interpretation Act* 35(1)"writing".

Notes: Reg. 7400 added by P.C. 2007-205, this version effective for dispositions of property after 2007.

Former Reg. 7400 repealed by P.C. 2001-1378, effective Aug. 15, 2001. It applied to former ITA 115.1, which was repealed in 1993 retroactive to 1985 and replaced with a more general version.

Proposed Reg. 7400 in the Sept. 16, 2004 draft regulations, prescribing Canadian Forces missions, was extended and enacted as Reg. 7500 (below).

PART LXXV — [7500] PRESCRIBED MISSIONS

7500. [Repealed]

Notes: See Notes to ITA 110(1.3). Reg. 7500 (Part LXXV) repealed by 2013 budget bill #1, for missions initiated after Sept. 2012. The list of prescribed missions was replaced by designations by the Minister of Finance under ITA 110(1.3). Missions initiated before Oct. 2012 that were listed in Reg. 7500 remain prescribed, and the former version of ITA 110(1)(f)(v)(A) continues to apply to them. Reg. 7500 read:

7500. For the purposes of subclause 110(1)(f)(v)(A)(II) of the Act, the following are prescribed missions:

(a) Operation Palladium (Bosnia-Herzegovina);

(b) Operation Halo (Haiti);

(c) Operation Danaca (Middle East — Golan Heights);

(d) Operation Calumet (Middle East — Sinai);

(e) Operation Jade (Middle East — Jerusalem, Damascus and Egypt);

(f) Operation Iraqi Freedom (Kuwait);

(g) Operation Solitude (Senegal);

(h) Operation Altair (Persian Gulf);

(i) Operation Hamlet (Haiti);

(j) Operation Structure (Sri Lanka);

(k) Operation Habitation (Haiti);

(l) Operation Augural (Sudan — Kartoum);

(m) Operation Bronze (Bosnia-Herzegovina — North Atlantic Treaty Organization Stabilisation Force);

(n) Operation Boreas (Bosnia-Herzegovina — European Union Force);

(o) Operation Safari (Sudan — Kartoum);

(p) Operation Gladius (Golan Heights);

(q) Operation Augural (Ethiopia — Addis Ababa);

(r) United Nations Mission in the Sudan — Civilian Policing Component (Sudan — Kartoum);

(s) Operation Caribbe (Curacao);

(t) Operation Kobold (Balkans — Pristina);

(u) Operation Saturn (Ethiopia — Addis Ababa);

(v) Operation Enduring Freedom (Kuwait);

(w) Seventh Airlift Squadron Operation (Kyrgyzstan); and

(x) Operation Slipper (United Arab Emirates).

Reg. 7500(s)-(x) added by P.C. 2013-144, effective Oct. 30, 2007 (para. (s)), Sept. 1, 2008 ((t), (u)), Feb. 23/09 ((v)), Feb. 28/09 ((w)) and April 14/09 (para. (x)).

Reg. 7500 added by P.C. 2008-410, for 2004 and later tax years. The addition of Bosnia and Haiti was first announced by then-Prime Minister Paul Martin: Drache, "Tax Relief By Way of Prime Ministerial Speech", xxvi(10) *The Canadian Taxpayer* (Carswell) 75 (May 11, 2004).

Former Reg. 7500 repealed by P.C. 2001-1378, effective Aug. 15, 2001. It defined "prescribed film production" and "prescribed revenue guarantee" for ITA 96(2)(d)(ii), which before 1996 excluded prescribed revenue guarantees for prescribed film productions from the at-risk rules, thus allowing films to be tax shelters. (A credit is now provided directly to film producers in ITA 125.4.)

PART LXXVI — [7600] CARVED-OUT PROPERTY EXCLUSION

7600. [Prescribed property] — For the purposes of paragraph (g) of the definition "carved-out property" in subsection 209(1) of the Act, a prescribed property at any time is

(a) any right, licence or privilege to prospect, explore, drill or mine for minerals in a mineral resource (other than a bituminous sands deposit, oil sands deposit or oil shale deposit) in Canada;

(b) any rental or royalty computed by reference to the amount or value of production of minerals from a mineral resource (other than a bituminous sands deposit, oil sands deposit or oil shale deposit) in Canada;

(c) any real property in Canada the principal value of which depends on its mineral resource content (other than a bituminous sands deposit, oil sands deposit or oil shale deposit);

(d) any right to or interest in any property described in any of paragraphs (a) to (c); or

(e) a property acquired before that time by a taxpayer in the circumstances described in paragraph (c) of the definition "carved-out property" in subsection 209(1) of the Act, except where it is reasonable to consider that one of the main reasons for the acquisition of the property, or any series of transactions or events in which the property was acquired, by the taxpayer was to reduce or postpone tax that would, but for this paragraph, be payable by another taxpayer under Part XII.1 of the Act.

Related Provisions: ITA 248(10) — Series of transactions.

Notes: For the meaning of "right, licence or privilege" in para. (a), see Notes to ITA 66(15)"Canadian resource property". For the meaning of "one of the main reasons" in para. (e), see Notes to ITA 83(2.1).

Definitions [Reg. 7600]: "amount", "bituminous sands" — ITA 248(1); "Canada" — ITA 255, *Interpretation Act* 35(1); "mineral", "mineral resource", "prescribed", "property" — ITA 248(1); "series" — ITA 248(10); "taxpayer" — ITA 248(1).

PART LXXVII — [7700] PRESCRIBED PRIZES

7700. [Prescribed prize] — For the purposes of subparagraph 56(1)(n)(i) of the Act, a prescribed prize is any prize that is recognized by the general public and that is awarded for meritorious achievement in the arts, the sciences or service to the public but does not include any amount that can reasonably be regarded as having been received as compensation for services rendered or to be rendered.

Notes: The concept of prescribed prize was introduced by the 1987 budget, retroactive to 1983, after a Canadian (John Polanyi) won a Nobel prize in 1986 and questions arose as to whether it was taxable.

The TCC has held the following to be prescribed prizes: international accounting case writing competition (*Labelle*, 1994 CarswellNat 1934); Music Spirit East Award and Ultimate Deal Award for outstanding achievement in music (*Foulds*, [1997] 2 C.T.C. 2660); Gerda Lissner Foundation opera-singer competition, paying $81,000 over 10 years to cover the cost of singing coaches, training, accommodation, travel and a monthly stipend (*Knapik-Sztramko*, [2014] 1 C.T.C. 2066). In light of the last case, some of the negative CRA interpretations below could be wrong.

CRA states in VIEWS docs 2013-0475531E5 and 2013-0478391E5 that it will consider "evidence that suggests a high level of public awareness of the prize which could include the extent to which any public announcement or receipt of the prize is widely publicized by the media and whether the prize was available to a broad base of applicants", and that the paying entity, in conjunction with the recipient, should determine whether a prize "can be regarded as compensation for services rendered".

CRA has stated that the following are prescribed prizes: Agri-Food Innovation Excellence awards (VIEWS doc 2006-0202931E5); some Canada Council awards (former IT-257R para. 9, but for exclusions see Income Tax Folio S4-F14-C1 ¶1.27, 1.29, 1.44; docs 933395, 2000-0002565, 2001-0077455, 2004-0076661E5); Carnegie Hero Fund Commission Prize (2002-0142187); CEAD [Centre des auteurs dramatiques] Diffusion prizes to French-Canadian playwrights (2009-0344681E5); Governor General's Performing Arts Awards (9300075); Hnatyshyn Foundation Visual Arts Award (2007-0224981E5); "INDEX:" Award (2008-0265731E5); Kobzar Literary Award (2006-0179911E5); Leadership in Faculty Teaching Award (2007-0245311I7); Margaret Sinclair Memorial Award from the Fields Institute (2013-0475531E5, though the institute, award name and subject matter were blanked out); Millennium Prize awarded by National Gallery of Canada Foundation (2001-0072015); Polanyi Prizes, likely (2015-0595091E5); Prime Minister's Award for Teaching Excellence in Science, Technology and Math (9514155); Prix du ministre de l'Éducation du Québec (2005-015171117); Prix québécois de citoyenneté (2009-0349421E5); unnamed prize administered by a university (2010-0374461E5); unnamed prize for achievement in sciences (2005-0145751E5); unnamed prize for achievement in unstated field (2013-0478391E5, 2015-061046117, 2017-0715041E5, 2019-0811441E5); unnamed prize for emerging artists (2018-0780601E5); unnamed prize in competition to present sustainable business practice (2012-0438891E5).

CRA says that Olympic medals and Canadian Olympic Committee prize money for winning them are taxable: VIEWS docs 2004-0098691E5, 2008-0300071M4, 2012-0458181M4, 2012-0460111M4, 2013-0477251M4, 2014-0521731M4, 2016-0664861M4. This may be correct, as competing in the Olympics might not be a "service to the public". *Contra*, see William Innes, "No Medal for CRA's Questionable Treatment of Canadian Olympic Medalists", Carswell *Tax and Estate Planning Centre*, Aug. 14, 2012; Donalee Moulton, "Taxing questions for Olympic medalists", *The Bottom Line*, Mid-September 2012, pp. 1, 17.

CRA also says the following do not qualify: research grants; university awards for scholastic achievement (doc 9911565); some Canada Council awards (see above); John G. Diefenbaker Award and Canada-Germany Research Award (921002); prizes to high school students in an essay contest (2004-0084611E5); award that appears to be a fellowship (2005-0127741E5); charitable foundation award connected to recipient's business or employment (2009-0313051E5); graduate level social-work award that appears to be a scholarship (2017-0715041E5).

CRA refused to opine whether awards would qualify in docs 2010-0362391E5 (awards in music competitions), 2010-0387711E5 (proposed prizes — insufficient info).

Definitions [Reg. 7700]: "amount", "prescribed" — ITA 248(1).

Income Tax Folios: S1-F2-C3: Scholarships, research grants and other education assistance [replaces IT-340R].

Interpretation Bulletins: IT-257R: Canada Council grants.

PART LXXVIII — [7800] SPECIFIED PENSION PLANS

Notes: Heading changed from "Prescribed Provincial Pension Plans" by 2011 budget bill #2, effective 2010.

7800. For the purposes of the definition "specified pension plan" in subsection 248(1) of the Act, a prescribed arrangement is the Saskatchewan Pension Plan established under *The Saskatchewan Pension Plan Act*, chapter S-32.2 of the Statutes of Saskatchewan, 1986, as amended from time to time.

Notes: See Notes to ITA 248(1)"specified pension plan", which replaced "prescribed provincial pension plan". Reg. 7800 amended by 2011 budget bill #2, effective 2010. Reg. 7800(1) amended by P.C. 2001-1378, effective Aug. 15, 2001.

Definitions [Reg. 7800]: "amount", "prescribed" — ITA 248(1); "taxation year" — ITA 249.

Interpretation Bulletins: IT-124R6: Contributions to registered retirement savings plans; IT-499R: Superannuation or pension benefits; IT-517R: Pension tax credit.

PART LXXIX — [7900] PRESCRIBED FINANCIAL INSTITUTIONS

7900. For the purposes of the definitions "excluded income" and "excluded revenue" and "specified deposit" in subsection 95(2.5) of the Act, each of the following is a prescribed financial institution:

(a) a member of the Canadian Payments Association; and

(b) a credit union that is a shareholder or member of a body corporate or organization that is a central for the purposes of the *Canadian Payments Act*.

Notes: Reg. 7900(2) repealed and 7900(1) renumbered 7900 and amended, by 2013 budget bill #1, for tax years that begin after March 20, 2013, to delete reference to ITA 33.1 from opening words and "other than an authorized foreign bank" from para. (a).

Reg. 7900 changed to 7900(1) by P.C. 2009-1869 effective 1998, last change effective 2008. From Oct. 24, 2001 through 2007, Reg. 7900(1) also applied to former ITA 212(1)(b)(iii)(D) and 212(1)(b)(xi). Before Oct. 24, 2001, Reg. 7900(1) read differently. Earlier amended by P.C. 1997-1670. Reg. 7900(2) added by P.C. 2009-1869 effective 1998, last change effective 2008. Before 2008, Reg. 7900(2) also applied to former ITA 212(1)(b)(iii)(D).

Definitions [Reg. 7900]: "corporation" — ITA 248(1), *Interpretation Act* 35(1); "credit union" — ITA 137(6), 248(1); "shareholder" — ITA 248(1).

PART LXXX — [8000–8007] PRESCRIBED RESERVE AMOUNT AND RECOVERY RATE

8000. [Prescribed reserve amount] — For the purpose of clause 20(1)(l)(ii)(C) of the Act, the prescribed reserve amount for a taxation year means the aggregate of

(a) where the taxpayer is a bank, an amount equal to the lesser of

(i) the amount of the reserve reported in its annual report for the year that is filed with and accepted by the relevant authority or, where the taxpayer was throughout the year subject to the supervision of the relevant authority but was not required to file an annual report for the year with the relevant authority, in its financial statements for the year, as general provisions or as specific provisions, in respect of exposures to designated countries in respect of loans or lending assets of the taxpayer made or acquired by it in the ordinary course of its business, and

(ii) an amount in respect of the loans or lending assets of the taxpayer at the end of the year that were made or acquired by the taxpayer in the ordinary course of its business and reported for the year by the taxpayer to the relevant authority, in accordance with the guidelines established by the relevant authority, as part of the taxpayer's total exposure to designated countries for the purpose of determining the taxpayer's general provisions or specific provisions referred to in subparagraph (i) or that were acquired by the taxpayer after August 16, 1990 and reported for the year by the taxpayer to the relevant authority, in accordance with the guidelines established by the relevant authority, as an exposure to a designated country (in this subparagraph referred to as the "loans") equal to the positive or negative amount, as the case may be, determined by the formula

$$45\% \ (A + B) - (B + C)$$

where

A is the aggregate of all amounts each of which is the amount that would be the amortized cost of a loan to the taxpayer at the end of the year if the definition "amortized cost" in section 248 of the Act were read without reference to paragraphs (e) and (i) thereof,

B is the aggregate of all amounts each of which is the amount, if any, by which the principal amount of a loan outstanding at the time it was acquired by the taxpayer exceeds the amortized cost of the loan to the taxpayer immediately after the time it was acquired by the taxpayer, and

C is the aggregate of all amounts each of which is

    (A) an amount deducted in respect of a loan under clause 20(1)(l)(ii)(B) of the Act in computing the taxpayer's income for the year, or

    (B) an amount in respect of a loan determined as the amount, if any, by which

        (I) the aggregate of all amounts in respect of the loan deducted under paragraph 20(1)(p) of the Act in computing the taxpayer's income for the year or a preceding taxation year

    exceeds

        (II) the aggregate of all amounts in respect of the loan included under paragraph 12(1)(i) of the Act in computing the taxpayer's income for the year or a preceding taxation year, and

(a.1) where the taxpayer is a bank, the positive or negative amount that would be determined under the formula in subparagraph (a)(ii) in respect of the specified loans owned by the taxpayer at the end of the year if that subparagraph applied to those loans.

(b) [Repealed]

Related Provisions: ITA 257 — Negative amounts in formulas.

Notes: Opening words of Reg. 8000 amended by P.C. 1999-195 to change reference from 20(1)(l)(ii)(A) to 20(1)(l)(ii)(C), effective on the same basis as the 1995-97 technical bill amendments to ITA 20(1)(l).

Reg. 8000(a.1) added by P.C. 1999-195, effective for the 1997 and later taxation years (and 1992-96 by election).

Reg. 8000(b) repealed by P.C. 1999-195, effective on the same basis as the 1995-97 technical bill amendments to ITA 20(1)(l).

Definitions [Reg. 8000]: "amortized cost", "amount" — ITA 248(1); "bank" — ITA 248(1), *Interpretation Act* 35(1); "business" — ITA 248(1); "designated country", "exposure to a designated country", "general provisions" — Reg. 8006; "lending asset" — ITA 248(1); "loans" — Reg. 8000(a)(ii); "loans or lending assets" — Reg. 8003; "prescribed", "principal amount" — ITA 248(1); "principal amount outstanding" — Reg. 8002(a); "relevant authority", "specific provisions", "specified loan" — Reg. 8006; "taxation year" — ITA 249; "taxpayer" — ITA 248(1).

8001. [Repealed]

Notes: Reg. 8001 repealed by P.C. 1999-195, effective on the same basis as the 1995-97 technical bill amendments to ITA 20(1)(l).

8002. [Principal amount, amortized cost] — For the purposes of paragraph 8000(a),

(a) the principal amount outstanding at any time of a lending asset of a taxpayer that is a share of the capital stock of a corporation is the part of the consideration received by the corporation for the issue of the share that is outstanding at that time;

(b) where

    (i) a taxpayer realizes a loss from the disposition of a loan or lending asset described in subparagraph 8000(a)(ii) or a spec-

ified loan described in paragraph 8000(a.1) (in this paragraph referred to as the "former loan") for consideration that included another loan or lending asset that was a loan or lending asset described in subparagraph 8000(a)(ii) or paragraph 8000(a.1) (in this paragraph referred to as the "new loan"), and

    (ii) in the case of a former loan that is not a specified loan, the loss is included in computing the taxpayer's provisionable assets as reported for the year to the relevant authority, in accordance with the guidelines established by the relevant authority, for the purpose of determining the taxpayer's general provisions or specific provisions in respect of exposures to designated countries,

the principal amount of the new loan outstanding at the time it was acquired by the taxpayer is deemed to be equal to the principal amount of the former loan outstanding immediately before that time; and

(c) where at the end of a particular taxation year a taxpayer owns a specified loan that, at the end of the preceding taxation year, was described in an inventory of the taxpayer, the amortized cost of the specified loan to the taxpayer at the end of the particular year is its value determined under section 10 of the Act at the end of the preceding year for the purpose of computing the taxpayer's income for the preceding year.

Notes: Reg. 8002(b) amended and (c) added by P.C. 1999-195, effective on the same basis as the addition of Reg. 8000(a.1).

Definitions [Reg. 8002]: "amortized cost" — Reg. 8002(c), ITA 248(1); "corporation" — ITA 248(1), *Interpretation Act* 35(1); "designated country" — Reg. 8006; "disposition" — ITA 248(1); "exposure to a designated country" — Reg. 8006; "former loan" — Reg. 8002(b)(i); "general provisions" — Reg. 8006; "inventory", "lending asset" — ITA 248(1); "new loan" — Reg. 8002(b)(i); "principal amount" — Reg. 8002, ITA 248(1); "provisionable assets", "relevant authority" — Reg. 8006; "share" — ITA 248(1); "specific provisions", "specified loan" — Reg. 8006; "taxation year" — ITA 249; "taxpayer" — ITA 248(1).

8003. [Election] — Where a taxpayer elects to have this section apply by notifying the Minister in writing within 90 days after the day on which this section is published in the *Canada Gazette*, the loans or lending assets of the taxpayer that are described in subparagraph 8000(a)(ii) shall not include any loan or lending asset acquired by the taxpayer before November 1988 from a person with whom the taxpayer was dealing at arm's length.

Notes: Jan. 16, 1991 was the date on which Reg. 8003 (along with the rest of Part LXXX) was published in the *Canada Gazette*.

Definitions [Reg. 8003]: "arm's length" — ITA 251(1); "Canada" — ITA 255, *Interpretation Act* 35(1); "lending asset", "Minister", "person", "taxpayer" — ITA 248(1); "writing" — *Interpretation Act* 35(1).

8004. [Repealed]

Notes: Reg. 8004 repealed by P.C. 1999-195, effective on the same basis as the 1995-97 technical bill amendments to ITA 20(1)(l).

8005. [Rules — loans and lending assets] — For the purposes of subparagraph 8000(a)(ii), where a loan or lending asset of a person (in this section referred to as the **"holder"**) related to a taxpayer

(a) was reported for the year by the taxpayer to the relevant authority, in accordance with the guidelines established by the relevant authority, as an exposure to a designated country,

(b) was acquired by the holder or another person related to the taxpayer after August 16, 1990 as part of a series of transactions or events in which the taxpayer or a person related to the taxpayer disposed of a loan or lending asset that

    (i) for the taxation year immediately preceding the particular year in which it was disposed of, was a loan or lending asset that was reported by the taxpayer to the relevant authority, in accordance with the guidelines established by the relevant authority, as an exposure to a designated country, and

    (ii) was a loan or lending asset a loss arising on the disposition of which would be a loss in respect of which a deduction is permitted under Part I of the Act to the taxpayer or a person related to the taxpayer, and

(c) had an amortized cost to the holder, immediately after the time it was acquired by the holder, that was less than 55 per cent of its principal amount,

the following rules apply:

(d) the loan or lending asset shall be deemed

(i) to be a loan or lending asset of the taxpayer at the end of the year,

(ii) to be a loan or lending asset of the taxpayer that was acquired by the taxpayer at the time it was acquired by the holder, and

(iii) to have an amortized cost to the taxpayer, at any time, that is equal to its amortized cost to the holder at that time, and

(e) any amount in respect of the loan or lending asset deducted under paragraph 20(1)(p) of the Act or included under paragraph 12(1)(i) of the Act in computing the holder's income for a particular year shall be deemed to have been so deducted or included, as the case may be, in computing the income of the taxpayer for the year in which the particular year ends.

Related Provisions: ITA 248(10) — Series of transactions.

Definitions [Reg. 8005]: "amortized cost", "amount" — ITA 248(1); "disposed" — ITA 248(1)"disposition"; "disposition" — ITA 248(1); "exposure to a designated country" — Reg. 8006; "holder" — Reg. 8005; "lending asset", "person", "principal amount" — ITA 248(1); "related" — ITA 251(2)–(6); "relevant authority" — Reg. 8006; "series" — ITA 248(10); "taxation year" — ITA 249; "taxpayer" — ITA 248(1).

8006. For the purposes of this Part,

"designated country" has the same meaning as in the Guidelines for banks established pursuant to section 175 of the *Bank Act*, as that section read on May 31, 1992, and issued by the Office of the Superintendent of Financial Institutions, as amended from time to time;

"exposure to a designated country" has the same meaning as in the Guidelines for banks established pursuant to section 175 of the *Bank Act*, as that section read on May 31, 1992, and issued by the Office of the Superintendent of Financial Institutions, as amended from time to time;

"general provisions" has the same meaning as the expression "general country risk provisions" in the Guidelines for banks established pursuant to section 175 of the *Bank Act*, as that section read on May 31, 1992, and issued by the Office of the Superintendent of Financial Institutions, as amended from time to time;

"provisionable assets" has the same meaning as in the Guidelines for banks established pursuant to section 175 of the *Bank Act*, as that section read on May 31, 1992, and issued by the Office of the Superintendent of Financial Institutions, as amended from time to time;

"relevant authority" means the Superintendent of Financial Institutions;

"specific provisions" has the same meaning as in the Guidelines for banks established pursuant to section 175 of the *Bank Act*, as that section read on May 31, 1992, and issued by the Office of the Superintendent of Financial Institutions, as amended from time to time.

"specified loan" means

(a) a United Mexican States Collateralized Par Bond due in 2019, or

(b) a United Mexican States Collateralized Discount Bond due in 2019;

Notes: These Mexican bonds are known as "Brady bonds". Definition "specified loan" added by P.C. 1995-195, effective on the same basis as Reg. 8000(a.1).

Notes [Reg. 8006]: Reg. 8006 added by P.C. 1992-2335, effective for taxation years and fiscal period beginning after June 17, 1987 and ending after 1987.

Definitions [Reg. 8006]: "bank" — ITA 248(1), *Interpretation Act* 35(1).

8007. [Repealed]

Notes: Reg. 8007 added and repealed by P.C. 1999-195. It was effective only for tax years that ended after 1991 and before Oct. 1997 and only by election. It provided that Reg. 8000(b) does not apply to a specified loan of a bank.

PART LXXXI — [8100–8105] [REPEALED]

8100–8105. [Repealed]

Notes: Part LXXXI (Reg. 8100-8105, 1994 transitional rules for life insurers' reserves) repealed by 2002-2013 technical bill, for tax years that begin after Oct. 2011.

PART LXXXII — [8200–8201.1] PRESCRIBED PROPERTIES AND PERMANENT ESTABLISHMENTS

8200. Prescribed properties [for leasing rules] — For the purposes of subsection 16.1(1) of the Act, "prescribed property" means

(a) exempt property, within the meaning assigned by paragraph 1100(1.13)(a), other than property leased on or before February 2, 1990 that is

(i) a truck or tractor that is designed for use on highways and has a "gross vehicle weight rating" (within the meaning assigned that expression by the *Motor Vehicle Safety Regulations*) of 11,778 kilograms or more,

(ii) a trailer that is designed for use on highways and is of a type designed to be hauled under normal operating conditions by a truck or tractor described in subparagraph (i), or

(iii) a railway car,

(b) property that is the subject of a lease where the tangible property, other than exempt property (within the meaning assigned by paragraph 1100(1.13)(a)), that was the subject of the lease had, at the time the lease was entered into, an aggregate fair market value not in excess of $25,000, and

(c) intangible property.

Notes: A transport truck is "exempt property" under Reg. 1100(1.13)(a) and thus is prescribed property: VIEWS doc 2015-0566011E5; but a logging truck is not: 2014-0548041E5.

Reg. 8200 added by P.C. 1991-465, for leases entered into after 10pm EDT April 26, 1989, with certain grandfathering for earlier leases.

Definitions [Reg. 8200]: "fair market value" — see ITA 69(1) Notes; "property" — ITA 248(1).

8200.1 [Prescribed energy conservation property] — For the purposes of subsection 13(18.1), the definition "Canadian renewable and conservation expense" in subsection 66.1(6) and subparagraph 241(4)(d)(vi.1) of the Act, "prescribed energy conservation property" means property described in Class 43.1 or 43.2 in Schedule II.

Related Provisions: ITA 13(18.1) — Dept. of Natural Resources "Technical Guide to Class 43.1" to be determinative.

Notes: Reg. 8200.1 amended by 2013 budget bill #2, effective Dec. 21, 2012, to apply to ITA 66.1(6)"Canadian renewable and conservation expense".

Reg. 8200.1 added by P.C. 1997-1033 effective Feb. 22, 1994, and amended to add reference to Class 43.2 by P.C. 2006-329, effective Feb. 23, 2005.

Definitions [Reg. 8200.1]: "prescribed", "property" — ITA 248(1).

8201. [Permanent establishment] — For the purposes of subsection 16.1(1), the definition "outstanding debts to specified non-residents" in subsection 18(5), subsections 100(1.3) and 112(2), the definition "qualified Canadian transit organization" in subsection 118.02(1), subsections 125.4(1) and 125.5(1), the definition "taxable supplier" in subsection 127(9), subparagraph 128.1(4)(b)(ii), paragraphs 181.3(5)(a) and 190.14(2)(b), section 233.8, the definitions "Canadian banking business" and "tax-indifferent investor" in subsection 248(1) and paragraph 260(5)(a) of the Act, a "permanent establishment" of a person or partnership (either of whom is referred to in this section as the "person") means a fixed place of business of the person, including an office, a branch, a mine, an oil well, a farm, a timberland, a factory, a workshop or a warehouse if the person has a fixed place of business and, where the person does not have any fixed place of business, the principal place at which the person's business is conducted, and

(a) where the person carries on business through an employee or agent, established in a particular place, who has general authority to contract for the person or who has a stock of merchandise owned by the person from which the employee or agent regularly fills orders, the person shall be deemed to have a permanent establishment at that place,

(b) where the person is an insurance corporation, the person is deemed to have a permanent establishment in each country in which the person is registered or licensed to do business,

(c) where the person uses substantial machinery or equipment at a particular place at any time in a taxation year, the person shall be deemed to have a permanent establishment at that place,

(d) the fact that the person has business dealings through a commission agent, broker or other independent agent or maintains an office solely for the purchase of merchandise shall not of itself be held to mean that the person has a permanent establishment, and

(e) where the person is a corporation, the fact that the person has a subsidiary controlled corporation at a place or a subsidiary controlled corporation engaged in trade or business at a place shall not of itself be held to mean that the person is operating a permanent establishment at that place,

except that, where the person is resident in a country with which the Government of Canada has concluded a tax treaty in which the expression "permanent establishment" is given a particular meaning, that meaning shall apply.

Related Provisions: ITA 56.4(1)"permanent establishment" — Definition applies for restrictive covenants (non-competition agreements); Reg. 5906(2) — Definition for FAPI and related purposes.

Notes: For the meaning of "substantial machinery or equipment" in Reg. 8201(c), see Notes to Reg. 400(2).

Reg. 8201(1) opening words amended by 2016 budget bill #2, effective 2016, to add 233.8.

Reg. 8201 earlier amended by 2016 budget bill #1 (effective April 22, 2015, to add 248(1)"tax-indifferent investor"), 2002-2013 technical bill, 2012 budget bill #2; P.C. 2010-548, 2005-1508, 2000-183. Added by P.C. 1994-139.

Definitions [Reg. 8201]: "business" — ITA 248(1); "Canada" — ITA 255, *Interpretation Act* 35(1); "corporation" — ITA 248(1), *Interpretation Act* 35(1); "employee", "insurance corporation", "office" — ITA 248(1); "partnership" — see ITA 96(1) Notes; "person" — ITA 248(1); "resident" — ITA 250; "subsidiary controlled corporation", "tax treaty" — ITA 248(1); "taxation year" — ITA 249.

I.T. Technical News: 33 (permanent establishment — the *Dudney* case update).

Application Policies: SR&ED 2002-02R2: Experimental production and commercial production with experimental development work — allowable SR&ED expenditures.

Forms: T2 Sched. 305: Newfoundland and Labrador capital tax on financial institutions.

8201.1 [Repealed]

Notes: Reg. 8201.1 added and repealed by P.C. 2000-183, effective only from Dec. 5, 1985 through the 1994 taxation year. It defined "permanent establishment" for ITA 206(1.3), later moved to Reg. 8201.

Proposed Reg. 8202 (Feb. 27, 2004 draft), which would have defined "permanent establishment" for various purposes in ss. 90-95, has been replaced by Reg. 5906(2)(b) (Dec. 18, 2009 draft).

PART LXXXIII — [8300–8311] PENSION ADJUSTMENTS, PAST SERVICE PENSION ADJUSTMENTS, PENSION ADJUSTMENT REVERSALS AND PRESCRIBED AMOUNTS

8300. Interpretation — (1) In this Part,

"certifiable past service event", with respect to an individual means a past service event that is required, by reason of subsection 147.1(10) of the Act, to be disregarded, in whole or in part, in determining the benefits to be paid under a registered pension plan with respect to the individual until a certification of the Minister in respect of the event has been obtained;

Registered Pension Plans Technical Manual: §1.10 (certifiable past service event).

"complete period of reduced services" of an individual means a period of reduced services of the individual that is not part of a longer period of reduced services of the individual;

Registered Pension Plans Technical Manual: §1.13 (complete period of reduced services).

"designated savings arrangement" of an individual means a RRIF or RRSP under which the individual is the annuitant, or the individual's account under a money purchase provision of a registered pension plan;

Notes: Definition added by 2011 budget bill #2, effective March 23, 2011.

"excluded contribution" to a registered pension plan means an amount that is transferred to the plan in accordance with any of subsections 146(16), 146.3(14.1), 147(19), 147.3(1) to (4) and 147.3(5) to (7) of the Act;

Notes: Definition amended by P.C. 2005-1508, effective 2004, to add reference to ITA 146.3(14.1).

References to ITA 147.3 amended by P.C. 1995-17, retroactive to transfers in 1991 or later, so that a transfer under ITA 147.1(4.1) is not an excluded contribution.

In its application in respect of amounts paid to pension plans before 1991, read the definition to include amounts deductible under ITA 60(j) or (j.1).

"flat benefit provision" of a pension plan means a defined benefit provision of the plan under which the amount of lifetime retirement benefits provided to each member is based on the aggregate of all amounts each of which is the product of a fixed rate and either the duration of service of the member or the number of units of output of the member, and, for the purposes of this definition, where

(a) the amount of lifetime retirement benefits provided under a defined benefit provision to each member is subject to a limit based on the remuneration received by the member, and

(b) the limit may reasonably be considered to be included to ensure that the amount of lifetime retirement benefits provided to each member does not exceed the maximum amount of such benefits that may be provided by a registered pension plan,

the limit shall be disregarded for the purpose of determining whether the provision is a flat benefit provision;

"individual pension plan", in respect of a calendar year, means a registered pension plan that contains a defined benefit provision if, at any time in the year or a preceding year, the plan

(a) has fewer than four members and at least one of them is related to a participating employer in the plan, or

(b) is a designated plan and it is reasonable to conclude that the rights of one or more members to receive benefits under the plan exist primarily to avoid the application of paragraph (a);

Related Provisions: Reg. 8300(1.1) — Minister may waive definition; Reg. 8304(10), (11) — Past service event in relation to individual pension plan; Reg. 8500(1)"IPP minimum amount" — Definition; Reg. 8502(d)(x) — Permissible distributions — IPP minimum amount; Reg. 8503(26) — IPP — minimum withdrawal; Reg. 8515 — Special rules for designated plans.

Notes: For discussion of IPPs see Notes to Reg. 8515(1).

Definition added by 2011 budget bill #2, effective March 23, 2011.

Registered Plans Directorate Newsletters: 14-1 (reviewing earnings and service for IPPs).

"member", in relation to a deferred profit sharing plan or a benefit provision of a registered pension plan, means an individual who has a right (either immediate or in the future and either absolute or contingent) to receive benefits under the plan or the provision, as the case may be, other than an individual who has such a right only because of the participation of another individual in the plan or under the provision, as the case may be;

Related Provisions: ITA 147.1(1)"member" — Similar definition in the Act.

Notes: Definition "member" added by P.C. 1998-2256, effective 1990.

Registered Pension Plans Technical Manual: §1.29 (member).

"PA offset" for a calendar year means

(a) for years before 1997, $1,000, and

(b) for years after 1996, $600;

Notes: See Notes to ITA 248(1)"pension adjustment". Definition "PA offset" added by P.C. 1998-2256, effective 1990.

"past service event" means any transaction, event or circumstance that occurs after 1989 and as a consequence of which

(a) retirement benefits become provided to an individual under a defined benefit provision of a pension plan in respect of a period before the time that the transaction, event or circumstance occurs,

(b) there is a change to the way in which retirement benefits provided to an individual under a defined benefit provision of a pension plan in respect of a period before the time that the transaction, event or circumstance occurs are determined, including a change that is applicable only in specified circumstances, or

(c) there is a change in the value of an indexing or other automatic adjustment that enters into the determination of the amount of an individual's retirement benefits under a defined benefit provision of a pension plan in respect of a period before the time that the value of the adjustment changes;

Related Provisions: Reg. 8300(2) — Definition applies to ITA 147.1(1).

Registered Pension Plans Technical Manual: §1.34 (past service event).

"period of reduced services" of an individual means, in connection with a benefit provision of a registered pension plan, a period that consists of one or more periods each of which is

(a) an eligible period of reduced pay or temporary absence of the individual with respect to an employer who participates under the provision, or

(b) a period of disability of the individual;

Notes: Opening words of definition amended by P.C. 2007-849, effective June 13, 2007.

"refund benefit" means

(a) with respect to an individual and a benefit provision of a pension plan, a return of contributions made by the individual under the provision, and

(b) with respect to an individual and a deferred profit sharing plan, a return of contributions made by the individual to the plan,

and includes any interest (computed at a rate not exceeding a reasonable rate) payable in respect of those contributions;

Notes: Para. (a) amended by P.C. 2007-849, effective June 13, 2007, to change "money purchase or defined benefit provision" to "benefit provision".

"resident compensation" of an individual from an employer for a calendar year means the amount that would be the individual's compensation from the employer for the year if the definition "compensation" in subsection 147.1(1) of the Act were read without reference to paragraphs (b) and (c) of that definition.

Notes: Definition "resident compensation" added by P.C. 1998-2256, effective 1990.

(1.1) The Minister may waive in writing the application of the definition "individual pension plan" in subsection (1) if is just and equitable to do so having regard to all the circumstances.

Notes: For the meaning of "just and equitable", see Notes to ITA 85(7.1).

Reg. 8300(1.1) added by 2011 budget bill #2, effective March 23, 2011.

(2) The definition "past service event" in subsection (1) is applicable for the purposes of subsection 147.1(1) of the Act.

Registered Pension Plans Technical Manual: §1.34 (past service event).

(3) All words and expressions used in this Part that are defined in sections 147 or 147.1 of the Act or in Part LXXXV have the meanings assigned in those provisions unless a definition in this Part is applicable.

Related Provisions: Reg. 8500(2) — Mirror image rule causing terms in Reg. 8300(1) to be defined for purposes of Part 85.

(4) For the purposes of this Part, an officer who receives remuneration for holding an office shall, for any period that the officer holds the office, be deemed to render services to, and to be in the service of, the person from whom the officer receives the remuneration.

(5) For the purposes of this Part (other than the definition "member" in subsection (1)), where an individual has received an interest in an annuity contract in full or partial satisfaction of the individual's entitlement to benefits under a defined benefit provision of a pension plan, any rights of the individual under the contract are deemed to be rights under the defined benefit provision.

Notes: Reg. 8300(5) amended by P.C. 1998-2256, effective 1990.

(6) For the purposes of this Part and subsection 147.1(10) of the Act, and subject to subsection 8308(1), the following rules apply in respect of the determination of the benefits that are provided to an individual under a defined benefit provision of a pension plan at a particular time:

(a) where a term of the defined benefit provision, or an amendment to a term of the provision, is not applicable with respect to the individual before a specified date, the term shall be considered to have been added to the provision, or the amendment shall be considered to have been made to the term, on the specified date;

(b) where an alteration to the benefits provided to the individual is conditional on the requirements of subsection 147.1(10) of the Act being met, those requirements shall be assumed to have been met;

(c) benefits that will be reinstated if the individual returns to employment with an employer who participates in the plan shall be considered not to be provided until the individual returns to employment; and

(d) where benefits under the provision depend on the individual's job category or other circumstances, the only benefits provided to the individual are the benefits that are relevant to the individual's circumstances at the particular time.

(7) For the purposes of subsections 8301(3) and (8), paragraph 8302(3)(c), subsections 8302(5) and 8304(5) and (5.1), paragraphs 8304.1(10)(c) and (11)(c), subparagraph 8306(4)(a)(ii) and subsection 8308(3), the benefits to which an individual is entitled at any time under a deferred profit sharing plan or pension plan include benefits to which the individual has only a contingent right because a condition for the vesting of the benefits has not been satisfied.

Notes: Reg. 8300(7) amended by P.C. 1998-2256, effective 1990, to add references to Reg. 8304(5.1), 8304.1, 8306 and 8308.

(8) For the purposes of this Part, such portion of an amount allocated to an individual at any time under a money purchase provision of a registered pension plan as

(a) is attributable to

(i) forfeited amounts under the provision or earnings of the plan that are reasonably attributable to those amounts,

(ii) a surplus under the provision,

(iii) property transferred to the provision in respect of the actuarial surplus under a defined benefit provision of the plan or another registered pension plan, or

(iv) property transferred to the provision in respect of the surplus under another money purchase provision of the plan or under a money purchase provision of another registered pension plan, and

Regulations

(b) can reasonably be considered to be allocated in lieu of a contribution that would otherwise have been made under the provision by an employer in respect of the individual

shall be deemed to be a contribution made under the provision by the employer with respect to the individual at that time and not to be an amount attributable to anything referred to in paragraph (a).

Notes: Reg. 8300(8)(a)(iv) added by P.C. 2003-1497, for allocations after 1998. It is consequential on the introduction of ITA 147.3(7.1).

Reg. 8300(8) added by P.C. 1995-17, for amounts allocated after April 5, 1994.

(9) For the purposes of this Part and Part LXXXV, where property held in connection with a particular benefit provision of a pension plan is made available at any time to pay benefits under another benefit provision of the plan, the property is deemed to be transferred at that time from the particular benefit provision to the other benefit provision.

Notes: Reg. 8300(9) added by P.C. 1998-2256, effective 1990.

(10) For the purposes of this Part and Parts LXXXIV and LXXXV, and subject to subsection (11), an individual is considered to have terminated from a deferred profit sharing plan or a benefit provision of a registered pension plan when the individual has ceased to be a member in relation to the plan or the provision, as the case may be.

Notes: Reg. 8300(10) added by P.C. 1998-2256, effective 1990.

(11) Where the benefits provided with respect to an individual under a particular defined benefit provision of a registered pension plan depend on benefits provided with respect to the individual under one or more other defined benefit provisions of registered pension plans (each of the particular provision and the other provisions being referred to in this subsection as a "related provision"), for the purposes of this Part and Parts LXXXIV and LXXXV,

(a) if the individual ceases, at any particular time after 1996, to be a member in relation to a specific related provision and is, at the particular time, a member in relation to another related provision, the individual is deemed

(i) not to terminate from the specific provision at the particular time, and

(ii) to terminate from the specific provision at the earliest subsequent time when the individual is no longer a member in relation to any of the related provisions;

(b) if the conditions in subsection 8304.1(14) (read without reference to the words "after 1996 and") are not satisfied with respect to the individual's termination from a related provision, the conditions in that subsection are deemed not to be satisfied with respect to the individual's termination from each of the other related provisions; and

(c) a specified distribution (as defined in subsection 8304.1(8)) made at any particular time in respect of the individual and a related provision is deemed, for the purpose of subsection 8304.1(5), also to be a specified distribution made at the particular time in respect of the individual and each of the other related provisions, except to the extent that the Minister has waived the application of this paragraph with respect to the distribution.

Notes: Reg. 8300(11) added by P.C. 1998-2256, effective 1990.

(12) For the purposes of this Part, where

(a) all or any part of the amounts payable to an individual under a deferred profit sharing plan are paid by a trustee under the plan to a licensed annuities provider to purchase for the individual an annuity described in subparagraph 147(2)(k)(vi) of the Act, or

(b) an individual has acquired, in full or partial satisfaction of the individual's entitlement to benefits under a benefit provision of a registered pension plan (other than benefits to which the individual was entitled only because of the participation of another individual under the provision), an interest in an annuity contract (other than as a consequence of a transfer of property from the provision to a registered retirement savings plan or a registered retirement income fund under which the individual is the annuitant),

the individual is deemed to continue, from the time of the payment or acquisition, as the case may be, until the individual's death, to be a member in relation to the plan or provision, as the case may be.

Related Provisions: ITA 146(21.2) — Saskatchewan Pension Plan account deemed to be RRSP for purposes of regulations; ITA 147.5(12) — Pooled registered pension plan deemed to be RRSP for purposes of regulations.

Notes: Reg. 8300(12) added by P.C. 1998-2256, effective 1990.

(13) For the purposes of this Part and Part LXXXV, where a benefit is to be provided, or may be provided, to an individual under a defined benefit provision of a registered pension plan as a consequence of an allocation that is to be made, or may be made, to the individual of all or part of an actuarial surplus under the provision, the individual is considered not to have any right to receive the benefit under the provision until the time at which the benefit becomes provided under the provision.

Notes [Reg. 8300(13)]: Reg. 8300(13) added by P.C. 1998-2256, effective 1990.

Definitions [Reg. 8300]: "amount", "annuity" — ITA 248(1); "benefit provision" — Reg. 8300(3), 8500(1); "benefits" — Reg. 8300(3), 8501(5)(c); "calendar year" — *Interpretation Act* 37(1)(a); "contribution" — Reg. 8300(8), 8302(11), (12); "deferred profit sharing plan" — ITA 147(1), 248(1); "defined benefit provision" — ITA 147.1(1), Reg. 8300(3); "designated plan" — Reg. 8300(3), 8500(1), 8515; "eligible period of reduced pay" — Reg. 8300(3), 8500(1); "employer", "employment" — ITA 248(1); "flat benefit provision" — Reg. 8500(1); "individual" — ITA 248(1); "individual pension plan" — Reg. 8300(1); "lifetime retirement benefits" — Reg. 8300(3), 8500(1); "Minister" — ITA 248(1); "money purchase provision" — ITA 147.1(1); "office", "officer" — ITA 248(1); "offset provision" — Reg. 8300(11)(b); "past service event" — Reg. 8301, 8308.1(2)–(4), 8308.3(2), (3); "period of disability" — Reg. 8300(3), 8500(1); "period of reduced services" — Reg. 8300(1); "person", "property" — ITA 248(1); "RRIF" — ITA 248(1)"registered retirement income fund"; "RRSP" — ITA 248(1)"registered retirement savings plan"; "registered pension plan" — ITA 248(1); "related" — ITA 251(2)–(6); "related provision" — Reg. 8300(12); "registered retirement income fund" — ITA 146.3(1), 248(1); "registered retirement savings plan" — ITA 146(1), (21.2), 147.5(12), 248(1); "render services" — Reg. 8300(4); "retirement benefits" — Reg. 8300(3), 8500(1); "specified distribution" — Reg. 8304.1(8); "surplus" — Reg. 8300(3), 8500(1); "temporary absence" — Reg. 8300(3), 8500(1)"eligible period of temporary absence"; "writing" — *Interpretation Act* 35(1).

8301. Pension adjustment — (1) Pension adjustment with respect to employer

— For the purpose of subsection 248(1) of the Act, "pension adjustment" of an individual for a calendar year with respect to an employer means, subject to paragraphs 8308(4)(d) and (5)(c), the total of all amounts each of which is

(a) the individual's pension credit for the year with respect to the employer under a deferred profit sharing plan or under a benefit provision of a registered pension plan;

(b) the individual's pension credit for the year with respect to the employer under a foreign plan, determined under section 8308.1; or

(c) the individual's pension credit for the year with respect to the employer under a specified retirement arrangement, determined under section 8308.3.

Related Provisions: Reg. 8301(2) — Pension credit — deferred profit sharing plan; Reg. 8301(3) — Non-vested termination from DPSP; Reg. 8301(4) — Pension credit — money purchase provision; Reg. 8500(8)(c) — Non-member benefits ignored in determining pension adjustment.

Notes: See Notes to ITA 248(1)"pension adjustment" and 147.1(2). On whether the PA must reduce the RRSP deduction, see ITA 146(1)"RRSP deduction limit" Notes.

Reg. 8301(1)(b) and (c) added by P.C. 1996-911, for 1992 and later years.

Interpretation Bulletins: IT-124R6: Contributions to registered retirement savings plans; IT-307R4: Spousal or common-law partner registered retirement savings plans; IT-363R2: Deferred profit sharing plans — deductibility of employer contributions and taxation of amounts received by a beneficiary (archived).

Registered Plans Compliance Bulletins: 1 (pension adjustments).

Forms: T1 General return, Line 20600 [former 206]; T4084: Pension adjustment guide.

(2) Pension credit — deferred profit sharing plan

— For the purposes of subsection (1) and Part LXXXV and subsection 147(5.1) of the Act, and subject to subsection 8304(2), an individual's pension credit for a calendar year with respect to an employer under a deferred profit sharing plan is the amount determined by the formula

A – B

where

A is the total of all amounts each of which is

(a) a contribution made to the plan in the year by the employer with respect to the individual, or

(b) the portion of an amount allocated in the year to the individual that is attributable to forfeited amounts under the plan or to earnings of the plan in respect of forfeited amounts, except to the extent that the portion

(i) is included in determining the individual's pension credit for the year with respect to any other employer who participates in the plan, or

(ii) is paid to the individual in the year; and

B is nil, unless the conditions in subsection (2.1) are satisfied, in which case it is the total referred to in paragraph (2.1)(b).

Related Provisions: ITA 257 — Negative amounts in formulas; Reg. 8311 — Pension credit rounded to nearest dollar.

Notes: It is common for an employer to contribute to a DPSP after fiscal year-end. This can result in contributions based on employees' previous-year earnings, but included in the employees' current-year pension credits. This gives rise to excess DPSP contributions if an employee's compensation for the current year is insufficient to support the pension credit (e.g., if the employee goes on leave without pay later in the year). Reg. 8301(2) provides a mechanism to deal with such over-contributions. It allows them to be ignored when determining the DPSP pension credit, provided the excess is refunded from the plan in the year or by the following February. It also covers employees who terminate employment, previously covered by former ITA 147(5.11).

Reg. 8301(2) amended by P.C. 2005-1508, effective for determining pension credits for 2002 and later calendar years. See up to PITA 35th ed. for credits for earlier years.

Interpretation Bulletins: IT-124R6: Contributions to registered retirement savings plans; IT-363R2: Deferred profit sharing plans — deductibility of employer contributions and taxation of amounts received by a beneficiary (archived).

(2.1) Conditions re — description of B in subsec. (2) — The following are conditions for the purpose of the description of B in subsection (2):

(a) the total of all amounts, each of which would be the individual's pension credit for the calendar year with respect to the employer under a deferred profit sharing plan if the description of B in subsection (2) were read as "is nil.", is

(i) equal to, or less than, 50% of the money purchase limit for the year,

(ii) greater than 18% of the amount that would be the individual's compensation from the employer for the year if the definition "compensation" in subsection 147.1(1) of the Act were read without reference to paragraph (b) of that definition, and

(iii) equal to, or less than, 18% of the amount that would be the individual's compensation from the employer for the preceding year if the definition "compensation" in subsection 147.1(1) of the Act were read without reference to paragraph (b) of that definition; and

(b) the total of all amounts, each of which is an amount that is paid from the plan to the individual or the employer in the calendar year or in the first two months of the following year that can reasonably be considered to derive from an amount included in the value of A in subsection (2) with respect to the individual and the employer for the year, is greater than nil.

Related Provisions: Reg. 8301(15) — Transferred amounts deemed not paid.

Notes: Reg. 8301(2.1) added by P.C. 2005-1508, effective for determining pension credits for 2002 and later calendar years.

(3) Non-vested termination from DPSP — For the purposes of subsection (1) and Part LXXXV and subsection 147(5.1) of the Act, where

(a) an individual ceased in a calendar year after 1989 and before 1997 to be employed by an employer who participated in a deferred profit sharing plan for the benefit of the individual,

(b) as a consequence of the termination of employment, the individual ceased in the year to have any rights to benefits (other than a right to a refund benefit) under the plan,

(c) the individual was not entitled to benefits under the plan at the end of the year, or was entitled only to a refund benefit, and

(d) no benefit has been paid under the plan with respect to the individual, other than a refund benefit,

the individual's pension credit under the plan for the year with respect to the employer is nil.

Related Provisions: Reg. 8300(7) — Benefits include contingent benefits.

Notes: Reg. 8301(3)(a) amended by P.C. 1998-2256, retroactive to 1990, to add "and before 1997".

Before 1991, ignore the words "and subsection 147(5.1) of the Act" in the opening words of Reg. 8301(3). See Notes to Reg. 8311.

Interpretation Bulletins: IT-124R6: Contributions to registered retirement savings plans.

(4) Pension credit — money purchase provision — For the purposes of subsection (1) and Part LXXXV and subsection 147.1(9) of the Act, and subject to subsections (4.1) and (8) and 8304(2), an individual's pension credit for a calendar year with respect to an employer under a money purchase provision of a registered pension plan is the total of all amounts each of which is

(a) a contribution (other than an additional voluntary contribution made by the individual in 1990, an excluded contribution or a contribution described in paragraph 8308(6)(e) or (g)) made under the provision in the year by

(i) the individual, except to the extent that the contribution was not made in connection with the individual's employment with the employer and is included in determining the individual's pension credit for the year with respect to any other employer who participates in the plan, or

(ii) the employer with respect to the individual, or

(b) such portion of an amount allocated in the year to the individual as is attributable to

(i) forfeited amounts under the provision or earnings of the plan in respect thereof,

(ii) a surplus under the provision,

(ii.1) property transferred to the provision in respect of the actuarial surplus under a defined benefit provision of the plan or another registered pension plan, or

(ii.2) property transferred to the provision in respect of the surplus under another money purchase provision of the plan or under a money purchase provision of another registered pension plan,

except to the extent that that portion is

(iii) included in determining the individual's pension credit for the year with respect to any other employer who participates in the plan,

(iv) paid to the individual in the year, or

(v) where the year is 1990, attributable to amounts forfeited before 1990 or earnings of the plan in respect thereof,

except that the individual's pension credit is nil where the year is before 1990, and, for the purposes of this subsection, the plan administrator shall determine the portion of a contribution made by an individual or an amount allocated to the individual that is to be included in determining the individual's pension credit with respect to each employer.

Related Provisions: Reg. 8301(15) — Transferred amounts deemed not paid; Reg. 8311 — Pension credit rounded to nearest dollar; Reg. 8506(11)(c) — Recontribution for 2015 due to reduction in minimum withdrawal.

Notes: Reg. 8301(4)(b)(ii.2) added by P.C. 2003-1497, for pension for 1999 and later years. It is consequential on the introduction of ITA 147.3(7.1).

Opening words of Reg. 8301(4) and of Reg. 8301(4)(a) amended by P.C. 1995-17, this version effective for the determination of pension credits for 1993 and later years.

Reg. 8301(4)(b)(ii.1) added by P.C. 1995-17, effective for the determination of pension credits for 1991 and later years.

Interpretation Bulletins: IT-124R6: Contributions to registered retirement savings plans.

Registered Plans Directorate Newsletters: 91-4R (registration rules for money purchase provisions).

(4.1) Money purchase pension credits based on amounts allocated — Where,

(a) under the terms of a money purchase provision of a pension plan, the method for allocating contributions is such that contributions made by an employer with respect to a particular individual may be allocated to another individual, and

(b) the Minister has, on the written application of the administrator of the plan, approved in writing a method for determining pension credits under the provision that, for each individual, takes into account amounts allocated to the individual,

each pension credit under the provision is the amount determined in accordance with the method approved by the Minister.

Notes: Reg. 8301(4.1) added by P.C. 1995-17, for pension for 1993 and later years.

(5) Pension credit — defined benefit provision of a specified multi-employer plan — For the purposes of this Part and Part LXXXV and subsection 147.1(9) of the Act, an individual's pension credit for a calendar year with respect to an employer under a defined benefit provision of a registered pension plan that is, in the year, a specified multi-employer plan is the aggregate of

(a) the aggregate of all amounts each of which is a contribution (other than an excluded contribution) made under the provision by the individual

(i) in the year, in respect of

(A) the year, or

(B) a plan year ending in the year (other than in respect of such portion of a plan year as is before 1990), or

(ii) in January of the year (other than in January 1990) in respect of the immediately preceding calendar year,

except to the extent that the contribution was not made in connection with the individual's employment with the employer and is included in determining the individual's pension credit for the year with respect to any other employer who participates in the plan,

(b) the aggregate of all amounts each of which is a contribution made in the year by the employer in respect of the provision, to the extent that the contribution may reasonably be considered to be determined by reference to the number of hours worked by the individual or some other measure that is specific to the individual, and

(c) the amount determined by the formula

$$(A / B) \times (C - B)$$

where

A is the amount determined under paragraph (b) for the purpose of computing the individual's pension credit,

B is the aggregate of all amounts each of which is the amount determined under paragraph (b) for the purpose of computing the pension credit of an individual for the year with respect to the employer under the provision, and

C is the aggregate of all amounts each of which is a contribution made in the year by the employer in respect of the provision,

except that, where the year is before 1990, the individual's pension credit is nil.

Related Provisions: ITA 257 — Negative amounts in formulas; Reg. 8311 — Pension credit rounded to nearest dollar.

Registered Plans Compliance Bulletins: 7 (making contributions and calculating and reporting pension adjustment for SMEPs).

(6) Pension credit — defined benefit provision — Subject to subsections (7), (8) and (10) and sections 8304 and 8308, for the purposes of this Part and Part LXXXV and subsection 147.1(9) of the Act, an individual's pension credit for a calendar year with respect to an employer under a defined benefit provision of a particular registered pension plan (other than a plan that is, in the year, a specified multi-employer plan) is

(a) if the year is after 1989, the amount determined by the formula

$$A - B$$

where

A is 9 times the individual's benefit entitlement under the provision with respect to the employer and the year, and

B is the amount, if any, by which the PA offset for the year exceeds the total of all amounts each of which is the value of B determined under this paragraph for the purpose of computing the individual's pension credit for the year

(i) with respect to the employer under any other defined benefit provision of a registered pension plan,

(ii) with respect to any other employer who at any time in the year does not deal at arm's length with the employer, under a defined benefit provision of a registered pension plan, or

(iii) with respect to any other employer under a defined benefit provision of the particular plan; and

(b) if the year is before 1990, nil.

Related Provisions: ITA 257 — Negative amounts in formulas; Reg. 8302(1) — Benefit entitlement is portion attributable to employer; Reg. 8311 — Pension credit rounded to nearest dollar.

Notes: See Notes to ITA 248(1)"pension adjustment".

Reg. 8301(6) amended by P.C. 1998-2256, retroactive to 1990, effectively to change $1,000 to "the PA offset", now defined in Reg. 8300(1).

Interpretation Bulletins: IT-124R6: Contributions to registered retirement savings plans.

Registered Plans Compliance Bulletins: 1 (pension adjustments).

Registered Plans Directorate Actuarial Bulletins: 1R1 (calculating actuarial increase where pension start postponed beyond age 65).

Registered Plans Frequently Asked Questions: RPFAQ-2 (RPPs), q. 25 (designated status where specified individuals have no further defined benefit credits).

(7) Pension credit — defined benefit provision of a multi-employer plan — Where a registered pension plan is a multi-employer plan (other than a specified multi-employer plan) in a calendar year, the following rules apply, except to the extent that the Minister has waived in writing their application in respect of the plan, for the purpose of determining the pension credit of an individual for the year under a defined benefit provision of the plan:

(a) where the individual is employed in the year by more than one participating employer, the pension credit of the individual for the year under the provision with respect to a particular employer shall be determined as if the individual were not employed by any other participating employer;

(b) the description of B in paragraph (6)(a) shall be read as

"B is the amount determined by the formula

$$(C \times D) - E$$

where

C is the PA offset for the year,

D is

(i) where the member rendered services on a full-time basis throughout the year to the employer, one, and

(ii) in any other case, the fraction (not greater than one) that measures the services that, for the purpose of determining the member's lifetime retirement benefits under the provision, the member is treated as having rendered in the year to the employer, expressed as a proportion of the services that would have been rendered by the member in the year to the employer if the member had rendered services to the employer on a full-time basis throughout the year, and

E is the total of all amounts each of which is the value of B determined under this paragraph for the purpose of computing the individual's pension credit for the year with respect to the employer under any other defined benefit provision of the plan; and";

(c) where a period in the year is a period of reduced services of the individual, the pension credit of the individual for the year under the provision with respect to each participating employer shall be determined as the aggregate of

(i) the pension credit that would be determined if no benefits (other than benefits attributable to services rendered by the individual) had accrued to the individual in respect of periods of reduced services, and

(ii) the pension credit that would be determined if the only benefits that had accrued to the individual were benefits in respect of periods of reduced services, other than benefits attributable to services rendered by the individual during such periods; and

(d) subsection (10) shall not apply.

Related Provisions: ITA 257 — Negative amounts in formulas; Reg. 8311 — Pension credit rounded to nearest dollar.

Notes: Reg. 8301(7)(b) amended by P.C. 1998-2256, effective 1990, to change $1,000 to "the PA offset", now defined in Reg. 8300(1). See also Notes to Reg. 8301(6).

(8) Non-vested termination from RPP — For the purposes of this Part and Part LXXXV and subsection 147.1(9) of the Act, and subject to subsection (9), where

(a) an individual ceased in a calendar year after 1989 and before 1997 to be employed by an employer who participated in a registered pension plan for the benefit of the individual,

(b) as a consequence of the termination of employment, the individual ceased in the year to have any rights to benefits (other than a right to a refund benefit) under a benefit provision of the plan,

(c) the individual was not entitled to benefits under the provision at the end of the year, or was entitled only to a refund benefit, and

(d) no benefit has been paid under the provision with respect to the individual, other than a refund benefit,

the individual's pension credit under the provision for the year with respect to the employer is

(e) where the provision is a money purchase provision, the total of all amounts each of which is a contribution (other than an additional voluntary contribution made by the individual in 1990, an excluded contribution or a contribution described in paragraph 8308(6)(e)) made under the provision in the year by the individual, except to the extent that the contribution was not made in connection with the individual's employment with the employer and is included in determining the individual's pension credit for the year with respect to any other employer who participates in the plan, and

(f) where the provision is a defined benefit provision, the lesser of

(i) the pension credit that would be determined if this subsection were not applicable, and

(ii) the aggregate of all amounts each of which is a contribution (other than an excluded contribution) made under the provision by the individual in, and in respect of, the year, except to the extent that the contribution was not made in connection with the individual's employment with the employer and is included in determining the individual's pension credit for the year with respect to any other employer who participates in the plan.

Related Provisions: Reg. 8300(7) — Benefits include contingent benefits.

Notes: Reg. 8301(8)(b) amended by P.C. 2007-849, effective June 13, 2007, to change "money purchase or defined benefit provision" to "benefit provision". Reg. 8301(8) earlier amended by P.C. 1998-2256 and P.C. 1995-17, both retroactive to 1990.

Interpretation Bulletins: IT-124R6: Contributions to registered retirement savings plans.

(9) Multi-employer plans — Subsection (8) is not applicable in respect of a registered pension plan that is a multi-employer plan in a calendar year except, where

(a) the plan is not a specified multi-employer plan in the year;

(b) if the plan contains a defined benefit provision, the Minister has waived in writing the application of paragraph (7)(b) in respect of the plan for the year; and

(c) the Minister has approved in writing the application of subsection (8) in respect of the plan for the year.

Interpretation Bulletins: IT-124R6: Contributions to registered retirement savings plans.

(10) Transition rule — money purchase offsets — Where,

(a) throughout the period beginning on January 1, 1981 and ending on December 31 of a particular calendar year after 1989 and before 2000, there has been subtracted, in determining the amount of lifetime retirement benefits under a defined benefit provision of a registered pension plan (other than a specified multi-employer plan), the amount of lifetime retirement benefits under a money purchase provision of the plan or of another registered pension plan,

(b) lifetime retirement benefits under the defined benefit provision are determined, at the end of the particular year, in substantially the same manner as they were determined at the end of 1989, and

(c) for each individual and each calendar year before 1990, the amount of employer contributions made under the money purchase provision for the year with respect to the individual did not exceed $3,500,

the pension credit of an individual for the particular year with respect to an employer under the defined benefit provision is equal to the amount, if any, by which

(d) the amount that would, but for this subsection, be the individual's pension credit

exceeds

(e) the lesser of

(i) $2,500, and

(ii) the amount determined by the formula

$$1/10 \times (A - (B \times C))$$

where

A is the balance in the individual's account under the money purchase provision at the end of 1989,

B is the aggregate of all amounts each of which is the duration (measured in years, including any fraction of a year) of a period ending before 1990 that is pensionable service of the individual under the defined benefit provision and that is not part of a longer period ending before 1990 that is pensionable service of the individual under the provision, and

C is the amount that would be the individual's pension credit for 1989 with respect to the employer under the defined benefit provision if subsection (6) were read without reference to the words "if the year is after 1989" in paragraph (6)(a) and without reference to paragraph (6)(b).

Related Provisions: ITA 257 — Negative amounts in formulas; Reg. 8301(7)(d) — Provisions inapplicable in determining pension credit in multi-employer plan.

Notes: Reg. 8301(10)(e)(ii)C amended by P.C. 1998-2256, retroactive to 1990, consequential on amendments to Reg. 8301(6).

(11) Timing of contributions — Subject to paragraph (12)(b), for the purposes of this Part, a contribution made by an employer in the first two months of a calendar year to a deferred profit sharing

plan, in respect of a money purchase provision of a registered pension plan, or in respect of a defined benefit provision of a registered pension plan that was, in the immediately preceding calendar year, a specified multi-employer plan, shall be deemed to have been made by the employer at the end of the immediately preceding calendar year and not to have been made in the year, to the extent that the contribution can reasonably be considered to relate to a preceding calendar year.

Notes: Reg. 8301(11) applies to contributions that relate to any preceding calendar year (rather than just the immediately preceding year). This ensures, for example, that a contribution made in January or February of 2006 that relates to a fiscal year starting in 2004 and ending in 2005 will be treated, for PA purposes, as though it were made entirely in 2005. Thus, it will be reflected entirely in the individual's 2005 PA.

Information Circulars: 98-2: Prescribed compensation for RPPs, para. 25.

(12) Indirect contributions — For the purposes of this Part and Part LXXXIV, where a trade union or association of employers (in this subsection and subsections (13) and (14) referred to as the "contributing entity") makes contributions to a registered pension plan,

(a) such portion of a payment made to the contributing entity by an employer or an individual as may reasonably be considered to relate to the plan (determined in accordance with subsection (13), where that subsection is applicable) shall be deemed to be a contribution made to the plan by the employer or individual, as the case may be, at the time the payment was made to the contributing entity; and

(b) subsection (11) shall not apply in respect of a contribution deemed by paragraph (a) to have been made to the plan.

(13) Apportionment of payments — For the purposes of subsection (12), where employers or individuals make payments in a calendar year to a contributing entity to enable the contributing entity to make contributions to a registered pension plan and the payments are not made solely for the purpose of being contributed to the plan, the contributing entity shall

(a) determine, in a manner that is reasonable in the circumstances, the portion of each payment that relates to the plan;

(b) make the determination in such a manner that all contributions made by the contributing entity to the plan, other than contributions made by the contributing entity as an employer or former employer of members of the plan, are considered to be funded by payments made to the contributing entity by employers or individuals;

(c) in the case of payments remitted to the contributing entity by an employer, notify the employer in writing, by January 31 of the immediately following calendar year, of the portion, or of the method for determining the portion, of each such payment that relates to the plan; and

(d) in the case of payments remitted to the contributing entity by an individual, notify the administrator of the plan in writing, by January 31 of the immediately following calendar year, of the total amount of payments made in the year by the individual that relate to the plan.

(14) Non-compliance by contributing entity — Where a contributing entity does not comply with the requirements of subsection (13) as they apply in respect of payments made to the contributing entity in a calendar year to enable the contributing entity to make contributions to a registered pension plan,

(a) the plan becomes, on February 1 of the immediately following calendar year, a revocable plan; and

(b) the Minister may make any determinations referred to in subsection (13) that the contributing entity failed to make, or failed to make in accordance with that subsection.

Related Provisions: ITA 147.1(8), (9), 147.3(12), Reg. 8305(2)(a), 8408(2), 8501(2), 8503(11), (15), 8506(4), 8511(2), 8515(9) — Other ways plan becomes revocable plan; Reg. 8301(12) — Meaning of contributing entity.

(15) Transferred amounts — For the purposes of subparagraph (b)(ii) of the description of A in subsection (2), paragraph (2.1)(b)

and subparagraph (4)(b)(iv), an amount transferred for the benefit of an individual from a registered pension plan or a deferred profit sharing plan directly to a registered pension plan, a registered retirement savings plan, a registered retirement income fund or a deferred profit sharing plan is deemed to be an amount that was not paid to the individual.

Related Provisions: ITA 146(21.2) — Sask. Pension Plan account deemed to be RRSP for purposes of regulations; ITA 147.5(12) — PRPP deemed to be RRSP for regulations.

Notes: Reg. 8301(15) amended by P.C. 2005-1508, effective for determining pension credits for 2002 and later calendar years.

Reg. 8301(15) amended by P.C. 1995-17, effective for transfers after August 29, 1990, to add reference to transfers to RRIFs.

(16) Subsequent events — Except as otherwise expressly provided in this Part, each pension credit of an individual for a calendar year shall be determined without regard to transactions, events and circumstances that occur subsequent to the year.

Definitions [Reg. 8301]: "additional voluntary contribution", "amount" — ITA 248(1); "arm's length" — ITA 251(1); "benefit provision" — Reg. 8300(3), 8500(1); "benefits" — Reg. 8300(7); "calendar year" — *Interpretation Act* 37(1)(a); "contributing entity" — Reg. 8301(12); "contribution" — Reg. 8300(8), 8302(11), (12); "deferred profit sharing plan" — ITA 147(1), 248(1); "defined benefit provision" — ITA 147.1(1), Reg. 8300(3); "employed", "employer", "employment" — ITA 248(1); "excluded contribution" — Reg. 8300(1); "individual" — ITA 248(1); "lifetime retirement benefits" — Reg. 8300(3), 8500(1); "Minister" — ITA 248(1); "money purchase limit" — ITA 147.1(1), 248(1); "month" — *Interpretation Act* 35(1); "multi-employer plan" — Reg. 8300(3), 8500(1); "PA offset" — Reg. 8300(1); "participating employer" — ITA 147.1(1); "pension credit" — Reg. 8301, 8308.1(2)–(4), 8308.3(2), (3); "pensionable service" — Reg. 8300(3), 8500(1); "period of reduced services" — Reg. 8300(1); "property" — ITA 248(1); "refund benefit" — Reg. 8300(1); "registered pension plan" — ITA 248(1); "registered retirement income fund" — ITA 146.3(1), 248(1); "registered retirement savings plan" — ITA 146(1), (21.2), 147.5(12), 248(1); "revocable plan" — 147.1(8), (9), 147.3(12), Reg. 8301(14)(a), 8305(2), 8408(2), 8501(2), 8503(11), (15), 8506(4), 8511(2), 8515(9); "specified multi-employer plan" — ITA 147.1(1), Reg. 8510(2), (3); "surplus" — Reg. 8300(3), 8500(1); "written" — *Interpretation Act* 35(1)"writing".

8302. Benefit entitlement — **(1)** For the purposes of subsection 8301(6), the benefit entitlement of an individual under a defined benefit provision of a registered pension plan in respect of a calendar year and an employer is the portion of the individual's benefit accrual under the provision in respect of the year that can reasonably be considered to be attributable to the individual's employment with the employer.

Related Provisions: Reg. 8302(2) — Meaning of benefit accrual.

(2) Benefit accrual for year — For the purposes of subsection (1), and subject to subsections (6), (8) and (9), the benefit accrual of an individual under a defined benefit provision of a registered pension plan in respect of a calendar year is the amount computed in accordance with the following rules:

(a) determine the portion of the individual's normalized pension under the provision at the end of the year that can reasonably be considered to have accrued in respect of the year;

(b) where the year is after 1989 and before 1995, determine the lesser of the amount determined under paragraph (a) and

(i) for 1990, $1,277.78,

(ii) for 1991 and 1992, $1,388.89,

(iii) for 1993, $1,500.00, and

(iv) for 1994, $1,611.11; and

(c) where, in determining the amount of lifetime retirement benefits payable to the individual under the provision, there is deducted from the amount of those benefits that would otherwise be payable the amount of lifetime retirement benefits payable to the individual under a money purchase provision of a registered pension plan or the amount of a lifetime annuity payable to the individual under a deferred profit sharing plan, reduce the amount that would otherwise be determined under this subsection by $1/9$ of the total of all amounts each of which is the pension credit of the individual for the year under such a money purchase provision or deferred profit sharing plan.

Related Provisions: Reg. 8302(3) — Meaning of normalized pension.

Notes: Reg. 8302(2)(b) and (c) amended by P.C. 1995-17, effective 1992, to postpone the scheduled increase from 1991 by one year (see Notes to ITA 147.1(1)"money purchase limit").

(3) Normalized pensions — For the purposes of paragraph (2)(a), and subject to subsection (11), the normalized pension of an individual under a defined benefit provision of a registered pension plan at the end of a particular calendar year is the amount (expressed on an annualized basis) of lifetime retirement benefits that would be payable under the provision to the individual immediately after the end of the particular year if

(a) where lifetime retirement benefits have not commenced to be paid under the provision to the individual before the end of the particular year, they commenced to be paid immediately after the end of the year;

(b) where the individual had not attained 65 years of age before the time at which lifetime retirement benefits commenced to be paid (or are assumed by reason of paragraph (a) to have commenced to be paid) to the individual, the individual attained that age at that time;

(c) all benefits to which the individual is entitled under the provision were fully vested;

(d) where the amount of the individual's lifetime retirement benefits would otherwise be determined with a reduction computed by reference to the individual's age, duration of service or both, or with any other similar reduction, no such reduction were applied;

(d.1) no reduction in the amount of the individual's lifetime retirement benefits were applied in respect of benefits described in any of clauses 8503(2)(a)(vi)(A) to (C);

(d.2) no adjustment that is permissible under subparagraph 8503(2)(a)(ix) were made to the amount of the individual's lifetime retirement benefits;

(e) where the amount of the individual's lifetime retirement benefits depends on the remuneration received by the individual in a calendar year (in this paragraph referred to as the "other year") other than the particular year, the remuneration received by the individual in the other year were determined in accordance with the following rules:

(i) where the individual was remunerated for both the particular year and the other year as a person who rendered services on a full-time basis throughout each of the years, the remuneration received by the individual in the other year is identical to the remuneration received by the individual in the particular year,

(ii) where subparagraph (i) is not applicable and the individual rendered services in the particular year, the remuneration received by the individual in the other year is the remuneration that the individual would have received in the other year (or a reasonable estimate thereof determined by a method acceptable to the Minister) had the individual's rate of remuneration in the other year been the same as the individual's rate of remuneration in the particular year, and

(iii) where subparagraph (i) is not applicable and the individual did not render services in the particular year, the remuneration received by the individual in the other year is the remuneration that the individual would have received in the other year (or a reasonable estimate thereof determined by a method acceptable to the Minister) had the individual's rate of remuneration in the other year been the amount that it is reasonable to consider would have been the individual's rate of remuneration in the particular year had the individual rendered services in the particular year;

(f) where the amount of the individual's lifetime retirement benefits depends on the individual's remuneration and all or a portion of the remuneration received by the individual in the particular year is treated under the provision as if it were remuneration received in a calendar year preceding the particular year for ser-

vices rendered in that preceding year, that remuneration were remuneration for services rendered in the particular year;

(g) where the amount of the individual's lifetime retirement benefits depends on the individual's remuneration and the particular year is after 1989 and before 1995, benefits, to the extent that they can reasonably be considered to be in respect of the following range of annual remuneration, were excluded:

(i) where the particular year is 1990, the range from $63,889 to $86,111,

(ii) where the particular year is 1991 or 1992, the range from $69,444 to $86,111,

(iii) where the particular year is 1993, the range from $75,000 to $86,111, and

(iv) where the particular year is 1994, the range from $80,556 to $86,111;

(h) where

(i) the amount of the individual's lifetime retirement benefits depends on the individual's remuneration,

(ii) the formula for determining the amount of the individual's lifetime retirement benefits includes an adjustment to the individual's remuneration for one or more calendar years,

(iii) the adjustment to the individual's remuneration for a year (in this paragraph referred to as the "specified year") consists of multiplying the individual's remuneration for the specified year by a factor that does not exceed the ratio of the average wage for the year in which the amount of the individual's lifetime retirement benefits is required to be determined to the average wage for the specified year (or a substantially similar measure of the change in the wage measure), and

(iv) the adjustment may reasonably be considered to be made to increase the individual's remuneration for the specified year to reflect, in whole or in part, increases in average wages and salaries from that year to the year in which the amount of the individual's lifetime retirement benefits is required to be determined,

the formula did not include the adjustment to the individual's remuneration for the specified year;

(i) where the amount of the individual's lifetime retirement benefits depends on the Year's Maximum Pensionable Earnings for calendar years other than the particular year, the Year's Maximum Pensionable Earnings for each such year were equal to the Year's Maximum Pensionable Earnings for the particular year;

(j) if the amount of the individual's lifetime retirement benefits depends solely on the actual amount of the pension (in this paragraph referred to as the "statutory pension") payable to the individual under paragraph 46(1)(a) of the *Canada Pension Plan* or a similar provision of a "provincial pension plan" (as defined in section 3 of that Act), the amount of statutory pension (expressed on an annualized basis) were equal to

(i) 25 per cent of the lesser of the Year's Maximum Pensionable Earnings for the particular year and,

(A) in the case of an individual who renders services throughout the particular year on a full-time basis to employers who participate in the plan, the aggregate of all amounts each of which is the individual's remuneration for the particular year from such an employer, and

(B) in any other case, the amount that it is reasonable to consider would be determined under clause (A) if the individual had rendered services throughout the particular year on a full-time basis to employers who participate in the plan, or

(ii) at the option of the plan administrator, any other amount determined in accordance with a method for estimating the statutory pension that can be expected to result in amounts substantially similar to amounts determined under subparagraph (i);

(j.1) if the amount of the individual's lifetime retirement benefits depends on the actual amount of the pension (in this paragraph referred to as the "statutory pension") payable to the individual under paragraphs 46(1)(a) and (b) of the *Canada Pension Plan* or a similar provision of a "provincial pension plan" (as defined in section 3 of that Act), the amount of statutory pension (expressed on an annualized basis) were equal to

(i) the amount determined by the formula

$$A \times B$$

where

A is

(A) for 2018 and preceding years, 0.25,

(B) for 2019, 0.2625,

(C) for 2020, 0.275,

(D) for 2021, 0.29165,

(E) for 2022, 0.3125, and

(F) for 2023 and subsequent years, ⅓, and

B is the lesser of the Year's Maximum Pensionable Earnings for the particular year and,

(A) in the case of an individual who renders services throughout the particular year on a full-time basis to employers who participate in the plan, the aggregate of all amounts each of which is the individual's remuneration for the particular year from such an employer, and

(B) in any other case, the amount that it is reasonable to consider would be determined under clause (A) if the individual had rendered services throughout the particular year on a full-time basis to employers who participate in the plan, or

(ii) at the option of the plan administrator, any other amount determined in accordance with a method for estimating the statutory pension that can be expected to result in amounts substantially similar to amounts determined under subparagraph (i);

(k) where the amount of the individual's lifetime retirement benefits depends on a pension (in this paragraph referred to as the "statutory pension") payable to the individual under Part I of the *Old Age Security Act*, the amount of statutory pension payable for each calendar year were equal to the aggregate of all amounts each of which is the the full monthly pension payable under Part I of the *Old Age Security Act* for a month in the particular year;

(l) except as otherwise expressly permitted in writing by the Minister, where the amount of the individual's lifetime retirement benefits depends on the amount of benefits (other than public pension benefits or similar benefits of a country other than Canada) payable under another benefit provision of a pension plan or under a deferred profit sharing plan, the amounts of the other benefits were such as to maximize the amount of the individual's lifetime retirement benefits;

(m) where the individual's lifetime retirement benefits would otherwise include benefits that the plan is required to provide by reason of a designated provision of the law of Canada or a province (within the meaning assigned by section 8513), or that the plan would be required to provide if each such provision were applicable to the plan with respect to all its members, such benefits were not included;

(n) where

(i) the individual attained 65 years of age before lifetime retirement benefits commenced to be paid (or are to be assumed by reason of paragraph (a) to have commenced to be paid) to the individual, and

(ii) an adjustment is made in determining the amount of those benefits for the purpose of offsetting, in whole or in part, the decrease in the value of lifetime retirement benefits that would otherwise result by reason of the deferral of those benefits after the individual attained 65 years of age,

that adjustment were not made, except to the extent that the adjustment exceeds the adjustment that would be made on an actuarially equivalent basis;

(o) except as otherwise provided by subsection (4), where the amount of the individual's lifetime retirement benefits depends on

(i) the form of benefits provided with respect to the individual under the provision (whether or not at the option of the individual), including

(A) the benefits to be provided after the death of the individual,

(B) the amount of retirement benefits, other than lifetime retirement benefits, provided to the individual, or

(C) the extent to which the lifetime retirement benefits will be adjusted to reflect changes in the cost of living, or

(ii) circumstances that are relevant in determining the form of benefits,

the form of benefits and the circumstances were such as to maximize the amount of the individual's lifetime retirement benefits on commencement of payment;

(p) where the amount of the individual's lifetime retirement benefits depends on whether the individual is totally and permanently disabled at the time at which retirement benefits commence to be paid to the individual, the individual were not so disabled at that time; and

(q) where lifetime retirement benefits have commenced to be paid under the provision to the individual before the end of the particular year, benefits payable as a consequence of cost-of-living adjustments described in paragraph 8303(5)(k) were disregarded.

Related Provisions: Reg. 8300(4) — Officer deemed to render services to employer; Reg. 8300(7) — Benefits include contingent benefits; Reg. 8302(5) — Benefit entitlement terminated — normalized pension calculations; Reg. 8503(2) — Permissible benefits; Reg. 8513 — Designate provision of the law of Canada or a province.

Notes: For the Year's Maximum Pensionable Earnings for Reg. 8302(3)(i), see Table I-8 in the introductory pages.

Reg. 8302(3)(j) opening words amended and (j.1) added by 2019 budget bill #1, effective 2019, to add (in (j)) "solely" and change "under the *Canada Pension Plan* or a provincial plan" to "under paragraph 46(1)(a) of the *Canada Pension Plan* or a similar provision of a "provincial pension plan" ". Para. (j) now applies to an RPP whose defined benefits payable to a plan member are offset solely by reference to "base CPP" payments (i.e., payable pursuant to *CPP* para. 46(1)(a)) to the plan member. New (j.1) applies to an RPP whose defined benefits payable to a plan member are offset by reference to full CPP payments to the plan member. The references to *CPP* paras. 46(1)(a) and (b) effectively refer to both base CPP payments and enhanced CPP payments.

Reg. 8302(3) amended by P.C. 2001-153 (for pension credits for 1990 and later years), P.C. 1995-17 (effective 1992).

Registered Plans Directorate Actuarial Bulletins: 1R1 (calculating actuarial increase where pension start postponed beyond age 65).

(4) Optional forms — Where the terms of a defined benefit provision of a registered pension plan permit a member to elect to receive additional lifetime retirement benefits in lieu of benefits that would, in the absence of the election, be payable after the death of the member if the member dies after retirement benefits under the provision commence to be paid to the member, paragraph (3)(o) applies as if the following elections were not available to the member:

(a) an election to receive additional lifetime retirement benefits, not exceeding additional benefits determined on an actuarially equivalent basis, in lieu of all or any portion of a guarantee that retirement benefits will be paid for a minimum period of 10 years or less, and

(b) an election to receive additional lifetime retirement benefits in lieu of retirement benefits that would otherwise be payable to an individual who is a spouse or common-law partner or former spouse or common-law partner of the member for a period beginning after the death of the member and ending with the death of the individual, where

(i) the election may be made only if the life expectancy of the individual is significantly shorter than normal and has been so certified in writing by a medical doctor or a nurse practitioner licensed to practise under the laws of a province or of the place where the individual resides, and

(ii) the additional benefits do not exceed additional benefits determined on an actuarially equivalent basis and on the assumption that the individual has a normal life expectancy.

Notes: Reg. 8302(4)(b)(i) amended by 2017 budget bill #2 to add "or a nurse practitioner", for certifications made after Sept. 7, 2017.

Reg. 8302(4)(b) amended by P.C. 2001-957, effective 2001 or earlier.

(5) Termination of entitlement to benefits — For the purposes of subsection (3), where an individual ceased in a calendar year to be entitled to all or part of the lifetime retirement benefits provided to the individual under a defined benefit provision of a registered pension plan, the normalized pension of the individual under the provision at the end of the year shall be determined on the assumption that the individual continued to be entitled to those benefits immediately after the end of the year.

Related Provisions: Reg. 8300(7) — Benefits include contingent benefits.

(6) Defined benefit offset — Where the amount of lifetime retirement benefits provided under a particular defined benefit provision of a registered pension plan to a member of the plan depends on the amount of lifetime retirement benefits provided to the member under one or more other defined benefit provisions of registered pension plans, the benefit accrual of the member under the particular provision in respect of a calendar year is the amount, if any, by which

(a) the amount that would, but for this subsection, be the benefit accrual of the member under the particular provision in respect of the year if the benefits provided under the other provisions were provided under the particular provision

exceeds

(b) the amount that would be the benefit accrual of the member under the other provisions in respect of the year if the other provisions were a single provision.

(7) Offset of specified multi-employer plan benefits — Where the amount of an individual's lifetime retirement benefits under a defined benefit provision (in this subsection referred to as the "supplemental provision") of a registered pension plan depends on the amount of benefits payable under a defined benefit provision of a specified multi-employer plan, the defined benefit provision of the specified multi-employer plan shall be deemed to be a money purchase provision for the purpose of determining the benefit accruals of the individual under the supplemental provision.

(8) Transition rule — career average benefits — Where

(a) on March 27, 1988 lifetime retirement benefits under a defined benefit provision of a pension plan were determined as the greater of benefits computed on a career average basis and benefits computed on a final or best average earnings basis,

(b) the method for determining lifetime retirement benefits under the provision has not been amended after March 27, 1988 and before the end of a particular calendar year, and

(c) it was reasonable to expect, on January 1, 1990, that the lifetime retirement benefits to be paid under the provision to at least 75 per cent of the members of the plan on that date (other than members to whom benefits do not accrue under the provision after that date) will be determined on a final or best average earnings basis,

at the option of the plan administrator, benefit accruals under the provision in respect of the particular year may, where the particular year is before 1992, be determined without regard to the career average formula.

(9) Transition rule — benefit rate greater than 2 per cent — Subject to subsection (6), where

(a) the amount of lifetime retirement benefits provided under a defined benefit provision of a registered pension plan to a member of the plan is determined, in part, by multiplying the member's remuneration (or a function of the member's remuneration) by one or more benefit accrual rates, and

(b) the largest benefit accrual rate that may be applicable is greater than 2 per cent,

the member's benefit accrual under the provision in respect of 1990 or 1991 is the lesser of

(c) the member's benefit accrual otherwise determined, and

(d) 2 per cent of the aggregate of all amounts each of which is the amount that would, if the definition "compensation" in subsection 147.1(1) of the Act were read without reference to subparagraphs (a)(iii) and (iv) and paragraphs (b) and (c) thereof, be the member's compensation for the year from an employer who participated in the plan in the year for the benefit of the member.

Related Provisions: Reg. 8302(10) — Period of reduced remuneration.

(10) Period of reduced remuneration — For the purposes of paragraph (9)(d), where a member of a registered pension plan is provided with benefits under a defined benefit provision of the plan in respect of a period in 1990 or 1991

(a) throughout which, by reason of disability, leave of absence, lay-off or other circumstance, the member rendered no services, or rendered a reduced level of services, to employers who participate in the plan, and

(b) throughout which the member received no remuneration, or a reduced rate of remuneration,

the member's compensation shall be determined on the assumption that the member received remuneration for the period equal to the amount of remuneration that it is reasonable to consider the member would have received if the member had rendered services throughout the period on a regular basis (having regard to the services rendered by the member before the period) and the member's rate of remuneration had been commensurate with the member's rate of remuneration when the member did render services on a regular basis.

(11) Anti-avoidance — Where the terms of a defined benefit provision of a registered pension plan can reasonably be considered to have been established or modified so that a pension credit of an individual for a calendar year under the provision would, but for this subsection, be reduced as a consequence of the application of paragraph (3)(g), that paragraph shall not apply in determining the individual's normalized pension under the provision in respect of the year.

Definitions [Reg. 8302]: "amount", "annuity" — ITA 248(1); "benefit accrual" — Reg. 8302(2); "benefit entitlement" — Reg. 8302(1); "benefit provision" — Reg. 8300(3), 8500(1); "benefits" — Reg. 8300(7); "calendar year" — *Interpretation Act* 37(1)(a); "Canada" — ITA 255, *Interpretation Act* 35(1); "commencement" — *Interpretation Act* 35(1); "contributing entity" — Reg. 8302(12); "deferred profit sharing plan" — ITA 147(1), 248(1); "defined benefit provision" — ITA 147.1(1), Reg. 8300(3); "designated provision of the law of Canada or a province" — Reg. 8513; "employer", "employment", "individual" — ITA 248(1); "lifetime retirement benefits" — Reg. 8300(3), 8500(1); "member's compensation" — Reg. 8302(10); "Minister" — ITA 248(1); "month" — *Interpretation Act* 35(1); "normalized pension" — Reg. 8302(3), (5); "other year" — Reg. 8302(3)(e); "pension credit" — Reg. 8301, 8308.1(2)–(4), 8308.3(2), (3); "person" — ITA 248(1); "province" — *Interpretation Act* 35(1); "provincial pension plan" — *Canada Pension Plan* s. 3; "public pension benefits" — Reg. 8300(3), 8500(1); "registered pension plan" — ITA 248(1); "render services" — Reg. 8300(4); "retirement benefits" — Reg. 8300(3), 8500(1); "specified multi-employer plan" — ITA 147.1(1), Reg. 8510(2), (3); "specified year" — Reg. 8302(3)(h)(3); "spouse" — Reg. 8302(4)(b); "statutory pension" — Reg. 8302(3)(j), (k); "supplemental provision" — Reg. 8302(7); "totally and permanently disabled" — Reg. 8300(3), 8500(1); "writing" — *Interpretation Act* 35(1); "Year's Maximum Pensionable Earnings" — Reg. 8300(3), 8500(1).

8303. Past service pension adjustment — (1) PSPA with respect to employer — For the purpose of subsection 248(1) of the Act, "past service pension adjustment" of an individual for a calendar year in respect of an employer means the total of

(a) the accumulated past service pension adjustment (in this Part referred to as "accumulated PSPA") of the individual for the year with respect to the employer, determined as of the end of the year,

(b) the total of all amounts each of which is the foreign plan PSPA (determined under subsection 8308.1(5) or (6)) of the individual with respect to the employer associated with a modification of benefits in the year under a foreign plan (as defined in subsection 8308.1(1)), and

(c) the total of all amounts each of which is the specified retirement arrangement PSPA (determined under subsection 8308.3(4) or (5)) of the individual with respect to the employer associated with a modification of benefits in the year under a specified retirement arrangement (as defined in subsection 8308.3(1)).

Related Provisions: ITA 252.1(a) — All union locals deemed to be one employer.

Notes: For explanation of PSPA see CRA guide T4104; Willis Towers Watson, *Canadian Pensions and Retirement Income Planning*, 6th ed. (LexisNexis, 2017), chap. 10; Millard & Théroux, "Private Health Services Plans and Pension Arbitrage", 2004 Cdn Tax Foundation conference report, at 12:25-46.

In *Moors*, 2015 FC 446, the Court upheld a Canadian Human Rights Commission ruling that the PSPA for a woman on maternity leave did not discriminate against her under the *Charter of Rights*.

Reg. 8303(1)(b) and (c) added by P.C. 1996-911, effective for the determination of past service adjustments for 1993 and later years.

Registered Plans Compliance Bulletins: 1 (calculation of past service pension adjustment).

Forms: T4104: Past service pension adjustment guide.

(2) Accumulated PSPA for year — For the purposes of this Part, the accumulated PSPA of an individual for a calendar year with respect to an employer, determined as of any time, is the total of all amounts each of which is the individual's provisional past service pension adjustment (in this Part referred to as "provisional PSPA") with respect to the employer that is associated with

(a) a past service event (other than a certifiable past service event with respect to the individual) that occurred in the preceding year; or

(b) a certifiable past service event with respect to the individual where the Minister has, in the year and before that time, issued a certification for the purposes of subsection 147.1(10) of the Act in respect of the event and the individual.

Related Provisions: Reg. 8303(2.1) — 1991 past service events and certifications; Reg. 8311 — Provisional PSPA rounded to nearest dollar.

Notes: Reg. 8303(2)(a) amended by P.C. 2001-153, for past service events after 2000.

Opening words of Reg. 8303(2) amended by P.C. 1998-2256, effective 1996, to remove its application to ITA 204.2(1.3).

(2.1) 1991 past service events and certifications — For the purposes of subsection (2),

(a) a past service event that occurred in 1991 (including, for greater certainty, a past service event that is deemed by paragraph 8304(3)(b) to have occurred immediately after the end of 1990) shall be deemed to have occurred on January 1, 1992 and not to have occurred in 1991; and

(b) a certification issued by the Minister in 1991 shall be deemed to have been issued on January 1, 1992 and not to have been issued in 1991.

Notes: Reg. 8303(2.1) added by P.C. 1995-17, effective 1991. Its effect is to make 1992 the first year for which PSPAs were reported; thus, RRSP deduction room is first reduced by PSPAs in 1992.

(3) Provisional PSPA — Subject to subsections (8) and (10) and sections 8304 and 8308, for the purposes of this Part, the provisional PSPA of an individual with respect to an employer that is associated with a past service event that occurs at a particular time in a particular calendar year is the amount determined by the formula

$$A - B - C + D$$

where

A is the aggregate of all amounts each of which is, in respect of a calendar year after 1989 and before the particular year, the amount that would have been the individual's pension credit for the year with respect to the employer under a defined benefit provision of a registered pension plan (other than a plan that is, at the particular time, a specified multi-employer plan) had the individual's benefit entitlement under the provision in respect of the year and the employer been equal to the individual's redetermined benefit entitlement (determined as of the particular time) under the provision in respect of the year and the employer,

B is the aggregate that would be determined for A if the reference in the description of A to "determined as of the particular time" were read as a reference to "determined as of the time immediately before the particular time",

C is such portion of the amount of the individual's qualifying transfers made in connection with the past service event as is not deducted in computing the provisional PSPA of the individual with respect to any other employer, and

D is the total of all amounts each of which is an excess money purchase transfer in relation to the individual and the past service event that is not included in determining any other provisional PSPA of the individual that is associated with the past service event.

Related Provisions: ITA 257 — Negative amounts in formulas; Reg. 8303(4) — Meaning of redetermined benefit entitlement; Reg. 8303(6) — Meaning of qualifying transfers; Reg. 8303(7.1) — Excess money purchase transfer amount; Reg. 8500(8)(c) — Non-member benefits ignored in determining pension adjustment.

Notes: D added by P.C. 1998-2256, for past service events after 1997.

Forms: T1004: Applying for the certification of a provisional PSPA.

(4) Redetermined benefit entitlement — For the purposes of the description of A in subsection (3), an individual's redetermined benefit entitlement under a defined benefit provision of a registered pension plan in respect of a calendar year and an employer, determined as of a particular time, is the amount that would be determined under section 8302 to be the individual's benefit entitlement under the provision in respect of the year and the employer if, for the purpose of computing the benefit accrual of the individual in respect of the year under the provision and, where subsection 8302(6) is applicable, under any other defined benefit provision, the amount determined under paragraph 8302(2)(a) in respect of a specific provision were equal to such portion of the individual's normalized pension (computed in accordance with subsection (5)) under the specific provision at the particular time, determined with reference to the year, as may reasonably be considered to have accrued in respect of the year.

(5) Normalized pension — For the purposes of subsection (4), the normalized pension of an individual under a defined benefit provision of a registered pension plan at a particular time, determined with reference to a calendar year (in this subsection referred to as the "pension credit year"), is the amount (expressed on an annualized basis) of lifetime retirement benefits, other than excluded benefits, that would be payable to the individual under the provision immediately after the particular time if

(a) where lifetime retirement benefits have not commenced to be paid under the provision to the individual before the particular time, they commenced to be paid immediately after the particular time,

(b) where the individual had not attained 65 years of age before the time at which lifetime retirement benefits commenced to be paid (or are assumed by reason of paragraph (a) to have commenced to be paid) to the individual, the individual attained that age at that time,

(c) the amount of the individual's lifetime retirement benefits were determined with regard to all past service events occurring at or before the particular time and without regard to past service events occurring after the particular time,

(d) paragraphs 8302(3)(c) to (p) (other than paragraph 8302(3)(g), where subsection 8302(11) was applicable in respect of the pension credit year and the provision or would have been applicable had all benefits provided as a consequence of past service events become provided in the pension credit year) were applied for the purpose of determining the amount of the individual's lifetime retirement benefits and, for the purpose of those paragraphs, the pension credit year were the particular year referred to in those paragraphs, and

(e) where

(i) the amount of the individual's lifetime retirement benefits under the provision depends on the individual's remuneration, and

(ii) all or any part of the individual's lifetime retirement benefits in respect of the pension credit year became provided as a consequence of a past service event, pursuant to terms of the provision that enable benefits to be provided to members of the plan in respect of periods of employment with employers who have not participated under the provision,

the remuneration received by the individual from each such employer in respect of a period of employment in respect of which the individual is provided with benefits under the provision were remuneration received from an employer who has participated under the provision for the benefit of the individual,

and, for the purposes of this subsection, the following benefits are excluded benefits:

(f) where the formula for determining the amount of lifetime retirement benefits payable under the provision to the individual requires the calculation of an amount that is the product of a fixed rate and the duration of all or part of the individual's pensionable service, benefits payable as a direct consequence of an increase in the value of the fixed rate at any time (in this paragraph referred to as the "time of increase") after the pension credit year, other than benefits

(i) provided as a consequence of a second or subsequent increase in the value of the fixed rate after the time that retirement benefits under the provision commenced to be paid to the individual, or

(ii) that would not have become provided had the value of the fixed rate been increased to the amount determined by the formula

$$A \times B / C$$

where

A is the value of the fixed rate immediately before the time of the increase,

B is the average wage for the calendar year that includes the time of the increase, and

C is

(A) if the value of the fixed rate was last increased or established in the calendar year that includes the time of the increase, the average wage for that year, or

(B) otherwise, the average wage for the year immediately preceding the calendar year that includes the time of increase,

(f.1) where the formula for determining the amount of lifetime retirement benefits payable under the provision to the individual includes a limit that is the product of the duration of the individual's pensionable service and the lesser of a percentage of the individual's remuneration and a fixed rate, and the value of the fixed rate is increased after the pension credit year to an amount equal to the defined benefit limit for the earlier of the year in which the increase occurs and the year in which retirement benefits under the provision commenced to be paid to the individual, the portion of the benefits payable as a direct consequence of the increase that would not have become provided had the value of

the fixed rate been set at the defined benefit limit for the pension credit year, if

(i) the value of the fixed rate was, immediately before the increase, equal to the defined benefit limit for the year in which the value of the fixed rate was last established, and

(ii) where the year in which the value of the fixed rate was last established precedes the year immediately preceding the year in which the increase occurs,

(A) the Minister has approved in writing the application of this paragraph in respect of the past service event,

(B) there are more than nine active members (within the meaning assigned by paragraph 8306(4)(a)) under the provision, and

(C) the plan is not a designated plan,

(f.2) where the formula for determining the amount of lifetime retirement benefits payable under the provision to the individual includes a limit that is the product of the duration of the individual's pensionable service and the lesser of a percentage of the individual's remuneration and a fixed rate the value of which can reasonably be considered to be fixed each year as a portion of the defined benefit limit for that year, benefits payable as a direct consequence of an increase, after the pension credit year, in the value of the fixed rate to reflect the defined benefit limit for the year in which the increase occurs, if

(i) except as otherwise expressly permitted by the Minister, it is reasonable to consider that, for years after 1989, the ratio of the fixed rate to the defined benefit limit has been, and will remain, constant,

(ii) the benefits are not provided as a consequence of a second or subsequent increase in the value of the fixed rate after the time that retirement benefits under the provision commenced to be paid to the individual,

(iii) the Minister has approved in writing the application of this paragraph in respect of the past service event, and

(iv) the plan is not a designated plan,

(g) where

(i) the provision is a flat benefit provision,

(ii) at the particular time, the amount (expressed on an annual basis) of lifetime retirement benefits provided under the provision to each member in respect of pensionable service in each calendar year does not exceed 40 per cent of the defined benefit limit for the year that includes the particular time,

(iii) the conditions in subsection 8306(2) are satisfied in respect of the provision and the past service event in connection with which the normalized pension is being calculated, and

(iv) only one fixed rate is applicable in determining the amount of the individual's lifetime retirement benefits,

benefits provided as a direct consequence of an increase in the value of the fixed rate at any time (in this paragraph referred to as the "time of increase") after the pension credit year, other than benefits

(v) provided as a consequence of a second or subsequent increase in the value of the fixed rate after the time that retirement benefits under the provision commenced to be paid to the individual, or

(vi) that would not have become provided had the value of the fixed rate been increased to the greater of

(A) the greatest of all amounts each of which is an amount determined by the formula

$$A \times B / C$$

where

A is a value of the fixed rate in the period beginning on January 1, 1984 and ending immediately before the time of increase,

B is the average wage for the calendar year that includes the time of increase, and

C is the average wage for the later of 1984 and the calendar year in which the value of the fixed rate used for A was first effective, and

(B) the amount determined by the formula

$$D + (E \times F)$$

where

D is the value of the fixed rate immediately before the time of increase,

E is the amount by which the value of the fixed rate used for D would have to be increased to provide an increase in the individual's annual lifetime retirement benefits equal to $18 for each year of pensionable service, and

F is the duration (measured in years, including any fraction of a year) of the period beginning on the later of January 1, 1984 and the day on which the value of the fixed rate used for D was first effective and ending on the day that includes the time of increase;

(h) where the provision is a flat benefit provision, benefits provided as a direct consequence of an increase at any time (in this paragraph referred to as the "time of increase") after the pension credit year in the value of a fixed rate under the provision where

(i) the value of the fixed rate was increased pursuant to an agreement made before 1992, and

(ii) at the time the agreement was made, it was reasonable to expect that the percentage increase in the value of the fixed rate would approximate or be less than the percentage increase in the average wage from the calendar year in which the value of the fixed rate was last increased before the time of increase (or, if the increase is the first increase, the calendar year in which the initial value of the fixed rate was first applicable) to the calendar year that includes the time of increase,

(i) where the provision is a flat benefit provision under which the amount of each member's retirement benefits depends on the member's job category or rate of pay in such a manner that the ratio of the amount of lifetime retirement benefits to remuneration does not significantly increase as remuneration increases, benefits provided as a direct consequence of a change, after the pension credit year, in the individual's job category or rate of pay,

(j) where

(i) the individual's pensionable service under the provision ends before the particular time,

(ii) the individual's lifetime retirement benefits under the provision have been adjusted by a cost-of-living or similar adjustment in respect of the period (in this paragraph referred to as the "deferral period") beginning at the latest of

(A) the time at which the individual's pensionable service under the provision ends,

(B) if the amount of the individual's lifetime retirement benefits depends on the individual's remuneration, the end of the most recent period for which the individual received remuneration that is taken into account in determining the individual's lifetime retirement benefits,

(C) if the amount of the individual's lifetime retirement benefits depends on the individual's remuneration and the remuneration is adjusted as described in paragraph 8302(3)(h), the end of the period in respect of which the adjustment is made, and

(D) if the formula for determining the amount of the individual's lifetime retirement benefits requires the calculation of an amount that is the product of a fixed rate and the duration of all or part of the individual's pensionable

service (or other measure of services rendered by the individual), the time as of which the value of the fixed rate applicable with respect to the individual was established,

and ending at the earlier of the particular time and the time, if any, at which lifetime retirement benefits commenced to be paid under the provision to the individual, and

(iii) the adjustment is warranted, having regard to all prior such adjustments, by the increase in the Consumer Price Index or in the wage measure from the commencement of the deferral period to the time the adjustment was made,

benefits payable as a consequence of the adjustment,

(k) benefits payable as a consequence of a cost-of-living adjustment made after the time lifetime retirement benefits commenced to be paid under the provision to the individual, where the adjustment

(i) is warranted, having regard to all prior such adjustments, by the increase in the Consumer Price Index from that time to the time at which the adjustment was made, or

(ii) is a periodic adjustment described in subparagraph 8503(2)(a)(ii), and

(l) such portion of the individual's lifetime retirement benefits as

(i) would not otherwise be excluded in determining the individual's normalized pension,

(ii) may reasonably be considered to be attributable to cost-of-living adjustments or to adjustments made by reason of increases in a general measure of salaries and wages (other than increases in such a measure after the time at which lifetime retirement benefits commenced to be paid under the provision to the individual), and

(iii) is acceptable to the Minister.

Related Provisions: ITA 257 — Negative amounts in formulas.

Notes: CRA states in q.6 of "Frequently Asked Questions — Past Service Pension Adjustments" (tinyurl.com/faqs-cra) that the PSPA benefit exclusion under Reg. 8303(5)(f) is not available if the value of the fixed rate is increased in the same year the plan is established. To eliminate the unintended benefit exclusion, CRA uses its authority under Reg. 8310(2) to require a modified calculation (for amendments submitted after June 27, 2007), resulting in no benefit exclusion, so that PSPA must be reported for the increase in the fixed rate. The calculation in such cases uses the average wage for the calendar year of the increase for cl. (f)(ii)C(A).

Reg. 8303(5)(f)(ii)C(A) amended to change "has previously been increased" to "was last increased or established" by Reg. 2011-936, effective for past service events that occur after Feb. 18, 2011.

Reg. 8303(5)(f.1)(ii)(C) and (f.2)(iv) amended by 2007 budget bill #2, effective for past service events that occur after 2007, to change "designated plan under section 8515" to "designated plan" (non-substantive amendment: definition is now in Reg. 8500(1) and applies via Reg. 8300(3)).

Reg. 8303(5)(f.1), (f.2) added by P.C. 2005-1508, effective 2004, but in respect of past service events that occur before 2006, ignore 8303(5)(f.1)(i) and (ii).

Registered Plans Directorate Actuarial Bulletins: 1R1 (calculating actuarial increase where pension start postponed beyond age 65).

(6) Qualifying transfers

(6) **Qualifying transfers** — For the purposes of subsections (3) and 8304(5), (7) and (10), and subject to subsection (6.1) and paragraph 8304(2)(h), the amount of an individual's qualifying transfers made in connection with a past service event is the total of all amounts each of which is

(a) the portion of an amount transferred to a registered pension plan

(i) in accordance with any of subsections 146(16), 147(19) and 147.3(2), (5) and (7) of the Act, or

(ii) from a specified multi-employer plan in accordance with subsection 147.3(3) of the Act

that is transferred to fund benefits provided to the individual as a consequence of the past service event; or

(b) the amount of any property held in connection with a benefit provision of a registered pension plan that is made available to fund benefits provided to the individual under another benefit provision of the plan as a consequence of the past service event, where the transaction by which the property is made so available is such that, if the benefit provisions were in separate registered pension plans, the transaction would constitute a transfer of property from one plan to the other in accordance with any of subsections 147.3(2), (5) and (7) of the Act.

Notes: Reg. 8303(6) opening words amended by 2011 budget bill #2, effective March 23, 2011, to add reference to Reg. 8304(10).

Reg. 8303(6) earlier amended by P.C. 2001-153 (effective for determining qualifying transfers that occur after April 18, 2000) and P.C. 1998-2256.

Registered Pension Plans Technical Manual: §6.1 (qualifying transfers).

(6.1) Exclusion for pre-1990 benefits — The amount of an individual's qualifying transfers made in connection with a past service event shall be determined under subsection (6) without regard to the portion, if any, of amounts transferred or property made available, as the case may be, that can reasonably be considered to have been transferred or made available to fund benefits provided in respect of periods before 1990.

Notes: Reg. 8303(6.1) added by P.C. 1998-2256, effective for the determination of qualifying transfers that occur after June 25, 1998.

(7) Deemed payment — Where

(a) an individual has given an irrevocable direction that

(i) an amount be paid to a registered pension plan, or

(ii) property held in connection with a benefit provision of a registered pension plan be made available to fund benefits provided to the individual under another benefit provision of the plan

in the event that the Minister issues a certification for the purposes of subsection 147.1(10) of the Act with respect to the individual and to benefits provided under a defined benefit provision of the plan as a consequence of a past service event, and

(b) the amount is to be paid or the property is to be made available, as the case may be,

(i) where subparagraph (ii) does not apply, on or before the day that is 90 days after the day on which the certification is received by the administrator of the plan, and

(ii) where the plan was deemed by paragraph 147.1(3)(a) of the Act to be a registered pension plan at the time the direction was given, on or before the day that is 90 days after the later of

(A) the day on which the certification is received by the administrator of the plan, and

(B) the day on which the administrator of the plan receives written notice from the Minister of the registration of the plan for the purposes of the Act,

the amount or property, as the case may be, is deemed, for the purpose of subsection (6), to have been paid or made available, as the case may be, at the time the direction was given.

Notes: Reg. 8303(7) amended to add (a)(ii) and (b)(ii) by P.C. 1998-2256, effective on the same basis as the amendments to Reg. 8303(6).

Registered Pension Plans Technical Manual: §6.2 (deemed payment).

Registered Plans Compliance Bulletins: 2 (qualifying transfers).

(7.1) Excess money purchase transfer — Where lifetime retirement benefits have, as a consequence of a past service event, become provided to an individual under a defined benefit provision of a registered pension plan (other than a specified multi-employer plan) in respect of a period (in this subsection referred to as the "past service period") that

(a) was previously pensionable service of the individual under a particular defined benefit provision of a registered pension plan (other than a specified multi-employer plan),

(b) ceased to be pensionable service of the individual under the particular provision as a result of the payment of a single amount, all or part of which was transferred on behalf of the individual from the particular provision to a registered retirement savings plan, a registered retirement income fund, a money purchase provision of a registered pension plan or a defined ben-

efit provision of a registered pension plan that was, at the time of the transfer, a specified multi-employer plan,

(c) has not, at any time after the payment of the single amount and before the past service event, been pensionable service of the individual under any defined benefit provision of a registered pension plan (other than a specified multi-employer plan), and

(d) is not, for the purpose of subsection 8304(5), a qualifying past service period in relation to the individual and the past service event,

the amount determined by the formula

$$A - B$$

is, for the purpose of the description of D in subsection (3), an excess money purchase transfer in relation to the individual and the past service event, where

A is the portion of the amount transferred, as described in paragraph (b), that can reasonably be considered to be attributable to benefits in respect of the portion of the past service period that is after 1989, and

B is the total of all amounts each of which is the portion of a pension credit, or the grossed-up amount of a provisional PSPA, of the individual that can reasonably be considered to be attributable to benefits previously provided under the particular provision in respect of the past service period.

Related Provisions: ITA 146(21.2) — Saskatchewan Pension Plan account deemed to be RRSP for purposes of regulations; ITA 147.5(12) — Pooled registered pension plan deemed to be RRSP for purposes of regulations; ITA 257 — Negative amounts in formulas; Reg. 8304.1(7) — Meaning of grossed-up amount of provisional PSPA.

Notes: Reg. 8303(7.1) added by P.C. 1998-2256, for past service events after 1997.

(8) Specified multi-employer plan — Where, in a calendar year, an individual makes a contribution (other than an excluded contribution) in respect of a defined benefit provision of a registered pension plan that is, in the year, a specified multi-employer plan, and the contribution

(a) is made in respect of a period after 1989 and before the year, and

(b) is not included in determining the individual's pension credit for the year with respect to any employer under the provision,

the individual's provisional PSPA with respect to an employer who participates in the plan, associated with the payment of the contribution, is the portion of the contribution that is not included in the individual's provisional PSPA with respect to any other employer who participates in the plan, and, for the purpose of this subsection, the plan administrator shall determine the portion of the contribution to be included in the provisional PSPA of the individual with respect to each employer.

Related Provisions: Reg. 8303(9) — Contributions include conditional contributions.

(9) Conditional contributions — For the purpose of subsection (8), a contribution includes an amount paid to a registered pension plan where the right of any person to retain the amount on behalf of the plan is conditional on the Minister issuing a certification for the purposes of subsection 147.1(10) of the Act as it applies with respect to the individual and to benefits provided as a consequence of the payment.

(10) Benefits in respect of foreign service — Where as a consequence of a past service event, benefits become provided to an individual under a defined benefit provision of a registered pension plan in respect of a period throughout which the individual was employed outside Canada, and the Minister has consented in writing to the application of this subsection, each provisional PSPA of the individual associated with the past service event shall be determined on the assumption that no benefits were provided in respect of the period.

Related Provisions: ITA 252.1 — All union locals deemed to be one employer; Reg. 8503(3)(a)(vii) — Eligible service outside Canada.

Registered Pension Plans Technical Manual: §6.3 (benefits in respect of foreign service).

Registered Plans Directorate Newsletters: 93-2 (foreign service newsletter); 2000-1 (foreign service newsletter update).

Definitions [Reg. 8303]: "accumulated PSPA" — Reg. 8303(1)(a), 8303(2); "active member" — Reg. 8300(3), 8500(1); "amount" — ITA 248(1); "associated" — ITA 256; "calendar year" — *Interpretation Act* 37(1)(a); "Canada" — ITA 255, *Interpretation Act* 35(1); "certifiable past service event" — Reg. 8300(1); "certification" — Reg. 8303(2.1)(b); "commencement" — *Interpretation Act* 35(1); "Consumer Price Index" — Reg. 8300(3), 8500(1); "contribution" — Reg. 8303(9); "deferral period" — Reg. 8303(5)(j)(ii); "defined benefit limit" — Reg. 8300(3), 8500(1); "defined benefit provision" — ITA 147.1(1), Reg. 8300(3); "designated plan" — Reg. 8300(3), 8500(1), 8515; "employed", "employer", "employment" — ITA 248(1); "excluded contribution", "flat benefit provision" — Reg. 8300(1); "grossed-up amount" — Reg. 8304(7); "individual" — ITA 248(1); "lifetime retirement benefits" — Reg. 8300(3), 8500(1); "Minister" — ITA 248(1); "normalized pension" — Reg. 8303(5); "past service event" — Reg. 8300(1), 8303(2.1)(a); "past service pension adjustment" — ITA 248(1), Reg. 8303(1); "past service period" — Reg. 8303(7.1); "pension credit" — Reg. 8301, 8308.1(2)–(4), 8308.3(2), (3); "pension credit year" — Reg. 8303(5); "pensionable service" — Reg. 8300(3), 8500(1); "person", "property" — ITA 248(1); "provisional PSPA" — Reg. 8303(2), (3), 8308(4)(e); "qualifying transfers" — Reg. 8303(6); "redetermined benefit entitlement" — Reg. 8303(4); "registered pension plan" — ITA 248(1); "registered retirement income fund" — ITA 146.3(1), 248(1); "registered retirement savings plan" — ITA 146(1), (21.2), 147.5(12), 248(1); "retirement benefits" — Reg. 8300(3), 8500(1); "specified multi-employer plan" — ITA 147.1(1), Reg. 8510(2), (3); "time of increase" — Reg. 8303(5)(g), (h); "written", "writing" — *Interpretation Act* 35(1)"writing".

Interpretation Bulletins [Reg. 8303]: IT-124R6: Contributions to registered retirement savings plans.

8304. Past service benefits — Additional rules — (1) Replacement of defined benefits — Where

(a) an individual ceased, at any time in a calendar year, to have any rights to benefits under a defined benefit provision of a registered pension plan (in this subsection referred to as the "former provision"),

(b) benefits became provided at that time to the individual under another defined benefit provision of a registered pension plan (in this subsection referred to as the "current provision") in lieu of the benefits under the former provision,

(c) the benefits that became provided at that time to the individual under the current provision in respect of the period in the year before that time are attributable to employment with the same employers as were the individual's benefits in respect of that period under the former provision,

(d) no amount was transferred in the year on behalf of the individual from the former provision to a registered retirement savings plan, a registered retirement income fund or a money purchase provision of a registered pension plan, and

(e) no benefits became provided under the former provision to the individual in the year and after that time,

each pension credit of the individual under the former provision for the year is nil.

Related Provisions: ITA 146(21.2) — Saskatchewan Pension Plan account deemed to be RRSP for purposes of regulations; ITA 147.5(12) — Pooled registered pension plan deemed to be RRSP for purposes of regulations.

Notes: Reg. 8304(1)(d) amended by P.C. 1995-17, effective for the determination of pension credits for 1990 and later years, to add reference to transfers to a RRIF.

Interpretation Bulletins: IT-124R6: Contributions to registered retirement savings plans; IT-528: Transfers of funds between registered plans.

Forms: T4104: Past service pension adjustment guide.

(2) Replacement of money purchase benefits — Where

(a) an individual ceased, at any time in a calendar year, to have any rights to benefits under a money purchase provision of a registered pension plan or under a deferred profit sharing plan (in this subsection referred to as the "former provision"),

(b) benefits became provided at that time to the individual under a defined benefit provision of a registered pension plan (in this subsection referred to as the "current provision") in lieu of benefits under the former provision,

(c) the benefits that became provided at that time to the individual under the current provision in respect of the period in the year before that time are attributable to employment with the same employers who made contributions under the former provision in respect of that period on behalf of the individual,

(d) no amount was transferred in the year on behalf of the individual from the former provision to a registered retirement savings plan, a registered retirement income fund, a money purchase provision of a registered pension plan or a deferred profit sharing plan,

(e) no contributions were made under the former provision by or on behalf of the individual, and no other amounts were allocated under the former provision to the individual, in the year and after that time, and

(f) it is reasonable to consider that no excess would, if this subsection did not apply and if the year ended at that time, be determined under any of paragraphs 147(5.1)(a) to (c), 147.1(8)(a) and (b) and (9)(a) and (b) of the Act with respect to the individual for the year,

the following rules apply:

(g) each pension credit of the individual under the former provision for the year is nil, and

(h) the amount, if any, of the individual's qualifying transfers made in connection with the replacement of the individual's benefits shall be determined under subsection 8303(6) without regard to the portion, if any, of amounts transferred from the former provision to the current provision that can reasonably be considered to relate to an amount that, but for paragraph (g), would have been included in determining the individual's pension credit under the former provision for the year.

Related Provisions: ITA 146(21.2) — Saskatchewan Pension Plan account deemed to be RRSP for purposes of regulations; ITA 147.5(12) — Pooled registered pension plan deemed to be RRSP for purposes of regulations; Reg. 8301(2) — Pension credit — DPSP; Reg. 8301(4) — Pension credit — money purchase RPP.

Notes: Reg. 8304(2) amended by P.C. 2001-153 (for pension credits for 2000 and later years and qualifying transfers after April 18, 2000), 1995-17.

(3) Past service benefits in year of past service event — Subject to subsection (4), where, as a consequence of a past service event that occurs at a particular time in a calendar year, benefits (in this subsection and subsection (4) referred to as "past service benefits") become provided to an individual under a defined benefit provision of a registered pension plan in respect of a period in the year and before the particular time that, immediately before the past service event, was not pensionable service of the individual under the provision, the following rules apply, except to the extent that the Minister has waived in writing their application in respect of the plan:

(a) each pension credit of the individual under the provision for the year shall be determined as if the past service benefits had not become provided to the individual;

(b) where the year is 1990, the past service event shall be deemed, for the purposes of this Part, to have occurred immediately after the end of the year;

(c) where the year is after 1990, each provisional PSPA of the individual associated with the past service event as a consequence of which the past service benefits became provided shall be determined as if the past service event had occurred immediately after the end of the year;

(d) where information that is required for the computation of a provisional PSPA referred to in paragraph (c) is not determinable until after the time at which the provisional PSPA is computed, reasonable assumptions shall be made in respect of such information; and

(e) subsection 147.1(10) of the Act shall apply in respect of the past service benefits to the extent that that subsection would apply if the past service event had occurred immediately after the end of the year.

(4) Exceptions — Subsection (3) does not apply where

(a) the past service benefits become provided in circumstances where subsection (1) or (2) is applicable; or

(b) the period in respect of which the past service benefits are provided was not, at any time before the past service event,

(i) pensionable service of the individual under a defined benefit provision of a registered pension plan, or

(ii) a period in respect of which a contribution was made on behalf of, or an amount (other than an amount in respect of earnings of a plan) was allocated to, the individual under a money purchase provision of a registered pension plan or under a deferred profit sharing plan.

(c) [Repealed]

Notes: Reg. 8304(4) amended by P.C. 1998-2256 (for past service events after 1996), 1995-17.

(5) Modified PSPA calculation — Subject to subsection (10), if

(a) lifetime retirement benefits have, as a consequence of a past service event, become provided to an individual under a defined benefit provision of a registered pension plan in respect of one or more qualifying past service periods in relation to the individual and the past service event, and

(b) the benefits are considered to be attributable to employment of the individual with a single employer,

the provisional PSPA of the individual with respect to the employer that is associated with the past service event is the amount determined by the formula

$$A + B + C - D$$

where

A is the provisional PSPA that would be determined if

(a) this subsection did not apply,

(b) all former benefits in relation to the individual and the past service event had ceased to be provided at the time the past service event occurred,

(c) all former benefits in relation to the individual and the past service event were considered to be attributable to employment of the individual with the employer, and

(d) the value of C in subsection 8303(3) were nil;

B is the total of all amounts each of which is a non-vested PA amount in respect of the individual and the past service event;

C is the total of all amounts each of which is a money purchase transfer in relation to the individual and the past service event; and

D is the amount of the individual's qualifying transfers made in connection with the past service event.

Related Provisions: ITA 257 — Negative amounts in formulas; Reg. 8300(7) — Benefits include contingent benefits; Reg. 8303(6) — Meaning of qualifying transfers.

Notes: Reg. 8304(5) opening words amended by 2011 budget bill #2, for past service events occurring after March 22, 2011, to add "Subject to subsection (10)".

(5.1) Definitions for subsection (5) — For the purpose of subsection (5), where

(a) lifetime retirement benefits (in this subsection referred to as "past service benefits") have, as a consequence of a past service event occurring at a particular time, become provided to an individual under a defined benefit provision of a registered pension plan in respect of a period that

(i) immediately before the particular time, was not pensionable service of the individual under the provision, and

(ii) is, or was, pensionable service of the individual under another defined benefit provision (in this subsection referred to as the "former provision") of a registered pension plan,

(b) either

(i) the individual has not, at any time after 1996 and before the particular time, been a member in relation to the former provision,

(ii) the individual ceased, at the particular time, to be a member in relation to the former provision, or

(iii) the past service event is a certifiable past service event and the individual is to cease being a member in relation to the former provision no later than 90 days after the day on which a certification of the Minister is issued for the purposes of subsection 147.1(10) of the Act in respect of the past service benefits, and

(c) lifetime retirement benefits to which the individual is or was entitled under the former provision in respect of the period have not been taken into account under subsection (5) as former benefits in determining a provisional PSPA of the individual that is associated with any other past service event,

the following rules apply:

(d) the period is a qualifying past service period in relation to the individual and the past service event,

(e) lifetime retirement benefits to which the individual is or was entitled under the former provision in respect of the period are former benefits in relation to the individual and the past service event,

(f) where subsection 8301(8) has applied in respect of the determination of a pension credit of the individual under the former provision with respect to an employer for a year that includes any part of the period, the amount determined by the formula

$$A - B$$

is a non-vested PA amount in respect of the individual and the past service event, where

A is the amount that would have been the individual's pension credit under the former provision for the year with respect to the employer if subsection 8301(8) had not applied, and

B is the individual's pension credit under the former provision for the year with respect to the employer, and

(g) the amount determined by the formula

$$A - B$$

is a money purchase transfer in relation to the individual and the past service event, where

A is the total of all amounts each of which is

(i) an amount that was transferred, at or before the particular time, on behalf of the individual from the former provision to a registered retirement savings plan, a registered retirement income fund, a money purchase provision of a registered pension plan or a defined benefit provision of a registered pension plan that was, at the time of the transfer, a specified multi-employer plan, or

(ii) an amount that is to be paid or otherwise made available under the former provision with respect to the individual after the particular time, other than an amount that is to be transferred to fund the past service benefits or paid directly to the individual,

to the extent that the amount can reasonably be considered to be attributable to benefits in respect of the portion of the period that is after 1989, and

B is the total of all amounts each of which is, in respect of an employer with respect to which a provisional PSPA of the individual that is associated with the past service event is determined under subsection (5), the amount, if any, by which

(i) the portion of the value determined for B in subsection 8303(3), for the purpose of determining the individual's provisional PSPA with respect to the employer, that can reasonably be considered to be attributable to benefits provided in respect of the period

exceeds

(ii) the portion of the value determined for A in subsection 8303(3), for the purpose of determining the individual's provisional PSPA with respect to the employer, that can reasonably be considered to be attributable to benefits provided in respect of the period.

Related Provisions: ITA 146(21.2) — Saskatchewan Pension Plan account deemed to be RRSP for purposes of regulations; ITA 147.5(12) — Pooled registered pension plan deemed to be RRSP for purposes of regulations; ITA 257 — Negative amounts in formulas; Reg. 8300(7) — Benefits include contingent benefits.

Notes: Reg. 8304(5.1) added by P.C. 1998-2256, effective for the determination of provisional PSPAs that are associated with past service events that occur after 1997.

(6) Reinstatement of pre-1997 benefits — Where lifetime retirement benefits have, as a consequence of a past service event, become provided to an individual under a defined benefit provision of a registered pension plan in respect of a period that

(a) was previously pensionable service of the individual under the provision,

(b) ceased to be pensionable service of the individual under the provision as a consequence of the individual ceasing before 1997 to be a member in relation to the provision, and

(c) has not, at any time after 1996 and before the past service event, been pensionable service of the individual under a defined benefit provision of a registered pension plan,

each provisional PSPA of the individual that is associated with the past service event shall be determined as if all benefits provided to the individual under the provision before 1997 in respect of the period had been provided to the individual under another defined benefit provision of a registered pension plan in relation to which the individual has not, at any time after 1996, been a member.

Notes: Reg. 8304(6) amended by P.C. 1998-2256, for provisional PSPAs that are associated with past service events after 1997.

(7) Two or more employers — Where

(a) lifetime retirement benefits (in this subsection referred to as "past service benefits") provided to an individual under a defined benefit provision of a registered pension plan as a consequence of a past service event are attributable to employment of the individual with two or more employers (each of which is, in this subsection, referred to as a "current employer"), and

(b) subsection (5) would, but for paragraph (5)(b), apply in respect of the determination of each provisional PSPA of the individual that is associated with the past service event,

each such provisional PSPA shall be determined in accordance with the formula set out in subsection (5), except that

(c) in determining the amount A,

(i) the former benefits of the individual shall be considered to be attributable to employment of the individual with the individual's current employers, and

(ii) the portion of the former benefits attributable to employment with each current employer shall be determined by the administrator of the pension plan under which the past service benefits are provided in a manner that is consistent with the association of the past service benefits with each current employer,

(d) the amounts B and C shall be included in computing only one provisional PSPA of the individual, as determined by the administrator of the pension plan under which the past service benefits are provided, and

(e) the amount D that is deducted in computing the individual's provisional PSPA with respect to a particular employer shall equal such portion of the individual's qualifying transfers made in connection with the past service event as is not deducted in computing the provisional PSPA of the individual with respect to any other employer.

Related Provisions: Reg. 8303(6) — Meaning of qualifying transfers.

Notes: Reg. 8304(7)(b) amended by P.C. 1998-2256, effective for the determination of provisional PSPAs that are associated with past service events that occur after 1997, to change "but for the condition in paragraph (5)(c)" to "but for paragraph (5)(b)".

(8) [Repealed]

Notes: Reg. 8304(8), "Additional rules re calculation of PSPA", repealed by P.C. 1998-2256, for provisional PSPAs associated with past service events after 1997.

(9) Specified multi-employer plans — Except in subparagraph (4)(b)(i), a reference in this section to a defined benefit provision of a registered pension plan at any time does not, unless expressly provided, include a defined benefit provision of a plan that is, at that time, a specified multi-employer plan.

(10) Individual pension plans — If there is a past service event in relation to a defined benefit provision under an individual pension plan, the provisional PSPA of an individual with respect to an employer that is associated with the past service event is the amount, if any, determined by the formula

$$A - B$$

where

A is the greater of

(a) the provisional PSPA that would be determined if

(i) this subsection did not apply,

(ii) the value of C in subsection 8303(3) were nil, and

(iii) the value of D in subsection 8304(5) were nil, and

(b) the lesser of

(i) the total of

(A) the proportion of the fair market value of all property held in connection with the individual's designated savings arrangements at the time of the past service event, that

(I) the total of all amounts each of which is the duration (measured in years, including any fraction of a year) of a period that is pensionable service of the individual under the provision

is of

(II) the lesser of 35 and the number of years by which the individual's age in whole years at the time of the past service event exceeds 18, and

(B) the individual's unused RRSP deduction room at the end of the year immediately preceding the calendar year that includes the past service event, and

(ii) the actuarial liabilities of the retirement benefits associated with the past service event, determined on the basis of the funding assumptions specified under subsections 8515(6) and (7), at the same effective date as the actuarial valuation that forms the basis for the recommendation referred to in subsection 147.2(2) of the Act that is not earlier than the calendar year of the past service event; and

B is the amount of the individual's qualifying transfers made in connection with the past service event.

Related Provisions: ITA 257 — Negative amounts in formulas; Reg. 8304(11) — Restriction on subsec. (10) applying.

Notes: On interaction with provincial pension legislation see VIEWS doc 2012-0435731C6. On documenting qualifying transfers see 2015-0573331C6 [2015 CLHIA q.6].

Reg. 8304(10) added by 2011 budget bill #2, for past service events after March 22, 2011.

(11) Subsection (10) does not apply to a past service event in relation to an individual pension plan if the provisional PSPA of the member determined under subsections 8303(3) and 8304(5) would be nil if no qualifying transfers were made in connection with the past service event, unless it is a past service event that results from the establishment of the plan or from an amendment to the plan to provide additional retirement benefits.

Notes: Reg. 8304(11) added by 2011 budget bill #2, for past service events after March 22, 2011.

Definitions [Reg. 8304]: "amount" — ITA 248(1); "associated" — ITA 256; "benefits" — Reg. 8300(7); "calendar year" — *Interpretation Act* 37(1)(a); "certifiable past service event" — Reg. 8300(1); "contribution" — Reg. 8300(8), 8302(11), (12); "current employer" — Reg. 8304(5)(c), (7)(a); "current provision" — Reg. 8304(1)(b), (2)(b), (5)(a); "deferred profit sharing plan" — ITA 147(1), 248(1); "defined benefit provision" — ITA 147.1(1), Reg. 8300(3), 8304(9); "designated savings arrangement" — Reg. 8300(1); "employer", "employment" — ITA 248(1); "fair market value" — see ITA 69(1) Notes; "former benefits" — Reg. 8304(5)(d), (5.1)(e); "former provision" — Reg. 8304(1)(a), (2)(a), (5)(a)(ii), (5.1)(a)(ii); "individual" — ITA 248(1); "individual pension plan" — Reg. 8300(1); "lifetime retirement benefits" — Reg. 8300(3), 8500(1); "Minister" — ITA 248(1); "past service benefits" — Reg. 8304(3), (5.1)(a), (7)(a); "past service event" — Reg. 8300(1); "pension credit" — Reg. 8301, 8308.1(2)–(4), 8308.3(2), (3); "pensionable service" — Reg. 8300(3), 8500(1); "property" — ITA 248(1); "provision" — Reg. 8300(12)(c); "provisional PSPA" — Reg. 8303(2), (3), 8308(4)(e); "qualifying transfers" — Reg. 8303(6); "registered pension plan" — ITA 248(1); "registered retirement income fund" — ITA 146.3(1), 248(1); "registered retirement savings plan" — ITA 146(1), (21.2), 147.5(12), 248(1); "retirement benefits" — Reg. 8300(3), 8500(1); "specified multi-employer plan" — ITA 147.1(1), Reg. 8510(2), (3); "unused RRSP deduction room" — ITA 146(1), 248(1); "writing" — *Interpretation Act* 35(1).

Interpretation Bulletins [Reg. 8304]: IT-124R6: Contributions to registered retirement savings plans.

8304.1 Pension adjustment reversal — (1) Total pension adjustment reversal
— For the purpose of subsection 248(1) of the Act, an individual's "total pension adjustment reversal" for a calendar year means the total of all amounts each of which is the pension adjustment reversal (in this Part and Part LXXXIV referred to as "PAR") determined in connection with the individual's termination in the year from a deferred profit sharing plan or from a benefit provision of a registered pension plan.

Related Provisions: Reg. 8304.1(2) — Termination during 1997 deemed to be in 1998; Reg. 8311 — PAR rounded to nearest dollar.

Notes: See Notes at end of Reg. 8304.1.

Forms: RC4137: Pension adjustment reversal guide; T4104: Past service pension adjustment guide.

(2) Termination in 1997 — For the purpose of subsection (1) and the description of R in paragraph 8307(2)(b), where an individual terminates in 1997 from a deferred profit sharing plan or from a benefit provision of a registered pension plan, the termination is deemed to have occurred in 1998.

Related Provisions: Reg. 8311 — PAR rounded to nearest dollar.

(3) PAR — deferred profit sharing plan — For the purposes of this Part and Part LXXXIV and subject to subsection (12), an individual's PAR determined in connection with the individual's termination from a deferred profit sharing plan is

(a) if the conditions in subsection (13) are satisfied with respect to the termination, the total of all amounts each of which is an amount

(i) included in determining a pension credit of the individual under the plan, and

(ii) to which the individual has ceased, at or before the time of the termination, to have any rights,

but does not include any amount to which a spouse or common-law partner or former spouse or common-law partner of the individual has acquired rights as a consequence of a breakdown of their marriage or common-law partnership; and

(b) in any other case, nil.

Related Provisions: Reg. 8311 — PAR rounded to nearest dollar.

Notes: Reg. 8304.1(3)(a) amended by P.C. 2001-957, effective 2001 or earlier.

See Notes at end of Reg. 8304.1.

(4) PAR — money purchase provision — For the purposes of this Part and Part LXXXIV and subject to subsection (12), an individual's PAR determined in connection with the individual's termi-

nation from a money purchase provision of a registered pension plan is

(a) if the conditions in subsection (14) are satisfied with respect to the termination, the total of all amounts each of which is an amount

(i) included in determining a pension credit of the individual under the provision, and

(ii) to which the individual has ceased, at or before the time of the termination, to have any rights,

but does not include any amount to which a spouse or common-law partner or former spouse or common-law partner of the individual has acquired rights as a consequence of a breakdown of their marriage or common-law partnership; and

(b) in any other case, nil.

Related Provisions: Reg. 8500(8)(c) — Non-member benefits ignored in determining pension adjustment; Reg. 8311 — PAR rounded to nearest dollar.

Notes: Reg. 8304.1(4)(a) amended by P.C. 2001-957 to add references to common-law partner, generally effective 2001.

See Notes at end of Reg. 8304.1.

(5) PAR — defined benefit provision — For the purposes of this Part and Part LXXXIV and subject to subsections (6) and (12), an individual's PAR determined in connection with the individual's termination from a defined benefit provision of a registered pension plan is

(a) where the conditions in subsection (14) are satisfied with respect to the termination, the amount determined by the formula

$$A + B - C - D$$

where

A is the total of all amounts each of which is, in respect of a particular year that is the year in which the termination occurs or that is a preceding year, the lesser of

(i) the total of all amounts each of which is the pension credit of the individual under the provision for the particular year with respect to an employer, and

(ii) the RRSP dollar limit for the year following the particular year,

B is the total of all amounts each of which is the portion of the grossed-up amount of a provisional PSPA (other than a provisional PSPA determined in accordance with subsection 8303(8)) of the individual that is associated with a past service event occurring before the time of the termination that can reasonably be considered to be attributable to benefits provided under the provision,

C is the total of all amounts each of which is a specified distribution made in respect of the individual and the provision at or before the time of the termination, and

D is the total of all amounts each of which is a PA transfer amount in relation to the individual's termination from the provision; and

(b) in any other case, nil.

Related Provisions: ITA 257 — Negative amounts in formulas; Reg. 8300(11)(c) — Deemed specified distribution; Reg. 8304.1(6) — Defined benefit pension credits; Reg. 8304.1(7) — Meaning of grossed-up amount of provisional PSPA; Reg. 8304.1(8) — Meaning of specified distribution; Reg. 8304.1(10) — PA transfer amount; Reg. 8304.1(11) — Special 1997 PA transfer amount; Reg. 8304.1(14) — Terminations conditions; Reg. 8500(8)(c) — Non-member benefits ignored in determining pension adjustment.

Notes: See Notes at end of Reg. 8304.1.

(6) Defined benefit pension credits — For the purpose of subparagraph (i) of the description of A in paragraph (5)(a), in determining an individual's PAR in connection with the individual's termination from a defined benefit provision of a registered pension plan,

(a) the individual's pension credits under the provision for the year in which the termination occurs shall be determined without regard to benefits provided after the time of the termination; and

(b) the individual's pension credits under the provision for each year in which the plan was a specified multi-employer plan are deemed to be nil.

(7) Grossed-up PSPA amount — For the purposes of the descriptions of B in subsection 8303(7.1) and paragraph (5)(a), the grossed-up amount of an individual's provisional PSPA with respect to an employer that is associated with a past service event is the amount that would be the provisional PSPA if

(a) the values of C and D in subsections 8303(3) and 8304(5) were nil; and

(b) the words "at the time the past service event occurred" in paragraph (b) of the description of A in subsection 8304(5) were read as "immediately before the time the past service event occurred".

(8) Specified distribution — For the purpose of the description of C in paragraph (5)(a), an amount paid under a defined benefit provision of a registered pension plan with respect to an individual is a specified distribution made in respect of the individual and the provision at the time it is paid, except to the extent that

(a) it can reasonably be considered to be a payment of benefits in respect of any period before 1990;

(b) it is transferred to another registered pension plan (other than a plan that is, at the time of the transfer, a specified multi-employer plan) in accordance with subsection 147.3(3) of the Act;

(c) it is transferred to another defined benefit provision of the plan where the transfer would, if the provision and the other provision were in separate registered pension plans, constitute a transfer in accordance with subsection 147.3(3) of the Act;

(d) it is a payment in respect of an actuarial surplus;

(e) it is

(i) a return of contributions made by the individual under the provision, where the contributions are returned pursuant to an amendment to the plan that also reduces the future contributions that would otherwise be required to be made under the provision by members of the plan and that does not reduce benefits provided under the provision, or

(ii) a payment of interest in respect of contributions that are returned as described in subparagraph (i);

(f) it can reasonably be considered to be a payment of benefits provided in respect of a period throughout which the plan was a specified multi-employer plan; or

(g) it can reasonably be considered to be a payment of benefits provided in respect of a period throughout which the individual was employed outside Canada, where the benefits became provided as a consequence of a past service event in respect of which the Minister had consented to the application of subsection 8303(10) for the purpose of determining the individual's provisional PSPAs.

Related Provisions: Reg. 8304.1(9) — Property made available deemed to be paid; Reg. 8304.1(15) — Marriage breakdown — benefits acquired by spouse.

(9) Property made available — Where property held in connection with a particular defined benefit provision of a pension plan is made available at any time to provide benefits with respect to an individual under another benefit provision of a pension plan, subsection (8) applies as if the amount of the property had been paid under the particular provision at that time with respect to the individual.

(10) PA transfer amount — Where

(a) an individual has terminated, at a particular time after 1996, from a defined benefit provision (in this subsection referred to as the "former provision") of a registered pension plan,

(b) lifetime retirement benefits (in this subsection referred to as the "past service benefits") have, as a consequence of a past ser-

vice event occurring at or before the particular time, become provided to the individual under another defined benefit provision of a registered pension plan in respect of a period that is or was pensionable service of the individual under the former provision, and

(c) lifetime retirement benefits to which the individual is or was entitled under the former provision in respect of the period have, under subsection 8304(5), been taken into account as former benefits in determining a provisional PSPA of the individual that is associated with the past service event,

for the purposes of subsection 8406(5) and the description of D in paragraph (5)(a), the lesser of

(d) the portion of the value determined for A in subsection 8303(3), for the purpose of determining the provisional PSPA, that can reasonably be considered to be attributable to the past service benefits, and

(e) the portion of the value determined for B in subsection 8303(3), for the purpose of determining the provisional PSPA, that can reasonably be considered to be attributable to the former benefits

is a PA transfer amount in relation to the individual's termination from the former provision.

Related Provisions: Reg. 8300(7) — Benefits include contingent benefits; Reg. 8304.1(11) — Special 1997 PA transfer amount.

Notes: See Notes at end of Reg. 8304.1.

(11) Special 1997 PA transfer amount — Where

(a) an individual has terminated, at a particular time in 1997, from a particular defined benefit provision of a registered pension plan,

(b) lifetime retirement benefits (in this subsection referred to as the "past service benefits") have, as a consequence of a past service event that occurred after the particular time and before 1998, become provided to the individual under the particular provision, or under another defined benefit provision of a registered pension plan, in respect of a period that was previously pensionable service of the individual under the particular provision, and

(c) lifetime retirement benefits to which the individual was previously entitled under the particular provision in respect of the period have, under subsection 8304(5), been taken into account as former benefits in determining a provisional PSPA of the individual that is associated with the past service event,

for the purposes of subsection 8406(5) and the description of D in paragraph (5)(a), the lesser of

(d) the portion of the value determined for A in subsection 8303(3), for the purpose of determining the provisional PSPA, that can reasonably be considered to be attributable to the past service benefits, and

(e) the portion of the value determined for B in subsection 8303(3), for the purpose of determining the provisional PSPA, that can reasonably be considered to be attributable to the former benefits

is a PA transfer amount in relation to the individual's termination from the particular provision at the particular time.

Related Provisions: Reg. 8300(7) — Benefits include contingent benefits.

(12) Subsequent membership — Where an individual has ceased at a particular time to be a member in relation to a deferred profit sharing plan or a benefit provision of a registered pension plan and subsequently becomes a member in relation to the plan or the provision, as the case may be, the following rules apply in determining the individual's PAR in connection with any subsequent termination from the plan or the provision, as the case may be:

(a) in the case of a deferred profit sharing plan or money purchase provision, any amounts included in a pension credit of the individual under the plan or provision because of an allocation to the individual before the particular time shall be disregarded; and

(b) in the case of a defined benefit provision,

(i) the value of A in paragraph (5)(a) shall be determined without regard to any pension credit, or portion of a pension credit, that is attributable to benefits provided under the provision before the particular time,

(ii) the value of B in paragraph (5)(a) shall be determined without regard to any provisional PSPA that is associated with a past service event that occurred before the particular time, and

(iii) the value of C in paragraph (5)(a) shall be determined without regard to any specified distribution (as defined in subsection (8)) made at or before the particular time.

(13) Termination conditions — deferred profit sharing plan — For the purpose of paragraph (3)(a), the conditions with respect to an individual's termination from a deferred profit sharing plan are the following

(a) the termination occurs after 1996 and otherwise than because of death; and

(b) no payments described in subparagraph 147(2)(k)(v) of the Act have been made out of or under the plan with respect to the individual.

(14) Termination conditions — registered pension plan — For the purposes of paragraphs (4)(a) and (5)(a), the conditions with respect to an individual's termination from a benefit provision of a registered pension plan are the following:

(a) the termination occurs after 1996 and otherwise than because of death; and

(b) no retirement benefits have been paid under the provision with respect to the individual (other than retirement benefits paid with respect to the individual's spouse or common-law partner or former spouse or common-law partner as a consequence of a breakdown of their marriage or common-law partnership).

Related Provisions: Reg. 8300(11)(b) — Termination conditions deemed not satisfied.

Notes: Reg. 8304.1(14)(b) amended by P.C. 2001-957 to add references to common-law partner and common-law partnership, effective as per Notes to ITA 248(1)"common-law partner".

(15) Breakdown of marriage or common-law partnership — Where

(a) before a member terminates from a defined benefit provision of a registered pension plan, there has been a breakdown of the member's marriage or common-law partnership, and

(b) as a consequence of the breakdown,

(i) the member has ceased to have rights to all or a portion of the benefits provided under the provision with respect to the member, and

(ii) an individual who is the member's spouse or common-law partner or former spouse or common-law partner has acquired rights under the provision in respect of those benefits,

for the purpose of subsection (8),

(c) any amount paid under the provision with respect to the rights acquired by the individual (other than a single amount paid under the provision at or before the time of the member's termination in full satisfaction of the rights acquired by the individual) is deemed not to have been paid with respect to the member, and

(d) unless a single amount has been paid under the provision at or before the time of the member's termination in full satisfaction of the rights acquired by the individual, a single amount equal to the present value (at the time the member terminates from the provision) of the benefits to which the member has ceased to have rights as a consequence of the breakdown is

deemed to have been paid to the member at that time under the provision in full satisfaction of those benefits.

Notes: Reg. 8304.1(15) amended by P.C. 2001-957, effective 2001 or earlier.

Notes [Reg. 8304.1]: Reg. 8304.1 implements the pension adjustment reversal (PAR) calculation, for ITA 248(1)"total pension adjustment reversal" and 146(1)"RRSP deduction limit"R.

PAR was to be part of the new RRSP system introduced by the 1989 Budget, but was removed before enactment to make the rules simpler. It was reintroduced in 1997 to make the rules fairer. By reducing the PA, it allows more RRSP contribution room.

There is generally PAR when X ceases, before retirement, to be entitled to benefits under an RPP or DPSP (usually by terminating employment). PAR under a defined benefit RPP is generally the total of X's pension credits and PSPAs since 1990, minus any lump sum amounts paid out or transferred to an RRSP or other money purchase plan, in respect of X's post-1989 benefits under the RPP. PAR under a DPSP or money purchase RPP is the pension credits included under the plan or provision since 1990 but not vested in X.

See Guide RC4137, and Willis Towers Watson, *Canadian Pensions and Retirement Income Planning*, 6th ed. (LexisNexis, 2017), chap. 11.

For PAR reporting requirements, see Reg. 8402.01.

See also VIEWS docs 2004-0092601E5 (PAR is calculated when pension plan participation ends, not when employment ends; the RRSP room created may not be usable until the next year); 2006-0165431E5 (status Indian's PAR is not reduced by exempt income); 2008-0273681E5 (there is no similar rule for amounts withdrawn from an RRSP).

Reg. 8304.1 added by P.C. 1998-2256, effective 1997.

Definitions [Reg. 8304.1]: "amount" — Reg. 8304(16)(c), (d); "annuity" — ITA 248(1); "associated" — ITA 256; "benefit provision" — Reg. 8300(3), 8500(1); "calendar year" — *Interpretation Act* 37(1)(a); "Canada" — ITA 255, *Interpretation Act* 35(1); "common-law partnership" — ITA 248(1); "contribution" — Reg. 8300(8), 8302(11), (12); "deferred profit sharing plan" — ITA 147(1), 248(1); "defined benefit provision" — ITA 147.1(1), Reg. 8300(3); "employed", "employer" — ITA 248(1); "excess money purchase offset" — Reg. 8304.1(12); "former provision" — Reg. 8304.1(10)(a); "grossed-up amount" — Reg. 8304.1(7); "individual" — ITA 248(1); "lifetime retirement benefits" — Reg. 8300(3), 8500(1); "Minister" — ITA 248(1); "offset provision" — Reg. 8304.1(12)(b); "PA transfer amount" — Reg. 8304.1(10), (11); "PAR" — Reg. 8304.1(1), (3)–(6); "past service benefits" — Reg. 8304.1(10)(b), (11)(b); "past service event" — Reg. 8300(1); "pension adjustment" — Reg. 8308(5)(c), 8308(8); "pension credit" — Reg. 8301, 8308.1(2)–(4), 8308.3(2), (3); "pensionable service" — Reg. 8300(3), 8500(1); "property" — ITA 248(1); "provisional PSPA" — Reg. 8303(2), (3), 8308(4)(e); "registered pension plan" — ITA 248(1); "registered retirement income fund" — ITA 146.3(1), 248(1); "registered retirement savings plan" — ITA 146(1), (21.2), 147.5(12), 248(1); "retirement benefits" — Reg. 8300(3), 8500(1); "specified distribution" — Reg. 8304.1(8); "specified multi-employer plan" — ITA 147.1(1), Reg. 8510(2), (3); "spouse" — Reg. 8304.1(16)(b)(ii); "termination" — Reg. 8304.1(2), (15).

Forms [Reg. 8304.1]: RC4137: Pension adjustment reversal guide.

8305. Association of benefits with employers — **(1)** Where, for the purposes of this Part, it is necessary to determine the portion of an amount of benefits provided with respect to a member of a registered pension plan under a defined benefit provision of the plan that is attributable to the member's employment with a particular employer, the following rules apply, subject to subsection 8308(7):

(a) the determination shall be made by the plan administrator;

(b) benefits provided as a consequence of services rendered by the member to an employer who participates in the plan shall be regarded as attributable to employment with that employer, whether the benefits become provided at the time the services are rendered or at a subsequent time; and

(c) the determination shall be made in a manner that

(i) is reasonable in the circumstances,

(ii) is not inconsistent with such determinations made previously, and

(iii) results in the full amount of benefits being attributed to employment with one or more employers who participate in the plan.

(2) Where the administrator of a registered pension plan does not comply with the requirements of subsection (1) in connection with the determination of an amount under this Part at any time,

(a) the plan becomes, at that time, a revocable plan; and

Regulations

(b) the Minister shall make any determinations referred to in subsection (1) that the administrator fails to make, or fails to make in accordance with that subsection.

Related Provisions: ITA 147.1(8), (9), 147.3(12), Reg. 8301(14)(a), 8408(2), 8501(2), 8503(11), (15), 8506(4), 8511(2), 8515(9) — Other ways plan becomes revocable plan.

Definitions [Reg. 8305]: "amount" — ITA 248(1); "defined benefit provision" — ITA 147.1(1), Reg. 8300(3); "employer", "employment", "Minister", "registered pension plan" — ITA 248(1); "revocable plan" — ITA 147.1(8), (9), 147.3(12), Reg. 8301(14)(a), 8305(2), 8408(2), 8501(2), 8503(11), (15), 8506(4), 8511(2), 8515(9).

8306. Exemption from certification — **(1)** For the purposes of subsection 147.1(10) of the Act as it applies in respect of a past service event and the benefits provided under a defined benefit provision of a registered pension plan with respect to a particular member of the plan, a certification of the Minister is not required where

(a) each provisional PSPA of the member that is associated with the past service event is nil;

(b) the conditions in subsection (2) or (3) are satisfied;

(c) the conditions in subsection (2) or (3) are substantially satisfied and the Minister waives in writing the requirement for certification;

(c.1) paragraph 8303(5)(f.1) was applicable in determining the provisional PSPA of the member that is associated with the past service event; or

(d) the past service event is deemed by paragraph 8304(3)(b) to have occurred immediately after the end of 1990.

Notes: Reg. 8306(1)(c.1) added by P.C 2005-1508, for past service events after 2005 (after 2003 if the value of the fixed rate immediately before the past service event was at least $1,715).

(2) The following are conditions for the purposes of paragraphs (1)(b) and (c) and 8303(5)(g):

(a) there are more than 9 active members under the provision,

(b) no more than 25 per cent of the active members under the provision are specified active members under the provision;

(c) for all or substantially all of the active members under the provision, the amount of lifetime retirement benefits accrued under the provision has increased as a consequence of the past service event;

(d) where there is a specified active member under the provision;

(i) the amounts C and D in subparagraph (ii) are greater than nil, and

(ii) the amount determined by the formula A/C does not exceed the amount determined by the formula

$$B/D$$

where

A is the aggregate of all amounts each of which is the amount of lifetime retirement benefits accrued under the provision, immediately after the past service event, to a specified active member under the provision,

B is the aggregate of all amounts each of which is the amount of lifetime retirement benefits accrued under the provision, immediately after the past service event, to an active member (other than a specified active member) under the provision,

C is the aggregate of all amounts each of which is the amount of lifetime retirement benefits accrued under the provision, immediately before the past service event, to a specified active member under the provision, and

D is the aggregate of all amounts each of which is the amount of lifetime retirement benefits accrued under the provision, immediately before the past service event, to an active member (other than a specified active member) under the provision; and

(e) the benefits provided under the provision as a consequence of the past service event to members of the plan who are not active members under the provision are not more advantageous than such benefits provided to active members under the provision.

Related Provisions: Reg. 8306(4) — Meaning of active member and specified active member.

Notes: CRA considers that "substantially all", used in para. (c), means 90% or more.

(3) The following are conditions for the purposes of paragraphs (1)(b) and (c):

(a) the past service event consists of the establishment of the provision;

(b) there are more than 9 active members under the provision;

(c) no more than 25 per cent of the active members under the provision are specified active members under the provision;

(d) the member is not a specified active member under the provision;

(e) if the member is not an active member under the provision, for each of the 5 years immediately preceding the calendar year in which the past service event occurs,

(i) the member was not connected at any time in the year with an employer who participates in the plan, and

(ii) the aggregate of all amounts each of which is the remuneration of the member for the year from an employer who participates in the plan did not exceed $2\frac{1}{2}$ times the Year's Maximum Pensionable Earnings for the year; and

(f) the aggregate of all amounts each of which is a provisional PSPA of the member associated with the past service event does not exceed $\frac{7}{2}$ of the money purchase limit for the year in which the past service event occurs.

Related Provisions: Reg. 8306(4) — Meaning of active member and specified active member.

(4) For the purposes of this section as it applies in respect of a past service event,

(a) a member of a pension plan is an active member under a defined benefit provision of the plan if

(i) lifetime retirement benefits accrue under the provision to the member in respect of a period that immediately follows the time the past service event occurs, or

(ii) the member is entitled, immediately after the time the past service event occurs, to lifetime retirement benefits under the provision in respect of a period before that time and it is reasonable to expect, at that time, that lifetime retirement benefits will accrue under the provision to the member in respect of a period after that time; and

(b) an active member under a defined benefit provision of a pension plan is a specified active member under the provision if

(i) the member is connected, at the time of the past service event, with an employer who participates in the plan, or

(ii) it is reasonable to expect, at the time of the past service event, that the aggregate of all amounts each of which is the remuneration of the member for the calendar year in which the past service event occurs from an employer who participates in the plan will exceed $2\frac{1}{2}$ times the Year's Maximum Pensionable Earnings for the year.

Related Provisions: Reg. 8300(7) — Benefits include contingent benefits.

Definitions [Reg. 8306]: "active member" — Reg. 8306(4)(a); "amount" — ITA 248(1); "associated" — ITA 256; "benefits" — Reg. 8300(7); "calendar year" — *Interpretation Act* 37(1)(a); "defined benefit provision" — ITA 147.1(1), Reg. 8300(3); "employer" — ITA 248(1); "lifetime retirement benefits" — Reg. 8300(3), 8500(1); "Minister" — ITA 248(1); "money purchase limit" — ITA 147.1(1), 248(1); "past service event" — Reg. 8300(1); "provisional PSPA" — Reg. 8303(2), (3), 8308(4)(e); "registered pension plan" — ITA 248(1); "specified active member" — Reg. 8306(4)(b); "writing" — *Interpretation Act* 35(1); "Year's Maximum Pensionable Earnings" — Reg. 8300(3), 8500(1).

Forms: T215: Past service pension adjustments exempt from certification; T215 Segment; T215 Summ: Summary of past service pension adjustments exempt from certification.

8307. Certification in respect of past service events — (1) Application for certification — Application for a certification of the Minister for the purposes of subsection 147.1(10) of the Act shall be made in prescribed form by the administrator of the registered pension plan to which the certification relates.

Forms: T1004: Applying for the certification of a provisional PSPA.

(2) Prescribed condition — For the purposes of subsection 147.1(10) of the Act in respect of a past service event and benefits with respect to a particular member of a registered pension plan, the prescribed condition is that, at the particular time the Minister issues the certification,

(a) the aggregate of all amounts each of which is the member's provisional PSPA with respect to an employer associated with the past service event

does not exceed

(b) the amount determined by the formula

$$\$8,000 + A + B + C - D + R$$

where

A is the member's unused RRSP deduction room at the end of the year immediately preceding the calendar year (in this paragraph referred to as the "particular year") that includes the particular time,

B is the amount of the member's qualifying withdrawals made for the purposes of the certification, determined as of the particular time,

C is the amount of the member's PSPA withdrawals for the particular year, determined as of the particular time, and

D is the aggregate of all amounts each of which is the accumulated PSPA of the member for the particular year with respect to an employer, determined as of the particular time.

R is the total of all amounts each of which is a PAR determined in connection with the individual's termination in the particular year from a deferred profit sharing plan, or from a benefit provision of a registered pension plan, and in respect of which an information return has been filed under section 8402.01 with the Minister before the particular time.

Related Provisions: ITA 257 — Negative amounts in formulas; Reg. 8304.1(2) — Termination during 1997 deemed to be in 1998; Reg. 8307(3) — Meaning of qualifying withdrawals; Reg. 8307(5) — PSPA withdrawals.

Notes: Formula element R added by P.C. 1998-2256, for 1998 and later calendar years. See Notes at end of Reg. 8304.1.

(3) Qualifying withdrawals — For the purposes of paragraph (5)(a) and the description of B in paragraph (2)(b), the amount of an individual's qualifying withdrawals made for the purposes of a certification in respect of a past service event, determined as of a particular time, is the lesser of

(a) the aggregate of all amounts each of which is such portion of an amount withdrawn by the individual from a registered retirement savings plan under which the individual was the annuitant (within the meaning assigned by subsection 146(1) of the Act) at the time of the withdrawal as

(i) is eligible, pursuant to subsection (4), to be designated for the purposes of the certification, and

(ii) is designated by the individual for the purposes of the certification by filing a prescribed form containing prescribed information with the Minister before the particular time, and

(b) the amount, if any, by which

(i) the aggregate of all amounts each of which is the provisional PSPA of the individual with respect to an employer associated with the past service event

exceeds

(ii) the amount, positive or negative, determined by the formula

$$A + C - D + R$$

where A, C, D and R have the same values as they have at the particular time for the purposes of the formula in paragraph (2)(b).

Related Provisions: ITA 146(21.2) — Sask. Pension Plan account deemed to be RRSP for purposes of regulations; ITA 147.5(12) — Pooled registered pension plan deemed to be RRSP for purposes of regulations; ITA 257 — Negative amounts in formulas.

Notes: For CRA interpretation see VIEWS doc 2012-0469961E5.

Interpretation Bulletins: IT-124R6: Contributions to registered retirement savings plans.

Forms: T1006: Designating an RRSP, an PRPP or an SPP withdrawal as a qualifying withdrawal.

(4) Eligibility of withdrawn amount for designation — An amount withdrawn by an individual from a registered retirement savings plan is eligible to be designated for the purposes of a certification, except to the extent that the following rules provide otherwise:

(a) the amount is not eligible to be designated if the amount was

(i) withdrawn from a registered retirement savings plan in a calendar year other than the year in which the designation would be filed with the Minister or either of the 2 immediately preceding calendar years, or

(ii) withdrawn in circumstances that entitle the individual to a deduction under paragraph 60(l) of the Act; and

(b) the amount is not eligible to be designated to the extent that the amount was

(i) designated by the individual for the purposes of any other certification, or

(ii) deducted under section 60.2 or subsection 146(8.2) or 147.3(13.1) of the Act in computing the individual's income for any taxation year.

Related Provisions: ITA 146(21.2) — Sask. Pension Plan account deemed to be RRSP; ITA 147.5(12) — Pooled registered pension plan deemed to be RRSP.

Notes: Reg. 8307(4)(b)(ii) amended by P.C. 2001-153 to add reference to 147.3(13.1), for 1992 and later tax years.

(5) PSPA withdrawals — For the purposes of the description of C in paragraph (2)(b) and the description of G in the definition "net past service pension adjustment" in subsection 146(1) of the Act, the amount of an individual's PSPA withdrawals for a calendar year, determined as of a particular time, is

(a) if the Minister has issued, in the year and before the particular time, a certification for the purposes of subsection 147.1(10) of the Act with respect to the individual, the aggregate of all amounts each of which is the amount of the individual's qualifying withdrawals made for the purposes of a certification that the Minister has issued in the year and before the particular time; and

(b) in any other case, nil.

Related Provisions: Reg. 8307(3) — Meaning of qualifying withdrawals.

Notes: Opening words of Reg. 8307(5) amended by P.C. 1998-2256, effective 1996, to remove its application to ITA 204.2(1.3).

Interpretation Bulletins: IT-124R6: Contributions to registered retirement savings plans.

(6) Prescribed withdrawal — For the purposes of subsection (7) and subsections 146(8.2) and 147.3(13.1) of the Act, a prescribed withdrawal is the portion of an amount withdrawn by an individual from a registered retirement savings plan under which the individual is the annuitant (within the meaning assigned by subsection 146(1) of the Act) that is designated in accordance with subparagraph (3)(a)(ii) for the purposes of a certification in respect of the individual.

Related Provisions: ITA 146(21.2) — Saskatchewan Pension Plan account deemed to be RRSP for purposes of regulations; ITA 147.5(12) — Pooled registered pension plan deemed to be RRSP for purposes of regulations.

Notes: Reg. 8307(6) amended by P.C. 2001-153, effective for 1992 and later taxation years, to add reference to 147.3(13.1) and correct an incorrect reference to (3)(a)(ii).

Reg. 8307(6) is effective 1991. (See Notes at end of Reg. 8300–8311.)

Interpretation Bulletins: IT-124R6: Contributions to registered retirement savings plans; IT-528: Transfers of funds between registered plans.

(7) Prescribed premium — For the purpose of subsection 146(6.1) of the Act, a premium paid by a taxpayer under a registered retirement savings plan under which the taxpayer is the annuitant (within the meaning assigned by subsection 146(1) of the Act) at the time the premium is paid is a prescribed premium for a particular taxation year of the taxpayer where the following conditions are satisfied:

(a) the taxpayer withdrew an amount (in this subsection referred to as the "withdrawn amount") in the particular year from a registered retirement savings plan for the purposes of a certification in respect of a past service event;

(b) all or part of the withdrawn amount is a prescribed withdrawal pursuant to subsection (6);

(c) it is subsequently determined that

(i) as a consequence of reasonable error, the taxpayer withdrew a greater amount than necessary for the purposes of the certification, or

(ii) as a consequence of the application of paragraph 147.1(3)(b) of the Act, it was not necessary for the taxpayer to withdraw any amount;

(d) the premium is paid by the taxpayer in the 12-month period immediately following the time at which the determination referred to in paragraph (c) is made;

(e) the amount of the premium does not exceed such portion of the withdrawn amount as is a prescribed withdrawal pursuant to subsection (6) and is determined to have been an unnecessary withdrawal;

(f) the taxpayer files with the Minister, on or before the day on or before which the taxpayer is required (or would be required if tax under Part I of the Act were payable by the taxpayer for the taxation year in which the taxpayer pays the premium) by section 150 of the Act to file a return of income for the taxation year in which the taxpayer pays the premium, a written notice in which the taxpayer designates the premium as a recontribution of all or any portion of the withdrawn amount; and

(g) the taxpayer has not designated, pursuant to paragraph (f), any other premium as a recontribution of all or any portion of the withdrawn amount.

Related Provisions: ITA 146(21.2) — Saskatchewan Pension Plan account deemed to be RRSP for purposes of regulations; ITA 147.5(12) — Pooled registered pension plan deemed to be RRSP for purposes of regulations.

Definitions [Reg. 8307]: "accumulated PSPA" — Reg. 8303(1)(a), 8303(2); "amount" — ITA 248(1); "associated" — ITA 256; "benefit provision" — Reg. 8300(3), 8500(1); "calendar year" — *Interpretation Act* 37(1)(a); "employer", "individual", "Minister" — ITA 248(1); "PAR" — Reg. 8304.1(1), (3)–(6); "particular year" — Reg. 8307(2)(b)(A); "past service event" — Reg. 8300(1); "prescribed" — ITA 248(1); "prescribed withdrawal" — Reg. 8307(6); "provisional PSPA" — Reg. 8303(2), (3), 8308(4)(e); "PSPA withdrawal" — Reg. 8307(5); "qualifying withdrawal" — Reg. 8307(3); "registered pension plan" — ITA 248(1); "registered retirement savings plan" — ITA 146(1), (21.2), 147.5(12), 248(1); "taxation year" — ITA 249; "taxpayer" — ITA 248(1); "unused RRSP deduction room" — ITA 146(1), 248(1); "withdrawn amount" — Reg. 8307(7)(a); "written" — *Interpretation Act* 35(1)"writing".

Interpretation Bulletins: IT-124R6: Contributions to registered retirement savings plans.

8308. Special rules — (1) Benefits provided before registration — For the purposes of this Part and subsection 147.1(10) of the Act, benefits that became provided under a defined benefit provision of a pension plan before the day as of which the plan becomes a registered pension plan shall be deemed to have become provided as a consequence of an event occurring on that day and not to have been provided before that day.

(2) Prescribed amount for connected persons — Where

(a) at any particular time in a calendar year after 1990,

(i) an individual becomes a member of a registered pension plan, or

(ii) lifetime retirement benefits commence to accrue to the individual under a defined benefit provision of a registered pension plan following a period in which lifetime retirement benefits did not accrue to the individual,

(b) the individual is connected at the particular time, or was connected at any time after 1989, with an employer who participates in the plan for the benefit of the individual,

(c) the individual did not have a pension adjustment for 1990 that was greater than nil, and

(d) this subsection did not apply before the particular time to prescribe an amount with respect to the individual,

an amount equal to the lesser of $11,500 and 18% of the individual's earned income (as defined in subsection 146(1) of the Act) for 1990 is prescribed with respect to the individual for the calendar year that includes the particular time for the purposes of the descriptions of B in the definitions "RRSP deduction limit" and "unused RRSP deduction room" in subsection 146(1) of the Act and the description of B in paragraph 204.2(1.1)(b) of the Act.

Notes: Reg. 8308(2) amended by P.C. 2007-849, effective June 13, 2007.

Interpretation Bulletins: IT-124R6: Contributions to registered retirement savings plans.

(3) Remuneration for prior years — Where an individual who is entitled to benefits under a defined benefit provision of a registered pension plan receives remuneration at a particular time in a particular calendar year no part of which is pensionable service of the individual under the provision and the remuneration is treated for the purpose of determining benefits under the provision as if it were remuneration received in one or more calendar years preceding the particular calendar year for services rendered in those preceding years, the following rules apply:

(a) such portion of the remuneration as is treated under the provision as if it were remuneration received in a preceding calendar year for services rendered in that preceding year shall be deemed, for the purpose of determining, as of the particular time and any subsequent time, a redetermined benefit entitlement of the individual under the provision, to have been received in that preceding year for services rendered in that preceding year; and

(b) the pension credit of the individual for the particular year under the provision with respect to an employer is the aggregate of

(i) the amount that would otherwise be the individual's pension credit for the particular year, and

(ii) the amount that would, if the payment of the remuneration were a past service event, be the provisional PSPA (or a reasonable estimate thereof determined in a manner acceptable to the Minister) of the individual with respect to the employer that is associated with the payment of the remuneration.

Related Provisions: Reg. 8300(7)) — Benefits include contingent benefits.

(4) Period of reduced services — retroactive benefits — Where,

(a) as a consequence of a past service event, retirement benefits (in this subsection referred to as "retroactive benefits") become provided under a defined benefit provision of a registered pension plan (other than a plan that is a specified multi-employer plan) to an individual in respect of a period of reduced services of the individual,

(b) the period of reduced services was not, before the past service event, pensionable service of the individual under the provision, and

(c) the past service event occurs on or before April 30 of the year immediately following the calendar year in which ends the complete period of reduced services of the individual that includes the period of reduced services,

the following rules apply:

(d) each pension adjustment of the individual with respect to an employer for a year before the calendar year in which the past service event occurs shall be deemed to be, and to always have been, the aggregate of

(i) the amount that would otherwise be the individual's pension adjustment with respect to the employer for the year, and

(ii) such portion of the provisional PSPA of the individual with respect to the employer that is associated with the past service event as may reasonably be considered to be attributable to the provision of retroactive benefits in respect of the year, and

(e) each provisional PSPA of the individual with respect to an employer that is associated with the past service event shall be deemed (except for the purposes of this subsection) to be such portion of the amount that would otherwise be the individual's provisional PSPA as may reasonably be considered not to be attributable to the provision of retroactive benefits.

Related Provisions: Reg. 8308(4.1) — COVID-19 extension of time in 2020.

Interpretation Bulletins: IT-363R2: Deferred profit sharing plans — deductibility of employer contributions and taxation of amounts received by a beneficiary (archived).

Information Circulars: 98-2: Prescribed compensation for RPPs, paras. 23–25.

(4.1) COVID-19 — retroactive benefits — Paragraph (4)(c), in its application to a complete period of reduced services that ended in 2019, is to be read as follows:

(c) the past service event occurs on or before June 1, 2020 or such later date as is acceptable to the Minister,

Notes: See Notes to Reg. 6801.1. Reg. 8308(4.1) added by P.C. 2021-522, effective June 10, 2021.

(5) Period of reduced services — retroactive contributions — Where

(a) a contribution (in this subsection referred to as a "retroactive contribution") is made by an individual, or by an employer with respect to the individual, under a money purchase provision of a registered pension plan in respect of a period in a particular calendar year that is a period of reduced services of the individual, and

(b) the retroactive contribution is made after the particular year and on or before April 30 of the year immediately following the calendar year in which ends the complete period of reduced services of the individual that includes the period of reduced services,

the following rules apply:

(c) each pension adjustment of the individual for the particular year with respect to an employer shall be deemed to be, and to always have been, the amount that it would have been had the retroactive contribution been made at the end of the particular year, and

(d) the retroactive contribution shall be deemed, for the purpose of determining pension adjustments of the individual for any year after the particular year, to have been made at the end of the particular year and not to have been made at any subsequent time.

Related Provisions: Reg. 8308(5.1) — COVID-19 extension of time in 2020.

Interpretation Bulletins: IT-363R2: Deferred profit sharing plans — deductibility of employer contributions and taxation of amounts received by a beneficiary (archived).

Information Circulars: 98-2: Prescribed compensation for RPPs, paras. 23–25.

(5.1) COVID-19 — retroactive contributions — Paragraph (5)(b), in its application to a complete period of reduced services that ended in 2019, is to be read as follows:

(b) the retroactive contribution is made after 2019 and on or before June 1, 2020 or such later date as is acceptable to the Minister,

Related Provisions: Reg. 8308(5.2), (5.3) — Retroactive contributions for 2020.

Notes: See Notes to Reg. 6801.1. Reg. 8308(5.1) added by P.C. 2021-522, effective June 10, 2021.

(5.2) Conditions — retroactive contributions — Subsection (5.3) applies in respect of a contribution made with respect to an individual under a money purchase provision of a registered pension plan (in this subsection and in subsection (5.3) referred to as a **"retroactive contribution"**), if

(a) in the case of a contribution payable by an individual,

(i) the individual makes the retroactive contribution after 2020 and on or before April 30, 2022, or

(ii) the individual makes a written commitment, on or before April 30, 2022, to the plan administrator, or to a participating employer of the plan, to make the retroactive contribution;

(b) in the case of a contribution payable by a participating employer,

(i) the employer makes the retroactive contribution after 2020 and on or before April 30, 2022, or

(ii) it is conditional on the individual making the retroactive contribution that the individual has committed to pay under subparagraph (a)(ii); and

(c) the retroactive contribution replaces, in whole or in part, a contribution that would have been required to be made to the plan in the calendar year 2020 or 2021 but for an amendment made to the plan under sections 8511 and 8512 that reduced the contributions required to be made.

Notes: See Notes to Reg. 6801.1. Reg. 8308(5.2) added by P.C. 2021-522, effective June 10, 2021.

(5.3) COVID-19 — retroactive contributions — If this subsection applies in respect of a retroactive contribution,

(a) each pension adjustment of the individual for the 2020 or 2021 calendar year with respect to an employer is deemed to be, and to always have been, the amount that it would have been had the retroactive contribution been made at the end of 2020 or 2021, as the case may be; and

(b) the retroactive contribution is deemed, for the purpose of determining pension adjustments of the individual for any calendar year after the year referred to in paragraph (5.2)(c), to have been made at the end of that year and not to have been made at any subsequent time.

Related Provisions: Reg. 8308(5.2) — Conditions for (5.3) to apply.

Notes: See Notes to Reg. 6801.1. Reg. 8308(5.3) added by P.C. 2021-522, effective June 10, 2021.

(6) Commitment to make retroactive contributions — Where

(a) an individual enters into a written commitment to make a contribution under a money purchase provision of a registered pension plan,

(b) the commitment is made to the administrator of the plan or to an employer who participates in the plan, and

(c) the rules in subsection (5) would apply in respect of the contribution if the contribution were made at the time at which the individual enters into the commitment,

the following rules apply for the purposes of this Part:

(d) the individual shall be deemed to have made the contribution to the plan at the time at which the individual enters into the commitment,

(e) if the individual subsequently pays all or a part of the contribution to the plan pursuant to the commitment, the amount paid

Regulations

to the plan is, for the purposes of paragraphs 8301(4)(a) and (8)(e), a contribution described in this paragraph,

(f) any contribution that an employer is required to make under the money purchase provision conditional on the individual making the contribution that the individual has committed to pay and in respect of which subsection (5) would apply if the contribution were made by the employer at the time the individual enters into the commitment shall be deemed to have been made by the employer at that time, and

(g) if an employer subsequently pays to the plan all or a part of a contribution in respect of which paragraph (f) applies, the amount paid to the plan is, for the purposes of paragraph 8301(4)(a), a contribution described in this paragraph.

Notes: Reg. 8308(6)(e) and (g) amended by P.C. 1995-17, for amounts paid to RPPs after 1989, to refer to Reg. 8301(4)(a) and (8)(e) and thus modify the way in which contributions made under a commitment are excluded in determining pension credits for the year of contribution.

Information Circulars: 98-2: Prescribed compensation for RPPs, paras. 23–25.

(7) Loaned employees — Where, pursuant to an arrangement between an employer (in this subsection referred to as the "lending employer") who is a participating employer in relation to a pension plan and an employer (in this subsection referred to as the "borrowing employer") who, but for this subsection, would not be a participating employer in relation to the plan,

(a) an employee of the lending employer renders services to the borrowing employer for which the employee receives remuneration from the borrowing employer, and

(b) while the employee renders services to the borrowing employer, benefits continue to accrue under a defined benefit provision of the plan to the employee, or the lending employer continues to make contributions under a money purchase provision of the plan with respect to the employee,

the following rules apply:

(c) for the purpose of the definition "participating employer" in subsection 147.1(1) of the Act as it applies in respect of the plan, the borrowing employer is a prescribed employer,

(d) the determination, for the purposes of this Part, of the portion of the employee's benefit accrual under a defined benefit provision of the plan in respect of a year that can reasonably be considered to be attributable to the employee's employment with each of the lending and borrowing employers shall be made with regard to the remuneration received by the employee for the year from each employer, and

(e) such portion of the contributions made under a money purchase provision of the plan by the lending employer as may reasonably be considered to be in respect of the employee's remuneration from the borrowing employer shall be deemed, for the purposes of this Part, to be contributions made by the borrowing employer.

Related Provisions: Reg. 8507(5)E(a) — Additional compensation fraction.

Registered Pension Plans Technical Manual: §6.4 (loaned employees).

(8) Successor plans — Notwithstanding any other provisions of this Part, other than section 8310, where

(a) all benefits with respect to an individual under a defined benefit provision (in this subsection referred to as the "former provision") of a registered pension plan are replaced in a calendar year by identical benefits under a defined benefit provision of another registered pension plan,

(b) the replacement of benefits is consequent on a transfer of the individual's employment from one employer (in this subsection referred to as the "former employer") to another employer (in this subsection referred to as the "successor employer"), and

(c) the Minister consents in writing to the application of this subsection in respect of that replacement of benefits,

the individual's pension adjustments for the year with respect to the former employer and the successor employer shall be the amounts that they would be if all benefits with respect to the individual

under the former provision had been attributable to employment with the successor employer and not to employment with the former employer.

(9) Special downsizing benefits — Where

(a) lifetime retirement benefits that do not comply with the condition in paragraph 8503(3)(a) are provided to an individual under a defined benefit provision of a registered pension plan, and

(b) the benefits are permissible only by reason of subsection 8505(3),

each pension credit of the individual under the provision and each provisional PSPA of the individual shall be determined without regard to the lifetime retirement benefits.

Definitions [Reg. 8308]: "amount" — ITA 248(1); "associated" — ITA 256; "benefits" — Reg. 8300(7); "borrowing employer" — Reg. 8308(7); "calendar year" — *Interpretation Act* 37(1)(a); "complete period of reduced services" — Reg. 8300(1); "contribution" — Reg. 8300(8), 8302(11), (12); "defined benefit provision" — ITA 147.1(1), Reg. 8300(3); "employee", "employer", "employment" — ITA 248(1); "former employer" — Reg. 8308(8)(b); "former provision" — Reg. 8308(8)(a); "individual" — ITA 248(1); "lending employer" — Reg. 8308(7); "lifetime retirement benefits" — Reg. 8300(3), 8500(1); "Minister" — ITA 248(1); "participating employer" — ITA 147.1(1); "past service event" — Reg. 8300(1); "pension adjustment" — Reg. 8308(5)(c), 8308(8); "pension credit" — Reg. 8301, 8308.1(2)–(4), 8308.3(2), (3); "pensionable service" — Reg. 8300(3), 8500(1); "period of reduced services" — Reg. 8300(1); "prescribed" — ITA 248(1); "provisional PSPA" — Reg. 8303(2), (3), 8308(4)(e); "registered pension plan" — ITA 248(1); "retirement benefits" — Reg. 8300(3), 8500(1); "retroactive benefits" — Reg. 8308(4)(a); "retroactive contribution" — Reg. 8308(5)(a); "specified multi-employer plan" — ITA 147.1(1), Reg. 8510(2), (3); "successor employer" — Reg. 8308(8)(b); "written" — *Interpretation Act* 35(1)"writing".

Interpretation Bulletins: IT-528: Transfers of funds between registered plans.

8308.1 Foreign plans — (1) Definitions — In this section, **"foreign plan"** means a plan or arrangement (determined without regard to subsection 207.6(5) of the Act) that would, but for paragraph (l) of the definition "retirement compensation arrangement" in subsection 248(1) of the Act, be a retirement compensation arrangement.

(2) Pension credit — Subject to subsections (3) to (4.1), the pension credit of an individual for a calendar year with respect to an employer under a foreign plan is

(a) where paragraph (b) does not apply, nil; and

(b) where

(i) the year is 1992 or a subsequent year,

(ii) the individual became entitled in the year, either absolutely or contingently, to benefits under the foreign plan in respect of services rendered to the employer in a period throughout which the individual was resident in Canada and rendered services to the employer that were primarily services rendered in Canada or services rendered in connection with a business carried on by the employer in Canada, or a combination of those services,

(iii) the individual continued to be entitled at the end of the year, either absolutely or contingently, to all or part of the benefits, and

(iv) either

(A) no contribution was made under the foreign plan in the year in respect of the individual, except where

(I) no contribution was made because the foreign plan had an actuarial surplus, and

(II) had a contribution been made in respect of the benefits referred to in subparagraph (ii), it would have been a resident's contribution (as defined in subsection 207.6(5.1) of the Act), or

(B) a contribution that is not a resident's contribution was made under the foreign plan in the year in respect of the individual, the lesser of

(v) the amount, if any, by which 18% of the individual's resident compensation from the employer for the year exceeds the PA offset for the year, and

(vi) the amount by which the money purchase limit for the year exceeds the PA offset for the year.

Notes: The calculations in Reg. 8308.1 and 8308.2 are mutually exclusive, and cannot be prorated by an employee who participates in a US pension plan, so only 8308.1 applies: VIEWS doc 2010-0388731E5.

Reg. 8308.1(2) amended by P.C. 1998-2256, retroactive to its introduction in 1992, to make the opening words subject to subsec. (4.1) and to change everything after subpara. (iv) to use "the PA offset" (now defined in Reg. 8300(1)) instead of $1,000.

(2.1) Pension credit — tax treaty — For the purposes of applying subsection (2) in determining an individual's pension credit for a calendar year with respect to an employer under a foreign plan, if any contributions made to, or benefits accruing under, the plan in respect of the individual and the calendar year benefit from the application of paragraph 8 of Article XVIII of the *Canada-United States Tax Convention* signed at Washington on September 26, 1980, or from the application of a similar provision in another tax treaty,

(a) subparagraph (2)(b)(ii) shall be read without reference to the words "was resident in Canada and"; and

(b) the portion of subsection (2) after subparagraph (2)(b)(iv) shall be read as "the lesser of the money purchase limit for the year and 18% of the individual's resident compensation from the employer for the year".

Notes: Canada-U.S. Tax Treaty:Art. XVIII:8 extends benefits to, for example, individuals who continue coverage under their US pension plan while on short-term assignment in Canada. To ensure appropriate recognition of such pension contributions, the tax relief under Art. XVIII:8 generally applies only if the individual's employment in Canada does not give rise to tax-deferred retirement savings opportunities under the Canadian system. Reg. 8308.1(2.1) therefore imposes special rules to ensure that an individual who deducts foreign pension plan contributions because of Art. XVIII:8, or a similar provision in another treaty, does not accrue RRSP room in respect of that same employment. (Finance Technical Notes)

Reg. 8308.1(2.1) added by 2008 budget bill #2, effective on determining pension credits for 2009 and later tax years.

(3) Pension credit — alternative determination — Subject to subsection (4), where the Minister has, on the written application of an employer, approved in writing a method for determining pension credits for a year with respect to the employer under a foreign plan, the pension credits shall be determined in accordance with that method.

(4) Pension credits for 1992, 1993 and 1994 — The pension credit of an individual for 1992, 1993 or 1994 with respect to an employer under a foreign plan is the lesser of

(a) the amount that would, but for this subsection, be determined as the pension credit for the year, and

(b) the amount, if any, by which the lesser of

(i) 18% of the amount that would be the individual's compensation from the employer for the year if the definition "compensation" in subsection 147.1(1) of the Act were read without reference to paragraphs (b) and (c) of that definition, and

(ii) the money purchase limit for the year

exceeds the total of

(iii) $1,000, and

(iv) the amount that would be the pension adjustment of the individual for the year with respect to the employer if subsection 8301(1) were read without reference to paragraph (b) of that subsection.

Notes: The money purchase limit for 2002 is deemed to be $14,500 for Reg. 8308.1. See Notes to ITA 147.1(1)"money purchase limit".

(4.1) Pension credits — 1996 to 2002 — For the purpose of determining the pension credit of an individual for a calendar year

after 1995 and before 2003 with respect to an employer under a foreign plan, subparagraph (2)(b)(vi) shall be read as

"(vi) the money purchase limit for the year.".

Notes: Reg. 8308.1(4.1) amended by P.C. 2005-1508, effective 2003, to change "2004" to "2003". For 2002, see Notes to ITA 147.1(1)"money purchase limit". Reg. 8308.1(4.1) added by P.C. 1998-2256, retroactive to 1992.

(5) Foreign plan PSPA — Subject to subsection (6), where the benefits to which an individual is entitled, either absolutely or contingently, under a foreign plan are modified, the foreign plan PSPA of the individual with respect to an employer associated with the modification of benefits is the amount, if any, by which

(a) the total of all amounts each of which is the amount that, if this section were read without reference to subsection (3), would be the pension credit of the individual with respect to the employer under the foreign plan for a calendar year before the year in which the individual's benefits are modified

exceeds the total of all amounts each of which is

(b) the pension credit of the individual with respect to the employer under the foreign plan for a calendar year before the year in which the individual's benefits are modified, or

(c) the foreign plan PSPA of the individual with respect to the employer associated with a previous modification of the individual's benefits under the foreign plan.

(6) Foreign plan PSPA — alternative determination — Where the Minister has, on the written application of an employer, approved in writing a method for determining the foreign plan PSPA of an individual with respect to the employer associated with a modification of the individual's benefits under a foreign plan, the individual's foreign plan PSPA shall be determined in accordance with that method.

Notes: Reg. 8308.1 added by P.C. 1996-911, effective 1992.

Definitions [Reg. 8308.1]: "amount" — ITA 248(1); "associated" — ITA 256; "business" — ITA 248(1); "calendar year" — *Interpretation Act* 37(1)(a); "Canada" — ITA 255, *Interpretation Act* 35(1); "contribution" — Reg. 8300(8), 8302(11), (12); "employer" — ITA 248(1); "foreign plan" — Reg. 8308.1(1); "individual", "Minister" — ITA 248(1); "money purchase limit" — ITA 147.1(1), 248(1); "PA offset" — Reg. 8300(1); "pension adjustment" — Reg. 8308(5)(c), 8308(8); "pension credit" — Reg. 8301, 8308.1(2)–(4), 8308.3(2), (3); "resident compensation" — Reg. 8300(1); "resident in Canada" — ITA 250; "retirement compensation arrangement", "tax treaty" — ITA 248(1); "written" — *Interpretation Act* 35(1)"writing".

8308.2 (1) For the purposes of the descriptions of B in the definitions "RRSP deduction limit" and "unused RRSP deduction room" in subsection 146(1) of the Act and the description of B in paragraph 204.2(1.1)(b) of the Act, there is prescribed in respect of an individual for a calendar year the lesser of the money purchase limit for the preceding calendar year (in this section referred to as the "service year") and the amount determined by subsection (2), if the individual

(a) rendered services to an employer (excluding services that were primarily services rendered in Canada or services rendered in connection with a business carried on by the employer in Canada, or a combination of those services) throughout a period in the service year in which the individual was resident in Canada;

(b) became entitled, either absolutely or contingently, in the service year to benefits under a foreign plan (as defined in subsection 8308.1(1)) in respect of the services; and

(c) continued to be entitled at the end of the service year, either absolutely or contingently, to all or part of the benefits.

Notes: See Notes to Reg. 8308.1(2) re overlap of 8308.1 and 8308.2.

Reg. 8308.2(1) added by P.C. 1998-2256, retroactive to 1992.

(2) The amount determined for the purpose of subsection (1) is,

(a) if the only benefits to which the individual became entitled in the service year under the foreign plan were provided under one or more money purchase provisions of the foreign plan, the total of all amounts each of which is the individual's pension credit for the service year with respect to the employer under a money purchase provision of the foreign plan, determined

(i) as though the foreign plan were a registered pension plan,

(ii) without regard to any contributions made by the individual, and

(iii) if, under the laws of the country in which the foreign plan is established, any contributions made after the end of the service year are treated as having been made in the service year, as though those contributions were made in the service year and not when the contributions were actually made; and

(b) in any other case, the greater of

(i) the total that would be determined under paragraph (a) if the individual had not become entitled in the service year to any benefits under a defined benefit provision of the foreign plan, and

(ii) 10% of the portion of the individual's resident compensation from the employer for the service year that is attributable to services rendered to the employer and included under paragraph (1)(a).

Notes: Reg. 8308.2 amended by 2008 budget bill #2, for 2009 and later calendar years except that in determining prescribed amounts for 2009, the money purchase limit for 2008 is reduced by $600.

Reg. 8308.2(2) amended by P.C. 2005-1508, effective 2003, to change "2005" to "2004". Reg. 8308.2(2) added by P.C. 1998-2256, retroactive to 1992.

Definitions [Reg. 8308.2]: "amount", "business" — ITA 248(1); "calendar year" — *Interpretation Act* 37(1)(a); "Canada" — ITA 255, *Interpretation Act* 35(1); "contribution" — Reg. 8300(8), 8302(11), (12); "defined benefit provision" — ITA 147.1(1), Reg. 8300(3); "employer" — ITA 248(1); "foreign plan" — Reg. 8308.1(1); "individual" — ITA 248(1); "money purchase limit" — ITA 147.1(1), 248(1); "pension credit" — Reg. 8301, 8308.1(2)–(4), 8308.3(2), (3); "prescribed", "registered pension plan" — ITA 248(1); "resident compensation" — Reg. 8300(1); "resident in Canada" — ITA 250; "service year" — Reg. 8308.2(1).

8308.3 Specified retirement arrangements — (1) Definition

— In this section, "specified retirement arrangement" means, in respect of an individual and an employer, a plan or arrangement under which payments that are attributable to the individual's employment with the employer are to be, or may be, made to or for the benefit of the individual after the termination of the individual's employment with the employer, but does not include

(a) a plan or arrangement referred to in any of paragraphs (a) to (k), (m) and (n) of the definition "retirement compensation arrangement" in subsection 248(1) of the Act;

(b) [Repealed]

(c) a plan or arrangement that does not provide in any circumstances for payments to be made to or for the benefit of the individual after the later of the last day of the calendar year in which the individual attains 71 years of age and the day that is 5 years after the day of termination of the individual's employment with the employer;

(d) a plan or arrangement (in this paragraph referred to as the "arrangement") that is, or would be, but for paragraph (l) of the definition "retirement compensation arrangement" in subsection 248(1) of the Act, a retirement compensation arrangement where

(i) the funding of the arrangement is subject to the *Pension Benefits Standards Act, 1985* or a similar law of a province, or

(ii) the arrangement is funded substantially in accordance with the funding requirements that would apply if the arrangement were subject to the *Pension Benefits Standards Act, 1985*;

(e) a plan or arrangement that is deemed by subsection 207.6(6) of the Act to be a retirement compensation arrangement; or

(f) an arrangement established by the *Judges Act* or the *Lieutenant Governors Superannuation Act*.

Notes: Reg. 8308.3(1)(c) amended by 2007 budget bill #1 to change "69" to "71" effective 2007 (in conjunction with increase in the RRSP age limit to 71: see ITA 146(2)(b.4)).

Reg. 8308.3(1)(c) amended by P.C. 1998-2256, effective 1998, to change "the day on which the individual attains 71 years" to "the last day . . . 69 years"; but new para. (c) does not apply in respect of an individual who turned 69 before 1998.

Reg. 8308.3(1) amended by P.C. 1998-2256, retroactive to 1992.

(2) Pension credit — Subject to subsections (3) and (3.1), the pension credit of an individual for a calendar year with respect to an employer under a specified retirement arrangement is

(a) where paragraph (b) does not apply, nil; and

(b) where

(i) the year is 1993 or a subsequent year,

(ii) the employer is, at any time in the year,

(A) a person who is exempt, because of section 149 of the Act, from tax under Part I of the Act on all or part of the person's taxable income, or

(B) the Government of Canada or the government of a province,

(iii) the individual became entitled in the year, either absolutely or contingently, to benefits under the arrangement in respect of employment with the employer,

(iv) at the end of the year, the individual is entitled, either absolutely or contingently, to benefits under the arrangement, and

(v) the amount determined by the formula

$$0.85A - B$$

is greater than nil where

A is the lesser of

(A) the amount, if any, by which 18% of the individual's resident compensation from the employer for the year exceeds the PA offset for the year, and

(B) the amount by which the money purchase limit for the year exceeds the PA offset for the year, and

B is the amount that would be the pension adjustment of the individual for the year with respect to the employer if subsection 8301(1) were read without reference to paragraph (c) of that subsection,

the amount that would be determined by the formula in subparagraph (v) if the reference to "0.85" in the formula were replaced by a reference to "1".

Related Provisions: ITA 257 — Negative amounts in formulas.

Notes: The money purchase limit for 2002 was $14,500 for purposes of Reg. 8308.3. See Notes to ITA 147.1(1)"money purchase limit".

Reg. 8308.3(2) amended by P.C. 1998-2256, retroactive to 1992.

(3) Pension credit — alternative determination — Where the Minister has, on the written application of an employer, approved in writing a method for determining pension credits for a year with respect to the employer under a specified retirement arrangement, the pension credits shall be determined in accordance with that method.

(3.1) Pension credits — 1996 to 2002 — For the purpose of determining the pension credit of an individual for a calendar year after 1995 and before 2003 with respect to an employer under a specified retirement arrangement, the portion of paragraph (2)(b) after subparagraph (iv) shall be read as

"(v) the amount determined by the formula

$$0.85A - B$$

is greater than nil where

A is the lesser of

(A) the amount, if any, by which 18% of the individual's resident compensation from the employer for the year exceeds the PA offset for the year, and

(B) the amount by which $15,500 exceeds the PA offset for the year, and

B is the amount that would be the pension adjustment of the individual for the year with respect to the employer if subsection 8301(1) were read without reference to paragraph (c),

the amount that would be determined by the formula in subparagraph (v) if

(vi) the reference to "0.85A" in that formula were read as a reference to "A", and

(vii) clause (B) of the description of A in that subparagraph were read as

"(B) the money purchase limit for the year, and".".

Related Provisions: ITA 257 — Negative amounts in formulas.

Notes: Reg. 8308.3(3.1) amended by P.C. 2005-1508, effective 2003. Added by P.C. 1998-2256, effective 1992.

(4) Specified retirement arrangement PSPA — Subject to subsection (5), where the benefits to which an individual is entitled, either absolutely or contingently, under a specified retirement arrangement are modified, the specified retirement arrangement PSPA of the individual with respect to an employer associated with the modification of benefits is the amount, if any, by which

(a) the total of all amounts each of which is the amount that, if this section were read without reference to subsection (3), would be the pension credit of the individual with respect to the employer under the arrangement for a calendar year before the year in which the individual's benefits are modified

exceeds the total of all amounts each of which is

(b) the pension credit of the individual with respect to the employer under the arrangement for a calendar year before the year in which the individual's benefits are modified, or

(c) the specified retirement arrangement PSPA of the individual with respect to the employer associated with a previous modification of the individual's benefits under the arrangement.

(5) Specified retirement arrangement PSPA — alternative determination — Where the Minister has, on the written application of an employer, approved in writing a method for determining the specified retirement arrangement PSPA of an individual with respect to the employer associated with a modification of the individual's benefits under a specified retirement arrangement, the individual's specified retirement arrangement PSPA shall be determined in accordance with that method.

Notes: Reg. 8308.3 added by P.C. 1996-911, this version effective 1996.

Definitions [Reg. 8308.3]: "amount" — ITA 248(1); "arrangement" — Reg. 8308.3(1)(d); "associated" — ITA 256; "calendar year" — *Interpretation Act* 37(1)(a); "Canada" — ITA 255, *Interpretation Act* 35(1); "employer", "employment" — ITA 248(1); "Governor" — *Interpretation Act* 35(1); "individual", "Minister" — ITA 248(1); "money purchase limit" — ITA 147.1(1), 248(1); "PA offset" — Reg. 8300(1); "pension adjustment" — Reg. 8308(5)(c), 8308(8); "pension credit" — Reg. 8301, 8308.1(2)–(4), 8308.3(2), (3); "person" — *Interpretation Act* 35(1); "province" — *Interpretation Act* 35(1); "resident compensation" — Reg. 8300(1); "retirement compensation arrangement", "taxable income" — ITA 248(1); "written" — *Interpretation Act* 35(1) "writing".

8308.4 Government-sponsored retirement arrangements — **(1) Definitions** — The definitions in this subsection apply in this section.

"administrator" means, in respect of a government-sponsored retirement arrangement, the government or other entity that has ultimate responsibility for the administration of the arrangement.

"government-sponsored retirement arrangement" means a plan or arrangement established to provide pensions directly or indirectly from the public money of Canada or a province to one or more individuals each of whom renders services in respect of which amounts that are included in computing the income from a business of any person or partnership are paid directly or indirectly from the public money of Canada or a province.

Notes: For the meaning of "indirectly", see Notes to ITA 17.1(1).

Notes: See at end of Reg. 8308.4.

(2) Prescribed amount — Where

(a) in a particular calendar year after 1992 an individual renders services in respect of which an amount that is included in computing the income from a business of any person was payable directly or indirectly by the Government of Canada or of a province, and

(b) at the end of the particular year, the individual is entitled, either absolutely or contingently, to benefits under a government-sponsored retirement arrangement that provides benefits in connection with such services,

there is prescribed in respect of the individual for the year following the particular year, for the purposes of the descriptions of B in the definitions "RRSP deduction limit" and "unused RRSP deduction room" in subsection 146(1) of the Act and the description of B in paragraph 204.2(1.1)(b) of the Act,

(c) where the particular year is before 1996, the amount by which the RRSP dollar limit for that following year exceeds $1,000, and

(d) in any other case, the RRSP dollar limit for that following year.

Notes: For meaning of "indirectly" in para. (a), see Notes to ITA 17.1(1).

Notes: Reg. 8308.4 added by P.C. 1996-911, effective 1993; and subsec. (2) amended retroactive to its introduction by P.C. 1998-2256. The substance of the amendment is that for years after 1996, the prescribed amount is determined without subtracting $1,000 from the RRSP dollar limit; thus, individuals participating in government-sponsored retirement arrangements will have no RRSP deduction room.

Definitions [Reg. 8308.4]: "administrator" — Reg. 8308.4(1); "amount", "business" — ITA 248(1); "calendar year" — *Interpretation Act* 37(1)(a); "Canada" — ITA 255, *Interpretation Act* 35(1); "government-sponsored retirement arrangement" — Reg. 8308.4(1); "individual" — ITA 248(1); "partnership" — see ITA 96(1) Notes; "person", "prescribed" — ITA 248(1); "province" — *Interpretation Act* 35(1); "RRSP dollar limit" — ITA 146(1), 248(1).

Registered Plans Directorate Newsletters: 91-4R (registration rules for money purchase provisions).

8309. Prescribed amount for lieutenant governors and judges — **(1)** Subject to subsection (3), where an individual is, at any time in a particular calendar year after 1989, a lieutenant governor of a province (other than a lieutenant governor who is not a contributor as defined in section 2 of the *Lieutenant Governors Superannuation Act*), there is prescribed in respect of the individual for the year following the particular year, for the purposes of the descriptions of B in the definitions "RRSP deduction limit" and "unused RRSP deduction room" in subsection 146(1) of the Act and the description of B in paragraph 204.2(1.1)(b) of the Act, the lesser of

(a) the amount, if any, by which 18% of the salary received by the individual for the particular year as a lieutenant governor exceeds the PA offset for the particular year, and

(b) the amount by which the money purchase limit for the particular year exceeds the PA offset for the particular year.

Notes: The money purchase limit for 2002 is deemed to be $14,500 for purposes of Reg. 8309. See Notes to ITA 147.1(1) "money purchase limit".

Reg. 8309(1) amended by P.C. 1998-2256, retroactive to 1990.

(2) Subject to subsection (3), where an individual is, at any time in a particular calendar year after 1990, a judge in receipt of a salary under the *Judges Act*, there is prescribed in respect of the individual for the year following the particular year, for the purposes of the descriptions of B in the definitions "RRSP deduction limit" and "unused RRSP deduction room" in subsection 146(1) of the Act and the description of B in paragraph 204.2(1.1)(b) of the Act, the lesser of

(a) the amount, if any, by which 18% of the portion of the salary received by the individual for the particular year under the *Judges Act* in respect of which contributions are required under subsection 50(1) or (2) of that Act exceeds the PA offset for the particular year; and

(b) the amount determined by the formula

$$A \times \frac{B}{12}$$

where

A is the amount by which the money purchase limit for the particular year exceeds the PA offset for the particular year, and

B is the number of months, in the particular year, for which the individual received salary in respect of which contributions were required under subsection 50(1) or (2) of the *Judges Act*.

Notes: For explanation of Reg. 8309(2) see VIEWS doc 2004-0078271E5.

The money purchase limit for 2002 is deemed to be $14,500 for purposes of Reg. 8309. See Notes to ITA 147.1(1)"money purchase limit".

Reg. 8309(2)(a) and (b) amended by P.C. 2001-1634, effective for determining prescribed amounts for 2001 and later taxation years. The amendment responds to the May 31, 2000 report of the Judicial Compensation and Benefits Commission. The SCC had held in *Reference re Remuneration of Judges*, [1998] 1 S.C.R. 3, that every Canadian jurisdiction must have an independent commission to make recommendations on judges' compensation. The amendment allows judges to contribute to an RRSP starting in the year following the year in which their contributions to the judicial annuity scheme are reduced from 7% of salary to 1% under subsec. 50(2.1) of the *Judges Act*.

Reg. 8309(2) amended by P.C. 1998-2256, retroactive to 1990, to use "the PA offset" (see Reg. 8300(1)) in place of $1,000.

(3) For the purpose of determining the amount prescribed under subsection (1) or (2) in respect of an individual for a calendar year after 2000 and before 2004,

(a) paragraph (1)(b) shall be read as follows:

"(b) the money purchase limit for the particular year.", and

(b) the description of A in paragraph (2)(b) shall be read as follows:

"A is the money purchase limit for the particular year, and".

Notes: Reg. 8309(3) amended by P.C. 2005-1508, effective 2003, to change "2005" to "2004".

Reg. 8309(3) amended by P.C. 2001-1634, for 2001 and later tax years. See Notes to Reg. 8309(2). Added by P.C. 1998-2256, retroactive to 1990.

Definitions [Reg. 8309]: "amount" — ITA 248(1); "calendar year" — *Interpretation Act* 37(1)(a); "Governor" — *Interpretation Act* 35(1); "individual" — ITA 248(1); "lieutenant governor" — *Interpretation Act* 35(1); "money purchase limit" — ITA 147.1(1), 248(1); "PA offset" — Reg. 8300(1); "prescribed" — ITA 248(1); "province" — *Interpretation Act* 35(1).

8310. Minister's powers — **(1)** Where more than one method for determining an amount under this Part complies with the rules in this Part, only such of those methods as are acceptable to the Minister shall be used.

(2) Where, in a particular case, the rules in this Part require the determination of an amount in a manner that is not appropriate having regard to the provisions of this Part read as a whole and the purposes for which the amount is determined, the Minister may permit or require the amount to be determined in a manner that, in the Minister's opinion, is appropriate.

Notes: For an example of CRA using its power under Reg. 8310(2) see Notes to Reg. 8303(5).

Registered Pension Plans Technical Manual: §6.1 (qualifying transfers).

(3) Where, pursuant to subsection (2), the Minister gives permission or imposes a requirement, the permission or requirement is not effective unless it is given or imposed in writing.

Definitions [Reg. 8310]: "amount", "Minister" — ITA 248(1); "writing" — *Interpretation Act* 35(1).

8311. Rounding of amounts — Where a pension credit, provisional PSPA or PAR of an individual is not a multiple of one dollar, it shall be rounded to the nearest multiple of one dollar or, if it is equidistant from 2 such consecutive multiples, to the higher of the two multiples.

Notes: Reference to PAR (pension adjustment reversal; see Reg. 8304.1) added to Reg. 8311 by P.C. 1998-2256, effective 1997.

Definitions [Reg. 8311]: "individual" — ITA 248(1); "PAR" — Reg. 8304.1(1), (3)–(5); "pension credit" — Reg. 8301, 8308.1(2)–(4), 8308.3(2), (3); "provisional PSPA" — Reg. 8303(2), (3), 8308(4)(e).

Notes [Reg. 8300–8311]: Part LXXXIII added by P.C. 1991-2540, effective 1990, with some different application for 1991.

The PAR was originally included in the pension regulations before they were passed into force, and deleted in 1990 on the grounds that the system was too complicated. See Reg. 8304 in the Dec. 11, 1989 draft regulations.

PART LXXXIV — [8400–8410] RETIREMENT AND PROFIT SHARING PLANS — REPORTING AND PROVISION OF INFORMATION

8400. Definitions — **(1)** All words and expressions used in this Part that are defined in subsection 8300(1), 8308.4(1) or 8500(1) or in subsection 147.1(1) of the Act have the meanings assigned in those provisions.

Notes: Reference to 8308.4(1) added by P.C. 1996-911, effective 1993.

(2) A reference in this Part to a pension credit of an individual means a pension credit of the individual as determined under Part LXXXIII.

(3) For the purposes of this Part, where the administrator of a pension plan is not otherwise a person, the administrator shall be deemed to be a person.

Definitions [Reg. 8400]: "administrator" — ITA 147.1(1), Reg. 8308.4(1); "individual" — ITA 248(1); "pension credit" — Reg. 8301, 8308.1(2)–(4), 8308.3(2), (3), Reg. 8400(2); "person" — ITA 248(1).

8401. Pension adjustment — **(1)** Where the pension adjustment of an individual for a calendar year with respect to an employer is greater than nil, the employer shall, on or before the last day of February in the immediately following calendar year, file with the Minister an information return in prescribed form reporting the pension adjustment, other than the portion, if any, required by subsection (2) or (3) to be reported by the administrator of a registered pension plan.

(2) Where an individual makes a contribution in a particular calendar year to a registered pension plan that is a specified multi-employer plan in the year and the contribution is not remitted to the plan by any participating employer on behalf of the individual, the plan administrator shall, on or before the last day of February in the immediately following calendar year, file with the Minister an information return in prescribed form reporting the aggregate of all amounts each of which is the portion, if any, of the individual's pension adjustment for the particular year with respect to an employer that may reasonably be considered to result from the contribution.

(3) Where the portion of a pension credit of an individual for a calendar year that, pursuant to subsection (4), is reportable by the administrator of a registered pension plan is greater than nil, the administrator shall, on or before the last day of February in the immediately following calendar year, file with the Minister an information return in prescribed form reporting that portion of the pension credit.

(4) For the purpose of subsection (3), where, on application by the administrator of a registered pension plan that is, in a calendar year, a multi-employer plan (other than a specified multi-employer plan), the Minister consents in writing to the application of this subsection with respect to the plan in the year, such portion of each pension credit for the year under a defined benefit provision of the plan as may reasonably be considered to be attributable to benefits provided in respect of a period of reduced services or disability of an individual is, to the extent permitted by the Minister, reportable by the administrator.

(5) Subsections (1) to (3) do not apply to require the reporting of amounts with respect to an individual for the calendar year in which the individual dies.

(6) Where the pension adjustment of an individual for a calendar year with respect to an employer is altered by reason of the application of paragraph 8308(4)(d) or (5)(c) and the amount (in this subsection referred to as the "redetermined amount") that a person would have been required to report based on the pension adjustment as altered exceeds

(a) if the person has not previously reported an amount in respect of the individual's pension adjustment, nil, and

(b) otherwise, the amount reported by the person in respect of the individual's pension adjustment,

the person shall, within 60 days after the day on which paragraph 8308(3)(c) or (5)(c), as the case may be, applies to alter the pension adjustment, file with the Minister an information return in prescribed form reporting the redetermined amount.

Related Provisions: *Interpretation Act* 27(5) — Meaning of "within 60 days".

Definitions [Reg. 8401]: "administrator" — ITA 147.1(1), Reg. 8308.4(1); "amount" — ITA 248(1); "calendar year" — *Interpretation Act* 37(1)(a); "contribution" — Reg. 8302(12); "defined benefit provision" — ITA 147.1(1), Reg. 8400(1); "employer", "individual", "Minister" — ITA 248(1); "multi-employer plan", "participating employer" — ITA 147.1(1); "pension adjustment" — ITA 248(1); "pension credit" — Reg. 8301, 8308.1(2)–(4), 8308.3(2), (3), Reg. 8400(2); "person" — ITA 248(1), Reg. 8400(3); "prescribed" — ITA 248(1); "redetermined amount" — Reg. 8401(6); "registered pension plan" — ITA 248(1); "specified multi-employer plan" — ITA 147.1(1), Reg. 8510(2), (3); "writing" — *Interpretation Act* 35(1).

8402. Past service pension adjustment — (1) Where a provisional PSPA (computed under section 8303, 8304 or 8308) of an individual with respect to an employer that is associated with a past service event (other than a certifiable past service event) is greater than nil, the administrator of each registered pension plan to which the past service event relates shall, within 120 days after the day on which the past service event occurs, file with the Minister an information return in prescribed form reporting such portion of the aggregate of all amounts each of which is the individual's PSPA with respect to an employer that is associated with the past service event as may reasonably be considered to be attributable to benefits provided under the plan, except that a return is not required to be filed by an administrator if the amount that would otherwise be reported by the administrator is nil.

Related Provisions: *Interpretation Act* 27(5) — Meaning of "within 120 days".

Notes: Reg. 8402(1) amended by P.C. 2005-694, effective May 18, 2005, to change "60 days" to "120 days". See also Notes at end of Reg. 8402.

(2) Where a foreign plan PSPA (computed under subsection 8308.1(5) or (6)) of an individual with respect to an employer associated with a modification of benefits under a foreign plan (as defined by subsection 8308.1(1)) is greater than nil, the employer shall, on or before the last day of February in the year following the calendar year in which the individual's benefits were modified, file with the Minister an information return in prescribed form reporting the foreign plan PSPA.

(3) Where a specified retirement arrangement PSPA (computed under subsection 8308.3(4) or (5)) of an individual with respect to an employer associated with a modification of benefits under a specified retirement arrangement (as defined by subsection 8308.3(1)) is greater than nil, the employer shall, on or before the last day of February in the calendar year following the calendar year in which the individual's benefits were modified, file with the Minister an information return in prescribed form reporting the specified retirement arrangement PSPA.

Notes: Reg. 8402 renumbered as 8402(1), and 8402(2) and (3) added, by P.C. 1996-911, effective 1992. See also Notes after Reg. 8410.

Definitions [Reg. 8402]: "administrator" — ITA 147.1(1), Reg. 8308.4(1); "amount" — ITA 248(1); "associated" — ITA 256; "calendar year" — *Interpretation Act* 37(1)(a); "certifiable past service event" — Reg. 8300(1); "employer", "individual", "Minister" — ITA 248(1); "past service event" — ITA 147.1(1), Reg. 8300(1); "prescribed", "registered pension plan" — ITA 248(1).

8402.01 Pension adjustment reversal — (1) Deferred profit sharing plan — Where the PAR determined in connection with an individual's termination from a deferred profit sharing plan is greater than nil, each trustee under the plan shall file with the Minister an information return in prescribed form reporting the PAR

(a) where the termination occurs in the first, second or third quarter of a calendar year, on or before the day that is 60 days after the last day of the quarter in which the termination occurs, and

(b) where the termination occurs in the fourth quarter of a calendar year, before February of the following calendar year,

and, for this purpose, an information return filed by a trustee under a deferred profit sharing plan is deemed to have been filed by each trustee under the plan.

Related Provisions: Reg. 8404(2) — Copy of return must be provided to taxpayer.

Notes: See at end of Reg. 8402.01.

Forms: T10: Pension adjustment reversal; T10 Segment; T10 Summ: Summary of PARs.

(2) Deferred profit sharing plan — employer reporting — Where an amount included in an individual's pension credit in respect of an employer under a deferred profit sharing plan is included in determining a PAR in connection with the individual's termination from the plan, the employer is deemed to be a trustee under the plan for the purpose of reporting the PAR.

Related Provisions: Reg. 8404(2) — Copy of return must be provided to taxpayer.

(3) Benefit provision of a registered pension plan — Subject to subsection (4), where the PAR determined in connection with an individual's termination from a benefit provision of a registered pension plan is greater than nil, the administrator of the plan shall file with the Minister an information return in prescribed form reporting the PAR

(a) where the termination occurs in the first, second or third quarter of a calendar year, on or before the day that is 60 days after the last day of the quarter in which the termination occurs; and

(b) where the termination occurs in the fourth quarter of a calendar year, before February of the following calendar year.

Related Provisions: Reg. 8404(2) — Copy of return must be provided to taxpayer.

Notes: See Notes at end of Reg. 8402.01.

(4) Extended deadline — PA transfer amount — Where, in determining an individual's PAR in connection with the individual's termination from a defined benefit provision of a registered pension plan, it is reasonable for the administrator of the plan to conclude, on the basis of information provided to the administrator by the administrator of another pension plan or by the individual, that the value of D in paragraph 8304.1(5)(a) in respect of the termination may be greater than nil, the administrator shall file with the Minister an information return in prescribed form reporting the PAR, if it is greater than nil, on or before the later of

(a) the day on or before which it would otherwise be required to be filed; and

(b) the day that is 60 days after the earliest day on which the administrator has all the information required to determine that value.

Notes: See at end of Reg. 8402.01.

(5) Calendar year quarter — For the purposes of this section,

(a) the first quarter of a calendar year is the period beginning on January 1 and ending on March 31 of the calendar year;

(b) the second quarter of a calendar year is the period beginning on April 1 and ending on June 30 of the calendar year;

(c) the third quarter of a calendar year is the period beginning on July 1 and ending on September 30 of the calendar year; and

(d) the fourth quarter of a calendar year is the period beginning on October 1 and ending on December 31 of the calendar year.

Regulations

Notes [Reg. 8402.01]: Reg. 8402.01 added by P.C. 1998-2256, effective 1997, except that the deadline for any return required by it is extended to March 31, 1999 for 1997 or 1998 terminations (60 days after publication in the *Canada Gazette*, which was Jan. 6, 1999) and Sept. 30, 1999 for 1999 terminations. It sets out the reporting requirements for PARs (pension adjustment reversals); see Reg. 8304.1.

Definitions [Reg. 8402.01]: "administrator" — ITA 147.1(1), Reg. 8308.4(1); "benefit provision" — ITA 147.1(1); "calendar year" — *Interpretation Act* 37(1)(a); "deferred profit sharing plan" — ITA 147(1), 248(1); "defined benefit provision" — ITA 147.1(1), Reg. 8400(1); "individual", "Minister" — ITA 248(1); "PAR" — Reg. 8304.1(1), (3)–(5); "prescribed" — ITA 248(1); "quarter" — Reg. 4300; "registered pension plan" — ITA 248(1).

8402.1 Where an amount is prescribed by subsection 8308.4(2) in respect of an individual for a calendar year because of the individual's entitlement (either absolute or contingent) to benefits under a government-sponsored retirement arrangement (as defined in subsection 8308.4(1)), the administrator of the arrangement shall, on or before the last day of February in the year, file with the Minister an information return in prescribed form reporting the prescribed amount.

Notes: Reg. 8402.1 added by P.C. 1996-911, effective 1993.

Definitions [Reg. 8402.1]: "administrator" — ITA 147.1(1), Reg. 8308.4(1); "amount", "individual", "Minister", "prescribed" — ITA 248(1).

8403. Connected persons — Where, at any particular time after 1990,

(a) an individual becomes a member of a registered pension plan, or

(b) lifetime retirement benefits commence to accrue to the individual under a defined benefit provision of a registered pension plan following a period in which lifetime retirement benefits did not accrue to the individual,

each employer who participates in the plan for the benefit of the individual and with whom the individual is connected (within the meaning assigned by subsection 8500(3)) at the particular time, or was connected at any time after 1989, shall, within 60 days after the particular time, file with the Minister an information return in prescribed form containing prescribed information with respect to the individual unless the employer has previously filed an information return under this section with respect to the individual.

Related Provisions: *Interpretation Act* 27(5) — Meaning of "within 60 days".

Notes: See Notes to Reg. 8410.

Definitions [Reg. 8403]: "defined benefit provision" — ITA 147.1(1), Reg. 8400(1); "employer", "individual" — ITA 248(1); "lifetime retirement benefits" — Reg. 8500(1); "Minister", "prescribed", "registered pension plan" — ITA 248(1).

Registered Plans Directorate Newsletters: 98-1 (simplified pension plans).

Forms: T1007: Connected person information return.

8404. Reporting to individuals — **(1)** Every person who is required by section 8401 or 8402.1 to file an information return with the Minister shall, on or before the day on or before which the return is required to be filed with the Minister, send to each individual to whom the return relates, two copies of the portion of the return that relates to the individual.

Notes: Reference to 8402.1(1) added by P.C. 1996-911, and changed to (all of) 8402.1 by P.C. 1998-2256, both effective 1993.

(2) Every person who is required by section 8402, 8402.01 or 8403 to file an information return with the Minister shall, on or before the day on or before which the return is required to be filed with the Minister, send to each individual to whom the return relates, one copy of the portion of the return that relates to the individual.

Notes: Reference to 8402.1(2) added by P.C. 1996-911, effective 1993, and changed to 8402.01 by P.C. 1998-2256, effective 1997.

(3) Every person who obtains a certification from the Minister for the purposes of subsection 147.1(10) of the Act in respect of a past service event and an individual shall, within 60 days after receiving from the Minister the form submitted to the Minister pursuant to subsection 8307(1) in respect of the past service event and the individual, forward to the individual one copy of the form as returned by the Minister.

Related Provisions: *Interpretation Act* 27(5) — Meaning of "within 60 days".

(4) Every person required by subsection (1), (2) or (3) to forward a copy of an information return or a form to an individual shall send the copy to the individual at the individual's last known address or shall deliver the copy to the individual in person.

Definitions [Reg. 8404]: "individual", "Minister" — ITA 248(1); "past service event" — ITA 147.1(1), Reg. 8300(1); "person" — ITA 248(1), Reg. 8400(3).

8405. Discontinuance of business — Subsection 205(2) and section 206 are applicable, with such modifications as the circumstances require, in respect of returns required to be filed under this Part.

8406. Provision of information — **(1)** Where a person who is required to file an information return under section 8401 requires information from another person in order to determine an amount that is to be reported or to otherwise complete the return and makes a written request to the other person for the information, the other person shall provide the person with the information that is available to that other person,

(a) where the information return is required to be filed in the calendar year in which the request is received, within 30 days after receipt of the request; or

(b) in any other case, by January 31 of the year immediately following the calendar year in which the request is received.

Related Provisions: *Interpretation Act* 27(5) — Meaning of "within 30 days".

(2) Where the administrator of a registered pension plan requires information from a person in order to determine a provisional PSPA of an individual under section 8303, 8304 or 8308 and makes a written request to the person for the information, the person shall, within 30 days after receipt of the request, provide the administrator with the information that is available to the person.

Related Provisions: *Interpretation Act* 27(5) — Meaning of "within 30 days".

(3) Where the administrator of a registered pension plan requires information from a person in order to complete an information return required to be filed under section 8409 and makes a written request to the person for the information, the person shall, within 30 days after receipt of the request, provide the administrator with the information that is available to that person.

Related Provisions: *Interpretation Act* 27(5) — Meaning of "within 30 days".

(4) Where a person requires information from another person in order to determine a PAR under section 8304.1 in connection with an individual's termination in a calendar year from a deferred profit sharing plan or from a benefit provision of a registered pension plan (other than information that the other person is required to provide to the person under subsection (5)) and makes a written request to the other person for the information, the other person shall provide the person with the information that is available to the other person on or before

(a) if the request is received before December 17 of the year, the day that is 30 days after the day on which the request is received; and

(b) in any other case, the later of the day that is 15 days after the day on which the request is received and January 15 of the year following the year.

Notes: Reg. 8406(4) added by P.C. 1998-2256, effective 1997, except that the deadline for notification was extended to March 7, 1999.

(5) Where benefits provided to an individual under a registered pension plan (in this subsection referred to as the "importing plan") as a consequence of a past service event result in a PA transfer amount in relation to the individual's termination from a defined benefit provision of another registered pension plan (in this subsection referred to as the "exporting plan"),

(a) the administrator of the importing plan shall, in writing on or before the day that is 30 days after the day on which the past service event occurred, notify the administrator of the exporting plan of the occurrence of the past service event and of its relevance in determining the individual's PAR in connection with the individual's termination from the defined benefit provision; and

(b) the administrator of the importing plan shall notify the administrator of the exporting plan of the PA transfer amount in writing on or before the day that is 60 days after

(i) in the case of a certifiable past service event, the day on which the Minister issues a certification for the purposes of subsection 147.1(10) of the Act in respect of the past service event and the individual, and

(ii) in any other case, the day on which the past service event occurred.

Related Provisions: Reg. 8304.1(10) — PA transfer amount; Reg. 8304.1(11) — Special 1997 PA transfer amount.

Notes: Reg. 8406(5) added by P.C. 1998-2256, effective 1997.

Definitions [Reg. 8406]: "administrator" — ITA 147.1(1), Reg. 8308.4(1); "amount" — ITA 248(1); "calendar year" — *Interpretation Act* 37(1)(a); "certifiable past service event" — Reg. 8300(1); "defined benefit provision" — ITA 147.1(1), Reg. 8400(1); "exporting plan", "importing plan" — Reg. 8406(4); "individual", "Minister" — ITA 248(1); "PA transfer amount" — Reg. 8304.1(10), (11); "PAR" — Reg. 8304.1(1), (3)–(5); "past service event" — ITA 147.1(1), Reg. 8300(1); "person" — ITA 248(1), Reg. 8400(3); "registered pension plan" — ITA 248(1); "written" — *Interpretation Act* 35(1)"writing".

8407. Qualifying withdrawals — Where

(a) an individual who has withdrawn an amount from a registered retirement savings plan under which the individual was, at the time of the withdrawal, the annuitant (as defined in subsection 146(1) of the Act) provides to the issuer (as defined by subsection 146(1) of the Act) of the plan, in the calendar year in which the amount was withdrawn or one of the two immediately following calendar years, the prescribed form referred to in subparagraph 8307(3)(a)(ii) accompanied by a request that the issuer complete the form in respect of the withdrawal, and

(b) the issuer has not, at the time of receipt of the request, forwarded to the individual 2 copies of the information return required by subsection 214(1) to be made by the issuer in respect of the withdrawal, and does not, within 30 days after receipt of the request, forward to the individual 2 copies of that return,

the issuer shall, within 30 days after receipt of the request, complete those portions of the form that the form indicates are required to be completed by the issuer in respect of the withdrawal and return the form to the individual.

Related Provisions: ITA 146(21.2) — Saskatchewan Pension Plan account deemed to be RRSP for purposes of regulations; ITA 147.5(12) — Pooled registered pension plan deemed to be RRSP for purposes of regulations; *Interpretation Act* 27(5) — Meaning of "within 30 days".

Notes: Reg. 8407(a) amended by P.C. 2007-849, effective June 13, 2007.

Definitions [Reg. 8407]: "amount" — ITA 248(1); "calendar year" — *Interpretation Act* 37(1)(a); "individual", "prescribed" — ITA 248(1); "registered retirement savings plan" — ITA 146(1), (21.2), 147.5(12), 248(1).

Forms: T1006: Designating an RRSP, an PRPP or an SPP withdrawal as a qualifying withdrawal.

8408. Requirement to provide Minister with information —

(1) The Minister may, by notice served personally or by registered or certified mail, require that a person provide the Minister, within such reasonable time as is stipulated in the notice, with

(a) information relating to the determination of amounts under Part LXXXIII;

(b) where the person claims that paragraph 147.1(10)(a) of the Act is not applicable with respect to an individual and a past service event by reason of an exemption provided by regulation, information relevant to the claim; or

(c) information for the purpose of determining whether the registration of a pension plan may be revoked.

(2) Where a person fails to provide the Minister with information pursuant to a requirement under subsection (1), each registered pension plan and deferred profit sharing plan to which the information

relates becomes a revocable plan as of the day on or before which the information was required to be provided.

Related Provisions: ITA 147(21), 147.1(8), (9), 147.3(12), Reg. 8301(14)(a), 8305(2)(a), 8501(2), 8503(11), (15), 8506(4), 8511(2), 8515(9) — Other ways plan becomes revocable plan.

Definitions [Reg. 8408]: "amount" — ITA 248(1); "deferred profit sharing plan" — ITA 147(1), 248(1); "individual", "Minister" — ITA 248(1); "past service event" — ITA 147.1(1), Reg. 8300(1); "person" — ITA 248(1), Reg. 8400(3); "registered pension plan" — ITA 248(1); "revocable plan" — ITA 147.1(8), (9), 147.3(12), Reg. 8301(14)(a), 8305(2), 8408(2), 8501(2), 8503(11), (15), 8506(4), 8511(2), 8515(9).

8409. Annual information returns — (1) The administrator of a registered pension plan that is administered under the supervision of a government regulator shall file an information return for a fiscal period of the plan in prescribed form and containing prescribed information

(a) where an agreement concerning annual information returns has been entered into by the Minister and the regulator, as identified in subsection (2),

(i) in the case of the agreement with the Pension Commission of Ontario, with the Taxation Data Centre of the Ministry of Finance of Ontario, and

(ii) in any other case, with that regulator,

on or before the day that an information return required by that regulator is to be filed for the fiscal period; and

(b) in any other case, with the Minister on or before the day that is 180 days after the end of the fiscal period.

Announced Administrative Change — T244 filing deadline in 2021

CRA news release, June 25, 2021: *Registered Pension Plans (RPPs) — What's new*

Due to a legislative change that the Financial Services Regulatory Authority of Ontario (FSRA) enacted in December 2020, individual pension plans and designated plans can file an election to be exempt from the application of Ontario's *Pension Benefits Act*. Plans for which this election is approved, would be required to file the Form T244, *Annual Information Return* 180 days after the plan's fiscal year end. The Registered Plans Directorate is providing a one-time filing extension, to September 30, 2021, for all plans with a December to March year end that are affected by the FSRA change. This will preserve, or in some cases shorten, the filing deadline that these plans would otherwise have had. In future years, all plans will be required to respect the Canada Revenue Agency deadline.

More information on filing dates and penalties can be found in Newsletter 16-2, *Annual Information Return — reminder of filing obligation and late-filing penalties*. Electronic filing options can be found on "Filing forms with the Registered Plans Directorate".

Notes: See Notes at end of Reg. 8409.

Registered Pension Plans Technical Manual: §6.5 (annual information returns).

Registered Plans Directorate Newsletters: 16-2 (annual information return).

Forms: RC154: Schedule of required information for the CRA (for Quebec); T244: Registered pension plan annual information return.

(2) For the purposes of paragraph (1)(a), the following government regulators have entered into an agreement concerning annual information returns with the Minister:

(a) the Pension Commission of Ontario, Province of Ontario;

(b) the Superintendent of Pensions, Province of Nova Scotia;

(c) the Superintendent of Pensions, Province of New Brunswick;

(d) the Superintendent of Pensions, Province of Manitoba; and

(e) the Superintendent of Pensions, Province of British Columbia.

Proposed Amendment — Reg. 8409(2)

CCRA, Registered Plans Directorate Newsletter No. 03-1 (June 27, 2003): *Joint Annual Information Return — New Participating Pension Supervisory Authority*

Further to our Newsletter No. 95-4, *New Filing Requirements for the Registered Pension Plan Annual Information Return*, and our Newsletter No. 01-2, *Joint Annual Information Return — New Participating Pension Supervisory Authorities*, the CCRA has developed a new joint annual information return with the Régie des rentes du Québec....

In creating the joint annual information return with the Régie des rentes du Québec, we created a new schedule to include with Quebec's annual information return. The new

Registered Pension Plans Technical Manual: §6.5 (annual information returns).

Registered Plans Directorate Newsletters: 03-1 (joint annual information return — new participating pension supervisory authority).

(3) The administrator of a registered pension plan shall, within 60 days after the final distribution of property held in connection with the plan, notify the Minister in writing of the date of the distribution and the method of settlement.

Related Provisions: *Interpretation Act* 27(5) — Meaning of "within 60 days".

Registered Plans Compliance Bulletins: 1 (terminating registered pension plans).

Notes [Reg. 8409]: Reg. 8409 replaced by P.C. 1996-213, for fiscal periods that end after Dec. 30, 1994. See also Notes after Reg. 8410.

The 1996 amendments implemented changes announced by Revenue Canada press releases on Dec. 20, 1994 ("Simplified Filing Requirements for Registered Pension Plan Annual Information Returns"); Feb. 9, 1995 ("Ottawa and New Brunswick Combine Filing Requirements for Registered Pension Plans"); April 6, 1995 ("Ottawa and Nova Scotia Combine ..."); and May 19, 1995 ("Ottawa and British Columbia Combine ..."). The information return can now be filed with the provincial or federal regulator responsible for the supervision of the RPP if the regulator has entered into an agreement with CRA regarding such information returns. Reg. 8409(2) lists the regulators that have entered into such an agreement.

CRA indicates in Registered Plans Directorate Newsletter 96-2 (June 17, 1996) the circumstances in which it will waive the Reg. 8409 filing obligation for inactive plans. See the Newsletter, or contact the Registered Plans Directorate at (613) 954-0419.

Definitions [Reg. 8409]: "administrator" — ITA 147.1(1), Reg. 8308.4(1); "fiscal period" — ITA 249.1; "Minister", "prescribed", "property", "registered pension plan" — ITA 248(1); "writing" — *Interpretation Act* 35(1).

Registered Plans Directorate Newsletters: 95-4 (new filing requirements for the registered pension plan annual information return); 95-7 (Quebec simplified pension plans); 96-2 (waiving the requirement to file a registered pension plan annual information return for an inactive plan); 01-2 (joint annual information return — new participating pension supervisory authorities).

8410. Actuarial reports — The administrator of a registered pension plan that contains a defined benefit provision shall, on demand from the Minister served personally or by registered or certified mail and within such reasonable time as is stipulated in the demand, file with the Minister a report prepared by an actuary on the basis of reasonable assumptions and in accordance with generally accepted actuarial principles and containing such information as is required by the Minister in respect of the defined benefit provisions of the plan.

Notes [Reg. 8400–8410]: Part LXXXIV added by P.C. 1991-2540, Reg. 8400 to 8405, 8409 and 8410 effective 1990, with grandfathering of filing dates to February 28, 1991 (for Reg. 8405) and to March 15, 1992 (for deadlines under Reg. 8402, 8403, 8404(2), (3) and 8409(1) and (3)).

Definitions [Reg. 8410]: "actuary" — ITA 147.1(1); "administrator" — ITA 147.1(1), Reg. 8308.4(1); "defined benefit provision" — ITA 147.1(1), Reg. 8400(1); "Minister", "registered pension plan" — ITA 248(1).

Registered Plans Compliance Bulletins: 1 (terminating registered pension plans).

Registered Plans Directorate Newsletters: 95-3 (actuarial report content); 95-5 (conversion of a defined benefit provision to a money purchase provision).

PART LXXXV — [8500–8520] REGISTERED PENSION PLANS

8500. Interpretation — (1) [Definitions] — In this Part,

"active member" of a pension plan in a calendar year means a member of the plan to whom benefits accrue under a defined benefit provision of the plan in respect of all or any portion of the year or who makes contributions, or on whose behalf contributions are made, in relation to the year under a money purchase provision of the plan;

Related Provisions: ITA 147.1(1)"member" — Similar definition in the Act; Reg. 8500(7) — Amount allocated under money purchase provision deemed to be contribution.

Registered Pension Plans Technical Manual: §1.2 (active member).

"average Consumer Price Index" for a calendar year means the amount that is obtained by dividing by 12 the aggregate of all amounts each of which is the Consumer Price Index for a month in the 12-month period ending on September 30 of the immediately preceding calendar year;

Registered Pension Plans Technical Manual: §1.5 (average Consumer Price Index).

"beneficiary" of an individual means a person who has a right, by virtue of the participation of the individual in a pension plan, to receive benefits under the plan after the death of the individual;

Registered Pension Plans Technical Manual: §1.7 (beneficiary).

"benefit provision" of a pension plan means a money purchase or defined benefit provision of the plan;

Registered Pension Plans Technical Manual: §1.8 (benefit provision).

"bridging benefits" provided to a member under a benefit provision of a pension plan means retirement benefits payable to the member under the provision for a period ending no later than a date determinable at the time the benefits commence to be paid;

Related Provisions: ITA 118(8.1) — Pension income credit for bridging benefits.

Registered Pension Plans Technical Manual: §1.9 (bridging benefits).

"Consumer Price Index" for a month means the Consumer Price Index for the month as published by Statistics Canada under the authority of the *Statistics Act*;

Registered Pension Plans Technical Manual: §1.15 (Consumer Price Index).

"defined benefit limit" for a calendar year means the greater of

(a) $1,722.22, and

(b) 1/9 of the money purchase limit for the year;

Notes: The limit is: 1990-2003: $1,722.22; 2004: $1,833.33; 2005: $2,000; 2006: $2,111.11; 2007: $2,222.22; 2008: $2,333.33; 2009: $2,444.44; 2010: $2,494.44; 2011: $2,552.22; 2012: $2,646.67; 2013: $2,696.67; 2014: $2,770.00; 2015: $2,818.89; 2016: $2,890.00; 2017: $2,914.44; 2018: $2,944.44; 2019: $3,025.56; 2020: $3,092.22; 2021: $3,245.56.

See also Reg. 8509(13) and 8516(9), which contain grandfathering provisions for certain RPP benefits and contributions based on indexing of the DBL before 2005.

Definition amended by P.C. 1998-2256, last change effective 1997. Since $1,722.22 is 1/9 of $15,500, the limit was frozen at $1,722.22 until the ITA 147.1(1) money purchase limit exceeded $15,500. Earlier amended by P.C. 1995-17, effective 1992.

Registered Pension Plans Technical Manual: §1.17 (defined benefit limit).

"dependant" of an individual at the time of the individual's death means a parent, grandparent, brother, sister, child or grandchild of the individual who, at that time, is both dependent on the individual for support and

(a) under 19 years of age and will not attain 19 years of age in the calendar year that includes that time,

(b) in full-time attendance at an educational institution, or

(c) dependent on the individual by reason of mental or physical infirmity;

Registered Pension Plans Technical Manual: §1.19 (dependant).

"designated plan" has the meaning assigned by section 8515;

Notes: Reg. 8500(1)"designated plan" added by 2007 budget bill #2, effective 2008.

"disabled" means, in relation to an individual, suffering from a physical or mental impairment that prevents the individual from performing the duties of the employment in which the individual was engaged before the commencement of the impairment;

Registered Pension Plans Technical Manual: §1.21 (disabled).

"eligible period of reduced pay" of an employee with respect to an employer means a period (other than a period in which the employee is, at any time after 1990, connected with the employer or a period any part of which is a period of disability of the employee)

(a) that begins after the employee has been employed by the employer or predecessor employers to the employer for not less than 36 months,

(b) throughout which the employee renders services to the employer, and

(c) throughout which the remuneration received by the employee from the employer is less than the remuneration that it is reasonable to expect the employee would have received from the employer had the employee rendered services throughout the period on a regular basis (having regard to the services rendered by the employee to the employer before the period) and had the employee's rate of remuneration been commensurate with the employee's rate of remuneration before the period;

Related Provisions: Reg. 8500(1.3) — COVID-19 relief for 2020-21; Reg. 8508(a) — Sabbatical arrangement deemed to be eligible period of reduced pay.

Information Circulars: 98-2: Prescribed compensation for RPPs, para. 10.

Registered Pension Plans Technical Manual: §1.22 (eligible period of reduced pay).

"eligible period of temporary absence" of an individual with respect to an employer means a period throughout which the individual does not render services to the employer by reason of leave of absence, layoff, strike, lock-out or any other circumstance acceptable to the Minister, other than a period

(a) a part of which is a period of disability of the individual, or

(b) in which the individual is, at any time after 1990, connected with the employer;

Registered Pension Plans Technical Manual: §1.23 (eligible period of temporary absence).

"eligible survivor benefit period" in relation to a person who is a dependant of an individual at the time of the individual's death, means the period beginning on the day of death of the individual and ending on the latest of

(a) where the dependant is under 19 years of age throughout the calendar year that includes the day of death of the individual, the earlier of

(i) December 31 of the calendar year in which the dependant attains 18 years of age, and

(ii) the day of death of the dependant,

(b) where the dependant is in full-time attendance at an educational institution on the later of the day of death of the individual and December 31 of the calendar year in which the dependant attains 18 years of age, the day on which the dependant ceases to be in full-time attendance at an educational institution, and

(c) where the dependant is dependent on the individual at the time of the individual's death by reason of mental or physical infirmity, the day on which the dependant ceases to be infirm or, if there is no such day, the day of death of the dependant;

Registered Pension Plans Technical Manual: §1.24 (eligible survivor benefit period).

"existing plan" means a pension plan that was a registered pension plan on March 27, 1988 or in respect of which an application for registration was made to the Minister before March 28, 1988, and includes a pension plan that was established before March 28, 1988 pursuant to an Act of Parliament that deems member contributions to be contributions to a registered pension plan;

"forfeited amount" under a money purchase provision of a pension plan means an amount to which a member of the plan has ceased to have any rights, other than the portion thereof, if any, that is payable

(a) to a beneficiary of the member as a consequence of the member's death, or

(b) to a spouse or common-law partner or former spouse or common-law partner of the member as a consequence of the breakdown of their marriage or common-law partnership;

Notes: Para. (b) amended by P.C. 2001-957 to add references to common-law partner, effective as per Notes to ITA 248(1)"common-law partner".

"grandfathered plan" means

(a) an existing plan that, on March 27, 1988, contained a defined benefit provision, or

(b) a pension plan that was established to provide benefits under a defined benefit provision to one or more individuals in lieu of benefits to which the individuals were entitled under a defined benefit provision of another pension plan that is a grandfathered plan, whether or not benefits are also provided to other individuals;

Related Provisions: Reg. 8509(13) — Grandfathering where plan complied before March 1996 budget date.

Registered Pension Plans Technical Manual: §1.25 (grandfathered plan).

"IPP minimum amount", for a year, for a person who is a member of an individual pension plan (or a beneficiary, in respect of the plan, who was, at the time of the member's death, a spouse or common-law partner of the member) means

(a) if there is only one such person in respect of the plan, the minimum amount that would be determined under subsection 146.3(1) of the Act for the year in respect of the plan if the plan were a registered retirement income fund that held the same property as the property held by the plan and the person were the annuitant of the fund, and

(b) in any other case, the minimum amount that would be determined under subsection 146.3(1) of the Act if the person were the annuitant of a registered retirement income fund and the fair market value of the property held in connection with the fund at the beginning of the year were determined by the formula

$$A \times B/C$$

where

A is the fair market value of all property held in connection with the plan at the beginning of the year,

B is the amount of the actuarial liabilities in respect of the benefits payable to the person under the terms of the plan at the beginning of the year, and

C is the amount of the actuarial liabilities in respect of all benefits payable under the terms of the plan at the beginning of the year;

Related Provisions: Reg. 8502(d)(x) — Permissible distributions; Reg. 8503(26) — IPP — minimum withdrawal.

Notes: See Notes to Reg. 8515(1). Definition added by 2011 budget bill #2, effective for 2012 and later taxation years.

Registered Plans Directorate Newsletters: 14-2 (IPP minimum amount).

"lifetime retirement benefits" provided to a member under a benefit provision of a pension plan means

(a) retirement benefits provided to the member under the provision that, after they commence to be paid, are payable to the member until the member's death, unless the benefits are commuted or payment of the benefits is suspended, and

(b) for greater certainty, retirement benefits provided to the member under the provision in accordance with paragraph 8506(1)(e.1);

Related Provisions: Reg. 8504(6) — Pre-1990 benefits.

Notes: Para. (b) added by P.C. 2005-1508, effective 2004.

Registered Pension Plans Technical Manual: §1.28 (lifetime retirement benefits).

"multi-employer plan" in a calendar year means

(a) a pension plan in respect of which it is reasonable to expect, at the beginning of the year (or at the time in the year when the plan is established, if later), that at no time in the year will more than 95 per cent of the active members of the plan be employed by a single participating employer or by a related group of participating employers, other than a plan where it is reasonable to consider that one of the main reasons there is more than one employer participating in the plan is to obtain the benefit of any of the provisions of the Act or these Regulations that are applicable only with respect to multi-employer plans, or

(b) a pension plan that is, in the year, a specified multi-employer plan,

and, for the purposes of this definition, 2 corporations that are related to each other solely by reason that they are both controlled by Her Majesty in right of Canada or a province shall be deemed not to be related persons;

Related Provisions: ITA 252.1 — Trade union locals and branches deemed to be a single employer; ITA 256(6), (6.1) — Meaning of "controlled".

Notes: For interpretation see VIEWS doc 2004-0093911E5. For the meaning of "one of the main reasons" in para. (a), see Notes to ITA 83(2.1).

For PSPA and PAR for multi-employer plans, see Willis Towers Watson, *Canadian Pensions and Retirement Income Planning*, 6th ed. (LexisNexis, 2017), chap. 12.

Regulations: 8510(2), (3) (meaning of "specified multi-employer plan").

Registered Pension Plans Technical Manual: §1.32 (multi-employer plan).

Registered Plans Frequently Asked Questions: RPFAQ-2 (RPPs), q. 13 (what is a MEP?).

"pensionable service" of a member of a pension plan under a defined benefit provision of the plan means the periods in respect of which lifetime retirement benefits are provided to the member under the provision;

Registered Pension Plans Technical Manual: §1.35 (pensionable service).

"period of disability" of an individual means a period throughout which the individual is disabled;

Registered Pension Plans Technical Manual: §1.36 (period of disability).

"predecessor employer" means, in relation to a particular employer, an employer (in this definition referred to as the "vendor") who has sold, assigned or otherwise disposed of all or part of the vendor's business or undertaking or all or part of the assets of the vendor's business or undertaking to the particular employer or to another employer who, at any time after the sale, assignment or other disposition, becomes a predecessor employer in relation to the particular employer, if all or a significant number of employees of the vendor have, in conjunction with the sale, assignment or disposition, become employees of the employer acquiring the business, undertaking or assets;

Related Provisions: Reg. 8500(1.2) — Definition applies for purposes of ITA 147.2(8); Reg. 8504(2.1) — Employment with predecessor employer included in calculation of maximum benefits.

Notes: Definition amended to change "one or more employees" to "all or a significant number of employees" by 2002-2013 technical bill (Part 5 — technical), effective Nov. 6, 2010, but the amendment does not apply in respect of a sale, assignment or disposition of a business or undertaking that occurred before that date.

Registered Plans Directorate Newsletters: 14-1 (reviewing earnings and service for IPPs).

"public pension benefits" means amounts payable on a periodic basis under the *Canada Pension Plan*, a provincial pension plan as defined in section 3 of the *Canada Pension Plan*, or Part I of the *Old Age Security Act*, but does not include disability, death or survivor benefits provided under those Acts;

"public safety occupation" means the occupation of

(a) firefighter,

(b) police officer,

(c) corrections officer,

(d) air traffic controller,

(e) commercial airline pilot, or

(f) paramedic;

Notes: Para. (f), paramedic, added by P.C. 2005-1508, effective 2005, as proposed in the February 2005 budget. Public safety workers, due to their jobs' physical requirements, can retire 5 years early with full pension. See Reg. 8503(3)(c)(i) and (g)(i).

Registered Pension Plans Technical Manual: §1.39 (public safety occupation).

"retirement benefits" provided to an individual under a benefit provision of a pension plan means benefits provided to the individual under the provision that are payable on a periodic basis;

Related Provisions: ITA 60.021(4)(b) — Definition applies to 2008 RRIF minimum amount reduction; ITA 60.022(5)(b) — Definition applies to ITA 60.022.

Registered Pension Plans Technical Manual: §1.40 (retirement benefits).

"surplus" under a money purchase provision of a pension plan at any time means such portion, if any, of the amount held at that time in respect of the provision as has not been allocated to members and is not reasonably attributable to

(a) forfeited amounts under the provision or earnings of the plan that are reasonably attributable to those amounts,

(b) contributions made under the provision by an employer that will be allocated to members as part of the regular allocation of such contributions, or

(c) earnings of the plan (other than earnings that are reasonably attributable to the surplus under the provision before that time) that will be allocated to members as part of the regular allocation of such earnings;

Related Provisions: Reg. 8500(1.1) — Definition applies to ITA 147.3(7.1).

Registered Pension Plans Technical Manual: §1.44 (surplus).

"totally and permanently disabled" means, in relation to an individual, suffering from a physical or mental impairment that prevents the individual from engaging in any employment for which the individual is reasonably suited by virtue of the individual's education, training or experience and that can reasonably be expected to last for the remainder of the individual's lifetime;

Registered Pension Plans Technical Manual: §1.45 (totally and permanently disabled).

"Year's Maximum Pensionable Earnings" for a calendar year has the meaning assigned by section 18 of the *Canada Pension Plan*.

Notes: See Table I-8 at beginning of book for the YMPE.

Interpretation Bulletins: IT-124R6: Contributions to registered retirement savings plans.

Registered Pension Plans Technical Manual: §1.47 (Year's Maximum Pensionable Earnings).

Registered Plans Directorate Newsletters [Reg. 8500(1)]: 91-4R (registration rules for money purchase provisions); 96-1 (changes to retirement savings limits).

(1.1) [Application of "surplus"] — The definition "surplus" in subsection (1) applies for the purpose of subsection 147.3(7.1) of the Act.

Notes: Reg. 8500(1.1) added by P.C. 2003-1497, effective 1999.

Registered Pension Plans Technical Manual: §1.44 (surplus).

(1.2) [Application of "predecessor employer"] — The definition "predecessor employer" in subsection (1) applies for the purpose of subsection 147.2(8) of the Act.

Notes: Reg. 8500(1.2) added by 2002-2013 technical bill (Part 5 — technical), effective for contributions made after 1990.

(1.3) [Eligible period of reduced pay for 2020-21 — COVID-19] — For the purpose of determining under subsection 8507(3) whether a period in a calendar year is a qualifying period of an individual in the year with respect to an employer, the definition "eligible period of reduced pay" in subsection (1) is, in respect of the individual and the employer for the calendar year 2020 or 2021, modified as follows:

(a) it is to be read without reference to its paragraph (a); and

(b) its paragraph (c) is to be read as follows:

(c) throughout which the remuneration received by the employee from the employer is less than the remuneration so received before the period;

Notes: See Notes to Reg. 6801.1. Reg. 8500(1.3) added by P.C. 2021-522, effective June 10, 2021.

(2) [Terms defined in ITA 147.1(1) and Part 83] — All words and expressions used in this Part that are defined in subsection 147.1(1) of the Act or in Part LXXXIII have the meanings assigned in those provisions.

Related Provisions: Reg. 8300(3) — Mirror image rule causing terms in Reg. 8500(1) to be defined for purposes of Part 83.

Notes: Reg. 8500(2) amended by 2007 budget bill #2, effective 2008, to add reference to Part LXXXIII.

(3) ["Connected"] — For the purposes of this Part, a person is connected with an employer at any time where, at that time, the person

(a) owns, directly or indirectly, not less than 10 per cent of the issued shares of any class of the capital stock of the employer or of any other corporation that is related to the employer,

(b) does not deal at arm's length with the employer, or

(c) is a specified shareholder of the employer by reason of paragraph (d) of the definition "specified shareholder" in subsection 248(1) of the Act,

and, for the purposes of this subsection,

(d) a person shall be deemed to own, at any time, each share of the capital stock of a corporation owned, at that time, by a person with whom the person does not deal at arm's length,

(e) where shares of the capital stock of a corporation are owned at any time by a trust,

(i) if the share of any beneficiary in the income or capital of the trust depends on the exercise by any person of, or the failure by any person to exercise, any discretionary power, each beneficiary of the trust shall be deemed to own, at that time, all the shares owned by the trust, and

(ii) in any other case, each beneficiary of a trust shall be deemed to own, at that time, that proportion of the shares owned by the trust that the fair market value at that time of the beneficiary's beneficial interest in the trust is of the fair market value at that time of all beneficial interests in the trust,

(f) each member of a partnership shall be deemed to own, at any time, that proportion of all shares of the capital stock of a corporation that are property of the partnership at that time that the fair market value at that time of the member's interest in the partnership is of the fair market value at that time of the interests of all members in the partnership, and

(g) a person who, at any time, has a right under a contract, in equity or otherwise, either immediately or in the future and either absolutely or contingently, to, or to acquire, shares of the capital stock of a corporation shall be deemed to own, at that time, those shares if one of the main reasons for the existence of the right may reasonably be considered to be that the person not be connected with an employer.

Notes: For the meaning of "one of the main reasons" in para. (g), see Notes to ITA 83(2.1).

Interpretation Bulletins: IT-124R6: Contributions to registered retirement savings plans.

Registered Pension Plans Technical Manual: §1.14 (connected person).

Registered Plans Directorate Newsletters: 91-4R (registration rules for money purchase provisions).

(4) [Offices] — For the purposes of this Part, an officer who receives remuneration for holding an office shall, for any period that the officer holds the office, be deemed to render services to, and to be in the service of, the person from whom the officer receives the remuneration.

Interpretation Bulletins: IT-167R6: Registered pension plans — employee's contributions.

(5) ["Spouse" and "former spouse"] — For the purpose of this Part, "spouse" and "former spouse" of a particular individual

include another individual who is a party to a void or voidable marriage with the particular individual.

Notes: Reg. 8500(5) amended by P.C. 2007-849, effective June 13, 2007, to delete "of the opposite sex", consistent with 2005 same-sex marriage bill, and to add "former spouse".

Reg. 8500(5) amended by P.C. 2001-957, effective as per Notes to ITA 248(1)"common-law partner".

Registered Pension Plans Technical Manual: §1.43 (spouse).

Registered Plans Directorate Newsletters: 91-4R (registration rules for money purchase provisions).

(6) [Combining periods] — Where this Part provides that an amount is to be determined by aggregating the durations of periods that satisfy specified conditions, a period shall be included in determining the aggregate only if it is not part of a longer period that satisfies the conditions.

(7) [Deemed contributions] — For the purposes of the definition "active member" in subsection (1), subparagraph 8503(3)(a)(v) and paragraphs 8504(7)(d), 8506(2)(c.1) and 8507(3)(a), the portion of an amount allocated to an individual at any time under a money purchase provision of a registered pension plan that is attributable to

(a) forfeited amounts under the provision or earnings of the plan that are reasonably attributable to those amounts,

(b) a surplus under the provision,

(c) property transferred to the provision in respect of the actuarial surplus under a defined benefit provision of the plan or another registered pension plan, or

(d) property transferred to the provision in respect of the surplus under another money purchase provision of the plan or under a money purchase provision of another registered pension plan

shall be deemed to be a contribution made under the provision on behalf of the individual at that time.

Notes: Opening words of Reg. 8500(7) amended by P.C. 2005-1508 to add reference to Reg. 8506(2)(c.1), effective 2004.

Reg. 8500(7)(d) added by P.C. 2003-1497, effective for allocations that occur after 1998. It is consequential on the introduction of ITA 147.3(7.1).

Reg. 8500(7) added by P.C. 1995-17, this version effective for amounts allocated after April 5, 1994. (The rule in Reg. 8500(7) was formerly in the closing words of Reg. 8507(3)(a).)

Registered Pension Plans Technical Manual: §1.2 (active member); §1.16 (deemed contributions).

(8) [Member and non-member benefits] — Where an individual who is entitled to receive benefits (in this subsection referred to as "member benefits") under a pension plan because of the individual's membership in the plan is also entitled to receive other benefits (in this subsection referred to as "non-member benefits") under the plan or under any other pension plan solely because of the participation of another individual in the plan or in the other plan, the following rules apply:

(a) for the purpose of determining whether the member benefits are permissible under this Part, the non-member benefits shall be disregarded;

(b) for the purpose of determining whether the non-member benefits are permissible under this Part, the member benefits shall be disregarded; and

(c) for the purpose of determining a pension adjustment, pension adjustment reversal or provisional past service pension adjustment of the individual under Part LXXXIII, the non-member benefits shall be disregarded.

Notes: Reg. 8500(8) added by P.C. 2001-153, effective 1989, except that before 1997, ignore the words "pension adjustment reversal" in para. (c).

(9) [Transfer of significant number of members to new plan] — For the purposes of paragraph 147.3(6)(b) of the Act and subparagraphs 8502(d)(iv) and 8503(2)(h)(iii), if an amount is transferred in accordance with subsection 147.3(3) of the Act to a defined benefit provision (referred to in this subsection as the "current provision") of a registered pension plan from a defined benefit

Regulations

provision (referred to in this subsection as the "former provision") of another registered pension plan on behalf of all or a significant number of members whose benefits under the former provision are replaced by benefits under the current provision, each current service contribution made at a particular time under the former provision by a member whose benefits are so replaced is deemed to be a current service contribution made at that particular time under the current provision by the member.

Notes: Reg. 8500(9) added by 2002-2013 technical bill, effective 2000.

Definitions [Reg. 8500]: "active member" — Reg. 8500(1); "amount" — ITA 248(1); "arm's length" — ITA 251(1); "beneficiary", "benefit provision" — Reg. 8500(1); "benefits" — Reg. 8501(5)(c); "business" — ITA 248(1); "calendar year" — *Interpretation Act* 37(1)(a); "Canada" — ITA 255, *Interpretation Act* 35(1); "child" — ITA 252(1); "commencement" — *Interpretation Act* 35(1); "common-law partner", "common-law partnership" — ITA 248(1); "connected" — Reg. 8500(3); "consequence of the member's death" — 248(8); "Consumer Price Index" — Reg. 8500(1); "contribution" — Reg. 8500(7), 8501(6); "controlled" — ITA 256(6), (6.1); "corporation" — ITA 248(1), *Interpretation Act* 35(1); "defined benefit provision" — ITA 147.1(1), Reg. 8500(2); "dependant", "disabled" — Reg. 8500(1); "disposed" — ITA 248(1)"disposition"; "employed", "employee", "employer", "employment" — ITA 248(1); "existing plan" — Reg. 8500(1); "fair market value" — see ITA 69(1) Notes; "forfeited amount", "grandfathered plan" — Reg. 8500(1); "Her Majesty" — *Interpretation Act* 35(1); "individual" — ITA 248(1); "individual pension plan" — Reg. 8300(1), 8500(2); "lifetime retirement benefits" — Reg. 8500(1); "member" — ITA 147.1(1), Reg. 8300(1), 8500(2); "minimum amount" — ITA 146.3(1); "Minister" — ITA 248(1); "money purchase limit", "money purchase provision" — ITA 147.1(1); "month" — *Interpretation Act* 35(1); "office" — ITA 248(1); "officer" — Reg. 8500(4); "own" — Reg. 8500(3)(d)–(g); "Parliament" — *Interpretation Act* 35(1); "participating employer" — ITA 147.1(1); "partnership" — see ITA 96(1) Notes; "past service pension adjustment" — ITA 248(1), Reg. 8303(1); "pension adjustment" — ITA 248(1); "period of disability" — Reg. 8500(1); "person" — ITA 248(1); "predecessor employer" — Reg. 8500(1); "property" — ITA 248(1); "province" — *Interpretation Act* 35(1); "provincial pension plan", "provincial plan" — *Canada Pension Plan* s. 3; "provisional past service pension adjustment" — Reg. 8303(2); "registered pension plan" — ITA 248(1); "registered retirement income fund" — ITA 146.3(1), 248(1); "related" — ITA 251(2)–(6), Reg. 8500(1)"multi-employer plan"; "retirement benefits" — Reg. 8500(1); "share" — ITA 248(1); "specified multi-employer plan" — ITA 147.1(1), Reg. 8510(2), (3); "specified shareholder" — ITA 248(1); "spouse" — Reg. 8500(5); "surplus" — Reg. 8500(1); "taxpayer" — ITA 248(1); "trust" — ITA 104(1), 248(1), (3).

8501. Prescribed conditions for registration and other conditions applicable to registered pension plans — (1) Conditions for registration — For the purposes of section 147.1 of the Act, and subject to sections 8509 and 8510, the prescribed conditions for the registration of a pension plan are

(a) the conditions in paragraphs 8502(a), (c), (e), (f) and (l),

(b) if the plan contains a defined benefit provision, the conditions in paragraphs 8503(4)(a) and (c), and

(c) if the plan contains a money purchase provision, the conditions in paragraphs 8506(2)(a) and (d),

and the following conditions:

(d) there is no reason to expect, on the basis of the documents that constitute the plan and establish the funding arrangements, that

(i) the plan may become a revocable plan pursuant to subsection (2), or

(ii) the conditions in subsection 147.1(10) of the Act may not be complied with, and

(e) there is no reason to expect that the plan may become a revocable plan under subsection 147.1(8) or (9) of the Act or subsections 8503(15) or (26) or 8506(4).

Related Provisions: Reg. 8501(3) — Conditions inapplicable where inconsistent with 8503(6) and (8) and 8505(3) and (4); Reg. 8501(6) — Rule where contributions made through employer association or trade union from employer or individual.

Notes: See Notes to 147.1(2).

Reg. 8501(1)(e) amended by 2011 budget bill #2, for 2012 and later tax years.

Reg. 8501(1)(e) amended by P.C. 2005-1508 to refer to Reg. 8506(4), effective 2004.

Information Circulars: 98-2: Prescribed compensation for RPPs, paras. 19, 30.

Registered Pension Plans Technical Manual: §7.1 (conditions for registration).

Registered Plans Compliance Bulletins: 5 (reminder of primary purpose requirement for RPPs).

Registered Plans Directorate Newsletters: 91-4R (registration rules for money purchase provisions).

(2) Conditions applicable to registered pension plans — For the purposes of paragraph 147.1(11)(c) of the Act, and subject to sections 8509 and 8510, a registered pension plan becomes a revocable plan at any time that it fails to comply with

(a) a condition set out in any of paragraphs 8502(b), (d), (g) to (k) and (m);

(b) where the plan contains a defined benefit provision, a condition set out in paragraph 8503(3)(a), (b), (d), (j), (k) or (l) or (4)(b), (d), (e) or (f); or

(c) where the plan contains a money purchase provision, a condition set out in any of paragraphs 8506(2)(b) to (c.1) and (e) to (i).

Related Provisions: ITA 147.1(8), (9), 147.3(12), Reg. 8301(14)(a), 8305(2), 8408(2), 8503(11), (15), 8506(4), 8511(2), 8515(9) — Other ways plan becomes revocable plan; Reg. 8501(3) — Conditions inapplicable where inconsistent with 8503(6) and (8) and 8505(3) and (4); Reg. 8501(6) — Rule where contributions made through employer association or trade union from employer or individual.

Notes: See Notes to ITA 147.1(2).

Reg. 8501(2)(c) amended by P.C. 2005-1508, effective 2004. Reg. 8501(2) earlier amended by P.C. 1996-911 (effective 1994) and P.C. 1995-17 (effective April 6, 1994).

Registered Pension Plans Technical Manual: §7.2 (conditions applicable to RPPs).

Registered Plans Compliance Bulletins: 8 (over-contributions to an RPP).

Registered Plans Directorate Newsletters: 91-4R (registration rules for money purchase provisions).

(3) Permissive rules — The conditions in this Part do not apply in respect of a pension plan to the extent that they are inconsistent with the provisions of subsections 8503(6) and (8) and 8505(3) and (4).

Notes: Reg. 8501(3) amended by P.C. 1995-17, retroactive to its introduction (1989), to add reference to Reg. 8505(4).

Registered Pension Plans Technical Manual: §7.3 (permissive rules).

(4) Supplemental plans — Where

(a) the benefits provided under a pension plan (in this subsection referred to as the "supplemental plan") that contains one defined benefit provision and no money purchase provisions may reasonably be considered to be supplemental to the benefits provided under a defined benefit provision (in this subsection referred to as the "base provision") of another pension plan,

(b) the supplemental plan does not otherwise comply with the condition set out in paragraph 8502(a) or the condition in paragraph 8502(c), and

(c) the Minister has approved the application of this subsection, which approval has not been withdrawn,

for the purpose of determining whether the supplemental plan complies with the conditions in paragraphs 8502(a) and (c), the benefits provided under the base provision shall be considered to be provided under the supplemental plan.

Registered Pension Plans Technical Manual: §7.4 (supplemental plans).

(5) Benefits payable after the breakdown of the marriage or common-law partnership — Where

(a) an individual who is a spouse or common-law partner or former spouse or common-law partner of a member of a registered pension plan is entitled to receive all or a portion of the benefits that would otherwise be payable under the plan to the member, and

(b) the entitlement was created

(i) by assignment of benefits by the member, on or after the breakdown of their marriage or common-law partnership, in settlement of rights arising out of their marriage or common-law partnership, or

(ii) by a provision of the law of Canada or a province applicable in respect of the division of property between the member and the individual, on or after the breakdown of their marriage or common-law partnership, in settlement of rights arising out of their marriage or common-law partnership,

the following rules apply:

(c) except where paragraph (d) applies, the benefits to which the individual is entitled are, for the purposes of this Part, deemed to be benefits provided and payable to the member, and

(d) the benefits to which the individual is entitled are, for the purposes of this Part, deemed to be benefits provided and payable to the individual and not provided or payable to the member where

(i) the entitlement of the individual was created by a provision of the law of Canada or a province described in subparagraph (b)(ii), and

(ii) that provision

(A) requires that benefits commence to be paid to the individual at a time that may be different from the time benefits commence to be paid to the member, or

(B) gives the individual any rights in respect of the benefits to which the individual is entitled in addition to the rights that the individual would have as a consequence of an assignment by the member, in whole or in part, of the member's right to benefits under the plan.

Notes: Reg. 8501(5) amended by P.C. 2001-957, effective as per Notes to ITA 248(1)"common-law partner".

Registered Pension Plans Technical Manual: §7.5 (benefits payable after breakdown of marriage).

Registered Plans Frequently Asked Questions: RPFAQ-2 (RPPs), q. 19 (interaction with Ontario rule for pension benefits for ex-spouse).

(6) Indirect contributions — Where an employer or an individual makes payments to a trade union or an association of employers (in this subsection referred to as the "contributing entity") to enable the contributing entity to make contributions to a pension plan, such portion of a contribution made by the contributing entity to the plan as is reasonably attributable to a payment made to the contributing entity by an employer or individual shall, for the purposes of the conditions in this Part, be considered to be a contribution made by the employer or individual, as the case may be, and not by the contributing entity.

Registered Pension Plans Technical Manual: §7.6 (indirect contributions).

(6.1) Member contributions for unfunded liability — For the purposes of the conditions in this Part (other than subparagraph 8510(9)(b)(i)), a contribution made by a member of a pension plan in respect of a defined benefit provision of the plan is deemed to be a current service contribution made by the member in respect of the member's benefits under the provision if

(a) the contribution cannot, but for this subsection, reasonably be considered to be made in respect of the member's benefits under the provision;

(b) the contribution is determined by reference to the actuarial liabilities under the provision in respect of periods before the time of the contribution; and

(c) the contribution is made pursuant to an arrangement

(i) under which all, or a significant number, of the active members of the plan are required to make similar contributions,

(ii) the main purpose of which is to ensure that the plan has sufficient assets to pay benefits under the provision, and

(iii) that is approved by the Minister.

Related Provisions: Reg. 8501(6.2) — Contribution is a prescribed eligible contribution.

Notes: Opening words amended by P.C. 2007-1443, effective June 24, 2007.

Reg. 8501(6.1) added by P.C. 2003-1497, for contributions made after 1990. It and (6.2) accommodate arrangements under defined benefit RPPs that require plan members to share in the funding of an unfunded liability.

Registered Pension Plans Technical Manual: §7.7 (member contributions for unfunded liability).

Registered Plans Directorate Actuarial Bulletins: 3R1 (what information to send when requesting Reg. 8503(5) waiver).

(6.2) Prescribed eligible contributions — For the purpose of paragraph 147.2(4)(a) of the Act, a contribution described in subsection (6.1) is a prescribed eligible contribution.

Notes: Reg. 8501(6.2) added by P.C. 2003-1497, for contributions made after 1990.

Registered Pension Plans Technical Manual: §7.7 (member contributions for unfunded liability).

(7) Benefits provided with surplus on plan wind-up — Where

(a) a single amount is paid in full or partial satisfaction of an individual's entitlement to retirement benefits (in this subsection referred to as the "commuted benefits") under a defined benefit provision of a registered pension plan,

(b) other benefits are subsequently provided to the individual under the provision as a consequence of an allocation, on full or partial wind-up of the plan, of an actuarial surplus under the provision,

(c) the other benefits include benefits (in this subsection referred to as "ancillary benefits") that, but for this subsection, would not be permissible under this Part,

(d) if the individual had previously terminated from the provision and the conditions in subsection 8304.1(14) were satisfied with respect to the termination, it is reasonable to consider that all of the ancillary benefits are in respect of periods before 1990, and

(e) the Minister has approved the application of this subsection in respect of the ancillary benefits,

for the purpose of determining whether the ancillary benefits are permissible under this Part, the individual is considered to have an entitlement under the provision to the commuted benefits.

Notes: Reg. 8501(7) added by P.C. 1998-2256, for benefits provided after 1996.

Registered Pension Plans Technical Manual: §7.8 (benefits provided with surplus on plan wind-up).

Registered Plans Frequently Asked Questions: RPFAQ-2 (RPPs), q. 5 (transfer of ancillary benefits to RRSP after commuted value transferred).

Definitions [Reg. 8501]: "active member" — Reg. 8500(1); "benefits" — Reg. 8501(5)(c); "Canada" — ITA 255, *Interpretation Act* 35(1); "common-law partnership" — ITA 248(1); "contributing entity" — Reg. 8501(6); "contribution" — Reg. 8501(6), (7); "defined benefit provision" — ITA 147.1(1), Reg. 8500(2); "employer", "individual" — ITA 248(1); "member" — ITA 147.1(1), Reg. 8300(1), 8500(2); "Minister" — ITA 248(1); "money purchase provision" — ITA 147.1(1); "prescribed", "property" — ITA 248(1); "province" — *Interpretation Act* 35(1); "registered pension plan" — ITA 248(1); "retirement benefits" — Reg. 8500(1); "revocable plan" — ITA 147.1(8), (9), 147.3(12), Reg. 8301(14)(a), 8305(2), 8408(2), 8501(2), 8503(11), (15), 8506(4), 8511(2), 8515(9); "single amount" — ITA 147.1(1); "spouse" — Reg. 8500(5); "supplemental plan" — Reg. 8501(4)(a); "surplus" — Reg. 8500(1).

8502. Conditions applicable to all plans — For the purposes of section 8501, the following conditions are applicable in respect of a pension plan:

(a) **primary purpose** — the primary purpose of the plan is to provide periodic payments to individuals after retirement and until death in respect of their service as employees;

Notes: See Notes to ITA 147.1(11) for pension plans revoked for not complying with Reg. 8502(a).

Where a self-employed professional incorporates, the plan can recognize service only from the incorporation date. Before incorporation there was no employer-employee relationship, and such period is not eligible service under Reg. 8503(3)(a): tinyurl.com/rpd-consults, "Questions from the Industry" 2003 q.3. (The person would have RRSP contribution room under ITA 146(1) instead.)

A plan for an incorporated employee can qualify: VIEWS doc 2005-0122731I7.

Registered Pension Plans Technical Manual: §8.1 (primary purpose).

(b) **permissible contributions** — each contribution made to the plan after 1990 is an amount that

(i) is paid by a member of the plan in accordance with the plan as registered, where the amount is credited to the member's account under a money purchase provision of the plan, or is paid in respect of the member's benefits under a defined benefit provision of the plan,

(ii) is paid in accordance with a money purchase provision of the plan as registered, by an employer with respect to the employer's employees or former employees,

(iii) is an eligible contribution that is paid in respect of a defined benefit provision of the plan by an employer with respect to the employer's employees or former employees,

(iv) is transferred to the plan in accordance with any of subsections 146(16), 146.3(14.1), 147(19), 147.3(1) to (8) and 147.5(21) of the Act,

(v) is acceptable to the Minister and that is transferred to the plan from a pension plan that is maintained primarily for the benefit of non-residents in respect of services rendered outside Canada, or

(v.1) is paid by the trustee of a trust described in paragraph 6802(h), where the amount would have been an eligible contribution if the amount had been paid in respect of a defined benefit provision of the plan by an employer with respect to the employer's employees or former employees,

and, for the purposes of this paragraph,

(vi) an eligible contribution is a contribution that is paid by an employer in respect of a defined benefit provision of a pension plan is where it is an eligible contribution under subsection 147.2(2) of the Act or, in the case of a plan in which Her Majesty in right of Canada or a province is a participating employer, would be an eligible contribution under subsection 147.2(2) of the Act if all amounts held to the credit of the plan in the accounts of Canada or the province were excluded from the assets of the plan, and

(vii) the portion of each contribution that is made by Her Majesty in right of Canada or of a province, or by a person described in paragraph 4802(1)(d), in respect of a defined benefit provision of the plan and that can reasonably be considered to be made with respect to one or more employees or former employees of another person is deemed to be a contribution made by that other person;

(c) **permissible benefits** — the plan does not provide for, and its terms are such that it will not under any circumstances provide for, any benefits other than benefits

(i) that are provided under one or more defined benefit provisions and are in accordance with subsection 8503(2), paragraphs 8503(3)(c) and (e) to (i) and section 8504,

(ii) that are provided under one or more money purchase provisions and are in accordance with subsection 8506(1),

(iii) that the plan is required to provide by reason of a designated provision of the law of Canada or a province, or that the plan would be required to provide if each such provision were applicable to the plan with respect to all its members, and

(iv) that the plan is required to provide to an individual who is a spouse or common-law partner or former spouse or common-law partner of a member of the plan by reason of a provision of the law of Canada or a province applicable in respect of the division of property between the member and the individual, on or after the breakdown of their marriage or common-law partnership, in settlement of rights arising out of their marriage or common-law partnership;

(d) **permissible distributions** — each distribution that is made from the plan is

(i) a payment of benefits in accordance with the plan as registered,

(ii) a transfer of property held in connection with the plan where the transfer is made in accordance with subsection 147.3(3), (4.1), (7.1) or (8) of the Act,

(iii) a return of all or a portion of the contributions made by a member of the plan or an employer who participates in the plan, where the payment is made to avoid the revocation of the registration of the plan,

(iv) a return of all or a portion of the contributions made by a member of the plan under a defined benefit provision of the plan, where the return of contributions is pursuant to an amendment to the plan that also reduces the future contributions that would otherwise be required to be made under the provision by members,

(v) a payment of interest (computed at a rate not exceeding a reasonable rate) in respect of contributions that are returned as described in subparagraph (iv),

(vi) a payment in full or partial satisfaction of the interests of a person in an actuarial surplus that relates to a defined benefit provision of the plan,

(vii) a payment to an employer of property held in connection with a money purchase provision of the plan,

(viii) where the Minister has, under subsection 8506(2.1), waived the application of the condition in paragraph 8506(2)(b.1) in respect of a money purchase provision of the plan, a payment under the provision of an amount acceptable to the Minister,

(ix) a payment, other than a payment described in subparagraph (i), with respect to a member of a single amount that the plan is required to make because of the *Pension Benefits Standards Act, 1985* or a similar law of a province, where the single amount is not transferred directly to another registered pension plan, a registered retirement savings plan or a registered retirement income fund, or

(x) the portion of the IPP minimum amount for an individual that is not described in subparagraph (i).

Notes: For purposes of (d)(v), CRA will accept any reasonable method used to credit interest: tinyurl.com/rpd-consults, "Questions from the Industry" 2003 q.10. However, this question has now been removed.

Where the value of a defined-benefit plan exceeds the cost of an annuity with the same payout, it can be paid out as a taxable lump-sum: VIEWS doc 2012-0435781C6.

CRA announced on May 15, 2009 that it was considering allowing lump-sum payments for missed pension benefits without prior CRA approval, and invited comments until May 29/09. Its revised position was announced in RPD newsletter 09-1.

Reg. 8502(d) amended by 2011 budget bill #2 (for 2012 and later tax years); P.C. 2007-1443, 2003-1497, 1995-17.

Registered Pension Plans Technical Manual: §8.4 (permissible distributions).

Registered Plans Compliance Bulletins: 8 (over-contributions to an RPP).

Registered Plans Directorate Newsletters: 91-4R (registration rules for money purchase provisions); 96-3 (flexible pension plans); 09-1 (administrative relief procedures for retroactive lump-sum catch-up payments); 20-1 (RPP annuity contracts).

(e) **payment of pension** — the plan

(i) requires that the retirement benefits of a member under each benefit provision of the plan begin to be paid not later than the end of the calendar year in which the member attains 71 years of age except that,

(A) in the case of benefits provided under a defined benefit provision, the benefits may begin to be paid at any later time that is acceptable to the Minister, if the amount of benefits (expressed on an annualized basis) payable does not exceed the amount of benefits that would be payable if payment of the benefits began at the end of the calendar year in which the member attains 71 years of age,

(B) in the case of benefits provided under a money purchase provision in accordance with paragraph 8506(1)(e.1), the benefits may begin to be paid not later than the end of the calendar year in which the member attains 72 years of age, and

(C) in the case of benefits provided under a money purchase provision in accordance with paragraph 8506(1)(e.2), the benefits may begin to be paid not later than the later of

(I) the end of the calendar year in which the member attains 71 years of age, and

(II) the end of the calendar year in which a transfer was made from the member's account to acquire rights under the VPLA fund, and

(ii) provides that retirement benefits under each benefit provision are payable not less frequently than annually;

Notes: Reg. 8502(e)(i)(C) added by 2021 budget bill #1, effective 2020. Reg. 8502(e) earlier amended by 2007 budget bill #1 (effective 2007), P.C. 2004-1508, 1998-2256.

Registered Pension Plans Technical Manual: §8.5 (payment of pension).

Registered Plans Directorate Newsletters: 91-4R (registration rules for money purchase provisions).

(f) **assignment of rights** — the plan includes a stipulation that no right of a person under the plan is capable of being assigned, charged, anticipated, given as security or surrendered, and, for the purposes of this condition,

(i) assignment does not include

(A) assignment pursuant to a decree, order or judgment of a competent tribunal or a written agreement in settlement of rights arising out of a marriage or common-law partnership between an individual and the individual's spouse or common-law partner or former spouse or common-law partner, on or after the breakdown of their marriage or common-law partnership, or

(B) assignment by the legal representative of a deceased individual on the distribution of the individual's estate, and

(ii) surrender does not include a reduction in benefits to avoid the revocation of the registration of the plan;

Related Provisions: ITA 147(2)(e) — Parallel rules for DPSPs.

Notes: Reg. 8502(f)(i)(A) amended by P.C. 2001-957, effective on the same basis as the addition of ITA 248(1)"common-law partner".

Registered Pension Plans Technical Manual: §8.6 (assignment of rights).

Registered Plans Directorate Newsletters: 91-4R (registration rules for money purchase provisions).

(g) **funding media** — the arrangement under which property is held in connection with the plan is acceptable to the Minister;

Related Provisions: Reg. 8501(2)(a) — Revocation of plan for failure to comply with conditions.

Notes: For an example of an unacceptable arrangement see VIEWS doc 2008-0274281E5.

Registered Pension Plans Technical Manual: §8.7 (funding media).

Registered Plans Directorate Newsletters: 91-4R (registration rules for money purchase provisions); 98-1 (simplified pension plans).

(h) **investments** — the property that is held in connection with the plan does not include

(i) a prohibited investment under subsection 8514(1),

(ii) at any time that the plan is subject to the *Pension Benefits Standards Act, 1985* or a similar law of a province, an investment that is not permitted at that time under such laws as apply to the plan, or

(iii) at any time other than a time referred to in subparagraph (ii), an investment that would not be permitted were the plan subject to the *Pension Benefits Standards Act, 1985*;

Related Provisions: Reg. 8501(2)(a) — Revocation of plan for failure to comply with conditions.

Notes: See Genest, "Quebec Individual Pension Plans", 19(5) *Taxation of Executive Compensation & Retirement* (Federated Press) 935-38 (Dec./Jan. 2008).

Registered Pension Plans Technical Manual: §8.8 (investments).

Registered Plans Directorate Newsletters: 91-4R (registration rules for money purchase provisions).

(i) **borrowing** — a trustee or other person who holds property in connection with the plan does not borrow money for the purposes of the plan, except where

(i) the borrowing is for a term not exceeding 90 days,

(ii) the borrowing is not part of a series of loans or other transactions and repayments, and

(iii) none of the property that is held in connection with the plan is used as security for the borrowed money (except where the borrowing is necessary to provide funds for the current payment of benefits or the purchase of annuities under the plan without resort to a distressed sale of the property that is held in connection with the plan),

or where

(iv) the money is borrowed for the purpose of acquiring real property that may reasonably be considered to be acquired for the purpose of producing income from property,

(v) the aggregate of all amounts borrowed for the purpose of acquiring the property and any indebtedness incurred as a consequence of the acquisition of the property does not exceed the cost to the person of the property, and

(vi) none of the property that is held in connection with the plan, other than the real property, is used as security for the borrowed money;

Related Provisions: ITA 248(10) — Series of transactions; Reg. 8501(2)(a) — Revocation of plan for failure to comply with conditions; Reg. 8502(i.1) — COVID-19 relief from Reg. 8502(i)(i) and (ii) in 2020-22.

Notes: See VIEWS docs 2016-0644761I7 (RPP was in violation of Reg. 8502(i); proposed cure was acceptable); 2020-0850981E5 (RPP participating in Canada Emergency Commercial Rent Assistance Program (COVID-19) violates 8502(i) but will not be revoked for this [see also Reg. 8502(i.1)]).

Registered Pension Plans Technical Manual: §8.9 (borrowing).

(i.1) **COVID-19 — borrowing** — in their application to loans that are entered into after April 2020 and before February 2022, subparagraphs (i)(i) and (ii) are to be read as follows:

(i) the loan or, if the loan is part of a series of loans or repayments, the series of loans and repayments is repaid no later than April 30, 2022, and

Notes: See Notes to Reg. 6801.1. Reg. 8502(i.1) added by P.C. 2021-522, effective June 10, 2021.

(j) **determination of amounts** — except as otherwise provided in this Part, each amount that is determined in connection with the plan is determined, where the amount is based on assumptions, using such reasonable assumptions as are acceptable to the Minister, and, where actuarial principles are applicable to the determination, in accordance with generally accepted actuarial principles;

Related Provisions: Reg. 8501(2)(a) — Revocation of plan for failure to comply with conditions.

Registered Pension Plans Technical Manual: §8.10 (determination of amounts).

Registered Plans Directorate Newsletters: 91-4R (registration rules for money purchase provisions); 94-3R1 (using assumptions to compute the present value of benefits); 95-5 (conversion of a defined benefit provision to a money purchase provision); 96-3 (flexible pension plans).

(k) **transfer of property between provisions** — property that is held in connection with a benefit provision of the plan is not made available to pay benefits under another benefit provision of the plan (including another benefit provision that replaces the first benefit provision), except where the transaction by which the property is made so available is such that if the benefit provisions were in separate registered pension plans, the transaction would constitute a transfer of property from one plan to the other in accordance with any of subsections 147.3(1) to (4.1), (6), (7.1) and (8) of the Act;

Related Provisions: Reg. 8501(2)(a) — Revocation of plan for failure to comply with conditions.

Notes: Reg. 8502(k) amended by P.C. 1995-17, for transactions in 1991 or later; and by P.C. 2003-1497, for distributions that occur after 1998, to refer to 147.3(7.1).

Registered Pension Plans Technical Manual: §6.1 (qualifying transfers); §8.11 (transfer of property between provisions).

Registered Plans Directorate Newsletters: 95-5 (conversion of a defined benefit provision to a money purchase provision); 04-1 (transfer from a defined benefit provision).

(l) **appropriate pension adjustments** — the plan terms are not such that an amount that is determined under Part LXXXIII in respect of the plan would be inappropriate having regard to the provisions of that Part read as a whole and the purposes for which the amount is determined; and

Registered Pension Plans Technical Manual: §8.12 (appropriate pension adjustments).

Registered Plans Directorate Newsletters: 91-4R (registration rules for money purchase provisions); 01-3 (tailored individual pension plan).

(m) **participants in GSRAs** — no individual who, at any time after 1993, is entitled, either absolutely or contingently, to benefits under the plan by reason of employment with an employer with whom the individual is connected is entitled at that time, either absolutely or contingently, to benefits under a government-sponsored retirement arrangement (as defined in subsection 8308.4(1)).

Related Provisions: Reg. 8501(2)(a) — Revocation of plan for failure to comply with conditions.

Notes: Reg. 8502(m) added by P.C. 1996-911, effective 1994.

Registered Pension Plans Technical Manual: §8.13 (participants in GSRAs).

Registered Plans Directorate Newsletters: 91-4R (registration rules for money purchase provisions).

Definitions [Reg. 8502]: "amount", "annuity" — ITA 248(1); "benefit provision" — Reg. 8500(1); "benefits" — Reg. 8501(5)(c); "borrowed money" — ITA 248(1); "calendar year" — *Interpretation Act* 37(1)(a); "Canada" — ITA 255, *Interpretation Act* 35(1); "common-law partnership" — ITA 248(1); "connected" — Reg. 8500(3); "contribution" — Reg. 8501(6); "defined benefit provision" — ITA 147.1(1), Reg. 8500(2);

"designated provision of the law of Canada or a province" — Reg. 8513; "eligible contribution" — Reg. 8502(b)(vi), 8510(6)(a); "employee", "employer", "employment" — ITA 248(1); "Her Majesty" — *Interpretation Act* 35(1); "IPP minimum amount" — Reg. 8500(1); "individual" — ITA 248(1); "member" — ITA 147.1(1), Reg. 8300(1), 8500(2); "Minister" — ITA 248(1); "money purchase provision" — ITA 147.1(1); "non-resident" — ITA 248(1); "participating employer" — ITA 147.1(1); "person" — ITA 248(1); "plan as registered" — ITA 147.1(15); "prohibited investment" — Reg. 8514(1); "property" — ITA 248(1); "province" — *Interpretation Act* 35(1); "registered pension plan" — ITA 248(1); "registered retirement income fund" — ITA 146.3(1), 248(1); "registered retirement savings plan" — ITA 146(1), (21.2), 147.5(12), 248(1); "retirement benefits" — Reg. 8500(1); "security" — *Interpretation Act* 35(1); "series" — ITA 248(10); "spouse" — Reg. 8500(5); "surplus" — Reg. 8500(1); "written" — *Interpretation Act* 35(1) "writing".

8503. Defined benefit provisions — (1) Net contribution accounts

— In this section and subsection 8517(2), the net contribution account of a member of a pension plan in relation to a defined benefit provision of the plan is an account that is

(a) credited with

(i) the amount of each contribution that is made by the member to the plan in respect of the provision,

(ii) each amount that is transferred on behalf of the member to the plan in respect of the provision in accordance with any of subsections 146(16), 147(19) and 147.3(2) and (5) to (7) of the Act,

(iii) such portion of each amount that is transferred to the plan in respect of the provision in accordance with subsection 147.3(3) of the Act as may reasonably be considered to derive from contributions that are made by the member to a registered pension plan or interest (computed at a reasonable rate) in respect of such contributions,

(iv) the amount of any property that was held in connection with another benefit provision of the plan and that has been made available to provide benefits under the provision, to the extent that if the provisions were in separate registered pension plans, the amount would be included in the member's net contribution account by reason of subparagraph (ii) or (iii), and

(v) interest (computed at a reasonable rate determined by the plan administrator) in respect of each period throughout which the account has a positive balance; and

(b) charged with

(i) each amount that is paid under the provision with respect to the member, otherwise than in respect of an actuarial surplus under the provision,

(ii) the amount of any property that is held in connection with the provision (other than property that is in respect of an actuarial surplus under the provision) and that is made available to provide benefits with respect to the member under another benefit provision of the plan, and

(iii) interest (computed at a reasonable rate determined by the plan administrator) in respect of each period throughout which the account has a negative balance.

Notes: Reg. 8503(1)(b)(i) and (ii) amended by P.C. 1995-17, retroactive to 1989, so that a member's net contribution account is not charged with payments made in respect of an actuarial surplus under the provision.

Registered Pension Plans Technical Manual: §9.1 (net contribution account).

Registered Plans Directorate Newsletters: 04-1 (transfer from a defined benefit provision).

(2) Permissible benefits — For the purposes of paragraph 8502(c), the following benefits may, subject to the conditions set out in respect of each benefit, be provided under a defined benefit provision of a pension plan:

(a) **lifetime retirement benefits** — lifetime retirement benefits provided to a member where the benefits are payable in equal periodic amounts, or are not so payable only by reason that

(i) the benefits payable to a member after the death of the member's spouse or common-law partner are less than the benefits that would be payable to the member were the member's spouse or common-law partner alive,

(ii) the plan provides for periodic cost-of-living adjustments to be made to the benefits, where the adjustments

(A) are determined in such a manner that they do not exceed cost-of-living adjustments warranted by increases in the Consumer Price Index after the benefits commence to be paid,

(B) consist of periodic increases at a rate not exceeding 4 per cent per annum after the time the benefits commence to be paid,

(C) are based on the rates of return on a specified pool of assets after the benefits commence to be paid, or

(D) consist of any combination of adjustments described in clauses (A) to (C),

and, in the case of adjustments described in clauses (C) and (D), the present value (at the time the member's benefits commence to be paid) of additional benefits that can reasonably be expected to be paid as a consequence of the adjustments does not exceed the greater of

(E) the present value (at the time the member's benefits commence to be paid) of additional benefits that could reasonably be expected to be paid as a consequence of adjustments warranted by increases in the Consumer Price Index after the member's benefits commence to be paid, and

(F) the present value (at the time the member's benefits commence to be paid) of additional benefits that would be paid as a consequence of adjustments at a fixed rate of 4 per cent per annum after the time the member's benefits commence to be paid,

(iii) where the plan does not provide for periodic cost-of-living adjustments to be made to the benefits, or provides only for such adjustments as are described in clause (ii)(A) or (B), the plan provides for cost-of-living adjustments to be made to the benefits from time to time at the discretion of any person, where the adjustments, together with periodic cost-of-living adjustments, if any, are warranted by increases in the Consumer Price Index after the benefits commence to be paid,

(iv) the amount of the benefits is increased as a consequence of additional lifetime retirement benefits becoming provided to the member under the provision,

(v) the amount of the benefits is determined with a reduction computed by reference to the member's age, duration of service, or both (or with any other similar reduction), and the amount is subsequently adjusted to reduce or eliminate the portion, if any, of the reduction that is not required for the benefits to comply with the conditions in paragraph (3)(c),

(vi) the amount of the benefits is determined with a reduction computed by reference to the following benefits and the amount is subsequently adjusted to reduce or eliminate the reduction:

(A) disability benefits to which the member is entitled under the *Canada Pension Plan* or a provincial pension plan as defined in section 3 of that Act,

(B) benefits to which the member is entitled under an employees' or workers' compensation law of Canada or a province in respect of an injury or disability, or

(C) benefits to which the member is entitled pursuant to a sickness or accident insurance plan or a disability insurance plan,

(vii) the amount of the benefits is determined with a reduction computed by reference to other benefits provided under the provision in respect of the member that are permissible under paragraph (c), (d), (k) or (n), and the amount is subsequently adjusted to reduce or eliminate the reduction,

(viii) the amount of the benefits is reduced as a consequence of benefits that are permissible under paragraph (c), (d), (k) or (n) becoming provided under the provision in respect of the member,

(ix) the amount of the benefits payable to the member while the member is in receipt of remuneration from a participating employer is less than the amount of the benefits that would otherwise be payable to the member if the member were not in receipt of the remuneration, or

(x) the amount of the benefits is adjusted in accordance with plan terms that were submitted to the Minister before April 19, 2000, where the benefits have commenced to be paid before 2003 and the adjustment is approved by the Minister;

(b) **bridging benefits** — bridging benefits provided to a member where

(i) the bridging benefits are payable for a period beginning no earlier than the time lifetime retirement benefits commence to be paid under the provision to the member and ending no later than the end of the month immediately following the month in which the member attains 65 years of age, and

(ii) the amount of the bridging benefits payable for a particular month does not exceed the amount that is determined for that month by the formula

$$A \times (1 - .0025 \times B) \times C \times D / 10$$

where

A is the amount (or a reasonable estimate thereof) of public pension benefits that would be payable to the member for the month in which the bridging benefits commence to be paid to the member if

(A) the member were 65 years of age throughout that month,

(B) that month were the first month for which public pension benefits were payable to the member,

(C) the member were entitled to the maximum amount of benefits payable under the *Old Age Security Act*, and

(D) the member were entitled to that proportion, not exceeding 1, of the maximum benefits payable under the *Canada Pension Plan* (or a provincial plan as defined in section 3 of the *Canada Pension Plan*) that the total of the member's remuneration for the 3 calendar years in which the remuneration is the highest is of the total of the Year's Maximum Pensionable Earnings for those 3 years (or such other proportion of remuneration to Year's Maximum Pensionable Earnings as is acceptable to the Minister),

B is

(A) except where clause (B) is applicable, the number of months, if any, from the date on which the bridging benefits commence to be paid to the member to the date on which the member attains 60 years of age, and

(B) where the member is totally and permanently disabled at the time the bridging benefits commence to be paid to the member and the member was not, at any time after 1990, connected with an employer who has participated in the plan, nil,

C is the greatest of all amounts each of which is the ratio of the Consumer Price Index for a month not before the month in which the bridging benefits commence to be paid to the member and not after the particular month, to the Consumer Price Index for the month in which the bridging benefits commence to be paid to the member, and

D is

(A) except where clause (B) is applicable, the lesser of 10 and

(I) where the member was not, at any time after 1990, connected with an employer who has participated in the plan, the aggregate of all amounts each of which is the duration (measured in years, including any fraction of a year) of a period that is pensionable service of the member under the provision, and

(II) in any other case, the aggregate that would be determined under subclause (I) if the duration of each period were multiplied by a fraction (not greater than 1) that measures the services rendered by the member throughout the period to employers who participate in the plan as a proportion of the services that would have been rendered by the member throughout the period to such employers had the member rendered services on a full-time basis, and

(B) where the member is totally and permanently disabled at the time at which the bridging benefits commence to be paid to the member and the member was not, at any time after 1990, connected with an employer who has participated in the plan, 10;

(c) **guarantee period** — retirement benefits (in this paragraph referred to as "continued retirement benefits") provided to one or more beneficiaries of a member who dies after retirement benefits under the provision commence to be paid to the member where

(i) the continued retirement benefits are payable for a period beginning after the death of the member and ending

(A) if retirement benefits permissible under paragraph (d) are provided under the provision to a spouse or common-law partner or former spouse or common-law partner of the member, no later than five years, and

(B) in any other case, no later than 15 years

after the day on which retirement benefits commence to be paid under the provision to the member, and

(ii) the aggregate amount of continued retirement benefits payable under the provision for each month does not exceed the amount of retirement benefits that would have been payable under the provision for the month to the member if the member were alive;

(d) **post-retirement survivor benefits** — retirement benefits (in this paragraph referred to as "survivor retirement benefits") provided to one or more beneficiaries of a member who dies after retirement benefits under the provision commence to be paid to the member where

(i) each beneficiary is, at the time of the member's death, a spouse, a common-law partner, a former spouse, a former common-law partner or a dependant, of the member,

(ii) the survivor retirement benefits provided to a spouse or common-law partner or former spouse or common-law partner are payable for a period beginning after the death of the member and ending with the death of the spouse or common-law partner or former spouse or common-law partner,

(iii) the survivor retirement benefits provided to a dependant are payable for a period beginning after the death of the member and ending no later than at the end of the dependant's eligible survivor benefit period,

(iv) the amount of survivor retirement benefits payable for each month to a beneficiary does not exceed 66⅔ per cent of the amount of retirement benefits that would have been payable under the provision for the month to the member if the member were alive, and

(v) the aggregate amount of survivor retirement benefits and other retirement benefits payable under the provision for each month to beneficiaries of the member does not exceed the amount of retirement benefits that would have been paya-

ble under the provision for the month to the member if the member were alive;

(e) **pre-retirement survivor benefits** — retirement benefits (in this paragraph referred to as "survivor retirement benefits") provided to one or more beneficiaries of a member who dies before retirement benefits under the provision commence to be paid to the member where

(i) no other benefits (other than benefits permissible under paragraph (g), (j), (l.1) or (n)) are payable as a consequence of the member's death,

(ii) each beneficiary is, at the time of the member's death, a spouse, a common-law partner, a former spouse, a former common-law partner or a dependant, of the member,

(iii) the survivor retirement benefits provided to a spouse or common-law partner are payable for a period beginning after the death of the member and ending with the death of the spouse or common-law partner or former spouse or common-law partner,

(iv) the survivor retirement benefits provided to a dependant are payable for a period beginning after the death of the member and ending no later than at the end of the dependant's eligible survivor benefit period,

(v) the amount of survivor retirement benefits payable for a month to a beneficiary does not exceed 66⅔ per cent of the amount that is determined in respect of the month by the formula set out in subparagraph (vi), and

(vi) the aggregate amount of survivor retirement benefits payable under the provision for a particular month to beneficiaries of the member does not exceed the amount that is determined for the particular month by the formula

$$\frac{(A + B)}{12} \times C$$

where

A is the amount (expressed on an annualized basis) of lifetime retirement benefits that accrued under the provision to the member as of the member's day of death, determined without any reduction computed by reference to the member's age, duration of service, or both, and without any other similar reduction,

B is, in the case of a member who attains 65 years of age before the member's death or who was, at any time after 1990, connected with an employer who has participated in the plan, nil, and, otherwise, the amount, if any, by which the lesser of

(A) the amount (expressed on an annualized basis) of lifetime retirement benefits that could reasonably be expected to have accrued to the member to the day on which the member would have attained 65 years of age if the member had survived to that day and continued in employment and if the member's rate of remuneration had not increased after the member's day of death, and

(B) the amount, if any, by which ½ of the Year's Maximum Pensionable Earnings for the calendar year in which the member dies exceeds such amount as is required by the Minister to be determined in respect of benefits provided, as a consequence of the death of the member, under other benefit provisions of the plan and under benefit provisions of other registered pension plans

exceeds the amount determined for A, and

C is the greatest of all amounts each of which is the ratio of the Consumer Price Index for a month not before the month in which the member dies and not after the particular month, to the Consumer Price Index for the month in which the member dies;

(f) **pre-retirement survivor benefits — alternative rule** — retirement benefits (in this paragraph referred to as "survivor benefits") provided to a beneficiary of a member who dies before retirement benefits under the defined benefit provision commence to be paid to the member where

(i) no other benefits (other than benefits permissible under paragraph (g), (j), (l.1) or (n)) are payable as a consequence of the member's death,

(ii) the beneficiary is a spouse or common-law partner or former spouse or common-law partner of the member,

(iii) the survivor benefits are payable for a period beginning not later than the later of

(A) the day that is one year after the day of death of the member, and

(B) the end of the calendar year in which the beneficiary attains 71 years of age,

and ending with the death of the beneficiary,

(iv) the survivor benefits would be in accordance with paragraph (a) if the beneficiary were a member of the plan, and

(v) the present value (at the time of the member's death) of all benefits provided as a consequence of the member's death does not exceed the present value (immediately before the member's death) of all benefits that have accrued under the provision with respect to the member to the day of the member's death;

(g) **pre-retirement survivor benefits — guarantee period** — retirement benefits provided to one or more individuals as a consequence of the death of a person who

(i) is a beneficiary of a member who died before retirement benefits under the provision commenced to be paid to the member,

(ii) was, at the time of the member's death, a spouse or common-law partner or former spouse or common-law partner of the member, and

(iii) dies after the member's death,

where the benefits would be in accordance with paragraph (c) if the person were a member of the plan;

(h) **lump-sum payments on termination** — the payment, with respect to a member in connection with the member's termination from the plan (otherwise than by reason of death), of one or more single amounts where

(i) the payments are the last payments to be made under the provision with respect to the member,

(ii) if subparagraph (iii) is not applicable, each single amount does not exceed the balance in the member's net contribution account immediately before the time of payment of the single amount, and

(iii) if

(A) the Minister has, pursuant to subsection (5), waived the application of the conditions in paragraph (4)(a) in respect of the provision, or

(B) the member's contributions under the provision for each calendar year after 1990 would have been in accordance with paragraph (4)(a) if the reference in clause (i)(B) thereof to "70 per cent" were read as a reference to "50 per cent",

each single amount does not exceed the amount that would be the balance in the member's net contribution account immediately before the time of the payment of the single amount if, for each current service contribution made by the member under the provision, the account were credited at the time of the contribution with an additional amount equal to the amount of the contribution (other than the portion of the contribution, if any, paid in respect of one or more periods that were not periods of regular employment and that would

not have been required to be paid by the member if the periods were periods of regular employment);

(i) **payment of commuted value of benefits on death before retirement** — the payment of one or more single amounts to one or more beneficiaries of a member who dies before retirement benefits under the provision commence to be paid to the member where

(i) no retirement benefits are payable as a consequence of the member's death, and

(ii) the aggregate of all amounts, each of which is such a single amount (other than the portion thereof, if any, that can reasonably be considered to be interest, computed at a rate not exceeding a reasonable rate, in respect of the period from the day of death of the member to the day the single amount is paid), does not exceed the present value, immediately before the death of the member, of all benefits that have accrued under the provision with respect to the member to the day of the member's death;

(j) **lump sum payments on death** — the payment of one or more single amounts after the death of a member where

(i) the payments are the last payments to be made under the provision with respect to the member,

(ii) if the member dies before retirement benefits under the provision commence to be paid to the member and no retirement benefits are payable as a consequence of the member's death, the aggregate amount to be paid at any time complies with whichever of the conditions in subparagraphs (h)(ii) and (iii) would be applicable if the single amounts were paid in connection with the member's termination from the plan otherwise than by reason of death, and

(iii) if subparagraph (ii) is not applicable, the aggregate amount to be paid at any time does not exceed the balance, immediately before that time, in the member's net contribution account in relation to the provision;

(k) **additional post-retirement death benefits** — retirement benefits (in this paragraph referred to as "additional death benefits") payable after the death of a member who dies after retirement benefits under the provision commence to be paid to the member where the additional death benefits are

(i) retirement benefits provided to a spouse or common-law partner or former spouse or common-law partner of the member that are in excess of the benefits that are permissible under paragraph (d), but that would be permissible under that paragraph if the reference in subparagraph (d)(iv) to "66⅔ per cent" were read as a reference to "100 per cent",

(ii) retirement benefits provided to one or more beneficiaries of the member that are in excess of the benefits that are permissible under paragraph (c), but that would be permissible under that paragraph if it were read without reference to clause (i)(A) thereof, or

(iii) a combination of retirement benefits described in subparagraphs (i) and (ii),

and where

(iv) the additional death benefits are provided in lieu of a proportion of the lifetime retirement benefits that would otherwise be payable under the provision to the member, and

(v) the present value of all benefits provided under the provision with respect to the member does not exceed the present value of the benefits that would be provided if

(A) the amount of the member's lifetime retirement benefits were determined without any reduction dependent on the benefits payable after the death of the member or on circumstances that are relevant in determining such death benefits,

(B) the maximum amount of retirement benefits that are permissible under paragraph (d) were payable to the member's spouse or common-law partner or former

Regulations

spouse or common-law partner after the death of the member, and

(C) those present values were determined as of

(I) except where subclause (II) applies, the particular time at which retirement benefits under the provision commence to be paid to the member, and

(II) where the additional death benefits become provided after the particular time, the time at which the additional death benefits become provided;

(l) **additional bridging benefits** — bridging benefits in excess of bridging benefits that are permissible under paragraph (b) (referred to in this paragraph as "additional bridging benefits") provided to a member where

(i) the additional bridging benefits would be permissible under paragraph (b) if

(A) the formula in subparagraph (b)(ii) were replaced by the formula "A/12 × C", and

(B) the description of A in subparagraph (b)(ii) were read as follows:

"A is 40% of the Year's Maximum Pensionable Earnings for the year in which the bridging benefits commence to be paid to the member,"

(ii) the additional bridging benefits are provided in lieu of all or a proportion of the benefits that would otherwise be payable under the provision with respect to the member, and

(iii) the present value (at the time retirement benefits under the provision commence to be paid to the member) of all benefits provided under the provision with respect to the member does not exceed the present value (at that time) of the benefits that would be so provided if the additional bridging benefits were not provided;

(l.1) **survivor bridging benefits** — retirement benefits (in this paragraph referred to as "survivor bridging benefits") provided to a beneficiary of a member after the death of the member where

(i) the beneficiary is a spouse or common-law partner or former spouse or common-law partner of the member,

(ii) the survivor bridging benefits are payable at the election of the beneficiary, and

(iii) the survivor bridging benefits would be in accordance with paragraph (l) if the beneficiary were a member of the plan;

(m) **commutation of benefits** — the payment with respect to a member of a single amount in full or partial satisfaction of the member's entitlement to other benefits under the provision, where the single amount does not exceed the total of

(i) the present value (at the particular time determined in accordance with subsection (2.1)) of

(A) the other benefits that, as a consequence of the payment, cease to be provided, and

(B) benefits, other than benefits referred to in clause (A), that it is reasonable to consider would cease to be provided as a consequence of the payment if

(I) where retirement benefits have not commenced to be paid under the provision to the member at the particular time, the plan provided for the retirement benefits that accrued to the member under the provision to be adjusted to reflect the increase in a general measure of wages and salaries from the particular time to the day on which the benefits commence to be paid, and

(II) the plan provided for periodic cost-of-living adjustments to be made to the retirement benefits payable under the provision to the member to reflect increases in the Consumer Price Index after the retirement benefits commence to be paid (other than increases before the particular time), and

(ii) interest (computed at a reasonable rate) from the particular time to the time the single amount is paid; and

(n) **[commutation of benefits]** — the payment, with respect to an individual after the death of a member, of a single amount in full or partial satisfaction of the individual's entitlement to other benefits under the provision, where

(i) the individual is a beneficiary of the member,

(ii) the single amount does not exceed the total of

(A) the present value (at the particular time determined in accordance with subsection (2.1)) of the other benefits that, as a consequence of the payment, cease to be provided, and

(B) interest (computed at a reasonable rate) from the particular time to the time the single amount is paid, and

(iii) if the other benefits in respect of which the single amount is paid include benefits described in paragraph (e) and the beneficiary was a spouse or common-law partner or former spouse or common-law partner of the member at the time of the member's death, the single amount is not transferred from the plan directly to another registered pension plan, a registered retirement savings plan or a registered retirement income fund except with the approval of the Minister.

Related Provisions: ITA 146(21.2) — Saskatchewan Pension Plan account deemed to be RRSP for purposes of regulations; ITA 147.5(12) — Pooled registered pension plan deemed to be RRSP for purposes of regulations; Reg. 8500(9) — Transfer of significant number of members to new pension plan; Reg. 8302(3) — Normalized pensions; Reg. 8503(2.1) — Rule for commutation of benefits under (2)(m) or (n); Reg. 8503(7.1) — Bridging benefits election; Reg. 8503(16)–(25) — Phased retirement.

Notes: See Notes to ITA 147.1(2).

"Following the release of Flexible Pension Plans Newsletter 96-3, interest in allowing employer funded optional ancillary benefits became apparent. In response, the Directorate undertook to evaluate how these changes might be achieved within the current defined benefit rules. While much analysis and discussion occurred, our effort was halted in 2005 until such time as a solution is proposed that can be accommodated by all jurisdictions. To date, there has been little progress on this issue. Consequently, the Directorate confirms that the terms of Newsletter 96-3 remain valid and in force. Newsletter 96-3 will continue to be applied to flexible plans providing Optional Ancillary Benefits to a member." (Registered Plans Administrators Notice, Oct. 29, 2009)

In (b)(ii)A(D), "provincial plan" should be "provincial pension plan". This has been pointed out to Finance.

Reg. 8503(2)(f)(iii)(B) amended by 2007 budget bill #1 to change "69" to "71" effective 2007 (in conjunction with RRSP age limit increase to 71: see ITA 146(2)(b.4)).

Reg. 8503(2) earlier amended by P.C. 2001-957 (effective 2001), P.C. 2001-153, 1998-2256 and 1995-17.

Registered Pension Plans Technical Manual: §9.2–§9.17 (permissible benefits).

Registered Plans Directorate Newsletters: 96-3 (flexible pension plans); 98-2 (treating excess member contributions under a registered pension plan); 04-1 (transfer from a defined benefit provision); 09-1 (administrative relief procedures for retroactive lump-sum catch-up payments).

Registered Plans Frequently Asked Questions: RPFAQ-2 (RPPs), q. 3 (increase to survivor pension after benefits begin); q. 10 (plan amendment altering benefits paid to retired members); q. 12 (guarantee period combined with joint survivor option); q. 15 (plan amendments to incorporate Quebec supplemental pension plan).

(2.1) Rule for commutation of benefits — For the purpose of determining the limit on a single amount that can be paid with respect to an individual under paragraph (2)(m) or (n), the particular time referred to in that paragraph is

(a) except where paragraph (b) applies, the time the single amount is paid; and

(b) an earlier time than the time the single amount is paid, where

(i) the amount is based on a determination of the actuarial value (at the earlier time) of the individual's benefits,

(ii) the use of the earlier time in determining the actuarial value

(A) is required by the *Pension Benefits Standards Act, 1985* or a similar law of a province, or

(B) is reasonable having regard to accepted actuarial practice and the circumstances in which the individual acquires the right to the payment, and

(iii) except where clause (ii)(A) applies, the earlier time is no more than two years before the time the single amount is paid.

Notes: Reg. 8503(2.1) added by P.C. 2001-153, effective 1989.

Registered Pension Plans Technical Manual: §9.18 (rule for commutation of benefits).

(3) Conditions applicable to benefits — For the purposes of subsection 8501(2) and subparagraph 8502(c)(i), the following conditions are applicable with respect to the benefits provided under each defined benefit provision of a pension plan:

(a) **eligible service** — the only lifetime retirement benefits provided under the provision to a member (other than additional lifetime retirement benefits provided to a member because the member is totally and permanently disabled at the time the member's retirement benefits commence to be paid) are lifetime retirement benefits provided in respect of one or more of the following periods (other than the portion of a period that is after the calendar year in which the member attains 71 years of age), namely,

(i) a period throughout which the member is employed in Canada by, and receives remuneration from, an employer who participates in the plan,

(ii) a period throughout which the member was employed in Canada by, and received remuneration from, a predecessor employer to an employer who participates in the plan,

(iii) an eligible period of temporary absence of the member with respect to an employer who participates in the plan or a predecessor employer to such an employer,

(iv) a period of disability of the member subsequent to a period described in subparagraph (i) where, throughout such part of the period of disability as is after 1990, the member is not connected with an employer who participates in the plan,

(v) a period in respect of which

(A) unless the provision is a provision of an individual pension plan,

(I) subparagraph (v.1) does not apply, and

(II) benefits that are attributable to employment of the member with a former employer accrued to the member under a defined benefit provision of another registered pension plan, or

(B) contributions were made by or on behalf of the member under a money purchase provision of another registered pension plan,

where the member has ceased to be a member of that other plan,

(v.1) unless the provision is a provision of an individual pension plan, a portion — determined by reference to the proportion of property that has been transferred, as described in clause (B) — of a period in respect of which

(A) benefits that are attributable to employment of the member with a former employer accrued to the member under a defined benefit provision of another registered pension plan, and

(B) pursuant to the *Pension Benefits Standards Act, 1985* or a similar law of a province, a portion of property held in connection with the benefits described in clause (A) has been transferred to the provision and the balance of property is required to be transferred to the provision at a later date,

(vi) unless the provision is a provision of an individual pension plan, a period throughout which the member was employed in Canada by a former employer where the period

was an eligibility period for the participation of the member in another registered pension plan, and

(vii) a period acceptable to the Minister throughout which the member is employed outside Canada;

(b) **benefit accruals after pension commencement** — benefits are not provided under the provision (in this paragraph referred to as the "particular provision") to a member in respect of a period that is after the day on which retirement benefits commence to be paid to the member under a defined benefit provision of

(i) the plan, or

(ii) any other registered pension plan if

(A) an employer who participated under the particular provision for the benefit of the member, or

(B) an employer who does not deal at arm's length with an employer referred to in clause (A)

has participated under the defined benefit provision of the other plan for the benefit of the member;

(c) **early retirement** — where lifetime retirement benefits commence to be paid under the provision to a member at any time before

(i) in the case of a member whose benefits are provided in respect of employment in a public safety occupation, the earliest of

(A) the day on which the member attains 55 years of age,

(B) the day on which the member has 25 years of early retirement eligibility service in relation to the provision,

(C) the day on which the aggregate of the member's age (measured in years, including any fraction of a year) and years of early retirement eligibility service in relation to the provision is equal to 75, and

(D) if the member was not, at any time after 1990, connected with any employer who has participated in the plan, the day on which the member becomes totally and permanently disabled, and

(ii) in any other case, the earliest of

(A) the day on which the member attains 60 years of age,

(B) the day on which the member has 30 years of early retirement eligibility service in relation to the provision,

(C) the day on which the aggregate of the member's age (measured in years, including any fraction of a year) and years of early retirement eligibility service in relation to the provision is equal to 80, and

(D) if the member was not, at any time after 1990, connected with any employer who has participated in the plan, the day on which the member becomes totally and permanently disabled,

the amount (expressed on an annualized basis) of lifetime retirement benefits payable to the member for each calendar year does not exceed the amount determined for the year by the formula

$$X \times (1 - .0025 \times Y)$$

where

X is the amount (expressed on an annualized basis) of lifetime retirement benefits that would be payable to the member for the year if the benefits were determined without a reduction computed by reference to the member's age, duration of service, or both, and without any other similar reduction, and

Y is the number of months in the period from the day on which lifetime retirement benefits commence to be paid to the member to the earliest of the days that would be determined under clauses (i)(A) to (C) or (ii)(A) to (C), as the case may be, if the member continued in employment with an employer who participates in the plan,

Regulations

and, for the purposes of this paragraph,

(iii) "early retirement eligibility service" of a member in relation to a defined benefit provision of a pension plan means one or more periods each of which is

(A) a period that is pensionable service of the member under the provision, or

(B) a period throughout which the member was employed by an employer who has participated in the plan or by a predecessor employer to such an employer, and

(iv) "years of early retirement eligibility service" of a member in relation to a defined benefit provision of a pension plan means the aggregate of all amounts each of which is the duration (measured in years, including any fraction of a year) of a period that is early retirement eligibility service of the member in relation to the provision;

(d) **increased benefits for disabled member** — where the amount of lifetime retirement benefits provided under the provision to a member depends on whether the member is physically or mentally impaired at the time (in this paragraph referred to as the "time of commencement") at which retirement benefits under the provision commence to be paid to the member,

(i) the amount of lifetime retirement benefits payable if the member

(A) is not totally and permanently disabled at the time of commencement, or

(B) is totally and permanently disabled at the time of commencement and was, at any time after 1990, connected with an employer who has participated in the plan

satisfies the limit that would be determined by the formula set out in paragraph (c) if the member were not impaired at the time of commencement, and

(ii) the amount of lifetime retirement benefits payable for a particular month to the member if subparagraph (i) is not applicable does not exceed the amount that is determined for the particular month by the formula

$$\frac{(A + B)}{12} \times C$$

where

A   is the amount (expressed on an annualized basis) of lifetime retirement benefits that have accrued under the provision to the member to the time of commencement, determined as if the member were not impaired at the time of commencement and without any reduction computed by reference to the member's age, duration of service, or both, and without any other similar reduction,

B   is, in the case of a member who attains 65 years of age before the time of commencement, nil, and, otherwise, the amount, if any, by which the lesser of

(A) the amount (expressed on an annualized basis) of lifetime retirement benefits that could reasonably be expected to have accrued to the member to the day on which the member would have attained 65 years of age if the member had survived to that day and continued in employment and if the member's rate of remuneration had not increased after the time of commencement, and

(B) the amount, if any, by which the Year's Maximum Pensionable Earnings for the calendar year that includes the time of commencement exceeds such amount as is required by the Minister to be determined in respect of benefits provided to the member under other benefit provisions of the plan and under benefit provisions of other registered pension plans

exceeds the amount determined for A, and

C   is the greatest of all amounts each of which is the ratio of the Consumer Price Index for a month not before the

month that includes the time of commencement and not after the particular month, to the Consumer Price Index for the month that includes the time of commencement;

(e) **pre-1991 benefits** — all benefits provided under the provision in respect of periods before 1991 are acceptable to the Minister and, for the purposes of this condition, any benefits in respect of periods before 1991 that become provided after 1988 with respect to a member who is connected with an employer who participates in the plan or was so connected at any time before the benefits become provided shall, unless the Minister is notified in writing that the benefits are provided with respect to the member, be deemed to be unacceptable to the Minister;

(f) **determination of retirement benefits** — the amount of retirement benefits provided under the provision to a member is determined in such a manner that the member's pension credit (as determined under Part LXXXIII) under the provision for a calendar year with respect to an employer is determinable at the end of the year;

(g) **benefit accrual rate** — if the amount of lifetime retirement benefits provided under the provision to a member is determined, in part, by multiplying the member's remuneration (or a function of the member's remuneration) by an annual benefit accrual rate, or in a manner that is equivalent to that calculation, the annual benefit accrual rate or the equivalent annual benefit accrual rate does not exceed

(i) in the case of a member whose benefits are provided in respect of employment in a public safety occupation and for whom the formula for determining the amount of the lifetime retirement benefits can reasonably be considered to take into account public pension benefits, 2.33 per cent, and

(ii) in any other case, 2 per cent;

(h) **increase in accrued benefits** — where the amount of lifetime retirement benefits provided to a member in respect of a calendar year depends on

(i) the member's remuneration in subsequent years, or

(ii) the average wage (or other general measure of wages and salaries) for subsequent years,

and this condition has not been waived by the Minister, the formula for determining the amount of lifetime retirement benefits is such that

(iii) the percentage increase from year to year in the amount of lifetime retirement benefits that accrued to the member in respect of the year can reasonably be expected to approximate or be less than the percentage increase from year to year in the member's remuneration or in the average wage (or other general measure of wages and salaries), as the case may be, or

(iv) the condition in subparagraph (iii) is not satisfied only by reason that the formula can reasonably be considered to have been designed taking into account the public pension benefits payable to members,

and, for the purposes of this condition, where in determining the amount of lifetime retirement benefits provided under the provision to a member there is deducted an amount described in subparagraph (j)(i), it shall be assumed that the amount so deducted is nil;

(i) where the amount of lifetime retirement benefits provided to a member in respect of a calendar year depends on the member's remuneration in other years, the formula for determining the amount of the lifetime retirement benefits is such that any increase in the amount of lifetime retirement benefits that accrued to the member in respect of the year that is attributable to increased remuneration is primarily attributable to an increase in the rate of the member's remuneration;

(j) **offset benefits** — where

(i) in determining the amount of lifetime retirement benefits provided under the provision to a member there is deducted

(A) the amount of lifetime retirement benefits provided to the member under a benefit provision of a registered pension plan, or

(B) the amount of a lifetime annuity that is provided to the member under a deferred profit sharing plan, and

(ii) a single amount is paid in full or partial satisfaction of the member's entitlement to benefits under the benefit provision referred to in clause (i)(A) or the deferred profit sharing plan referred to in clause (i)(B),

the amount that is so deducted in determining the amount of the member's lifetime retirement benefits under the defined benefit provision includes the amount of lifetime retirement benefits or lifetime annuity that may reasonably be considered to have been forgone as a consequence of the payment of the single amount;

(k) **bridging benefits — cross-plan restriction** — bridging benefits are not paid under the provision to a member who receives bridging benefits under another defined benefit provision of the plan (in this paragraph referred to as the "particular plan") or under a defined benefit provision of another registered pension plan, except that this condition is not applicable where it is waived by the Minister or where

(i) bridging benefits are paid to the member under only one defined benefit provision of the particular plan,

(ii) the decision to provide bridging benefits under the particular plan to the member was not made by the member, by persons with whom the member does not deal at arm's length or by the member and such persons, and

(iii) each employer who has participated in any registered pension plan (other than the particular plan) under a defined benefit provision of which the member receives bridging benefits

(A) has not participated in the particular plan, and

(B) has always dealt at arm's length with each employer who has participated in the particular plan,

and, for the purposes of this paragraph, bridging benefits provided under a defined benefit provision of a registered pension plan to the member do not include benefits that are provided on a basis no more favourable than an actuarially equivalent basis in lieu of all or a proportion of the benefits that would otherwise be payable under the provision with respect to the member; and

(l) **division of benefits on breakdown of the marriage or common-law partnership** — if, by reason of a provision of a law described in subparagraph 8501(5)(b)(ii), an individual who is a spouse or common-law partner or former spouse or common-law partner of a member becomes entitled to receive all or a portion of the benefits that would otherwise be payable under the defined benefit provision to the member, and paragraph 8501(5)(d) applies with respect to the benefits,

(i) the present value of benefits provided under the provision with respect to the member (including, for greater certainty, benefits provided with respect to the individual) is not increased as a consequence of the individual becoming so entitled to benefits, and

(ii) the benefits provided under the provision to the member are not, at any time, adjusted to replace, in whole or in part, the portion of the member's benefits to which the individual has become entitled.

Related Provisions: Reg. 8500(7) — Amounts allocated under money purchase provision deemed to be contribution; Reg. 8501(2)(b) — Revocation of plan for failure to comply with conditions; Reg. 8503(13) — Statutory pension plans — special rules; Reg. 8503(16)–(25) — Phased retirement; Reg. 8510(5) — Special rules — multi-employer plan; Reg. 8510(6) — Special rules — specified multi-employer plan; Reg. 8510(8) — Purchase of additional benefits — specified multi-employer plan.

Notes: Determining whether an employee can purchase past service is a question of fact, which requires review of the RPP and finding an employer-employee relationship: VIEWS doc 2003-0046891E5.

Incorporated professionals: see Reg. 8502(a) Notes. Phased retirement: see Reg. 8503(19) Notes.

Reg. 8503(3) opening words: eligible service may not include any portion of a period that is after the calendar year in which the member turns 71 (Reg. 8502(e) pension commencement deadline). This is consequential on Reg. 8503(19), which allows for continued defined benefit accruals after pension commencement (phased retirement). It is also consistent with a similar restriction on contributions under a money purchase provision in Reg. 8506(2)(c.1).

Reg. 8503(3)(a)(i): see VIEWS docs 2009-0326971C6, 2009-0326981C6.

Reg. 8503(3)(a)(vii): lifetime retirement benefits may be provided for foreign service only to the extent acceptable to CRA. See Information Circular 72-13R8, para. 8(e); Registered Plans Division Newsletter 2001-1; Whiston, "Foreign Service Finally Increases to Five Years", 11(6) *Taxation of Executive Compensation and Retirement [TECR]* (Federated Press) 239-44 (Feb. 2000).

Reg. 8503(3)(e): for the administrative conditions "acceptable to the Minister", see Registered Plans Division Newsletter 99-1; Woodhead, "Revenue Canada Imposes New Restrictions on Past Service Benefits", 10(9) *TECR* 140-43 (May 1999).

Reg. 8503(3)(g): With the higher accrual rate, a pension plan for a "public safety occupation" (Reg. 8500(1)) can allow PSO employees to retire 5 years earlier than other plan members (see also Reg. 8503(3)(c)(i)). First added in 2003 to allow pension benefits for firefighters to be increased within an integrated plan structure.

Reg. 8503(3) amended by 2021 budget bill #1, effective March 19, 2019, but the changes do not apply to a period that was pensionable service (as defined in Reg. 8500(1)) in respect of a member under a defined benefit provision of an individual pension plan before March 19, 2019: "unless the provision is a provision of an individual pension plan" added to (a)(v)(A) opening words (replacing "both"), and to (a)(v.1) and (a)(vi) opening words.

Reg. 8503(3)(a)(v)(A)(I) and (a)(v.1) added by 2017 budget bill #2, for transfers of property after 2012. Reg. 8503(3) earlier amended by 2007 budget bill #2, P.C. 2005-150, 2003-1920, 2001-957, 2001-153.

Information Circulars: 72-13R8: Employees' pension plans; 98-2: Prescribed compensation for RPPs, paras. 8, 32.

Registered Pension Plans Technical Manual: §1.45 (totally and permanently disabled); §10.1–§10.12 (conditions applicable to benefits).

Registered Plans Directorate Newsletters: 92-8R (eligible service); 92-12 (commutation and opting out of a pension plan); 93-2 (foreign service newsletter); 99-1 (proportionality condition for pre-1990 pension benefits); 2000-1 (foreign service newsletter update); 14-1 (reviewing earnings and service for IPPs).

Registered Plans Frequently Asked Questions: RPFAQ-2 (RPPs), q. 1 ("growing in" rule and Reg. 8503(3)(c)); q. 2 ("early retirement eligibility service" in Reg. 8503(3)(c)(iii)); q. 4 (application of Reg. 8503(3)(g)); q. 15 (plan amendments to incorporate Quebec supplemental pension plan); q. 16 (benefit accrual rates).

(4) Additional conditions — For the purposes of section 8501, the following conditions are applicable in respect of each defined benefit provision of a pension plan:

(a) **member contributions** — where members are required or permitted to make contributions under the provision,

(i) the aggregate amount of current service contributions to be made by a member in respect of a calendar year after 1990, no part of which is a period of disability or an eligible period of reduced pay or temporary absence of the member, does not exceed the lesser of

(A) 9 per cent of the aggregate of all amounts each of which is the member's compensation for the year from an employer who participates in the plan in the year for the benefit of the member, and

(B) the aggregate of $1,000 and 70 per cent of the aggregate of all amounts each of which is the amount that would be the member's pension credit (as determined under Part LXXXIII) for the year under the provision with respect to an employer if section 8302 were read without reference to paragraphs (2)(b) and (3)(g) thereof,

(ii) the method for determining current service contributions to be made by a member in respect of a calendar year that includes a period of disability or an eligible period of reduced pay or temporary absence of the member (referred to in this subparagraph as a "period of reduced services") is consistent with that used for determining contributions in respect of years described in subparagraph (i), except that the

Regulations

member may be permitted or required to make, in respect of a period of reduced services, current service contributions not exceeding the amount reasonably necessary to fund the member's benefits in respect of the period of reduced services, and

(iii) the aggregate amount of contributions to be made by a member in connection with benefits that, as a consequence of a transaction, event or circumstance occurring at a particular time, become provided under the provision in respect of periods before that time does not exceed the amount reasonably necessary to fund such benefits;

(b) **pre-payment of member contributions** — the contributions that are made under the provision by a member in respect of a calendar year are not paid before the year;

(c) **reduction in benefits and return of contributions** — where the plan is not established by an enactment of Canada or a province, it includes a stipulation that permits, for the purpose of avoiding revocation of the registration of the plan,

(i) the plan to be amended at any time to reduce the benefits provided under the provision with respect to a member, and

(ii) a contribution that is made under the provision by a member or an employer to be returned to the person who made the contribution

which stipulation may provide that an amendment to the plan, or a return of contributions, is subject to the approval of the authority administering the *Pension Benefits Standards Act, 1985* or a similar law of a province;

(d) **undue deferral of payment** — each single amount that is payable after the death of a member is paid as soon as is practicable after the member's death (or, in the case of a single amount permitted by reason of paragraph (2)(j), after all other benefits have been paid);

(e) where additional lifetime retirement benefits are provided under the provision to a member because the member is totally and permanently disabled, the additional benefits are not paid before the plan administrator has received from a medical doctor or a nurse practitioner who is licensed to practise under the laws of a province or of the place where the member resides a written report providing the information on the medical condition of the member taken into account by the administrator in determining that the member is totally and permanently disabled; and

(f) where lifetime retirement benefits are provided under the provision to a member in respect of a period of disability of the member, the benefits, to the extent that they would not be in accordance with paragraph (3)(a) if that paragraph were read without reference to subparagraph (iv) thereof, are not paid before the plan administrator has received from a medical doctor or a nurse practitioner who is licensed to practise under the laws of a province or of the place where the member resides a written report providing the information on the medical condition of the member taken into account by the administrator in determining that the period is a period of disability.

Related Provisions: Reg. 8501(2)(b) — Revocation of plan for failure to comply with conditions; Reg. 8503(5) — Minister may waive member contribution conditions; Reg. 8509(10.1) — Conditions inapplicable for pre-1992 plans; Reg. 8510(6) — Special rules — specified multi-employer plan.

Notes: Reg. 8503(4)(e) and (f) amended by 2017 budget bill #2 to add "or a nurse practitioner", for reports made after Sept. 7, 2017.

Reg. 8503(4)(c) amended by P.C. 1995-17, retroactive to 1989, to exempt legislated plans from the stipulation, and to allow the stipulation to provide that an amendment or return of contribution is subject to the approval of the authority administering the pension benefit standards legislation. (Reg. 8509(10.1) exempts pre-1992 plans and replacement plans from the stipulation.)

Original Reg. 8503(4)(e) and (f) repealed by P.C. 1995-17 retroactive to their introduction (1989), and new Reg. 8503(4)(e) and (f) added effective for benefits that begin to be paid after April 5, 1994.

Registered Pension Plans Technical Manual: §1.22 (eligible period of reduced pay); §11.1–§11.5 (additional contributions).

Registered Plans Directorate Actuarial Bulletins: 3R1 (what information to send when requesting Reg. 8503(5) waiver).

Registered Plans Directorate Newsletters: 96-3 (flexible pension plans); 04-1 (transfer from a defined benefit provision).

(5) Waiver of member contribution conditions — The Minister may waive the conditions in paragraph (4)(a) where member contributions under a defined benefit provision of a pension plan are determined in a manner acceptable to the Minister and it is reasonable to expect that, on a long-term basis, the aggregate of the regular current service contributions made under the provision by all members will not exceed ½ of the amount that is required to fund the aggregate benefits in respect of which those contributions are made.

Registered Pension Plans Technical Manual: §11.6 (waiver of member contribution condition).

Registered Plans Directorate Actuarial Bulletins: 3R1 (what information to send when requesting Reg. 8503(5) waiver).

(6) Pre-retirement death benefits — A pension plan may provide, in the case of a member who dies before retirement benefits under a defined benefit provision of the plan commence to be paid to the member but after becoming eligible to have retirement benefits commence to be paid, benefits under the provision to the beneficiaries of the member where the benefits would be in accordance with subsection (2) if retirement benefits under the provision had commenced to be paid to the member immediately before the member's death.

Related Provisions: Reg. 8501(3) — Conditions inapplicable where inconsistent with 8503(6).

Registered Pension Plans Technical Manual: §11.7 (pre-retirement death benefits).

(7) Commutation of lifetime retirement benefits — Where a pension plan permits a member to receive a single amount in full or partial satisfaction of the member's entitlement to lifetime retirement benefits under a defined benefit provision of the plan, the following rules apply:

(a) the condition in subparagraph (2)(b)(i) that the payment of bridging benefits under the provision not commence before lifetime retirement benefits commence to be paid under the provision to the member is not applicable where, before the member's lifetime retirement benefits commence to be paid, a single amount is paid in full satisfaction of the member's entitlement to the lifetime retirement benefits; and

(b) such part of the member's lifetime retirement benefits as remains payable after a single amount is paid in full satisfaction of the member's entitlement to lifetime retirement benefits that would otherwise be payable after the member attains a particular age shall be deemed, for the purposes of the conditions in this section, to be lifetime retirement benefits and not to be bridging benefits.

Registered Pension Plans Technical Manual: §11.8 (commutation of lifetime retirement benefits).

(7.1) Bridging benefits and election — Where a pension plan permits a member, or a spouse or common-law partner or former spouse or common-law partner of the member, to elect to receive benefits described in any of paragraphs (2)(b), (l) or (l.1) under a defined benefit provision of the plan on a basis no more favourable than an actuarially equivalent basis in lieu of all or a proportion of the benefits that would otherwise be payable under the provision with respect to the member, the following rules apply:

(a) the condition in subparagraph (2)(b)(i) that the payment of bridging benefits under the provision not commence before lifetime retirement benefits commence to be paid under the provision to the member does not apply if, as a consequence of the election, no lifetime retirement benefits remain payable under the provision to the member; and

(b) for the purpose of determining whether retirement benefits provided under the provision to beneficiaries of the member are in accordance with paragraphs (2)(c), (d) and (k), the election may be disregarded.

Notes: Reg. 8503(7.1) added by P.C. 2001-153, effective June 5, 1997.

Opening words of Reg. 8503(7.1) amended by P.C. 2001-957 to add reference to "common-law partner", effective as per Notes to ITA 248(1)"common-law partner".

Registered Pension Plans Technical Manual: §11.9 (bridging benefits and elections).

(8) Suspension or cessation of pension — A pension plan may provide for

(a) the suspension of payment of a member's retirement benefits under a defined benefit provision of the plan where

(i) the retirement benefits payable to the member after the suspension are not altered by reason of the suspension, or

(ii) subsection (9) is applicable in respect of the member's retirement benefits; and

(b) the cessation of payment of any additional benefits that are payable to a member under a defined benefit provision of the plan because of a physical or mental impairment of the member or the termination of the member's employment under a downsizing program (within the meaning assigned by subsection 8505(1)).

Related Provisions: Reg. 8501(3) — Conditions inapplicable where inconsistent with 8503(8).

Notes: Reg. 8503(8)(b) amended by P.C. 1995-17, retroactive to 1989, to add reference to termination under a downsizing program.

Registered Pension Plans Technical Manual: §11.10 (suspension or cessation of pension).

(9) Re-employed member — Subject to subsection (10), where a pension plan provides, in the case of a member who becomes an employee of a participating employer after the member's retirement benefits under a defined benefit provision of the plan have commenced to be paid, that

(a) payment of the member's retirement benefits under the provision is suspended while the member is employed by a participating employer, and

(b) the amount of retirement benefits payable to the member after the suspension is redetermined

(i) to include benefits in respect of all or any part of the period throughout which payment of the member's benefits was suspended,

(i.1) where the retirement benefits payable under the provision to the member after the suspension are not adjusted by any cost-of-living or similar adjustments in respect of the period throughout which payment of the member's benefits was suspended, to take into account the member's remuneration from the employer for the period throughout which payment of the benefits was suspended,

(ii) where the member was totally and permanently disabled at the time the member's retirement benefits commenced to be paid, to include benefits in respect of all or a part of the period of disability of the member,

(iii) where the amount of the member's retirement benefits was previously determined with a reduction computed by reference to the member's age, duration of service, or both, or with any other similar reduction, by redetermining the amount of the reduction, or

(iv) where payment of the member's retirement benefits resumes after the member attains 65 years of age, by applying an adjustment for the purpose of compensating, in whole or in part, for the payments forgone by the member after attaining 65 years of age,

the following rules apply:

(c) the condition in paragraph (3)(b) is not applicable in respect of benefits provided under the provision to the member in respect of a period throughout which payment of the member's benefits is suspended,

(d) where the member was totally and permanently disabled at the time the member's retirement benefits commenced to be paid, the condition in paragraph (3)(b) is not applicable in respect of benefits provided under the provision to the member in respect of a period of disability of the member,

(e) the conditions in paragraphs (2)(b) and (3)(c) and (d) and section 8504 are applicable in respect of benefits payable under the provision to the member after a suspension of the member's retirement benefits as if the member's retirement benefits had not previously commenced to be paid,

(f) for the purpose of paragraph 8502(c) as it applies in respect of benefits provided under the provision on the death of the member during or after a period throughout which payment of the member's benefits is suspended, subsections (2) and (6) are applicable as if the member's retirement benefits had not commenced to be paid before the period, and

(g) the provisions in paragraph (2)(m), Part LXXXIII and subsection 8517(4) that depend on whether the member's retirement benefits have commenced to be paid apply to past service events, commutations and transfers occurring in the period in which the member's benefits are suspended as if the member's benefits had not previously commenced to be paid.

Related Provisions: Reg. 8503(11.1) — Rules for member aged 70–71 in 2007.

Notes: Reg. 8503(9)(g) added by 2007 budget bill #2, for benefits provided or payable after 2007.

Reg. 8503(9)(b)(i.1) added by P.C. 1995-17, retroactive to 1989.

Registered Pension Plans Technical Manual: §11.11 (re-employed member).

(10) Re-employed member — special rules not applicable — Subsection (9) does not apply in respect of benefits provided under a defined benefit provision of a pension plan to a member unless the terms of the plan that provide for the redetermination of the amount of the member's retirement benefits do not apply where retirement benefits have, at any time, been paid under the provision to the member while the member was an employee of a participating employer.

Related Provisions: Reg. 8503(11.1) — Rules for member aged 70–71 in 2007.

Registered Pension Plans Technical Manual: §11.12 (re-employed member — rules not applicable).

(11) Re-employed member — anti-avoidance — Where a member of a registered pension plan has become an employee of a participating employer after the member's retirement benefits under a defined benefit provision of the plan have commenced to be paid and it is reasonable to consider that one of the main reasons for the employment of the member is to enable the member to benefit from terms of the plan that provide for a redetermination of the amount of the member's retirement benefits provided in respect of a period before the benefits commenced to be paid, the plan becomes a revocable plan at the time the payment of the member's benefits resumes.

Related Provisions: ITA 147.1(8), (9), 147.3(12), Reg. 8301(14)(a), 8305(2), 8408(2), 8501(2), 8503(15), 8506(4), 8511(2), 8515(9) — Other ways plan becomes revocable plan; Reg. 8503(11.1) — Special rules for member aged 70–71 in 2007.

Notes: For the meaning of "one of the main reasons" see Notes to ITA 83(2.1).

Registered Pension Plans Technical Manual: §11.13 (re-employed member — anti-avoidance).

(11.1) Special rules for member aged 70 or 71 in 2007 — Where

(a) a member of a registered pension plan attained 69 years of age in 2005 or 2006,

(b) the member's retirement benefits under a defined benefit provision of the plan commenced to be paid to the member in the year in which the member attained 69 years of age,

(c) the member's retirement benefits are suspended as of any particular time in 2007, and

(d) the member was employed with a participating employer from the time the member's retirement benefits commenced to be paid to the particular time,

Regulations

the following rules apply:

(e) subsections (9) and (11) shall apply with respect to the member as though the member became an employee of the participating employer at the particular time, and

(f) for the purpose of subsection (10), retirement benefits paid under the provision to the member before the particular time shall be disregarded.

Notes: Reg. 8503(11.1) added by 2007 budget bill #1, effective 2007. It relates to the increase in RRSP age limit from 69 to 71 (see ITA 146(2)(b.4)).

(12) Limits dependent on Consumer Price Index — Benefits provided under a defined benefit provision of a pension plan that are benefits to which a condition in any of subparagraphs (2)(b)(ii) and (e)(v) and (vi) and (3)(d)(ii) is applicable shall be deemed to comply with the condition where they would so comply if the Consumer Price Index ratio computed as part of the formula that applies for the purpose of the condition were replaced by a substantially similar measure of the change in the Consumer Price Index.

Registered Pension Plans Technical Manual: §11.14 (limits dependent on Consumer Price Index).

(13) Statutory plans — special rules — Notwithstanding subsection (3),

(a) for the purposes of the condition in paragraph (3)(b) as it applies in respect of benefits provided under the pension plan established by the *Public Service Superannuation Act*, the reference to "any other registered pension plan" in subparagraph (3)(b)(ii) does not include the pension plans established by the *Canadian Forces Superannuation Act* and the *Royal Canadian Mounted Police Superannuation Act*; and

(b) the condition in paragraph (3)(c) does not apply in respect of benefits provided under the pension plan established by the *Canadian Forces Superannuation Act*.

Registered Pension Plans Technical Manual: §11.15 (statutory plans — special rules).

(14) Artificially reduced pension adjustment — Where

(a) the amount of lifetime retirement benefits provided under a defined benefit provision of a registered pension plan to a member depends on the member's remuneration,

(b) remuneration (in this subsection referred to as "excluded remuneration") of certain types is disregarded for the purpose of determining the amount of the member's lifetime retirement benefits, and

(c) it can reasonably be considered that one of the main reasons that remuneration in the form of excluded remuneration was paid to the member by an employer at any time was to artificially reduce a pension credit of the member under the provision with respect to the employer,

the following rules apply for the purposes of the conditions in subsection 8504(1):

(d) the member shall be deemed to have been connected with the employer while the member was employed by the employer, and

(e) the member shall be deemed not to have received such remuneration as is excluded remuneration.

Notes: For the meaning of "one of the main reasons" in para. (c), see Notes to ITA 83(2.1).

Registered Pension Plans Technical Manual: §1.14 (connected person); §11.16 (artificially reduced pension adjustment).

(15) Past service employer contributions — Where

(a) a contribution that is made by an employer to a registered pension plan is made, in whole or in part, in respect of benefits (in this subsection referred to as "past service benefits") provided under the plan to a member in respect of a period before 1990 and before the calendar year in which the contribution is made,

(b) the contribution is made

(i) after December 10, 1989, or

(ii) before December 10, 1989 where the contribution has not, before that date, been approved by the Minister under paragraph 20(1)(s) of the Act, and

(c) it is reasonable to consider that all or substantially all of such portion of the contribution as is in respect of past service benefits was paid by the employer, with the consent of the member, in lieu of a payment or other benefit to which the member would otherwise be entitled,

the plan becomes, for the purposes of paragraph 147.1(11)(c) of the Act, a revocable plan on the later of December 11, 1989 and the day immediately before the day on which the contribution is made.

Related Provisions: ITA 147.1(8), (9), 147.3(12), Reg. 8301(14)(a), 8305(2), 8408(2), 8501(2) 8503(11), 8506(4), 8511(2), 8515(9) — Other ways plan becomes revocable plan; Reg. 8505(8) — Exemption from past service contribution rule.

Notes: CRA considers that "substantially all" means 90% or more.

For discussion of Reg. 8503(15), see Randy Bauslaugh & Barbara Austin, "Trading Surplus and Other Benefits for Pension Benefits", 9(6) *Taxation of Executive Compensation and Retirement* (Federated Press) 91–95 (Feb. 1998).

Registered Pension Plans Technical Manual: §11.17 (past service employer contribution).

(16) [Phased retirement benefits] Definitions — The following definitions apply in this subsection and in subsections (17) to (23).

"qualifying period" of a member under a defined benefit provision of a pension plan means a period throughout which the member is employed by an employer who participates in the plan but does not include any period that is before the day that is the first day, on or after the later of the following days, in respect of which retirement benefits are provided under the provision to the member:

(a) the day on which retirement benefits first commenced to be paid to the member under the provision; and

(b) the member's specified eligibility day under the provision.

"specified eligibility day" of a member under a defined benefit provision of a pension plan means the earlier of

(a) the later of

(i) the day on which the member attains 55 years of age, and

(ii) the day on which the member attains the earliest age at which payment of the member's lifetime retirement benefits may commence under the terms of the provision without a reduction computed by reference to the member's age, duration of service, or both (and without any other similar reduction), otherwise than because of the member being totally and permanently disabled; and

(b) the day on which the member attains 60 years of age.

Notes: See Notes to Reg. 8503(19). Reg. 8503(16) added by 2007 budget bill #2, effective for benefits that are provided or payable after 2007.

Registered Pension Plans Technical Manual: §11.18 (definitions for purpose of phased retirement benefits).

(17) Bridging benefits payable on a stand-alone basis — The condition in subparagraph (2)(b)(i) that bridging benefits be payable to a member under a defined benefit provision of a pension plan for a period beginning no earlier than the time lifetime retirement benefits commence to be paid under the provision to the member does not apply where the following conditions are satisfied:

(a) the bridging benefits do not commence to be paid before the member's specified eligibility day under the provision;

(b) the plan provides that bridging benefits are payable under the provision to the member only for calendar months

(i) at any time in which the member is employed by an employer who participates in the plan, or

(ii) that begin on or after the time the member's lifetime retirement benefits under the provision commence to be paid;

(c) the member was not, at any time before the time at which the bridging benefits commence to be paid, connected with an employer who participates in the plan; and

(d) the plan is not a designated plan.

Related Provisions: Reg. 8503(18) — Application rules; Reg. 8503(23) — Cross-plan rules; Reg. 8507(3)(a)(vii)(A) — Periods of parenting.

Notes: Reg. 8503(17) added by 2007 budget bill #2, effective for benefits that are provided or payable after 2007. See Notes to Reg. 8503(19).

Registered Pension Plans Technical Manual: §11.19 (bridging benefits payable on a stand-alone basis).

(18) Rules of application — Where bridging benefits under a defined benefit provision of a pension plan commence to be paid to a member in circumstances to which subsection (17) applies, the following rules apply:

(a) if the member dies before lifetime retirement benefits under the provision commence to be paid to the member, subsections (2) and (6) apply in respect of benefits provided under the provision on the death of the member as if the bridging benefits had not commenced to be paid before the member's death; and

(b) the provisions in paragraph (2)(m), Part LXXXIII and subsection 8517(4) that depend on whether the member's retirement benefits have commenced to be paid apply to past service events, commutations and transfers occurring before lifetime retirement benefits under the provision commence to be paid to the member as if the bridging benefits had not commenced to be paid.

Notes: Reg. 8503(18) added by 2007 budget bill #2, for benefits provided or payable after 2007.

Registered Pension Plans Technical Manual: §11.20 (rules of application).

(19) Benefit accruals after pension commencement [phased retirement] — Paragraph (3)(b) does not apply to retirement benefits (in this subsection and in subsections (20) and (21) referred to as "additional benefits") provided under a defined benefit provision of a pension plan to a member of the plan if the following conditions are satisfied:

(a) the additional benefits are provided in respect of all or part of a qualifying period of the member under the provision;

(b) the amount of retirement benefits payable to the member under the provision for each whole calendar month in the qualifying period does not exceed 5% of the amount (expressed on an annualized basis) of retirement benefits that have accrued under the provision to the member to the beginning of the month, determined without a reduction computed by reference to the member's age, duration of service, or both, and without any other similar reduction (except that, if the plan limits the amount of pensionable service of a member or prohibits the provision of benefits in respect of periods after a member attains a specific age or combination of age and pensionable service, this condition does not apply to any calendar month in respect of which no benefits can be provided to the member because of the limit or prohibition, as the case may be);

(c) no part of the additional benefits are provided as a consequence of a past service event, unless the benefits are provided in circumstances to which subsection 8306(1) would apply if no qualifying transfers were made in connection with the past service event;

(d) the member was not, at any time before the additional benefits become provided, connected with an employer who participates in the plan; and

(e) the plan is not a designated plan.

Related Provisions: Reg. 8503(23) — Cross-plan rules; Reg. 8507(3)(a)(vii)(B) — Periods of parenting.

Notes: Reg. 8503(16)-(25) are part of the rules for "phased retirement", announced in the March 19, 2007 federal budget. The pension side of these rules is in s. 16.1 of the *Pension Benefit Standards Act, 1985*, enacted by 2007 budget bill #2, Part 7. Employees under provincial jurisdiction (as most are) must wait until their province makes similar amendments to its *Pension Benefits Standards Act*.

See "What is phased retirement?", tinyurl.com/phased-retire.

See also Marcel Théroux, "Phased Retirement Regs", 16(2) *Canadian Tax Highlights* (ctf.ca) 3-4 (Feb. 2008).

Reg. 8503(19) added by 2007 budget bill #2, effective for benefits that are provided or payable after 2007.

Registered Pension Plans Technical Manual: §11.21 (benefit accruals after pension commitment).

Registered Plans Frequently Asked Questions: RPFAQ-2 (RPPs), q. 26 (phased retirement).

(20) Redetermination of benefits — Where the amount of retirement benefits payable under a defined benefit provision of a pension plan to a member is redetermined to include additional benefits provided to the member in respect of a qualifying period of the member under the provision, the conditions in paragraph (2)(b) and section 8504 apply in respect of benefits payable under the provision to the member after the redetermination as if the member's retirement benefits had first commenced to be paid at the time of the redetermination.

Related Provisions: Reg. 8503(19) — Meaning of "additional benefits"; Reg. 8503(22) — Anti-avoidance.

Notes: Reg. 8503(20) added by 2007 budget bill #2, for benefits provided or payable after 2007. See Notes to Reg. 8503(19).

Registered Pension Plans Technical Manual: §11.22 (redetermination of benefits).

(21) Rules of application — Where additional benefits are provided under a defined benefit provision of a pension plan to a member in respect of a qualifying period of the member under the provision, the following rules apply:

(a) if the qualifying period ends as a consequence of the member's death, subsections (2) and (6) apply in respect of benefits provided under the provision on the death of the member as if the member's retirement benefits had not commenced to be paid before the member's death; and

(b) the provisions in paragraph (2)(m), Part LXXXIII and subsection 8517(4) that depend on whether the member's retirement benefits have commenced to be paid apply to past service events, commutations and transfers occurring in the qualifying period as if the member's retirement benefits had not commenced to be paid.

Related Provisions: Reg. 8503(19) — Meaning of "additional benefits"; Reg. 8503(22) — Anti-avoidance.

Notes: Reg. 8503(21) added by 2007 budget bill #2, for benefits provided or payable after 2007.

Registered Pension Plans Technical Manual: §11.23 (rules of application).

(22) Anti-avoidance — Subsections (20) and (21) do not apply where it is reasonable to consider that one of the main reasons for the provision of additional benefits to the member is to obtain the benefit of any of those subsections.

Notes: For the meaning of "one of the main reasons" see Notes to ITA 83(2.1).

Reg. 8503(22) added by 2007 budget bill #2, for benefits provided or payable after 2007.

Registered Pension Plans Technical Manual: §11.24 (anti-avoidance).

(23) Cross-plan rules — Where a member is provided with benefits under two or more associated defined benefit provisions, the determination of whether the conditions in subsections (17) and (19) are satisfied in respect of benefits payable or provided to the member under a particular associated provision shall be made on the basis of the following assumptions:

(a) benefits payable to the member under each of the other associated provisions were payable under the particular associated provision;

(b) if, before the member's specified eligibility day (determined without reference to this paragraph) under the particular associated provision, the member had commenced to receive retirement benefits under another associated provision on or after the member's specified eligibility day under that provision, the member's specified eligibility day under the particular associated provision were the member's specified eligibility day under that other associated provision; and

(c) if one or more of the other associated provisions is in a designated plan, the plan that includes the particular provision were also a designated plan.

Related Provisions: Reg. 8503(24), (25) — Meaning of "associated".

Notes: Reg. 8503(23) added by 2007 budget bill #2, effective for benefits that are provided or payable after 2007. See Notes to Reg. 8503(19).

Registered Pension Plans Technical Manual: §11.25 (cross-plan rules).

(24) Associated defined benefit provisions — For the purpose of subsection (23), a defined benefit provision is associated with another defined benefit provision (other than a provision that is not in a registered pension plan) if

(a) the provisions are in the same pension plan; or

(b) the provisions are in separate pension plans and

(i) there is an employer who participates in both plans, or

(ii) an employer who participates in one of the plans does not deal at arm's length with an employer who participates in the other plan.

Related Provisions: Reg. 8503(25) — Exception.

Notes: Reg. 8503(24) added by 2007 budget bill #2, effective for benefits that are provided or payable after 2007.

Registered Pension Plans Technical Manual: §11.26 (associated defined benefit provisions).

(25) Subsec. (24) not applicable — A particular defined benefit provision of a pension plan is not associated with a defined benefit provision of another pension plan if it is unreasonable to expect the benefits under the particular provision to be coordinated with the benefits under the other provision and the Minister has agreed not to treat the particular provision as being associated with the other provision.

Notes: Reg. 8503(25) added by 2007 budget bill #2, effective for benefits that are provided or payable after 2007. See Notes to Reg. 8503(19).

Registered Pension Plans Technical Manual: §11.26 (associated defined benefit provisions).

(26) IPP — minimum withdrawal — An individual pension plan becomes a revocable plan at the end of a year if

(a) a person who is a member or a beneficiary, in respect of the plan, who was, at the time of the member's death, a spouse or common-law partner of the member, is in receipt of retirement benefits under the terms of the plan;

(b) the person has attained 71 years of age before the year; and

(c) the plan has not paid in the year an amount to the person equal to the greater of the retirement benefits payable to the person for the year and the IPP minimum amount for the person for the year.

Notes: See Notes to Reg. 8515(1) re IPPs. On interaction with provincial pension legislation see VIEWS doc 2012-0435731C6.

Reg. 8503(26) added by 2011 budget bill #2, for 2012 and later taxation years.

Registered Plans Directorate Newsletters: 14-2 (IPP minimum amount).

Registered Pension Plans Technical Manual: §11.27 (IPP — minimum withdrawal).

Definitions [Reg. 8503]: "additional bridging benefits" — Reg. 8503(2)(l); "additional death benefits" — Reg. 8503(2)(k); "administrator" — ITA 147.1(1); "aggregate" — Reg. 8509(2)(c)(i); "amount" — Reg. 8509(2)(o)(ii); "annuity" — ITA 248(1); "any other registered pension plan" — Reg. 8503(13)(a); "arm's length" — ITA 251(1); "associated" — Reg. 8503(24), (25); "average wage" — ITA 147.1(1); "beneficiary", "benefit provision" — Reg. 8500(1); "benefit year" — Reg. 8504(6); "benefits" — Reg. 8501(5)(c); "bridging benefits" — Reg. 8500(1), 8503(7)(b); "bridging period" — Reg. 8504(5); "calendar year" — Interpretation Act 37(1)(a); "Canada" — ITA 255, Interpretation Act 35(1); "commencement" — Interpretation Act 35(1); "common-law partner" — ITA 248(1); "compensation" — ITA 147.1(1); "compensation year" — Reg. 8504(2)(b)J; "connected" — Reg. 8500(3); "consequence of the death", "consequence of the member's death" — ITA 248(8); "Consumer Price Index" — Reg. 8500(1); "continued retirement benefits" — Reg. 8503(2)(c); "contribution" — Reg. 8501(6), (7); "death benefit" — ITA 248(1); "deferred profit sharing plan" — ITA 147(1), 248(1); "defined benefit limit" — ITA 147.1(1), Reg. 8500(2); "dependant", "designated plan" — Reg. 8500(1); "early retirement eligibility service" — Reg. 8503(3)(c)(iii); "eligible period of reduced pay", "eligible period of temporary absence", "eligible survivor benefit period" — Reg. 8500(1); "employed", "employee", "employer", "employment" — ITA 248(1); "excluded remuneration" —

Reg. 8503(14)(b); "highest average compensation" — Reg. 8504(2); "IPP minimum amount" — Reg. 8500(1); "individual" — ITA 248(1); "individual pension plan" — Reg. 8300(1), 8500(2); "lifetime retirement benefits" — Reg. 8500(1); "member" — ITA 147.1(1), Reg. 8300(1), 8500(2); "member's total indexed compensation" — Reg. 8504(2); "Minister" — ITA 248(1); "money purchase provision" — ITA 147.1(1); "month" — Interpretation Act 35(1); "net contribution account" — Reg. 8503(1); "participating employer" — ITA 147.1(1); "particular plan" — Reg. 8503(3)(k); "particular provision" — Reg. 8503(3)(b); "past service benefits" — Reg. 8503(15)(a); "past service event" — ITA 147.1(1), Reg. 8300(1), (2), 8500(2); "payment year" — Reg. 8504(6)(a); "pension credit" — Reg. 8301, 8308.1(2)–(4), 8308.3(2), (3); "pensionable service", "period of disability" — Reg. 8500(1); "period of reduced services" — Reg. 8503(4)(a)(ii); "person" — ITA 248(1); "predecessor employer" — Reg. 8500(1); "property" — ITA 248(1); "province" — Interpretation Act 35(1); "provincial pension plan", "provincial plan" — Canada Pension Plan s. 3; "public health benefits", "public safety occupation" — Reg. 8500(1); "qualifying period" — Reg. 8503(16); "registered pension plan" — ITA 248(1); "registered retirement income fund" — ITA 146.3(1), 248(1); "registered retirement savings plan" — ITA 146(1), (21.2), 147.5(12), 248(1); "related" — ITA 251(2)–(6); "retirement benefits" — Reg. 8500(1); "revocable plan" — ITA 147.1(8), (9), 147.3(12), Reg. 8301(14)(a), 8305(2), 8408(2), 8501(2), 8503(11), (15), 8506(4), 8511(2), 8515(9); "single amount" — ITA 147.1(1); "specified eligibility day" — Reg. 8503(16); "specified year" — Reg. 8504(1)(a)(i); "spouse" — Reg. 8500(5); "surplus" — Reg. 8500(1); "surviving spouse benefits" — Reg. 8503(2)(f); "survivor retirement benefits" — Reg. 8503(2)(d), (e); "temporary absence" — Reg. 8500(1)"eligible period of temporary absence"; "time of commencement" — Reg. 8503(3)(d); "totally and permanently disabled" — Reg. 8500(1); "writing" — Interpretation Act 35(1); "written" — Interpretation Act 35(1)"writing"; "year of commencement" — Reg. 8504(1)(a), 8504(2); "Year's Maximum Pensionable Earnings" — Reg. 8500(1); "years of early retirement eligibility service" — Reg. 8503(3)(c)(iv).

8504. Maximum benefits — (1) Lifetime retirement benefits — For the purposes of subparagraph 8502(c)(i), the following conditions are applicable in respect of the lifetime retirement benefits provided to a member under a defined benefit provision of a pension plan:

(a) the amount (expressed on an annualized basis) of lifetime retirement benefits payable to the member for the calendar year (in this paragraph referred to as the "year of commencement") in which the lifetime retirement benefits commence to be paid does not exceed the aggregate of

(i) the aggregate of all amounts each of which is, in respect of a calendar year after 1990 (in this paragraph referred to as a "specified year") in which the member was, at any time, connected with an employer who participated in the plan in the year for the benefit of the member, the lesser of

(A) the amount determined by the formula

$$.02 \times A \times B / C$$

where

A is the aggregate of all amounts each of which is the member's compensation for the specified year from an employer who participated under the provision in the year for the benefit of the member,

B is the greatest of all amounts each of which is the average wage for a calendar year not before the specified year and not after the year of commencement, and

C is the average wage for the specified year, and

(B) the amount determined by the formula

$$D \times E$$

where

D is the defined benefit limit for the year of commencement, and

E is the fraction of the specified year that is pensionable service of the member under the provision, and

(ii) the amount determined by the formula

$$F \times G$$

where

F is the lesser of

(A) 2 per cent of the member's highest average compensation (computed under subsection (2)) for the purpose of the provision, indexed to the year of commencement, and

    (B) the defined benefit limit for the year of commencement, and;

G is the aggregate of all amounts each of which is the duration (measured in years, including any fraction of a year) of a period that is pensionable service of the member under the provision and no part of which is in a specified year; and

(b) the amount of lifetime retirement benefits payable to the member for a particular calendar year after the year in which the lifetime retirement benefits commence to be paid does not exceed the product of

    (i) the aggregate of the amounts determined under subparagraphs (a)(i) and (ii), and

    (ii) the greatest of all amounts each of which is the ratio of

        (A) the average Consumer Price Index for a calendar year not earlier than the calendar year in which the lifetime retirement benefits commence to be paid and not later than the particular year

to

        (B) the average Consumer Price Index for the calendar year in which the lifetime retirement benefits commence to be paid.

Related Provisions: Reg. 8503(14) — Rules applicable where pension credit artificially reduced; Reg. 8504(2) — Meaning of highest average compensation; Reg. 8504(3) — Alternative compensation rules; Reg. 8504(4) — Part-time employees; Reg. 8504(10) — Excluded benefits; Reg. 8504(13) — Alternative CPI indexing; Reg. 8505(7) — Exclusion from maximum pension rules; Reg. 8510(5) — Special rules — multi-employer plan.

Notes: Where a member of a defined benefit RPP leaves employment and elects to receive a deferred pension, it is limited by the defined benefit limit for the year the pension starts (not the year of leaving employment): VIEWS doc 2004-0059381E5.

Pre-1991 service is limited to 35 years: Information Circular 72-13R8 paras. 2, 9(g).

Information Circulars: 98-2: Prescribed compensation for RPPs.

Registered Pension Plans Technical Manual: §12.1 (lifetime retirement benefits).

Registered Plans Directorate Actuarial Bulletins: 1R1 (calculating actuarial increase where pension start postponed beyond age 65).

Registered Plans Frequently Asked Questions: RPFAQ-2 (RPPs), q. 14 (indexing accrued benefits during pre-retirement deferral period).

(2) Highest average compensation — For the purposes of subsection (1) and paragraph 8505(3)(d), the highest average compensation of a member of a pension plan for the purpose of a defined benefit provision of the plan, indexed to the calendar year (in this subsection referred to as the "year of commencement") in which the member's lifetime retirement benefits under the provision commence to be paid, is,

(a) in the case of a member who has been employed for 3 non-overlapping periods of 12 consecutive months each by employers who participated under the provision for the benefit of the member, $\frac{1}{3}$ of the greatest of all amounts each of which is the aggregate of the member's total indexed compensation for the purpose of the provision for each of the 36 months in 3 such periods throughout which the member was so employed, and

(b) in any other case, the amount determined by the formula

$$12 \times H / I$$

where

H is the aggregate of all amounts each of which is the member's total indexed compensation for the purpose of the provision for a month throughout which the member was employed by an employer who participated under the provision for the benefit of the member, and

I is the number of months for which total indexed compensation is included in the amount determined for H,

and, for the purposes of this subsection, the member's total indexed compensation for a month for the purpose of the provision is the amount determined by the formula

$$J \times K / L$$

where

J is the aggregate of all amounts each of which is such portion of the member's compensation for the calendar year (in this subsection referred to as the "compensation year") that includes the month from an employer who participated under the provision for the benefit of the member as may reasonably be considered to have been received in the month or to otherwise relate to the month,

K is the greatest of all amounts each of which is the average wage for a calendar year not before the later of the compensation year and 1986 and not after the year of commencement, and

L is the average wage for the later of the compensation year and 1986.

Related Provisions: Reg. 8504(2.1) — Employment with predecessor employer included; Reg. 8504(3) — Alternative compensation rules; Reg. 8504(4) — Part-time employees.

Notes: Reg. 8504(2) opening words amended by 2007 budget bill #2, effective for 2008 and later calendar years, to change "retirement benefits" to "lifetime retirement benefits". This is consequential on new Reg. 8503(17), which enables an RPP to provide for payment of bridging benefits on a stand-alone basis (without simultaneous payment of lifetime retirement benefits) to qualifying employees. Bridging benefits are considered to be retirement benefits. The amendment ensures that, in computing the highest average indexed compensation of a member who has received stand-alone bridging benefits, compensation can be indexed to the year in which lifetime retirement benefits begin, rather than the possibly earlier year when the bridging benefits began.

Registered Pension Plans Technical Manual: §12.2 (highest average compensation).

(2.1) Predecessor employer — For the purposes of subsection (2), if the pensionable service of the member under the provision includes a period throughout which the member was employed by a predecessor employer to an employer who participates in the plan, the predecessor employer is deemed to have participated under the provision for the benefit of the member.

Notes: Reg. 8504(2.1) added by 2002-2013 technical bill (Part 5 — technical), effective 1991.

Registered Pension Plans Technical Manual: §12.3 (predecessor employer).

(3) Alternative compensation rules — Lifetime retirement benefits provided to a member under a defined benefit provision of a pension plan shall be deemed to comply with the conditions in subsection (1) where they would so comply if either or both of the following rules were applicable:

(a) determine, for the purpose of subsection (2), the member's compensation from an employer for a calendar year by adding to the compensation otherwise determined such portion of the amount of each bonus and retroactive increase in remuneration paid by the employer to the member after the year as may reasonably be considered to be in respect of the year and by deducting therefrom such portion of the amount of each bonus and retroactive increase in remuneration paid by the employer to the member in the year as may reasonably be considered to be in respect of a preceding year; and

(b) determine, for the purpose of computing the amount J in subsection (2), the portion of the member's compensation from an employer for a calendar year that may reasonably be considered to relate to a month in the year by apportioning the compensation uniformly over the period in the year in respect of which it was paid.

Registered Pension Plans Technical Manual: §12.4 (alternative compensation rules).

(4) Part-time employees — Where the pensionable service of a member under a defined benefit provision of a pension plan includes a period throughout which the member rendered services on a part-time basis to an employer who participates in the plan, the lifetime retirement benefits provided under the provision to the

Regulations

member shall be deemed to comply with the conditions in subsection (1) where they would so comply or be deemed by subsection (3) to so comply if

(a) for the purpose of determining the amount J in subsection (2), the member's compensation from an employer for a calendar year in which the member rendered services on a part-time basis to the employer were the amount that it is reasonable to expect would have been the member's compensation for the year from the employer if the member had rendered services to the employer on a full-time basis throughout the period or periods in the year throughout which the member rendered services to the employer, and

(b) in determining the amount G in subparagraph (1)(a)(ii), the duration of each period were multiplied by a fraction (not greater than 1) that measures the services rendered by the member throughout the period to employers who participate in the plan as a proportion of the services that would have been rendered by the member throughout the period to such employers had the member rendered services on a full-time basis,

and, for the purposes of this subsection,

(c) where a member of a pension plan has rendered services throughout a period to 2 or more employers who participate in the plan, the employers shall be deemed to be, throughout the period, the same employer, and

(d) where a period is

(i) an eligible period of reduced pay or temporary absence of a member of a pension plan with respect to an employer, or

(ii) a period of disability of the member,

the member shall be deemed to have

(iii) rendered services throughout the period on a regular basis (having regard to the services rendered by the employee before the period) to the employer or employers by whom the member was employed before the period, and

(iv) received remuneration throughout the period at a rate commensurate with the member's rate of remuneration before the period.

Registered Pension Plans Technical Manual: §12.5 (part-time employees).

Registered Plans Frequently Asked Questions: RPFAQ-2 (RPPs), q. 9 (where T10 returned due to incorrect address).

(5) Retirement benefits before age 65 — For the purposes of subparagraph 8502(c)(i), the following conditions are applicable in respect of retirement benefits payable under a defined benefit provision of a pension plan to a member of the plan for the period (in this subsection referred to as the "bridging period") from the time the benefits commence to be paid to the time the member attains 65 years of age:

(a) the amount (expressed on an annualized basis) of retirement benefits payable to the member for that part of the bridging period that is in the calendar year in which the benefits commence to be paid does not exceed the amount determined by the formula

$$(A \times B) + \left(0.25 \times C \times \frac{D}{35}\right)$$

where

A is the defined benefit limit for the calendar year in which the benefits commence to be paid,

B is the aggregate of all amounts each of which is the duration (measured in years, including any fraction of a year) of a period that is pensionable service of the member under the provision,

C is the average of the Year's Maximum Pensionable Earnings for the year in which the benefits commence to be paid and for each of the 2 immediately preceding years, and

D is the lesser of 35 and the amount determined for B; and

(b) the amount of retirement benefits (expressed on an annualized basis) payable to the member for that part of the bridging period that is in a particular calendar year after the year in which the retirement benefits commence to be paid does not exceed the product of

(i) the amount determined by the formula set out in paragraph (a), and

(ii) the greatest of all amounts each of which is the ratio of

(A) the average Consumer Price Index for a calendar year not earlier than the calendar year in which the retirement benefits commence to be paid and not later than the particular year

to

(B) the average Consumer Price Index for the calendar year in which the retirement benefits commence to be paid.

Related Provisions: Reg. 8504(8) — Rule where benefits provided under multiple plans; Reg. 8504(11) — Excluded benefits; Reg. 8504(14) — Alternative CPI indexing; Reg. 8505(7) — Exclusion from maximum pension rules.

Registered Pension Plans Technical Manual: §12.6 (retirement benefits before age 65).

(6) Pre-1990 benefits — For the purposes of subparagraph 8502(c)(i), and subject to subsection (7), the lifetime retirement benefits provided under a defined benefit provision of a pension plan to a member of the plan in respect of pensionable service in a particular calendar year before 1990 (in this subsection referred to as the "benefit year") are subject to the condition that

(a) the amount (expressed on an annualized basis) of such lifetime retirement benefits payable to the member for a particular calendar year (in this subsection referred to as the "payment year")

does not exceed

(b) the amount determined by the formula

$$\frac{2}{3} \times A \times B \times C$$

where

A is the greater of $1,725 and the defined benefit limit for the year in which the benefits commence to be paid,

B is the aggregate of all amounts each of which is the duration (measured as a fraction of a year) of a period in the benefit year that is pensionable service of the member under the provision, and

C is the greatest of all amounts each of which is the ratio of

(i) the average Consumer Price Index for a calendar year not earlier than the calendar year in which the lifetime retirement benefits commence to be paid and not later than the payment year

to

(ii) the average Consumer Price Index for the calendar year in which the lifetime retirement benefits commence to be paid.

Related Provisions: Reg. 8504(8) — Rule where benefits provided under multiple plans; Reg. 8504(12) — Excluded benefits; Reg. 8504(15) — Alternative CPI indexing.

Registered Pension Plans Technical Manual: §12.7 (pre-1990 benefits).

Registered Plans Directorate Newsletters: 95-3 (actuarial report content).

(7) Limit not applicable — The condition in subsection (6) is not applicable with respect to lifetime retirement benefits provided to an individual in respect of periods of pensionable service in a particular calendar year if

(a) at any time before June 8, 1990, a period in the particular year was pensionable service of the individual under a defined benefit provision of a registered pension plan;

(b) on June 7, 1990, the individual was entitled, pursuant to an arrangement in writing, to be provided with lifetime retirement benefits under a defined benefit provision of a registered pension plan in respect of a period in the particular year, whether or not the individual's entitlement was conditional upon the individual making contributions under the provision;

(c) at the commencement of the particular year, a period in a preceding year was pensionable service of the individual under a defined benefit provision of a registered pension plan, and the individual did not, by reason of disability or leave of absence, render services in the particular year to an employer who participated in the plan with respect to the individual;

(d) contributions were made before June 8, 1990 by or on behalf of the individual under a money purchase provision of a registered pension plan in respect of the year; or

(e) contributions were made in the year by or on behalf of the individual to a deferred profit sharing plan.

Related Provisions: Reg. 8500(7) — Amounts allocated under money purchase provision deemed to be contribution.

Registered Pension Plans Technical Manual: §12.8 (limit not applicable).

(8) Cross-plan restrictions — Where an individual is provided with benefits under more than one defined benefit provision, the determination of whether the benefits provided to the individual under a particular defined benefit provision comply with the conditions in subsections (5) and (6) shall be made on the assumption that benefits provided to the individual under each other defined benefit provision (other than a provision that is not included in a registered pension plan) associated with the particular provision were provided under the particular provision.

Related Provisions: Reg. 8504(9) — Associated defined benefit provisions; Reg. 8510(5) — Special rules — multi-employer plan.

Registered Pension Plans Technical Manual: §12.9 (cross-plan restrictions).

(9) Associated defined benefit provisions — For the purposes of subsection (8), a defined benefit provision is associated with a particular defined benefit provision if

(a) the provisions are in the same pension plan, or

(b) the provisions are in separate pension plans and

(i) there is an employer who participates in both plans,

(ii) an employer who participates in one of the plans does not deal at arm's length with an employer who participates in the other plan, or

(iii) there is an individual who is provided with benefits under both provisions and the individual, or a person with whom the individual does not deal at arm's length, has the power to determine the benefits that are provided under the particular provision,

unless it is unreasonable to expect the benefits under the particular provision to be coordinated with the benefits under the other provision and the Minister has agreed not to treat the other provision as being associated with the particular provision.

Registered Pension Plans Technical Manual: §12.10 (associated defined benefit provisions).

(10) Excluded benefits — For the purpose of determining whether lifetime retirement benefits provided under a defined benefit provision of a pension plan comply with the conditions in subsection (1), the following benefits shall be disregarded:

(a) additional lifetime retirement benefits payable to a member because the member is totally and permanently disabled at the time the member's retirement benefits commence to be paid; and

(b) additional lifetime retirement benefits payable to a member whose retirement benefits commence to be paid after the member attains 65 years of age, where the additional benefits result from an adjustment that is made to offset, in whole or in part, the decrease in the value of lifetime retirement benefits that would otherwise result by reason of the deferral of such benefits after the member attains 65 years of age and the adjustment is

not more favourable than such an adjustment made on an actuarially equivalent basis.

Related Provisions: Reg. 8504(11), (12) — Benefits to be disregarded.

Registered Pension Plans Technical Manual: §12.11 (excluded benefits).

Registered Plans Directorate Actuarial Bulletins: 1R1 (calculating actuarial increase where pension start postponed beyond age 65).

(11) [Excluded benefits] — For the purpose of determining whether retirement benefits provided under a defined benefit provision of a pension plan comply with the conditions in subsection (5), the following benefits shall be disregarded:

(a) additional lifetime retirement benefits described in paragraph (10)(a); and

(b) bridging benefits payable at the election of a member, where the benefits are provided on a basis that is not more favourable than an actuarially equivalent basis in lieu of all or a proportion of the benefits that would otherwise be payable under the provision with respect to the member.

Notes: Reg. 8504(11)(b) amended by P.C. 2001-153, effective June 5, 1997.

Registered Pension Plans Technical Manual: §12.12 (excluded benefits).

(12) [Excluded benefits] — For the purpose of determining whether lifetime retirement benefits provided under a defined benefit provision of a pension plan comply with the condition in subsection (6), additional lifetime retirement benefits that are described in paragraph (10)(b) shall be disregarded.

Registered Pension Plans Technical Manual: §12.13 (excluded benefits).

(13) Alternative CPI indexing — The lifetime retirement benefits provided to a member under a defined benefit provision of a pension plan shall be deemed to comply with the condition in paragraph (1)(b) where they would so comply, or would be deemed by subsection (3) or (4) to so comply, if the ratio that is determined under subparagraph (1)(b)(ii) were replaced by a substantially similar measure of the change in the Consumer Price Index.

Registered Pension Plans Technical Manual: §12.14 (alternative CPI indexing).

(14) [Idem] — The retirement benefits provided to a member under a defined benefit provision of a pension plan shall be deemed to comply with the condition in paragraph (5)(b) where they would so comply if the ratio that is determined under subparagraph (5)(b)(ii) were replaced by a substantially similar measure of the change in the Consumer Price Index.

(15) [Idem] — The lifetime retirement benefits provided to a member under a defined benefit provision of a pension plan shall be deemed to comply with the condition in subsection (6) where they would so comply if the amount C in the formula set out in paragraph (6)(b) were replaced by a substantially similar measure of the change in the Consumer Price Index.

Definitions [Reg. 8504]: "amount" — ITA 248(1); "arm's length" — ITA 251(1); "associated" — Reg. 8504(9); "average Consumer Price Index" — Reg. 8500(1); "average wage" — ITA 147.1(1); "benefits" — Reg. 8501(5)(c); "bridging benefits" — Reg. 8500(1); "calendar year" — Interpretation Act 37(1)(a); "commencement" — Interpretation Act 35(1); "compensation" — ITA 147.1(1); "connected" — Reg. 8500(3); "Consumer Price Index" — Reg. 8500(1); "contribution" — Reg. 8501(6), (7); "deferred profit sharing plan" — ITA 147(1), 248(1); "defined benefit limit" — Reg. 8500(1); "defined benefit provision" — ITA 147.1(1), Reg. 8500(2); "eligible period of reduced pay" — Reg. 8500(1); "employed", "employee" — ITA 248(1); "employer" — ITA 248(1), Reg. 8504(4)(c); "highest average compensation" — Reg. 8504(2); "individual" — ITA 248(1); "lifetime retirement benefits" — Reg. 8500(1); "member" — ITA 147.1(1), Reg. 8300(1), 8500(2); "Minister" — ITA 248(1); "money purchase provision" — ITA 147.1(1); "month" — Interpretation Act 35(1); "pensionable service", "period of disability" — Reg. 8500(1); "person" — ITA 248(1); "predecessor employer" — Reg. 8500(1); "registered pension plan" — ITA 248(1); "related" — ITA 251(2)–(6); "retirement benefits" — Reg. 8500(1); "specified year" — Reg. 8504(a)(i); "temporary absence" — Reg. 8500(1) "eligible period of temporary absence"; "totally and permanently disabled" — Reg. 8500(1); "writing" — Interpretation Act 35(1); "Year's Maximum Pensionable Earnings" — Reg. 8500(1).

Registered Plans Directorate Newsletters: 96-1 (changes to retirement savings limits).

8505. Additional benefits on downsizing — (1) Downsizing program — For the purposes of this section, "downsizing program" means the actions that are taken by an employer to bring about a reduction in the employer's workforce, including

(a) the termination of the employment of employees; and

(b) the payment of amounts and the provision of special benefits to employees who elect to or are required to terminate their employment.

Registered Pension Plans Technical Manual: §13.1 (downsizing program).

(2) Applicability of downsizing rules — For the purposes of this section,

(a) a downsizing program is an approved downsizing program if the Minister has approved in writing the application of this section in respect of the program;

(b) subject to subsection (2.1), an individual is a qualifying individual in relation to an approved downsizing program if

(i) the employment of the individual is terminated while the downsizing program is in effect,

(ii) the individual was not, at any time before the termination of employment, connected with the employer from whom the individual terminated employment, and

(iii) the Minister has approved in writing the application of this section to the individual; and

(c) the specified day is, in respect of an approved downsizing program,

(i) the day that is designated by the Minister in writing for the purpose of subparagraph (3)(c)(ii), and

(ii) if no such day has been designated, the day that is 2 years after the day on which the Minister approves the application of this section in respect of the downsizing program.

Notes: Reference to Reg. 8505(2.1) added to opening words of Reg. 8505(2)(b) by P.C. 1995-17, effective on the same basis as the addition of Reg. 8505(2.1).

Registered Pension Plans Technical Manual: §13.2 (applicability of downsizing rules).

(2.1) Qualifying individual — exclusion — An individual whose employment is terminated under an approved downsizing program is not a qualifying individual in relation to the program if, at the time the individual's employment is terminated, it is reasonable to expect that

(a) the individual will become employed by, or provide services to,

(i) a person or body of persons from whom the individual terminated employment under the downsizing program, or

(ii) a person or body of persons that does not deal at arm's length with a person or body of persons referred to in subparagraph (i), or

(b) a corporation with which the individual is connected will provide services to a person or body of persons referred to in paragraph (a) and the individual will be directly involved in the provision of the services,

except that this subsection does not apply with respect to an individual where

(c) it is reasonable to expect that

(i) the individual will not be employed or provide services, or

(ii) if paragraph (b) is applicable, the corporation will not provide services,

for a period exceeding 12 months, and

(d) the Minister has waived the application of this subsection with respect to the individual.

Notes: Reg. 8505(2.1) added by P.C. 1995-17, for termination after Feb. 14, 1992. However, it does not apply if the individual was notified by that date that employment would be terminated or if the individual elected by that date to terminate employment.

Registered Pension Plans Technical Manual: §13.3 (qualifying individual — exclusion).

(3) Additional lifetime retirement benefits — Lifetime retirement benefits (in this section referred to as "special retirement be-

nefits") that do not comply with the condition in paragraph 8503(3)(a) may be provided under a defined benefit provision of a pension plan to a member of the plan who terminates employment after attaining 55 years of age where the following conditions are satisfied:

(a) the special retirement benefits are provided pursuant to an approved downsizing program;

(b) the member is a qualifying individual in relation to the downsizing program;

(c) under the terms of the provision,

(i) retirement benefits will not commence to be paid to the member until the member ceases to be employed by all employers who participate in the plan, and

(ii) retirement benefits will commence to be paid to the member no later than on the specified day;

(d) the amount (expressed on an annualized basis) of special retirement benefits payable to the member for a particular calendar year does not exceed the amount that is determined by the formula

$$A \times B \times C$$

where

A is the lesser of

(i) 2 per cent of the member's highest average compensation (computed under subsection 8504(2)) for the purpose of the provision, indexed to the calendar year (in this paragraph referred to as the "year of commencement") in which retirement benefits commence to be paid under the provision to the member, and

(ii) the defined benefit limit for the year of commencement,

B is the lesser of 7 and the amount, if any, by which 65 exceeds the member's age (expressed in years, including any fraction of a year) at termination of employment, and

C is the greatest of all amounts each of which is the ratio of

(i) the average Consumer Price Index for a calendar year not earlier than the year of commencement and not later than the particular year

to

(ii) the average Consumer Price Index for the year of commencement;

(e) [Repealed]

(f) the plan

(i) does not permit the commutation of retirement benefits payable to the member, or

(ii) permits the commutation of retirement benefits payable to the member only if the life expectancy of the member is significantly shorter than normal; and

(g) lifetime retirement benefits that are permissible only by reason of this subsection are not provided to the member under any other defined benefit provision, unless this condition has been waived by the Minister.

Related Provisions: Reg. 8501(3) — Conditions inapplicable where inconsistent with 8505(3); Reg. 8505(6) — Alternative CPI indexing.

Notes: Reg. 8505(3)(e) repealed retroactive to its introduction (1989) by P.C. 1995-17. (This was a requirement that the additional lifetime retirement benefits terminate if the individual subsequently became employed or otherwise rendered services as described in Reg. 8505(5), as it then read.)

Information Circulars: 98-2: Prescribed compensation for RPPs, para. 29.

Registered Pension Plans Technical Manual: §13.4 (additional lifetime retirement benefits).

(3.1) Re-employed members — Where

(a) a member of a pension plan becomes an employee of a participating employer after lifetime retirement benefits that are permissible only by reason of subsection (3) have commenced to be paid under a defined benefit provision of the plan to the member, and

(b) payment of the member's retirement benefits under the provision is suspended while the member is so employed,

the condition in paragraph (3)(d) is applicable in respect of benefits payable under the provision to the member after the suspension as if

(c) the member had not become so employed, and

(d) payment of the member's retirement benefits had not been suspended.

Notes: Reg. 8505(3.1) added by P.C. 1995-17, effective 1989.

Registered Pension Plans Technical Manual: §13.5 (re-employed members).

(4) Early retirement reduction — Where a member of a pension plan is a qualifying individual in relation to an approved downsizing program, the terms of a defined benefit provision of the plan that determine the amount by which the member's lifetime retirement benefits under the provision are reduced because of the early commencement of the benefits may, under the downsizing program, be modified in such a way that the benefits do not comply with the condition in paragraph 8503(3)(c) but would so comply if the member's benefits were provided in respect of employment in a public safety occupation.

Related Provisions: Reg. 8501(3) — Conditions inapplicable where inconsistent with 8505(4); Reg. 8505(5) — Exception for future benefits.

Notes: Reg. 8505(4) amended by P.C. 1995-17, effective 1989. (The change eliminated a requirement that the early retirement reduction be redetermined so as to comply with Reg. 8503(3)(c) if the individual subsequently became re-employed or otherwise rendered services as described in Reg. 8505(5), as it then read.)

Registered Pension Plans Technical Manual: §13.6 (early retirement reduction).

(5) Exception for future benefits — Subsection (4) does not apply with respect to benefits that are provided to an individual in respect of a period that is after the day on which the individual's employment was terminated under an approved downsizing program.

Notes: Reg. 8505(5) amended by P.C. 1995-17, effective 1989. (The former version described the re-employment circumstances under which special benefits provided to an individual under a downsizing program must terminate. It was repealed due to the elimination of the requirements in Reg. 8505(3)(e) and (4)(c), and replaced by the present rule, which sets out an exception to Reg. 8505(4).)

Registered Pension Plans Technical Manual: §13.7 (exception for future benefits).

(6) Alternative CPI indexing — Special retirement benefits provided to a member under a defined benefit provision of a pension plan shall be deemed to comply with the condition in paragraph (3)(d) where they would so comply if the amount C in that paragraph were replaced by a substantially similar measure of the change in the Consumer Price Index.

Registered Pension Plans Technical Manual: §13.8 (alternative CPI indexing).

(7) Exclusion from maximum pension rules — For the purpose of determining whether retirement benefits provided under a defined benefit provision of a pension plan comply with the conditions in subsections 8504(1) and (5), lifetime retirement benefits that are permissible only by reason of subsection (3) shall be disregarded.

Registered Pension Plans Technical Manual: §13.9 (exclusion from maximum pension rules).

(8) Exemption from past service contribution rule — Subsection 8503(15) does not apply in respect of a contribution that is made in respect of benefits provided to a qualifying individual pursuant to an approved downsizing program.

Registered Pension Plans Technical Manual: §13.10 (exemption from past service contribution rule).

Definitions [Reg. 8505]: "amount" — ITA 248(1); "approved downsizing program" — Reg. 8505(2)(a); "arm's length" — ITA 251(1); "average Consumer Price Index" — Reg. 8500(1); "benefits" — Reg. 8501(1)(c); "calendar year" — *Interpretation Act* 37(1)(a); "commencement" — *Interpretation Act* 35(1); "compensation" — ITA 147.1(1); "connected" — Reg. 8500(3); "Consumer Price Index" — Reg. 8500(1); "contribution" — Reg. 8501(6); "corporation" — ITA 248(1), *Interpretation Act* 35(1); "defined benefit limit" — Reg. 8500(1); "defined benefit provision" — ITA 147.1(1),

Reg. 8500(2); "downsizing program" — Reg. 8505(1); "employed", "employee", "employer", "employment" — ITA 248(1); "highest average compensation" — Reg. 8504(2); "individual" — ITA 248(1); "lifetime retirement benefits" — Reg. 8500(1); "member" — ITA 147.1(1), Reg. 8300(1), 8500(2); "Minister" — ITA 248(1); "month" — *Interpretation Act* 35(1); "participating employer" — ITA 147.1(1); "person" — ITA 248(1); "public safety occupation" — Reg. 8500(1); "qualifying individual" — Reg. 8505(2)(b), 8505(2.1); "retirement benefits" — Reg. 8500(1); "special retirement benefits" — Reg. 8505(3); "specified day" — Reg. 8505(2)(c); "writing" — *Interpretation Act* 35(1); "year of commencement" — Reg. 8505(3)(d)(i).

8506. Money purchase provisions — (1) Permissible benefits — For the purposes of paragraph 8502(c), the following benefits may, subject to the conditions specified in respect of each benefit, be provided under a money purchase provision of a pension plan:

(a) **lifetime retirement benefits** — lifetime retirement benefits provided to a member where the benefits are payable in equal periodic amounts or are not so payable only by reason that

(i) the benefits payable to a member after the death of the member's spouse or common-law partner are less than the benefits that would be payable to the member were the member's spouse or common-law partner alive, or

(ii) the benefits are adjusted, after they commence to be paid, where those adjustments would be in accordance with any of subparagraphs 146(3)(b)(iii) to (v) of the Act if the annuity by means of which the lifetime retirement benefits are provided were an annuity under a retirement savings plan;

(b) **bridging benefits** — bridging benefits provided to a member where the bridging benefits are payable for a period ending no later than the end of the month following the month in which the member attains 65 years of age;

(c) **guarantee period** — retirement benefits (in this paragraph referred to as "continued retirement benefits") provided to one or more beneficiaries of a member who dies after retirement benefits under the provision commence to be paid to the member where

(i) the continued retirement benefits are payable for a period beginning after the death of the member and ending no later than 15 years after the day on which retirement benefits commence to be paid under the provision to the member, and

(ii) the total amount of continued retirement benefits payable under the provision for each month does not exceed the amount of retirement benefits (other than benefits permissible under paragraph (e.1)) that would have been payable under the provision for the month to the member if the member were alive;

(d) **post-retirement survivor benefits** — retirement benefits (in this paragraph referred to as "survivor retirement benefits") provided to a beneficiary of a member who dies after retirement benefits under the provision commence to be paid to the member where

(i) the beneficiary is a spouse or common-law partner or former spouse or common-law partner of the member at the time the member's retirement benefits commence to be paid,

(ii) the survivor retirement benefits are payable for a period beginning after the death of the member and ending with the death of the beneficiary, and

(iii) the total amount of survivor retirement benefits and other retirement benefits (other than benefits permissible under paragraph (e.1)) payable under the provision for each month to beneficiaries of the member does not exceed the amount of retirement benefits (other than benefits permissible under paragraph (e.1)) that would have been payable under the provision for the month to the member if the member were alive;

(e) **pre-retirement survivor benefits** — retirement benefits provided to a beneficiary of a member who dies before retirement benefits under the provision commence to be paid to the member, and benefits provided to other individuals after the death of the beneficiary, where

(i) the beneficiary is a spouse or common-law partner or former spouse or common-law partner of the member at the time of the member's death,

(ii) the benefits would be permissible under paragraphs (a) to (c) if the beneficiary were a member of the plan, and

(iii) the retirement benefits are payable to the beneficiary beginning no later than on the later of one year after the day of death of the member and the end of the calendar year in which the beneficiary attains 71 years of age;

(e.1) **variable benefits** — retirement benefits (in this paragraph referred to as "variable benefits"), other than benefits permissible under any of paragraphs (a) to (e) and (e.2), provided to a member and, after the death of the member, to one or more beneficiaries of the member if

(i) the variable benefits are paid from the member's account,

(ii) the variable benefits provided to the member or a beneficiary (other than a beneficiary who is the specified beneficiary of the member in relation to the provision) are payable for a period ending no later than the end of the calendar year following the calendar year in which the member dies,

(iii) the variable benefits provided to a beneficiary who is the specified beneficiary of the member in relation to the provision are payable for a period ending no later than the end of the calendar year in which the specified beneficiary dies, and

(iv) the amount of variable benefits payable to the member and beneficiaries of the member for each calendar year is not less than the minimum amount for the member's account under the provision for the calendar year;

> ### Proposed Amendment — Reg. 8506(1)(e.1) — Variable benefits under Sask. Pension Plan
>
> **Letter from Dept. of Finance, May 11, 2018**: See under ITA 118(7) "pension income".

(e.2) **variable payment life annuity [VPLA]** — retirement benefits (referred to in this paragraph as "VPLA benefits"), other than benefits permissible under any of paragraphs (a) to (e.1), provided to a member and, after the death of the member, to one or more beneficiaries of the member if

(i) the VPLA benefits are paid from a VPLA fund,

(ii) the VPLA benefits are provided to the member (or, after the death of the member, to one or more beneficiaries of the member) because of a transfer of one or more amounts from the member's account to the VPLA fund,

(iii) each VPLA benefit is any of the following:

(A) a retirement benefit described in any of paragraphs (b) to (e), (g) and (i),

(B) in the case of the wind-up of the VPLA fund, a payment described in paragraph (h), and

(C) a retirement benefit that would be described in paragraph (a) if its subparagraph (ii) read as follows:

(ii) the benefits are adjusted annually, after they commence to be paid, in whole or in part to reflect

(A) increases in the Consumer Price Index, as published by Statistics Canada under the authority of the *Statistics Act*, or

(B) increases at a rate specified under the terms of the plan not exceeding 2% per annum;

(iv) the VPLA benefits are increased or decreased to the extent that the following differ materially from the actuarial assumptions used to determine the VPLA benefits:

(A) the amount or rate of return earned by the VPLA fund, or

(B) the rate of mortality of the members and beneficiaries who are entitled to receive the VPLA benefits;

(f) **payment from account** — the payment with respect to a member of a single amount from the member's account under the provision;

(g) **payment from account after death** — the payment, with respect to one or more beneficiaries of a member, of one or more single amounts from the member's account under the provision;

(h) **commutation of benefits** — the payment with respect to a member of a single amount in full or partial satisfaction of the member's entitlement to other benefits under the provision, where the single amount does not exceed the present value (at the time the single amount is paid) of the other benefits that, as a consequence of the payment, cease to be provided; and

(i) the payment, with respect to an individual after the death of a member, of a single amount in full or partial satisfaction of the individual's entitlement to other benefits under the provision, where the individual is a beneficiary of the member and the single amount does not exceed the present value (at the time the single amount is paid) of the other benefits that, as a consequence of the payment, cease to be provided.

Related Provisions: Reg. 8502(e)(i)(C) — Conditions for plan to permit VPLA under Reg. 8506(1)(e.2); Reg. 8506(5) — Minimum amount for (e.1); Reg. 8506(8) — Specified beneficiary for (e.1).

Notes: Reg. 8506(1)(e.2) added and (e.1) amended to refer to it, by 2021 budget bill #1, effective 2020, implementing a 2019 Budget proposal. A variable payment life annuity provides payments that vary based on the investment performance of the underlying annuities fund and on the mortality experience of VPLA annuitants.

Reg. 8506(1)(e)(iii) amended by 2007 budget bill #1 to change "69" to "71", effective 2007 (in sync with increase in the RRSP age limit to 71: see ITA 146(2)(b.4)).

Reg. 8506(1)(a)(ii), (c)(ii), (d)(iii) and (g) amended, and (e.1) added, by P.C. 2005-1508, effective 2004, except that, in respect of retirement benefits provided under a money purchase provision under an arrangement that was accepted for the purpose of Reg. 8506(2)(g) before Feb. 27, 2004, read Reg. 8506(1)(a)(ii) as:

(ii) the benefits are adjusted, after they commence to be paid, where those adjustments are acceptable to the Minister and are similar in nature to the adjustments described in any of subparagraphs 146(3)(b)(iii) to (v) of the Act;

Reg. 8506(1)(a)(i), (d)(i) and (e)(i) amended by P.C. 2001-957, effective 2001 or earlier.

Registered Pension Plans Technical Manual: §14.1 (money purchase provisions — permissible benefits).

Registered Plans Directorate Newsletters: 91-4R (registration rules for money purchase provisions).

Registered Plans Frequently Asked Questions: RPFAQ-2 (RPPs), q. 17 (variable benefits).

(2) Additional conditions — For the purposes of section 8501, the following conditions are applicable with respect to each money purchase provision of a pension plan:

(a) **employer contributions acceptable to minister** — the amount of contributions that are to be made under the provision by each employer who participates in the plan is determined in a manner acceptable to the Minister;

(b) **employer contributions with respect to particular members** — each contribution that is made under the provision by an employer consists only of amounts each of which is an amount that is paid by the employer with respect to a particular member;

(b.1) **allocation of employer contributions** — each contribution that is made under the provision by an employer is allocated to the member with respect to whom it is made;

(c) **employer contributions not permitted** — contributions are not made under the provision by an employer, and property is not transferred to the provision in respect of the actuarial surplus under a defined benefit provision of the plan or another registered pension plan,

(i) at a time when there is a surplus under the provision, or

(ii) at a time after 1991 when an amount that became a forfeited amount under the provision before 1990, or any earnings of the plan that are reasonably attributable to that amount, is being held in respect of the provision and has not been reallocated to members of the plan;

(c.1) **contributions not permitted** — no contribution is made under the provision with respect to a member, and no amount is transferred for the benefit of a member to the provision from another benefit provision of the plan, at any time after the calendar year in which the member attains 71 years of age, other than an amount that is transferred for the benefit of the member to the provision

(i) in accordance with subsection 146.3(14.1) or 147.3(1) or (4) of the Act, or

(ii) from another benefit provision of the plan, where the amount so transferred would, if the benefit provisions were in separate registered pension plans, be in accordance with subsection 147.3(1) or (4) of the Act;

(d) **return of contributions** — where the plan is not established by an enactment of Canada or a province, it includes a stipulation that permits, for the purpose of avoiding revocation of the registration of the plan, a contribution made under the provision by a member or by an employer to be returned to the person who made the contribution, which stipulation may provide that a return of contributions is subject to the approval of the authority administering the *Pension Benefits Standards Act, 1985* or a similar law of a province;

(e) **allocation of earnings** — the earnings of the plan, to the extent that they relate to the provision and are not reasonably attributable to forfeited amounts or a surplus under the provision, are allocated to plan members on a reasonable basis and no less frequently than annually;

(f) **payment or reallocation of forfeited amounts** — each forfeited amount under the provision (other than an amount forfeited before 1990) and all earnings of the plan that are reasonably attributable to the forfeited amount are

(i) paid to participating employers,

(ii) reallocated to members of the plan, or

(iii) paid as or on account of administrative, investment or similar expenses incurred in connection with the plan

on or before December 31 of the year immediately following the calendar year in which the amount is forfeited, or such later time as is permitted by the Minister under subsection (3);

(g) **retirement benefits** — retirement benefits (other than benefits permissible under paragraph (1)(e.1) or (e.2)) under the provision are provided by means of annuities that are purchased from a licensed annuities provider;

(h) **undue deferral of payment — death of member** — each single amount that is payable after the death of a member (other than a single amount that is payable after the death of the specified beneficiary of the member in relation to the provision) is paid as soon as is practicable after the member's death; and

(i) **undue deferral of payment — death of specified beneficiary** — each single amount that is payable after the death of the specified beneficiary of a member in relation to the provision is paid as soon as is practicable after the specified beneficiary's death.

Related Provisions: Reg. 8500(7) — Amount allocated under money purchase provision deemed to be contribution; Reg. 8501(2)(c) — Revocation of plan for failure to comply with conditions; Reg. 8506(8) — Specified beneficiary; Reg. 8506(11)(b) — Recontribution for 2015 due to reduction in minimum withdrawal; Reg. 8509(10.1) — Conditions inapplicable to pre-1992 plans.

Notes: Minimum acceptable contributions under Reg. 8506(2)(a) are normally 1% of total pensionable earnings of active members: Registered Plans Directorate Newsletter 91-4R; *RPP Technical Manual* §14.2.1.

Registered Plans Directorate Newsletter 91-4R states that a money purchase (MP) provision must require employers to contribute at least 1% of total pensionable earnings of all active members participating under the provision annually. This rule applies only to an MP provision of an RPP in which members' benefits are provided exclusively on a MP basis. In light of COVID-19, CRA waived the 1% rule from May 5 to Dec. 31, 2020 if the plan was amended to suspend accruals for the year, meaning that there

would be no employer or employee contributions made to the plan or provision following the amendment. (CRA Registered Plans Division announcement, May 5, 2020)

See VIEWS docs 2008-0271871E5, 2008-0276471E5 where an RPP forfeiture is allocated to an employer.

The Feb. 27, 2004 draft regulations proposed to change para. (e) from "annually" to "monthly". This was dropped from the final amendments (P.C. 2005-698). "Instead, the minimum withdrawal rules for variable benefits take into account unallocated earnings" (Regulatory Impact Analysis Statement).

Reg. 8506(2)(g) amended to refer to (1)(e.2) by 2021 budget bill #1, effective 2020. Reg. 8506(2) earlier amended by 2007 budget bill #1 (effective 2007), P.C. 2005-1508, 1995-17.

Registered Pension Plans Technical Manual: §14.2 (additional conditions).

Registered Plans Directorate Newsletters: 91-4R (registration rules for money purchase provisions).

Registered Plans Frequently Asked Questions: RPFAQ-2 (RPPs), q. 17 (variable benefits).

(2.1) Alternative method for allocating employer contributions — The Minister may, on the written application of the administrator of a pension plan, waive the application of the condition in paragraph (2)(b.1) in respect of a money purchase provision of the plan where contributions made under the provision by an employer are allocated to members of the plan in a manner acceptable to the Minister.

Notes: Reg. 8506(2.1) added by P.C. 1995-17, effective April 6, 1994.

Registered Pension Plans Technical Manual: §14.3 (alternative method for allocating employer conditions).

(3) Reallocation of forfeitures — The Minister may, on the written application of the administrator of a registered pension plan, extend the time for satisfying the requirements of paragraph (2)(f) where

(a) the aggregate of the forfeited amounts that arise in a calendar year is greater than normal because of unusual circumstances; and

(b) the forfeited amounts are to be reallocated on a reasonable basis to a majority of plan members or paid as or on account of administrative, investment or similar expenses incurred in connection with the plan.

Notes: Reg. 8506(3)(b) amended by P.C. 1995-17, to add everything from "or paid as or on account of ...", effective on the same basis as Reg. 8506(2)(f)(iii) (see Notes to 8506(2)).

Registered Pension Plans Technical Manual: §14.4 (reallocation of forfeitures).

Registered Plans Directorate Newsletters: 91-4R (registration rules for money purchase provisions).

(4) Non-payment of minimum amount — plan revocable — A registered pension plan that contains a money purchase provision becomes, for the purposes of paragraph 147.1(11)(c) of the Act, a revocable plan at the beginning of a calendar year if the total amount of retirement benefits (other than retirement benefits permissible under any of paragraphs (1)(a) to (e)) paid from the plan in the calendar year in respect of a member's account under the provision is less than the minimum amount for the account for the calendar year.

Related Provisions: ITA 147.1(8), (9), 147.3(12), Reg. 8301(14)(a), 8305(2), 8408(2), 8501(2) 8503(11), (15), 8511(2), 8515(9) — Other ways plan becomes revocable plan; Reg. 8506(5) — Minimum amount.

Notes: Reg. 8506(4) added by P.C. 2005-1508, effective 2004.

Registered Pension Plans Technical Manual: §14.5 (non-payment of minimum amount — plan revocable).

(5) Minimum amount — For the purposes of paragraph (1)(e.1) and subsection (4), but subject to subsection (7), the minimum amount for a member's account under a money purchase provision of a registered pension plan for a calendar year is the amount determined by the formula

$$A \times B$$

where

A is the balance in the account at the beginning of the year; and

B is

(a) if there is a specified beneficiary of the member for the year in relation to the provision, the factor designated under subsection 7308(4) for the year in respect of the specified beneficiary,

(b) if paragraph (a) does not apply for the year, the factor designated under subsection 7308(4) for the year in respect of an individual where

(i) the individual was, at the time the designation referred to in subparagraph (ii) was made, the member's spouse or common-law partner,

(ii) the member had, before the beginning of the year, provided the administrator of the plan with a written designation of the individual for the purpose of this paragraph in relation to the provision, and

(iii) the member had not, before the beginning of the year, revoked the designation, and

(c) in any other case, the factor designated under subsection 7308(4) for the year in respect of the member.

Related Provisions: ITA 60.021(4)(c) — Determination applies to 2008 RRIF minimum amount reduction; ITA 146.3(1)"minimum amount" — Parallel minimum for RRIF; ITA 147.5(4) — Pooled registered pension plan becomes revocable if less than minimum amount is distributed; Reg. 8506(6) — Determination of account balance; Reg. 8506(7) — Minimum amount nil before age 69; Reg. 8506(7.1) — Minimum amount for 2020; Reg. 8506(8) — Specified beneficiary.

Notes: Reg. 8506(5) added by P.C. 2005-1508, effective 2004.

Registered Pension Plans Technical Manual: §14.6 (minimum amount).

(6) Determination of account balance — For the purpose of the description of A in subsection (5), the balance in a member's account at the beginning of a calendar year (in this subsection referred to as the "current year") is to be determined in accordance with the following rules:

(a) the determination is to be made in a manner that reasonably reflects the fair market value of the property held in connection with the account at the beginning of the current year, including an estimate of the portion of any unallocated earnings of the plan that arose in the preceding calendar year and that can reasonably be expected to be allocated to the account in the current year; and

(b) if retirement benefits (other than benefits permissible under paragraph (1)(e.1)) provided under the provision with respect to the member had commenced to be paid before the current year and continue to be payable in the current year, the determination is to be made without regard to the value of any property held in connection with those benefits.

Notes: Reg. 8506(6) added by P.C. 2005-1508, effective 2004.

Registered Pension Plans Technical Manual: §14.7 (determination of account balance).

(7) Special rules for minimum amount — The minimum amount for a member's account under a money purchase provision of a registered pension plan for a calendar year is

(a) nil, if an individual who is either the member or the specified beneficiary of the member for the year in relation to the provision

(i) is alive at the beginning of the year, and

(ii) had not attained 71 years of age at the end of the preceding calendar year; and

(b) if paragraph (a) does not apply and the year is 2008, 75 per cent of the amount that would, in the absence of this subsection, be the minimum amount for the account for the year.

Related Provisions: ITA 146.3(1.1) — Parallel rule for 2008 for RRIF; Reg. 8506(7.1) — Minimum amount for 2020; Reg. 8506(9), (10) — Recontribution of overwithdrawn amount for 2008.

Notes: Reg. 8506(7) amended, effectively to add para. (b), by 2008 budget bill #2, effective March 12, 2009. (See Notes to ITA 60.021.)

Reg. 8506(7)(b) amended by 2007 budget bill #1 to change "69" to "71", effective 2007 (in conjunction with increase in the RRSP age limit to 71: see ITA 146(2)(b.4)).

Reg. 8506(7) added by P.C. 2005-1508, effective 2004.

Registered Pension Plans Technical Manual: §14.8 (when the minimum amount is nil).

(7.1) [Minimum amount for 2020] — The minimum amount for a member's account under a money purchase provision of a registered pension plan for 2020 is 75% of the amount that would, in the absence of this subsection, be the minimum amount for the account for the year.

Related Provisions: ITA 146.3(1.4) — Parallel rule for 2020 for RRIF.

Notes: Reg. 8506(7.1) added by 2020 COVID bill #1, effective March 25, 2020. See Notes to ITA 146.3(1.4).

(8) Specified beneficiary — In this section, an individual is the specified beneficiary of a member for a calendar year in relation to a money purchase provision of a registered pension plan if

(a) the member died before the beginning of the year;

(b) the individual is a beneficiary of the member and was, immediately before the member's death, the member's spouse or common-law partner; and

(c) the member or the member's legal representative had, before the beginning of the year, provided the administrator of the plan with a written designation of the individual (and of no other individual) as the specified beneficiary of the member for the calendar year in relation to the provision.

Notes: Reg. 8506(8) added by P.C. 2005-1508, effective 2004.

Registered Pension Plans Technical Manual: §14.9 (specified beneficiary).

(9) Recontribution — adjusted minimum amount for 2008 — If a contribution made by a member of a registered pension plan and credited to the member's account under a money purchase provision of the plan complies with the conditions in subsection (10), the contribution

(a) is deemed to have been made in accordance with the plan as registered;

(b) is to be disregarded for the purposes of paragraph (2)(c.1); and

(c) is deemed to be an excluded contribution for the purposes of paragraph 8301(4)(a).

Related Provisions: ITA 60.021 — Parallel rule for RRIF; Reg. 8506(9), (10) — Recontribution of overwithdrawn amount for 2008.

Notes: Reg. 8506(9) added by 2008 budget bill #2, effective March 12, 2009 (and see Notes to Reg. 8506(10)). See Notes to ITA 60.021.

Registered Pension Plans Technical Manual: §14.10 (adjusted minimum amount for 2008).

(10) Conditions referred to in subsec. (9) — The conditions referred to in subsection (9) are as follows:

(a) the contribution is made in 2008;

(b) the contribution is designated for the purposes of this subsection in a manner acceptable to the Minister; and

(c) the amount of the contribution does not exceed the amount determined by the formula

$$A - B - C$$

where

A is the lesser of

(i) the total of all amounts each of which is the amount of a retirement benefit (other than a retirement benefit permissible under any of paragraphs (1)(a) to (e)) paid from the plan in 2008 in respect of the account and included, because of paragraph 56(1)(a) of the Act, in computing the taxpayer's income for the taxation year, and

(ii) the amount that would, in the absence of paragraph (7)(b), be the minimum amount for the account for 2008,

B is the minimum amount for the account for 2008, and

C is the total of all other contributions made by the member under the money purchase provision at or before the time of the contribution and designated for the purposes of this subsection.

Related Provisions: ITA 257 — Negative amounts in formulas.

Notes: Reg. 8506(10) added by 2008 budget bill #2, effective March 12, 2009. Contributions described in Reg. 8506(9)-(10) that are made from Jan. 1, 2009 through April 11, 2009 (or such longer period as is acceptable to the Minister of National Revenue) are deemed for the purpose of Reg. 8506(10) to have been made on Dec. 31, 2008 and not when they were actually made, except that the amounts so deemed shall not exceed the amount that would be determined in respect of the account under Reg. 8506(10)(c), if the value of C in the formula in that para. were nil.

Registered Pension Plans Technical Manual: §14.10 (adjusted minimum amount for 2008).

(11) Recontribution for 2015 — If a contribution made by a member of a registered pension plan and credited to the member's account under a money purchase provision of the plan complies with the conditions in subsection (12), the contribution

(a) is deemed to have been made in accordance with the plan as registered;

(b) is to be disregarded for the purposes of paragraph (2)(c.1); and

(c) is deemed to be an excluded contribution for the purposes of paragraph 8301(4)(a).

Notes: Reg. 8506(11)-(12), added by 2015 Budget bill effective June 23, 2015, allow recontribution of certain variable benefit payments to an RPP where a member received in 2015 more than the minimum amount determined using the reduced factors in Reg. 7308 (e.g. because payment was made before the April 2015 announcement of the reductions). See Notes to ITA 60.022(1), the parallel rule for RRIFs.

(12) Conditions referred to in subsec. (11) — The conditions referred to in subsection (11) are as follows:

(a) the contribution is made after December 31, 2014 and before March 1, 2016;

(b) the contribution is designated for the purposes of this subsection in a manner acceptable to the Minister; and

(c) the amount of the contribution does not exceed the amount determined by the formula

$$A - B - C$$

where

A   is the lesser of

(i) the total of all amounts each of which is the amount of a retirement benefit (other than a retirement benefit permissible under any of paragraphs (1)(a) to (e)) paid from the plan in 2015 in respect of the account and included, because of paragraph 56(1)(a) of the Act, in computing the taxpayer's income for the taxation year, and

(ii) the amount that would be the minimum amount for the account for 2015 if it were determined using the factor designated under subsection 7308(4) as it read on December 31, 2014,

B   is the minimum amount for the account for 2015, and

C   is the total of all other contributions made by the member under the money purchase provision at or before the time of the contribution and designated for the purposes of this subsection.

Related Provisions: ITA 60.022 — Parallel rule for RRIF; ITA 257 — Negative amounts in formulas.

Notes: See Notes to Reg. 8506(11).

(13) VPLA fund — For the purposes of paragraph (1)(e.2) and clause 8502(e)(i)(C), a VPLA fund under a money purchase provision of a pension plan is an arrangement that meets the following conditions:

(a) no amounts are contributed to the arrangement other than amounts that are transferred from accounts of the members of the plan;

(b) the arrangement has at least 10 members at the time it is established and, at all times after it is established, it is reasona-

ble to expect that the arrangement will have at least 10 members on an ongoing basis; and

(c) no benefit may be paid from the arrangement other than retirement benefits described in subparagraph (1)(e.2)(iii).

Notes: Reg. 8506(13) added by 2021 budget bill #1, effective 2020, implementing a 2019 Budget proposal (see also Reg. 8506(1)(e.2)).

Definitions [Reg. 8506]: "administrator" — ITA 147.1(1); "amount", "annuity" — ITA 248(1); "beneficiary", "benefit provision" — Reg. 8500(1); "benefits" — Reg. 8501(5)(c); "bridging benefits" — Reg. 8500(1); "business" — ITA 248(1); "calendar year" — *Interpretation Act* 37(1)(a); "Canada" — ITA 255, *Interpretation Act* 35(1); "common-law partner" — ITA 248(1); "continued retirement benefits" — Reg. 8506(1)(c); "contribution" — Reg. 8501(6); "defined benefit provision" — ITA 147.1(1), Reg. 8500(2); "employer" — ITA 248(1); "excluded contribution" — Reg. 8300(1), 8500(2); "fair market value" — see ITA 69(1) Notes; "forfeited amount" — Reg. 8500(1); "individual", "legal representative" — ITA 248(1); "licensed annuities provider" — ITA 147(1), 248(1); "lifetime retirement benefits" — Reg. 8500(1); "member" — ITA 147.1(1), Reg. 8300(1), 8500(2); "minimum amount" — Reg. 8506(5), (7); "Minister" — ITA 248(1); "money purchase provision" — ITA 147.1(1); "month" — *Interpretation Act* 35(1); "participating employer" — ITA 147.1(1); "person" — ITA 248(1); "plan as registered" — ITA 147.1(15); "property" — ITA 248(1); "province" — *Interpretation Act* 35(1); "registered pension plan" — ITA 248(1); "retirement benefits" — Reg. 8500(1); "retirement savings plan" — ITA 146(1), 248(1); "revocable plan" — ITA 147.1(8), (9), 147.3(12), Reg. 8301(14)(a), 8305(2), 8408(2), 8501(2), 8503(11), (15), 8506(4), 8511(2), 8515(9); "single amount" — ITA 147.1(1); "specified beneficiary" — Reg. 8506(8); "spouse" — Reg. 8500(5); "surplus" — Reg. 8500(1); "survivor retirement benefits" — Reg. 8506(1)(d); "taxation year" — ITA 249; "taxpayer" — ITA 248(1); "VPLA fund" — Reg. 8506(13); "variable benefits" — Reg. 8506(1)(e.1); "written" — *Interpretation Act* 35(1)"writing".

8507. Periods of reduced pay — (1) Prescribed compensation — For the purposes of paragraph (b) of the definition "compensation" in subsection 147.1(1) of the Act, there is prescribed for inclusion in the compensation of an individual from an employer for a calendar year after 1990

(a) where the individual has a qualifying period in the year with respect to the employer, the amount that is determined under subsection (2) in respect of the period; and

(b) where the individual has a period of disability in the year, the amount that would be determined under paragraph (2)(a) in respect of the period if the period were a qualifying period of the individual with respect to the employer.

Related Provisions: Reg. 8508 — Salary deferral leave plan.

Interpretation Bulletins: IT-363R2: Deferred profit sharing plans — deductibility of employer contributions and taxation of amounts received by a beneficiary (archived).

Information Circulars: 98-2: Prescribed compensation for RPPs.

Registered Pension Plans Technical Manual: §1.22 (eligible period of reduced pay); §15 (periods of reduced pay and salary deferral leave plan); §15.1 (prescribed compensation).

(2) Additional compensation in respect of qualifying period — For the purposes of paragraph (1)(a) and subsection (5), the amount that is determined in respect of a period in a calendar year that is a qualifying period of an individual with respect to an employer is the lesser of

(a) the amount, if any, by which

(i) the amount that it is reasonable to consider would have been the remuneration of the individual for the period from the employer if the individual had rendered services to the employer throughout the period on a regular basis (having regard to the services rendered by the individual to the employer before the complete period of reduced pay of which the period is a part) and the individual's rate of remuneration had been commensurate with the individual's rate of remuneration before the beginning of the complete period of reduced pay

exceeds

(ii) the remuneration of the individual for the period from the employer, and

(b) the amount determined by the formula

$$(5 + A + B - C) \times D$$

where

A is the lesser of 3 and the amount that would be the cumulative additional compensation fraction of the individual with respect to the employer, determined to the time that is immediately before the end of the period, if the individual's only qualifying periods had been periods that are also periods of parenting,

B is

(i) if no part of the period is a period of parenting, nil, and

(ii) otherwise, the lesser of

(A) the amount, if any, by which 3 exceeds the amount determined for A, and

(B) the ratio of

(I) the amount that would be determined under paragraph (a) if the remuneration referred to in subparagraphs (a)(i) and (ii) were the remuneration for such part of the period as is a period of parenting

to

(II) the amount determined for D,

C is the cumulative additional compensation fraction of the individual with respect to the employer, determined to the time that is immediately before the end of the period, and

D is the amount that it is reasonable to consider would have been the individual's remuneration for the year from the employer if the individual had rendered services to the employer on a full-time basis throughout the year and the individual's rate of remuneration had been commensurate with the individual's rate of remuneration before the beginning of the complete period of reduced pay of which the period is a part.

Related Provisions: ITA 257 — Negative amounts in formulas; Reg. 8507(7) — Complete period of reduced pay.

Information Circulars: 98-2: Prescribed compensation for RPPs.

Registered Pension Plans Technical Manual: §1.23 (eligible period of temporary absence); §15.2 (additional compensation in respect of qualifying period).

(3) Qualifying periods and periods of parenting — For the purposes of this section,

(a) a period in a calendar year is a qualifying period of an individual in the year with respect to an employer if

(i) the period is an eligible period of reduced pay or temporary absence of the individual in the year with respect to the employer,

(ii) either

(A) lifetime retirement benefits are provided to the individual under a defined benefit provision of a registered pension plan (other than a plan that is, in the year, a specified multi-employer plan) in respect of the period, or

(B) contributions are made by or on behalf of the individual under a money purchase provision of a registered pension plan (other than a plan that is, in the year, a specified multi-employer plan) in respect of the period,

pursuant to terms of the plan that apply in respect of periods that are not regular periods of employment,

(iii) the lifetime retirement benefits or the contributions, as the case may be, exceed the benefits that would otherwise be provided or the contributions that would otherwise be made if the benefits or contributions were based on the services actually rendered by the individual and the remuneration actually received by the individual,

(iv) the individual's pension adjustment for the year with respect to the employer includes an amount in respect of the lifetime retirement benefits or the contributions, as the case may be,

(v) no benefits are provided in respect of the period to the individual under a defined benefit provision of any registered pension plan in which the employer does not participate,

(vi) no contributions are made by or on behalf of the individual in respect of the period under a money purchase provision of a registered pension plan or a deferred profit sharing plan in which the employer does not participate,

(vii) no part of the period is after the earlier of

(A) the time at which bridging benefits commence to be paid to the individual in circumstances to which subsection 8503(17) applied, and

(B) the earliest day in respect of which benefits have been provided to the individual in circumstances to which subsection 8503(19) applied; and

(b) a period of parenting of an individual is all or a part of a period that begins

(i) at the time of the birth of a child of whom the individual is a natural parent, or

(ii) at the time the individual adopts a child,

and ends 12 months after that time.

Related Provisions: Reg. 8500(1.3) — Eligible period of reduced pay for 2020-21 (COVID-19); Reg. 8500(7) — Amounts allocated under money purchase provision deemed to be contribution.

Notes: Prescribed compensation for maternity or parental leave is generally the amount the individual would have received had they worked on a regular basis throughout the period: tinyurl.com/rpd-consults, "Questions from the Industry" 2003 q.6. However, this question has now been removed.

Reg. 8507(3)(a)(vii) added by 2007 budget bill #2, for calendar years after 2007.

Closing words of Reg. 8507(3)(a) repealed by P.C. 1995-17, retroactive to their introduction (1989). They provided that if an amount attributable to forfeitures or surplus was allocated to an individual under a money purchase provision, the amount was deemed to be a contribution made to the provision on behalf of the individual. This rule is now in Reg. 8500(7).

Information Circulars: 98-2: Prescribed compensation for RPPs.

Registered Pension Plans Technical Manual: §15.3 (qualifying periods and periods of parenting).

(4) Cumulative additional compensation fraction — For the purposes of this section, the cumulative additional compensation fraction of an individual with respect to an employer, determined to any time, is the aggregate of all amounts each of which is the additional compensation fraction that is associated with a period that ends at or before that time and that is a qualifying period of the individual in a calendar year after 1990 with respect to

(a) the employer;

(b) any other employer who does not deal at arm's length with the employer; or

(c) any other employer who participates in a registered pension plan in which the employer participates for the benefit of the individual.

Related Provisions: Reg. 8507(5) — Additional compensation fraction.

Registered Pension Plans Technical Manual: §15.4 (cumulative additional compensation fraction).

(5) Additional compensation fraction — For the purposes of subsection (4), the additional compensation fraction associated with a qualifying period of an individual in a calendar year with respect to a particular employer is the amount determined by the formula

$$E / D$$

where

D is the amount determined for D under paragraph (2)(b) in respect of the qualifying period, and

E is

(a) if

(i) all or a part of the qualifying period is a period throughout which the individual renders services to another employer pursuant to an arrangement in respect of which subsection 8308(7) is applicable,

(ii) the particular employer is a lending employer for the purposes of subsection 8308(7) as it applies in respect of the arrangement, and

(iii) the particular employer and the other employer deal with each other at arm's length,

the amount that would be determined under subsection (2) in respect of the qualifying period if, in the determination of the amount under paragraph (2)(a), no remuneration were included in respect of the portion of the qualifying period referred to in subparagraph (a)(i), and

(b) otherwise, the amount that is determined under subsection (2) in respect of the qualifying period.

Information Circulars: 98-2: Prescribed compensation for RPPs, para. 21.

Registered Pension Plans Technical Manual: §15.5 (additional compensation fraction).

(6) Exclusion of subperiods — A reference in this section to a qualifying period of an individual in a calendar year with respect to an employer or to a period of disability of an individual in a calendar year does not include a period that is part of a longer such period.

Registered Pension Plans Technical Manual: §15.6 (exclusion of subperiods).

(7) Complete period of reduced pay — In subsection (2), "complete period of reduced pay" of an individual with respect to an employer means a period that consists of one or more periods each of which is

(a) a period of disability of the individual, or

(b) an eligible period of reduced pay or temporary absence of the individual with respect to the employer,

and that is not part of a longer such period.

Registered Pension Plans Technical Manual: §15.7 (complete period of reduced pay).

Definitions [Reg. 8507]: "additional compensation fraction" — Reg. 8507(5); "amount" — ITA 248(1); "arm's length" — ITA 251(1); "associated" — ITA 256; "benefits" — Reg. 8501(5)(c); "calendar year" — *Interpretation Act* 37(1)(a); "child" — ITA 252(1); "compensation" — ITA 147.1(1); "complete period of reduced pay" — Reg. 8507(7); "contribution" — Reg. 8501(6), (7); "cumulative additional compensation fraction" — Reg. 8507(4); "deferred profit sharing plan" — ITA 147(1), 248(1); "defined benefit provision" — ITA 147.1(1), Reg. 8500(2); "eligible period of reduced pay" — Reg. 8500(1), (1.3); "employer", "employment", "individual" — ITA 248(1); "lifetime retirement benefits" — Reg. 8500(1); "money purchase provision" — ITA 147.1(1); "month" — *Interpretation Act* 35(1); "pension adjustment" — ITA 248(1); "period of disability" — Reg. 8500(1); "prescribed" — ITA 248(1); "qualifying period" — Reg. 8507(3)(a), 8507(6); "registered pension plan" — ITA 248(1); "specified multi-employer plan" — ITA 147.1(1), Reg. 8510(2), (3); "temporary absence" — Reg. 8500(1)"eligible period of temporary absence".

Interpretation Bulletins [Reg. 8507]: IT-363R2: Deferred profit sharing plans — deductibility of employer contributions and taxation of amounts received by a beneficiary (archived).

Registered Plans Directorate Newsletters [Reg. 8507]: 91-4R (registration rules for money purchase provisions).

8508. Salary deferral leave plan — Where an employee and an employer enter into an arrangement in writing described in paragraph 6801(a) or (b),

(a) the period throughout which the employee defers salary or wages pursuant to the arrangement shall be deemed to be an eligible period of reduced pay of the employee with respect to the employer; and

(b) for the purposes of section 8507, the amount that it is reasonable to consider would have been the remuneration of the employee for any period from the employer shall be determined on the basis that the employee's rate of remuneration was the amount that it is reasonable to consider would, but for the arrangement, have been the employee's rate of remuneration.

Definitions [Reg. 8508]: "amount" — ITA 248(1); "eligible period of reduced pay" — Reg. 8500(1); "employee", "employer", "salary or wages" — ITA 248(1); "writing" — *Interpretation Act* 35(1).

Information Circulars: 98-2: Prescribed compensation for RPPs, para. 22.

Registered Pension Plans Technical Manual: §15 (periods of reduced pay and salary deferral leave plan); §15.8 (salary deferral leave plan).

8509. Transition rules — (1) Prescribed conditions applicable before 1992 to grandfathered plan — The prescribed conditions for the registration of a grandfathered plan are, before 1992,

(a) the condition set out in paragraph 8502(a),

(b) the condition set out in paragraph 8502(c), but only in respect of benefits provided under a money purchase provision of the plan, and

(c) if the plan contains a money purchase provision, the condition set out in paragraph 8506(2)(a),

and the following conditions:

(d) the benefits provided under each defined benefit provision of the plan are acceptable to the Minister and, for the purposes of this condition, any benefits in respect of periods before 1991 that become provided after 1988 with respect to a member who is connected with an employer who participates in the plan, or was so connected at any time before the benefits become provided, shall, unless the Minister is notified in writing that the benefits are provided with respect to the member, be deemed to be unacceptable to the Minister, and

(e) the plan contains such terms as may be required by the Minister.

Registered Pension Plans Technical Manual: §16.1 (prescribed conditions applicable before 1992 to grandfathered plans).

(2) Conditions applicable after 1991 to benefits under grandfathered plan — For the purpose of the condition in paragraph 8502(c) as it applies after 1991 in respect of a grandfathered plan,

(a) the condition in subparagraph 8503(2)(b)(ii) is replaced by the condition that the amount of bridging benefits payable to a member for a particular month does not exceed the amount that is determined in respect of the month by the formula

$$(A \times C \times (E/F)) + (G \times (1 - (E/F)))$$

where

A is the amount determined for A under subparagraph 8503(2)(b)(ii) with respect to the member for the month,

C is the amount determined for C under subparagraph 8503(2)(b)(ii) with respect to the member for the month,

E is the aggregate of all amounts each of which is the duration (measured in years, including any fraction of a year) of a period ending before 1992 that is pensionable service of the member under the provision,

F is the aggregate of all amounts each of which is the duration (measured in years, including any fraction of a year) of a period that is pensionable service of the member under the provision, and

G is the amount determined with respect to the member for the month by the formula in subparagraph 8503(2)(b)(ii);

(b) the conditions in paragraphs 8503(3)(c), (h) and (i) and 8504(1)(a) and (b) apply only in respect of lifetime retirement benefits provided in respect of periods after 1991; and

(c) for the purposes of the conditions in paragraphs 8504(1)(a) and (b),

(i) the aggregate that is determined under subparagraph 8504(1)(a)(i) does not include an amount in respect of 1991, and

(ii) the amount that is determined for G under subparagraph 8504(1)(a)(ii) is based only on periods of pensionable service after 1991.

Related Provisions: ITA 257 — Negative amounts in formulas.

Registered Pension Plans Technical Manual: §16.2 (post-91 conditions for grandfathered plan).

(3) Additional prescribed condition for grandfathered plan after 1991 — The prescribed conditions for the registration of a grandfathered plan include, after 1991, the condition that all benefits provided under each defined benefit provision of the plan in respect of periods before 1992 are acceptable to the Minister.

Registered Pension Plans Technical Manual: §16.3 (additional prescribed conditions for grandfathered plan after 1991).

(4) Defined benefits under grandfathered plan exempt from conditions — The Minister may, after 1991, exempt from the condition in paragraph 8502(c) the following benefits provided under a defined benefit provision of a grandfathered plan:

(a) benefits that are payable after the death of a member, to the extent that the benefits can reasonably be considered to relate to lifetime retirement benefits provided to the member in respect of periods before 1992; and

(b) bridging benefits in excess of bridging benefits that are permissible under paragraph 8503(2)(b), to the extent that the excess bridging benefits are vested in a member on December 31, 1991.

Registered Pension Plans Technical Manual: §16.4 (defined benefits under grandfathered plan exempt from conditions).

(4.1) Benefits under grandfathered plan — pre-1992 disability — Where benefits are provided under a defined benefit provision of a grandfathered plan to a member of the plan as a consequence of the member having become, before 1992, physically or mentally impaired, the following rules apply:

(a) the conditions in this Part (other than the condition in paragraph (b)) do not apply in respect of the benefits;

(b) the prescribed conditions for the registration of the plan include the condition that the benefits are acceptable to the Minister; and

(c) subsections 147.1(8) and (9) of the Act do not apply to render the plan a revocable plan where those subsections would not so apply if the member's pension credits under the provision were determined without regard to the benefits.

Notes: Reg. 8509(4.1) added by P.C. 1995-17, effective 1989.

Registered Pension Plans Technical Manual: §16.4 (defined benefits under grandfathered plan exempt from conditions); §16.5 (benefits under grandfathered plan — pre-1992 disability).

(5) Conditions not applicable to grandfathered plan — Where a pension plan is a grandfathered plan,

(a) the conditions referred to in paragraph 8501(2)(b) do not apply before 1992 in respect of the plan;

(b) the condition in paragraph 8502(d) does not apply in respect of distributions that are made before 1992 under a defined benefit provision of the plan; and

(c) the conditions in paragraphs 8503(3)(a) and (b) do not apply in respect of benefits provided under a defined benefit provision of the plan in respect of periods before 1992.

Registered Pension Plans Technical Manual: §16.6 (conditions not applicable to grandfathered plan).

(6) PA limits for grandfathered plan for 1991 — Subsections 147.1(8) and (9) of the Act do not apply in respect of a grandfathered plan for a calendar year before 1992 if

(a) the plan does not contain a money purchase provision in that year; or

(b) no contributions are made in respect of that year under the money purchase provisions of the plan.

Registered Pension Plans Technical Manual: §16.7 (PA limits for grandfathered plan for 1991).

(7) Limit on pre-age 65 benefits — Where a pension plan is a grandfathered plan or would be a grandfathered plan if the references to "March 27, 1988" in the definitions "existing plan" and "grandfathered plan" in subsection 8500(1) were read as references to "June 7, 1990" and the references to "March 28, 1988" in the

definition "existing plan" in that subsection were read as references to "June 8, 1990",

(a) the conditions in paragraphs 8504(5)(a) and (b) apply only in respect of retirement benefits provided in respect of periods after 1991; and

(b) the amounts that are determined for B and D under paragraph 8504(5)(a) are based only on periods of pensionable service after 1991.

Registered Pension Plans Technical Manual: §16.8 (limit on pre-age 65 benefits).

(8) Benefit accrual rate greater than 2 per cent — Where a pension plan is a grandfathered plan or would be a grandfathered plan if the references to "March 27, 1988" in the definitions "existing plan" and "grandfathered plan" in subsection 8500(1) were read as references to "July 31, 1991" and the references to "March 28, 1988" in the definition "existing plan" in that subsection were read as references to "August 1, 1991",

(a) the condition in paragraph 8503(3)(g) applies only in respect of lifetime retirement benefits provided under a defined benefit provision of the plan in respect of periods after 1994; and

(b) subparagraph 8503(3)(h)(iv) is not applicable in respect of lifetime retirement benefits provided under a defined benefit provision of the plan to a member unless the formula for determining the amount of the member's lifetime retirement benefits complies with the condition in paragraph 8503(3)(g) as that condition would, but for this subsection, apply.

Registered Pension Plans Technical Manual: §16.9 (benefit accrual rate greater then 2%).

(9) Benefits under plan other than grandfathered plan — The following rules apply in respect of the benefits provided under a defined benefit provision of a pension plan that is not a grandfathered plan:

(a) the condition in paragraph 8502(c) does not apply in respect of benefits provided with respect to an individual

(i) to whom retirement benefits have commenced to be paid under the provision before 1992, or

(ii) who has died before 1992; and

(b) the prescribed conditions for the registration of the plan include the condition that all benefits referred to in paragraph (a) are acceptable to the Minister.

Registered Pension Plans Technical Manual: §16.10 (benefits under plan other than grandfathered plan).

(10) Money purchase benefits exempt from conditions — The Minister may exempt from the condition in paragraph 8502(c) all or a portion of the benefits provided under a money purchase provision of a pension plan with respect to a member that may reasonably be considered to derive from contributions made before 1992 under a money purchase provision of a registered pension plan.

Registered Pension Plans Technical Manual: §1.31 (money purchase provision); §16.11 (money purchase benefits exempt from conditions).

Registered Plans Directorate Newsletters: 91-4R (registration rules for money purchase provisions).

(10.1) Stipulation not required for pre-1992 plans — The conditions in paragraphs 8503(4)(c) and 8506(2)(d) do not apply in respect of a pension plan

(a) that was a registered pension plan on December 31, 1991,

(b) in respect of which an application for registration was made to the Minister before 1992, or

(c) that was established to provide benefits to one or more individuals in lieu of benefits to which the individuals were entitled under another pension plan that is a plan described in paragraph (a) or (b) or this paragraph, whether or not benefits are also provided to other individuals.

Notes: Reg. 8509(10.1) added by P.C. 1995-17, effective 1989. (This exemption recognizes that many of these plans either cannot be amended to add the stipulation or can be amended only with the consent of plan members as well as court approval.)

Registered Pension Plans Technical Manual: §16.12 (stipulation not required for pre-1992 plans).

Registered Plans Directorate Newsletters: 91-4R (registration rules for money purchase provisions).

(11) Benefits acceptable to Minister — For greater certainty, where benefits under a defined benefit provision of a pension plan are, by reason of paragraph 8503(3)(e) or subsection (3), subject to the condition that they be acceptable to the Minister, the provisions of this section shall not be considered to limit in any way the requirements that may be imposed by the Minister in respect of the benefits.

Registered Pension Plans Technical Manual: §16.13 (benefits acceptable to Minister).

(12) PA limits — 1996 to 2002 — Neither subsection 147.1(8) nor (9) of the Act applies to render a registered pension plan a revocable plan at the end of any calendar year after 1995 and before 2003 solely because a pension adjustment, a total of pension adjustments or a total of pension credits of an individual for the year (each of which is, in this subsection, referred to as a "test amount") is excessive where the subsection would not apply to render the plan a revocable plan at the end of the year if each test amount were decreased by the lesser of

(a) the amount, if any, by which the lesser of

   (i) the total of all amounts each of which is

      (A) a pension credit under a defined benefit provision of a registered pension plan that is included in determining the test amount, or

      (B) a pension credit under a money purchase provision of a registered pension plan or under a deferred profit sharing plan that is included in determining the test amount and that is taken into account, under paragraph 8302(2)(c), in determining a pension credit referred to in clause (A), and

   (ii) $15,500

exceeds the money purchase limit for the year, and

(b) the total of all amounts each of which is a pension credit referred to in clause (a)(i)(A).

Notes: Reg. 8509(12) amended by P.C. 2005-1508, effective 2003, to change "2004" to "2003". Added by P.C. 1998-2256, effective 1996.

Registered Pension Plans Technical Manual: §16.14 (PA limits — 1996 to 2002).

Registered Plans Directorate Newsletters: 96-1 (changes to retirement savings limits).

(13) Maximum benefits indexed before 2005 — Where

(a) a pension plan is a grandfathered plan or would be a grandfathered plan if the references to "March 27, 1988" in the definitions "existing plan" and "grandfathered plan" in subsection 8500(1) were read as references to "March 5, 1996" and the references to "March 28, 1988" in the definition "existing plan" in that subsection were read as references to "March 6, 1996",

(b) under the terms of the plan as they read immediately before March 6, 1996, the plan provided for benefits that are benefits to which a condition in any of subsections 8504(1), (5) and (6) and paragraph 8505(3)(d) applies and, at that time, the benefits complied with the condition, and

(c) as a consequence of the change in the defined benefit limit effective March 6, 1996, the benefits would, if this Part were read without reference to this subsection, cease to comply with the condition,

the following rules apply:

(d) for the purpose of determining at any time after March 5, 1996 and before 1998 whether the benefits comply with the condition, the defined benefit limit for each year after 1995 is deemed to be the amount that it would be if the definition

"money purchase limit" in subsection 147.1(1) of the Act were applied as it read on December 31, 1995, and

(e) for the purpose of determining at any time after 1997 whether the benefits comply with the condition, the defined benefit limit for 1996 and 1997 is deemed to be the amount that it would be if it were determined in accordance with paragraph (d).

Notes: Reg. 8509(13) added by P.C. 1998-2256, effective March 6, 1996, except that where

(a) the retirement benefits provided to an individual under a pension plan are provided by means of an annuity contract issued before March 6, 1996, and

(b) under the terms and conditions of the contract as they read immediately before March 6, 1996,

   (i) the day on which annuity payments are to begin under the contract is fixed and determined and is after 1997, and

   (ii) the amount and timing of each annuity payment are fixed and determined,

ignore para. (e) and the words "and before 1998" in para. (d).

Definitions [Reg. 8509]: "amount" — ITA 248(1); "benefits" — Reg. 8501(5)(c); "bridging benefits" — Reg. 8500(1); "calendar year" — *Interpretation Act* 37(1)(a); "connected" — Reg. 8500(3); "contribution" — Reg. 8501(6); "deferred profit sharing plan" — ITA 147(1), 248(1); "defined benefit limit" — Reg. 8500(1); "defined benefit provision" — ITA 147.1(1), Reg. 8500(2); "employer" — ITA 248(1); "grandfathered plan" — Reg. 8500(1); "individual" — ITA 248(1); "lifetime retirement benefits" — Reg. 8500(1); "member" — ITA 147.1(1), Reg. 8300(1), 8500(2); "Minister" — ITA 248(1); "money purchase limit", "money purchase provision" — ITA 147.1(1); "month" — *Interpretation Act* 35(1); "pension adjustment" — ITA 248(1); "pension credit" — Reg. 8301, 8308.1(2)–(4), 8308.3(2), (3); "pensionable service" — Reg. 8500(1); "prescribed", "registered pension plan" — ITA 248(1); "retirement benefits" — Reg. 8500(1); "revocable plan" — ITA 147.1(8), (9), 147.3(12), Reg. 8301(14)(a), 8305(2), 8408(2), 8501(2), 8503(11), (15), 8506(4), 8511(2), 8515(9); "test amount" — Reg. 8509(12); "writing" — *Interpretation Act* 35(1).

8510. Multi-employer plans and other special plans —

Notes: Heading changed from "Multi-employer plans and specified multi-employer plans" by P.C. 2007-1443, effective June 24, 2007.

(1) Definition of "multi-employer plan" — The definition "multi-employer plan" in subsection 8500(1) is applicable for the purposes of subsection 147.1(1) of the Act.

Registered Pension Plans Technical Manual: §1.32 (multi-employer plan); §17.1 (definition of a multi-employer plan (MEP)).

(2) Definition of "specified multi-employer plan" — For the purposes of this Part and subsection 147.1(1) of the Act, "specified multi-employer plan" in a calendar year means a pension plan

(a) in respect of which the conditions in subsection (3) are satisfied at the beginning of the year (or at the time in the year when the plan is established, if later),

(b) that has, on application by the plan administrator, been designated in writing by the Minister to be a specified multi-employer plan in the year, or

(c) that was, by reason of paragraph (a), a specified multi-employer plan in the immediately preceding calendar year (where that year is after 1989),

but does not include a pension plan where the Minister has, before the beginning of the year, given notice by registered mail to the plan administrator that the plan is not a specified multi-employer plan.

Related Provisions: Reg. 8510(4) — Minister's notice concerning specified multi-employer plans.

Registered Pension Plans Technical Manual: §1.42 (specified multi-employer plan); §17.2 (definition of a SMEP).

Registered Plans Frequently Asked Questions: RPFAQ-2 (RPPs), q. 13 (what is a SMEP?).

(3) Qualification as a specified multi-employer plan — The conditions referred to in paragraph (2)(a) are the following:

(a) it is reasonable to expect that at no time in the year will more than 95 per cent of the active members of the plan be employed by a single participating employer or by a related group of participating employers;

(b) where the year is 1991 or a subsequent year, it is reasonable to expect that

(i) at least 15 employers will contribute to the plan in respect of the year, or

(ii) at least 10 per cent of the active members of the plan will be employed in the year by more than one participating employer,

and, for the purposes of this condition, all employers who are related to each other shall be deemed to be a single employer;

(c) employers participate in the plan pursuant to a collective bargaining agreement;

(d) all or substantially all of the employers who participate in the plan are persons who are not exempt from tax under Part I of the Act;

(e) contributions are made by employers in accordance with a negotiated contribution formula that does not provide for any variation in contributions determined by reference to the financial experience of the plan;

(f) the contributions that are to be made by each employer in the year are determined, in whole or in part, by reference to the number of hours worked by individual employees of the employer or some other measure that is specific to each employee with respect to whom contributions are made to the plan;

(g) the administrator is a board of trustees or similar body that is not controlled by representatives of employers; and

(h) the administrator has the power to determine the benefits to be provided under the plan, whether or not that power is subject to the terms of a collective bargaining agreement.

Notes: CRA considers that "substantially all", used in para. (d), means 90% or more.

Registered Pension Plans Technical Manual: §1.42 (specified multi-employer plan); §17.3 (qualification as a specified multi-employer plan).

Registered Plans Frequently Asked Questions: RPFAQ-2 (RPPs), q. 13 (what is a SMEP?).

(4) Minister's notice — For the purpose of subsection (2), the Minister may give notice that a plan is not a specified multi-employer plan only if the Minister is satisfied that participating employers will be able to comply with all reporting obligations imposed by Part LXXXIV in respect of the plan if it is not a specified multi-employer plan, and

(a) the notice is given at or after a time when the conditions in subsection (3) are not satisfied in respect of the plan; or

(b) the plan administrator has applied to the Minister for the notice.

Registered Pension Plans Technical Manual: §17.4 (Minister's notice).

(5) Special rules — multi-employer plan — Where a pension plan is a multi-employer plan in a calendar year,

(a) each member of the plan who is connected at any time in the year with an employer who participates in the plan shall be deemed, for the purposes of applying the conditions in sections 8503 and 8504 in respect of the plan in the year and in each subsequent year, not to be so connected in the year;

(b) paragraph 8503(3)(b) shall, in its application in respect of benefits provided under a defined benefit provision of the plan in respect of a period in the year, be read without reference to subparagraph (ii) thereof; and

(c) the condition in paragraph 8503(3)(k) and the rule in subsection 8504(8) shall apply in the year in respect of the plan without regard to benefits provided under any other pension plan.

Related Provisions: Reg. 8510(7) — Additional prescribed conditions.

Registered Pension Plans Technical Manual: §17.5 (special rules — MEPs).

(6) Special rules — specified multi-employer plan — Where a pension plan is a specified multi-employer plan in a calendar year,

(a) a contribution that is made in the year in respect of a defined benefit provision of the plan by an employer with respect to the employer's employees or former employees in accordance with the plan as registered shall be deemed, for the purpose of paragraph 8502(b), to be an eligible contribution;

(b) subparagraph 8502(c)(i) shall, in its application in the year in respect of the plan, be read as follows:

"(i) benefits that are in accordance with subsection 8503(2), paragraphs 8503(3)(c), (e) and (g) and subsections 8504(5) and (6)";

(c) the conditions in paragraphs 8503(3)(j) and (4)(a) do not apply in the year in respect of the plan; and

(d) a payment made in the year under a defined benefit provision of the plan with respect to a member is deemed to comply with the conditions in paragraph 8503(2)(h) (in the case of a payment made in connection with the member's termination from the plan otherwise than by reason of death) or (j) (in the case of a payment made after the death of the member) where it would comply if paragraph 8503(2)(h) were read as follows:

"(h) the payment, with respect to a member in connection with the member's termination from the plan (otherwise than by reason of death), of one or more single amounts where

(i) the payments are the last payments to be made under the provision with respect to the member, and

(ii) each single amount does not exceed the amount that would be the balance in the member's net contribution account immediately before the time of payment of the single amount if, for each contribution that is a specified contribution, the account were credited at the time of the specified contribution with an additional amount equal to the amount of the specified contribution and, for this purpose, a specified contribution is

(A) a contribution included in determining a pension credit of the member under the provision because of paragraph 8301(5)(b), or

(B) a contribution made before 1990 in respect of the provision by a participating employer, to the extent that the contribution can reasonably be considered to have been determined by reference to the number of hours worked by the member or some other measure specific to the member;".

Related Provisions: Reg. 8510(7) — Additional prescribed conditions.

Notes: Reg. 8510(6)(d) added by P.C. 2001-153, effective 1989.

Registered Pension Plans Technical Manual: §17.6 (special rules — SMEPs).

Registered Plans Compliance Bulletins: 7 (making contributions and calculating and reporting pension adjustment for SMEPs).

(7) Additional prescribed conditions — Where a pension plan is a specified multi-employer plan in a calendar year, the prescribed conditions for the registration of the plan include, in that year, the following conditions:

(a) when employer and member contribution rates under the plan were last established, it was reasonable to expect that, for each calendar year beginning with the year in which the contribution rates were last established,

(i) the aggregate of all amounts each of which is the pension credit of an individual for the year with respect to an employer under a benefit provision of the plan

would not exceed

(ii) 18 per cent of the aggregate of all amounts each of which is, for an individual and an employer where the pension credit of the individual for the year with respect to the employer under a benefit provision of the plan is greater than nil, the compensation of the individual from the employer for the year,

except that this condition does not apply for years before 1992 in the case of a pension plan that is a grandfathered plan;

(b) where the plan contains a money purchase provision,

(i) the plan terms are such that, if subsection 147.1(9) of the Act were applicable in respect of the plan, the plan would not under any circumstances become a revocable plan at the end of the year pursuant to that subsection, or

(ii) if the plan terms do not comply with the condition in subparagraph (i), the only circumstances that would result in the plan becoming a revocable plan at the end of the year pursuant to subsection 147.1(9) of the Act, if that subsection were applicable in respect of the plan, are circumstances acceptable to the Minister; and

(c) no contributions are made

(i) to the plan with respect to a member at any time after the end of the calendar year in which the member attains 71 years of age, or

(ii) to a defined benefit provision of the plan with respect to a member during a period (other than a "qualifying period", as defined in subsection 8503(16)) in which the member is in receipt of retirement benefits from a defined benefit provision of the plan.

Notes: Reg. 8510(7)(c) added by 2021 budget bill #1, for contributions made pursuant to any collective bargaining agreement entered into after 2019, except that it does not apply in respect of contributions made by the date the agreement is entered into. It implements a March 2019 Budget proposal, "Contributions to Specified Multi-Employer Plan for Older Members".

Information Circulars: 98-2: Prescribed compensation for RPPs, para. 6.

Registered Pension Plans Technical Manual: §17.7 (additional prescribed conditions).

Registered Plans Compliance Bulletins: 7 (making contributions and calculating and reporting pension adjustment for SMEPs).

(8) Purchase of additional benefits — Where, in the case of a pension plan that is a specified multi-employer plan in a calendar year,

(a) the amount of lifetime retirement benefits provided under a defined benefit provision of the plan to each member is determined by reference to the hours of employment of the member with participating employers,

(b) the plan permits a member whose actual hours of employment in a period are fewer than a specified number of hours for the period to make contributions to the plan in order to increase, to an amount not exceeding the specified number of hours for the period, the number of hours that are treated under the provision as hours of employment of the member in the period, and

(c) the specified number of hours for a period does not exceed a reasonable measure of the actual hours of employment of members who render services throughout the period on a full-time basis,

the condition in paragraph 8503(3)(a) does not apply in respect of such portion of the lifetime retirement benefits provided under the provision to a member as is determined by reference to hours acquired by the member as a consequence of contributions made to the plan in the year by the member, as described in paragraph (b).

Registered Pension Plans Technical Manual: §17.8 (purchase of additional benefits).

(9) Special rules — member-funded pension plans — Where a pension plan (other than a specified multi-employer plan) is a member-funded pension plan for the purposes of Division IX of the *Regulation respecting the exemption of certain categories of pension plans from the provisions of the Supplemental Pension Plans Act* of Quebec (R.Q., c. R.-15.1, r. 2), as amended from time to time,

(a) paragraph 8502(c) shall in its application in respect of the plan be read without reference to subparagraph (iii);

(b) the prescribed conditions for the registration of the plan include the following conditions:

(i) the plan terms are such that each contribution to be made by a member under a defined benefit provision of the plan

would be an eligible contribution under subsection 147.2(2) of the Act if

(A) the contribution were made by an employer who participates in the plan for the benefit of the member, and

(B) this subsection were read without reference to paragraph (c),

(ii) unless this condition is waived by the Minister, the plan is maintained pursuant to a collective bargaining agreement,

(iii) the plan is not, and it is reasonable to expect that the plan will not become, a designated plan, and

(iv) the amount of benefits provided to members, the amount of contributions required to be made by members and the entitlement of members' to benefit from actuarial surplus are determined in a manner that is

(A) clearly established in the plan terms, and

(B) not more advantageous for members who, at any time after the plan is established, are specified individuals (within the meaning assigned by subsection 8515(4)) under the plan than for members who are not specified individuals; and

(c) a contribution made by an employer to the plan is a prescribed contribution for the purposes of subsection 147.2(2) of the Act if

(i) the contribution is a current service contribution that would be an eligible contribution under subsection 147.2(2) of the Act if no contributions were prescribed for the purposes of that subsection and if that subsection were read without reference to its subparagraph (d)(ii), and

(ii) the recommendation pursuant to which the contribution is made is such that the current service contributions to be made by the employer do not exceed,

(A) where the amount of actuarial surplus in respect of the employer is greater than the amount determined under subparagraph 147.2(2)(d)(ii) of the Act, 50% of the current service contribution that would be required to be made by the employer if there were no actuarial surplus under the provisions, and

(B) in any other case, the current service contributions that would be required to be made by the employer if there were no actuarial surplus under the provisions.

Notes: Member-funded pension plans are a kind of plan introduced by the Régie des rentes du Québec, which governs pension plans in Quebec.

Reg. 8510(9)(c)(i) and (ii)(A) amended by 2010 budget bill #1 to delete references to ITA 147.2(2)(d)(iii), effective for contributions made after 2009 to fund benefits provided in respect of periods of pensionable service after 2009.

Reg. 8510(9) added by P.C. 2007-1443, effective June 24, 2007.

Registered Pension Plans Technical Manual: §17.9 (special rules — member-funded pension plans).

Definitions [Reg. 8510]: "active member" — Reg. 8500(1); "administrator" — ITA 147.1(1); "amount" — ITA 248(1); "benefit provision" — Reg. 8500(1); "benefits" — Reg. 8501(5)(c); "calendar year" — *Interpretation Act* 37(1)(a); "compensation" — ITA 147.1(1); "connected" — Reg. 8500(3); "contribution" — Reg. 8501(6); "defined benefit provision" — ITA 147.1(1), Reg. 8500(2); "employed", "employee", "employer", "employment" — ITA 248(1); "grandfathered plan" — Reg. 8500(1); "individual" — ITA 248(1); "lifetime retirement benefits" — Reg. 8500(1); "member" — ITA 147.1(1), Reg. 8300(1), 8500(2); "Minister" — ITA 248(1); "money purchase provision" — ITA 147.1(1); "multi-employer plan" — ITA 147.1(1), Reg. 8500(1); "participating employer" — ITA 147.1(1); "pension credit" — Reg. 8301, 8308.1(2)–(4), 8308.3(2), (3); "person" — ITA 248(1); "plan as registered" — ITA 147.1(15); "prescribed" — ITA 248(1); "qualifying period" — Reg. 8503(16); "related" — ITA 251(2)–(6); "retirement benefits" — Reg. 8500(1); "single amount" — ITA 147.1(1); "specified multi-employer plan" — ITA 147.1(1), Reg. 8510(2), (3); "writing" — *Interpretation Act* 35(1).

8511. Conditions applicable to amendments — **(1)** For the purposes of paragraph 147.1(4)(c) of the Act, the following conditions are prescribed in respect of an amendment to a registered pension plan:

(a) where the amendment increases the accrued lifetime retirement benefits provided to a member under a defined benefit provision of the plan, the increase is not, in the opinion of the Minister, inconsistent with the conditions in paragraphs 8503(3)(h) and (i); and

(b) where the plan is a grandfathered plan and the amendment increases the bridging benefits provided to a member under a defined benefit provision of the plan, the member's bridging benefits, as amended, comply with the condition in subparagraph 8503(2)(b)(ii) that would apply if the plan were not a grandfathered plan.

Registered Pension Plans Technical Manual: §18.1 (conditions applicable to amendments).

(2) Where an amendment to a registered pension plan provides for the return to a member of all or a part of the contributions made by the member under a defined benefit provision of the plan, the plan becomes a revocable plan at any time that an amount (other than an amount that may be transferred from the plan in accordance with subsection 147.3(6) of the Act) that is payable to the member as a consequence of the amendment is not paid to the member as soon after the amendment as is practicable.

Related Provisions: ITA 147.1(8), (9), 147.3(12), Reg. 8301(14)(a), 8305(2), 8408(2), 8501(2) 8503(11), (15), 8506(4), 8515(9) — Other ways plan becomes revocable plan.

Notes: Reg. 8511(2) amended by P.C. 1995-17, retroactive to its introduction (1989).

Registered Pension Plans Technical Manual: §18.2 (conditions applicable to amendments).

Definitions [Reg. 8511]: "amount" — ITA 248(1); "bridging benefits" — Reg. 8500(1); "contribution" — Reg. 8501(6); "defined benefit provision" — ITA 147.1(1), Reg. 8500(2); "grandfathered plan", "lifetime retirement benefits" — Reg. 8500(1); "member" — ITA 147.1(1), Reg. 8300(1), 8500(2); "Minister", "prescribed", "registered pension plan" — ITA 248(1); "revocable plan" — ITA 147.1(8), (9), 147.3(12), Reg. 8301(14)(a), 8305(2), 8408(2), 8501(2), 8503(11), (15), 8506(4), 8511(2), 8515(9).

8512. Registration and amendment — **(1)** For the purpose of subsection 147.1(2) of the Act, an application for registration of a pension plan shall be made by sending the following documents by registered mail to the Commissioner of Revenue at Ottawa:

(a) an application in prescribed form containing prescribed information;

(b) certified copies of the plan text and any other documents that contain terms of the plan;

(c) certified copies of all trust deeds, insurance contracts and other documents that relate to the funding of benefits under the plan;

(d) certified copies of all agreements that relate to the plan; and

(e) certified copies of all resolutions and by-laws that relate to the documents referred to in paragraphs (b) to (d).

Notes: Reg. 8512(1) opening words amended by P.C. 2007-849, effective June 13, 2007, to change "forwarding by registered mail to the Deputy Minister of National Revenue for Taxation at Ottawa the following documents" to "sending the following documents by registered mail to the Commissioner of Revenue at Ottawa".

Reg. 8512(1) applies as of Jan. 15, 1992. See Notes to Reg. 8520.

Registered Pension Plans Technical Manual: §18.3 (registration).

Registered Plans Directorate Newsletters: 91-4R (registration rules for money purchase provisions); 04-2R (RPP applications — processing an incomplete application).

Registered Plans Frequently Asked Questions: RPFAQ-2 (RPPs), q. 22 (what is a complete application for registering a pension plan?).

Forms: T510: Application to register a pension plan.

(2) Where an amendment is made to a registered pension plan, to the arrangement for funding benefits under the plan or to a document that has been filed with the Minister in respect of the plan, within 60 days after the day on which the amendment is made, the plan administrator shall send to the Commissioner of Revenue at Ottawa

(a) a prescribed form containing prescribed information; and

(b) certified copies of all documents that relate to the amendment.

Related Provisions: *Interpretation Act* 27(5) — Meaning of "within 60 days".

Notes: Reg. 8512(2) opening words amended by P.C. 2007-849, effective June 13, 2007, to change "Deputy Minister of National Revenue for Taxation" to "Commissioner of Revenue".

Registered Plans Compliance Bulletins: 1 (terminating registered pension plans).

Registered Plans Directorate Newsletters: 96-1 (changes to retirement savings limits); 04-2R (RPP applications — processing an incomplete application).

Registered Plans Frequently Asked Questions: RPFAQ-2 (RPPs), q. 23 (what is a complete application for amending an RPP?); q. 24 (what is a complete application for terminating an RPP?).

Registered Pension Plans Technical Manual: §18.4 (amendment).

Forms: T920: Application to amend an RPP.

(3) For the purpose of subsection 147.1(4) of the Act, an application for the acceptance of an amendment to a registered pension plan is made in prescribed manner if the documents that are required by subsection (2) are sent by registered mail to the Commissioner of Revenue at Ottawa.

Notes: Reg. 8512(3) amended by P.C. 2007-849, effective June 13, 2007, to change "where" to "if", "forwarded" to "sent", and "Deputy Minister of National Revenue for Taxation" to "Commissioner of Revenue".

Registered Pension Plans Technical Manual: §18.4 (amendment).

Registered Plans Directorate Newsletters: 04-2R (RPP applications — processing an incomplete application).

Definitions [Reg. 8512]: "administrator" — ITA 147.1(1); "benefits" — Reg. 8501(5)(c); "Minister", "prescribed", "registered pension plan" — ITA 248(1); "trust" — ITA 104(1), 248(1), (3).

8513. Designated laws — For the purposes of paragraph 8302(3)(m), subparagraph 8502(c)(iii) and paragraph 8517(5)(f), "designated provision of the law of Canada or a province" means subsection 21(2) of the *Pension Benefits Standards Act, 1985* and any provision of a law of a province that is similar to that subsection.

Definitions [Reg. 8513]: "province" — *Interpretation Act* 35(1).

Registered Pension Plans Technical Manual: §18.5 (designated laws).

Registered Plans Directorate Newsletters: 91-4R (registration rules for money purchase provisions).

8514. Prohibited investments — **(1)** For the purposes of subparagraph 8502(h)(i) and subject to subsections (2), (2.1) and (3), a prohibited investment in respect of a registered pension plan is a share of the capital stock of, an interest in, or a debt of

(a) an employer who participates in the plan,

(b) a person who is connected with an employer who participates in the plan,

(c) a member of the plan,

(d) a person or partnership that controls, directly or indirectly, in any manner whatever, a person or partnership referred to in paragraph (a) or (b), or

(e) a person or partnership that does not deal at arm's length with a person or partnership referred to in paragraph (a), (b), (c) or (d),

or an interest in, or a right to acquire, such a share, interest or debt.

Proposed Amendment — Reg. 8514(1)

Letter from Dept. of Finance, June 12, 2017: Mr. Jack A. Silverson, Osler, Hoskin & Harcourt LLP, Toronto; Mr. Vince F. Imerti, Stikeman Elliott LLP, Toronto

Dear Mr. Silverson and Mr. Imerti:

I am writing in response to your letter of November 23, 2016 and further discussions in which you outline proposed transactions and identify certain technical issues with the income tax rules that would apply to the transactions.

In your letter, you advise that [xxx]

- [xxx] a corporation without share capital, was established to provide investment management services and investment advisory services to its members.

- The initial members of [xxx]

- For the purposes of subsection 8514(1) of the *Income Tax Regulations* (the "Regulations"), none of the members have an "interest" in [xxx]

- The members may enter into investment management agreements with [xxx] if they wish to invest plan assets ([xxx])

I understand that [xxx] employees accrue pensionable service under the [xxx] and that some [xxx] employees will transfer their employment to [xxx]. It is contemplated that [xxx] will become a participating employer under the [xxx] so that, among other things, the transferred employees will benefit from uninterrupted pension coverage.

I also understand that [xxx] will manage the investment of [xxx] assets in certain pooled investment corporations, pooled investment partnerships and pooled investment trusts (collectively the "Pooled Vehicles"). [xxx] interest in any Pooled Vehicle would be limited to that consistent with its role as investment manager and advisor. You have indicated that by virtue of its role as investment manager and advisor, [xxx] is expected to factually not deal at arm's length with the Pooled Vehicles. As a result, if [xxx] were a participating employer under the [xxx] an investment in a Pooled Vehicle would be a prohibited investment described in paragraph 8514(1)(e) of the Regulations for the [xxx].

In this context, you have requested that we recommend amendments to section 8514 of the Regulations to permit [xxx] to be a participating employer under the [xxx] without causing the Pooled Vehicles to be prohibited investments for [xxx]. We agree that the proposed transactions do not raise income tax policy concerns. In Particular, we understand that, but for [xxx] being a participating employer, the Pooled Vehicles would not be prohibited investments under the Regulations and would adhere to investment restrictions under [xxx].

We are prepared to recommend that a recommendation be made to the Governor General in Council that amendments to section 8514 of the Regulations be made such that a person or partnership in which a registered pension plan invests would not be a prohibited investment to the plan solely because the person or partnership does not deal at arm's length with a participating employer whose main object is the management of, and/or the provision of investment advice in respect of, the fund of a registered pension plan, Her Majesty in right of Canada, Her Majesty in right of a province, or an entity described in any of paragraphs 149(1)(c) and (d) to (d.4) of the *Income Tax Act*.

We would also recommend that the proposed amendments apply in respect of investments made after May 2017.

While I cannot offer any assurance that the Governor General in Council will agree with our recommendations, I hope that this statement of our intention is helpful to you.

Thank you for writing to us on this matter.

Yours sincerely,

Brian Ernewein, General Director, Legislation, Tax Policy Branch

Notes: Opening words of Reg. 8514(1) amended by P.C. 2001-153 to add reference to (2.1), effective for property acquired after September 1999.

Registered Pension Plans Technical Manual: §18.6 (prohibited investments).

(2) A prohibited investment does not include

(a) a debt obligation described in paragraph (a) of the definition "fully exempt interest" in subsection 212(3) of the Act;

(b) a share listed on a designated stock exchange;

(c) a bond, debenture, note or similar obligation of a corporation any shares of which are listed on a designated stock exchange;

(d) an interest in, or a right to acquire, property referred to in paragraph (b) or (c); or

(e) a mortgage in respect of real property situated in Canada that

(i) where this condition has not been waived by the Minister and the amount paid for the mortgage, together with the amount of any indebtedness outstanding at the time the mortgage was acquired under any mortgage or hypothec that ranks equally with or superior to the mortgage, exceeds 75 per cent of the fair market value, at that time, of the real property that is subject to the mortgage, is insured under the *National Housing Act* or by a corporation that offers its services to the public in Canada as an insurer of mortgages,

(ii) where the registered pension plan in connection with which the mortgage is held would be a designated plan for the purposes of subsection 8515(5) if subsection 8515(4) were read without reference to paragraph (b) thereof, is administered by an approved lender under the *National Housing Act*, and

(iii) bears a rate of interest that would be reasonable in the circumstances if the mortgagor dealt with the mortgagee at arm's length.

Notes: Reg. 8514(2)(a) changed from "a bond, debenture, note, mortgage or similar obligation described in clause 212(1)(b)(ii)(C) of the Act" by 2007 budget bill #2, effective 2008 (due to changes to ITA 212(1)(b)).

Reg. 8514(2)(b), (c) amended by 2007 budget bill #2, effective Dec. 14, 2007, to change "stock exchange referred to in section 3200 or 3201" to "designated stock exchange".

Reg. 8514(2)(a) amended to change "mortgage, hypothec" to "mortgage" by P.C. 1994-1817, effective Nov. 30, 1994. This change was intended to be non-substantive.

Registered Pension Plans Technical Manual: §18.7 (mortgages).

(2.1) [Multi-employer plan] — Where a share of the capital stock of, an interest in or a debt of, a person who is connected with a particular employer who participates in a registered pension plan that is a multi-employer plan would, but for this subsection, be a prohibited investment in respect of the plan, the property is not a prohibited investment in respect of the plan if

(a) the plan contains no money purchase provision other than a money purchase provision under which each member account is credited, on a reasonable basis and no less frequently than annually, an amount based on the income earned, losses incurred and capital gains and capital losses realized, on all of the property held by the plan;

(b) at the time the property is acquired by the plan, there are at least 15 employers who participate in the plan, and, for this purpose,

(i) all employers who are related to each other are deemed to be a single employer, and

(ii) all the structural units of a trade union, including each local, branch, national and international unit, are deemed to be a single employer;

(c) at the time the property is acquired by the plan, no more than 10% of the active members of the plan are employed by the particular employer or by any person related to the particular employer;

(d) the property would not be a prohibited investment in respect of the plan if subsection (1) were read without reference to paragraph (1)(b); and

(e) immediately after the time the property is acquired by the plan, the total of all amounts each of which is the cost amount to a person of a property held in connection with the plan that would, but for this subsection, be a prohibited investment in respect of the plan does not exceed 10% of the total of all amounts each of which is the cost amount to a person of a property held in connection with the plan.

Related Provisions: Reg. 8514(2.2) — Whether Crown corporations "related" to each other.

Notes: Reg. 8514(2.1)(a) changed from "the plan does not contain a money purchase provision" by 2002-2013 technical bill (Part 5 — technical), effective 2011.

Reg. 8514(2.1) added by P.C. 2001-153, effective for property acquired after September 1999.

Registered Pension Plans Technical Manual: §18.8 (prohibited investments — MEP).

(2.2) [Crown corporations — whether related] — For the purposes of the conditions in paragraphs (2.1)(b) and (c), two corporations that are related to each other solely because they are both controlled by Her Majesty in right of Canada or a province are deemed not to be related to each other.

Notes: Reg. 8514(2.2) added by P.C. 2001-153, effective for property acquired after September 1999.

(3) A prohibited investment in respect of a registered pension plan does not include an investment that was acquired by the plan before March 28, 1988.

Related Provisions: Reg. 8514(4) — When debt obligation deemed to be issued.

(4) For the purposes of subsection (3), where at any time after March 27, 1988, the principal amount of a bond, debenture, note, mortgage or similar obligation increases as a consequence of the advancement or lending of additional amounts, or the maturity date of such an obligation is extended, the obligation shall, after that time, be deemed to have been issued at that time.

Notes: Reg. 8514(4) amended to change "mortgage, hypothec" to "mortgage" by P.C. 1994-1817, effective Nov. 30, 1994. This change was intended to be non-substantive.

Definitions [Reg. 8514]: "active member" — Reg. 8500(1); "amount" — ITA 248(1); "arm's length" — ITA 251(1); "Canada" — ITA 255, *Interpretation Act* 35(1); "connected" — Reg. 8500(3); "corporation" — ITA 248(1), *Interpretation Act* 35(1); "cost amount" — ITA 248(1); "designated stock exchange" — ITA 248(1), 262; "employed", "employer" — ITA 248(1); "fair market value" — see ITA 69(1) Notes; "fully exempt interest" — ITA 212(3); "Her Majesty" — *Interpretation Act* 35(1); "insurer" — ITA 248(1); "member" — ITA 147.1(1), Reg. 8300(1), 8500(2); "Minister" — ITA 248(1); "money purchase provision" — ITA 147.1(1); "multi-employer plan" — ITA 147.1(1), Reg. 8500(1); "partnership" — see ITA 96(1) Notes; "person", "principal amount", "property" — ITA 248(1); "province" — *Interpretation Act* 35(1); "registered pension plan" — ITA 248(1); "related" — ITA 251(2)–(6), Reg. 8514(2.2); "share" — ITA 248(1).

8515. Special rules for designated plans [Individual Pension Plans] — (1) Designated plans — For the purposes of subsections (5) and (9), and subject to subsection (3), a registered pension plan that contains a defined benefit provision is a designated plan throughout a calendar year if the plan is not maintained pursuant to a collective bargaining agreement and

(a) the aggregate of all amounts each of which is a pension credit (as determined under Part LXXXIII) for the year of a specified individual under a defined benefit provision of the plan

exceeds

(b) 50 per cent of the aggregate of all amounts each of which is a pension credit (as determined under Part LXXXIII) for the year of an individual under a defined benefit provision of the plan.

Related Provisions: ITA 147.3(3)(c) — IPP excluded from defined-benefit RPP transfer rule; Reg. 8300(1)"individual pension plan" — Definition; Reg. 8500(1)"designated plan" — Definition applies to all of Part 85; Reg. 8503(26) — IPP minimum withdrawal; Reg. 8515(3) — Exceptions; Reg. 8515(4) — Specified individual.

Notes: Reg. 8515 provides for an Individual Pension Plan (IPP). See Merrick, *The Essential Individual Pension Plan Handbook* (LexisNexis, 2007, 350pp.); Théroux & Rowse, "Individual Pension Plans", 1991 Corporate Management Tax Conference (ctf.ca) 8:1-65 and 1991 BC Tax Conf (ctf.ca) 11:1-152; Gasparro, "Current Issues", 2011 Ontario Tax Conf (ctf.ca), 1B:1-27; Gosselin & Laporte, "A Review of Individual Pension Plans", 61(1) *Canadian Tax Journal* 257-278 (2013); Koiv et al, "Individual Pension Plans", 2018 STEP Canada conference, 40pp (contact memberservices@step.ca); Antel, "An Owner-Manager Remuneration Perspective on IPPs and RCAs", 2018 Prairie Provinces Tax Conf.

ITA 147.3(3)(c) was amended in 2021 to prevent plans that would transfer excessive pension to an IPP sponsored by a different employer.

Shorter articles on IPPs: Baston, "IPPs Revisited", 6(2) *Taxation of Executive Compensation & Retirement [TECR]* (Federated Press) 19-22 (Sept. 1994); Casanova, "Portability and Proportionality of IPPs", 11(1) *TECR* 174-76 (July-Aug. 1999); Belley, "Owner-Manager Compensation 3: IPPs", 2(1) *Tax for the Owner-Manager* (ctf.ca) 5-6 (Jan. 2002); Anderson, " 'Super-sized' Retirement Plan", 19(1) *TECR* 864-70 (July/Aug. 2007); Bullock, "Changes for Individual Pension Plans Proposed", 22(8) *TECR* 1396-97 (April 2011); Peermohamed, "Individual Pension Plans: Non-Compliance with the Primary Purpose Test", 3(2) *Canadian Tax Focus* (ctf.ca) 7-8 (May 2013); Koiv & Kennedy, "Why IPPs can help more business owners than you'd expect", tinyurl.com/ipp-koiv; Koiv & Lesniewski, "What the IPP Numbers Look Like in 2018", tinyurl.com/ipp-numbers; Marta & Maguire, "Individual Pension Plans as Executive Compensation and Considerations in Corporate Transactions", XXVIII(2) *TECR* 9-16 (2020). On Ontario relaxing IPP rules in 2020: tinyurl.com/osler-213.

CRA discussion: Registered Plans Directorate newsletters 01-3, 04-1, 14-1, 14-2, 16-1, 16-3, 21-1; docs 9310360, 2009-0326971C6, 2009-0326981C6, 2012-0435731C6, 2014-0553991E5, 2016-066593117. See also Reg. 8502(h) Notes; and the 2021 budget bill #1 amendments to Reg. 8503(3)(a)(v), (v.1) and (vi).

"Tailored" IPPs are not acceptable: RPD newsletter 01-3. A pension plan for employees of a partnership is acceptable: VIEWS doc 9218566. IPPs that are designed to extract public service pension rather than to provide retirement benefits for new employment have been revoked by CRA: see Notes to 147.1(11).

For CRA interpretations on deductibility of employer contributions to an IPP see docs 2008-0284471C6 (where corp year-end and actuarial period do not match); 2016-0627311E5 (where employer contributing to RCA and IPP using employee's years of service).

For another option see Tehranchian, "Personal Pension Plans", 11(2) *Taxes & Wealth Management* (Carswell) 9-11 (March 2018) (also in *Canadian Bushiness Journal*, Feb. 2018).

See also Reg. 8300(1)"individual pension plan" and the provisions listed in the Related Provisions annotation to that definition, introduced by the 2011 Budget.

For an ongoing lawsuit against a planner that set up a bad IPP, see *Nelson v. Lavoie*, 2019 ONCA 431 (limitation period met).

Registered Pension Plans Technical Manual: §19.1 (designated plan).

Registered Plans Compliance Bulletins: 2 (funding designated RPPs).

Registered Plans Directorate Actuarial Bulletins: 2 (designated plans — funding issues).

Registered Plans Directorate Newsletters: 01-3 (tailored individual pension plan); 04-1 (pitfalls to avoid); 14-1 (reviewing earnings and service for IPPs); 14-2 (IPP minimum amount); 16-1 (qualifying transfers to IPPs); 16-3 (transfers from underfunded IPPs); 21-1 (additional conditions for IPPs and designated plans).

Registered Plans Frequently Asked Questions: RPFAQ-2 (RPPs), q. 11 (IPPs established primarily to transfer funds from an existing RPP); q. 25 (designated status where specified individuals have no further defined benefit credits).

(2) Designated plan in previous year — For the purposes of subsections (5) and (9), a registered pension plan is a designated plan throughout a particular calendar year after 1990 if the plan was a designated plan at any time in the immediately preceding year, except where the Minister has waived in writing the application of this subsection in respect of the plan.

Related Provisions: Reg. 8500(1)"designated plan" — Definition applies to all of Part 85.

Notes: The purpose of Reg. 8515(2) is to prevent a plan from moving in and out of the "designated plan" category. CRA may waive Reg. 8515(2) if the RPP is unlikely to become a designated plan. This condition is considered to be met for a year in which no more pension credits accrue under a defined-benefit provision and there are no more restricted-funding members per Reg. 8515(8). (tinyurl.com/rpp-faqs, q.25)

Registered Pension Plans Technical Manual: §19.2 (designated plan in previous year).

Registered Plans Frequently Asked Questions: RPFAQ-2 (RPPs), q. 25 (designated status where specified individuals have no further defined benefit credits).

(3) Exceptions — A registered pension plan is not a designated plan in a calendar year pursuant to subsection (1) if

(a) the plan would not be a designated plan in the year pursuant to that subsection if the reference in paragraph (1)(b) to "50 per cent" were read as a reference to "60 per cent",

(b) the plan was established before the year, and

(c) the amount determined under paragraph (1)(a) in respect of the plan for the immediately preceding year did not exceed the amount determined under paragraph (1)(b).

Related Provisions: Reg. 8515(3.1) — Where plan has more than 9 active members.

Notes: Reg. 8515(3) amended by P.C. 2011-936, effective Feb. 20, 2011, to delete an alternate test of more than 9 active members and notice from the Minister that the plan is not a designated plan in the year (see now Reg. 8515(3.1)).

Registered Pension Plans Technical Manual: §19.3 (exceptions).

(3.1) If a designated plan has more than nine active members, the Minister may waive the application of any provision of this Part or Part LXXXIII that would otherwise apply to the designated plan because of its status as a designated plan.

Notes: Reg. 8515(3.1) added by P.C. 2011-936, effective Feb. 20, 2011.

Registered Pension Plans Technical Manual: §19.4 (exceptions).

(4) Specified individuals — An individual is a specified individual for the purposes of paragraph (1)(a) in respect of a pension plan and a particular calendar year if

(a) the individual was connected at any time in the year with an employer who participates in the plan; or

(b) the aggregate of all amounts each of which is the remuneration of the individual for the year from an employer who participates in the plan, or from an employer who does not deal at arm's length with a participating employer, exceeds 2½ times the Year's Maximum Pensionable Earnings for the year.

Registered Pension Plans Technical Manual: §19.5 (specified individual).

Registered Plans Frequently Asked Questions: RPFAQ-2 (RPPs), q. 25 (designated status where specified individuals have no further defined benefit credits).

(5) Eligible contributions — For the purpose of determining whether a contribution made by an employer to a registered pension plan at a time when the plan is a designated plan is an eligible contribution under subsection 147.2(2) of the Act, a prescribed condition is that

(a) the contribution satisfies the condition in subsection (6), or

(b) the contribution would satisfy the condition in subsection (6) if

(i) paragraph (6)(b) and subparagraph (7)(e)(i) were applicable only in respect of retirement benefits that became provided under the plan after 1990,

(ii) paragraph (6)(c) were applicable only in respect of those benefits payable after the death of a member that relate to retirement benefits that became provided under the plan to the member after 1990, and

(iii) the assumption as to the time retirement benefits (other than retirement benefits that became provided after 1990) will commence to be paid is the same for the purposes of the maximum funding valuation as for the purposes of the actuarial valuation that forms the basis for the recommendation referred to in subsection 147.2(2) of the Act pursuant to which the contribution is made.

Related Provisions: ITA 147.2(7) — Amount paid by letter-of-credit issuer deemed to be eligible contribution; Reg. 8515(1)–(3) — Designated plans.

Notes: Reg. 8515(5) applies to contributions made after 1991 to a pension plan that was registered by July 31, 1991, and to contributions made after 1990 if the pension plan was registered after July 1991.

Registered Pension Plans Technical Manual: §19.6 (eligible contributions).

Registered Plans Directorate Actuarial Bulletins: 2 (eligible employer contributions to a designated plan).

(6) Funding restriction — The condition referred to in subsection (5) is that the contribution would be required to be made for the plan to have sufficient assets to pay benefits under the defined benefit provisions of the plan, as registered, with respect to the employees and former employees of the employer if

(a) required contributions were determined on the basis of a maximum funding valuation prepared as of the same effective date as the actuarial valuation that forms the basis for the recommendation referred to in subsection 147.2(2) of the Act pursuant to which the contribution is made;

(a.1) each defined benefit provision of the plan provided that, with respect to restricted-funding members, retirement benefits are payable monthly in advance;

(b) each defined benefit provision of the plan provided that, after retirement benefits commence to be paid with respect to a restricted-funding member, the benefits are adjusted annually by a percentage increase for each year that is 1 percentage point less than the percentage increase in the Consumer Price Index for the year, in lieu of any cost-of-living adjustments actually provided;

(c) each defined benefit provision of the plan provided the following benefits after the death of a restricted-funding member who dies after retirement benefits under the provision have commenced to be paid to the member, in lieu of the benefits actually provided:

(i) where the member dies within 5 years after retirement benefits commence to be paid under the provision, the continuation of the retirement benefits for the remainder of the 5 years as if the member were alive, and

(ii) where an individual who is a spouse or common-law partner of the member when retirement benefits commence to be paid under the provision to the member is alive on the later of the day of death of the member and the day that is 5 years after the day on which the member's retirement benefits commence to be paid, retirement benefits payable to the individual for the duration of the individual's life, with the amount of the benefits payable for each month equal to $66\frac{2}{3}$ per cent of the amount of retirement benefits that would have been payable under the provision for the month to the member if the member were alive;

(d) where more than one employer participates in the plan, assets and actuarial liabilities were apportioned in a reasonable manner among participating employers with respect to their employees and former employees; and

(e) the rule in paragraph 147.2(2)(d) of the Act that provides for the disregard of a portion of the assets of the plan apportioned to the employer with respect to the employer's employees and former employees were applicable for the purpose of determining required contributions pursuant to this subsection.

Related Provisions: Reg. 8515(7) — Maximum funding valuation; Reg. 8515(8) — Restricted-funding member.

Notes: Reg. 8515(6)(c)(ii) amended by P.C. 2001-957 to add reference to "common-law partner", effective as per Notes to ITA 248(1)"common-law partner".

Registered Pension Plans Technical Manual: §19.7 (funding restriction).

Registered Plans Directorate Actuarial Bulletins: 2 (eligible employer contributions to a designated plan).

(7) Maximum funding valuation — For the purposes of subsection (6), a maximum funding valuation is a valuation prepared by an actuary in accordance with the following rules:

(a) the projected accrued benefit method is used for the purpose of determining actuarial liabilities and current service costs;

(b) the valuation rate of interest is 7.5 per cent per annum;

(c) it is assumed that

(i) the rate of increase in general wages and salaries and in each member's rate of remuneration will be 5.5 per cent per annum, and

(ii) the rate of increase in the Consumer Price Index will be 4 per cent per annum;

(d) each assumption made in respect of economic factors other than those referred to in paragraph (c) is consistent with the assumptions in that paragraph;

(e) in the case of a restricted-funding member, it is assumed that

(i) retirement benefits will commence to be paid to the member no earlier than the day on which the member attains 65 years of age,

(ii) the member will survive to the time the member's retirement benefits commence to be paid,

(iii) where the member is employed by a participating employer as of the effective date of the valuation, the member will continue in employment until the time when the member's retirement benefits commence to be paid, and

(iv) when the member's retirement benefits commence to be paid, the member will be married to a person who is the same age as the member;

(f) the rate of mortality at each age is equal to

(i) in the case of a restricted-funding member, 80 per cent of the average of the rates at that age for males and females in the *1983 Group Annuity Mortality Table*, as published in Volume XXXV of the *Transactions of the Society of Actuaries*, and

(ii) in the case of any other member, 80 per cent of the rate at that age in the mortality table referred to in subparagraph (i) for individuals of the same sex as the member;

(g) it is assumed that where a member has a choice between receiving retirement benefits or a lump sum payment, retirement benefits will be paid to the member; and

(h) the plan's assets are valued at an amount equal to their fair market value as of the effective date of the valuation.

Related Provisions: Reg. 8515(8) — Restricted-funding member.

Notes: Despite low interest rates, a change in the fixed 7.5% interest rate assumption is not being pursued, but exemption can be requested using the waiver provisions: tinyurl.com/rpd-consults, "Questions from the Industry" 2003 q.8. However, this question has now been removed.

Reg. 8515(7)(e)(i) amended by P.C. 1995-17, retroactive to its introduction (1989), to delete an assumption that the member's pension would begin to be paid on the later of the effective date of the valuation and the member's 65th birthday, if the pension had not begun by the time the valuation was prepared. This assumption is inappropriate if the member continues to accrue benefits after age 65.

Reg. 8515(7)(f) amended by P.C. 1995-17, to limit subpara. (i) to a restricted-funding member and add subpara. (ii). For female members, the amendment is retroactive to the introduction of the rules limiting contributions to designated plans (1989). However, for a contribution made by June 4, 1994, or pursuant to a valuation report filed with Revenue Canada under ITA 147.2(3) by June 4, 1994, subpara. (i) applies to a male member who is not a restricted-funding member.

Registered Pension Plans Technical Manual: §19.8 (maximum funding valuation).

Registered Plans Directorate Actuarial Bulletins: 2 (eligible employer contributions to a designated plan).

(8) Restricted-funding members — For the purposes of subsections (6) and (7) as they apply in respect of a contribution made to a registered pension plan, a member of the plan is a restricted-funding member if, at the time the maximum funding valuation is prepared,

(a) the member has a right, whether absolute or contingent, to receive retirement benefits under a defined benefit provision of the plan and the benefits have not commenced to be paid; or

(b) the payment of retirement benefits under a defined benefit provision of the plan to the member has been suspended.

Registered Pension Plans Technical Manual: §19.9 (restricted-funding members).

Registered Plans Directorate Actuarial Bulletins: 2 (eligible employer contributions to a designated plan).

Registered Plans Frequently Asked Questions: RPFAQ-2 (RPPs), q. 25 (designated status where specified individuals have no further defined benefit credits).

(9) Member contributions — Where

(a) a member of a registered pension plan makes a contribution to the plan to fund benefits that have become provided at a particular time under a defined benefit provision of the plan in respect of periods before that time,

(b) the contribution is made at a time when the plan is a designated plan, and

(c) the contribution would not be an eligible contribution under subsection 147.2(2) of the Act if it were made by an employer who participates in the plan on behalf of the member,

the plan becomes, for the purposes of paragraph 147.1(11)(c) of the Act, a revocable plan immediately before the time the contribution is made.

Related Provisions: ITA 147.1(8), (9), 147.3(12), Reg. 8301(14)(a), 8305(2), 8408(2), 8501(2) 8503(11), (15), 8506(4), 8511(2) — Other ways plan becomes revocable plan; Reg. 8515(1)–(3) — Designated plans.

Registered Pension Plans Technical Manual: §19.10 (member contributions).

Definitions [Reg. 8515]: "active member" — Reg. 8500(1); "actuary", "administrator" — ITA 147.1(1); "amount" — ITA 248(1); "arm's length" — ITA 251(1); "benefits" — Reg. 8501(5)(c); "calendar year" — *Interpretation Act* 37(1)(a); "connected" — Reg. 8500(3); "Consumer Price Index" — Reg. 8500(1); "contribution" — Reg. 8501(6); "defined benefit provision" — ITA 147.1(1), Reg. 8500(2); "designated plan" — Reg. 8515(1)–(3); "employed", "employee", "employer", "employment" — ITA 248(1); "fair market value" — see ITA 69(1) Notes; "individual" — ITA 248(1); "maximum funding valuation" — Reg. 8515(7); "member" — ITA 147.1(1); "Minister" — ITA 248(1); "month" — *Interpretation Act* 35(1); "participating employer" — ITA 147.1(1); "pension credit" — Reg. 8301, 8308.1(2)–(4), 8308.3(2), (3); "person" — ITA 248(1); "plan as registered" — ITA 147.1(15); "prescribed" — ITA 248(1); "registered pension plan" — Reg. 8515(1), (2); "restricted-funding member" — Reg. 8515(8); "retirement benefits" — Reg. 8500(1); "revocable plan" — ITA 147.1(8), (9), 147.3(12), Reg. 8301(14)(a), 8305(2), 8408(2), 8501(2), 8503(11), (15), 8506(4), 8511(2), 8515(9); "specified individual" — Reg. 8515(4); "spouse" — Reg. 8500(5); "writing" — *Interpretation Act* 35(1); "written" — *Interpretation Act* 35(1)"writing"; "Year's Maximum Pensionable Earnings" — Reg. 8500(1).

8516. Eligible contributions — (1) Prescribed contribution — For the purposes of subsection 147.2(2) of the Act, a contribution described in subsection (2) or (3) is a prescribed contribution.

Related Provisions: Reg. 8510(9) — Member-funded pension plans.

Notes: See Notes at end of Reg. 8516.

Reg. 8516(1) amended by 2010 budget bill #1 to delete reference to (repealed) subsec. (4), effective for contributions made after 2009 to fund benefits provided in respect of periods of pensionable service after 2009.

Registered Pension Plans Technical Manual: §19.11 (prescribed contribution).

(2) Funding on termination basis — A contribution that is made by an employer to a registered pension plan is described in this subsection if

(a) the contribution is made pursuant to a recommendation by an actuary in whose opinion the contribution is required to be made so that, if the plan is terminated immediately after the contribution is made, it will have sufficient assets to pay benefits accrued under the defined benefit provisions of the plan, as registered, to the time the contribution is made;

(b) the recommendation is based on an actuarial valuation that complies with the following conditions:

(i) the effective date of the valuation is not more than four years before the day on which the contribution is made,

(ii) all assumptions made for the purposes of the valuation are reasonable at the time the valuation is prepared and at the time the contribution is made,

(iii) the valuation is prepared in accordance with generally accepted actuarial principles applicable with respect to a valuation prepared on the basis that a plan will be terminated, and

(iv) where more than one employer participates in the plan, assets and actuarial liabilities are apportioned in a reasonable manner among participating employers;

(c) the recommendation is approved by the Minister; and

(d) at the time the contribution is made, the plan is not a designated plan.

Notes: See at end of Reg. 8516.

Registered Pension Plans Technical Manual: §19.12 (funding on termination basis).

Registered Plans Directorate Actuarial Bulletins: 2 (eligible employer contributions to a designated plan).

(3) Contributions required by pension benefits legislation — A contribution that is made by an employer to a registered pension plan is described in this subsection if

(a) the contribution

(i) is required to be made to comply with the *Pension Benefits Standards Act, 1985* or a similar law of a province,

(ii) is made in respect of benefits under the defined benefit provisions of the plan as registered, and

(iii) is made pursuant to a recommendation by an actuary;

(b) the recommendation is based on an actuarial valuation that complies with the following conditions:

(i) the effective date of the valuation is not more than four years before the day on which the contribution is made,

(ii) all assumptions made for the purposes of the valuation are reasonable at the time the valuation is prepared and at the time the contribution is made, and

(iii) where more than one employer participates in the plan, assets and actuarial liabilities are apportioned in a reasonable manner among participating employers;

(c) the recommendation is approved by the Minister; and

(d) at the time the contribution is made, the plan is not a designated plan.

Notes: See at end of Reg. 8516.

Registered Pension Plans Technical Manual: §19.13 (contributions required by pension benefits legislation).

Registered Plans Directorate Actuarial Bulletins: 2 (eligible employer contributions to a designated plan).

(4) [Repealed]

Notes: Reg. 8516(4), "Shared funding arrangement", repealed by 2010 budget bill #1, for contributions after 2009 to fund benefits provided in respect of periods of pensionable service after 2009. See Notes to ITA 147.2(2).

Reg. 8516(2)(d), (3)(d) and (4)(e) amended by 2007 budget bill #2, effective 2008.

Reg. 8516 amended by P.C. 2003-1497, for contributions made after 2002. Reg. 8516(4) provided more flexibility to RPPs that implemented funding arrangements requiring participating employers and members to share entitlement to surplus and liability for actuarial deficiencies. They permitted employer contributions to be made to such a plan as follows where the contributions would not otherwise be allowed by former ITA 147.2(2) because the plan's funding ratio exceeded 110%:

Funding ratio	Total employer + employee current service contributions
>110% and ≤ 115%	75% of current service costs
>115% and ≤ 120%	50% of current service costs
>120% and ≤ 125%	25% of current service costs
>125%	nil

Reg. 8516 added by P.C. 1995-17, effective 1989; Reg. 8516(9) added by P.C. 1998-2256, effective 1996.

Definitions [Reg. 8516]: "actuary" — ITA 147.1(1); "amount" — ITA 248(1); "benefits" — Reg. 8501(5)(c); "contribution" — Reg. 8501(6); "defined benefit provision" — ITA 147.1(1), Reg. 8500(2); "designated plan" — Reg. 8500(1); "employee", "employer" — ITA 248(1); "member" — ITA 147.1(1); "Minister" — ITA 248(1); "participating employer" — ITA 147.1(1); "plan as registered" — ITA 147.1(15); "prescribed" — ITA 248(1); "province" — *Interpretation Act* 35(1); "registered pension plan" — ITA 248(1); "surplus" — Reg. 8500(1).

8517. Transfer — defined benefit to money purchase — (1) Prescribed amount

— Subject to subsections (2) to (3.1), for the purpose of applying paragraph 147.3(4)(c) of the Act to the transfer of an amount on behalf of an individual in full or partial satisfaction of the individual's entitlement to benefits under a defined benefit provision of a registered pension plan, the prescribed amount is the amount that is determined by the formula

$$A \times B$$

where

A is the amount of the individual's lifetime retirement benefits under the provision commuted in connection with the transfer, as determined under subsection (4), and

B is

(a) the present value factor that corresponds to the age attained by the individual at the time of the transfer, determined pursuant to the table to this subsection, or

(b) where the present value factor referred to in paragraph (a) is less than the present value factor that corresponds to the next higher age, the present value factor determined by interpolation between those two factors on the basis of the age (expressed in years, including any fraction of a year) of the individual.

Attained Age	Present Value Factor	Attained Age	Present Value Factor
Under 50	9.0	73	9.8
50	9.4	74	9.4
51	9.6	75	9.1
52	9.8	76	8.7
53	10.0	77	8.4
54	10.2	78	8.0
55	10.4	79	7.7
56	10.6	80	7.3
57	10.8	81	7.0
58	11.0	82	6.7
59	11.3	83	6.4
60	11.5	84	6.1
61	11.7	85	5.8
62	12.0	86	5.5
63	12.2	87	5.2
64	12.4	88	4.9

Attained Age	Present Value Factor	Attained Age	Present Value Factor
65	12.4	89	4.7
66	12.0	90	4.4
67	11.7	91	4.2
68	11.3	92	3.9
69	11.0	93	3.7
70	10.6	94	3.5
71	10.3	95	3.2
72	10.1	96 or over	3.0

Related Provisions: Reg. 8517(3.01) — Transfer of commuted pension where employer insolvent.

Notes: See the *Yudelson* case in Notes to ITA 147.3(4).

Reg. 8517(1) opening words amended by P.C. 1998-2256, effective for amounts transferred in respect of benefits provided after 1996, to make it subject to subsec. (3.1).

Table amended by P.C. 1998-2256, for transfers that occur after 1995. The former table used the same numbers for ages 50-71, but read "0.0" for age 72 or over. The change allows a person over 72 to transfer a single amount from a defined benefit RPP to a RRIF (if permitted by the plan to do so), without the negative consequences of ITA 147.3(10) (income inclusion, possible RRSP overcontributions penalty tax) and (12) (potential revocation of the plan's registration). Such a transfer cannot be made to an RRSP or money purchase provision of an RPP because of the registration rules that apply to such plans.

Interpretation Bulletins: IT-528: Transfers of funds between registered plans.

Registered Pension Plans Technical Manual: §20.1 (prescribed amount).

Registered Plans Compliance Bulletins: 8 (transfers from an RPP when the plan is underfunded at termination).

Registered Plans Directorate Newsletters: 04-1 (transfer from a defined benefit provision).

Forms: T2151: Direct transfer of a single amount under subsec. 147(19) or s. 147.3.

(2) Minimum prescribed amount — Where an amount is transferred in full satisfaction of an individual's entitlement to benefits under a defined benefit provision of a registered pension plan, the prescribed amount for the purposes of paragraph 147.3(4)(c) of the Act in respect of the transfer is the greater of the amount that would, but for this subsection, be the prescribed amount, and the balance, at the time of the transfer, in the individual's net contribution account (within the meaning assigned by subsection 8503(1)) in relation to the provision.

Registered Pension Plans Technical Manual: §20.2 (minimum prescribed amount).

Registered Plans Directorate Newsletters: 04-1 (transfer from a defined benefit provision).

(3) Underfunded pension [conditions for 8517(3.01)] — Subsection (3.01) applies in respect of a transfer of an amount on behalf of an individual in full or partial satisfaction of the individual's entitlement to benefits under a defined benefit provision of a registered pension plan if

(a) the individual is an employee or a former employee of an employer (or a predecessor employer of the employer);

(b) the employer

(i) was a participating employer under the provision,

(ii) is the subject of proceedings commenced under the *Bankruptcy and Insolvency Act* or the *Companies' Creditors Arrangement Act*, and

(iii) has ceased making regular contributions under the provision;

(c) after the commencement of the proceedings, lifetime retirement benefits paid or payable to the individual under the provision have been reduced because the assets of the plan are insufficient to pay the benefits provided under the provision of the plan as registered;

(d) the plan is not a designated plan; and

(e) the Minister has approved the application of subsection (3.01) in respect of the transfer.

Notes: Reg. 8517(3) replaced by 2011 budget bill #2, effective 2011. See Notes to ITA 146(5.2); and CRA Q&A "Measure for Members of Registered Pension Plans Sponsored by Employers who have Commenced Bankruptcy and Insolvency Proceedings" (April 4, 2012) at tinyurl.com/cra-rpp-bankrupt.

Registered Pension Plans Technical Manual: §20.3 (underfunded pension).

(3.001) [Rollover of commuted pension where employer insolvent] — Subsection (3.01) applies in respect of a transfer of an amount on behalf of an individual in full or partial satisfaction of the individual's entitlement to benefits under a defined benefit provision of a registered pension plan if

(a) the individual is an employee or a former employee of an employer (or a predecessor employer of the employer) that was a participating employer under the provision;

(b) lifetime retirement benefits paid or payable to the individual under the provision have been reduced because the assets of the plan are insufficient to pay the benefits provided under the provision of the plan as registered;

(c) the Minister has approved the application of subsection (3.01) in respect of the transfer; and

(d) either

(i) the plan is not an individual pension plan and the reduction in the lifetime retirement benefits paid or payable to the individual has been approved under the *Pension Benefits Standards Act, 1985* or a similar law of a province, or

(ii) the plan is an individual pension plan, the amount transferred from the plan on behalf of the individual is the last payment from the plan to the individual and all the property held in connection with the plan is distributed from the plan on behalf of plan members within 90 days of the transfer.

Notes: See Notes to Reg. 8517(3.01). Reg. 8517(3.001), and reference to it in (3.01), added by 2014 budget bill #1, effective for transfers from registered pension plans made after 2012. This implements two Aug. 23, 2013 comfort letters and a Feb. 2014 Budget proposal. For CRA policy see Registered Plans Directorate Newsletter 16-3.

Registered Plans Directorate Newsletters: 16-3 (transfers from underfunded IPPs).

(3.01) [Rollover of commuted pension where employer insolvent] — If this subsection applies, the description of A in subsection (1) is to be read as follows in respect of the transfer:

A is the amount of the individual's lifetime retirement benefits under the provision commuted in connection with the transfer, as determined under subsection (4), but without reference to the benefit reduction referred to in paragraph (3)(c) or (3.001)(b), as the case may be; and

Related Provisions: ITA 146(5.2), (5.201) — Rollover to RRSP; Reg. 8517(3) — Conditions for Reg. 8517(3.01) to apply; Reg. 8517(3.02) — Prescribed amount for ITA 147.3(4)(c).

Notes: Reg. 8517(3)-(3.02) implement comfort letters of Nov. 16, 2010 and March 8, 2011 to allow the transfer of a commuted pension when the employer is insolvent. See Notes to ITA 146(5.2).

Reg. 8517(3.01) added by 2011 budget bill #2, effective 2011. See also Notes to Reg. 8517(3.001).

Registered Pension Plans Technical Manual: §20.3 (underfunded pension).

Registered Plans Compliance Bulletins: 8 (transfers from an RPP when the plan is underfunded at termination).

Registered Plans Directorate Newsletters: 16-3 (transfers from underfunded IPPs).

(3.02) [Prescribed amount for ITA 147.3(4)(c)] — If a particular amount is transferred in full or partial satisfaction of an individual's entitlement to benefits under a defined benefit provision of a registered pension plan and subsection (3.01) had applied in respect of a transfer (in this subsection referred to as the "initial transfer") of an amount on behalf of the individual under the provision, for the purpose of paragraph 147.3(4)(c) of the Act the prescribed amount in respect of the transfer of the particular amount is the lesser of

(a) the particular amount, and

(b) the amount, if any, by which the prescribed amount in respect of the initial transfer exceeds the total of all amounts each of which is the amount of a previous transfer to which this sub-

section or subsection (3.01) applied in respect of the individual's entitlement to benefits under the provision.

Notes: Reg. 8517(3.02) added by 2011 budget bill #2, effective 2011.

Registered Pension Plans Technical Manual: §20.3 (underfunded pension).

(3.1) Benefits provided with surplus on plan wind-up — Where an amount is transferred in full or partial satisfaction of an individual's entitlement to benefits under a defined benefit provision of a registered pension plan and the benefits include benefits (in this subsection referred to as "ancillary benefits") that are permissible solely because of subsection 8501(7), the prescribed amount for the purpose of paragraph 147.3(4)(c) of the Act in respect of the transfer is the total of

(a) the amount that would, but for this subsection, be the prescribed amount, and

(b) an amount approved by the Minister not exceeding the lesser of

(i) the present value (at the time of the transfer) of the ancillary benefits that, as a consequence of the transfer, cease to be provided, and

(ii) the total of all amounts each of which is, in respect of a previous transfer from the provision to a money purchase provision of a registered pension plan, a registered retirement savings plan or a registered retirement income fund in full or partial satisfaction of the individual's entitlement to other benefits under the defined benefit provision, the amount, if any, by which

(A) the prescribed amount for the purpose of paragraph 147.3(4)(c) of the Act in respect of the previous transfer exceeds

(B) the amount of the previous transfer.

Related Provisions: ITA 146(21.2) — Saskatchewan Pension Plan account deemed to be RRSP for purposes of regulations; ITA 147.5(12) — Pooled registered pension plan deemed to be RRSP for purposes of regulations.

Notes: Reg. 8517(3.1) added by P.C. 1998-2256, effective for amounts transferred in respect of benefits provided after 1996.

Registered Pension Plans Technical Manual: §20.4 (benefits provided with surplus on wind-up).

Registered Plans Directorate Newsletters: 04-1 (transfer from a defined benefit provision).

Registered Plans Frequently Asked Questions: RPFAQ-2 (RPPs), q. 5 (transfer of ancillary benefits to RRSP after commuted value transferred).

(4) Amount of lifetime retirement benefits commuted — For the purposes of subsection (1), and subject to subsection (7), the amount of an individual's lifetime retirement benefits under a defined benefit provision of a registered pension plan commuted in connection with the transfer of an amount on behalf of the individual in full or partial satisfaction of the individual's entitlement to benefits under the provision is the aggregate of

(a) where retirement benefits have commenced to be paid under the provision to the individual, the amount (expressed on an annualized basis) by which the individual's lifetime retirement benefits under the provision are reduced as a result of the transfer,

(b) where retirement benefits have not commenced to be paid under the provision to the individual, the amount (expressed on an annualized basis) by which the individual's normalized pension (computed in accordance with subsection (5)) under the provision at the time of the transfer is reduced as a result of the transfer, and

(c) where, in conjunction with the transfer, any other payment (other than an amount that is transferred in accordance with subsection 147.3(5) of the Act or that is transferred after 1991 in accordance with subsection 147.3(3) of the Act) is made from the plan in partial satisfaction of the individual's entitlement to benefits under the provision, the amount (expressed on an annualized basis) by which

(i) if paragraph (a) is applicable, the individual's lifetime retirement benefits under the provision are reduced, and

(ii) if paragraph (b) is applicable, the individual's normalized pension (computed in accordance with subsection (5)) under the provision at the time of the payment is reduced,

as a result of the payment, except to the extent that such reduction is included in determining, for the purposes of subsection (1), the amount of the individual's lifetime retirement benefits under the provision commuted in connection with the transfer of another amount on behalf of the individual.

Notes: See the *Yudelson* case in Notes to ITA 147.3(4).

Registered Pension Plans Technical Manual: §20.5 (amounts of lifetime retirement benefits commuted).

(5) Normalized pensions — For the purposes of subsection (4), the normalized pension of an individual under a defined benefit provision of a registered pension plan at a particular time is the amount (expressed on an annualized basis) of lifetime retirement benefits that would be payable under the provision at the particular time if

(a) lifetime retirement benefits commenced to be paid to the individual at the particular time;

(b) where the individual has not attained 65 years of age before the particular time, the individual attained that age at the particular time;

(c) all benefits to which the individual is entitled under the provision were fully vested;

(d) where the amount of the individual's lifetime retirement benefits would otherwise be determined with a reduction computed by reference to the individual's age, duration of service, or both, or with any other similar reduction, no such reduction were applied;

(e) where the amount of the individual's lifetime retirement benefits depends on the amount of benefits provided under another benefit provision of the plan or under another plan or arrangement, a reasonable estimate were made of those other benefits;

(f) where the individual's lifetime retirement benefits would otherwise include benefits that the plan is required to provide by reason of a designated provision of the law of Canada or a province, or that the plan would be required to provide if each such provision were applicable to the plan with respect to all its members, such benefits were not included; and

(g) except as otherwise provided by subsection (6), where the amount of the individual's lifetime retirement benefits depends on

(i) the form of benefits provided with respect to the individual under the provision (whether or not at the option of the individual), including

(A) the benefits to be provided after the death of the individual,

(B) the amount of retirement benefits, other than lifetime retirement benefits, provided to the individual, or

(C) the extent to which the lifetime retirement benefits will be adjusted to reflect changes in the cost of living, or

(ii) circumstances that are relevant in determining the form of benefits,

the form of benefits and the circumstances were such as to maximize the amount of the individual's lifetime retirement benefits on commencement of payment.

Related Provisions: Reg. 8513 — Designated provision of the law of Canada or a province.

Registered Pension Plans Technical Manual: §20.6 (normalized pension).

Registered Plans Directorate Newsletters: 98-2 (treating excess member contributions under a registered pension plan); 04-1 (transfer from a defined benefit provision).

(6) Optional forms — Where

(a) the terms of a defined benefit provision of a registered pension plan permit an individual to elect to receive additional lifetime retirement benefits in lieu of benefits that would, in the absence of the election, be payable after the death of the individual

if the individual dies after retirement benefits under the provision commence to be paid to the individual, and

(b) the elections available to the individual include an election

(i) to receive additional lifetime retirement benefits, not exceeding additional benefits determined on an actuarially equivalent basis, in lieu of all or a portion of a guarantee that retirement benefits will be paid for a minimum period of 10 years or less, or

(ii) to receive additional lifetime retirement benefits in lieu of retirement benefits that would otherwise be payable to a person who is a spouse or common-law partner or former spouse or common-law partner of the individual for a period beginning after the death of the individual and ending with the death of the person, where

(A) the election may be made only if the life expectancy of the person is significantly shorter than normal and has been so certified in writing by a medical doctor or a nurse practitioner licensed to practise under the laws of a province or of the place where the person resides, and

(B) the additional benefits do not exceed additional benefits determined on an actuarially equivalent basis and on the assumption that the person has a normal life expectancy,

paragraph (5)(g) applies as if

(c) the election described in subparagraph (b)(i) were not available to the individual, and

(d) where the particular time the normalized pension of the individual is determined under subsection (5) is after 1991, the election described in subparagraph (b)(ii) were not available to the individual.

Notes: Reg. 8517(6)(b)(ii)(A) amended by 2017 budget bill #2 to add "or a nurse practitioner", for certifications made after Sept. 7, 2017.

Reg. 8517(6)(b)(ii) amended by P.C. 2001-957, effective as per Notes to ITA 248(1)"common-law partner".

(7) Replacement benefits — Where

(a) an amount is transferred on behalf of an individual in full or partial satisfaction of the individual's entitlement to benefits under a defined benefit provision (in this subsection referred to as the "particular provision") of a registered pension plan,

(b) in conjunction with the transfer, benefits become provided to the individual under another defined benefit provision of the plan or under a defined benefit provision of another registered pension plan, and

(c) an employer who participated under the particular provision for the benefit of the individual also participates under the other provision for the individual's benefit,

the amount of the individual's lifetime retirement benefits under the particular provision commuted in connection with the transfer is the amount that would be determined under subsection (4) if the benefits provided under the other provision were provided under the particular provision.

Definitions [Reg. 8517]: "amount" — ITA 248(1); "ancillary benefits" — Reg. 8517(3.1); "benefit provision" — Reg. 8500(1); "benefits" — Reg. 8501(5)(c); "Canada" — ITA 255, *Interpretation Act* 35(1); "commencement" — *Interpretation Act* 35(1); "contribution" — Reg. 8501(6); "defined benefit provision" — ITA 147.1(1), Reg. 8500(2); "designated plan" — Reg. 8500(1); "designated provision of the law of Canada or a province" — Reg. 8513; "employee", "employer", "individual" — ITA 248(1); "lifetime retirement benefits" — Reg. 8500(1), 8517(4); "member" — ITA 147.1(1), Reg. 8300(1), 8500(2); "Minister" — ITA 248(1); "money purchase provision" — ITA 147.1(1); "net contribution account" — Reg. 8503(1); "normalized pension" — Reg. 8517(5); "participating employer" — ITA 147.1(1); "particular provision" — Reg. 8517(7)(a); "plan as registered" — ITA 147.1(15); "predecessor employer" — Reg. 8500(1); "prescribed", "property" — ITA 248(1); "province" — *Interpretation Act* 35(1); "registered pension plan" — ITA 248(1); "registered retirement savings plan" — ITA 146(1), (21.2), 147.5(12), 248(1); "registered retirement savings plan" — ITA 146(1), (21.2), 147.5(12), 248(1); "retirement benefits" — Reg. 8500(1); "spouse" — Reg. 8500(5); "time of termination" — Reg. 8517(3)(a); "writing" — *Interpretation Act* 35(1).

Interpretation Bulletins: IT-528: Transfers of funds between registered plans.

Registered Plans Directorate Newsletters: 95-5 (conversion of a defined benefit provision to a money purchase provision).

8518. [Repealed]

Notes: Reg. 8518 repealed by P.C. 2005-1508, effective Sept. 21, 2005. It provided that ITA 147.1(8) did not apply as a result of certain pension adjustments resulting from DPSP pension credits.

8519. Association of benefits with time periods — Where, for the purposes of Part LXXXIII or this Part or subsection 147.1(10) of the Act, it is necessary to associate benefits provided under a defined benefit provision of a pension plan with periods of time, the association shall be made in a manner acceptable to the Minister.

Definitions [Reg. 8519]: "benefits" — Reg. 8501(5)(c); "defined benefit provision" — ITA 147.1(1), Reg. 8500(2); "Minister" — ITA 248(1).

8520. Minister's actions — For the purposes of this Part, a waiver, extension of time or other modification of the requirements of this Part granted by the Minister or an approval by the Minister in respect of any matter is not effective unless it is in writing and expressly refers to the requirement that is modified or the matter in respect of which the approval is given.

Notes [Reg. 8500–8520]: Part LXXXV added by P.C. 1991-2540, effective 1989, with certain grandfathering for 1990-92.

Definitions [Reg. 8520]: "Minister" — ITA 248(1); "writing" — *Interpretation Act* 35(1).

PART LXXXVI — [8600–8605] TAXABLE CAPITAL EMPLOYED IN CANADA

8600. [Definitions] — For the purposes of this Part and Part I.3 of the Act,

"attributed surplus" of a non-resident insurer for a taxation year has the meaning assigned by subsection 2400(1);

Notes: Definition amended by P.C. 2000-1714, for 1999 and later taxation years.

"Canadian assets" of a corporation that is a financial institution (as defined in subsection 181(1) of the Act) at any time in a taxation year means, in respect of the year, the amount, if any, by which

(a) the total of all amounts each of which is the amount at which an asset of the corporation (which asset is required, or, if the corporation were a bank to which the *Bank Act* applied, would be required, to be reflected in a return under subsection 223(1) of the *Bank Act*, as that Act read on May 31, 1992, if that return were prepared on a non-consolidated basis) would be shown on the corporation's balance sheet at the end of the year if its balance sheet were prepared on a non-consolidated basis

exceeds

(b) the investment allowance of the corporation for the year determined under subsection 181.3(4) of the Act;

Notes: Para. (c) repealed, and "exceeds the total of" before para. (b) changed to "exceeds", by 2013 budget bill #1, for taxation years that begin after March 20, 2013 (consequential on the elimination of international banking centres in ITA 33.1).

"Canadian premiums" for a taxation year, in respect of an insurance corporation that was resident in Canada at any time in the year and throughout the year did not carry on a life insurance business, means the total of the insurance corporation's net premiums for the year

(a) in respect of insurance on property situated in Canada, and

(b) in respect of insurance, other than on property, from contracts with persons resident in Canada,

and, for the purposes of this definition, "net premiums" has the same meaning as in subsection 403(2), and subsection 403(3) applies as if the references therein to "province" were read as references to "country";

"Canadian reserve liabilities" of an insurer as at the end of a taxation year has the meaning assigned by subsection 2400(1);

Notes: Definition amended by P.C. 2000-1714, for 1999 and later taxation years.

"permanent establishment" has the same meaning as in subsection 400(2);

"total assets" of a corporation that is a financial institution (as defined in subsection 181(1) of the Act) at any time in a taxation year means, in respect of that year, the amount, if any, by which

(a) the total of all amounts each of which is the amount at which an asset of the corporation would be shown on the corporation's balance sheet at the end of the year if its balance sheet were prepared on a non-consolidated basis

exceeds

(b) the investment allowance of the corporation for the year determined under subsection 181.3(4) of the Act;

"total premiums" for a taxation year, in respect of an insurance corporation that was resident in Canada at any time in the year and throughout the year did not carry on a life insurance business, means the total of the corporation's net premiums for the year (as defined in subsection 403(2)) that are included in computing its income under Part I of the Act;

"total reserve liabilities" of an insurer as at the end of a taxation year means the amount determined by the formula

$$A - B$$

where

A is the total amount as at the end of the year of the insurer's liabilities and reserves (other than liabilities and reserves in respect of a segregated fund within the meaning assigned by subsection 138(12) of the Act) in respect of all its insurance policies, as determined for the purposes of the Superintendent of Financial Institutions, if the insurer is required by law to report to the Superintendent of Financial Institutions, or, in any other case, the superintendent of insurance or other similar officer or authority of the province under the laws of which the insurer is incorporated, and

B is the total of the reinsurance recoverable (within the meaning assigned by subsection 2400(1)) reported as a reinsurance asset by the insurer as at the end of the year relating to its liabilities and reserves in A.

Related Provisions: ITA 248(1) — "Insurance policy" includes "life insurance policy"; ITA 257 — Negative amounts in formulas.

Notes: See VIEWS doc 2007-0240221C6.

Reg. 8600 "total reserve liabilities" amended by 2010 budget bill #2, effective for taxation years that begin after 2010. Earlier amended by P.C. 2000-1714.

Notes [Reg. 8600]: Reg. 8600 added by P.C. 1994-556, effective for taxation years that end after June 1989.

Definitions [Reg. 8600]: "amount" — ITA 248(1); "attributed surplus" — Reg. 2400(1), 8600; "bank" — ITA 248(1), *Interpretation Act* 35(1); "Canada" — ITA 255, *Interpretation Act* 35(1); "corporation" — ITA 248(1), *Interpretation Act* 35(1); "insurance corporation", "insurance policy", "insurer", "life insurance business" — ITA 248(1); "net premiums" — Reg. 403(2), (3), Reg. 8600 "Canadian premiums"; "non-resident", "officer", "person", "property" — ITA 248(1); "province" — *Interpretation Act* 35(1); "reinsurance recoverable" — Reg. 2400(1); "resident in Canada" — ITA 250; "segregated fund" — ITA 138(12); "taxation year" — ITA 249.

8601. [Prescribed proportion of taxable capital] — For the purpose of determining the taxable capital employed in Canada of a corporation for a taxation year under subsection 181.2(1) of the Act, the prescribed proportion of the corporation's taxable capital (as determined under Part I.3 of the Act) for the year is the amount determined by the formula

$$A \times B / C$$

where

A is the taxable capital (as determined under Part I.3 of the Act) of the corporation for the year,

B is the total of all amounts each of which is the amount, determined in accordance with Part IV (or, in the case of an airline corporation, that would be so determined if the corporation had a permanent establishment in every province and if paragraphs 407(1)(a) and (b) were read without reference to the words "in Canada"), of the corporation's taxable income earned in the year in a particular province or the amount of its taxable income that would, pursuant to that Part, be earned in the year in a province if all permanent establishments of the corporation in Canada were in a province, and

C is the corporation's taxable income for the year,

except that, where the corporation's taxable income for the year is nil, the corporation shall, for the purposes of this section, be deemed to have a taxable income for the year of $1,000.

Notes: Reg. 8601 added by P.C. 1994-556, for taxation years that end after June 1989.

Definitions [Reg. 8601]: "amount" — ITA 248(1); "Canada" — ITA 255, *Interpretation Act* 35(1); "corporation" — ITA 248(1), *Interpretation Act* 35(1); "employed" — ITA 248(1); "permanent establishment" — Reg. 400(2), 8600; "prescribed" — ITA 248(1); "province" — *Interpretation Act* 35(1); "taxable income" — ITA 248(1); "taxation year" — ITA 249.

8602. [No longer relevant]

Notes: Reg. 8602, added by P.C. 1994-556 for tax years that end after June 1989, prescribes an amount for ITA 125.3, which is obsolete.

8603. [Definitions] — For the purposes of Part VI [ss. 190–190.211] of the Act,

(a) "Canadian assets" of a corporation that is a financial institution (as defined in subsection 190(1) of the Act) at any time in a taxation year means, in respect of that year, the amount that would be determined under the definition "Canadian assets" in section 8600 in respect of the corporation for the year if the reference in that definition to "subsection 181(1)" were read as a reference to "subsection 190(1)" and paragraph (b) of that definition were read as follows:

"(b) the total determined under section 190.14 of the Act in respect of the corporation's investments for the year in financial institutions related to it;";

(b) "total assets" of a corporation that is a financial institution (as defined in subsection 190(1) of the Act) at any time in a taxation year means, in respect of that year, the amount that would be determined under the definition "total assets" in section 8600 in respect of the corporation for the year if the reference in that definition to "subsection 181(1)" were read as a reference to "subsection 190(1)" and paragraph (b) of that definition were read as follows:

"(b) the total determined under section 190.14 of the Act in respect of the corporation's investments for the year in financial institutions related to it;"; and

(c) "attributed surplus", "Canadian reserve liabilities" and "total reserve liabilities" have the same respective meanings as in section 8600.

Notes: Reg. 8603(a) amended by 2013 budget bill #1, for tax years that begin after March 20, 2013. Reg. 8603 added by P.C. 1994-556, for 1990 and later tax years.

Definitions [Reg. 8603]: "amount" — ITA 248(1); "corporation" — ITA 248(1), *Interpretation Act* 35(1); "related" — ITA 251(2)–(6); "taxation year" — ITA 249.

8604. [Repealed]

Notes: Reg. 8604 repealed by 2002-2013 technical bill, effective Dec. 20, 2002. It prescribed corporations for ITA 181(1)"financial institution"(g). Such corps were also deemed to be RFIs by ITA 248(1)"restricted financial institution"(e.1); SFIs by ITA 248(1)"specified financial institution"(e.1); and FIs by ITA 142.2(1)"financial institution"(a)(i). The list was moved to a Schedule to the ITA (see after ITA s. 281).

Reg. 8604 previously amended by S.C. 2001 c. 22 and P.C. 1998-2046, 1994-556.

8605. (1) For the purposes of subclause 181.3(1)(c)(ii)(A)(II) and clause 190.11(b)(i)(B) of the Act, the amount prescribed in respect of a particular corporation for a taxation year ending at a particular time is the total of all amounts each of which is the amount deter-

mined in respect of a corporation that is, at the particular time, a foreign insurance subsidiary of the particular corporation, equal to the amount, if any, by which

(a) the amount by which the total, at the end of the subsidiary's last taxation year ending at or before the particular time, of

(i) the amount of the subsidiary's long-term debt, and

(ii) the amount of the subsidiary's capital stock (or, in the case of an insurance corporation incorporated without share capital, the amount of its member's contributions), retained earnings, contributed surplus and any other surpluses

exceeds the total of

(iii) the amount of the subsidiary's deferred tax debit balance at the end of the year, and

(iv) the amount of any deficit deducted in computing the subsidiary's shareholders' equity at the end of the year

exceeds the total of all amounts each of which is

(b) the carrying value to its owner at the particular time for the taxation year that includes the particular time of a share of the subsidiary's capital stock or its long term debt that is owned at the particular time by

(i) the particular corporation,

(ii) a subsidiary of the particular corporation,

(iii) a corporation

(A) that is resident in Canada,

(B) that carried on a life insurance business in Canada at any time in its taxation year ending at or before the particular time, and

(C) that is

(I) a corporation of which the particular corporation is a subsidiary, or

(II) a subsidiary of a corporation described in subclause (I), or

(iv) a subsidiary of a corporation described in subparagraph (iii), or

(c) an amount included under paragraph (a) in respect of any surplus of the subsidiary contributed by a corporation described in any of subparagraphs (b)(i) to (iv), other than an amount included under paragraph (b).

(d) [Repealed]

Notes: Reg. 8605(1) amended by P.C. 1998-2046, retroactive to 1991.

(2) For the purposes of subclause 181.3(1)(c)(ii)(A)(III) and clause 190.11(b)(i)(C) of the Act, the amount prescribed in respect of a particular corporation for a taxation year ending at a particular time is the total of all amounts each of which is the amount determined in respect of a corporation that is, at the particular time, a foreign insurance subsidiary of the particular corporation, equal to the amount, if any, by which

(a) the total of the amounts determined under paragraphs (1)(b) and (c) in respect of the subsidiary for the year

exceeds

(b) the amount determined under paragraph (1)(a) in respect of the subsidiary for the year.

(3) For the purposes of subclause 181.3(1)(c)(ii)(A)(V) and clause 190.11(b)(i)(E) of the Act, the amount prescribed in respect of a particular corporation for a taxation year ending at a particular time means the total of all amounts each of which would be the total reserve liabilities of a foreign insurance subsidiary of the particular corporation as at the end of the subsidiary's last taxation year ending at or before the particular time if the subsidiary were required by law to report to the Superintendent of Financial Institutions for that year.

Notes: Reg. 8605(3) amended by P.C. 2000-1714, for 1999 and later tax years.

(4) The definitions in this subsection apply in this section.

"**foreign insurance subsidiary**" of a particular corporation at any time means a non-resident corporation that

(a) carried on a life insurance business throughout its last taxation year ending at or before that time,

(b) did not carry on a life insurance business in Canada at any time in its last taxation year ending at or before that time, and

(c) is at that time

(i) a subsidiary of the particular corporation, and

(ii) not a subsidiary of any corporation that

(A) is resident in Canada,

(B) carried on a life insurance business in Canada at any time in its last taxation year ending at or before that time, and

(C) is a subsidiary of the particular corporation.

"**subsidiary**" of a corporation (in this definition referred to as the "parent corporation") means a corporation controlled by the parent corporation where shares of each class of the capital stock of the corporation having a fair market value of not less than 75% of the fair market value of all of the issued and outstanding shares of that class belong to

(a) the parent corporation,

(b) a corporation that is a subsidiary of the parent corporation, or

(c) any combination of corporations each of which is a corporation referred to in paragraph (a) or described in paragraph (b).

Related Provisions: Reg. 8500(1.1) — Definition applies to ITA 147.3(7.1).

Notes [Reg. 8605]: Reg. 8605(3) amended by P.C. 2000-1714, for 1999 and later tax years. Reg. 8605 added by P.C. 1996-1597, for 1991 and later tax years.

Definitions [Reg. 8605]: "amount" — ITA 248(1); "Canada" — ITA 255, *Interpretation Act* 35(1); "carrying value" — ITA 181(3), 190(2); "controlled" — ITA 256(6), (6.1); "corporation" — ITA 248(1), *Interpretation Act* 35(1); "fair market value" — see ITA 69(1) Notes; "foreign insurance subsidiary" — Reg. 8605(4); "insurance corporation", "life insurance business", "non-resident" — ITA 248(1); "parent corporation" — Reg. 8605(4)"subsidiary"; "prescribed" — ITA 248(1); "resident in Canada" — ITA 250; "share" — ITA 248(1); "subsidiary" — Reg. 8605(4); "taxation year" — ITA 249; "total reserve liabilities" — Reg. 8600.

PART LXXXVII — [8700] NATIONAL ARTS SERVICE ORGANIZATIONS

8700. [Prescribed conditions] — For the purposes of paragraph 149.1(6.4)(d) of the Act, the following conditions are prescribed for a national arts service organization:

(a) the organization is an organization

(i) that is, because of paragraph 149(1)(l) of the Act, exempt from tax under Part I of the Act,

(ii) that represents, in an official language of Canada, a community of artists from one or more of the following sectors of activity in the arts community, that is, theatre, opera, music, dance, painting, sculpture, drawing, crafts, design, photography, the literary arts, film, sound recording and other audiovisual arts,

(iii) no part of the income of which may be payable to, or otherwise available for the personal benefit of, any proprietor, member, shareholder, trustee, or settlor of the organization, except where the payment is for services rendered or is an amount to which paragraph 56(1)(n) of the Act applies in respect of the recipient,

(iv) all of the resources of which are devoted to the activities and objects described in its application for its last designation by the Minister of Canadian Heritage pursuant to paragraph 149.1(6.4)(a) of the Act,

(v) more than 50 per cent of the directors, trustees, officers or other officials of which deal with each other at arm's length, and

(vi) no more than 50% of the property of which at any time has been contributed or otherwise paid into the organization by one person or members of a group of persons who do not deal with each other at arm's length and, for the purpose of this subparagraph, a reference to any person or to members of a group does not include a reference to Her Majesty in Right of Canada or a province, a municipality, a registered charity that is not a private foundation or any club, society or association described in paragraph 149(1)(l) of the Act; and

(b) the activities of the organization (which may include collective bargaining on behalf of its sector of activity under the *Status of the Artist Act*, provided it is not the organization's primary activity) are confined to one or more of

(i) promoting one or more art forms,

(ii) conducting research into one or more art forms,

(iii) sponsoring arts exhibitions or performances,

(iv) representing interests of the arts community or a sector thereof (but not of individuals) before governmental, judicial, quasi-judicial or other public bodies,

(v) conducting workshops, seminars, training programs and similar development programs relating to the arts for members of the organization, in respect of which the value of benefits received or enjoyed by members of the organization is required by paragraph 56(1)(aa) [now 56(1)(z.1) — ed.] of the Act to be included in computing the incomes of those members,

(vi) educating the public about the arts community or the sector represented by the organization,

(vii) organizing and sponsoring conventions, conferences, competitions and special events relating to the arts community or the sector represented by the organization,

(viii) conducting arts studies and surveys of interest to members of the organization relating to the arts community or the sector represented by the organization,

(ix) acting as an information centre by maintaining resource libraries and data bases relating to the arts community or the sector represented by the organization,

(x) disseminating information relating to the arts community or the sector represented by the organization, and

(xi) paying amounts to which paragraph 56(1)(n) of the Act applies in respect of the recipient and which relate to the arts community or the sector represented by the organization.

Notes: For background to the reference to collective bargaining in para. (b), see Drache, "All it Takes is (Lots and Lots) of Time", xxxiii(6) *The Canadian Taxpayer* (Carswell) 47-48 (March 25, 2011).

Reg. 8700(a)(ii) and (iv), and opening words of Reg. 8700(b), amended by P.C. 2011-936, effective Feb. 20, 2011.

Reg. 8700(a)(vi) previously amended by P.C. 2007-849.

Reg. 8700 added by P.C. 1994-139, effective July 14, 1990.

Definitions [Reg. 8700]: "amount" — ITA 248(1); "arm's length" — ITA 251(1); "Canada" — ITA 255, *Interpretation Act* 35(1); "Her Majesty" — *Interpretation Act* 35(1); "individual", "Minister", "officer", "person", "prescribed" — ITA 248(1); "private foundation" — ITA 149.1(1), "property" — ITA 248(1); "province" — *Interpretation Act* 35(1); "registered charity" — ITA 248(1); "related" — ITA 251(2)–(6); "shareholder" — ITA 248(1).

PART LXXXVIII — [8800–8801] DISABILITY-RELATED MODIFICATIONS AND APPARATUS

8800. [Prescribed renovations and alterations] — The renovations and alterations that are prescribed for the purposes of paragraph 20(1)(qq) of the Act are

(a) the installation of

(i) an interior or exterior ramp; or

(ii) a hand-activated electric door opener; and

(b) a modification to a bathroom, elevator or doorway to accommodate its use by a person in a wheelchair.

Notes: Reg. 8800 added by P.C. 1993-2026, for renovations and alterations after 1990.

Definitions [Reg. 8800]: "person", "prescribed" — ITA 248(1).

8801. [Prescribed devices and equipment] — The devices and equipment that are prescribed for the purposes of paragraph 20(1)(rr) of the Act are

(a) an elevator car position indicator, such as a braille panel or an audio signal, for individuals having a sight impairment;

(b) a visual fire alarm indicator, a listening device for group meetings or a telephone device, for individuals having a hearing impairment; and

(c) a disability-specific computer software or hardware attachment.

Notes: Reg. 8801 added by P.C. 1993-2026 and para. (c) added by P.C. 1995-579, both for amounts paid after Feb. 25, 1992.

Definitions [Reg. 8801]: "individual", "prescribed" — ITA 248(1).

PART LXXXIX — [8900–8901] ENTITIES PRESCRIBED WITH RESPECT TO CERTAIN RULES

8900. (1) International organizations — For the purposes of subparagraph 110(1)(f)(iii) and paragraph 126(3)(a) of the Act, the following international organizations are prescribed:

(a) the United Nations; and

(b) each international organization that is a specialized agency brought into relationship with the United Nations in accordance with Article 63 of the Charter of the United Nations.

Notes: See Notes to ITA 110(1)(f). The UN Population Fund (UNFPA) is included as part of the UN: VIEWS doc 2006-0200231E5. The "specialized agencies" are listed in 2010-0371291I7. They include the World Bank (2007-0262311E5); but only employment income is exempted, not pensions: 2004-0101881E5. See also 2004-0085861I7, 2005-0132721I7, 2007-0248321E5, 2008-0303191E5 and 2012-0461051E5 on "specialized agency...". The OAS and Inter-American Institute for Cooperation on Agriculture are not prescribed international organizations: 2000-0054485. Nor is the Inter-American Development Bank: 2011-0410811E5. In some cases, "by the terms of the constating documents of an organization, the member countries who establish the organization agree not to tax the salaries ... of employees. You can contact organizations ... directly to make such enquiries": 2010-0362631M4.

Reg. 8900(1) opening words amended to apply to ITA 126(3)(a) by 2013 budget bill #2, effective for 2013 and later taxation years.

(2) International non-governmental organizations — For the purpose of subparagraph 110(1)(f)(iv) of the Act, the following international non-governmental organizations are prescribed:

(a) the International Air Transport Association;

(b) the Société internationale de télécommunications aéronautiques; and

(c) the World Anti-Doping Agency.

Notes: Reg. 8900(2) amended by P.C. 2003-266, for 2001 and later taxation years.

Reg. 8900 added by P.C. 1995-663, para. (a) effective 1991 and (b) effective 1993.

Definitions [Reg. 8900]: "prescribed" — ITA 248(1).

8901. [Repealed]

Notes: Reg. 8901 repealed by 2002-2013 technical bill (Part 5 — technical), for fiscal periods that begin after June 26, 2013. It prescribed Gaz Métropolitain LP for ITA 249.1(1)(b). Added by P.C. 2003-266, for fiscal periods that begin after 1994. The effect was that the fiscal period of the LP could end up to 12 months after it began in a year rather than at the end of December of each calendar year.

Reg. 8901.1 and 8901.2, which (from their numbering) should be in this Part, were incorrectly added as Part LXXXIX.1 (89.1), below.

PART LXXXIX.1 — [8901.1, 8901.2] COVID-19 WAGE AND RENT SUBSIDIES

Notes: This Part should not have been numbered LXXXIX.1 [89.1], with section 8901.1, as it messes up the section numbering. If a new section were added to Part

LXXXIX [89], it would be 8902, yet would appear before 8901.1! Conceptually the first section of Part LXXXIX.1 [89.1] should be 89.100, which also does not fit numerically. Better would have been to add a new section 8902 to existing Part LXXXIX [89], add a new Part XCVII [97], or replace a long-unused Part such as XIX [19] or XXV [25].

8901.1 [Prescribed eligible entities] — For the purposes of paragraph (f) of the definition "eligible entity" in subsection 125.7(1) of the Act, the following entities are prescribed:

(a) a corporation that meets the following conditions:

(i) it is described in paragraph 149(1)(d.5) of the Act,

(ii) not less than 90% of the shares, or the capital, of the corporation are owned by one or more "Aboriginal governments" (as defined in subsection 241(10) of the Act) — or similar Indigenous governing bodies — described in paragraph 149(1)(c) of the Act, and

(iii) it carries on a business;

(b) a corporation that meets the following conditions:

(i) it is described in paragraph 149(1)(d.6) of the Act,

(ii) all of the shares (except directors' qualifying shares), or the capital, of the corporation are owned by one or more of

(A) an "Aboriginal government" (as defined in subsection 241(10) of the Act) — or a similar Indigenous governing body — described in paragraph 149(1)(c) of the Act, or

(B) a corporation described in this paragraph or paragraph (a), and

(iii) it carries on a business;

(c) a partnership, each member of which is

(i) an eligible entity, or

(ii) an "Aboriginal government" (as defined in subsection 241(10) of the Act) — or a similar Indigenous governing body — described in paragraph 149(1)(c) of the Act;

(d) a partnership, in respect of a qualifying period, if throughout the qualifying period it is the case that

$$A \leq 0.5B$$

where

A is the total of all amounts, each of which is the fair market value of an interest in the partnership held — directly or indirectly, through one or more partnerships — by a person or partnership other than an eligible entity, and

B is the total fair market value of all interests in the partnership;

(e) a person described in paragraph 149(1)(g) or (h) of the Act; and

(f) a person or partnership that operates a private school or private college.

Notes: See Finance news release and Backgrounder, in Notes to ITA 125.7(2).

Reg. 8901.1 added by P.C. 2020-331, effective April 11, 2020.

Definitions [Reg. 8901.1]: "Aboriginal government" — ITA 241(10); "amount", "business" — ITA 248(1); "corporation" — ITA 248(1), *Interpretation Act* 35(1); "fair market value" — see ITA 69(1) Notes; "partnership" — see ITA 96(1) Notes; "person", "prescribed", "share" — ITA 248(1).

8901.2 [CEWS — furloughed employees] — The amount determined by regulation in respect of a qualifying entity for the purposes of clause (b)(iv)(B) of the description of A in subsection 125.7(2) of the Act for a week in a qualifying period is

(a) for the seventh qualifying period and the eighth qualifying period, the greater of

(i) the amount determined for the week under subparagraph (a)(i) of the description of A in subsection 125.7(2) of the Act, and

(ii) the amount determined for the week under subparagraph (a)(ii) of the description of A in subsection 125.7(2) of the Act;

(b) for the ninth qualifying period and the tenth qualifying period, the greater of

(i) $500, and

(ii) the lesser of

(A) 55% of "baseline remuneration" (as defined in subsection 125.7(1) of the Act) in respect of the eligible employee determined for that week, and

(B) $573;

(c) for any of the eleventh qualifying period to the nineteenth qualifying period, the greater of

(i) $500, and

(ii) the lesser of

(A) 55% of "baseline remuneration" (as defined in subsection 125.7(1) of the Act) in respect of the eligible employee determined for that week, and

(B) $595; and

(d) for the twentieth qualifying period and any subsequent qualifying period, nil.

Notes [Reg. 8901.2]: This Reg. 8901.2 is different from Reg. 8901.2 in Part LXXXIX.2 [89.2], passed June 7, 2020 but then repealed retroactive to its introduction. That one prescribed different CEWS amounts that were later replaced retroactively by legislation. See Part LXXXIX.2 below.

Reg. 8901.2(1)-(6) repealed, and (7) renumbered Reg. 8901.2, by 2021 budget bill #1, effective June 29, 2021. Reg. 8901.2(1)-(6) all prescribed percentages and periods for ITA 125.7 for **Periods 11-16 (Dec. 20/20-June 5/21)** [see 125.7(1) "qualifying period" for the period numbers]; these were all moved inside ITA 125.7. Reg. 8901.2(7) became simply Reg. 8901.2. Before these amendments:

Reg. 8901.2(1) prescribed the "qualifying periods" for Periods 11-16:

(1) [CEWS/CERS — prescribed qualifying periods] — For the purposes of paragraph (d) of the definition "qualifying period" in subsection 125.7(1) of the Act, the prescribed periods are

(a) the period that begins on December 20, 2020 and ends on January 16, 2021;

(b) the period that begins on January 17, 2021 and ends on February 13, 2021;

(c) the period that begins on February 14, 2021 and ends on March 13, 2021;

(d) the period that begins on March 14, 2021 and ends on April 10, 2021;

(e) the period that begins on April 11, 2021 and ends on May 8, 2021; and

(f) the period that begins on May 9, 2021 and ends on June 5, 2021.

Paras. (d)-(f) added by P.C. 2021-214, effective March 14, 2021.

Reg. 8901.2(2) prescribed the "base percentage" for Periods 11-16:

(2) [CEWS/CERS — prescribed base percentage] — For the purposes of paragraph (g) of the definition "base percentage" in subsection 125.7(1) of the Act, the percentages determined by regulation in respect of an "eligible entity", as defined in that subsection, for each of the qualifying periods referred to in paragraphs (1)(a) to (f) are

(a) if the entity's "revenue reduction percentage" (as defined in subsection 125.7(1) of the Act) is greater than or equal to 50%, 40%; and

(b) in any other case, 0.8 multiplied by the "revenue reduction percentage" (as defined in subsection 125.7(1) of the Act).

This means 0.8 times the revenue reduction percentage, max 40%, for Dec. 20/20 to March 13/21 (Periods 11-13).

Opening words amended by P.C. 2021-214, effective March 14, 2021, to change "(1)(a), (b) and (c)" to "(1)(a) to (f)".

Reg. 8901.2(3) prescribed the "current reference period" for Periods 11-16:

(3) [CEWS/CERS — prescribed current reference period] — For the purposes of paragraph (d) of the definition "current reference period" in subsection 125.7(1) of the Act, the prescribed current reference periods are

(a) for the qualifying period referred to in paragraph (1)(a), December 2020;

(b) for the qualifying period referred to in paragraph (1)(b), January 2021;

(c) for the qualifying period referred to in paragraph (1)(c), February 2021;

(d) for the qualifying period referred to in paragraph (1)(d), March 2021;

(e) for the qualifying period referred to in paragraph (1)(e), April 2021; and

(f) for the qualifying period referred to in paragraph (1)(f), May 2021.

Paras. (d)-(f) added by P.C. 2021-214, effective March 14, 2021.

Reg. 8901.2(4) prescribed the "prior reference period" for Periods 11-16:

(4) [CEWS/CERS — prescribed prior reference period] — For the purposes of paragraph (c) of the definition "prior reference period" in subsection 125.7(1) of the Act, the prescribed prior reference periods are

(a) for the qualifying period referred to in paragraph (1)(a), December 2019;

(b) for the qualifying period referred to in paragraph (1)(b), January 2020;

(c) for the qualifying period referred to in paragraph (1)(c), February 2020;

(d) for the qualifying period referred to in paragraph (1)(d), March 2019;

(e) for the qualifying period referred to in paragraph (1)(e), April 2019; and

(f) for the qualifying period referred to in paragraph (1)(f), May 2019.

For months in 2021, the prior reference period (baseline for comparing revenues to a "normal" year) was in 2020 up to March 2020, when things were reasonably normal. For April-June 2021, the prior reference period needs to be from 2019, because COVID-19 was already causing reduced revenues in those months in 2020.

Paras. (d)-(f) added by P.C. 2021-214, effective March 14, 2021.

Reg. 8901.2(5) prescribed the "rent subsidy percentage" for Periods 11-16:

(5) [CERS — prescribed rent subsidy percentage] — For the purposes of paragraph (b) of the definition "rent subsidy percentage" in subsection 125.7(1) of the Act, the percentages determined by regulation in respect of an "eligible entity", as defined in that subsection, for each of the qualifying periods referred to in paragraphs (1)(a) to (f) are

(a) if the eligible entity's "revenue reduction percentage" (as defined in subsection 125.7(1) of the Act) is greater than or equal to 70%, 65%;

(b) if the eligible entity's "revenue reduction percentage" (as defined in subsection 125.7(1) of the Act) is greater than or equal to 50% but less than 70%, the percentage determined by the formula

$$40\% + (A - 50\%) \times 1.25$$

where

A is the eligible entity's "revenue reduction percentage" (as defined in subsection 125.7(1) of the Act); and

(c) if the eligible entity's "revenue reduction percentage" (as defined in subsection 125.7(1) of the Act) is less than 50%, the percentage determined by the formula

$$0.8 \times B$$

where

B is the eligible entity's "revenue reduction percentage" (as defined in subsection 125.7(1) of the Act).

Opening words amended by P.C. 2021-214, effective March 14, 2021, to change "(1)(a), (b) and (c)" to "(1)(a) to (f)".

Reg. 8901.2(6) prescribed the "top-up percentage" for Periods 11-16:

(6) [CEWS — prescribed top-up percentage] — For the purposes of the definition "top-up percentage" in subsection 125.7(1) of the Act, the percentage determined by regulation for the qualifying periods referred to in paragraphs (1)(a) to (f) is the lesser of 35% and the percentage determined by the formula

$$1.75 \times (A - 50\%)$$

where

A is the entity's top-up "revenue reduction percentage" (as defined in subsection 125.7(1) of the Act) for the qualifying period.

Opening words amended by P.C. 2021-214, effective March 14, 2021, to change "(1)(a), (b) and (c)" to "(1)(a) to (f)".

Reg. 8901.2(7) was identical to what is now Reg. 8901.2. It replaced what was all of Reg. 8901.2 before Dec. 20, 2020. It works differently over different periods:

August 30 to October 24, 2020 (Periods 7-8)

Reg. 8901.2 added by P.C. 2020-673, effective Aug. 30, 2020. From Aug. 30 to Sept. 26, read:

8901.2 The amount determined by regulation in respect of a qualifying entity for the purposes of clause (b)(iv)(B) of the description of A in subsection 125.7(2) of the Act for a week in the qualifying period described in paragraph (c.4) of the definition "qualifying period" in subsection 125.7(1) of the Act is the greater of

(a) the amount determined for the week under subparagraph (a)(i) of the description of A in subsection 125.7(2) of the Act, and

(b) the amount determined for the week under subparagraph (a)(ii) of the description of A in subsection 125.7(2) of the Act.

The introduction of Reg. 8901.2 (P.C. 2020-673) implemented an Aug. 21, 2020 Finance news release *Government extends Canada Emergency Wage Subsidy support for furloughed employees for four weeks*: "the government proposes to extend the current treatment of furloughed employees under the CEWS program by 4 weeks — from August 30 to September 26".

Amended by P.C. 2020-805, effective Sept. 27, 2020. From Sept. 27 to Oct. 24, read as above, but in the opening words, after "paragraph (c.4)", add "or (c.5)". This extension implemented a Sept. 25, 2020 Finance news release *Government provides update on support for furloughed employees under the Canada Emergency Wage Subsidy.*

In effect, this rule amended ITA 125.7(2)A(b)(iii) to apply to 125.7(1)"qualifying period"(c.4) and (c.5), and amended 125.7(2)A(b)(iv) to apply from "qualifying period"(c.6). Reg 8901.2(a)(i) and (ii) implement the ITA 125.7(2)A(b)(iii)(B) rule for periods (c.4) [Period 7, Aug. 30-Sept. 26] and (c.5) [Period 8, Sept. 27-Oct. 24].

October 25 to December 19, 2020 (Periods 9-10)

Reg. 8901.2 amended by P.C. 2020-877, effective Oct. 25, 2020. From Oct. 25 to Dec. 19, it read (identical to what is now Reg. 8901.2(a)-(b)):

8901.2 The amount determined by regulation in respect of a qualifying entity for the purposes of clause (b)(iv)(B) of the description of A in subsection 125.7(2) of the Act for a week in a qualifying period described in

(a) paragraph (c.4) or (c.5) of the definition qualifying period in subsection 125.7(1) of the Act is the greater of

(i) the amount determined for the week under subparagraph (a)(i) of the description of A in subsection 125.7(2) of the Act, and

(ii) the amount determined for the week under subparagraph (a)(ii) of the description of A in subsection 125.7(2) of the Act; and

(b) paragraph (c.6) or (c.7) of the definition qualifying period in subsection 125.7(1) of the Act is the greater of

(i) $500, and

(ii) the lesser of

(A) 55% of baseline remuneration in respect of the eligible employee determined for that week, and

(B) $573.

In effect, Reg 8901.2(a) amended ITA 125.7(2)A(b)(iii) to apply to 125.7(1)"qualifying period"(c.4) and (c.5), and amended 125.7(2)A(b)(iv) to apply from "qualifying period"(c.6). Reg 8901.2(a)(i) and (ii) implemented the ITA 125.7(2)A(b)(iii)(B) rule for periods (c.4) [Period 7, Aug. 30-Sept. 26] and (c.5) [Period 8, Sept. 27-Oct. 24].

Reg. 8901.2(b) prescribed the amounts for periods (c.6) [Period 9, Oct. 25-Nov. 21] and (c.7) [Period 10, Nov. 22-Dec. 19].

December 20, 2020 to March 13, 2021 (Periods 11-13)

Reg. 8901.2 rewritten by P.C. 2020-1124, effective Dec. 20, 2020. Reg. 8901.2(7) replaced what had been Reg. 8901.2. Paras. 8901.2(7)(a)-(b) were the former 8901.2(a)-(b), and still apply to Periods 7-10 [ITA 125.7(1)"qualifying period"(c.4)-(c.7)], from Aug. 30 to Dec. 19.

Reg. 8901.2(7)(c) applied to the periods listed in new Reg. 8901.2(1)(a)-(f): Period 11 (Dec. 20, 2020-Jan. 16, 2021), Period 12 (Jan. 17-Feb. 13); Period 13 (Feb. 14-March 13); Period 14 (March 14-April 10); Period 15 (April 11-May 8); and Period 16 (May 9-June 5, 2021). The maximum weekly amount (Reg. 8901.2(7)(c)(ii)(B)) is $595.

Opening words amended by P.C. 2021-214, effective March 14, 2021, to change "(1)(a), (b) and (c)" to "(1)(a) to (f)".

Definitions [Reg. 8901.2]: "amount" — ITA 248(1); "baseline remuneration" — ITA 125.7(1); "eighth qualifying period" — ITA 125.7(1)"qualifying period"(c.5); "eleventh qualifying period" — ITA 125.7(1)"qualifying period"(c.8); "eligible employee" — ITA 125.7(1); "employee" — ITA 248(1); "nineteenth qualifying period" — ITA 125.7(1)"qualifying period"(c.97); "ninth qualifying period" — ITA 125.7(1)"qualifying period"(c.6); "qualifying entity", "qualifying period" — ITA 125.7(1); "regulation" — ITA 248(1); "seventh qualifying period" — ITA 125.7(1)"qualifying period"(c.4); "tenth qualifying period" — ITA 125.7(1)"qualifying period"(c.7); "twentieth qualifying period" — ITA 125.7(1)"qualifying period"(c.98).

PART LXXXIX.2 — [8901.2 — REPEALED] QUALIFYING PERIODS PRESCRIBED FOR COVID-19 WAGE SUBSIDY

Notes: Former Part LXXXIX.2 (89.2) with one section, Reg. 8901.2, added by P.C. 2020-516, effective June 7, 2020, and then repealed by 2020 COVID bill #3 retroactive to its introduction, as that bill directly amended 125.7(1)"current reference period", "prior reference period" and "qualifying period" instead. It provided:

8901.2 [Canada Emergency Wage Subsidy] — (1) [Current reference period] — For the purposes of paragraph (d) of the definition "current reference period" in subsection 125.7(1) of the Act, in respect of the qualifying period prescribed in subsection (3), the prescribed period is June 2020.

(2) [Prior reference period] — For the purposes of paragraph (c) of the definition "prior reference period" in subsection 125.7(1) of the Act, in respect of the qualifying period prescribed in subsection (3),

(a) if the eligible entity has met the condition described in subparagraph (b)(i) of that definition or has made an election under subparagraph (b)(ii) of that definition, January and February 2020 is the prescribed period; and

(b) in any other case, June 2019 is the prescribed period.

(3) [Qualifying period] — For the purposes of paragraph (d) of the definition "qualifying period" in subsection 125.7(1) of the Act, the prescribed period is the period that begins on June 7, 2020 and ends on July 4, 2020.

(4) [Specified percentage] — For the purposes of paragraph (c) of the definition "specified percentage" in subsection 125.7(1) of the Act, in respect of the qualifying period prescribed in subsection (3), the prescribed percentage is 70%.

In any event, this should never have been numbered Part LXXXIX.2 [89.2], with section 8901.2, as it messes up the section numbering, and no new Part was needed. See Notes preceding Reg. 8901.1 above. Both Reg. 8901.1 and 8901.2 should simply have been added to Part LXXXIX (89).

A new Reg. 8901.2 was passed on Sept. 20, 2020. It is in Part LXXXIX.1 (89.1) above.

PART XC — [9000–9006] FINANCIAL INSTITUTIONS — PRESCRIBED ENTITIES AND PROPERTIES

9000. Prescribed person not a financial institution — For the purposes of paragraph (e) of the definition "financial institution" in subsection 142.2(1) of the Act, the following are prescribed persons:

(a) the Business Development Bank of Canada;

(b) BDC Capital Inc.; and

(c) a trust, at any particular time, if at that particular time

(i) the trust is a related segregated fund trust (within the meaning assigned by paragraph 138.1(1)(a) of the Act),

(ii) the trust is deemed, under paragraph 138.1(1)(a) of the Act, to have been created at a time that is not more than two years before that particular time, and

(iii) the cost of the trustee's interest (as determined by paragraph 138.1(1)(c) and (d) of the Act) in the trust does not exceed $5,000,000.

Proposed Addition — Reg. 9000 — Farm Credit Canada

Letter from Dept. of Finance, June 18, 2018: Mr. Gregory Willner, Executive Vice-President, Law and Corporate Secretary, Farm Credit Canada, Regina, SK

Dear Mr. Willner:

I am writing in respect of an issue raised in discussions between you and officials of the Department concerning the role of Farm Credit Canada (FCC) in promoting capital investments in the agricultural sector. As part of its mandate, FCC supports venture capital funds (the Funds), structured as partnerships, that seek to ensure that higher risk venture capital is available to innovative agricultural firms.

The issue you raised concerns the potential tax implications of FCC's involvement in the Funds for private sector investors in the Funds. Specifically, there is a concern that FCC's participation in the Funds, as an investor, would engage several aspects of the mark-to-market rules in the *Income Tax Act* (the Act). In general terms, the mark-to-market rules provide certainty in respect of the character and timing of gain and loss recognition on certain investment property owned by financial institutions. Under these rules, the increase or decrease in the value of this investment property each taxation year must be recognized as income or as a loss for income tax purposes in the year.

You have noted that FCC would be characterized as a "financial institution" as that term is defined in subsection 142.2(1) of the Act, and that it would therefore be subject to the mark-to-market rules. You have also indicated that FCC is, at least in the early years of the Funds, expected to hold over 50% of the fair market value of all interests in each of the Funds. Since paragraph (b) of the definition "financial institution" refers to a trust or partnership more than 50% of the fair market value of all interests in which are held at any time by one or more financial institutions, you have concluded that the Funds (at least in their early years) would also be characterized as financial institutions under the mark-to-market rules because of FCC's participation. As such, they would be required to recognize in each taxation year the increase or decrease in the value of their "mark-to-market property" (as defined in subsection 142.2(1) of the Act).

You are concerned that some private sector investors in the Funds, while not characterized as financial institutions under the mark-to-market rules, might still indirectly be impacted by the rules by virtue of the Funds being financial institutions. Specifically, since the Funds are structured as partnerships, all taxable investors in the Funds would be required to include in their income each year all accrued gains allocated to them for that year. You have noted that FCC is a tax-exempt corporation under subsection 149(1) of the Act and that its tax position is therefore not impacted by the mark-to-market rules. As such, you question whether it is appropriate in tax policy terms for the status of a corporation that is itself exempt from tax to influence the tax position of other entities by virtue of the mark-to-market rules.

Based on the foregoing, we agree that FCC's participation in the Funds should not give rise to the application of the mark-to-market rules to the Funds. Accordingly, we are prepared to recommend to the Minister of Finance an amendment that would prevent FCC from being treated as a financial institution for the purposes of the mark-to-market rules.

We would recommend that this amendment apply to the 2016 and subsequent taxation years.

While I cannot offer any assurance that the Minister will agree with our recommendation, I hope that that this statement of our intention is helpful to you.

Yours sincerely,

Brian Ernewein, General Director — Legislation, Tax Policy Branch

Notes: This is expected to be done by adding FCC to Reg. 9000.

Notes: Reg. 9000(a) and (b) added by 2014 budget bill #1, effective for taxation years ending after Nov. 29, 2013. Before the amendment, (c)(i)-(iii) were (a)-(c).

Reg. 9000 added by 2008 budget bill #2, for tax years that end after Feb. 22, 1994.

Definitions [Reg. 9000]: "person", "prescribed" — ITA 248(1); "related segregated fund trust" — ITA 138.1(1)(a); "trust" — ITA 104(1), 248(1), (3).

9001. Prescribed property not mark-to-market property —
(1) In this section, "qualified small business corporation", at any time, means a corporation in respect of which the following conditions are satisfied at that time:

(a) the corporation is a Canadian-controlled private corporation;

(b) the corporation either is an eligible corporation (as defined in subsection 5100(1)) or would be an eligible corporation if the definition "eligible corporation" in subsection 5100(1) were read without reference to its paragraph (e);

(c) the carrying value of the total assets of the corporation and all corporations related to it (determined in accordance with generally accepted accounting principles on a consolidated or combined basis, where applicable) does not exceed $50,000,000; and

(d) the number of employees of the corporation and all corporations related to it does not exceed 500.

Notes: See Notes at end of Reg. 9001.

(2) For the purpose of paragraph (e) of the definition "excluded property" in subsection 142.2(1) of the Act, a share of the capital stock of a corporation is a prescribed property of a taxpayer if

(a) immediately after the time at which the taxpayer acquired the share, the corporation was a qualified small business corporation, and

(i) the corporation continued to be a qualified small business corporation for one year after that time, or

(ii) the taxpayer could not reasonably expect at that time that the corporation would cease to be a qualified small business corporation within one year after that time; or

(b) the share was issued to the taxpayer in exchange for one or more shares of the capital stock of the corporation that were, at the time of the exchange, prescribed property of the taxpayer under this subsection.

Notes: Reg. 9001 added by 2008 budget bill #2, effective for taxation years that end after Feb. 22, 1994, but for taxation years that began before October 2006, read "excluded property" as "mark-to-market property".

Definitions [Reg. 9001]: "business" — ITA 248(1); "Canadian-controlled private corporation" — ITA 125(7), 248(1); "corporation" — ITA 248(1), *Interpretation Act* 35(1); "eligible corporation" — Reg. 5100(1); "employee", "prescribed", "property" — ITA 248(1); "qualified small business corporation" — Reg. 9001(1); "related" — ITA 251(2)–(6); "share", "small business corporation", "taxpayer" — ITA 248(1).

9002. Prescribed property not mark-to-market property —
(1) For the purposes of paragraph (e) of the definition "excluded property" in subsection 142.2(1) of the Act, and of subparagraph 142.6(4)(a)(ii) of the Act, a debt obligation held by a bank is a prescribed property of the bank if the obligation is

(a) an exposure to a designated country (within the meaning assigned by section 8006); or

(b) a United Mexican States Collateralized Par Bond due 2019; or

(c) a United Mexican States Collateralized Discount Bond due 2019.

Notes: Reg. 9002(1) added by 2008 budget bill #2, last change effective for tax years that end after Sept. 2006.

A bond referred to in Reg. 9002(1)(d) is also known as a "Brady bond".

(2) For the purpose of paragraph (e) of the definition "excluded property" in subsection 142.2(1) of the Act, a share is a prescribed property of a taxpayer for a taxation year if

(a) the share is a lending asset of the taxpayer in the year; or

(b) the share was, immediately after its issuance, a share described in paragraph (e) of the definition "term preferred share" in subsection 248(1) of the Act, and the share would, at any time in the year, be a term preferred share if

(i) that definition were read without reference to the portion following paragraph (b), and

(ii) where the share was issued or acquired on or before June 28, 1982, it were issued or acquired after that day.

Notes: Reg. 9002(2) added by 2008 budget bill #2, last change effective for tax years that end after Sept. 2006.

(3) For the purpose of paragraph (e) of the definition "excluded property" in subsection 142.2(1) of the Act, a share of the capital stock of a corporation that is held by a credit union is a prescribed property of the credit union for a taxation year if, throughout the period (referred to in this subsection as the "holding period") in that taxation year during which the credit union holds the share

(a) the corporation is a credit union; or

(b) the following conditions are satisfied:

(i) credit unions hold shares of the corporation that

(A) give those credit unions at least 50% of the votes that could be cast under all circumstances at an annual meeting of shareholders of the corporation, and

(B) have a fair market value of at least 50% of the fair market value of all the issued shares of the corporation,

(ii) the corporation is not controlled, directly or indirectly in any manner whatever, by any person that is not a credit union, and

(iii) the corporation would not be controlled by a person that is not a credit union if each share of the corporation that is not owned at any time in the holding period by a credit union were owned, at that time, by the person.

Notes: Reg. 9002(3) added by 2008 budget bill #2, this version effective for tax years that begin after Feb. 2, 2009, and also, by election, for earlier tax years that end after 2002.

Definitions [Reg. 9002]: "bank" — ITA 248(1), *Interpretation Act* 35(1); "controlled" — ITA 256(5.1)–(6); "corporation" — ITA 248(1), *Interpretation Act* 35(1); "credit union" — ITA 137(6), 248(1); "excluded property" — ITA 142.2(1); "fair market value" — see ITA 69(1) Notes; "lending asset", "person", "prescribed", "property", "share", "shareholder" — ITA 248(1); "taxation year" — ITA 249; "taxpayer", "term preferred share" — ITA 248(1).

9002.1 Prescribed payment card corporation share not mark-to-market property —
For the purpose of paragraph (b) of the definition "excluded property" in subsection 142.2(1) of the Act, a prescribed payment card corporation share of a taxpayer at any time means a share of the capital stock of a particular corporation if, at that time,

(a) the particular corporation is any one of the following

(i) MasterCard International Incorporated,

(ii) MasterCard Incorporated, or

(iii) Visa Inc.; and

(b) the share

(i) is of a class of shares that is not listed on a stock exchange,

(ii) is not convertible into or exchangeable for a share of the class of the capital stock of a corporation that is listed on a stock exchange, and

(iii) was issued by the particular corporation to the taxpayer or to a person related to the taxpayer.

Proposed Amendment — Reg. 9002.1

Letter from Dept. of Finance, Jan. 30, 2018: Mr. Ash Gupta, Gowling WLG (Canada) LLP, Toronto, ON

Dear Mr. Gupta:

I am writing further to your request that section 9002.1 of the *Income Tax Regulations* (the "Regulations") be amended so that shares of Interac Corp. ("Newco") that will be held by financial institutions as the result of a corporate reorganization will be prescribed payment card corporation shares for the purposes of paragraph (b) of the definition "excluded property" in subsection 142.2(1) of the *Income Tax Act*.

Our understanding of the request for relief and the facts relevant to the request is based on correspondence, and discussions, between you and officials of the Department of Finance, including with respect to the Amended and Restated Consent Agreement of the Competition Tribunal dated October 20, 2017 (the "Consent Agreement") and [xxx].

You describe a scenario in which your clients, Interac Inc., Acxsys Corporation, and ACX Corporation (the "Entities"), intend to participate in a proposed reorganization permitted under the terms of the Consent Agreement. As part of the reorganization, current shareholders of the Entities will exchange their shares of the Entities for common shares of a new corporation, Newco. In addition, members of the Interac Association (the "Association") will exchange certain rights as members of the Association for common shares of Newco. Common shares will be the only class of share issued by Newco.

The current shareholders of the Entities, and a number of the other taxpayers that will become shareholders of Newco, are financial institutions as defined in subsection 142.2(1). You have advised that, in the absence of the requested relief, the shares of Newco will be mark-to-market property of certain shareholders following the proposed reorganization.

You indicate that the Entities, together with the Association, develop and provide network services that facilitate payments, and develop and license software related thereto. [xxx] None of the shares of any of the Entities have ever been listed on a stock exchange.

You also indicate that Newco will generally be restricted to carrying on the same business as that carried on by the Entities and the Association prior to the reorganization. The initial shareholders of Newco will consist of the members of the Association immediately prior to the reorganization. The shares of Newco will be subject to ongoing transfer restrictions and will neither be listed on a stock exchange nor exchangeable for shares listed on a stock exchange. [xxx]

In your view, based on the above, including the restrictions imposed on Newco and its shareholders by the Consent Agreement and [xxx] shares of the capital stock of Newco will form part of the organizational infrastructure of its shareholders and will not be acquired or held by those shareholders in the ordinary course of their business. Your view is that the shares of Newco should be excluded property as defined in subsection 142.2(1).

As a result of your submissions and our own analysis, we have concluded that the proposed amendment would be consistent with the tax policy behind the mark-to-market rules. Therefore, we are prepared to recommend to the Minister of Finance that paragraph 9002.1(a) of the Regulations be amended so that a share of Newco may qualify as a "prescribed payment card corporation share" for purposes of the definition "excluded property" in subsection 142.2(1). The current requirements in paragraph 9002.1(b) of the Regulations would apply to the shares of Newco.

While we cannot offer any assurance that either the Minister of Finance or Parliament will agree with our recommendation in respect of this matter, we hope that this statement of our intention is helpful.

Yours sincerely,

Brian Ernewein, General Director, Legislation, Tax Policy Branch

Notes: This was added because financial institutions had significant holdings in MasterCard and VISA after they went public.

The draft regulations of Nov. 7/07 had Reg. 9002.1 and 9002.2 reversed from what they are now, and each had lengthy rules. The new version simply lists the qualifying entities by name.

Reg. 9002.1 added by 2008 budget bill #2, last change effective for tax years that end after Sept. 2006.

Definitions [Reg. 9002.1]: "class of shares" — ITA 248(6); "corporation" — ITA 248(1), *Interpretation Act* 35(1); "person", "prescribed" — ITA 248(1); "public corporation" — ITA 89(1), 248(1); "share", "taxpayer" — ITA 248(1).

9002.2 [Repealed]

Notes: Reg. 9002.2 added and repealed by 2008 budget bill #2. It applied for taxation years that began after 1998 and before 2008. It prescribed the TSX, Bourse de Montréal and Cdn Venture Exchange companies for ITA 142.2(1)"excluded property"(c). This was done because investment dealers had significant holdings in these exchanges after they went public. See also Notes to Reg. 9002.1.

9003. Significant interest in a corporation — For the purpose of paragraph 142.2(3)(c) of the Act, a share described in paragraph 9002(2)(b) is prescribed in respect of all taxpayers.

Notes: Reg. 9003 added by 2008 budget bill #2, effective for taxation years that end after Feb. 22, 1994.

Definitions [Reg. 9003]: "prescribed", "share", "taxpayer" — ITA 248(1).

9004. Financing arrangement not a specified debt obligation — For the purpose of paragraph (c) of the definition "specified debt obligation" in subsection 142.2(1) of the Act, a property is a prescribed property throughout a taxation year if

(a) the property is a direct financing lease, or any other financing arrangement, of a taxpayer that is reported as a loan in the taxpayer's financial statements for the year prepared in accordance with generally accepted accounting principles; and

(b) in computing the taxpayer's income for the year, an amount is deductible under paragraph 20(1)(a) of the Act in respect of the property that is the subject of the arrangement.

Notes: Reg. 9004 amended by 2008 budget bill #2, effective for taxation years that begin after Feb. 2, 2009. The changes were non-substantive.

Reg. 9004 added by P.C. 1995-195, effective on the same basis as the 1995-97 technical bill amendments to ITA 20(1)(l).

Definitions [Reg. 9004]: "amount", "prescribed", "property" — ITA 248(1); "taxation year" — ITA 249; "taxpayer" — ITA 248(1).

9005. Prescribed non-reporting financial institution — For the purposes of the definition "non-reporting financial institution" in subsection 270(1) of the Act, the following entities are prescribed:

(a) a labour-sponsored venture capital corporation as prescribed in section 6701;

(b) a registered retirement savings plan;

(c) a registered retirement income fund;

(d) a pooled registered pension plan;

(e) a deferred profit sharing plan;

(f) a registered disability savings plan;

(g) a registered education savings plan;

(h) a registered pension plan;

(i) a trust governed by a registered pension plan;

(j) a trust described in paragraph 149(1)(o.4) of the Act, if all of the interests in the trust as a beneficiary are held by one or more registered pension plans;

(k) a corporation described in clause 149(1)(o.1)(i)(A) or subparagraph 149(1)(o.1)(ii) or (o.2)(i) of the Act;

(l) a corporation described in any of subparagraphs 149(1)(o.2)(ii) to (iii) of the Act, if all of the shares of the corporation are held by

(i) one or more registered pension plans or trusts governed by registered pension plans,

(ii) one or more trusts described in paragraph (j), or

(iii) one or more corporations described in this paragraph or paragraph (k);

(m) a trust, if all of the interests in the trust as a beneficiary are held by one or more plans, trusts or corporations described in paragraph (i), (k) or (l);

(n) a "central cooperative credit society", as defined in section 2 of the *Cooperative Credit Associations Act* and whose accounts are maintained for member financial institutions; and

(o) a TFSA.

Notes: Reg. 9005 added by 2016 budget bill #2, effective July 2017. See ITA 281 Notes.

Definitions [Reg. 9005]: "corporation" — ITA 248(1), *Interpretation Act* 35(1); "deferred profit sharing plan" — ITA 147(1), 248(1); "pooled registered pension plan" — ITA 147.5(1), 248(1); "prescribed" — ITA 248(1); "registered disability savings plan" — ITA 146.4(1), 248(1); "registered education savings plan" — ITA 146.1(1), 248(1); "registered pension plan" — ITA 248(1); "registered retirement income fund" — ITA 146,3(1), 248(1); "registered retirement savings plan" — ITA 146(1), 248(1); "share", "TFSA" — ITA 248(1); "trust" — ITA 104(1), 248(1), (3).

9006. Prescribed excluded accounts — For the purposes of the definition "excluded account" in subsection 270(1) of the Act, the following accounts are prescribed:

(a) a registered retirement savings plan;

(b) a registered retirement income fund;

(c) a pooled registered pension plans;

(d) a registered pension plan;

(e) a registered disability savings plan;

(f) a registered education savings plan;

(g) a deferred profit sharing plan;

(h) a net income stabilization account, including a NISA Fund No. 2;

(i) an eligible funeral arrangement;

(j) a dormant account if the balance or value of the account does not exceed 1,000 USD; and

(k) a TFSA.

Notes: Reg. 9006 added by 2016 budget bill #2, effective July 2017. See ITA 281 Notes.

Definitions [Reg. 9006]: "deferred profit sharing plan" — ITA 147(1), 248(1); "eligible funeral arrangement" — ITA 148.1(1), 248(1); "net income stabilization account" — ITA 248(1); "pooled registered pension plan" — ITA 147.5(1), 248(1); "prescribed" — ITA 248(1); "registered disability savings plan" — ITA 146.4(1), 248(1); "registered education savings plan" — ITA 146.1(1), 248(1); "registered pension plan" — ITA 248(1); "registered retirement income fund" — ITA 146.3(1), 248(1); "registered retirement savings plan" — ITA 146(1), 248(1); "TFSA" — ITA 248(1).

PART XCI — [9100–9104] FINANCIAL INSTITUTIONS — INCOME FROM SPECIFIED DEBT OBLIGATIONS

9100. Interpretation — Definitions — The following definitions apply in this Part.

"fixed payment obligation", of a taxpayer, means a specified debt obligation under which

(a) the amount and timing of each payment (other than a fee or similar payment or an amount payable because of a default by the debtor) to be made by the debtor were fixed when the taxpayer acquired the obligation and have not been changed; and

(b) all payments are to be made in the same currency.

"primary currency", of a specified debt obligation, means

(a) the currency with which the obligation is primarily connected; and

(b) if there is no such currency, Canadian currency.

Notes: The draft regulations of June 1/95 included a definition of "specified debt obligation" here, referring to ITA 142.2(1). It is not needed because Reg. 9100-9104 are made for purposes of ITA 142.3, and the definitions in ITA 142.2(1) already apply to ITA 142.3 (see *Interpretation Act* s. 16).

"tax basis", of a specified debt obligation at any time to a taxpayer, has the meaning assigned by subsection 142.4(1) of the Act.

"total return", of a taxpayer from a fixed payment obligation, means the amount, measured in the primary currency of the obligation, by which

(a) the total of all amounts each of which is the amount of a payment (other than a fee or similar payment) required to be made by the debtor under the obligation after its acquisition by the taxpayer

exceeds

(b) the cost to the taxpayer of the obligation.

Notes [Reg. 9100]: Reg. 9100 (and all of Parts XCI, XCII) added by P.C. 2009-1212, effective for taxation years ending after Oct. 30, 1994.

Definitions [Reg. 9100]: "amount" — ITA 248(1); "fixed payment obligation", "primary currency" — Reg. 9100; "specified debt obligation" — ITA 142.2(1); "taxpayer" — ITA 248(1).

9101. Prescribed inclusions and deductions — (1) Inclusion — For the purpose of paragraph 142.3(1)(a) of the Act, where a taxpayer holds a specified debt obligation at any time in a taxation year, the amount prescribed in respect of the obligation for the year is the total of

(a) the taxpayer's accrued return from the obligation for the year,

(b) if the taxpayer's accrual adjustment determined under section 9102 in respect of the obligation for the year is greater than nil, the amount of the adjustment, and

(c) if a foreign exchange adjustment is determined under section 9104 in respect of the obligation for the year and is greater than nil, the amount of the adjustment.

(2) Deduction — For the purpose of paragraph 142.3(1)(b) of the Act, where a taxpayer holds a specified debt obligation at any time in a taxation year, the amount prescribed in respect of the obligation is the total of

(a) if the taxpayer's accrual adjustment determined under section 9102 in respect of the obligation for the year is less than nil, the absolute value of the amount of the adjustment, and

(b) if a foreign exchange adjustment is determined under section 9104 in respect of the obligation for the year and is less than nil, the absolute value of the amount of the adjustment.

Notes [Reg. 9101]: Reg. 9101 added by P.C. 2009-1212, for tax years ending after Oct. 30, 1994.

Definitions [Reg. 9101]: "accrual adjustment" — Reg. 9102(4), (5); "accrued return" — Reg. 9102(3); "amount" — ITA 248(1); "foreign exchange adjustment" — Reg. 9104(1); "prescribed" — ITA 248(1); "specified debt obligation" — ITA 142.2(1); "taxation year" — ITA 249; "taxpayer" — ITA 248(1).

9102. General accrual rules — (1) Fixed payment obligation not in default — For the purpose of paragraph 9101(1)(a), a taxpayer's accrued return for a taxation year from a fixed payment obligation, under which each payment required to be made before the end of the year was made by the debtor when it was required to be made, shall be determined in accordance with the following rules:

(a) determine, in the primary currency of the obligation, the portion of the taxpayer's total return from the obligation that is allocated to each day in the year using

(i) the level-yield method described in subsection (2), or

(ii) any other reasonable method that is substantially similar to the level-yield method;

(b) if the primary currency of the obligation is not Canadian currency, translate to Canadian currency the amount allocated to each day in the year, using a reasonable method of translation; and

(c) determine the total of all amounts each of which is the Canadian currency amount allocated to a day, in the year, at the beginning of which the taxpayer holds the obligation.

(2) Level-yield method — For the purpose of subsection (1), the level-yield method for allocating a taxpayer's total return from a fixed payment obligation is the method that allocates, to each particular day in the period that begins on the day following the day on which the taxpayer acquired the obligation and that ends on the day on which the obligation matures, the amount determined by the formula

$$(A + B - C) \times D$$

where

A is the cost of the obligation to the taxpayer (expressed in the primary currency of the obligation);

B is the total of all amounts each of which is the portion of the taxpayer's total return from the obligation that is allocated to a day before the particular day;

C is the total of all payments required to be made under the obligation after it was acquired by the taxpayer and before the particular day; and

D is the rate of interest per day that, if used in computing the present value (as of the end of the day on which the taxpayer acquired the obligation and based on daily compounding) of all payments to be made under the obligation after it was acquired by the taxpayer, produces a present value equal to the cost to the taxpayer of the obligation (expressed in the primary currency of the obligation).

Related Provisions: ITA 257 — Negative amounts in formulas.

(3) Other specified debt obligations — For the purpose of paragraph 9101(1)(a), a taxpayer's accrued return for a taxation year from a specified debt obligation, other than an obligation to which subsection (1) applies, shall be determined

(a) using a reasonable method that,

(i) taking into account the extent to which the obligation differs from fixed payment obligations, is consistent with the principles implicit in the methods that can be used under subsection (1) for fixed payment obligations, and

(ii) is in accordance with generally accepted accounting practice for the measurement of profit from debt obligations; and

(b) on the basis of reasonable assumptions with respect to the timing and amount of any payments to be made by the debtor under the obligation that are not fixed in their timing or amount (measured in the primary currency of the obligation).

(4) Accrual adjustment nil — For the purposes of paragraphs 9101(1)(b) and (2)(a), if subsection 142.3(1) of the Act applies to a taxpayer for a particular taxation year in respect of a specified debt obligation and either the subsection did not apply in respect of the obligation for the taxpayer's immediately preceding taxation year or the taxpayer did not own the obligation at the end of that immediately preceding taxation year, the taxpayer's accrual adjustment in respect of the obligation for the particular taxation year is nil.

(5) Accrual adjustment — For the purposes of paragraphs 9101(1)(b) and (2)(a), if subsection (4) does not apply to determine a taxpayer's accrual adjustment in respect of a specified debt obligation for a particular taxation year, the taxpayer's accrual adjustment is the positive or negative amount determined by the formula

$$A - B$$

where

A is the total of all amounts each of which is the amount that would be the taxpayer's accrued return from the obligation for a taxation year, before the particular taxation year, for which subsection 142.3(1) of the Act applied to the taxpayer in respect of the obligation if the accrued return were redetermined on the basis of

(a) the information available at the end of the particular year, and

(b) the assumptions, if any, with respect to the timing and amount of payments to be made under the obligation after the particular taxation year that were used for the purpose of determining the taxpayer's accrued return from the obligation for the particular taxation year; and

B is the total of

(a) the amount included under paragraph 9101(1)(a) as the taxpayer's accrued return from the obligation for the taxation year immediately preceding the particular taxation year, and

(b) if the taxpayer's accrual adjustment in respect of the obligation for that immediately preceding taxation year was determined under this subsection, the value of A for the purpose of determining that accrual adjustment.

Related Provisions: ITA 257 — Negative amounts in formulas.

(6) Special cases and transition — The rules in this section for determining accrued returns and accrual adjustments are subject to section 9103.

Notes [Reg. 9102]: Reg. 9102 added by P.C. 2009-1212, for tax years ending after Oct. 30, 1994.

Definitions [Reg. 9102]: "amount" — ITA 248(1); "fixed payment obligation" — Reg. 9100; "level-yield method" — Reg. 9102(2); "primary currency" — Reg. 9100; "specified debt obligation" — ITA 142.2(1); "taxation year" — ITA 249; "taxpayer" — ITA 248(1); "total return" — Reg. 9100.

9103. Accrual rules — special cases and transition — (1) Convertible obligation — For the purposes of section 9102, if the terms of a specified debt obligation of a taxpayer give the taxpayer the right to exchange the obligation for shares of the debtor or of a corporation related to the debtor

(a) subject to paragraph (b), the right shall be disregarded (whether it has been exercised or not); and

(b) if 5% or more of the cost of the obligation to the taxpayer is attributable to the right, the cost is deemed to equal the amount by which the cost exceeds the portion of the cost attributable to the right.

(2) [Repealed]

Notes: Reg. 9103(2), "Default by debtor", repealed by P.C. 2009-1212 (after adding it for tax years ending after Oct. 30, 1994), effective for tax years that end after Sept. 1997, or after 1995 if an election was filed by Sept. 30, 1998.

(3) Amendment of obligation — If the terms of a specified debt obligation of a taxpayer are amended at any time in a taxation year of the taxpayer to change the timing or amount of any payment to be made, at or after that time, under the obligation, the taxpayer's accrued returns for the taxation year and for each subsequent taxation year are to be redetermined under section 9102 using a reasonable method that fully gives effect, in those accrued returns, to the alteration to the payments under the obligation.

Notes: Reg. 9103(3) added by P.C. 2009-1212, this version effective for taxation years beginning after April 10, 2009.

(4) Obligations acquired before financial institution rules apply — If a taxpayer held a specified debt obligation at the beginning of the taxpayer's first taxation year (in this subsection referred to as the "initial year") for which subsection 142.3(1) of the Act applied to the taxpayer in respect of the obligation, the following rules apply:

(a) the taxpayer's accrued return from the obligation for the initial year or a subsequent taxation year shall not include an amount to the extent that the amount was included in computing the taxpayer's income for a taxation year preceding the initial year; and

(b) if interest on the obligation in respect of a period before the initial year becomes receivable or is received by the taxpayer in a particular taxation year that is the initial year or a subsequent taxation year, and all or part of the interest would not, but for this paragraph, be included in computing the taxpayer's income for any taxation year, there shall be included in determining the taxpayer's accrued return from the obligation for the particular taxation year the amount, if any, by which

(i) the portion of the interest that would not otherwise be included in computing the taxpayer's income for any taxation year

exceeds

(ii) the portion of the cost of the obligation to the taxpayer that is reasonably attributable to that portion of the interest.

(5) Prepaid interest — transition rule — If, before November 1994 and in a taxation year that ended after February 22, 1994, a taxpayer received an amount under a specified debt obligation in satisfaction, in whole or in part, of the debtor's obligation to pay interest in respect of a period after the taxation year,

(a) the amount may, at the election of the taxpayer, be included in determining the taxpayer's accrued return for the taxation year from the obligation; and

(b) if the amount is so included, the taxpayer's accrued returns for subsequent taxation years from the obligation shall not include any amount in respect of interest that, because of the payment of the amount, the debtor is no longer required to pay.

Notes [Reg. 9103]: Reg. 9103 added by P.C. 2009-1212, for tax years ending after Oct. 30, 1994, but see also Notes to Reg. 9103(2) and (3).

Definitions [Reg. 9103]: "amount" — ITA 248(1); "corporation" — ITA 248(1), *Interpretation Act* 35(1); "initial year" — Reg. 9103(4); "related" — ITA 251(2)–(6); "share" — ITA 248(1); "specified debt obligation" — ITA 142.2(1); "taxation year" — ITA 249; "taxpayer" — ITA 248(1).

9104. Foreign exchange adjustment — (1) Obligations held at end of taxation year — For the purposes of paragraphs 9101(1)(c) and (2)(b), if, at the end of a taxation year, a taxpayer holds a specified debt obligation the primary currency of which is not Canadian currency, the taxpayer's foreign exchange adjustment in respect of the obligation for the taxation year is the positive or negative amount determined by the formula

$$(A \times B) - C$$

where

A is the amount that would be the tax basis of the obligation to the taxpayer at the end of the year if

(a) the tax basis were determined using the primary currency of the obligation as the currency in which all amounts are expressed,

(b) the definition "tax basis" in subsection 142.4(1) of the Act were read without reference to paragraphs (f), (h), (o) and (q), and

(c) the taxpayer's foreign exchange adjustment in respect of the obligation for each year were nil;

B is the rate of exchange at the end of the year of the primary currency of the obligation into Canadian currency; and

C is the amount that would be the tax basis of the obligation to the taxpayer at the end of the year if

(a) the definition "tax basis" in subsection 142.4(1) of the Act were read without reference to paragraphs (h) and (q), and

(b) the taxpayer's foreign exchange adjustment in respect of the obligation for the year were nil.

Related Provisions: ITA 257 — Negative amounts in formulas.

I.T. Technical News: 15 (tax consequences of the adoption of the "euro" currency).

(2) Disposition of obligation — If a taxpayer disposes of a specified debt obligation the primary currency of which is not Canadian currency, the taxpayer's foreign exchange adjustment in respect of the obligation for the taxation year in which the disposition occurs is the amount that would be the foreign exchange adjustment if the taxation year had ended immediately before the disposition.

(3) Disposition of obligation before 1996 — At the election of a taxpayer, subsection (2) does not apply to specified debt obligations disposed of by the taxpayer before 1996.

Notes [Reg. 9104]: Reg. 9104 added by P.C. 2009-1212, effective for taxation years ending after Oct. 30, 1994.

Definitions [Reg. 9104]: "amount" — ITA 248(1); "disposed", "disposes" — ITA 248(1)"disposition"; "disposition" — ITA 248(1); "primary currency" — Reg. 9100; "specified debt obligation" — ITA 142.2(1); "tax basis" — ITA 142.4(1), Reg. 9100; "taxation year" — ITA 249; "taxpayer" — ITA 248(1).

PART XCII — [9200–9204] FINANCIAL INSTITUTIONS — DISPOSITION OF SPECIFIED DEBT OBLIGATIONS

9200. Interpretation — (1) Definitions — The following definitions apply in this Part.

"gain", of a taxpayer from the disposition of a specified debt obligation, means the gain from the disposition determined under paragraph 142.4(6)(a) of the Act.

"loss", of a taxpayer from the disposition of a specified debt obligation, means the loss from the disposition determined under paragraph 142.4(6)(b) of the Act.

"residual portion", of a taxpayer's gain or loss from the disposition of a specified debt obligation, means the amount determined under subsection 142.4(8) of the Act in respect of the disposition.

(2) Amortization date — For the purposes of this Part, the amortization date for a specified debt obligation disposed of by a taxpayer is the day determined as follows:

(a) subject to paragraphs (b) to (d), the amortization date is the later of the day of disposition and the day on which the debtor is required to make the final payment under the obligation, determined without regard to any option respecting the timing of payments under the obligation (other than an option that was exercised before the disposition);

(b) subject to paragraphs (c) and (d), the amortization date is the day of disposition if the day on which the debtor is required to make the final payment under the obligation is not determinable for the purpose of paragraph (a);

(c) subject to paragraph (d), the amortization date is the first day, if any, after the disposition on which the interest rate could change, if the obligation is one in respect of which the following conditions are satisfied:

(i) the obligation provides for stipulated interest payments,

(ii) the rate of interest for one or more periods after the issuance of the obligation was not fixed on the day of issue, and

(iii) when the obligation was issued, it was reasonable to expect that the interest rate for each period would equal or approximate a reasonable market rate of interest for that period; and

(d) if, for purposes of its financial statements, the taxpayer had a gain or loss from the disposition that is being amortized to profit, the amortization date is the last day of the amortization period.

Notes [Reg. 9200]: Reg. 9200 added by P.C. 2009-1212, for tax years ending after Oct. 30, 1994.

Definitions [Reg. 9200]: "amortization date" — Reg. 9200(2); "amount" — ITA 248(1); "disposed" — ITA 248(1)"disposition"; "disposition" — ITA 248(1); "gain", "loss" — Reg. 9200(1); "specified debt obligation" — ITA 142.2(1); "taxpayer" — ITA 248(1).

9201. Transition amount — For the purpose of subsection 142.4(1) of the Act, "transition amount", of a taxpayer in respect of the disposition of a specified debt obligation, means,

(a) if neither paragraph (b) nor (c) applies, nil;

(b) if

(i) the taxpayer acquired the obligation before its taxation year that includes February 23, 1994,

(ii) neither paragraph 7000(2)(a) nor (b) has applied to the obligation, and

(iii) the principal amount of the obligation exceeds the cost of the obligation to the taxpayer (which excess is referred to in this paragraph as the "discount"),

the amount determined by the formula

$$A - B$$

where

A is the total of all amounts each of which is the amount included in respect of the discount in computing the taxpayer's profit for a taxation year that ended before February 23, 1994, and

B is the total of all amounts each of which is the amount included in respect of the discount in computing the taxpayer's income for a taxation year that ended before February 23, 1994; and

(c) where

(i) the conditions in subparagraphs (b)(i) and (ii) are satisfied, and

(ii) the cost of the obligation to the taxpayer exceeds the principal amount of the obligation (which excess is referred to in this paragraph as the "premium"),

the negative of the amount determined by the formula

$$A - B$$

where

A is the total of all amounts each of which is the amount deducted in respect of the premium in computing the taxpayer's profit for a taxation year that ended before February 23, 1994, and

B is the total of all amounts each of which is the amount deducted in respect of the premium in computing the taxpayer's income for a taxation year that ended before February 23, 1994.

Related Provisions: ITA 257 — Negative amounts in formulas.

Notes [Reg. 9201]: Reg. 9201 added by P.C. 2009-1212, for tax years ending after Oct. 30, 1994.

Definitions [Reg. 9201]: "amount" — ITA 248(1); "discount" — Reg. 9201(b)(iii); "disposition" — ITA 248(1); "premium" — Reg. 9201(c)(ii); "principal amount" — ITA 248(1); "specified debt obligation" — ITA 142.2(1); "taxation year" — ITA 249; "taxpayer" — ITA 248(1).

9202. Prescribed debt obligations — (1) Application of related election — The following rules apply with respect to an election made under subsection (3) or (4) by a taxpayer:

(a) the election applies only if

(i) it is in writing,

(ii) it specifies the first taxation year (in this subsection referred to as the "initial year") of the taxpayer to which it is to apply, and

(iii) either it is received by the Minister within six months after the end of the initial year, or the Minister has expressly accepted the later filing of the election;

(b) subject to paragraph (c), the election applies to dispositions of specified debt obligations in the initial year and subsequent taxation years; and

(c) if the Minister has approved, on written application by the taxpayer, the revocation of the election, the election does not apply to dispositions of specified debt obligations in the taxation year specified in the application and in subsequent taxation years.

Related Provisions: *Interpretation Act* 27(5) — Meaning of "within six months".

(2) Prescribed specified debt obligation — For the purpose of subparagraph 142.4(5)(a)(ii) of the Act, a specified debt obligation disposed of by a taxpayer in a taxation year is prescribed in respect of the taxpayer if the amortization date for the obligation is not more than two years after the end of the taxation year.

(3) Prescribed specified debt obligation — exception — Subsection (2) does not apply in respect of a taxpayer for a taxation year if

(a) generally accepted accounting principles require that the taxpayer's gains and losses arising on the disposition of a class of debt obligations be amortized to profit for the purpose of the taxpayer's financial statements;

(b) the taxpayer has elected not to have subsection (2) apply; and

(c) the election applies to dispositions in the year.

(4) Prescribed specified debt obligation — For the purpose of subparagraph 142.4(5)(a)(ii) of the Act, a specified debt obligation disposed of by a taxpayer in a taxation year is prescribed in respect of the taxpayer if

(a) the taxpayer has elected to have this subsection apply;

(b) the election applies to dispositions in the year; and

(c) the absolute value of the positive or negative amount determined by the formula (A – B) does not exceed the lesser of $5,000 and the amount, if any, specified in the election, where

A is the total of all amounts each of which is the residual portion of the taxpayer's gain from the disposition of the obligation or any other specified debt obligation disposed of in the same transaction, and

B is the total of all amounts each of which is the residual portion of the taxpayer's loss from the disposition of the obligation or any other specified debt obligation disposed of in the same transaction.

Related Provisions: ITA 257 — Negative amounts in formulas.

(5) Prescribed specified debt obligation — For the purpose of subparagraph 142.4(5)(a)(ii) of the Act, a specified debt obligation disposed of by a taxpayer in a taxation year is prescribed in respect of the taxpayer if

(a) the disposition resulted in an extinguishment of the obligation, other than an extinguishment that occurred because of a purchase of the obligation by the debtor in the open market;

(b) the taxpayer had the right to require the obligation to be settled at any time; or

(c) the debtor had the right to settle the obligation at any time.

Notes [Reg. 9202]: Reg. 9202 added by P.C. 2009-1212, effective for taxation years ending after Oct. 30, 1994.

Definitions [Reg. 9202]: "amortization date" — Reg. 9200(2); "amount" — ITA 248(1); "disposed" — ITA 248(1)"disposition"; "disposition" — ITA 248(1); "election" — Reg. 9202(1); "gain" — Reg. 9200(1); "initial year" — Reg. 9202(1)(a)(ii); "loss" — Reg. 9200(1); "Minister" — ITA 248(1); "month" — *Interpretation Act* 35(1); "prescribed" — ITA 248(1); "residual portion" — Reg. 9200(1); "specified debt obligation" — ITA 142.2(1); "taxation year" — ITA 249; "taxpayer" — ITA 248(1); "writing" — *Interpretation Act* 35(1); "written" — *Interpretation Act* 35(1)"writing".

9203. Residual portion of gain or loss — (1) Allocation of residual portion — Subject to section 9204, if subsection 142.4(4) of the Act applies to the disposition of a specified debt obligation by a taxpayer, the amount allocated to each taxation year in respect of the residual portion of the gain or loss from the disposition shall be determined, for the purpose of that subsection,

(a) by a method that complies with, or is substantially similar to a method that complies with, subsection (2); or

(b) if gains and losses from the disposition of debt obligations are amortized to profit for the purpose of the taxpayer's financial statements, by the method used for the purpose of the taxpayer's financial statements.

(2) Proration method — For the purpose of subsection (1), a method for allocating to taxation years the residual portion of a taxpayer's gain or loss from the disposition of a specified debt obligation complies with this subsection if the amount allocated to each taxation year is determined by the formula

$$A \times B / C$$

where

A is the residual portion of the taxpayer's gain or loss;

B is the number of days in the taxation year that are in the period referred to in the description of C; and

C is the number of days in the period that,

> (a) where subsection (3) applies in respect of the obligation, is determined under that subsection, and
>
> (b) in any other case,
>
>> (i) begins on the day on which the taxpayer disposed of the obligation, and
>>
>> (ii) ends on the earlier of
>>
>>> (A) the amortization date for the obligation, and
>>>
>>> (B) the day that is 20 years after the day on which the taxpayer disposed of the obligation.

(3) Single proration period — This subsection applies in respect of specified debt obligations disposed of by a taxpayer in a transaction in a taxation year, and the period determined under this subsection in respect of the obligations is the period that begins on the day of disposition and ends on the weighted average amortization date for those obligations so disposed of to which subsection 142.4(4) of the Act applies, if

> (a) the taxpayer has elected in its return of income for the taxation year to have this subsection apply in respect of the obligations so disposed of;
>
> (b) all the obligations so disposed of were disposed of at the same time; and
>
> (c) the number of the obligations so disposed of to which subsection 142.4(4) of the Act applies is at least 50.

(4) Weighted average amortization date — For the purpose of subsection (3), the weighted average amortization date for a group of specified debt obligations disposed of on the same day by a taxpayer is,

> (a) if paragraph (b) does not apply, the day that is the number of days after the day of disposition equal to the total of the number of days determined in respect of each obligation by the formula

$$A \times B / C$$

where

A is the number of days from the day of disposition to the amortization date for the obligation,

B is the residual portion of the gain or loss from the disposition of the obligation, and

C is the total of all amounts each of which is the residual portion of the gain or loss from the disposition of an obligation in the group; and

> (b) the day that the taxpayer determines using a reasonable method for estimating the day determined under paragraph (a).

Notes [Reg. 9203]: Reg. 9203 added by P.C. 2009-1212, effective for taxation years ending after Oct. 30, 1994.

Definitions [Reg. 9203]: "amortization date" — Reg. 9200(2); "amount" — ITA 248(1); "disposed" — ITA 248(1) "disposition"; "disposition" — ITA 248(1); "gain", "loss" — Reg. 9200(1); "residual portion" — Reg. 9200(1), 9203(2); "specified debt obligation" — ITA 142.2(1); "taxation year" — ITA 249; "taxpayer" — ITA 248(1); "weighted average amortization date" — Reg. 9203(4).

9204. Special rules for residual portion of gain or loss —
(1) Application — This section applies for the purposes of subparagraphs 142.4(4)(c)(ii) and (d)(ii) of the Act.

(2) Winding-up — If subsection 88(1) of the Act has applied to the winding-up of a taxpayer (in this subsection referred to as the "subsidiary"), the following rules apply in respect of the residual portion of a gain or loss of the subsidiary from the disposition of a specified debt obligation to which subsection 142.4(4) of the Act applies:

> (a) the amount of that residual portion allocated to the taxation year of the subsidiary in which its assets were distributed to its parent on the winding-up shall be determined on the assumption that the taxation year ended when the assets were distributed to its parent;

> (b) no amount shall be allocated in respect of that residual portion to any taxation year of the subsidiary after its taxation year in which its assets were distributed to its parent; and

> (c) the amount of that residual portion allocated to the taxation year of the parent in which the subsidiary's assets were distributed to it shall be determined on the assumption that the taxation year began when the assets were distributed to it.

Related Provisions: Reg. 9204(2.1) — Winding-up into authorized foreign bank.

(2.1) [Repealed]

Notes: Reg. 9204(2.1) added and repealed by P.C. 2009-1869, effective from June 27, 1999 (but before Aug. 9, 2000 it applied only in respect of authorized foreign banks) and repealed for windings-up that occur after June 14, 2004 (see ITA 142.7).

(3) Transfer of an insurance business — No amount in respect of the residual portion of a gain or loss of an insurer from the disposition of a specified debt obligation to which subsection 142.4(4) of the Act applies shall be allocated to any taxation year of the insurer that ends after the insurer ceased to carry on all or substantially all of an insurance business, if

> (a) subsection 138(11.5) or (11.94) of the Act has applied to the transfer of that business; and

> (b) the person to whom that business was transferred is considered, because of paragraph 138(11.5)(k) of the Act, to be the same person as the insurer in respect of that residual portion.

Notes: CRA considers that "substantially all" means 90% or more.

(4) Transfer to new partnership — If subsection 98(6) of the Act deems a partnership (in this subsection referred to as the "new partnership") to be a continuation of another partnership (in this subsection referred to as the "predecessor partnership"), the following rules apply in respect of the residual portion of a gain or loss of the predecessor partnership from the disposition of a specified debt obligation to which subsection 142.4(4) of the Act applies:

> (a) the amount of that residual portion allocated to the taxation year of the predecessor partnership in which its property was transferred to the new partnership shall be determined on the assumption that the taxation year ended when the property was transferred;

> (b) no amount shall be allocated in respect of that residual portion to any taxation year of the predecessor partnership after its taxation year in which its property was transferred to the new partnership; and

> (c) the amount of that residual portion allocated to the taxation year of the new partnership in which the predecessor partnership's property was transferred to it shall be determined on the assumption that the taxation year began when the property was transferred to it.

(5) Ceasing to carry on business — There shall be allocated to a particular taxation year of a taxpayer the part, if any, of the residual portion of the taxpayer's gain or loss that is from a disposition of a specified debt obligation to which subsection 142.4(4) of the Act applies and that was not allocated to a preceding taxation year, if

> (a) at any time in the particular taxation year the taxpayer ceases to carry on all or substantially all of a business, otherwise than as a result of a merger to which subsection 87(2) of the Act applies, a winding-up to which subsection 88(1) of the Act applies or a transfer of the business to which subsection 98(6) or 138(11.5) or (11.94) of the Act applies;

> (b) the disposition occurred before that time; and

> (c) the specified debt obligation was property used in the business.

Related Provisions: Reg. 9204(2.1)(b) — Application of ITA 142.7(13) until June 14/04 to windup of entrant bank; Reg. 9204(5.1) — When non-resident taxpayer deemed to cease carrying on business.

Notes: The Aug. 8/00 draft regulations proposed to amend Reg. 9204(5) to add a reference to ITA 142.7(13). This was moved to temporary Reg. 9204(2.1)(b) instead.

CRA considers that "substantially all" means 90% or more.

(5.1) Non-resident taxpayer — For the purpose of subsection (5), a non-resident taxpayer is considered to cease to carry on all or substantially all of a business if the taxpayer ceases to carry on, or ceases to carry on in Canada, all or substantially all of the part of the business that was carried on in Canada.

Notes: The CRA interprets "substantially all" as meaning 90% or more.

Reg. 9204(5.1) added by P.C. 2009-1869, effective June 27, 1999, except that before Aug. 9, 2000 it applied only in respect of authorized foreign banks.

(6) Ceasing to be a financial institution — There shall be allocated to a particular taxation year of a taxpayer the part, if any, of the residual portion of the taxpayer's gain or loss that is from a disposition of a specified debt obligation to which subsection 142.4(4) of the Act applies and that was not allocated to a preceding taxation year, if

(a) the particular taxation year ends immediately before the time at which the taxpayer ceases to be a financial institution, otherwise than because it has ceased to carry on a business; and

(b) the disposition occurred before that time.

Notes [Reg. 9204]: Reg. 9204 (and all of Parts XCI, XCII) added by P.C. 2009-1212, effective for taxation years ending after Oct. 30, 1994.

Definitions [Reg. 9204]: "amount", "business" — ITA 248(1); "Canada" — ITA 255, *Interpretation Act* 35(1); "Canadian affiliate" — ITA 142.7(1); "disposed" — ITA 248(1) "disposition"; "disposition" — ITA 248(1); "entrant bank" — ITA 142.7(1); "financial institution" — ITA 142.2(1); "gain" — Reg. 9200(1); "insurer" — ITA 248(1); "loss" — Reg. 9200(1); "new partnership" — Reg. 9204(4); "non-resident" — ITA 248(1); "partnership" — see ITA 96(1) Notes; "person" — ITA 248(1); "predecessor partnership" — Reg. 9204(4); "property" — ITA 248(1); "residual portion" — Reg. 9200(1); "specified debt obligation" — ITA 142.2(1); "subsidiary" — Reg. 9204(2); "taxation year" — ITA 249; "taxpayer" — ITA 248(1).

PART XCIII — [9300] FILM OR VIDEO PRODUCTION SERVICES TAX CREDIT

9300. Accredited production — **(1)** Subject to subsection (2), for the purpose of section 125.5 of the Act, accredited production means

(a) a film or video production in respect of which the aggregate expenditures, included in the cost of the production, in the period that ends 24 months after the time that the principal filming or taping of the production began, exceeds $1,000,000; and

(b) a film or video production that is part of a series of television productions that has two or more episodes, or is a pilot program for such a series of episodes, in respect of which the aggregate expenditures included in the cost of each episode in the period that ends 24 months after the time that the principal filming or taping of the production began exceeds

(i) in the case of an episode whose running time is less than 30 minutes, $100,000, and

(ii) in any other case, $200,000.

Proposed Amendments — Reg. 9300(1) — Extended timelines due to COVID-19

Federal Budget, Supplementary Information, April 19, 2021: See under Reg. 1106(1) "application for a certificate of completion".

Notes: See Notes at end of Reg. 9300.

(2) An accredited production does not include a production that is any of the following:

(a) news, current events or public affairs programming, or a programme that includes weather or market reports;

(b) a talk show;

(c) a production in respect of a game, questionnaire or contest;

(d) a sports event or activity;

(e) a gala presentation or awards show;

(f) a production that solicits funds;

(g) reality television;

(h) pornography;

(i) advertising; and

(j) a production produced primarily for industrial, corporate or institutional purposes.

Notes: Reg. 9300 (Part XCIII) added by P.C. 2005-698, effective for taxation years that end after October 1997.

Forms [Reg. 9300]: T1177: Film or video production services tax credit.

Definitions [Reg. 9300]: "month" — *Interpretation Act* 35(1).

PART XCIV — [9400–9401] [REPEALED]

Notes [Part XCIV]: Part XCIV (Reg. 9400-9401) repealed by 2016 budget bill #1, effective 2017. It prescribed programs for the (now repealed) Child Fitness Credit in ITA 118.03 (2007-13) and 122.8 (2015-16) and Children's Arts Credit in ITA 118.031 (2015-16).

PART XCV — [9500] EMPLOYEE LIFE AND HEALTH TRUSTS

9500. Prescribed rights — For the purpose of subparagraph 144.1(2)(g)(iii) of the Act, prescribed payments are payments to General Motors of Canada Limited or Chrysler Canada Inc. by the employee life and health trust established for the benefit of retired automobile industry workers by the Canadian Auto Workers' Union that

(a) are reasonable in the circumstances;

(b) are made as consideration for administrative services provided to or on behalf of the trust or its beneficiaries, or as reimbursement for employee benefit payments made on behalf of, or in contemplation of the establishment of, the trust; and

(c) the recipient acknowledges in writing shall be included in computing the recipient's income in the year that they are receivable, to the extent that the recipient deducts in the year, or deducted in a prior year, in computing its income amounts in respect of the services or benefit payments described in paragraph (b).

Notes: Reg. 9500 added by 2010 budget bill #2, effective 2010.

Definitions [Reg. 9500]: "automobile" — ITA 248(1) *(not intended to apply here)*; "employee", "prescribed" — ITA 248(1); "trust" — ITA 104(1), 248(1), (3); "writing" — *Interpretation Act* 35(1).

PART XCVI — [9600] SCHOOL SUPPLIES TAX CREDIT

9600. Prescribed durable goods — For the purpose of the definition "teaching supplies" in subsection 122.9(1) of the Act, the following are prescribed durable goods:

(a) books;

(b) games and puzzles;

(c) containers (such as plastic boxes or banker boxes); and

(d) educational support software.

Notes: Reg. 9600 added by 2016 budget bill #1, for 2016 and later tax years.

Definitions [Reg. 9600]: "prescribed" — ITA 248(1).

SCHEDULE I — (SECS. 100, 102 AND 106) RANGES OF REMUNERATION AND OF TOTAL REMUNERATION

1. For the purposes of paragraph 102(1)(c), the ranges of remuneration for each pay period in a taxation year shall be determined as follows:

(a) in respect of a daily pay period, the ranges of remuneration shall commence at $44 and increase in increments of $2 for each range up to and including $151.99;

(b) in respect of a weekly pay period, the ranges of remuneration shall commence at $202 and increase in increments of

(i) $2 for each range up to and including $309.99,

(ii) $4 for each range from $310 to $529.99,

(iii) $8 for each range from $530 to $969.99,

(iv) $12 for each range from $970 to $1,629.99,

(v) $16 for each range from $1,630 to $2,509.99,

(vi) $20 for each range from $2,510 to $3,609.99;

(c) in respect of a bi-weekly pay period, the ranges of remuneration shall commence at $403 and increase in increments of

(i) $4 for each range up to and including $618.99,

(ii) $8 for each range from $619 to $1,058.99,

(iii) $16 for each range from $1,059 to $1,938.99,

(iv) $24 for each range from $1,939 to $3,258.99,

(v) $32 for each range from $3,259 to $5,018.99,

(vi) $40 for each range from $5,019 to $7,218.99;

(d) in respect of a semi-monthly pay period, the ranges of remuneration shall commence at $437 and increase in increments of

(i) $4 for each range up to and including $652.99,

(ii) $8 for each range from $653 to $1,092.99,

(iii) $18 for each range from $1,093 to $2,082.99,

(iv) $26 for each range from $2,083 to $3,512.99,

(v) $34 for each range from $3,513 to $5,382.99,

(vi) $44 for each range from $5,383 to $7,802.99;

(e) in respect of 12 monthly pay periods, the ranges of remuneration shall commence at $873 and increase in increments of

(i) $8 for each range up to and including $1,304.99,

(ii) $18 for each range from $1,305 to $2,294.99,

(iii) $34 for each range from $2,295 to $4,164.99,

(iv) $52 for each range from $4,165 to $7,024.99,

(v) $70 for each range from $7,025 to $10,874.99,

(vi) $86 for each range from $10,875 to $15,604.99;

(f) in respect of 10 monthly pay periods, the ranges of remuneration shall commence at $1,048 and increase in increments of

(i) $10 for each range up to and including $1,587.99,

(ii) $20 for each range from $1,588 to $2,687.99,

(iii) $42 for each range from $2,688 to $4,997.99,

(iv) $62 for each range from $4,998 to $8,407.99,

(v) $84 for each range from $8,408 to $13,027.99,

(vi) $104 for each range from $13,028 to $18,747.99;

(g) in respect of four-week pay periods, the ranges of remuneration shall commence at $806 and increase in increments of

(i) $8 for each range up to and including $1,237.99,

(ii) $16 for each range from $1,238 to $2,117.99,

(iii) $32 for each range from $2,118 to $3,877.99,

(iv) $48 for each range from $3,878 to $6,517.99,

(v) $64 for each range from $6,518 to $10,037.99,

(vi) $80 for each range from $10,038 to $14,437.99;

(h) in respect of 22 pay periods per annum, the ranges of remuneration shall commence at $477 and increase in increments of

(i) $6 for each range up to and including $800.99,

(ii) $10 for each range from $801 to $1,350.99,

(iii) $18 for each range from $1,351 to $2,340.99,

(iv) $28 for each range from $2,341 to $3,880.99,

(v) $38 for each range from $3,881 to $5,970.99,

(vi) $48 for each range from $5,971 to $8,610.99.

Notes: S. 1 amended (for 2004-07) by P.C. 2007-974, this version effective 2007. Earlier amended by P.C. 2005-1133, 2005-694, 2001-1115, 1999-2205, 1998-2771, 1996-501, 1994-1370, 1992-2347 and 1992-291.

Definitions: "pay period", "remuneration" — Reg. 100(1); "taxation year" — ITA 249.

2. For the purposes of paragraph 102(1)(d), the mid-point of the range of amount of personal credits for a taxation year shall be as follows:

(a) from $0 to $8,929, $8,929;

(b) from $8,929.01 to $10,817, $9,873.00;

(c) from $10,817.01 to $12,705, $11,761.00;

(d) from $12,705.01 to $14,593, $13,649.00;

(e) from $14,593.01 to $16,481, $15,537.00;

(f) from $16,481.01 to $18,369, $17,425.00;

(g) from $18,369.01 to $20,257, $19,313.00;

(h) from $20,257.01 to $22,145, $21,201.00;

(i) from $22,145.01 to $24,033, $23,089.00;

(j) from $24,033.01 to $25,921, $24,977.00;

(k) for amounts in excess of $25,921, the amount of the personal credits.

Notes: S. 2 amended (for 2004-07) by P.C. 2007-974, this version effective 2007. Earlier amended by P.C. 2005-1133, 2005-694, 2001-1115, 1999-2205, 1998-2771, 1996-501, 1992-2347 and 1992-291.

Definitions: "remuneration" — Reg. 100(1); "taxation year" — ITA 249.

3. [Repealed]

Notes: S. 3 repealed by P.C. 2001-1115, for 2001 and later taxation years.

SCHEDULE II — CAPITAL COST ALLOWANCES

Class 1 — (4%+)

[Reg. 1100(1)(a)(i), 1100(1)(a.1)-(a.3), 1100(1)(za.1), (zc)(i)(A), (B)]

Property not included in any other class that is

(a) a bridge;

(b) a canal;

(c) a culvert;

(d) a dam;

(e) a jetty acquired before May 26, 1976;

(f) a mole acquired before May 26, 1976;

(g) a road, sidewalk, airplane runway, parking area, storage area or similar surface construction, acquired before May 26, 1976;

(h) railway track and grading, including components such as rails, ballast, ties and other track material,

(i) that is not part of a railway system, or

(ii) that was acquired after May 25, 1976;

(i) railway traffic control or signalling equipment, acquired after May 25, 1976, including switching, block signalling, interlocking, crossing protection, detection, speed control or retarding equipment, but not including property that is principally electronic equipment or systems software therefor;

(j) a subway or tunnel, acquired after May 25, 1976.

(k) electrical generating equipment (except as specified elsewhere in this Schedule);

(l) a pipeline, other than

(i) a pipeline that is gas or oil well equipment, and

(ii) a pipeline that is for oil or natural gas if the Minister, in consultation with the Minister of Natural Resources, is or has been satisfied that the main source of supply for the pipeline is or was likely to be exhausted within 15 years after the date on which the operation of the pipeline commenced;

(m) the generating or distributing equipment and plant (including structures) of a producer or distributor of electrical energy;

(n) manufacturing and distributing equipment and plant (including structures) acquired primarily for the production or distribution of gas, except

(i) a property acquired for the purpose of producing or distributing gas that is normally distributed in portable containers,

(ii) a property acquired for the purpose of processing natural gas, before the delivery of such gas to a distribution system, or

(iii) a property acquired for the purpose of producing oxygen or nitrogen;

(o) the distributing equipment and plant (including structures) of a distributor of water;

(p) the production and distributing equipment and plant (including structures) of a distributor of heat; or

(q) a building or other structure, or a part of it, including any component parts such as electric wiring, plumbing, sprinkler systems, air-conditioning equipment, heating equipment, lighting fixtures, elevators and escalators (except property described in any of paragraphs (k) and (m) to (p) of this Class or in any of paragraphs (a) to (e) of Class 8).

Related Provisions [Cl. 1]: Reg. 1100(1)(a.1) — Additional 6% allowance where building used in manufacturing or processing and election made; Reg. 1100(1)(a.2) — Additional 2% allowance for non-residential where election made; Reg. 1101(5b.1) — Election for separate class for eligible non-residential building; Reg. 1101(5e), (5e.1) — Separate classes; Reg. 1102(2) — Land excluded from value of building; Reg. 4600(1)(a), 4600(2)(a) — Qualified property for investment tax credit; Reg. Sch. II:Cl. 7(k) — Pumping or compression equipment for CO2 pipeline; Reg. Sch. II:Cl. 43.1 — Energy generation property; Reg. Sch. II:Cl. 47 — Electricity transmission equipment; Reg. Sch. II:Cl. 49 — Pipeline.

Notes [Cl. 1]: *1(a)* will cover a portable steel bridge rented by the taxpayer to others: VIEWS doc 2003-0017365.

For *1(g)* now, see Notes to Class 17.

1(k) amended by P.C. 1997-1033, retroactive to property acquired after 1987, to add the parenthetical exclusion.

"Pipeline" (*1(l)*) is defined administratively in IT-482R para. 1. 1(l) amended by P.C. 2006-329, effective Feb. 23, 2005, to reformat as subparagraphs and change "Energy, Mines and Resources" to "Natural Resources".

1(n) can cover natural gas transmission pipeline appendage equipment: IT-476R para. 24; VIEWS doc 2004-0057561I7. The terms "distributing" and "distribution" in 1(n) should be interpreted in the broad and general sense and not in the restrictive sense used by the natural gas industry: *Northern and Central Gas*, [1987] 2 C.T.C. 241 (FCA). See also IT-482R para. 2. In *Repsol Canada*, 2017 FCA 193, a LNG terminal (pre-2007) was Class 43, not 1(n).

1(q) includes certain wellsite trailers: VIEWS doc 2017-073397117. "Component parts" of a building include parking lots in an underground garage (2008-026753117); and ozone equipment to treat chicken barn water, because it is permanently installed and attached to the building (2006-0201091E5). The phrase may include an oil separator for a garage (2012-0432101E5). It did not include a water well and pump even though they were essential for the house, since the well was a separate Class 8 structure: *Henkels*, 2009 TCC 558. A demountable partition wall system is considered an integral part of a building and included in the same class as the building: 2012-0441991E5. An arena is in 1(q) unless it falls into Class 6: 2013-0560281E5. 1(q) can include waste water treatment equipment: 2012-0469941E5. In *Adélard Soucy*, 2019 QCCQ 6956, a preassembled building to keep machining equipment warm at a mine site was Class 8(a) and 29, not 1(q). For the meaning of "building or other structure", see *British Columbia Forest*, [1971] C.T.C. 270 (SCC). Note that the land value must be deducted in determining cost: Reg. 1102(2).

Mobile homes were "trailers" (Cl. 10(e)) and not "structures": *Lansdowne Equity Ventures*, 2006 TCC 565. A mobile home that is permanently attached to a foundation is Class 1 but if not is Class 10(e): VIEWS docs 2008-029653117, 2009-0332411M4.

1(q) amended by P.C. 2005-2186, for property acquired after 1987, to add the parenthesized exclusion.

Definitions [Cl. 1]: "building" — Reg 1102(5), (5.1); "class" — Reg. 1102 (1)–(3), (14), (14.1); "gas or oil well equipment" — Reg. 1104(2); "Minister", "property" — ITA 248(1); "railway system" — Reg. 1104(2); "structure" — Reg 1102(5), (5.1); "systems software" — Reg. 1104(2).

Income Tax Folios: S3-F4-C1: General discussion of CCA.

Interpretation Bulletins: IT-79R3: CCA — Buildings or other structures; IT-195R4: Rental property — CCA restrictions; IT-304R2: Condominiums; IT-367R3: CCA —

multiple-unit residential buildings (archived); IT-476R: CCA — Equipment used in petroleum and natural gas activities; IT-482R: Pipelines.

Class 2 — (6%)
[Reg. 1100(1)(a)(ii)]

Property that is

(a) electrical generating equipment (except as specified elsewhere in this Schedule);

(b) a pipeline, other than gas or oil well equipment, unless, in the case of a pipeline for oil or natural gas, the Minister in consultation with the Minister of Energy, Mines and Resources, is or has been satisfied that the main source of supply for the pipeline is or was likely to be exhausted within 15 years from the date on which operation of the pipeline commenced;

(c) the generating or distributing equipment and plant (including structures) of a producer or distributor of electrical energy, except a property included in Class 10, 13, 14, 26 or 28;

(d) manufacturing and distributing equipment and plant (including structures) acquired primarily for the production or distribution of gas, except

(i) a property included in Class 10, 13 or 14

(ii) a property acquired for the purpose of producing or distributing gas that is normally distributed in portable containers,

(iii) a property acquired for the purpose of processing natural gas, before delivery of such gas to a distribution system, or

(iv) a property acquired for the purpose of producing oxygen or nitrogen;

(e) the distributing equipment and plant (including structures) of a distributor of water, except a property included in Class 10, 13 or 14; or

(f) the production and distributing equipment and plant (including structures) of a distributor of heat, except a property included in Class 10, 13 or 14

acquired by the taxpayer

(g) before 1988, or

(h) before 1990

(i) pursuant to an obligation in writing entered into by the taxpayer before June 18, 1987,

(ii) that was under construction by or on behalf of the taxpayer on June 18, 1987, or

(iii) that is machinery or equipment that is a fixed and integral part of a building, structure, plant facility or other property that was under construction by or on behalf of the taxpayer on June 18, 1987.

Related Provisions: Reg. 1101(5i) — Separate class for certain pipelines; 1103(2), 4600(2)(a) — Qualified property for investment tax credit; Reg. Sch. II:Cl. 43.1 — Energy generation property; Reg. Sch. II:Cl. 49 — Pipeline.

Definitions [Cl. 2]: "building" — Reg 1102(5), (5.1); "gas or oil well equipment" — Reg. 1104(2); "Minister", "property" — ITA 248(1); "structure" — Reg 1102(5), (5.1); "taxpayer" — ITA 248(1); "writing" — *Interpretation Act* 35(1).

Income Tax Folios: S3-F4-C1: General discussion of CCA.

Class 3 — (5%+)
[Reg. 1100(1)(a)(iii), (sb), (za.2), (zc)(i)(C)]

Property not included in any other class that is

(a) a building or other structure, or part thereof, including component parts such as electric wiring, plumbing, sprinkler systems, air-conditioning equipment, heating equipment, lighting fixtures, elevators and escalators, acquired by the taxpayer

(i) before 1988, or

(ii) before 1990

(A) pursuant to an obligation in writing entered into by the taxpayer before June 18, 1987,

(B) that was under construction by or on behalf of the taxpayer on June 18, 1987, or

(C) that is a component part of a building that was under construction by or on behalf of the taxpayer on June 18, 1987;

(b) a breakwater;

(c) a dock;

(d) a trestle;

(e) a windmill;

(f) a wharf;

(g) an addition or alteration, made during the period that is after March 31, 1967 and before 1988, to a building that would have been included in this class during that period but for the fact that it was included in Class 20;

(h) a jetty acquired after May 25, 1976;

(i) a mole acquired after May 25, 1976;

(j) telephone, telegraph or data communication equipment, acquired after May 25, 1976, that is a wire or cable;

(k) an addition or alteration, other than an addition or alteration described in paragraph (k) of Class 6, made after 1987, to a building included, in whole or in part,

(i) in this class,

(ii) in Class 6 by virtue of subparagraph (a)(viii) thereof, or

(iii) in Class 20,

to the extent that the aggregate cost of all such additions or alterations to the building does not exceed the lesser of

(iv) $500,000, and

(v) 25 per cent of the aggregate of the amounts that would, but for this paragraph, be the capital cost of the building and any additions or alterations thereto included in this class or Class 6 or 20; or

(l) ancillary to a wire or cable referred to in paragraph (j) or Class 42 and that is supporting equipment such as a pole, mast, tower, conduit, brace, crossarm, guy or insulator.

Related Provisions: Reg. 1101(5e.2), (5f) — Railway trestles — separate classes; Reg. 1102(15)(a), 1103(2f); Reg. 4600(1)(a) — Qualified property for investment tax credit; Reg. Sch. II:Cl. 42 — Fibre optic cable or telecom cable.

Notes: Multi-use communication cable can fall into either 3(j) or 10(f) depending on the facts: VIEWS doc 2002-0127845.

In *Repsol Canada*, 2017 FCA 193, a LNG jetty (pre-2007) was Class 43, not 3(h).

3(j) amended by P.C. 1994-139, effective for property acquired after Dec. 23, 1991, other than pursuant to an agreement in writing entered into by that date.

3(l) added by P.C. 1994-139, for property acquired after Dec. 23, 1991, other than property acquired pursuant to an agreement in writing entered into by the taxpayer before Dec. 24, 1991. However, if the taxpayer so elected in a letter filed with Revenue Canada by Aug. 8, 1994 or in a letter filed with the taxpayer's return for the first taxation year ending after Dec. 23, 1991, then Reg. 1100(1)(a)(xxviii), amended Classes 3(j) and (l) and Class 42 apply to property acquired after the beginning of that taxation year. If the taxpayer makes such election, ignore the words "or Class 42" in 3(l) and ignore Class 42, with respect to property acquired before Dec. 24, 1991. In any event, with respect to property acquired from Dec. 24, 1991 through Feb. 8, 1994, ignore the words "or Class 42" in 3(l).

Definitions [Cl. 3]: "amount" — ITA 248(1); "building" — Reg 1102(5), (5.1); "class" — Reg. 1102 (1)–(3), (14), (14.1); "property" — ITA 248(1); "structure" — Reg 1102(5), (5.1); "taxpayer" — ITA 248(1); "telegraph" — *Interpretation Act* 36; "writing" — *Interpretation Act* 35(1).

Income Tax Folios: S3-F4-C1: General discussion of CCA.

Interpretation Bulletins: IT-79R3: CCA — buildings or other structures; IT-195R4: Rental property — CCA restrictions; IT-367R3: CCA — multiple-unit residential buildings (archived).

Class 4 — (6%)
[Reg. 1100(1)(a)(iv)]

Property that would otherwise be included in another class in this Schedule that is

(a) a railway system or a part thereof, except automotive equipment not designed to run on rails or tracks, that was acquired

after the end of the taxpayer's 1958 taxation year and before May 26, 1976; or

(b) a tramway or trolley bus system or a part thereof, except property included in class 10, 13 or 14.

Related Provisions: Reg. 1103(2), 1104(2)"tramway or trolley bus system".

Notes: The "acquired after 1958" condition in 4(a) applies only to the exclusion for automotive equipment, so a railway acquired before 1958 is in Class 4 in CRA's view: doc 2009-0313081E5.

Definitions [Cl. 4]: "class" — Reg. 1102 (1)–(3), (14), (14.1); "property" — ITA 248(1); "railway system" — Reg. 1104(2); "taxation year" — ITA 249; "taxpayer" — ITA 248(1); "tramway or trolley bus system" — Reg. 1104(2).

Income Tax Folios: S3-F4-C1: General discussion of CCA.

Class 5 — (10%)
[Reg. 1100(1)(a)(v)]

[Applies only to property acquired before 1963 — ed.]

Class 6 — (10%+)
[Reg. 1100(1)(a)(vi), (sb), (zc)(i)(D)]

Property not included in any other class that is

(a) a building of

(i) frame,

(ii) log,

(iii) stucco on frame,

(iv) galvanized iron, or

(v) corrugated metal,

construction, including component parts such as electric wiring, plumbing, sprinkler systems, air-conditioning equipment, heating equipment, lighting fixtures, elevators and escalators, if the building

(vi) is used by the taxpayer for the purpose of gaining or producing income from farming or fishing,

(vii) has no footings or any other base support below ground level,

(viii) was acquired by the taxpayer before 1979 and is not a building described in subparagraph (vi) or (vii),

(ix) was acquired by the taxpayer after 1978 under circumstances such that

(A) he was obligated to acquire the building under the terms of an agreement in writing entered into before 1979, and

(B) the installation of footings or any other base support of the building was commenced before 1979, or

(x) was acquired by the taxpayer after 1978 under circumstances such that

(A) he commenced construction of the building before 1979, or

(B) the construction of the building was commenced under the terms of an agreement in writing entered into by him before 1979, and

the installation of footings or any other base support of the building was commenced before 1979;

(b) a wooden breakwater;

(c) a fence;

(d) a greenhouse;

(e) an oil or water storage tank;

(f) a railway tank car acquired before May 26, 1976;

(g) a wooden wharf;

(h) an aeroplane hangar acquired after the end of the taxpayer's 1958 taxation year;

(i) an addition or alteration, made

(A) during the period that is after March 31, 1967 and before 1979, or

(B) after 1978 if the taxpayer was obligated to have it made under the terms of an agreement in writing entered into before 1979,

to a building that would have been included in this class during that period but for the fact that it was included in Class 20;

(j) a railway locomotive that is acquired after May 25, 1976 and before February 26, 2008 and that is not an automotive railway car;

(k) an addition or alteration, made after 1978 to a building included in this class by virtue of subparagraph (a)(viii), to the extent that the aggregate cost of all such additions and alterations to the building does not exceed $100,000.

Related Provisions: Reg. 1102(2) — Land excluded from value of building; Reg. 1102(15)(a), 1103(2f); Reg. 4600(1)(a) — Qualified property for investment tax credit; Reg. Sch. II:Cl. 10(y) — New railway locomotive.

Notes: For "component parts" of a building in 6(a), see Notes to Cl. 1 re 1(q). Note that the land value must be excluded: Reg. 1102(2).

Wellsite trailers may be Class 6: VIEWS doc 2017-0733971I7.

"Water storage tank" in 6(e) includes golf course pools (*Oriole Park Fairways* (1956), 16 Tax A.B.C. 92), an artificial lake (VIEWS docs 2007-0220121E5, 2013-0479421E5), and a man-made reservoir or farm dugout (doc 2003-0033707).

Cl. 6 amended by P.C. 2009-660 (for property acquired after Feb. 25, 2008), 1994-139.

Definitions [Cl. 6]: "building" — Reg 1102(5), (5.1); "class" — Reg. 1102 (1)–(3), (14), (14.1); "farming", "fishing", "property" — ITA 248(1); "taxation year" — ITA 249; "taxpayer" — ITA 248(1); "writing" — *Interpretation Act* 35(1).

Income Tax Folios: S3-F4-C1: General discussion of CCA.

Interpretation Bulletins: IT-79R3: CCA — buildings or other structures; IT-195R4: Rental property — CCA restrictions; IT-367R3: CCA — multiple-unit residential buildings (archived); IT-476R: CCA — Equipment used in petroleum and natural gas activities.

Class 7 — (15%)
[Reg. 1100(1)(a)(vii)]

Property that is

(a) a canoe or rowboat;

(b) a scow;

(c) a vessel, but not including a vessel

(i) of a separate class prescribed by subsection 1101(2a), or

(ii) included in Class 41;

(d) furniture, fittings and equipment attached to a property included in this class, but not including radiocommunication equipment;

(e) a spare engine for a property included in this class;

(f) a marine railway;

(g) a vessel under construction, other than a vessel included in Class 41;

(h) subject to an election made under subsection 1103(2i), property acquired after February 27, 2000 that is

(i) a rail suspension device designed to carry trailers that are designed to be hauled on both highways and railway tracks, or

(ii) a railway car;

(i) property that is acquired after February 27, 2000 (other than property included in paragraph (y) of Class 10), that is a railway locomotive and that is not an automotive railway car;

(j) pumping or compression equipment, including equipment ancillary to pumping and compression equipment, acquired after February 22, 2005 if the equipment pumps or compresses petroleum, natural gas or a related hydrocarbon for the purpose of moving it

(i) through a transmission pipeline,

(ii) from a transmission pipeline to a storage facility, or

(iii) to a transmission pipeline from a storage facility; or

(k) pumping or compression equipment that is acquired after February 25, 2008, including equipment ancillary to pumping

and compression equipment, that is on a pipeline and that pumps or compresses carbon dioxide for the purpose of moving it through the pipeline.

Related Provisions: ITA 13(13), Reg. 1101(2)–(2b) — Separate class for certain Class 7 property; ITA 13(16) — Election on disposition of vessel; Reg. 1101(5u) — Election for separate class for property in 7(j) or (k); Reg. 1103(2i) — Election to include Class 7(h) property in Class 35; Reg. Sch. II:Cl. 10(y) — New railway locomotive.

Notes: A boat with its motor removed and moored where it will be used as a business (e.g. a restaurant) is still Class 7 property: VIEWS doc 2010-0377841E5. So is a floating home: 2011-0431631I7.

7(i) amended to add exclusion for Cl. 10(y), and 7(k) added, by P.C. 2009-660, for property acquired after Feb. 25, 2008.

7(h) and (i) added by P.C. 2005-2186, for property acquired after Feb. 27, 2000. See Notes to Reg. 1103(2i).

7(j) added by P.C. 2006-329, effective Feb. 23, 2005.

Definitions [Cl. 7]: "class" — Reg. 1102(1)–(3), (14), (14.1); "prescribed", "property" — ITA 248(1).

Income Tax Folios: S3-F4-C1: General discussion of CCA.

Interpretation Bulletins: IT-267R2: CCA — vessels; IT-317R: Radio and television equipment; IT-476R: CCA — Equipment used in petroleum and natural gas activities.

Class 8 — (20%+)
[Reg. 1100(1)(a)(viii), 1100(1)(sb), (zc)(i)(E), (F)]

Property not included in Class 1, 2, 7, 9, 11, 17 or 30 that is

(a) a structure that is manufacturing or processing machinery or equipment;

(b) tangible property attached to a building and acquired solely for the purpose of

(i) servicing, supporting, or providing access to or egress from, machinery or equipment,

(ii) manufacturing or processing, or

(iii) any combination of the functions described in subparagraphs (i) and (ii);

(c) a building that is a kiln, tank or vat, acquired for the purpose of manufacturing or processing;

(d) a building or other structure, acquired after February 19, 1973, that is designed for the purpose of preserving ensilage on a farm;

(e) a building or other structure, acquired after February 19, 1973, that is

(i) designed to store fresh fruits or fresh vegetables at a controlled level of temperature and humidity, and

(ii) to be used principally for the purpose of storing fresh fruits or fresh vegetables by or for the person or persons by whom they were grown;

(f) electrical generating equipment acquired after May 25, 1976, if

(i) the taxpayer is not a person whose business is the production for the use of or distribution to others of electrical energy,

(ii) the equipment is auxiliary to the taxpayer's main power supply, and

(iii) the equipment is not used regularly as a source of supply;

(g) electrical generating equipment, acquired after May 25, 1976, that has a maximum load capacity of not more than 15 kilowatts;

(h) portable electrical generating equipment acquired after May 25, 1976;

(i) a tangible capital property that is not included in another class in this Schedule except

(i) land or any part thereof or any interest therein,

(ii) an animal,

(iii) a tree, shrub, herb or similar growing thing,

(iv) an oil or gas well,

(v) a mine,

(vi) a specified temporary access road of the taxpayer,

(vii) radium,

(viii) a right of way,

(ix) a timber limit,

(x) a tramway track, or

(xi) property of a separate class prescribed by subsection 1101(2a);

(j) property not included in any other class that is radiocommunication equipment acquired after May 25, 1976;

(k) a rapid transit car that is used for the purpose of public transportation within a metropolitan area and is not part of a railway system;

(l) an outdoor advertising poster panel or bulletin board; or

(m) a greenhouse constructed of a rigid frame and a replaceable, flexible plastic cover.

Related Provisions: Reg. 1100(1.13)(a)(i) — Furniture and equipment costing over $1 million subject to specified leasing property rules; Reg. 1101(5l), (5p), 1103(2g) — Separate class for certain equipment; Reg. 1102(2) — Land excluded from value of building; Reg. 1102(15)(b), 1103(2a) — Election to include property in Class 8; 1104(2) — Definition of "specified temporary access road"; 4600(2)(c) — Qualified property for investment tax credit; Reg. Sch. II Cl. 1(q) — Class 8(a)–(e) takes priority over Class 1(q); Reg. Sch. II:Cl. 30 — Television set-top boxes; Reg. Sch. II:Cl. 43.1 — Energy generation property; Reg. Sch. II:Cl. 46 — Data network infrastructure equipment; Reg. Sch. II:Cl. 49 — Pipeline; *Interpretation Act* 35(1) — Definition of "radiocommunication".

Notes: *8(a)* included a preassembled building to keep machining equipment warm at a mine site in *Adélard Soucy*, 2019 QCCQ 6956. See ITA 125.1(3)"manufacturing or processing" Notes re that term.

8(i) is the "catch-all" for property (such as furniture) not listed in any other class. IT-472 para. 8 lists some examples, including advertising signs, artificial snow making equipment, auto-refractor eye-testing equipment, bedding (but not "linen"), bowling alleys, cable reels and paper cores, carpets, Cobalt 60, cold storage refrigeration equipment, display mannequins, fabric "buildings", filmstrips (anyone remember those?), grain handling equipment, greenhouse steam plants, kitchen utensils and medical/dentist instruments costing over $500 [see Cl. 12(c)], liquid storage tank (but not for oil or water), mattresses, musician's sheet music or master tape, oil pipeline pumping equipment, professionals' libraries, returnable containers including pallets, short-life pipelines, swimming pool filtration and lighting systems, telephone switching equipment, tile drainage (but see ITA 30), utility systems and water well equipment. It also includes: air ozone treatment equipment (VIEWS doc 2006-0201091E5); charging station for electric vehicles (2014-0549331E5); computer telephone system (2010-0362061E5); cushion gas (2007-0257121I7); genealogical database licensed to others (*Pépin*, 2011 CarswellNat 5869 (TCC) (appeal to FCA discontinued: A-381-11), para. 31); grain silo (2006-0214111E5); indoor golf simulator (2010-0376141E5); irrigation system for cranberry farm (2013-0479421E5); master recordings of music (2007-024069117, but *Unidisc*, 2021 QCCA 393 (leave to appeal to SCC requested) says they are eligible capital property, now Class 14.1); oil separator for a garage, where not a "component part" of the building (2012-0432101E5); portable oxygen concentrators, cylinders and regulators (2009-0333861E5); skateboard park ramps (2014-0560281E5); waste water treatment equipment, where not part of a building or other structure (2012-0469941E5); water well and pump (*Henkels*, [2010] 1 C.T.C. 2438 (TCC)); water pipes, electrical wiring and sewage lines (2012-0442571E5).

"Land" in 8(i)(i) might include buildings: see ITA 70(5.2) Notes.

8(i)(ii) excludes an animal, so no CCA can be claimed on zoo animals, which are capital assets: VIEWS doc 2014-0527651E5. (It is not clear if an animal's cost can be written off when it dies.)

A barrister's robes are in Cl. 12 rather than Cl. 8: *Desgagné*, 2012 TCC 63.

Opening words of Cl. 8 amended by P.C. 1997-1033, retroactive to property acquired after 1987, to refer to Cl. 1 (see 1(k)), and by P.C. 2005-2186, effective for property acquired after February 27, 2000, to refer to Cl. 17 (see 17(a.1)).

8(i)(iv) amended by P.C. 1999-629, for property acquired after March 6, 1996, to change "gas well" to "oil or gas well". ("Oil well" was formerly in 8(1)(vi).)

8(i)(vi) amended by P.C. 1999-629, for property acquired after March 6, 1996, to change "oil well" to "specified temporary access road of the taxpayer". ("Oil well" was moved to 8(1)(iv).) See Reg. 1104(2)"specified temporary access road".

8(m) added by P.C. 1994-139, for 1989 and later tax years, for property acquired after 1987.

Definitions [Cl. 8]: "building" — Reg 1102(5), (5.1); "business" — ITA 248(1); "capital property" — ITA 54, 248(1); "class" — Reg. 1102 (1)–(3), (14), (14.1); "land" — see Notes to ITA 70(5.2); "oil or gas well", "person", "prescribed", "pro-

perty" — ITA 248(1); "railway system" — Reg. 1104(2); "specified temporary access road" — Reg. 1104(2); "structure" — Reg 1102(5), (5.1); "taxpayer" — ITA 248(1).

Income Tax Folios: S3-F4-C1: General discussion of CCA.

Interpretation Bulletins: IT-79R3: CCA — buildings and other structures; IT-283R2: CCA — Videotapes, videotape cassettes, films, computer software and master recording media (archived); IT-317R: Radio and television equipment; IT-472: Class 8 property; IT-476R: CCA — Equipment used in petroleum and natural gas activities; IT-482R: Pipelines.

Class 9 — (25%)
[Reg. 1100(1)(a)(ix)]

Property acquired before May 26, 1976, other than property included in Class 30, that is

(a) electrical generating equipment, if

(i) the taxpayer is not a person whose business is the production for the use of or distribution to others of electrical energy,

(ii) the equipment is auxiliary to the taxpayer's main power supply, and

(iii) the equipment is not used regularly as a source of supply,

(b) radar equipment,

(c) radio transmission equipment,

(d) radio receiving equipment,

(e) electrical generating equipment that has a maximum load capacity of not more than 15 kilowatts, or

(f) portable electrical generating equipment,

and property acquired after May 25, 1976 that is

(g) an aircraft;

(h) furniture, fittings or equipment attached to an aircraft; or

(i) a spare part for an aircraft, or for furniture, fittings or equipment attached to an aircraft.

Related Provisions: Reg. 4600(2)(i) — Qualified property for investment tax credit; *Interpretation Act* 35(1) — Definition of "radio".

Notes: For the meaning of "aircraft" see Notes to ITA 8(1)(j). For interpretation of aircraft "spare parts" for 9(i), see VIEWS doc 2012-0461421E5.

For a ruling on a public company that sets up a subsidiary to own a company aircraft, see VIEWS doc 2006-0211021R3.

Definitions [Cl. 9]: "business", "person", "property" — ITA 248(1); "radio" — *Interpretation Act* 35(1); "taxpayer" — ITA 248(1).

Income Tax Folios: S3-F4-C1: General discussion of CCA.

Interpretation Bulletins: IT-317R: Radio and television equipment.

Class 10 — (30%+)
[Reg. 1100(1)(a)(x), 1100(1)(zc)(i)(G)]

Property not included in any other class that is

(a) automotive equipment, including a trolley bus, but not including

(i) an automotive railway car acquired after May 25, 1976,

(ii) a railway locomotive, or

(iii) a tramcar,

(b) a portable tool acquired after May 25, 1976, for the purpose of earning rental income for short terms, such as hourly, daily, weekly or monthly, except a property described in Class 12,

(c) harness or stable equipment,

(d) a sleigh or wagon,

(e) a trailer, including a trailer designed to be hauled on both highways and railway tracks,

(f) general-purpose electronic data processing equipment and systems software for that equipment, including ancillary data processing equipment, acquired after May 25, 1976 and before March 23, 2004 (or after March 22, 2004 and before 2005 if an election in respect of the property is made under subsection

1101(5q)), but not including property that is principally or is used principally as

(i) electronic process control or monitor equipment,

(ii) electronic communications control equipment,

(iii) systems software for a property referred to in subparagraph (i) or (ii), or

(iv) data handling equipment unless it is ancillary to general-purpose electronic data processing equipment,

(f.1) a designated underground storage cost, or

(f.2) an unmanned telecommunication spacecraft designed to orbit above the earth,

and property (other than property included in Class 41, 41.1 or 41.2 or property included in Class 43 that is described in paragraph (b) of that Class) that would otherwise be included in another Class in this Schedule, that is

(g) a building or other structure (other than property described in paragraph (l) or (m)) that would otherwise be included in Class 1, 3 or 6 and that was acquired for the purpose of gaining or producing income from a mine, except

(i) a property included in Class 28,

(ii) a property acquired principally for the purpose of gaining or producing income from the processing of ore from a mineral resource that is not owned by the taxpayer,

(iii) an office building not situated on the mine property, or

(iv) a refinery that was acquired by the taxpayer

(A) before November 8, 1969, or

(B) after November 7, 1969 and that had been used before November 8, 1969 by any person with whom the taxpayer was not dealing at arm's length;

(h) contractor's movable equipment, including portable camp buildings, acquired for use in a construction business or for lease to another taxpayer for use in that other taxpayer's construction business, except a property included in

(i) this Class by virtue of paragraph (t),

(ii) a separate class prescribed by subsection 1101(2b), or

(iii) Class 22 or 38;

(i) a floor of a roller skating rink;

(j) gas or oil well equipment;

(k) property (other than a property included in Class 28 or property described in paragraph (l) or (m)) that was acquired for the purpose of gaining or producing income from a mine and that is

(i) a structure that would otherwise be included in Class 8, or

(ii) machinery or equipment,

except a property acquired before May 9, 1972 for the purpose of gaining or producing income from the processing of ore after extraction from a mineral resource that is not owned by the taxpayer;

(l) property acquired after the 1971 taxation year for the purpose of gaining or producing income from a mine and providing services to the mine or to a community where a substantial proportion of the persons who ordinarily work at the mine reside, if such property is

(i) an airport, dam, dock, fire hall, hospital, house, natural gas pipeline, power line, recreational facility, school, sewage disposal plant, sewer, street lighting system, town hall, water pipeline, water pumping station, water system, wharf or similar property,

(ii) a road, sidewalk, aeroplane runway, parking area, storage area or similar surface construction, or

(iii) machinery or equipment ancillary to any of the property described in subparagraph (i) or (ii),

but is not

(iv) a property included in Class 28, or

(v) a railway not situated on the mine property;

(m) property acquired after March 31, 1977, principally for the purpose of gaining or producing income from a mine, if such property is

(i) railway track and grading including components such as rails, ballast, ties and other track material,

(ii) property ancillary to the track referred to in subparagraph (i) that is

(A) railway traffic control or signalling equipment, including switching, block signalling, interlocking, crossing protection, detection, speed control or retarding equipment, or

(B) a bridge, culvert, subway, trestle or tunnel,

(iii) machinery or equipment ancillary to any of the property referred to in subparagraph (i) or (ii), or

(iv) conveying, loading, unloading or storing machinery or equipment, including a structure, acquired for the purpose of shipping output from the mine by means of the track referred to in subparagraph (i),

but is not

(v) property included in Class 28, or

(vi) for greater certainty, rolling stock;

(n) property that was acquired for the purpose of cutting and removing merchantable timber from a timber limit and that will be of no further use to the taxpayer after all merchantable timber that the taxpayer is entitled to cut and remove from the limit has been cut and removed, unless the taxpayer has elected to include another property of this kind in another class in this Schedule;

(o) mechanical equipment acquired for logging operations, except a property included in Class 7;

(p) an access road or trail for the protection of standing timber against fire, insects or disease;

(q) property acquired for a motion picture drive-in theatre;

(r) property included in this class by virtue of subsection 1102(8) or (9), except a property included in Class 28;

(s) a motion picture film or video tape acquired after May 25, 1976, except a property included in paragraph (w) or (x) or in Class 12;

(t) a property acquired after May 22, 1979 that is designed principally for the purpose of

(i) determining the existence, location, extent or quality of accumulations of petroleum or natural gas,

(ii) drilling oil or gas wells, or

(iii) determining the existence, location, extent or quality of mineral resources,

except a property included in a separate class prescribed by subsection 1101(2b);

(u) property acquired after 1980 to be used primarily in the processing in Canada of heavy crude oil recovered from a natural reservoir in Canada to a stage that is not beyond the crude oil stage or its equivalent that is

(i) property that would otherwise be included in Class 8 except railway rolling stock or a property described in paragraph (j) of Class 8,

(ii) an oil or water storage tank,

(iii) a powered industrial lift truck that would otherwise be included in paragraph (a), or

(iv) property that would otherwise be included in paragraph (f);

(v) property acquired after August 31, 1984 (other than property that is included in Class 30) that is equipment used for the purpose of effecting an interface between a cable distribution system and electronic products used by consumers of that system and that is designed primarily

(i) to augment the channel capacity of a television receiver or radio,

(ii) to decode pay television or other signals provided on a discretionary basis, or

(iii) to achieve any combination of functions described in subparagraphs (i) and (ii);

(w) a certified production acquired after 1987 and before March 1996;

(x) a Canadian film or video production; or

(y) a railway locomotive that is not an automotive railway car and that was not used or acquired for use for any purpose by any taxpayer before February 26, 2008.

Related Provisions: ITA 127.52(1)(c) — Add-back of CCA on film properties for minimum tax purposes; Reg. 1100(1)(m) — Additional allowance — Canadian film or video production; Reg. 1100(1)(zg) — accelerated CCA for year 2000 compliant hardware; Reg. 1100(1.13)(a)(i) — Equipment in Cl. 10(f) costing over $1 million subject to specified leasing property rules; Reg. 1100(21), (21.1) — Certified films and video tapes; Reg. 1101(5a) — Separate class for spacecraft under Class 10(f.2); Reg. 1101(5k) — Separate class for property under Class 10(w); Reg. 1101(5k.1) — Separate class for certain property under Class 10(x); Reg. 1101(5p), 1103(2g) — Separate class for certain equipment under Class 10(f); Reg. 1102(8)(c), 1102(9)(c) — Generating equipment; Reg. 1102(18), 1103(2e) — Townsite costs; Reg. 1102(19.1), (19.2) — Property incorporated into railway locomotive on refurbishment or reconditioning; Reg. 1104(2) — Definitions; Reg. 1104(5), (6) — Income from a mine; Reg. 1106 — Certificate for Class 10(x); Reg. 1206(1)"enhanced recovery equipment"(a), 1206(1)"processing property", 1206(1)"tertiary recovery equipment"; Reg. 4600(1)(a), 4600(2)(e), (g), (h) — Qualified property for investment tax credit; Reg. Sch. II Cl. 10.1 — Automobile costing over $30,000; Reg. Sch. II Cl. 16(g) — Large trucks and tractors; Reg. Sch. II Cl. 29(b)(iv) — Property in Class 10(f) used in M&P; Reg. Sch. II Cl. 41; Reg. Sch. II:Cl. 50 — Computers acquired after March 18, 2007; Reg. Sch. II:Cl. 54 — Zero-emission vehicle acquired before 2028.

Notes: *10(a)* covers cars, but not those costing over $30,000, which are in Class 10.1, or electric or hybrid cars, which are in Class 54. (Taxis and rental cars are in Class 16.). It includes a motor home (which is not an "automobile"): VIEWS doc 2003-0045525, and an an all-terrain vehicle: doc 2002-0141367. The term "automotive equipment" is interpreted broadly, and includes outboard motors and hovercraft (Income Tax Folio S3-F4-C1 ¶1.118) and a self-propelled sprayer (2011-0402501E5).

10(e) changed from simply "a trailer" to current wording by P.C. 1994-139, effective for property acquired after December 23, 1991.

Mobile homes were "trailers" for 10(e): *Lansdowne Equity Ventures*, 2006 TCC 565. A mobile home that is permanently attached to a foundation is Class 1 but if not is Class 10(e): VIEWS docs 2008-029653117, 2009-0332411M4. Wellsite trailers that are frequently moved are 10(e): 2017-073397117.

Multi-use communication cable can fall into either *10(f)* or 3(j) depending on the facts: VIEWS doc 2002-0127845. Internet equipment used in the telecommunications industry (hubs, routers, servers, switches, etc.) is generally excluded from 10(f) due to 10(f)(ii); see VIEWS doc 2003-0015997, but see now Class 46 and Reg. 1104(2)"data network infrastructure equipment". See also Notes to Reg. 1104(2)"general purpose electronic data processing equipment".

10(f) amended by P.C. 2005-2286, effective March 23, 2004, to add "and before March 23, 2004" and grandfathering for before 2005. See now Class 50 (55% CCA) for computers.

Text *before para. (g)* amended to refer to Class 41.1 by P.C. 2011-44, for property acquired after March 18, 2007; to Class 41.2 by 2013 budget bill #2, for property acquired after March 20, 2013; to Class 43(b) by P.C. 1994-230, for property acquired after Feb. 25, 1992.

10(g)(ii): see Michael Colborne, "Class 10(g) and the Ownership of Mineral Resources", II(1) *Resource Sector Taxation* (Federated Press) 105-07 (2003).

Opening words of *10(h)* amended by P.C. 1994-139, effective for property acquired after December 23, 1991, other than property acquired before 1993 pursuant to an agreement in writing entered into by that date, or that was under construction by or on behalf of the taxpayer on that date. For earlier acquisitions, read "(h) contractor's movable equipment, including portable camp buildings, except a property included in".

10(l)(ii): for "similar surface construction", see Notes to Class 17.

10(n) amended by P.C. 1994-139, effective for 1986 and later taxation years, to add the words "that the taxpayer is entitled to cut and remove". Thus, it can apply where the taxpayer has the right to remove some but not all of the timber from the timber limit.

10(s) amended by P.C. 2005-698, effective for 1995 and later taxation years, to add reference to 10(x).

10(u): For the meaning of "used primarily" see Notes to ITA 73(3).

10(v) opening words amended by 2010 budget bill #2, effective for taxation years that end after March 4, 2010, to add exclusion for Class 30 property.

10(w) amended by P.C. 2005-698, effective for 1995 and later taxation years, to add "and before March 1996".

10(x) added by P.C. 2005-698, effective for 1995 and later taxation years.

10(y) added by P.C. 2009-660, effective for property acquired after Feb. 25, 2008.

Definitions [Cl. 10]: "arm's length" — ITA 251(1); "building" — Reg 1102(5), (5.1); "business" — ITA 248(1); "Canada" — ITA 255, *Interpretation Act* 35(1); "Canadian film or video production" — Reg. 1106(4); "certified production" — Reg. 1104(2); "class" — Reg. 1102 (1)–(3), (14), (14.1); "designated underground storage cost", "gas or oil well equipment", "general-purpose electronic data processing equipment" — Reg. 1104(2); "income from a mine" — Reg. 1104(5), (6), (6.1)(a), (b); "mine" — Reg. 1104(6)(b); "mineral resource", "office", "oil or gas well", "person", "prescribed", "property" — ITA 248(1); "radio" — *Interpretation Act* 35(1); "structure" — Reg 1102(5), (5.1); "systems software" — Reg. 1104(2); "taxation year" — ITA 249; "taxpayer" — ITA 248(1).

Income Tax Folios: S3-F4-C1: General discussion of CCA.

Interpretation Bulletins: IT-283R2: CCA — Videotapes, videotape cassettes, films, computer software and master recording media (archived); IT-306R2: Contractor's movable equipment; IT-501: Logging assets.

I.T. Technical News: 14 (millennium bug expenditures).

Class 10.1 — (30%)
[Reg. 1100(1)(a)(x.1)]

Property that would otherwise be included in Class 10 that is a passenger vehicle, the cost of which to the taxpayer exceeds $20,000 or such other amount as may be prescribed for the purposes of subsection 13(2) of the Act.

Related Provisions: Reg. 1101(1af) — Separate class; Reg. 1100(2.5) — 50% CCA in year of disposition; Reg. 7307 — Prescribed amount; Reg. Sch. II:Cl. 54 — Zero-emission vehicle acquired before 2028.

Notes: The $20,000 is actually $30,000. See Notes to ITA 13(7)(g) and 248(1)"automobile". Each car in this class is deemed to be a separate class by Reg. 1101(1af).

Definitions [Cl. 10.1]: "amount", "passenger vehicle", "prescribed", "property", "taxpayer" — ITA 248(1).

Income Tax Folios: S3-F4-C1: General discussion of CCA.

Interpretation Bulletins: IT-521R: Motor vehicle expenses claimed by self-employed individuals; IT-522R: Vehicle, travel and sales expenses of employees.

I.T. Technical News: 10 (1997 deduction limits and benefit rates for automobiles).

Class 11 — (35%)
[Reg. 1100(1)(a)(xi)]

Property not included in any other class that is used to earn rental income and that is

(a) an electrical advertising sign owned by the manufacturer thereof, acquired before May 26, 1976; or

(b) an outdoor advertising poster panel or bulletin board acquired by the taxpayer

(i) before 1988, or

(ii) before 1990

(A) pursuant to an obligation in writing entered into by the taxpayer before June 18, 1987, or

(B) that was under construction by or on behalf of the taxpayer on June 18, 1987.

Definitions [Cl. 11]: "class" — Reg. 1102 (1)–(3), (14), (14.1); "property", "taxpayer" — ITA 248(1); "writing" — *Interpretation Act* 35(1).

Class 12 — (100%)
[Reg. 1100(1)(a)(xii), 1100(1)(l)]

Property not included in any other class that is

(a) a book that is part of a lending library;

(b) chinaware, cutlery or other tableware;

(c) a kitchen utensil costing less than

(i) $100, if acquired before May 26, 1976,

(ii) $200, if acquired after May 25, 1976, and before May 2, 2006, or

(iii) $500, if acquired after May 1, 2006;

(d) a die, jig, pattern, mould or last;

(e) a medical or dental instrument costing less than

(i) $100, if acquired before May 26, 1976,

(ii) $200, if acquired after May 25, 1976, and before May 2, 2006, or

(iii) $500, if acquired after May 1, 2006;

(f) a mine shaft, main haulage way or similar underground work designed for continuing use, or any extension thereof, sunk or constructed after the mine came into production, to the extent that the property was acquired before 1988;

(g) linen;

(h) a tool (other than an electronic communication device or electronic data processing equipment that is acquired after May 1, 2006 and that can be used for a purpose other than any of measuring, locating and calculating) costing less than

(i) $100, if acquired before May 26, 1976,

(ii) $200, if acquired after May 25, 1976, and before May 2, 2006, or

(iii) $500, if acquired after May 1, 2006;

(i) a uniform;

(j) the cutting or shaping part in a machine;

(k) apparel or costume, including accessories used therewith, used for the purpose of earning rental income;

(l) a video tape acquired before May 26, 1976;

(m) a motion picture film or video tape that is a television commercial message;

(n) a certified feature film or certified production;

(o) computer software acquired after May 25, 1976, but not including systems software and property that is described in paragraph (s);

(p) a metric scale or a scale designed for ready conversion to metric weighing, acquired after March 31, 1977 and before 1984 for use in a retail business and having a maximum weighing capacity of 100 kilograms;

(q) a designated overburden removal cost; or

(r) a video-cassette, a video-laser disk or a digital video disk, that is acquired for the purpose of renting and that is not expected to be rented to any one person for more than 7 days in any 30-day period;

and property that would otherwise be included in another class in this Schedule that is

(s) acquired by the taxpayer after August 8, 1989 and before 1993, for use in a business of selling goods or providing services to consumers that is carried on in Canada, or for lease to another taxpayer for use by that other taxpayer in such a business, and that is

(i) electronic bar code scanning equipment designed to read bar codes applied to goods held for sale in the ordinary course of the business,

(ii) a cash register or similar sales recording device designed with the capability of calculating and recording sales tax imposed by more than one jurisdiction in respect of the same sale,

(iii) equipment or computer software that is designed to convert a cash register or similar sales recording device to one having the capability of calculating and recording sales tax imposed by more than one jurisdiction in respect of the same sale, or

(iv) electronic equipment or computer software that is ancillary to property described in subparagraph (i), (ii) or (iii) and all or substantially all the use of which is in conjunction with that property.

Proposed Amendment — 100% deduction for any property, for CCPC (up to $1.5 million)

Federal Budget, Supplementary Information, April 19, 2021: See under Reg. 1100(1)(a) opening words.

Related Provisions: ITA 127.52(1)(c) — Add-back of CCA on film properties for minimum tax purposes; ITA 237.1 — Tax shelters; Reg. 1100(2)C:F(b)(i) — Year of acquisition — no 50% reduction on most Class 12 property; Reg. 1100(20.1) — Limitation on CCA claim for computer software tax shelter property; Reg. 1100(21), (21.1) — Certified films and video tapes; Reg. 1101(5r) — Separate class for all computer software tax shelter property; Reg. 1104(2), (7) — Definitions; Reg. Sch. II:Cl. 52 — Software acquired from Jan. 28/09 to Jan. 31/10 (100% with no half-year rule).

Notes: Cl. 12(a)-(c), (e)-(i), (k)-(l), (p)-(s) are excluded from the rule limiting CCA to 50% for the acquisition year (Reg. 1100(2)C:F(b)(i)), so 100% can be deducted, either as CCA or as an expense: VIEWS doc 2019-0821671M4.

12(a) does not include an audio book in CRA's view: doc 2008-0268131E5.

12(c) covered restaurant cutlery in *Driver*, 2011 TCC 444.

12(d): A mould can also fall in Cl. 29 or 43: VIEWS doc 2010-0358811E5.

12(e): Portable oxygen concentrators, cylinders and regulators are not considered "medical or dental instruments", but are in Cl. 8(i): VIEWS doc 2009-0333861E5.

12(g) covered restaurant linens in *Driver*, 2011 TCC 444.

12(h): for the meaning of "tools", see IT-422. The CCA claim must be reduced for personal use of the tools: doc 2011-0392441E5.

12(i) includes a barrister's gown: *Desgagné*, 2012 TCC 63.

12(o) sparked an industry of software shelters until Reg. 1100(20.1) was announced in 1997. CRA vigorously attacked such shelters, alleging: little or no economic activity; no businesses carried on; inflated costs; over-valuation of assets; promissory notes with only contingent liability; circumvention of the "at-risk" rules; and that arrangements crossed the line into abusive tax planning. Substantive decisions include: *Brown*, 2003 FCA 192 (leave to appeal denied 2004 CarswellNat 84 (SCC)) (American Softworks: promissory note was contingent liability; partnership was limited partnership so "at-risk" rules applied; partnership and software vendor did not deal at arm's length; software valuation was too high; partnership had reasonable expectation of profit; software was available for use); *CIT Financial*, 2004 FCA 201 (leave to appeal denied 2004 CarswellNat 4370) (GAAR did not apply; value of software reduced); *Morley*, 2006 FCA 171 (leave to appeal denied 2006 CarswellNat 3839) (Agensys: promissory note was a sham); *Baxter*, 2007 FCA 172 (leave to appeal denied 2007 CarswellNat 3625) (Trafalgar: unregistered "tax shelter" so no CCA); *Tolhoek*, 2008 FCA 128 (Trafalgar/Icon: unpaid indebtedness with revenue guarantee was limited-recourse amount under 143.2(7) and (13), deduction limited to cash put in; assessment could be issued late due to 143.2(15)); *Sherman*, 2009 FCA 9 (business acquisition held to be solely tax-motivated, CCA disallowed); *Krumm*, 2021 FCA 78 (unregistered "tax shelter" so no deduction); *McCoy*, 2003 TCC 332 (Trafalgar/MarketVision: software valuation); *Drouin*, 2013 TCC 139 (Prospector Networks franchises: deductions allowed, as there was a real business and agreements were not shams); *Lee*, 2020 QCCQ 780 (Prospector Networks: Quebec equivalents of ITA 237.1(6.1), 143.2(6) and Reg. 1100(20.1) applied). **Procedural decisions**: *Loewen*, 2004 FCA 146 (leave to appeal denied 2004 CarswellNat 5843) (AIRS II); *Gamble*, 2011 TCC 244 (extension of time to appeal allowed); *Romanuk*, 2013 FCA 133 (leave to appeal denied 2013 CarswellNat 4317) (Softcom Solutions: CRA audit requests did not violate *Charter* [see also *Softcom Solutions*, 2020 ONSC 3290]); *Advantex Marketing*, 2014 TCC 21 (order that Advantex provide person to be examined for discovery by Crown); *Woessner*, 2017 TCC 124 (American Softworks: counsel removed for conflict of interest). There were also fraudulent schemes: *Viccars*, 2010 ABPC 351 (3-year jail term for lawyer).

Some of these shelters, which avoided the "leasing property" rules in Reg. 1100(17) by planning for business income rather than property income from the software, were shut down by the Aug. 6, 1997 news release and accompanying draft regs (unless no representations are made so they are not "tax shelters" as described). See Reg. 1100(20.1) and (20.2); and now the "matchable expenditure" rules in ITA 18.1. See also Notes to 143.2 and 237.1(1)"tax shelter".

12(o) includes a right to use software for 36 months: VIEWS doc 2004-0071561E5.

Cl. 12 amended by P.C. 2011-935 (effective May 2, 2006), 2010-548 (effective May 12, 2010), 2005-698.

Definitions [Cl. 12]: "business" — ITA 248(1); "Canada" — ITA 255, *Interpretation Act* 35(1); "certified feature film", "certified production" — Reg. 1104(2); "class" — Reg. 1102 (1)–(3), (14), (14.1); "computer software", "designated overburden removal cost" — Reg. 1104(2); "mine" — Reg. 1104(7)(a); "person", "property" — ITA 248(1); "systems software" — Reg. 1104(2); "taxpayer" — ITA 248(1); "television commercial message" — Reg. 1104(2).

Income Tax Folios: S3-F4-C1: General discussion of CCA.

Interpretation Bulletins: IT-283R2: CCA — Videotapes, videotape cassettes, films, computer software and master recording media (archived); IT-422: Definition of tools; IT-441: Certified feature productions (archived).

I.T. Technical News: 12 (millennium bug expenditures); 14 (millennium bug expenditures).

Class 13
[Reg. 1100(1)(b), Schedule III]

Property that is a leasehold interest and property acquired by a taxpayer that would, if that property had been acquired by a person with whom the taxpayer was not dealing at arm's length at the time the property was acquired by the taxpayer, be a leasehold interest of that person, except

(a) an interest in minerals, petroleum, natural gas, other related hydrocarbons or timber and property relating thereto or in respect of a right to explore for, drill for, take or remove minerals, petroleum, natural gas, other related hydrocarbons or timber;

(b) that part of the leasehold interest that is included in another class in this Schedule by reason of subsection 1102(5) or (5.1); or

(c) a property that is included in Class 23.

Related Provisions: Reg. 1100(1)(b) — Additional allowance; Reg. 1100(2)C:F(b)(ii) — Year of acquisition — no 50% reduction on Class 13 property; Reg. 1700(4) — CCA — Farming/fishing property owned since before 1972: leasehold interests.

Notes: TV monitors installed in railway stations and transit terminals are not Class 13 property: VIEWS doc 2006-0175611E5. A licence of space to operate a daycare facility is a Class 14 license, not a Class 13 leasehold interest: doc 2006-0199451E5.

Opening words of Class 13 changed from "Property that is a leasehold interest, except", and reference to Reg. 1102(5.1) added to Class 13(b), by P.C. 1994-139, effective for property acquired after Dec. 23, 1991 (with grandfathering).

Definitions [Cl. 13]: "arm's length" — ITA 251(1); "class" — Reg. 1102 (1)–(3), (14), (14.1); "mineral" — Reg. 1104(3); "person", "property" — ITA 248(1); "related" — ITA 251(2)–(6); "taxpayer" — ITA 248(1).

Income Tax Folios: S3-F4-C1: General discussion of CCA.

Interpretation Bulletins: IT-195R4: Rental property — CCA restrictions; IT-324: Emphyteutic lease (archived).

Class 14
[Reg. 1100(1)(c) — apportioned over the life of the property (see also Class 44)]

Property that is a patent, franchise, concession or licence for a limited period in respect of property, except

(a) a franchise, concession or licence in respect of minerals, petroleum, natural gas, other related hydrocarbons or timber and property relating thereto (except a franchise for distributing gas to consumers or a licence to export gas from Canada or from a province) or in respect of a right to explore for, drill for, take or remove minerals, petroleum, natural gas, other related hydrocarbons or timber;

(b) a leasehold interest;

(c) a property that is included in Class 23;

(d) a licence to use computer software; or

(e) a property that is included in Class 44.

Related Provisions: Reg. 1100(1)(c) — Additional allowance; Reg. 1100(2)C:F(b)(ii) — Year of acquisition — no 50% reduction on Class 14 property; Reg. 1103(2h) — Election for patent to be in Class 14 instead of Class 44; Reg. Sch. II Cl. 44 — Patent or right to use patented information.

Notes: Class 14 assets are written off over the life of the property: see Reg. 1100(1)(c). IT-477 sets out CRA policy. Generally, a Class 14 asset will be written off on an equal basis over the life of the asset, but another basis may be used where legal agreements and other relevant factors indicate that such is reasonable. Where a franchise agreement terminates early, see VIEWS doc 2010-0382581E5.

Class 14 property includes: right to cut Christmas trees over 10 years (VIEWS doc 2011-042464117); license to market customer loyalty cards in a particular territory (*Madell*, 2009 FCA 193; also *Caputo*, 2008 TCC 263, *Falkenberg*, 2008 TCC 265, and *Storwick*, 2008 TCC 268 — FCA appeals discontinued); licence of space to operate daycare facility (2006-0199451E5); licence to construct and operate a facility (2006-0218781R3, 2013-0487301E5); franchise for a limited period (2010-0365771E5); film distribution licence (2010-0374221R3). In *568864 B.C.*, 2014 TCC 373, patents held as loan security and seized when the loan went bad were Class 14 assets.

Class 14 property does not include a fishing licence, which is Class 14.1 (eligible capital property before 2017) in CRA's view: doc 2000-0038827 (but see Notes to 248(1)"property" re whether a fishing licence is property). It does not include a licence that includes a renewal term that is reasonably expected to be exercised: 2014-0552041E5. See also Notes to Class 14.1.

Para. 14(e) added by P.C. 1994-231, for property acquired after April 26, 1993.

Definitions [Cl. 14]: "Canada" — ITA 255, *Interpretation Act* 35(1); "computer software" — Reg. 1104(2); "mineral" — Reg. 1104(3); "property" — ITA 248(1); "province" — *Interpretation Act* 35(1); "related" — ITA 251(2)–(6).

Income Tax Folios: S3-F4-C1: General discussion of CCA.

Interpretation Bulletins: IT-143R3: Meaning of eligible capital expenditure; IT-283R2: CCA — Videotapes, videotape cassettes, films, computer software and master recording media (archived); IT-477: Patents, franchises, concessions and licences.

Class 14.1 — (5%+)
[Reg. 1100(1)(a)(xii.1), 1100(1)(c.1)]

Property of a taxpayer that, in respect of a business of the taxpayer,

(a) is goodwill;

(b) was eligible capital property of the taxpayer immediately before January 1, 2017 and is owned by the taxpayer at the beginning of that day; or

(c) is acquired after 2016, other than

(i) property that is tangible or, for civil law, corporeal property,

(ii) property that is not acquired for the purpose of gaining or producing income from business,

(iii) property in respect of which any amount is deductible (otherwise than as a result of being included in this class) in computing the taxpayer's income from the business,

(iv) property in respect of which any amount is not deductible in computing the taxpayer's income from the business because of any provision of the Act (other than paragraph 18(1)(b)) or these Regulations,

(v) an interest in a trust,

(vi) an interest in a partnership,

(vii) a share, bond, debenture, mortgage, hypothecary claim, note, bill or other similar property, or

(viii) property that is an interest in, or for civil law a right in, or a right to acquire, a property described in any of subparagraphs (i) to (vii).

Related Provisions: ITA 13(34)–(37) — Increases and decreases to goodwill based on outlays and receipts; ITA 13(36) — Class 14.1 property ("CFP") does not include cost of shares, or of cancelling an obligation to pay such cost; ITA 13(38)–(42), 40(13)–(16) — Transition from pre-2017 eligible capital property; ITA 20(1)(b) — Incorporation expense deductible up to $3,000; ITA 20(16.1)(c) — No terminal loss on CFP unless taxpayer ceases to carry on the business; ITA 24(2) — Where taxpayer ceases business and spouse or controlled corp starts to carry it on; ITA 70(5.1) — Transfer of CFP on death; ITA 128.1(1)(b)(iii) — no step-up of CFP on emigration from Canada; ITA 128.1(4)(b)(ii) — no deemed disposition of CFP on immigration to Canada; ITA 248(1)"taxable Canadian property"(b) — CFP is generally TCP; ITA 248(1)"property"(e) — Goodwill is property.

Notes: Generally, Class 14.1 is goodwill and other intangibles that before 2017 were eligible capital property (ECP). See Notes to ITA 20(1)(b) for what was ECP (also re the 2017 changes, and deducting incorporation expenses). Due to 14.1(c)(iii), property that can fall into another Class (e.g., a Class 14 patent) is not Class 14.1.

The multiple negatives in (c)(iv), including the opening words of para. (c), make it hard to read. It *excludes* from Class 14.1 any property where another provision prohibits its deduction (e.g., 18(1)(l) — club membership), *except for* 18(1)(b), which prohibits deduction of capital expenses and requires CCA instead.

The base CCA for Class 14.1 is 5% of the declining balance, under Reg. 1100(1)(a)(xii.1). A further 2% for pre-2017 ECP, topped up to $500 to clear out small balances, is allowed under Reg. 1100(1)(c.1) until 2026.

The word "property" at beginning of Cl. 14.1 does not restrict the Class (see 248(1)"property"(e)), so legal and accounting fees paid on an aborted share acquisition can qualify: docs 2017-0727041E5, 2018-0780011C6 [2018 CTF q.15].

Class 14.1 added by 2016 budget bill #2, effective 2017.

Definitions [Cl. 14.1]: "amount", "business" — ITA 248(1); "class" — Reg. 1101(6), 1102(1)–(3), (14), (14.1); "eligible capital property" — ITA 54, 248(1); "goodwill" — ITA 13(34); "partnership" — see ITA 96(1) Notes; "property", "share", "taxpayer" — ITA 248(1); "trust" — ITA 104(1), 248(1), (3).

Class 15
[Reg. 1100(1)(f)]

Property that would otherwise be included in another class in this Schedule and that

(a) was acquired for the purpose of cutting and removing merchantable timber from a timber limit, and

(b) will be of no further use to the taxpayer after all merchantable timber that the taxpayer is entitled to cut and remove from the limit has been cut and removed,

except

(c) property that the taxpayer has, in the taxation year or a preceding taxation year, elected not to include in this class, or

(d) a timber resource property.

Related Provisions: Reg. 1100(2)C:F(b)(ii) — Year of acquisition — no 50% reduction on Class 15 property; Reg. Sch. IV — Class 15 CCA.

Notes: For CRA interpretation see VIEWS doc 2014-0528021E5. For the meaning of "timber limit" see Notes to ITA 13(21)"timber resource property".

Class 15 amended by P.C. 1994-139, for 1986 and later tax years, so it can apply to a right to remove *some* but not *all* of the timber from the timber limit.

Definitions [Cl. 15]: "class" — Reg. 1102 (1)–(3), (14), (14.1); "property" — ITA 248(1); "taxation year" — ITA 249; "taxpayer" — ITA 248(1); "timber resource property" — ITA 13(21), 248(1).

Income Tax Folios: S3-F4-C1: General discussion of CCA.

Interpretation Bulletins: IT-501: Logging assets.

Class 16 — (40%)
[Reg. 1100(1)(a)(xiii)]

Property acquired before May 26, 1976 that is

(a) an aircraft,

(b) furniture, fittings or equipment attached to an aircraft, or

(c) a spare part for a property included in this class,

property acquired after May 25, 1976 that is

(d) a taxicab,

property acquired after November 12, 1981 that is

(e) a motor vehicle that

(i) would be an automobile as that term is defined in subsection 248(1) of the Act, if that definition were read without reference to paragraph (d) thereof,

(ii) was acquired for the purpose of renting or leasing, and

(iii) is not expected to be rented or leased to any person for more than 30 days in any 12 month period,

property acquired after February 15, 1984 that is

(f) a coin-operated video game or pinball machine,

and property acquired after December 6, 1991 that is

(g) a truck or tractor designed for hauling freight, and that is primarily so used by the taxpayer or a person with whom the taxpayer does not deal at arm's length in a business that includes hauling freight, and that has a "gross vehicle weight rating" (as that term is defined in subsection 2(1) of the *Motor Vehicle Safety Regulations*) in excess of 11,788 kg.

Related Provisions: Reg. Sch. II:Cl. 55 — Zero-emission vehicle acquired before 2028.

Notes: 16(e) does not cover rental vans if 248(1)"automobile"(e)(ii) excludes them from being "automobiles", so they go into Class 10: VIEWS doc 2009-0344861E5. Electric and hybrid rental cars go into Class 55.

16(g) generally applies to large trucks and tractors used by the trucking sector for hauling freight, but it might also apply to a taxpayer that hauls its own freight: VIEWS doc 2003-0019495. Garbage trucks qualify: 2009-0330041C6.

16(e)(i) amended by P.C. 1994-139, for tax years and fiscal periods that begin after June 17, 1987 and end after 1987. 16(g) added by P.C. 1994-139.

Definitions [Cl. 16]: "arm's length" — ITA 251(1); "automobile", "business" — ITA 248(1); "class" — Reg. 1102 (1)–(3), (14), (14.1); "month" — *Interpretation Act* 35(1); "motor vehicle", "person", "property", "taxpayer" — ITA 248(1).

Income Tax Folios: S3-F4-C1: General discussion of CCA.

Interpretation Bulletins: IT-317R: Radio and television equipment.

Class 17 — (8%)
[Reg. 1100(1)(a)(xiv)]

Property that would otherwise be included in another class in this Schedule that is

(a) a telephone system, telegraph system, or a part thereof, acquired before May 26, 1976, except

(i) radiocommunication equipment, or

(ii) a property included in Class 10, 13, 14 or 28, or

(a.1) property (other than a building or other structure) acquired after February 27, 2000 that has not been used for any purpose before February 28, 2000 and is

(i) electrical generating equipment (other than electrical generating equipment described in Class 43.1, 43.2 or 48 or in Class 8 because of paragraph (f), (g) or (h) of that Class), or

(ii) production and distribution equipment of a distributor of water or steam (other than such property described in Class 43.1 or 43.2) used for heating or cooling (including, for this purpose, pipe used to collect or distribute an energy transfer medium but not including equipment or pipe used to distribute water that is for consumption, disposal or treatment),

and property not included in any other class, acquired after May 25, 1976, that is

(b) telephone, telegraph or data communication switching equipment, except

(i) equipment installed on customers' premises, or

(ii) property that is principally electronic equipment or systems software therefor; or

(c) a road (other than a specified temporary access road of the taxpayer), sidewalk, airplane runway, parking area, storage area or similar surface construction.

Related Provisions: ITA 127(9)"qualified property"(b.1) — Property in Cl. 17(a.1)(i) to be prescribed energy generation and conservation property for Atlantic investment tax credit; Reg. 1103(2), 1104(2)"specified temporary access road", "telegraph system", "telephone system"; Reg. 4600(3) — Prescribed energy generation and conservation property; Reg. Sch. II:Cl. 29; Reg. Sch. II:Cl. 43.1 — Property that would otherwise be in 17(a.1).

Notes: For (a.1), property can be used as long as it was not used before Feb. 28, 2000: VIEWS doc 2011-0429081E5.

"Similar surface construction" in (c) requires: a clearly discernable change in the land from its natural state; a circumscribed space with the construction visible; and a recurring need for maintenance: *Mont-Sutton Inc.*, [2000] 1 C.T.C. 311 (FCA). Thus, it includes: campsites (VIEWS doc 2007-025488117); cross-country ski trails (2005-0111301E5); pond construction for a cranberry farm (2013-0479421E5); ski slopes (*Mont-Sutton*). It does not include: golf greens and tees (*Hampton Golf Club*, [1986] 2 C.T.C. 403 (FCTD)); underground garage parking spaces (2008-026753117). See also 2012-0442571E5.

Driveway paving costs were Class 17 in *Henkels*, [2010] 1 C.T.C. 2438 (TCC).

17(a.1) added by P.C. 2005-2186, effective for property acquired after February 27, 2000; and amended by P.C. 2006-329, effective Feb. 23, 2005, to add references to Classes 43.1, 43.2 and 48.

17(c) amended by P.C. 1999-629, for property acquired after March 6, 1996, to refer to a specified temporary access road. See Notes to Reg. 1104(2)"specified temporary access road".

Definitions [Cl. 17]: "class" — Reg. 1102 (1)–(3), (14), (14.1); "property" — ITA 248(1); "specified temporary access road" — Reg. 1104(2); "systems software" — Reg. 1104(2); "taxpayer" — ITA 248(1); "telegraph system" — Reg. 1104(2), *Interpretation Act* 36; "telephone system" — Reg. 1104(2).

Income Tax Folios: S3-F4-C1: General discussion of CCA.

Interpretation Bulletins: IT-476R: CCA — Equipment used in petroleum and natural gas activities; IT-482R: Pipelines; IT-485: Cost of clearing or levelling land [to be amended re golf courses, per I.T. Technical News 20].

I.T. Technical News: 20 (tax treatment of golf courses).

Class 18 — (60%)
[Reg. 1100(1)(a)(xv)]

[Applies only to a film acquired before May 26, 1976 — ed.]

Class 19 — (50% or 20%)
[Reg. 1100(1)(n), (o)]

[Applies only to property acquired before 1967 — ed.]

Class 20 — (20%)
[Reg. 1100(1)(p)]

[Applies to property acquired before April 1967 or covered by the *Area Development Incentives Act*, repealed decades ago — ed.]

Class 21 — (50%)
[Reg. 1100(1)(q)]

[Applies to property acquired before April 1967 or covered by the *Area Development Incentives Act*, repealed decades ago — ed.]

Class 22 — (50%)
[Reg. 1100(1)(a)(xvi)]

Property acquired by the taxpayer after March 16, 1964 and

(a) before 1988, or

(b) before 1990

(i) pursuant to an obligation in writing entered into by the taxpayer before June 18, 1987, or

(ii) that was under construction by or on behalf of the taxpayer on June 18, 1987

that is power-operated movable equipment designed for the purpose of excavating, moving, placing or compacting earth, rock, concrete or asphalt, except a property included in Class 7.

Notes: This text is still needed for Cl. 38.

In *Nomad Sand*, 1990 CarswellNat 504 (FCA), front-end loaders for a sand and gravel pit were Class 22.

Class 23 — (100%)
[Reg. 1100(1)(a)(xvii)]

[Applies to leasehold interests and buildings for Expo '67 in Montreal and Expo '86 in Vancouver — ed.]

Class 24 — (50%+)
[Reg. 1100(1)(ta)]

[Applies only to property acquired before 1999 — ed.]

Class 25 — (100%)
[Reg. 1100(1)(a)(xviii)]

[Applies only to property acquired before 1974 — ed.]

Class 26 — (5%)
[Reg. 1100(1)(a)(xix)]

Property that is

(a) a catalyst; or

(b) deuterium enriched water (commonly known as "heavy water") acquired after May 22, 1979.

Notes: The rate for refinery catalysts may be too low, but this can be fixed only by Finance: VIEWS doc 2017-0695131C6 [2017 CPTS q.7].

Definitions [Cl. 26]: "property" — ITA 248(1).

Class 27 — (50%+)
[Reg. 1100(1)(ta)]

[Applies only to property acquired before 1999 — ed.]

Class 28 — (30%+)
[Reg. 1100(1)(a)(xx), 1100(1)(w), (zc)(i)(H)]

Property situated in Canada that would otherwise be included in another class in this Schedule that

(a) was acquired by the taxpayer

(i) before 1988, or

(ii) before 1990

(A) pursuant to an obligation in writing entered into by the taxpayer before June 18, 1987,

(B) that was under construction by or on behalf of the taxpayer on June 18, 1987, or

(C) that is machinery or equipment that is a fixed and integral part of a building, structure, plant facility or other property that was under construction by or on behalf of the taxpayer on June 18, 1987,

and that

(b) was acquired by the taxpayer principally for the purpose of gaining or producing income from one or more mines operated by the taxpayer and situated in Canada and each of which

(i) came into production in reasonable commercial quantities after November 7, 1969, or

(ii) was the subject of a major expansion after November 7, 1969

(A) whereby the greatest designed capacity, measured in weight of input of ore, of the mill that processed the ore from the mine was not less than 25% greater in the year following the expansion than it was in the year preceding the expansion, or

(B) where in the one-year period preceding the expansion,

(I) the Minister, in consultation with the Minister of Natural Resources, determines that the greatest designed capacity of the mine, measured in weight of output of ore, immediately after the expansion was not less than 25% greater than the greatest designed capacity of the mine immediately before the expansion, and

(II) either

1. no mill processed the ore from the mine at any time, or

2. the mill that processed the ore from the mine processed other ore,

(c) was acquired by the taxpayer

(i) after November 7, 1969,

(ii) before the coming into production of the mine or the completion of the expansion of the mine referred to in subparagraph (b)(i) or (ii), as the case may be, and

(iii) in the case of a mine that was the subject of a major expansion described in subparagraph (b)(ii), in the course of and principally for the purposes of the expansion,

(d) had not, before it was acquired by the taxpayer, been used for any purpose whatever by any person with whom the taxpayer was not dealing at arm's length, and

(e) is any of the following, namely,

(i) property that was acquired before the mine came into production and that would, but for this class, be included in Class 10 by virtue of paragraph (g), (k), (l) or (r) of that class or would have been so included in that class if it had been acquired after the 1971 taxation year,

(ii) property that was acquired before the mine came into production and that would, but for this class, be included in Class 10 by virtue of paragraph (m) of that class, or

(iii) property that was acquired after the mine came into production and that would, but for this class, be included in Class 10 by virtue of paragraph (g), (k), (l) or (r) of that class,

or that would be described in paragraphs (b) to (e) if in those paragraphs each reference to a "mine" were read as a reference to a "mine that is a location in a bituminous sands deposit, oil sands deposit or oil shale deposit from which material is extracted", and each reference to "after November 7, 1969" were read as "before November 8, 1969".

Related Provisions: Reg. 1101(4a), (4b) — Separate class for certain property under Class 28; Reg. 1104(5) — Income from a mine; Reg. 1104(7) — Meaning of "mine"; Reg. 1104(8.1) — Production in paras. (c) and (e) means production in reasonable commercial quantities; Reg. 4600(1)(b), 4600(2)(j) — Qualified property for investment tax credit.

Notes: See Notes to Class 41.

28(b)(ii) amended by P.C. 2000-1331 for expansions commencing after Sept. 13, 2000; and by P.C. 1994-139 for expansions that begin after June 18, 1987.

Definitions [Cl. 28]: "arm's length" — ITA 251(1); "bituminous sands" — ITA 248(1); "building" — Reg 1102(5), (5.1); "Canada" — ITA 255, *Interpretation Act* 35(1); "class" — Reg. 1102 (1)–(3), (14), (14.1); "income from a mine" — Reg. 1104(5), (6.1)(a); "mine" — Reg. 1104(7)(a); "Minister", "person" — ITA 248(1); "production" — Reg. 1104(8.1); "property" — ITA 248(1); "structure" — Reg 1102(5), (5.1); "taxation year" — ITA 249; "taxpayer" — ITA 248(1); "writing" — *Interpretation Act* 35(1).

Class 29 — (25%-50%-25%)
[Reg. 1100(1)(ta)]

Property (other than property included in Class 41 solely because of paragraph (c) or (d) of that Class or property included in Class 47 because of paragraph (b) of that Class) that would otherwise be included in another class in this Schedule

(a) that is property manufactured by the taxpayer, the manufacture of which was completed by him after May 8, 1972, or other property acquired by the taxpayer after May 8, 1972,

(i) to be used directly or indirectly by him in Canada primarily in the manufacturing or processing of goods for sale or lease, or

(ii) to be leased, in the ordinary course of carrying on a business in Canada of the taxpayer, to a lessee who can reasonably be expected to use, directly or indirectly, the property in Canada primarily in Canadian field processing carried on by the lessee or in the manufacturing or processing by the lessee of goods for sale or lease, if the taxpayer is a corporation whose principal business is

(A) leasing property,

(B) manufacturing property that it sells or leases,

(C) the lending of money,

(D) the purchasing of conditional sales contracts, accounts receivable, bills of sale, chattel mortgages, bills of exchange or other obligations representing part or all of the sale price of merchandise or services, or

(E) selling or servicing a type of property that it also leases,

or any combination thereof, unless use of the property by the lessee commenced before May 9, 1972;

(b) that is

(i) property that, but for this class, would be included in Class 8, except railway rolling stock or a property described in paragraph (j) of Class 8,

(ii) an oil or water storage tank,

(iii) a powered industrial lift truck,

(iv) electrical generating equipment described in Class 9,

(v) property that is described in paragraph (b) or (f) of Class 10, or

(vi) property that would be described in paragraph (f) of Class 10 if the portion of that paragraph before subparagraph (i) read as follows:

"(f) general-purpose electronic data processing equipment and systems software for that equipment, including ancillary data processing equipment, acquired after March 18, 2007 and before January 28, 2009, but not including property that is principally or is used principally as";

and

(c) that is property acquired by the taxpayer

(i) before 1988,

(ii) before 1990

(A) pursuant to an obligation in writing entered into by the taxpayer before June 18, 1987,

(B) that was under construction by or on behalf of the taxpayer on June 18, 1987, or

(C) that is machinery or equipment that is a fixed and integral part of a building, structure, plant facility or other property that was under construction by or on behalf of the taxpayer on June 18, 1987, or

(iii) after March 18, 2007 and before 2016 if the property is machinery, or equipment,

(A) that would be described in paragraph (a) if subparagraph (a)(ii) were read without reference to "in Canadian field processing carried on by the lessee or,", and

(B) that is described in any of subparagraphs (b)(i) to (iii) and (vi),

Related Provisions: Reg. 1100(1)(ta) — CCA calculation; Reg. 1100(2)C:F(b)(ii) — Year of acquisition — no 50% reduction on Class 29 property; Reg. 1104(9) — Definition of manufacturing or processing; Reg. 4600(2)(k) — Qualified property for investment tax credit; Reg. Sch. II:Cl. 43 — Class property acquired since 1988.

Notes: See Notes to Reg. 1100(1)(ta), which allows Cl. 29 at 25%, 50%, 25% straight-line over 3 years: tinyurl.com/class29-cra. However, see also Reg. 1100(2) for the Accelerated Investment Incentive (property acquired after Nov. 21, 2018).

Some Class 29 property now falls under Class 43, and some is subject to a 50% rate again since the March 19, 2007 budget. For an example of reclassifying property from Cl. 43 to 29 see VIEWS doc 2010-0365171M4. No election is required for property acquired before 2014 to be in 29(c)(iii): 2012-0433141E5. See also 2013-0515361E5 (general discussion).

Para. (a): For "used primarily in the manufacturing or processing of goods for sale or lease", see ITA 127(9)"qualified property" Notes and VIEWS doc 2019-0816111C6 [2019 CPTS], q.2. For "indirectly" see ITA 17.1(1) Notes. For "principal business" see ITA 20(1)(bb) Notes.

A container and shearing machine may fall under Cl. 29: doc 2011-0426341E5, as may machinery for applying an alloy to steel rods: 2014-0548101E5. Steel tank and oak barrels used for winemaking can fall into Cl. 29: 2013-0503311E5, 2013-0510351E5.

An artificial lake is not in Cl. 29 but in Cl. 6: VIEWS doc 2007-0220121E5. A freezer plant may be: 2008-0293291E5. See also 2009-0324801E5 (specific goods).

Computer equipment acquired for use in manufacturing falls under Class 50, not Class 29: doc 2013-0498331E5.

In *Coop Belle-de-Jour*, 2019 QCCQ 6609, a biomass system for heating greenhouses qualified, as the greenhouses were used primarily for floral arranging. In *Adélard Soucy*, 2019 QCCQ 6956, a preassembled building to keep machining equipment warm at a mine site qualified.

Where Cl. 29 property is transferred not at arm's length, see VIEWS doc 2018-0785371E5.

Cl. 29 amended by 2013 budget bill #1 (effective March 21, 2013), 2011 budget bill #2, P.C. 2009-660, 2009-581, 1999-629.

Definitions [Cl. 29]: "building" — Reg 1102(5), (5.1); "business" — ITA 248(1); "Canada" — ITA 255, *Interpretation Act* 35(1); "Canadian field processing" — ITA 248(1); "carrying on a business in Canada" — ITA 253; "class" — Reg. 1102 (1)–(3), (14), (14.1); "corporation" — ITA 248(1), *Interpretation Act* 35(1); "manufacturing or processing" — Reg. 1104(9); "property" — ITA 248(1); "structure" — Reg 1102(5), (5.1); "taxpayer" — ITA 248(1); "writing" — *Interpretation Act* 35(1).

Income Tax Folios: S3-F4-C1: General discussion of CCA; S4-F15-C1: Manufacturing and processing [replaces IT-147R3].

Interpretation Bulletins: IT-283R2: CCA — Videotapes, videotape cassettes, films, computer software and master recording media (archived); IT-411R: Meaning of "construction".

Class 30 — (40%)
[Reg. 1100(1)(a)(xxi)]

Property of a taxpayer that is

(a) an unmanned telecommunication space-craft that was designed to orbit above the earth and that was acquired by the taxpayer

(i) before 1988, or

(ii) before 1990

(A) pursuant to an obligation in writing entered into by the taxpayer before June 18, 1987, or

(B) that was under construction by or on behalf of the taxpayer on June 18, 1987; or

(b) equipment used for the purpose of effecting an interface between a cable or satellite distribution system (other than a satellite radio distribution system) and electronic products used by consumers of that system if the equipment

(i) is designed primarily

(A) to augment the channel capacity of a television receiver, or

(B) to decode pay television or other signals provided on a discretionary basis,

(ii) is acquired by the taxpayer after March 4, 2010, and

(iii) has not been used or acquired for use for any purpose by any taxpayer before March 5, 2010.

Related Provisions: Reg. 1101(5a) — Separate class.

Notes: Cl. 30(b), for television set-top boxes, added (and "of a taxpayer" added to opening words) by 2010 budget bill #2, for tax years that end after March 4, 2010.

Definitions [Cl. 30]: "property" — ITA 248(1); "radio" — *Interpretation Act* 35(1); "taxpayer" — ITA 248(1); "writing" — *Interpretation Act* 35(1).

Class 31 — (5%)
[Reg. 1100(1)(a)(xxii)]

[Applies only to a multiple-unit residential building (MURB) begun before 1982 and acquired by June 17, 1987 or under an obligation entered into by that date — ed.]

Class 32 — (10%)
[Reg. 1100(1)(a)(xxiii)]

[Applies only to a multiple-unit residential building (MURB) acquired before 1980 — ed.]

Class 33 — (15%)
[Reg. 1100(1)(a)(xxiv)]

Property that is a timber resource property.

Notes: See VIEWS doc 2009-0343311E5 and ITA 13(21)"timber resource property" Notes.

Definitions [Cl. 33]: "property" — ITA 248(1); "timber resource property" — ITA 13(21), 248(1).

Income Tax Folios: S3-F4-C1: General discussion of CCA.

Interpretation Bulletins: IT-481: Timber resource property and timber limits.

Class 34 — (50%+)
[Reg. 1100(1)(ta)]

[Applies only to electrical and steam generating equipment, or heat equipment, acquired before Feb. 22, 1994 (unless grandfathered by certain agreements or arrangements made before that date), or under a certificate issued before 1996 — ed.]

Class 35 — (7%+)
[Reg. 1100(1)(a)(xxv), 1100(1)(z.1b), 1100(1)(z.1c), 1100(1)(zc)(i)(I)]

Property not included in any other class that is

(a) a railway car acquired after May 25, 1976; or

(b) a rail suspension device designed to carry trailers that are designed to be hauled on both highways and railway tracks.

Related Provisions: Reg. 1100(1)(z.1c) — Additional CCA for railway common carriers; Reg. 1100(1.13)(a)(viii) — Exclusion from specified leasing property rules; Reg. 1101(5d)–(5d.2) — Separate classes; Reg. 1103(2i) — Election to include Class 7(h) property in Class 35.

Notes: 35(b) added by P.C. 1994-139, for property acquired after Dec. 23, 1991 (after 1992 in some cases).

Definitions [Cl. 35]: "class" — Reg. 1102 (1)–(3), (14), (14.1); "property" — ITA 248(1).

Class 36

Property acquired after December 11, 1979 that is deemed to be depreciable property by virtue of paragraph 13(5.2)(c) of the Act.

Related Provisions: Reg. 1101(5g) — Separate class.

Definitions [Cl. 36]: "property" — ITA 248(1).

Class 37 — (15%)
[Reg. 1100(1)(a)(xxvi)]

Property that would otherwise be included in another class in this Schedule that is property used in connection with an amusement park, including

(a) land improvements (other than landscaping) for or in support of park activities, including

(i) roads, sidewalks, parking areas, storage areas, or similar surface constructions, and

(ii) canals,

(b) buildings (other than warehouses, administration buildings, hotels or motels), structures and equipment (other than automotive equipment), including

(i) rides, attractions and appurtenances associated with a ride or attraction, ticket booths and facades,

(ii) equipment, furniture and fixtures, in or attached to a building included in this class,

(iii) bridges, and

(iv) fences or similar perimeter structures, and

(c) automotive equipment (other than automotive equipment designed for use on highways or streets),

and property not included in another class in this Schedule that is a waterway or a land improvement (other than landscaping, clearing or levelling land) used in connection with an amusement park.

Related Provisions: Reg. 1103(2b) — Election to include earlier property in Class 37; Reg. 1104(12) — Meaning of "amusement park".

Notes: For "similar surface construction" in 37(a)(i), see Notes to Class 17.

Definitions [Cl. 37]: "amusement park" — Reg. 1104(12); "associated" — ITA 256; "building" — Reg 1102(5), (5.1); "class" — Reg. 1102 (1)–(3), (14), (14.1); "property" — ITA 248(1); "structure" — Reg 1102(5), (5.1).

Class 38
[Reg. 1100(1)(zd)]

Property not included in Class 22 but that would otherwise be included in that class if that class were read without reference to paragraphs (a) and (b) thereof.

Related Provisions: Reg. 1101(5l) — Election for separate class; Reg. 4600(2)(e) — Qualified property for investment tax credit.

Definitions [Cl. 38]: "class" — Reg. 1102 (1)–(3), (14), (14.1); "property" — ITA 248(1).

Income Tax Folios: S3-F4-C1: General discussion of CCA.

Interpretation Bulletins: IT-411R: Meaning of "contruction"; IT-469R: CCA — Earth-moving equipment.

Class 39
[Reg. 1100(1)(ze)]

[Applies only to property acquired before 1992 — ed.]

Class 40
[Reg. 1100(1)(zf)]

[Applies only to property acquired before 1990 — ed.]

Class 41 — (25%+)
[Reg. 1100(1)(a)(xxvii), 1100(1)(y), (ya)]

Property (other than property included in Class 41.1 or 41.2)

(a) not included in Class 28 that would otherwise be included in that class if that Class were read without reference to paragraph

(a) of that Class, and if subparagraphs (e)(i) to (iii) of that Class were read as follows:

"(i) property that was acquired before the mine came into production and that would, but for this Class, be included in Class 10 because of paragraph (g), (k), (l) or (r) of that class or would have been so included in that class if it had been acquired after the 1971 taxation year, and property that would, but for this class, be included in Class 41 because of subsection 1102(8) or (9),

(ii) property that was acquired before the mine came into production and that would, but for this Class, be included in Class 10 because of paragraph (m) of that Class, or

(iii) property that was acquired after the mine came into production and that would, but for this Class, be included in Class 10 because of paragraph (g), (k), (l) or (r) of that Class, and property that would, but for this Class, be included in Class 41 because of subsection 1102(8) or (9);"

(a.1) that is the portion, expressed as a percentage determined by reference to capital cost, of property that

(i) would, but for this Class, be included in Class 10 because of paragraph (g), (k), or (l) of that Class, or that is included in this Class because of subsection 1102(8) or (9),

(ii) is not described in paragraph (a) or (a.2),

(iii) was acquired by the taxpayer principally for the purpose of gaining or producing income from one or more mines that are operated by the taxpayer and situated in Canada, and that became available for use for the purpose of subsection 13(26) of the Act in a taxation year, and

(iv) had not, before it was acquired by the taxpayer, been used for any purpose by any person or partnership with whom the taxpayer was not dealing at arm's length,

where that percentage is determined by the formula

$$100 \times \frac{[A - (B \times 365/C)]}{A}$$

where

A   is the total of all amounts each of which is the capital cost of a property of the taxpayer that became available for use for the purpose of subsection 13(26) of the Act in the year and that is described in subparagraphs (i) to (iv) in respect of the mine or mines, as the case may be,

B   is 5% of the taxpayer's gross revenue from the mine or mines, as the case may be, for the year, and

C   is the number of days in the year;

(a.2) that

(i) is property that would, but for this Class, be included in Class 10 because of paragraph (g), (k), or (l) of that Class or that is included in this Class because of subsection 1102(8) or (9),

(ii) was acquired by the taxpayer in a taxation year principally for the purpose of gaining or producing income from one or more mines each of which

(A) is one or more wells operated by the taxpayer for the extraction of material from a deposit of bituminous sands or oil shales, operated by the taxpayer and situated in Canada,

(B) was the subject of a major expansion after March 6, 1996, and

(C) is a mine in respect of which the Minister, in consultation with the Minister of Natural Resources, determines that the greatest designed capacity of the mine, measured in volume of oil that is not beyond the crude oil stage or its equivalent, immediately after the expansion was not less than 25% greater than the greatest designed capacity of the mine immediately before the expansion,

(iii) was acquired by the taxpayer

(A) after March 6, 1996,

(B) before the completion of the expansion, and

(C) in the course of and principally for the purposes of the expansion, and

(iv) had not, before it was acquired by the taxpayer, been used for any purpose by any person or partnership with whom the taxpayer was not dealing at arm's length;

(a.3) that is property included in this Class because of subsection 1102(8) or (9), other than property described in paragraph (a) or (a.2) or the portion of property described in paragraph (a.1);

(b) that is property, other than property described in subsection 1101(2c),

(i) described in paragraph (f.1), (g), (j), (k), (l), (m), (r), (t) or (u) of Class 10 that would be included in that Class if this Schedule were read without reference to this paragraph; or

(ii) that is a vessel, including the furniture, fittings, radio communication equipment and other equipment attached thereto, that is designed principally for the purpose of

(A) determining the existence, location, extent or quality of accumulations of petroleum, natural gas or mineral resources, or

(B) drilling oil or gas wells,

and that was acquired by the taxpayer after 1987 other than property that was acquired before 1990

(iii) pursuant to an obligation in writing entered into by the taxpayer before June 18, 1987,

(iv) that was under construction by or on behalf of the taxpayer on June 18, 1987, or

(v) that is machinery and equipment that is a fixed and integral part of property that was under construction by or on behalf of the taxpayer on June 18, 1987;

(c) acquired by the taxpayer after May 8, 1972, to be used directly or indirectly by the taxpayer in Canada primarily in Canadian field processing, where the property would be included in Class 29 if

(i) Class 29 were read without reference to

(A) the words "property included in Class 41 solely because of paragraph (c) or (d) of that Class or",

(B) its subparagraphs (b)(iii) and (v), and

(C) its paragraph (c),

(ii) subsection 1104(9) were read without reference to paragraph (k) of that subsection, and

(iii) this Schedule were read without reference to this Class, Class 39 and Class 43; or

(d) acquired by the taxpayer after December 5, 1996 (otherwise than pursuant to an agreement in writing made before December 6, 1996) to be leased, in the ordinary course of carrying on a business in Canada of the taxpayer, to a lessee who can reasonably be expected to use, directly or indirectly, the property in Canada primarily in Canadian field processing carried on by the lessee, where the property would be included in Class 29 if

(i) Class 29 were read without reference to

(A) the words "property included in Class 41 solely because of paragraph (c) or (d) of that Class or",

(B) its subparagraphs (b)(iii) and (v), and

(C) its paragraph (c), and

(ii) this Schedule were read without reference to this Class, Class 39 and Class 43.

Related Provisions: ITA 13(5) — Reclassification of property as a result of change in regulations; ITA 257 — Negative amounts in formulas; Reg. 1101(4c), (4d) — Separate class for certain property under (a)–(a.2); Reg. 1102(8)(d), 1102(9)(d) — Electrical plant used for mining; Reg. 1102(14.11) — Effect of transfer of oil sands property on reorganization; Reg. 1102(14.12) — Rules where property acquired by transfer, amalgamation or windup; Reg. 1102(18) — Townsite costs; Reg. 1104(5) — Income from a mine; Reg. 1104(5.1), (5.2) — Gross revenue from a mine; Reg. 1104(7) — Meaning of "mine"; Reg. 1104(8.1) — Production in para. (a) means production in reasonable commercial quantities; Reg. 1206(1)"bituminous sands equipment", "tertiary recovery equipment"; Reg. 4600(1)(b), 4600(2)(g), (j) — Qualified property for investment tax credit; Reg. Sch. II:Cl. 41.1 — Oil sands property acquired after March 18/07; Reg. Sch. II:Cl. 41.2 — Property in 41(a) or (a.1) now deemed to be Class 41.2; Reg. Sch. II:Cl. 43 — Class property acquired since 1988.

Notes: See Tom Stack, "Overview of Capital Cost Allowance Classifications for Mining Assets", VI(2) *Resource Sector Taxation* (Federated Press) 436-438 (2008).

"Designed capacity" in 41(a.2)(ii)(C) means "what an existing thing ... was designed to theoretically achieve, not what it is capable of doing in the design phase": *Thompson Creek Mining*, 2017 BCSC 1128 (under BC *Mineral Tax Act*).

Property for a new sylvite (potash ore) mine qualified under 41(a): VIEWS doc 2006-0197591E5. Property related to a bituminous sands project qualified in 2004-0106281R3, 2006-0188921R3, 2007-0222741R3, 2007-0251451R3. See also Cl. 41.1 Notes.

For the meaning of "indirectly" in 41(c) and (d), see Notes to ITA 17.1(1).

Opening words amended to exclude Class 41.1 property by P.C. 2011-44, for property acquired after March 18, 2007, and to exclude Class 41.2 property by 2013 budget bill #2, for property acquired after March 20, 2013.

41(a) amended by P.C. 2001-1378 effective August 15, 2001, and by P.C. 1998-49 effective for property acquired after March 6, 1996.

41(a.1), added by P.C. 1998-49 effective for property acquired after March 6, 1996, implements a 1996 budget proposal for accelerated CCA for Cl. 41 property, that becomes available for use in respect of a mine in a year, in excess of 5% of the gross revenue from the mine for the year. See Reg. 1104(5.1)–(5.2).

41(a.2), added by P.C. 1998-49 effective for property acquired after March 6, 1996, implements a 1996 budget proposal to treat oil sands in-situ projects as mines for CCA purposes. It provides a "major mine expansion" test for in-situ projects, analogous to the test in Class 28, to determine eligibility for accelerated CCA.

41(a.2)(ii)(C) amended by P.C. 2000-1331, for expansions that begin after Sept. 13, 2000.

41(a.3), added by P.C. 1998-49 effective for property acquired after 1987, provides a cross-reference for property included in 41 by Reg. 1102(8) and (9) (electrical plant for mining) This property is not eligible for accelerated CCA, but is given the same 25% rate as property in 41(b).

41(b) opening words amended by P.C. 2005-2186 to add exclusion for Reg. 1101(2c), effective Nov. 7, 2001. 41(b)(i) amended by P.C. 1994-230 and P.C. 1997-1033, effective for property acquired after February 25, 1992.

41(c)(i)(A), (d)(i)(A) added by P.C. 2009-581, for property acquired after March 18, 2007.

41(c) and (d) added by P.C. 1999-629, for taxation years that begin after 1996.

Definitions [Cl. 41]: "amount" — ITA 248(1); "arm's length" — ITA 251(1); "bituminous sands", "business" — ITA 248(1); "Canada" — ITA 255, *Interpretation Act* 35(1); "Canadian field processing" — ITA 248(1); "carrying on a business in Canada" — ITA 253; "class" — Reg. 1102(1)–(3), (14), (14.1); "gross revenue" — ITA 248(1); "gross revenue from a mine" — Reg. 1104(5.1); "income from one or more mines" — Reg. 1104(5), (6.1); "mine" — Reg. 1104(7)(a); "mineral resource", "Minister", "oil or gas well" — ITA 248(1); "partnership" — see ITA 96(1) Notes; "person" — ITA 248(1); "production" — Reg. 1104(8.1); "property" — ITA 248(1); "radio" — *Interpretation Act* 35(1); "taxation year" — ITA 249; "taxpayer" — ITA 248(1); "writing" — *Interpretation Act* 35(1).

Income Tax Folios: S3-F4-C1: General discussion of CCA.

Interpretation Bulletins: IT-267R2: CCA — vessels; IT-476R: CCA — Equipment used in petroleum and natural gas activities; IT-482R: Pipelines.

Class 41.1 — (25%+)
[Reg. 1100(1)(a)(xxvii.1), 1100(1)(y.1), (ya.1)]

Oil sands property (other than specified oil sands property) that,

(a) is acquired by a taxpayer after March 18, 2007 and before 2016 and that if acquired before March 19, 2007, would be included in paragraphs (a), (a.1) or (a.2) of Class 41, or

(b) is acquired by a taxpayer after 2015 and that if acquired before March 19, 2007 would be included in Class 41.

Related Provisions: ITA 13(5) — Reclassification of property due to change in regulations; Reg. 1100(1)(a)(xxvii.1), 110(1)(y.1), (ya.1) — CCA and additional allowances; Reg. 1101(4e), (4f) — Separate class for certain property under para. (a); Reg. 1102(8)(d), 1102(9)(d) — Electrical plant used for mining; Reg. 1104(5.1) — Gross revenue from a mine; Reg. 1104(7) — Meaning of "mine"; Reg. 1104(8.1) — Meaning of "production"; Reg. 4600(1)(b), 4600(2)(j) — Qualified property for investment tax credit.

Notes: For rulings that property is Cl. 41.1 see VIEWS docs 2009-0307841R3, 2009-0314541R3.

Class 41.1 added by P.C. 2011-44, for property acquired after March 18, 2007.

Definitions [Cl. 41.1]: "mine" — Reg. 1104(7); "oil sands property" — Reg. 1104(2); "production" — Reg. 1104(8.1); "property" — ITA 248(1); "specified oil sands property" — Reg. 1104(2); "taxpayer" — ITA 248(1).

Class 41.2 — (25%+)
[Reg. 1100(1)(a)(xxvii.2), 1100(1)(y.2), (ya.2)]

Property, other than an oil sands property or eligible mine development property,

(a) that is acquired by a taxpayer after March 20, 2013 and before 2021 and that, if acquired on March 20, 2013, would be included in paragraph (a) or (a.1) of Class 41; or

(b) that is acquired by a taxpayer after 2020 and that, if acquired on March 20, 2013, would be included in paragraph (a) or (a.1) of Class 41.

Related Provisions: Reg. 1100(1)(a)(xxvii.2) — Base CCA of 25%; Reg. 1100(1)(y.2), (ya.2) — Additional allowance until 2020; Reg. 1101(4g), (4h) — Separate classes; Reg. 1102(8)(d), (9)(d) — Electrical plant used for mining; Reg. 1102(14.12) — Rules where property acquired by transfer, amalgamation or windup; Reg. 1104(5) — Income from a mine; Reg. 1104(5.1) — Gross revenue from a mine; Reg. 1104(7) — Meaning of "mine"; Reg. 1104(8.1) — Meaning of "production"; Reg. 4600(1)(b), 4600(2)(j) — Qualified property for investment tax credit.

Notes: See Michael Colborne & Lana Paton, "2013 Mining Update", 2013 Cdn Tax Foundation conference report at 9:1-5.

Cl. 41.2 added by 2013 budget bill #2, effective March 21, 2013.

Definitions [Cl. 41.2]: "eligible mine development property", "oil sands property" — Reg. 1104(2); "property", "taxpayer" — ITA 248(1).

Class 42 — (12%)
[Reg. 1100(1)(a)(xxviii)]

Property that is

(a) fibre-optic cable; or

(b) telephone, telegraph or data communication equipment that is a wire or cable (other than a cable included in this class because of paragraph (a)), acquired after February 22, 2005, and that has not been used, or acquired for use, for any purpose before February 23, 2005.

Related Provisions: Reg. Sch. II:Cl. 3(l)–Supporting equipment.

Notes: 42(b) added by P.C. 2006-329, effective Feb. 23, 2005.

Class 42 (now 42(a)) added by P.C. 1994-139, for property acquired after Dec. 23, 1991, with certain grandfathering.

Definitions [Cl. 42]: "income from a mine" — Reg. 1104(5); "mine" — Reg. 1104(7); "oil sands property" — Reg. 1104(2); "property", "taxpayer" — ITA 248(1).

Class 43 — (30%)
[Reg. 1100(1)(a)(xxix)]

Property acquired after February 25, 1992 that

(a) is not included in Class 29 or 53, but that would otherwise be included in Class 29 if that Class were read without reference to its subparagraphs (b)(iii) and (v) and paragraph (c); or

(b) is property

(i) that is described in paragraph (k) of Class 10 and that would be included in that Class if this Schedule were read without reference to this paragraph and paragraph (b) of Class 41, and

(ii) that, at the time of its acquisition, can reasonably be expected to be used entirely in Canada and primarily for the purpose of processing ore extracted from a mineral resource located in a country other than Canada.

Related Provisions: Reg. 1100(2)A(d) (after 2025) — Amount deductible in first year property is available for use; Reg. 1101(5s) — Election for separate class for para. (a) property costing at least $1,000; Reg. 1102(16.1) — Election to include Class 43.1 or 43.2 property in Class 29 or 43; Reg. 4600(2)(k) — Investment tax credit.

Notes: The following can fall into Class 43: grain silo (VIEWS docs 2005-0112831E5, 2006-0214111E5); hydraulic punch (2008-0268021E5); laser cutting machine (2010-0386381E5). Some Cl. 43 property acquired before 2014 is now in Cl. 29(c)(iii).

Assets were held to be Cl. 43 in: *Ateliers Ferroviaires*, 2011 TCC 352, para. 5 (equipment used to manufacture steel parts for repairing railway structures); *Repsol Canada*,

2017 FCA 193 (LNG terminal and jetty, pre-2007); *Stark International*, 2019 TCC 248 (oil processing equipment for transformers; safety equipment did not qualify [para. 50]).

See also VIEWS docs 2009-0324801E5 (specific goods), 2010-0365171M4 (property reclassified to Cl. 29).

43(a) amended by 2015 Budget bill, effective June 23, 2015, to refer to Class 53.

Class 43 added by P.C. 1994-230, for property acquired after Feb. 25, 1992, and para. 43(b) amended retroactive to its introduction by P.C. 1997-1033.

Definitions [Cl. 43]: "Canada" — ITA 255, *Interpretation Act* 35(1); "mineral resource", "property" — ITA 248(1).

Income Tax Folios: S3-F4-C1: General discussion of CCA; S4-F15-C1: Manufacturing and processing [replaces IT-147R3].

Interpretation Bulletins: IT-411R: Meaning of "construction"; IT-476R: CCA — Equipment used in petroleum and natural gas activities; IT-482R: Pipelines.

Class 43.1 — (30%)

[Reg. 1100(1)(a)(xxix.1), 1100(2)A(b)]

Property, other than reconditioned or remanufactured equipment, that would otherwise be included in Class 1, 2, 8 or 48 or in Class 17 because of paragraph (a.1) of that Class

(a) that is

(i) electrical generating equipment, including any heat generating equipment used primarily for the purpose of producing heat energy to operate the electrical generating equipment,

(ii) equipment that generates both electrical and heat energy other than, for greater certainty, fuel cell equipment,

(ii.1) fixed location fuel cell equipment that uses hydrogen generated only from internal, or ancillary, fuel reformation equipment,

(iii) heat recovery equipment used primarily for the purpose of conserving energy, or reducing the requirement to acquire energy, by extracting for reuse thermal waste that is generated by equipment referred to in subparagraph (i) or (ii),

(iii.1) district energy equipment that is part of a district energy system that uses thermal energy that is primarily supplied by electrical cogeneration equipment that would be property described in paragraphs (a) to (c) if read without reference to this subparagraph,

(iv) control, feedwater and condensate systems and other equipment, if that property is ancillary to equipment described in any of subparagraphs (i) to (iii), or

(v) an addition to a property described in any of subparagraphs (i) to (iv),

other than buildings or other structures, heat rejection equipment (such as condensers and cooling water systems), transmission equipment, distribution equipment, fuel handling equipment that is not used to upgrade the combustible portion of the fuel and fuel storage facilities,

(b) that

(i) is situated in Canada,

(ii) is

(A) acquired by the taxpayer for use by the taxpayer for the purpose of gaining or producing income from a business carried on in Canada or from property situated in Canada, or

(B) leased by the taxpayer to a lessee for the use by the lessee for the purpose of gaining or producing income from a business carried on in Canada or from property situated in Canada, and

(iii) has not been used for any purpose before it was acquired by the taxpayer unless

(A) the property was depreciable property that

(I) was included in Class 34, 43.1 or 43.2 of the person from whom it was acquired, or

(II) would have been included in Class 34, 43.1 or 43.2 of the person from whom it was acquired had the

person made a valid election to include the property in Class 43.1 or 43.2, as the case may be, under paragraph 1102(8)(d) or 1102(9)(d), and

(B) the property was acquired by the taxpayer not more than five years after the time it is considered to have become available for use, for the purpose of subsection 13(26) of the Act, by the person from whom it was acquired and remains at the same site in Canada as that at which that person used the property, and

(c) that is

(i) part of a system (other than an enhanced combined cycle system) that

(A) is used by the taxpayer, or by a lessee of the taxpayer, to generate electrical energy, or both electrical and heat energy, using only fuel that is eligible waste fuel, fossil fuel, producer gas, spent pulping liquor or any combination of those fuels, and

(B) has a heat rate attributable to fossil fuel (other than solution gas) not exceeding 6,000 BTU per kilowatt-hour of electrical energy generated by the system, which heat rate is calculated as the fossil fuel (expressed as the high heat value of the fossil fuel) used by the system that is chargeable to gross electrical energy output on an annual basis,

(ii) part of an enhanced combined cycle system that

(A) is used by the taxpayer, or by a lessee of the taxpayer, to generate electrical energy using only a combination of natural gas and thermal waste from one or more natural gas compressor systems located on a natural gas pipeline,

(B) has an incremental heat rate not exceeding 6,700 BTU per kilowatt-hour of electricity generated by the system, which heat rate is calculated as the natural gas (expressed as its high heat value) used by the system that is chargeable to gross electrical energy output on an annual basis, and

(C) does not have economically viable access to a steam host, or

(iii) equipment that is used by the taxpayer, or by a lessee of the taxpayer, to generate electrical energy in a process all or substantially all of the energy input of which is thermal waste, other than

(A) equipment that uses heat produced by a gas turbine that is part of the first stage of a combined cycle system, and

(B) equipment that, on the date of its acquisition, uses chlorofluorocarbons (CFCs) or hydrochlorofluorocarbons (HCFCs), within the meaning assigned by the *Ozone-Depleting Substances Regulations, 1998*,

and property, other than reconditioned or remanufactured equipment, that would otherwise be included in another Class in this Schedule

(d) that is

(i) property that meets the following conditions:

(A) it is used by the taxpayer, or by a lessee of the taxpayer, primarily for the purpose of heating an actively circulated liquid or gas and is

(I) active solar heating equipment, including such equipment that consists of above ground solar collectors, solar energy conversion equipment, solar water heaters, thermal energy storage equipment, control equipment and equipment designed to interface solar heating equipment with other heating equipment, or

(II) equipment that is part of a ground source heat pump system that transfers heat to or from the ground or groundwater (but not to or from surface water such as a river, a lake or an ocean) and that, at the time of

Regulations

installation, meets the standards set by the Canadian Standards Association for the design and installation of earth energy systems, including such equipment that consists of piping (including above or below ground piping and the cost of drilling a well, or trenching, for the purpose of installing that piping), energy conversion equipment, thermal energy storage equipment, control equipment and equipment designed to enable the system to interface with other heating or cooling equipment, and

(B) it is not a building, part of a building (other than a solar collector that is not a window and that is integrated into a building), equipment used to heat water for use in a swimming pool, energy equipment that backs up equipment described in subclause (A)(I) or (II) nor equipment that distributes heated or cooled air or water in a building,

(ii) a hydro-electric installation of a producer of hydro-electric energy, where that installation

(A) has, if acquired after February 21, 1994 and before December 11, 2001, an annual average generating capacity not exceeding 15 megawatts upon completion of the site development, or, if acquired after December 10, 2001, a rated capacity at the hydro-electric installation site that does not exceed 50 megawatts, and

(B) is the electrical generating equipment and plant (including structures) of that producer including a canal, a dam, a dyke, an overflow spillway, a penstock, a powerhouse (complete with electrical generating equipment and other ancillary equipment), control equipment, fishways or fish bypasses, and transmission equipment,

other than distribution equipment, property otherwise included in Class 10 and property that would be included in Class 17 if that Class were read without reference to its subparagraph (a.1)(i),

(iii) an addition or alteration, which is acquired after February 21, 1994 and before December 11, 2001, to a hydro-electric installation that is described in subparagraph (ii) or that would be so described if that installation were acquired by the taxpayer after February 21, 1994, and which results in an increase in generating capacity, if the resulting annual average generating capacity of the hydro-electric installation does not exceed 15 megawatts,

(iii.1) an addition or alteration, which is acquired after December 10, 2001, to a hydro-electric installation that is described in subparagraph (ii) or that would be so described if that installation were acquired by the taxpayer after February 21, 1994, and which results in an increase in generating capacity, if the resulting rated capacity at the hydro-electric installation site does not exceed 50 megawatts,

(iv) heat recovery equipment used by the taxpayer, or by a lessee of the taxpayer, primarily for the purpose of conserving energy, reducing the requirement to acquire energy or extracting heat for sale, by extracting for reuse thermal waste that is generated directly in an industrial process (other than an industrial process that generates or processes electrical energy), including such equipment that consists of heat exchange equipment, compressors used to upgrade low pressure steam, vapour or gas, waste heat boilers and other ancillary equipment such as control panels, fans, instruments or pumps, but not including property that is employed in reusing the recovered heat (such as property that is part of the internal heating or cooling system of a building or electrical generating equipment), is a building or is equipment that recovers heat primarily for use for heating water in a swimming pool,

(v) a fixed location device that is a wind energy conversion system that

(A) is used by the taxpayer, or by a lessee of the taxpayer, primarily for the purpose of generating electrical energy, and

(B) consists of a wind-driven turbine, electrical generating equipment and related equipment, including

(I) control and conditioning equipment,

(II) support structures,

(III) a powerhouse complete with other ancillary equipment, and

(IV) transmission equipment,

other than distribution equipment, auxiliary electrical generating equipment, property otherwise included in Class 10 and property that would be included in Class 17 if that Class were read without reference to its subparagraph (a.1)(i),

(vi) fixed location photovoltaic equipment that is used by the taxpayer, or a lessee of the taxpayer, primarily for the purpose of generating electrical energy from solar energy if the equipment consists of solar cells or modules and related equipment including inverters, control and conditioning equipment, support structures and transmission equipment, but not including

(A) a building or a part of a building (other than a solar cell or module that is integrated into a building),

(B) auxiliary electrical generating equipment, property otherwise included in Class 10 and property that would be included in Class 17 if that Class were read without reference to its subparagraph (a.1)(i), and

(C) distribution equipment,

(vii) equipment used by the taxpayer, or by a lessee of the taxpayer, primarily for the purpose of generating electrical energy or heat energy, or both electrical and heat energy, solely from geothermal energy, including such equipment that consists of piping (including above or below ground piping and the cost of completing a well (including the wellhead and production string), or trenching, for the purpose of installing that piping), pumps, heat exchangers, steam separators, electrical generating equipment and ancillary equipment used to collect the geothermal heat, but not including buildings, distribution equipment, equipment used to heat water for use in a swimming pool, equipment described in subclause (i)(A)(II), property otherwise included in Class 10 and property that would be included in Class 17 if that Class were read without reference to its paragraph (a.1),

(viii) equipment used by the taxpayer, or by a lessee of the taxpayer, primarily for the purpose of collecting landfill gas or digester gas, including such equipment that consists of piping (including above or below ground piping and the cost of drilling a well, or trenching, for the purpose of installing that piping), fans, compressors, storage tanks, heat exchangers and related equipment used to collect gas, to remove non-combustibles and contaminants from the gas or to store the gas, but not including property otherwise included in Class 10 or 17,

(ix) equipment used by the taxpayer, or by a lessee of the taxpayer, for the sole purpose of generating heat energy, primarily from the consumption of eligible waste fuel, producer gas or a combination of those fuels and not using any fuel other than eligible waste fuel, fossil fuel or producer gas, including such equipment that consists of fuel handling equipment used to upgrade the combustible portion of the fuel and control, feedwater and condensate systems, and other ancillary equipment, but not including equipment used for the purpose of producing heat energy to operate electrical generating equipment, buildings or other structures, heat rejection equipment (such as condensers and cooling water systems), fuel storage facilities, other fuel handling equipment and property otherwise included in Class 10 or 17,

(x) an expansion engine with one or more turbines, or cylinders, that convert the compression energy in pressurized natural gas into shaft power that generates electricity, including the related electrical generating equipment and ancillary controls, where the expansion engine

(A) is part of a system that is installed

(I) on a distribution line of a distributor of natural gas, or

(II) on a branch distribution line of a taxpayer primarily engaged in the manufacturing or processing of goods for sale or lease if the branch line is used to deliver natural gas directly to the taxpayer's manufacturing or processing facility,

(B) is used instead of a pressure reducing valve,

(xi) equipment used by the taxpayer, or by a lessee of the taxpayer, in a system that converts wood waste or plant residue into bio-oil, if that bio-oil is used primarily for the purpose of generating heat that is used directly in an industrial process or a greenhouse, generating electricity or generating electricity and heat, other than equipment used for the collection, storage or transportation of wood waste or plant residue, buildings or other structures and property otherwise included in Class 10 or 17,

(xii) fixed location fuel cell equipment used by the taxpayer, or by a lessee of the taxpayer, that uses hydrogen generated only from ancillary electrolysis equipment (or, if the fuel cell is reversible, the fuel cell itself) using electricity all or substantially all of which is generated by using kinetic energy of flowing water or wave or tidal energy (otherwise than by diverting or impeding the natural flow of the water or by using physical barriers or dam-like structures) or by geothermal, photovoltaic, wind energy conversion, or hydro-electric equipment, of the taxpayer or the lessee, and equipment ancillary to the fuel cell equipment other than buildings or other structures, transmission equipment, distribution equipment, auxiliary electrical generating equipment and property otherwise included in Class 10 or 17,

(xiii) property that is part of a system that is used by the taxpayer, or by a lessee of the taxpayer, primarily to produce and store biogas, including equipment that is an anaerobic digester reactor, a buffer tank, a pre-treatment tank, biogas piping, a fan, a compressor, a heat exchanger, a biogas storage tank and equipment used to remove non-combustibles and contaminants from the gas, but not including

(A) property (other than a buffer tank) that is used to collect, move or store organic waste,

(B) equipment used to process the residue after digestion or to treat recovered liquids,

(C) buildings or other structures, and

(D) property otherwise included in Class 10 or 17,

(xiv) property that is used by the taxpayer, or by a lessee of the taxpayer, primarily for the purpose of generating electricity using kinetic energy of flowing water or wave or tidal energy (otherwise than by diverting or impeding the natural flow of the water or by using physical barriers or dam-like structures), including support structures, control and conditioning equipment, submerged cables and transmission equipment, but not including buildings, distribution equipment, auxiliary electricity generating equipment, property otherwise included in Class 10 and property that would be included in Class 17 if that class were read without reference to its subparagraph (a.1)(i),

(xv) district energy equipment that

(A) is used by the taxpayer or by a lessee of the taxpayer,

(B) is part of a district energy system that uses thermal energy that is primarily supplied by equipment that is described in subparagraphs (i), (iv), (vii) or (ix) or would be described in those subparagraphs if owned by the taxpayer, and

(C) is not a building,

(xvi) equipment used by the taxpayer, or by a lessee of the taxpayer, primarily for the purpose of generating producer gas (other than producer gas that is to be converted into liquid biofuels or chemicals), including related piping (including fans and compressors), air separation equipment, storage equipment, equipment used for drying or shredding eligible waste fuel, ash-handling equipment, equipment used to upgrade the producer gas into biomethane and equipment used to remove non-combustibles and contaminants from the producer gas, but not including buildings or other structures, heat rejection equipment (such as condensers and cooling water systems), equipment used to convert producer gas into liquid biofuels or chemicals and property otherwise included in Class 10 or 17,

(xvii) equipment used by the taxpayer, or by a lessee of the taxpayer, for the purpose of charging electric vehicles, including charging stations, transformers, distribution and control panels, circuit breakers, conduits and related wiring, if

(A) the equipment is situated

(I) on the load side of an electricity meter used for billing purposes by a power utility, or

(II) on the generator side of an electricity meter used to measure electricity generated by the taxpayer or the lessee, as the case may be,

(B) more than 75 per cent of the electrical equipment capacity is dedicated to charging electric vehicles, and

(C) the equipment is

(I) an electric vehicle charging station (other than a building) that supplies more than 10 kilowatts of continuous power, or

(II) used primarily in connection with one or more electric vehicle charging stations (other than buildings) each of which supplies more than 10 kilowatts of continuous power, or

(xviii) fixed location energy storage property that

(A) is used by the taxpayer, or by a lessee of the taxpayer, primarily for the purpose of storing electrical energy

(I) including batteries, compressed air energy storage, flywheels, ancillary equipment (including control and conditioning equipment) and related structures, and

(II) not including buildings, pumped hydroelectric storage, hydro electric dams and reservoirs, property used solely for backup electrical energy, batteries used in motor vehicles, fuel cell systems where the hydrogen is produced via steam reformation of methane and property otherwise included in Class 10 or 17, and

(B) either

(I) if the electrical energy to be stored is used in connection with property of the taxpayer or a lessee of the taxpayer, as the case may be, is described in paragraph (c) or would be described in this paragraph if it were read without reference to this subparagraph, or

(II) meets the condition that the efficiency of the electrical energy storage system that includes the property — computed by reference to the quantity of electrical energy supplied to and discharged from the electrical energy storage system — is greater than 50%, and

(e) that

(i) is situated in Canada,

(ii) is

(A) acquired by the taxpayer for use by the taxpayer for the purpose of gaining or producing income from a business carried on in Canada or from property situated in Canada, or

(B) leased by the taxpayer to a lessee for the use by the lessee for the purpose of gaining or producing income from a business carried on in Canada or from property situated in Canada, and

(iii) has not been used for any purpose before it was acquired by the taxpayer unless

(A) the property was depreciable property that was

(I) was included in Class 34, 43.1 or 43.2 of the person from whom it was acquired, or

(II) would have been included in Class 34, 43.1 or 43.2 of the person from whom it was acquired had the person made a valid election to include the property in Class 43.1 or 43.2, as the case may be, under paragraph 1102(8)(d) or 1102(9)(d), and

(B) the property was acquired by the taxpayer not more than five years after the time it is considered to have become available for use, for the purpose of subsection 13(26) of the Act, by the person from whom it was acquired and remains at the same site in Canada as that at which that person used the property.

Proposed Amendments — Classes 43.1 and 43.2

Federal Budget, Supplementary Information, April 19, 2021: *Capital Cost Allowance for Clean Energy Equipment*

Under the *Income Tax Act* taxpayers are entitled to deduct a portion of the capital cost of a depreciable property, as capital cost allowance (CCA), in computing their income for each taxation year [ITA 20(1)(a) — ed.]. With some exceptions, CCA deductions are claimed by class of property [Reg. 1100(1)(a) — ed.] and are calculated on a declining-balance basis.

Under the CCA regime, Classes 43.1 and 43.2 of Schedule II to the *Income Tax Regulations* provide accelerated CCA rates (30% and 50%, respectively) for investments in specified clean energy generation and energy conservation equipment. Class 43.2 generally includes property that would otherwise be included in Class 43.1, except that in certain cases Class 43.2 imposes stricter eligibility criteria. In addition, property in these classes that is acquired after November 20, 2018 and that becomes available for use before 2024 is eligible for immediate expensing while property that becomes available for use after 2023 and before 2028 is subject to a phase-out from these immediate expensing rules.

Providing accelerated CCA is an exception to the general practice of setting CCA rates based on the useful life of assets. Accelerated CCA provides a financial benefit by deferring taxation.

In addition, if the majority of the tangible property in a project is eligible for inclusion in Class 43.1 or 43.2, certain intangible project start-up expenses (e.g., engineering and design work, and feasibility studies) are treated as Canadian Renewable and Conservation Expenses. These expenses can be deducted in full in the year incurred, carried forward indefinitely for use in future years, or transferred to investors using flow-through shares.

To support investment in clean technologies, Budget 2021 proposes to expand Classes 43.1 and 43.2 to include the following:

- pumped hydroelectric storage equipment;
- electricity generation equipment that uses physical barriers or dam-like structures to harness the kinetic energy of flowing water or wave or tidal energy;
- active solar heating systems, ground source heat pump systems, and geothermal energy systems that are used to heat water for a swimming pool;
- equipment used to produce solid and liquid fuels (e.g., wood pellets and renewable diesel) from specified waste material or carbon dioxide;
- a broader range of equipment used for the production of hydrogen by electrolysis of water; and
- equipment used to dispense hydrogen for use in hydrogen-powered automotive equipment and vehicles.

Accelerated CCA would be available in respect of these types of property only if, at the time the property becomes available for use, the requirements of all Canadian environmental laws, by-laws and regulations applicable in respect of the property have been met.

Classes 43.1 and 43.2 currently include certain systems that burn fossil fuels and/or waste fuels to produce either electricity or heat, or both. The eligibility criteria for these systems have not been modified since they were first set approximately 25 and 15 years ago, for Classes 43.1 and 43.2 respectively. Additionally, Classes 43.1 and 43.2 include certain systems that derive up to one half of their fuel energy input from fossil fuels.

To ensure the incentive provided by Classes 43.1 and 43.2 is consistent with the government's current environmental objectives, Budget 2021 proposes changes in the eligibility criteria for the following types of equipment:

- fossil-fuelled cogeneration systems;
- fossil-fuelled enhanced combined cycle systems;
- specified waste-fuelled electrical generation systems with an electrical capacity greater than 3 megawatts;
- specified waste-fuelled heat production equipment for which more than one quarter of the total fuel energy input is from fossil fuels; and
- producer gas generating equipment for which more than one quarter of the total fuel energy input is from fossil fuels.

Each of these measures is discussed in more detail below.

Pumped Hydroelectric Energy Storage Equipment

Pumped hydroelectric storage is one type of electrical energy storage system that uses electricity to pump water uphill into a reservoir, where it can be held until needed and released for the generation of electricity. This form of storage can provide environmental benefits by displacing fossil-fuelled power generation when demand is highest and by facilitating the integration of electricity generated from intermittent renewable energy sources. A range of electrical energy storage equipment, other than pumped hydroelectric storage, is currently eligible under Classes 43.1 and 43.2.

Budget 2021 proposes to expand Class 43.1 and 43.2 eligibility for electrical energy storage property by removing the exclusion for pumped hydroelectric storage. Eligible pumped hydroelectric storage property would include reversing turbines, transmission equipment, dams, reservoirs and related structures, but not buildings or property used solely for backup electrical energy.

Water Current, Wave or Tidal Energy Technologies Using Physical Barriers

The current rules generally include in Class 43.1 and 43.2 equipment that generates electricity using kinetic energy of flowing water or wave or tidal energy. Equipment that generates electricity by diverting or impeding the natural flow of water, or by using physical barriers or dam-like structures, is currently ineligible.

Budget 2021 proposes to expand Class 43.1 and 43.2 eligibility by removing these restrictions.

Active Solar Heating, Ground Source Heat Pump and Geothermal Energy Systems Used to Heat a Swimming Pool

Ground source heat pump, active solar heating and geothermal energy systems can provide renewable energy for various residential, commercial and industrial applications, such as water or space heating. Active solar heating systems use a solar collector to heat an actively circulated liquid or gas medium. Ground source heat pump systems exchange heat with the earth at depths of tens of metres while geothermal energy systems extract steam or hot water directly from the earth through wells drilled to depths of up to several thousand metres. Most active solar heating, ground source heat pump and geothermal energy systems are eligible under Classes 43.1 and 43.2, other than systems used to heat water for use in a swimming pool.

Budget 2021 proposes to expand Class 43.1 and 43.2 eligibility by removing the exclusion of active solar heating and ground-source heat pump systems used to heat swimming pools. Similarly, it is proposed to remove the exclusion for geothermal energy systems used to heat swimming pools, except where geothermal water is used directly in a pool or spa.

Equipment Used to Produce Fuel from Specified Waste Material or Carbon Dioxide

Solid, liquid and gaseous renewable fuels may be derived from organic material through a broad range of mechanical, bio-chemical and thermo-chemical processes. It is also possible to produce liquid synthetic fuels from carbon dioxide. Depending on the type of fuels, different applications are possible, for example: direct combustion to generate electricity or heat; injection into natural gas distribution networks; and fuelling vehicles. Equipment used for the production of gaseous renewable fuels (e.g., biogas and producer gas) from certain waste material (e.g., wood, food and animal waste) is generally eligible under Class 43.1 and 43.2. Certain equipment used to produce liquid renewable fuels is eligible under Class 43.1 and 43.2 if it is used to convert wood waste or plant residue into bio-oil that is used primarily for the purpose of generating heat used directly in an industrial process or a greenhouse, generating electricity, or generating electricity and heat.

Budget 2021 proposes to expand eligibility under Class 43.1 and 43.2 to equipment used to convert specified waste material into bio-coal or pellets (including torrefied pellets), but excluding standard equipment used to make wood chips, hog fuel and black liquor. Eligible property would include equipment where all or substantially all of the use of the equipment is in a system that produces bio-coal or pellets (including torrefied pellets) from specified waste material, including storage equipment, materials handling equipment and ash-handling equipment. However, eligible property would not include the following:

- equipment used for shredding, drying or cutting organic material (other than equipment all or substantially all of the use of which is to produce fuel for sale);
- vehicles; and
- buildings or other structures.

Budget 2021 also proposes to expand eligibility under Class 43.1 and 43.2 to a broader range of equipment used to produce liquid biofuels (e.g., ethanol, biodiesel and renewable diesel) from specified waste material or carbon dioxide. Eligible property would include equipment where all or substantially all of the use of the equipment is to produce liquid fuels from specified waste material, including related piping, storage equipment, materials handling equipment, ash-handling equipment and equipment used to remove non-combustibles and contaminants from the fuels produced. However, eligible property would not include the following:

- equipment used to produce spent pulping liquor;
- vehicles; and
- buildings or other structures.

For all of these proposed changes, "specified waste material" would include wood waste, municipal waste, sludge from an eligible sewage treatment facility, plant residue, spent pulping liquor, food and animal waste, manure, pulp and paper by-product, and separated organics.

Hydrogen Production by Electrolysis of Water

Hydrogen can provide a clean source of energy with which to generate electricity or heat, or to fuel zero-emission vehicles, and it can also be used in a variety of industrial processes. Currently, hydrogen is mainly produced by steam methane reformation, but it can also be produced by electrolysis of water. When powered by renewable energy, hydrogen produced by electrolysis of water maximizes the environmental benefits of using hydrogen as an energy supply by minimizing its lifecycle carbon intensity. Equipment used to produce hydrogen by electrolysis of water is eligible under Classes 43.1 and 43.2 when it is ancillary to a fixed-location fuel cell and all or substantially all of the electricity used to power the production process is generated using specified renewable energy sources. These renewable energy sources include: the kinetic energy of flowing water; wave or tidal energy; geothermal, photovoltaic or wind energy conversion; and hydroelectric equipment.

Budget 2021 proposes to expand eligibility under Classes 43.1 and 43.2 to include a broader range of equipment used to produce hydrogen by electrolysis of water. Eligible property would include: equipment where all or substantially all of the use of the equipment is to produce hydrogen by electrolysis of water, including electrolysers, rectifiers and other ancillary electrical equipment; water treatment and conditioning equipment; and equipment used for hydrogen compression and storage. Eligible property would not include:

- hydrogen transmission or distribution equipment;
- electrical transmission or distribution equipment;
- vehicles or auxiliary electrical generating equipment; and
- buildings or other structures.

For greater certainty, eligible property would not be required to be powered by renewable energy sources eligible for inclusion in Class 43.1 or 43.2.

Hydrogen Refuelling Equipment

Hydrogen fuel cell electric vehicles are a nascent zero-emission mode of transportation in Canada that require specific refuelling infrastructure. In Budget 2016, the government announced support for business investments in electric vehicle charging infrastructure by expanding Class 43.1 to include electric vehicle charging stations capable of supplying more than 10 kilowatts of continuous power, and by expanding Class 43.2 to include such stations that are capable of supplying at least 90 kilowatts of continuous power.

To support greater use of hydrogen-powered vehicles, Budget 2021 proposes to expand eligibility under Classes 43.1 and 43.2 to include hydrogen refuelling equipment. Eligible property would include equipment used to dispense hydrogen for use in hydrogen-powered automotive equipment and vehicles, including vaporization, compression, storage and cooling equipment. Eligible property would not include:

- hydrogen production equipment;
- hydrogen transmission equipment;
- electrical transmission and distribution equipment;
- vehicles or auxiliary electrical generating equipment; and
- buildings or other structures.

Fossil-Fuelled Cogeneration Systems

Fossil-fuelled cogeneration systems generate both electricity and useful heat using fossil fuels as the energy source (typically natural gas). Due to the use of heat that would otherwise be wasted, these systems offer an efficient use of fossil fuels. However, they still produce greenhouse gas emissions and, as such, cannot achieve net-zero emissions on a lifecycle basis.

Budget 2021 proposes to remove these systems from Classes 43.1 and 43.2.

Fossil-Fuelled Enhanced Combined Cycle Systems

A combined cycle system uses two different heat engines simultaneously to produce electricity. It is usually composed of a gas turbine and a steam turbine, where the residual heat from the gas turbine is used to generate steam to drive the steam turbine, resulting in higher efficiency than using the gas turbine alone. An "enhanced combined cycle system" is a type of combined cycle system in which thermal waste from one or more natural gas compressor systems is recovered and used to contribute at least 20% of the energy input of a combined cycle process in order to enhance the generation of electricity.

These systems burn natural gas as a fuel and must be located where there is no other viable host for the waste heat. Similar to fossil-fuelled cogeneration systems, enhanced combined cycle systems offer an efficient use of fossil fuels but cannot achieve net-zero emissions on a lifecycle basis.

Budget 2021 proposes to remove these systems from Classes 43.1 and 43.2.

Specified Waste-Fuelled Electrical Generation Systems

Specified waste-fuelled electrical generation systems generate electricity (and, in the case of cogeneration systems, electricity and useful heat) using certain specified waste fuels, or a mix of specified waste fuels and fossil fuels (co-fired systems). These specified waste fuels include "eligible waste fuel" (biogas, bio-oil, digester gas, landfill gas, municipal waste, plant residue, pulp and paper waste, and wood waste), producer gas and spent pulping liquor. The co-firing of specified waste fuels with fossil fuels may be done for technical, economic, or fuel availability reasons.

Budget 2021 proposes to remove from Classes 43.1 and 43.2 specified waste-fuelled electrical generation systems for which more than one quarter of their total fuel energy input is from fossil fuels, determined on an annualized basis.

Classes 43.1 and 43.2 apply energy efficiency requirements for specified waste-fuelled electrical generation systems that co-fire with fossil fuels. These energy efficiency requirements are expressed in the form of maximum heat rate thresholds, which are defined as the ratio of the fuel energy input over the electrical and heat energy output. In contrast, there are no heat rate thresholds for systems that burn only specified waste fuels.

To promote the efficient use of waste fuels, Budget 2021 proposes that eligibility for Classes 43.1 and 43.2 for all specified waste-fuelled electrical generation systems be subject to a heat rate threshold. Systems with an electrical output capacity of three megawatts or less will be exempt from this requirement.

Eligible specified waste-fuelled electrical generation systems would be those that do not exceed a heat rate threshold of 11,000 BTU per kilowatt-hour. The heat rate would be calculated as shown below:

$$\text{Heat Rate} = \frac{(2 \times F_{fossil}) + F_{waste}}{E + (H \div 3412)}$$

where:

- F_{fossil} is the energy content of the fossil fuel consumed by the system in a year in BTU (excluding solution gas), calculated based on the fuel's higher heating value;
- F_{waste} is the energy content of the specified waste fuel consumed by the system in a year in BTU, calculated based on the fuel's higher heating value;
- E is the gross electrical energy produced by the system in a year in kilowatt-hours; and
- H is the net useful energy in the form of heat exported from the system to a thermal host in a year in BTU.

Specified Waste-Fuelled Heat Production Equipment

Specified waste-fuelled heat production equipment produces heat primarily from eligible waste fuel or producer gas, meaning that more than half of the total fuel energy input must be eligible waste fuel or producer gas. The remaining fuel energy input may be from fossil fuels.

To align with the changes proposed to the eligibility requirements for specified waste-fuelled electrical generation systems, Budget 2021 proposes to remove from Classes 43.1 and 43.2 specified waste-fuelled heat production equipment for which more than one quarter of the total fuel energy input is from fossil fuels, determined on an annualized basis.

Producer Gas Generating Equipment

Producer gas generating equipment generates producer gas from eligible waste fuel using a thermo-chemical conversion process (generally referred to as "gasification"). More than half of the total fuel energy input must be eligible waste fuel, while the remaining fuel energy input may be from fossil fuels.

To align with the changes proposed to the eligibility requirements for specified waste-fuelled electrical generation systems and specified waste-fuelled heat production equipment, Budget 2021 proposes to exclude from Classes 43.1 and 43.2 producer gas generating equipment for which more than one quarter of the total fuel energy input is from fossil fuels, determined on an annualized basis.

Similarly, there is currently a requirement for producer gas to be generated primarily from eligible waste fuel for it to be an eligible fuel for specified waste-fuelled electrical generation systems and for specified waste-fuelled heat production equipment.

For specified waste-fuelled electrical generation systems and specified waste-fuelled heat production equipment, Budget 2021 proposes to remove from the eligible fuels producer gas generated from more than one-quarter fossil fuel energy input.

Timing of Changes

The expansion of Classes 43.1 and 43.2 would apply in respect of property that is acquired and that becomes available for use on or after April 19, 2021, where it has not been used or acquired for use for any purpose before April 19, 2021.

The removal of certain property from eligibility for Classes 43.1 and 43.2, as well as the application of the new heat rate threshold for specified waste-fuelled electrical generation systems, would apply in respect of property that becomes available for use after 2024.

Regulations

Strategic Environmental Assessment Statement

These measures are expected to have a positive environmental impact by encouraging investment in technologies that would reduce emissions of greenhouse gases and air pollutants. This would help advance the government's commitments to exceed Canada's target of reducing total greenhouse gas emissions by 30 per cent relative to 2005 levels by 2030, and to achieve net-zero greenhouse gas emissions by 2050. These measures would also contribute to the Federal Sustainable Development Strategy goals of growing the clean technology industry in Canada, and ensuring all Canadians have access to affordable, reliable and sustainable energy.

Federal Budget, Chapter 5, April 19, 2021: *Accelerating Investment in Clean Energy Technologies*

In 2018, Canada introduced tax incentives to encourage businesses to invest in clean energy generation and energy efficiency equipment. In particular, this included a time-limited measure allowing businesses to immediately write off the full cost of investments in certain clean energy technologies. To support clean tech jobs, help Canadian companies adopt more clean technologies, and fight climate change:

Budget 2021 proposes to expand the list of eligible equipment to include equipment used in pumped hydroelectric energy storage, renewable fuel production, hydrogen production by electrolysis of water, and hydrogen refueling. Certain existing restrictions related to investments in water-current, wave and tidal energy, active solar heating, and geothermal energy technologies would also be removed.

To ensure this tax incentive remains consistent with the government's environmental objectives:

Budget 2021 proposes to update the eligibility criteria such that certain fossil-fuelled and low efficiency waste-fuelled electrical generation equipment will no longer be eligible after 2024. Reforming eligibility for this tax incentive will help reduce pollution and greenhouse gas emissions in Canada. It is estimated that these measures will reduce federal revenues by $142 million over five years starting in 2021-22.

Notes: See also Proposed Amendment under ITA 123.4, reducing the tax rate on income from manufacturing clean tech products.

Budget Table 1 projects that these measures will cost the federal government $14 million in 2021-22, $22m in 2022-23, $30m in 2023-24, $34m in 2024-25 and $42m in 2025-26.

Related Provisions: ITA 13(18.1) — Energy, Mines and Resources "Technical Guide to Class 43.1" to be determinative; ITA 66(15)"principal-business corporation"(h), (i) — Corporation whose business uses property in Cl. 43.1 or 43.2; ITA 127(9)"qualified property"(b.1) — Property in Cl. 43.1 to be prescribed energy generation and conservation property for Atlantic investment tax credit; Reg. 1100(2)A(b) — Amount deductible in first year property is available for use; Reg. 1100(24), (25) — Limitation on deduction for specified energy property; Reg. 1102(8)(d), 1102(9)(d) — Generating equipment — election for Class 43.1; Reg. 1102(16.1) — Election to include Class 43.1 property in Class 29 or 43; Reg. 1102(21) — Limitation where Cl. 43.1(b)(iii)(A) or (B) or 43.1(e)(iii)(A) or (B) applies; Reg. 1104(13) — Definitions; Reg. 1104(14), (15) — Where Cl. 43.1(c) not operating due to deficiency, failing or shutdown; Reg. 1104(17) — Certain property must satisfy all applicable environmental laws and regulations; Reg. 1219 — Canadian renewable and conservation expense; Reg. 1219(1)(f) — Well for installation of underground piping under Cl. 43.1(d) excluded from CRCE; Reg. 4600(2)(m) — Qualified property for investment tax credit; Reg. 4600(3) — Prescribed energy generation and conservation property; Reg. 8200.1 — Cl. 43.1 property is prescribed energy conservation property; Reg. Sch. II:Cl. 43.2 — Certain property acquired after Feb. 22, 2005 and before 2025.

Notes: Much Class 43.1 property actually falls into Class 43.2 instead. Systems referred to in 43.1(c)(i) may be called "cogeneration" (co-gen) systems.

See generally Income Tax Folio S3-F8-C2. For the *Class 43.1 and 43.2 Technical Guide* (binding for certain purposes: ITA 13(18.1)), see tinyurl.com/43-1guide.

For CRA opinions on Cl. 43.1 see docs 2002-0155165 (solar panels, heat pumps); 2002-0180955 (co-gen system installed in greenhouse is eligible; active solar system ineligible before 2003 amendments); 2003-0034691E5 (wood waste system); 2003-0051021E5 (ground source heat pump [GSHP] to heat residential units is not use in "industrial process"); 2003-0051031E5 (GSHP to heat greenhouse is eligible); 2004-0072611E5 (biogas system); 2004-0085911E5 (solution gas facilities); 2004-0096611E5, 2005-0113341E5, 2005-0140801E5, 2006-0169361E5, 2006-0216881E5, 2007-0252721E5 and 2014-0543041E5 (photovoltaic systems); 2005-0151611E5 (boiler fuelled by wood pellets to heat greenhouse); 2005-0146771M4 (equipment to produce biogas from non-anaerobic digestion of manure is ineligible); 2005-0150711E5, 2006-0195841E5 and 2006-0207801E5 (wind turbines); 2005-0156291E5 (co-gen facility); 2005-0162341E5 (small hydro installation); 2006-0190041E5 (biogas digester, and purification of biogas into methane); 2007-0225661E5 (detailed discussion of 43.1(d)); 2007-0261111E5 (geoexchange equipment); 2008-0301331E5 (solar water heater); 2009-0341721E5, 2009-0343551E5, 2009-0343881E5, 2010-0356431E5, 2011-0424381E5 and 2012-0435151E5 (solar panels on rooftops or farm); 2011-0398851M4 (equipment in co-gen system that uses straw as feedstock); 2011-0427561E5 (geothermal well drilling and completion costs); 2011-0430431E5 (GSHP); 2012-0460711M4 (solar panels: application of specified energy property rules); 2012-0469941E5 (waste water treatment equipment does not qualify); 2013-0486441E5 (anaerobic digester); 2013-0509801E5 (solar photovoltaic system components); 2014-0521261I7 (biomass electrical facility owned by First Nation); 2014-0547911E5 (heat recovery application); 2016-0635031E5 (geothermal energy). See also Cl. 43.2 Notes.

Taxpayers cannot classify equipment as Cl. 8 instead of 43.1 to avoid the "specified energy property" rules (Reg. 1100(25)): VIEWS doc 2008-0265011E5.

CRA interprets "substantially all", used in (c)(iii) and (d)(xii), as 90% or more.

See also Hay, "Federal Income Tax Incentives for Independent Power Generation", VII(3) *Business Vehicles* (Federated Press) 342-50 (2001); Shannon, "Canadian Renewable and Conservation Expense Clean Energy Tax Incentives", 9(2) *Taxes & Wealth Management* (Carswell) 14-17 (May 2016).

43.1(d) amended by 2019 budget bill #1, for property acquired after March 21, 2016 that has not been used or acquired for use by that date: to change "energy storage equipment" to "thermal energy storage equipment" in (i)(A)(I) and (II); to change "control, conditioning and battery storage equipment" to "control and conditioning equipment" in (d)(v)(B)(I), (d)(vi) and (d)(xiv); to add "using kinetic energy ... or by geothermal", in (d)(xii); and to add (d)(xvii), (xviii).

43.1(d)(vii) amended by 2019 budget bill #1, for property acquired after March 21, 2016 that has not been used or acquired for use by that date, and then amended by same bill, for property acquired for use after March 21, 2017 that has not been used or acquired for use by that date, to restore the version enacted by 2017 budget bill #2. For property acquired after March 21, 2016 and before March 22, 2017, read:

> (vii) equipment used by the taxpayer, or by a lessee of the taxpayer, primarily for the purpose of generating electrical energy solely from geothermal energy, including such equipment that consists of piping (including above or below ground piping and the cost of drilling a well, or trenching, for the purpose of installing that piping), pumps, heat exchangers, steam separators, electrical generating equipment and ancillary equipment used to collect the geothermal heat, but not including buildings, transmission equipment, distribution equipment, property otherwise included in Class 10 and property that would be included in Class 17 if that Class were read without reference to its subparagraph (a.1)(i),

43.1(d)(iv) amended by 2017 budget bill #2, for property acquired after March 3, 2010, to add "or extracting heat for sale".

43.1(d)(xv)(B) amended by 2017 budget bill #2 to add reference to para. (vii), for property acquired after March 21, 2017 that has not been used or acquired for use before that date.

43.1 earlier amended by 2014, 2013, 2012, 2011 and 2010 budget bills #2; P.C. 2009-581, 2006-1103, 2006-329, 2005-2287, 2005-2186, 2001-1378. 2000-1331. For details see these Notes up to PITA 58th ed. Class 43.1 added by P.C. 1997-1033.

Definitions [Cl. 43.1]: "biogas", "bio-oil" — Reg. 1104(13); "building" — Reg 1102(5), (5.1); "business" — ITA 248(1); "Canada" — ITA 255, *Interpretation Act* 35(1); "class" — Reg. 1101(6), 1102(1)–(3), (14), (14.1); "depreciable property" — ITA 13(21), 248(1); "digester gas", "distribution equipment", "district energy equipment", "district energy system", "eligible waste fuel", "enhanced combined cycle system", "fossil fuel", "landfill gas" — Reg. 1104(13); "motor vehicle" — ITA 248(1); "municipal waste" — Reg. 1104(13); "person" — ITA 248(1); "plant residue", "producer gas" — Reg. 1104(13); "property" — ITA 248(1); "solution gas", "spent pulping liquor" — Reg. 1104(13); "structure" — Reg. 1102(5), (5.1); "taxpayer" — ITA 248(1); "thermal waste", "transmission equipment", "wood waste" — Reg. 1104(13).

Income Tax Folios: S3-F4-C1: General discussion of CCA.

Interpretation Bulletins: IT-482R: Pipelines.

Class 43.2 — (50%)
[Reg. 1100(1)(a)(xxix.2), 1100(2)A(c)]

Property that is acquired after February 22, 2005 and before 2025 (other than property that was included, before it was acquired, in another class in this Schedule by any taxpayer) and that is property that would otherwise be included in Class 43.1

(a) otherwise than because of paragraph (d) of that Class, if the expression "6,000 BTU" in clause (c)(i)(B) of that Class were read as "4,750 BTU"; or

(b) because of paragraph (d) of that Class, if

(i) the expression "6,000 BTU" in clause (c)(i)(B) of that Class were read as "4,750 BTU",

(ii) subclauses (d)(xvii)(C)(I) and (II) of that Class were read as follows:

(I) an electric vehicle charging station (other than a building) that supplies at least 90 kilowatts of continuous power, or

(II) used

1 primarily in connection with one or more electric vehicle charging stations (other than buildings) each of which supplies more than 10 kilowatts of continuous power, and

2 in connection with one or more electric vehicle charging stations (other than buildings) each of which supplies at least 90 kilowatts of continuous power, or and

(iii) clause (d)(xviii)(B) of that Class were read without reference to its subclause (II).

Proposed Amendments — Classes 43.1 and 43.2

Federal Budget, Supplementary Information, April 19, 2021: See under Class 43.1.

Related Provisions: ITA 127(9)"qualified property"(b.1) — Property in Cl. 43.2 to be prescribed energy generation and conservation property for Atlantic investment tax credit; Reg. 1100(2)A(c) — Amount deductible in first year property is available for use; Reg. 1102(16.1) — Election to include Class 43.2 property in Class 29 or 43; Reg. 1104(13) — Definitions; Reg. 1104(17) — Certain property must satisfy all applicable environmental laws and regulations; Reg. 1219(1)(f) — Well for installation of underground piping under Cl. 43.2(b) excluded from CRCE; Reg. 4600(2)(n) — Qualified property for investment tax credit. See also Related Provisions annotation to Class 43.1; Reg. 4600(3) — Prescribed energy generation and conservation property.

Notes: For CRA interpretation see *Technical Guide to Class 43.1 and 43.2* (tinyurl.com/43-1guide); VIEWS docs 2006-0195481E5, 2006-0207801E5 and 2011-0409111E5 (wind turbines); 2007-0225661E5 (general discussion); 2008-0275351E5, 2008-0287671E5, 2009-0341721E5, 2009-0342121E5, 2009-0343551E5, 2010-0353421E5, 2010-0356431E5, 2010-0361131E5, 2011-0396841E5, 2011-0424381E5 and 2012-0435151E5 (home or farm rooftop solar panels); 2008-0276761 (wood waste fuelled heat production system and ground source heat pump); 2009-0352781E5 (ground mount solar tracker); 2010-0373951E5 (wind energy conversion system); 2010-0385231E5 (digester producing biogas from sludge); 2011-0430431E5 (ground source heat pump); 2012-0433611E5 (purchase of building with geothermal heating/cooling system: parts integral to the building are excluded); 2015-0565761E5 (cogeneration equipment); 2015-0565841M4 (general information); 2015-0568271E5 (solar thermal system); 2016-0670661E5 (de-icing equipment for solar panels); 2018-0768241E5 (equipment used to produce biofuels); 2019-0797491E5 (equipment used to produce biofuels and chemicals from municipal solid waste). See also Cl. 43.1 Notes.

See also Bernstein & Worndl, "Structuring Solar Projects in Canada", 2061 *Tax Topics* (CCH) 1-3 (Sept. 8, 2011).

43.2(a), (b) amended by 2019 budget bill #1, for property acquired after March 21, 2016 that has not been used or acquired for use by that date, to add "otherwise than because of paragraph (d) of that Class" to (a), and "if" and subparas. (i)-(iii) to (b).

43.2 opening words amended by 2018 budget bill #1, effective June 21, 2018, to change "before 2020" to "before 2025". This extends the "clean energy" incentives through 2024. Amended by P.C. 2009-581, effective March 19, 2007, to change "before 2012" to "before 2020".

Cl. 43.2 added by P.C. 2006-329, effective Feb. 23, 2005; but for property acquired before Dec. 10, 2005, ignore "(other than property that was included, before it was acquired, in another Class in this Schedule by any taxpayer)".

Definitions [Cl. 43.2]: "class" — Reg. 1101(6), 1102(1)–(3), (14), (14.1); "property", "taxpayer" — ITA 248(1).

Class 44 — (25%+)
[Reg. 1100(1)(a)(xxx), 1100(9.1), 1103(2h)]

Property that is a patent, or a right to use patented information for a limited or unlimited period.

Related Provisions: Reg. 1103(2h) — Election not to include property in Class 44; Reg. Sch. II:Cl. 14 — Patent for a limited period.

Notes: For a ruling on Cl. 44 property see VIEWS doc 2010-0365861R3.

Class 44 added by P.C. 1994-231, effective for property acquired after April 26, 1993.

Definitions [Cl. 44]: "property" — ITA 248(1).

Class 45 — (45%)
[Reg. 1100(1)(a)(xxxi)]

Property acquired after March 22, 2004 and before March 19, 2007 (other than property acquired before 2005 in respect of which an election is made under subsection 1101(5q)) that is general-purpose electronic data processing equipment and systems software for that equipment, including ancillary data processing equipment, but not including property that is principally or is used principally as

(a) electronic process control or monitor equipment;

(b) electronic communications control equipment;

(c) systems software for equipment referred to in paragraph (a) or (b); or

(d) data handling equipment (other than data handling equipment that is ancillary to general-purpose electronic data processing equipment).

Related Provisions: Reg. 1100(1.13)(a)(i.1) — Property costing over $1 million subject to specified leasing property rules; Reg. Sch. II:Cl. 50, 52 — Computers acquired after March 18, 2007.

Notes: Cl. 45 was the general category for computers and system software acquisitions until March 18/07; after that date see Classes 50 and 52. For application software see Cl. 12(o). Small and medium-size printers are Cl. 45 as "ancillary data processing equipment", but large printers are likely Cl. 8 (publishing equipment): VIEWS doc 2005-016333117. See also Notes to Reg. 1104(2)"general-purpose electronic data processing equipment".

Cl. 45 opening words amended by P.C. 2009-581, effective March 19, 2007, to add "and before March 19, 2007".

Cl. 45 added by P.C. 2005-2286, effective March 23, 2004. For property acquired before that date, see Cl. 10(f) and Reg. 1101(5p).

Definitions [Cl. 45]: "general-purpose electronic data processing equipment" — Reg. 1104(2); "property" — ITA 248(1); "systems software" — Reg. 1104(2).

Class 46 — (30%)
[Reg. 1100(1)(a)(xxxii)]

Property acquired after March 22, 2004 that is data network infrastructure equipment, and systems software for that equipment, that would, but for this Class, be included in Class 8 because of paragraph (i) of that Class.

Notes: IP (VoIP) telephone is excluded from Cl. 46 in CRA's view: VIEWS docs 2007-0243381C6, 2010-0362061E5.

Cl. 46 added by P.C. 2005-2286, effective March 23, 2004. See Reg. 1104(2)"data network infrastructure equipment".

Definitions [Cl. 46]: "data network infrastructure equipment" — Reg. 1104(2); "property" — ITA 248(1); "systems software" — Reg. 1104(2).

Class 47 — (8%+)
[Reg. 1100(1)(a)(xxxiii), 1100(1)(yb)]

Property that is

(a) transmission or distribution equipment (which may include for this purpose a structure) acquired after February 22, 2005 and that is used for the transmission or distribution of electrical energy, other than

(i) property that is a building, and

(ii) property that has been used or acquired for use for any purpose by any taxpayer before February 23, 2005; or

(b) equipment acquired after March 18, 2007 that is part of a liquefied natural gas facility that liquefies or regasifies natural gas, including controls, cooling equipment, compressors, pumps, storage tanks, vaporizers and ancillary equipment, loading and unloading pipelines on the facility site used to transport liquefied natural gas between a ship and the facility, and related structures, other than property that is

(i) acquired for the purpose of producing oxygen or nitrogen,

(ii) a breakwater, a dock, a jetty, a wharf, or a similar structure, or

(iii) a building.

Related Provisions: Reg. 1100(1)(a.3), (yb) — Additional allowances; Reg. 1100(24), (25) — Limitation on deduction for specified energy property; Reg. 1101(4i) — Separate class for certain Class 47 equipment.

Notes: Cl. 47 amended by P.C. 2009-581, effective March 19, 2007.

Cl. 47 added by P.C. 2006-329, effective Feb. 23, 2005.

Definitions [Cl. 47]: "property", "taxpayer" — ITA 248(1).

Class 48 — (15%)
[Reg. 1100(1)(a)(xxxiv)]

Property acquired after February 22, 2005 that is a combustion turbine (including associated burners and compressors) that generates electrical energy, other than

(a) electrical generating equipment described in any of paragraphs (f) to (h) of Class 8;

(b) property acquired before 2006 in respect of which an election is made under subsection 1101(5t); and

(c) property that has been used or acquired for use for any purpose by any taxpayer before February 23, 2005.

Related Provisions: ITA 127(9)"qualified property"(b.1) — Property in Cl. 48 to be prescribed energy generation and conservation property for Atlantic investment tax credit; Reg. 1100(24), (25) — Limitation on deduction for specified energy property; Reg. 4600(3) — Prescribed energy generation and conservation property; Reg. Sch. II:Cl. 43.1 — Energy generation property.

Notes: Cl. 48 added by P.C. 2006-329, effective Feb. 23, 2005.

Definitions [Cl. 48]: "property", "taxpayer" — ITA 248(1).

Class 49 — (8%)
[Reg. 1100(1)(a)(xxxv)]

Property that is a pipeline, including control and monitoring devices, valves and other equipment ancillary to the pipeline, that

(a) is acquired after February 22, 2005, is used for the transmission (but not the distribution) of petroleum, natural gas or related hydrocarbons, and is not

(i) a pipeline described in subparagraph (l)(ii) of Class 1,

(ii) property that has been used or acquired for use for any purpose by any taxpayer before February 23, 2005,

(iii) equipment included in Class 7 because of paragraph (j) of that Class, or

(iv) a building or other structure; or

(b) is acquired after February 25, 2008, is used for the transmission of carbon dioxide, and is not

(i) equipment included in Class 7 because of paragraph (k) of that Class, or

(ii) a building or other structure.

Related Provisions: Reg. 1101(5v) — Election for separate class for property in Class 49.

Notes: CRA has no specific policy on allocating costs between a pipeline (Class 49) and its appendages (Class 7): VIEWS doc 2017-0695131C6 [2017 CPTS q.8].

Cl. 49 amended by P.C. 2009-660, for property acquired after Feb. 25, 2008, effectively to add 49(b).

Cl. 49 added by P.C. 2006-329, effective Feb. 23, 2005.

Definitions [Cl. 49]: "property", "taxpayer" — ITA 248(1).

Income Tax Folios: S3-F4-C1: General discussion of CCA.

Interpretation Bulletins: IT-476R: CCA — Equipment used in petroleum and natural gas activities.

Class 50 — (55%)
[Reg. 1100(1)(a)(xxxvi)]

Property acquired after March 18, 2007 that is general-purpose electronic data processing equipment and systems software for that equipment, including ancillary data processing equipment, but not including property that is included in Class 52 or that is principally or is used principally as

(a) electronic process control or monitor equipment;

(b) electronic communications control equipment;

(c) systems software for equipment referred to in paragraph (a) or (b); or

(d) data handling equipment (other than data handling equipment that is ancillary to general-purpose electronic data processing equipment).

Related Provisions: Reg. 4600(2)(k) — Qualified property for investment tax credit; Reg. Sch. II:Cl. 52 — 100% CCA for computers acquired Jan. 28/09 to Jan. 31/10.

Notes: See Notes to Reg. 1104(2)"general-purpose electronic data processing equipment" for the meaning of that term. From Jan. 27/09 to Jan. 31/11 see Cl. 52; before March 19/07 see Cl. 45.

Computer equipment acquired for use in manufacturing falls under Class 50, not Class 29: doc 2013-0498331E5.

Cl. 50 opening words amended by P.C. 2009-660, effective for property acquired after Jan. 27, 2009, to refer to Class 52 (which provides a temporary 100% writeoff). Cl. 50 added by P.C. 2009-581, effective March 19, 2007.

Class 51 — (6%)
[Reg. 1100(1)(a)(xxxvii)]

Property acquired after March 18, 2007 that is a pipeline, including control and monitoring devices, valves and other equipment ancillary to the pipeline, used for the distribution (but not the transmission) of natural gas, other than

(a) a pipeline described in subparagraph (l)(ii) of Class 1 or in Class 49;

(b) property that has been used or acquired for use for any purpose by a taxpayer before March 19, 2007; and

(c) a building or other structure.

Related Provisions: Reg. 1100(1.13)(a)(i.1) — Property costing over $1 million subject to specified leasing property rules.

Notes: Cl. 51 added by P.C. 2009-581, effective March 19, 2007.

Definitions [Cl. 51]: "property", "taxpayer" — ITA 248(1).

Class 52 — (100%)
[Reg. 1100(1)(a)(xxxviii)]

Property acquired by a taxpayer after January 27, 2009 and before February 2011 that

(a) is general-purpose electronic data processing equipment and systems software for that equipment, including ancillary data processing equipment, but not including property that is principally or is used principally as

(i) electronic process control or monitor equipment,

(ii) electronic communications control equipment,

(iii) systems software for equipment referred to in paragraph (i) or (ii), or

(iv) data handling equipment (other than data handling equipment that is ancillary to general-purpose electronic data processing equipment);

(b) is situated in Canada;

(c) has not been used, or acquired for use, for any purpose whatever before it is acquired by the taxpayer; and

(d) is acquired by the taxpayer

(i) for use in a business carried on by the taxpayer in Canada or for the purpose of earning income from property situated in Canada, or

(ii) for lease by the taxpayer to a lessee for use by the lessee in a business carried on by the lessee in Canada or for the purpose of earning income from property situated in Canada.

Related Provisions: Reg. 1100(1)(ta) — CCA calculation; Reg. 1100(2)C:F(b)(ii) — Year of acquisition — no 50% reduction on Class 52 property; Reg. 4600(2)(k) — Qualified property for investment tax credit; Reg. Sch. II:Cl. 50 — 55% CCA rate for computers acquired at other times.

Notes: See Notes to Reg. 1104(2)"general-purpose electronic data processing equipment" for the meaning of that term. After Jan. 2011 and before Jan. 27/09 see Cl. 50; before March 19/07 see Cl. 45.

A used computer is in class 50 (including a refurbished computer and one changed from personal to business use): VIEWS docs 2009-034417117, 2011-0392831M4.

Cl. 52 added by P.C. 2009-660, for property acquired after Jan. 27, 2009, and corrected by P.C. 2009-847 (May 28, 2009).

Class 53 — (50%)
[Reg. 1100(1)(a)(xxxix), 1100(2)A(d)]

Property acquired after 2015 and before 2026 that is not included in Class 29, but that would otherwise be included in that Class if

(a) subparagraph (a)(ii) of that Class were read without reference to "in Canadian field processing carried on by the lessee or"; and

(b) that Class were read without reference to its subparagraphs (b)(iv) to (vi) and paragraph (c).

Related Provisions: Reg. 1100(2)A(d) — Amount deductible in first year property is available for use.

Notes: Cl. 53 (added by 2015 Budget bill effective June 23, 2015) implements the April 2015 Budget proposal to extend for 10 years the accelerated CCA for manufacturing and processing machinery and equipment (with some exclusions), which under Cl. 29(c)(iii) had to be acquired by the end of 2015.

For acquisitions after Nov. 20, 2018, 100% deduction is now allowed in the year of acquisition, due to Reg. 1100(2)A(d).

For earlier acquisitions, under Reg. 1100(1)(a)(xxxix), the rate for Cl. 53 is 50% on a declining-balance basis with the half-year rule in Reg. 1100(2) applying, thus 25% in Y1, 37.5% (of original cost) in Y2, 18.75% in Y3, 9.375% in Y4, etc.

Such property acquired after 2025 will be in Class 43 (30% declining balance rate).

See also VIEWS doc 2018-0768241E5 (equipment used to produce biofuels).

Income Tax Folios [Cl. 53]: S4-F15-C1: Manufacturing and processing [replaces IT-147R3].

Class 54 — (30% to 100%)
[Reg. 1100(1)(a)(xl), 1100(2)A(e)]

Property that is a zero-emission vehicle that is not included in Class 16 or 55.

Related Provisions: ITA 13(7)(i) — Cost of ZEPV capped at $55,000; ITA 248(1)"zero-emission passenger vehicle" — Class 54 automobile is ZEPV; Reg. 1100(2)A(e) — Amount deductible in first year property is available for use; Reg. 1102(14.13) — Class 54 not preserved on reorganization or non-arm's length transfer; Reg. 1103(2j) — Election not to include property in Class 54.

Notes: See Notes to ITA 248(1)"zero-emission vehicle" and Reg. 1100(2).

Unlike Class 10.1, Class 54 does not establish a separate class for each vehicle whose cost exceeds the $55,000 threshold. Also, Class 54 can include zero-emission passenger vehicles that both do and do not exceed the $55,000.

Cl. 54 added by 2019 budget bill #1, effective March 19, 2019.

Definitions: "zero-emission vehicle" — ITA 248(1).

Class 55 — (40% to 100%)
[Reg. 1100(1)(a)(xli), 1100(2)A(f)]

Property that is a zero-emission vehicle that would otherwise be included in Class 16.

Related Provisions: Reg. 1100(2)A(f) — Amount deductible in first year property is available for use; Reg. 1102(14.13) — Cl. 55 not preserved on reorganization or non-arm's length transfer; Reg. 1103(2j) — Election not to include property in Cl. 55.

Notes: See Notes to ITA 248(1)"zero-emission passenger vehicle" and Reg. 1100(2). Cl. 55 added by 2019 budget bill #1, effective March 19, 2019.

Definitions: "zero-emission vehicle" — ITA 248(1).

Class 56 — (30% to 100%)
[Reg. 1100(1)(a)(xlii), 1100(2)A(e)]

Property that is acquired, and becomes available for use, by a taxpayer after March 1, 2020 and before 2028, if the property

(a) is either

(i) automotive equipment (other than a motor vehicle) that is fully electric or powered by hydrogen, or

(ii) an addition or alteration made by the taxpayer to automotive equipment (other than a motor vehicle) to the extent it causes the automotive equipment to become fully electric or powered by hydrogen; and

(b) would be accelerated investment incentive property of the taxpayer if subsection 1104(4) were read without its exclusion for property included in Class 56.

Related Provisions: Reg. 1100(2)A(e) — Amount deductible in first year property is available for use; Reg. 1102(14.13) — Class 56 not preserved on reorganization or non-arm's length transfer; Reg. 1103(2j) — Election to not include property in Cl. 56.

Notes: Class 56 added by 2021 budget bill #1, effective June 29, 2021. It covers off-road zero-emission vehicles. It was proposed in a Finance news release of Dec 15, 2020 and a Prime Minister's Office news release of March 2, 2020.

Definitions: "accelerated investment incentive property" — Reg. 1104(4), (4.1); "motor vehicle", "property", "taxpayer" — ITA 248(1).

Notes [Sch. II]: A Dept. of Finance discussion paper, *Consultations on Accelerated Capital Cost Allowance for Carbon Capture and Storage Assets* (April 17, 2009), reproduced here as a Possible Future Amendment in the 36th-45th eds., did not proceed, as this issue was addressed through direct funding via the Clean Energy Fund. See also the 2021 Budget proposal to provide a new investment tax credit for investment in carbon capture and stores, under ITA 127(9)"investment tax credit".

SCHEDULE III — CAPITAL COST ALLOWANCES, CLASS 13

1. For the purposes of paragraph 1100(1)(b), the amount that may be deducted in computing the income of a taxpayer for a taxation year in respect of the capital cost to him of property of Class 13 in Schedule II is the lesser of

(a) the aggregate of each amount determined in accordance with section 2 of this Schedule that is a prorated portion of the part of the capital cost to him, incurred in a particular taxation year, of a particular leasehold interest; and

(b) the undepreciated capital cost to the taxpayer as of the end of the taxation year (before making any deduction under section 1100) of property of the class.

Notes: For CRA discussion of the application of Sch. III in various situations, see VIEWS doc 2004-0071821E5.

Definitions: "amount" — ITA 248(1); "capital cost" — Reg. 1100(1)(b); "property" — ITA 248(1); "taxation year" — ITA 249; "taxpayer" — ITA 248(1); "undepreciated capital cost" — ITA 13(21), 248(1).

2. Subject to section 3 of this Schedule, the prorated portion for the year of the part of the capital cost, incurred in a particular taxation year, of a particular leasehold interest is the lesser of

(a) $\frac{1}{5}$ of that part of the capital cost; and

(b) the amount determined by dividing that part of the capital cost by the number of 12-month periods (not exceeding 40 such periods) falling within the period commencing with the beginning of the particular taxation year in which the capital cost was incurred and ending with the day the lease is to terminate.

Definitions: "amount" — ITA 248(1); "capital cost" — Reg. 1100(1)(b); "taxation year" — ITA 249.

3. For the purpose of determining, under section 2 of this Schedule, the prorated portion for the year of the part of the capital cost, incurred in a particular taxation year, of a particular leasehold interest, the following rules apply:

(a) where an item of the capital cost of a leasehold interest was incurred before the taxation year in which the interest was acquired, it shall be deemed to have been incurred in the taxation year in which the interest was acquired;

(b) where, under a lease, a tenant has a right to renew the lease for an additional term, or for more than one additional term, after the term that includes the end of the particular taxation year in which the capital cost was incurred, the lease shall be deemed to terminate on the day on which the term next succeeding the term in which the capital cost was incurred is to terminate;

(c) the prorated portion for the year of the part of the capital cost, incurred in a particular taxation year, of a particular leasehold interest shall not exceed the amount, if any, remaining after deducting from that part of the capital cost the aggregate of the amounts claimed and deductible in previous years in respect thereof;

(d) where, at the end of a taxation year, the aggregate of

(i) the amounts claimed and deductible in previous taxation years in respect of a particular leasehold interest, and

(ii) the proceeds of disposition, if any, of part or all of that interest

equals or exceeds the capital cost as of that time of the interest, the prorated portion of any part of that capital cost shall, for all subsequent years, be deemed to be nil; and

(e) where, at the end of a taxation year, the undepreciated capital cost to the taxpayer of property of Class 13 in Schedule II is nil, the prorated portion of any part of the capital cost as of that time shall, for all subsequent years, be deemed to be nil.

Definitions: "amount" — ITA 248(1); "capital cost" — Reg. 1100(1)(b); "property" — ITA 248(1); "taxation year" — ITA 249; "taxpayer" — ITA 248(1); "undepreciated capital cost" — ITA 13(21), 248(1).

Interpretation Bulletins: IT-324: CCA — Emphyteutic lease (archived); IT-464R: CCA — Leasehold interests.

4. Where a taxpayer has acquired a property that would, if the property had been acquired by a person with whom the taxpayer was not dealing at arm's length at the time the property was acquired, be a leasehold interest of that person, a reference in this Schedule to a leasehold interest shall, in respect of the taxpayer, include a reference to that property, and the terms and conditions of the leasehold interest of that property in respect of the taxpayer shall be deemed to be the same as those that would have applied in respect of that person had that person acquired the property.

Notes: S. 4 added by P.C. 1994-139, effective for property acquired after December 23, 1991, other than property acquired before 1993

(a) pursuant to an agreement in writing entered into before December 24, 1991, or

(b) that was under construction by or on behalf of the taxpayer on December 23, 1991.

Definitions: "arm's length" — ITA 251(1); "person", "property", "taxpayer" — ITA 248(1).

SCHEDULE IV — CAPITAL COST ALLOWANCES, CLASS 15

1. For the purposes of paragraph 1100(1)(f), the amount that may be deducted in computing the income of a taxpayer for a taxation year in respect of property described in Class 15 in Schedule II is the lesser of

(a) an amount equal to

(i) if the property is an accelerated investment incentive property acquired in the year,

(A) if the property is acquired before 2024, 1.5 times an amount computed on the basis of a rate per cord, board foot or cubic metre cut in the taxation year, and

(B) if the property is acquired after 2023, 1.25 times an amount computed on the basis of a rate per cord, board foot or cubic metre cut in the taxation year, and

(ii) in any other case, an amount computed on the basis of a rate per cord, board foot or cubic metre cut in the taxation year, and

(b) the undepreciated capital cost to the taxpayer as of the end of the taxation year (before making any deduction under section 1100 for the taxation year) of property of that class.

Notes: 1(a)(i) added by 2019 budget bill #1, effective June 21, 2019. Before that date, read simply:

(a) an amount computed on the basis of a rate per cord, board foot or cubic metre cut in the taxation year; and

Reference to "cubic metre" added to 1(a) by P.C. 1994-139, effective for 1986 and later taxation years.

Definitions: "accelerated investment incentive property" — Reg. 1104(4), (4.1); "amount", "property", "taxpayer" — ITA 248(1); "undepreciated capital cost" — ITA 13(21), 248(1).

2. Where all the property of the class is used in connection with one timber limit or section thereof, the rate per cord, board foot or cubic metre is the amount determined by dividing

(a) the undepreciated capital cost to the taxpayer as of the end of the taxation year (before making any deduction under section 1100 for the taxation year and computed as if subparagraph 1(a)(i) did not apply) of the property

by

(b) the number of cords, board feet or cubic metres of timber in the limit or section thereof as of the commencement of the taxation year, obtained by deducting the quantity cut up to that time from the amount shown by the latest cruise.

Notes: 2(a) amended by 2019 budget bill #1, effective June 21, 2019, to add "and computed as if subparagraph 1(a)(i) did not apply".

Reference to "cubic metres" added to s. 2 by P.C. 1994-139, effective for 1986 and later taxation years.

3. Where a part of the property of the class is used in connection with one timber limit or a section thereof and a part is used in connection with another limit or section thereof, a separate rate shall be computed for each part of the property, in the manner provided in section 2 of this Schedule, as though each part of the property were the taxpayer's only property of that class.

Definitions: "property", "taxpayer" — ITA 248(1).

SCHEDULE V — CAPITAL COST ALLOWANCES, INDUSTRIAL MINERAL MINES

1. For the purposes of paragraph 1100(1)(g), the amount that may be deducted in computing the income of a taxpayer for a taxation year in respect of a property described in that paragraph that is an industrial mineral mine or a right to remove industrial minerals from an industrial mineral mine is the lesser of

(a) an amount computed on the basis of a rate (computed under section 2 or 3 of this Schedule, as the case may be) per unit of mineral mined in the taxation year; and

(b) the undepreciated capital cost to the taxpayer as of the end of the taxation year (before making any deduction under section 1100) of the mine or right.

Notes: For the meaning of "industrial minerals" see Notes to ITA 125.3(1)"manufacturing or processing". For "industrial mineral mine", see definition in Reg. 1104(3).

Definitions: "amount" — ITA 248(1); "industrial mineral mine", "mineral" — Reg. 1104(3); "property" — ITA 248(1); "taxation year" — ITA 249; "taxpayer" — ITA 248(1); "undepreciated capital cost" — ITA 13(21), 248(1).

2. If the taxpayer has not been granted an allowance in respect of the mine or right for a previous taxation year, the rate for a taxation year is determined by the formula

$$A(B - C)/D$$

where

A is

(a) 1.5, if the property is an accelerated investment incentive property acquired before 2024,

(b) 1.25, if the property is an accelerated investment incentive property acquired after 2023, and

(c) 1, in any other case;

B is the capital cost of the mine or right to the taxpayer;

C is the residual value, if any, of the mine or right; and

D is

(a) if the taxpayer has acquired a right to remove only a specified number of units, the specified number of units of material that the taxpayer acquired a right to remove, and

(b) in any other case, the number of units of commercially mineable material estimated as being in the mine when the mine or right was acquired.

Related Provisions: ITA 257 — Negative amounts in formulas; Reg. 1104(4) — Accelerated investment incentive property.

Notes: For a numerical example of s. 2 see VIEWS doc 2020-0850001E5.

S. 2 amended by 2019 budget bill #1, effective June 21, 2019. Before that date, read:

2. Where the taxpayer has not been granted an allowance in respect of the mine or right for a previous taxation year, the rate for a taxation year is an amount determined by dividing the capital cost of the mine or right to the taxpayer minus the residual value, if any, by

(a) in any case where the taxpayer has acquired a right to remove only a specified number of units, the specified number of units of material that he acquired a right to remove; and

(b) in any other case, the number of units of commercially mineable material estimated as being in the mine when the mine or right was acquired.

Definitions: "accelerated investment incentive property" — Reg. 1104(4), (4.1); "amount", "property" — ITA 248(1); "residual value" — Reg. Sch. V s. 5; "taxation year" — ITA 249; "taxpayer" — ITA 248(1).

3. Where the taxpayer has been granted an allowance in respect of the mine or right in a previous taxation year, the rate for the taxation year is

(a) if paragraph (b) does not apply,

(i) if section 2 applied in the previous year to determine the rate employed to determine the allowance for the year, the rate that would have been determined under section 2 if paragraph (c) of the description of A in that section applied, and

(ii) in any other case, the rate employed to determine the allowance for the most recent year for which an allowance was granted; and

(b) where it has been established that the number of units of material remaining to be mined in the previous taxation year was in fact different from the quantity that was employed in determining the rate for the previous year referred to in paragraph (a), or where it has been established that the capital cost of the mine or right is substantially different from the amount that was employed in determining the rate for that previous year, a rate determined by dividing the amount that would be the undepreciated capital cost to the taxpayer of the mine or right as of the commencement of the year if paragraph (c) of the description of A in section 2 had applied in respect of each previous taxation year minus the residual value, if any, by

(i) in any case where the taxpayer has acquired a right to remove only a specified number of units, the number of units of commercially mineable material that, at the commencement of the year, he had a right to remove, and

(ii) in any other case, the number of units of commercially mineable material estimated as remaining in the mine at the commencement of the year.

Notes: 3(a)(i) added by 2019 budget bill #1, effective June 21, 2019. Before that date, read simply:

(a) where paragraph (b) does not apply, the rate employed to determine the allowance for the most recent year for which an allowance was granted; and

Para. 3(b) opening words amended by 2019 budget bill #1, effective June 21, 2019, to change "by dividing the undepreciated capital cost" to "by dividing the amount that would be the undepreciated capital cost" and to add "if paragraph (c) of the description of A in section 2 had applied in respect of each previous taxation year" at end of para.

Definitions: "amount" — ITA 248(1); "residual value" — Reg. Sch. V s. 5; "taxation year" — ITA 249; "taxpayer" — ITA 248(1); "undepreciated capital cost" — ITA 13(21), 248(1).

4. In lieu of the aggregate of deductions otherwise allowable under this Schedule, a taxpayer may elect that the deduction for the taxation year be the lesser of

(a) $100; and

(b) the amount received by him in the taxation year from the sale of mineral.

Definitions: "amount" — ITA 248(1); "mineral" — Reg. 1104(3); "taxation year" — ITA 249; "taxpayer" — ITA 248(1).

5. In this Schedule, "residual value" means the estimated value of the property if all commercially mineable material were removed.

Definitions: "property" — ITA 248(1).

Interpretation Bulletins [Schedule V]: IT-423: Sale of sand, gravel or topsoil (archived); IT-492: Industrial mineral mines.

SCHEDULE VI — CAPITAL COST ALLOWANCES, TIMBER LIMITS AND CUTTING RIGHTS

1. For the purposes of paragraph 1100(1)(e), the amount that may be deducted in computing the income of a taxpayer for a taxation year in respect of the capital cost to him of a property, other than a timber resource property, that is a timber limit or a right to cut timber from a limit is the lesser of

(a) the aggregate of

(i) an amount computed on the basis of a rate (determined under section 2 or 3 of this Schedule) per cord, board foot or cubic metre cut in the year, and

(ii) the lesser of

(A) ¹/₁₀ of the amount expended by the taxpayer after the commencement of his 1949 taxation year that is included in the capital cost to him of the timber limit or right, for surveys, cruises or preparation of prints, maps or plans for the purpose of obtaining a licence or right to cut timber, and

(B) the amount expended as described in clause (A) minus the aggregate of amounts deducted under this subparagraph in computing the income of the taxpayer in previous years; and

(b) the undepreciated capital cost to the taxpayer as of the end of the year (before making any deduction under section 1100 for the year) of the timber limit or right.

Notes: For discussion of this section see the footnotes in *Myles*, [2002] 1 C.T.C. 2570 (TCC). See also Notes to ITA 13(21)"timber resource property" re the meaning of "timber limit".

Reference to "cubic metre" added to 1(a)(i) by P.C. 1994-139, effective for 1986 and later taxation years.

Definitions: "amount", "property" — ITA 248(1); "taxation year" — ITA 249; "taxpayer" — ITA 248(1); "timber resource property", "undepreciated capital cost" — ITA 13(21), 248(1).

2. If the taxpayer has not been granted an allowance in respect of the limit or right for a previous taxation year, the rate for a taxation year is an amount determined by the formula

$$A(B - (C + D))/E$$

where

A is

(a) 1.5, if the property is an accelerated investment incentive property acquired before 2024,

(b) 1.25, if the property is an accelerated investment incentive property acquired after 2023, and

(c) 1, in any other case;

B is the capital cost of the mine or right to the taxpayer;

C is the residual value of the timber limit;

D is the total of all amounts expended by the taxpayer after the commencement of the taxpayer's 1949 taxation year that are included in the capital cost to the taxpayer of the timber limit or right, for surveys, cruises or preparation of prints, maps or plans for the purpose of obtaining a licence or right to cut timber; and

E is the quantity of timber in the limit or the quantity of timber the taxpayer has obtained a right to cut, as the case may be, (expressed in cords, board feet or cubic metres) as shown by a cruise.

Related Provisions: ITA 257 — Negative amounts in formulas; Reg. 1104(4) — Accelerated investment incentive property.

Notes: S. 2 amended by 2019 budget bill #1, effective June 21, 2019. Before then, read:

2. If the taxpayer has not been granted an allowance in respect of the limit or right for a previous taxation year, the rate for a taxation year is an amount determined by dividing

(a) the capital cost of the limit or right to the taxpayer, minus the aggregate of the residual value of the timber limit and any amount expended by the taxpayer after the commencement of his 1949 taxation year that is included in the capital cost to him of the timber limit or right, for surveys, cruises or preparation of prints, maps or plans for the purpose of obtaining a licence or right to cut timber,

Regulations

by

(b) the quantity of timber in the limit or the quantity of timber the taxpayer has obtained a right to cut, as the case may be, (expressed in cords, board feet or cubic metres) as shown by a cruise.

Reference to "cubic metres" added to 2(b) and "bona fide cruise" changed to "cruise", by P.C. 1994-139, effective for 1986 and later taxation years.

Definitions: "accelerated investment incentive property" — Reg. 1104(4), (4.1); "amount", "property" — ITA 248(1); "residual value" — Reg. Sch. VI s. 5; "taxation year" — ITA 249; "taxpayer" — ITA 248(1).

3. If the taxpayer has been granted an allowance in respect of the limit or right in a previous taxation year, the rate for a taxation year is

(a) if paragraph (b) does not apply,

(i) if section 2 applied in the previous year to determine the rate employed to determine the allowance for the year, the rate that would have been determined under section 2 if paragraph (c) of the description of A in that section applied, and

(ii) in any other case, the rate employed to determine the allowance for the most recent year for which an allowance was granted; and

(b) where it has been established that the quantity of timber that was in the limit or that the taxpayer had a right to cut was in fact substantially different from the quantity that was employed in determining the rate for the previous year referred to in paragraph (a), or where it has been established that the capital cost of the limit or right is substantially different from the amount that was employed in determining the rate for that previous year, a rate determined by dividing

(i) the amount that would be the undepreciated capital cost to the taxpayer of the limit or right as of the commencement of the year if paragraph (c) of the description of A in section 2 had applied in respect of each previous taxation year, minus the residual value,

by

(ii) the estimated remaining quantity of timber that is in the limit or that the taxpayer has a right to cut, as the case may be, (expressed in cords, board feet or cubic metres) at the commencement of the year.

Notes: 3(a)(i) added by 2019 budget bill #1, effective June 21, 2019. Before the amendment, read simply:

(a) where paragraph (b) does not apply, the rate employed to determine the allowance for the most recent year for which an allowance was granted; and

3(b)(i) amended by 2019 budget bill #1, effective June 21, 2019, to change "the undepreciated capital cost" to "the amount that would be the undepreciated capital cost" and add "if paragraph (c) of the description of A in section 2 had applied in respect of each previous taxation year".

Reference to "cubic metres" added to 3(b)(ii) by P.C. 1994-139, effective for 1986 and later taxation years.

Definitions: "amount" — ITA 248(1); "residual value" — Reg. Sch. VI s. 5; "taxation year" — ITA 249; "taxpayer" — ITA 248(1); "undepreciated capital cost" — ITA 13(21), 248(1).

4. In lieu of the deduction otherwise determined under this Schedule, a taxpayer may elect that the deduction for a taxation year to be the lesser of

(a) $100; and

(b) the amount received by him in the taxation year from the sale of timber.

Definitions: "amount" — ITA 248(1); "taxation year" — ITA 249; "taxpayer" — ITA 248(1).

5. In this Schedule, **"residual value"** means the estimated value of the property if the merchantable timber were removed.

Definitions: "property" — ITA 248(1).

Interpretation Bulletins: IT-481: Timber limits and cutting rights.

SCHEDULE VII — PUBLICLY-TRADED SHARES OR SECURITIES
[Reg. 4400]

Notes: Schedule VII lists the values of publicly-traded shares on valuation day (V-Day), Dec. 22, 1971. That date was used because, at the time, settlement of publicly traded shares normally occurred five business days after sale. Sch. VII is needed where a taxpayer disposes of publicly-traded shares held continuously since before 1972. Only the gain since V-Day is a capital gain: see ITAR 26(3), 26(11).

Schedule VII, which fills 20 pages, is not reproduced in the *Practitioner's Income Tax Act* because it is no longer relevant to most taxpayers. For a copy see canLii.org.

SCHEDULE VIII — UNIVERSITIES OUTSIDE CANADA [REPEALED]

1–25. [Repealed]

Notes [Sch. VIII]: Sch. VIII repealed by 2018 budget bill #1, effective Feb. 27, 2018. The list of foreign universities that qualify for charitable donations as though they were Canadian charities is now maintained by CRA (tinyurl.com/univs-cra) rather than prescribed in Sch. VIII. See Notes to ITA 149.1(1)"qualified donee" (re (a)(iv)).

Sch. VIII read (still relevant indefinitely due to the 2018 in-force rule for ITA 149.1(1)"qualified donee"(a)(iv)):

SCHEDULE VIII — UNIVERSITIES OUTSIDE CANADA

1. The universities situated in the United States of America that are prescribed by section 3503 are the following:

Abilene Christian University, Abilene, Texas
Academy of the New Church, The, Bryn Athyn, Pennsylvania
Adams State College, Alamosa, Colorado
Adler School of Professional Psychology, Chicago, Illinois
Albany College of Pharmacy and Health Sciences, Albany, New York
Alfred University, Alfred, New York
American Film Institute, Los Angeles, California
American Film Institute Center for Advanced Film and Television Studies, Los Angeles, California
American International College, Springfield, Massachusetts
American Jewish University, Bel Air, California
American University, The, Washington, District of Columbia
American University in Cairo, The, New York, New York
Amherst College, Amherst, Massachusetts
Anabaptist Mennonite Biblical Seminary, Elkhart, Indiana
Anderson College, Anderson, South Carolina
Andover Newton Theological School, Newton Centre, Massachusetts
Andrews University, Berrien Springs, Michigan
Antioch College, Yellow Springs, Ohio
Arizona State University, Tempe, Arizona
Asbury Theological Seminary, Wilmore, Kentucky
Atlantic Union College, South Lancaster, Massachusetts
Aurora University, Aurora, Illinois
Azusa Pacific College, Azusa, California
Babson College, Babson Park, Massachusetts
Bacone College, Muskogee, Oklahoma
Bard College, Annandale-on-Hudson, New York
Barnard College, New York, New York
Bates College, Lewiston, Maine
Bastyr University, Seattle, Washington
Baylor College of Medicine, Houston, Texas
Baylor University, Waco, Texas
Bemidji State University, Bemidji, Minnesota
Bentley College, Waltham, Massachusetts
Berklee College of Music, Boston, Massachusetts
Beth Medrash Govoha, Lakewood, New Jersey
Biola University, LaMirada, California
Bob Jones University, Greenville, South Carolina
Boston University, Boston, Massachusetts
Bowdoin College, Brunswick, Maine
Bowling Green State University, Bowling Green, Ohio
Brandeis University, Waltham, Massachusetts
Brigham Young University, Provo, Utah
Brigham Young University — Hawaii Campus, Laie, Hawaii
Brigham Young University — Idaho, Rexburg, Idaho
Brown University, Providence, Rhode Island
Bryn Mawr College, Bryn Mawr, Pennsylvania
Bucknell University, Lewisburg, Pennsylvania
California College of the Arts, San Francisco, California
California Institute of Technology, Pasadena, California

California Institute of the Arts, Valencia, California
California Lutheran University, Thousand Oaks, California
Calvin College, Grand Rapids, Michigan
Calvin Theological Seminary, Grand Rapids, Michigan
Canisius College, Buffalo, New York
Carleton College, Northfield, Minnesota
Carnegie-Mellon University, Pittsburgh, Pennsylvania
Carroll College, Helena, Montana
Case Western Reserve University, Cleveland, Ohio
Catholic University of America, The, Washington, District of Columbia
Cedarville College, Cedarville, Ohio
Centenary College, Hackettstown, New Jersey
Central Michigan University, Mount Pleasant, Michigan
Central Yeshiva Tomchei Tmimim-Lubavitch, Brooklyn, New York
Christendom College, Front Royal, Virginia
City University of New York, The, John Jay College of Criminal Justice, New York, New York
City University of Seattle, Bellevue, Washington
Claremont McKenna College, Claremont, California
Clark University, Worcester, Massachusetts
Clarkson University, Potsdam, New York
Colby College, Waterville, Maine
Colby-Sawyer College, New London, New Hampshire
Colgate University, Hamilton, New York
Colgate-Rochester Divinity School, The, Rochester, New York
College of William and Mary, Williamsburg, Virginia
Colorado College, The, Colorado Springs, Colorado
Colorado School of Mines, Golden, Colorado
Colorado State University, Fort Collins, Colorado
Columbia International University, Columbia, South Carolina
Columbia Union College, Takoma Park, Maryland
Columbia University in the City of New York, New York, New York
Concordia College, Moorhead, Minnesota
Concordia University, Mequon, Wisconsin
Connecticut College, New London, Connecticut
Conway School of Landscape Design, Conway, Massachusetts
Cooper Union for the Advancement of Science and Art, The, New York, New York
Cornell University, Ithaca, New York
Cornerstone College and Grand Rapids Baptist Seminary, Grand Rapids, Michigan
Covenant College, Lookout Mountain, Tennessee
Cranbrook Academy of Art, Bloomfield Hills, Michigan
Creighton University, Omaha, Nebraska
Curtis Institute of Music, The, Philadelphia, Pennsylvania
Dallas Theological Seminary, Dallas, Texas
Dartmouth College, Hanover, New Hampshire
Denison University, Granville, Ohio
De Paul University, Chicago, Illinois
Dordt College, Sioux Center, Iowa
Drake University, Des Moines, Iowa
Drew University, Madison, New Jersey
Drury College, Springfield, Missouri
Duke University, Durham, North Carolina
Duquesne University, Pittsburgh, Pennsylvania
D'Youville College, Buffalo, New York
Eastern College, St. Davids, Pennsylvania
Eastern Mennonite University, Harrisonburg, Virginia
Eastern Washington University, Cheney, Washington
Eckerd College, St. Petersburg, Florida
Ecumenical Theological Center, Detroit, Michigan
Elmira College, Elmira, New York
Embry-Riddle Aeronautical University, Daytona Beach, Florida
Emerson College, Boston, Massachusetts
Emmanuel School of Religion, Johnson City, Tennessee
Emmaus Bible College, Dubuque, Iowa
Emory University, Atlanta, Georgia
Emporia State University, Emporia, Kansas
Fairleigh Dickinson University, Teaneck, New Jersey
Ferris State University, Big Rapids, Michigan
Finlandia University, Hancock, Michigan
Florida Atlantic University, Boca Raton, Florida
Florida Gulf Coast University, Fort Myers, Florida
Florida State University, Tallahassee, Florida
Fordham University, New York, New York
Franciscan University of Steubenville, Steubenville, Ohio
Freed-Hardeman University, Henderson, Tennessee
Fresno Pacific College, Fresno, California
Fuller Theological Seminary, Pasadena, California
Gallaudet College, Washington, District of Columbia
Geneva College, Beaver Falls, Pennsylvania
George Washington University, The, Washington, District of Columbia
Georgetown University, Washington, District of Columbia

Georgia Institute of Technology, Atlanta, Georgia
Goddard College, Plainfield, Vermont
God's Bible School and College, Cincinnati, Ohio
Gonzaga University, Spokane, Washington
Gordon College, Wenham, Massachusetts
Gordon-Conwell Theological Seminary, South Hamilton, Massachusetts
Goshen College, Goshen, Indiana
Grace University, Omaha, Nebraska
Graceland College, Lamoni, Iowa
Greenville College, Greenville, Illinois
Grinnell College, Grinnell, Iowa
Hamilton College, Clinton, New York
Hampshire College, Amherst, Massachusetts
Harvard University, Cambridge, Massachusetts
Haverford College, Haverford, Pennsylvania
Hawaii Pacific University, Honolulu, Hawaii
Hebrew Union College — Jewish Institute of Religion, Cincinnati, Ohio
Herman M. Finch University of Health Sciences, The/The Chicago Medical School, North Chicago, Illinois
Hillsdale College, Hillsdale, Michigan
Hobart and William Smith Colleges, Geneva, New York
Holy Trinity Orthodox Seminary, The, Jordanville, New York
Hope College, Holland, Michigan
Houghton College, Houghton, New York
Howard University, Washington, District of Columbia
Huntington University, Huntington, Indiana
Idaho State University, Pocatello, Idaho
Illinois Institute of Technology, Chicago, Illinois
Illinois State University, Normal, Illinois
Indiana University, Bloomington, Indiana
Iowa State University of Science and Technology, Ames, Iowa
Ithaca College, Ithaca, New York
Jacksonville State University, Jacksonville, Alabama
Jamestown College, Jamestown, North Dakota
Jewish Theological Seminary of America, The, New York, New York
John Brown University, Siloam Springs, Arkansas
Johns Hopkins University, The, Baltimore, Maryland
Juilliard School, The, New York, New York
Kansas State University, Manhattan, Kansas
Kent State University, Kent, Ohio
Kenyon College, Gambier, Ohio
Kettering University, Flint, Michigan
Kuyper College, Grand Rapids, Michigan
Lafayette College, Easton, Pennsylvania
Lake Superior State University, Sault Ste. Marie, Michigan
Lawrence Technological University, Southfield, Michigan
Lehigh University, Bethlehem, Pennsylvania
Leland Stanford Junior University (Stanford University), Stanford, California
Le Moyne College, Syracuse, New York
Le Tourneau College, Longview, Texas
Liberty University, Lynchburg, Virginia
Life Chiropractic College West, Hayward, California
Life University, Marietta, Georgia
Limestone College, Gaffney, South Carolina
Logan College of Chiropractic, St. Louis, Missouri
Loma Linda University, Loma Linda, California
Louisiana State University and Agricultural and Mechanical College, Baton Rouge, Louisiana
Loyola Marymount University, Los Angeles, California
Loyola University, Chicago, Illinois
Macalester College, St. Paul, Minnesota
Magdalen College, Warner, New Hampshire
Maharishi University of Management, Fairfield, Iowa
Manchester College, North Manchester, Indiana
Manhattanville College, Purchase, New York
Mankato State University, Mankato, Minnesota
Marantha Baptist Bible College, Watertown, Wisconsin
Marian University, Fond du Lac, Wisconsin
Marquette University, Milwaukee, Wisconsin
Massachusetts Institute of Technology, Cambridge, Massachusetts
Mayo Foundation, Rochester, Minnesota
Mayo Graduate School of Medicine, Rochester, Minnesota
Meadville-Lombard Theological School, Chicago, Illinois
Medaille College, Buffalo, New York
Medical College of Ohio, Toledo, Ohio
Medical University of South Carolina, Charleston, South Carolina
Mercyhurst College, Erie, Pennsylvania
Mesivta Torah Vodaath Rabbinical Seminary, Brooklyn, New York
Mesivta Yeshiva Rabbi Chaim Berlin, Brooklyn, New York
Messiah College, Grantham, Pennsylvania
Miami University, Oxford, Ohio
Michigan State University, East Lansing, Michigan

Michigan State University College of Law, East Lansing, Michigan
Michigan Technological University, Houghton, Michigan
Middlebury College, Middlebury, Vermont
Minot State University, Minot, North Dakota
Mirrer Yeshiva Central Institute, Brooklyn, New York
Montana State University, Bozeman, Montana
Montana Tech of the University of Montana, Butte, Montana
Moody Bible Institute, Chicago, Illinois
Moravian College, Bethlehem, Pennsylvania
Mount Holyoke College, South Hadley, Massachusetts
Mount Ida College, Newton Centre, Massachusetts
Mount Sinai School of Medicine, New York, New York
Multnomah Bible College, Portland, Oregon
Naropa University, Boulder, Colorado
National College of Chiropractic, The, Lombard, Illinois
Nazarene Theological Seminary, Kansas City, Missouri
Ner Israel Rabbinical College, Baltimore, Maryland
New England College, Henniker, New Hampshire
New School University, New York, New York
New York University, New York, New York
Niagara University, Niagara, New York
North American Baptist Seminary, Sioux Falls, South Dakota
North Carolina State University at Raleigh, Raleigh, North Carolina
North Dakota State University of Agriculture and Applied Science, Fargo, North Dakota
Northeastern University, Boston, Massachusetts
Northern Michigan University, Marquette, Michigan
Northwestern College, Orange City, Iowa
Northwestern College, St. Paul, Minnesota
Northwestern University, Evanston, Illinois
Northwood University, Midland, Michigan
Nova Southeastern University, Fort Lauderdale, Florida
Nyack Missionary College, Nyack, New York
Oakland University, Rochester, Michigan
Oakwood College, Huntsville, Alabama
Oberlin College, Oberlin, Ohio
Ohio State University, The, Columbus, Ohio
Ohio University, Athens, Ohio
Ohr Somayach/Joseph Tanenbaum Educational Center, Monsey, New York
Old Dominion University, Norfolk, Virginia
Olivet Nazarene University, Bourbonnais, Illinois
Oral Roberts University, Tulsa, Oklahoma
Oregon State University, Corvallis, Oregon
Pace University, New York, New York
Pacific Graduate School of Psychology, Menlo Park, California
Pacific Lutheran University, Tacoma, Washington
Pacific Union College, Angwin, California
Pacific University, Forest Grove, Oregon
Palm Beach Atlantic University, West Palm Beach, Florida
Palmer College of Chiropractic, Davenport, Iowa
Palmer College of Chiropractic-West, San Jose, California
Park University, Parkville, Missouri
Pennsylvania State University, The, University Park, Pennsylvania
Pepperdine University, Malibu, California
Philadelphia Biblical University, Langhorne, Pennsylvania
Pomona College, Claremont, California
Princeton Theological Seminary, Princeton, New Jersey
Princeton University, Princeton, New Jersey
Principia College, The, Elsah, Illinois
Providence College, Providence, Rhode Island
Purdue University, Lafayette, Indiana
Rabbinical College Bobover Yeshiva Bnei Zion, Brooklyn, New York
Rabbinical College of America, Morristown, New Jersey
Rabbinical College of Long Island, Long Beach, New York
Rabbinical Seminary of America, Forest Hills, New York
Reed College, Portland, Oregon
Reformed Theological Seminary, Jackson, Mississippi
Rensselaer Polytechnic Institute, Troy, New York
Rice University, Houston, Texas
Rio Grande Bible Institute, Edinburg, Texas
Roberts Wesleyan College, North Chili, New York
Rockefeller University, New York, New York
Rollins College, Winter Park, Florida
Rush University, Chicago, Illinois
Rutgers — The State University, New Brunswick, New Jersey
St. Bonaventure University, St. Bonaventure, New York
St. John's College, Annapolis, Maryland
St. John's College, Santa Fe, New Mexico
Saint John's University, Collegeville, Minnesota
St. John's University, Jamaica, New York
St. Lawrence University, Canton, New York
Saint Louis University, St. Louis, Missouri
Saint Mary's University of Minnesota, Winona, Minnesota

St. Mary's University of San Antonio, San Antonio, Texas
Saint Olaf College, Northfield, Minnesota
St. Vladimir's Orthodox Theological Seminary, Crestwood, New York
San Francisco State College, San Francisco, California
San José State University, San José, California
Santa Clara University, Santa Clara, California
Sarah Lawrence College, Bronxville, New York
Scripps College, Claremont, California
Scripps Research Institute, The, La Jolla, California
Seattle Pacific University, Seattle, Washington
Seattle University, Seattle, Washington
Simpson College, Indianola, Iowa
Simpson College, Redding, California
Skidmore College, Saratoga Springs, New York
Smith College, The, Northampton, Massachusetts
Southeastern University, Lakeland, Florida
Southern Adventist University, Collegedale, Tennessee
Southern Methodist University, Dallas, Texas
Southwestern Adventist University, Keene, Texas
Spring Arbor College, Spring Arbor, Michigan
State University College at Oswego, Oswego, New York
State University College at Potsdam, Potsdam, New York
State University of New York at Binghamton, Binghamton, New York
State University of New York at Buffalo, Buffalo, New York
State University of New York at Geneseo, Geneseo, New York
State University of New York College of Arts and Science at Plattsburgh, Plattsburgh, New York
Stephens College, Columbia, Missouri
Swarthmore College, Swarthmore, Pennsylvania
Syracuse University, Syracuse, New York
Tabor College, Hillsboro, Kansas
Talmudical Yeshiva of Philadelphia, Philadelphia, Pennsylvania
Taylor University, Upland, Indiana
Teachers College, Columbia University, New York, New York
Telshe Yeshiva Rabbinical College of Telshe, Inc., Wickliffe, Ohio
Telshe Yeshiva-Chicago, Rabbinical College of Telshe-Chicago, Inc., Chicago, Illinois
Temple University, Philadelphia, Pennsylvania
Temple University School of Podiatric Medicine, Philadelphia, Pennsylvania
Texas A&M University, College Station, Texas
Texas Chiropractic College, Pasadena, Texas
Texas Woman's University, Denton, Texas
Thomas Aquinas College, Santa Paula, California
Thunderbird School of Global Management, Glendale, Arizona
Touro College, New York, New York
Trinity Bible College, Ellendale, North Dakota
Trinity Christian College, Palos Heights, Illinois
Trinity College, Hartford, Connecticut
Trinity Episcopal School for Ministry, Ambridge, Pennsylvania
Trinity Evangelical Divinity School, Deerfield, Illinois
Trinity Lutheran College, Issaquah, Washington
Trinity University, San Antonio, Texas
Tufts University, Medford, Massachusetts
Tulane University, New Orleans, Louisiana
Union College, Lincoln, Nebraska
Union College, Schenectady, New York
Union Institute & University, Cincinnati, Ohio
Union University, Jackson, Tennessee
University at Albany, State University of New York, Albany, New York
University of Alabama at Birmingham, The, Birmingham, Alabama
University of Alabama in Huntsville, Huntsville, Alabama
University of Arizona, The, Tucson, Arizona
University of California, Berkeley, California
University of California, Davis, California
University of California, Irvine, California
University of California, Los Angeles, California
University of California, Riverside, California
University of California, San Diego, California
University of California, San Francisco, California
University of California, Santa Barbara, California
University of California, Santa Cruz, California
University of Central Florida, Orlando, Florida
University of Chicago The, Chicago, Illinois
University of Cincinnati, Cincinnati, Ohio
University of Colorado, Boulder, Colorado
University of Delaware, Newark, Delaware
University of Denver, Denver, Colorado
University of Detroit Mercy, Detroit, Michigan
University of Findlay, The, Findlay, Ohio
University of Florida, Gainesville, Florida
University of Georgia, The, Athens, Georgia
University of Houston, Houston, Texas
University of Idaho, Moscow, Idaho

University of Illinois, Urbana, Illinois
University of Kansas, Lawrence, Kansas
University of Kentucky, Lexington, Kentucky
University of Louisville, Louisville, Kentucky
University of Maine, Orono, Maine
University of Maryland, College Park, Maryland
University of Massachusetts at Amherst, Amherst, Massachusetts
University of Miami, Coral Gables, Florida
University of Michigan, The, Ann Arbor, Michigan
University of Minnesota, Minneapolis, Minnesota
University of Mississippi, The, Oxford, Mississippi
University of Missouri, Columbia, Missouri
University of Montana-Missoula, The, Missoula, Montana
University of Nebraska, The, Lincoln, Nebraska
University of Nevada-Reno, Reno, Nevada
University of North Carolina at Chapel Hill, Chapel Hill, North Carolina
University of North Dakota, Grand Forks, North Dakota
University of North Texas, Denton, Texas
University of Notre Dame du Lac, Notre Dame, Indiana
University of Oklahoma, Norman, Oklahoma
University of Oregon, Eugene, Oregon
University of Pennsylvania, Philadelphia, Pennsylvania
University of Pittsburgh, Pittsburgh, Pennsylvania
University of Portland, Portland, Oregon
University of Rhode Island, Kingston, Rhode Island
University of Rochester, Rochester, New York
University of St. Thomas, Houston, Texas
University of St. Thomas, St. Paul, Minnesota
University of San Diego, San Diego, California
University of Southern California, Los Angeles, California
University of Southern Mississippi, The, Hattiesburg, Mississippi
University of Tennessee, The, Knoxville, Tennessee
University of Texas, Austin, Texas
University of Texas at Arlington, Arlington, Texas
University of Texas Health Science Center at Houston, Houston, Texas
University of Texas Southwestern Medical Center at Dallas, The, Dallas, Texas
University of the Pacific, Stockton, California
University of Tulsa, Tulsa, Oklahoma
University of Utah, Salt Lake City, Utah
University of Vermont, Burlington, Vermont
University of Virginia, Charlottesville, Virginia
University of Washington, Seattle, Washington
University of Western States, Portland, Oregon
University of Wisconsin, Madison, Wisconsin
University of Wisconsin-Milwaukee, Milwaukee, Wisconsin
University of Wyoming, The, Laramie, Wyoming
Utah State University of Agriculture and Applied Science, Logan, Utah
Utah Valley University, Orem, Utah
Valparaiso University, Valparaiso, Indiana
Vanderbilt University, Nashville, Tennessee
Vassar College, Poughkeepsie, New York
Villanova University, Villanova, Pennsylvania
Wake Forest University, Winston-Salem, North Carolina
Walla Walla University, College Place, Washington
Washington and Lee University, Lexington, Virginia
Washington State University, Pullman, Washington
Washington University, St. Louis, Missouri
Wayne State University, Detroit, Michigan
Welch College, Nashville, Tennessee
Wellesley College, Wellesley, Massachusetts
Wesleyan University, Middleton, Connecticut
West Virginia University, Morgantown, West Virginia
Western Illinois University, Macomb, Illinois
Western Seminary, Portland, Oregon
Western University of Health Sciences, Pomona, California
Western Washington University, Bellingham, Washington
Westminster Theological Seminary, Philadelphia, Pennsylvania
Wheaton College, Norton, Massachusetts
Wheaton College, Wheaton, Illinois
Whitman College, Walla Walla, Washington
Whittier College, Whittier, California
Whitworth College, Spokane, Washington
Williams College, Williamstown, Massachusetts
Wittenberg University, Springfield, Ohio
Woods Hole Oceanographic Institution, Woods Hole, Massachusetts
Yale University, New Haven, Connecticut
Yeshiva Ohr Elchonon Chabad/West Coast Talmudic Seminary, Los Angeles, California
Yeshiva University, New York, New York

Notes [former s. 1]: S. 1 amended by P.C. 2015-862 (last change effective July 2015), 2014-358, 2012-1330, 2010-551, 2006-997, 2006-815, 2005-1133, 2005-694, 2002-2169, 2001-829, 2000-726, 1997-1041, 1996-632, 1995-581, 1994-866, 1993-901, 1992-1108.

2. The universities situated in the United Kingdom of Great Britain and Northern Ireland that are prescribed by section 3503 are the following:

Aston University, Birmingham, England
Brunel University, Uxbridge, England
City University London, London, England
Cranfield University, Bedfordshire, England
Gateshead Talmudical College, Gateshead, England
Heriot-Watt University, Edinburgh, Scotland
Imperial College of Science, Technology and Medicine, London, England
King's College London, London, England
London Business School, London, England
London School of Economics and Political Science, The, London, England
London School of Hygiene & Tropical Medicine, London, England
Loughborough University, Leicestershire, England
Queen's University of Belfast, The, Belfast, Northern Ireland
Swansea University, Swansea, Wales
University College London, London, England
University of Aberdeen, Aberdeen, Scotland
University of Bath, The, Bath, England
University of Birmingham, Birmingham, England
University of Bradford, Bradford, England
University of Bristol, Bristol, England
University of Buckingham, The, Buckingham, England
University of Cambridge, Cambridge, England
University of Dundee, The, Dundee, Scotland
University of Durham, Durham, England
University of Edinburgh, Edinburgh, Scotland
University of Exeter, Exeter, England
University of Glasgow, Glasgow, Scotland
University of Keele, Keele, England
University of Kent, Canterbury, England
University of Leeds, Leeds, England
University of Liverpool, Liverpool, England
University of London, London, England
University of Manchester, The, Manchester, England
University of Newcastle, The, Newcastle upon Tyne, England
University of Nottingham, The, Nottingham, England
University of Oxford, Oxford, England
University of Reading, Reading, England
University of St. Andrews, St. Andrews, Scotland
University of Sheffield, Sheffield, England
University of Southampton, Southampton, England
University of Strathclyde, Glasgow, Scotland
University of Surrey, Guildford, Surrey, England
University of Sussex, Brighton, England
University of Ulster, Newtonabbey, Northern Ireland
University of Wales, Cardiff, Wales
University of York, York, England

Notes [former s. 2]: S. 2 amended by P.C. 2015-862 (last change effective 2014), 2014-358, 2012-1330, 2010-551, 2006-815, 2002-2169, 2001-829, 2000-726, 1996-632, 1994-866, 1992-1108.

3. The universities situated in France that are prescribed by section 3503 are the following:

American University in Paris, Paris
Catholic Faculties of Lyon, Lyon
Catholic Institute of Paris, Paris
Catholic University of Lille, The, Lille
École Nationale des Ponts et Chaussées, Paris
European Institute of Business Administration (INSEAD), Fontainebleau
Hautes Études Commerciales, Paris

Notes [former s. 3]: S. 3 amended by P.C. 2014-358 (effective April 23/14), 2000-829, 2000-726, 1994-866.

4. The universities situated in Austria that are prescribed by section 3503 are the following:

WU Vienna University of Economics and Business, Vienna

Notes [former s. 4]: U of Vienna deleted by P.C. 2012-1330 effective Oct. 24, 2012. WU Vienna U of Economics added by P.C. 2010-551, effective 2007.

5. The universities situated in Belgium that are prescribed by section 3503 are the following:

Catholic University of Louvain, Louvain

Notes [former s. 5]: Free U of Brussels deleted by P.C. 2000-726, effective June 7/00.

6. The universities situated in Switzerland that are prescribed by section 3503 are the following:

Franklin College of Switzerland, Sorengo (Lugano)

University of Lausanne, Lausanne

Notes [former s. 6]: S. 6 amended by P.C. 2014-358 to delete U of Geneva (Geneva) effective April 23/14. Earlier amended by P.C. 2000-829, 1992-1108.

7. [Repealed]

Notes [former s. 7]: S. 7, prescribing Pontifical Gregorian U in Vatican City, repealed by P.C. 2014-358 effective April 23/14.

8. The universities situated in Israel that are prescribed by section 3503 are the following:

Bar-Ilan University, Ramat-Gan
Ben Gurion University of the Negev, Beersheba
École biblique et archéologique française, Jerusalem
Hebrew University of Jerusalem, The, Jerusalem
Interdisciplinary Center, The, Herzliya, Israel
Jerusalem College for Women, Bayit-Vegan, Jerusalem
Jerusalem College of Technology, Jerusalem
Technion-Israel Institute of Technology, Haifa
Tel-Aviv University, Tel-Aviv
University of Haifa, Haifa
Weizmann Institute of Science, Rehovot, Israel
Yeshivat Aish Hatorah, Jerusalem

Notes [former s. 8]: S. 8 amended by P.C. 2014-358 (last change effective 2013), 2012-1330, 2000-829, 1996-632, 1994-866.

9. The universities situated in Lebanon that are prescribed by section 3503 are the following:

American University of Beirut, Riad El Solh, Beirut
St. Joseph University, Beirut

Notes [former s. 9]: American U of Beirut deleted by P.C. 2000-726, effective June 7/00, and reinstated by P.C. 2006-815 effective 2003.

10. The universities situated in Ireland that are prescribed by section 3503 are the following:

National University of Ireland, Dublin
Royal College of Surgeons in Ireland, Dublin
University of Dublin, The, Trinity College, Dublin

Notes [former s. 10]: U of Dublin changed to U of Dublin, Trinity Coll. by P.C. 2006-997, effective 2005.

11. The universities situated in the Federal Republic of Germany that are prescribed by section 3503 are the following:

Ukrainian Free University, Munich
University of Heidelberg, Heidelberg

Notes [former s. 11]: Ruprecht-Karls-Universität Heidenberg added by P.C. 1996-632, effective 1995, and changed to U of Heidelberg by P.C. 2006-997 retroactive to 1995.

12. The universities situated in Poland that are prescribed by section 3503 are the following:

Catholic University of Lublin, Lublin
Jagiellonian University, Krakow

Notes [former s. 12]: Jagiellonian U added by P.C. 2000-726, effective 1998.

13. The universities situated in Spain that are prescribed by section 3503 are the following:

University of Navarra, Pamplona

14. The universities situated in the People's Republic of China that are prescribed by section 3503 are the following:

Nanjing University, Nanjing
Peking University, Beijing

Notes [former s. 14]: S. 14 amended to add Peking U by P.C. 2012-1330, effective 2010. Earlier amended by P.C. 2001-829, 2000-829.

15. The universities situated in Jamaica that are prescribed for the purposes of section 3503 are the following:

University of the West Indies, Mona Campus, Kingston

16. For the purposes of section 3503, the university situated in Italy is the following:

John Cabot University, Rome
Pontifical University of the Holy Cross, Rome

Notes [former s. 16]: S. 16 added by P.C. 2010-551, effective 2008; Pontifical U added by P.C. 2012-1330 effective 2010.

Former s. 16 (Universita Karlova, Prague, Czech and Slovak Federal Republic) added by P.C. 1992-1108, repealed by P.C. 2001-829 effective May 23/01.

17. The universities situated in Australia that are prescribed by section 3503 are the following:

Adelaide University, Adelaide
Australian National University, Canberra
Avondale College, Cooranbong
Monash University, Victoria
University of Melbourne, The, Parkville
University of Tasmania, Hobart

Notes [former s. 17]: S. 17 amended by P.C. 2014-358 (effective April 23/14), 2012-1330, 2002-2169, 2001-829, 2000-726, 1996-632, 1994-866, 1993-901.

18. [Repealed]

Notes [former s. 18]: S. 18, prescribing U of Zagreb in Croatia, added by P.C. 1994-866 effective 1993 and repealed by P.C. 2012-1330 effective Oct. 24, 2012.

19. The universities situated in South Africa that are prescribed by section 3503 are the following:

University of Cape Town, Rondebosch
University of KwaZulu-Natal, Durban

Notes [former s. 19]: S. 19 amended by P.C. 2014-358 (effective April 23/14), 2012-1330, 2006-815, 2001-829, 1995-581 (added).

20. For the purposes of section 3503 the universities situated in the Netherlands are the following:

Leiden University, Leiden
Nyenrode University, Breukelen
University of Groningen, Groningen

Notes [former s. 20]: S. 20 amended by P.C. 2002-2169 (effective 2001), 2000-726, 1996-632 (added).

21. For the purposes of section 3503 the universities situated in Hong Kong are the following:

Chinese University of Hong Kong, The, Shatin, New Territories
Hong Kong University of Science and Technology, The, Kowloon
University of Hong Kong, The, Hong Kong

Notes [former s. 21]: Chinese U of HK added by P.C. 2010-551 effective 2007. S 21 earlier amended by P.C. 2002-2169; added by 1996-632.

22. The universities situated in New Zealand that are prescribed by section 3503 are the following:

University of Auckland, The, Auckland
University of Otago, Dunedin

Notes [former s. 22]: S. 22 amended by P.C. 2014-358 to delete Victoria U of Wellington (Wellington) effective April 23/14. Earlier amended by P.C. 2006-815, 2005-694, 2000-726.

23. The university situated in Hungary that is prescribed by section 3503 is the following:

Central European University, Budapest

Notes [former s. 23]: S. 23 added by P.C. 2001-829, effective 1999.

24. [Repealed]

Notes [former s. 24]: S. 24, prescribing Panjab U (Chandigarh) in India, added by P.C. 1994-866 effective 1993 and repealed by P.C. 2014-358 effective April 23/14.

25. The university situated in Estonia that is prescribed by section 3503 is the following:

University of Tartu, Tartu

Notes [former s. 25]: S. 25 added by P.C. 2006-815, effective 2004.

Income Tax Folios [former Sch. VIII]: S1-F2-C2: Tuition tax credit [replaces IT-516R2]

Forms [former Sch. VIII]: RC191: Donations to prescribed universities outside Canada [info sheet]

SCHEDULES IX, X
[Revoked]

Notes: Schedules IX and X revoked by P.C. 1993-1688, for 1993 and later taxation years. Schedule IX listed prescribed areas under Reg. 7303 for purposes of the northern residents deduction under ITA 110.7. Schedule X contained climatological maps used for the northern residents deduction under Reg. 7303.

SELECTED REMISSION ORDERS

Notes: A remission order is a mechanism by which the federal Cabinet (technically the "Governor in Council") can "remit" tax or other amounts such as interest and penalties – i.e., pay such amount back to a taxpayer or cancel the taxpayer's obligation to pay.

Remission orders are issued under the authority of *Financial Administration Act* s. 23(2), "where the Governor in Council considers that the collection of the tax or the enforcement of the penalty is unreasonable or unjust or that it is otherwise in the public interest to remit the tax or penalty". Like regulations, they are passed as "orders in council" by Cabinet. Some are for specific taxpayers or groups of taxpayers; others are for all taxpayers affected by a specific issue or transaction. (Remission orders for Customs duties can be granted under *Customs Tariff* s. 115 rather than the FAA.)

How to apply: The process is rarely successful and takes years. Send a letter to the Director of the taxpayer's Tax Services Office (there is no prescribed form). (CRA may treat a letter seeking relief that cannot legally be granted as a remission order request, e.g. doc 2018-0789661M4.) The Director (on advice from subordinates) will recommend for or against remission. The request then goes to the Headquarters Remission Committee in Ottawa, which makes a further recommendation. A formal decision on recommending remission is then made by the Assistant Commissioner, Legislative Policy and Regulatory Affairs. If that decision is positive, the matter goes to the Commissioner, then the Minister, then Cabinet, which makes the final decision. (The initial request can also be made directly to HQ, but it will be referred back to the local office for a recommendation, so the process is the same.) As of fall 2020, the Committee members (for both income tax and GST/HST) are: Lynn Laplante [Chair, 613-670-7385] (Manager, Remissions & Delegations, Legislative Policy & Regulatory Affairs Branch (LPRA)); Cornelis (Kees) Rystenbil (Manager, Provincial Legislative Amendments, LPRA); Catherine Seguin (Asst Director, Financial Institution & Real Property Division, LPRA); Mark Van Helvoirt (A/Manager, Quality Assurance, Collections & Verification Branch); Ken Mathews (Manager, Commodity Tax Legislative Amendments, LPRA). In 2010-11, the Committee considered 44 cases and recommended remission in 14. It considered 6 cases in 2013-14, 21 in 2014-15, 26 in 2016-17, 19 in 2017-18, 18 in 2018-19 and 25 in 2019-20, with no disclosure as to how many recommendations it made for remission, but one can see from the *Canada Gazette* how many remission orders are granted each year. (*Access to Information Act* disclosure)

A remission order request has best chance of success if it is based on the Remission Guidelines in section III of the *CRA Remission Guide* (Oct. 2014; on *TaxPartner* and *Taxnet Pro*). The stated categories of relief are: (1) extreme hardship; (2) financial setback coupled with extenuating factors (e.g., conditions beyond a person's control, or taxpayer error); (3) incorrect CRA action or advice; and (4) unintended results of the legislation. (These are also cited in *Coulter*, [2004] 4 C.T.C. 2374 (TCC), para. 30, and *Frank Arthur Investments*, 2014 CarswellNat 1057 (FC), paras. 29-30.) The CRA *National Collections Manual* (2015, on *TaxPartner* and *Taxnet Pro*), under "Remission — Tax programs", contains basic information on how to process a remission request.

Using the Courts: The Courts have no authority to order that a remission order be granted, even if one was promised by CRA officials: *Superior Auto Sales*, [1997] 3 C.T.C. 274 (FCTD). The Federal Court has judicial-review (JR) jurisdiction (see Notes to ITA 171(1) and 220(3.1)) over a CRA decision not to recommend a remission order, but not over a Cabinet decision not to pass one. To date all JR applications but one on CRA "refusals to recommend" have been dismissed: *Waycobah First Nation*, 2011 FCA 191 (GST); *Twentieth Century Fox*, 2013 FCA 25 (GST); *Desgagnés Transarctik*, 2014 FCA 14 (Customs duties remission not recommended by CBSA); *Fink*, 2019 FCA 276; *Deshaies*, 2019 FCA 300; *Escape Trailer*, 2020 FCA 54 (GST); *Axa Canada*, 2006 FC 17 (GST); *Germain*, 2012 FC 768; *Frank Arthur Investments*, 2014 FC 336 (pre-1991 Federal Sales Tax); *Jarrold*, 2015 FC 153 (GST); *Matthew*, 2017 FC 538; *Pay Audio*, 2018 FC 494 (GST); *Boivin*, 2019 FC 210; *Internorth*, 2019 FC 574; *Meleca*, 2020 FC 1159. Similarly, in *St-Laurent [Simard]*, 2009 FCA 379, para. 25, a Tax Court judge could not be faulted for refusing to recommend a remission order. Even if the Court agrees CRA's decision was unreasonable, its only remedy is to send the matter back to CRA for a new decision: *Pay Audio*, para. 40. However, since the 2019 Supreme Court of Canada decision in *Vavilov*, CRA may be required to provide a more reasoned explanation for refusing to recommend remission; see Notes to ITA 220(3.1). The one successful JR application to date is *Mokrycke*, 2020 FC 1027: based on *Vavilov*, CRA's decision was not justified and was sent back for a new decision. M challenged CRA's audit reassessments of 2005-06 as incorrect; he had not appealed to the TCC in time due to personal circumstances, and claimed his accountant had failed to appeal for him [but note that his accountant, not being a lawyer, could not have!].

The Federal Court has judicial-review jurisdiction over how remission is calculated under a remission order, e.g. *Imperial Oil Resources*, 2014 FC 838 (not appealed).

The Tax Court sometimes recommends a remission order be granted, or at least suggests the taxpayer apply for one. See *Chalifoux*, [1991] 2 C.T.C. 2243; *Khan*, [2002] 4 C.T.C. 2444; *Cameron*, 2006 TCC 588; *Schoenne*, 2011 TCC 189; *Kwangwari*, 2013 TCC 302; *Demers*, 2014 TCC 368, para. 70; *Chitalia*, 2017 TCC 227, para. 24. The Court has also recommended remission orders in many GST appeals: *Musselman*, [1995] G.S.T.C. 60; *Clear Customs Brokers*, [1996] G.S.T.C. 46; *Drover*, [1997] G.S.T.C. 26; *Westcan Malting*, [1998] G.S.T.C. 34; *Sterling Business*, [1998] G.S.T.C. 130; *Evergreen Forestry*, [1999] G.S.T.C. 35; *Didkowski*, [2001] G.S.T.C. 22 (remission order was later granted); *Danette Electronical Engineering*, [2001] G.S.T.C. 71 (later granted); *Snider*, [2002] G.S.T.C. 44; *Nelson Consulting*, [2002] G.S.T.C. 122 (later granted); *Hallmark Poultry*, [2003] G.S.T.C. 69; *Lair*, 2003 TCC 929; *Zubic*, 2004 TCC 533; *Thompson*, 2003 TCC 119; *Hrenchuk*, [2005] G.S.T.C. 136; *Slovack*, 2006 TCC 687; *Evasion Hors Piste*, 2006 TCC 477 (later granted); *de Moissac*, [2007] 1 C.T.C. 2001; *Nimis*, 2007 TCC 10; *Beutler*, 2007 TCC 371; *Vescio*, 2007 TCC 690; *Gagné-Lessard Sports*, 2007 TCC 300 (later granted); *Smart Net Systems*, 2013 TCC 212 (later granted); *A OK Payday Loans*, 2013 TCC 217; *Cassidy*, 2020 TCC 1, para. 14; *1089391 Ontario*, 2020 TCC 129, para. 56.

Effect of a remission order: A remission order "cannot affect the correctness of an income tax assessment, which must be determined solely on the basis of the *Income Tax Act* and *Income Tax Regulations*. A tax remission order applies at the collection stage. It can do no more than relieve a person from a tax debt or oblige the Crown to refund a tax debt that has been paid": *Imperial Oil Resources*, 2009 FCA 325, para. 27; *Perley*, [1999] 3 C.T.C. 180 (FCA). Thus, the Tax Court does not have jurisdiction to apply an existing remission order to a subsequent assessment: *Perley*.

A federal remission order cannot remit provincial tax, but the province may have such a process, e.g. Ontario *Financial Administration Act* s. 5.1, which authorizes the Ontario Cabinet to remit tax but also gives the Ontario Minister of Finance authority to remit up to $10,000 without asking Cabinet.

There is no time limit to apply for a refund under a remission order that does not specify a deadline: VIEWS doc 2005-0129791I7.

Interest does not run on a remission order if the CRA does not refund the tax promptly: *Pacific Vending*, [2001] G.S.T.C. 66 (TCC); *Imperial Oil Resources*, 2016 FCA 139.

See also: H. Arnold Sherman and Jeffrey D. Sherman, "Income Tax Remission Orders: The Tax Planner's Last Resort or the Ultimate Weapon?", 34(4) *Canadian Tax Journal* 801-27 (July-Aug. 1986); Joanne Swystun & Maryam Mohajer, "Remission Orders Under the Financial Administration Act", X(2) *Tax Litigation* (Federated Press) 624-28 (2002); "Remission Orders", 1948 *Tax Topics* (CCH) 1-4 (July 9, 2009); Mike Harris, "Remission Orders and the Exercise of Discretion", 2063 *Tax Topics* 1-5 (Sept. 22, 2011); Rahul Sharma, "A Taxpayer's Last Resort: The Remission Order", 7(2) *Taxes & Wealth Management* (Carswell) 17-18 (May 2014); Maria Severino & Clara Pham, "FCA emphasizes sparing use of tax remission orders in Internorth case", 2019(16) *Tax Times* (Carswell) 1-2 (Aug. 23, 2019); David Sherman's Analysis to *Excise Tax Act* s. 165 in the *Canada GST Service*, *GST Partner* or *Taxnet Pro*.

Not all income tax remission orders are reproduced below. The Editor has selected ones that are of continuing application, of general interest, or are useful examples.

General Remission Orders

Private Remission Orders

INCOME TAX REMISSION ORDERS

REMISSION ORDERS — GENERAL

[These remission orders are of general interest and applicable to groups of taxpayers. For remission orders applying to a particular individual or corporation (but still of some general interest) see the "Private" remission orders further below — ed.]

BRITISH COLUMBIA FORESTRY REVITALIZATION REMISSION ORDER
P.C. 2013-2, January 11, 2013 (SI/2013-1)

Interpretation

1. (1) The following definitions apply in this Order.

"Act" means the *Income Tax Act*.

"declaration of Subtrust" means the declaration, dated January 3, 2012, that sets out the terms and conditions of the Subtrust.

"eligible amount", in respect of an eligible taxpayer, means an amount paid by the Subtrust in respect of the eligible taxpayer's Eligible Income Tax, within the meaning assigned by section 2.02 of the declaration of Subtrust, that is attributable to an FRT Contractor Mitigation Amount.

"eligible taxpayer" has the meaning assigned by section 2.04 of the declaration of Subtrust.

"FRT Contractor Mitigation Amount" has the meaning assigned by section 2.01 of the declaration of Subtrust.

"Subtrust" means the 2011 Contractor Mitigation Account Subtrust that was established on January 3, 2012, and is a subtrust of the BC Forestry Revitalization Trust II.

(2) **Application of meanings in Act** — Unless the context otherwise requires, words and expressions used in this Order have the same meaning as in the Act.

Remission

2. **Eligible Amount** — Remission is granted to each eligible taxpayer of the income tax paid or payable under Part I of the Act for a taxation year, and of any related interest and penalties, that are attributable to an eligible amount paid in the year by the Subtrust to, or for the benefit of, the eligible taxpayer.

3. **FRT Contractor Mitigation Amount** — Remission is granted to each eligible taxpayer in respect of whom an eligible amount has been paid by the Subtrust of the amount of any interest and penalties paid or payable to the extent that they relate to income tax under Part I of the Act that is attributable to an FRT Contractor Mitigation Amount paid to, or for the benefit of, the eligible taxpayer.

Explanatory Note [not part of the Order]: The Order provides, first, for the remission to each eligible taxpayer of taxes paid or payable by the taxpayer under the *Income Tax Act* as a result of payments from the 2011 Contractor Mitigation Account Subtrust (the Subtrust), second for the remission of interest and penalties related to income taxes in respect of the previous payments from the BC Forest Revitalization Trust and the BC Forestry Revitalization Trust II (the Trusts), as well as in respect of the payments from the Subtrust.

Objective: To serve the public interest.

Background: In 2003 and 2008, the Province of British Columbia (the Province) created the Trusts to compensate eligible contractors for the loss of their contractual rights because of timber reallocation resulting from the restructuring of the Province's forestry sector under its *Forestry Revitalization Act*. Because of this restructuring, contractors suffered financial hardship. A purpose of the Trusts was to mitigate the adverse financial impacts that they suffered. The amount of compensation received by contractors was generally related to the value of lost contracts and redundant equipment. This amount was included in computing the income of contractors under Part I of the *Income Tax Act* and the net benefits to them were consequently lower. On the initiative of the Province, the Subtrust was created to make new payments to the contractors, or to the Receiver General for Canada for the benefit of contractors, to compensate for income taxes paid or payable by the contractors in respect of the previous payments from the Trusts.

Implications: The cost of this Remission Order is estimated to be $2.5 million. This cost includes the remission of taxes payable in respect of payments from the Subtrust (i.e. to compensate the tax paid or payable in respect of payments from the Trusts). The cost also includes interest and penalties in respect of income taxes payable on payments from the Trusts and the Subtrust.

Departmental contact: Ève Pentassuglia, Tax Legislation Division, Department of Finance, 140 O'Connor Street, Ottawa, Ontario K1A 0G5, Telephone: 613-992-5636.

Notes: This remission order was proposed in a letter from the Minister of Finance dated March 25, 2011 (published here in PITA 40th-42nd ed.).

CAMP IPPERWASH INDIAN SETTLEMENT REMISSION ORDER, 2003
P.C. 2003-989, June 18, 2003 (SI/2003-133)

1. **Interpretation** — The following definitions apply in this Order.

"band" has the same meaning as in subsection 2(1) of the *Indian Act*.

"Indian" has the same meaning as in subsection 2(1) of the *Indian Act*.

"Indian Settlement" means the settlement named, and constituting the lands described, in the schedule.

"reserve" has the same meaning as in subsection 2(1) of the *Indian Act*.

2. **Application** — This Order applies in respect of the Indian Settlement until lands constituting that Indian settlement are set apart as a reserve by an order of the Governor in Council.

Part 1 — Income Tax

3. **Interpretation** — In this Part,

(a) **"tax"** means a tax imposed under Part I, I.1 or I.2 of the *Income Tax Act*; and

(b) all other words and expressions not otherwise defined in section 1 have the same meaning as in the *Income Tax Act*.

4. **Remission of Income Tax** — Remission is hereby granted to an Indian, or a band, with income situated on the Indian Settlement, in respect of each taxation year or fiscal period beginning during or after the calendar year 1985, of the amount, if any, by which

(a) the taxes, interest and penalties paid or payable by the Indian or band, as the case may be, for the taxation year or fiscal period exceed

(b) the taxes, interest and penalties that would have been payable by that Indian or band for the taxation year or fiscal period if the Indian Settlement had been a reserve throughout that taxation year or fiscal period.

Part 2 — Goods and Services Tax

5. **Interpretation** — In this Part,

(a) **"tax"** means the goods and services tax imposed under subsection 165(1) of the *Excise Tax Act*; and

(b) all other words and expressions not otherwise defined in section 1 have the same meaning as in Part IX of the *Excise Tax Act*.

6. **Remission of the Goods and Services Tax** — Subject to sections 7 and 8, remission is hereby granted to an Indian or a band that is the recipient of a taxable supply made on or delivered to the Indian Settlement on or after the day on which this Order comes into force in the case of an Indian, and January 1, 1991 in the case of a band, of the amount, if any, by which

(a) the tax paid or payable by the recipient

exceeds

(b) the tax that would have been payable by the recipient if the Indian Settlement had been a reserve at the time the supply was made or delivered.

7. **Conditions** — Remission granted to an Indian under section 6 is on condition that

(a) the tax paid or payable has not otherwise been rebated, credited, refunded or remitted under Part IX of the *Excise Tax Act* or under the *Financial Administration Act*; and

(b) in respect of tax paid, a written claim for the remission is made to the Minister of National Revenue within two years after the day on which the tax was paid.

8. Remission granted to a band under section 6 is on condition that

(a) the tax paid or payable has not otherwise been rebated, credited, refunded or remitted under Part IX of the *Excise Tax Act* or under the *Financial Administration Act*;

(b) in respect of tax paid on or after January 1, 1991 but before the day on which this Order comes into force, a written claim for the remission is made to the Minister of National Revenue within two years after the day on which this Order comes into force; and

(c) in respect of tax paid on or after the day on which this Order comes into force, a written claim for the remission is made to the Minister of National Revenue within two years after the day on which the tax was paid.

Schedule *(Section 1)*

Settlement	Legal Description of Settlement Lands
Camp Ipperwash	Those lands in the Township of Bosanquet, County of Lambton, Province of Ontario, more particularly described as follows:
	Part of Lots 1 and 2, all of Lots 3 to 7 inclusive, Concession A;
	Part of Lots 1 and 2, all of Lots 3 to 8 inclusive, Concession B;
	Part of Lots 1 and 2, all of Lots 3 to 8 inclusive, Concession C;
	Part of Lots 1, 2 and 8, all of Lots 3 to 7 inclusive, Concession D.
	All according to Registered Plan No. 23, and designated as Part 1 on a plan deposited in the Land Registry Office for the Registry Division of Lambton (No. 25) as Plan 25R-3072.
	Save and except part of Lots 4, 5 and 6, Concession A, and road allowances, all according to Registered Plan No. 23, and designated as Part 5 on a plan deposited in the Land Registry Office for the Registry Division of Lambton (No. 25) as Plan 25R-3320.

Explanatory Note [not part of the Order]: The purpose of this Order is to provide relief from federal income tax and the goods and services tax to Indians and Indian Bands on Camp Ipperwash that would be available if that land were a reserve under the *Indian Act*. The Government of Canada has made a public commitment to grant reserve status under the *Indian Act* to that land.

CHILD CARE EXPENSE AND MOVING EXPENSE REMISSION ORDER

ORDER RESPECTING THE REMISSION OF INCOME TAX PAYABLE BY CERTAIN CANADIAN RESIDENTS INCURRING CHILD CARE EXPENSES OUTSIDE CANADA OR INCURRING MOVING EXPENSES WHEN MOVING TO OR FROM A LOCATION OUTSIDE CANADA

P.C. 1991-257, February 14, 1991 (SI/91-23), as amended by P.C. 1994-328, February 24, 1994 (SI/94-26).

[Applies to taxation years 1984-88, with application deadline Dec. 31, 1995 — ed.]

CHURCHILL FALLS (LABRADOR) CORPORATION REMISSION ORDER
P.C. 1968-832, April 30, 1968

Whereas it has been made to appear that

1. Churchill Falls (Labrador) Corporation is undertaking a very large investment to develop facilities at Churchill Falls in Labrador to produce very large amounts of electric power for sale to provincially-owned power corporations;

2. The said Corporation proposes to finance the construction of facilities to produce and transmit power in part by means of the sale of first mortgage bonds,[1] of which an aggregate principal amount exceeding four hundred million Canadian dollars is expected to be sold in the United States in denominations of United States dollars;

3. The sale of an issue of bonds of this size might well be prevented by the imposition of a Canadian withholding tax on the interest payable on such bonds, since such a large issue must be sold to many institutions which would neither be exempt from tax nor able to offset it against taxes payable to the United States, or if it were not prevented, the rate of interest required to be paid by the Corporation would be significantly increased, in turn materially increasing the cost of power to the provincially-owned power corporations;

4. Interest paid on bonds issued by the provincially-owned power corporations is not subject to Canadian withholding tax, and the Government of Canada has long followed the policy, most recently expressed in the *Public Utilities Income Tax Transfer Act*, of effectively removing or reducing those federal taxes on investor-owned power corporations that materially affect their position *vis-à-vis* provincially-owned power corporations; and

5. The said issue of first mortgage bonds can be sold in the United States exempt from the Interest Equalization Tax of the United States;

And whereas the Governor in Council considers it to be in the public interest that the first mortgage bonds of the said Corporation may be sold in the United States exempt from withholding tax;

Therefore, His Excellency the Governor General in Council on the recommendation of the Treasury Board, pursuant to section 22 of the *Financial Administration Act*, is pleased hereby to remit

(a) the amount of any tax payable by a person under Part III of the *Income Tax Act* on, or such part of the amount of any tax that is or, but for this Order, would be payable by a person under that Part as may reasonably be regarded as attributable to, amounts paid or credited or deemed to have been paid or credited to that person as, on account or in lieu of payment of, or in satisfaction of, interest on first mortgage bonds issued by Churchill Falls (Labrador) Corporation Limited on or after the date of this Order,

(i) that are in denominations of United States dollars, and

(ii) that are identified in a manner prescribed by the Minister of Finance for the purposes of this Order as comprising, or as having been issued in exchange or substitution or partial exchange or substitution for bonds comprising, part of a series of first mortgage bonds issued or covenanted to be issued by Churchill Falls (Labrador) Corporation Limited whether in denominations of United States dollars or otherwise, the aggregate principal amount of which (expressed in terms of Canadian dollars) when added to the aggregate principal amount similarly so expressed of all first mortgage bonds previously issued or covenanted to be issued by Churchill Falls (Labrador) Corporation Limited whether in denominations of United States dollars or otherwise, does not exceed six hundred million dollars; and

(b) any tax or penalty payable by a person under the *Income Tax Act* as a result of the failure of such person to deduct or withhold an amount as required by section 109 of that Act from any amount paid or credited or deemed to have been paid or credited by him as, on account or in lieu of payment of, or in satisfaction of, interest as described in paragraph (a).

[Note: The reference in this Order in Council to Section 22 of the *Financial Administration Act* and to section 109 and Part III of the *Income Tax Act* should be construed as references to sections 23 and 215 and Part XIII, respectively, of the present statutes.]

FARMERS' INCOME TAXES REMISSION ORDER
P.C. 1993-1647, August 4, 1993 (SI/93-164)

[Applies to the 1992 taxation year — ed.]

GOVERNMENT AND LONG-TERM CORPORATE DEBT OBLIGATIONS REMISSION ORDER

ORDER RESPECTING THE REMISSION OF CERTAIN INCOME TAXES PAID OR PAYABLE BY CERTAIN PERSONS IN RESPECT OF INTEREST FROM GOVERNMENT AND LONG-TERM CORPORATE DEBT OBLIGATIONS
P.C. 1985-3480, November 28, 1985 (SI/85-214)

1. **Short Title** — This Order may be cited as the *Government and Long-Term Corporate Debt Obligations Remission Order*.
2. **Interpretation** — In this Order, "Act" means the *Income Tax Act*.

Remission

3. Remission is hereby granted to each non-resident person who is liable for tax under Part XIII of the Act in respect of any amount paid or credited to him as, on account or in lieu of payment of, or in satisfaction of, interest of an amount equal to the amount, if any, by which

(a) the tax payable by the non-resident person under Part XIII of the Act in respect of the amount so paid or credited

---

[1] Maturity date of the mortgage bonds is in the year 2007.

exceeds

(b) the tax that would be payable by the non-resident person under Part XIII of the Act in respect of the amount so paid or credited if the references to "1986" in subparagraphs 212(1)(b)(ii) and (vii) of the Act were read as references to "1987".

4. Where a person required to deduct or withhold a tax payable by a non-resident person under Part XIII of the Act is liable to pay as tax under Part XIII on behalf of the non-resident person the whole of the amount that should have been deducted or withheld, remission is hereby granted to that person of an amount equal to the amount, if any, by which

(a) the tax payable by the person so required to deduct or withhold under Part XIII of the Act

exceeds

(b) the tax that would be payable by the person so required to deduct or withhold under Part XIII of the Act if the references to "1986" in subparagraphs 212(1)(b)(ii) and (vii) of the Act were read as references to "1987".

Explanatory Note [not part of the Order]: This Order remits income tax payable on interest income received by non-resident persons from residents of Canada in respect of government and long-term corporate debt obligations issued in 1986.

ICE STORM EMPLOYEE BENEFITS REMISSION ORDER

P.C. 1998-2047, November 19, 1998 (SI/98-119)

[Applies to the 1998 year only — ed.]

INCOME EARNED IN QUEBEC INCOME TAX REMISSION ORDER, 1988

ORDER RESPECTING THE REMISSION OF INCOME TAX IN RESPECT OF CERTAIN INCOME OF INDIVIDUALS EARNED IN THE PROVINCE OF QUEBEC (1988)

P.C. 1989-1204, June 22, 1989 (SI/89-157), as amended by P.C. 1991-1661, September 5, 1991 (SI/91-116); P.C. 1992-2593, December 11, 1992 (SI/92-230); P.C. 1994-567, April 14, 1994 (SI/94-43); P.C. 1998-396, March 19, 1998 (SI/98-47).

1. **Short Title** — This Order may be cited as the *Income Earned in Quebec Income Tax Remission Order, 1988.*
2. **Interpretation** — In this Order,

"**Act**" means the *Income Tax Act*;

"**Regulations**" means the *Income Tax Regulations*.

Remission to Individuals Who Did Not Reside in Canada at any Time in a Taxation Year

3. Remission is hereby granted to any individual who did not reside in Canada at any time in a taxation year of the amount, if any, by which

(a) the tax, interest and penalties paid or payable under the Act by that individual in respect of that taxation year

exceeds

(b) the tax, interest and penalties that would have been payable by that individual under the Act in respect of that taxation year if, for the purpose of determining that person's income earned in that year in the Province of Quebec, section 2602 of the Regulations read as follows:

"2602. (1) Except as provided in subsection (2), where an individual did not reside in Canada at any time in a taxation year, his income earned in the taxation year in a particular province is the aggregate of

(a) that part of the amount of his income from an office or employment that is included in computing his taxable income earned in Canada for the year by virtue of subparagraph 115(1)(a)(i) of the Act that is reasonably attributable to the duties performed by him in the province,

(b) his income for that year earned in the province as determined in the manner set forth in section 4 of the *Income Earned in Quebec Income Tax Remission Order, 1988,*

(c) his income for that year from carrying on business earned in the province, determined as hereinafter set forth in this Part,

(d) the taxable capital gains in the province included in computing his taxable income earned in Canada for the year by virtue of subparagraph 115(1)(a)(iii) of the Act from dispositions of property, each of which was a disposition of a property or an interest therein that was

(i) real property situated in the province or an option in respect thereof, or

(ii) any other capital property used by him in carrying on a business in the province,

determined as hereinafter set forth in this Part, and

(e) the income of the individual for that year from the disposition of a life insurance policy under which a person resident in the province is, at the time the policy was issued or effected, the person whose life was insured.

(2) Where the aggregate of the amount of an individual's income as determined under subsection (1) for all provinces for a taxation year exceeds his income described in subsection 115(1) of the Act, the amount of his income earned in the taxation year in a particular province shall be that proportion of his income so described that the amount of his income earned in the taxation year in the province as determined under subsection (1) is of the aggregate of all those amounts.

(3) Where, in a taxation year, a non-resident individual has disposed of real property situated in a particular province or an interest therein, or an option in respect thereof, any taxable capital gain from that disposition shall be a taxable capital gain in that particular province.

(4) Except as provided in subsection (5), where, in a taxation year, a non-resident individual has disposed of any capital property, other than property referred to in subsection (3), used by him in carrying on a business in Canada, the proportion of any taxable capital gain from that disposition that

(a) his income for the year from carrying on that business in a particular province

is of

(b) his income for the year from carrying on that business in Canada,

2136

shall be a taxable capital gain in that particular province.

(5) Where in a taxation year a non-resident individual

(a) had no permanent establishment in Canada, and

(b) disposed of any capital property, other than property referred to in subsection (3), used by him in a previous year in carrying on a business in Canada,

the proportion of any taxable capital gain from that disposition that

(c) his income from carrying on that business in a particular province for the last preceding taxation year in which he had income from carrying on that business in a province

is of

(d) his income for the year referred to in paragraph (c), from carrying on that business in Canada,

shall be a taxable capital gain in the particular province."

4. Where an individual who did not reside in Canada at any time in a taxation year was

(a) a student in full-time attendance at an educational institution in the Province of Quebec that is a university, college or other educational institution providing courses at a post-secondary school level,

(b) a student attending, or a teacher teaching at, an educational institution outside Canada that is a university, college or other educational institution providing courses at a post-secondary school level who had, in any previous year, ceased to be resident in the Province of Quebec in the course of or subsequent to moving to attend or to teach at, as the case may be, that institution,

(c) an individual who had, in any previous year, ceased to be resident in the Province of Quebec in the course of or subsequent to moving to carry on research or any similar work under a grant received by him to enable him to carry on that research or work, or

(d) an individual who had, in any previous year, ceased to be resident in the Province of Quebec and who was, in the taxation year, in receipt of remuneration in respect of an office or employment that was paid to him directly or indirectly by

(i) the Province of Quebec,

(ii) any corporation, commission or association the shares, capital or property of which were at least 90 per cent owned by the Province of Quebec, or a wholly-owned subsidiary corporation to such a corporation, commission or association, on condition that no person other than Her Majesty in right of the Province of Quebec had any right to the shares, capital or property of that corporation, commission, association or subsidiary or a right to acquire the shares, capital or property,

(iii) an educational institution, other than an educational institution of the Government of Canada, in the Province of Quebec that was

(A) a university, college or other educational institution providing courses at a post-secondary school level that received or was entitled to receive financial support from the Province of Quebec,

(B) a school operated by the Province of Quebec, or by a municipality thereof or by a public body thereof performing a function of government, or a school operated on behalf of that Province, municipality or public body, or

(C) a secondary school providing courses leading to a certificate or diploma that is a requirement for entrance to a college or university, or

(iv) an institution in the Province of Quebec, other than an institution of the Government of Canada, supplying health services or social services, or both, that received or was entitled to receive financial support from the Province of Quebec,

there shall be included, for the purposes of this Order, in computing his income earned in the taxation year in the Province of Quebec the aggregate of

(e) the amount of any remuneration in respect of an office or employment that was paid to him directly or indirectly by the Province of Quebec or any corporation, commission, association or institution referred to in paragraph (d), other than an institution of the Government of Canada, or by a wholly-owned corporation subsidiary to such corporation, commission or association, and that was received by the individual who did not reside in Canada in the year, except to the extent that such remuneration was attributable to the duties of an office or employment performed by him outside Canada, and that is

(i) is subject to an income or profits tax imposed by the government of a country other than Canada, or

(ii) is paid in connection with the selling of property, the negotiating of contracts or the rendering of services for his employer, or a foreign affiliate of his employer, or any other person with whom his employer does not deal at arm's length, in the ordinary course of a business carried on by his employer, that foreign affiliate or that other person,

(f) amounts that would be required by paragraph 56(1)(n) or (o) of the Act to be included in computing the individual's income for the year if

(i) the individual were resident in Canada throughout the year,

(ii) the references in subparagraph 56(1)(n)(i) and paragraph 56(1)(o) of the Act to "received by the taxpayer in the year" were read as references to "received by the taxpayer in the year from the Province of Quebec or any corporation, commission, association or institution referred to in paragraph 4(d) of the *Income Earned in Quebec Income Tax Remission Order, 1988*, other than an institution of the Government of Canada, or from a wholly-owned corporation subsidiary to such corporation, commission or association", and

(iii) the reference to "$500" in paragraph 56(1)(n) of the Act were read as a reference to "the proportion of $500 that the amount determined under subparagraph (i) is of the amount that would be so determined if the requirements of subparagraphs 4(f)(i) and (ii) of the *Income Earned in Quebec Income Tax Remission Order, 1988* were not taken into account",

(g) amounts that would be required by subsection 56(8) of the Act to be included in computing the individual's income for the year if the individual were resident in Canada throughout the year, and

(h) amounts that would be required by paragraph 56(1)(q) of the Act to be included in computing his income for the year if he were resident in Canada throughout the year, minus the amount that would be deductible in computing his income for the year by virtue of section 62 of the Act if

(i) that section were read without reference to paragraph (1)(a) thereof,

(j) that section were applicable in computing the taxable income of individuals who did not reside in Canada, and

(k) the amounts described in subparagraph (1)(f)(ii) thereof were the amounts described in paragraph (f).

Remission to Individuals Who Did Not Reside in a Province, the Northwest Territories or the Yukon Territory on the Last Day of the Taxation Year

5.(1) Subject to subsection (2), remission is hereby granted to any individual who did not reside in a province on the last day of a taxation year of the amount, if any, by which

(a) income tax, interest and penalties paid or payable under the Act by that individual in respect of that taxation year,

exceeds

(b) the tax, interest and penalties that would have been payable by that individual under the Act in respect of that taxation year if the individual had resided in the Province of Quebec on the last day of the taxation year.

(2) Subsection (1) is applicable to an individual who

(a) sojourned in the Province of Quebec for a period of, or periods the aggregate of which is, 183 days or more and was ordinarily resident outside Canada;

(b) was at any time in the year an agent-general, officer or servant of the Province of Quebec and was resident in that Province immediately prior to his appointment or employment by that Province;

(c) performed services at any time in the year under an international development assistance program prescribed under Part XXXIV of the Regulations and was at any time

(i) in the three month period preceding the day on which those services commenced, resident in the Province of Quebec, and

(ii) in the six month period preceding the day on which those services commenced, an officer or servant of

(A) the Province of Quebec,

(B) any corporation, commission or association the shares, capital or property of which were at least 90 per cent owned by the Province of Quebec, or a wholly-owned corporation subsidiary to such a corporation, commission or association, on condition that no person other than Her Majesty in right of the Province of Quebec had any right to those shares or that capital or property of such corporation, commission, association or subsidiary or a right to acquire those shares or that capital or property,

(C) an educational institution, other than an educational institution of the Government of Canada, in the Province of Quebec that was

(I) a university, college or other educational institution providing courses at a post-secondary school level that received or was entitled to receive financial support from the Province of Quebec,

(II) a school operated by the Province of Quebec, or by a municipality thereof or by a public body thereof performing a function of government, or a school operated on behalf of that Province, municipality or public body, or

(III) a secondary school providing courses leading to a certificate or diploma that is a requirement for entrance to a college or university, or

(D) an institution in the Province of Quebec, other than an institution of the Government of Canada, supplying health services or social services, or both, that received or was entitled to receive financial support from the Province of Quebec;

(d) was resident in Canada in any previous year and was, at any time in the year, the spouse of a person described in paragraph (b) or (c) living with that person; or

(e) was, at any time in the year, a child of a person described in paragraph (b) or (c) and was living with the person in a self-contained domestic establishment that the person, whether alone or jointly with one or more persons, maintained and in which the person lived and actually supported the child who, at that time, was

(i) wholly dependent for support on the person, or the person and the other person or persons, and

(ii) either under 18 years of age or so dependent by reason of mental or physical infirmity.

(3) Paragraph (2)(d) is not applicable where the spouse of an individual described in paragraph (2)(c) is also an individual described in paragraph (2)(c).

Remission to Individuals Who Resided in the Province of Quebec on the Last Day of a Taxation Year

6.(1) Remission is hereby granted to any individual who resided in the Province of Quebec on the last day of a taxation year of the amount, if any, by which

(a) the tax, interest and penalties payable under the Act by that individual in respect of that taxation year,

exceeds

(b) the tax, interest and penalties that would have been payable by that individual in respect of that taxation year if

(i) if subsections 2601(1) and (2) of the Regulations read as follows:

"2601. (1) Notwithstanding subsection (4) and section 2603, where an individual resided in a particular province on the last day of a taxation year and had no income for the year from a business with a permanent establishment in another province, his income earned in the taxation year in the province is his income for the year.

(2) Notwithstanding subsection (4) and section 2603, where an individual resided in a particular province on the last day of a taxation year and had income for the year from a business with a permanent establishment in any other province, his income earned in the taxation year in the province is the amount, if any, by which

(a) his income for the year

exceeds

(b) the aggregate of his income for the year from carrying on business earned in each other province, determined as hereinafter set forth in this Part.",

(ii) if the definition "business-income tax" in subsection 126(7) of the Act read as follows:

" "business-income tax" paid by a taxpayer for a taxation year in respect of businesses carried on by the taxpayer in a country other than Canada (in this definition referred to as the "business country") means such portion of 55% of any income or profits tax paid by the taxpayer for the year to the government of any country other than Canada or to the government of a state, province or other political subdivision of any such country as can reasonably be regarded as tax in respect of the income of the taxpayer from any business carried on by the taxpayer in the business country, but does not include a tax, or the portion of a tax, that can reasonably be regarded as relating to an amount that

(a) any other person or partnership has received or is entitled to receive from that government, or

(b) was deductible under subparagraph 110(1)(f)(i) in computing the taxpayer's taxable income for the year;", and

(iii) if the definition "tax for the year otherwise payable under this Part" in subsection 126(7) of the Act read as follows:

" "tax for the year otherwise payable under this Part" means the the amount determined by the formula

$$A - B$$

where

A is the tax payable under this Part for the year after taking into account the requirements of subparagraph 6(1)(b)(i) of the *Income Earned in Quebec Income Tax Remission Order, 1988*, but before making any deduction under any of sections 121, 122.3, 126.1, 127 and 127.2 to 127.4 and this section, and

B is the amount, if any, deemed by subsection 120(2) to have been paid on account of tax payable under this Part for the year after taking into account the requirements of subparagraph 6(1)(b)(i) of the *Income Earned in Quebec Income Tax Remission Order, 1988*;".

(2) In subsection (1), a reference to the last day of a taxation year shall, in the case of an individual who resided in the Province of Quebec at any time in the year and ceased to reside in Canada before the end of the year, be deemed to be a reference to the last day in the year on which the individual resided in Canada.

Deductions and Remittances

7. Notwithstanding paragraph 102(1)(a), subsection 102(2), paragraph 103(1)(m) and subparagraphs 103(4)(a)(xiii), (b)(xiii) and (c)(xiii) of the Regulations, the amount to be deducted or withheld by an employer and remitted to the Receiver General pursuant to Part I of the Regulations shall, in the case of

(a) an individual referred to in section 4 in respect of the remuneration referred to in paragraph 4(e), and

(b) an individual referred to in paragraph 5(2)(b), (c), (d) or (e) in respect of remuneration received from the Province of Quebec or from any corporation, commission, association or institution referred to in paragraph 5(2)(c), other than an institution of the Government of Canada, or from a wholly-owned corporation subsidiary to such corporation, commission or association,

be determined as if the employee reported for work at an establishment of the employer in Quebec.

7.1 Every individual to whom an amount was remitted under section 5 for a taxation year shall reimburse that amount, plus interest thereon to the day of payment, to Her Majesty in right of Canada to the extent of the amount of tax payable under the *Taxation Act*, R.S.Q., c. I-3, for that year that the individual, as a result of an objection served on the Minister of Revenue of the Province of Quebec, a claim filed in any court or a complaint made to any tribunal, was declared not to be liable to pay on the ground that the individual was not subject to the tax levied under that Act because of the individual's place of residence.

8.(1) Sections 3 to 6 apply to the 1983 to 1996 taxation years.

(2) Section 7 is applicable in respect of the 1989 and subsequent taxation years.

Explanatory Note [not part of the Order]: This Order

(a) defines the expression "income earned in the year in Quebec" for the purposes of the *Income Tax Act*;

(b) remits to certain individuals who are deemed to be resident in Canada, to non-residents who realized capital gains in Quebec and to Quebec residents who earned business income from a foreign source, the additional tax, interest and penalty arising both from the imposition of the 43 per cent federal surtax and from the loss of the federal tax abatement in respect of income earned in Quebec; and

(c) applies in respect of the 1983 to 1988 taxation years in the case of sections 3 to 6 and section 7 applies in respect of the 1989 and subsequent taxation years.

Explanatory Note to Amending Order (P.C. 1991-1661): This Order extends the application of the *Income Earned in Quebec Income Tax Remission Order, 1988* with respect to the 1989 to 1991 taxation years in the case of sections 3 to 6 of that Order. The federal surtax and the federal tax abatement in respect of income earned in Quebec are respectively 52% for the 1990 and subsequent taxation years (49.5% for the 1989 taxation year) and 16.5%.

Explanatory Note to Amending Order (P.C. 1992-2593): This Order extends the application of the *Income Earned in Quebec Income Tax Remission Order, 1988* with respect to the 1992 taxation year in the case of sections 3 to 6 of that Order. The federal surtax and the federal tax abatement in respect of income earned in Quebec are respectively 52% and 16.5%.

Explanatory Note to Amending Order (P.C. 1994-567): This amendment extends the application of sections 3 to 6 of the Order to the 1993 taxation year. The federal surtax and the federal tax abatement in respect of income earned in Quebec are 52% and 16.5%, respectively.

Explanatory Note to Amending Order (P.C. 1998-396): This Order extends, with the necessary changes, the application of the *Income Earned in Quebec Income Tax Remission Order, 1988* with respect to the 1994, 1995 and 1996 taxation years in the case of sections 3 to 6 of that Order. The federal surtax and the federal tax abatement in respect of income earned in Quebec are respectively 52% and 16.5%.

Notes: This remission order is designed to prevent double tax on certain non-residents. It will be extended to years after 1996. See VIEWS doc 2009-0330381C6.

INCOME TAX ON PENSIONS PAID TO NON-RESIDENTS REMISSION ORDER

P.C. 1994-1780, November 16, 1994 (SI/94-129)

[Applies to tax payable under ITA 217(c) for 1991 and 1992 — ed.]

INCOME TAX PAID BY INVESTORS, OTHER THAN PROMOTERS REMISSION ORDER

P.C. 1996-1274, August 7, 1996 (SI/96-80)

His Excellency the Governor General in Council, considering that is in the public interest to do so, on the recommendation of the Minister of National Revenue, pursuant to subsection 23(2) of the *Financial Administration Act*, hereby remits to each taxpayer, other than a promoter, who has delivered or delivers to the Minister a timely and duly executed agreement letter (referred to in the details of the settlement project regarding general partnerships used as SR&ED tax shelters issued by the Minister on June 30, 1995) accepted by the Minister, amounts payable under the *Income Tax Act* by the taxpayer equal to

(1) the difference between

(a) 50% of the product of each payment made before executing the agreement on account of the tax liability resulting from adjustments made by the Minister to the taxpayer's claim in respect of the tax shelter and the prescribed rate of interest for income tax refunds, for the period from the date of the payment to the date of the assessment of the tax liability made as a result of the agreement, compounded daily, and

(b) refund interest in respect of any such payment,

(2) 50% of the product of that difference and that rate, for the period from the said date of assessment to the date this Order is implemented, so compounded, and

(3) amounts that would not be payable if there were no such refund interest or if this Order were not made.

Explanatory Note [not part of the Order]: This Order remits amounts of income tax paid by taxpayers who made payments on account of their tax assessments before executing agreement letters (referred to in the details of the settlement project regarding general partnerships used as SR&ED tax shelters issued by Revenue Canada on June 30, 1995), in order that those taxpayers be on even terms with taxpayers who had not made such payments.

Notes: Documents obtained under the *Access to Information Act* reveal that this remission order deals with a group of approximately 8,000 taxpayers in Quebec who invested in scientific research partnership tax shelters from 1989-94 and claimed an investment tax credit (ITC) and a partnership loss. Most of these investors disposed of their partnership interest in the year following the year of purchase. Revenue Canada concluded that the investors were not entitled to any ITC or partnership loss.

Under the settlement project, Revenue Canada (and Revenu Québec) allowed the investors an income loss on the disposal of the partnership interest, and, for an investor who was not a promoter, will cancel the interest owing on the unpaid tax. This proposal applied also to taxpayers who did not file an objection or who had paid their tax debt in full. The settlement proposal was sent to the investors' representatives (over 100 in total) on June 30, 1995, and was to be accepted by September 30, 1995, although it appears that it was still open for acceptance much later.

The total number of taxpayers involved in the settlement is 7,556. Some $103 million of federal tax and interest was at stake, of which about $45.9 million would be eliminated if all taxpayers accept the settlement.

The remission order gives effect to the settlement project, to the extent Revenue Canada was not otherwise authorized under the *Income Tax Act* to implement the settlement. The remission order was expected to apply to 3,282 taxpayers, and would remit a total of approximately $900,000.

For more on the history of this dispute see *Moledina*, 2007 TCC 354; *St-Laurent [Simard]*, 2009 FCA 379.

INCOME TAX REMISSION ORDER (CANADA PENSION PLAN)

P.C. 1995-201, February 22, 1995 (SI/95-21)

His Excellency the Governor General in Council, considering that the collection of the tax is unjust, on the recommendation of the Minister of National Revenue, pursuant to subsection 23(2) of the *Financial Administration Act*, is pleased hereby to remit the net total of the taxes payable under Parts I and I.1 of the *Income Tax Act* for the 1987 to 1995 taxation years that, without regard to sections 122.2 and 122.4 to 122.64 thereof as they read at any time, would not be payable by a taxpayer if the part of any amount received by the taxpayer after 1987 and before 1996 by reason of section 63.1 of the *Canada Pension Plan* that was payable for a month in a year preceding the year in which it was received had been received in that preceding year, and all relevant penalties and interest.

INCOME TAX REMISSION ORDER (YUKON TERRITORY LANDS)

ORDER RESPECTING THE REMISSION OF INCOME TAX IN RELATION TO CERTAIN LANDS IN THE YUKON TERRITORY

P.C. 1995-197, February 7, 1995 (SI/95-18)

1. **Short Title** — This Order may be cited as the *Income Tax Remission Order (Yukon Territory Lands)*.

2. **Interpretation** — In this Order,

"**Act**" means the *Yukon First Nations Self-Government Act*;

"**reserve**" has the same meaning as in subsection 2(1) of the *Indian Act*.

3. **Remission** — Remission is hereby granted of amounts payable under the *Income Tax Act* that would not be payable if the lands in the Yukon Territory

(a) that are reserved or set aside, as at the day on which this Order comes into force, by notation in the property records of the Department of Indian Affairs and Northern Development, for the use of its Indian and Inuit Affairs Program, were reserves for the period beginning after 1984 and ending on the expiration of the third calendar year after the calendar year in which the Act comes into force;

(b) that were so notated for a period beginning after 1984 and ending before the day on which this Order comes into force, had been a reserve throughout each calendar year of that period; and

(c) that are so notated for a period beginning after the day on which this Order comes into force and ending before the expiration of the third calendar year after the calendar year in which the Act comes into force, were a reserve throughout each calendar year of that period.

INDIAN INCOME TAX REMISSION ORDER [MARCH 1993]

ORDER RESPECTING THE REMISSION OF INCOME TAX PAID OR PAYABLE ON INCOME FROM EMPLOYERS RESIDING ON RESERVES AND INDIAN SETTLEMENTS AND ON CERTAIN UNEMPLOYMENT INSURANCE BENEFITS RECEIVED BY INDIANS

P.C. 1993-523, March 16, 1993 (SI/93-44), as amended by P.C. 1994-799, May 12, 1994 (SI/94-69)

[Applies to taxation years 1985-93 to give retroactive effect to the *Williams* decision; see Notes to ITA 81(1)(a) — ed.]

INDIAN INCOME TAX REMISSION ORDER [AUGUST 1993]

P.C. 1993-1649, August 4, 1993 (SI/93-166)

[Extends the 1985-91 relief given by the *Indian Income Tax Remission Order* to unemployment insurance benefits exempt under the *Cree-Naskapi (of Quebec) Act* and the *Sechelt Indian Band Self-Government Act* — ed.]

INDIAN SETTLEMENTS REMISSION ORDER (2000)

P.C. 2000-1112, July 27, 2000 (SI/2000-69)

1. **Interpretation** — The following definitions apply in this Order.

   "Indian Settlement" means a settlement named in column 1 of Schedule 1 and described in column 2 of that Schedule.

   "reserve" has the same meaning as in subsection 2(1) of the *Indian Act*.

2. **Application** — This Order applies in respect of an Indian Settlement until all or part of the lands constituting that Indian Settlement are set apart as a reserve by an order of the Governor in Council.

Part 1 — Income Tax

3. **Interpretation** — In this Part,

   (a) **"tax"** means a tax imposed under Part I, I.1 or I.2 of the *Income Tax Act*; and

   (b) all other words and expressions not otherwise defined in section 1 have the same meaning as in the *Income Tax Act*.

4. **Remission of Income Tax** — Remission is hereby granted to a taxpayer whose income is situated on an Indian Settlement, in respect of each taxation year or fiscal period beginning during or after the year set out in column 2 of Schedule 2 in respect of that Indian Settlement, of any amount by which

   (a) the taxes, interest and penalties paid or payable by the taxpayer for the taxation year or fiscal period

exceed

   (b) the taxes, interest and penalties that would have been payable by the taxpayer for the taxation year or fiscal period if the Indian Settlement had been a reserve throughout that taxation year or fiscal period.

Part 2 — Goods and Services Tax

5. **Interpretation** — In this Part,

   (a) **"tax"** means the goods and services tax imposed under Division II of Part IX of the *Excise Tax Act*; and

   (b) all other words and expressions not otherwise defined in section 1 have the same meaning as in Part IX of the *Excise Tax Act*.

6. **Remission of the Goods and Services Tax** — Subject to sections 7 and 8, remission is hereby granted to a recipient of a taxable supply made on or delivered to an Indian Settlement on or after the date set out in column 3 or 4 of an item of Schedule 2, as the case may be, of tax paid or payable by that person in an amount equal to any amount by which

   (a) the tax paid or payable by the recipient

exceeds

   (b) the tax that would have been payable by the recipient if the Indian Settlement had been a reserve.

Conditions

7. Remission under section 6 is granted to an individual if

   (a) the tax paid or payable has not otherwise been rebated, credited, refunded or remitted under Part IX of the *Excise Tax Act* or the *Financial Administration Act*; and

   (b) a claim for the remission is made to the Minister of National Revenue within two years after the day on which the tax was paid or became payable.

8. Remission under section 6 is granted to a person other than an individual if

   (a) the tax paid or payable has not otherwise been rebated, credited, refunded or remitted under Part IX of the *Excise Tax Act* or the *Financial Administration Act*;

   (b) in respect of tax paid on or after the date set out in column 4 of an item of Schedule 2 but before the date set out in column 3 of that item, a claim for the remission is made to the Minister of National Revenue within two years after the latter date; and

(c) in respect of tax paid on or after the date set out in column 3 of an item of Schedule 2, a claim for the remission is made to the Minister of National Revenue within two years after the date on which the tax was paid.

Schedule 1

[Specifies precise survey locations for Alexander Settlement, Fox Creek Settlement, Fort Assiniboine Settlement, Loon River Settlement — ed.]

Schedule 2

(Section 4, 6 and 8)

Item	Column 1 Indian Settlement	Column 2 Taxation Year	Column 3 Date for Remission of Goods and Services Tax for Individuals	Column 4 Date for Remission of Goods and Services Tax for Persons other than Individuals
1.	Alexander Settlement	1998	July 27, 2000	January 1, 1998
2.	Fox Creek Settlement	1998	July 27, 2000	January 1, 1998
3.	Fort Assiniboine Settlement	1998	July 27, 2000	January 1, 1998
4.	Loon River Settlement	1994	July 27, 2000	January 1, 1994
5.	Loon Prairie Settlement	1994	July 27, 2000	January 1, 1994

Explanatory Note [not part of the Order]: The purpose of this Order is to provide the benefits of relief from income tax and the goods and services tax to Indians, Indian Bands and qualifying band corporations on specified Indian Settlements that would be accorded if those settlements were reserves. These Indian Settlements are those for which a public commitment has been made by the Government of Canada to grant reserve status under the *Indian Act*.

INDIANS AND BANDS ON CERTAIN INDIAN SETTLEMENTS REMISSION ORDER

ORDER RESPECTING THE REMISSION OF CERTAIN INCOME TAXES PAYABLE BY INDIANS AND OF THE GOODS AND SERVICES TAX PAYABLE BY INDIANS OR BY BANDS OR DESIGNATED CORPORATIONS ON CERTAIN INDIAN SETTLEMENTS

P.C. 1992-1052, June 3, 1992 (SI/92-102), as amended by P.C. 1994-2096, December 28, 1994 (SI/94-145)

1. **Short Title** — This Order may be cited as the *Indians and Bands on certain Indian Settlements Remission Order*.

2. **Interpretation** — In this Order,

"**band**" has the same meaning as in subsection 2(1) of the *Indian Act*;

"**designated corporation**" means the Ouje-Bougoumou Development Corporation or the Ouje-Bougoumou Eenuch Association;

"**Indian**" has the same meaning as in subsection 2(1) of the *Indian Act*;

"**Indian settlement**" means an area that is named and described in the schedule but does not include an area that is

(a) a reserve within the meaning of the *Indian Act*, or

(b) Category IA land within the meaning of the *Cree-Naskapi (of Quebec) Act*;

"**reserve**" has the same meaning as in subsection 2(1) of the *Indian Act*.

Part I — Income Taxes

3. **Interpretation** — (1) For the purposes of this Part,

"**Act**" means the *Income Tax Act*;

"**tax**" means tax under Parts I, I.1 and I.2 of the Act.

(2) All other words and expressions used in this part have the same meaning as in the Act.

4. **Remission of Income Tax** — Remission is hereby granted to a taxpayer who is an Indian in respect of each taxation year after 1992 of the amount, if any, by which the taxes, interest and penalties payable by the taxpayer for the taxation year under the Act exceed the taxes, interest and penalties that would have been payable by the taxpayer for the year under the Act if the Indian settlements were reserves throughout the year.

Part II — Goods and Services Tax

5. **Interpretation** — (1) For the purposes of this Part,

"**Act**" means the *Excise Tax Act;*

"**tax**" means the goods and services tax imposed under Division II of Part IX of the Act.

(2) All other words and expressions used in this Part have the same meaning as in Part IX of the Act.

6. **Remission of the Goods and Services Tax** — Subject to section 8, remission of the tax paid or payable on or after the day on which this Order comes into force is hereby granted to an individual who is an Indian and who is the recipient of a taxable supply, in an amount equal to the amount, if any, by which

(a) the tax paid or payable by the individual under the Act

exceeds

(b) the tax that would have been payable by the individual if the Indian settlements were reserves.

7. Subject to section 8, remission of the tax paid or payable on or after January 1, 1991 is hereby granted to a band or a designated corporation that is the recipient of a taxable supply, in an amount equal to the amount, if any, by which

(a) the tax paid or payable by the band or designated corporation under the Act

exceeds

(b) the tax that would have been payable by the band or designated corporation if the Indian settlements were reserves.

8. **Condition** — Remission under sections 6 and 7 in respect of tax paid is granted on condition that an application in writing for the remission be submitted to the Minister of National Revenue within four years after the day on which the tax was paid.

Schedule — Indian Settlements

(Section 2)

1. — Ouje-Bougoumou, Quebec

The settlement is situated on the north shore of Lake Opémisca, 32 km northwest of Chibougamau, Quebec, in Cuvier Township at 49°55' latitude and 74°49' longitude and has an area of 100 km².

2. — Kanesatake (Oka), Quebec

The settlement is situated 25 km northwest of Montreal, on the north side of Des Deux Montagnes Lake, and, for the purposes of this Order, comprises the Village of Oka and the areas in the western portion of the Parish of Oka, known as Côte Sainte-Philomène, Côte Saint-Jean, Côte Saint-Ambroise and Côte Sainte-Germaine-Côte-Sud.

3. — Kee-Way-Win Settlement, Ontario

The settlement is situated on the south side of Sandy Lake, in the District of Kenora, Patricia Portion, at 53°4' latitude and 92°45' longitude, and has an area of approximately 19,030 hectares.

4. — Savant Lake Settlement, Ontario

The settlement is situated on the north side of Kasheweogama Lake in the Township of McCubbin, District of Thunder Bay, at 50°4' latitude and 90°43' longitude, and has an area of approximately 5,890 hectares.

5. — Long Dog Lake Settlement, Ontario

The settlement is situated on the south side of Long Dog Lake, District of Kenora, Patricia Portion, at 52°28' latitude and 90°43' longitude, and has an area of 5,305 hectares.

6. — MacDowell Lake Settlement, Ontario

The settlement is situated at the southwest end of MacDowell Lake, District of Kenora, Patricia Portion, at 52°11' latitude and 92°45' longitude, and has an area of approximately 4,455 hectares.

7. — Slate Falls Settlement, Ontario

The settlement is situated on the northeast end of North Bamaji Lake, District of Kenora, Patricia Portion, at 51°11' latitude and 91°35' longitude, and has an area of approximately 6,870 hectares.

8. — Aroland Settlement, Ontario

The settlement is situated on both the north and south sides of King's Highway 643 at Aroland rural community in the Township of Danford, District of Thunder Bay, at 50°14' latitude and 86°59' longitude, extends northwards west and north of Esnagami Lake and has an area of approximately 18,130 hectares.

9. — Grandmother's Point Settlement, Ontario

The settlement is situated at the southwest end of Attawapiskat Lake, in the District of Kenora, Patricia Portion, at 52°14' latitude and 87°53' longitude, and has an area of approximately 855 hectares.

10. — Cadotte Lake Settlement, Alberta

The settlement is situated 40 miles east of Peace River, Alberta at Cadotte Lake, on highway 686, comprises portions of Townships 86 and 87, within ranges 15, 16 and 17, and also land bordering on Marten Lake in Townships 86 and 87 within ranges 13 and 14, west of the 5th meridian (but excluding all mines and minerals and the beds and shores of the Cadotte and Otter Rivers), and has an area of approximately 14,245 hectares.

11. — Fort MacKay, Alberta

The settlement is situated 105 km northwest of Fort McMurray, and comprises the areas of Namur Lake, Namur River and portions of the Hamlet of Fort MacKay. The Hamlet of Fort MacKay is situated on the west side of the Athabaska River and the Fort MacKay Band occupies an area that includes Lots 1 to 7 on Plan 9022250 (but excluding all mines and minerals), as well as a small portion of the East-West Government Road allowance. The Indian settlement has an area of approximately 86.6 hectares.

12. — Little Buffalo Settlement, Alberta

The settlement is situated in north central Alberta and surrounding Lubicon Lake, and has an area of approximately 24,505 hectares.

Notes: See also the *Indians and the War Lake First Nation Band on the Ilford Indian Settlement Remission Order*.

INDIANS AND BANDS ON CERTAIN INDIAN SETTLEMENTS REMISSION ORDER (1997)

P.C. 1997-1529, October 23, 1997 (SI/97-127)

1. **Interpretation** — The definitions in this section apply in this Order.

"**band**" has the same meaning as in subsection 2(1) of the *Indian Act*.

"**Indian**" has the same meaning as in subsection 2(1) of the *Indian Act*.

"**Indian Settlement**" means an area that is named and described in column 2 of the schedule.

"**reserve**" has the same meaning as in subsection 2(1) of the *Indian Act*.

2. **Application** — This Order applies to any Indian Settlement until the time when the area of that Indian Settlement is set aside, in whole or in part, as a reserve by Order of the Governor in Council.

Part 1 — Income Tax

3. **Interpretation** — (1) For the purposes of this Part, "tax" means tax imposed under Parts I, I.1 and I.2 of the *Income Tax Act*.

(2) Subject to section 1, all other words and expressions used in this Part have the same meaning as in the *Income Tax Act*.

4. **Remission of Income Tax** — Remission is hereby granted to a taxpayer who is an Indian whose income is situated on an Indian Settlement, in respect of the taxation year set out in column 3 of the schedule in relation to that Indian Settlement and each taxation year after that year, of the amount, if any, by which

(a) the taxes, interest and penalties paid or payable by the taxpayer for the taxation year under the *Income Tax Act*

exceed

(b) the taxes, interest and penalties that would have been payable by the taxpayer for the taxation year under that Act if the Indian Settlement were a reserve throughout the year.

Part 2 — Goods and Services Tax

5. (1) **Interpretation** — (1) For the purposes of this Part, "tax" means the goods and services tax imposed under Division II of Part IX of the *Excise Tax Act*.

(2) Subject to section 1, all other words and expressions used in this Part have the same meaning as in Part IX of the *Excise Tax Act*.

Remission of the Goods and Services Tax

6. Subject to section 8, remission of the tax paid or payable is hereby granted to an individual who is an Indian who resides on an Indian Settlement and who is the recipient of a taxable supply made on or after the date for remission of the tax set out in column 4 of the schedule, in an amount equal to the amount, if any, by which

(a) the tax paid or payable by the individual

exceeds

(b) the tax that would have been payable by the individual if the Indian Settlement were a reserve.

7. Subject to section 9, remission of the tax paid or payable is hereby granted to a band that is established on an Indian Settlement and is the recipient of a taxable supply made on or after the date for remission of the tax set out in column 5 of the schedule, in an amount equal to the amount, if any, by which

(a) the tax paid or payable by the band

exceeds

(b) the tax that would have been payable by the band if the Indian Settlement were a reserve.

8. Remission under section 6 in respect of tax paid is granted on the condition that an application in writing for the remission be submitted to the Minister of National Revenue within two years after the date on which the tax was paid.

9. Remission under section 7 in respect of tax paid is granted on the condition that an application in writing for the remission be submitted to the Minister of National Revenue

(a) for tax paid on or after the date for remission of the tax set out in column 5 of the schedule but before the date for remission of the tax set out in column 4, within two years after the latter date; and

(b) for tax paid on or after the date for remission of the tax set out in column 4 of the schedule, within two years after the date on which the tax was paid.

Schedule

(Sections 1, 4, 6, 7 and 9)

Item	Column 1 Band	Column 2 Indian Settlement and Legal Description of Settlement Lands	Column 3 Taxation Year	Column 4 Date for Remission of GST for Individual Indians	Column 5 Date for Remission of GST for Bands
1.	Nibinamik First Nation	Summer Beaver, Ontario: District of Nakina, Ontario (52 degrees 45 minutes north latitude, 88 degrees 35 minutes west longitude) having an area of approximately 3.5 square miles. (Excluded are locations SN 160 and CL 6298, the sites of the old and new schools.)	1995	October 23, 1997	January 1, 1995
2.	Long Point First Nation	Winneway, Quebec: North-half portion of Lots 50 and 51 Range 8, the whole of Lot 46-5 Range 9 and South-east corner of Lot 47 Range 9, 51770 CLSR, and 59890 CLSR, Township of Devlin, having an area of approximately 47 hectares.	1996	October 23, 1997	January 1, 1996
3.	God's River First Nation	God's River, Manitoba: Parcel 5, Plan 4955 NLTO (situated in projected Township 67, Range 23, East of the principal meridian) having an area of approximately 2.83 acres	1993	October 23, 1997	January 1, 1993

Explanatory Note [not part of the Order]: The purpose of this Order is to extend the benefits of relief from income tax and the goods and services tax (GST) to Indians, as though the specified Indian settlements were reserves. This Order applies to settlements for which a public commitment has been made by the Government of Canada to grant reserve status under the Indian Act. The Department of Indian and Northern Affairs has advised the Department of National Revenue of the settlements that have identified boundaries that should be included in this Order.

With respect to income tax, this Order places Indian individuals in the tax position that they would have been in had the Indian settlements been granted reserve status. With respect to the GST, the same relief that has been afforded to Indian individuals and Indian bands for on-reserve and certain off-reserve acquisitions of taxable supplies has also been extended to similar acquisitions made by Indian individuals or bands on or outside of the specified Indian settlements.

INDIANS AND THE WAR LAKE FIRST NATION BAND ON THE ILFORD INDIAN SETTLEMENT REMISSION ORDER

Order Respecting the Remission of Certain Income Taxes Paid or Payable by Indians and the Goods and Services Tax Paid or Payable by Indians or by the War Lake First Nation Band on the Ilford Indian Settlement

P.C. 1994-801, May 12, 1994 (SI/94-71)

1. **Short Title** — This Order may be cited as the *Indians and the War Lake First Nation Band on the Ilford Indian Settlement Remission Order*.

2. **Interpretation** — In this Order,

"**band**" has the same meaning as in subsection 2(1) of the *Indian Act*;

"**Ilford Indian Settlement**" means the settlement that is situated near Ilford in the Province of Manitoba, consisting of parcels of land lettered "A" and "B", which parcels are shown on a plan of survey of part of unsurveyed township 81 in Range 12, east of the principal meridian and contain 2.89 hectares and 3.89 hectares, respectively, and that is not a reserve;

"**Indian**" has the same meaning as in subsection 2(1) of the *Indian Act*;

"**reserve**" has the same meaning as in subsection 2(1) of the *Indian Act*.

Part I — Income Tax

3. **Interpretation** — (1) For the purposes of this Part, "tax" means tax under Parts I, I.1 and I.2 of the *Income Tax Act*.

(2) Subject to section 2, all other words and expressions used in this Part have the same meaning as in the *Income Tax Act*.

4. **Remission of Income Tax** — Remission is hereby granted to a taxpayer who is an Indian in respect of the 1992 taxation year and each taxation year following that year of the amount, if any, by which the taxes, interest and penalties paid or payable by the taxpayer for the taxation year under the *Income Tax Act* exceed the taxes, interest and penalties that would have been payable by the taxpayer for the year under the Act if the Ilford Indian Settlement were a reserve throughout the year.

Part II — Goods and Services Tax

5. **Interpretation** — (1) For the purposes of this Part, "tax" means the goods and services tax imposed under Division II of Part IX of the *Excise Tax Act*.

(2) Subject to section 2, all other words and expressions used in this Part have the same meaning as in Part IX of the *Excise Tax Act*.

6. **Remission of the Goods and Services Tax** — Subject to section 8, remission is hereby granted to an individual who is an Indian and who is the recipient of a taxable supply made on or after the day on which this Order comes into force of the tax paid or payable, in an amount equal to the amount, if any, by which

(a) the tax paid or payable by the individual

exceeds

(b) the tax that would have been payable by the individual if the Ilford Indian Settlement were a reserve.

7. Subject to section 8, remission is hereby granted to the War Lake First Nation Band of the tax paid or payable, where the band is the recipient of a taxable supply made on or after January 1, 1992, in an amount equal to the amount, if any, by which

(a) the tax paid or payable by the band

exceeds

(b) the tax that would have been payable by the band if the Ilford Indian Settlement were a reserve.

8. Condition — Remission under sections 6 and 7 in respect of tax paid is granted on condition that an application in writing for the remission be submitted to the Minister of National Revenue within four years after the day on which the tax was paid.

Explanatory Note [not part of the Order]: The purpose of this Order is to extend the benefits of relief from income tax and the goods and services tax (GST) to Indians present at the Ilford Indian Settlement, as though this settlement were a reserve. On July 6, 1990, approval in principle to establish a reserve for the War Lake Band was given by the Department of Indian Affairs and Northern Development. The Province of Manitoba subsequently agreed to relinquish lands for the purpose of creating a reserve. On October 6, 1992, the province agreed to the boundaries of the proposed reserve and gave permission to survey the lands in question. The agreement to transfer the lands was signed on December 7, 1992 by all of the parties concerned.

With respect to income tax, this Order places Indians on the Ilford Settlement in the same tax position that they would have been in had the Ilford Indian Settlement been granted reserve status. With respect to the GST, the same relief that applies to Indian individuals and bands for on-reserve and certain off-reserve acquisitions of taxable supplies has also been extended to similar acquisitions made by Indians and the War Lake First Nation Band on the Ilford Indian Settlement.

LABRADOR INNU SETTLEMENTS REMISSION ORDER, 2003

P.C. 2003-990, June 18, 2003 (SI/2003-134), as amended by P.C. 2005-1654, September 26, 2005 (SI/2005-88); P.C. 2007-1640, October 25, 2007 (SI/2007-100).

1. Interpretation — The following definitions apply in this Order.

"**band**" has the same meaning as in subsection 2(1) of the *Indian Act*.

"**Indian**" has the same meaning as in subsection 2(1) of the *Indian Act*.

"**Innu**" means a person described in section 3 of the *Sheshatshiu Innu First Nation Band Order* or section 3 of the *Mushuau Innu First Nation Band Order*.

"**Innu First Nations**" means those bodies described in section 2 of the *Sheshatshiu Innu First Nation Band Order* and section 2 of the *Mushuau Innu First Nation Band Order*.

"**Innu Settlement**" means a settlement named, and constituting the corresponding lands described, in the schedule.

"**reserve**" has the same meaning as in subsection 2(1) of the *Indian Act*.

2. Application — This Order applies in respect of an Innu Settlement until lands constituting that Innu Settlement are set apart as a reserve by an order of the Governor in Council.

Part 1 — Income Tax

3. Interpretation — In this Part,

(a) "**tax**" means a tax imposed under Part I or I.2 of the *Income Tax Act*; and

(b) all other words and expressions not otherwise defined in section 1 have the same meaning as in the *Income Tax Act*.

4. Remission of Income Tax — Remission is hereby granted to an Innu, or an Innu First Nation, with income situated on an Innu Settlement, in respect of the taxation year 2002 or any fiscal period beginning during the calendar year 2002, of the amount, if any, by which

(a) the taxes, interest and penalties paid or payable by the Innu or Innu First Nation, as the case may be, for that taxation year or fiscal period

exceed

(b) the taxes, interest and penalties that would have been payable by that Innu or Innu First Nation for that taxation year or fiscal period if, throughout that year or fiscal period

(i) the Innu Settlement had been a reserve,

(ii) in the case of an Innu, that Innu had been an Indian, and

(iii) in the case of an Innu First Nation, that Innu First Nation had been a band.

5. Remission is hereby granted to an Indian, or a band, with income situated on an Innu Settlement, in respect of each taxation year or fiscal period beginning during or after the calendar year 2002 of the amount, if any, by which

(a) the taxes, interest and penalties paid or payable by the Indian or band, as the case may be, for the taxation year or fiscal period

exceed

(b) the taxes, interest and penalties that would have been payable by that Indian or band for the taxation year or fiscal period if, throughout that taxation year or fiscal period the Innu Settlement had been a reserve.

Part 2 — Goods and Services Tax

6. Interpretation — In this Part,

(a) "**tax**" means the goods and services tax imposed under subsection 165(1) of the *Excise Tax Act*; and

(b) all other words and expressions not otherwise defined in section 1 have the same meaning as in Part IX of the *Excise Tax Act*.

7. Remission of the Goods and Services Tax — Subject to section 9, remission is hereby granted to an Innu First Nation that is the recipient of a taxable supply made on or delivered to an Innu Settlement on or after January 1, 2002 and on or before November 20, 2002 of the amount, if any, by which

(a) the tax paid or payable by the recipient

exceeds

(b) the tax that would have been payable by the recipient if, at the time when the supply was made or delivered,

(i) the Innu Settlement had been a reserve, and

(ii) the Innu First Nation had been a band.

8. Subject to section 9, remission is hereby granted to an Indian or a band that is the recipient of a taxable supply made on or delivered to an Innu Settlement on or after November 21, 2002 in the case of an Indian, and on or after January 1, 2002 in the case of a band, of the amount, if any, by which

(a) the tax paid or payable by the recipient

exceeds

(b) the tax that would have been payable by the recipient if, at the time when the supply was made or delivered, the Innu Settlement had been a reserve.

9. **Conditions** — Remission granted under sections 7 and 8 is on condition that

(a) the tax paid or payable has not otherwise been rebated, credited, refunded or remitted under Part IX of the *Excise Tax Act* or under the *Financial Administration Act*; and

(b) in respect of tax paid, a written claim for the remission is made to the Minister of National Revenue within two years after the later of

(i) the day on which the tax was paid, and

(ii) the day on which this Order comes into force.

Part 3 — Tax in a Participating Province

10. **Interpretation** — In this Part,

(a) "**tax**" means the tax in a participating province imposed under subsection 165(2) of the *Excise Tax Act*; and

(b) all other words and expressions not otherwise defined in section 1 have the same meaning as in Part IX of the *Excise Tax Act*.

11. **Remission of the Tax in a Participating Province** — Subject to section 12, remission is hereby granted to an Indian or a band that is the recipient of a taxable supply made on or delivered to the Natuashish Settlement named in the schedule during the period beginning on January 1, 2003 and ending on December 10, 2003 of the amount, if any, by which

(a) the tax paid or payable by the recipient

exceeds

(b) the tax that would have been payable by the recipient if, at the time when the supply was made or delivered, the Natuashish Settlement had been a reserve.

11.1 Subject to section 12, remission is hereby granted to an Indian or a band that is the recipient of a taxable supply made on or delivered to the Sheshatshiu Settlement described in the schedule during the period beginning on January 1, 2006 and ending on November 22, 2006 of the amount, if any, by which

(a) the tax paid or payable by the recipient

exceeds

(b) the tax that would have been payable by the recipient if, at the time when the supply was made or delivered, the Sheshatshiu Settlement had been a reserve.

12. **Conditions** — The remission granted under section 11 or 11.1 is on condition that

(a) the tax paid or payable has not otherwise been rebated, credited, refunded or remitted under Part IX of the *Excise Tax Act* or under the *Financial Administration Act*; and

(b) in respect of tax paid, a written claim for the remission is made to the Minister of National Revenue within two years after the later of

(i) the day on which the tax was paid, and

(ii) the day on which this Part comes into force.

Schedule *(Sections 1, 11 and 11.1)*

Sheshatshiu Settlement

All that parcel of land situated and being in the Electoral District of Lake Melville in the Province of Newfoundland and Labrador as shown on a plan of survey certified by Neil E. Parrott, CLS, NLS, dated March 31, 2000, a copy of which is recorded in the Atlantic Office of Natural Resources Canada, Legal Surveys Division as Plan No. 2001-002 RSAtl.; said parcel being more precisely described as follows:

[Specifics omitted since the 35th edition — ed.]

Natuashish Settlement

Parcel 1

All that parcel of land situated and being at Sango Bay in the Electoral District of Torngat Mountains, in the Province of Newfoundland and Labrador, as shown on a plan of survey prepared by N. E. Parrott, CLS, NLS, dated November 30, 2001 and being bound and abutted as follows:

[Specifics omitted since the 35th edition — ed.]

Parcel 2

All that parcel of land situate and being at Sango Bay in the Electoral District of Torngat Mountains, in the Province of Newfoundland and Labrador, shown as Lot 6 on a plan of survey prepared by N. E. Parrott, CLS, NLS, dated March 01, 2002 and being bound and abutted as follows:

[Specifics omitted since the 35th edition — ed.]

Explanatory Note [not part of the Order]: The purpose of this Order is to provide the relief from federal income tax and the federal portion of the Harmonized Sales Tax to the Sheshatshiu and Mushuau Innu First Nations and their members — and to other Indians and bands — on the two specified Innu Settlements that would be available if those settlements were reserves.

The two Innu Settlements specified in the order are settlements in respect of which a public commitment has been made by the Government of Canada to grant reserve status under the *Indian Act*. The specified Innu First Nations members are individuals who became entitled to be registered as Indians under the *Indian Act* pursuant to the *Sheshatshiu Innu First Nation Band Order* and the *Mushuau Innu First Nation Band Order* that came into force on November 21, 2002. Those Orders also declared the Sheshatshiu and Mushuau Innu First Nations to be bands for the purposes of the *Indian Act*.

This Order provides income tax relief as if, since January 1, 2002, the specified Innu Settlements had been reserves under the *Indian Act*, the specified Innu First Nations members had been Indians as that term is defined in the *Indian Act*, and the specified Innu First Nations had been bands under the Indian Act. Similarly, the order provides relief from federal goods and services tax to the specified Innu First Nations beginning on January 1, 2002 and to the specified Innu First Nations members beginning on November 21, 2002. Similar tax relief is extended to other Indians and bands in respect of income on, or taxable supplies made on or delivered to, the lands in question.

Explanatory Note to Amending Order (P.C. 2005-1654): The Order amends the *Labrador Innu Settlements Remission Order, 2003*, which provides relief from federal income tax and the federal portion of the harmonized sales tax (HST) to the Sheshatshiu and Mushuau Innu First Nations and their members — and to other Indians and bands — on the two specified Innu Settlements that would be available if those settlements were reserves.

The amendment provides relief from the provincial component of the HST to the Mushuau Innu First Nation and its members — and to other Indians and bands — for the period beginning on January 1, 2003 and ending on the date of establishment of Natuashish Indian Reserve No. 2 on December 11, 2003.

Explanatory Note to Amending Order (P.C. 2007-1640): This Order further amends the *Labrador Innu Settlements Remission Order, 2003*, which provides relief from federal income tax and the federal portion of the harmonized sales tax (HST) to the Sheshatshiu and Mushuau Innu First Nations and their members — and to other Indians and bands — on the two specified Innu Settlements that would have been available [if] those settlements were reserves.

The amendment provides relief from the provincial component of the HST to the Sheshatshiu Innu First Nation and its members — and to other Indians and bands — for the period beginning on January 1, 2006 and ending on November 22, 2006, that period ending the day before the date of establishment of Sheshatshiu Indian Reserve No. 3 on November 23, 2006.

LIONAIRD CAPITAL CORPORATION NOTES REMISSION ORDER
P.C. 1999-737, April 22, 1999 (SI/99-45)

[Applies to the 1997 and 1998 taxation years — ed.]

LOCALLY ENGAGED EMPLOYEES OF THE CANADIAN EMBASSY AND CONSULATES IN THE UNITED STATES REMISSION ORDER
P.C. 2018-345, April 18, 2018 (SI/2018-30)

Her Excellency the Governor General in Council, considering that it is in the public interest to do so, on the recommendation of the Minister of Finance, pursuant to subsection 23(2) of the *Financial Administration Act*, makes the annexed *Locally Engaged Employees of the Canadian Embassy and Consulates in the United States Remission Order*.

Interpretation

1. (1) **Definitions** — The following definitions apply in this Order.

"**Act**" means the *Income Tax Act*.

"**Canada-US Tax Convention**" means the convention, as defined in the *Canada-United States Tax Convention Act, 1984*.

"**Embassy or Consulate**" means the Embassy of Canada located in Washington, D.C., United States or any one or more of the offices of the Consulate General of Canada that are located in the United States.

"**locally engaged employee**" means an individual who during the taxation year

(a) is a non-resident of Canada;

(b) is a Canadian citizen; and

(c) is paid by the government of Canada for services rendered by the individual in the discharge of functions of a governmental nature at an Embassy or Consulate.

(2) **Application of meanings in Act** — Unless the context otherwise requires, words and expressions used in this Order have the same meaning as in the Act.

Remission

2. **Remission of Income Tax** — Subject to sections 3 and 4, remission is granted to each locally engaged employee with respect to tax payable under the Act for taxation years that begin after 2016 of the lesser of, in respect of remuneration that is taxable in Canada, and not in the United States, because of Article XIX of the Canada-US Tax Convention,

(a) the amount added to the tax payable under Part I of the Act by the employee under subsection 120(1) of the Act for the taxation year, and

(b) the amount, if any, of United States state-level income tax paid by the employee for the taxation year.

Conditions

3. **Amount not otherwise claimed** — Remission is granted only to the extent the amount remitted has not otherwise been rebated, remitted, credited or refunded to any person under the Act, the *Financial Administration Act* or any other Act of Parliament.

4. **Timing and Documentation** — Remission is granted to a locally engaged employee in respect of a taxation year on the condition that

(a) the locally engaged employee applies for the remission in writing to the Minister on or before the day that is two years after their filing-due date for the taxation year; and

(b) the application is accompanied by the documentation required to determine both the eligibility for and the amount of the remission.

Coming into Force

5. **Coming into force** — This Order comes into force on the day on which it is made.

Objective: The objective of this Order is to relieve double taxation, to the extent that it arises, with respect to the tax liability of Canadian citizens who are locally engaged at the Canadian embassy in Washington, D.C. or at a Canadian consular office in the United States (the "Embassy or Consulate") on account of U.S. state-level income tax paid in addition to the "additional tax" that is payable in Canada, with respect to taxation years commencing on or after January 1, 2017.

Background: Under Article XIX of the *Convention between Canada and the United States of America with Respect to Taxes on Income and on Capital signed at Washington on September 26, 1980, as amended by the Protocols signed on June 14, 1983, March 28, 1984, March 17, 1995, July 29, 1997, and September 21, 2007* (the "Canada-US Tax Convention"), Canadian citizens who are locally engaged by the Embassy or Consulate are, by virtue of their status as Canadian citizens, taxable exclusively in Canada. This is a departure from the general rule that residence (as opposed to citizenship) is the criterion establishing an individual's liability for tax in a jurisdiction.

A locally engaged employee is an individual who during a taxation year commencing on or after January 1, 2017 is (i) a non-resident of Canada; (ii) a Canadian citizen; and (iii) paid by the government of Canada for services rendered in the discharge by the individual of functions of a governmental nature to an Embassy or a Consulate.

As a result of the provisions of Article XIX, locally engaged employees of the Embassy or Consulate do not pay U.S. federal tax. They are instead fully liable for Canadian federal tax. Included in their Canadian federal tax liability is an "additional tax" that is levied under subsection 120(1) of the *Income Tax Act*. Usually, when an individual is not resident in a province or territory, they are not liable for provincial or territorial tax.

In this particular case, the federal additional tax becomes payable. It is calculated to approximate the provincial or territorial tax that would otherwise be payable. The federal additional tax ensures that all individual Canadian taxpayers face a broadly comparable total income tax burden even in the case that they are not a resident of, and hence taxable in, any province or territory. Since locally engaged employees are not residents of any Canadian province or territory, they are not liable for any provincial or territorial tax. However, they are liable for the additional tax.

Some U.S. states levy an income tax against such employees. As a result these locally engaged employees are subject to double taxation because they are liable for both the Canadian federal additional tax and U.S. state-level income tax.

This Order does not apply to any sub-national level of tax liabilities other than state-level income tax.

Implications: The Remission Order applies to the 2017 taxation year and any subsequent taxation year; for 2017, this Order is expected to remit approximately $200,000 in federal income tax. The source of funds for the amounts remitted through this Order is the fiscal framework.

To obtain relief from double taxation under this Remission Order, locally engaged employees must apply in writing to the Minister of National Revenue on or before the day that is two years after their filing-due date for any given taxation year. The application must be accompanied by the documentation needed to determine both the eligibility for and the amount of the remission.

The Canada Revenue Agency will administer this Remission Order.

Consultation: No external consultations have been conducted. Global Affairs Canada will inform locally engaged employees working in the Embassy or Consulate of the implementation of this Remission Order.

Departmental contact: Stephanie Smith. Senior Director, Tax Treaties, Tax Legislation Division, Tax Policy Branch, Department of Finance, Telephone: 613-369-4081, Email: stephanie.smith@canada.ca.

MAINTENANCE PAYMENTS REMISSION ORDER

ORDER RESPECTING THE REMISSION OF INCOME TAX PAYABLE BY CERTAIN TAXPAYERS WHO HAVE MADE MAINTENANCE PAYMENTS

P.C. 1991-256, February 14, 1991 (SI/91-22), as amended by P.C. 1994-622, April 21, 1994 (SI/94-51)

[Applies to the 1979-88 taxation years, with latest application deadline Dec. 31, 1995 — ed.]

MCINTYRE LANDS INCOME TAX REMISSION ORDER

P.C. 2005-2230, November 28, 2005 (SI/2005-128).

1. The following definitions apply in this Order.

"**Indian**" has the same meaning as in subsection 2(1) of the *Indian Act*.

"**McIntyre Lands**" means the lands described in the Schedule.

"**reserve**" has the same meaning as in subsection 2(1) of the *Indian Act*.

"**Yukon First Nation Final Agreement**" means a land claims agreement that is in effect pursuant to the *Yukon First Nations Land Claims Settlement Act*.

2. Subject to section 3, remission is hereby granted to an Indian in respect of each taxation year from 1999 to 2005 of the amount, if any, by which

(a) the tax, interest and penalties paid or payable by the Indian under Parts I, I.1 and I.2 of the *Income Tax Act* for the year

exceeds

(b) the tax, interest and penalties that would have been payable by the Indian if the McIntyre Lands had been a reserve throughout that year.

3. This Order does not apply to an Indian who is enrolled throughout a taxation year referred to in section 2 under a Yukon First Nation Final Agreement.

Schedule *(Section 1)*

McIntyre Lands

[Specifies precise locations in the Hillcrest McIntyre subdivision in Whitehorse, Yukon — ed.]

OVERPAYMENTS OF CANADA EDUCATION SAVINGS GRANTS REMISSION ORDER

P.C. 2008-1053, June 12, 2008 (SI/2008-69)

1. Remission — Remission is hereby granted to any beneficiary of an overpayment in respect of a Canada Education Savings grant paid under the *Canada Education Savings Act* and the *Canada Education Savings Regulations* during the period beginning on January 1, 1998 and ending on June 30, 2005.

2. Conditions — The remission is granted on the condition that

(a) the beneficiary is a person so designated in respect of a registered education savings plan within the meaning of section 146.1 of the *Income Tax Act*;

(b) the grant was paid to or for the benefit of the beneficiary during the period specified in section 1;

(c) the grant has not been repaid; and

(d) the minimum contributions under subparagraph 4(1)(c)(i) or (ii) of the *Canada Education Savings Regulations* were not made to the registered education savings plan in respect of the beneficiary.

Explanatory Note [not part of the Order]: The Order remits overpayments to certain beneficiaries in respect of a Canada Education Savings grant paid under the *Canada Education Savings Act* and the *Canada Education Savings Regulations*, during the period beginning on January 1, 1998 and ending on June 30, 2005.

It remits an amount equal to the Canada Education Savings grant — in respect of a contribution made to a registered education savings plan — that was paid to a beneficiary 16 or 17 years of age in the year in which the contribution was made and for whom the minimum contributions set out in the *Canada Education Savings Regulations* were not made to the registered education savings plan before the beneficiary attained 16 years of age.

PAYMENTS RECEIVED UNDER THE ATLANTIC GROUNDFISH LICENCE RETIREMENT PROGRAM REMISSION ORDER

P.C. 2013-936, September 27, 2013 (SI/2013-104)

1. Remission — Remission is granted, in respect of a portion of the payment received on the disposition of a fishing licence under the Atlantic Groundfish Licence Retirement Program, for the 1998, 1999, 2000, 2001 or 2002 tax year, as the case may be, to each person whose name is set out in column 1 of the schedule, of

(a) the amount set out in column 2 of the schedule, which represents a portion of the federal income tax and any applicable penalty for the late filing of an income tax return paid or payable under the *Income Tax Act* and, if applicable, a portion of an amount of employment insurance benefits repayment paid or payable under Part VII of the *Employment Insurance Act*; and

(b) all interest paid or payable on the amount set out in column 2 of the schedule.

Schedule *(Section 1)*

[Lists 156 taxpayers — ed.]

Explanatory Note [not part of the Order]: The Order remits a portion of the federal income tax, late-filing penalties, employment insurance benefits repayments, and interest paid or payable thereon, in respect of the 1998, 1999, 2000, 2001 or 2002 tax year, as the case may be, by fishers who received payments under the Atlantic Groundfish Licence Retirement Program (AGLRP).

The portion remitted is calculated as if one-half of the payment received from the retirement of the fishing licence under the AGLRP had been non-taxable and the remaining one-half had been a taxable capital gain to an individual licence holder in the tax year in which the AGLRP payment was received.

PAYMENTS RECEIVED UNDER THE ATLANTIC GROUNDFISH LICENCE RETIREMENT PROGRAM REMISSION ORDER, NO. 2

P.C. 2016-869, October 19, 2016 (SI/2016-59)

1. Remission — Remission is granted, in respect of a portion of the payment received on the disposition of a fishing licence under the Atlantic Groundfish Licence Retirement Program, for the 1999 tax year, to each person whose name is set out in column 1 of the schedule, of

(a) the amount set out in column 2 of the schedule, which represents a portion of the federal income tax paid or payable under the *Income Tax Act* and, if applicable, a portion of an amount of employment insurance benefits repayment paid or payable under Part VII of the *Employment Insurance Act*; and

(b) all interest paid or payable on the amount set out in column 2 of the schedule.

Schedule *(Section 1)*

[Not reproduced: lists Stanley Fraser, Gerard Green, David Newell, Anthony Sexton, Morgan Sheppard, John Woodrow — ed.]

Explanatory Note [not part of the Order]: The Order remits a portion of the federal income tax, employment insurance benefits repayments, where applicable, and interest paid or payable thereon, in respect of the 1999 tax year, by fishers who received payments under the Atlantic Groundfish Licence Retirement Program (AGLRP).

The portion remitted is calculated as if one-half of the payment received from the retirement of the fishing licence under the AGLRP had been non-taxable and the remaining one-half had been a taxable capital gain to an individual licence holder in the tax year in which the AGLRP payment was received.

PRESCRIBED AREAS FORWARD AVERAGING REMISSION ORDER

ORDER RESPECTING THE REMISSION OF INCOME TAX AND PENALTIES, AND INTEREST THEREON, PAYABLE BY CERTAIN RESIDENTS OF PRESCRIBED AREAS WHO FILED FORWARD AVERAGING ELECTIONS IN RESPECT OF THE 1987 TAXATION YEAR

P.C. 1994-109, January 20, 1994 (SI/94-16)

[Applies to the 1987 taxation year, with application deadline Dec. 31, 1995 — ed.]

QUEBEC DOMESTIC HELP CHARITIES REMISSION ORDER

P.C. 2011-1323, November 17, 2011 (SI/2011-100)

1. **Interpretation** — The following definitions apply in this Order.

   "registered charity" has the same meaning as in subsection 248(1) of the *Income Tax Act*.

   "revocation tax" has the meaning assigned by subsection 188(1.1) of the *Income Tax Act*.

2. **Remission** — Remission of the revocation tax paid or payable is granted to a person on the condition that the person

   (a) was a registered charity before the coming into force of this Order;

   (b) was a participant in the Financial Assistance Program for Domestic Help Services, established by the Quebec Department of Health and Social Services, before the coming into force of this Order;

   (c) makes a written application for revocation of its registration as a registered charity to the Minister of National Revenue within nine months after the day on which this Order comes into force; and

   (d) makes a written application for remission under this Order to the Minister of National Revenue within nine months after the day on which this Order comes into force.

Notes: This Order entered into force on Dec. 7, 2011 (upon publication in the *Canada Gazette*, Part II), so the application deadline under 2(d) is Sept. 7, 2012.

Explanatory Note [not part of the Order]: The Order remits the revocation tax paid or payable under subsection 188(1.1) of the *Income Tax Act* to certain charities that were, in addition to being a registered charity for the purposes of the *Income Tax Act*, concurrently participating in the *Programme d'exonération financière pour les services d'aide domestique* to provide subsidized domestic help services to residents of Quebec. Due to the requirements of the *Income Tax Act*, the organizations in question cannot retain their status as a registered charity and continue to participate in the program.

REMISSION ORDER IN RESPECT OF A TRANSFER OF A SAHTU DENE AND METIS SETTLEMENT CORPORATION'S ASSETS UNDER A SELF-GOVERNMENT AGREEMENT

P.C. 2015-637, June 17, 2015 (SI/2015-45)

1. **Interpretation** — (1) **Definitions** — The following definitions apply in this Order.

   "Act" means the *Income Tax Act*.

   "Sahtu Dene and Metis Comprehensive Land Claim Agreement" means the Comprehensive Land Claim Agreement entered into by Her Majesty the Queen in right of Canada and the Sahtu Dene and Metis, as represented by the Sahtu Tribal Council, signed on September 6, 1993, as amended from time to time.

   "Sahtu Dene and Metis First Nation Government" has the meaning assigned by 2.1 of Appendix B of the Sahtu Dene and Metis Comprehensive Land Claim Agreement.

   "self-government agreement" has the meaning assigned by 2.1 of Appendix B of the Sahtu Dene and Metis Comprehensive Land Claim Agreement.

   "settlement corporation" has the meaning assigned by 11.3.1 of the Sahtu Dene and Metis Comprehensive Land Claim Agreement.

   (2) **Application of meanings in Act** — Any word or expression used in this Order and not defined in subsection (1) has the same meaning as in the Act.

2. **Remission** — Remission is granted of

   (a) the tax payable under the Act by a settlement corporation in respect of the settlement corporation ceasing to exist and all of its assets being transferred to, by way of vesting in, a Sahtu Dene and Metis First Nation Government under the self-government agreement that creates the Sahtu Dene and Metis First Nation Government;

   (b) any penalties payable under the Act in respect of the settlement corporation ceasing to exist and all of its assets being transferred to, by way of vesting in, a Sahtu Dene and Metis First Nation Government under the self-government agreement that creates the Sahtu Dene and Metis First Nation Government; and

   (c) any interest payable in respect of that tax and those penalties.

3. **Condition** — Remission is granted of an amount under this Order to a person on condition that

   (a) the amount has not otherwise been rebated, credited, refunded or remitted to the person or any other person under the Act, the *Financial Administration Act* or any other Act of the Parliament of Canada; and

   (b) the person applies in writing to the Minister of National Revenue for remission under this Order in respect of the transfer before the later of

   (i) the day that is eighteen months after the day on which this order is made, and

   (ii) the filing-due date of the person's taxation year in which the transfer occurs.

Explanatory Note [not part of the Order]: *Proposal*

To make the annexed *Remission Order in Respect of a Transfer of a Sahtu Dene and Metis Settlement Corporation's Assets under a Self-Government Agreement.*

Objective

The objective of the Order is to enable a settlement corporation within the meaning of the Sahtu Dene and Metis Comprehensive Land Claim Agreement to cease to exist and all of its assets to be transferred to a Sahtu Dene and Metis First Nation Government under the self-government agreement that creates the Sahtu Dene and Metis First Nation Government, without tax implications.

Background

Canada and the Sahtu Dene and Metis entered into the Sahtu Dene and Metis Comprehensive Land Claim Agreement in 1993. Under the Sahtu Dene and Metis Comprehensive Land Claim Agreement, the Sahtu Dene and Metis received title to lands, financial payments, confirmation of harvesting rights, and guaranteed participation in specified land and resource management regimes. The Sahtu Dene and Metis Comprehensive Land Claim Agreement provides for rights to be exercised by and responsibilities to be performed by organizations referred to as "designated Sahtu organizations."

Under the Sahtu Dene and Metis Comprehensive Land Claim Agreement, a "settlement corporation" is a corporation that, among other things, is a designated Sahtu organization, has received no contributions of capital other than financial payments under the Sahtu Dene and Metis Comprehensive Land Claim Agreement, devotes all or substantially all of its resources to making permitted investments and carrying out permitted activities, has filed an election with the Minister of National Revenue to be a "settlement corporation" and has not had its status as a "settlement corporation" terminated.

Under chapter 11 of the Sahtu Dene and Metis Comprehensive Land Claim Agreement, a settlement corporation is exempt from federal and territorial income tax except as provided in that chapter. Under chapter 11, a settlement corporation is liable to pay federal and territorial income tax in certain circumstances. For example, it is liable to pay federal and territorial tax on any income it derives from a property that is not a permitted investment or acquired in the course of carrying on a permitted activity. It is also liable to pay federal and territorial tax in respect of any payment it makes that is not a permitted investment or made in the course of carrying on a permitted activity. In addition, if the settlement corporation commences to be wound-up, it is liable to pay federal and territorial income tax on the amount distributed on the winding-up, less the aggregate of the amount disbursed or expended in the course of the winding-up on its permitted activities, all amounts that may reasonably be considered to be original contributed capital and that are transferred to a designated settlement corporation or to another settlement corporation, and all other amounts transferred to another settlement corporation.

The Sahtu Dene and Metis Comprehensive Land Claim Agreement also provides for the negotiation of self-government agreements between Canada and the Government of the Northwest Territories and each of the five Sahtu Dene and Metis communities (Colville Lake, Déline, Fort Good Hope, Norman Wells and Tulita).

On February 18, 2015, Canada, the Government of the Northwest Territories and the Sahtu Dene and Metis of Déline signed the Déline Final Self-Government Agreement. The Déline Final Self-Government Agreement provides that, on the effective date of that agreement, the Déline Financial Corporation (a settlement corporation) will cease to exist and all of its claims, rights, titles, interests, assets, obligations and liabilities will vest in the Déline Got'ine Government (the government to be created by the Déline Final Self-Government Agreement).

The Déline Final Self-Government Agreement provides that a transfer of assets to the Déline Got'ine Government under the Déline Final Self-Government Agreement is not taxable. However, due to the conflict rules in the Sahtu Dene and Metis Comprehensive Land Claim Agreement, in the case of a conflict, the provisions of the Sahtu Dene and Metis Comprehensive Land Claim Agreement in respect of the taxation of settlement corporations would prevail over the provision of the Déline Final Self-Government Agreement providing that no transfer of assets to the Déline Got'ine Government under the Déline Final Self- Government Agreement is taxable.

The purpose of the Order is to ensure that the proposed transfer of assets by the Déline Financial Corporation to the Déline Got'ine Government under the Déline Final Self-Government Agreement, and any similar transfer of assets by a settlement corporation to a Sahtu Dene and Metis First Nation Government under a Sahtu Dene and Metis self-government agreement with another Sahtu Dene and Metis community, will not result in an obligation to pay income tax. The rationale for relieving the tax in these circumstances is two-fold. First, the tax provisions of the Sahtu Dene and Metis Comprehensive Land Claim Agreement were not intended to apply to a transfer under a self-government agreement. Second, it is in the public interest to enable the parties to determine the government structure on efficiency and other grounds, rather than tax considerations.

Implications

The Order remits the income tax payable, and any related penalties and interest, in respect of a settlement corporation ceasing to exist and all of its assets vesting in a Sahtu Dene and Metis First Nation Government under a self-government agreement. As a result, the Order permits the parties to a self-government negotiation to determine the most appropriate government structure based on efficiency and other grounds, rather than based on tax considerations. The cost of the Order is estimated to be nil because it is not expected that the parties to a self-government agreement would agree on the merger of a settlement corporation and a new government body created by the self-government agreement in the absence of the Order.

Consultation

The Government of the Northwest Territories and the Sahtu Secretariat Incorporated, which represents the Sahtu Dene and Metis, were consulted in relation to the proposal.

Departmental contact

For more information, please contact Sara Gill, Senior Tax Policy Officer, Tax Policy Branch, Department of Finance, Telephone: 613-369-3808.

RESIDENTS OF INDIA REMISSION ORDER

ORDER RESPECTING THE REMISSION OF INCOME TAX, INTEREST AND PENALTIES ON ROYALTIES OR FEES RECEIVED FROM CANADA BY RESIDENTS OF INDIA FOR TECHNICAL SERVICES

P.C. 1991-1953, October 23, 1991 (SI/91-137)

1. **Short Title** — This Order may be cited as the *Residents of India Remission Order*.

2. **Interpretation** — In this Order,

"**Act**" means the *Income Tax Act*;

"**Agreement**" means the *Agreement between the Government of Canada and the Government of India for the Avoidance of Double Taxation and the Prevention of Fiscal Evasion with respect to Taxes on Income* set out in Schedule III to chapter 7 of the Statutes of Canada, 1986;

"**person**" has the meaning assigned by paragraph 1(c) of Article 3 of the Agreement.

3. **Remission** — Remission is hereby granted to any person who is a resident of India, within the meaning of the Agreement, for any amount paid or credited to that person in respect of royalties in relation to a right or property that is granted after December 12, 1988 or in respect of fees for technical services under a contract that is signed after that date, of an amount equal to the amount by which

(a) the aggregate of the taxes, interest and penalties payable by that person under the Act with respect to the amount so paid or credited

exceeds

(b) the aggregate of the taxes, interest and penalties that would have been payable by that person under the Act with respect to the amount so paid or credited, if the reference to a rate of 30 per cent in paragraph 2 of Article 13 of the Agreement were read as a reference to a rate of 20 per cent.

SAGUENAY RIVER REMISSION ORDER

INCOME TAX AS WELL AS CANADA PENSION PLAN AND EMPLOYMENT INSURANCE PREMIUMS REMISSION ORDER

P.C. 1997-201, February 11, 1997 (SI/97-26)

His Excellency the Governor General in Council, considering that it is in the public interest to do so, on the recommendation of the Minister of National Revenue and the Treasury Board, pursuant to subsections 23(2) and 23(2.1) of the *Financial Administration Act*, hereby remits amounts payable under the *Income Tax Act*, the *Canada Pension Plan* and the *Employment Insurance Act* as a result of an amount paid as relief for loss because of torrential rains and wind in or near the region along the Saguenay River on or about July 20, 1996, that is required to be included in the income from employment of a taxpayer by virtue of paragraph 6(1)(a) or (b) of the *Income Tax Act*, where the payment is voluntary, reasonable and bona fide, is not based on employment factors such as performance, position or years of service and is not made in exchange for past or future services or to compensate for loss of income, plus relevant interest and penalties, on condition that the taxpayer waive any benefit or right accruing under the said Acts as a result of the payment.

SASKATCHEWAN INDIAN FEDERATED COLLEGE REMISSION ORDER, 2003

P.C. 2003-910, June 12, 2003 (SI/2003-122)

1. **Interpretation** — The following definitions apply in this Order.

   "band" has the same meaning as in subsection 2(1) of the *Indian Act*.

   "Indian" has the same meaning as in subsection 2(1) of the *Indian Act*.

   "Indian Settlement" means the settlement named, and constituting the lands described, in the schedule.

   "reserve" has the same meaning as in subsection 2(1) of the *Indian Act*.

2. **Application** — This Order applies in respect of the Indian Settlement until lands constituting that Indian Settlement are set apart as a reserve by an order of the Governor in Council.

Part 1 — Income Tax

3. **Interpretation** — In this Part,

   (a) **"tax"** means a tax imposed under Part I, I.1 or I.2 of the *Income Tax Act*; and

   (b) all other words and expressions not otherwise defined in section 1 have the same meaning as in the *Income Tax Act*.

4. **Remission of Income Tax** — Remission is hereby granted to an Indian, or a band, with income situated on the Indian Settlement, in respect of each taxation year or fiscal period beginning during or after the calendar year 2000, of the amount, if any, by which

   (a) the taxes, interest and penalties paid or payable by the Indian or band, as the case may be, for the taxation year or fiscal period exceed

   (b) the taxes, interest and penalties that would have been payable by that Indian or band for the taxation year or fiscal period if the Indian Settlement had been a reserve throughout that taxation year or fiscal period.

Part 2 — Goods and Services Tax

5. **Interpretation** — In this Part,

   (a) **"tax"** means the goods and services tax imposed under subsection 165(1) of the *Excise Tax Act*; and

   (b) all other words and expressions not otherwise defined in section 1 have the same meaning as in Part IX of the *Excise Tax Act*.

6. **Remission of the Goods and Services Tax** — Subject to sections 7 and 8, remission is hereby granted to an Indian or a band that is the recipient of a taxable supply made on or delivered to the Indian Settlement on or after the day on which this Order comes into force in the case of an Indian, and January 1, 2000 in the case of a band, of the amount, if any, by which

   (a) the tax paid or payable by the recipient exceeds

   (b) the tax that would have been payable by the recipient if the Indian Settlement had been a reserve at the time the supply was made or delivered.

7. **Conditions** — Remission granted to an Indian under section 6 is on condition that

   (a) the tax paid or payable has not otherwise been rebated, credited, refunded or remitted under Part IX of the *Excise Tax Act* or under the *Financial Administration Act*; and

   (b) in respect of tax paid, a written claim for the remission is made to the Minister of National Revenue within two years after the day on which the tax was paid.

8. Remission granted to a band under section 6 is on condition that

   (a) the tax paid or payable has not otherwise been rebated, credited, refunded or remitted under Part IX of the *Excise Tax Act* or under the *Financial Administration Act*;

   (b) in respect of tax paid on or after January 1, 2000 but before the day on which this Order comes into force, a written claim for the remission is made to the Minister of National Revenue within two years after the day on which this Order comes into force; and

   (c) in respect of tax paid on or after the day on which this Order comes into force, a written claim for the remission is made to the Minister of National Revenue within two years after the day on which the tax was paid.

Schedule *(Section 1)*

Settlement	Legal Description of Settlement Lands
Saskatchewan Indian Federated College Campus	In the City of Regina, in the North East and South East Quarters of Section 8, in Township 17, Range 19 West of the Second Meridian, Saskatchewan, all that portion shown as Block B on a Plan of record in the Saskatchewan Land Surveys Directory as No. 99RA08587, as amended by Master of Titles Order No. 01RA01057, containing 13.153 hectares (32.503 acres) more or less.

Explanatory Note [not part of the Order]: The purpose of this Order is to provide relief from federal income tax and the goods and services tax to Indians and Indian Bands on the campus of the Saskatchewan Indian Federated College that would be available if that campus were a reserve under the *Indian Act*. The Government of Canada has made a public commitment to grant reserve status under the *Indian Act* to that land.

SYNCRUDE REMISSION ORDER

ORDER RESPECTING THE REMISSION OF INCOME TAX FOR THE SYNCRUDE PROJECT
P.C. 1976-1026, May 6, 1976 (C.R.C. 1978, Vol. VII, c. 794)

1. **Short title** — This Order may be cited as the *Syncrude Remission Order*.

2. **Interpretation** — In this Order,

"**barrels**" means barrels of synthetic crude oil from Leases 17 and 22 pursuant to the Syncrude Project;

"**condition**" means that the fiscal programs as they relate to the Syncrude Project in effect at the commencement of the Syncrude Project have been revised in such a manner as to have significant adverse economic effect on the Syncrude Project;

"**Crown**" means Her Majesty in right of the Province of Alberta;

"**leased substances**" means all substances the participant has recovered pursuant to Leases 17 and 22;

"**Leases 17 and 22**" means Government of Alberta Bituminous Sands Leases Nos 17 and 22, excluding that portion of Lease No 17 that is subject to an Agreement dated September 20, 1972 as amended by an Agreement dated September 26, 1972 whereby Great Canadian Oil Sands Limited was granted a sublease of lands contained in Lease No 17 and includes any other documents or titles that extend the duration of Leases 17 and 22;

"**participant**" means

(a) Canada-Cities Service Ltd, a body corporate, incorporated under the laws of Canada and having its head office at the City of Calgary, in the Province of Alberta,

(b) Imperial Oil Limited, a body corporate, incorporated under the laws of Canada and having its head office at the municipality of Metropolitan Toronto, in the Province of Ontario,

(c) Gulf Oil Canada Limited, a body corporate, incorporated under the laws of Canada and having its head office at the City of Toronto, in the Province of Ontario,

(d) the Crown as represented by the Minister of Energy and Resources for the Province of Alberta,

(e) Her Majesty in right of Canada as represented by the Minister of Energy, Mines and Resources for Canada, and

(f) Ontario Energy Corporation, a body corporate, incorporated by Special Act of the Legislature of the Province of Ontario and having its head office at the City of Toronto, in the Province of Ontario,

or any or all of them or their successors or assignees as long as they retain a share in the Syncrude Project;

"**royalty provisions**" means the provisions contained in paragraphs 12(1)(o) and 18(1)(m), and subsection 69(6) to (10) of the *Income Tax Act*;

"**Syncrude Project**" means the scheme of the participant for the recovery of leased substances from Leases 17 and 22;

"**synthetic crude oil**" means a mixture, mainly of pentanes and heavier hydrocarbons, that may contain sulphur compounds, that is derived from crude bitumen and that is liquid at the time its volume is measured or estimated.

3. **Remission** — (1) Subject to subsection (2), remission is hereby granted to each participant of any tax payable for a taxation year pursuant to Part I of the *Income Tax Act* as a result of the royalty provisions being applicable to

(a) amounts receivable and the fair market value of any property receivable by the Crown as a royalty, tax, rental or levy with respect to the Syncrude Project, or as an amount however described, that may reasonably be regarded as being in lieu of any of the preceding amounts;

(b) dispositions of leased substances to the Crown by the participant; and

(c) acquisitions of leased substances from the Crown by the participant.

(2) No remission shall be granted pursuant to this Order to a participant in respect of a taxation year of that participant that commences after

(a) the recovery of 1.1 billion barrels, where the Governor in Council revokes this Order upon being satisfied on the report of the Minister of Finance that the condition exists prior to the recovery of 1.1 billion barrels,

(b) the recovery of the number of barrels recovered on the date the Governor in Council revokes this Order upon being satisfied on the report of the Minister of Finance that the condition exists if that date is after the recovery of more than 1.1 billion barrels and less than 2.1 billion barrels,

(c) the recovery of 2.1 billion barrels, or

(d) December 31, 2003,

whichever first occurs.

Related Provisions [s. 3]: Reg. 1204(4), (5) — Syncrude royalties excluded from resource profits while remission order in force.

Notes: Remission under this remission order was reduced by a parallel Alberta incentive: *Imperial Oil Resources*, 2010 FCA 325 (leave to appeal denied 2010 CarswellNat 1313 (SCC)). In *Imperial Oil Resources*, 2014 FC 838 (not appealed), remission entitlement was held to be based on actual royalties paid to Alberta, not reduced by an (unsuccessful) application to reduce those royalties. In *Imperial Oil Resources*, 2016 FCA 139, no interest was payable by the CRA on late payment under this remission order.

REMISSION ORDERS — PRIVATE

[These remission orders apply to a single individual or corporation, or a named group, but are still of general interest. For remission orders that apply more widely to groups or classes of persons, see the "General" remission orders above — ed.]

RON ADAMS REMISSION ORDER
P.C. 2014-1129, November 5, 2014 (SI/2014-93)

His Excellency the Governor General in Council, considering that the collection of the interest is unjust, on the recommendation of the Minister of National Revenue, pursuant to subsection 23(2) of the *Financial Administration Act*, remits interest in the amount of $8,765.57 calculated as of April 9, 2013, paid or payable under Part I of the *Income Tax Act* by Ron Adams for a pre-1986 taxation year, and all relevant interest on that interest.

Explanatory Note [not part of the Order]: This Order remits a portion of the interest, and all relevant interest thereon, paid or payable by Ron Adams in respect of a pre-1986 tax year.

Mr. Adams was unable to address his income tax debt due to financial difficulties. Interest charges have increased the debt to a level where paying it would cause continued extreme hardship for Mr. Adams.

ROSA AMORIM REMISSION ORDER
P.C. 2009-1224, July 30, 2009 (SI/2009-69)

Her Excellency the Governor General in Council, considering that the collection of the tax is unjust, on the recommendation of the Minister of National Revenue, pursuant to subsection 23(2) of the *Financial Administration Act*, hereby remits tax in the amount of $2,839.00, a penalty of $1,422.85 and all arrears interest, paid or payable under Part I of the *Income Tax Act* by Rosa Amorim for the 1991 taxation year.

Explanatory Note [not part of the Order]: The Order remits a portion of the income tax, the late filing penalty and all the interest, paid or payable, by Rosa Amorim in respect of the 1991 taxation year.

The amount of tax remitted represents the additional tax incurred by Ms. Amorim due to an error the Canada Revenue Agency made in the way the tax was calculated under section 120.3 of the *Income Tax Act*. The penalty is being remitted because it represents a significant financial setback to Ms. Amorim and the return was filed late due to circumstances beyond her control. Interest is being remitted due to incorrect action on the part of federal government officials.

GINETTE ARCHAMBAULT INCOME TAX REMISSION ORDER
P.C. 2010-273, March 11, 2010 (SI/2010-27)

1. **Remission** — Remission is hereby granted of a portion of the tax paid or payable by Ginette Archambault under Part I of the *Income Tax Act* in the amounts of $3,362.93 and $2,729.75 for the 1999 and 2000 taxation years, respectively, and all interest paid or payable on that tax.

2. **Condition** — The remission is granted on the condition that Ginette Archambault does not claim a deduction under paragraph 111(1)(a) of the *Income Tax Act* for any portion of her non-capital loss relating to the repayment in 2004 of wage loss replacement benefits to her employer.

Explanatory Note [not part of the Order]: The Order remits a portion of the income tax, and all relevant interest on that tax, paid or payable by Ginette Archambault for the 1999 and 2000 taxation years.

The amounts remitted represent the additional tax paid or payable by Ms. Archambault as a result of circumstances that were beyond her control. The payment of these amounts represents a financial setback for Ms. Archambault.

ALFO BACCI TAX REMISSION ORDER
P.C. 2012-33, February 2, 2012 (SI/2012-6)

His Excellency the Governor General in Council, considering that the collection of the interest is unjust, on the recommendation of the Minister of National Revenue, pursuant to subsection 23(2) of the *Financial Administration Act*, hereby remits interest in the amount of $10,500.00 that accrued during the period beginning on January 15, 1993 and ending on July 4, 2006, paid or payable by Alfo Bacci or his estate for a pre-1986 taxation year and the 1987, 1988 and 1991 taxation years under Part I of the *Income Tax Act*.

Explanatory Note [not part of the Order]: The Order remits arrears interest in respect of pre-1986, 1987, 1988 and 1991 debt for the period of January 15, 1993, to July 4, 2006, paid or payable, by Alfo Bacci or his estate.

The arrears interest is being remitted because payment of this amount represents a significant financial setback for Mr. Bacci's estate and it arose due to circumstances beyond his control.

JACQUES BEAUVAIS REMISSION ORDER
P.C. 2006-406, May 18, 2006 (SI/2006-88)

Her Excellency the Governor General in Council, considering that the collection of the tax is unjust, on the recommendation of the Minister of National Revenue, pursuant to subsection 23(2) of the *Financial Administration Act*, hereby remits tax under Part I.2 of the *Income Tax Act* in the amount of $4,393.75 for the 2003 taxation year, and all relevant interest thereon, paid or payable by Jacques Beauvais.

Explanatory Note [not part of the Order]: This Order remits a portion of income tax and all relevant interest paid or payable thereon by Jacques Beauvais in respect of the 2003 taxation year.

In 2003, Mr. Beauvais received a lump sum payment from a government agency which he was entitled to receive in the years from 1997 to 2002. As a result of the income inclusion in 2003, Mr. Beauvais was required to repay his Old Age Security pension and Guaranteed Income Supplement benefits for that year. The amount remitted represents the additional tax liability incurred by Mr. Beauvais as a result of the lengthy delay by the government agency in paying him the amounts to which he was entitled in the relevant years.

TONELE BENOIT REMISSION ORDER
P.C. 2019-1145, August 7, 2019 (SI/2019-84)

Whereas the Treasury Board has delegated to the President of the Treasury Board, pursuant to subsection 6(4) of the *Financial Administration Act*, its power to make a recommendation in respect of remission orders in amounts of less than $25,000 for other debts that are under the responsibility of the Minister of National Revenue;

Therefore, Her Excellency the Governor General in Council, considering that the collection of the amounts is unjust, on the recommendation of the Minister of Employment and Social Development, the Minister of National Revenue and the President of the Treasury Board, pursuant to subsection 23(2.1) of the *Financial Administration Act*, remits the following amounts to Tonele Benoit:

(a) the amounts of $873 and $6,400 that were paid or payable by her under Part I of the *Income Tax Act* as repayment of Canada child tax benefits received with respect to the 2014 base taxation year and Canada child benefits received with respect to the 2015 base taxation year, respectively;

(b) the amounts of $35.75, $145 and $73.50 that were paid or payable by her under Part I of the *Income Tax Act* as repayment of the goods and services tax/harmonized sales tax credit received with respect to the 2014, 2015 and 2016 base taxation years, respectively; and

(c) the amount of $480 that was paid or payable by her under the *Universal Child Care Benefit Act* as repayment of benefits received with respect to the 2016 taxation year.

Explanatory Note [not part of the Order]: The Order remits a total of $8,007.25 with respect to Canada child tax benefits, Canada child benefits, goods and services tax/harmonized sales tax credit and universal child care benefits received by Tonele Benoit, to which she was not entitled. Remission is based on extreme hardship and incorrect action on the part of Canada Revenue Agency officials.

NELLY BITUALA-MAYALA REMISSION ORDER
P.C. 2009-968, June 11, 2009 (SI/2009-55)

Her Excellency the Governor General in Council, considering that the collection of the amount is unjust, on the recommendation of the Minister of National Revenue and the Treasury Board, pursuant to subsection 23(2.1) of the *Financial Administration Act* hereby remits to Nelly Bituala-Mayala the amount of $16,143, paid or payable by her as repayment of Canada child tax benefits with respect to the 2003 and 2004 base taxation years under Part I of the *Income Tax Act*.

Explanatory Note [not part of the Order]: The Order remits the amount of $16,143 with respect to Canada child tax benefits received by Nelly Bituala-Mayala in error, for the 2003 and 2004 base taxation years, to which she was not entitled. The remission is based on extreme hardship and an error on the part of the Canada Revenue Agency as to her entitlement to the benefits for that period.

BLACKBERRY LIMITED INCOME TAX REMISSION ORDER
P.C. 2013-1404, December 12, 2013 (SI/2014-1)

1. **Interpretation — (1) Definitions** — The following definitions apply in this Order.

"**Act**" means the *Income Tax Act*.

"**Minister**" means the Minister of National Revenue.

(2) **Application of meanings in Act** — Unless the context otherwise requires, words and expressions used in this Order have the same meaning as in the Act.

2. **Remission** — Subject to section 3, remission is granted to BlackBerry Limited, in respect of tax paid for its 2009 to 2012 taxation years, of an amount equal to the amount by which

(a) the total tax and interest payable under the Act by BlackBerry Limited for those years

exceeds

(b) the total tax and interest that would be payable under the Act by BlackBerry Limited for those years if

(i) the reference to "3 taxation years" in paragraph 111(1)(a) of the Act were a reference to "4 taxation years" and BlackBerry Limited had, in computing taxable income for each of its 2011 and 2012 taxation years, claimed the lesser of

(A) the deduction that would have been available under that paragraph as a consequence, and

(B) the amount, if any, specified by BlackBerry Limited,

(ii) BlackBerry Limited had, in computing tax payable for each of its 2009 and 2010 taxation years, claimed the lesser of

(A) the deduction that would have been available under subsection 127(5) of the Act as a consequence of the deduction referred to or amount specified, as the case may be, in subparagraph (i), and

(B) the amount, if any, specified by BlackBerry Limited, and

(iii) the reference to "3 taxation years" in paragraph (c) of the definition "investment tax credit" in subsection 127(9) of the Act were a reference to "4 taxation years" and BlackBerry Limited had, in computing tax payable for each of its 2011 and 2012 taxation years, claimed the lesser of

(A) the deduction that would have been available under subsection 127(5) of the Act as a consequence, and

(B) the amount, if any, specified by BlackBerry Limited.

3. **Conditions** — Remission is granted under section 2 on condition that BlackBerry Limited

(a) has at least two taxation years that end after October 2013 and before March 2, 2014;

(b) files a waiver with the Minister under subparagraph 152(4)(a)(ii) of the Act with respect to each of its taxation years that end after 2010 and before March 1, 2015 and does not revoke any of them before 2020;

(c) does not claim, in computing its taxable income under the Act for any taxation year, a deduction in respect of any portion of a non-capital loss to the extent that the portion has resulted in an amount of tax being remitted under this Order;

(d) does not deduct, in computing its tax payable under the Act for any taxation year, an amount in respect of an investment tax credit to the extent that the amount has resulted in an amount of tax being remitted under this Order;

(e) for any amount specified under clause 2(b)(i)(B) or (iii)(B) that relates to the computation of taxable income or tax payable for its 2011 taxation year, provides that amount in writing to the Minister on or before the filing-due date for its second taxation year ending after October 2013;

(f) for any amount specified under clause 2(b)(ii)(B) that relates to the computation of tax payable for its 2009 taxation year, provides that amount in writing to the Minister on or before the filing-due date for its second taxation year ending after October 2013;

(g) for any amount specified under clause 2(b)(i)(B) or (iii)(B) that relates to the computation of taxable income or tax payable for its 2012 taxation year, provides that amount in writing to the Minister on or before the filing-due date for its third taxation year ending after October 2013; and

(h) for any amount specified under clause 2(b)(ii)(B) that relates to the computation of tax payable for its 2010 taxation year, provides that amount in writing to the Minister on or before the filing-due date for its third taxation year ending after October 2013.

Explanatory Note [not part of the Order]: The Order makes a remission to BlackBerry Limited of taxes paid for the 2009 to 2012 taxation years. In effect, it enables the company to have undertaken a transaction to obtain early a portion of a refund that otherwise would have been received after its March 1, 2014, year-end without reducing the total amount of that refund.

Background

A transaction entered into by BlackBerry Limited resulted in it having a taxation year ending on November 3, 2013. This taxation year end enabled the company to apply the non-capital losses realized up to that date against taxable income earned in a prior year and obtain a refund of income tax paid for that prior year. If not for the transaction, its taxation year would have ended on March 1, 2014.

As a result of the transaction, BlackBerry Limited lost the ability it would otherwise have had under the *Income Tax Act* to apply non-capital losses and investment tax credits, that might be realized during the period from November 4, 2013, to March 1, 2014, against its taxable income and income tax payable, respectively, for its 2011 taxation year. BlackBerry Limited similarly lost the ability to apply, against its taxable income and income tax payable for the 2012 taxation year, non-capital losses and investment tax credits that might be realized in its second taxation year ending after November 3, 2013.

As a result of the inability to carry back these non-capital losses to its 2011 and 2012 taxation years, Blackberry Limited lost the ability to apply all or a portion of investment tax credits that it realized for its 2011 and 2012 taxation years against tax payable for its 2009 and subsequent taxation years.

The Order effectively preserves the carry-back abilities that would have existed had the company not undertaken the transaction to cause an early taxation year-end on November 3, 2013.

Financial implications

The Order in effect allows BlackBerry Limited to have undertaken a transaction to obtain an early refund of tax associated with the non-capital losses accrued over the first eight months of its taxation year beginning March 3, 2013, without losing the ability to carry back (to the extent that otherwise would have been permitted) any losses incurred and investment tax credits earned over the following four months. The transaction has enabled the company to obtain a portion of its anticipated tax refund earlier than normal. However, the Order will not result in the company receiving a total amount of tax refunds in excess of the amount that would have been obtained had the company not undertaken the transaction but instead had waited and claimed a refund following its normal taxation year end on March 1, 2014.

The Order will not have any impact on the amount of government tax revenues.

Consultation

The Canada Revenue Agency was consulted in relation to the proposal.

Departmental contact

Tobias Witteveen, Tax Legislation Division, Department of Finance, L'Esplanade Laurier, 140 O'Connor Street, Ottawa, Ontario K1A 0G5, Telephone: 613-992-4859.

Notes: See Amanda Doucette, "Remission Order Advances Payment of BlackBerry Tax Refund", 4(2) *Canadian Tax Focus* (ctf.ca) 2-3 (May 2014); and Feb. 5, 2014 Finance comfort letter in [2004] 4 *Tax Times* (Carswell) 4-5 (Feb. 28, 2014).

CATHERINE BLAND REMISSION ORDER
P.C. 2009-170, February 5, 2009 (SI/2009-7)

Her Excellency the Governor General in Council, considering that the collection of the tax is unjust, on the recommendation of the Minister of National Revenue, pursuant to subsection 23(2) of the *Financial Administration Act*, hereby remits tax in the amount of $527.91, and all relevant interest on it, paid or payable by Catherine Bland, for the 1990 taxation year, under Part I of the *Income Tax Act*.

Explanatory Note [not part of the Order]: This Order remits a portion of the income tax in respect of the 1990 taxation year, and all relevant interest on it paid or payable by Catherine Bland.

Ms. Bland was unable to address her income tax debt for the 1990 taxation year due to financial difficulties. Interest charges have increased the debt to a level where paying it would cause extreme hardship for Ms. Bland.

LÉOPOLD BOUCHARD REMISSION ORDER
P.C. 2007-562, April 19, 2007 (SI/2007-52)

Her Excellency the Governor General in Council, considering that the collection of the tax is unjust, on the recommendation of the Minister of National Revenue, pursuant to subsection 23(2) of the *Financial Administration Act*, hereby remits tax under Part I of the *Income Tax Act* in the amount of $1,233.93 for the 1993 taxation year, and all relevant interest thereon, paid or payable by Léopold Bouchard.

Explanatory Note [not part of the Order]: This Order remits a portion of income tax and all relevant penalties and interest paid or payable thereon by Léopold Bouchard in respect of the 1993 taxation year.

In 1993, Mr. Bouchard fell seriously ill and became unable to continue to work. Having fallen ill, he did not file his 1993 income tax return until several years later and was assessed tax of $1,233.93 and related penalties and interest. He began receiving social assistance in 1995 and continues to receive these long-term disability benefits. Mr. Bouchard's income is at a level where paying this debt would cause him extreme hardship.

DOINA-FLORICA CALIN REMISSION ORDER

P.C. 2007-563, April 19, 2007 (SI/2007-53)

Her Excellency the Governor General in Council, considering that the collection of the tax is unjust, on the recommendation of the Minister of National Revenue, pursuant to subsection 23(2) of the *Financial Administration Act*, hereby remits tax under Part I of the *Income Tax Act* in the amount of $17,100.57 for the 2000 taxation year, and all relevant interest thereon, paid or payable by Doina-Florica Calin.

Explanatory Note [not part of the Order]: This Order remits a portion of income tax and all relevant interest paid or payable thereon by Doina-Florica Calin in respect of her final return.

The exectuor of the estate was unable to take advantage of alleviating legislative provisions because he forfeited options after the legislated timeframe (first taxation year of the estate). The executor missed this deadline due to serious health problems.

CYNTHIA CARLSON REMISSION ORDER

P.C. 2010-1594, December 9, 2010 (SI/2010-93)

His Excellency the Governor General in Council, considering that the collection of the interest is unjust, on the recommendation of the Minister of National Revenue, pursuant to subsection 23(2) of the *Financial Administration Act*, hereby remits interest in the amount of $2,971.35, paid or payable under Part I of the *Income Tax Act* by Cynthia Carlson, having accrued during the period beginning on January 1, 1986 and ending on January 1, 2001, and all relevant interest on it.

Explanatory Note [not part of the Order]: The Order remits to Cynthia Carlson $2,971.35, which represents a portion of the interest charges on arrears of an income tax debt relating to the 1986 taxation year.

The interest accrued due to circumstances beyond her control and caused a significant financial setback for Ms. Carlson.

Notes: See Notes to the *Mildred Jacobs Remission Order* below.

CERTAIN FORMER EMPLOYEES OF SDL OPTICS, INC. REMISSION ORDER

P.C. 2007-1635, October 25, 2007 (SI/2007-99), as amended by Errata, *Canada Gazette* Part II, Vol. 142, No. 3, February 6, 2008

Her Excellency the Governor General in Council, considering that it is in the public interest to do so, on the recommendation of the Minister of National Revenue, pursuant to subsection 23(2) of the *Financial Administration Act*, hereby makes the annexed *Certain Former Employees of SDL Optics, Inc. Remission Order*.

1. **Interpretation** — In this Order, "employment benefit" means a benefit under subsection 7(1) of the *Income Tax Act* in respect of the acquisition of shares, in 1999 and 2000, through the stock purchase plan for employees of SDL Optics, Inc.

2. **Remission** — Remission is granted to the taxpayers set out in column 1 of the schedule for the amount set out in column 2, in respect of the 1999 or 2000 taxation years, as the case may be, which represents,

   (a) for those taxpayers set out in items 1 to 21 of the schedule, all or a portion of tax paid or payable under Part I of the *Income Tax Act* in respect of an employment benefit; or

   (b) for those taxpayers set out in items 22 to 42 of the schedule, all or a portion of interest paid or payable under Part I of that Act, on tax paid or payable under that Part in respect of an employment benefit.

3. **Condition** — The remission set out in paragraph 2(a) is granted with one of the following conditions:

   (a) in respect of those taxpayers set out in items 1, 4 to 11, 13, 15, and 17 to 19 of the schedule, that the taxpayer agrees to reduce the adjusted cost base of any shares held at the close of the stock markets on December 29, 2006 that were, or are identical to those, purchased in 1999 or 2000 through the stock purchase plan for employees of SDL Optics, Inc. by the amount set out in column 2 of the schedule, divided by the taxpayer's effective federal tax rate on the employment benefit; and

   (b) in respect of those taxpayers set out in item 2, 3, 12, 14, 20 and 21 of the schedule, that the taxpayer agrees not to claim a deduction in respect of net capital losses, equal to one-half the amount set out in column 2 of the schedule, divided by the taxpayer's effective federal tax rate on the employment benefit.

Schedule *(Sections 2 and 3)*

[Not reproduced: lists 42 employees and amounts — ed.]

Explanatory Note [not part of the Order]: The Order remits all or a portion of federal income tax paid or payable in respect of the 1999 or 2000 taxation years, as the case may be, by certain former employees of SDL Optics, Inc. Those individuals qualify for tax remission if the tax assessed on the employment benefit associated with shares acquired in 1999 or 2000 through the stock purchase plan for employees of SDL Optics, Inc. exceeds the total of the proceeds of disposition realized on the disposition of those shares and the market value of any of those shares held at the close of stock markets on December 29, 2006. The amount remitted is subject to certain conditions and adjustments.

The Order also remits, to certain former employees of SDL Optics, Inc., all or a portion of interest paid or payable on tax paid or payable on an employment benefit in respect of shares acquired in 1999 or 2000 through the stock purchase plan for employees of SDL Optics, Inc.

Notes: This remission order provides relief for underwater stock options to certain employees of JDS Uniphase in Saanich, BC. See Notes to ITA 7(1). Para. 3(a) and item 25 in column 2 amended by Errata, *Canada Gazette* Part II, Vol. 141, No. 23, February 6, 2008.

CERTAIN FORMER EMPLOYEES OF SDL OPTICS, INC. REMISSION ORDER NO. 2
P.C. 2008-975, May 29, 2008 (SI/2008-60)

Her Excellency the Governor General in Council, considering that it is in the public interest to do so, on the recommendation of the Minister of National Revenue, pursuant to subsection 23(2) of the *Financial Administration Act*, hereby makes the annexed *Certain Former Employees of SDL Optics, Inc. Remission Order No. 2.*

1. **Interpretation** — In this Order, **"employment benefit"** means a benefit under subsection 7(1) of the *Income Tax Act* in respect of the acquisition of shares, in 1999 and 2000, through the stock purchase plan for employees of SDL Optics, Inc.

2. **Remission** — Remission is granted to the taxpayers set out in column 1 of the schedule for the amount set out in column 2, in respect of the 1999 or 2000 taxation years, as the case may be, which represents all or a portion of tax paid or payable under Part I of the *Income Tax Act* in respect of an employment benefit.

3. **Condition** — The remission set out in section 2 is granted on the condition that the taxpayer agrees to reduce the adjusted cost base of any shares held at the close of the stock markets on December 29, 2006 that were, or are identical to those, purchased in 1999 or 2000 through the stock purchase plan for employees of SDL Optics, Inc. by the amount set out in column 2 of the schedule, divided by the taxpayer's effective federal tax rate on the employment benefit.

Schedule *(Sections 2 and 3)*

[Not reproduced: lists Jingjing Liu, Mandeep Saini and Shanna Wong — ed.]

Explanatory Note [not part of the Order]: The Order remits all or a portion of federal income tax paid or payable in respect of the 1999 or 2000 taxation years, as the case may be, by certain former employees of SDL Optics, Inc. Those individuals qualify for tax remission if the tax assessed on the employment benefit associated with shares acquired in 1999 or 2000 through the stock purchase plan for employees of SDL Optics, Inc. exceeds the total of the proceeds of disposition realized on the disposition of those shares and the market value of any of those shares held at the close of stock markets on December 29, 2006. The remission is conditional and the amount remitted is subject to certain adjustments.

Notes: See Notes to the "Certain Former Employees of SDL Optics, Inc. Remission Order" above.

CERTAIN TAXPAYERS REMISSION ORDER, 1997-3
P.C. 1997-1066, July 25, 1997 (SI/97-95)

1. Remission is hereby granted to the taxpayers named in column I of an item of the schedule of the amount set out in column II of that item, which represents tax, including any interest payable thereon, under the *Income Tax Act*, in respect of the taxation year set out in column III of that item.

2. Remission is hereby granted of amounts payable by Julius Uzoaba under the *Income Tax Act* for or in respect of 1995, not exceeding $29,217.86 plus relevant interest, that would not be payable if each portion of a lump-sum received in 1995 as a result of a decision in respect of wages and the relevant interest for or in respect of a previous year had been received in that previous year, on condition that he forthwith file with the Minister a document, in a form under seal acceptable to the Minister, in which he undertakes to withdraw and not to institute or proceed with any relevant action, objection, appeal, application or other proceeding of any kind if there is a corresponding provincial remission and in which he agrees that, notwithstanding any such proceeding and any consequent assessment, subject to this remission, the federal taxes payable are to be computed on the basis that the said wages and related interest must be included in computing income for 1995.

Schedule

[Not reproduced — 48 entries showing name, amount and taxation year]

Explanatory Note [not part of the Order]: This Order remits income tax, including interest thereon, on the basis of extreme hardship or serious financial setback coupled with conditions beyond the taxpayer's control that gave rise to unintended results, including incomes below the poverty line, serious illness, and the receipt of retroactive lump-sum payments.

CERTAIN TAXPAYERS REMISSION ORDER, 1998-2
P.C. 1998-2092, November 26, 1998 (SI/98-121)

1. Remission is hereby granted to the taxpayers named in column I of an item of the schedule of the amount set out in column II of that item, which represents tax, penalties and interest, including any interest payable thereon, under the *Income Tax Act*, in respect of the taxation year set out in column III of that item.

2. Remission is hereby granted of amounts payable under the *Income Tax Act* by a taxpayer who is or was a judge of the Court of Québec, who made an excess contribution not exceeding $7,500 in 1989 or 1990 to a registered retirement savings plan, the deduction of which was disallowed by assessment and that, within one year of the date of this Order, is withdrawn, or has been withdrawn, from the plan, or the judge's spouse, that would not be payable if the excess contribution had not been made and the amount of the withdrawal were not required to be included in computing income, on condition that the taxpayer discontinue or have discontinued all relevant proceedings and undertake forthwith, in a form filed with and acceptable to the Minister of National Revenue, not to institute or proceed with any action, objection, appeal, application or other proceeding of any kind in respect of any contribution in 1989 or 1990 to such a plan.

3. Remission is hereby granted of amounts payable under the *Income Tax Act* by Andrew Gorgichuk and Joachim Gorgichuk that would not be payable if expenditures after 1996 and before the 121st day hereafter (not exceeding $62,230) made by their partnership, in the income of which for its 1996 taxation year $62,230 was included contrary to information received from an appropriate official, had been made by it in that 1996 taxation year and not in any other year and such deductions or other claims in respect of the expenditures that would have been permitted under the said Act as the taxpayers may jointly and not severally describe in the form had been made, on

condition that they undertake forthwith, in a form filed with and acceptable to the Minister of National Revenue (the "form"), not to make any claim or deduction in respect of any such expenditures in any taxation year or that is inconsistent with this remission.

Schedule

[Not reproduced]

Explanatory Note [not part of the Order]: This Order remits income tax and interest on the basis of extreme hardship or financial setback coupled with conditions over which the taxpayer had no control that gave rise to unintended results, including incomes slightly above and below the poverty line, old age, illness, departmental error or delay, and the receipt of retroactive lump-sum payments, such as pension and disability benefits, which, if received in the years in respect of which they were paid, would have resulted in less or no tax liability.

Section 2 of the Order remits tax and interest resulting from 1989 or 1990 excess RRSP contributions by some judges of the Court of Québec who claim discrimination in that Federal judges can contribute greater amounts to RRSPs. One judge has appealed to the Federal Court but some of the judges wish to discontinue their objections if remission is granted provided that the excess contributions be withdrawn.

Section 3 reallocates farm expenses so as to offset farm income which a partnership believed was not taxable on the basis of information furnished by a departmental official.

CERTAIN TAXPAYERS REMISSION ORDER, 1999-2
P.C. 1999-1855, October 21, 1999 (SI/99-124)

1. Remission is hereby granted to the taxpayers named in column I of an item of the schedule of the amount set out in column II of that item, which represents tax, penalties and interest, including any interest payable thereon, under the *Income Tax Act*, in respect of the taxation year set out in column III of that item.

2. Remission is hereby granted to Florence Currie of $12,445 payable by her under the *Income Tax Act* for 1997, plus any interest payable thereon, subject to a deduction therefrom required by the Minister of National Revenue (the "Minister") in respect of any deduction claimed or allowed in respect of a relevant retroactive pension payment, on condition that any other relevant relief is waived in a form filed with and acceptable to the Minister.

3. Remission is hereby granted of amounts payable under the *Income Tax Act* by a taxpayer who is or was a judge of the Court of Québec, who made an excess contribution not exceeding $7,500 in 1989 or 1990 to a registered retirement savings plan, the deduction of which was disallowed by assessment and that, within one year of the date of this Order, is withdrawn, or has been withdrawn, from a plan or fund to which it was transferred as provided in subsection 146(16) or 146.3(14) of that Act, or the judge's spouse, that would not be payable if the excess contribution had not been made and the amount of the withdrawal were not required to be included in computing income, on condition that the taxpayer discontinue or have discontinued all relevant proceedings and undertake forthwith, in a form filed with and acceptable to the Minister of National Revenue, not to institute or proceed with any action, objection, appeal, application or other proceeding of any kind in respect of any contribution in 1989 or 1990 to such a plan.

Schedule

[Not reproduced]

Explanatory Note [not part of the Order]: This Order remits income tax and interest on the basis of extreme hardship or financial setback coupled with conditions over which the taxpayer had no control that gave rise to unintended results, including incomes slightly above and below the poverty line, old age, illness, and the receipt of retroactive lump-sum payments due to processing delays, such as pension and disability benefits, which, if received in the years in respect of which they were paid, would have resulted in less or no tax liability.

Section 3 of the Order remits tax and interest resulting from 1989 or 1990 excess RRSP contributions by some judges of the Court of Québec who claim discrimination in that Federal judges can contribute greater amounts to RRSPs. Remission has already been granted to the judges providing for withdrawals from their RRSPs, but they failed to request a remission providing for withdrawals from their RRIFs (*cf.* SI/98-121).

CERTAIN TAXPAYERS REMISSION ORDER, 2000-3
P.C. 2001-429, March 22, 2001 (SI/2001-45)

1. Remission is hereby granted of amounts payable under the *Income Tax Act* by a person who was a member of the *Newfoundland Association of Public Employees* where those amounts would not be payable if the contributions paid by the person in respect of non-existent service pursuant to section 32 of the *Public Service (Pensions) Act*, R.S.N. 1970, c. 319, and the regulations made under that section, were deductible under the *Income Tax Act*, and where the following conditions are met:

(a) the contributions for non-existent service were made pursuant to an agreement entered into prior to 1991,

(b) the contributions were made in accordance with the pension plan as registered,

(c) the contributions have not been deducted from income in prior years, and

(d) the person applies for this relief, in writing, to the Minister of National Revenue before January 1, 2002.

Explanatory Note [not part of the Order]: This Order remits amounts payable under the *Income Tax Act* resulting from the disallowance of the deduction from income of pension contributions made in respect of non-existent service, as previously provided for under the *Newfoundland Association of Public Employees* pension plan.

CERTAIN TAXPAYERS REMISSION ORDER, 2001-1
P.C. 2001-691, April 26, 2001 (SI/2001-58)

1. Remission is hereby granted to the taxpayers named in column 1 of an item of the schedule of the amount set out in column 2 of that item, which represents arrears interest payable under the *Income Tax Act* in respect of the taxation year set out in column 3 of that item.

Schedule *(Section 1)*

[Not reproduced: lists Josette, Dominique and Josée Bédard — ed.]

Explanatory Note [not part of the Order]: This Order remits arrears interest that became payable following a court decision issued in 1998.

The taxpayers had initially included in their tax returns amounts received as dividends from a non-arm's length corporation. Revenue Canada (now the Canada Customs and Revenue Agency) later issued reassessments excluding the dividend income from the taxpayers' income and including it in the income of an individual related to the taxpayers. The courts subsequently found, in a similar situation, that the amounts should not have been included in the income of the individual related to the taxpayer. Hence, the taxpayers' initial position was correct. As a result, the dividends were once again included in the taxpayers' income for the relevant taxation years, and interest was computed on the assessed tax arrears. However, given that the taxpayers had initially included those amounts in their tax returns and that their exclusion was the direct result of actions taken by Revenue Canada, the collection of arrears interest is considered unreasonable in this case.

Notes: Interest can be waived under ITA 220(3.1), but only in respect of 1985 and later taxation years.

CERTAIN TAXPAYERS REMISSION ORDER, 2003-1

P.C. 2003-912, June 12, 2003 (SI/2003-123)

1. **Remission** — Subject to section 2, remission is hereby granted of amounts payable under the *Income Tax Act* by a person who is or was a member of the *Memorial University Pension Plan* where those amounts would not be payable if the contributions paid by the person in respect of non-existent service pursuant to regulations made under section 29 of *The Memorial University (Pensions) Act*, R.S.N. 1970, c. 232, were deductible under the *Income Tax Act*.

2. **Conditions** — Remission is granted if the following conditions are met:

   (a) the contributions for non-existent service were made pursuant to an agreement entered into prior to 1990;

   (b) the contributions were made in accordance with the pension plan as registered;

   (c) the contributions have not been deducted from income in prior years; and

   (d) the person applies for this relief, in writing, to the Minister of National Revenue before January 1, 2004.

Explanatory Note [not part of the Order]: This Order remits amounts payable under the *Income Tax Act* resulting from the disallowance of the deduction from income of pension contributions made in respect of the purchase of non-existent service, as provided for under the Memorial University Pension Plan at the time of purchase.

MURRAY CHALMERS REMISSION ORDER

P.C. 2007-254, March 1, 2007 (SI/2007-33)

Her Excellency the Governor General in Council, considering that the collection of the tax is unjust, on the recommendation of the Minister of National Revenue, pursuant to subsection 23(2) of the *Financial Administration Act*, hereby remits tax under Part I.2 of the *Income Tax Act* in the amount of $685.95 for the 2004 taxation year, and all relevant interest thereon, paid or payable by Murray Chalmers.

Explanatory Note [not part of the Order]: This Order remits a portion of income tax and all relevant interest paid or payable thereon by Murray Chalmers in respect of the 2004 taxation year.

In 2004, Mr. Chalmers received a taxable lump sum payment from a government agency, which he was entitled to receive in the years from 1976 to 2004. As a result of the income inclusion in 2004, Mr. Chalmers was required to repay his Old Age Security pension for that year. The amount remitted represents the additional tax liability incurred by Mr. Chalmers as a result of the lengthy delay by the government agency in paying him the amounts to which he was entitled in the relevant years.

JANET DE LA TORRE REMISSION ORDER

P.C. 2017-1506, December 13, 2017 (SI/2017-81)

Whereas the Treasury Board has delegated to the President of the Treasury Board, pursuant to subsection 6(4) of the *Financial Administration Act*, its power to make a recommendation in respect of remission orders in amounts of less than $25,000 for other debts that are under the responsibility of the Minister of National Revenue;

Therefore, Her Excellency the Governor General in Council, considering that the collection of the amounts is unjust, on the recommendation of the Minister of Employment and Social Development, the Minister of National Revenue and the President of the Treasury Board, pursuant to subsection 23(2.1) of the *Financial Administration Act*, remits the following amounts to Janet De La Torre:

   (a) the amount of $1,263.12 that was paid or payable by her as repayment of Canada child tax benefits with respect to the 2012 base taxation year under Part I of the *Income Tax Act*; and

   (b) the amount of $500.00 that was paid or payable by her as repayment of benefits received in the 2013 and 2014 taxation years under the *Universal Child Care Benefit Act*.

Explanatory Note [not part of the Order]: The Order remits a total of $1,763.12 with respect to Canada child tax benefits and universal child care benefits received by Janet De La Torre, to which she was not entitled. The remission is based on extreme hardship.

MARIE-ROSE DENIS INCOME TAX REMISSION ORDER

P.C. 2017-163, March 8, 2017 (SI/2017-18)

His Excellency the Governor General in Council, considering that the collection of the tax referred to in the annexed Order is unjust, on the recommendation of the Minister of National Revenue, pursuant to subsection 23(2) of the *Financial Administration Act*, makes the annexed *Marie-Rose Denis Income Tax Remission Order*.

Remission

1. Remission is granted of the tax paid or payable by Marie-Rose Denis under Part I of the *Income Tax Act* in the amounts of $1,502.94, $3,042.53 and $2,991.91 for the 2007, 2008 and 2009 taxation years, respectively, and all relevant interest on that tax.

Condition

2. The remission is granted on the condition that Marie-Rose Denis does not claim a deduction under paragraph 111(1)(a) of the *Income Tax Act* for any portion of her non-capital loss relating to the repayment in 2013 of wage-loss replacement benefits to the Centre de santé et de services sociaux de la Baie-des-Chaleurs.

Explanatory Note [not part of the Order]: The Order remits income tax, and all relevant interest on it, paid or payable by Marie-Rose Denis for the 2007 to 2009 taxation years.

The amount remitted represents the additional tax incurred by Ms. Denis as a result of circumstances that were not within her control. The payment of these amounts caused a financial setback for Ms. Denis.

JACQUELINE DOSKOCH REMISSION ORDER

P.C. 2010-1595, December 9, 2010 (SI/2010-94)

His Excellency the Governor General in Council, considering that the collection of the interest is unjust, on the recommendation of the Minister of National Revenue, pursuant to subsection 23(2) of the *Financial Administration Act*, hereby remits all interest — calculated as of September 14, 2010 to be in the amounts of $64.77, $5,472.55, $20,759.78, $6,526.56 and $693.73 — and all relevant interest on that interest, paid or payable under Part I of the *Income Tax Act* by Jacqueline Doskoch for the 1980, 1981, 1983, 1984 and 1985 taxation years, respectively.

Explanatory Note [not part of the Order]: The Order remits interest, and all relevant interest on it, paid or payable by Jacqueline Doskoch for the 1980, 1981, 1983, 1984 and 1985 taxation years.

The interest accrued due to a circumstance beyond her control and caused a significant financial setback for Ms. Doskoch.

Notes: See Notes to the *Mildred Jacobs Remission Order* below.

WENDY DREVER REMISSION ORDER

P.C. 2009-299, February 26, 2009 (SI/2009-17)

Her Excellency the Governor General in Council, considering that the collection of the tax is unjust, on the recommendation of the Minister of National Revenue, pursuant to subsection 23(2) of the *Financial Administration Act*, hereby remits tax in the amount of $2,891.00, and all relevant interest on it, paid or payable by Wendy Drever, for the 2002 taxation year, under Part I of the *Income Tax Act*.

Explanatory Note [not part of the Order]: This Order remits a portion of income tax and all relevant interest paid or payable by Wendy Drever in respect of the 2002 taxation year.

Ms. Drever has been receiving taxable wage loss replacement benefits since 1995. In 2002, she received a retroactive lump sum disability payment from the Canada Pension Plan (CPP). This amount reduced her wage loss replacement benefit entitlements and she was required to repay the CPP lump sum payment to the wage loss replacement provider. She was taxed on the lump sum payment in 2002 and received a deduction from 2003 income for the repayment amount. Due to delays that were not within her control, the transaction bridged two taxation years. The amount remitted represents the additional tax liability incurred by Ms. Drever because of this timing difference.

MARY DUNCAN REMISSION ORDER

P.C. 2016-821, October 5, 2016 (SI/2016-52)

His Excellency the Governor General in Council, considering that the collection of the tax and the enforcement of the penalty are unjust, on the recommendation of the Minister of National Revenue, pursuant to subsection 23(2) of the *Financial Administration Act*, remits to Mary Duncan the following amounts paid or payable under Part I of the *Income Tax Act*:

(a) tax in the amount of $720.47 for the 1999 taxation year;

(b) late-filing penalty in the amount of $1,346.37 for the 1999 taxation year; and

(c) interest in the amount of $4,790.99 having accrued during the period beginning on January 1, 1999 and ending on December 31, 2000, for the 1993 to 1997 and 1999 taxation years.

Explanatory Note [not part of the Order]: This Order remits tax and a late-filing penalty in respect of the 1999 taxation year and arrears interest for the 1993, 1994, 1995, 1996, 1997 and 1999 taxation years, paid or payable by Mary Duncan.

The amounts remitted represent the additional liabilities incurred by Ms. Duncan as a result of circumstances that were beyond her control.

PIERRE DUPUIS INCOME TAX REMISSION ORDER, NO. 2

P.C. 2011-489, March 25, 2011 (SI/2011-27)

His Excellency the Governor General in Council, considering that the collection of the tax and penalty is unjust, on the recommendation of the Minister of National Revenue, pursuant to subsection 23(2) of the *Financial Administration Act*, hereby makes the annexed *Pierre Dupuis Income Tax Remission Order, No. 2*.

1. **Remission** — Remission is hereby granted of the tax paid or payable by Pierre Dupuis under Part I of the *Income Tax Act* in the amounts of $324.10, $298.72, $1,244.29 and $201.29 for the 1995, 1996, 1997 and 1999 taxation years, respectively, and a penalty of $16.76 paid or payable for the 1997 taxation year and all relevant interest on that tax and penalty.

2. **Condition** — The remission is granted on the condition that Pierre Dupuis does not claim a deduction under paragraph 111(1)(a) of the *Income Tax Act* for any portion of his non-capital loss relating to the repayment in 2003 of wage loss replacement benefits to Standard Life Assurance Company or to the repayment in 2003 of disability benefits to the Quebec Pension Plan.

Explanatory Note [not part of the Order]: The Order remits the income tax, the late-filing penalty and all relevant interest on these amounts, paid or payable by Pierre Dupuis for the 1995, 1996, 1997 and 1999 taxation years.

The amounts remitted represent the additional tax and penalty paid or payable by Mr. Dupuis as a result of circumstances that were beyond his control. The payment of these amounts represents a financial setback for Mr. Dupuis.

RONALD FRANCOEUR REMISSION ORDER

P.C. 2006-503, June 8, 2006 (SI/2006-94)

Her Excellency the Governor General in Council, considering that the collection of the tax is unjust, on the recommendation of the Minister of National Revenue, pursuant to subsection 23(2) of the *Financial Administration Act*, hereby remits tax and penalties under Part I of the *Income Tax Act* in the amount of $764.21 for the 1999 taxation year, and all relevant interest on that amount, paid or payable by Ronald Francoeur.

Explanatory Note [not part of the Order]: The Order remits a portion of income tax and all relevant interest paid or payable on that amount by Ronald Francoeur in respect of the 1999 taxation year.

In 2002, Mr. Francoeur repaid Employment Insurance (EI) benefits that he had received in 1999 but was unable to deduct the repayment amount in 2002. The amount of taxes paid in relation to the 1999 EI benefits represents an inequitable outcome beyond the control of Mr. Francoeur.

DANIELLE GAREAU REMISSION ORDER

P.C. 2003-774, May 29, 2003 (SI/2003-113)

Her Excellency the Governor General in Council, considering that the collection of the tax is unjust, on the recommendation of the Minister of National Revenue, pursuant to subsection 23(2) of the *Financial Administration Act*, hereby remits tax under Part I of the *Income Tax Act* in the amount of $155.10 for the 1998 taxation year, and all relevant interest thereon, paid or payable by Danielle Gareau.

Explanatory Note [not part of the Order]: This Order remits a portion of the income tax and all relevant interest paid or payable thereon by Danielle Gareau in respect of the 1998 taxation year.

In 1998, Ms. Gareau received Employment Insurance (EI) benefits in excess of her entitlements. She repaid some of the excess in 1998 and, on the advice of officials of the Department of Human Resources Development, she repaid the balance by installments in 1999. Repayments of benefits may be deducted from income in the year of repayment. Thus, Ms. Gareau was entitled to deduct her repayment from her 1999 income. However, she had no income in 1999 from which to deduct it. As a result, she has been taxed in 1998 on EI benefits that she repaid in 1999. The inclusion in income of EI benefits in 1998 that were later repaid unfairly caused Danielle Gareau additional tax liability.

SUSAN GILL REMISSION ORDER

P.C. 2011-279, March 3, 2011 (SI/2011-19)

His Excellency the Governor General in Council, considering that the collection of the interest is unjust, on the recommendation of the Minister of National Revenue, pursuant to subsection 23(2) of the *Financial Administration Act*, hereby remits interest in the amount of $12,592.51, paid or payable under Part I of the *Income Tax Act* by Susan Gill for the 1982, 1983 and 1984 taxation years, having accrued during the period beginning on January 1, 1987 and ending on December 31, 2000, and all relevant interest on it.

Explanatory Note [not part of the Order]: The Order remits a portion of the interest, and all relevant interest on it, paid or payable by Susan Gill for the 1982, 1983 and 1984 taxation years.

The interest accrued in part due to circumstances beyond her control and would create a significant financial setback for Ms. Gill. The payment of this amount would produce an inequitable amount for Ms. Gill.

Notes: See Notes to the *Mildred Jacobs Remission Order* below.

PIERRE GOSSELIN REMISSION ORDER

P.C. 2009-951, June 11, 2009 (SI/2009-51)

Her Excellency the Governor General in Council, considering that the collection of the tax is unjust, on the recommendation of the Minister of National Revenue, pursuant to subsection 23(2) of the *Financial Administration Act*, hereby remits tax

(a) in the amount of $2,798.63, $2,755.07, $5,197.06, $1,891.79, $2,176.76, $2,613.95, $1,583.89, $1,889.86, $2,239.50, $1,117.15, $167.79 and $201.04, and all relevant interest on it, paid or payable under Part I of the *Income Tax Act* by Pierre Gosselin or his estate for the 1991, 1992, 1993, 1994, 1995, 1996, 1997, 1998, 1999, 2000, 2003 and 2004 taxation years, respectively, and

(b) in the amount of $2,576.55, and all relevant interest on it, paid or payable under Part I.2 of the *Income Tax Act* by Pierre Gosselin or his estate for the 2005 taxation year.

Explanatory Note [not part of the Order]: The Order remits a portion of the income tax and all relevant interest paid or payable by Pierre Gosselin or his estate for the 1991 to 2000 and 2003 to 2005 taxation years.

The amount remitted represents the additional tax incurred by Mr. Gosselin as a result of circumstances that were not within his control. The payment of that amount caused a significant financial setback for Mr. Gosselin.

JANET HALL REMISSION ORDER

P.C. 2004-1336, November 16, 2004 (SI/2004-154)

Her Excellency the Governor General in Council, considering that the collection of the tax is unjust, on the recommendation of the Minister of National Revenue, pursuant to subsection 23(2) of the *Financial Administration Act*, hereby remits tax under Part I of the *Income Tax Act* in the amount of $4,648.90 for the 2001 taxation year, and all relevant interest thereon, paid or payable by Janet Hall.

Explanatory Note [not part of the Order]: This Order remits a portion of income tax and all relevant interest paid or payable thereon by Janet Hall in respect of the 2001 taxation year.

Ms. Hall has been receiving taxable wage loss replacement benefits since 1994. In 2001 she received a retroactive lump sum disability payment from the Canada Pension Plan (CPP). This amount reduced her wage loss replacement entitlements and she was required to repay approximately 95% of the CPP lump sum to the wage loss replacement provider. She was taxed on the lump sum payment in 2001 and received a deduction from 2002 income for the repayment amount. Due to delays that were not within her control, the transaction bridged two taxation years. The additional tax assessed because of the timing difference represents a significant financial setback for Ms. Hall.

CÉLINE HAMEL INCOME TAX REMISSION ORDER

P.C. 2015-839, July 1, 2015 (SI/2015-56)

His Excellency the Governor General in Council, considering that the collection of tax in question is unjust, on the recommendation of the Minister of National Revenue, pursuant to subsection 23(2) of the *Financial Administration Act*, makes the annexed *Céline Hamel Income Tax Remission Order*.

Remission

1. Remission is granted of the tax paid or payable by Céline Hamel under Part I of the *Income Tax Act* in the amounts of $1,034.87, $98.87 and $201.95 for the 2005, 2006 and 2007 taxation years, respectively, and all relevant interest on those amounts.

Condition

2. The remission is granted on the condition that Céline Hamel does not claim a deduction under paragraph 111(1)(a) of the *Income Tax Act* for any portion of her non-capital loss relating to the repayment, in 2011, of wage-loss replacement benefits and disability benefits by her to the Centre de santé et de services sociaux de Gatineau and to the Régie des rentes du Québec, respectively.

Explanatory Note [not part of the Order]: The Order remits income tax, and all relevant interest on it, paid or payable by Céline Hamel for the 2005, 2006 and 2007 taxation years.

The amount remitted represents the additional tax incurred by Ms. Hamel as a result of circumstances that were not within her control. The payment of these amounts caused a financial setback for Ms. Hamel.

VERA HENDERSON INCOME TAX REMISSION ORDER

P.C. 2008-983, May 29, 2008 (SI/2008-62)

Her Excellency the Governor General in Council, considering that the collection of tax is unjust, on the recommendation of the Minister of Finance, pursuant to subsection 23(2) of the *Financial Administration Act*, hereby makes the annexed *Vera Henderson Income Tax Remission Order*.

1. **Remission** — Remission is hereby granted of the tax paid by Vera Henderson under Part I of the *Income Tax Act* in the amount of $4,000.70 for the 2001 taxation year.

2. **Condition** — The remission is granted on the condition that Vera Henderson does not claim a deduction under subsection 120.2(1) of the *Income Tax Act* in respect of the amount remitted.

Explanatory Note [not part of the Order]: The Order remits $4,000.70 paid by Vera Henderson as income tax for the 2001 taxation year.

The amount remitted represents the additional tax paid by Mrs. Henderson due to unintended results of the legislation.

XIU QUE HONG REMISSION ORDER

P.C. 2013-39, January 31, 2013 (SI/2013-10)

His Excellency the Governor General in Council, considering that the collection of the amount is unjust, on the recommendation of the Minister of National Revenue and the Treasury Board, pursuant to subsection 23(2.1) of the *Financial Administration Act*, remits the amount of $8,060.90 paid or payable by Xiu Que Hong as repayment of Canada child tax benefits under Part I of the *Income Tax Act* with respect to the 2005 and 2006 base taxation years.

Explanatory Note [not part of the Order]: The Order remits the amount of $8,060.90 with respect to Canada child tax benefits received by Xiu Que Hong, for the 2005 and 2006 base taxation years, to which she was not entitled. The remission is based on extreme hardship and financial setback with an extenuating circumstance.

INVESTORS IN THE NORBOURG AND EVOLUTION FUNDS REMISSION ORDER

P.C. 2012-816, June 19, 2012 (SI/2012-43)

His Excellency the Governor General in Council, considering that it is in the public interest to do so, on the recommendation of the Minister of National Revenue, pursuant to subsection 23(2) of the *Financial Administration Act*, hereby makes the annexed *Investors in the Norbourg and Evolution Funds Remission Order*.

1. **Interpretation** — The following definitions apply in this Order.

"**dividend**" means funds to be distributed to creditors in accordance with sections 148 and 151 of the *Bankruptcy and Insolvency Act*.

"**Groupe Norbourg**" means the five companies set out below that were controlled by Vincent Lacroix, that managed securities and investments including Norbourg and Evolution funds, and that made assignments in bankruptcy which were filed under section 49 of the *Bankruptcy and Insolvency Act*:

    (a) Norbourg Groupe Financier inc;

    (b) Ascencia Capital inc;

    (c) Norbourg Gestion d'actif inc;

    (d) Fonds Évolution inc;

    (e) Gestion d'actifs Perfolio inc.

"**Groupe Norbourg trustee**" means RSM Richter Inc. in its capacity as trustee in bankruptcy of Groupe Norbourg under subsection 49(4) of the *Bankruptcy and Insolvency Act*.

"**investor**" means a unit holder who, on August 25, 2005, held units in one or more of the Norbourg or Evolution funds set out in the schedule, and who made a claim against any of these funds.

"Lacroix trustee" means Ernst & Young Inc. in its capacity as trustee in bankruptcy of Vincent Lacroix under subsection 43(9) of the *Bankruptcy and Insolvency Act*.

"liquidator" means Martin Daigneault of Ernst & Young Inc. in his capacity as liquidator under the *Securities Act*, R.S.Q., c. V-11, of the mutual funds managed by Groupe Norbourg.

2. **Remission** — Subject to section 3, remission is granted to the Lacroix trustee of an amount, not exceeding $256,000, that is equal to the estimated bankruptcy dividend payment in respect of tax payable by Vincent Lacroix, a bankrupt, under Part I of the *Income Tax Act* for the 2005 taxation year.

3. **Conditions** — The remission is granted subject to the following conditions:

(a) the liquidator or the Groupe Norbourg trustee files a claim in the Vincent Lacroix bankruptcy for funds misappropriated from investments and securities managed by the Groupe Norbourg;

(b) the Lacroix trustee accepts the validity of the claim by the liquidator or the Groupe Norbourg trustee in the Vincent Lacroix bankruptcy or accepts that the claim be recognized as valid by a tribunal;

(c) the assets in the bankruptcy estate of Vincent Lacroix do not permit settlement of the claim of the liquidator or of the Groupe Norbourg trustee at the time of distribution;

(d) in accordance with instructions from the Crown, the amount of dividend described in section 2 will be remitted by the Lacroix trustee to the liquidator;

(e) the liquidator accepts the amount of dividend and accepts to distribute it to the investors in accordance with the directives of the tribunal having jurisdiction;

(f) once the claims of all investors have been fully met, any remaining part of the amount described in section 2 is returned by the liquidator to the Crown as soon as possible;

(g) upon request from the Crown, the liquidator undertakes to provide a final report to the Crown of the distribution to investors of the amount described in section 2;

(h) the Crown is not liable for any fees related to the determination and the distribution of the amounts distributed to the investors; and

(i) the Crown has the right to require an investor to repay any amount received by the investor under this Remission Order to the extent that the total compensation paid to satisfy the investor's claim exceeds the amount of that claim.

Schedule

(Section 1)

Evolution Funds

Evolution American Fund	Evolution Money Market Fund
Evolution American RSP Fund	Evolution Perfolio Balanced Fund
Evolution Asset Management Global Industries of the Future Fund	Evolution Perfolio Diversified Revenue Fund
Evolution Balanced Fund	Evolution Perfolio Global Fund
Evolution Bond Fund	Evolution Perfolio Growth Fund
Evolution Canadian Asset Allocation Fund	Evolution Quebec Expansion Fund
Evolution Canadian Demographic Fund	Evolution QSSP Fund
Evolution Canadian Equity — Large Cap Fund	Evolution Selection ETF Fund
Evolution Canadian Equity — Value Fund	Evolution World Leaders Fund
Evolution Demographic Trends Fund	Evolution World Leaders RSP Fund
Evolution Finance and Technology Fund	

Norbourg Funds

Norbourg Balanced Fund	Norbourg Fixed Income Fund
Norbourg Canadian Tactical Asset Allocation Fund	Norbourg International Balanced Fund
Norbourg Convertible Debentures Fund	Norbourg Money Market Fund
Norbourg Emerging Growth Companies Fund	Norbourg Equity — Special Situations Fund

Explanatory Note [not part of the Order]: This Order grants remission and waives receipt of an amount not exceeding $256,000, which amount is equal to the estimated dividend bankruptcy payment in respect of tax pursuant to Part I of the *Income Tax Act* payable by Vincent Lacroix, a bankrupt person, for the 2005 taxation year.

The remission and waiver are subject to conditions that, if met, will permit the distribution of the amount to investors in the Norbourg and Evolution funds as partial settlement of funds misappropriated by the tax debtor Vincent Lacroix.

MILDRED JACOBS REMISSION ORDER
P.C. 2011-482, March 25, 2011 (SI/2011-24)

His Excellency the Governor General in Council, considering that the collection of the penalty and interest is unjust, on the recommendation of the Minister of National Revenue, pursuant to subsection 23(2) of the *Financial Administration Act*, hereby remits a penalty of $16,786.79 and arrears interest of $131,703 as of December 11, 2007, and all interest on that penalty and interest, paid or payable under Part I of the *Income Tax Act* by Mildred Jacobs or her estate for the 1994 taxation year.

Explanatory Note [not part of the Order]: The Order remits the late filing penalty and a portion of the arrears interest for the 1994 tax year, paid or payable, by Mildred Jacobs or her estate.

The penalty and arrears interest are being remitted because collection of these amounts is unreasonable and unjust based on the circumstances of her case.

Notes: Since *Bozzer*, 2011 FCA 186, remission orders like this that waive only interest and penalty are no longer needed for interest accruing within the 10 years before CRA is asked to provide relief, as CRA can do this under ITA 220(3.1). They are still needed for interest accruing earlier.

DEBBIE JOHNSTON REMISSION ORDER

P.C. 2013-38, January 31, 2013 (SI/2013-9)

His Excellency the Governor General in Council, considering that the collection of the debt is unjust, on the recommendation of the Minister of National Revenue and the Treasury Board, pursuant to subsection 23(2.1) of the *Financial Administration Act*, remits the amount of $1,408.60, paid or payable under Part I of the *Income Tax Act* by Debbie Johnston, as repayment of goods and services tax credits with respect to the 1994 and 1995 base taxation years.

Explanatory Note [not part of the Order]: The Order remits the amount of $1,408.60 with respect to the goods and services tax credits that were determined to be in excess of Debbie Johnston's entitlement for the 1994 and 1995 base taxation years. The remission is based on financial setback with extenuating circumstances.

KEITH KIRBY REMISSION ORDER

P.C. 2005-1533, August 31, 2005 (SI/2005-79)

Her Excellency the Governor General in Council, considering that the collection of the tax is unjust, on the recommendation of the Minister of National Revenue, pursuant to subsection 23(2) of the *Financial Administration Act*, hereby remits tax under Part I.2 of the *Income Tax Act* in the amount of $2,167.41 for the 1999 taxation year, and all relevant interest thereon, paid or payable by Keith Kirby.

Explanatory Note [not part of the Order]: This Order remits a portion of income tax and all relevant interest paid or payable thereon by Keith Kirby in respect of the 1999 taxation year.

In 1999, Mr. Kirby received a lump sum payment from a government agency, a portion of which he was entitled to receive in the years from 1996 to 1998. As a result of the income inclusion in 1999, Mr. Kirby was required to repay a significant portion of his Old Age Security benefits for that year and was not entitled to claim the age amount. The amount remitted represents the additional tax liability incurred by Mr. Kirby as a result of the delay by the government agency in paying him the amounts to which he was entitled in the relevant years.

WESLEY KOOL REMISSION ORDER

P.C. 2006-1277, November 2, 2006 (SI/2006-131)

Her Excellency the Governor General in Council, considering that the collection of the tax is unjust, on the recommendation of the Minister of National Revenue, pursuant to subsection 23(2) of the *Financial Administration Act*, hereby remits tax under Part I.2 of the *Income Tax Act* in the amount of $761.18 for the 2004 taxation year, and all relevant interest thereon, paid or payable by Wesley Kool.

Explanatory Note [not part of the Order]: This Order remits a portion of income tax and all relevant interest paid or payable thereon by Wesley Kool in respect of the 2004 taxation year.

In 2004, Mr. Kool received a taxable lump sum payment from a government agency, a portion of which he was entitled to receive in the years from 1983 to 2003. As a result of the income inclusion in 2004, Mr. Kool was required to repay Old Age Security benefits for that year. The amount remitted represents the additional tax liability incurred by Mr. Kool as a result of the lengthy delay by the government agency in paying him the amounts to which he was entitled in the relevant years.

MILCA KWANGWARI REMISSION ORDER

P.C. 2017-1507, December 13, 2017 (SI/2017-82)

Whereas the Treasury Board has delegated to the President of the Treasury Board, pursuant to subsection 6(4) of the *Financial Administration Act*, its power to make a recommendation in respect of remission orders in amounts of less than $25,000 for other debts that are under the responsibility of the Minister of National Revenue;

Therefore, Her Excellency the Governor General in Council, considering that the collection of the amounts is unjust, on the recommendation of the Minister of Employment and Social Development, the Minister of National Revenue and the President of the Treasury Board, pursuant to subsection 23(2.1) of the *Financial Administration Act*, remits the following amounts to Milca Kwangwari:

(a) $1,034.34 and $413.56, paid or payable by her under Part I of the *Income Tax Act* as a repayment of Canada child tax benefits for the 2008 and 2009 base taxation years, respectively; and

(b) $523.36 and $962.74, paid or payable by her under the *Universal Child Care Benefit Act* as a repayment of benefits for the 2009 and 2010 taxation years, respectively.

Explanatory Note [not part of the Order]: The Order remits a total of $2,934 with respect to Canada child tax benefits and universal child care benefits received by Milca Kwangwari, to which she was not entitled. The remission is based on incorrect action on the part of Canada Revenue Agency officials.

TRENA LAHAYE REMISSION ORDER

P.C. 2016-868, October 19, 2016 (SI/2016-58)

Whereas the recommendation of the Treasury Board is required for the remission of other debts under subsection 23(2.1) of the *Financial Administration Act*, and the Treasury Board has delegated to the President of the Treasury Board, pursuant to subsection 6(4) of that Act, its power to make that recommendation in respect of remission orders in amounts of less than $25,000 for other debts that are under the responsibility of the Minister of National Revenue;

Therefore, His Excellency the Governor General in Council, considering that the collection of the amounts is unjust, on the recommendation of the Minister of National Revenue and the President of the Treasury Board, pursuant to subsection 23(2.1) of the *Financial Administration Act*, remits to Trena LaHaye the following amounts paid or payable under Part I of the *Income Tax Act* for the 2010 to 2012 base taxation years:

(a) $6,272.10 as repayment of Canada child tax benefits; and

(b) $270.55 as repayment of the goods and services tax/harmonized sales tax credit.

Explanatory Note [not part of the Order]: The Order remits $6,272.10 with respect to Canada child tax benefits and $270.55 with respect to the goods and services tax/Harmonized sales tax credit received by Trena LaHaye in error to which she was not entitled. The remission is based on incorrect action on the part of Canada Revenue Agency officials.

LINE LAJEUNESSE AND EDUARDUS A.T. MERKS REMISSION ORDER

P.C. 2002-1895, November 7, 2002 (SI/2002-148)

1. **Remission to Line Lajeunesse** — Remission is hereby granted to Line Lajeunesse of tax paid under the *Income Tax Act* in the amount determined by the formula

$$[A \times B] - C] + [A \times (D + E)]$$

where

A is 0.44195,

B is the previous contribution of $16,502 to a registered retirement saving plan, on the condition that the income tax deduction claimed by Line Lajeunesse in respect of that contribution is cancelled,

C is the income tax saved by Line Lajeunesse due to the deduction from income referred to in the description of B of this formula,

D is the amount, up to a maximum of $41,292.62, that Line Lajeunesse will contribute to a registered retirement plan within three months after the date of coming into force of this Order, on the condition that she never claims a deduction from income in respect of that amount, and

E is the contribution of $5,000 made by Line Lajeunesse to a registered retirement savings plan in January 2001, on the condition that she never claims a deduction from income in respect of that amount and that she remits to the Canada Customs and Revenue Agency the related income tax receipt.

2. **Remission to Eduardus A.T. Merks** — Remission is hereby granted to Eduardus A.T. Merks in the amount of $2,978.68, which represents tax paid under the *Income Tax Act*.

Explanatory Note [not part of the Order]: This Order remits income tax to Ms. Lajeunesse as if she were entitled to receive tax-free amounts transferred from a registered retirement savings plan.

This Order also remits to Mr. Merks $2,978.68 as if he were entitled to a tax deduction in respect of medical expenses.

YOLANDE LAURENCE REMISSION ORDER

P.C. 2014-952, September 18, 2014 (SI/2014-77)

His Excellency the Governor General in Council, considering that the collection of the amounts is unjust, on the recommendation of the Minister of National Revenue and the Treasury Board, pursuant to subsection 23(2.1) of the *Financial Administration Act*, remits the amount of $5,069.81 paid or payable by Yolande Laurence, as repayment of Canada child tax benefits under Part I of the *Income Tax Act*, with respect to the 2004, 2005 and 2006 base taxation years, and $250, paid or payable by her, as repayment of an energy cost benefit under the *Energy Costs Assistance Measures Act*, with respect to the 2004 base taxation year.

Explanatory Note [not part of the Order]: The Order remits $5,069.81 with respect to Canada child tax benefits and $250 with respect to the energy cost benefit received by Yolande Laurence in error, to which she was not entitled. The remission is based on incorrect action on the part of federal government officials.

DAVID LYNDS INCOME TAX REMISSION ORDER

P.C. 2005-707, May 3, 2005 (SI/2005-40)

1. **Interpretation** — In this Order, **"non-capital loss"** has the meaning assigned by subsection 111(8) of the *Income Tax Act*.

2. **Remission** — Remission is hereby granted of the tax paid or payable by David Lynds under Part I of the *Income Tax Act* in the amount of $303.45, $5,050.75, $1,464.72, $2,783.04, $2,825.00 and $2,712.44 for the 1992, 1993, 1994, 1995, 1996 and 1997 taxation years respectively, and all interest paid or payable on it.

3. **Condition** — The remission is granted on the condition that David Lynds does not claim a deduction for any portion of his non-capital loss relating to the repayment in 2001 of wage loss replacement benefits to Manulife Financial.

Explanatory Note [not part of the Order]: The Order remits to David Lynds $15,139.40, which represents a portion of the tax paid or payable by Mr. Lynds under Part I of the *Income Tax Act* for the taxation years 1992 through 1997 and all interest paid or payable on it.

The amount remitted represents the additional tax liability incurred by Mr. Lynds as a result of the lengthy adjudication period involved in obtaining a workers' compensation award.

MICHELINE MALENFANT AND ROCH MALENFANT REMISSION ORDER

P.C. 2005-1732, October 4, 2005 (SI/2005-93)

Her Excellency the Governor General in Council, considering that the collection of the tax is unjust, on the recommendation of the Minister of National Revenue, pursuant to subsection 23(2) of the *Financial Administration Act*, hereby remits tax under Part I of the *Income Tax Act* in the amounts of $434.21 and $840.79 for the 2001 taxation year, and all relevant interest thereon, paid or payable by Micheline Malenfant and Roch Malenfant, respectively.

Explanatory Note [not part of the Order]: This Order remits a portion of income tax and all relevant interest paid or payable thereon by Micheline Malenfant and Roch Malenfant in respect of the 2001 taxation year.

In 2002, Ms. Malenfant repaid Employment Insurance (EI) benefits that she had received in 2001, but she was unable to deduct the repayment amount in 2002. This situation also created an additional tax liability in 2001 for Mr. Malenfant as he became unable to claim a tax credit to which he would otherwise have been entitled. The amount of taxes paid in relation to the 2001 EI benefits represents an inequitable outcome beyond the control of the Malenfants.

JERRY MATHEWS REMISSION ORDER

P.C. 2006-446, June 1, 2006 (SI/2006-92)

Her Excellency the Governor General in Council, considering that the collection of the amount is unjust, on the recommendation of the Minister of National Revenue and the Treasury Board, pursuant to subsection 23(2.1) of the *Financial Administration Act*, hereby remits interest charged under Part I of the *Income Tax Act* in the amount of $4,382.01 as of April 5, 2004, and all interest on that interest, paid or payable by Jerry Mathews.

Explanatory Note [not part of the Order]: This Order remits to Jerry Mathews $4,382.01, which represents interest charges on arrears of a 1983 income tax debt.

Mr. Mathews filed his 1980 to 1985 tax returns in 2000. He owed a tax balance for 1983; however, a subsequent year loss carryback eliminated the tax debt. While the taxes were eliminated, the interest that had accrued on that debt remained and arrears interest continued to accrue on that balance.

Having regard to the length of time that had elapsed and the fact that no income tax liability arose as a result of the late filings, it is just to remit the accumulated interest charges.

ESTATES OF KATHLEEN McGOWAN AND WILLIAM F. McGOWAN REMISSION ORDER

P.C. 2014-1477, December 31, 2014 (SI/2014-111)

His Excellency the Governor General in Council, considering that the collection of the penalties and interest is unjust, on the recommendation of the Minister of National Revenue, pursuant to subsection 23(2) of the *Financial Administration Act*, makes the annexed *Estates of Kathleen McGowan and William F. McGowan Remission Order*.

1. (1) Remission is granted of the amounts set out in column 1 of Schedule 1, which represent penalties paid or payable by the Estate of Kathleen McGowan under Part I of the *Income Tax Act* for the taxation years listed in column 2, and all relevant interest on those amounts.

(2) Remission, in the amount of $7,660.97, is granted of interest paid or payable by the Estate of Kathleen McGowan under Part I of the *Income Tax Act* for the 1996, 1997, 1998 and 1999 taxation years, having accrued during the period beginning on January 23, 1997 and ending on December 31, 2000, and all relevant interest on that amount.

2. (1) Remission is granted of the amounts set out in column 1 of Schedule 2, which represent penalties paid or payable by the Estate of William F. McGowan under Part I of the *Income Tax Act* for the taxation years listed in column 2, and all relevant interest on those amounts.

(2) Remission, in the amount of $132.67, is granted of interest paid or payable by the Estate of William F. McGowan under Part I of the *Income Tax Act* for the 2000 taxation year, having accrued during the period beginning on June 4, 2000 and ending on December 31, 2000, and all relevant interest on that amount.

Schedules 1 and 2 — *(Subsections 1(1), 2(1))*

[Not reproduced]

Explanatory Note [not part of the Order]: This Order remits a portion of the arrears interest in respect of the 1996, 1997, 1998, 1999 and 2000 taxation years, and late-filing penalties in respect of the 1996, 1997, 1998, 1999, 2000, 2001, 2002 and 2003 taxation years and all relevant interest paid or payable thereon by the estates of Kathleen and William F. McGowan.

The amounts remitted represent the additional liabilities incurred by the estates as a result of circumstances that were beyond the executor's control.

OAK RIDGES MORAINE LAND EXCHANGE INCOME TAX REMISSION ORDER

P.C. 2010-218, February 23, 2010 (SI/2010-17), as amended by P.C. 2018-610, June 13, 2018 (SI/2018-41)

1. **Interpretation** — (1) **Definitions** — The following definitions apply in this Order.

"**Act**" means the *Income Tax Act*.

"**Agreement**" means the agreement entered into on July 5, 2004 between the Province of Ontario, as represented by the Minister of Municipal Affairs and Housing, and certain parties including transferor corporations and members.

"**Drynoch Partnership**" means the Village of Drynoch Partnership formed under the laws of Ontario.

"**eligible amount**", in respect of an eligible person, means an amount equal to the amount determined under subsection 2(1) for the eligible person.

"**eligible person**" means a transferor corporation or a member.

"**member**" means a person that is listed in any of Parts 1, 2 and 3 of Schedule 1 and that on August 14, 2007 was, or was a beneficiary of a bare trust that was, a partner of one or both of the Drynoch Partnership and the transferor partnership.

"**North Pickering Land**", in respect of a transferor corporation or the transferor partnership, means any interest in land that the transferor corporation or the transferor partnership, as the case may be, acquired on August 14, 2007 under the Agreement.

"**Oak Ridges Moraine Land**", in respect of a transferor corporation or the transferor partnership, means any interest in land that the transferor corporation or the transferor partnership, as the case may be, disposed of on August 14, 2007 under the Agreement.

"**payment year**", in respect of an eligible person, means the eligible person's specified taxation year and each of the eligible person's nine taxation years following that specified taxation year.

"**specified taxation year**", in respect of an eligible person, means the eligible person's taxation year that

(a) in the case of a transferor corporation, includes August 14, 2007; and

(b) in the case of a member, includes December 31, 2007.

"**transferor corporation**" means a corporation listed in Schedule 2.

"**transferor partnership**" means the MacLeod Landing Partnership formed under the laws of Ontario.

(2) **Application of rules under Act** — For greater certainty,

(a) for the purpose of this Order a disposition includes a deemed disposition under the Act; and

(b) if under the Act the transferor partnership or the Drynoch Partnership is continued or ceases to exist, or is deemed to be continued or to cease to exist, for the purpose of this Order the transferor partnership or the Drynoch Partnership, as the case may be, is continued or ceases to exist, or is deemed to be continued or to cease to exist.

(3) **Application of meanings in Act** — Unless the context otherwise requires, words and expressions used in this Order have the same meaning as in the Act.

(4) **Transferor corporation that is member** — For the purposes of this Order, if a transferor corporation is also a member, the transferor corporation is deemed to be a separate and distinct eligible person from the member.

2. **Remission** — (1) **Income tax remitted** — Subject to sections 3 to 5, remission is granted to each eligible person for their specified taxation year of the amount, if any, by which

(a) the income tax payable under Part I of the Act by the eligible person for their specified taxation year

exceeds

(b) the income tax that would have been payable under Part I of the Act by the eligible person for their specified taxation year, if the transferor corporation's or the transferor partnership's, as the case may be, proceeds from the disposition of their Oak Ridges Moraine Land had been equal to the cost amount to the transferor corporation or the transferor partnership, as the case may be, of their Oak Ridges Moraine Land immediately before the disposition.

(2) **Income tax remitted** — If at a particular time an eligible person does not meet one or more of the conditions set out in section 4 (other than the condition set out in paragraph 4(a)), but has paid an amount before the particular time that was required to be paid under section 5 before the particular time, remission is granted to the eligible person of the tax payable under Part I of the Act in respect of the eligible person's specified taxation year to the extent of the amount so paid by the eligible person.

(3) **Penalty and interest remitted** — Remission is granted to an eligible person of the amount of any interest or penalty payable under the Act on any amount remitted under this section.

Conditions

3. **Inventory requirement** — No remission is granted to an eligible person under section 2 unless,

(a) if the eligible person is a transferor corporation, that transferor corporation's Oak Ridges Moraine Land was described, immediately before its disposition on August 14, 2007, in an inventory of that transferor corporation; and

(b) if the eligible person is a member, the transferor partnership's Oak Ridges Moraine Land was described, immediately before its disposition on August 14, 2007, in an inventory of the transferor partnership.

4. **Application, payments and acknowledgements** — A remission referred to in subsection 2(1) is granted to an eligible person on the condition that

(a) the eligible person applies to the Minister in writing for remission under this Order at a time (in this section referred to as the "application time") that is before the last day of the sixth month that follows the month in which this Order is published in the *Canada Gazette*, Part II;

(b) the eligible person pays to the Receiver General for Canada, on or before the date provided under section 5 for its payment, each amount, if any, that the eligible person is required to pay under that section; and

(c) the eligible person provides to the Minister,

(i) with the application described in paragraph (a), an acknowledgement in writing specifying the amount, if any, that the eligible person is required to pay under section 5 as of the application time,

(ii) on or before each day that is the eligible person's filing-due date for a particular payment year that ends after the application time, an acknowledgement in writing specifying the amount, if any, that remains to be paid under section 5 for the payment years that follow the particular payment year; and

(iii) with the application described in paragraph (a) and any acknowledgement referred to in subparagraph (i), an acknowledgement in writing that, if the eligible person does not meet the conditions set out in this section at a particular time that is after the application time, it owes at the particular time, under the Act, an amount equal to the total of

(A) the particular amount, if any, by which the eligible amount exceeds the total of all amounts paid by the eligible person under section 5 before the particular time, and

(B) the total of the interest and penalties payable under the Act in respect of the particular amount.

5. (1) **Disposition of North Pickering Land by a Transferor Corporation** — If, in a payment year, a transferor corporation disposes of North Pickering Land, the transferor corporation must pay the amount determined by the formula

$$A \times (B/C)$$

where

A is the eligible amount of the transferor corporation;

B is the fair market value, on August 14, 2007, of the North Pickering Land disposed of by the transferor corporation in the payment year; and

C is the fair market value, on August 14, 2007, of all of the North Pickering Land of the transferor corporation.

(2) **Disposition of North Pickering Land by the Transferor Partnership** — If, in a fiscal period of the transferor partnership that ends in a payment year of a member, the transferor partnership disposes of North Pickering Land, the member must pay the amount determined by the formula

$$A \times (B/C) \times (D/E)$$

where

A is the eligible amount of the member;

B is the fair market value, at the end of August 14, 2007, of the North Pickering Land disposed of by the transferor partnership in the fiscal period;

C is the fair market value, on August 14, 2007, of all of the North Pickering Land of the transferor partnership;

D is the lesser of E and the proportion (expressed as a percentage) of the interests in the transferor partnership that may reasonably be considered to be held by the member directly, or indirectly through the Drynoch partnership or a bare trustee, at the end of the payment year; and

E is the proportion (expressed as a percentage) of the interests in the transferor partnership that may reasonably be considered to have been held by the member directly, or indirectly through the Drynoch partnership or a bare trustee, on August 14, 2007.

(3) **Disposition of partnership interest** — A member must pay, in addition to any amount payable by the member under subsection (2), in respect of a particular payment year the total of,

(a) if the member disposes, at any time in the particular payment year, of all or part of the member's direct interest in a particular partnership that is the transferor partnership or the Drynoch Partnership, the positive amount, if any, determined by the formula

$$(A - B) \times [(C - D)/E]$$

where

A is the eligible amount of the member;

B is the total of all amounts each of which is an amount payable by the member

(i) under this subsection for a previous payment year, or

(ii) under subsection (2) for a previous payment year or the particular payment year;

C is the lesser of the proportion (expressed as a percentage) of the interests in the particular partnership that may reasonably be considered to have been held directly by the member on August 14, 2007 and the proportion (expressed as a percentage) of the interests in the particular partnership that may reasonably be considered to be held directly by the member at the beginning of the particular payment year;

D is the lesser of E and the proportion (expressed as a percentage) of the interests in the particular partnership that may reasonably be considered to be held directly by the member at the end of the particular payment year, and

E is the proportion (expressed as a percentage) of the interest in the particular partnership that may reasonably be considered to have been held directly by the member on August 14, 2007, and

(b) if the member is mentioned in Part 1 or 3 of Schedule 1 and the particular payment year includes the end of a fiscal period of the Drynoch partnership during which the Drynoch partnership disposes of all or part of its interests in the transferor partnership, the positive amount, if any, determined by the formula

$$(A - B) \times [(C - D)/E]$$

where

A is the eligible amount of the member;

B is the total of all amounts each of which is an amount payable by the member

(i) under paragraph (a) for the particular payment year,

(ii) under this subsection for a previous payment year, or

(iii) under subsection (2) for a previous payment year or the particular payment year;

C is the lesser of

(i) the proportion (expressed as a percentage) of the interests in the transferor partnership that may reasonably be considered to have been held by the Drynoch Partnership on August 14, 2007, and

(ii) the proportion (expressed as a percentage) of the interests in the transferor partnership that may reasonably be considered to have been held by the Drynoch Partnership at the end of its fiscal period that ends in the member's taxation year that immediately precedes the particular payment year;

D is the lesser of C and the proportion (expressed as a percentage) of the interests in the transferor partnership that may reasonably be considered to have been held by the Drynoch Partnership at the end of its fiscal period that ends in the particular payment year; and

E is the proportion (expressed as a percentage) of the interests in the transferor partnership that was held by the Drynoch Partnership at the end of August 14, 2007.

Related Provisions: ITA 257 — Negative amounts in formulas.

(4) **Timing of payment** — An amount payable by an eligible person under any of subsections (1) to (3) in respect of a payment year must be paid on or before the filing-due date for the later of

(a) the eligible person's first taxation year that ends on or after the day on which this Order is published in the *Canada Gazette*, Part II; and

(b) the eligible person's taxation year that corresponds to the payment year.

(5) **Final payment** — Each eligible person must pay on or before the eligible person's filing-due date for the twentieth taxation year following their specified taxation year, the amount determined by the formula

$$A - B$$

where

A is the eligible amount of the eligible person; and

B is the total of all amounts each of which is an amount payable under any of subsections (1) to (3) by the eligible person.

Related Provisions: ITA 257 — Negative amounts in formulas.

Notes: 5(5) amended by P.C. 2018-610 to change "tenth" to "twentieth", to defer tax for a further 10 years.

(6) Maximum — The total of all amounts, each of which is an amount payable by an eligible person under this section, may not exceed the amount obtained by subtracting one dollar from the eligible amount of the eligible person.

Schedules

[Not reproduced: lists 15 members of partnerships and 12 transferor corporations — ed.]

Explanatory Note [not part of the Order]: In July 2004, certain landowners (the "Landowners") of the Richmond Hill Land portion of the Oak Ridges Moraine agreed with the Province of Ontario (the "Province") to exchange environmentally-sensitive lands for lands owned by the Province in North Pickering, Ontario.

The Remission Order provides for the remission to each eligible person of taxes payable by the person under the *Income Tax Act* arising as a result of the exchange, while imposing conditions for the remission, one of which is the payment of certain amounts. The amounts become payable to the Receiver General for Canada progressively on the disposition of all or a part of the North Pickering lands and any amount still owing whether or not the lands have been disposed of is payable at the end of the 10th taxation year following the taxation year affected by the exchange.

The cost of this Remission Order is estimated to be between $5.2 million and $9.1 million. It is difficult to make a more precise estimate because of variables such as the different tax rates applicable to each eligible person, the timing of payments required to be made under the Remission Order and interest rate assumptions.

Dept. of Finance comfort letter, Jan. 9, 2018 [not part of the Order]: Mr. Ronald Appleby, Robins Appleby LLP, Toronto, ON

Dear Mr. Appleby:

I am writing in response to your correspondence of November 9, 2016, in which you request an extension of the remission order that was issued for the benefit of certain taxpayers (the "Landowners") that you represent.

On August 14, 2007, the Landowners exchanged their environmentally sensitive land in the Oak Ridges Moraine for development land in North Pickering ("North Pickering Lands") pursuant to an agreement with the Province of Ontario. A remission of federal taxes for a period of up to 10 years was provided to the Landowners and, for most Landowners, the 10-year period will expire at the end of 2017. Ontario also provided a remission of provincial income taxes until such time as the North Pickering Lands are sold.

In your correspondence, you have requested that the terms of the remission order be changed to allow for remission of federal income taxes until such time as the North Pickering Lands are sold by the Landowners, which would be consistent with Ontario's remission order.

It is my understanding that the Landowners have been unable to proceed with the development of the North Pickering Lands due to certain regulatory delays beyond their control. There have been numerous lengthy delays in obtaining certain approvals for the development of the North Pickering Lands. Given that the delays in the regulatory process appear to either have been cleared or will soon be cleared, it is reasonable to expect that the Landowners will now proceed with the development of the North Pickering Lands and be in a position to sell the North Pickering Lands.

The underlying tax obligations arose because of the exchange of the environmentally sensitive lands with Ontario. The preservation of the environmentally sensitive lands in the Oak Ridges Moraine is important to protect the water supply of the many small towns in and around the northern Toronto region.

Given these facts, I will recommend to the Governor General in Council that the Oak Ridges Moraine Remission Order be amended to grant an extension of the deferral of taxes provided there in. In particular, I will recommend, as was the case previously, that the deferral of taxes be provided until the earlier of such time as the North Pickering Lands are sold or 10 taxation years.

Thank you for bringing this matter to my attention.

Yours sincerely,

The Honouorable [*sic*] Bill Morneau, P.C., M.P.

Explanatory Note to Amending Order (P.C. 2018-610) [not part of the Order]: **Proposal**: Pursuant to section 23 of the *Financial Administration Act*, this Order amends the *Oak Ridges Moraine Land Exchange Income Tax Remission Order* (the "Remission Order") to extend the deferral of taxes it provides for another 10 years.

Objective: The purpose of this Order is to extend the tax relief provided by the original Remission Order, which would otherwise end on the filing-due date for the 2017 taxation year, for another 10 years.

Background: In July 2004, certain landowners of the Oak Ridges Moraine (the "Landowners") agreed with the Government of Ontario to exchange environmentally sensitive lands for lands owned by Ontario. Pursuant to the 2004 agreement, on August 14, 2007, the Landowners exchanged their environmentally sensitive land in the Oak Ridges Moraine for development land in North Pickering ("North Pickering Lands"). A remission of federal taxes for a period of up to 10 years was provided to the Landowners, until the filing-due date for their 2017 taxation year.

There have been a number of delays in obtaining certain approvals for the development of the North Pickering Lands. As a result, the first occupancies of homes built on the North Pickering Lands are presently scheduled for 2019. They were originally scheduled for 2011, representing a delay of eight years.

As a result of the extension of the Remission Order to 20 years from 10 years, the deferred taxes will become payable to the Receiver General for Canada progressively on the disposition of all or a part of the North Pickering Lands and any amount still owing, whether or not the lands have been disposed of, is payable by the filing-due date for the 20th taxation year (generally 2027) following the taxation year in which the land exchange took place. [Disposition has a specific meaning in tax terms. For example, land can be sold, transferred, or one could dispose of land without selling it (e.g. in the event of an individual's death, all of his or her assets are deemed to have been disposed of immediately before death).]

Implications: The underlying tax obligations arose because of the exchange of the environmentally sensitive lands with Ontario. The preservation of the environmentally sensitive lands in the Oak Ridges Moraine is important to protect the water supply of many communities in and around the northern Greater Toronto region.

The total tax deferred under the Remission Order is approximately $17.4 million. The cost to the government to borrow $17.4 million is approximately $400,000 per year. The cost of deferring receipt of the tax revenue for 10 years would be approximately $3.6 million, on a net present value basis, calculated based on the yield on Government of Canada 10-year bonds on October 18, 2017, of 2.30% per annum.

Consultations: The beneficiaries of this amending Order (i.e. the Landowners) are aware of the proposed extension of the tax deferral. Other than the request for an extension of the Remission Order by the representative of the Landowners, and subsequent clarifying communication with the representative, no other consultations have been undertaken. As a result of this communication, the amending Order also corrects typographical errors in the last name of the two individual beneficiaries listed in Part 1 of Schedule 1 of the Remission Order.

Departmental contact: Gurinderpal Grewal, Senior Advisor, Tax Policy Branch, James Michael Flaherty Building, 90 Elgin Street, 11th Floor, Ottawa, Ontario K1A 0G5, Telephone: 613-369-3667, Email: Gurinderpal.Grewal@canada.ca

JOSEPHINE PASTORIOUS REMISSION ORDER
P.C. 2005-1534, August 31, 2005 (SI/2005-80)

Her Excellency the Governor General in Council, considering that the collection of the tax is unjust, on the recommendation of the Minister of National Revenue, pursuant to subsection 23(2) of the *Financial Administration Act*, hereby remits tax under Part I.2 of the *Income Tax Act* in the amount of $3,568.00 for the 2001 taxation year, and all relevant interest thereon, paid or payable by Josephine Pastorious.

Explanatory Note [not part of the Order]: This Order remits a portion of income tax and all relevant interest paid or payable thereon by Josephine Pastorious in respect of the 2001 taxation year..

In 2001, Ms. Pastorious received a lump sum payment from a government agency, representing retroactive benefits back to 1978. As a result of the income inclusion in 2001, Ms. Pastorious was required to repay a significant portion of her Old Age Security benefits for that year and was not entitled to claim the age amount. The amount remitted represents the additional tax liability incurred by Ms. Pastorious as a result of the lengthy delay by the government agency in paying her amounts to which she was entitled in the relevant years.

TOBIE PELLETIER REMISSION ORDER

P.C. 2011-846, July 29, 2011 (SI/2011-65)

His Excellency the Governor General in Council, considering that the collection of the tax is unjust, on the recommendation of the Minister of National Revenue, pursuant to subsection 23(2) of the *Financial Administration Act*, hereby remits tax in the amount of $8,387, and all relevant interest on it, paid or payable under Part I.2 of the *Income Tax Act* by Tobie Pelletier for the 2008 taxation year.

Explanatory Note [not part of the Order]: This Order remits a portion of income tax and all relevant interest paid or payable thereon by Tobie Pelletier in respect of the 2008 taxation year.

In 2008, Mr. Pelletier received a lump sum payment from a government agency, which he was entitled to receive in the years from 1999 to 2008. As a result of the income inclusion in 2008, Mr. Pelletier was required to repay his Old Age Security pension and net federal supplements for that year. The amount remitted represents the additional tax liability incurred by Mr. Pelletier as a result of the lengthy delay by the government agency in paying him the amounts to which he was entitled in the relevant years.

KEITH PHILLIPS REMISSION ORDER

P.C. 2013-40, January 31, 2013 (SI/2013-11)

His Excellency the Governor General in Council, considering that the collection of the amounts is unjust, on the recommendation of the Minister of National Revenue and the Treasury Board, pursuant to subsection 23(2.1) of the *Financial Administration Act*, remits to Keith Phillips the amounts of $3,380.12 and $4,418.90, paid or payable by him as repayment of an unwarranted refund with respect to the 1995 and 1996 taxation years, respectively, under Part I of the *Income Tax Act* and, on the recommendation of the Minister of National Revenue, pursuant to subsection 23(2) of the *Financial Administration Act*, remits tax in the amounts of $1,699.40, $2,492 and $1,822.10 for the 1995, 1996 and 1997 taxation years, respectively, and penalties in the amounts of $2,276.06, $2,927.83 and $2,843.04, paid or payable by him for the 1995, 1996 and 1997 taxation years, respectively, under Part I of the *Income Tax Act*, and all relevant interest on those amounts.

Explanatory Note [not part of the Order]: The Order remits certain amounts paid or payable by Mr. Phillips for the 1995 to 1997 years.

The payment of those amounts, incurred as a result of extenuating factors, would cause a significant financial setback for Mr. Phillips.

DANE POCRNIC REMISSION ORDER

P.C. 2005-624, April 19, 2005 (SI/2005-38)

Her Excellency the Governor General in Council, considering that the collection of the tax is unjust, on the recommendation of the Minister of National Revenue, pursuant to subsection 23(2) of the *Financial Administration Act*, hereby remits tax under Part I.2 of the *Income Tax Act* in the amount of $3,161 for the 1999 taxation year, and all relevant interest thereon, paid or payable by Dane Pocrnic.

Explanatory Note [not part of the Order]: This Order remits a portion of income tax and all relevant interest paid or payable thereon by Dane Pocrnic in respect of the 1999 taxation year.

In 1999, Mr. Pocrnic received a taxable lump sum payment from a government agency, a portion of which he was entitled to receive in the years from 1992 to 1998. As a result of the income inclusion in 1999, Mr. Pocrnic was required to repay a significant portion of his Old Age Security benefits for that year. The amount remitted represents the additional tax liability incurred by Mr. Pocrnic as a result of the lengthy delay by the government agency in paying him the amounts to which he was entitled in the relevant years.

Notes: See *Pelletier*, 2010 CarswellNat 4258 (TCC), and Notes at end of ITA 180.2.

DONALD POTTER INCOME TAX REMISSION ORDER

P.C. 2004-264, March 23, 2004 (SI/2004-32)

1. **Interpretation** — In this Order, **"registered retirement savings plan"** has the meaning assigned by subsection 146(1) of the *Income Tax Act*.

2. **Remission** — Subject to section 3, remission is hereby granted of the tax paid or payable by Donald Potter under Part I of the *Income Tax Act* in the amount of $2,517.61 for the 2001 taxation year and all interest paid or payable in respect of that tax.

3. **Condition** — The remission referred to in section 2 is granted on condition that Donald Potter does not institute or proceed with any action, objection, appeal, application or other proceeding of any kind in respect of the taxation of funds withdrawn from his registered retirement savings plans in 2001.

Explanatory Note [not part of the Order]: This Order remits $2,517.61, representing a portion of the tax paid or payable by Donald Potter under Part I of the *Income Tax Act* for the 2001 taxation year and all interest paid or payable in respect of that portion.

The amount remitted is in relation to funds withdrawn by Mr. Potter from registered retirement savings plans based on incorrect information regarding the amount of non-capital losses he had available to be carried forward to the 2001 taxation year. The incorrect information was provided in writing by a Canada Customs and Revenue Agency (CCRA) official who also sent letters of authority to the financial institutions who issued those plans permitting them to pay the funds to Mr. Potter without withholding the required tax.

The amount remitted corresponds to the additional tax liability incurred by Mr. Potter in respect of the 2001 taxation year as a result of his reliance on the incorrect information provided by the CCRA official.

ALLAN PYSHER INCOME TAX REMISSION ORDER

P.C. 2015-54, January 29, 2015 (SI/2015-7)

1. Remission — Remission is granted of the tax paid or payable by Allan Pysher under Part I of the *Income Tax Act* in the amounts of $4,211.51, $4,570.30, $4,295.60, $4,544.46, $4,698.60, $4,139.52, $4, 553.92, $2,568.70, $3,529.32, $4,260.93 and $3,741.86 for the 1999 to 2008 and 2011 taxation years, respectively, and all relevant interest on that tax.

2. Condition — The remission is granted on the condition that Allan Pysher does not claim a deduction under paragraph 111(1)(a) of the *Income Tax Act* for any portion of his non-capital loss relating to the repayment in 2012 of disability benefits to Great-West Life Assurance Company.

Explanatory Note [not part of the Order]: The Order remits income tax, and all relevant interest on it, paid or payable by Allan Pysher for the 1999 to 2008 and 2011 taxation years.

The amount remitted represents the additional tax incurred by Mr. Pysher as a result of circumstances that were not within his control. The payment of these amounts caused a financial setback for Mr. Pysher.

CLARA REID REMISSION ORDER
P.C. 2006-372, May 11, 2006 (SI/2006-78)

Her Excellency the Governor General in Council, considering that the collection of the tax is unjust, on the recommendation of the Minister of National Revenue, pursuant to subsection 23(2) of the *Financial Administration Act*, hereby remits tax under Part I of the *Income Tax Act* in the amount of $1,335.60 for the 2003 taxation year, and all relevant interest thereon, paid or payable by Clara Reid.

Explanatory Note [not part of the Order]: This Order remits a portion of income tax and all relevant interest paid or payable thereon by Clara Reid in respect of the 2003 taxation year.

In 2003 Ms. Reid received Employment Insurance (EI) benefits. She reported them as income on her 2003 return and paid the applicable tax. In 2004 her claim for long-term disability payments was approved retroactive to 2003. Since the benefit periods overlapped, she was required to repay the EI benefits. She repaid the full amount.

In 2004 she was entitled to a deduction from income for the amount of the repayment. However, she had no income in 2004 from which to deduct it. As a result, she has been taxed in 2003 on benefits that she repaid in 2004. The inclusion in income of the EI beenfits in 2003 that were later repaid unfairly caused Clara Reid an additional tax liability.

BELA REVI TAX REMISSION ORDER
P.C. 2011-1140, September 29, 2011 (SI/2011-83)

His Excellency the Governor General in Council, considering that the collection of the tax is unjust, on the recommendation of the Minister of National Revenue, pursuant to subsection 23(2) of the *Financial Administration Act*, hereby remits tax in the amount of $2,450.85, and all relevant interest on it, paid or payable under Part I.2 of the *Income Tax Act* by Bela Revi for the 2008 taxation year.

Explanatory Note [not part of the Order]: This Order remits a portion of income tax and all relevant interest paid or payable thereon by Bela Revi in respect of the 2008 taxation year.

In 2008, Mr. Revi received a lump sum payment by a government agency that related to the 1996 to 2008 years. As a result of the payment, he was required to repay a portion of his Old Age Security pension for that year. The amount remitted represents the additional tax liability incurred by Mr. Revi as a result of the payment not having been made earlier.

RAM SEWAK REMISSION ORDER
P.C. 2006-445, June 1, 2006 (SI/2006-91)

Her Excellency the Governor General in Council, considering that the collection of the tax is unjust, on the recommendation of the Minister of National Revenue, pursuant to subsection 23(2) of the *Financial Administration Act*, hereby remits tax and penalties under Part I of the *Income Tax Act* in the amount of $989.80 for the 1977 taxation year, and all relevant interest thereon, paid or payable by Ram Sewak.

Explanatory Note [not part of the Order]: This Order remits a portion of income tax and all relevant penalties and interest paid or payable thereon by Ram Sewak in respect of the 1977 taxation year.

In 2001, Mr. Sewak returned to Canada to find out he had an income tax debt dating back to 1978, the year he left Canada. Interest charges have increased the debt to a level where paying it would cause exereme hardship for Mr. Sewak.

EUGENE SKRIPKARIUK REMISSION ORDER
P.C. 2009-169, February 5, 2009 (SI/2009-6)

Her Excellency the Governor General in Council, considering that the collection of the tax is unjust, on the recommendation of the Minister of National Revenue, pursuant to subsection 23(2) of the *Financial Administration Act*, hereby remits tax in the amount of $3,332.42, and all relevant interest on it, paid or payable under Part I of the *Income Tax Act* by Eugene Skripkariuk for the 2003 taxation year.

Explanatory Note [not part of the Order]: This Order remits a portion of the income tax, and all relevant interest on it, paid or payable by Eugene Skripkariuk for the 2003 taxation year.

The amount remitted represents the amount of tax that is the result of an error committed by Mr. Skripkariuk when filing his 2003 income tax return that would have been detected by the Canada Revenue Agency if proper procedures had been followed. The payment of that amount would cause significant financial hardship for Mr. Skripkariuk.

KAREN SMEDLEY AND GEORGE SMEDLEY REMISSION ORDER
P.C. 2004-265, March 23, 2004 (SI/2004-33)

Her Excellency the Governor General in Council, considering that the collection of the tax is unjust, on the recommendation of the Minister of National Revenue, pursuant to subsection 23(2) of the *Financial Administration Act*, hereby remits tax under Part I of the *Income Tax Act* in the amounts of $8,725.16 and $11,190.65 for the 1994 taxation year, and all relevant interest thereon, paid or payable by Karen Smedley and George Smedley, respectively.

Explanatory Note [not part of the Order]: This Order remits a portion of income tax and all relevant interest paid or payable thereon by Karen Smedley and George Smedley in respect of the 1994 taxation year.

During the course of an audit in 1996 by Revenue Canada a portion of the Smedleys' 1994 claim for the capital gains exemption was disallowed because the disposition occurred after February 22, 1994. The Smedleys disputed the disposition date in court and were unsuccessful.

Both had already filed an "Election to Report a Capital Gain on Property Owned at the end of February 24, 1994" in respect of a similar property. The Revenue Canada auditor failed to advise the Smedleys that they could have amended their elections to include the first property and thereby take advantage of the capital gains exemption on its disposition. Incorrect action on the part of the auditor caused the Smedleys substantial additional tax liability.

LAURA SPEAKMAN REMISSION ORDER
P.C. 2010-1593, December 9, 2010 (SI/2010-92)

His Excellency the Governor General in Council, considering that the collection of the penalties and interest is unjust, on the recommendation of the Minister of National Revenue, pursuant to subsection 23(2) of the *Financial Administration Act*, hereby remits penalties in the amounts of $11.20 and $19.16 for the 1995 and 1998 taxation years, respectively, and arrears interest in the amounts of $907.45, $2,852.15, $449.25, $683.10 and $131.91 for the 1992, 1993, 1995, 1997 and 1998 taxation years, respectively, and all interest on the penalties and interest, paid or payable under Part I of the *Income Tax Act* by Laura Speakman.

Explanatory Note [not part of the Order]: The Order remits late filing penalties for the 1995 and 1998 tax years and all arrears interest for the 1992, 1993, 1995, 1997 and 1998 tax years, paid or payable, by Laura Speakman.

The penalties and arrears interest are being remitted because payment of these amounts represents a significant financial setback for Ms. Speakman and they arose due to circumstances beyond her control. The remission is also based on incorrect action on the part of Canada Revenue Agency officials.

KATHRYN STRIGNER TAX REMISSION ORDER
P.C. 2011-488, March 25, 2011 (SI/2011-26)

1. **Interpretation** — In this Order, "non-capital loss" has the same meaning as in subsection 111(8) of the *Income Tax Act*.

2. **Remission** — Remission is hereby granted of a portion of the tax paid or payable by Kathryn Strigner under Part I of the *Income Tax Act* in the amounts of $5,096.49, $4,865.50, $3,271.33, $1,387.27, $3,200.41, $2,922.58, $2,893.81, $2,674.53, $2,699.28, $2,865.26, and $1,414.37 for the 1993 to 2003 taxation years, respectively, and all relevant interest on those amounts.

3. **Condition** — The remission is granted on the condition that Kathryn Strigner does not claim a deduction for any portion of her unused non-capital loss of $236,755 relating to the repayment in 2008 of disability income replacement benefits to Sun Life Assurance Company of Canada.

Explanatory Note [not part of the Order]: The Order remits a portion of the income tax and all relevant interest on that tax, paid or payable by Kathryn Strigner for the 1993 to 2003 taxation years.

The amounts remitted represent the additional tax paid or payable by Ms. Strigner as a result of circumstances that were beyond her control. The payment of these amounts represents a financial setback for Ms. Strigner.

RITA S. SWEET REMISSION ORDER
P.C. 2016-1052, December 14, 2016 (SI/2016-65)

His Excellency the Governor General in Council, considering that the collection of the tax is unjust, on the recommendation of the Minister of National Revenue, pursuant to subsection 23(2) of the *Financial Administration Act*, remits tax in the amounts of $20.39, $891.63, $906.22, $949.40, $1,278.50, $1,247.53, $3,373.97, $1,297.18, $976.10, $1,479.60, $1,916.36, $2,095.10, $2,051.65, $1,984.90 and $1,542.44 paid or payable by Rita S. Sweet under Part I of the *Income Tax Act* for the 1989, 1990, 1991, 1992, 1993, 1994, 1995, 1996, 1997, 1998, 1999, 2000, 2001, 2002, and 2003 taxation years, respectively.

Explanatory Note [not part of the Order]: The Order remits a portion of the income tax paid or payable by Rita S. Sweet for the 1989 to 2003 taxation years.

The amount remitted represents the amount of tax that is the result of incorrect action by a federal government authority.

TELESAT CANADA REMISSION ORDER
P.C. 1999-1335, July 28, 1999 (SI/99-82)

1. **Interpretation** — The definitions in this section apply in this Order.

"**Act**" means the *Income Tax Act*.

"**former property**" means the Anik E1 satellite in respect of which Telesat Canada has received proceeds of disposition referred to in paragraph 13(4)(a) of the Act.

"**replacement property**" means the property acquired as a replacement for the former property and to which subsection 13(4) of the Act would apply if it were read in accordance with paragraph 2(b) of this Order and if Telesat Canada had made an election under subsection 13(4) of the Act with respect to the replacement property in its return of income for the taxation year in which it acquired the property.

2. **Remission** — Subject to section 3, remission is hereby granted to Telesat Canada in respect of each of the 1996 and subsequent taxation years, of an amount equal to the amount, if any, by which

(a) the total of the tax payable under Part I and Part I.3 of the Act by Telesat Canada for the year and the interest and penalties in respect thereof payable by it under the Act for the year

exceeds

(b) the total of the tax that would be payable under Part I and Part I.3 of the Act by Telesat Canada for the year and the interest and penalties in respect thereof that would be payable by it under the Act for the year if the expression "the second taxation year following the initial year" in clause 13(4)(c)(ii)(A) and paragraph 44(1)(c) of the Act were read as "the taxation year that includes December 31,

1999" and if Telesat Canada had made an election, as and when required, under subsection 13(4) of the Act, with respect to the disposition of the former property and the acquisition of the replacement property.

3. **Conditions** — Remission is granted under section 2 on condition that

(a) in calculating the income or loss of Telesat Canada under the Act in respect of the 1996 and subsequent taxation years, no deduction in respect of the cost of the replacement property is claimed except to the extent that would be allowed if subsection 13(4) and section 44 of the Act were read in accordance with paragraph 2(b) of this Order and if Telesat Canada had made a valid election under subsection 13(4) of the Act with respect to the disposition of the former property and the acquisition of the replacement property; and

(b) if there is a disposition of the replacement property, the Act is treated by Telesat Canada and the person or partnership that acquired the replacement property as applying as if subsection 13(4) and section 44 of the Act were read in accordance with paragraph 2(b) of this Order and as if Telesat Canada had made a valid election under subsection 13(4) of the Act with respect to the disposition of the former property and the acquisition of the replacement property.

Explanatory Note [not part of the Order]: This Order defers income tax that would otherwise be payable on insurance proceeds received by Telesat Canada in respect of a damaged satellite, by remitting income tax otherwise payable on the initial receipt of those proceeds on the condition that Telesat Canada reduce its adjusted cost base and capital cost in respect of the replacement satellite, in accordance with the replacement property rules in the *Income Tax Act*.

The present value of the net benefit of the Order is approximately $14 million. This is the amount by which the income tax remitted exceeds the present value of future capital cost allowance deductions that would have been available if the replacement satellite were not treated as a replacement property.

WILLARD THORNE REMISSION ORDER
P.C. 2002-2177, December 12, 2002 (SI/2003-1)

Her Excellency the Governor General in Council, considering that the collection of the tax is unjust, on the recommendation of the Minister of National Revenue, pursuant to subsection 23(2) of the *Financial Administration Act*, hereby remits tax under Part I of the *Income Tax Act* in the amount of $819.40 for the 1987 taxation year, and all relevant interest thereon, paid or payable by Willard Thorne.

Explanatory Note [not part of the Order]: This Order remits the income tax and all relevant interest paid or payable by Mr. Willard Thorne in respect of the 1987 taxation year.

In 1987, Mr. Thorne received a retroactive lump sum payment of benefits under the Canada Pension Plan, covering the period of 1985 to 1987. The inclusion of the lump sum amount in his income caused Mr. Thorne a tax liability in 1987. However, had there not been a delay in the payments of benefits to which he was entitled, Mr. Thorne would not have had any tax liability in either year.

Notes: 1985-87 preceded the availability of the averaging provided by ITA 56(8) and 120.3.

JARED TORGERSON REMISSION ORDER
P.C. 2009-878, June 4, 2009 (SI/2009-44)

Her Excellency the Governor General in Council, considering that the collection of the tax is unjust, on the recommendation of the Minister of National Revenue, pursuant to subsection 23(2) of the *Financial Administration Act*, hereby remits tax in the amount of $588, and all relevant interest on it, paid or payable under Part I of the *Income Tax Act* by Jared Torgerson for the 1992 taxation year.

Explanatory Note [not part of the Order]: The Order remits the income tax, and all relevant interest on it, paid or payable by Jared Torgerson for the 1992 taxation year.

The amount remitted represents the amount of tax that is the result of an error committed by a Canada Revenue Agency official when Mr. Torgerson's 1992 income tax return was assessed in June 1993. Because of circumstances beyond his control, Mr. Torgerson could not take the appropriate steps to have the error corrected at the time.

YVONNE TOWNSHEND REMISSION ORDER
P.C. 2007-1776, November 22, 2007 (SI/2007-107)

Her Excellency the Governor General in Council, considering that the collection of the tax is unjust, on the recommendation of the Minister of National Revenue, pursuant to subsection 23(2) of the *Financial Administration Act*, hereby remits tax under Part I of the *Income Tax Act* in the amounts of $939.75, $1,233.14 and $634.93 for the 1996, 1997 and 1998 taxation years, respectively, and all relevant interest thereon, paid or payable by Yvonne Townshend.

Explanatory Note [not part of the Order]: This Order remits a portion of income tax and all relevant interest paid or payable thereon by Yvonne Townshend in respect of the 1996, 1997 and 1998 taxation years.

The amount remitted represents the additional tax that is causing a significant financial setback for Ms. Townshend. The difficulty in paying the tax is due to circumstances beyond her control. The remission is also based on extreme hardship.

JOHN WAGONTALL REMISSION ORDER
P.C. 2014-1131, November 5, 2014 (SI/2014-95)

His Excellency the Governor General in Council, considering that the collection of the tax is unjust, on the recommendation of the Minister of National Revenue, pursuant to subsection 23(2) of the *Financial Administration Act*, makes the annexed *John Wagontall Remission Order*.

1. Remission — Remission is granted of the tax paid or payable by John Wagontall under Part I of the *Income Tax Act* in the amounts of $252.71, $5,614.70, $6,963.09, $4,918.62, $832.15 and $809.75 for the 2004, 2005, 2006, 2007, 2008 and 2010 taxation years, respectively, and all relevant interest on those amounts.

2. Condition — The remission is granted on the condition that John Wagontall does not claim a deduction under paragraph 111(1)(a) of the *Income Tax Act* for any portion of his non-capital loss relating to the repayment in 2011 of disability benefits to the City of Lethbridge and to the Co-operators Life Insurance Company.

Explanatory Note [not part of the Order]: The Order remits income tax, and all relevant interest on it, paid or payable by John Wagontall for the 2004 to 2008 and 2010 taxation years.

The amount remitted represents the additional tax incurred by Mr. Wagontall as a result of circumstances that were not within his control. The payment of these amounts caused a financial setback for Mr. Wagontall.

EVAN WARDEN REMISSION ORDER
P.C. 2010-1596, December 9, 2010 (SI/2010-95)

His Excellency the Governor General in Council, considering that the collection of the interest is unjust, on the recommendation of the Minister of National Revenue, pursuant to subsection 23(2) of the *Financial Administration Act*, hereby remits interest in the amount of $2,287.32, paid or payable under Part I of the *Income Tax Act* by Evan Warden for the 1997 taxation year, and all relevant interest on it.

Explanatory Note [not part of the Order]: The Order remits a portion of the interest, and any interest thereon, paid or payable by Evan Warden for the 1997 taxation year.

The remission is based on incorrect action on the part of Canada Revenue Agency officials.

Notes: See Notes to the *Mildred Jacobs Remission Order* above.

INCOME TAX CONVENTIONS INTERPRETATION ACT

An Act respecting the interpretation of Canada's international conventions relating to income tax and the Acts implementing such conventions.

R.S.C. 1985, c. I-4, AS AMENDED

Short Title

Notes [ITCIA]: For principles of tax treaty interpretation as well as the ITCIA, see:

- *Books*: Marwah Rizqy, "History of Tax Treaties", chap. 3 of Vidal, *Introduction to International Tax in Canada* (Carswell, 8th ed., 2020); Sophie Chatel, "Tax Treaties", *ibid.* chap. 4; Michael Lang, *Introduction to the Law of Double Taxation Conventions* (IBFD, 2010, 222pp); Jonathan Schwarz, *Schwarz on Tax Treaties* (WoltersKluwer UK, 5th ed., 2018); David Ward et al., *The Interpretation of Income Tax Treaties with Particular Reference to the Commentaries on the OECD Model* (International Fiscal Assn & International Bureau of Fiscal Documentation, 2005, 350pp.); Li & Cockfield, *International Taxation in Canada*, 4th ed. (Lexis-Nexis, 2018), section 2:F, "Interpretation of Tax Treaties"; *Courts and Tax Treaty Law* (IBFD, ibfd.org, 2007, 412pp.).

- *Articles*: Richardson & Welkoff, "The Interpretation of Tax Conventions in Canada", 43(5) *Canadian Tax Journal [CTJ]* 1759-191 (1995); Li & Sandler, "The Relationship Between Domestic Anti-Avoidance Legislation and Tax Treaties", 45(5) *CTJ* 891-958 (1997); David Ward, "Tax Treaties: An Eroding Set of Rules", 1999 Cdn Tax Foundation conference report, 41:1-21; Ward & Ruby, "Tax Treaty Cases, 1965-2008", 58(Supp.[Bowman]) *CTJ* 111-26 (2010); Nitikman et al., "Treaty Interpretation: Contrasting Views", 2010 conference report, 15:1-18; Arnold, Richardson & Walker, "Judicial Approaches to Treaty Interpretation", 2012 conference report, 29:1-77.

For a comprehensive database of cases interpreting the provisions of tax treaties, see the Tax Treaty Case Law database maintained by the International Bureau of Fiscal Documentation (ibfd.org). See also Eduardo Baistrocchi, *A Global Analysis of Tax Treaty Disputes* (Cambridge Univ. Press, 2017, 2 vols., 1588pp), reviewed at 66(2) *Canadian Tax Journal* 507-08 (2018).

"Contrary to an ordinary taxing statute a tax treaty must be given a liberal interpretation with a view of implementing the true intentions of the parties. A literal or legalistic interpretation must be avoided when the basic object of the treaty might be defeated or frustrated in so far as the particular item under consideration is concerned": *Gladden Estate*, [1985] 1 C.T.C. 163 (FCTD), approved in *Crown Forest*, [1995] 2 C.T.C. 64 (SCC), and *Allchin*, 2004 FCA 206.

"Parties to a tax treaty are presumed to know the other country's tax system when they negotiate a tax treaty", so the Canada-Luxembourg treaty allowing a capital gain to escape both countries' tax was acceptable: *Alta Energy Luxembourg*, 2018 TCC 152, para. 84; aff'd 2020 FCA 43; SCC appeal heard March 19/21 (and a treaty exemption that does not appear in Canada's other treaties should not be restricted by those other treaties: FCA para. 30) [see Notes to ITA 245(2) for commentary].

For more on interpreting tax treaties see *Société Générale Valeurs*, 2016 TCC 131; aff'd 2017 FCA 3.

For treaty interpretation during COVID-19, see OECD, *Updated guidance on tax treaties and the impact of the COVID-19 pandemic* (Jan. 2021, 22pp), tinyurl.com/covid-treaty.

Where the French and English text of a treaty differ and both are "equally authentic", the version giving taxpayers a more favourable result applies (and the German version of the Canada-Switzerland treaty is not official): VIEWS doc 2015-0581521C6 [2015 IFA q.12].

See also Notes at the beginning of the Canada-U.S. tax treaty, below.

See after this Act for the Multilateral Instrument (MLI), which effectively amends most of Canada's tax treaties (but not the Canada-US treaty) starting 2020 or later.

Note that almost every tax-treaty-implementing statute in Canada (e.g., *Canada-United States Tax Convention Act, 1984*, S.C. 1984, c. 20, s. 3(2.1)) contains a provision stating: "In the event of any inconsistency between the provisions of the *Income Tax Conventions Interpretation Act* and the provisions of the Convention, and the provisions of any other law, the provisions of that Act prevail to the extent of the inconsistency." See also s. 4(2) of the statute enacting the MLI (reproduced after this Act), which provides that the ITCIA prevails over the MLI in the event of inconsistency.

On negotiating treaties see *The Platform for Collaboration on Tax: Toolkit on Tax Treaty Negotiations* (IMF, OECD, UN and World Bank Group), March 2001, 26pp.

CRA Audit Manual [ITCIA]: 15.11.0: Tax treaties.

1. Short title — This Act may be cited as the *Income Tax Conventions Interpretation Act*.

Definition

2. Definition of "convention" — In this Act, **"convention"** means any convention or agreement between Canada and another state relating to tax on income, and includes any protocol or supplementary convention or agreement relating thereto.

Interpretation

3. Meaning of undefined terms — Notwithstanding the provisions of a convention or the Act giving the convention the force of law in Canada, it is hereby declared that the law of Canada is that, to the extent that a term in the convention is

(a) not defined in the convention,

(b) not fully defined in the convention, or

(c) to be defined by reference to the laws of Canada,

that term has, except to the extent that the context otherwise requires, the meaning it has for the purposes of the *Income Tax Act*, as amended from time to time, and not the meaning it had for the purposes of the *Income Tax Act* on the date the convention was entered into or given the force of law in Canada if, after that date, its meaning for the purposes of the *Income Tax Act* has changed.

Notes: S. 3 was introduced to overrule *Melford Developments*, [1982] C.T.C. 330 (SCC), where the Supreme Court ruled that an undefined term was to be interpreted as having the meaning it had under the ITA at the time the convention was adopted.

For Canada's interpretation of "royalty", see *Income Tax Technical News* 23.

I.T. Technical News: 18 (*Cudd Pressure* case).

4. Permanent establishments in Canada — Notwithstanding the provisions of a convention or the Act giving the convention the force of law in Canada, it is hereby declared that the law of Canada is that where, for the purposes of the application of the convention, the profits from a business activity, including an industrial or commercial activity, attributable or allocable to a permanent establishment in Canada are to be determined for any period,

(a) there shall, except where the convention expressly otherwise provides, be included in the determination of those profits all amounts with respect to that activity that are attributable or allocable to the permanent establishment and that would be required to be included under the *Income Tax Act*, as amended from time to time, by a person resident in Canada carrying on the activity in Canada in the computation of his income from a business for that period; and

(b) there shall, except to the extent that an agreement between the competent authorities of the parties to the convention expressly otherwise provides, not be deducted in the determination of those profits any amount with respect to that activity that is attributable or allocable to the permanent establishment and that would not be deductible under the *Income Tax Act*, as amended from time to time, by a person resident in Canada carrying on the activity in Canada in the computation of his income from a business for that period.

Notes: See *Cudd Pressure*, [1999] 1 C.T.C. 1 (FCA), where a PE in Canada was not allowed to deduct notional rent of equipment from head office due to para. 4(b). For CRA interpretation see doc 2004-0078321E5 (branch profits of foreign bank in Canada) and Notes to Canada-US treaty Art. VII:2.

4.1 Application of s. 245 of the *Income Tax Act* — Notwithstanding the provisions of a convention or the Act giving the convention the force of law in Canada, it is hereby declared that the law of Canada is that section 245 of the *Income Tax Act* applies to any benefit provided under the convention.

Notes: See Mark Meredith, "Treaty Interpretation and Assertions of Abuse", 2008 Cdn Tax Foundation conference report, 20:1-14.

4.1 applies even to a treaty whose enabling legislation does not make it subject to the ITCIA, as 4.1 was enacted later and is "crystal clear as to its intent and effect": *Antle*, 2009 TCC 465, para. 87 [affirmed on other grounds 2010 FCA 280; leave to appeal denied 2011 CarswellNat 1491 (SCC); motion for reconsideration dismissed 2012 CarswellNat 183]. See also 4.3 Notes.

4.1 added by 2004 Budget, for transactions after Sept. 1988. See Notes to ITA 245(4).

4.2 Stock exchanges — Notwithstanding the provisions of a convention or the Act giving the convention the force of law in Canada, each reference in a convention to a stock exchange that is prescribed under, or for the purposes of, the *Income Tax Act* shall be read as a reference to a designated stock exchange, as defined in the *Income Tax Act*.

Notes: 4.2 added by 2007 Budget second bill, effective Dec. 14, 2007, due to replacement of "prescribed stock exchange" throughout the ITA with "designated stock exchange" (see ITA 248(1) and 262).

Definitions [s. 4.2]: "convention" — ITCIA 2; "designated stock exchange" — ITA 248(1), 262.

4.3 Application of s. 94 of the *Income Tax Act* — Notwithstanding the provisions of a convention or the Act giving the convention the force of law in Canada, if a trust is deemed by subsection 94(3) of the *Income Tax Act* to be resident in Canada for a taxation year for the purposes of computing its income, the trust is deemed to be a resident of Canada, and not a resident of the other contracting state, for the purposes of applying the convention

(a) in respect of the trust for that taxation year; and

(b) in respect of any other person for any period that includes all or part of that taxation year.

Notes: This provision, part of the "non-resident trust" package (ITA s. 94), was first introduced in the Aug. 27/10 draft legislation, to overrule the TCC's ruling in *Antle* (see Notes to ITCIA 4.1). It overrides Canada's tax treaties by giving precedence to ITA 94(3) in deeming a trust to be resident in Canada. See Halvorson, "Unilateral Treaty Override", 18(10) *Canadian Tax Highlights* (ctf.ca) 2-3 (Oct. 2010); VIEWS doc 2013-0492821C6 [2013 APFF q.3]; Doobay, "Dual-Resident Estate", 25(10) *Canadian Tax Highlights* (ctf.ca) 4-5 (Oct. 2017); VIEWS doc 2017-0693451C6 [2017 STEP q.3]. See also Notes above at beginning of this Act.

4.3 added by 2002-2013 technical bill (Part 1 — NRTs), effective March 5, 2010.

Definitions [s. 4.3]: "Canada" — ITCIA 5; "convention" — ITCIA 2; "person" — ITA 248(1); "taxation year" — ITA 249; "trust" — ITA 104(1), 248(1), (3).

5. Definitions — Notwithstanding the provisions of a convention or the Act giving the convention the force of law in Canada, in this section and in the convention,

"annuity" does not include any pension payment or any payment under a plan, arrangement or contract described in subparagraphs (a)(i) to (ix) of the definition "pension";

Notes: Definition amended by 1998 Budget to delete "(other than a periodic pension payment) arising in Canada" from the end, effective for amounts paid after 1996.

Definition "annuity" added by 1992 technical bill, for amounts paid after 1991. It ensures that pension payments that are specifically excluded from the definition of "periodic pension payment" are not eligible for the reduced rate of withholding tax that applies to annuity payments under many of Canada's tax treaties.

See 5.1 below for the meaning of "pension" for purposes of this definition.

"Canada" means the territory of Canada, and includes

(a) every area beyond the territorial seas of Canada that, in accordance with international law and the laws of Canada, is an area in respect of which Canada may exercise rights with respect to the seabed and subsoil and their natural resources, and

(b) the seas and airspace above every area described in paragraph (a);

"immovable property" and **"real property"**, with respect to such property in Canada, are hereby declared to include

(a) any right to explore for or exploit mineral deposits and sources in Canada and other natural resources in Canada, and

(b) any right to an amount computed by reference to the production, including profit, from, or to the value of production from, mineral deposits and sources in Canada and other natural resources in Canada;

Definitions [s. 5"immovable property"]: "immovable" — Quebec *Civil Code* art. 900-907.

"pension" means, in respect of payments that arise in Canada,

(a) if the convention does not include a definition "pension", a payment under any plan, arrangement or contract that is

(i) a registered pension plan,

(ii) a registered retirement savings plan,

(iii) a registered retirement income fund,

(iv) a retirement compensation arrangement,

(v) a deferred profit sharing plan,

(vi) a plan that is deemed by subsection 147(15) of the *Income Tax Act* not to be a deferred profit sharing plan,

(vii) an annuity contract purchased under a plan referred to in subparagraph (v) or (vi),

(viii) an annuity contract where the amount paid by or on behalf of an individual to acquire the contract was deductible under paragraph 60(l) of the *Income Tax Act* in computing the individual's income for any taxation year (or would have been so deductible if the individual had been resident in Canada), or

(ix) a superannuation, pension or retirement plan not otherwise referred to in this paragraph, and

(b) if the convention includes a definition "pension", a payment that is a pension for the purposes of the convention or a payment (other than a payment of social security benefits) that would be a periodic pension payment if the convention did not include a definition "pension";

Related Provisions: 5"annuity" — Annuity excludes pension payments and certain other payments.

Notes: See Ross, "Withholding Taxes on Retirement Compensation Arrangements", 20(4) *Taxation of Executive Compensation & Retirement* (Federated Press) 1074-76 (Nov. 2008).

Definition "pension" added by 1998 Budget, for amounts paid after 1996. Before 1997, see 5.1.

"periodic pension payment" means, in respect of payments that arise in Canada, a pension payment other than

(a) a lump sum payment, or a payment that can reasonably be considered to be an instalment of a lump sum amount, under a registered pension plan,

(b) a payment before maturity, or a payment in full or partial commutation of the retirement income, under a registered retirement savings plan,

(c) a payment at any time in a calendar year under a registered retirement income fund, where the total of all payments (other than the specified portion of each such payment) made under the fund at or before that time and in the year exceeds the total of

(i) the amount that would be the greater of

(A) twice the amount that, if the value of C in the definition "minimum amount" in subsection 146.3(1) of the *Income Tax Act* were nil, would be the minimum amount under the fund for the year, and

(B) 10% of the fair market value of the property (other than annuity contracts that, at the beginning of the year, are not described in paragraph (b.1) of the definition "qualified investment" in subsection 146.3(1) of the *Income Tax Act*) held in connection with the fund at the beginning of the year if all property transferred in the year and before that time to the carrier of the fund as consideration for the carrier's undertaking to make payments under the fund had been so transferred immediately before the beginning of the year and if the definition "minimum amount" in subsection 146.3(1) of the *Income Tax Act* applied with respect to all registered retirement income funds, and

(ii) the total of all amounts each of which is an annual or more frequent periodic payment under an annuity contract that is a qualified investment, as defined in subsection 146.3(1) of the *Income Tax Act*, (other than an annuity contract the fair market value of which is taken into account under clause (i)(B)) held by a trust governed by the fund that was paid into the trust in the year and before that time, or

(d) a payment to a recipient at any time in a calendar year under an arrangement, other than a plan or fund referred to in paragraphs (a) to (c), where

(i) the payment is not

(A) one of a series of annual or more frequent payments to be made over the lifetime of the recipient or over a period of at least 10 years,

(B) one of a series of annual or more frequent payments each of which is contingent on the recipient continuing to suffer from a physical or mental impairment, or

(C) a payment to which the recipient is entitled as a consequence of the death of an individual who was in receipt of periodic pension payments under the arrangement, and that is made under a guarantee that a minimum number of payments will be made in respect of the individual, or

(ii) at the time the payment is made, it may reasonably be concluded that

(A) the total amount of payments (other than excluded payments) under the arrangement to the recipient in the year will exceed twice the total amount of payments (other than excluded payments) made under the arrangement to the recipient in the immediately preceding year, otherwise than because of the fact that payments commenced to be made to the recipient in the preceding year and were made for a period of less than twelve months in that year, or

(B) the total amount of payments (other than excluded payments) under the arrangement to the recipient in the year will exceed twice the total amount of payments (other than excluded payments) to be made under the arrangement to the recipient in any subsequent year, otherwise than because of the termination of the series of payments or the reduction in the amount of payments to be made after the death of any individual,

and, for the purposes of this subparagraph, "excluded payment" means a payment that is neither a periodic payment nor a payment described in any of clauses (i)(A) to (C).

Related Provisions: ITA 146.3(1.3) — RRIF minimum amount for 2015.

Notes: A "periodic pension payment" (PPP) can have reduced or no withholding by treaty, e.g. Canada-US Treaty Art. XVIII:2(a); Canada-UK Treaty Art. 17:1. Taxpayers leaving Canada permanently when under 71, and moving to a country that has such a treaty term with Canada and that will not tax their Canadian pension payments, can benefit from converting their RRSP to a RRIF, so that, starting the next year, at least 10% can be withdrawn annually at the reduced treaty withholding rate for pensions (see (c)(i)(B)).

PPP excludes the payments listed in (a)-(d). These do not qualify for reduced withholding tax, or the reduced rate on annuity payments (see 5"annuity"). Thus, transfer of an entire RRSP or LIRA to a UK pension plan is subject to withholding tax: VIEWS doc 2013-0479901E5. A surplus distribution on Individual Pension Plan windup is not a PPP: 2017-0732681E5.

See 5 and 5.1 for the meaning of "pension" and "specified portion" for this definition.

Definition amended by 1998 Budget (for amounts paid after 1996) and 1995-97 technical bill (for amounts paid after 1997). Added by 1992 technical bill.

"real property" — [see under "immovable" above — ed.]

Definitions [s. 5]: "fair market value" — see Notes to ITA 69(1); "minimum amount" — ITA 146.3(1).

5.1 (1) [Repealed]

Notes: 5.1(1) repealed by 1998 Budget, effective for amounts paid after 1996.

See now 5"pension".

(2) Definition of "specified portion" — For the purpose of the definition "periodic pension payment" in section 5, the "specified portion" of a payment means the total of

(a) the portion of the payment that is not required by section 146.3 of the *Income Tax Act* to be included in computing the income of any person and that is not included under paragraph 212(1)(q) of that Act in respect of any person; and

(b) the portion of the payment in respect of which a deduction is available under paragraph 60(l) of the *Income Tax Act* in computing the income of any person.

Notes: 5.1(2) added by the 1995-97 technical bill, for amounts paid after 1997.

6. Meaning of "interest" — Notwithstanding section 3, the meaning of the term "interest" in any convention given the force of law in Canada before November 19, 1974 does not include any amount paid or credited, pursuant to an agreement in writing entered into before June 23, 1983, as consideration for a guarantee referred to in paragraph 214(15)(a) of the *Income Tax Act*.

6.1 Transitional — [Deals with 1983 taxation year only]

6.2 Partnerships — Notwithstanding the provisions of a convention between Canada and another state or the Act giving it the force of law in Canada, it is hereby declared that the law of Canada is that, for the purposes of the application of the convention and the *Income Tax Act* to a person who is a resident of Canada, a partnership of which that person is a member is neither a resident nor an enterprise of that other state.

Notes: 6.2 added by 1991 technical bill, effective 1983. It was enacted to preclude the application in Canada of the reasoning of the English Court of Appeal in *Padmore*, [1989] STC 493, 62 TC 383. It clarifies that the tax treatment of a Canadian resident partner's share of the income of a partnership is not affected by the fact that a partnership may be considered a resident or enterprise of another country under one of Canada's tax treaties.

See Tanvi Vithlani, "The Application of Treaty Benefits to Partnerships: Characterization of a Foreign Entity", 52(1) *Canadian Tax Journal* 294-314 (2004).

6.3 Gains arising in Canada — Except where a convention expressly otherwise provides, any amount of income, gain or loss in respect of the disposition of a property that is taxable Canadian property within the meaning assigned by the *Income Tax Act* is deemed to arise in Canada.

Notes: 6.3 added by 1998 Budget, effective for dispositions that occur after Feb. 23, 1998. Before its enactment, residents of Australia, New Zealand or Japan who disposed of taxable Canadian property (TCP) could arrange, in some cases, for the sale to be outside Canada and thus not taxed in Canada due to the treaties with those countries. For CRA interpretation see docs 2000-0024247, 2007-0259991E5, 2014-0555061E5.

Other than for gains on TCP, "arising" is not generally defined for tax-treaty purposes. For its meaning, see Notes to Canada-US treaty Art. XXI:7.

Definitions [s. 6.3]: "convention" — ITCIA 2; "taxable Canadian property" — ITA 248(1).

Application

7. Application — This Act applies

(a) in the case of tax under Part XIII of the *Income Tax Act*, to amounts paid or credited after June 23, 1983; and

(b) in all other cases, to taxation years ending after June 23, 1983.

MLI — Multilateral Convention to Implement Tax Treaty Related Measures to Prevent Base Erosion and Profit Shifting [S.C. 2019, c. 12, Schedule]

Notes: This Convention, known more commonly as the Multilateral Instrument or "**MLI**", was signed by Canada on June 7, 2017 and is enacted in Canada by the *Multilateral Instrument in Respect of Tax Conventions Act*, S.C. 2019, c. 12 (Bill C-82), Royal Assent June 21, 2019. The relevant portions for Canada are reproduced below. For the full text of the MLI (49 pages), see tinyurl.com/mli-fulltext; for the OECD's Explanatory Notes to each paragraph see tinyurl.com/mli-expl (85 pages).

The MLI is a novel approach to amending tax treaties, far quicker than each country renegotiating each of its treaties with each other country, which would take decades. It effectively amends Canada's tax treaties with each other country that has signed onto the MLI, once ratified by both countries and once "instruments of ratification" are deposited with the OECD (the "Depositary" under Art. 39) under which each country lists the other as a country for which it wishes to amend the treaty (see Art. 2:1(a)(ii)). See tinyurl.com/oecd-mli for the official MLI website.

Canada ratified the MLI on June 21, 2019 (Royal Assent to S.C. 2019, c. 12), and deposited its instruments of ratification on Aug. 29, 2019. As a result, the MLI came into force in Canada on Dec. 1, 2019 (Art. 34:1), and the withholding tax changes are in effect since Jan. 1, 2020 (Art. 35:1) for 24 of Canada.s treaties, including those with Australia, France, India, Japan, Luxembourg, Netherlands and the UK. Other changes take effect as per Art. 35:2.

As of May 2021, 95 jurisdictions had signed the MLI and 64 had deposited instruments of ratification.

The **United States has not signed on**, so the MLI does not affect the Canada-US treaty. Pursuant to tinyurl.com/canada-mli, Canada wishes the following treaties to be covered (note that Canada's country numbering is different in French):

1. Algeria	43. Latvia
2. Argentina	44. Lithuania
3. Armenia	45. Luxembourg
4. Australia	46. Malaysia
5. Austria	47. Malta
6. Azerbaijan	48. Mexico
7. Bangladesh	49. Moldova
8. Barbados	50. Mongolia
9. Belgium	51. Morocco
10. Brazil	52. Netherlands
11. Bulgaria	53. New Zealand
12. Cameroon	54. Nigeria
13. Chile	55. Norway
14. China	56. Oman
15. Colombia	57. Pakistan
16. Croatia	58. Papua New Guinea
17. Cyprus	59. Peru
18. Czech Republic	60. Philippines
19. Denmark	61. Poland
20. Dominican Republic	62. Portugal
21. Egypt	63. Romania
22. Estonia	64. Russia
23. Finland	65. Senegal
24. France	66. Serbia
25. Gabon	67. Singapore
26. Greece	68. Slovak Republic
27. Hong Kong	69. Slovenia
28. Hungary	70. South Africa
29. Iceland	71. Spain
30. India	72. Sri Lanka
31. Indonesia	73. Sweden
32. Ireland	74. Tanzania
33. Israel	75. Thailand
34. Italy	76. Trinidad and Tobago
35. Ivory Coast	77. Tunisia
36. Jamaica	78. Turkey
37. Japan	79. Ukraine
38. Jordan	80. United Arab Emirates
39. Kazakhstan	81. United Kingdom
40. Kenya	82. Vietnam
41. Korea, Republic of	83. Zambia
42. Kuwait	84. Zimbabwe

See "Current Status of Tax Treaties" Table T-1 below, after the Canada-UK treaty, for the MLI ratification date of those countries that have ratified the MLI.

Germany and **Switzerland** are not on Canada's list because Canada is in the process of renegotiating its treaties with those countries, and will incorporate the necessary provisions in the new treaty. **Brazil** is on the list but has not signed the MLI, so in current negotiations Canada will aim to incorporate the provisions (Finance update, 2020 IFA webinar, Sept. 15, 2020). The other countries with which Canada has treaties but are not on the above list, because as of Jan. 2020 they had not signed the MLI, are: Ecuador, Guyana, Kyrgyzstan, Taiwan, Uzbekistan, Venezuela.

The UK deposited instruments of ratification on June 29, 2018 and included Canada on its list of treaties that it wishes to be covered, so the Canada-UK tax treaty (reproduced after the Canada-US treaty) is affected by the MLI, and we have annotated it accordingly. The UK has also produced a "synthesized" revised version of this treaty, as it has done for its other treaties, as an unofficial guideline to understanding how the MLI amends the treaty. (Finance Canada may publish one as well, or might announce that it agrees with the UK's version.)

Effect of the MLI applying

Once the MLI applies to two countries, their bilateral tax treaty is effectively amended, for the "minimum provisions" that all signatories agree to, as well as for any additional provisions that both countries have opted into. This is made more complex by the fact that a country may agree to apply a provision only for its treaties with specific countries; and that some provisions contain multiple options to choose from: one may have to determine from the MLI whether the provision has any effect if country X chooses option A and country Y chooses option B for the same provision.

The MLI does not *amend* the treaties to which it applies. Rather, it provides rules that replace or interpret existing provisions, and that exist alongside the treaty.

To determine which options a country has chosen, see the **"reservations and notifications"** by that country. (A "reservation" means the country chooses *not* to apply the provision in question.) To find this, go to tinyurl.com/oecd-mli, click on Signatories and Parties, which opens (or saves) a PDF file listing all signatories. In that file, click on the country's ratification date (or signature date, if not yet ratified), and that will bring up another PDF with the country's Reservations and Notifications. For Canada's list (43 pages in each language), see **tinyurl.com/canada-mli**. Per Art. 28:5, reservations must be made by the time instruments of ratification are deposited (except where an Article specifically permits a later reservation), so a country cannot withdraw from an MLI Article later. However, a country can withdraw a *reservation* at any time: Art. 28:9. Finance says (Brian Ernewein, 2020 IFA webinar, Sept. 15, 2020) that Canada's reservations are not necessarily rejections, and some may be withdrawn in the future, or incorporated into future treaty negotiations.

One can also use the OECD's "MLI Matching Database" (tinyurl.com/mli-match), which shows which provisions of the MLI apply to the treaty between any given pair of signatories.

The Dept. of Finance (Ted Cook) announced at the 2019 Cdn Tax Foundation annual conference (Dec. 3, 2019) that it would begin posting "synthesized texts" of Canada's MLI-affected treaties in early 2020. This was delayed due to COVID-19, but is still planned. (The UK released its synthesized version of the Canada-UK treaty in Nov. 2019. The Netherlands released a synthesized version of the Canada-Netherlands treaty in June 2021.)

MLI provisions applying to Canada

The **"minimum provisions"** to which all MLI signatories agree are (full text reproduced below):

- **Article 6** — amends treaty preamble to include a purpose that the treaty not create "opportunities for non-taxation or reduced taxation through tax evasion or avoidance (including through treaty-shopping arrangements)".

- **Article 7** — prevents treaty shopping. Canada has opted for the "principal purpose" test in Art. 7:1 rather than a "limitation on benefits" rule.

- **Article 16** — Mutual Agreement Procedure for dispute resolution.

- **Article 17** — "corresponding adjustments" to match a transfer pricing-assessment in the other country.

Canada has further agreed (in tinyurl.com/canada-mli) to the following (for treaties where the other country has signed on to the same change):

- **Article 4** — provision for resolving dual resident entity cases, for persons other than individuals
- **Article 5** — application of methods for elimination of double taxation (only for Gabon, Ivory Coast, Morocco and Poland)
- **Article 8** — 365-day holding period requirement for a non-resident company holding shares of a Canadian company, to apply a lower treaty-based rate of withholding tax on dividends where the shareholder owns a minimum percentage of the shares
- **Article 9** — 365-day look-back rule for non-residents who realize capital gains on disposition of shares or other interests that derive their value from Canadian real property (see Notes to ITA 248(1)"taxable Canadian property")
- **Articles 18-26** — arbitration

Priority over ITA but not ITCIA

Section 4 of S.C. 2019, c. 12 (the enacting bill) provides:

4. (1) Inconsistent laws — general rule — Subject to subsection (2), in the event of any inconsistency between the provisions of this Act or the multilateral instrument and the provisions of any other law, the provisions of this Act and the multilateral instrument prevail to the extent of the inconsistency.

(2) Inconsistent laws — exception — In the event of any inconsistency between the provisions of the multilateral instrument and the provisions of the *Income Tax Conventions Interpretation Act*, the provisions of that Act prevail to the extent of the inconsistency.

(The reason for subsec. 4(2) is presumably that since the ITCIA prevails over Canada's tax treaties (as provided by the implementing statute for each treaty), the ITCIA should also prevail over each treaty as amended by the MLI.)

Further information

CRA discussion (in addition to docs listed under the Articles below: VIEWS doc 2018-0779891C6 [2018 CTF q.3] (general discussion of MLI); Information Circular 71-17R6, paras. 118-120.

Dept. of Finance news releases:

- June 7, 2017, "Canada Signs Agreement to Combat International Tax Avoidance", and accompanying Backgrounder
- May 28, 2018, "Canada Takes Next Step in Fight Against Aggressive International Tax Avoidance", and accompanying Backgrounder
- Aug. 29, 2019, "Canada Ratifies the Multilateral Convention to Implement Tax Treaty Related Measures to Prevent Base Erosion and Profit Shifting"

Books and major articles (earliest first):

- Bradley & Bright, "State Sovereignty and the Multilateral Instrument", 64(2) *Canadian Tax Journal* 465-86 (2016)
- "The Multilateral Instrument" panel discussions, 2017 Cdn Tax Foundation conference report, 15:1-19 and 16:1-16
- Rizqy & Shearmur, "Multilateral Instrument", chap. 27 of Vidal, *Introduction to International Tax in Canada* (Carswell, 8th ed., 2020)
- Whitmore & Strychun, "Canadian Inbound Investment After the MLI", 67(3) *Canadian Tax Journal* 831-80 (2019)

Shorter articles (earliest first):

- Boidman & Kandev, "Canada's Limited Approach to the OECD's Multilateral Instrument", 87(1) *Tax Notes International* (taxanalysts.org) 63-69 (July 3, 2017)
- Abitbol, "Canada Goes Beyond the MLI's Minimum Standards", 8(3) *Canadian Tax Focus* (ctf.ca) 3-4 (Aug. 2018)
- D'Avignon & Guenther, "Changes to Canada's International Tax Treaty Landscape", XIII(2) *Resource Sector Taxation* (Federated Press) 9-11 (2019)
- Johnson et al., "The Multilateral Instrument and Canadian Tax Planning Considerations", tinyurl.com/mli-plan (July 20, 2020)
- KPMG *TaxNewsFlash* #2021-28, "MLI Update" (May 25, 2021)

See also Notes to specific paragraphs of the Articles below for further references.

Possible Future Amendment — International Tax Anti-avoidance

Prime Minister's mandate letter to Minister of Finance, Dec. 2019: I will expect you to work with your colleagues and through established legislative, regulatory and Cabinet processes to deliver on your top priorities. In particular, you will:. . .

- Modernize anti-avoidance rules to stop large multinational companies from being able to shop for lower tax rates by constructing complex schemes between countries.

Liberal.ca election platform, Oct. 2019: We will: ... modernize anti-avoidance rules to stop large multinational companies from being able to shop for lower tax rates by constructing complex schemes between countries; ...

Notes: It is unclear whether this means anything beyond applying MLI Articles 6 and 7.

The Parties to this Convention,

Recognising that governments lose substantial corporate tax revenue because of aggressive international tax planning that has the effect of artificially shifting profits to locations where they are subject to non-taxation or reduced taxation;

Mindful that base erosion and profit shifting (hereinafter referred to as "BEPS") is a pressing issue not only for industrialised countries but also for emerging economies and developing countries;

Recognising the importance of ensuring that profits are taxed where substantive economic activities generating the profits are carried out and where value is created;

Welcoming the package of measures developed under the OECD/G20 BEPS project (hereinafter referred to as the "OECD/G20 BEPS package");

Noting that the OECD/G20 BEPS package included tax treaty-related measures to address certain hybrid mismatch arrangements, prevent treaty abuse, address artificial avoidance of permanent establishment status, and improve dispute resolution;

Conscious of the need to ensure swift, co-ordinated and consistent implementation of the treaty-related BEPS measures in a multilateral context;

Noting the need to ensure that existing agreements for the avoidance of double taxation on income are interpreted to eliminate double taxation with respect to the taxes covered by those agreements without creating opportunities for non-taxation or reduced taxation through tax evasion or avoidance (including through treaty-shopping arrangements aimed at obtaining reliefs provided in those agreements for the indirect benefit of residents of third jurisdictions);

Recognising the need for an effective mechanism to implement agreed changes in a synchronised and efficient manner across the network of existing agreements for the avoidance of double taxation on income without the need to bilaterally renegotiate each such agreement;

Have agreed as follows:

Notes: For the OECD's Explanatory Notes to each Article below, see tinyurl.com/mli-expl.

PART I.

SCOPE AND INTERPRETATION OF TERMS

Article 1 — Scope of the Convention

This Convention modifies all Covered Tax Agreements as defined in subparagraph a) of paragraph 1 of Article 2 (Interpretation of Terms).

Article 2 — Interpretation of Terms

1. For the purpose of this Convention, the following definitions apply:

a) The term **"Covered Tax Agreement"** means an agreement for the avoidance of double taxation with respect to taxes on income (whether or not other taxes are also covered):

i) that is in force between two or more:

A) Parties; and/or

B) jurisdictions or territories which are parties to an agreement described above and for whose international relations a Party is responsible; and

ii) with respect to which each such Party has made a notification to the Depositary listing the agreement as well as any amending or accompanying instruments thereto (identified by title, names of the parties, date of signature, and, if applicable at the time of the notification, date of entry into force) as an agreement which it wishes to be covered by this Convention.

b) The term **"Party"** means:

i) A State for which this Convention is in force pursuant to Article 34 (Entry into Force); or

ii) A jurisdiction which has signed this Convention pursuant to subparagraph b) or c) of paragraph 1 of Article 27 (Signature and Ratification, Acceptance or Approval) and for which this Convention is in force pursuant to Article 34 (Entry into Force).

c) The term **"Contracting Jurisdiction"** means a party to a Covered Tax Agreement.

d) The term **"Signatory"** means a State or jurisdiction which has signed this Convention but for which the Convention is not yet in force.

2. As regards the application of this Convention at any time by a Party, any term not defined herein shall, unless the context otherwise requires, have the meaning that it has at that time under the relevant Covered Tax Agreement.

PART II.

HYBRID MISMATCHES

Article 3 — Transparent Entities

[Not relevant in Canada — ed.]

Notes: In tinyurl.com/canada-mli, Canada "reserves the right for the entirety of Article 3 not to apply to its Covered Tax Agreements", meaning that Article 3 does not apply.

Article 4 — Dual Resident Entities

1. Where by reason of the provisions of a Covered Tax Agreement a person other than an individual is a resident of more than one Contracting Jurisdiction, the competent authorities of the Contracting Jurisdictions shall endeavour to determine by mutual agreement the Contracting Jurisdiction of which such person shall be deemed to be a resident for the purposes of the Covered Tax Agreement, having regard to its place of effective management, the place where it is incorporated or otherwise constituted and any other relevant factors. In the absence of such agreement, such person shall not be entitled to any relief or exemption from tax provided by the Covered Tax Agreement except to the extent and in such manner as may be agreed upon by the competent authorities of the Contracting Jurisdictions.

Notes: This applies to all of Canada's treaties to which the MLI applies, but only to a "person other than an individual". See Notes to para. 3 below.

2. Paragraph 1 shall apply in place of or in the absence of provisions of a Covered Tax Agreement that provide rules for determining whether a person other than an individual shall be treated as a resident of one of the Contracting Jurisdictions in cases in which that person would otherwise be treated as a resident of more than one Contracting Jurisdiction. Paragraph 1 shall not apply, however, to provisions of a Covered Tax Agreement specifically addressing the residence of companies participating in dual-listed company arrangements.

Notes: See Notes to para. 3 below.

3. A Party may reserve the right:

a) for the entirety of this Article not to apply to its Covered Tax Agreements;

b) for the entirety of this Article not to apply to its Covered Tax Agreements that already address cases where a person other than an individual is a resident of more than one Contracting Jurisdiction by requiring the competent authorities of the Contracting Jurisdictions to endeavour to reach mutual agreement on a single Contracting Jurisdiction of residence;

c) for the entirety of this Article not to apply to its Covered Tax Agreements that already address cases where a person other than an individual is a resident of more than one Contracting Jurisdiction by denying treaty benefits without requiring the competent authorities of the Contracting Jurisdictions to endeavour to reach

mutual agreement on a single Contracting Jurisdiction of residence;

d) for the entirety of this Article not to apply to its Covered Tax Agreements that already address cases where a person other than an individual is a resident of more than one Contracting Jurisdiction by requiring the competent authorities of the Contracting Jurisdictions to endeavour to reach mutual agreement on a single Contracting Jurisdiction of residence, and that set out the treatment of that person under the Covered Tax Agreement where such an agreement cannot be reached;

e) to replace the last sentence of paragraph 1 with the following text for the purposes of its Covered Tax Agreements: "In the absence of such agreement, such person shall not be entitled to any relief or exemption from tax provided by the Covered Tax Agreement.";

f) for the entirety of this Article not to apply to its Covered Tax Agreements with Parties that have made the reservation described in subparagraph e).

Notes: In tinyurl.com/canada-mli, Canada states that all 84 of its MLI-affected treaties "contain a provision described in Article 4(2) that is not subject to a reservation under Article 4(3)(b) through (d)", listing the provision in each case (e.g., Canada-UK Treaty Art. 4(3)). Thus, Canada is not applying a reservation, and agrees that para. 1 applies to corporations and other non-individuals for all its MLI-affected treaties.

4. Each Party that has not made a reservation described in subparagraph a) of paragraph 3 shall notify the Depositary of whether each of its Covered Tax Agreements contains a provision described in paragraph 2 that is not subject to a reservation under subparagraphs b) through d) of paragraph 3, and if so, the article and paragraph number of each such provision. Where all Contracting Jurisdictions have made such a notification with respect to a provision of a Covered Tax Agreement, that provision shall be replaced by the provisions of paragraph 1. In other cases, paragraph 1 shall supersede the provisions of the Covered Tax Agreement only to the extent that those provisions are incompatible with paragraph 1.

Notes: See Notes to para. 3 above.

Article 5 — Application of Methods for Elimination of Double Taxation

[Mostly not relevant in Canada — ed.]

Notes: In tinyurl.com/canada-mli, Canada "reserves the right for the entirety of Article 5 not to apply with respect to the following Covered Tax Agreements", and then lists all MLI-affected treaties except #25, 35, 51, 61 — Gabon, Ivory Coast, Morocco and Poland. Thus, Article 5 can apply only to these treaties, and even for those, Canada has not selected an option under Art. 5:10. For the text, see tinyurl.com/mli-fulltext.

PART III.

TREATY ABUSE

Article 6 — Purpose of a Covered Tax Agreement

1. A Covered Tax Agreement shall be modified to include the following preamble text:

"Intending to eliminate double taxation with respect to the taxes covered by this agreement without creating opportunities for non-taxation or reduced taxation through tax evasion or avoidance (including through treaty-shopping arrangements aimed at obtaining reliefs provided in this agreement for the indirect benefit of residents of third jurisdictions),"

Notes: This applies to all MLI-affected treaties, once the other country has deposited its instruments of ratification (see Notes above at beginning of the MLI). Note that the specific extension to treaty-shopping applies only if there is a "resident of a third jurisdiction" involved. See also the articles cited in Notes at beginning of the MLI.

2. The text described in paragraph 1 shall be included in a Covered Tax Agreement in place of or in the absence of preamble language of the Covered Tax Agreement referring to an intent to eliminate double taxation, whether or not that language also refers to the intent not to create opportunities for non-taxation or reduced taxation.

3. A Party may also choose to include the following preamble text with respect to its Covered Tax Agreements that do not contain pre-

amble language referring to a desire to develop an economic relationship or to enhance co-operation in tax matters:

"Desiring to further develop their economic relationship and to enhance their co-operation in tax matters,"

Notes: Tinyurl.com/canada-mli does not state an intention by Canada to add this to any of Canada's treaties.

4. A Party may reserve the right for paragraph 1 not to apply to its Covered Tax Agreements that already contain preamble language describing the intent of the Contracting Jurisdictions to eliminate double taxation without creating opportunities for non-taxation or reduced taxation, whether that language is limited to cases of tax evasion or avoidance (including through treaty-shopping arrangements aimed at obtaining reliefs provided in the Covered Tax Agreement for the indirect benefit of residents of third jurisdictions) or applies more broadly.

Notes: Tinyurl.com/canada-mli does not state that Canada reserves its right for Canada not to apply para. 1 to any of its treaties.

5. Each Party shall notify the Depositary of whether each of its Covered Tax Agreements, other than those that are within the scope of a reservation under paragraph 4, contains preamble language described in paragraph 2, and if so, the text of the relevant preambular paragraph. Where all Contracting Jurisdictions have made such a notification with respect to that preamble language, such preamble language shall be replaced by the text described in paragraph 1. In other cases, the text described in paragraph 1 shall be included in addition to the existing preamble language.

6. Each Party that chooses to apply paragraph 3 shall notify the Depositary of its choice. Such notification shall also include the list of its Covered Tax Agreements that do not already contain preamble language referring to a desire to develop an economic relationship or to enhance co-operation in tax matters. The text described in paragraph 3 shall be included in a Covered Tax Agreement only where all Contracting Jurisdictions have chosen to apply that paragraph and have made such a notification with respect to the Covered Tax Agreement.

Article 7 — Prevention of Treaty Abuse

1. Notwithstanding any provisions of a Covered Tax Agreement, a benefit under the Covered Tax Agreement shall not be granted in respect of an item of income or capital if it is reasonable to conclude, having regard to all relevant facts and circumstances, that obtaining that benefit was one of the principal purposes of any arrangement or transaction that resulted directly or indirectly in that benefit, unless it is established that granting that benefit in these circumstances would be in accordance with the object and purpose of the relevant provisions of the Covered Tax Agreement.

Notes: Para. 1 applies the principal-purpose text (PPT). Tinyurl.com/canada-mli states that while Canada accepts para. 1 as an interim measure, it intends where possible to adopt a limitation-on-benefits (LOB) provision, in addition to or in replacement of para. 1, through bilateral treaty negotiations (Art. 7:7(a)).

Note that MLI Art. 6 adds a purpose to each treaty as a whole. It is unclear whether it also affects the "object and purpose of the relevant provisions", such as a provision providing a reduced withholding tax in particular circumstances.

In interpreting "benefit" in the PPT, see the commentary to the 2017 OECD Model Treaty (tinyurl.com/oecd-model).

CRA (limited) interpretation of the PPT: VIEWS docs 2017-0724151C6 [2017 CTF q.8], 2018-0749181C6 [IFA 2018 q.2]; 2020-0862471C6 [2020 CTF q.6] (contains list of questions CRA will consider) [tinyurl.com/osler-mli, "Continued uncertainty following recent CRA position on Tax Treaty anti-avoidance rule"].

CRA announced at 2019 CTF conf q.1 [VIEWS doc 2019-0824551C6] that to ensure consistency in application of the PPT it is creating a "Treaty Abuse Prevention Committee", chaired by the Director of the Income Tax Rulings International Division, and including members from Legislative Policy, Tax Avoidance, International Tax, Finance and Justice. Like the GAAR committee(see Notes to ITA 245(2)), the TAP Committee will make recommendations to Rulings and Audit on whether to apply the PPT (including on whether GAAR applies to a tax benefit arising from a treaty).

See also Duff, "Tax Treaty Abuse and the Principal Purpose Test", 66(3) *Canadian Tax Journal* 619-77 and 66(4) 947-1011 (2018); Woolford & MacDonald, "The Multilateral Instrument and Principal Purpose Test", XXI(1) *Corporate Finance* (Federated Press) 6-16 (2018); Kandev and Lennard, "Interpreting the Expression 'Arrangement or Transaction' in the Principal Purpose Test", 106 *International Tax* (CCH) 1-4 (June 2019); Boidman & Kandev, "Canada Enacts Multilateral Instrument", 95(4) *Tax Notes*

International (taxanalysts.org) 315-21 (July 22, 2019); Woolford, Schwarz & Smith, "Implementation of the Principal-Purpose Test", 2019 Cdn Tax Foundation conference report, 28:1-17; Kandev & Lennard, "The OECD Multilateral Instrument: A Canadian Perspective on the Principal Purpose Test", 74(1) *Bulletin for International Taxation* (ibfd.org) 54-60 (Jan. 2020) (discusses the relationship to GAAR); Gagnon, Heale & Tonkovich, "The Multilateral Instrument's Principal Purpose Test", XXIII(2) *Tax Litigation* (Federated Press) 2-11 (2020); Baxter, "Modern Day Treaty Shopping Restricted", 17(6) *Tax Hyperion* (Carswell) 5-8 (Nov-Dec 2020).

2. Paragraph 1 shall apply in place of or in the absence of provisions of a Covered Tax Agreement that deny all or part of the benefits that would otherwise be provided under the Covered Tax Agreement where the principal purpose or one of the principal purposes of any arrangement or transaction, or of any person concerned with an arrangement or transaction, was to obtain those benefits.

Notes: See Notes to para. 15.

3. A Party that has not made the reservation described in subparagraph a) of paragraph 15 may also choose to apply paragraph 4 with respect to its Covered Tax Agreements.

4. *[Not applicable in Canada — ed.]* Where a benefit under a Covered Tax Agreement is denied to a person under provisions of the Covered Tax Agreement (as it may be modified by this Convention) that deny all or part of the benefits that would otherwise be provided under the Covered Tax Agreement where the principal purpose or one of the principal purposes of any arrangement or transaction, or of any person concerned with an arrangement or transaction, was to obtain those benefits, the competent authority of the Contracting Jurisdiction that would otherwise have granted this benefit shall nevertheless treat that person as being entitled to this benefit, or to different benefits with respect to a specific item of income or capital, if such competent authority, upon request from that person and after consideration of the relevant facts and circumstances, determines that such benefits would have been granted to that person in the absence of the transaction or arrangement. The competent authority of the Contracting Jurisdiction to which a request has been made under this paragraph by a resident of the other Contracting Jurisdiction shall consult with the competent authority of that other Contracting Jurisdiction before rejecting the request.

Notes: Para. 4 does not apply unless a party has "chosen" under para. 3 to have it apply, and has notified the depositary (see para. 17(b) of this Article). Canada has not chosen to apply it, even though it has not made any reservations under para. 15(a).

5. Paragraph 4 shall apply to provisions of a Covered Tax Agreement (as it may be modified by this Convention) that deny all or part of the benefits that would otherwise be provided under the Covered Tax Agreement where the principal purpose or one of the principal purposes of any arrangement or transaction, or of any person concerned with an arrangement or transaction, was to obtain those benefits.

6. A Party may also choose to apply the provisions contained in paragraphs 8 through 13 (hereinafter referred to as the "Simplified Limitation on Benefits Provision") to its Covered Tax Agreements by making the notification described in subparagraph c) of paragraph 17. The Simplified Limitation on Benefits Provision shall apply with respect to a Covered Tax Agreement only where all Contracting Jurisdictions have chosen to apply it.

7. In cases where some but not all of the Contracting Jurisdictions to a Covered Tax Agreement choose to apply the Simplified Limitation on Benefits Provision pursuant to paragraph 6, then, notwithstanding the provisions of that paragraph, the Simplified Limitation on Benefits Provision shall apply with respect to the granting of benefits under the Covered Tax Agreement:

a) by all Contracting Jurisdictions, if all of the Contracting Jurisdictions that do not choose pursuant to paragraph 6 to apply the Simplified Limitation on Benefits Provision agree to such application by choosing to apply this subparagraph and notifying the Depositary accordingly; or

b) only by the Contracting Jurisdictions that choose to apply the Simplified Limitation on Benefits Provision, if all of the Contracting Jurisdictions that do not choose pursuant to paragraph 6 to apply the Simplified Limitation on Benefits Provision agree to such application by choosing to apply this subparagraph and notifying the Depositary accordingly.

Simplified Limitation on Benefits Provision

8. Except as otherwise provided in the Simplified Limitation on Benefits Provision, a resident of a Contracting Jurisdiction to a Covered Tax Agreement shall not be entitled to a benefit that would otherwise be accorded by the Covered Tax Agreement, other than a benefit under provisions of the Covered Tax Agreement:

a) which determine the residence of a person other than an individual which is a resident of more than one Contracting Jurisdiction by reason of provisions of the Covered Tax Agreement that define a resident of a Contracting Jurisdiction;

b) which provide that a Contracting Jurisdiction will grant to an enterprise of that Contracting Jurisdiction a corresponding adjustment following an initial adjustment made by the other Contracting Jurisdiction, in accordance with the Covered Tax Agreement, to the amount of tax charged in the first-mentioned Contracting Jurisdiction on the profits of an associated enterprise; or

c) which allow residents of a Contracting Jurisdiction to request that the competent authority of that Contracting Jurisdiction consider cases of taxation not in accordance with the Covered Tax Agreement,

unless such resident is a "qualified person", as defined in paragraph 9 at the time that the benefit would be accorded.

9. A resident of a Contracting Jurisdiction to a Covered Tax Agreement shall be a qualified person at a time when a benefit would otherwise be accorded by the Covered Tax Agreement if, at that time, the resident is:

a) an individual;

b) that Contracting Jurisdiction, or a political subdivision or local authority thereof, or an agency or instrumentality of any such Contracting Jurisdiction, political subdivision or local authority;

c) a company or other entity, if the principal class of its shares is regularly traded on one or more recognised stock exchanges;

d) a person, other than an individual, that:

   i) is a non-profit organisation of a type that is agreed to by the Contracting Jurisdictions through an exchange of diplomatic notes; or

   ii) is an entity or arrangement established in that Contracting Jurisdiction that is treated as a separate person under the taxation laws of that Contracting Jurisdiction and:

      A) that is established and operated exclusively or almost exclusively to administer or provide retirement benefits and ancillary or incidental benefits to individuals and that is regulated as such by that Contracting Jurisdiction or one of its political subdivisions or local authorities; or

      B) that is established and operated exclusively or almost exclusively to invest funds for the benefit of entities or arrangements referred to in subdivision A);

e) a person other than an individual, if, on at least half the days of a twelve-month period that includes the time when the benefit would otherwise be accorded, persons who are residents of that Contracting Jurisdiction and that are entitled to benefits of the Covered Tax Agreement under subparagraphs a) to d) own, directly or indirectly, at least 50 per cent of the shares of the person.

10.

a) A resident of a Contracting Jurisdiction to a Covered Tax Agreement will be entitled to benefits of the Covered Tax Agreement with respect to an item of income derived from the other Contracting Jurisdiction, regardless of whether the resident is a qualified person, if the resident is engaged in the active conduct of a business in the first-mentioned Contracting Jurisdiction, and the income derived from the other Contracting Jurisdiction emanates from, or is incidental to, that business. For purposes of the Simplified Limitation on Benefits Provision, the term "active conduct of a business" shall not include the following activities or any combination thereof:

   i) operating as a holding company;

   ii) providing overall supervision or administration of a group of companies;

   iii) providing group financing (including cash pooling); or

   iv) making or managing investments, unless these activities are carried on by a bank, insurance company or registered securities dealer in the ordinary course of its business as such.

b) If a resident of a Contracting Jurisdiction to a Covered Tax Agreement derives an item of income from a business activity conducted by that resident in the other Contracting Jurisdiction, or derives an item of income arising in the other Contracting Jurisdiction from a connected person, the conditions described in subparagraph a) shall be considered to be satisfied with respect to such item only if the business activity carried on by the resident in the first-mentioned Contracting Jurisdiction to which the item is related is substantial in relation to the same activity or a complementary business activity carried on by the resident or such connected person in the other Contracting Jurisdiction. Whether a business activity is substantial for the purposes of this subparagraph shall be determined based on all the facts and circumstances.

c) For purposes of applying this paragraph, activities conducted by connected persons with respect to a resident of a Contracting Jurisdiction to a Covered Tax Agreement shall be deemed to be conducted by such resident.

11. A resident of a Contracting Jurisdiction to a Covered Tax Agreement that is not a qualified person shall also be entitled to a benefit that would otherwise be accorded by the Covered Tax Agreement with respect to an item of income if, on at least half of the days of any twelve-month period that includes the time when the benefit would otherwise be accorded, persons that are equivalent beneficiaries own, directly or indirectly, at least 75 per cent of the beneficial interests of the resident.

12. If a resident of a Contracting Jurisdiction to a Covered Tax Agreement is neither a qualified person pursuant to the provisions of paragraph 9, nor entitled to benefits under paragraph 10 or 11, the competent authority of the other Contracting Jurisdiction may, nevertheless, grant the benefits of the Covered Tax Agreement, or benefits with respect to a specific item of income, taking into account the object and purpose of the Covered Tax Agreement, but only if such resident demonstrates to the satisfaction of such competent authority that neither its establishment, acquisition or maintenance, nor the conduct of its operations, had as one of its principal purposes the obtaining of benefits under the Covered Tax Agreement. Before either granting or denying a request made under this paragraph by a resident of a Contracting Jurisdiction, the competent authority of the other Contracting Jurisdiction to which the request has been made shall consult with the competent authority of the first-mentioned Contracting Jurisdiction.

13. For the purposes of the Simplified Limitation on Benefits Provision:

a) the term "recognised stock exchange" means:

   i) any stock exchange established and regulated as such under the laws of either Contracting Jurisdiction; and

   ii) any other stock exchange agreed upon by the competent authorities of the Contracting Jurisdictions;

b) the term "principal class of shares" means the class or classes of shares of a company which represents the majority of the aggregate vote and value of the company or the class or classes of beneficial interests of an entity which represents in the aggregate a majority of the aggregate vote and value of the entity;

c) the term "equivalent beneficiary" means any person who would be entitled to benefits with respect to an item of income accorded by a Contracting Jurisdiction to a Covered Tax Agreement under the domestic law of that Contracting Jurisdiction, the Covered Tax Agreement or any other international instrument which are equivalent to, or more favourable than, benefits to be accorded to that item of income under the Covered Tax Agreement; for the purposes of determining whether a person is an equivalent beneficiary with respect to dividends, the person shall be deemed to hold the same capital of the company paying the dividends as such capital the company claiming the benefit with respect to the dividends holds;

d) with respect to entities that are not companies, the term "shares" means interests that are comparable to shares;

e) two persons shall be "connected persons" if one owns, directly or indirectly, at least 50 per cent of the beneficial interest in the other (or, in the case of a company, at least 50 per cent of the aggregate vote and value of the company's shares) or another person owns, directly or indirectly, at least 50 per cent of the beneficial interest (or, in the case of a company, at least 50 per cent of the aggregate vote and value of the company's shares) in each person; in any case, a person shall be connected to another if, based on all the relevant facts and circumstances, one has control of the other or both are under the control of the same person or persons.

14. The Simplified Limitation on Benefits Provision shall apply in place of or in the absence of provisions of a Covered Tax Agreement that would limit the benefits of the Covered Tax Agreement (or that would limit benefits other than a benefit under the provisions of the Covered Tax Agreement relating to residence, associated enterprises or non-discrimination or a benefit that is not restricted solely to residents of a Contracting Jurisdiction) only to a resident that qualifies for such benefits by meeting one or more categorical tests.

15. A Party may reserve the right:

a) for paragraph 1 not to apply to its Covered Tax Agreements on the basis that it intends to adopt a combination of a detailed limitation on benefits provision and either rules to address conduit financing structures or a principal purpose test, thereby meeting the minimum standard for preventing treaty abuse under the OECD/G20 BEPS package; in such cases, the Contracting Jurisdictions shall endeavour to reach a mutually satisfactory solution which meets the minimum standard;

b) for paragraph 1 (and paragraph 4, in the case of a Party that has chosen to apply that paragraph) not to apply to its Covered Tax Agreements that already contain provisions that deny all of the benefits that would otherwise be provided under the Covered Tax Agreement where the principal purpose or one of the principal purposes of any arrangement or transaction, or of any person concerned with an arrangement or transaction, was to obtain those benefits;

c) for the Simplified Limitation on Benefits Provision not to apply to its Covered Tax Agreements that already contain the provisions described in paragraph 14.

Notes: Tinyurl.com/canada-mli states that its treaties with the following countries are not subject to a reservation under para. 15(b) and contain a provision described in para. 2: #13, 15, 22, 26, 27, 33, 39, 43, 44, 48, 53, 54, 56, 59, 61, 79 and 81 — Chile, Colombia, Estonia, Greece, Hong Kong, Israel, Kazakhstan, Latvia, Lithuania, Mexico, New Zealand, Nigeria, Oman, Peru, Poland, Ukraine and UK.

16. Except where the Simplified Limitation on Benefits Provision applies with respect to the granting of benefits under a Covered Tax Agreement by one or more Parties pursuant to paragraph 7, a Party that chooses pursuant to paragraph 6 to apply the Simplified Limitation on Benefits Provision may reserve the right for the entirety of this Article not to apply with respect to its Covered Tax Agreements for which one or more of the other Contracting Jurisdictions has not chosen to apply the Simplified Limitation on Benefits Provision. In such cases, the Contracting Jurisdictions shall endeavour to reach a mutually satisfactory solution which meets the minimum standard for preventing treaty abuse under the OECD/G20 BEPS package.

17.

a) Each Party that has not made the reservation described in subparagraph a) of paragraph 15 shall notify the Depositary of whether each of its Covered Tax Agreements that is not subject to a reservation described in subparagraph b) of paragraph 15 contains a provision described in paragraph 2, and if so, the article and paragraph number of each such provision. Where all Contracting Jurisdictions have made such a notification with respect to a provision of a Covered Tax Agreement, that provision shall be replaced by the provisions of paragraph 1 (and where applicable, paragraph 4). In other cases, paragraph 1 (and where applicable, paragraph 4) shall supersede the provisions of the Covered Tax Agreement only to the extent that those provisions are incompatible with paragraph 1 (and where applicable, paragraph 4). A Party making a notification under this subparagraph may also include a statement that while such Party accepts the application of paragraph 1 alone as an interim measure, it intends where possible to adopt a limitation on benefits provision, in addition to or in replacement of paragraph 1, through bilateral negotiation.

b) Each Party that chooses to apply paragraph 4 shall notify the Depositary of its choice. Paragraph 4 shall apply to a Covered Tax Agreement only where all Contracting Jurisdictions have made such a notification.

c) Each Party that chooses to apply the Simplified Limitation on Benefits Provision pursuant to paragraph 6 shall notify the Depositary of its choice. Unless such Party has made the reservation described in subparagraph c) of paragraph 15, such notification shall also include the list of its Covered Tax Agreements which contain a provision described in paragraph 14, as well as the article and paragraph number of each such provision.

d) Each Party that does not choose to apply the Simplified Limitation on Benefits Provision pursuant to paragraph 6, but chooses to apply either subparagraph a) or b) of paragraph 7 shall notify the Depositary of its choice of subparagraph. Unless such Party has made the reservation described in subparagraph c) of paragraph 15, such notification shall also include the list of its Covered Tax Agreements which contain a provision described in paragraph 14, as well as the article and paragraph number of each such provision.

e) Where all Contracting Jurisdictions have made a notification under subparagraph c) or d) with respect to a provision of a Covered Tax Agreement, that provision shall be replaced by the Simplified Limitation on Benefits Provision. In other cases, the Simplified Limitation on Benefits Provision shall supersede the provisions of the Covered Tax Agreement only to the extent that those provisions are incompatible with the Simplified Limitation on Benefits Provision.

Notes: See Notes to para. 1.

Article 8 — Dividend Transfer Transactions

1. Provisions of a Covered Tax Agreement that exempt dividends paid by a company which is a resident of a Contracting Jurisdiction from tax or that limit the rate at which such dividends may be taxed, provided that the beneficial owner or the recipient is a company which is a resident of the other Contracting Jurisdiction and which owns, holds or controls more than a certain amount of the capital, shares, stock, voting power, voting rights or similar ownership interests of the company paying the dividends, shall apply only if the ownership conditions described in those provisions are met throughout a 365 day period that includes the day of the payment of the dividends (for the purpose of computing that period, no account shall be taken of changes of ownership that would directly result from a corporate reorganisation, such as a merger or divisive reorganisation, of the company that holds the shares or that pays the dividends).

Notes: This adds a 365-day holding requirement to treaty provisions (such as Canada-UK Treaty Art. 10(2)(a)) that reduce the withholding tax rate on dividends for a shareholder that owns a minimum percentage of the paying corporation's shares. See Notes to para. 3 for the treaties to which this does not apply.

Note that the 365 days need only *include* the dividend payment date; there is no requirement to have held the shares for a year before receiving the dividend. However, a payor who withholds and remits withholding tax at the lower rate, when the shareholder has held the share for less than one year, takes the risk that the shareholder could dispose of the share before the 365 days are up.

2. The minimum holding period provided in paragraph 1 shall apply in place of or in the absence of a minimum holding period in provisions of a Covered Tax Agreement described in paragraph 1.

3. A Party may reserve the right:

a) for the entirety of this Article not to apply to its Covered Tax Agreements;

b) for the entirety of this Article not to apply to its Covered Tax Agreements to the extent that the provisions described in paragraph 1 already include:

i) a minimum holding period;

ii) a minimum holding period shorter than a 365 day period; or

iii) a minimum holding period longer than a 365 day period.

Notes: Tinyurl.com/canada-mli lists the MLI-affected treaties containing a provision described in Art. 8:1, and that is not subject to a reservation described in Art. 8:3(b). All treaties are listed except for #1, 7, 8, 12, 17, 20, 21, 25, 35, 46, 47, 51, 58, 65, 67, 72, 77 and 83. Thus, Art. 8:1 can apply to all treaties except those with Algeria, Bangladesh, Barbados, Cameroon, Cyprus, Dominican Republic, Egypt, Gabon, Ivory Coast, Malaysia, Malta, Morocco, Papua New Guinea, Senegal, Singapore, Sri Lanka, Tunisia and Zambia, as these treaties do not have a reduced-tax rate for a shareholder owning a minimum percentage of the shares. (Of course, Art 8 does not apply unless the other country has opted into it, so, for example, it does not apply to the Canada-UK treaty since the UK has "reserved" on this Article.)

4. Each Party that has not made a reservation described in subparagraph a) of paragraph 3 shall notify the Depositary of whether each of its Covered Tax Agreements contains a provision described in paragraph 1 that is not subject to a reservation described in subparagraph b) of paragraph 3, and if so, the article and paragraph number of each such provision. Paragraph 1 shall apply with respect to a provision of a Covered Tax Agreement only where all Contracting Jurisdictions have made such a notification with respect to that provision.

Notes: See Notes to para. 3.

Article 9 — *Capital Gains from Alienation of Shares or Interests of Entities Deriving their Value Principally from Immovable Property*

1. Provisions of a Covered Tax Agreement providing that gains derived by a resident of a Contracting Jurisdiction from the alienation of shares or other rights of participation in an entity may be taxed in the other Contracting Jurisdiction provided that these shares or rights derived more than a certain part of their value from immovable property (real property) situated in that other Contracting Jurisdiction (or provided that more than a certain part of the property of the entity consists of such immovable property (real property)):

a) shall apply if the relevant value threshold is met at any time during the 365 days preceding the alienation; and

b) shall apply to shares or comparable interests, such as interests in a partnership or trust (to the extent that such shares or interests are not already covered) in addition to any shares or rights already covered by the provisions.

Notes: Para. 1(a) adds a 365-day look-back rule to treaty provisions that allow Canada to tax a gain, realized by a resident of the other country, on shares whose value is primarily attributable to real property in Canada. (The UK has "reserved" for MLI Art. 9 not to apply to its treaties, so this does not apply to the Canada-UK treaty.) If the test was met anytime within 365 days before the sale, the rule applies and Canada can tax the gain (and conversely for the other country taxing a gain by a Canadian resident). Tinyurl.com/canada-mli lists the MLI-affected treaties to which this applies; the only ones not listed are #2, 10, 12, 13, 30, 37, 38, 54, 72, 76, 82 (because the treaties do not contain such a rule): Argentina, Brazil, Cameroon, Chile, India, Japan, Jordan, Nigeria, Sri Lanka, Trinidad & Tobago, Vietnam. See however Notes to para. 4 below.

Para. 1(b) extends treaty provisions that allow Canada to tax a gain on shares whose value is primarily attributable to real property in Canada, to apply to partnership and trust interests. However, most of Canada's treaties already do this: e.g., Canada-UK treaty Art. 13(5)(b). Tinyurl.com/canada-mli lists the MLI-affected treaties that contain such a provision; the only ones *not* listed are those not listed for 1(a) above, plus #14 (China). Thus, the treaty with China is the only one for which para. 1(b) actually has any effect. See also Notes to para. 4.

2. The period provided in subparagraph a) of paragraph 1 shall apply in place of or in the absence of a time period for determining whether the relevant value threshold in provisions of a Covered Tax Agreement described in paragraph 1 was met.

3. A Party may also choose to apply paragraph 4 with respect to its Covered Tax Agreements.

4. For purposes of a Covered Tax Agreement, gains derived by a resident of a Contracting Jurisdiction from the alienation of shares or comparable interests, such as interests in a partnership or trust, may be taxed in the other Contracting Jurisdiction if, at any time during the 365 days preceding the alienation, these shares or comparable interests derived more than 50 per cent of their value directly or indirectly from immovable property (real property) situated in that other Contracting Jurisdiction.

Notes: Tinyurl.com/canada-mli states that Canada chooses to apply para. 4. Thus, per para. 5, Canada can tax a gain on shares (or a partnership or trust interest) whose value is primarily attributable to real property in Canada, or was within the past 365 days. As per Notes to para. 1 above, this is already the case under the text of many of Canada's treaties.

See also Kelsey Horning, "Countries Adopt MLI's Lookback for Interests in Real Property", 10(2) *Canadian Tax Focus* (ctf.ca) 11 (May 2020).

5. Paragraph 4 shall apply in place of or in the absence of provisions of a Covered Tax Agreement providing that gains derived by a resident of a Contracting Jurisdiction from the alienation of shares or other rights of participation in an entity may be taxed in the other Contracting Jurisdiction provided that these shares or rights derived more than a certain part of their value from immovable property (real property) situated in that other Contracting Jurisdiction, or provided that more than a certain part of the property of the entity consists of such immovable property (real property).

Notes: See Notes to para. 4.

6. A Party may reserve the right:

a) for paragraph 1 not to apply to its Covered Tax Agreements;

b) for subparagraph a) of paragraph 1 not to apply to its Covered Tax Agreements;

c) for subparagraph b) of paragraph 1 not to apply to its Covered Tax Agreements;

d) for subparagraph a) of paragraph 1 not to apply to its Covered Tax Agreements that already contain a provision of the type described in paragraph 1 that includes a period for determining whether the relevant value threshold was met;

e) for subparagraph b) of paragraph 1 not to apply to its Covered Tax Agreements that already contain a provision of the type described in paragraph 1 that applies to the alienation of interests other than shares;

f) for paragraph 4 not to apply to its Covered Tax Agreements that already contain the provisions described in paragraph 5.

Notes: See Notes to para. 1 for the reservations under para. 6(e).

7. Each Party that has not made the reservation described in subparagraph a) of paragraph 6 shall notify the Depositary of whether each of its Covered Tax Agreements contains a provision described in paragraph 1, and if so, the article and paragraph number of each such provision. Paragraph 1 shall apply with respect to a provision of a Covered Tax Agreement only where all Contracting Jurisdictions have made a notification with respect to that provision.

Notes: See Notes to para. 1 for the notification.

8. Each Party that chooses to apply paragraph 4 shall notify the Depositary of its choice. Paragraph 4 shall apply to a Covered Tax Agreement only where all Contracting Jurisdictions have made such a notification. In such case, paragraph 1 shall not apply with respect to that Covered Tax Agreement. In the case of a Party that has not made the reservation described in subparagraph a) of paragraph 6 and has made the reservation described in subparagraph a) of paragraph 6, such notification shall also include the list of its Covered Tax Agreements which contain a provision described in paragraph 5, as well as the article and paragraph number of each such provision. Where all Contracting Jurisdictions have made a notification with respect to a provision of a Covered Tax Agreement under this

paragraph or paragraph 7, that provision shall be replaced by the provisions of paragraph 4. In other cases, paragraph 4 shall supersede the provisions of the Covered Tax Agreement only to the extent that those provisions are incompatible with paragraph 4.

Notes: See Notes to para. 4 for the notification.

Article 10 — Anti-abuse Rule for Permanent Establishments Situated in Third Jurisdictions

[Not relevant in Canada — ed.]

Notes: In tinyurl.com/canada-mli, Canada "reserves the right for the entirety of Article 10 not to apply to its Covered Tax Agreements", meaning that Article 10 does not apply.

Article 11 — Application of Tax Agreements to Restrict a Party's Right to Tax its Own Residents

[Not relevant in Canada — ed.]

Notes: In tinyurl.com/canada-mli, Canada "reserves the right for the entirety of Article 11 not to apply to its Covered Tax Agreements", meaning that Article 11 does not apply.

PART IV.

AVOIDANCE OF PERMANENT ESTABLISHMENT STATUS

Article 12 — Artificial Avoidance of Permanent Establishment Status through Commissionnaire Arrangements and Similar Strategies

[Not relevant in Canada — ed.]

Notes: In tinyurl.com/canada-mli, Canada "reserves the right for the entirety of Article 12 not to apply to its Covered Tax Agreements", meaning that Article 12 does not apply.

Article 13 — Artificial Avoidance of Permanent Establishment Status through the Specific Activity Exemptions

[Not relevant in Canada — ed.]

Notes: In tinyurl.com/canada-mli, Canada "reserves the right for the entirety of Article 13 not to apply to its Covered Tax Agreements", meaning that Article 13 does not apply.

Article 14 — Splitting-up of Contracts

[Not relevant in Canada — ed.]

Notes: In tinyurl.com/canada-mli, Canada "reserves the right for the entirety of Article 14 not to apply to its Covered Tax Agreements", meaning that Article 14 does not apply.

Article 15 — Definition of a Person Closely Related to an Enterprise

[Not relevant in Canada — ed.]

Notes: In tinyurl.com/canada-mli, Canada "reserves the right for the entirety of Article 15 not to apply to the Covered Tax Agreements to which the reservations described in Article 12(4), 13(6)(a) or (c) and Article 14(3)(a) apply", meaning that Article 15 does not apply.

PART V.

IMPROVING DISPUTE RESOLUTION

Article 16 — Mutual Agreement Procedure

1. Where a person considers that the actions of one or both of the Contracting Jurisdictions result or will result for that person in taxation not in accordance with the provisions of the Covered Tax Agreement, that person may, irrespective of the remedies provided by the domestic law of those Contracting Jurisdictions, present the case to the competent authority of either Contracting Jurisdiction. The case must be presented within three years from the first notification of the action resulting in taxation not in accordance with the provisions of the Covered Tax Agreement.

Notes: In tinyurl.com/canada-mli, Canada "reserves the right for the first sentence of Article 16(1) not to apply to its Covered Tax Agreements on the basis that it intends..." [quoting Art. 16:5(a) verbatim], meaning the first sentence does not apply. However, see para. 4(a) below.

Tinyurl.com/canada-mli also states that all of Canada's MLI-affected treaties "contain a provision that provides that a case referred to in the first sentence of Article 16(1) must be presented within a specific time period that is shorter than three years", with the exception of #4, 10, 13, 14, 15, 19, 23, 26, 27, 33, 41, 48, 53, 61, 66, 71, 73 and 81. Thus, the following treaties *do not* have such a shorter limitation period: Australia, Brazil, Chile, China, Colombia, Denmark, Finland, Greece, Hong Kong, Israel, Korea, Mexico, New Zealand, Poland, Serbia, Spain, Sweden and the UK. All the others may have the deadline extended to 3 years: see Art. 16:6(b).

Tinyurl.com/canada-mli also states (for Art. 16:6(b)(ii)) that the following treaties "contain a provision that provides that a case referred to in the first sentence of Article 16(1) must be presented within a specific time period that is at least three years": #15, 23, 26, 27, 33, 41, 48, 53, 61, 66, 71 and 81. Thus, the following treaties already have at least a 3-year limitation period: Colombia, Finland, Greece, Hong Kong, Israel, Korea, Mexico, New Zealand, Poland, Serbia, Spain and the UK.

2. The competent authority shall endeavour, if the objection appears to it to be justified and if it is not itself able to arrive at a satisfactory solution, to resolve the case by mutual agreement with the competent authority of the other Contracting Jurisdiction, with a view to the avoidance of taxation which is not in accordance with the Covered Tax Agreement. Any agreement reached shall be implemented notwithstanding any time limits in the domestic law of the Contracting Jurisdictions.

Notes: In tinyurl.com/canada-mli, Canada "reserves the right for the second sentence of Article 16(2) not to apply to its Covered Tax Agreements on the basis that for the purposes of all of its Covered Tax Agreements it intends..." [quoting Art. 16:5(c)(ii) verbatim], meaning the second sentence does not apply.

3. The competent authorities of the Contracting Jurisdictions shall endeavour to resolve by mutual agreement any difficulties or doubts arising as to the interpretation or application of the Covered Tax Agreement. They may also consult together for the elimination of double taxation in cases not provided for in the Covered Tax Agreement.

4.

a)

i) The first sentence of paragraph 1 shall apply in place of or in the absence of provisions of a Covered Tax Agreement (or parts thereof) that provide that where a person considers that the actions of one or both of the Contracting Jurisdiction result or will result for that person in taxation not in accordance with the provisions of the Covered Tax Agreement, that person may, irrespective of the remedies provided by the domestic law of those Contracting Jurisdictions, present the case to the competent authority of the Contracting Jurisdiction of which that person is a resident including provisions under which, if the case presented by that person comes under the provisions of a Covered Tax Agreement relating to non-discrimination based on nationality, the case may be presented to the competent authority of the Contracting Jurisdiction of which that person is a national.

ii) The second sentence of paragraph 1 shall apply in place of provisions of a Covered Tax Agreement that provide that a case referred to in the first sentence of paragraph 1 must be presented within a specific time period that is shorter than three years from the first notification of the action resulting in taxation not in accordance with the provisions of the Covered Tax Agreement, or in the absence of a provision of a Covered Tax Agreement describing the time period within which such a case must be presented.

b)

i) The first sentence of paragraph 2 shall apply in the absence of provisions of a Covered Tax Agreement that provide that the competent authority that is presented with the case by the person referred to in paragraph 1 shall endeavour, if the objection appears to it to be justified and if it is not itself able to arrive at a satisfactory solution, to resolve the case by mutual agreement with the competent authority of the other Contracting Jurisdiction, with a view to the avoidance of taxation which is not in accordance with the Covered Tax Agreement.

ii) The second sentence of paragraph 2 shall apply in the absence of provisions of a Covered Tax Agreement providing that any agreement reached shall be implemented notwithstanding any time limits in the domestic law of the Contracting Jurisdictions.

c)

i) The first sentence of paragraph 3 shall apply in the absence of provisions of a Covered Tax Agreement that provide that the competent authorities of the Contracting Jurisdictions shall endeavour to resolve by mutual agreement any difficulties or doubts arising as to the interpretation or application of the Covered Tax Agreement.

ii) The second sentence of paragraph 3 shall apply in the absence of provisions of a Covered Tax Agreement that provide that the competent authorities of the Contracting Jurisdictions may also consult together for the elimination of double taxation in cases not provided for in the Covered Tax Agreement.

Notes: For 4(c), see Notes to para. 6 below.

5. A Party may reserve the right:

a) for the first sentence of paragraph 1 not to apply to its Covered Tax Agreements on the basis that it intends to meet the minimum standard for improving dispute resolution under the OECD/G20 BEPS Package by ensuring that under each of its Covered Tax Agreements (other than a Covered Tax Agreement that permits a person to present a case to the competent authority of either Contracting Jurisdiction), where a person considers that the actions of one or both of the Contracting Jurisdictions result or will result for that person in taxation not in accordance with the provisions of the Covered Tax Agreement, irrespective of the remedies provided by the domestic law of those Contracting Jurisdictions, that person may present the case to the competent authority of the Contracting Jurisdiction of which the person is a resident or, if the case presented by that person comes under a provision of a Covered Tax Agreement relating to non-discrimination based on nationality, to that of the Contracting Jurisdiction of which that person is a national; and the competent authority of that Contracting Jurisdiction will implement a bilateral notification or consultation process with the competent authority of the other Contracting Jurisdiction for cases in which the competent authority to which the mutual agreement procedure case was presented does not consider the taxpayer's objection to be justified;

b) for the second sentence of paragraph 1 not to apply to its Covered Tax Agreements that do not provide that the case referred to in the first sentence of paragraph 1 must be presented within a specific time period on the basis that it intends to meet the minimum standard for improving dispute resolution under the OECD/G20 BEPS package by ensuring that for the purposes of all such Covered Tax Agreements the taxpayer referred to in paragraph 1 is allowed to present the case within a period of at least three years from the first notification of the action resulting in taxation not in accordance with the provisions of the Covered Tax Agreement;

c) for the second sentence of paragraph 2 not to apply to its Covered Tax Agreements on the basis that for the purposes of all of its Covered Tax Agreements:

i) any agreement reached via the mutual agreement procedure shall be implemented notwithstanding any time limits in the domestic laws of the Contracting Jurisdictions; or

ii) it intends to meet the minimum standard for improving dispute resolution under the OECD/G20 BEPS package by accepting, in its bilateral treaty negotiations, a treaty provision providing that:

A) the Contracting Jurisdictions shall make no adjustment to the profits that are attributable to a permanent establishment of an enterprise of one of the Contracting Jurisdictions after a period that is mutually agreed between both Contracting Jurisdictions from the end of the taxable year in which the profits would have been attributable to the permanent establishment (this provision shall not apply in the case of fraud, gross negligence or wilful default); and

B) the Contracting Jurisdictions shall not include in the profits of an enterprise, and tax accordingly, profits that would have accrued to the enterprise but that by reason of the conditions referred to in a provision in the Covered Tax Agreement relating to associated enterprises have not so accrued, after a period that is mutually agreed between both Contracting Jurisdictions from the end of the taxable year in which the profits would have accrued to the enterprise (this provision shall not apply in the case of fraud, gross negligence or wilful default).

Notes: Canada has reserved under both 5(a) and 5(c)(ii). See Notes to paras. 1 and 2.

6.

a) Each Party that has not made a reservation described in subparagraph a) of paragraph 5 shall notify the Depositary of whether each of its Covered Tax Agreements contains a provision described in clause i) of subparagraph a) of paragraph 4, and if so, the article and paragraph number of each such provision. Where all Contracting Jurisdictions have made a notification with respect to a provision of a Covered Tax Agreement, that provision shall be replaced by the first sentence of paragraph 1. In other cases, the first sentence of paragraph 1 shall supersede the provisions of the Covered Tax Agreement only to the extent that those provisions are incompatible with that sentence.

b) Each Party that has not made the reservation described in subparagraph b) of paragraph 5 shall notify the Depositary of:

i) the list of its Covered Tax Agreements which contain a provision that provides that a case referred to in the first sentence of paragraph 1 must be presented within a specific time period that is shorter than three years from the first notification of the action resulting in taxation not in accordance with the provisions of the Covered Tax Agreement, as well as the article and paragraph number of each such provision; a provision of a Covered Tax Agreement shall be replaced by the second sentence of paragraph 1 where all Contracting Jurisdictions have made such a notification with respect to that provision; in other cases, subject to clause ii), the second sentence of paragraph 1 shall supersede the provisions of the Covered Tax Agreement only to the extent that those provisions are incompatible with the second sentence of paragraph 1;

ii) the list of its Covered Tax Agreements which contain a provision that provides that a case referred to in the first sentence of paragraph 1 must be presented within a specific time period that is at least three years from the first notification of the action resulting in taxation not in accordance with the provisions of the Covered Tax Agreement, as well as the article and paragraph number of each such provision; the second sentence of paragraph 1 shall not apply to a Covered Tax Agreement where any Contracting Jurisdiction has made such a notification with respect to that Covered Tax Agreement.

c) Each Party shall notify the Depositary of:

i) the list of its Covered Tax Agreements which do not contain a provision described in clause i) of subparagraph b) of paragraph 4; the first sentence of paragraph 2 shall apply to a Covered Tax Agreement only where all Contracting Jurisdictions have made such a notification with respect to that Covered Tax Agreement;

ii) in the case of a Party that has not made the reservation described in subparagraph c) of paragraph 5, the list of its Covered Tax Agreements which do not contain a provision described in clause ii) of subparagraph b) of paragraph 4; the second sentence of paragraph 2 shall apply to a Covered Tax Agreement only where all Contracting Jurisdictions have made such a notification with respect to that Covered Tax Agreement.

d) Each Party shall notify the Depositary of:

i) the list of its Covered Tax Agreements which do not contain a provision described in clause i) of subparagraph c) of paragraph 4; the first sentence of paragraph 3 shall apply to a Covered Tax Agreement only where all Contracting Jurisdictions have made such a notification with respect to that Covered Tax Agreement;

ii) the list of its Covered Tax Agreements which do not contain a provision described in clause ii) of subparagraph c) of paragraph 4; the second sentence of paragraph 3 shall apply to a Covered Tax Agreement only where all Contracting Jurisdictions have made such a notification with respect to that Covered Tax Agreement.

Notes: For Canada's notifications under 6(b)(i) and (ii), see Notes to para. 1 above.

For 6(d)(i), tinyurl.com/canada-mli states that Canada considers that the treaties with Australia and France *do not* contain a provision described in 4(c)(i).

For 6(d)(ii), Canada states that it considers that the following treaties *do not* contain a provision described in 4(c)(ii): #5, 9, 13, 24, 31, 32, 35, 36, 46, 48, 57, 62, 67 — Austria, Belgium, Chile, France, Indonesia, Ireland, Ivory Cost, Jamaica, Malaysia, Mexico, Pakistan, Portugal and Singapore.

Article 17 — Corresponding Adjustments

1. Where a Contracting Jurisdiction includes in the profits of an enterprise of that Contracting Jurisdiction — and taxes accordingly — profits on which an enterprise of the other Contracting Jurisdiction has been charged to tax in that other Contracting Jurisdiction and the profits so included are profits which would have accrued to the enterprise of the first-mentioned Contracting Jurisdiction if the conditions made between the two enterprises had been those which would have been made between independent enterprises, then that other Contracting Jurisdiction shall make an appropriate adjustment to the amount of the tax charged therein on those profits. In determining such adjustment, due regard shall be had to the other provisions of the Covered Tax Agreement and the competent authorities of the Contracting Jurisdictions shall if necessary consult each other.

Notes: See Notes to para. 2 below.

2. Paragraph 1 shall apply in place of or in the absence of a provision that requires a Contracting Jurisdiction to make an appropriate adjustment to the amount of the tax charged therein on the profits of an enterprise of that Contracting Jurisdiction where the other Contracting Jurisdiction includes those profits in the profits of an enterprise of that other Contracting Jurisdiction and taxes those profits accordingly, and the profits so included are profits which would have accrued to the enterprise of that other Contracting Jurisdiction if the conditions made between the two enterprises had been those which would have been made between independent enterprises.

Notes: In tinyurl.com/canada-mli, Canada "reserves the right for the entirety of Article 17 not to apply to its Covered Tax Agreements that already contain a provision described in Article 17(2)", meaning that Art. 17 does not apply to those treaties. The only MLI-affected treaties not listed are #5, 10, 12, 14, 16, 24, 25, 31, 39, 46, 50, 51, 55, 57 and 67 — Austria, Brazil, Cameroon, China, Croatia, France, Gabon, Indonesia, Kazakhstan, Malaysia, Mongolia, Morocco, Norway, Pakistan and Singapore. See also Notes to para. 3 below for an additional reservation.

Thus, it appears that MLI Art. 17 may not actually have any impact in Canada.

3. A Party may reserve the right:

a) for the entirety of this Article not to apply to its Covered Tax Agreements that already contain a provision described in paragraph 2;

b) for the entirety of this Article not to apply to its Covered Tax Agreements on the basis that in the absence of a provision referred to in paragraph 2 in its Covered Tax Agreement:

i) it shall make the appropriate adjustment referred to in paragraph 1; or

ii) its competent authority shall endeavour to resolve the case under the provisions of a Covered Tax Agreement relating to mutual agreement procedure;

c) in the case of a Party that has made a reservation under clause ii) of subparagraph c) of paragraph 5 of Article 16 (Mutual Agreement Procedure), for the entirety of this Article not to apply to its Covered Tax Agreements on the basis that in its bilateral treaty negotiations it shall accept a treaty provision of the type contained in paragraph 1, provided that the Contracting Jurisdictions were able to reach agreement on that provision and on the provisions described in clause ii) of subparagraph c) of paragraph 5 of Article 16 (Mutual Agreement Procedure).

Notes: In tinyurl.com/canada-mli, per para. 3(c), Canada "reserves the right for the entirety of Article 17 not to apply to its Covered Tax Agreements on the basis that in its bilateral treaty negotiations it shall accept a treaty provision of the type contained in Article 17(1), provided that the Contracting Jurisdictions were able to reach agreement on that provision and on the provisions described in Article 16(5)(c)(ii)".

4. Each Party that has not made a reservation described in paragraph 3 shall notify the Depositary of whether each of its Covered Tax Agreements contains a provision described in paragraph 2, and if so, the article and paragraph number of each such provision. Where all Contracting Jurisdictions have made such a notification with respect to a provision of a Covered Tax Agreement, that provision shall be replaced by the provisions of paragraph 1. In other cases, paragraph 1 shall supersede the provisions of the Covered Tax Agreement only to the extent that those provisions are incompatible with paragraph 1.

PART VI.

ARBITRATION

Article 18 — Choice to Apply Part VI

A Party may choose to apply this Part with respect to its Covered Tax Agreements and shall notify the Depositary accordingly. This Part shall apply in relation to two Contracting Jurisdictions with respect to a Covered Tax Agreement only where both Contracting Jurisdictions have made such a notification.

Notes: In tinyurl.com/canada-mli, Canada "chooses to apply Part VI". See however Notes to Art. 23:7, 26:4 and 28:2. See Art. 36 re when Part VI comes into effect.

Article 19 — Mandatory Binding Arbitration

1. Where:

a) under a provision of a Covered Tax Agreement (as it may be modified by paragraph 1 of Article 16 (Mutual Agreement Procedure)) that provides that a person may present a case to a competent authority of a Contracting Jurisdiction where that person considers that the actions of one or both of the Contracting Jurisdictions result or will result for that person in taxation not in accordance with the provisions of the Covered Tax Agreement (as it may be modified by the Convention), a person has presented a case to the competent authority of a Contracting Jurisdiction on the basis that the actions of one or both of the Contracting Jurisdictions have resulted for that person in taxation not in accordance with the provisions of the Covered Tax Agreement (as it may be modified by the Convention); and

b) the competent authorities are unable to reach an agreement to resolve that case pursuant to a provision of a Covered Tax Agreement (as it may be modified by paragraph 2 of Article 16 (Mutual Agreement Procedure)) that provides that the competent authority shall endeavour to resolve the case by mutual agreement with the competent authority of the other Contracting Jurisdiction, within a period of two years beginning on the start date referred to in paragraph 8 or 9, as the case may be (unless, prior to the expiration of that period the competent authorities of the Contracting Jurisdictions have agreed to a different time period with respect to that case and have notified the person who presented the case of such agreement),

any unresolved issues arising from the case shall, if the person so requests in writing, be submitted to arbitration in the manner described in this Part, according to any rules or procedures agreed upon by the competent authorities of the Contracting Jurisdictions pursuant to the provisions of paragraph 10.

2. Where a competent authority has suspended the mutual agreement procedure referred to in paragraph 1 because a case with re-

spect to one or more of the same issues is pending before court or administrative tribunal, the period provided in subparagraph b) of paragraph 1 will stop running until either a final decision has been rendered by the court or administrative tribunal or the case has been suspended or withdrawn. In addition, where a person who presented a case and a competent authority have agreed to suspend the mutual agreement procedure, the period provided in subparagraph b) of paragraph 1 will stop running until the suspension has been lifted.

3. Where both competent authorities agree that a person directly affected by the case has failed to provide in a timely manner any additional material information requested by either competent authority after the start of the period provided in subparagraph b) of paragraph 1, the period provided in subparagraph b) of paragraph 1 shall be extended for an amount of time equal to the period beginning on the date by which the information was requested and ending on the date on which that information was provided.

4.

a) The arbitration decision with respect to the issues submitted to arbitration shall be implemented through the mutual agreement concerning the case referred to in paragraph 1. The arbitration decision shall be final.

b) The arbitration decision shall be binding on both Contracting Jurisdictions except in the following cases:

i) if a person directly affected by the case does not accept the mutual agreement that implements the arbitration decision. In such a case, the case shall not be eligible for any further consideration by the competent authorities. The mutual agreement that implements the arbitration decision on the case shall be considered not to be accepted by a person directly affected by the case if any person directly affected by the case does not, within 60 days after the date on which notification of the mutual agreement is sent to the person, withdraw all issues resolved in the mutual agreement implementing the arbitration decision from consideration by any court or administrative tribunal or otherwise terminate any pending court or administrative proceedings with respect to such issues in a manner consistent with that mutual agreement.

ii) if a final decision of the courts of one of the Contracting Jurisdictions holds that the arbitration decision is invalid. In such a case, the request for arbitration under paragraph 1 shall be considered not to have been made, and the arbitration process shall be considered not to have taken place (except for the purposes of Articles 21 (Confidentiality of Arbitration Proceedings) and 25 (Costs of Arbitration Proceedings)). In such a case, a new request for arbitration may be made unless the competent authorities agree that such a new request should not be permitted.

iii) if a person directly affected by the case pursues litigation on the issues which were resolved in the mutual agreement implementing the arbitration decision in any court or administrative tribunal.

5. The competent authority that received the initial request for a mutual agreement procedure as described in subparagraph a) of paragraph 1 shall, within two calendar months of receiving the request:

a) send a notification to the person who presented the case that it has received the request; and

b) send a notification of that request, along with a copy of the request, to the competent authority of the other Contracting Jurisdiction.

6. Within three calendar months after a competent authority receives the request for a mutual agreement procedure (or a copy thereof from the competent authority of the other Contracting Jurisdiction) it shall either:

a) notify the person who has presented the case and the other competent authority that it has received the information necessary to undertake substantive consideration of the case; or

b) request additional information from that person for that purpose.

7. Where pursuant to subparagraph b) of paragraph 6, one or both of the competent authorities have requested from the person who presented the case additional information necessary to undertake substantive consideration of the case, the competent authority that requested the additional information shall, within three calendar months of receiving the additional information from that person, notify that person and the other competent authority either:

a) that it has received the requested information; or

b) that some of the requested information is still missing.

8. Where neither competent authority has requested additional information pursuant to subparagraph b) of paragraph 6, the start date referred to in paragraph 1 shall be the earlier of:

a) the date on which both competent authorities have notified the person who presented the case pursuant to subparagraph a) of paragraph 6; and

b) the date that is three calendar months after the notification to the competent authority of the other Contracting Jurisdiction pursuant to subparagraph b) of paragraph 5.

9. Where additional information has been requested pursuant to subparagraph b) of paragraph 6, the start date referred to in paragraph 1 shall be the earlier of:

a) the latest date on which the competent authorities that requested additional information have notified the person who presented the case and the other competent authority pursuant to subparagraph a) of paragraph 7; and

b) the date that is three calendar months after both competent authorities have received all information requested by either competent authority from the person who presented the case.

If, however, one or both of the competent authorities send the notification referred to in subparagraph b) of paragraph 7, such notification shall be treated as a request for additional information under subparagraph b) of paragraph 6.

10. The competent authorities of the Contracting Jurisdictions shall by mutual agreement (pursuant to the article of the relevant Covered Tax Agreement regarding procedures for mutual agreement) settle the mode of application of the provisions contained in this Part, including the minimum information necessary for each competent authority to undertake substantive consideration of the case. Such an agreement shall be concluded before the date on which unresolved issues in a case are first eligible to be submitted to arbitration and may be modified from time to time thereafter.

11. For purposes of applying this Article to its Covered Tax Agreements, a Party may reserve the right to replace the two-year period set forth in subparagraph b) of paragraph 1 with a three-year period.

12. A Party may reserve the right for the following rules to apply with respect to its Covered Tax Agreements notwithstanding the other provisions of this Article:

a) any unresolved issue arising from a mutual agreement procedure case otherwise within the scope of the arbitration process provided for by this Convention shall not be submitted to arbitration, if a decision on this issue has already been rendered by a court or administrative tribunal of either Contracting Jurisdiction;

b) if, at any time after a request for arbitration has been made and before the arbitration panel has delivered its decision to the competent authorities of the Contracting Jurisdictions, a decision concerning the issue is rendered by a court or administrative tribunal of one of the Contracting Jurisdictions, the arbitration process shall terminate.

Notes: In tinyurl.com/canada-mli, Canada "reserves the right for the following rules to apply..." [quotes the rest of para. 12 verbatim]. See also Notes to Art. 28:2.

Article 20 — Appointment of Arbitrators

1. Except to the extent that the competent authorities of the Contracting Jurisdictions mutually agree on different rules, paragraphs 2 through 4 shall apply for the purposes of this Part.

2. The following rules shall govern the appointment of the members of an arbitration panel:

a) The arbitration panel shall consist of three individual members with expertise or experience in international tax matters.

b) Each competent authority shall appoint one panel member within 60 days of the date of the request for arbitration under paragraph 1 of Article 19 (Mandatory Binding Arbitration). The two panel members so appointed shall, within 60 days of the latter of their appointments, appoint a third member who shall serve as Chair of the arbitration panel. The Chair shall not be a national or resident of either Contracting Jurisdiction.

c) Each member appointed to the arbitration panel must be impartial and independent of the competent authorities, tax administrations, and ministries of finance of the Contracting Jurisdictions and of all persons directly affected by the case (as well as their advisors) at the time of accepting an appointment, maintain his or her impartiality and independence throughout the proceedings, and avoid any conduct for a reasonable period of time thereafter which may damage the appearance of impartiality and independence of the arbitrators with respect to the proceedings.

3. In the event that the competent authority of a Contracting Jurisdiction fails to appoint a member of the arbitration panel in the manner and within the time periods specified in paragraph 2 or agreed to by the competent authorities of the Contracting Jurisdictions, a member shall be appointed on behalf of that competent authority by the highest ranking official of the Centre for Tax Policy and Administration of the Organisation for Economic Co-operation and Development that is not a national of either Contracting Jurisdiction.

4. If the two initial members of the arbitration panel fail to appoint the Chair in the manner and within the time periods specified in paragraph 2 or agreed to by the competent authorities of the Contracting Jurisdictions, the Chair shall be appointed by the highest ranking official of the Centre for Tax Policy and Administration of the Organisation for Economic Co-operation and Development that is not a national of either Contracting Jurisdiction.

Article 21 — Confidentiality of Arbitration Proceedings

1. Solely for the purposes of the application of the provisions of this Part and of the provisions of the relevant Covered Tax Agreement and of the domestic laws of the Contracting Jurisdictions related to the exchange of information, confidentiality, and administrative assistance, members of the arbitration panel and a maximum of three staff per member (and prospective arbitrators solely to the extent necessary to verify their ability to fulfil the requirements of arbitrators) shall be considered to be persons or authorities to whom information may be disclosed. Information received by the arbitration panel or prospective arbitrators and information that the competent authorities receive from the arbitration panel shall be considered information that is exchanged under the provisions of the Covered Tax Agreement related to the exchange of information and administrative assistance.

2. The competent authorities of the Contracting Jurisdictions shall ensure that members of the arbitration panel and their staff agree in writing, prior to their acting in an arbitration proceeding, to treat any information relating to the arbitration proceeding consistently with the confidentiality and nondisclosure obligations described in the provisions of the Covered Tax Agreement related to exchange of information and administrative assistance and under the applicable laws of the Contracting Jurisdictions.

Article 22 — Resolution of a Case Prior to the Conclusion of the Arbitration

For the purposes of this Part and the provisions of the relevant Covered Tax Agreement that provide for resolution of cases through mutual agreement, the mutual agreement procedure, as well as the arbitration proceeding, with respect to a case shall terminate if, at any time after a request for arbitration has been made and before the arbitration panel has delivered its decision to the competent authorities of the Contracting Jurisdictions:

a) the competent authorities of the Contracting Jurisdictions reach a mutual agreement to resolve the case; or

b) the person who presented the case withdraws the request for arbitration or the request for a mutual agreement procedure.

Article 23 — Type of Arbitration Process

1. Except to the extent that the competent authorities of the Contracting Jurisdictions mutually agree on different rules, the following rules shall apply with respect to an arbitration proceeding pursuant to this Part:

a) After a case is submitted to arbitration, the competent authority of each Contracting Jurisdiction shall submit to the arbitration panel, by a date set by agreement, a proposed resolution which addresses all unresolved issue(s) in the case (taking into account all agreements previously reached in that case between the competent authorities of the Contracting Jurisdictions). The proposed resolution shall be limited to a disposition of specific monetary amounts (for example, of income or expense) or, where specified, the maximum rate of tax charged pursuant to the Covered Tax Agreement, for each adjustment or similar issue in the case. In a case in which the competent authorities of the Contracting Jurisdictions have been unable to reach agreement on an issue regarding the conditions for application of a provision of the relevant Covered Tax Agreement (hereinafter referred to as a "threshold question"), such as whether an individual is a resident or whether a permanent establishment exists, the competent authorities may submit alternative proposed resolutions with respect to issues the determination of which is contingent on resolution of such threshold questions.

b) The competent authority of each Contracting Jurisdiction may also submit a supporting position paper for consideration by the arbitration panel. Each competent authority that submits a proposed resolution or supporting position paper shall provide a copy to the other competent authority by the date on which the proposed resolution and supporting position paper were due. Each competent authority may also submit to the arbitration panel, by a date set by agreement, a reply submission with respect to the proposed resolution and supporting position paper submitted by the other competent authority. A copy of any reply submission shall be provided to the other competent authority by the date on which the reply submission was due.

c) The arbitration panel shall select as its decision one of the proposed resolutions for the case submitted by the competent authorities with respect to each issue and any threshold questions, and shall not include a rationale or any other explanation of the decision. The arbitration decision will be adopted by a simple majority of the panel members. The arbitration panel shall deliver its decision in writing to the competent authorities of the Contracting Jurisdictions. The arbitration decision shall have no precedential value.

2. For the purpose of applying this Article with respect to its Covered Tax Agreements, a Party may reserve the right for paragraph 1 not to apply to its Covered Tax Agreements. In such a case, except to the extent that the competent authorities of the Contracting Jurisdictions mutually agree on different rules, the following rules shall apply with respect to an arbitration proceeding:

a) After a case is submitted to arbitration, the competent authority of each Contracting Jurisdiction shall provide any information that may be necessary for the arbitration decision to all panel members without undue delay. Unless the competent authorities of the Contracting Jurisdictions agree otherwise, any information that was not available to both competent authorities before the request for arbitration was received by both of them shall not be taken into account for purposes of the decision.

b) The arbitration panel shall decide the issues submitted to arbitration in accordance with the applicable provisions of the Covered Tax Agreement and, subject to these provisions, of those of the domestic laws of the Contracting Jurisdictions. The panel members shall also consider any other sources which the competent authorities of the Contracting Jurisdictions may by mutual agreement expressly identify.

c) The arbitration decision shall be delivered to the competent authorities of the Contracting Jurisdictions in writing and shall indicate the sources of law relied upon and the reasoning which led to its result. The arbitration decision shall be adopted by a simple majority of the panel members. The arbitration decision shall have no precedential value.

3. A Party that has not made the reservation described in paragraph 2 may reserve the right for the preceding paragraphs of this Article not to apply with respect to its Covered Tax Agreements with Parties that have made such a reservation. In such a case, the competent authorities of the Contracting Jurisdictions of each such Covered Tax Agreement shall endeavour to reach agreement on the type of arbitration process that shall apply with respect to that Covered Tax Agreement. Until such an agreement is reached, Article 19 (Mandatory Binding Arbitration) shall not apply with respect to such a Covered Tax Agreement.

Notes: In tinyurl.com/canada-mli, Canada "reserves the right for Article 23(1) and (2) not to apply with respect to its Covered Tax Agreements with Parties that have made the reservation described in Article 23(2)".

4. A Party may also choose to apply paragraph 5 with respect to its Covered Tax Agreements and shall notify the Depositary accordingly. Paragraph 5 shall apply in relation to two Contracting Jurisdictions with respect to a Covered Tax Agreement where either of the Contracting Jurisdictions has made such a notification.

Notes: In tinyurl.com/canada-mli, Canada "chooses to apply Article 23(5)".

5. Prior to the beginning of arbitration proceedings, the competent authorities of the Contracting Jurisdictions to a Covered Tax Agreement shall ensure that each person that presented the case and their advisors agree in writing not to disclose to any other person any information received during the course of the arbitration proceedings from either competent authority or the arbitration panel. The mutual agreement procedure under the Covered Tax Agreement, as well as the arbitration proceeding under this Part, with respect to the case shall terminate if, at any time after a request for arbitration has been made and before the arbitration panel has delivered its decision to the competent authorities of the Contracting Jurisdictions, a person that presented the case or one of that person's advisors materially breaches that agreement.

Notes: See Notes to para. 4.

6. Notwithstanding paragraph 4, a Party that does not choose to apply paragraph 5 may reserve the right for paragraph 5 not to apply with respect to one or more identified Covered Tax Agreements or with respect to all of its Covered Tax Agreements.

Notes: See Notes to para. 7.

7. A Party that chooses to apply paragraph 5 may reserve the right for this Part not to apply with respect to all Covered Tax Agreements for which the other Contracting Jurisdiction makes a reservation pursuant to paragraph 6.

Notes: In tinyurl.com/canada-mli, Canada "reserves the right for Part VI not to apply with respect to all Covered Tax Agreements for which the other Contracting Jurisdiction makes a reservation pursuant to Article 23(6)".

Article 24 — Agreement on a Different Resolution

1. For purposes of applying this Part with respect to its Covered Tax Agreements, a Party may choose to apply paragraph 2 and shall notify the Depositary accordingly. Paragraph 2 shall apply in relation to two Contracting Jurisdictions with respect to a Covered Tax Agreement only where both Contracting Jurisdictions have made such a notification.

2. Notwithstanding paragraph 4 of Article 19 (Mandatory Binding Arbitration), an arbitration decision pursuant to this Part shall not be binding on the Contracting Jurisdictions to a Covered Tax Agreement and shall not be implemented if the competent authorities of the Contracting Jurisdictions agree on a different resolution

of all unresolved issues within three calendar months after the arbitration decision has been delivered to them.

3. A Party that chooses to apply paragraph 2 may reserve the right for paragraph 2 to apply only with respect to its Covered Tax Agreements for which paragraph 2 of Article 23 (Type of Arbitration Process) applies.

Article 25 — Costs of Arbitration Proceedings

In an arbitration proceeding under this Part, the fees and expenses of the members of the arbitration panel, as well as any costs incurred in connection with the arbitration proceedings by the Contracting Jurisdictions, shall be borne by the Contracting Jurisdictions in a manner to be settled by mutual agreement between the competent authorities of the Contracting Jurisdictions. In the absence of such agreement, each Contracting Jurisdiction shall bear its own expenses and those of its appointed panel member. The cost of the chair of the arbitration panel and other expenses associated with the conduct of the arbitration proceedings shall be borne by the Contracting Jurisdictions in equal shares.

Article 26 — Compatibility

1. Subject to Article 18 (Choice to Apply Part VI), the provisions of this Part shall apply in place of or in the absence of provisions of a Covered Tax Agreement that provide for arbitration of unresolved issues arising from a mutual agreement procedure case. Each Party that chooses to apply this Part shall notify the Depositary of whether each of its Covered Tax Agreements, other than those that are within the scope of a reservation under paragraph 4, contains such a provision, and if so, the article and paragraph number of each such provision. Where two Contracting Jurisdictions have made a notification with respect to a provision of a Covered Tax Agreement, that provision shall be replaced by the provisions of this Part as between those Contracting Jurisdictions.

Notes: In tinyurl.com/canada-mli, Canada "considers that the following agreements are not within the scope of a reservation under Article 26(4) and contain a provision that provides for arbitration of unresolved issues arising from a mutual agreement procedure case": #13, 24, 26, 29, 32, 34, 39, 48, 49, 50, 52, 59, 70 — Chile, France, Greece, Iceland, Ireland, Italy, Kazakhstan, Mexico, Moldova, Mongolia, Netherlands, Peru, South Africa.

2. Any unresolved issue arising from a mutual agreement procedure case otherwise within the scope of the arbitration process provided for in this Part shall not be submitted to arbitration if the issue falls within the scope of a case with respect to which an arbitration panel or similar body has previously been set up in accordance with a bilateral or multilateral convention that provides for mandatory binding arbitration of unresolved issues arising from a mutual agreement procedure case.

3. Subject to paragraph 1, nothing in this Part shall affect the fulfilment of wider obligations with respect to the arbitration of unresolved issues arising in the context of a mutual agreement procedure resulting from other conventions to which the Contracting Jurisdictions are or will become parties.

4. A Party may reserve the right for this Part not to apply with respect to one or more identified Covered Tax Agreements (or to all of its Covered Tax Agreements) that already provide for mandatory binding arbitration of unresolved issues arising from a mutual agreement procedure case.

Notes: In tinyurl.com/canada-mli, Canada "reserves the right for Part VI not to apply" (meaning Part VI does not apply) to the treaty with the United Kingdom, since it already provides for mandatory binding arbitration (see Canada-UK treaty Art. 23(6), (7)).

PART VII.

FINAL PROVISIONS

Article 27 — Signature and Ratification, Acceptance or Approval

1. As of 31 December 2016, this Convention shall be open for signature by:

a) all States;

b) Guernsey (the United Kingdom of Great Britain and Northern Ireland); Isle of Man (the United Kingdom of Great Britain and Northern Ireland); Jersey (the United Kingdom of Great Britain and Northern Ireland); and

c) any other jurisdiction authorised to become a Party by means of a decision by consensus of the Parties and Signatories.

2. This Convention is subject to ratification, acceptance or approval.

Article 28 — Reservations

1. Subject to paragraph 2, no reservations may be made to this Convention except those expressly permitted by:

a) Paragraph 5 of Article 3 (Transparent Entities);

b) Paragraph 3 of Article 4 (Dual Resident Entities);

c) Paragraphs 8 and 9 of Article 5 (Application of Methods for Elimination of Double Taxation);

d) Paragraph 4 of Article 6 (Purpose of a Covered Tax Agreement);

e) Paragraphs 15 and 16 of Article 7 (Prevention of Treaty Abuse);

f) Paragraph 3 of Article 8 (Dividend Transfer Transactions);

g) Paragraph 6 of Article 9 (Capital Gains from Alienation of Shares or Interests of Entities Deriving their Value Principally from Immovable Property);

h) Paragraph 5 of Article 10 (Anti-abuse Rule for Permanent Establishments Situated in Third Jurisdictions);

i) Paragraph 3 of Article 11 (Application of Tax Agreements to Restrict a Party's Right to Tax its Own Residents);

j) Paragraph 4 of Article 12 (Artificial Avoidance of Permanent Establishment Status through Commissionnaire Arrangements and Similar Strategies);

k) Paragraph 6 of Article 13 (Artificial Avoidance of Permanent Establishment Status through the Specific Activity Exemptions);

l) Paragraph 3 of Article 14 (Splitting-up of Contracts);

m) Paragraph 2 of Article 15 (Definition of a Person Closely Related to an Enterprise);

n) Paragraph 5 of Article 16 (Mutual Agreement Procedure);

o) Paragraph 3 of Article 17 (Corresponding Adjustments);

p) Paragraphs 11 and 12 of Article 19 (Mandatory Binding Arbitration);

q) Paragraphs 2, 3, 6, and 7 of Article 23 (Type of Arbitration Process);

r) Paragraph 3 of Article 24 (Agreement on a Different Resolution);

s) Paragraph 4 of Article 26 (Compatibility);

t) Paragraphs 6 and 7 of Article 35 (Entry into Effect); and

u) Paragraph 2 of Article 36 (Entry into Effect of Part VI).

2.

a) Notwithstanding paragraph 1, a Party that chooses under Article 18 (Choice to Apply Part VI) to apply Part VI (Arbitration) may formulate one or more reservations with respect to the scope of cases that shall be eligible for arbitration under the provisions of Part VI (Arbitration). For a Party which chooses under Article 18 (Choice to Apply Part VI) to apply Part VI (Arbitration) after it has become a Party to this Convention, reservations pursuant to this subparagraph shall be made at the same time as that Party's notification to the Depositary pursuant to Article 18 (Choice to Apply Part VI).

b) Reservations made under subparagraph a) are subject to acceptance. A reservation made under subparagraph a) shall be considered to have been accepted by a Party if it has not notified the Depositary that it objects to the reservation by the end of a period of twelve calendar months beginning on the date of notification of the reservation by the Depositary or by the date on which it deposits its instrument of ratification, acceptance, or approval, whichever is later. For a Party which chooses under Article 18 (Choice to Apply Part VI) to apply Part VI (Arbitration)

after it has become a Party to this Convention, objections to prior reservations made by other Parties pursuant to subparagraph a) can be made at the time of the first-mentioned Party's notification to the Depositary pursuant to Article 18 (Choice to Apply Part VI). Where a Party raises an objection to a reservation made under subparagraph a), the entirety of Part VI (Arbitration) shall not apply as between the objecting Party and the reserving Party.

Notes: In tinyurl.com/canada-mli, pursuant to para. 2(a), Canada "formulates the following reservations with respect to the scope of cases that shall be eligible for arbitration under the provisions of Part VI":

1. Canada reserves the right to limit the scope of issues eligible for arbitration under the Convention to the following:

(a) Issues arising under provisions akin to Article 4 (Resident) of the OECD Model Tax Convention, but only insofar as the issue relates to the residence of an individual;

(b) Issues arising under provisions akin to Article 5 (Permanent Establishment) of the OECD Model Tax Convention;

(c) Issues arising under provisions akin to Article 7 (Business Profits) of the OECD Model Tax Convention;

(d) Issues arising under provisions akin to Article 9 (Associated Enterprises) of the OECD Model Tax Convention;

(e) Issues arising under provisions akin to Article 12 (Royalties) of the OECD Model Tax Convention, but only insofar as such a provision might apply in transactions involving related persons to which provisions akin to Article 9 of the OECD Model Tax Convention might apply; and

(f) Any other provisions subsequently agreed by the Contracting Jurisdictions through an exchange of diplomatic notes.

2. Canada reserves the right to exclude from the scope of the arbitration provisions of the Convention issues pertaining to the application of anti-abuse provisions whether contained in the Convention, a Covered Tax Agreement, or the domestic law of a Contracting Jurisdiction.

3. Unless explicitly provided otherwise in the relevant provisions of this Convention, a reservation made in accordance with paragraph 1 or 2 shall:

a) modify for the reserving Party in its relations with another Party the provisions of this Convention to which the reservation relates to the extent of the reservation; and

b) modify those provisions to the same extent for the other Party in its relations with the reserving Party.

4. Reservations applicable to Covered Tax Agreements entered into by or on behalf of a jurisdiction or territory for whose international relations a Party is responsible, where that jurisdiction or territory is not a Party to the Convention pursuant to subparagraph b) or c) of paragraph 1 of Article 27 (Signature and Ratification, Acceptance or Approval), shall be made by the responsible Party and can be different from the reservations made by that Party for its own Covered Tax Agreements.

5. Reservations shall be made at the time of signature or when depositing the instrument of ratification, acceptance or approval, subject to the provisions of paragraphs 2, 6 and 9 of this Article, and paragraph 5 of Article 29 (Notifications). However, for a Party which chooses under Article 18 (Choice to Apply Part VI) to apply Part VI (Arbitration) after it has become a Party to this Convention, reservations described in subparagraphs p), q), r) and s) of paragraph 1 of this Article shall be made at the same time as that Party's notification to the Depositary pursuant to Article 18 (Choice to Apply Part VI).

6. If reservations are made at the time of signature, they shall be confirmed upon deposit of the instrument of ratification, acceptance or approval, unless the document containing the reservations explicitly specifies that it is to be considered definitive, subject to the provisions of paragraphs 2, 5 and 9 of this Article, and paragraph 5 of Article 29 (Notifications).

7. If reservations are not made at the time of signature, a provisional list of expected reservations shall be provided to the Depositary at that time.

8. For reservations made pursuant to each of the following provisions, a list of agreements notified pursuant to clause ii) of subparagraph a) of paragraph 1 of Article 2 (Interpretation of Terms) that

are within the scope of the reservation as defined in the relevant provision (and, in the case of a reservation under any of the following provisions other than those listed in subparagraphs c), d) and n), the article and paragraph number of each relevant provision) must be provided when such reservations are made:

a) Subparagraphs b), c), d), e) and g) of paragraph 5 of Article 3 (Transparent Entities);

b) Subparagraphs b), c) and d) of paragraph 3 of Article 4 (Dual Resident Entities);

c) Paragraphs 8 and 9 of Article 5 (Application of Methods for Elimination of Double Taxation);

d) Paragraph 4 of Article 6 (Purpose of a Covered Tax Agreement);

e) Subparagraphs b) and c) of paragraph 15 of Article 7 (Prevention of Treaty Abuse);

f) Clauses i), ii), and iii) of subparagraph b) of paragraph 3 of Article 8 (Dividend Transfer Transactions);

g) Subparagraphs d), e) and f) of paragraph 6 of Article 9 (Capital Gains from Alienation of Shares or Interests of Entities Deriving their Value Principally from Immovable Property);

h) Subparagraphs b) and c) of paragraph 5 of Article 10 (Anti-abuse Rule for Permanent Establishments Situated in Third Jurisdictions);

i) Subparagraph b) of paragraph 3 of Article 11 (Application of Tax Agreements to Restrict a Party's Right to Tax its Own Residents);

j) Subparagraph b) of paragraph 6 of Article 13 (Artificial Avoidance of Permanent Establishment Status through the Specific Activity Exemptions);

k) Subparagraph b) of paragraph 3 of Article 14 (Splitting-up of Contracts);

l) Subparagraph b) of paragraph 5 of Article 16 (Mutual Agreement Procedure);

m) Subparagraph a) of paragraph 3 of Article 17 (Corresponding Adjustments);

n) Paragraph 6 of Article 23 (Type of Arbitration Process); and

o) Paragraph 4 of Article 26 (Compatibility).

The reservations described in subparagraphs a) through o) above shall not apply to any Covered Tax Agreement that is not included on the list described in this paragraph.

9. Any Party which has made a reservation in accordance with paragraph 1 or 2 may at any time withdraw it or replace it with a more limited reservation by means of a notification addressed to the Depositary. Such Party shall make any additional notifications pursuant to paragraph 6 of Article 29 (Notifications) which may be required as a result of the withdrawal or replacement of the reservation. Subject to paragraph 7 of Article 35 (Entry into Effect), the withdrawal or replacement shall take effect:

a) with respect to a Covered Tax Agreement solely with States or jurisdictions that are Parties to the Convention when the notification of withdrawal or replacement of the reservation is received by the Depositary:

i) for reservations in respect of provisions relating to taxes withheld at source, where the event giving rise to such taxes occurs on or after 1 January of the year next following the expiration of a period of six calendar months beginning on the date of the communication by the Depositary of the notification of withdrawal or replacement of the reservation; and

ii) for reservations in respect of all other provisions, for taxes levied with respect to taxable periods beginning on or after 1 January of the year next following the expiration of a period of six calendar months beginning on the date of the communication by the Depositary of the notification of withdrawal or replacement of the reservation; and

b) with respect to a Covered Tax Agreement for which one or more Contracting Jurisdictions becomes a Party to this Convention af-

ter the date of receipt by the Depositary of the notification of withdrawal or replacement: on the latest of the dates on which the Convention enters into force for those Contracting Jurisdictions.

Article 29 — Notifications

1. Subject to paragraphs 5 and 6 of this Article, and paragraph 7 of Article 35 (Entry into Effect), notifications pursuant to the following provisions shall be made at the time of signature or when depositing the instrument of ratification, acceptance or approval:

a) Clause ii) of subparagraph a) of paragraph 1 of Article 2 (Interpretation of Terms);

b) Paragraph 6 of Article 3 (Transparent Entities);

c) Paragraph 4 of Article 4 (Dual Resident Entities);

d) Paragraph 10 of Article 5 (Application of Methods for Elimination of Double Taxation);

e) Paragraphs 5 and 6 of Article 6 (Purpose of a Covered Tax Agreement);

f) Paragraph 17 of Article 7 (Prevention of Treaty Abuse);

g) Paragraph 4 of Article 8 (Dividend Transfer Transactions);

h) Paragraphs 7 and 8 of Article 9 (Capital Gains from Alienation of Shares or Interests of Entities Deriving their Value Principally from Immovable Property);

i) Paragraph 6 of Article 10 (Anti-abuse Rule for Permanent Establishments Situated in Third Jurisdictions);

j) Paragraph 4 of Article 11 (Application of Tax Agreements to Restrict a Party's Right to Tax its Own Residents);

k) Paragraphs 5 and 6 of Article 12 (Artificial Avoidance of Permanent Establishment Status through Commissionnaire Arrangements and Similar Strategies);

l) Paragraphs 7 and 8 of Article 13 (Artificial Avoidance of Permanent Establishment Status through the Specific Activity Exemptions);

m) Paragraph 4 of Article 14 (Splitting-up of Contracts);

n) Paragraph 6 of Article 16 (Mutual Agreement Procedure);

o) Paragraph 4 of Article 17 (Corresponding Adjustments);

p) Article 18 (Choice to Apply Part VI);

q) Paragraph 4 of Article 23 (Type of Arbitration Process);

r) Paragraph 1 of Article 24 (Agreement on a Different Resolution);

s) Paragraph 1 of Article 26 (Compatibility); and

t) Paragraphs 1, 2, 3, 5 and 7 of Article 35 (Entry into Effect).

2. Notifications in respect of Covered Tax Agreements entered into by or on behalf of a jurisdiction or territory for whose international relations a Party is responsible, where that jurisdiction or territory is not a Party to the Convention pursuant to subparagraph b) or c) of paragraph 1 of Article 27 (Signature and Ratification, Acceptance or Approval), shall be made by the responsible Party and can be different from the notifications made by that Party for its own Covered Tax Agreements.

3. If notifications are made at the time of signature, they shall be confirmed upon deposit of the instrument of ratification, acceptance or approval, unless the document containing the notifications explicitly specifies that it is to be considered definitive, subject to the provisions of paragraphs 5 and 6 of this Article, and paragraph 7 of Article 35 (Entry into Effect).

4. If notifications are not made at the time of signature, a provisional list of expected notifications shall be provided at that time.

5. A Party may extend at any time the list of agreements notified under clause ii) of subparagraph a) of paragraph 1 of Article 2 (Interpretation of Terms) by means of a notification addressed to the Depositary. The Party shall specify in this notification whether the agreement falls within the scope of any of the reservations made by the Party which are listed in paragraph 8 of Article 28 (Reserva-

tions). The Party may also make a new reservation described in paragraph 8 of Article 28 (Reservations) if the additional agreement would be the first to fall within the scope of such a reservation. The Party shall also specify any additional notifications that may be required under subparagraphs b) through s) of paragraph 1 to reflect the inclusion of the additional agreements. In addition, if the extension results for the first time in the inclusion of a tax agreement entered into by or on behalf of a jurisdiction or territory for whose international relations a Party is responsible, the Party shall specify any reservations (pursuant to paragraph 4 of Article 28 (Reservations)) or notifications (pursuant to paragraph 2 of this Article) applicable to Covered Tax Agreements entered into by or on behalf of that jurisdiction or territory. On the date on which the added agreement(s) notified under clause ii) of subparagraph a) of paragraph 1 of Article 2 (Interpretation of Terms) become Covered Tax Agreements, the provisions of Article 35 (Entry into Effect) shall govern the date on which the modifications to the Covered Tax Agreement shall have effect.

6. A Party may make additional notifications pursuant to subparagraphs b) through s) of paragraph 1 by means of a notification addressed to the Depositary. These notifications shall take effect:

a) with respect to Covered Tax Agreements solely with States or jurisdictions that are Parties to the Convention when the additional notification is received by the Depositary:

i) for notifications in respect of provisions relating to taxes withheld at source, where the event giving rise to such taxes occurs on or after 1 January of the year next following the expiration of a period of six calendar months beginning on the date of the communication by the Depositary of the additional notification; and

ii) for notifications in respect of all other provisions, for taxes levied with respect to taxable periods beginning on or after 1 January of the year next following the expiration of a period of six calendar months beginning on the date of the communication by the Depositary of the additional notification; and

b) with respect to a Covered Tax Agreement for which one or more Contracting Jurisdictions becomes a Party to this Convention after the date of receipt by the Depositary of the additional notification: on the latest of the dates on which the Convention enters into force for those Contracting Jurisdictions.

Article 30 — Subsequent Modifications of Covered Tax Agreements

The provisions in this Convention are without prejudice to subsequent modifications to a Covered Tax Agreement which may be agreed between the Contracting Jurisdictions of the Covered Tax Agreement.

Article 31 — Conference of the Parties

1. The Parties may convene a Conference of the Parties for the purposes of taking any decisions or exercising any functions as may be required or appropriate under the provisions of this Convention.

2. The Conference of the Parties shall be served by the Depositary.

3. Any Party may request a Conference of the Parties by communicating a request to the Depositary. The Depositary shall inform all Parties of any request. Thereafter, the Depositary shall convene a Conference of the Parties, provided that the request is supported by one-third of the Parties within six calendar months of the communication by the Depositary of the request.

Article 32 — Interpretation and Implementation

1. Any question arising as to the interpretation or implementation of provisions of a Covered Tax Agreement as they are modified by this Convention shall be determined in accordance with the provision(s) of the Covered Tax Agreement relating to the resolution by mutual agreement of questions of interpretation or application of the Covered Tax Agreement (as those provisions may be modified by this Convention).

2. Any question arising as to the interpretation or implementation of this Convention may be addressed by a Conference of the Parties convened in accordance with paragraph 3 of Article 31 (Conference of the Parties).

Article 33 — Amendment

1. Any Party may propose an amendment to this Convention by submitting the proposed amendment to the Depositary.

2. A Conference of the Parties may be convened to consider the proposed amendment in accordance with paragraph 3 of Article 31 (Conference of the Parties).

Article 34 — Entry into Force

1. This Convention shall enter into force on the first day of the month following the expiration of a period of three calendar months beginning on the date of deposit of the fifth instrument of ratification, acceptance or approval.

Notes: The MLI came into force July 1, 2018, after the first five parties (Austria, Isle of Man, Jersey, Poland and Slovenia) had deposited instruments of ratification.

2. For each Signatory ratifying, accepting, or approving this Convention after the deposit of the fifth instrument of ratification, acceptance or approval, the Convention shall enter into force on the first day of the month following the expiration of a period of three calendar months beginning on the date of the deposit by such Signatory of its instrument of ratification, acceptance or approval.

Related Provisions: Art. 35:1 — When MLI enters into effect for Canada.

Notes: Canada deposited instruments of ratification on Aug. 29, 2019, so the MLI enters into force for Canada on Dec. 1, 2019.

Article 35 — Entry into Effect

1. The provisions of this Convention shall have effect in each Contracting Jurisdiction with respect to a Covered Tax Agreement:

a) with respect to taxes withheld at source on amounts paid or credited to non-residents, where the event giving rise to such taxes occurs on or after the first day of the next calendar year that begins on or after the latest of the dates on which this Convention enters into force for each of the Contracting Jurisdictions to the Covered Tax Agreement; and

b) with respect to all other taxes levied by that Contracting Jurisdiction, for taxes levied with respect to taxable periods beginning on or after the expiration of a period of six calendar months (or a shorter period, if all Contracting Jurisdictions notify the Depositary that they intend to apply such shorter period) from the latest of the dates on which this Convention enters into force for each of the Contracting Jurisdictions to the Covered Tax Agreement.

Related Provisions: Art. 34:2 — When MLI enters into force.

Notes: Canada deposited instruments of ratification on Aug. 29, 2019, so for treaties with countries that deposited by Sept. 30, 2019, the withholding tax changes are effective Jan. 1, 2020 (para. 1(a)). See also Art. 36.

2. Solely for the purpose of its own application of subparagraph a) of paragraph 1 and subparagraph a) of paragraph 5, a Party may choose to substitute "taxable period" for "calendar year", and shall notify the Depositary accordingly.

3. Solely for the purpose of its own application of subparagraph b) of paragraph 1 and subparagraph b) of paragraph 5, a Party may choose to replace the reference to "taxable periods beginning on or after the expiration of a period" with a reference to "taxable periods beginning on or after 1 January of the next year beginning on or after the expiration of a period", and shall notify the Depositary accordingly.

4. Notwithstanding the preceding provisions of this Article, Article 16 (Mutual Agreement Procedure) shall have effect with respect to a Covered Tax Agreement for a case presented to the competent authority of a Contracting Jurisdiction on or after the latest of the dates on which this Convention enters into force for each of the Contracting Jurisdictions to the Covered Tax Agreement, except for cases that were not eligible to be presented as of that date under the

Covered Tax Agreement prior to its modification by the Convention, without regard to the taxable period to which the case relates.

5. For a new Covered Tax Agreement resulting from an extension pursuant to paragraph 5 of Article 29 (Notifications) of the list of agreements notified under clause ii) of subparagraph a) of paragraph 1 of Article 2 (Interpretation of Terms), the provisions of this Convention shall have effect in each Contracting Jurisdiction:

a) with respect to taxes withheld at source on amounts paid or credited to non-residents, where the event giving rise to such taxes occurs on or after the first day of the next calendar year that begins on or after 30 days after the date of the communication by the Depositary of the notification of the extension of the list of agreements; and

b) with respect to all other taxes levied by that Contracting Jurisdiction, for taxes levied with respect to taxable periods beginning on or after the expiration of a period of nine calendar months (or a shorter period, if all Contracting Jurisdictions notify the Depositary that they intend to apply such shorter period) from the date of the communication by the Depositary of the notification of the extension of the list of agreements.

6. A Party may reserve the right for paragraph 4 not to apply with respect to its Covered Tax Agreements.

7.

a) A Party may reserve the right to replace:

i) the references in paragraphs 1 and 4 to "the latest of the dates on which this Convention enters into force for each of the Contracting Jurisdictions to the Covered Tax Agreement"; and

ii) the references in paragraph 5 to "the date of the communication by the Depositary of the notification of the extension of the list of agreements";

with references to "30 days after the date of receipt by the Depositary of the latest notification by each Contracting Jurisdiction making the reservation described in paragraph 7 of Article 35 (Entry into Effect) that it has completed its internal procedures for the entry into effect of the provisions of this Convention with respect to that specific Covered Tax Agreement";

iii) the references in subparagraph a) of paragraph 9 of Article 28 (Reservations) to "on the date of the communication by the Depositary of the notification of withdrawal or replacement of the reservation"; and

iv) the reference in subparagraph b) of paragraph 9 of Article 28 (Reservations) to "on the latest of the dates on which the Convention enters into force for those Contracting Jurisdictions";

with references to "30 days after the date of receipt by the Depositary of the latest notification by each Contracting Jurisdiction making the reservation described in paragraph 7 of Article 35 (Entry into Effect) that it has completed its internal procedures for the entry into effect of the withdrawal or replacement of the reservation with respect to that specific Covered Tax Agreement";

v) the references in subparagraph a) of paragraph 6 of Article 29 (Notifications) to "on the date of the communication by the Depositary of the additional notification"; and

vi) the reference in subparagraph b) of paragraph 6 of Article 29 (Notifications) to "on the latest of the dates on which the Convention enters into force for those Contracting Jurisdictions";

with references to "30 days after the date of receipt by the Depositary of the latest notification by each Contracting Jurisdiction making the reservation described in paragraph 7 of Article 35 (Entry into Effect) that it has completed its internal procedures for the entry into effect of the additional notification with respect to that specific Covered Tax Agreement";

vii) the references in paragraphs 1 and 2 of Article 36 (Entry into Effect of Part VI) to "the later of the dates on which this Convention enters into force for each of the Contracting Jurisdictions to the Covered Tax Agreement";

with references to "30 days after the date of receipt by the Depositary of the latest notification by each Contracting Jurisdiction making the reservation described in paragraph 7 of Article 35 (Entry into Effect) that it has completed its internal procedures for the entry into effect of the provisions of this Convention with respect to that specific Covered Tax Agreement"; and

viii) the reference in paragraph 3 of Article 36 (Entry into Effect of Part VI) to "the date of the communication by the Depositary of the notification of the extension of the list of agreements";

ix) the references in paragraph 4 of Article 36 (Entry into Effect of Part VI) to "the date of the communication by the Depositary of the notification of withdrawal of the reservation", "the date of the communication by the Depositary of the notification of replacement of the reservation" and "the date of the communication by the Depositary of the notification of withdrawal of the objection to the reservation"; and

x) the reference in paragraph 5 of Article 36 (Entry into Effect of Part VI) to "the date of the communication by the Depositary of the additional notification";

with references to "30 days after the date of receipt by the Depositary of the latest notification by each Contracting Jurisdiction making the reservation described in paragraph 7 of Article 35 (Entry into Effect) that it has completed its internal procedures for the entry into effect of the provisions of Part VI (Arbitration) with respect to that specific Covered Tax Agreement".

b) A Party making a reservation in accordance with subparagraph a) shall notify the confirmation of the completion of its internal procedures simultaneously to the Depositary and the other Contracting Jurisdiction(s).

c) If one or more Contracting Jurisdictions to a Covered Tax Agreement makes a reservation under this paragraph, the date of entry into effect of the provisions of the Convention, of the withdrawal or replacement of a reservation, of an additional notification with respect to that Covered Tax Agreement, or of Part VI (Arbitration) shall be governed by this paragraph for all Contracting Jurisdictions to the Covered Tax Agreement.

Article 36 — Entry into Effect of Part VI

1. Notwithstanding paragraph 9 of Article 28 (Reservations), paragraph 6 of Article 29 (Notifications), and paragraphs 1 through 6 of Article 35 (Entry into Effect), with respect to two Contracting Jurisdictions to a Covered Tax Agreement, the provisions of Part VI (Arbitration) shall have effect:

a) with respect to cases presented to the competent authority of a Contracting Jurisdiction (as described in subparagraph a) of paragraph 1 of Article 19 (Mandatory Binding Arbitration)), on or after the later of the dates on which this Convention enters into force for each of the Contracting Jurisdictions to the Covered Tax Agreement; and

b) with respect to cases presented to the competent authority of a Contracting Jurisdiction prior to the later of the dates on which this Convention enters into force for each of the Contracting Jurisdictions to the Covered Tax Agreement, on the date when both Contracting Jurisdictions have notified the Depositary that they have reached mutual agreement pursuant to paragraph 10 of Article 19 (Mandatory Binding Arbitration), along with information regarding the date or dates on which such cases shall be considered to have been presented to the competent authority of a Contracting Jurisdiction (as described in subparagraph a) of paragraph 1 of Article 19 (Mandatory Binding Arbitration)) according to the terms of that mutual agreement.

2. A Party may reserve the right for Part VI (Arbitration) to apply to a case presented to the competent authority of a Contracting Jurisdiction prior to the later of the dates on which this Convention enters into force for each of the Contracting Jurisdictions to the Cov-

ered Tax Agreement only to the extent that the competent authorities of both Contracting Jurisdictions agree that it will apply to that specific case.

3. In the case of a new Covered Tax Agreement resulting from an extension pursuant to paragraph 5 of Article 29 (Notifications) of the list of agreements notified under clause ii) of subparagraph a) of paragraph 1 of Article 2 (Interpretation of Terms), the references in paragraphs 1 and 2 of this Article to "the later of the dates on which this Convention enters into force for each of the Contracting Jurisdictions to the Covered Tax Agreement" shall be replaced with references to "the date of the communication by the Depositary of the notification of the extension of the list of agreements".

4. A withdrawal or replacement of a reservation made under paragraph 4 of Article 26 (Compatibility) pursuant to paragraph 9 of Article 28 (Reservations), or the withdrawal of an objection to a reservation made under paragraph 2 of Article 28 (Reservations) which results in the application of Part VI (Arbitration) between two Contracting Jurisdictions to a Covered Tax Agreement, shall have effect according to subparagraphs a) and b) of paragraph 1 of this Article, except that the references to "the later of the dates on which this Convention enters into force for each of the Contracting Jurisdictions to the Covered Tax Agreement" shall be replaced with references to "the date of the communication by the Depositary of the notification of withdrawal of the reservation", "the date of the communication by the Depositary of the notification of replacement of the reservation" or "the date of the communication by the Depositary of the notification of withdrawal of the objection to the reservation", respectively.

5. An additional notification made pursuant to subparagraph p) of paragraph 1 of Article 29 (Notifications) shall have effect according to subparagraphs a) and b) of paragraph 1, except that the references in paragraphs 1 and 2 of this Article to "the later of the dates on which this Convention enters into force for each of the Contracting Jurisdictions to the Covered Tax Agreement" shall be replaced with references to "the date of the communication by the Depositary of the additional notification".

Article 37 — Withdrawal

1. Any Party may, at any time, withdraw from this Convention by means of a notification addressed to the Depositary.

2. Withdrawal pursuant to paragraph 1 shall become effective on the date of receipt of the notification by the Depositary. In cases where this Convention has entered into force with respect to all Contracting Jurisdictions to a Covered Tax Agreement before the date on which a Party's withdrawal becomes effective, that Covered Tax Agreement shall remain as modified by this Convention.

Article 38 — Relation with Protocols

1. This Convention may be supplemented by one or more protocols.

2. In order to become a party to a protocol, a State or jurisdiction must also be a Party to this Convention.

3. A Party to this Convention is not bound by a protocol unless it becomes a party to the protocol in accordance with its provisions.

Article 39 — Depositary

1. The Secretary-General of the Organisation for Economic Co-operation and Development shall be the Depositary of this Convention and any protocols pursuant to Article 38 (Relation with Protocols).

2. The Depositary shall notify the Parties and Signatories within one calendar month of:

a) any signature pursuant to Article 27 (Signature and Ratification, Acceptance or Approval);

b) the deposit of any instrument of ratification, acceptance or approval pursuant to Article 27 (Signature and Ratification, Acceptance or Approval);

c) any reservation or withdrawal or replacement of a reservation pursuant to Article 28 (Reservations);

d) any notification or additional notification pursuant to Article 29 (Notifications);

e) any proposed amendment to this Convention pursuant to Article 33 (Amendment);

f) any withdrawal from this Convention pursuant to Article 37 (Withdrawal); and

g) any other communication related to this Convention.

3. The Depositary shall maintain publicly available lists of:

a) Covered Tax Agreements;

b) reservations made by the Parties; and

c) notifications made by the Parties.

In witness whereof the undersigned, being duly authorised thereto, have signed this Convention.

Done at Paris, the 24th day of November 2016, in English and French, both texts being equally authentic, in a single copy which shall be deposited in the archives of the Organisation for Economic Co-operation and Development.

CANADA–UNITED STATES TAX CONVENTION (1980)

Convention Between Canada and The United States of America With Respect to Taxes on Income and on Capital Signed on September 26, 1980, as Amended by the Protocols Signed on June 14, 1983, March 28, 1984, March 17, 1995, July 29, 1997 and September 21, 2007

Enacted in Canada by S.C. 1984, c. 20; 1995 Protocol by S.C. 1995, c. 34, Royal Assent November 8, 1995; 1997 Protocol by S.C. 1997, c. 38, Royal Assent December 10, 1997; 2007 Protocol by S.C. 2007, c. 32, Royal Assent December 14, 2007

Notes: The Income Tax Convention (tax treaty) between Canada and the United States was signed on Sept. 26, 1980 (replacing one signed in 1942), and amended before ratification by Protocols signed on June 14, 1983 and March 28, 1984. Instruments of ratification were exchanged on Aug. 16, 1984. A third Protocol, signed on March 17, 1995 (replacing one signed on Aug. 31, 1994), came into force with instruments of ratification exchanged on Nov. 9, 1995. A fourth Protocol, signed on July 29, 1997, came into force with instruments of ratification exchanged on Dec. 16, 1997. A fifth Protocol, signed on Sept. 21, 2007, came into force with instruments of ratification exchanged on Dec. 15, 2008 (Dept. of Finance news release 2008-104).

On the Fifth Protocol changes, see Cannon et al, "The Fifth Protocol to the Canada-U.S. Income Tax Convention", 2007 Cdn Tax Foundation conference report, 24:1-92; Biringer & Richardson, "The Fifth Protocol", XIV(3) *Corporate Finance* (Federated Press) 1498-1505 (2007).

The US does not intend to sign the *Multilateral Convention to Implement Tax Treaty Related Measures to Prevent Base Erosion and Profit Shifting* (MLI), which Canada has signed and ratified and which will effectively amend most of Canada's other treaties. (See immediately before this Treaty for the MLI.)

The US Treasury Department (ustreas.gov) released a Technical Explanation (TE) of the Convention (April 26, 1984), the 1995 Protocol (June 13, 1995), the 1997 Protocol (December 18, 1997) and the 2007 Protocol (July 11, 2008). In each case the Canadian Dept. of Finance issued a news release (Aug. 16, 1984; 95-048, June 13, 1995; 97-122, Dec. 18, 1998; 2008-052, July 10, 2008) stating that the TE "accurately reflects understandings reached in the course of negotiations with respect to the interpretation and application of the various provisions in" the treaty or Protocol. The relevant portion of the TE is reproduced below after each paragraph of the treaty. For discussion of the 2008 TE see Biringer & Richardson, "Fifth Protocol Close to Ratification?", XV(1) *Corporate Finance* 1586-90 (2008). The TE is not binding but may be used by the Courts as guidance: *Coblentz*, [1996] 3 C.T.C. 295 (FCA), *Kubicek*, [1997] 3 C.T.C. 435 (FCA); *Allchin*, 2004 FCA 206, para. 16. For more on this issue see the Introduction to David M. Sherman, *Department of Finance Technical Notes* (also at beginning of the Technical Notes database on *Taxnet Pro* and *TaxPartner*).

For discussion of each Article of this treaty see Kerzner, Timokhov & Chodikoff, *Tax Advisor's Guide to the Canada-U.S. Tax Treaty* (Carswell, looseleaf or *Taxnet Pro* Reference Centre); Vern Krishna, *The Canada-U.S. Tax Treaty: Text and Commentary* (LexisNexis Butterworths, 2004); CCH, *Canada-U.S. Tax Treaty: A Practical Interpretation* (2009); Rhoades & Langer, *U.S. International Taxation and Tax Treaties* (Matthew Bender, 6 vols. looseleaf). See also Tony Swiderski, "Interpreting the Canada-US Treaty: Too Unpredictable To Be Reliable?", 2006 Cdn Tax Foundation conference report, 13:1-25; and the OECD Model Tax Convention on Income and on Capital (International Bureau of Fiscal Documentation, ibfd.org). (All of Canada's tax treaties are based on the OECD Model Convention.)

A Canadian seeking treaty relief may need to file Form 8833 (www.irs.gov); severe penalties can apply for not filing. To obtain a reduced withholding rate under the treaty from a US payor, provide the payor with Form W8-BEN.

See also the Notes to the *Income Tax Conventions Interpretation Act* (ITCIA), reproduced on the preceding pages.

For information on US tax, see the Internal Revenue Service web site, www.irs.gov. For a general overview of issues relevant to US citizens in Canada, see Notes to ITA 128.1(1) and David M. Sherman, *The Lawyer's Guide to Income Tax and GST/HST* (2017), §3.5. See also Notes to ITA 233.3(3) re filing obligations for US citizens. The 2014 Canada-US Intergovernmental Agreement for FATCA (*Foreign Account Tax Compliance Act*) is reproduced after this treaty, and see ITA ss. 263-269, which implement it in Canada.

The Canada-US-Mexico Agreement (CUSMA or USMCA, enacted by S.C. 2020, c.1 to replace the North American Free Trade Agreement; in force July 1, 2020) does not apply to income tax matters (VIEWS doc 2004-0064481I7 re NAFTA). For reference to the Canada–United States Social Security Agreement, see CRA Information Circular 84-6.

The US is generally not taking part in the OECD BEPS changes (see at end of ITA 95).

CRA Audit Manual: 15.11.0: Tax treaties.

Table of Contents

Canada and the United States of America, desiring to conclude a Convention for the avoidance of double taxation and the prevention of fiscal evasion with respect to taxes on income and on capital, have agreed as follows:

Application of the 2007 Protocol: The coming into force of the Fifth Protocol (enacted in Canada by S.C. 2007, c. 32) is covered in article 27 of the Protocol. The latest any amendment came into force was Jan. 1, 2010. See up to PITA 51st ed.

Application of the 1995 Protocol: [Reproduced up to PITA 34th edition. The date of exchange of instruments of ratification was November 9, 1995.]

Article I — Personal Scope

This Convention is generally applicable to persons who are residents of one or both of the Contracting States.

Definitions: "person" — Art. III:1(e), ITCIA 3, *Interpretation Act* 35(1); "resident" — Art. IV.

Technical Explanation [1984]: Article I provides that the Convention is generally applicable to persons who are residents of either Canada or the United States or both

Canada and the United States. The word "generally" is used because certain provisions of the Convention apply to persons who are residents of neither Canada nor the United States.

Article II — Taxes Covered

1. This Convention shall apply to taxes on income and on capital imposed on behalf of each Contracting State, irrespective of the manner in which they are levied.

Technical Explanation [1984]: Paragraph 1 states that the Convention applies to taxes "on income and on capital" imposed on behalf of Canada and the United States, irrespective of the manner in which such taxes are levied. Neither Canada nor the United States presently impose taxes on capital. Paragraph 1 is not intended either to broaden or to limit paragraph 2, which provides that the Convention shall apply, in the case of Canada, to the taxes imposed by the Government of Canada under Parts I, XIII, and XIV of the *Income Tax Act* and, in the case of the United States, to the Federal income taxes imposed by the *Internal Revenue Code* ("the Code").

National taxes not generally covered by the Convention include, in the case of the United States, the estate, gift, and generation-skipping transfer taxes, the Windfall Profits Tax, Federal unemployment taxes, social security taxes imposed under sections 1401, 3101, and 3111 of the Code, and the excise tax on insurance premiums imposed under Code section 4371. The Convention also does not generally cover the Canadian excise tax on net insurance premiums paid by residents of Canada for coverage of a risk situated in Canada, the Petroleum and Gas Revenue Tax (PGRT) and the Incremental Oil Revenue Tax (IORT). However, the Convention has the effect of covering the Canadian social security tax in certain respects because under Canadian domestic tax law no such tax is due if there is no income subject to tax under the *Income Tax Act* of Canada. Taxes imposed by the states of the United States, and by the provinces of Canada, are not generally covered by the Convention. However, if such taxes are imposed in accordance with the provisions of the Convention, a foreign tax credit is ensured by paragraph 7 of Article XXIV (Elimination of Double Taxation).

2. Notwithstanding paragraph 1, the taxes existing on March 17, 1995 to which the Convention shall apply are:

(a) in the case of Canada, the taxes imposed by the Government of Canada under the *Income Tax Act*; and

(b) in the case of the United States, the Federal income taxes imposed by the *Internal Revenue Code* of 1986. However, the Convention shall apply to:

(i) the United States accumulated earnings tax and personal holding company tax, to the extent, and only to the extent, necessary to implement the provisions of paragraphs 5 and 8 of Article X (Dividends);

(ii) the United States excise taxes imposed with respect to private foundations, to the extent, and only to the extent, necessary to implement the provisions of paragraph 4 of Article XXI (Exempt Organizations);

(iii) the United States social security taxes, to the extent, and only to the extent, necessary to implement the provisions of paragraph 2 of Article XXIV (Elimination of Double Taxation) and paragraph 4 of Article XXIX (Miscellaneous Rules); and

(iv) the United States estate taxes imposed by the *Internal Revenue Code* of 1986, to the extent, and only to the extent, necessary to implement the provisions of paragraph 3(g) of Article XXVI (Mutual Agreement Procedure) and Article XXIX-B (Taxes Imposed by Reason of Death).

Related Provisions: Art. XXVI-A:9 — Cross-border collection assistance applies to other taxes as well.

Notes: Art. II:2 amended by 1995 Protocol.

Definitions: "Canada" — Art. III:1(a), ITCIA 5; "personal holding company" — *Internal Revenue Code* s. 542(a); "United States" — Art. III:1(b).

Technical Explanation [1995 Protocol]: Article 1 of the Protocol amends Article II (Taxes Covered) of the Convention. Article II identifies the taxes to which the Convention applies. Paragraph 1 of Article 1 replaces paragraphs 2 through 4 of Article II of the Convention with new paragraphs 2 and 3. For each Contracting State, new paragraph 2 of Article II specifies the taxes existing on the date of signature of the Protocol to which the Convention applies. New paragraph 3 provides that the Convention will also apply to taxes identical or substantially similar to those specified in paragraph 2, and to any new capital taxes, that are imposed after the date of signature of the Protocol.

New paragraph 2(a) of Article II describes the Canadian taxes covered by the Convention. As amended by the Protocol, the Convention will apply to all taxes imposed by the Government of Canada under the *Income Tax Act*.

New paragraph 2(b) of Article II amends the provisions identifying the U.S. taxes covered by the Convention in several respects. The Protocol incorporates into paragraph 2(b) the special rules found in paragraph 4 of Article II of the present Convention. New paragraph 2(b)(iii) conforms the rule previously found in paragraph 4(c) of Article II to the amended provisions of Article XXIV (Elimination of Double Taxation), under which Canada has agreed to grant a foreign tax credit for U.S. social security taxes. In addition, the Protocol adds a fourth special rule to reflect the addition to the Convention of new Article XXIX B (Taxes Imposed by Reason of Death) and related provisions in new paragraph 3(g) of Article XXVI (Mutual Agreement Procedure).

Article 1 of the Protocol also makes minor clarifying, non-substantive amendments to paragraphs 2 and 3 of the Article.

Technical Explanation [1984]: Paragraph 2 contrasts with paragraph 1 of the Protocol to the 1942 Convention, which refers to "Dominion income taxes." In addition, unlike the 1942 Convention, the Convention does not contain a reference to "surtaxes and excess-profits taxes."

3. The Convention shall apply also to:

(a) any taxes identical or substantially similar to those taxes to which the Convention applies under paragraph 2; and

(b) taxes on capital;

which are imposed after March 17, 1995 in addition to, or in place of, the taxes to which the Convention applies under paragraph 2.

Notes: Art. II:3 amended by 1995 Protocol, generally effective 1996.

Technical Explanation [1995 Protocol]: See under para. 2.

Technical Explanation [1984]: Paragraph 3 provides that the Convention also applies to any taxes identical or substantially similar to the taxes on income in existence on September 26, 1980 which are imposed in addition to or in place of the taxes existing on that date. Similarly, taxes on capital imposed after that date are to be covered.

It was agreed that Part I of the *Income Tax Act* of Canada is a covered tax even though Canada has made certain modifications in the *Income Tax Act* after the signature of the Convention and before the signature of the 1983 Protocol. In particular, Canada has enacted a low flat rate tax on petroleum production (the PGRT) which, at the time of the signature of the 1983 Protocol, is imposed generally at a statutory rate of 14.67% for the period June 1, 1982 to May 31, 1983, and at 16% thereafter, generally reduced to an effective rate of 11% or 12% after deducting a 25% resource allowance. The PGRT is not deductible in computing income for Canadian income tax purposes. This agreement is not intended to have implications for any other convention or for the interpretation of Code sections 901 and 903. Further, the PGRT and IORT are not taxes described in paragraphs 2 or 3.

4. [Repealed]

Notes: Art. II:4 repealed by 1995 Protocol, generally effective 1996.

Article III — General Definitions

1. For the purposes of this Convention, unless the context otherwise requires:

(a) when used in a geographical sense, the term **"Canada"** means the territory of Canada, including any area beyond the territorial seas of Canada which, in accordance with international law and the laws of Canada, is an area within which Canada may exercise rights with respect to the seabed and subsoil and their natural resources;

(b) the term **"United States"** means:

(i) the United States of America, but does not include Puerto Rico, the Virgin Islands, Guam or any other United States possession or territory; and

(ii) when used in a geographical sense, such term also includes any area beyond the territorial seas of the United States which, in accordance with international law and the laws of the United States, is an area within which the United States may exercise rights with respect to the seabed and subsoil and their natural resources;

(c) the term **"Canadian tax"** means the taxes referred to in Article II (Taxes Covered) that are imposed on income by Canada;

(d) the term **"United States tax"** means the taxes referred to in Article II (Taxes Covered), other than in subparagraph (b)(i) to

(iv) of paragraph 2 thereof, that are imposed on income by the United States;

(e) the term **"person"** includes an individual, an estate, a trust, a company and any other body of persons;

(f) the term **"company"** means any body corporate or any entity which is treated as a body corporate for tax purposes;

(g) the term **"competent authority"** means:

(i) in the case of Canada, the Minister of National Revenue or his authorized representative; and

(ii) in the case of the United States, the Secretary of the Treasury or his delegate;

(h) the term **"international traffic"** with reference to a resident of a Contracting State means any voyage of a ship or aircraft to transport passengers or property (whether or not operated or used by that resident) except where the principal purpose of the voyage is to transport passengers or property between places within the other Contracting State;

(i) the term **"State"** means any national State, whether or not a Contracting State; and

(j) the term **"the 1942 Convention"** means the Convention and Protocol between Canada and the United States for the Avoidance of Double Taxation and the Prevention of Fiscal Evasion in the case of Income Taxes signed at Washington on March 4, 1942, as amended by the Convention signed at Ottawa on June 12, 1950, by the Convention signed at Ottawa on August 8, 1956 and by the Supplementary Convention signed at Washington on October 25, 1966;

(k) the term **"national"** of a Contracting State means:

(i) any individual possessing the citizenship or nationality of that State; and

(ii) any legal person, partnership or association deriving its status as such from the laws in force in that State.

Related Provisions: ITCIA 3 — Terms have their meaning under the ITA as amended from time to time; 5 — Definitions of "annuity", "Canada", "immovable property", "real property", "periodic pension payment"; 6 — Definition of "interest".

Notes: See Notes to ITA 115.1 re the designated "competent authority".

A "company" can include a US partnership that "checks the box" to be taxable in the US as a corporation, and such a partnership can claim treaty benefits: VIEWS doc 2008-0278801C6 q.18 (2008 STEP conference).

Art. III:1(k) added by 2007 Protocol, generally for tax years beginning after 2008. Art. III:1(c), (d) amended by 1995 Protocol, generally effective 1996.

Definitions: "Canada" — Art. III:1(a), ITCIA 5; "estate", "individual" — ITCIA 3, ITA 248(1); "partnership" — see Notes to ITA 96(1); "person" — Art. III:1(e); "property" — ITCIA 3, ITA 248(1); "resident" — Art. IV; "State" — Art. III:1(i); "trust" — ITCIA 3, ITA 104(1), 248(1), (3); "United States" — Art. III:1(b).

Technical Explanation [2007 Protocol]: Article 1 of the Protocol adds subparagraph 1(k) to Article III (General Definitions) to address the definition of "national" of a Contracting State as used in the Convention. The Contracting States recognize that Canadian tax law does not draw distinctions based on nationality as such. Nevertheless, at the request of the United States, the definition was added and contains references to both citizenship and nationality. The definition includes any individual possessing the citizenship or nationality of a Contracting State and any legal person, partnership or association whose status is determined by reference to the laws in force in a Contracting State. The existing Convention contains one reference to the term "national" in paragraph 1 of Article XXVI (Mutual Agreement Procedure). The Protocol adds another reference in paragraph 1 of Article XXV (Non-Discrimination) to ensure that nationals of the United States are covered by the non-discrimination provisions of the Convention. The definition added by the Protocol is consistent with the definition provided in other U.S. tax treaties.

Technical Explanation [1995 Protocol]: This Article of the Protocol amends paragraphs 1(c) and 1(d) of Article III (General Definitions) of the Convention. These paragraphs define the terms "Canadian tax" and "United States tax," respectively. The present Convention defines "Canadian tax" to mean the Canadian taxes specified in paragraph 2(a) or 3(a) of Article II (Taxes Covered), i.e., Canadian income taxes. It similarly defines the term "United States tax" to mean the U.S. taxes specified in paragraph 2(b) or 3(b) of Article II, i.e., U.S. income taxes.

As amended by the Protocol, paragraph 2(a) of Article II of the Convention covers all taxes imposed by Canada under its *Income Tax Act*, including certain taxes that are not income taxes. As explained below, paragraph 2(b) is similarly amended by the Protocol to include certain U.S. taxes that are not income taxes. It was, therefore, necessary to amend the terms "Canadian tax" and "United States tax" so that they would continue to

refer exclusively to the income taxes imposed by each Contracting State. The amendment to the definition of the term "Canadian tax" ensures, for example, that the Protocol will not obligate the United States to give a foreign tax credit under Article XXIV (Elimination of Double Taxation) for covered taxes other than income taxes.

The definition of "United States tax," as amended, excludes certain United States taxes that are covered in Article II only for certain limited purposes under the Convention. These include the accumulated earnings tax, the personal holding company tax, foundation excise taxes, social security taxes, and estate taxes. To the extent that these are to be creditable taxes in Canada, that fact is specified elsewhere in the Convention. A Canadian income tax credit for U.S. social security taxes is provided in new paragraph 2(a)(ii) of Article XXIV (Elimination of Double Taxation). A Canadian income tax credit for the U.S. estate taxes is provided in paragraph 6 of new Article XXIX B (Taxes Imposed by Reason of Death).

Technical Explanation [1984]: Article III provides definitions and general rules of interpretation for the Convention. Paragraph 1(a) states that the term "Canada," when used in a geographical sense, means the territory of Canada, including any area beyond the territorial seas of Canada which, under international law and the laws of Canada, is an area within which Canada may exercise rights with respect to the seabed and subsoil and their natural resources. This definition differs only in form from the definition of Canada in the 1942 Convention; paragraph 1(a) omits the reference in the 1942 Convention to "the Provinces, the Territories and Sable Island" as unnecessary.

Paragraph 1(b)(i) defines the term "United States" to mean the United States of America. The term does not include Puerto Rico, the Virgin Islands, Guam, or any other United States possession or territory.

Paragraph 1(b)(ii) states that when the term "United States" is used in a geographical sense the term also includes any area beyond the territorial seas of the United States which, under international law and the laws of the United States, is an area within which the United States may exercise rights with respect to the seabed and subsoil and their natural resources.

Paragraph 1(c) defines the term "Canadian tax" to mean the taxes imposed by the Government of Canada under Parts I, XIII, and XIV of the *Income Tax Act* as in existence on September 26, 1980 and any identical or substantially similar taxes on income imposed by the Government of Canada after that date and which are in addition to or in place of the then existing taxes. The term does not extend to capital taxes, if and when such taxes are ever imposed by Canada.

Paragraph 1(d) defines the term "United States tax" to mean the Federal income taxes imposed by the *Internal Revenue Code* as in existence on September 26, 1980 and any identical or substantially similar taxes on income imposed by the United States after that date in addition to or in place of the then existing taxes. The term does not extend to capital taxes, nor to the United States taxes identified in paragraph 4 of Article II (Taxes Covered).

Paragraph 1(e) provides that the term "person" includes an individual, an estate, a trust, a company, and any other body of persons. Although both the United States and Canada do not regard partnerships as taxable entities, the definition in the paragraph is broad enough to include partnerships where necessary.

Paragraph 1(f) defines the term "company" to mean any body corporate or any entity which is treated as a body corporate for tax purposes.

The term "competent authority" is defined in paragraph 1(g) to mean, in the case of Canada, the Minister of National Revenue or his authorized representative and, in the case of the United States, the Secretary of the Treasury or his delegate. The Secretary of the Treasury has delegated the general authority to act as competent authority to the Commissioner of the Internal Revenue Service, who has redelegated such authority to the Associate Commissioner (Operations). The Assistant Commissioner (Examination) has been delegated the authority to administer programs for simultaneous, spontaneous and industrywide exchanges of information. The Director, Foreign Operations District, has been delegated the authority to administer programs for routine and specific exchanges of information and mutual assistance in collection. The Assistant Commissioner (Criminal Investigations) has been delegated the authority to administer the simultaneous criminal investigation program with Canada.

Paragraph 1(h) defines the term "international traffic" to mean, with reference to a resident of a Contracting State, any voyage of a ship or aircraft to transport passengers or property (whether or not operated or used by that resident), except where the principal purpose of the voyage is transport between points within the other Contracting State. For example, in determining for Canadian tax purposes whether a United States resident has derived profits from the operation of ships or aircraft in international traffic, a voyage of a ship or aircraft (whether or not operated or used by that resident) that includes stops in both Contracting States will not be international traffic if the principal purpose of the voyage is to transport passengers or property from one point in Canada to another point in Canada.

Paragraph 1(i) defines the term "State" to mean any national State, whether or not a Contracting State.

Paragraph 1(j) establishes "the 1942 Convention" as the term to be used throughout the Convention for referring to the pre-existing income tax treaty relationship between the United States and Canada.

2. As regards the application of the Convention by a Contracting State any term not defined therein shall, unless the context otherwise requires and subject to the provisions of Article XXVI (Mutual

Agreement Procedure), have the meaning which it has under the law of that State concerning the taxes to which the Convention applies.

Related Provisions: ITCIA 3 — Terms have their meaning under the ITA as amended from time to time.

Notes: Fifth Protocol (2007), Annex B, states (see also s. 3 of the *Income Tax Conventions Interpretation Act*):

1. Meaning of undefined terms

For purposes of paragraph 2 of Article III (General Definitions) of the Convention, it is understood that, as regards the application at any time of the Convention, and any protocols thereto by a Contracting State, any term not defined therein shall, unless the context otherwise requires or the competent authorities otherwise agree to a common meaning pursuant to Article XXVI (Mutual Agreement Procedure), have the meaning which it has at that time under the law of that State for the purposes of the taxes to which the Convention, and any protocols thereto apply, any meaning under the applicable tax laws of that State prevailing over a meaning given to the term under other laws of that State.

See Michael Kandev, "Tax Treaty Interpretation: Determining Domestic Meaning Under Article 3(2) of the OECD Model", 55(1) *Canadian Tax Journal* 31-71 (2007).

Definitions: "State" — Art. III:1(i).

Technical Explanation [2007 Protocol]: The General Note provides that for purposes of paragraph 2 of Article III, as regards the application at any time of the Convention, any term not defined in the Convention shall, unless the context otherwise requires or the competent authorities otherwise agree to a common meaning pursuant to Article XXVI (Mutual Agreement Procedure), have the meaning which it has at that time under the law of that State for the purposes of the taxes to which the Convention apply, any meaning under the applicable tax laws of that State prevailing over a meaning given to the term under other laws of that State.

Technical Explanation [1984]: Paragraph 2 provides that, in the case of a term not defined in the Convention, the domestic tax law of the Contracting State applying to the Convention shall control, unless the context in which the term is used requires a definition independent of domestic tax law or the competent authorities reach agreement on a meaning pursuant to Article XXVI (Mutual Agreement Procedure). The term "context" refers to the purpose and background of the provision in which the term appears.

Pursuant to the provisions of Article XXVI, the competent authorities of the Contracting States may resolve any difficulties or doubts as to the interpretation or application of the Convention. An agreement by the competent authorities with respect to the meaning of a term used in the Convention would supersede conflicting meanings in the domestic laws of the Contracting States.

Article IV — Residence

1. For the purposes of this Convention, the term **"resident of a Contracting State"** means any person that, under the laws of that State, is liable to tax therein by reason of that person's domicile, residence, citizenship, place of management, place of incorporation or any other criterion of a similar nature, but in the case of an estate or trust, only to the extent that income derived by the estate or trust is liable to tax in that State, either in its hands or in the hands of its beneficiaries. For the purposes of this paragraph, an individual who is not a resident of Canada under this paragraph and who is a United States citizen or an alien admitted to the United States for permanent residence (a "green card" holder) is a resident of the United States only if the individual has a substantial presence, permanent home or habitual abode in the United States, and that individual's personal and economic relations are closer to the United States than to any third State. The term "resident" of a Contracting State is understood to include:

(a) the Government of that State or a political subdivision or local authority thereof or any agency or instrumentality of any such government, subdivision or authority, and

(b)

(i) a trust, organization or other arrangement that is operated exclusively to administer or provide pension, retirement or employee benefits; and

(ii) a not-for-profit organization

that was constituted in that State and that is, by reason of its nature as such, generally exempt from income taxation in that State.

Related Provisions: ITCIA 4.3 — Residence of trust; ITCIA 6.2 — Residence of partnership.

Notes: In Canada's tax treaties, the words "liable to tax" mean comprehensively liable to tax on world income: *Crown Forest*, [1995] 2 C.T.C. 64 (SCC) (US); *McFadyen*, [2000] 4 C.T.C. 2573 (TCC), para. 139 (Japan); *Denisov*, 2010 TCC 101, para. 42 (Russia); *Income Tax Technical News* 35; VIEWS doc 2009-0344111E5. However, for the UK, Japan, Cyprus, Malaysia, Barbados and some other countries, which tax non-residents on a "remittance" basis (on funds remitted back to that country), that basis is considered sufficient to establish "liable to tax": CRA response, "The Impact of Recent Cases", 1998 Cdn Tax Foundation conference report at 52:28-29. Note also that a temporary resident in Australia on a work visa is not taxed on world income (*Income Tax Assessment Act* s. 768-10(1)). See also Powrie, "Tax Avoidance and Tax Treaties", 2008 conference report at 19:1-5; Choudhury & Navkar, "No Treaty Exemption for a Non-resident Employee", 23(4) *Taxation of Executive Compensation & Retirement* (Federated Press) 1470-71 (Nov. 2011).

CRA will issue a Certificate of Residency to confirm that tax is being paid in Canada: tinyurl.com/cra-residency.

A corporation incorporated in a third country but continued in a US jurisdiction is considered "resident" in the US under para. 1: VIEWS doc 2002-0157355. An "S" corporation and a qualified subchapter S subsidiary may be considered resident in the US for purposes of para. 1: docs 2005-0144621E5, 2009-0352761E5.

For a US limited liability corporation (LLC) and other hybrid entities, see Art. IV:6 and 7. A US partnership that "checks the box" to be taxable in the US as a corporation is resident in the US and can claim treaty benefits: VIEWS doc 2008-0278801C6 q.18 (2008 STEP conference).

Art. IV:1 amended by 1995 Protocol, generally effective 1996.

Definitions: "Canada" — Art. III:1(a), ITCIA 5; "estate", "individual" — ITCIA 3, ITA 248(1); "person" — Art. III:1(e), ITCIA 3, *Interpretation Act* 35(1); "State" — Art. III:1(i); "trust" — ITCIA 3, ITA 104(1), 248(1), (3); "United States" — Art. III:1(b).

I.T. Technical News: 16 (*Crown Forest Industries* case; U.S. S-Corps and LLCs); 34 (treaty interpretation and the meaning of "liable to tax"); 35 (treaty residence — resident of convenience).

Technical Explanation [1995 Protocol]: Article 3 of the Protocol amends Article IV (Residence) of the Convention. It clarifies the meaning of the term "resident" in certain cases and adds a special rule, found in a number of recent U.S. treaties, for determining the residence of U.S. citizens and "green-card" holders.

The first sentence of paragraph 1 of Article IV sets forth the general criteria for determining residence under the Convention. It is amended by the Protocol to state explicitly that a person will be considered a resident of a Contracting State for purposes of the Convention if he is liable to tax in that Contracting State by reason of citizenship. Although the sentence applies to both Contracting States, only the United States taxes its non-resident citizens in the same manner as its residents. Aliens admitted to the United States for permanent residence ("green card" holders) continue to qualify as U.S. residents under the first sentence of paragraph 1, because they are taxed by the United States as residents, regardless of where they physically reside.

U.S. citizens and green card holders who reside outside the United States, however, may have relatively little personal or economic nexus with the United States. The Protocol adds a second sentence to paragraph 1 that acknowledges this fact by limiting the circumstances under which such persons are to be treated, for purposes of the Convention, as U.S. residents. Under that sentence, a U.S. citizen or green card holder will be treated as a resident of the United States for purposes of the Convention, and, thereby, be entitled to treaty benefits, only if (1) the individual has a substantial presence, permanent home, or habitual abode in the United States, and (2) the individual's personal and economic relations with the United States are closer than those with any third country. If, however, such an individual is a resident of both the United States and Canada under the first sentence of the paragraph, his residence for purposes of the Convention is determined instead under the "tie-breaker" rules of paragraph 2 of the Article.

The fact that a U.S. citizen who does not have close ties to the United States may not be treated as a U.S. resident under Article IV of the Convention does not alter the application of the saving clause of paragraph 2 of Article XXIX (Miscellaneous Rules) to that citizen. However, like any other individual that is a resident alien under U.S. law, a green card holder is treated as a resident of the United States for purposes of the saving clause only if he qualifies as such under Article IV.

New paragraph 1(a) confirms that the term "resident" of a Contracting State includes the Government of that State or a political subdivision or local authority of that State, as well as any agency or instrumentality of one of these governmental entities. This is implicit in the current Convention and in other U.S. and Canadian treaties, even where not specified.

New paragraph 1 also clarifies, in subparagraph (b), that trusts, organizations, or other arrangements operated exclusively to provide retirement or employee benefits, and other not-for-profit organizations, such as organizations described in section 501(c) of the *Internal Revenue Code*, are residents of a Contracting State if they are constituted in that State and are generally exempt from income taxation in that State by reason of their nature as described above. This change clarifies that the specified entities are to be treated as residents of one of the Contracting States. This corresponds to the interpretation that had previously been adopted by the Contracting States. Such entities, therefore, will be entitled to the benefits of the Convention with respect to the other Contracting State, provided that they satisfy the requirements of new Article XXIX A (Limitation on Benefits) (discussed below).

Technical Explanation [1984]: Article IV provides a detailed definition of the term "resident of a Contracting State." The definition begins with a person's liability to tax as a resident under the respective taxation laws of the Contracting States. A person who, under those laws, is a resident of one Contracting State and not the other need look no further. However, the Convention definition is also designed to assign residence to one State or the other for purposes of the Convention in circumstances where each of the Contracting States believes a person to be its resident. The Convention definition is, of course, exclusively for purposes of the Convention.

Paragraph 1 provides that the term "resident of a Contracting State" means any person who, under the laws of that State, is liable to tax therein by reason of his domicile, residence, place of management, place of incorporation, or any other criterion of a similar nature. The phrase "any other criterion of a similar nature" includes, for U.S. purposes, an election under the Code to be treated as a U.S. resident. An estate or trust is, however, considered to be a resident of a Contracting State only to the extent that income derived by such estate or trust is liable to tax in that State either in its hands or in the hands of its beneficiaries. To the extent that an estate or trust is considered a resident of a Contracting State under this provision, it can be a "beneficial owner" of items of income specified in other articles of the Convention — e.g. paragraph 2 of Article X (Dividends).

2. Where by reason of the provisions of paragraph 1 an individual is a resident of both Contracting States, then his status shall be determined as follows:

(a) he shall be deemed to be a resident of the Contracting State in which he has a permanent home available to him; if he has a permanent home available to him in both States or in neither State, he shall be deemed to be a resident of the Contracting State with which his personal and economic relations are closer (centre of vital interests);

(b) if the Contracting State in which he has his centre of vital interests cannot be determined, he shall be deemed to be a resident of the Contracting State in which he has an habitual abode;

(c) if he has an habitual abode in both States or in neither State, he shall be deemed to be a resident of the Contracting State of which he is a citizen; and

(d) if he is a citizen of both States or of neither of them, the competent authorities of the Contracting States shall settle the question by mutual agreement.

Related Provisions: ITA 250(5) — Person not resident in Canada under treaty is deemed not resident under ITA.

Notes: The rules in para. 2 (para. 3 for corporations) are called the "tie-breaker" rules. Once a person is found resident in both Canada and the US under para. 1, there should be a "liberal analysis" under these rules: *Allchin*, 2004 FCA 206; redetermined 2005 TCC 711, where even though A had not cut her ties with Canada, she was liable to pay US tax because she held a "green card", and her connections with the US were closer. A person found to be more closely connected to the US is deemed non-resident of Canada by ITA 250(5). See also ITA 250(1) Notes. If the person is resident in only one country under the common-law test, the tie-breaker rules are not relevant: *Vegh*, 2012 TCC 95, para. 36.

Note that being found resident in Canada under the tie-breaker rules excuses one from paying US tax, but *not* from having to file US returns (see Notes to ITA 128.1(1)) and FBAR forms (see Notes to ITA 233.3(3)); see also Arnold Sherman, "Risk of Deemed US Residence", 23(5) *Canadian Tax Highlights* (ctf.ca) 10-11 (May 2015).

"If a person who has a home in one state sets up a second in the other state while retaining the first, the fact that he retains the first in the environment where he has always lived, where he has worked, and where he has his family and possessions, can, together with other elements, go to demonstrate that he has retained his centre of vital interests in the first state": *Gaudreau*, 2005 TCC 840; aff'd 2005 FCA 388. For a ruling that a particular individual kept his centre of vital interests in Canada and so remained resident, see VIEWS doc 2004-0083621R3. See also 2012-0457311E5 (general discussion).

The tie-breaker rules were also applied in *Bujnowski*, 2006 FCA 32 (B resident in Canada); *Salt*, 2007 TCC 118 (S resident in Australia under Canada-Australia treaty, based on where permanent home available); *Garcia*, 2007 TCC 548 (G resident in Canada where only permanent home available); *Minin*, 2008 TCC 429 (M resident in Canada where permanent home available); *Lingle*, 2009 TCC 435; aff'd 2010 FCA 152 (detailed discussion by both Courts of "habitual abode", which was not in US despite spending every weekend with family in US); *Trieste*, 2012 FCA 320 (habitual abode was Canada, even though T returned to US monthly and for holidays); *Elliott (Dysert)*, 2013 TCC 57 (cost engineers working at Syncrude for 4 years, renting apartments in Edmonton, had permanent homes in both countries, but personal and economic relations were closer to US); *Davis*, 2018 TCC 110 (dual resident was moving to Canada but "habitual abode" was still in US on date of large withdrawal from retirement account); VIEWS doc 2014-0516451E5 (Canada-Israel treaty to BC venture capital corp). See also Notes to Reg. 2607.

See case law from other countries as well, e.g. *Pike*, [2020] FCAFC 159 (Australia) (habitual abode in both AU and Thailand but personal relations closer to AU).

For all of Canada's treaties, the tie-breaker rules are considered only if the evidence shows that the foreign country taxes the person comprehensively on worldwide income. See Notes to para. 1 above.

See also Bernstein, "Treaties: Residence Tiebreaker", 22(11) *Canadian Tax Highlights* (ctf.ca) 9-10 (Nov. 2014); Vithyananthan & Park, "Returning Snowbirds and US Filing Requirements", 12(1) *BorderCrossings* (Carswell) 1-5 (July 2019).

Definitions: "competent authority" — Art. III:1(g); "individual" — ITCIA 3, ITA 248(1); "resident" — Art. IV; "State" — Art. III:1(i).

Technical Explanation [1984]: Paragraphs 2, 3, and 4 provide rules to determine a single residence for purposes of the Convention for persons resident in both Contracting States under the rules set forth in paragraph 1. Paragraph 2 deals with individuals. A "dual resident" individual is initially deemed to be a resident of the Contracting State in which he has a permanent home available to him. If the individual has a permanent home available to him in both States or in neither, he is deemed to be a resident of the Contracting State with which his personal and economic relations are closer. If the personal and economic relations of an individual are not closer to one Contracting State than to the other, the individual is deemed to be a resident of the Contracting State in which he has a habitual abode. If he has such an abode in both States or in neither State, he is deemed to be a resident of the Contracting State of which he is a citizen. If the individual is a citizen of both States or of neither, the competent authorities are to settle the status of the individual by mutual agreement.

3. Where by reason of the provisions of paragraph 1, a company is a resident of both Contracting States, then

(a) if it is created under the laws in force in a Contracting State, but not under the laws in force in the other Contracting State, it shall be deemed to be a resident only of the first-mentioned State; and

(b) in any other case, the competent authorities of the Contracting States shall endeavor to settle the question of residency by mutual agreement and determine the mode of application of this Convention to the company. In the absence of such agreement, the company shall not be considered a resident of either Contracting State for purposes of claiming any benefits under this Convention.

Related Provisions: ITA 250(3) — Person not resident in Canada under treaty is not resident under ITA; ITA 250(5.1) — Continuation in other jurisdiction.

Notes: In *Landbouwbedrijf Backx*, 2021 TCC 2 (under appeal to FCA), para. 100, absent expert evidence on Dutch law, the TCC could not find that LB was both Canadian and Dutch resident, so this rule in Canada-Netherlands treaty art. 4(3) did not apply.

For an example of Art. IV:3 applying see VIEWS doc 2008-0270771E5.

Art. IV:3 amended by 2007 Protocol (generally for years beginning after 2008, and for corporate continuations after Sept. 17, 2000), 1995 Protocol.

Definitions: "company" — Art. III:1(f); "competent authority" — Art. III:1(g); "State" — Art. III:1(i).

Technical Explanation [2007 Protocol]: Article 2 of the Protocol replaces paragraph 3 of Article IV (Residence) of the existing Convention to address the treatment of so-called dual resident companies. Article 2 of the Protocol also adds new paragraphs 6 and 7 to Article IV to determine whether income is considered to be derived by a resident of a Contracting State when such income is derived through a fiscally transparent entity.

Paragraph 3 of Article IV — Dual resident companies

Paragraph 3, which addresses companies that are otherwise considered resident in each of the Contracting States, is replaced. The provisions of paragraph 3, and the date upon which these provisions are effective, are consistent with an understanding reached between the United States and Canada on September 18, 2000, to clarify the residence of a company under the Convention when the company has engaged in a so-called corporate "continuance" transaction. The paragraph applies only where, by reason of the rules set forth in paragraph 1 of Article IV (Residence), a company is a resident of both Contracting States.

Subparagraph 3(a) provides a rule to address the situation when a company is a resident of both Contracting States but is created under the laws in force in only one of the Contracting States. In such a case, the rule provides that the company is a resident only of the Contracting State under which it is created. For example, if a company is incorporated in the United States but the company is also otherwise considered a resident of Canada because the company is managed in Canada, subparagraph 3(a) provides that the company shall be considered a resident only of the United States for purposes of the Convention. Subparagraph 3(a) is intended to operate in a manner similar to the first sentence of former paragraph 3. However, subparagraph 3(a) clarifies that such a company must be considered created in only one of the Contracting States to fall within the scope of subparagraph 3(a). In some cases, a company may engage in a corporate continuance transaction and retain its charter in the Contracting State from which it continued, while also being considered as created in the State to which the company continued. In such cases, the provisions of subparagraph 3(a) shall not apply because the company would be considered created in both of the Contracting States.

Subparagraph 3(b) addresses all cases involving a dual resident company that are not addressed in subparagraph 3(a). Thus, subparagraph 3(b) applies to continuance transactions occurring between the Contracting States if, as a result, a company otherwise would be considered created under the laws of each Contracting State, *e.g.*, because the corporation retained its charter in the first State. Subparagraph 3(b) would also address so-called serial continuance transactions where, for example, a company continues from one of the Contracting States to a third country and then continues into the other Contracting State without having ceased to be treated as resident in the first Contracting State.

Subparagraph 3(b) provides that if a company is considered to be a resident of both Contracting States, and the residence of such company is not resolved by subparagraph 3(a), then the competent authorities of the Contracting States shall endeavor to settle the question of residency by a mutual agreement procedure and determine the mode of application of the Convention to such company. Subparagraph 3(b) also provides that in the absence of such agreement, the company shall not be considered a resident of either Contracting State for purposes of claiming any benefits under the Convention.

Technical Explanation [1995 Protocol]: Article 3 of the Protocol adds a sentence to paragraph 3 of Article IV of the current Convention to address the residence of certain dual resident corporations. Certain jurisdictions allow local incorporation of an entity that is already organized and incorporated under the laws of another country. Under Canadian law, such an entity is referred to as having been "continued" into the other country. Although the Protocol uses the Canadian term, the provision operates reciprocally. The new sentence states that such a corporation will be considered a resident of the State into which it is continued. Paragraph 5 of Article 21 of the Protocol governs the effective date of this provision.

Technical Explanation [1984]: Paragraph 3 provides that if, under the provisions of paragraph 1, a company is a resident of both Canada and the United States, then it shall be deemed to be a resident of the State under whose laws (including laws of political subdivisions) it was created. Paragraph 3 does not refer to the State in which a company is organized, thus making clear that the tie-breaker rule for a company is controlled by the State of the company's original creation. Various jurisdictions may allow local incorporation of an entity that is already organized and incorporated under the laws of another country. Paragraph 3 provides certainty in both the United States and Canada with respect to the treatment of such an entity for purposes of the Convention.

4. Where by reason of the provisions of paragraph 1 an estate, trust or other person (other than an individual or a company) is a resident of both Contracting States, the competent authorities of the States shall by mutual agreement endeavor to settle the question and to determine the mode of application of the Convention to such person.

Notes: CRA has received "very few requests" to use Art. IV:4 other than for s. 94 deemed trusts: VIEWS doc 2017-0693451C6 [2017 STEP q.3].

CRA will resist using this provision for deemed resident trusts. See Notes to ITA 94(3). In *Perry*, 2007 FC 1071; aff'd 2008 FCA 260, the Court would not order competent authority consideration because new s. 94 had not yet been enacted. Where a trust is deemed resident in Canada under ITA 94(3), CRA will consider that this overrides the treaty due to ITCIA s. 4.3: 2013-0492821C6 [2013 APFF q.3].

Definitions: "company" — Art. III:1(f); "competent authority" — Art. III:1(g); "estate", "individual" — ITCIA 3, ITA 248(1); "person" — Art. III:1(e), ITCIA 3, *Interpretation Act* 35(1); "State" — Art. III:1(i); "trust" — ITCIA 3, ITA 104(1), 248(1), (3).

I.T. Technical News: 38 (Canada-US treaty's competent authority provision).

Technical Explanation [1984]: Paragraph 4 provides that where, by reason of the provisions of paragraph 1, an estate, trust, or other person, other than an individual or a company, is a resident of both Contracting States, the competent authorities of the States shall by mutual agreement endeavor to settle the question and determine the mode of application of the Convention to such person. This delegation of authority to the competent authorities complements the provisions of Article XXVI (Mutual Agreement Procedure), which implicitly grant such authority.

5. Notwithstanding the provisions of the preceding paragraphs, an individual shall be deemed to be a resident of a Contracting State if:

(a) the individual is an employee of that State or of a political subdivision, local authority or instrumentality thereof rendering services in the discharge of functions or a governmental nature in the other Contracting State or in a third State; and

(b) the individual is subjected in the first-mentioned State to similar obligations in respect of taxes on income as are residents of the first-mentioned State.

The spouse and dependent children residing with such an individual and meeting the requirements of subparagraph (b) above shall also be deemed to be residents of the first-mentioned State.

Related Provisions: ITA 250(1)(c) — Residence of Canadian ambassador, etc., working outside Canada.

Definitions: "individual" — ITCIA 3, ITA 248(1); "resident" — Art. IV; "State" — Art. III:1(i).

Technical Explanation [1984]: Paragraph 5 provides a special rule for certain government employees, their spouses, and dependent children. An individual is deemed to be a resident of a Contracting State if he is an employee of that State or of a political subdivision, local authority, or instrumentality of that State, is rendering services in the discharge of functions of a governmental nature in any State, and is subjected in the first-mentioned State to "similar obligations" in respect of taxes on income as are residents of the first-mentioned State. Paragraph 5 provides further that a spouse and dependent children residing with a government employee and also subject to "similar obligations" in respect of income taxes as residents of the first-mentioned State are also deemed to be residents of that State. Paragraph 5 overrides the normal tie-breaker rule of paragraph 2. A U.S. citizen or resident who is an employee of the U.S. government in a foreign country or who is a spouse or dependent of such employee is considered to be subject in the United States to "similar obligations" in respect of taxes on income as those imposed on residents of the United States, notwithstanding that such person may be entitled to the benefits allowed by sections 911 or 912 of the Code.

6. An amount of income, profit or gain shall be considered to be derived by a person who is a resident of a Contracting State where:

(a) the person is considered under the taxation law of that State to have derived the amount through an entity (other than an entity that is a resident of the other Contracting State); and

(b) by reason of the entity being treated as fiscally transparent under the laws of the first-mentioned State, the treatment of the amount under the taxation law of that State is the same as its treatment would be if that amount had been derived directly by that person.

Notes: S. 6 accommodates a US limited liability corporation (LLC), so that its members are deemed to earn income earned through the LLC and can benefit from treaty reductions in withholding tax rates. Multiple levels of LLC are acceptable: Lawrence Purdy, Dept. of Finance, Cdn Tax Foundation annual conference, Nov. 27, 2007 (oral comments); and VIEWS doc 2009-0330491E5. See also the 2021 Budget proposals for "hybrid mismatch arrangements", under ITA 248(1)"corporation".

IRS regulations issued Dec. 2016 (amending Treasury Regulations 1.6038A-1, 1.6038A-2, 301.7701-2) require a foreign owner of a single-member US LLC (including one owned through multiple disregarded entities) to file a Form 5472, with a $10,000 penalty for not filing.

In *TD Securities*, 2010 TCC 186, a US LLC was held entitled to the 5% rate on branch tax (Art. X:6) even before Art. IV:6 was added. See Baker & McCracken, "US LLC a Treaty Resident", 18(5) *Canadian Tax Highlights [CTH]* (ctf.ca) 2-3 (May 2010); Milet, "Hybrid Foreign Entities", 59(1) *Canadian Tax Journal* 25-57 (2011). CRA states in VIEWS doc 2010-0369271C6 that in light of *TD* it will allow treaty benefits to certain LLCs, but restricts the scope of the case. LLCs seeking refunds based on *TD* can use 227(6) or Art. XXVI. See Halvorson & Rogers, "CRA on TD Securities", 18(8) *CTH* 1-2 (Aug. 2010); CRA Round Table, 2010 Cdn Tax Foundation conference report, q.13, p. 4:13-14; docs 2012-0457591C6 [2012 BC Tax Conf. q.10], 2012-0462881C6 [2012 Ontario Tax Conf. q.12]; *M.P.N. Holdings*, 2011 TCC 181 (late appeal to take advantage of *TD* rejected). In *CGI Holding*, 2016 FC 1086, CRA's refusal to pay a refund was upheld, as CRA considered the facts to be different from *TD*.

Where exempt surplus is inflated by using an LLC, the CRA may argue that the LLC is not a "foreign affiliate". See Notes to ITA 113(1).

For para. 6(b), a "fiscally transparent" (pass-through) entity in the US can include an LLC, grantor trust, investment trust under *Internal Revenue Code* §584, partnership and "S" corporation. (See the US Technical Explanation below.) This rule is not needed for Canadian partnerships, as the same rule is considered by the CRA to apply under the common law, since partners own the partnership's property (see Notes to ITA 96(1)).

The Dept. of Finance (Lawrence Purdy) confirmed (round table, Cdn Tax Foundation annual conference, Nov. 27, 2007) that Art. IV:6 overrides a second treaty or no treaty; e.g. if a US resident owns a foreign fiscally transparent entity which owns a Canco that pays a dividend to the entity, Art. IV:6 will entitle the US resident to the treaty withholding tax rate.

For discussion of Art. IV:6 see: Cardarelli, "The Fifth Protocol", 2008 Cdn Tax Foundation conference report, 26:1-7; Darmo & Nikolakakis, "The New Rules on Limitation on Benefits and Fiscally Transparent Entities", 2009 conference report, 26:15-80; Pantry & Morlock, "Pitfalls for Canadians Investing in U.S. LLCs", XVI(2) *Corporate Finance* (Federated Press) 1802-11 (2009); Horne, "Update on Hybrid Entity Rules", XV(3) *International Tax Planning* (Federated Press) 1052-59 (2010); Richardson & D'Avignon, "Hybrid Entity Issues", VII(3) *Resource Sector Taxation* (Federated Press) 522-28 (2010); Rautenberg & Morris, "The Same Treatment Requirement Under the Fifth Protocol", XIII(3) *Business Vehicles* (Federated Press) 690-97 (2010); Strawson, "The Canadian Tax Treatment of US LLCs and Their Members", 2010 conference report, 20:1-34; Lindsey & MacEachern, "The ULC PUC Increase Strategy", 11(3) *Tax for the Owner-Manager* (ctf.ca) 6-7 (July 2011); Cardarelli & Keenan, "Planning

Around the Anti-Hybrid Rules", 2013 conference report, 16:1-27; Bernstein, "Canada-US Tax Traps for LLCs", 22(2) *CTH* 11-12 (Feb. 2014); Colden & Lévesque, "An In-depth Look at the Hybrid Rules", 2017 conference report, 19:1-28; Berry & Walker, "Pitfalls for Canadians Offering Options in US LLCs", XXVII(1) *Taxation of Executive Compensation & Retirement* (Federated Press) 2-3 (2019).

See also *Income Tax Technical News* 41 (2008 Cdn Tax Foundation conference report, 3:22-23, q.28); *Technical News* 44 [2009 CTF conf.]; VIEWS docs 2007-0259011C6 (LLC income from business carried on in Canada, not through PE, may be exempt; LLC should file T2 to claim treaty exemption); 2007-0261901C6 (meaning of "fiscally transparent"); 2007-0261911C6 (S corp can be fiscally transparent); 2008-0272871C6 (US "master limited partnership" can qualify); 2009-0318491I7 (meaning of "same treatment"); 2009-0329511E5 (dividends paid by LLC owned by US S-Corp owned by US resident individual); 2009-0339191E5 (who should file 78(1)(b) agreement); 2009-0345351C6 (whether US LLC can claim benefits under Art. X or XI where amount paid is disregarded under US tax law or treatment differs from Canada); 2009-0345771I7 (LLC claiming artiste treatment under Art. XVI:1); 2010-0355661E5 (use US LLC's taxable year, not that of US resident corp that derives business income from the LLC); 2011-0416891R3 (ruling that Art. IV:6 applies); 2011-0428781E5 (how US LLC will be taxed in Canada); 2012-0434311E5 (application to ITA 214(3)(a) deemed dividend); 2012-0436221I7 (single-member LLC entitled to treaty benefit); 2012-0440101E5 (branch tax); 2012-0458361R3 (cross-border financing: IV:6 applies); 2013-0483801C6 [2013 IFA] (new issues); 2017-0724081C6 [2017 CTF q.11] (dividends paid by ULC to LLCs ineligible for treaty benefits); 2017-0693381C6 [2017 STEP q.8] (single-member US LLC with Cdn member, carrying on business in US but managed in Canada: no credit for US tax); 2017-0736531I7 (Cdn branch income derived by US-resident corp through multiple stacked LLCs); 2018-0744121C6 [STEP 2018 q.16] (LLC electing to be a corp for US tax purposes); 2018-0753621I7 (247(12) deemed dividend treatment under Art. IV:6); 2020-0864281C6 [2020 CTF q.5] (which treaty applies to Technical Notes example of French entity).

In *Swift*, [2010] UKFTT 88, the UK First Tier Tribunal held that a Delaware LLC was fiscally transparent. For discussion and analysis for Canada see 2010(9) *Tax Alert* (ey.com), March 2010.

Art. IV:6 added by 2007 Protocol, generally for taxable years beginning after 2008.

Definitions: "person" — Art. III:1(e); "State" — Art. III:1(i).

I.T. Technical News: 38 (limited liability company under the Protocol); 41 (5th protocol to the Canada-US Tax Convention — hybrid entities); 44 (payments by ULC; US LLC with a Canadian branch).

Forms: NR303: Declaration of eligibility for benefits (reduced tax) under a tax treaty for a hybrid entity.

Technical Explanation [2007 Protocol]: New paragraphs 6 and 7 are added to Article IV to provide specific rules for the treatment of amounts of income, profit or gain derived through or paid by fiscally transparent entities such as partnerships and certain trusts. Fiscally transparent entities, as explained more fully below, are in general entities the income of which is taxed at the beneficiary, member, or participant level. Entities that are subject to tax, but with respect to which tax may be relieved under an integrated system, are not considered fiscally transparent entities. Entities that are fiscally transparent for U.S. tax purposes include partnerships, common investment trusts under section 584, grantor trusts, and business entities such as a limited liability company ("LLC") that is treated as a partnership or is disregarded as an entity separate from its owner for U.S. tax purposes. Entities falling within this description in Canada are (except to the extent the law provides otherwise) partnerships and what are known as "bare" trusts.

United States tax law also considers a corporation that has made a valid election to be taxed under Subchapter S of Chapter 1 of the Internal Revenue Code (an "S corporation") to be fiscally transparent within the meaning explained below. Thus, if a U.S. resident derives income from Canada through an S corporation, the U.S. resident will under new paragraph 6 be considered for purposes of the Convention as the person who derived the income. Exceptionally, because Canada will ordinarily accept that an S corporation is itself resident in the United States for purposes of the Convention, Canada will allow benefits under the Convention to the S corporation in its own right. In a reverse case, however — that is, where the S corporation is owned by a resident of Canada and has U.S.-source income, profits or gains — the Canadian resident will not be considered as deriving the income by virtue of subparagraph 7 (a) as Canada does not see the S corporation as fiscally transparent.

Under both paragraph 6 and paragraph 7, it is relevant whether the treatment of an amount of income, profit or gain derived by a person through an entity under the tax law of the residence State is "the same as its treatment would be if that amount had been derived directly." For purposes of paragraphs 6 and 7, whether the treatment of an amount derived by a person through an entity under the tax law of the residence State is the same as its treatment would be if that amount had been derived directly by that person shall be determined in accordance with the principles set forth in Code section 894 and the regulations under that section concerning whether an entity will be treated as fiscally transparent with respect to an item of income received by the entity. Treas. Reg. section 1.894-1(d)(3)(iii) provides that an entity will be fiscally transparent under the laws of an interest holder's jurisdiction with respect to an item of income to the extent that the laws of that jurisdiction require the interest holder resident in that jurisdiction to separately take into account on a current basis the interest holder's respective share of the item of income paid to the entity, whether or not distributed to the interest holder, and the character and source of the item in the hands of the interest holder are determined as if such item were realized directly from the source from which realized by the entity. Although Canada does not have analogous provisions in its domestic law, it is anticipated that principles comparable to those described above will apply.

Paragraph 6

Under paragraph 6, an amount of income, profit or gain is considered to be derived by a resident of a Contracting State (residence State) if 1) the amount is derived by that person through an entity (other than an entity that is a resident of the other Contracting State (source State), and 2) by reason of that entity being considered fiscally transparent under the laws of the residence State, the treatment of the amount under the tax law of the residence State is the same as its treatment would be if that amount had been derived directly by that person. These two requirements are set forth in subparagraphs 6(a) and 6(b), respectively.

For example, if a U.S. resident owns a French entity that earns Canadian-source dividends and the entity is considered fiscally transparent under U.S. tax law, the U.S. resident is considered to derive the Canadian-source dividends for purposes of Article IV (and thus, the dividends are considered as being "paid to" the resident) because the U.S. resident is considered under the tax law of the United States to have derived the dividend through the French entity and, because the entity is treated as fiscally transparent under U.S. tax law, the treatment of the income under U.S. tax law is the same as its treatment would be if that amount had been derived directly by the U.S. resident. This result obtains even if the French entity is viewed differently under the tax laws of Canada or of France (*i.e.*, the French entity is treated under Canadian law or under French tax law as not fiscally transparent).

Similarly, if a Canadian resident derives U.S.-source income, profit or gain through an entity created under Canadian law that is considered a partnership for Canadian tax purposes but a corporation for U.S. tax purposes, U.S.-source income, profit or gain derived through such entity by the Canadian resident will be considered to be derived by the Canadian resident in considering the application of the Convention.

Application of paragraph 6 and related treaty provisions by Canada

In determining the entitlement of a resident of the United States to the benefits of the Convention, Canada shall apply the Convention within its own legal framework.

For example, assume that from the perspective of Canadian law an amount of income is seen as being paid from a source in Canada to USLLC, an entity that is entirely owned by U.S. persons and is fiscally transparent for U.S. tax purposes, but that Canada considers a corporation and, thus, under Canadian law, a taxpayer in its own right. Since USLLC is not itself taxable in the United States, it is not considered to be a U.S. resident under the Convention; but for new paragraph 6 Canada would not apply the Convention in taxing the income.

If new paragraph 6 applies in respect of an amount of income, profit or gain, such amount is considered as having been derived by one or more U.S. resident shareholders of USLLC, and Canada shall grant benefits of the Convention to the payment to USLLC and eliminate or reduce Canadian tax as provided in the Convention. The effect of the rule is to suppress Canadian taxation of USLLC to give effect to the benefits available under the Convention to the U.S. residents in respect of the particular amount of income, profit or gain.

However, for Canadian tax purposes, USLLC remains the only "visible" taxpayer in relation to this amount. In other words, the Canadian tax treatment of this taxpayer (USLLC) is modified because of the entitlement of its U.S. resident shareholders to benefits under the Convention, but this does not alter USLLC's status under Canadian law. Canada does not, for example, treat USLLC as though it did not exist, substituting the shareholders for it in the role of taxpayer under Canada's system.

Some of the implications of this are as follows. First, Canada will not require the shareholders of USLLC to file Canadian tax returns in respect of income that benefits from new paragraph 6. Instead, USLLC itself will file a Canadian tax return in which it will claim the benefit of the paragraph and supply any documentation required to support the claim. (The Canada Revenue Agency will supply additional practical guidance in this regard, including instructions for seeking to establish entitlement to Convention benefits in advance of payment.) Second, as is explained in greater detail below, if the income in question is business profits, it will be necessary to determine whether the income was earned through a permanent establishment in Canada. This determination will be based on the presence and activities in Canada of USLLC itself, not of its shareholders acting in their own right.

Determination of the existence of a permanent establishment from the business activities of a fiscally transparent entity

New paragraph 6 applies not only in respect of amounts of dividends, interest and royalties, but also profit (business income), gains and other income. It may thus be relevant in cases where a resident of one Contracting State carries on business in the other State through an entity that has a different characterization in each of the two Contracting States.

Application of new paragraph 6 and the provisions of Article V (Permanent Establishment) by Canada

Assume, for instance, that a resident of the United States is part owner of a U.S. limited liability company (USLLC) that is treated in the United States as a fiscally transparent entity, but in Canada as a corporation. Assume one of the other two shareholders of USLLC is resident in a country that does not have a tax treaty with Canada and that the remaining shareholder is resident in a country with which Canada does have a tax treaty, but that the treaty does not include a provision analogous to paragraph 6.

Assume further that USLLC carries on business in Canada, but does not do so through a permanent establishment there. (Note that from the Canadian perspective, the presence or absence of a permanent establishment is evaluated with respect to USLLC only, which Canada sees as a potentially taxable entity in its own right.) Regarding Canada's application of the provisions of the Convention, the portion of USLLC's profits that belongs to the U.S. resident shareholder will not be taxable in Canada, provided that the U.S. resident meets the Convention's limitation on benefits provisions. Under paragraph 6, that portion is seen as having been derived by the U.S. resident shareholder, who is entitled to rely on Article VII (Business Profits). The balance of USLLC's profits will, however, remain taxable in Canada. Since USLLC is not itself resident in the United States for purposes of the Convention, in respect of that portion of its profits that is not considered to have been derived by a U.S. resident (or a resident of another country whose treaty with Canada includes a rule comparable to paragraph 6) it is not relevant whether or not it has a permanent establishment in Canada.

Another example would be the situation where a USLLC that is wholly owned by a resident of the U.S. carries on business in Canada through a permanent establishment. If the USLLC is fiscally transparent for U.S. tax purposes (and therefore, the conditions for the application of paragraph 6 are satisfied) then the USLLC's profits will be treated as having been derived by its U.S. resident owner inclusive of all attributes of that income (*e.g.*, such as having been earned through a permanent establishment). However, since the USLLC remains the only "visible" taxpayer for Canadian tax purposes, it is the USLLC, and not the U.S. shareholder, that is subject to tax on the profits that are attributable to the permanent establishment.

Application of new paragraph 6 and the provisions of Article V (Permanent Establishment) by the United States

It should be noted that in the situation where a person is considered to derive income through an entity, the United States looks in addition to such person's activities in order to determine whether he has a permanent establishment. Assume that a Canadian resident and a resident in a country that does not have a tax treaty with the United States are owners of CanLP. Assume further that Can LP is an entity that is considered fiscally transparent for Canadian tax purposes but is not considered fiscally transparent for U.S. tax purposes, and that CanLP carries on business in the United States. If CanLP carries on the business through a permanent establishment, that permanent establishment may be attributed to the partners. Moreover, in determining whether there is a permanent establishment, the activities of both the entity and its partners will be considered. If CanLP does not carry on the business through a permanent establishment, the Canadian resident, who derives income through the partnership, may claim the benefits of Article VII (Business Profits) of the Convention with respect to such income, assuming that the income is not otherwise attributable to a permanent establishment of the partner. In any case, the third country partner cannot claim the benefits of Article VII of the Convention between the United States and Canada.

[See also Technical Explanation under para. 7 — ed.]

7. An amount of income, profit or gain shall be considered not to be paid to or derived by a person who is a resident of a Contracting State where:

(a) the person is considered under the taxation law of the other Contracting State to have derived the amount through an entity that is not a resident of the first-mentioned State, but by reason of the entity not being treated as fiscally transparent under the laws of that State, the treatment of the amount under the taxation law of that State is not the same as its treatment would be if that amount had been derived directly by that person; or

(b) the person is considered under the taxation law of the other Contracting State to have received the amount from an entity that is a resident of that other State, but by reason of the entity being treated as fiscally transparent under the laws of the first-mentioned State, the treatment of the amount under the taxation law of that State is not the same as its treatment would be if that entity were not treated as fiscally transparent under the laws of that State.

Notes: S. 7, which came into force Jan. 1, 2010, denies treaty benefits to hybrid entities. It covers Nova Scotia unlimited liability corporations (NSULCs) and other provinces' ULCs (see Notes to ITA 248(1)"corporation"). Para. 7(a) appears to target "synthetic NRO" financing structures that use "reverse hybrid" partnerships with US corporate partners (see ITA 133 Notes). S. 7 applies to both deductible and non-deductible interest, even though deductible interest was what was targeted. See also the 2021 Budget proposals for "hybrid mismatch arrangements", under ITA 248(1)"corporation".

For discussion of Art. IV:7 see Cannon et al., "The Fifth Protocol to the Canada-U.S. Income Tax Convention", 2007 Cdn Tax Foundation conference report, 24:15-24; Glicklich & Leitner, "New Canada-US Protocol Contains Hybrid Entity Surprises", 55(4) *Canadian Tax Journal* 935-46 (2007); Corrado Cardarelli, "The Fifth Protocol", 2008 conference report, 26:7-21; Stricof & Slaats, "Financing U.S. Subsidiaries of Canadian Companies", 2009 conference report, 21:9-14; Darmo & Nikolakakis, "The New Rules on Limitation on Benefits and Fiscally Transparent Entities", 2009 conference report, 26:15-80; Richardson & Wong, "Canadian Unlimited Liability Companies May Still Afford Benefits ...", XVI(2) *Corporate Finance* (Federated Press) 1790-97 (2009); Barry Horne, "Update on Hybrid Entity Rules", XV(3) *International Tax Plan-*

ning (Federated Press) 1052-59 (2010); Richardson & D'Avignon, "Hybrid Entity Issues and Recent Rulings", VII(3) *Resource Sector Taxation* (Federated Press) 522-28 (2010); Rautenberg & Morris, "The Same Treatment Requirement Under the Fifth Protocol", XIII(3) *Business Vehicles* (Federated Press) 690-97 (2010); Lindsey & MacEachern, "The ULC PUC Increase Strategy", 11(3) *Tax for the Owner-Manager* (ctf.ca) 6-7 (July 2011); Blucher, "ULCs, LLCs and the Anti-Hybrid Rule", 2010 conference report, 21:1-23; Charles Reagh, "Update on Unlimited Liability Companies", *Privately Held Companies & Taxes* Newsletter (Carswell *Taxnet Pro*), April 2013, pp. 10-17; Cardarelli & Keenan, "Planning Around the Anti-Hybrid Rules", 2013 conference report, 16:1-27; Bernstein, "Canada-US Tax Traps for LLCs", 22(2) *Canadian Tax Highlights* (ctf.ca) 11-12 (Feb. 2014); Thompson, "Canada-US Cross-Border Ventures", 2015 conference report, 28:1-27; Colden & Lévesque, "An In-depth Look at the Hybrid Rules", 2017 Cdn Tax Foundation conference report, 19:1-28.

For CRA rulings that para. 7(b) will not apply to an ITA 84(1) deemed dividend from a ULC on reduction of capital, see docs 2009-0341681R3, 2009-0348581R3, 2009-0350471R3, 2009-0350921R3, 2011-0439761R3, 2012-0471921R3, 2013-0491331R3 [Chong, "Partnerships and Treaty Article IV(7)(b)", 22(11) *Canadian Tax Highlights* (ctf.ca) 10-11 (Nov. 2014); Gamble, "Canada Revenue Agency Issues Favourable Unlimited Liability Company Ruling", XV(3) *International Tax Planning* (Federated Press) 1071-73 (2010)]; 2014-0534751R3 (deemed dividends from ULC holdco).

For more CRA interpretation see VIEWS docs 2009-031849117 (meaning of "same treatment"), 2009-0319481E5, 2009-0327031C6 (RRSPs and RCAs as fiscally transparent entities), 2009-0343641R3 (dividend paid by ULC to Dutch company); 2009-0348041R3 (interest paid by Canadian-resident ULC to US-resident corp whose subsidiary is sole shareholder of the ULC); 2009-0344201E5 (US charity receiving income from Canadian-resident ULC); 2009-0346291E5 (various scenarios); 2009-0345901R3 (Art. IV:7 does not apply to fees paid by a Canadian ULC to a US LP); 2010-0353101R3 and 2011-0429621R3 (restructuring to avoid Art. IV:7(b)); 2010-0359981R3 (licence and service fee payments); 2010-0360501R3 (Art. IV:7(b) and PUC increase); 2010-0361591R3 (Art. IV:7(b) restructuring); 2010-0364531R3 (deemed dividends derived by US residents); 2010-0372181R3 (Art. IV:7(b) does not apply to deemed interest and dividend); 2010-0375311R3 (Art. IV:7(b) restructuring); 2010-0376751E5 (where US individual owns two S Corps each of which owns part of Canadian ULC); 2010-0390141R3 (supplemental ruling); 2011-0399121R3 (Art. IV(7)(b) and PUC increase); 2011-0429261R3 (loan restructuring — Art. IV:7(b) does not apply); CRA Roundtable qq.4-7, 2009 Cdn Tax Foundation conference report, 3:5-9 [*Income Tax Technical News* ITTN-44] (PUC increase by ULC; Luxembourg intermediary; payments by ULC; payments in 2009); 2012-0434311E5 (application to ITA 214(3)(a) deemed dividend); 2012-0436221I7 (payments by ULC to US resident); 2012-0467721R3 (7(b) will not apply to PUC increase and reduction [see Chana & Roth, "Article IV(7)(b) Interpretation Confirmed", 21(11) *Canadian Tax Highlights* (ctf.ca) 10-11 (Nov. 2013)]); 2013-0483801C6 [2013 IFA] (new issues, including treaty-shopping concerns); 2013-0486931E5 (7(b) will apply to trust's distribution of dividend or deemed dividend from ULC to US-resident beneficiary); 2013-0511761R3 (7(b) does not apply to interest payments); 2016-0642131C6 [IFA 2016 q.9] (7(b) applies to interest paid by Canadian ULC (disregarded for US tax) to US S-corp that owns Qualified Subchapter S sub that owns the ULC); 2018-075362117 (247(12) deemed dividend treatment under Art. IV:7).

Art. IV:7 added by 2007 Protocol, effective 2010.

Definitions: "person" — Art. III:1(e); "State" — Art. III:1(i).

I.T. Technical News: 44 (paid-up capital increase by a ULC; Luxembourg intermediary; payments by ULC).

Technical Explanation [2007 Protocol]: Paragraph 7 addresses situations where an item of income, profit or gain is considered not to be paid to or derived by a person who is a resident of a Contracting State. The paragraph is divided into two subparagraphs.

Under subparagraph 7(a), an amount of income, profit or gain is considered not to be paid to or derived by a person who is a resident of a Contracting State (the residence State) if (1) the other Contracting State (the source State) views the person as deriving the amount through an entity that is not a resident of the residence State, and (2) by reason of the entity not being treated as fiscally transparent under the laws of the residence State, the treatment of the amount under the tax law of the residence State is not the same as its treatment would be if that amount had been derived directly by that person.

For example, assume USCo, a company resident in the United States, is a part owner of CanLP, an entity that is considered fiscally transparent for Canadian tax purposes, but is not considered fiscally transparent for U.S. tax purposes. CanLP receives a dividend from a Canadian company in which it owns stock. Under Canadian tax law USCo is viewed as deriving a Canadian-source dividend through CanLP. For U.S. tax purposes, CanLP, and not USCo, is viewed as deriving the dividend. Because the treatment of the dividend under U.S. tax law in this case is not the same as the treatment under U.S. law if USCo derived the dividend directly, subparagraph 7(a) provides that USCo will not be considered as having derived the dividend. The result would be the same if CanLP were a third-country entity that was viewed by the United States as not fiscally transparent, but was viewed by Canada as fiscally transparent. Similarly, income from U.S. sources received by an entity organized under the laws of the United States that is treated for Canadian tax purposes as a corporation and is owned by shareholders who are residents of Canada is not considered derived by the shareholders of that U.S. entity even if, under U.S. tax law, the entity is treated as fiscally transparent.

Subparagraph 7(b) provides that an amount of income, profit or gain is not considered to be paid to or derived by a person who is a resident of a Contracting State (the residence State) where the person is considered under the tax law of the other Contracting State (the source State) to have received the amount from an entity that is a resident of that other State (the source State), but by reason of the entity being treated as fiscally transparent under the laws of the Contracting State of which the person is resident (the residence State), the treatment of such amount under the tax law of that State (the residence State) is not the same as the treatment would be if that entity were not treated as fiscally transparent under the laws of that State (the residence State).

That is, under subparagraph 7(b), an amount of income, profit or gain is not considered to be paid to or derived by a resident of a Contracting State (the residence State) if: (1) the other Contracting State (the source State) views such person as receiving the amount from an entity resident in the source State; (2) the entity is viewed as fiscally transparent under the laws of the residence State; and (3) by reason of the entity being treated as fiscally transparent under the laws of the residence State, the treatment of the amount received by that person under the tax law of the residence State is not the same as its treatment would be if the entity were not treated as fiscally transparent under the laws of the residence State.

For example, assume that USCo, a company resident in the United States is the sole owner of CanCo, an entity that is considered under Canadian tax law to be a corporation that is resident in Canada but is considered under U.S. tax law to be disregarded as an entity separate from its owner. Assume further that USCo is considered under Canadian tax law to have received a dividend from CanCo.

In such a case, Canada, the source State, views USCo as receiving income (*i.e.*, a dividend) from a corporation that is a resident of Canada (CanCo), CanCo is viewed as fiscally transparent under the laws of the United States, the residence State, and by reason of CanCo being disregarded under U.S. tax law, the treatment under U.S. tax law of the payment is not the same as its treatment would be if the entity were regarded as a corporation under U.S. tax law. That is, the payment is disregarded for U.S. tax purposes, whereas if U.S. tax law regarded CanCo as a corporation, the payment would be treated as a dividend. Therefore, subparagraph 7(b) would apply to provide that the income is not considered to be paid to or derived by USCo.

The same result obtains if, in the above example, USCo is considered under Canadian tax law to have received an interest or royalty payment (instead of a dividend) from CanCo. Under U.S. law, because CanCo is disregarded as an entity separate from its owner, the payment is disregarded, whereas if CanCo were treated as not fiscally transparent, the payment would be treated as interest or a royalty, as the case may be. Therefore, subparagraph 7(b) would apply to provide that such amount is not considered to be paid to or derived by USCo.

The application of subparagraph 7(b) differs if, in the above example, USCo (as well as other persons) are owners of CanCo, a Canadian entity that is considered under Canadian tax law to be a corporation that is resident in Canada but is considered under U.S. tax law to be a partnership (as opposed to being disregarded). Assume that USCo is considered under Canadian tax law to have received a dividend from CanCo. Such payment is viewed under Canadian tax law as a dividend, but under U.S. tax law is viewed as a partnership distribution. In such a case, Canada views USCo as receiving income (*i.e.*, a dividend) from an entity that is a resident of Canada (CanCo), CanCo is viewed as fiscally transparent under the laws of the United States, the residence State, and by reason of CanCo being treated as a partnership under U.S. tax law, the treatment under U.S. tax law of the payment (as a partnership distribution) is not the same as the treatment would be if CanCo were not fiscally transparent under U.S. tax law (as a dividend). As a result, subparagraph 7(b) would apply to provide that such amount is not considered paid to or derived by the U.S. resident.

As another example, assume that CanCo, a company resident in Canada, is the owner of USLP, an entity that is considered under U.S. tax law (by virtue of an election) to be a corporation resident in the United States, but that is considered under Canadian tax law to be a branch of CanCo. Assume further that CanCo is considered under U.S. tax law to have received a dividend from USLP. In this case, the United States views CanCo as receiving income (*i.e.*, a dividend) from an entity that is resident in the United States (USLP), but by reason of USLP being a branch under Canadian tax law, the treatment under Canadian tax law of the payment is not the same as its treatment would be if USLP were a company under Canadian tax law. That is, the payment is treated as a branch remittance for Canadian tax purposes, whereas if Canadian tax law regarded USLP as a corporation, the payment would be treated as a dividend. Therefore, subparagraph 7(b) would apply to provide that the income is not considered to be paid to or derived by CanCo. The same result would obtain in the case of interest or royalties paid by USLP to CanCo.

Paragraphs 6 and 7 apply to determine whether an amount is considered to be derived by (or paid to) a person who is a resident of Canada or the United States. If, as a result of paragraph 7, a person is not considered to have derived or received an amount of income, profit or gain, that person shall not be entitled to the benefits of the Convention with respect to such amount. Additionally, for purposes of application of the Convention by the United States, the treatment of such payments under Code section 894(c) and the regulations thereunder would not be relevant.

New paragraphs 6 and 7 are not an exception to the saving clause of paragraph 2 of Article XXIX (Miscellaneous Rules). Accordingly, subparagraph 7(b) does not prevent a Contracting State from taxing an entity that is treated as a resident of that State under its tax law. For example, if a U.S. partnership with members who are residents of Canada elects to be taxed as a corporation for U.S. tax purposes, the United States will tax

that partnership on its worldwide income on a net basis, even if Canada views the partnership as fiscally transparent.

Interaction of paragraphs 6 and 7 with the determination of "beneficial ownership"

With respect to payments of income, profits or gain arising in a Contracting State and derived directly by a resident of the other Contracting State (and not through a fiscally transparent entity), the term "beneficial owner" is defined under the internal law of the country imposing tax (*i.e.*, the source State). Thus, if the payment arising in a Contracting State is derived by a resident of the other State who under the laws of the first-mentioned State is determined to be a nominee or agent acting on behalf of a person that is not a resident of that other State, the payment will not be entitled to the benefits of the Convention. However, payments arising in a Contracting State and derived by a nominee on behalf of a resident of that other State would be entitled to benefits. These limitations are confirmed by paragraph 12 of the Commentary to Article 10 of the OECD Model.

Special rules apply in the case of income, profits or gains derived through a fiscally transparent entity, as described in new paragraph 6 of Article IV. Residence State principles determine who derives the income, profits or gains, to assure that the income, profits or gains for which the source State grants benefits of the Convention will be taken into account for tax purposes by a resident of the residence State. Source country principles of beneficial ownership apply to determine whether the person who derives the income, profits or gains, or another resident of the other Contracting State, is the beneficial owner of the income, profits or gains. The source State may conclude that the person who derives the income, profits or gains in the residence State is a mere nominee, agent, conduit, etc., for a third country resident and deny benefits of the Convention. If the person who derives the income, profits or gains under paragraph 6 of Article IV would not be treated under the source State's principles for determining beneficial ownership as a nominee, agent, custodian, conduit, etc., that person will be treated as the beneficial owner of the income, profits or gains for purposes of the Convention.

Assume, for instance, that interest arising in the United States is paid to CanLP, an entity established in Canada which is treated as fiscally transparent for Canadian tax purposes but is treated as a company for U.S. tax purposes. CanCo, a company incorporated in Canada, is the sole interest holder in CanLP. Paragraph 6 of Article IV provides that CanCo derives the interest. However, if under the laws of the United States regarding payments to nominees, agents, custodians and conduits, CanCo is found be a nominee, agent, custodian or conduit for a person who is not a resident of Canada, CanCo will not be considered the beneficial owner of the interest and will not be entitled to the benefits of Article XI with respect to such interest. The payment may be entitled to benefits, however, if CanCo is found to be a nominee, agent, custodian or conduit for a person who is a resident of Canada.

With respect to Canadian-source income, profit or gains, beneficial ownership is to be determined under Canadian law. For example, assume that LLC, an entity that is treated as fiscally transparent for U.S. tax purposes, but as a corporation for Canadian tax purposes, is owned by USCo, a U.S. resident company. LLC receives Canadian-source income. The question of the beneficial ownership of the income received by LLC is determined under Canadian law. If LLC is considered the beneficial owner of the income under Canadian law, paragraph 6 shall apply to extend benefits of the Convention to the income received by LLC to the extent that the Canadian-source income is derived by U.S. resident members of LLC.

Article V — Permanent Establishment

1. For the purposes of this Convention, the term **"permanent establishment"** means a fixed place of business through which the business of a resident of a Contracting State is wholly or partly carried on.

Related Provisions: Reg. 5906(2)(a)(i), 5906(2)(b)(i) — Treaty definition applies for certain purposes; Art. V, ss. 2–10 — Extensions to definition of "permanent establishment".

Notes: See Notes to para. 2 below and to Art. VII:1.

Definitions: "business" — ITCIA 3, ITA 248(1); "resident" — Art. IV.

I.T. Technical News: See under para. 2 below.

CRA Audit Manual: 15.6.0: Permanent establishment; 15.11.6: Tax treaties — permanent establishment.

Technical Explanation [1984]: Paragraph 1 provides that for the purposes of the Convention the term "permanent establishment" means a fixed place of business through which the business of a resident of a Contracting State is wholly or partly carried on. Article V does not use the term "enterprise of a Contracting State," which appears in the 1942 Convention. Thus, paragraph 1 avoids introducing an additional term into the Convention. The omission of the term is not intended to have any implications for the interpretation of the 1942 Convention.

2. The term "permanent establishment" shall include especially:

(a) a place of management;

(b) a branch;

(c) an office;

(d) a factory;

(e) a workshop; and

(f) a mine, an oil or gas well, a quarry or any other place of extraction of natural resources.

Announced Administrative Change — COVID-19 — Permanent Establishment

CRA notice (tinyurl.com/cra-internat, April 27, 2021): [CRA will generally not consider a PE to be created by a foreign company's employees who are forced by COVID-19 to remain in Canada. See under ITA 250(1)(a), sections II "Carrying on business in Canada/Permanent establishment" and VII.B "Permanent establishment" — ed.]

Proposed Amendment — Digital Services Tax on large non-resident businesses

Federal Budget, Annex 7, April 19, 2021: See under ITA 115(1) for this proposal, which starting in 2022 will tax certain non-resident businesses on revenue from digital services, even if they have no permanent establishment in Canada.

Related Provisions: Art. V:3 — Building site or construction or installation project.

Notes: A US resident with no "permanent establishment" (PE) in Canada is not subject to Canadian tax: Art. VII:1 (but see Notes to Art. VII:1). Cases on PE include: *Sunbeam Corp.*, [1962] C.T.C. 657 (SCC) (sales representative with access to SC's stock for promotional and display purposes did not create a PE); *Tara Exploration*, [1972] C.T.C. 328 (SCC) (TE's head office in Canada with no employees was not a PE); *Dudney*, [2000] 2 C.T.C. 56 (FCA); leave to appeal denied 2000 CarswellNat 2662 (SCC)) (consultant providing services in Canada did not have PE on client's premises; but see now Art. V:9); *Toronto Blue Jays*, 2005 CarswellOnt 504 (Ont CA; leave to appeal denied 2005 CarswellOnt 4534) (team's away-game locker rooms not PE); *Panther Oil*, [1961] C.T.C. 363 (Exch.) (Quebec manager who filled orders for Ont. corp's goods was a PE in Quebec); *Fowler*, [1990] 2 C.T.C. 2351 (TCC) (booth operated at exhibition in Canada for 3 weeks annually for 15 years was a PE); *American Income Life* and *Knights of Columbus*, 2008 TCC 306 and 307 (insurance companies' agents in Canada were independent); *Taisei Fire* (1995), 104 T.C. 535 (US Tax Court) (insurance co acting as agent for Japanese insurers did not cause them to have PE in the US). Note that the PE definition varies among treaties, Regulations (Reg. 400, 2600, 8201) and for GST/HST purposes (*Excise Tax Act* 123(1), 132.1(2)).

For software that assists in determining whether there is a PE, see *Permanent Establishment Classifier* at taxforesight.com.

See also Vidal, *Introduction to International Tax in Canada* (Carswell, 8th ed., 2020), chap. 8; Krishna, "Permanent Establishments in Electronic Commerce", 2001 Prairie Provinces Tax Conference (ctf.ca), 9:1-28; Evans, "Leased Equipment: When Does a PE Exist?", 50(2) *Canadian Tax Journal [CTJ]* 489-523 (2002); Milet, "Permanent Establishments Through Related Corporations Under the OECD Model Treaty", 55(2) *CTJ* 289-330 (2007); Taylor, Davies & McCart, "Policy Forum: A Subsidiary as a PE of its Parent", *ibid.* 333-345; Mirandola, "Canadian Tax Courts Provide Guidance on 'PE' ", XV(2) *Corporate Finance* (Federated Press) 1660-63 (2008) (discusses *American Income Life* and *Knights of Columbus*); Nitikman, "The Painter and the PE", 57(2) *CTJ* 213-58 (2009); Krauze, "Impact of Cloud Computing on PE Under the OECD Model Tax Convention", 44(3) *Tax Management International Journal* (Bloomberg BNA) 131-56 (March 13, 2015); Gelineck, "Permanent Establishments and the Offshore Oil and Gas Industry", 70(4) *Bulletin for International Taxation* (ibfd.org) 208-18 (April 2016) and 70(5) 259-65; Oppenheimer, "Canadian Business: US PE?", 24(8) *Canadian Tax Highlights [CTH]* (ctf.ca) 6-7 (Aug. 2016); Barrett & McLaren, "Onshoring — A Possible Strategy for Shoring up Tax Position in E-Commerce", XXI(1) *International Tax Planning* (Federated Press) 12-17 (2017); Bellemare, "Evolution of the PE Concept", 65(3) *CTJ* 725-46 (2017); Bandoblu, "IRS Scrutinizes US PE Positions Under Treaty", 127(3) *CTH* 4-5 (March 2019).

For CRA interpretation see *Income Tax Technical News* 33; VIEWS docs 9801607 (exercising management functions in Canada: likely PE); 2006-0165421E5 (pipeline may be PE); 2006-019443117 (soliciting orders through offices leased in Canada, to sell goods the US company does not manufacture, is PE); 2010-0381951E5 (soliciting orders and installing equipment in Canada: various); 2011-0396421R3 (no PE where parent's activities partly subcontracted to Canadian subsidiary [Perron, "Permanent Establishments", 1(3) *Canadian Tax Focus* (ctf.ca) 6 (Nov. 2011)]); 2011-0421371E5 (providing temporary computer consulting staff in Canada: no PE); 2011-0427551E5 (mere presence of employee is not PE); 2011-0429361E5 (contracting advertising services in Canada for condominiums in India: no PE); 2012-0432141R3 (website hosting does not create PE); 2014-0542411R3 (secondment arrangement where non-resident corp does not charge a markup: no PE); 2014-0550611R3 (hiring Canadian resident employee to do marketing from his home: no PE); 2017-0713071R3 (US LLC where member emigrates to Canada: no PE); 2019-0798751C5 [2019 IFA q.2] (shared workspace can be a PE).

I.T. Technical News: 18 (*Dudney* case); 25 (e-commerce — whether web site is PE); 33 (PE — the *Dudney* case update); 34 (PE — *Toronto Blue Jays* case).

Transfer Pricing Memoranda: TPM-08: The *Dudney* decision: effects on fixed base or permanent establishment audits and Reg. 105 treaty-based waiver guidelines.

CRA Audit Manual: 15.6.0: Permanent establishment.

Technical Explanation [1984]: Paragraph 2 provides that the term "permanent establishment" includes especially a place of management, a branch, an office, a factory, a workshop, and a mine, oil or gas well, quarry, or any other place of extraction of natural resources.

3. A building site or construction or installation project constitutes a permanent establishment if, but only if, it lasts more than 12 months.

Notes: CRA's view is that para. 3 is a stand-alone rule rather than merely an exception to para. 2: VIEWS doc 2010-038790117. The same rule in the Canada-France treaty was considered to apply to specialized equipment installation services (including preparation of specifications, and final testing): 2013-047485117. Repair work on the Canadian side of an international bridge will create a PE if it takes more than 12 months, including winter "unworkable" time: 2010-0359261E5. For detailed discussion see 2013-047516117 (on-site planning and supervision are included in the determination; services rendered offsite do not count). Dismantling and decommissioning a structure can be "construction", and different projects forming a "coherent whole" can run for the 12 months: 2016-0655701E5.

See also Hourdin, "Is the Construction PE Clause in the OECD Model Treaty Satisfactory?", 75(3) *Tax Notes International* (taxnotes.com) 229-46 (July 21, 2014).

Technical Explanation [1984]: Paragraph 3 adds that a building site or construction or installation project constitutes a permanent establishment if and only if it lasts for more than 12 months.

4. The use of an installation or drilling rig or ship in a Contracting State to explore for or exploit natural resources constitutes a permanent establishment if, but only if, such use is for more than three months in any twelve-month period.

Technical Explanation [1984]: Paragraph 4 provides that a permanent establishment exists in a Contracting State if the use of an installation or drilling rig or drilling ship in that State to explore for or exploit natural resources lasts for more than 3 months in any 12 month period, but not if such activity exists for a lesser period of time. The competent authorities have entered into an agreement under the 1942 Convention setting forth guidelines as to certain aspects of Canadian taxation of drilling rigs owned by U.S. persons that constitute Canadian permanent establishments. The agreement will be renewed when this Convention enters into force.

5. A person acting in a Contracting State on behalf of a resident of the other Contracting State — other than an agent of an independent status to whom paragraph 7 applies — shall be deemed to be a permanent establishment in the first-mentioned State if such person has, and habitually exercises in that State, an authority to conclude contracts in the name of the resident.

Notes: See Ehlermann & Castelon, "When Does a Dependent Agent Act Habitually?", 83(13) *Tax Notes International* (taxnotes.com) 1141-45 (Sept. 26, 2016). See also Notes to Art. V:7.

Definitions: "person" — Art. III:1(e), ITCIA 3, *Interpretation Act* 35(1); "State" — Art. III:1(i).

Technical Explanation [1984]: Paragraph 5 provides that a person acting in a Contracting State on behalf of a resident of the other Contracting State is deemed to be a permanent establishment of the resident if such person has and habitually exercises in the first-mentioned State the authority to conclude contracts in the name of the resident. This rule does not apply to an agent of independent status, covered by paragraph 7. Under the provisions of paragraph 5, a permanent establishment may exist even in the absence of a fixed place of business. If, however, the activities of a person described in paragraph 5 are limited to the ancillary activities described in paragraph 6, then a permanent establishment does not exist solely on account of the person's activities.

There are a number of minor differences between the provisions of paragraphs 1 through 5 and the analogous provisions of the 1942 Convention. One important deviation is elimination of the rule of the 1942 Convention which deems a permanent establishment to exist in any circumstance where a resident of one State uses substantial equipment in the other State for any period of time. The Convention thus generally raises the threshold for source basis taxation of activities that involve substantial equipment (and that do not otherwise constitute a permanent establishment). Another deviation of some significance is elimination of the rule of the 1942 Convention that considers a permanent establishment to exist where a resident of one State carries on business in the other State through an agent or employee who has a stock of merchandise from which he regularly fills orders that he receives. The Convention provides that a person other than an agent of independent status who is engaged solely in the maintenance of a stock of goods or merchandise belonging to a resident of the other State for the purpose of storage, display or delivery does not constitute a permanent establishment.

6. Notwithstanding the provisions of paragraphs 1, 2, 5 and 9, the term "permanent establishment" shall be deemed not to include a fixed place of business used solely for, or a person referred to in paragraph 5 engaged solely in, one or more of the following activities:

(a) the use of facilities for the purpose of storage, display or delivery of goods or merchandise belonging to the resident;

(b) the maintenance of a stock of goods or merchandise belonging to the resident for the purpose of storage, display or delivery;

(c) the maintenance of a stock of goods or merchandise belonging to the resident for the purpose of processing by another person;

(d) the purchase of goods or merchandise, or the collection of information, for the resident; and

(e) advertising, the supply of information, scientific research or similar activities which have a preparatory or auxiliary character, for the resident.

Notes: A third-party storage facility is not a PE due to para. 6(a): VIEWS doc 2010-0384901E5. For a ruling that activities carried on by a foreign bank in Canada through a representative office have a "preparatory or auxiliary character" for para. 6(e), see 2006-0173601R3. See also 2012-0438691E5 (6(a)-(c) may apply).

Art. V:6 amended to refer to para. V:9 by 2007 Protocol, effective on the same basis as the addition of para. V:9.

Definitions: "person" — Art. III:1(e), ITCIA 3, *Interpretation Act* 35(1).

Technical Explanation [2007 Protocol]: Article 3 of the Protocol amends Article V (Permanent Establishment) of the Convention. Paragraph 1 of Article 3 of the Protocol adds a reference in Paragraph 6 of Article IV to new paragraph 9 of Article V. Paragraph 2 of Article 3 of the Protocol sets forth new paragraphs 9 and 10 of Article V.

Technical Explanation [1984]: Paragraph 6 provides that a fixed place of business used solely for, or an employee described in paragraph 5 engaged solely in, certain specified activities is not a permanent establishment, notwithstanding the provisions of paragraphs 1, 2, and 5. The specified activities are: a) the use of facilities for the purpose of storage, display, or delivery of goods or merchandise belonging to the resident whose business is being carried on; b) the maintenance of a stock of goods or merchandise belonging to the resident for the purpose of storage, display, or delivery; c) the maintenance of a stock of goods or merchandise belonging to the resident for the purpose of processing by another person; d) the purchase of goods or merchandise, or the collection of information, for the resident; and e) advertising, the supply of information, scientific research, or similar activities which have a preparatory or auxiliary character, for the resident. Combinations of the specified activities have the same status as any one of the activities. Thus, unlike the OECD Model Convention, a combination of the activities described in subparagraphs 6(a) through 6(e) need not be of a preparatory or auxiliary character (except as required by subparagraph 6(e)) in order to avoid the creation of a permanent establishment. The reference in paragraph 6(e) to specific activities does not imply that any other particular activities — for example, the servicing of a patent or a know-how contract or the inspection of the implementation of engineering plans — do not fall within the scope of paragraph 6(e) provided that, based on the facts and circumstances, such activities have a preparatory or auxiliary character.

7. A resident of a Contracting State shall not be deemed to have a permanent establishment in the other Contracting State merely because such resident carries on business in that other State through a broker, general commission agent or any other agent of an independent status, provided that such persons are acting in the ordinary course of their business.

Notes: "Generally, in order for Canco to be an independent agent acting in the ordinary course of its business, Canco must be independent both legally and economically and acting in the ordinary course of its business when acting on behalf of USco": VIEWS doc 2004-0070351E5.

In *ValueClick* (Supreme Court of France, 2021, tinyurl.com/valclick), an Irish company had a PE in France because its related French company, an allegedly "independent" agent, handled marketing, administration and support in France.

Definitions: "business" — ITCIA 3, ITA 248(1); "person" — Art. III:1(e), ITCIA 3, *Interpretation Act* 35(1); "resident" — Art. IV.

Technical Explanation [1984]: Paragraph 7 provides that a resident of a Contracting State is not deemed to have a permanent establishment in the other Contracting State merely because such resident carries on business in the other State through a broker, general commission agent, or any other agent of independent status, provided that such persons are acting in the ordinary course of their business.

8. The fact that a company which is a resident of a Contracting State controls or is controlled by a company which is a resident of the other Contracting State, or which carries on business in that other State (whether through a permanent establishment or other-

wise), shall not constitute either company a permanent establishment of the other.

Definitions: "business" — ITCIA 3, ITA 248(1); "company" — Art. III:1(f); "resident" — Art. IV.

Technical Explanation [1984]: Paragraph 8 states that the fact that a company which is a resident of one Contracting State controls or is controlled by a company which is either a resident of the other Contracting State or which is carrying on a business in the other State, whether through a permanent establishment or otherwise, does not automatically render either company a permanent establishment of the other.

9. Subject to paragraph 3, where an enterprise of a Contracting State provides services in the other Contracting State, if that enterprise is found not to have a permanent establishment in that other State by virtue of the preceding paragraphs of this Article, that enterprise shall be deemed to provide those services through a permanent establishment in that other State if and only if:

(a) those services are performed in that other State by an individual who is present in that other State for a period or periods aggregating 183 days or more in any twelve-month period, and, during that period or periods, more than 50 percent of the gross active business revenues of the enterprise consists of income derived from the services performed in that other State by that individual; or

(b) the services are provided in that other State for an aggregate of 183 days or more in any twelve-month period with respect to the same or connected project for customers who are either residents of that other State or who maintain a permanent establishment in that other State and the services are provided in respect of that permanent establishment.

Announced Administrative Change — Art. V:9(a) — COVID-19

CRA notice (tinyurl.com/cra-internat, April 27, 2021): [CRA will generally exclude from the 183-test any days of physical presence in Canada due to COVID-19 travel restrictions. See under ITA 250(1)(a), sections II "Carrying on business in Canada/Permanent establishment" and VII.B "Permanent establishment" — ed.]

Notes: Para. 9 overrides *Dudney*, [2000] 2 C.T.C. 56 (FCA) and similar cases (see Notes to para. 2 above). See Cannon *et al.*, "The Fifth Protocol to the Canada-U.S. Income Tax Convention", 2007 Cdn Tax Foundation conference report at 24:47-58; Cardarelli, "The Fifth Protocol", 2008 conference report at 26:21-26; Sinclair, "The Services PE Provision", 2009 conference report, 22:1-29; Reid, "The New Services Provision", 58(4) *Canadian Tax Journal* 845-96 (2010); Nitikman, "More on Services PEs — What is a Connected Project?", 62(2) *CTJ* 317-82 (2014).

Para. 9(a) applied in *Wolf*, 2019 FCA 283 [Wen, "FCA Surprise", 10(1) *Canadian Tax Focus* (ctf.ca) 2 (Feb. 2020)].

When para. 9 applies, there may be no provincial PE so ITA 120(1) applies instead of provincial tax: Kevyn Nightingale, "A Federal Permanent Establishment, But Not a Provincial One", 2330 *Tax Topics* (CCH) 1-4 (Nov. 3, 2016).

Fifth Protocol (2007), Annex B, states:

2. Meaning of connected projects

For the purposes of applying subparagraph (b) of paragraph 9 of Article V (Permanent Establishment) of the Convention, it is understood that projects shall be considered to be connected if they constitute a coherent whole, commercially and geographically.

For CRA interpretation of "third parties" (in the Technical Explanation), "enterprise" and "same or connected", see VIEWS docs 2008-0300941C6, 2009-0319441C6, 2013-047516I7.

For more CRA interpretation see CRA Roundtables, 2009 Cdn Tax Foundation conference report qq.18-20 (p.3:18-20) [*IT Technical News* 44]; VIEWS docs 2010-0387091C6 [2010 CTF conf. report p. 4:9-10, q.9] (on retroactive application of deemed PE, CRA will consider waiving interest and penalties), 2010-0382801E5 (general comments), 2010-0391541E5 (re para. 9(b): for criticism see tinyurl.com/gowlings-V9), 2011-0402471E5 (whether 2 separate periods would both be counted); 2011-0426591C6 [2011 CTF conf. report q.1-4, p.4:1-3] ("provides" services does not require that USCo's own employees perform the services); 2012-0433791E5 (computation of days); 2013-0483801C6 [2013 IFA] (new issues); 2014-055866I17 (application to partnership based on total Canadian activities of partners); 2017-0709041C6 [2017 APFF q.6] (12-month period need not correspond to fiscal year).

Art. V:9 added by 2007 Protocol (former para. 9 was renumbered 10), effective as of the third taxable year that ends after Dec. 15, 2008, but in no event shall it apply to include, in the determination of whether an enterprise is deemed to provide services through a permanent establishment under para. 9, any days of presence, services rendered, or gross active business revenues that occur or arise prior to Jan. 1, 2010.

Definitions: "individual" — ITCIA 3, ITA 248(1); "resident" — Art. IV; "State" — Art. III:1(i).

I.T. Technical News: 44 (services provided by. . .[3 articles]).

Technical Explanation [2007 Protocol]: New paragraph 9 provides a special rule (subject to the provisions of paragraph 3) for an enterprise of a Contracting State that provides services in the other Contracting State, but that does not have a permanent establishment by virtue of the preceding paragraphs of the Article. If (and only if) such an enterprise meets either of two tests as provided in subparagraphs 9(a) and 9(b), the enterprise will be deemed to provide those services through a permanent establishment in the other State.

The first test as provided in subparagraph 9(a) has two parts. First, the services must be performed in the other State by an individual who is present in that other State for a period or periods aggregating 183 days or more in any twelve-month period. Second, during that period or periods, more than 50% of the gross active business revenues of the enterprise (including revenue from active business activities unrelated to the provision of services) must consist of income derived from the services performed in that State by that individual. If the enterprise meets both of these tests, the enterprise will be deemed to provide the services through a permanent establishment. This test is employed to determine whether an enterprise is deemed to have a permanent establishment by virtue of the presence of a single individual (*i.e.*, a natural person).

For the purposes of subparagraph 9(a), the term "gross active business revenues" shall mean the gross revenues attributable to active business activities that the enterprise has charged or should charge for its active business activities, regardless of when the actual billing will occur or of domestic law rules concerning when such revenues should be taken into account for tax purposes. Such active business activities are not restricted to the activities related to the provision of services. However, the term does not include income from passive investment activities.

As an example of the application of subparagraph 9(a), assume that Mr. X, an individual resident in the United States, is one of the two shareholders and employees of USCo, a company resident in the United States that provides engineering services. During the 12-month period beginning December 20 of Year 1 and ending December 19 of Year 2, Mr. X is present in Canada for periods totaling 190 days, and during those periods, 70% of all of the gross active business revenues of USCo attributable to business activities are derived from the services that Mr. X performs in Canada. Because both of the criteria of subparagraph 9(a) are satisfied, USCo will be deemed to have a permanent establishment in Canada by virtue of that subparagraph.

The second test as provided in subparagraph 9(b) provides that an enterprise will have a permanent establishment if the services are provided in the other State for an aggregate of 183 days or more in any twelve-month period with respect to the same or connected projects for customers who either are residents of the other State or maintain a permanent establishment in the other State with respect to which the services are provided. The various conditions that have to be satisfied in order for subparagraph 9(b) to have application are described in detail below.

In addition to meeting the 183-day threshold, the services must be provided for customers who either are residents of the other State or maintain a permanent establishment in that State. The intent of this requirement is to reinforce the concept that unless there is a customer in the other State, such enterprise will not be deemed as participating sufficiently in the economic life of that other State to warrant being deemed to have a permanent establishment.

Assume for example, that CanCo, a Canadian company, wishes to acquire USCo, a company in the United States. In preparation for the acquisition, CanCo hires Canlaw, a Canadian law firm, to conduct a due diligence evaluation of USCo's legal and financial standing in the United States. Canlaw sends a staff attorney to the United States to perform the due diligence analysis of USCo. That attorney is present and working in the United States for greater than 183 days. If the remuneration paid to Canlaw for the attorney's services does not constitute more than 50% of Canlaw's gross active business revenues for the period during which the attorney is present in the United States, Canlaw will not be deemed to provide the services through a permanent establishment in the United States by virtue of subparagraph 9(a). Additionally, because the services are being provided for a customer (CanCo) who neither is a resident of the United States nor maintains a permanent establishment in the United States to which the services are provided, Canlaw will also not have a permanent establishment in the United States by virtue of subparagraph 9(b).

Paragraph 9 applies only to the provision of services, and only to services provided by an enterprise to third parties. Thus, the provision does not have the effect of deeming an enterprise to have a permanent establishment merely because services are provided to that enterprise. Paragraph 9 only applies to services that are performed or provided by an enterprise of a Contracting State within the other Contracting State. It is therefore not sufficient that the relevant services be merely furnished to a resident of the other Contracting State. Where, for example, an enterprise provides customer support or other services by telephone or computer to customers located in the other State, those would not be covered by paragraph 9 because they are not performed or provided by that enterprise within the other State. Another example would be that of an architect who is hired to design blueprints for the construction of a building in the other State. As part of completing the project, the architect must make site visits to that other State, and his days of presence there would be counted for purposes of determining whether the 183-day threshold is satisfied. However, the days that the architect spends working on the blueprint in his home office shall not count for purposes of the 183-day threshold, because the architect is not performing or providing those services within the other State.

For purposes of determining whether the time threshold has been met, subparagraph 9(b) permits the aggregation of services that are provided with respect to connected projects. Paragraph 2 of the General Note provides that for purposes of subparagraph 9(b), projects shall be considered to be connected if they constitute a coherent whole, commercially and geographically. The determination of whether projects are connected should be determined from the point of view of the enterprise (not that of the customer), and will depend on the facts and circumstances of each case. In determining the existence of commercial coherence, factors that would be relevant include: 1) whether the projects would, in the absence of tax planning considerations, have been concluded pursuant to a single contract; 2) whether the nature of the work involved under different projects is the same; and 3) whether the same individuals are providing the services under the different projects. Whether the work provided is covered by one or multiple contracts may be relevant, but not determinative, in finding that projects are commercially coherent.

The aggregation rule addresses, for example, potentially abusive situations in which work has been artificially divided into separate components in order to avoid meeting the 183-day threshold. Assume for example, that a technology consultant has been hired to install a new computer system for a company in the other country. The work will take ten months to complete. However, the consultant purports to divide the work into two five-month projects with the intention of circumventing the rule in subparagraph 9(b). In such case, even if the two projects were considered separate, they will be considered to be commercially coherent. Accordingly, subject to the additional requirement of geographic coherence, the two projects could be considered to be connected, and could therefore be aggregated for purposes of subparagraph 9(b). In contrast, assume that the technology consultant is contracted to install a particular computer system for a company, and is also hired by that same company, pursuant to a separate contract, to train its employees on the use of another computer software that is unrelated to the first system. In this second case, even though the contracts are both concluded between the same two parties, there is no commercial coherence to the two projects, and the time spent fulfilling the two contracts may not be aggregated for purposes of subparagraph 9(b). Another example of projects that do not have commercial coherence would be the case of a law firm which, as one project provides tax advice to a customer from one portion of its staff, and as another project provides trade advice from another portion of its staff, both to the same customer.

Additionally, projects, in order to be considered connected, must also constitute a geographic whole. An example of projects that lack geographic coherence would be a case in which a consultant is hired to execute separate auditing projects at different branches of a bank located in different cities pursuant to a single contract. In such an example, while the consultant's projects are commercially coherent, they are not geographically coherent and accordingly the services provided in the various branches shall not be aggregated for purposes of applying subparagraph 9(b). The services provided in each branch should be considered separately for purposes of subparagraph 9(b).

The method of counting days for purposes of subparagraph 9(a) differs slightly from the method for subparagraph 9(b). Subparagraph 9(a) refers to days in which an individual is present in the other country. Accordingly, physical presence during a day is sufficient. In contrast, subparagraph 9(b) refers to days during which services are provided by the enterprise in the other country. Accordingly, non-working days such as weekends or holidays would not count for purposes of subparagraph 9(b), as long as no services are actually being provided while in the other country on those days. For the purposes of both subparagraphs, even if the enterprise sends many individuals simultaneously to the other country to provide services, their collective presence during one calendar day will count for only one day of the enterprise's presence in the other country. For instance, if an enterprise sends 20 employees to the other country to provide services to a client in the other country for 10 days, the enterprise will be considered present in the other country only for 10 days, not 200 days (20 employees x 10 days).

By deeming the enterprise to provide services through a permanent establishment in the other Contracting State, paragraph 9 allows the application of Article VII (Business Profits), and accordingly, the taxation of the services shall be on a net-basis. Such taxation is also limited to the profits attributable to the activities carried on in performing the relevant services. It will be important to ensure that only the profits properly attributable to the functions performed and risks assumed by provision of the services will be attributed to the deemed permanent establishment.

In addition to new paragraph 9, Article 3 of the Protocol amends paragraph 6 of Article V of the Convention to include a reference to paragraph 9. Therefore, in no case will paragraph 9 apply to deem services to be provided through a permanent establishment if the services are limited to those mentioned in paragraph 6 which, if performed through a fixed place of business, would not make the fixed place of business a permanent establishment under the provisions of that paragraph.

The competent authorities are encouraged to consider adopting rules to reduce the potential for excess withholding or estimated tax payments with respect to employee wages that may result from the application of this paragraph. Further, because paragraph 6 of Article V applies notwithstanding paragraph 9, days spent on preparatory or auxiliary activities shall not be taken into account for purposes of applying subparagraph 9(b).

10. For the purposes of the Convention, the provisions of this Article shall be applied in determining whether any person has a permanent establishment in any State.

Notes: Art. V:9 renumbered as 10 by 2007 Protocol, effective on the same basis as the addition of new para. 9.

Definitions: "person" — Art. III:1(e), ITCIA 3, *Interpretation Act* 35(1); "State" — Art. III:1(i).

Technical Explanation [2007 Protocol]: Paragraph 2 of Article 3 of the Protocol also sets forth new paragraph 10 of Article V. The provisions of new paragraph 10 are identical to paragraph 9 of Article V as it existed prior to the Protocol. New paragraph 10 provides that the provisions of Article V shall be applied in determining whether any person has a permanent establishment in any State.

Technical Explanation [1984]: Paragraph 9 [now 10 — ed.] provides that, for purposes of the Convention, the provisions of Article V apply in determining whether any person has a permanent establishment in any State. Thus, these provisions would determine whether a person other than a resident of Canada or the United States has a permanent establishment in Canada or the United States, and whether a person resident in Canada or the United States has a permanent establishment in a third State.

Related Provisions [Art. V]: ITCIA 4 — Permanent establishment in Canada.

Interpretation Bulletins [Art. V]: IT-173R2: Capital gains derived in Canada by residents of the United States.

Article VI — Income from Real Property

1. Income derived by a resident of a Contracting State from real property (including income from agriculture, forestry or other natural resources) situated in the other Contracting State may be taxed in that other State.

Definitions: "real property" — Art. VI:2, ITCIA 5; "resident" — Art. IV; "State" — Art. III:1(i).

CRA Audit Manual: 15.11.7: Tax treaties — income from real property.

Technical Explanation [1984]: Paragraph 1 provides that income derived by a resident of a Contracting State from real property situated in the other Contracting State may be taxed by that other State. Income from real property includes, for purposes of Article VI, income from agriculture, forestry or other natural resources. Also, while "income derived ... from real property" includes income from rights such as an overriding royalty or a net profits interest in a natural resource, it does not include income in the form of rights to explore for or exploit natural resources which a party receives as compensation for services (e.g., exploration services); the latter income is subject to the provisions of Article VII (Business Profits), XIV (Independent Personal Services), or XV (Dependent Personal Services), as the case may be. As provided by paragraph 3, paragraph 1 applies to income derived from the direct use, letting or use in any other form of real property and to income from the alienation of such property.

2. For the purposes of this Convention, the term **"real property"** shall have the meaning which it has under the taxation laws of the Contracting State in which the property in question is situated and shall include any option or similar right in respect thereof. The term shall in any case include usufruct of real property, rights to explore for or to exploit mineral deposits, sources and other natural resources and rights to amounts computed by reference to the amount or value of production from such resources; ships and aircraft shall not be regarded as real property.

Related Provisions: ITCIA 5 — Definition of "immovable property" and "real property".

Notes: CRA says oil royalties fall under this para.: doc 2011-0431571E5. Gravel extraction payments fall under the parallel para. of another treaty: 2010-0382231I7.

A purchaser's right under an Agreement of Purchase and Sale is likely an "option or similar right" (see ITA 116(1) Notes); a CRA answer to the author on this point will be in doc 2014-0547171E5, which CRA confirmed in July 2020 is still to be issued.

Definitions: "mineral", "property" — ITCIA 3, ITA 248(1); "usufruct" — Quebec *Civil Code* art. 1120-1171.

Technical Explanation [1984]: Generally speaking, the term "real property" has the meaning which it has under the taxation laws of the Contracting State in which the property in question is situated, in accordance with paragraph 2. In any case, the term includes any option or similar right in respect of real property, the usufruct of real property, and rights to explore for or to exploit mineral deposits, sources, and other natural resources. The reference to "rights to explore for or to exploit mineral deposits, sources and other natural resources" includes rights generating either variable (e.g., computed by reference to the amount of value or production) or fixed payments. The term "real property" does not include ships and aircraft.

3. The provisions of paragraph 1 shall apply to income derived from the direct use, letting or use in any other form of real property and to income from the alienation of such property.

Definitions: "property" — ITCIA 3, ITA 248(1); "real property" — Art. VI:2, ITCIA 5.

Technical Explanation [1984]: Unlike Article XIII A of the 1942 Convention, Article VI does not contain an election to allow a resident of a Contracting State to compute tax on income from real property situated in the other State on a net basis. Both the *Internal Revenue Code* and the *Income Tax Act* of Canada generally allow for net basis taxation with respect to real estate rental income, although Canada does not permit such an election for natural resource royalties. Also, unlike the 1942 Convention which in Article XI imposes a 15% limitation on the source basis taxation of rental or royalty income from real property, Article VI of the Convention allows a Contracting State to impose tax on such income under its internal law. In Canada the rate of tax on resource royalties is 25% of the gross amount of the royalty, if the income is not attributable to a business carried on in Canada. In an exchange of notes to the Protocol, the United States and Canada agreed to resume negotiations, upon request by either country, to provide an appropriate limit on taxation in the State of source if either country subsequently increases its statutory tax rate now applicable to such royalties (25% in the case of Canada and 30% in the case of the United States).

Interpretation Bulletins [Art. VI]: IT-173R2: Capital gains derived in Canada by residents of the United States.

Article VII — Business Profits

1. The business profits of a resident of a Contracting State shall be taxable only in that State unless the resident carries on business in the other Contracting State through a permanent establishment situated therein. If the resident carries on, or has carried on, business as aforesaid, the business profits of the resident may be taxed in the other State but only so much of them as is attributable to that permanent establishment.

Related Provisions: ITA 248(1)"treaty-protected business" — Business not subject to Canadian tax because of treaty; Art. V — Permanent establishment.

Notes: The worldwide approach of taxing a foreign resident's business income only if there is a "permanent establishment" may change: see OECD Proposed Amendments at end of s. 95, under "Action 1". See Art. V:2 Notes re whether there is a PE.

Fifth Protocol (2007), Annex B, states:

> *9. With reference to Article VII (Business Profits)*
>
> It is understood that the business profits to be attributed to a permanent establishment shall include only the profits derived from the assets used, risks assumed and activities performed by the permanent establishment. The principles of the OECD Transfer Pricing Guidelines shall apply for purposes of determining the profits attributable to a permanent establishment, taking into account the different economic and legal circumstances of a single entity. Accordingly, any of the methods described therein as acceptable methods for determining an arm's length result may be used to determine the income of a permanent establishment so long as those methods are applied in accordance with the Guidelines. In particular, in determining the amount of attributable profits, the permanent establishment shall be treated as having the same amount of capital that it would need to support its activities if it were a distinct and separate enterprise engaged in the same or similar activities. With respect to financial institutions other than insurance companies, a Contracting State may determine the amount of capital to be attributed to a permanent establishment by allocating the institution's total equity between its various offices on the basis of the proportion of the financial institution's risk-weighted assets attributable to each of them. In the case of an insurance company, there shall be attributed to a permanent establishment not only premiums earned through the permanent establishment, but that portion of the insurance company's overall investment income from reserves and surplus that supports the risks assumed by the permanent establishment.

(For interpretation of the "if it were a distinct and separate enterprise" test, see *Irish Bank Resolution*, [2020] EWCA Civ 1128 (England).)

On June 26, 2012, Canadian and US competent authorities signed the following:

> The competent authorities of the United States and Canada hereby enter into the following agreement regarding the application of Article VII (Business Profits) of the Convention between Canada and the United States of America with Respect to Taxes on Income and on Capital done at Washington on September 26, 1980, as amended by the Protocols done on June , 1983, March 28, 1994, March 17, 1995, July 29, 1997, and September 17, 2007 (the "Convention") in view of the agreed understanding set out in paragraph 9 of the Second Exchange of Notes to the Fifth Protocol to the Convention and annexed to the Convention as Annex B. This agreement is entered into under paragraph 3 of Article XXVI (Mutual Agreement Procedure) of the Convention.
>
> With reference to Article VII of the Convention, paragraph 9 of Annex B of the Convention refers to the applicability of the Organisation for Economic Cooperation and Development (the "OECD") Transfer Pricing Guidelines, by analogy, for the purposes of determining the business profits attributable to a permanent establishment. The OECD Report on the Attribution of Profits to Permanent Establishments (the "Report") was finalized in 2008 and revised in 2010 without change to the conclusions of the Report (the "authorized OECD approach" ("full AOA")). The competent authorities of the United States and Canada understand that paragraph 9 of Annex B of the Convention indicates that the principles of the full AOA as set out in the Report would apply without waiting for the Report to be finalized.

The competent authorities of the United States and Canada therefore agree that, under paragraph 9 of Annex B of the Convention, Article VII of the Convention is to be interpreted in a manner entirely consistent with the full AOA as set out in the Report. All other provisions of the Convention that require a determination of whether an asset or amount is effectively connected or attributable to a permanent establishment are also to be interpreted in a manner entirely consistent with the full AOA as set out in the Report. Further explanation of paragraph 9 and its effects on the interpretation and application of Article VII(2) and (3) of the Convention is found in the U.S. Treasury Department's Technical Explanation of the Fifth Protocol to the Convention, the contents with respect to which the Government of Canada subscribes.

The competent authorities understand that relief of double taxation continues to be subject to the provisions and limitations of each country's domestic law, as provided in Article XXIV (Elimination of Double Taxation).

This agreement generally applies to taxable years that begin on or after January 1, 2012; however, a taxpayer may choose to apply the entirety of this agreement in both Contracting States for all taxable years beginning after December 31, 2008.

For discussion of this agreement see Jim Wilson & Pierre Alary, "Canada and U.S. Announce Agreement Regarding PE Attribution of Income", tinyurl.com/pe-gowlings.

See also Vidal, *Introduction to International Tax in Canada* (Carswell, 8th ed., 2020), chap. 28, "e-Commerce"; Arnold et al., *The Taxation of Business Profits Under Tax Treaties* (ctf.ca, 2003); Metzler, "The US Taxation of Services Income", 2005 Cdn Tax Foundation conference report, 19:1-27.

A Canadian business that is exempt from US federal tax because it has no PE in the US still has US filing obligations: Form 1120-F (US Income Tax Return of a Foreign Corporation) and Form 8833 (Treaty-Based Return Position Disclosure). Each failure to file Form 8833 can lead to a US$10,000 fine. There may also be state income tax, capital tax and/or franchise tax: e.g., Lawrence, "New York Nexus Widens", 22(8) *Canadian Tax Highlights* (ctf.ca) 1-2 (Aug. 2014). Similarly, a US corp with no PE in Canada must file a T2SCH91: see Notes to ITA 150(1)(a).

See also VIEWS docs 2006-020417117 (insurance policy renewal commissions earned by non-resident insurance agent can be attributed to a prior PE that agent had while resident in Canada); 2017-070129117 (payment for exclusive distributorship rights is restrictive covenant subject to ITA 212(1)(i), but exempt due to Art. VII).

See also Art. V:9 Notes re services performed in the other country; ITA 253 Notes re carrying on business in Canada; and Art. VII:6 Notes where another provision applies as well as VII:1.

In *Vincent*, 2020 QCCQ 3605, a Quebec KPMG partner who moved to France but still received payments from KMPG Canada was held to be subject to Quebec tax under Quebec-France treaty Art. 7, since KPMG Canada had an office in Quebec.

Definitions: "business" — ITCIA 3, ITA 248(1); "permanent establishment" — Art. V:1; "resident" — Art. IV; "State" — Art. III:1(i).

I.T. Technical News: 18 (*Dudney* case); 25 (e-commerce).

CRA Audit Manual: 15.11.8: Tax treaties — business profits.

Technical Explanation [1984]: Paragraph 1 provides that business profits of a resident of a Contracting State are taxable only in that State unless the resident carries on business in the other Contracting State through a permanent establishment situated in that other State. If the resident carries on, or has carried on, business through such a permanent establishment, the other State may tax such business profits but only so much of them as are attributable to the permanent establishment. The reference to a prior permanent establishment ("or has carried on") makes clear that a Contracting State in which a permanent establishment existed has the right to tax the business profits attributable to that permanent establishment, even if there is a delay in the receipt or accrual of such profits until after the permanent establishment has been terminated.

Any business profits received or accrued in taxable years in which the Convention has effect, in accordance with Article XXX (Entry Into Force), which are attributable to a permanent establishment that was previously terminated are subject to tax in the Contracting State in which such permanent establishment existed under the provisions of Article VII.

2. Subject to the provisions of paragraph 3, where a resident of a Contracting State carries on, or has carried on, business in the other Contracting State through a permanent establishment situated therein, there shall in each Contracting State be attributed to that permanent establishment the business profits which it might be expected to make if it were a distinct and separate person engaged in the same or similar activities under the same or similar conditions and dealing wholly independently with the resident and with any other person related to the resident (within the meaning of paragraph 2 of Article IX (Related Persons)).

Notes: For discussion of paras. VII:2 and 3, see Ward, "Attribution of Income to Permanent Establishments", 48(3) *Canadian Tax Journal* 559-76 (2000); Arnold & Darmo, "Summary of Proceedings of an Invitational Seminar on the Attribution of Profits", 49(3) *CTJ* 525-52 (2001); Darmo, "OECD: Attribution of Profits", 1814 *Tax*

Topics (CCH) 1-5 (May 3/07); Cannon et al., "The Fifth Protocol", 2007 Cdn Tax Foundation conference report at 24:58-61.

In *Cudd Pressure*, [1999] 1 C.T.C. 1 (FCA), a PE in Canada could not deduct notional expenses paid to head office. CRA maintains this view despite new OECD model treaty commentary, except with respect to the US: VIEWS doc 2016-0642061C6 [2016 IFA q.2].

Art. VII:2 amended to add ", or has carried on," by 2007 Protocol, generally for taxable years beginning after 2008. Fifth Protocol (2007), Annex B, states:

> *5. Former permanent establishments and fixed bases*
>
> It is understood that the modifications of paragraph 2 of Article VII (Business Profits), paragraph 4 of Article X (Dividends), paragraph 3 of Article XI (Interest) and paragraph 5 of Article XII (Royalties) of the Convention to refer to business having formerly been carried on through a permanent establishment confirm the negotiators' shared understanding of the meaning of the existing provisions, and thus are clarifying only.

Definitions: "permanent establishment" — Art. V:1; "person" — Art. III:1(e), ITCIA 3, *Interpretation Act* 35(1); "resident" — Art. IV.

CRA Audit Manual: 15.11.8: Tax treaties — business profits.

Technical Explanation [2007 Protocol]: Article 4 of the Protocol replaces paragraph 2 of Article VII (Business Profits).

New paragraph 2 provides that where a resident of either Canada or the United States carries on (or has carried on) business in the other Contracting State through a permanent establishment in that other State, both Canada and the United States shall attribute to permanent establishments in their respective states those business profits which the permanent establishment might be expected to make if it were a distinct and separate person engaged in the same or similar activities under the same or similar conditions and dealing wholly independently with the resident and with any other person related to the resident. The term "related to the resident" is to be interpreted in accordance with paragraph 2 of Article IX (Related Persons). The reference to other related persons is intended to make clear that the test of paragraph 2 is not restricted to independence between a permanent establishment and a home office.

New paragraph 2 is substantially similar to paragraph 2 as it existed before the Protocol. However, in addition to the reference to a resident of a Contracting State who "carries on" business in the other Contracting State, the Protocol incorporates into the Convention the rule of Code section 864(c)(6) by adding "or has carried on" to address circumstances where, as a result of timing, income may be attributable to a permanent establishment that no longer exists in one of the Contracting States. In such cases, the income is properly within the scope of Article VII. Conforming changes are also made in the Protocol to Articles X (Dividends), XI (Interest), and XII (Royalties) of the Convention where Article VII would apply. As is explained in paragraph 5 of the General Note, these revisions to the Convention are only intended to clarify the application of the existing provisions of the Convention.

The following example illustrates the application of paragraph 2. Assume a company that is a resident of Canada and that maintains a permanent establishment in the United States winds up the permanent establishment's business and sells the permanent establishment's inventory and assets to a U.S. buyer at the end of year 1 in exchange for an installment obligation payable in full at the end of year 3. Despite the fact that the company has no permanent establishment in the United States in year 3, the United States may tax the deferred income payment recognized by the company in year 3.

The "attributable to" concept of paragraph 2 provides an alternative to the analogous but somewhat different "effectively connected" concept in Code section 864(c). Depending on the circumstances, the amount of income "attributable to" a permanent establishment under Article VII may be greater or less than the amount of income that would be treated as "effectively connected" to a U.S. trade or business under Code section 864. In particular, in the case of financial institutions, the use of internal dealings to allocate income within an enterprise may produce results under Article VII that are significantly different than the results under the effectively connected income rules. For example, income from interbranch notional principal contracts may be taken into account under Article VII, notwithstanding that such transactions may be ignored for purposes of U.S. domestic law. A taxpayer may use the treaty to reduce its taxable income, but may not use both treaty and Code rules where doing so would thwart the intent of either set of rules. See Rev. Rul. 84-17, 1984-1 C.B. 308.

The profits attributable to a permanent establishment may be from sources within or without a Contracting State. However, as stated in the General Note, the business profits attributable to a permanent establishment include only those profits derived from the assets used, risks assumed, and activities performed by the permanent establishment.

The language of paragraph 2, when combined with paragraph 3 dealing with the allowance of deductions for expenses incurred for the purposes of earning the profits, incorporates the arm's length standard for purposes of determining the profits attributable to a permanent establishment. The United States and Canada generally interpret the arm's length standard in a manner consistent with the OECD Transfer Pricing Guidelines.

Paragraph 9 of the General Note confirms that the arm's length method of paragraphs 2 and 3 consists of applying the OECD Transfer Pricing Guidelines, but taking into account the different economic and legal circumstances of a single legal entity (as opposed to separate but associated enterprises). Thus, any of the methods used in the Transfer Pricing Guidelines, including profits methods, may be used as appropriate and in accordance with the Transfer Pricing Guidelines. However, the use of the Transfer Pricing Guidelines applies only for purposes of attributing profits within the legal entity. It does not create legal obligations or other tax consequences that would result from transactions having independent legal significance. Thus, the Contracting States agree that the notional payments used to compute the profits that are attributable to a permanent establishment will not be taxed as if they were actual payments for purposes of other taxing provisions of the Convention, for example, for purposes of taxing a notional royalty under Article XII (Royalties).

One example of the different circumstances of a single legal entity is that an entity that operates through branches rather than separate subsidiaries generally will have lower capital requirements because all of the assets of the entity are available to support all of the entity's liabilities (with some exceptions attributable to local regulatory restrictions). This is the reason that most commercial banks and some insurance companies operate through branches rather than subsidiaries. The benefit that comes from such lower capital costs must be allocated among the branches in an appropriate manner. This issue does not arise in the case of an enterprise that operates through separate entities, since each entity will have to be separately capitalized or will have to compensate another entity for providing capital (usually through a guarantee).

Under U.S. domestic regulations, internal "transactions" generally are not recognized because they do not have legal significance. In contrast, the rule provided by the General Note is that such internal dealings may be used to attribute income to a permanent establishment in cases where the dealings accurately reflect the allocation of risk within the enterprise. One example is that of global trading in securities. In many cases, banks use internal swap transactions to transfer risk from one branch to a central location where traders have the expertise to manage that particular type of risk. Under paragraph 2 as set forth in the Protocol, such a bank may also use such swap transactions as a means of attributing income between the branches, if use of that method is the "best method" within the meaning of regulation section 1.482-1(c). The books of a branch will not be respected, however, when the results are inconsistent with a functional analysis. So, for example, income from a transaction that is booked in a particular branch (or home office) will not be treated as attributable to that location if the sales and risk management functions that generate the income are performed in another location.

The understanding in the General Note also affects the interpretation of paragraph 3 of Article VII. Paragraph 3 provides that in determining the business profits of a permanent establishment, deductions shall be allowed for the expenses incurred for the purposes of the permanent establishment, ensuring that business profits will be taxed on a net basis. This rule is not limited to expenses incurred exclusively for the purposes of the permanent establishment, but includes expenses incurred for the purposes of the enterprise as a whole, or that part of the enterprise that includes the permanent establishment. Deductions are to be allowed regardless of which accounting unit of the enterprise books the expenses, so long as they are incurred for the purposes of the permanent establishment. For example, a portion of the interest expense recorded on the books of the home office in one State may be deducted by a permanent establishment in the other. The amount of the expense that must be allowed as a deduction is determined by applying the arm's length principle.

As noted above, paragraph 9 of the General Note provides that the OECD Transfer Pricing Guidelines apply, by analogy, in determining the profits attributable to a permanent establishment. Accordingly, a permanent establishment may deduct payments made to its head office or another branch in compensation for services performed for the benefit of the branch. The method to be used in calculating that amount will depend on the terms of the arrangements between the branches and head office. For example, the enterprise could have a policy, expressed in writing, under which each business unit could use the services of lawyers employed by the head office. At the end of each year, the costs of employing the lawyers would be charged to each business unit according to the amount of services used by that business unit during the year. Since this has the characteristics of a cost-sharing arrangement and the allocation of costs is based on the benefits received by each business unit, such a cost allocation would be an acceptable means of determining a permanent establishment's deduction for legal expenses. Alternatively, the head office could agree to employ lawyers at its own risk, and to charge an arm's length price for legal services performed for a particular business unit. If the lawyers were under-utilized, and the "fees" received from the business units were less than the cost of employing the lawyers, then the head office would bear the excess cost. If the "fees" exceeded the cost of employing the lawyers, then the head office would keep the excess to compensate it for assuming the risk of employing the lawyers. If the enterprise acted in accordance with this agreement, this method would be an acceptable alternative method for calculating a permanent establishment's deduction for legal expenses.

The General Note also makes clear that a permanent establishment cannot be funded entirely with debt, but must have sufficient capital to carry on its activities as if it were a distinct and separate enterprise. To the extent that the permanent establishment has not been attributed capital for profit attribution purposes, a Contracting State may attribute such capital to the permanent establishment, in accordance with the arm's length principle, and deny an interest deduction to the extent necessary to reflect that capital attribution. The method prescribed by U.S. domestic law for making this attribution is found in Treas. Reg. section 1.882-5. Both section 1.882-5 and the method prescribed in the General Note start from the premise that all of the capital of the enterprise supports all of the assets and risks of the enterprise, and therefore the entire capital of the enterprise must be allocated to its various businesses and offices.

However, section 1.882-5 does not take into account the fact that some assets create more risk for the enterprise than do other assets. An independent enterprise would need less capital to support a perfectly-hedged U.S. Treasury security than it would need to support an equity security or other asset with significant market and/or credit risk. Accordingly, in some cases section 1.882-5 would require a taxpayer to allocate more

capital to the United States, and therefore would reduce the taxpayer's interest deduction more than is appropriate. To address these cases, the General Note allows a taxpayer to apply a more flexible approach that takes into account the relative risk of its assets in the various jurisdictions in which it does business. In particular, in the case of financial institutions other than insurance companies, the amount of capital attributable to a permanent establishment is determined by allocating the institution's total equity between its various offices on the basis of the proportion of the financial institution's risk-weighted assets attributable to each of them. This recognizes the fact that financial institutions are in many cases required to risk-weight their assets for regulatory purposes and, in other cases, will do so for business reasons even if not required to do so by regulators. However, risk-weighting is more complicated than the method prescribed by section 1.882-5. Accordingly, to ease this administrative burden, taxpayers may choose to apply the principles of Treas. Reg. section 1.882-5(c) to determine the amount of capital allocable to its U.S. permanent establishment, in lieu of determining its allocable capital under the risk-weighted capital allocation method provided by the General Note, even if it has otherwise chosen the principles of Article VII rather than the effectively connected income rules of U.S. domestic law. It is understood that this election is not binding for purposes of Canadian taxation unless the result is in accordance with the arm's length principle.

As noted in the Convention, nothing in paragraph 3 requires a Contracting State to allow the deduction of any expenditure which, by reason of its nature, is not generally allowed as a deduction under the tax laws in that State.

Technical Explanation [1984]: Paragraph 2 provides that where a resident of either Canada or the United States carries on business in the other Contracting State through a permanent establishment in that other State, both Canada and the United States shall attribute to that permanent establishment business profits which the permanent establishment might be expected to make if it were a distinct and separate person engaged in the same or similar activities under the same or similar conditions and dealing wholly independently with the resident and with any other person related to the resident. The term "related to the resident" is to be interpreted in accordance with paragraph 2 of Article IX (Related Persons). The reference to other related persons is intended to make clear that the test of paragraph 2 is not restricted to independence between a permanent establishment and a home office.

3. In determining the business profits of a permanent establishment, there shall be allowed as deductions expenses which are incurred for the purposes of the permanent establishment, including executive and general administrative expenses so incurred, whether in the State in which the permanent establishment is situated or elsewhere. Nothing in this paragraph shall require a Contracting State to allow the deduction of any expenditure which, by reason of its nature, is not generally allowed as a deduction under the taxation laws of that State.

Notes: See Notes to Art. VII:2.

Definitions: "permanent establishment" — Art. V:1; "State" — Art. III:1(i).

I.T. Technical News: 18 (*Cudd Pressure* case).

Technical Explanation [1984]: Paragraph 3 provides that, in determining business profits of a permanent establishment, there are to be allowed as deductions those expenses which are incurred for the purposes of the permanent establishment, including executive and administrative expenses, whether incurred in the State in which the permanent establishment is situated or in any other State. However, nothing in the paragraph requires Canada or the United States to allow a deduction for any expenditure which would not generally be allowed as a deduction under its taxation laws. The language of this provision differs from that of paragraph 1 of Article III of the 1942 Convention, which states that in the determination of net industrial and commercial profits of a permanent establishment there shall be allowed as deductions "all expenses, wherever incurred" as long as such expenses are reasonably allocable to the permanent establishment. Paragraph 3 of Article VII of the Convention is not intended to have any implications for interpretation of the 1942 Convention, but is intended to assure that under the Convention deductions are allowed by a Contracting State which are generally allowable by that State.

4. No business profits shall be attributed to a permanent establishment of a resident of a Contracting State by reason of the use thereof for either the mere purchase of goods or merchandise or the mere provision of executive, managerial or administrative facilities or services for such resident.

Definitions: "permanent establishment" — Art. V:1; "resident" — Art. IV.

Technical Explanation [1984]: Paragraph 4 provides that no business profits are to be attributed to a permanent establishment of a resident of a Contracting State by reason of the use of the permanent establishment for merely purchasing goods or merchandise or merely providing executive, managerial, or administrative facilities or services for the resident. Thus, if a company resident in a Contracting State has a permanent establishment in the other State, and uses the permanent establishment for the mere performance of stewardship or other managerial services carried on for the benefit of the resident, this activity will not result in profits being attributed to the permanent establishment.

5. For the purposes of the preceding paragraphs, the business profits to be attributed to a permanent establishment shall be determined by the same method year by year unless there is good and sufficient reason to the contrary.

Definitions: "permanent establishment" — Art. V:1.

Technical Explanation [1984]: Paragraph 5 provides that business profits are to be attributed to a permanent establishment by the same method in every taxable period unless there is good and sufficient reason to change such method. In the United States, such a change may be a change in accounting method requiring the approval of the Internal Revenue Service.

6. Where business profits include items of income which are dealt with separately in other Articles of this Convention, then the provisions of those Articles shall not be affected by the provisions of this Article.

Notes: This means that other Articles take precedence, but if a royalty payment taxed under 212(1)(d) is not "royalties" as defined in the treaty, Art. XII does not apply so Art. VII:1 exempts the payment if the USCo has no PE in Canada: VIEWS doc 2011-0416181E5.

Technical Explanation [1984]: Paragraph 6 explains the relationship between the provisions of Article VII and other provisions of the Convention. Where business profits include items of income which are dealt with separately in other Articles of the Convention, those other Articles are controlling.

7. For the purposes of the Convention, the business profits attributable to a permanent establishment shall include only those profits derived from the assets or activities of the permanent establishment.

Definitions: "permanent establishment" — Art. V:1.

Technical Explanation [1984]: Paragraph 7 provides a definition for the term "attributable to." Profits "attributable to" a permanent establishment are those derived from the assets or activities of the permanent establishment. Paragraph 7 does not preclude Canada or the United States from using appropriate domestic tax law rules of attribution. The "attributable to" definition does not, for example, preclude a taxpayer from using the rules of section 1.864-4(c)(5) of the Treasury Regulations to assure for U.S. tax purposes that interest arising in the United States is attributable to a permanent establishment in the United States. (Interest arising outside the United States is attributable to a permanent establishment in the United States based on the principles of Regulations sections 1.864-5 and 1.864-6 and Revenue Ruling 75-253, 1975-2 C.B. 203.) Income that would be taxable under the Code and that is "attributable to" a permanent establishment under paragraph 7 is taxable pursuant to Article VII, however, even if such income might under the Code be treated as fixed or determinable annual or periodical gains or income not effectively connected with the conduct of a trade or business within the United States. The "attributable to" definition means that the limited "force-of-attraction" rule of Code section 864(c)(3) does not apply for U.S. tax purposes under the Convention.

Article VIII — Transportation

1. Notwithstanding the provisions of Articles VII (Business Profits), XII (Royalties) and XIII (Gains), profits derived by a resident of a Contracting State from the operation of ships or aircraft in international traffic, and gains derived by a resident of a Contracting State from the alienation of ships, aircraft or containers (including trailers and related equipment for the transport of containers) used principally in international traffic, shall be exempt from tax in the other Contracting State.

Related Provisions: Art. III:1(h) — Meaning of "international traffic"; ITA 81(1)(c) — Exemption for income from ship or aircraft in international traffic.

Notes: See Notes to ITA 248(1) "taxable Canadian property" re its subpara. (b)(ii).

Definitions: "international traffic" — Art. III:1(h); "resident" — Art. IV.

Technical Explanation [1984]: Paragraph 1 provides that profits derived by a resident of a Contracting State from the operation of ships or aircraft in international traffic are exempt from tax in the other Contracting State, even if, under Article VII (Business Profits), such profits are attributable to a permanent establishment. Paragraph 1 also provides that gains derived by a resident of a Contracting State from the alienation of ships, aircraft or containers (including trailers and related equipment for the transport of containers) used principally in international traffic are exempt from tax in the other Contracting State even if, under Article XIII (Gains), those gains would be taxable in that other State. These rules differ from Article V of the 1942 Convention, which conditions the exemption in the State of source on registration of the ship or aircraft in the other State. Paragraph 1 also applies notwithstanding the provisions of Article XII (Royalties). Thus, to the extent that profits described in paragraph 2 would also fall within Article XII (Royalties) (e.g., rent from the lease of a container), the provisions of Article VIII are controlling.

2. For the purposes of this Convention, profits derived by a resident of a Contracting State from the operation of ships or aircraft in international traffic include profits from:

(a) the rental of ships or aircraft operated in international traffic;

(b) the use, maintenance or rental of containers (including trailers and related equipment for the transport of containers) used in international traffic; and

(c) the rental of ships, aircraft or containers (including trailers and related equipment for the transport of containers) provided that such profits are incidental to profits referred to in paragraph 1, 2(a) or 2(b).

Related Provisions: Art. III:1(h) — Meaning of "international traffic".

Definitions: "international traffic" — Art. III:1(h); "resident" — Art. IV.

Technical Explanation [1984]: Paragraph 2(a) provides that profits covered by paragraph 1 include profits from the rental of ships or aircraft operated in international traffic. Such rental profits are included whether the rental is on a time, voyage, or bareboat basis, and irrespective of the State of residence of the operator.

Paragraph 2(b) provides that profits covered by paragraph 1 include profits derived from the use, maintenance or rental of containers, including trailers and related equipment for the transport of containers, if such containers are used in international traffic.

Paragraph 2(c) provides that profits covered by paragraph 1 include profits derived by a resident of a Contracting State from the rental of ships, aircraft, or containers (including trailers and related equipment for the transport of containers), even if not operated in international traffic, as long as such profits are incidental to profits of such person referred to in paragraphs 1, 2(a), or 2(b).

3. Notwithstanding the provisions of Article VII (Business Profits), profits derived by a resident of a Contracting State from a voyage of a ship where the principal purpose of the voyage is to transport passengers or property between places in the other Contracting State may be taxed in that other State.

Related Provisions: Art. XV:3 — Exemption for employees' income.

Definitions: "property" — ITCIA 3, ITA 248(1); "resident" — Art. IV; "State" — Art. III:1(i).

Technical Explanation [1984]: Paragraph 3 states that profits derived by a resident of a Contracting State from a voyage of a ship where the principal purpose of the voyage is to transport passengers or property between points in the other Contracting State is taxable in that other State, whether or not the resident maintains a permanent establishment there. Paragraph 3 overrides the provisions of Article VIII. Profits from such a voyage do not qualify for exemption under Article VIII by virtue of the definition of "international traffic" in paragraph 1(h) of Article III (General Definitions). However, profits from a similar voyage by aircraft are taxable in the Contracting State of source only if the profits are attributable to a permanent establishment maintained in that State.

4. Notwithstanding the provisions of Articles VII (Business Profits) and XII (Royalties), profits of a resident of a Contracting State engaged in the operation of motor vehicles or a railway as a common carrier or a contract carrier derived from:

(a) the transportation of passengers or property between a point outside the other Contracting State and any other point; or

(b) the rental of motor vehicles (including trailers) or railway rolling stock, or the use, maintenance or rental of containers (including trailers and related equipment for the transport of containers) used to transport passengers or property between a point outside the other Contracting State and any other point

shall be exempt from tax in that other Contracting State.

Related Provisions: Art. XV:3 — Exemption for employees' income.

Notes: See Notes to Art. VII:1; and VIEWS doc 2007-0238071E5, "Voiturier public".

Definitions: "motor vehicle", "property" — ITCIA 3, ITA 248(1); "resident" — Art. IV.

Technical Explanation [1984]: Paragraph 4 provides that profits derived by a resident of a Contracting State engaged in the operation of motor vehicles or a railway as a common carrier or contract carrier, and attributable to the transportation of passengers or property between a point outside the other Contracting State and any other point are exempt from tax in that other State. In addition, profits of such a person from the rental of motor vehicles (including trailers) or railway rolling stock, or from the use, maintenance, or rental of containers (including trailers and related equipment for the transport of containers) used to transport passengers or property between a point outside the other Contracting State and any other point are exempt from tax in that other State.

5. The provisions of paragraphs 1, 3 and 4 shall also apply to profits or gains referred to in those paragraphs derived by a resident of a Contracting State from the participation in a pool, a joint business or an international operating agency.

Definitions: "resident" — Art. IV.

Technical Explanation [1984]: Paragraph 5 provides that a resident of a Contracting State that participates in a pool, a joint business, or an international operating agency is subject to the provisions of paragraphs 1, 3, and 4 with respect to the profits or gains referred to in paragraphs 1, 3, and 4.

6. Notwithstanding the provisions of Article XII (Royalties), profits derived by a resident of a Contracting State from the use, maintenance or rental of railway rolling stock, motor vehicles, trailers or containers (including trailers and related equipment for the transport of containers) used in the other Contracting State for a period or periods not expected to exceed in the aggregate 183 days in any twelve-month period shall be exempt from tax in the other Contracting State except to the extent that such profits are attributable to a permanent establishment in the other State and liable to tax in the other State by reason of Article VII (Business Profits).

Notes: The 183-day test applies on a property-by-property basis: VIEWS doc 2011-0428531E5.

Definitions: "motor vehicle" — ITCIA 3, ITA 248(1); "permanent establishment" — Art. V:1; "resident" — Art. IV; "State" — Art. III:1(i).

Technical Explanation [1984]: Paragraph 6 states that profits derived by a resident of a Contracting State from the use, maintenance, or rental of railway rolling stock, motor vehicles, trailers, or containers (including trailers and related equipment for the transport of containers) used in the other Contracting State for a period not expected to exceed 183 days in the aggregate in any 12-month period are exempt from tax in that other State except to the extent that the profits are attributable to a permanent establishment, in which case the State of source has the right to tax under Article VII. The provisions of paragraph 6, unlike the provisions of paragraph 4, apply whether or not the resident is engaged in the operation of motor vehicles or a railway as a common carrier or contract carrier. Paragraph 6 overrides the provisions of Article XII (Royalties), which would otherwise permit taxation in the State of source in the circumstances described.

Gains from the alienation of motor vehicles and railway rolling stock derived by a resident of a Contracting State are not affected by paragraph 4 or 6. Such gains would be taxable in the other Contracting State, however, only if the motor vehicles or rolling stock formed part of a permanent establishment maintained there. See paragraphs 2 and 4 of Article XIII.

Article IX — Related Persons

1. Where a person in a Contracting State and a person in the other Contracting State are related and where the arrangements between them differ from those which would be made between unrelated persons, each State may adjust the amount of the income, loss or tax payable to reflect the income, deductions, credits or allowances which would, but for those arrangements, have been taken into account in computing such income, loss or tax.

Related Provisions: ITA 247 — Transfer pricing adjustments.

Notes: See Cannon, "Article IX of the Canada-U.S. Income Tax Convention: Limited Liability Corporations", 30 *McCarthy Tétrault on Tax Disputes* (CCH) 10-12 (June 2006).

For an example of Art. IX applying to a disallowance of interest expense under the thin capitalization rule (ITA 18(4)) see *Specialty Manufacturing*, [1999] 3 C.T.C. 82 (FCA).

In *Chrysler Canada*, 2008 FC 1049, the Federal Court ruled that it has jurisdiction to review a CRA decision to apply a transfer pricing adjustment, even though the resulting assessment could be appealed to the Tax Court.

Definitions: "person" — Art. III:1(e), ITCIA 3, *Interpretation Act* 35(1); "related" — Art. IX:2; "State" — Art. III:1(i).

Technical Explanation [1984]: Paragraph 1 authorizes Canada and the United States, as the case may be, to adjust the amount of income, loss, or tax payable by a person with respect to arrangements between that person and a related person in the other Contracting State. Such adjustment may be made when arrangements between related persons differ from those that would obtain between unrelated persons. The term "person" encompasses a company resident in a third State with, for example, a permanent establishment in a Contracting State.

2. For the purposes of this Article, a person shall be deemed to be related to another person if either person participates directly or indirectly in the management or control of the other, or if any third person or persons participate directly or indirectly in the management or control of both.

Definitions: "person" — Art. III:1(e), ITCIA 3, *Interpretation Act* 35(1).

Technical Explanation [1984]: Paragraph 2 provides that, for the purposes of Article IX, a person is deemed to be related to another person if either participates directly or indirectly in the management or control of the other or if any third person or persons participate directly or indirectly in the management or control of both. Thus, if a resident of any State controls directly or indirectly a company resident in Canada and a company resident in the United States, such companies are considered to be related persons for purposes of Article IX. Article IX and the definition of "related person" in paragraph 2 may encompass situations that would not be covered by provisions in the domestic laws of the Contracting States. Nor is the paragraph 2 definition controlling for the definition of "related person" or similar terms appearing in other Articles of the Convention. Those terms are defined as provided in paragraph 2 of Article III (General Definitions).

3. Where an adjustment is made or to be made by a Contracting State in accordance with paragraph 1, the other Contracting State shall (notwithstanding any time or procedural limitations in the domestic law of that other State) make a corresponding adjustment to the income, loss or tax of the related person in that other State if:

(a) it agrees with the first-mentioned adjustment; and

(b) within six years from the end of the taxable year to which the first-mentioned adjustment relates, the competent authority of the other State has been notified of the first-mentioned adjustment. The competent authorities, however, may agree to consider cases where the corresponding adjustment would not otherwise be barred by any time or procedural limitations in the other State, even if the notification is not made within the six-year period.

Notes: In *Teletech*, 2013 FC 572, CRA refused Competent Authority assistance on transfer pricing because the reporting that triggered the problem (increasing parent's US income and decreasing sub's Canadian income) was not initiated by CRA or the IRS. The Court dismissed an application for judicial review, as it was filed too late.

Art. IX:3 amended by 1995 Protocol, generally effective 1996.

Definitions: "competent authority" — Art. III:1(g); "person" — Art. III:1(e), ITCIA 3, *Interpretation Act* 35(1); "related" — Art. IX:2; "State" — Art. III:1(i).

Technical Explanation [1995 Protocol]: Article 4 of the Protocol amends paragraphs 3 and 4 of Article IX (Related Persons) of the Convention. Paragraph 1 of Article IX authorizes a Contracting State to adjust the amount of income, loss, or tax payable by a person with respect to arrangements between that person and a related person in the other Contracting State, when such arrangements differ from those that would obtain between unrelated persons. Under the present Convention, if an adjustment is made or to be made by a Contracting State under paragraph 1, paragraph 3 obligates the other Contracting State to make a corresponding adjustment if two conditions are satisfied: (1) the other Contracting State agrees with the adjustment made or to be made by the first Contracting State, and (2) the competent authority of the other Contracting State has received notice of the first adjustment within six years of the end of the taxable year to which that adjustment relates. If notice is not given within the six-year period, and if the person to whom the first adjustment relates is not notified of the adjustment at least six months prior to the end of the six-year period, paragraph 4 of Article IX of the present Convention requires that the first Contracting State withdraw its adjustment, to the extent necessary to avoid double taxation.

Article 4 of the Protocol amends paragraphs 3 and 4 of Article IX to prevent taxpayers from using the notification requirements of the present Convention to avoid adjustments. Paragraph 4, as amended, eliminates the requirement that a Contracting State withdraw an adjustment if the notification requirement of paragraph 3 has not been met. Paragraph 4 is also amended to delete the requirement that the taxpayer be notified at least six months before expiration of the six-year period specified in paragraph 3.

As amended by the Protocol, Article IX also explicitly authorizes the competent authorities to relieve double taxation in appropriate cases, even if the notification requirement is not satisfied. Paragraph 3 confirms that the competent authorities may agree to a corresponding adjustment if such an adjustment is not otherwise barred by time or procedural limitations such as the statute of limitations. Paragraph 4 provides that the competent authority of the State making the initial adjustment may grant unilateral relief from double taxation in other cases, although such relief is not obligatory.

Technical Explanation [1984]: Paragraph 3 provides that where, pursuant to paragraph 1, an adjustment is made or to be made by a Contracting State, the other Contracting State shall make a corresponding adjustment to the income, loss, or tax of the related person in that other State, provided that the other State agrees with the adjustment and, within six years from the end of the taxable year of the person in the first State to which the adjustment relates, the competent authority of the other State has been notified in writing of the adjustment. The reference to an adjustment which "is made or to be made" does not require a Contracting State to formally propose an adjustment before paragraph 3 becomes pertinent. The notification required by paragraph 3 may be made by any of the related persons involved or by the competent authority of the State which makes or is to make the initial adjustment. The notification must give details regarding the adjustment sufficient to apprise the competent authority receiving the notification of the nature of the adjustment. If the requirements of paragraph 3 are complied with, the corresponding adjustment will be made by the other Contracting State notwithstanding any time or procedural limitations in the domestic law of that State.

4. In the event that the notification referred to in paragraph 3 is not given within the time period referred to therein, and the competent authorities have not agreed to otherwise consider the case in accordance with paragraph 3(b), the competent authority of the Contracting State which has made or is to make the first-mentioned adjustment may provide relief from double taxation where appropriate.

Notes: Art. IX:4 amended by 1995 Protocol, generally effective 1996.

Definitions: "competent authority" — Art. III:1(g).

Technical Explanation [1995 Protocol]: See under para. 3.

Technical Explanation [1984]: Paragraph 4 provides that in a case where the other Contracting State has not been notified as provided in paragraph 3 and if the person whose income, loss, or tax is being adjusted has not received notification of the adjustment within five and one-half years from the end of its taxable year to which the adjustment relates, such adjustment shall not be made to the extent that the adjustment would give rise to double taxation between the United States and Canada. Again, the notification referred to in this paragraph need not be a formal adjustment, but it must be in writing and must contain sufficient details to permit the taxpayer to give the notification referred to in paragraph 3.

If, for example, the Internal Revenue Service proposes to make an adjustment to the income of a U.S. company pursuant to Code section 482, and the adjustment involves an allocation of income from a related Canadian company, the competent authority of Canada must receive written notification of the proposed IRS adjustment within six years from the end of the taxable year of the U.S. company to which the adjustment relates. If such notification is not received in a timely fashion and if the U.S. company does not receive written notification of the adjustment from the IRS within 5½ years from the end of its relevant taxable year, the IRS will unilaterally recede on the proposed section 482 adjustment to the extent that this adjustment would otherwise give rise to double taxation between the United States and Canada. The Internal Revenue Service will determine whether and to what extent the adjustment would give rise to double taxation with respect to income arising in Canada by examining the relevant facts and circumstances such as the amount of foreign tax credits attributable to Canadian taxes paid by the U.S. company, including any carryovers and credits for deemed paid taxes.

5. The provisions of paragraphs 3 and 4 shall not apply in the case of fraud, willful default or neglect or gross negligence.

Notes: For case law interpreting "fraud, wilful default or neglect", see under ITA 152(4)(a)(i). For "gross negligence", see Notes to ITA 163(2).

Technical Explanation [1984]: Paragraph 5 provides that neither a corresponding adjustment described in paragraph 3 nor the cancelling of an adjustment described in paragraph 4 will be made in any case of fraud, willful default, neglect, or gross negligence on the part of the taxpayer or any related person.

Paragraphs 3 and 4 of Article IX are exceptions to the "saving clause" contained in paragraph 2 of Article XXIX (Miscellaneous Rules), as provided in paragraph 3(a) of Article XXIX. Paragraphs 3 and 4 of Article IX apply to adjustments made or to be made with respect to taxable years for which the Convention has effect as provided in paragraphs 2 and 5 of Article XXX (Entry Into Force).

Article X — Dividends

1. Dividends paid by a company which is a resident of a Contracting State to a resident of the other Contracting State may be taxed in that other State.

Definitions: "company" — Art. III:1(f); "dividends" — Art. X:3; "resident" — Art. IV; "State" — Art. III:1(i).

Technical Explanation [1984]: Paragraph 1 allows a Contracting State to impose tax on its residents with respect to dividends paid by a company which is a resident of the other Contracting State.

2. However, such dividends may also be taxed in the Contracting State of which the company paying the dividends is a resident and according to the laws of that State; but if a resident of the other Contracting State is the beneficial owner of such dividends, the tax so charged shall not exceed:

(a) 5 per cent of the gross amount of the dividends if the beneficial owner is a company which owns at least 10 per cent of the

voting stock of the company paying the dividends (for this purpose, a company that is a resident of a Contracting State shall be considered to own the voting stock owned by an entity that is considered fiscally transparent under the laws of that State and that is not a resident of the Contracting State of which the company paying the dividends is a resident, in proportion to the company's ownership interest in that entity);

(b) 15 per cent of the gross amount of the dividends in all other cases.

This paragraph shall not affect the taxation of the company in respect of the profits out of which the dividends are paid.

Related Provisions: ITA 104(16) — Income trust distributions treated as dividends; ITA 126 — Foreign tax credit; ITA 260(8.2) — Payment under securities lending arrangement; Art. XXI:2 — No withholding tax on dividend payments to RRSP, RRIF or RPP; Art. XXIV:2 — Credit for underlying US tax paid; Art. XXIX-A — Limitation on benefits.

Notes: See Notes to ITA 212(2).

The term "beneficial owner" is designed to prevent treaty-shopping effected by inserting a nominal owner resident in a treaty country into a corporate ownership chain. However, as long as the recipient of the dividend (or royalties, for Art. XII:2) has genuine possession, use, control and risk, the fact it is part of a chain of payments to another country does not prevent it from being the "beneficial owner" and getting treaty relief: *Prévost Car*, 2009 FCA 57 (dividends); *Velcro Canada*, 2012 TCC 57 (royalties; such back-to-back payments are now caught by ITA 212(3.1)–(3.94)). CRA will continue to attack what it considers abusive treaty shopping through limitation-on-benefits provisions (see Art. XXIX-A), GAAR and specific anti-abuse rules (see Canada-UK treaty Art. 10:7, 11:11 and 12:8): VIEWS doc 2009-0321451C6; but it accepts *Prévost* and *Velcro*: 2012-0444041C6. However, starting 2020 or later, the Multilateral Instrument (MLI — see the pages before this treaty) effectively amends many of Canada's treaties (but not this treaty) to prevent certain treaty shopping. Also, back-to-back rules in ITA 212(3.1)-(3.94) now apply to both interest and royalties.

For more on beneficial ownership see Powrie, "Tax Avoidance and Tax Treaties", 2008 Cdn Tax Foundation conference report at 19:5-15; Krishna, "Using Beneficial Ownership", 56(7) *Tax Notes International [TNI]* (taxnotes.com) 537-50 (Nov. 16, 2009); Kandev & Peters, "Treaty Interpretation", 2011 conference report, 26:1-60; Watson & Baum, "Beneficial Ownership as a Treaty Anti-Avoidance Tool?", 60(1) *Canadian Tax Journal* 149-68 (2012); Buttenham & Johns, "Velcro Canada", XVII(4) *International Tax Planning* (Federated Press) 1200-03 (2012); Arnold et al., "Judicial Approaches to Treaty Interpretation", 2012 conference report, at 29:13-63; Slade, "Beneficial Ownership", XVIII(3) *Corporate Finance* (Federated Press) 2136-38 (2012); Weigl, "The Meaning of Beneficial Ownership", IV(2) *Personal Tax & Estate Planning* (Federated Press) 179-82 (2012); Yoshimura, "Clarifying the Meaning of 'Beneficial Owner'", 72(8) *TNI* 761-82 (Nov. 25, 2013).

"Fiscally transparent" in the US includes an LLC; see Notes to Art. IV:6 above. The 2007 Protocol amendment deems US members of an LLC (that has not elected to be taxed as a corporation) to own stock in a Canco held by LLC, so that if their ownership reaches 10% they are entitled to the 5% dividend rate (dividend income deemed earned by Art. IV:6). See also Cannon et al., "The Fifth Protocol to the Canada-U.S. Income Tax Convention", 2007 Cdn Tax Foundation conference report at 24:12-17.

Dividends payable to a pension plan, RRSP or RRIF are not subject to withholding tax: Art. XXI:2. This does not apply to a TFSA.

The tax on dividends to an S-corporation holding more than 10% of the payer's voting shares, where the dividend payer is fiscally transparent for US purposes, is 25% due to Art. IV:7: VIEWS doc 2009-0319481E5. For tiered partnerships, see doc 2009-0318701E5. For partnerships under the parallel provision of the Canada-Netherlands treaty, see 2013-0486011E5.

For a ruling (pre-2007 Protocol) that the 5% rate applies to dividends through a partnership to US partners that are issued more than 10% of the shares of the Canadian corporation paying the dividend, see VIEWS doc 2005-0153941R3. For a more recent ruling applying para. 2(a), see 2012-0435211R3.

See also Notes to para. 3 below.

Art. X:2(a) amended by 2007 Protocol to add the words in parentheses, effective for taxable years beginning after 2008, but in respect of taxes withheld at source, for amounts paid or credited after Jan. 2009.

Art. X:2(a) amended by 1995 Protocol, the 5% rate effective for amounts paid or credited after 1996. For 1996, the rate was 6%. From Oct. 1984-1995, it was 10%.

Definitions: "company" — Art. III:1(f); "dividends" — Art. X:3; "resident" — Art. IV; "State" — Art. III:1(i).

I.T. Technical News: 38 (limited liability company under the Protocol).

Forms: NR301: Declaration of eligibility for benefits under a tax treaty for a non-resident taxpayer.

Technical Explanation [2007 Protocol]: Article 5 makes a number of amendments to Article X (Dividends) of the existing Convention. As with other benefits of the Convention, the benefits of Article X are available to a resident of a Contracting State only if that resident is entitled to those benefits under the provisions of Article XXIX A (Limitation on Benefits).

See the Technical Explanation for new paragraphs 6 and 7 of Article IV(Residence) for discussion regarding the interaction between domestic law concepts of beneficial ownership and the treaty rules to determine when a person is considered to derive an item of income for purposes of obtaining benefits of the Convention such as withholding rate reductions.

Paragraph 1

Paragraph 1 of Article 5 of the Protocol replaces subparagraph 2(a) of Article X of the Convention. In general, paragraph 2 limits the amount of tax that may be imposed on dividends by the Contracting State in which the company paying the dividends is resident if the beneficial owner of the dividends is a resident of the other Contracting State. Subparagraph 2(a) limits the rate to 5% of the gross amount of the dividends if the beneficial owner is a company that owns 10% or more of the voting stock of the company paying the dividends.

The Protocol adds a parenthetical to address the determination of the requisite ownership set forth in subparagraph 2(a) when the beneficial owner of dividends receives the dividends through an entity that is considered fiscally transparent in the beneficial owner's Contracting State. The added parenthetical stipulates that voting stock in a company paying the dividends that is indirectly held through an entity that is considered fiscally transparent in the beneficial owner's Contracting State is taken into account, provided the entity is not a resident of the other Contracting State. The United States views the new parenthetical as merely a clarification.

For example, assume USCo, a U.S. corporation, directly owns 2% of the voting stock of CanCo, a Canadian company that is considered a corporation in the United States and Canada. Further, assume that USCo owns 18% of the interests in LLC, an entity that in turn owns 50% of the voting stock of CanCo. CanCo pays a dividend to each of its shareholders. Provided that LLC is fiscally transparent in the United States and not considered a resident of Canada, USCo's 9% ownership in CanCo through LLC (50% x 18%) is taken into account in determining whether USCo meets the 10% ownership threshold set forth in subparagraph 2(a). In this example, USCo may aggregate its voting stock interests in CanCo that it owns directly and through LLC to determine if it satisfies the ownership requirement of subparagraph 2(a). Accordingly, USCo will be entitled to the 5% rate of withholding on dividends paid with respect to both its voting stock held through LLC and its voting stock held directly. Alternatively, if, for example, all of the shareholders of LLC were natural persons, the 5% rate would not apply.

Technical Explanation [1995 Protocol]: See under para. 7.

Technical Explanation [1984]: Paragraph 2 limits the amount of tax that may be imposed on such dividends by the Contracting State in which the company paying the dividends is resident if the beneficial owner of the dividends is a resident of the other Contracting State. The limitation is 10% of the gross amount of the dividends if the beneficial owner is a company that owns 10% or more of the voting stock of the company paying the dividends; and 15% of the gross amount of the dividends in all other cases. Paragraph 2 does not impose any restrictions with respect to taxation of the profits out of which the dividends are paid.

3. For the purposes of this Article, the term **"dividends"** means income from shares or other rights, not being debt-claims, participating in profits, as well as income that is subjected to the same taxation treatment as income from shares under the laws of the State of which the payer is a resident.

Notes: "Dividend" includes a deemed dividend under ITA *84(1)* (VIEWS docs 2009-0341681R3, 2009-0348581R3, 2010-0364531R3, 2010-0390141R3, 2011-0439761R3, 2012-0471921R3), *84(3)* (2011-0424211R3), *214(3)(a)* (2012-0434311E5) or *219(5.3)* (2001-0106695).

Fifth Protocol (2007), Annex B, states:

3. Definition of the term "dividends"

It is understood that distributions from Canadian income trusts and royalty trusts that are treated as dividends under the taxation laws of Canada shall be considered dividends for the purposes of Article X (Dividends) of the Convention.

Art. X:3 amended by 2007 Protocol to refer to "payer" rather than "company making the distribution", effective for taxable years beginning after 2008, but in respect of taxes withheld at source, for amounts paid or credited after Jan. 2009.

Definitions: "resident" — Art. IV; "share" — ITCIA 3, ITA 248(1); "State" — Art. III:1(i).

Technical Explanation [2007 Protocol]: Paragraph 2 of Article 5 of the Protocol replaces the definition of the term "dividends" provided in paragraph 3 of Article X of the Convention. The new definition conforms to the U.S. Model formulation. Paragraph 3 defines the term dividends broadly and flexibly. The definition is intended to cover all arrangements that yield a return on an equity investment in a corporation as determined under the tax law of the source State, as well as arrangements that might be developed in the future.

The term dividends includes income from shares, or other corporate rights that are not treated as debt under the law of the source State, that participate in the profits of the company. The term also includes income that is subjected to the same tax treatment as income from shares by the law of the source State. Thus, for example, a constructive dividend that results from a non-arm's length transaction between a corporation and a related party is a dividend. In the case of the United States the term "dividend" includes amounts treated as a dividend under U.S. law upon the sale or redemption of shares or

upon a transfer of shares in a reorganization. See, *e.g.*, Rev. Rul. 92-85, 1992-2 C.B. 69 (sale of foreign subsidiary's stock to U.S. sister company is a deemed dividend to extent of the subsidiary's and sister company's earnings and profits). Further, a distribution from a U.S. publicly traded limited partnership that is taxed as a corporation under U.S. law is a dividend for purposes of Article X. However, a distribution by a limited liability company is not considered by the United States to be a dividend for purposes of Article X, provided the limited liability company is not characterized as an association taxable as a corporation under U.S. law.

Paragraph 3 of the General Note states that distributions from Canadian income trusts and royalty trusts that are treated as dividends as a result of changes to Canada's taxation of income and royalty trusts enacted in 2007 (S.C. 2007, c. 29) shall be treated as dividends for the purposes of Article X.

Additionally, a payment denominated as interest that is made by a thinly capitalized corporation may be treated as a dividend to the extent that the debt is recharacterized as equity under the laws of the source State. At the time the Protocol was signed, interest payments subject to Canada's thin-capitalization rules were not recharacterized as dividends.

Technical Explanation [1984]: Paragraph 3 defines the term "dividends," as the term is used in this Article. Each Contracting State is permitted to apply its domestic law rules for differentiating dividends from interest and other disbursements.

4. The provisions of paragraph 2 shall not apply if the beneficial owner of the dividends, being a resident of a Contracting State, carries on, or has carried on, business in the other Contracting State of which the company paying the dividends is a resident, through a permanent establishment situated therein, and the holding in respect of which the dividends are paid is effectively connected to such permanent establishment. In such case, the provisions of Article VII (Business Profits) shall apply.

Notes: See Notes to Art. VII:2 re the words "or has carried on".

Art. X:4 amended by 2007 Protocol, effective for taxable years beginning after 2008, but in respect of taxes withheld at source, for amounts paid or credited after Jan. 2009.

Definitions: "business" — ITCIA 3, ITA 248(1); "company" — Art. III:1(f); "dividends" — Art. X:3; "permanent establishment" — Art. V:1; "resident" — Art. IV; "State" — Art. III:1(i).

Technical Explanation [2007 Protocol]: Paragraph 3 of Article 5 of the Protocol replaces paragraph 4 of Article X. New paragraph 4 is substantially similar to paragraph 4 as it existed prior to the Protocol. New paragraph 4, however, adds clarifying language consistent with the changes made in Articles 4, 6, and 7 of the Protocol with respect to income attributable to a permanent establishment that has ceased to exist. Paragraph 4 provides that the limitations of paragraph 2 do not apply if the beneficial owner of the dividends carries on or has carried on business in the State in which the company paying the dividends is a resident through a permanent establishment situated there, and the stockholding in respect of which the dividends are paid is effectively connected to such permanent establishment. In such a case, the dividends are taxable pursuant to the provisions of Article VII (Business Profits). Thus, dividends paid in respect of holdings forming part of the assets of a permanent establishment or which are otherwise effectively connected to such permanent establishment will be taxed on a net basis using the rates and rules of taxation generally applicable to residents of the State in which the permanent establishment is situated.

To conform with Article 9 of the Protocol, which deletes Article XIV (Independent Personal Services) of the Convention, paragraph 4 of Article 5 of the Protocol also amends paragraph 5 of Article X by omitting the reference to a "fixed base."

Technical Explanation [1984]: Paragraph 4 provides that the limitations of paragraph 2 do not apply if the beneficial owner of the dividends carries on business in the State in which the company paying the dividends is a resident through a permanent establishment or fixed base situated there, and the stockholding in respect of which the dividends are paid is effectively connected with such permanent establishment or fixed base. In such a case, the dividends are taxable pursuant to the provisions of Article VII (Business Profits) or Article XIV (Independent Personal Services), as the case may be. Thus, dividends paid in respect of holdings forming part of the assets of a permanent establishment or fixed base or which are otherwise effectively connected with such permanent establishment or fixed base (i.e., dividends attributable to the permanent establishment or fixed base) will be taxed on a net basis using the rates and rules of taxation generally applicable to residents of the State in which the permanent establishment or fixed base is situated.

5. Where a company is a resident of a Contracting State, the other Contracting State may not impose any tax on the dividends paid by the company, except insofar as such dividends are paid to a resident of that other State or insofar as the holding in respect of which the dividends are paid is effectively connected with a permanent establishment situated in that other State, nor subject the company's undistributed profits to a tax, even if the dividends paid or the undistributed profits consist wholly or partly of profits or income arising in such other State.

Notes: Art. X:5 amended by 2007 Protocol to change "permanent establishment or a fixed base" to "permanent establishment", for taxable years beginning after 2008, but in respect of taxes withheld at source, for amounts paid or credited after Jan. 2009.

Definitions: "company" — Art. III:1(f); "dividends" — Art. X:3; "permanent establishment" — Art. V:1; "resident" — Art. IV; "State" — Art. III:1(i).

Technical Explanation [2007 Protocol]: To conform with Article 9 of the Protocol, which deletes Article XIV (Independent Personal Services) of the Convention, paragraph 4 of Article 5 of the Protocol amends paragraph 5 of Article X by omitting the reference to a "fixed base."

Technical Explanation [1984]: Paragraph 5 imposes limitations on the right of Canada or the United States, as the case may be, to impose tax on dividends paid by a company which is a resident of the other Contracting State. The State in which the company is not resident may not tax such dividends except insofar as they are paid to a resident of that State or the holding in respect of which the dividends are paid is effectively connected with a permanent establishment or fixed base in that State. In the case of the United States, such dividends may also be taxed in the hands of a U.S. citizen and certain former citizens, pursuant to the "saving clause" of paragraph 2 of Article XXIX (Miscellaneous Rules). In addition, the Contracting State in which the company is not resident may not subject such company's undistributed profits to any tax. See, however, paragraphs 6, 7, and 8 which, in certain circumstances, qualify the rules of paragraph 5. Neither paragraph 5 nor any other provision of the Convention restricts the ability of the United States to apply the provisions of the Code concerning foreign personal holding companies and controlled foreign corporations.

6. Nothing in this Convention shall be construed as preventing a Contracting State from imposing a tax on the earnings of a company attributable to permanent establishments in that State, in addition to the tax which would be chargeable on the earnings of a company which is a resident of that State, provided that any additional tax so imposed shall not exceed 5 per cent of the amount of such earnings which have not been subjected to such additional tax in previous taxation years. For the purposes of this paragraph, the term "earnings" means the amount by which the business profits attributable to permanent establishments in a Contracting State (including gains from the alienation of property forming part of the business property of such permanent establishments) in a year and previous years exceeds the sum of:

(a) business losses attributable to such permanent establishments (including losses from the alienation of property forming part of the business property of such permanent establishments) in such year and previous years;

(b) all taxes, other than the additional tax referred to in this paragraph, imposed on such profits in that State;

(c) the profits reinvested in that State, provided that where that State is Canada, such amount shall be determined in accordance with the existing provisions of the law of Canada regarding the computation of the allowance in respect of investment in property in Canada, and any subsequent modification of those provisions which shall not affect the general principle hereof; and

(d) five hundred thousand Canadian dollars ($500,000) or its equivalent in United States currency, less any amounts deducted by the company, or by an associated company with respect to the same or a similar business, under this subparagraph (d); for the purposes of this subparagraph (d) a company is associated with another company if one company directly or indirectly controls the other, or both companies are directly or indirectly controlled by the same person or persons, or if the two companies deal with each other not at arm's length.

Related Provisions: ITA 219 — Branch tax.

Notes: See Notes to ITA 219(1).

Opening words of Art. X:6 amended by 1995 Protocol, the 5% rate effective for taxable years beginning after 1996. For 1996, the rate was 6%; for 1985-1995, 10%.

Definitions: "arm's length" — ITCIA 3, ITA 251(1); "associated" — ITCIA 3, ITA 256; "Canada" — Art. III:1(a), ITCIA 5; "company" — Art. III:1(f); "permanent establishment" — Art. V:1; "person" — Art. III:1(e), ITCIA 3, *Interpretation Act* 35(1); "property" — ITCIA 3, ITA 248(1); "resident" — Art. IV; "State" — Art. III:1(i); "taxation year" — ITCIA 3, ITA 249; "United States" — Art. III:1(b).

Technical Explanation [1995 Protocol]: See under para. 7.

Technical Explanation [1984]: Paragraph 6 provides that, notwithstanding paragraph 5, a Contracting State in which is maintained a permanent establishment or permanent establishments of a company resident in the other Contracting State may impose tax on such company's earnings, in addition to the tax that would be charged on the earnings of a company resident in that State. The additional tax may not, however,

exceed 10% of the amount of the earnings which have not been subjected to such additional tax in previous taxation years. Thus, Canada, which has a branch profits tax in force, may impose that tax up to the 10% limitation in the case of a United States company with one or more permanent establishments in Canada. This branch profits tax may be imposed notwithstanding other rules of the Convention, including paragraph 6 of Article XXV (Non-Discrimination).

For purposes of paragraph 6, the term "earnings" means the excess of business profits attributable to all permanent establishments for a year and previous years over the sum of: a) business losses attributable to such permanent establishments for such years; b) all taxes on profits, whether or not covered by the Convention (e.g., provincial taxes on profits and provincial resource royalties (which Canada considers "taxes") in excess of the mineral resource allowance provided for under the law of Canada), other than the additional tax referred to in paragraph 6; c) profits reinvested in such State; and d) $500,000 (Canadian, or its equivalent in U.S. dollars) less any amounts deducted under paragraph 6(d) with respect to the same or a similar business by the company or an associated company. The deduction under paragraph 6(d) is available as of the first year for which the Convention has effect, regardless of the prior earnings and tax expenses, if any, of the permanent establishment. The $500,000 deduction is taken into account after other deductions, and is permanent. For the purpose of paragraph 6, references to business profits and business losses include gains and losses from the alienation of property forming part of the business property of a permanent establishment. The term "associated company" includes a company which directly or indirectly controls another company or two companies directly or indirectly controlled by the same person or persons, as well as any two companies that deal with each other not at arm's length. This definition differs from the definition of "related persons" in paragraph 2 of Article IX (Related Persons).

7. Notwithstanding the provisions of paragraph 2,

(a) dividends paid by a company that is a resident of Canada and a non-resident-owned investment corporation to a company that is a resident of the United States, that owns at least 10 per cent of the voting stock of the company paying the dividends and that is the beneficial owner of such dividends, may be taxed in Canada at a rate not exceeding 10 per cent of the gross amount of the dividends;

(b) paragraph 2(b) and not paragraph 2(a) shall apply in the case of dividends paid by a resident of the United States that is a Regulated Investment Company; and

(c) subparagraph 2(a) shall not apply to dividends paid by a resident of the United States that is a Real Estate Investment Trust (REIT), and subparagraph 2(b) shall apply only if:

(i) the beneficial owner of the dividends is an individual holding an interest of not more than 10 percent in the REIT;

(ii) the dividends are paid with respect to a class of stock that is publicly traded and the beneficial owner of the dividends is a person holding an interest of not more than 5 percent in any class of the REIT's stock; or

(iii) the beneficial owner of the dividends is a person holding an interest of not more than 10 percent in the REIT and the REIT is diversified.

Otherwise, the rate of tax applicable under the domestic law of the United States shall apply. Where an estate or testamentary trust acquired its interest in a REIT as a consequence of an individual's death, for purposes of this subparagraph the estate or trust shall for the five-year period following the death be deemed with respect to that interest to be an individual.

Related Provisions: ITA 134.1 — Transitional rule re elimination of NROs.

Notes: Art. X:7(c) amended by 2007 Protocol, for taxable years beginning after 2008; but in respect of taxes withheld at source, for amounts paid or credited after Jan. 2009.

Art. X:7 amended by 1995 Protocol, for amounts paid or credited in 1996 or later.

Definitions: "Canada" — Art. III:1(a), ITCIA 5; "company" — Art. III:1(f); "dividends" — Art. X:3; "estate", "individual" — ITCIA 3, 248(1); "non-resident-owned investment corporation" — ITCIA 3, ITA 133(8), 248(1); "real estate investment trust" — *Internal Revenue Code* s. 856(a); "regulated investment company" — *Internal Revenue Code* s. 851(a); "resident" — Art. IV; "testamentary trust" — ITCIA 3, ITA 248(1); "trust" — ITCIA 3, ITA 104(1), 248(1); "United States" — Art. III:1(b).

Technical Explanation [2007 Protocol]: Paragraph 5 of Article 5 of the Protocol replaces subparagraph 7(c) of Article X of the existing Convention. Consistent with current U.S. tax treaty policy, new subparagraph 7(c) provides rules that expand the application of subparagraph 2(b) for the treatment of dividends paid by a Real Estate Investment Trust (REIT). New subparagraph 7(c) maintains the rule of the existing Convention that dividends paid by a REIT are not eligible for the 5% maximum rate of withholding tax of subparagraph 2(a), and provides that the 15% maximum rate of withholding tax of subparagraph 2(b) applies to dividends paid by REITs only if one of three conditions is met.

First, the dividend will qualify for the 15% maximum rate if the beneficial owner of the dividend is an individual holding an interest of not more than 10% in the REIT. For this purpose, subparagraph 7(c) also provides that where an estate or testamentary trust acquired its interest in a REIT as a consequence of the death of an individual, the estate or trust will be treated as an individual for the five-year period following the death. Thus, dividends paid to an estate or testamentary trust in respect of a holding of less than a 10% interest in the REIT also will be entitled to the 15% rate of withholding, but only for up to five years after the death.

Second, the dividend will qualify for the 15% maximum rate if it is paid with respect to a class of stock that is publicly traded and the beneficial owner of the dividend is a person holding an interest of not more than 5% of any class of the REIT's stock.

Third, the dividend will qualify for the 15% maximum rate if the beneficial owner of the dividend holds an interest in the REIT of 10% or less and the REIT is "diversified." A REIT is diversified if the gross value of no single interest in real property held by the REIT exceeds 10% of the gross value of the REIT's total interest in real property. For purposes of this diversification test, foreclosure property is not considered an interest in real property, and a REIT holding a partnership interest is treated as owning its proportionate share of any interest in real property held by the partnership.

A resident of Canada directly holding U.S. real property would pay U.S. tax either at a 30% rate of withholding tax on the gross income or at graduated rates on the net income. By placing the real property in a REIT, the investor absent a special rule could transform real estate income into dividend income, taxable at the rates provided in Article X, significantly reducing the U.S. tax that otherwise would be imposed. Subparagraph 7(c) prevents this result and thereby avoids a disparity between the taxation of direct real estate investments and real estate investments made through REIT conduits. In the cases in which subparagraph 7(c) allows a dividend from a REIT to be eligible for the 15% maximum rate of withholding tax, the holding in the REIT is not considered the equivalent of a direct holding in the underlying real property.

Technical Explanation [1995 Protocol]: Article 5 of the Protocol amends Article X (Dividends) of the Convention. Paragraph 1 of Article 5 amends paragraph 2(a) of Article X to reduce from 10% to 5% the maximum rate of tax that may be imposed by a Contracting State on the gross amount of dividends beneficially owned by a company resident in the other Contracting State that owns at least 10% of the voting stock of the company paying the dividends. The rate at which the branch profits tax may be imposed under paragraph 6 is also reduced by paragraph 1 of Article 5 from 10% to 5%. Under the entry-into-force provisions of Article 21 of the Protocol, these reductions will be phased in over a three-year period.

Paragraph 2 of Article 5 of the Protocol replaces paragraph 7 of Article X of the Convention with a new paragraph 7. Paragraph 7 of the existing Convention is no longer relevant because it applies only in the case where a Contracting State does not impose a branch profits tax. Both Contracting States now do impose such a tax.

New paragraph 7 makes the 5% withholding rate of new paragraph 2(a) inapplicable in certain situations. Under new paragraph 7(b), dividends paid by U.S. regulated investment companies (RICs) are denied the 5% withholding rate even if the Canadian shareholder is a corporation that would otherwise qualify as a direct investor by satisfying the 10-percent ownership requirement. Consequently, all RIC dividends to Canadian beneficial owners are subjected to the 15% rate that applies to dividends paid to portfolio investors.

Dividends paid by U.S. real estate investment trusts (REITs) to Canadian beneficial owners are also denied the 5% rate under the rules of paragraph 7(c). REIT dividends paid to individuals who own less than a 10% interest in the REIT are subject to withholding at a maximum rate of 15%. Paragraph 7(c) also provides that dividend distributions by a REIT to an estate or a testamentary trust acquiring the interest in the REIT as a consequence of the death of an individual will be treated as distributions to an individual, for the five-year period following the death. Thus, dividends paid to an estate or testamentary trust in respect of a holding of less than a 10% interest in the REIT also will be entitled to the 15% rate of withholding, but only for up to five years after the death. REIT dividends paid to other Canadian beneficial owners are subject to the rate of withholding tax that applies under the domestic law of the United States (i.e., 30%).

The denial of the 5% withholding rate at source to all RIC and REIT shareholders, and the denial of the 15% rate to most shareholders of REITs, is intended to prevent the use of these non-taxable conduit entities to gain unjustifiable benefits for certain shareholders. For example, a Canadian corporation that wishes to hold a portfolio of U.S. corporate shares may hold the portfolio directly and pay a U.S. withholding tax of 15% on all of the dividends that it receives. Alternatively, it may place the portfolio of U.S. stocks in a RIC, in which the Canadian corporation owns more than 10% of the shares, but in which there are enough small shareholders to satisfy the RIC diversified ownership requirements. Since the RIC is a pure conduit, there are no U.S. tax costs to the Canadian corporation of interposing the RIC as an intermediary in the chain of ownership. It is unlikely that a 10% shareholding in a RIC will constitute a 10% shareholding in any company from which the dividends originate. In the absence of the special rules in paragraph 7(b), however, interposition of a RIC would transform what should be portfolio dividends into direct investment dividends taxable at source by the United States only at 5%. The special rules of paragraph 7 prevent this.

Similarly, a resident of Canada may hold U.S. real property directly and pay U.S. tax either at a 30% rate on the gross income or at the income tax rates specified in the *Internal Revenue Code* on the net income. By placing the real estate holding in a REIT, the Canadian investor could transform real estate income into dividend income and thus transform high-taxed income into much lower-taxed income. In the absence of the special rule, if the REIT shareholder were a Canadian corporation that owned at least a 10% interest in the REIT, the withholding rate would be 5%; in all other cases, it would be 15%. In either event, with one exception, a tax rate of 30% or more would be significantly reduced. The exception is the relatively small individual Canadian investor who might be subject to U.S. tax at a rate of only 15% on the net income even if he earned the real estate income directly. Under the rule in paragraph 7(c), such individuals, defined as those holding less than a 10% interest in the REIT, remain taxable at source at a 15% rate.

Subparagraph (a) of paragraph 7 provides a special rule for certain dividends paid by Canadian non-resident-owned investment corporations ("NROs"). The subparagraph provides for a maximum rate of 10% (instead of the standard rate of 5%) for dividends paid by NROs that are Canadian residents to a U.S. company that owns 10% or more of the voting stock of the NRO and that is the beneficial owner of the dividend. This rule maintains the rate available under the current Convention for dividends from NROs. Canada wanted the withholding rate for direct investment NRO dividends to be no lower than the maximum withholding rates under the Convention on interest and royalties, to make sure that a foreign investor cannot transform interest or royalty income subject to a 10% withholding tax into direct dividends qualifying for a 5% withholding tax by passing it through to an NRO.

Technical Explanation [1984]: Paragraph 7 provides that, notwithstanding paragraph 5, a Contracting State that does not impose a branch profits tax as described in paragraph 6 (i.e., under current law, the United States) may tax a dividend paid by a company which is a resident of the other Contracting State if at least 50% of the company's gross income from all sources was included in the computation of business profits attributable to one or more permanent establishments which such company had in the first-mentioned State. The dividend subject to such a tax must, however, be attributable to profits earned by the company in taxable years beginning after September 26, 1980 and the 50% test must be met for the three-year period preceding the taxable year of the company in which the dividend is declared (including years ending on or before September 26, 1980) or such shorter period as the company had been in existence prior to that taxable year. Dividends will be deemed to be distributed, for purposes of paragraph 7, first out of profits of the taxation year of the company in which the distribution is made and then out of the profits of the preceding year or years of the company. Paragraph 7 provides further that if a resident of the other Contracting State is the beneficial owner of such dividends, any tax imposed under paragraph 7 is subject to the 10 or 15% limitation of paragraph 2 or the rules of paragraph 4 (providing for dividends to be taxed as business profits or income from independent personal services), as the case may be.

8. Notwithstanding the provisions of paragraph 5, a company which is a resident of Canada and which has income subject to tax in the United States (without regard to the provisions of the Convention) may be liable to the United States accumulated earnings tax and personal holding company tax but only if 50 per cent or more in value of the outstanding voting shares of the company is owned, directly or indirectly, throughout the last half of its taxable year by citizens or residents of the United States (other than citizens of Canada who do not have immigrant status in the United States or who have not been residents in the United States for more than three taxable years) or by residents of a third state.

Definitions: "Canada" — Art. III:1(a), ITCIA 5; "company" — Art. III:1(f); "personal holding company" — *Internal Revenue Code* s. 542(a); "resident" — Art. IV; "share" — ITCIA 3, ITA 248(1); "United States" — Art. III:1(b).

Technical Explanation [1984]: Paragraph 8 provides that, notwithstanding paragraph 5, a company which is a resident of Canada and which, absent the provisions of the Convention, has income subject to tax by the United States may be liable for the United States accumulated earnings tax and personal holding company tax. These taxes can be applied, however, only if 50% or more in value of the outstanding voting shares of the company is owned, directly or indirectly, throughout the last half of its taxable year by residents of a third State or by citizens or residents of the United States, other than citizens of Canada who are resident in the United States but who either do not have immigrant status in the United States or who have not been resident in the United States for more than three taxable years. The accumulated earnings tax is applied to accumulated taxable income calculated without the benefits of the Convention. Similarly, the personal holding company tax is applied to undistributed personal holding company income computed as if the Convention had not come into force.

Article X does not apply to dividends paid by a company which is not a resident of either Contracting State. Such dividends, if they are income of a resident of one of the Contracting States, are subject to tax as provided in Article XXII (Other Income).

Information Circulars [Art. X]: 76-12R6: Applicable rate of part XIII tax on amounts paid or credited to persons in countries with which Canada has a tax convention.

Article XI — Interest

1. Interest arising in a Contracting State and beneficially owned by a resident of the other Contracting State may be taxed only in that other State.

Related Provisions: Art. XI:2 — Meaning of "interest"; Art. XI:3, 4 — No application if permanent establishment; Art. XXII:4 — No withholding tax on guarantee fees; Art. XXIX-A — Limitation on benefits.

Notes: The words "only in that other State" eliminate withholding tax imposed by the source country effective 2010, unless an exception in paras. 3-6 applies. See for example VIEWS doc 2014-0521831R3. For arm's length interest, ITA 212(1)(b) was amended to eliminate all Canadian withholding tax anyway since 2008, except for "participating debt interest" (ITA 212(3)). See Notes to ITA 212(1)(b).

For "treaty shopping" using this provision, including the meaning of "beneficially owned" [beneficial ownership], see Notes to Art. X:2 and XXIX-A:1. (For Canada's other treaties, see the Multilateral Instrument, reproduced before ths treaty.)

See also Dept. of Finance news release 2007-070 (Sept. 21, 2007) on fin.gc.ca.

Art. XI amended by 2007 Protocol, effective for taxable years beginning after 2008, but in respect of taxes withheld at source, for amounts paid or credited after Jan. 2009. For 2008-09, a transitional rule (reproduced here up to the 48th ed.) allowed withholding tax at 7% and 4% respectively on interest between related persons.

Definitions: "arising" — Art. XI:4; "interest" — Art. XI:2; "State" — Art. III:1(i).

Forms: NR301: Declaration of eligibility for benefits under a tax treaty for a non-resident taxpayer.

Technical Explanation [2007 Protocol]: Article 6 of the Protocol replaces Article XI (Interest) of the existing Convention. Article XI specifies the taxing jurisdictions over interest income of the States of source and residence and defines the terms necessary to apply Article XI. As with other benefits of the Convention, the benefits of Article XI are available to a resident of a Contracting State only if that resident is entitled to those benefits under the provisions of Article XXIX A (Limitation on Benefits).

New paragraph 1 generally grants to the residence State the exclusive right to tax interest beneficially owned by its residents and arising in the other Contracting State. See the Technical Explanation for new paragraphs 6 and 7 of Article IV (Residence) for discussion regarding the interaction between domestic law concepts of beneficial ownership and the treaty rules to determine when a person is considered to derive an item of income for purposes of obtaining benefits under the Convention such as withholding rate reductions.

Subparagraph 3(d) of Article 27 of the Protocol provides an additional rule regarding the application of paragraph 1 during the first two years that end after the Protocol's entry into force. This rule is described in detail in the Technical Explanation to Article 27.

2. The term **"interest"** as used in this Article means income from debt-claims of every kind, whether or not secured by mortgage, and whether or not carrying a right to participate in the debtor's profits, and in particular, income from government securities and income from bonds or debentures, including premiums or prizes attaching to such securities, bonds or debentures, as well as income assimilated to income from money lent by the taxation laws of the Contracting State in which the income arises. However, the term "interest" does not include income dealt with in Article X (Dividends).

Definitions: "arises" — Art. XI:4; "State" — Art. III:1(i).

Technical Explanation [2007 Protocol]: Paragraph 2 of new Article XI is substantially identical to paragraph 4 of Article XI of the existing Convention.

Paragraph 2 defines the term "interest" as used in Article XI to include, inter alia, income from debt claims of every kind, whether or not secured by a mortgage. Interest that is paid or accrued subject to a contingency is within the ambit of Article XI. This includes income from a debt obligation carrying the right to participate in profits. The term does not, however, include amounts that are treated as dividends under Article X (Dividends).

The term "interest" also includes amounts subject to the same tax treatment as income from money lent under the law of the State in which the income arises. Thus, for purposes of the Convention, amounts that the United States will treat as interest include (i) the difference between the issue price and the stated redemption price at maturity of a debt instrument (*i.e.*, original issue discount (OID)), which may be wholly or partially realized on the disposition of a debt instrument (section 1273), (ii) amounts that are imputed interest on a deferred sales contract (section 483), (iii) amounts treated as interest or OID under the stripped bond rules (section 1286), (iv) amounts treated as original issue discount under the below-market interest rate rules (section 7872), (v) a partner's distributive share of a partnership's interest income (section 702), (vi) the interest portion of periodic payments made under a "finance lease" or similar contractual arrangement that in substance is a borrowing by the nominal lessee to finance the acquisition of property, (vii) amounts included in the income of a holder of a residual interest in a real estate mortgage investment conduit (REMIC) (section 860E), because these amounts generally are subject to the same taxation treatment as interest under

U.S. tax law, and (viii) interest with respect to notional principal contracts that are re-characterized as loans because of a "substantial non-periodic payment."

3. The provisions of paragraph 1 shall not apply if the beneficial owner of the interest, being a resident of a Contracting State, carries on, or has carried on, business in the other Contracting State in which the interest arises, through a permanent establishment situated therein, and the debt-claim in respect of which the interest is paid is effectively connected with such permanent establishment. In such case the provisions of Article VII (Business Profits) shall apply.

Notes: See Art. VII:2 Notes re the words "or has carried on". See Art. X:2 Notes re "beneficial owner" and anti-avoidance rules.

Definitions: "arises" — Art. XI:4; "interest" — Art. XI:2; "permanent establishment" — Art. V; "resident of a Contracting State" — Art. IV; "State" — Art. III:1(i).

Technical Explanation [2007 Protocol]: Paragraph 3 is in all material respects the same as paragraph 5 of Article XI of the existing Convention. New paragraph 3 adds clarifying language consistent with the changes made in Articles 4, 5, and 7 of the Protocol with respect to income attributable to a permanent establishment that has ceased to exist. Also, consistent with the changes described in Article 9 of the Protocol, discussed below, paragraph 3 does not contain references to the performance of independent personal services through a fixed base.

Paragraph 3 provides an exception to the exclusive residence taxation rule of paragraph 1 in cases where the beneficial owner of the interest carries on business through a permanent establishment in the State of source and the interest is effectively connected to that permanent establishment. In such cases the provisions of Article VII(Business Profits) will apply and the source State will retain the right to impose tax on such interest income.

4. For the purposes of this Article, interest shall be deemed to arise in a Contracting State when the payer is that State itself, or a political subdivision, local authority or a resident of that State. Where, however, the person paying the interest, whether he is a resident of a Contracting State or not, has in a State other than that of which he is a resident a permanent establishment in connection with which the indebtedness on which the interest is paid was incurred, and such interest is borne by such permanent establishment, then such interest shall be deemed to arise in the State in which the permanent establishment is situated and not in the State of which the payer is a resident.

Definitions: "interest" — Art. XI:2; "permanent establishment" — Art. V; "person" — Art. III:1(e); "resident" — Art. IV; "State" — Art. III:1(i).

Technical Explanation [2007 Protocol]: Paragraph 4 is in all material respects the same as paragraph 6 of Article XI of the existing Convention. The only difference is that, consistent with the changes described below with respect to Article 9 of the Protocol, paragraph 4 does not contain references to a fixed base.

Paragraph 4 establishes the source of interest for purposes of Article XI. Interest is considered to arise in a Contracting State if the payer is that State, or a political subdivision, local authority, or resident of that State. However, in cases where the person paying the interest, whether a resident of a Contracting State or of a third State, has in a State other than that of which he is a resident a permanent establishment in connection with which the indebtedness on which the interest was paid was incurred, and such interest is borne by the permanent establishment, then such interest is deemed to arise in the State in which the permanent establishment is situated and not in the State of the payer's residence. Furthermore, pursuant to paragraphs 1 and 4, and Article XXII (Other Income), Canadian tax will not be imposed on interest paid to a U.S. resident by a company resident in Canada if the indebtedness is incurred in connection with, and the interest is borne by, a permanent establishment of the company situated in a third State. For the purposes of this Article, "borne by" means allowable as a deduction in computing taxable income.

5. Where, by reason of a special relationship between the payer and the beneficial owner or between both of them and some other person, the amount of the interest, having regard to the debt-claim for which it is paid, exceeds the amount which would have been agreed upon by the payer and the beneficial owner in the absence of such relationship, the provisions of this Article shall apply only to the last-mentioned amount. In such case the excess part of the payments shall remain taxable according to the laws of each Contracting State, due regard being had to the other provisions of this Convention.

Notes: See Notes to Art. X:2 re "beneficial owner".

Definitions: "interest" — Art. XI:2; "person" — Art. III:1(e); "State" — Art. III:1(i).

Technical Explanation [2007 Protocol]: Paragraph 5 is identical to paragraph 7 of Article XI of the existing Convention.

Paragraph 5 provides that in cases involving special relationships between the payer and the beneficial owner of interest income or between both of them and some other person, Article XI applies only to that portion of the total interest payments that would have been made absent such special relationships (*i.e.*, an arm's-length interest payment). Any excess amount of interest paid remains taxable according to the laws of the United States and Canada, respectively, with due regard to the other provisions of the Convention.

6. Notwithstanding the provisions of paragraph 1:

(a) interest arising in the United States that is contingent interest of a type that does not qualify as portfolio interest under United States law may be taxed by the United States but, if the beneficial owner of the interest is a resident of Canada, the gross amount of the interest may be taxed at a rate not exceeding the rate prescribed in subparagraph (b) of paragraph 2 of Article X (Dividends);

(b) interest arising in Canada that is determined with reference to receipts, sales, income, profits or other cash flow of the debtor or a related person, to any change in the value of any property of the debtor or a related person or to any dividend, partnership distribution or similar payment made by the debtor to a related person may be taxed by Canada, and according to the laws of Canada, but if the beneficial owner is a resident of the United States, the gross amount of the interest may be taxed at a rate not exceeding the rate prescribed in subparagraph (b) of paragraph 2 of Article X (Dividends); and

(c) interest that is an excess inclusion with respect to a residual interest in a real estate mortgage investment conduit may be taxed by each State in accordance with its domestic law.

Related Provisions: ITA 12(1)(g) — Income based on production or use of property; ITA 212(1)(b), 212(3)"participating debt interest" — Withholding tax imposed by Canada; Art. XXI:2 — No withholding tax on interest payments to RRSP, RRIF or RPP.

Notes: For an example of 6(b) applying see VIEWS doc 2013-0494211I7 (interest computed by reference to a public commodity index) [Lamarre, "Participating Debt Interest and the Scope of Article XI(6)(b)", XIX(4) *Corporate Finance* (Federated Press) 2685-88 (2015)]. Para. 6(b) applies based on "each amount of interest paid or credited", so later non-participating interest payments are not tainted: 2019-0798741C6 [2019 IFA q.3].

See Notes to Art. X:2 re "beneficial owner".

Definitions: "arising" — Art. XI:4; "interest" — Art. XI:2; "person" — Art. III:1(e); "related" — ITCIA 3, ITA 251; "resident" — Art. IV; "State" — Art. III:1(i); "United States" — Art. III:1(b).

Technical Explanation [2007 Protocol]: New paragraph 6 provides anti-abuse exceptions to exclusive residence State taxation in paragraph 1 for two classes of interest payments.

The first class of interest, dealt with in subparagraphs 6(a) and 6(b), is so-called "contingent interest." With respect to interest arising in the United States, subparagraph 6(a) refers to contingent interest of a type that does not qualify as portfolio interest under U.S. domestic law. The cross-reference to the U.S. definition of contingent interest, which is found in Code section 871(h)(4), is intended to ensure that the exceptions of Code section 871(h)(4)(C) will apply. With respect to Canada, such interest is defined in subparagraph 6(b) as any interest arising in Canada that is determined by reference to the receipts, sales, income, profits or other cash flow of the debtor or a related person, to any change in the value of any property of the debtor or a related person or to any dividend, partnership distribution or similar payment made by the debtor or a related person.* Any such interest may be taxed in Canada according to the laws of Canada.

Under subparagraph 6(a) or 6(b), if the beneficial owner is a resident of the other Contracting State, the gross amount of the "contingent interest" may be taxed at a rate not exceeding 15%.

The second class of interest is dealt with in subparagraph 6(c). This exception is consistent with the policy of Code sections 860E(e) and 860G(b) that excess inclusions with respect to a real estate mortgage investment conduit (REMIC) should bear full U.S. tax in all cases. Without a full tax at source, foreign purchasers of residual interests would have a competitive advantage over U.S. purchasers at the time these interests are initially offered. Also, absent this rule, the U.S. fisc would suffer a revenue loss with respect to mortgages held in a REMIC because of opportunities for tax avoidance created by differences in the timing of taxable and economic income produced by these interests.

Therefore, subparagraph 6(c) provides a bilateral provision that interest that is an excess inclusion with respect to a residual interest in a REMIC may be taxed by each State in accordance with its domestic law. While the provision is written reciprocally,

at the time the Protocol was signed, the provision had no application in respect of Canadian-source interest, as Canada did not have REMICs.

*New subparagraph 6(b) of Article XI erroneously refers to a "similar payment made by the debtor to a related person." The correct formulation, which the Contracting States agree to apply, is "similar payment made by the debtor or a related person."

7. Where a resident of a Contracting State pays interest to a person other than a resident of the other Contracting State, that other State may not impose any tax on such interest except insofar as it arises in that other State or insofar as the debt-claim in respect of which the interest is paid is effectively connected with a permanent establishment situated in that other State.

Definitions: "arises" — Art. XI:4; "interest" — Art. XI:2; "permanent establishment" — Art. V; "person" — Art. III:1(e); "resident" — Art. IV; "State" — Art. III:1(i).

Technical Explanation [2007 Protocol]: Paragraph 7 is in all material respects the same as paragraph 8 of Article XI of the existing Convention. The only difference is that, consistent with the changes made in Article 9 of the Protocol, paragraph 7 removes the references to a fixed base.

Paragraph 7 restricts the right of a Contracting State to impose tax on interest paid by a resident of the other Contracting State. The first State may not impose any tax on such interest except insofar as the interest is paid to a resident of that State or arises in that State or the debt claim in respect of which the interest is paid is effectively connected with a permanent establishment situated in that State.

Relationship to other Articles

Notwithstanding the foregoing limitations on source State taxation of interest, the saving clause of paragraph 2 of Article XXIX (Miscellaneous Rules) permits the United States to tax its residents and citizens, subject to the special foreign tax credit rules of paragraph 5 of Article XXIV (Elimination of Double Taxation), as if the Convention had not come into force.

8, 9. [Repealed]

Article XII — Royalties

1. Royalties arising in a Contracting State and paid to a resident of the other Contracting State may be taxed in that other State.

Definitions: "arising" — Art. XII:6; "royalties" — Art. XII:4; "State" — Art. III:1(i).

Technical Explanation [1984]: Generally speaking, under the 1942 Convention royalties, including royalties with respect to motion picture films, which are derived by a resident of one Contracting State from sources within the other Contracting State are taxed at a maximum rate of 15% in the latter State; copyright royalties are exempt from tax in the State of source, if the resident does not have a permanent establishment in that State. See Articles II, III, XIII C, and paragraph 1 of Article XI of the 1942 Convention, and paragraph 6(a) of the Protocol to the 1942 Convention.

Paragraph 1 of Article XII of the Convention provides that a Contracting State may tax its residents with respect to royalties arising in the other Contracting State. Paragraph 2 provides that such royalties may also be taxed in the Contracting State in which they arise, but that if a resident of the other Contracting State is the beneficial owner of the royalties the tax in the Contracting State of source is limited to 10% of the gross amount of the royalties.

2. However, such royalties may also be taxed in the Contracting State in which they arise, and according to the laws of that State; but if a resident of the other Contracting State is the beneficial owner of such royalties, the tax so charged shall not exceed 10 per cent of the gross amount of the royalties.

Related Provisions: ITA 212(1)(d) — Withholding tax on royalties; ITA 212(3.9)–(3.94) — Back-to-back rules; Art. XXIX-A — Limitation on benefits.

Notes: For the meaning of "resident" in this context, see Art. IV:1 Notes. For "beneficial owner", see Art. X:2 Notes.

See also Jovicic et al., "Blurred Lines: Cross-Border Rents and Royalties", 2013 Cdn Tax Foundation annual conference report, 22:1-36.

Definitions: "arise" — Art. XII:6; "royalties" — Art. XII:4; "State" — Art. III:1(i).

I.T. Technical News: 23 (computer software).

Forms: NR301: Declaration of eligibility for benefits under a tax treaty for a non-resident taxpayer.

Technical Explanation [1984]: See Article XII, para. 1.

3. Notwithstanding the provisions of paragraph 2,

(a) copyright royalties and other like payments in respect of the production or reproduction of any literary, dramatic, musical or artistic work (other than payments in respect of motion pictures and works on film, videotape or other means of reproduction for use in connection with television);

(b) payments for the use of, or the right to use, computer software;

(c) payments for the use of, or the right to use, any patent or any information concerning industrial, commercial or scientific experience (but not including any such information provided in connection with a rental or franchise agreement); and

(d) payments with respect to broadcasting as may be agreed for the purposes of this paragraph in an exchange of notes between the Contracting States;

arising in a Contracting State and beneficially owned by a resident of the other Contracting State shall be taxable only in that other State.

Notes: See Notes to ITA 212(1)(d) re 212(1)(d)(vi), which provides the same rule as 3(a) for Canadian withholding tax generally.

Fifth Protocol (2007), Annex B, states:

8. Royalties — information in connection with franchise agreement

It is understood that the reference in subparagraph 3(c) of Article XII (Royalties) of the Convention to information provided in connection with a franchise agreement shall generally refer only to information that governs or otherwise deals with the operation (whether by the payer or by another person) of the franchise, and not to other information concerning industrial, commercial or scientific experience that is held for resale or license.

For a thorough overview of these rules, see Catherine Brown, "The 1995 Canada-US Protocol: The Scope of the New Royalty Provisions", 43(3) *Canadian Tax Journal* 592-609 (1995). For a ruling approving the exemption under 3(a) see VIEWS doc 2011-0416891R3; under 3(c), see 2008-0284551R3, 2012-0457951E5. See also 2011-0431871I7 (procurement licence fee under franchise agreement); 2013-0475751E5 (general comments); 2013-0494251E5 (3(c) can exempt the income stream from sale of a client list [presumably as "information concerning commercial experience"]).

Copyright royalties for production and reproduction of motion pictures and other works for private home use are exempt under para. 3, but this is based on the 1984 Technical Explanation, and similar treaty wording does *not* give rise to exemption under the treaties with the UK, France and Thailand in CRA's view: doc 2010-0374421E5. See also 2011-0392761E5 re film distribution royalties.

For "treaty shopping" using this provision see also Notes to Art. X:2 and XXIX-A:1.

Art. XII:3 amended by 1995 Protocol (effectively to add paras. (b)–(d)), effective for amounts paid or credited in 1996 or later.

Definitions: "arising" — Art. XII:6; "royalties" — Art. XII:4.

I.T. Technical News: 23 (computer software).

Technical Explanation [1995 Protocol]: Article 7 of the Protocol modifies Article XII (Royalties) of the Convention by expanding the classes of royalties exempt from withholding of tax at source. Paragraph 3, as amended by the Protocol, identifies four classes of royalty payments arising in one Contracting State and beneficially owned by a resident of the other that are exempt at source: (1) subparagraph (a) preserves the exemption in paragraph 3 of the present Convention for copyright royalties in respect of literary and other works, other than certain such payments in respect of motion pictures, videotapes, and similar payments; (2) subparagraph (b) specifies that computer software royalties are also exempt; (3) subparagraph (c) adds royalties paid for the use of, or the right to use, patents and information concerning industrial, commercial, and scientific experience, other than payments in connection with rental or franchise agreements; and (4) subparagraph (d) allows the Contracting States to reach an agreement, through an exchange of diplomatic notes, with respect to the application of paragraph 3 of Article XII to payments in respect of certain live broadcasting transmissions.

The specific reference to software in subparagraph (b) is not intended to suggest that the United States views the term "copyright" as excluding software in other U.S. treaties (including the current treaty with Canada).

The negotiators agreed that royalties paid for the use of, or the right to use, designs or models, plans, secret formulas, or processes are included under subparagraph 3(c) to the extent that they represent payments for the use of, or the right to use, information concerning industrial, commercial, or scientific experience. In addition, they agreed that royalties paid for the use of, or the right to use, "know-how," as defined in paragraph 11 of the Commentary on Article 12 of the OECD Model Income Tax Treaty, constitute payments for the use of, or the right to use, information concerning industrial, commercial, or scientific experience. The negotiators further agreed that a royalty paid under a "mixed contract," package fee," or similar arrangement will be treated as exempt at source by virtue of paragraph 3 to the extent of any portion that is paid for the use of, or the right to use, property or information with respect to which paragraph 3 grants an exemption.

The exemption granted under subparagraph 3(c) does not, however, extend to payments made for information concerning industrial, commercial, or scientific experience that is provided in connection with a rental or franchise agreement. For this purpose, the negotiators agreed that a franchise is to be distinguished from other arrangements resulting

in the transfer of intangible property. They agreed that a license to use intangibles (whether or not including a trademark) in a territory, in and of itself, would not constitute a franchise agreement for purposes of subparagraph 3(c) in the absence of other rights and obligations in the license agreement or in any other agreement that would indicate that the arrangement in its totality constituted a franchise agreement. For example, a resident of one Contracting State may acquire a right to use a secret formula to manufacture a particular product (e.g., a perfume), together with the right to use a trademark for that product and to market it at a non-retail level, in the other Contracting State. Such an arrangement would not constitute a franchise in the absence of any other rights or obligations under that arrangement or any other agreement that would indicate that the arrangement in its totality constituted a franchise agreement. Therefore, the royalty payment under that arrangement would be exempt from withholding tax in the other Contracting State to the extent made for the use of, or the right to use, the secret formula or other information concerning industrial, commercial, or scientific experience; however, it would be subject to withholding tax at a rate of 10%, to the extent made for the use of, or the right to use, the trademark.

The provisions of paragraph 3 do not fully reflect the U.S. treaty policy of exempting all types of royalty payments from taxation at source, but Canada was not prepared to grant a complete exemption for all types of royalties in the Protocol. Although the Protocol makes several important changes to the royalty provisions of the present Convention in the direction of bringing Article XII into conformity with U.S. policy, the United States remains concerned about the imposition of withholding tax on some classes of royalties and about the associated administrative burdens. In this connection, the Contracting States have affirmed their intention to collaborate to resolve in good faith any administrative issues that may arise in applying the provisions of subparagraph 3(c). The United States intends to continue to pursue a zero rate of withholding for all royalties in future negotiations with Canada, including discussions under Article 20 of the Protocol, as well as in negotiations with other countries.

As noted above, new subparagraph 3(d) enables the Contracting States to provide an exemption for royalties paid with respect to broadcasting through an exchange of notes. This provision was included because Canada was not prepared at the time of the negotiations to commit to an exemption for broadcasting royalties. Subparagraph 3(d) was included to enable the Senate to give its advice and consent in advance to such an exemption, in the hope that such an exemption could be obtained without awaiting the negotiation of another full protocol. Any agreement reached under the exchange of notes authorized by subparagraph 3(d) would lower the withholding rate from 10% to zero and, thus, bring the Convention into greater conformity with established U.S. treaty policy.

Technical Explanation [1984]: Paragraph 3 provides that, notwithstanding paragraph 2, copyright royalties and other like payments in respect of the production or reproduction of any literary, dramatic, musical, or artistic work, including royalties from such works on videotape or other means of reproduction for private (home) use, if beneficially owned by a resident of the other Contracting State, may not be taxed by the Contracting State of source. This exemption at source does not apply to royalties in respect of motion pictures, and of works on film, videotape or other means of reproduction for use in connection with television broadcasting. Such royalties are subject to tax at a maximum rate of 10% in the Contracting State in which they arise, as provided in paragraph 2 (unless the provisions of paragraph 5, described below, apply).

4. The term **"royalties"** as used in this Article means payments of any kind received as a consideration for the use of, or the right to use, any copyright of literary, artistic or scientific work (including motion pictures and works on film, videotape or other means of reproduction for use in connection with television), any patent, trade mark, design or model, plan, secret formula or process, or for the use of, or the right to use, tangible personal property or for information concerning industrial, commercial or scientific experience, and, notwithstanding the provisions of Article XIII (Gains), includes gains from the alienation of any intangible property or rights described in this paragraph to the extent that such gains are contingent on the productivity, use or subsequent disposition of such property or rights.

Notes: Oil royalty payments are not considered "royalties" under this definition but fall under Art. VI:2 and are fully taxed: VIEWS doc 2011-0431571E5. Fees for advertising on a US website are not "royalties" and are thus exempt under Art. VII:1 if the USCo has no PE in Canada: 2011-0416181E5. See also Notes to ITA 212(1)(d); "literary, dramatic, musical and artistic" royalties are exempt under 212(1)(d)(vi), though ITA 212(5) taxes film and TV show royalties.

Definitions: "property" — ITCIA 3, ITA 248(1).

I.T. Technical News: 23 (computer software); 25 (e-commerce — payments for digital products not royalties).

Technical Explanation [1984]: Paragraph 4 defines the term "royalties" for purposes of Article XII. "Royalties" means payments of any kind received as consideration for the use of or the right to use any copyright of literary, artistic, or scientific work, including motion pictures, and works on film, videotape or other means of reproduction for use in connection with television broadcasting, any patent, trademark, design or model, plan, secret formula or process, or any payment for the use of or the right to use tangible personal property or for information concerning industrial, commercial, or scientific experience. The term "royalties" also includes gains from the alienation of any intangible property or rights described in paragraph 4 to the extent that such gains are contingent on the productivity, use, or subsequent disposition of such intangible property or rights. Thus, a guaranteed minimum payment derived from the alienation of (but not the use of) any right or property described in paragraph 4 is not a "royalty." Any amounts deemed contingent on use by reason of Code section 871(e) are, however, royalties under paragraph 2 of Article III (General Definitions), subject to Article XXVI (Mutual Agreement Procedure). The term "royalties" does not encompass management fees, which are covered by the provisions of Article VII (Business Profits) or XIV (Independent Personal Services), or payments under a bona fide cost-sharing arrangement. Technical service fees may be royalties in cases where the fees are periodic and dependent upon productivity or a similar measure.

5. The provisions of paragraphs 2 and 3 shall not apply if the beneficial owner of the royalties, being a resident of a Contracting State, carries on, or has carried on, business in the other Contracting State in which the royalties arise, through a permanent establishment situated therein, and the right or property in respect of which the royalties are paid is effectively connected to such permanent establishment. In such case the provisions of Article VII (Business Profits) shall apply.

Notes: See Notes to Art. VII:2 re the words "or has carried on".

Para. XII:5 amended by 2007 Protocol, generally for tax years beginning after 2008.

Definitions: "arise" — Art. XII:6; "business" — ITCIA 3, ITA 248(1); "permanent establishment" — Art. V:1; "property" — ITCIA 3, ITA 248(1); "resident" — Art. IV; "royalties" — Art. XII:4; "State" — Art. III:1(i).

Technical Explanation [2007 Protocol]: Article 7 of the Protocol amends Article XII (Royalties) of the existing Convention. As with other benefits of the Convention, the benefits of Article XII are available to a resident of a Contracting State only if that resident is entitled to those benefits under the provisions of Article XXIX A (Limitation on Benefits).

See the Technical Explanation for new paragraphs 6 and 7 of Article IV (Residence) for discussion regarding the interaction between domestic law concepts of beneficial ownership and the treaty rules to determine when a person is considered to derive an item of income for purposes of obtaining benefits of the Convention such as withholding rate reductions.

Paragraph 1 of Article 7 of the Protocol replaces paragraph 5 of Article XII of the Convention. In all material respects, new paragraph 5 is the same as paragraph 5 of Article XII of the existing Convention. However, new paragraph 5 adds clarifying language consistent with the changes made in Articles 4, 5, and 6 of the Protocol with respect to income attributable to a permanent establishment that has ceased to exist. To conform with Article 9 of the Protocol, which deletes Article XIV (Independent Personal Services) of the Convention, paragraph 1 of Article 7 of the Protocol also amends paragraph 5 of Article XII by omitting the reference to a "fixed base."

New paragraph 5 provides that the 10% limitation on tax in the source State provided by paragraph 2, and the exemption in the source State for certain royalties provided by paragraph 3, do not apply if the beneficial owner of the royalties carries on or has carried on business in the source State through a permanent establishment and the right or property in respect of which the royalties are paid is attributable to such permanent establishment. In such case, the royalty income would be taxable by the source State under the provisions of Article VII (Business Profits).

Technical Explanation [1984]: Paragraph 5 provides that the 10% limitation on tax in the Contracting State of source provided by paragraph 2, and the exemption in the Contracting State of source for certain copyright royalties provided by paragraph 3, do not apply if the beneficial owner of the royalties carries on business in the State of source through a permanent establishment or fixed base and the right or property in respect of which the royalties are paid is effectively connected with such permanent establishment or fixed base (i.e., the royalties are attributable to the permanent establishment or fixed base). In that event, the royalty income would be taxable under the provisions of Article VII (Business Profits) or XIV (Independent Personal Services), as the case may be.

6. For the purposes of this Article,

(a) royalties shall be deemed to arise in a Contracting State when the payer is a resident of that State. Where, however, the person paying the royalties, whether he is a resident of a Contracting State or not, has in a State a permanent establishment in connection with which the obligation to pay the royalties was incurred, and such royalties are borne by such permanent establishment, then such royalties shall be deemed to arise in the State in which the permanent establishment is situated and not in any other State of which the payer is a resident; and

(b) where subparagraph (a) does not operate to treat royalties as arising in either Contracting State and the royalties are for the use of, or the right to use, intangible property or tangible personal property in a Contracting State, then such royalties shall be deemed to arise in that State.

Notes: Where Art. XII:6(a) deems royalty payments to arise in the US (but not elsewhere), the CRA will consider them to be "other income" under Art. XXII:1, so that Canada cannot impose non-resident withholding tax: VIEWS doc 2006-0188131E5.

Art. XII:6(a) amended by 2007 Protocol, for tax years beginning after 2008, but in respect of taxes withheld at source, for amounts paid or credited after Jan. 2009.

Art. XII:6 amended by 1995 Protocol, for amounts paid or credited after 1995.

Definitions: "permanent establishment" — Art. V:1; "person" — Art. III:1(e), ITCIA 3, *Interpretation Act* 35(1); "property" — ITCIA 3, ITA 248(1); "resident" — Art. IV; "royalties" — Art. XII:4; "State" — Art. III:1(i).

Technical Explanation [2007 Protocol]: Paragraph 2 of Article 7 of the Protocol sets forth a new subparagraph 6(a) of Article XII that is in all material respects the same as subparagraph 6(a) of Article XII of the existing Convention. The only difference is that, consistent with the changes made in Article 9 of the Protocol, new subparagraph 6(a) omits references to a "fixed base."

Technical Explanation [1995 Protocol]: Paragraph 2 of Article 7 of the Protocol amends the rules in paragraph 6 of Article XII of the Convention for determining the source of royalty payments. Under the present Convention, royalties generally are deemed to arise in a Contracting State if paid by a resident of that State. However, if the obligation to pay the royalties was incurred in connection with a permanent establishment or a fixed base in one of the Contracting States that bears the expense, the royalties are deemed to arise in that State.

The Protocol continues to apply these basic rules but changes the scope of an exception provided under the present Convention. Under the present Convention, a royalty paid for the use of, or the right to use, property in a Contracting State is deemed to arise in that State. Under the Protocol, this "place of use" exception applies only if the Convention does not otherwise deem the royalties to arise in one of the Contracting States. Thus, the "place of use" exception will apply only if royalties are neither paid by a resident of one of the Contracting States nor borne by a permanent establishment or fixed base in either State. For example, if a Canadian resident were to grant franchise rights to a resident of Chile for use in the United States, the royalty paid by the Chilean resident to the Canadian resident for those rights would be U.S. source income under this Article, subject to U.S. withholding at the 10% rate provided in paragraph 2.

The rules of this Article differ from those provided under U.S. domestic law. Under U.S. domestic law, a royalty is considered to be from U.S. sources if it is paid for the use of, or the privilege of using, an intangible within the United States; the residence of the payor is irrelevant. If paid to a nonresident alien individual or other foreign person, a U.S. source royalty is generally subject to withholding tax at a rate of 30% under U.S. domestic law. By reason of paragraph 1 of Article XXIX (Miscellaneous Rules), a Canadian resident would be permitted to apply the rules of U.S. domestic law to its royalty income if those rules produced a more favorable result in its case than those of this Article. However, under a basic principle of tax treaty interpretation recognized by both Contracting States, the prohibition against so-called "cherry-picking," the Canadian resident would be precluded from claiming selected benefits under the Convention (e.g., the tax rates only) and other benefits under U.S. domestic law (e.g., the source rules only) with respect to its royalties. See, e.g., Rev. Rul. 84-17, 1984-1 C.B. 308. For example, if a Canadian company granted franchise rights to a resident of the United States for use 50% in the United States and 50% in Chile, the Convention would permit the Canadian company to treat all of its royalty income from that single transaction as U.S. source income entitled to the withholding tax reduction under paragraph 2. U.S. domestic law would permit the Canadian company to treat 50% of its royalty income as U.S. source income subject to a 30% withholding tax and the other 50% as foreign source income exempt from U.S. tax. The Canadian company could choose to apply either the provisions of U.S. domestic law or the provisions of the Convention to the transaction, but would not be permitted to claim both the U.S. domestic law exemption for 50% of the income and the Convention's reduced withholding rate for the remainder of the income.

Royalties generally are considered borne by a permanent establishment or fixed base if they are deductible in computing the taxable income of that permanent establishment or fixed base.

Since the definition of "resident" of a Contracting State in Article IV (Residence), as amended by Article 3 of the Protocol, specifies that this term includes the Contracting States and their political subdivisions and local authorities, the source rule does not include a specific reference to these governmental entities.

Technical Explanation [1984]: Paragraph 6 establishes rules to determine the source of royalties for purposes of Article XII. The first rule is that royalties arise in a Contracting State when the payer is that State, or a political subdivision, local authority, or resident of that State. Notwithstanding that rule, royalties arise not in the State of the payer's residence but in any State, whether or not a Contracting State, in which is situated a permanent establishment or fixed base in connection with which the obligation to pay royalties was incurred, if such royalties are borne by such permanent establishment or fixed base. Thus, royalties paid to a resident of the United States by a company resident in Canada for the use of property in a third State will not be subject to tax in Canada if the obligation to pay the royalties is incurred in connection with, and the royalties are borne by, a permanent establishment of the company in a third State. "Borne by" means allowable as a deduction in computing taxable income.

A third rule, which overrides both the residence rule and the permanent establishment rule just described, provides that royalties for the use of, or the right to use, intangible property or tangible personal property in a Contracting State arise in that State. Thus, consistent with the provisions of Code section 861(a)(4), if a resident of a third State pays royalties to a resident of Canada for the use of or the right to use intangible property or tangible personal property in the United States, such royalties are considered to arise in the United States and are subject to taxation by the United States consistent with the Convention. Similarly, if a resident of Canada pays royalties to a resident of a third State, such royalties are considered to arise in the United States and are subject to U.S. taxation if they are for the use of or the right to use intangible property or tangible personal property in the United States. The term "intangible property" encompasses all the items described in paragraph 4, other than tangible personal property.

7. Where, by reason of a special relationship between the payer and the beneficial owner or between both of them and some other person, the amount of the royalties, having regard to the use, right or information for which they are paid, exceeds the amount which would have been agreed upon by the payer and the beneficial owner in the absence of such relationship, the provisions of this Article shall apply only to the last-mentioned amount. In such case, the excess part of the payments shall remain taxable according to the laws of each Contracting State, due regard being had to the other provisions of this Convention.

Related Provisions: ITA 247 — Transfer pricing adjustments.

Definitions: "person" — Art. III:1(e), ITCIA 3, *Interpretation Act* 35(1); "royalties" — Art. XII:4.

Technical Explanation [1984]: Paragraph 7 provides that in cases involving special relationships between persons the benefits of Article XII do not apply to amounts in excess of the amount which would have been agreed upon between persons with no special relationship; any such excess amount remains taxable according to the laws of Canada and the United States, consistent with any relevant provisions of the Convention.

8. Where a resident of a Contracting State pays royalties to a person other than a resident of the other Contracting State, that other State may not impose any tax on such royalties except insofar as they arise in that other State or insofar as the right or property in respect of which the royalties are paid is effectively connected with a permanent establishment situated in that other State.

Notes: Art. XII:8 amended by 2007 Protocol to change "permanent establishment or a fixed base" to "permanent establishment", effective for taxable years beginning after 2008, but in respect of taxes withheld at source, for amounts paid or credited after Jan. 2009.

Definitions: "arise" — Art. XII:6; "permanent establishment" — Art. V:1; "person" — Art. III:1(e), ITCIA 3, *Interpretation Act* 35(1); "property" — ITCIA 3, ITA 248(1); "resident" — Art. IV; "royalties" — Art. XII:4; "State" — Art. III:1(i).

Technical Explanation [2007 Protocol]: Paragraph 3 of Article 7 of Protocol amends paragraph 8 of Article XII of the Convention to remove references to a "fixed base." In addition, paragraph 8 of the General Note confirms the intent of the Contracting States that the reference in subparagraph 3(c) of Article XII of the Convention to information provided in connection with a franchise agreement generally refers only to information that governs or otherwise deals with the operation (whether by the payer or by another person) of the franchise, and not to other information concerning industrial, commercial or scientific experience that is held for resale or license.

Technical Explanation [1984]: Paragraph 8 restricts the right of a Contracting State to impose tax on royalties paid by a resident of the other Contracting State. The first State may not impose any tax on such royalties except insofar as they arise in that State or they are paid to a resident of that State or the right or property in respect of which the royalties are paid is effectively connected with a permanent establishment or fixed base situated in that State. This rule parallels the rule in paragraph 8 of Article XI (Interest) and paragraph 5 of Article X (Dividends). Again, U.S. citizens remain subject to U.S. taxation on royalties received despite this rule, by virtue of paragraph 2 of Article XXIX (Miscellaneous Rules).

Information Circulars [Art. XII]: 77-16R4: Non-resident income tax.

Article XIII — Gains

1. Gains derived by a resident of a Contracting State from the alienation of real property situated in the other Contracting State may be taxed in that other State.

Related Provisions: ITA 115(1)(b) — Tax on disposition of taxable Canadian property; ITA 126(2.21), (2.22) — Foreign tax credit to emigrant for tax payable on gain accrued while resident in Canada; ITA 128.1(4)(b)(i) — Real property in Canada excluded from deemed disposition on emigration.

Notes: *Canadian residents holding US real property*: FIRPTA (*Foreign Investment Real Property Tax Act*) imposes 15% US withholding tax on the gross sale proceeds of US real property or of an interest in a US corp whose value is primarily US real pro-

perty (there are some exceptions). The vendor must also report and pay US tax on the gain; the FIRPTA withholding is offset against this tax. There is an exemption for a residence valued up to US$300,000 (*Internal Revenue Code* §1445(b)(5), Reg. 1.445-2(d)(i)), and a reduced 10% rate for a value up to $1m (§1445(c)(4), Reg. 1.445-2(b)(2)), both only if the purchaser plans to use the property as a residence for certain minimum periods. (FIRPTA also applies at up to 21% to some distributions made by corporations, estates, partnerships or trusts: §1445(e).)

See Wise & Naish, "US Real Property Gains of Foreign Persons: An Overview for the Canadian Tax Practitioner", 51(1) *Canadian Tax Journal* 669-98 (2003); Ibrahim et al., "Ownership of US Residential Property by Canadian Residents", 2005 Cdn Tax Foundation conference report, 7:1-27; Bernstein, "Canadians and US Real Estate", 14(9) *Canadian Tax Highlights [CTH]* (ctf.ca) 8-9 (Sept. 2006), "Residence Trusts", 16(8) 9-10 (Aug. 2008) and "Investing in US Realty", 21(11) 7-8 (Nov. 2013); Ibrahim et al., "Canadians Purchasing US Real Estate", 2012 conference report, 39:1-33; Nelson, "US Tax: US Real Estate", 22(6) *CTH* 9-11 (June 2014); Gluc, "US Tax Reform and US Real Estate", 26(10) *CTH* 1-2 (Oct. 2018); Kerzner, "New US Tax Challenges for Cross-Border Real Estate Investments", 11(4) *Taxes & Wealth Management [TWM]* (Carswell) 1-3 (Nov. 2018); Bercovici, "What You Need to Know About FIRPTA", 11(4) *TWM* 4-7; Castillo & Kirkpatrick, "Canadians looking to sell US real estate", tinyurl.com/moodys-usre (May 2020); Tippett, "Seller Beware: Tax Issues for Canadian Residents Selling US Real Estate", 2020(21) *Tax Times* (Carswell) 1-2 (Nov. 6, 2020). See also ITA 70(5) Notes at "US tax" re US estate tax; and to ITA 15(1) under "Where a single-purpose corporation" re US vacation properties.

A company that owns Florida real property and has had a change in control must notify the county property appraiser on Form DR-430: Florida Statutes §193.1554-1555.

Definitions: "real property situated in the other Contracting State" — Art. XIII:3; "resident" — Art. IV; "State" — Art. III:1(i).

Technical Explanation [1984]: Paragraph 1 provides that Canada and the United States may each tax gains from the alienation of real property situated within that State which are derived by a resident of the other Contracting State. The term "real property situated in the other Contracting State" is defined for this purpose in paragraph 3 of this article. The term "alienation" used in paragraph 1 and other paragraphs of Article XIII means sales, exchanges and other dispositions or deemed dispositions (e.g., change of use, gifts, distributions, death) that are taxable events under the taxation laws of the Contracting State applying the provisions of the Article.

2. Gains from the alienation of personal property forming part of the business property of a permanent establishment which a resident of a Contracting State has or had (within the twelve-month period preceding the date of alienation) in the other Contracting State, including such gains from the alienation of such a permanent establishment, may be taxed in that other State.

Notes: Art. XIII:2 amended by 2007 Protocol, generally effective for taxable years beginning after 2008.

Definitions: "permanent establishment" — Art. V:1; "property" — ITCIA 3, ITA 248(1); "resident" — Art. IV; "State" — Art. III:1(i).

Technical Explanation [2007 Protocol]: Paragraph 1 of Article 8 of the Protocol replaces paragraph 2 of Article XIII (Gains) of the existing Convention. Consistent with Article 9 of the Protocol, new paragraph 2 does not contain any reference to property pertaining to a fixed base or to the performance of independent personal services.

New paragraph 2 of Article XIII provides that the Contracting State in which a resident of the other Contracting State has or had a permanent establishment may tax gains from the alienation of personal property constituting business property if such gains are attributable to such permanent establishment. Unlike paragraph 1 of Article VII(Business Profits), paragraph 2 limits the right of the source State to tax such gains to a twelve-month period following the termination of the permanent establishment.

Technical Explanation [1984]: Paragraph 2 of Article XIII provides that the Contracting State in which a resident of the other Contracting State "has or had" a permanent establishment or fixed base may tax gains from the alienation of personal property constituting business property if such gains are attributable to such permanent establishment or fixed base. Unlike paragraph 1 of Article VII (Business Profits), paragraph 2 limits the right of the source State to tax such gains to a twelve-month period following the termination of the permanent establishment or fixed base.

3. For the purposes of this Article the term **"real property situated in the other Contracting State"**

    (a) in the case of real property situated in the United States, means a United States real property interest and real property referred to in Article VI (Income from Real Property) situated in the United States, but does not include a share of the capital stock of a company that is not a resident of the United States; and

    (b) in the case of real property situated in Canada means:

        (i) real property referred to in Article VI (Income from Real Property) situated in Canada;

(ii) a share of the capital stock of a company that is a resident of Canada, the value of whose shares is derived principally from real property situated in Canada; and

(iii) an interest in a partnership, trust or estate, the value of which is derived principally from real property situated in Canada.

Related Provisions: ITCIA 5 — Definition of "real property".

Notes: For CRA interpretation of 3(b)(ii), see VIEWS docs 2003-0029675 (whether to use gross asset valuation method); 2004-0055901R3 (leasehold interest in land in Canada is "real property (RP) situated in Canada"); 2011-0416521E5 ("share" does not include an option to acquire a share [Hickey, "Realtyco Share Option Not a Share for Canada-US Treaty", 20(10) *Canadian Tax Highlights* (ctf.ca) *[CTH]* 9 (Oct. 2012)]); 2013-0516151I7 (Canada can tax gain on shares of corporation that owns Canadian RP through partnership [Cepparo, "Treaty Looks Through Partnership to Realty", 22(10) *CTH* 13 (Oct. 2014)]); 2014-0542551E5, 2016-0658431E5 (cash from disposing of RP is not considered "derived" from RP). See also docs on this rule in other treaties: 2007-0259991E5 (Japan), 2008-030441I7 (Israel), 2011-0397191I7 (Germany), 2016-0668041E5 (UK).

See also Lindsey et al, "US Investment in Canadian Resource Property", XVI(3) *International Tax Planning* (Federated Press) 1124-28 (2011).

Para. 3(a) amended by 1997 Protocol to add everything from "but does not include ...", and subpara. 3(b)(ii) amended to add "that is a resident of Canada", both amendments effective April 26, 1995.

Definitions: "Canada" — Art. III:1(a), ITCIA 5; "company" — Art. III:1(f); "estate" — ITCIA 3, ITA 248(1); "real property" — Art. VI:2, ITCIA 5; "resident" — Art. IV; "share" — Art. IV, ITA 248(1); "trust" — ITCIA 3, ITA 104(1), 248(1); "United States" — Art. III:1(b).

Technical Explanation [1997]: Article 1 of the Protocol amends paragraph 3 of Article XIII (Gains) of the Convention. Paragraph 1 of Article XIII of the Convention provides that gains derived by a resident of a Contracting State from the alienation of real property situated within the other Contracting State may be taxed in that other State. The term "real property situated in the other Contracting State" is defined for this purpose in paragraph 3 of Article XIII of the Convention.

Under paragraph 3(a) of Article XIII of the Convention, real property situated in the United States includes real property (as defined in Article VI (Income from Real Property)) of the Convention) situated in the United States and a United States real property interest. Under section 897(c) of the *Internal Revenue Code* (the "Code") the term "United States real property interest" includes shares in a U.S. corporation that owns sufficient U.S. real property interests to satisfy an asset-ratio test on certain testing dates.

Under Paragraph 3(b) of Article XIII of the Convention, real property situated in Canada means real property (as defined in Article VI of the Convention) situated in Canada; shares of stock of a company, the value of whose shares consists principally of Canadian real property; and an interest in a partnership, trust or estate, the value of which consists principally of Canadian real property. The term "principally" means more than 50%.

Under the Code, stock of a foreign corporation is not considered a "United States real property interest." Therefore, the United States does not tax a resident of Canada on the sale of stock of a foreign corporation, regardless of the composition of the corporation's assets. Although the Convention permits Canada to tax a U.S. resident on the sale of stock of a company that is not a resident of Canada if the value of the company's shares consists principally of Canadian real property, Canada does not currently impose such a tax. However, on April 26, 1995, amendments were proposed to the Canadian Income Tax Act that would impose Canadian income tax on gains realized on stock of certain companies that are not residents of Canada if (i) more than 50% of the fair market value of all of the company's properties consists of any combination of taxable Canadian property, Canadian resource property, timber resource property in Canada and income interests in Canadian trusts, and (ii) more than 50% of the fair market value of the shares in question is derived directly or indirectly from any combination of real property located in Canada, Canadian resource property, and timber resource property in Canada. [See ITA 115(1)(b) — ed.] This amendment is proposed to be effective as of April 26, 1995 with proration for gains that accrued before that date. Although the Canadian Parliament was dissolved before these amendments were passed, they are expected to be re-introduced in the current session with the same effective date.

The Protocol amends paragraphs 3(a) and 3(b)(ii) of Article XIII of the Convention to limit each State's right to tax the gains of a resident of the other State from the sale of stock of a real property holding company to cases where the company is resident in that State. Although the United States does not impose and is not currently considering imposing a tax under the Code on gains from the sale of stock of non-resident real property holding companies, the Protocol nevertheless amends the Convention to prohibit the imposition of such a tax on Canadian residents. Although Canada is considering imposing such a tax on gains from the sale of shares of companies that are not residents of Canada, this Protocol provision will cause the proposed amendments to the Canadian *Income Tax Act* to be inapplicable to U.S. residents who derive gains from the sale of stock of real property holding companies that are not residents of Canada. This provision will be retroactively effective to April 26, 1995, the date the previous Canadian legislation was proposed to be effective.

Technical Explanation [1984]: Paragraph 3 provides a definition of the term "real property situated in the other Contracting State." Where the United States is the other Contracting State, the term includes real property (as defined in Article VI (Income from Real Property)) situated in the United States and a United States real property interest. Thus, the United States retains the ability to exercise its full taxing right under the *Foreign Investment in Real Property Tax Act* (Code section 897). (For a transition rule from the 1942 Convention, see paragraph 9 of this Article).

Where Canada is the other Contracting State, the term means real property (as defined in Article VI) situated in Canada; shares of stock of a company, the value of whose shares consists principally of Canadian real property; and an interest in a partnership, trust or estate, the value of which consists principally of Canadian real property. The term "principally" means more than 50%. Taxation in Canada is preserved through several tiers of entities if the value of the company's shares or the partnership, trust or estate is ultimately dependent principally upon real property situated in Canada.

4. Gains from the alienation of any property other than that referred to in paragraphs 1, 2 and 3 shall be taxable only in the Contracting State of which the alienator is a resident.

Related Provisions: ITA 248(1)"treaty-protected property" — Property whose gain is not subject to Canadian tax because of treaty.

Notes: Although shares of a corp whose value is primarily real property in Canada are "taxable Canadian property" (TCP; ITA 248(1)), Canada often cannot tax gains on such shares realized by a resident of a treaty country, due to this rule in other treaties (e.g., VIEWS docs 2011-0403291R3, 2013-0477241R3), but can under this treaty due to Art. XIII:3(b)(ii). See also Art. VI:2 Notes on the meaning of "real property".

Para. 4 overrides ITA 115(1)(b) for persons resident in the U.S. under the treaty tie-breaker rules (Art. IV). It also applies to a disposition of TCP by a US partnership that has elected to be treated as a corp for US tax purposes: VIEWS docs 2004-0109171E5, 2005-0140221R3, 2005-0155811R3, 2008-0272141R3.

See also doc 2013-051615117 [Cepparo, "Treaty Looks Through Partnership to Realty", 22(10) *Canadian Tax Highlights* (ctf.ca) 13 (Oct. 2014)].

In *MIL (Investments)*, 2007 FCA 236, a capital gain on Canadian public company shares was avoided when a corp transferred its residence to Luxembourg and claimed treaty protection.

Definitions: "property" — ITCIA 3, ITA 248(1); "resident" — Art. IV.

Advance Tax Rulings: ATR-43: Utilization of a non-resident-owned investment corporation as a holding corporation. However, see para. 5 below.

Technical Explanation [1984]: Paragraph 4 reserves to the Contracting State of residence the sole right to tax gains from the alienation of any property other than property referred to in paragraphs 1, 2, and 3.

5. The provisions of paragraph 4 shall not affect the right of a Contracting State to levy, according to its domestic law, a tax on gains from the alienation of any property derived by an individual who is a resident of the other Contracting State if:

(a) the individual was a resident of the first-mentioned State:

(i) for at least 120 months during any period of 20 consecutive years preceding the alienation of the property; and

(ii) at any time during the 10 years immediately preceding the alienation of the property; and

(b) the property (or property for which such property was substituted in an alienation the gain on which was not recognized for the purposes of taxation in the first-mentioned State):

(i) was owned by the individual at the time the individual ceased to be a resident of the first-mentioned State; and

(ii) was not a property that the individual was treated as having alienated by reason of ceasing to be a resident of the first-mentioned State and becoming a resident of the other Contracting State.

Notes: For discussion of the 2007 Protocol amendment, see Dept. of Finance news release 2007-070 (Sept. 21, 2007) on fin.gc.ca, under "Taxpayer migration — protection against double taxation".

Art. XIII:5 amended by 2007 Protocol, effective with respect to alienations of property that occur (including, for greater certainty, those deemed under the law of a Contracting State to occur) after Sept. 17, 2000.

Definitions: "individual", "property" — ITCIA 3, ITA 248(1); "resident" — Art. IV; "State" — Art. III:1(i); "substituted" — ITA 248(5).

Technical Explanation [2007 Protocol]: Paragraph 2 of Article 8 of the Protocol replaces paragraph 5 of Article XIII of the existing Convention. In general, new paragraph 5 provides an exception to the general rule stated in paragraph 4 that gains from the alienation of any property, other than property referred to in paragraphs 1, 2, and 3, shall be taxable only in the Contracting State of which the alienator is a resident. Paragraph 5 provides that a Contracting State may, according to its domestic law, impose tax on gains derived by an individual who is a resident of the other Contracting State if such individual was a resident of the first-mentioned State for 120 months (whether or not consecutive) during any period of 20 consecutive years preceding the alienation of the property, and was a resident of that State at any time during the 10-year period immediately preceding the alienation of the property. Further, the property (or property received in substitution in a tax-free transaction in the first-mentioned State) must have been owned by the individual at the time he ceased to be a resident of the first-mentioned State and must not have been property that the individual was treated as having alienated by reason of ceasing to be a resident of the first-mentioned State and becoming a resident of the other Contracting State.

The provisions of new paragraph 5 are substantially similar to paragraph 5 of Article XIII of the existing Convention. However, the Protocol adds a new requirement to paragraph 5 that the property not be "a property that the individual was treated as having alienated by reason of ceasing to be a resident of the first-mentioned State and becoming a resident of the other Contracting State." This new requirement reflects the fact that the main purpose of paragraph 5 — ensuring that gains that accrue while an individual is resident in a Contracting State remain taxable for the stated time after the individual has moved to the other State — is met if that pre-departure gain is taxed in the first State immediately before the individual's emigration. This rule applies whether or not the individual makes the election provided by paragraph 7 of Article XIII, as amended, which is described below.

Technical Explanation [1984]: Paragraph 5 states that, despite paragraph 4, a Contracting State may impose tax on gains derived by an individual who is a resident of the other Contracting State if such individual was a resident of the first-mentioned State for 120 months (whether or not consecutive) during any period of 20 consecutive years preceding the alienation of the property, and was a resident of that State at any time during the 10-year period immediately preceding the alienation of the property. The property (or property received in substitution in a tax-free transaction in the first-mentioned State) must have been owned by the individual at the time he ceased to be a resident of the first-mentioned State.

6. Where an individual (other than a citizen of the United States) who was a resident of Canada became a resident of the United States, in determining his liability to United States taxation in respect of any gain from the alienation of a principal residence in Canada owned by him at the time he ceased to be a resident of Canada, the adjusted basis of such property shall be no less than its fair market value at that time.

Definitions: "Canada" — Art. III:1(a), ITCIA 5; "individual" — ITCIA 3, ITA 248(1); "property" — ITCIA 3, ITA 248(1); "resident" — Art. IV; "United States" — Art. III:1(b).

Technical Explanation [1984]: Paragraph 6 provides a rule to coordinate Canadian and United States taxation of gains from the alienation of a principal residence situated in Canada. An individual (not a citizen of the United States) who was a resident of Canada and becomes a resident of the United States may determine his liability for U.S. income tax purposes in respect of gain from the alienation of a principal residence in Canada owned by him at the time he ceased to be a resident of Canada by claiming an adjusted basis for such residence in an amount no less than the fair market value of the residence at that time. Under paragraph 2(b) of Article XXX, the rule of paragraph 6 applies to gains realized for U.S. income tax purposes in taxable years beginning on or after the first day of January next following the date when instruments of ratification are exchanged, even if a particular individual described in paragraph 6 ceased to be a resident of Canada prior to such date. Paragraph 6 supplements any benefits available to a taxpayer pursuant to the provisions of the Code, e.g., section 1034.

7. Where at any time an individual is treated for the purposes of taxation by a Contracting State as having alienated a property and is taxed in that State by reason thereof, the individual may elect to be treated for the purposes of taxation in the other Contracting State, in the year that includes that time and all subsequent years, as if the individual had, immediately before that time, sold and repurchased the property for an amount equal to its fair market value at that time.

Notes: For discussion of the 2007 amendment, see Finance news release 2007-070 (Sept. 21, 2007), under "Taxpayer migration"; Nelson, "IRS Emigrants' Guidance", 18(5) *Canadian Tax Highlights* (ctf.ca) 1-2 (May 2010).

Art. XIII:7 amended by 2007 Protocol, for alienations of property after Sept. 17, 2000.

Definitions: "fair market value" — see Notes to ITA 69(1); "individual" — ITCIA 3, ITA 248(1); "property" — ITCIA 3, ITA 248(1); "State" — Art. III:1(i).

Technical Explanation [2007 Protocol]: Paragraph 3 of Article 8 of the Protocol replaces paragraph 7 of Article XIII.

The purpose of paragraph 7, in both its former and revised form, is to provide a rule to coordinate U.S. and Canadian taxation of gains in the case of a timing mismatch. Such a mismatch may occur, for example, where a Canadian resident is deemed, for Canadian tax purposes, to recognize capital gain upon emigrating from Canada to the United States, or in the case of a gift that Canada deems to be an income producing event for its tax purposes but with respect to which the United States defers taxation while as-

signing the donor's basis to the donee. The former paragraph 7 resolved the timing mismatch of taxable events by allowing the individual to elect to be liable to tax in the deferring Contracting State as if he had sold and repurchased the property for an amount equal to its fair market value at a time immediately prior to the deemed alienation.

The election under former paragraph 7 was not available to certain non-U.S. citizens subject to tax in Canada by virtue of a deemed alienation because such individuals could not elect to be liable to tax in the United States. To address this problem, the Protocol replaces the election provided in former paragraph 7, with an election by the taxpayer to be treated by a Contracting State as having sold and repurchased the property for its fair market value immediately before the taxable event in the other Contracting State. The election in new paragraph 7 therefore will be available to any individual who emigrates from Canada to the United States, without regard to whether the person is a U.S. citizen immediately before ceasing to be a resident of Canada. If the individual is not subject to U.S. tax at that time, the effect of the election will be to give the individual an adjusted basis for U.S. tax purposes equal to the fair market value of the property as of the date of the deemed alienation in Canada, with the result that only post-emigration gain will be subject to U.S. tax when there is an actual alienation. If the Canadian resident is also a U.S. citizen at the time of his emigration from Canada, then the provisions of new paragraph 7 would allow the U.S. citizen to accelerate the tax under U.S. tax law and allow tax credits to be used to avoid double taxation. This would also be the case if the person, while not a U.S. citizen, would otherwise be subject to taxation in the United States on a disposition of the property.

In the case of Canadian taxation of appreciated property given as a gift, absent paragraph 7, the donor could be subject to tax in Canada upon making the gift, and the donee may be subject to tax in the United States upon a later disposition of the property on all or a portion of the same gain in the property without the availability of any foreign tax credit for the tax paid to Canada. Under new paragraph 7, the election will be available to any individual who pays taxes in Canada on a gain arising from the individual's gifting of a property, without regard to whether the person is a U.S. taxpayer at the time of the gift. The effect of the election in such case will be to give the donee an adjusted basis for U.S. tax purposes equal to the fair market value as of the date of the gift. If the donor is a U.S. taxpayer, the effect of the election will be the realization of gain or loss for U.S. purposes immediately before the gift. The acceleration of the U.S. tax liability by reason of the election in such case enables the donor to utilize foreign tax credits and avoid double taxation with respect to the disposition of the property.

Generally, the rule does not apply in the case of death. Note, however, that Article XXIX B (Taxes Imposed by Reason of Death) of the Convention provides rules that coordinate the income tax that Canada imposes by reason of death with the U.S. estate tax.

If in one Contracting State there are losses and gains from deemed alienations of different properties, then paragraph 7 must be applied consistently in the other Contracting State within the taxable period with respect to all such properties. Paragraph 7 only applies, however, if the deemed alienations of the properties result in a net gain.

Taxpayers may make the election provided by new paragraph 7 only with respect to property that is subject to a Contracting State's deemed disposition rules and with respect to which gain on a deemed alienation is recognized for that Contracting State's tax purposes in the taxable year of the deemed alienation. At the time the Protocol was signed, the following were the main types of property that were excluded from the deemed disposition rules in the case of individuals (including trusts) who cease to be residents of Canada: real property situated in Canada; interests and rights in respect of pensions; life insurance policies (other than segregated fund (investment) policies); rights in respect of annuities; interests in testamentary trusts, unless acquired for consideration; employee stock options; property used in a business carried on through a permanent establishment in Canada (including intangibles and inventory); interests in most Canadian personal trusts; Canadian resource property; and timber resource property.

Technical Explanation [1984]: Paragraph 7 provides a rule to coordinate U.S. and Canadian taxation of gains in circumstances where an individual is subject to tax in both Contracting States and one Contracting State deems a taxable alienation of property by such person to have occurred, while the other Contracting State at that time does not find a realization or recognition of income and thus defers, but does not forgive, taxation. In such a case the individual may elect in his annual return of income for the year of such alienation to be liable to tax in the latter Contracting State as if he had sold and repurchased the property for an amount equal to its fair market value at a time immediately prior to the deemed alienation. The provision would, for example, apply in the case of a gift by a U.S. citizen or a U.S. resident individual which Canada deems to be an income producing event for its tax purposes but with respect to which the United States defers taxation while assigning the donor's basis to the donee. The provision would also apply in the case of a U.S. citizen who, for Canadian tax purposes, is deemed to recognize income upon his departure from Canada, but not to a Canadian resident (not a U.S. citizen) who is deemed to recognize such income. The rule does not apply in the case of death, although Canada also deems that to be a taxable event, because the United States in effect forgives income taxation of economic gains at death. If in one Contracting State there are losses and gains from deemed alienations of different properties, then paragraph 7 must be applied consistently in the other Contracting State within the taxable period with respect to all such properties. Paragraph 7 only applies, however, if the deemed alienations of the properties result in a net gain.

8. Where a resident of a Contracting State alienates property in the course of a corporate or other organization, reorganization, amalgamation, division or similar transaction and profit, gain or income with respect to such alienation is not recognized for the purpose of taxation in that State, if requested to do so by the person who acquires the property, the competent authority of the other Contracting State may agree, in order to avoid double taxation and subject to terms and conditions satisfactory to such competent authority, to defer the recognition of the profit, gain or income with respect to such property for the purpose of taxation in that other State until such time and in such manner as may be stipulated in the agreement.

Notes: For discussion of this provision, see Vincent, "U.S. Revenue Procedure 98-21 and Article XIII(8)", VI(2) *Corporate Finance* (Federated Press) 505-7 (1998).

Art. XIII:8 amended by 1995 Protocol, generally effective 1996.

Definitions: "competent authority" — Art. III:1(g); "person" — Art. III:1(e), ITCIA 3, *Interpretation Act* 35(1); "property" — ITCIA 3, ITA 248(1); "resident" — Art. IV; "State" — Art. III:1(i); "United States" — Art. III:1(b).

Technical Explanation [1995 Protocol]: Article 8 of the Protocol broadens the scope of paragraph 8 of Article XIII (Gains) of the Convention to cover organizations, reorganizations, amalgamations, and similar transactions involving either corporations or other entities. The present Convention covers only transactions involving corporations. The amendment is intended to make the paragraph applicable to transactions involving other types of entities, such as trusts and partnerships.

As in the case of transactions covered by the present Convention, the deferral allowed under this provision shall be for such time and under such other conditions as are stipulated between the person acquiring the property and the competent authority. The agreement of the competent authority of the State of source is entirely discretionary and, when granted, will be granted only to the extent necessary to avoid double taxation.

Technical Explanation [1984]: Paragraph 8 concerns the coordination of Canadian and U.S. rules with respect to the recognition of gain on corporate organizations, reorganizations, amalgamations, divisions, and similar transactions. Where a resident of a Contracting State alienates property in such a transaction, and profit, gain, or income with respect to such alienation is not recognized for income tax purposes in the Contracting State of residence, the competent authority of the other Contracting State may agree, pursuant to paragraph 8, if requested by the person who acquires the property, to defer recognition of the profit, gain, or income with respect to such property for income tax purposes. This deferral shall be for such time and under such other conditions as are stipulated between the person who acquires the property and the competent authority. The agreement of the competent authority of the State of source is entirely discretionary and will be granted only to the extent necessary to avoid double taxation of income. This provision means, for example, that the United States competent authority may agree to defer recognition of gain with respect to a transaction if the alienator would otherwise recognize gain for U.S. tax purposes and would not recognize gain under Canada's law. The provision only applies, however, if alienations described in paragraph 8 result in a net gain. In the absence of extraordinary circumstances the provisions of the paragraph must be applied consistently within a taxable period with respect to alienations described in the paragraph that take place within that period.

9. Where a person who is a resident of a Contracting State alienates a capital asset which may in accordance with this Article be taxed in the other Contracting State and

(a) that person owned the asset on September 26, 1980 and was resident in the first-mentioned State on that date; or

(b) the asset was acquired by that person in an alienation of property which qualified as a non-recognition transaction for the purposes of taxation in that other State;

the amount of the gain which is liable to tax in that other State in accordance with this Article shall be reduced by the proportion of the gain attributable on a monthly basis to the period ending on December 31 of the year in which the Convention enters into force, or such greater portion of the gain as is shown to the satisfaction of the competent authority of the other State to be reasonably attributable to that period. For the purposes of this paragraph the term **"non-recognition transaction"** includes a transaction to which paragraph 8 applies and, in the case of taxation in the United States, a transaction that would have been a non-recognition transaction but for Sections 897(d) and 897(e) of the *Internal Revenue Code*. The provisions of this paragraph shall not apply to

(c) an asset that on September 26, 1980 formed part of the business property of a permanent establishment of a resident of a Contracting State situated in the other Contracting State;

(d) an alienation by a resident of a Contracting State of an asset that was owned at any time after September 26, 1980 and before such alienation by a person who was not at all times after that date while the asset was owned by such person a resident of that State; or

(e) an alienation of an asset that was acquired by a person at any time after September 26, 1980 and before such alienation in a transaction other than a non-recognition transaction.

Notes: CRA's view (IT-173R2 para. 14; *Income Tax Technical News* 4) is that the proration under para. 9 applies only to the period since Jan. 1, 1972, since Canada did not tax capital gains accrued before that date (see Notes to ITAR 26(3)). This view has been upheld by the Courts: *Kubicek Estate*, [1997] 3 C.T.C. 435 (FCA) (reversing the TCC and also overruling *Kaplan Estate*, [1998] 2 C.T.C. 2538 (TCC)); *Haas Estate*, [2001] 1 C.T.C. 132 (FCA); leave to appeal to SCC denied 2001 CarswellNat 1009.

When a cottage was built onto land and is personal-use property, it becomes part of the land for purposes of para. 9: VIEWS doc 2013-048905117.

Art. XIII:9(c) amended by 2007 Protocol, for tax years beginning after 2008; but for taxes withheld at source, for amounts paid or credited after Jan. 2009.

Definitions: "competent authority" — Art. III:1(g); "permanent establishment" — Art. V:1; "person" — Art. III:1(e), ITCIA 3, *Interpretation Act* 35(1); "property" — ITCIA 3, ITA 248(1); "resident" — Art. IV; "State" — Art. III:1(i).

Interpretation Bulletins: IT-173R2: Capital gains derived in Canada by residents of the United States.

I.T. Technical News: 4 (article XIII:9 of the Canada–U.S. tax convention (1980).

Technical Explanation [2007 Protocol]: Consistent with the provisions of Article 9 of the Protocol, paragraph 4 of Article 8 of the Protocol amends subparagraph 9(c) of Article XIII of the existing Convention to remove the words "or pertained to a fixed base."

Relationship to other Articles

The changes to Article XIII set forth in paragraph 3 were announced in a press release issued by the Treasury Department on September 18, 2000. Consistent with that press release, subparagraph 3(e) of Article 27 of the Protocol provides that the changes, jointly effectuated by paragraphs 2 and 3, will be generally effective for alienations of property that occur after September 17, 2000.

Technical Explanation [1984]: Paragraph 9 provides a transitional rule reflecting the fact that under Article VIII of the 1942 Convention gains from the sale or exchange of capital assets are exempt from taxation in the State of source provided the taxpayer had no permanent establishment in that State. Paragraph 9 applies to deemed, as well as actual, alienations or dispositions. In addition, paragraph 9 applies to a gain described in paragraph 1, even though such gain is also income within the meaning of paragraph 3 of Article VI. Paragraph 9 will apply to transactions notwithstanding section 1125(c) of the *Foreign Investment in Real Property Tax Act*, Public Law 96-499 ("FIRPTA").

Paragraph 9 applies to capital assets alienated by a resident of a Contracting State if (a) that person owned the asset on September 26, 1980 and was a resident of that Contracting State on September 26, 1980 (and at all times after that date until the alienation), or (b) the asset was acquired by that person in an alienation of property which qualified as a non-recognition transaction for tax purposes in the other Contracting State. For purposes of subparagraph 9(b), a non-recognition transaction is a transaction in which gain resulting therefrom is, in effect, deferred for tax purposes, but is not permanently forgiven. Thus, in the United States, certain tax-free organizations, reorganizations, liquidations and like-kind exchanges will qualify as non-recognition transactions. However, a transfer of property at death will not constitute a non-recognition transaction, since any gain due to appreciation in the property is permanently forgiven in the United States due to the fair market value basis taken by the recipient of the property. If a transaction is a non-recognition transaction for tax purposes, the transfer of non-qualified property, or "boot," which may cause some portion of the gain on the transaction to be recognized, will not cause the transaction to lose its character as a non-recognition transaction for purposes of subparagraph 9(b). In addition, a transaction that would have been a non-recognition transaction in the United States but for the application of sections 897(d) and 897(e) of the Code will also constitute a non-recognition transaction for purposes of subparagraph 9(b). Further, a transaction which is not a non-recognition transaction under U.S. law, but to which non-recognition treatment is granted pursuant to the agreement of the competent authority under paragraph 8 of this Article, is a non-recognition transaction for purposes of subparagraph 9(b). However, a transaction which is not a non-recognition transaction under U.S. law does not become a non-recognition transaction for purposes of subparagraph 9(b) merely because the basis of the property in the hands of the transferee is reduced under section 1125(d) of FIRPTA.

The benefits of paragraph 9 are not available to the alienation or disposition by a resident of a Contracting State of an asset that (a) on September 26, 1980 formed part of the business property of a permanent establishment or pertained to a fixed base which a resident of that Contracting State had in the other Contracting State, (b) was alienated after September 26, 1980 and before the alienation in question in any transaction that was not a non-recognition transaction, as described above, or (c) was owned at any time prior to the alienation in question and after September 26, 1980 by a person who was not a resident of that same Contracting State after September 26, 1980 while such person held the asset. Thus, for example, in order for paragraph 9 to be availed of by a

Canadian resident who did not own the alienated asset on September 26, 1980, the asset must have been owned by other Canadian residents continuously after September 26, 1980 and must have been transferred only in transactions which were non-recognition transactions for U.S. tax purposes.

The availability of the benefits of paragraph 9 is illustrated by the following examples. It should be noted that the examples do not purport to fully describe the U.S. and Canadian tax consequences resulting from the transactions described therein. Any condition for the application of paragraph 9 which is not discussed in an example should be assumed to be satisfied.

Example 1.

A, an individual resident of Canada, owned an appreciated U.S. real property interest on September 26, 1980. On January 1, 1982, A transferred the U.S. real property interest to X, a Canadian corporation, in exchange for 100% of X's voting stock. A's gain on the transfer to X is exempt from U.S. tax under Article VIII of the 1942 Convention. Since the transaction qualifies as a non-recognition transaction for U.S. tax purposes, as described above, X is entitled to the benefits of paragraph 9, pursuant to subparagraph 9(b), upon a subsequent disposition of the U.S. real property interest occurring after the entry into force of this Convention. If A's transfer to X had instead occurred after the entry into force of this Convention, A would be entitled to the benefits of paragraph 9, pursuant to subparagraph 9(a), with respect to U.S. taxation of that portion of the gain resulting from the transfer to X that is attributable on a monthly basis to the period ending on December 31 of the year in which the Convention enters into force (or a greater portion of the gain as is shown to the satisfaction of the U.S. competent authority). X would be entitled to the benefits of paragraph 9 pursuant to subparagraph 9(b), upon a subsequent disposition of the U.S. real property interest.

Example 2.

The facts are the same as in Example 1, except that A is a corporation which is resident in Canada. Assuming that the transfer of the U.S. real property interest to X is a section 351 transaction or a tax-free reorganization for U.S. tax purposes, the results are the same as in Example 1.

Example 3.

The facts are the same as in Example 1, except that X is a U.S. corporation. If the transfer to X by A took place on January 1, 1982, A's gain on the transfer to X would be exempt from tax under Article VIII of the 1942 Convention and A would be entitled to the benefits of paragraph 9, pursuant to subparagraph 9(b), upon a subsequent disposition of the stock of X occurring after the entry into force of this Convention. If the transfer to X by A took place after the entry into force of this Convention, A would be entitled to the benefits of paragraph 9, pursuant to subparagraph 9(a), with respect to U.S. taxation (if any) of the gain resulting from the transfer to X, and would also be entitled to the benefits of paragraph 9, pursuant to subparagraph 9(b), upon a subsequent disposition of the stock of X. For several reasons, including the fact that X is a U.S. corporation, paragraph 9 has no impact on the U.S. tax consequences of a subsequent disposition by X of the U.S. real property interest in either case.

Example 4.

B, a corporation resident in Canada, owns all of the stock of C, which is also a corporation resident in Canada. C owns a U.S. real property interest. After the Convention enters into force, B liquidates C in a section 332 liquidation. The transaction is treated as a non-recognition transaction for U.S. tax purposes under the definition of a non-recognition transaction described above. C is entitled to the benefits of paragraph 9, pursuant to subparagraph 9(a), with respect to gain taxed (if any) under section 897(d), and B is entitled to the benefits of paragraph 9, pursuant to subparagraph 9(b), upon a subsequent disposition of the U.S. real property interest. Generally, the United States would not subject B to tax upon the liquidation of C.

Example 5.

The facts are the same as in Example 4, except that C is a U.S. corporation. B is entitled to the benefits of paragraph 9, pursuant to subparagraph 9(a), with respect to U.S. taxation (if any) of the gain resulting from the liquidation of C. B is not entitled to the benefits of paragraph 9 upon a subsequent disposition of the U.S. real property interest since that asset was held after September 26, 1980 by a person who was not a resident of Canada. The U.S. tax consequences to C are governed by the internal law of the United States.

Example 6.

D, an individual resident of the United States, owns Canadian real estate. On January 1, 1982, D transfers the Canadian real estate to E, a corporation resident in Canada, in exchange for all of E's stock. This transfer is treated as a taxable transaction under the *Income Tax Act* of Canada. However, D's gain on the transfer is exempt from Canadian tax under Article VIII of the 1942 Convention. D is not entitled to the benefits of subparagraph 9(b) upon a subsequent disposition of the stock of E since the stock was not transferred in a transaction which was a non-recognition transaction for Canadian tax purposes. E is not entitled to Canadian benefits under this paragraph since, *inter alia*, it is a Canadian resident. (However, under Canadian law, both D and E would have a basis for tax purposes equal to the fair market value of the property at the time of D's transfer). If the transfer to E had taken place after entry into force of this Convention, D would be entitled to the benefits of paragraph 9, pursuant to subparagraph 9(a), with respect to Canadian tax resulting from the transfer to E, but would not be entitled to the benefits of subparagraph 9(b) upon a subsequent disposition of the E stock. (Note that

E could seek to have the transaction treated as a non-recognition transaction under paragraph 8 of this Article, with the result that, if the competent authority agrees, D will take a carryover basis in the stock of E and be entitled to the benefits of subparagraph 9(b) upon a subsequent disposition thereof).

Example 7.

The facts are the same as in Example 6, except that E is a U.S. corporation. This transaction is also a recognition event under Canadian law at the shareholder level. The results are generally the same as in Example 6. However, if the transfer to E had been granted non-recognition treatment in Canada pursuant to paragraph 8, both D and E would be entitled to the benefits of paragraph 9 for Canadian tax purposes, pursuant to subparagraph 9(b), upon subsequent dispositions of the stock of E or the Canadian real estate, respectively.

Example 8.

F, an individual resident of the United States, owns all of the stock of G, a Canadian corporation, which in turn owns Canadian real estate. F causes G to be amalgamated in a merger with another Canadian corporation. This is a non-recognition transaction under Canadian law and F is entitled for Canadian tax purposes, to the benefits of paragraph 9, pursuant to subparagraph 9(b), upon a subsequent disposition of the stock of the other Canadian corporation.

Example 9.

H, a U.S. corporation, owns all of the stock of J, another U.S. corporation. J owns Canadian real estate. H liquidates J. For Canadian tax purposes, no tax is imposed on H as a result of the liquidation and H receives a fair market value basis in the Canadian real estate. Accordingly, since gain has been forgiven due to the fair market value basis (rather than postponed in a non-recognition transaction), H would not be entitled to the benefits of subparagraph 9(b) upon the subsequent disposition of the Canadian real estate. Canada would impose a tax on J, but J would be entitled to the benefits of paragraph 9, pursuant to subparagraph 9(a), with respect to Canadian tax imposed on the liquidation.

Example 10.

The facts are the same as in Example 9, except that J is a Canadian corporation. Paragraph 9 does not affect the Canadian taxation of J. While H is subject to Canadian tax on the liquidation of J, H is entitled to the benefits of paragraph 9, pursuant to subparagraph 9(a), with respect to such Canadian taxation. H will take a fair market value basis (rather than have gain postponed in a non-recognition transaction) in the Canadian real estate for Canadian tax purposes and is thus not entitled to the benefits of paragraph 9 upon a subsequent disposition of the Canadian real estate (since, *inter alia*, the gain has been forgiven due to the fair market value basis).

Example 11.

K, a U.S. corporation, owns the stock of L, another U.S. corporation, which in turn owns Canadian real estate. K causes L to be merged into another U.S. corporation. For Canadian tax purposes, such a transaction is treated as a recognition event, but Canada will not impose a tax on K under its internal law. Canada would impose a tax on L, but L is entitled to the benefits of paragraph 9, pursuant to subparagraph 9(a), with respect to Canadian taxation of gain resulting from the merger. The acquiring U.S. corporation would take a fair market value basis in the Canadian real estate, and would thus not be entitled to the benefits of subparagraph 9(b) upon a subsequent disposition of the real estate. (Note that the acquiring U.S. corporation could seek to obtain non-recognition treatment under paragraph 8 of this Article, with the result that, if approved by the competent authority, it would obtain a carryover basis in the property and be entitled to the benefits of subparagraph 9(b) upon a subsequent disposition of the Canadian real estate).

Paragraph 9 provides that where a resident of Canada or the United States is subject to tax pursuant to Article XIII in the other Contracting State on gains from the alienation of a capital asset, and if the other conditions of paragraph 9 are satisfied, the amount of the gain shall be reduced for tax purposes in that other State by the amount of the gain attributable to the period during which the property was held up to and including December 31 of the year in which the documents of ratification are exchanged. The gain attributable to such person[1] is normally determined by dividing the total gain by the number of full calendar months the property was held by such person, including, in the case of an alienation described in paragraph 9(b), the number of months in which a predecessor in interest held the property, and multiplying such monthly amount by the number of full calendar months ending on or before December 31 of the year in which the instruments of ratification are exchanged.

Upon a clear showing, however, a taxpayer may prove that a greater portion of the gain was attributable to the specified period. Thus, in the United States the fair market value of the alienated property at the treaty valuation date may be established under paragraph 9 in the manner and with the evidence that is generally required by U.S. Federal income, estate, and gift tax regulations. For this purpose a taxpayer may use valid appraisal techniques for valuing real estate such as the comparable sales approach (see Rev. Proc. 79-24, 1979-1 C.B. 565) and the reproduction cost approach. If more than one property is alienated in a single transaction each property will be considered individually.

A taxpayer who desires to make this alternate showing for U.S. tax purposes must so indicate on his U.S. income tax return for the year of the sale or exchange and must attach to the return a statement describing the relevant evidence. The U.S. competent

---

[1]*Sic.* Should read "period" — ed.

authority or his authorized delegate will determine whether the taxpayer has satisfied the requirements of paragraph 9.

The amount of gain which is reduced by reason of the application of paragraph 9 is not to be treated for U.S. tax purposes as an amount of "nontaxed gain" under section 1125(d)(2)(B) of FIRPTA, where that section would otherwise apply. (Note that gain not taxed by virtue of the 1942 Convention is "nontaxed gain").

U.S. residents, citizens and former citizens remain subject to U.S. taxation on gains as provided by the Code notwithstanding the provisions of Article XIII, other than paragraphs 6 and 7. See paragraphs 2 and 3(a) of Article XXIX (Miscellaneous Rules).

Article XIV — [Repealed]

Notes: Art. XIV, "Independent Personal Services", repealed by 2007 Protocol, for tax years beginning after 2008, but for taxes withheld at source, for amounts paid or credited after Jan. 2009. See now Art. V:9, deeming an individual performing services in the other country to have a permanent establishment if spending sufficient time there.

Fifth Protocol (2007), Annex B, states:

4. Deletion of Article XIV (Independent Personal Services)

It is understood that the deletion of Article XIV (Independent Personal Services) of the Convention confirms the negotiators' shared understanding that no practical distinction can be made between a "fixed base" and a "permanent establishment", and that independent personal services of a resident of a Contracting State, to the extent that such resident is found to have a permanent establishment in the other Contracting State with respect to those services, shall be subject to the provisions of Article VII (Business Profits).

See Nightingale, "The CRA Finally Asks for Water", 1859 *Tax Topics* (CCH) 1-4 (Oct. 25, 2007).

In *Dudney*, [2000] 2 C.T.C. 56 (FCA); leave to appeal denied 2000 CarswellNat 2662 (SCC), the term "fixed base" was interpreted to mean essentially the same as "permanent establishment". CRA accepts *Dudney* in cases where "the taxpayer does not have sufficient physical control of space to be carrying on his or her business in a particular place" (*Income Tax Technical News* 22). Art. V:9 now deems a person like Dudney to have a PE. See also VIEWS doc 2011-039345117.

Technical Explanation [2007 Protocol]: To conform with the current U.S. and OECD Model Conventions, Article 9 of the Protocol deletes Article XIV (Independent Personal Services) of the Convention. The subsequent articles of the Convention are not renumbered. Paragraph 4 of the General Note elaborates that current tax treaty practice omits separate articles for independent personal services because a determination of the existence of a fixed base is qualitatively the same as the determination of the existence of a permanent establishment. Accordingly, the taxation of income from independent personal services is adequately governed by the provisions of Articles V (Permanent Establishment) and VII (Business Profits).

Article XV — Income from Employment

Notes: Heading changed from "Dependent Personal Services" by 2007 Protocol.

1. Subject to the provisions of Articles XVIII (Pensions and Annuities) and XIX (Government Service), salaries, wages and other remuneration derived by a resident of a Contracting State in respect of an employment shall be taxable only in that State unless the employment is exercised in the other Contracting State. If the employment is so exercised, such remuneration as is derived therefrom may be taxed in that other State.

Notes: See Notes to Reg. 102(1) and Reg. 105.

Art. XV does not discriminate between Canadian and US citizens so as to violate the *Charter of Rights*: *Nightingale*, 2010 TCC 1.

Fifth Protocol (2007), Annex B, states (see Nijhawan, "Protocol to the Canada-US Tax Treaty", 18(10) *Taxation of Executive Compensation & Retirement* (Federated Press) 853-56 (June 2007)):

6. Stock options

For purposes of applying Article XV (Income from Employment) and Article XXIV (Elimination of Double Taxation) of the Convention to income of an individual in connection with the exercise or other disposal (including a deemed exercise or disposal) of an option that was granted to the individual as an employee of a corporation or mutual fund trust to acquire shares or units ("securities") of the employer (which is considered, for the purposes of this Note, to include any related entity) in respect of services rendered or to be rendered by such individual, or in connection with the disposal (including a deemed disposal) of a security acquired under such an option, the following principles shall apply:

(a) Subject to subparagraph 6(b) of this Note, the individual shall be deemed to have derived, in respect of employment exercised in a Contracting State, the same proportion of such income that the number of days in the period that begins on the day the option was granted, and that ends on the day the option was exercised or disposed of, on which the individual's principal

place of employment for the employer was situated in that Contracting State is of the total number of days in the period on which the individual was employed by the employer; and

(b) Notwithstanding subparagraph 6(a) of this Note, if the competent authorities of both Contracting States agree that the terms of the option were such that the grant of the option will be appropriately treated as transfer of ownership of the securities (e.g., because the options were in-the-money or not subject to a substantial vesting period), then they may agree to attribute income accordingly.

For CRA interpretation of "principal place of employment" and examples of applying the above see VIEWS docs 2008-0300631C6, 2012-044074117.

See Megoudis, "The Impact of the New Canada-United States Treaty Protocol on Cross-border Executives", 18(7) *Taxation of Executive Compensation & Retirement [TECR]* (Federated Press) 795-805 (March 2007); Nijhawan, "Protocol to the Canada-U.S. Tax Treaty: Implications for Cross-border Employment", 18(10) *TECR* (Federated Press) 853-56 (June 2007); Nijhawan & Kamath, "Amendments to Article XV of the Canada-U.S. Tax Convention", 19(10) *TECR* 1013-15 (June 2008); Finance news release 2007-070 (Sept. 21, 2007), under "Stock options — apportionment of taxing rights"; Sala, "US Parent Corporations Sending Employees to Quebec", 2306 *Tax Topics* (CCH) 1-7 (May 19, 2016).

In *Austin*, 2004 TCC 6, a Canadian Football League player played 3 or 4 of 18 games in a season in the US, and was paid per game. The Court held that the allocation of his income to the US was 3 or 4 out of 18, not 6 or 8 days out of 180 as claimed by CRA.

"Derived" in para. 1 means "having its source": *Garcia*, 2007 TCC 548, paras. 28-37 (see also ITA 18.1(12) Notes).

See also Notes to Canada-UK treaty Art. 15:1.

Art. XV:1 amended by 2007 Protocol, for tax years beginning after 2008, but in respect of taxes withheld at source, for amounts paid or credited after Jan. 2009.

Definitions: "employment" — ITCIA 3, ITA 248(1); "resident" — Art. IV; "State" — Art. III:1(i).

Technical Explanation [2007 Protocol]: Article 10 of the Protocol renames Article XV of the Convention as "Income from Employment" to conform with the current U.S. and OECD Model Conventions, and replaces paragraphs 1 and 2 of that renamed article consistent with the OECD Model Convention.

New paragraph 1 of Article XV provides that, in general, salaries, wages, and other remuneration derived by a resident of a Contracting State in respect of an employment are taxable only in that State unless the employment is exercised in the other Contracting State. If the employment is exercised in the other Contracting State, the entire remuneration derived therefrom may be taxed in that other State, subject to the provisions of paragraph 2.

New paragraph 1 of Article XV does not contain a reference to "similar" remuneration. This change was intended to clarify that Article XV applies to any form of compensation for employment, including payments in kind. This interpretation is consistent with paragraph 2.1 of the Commentary to Article 15 (Income from Employment) of the OECD Model and the Technical Explanation of the 2006 U.S. Model.

Technical Explanation [1984]: Paragraph 1 provides that, in general, salaries, wages, and other similar remuneration derived by a resident of a Contracting State in respect of an employment are taxable only in that State unless the employment is exercised in the other Contracting State. If the employment is exercised in the other Contracting State, the entire remuneration derived therefrom may be taxed in that other State but only if, as provided by paragraph 2, the recipient is present in the other State for a period or periods exceeding 183 days in the calendar year, or the remuneration is borne by an employer who is a resident of that other State or by a permanent establishment or fixed base which the employer has in that other State. However, in all cases where the employee earns $10,000 or less in the currency of the State of source, such earnings are exempt from tax in that State. "Borne by" means allowable as a deduction in computing taxable income. Thus, if a Canadian resident individual employed at the Canadian permanent establishment of a U.S. company performs services in the United States, the income earned by the employee from such services is not exempt from U.S. tax under paragraph 1 if such income exceeds $10,000 (U.S.) because the U.S. company is entitled to a deduction for such wages in computing its taxable income.

2. Notwithstanding the provisions of paragraph 1, remuneration derived by a resident of a Contracting State in respect of an employment exercised in the other Contracting State shall be taxable only in the first-mentioned State if:

(a) such remuneration does not exceed ten thousand dollars ($10,000) in the currency of that other State; or

(b) the recipient is present in that other State for a period or periods not exceeding in the aggregate 183 days in any twelve-month period commencing or ending in the fiscal year concerned, and the remuneration is not paid by, or on behalf of, a person who is a resident of that other State and is not borne by a permanent establishment in that other State.

Related Provisions: ITA 146(1)"earned income"(c) — Income exempted by tax treaty is not earned income of a non-resident for RRSP purposes.

Notes: The $10,000 is measured against *each* employment, not total employment in the other country: *Prescott*, [1995] 2 C.T.C. 2068 (TCC). Where the employee is resident in Canada only part of the year, the $10,000 is still measured for the entire year: VIEWS doc 2013-0484501E5.

Where the income exceeds $10,000, ensure CRA assesses the right provincial tax and not the high 120(1) tax: Kakkar, "Verifying the Basis for Taxing a Non-Resident's Income Earned in Canada", 12(4) *Tax for the Owner-Manager* (ctf.ca) 10 (Oct. 2012).

The term "permanent establishment" in para. 2(b) should be determined under the treaty between Canada and the *employee's* country of residence: VIEWS doc 2009-031995117. See also docs 2005-011852117 (US LLC can have PE in Canada), 2010-0382801E5 (general discussion), 2011-0393411E5 (stock option remuneration), 2011-0403541E5 ("person" in 2(b) refers to who exercises the functions of employer), 2011-0403551E5, 2011-0418281E5 (test is "who is exercising the functions of employer"), 2012-0464541E5 (interpretation of parallel provision in Canada-Germany treaty), 2012-045767117.

For discussion of the 2007 Protocol amendment see Teron, "Non-Resident Employee Stock Options", 16(1) *Canadian Tax Highlights* (ctf.ca) 7-8 (Jan. 2008); Nijhawan, "Protocol to the Canada-U.S. Tax Treaty", 18(10) *Taxation of Executive Compensation & Retirement* (Federated Press) 853-54 (June 2007); doc 2012-044074117.

Art. XV:2 amended by 2007 Protocol, for tax years beginning after 2008, but in respect of taxes withheld at source, for amounts paid or credited after Jan. 2009. Under the old wording, remuneration is "borne" by someone if they are charged directly or indirectly, through a management or administration fee or otherwise, even if the employee continues to be paid from the other country: 4(3) *Toronto Centre CRA & Professionals Consultation Group Newsletter* (Oct. 2005). The new wording is "paid by or on behalf of".

See also Notes to Art. XVI:1.

Definitions: "employment" — ITCIA 3, ITA 248(1); "permanent establishment" — Art. V:1; "resident" — Art. IV; "State" — Art. III:1(i).

Technical Explanation [2007 Protocol]: New paragraph 2 of Article XV provides two limitations on the right of a source State to tax remuneration for services rendered in that State. New paragraph 2 is divided into two subparagraphs that each sets forth a rule which, notwithstanding any contrary result due to the application of paragraph 1 of Article XV, prevents the source State from taxing income from employment in that State.

First, subparagraph 2(a) provides a safe harbor rule that the remuneration may not be taxed in the source State if such remuneration is $10,000 or less in the currency of the source State. This rule is identical to the rule in subparagraph 2(a) of Article XV of the existing Convention. It is understood that, consistent with the prior rule, the safe harbor will apply on a calendar-year basis.

Second, if the remuneration is not exempt from tax in the source State by virtue of subparagraph 2(a), subparagraph 2(b) provides an additional rule that the source State may not tax remuneration for services rendered in that State if the recipient is present in the source State for a period (or periods) that does not exceed in the aggregate 183 days in any twelve-month period commencing or ending in the fiscal year concerned, and the remuneration is not paid by or on behalf of a person who is a resident of that other State or borne by a permanent establishment in that other State. For purposes of this article, "borne by" means allowable as a deduction in computing taxable income.

Assume, for example, that Mr. X, an individual resident in Canada, is an employee of the Canadian permanent establishment of USCo, a U.S. company. Mr. X is sent to the United States to perform services and is present in the United States for less than 183 days. Mr. X receives more than $10,000 (U.S.) in the calendar year(s) in question. The remuneration paid to Mr. X for such services is not exempt from U.S. tax under paragraph 1, because his employer, USCo, is a resident of the United States and pays his remuneration. If instead Mr. X received less than $10,000 (U.S.), such earnings would be exempt from tax in the United States, because in all cases where an employee earns less than $10,000 in the currency of the source State, such earnings are exempt from tax in the source State.

As another example, assume Ms. Y, an individual resident in the United States is employed by USCo, a U.S. company. Ms. Y is sent to Canada to provide services in the Canadian permanent establishment of USCo. Ms. Y is present in Canada for less than 183 days. Ms. Y receives more than $10,000 (Canadian) in the calendar year(s) in question. USCo charges the Canadian permanent establishment with Ms. Y's remuneration, which the permanent establishment takes as a deduction in computing its taxable income. The remuneration paid to Ms. Y for such services is not exempt from Canadian tax under paragraph 1, because her remuneration is borne by the Canadian permanent establishment.

New subparagraph 2(b) refers to remuneration that is paid by or on behalf of a "person" who is a resident of the other Contracting State, as opposed to an "employer." This change is intended only to clarify that both the United States and Canada understand that in certain abusive cases, substance over form principles may be applied to recharacterize an employment relationship, as prescribed in paragraph 8 of the Com-

mentary to Article 15 (Income from Employment) of the OECD Model. Subparagraph 2(b) is intended to have the same meaning as the analogous provisions in the U.S. and OECD Models.

Paragraph 6 of the General Note

Paragraph 6 of the General Note contains special rules regarding employee stock options. There are no similar rules in the U.S. Model or the OECD Model, although the issue is discussed in detail in paragraph 12 of the Commentary to Article 15 (Income from Employment) of the OECD Model.

The General Note sets forth principles that apply for purposes of applying Article XV and Article XXIV (Elimination of Double Taxation) to income of an individual in connection with the exercise or other disposal (including a deemed exercise or disposal) of an option that was granted to the individual as an employee of a corporation or mutual fund trust to acquire shares or units ("securities") of the employer in respect of services rendered or to be rendered by such individual, or in connection with the disposal (including a deemed disposal) of a security acquired under such an option. For this purpose, the term "employer" is considered to include any entity related to the service recipient. The reference to a disposal (or deemed disposal) reflects the fact that under Canadian law and under certain provisions of U.S. law, income or gain attributable to the granting or exercising of the option may, in some cases, not be recognized until disposition of the securities.

Subparagraph 6(a) of the General Note provides a specific rule to address situations where, under the domestic law of the Contracting States, an employee would be taxable by both Contracting States in respect of the income in connection with the exercise or disposal of the option. The rule provides an allocation of taxing rights where (1) an employee has been granted a stock option in the course of employment in one of the Contracting States, and (2) his principal place of employment has been situated in one or both of the Contracting States during the period between grant and exercise (or disposal) of the option. In this situation, each Contracting State may tax as Contracting State of source only that proportion of the income that relates to the period or periods between the grant and the exercise (or disposal) of the option during which the individual's principal place of employment was situated in that Contracting State. The proportion attributable to a Contracting State is determined by multiplying the income by a fraction, the numerator of which is the number of days between the grant and exercise (or disposal) of the option during which the employee's principal place of employment was situated in that Contracting State and the denominator of which is the total number of days between grant and exercise (or disposal) of the option that the employee was employed by the employer.

If the individual is a resident of one of the Contracting States at the time he exercises the option, that Contracting State will have the right, as the State of residence, to tax all of the income under the first sentence of paragraph 1 of Article XV. However, to the extent that the employee renders his employment in the other Contracting State for some period of time between the date of the grant of the option and the date of the exercise (or disposal) of the option, the proportion of the income that is allocated to the other Contracting State under subparagraph 6(a) of the General Note will, subject to paragraph 2, be taxable by that other State under the second sentence of paragraph 1 of Article XV of the Convention. For this purpose, the tests of paragraph 2 of Article XV are applied to the year or years in which the relevant services were performed in the other Contracting State (and not to the year in which the option is exercised or disposed). To the extent the same income is subject to taxation in both Contracting States after application of Article XV, double taxation will be alleviated under the rules of Article XXIV (Elimination of Double Taxation).

Subparagraph 6(b) of the General Note provides that notwithstanding subparagraph 6(a), if the competent authorities of both Contracting States agree that the terms of the option were such that the grant of the option is appropriately treated as transfer of ownership of the securities (*e.g.*, because the options were in-the-money or not subject to a substantial vesting period), then they may agree to attribute income accordingly.

Technical Explanation [1984]: See Article XV, para. 1.

3. Notwithstanding the provisions of paragraphs 1 and 2, remuneration derived by a resident of a Contracting State in respect of an employment regularly exercised in more than one State on a ship, aircraft, motor vehicle or train operated by a resident of that Contracting State shall be taxable only in that State.

Related Provisions: Art. III:1(h) — Meaning of "international traffic"; ITA 146(1)"earned income"(c) — Income exempted by tax treaty is not earned income of a non-resident for RRSP purposes.

Definitions: "employment" — ITCIA 3, ITA 248(1); "resident" — Art. IV; "State" — Art. III:1(i).

Technical Explanation [1984]: Paragraph 3 provides that a resident of a Contracting State is exempt from tax in the other Contracting State with respect to remuneration derived in respect of an employment regularly exercised in more than one State on a ship, aircraft, motor vehicle, or train operated by a resident of the taxpayer's State of residence. The word "regularly" is intended to distinguish crew members from persons occasionally employed on a ship, aircraft, motor vehicle, or train. Only the Contracting State of which the employee and operator are resident has the right to tax such remuneration. However, this provision is subject to the "saving clause" of paragraph 2 of Article XXIX (Miscellaneous Rules), which permits the United States to tax its citizens despite paragraph 3.

Article XV states that its provisions are overridden by the more specific rules of Article XVIII (Pensions and Annuities) and Article XIX (Government Services).

Article XVI — Artistes and Athletes

1. Notwithstanding the provisions of Articles VII (Business Profits) and XV (Income from Employment), income derived by a resident of a Contracting State as an entertainer, such as a theatre, motion picture, radio or television artiste, or a musician, or as an athlete, from his personal activities as such exercised in the other Contracting State, may be taxed in that other State, except where the amount of the gross receipts derived by such entertainer or athlete, including expenses reimbursed to him or borne on his behalf, from such activities do not exceed fifteen thousand dollars ($15,000) in the currency of that other State for the calendar year concerned.

Related Provisions: ITA 146(1)"earned income"(c) — Income exempted by tax treaty is not earned income of a non-resident for RRSP purposes.

Notes: See Sprague, "Taxation of Professional Athletes", 54(2) *Canadian Tax Journal* 477-506 (2006); Jadd et al., "Performing in Canada", 56(3) *CTJ* 589-638 (2008); Feigenbaum, "The Price of Success", *Ameri-Can Tax Talk Newsletter* (Carswell *Taxnet Pro*), July 7, 2016; Bidner, "Non-Resident Entertainer Performing in Canada", 7(4) *Canadian Tax Focus* (ctf.ca) 4-5 (Nov. 2017); VIEWS docs 2008-0300871I7 (para. 1 applies independently of para. 2); 2008-0295951E5 (when para. 2 applies, first $15,000 is not exempt); 2009-034577II7 (limited-liability corp claiming Art. XVI:1 treatment); 2009-034695II7 (application of Reg. 400 to a corp under Art. XVI); 2015-0603271E5 (no late filing of an ITA 216.1 election).

In *Cheek*, [2002] 2 C.T.C. 2115 (TCC), Toronto Blue Jays broadcaster Tom Cheek was held not to be a "radio artiste", and thus was not subject to tax in Canada.

Art. XVI:1 amended by 2007 Protocol, for tax years beginning after 2008, but in respect of taxes withheld at source, for amounts paid or credited after Jan. 2009.

Definitions: "resident" — Art. IV; "State" — Art. III:1(i).

Technical Explanation [2007 Protocol]: Consistent with Article 9 and paragraph 1 of Article 10 of the Protocol, paragraphs 1, 2, and 3 of Article 11 of the Protocol revise paragraphs 1, 2, and 4 of Article XVI (Artistes and Athletes) of the existing Convention by deleting references to former Article XIV (Independent Personal Services) of the Convention and deleting and replacing other language in acknowledgement of the renaming of Article XV (Income from Employment).

Technical Explanation [1984]: Article XVI concerns income derived by a resident of a Contracting State as an entertainer, such as a theatre, motion picture, radio, or television artiste, or a musician, or as an athlete, from his personal activities as such exercised in the other Contracting State. Article XVI overrides Articles XIV (Independent Personal Services) and XV (Dependent Personal Services) to allow source basis taxation of an entertainer or athlete in cases where the latter Articles would not permit such taxation. Thus, paragraph 1 provides that certain income of an entertainer or athlete may be taxed in the State of source in all cases where the amount of gross receipts derived by the entertainer or athlete, including expenses reimbursed to him or borne on his behalf, exceeds $15,000 in the currency of that other State for the calendar year concerned. For example, where a resident of Canada who is an entertainer derives income from his personal activities as an entertainer in the United States, he is taxable in the United States on all such income in any case where his gross receipts are greater than $15,000 for the calendar year. Article XVI does not restrict the right of the State of source to apply the provisions of Articles XIV and XV. Thus, an entertainer or athlete resident in a Contracting State and earning $14,000 in wages borne by a permanent establishment in the other State may be taxed in the other State as provided in Article XV.

2. Where income in respect of personal activities exercised by an entertainer or an athlete in his capacity as such accrues not to the entertainer or athlete but to another person, that income may, notwithstanding the provisions of Articles VII (Business Profits) and XV (Income from Employment), be taxed in the Contracting State in which the activities of the entertainer or athlete are exercised. For the purposes of the preceding sentence, income of an entertainer or athlete shall be deemed not to accrue to another person if it is established that neither the entertainer or athlete, nor persons related thereto, participate directly or indirectly in the profits of such other person in any manner, including the receipt of deferred remuneration, bonuses, fees, dividends, partnership distributions or other distributions.

Notes: See Notes to para. 1.

Art. XVI:2 amended by 2007 Protocol, effective on the same basis as the amendment to para. 1.

Definitions: "person" — Art. III:1(e), ITCIA 3, *Interpretation Act* 35(1); "related" — ITCIA 3, ITA 251(2)–(6).

Technical Explanation [2007 Protocol]: See under Art. XVI:1 above.

Technical Explanation [1984]: Paragraph 2 provides that where income in respect of personal activities exercised by an entertainer or an athlete accrues not to the entertainer or athlete himself but to another person, that income may, notwithstanding the provisions of Article VII (Business Profits), Article XIV, and Article XV, be taxed in the Contracting State in which the activities are exercised. The anti-avoidance rule of paragraph 2 does not apply if it is established by the entertainer or athlete that neither he nor persons related to him participate directly or indirectly in the profits of the other person in any manner, including the receipt of deferred remuneration, bonuses, fees, dividends, partnership distributions, or other distributions.

Thus, if an entertainer who is a resident of Canada is under contract with a company and the arrangement between the entertainer and the company provides for payments to the entertainer based on the profits of the company, all of the income of the company attributable to the performer's U.S. activities may be taxed in the United States irrespective of whether the company maintains a permanent establishment in the United States. Paragraph 2 does not affect the rule of paragraph 1 that applies to the entertainer or athlete himself.

3. The provisions of paragraphs 1 and 2 shall not apply to the income of:

(a) an athlete in respect of his activities as an employee of a team which participates in a league with regularly scheduled games in both Contracting States; or

(b) a team described in subparagraph (a).

Notes: For discussion of para. 3 see Alan Macnaughton and Kim Wood, 'Should Provinces Tax Non-Resident Athletes?", 52(2) *Canadian Tax Journal* 428-83 (2004).

Definitions: "employee" — ITCIA 3, ITA 248(1).

Technical Explanation [1984]: Paragraph 3 provides that paragraphs 1 and 2 of Article XVI do not apply to the income of an athlete in respect of an employment with a team which participates in a league with regularly scheduled games in both Canada and the United States, nor do those paragraphs apply to the income of such a team. Such an athlete is subject to the rules of Article XV. Thus, the athlete's remuneration would be exempt from tax in the Contracting State of source if he is a resident of the other Contracting State and earns $10,000 or less in the currency of the State of source, or if he is present in that State for a period or periods not exceeding in the aggregate 183 days in the calendar year, and his remuneration is not borne by a resident of that State or a permanent establishment or fixed base in that State. In addition, a team described in paragraph 3 may not be taxed in a Contracting State under paragraph 2 of this Article solely by reason of the fact that a member of the team may participate in the profits of the team through the receipt of a bonus based, for example, on ticket sales. The employer may be taxable pursuant to other articles of the Convention, such as Article VII.

4. Notwithstanding the provisions of Articles VII (Business Profits) and XV (Income from Employment) an amount paid by a resident of a Contracting State to a resident of the other Contracting State as an inducement to sign an agreement relating to the performance of the services of an athlete (other than an amount referred to in paragraph 1 of Article XV (Income from Employment) may be taxed in the first-mentioned State, but the tax so charged shall not exceed 15 per cent of the gross amount of such payment.

Notes: See Scherer, Silber & Steinberg, "Auston Matthews Shoots and Scores Tax Savings", tinyurl.com/matthews-tax (2019).

Art. XVI:4 amended by 2007 Protocol to replace reference to Articles XIV and XV with VII and XV, effective on the same basis as the amendment to para. 1.

Definitions: "resident" — Art. IV; "State" — Art. III:1(i).

Technical Explanation [2007 Protocol]: See under Art. XVI:1 above.

Technical Explanation [1984]: Paragraph 4 provides that, notwithstanding Articles XIV and XV, an amount paid by a resident of a Contracting State to a resident of the other State as an inducement to sign an agreement relating to the performance of the services of an athlete may be taxed in the first-mentioned State. However, the tax imposed may not exceed 15% of the gross amount of the payment. The provision clarifies the taxation of signing bonuses in a manner consistent with their treatment under U.S. interpretations of the 1942 Convention. Amounts paid as salary or other remuneration for the performance of the athletic services themselves are not taxable under this provision, but are subject to the provisions of paragraphs 1 and 3 of this Article, or Articles XIV or XV, as the case may be. The paragraph covers all amounts paid (to the athlete or another person) as an inducement to sign an agreement for the services of an athlete, such as a bonus to sign a contract not to perform for other teams. An amount described in this paragraph is not to be included in determining the amount of gross receipts derived by an athlete in a calendar year for purposes of paragraph 1. Thus, if an athlete receives a $50,000 signing bonus and a $12,000 salary for a taxable year, the State of source would not be entitled to tax the salary portion of the receipt of the athlete for that year under paragraph 1 of this Article.

Article XVII — [Repealed]

Notes: Art. XVII, "Withholding of Taxes in Respect of Personal Services", repealed by 2007 Protocol, for tax years beginning after 2008, but in respect of taxes withheld at source, for amounts paid or credited after Jan. 2009.

Technical Explanation [2007 Protocol]: Article 12 of the Protocol deletes Article XVII (Withholding of Taxes in Respect of Personal Services) from the Convention. However, the subsequent Articles are not renumbered.

Article XVIII — Pensions and Annuities

1. Pensions and annuities arising in a Contracting State and paid to a resident of the other Contracting State may be taxed in that other State, but the amount of any such pension that would be excluded from taxable income in the first-mentioned State if the recipient were a resident thereof shall be exempt from taxation in that other State.

Notes: A US pension can be deducted under ITA 110(1)(f)(i) to reduce the 56(1)(a)(i) inclusion, to the extent it is non-taxable in the US: VIEWS doc 2014-0525681E5. US workers' compensation to an injured US federal government worker, which would be exempt in the US, is exempt under this para.: 2010-0389831E5.

In *Coblentz*, [1996] 3 C.T.C. 295 (FCA), the Court used the Technical Explanation (below) to assist in interpreting Art. XVIII:1, and ruled that a US itemized deduction was not a "personal allowance" as described in the Technical Explanation.

In *Korfage*, 2016 TCC 69, the excluded (exempt) portion under para. 1 had to be converted to C$ at the exchange rate for the year it was paid, even though the pension was fixed in C$ for all years at the time.

On conversion of a traditional IRA to a Roth IRA, see VIEWS doc 2011-0398691E5.

Where a Canadian individual inherits an IRA or US pension plan, US estate tax can be deducted against taxable income: VIEWS docs 2008-0304421I7 and 2009-0313171E5 (reversing 2003-0047151E5). See "Good news for Canadian residents who inherit a US pension plan of IRA", 4(1) *BorderCrossings* (Carswell) 1-2 (March 2011).

See also Notes to para. 7.

Definitions: "annuities" — Art. XVIII:4, ITCIA 5; "pension" — Art. XVIII:3, ITCIA 5; "State" — Art. III:1(i); "taxable income" — ITCIA 3, ITA 248(1).

Income Tax Folios: S5-F3-C1: Taxation of a Roth IRA.

Technical Explanation [1984]: Paragraph 1 provides that a resident of a Contracting State is taxable in that State with respect to pensions and annuities arising in the other Contracting State. However, the State of residence shall exempt from taxation the amount of any such pension that would be excluded from taxable income in the State of source if the recipient were a resident thereof. Thus, if a $10,000 pension payment arising in a Contracting State is paid to a resident of the other Contracting State and $5,000 of such payment would be excluded from taxable income as a return of capital in the first-mentioned State if the recipient were a resident of the first-mentioned State, the State of residence shall exempt from tax $5,000 of the payment. Only $5,000 would be so exempt even if the first-mentioned State would also grant a personal allowance as a deduction from gross income if the recipient were a resident thereof. Paragraph 1 imposes no such restriction with respect to the amount that may be taxed in the State of residence in the case of annuities.

2. However:

(a) pensions may also be taxed in the Contracting State in which they arise and according to the laws of that State; but if a resident of the other Contracting State is the beneficial owner of a periodic pension payment, the tax so charged shall not exceed 15 per cent of the gross amount of such payment; and

(b) annuities may also be taxed in the Contracting State in which they arise and according to the laws of that State; but if a resident of the other Contracting State is the beneficial owner of an annuity payment, the tax so charged shall not exceed 15 per cent of the portion of such payment that would not be excluded from taxable income in the first-mentioned State if the beneficial owner were a resident thereof.

Notes: See Notes to *Income Tax Conventions Interpretation Act* s. 5"periodic pension payment" and ITA 212(1)(l). CRA will not apply the "fiscally transparent" rules in Art. IV:7 to deny Art. XVIII treatment to RRSP and RCA payments: VIEWS doc 2009-0327031C6. In CRA's view, an RRIF lump-sum payment cannot be bifurcated to tax part of it at only 15%: 2007-0248991E5. For application to US tax on a pension, triggered by renouncing US citizenship, see 2013-0477121E5.

Definitions: "annuities", "annuity" — Art. XVIII:4, ITCIA 5; "pension" — Art. XVIII:3, ITCIA 5; "periodic pension payment" — ITCIA 5; "State" — Art. III:1(i); "taxable income" — ITCIA 3, ITA 248(1).

Information Circulars: 75-6R2: Required withholding from amounts paid to non-residents performing services in Canada.

Technical Explanation [1984]: Paragraph 2 provides rules with respect to the taxation of pensions and annuities in the Contracting State in which they arise. If the beneficial owner of a periodic pension payment is a resident of the other Contracting State, the tax imposed in the State of source is limited to 15% of the gross amount of such payment. Thus, the State of source is not required to allow a deduction or exclusion for a return of capital to the pensioner, but its tax is limited in amount in the case of a periodic payment. Other pension payments may be taxed in the State of source without limit.

In the case of annuities beneficially owned by a resident of a Contracting State, the Contracting State of source is limited to a 15% tax on the portion of the payment that would not be excluded from taxable income (i.e., as a return of capital) in that State if the beneficial owner were a resident thereof.

3. For the purposes of this Convention:

(a) the term **"pensions"** includes any payment under a superannuation, pension or other retirement arrangement, Armed Forces retirement pay, war veterans pensions and allowances and amounts paid under a sickness, accident or disability plan, but does not include payments under an income-averaging annuity contract or, except for the purposes of Article XIX (Government Service), any benefit referred to in paragraph 5; and

(b) the term **"pensions"** also includes a Roth IRA, within the meaning of section 408A of the Internal Revenue Code, or a plan or arrangement created pursuant to legislation enacted by a Contracting State after September 21, 2007 that the competent authorities have agreed is similar thereto. Notwithstanding the provisions of the preceding sentence, from such time that contributions have been made to the Roth IRA or similar plan or arrangement, by or for the benefit of a resident of the other Contracting State (other than rollover contributions from a Roth IRA or similar plan or arrangement described in the previous sentence that is a pension within the meaning of this subparagraph), to the extent of accretions from such time, such Roth IRA or similar plan or arrangement shall cease to be considered a pension for purposes of the provisions of this Article.

Related Provisions: ITA 94(1)"exempt foreign trust"(h)(ii)(D) — Roth IRA excluded from non-resident trust rules; ITCIA 5.1 — Definition of "pension".

Notes: US workers' compensation to an injured US federal government worker falls under 3(a): VIEWS doc 2010-0389831E5.

In *Watts*, 2004 TCC 535, CPP disability benefits paid to a US resident were held to be benefits under Canada's social security system under para. 5, and thus were excluded from this definition.

For para. (b) (Roth IRAs), see Notes to para. 7 below and to ITA 56(12).

Art. XVIII:3(b) added by 2007 Protocol, for tax years beginning after 2008, but in respect of taxes withheld at source, for amounts paid or credited after Jan. 2009. Earlier amended by 1997 and 1995 Protocols.

Definitions: "income-averaging annuity contract" — ITCIA 3, ITA 248(1); "pension" — ITCIA 5.

Income Tax Folios: S5-F3-C1: Taxation of a Roth IRA.

I.T. Technical News: 43 (taxation of Roth IRAs).

Technical Explanation [2007 Protocol]: Article 13 of the Protocol replaces paragraphs 3, 4, and 7 and adds paragraphs 8 through 17 to Article XVIII (Pensions and Annuities) of the Convention.

Roth IRAs

Paragraph 1 of Article 13 of the Protocol separates the provisions of paragraph 3 of Article XVIII into two subparagraphs. Subparagraph 3(a) contains the existing definition of the term "pensions," while subparagraph 3(b) adds a new rule to address the treatment of Roth IRAs or similar plan (as described below).

Subparagraph 3(a) of Article XVIII provides that the term "pensions" for purposes of the Convention includes any payment under a superannuation, pension, or other retirement arrangement, Armed-Forces retirement pay, war veterans pensions and allowances, and amounts paid under a sickness, accident, or disability plan, but does not include payments under an income-averaging annuity contract (which are subject to Article XXII (Other Income)) or social security benefits, including social security benefits in respect of government services (which are subject to paragraph 5 of Article XVIII). Thus, the term "pensions" includes pensions paid by private employers (including pre-tax and Roth 401(k) arrangements) as well as any pension paid in respect of government services. Further, the definition of "pensions" includes, for example, payments from individual retirement accounts (IRAs) in the United States and from registered retirement savings plans (RRSPs) and registered retirement income funds (RRIFs) in Canada.

Subparagraph 3(b) of Article XVIII provides that the term "pensions" generally includes a Roth IRA, within the meaning of Code section 408A (or a similar plan described below). Consequently, under paragraph 1 of Article XVIII, distributions from a

Roth IRA to a resident of Canada generally continue to be exempt from Canadian tax to the extent they would have been exempt from U.S. tax if paid to a resident of the United States. In addition, residents of Canada generally may make an election under paragraph 7 of Article XVIII to defer any taxation in Canada with respect to income accrued in a Roth IRA but not distributed by the Roth IRA, until such time as and to the extent that a distribution is made from the Roth IRA or any plan substituted therefore. Because distributions will be exempt from Canadian tax to the extent they would have been exempt from U.S. tax if paid to a resident of the United States, the effect of these rules is that, in most cases, no portion of the Roth IRA will be subject to taxation in Canada.

However, subparagraph 3(b) also provides that if an individual who is a resident of Canada makes contributions to his or her Roth IRA while a resident of Canada, other than rollover contributions from another Roth IRA (or a similar plan described below), the Roth IRA will cease to be considered a pension at that time with respect to contributions and accretions from such time and accretions from such time will be subject to tax in Canada in the year of accrual. Thus, the Roth IRA will in effect be bifurcated into a "frozen" pension that continues to be subject to the rules of Article XVIII and a savings account that is not subject to the rules of Article XVIII. It is understood by the Contracting States that, following a rollover contribution from a Roth 401(k) arrangement to a Roth IRA, the Roth IRA will continue to be treated as a pension subject to the rules of Article XVIII.

Assume, for example, that Mr. X moves to Canada on July 1, 2008. Mr. X has a Roth IRA with a balance of 1,100 on July 1, 2008. Mr. X elects under paragraph 7 of Article XVIII to defer any taxation in Canada with respect to income accrued in his Roth IRA while he is a resident of Canada. Mr. X makes no additional contributions to his Roth IRA until July 1, 2010, when he makes an after-tax contribution of 100. There are accretions of 20 during the period July 1, 2008 through June 30, 2010, which are not taxed in Canada by reason of the election under paragraph 7 of Article XVIII. There are additional accretions of 50 during the period July 1, 2010 through June 30, 2015, which are subject to tax in Canada in the year of accrual. On July 1, 2015, while Mr. X is still a resident of Canada, Mr. X receives a lump-sum distribution of 1,270 from his Roth IRA. The 1,120 that was in the Roth IRA on June 30, 2010 is treated as a distribution from a pension plan that, pursuant to paragraph 1 of Article XVIII, is exempt from tax in Canada provided it would be exempt from tax in the United States under the Internal Revenue Code if paid to a resident of the United States. The remaining 150 comprises the after-tax contribution of 100 in 2010 and accretions of 50 that were subject to Canadian tax in the year of accrual.

The rules of new subparagraph 3(b) of Article XVIII also will apply to any plan or arrangement created pursuant to legislation enacted by either Contracting State after September 21, 2007 (the date of signature of the Protocol) that the competent authorities agree is similar to a Roth IRA.

Technical Explanation [1997 Protocol]: Paragraph 1 of Article 2 of the Protocol amends paragraph 3 of Article XVIII (Pensions and Annuities) of the Convention to clarify that social security benefits paid by one Contracting State in respect of services rendered to that State or a subdivision or authority of that State are subject to the rules set forth in paragraph 5 of Article XVIII, and are not subject to Article XIX (Government Service). Thus, all social security benefits paid by a Contracting State will be subject to the same rules, regardless of whether the services were rendered to a private sector employer, the government, or both.

Technical Explanation [1995 Protocol]: Article 9 of the Protocol amends Article XVIII (Pensions and Annuities) of the Convention. Paragraph 3 of Article XVIII defines the term "pensions" for purposes of the Convention, including the rules for the taxation of cross-border pensions in paragraphs 1 and 2 of the Article, the rules in paragraphs 2 and 3 of Article XXI (Exempt Organizations) for certain income derived by pension funds, and the rules in paragraph 1(b)(i) of Article IV (Residence) regarding the residence of pension funds and certain other entities. The Protocol amends the present definition by substituting the phrase "other retirement arrangement" for the phrase "retirement plan." The purpose of this change is to clarify that the definition of "pensions" includes, for example, payments from Individual Retirement Accounts (IRAs) in the United States and to provide that "pensions" includes, for example, Registered Retirement Savings Plans (RRSPs) and Registered Retirement Income Funds (RRIFs) in Canada. The term "pensions" also would include amounts paid by other retirement plans or arrangements, whether or not they are qualified plans under U.S. domestic law; this would include, for example, plans and arrangements described in section 457 or 414(d) of the *Internal Revenue Code*.

Technical Explanation [1984]: Paragraph 3 defines the term "pensions" for purposes of the Convention to include any payment under a superannuation, pension, or retirement plan, Armed Forces retirement pay, war veterans pensions and allowances, and amounts paid under a sickness, accident, or disability plan. Thus, the term "pension" includes pensions paid by private employers as well as any pension paid by a Contracting State in respect of services rendered to that State. A pension for government service is covered. The term "pensions" does not include payments under an income averaging annuity contract or benefits paid under social security legislation. The latter benefits are taxed, pursuant to paragraph 5, only in the Contracting State paying the benefit. Income derived from an income averaging annuity contract is taxable pursuant to the provisions of Article XXII (Other Income).

4. For the purposes of this Convention:

(a) the term **"annuity"** means a stated sum paid periodically at stated times during life or during a specified number of years,

under an obligation to make the payments in return for adequate and full consideration (other than services rendered), but does not include a payment that is not a periodic payment or any annuity the cost of which was deductible for the purposes of taxation in the Contracting State in which it was acquired; and

(b) an annuity or other amount paid in respect of a life insurance or annuity contract (including a withdrawal in respect of the cash value thereof) shall be deemed to arise in a Contracting State if the person paying the annuity or other amount (in this subparagraph referred to as the "payer") is a resident of that State. However, if the payer, whether a resident of a Contracting State or not, has in a State other than that of which the payer is a resident a permanent establishment in connection with which the obligation giving rise to the annuity or other amount was incurred, and the annuity or other amount is borne by the permanent establishment, then the annuity or other amount shall be deemed to arise in the State in which the permanent establishment is situated and not in the State of which the payer is a resident.

Related Provisions: ITCIA 5 — Definition of "annuity".

Notes: "Annuity" excludes pension and similar payments: see ITCIA s. 5 (reproduced before this treaty). See also VIEWS doc 2015-0609951E5 ("annuity" in Canada-Turkey treaty can include payments subject to ITA 12.2 or 56(1)(d), but not RRSP payments dues to ITCIA 5).

Art. XVIII:4(b) added (and 4(a) changed from defining "annuities" to "annuity") by 2007 Protocol, effective for taxable years beginning after 2008, but in respect of taxes withheld at source, for amounts paid or credited after Jan. 2009.

Definitions: "annuity" — ITCIA 5.

Technical Explanation [2007 Protocol]: *Source of payments under life insurance and annuity contracts*

Paragraph 1 of Article 13 also replaces paragraph 4 of Article XVIII. Subparagraph 4(a) contains the existing definition of annuity, while subparagraph 4(b) adds a source rule to address the treatment of certain payments by branches of insurance companies.

Subparagraph 4(a) provides that, for purposes of the Convention, the term "annuity" means a stated sum paid periodically at stated times during life or during a specified number of years, under an obligation to make the payments in return for adequate and full consideration other than services rendered. The term does not include a payment that is not periodic or any annuity the cost of which was deductible for tax purposes in the Contracting State where the annuity was acquired. Items excluded from the definition of "annuity" and not dealt with under another Article of the Convention are subject to the rules of Article XXII (Other Income).

Under the existing Convention, payments under life insurance and annuity contracts to a resident of Canada by a Canadian branch of a U.S. insurance company are subject to either a 15-percent withholding tax under subparagraph 2(b) of Article XVIII or, unless dealt with under another Article of the Convention, an unreduced 30-percent withholding tax under paragraph 1 of Article XXII, depending on whether the payments constitute annuities within the meaning of paragraph 4 of Article XVIII.

On July 12, 2004, the Internal Revenue Service issued Revenue Ruling 2004-75, 2004-2 C.B. 109, which provides in relevant part that annuity payments under, and withdrawals of cash value from, life insurance or annuity contracts issued by a foreign branch of a U.S. life insurance company are U.S.-source income that, when paid to a nonresident alien individual, is generally subject to a 30-percent withholding tax under Code sections 871(a) and 1441. Revenue Ruling 2004-97, 2004-2 C.B. 516, provided that Revenue Ruling 2004-75 would not be applied to payments that were made before January 1, 2005, provided that such payments were made pursuant to binding life insurance or annuity contracts issued on or before July 12, 2004.

Under new subparagraph 4(b) of Article XVIII, an annuity or other amount paid in respect of a life insurance or annuity contract (including a withdrawal in respect of the cash value thereof), will generally be deemed to arise in the Contracting State where the person paying the annuity or other amount (the "payer") is resident. However, if the payer, whether a resident of a Contracting State or not, has a permanent establishment in a Contracting State other than a Contracting State in which the payer is a resident, the payment will be deemed to arise in the Contracting State in which the permanent establishment is situated if both of the following requirements are satisfied: (i) the obligation giving rise to the annuity or other amount must have been incurred in connection with the permanent establishment, and (ii) the annuity or other amount must be borne by the permanent establishment. When these requirements are satisfied, payments by a Canadian branch of a U.S. insurance company will be deemed to arise in Canada.

Technical Explanation [1984]: Paragraph 4 provides that, for purposes of the Convention, the term "annuities" means a stated sum paid periodically at stated times during life or during a specified number of years, under an obligation to make payments in return for adequate and full consideration other than services rendered. The term does not include a payment that is not periodic or any annuity the cost of which was deductible for tax purposes in the Contracting State where the annuity was acquired. Items excluded from the definition of "annuities" are subject to the rules of Article XXII.

5. Benefits under the social security legislation in a Contracting State (including tier 1 railroad retirement benefits but not including unemployment benefits) paid to a resident of the other Contracting State shall be taxable only in that other State, subject to the following conditions:

(a) a benefit under the social security legislation in the United States paid to a resident of Canada shall be taxable in Canada as though it were a benefit under the *Canada Pension Plan*, except that 15 per cent of the amount of the benefit shall be exempt from Canadian tax; and

(b) a benefit under the social security legislation in Canada paid to a resident of the United States shall be taxable in the United States as though it were a benefit under the Social Security Act, except that a type of benefit that is not subject to Canadian tax when paid to residents of Canada shall be exempt from United States tax.

Related Provisions: ITA 110(1)(h) — Reduction of income inclusion from 85% to 50% where benefits received since before 1996.

Notes: See Notes to para. 3 above.

The 15% exemption under 5(a) is done by 100% inclusion under ITA 56(1)(a)(i)(B) and 15% deduction under ITA 110(1)(f): VIEWS doc 2011-0392071E5.

The 15% exemption does not apply to private pension benefits: *Tingley*, [1999] 1 C.T.C. 2177 (TCC); *Bédard*, [1999] 2 C.T.C. 2671 (TCC); *Donnelly*, 2007 TCC 363. It does apply to *US Social Security Act* survivor benefits: VIEWS doc 2007-0228481E5; and to regular social security benefits reported on a Form SSA-1099: *Gravel*, 2007 TCC 646, para. 21.

Due to 5(a), the averaging election under ITA 56(8) and 120.3 can be made in respect of a retroactive lump-sum U.S. Social Security benefit: VIEWS docs 2010-0385701E5, 2011-0392071E5.

S.C. 1999, c. 22 (the 1999 Budget bill), s. 83, applicable to the 1996 and 1997 taxation years, provides special rules for the application of the 1997 Protocol to the Canada-U.S. Income Tax Convention. It creates a refundable credit of $50 to certain taxpayers. It was reproduced here up to the 25th edition.

Art. XVIII:5 amended by 1997 Protocol, generally retroactive to 1996, but with a number of transitional rules (reproduced here up to the 25th edition).

Art. XVIII:5 amended by 1995 Protocol, generally effective 1996.

Canada extended the 25% withholding tax under ITA 212(1)(h) to Old Age Security benefits and Canada Pension Plan/Quebec Pension Plan payments effective January 1, 1996. See the 1996 repeal of ITA 212(1)(h)(i) and (ii). However, the 1997 Protocol amendments effectively override this change for U.S. residents.

Definitions: "Canada" — Art. III:1(a), ITCIA 5; "Canadian tax" — Art. III:1(c); "resident" — Art. IV; "State" — Art. III:1(i); "United States" — Art. III:1(b); "United States tax" — Art. III:1(d).

Technical Explanation [1997 Protocol]: Paragraph 2 of Article 2 of the Protocol amends paragraph 5 of Article XVIII of the Convention, which provides rules for the taxation of social security benefits (including tier 1 railroad retirement benefits but not including unemployment benefits), and reverses changes made by the third protocol to the Convention, which was signed on March 17, 1995 and generally took effect as of January 1, 1996 (the "1995 Protocol"). Under the Convention prior to amendment by the 1995 Protocol, the State of residence of the recipient of social security benefits had the exclusive right to tax social security benefits paid by the other State on a net basis but exempted 50% of the benefit. This was changed by the 1995 Protocol. Under the 1995 Protocol, effective January 1, 1996 benefits paid under the U.S. or Canadian social security legislation to a resident of the other Contracting State (or, in the case of Canadian benefits, paid to a U.S. citizen) are taxable exclusively in the paying State.

Canada and the United States impose different source-basis taxing regimes on social security benefits. Under Code section 871(a)(3), 85% of social security benefits paid to a nonresident alien are includible in gross income. The taxable portion of social security benefits is subject to the regular 30% withholding tax, with the result that the gross social security benefit is subject to an effective tax rate of 25.5%. This is a final payment of tax and Canadian recipients of U.S. social security benefits, regardless of their level of income, may not elect to be taxed in the United States on a net basis at graduated rates.

In Canada, social security benefits paid to nonresidents are subject to a general withholding tax of 25%. However, Canada permits U.S. recipients of Canadian benefits to file a Canadian tax return and pay tax at regular graduated rates on their net income. As a result, low-income U.S. recipients of Canadian social security typically pay little or no tax on their benefits.

The Protocol returns to a system of residence-based taxation in which social security benefits are exclusively taxable in the State where the recipient lives. Social security benefits will generally be taxed as if they were benefits paid under the social security legislation in the residence State. Therefore, social security benefits will be taxed on a net basis at graduated rates and low-income recipients will not pay any tax on these benefits. However, the Protocol modifies the residence State's taxation of cross-border

benefits in order to take into account how the benefits would have been taxed in the source State if paid to a resident of that State.

In the case of Canadian recipients of U.S. social security benefits, the Protocol provides that only 85% of these benefits will be subject to tax in Canada. This reflects the fact that, although in Canada social security benefits are fully includible, a maximum of 85% of United States social security benefits are includible in income for U.S. tax purposes. See Code section 86. This is also consistent with the taxation of social security benefits under the Convention prior to the effective date of the 1995 Protocol, since at the time the pre-1996 rule was adopted the United States included a maximum of 50% of the social security benefits in income.

In the case of U.S. recipients of Canadian social security benefits, the Protocol provides that the benefits will be taxed as if they were payments under the *Social Security Act*. Therefore, a maximum of 85% of the Canadian benefits will be included in the gross income of a U.S. recipient, even though the entire benefit would have been taxed by Canada if received by a Canadian resident. However, if the Canadian benefit is of a type that is not subject to Canadian tax when paid to a resident of Canada, it will not be subject to U.S. tax when received by a resident of the United States. This provision is necessary to take into account certain proposed changes to Canada's Old Age Security benefits. At present, Old Age Security benefits paid to U.S. residents are subject to both ordinary Canadian income tax and an additional "recovery tax" that has the effect of means-testing the benefit. Canada has proposed to change the Old Age Security benefit system so that the benefit would be means-tested at source and not subject to the recovery tax. Because the amount of such future benefits will have already been reduced to take into account the recipient's income, it would not be appropriate to subject such benefits to additional U.S. tax.

[Application of the Protocol]

Article 3 of the Protocol contains the rules for bringing the Protocol into force and giving effect to its provisions.

Paragraph 1

Paragraph 1 provides for the ratification of the Protocol by both Contracting States according to their constitutional and statutory requirements and instruments of ratification will be exchanged as soon as possible.

In the United States, the process leading to ratification and entry into force is as follows: Once a protocol has been signed by authorized representatives of the two Contracting States, the Department of State sends the protocol to the President who formally transmits it to the Senate for its advice and consent to ratification, which requires approval by two-thirds of the Senators present and voting. Prior to this vote, however, it generally has been the practice for the Senate Committee on Foreign Relations to hold hearings on the protocol and make a recommendation regarding its approval to the full Senate. Both Government and private sector witnesses may testify at these hearings. After receiving the advice and consent of the Senate to ratification, the protocol is returned to the President for his signature on the ratification document. The President's signature on the document completes the process in the United States.

Paragraph 2

Paragraph 2 of Article 3 provides that the Protocol will enter into force on the date on which the instruments of ratification are exchanged. However, the date on which the Protocol enters into force will not be the date on which its provisions will take effect. Paragraph 2, therefore, also contains rules that determine when the provisions of the Protocol will have effect.

Under paragraph 2(a), Article 1 of the Protocol will have effect as of April 26, 1995. As discussed above, this is the date on which certain proposed amendments to Canadian law would be effective.

Under paragraph 2(b), Article 2 of the Protocol will have effect as of January 1, 1996, which is the date as of which the changes to the taxation of social security benefits that were implemented by the 1995 Protocol became effective. Consequently, the source-basis taxation of social security benefits that was implemented by the 1995 Protocol will be retroactively eliminated and recipients of cross-border social security benefits will be entitled to a refund of any source-State tax withheld on their benefits for 1996 and later years. This return to residence-basis taxation of social security benefits means that some high-income recipients of cross-border benefits may be required to pay additional taxes to their State of residence if their average tax rate on these benefits in their State of residence is higher than the current rate of source-State withholding tax. It is only for future years, however, that such high-income recipients of benefits will be subject to a higher rate of tax. No one will be subject to a higher rate of tax for the retroactive period. If, as a result of the change, the residence-State tax would exceed the amount of the refund otherwise due, there will be neither a refund of source-State tax nor the imposition of additional residence-State tax.

Subparagraphs (b)(i) and (ii) provide rules that determine how the retroactive effect of the Protocol will generally be implemented for the year in which the Protocol enters into effect. As discussed below, these rules are required as a result of administrative limitations on the ability of the relevant Government organizations to effect the payment of refunds. Withholding taxes imposed by the United States on cross-border social security benefits are collected and administered by the Social Security Administration (SSA), not the Internal Revenue Service (IRS). However, any refunds of withholding tax improperly collected on social security benefits are ordinarily paid by the IRS. If the Protocol enters into force prior to September 1 of a calendar year, it is possible for the SSA to pay refunds of the tax withheld for the entire year directly to the individual Canadian recipient. If the Protocol enters into force after August 31 of a calendar year, it will not be possible for SSA to pay refunds of tax withheld for that year and refunds must be paid through the IRS.

Paragraphs 3, 4 and 5 of Article 3 establish administrative procedures to govern the payment of refunds through the IRS, including rules to ensure that benefits will not be subject to a higher rate of tax in the residence State for the retroactive period. The taxes withheld on social security benefits paid for years after 1995 and prior to the calendar year in which the Protocol enters into force (referred to in the Protocol as "source-taxed benefits") will be subject to the refund procedures set forth in paragraphs 3, 4, and 5, regardless of when the Protocol enters into force. Social security benefits paid for calendar years beginning after the Protocol enters into force will not be subject to the refund procedures set forth in paragraphs 3, 4, and 5 because source State tax will not be withheld.

If the Protocol enters into force after August 31 of a calendar year, subparagraph (b)(i) provides that social security benefits paid during such calendar year will be treated as benefits paid for calendar years ending before the year in which the Protocol enters into force (and thus will be treated as "source-taxed benefits"). In this case, the taxes withheld on these benefits will be subject to the refund procedures set forth in paragraphs 3, 4, and 5 of Article 3 and these benefits will not be subject to a higher rate of residence-State tax. If the Protocol enters into force before September 1 of a calendar year, subparagraph (b)(ii) provides that social security benefits paid during such calendar year will be treated as benefits paid for calendar years beginning after the year in which the Protocol enters into force. In this case, the taxes withheld on these benefits will be directly and automatically refunded by the source State and the potentially higher rate of residence-State tax will apply.

Paragraph 3

Paragraph 3 of Article 3 of the Protocol provides rules governing the payment of refunds of source-State tax with respect to "source-taxed benefits." In general, all applications for refund must be made to the competent authority of the source State within three years of entry into force of the Protocol.

Except as set forth in subparagraph (b) of paragraph 2, the retroactive effect of the Protocol is elective and applies only if a recipient of benefits applies for a refund of the tax paid or withheld. Consequently, if a recipient of benefits does not apply for a refund of the tax paid or withheld, the Protocol will not be given retroactive effect, except as set forth in subparagraph (b) of paragraph 2. If the residence-State tax that would be imposed on such source-taxed benefits is greater than the source-State tax imposed on such benefits, it is assumed that the recipient will not apply for a refund of the source-State tax and such benefits will not be subject to the retroactive effect of the Protocol. Because the application for refund may be made on a year-by-year basis, the recipient may elect the most beneficial treatment for each year. Therefore, social security benefits will not be subject to a higher rate of tax for the retroactive period, except as set forth in subparagraph (b) of paragraph 2.

The refund procedure depends on the recipient's State of residence. In the case of U.S. residents who received Canadian social security benefits that were subject to Canadian tax, a U.S. resident who elects to have the Protocol apply retroactively will apply directly to the Canadian competent authority for the refund of any Canadian tax not previously refunded. On the receipt of such refund, the Canadian social security benefits will be includible in the U.S. resident's gross income for the years with respect to which the refund was paid. Consequently, the U.S. recipient may be required to file an amended U.S. income tax return for such years and pay U.S. tax on such benefits. Pursuant to Article XXVII (Exchange of Information) of the Convention, the Canadian competent authority will provide the U.S. competent authority with information regarding the payment of refunds.

In the case of Canadian residents who received U.S. social security benefits, the Canadian competent authority shall be the only person entitled to apply for a refund of the U.S. taxes withheld on such benefits. Individual residents of Canada will not apply directly to the IRS for refunds. However, the Canadian competent authority may base its applications on information received from individual Canadians, as well as on information to be provided by the United State competent authority. The Protocol provides that the Canadian competent authority shall apply for and receive all such refunds on behalf of individual residents of Canada and shall remit such refunds to individual residents of Canada after deducting any additional Canadian tax that may imposed as a result of such social security benefits being subject to tax in Canada. The Canadian competent authority shall make such application for refund on behalf of an individual resident of Canada only if the additional Canadian tax that would be imposed is less than the amount of the U.S. tax to be refunded. If, with respect to an individual resident of Canada, the additional Canadian tax that would be imposed on the individual's social security benefits is equal to or greater than the U.S. tax withheld, the Canadian competent authority shall not apply for a refund of the U.S. tax withheld on the individual's benefits. This provision ensures that refunds of U.S. tax will be paid only when the refund will benefit an individual resident of Canada. A refund of U.S. tax will not be paid if it would simply result in a payment from the U.S. Treasury to the Government of Canada without any portion of the refund being paid to an individual resident of Canada.

Paragraph 4

Paragraph 4 provides that all taxes refunded as a result of the Protocol will be refunded without interest. Correspondingly, any additional taxes assessed as a result of the Protocol will be assessed without interest provided that the additional taxes are paid in a timely manner. However, interest and penalties on underpayments may be assessed for periods beginning after December 31 of the year following the year in which the Protocol enters into force.

Paragraph 5

Paragraph 5 provides that the competent authorities shall establish procedures for making or revoking the application for refund provided for in paragraph 3 and such other procedures as are necessary to ensure the appropriate implementation of the Protocol. It will be necessary to establish procedures for a taxpayer to revoke his application for refund because a taxpayer may apply for a refund and then determine that the residence-State tax imposed on his social security benefits pursuant to Article 2 of the Protocol exceeds the amount of source-State tax refunded. Such a taxpayer (or, in the case of a Canadian resident, the Canadian competent authority acting on behalf of such taxpayer) will be permitted to revoke his application for refund provided that the taxpayer returns the source-State refund and the three-year period established in paragraph 3 has not expired as of the date on which the revocation is filed. The competent authorities will also establish procedures to ensure that duplicate refunds are not paid.

Technical Explanation [1995 Protocol]: Paragraph 2 of Article 9 of the Protocol amends paragraph 5 of Article XVIII to modify the treatment of social security benefits under the Convention. Under the amended paragraph, benefits paid under the U.S. or Canadian social security legislation to a resident of the other Contracting State, or, in the case of Canadian benefits, to a U.S. citizen, are taxable exclusively in the paying State. This amendment brings the Convention into line with current U.S. treaty policy. Social security benefits are defined, for this purpose, to include tier 1 railroad retirement benefits but not unemployment benefits (which therefore fall under Article XXII (Other Income) of the Convention). Pensions in respect of government service are covered not by this rule but by the rules of paragraphs 1 and 2 of Article XVIII.

The special rule regarding U.S. citizens is intended to clarify that only Canada, and not the United States, may tax a social security payment by Canada to a U.S. citizen not resident in the United States. This is consistent with the intention of the general rule, which is to give each Contracting State exclusive taxing jurisdiction over its social security payments. Since paragraph 5 is an exception to the saving clause, Canada will retain exclusive taxing jurisdiction over Canadian social security benefits paid to U.S. residents and citizens, and vice versa. It was not necessary to provide a special rule to clarify the taxation of U.S. social security payments to Canadian citizens, because Canada does not tax on the basis of citizenship and, therefore, does not include citizens within the scope of its saving clause.

Technical Explanation [1984]: Paragraph 5, as amended by the 1984 Protocol, provides that benefits under social security legislation in Canada or the United States paid to a resident of the other Contracting State are taxable only in the State in which the recipient is resident. However, the State of residence must exempt from taxation one-half of the total amount of such benefits paid in a taxable year. Thus, if U.S. social security benefits are paid to a resident of Canada, the United States will exempt such benefits from tax and Canada will exempt one-half of the benefits from taxation. The exemption of one-half of the benefits in the State of residence is an exception to the saving clause under subparagraph 3(a) of Article XXIX (Miscellaneous Rules). The United States will not exempt U.S. social security benefits from tax if the Canadian resident receiving such benefits is a U.S. citizen. If a U.S. citizen and resident receives Canadian social security benefits, Canada will not tax such benefits and the United States will exempt from tax one-half of the total amount of such benefits. The United States will also exempt one-half of Canadian social security benefits from tax if the recipient is a U.S. citizen who is a resident of Canada, under paragraph 7 of Article XXIX. Paragraph 5 encompasses benefits paid under social security legislation of a political subdivision, such as a province of Canada.

6. Alimony and other similar amounts (including child support payments) arising in a Contracting State and paid to a resident of the other Contracting State shall be taxable as follows:

(a) such amounts shall be taxable only in that other State;

(b) notwithstanding the provisions of subparagraph (a), the amount that would be excluded from taxable income in the first-mentioned State if the recipient were a resident thereof shall be exempt from taxation in that other State.

Notes: The 183-day test applies on a property-by-property basis: VIEWS doc 2011-0428531E5.

Canada repealed ITA 212(1)(f) effective May 1997, so no withholding tax applies to alimony or maintenance payments, even without treaty protection.

Definitions: "State" — Art. III:1(i); "taxable income" — ITCIA 3, ITA 248(1).

Technical Explanation [1984]: Paragraph 6(a) provides that only the State of which a person is resident has the right to tax alimony and other similar amounts (including child support payments) arising in the other Contracting State and paid to such person. However, under paragraph 6(b), the state of residence shall exempt from taxation the amount that would be excluded from taxable income in the State of source if the recipient were a resident thereof. Thus, if child support payments are made by a U.S. resident to a resident of Canada, Canada shall exempt from tax the amount of such payments which would be excluded from taxable income under section 71(b) of the *Internal Revenue Code*. Paragraph 6 does not define the term "alimony"; the term is defined pursuant to the provisions of paragraph 2 of Article III (General Definitions).

Article XVIII does not provide rules to determine the State in which pensions, annuities, alimony, and other similar amounts arise. The provisions of paragraph 2 of Article III are used to determine where such amounts arise for purposes of determining whether a Contracting State has the right to tax such amounts.

Paragraphs 1, 3, 4, 5(b) and 6(b) of Article XVIII are, by reason of paragraph 3(a) of Article XXIX (Miscellaneous Rules), exceptions to the "saving clause." Thus, the rules in those paragraphs change U.S. taxation of U.S. citizens and residents.

7. A natural person who is a citizen or resident of a Contracting State and a beneficiary of a trust, company, organization or other arrangement that is a resident of the other Contracting State, generally exempt from income taxation in that other State and operated exclusively to provide pension or employee benefits may elect to defer taxation in the first-mentioned State, subject to rules established by the competent authority of that State, with respect to any income accrued in the plan but not distributed by the plan, until such time as and to the extent that a distribution is made from the plan or any plan substituted therefor.

Notes: Amounts accruing in an IRA are not taxed until withdrawn, even without an election under para. 7: VIEWS doc 2015-0576551E5.

In *Rodrigue*, 2001 FCA 157, a contribution to a U.S. 401(k) plan was held non-deductible for Canadian tax purposes; the words "income accrued" in s. 7 were clearly meant to exempt only income earned on money in a plan and not contributions of capital made into the plan.

In *Natarajan*, 2010 TCC 582, CRA agreed that employment income paid by the employer to a US Deferred Income Plan was not taxable because it had not been "received" — effectively turning the US plan into an RRSP for Canadian tax purposes.

For Canadians with a 401(k) plan who are returning to Canada, see Faizal Valli, "Tax Implications of Canadians Transferring a U.S. Retirement Plan to Canada", 22(2) *Taxation of Executive Compensation & Retirement* (Federated Press) 1324-28 (Sept. 2010); Dario Bon, "Challenges Canadians face when transferring US retirement plans to an RRSP", tinyurl.com/moodys-401k.

US citizens or residents holding RRSPs or RRIFs can defer tax on amounts accruing in the plan: see IRS Rev. Proc. 2014-55 (Oct. 2014) on irs.gov, replacing 2002-23, which required annual filing of a Form 8891. However, to qualify the taxpayer must have satisfied some requirement for filing a US federal income tax return for *each* taxable year the person was a US citizen or resident; if not, they need permission from Treasury to make the election late, with costly user fees; and a $10,000 penalty may apply for not reporting the RRSP or RRIF on a Form 8938: Roy Berg, "IRS's new procedure for Canadian retirement plans: not all good news", tinyurl.com/irs-rrsp.

Note however that California taxes growth within an RRSP. See tinyurl.com/calif-rrsp.

US persons may also need to file various other forms: see Notes to 233.3(3).

Para. 7 can be used to defer Canadian tax on income of a Roth IRA (see ITA 56(12)) until it is distributed: VIEWS docs 2002-0152515, 2013-0476351E5; *Income Tax Technical News* 43. A contribution made while Canadian resident disqualifies the Roth IRA, and cannot be reversed: 2020-0846401E5. See also Cyna, "Taxpayers Need to Elect to Protect their Roth IRA", 7(11) *Tax Hyperion* (Carswell, Nov. 2010); Yager, "Roth IRAs", 18(11) *Canadian Tax Highlights* (ctf.ca) 9 (Nov. 2010). See also ITA 56(12) Notes. Para. 7 is not needed for a traditional IRA, which falls under ITA 248(1)"foreign retirement arrangement" and is not taxed until paid out: 2011-0404071E5.

Art. XVIII:7 amended by 2007 Protocol, for tax years beginning after 2008, but in respect of taxes withheld at source, for amounts paid or credited after Jan. 2009; added by 1995 Protocol. It is a more generic version of former Art. XXIX:5, which applied only to RRSPs.

Definitions: "company" — Art. III:1(f); "competent authority" — Art. III:1(g); "pension" — Art. XVIII:3, ITCIA 5; "person" — Art. III:1(e), ITCIA 3, *Interpretation Act* 35(1); "resident" — Art. IV; "State" — Art. III:1(i); "trust" — ITCIA 3, ITA 104(1), 248(1), (3).

Income Tax Folios: S5-F3-C1: Taxation of a Roth IRA.

I.T. Technical News: 43 (taxation of Roth IRAs).

Technical Explanation [2007 Protocol]: Paragraph 2 of Article 13 of the Protocol replaces paragraph 7 of Article XVIII of the existing Convention. Paragraph 7 continues to provide a rule with respect to the taxation of a natural person on income accrued in a pension or employee benefit plan in the other Contracting State. Thus, paragraph 7 applies where an individual is a citizen or resident of a Contracting State and is a beneficiary of a trust, company, organization, or other arrangement that is a resident of the other Contracting State, where such trust, company, organization, or other arrangement is generally exempt from income taxation in that other State, and is operated exclusively to provide pension, or employee benefits. In such cases, the beneficiary may elect to defer taxation in his State of residence on income accrued in the plan until it is distributed from the plan (or from another plan in that other Contracting State to which the income is transferred pursuant to the domestic law of that other Contracting State).

Paragraph 2 of Article 13 of the Protocol makes two changes to paragraph 7 of Article XVIII of the existing Convention. The first change is that the phrase "pension, retirement or employee benefits" is changed to "pension or employee benefits" solely to reflect the fact that in certain cases, discussed above, Roth IRAs will not be treated as pensions for purposes of Article XVIII. The second change is that "under" is changed to "subject to" to make it clear that an election to defer taxation with respect to undistributed income accrued in a plan may be made whether or not the competent authority of the first-mentioned State has prescribed rules for making an election. For the U.S.

rules, see Revenue Procedure 2002-23, 2002-1 C.B. 744. As of the date the Protocol was signed, the competent authority of Canada had not prescribed rules.

Technical Explanation [1995 Protocol]: A new paragraph 7 is added to Article XVIII by Article 9 of the Protocol. This paragraph replaces paragraph 5 of Article XXIX (Miscellaneous Rules) of the present Convention. The new paragraph makes reciprocal the rule that it replaced and expands its scope, so that it no longer applies only to residents and citizens of the United States who are beneficiaries of Canadian RRSPs. As amended, paragraph 7 applies to an individual who is a citizen or resident of a Contracting State and a beneficiary of a trust, company, organization, or other arrangement that is a resident of the other Contracting State and that is both generally exempt from income taxation in its State of residence and operated exclusively to provide pension, retirement, or employee benefits. Under this rule, the beneficiary may elect to defer taxation in his State of residence on income accrued in the plan until it is distributed or rolled over into another plan. The new rule also broadens the types of arrangements covered by this paragraph in a manner consistent with other pension-related provisions of the Protocol.

8. Contributions made to, or benefits accrued under, a qualifying retirement plan in a Contracting State by or on behalf of an individual shall be deductible or excludible in computing the individual's taxable income in the other Contracting State, and contributions made to the plan by the individual's employer shall be allowed as a deduction in computing the employer's profits in that other State, where:

(a) the individual performs services as an employee in that other State the remuneration from which is taxable in that other State;

(b) the individual was participating in the plan (or another similar plan for which this plan was substituted) immediately before the individual began performing the services in that other State;

(c) the individual was not a resident of that other State immediately before the individual began performing the services in that other State;

(d) the individual has performed services in that other State for the same employer (or a related employer) for no more than 60 of the 120 months preceding the individual's current taxation year;

(e) the contributions and benefits are attributable to the services performed by the individual in that other State, and are made or accrued during the period in which the individual performs those services; and

(f) with respect to contributions and benefits that are attributable to services performed during a period in the individual's current taxation year, no contributions in respect of the period are made by or on behalf of the individual to, and no services performed in that other State during the period are otherwise taken into account for purposes of determining the individual's entitlement to benefits under, any plan that would be a qualifying retirement plan in that other State if paragraph 15 of this Article were read without reference to subparagraphs (b) and (c) of that paragraph.

This paragraph shall apply only to the extent that the contributions or benefits would qualify for tax relief in the first-mentioned State if the individual was a resident of and performed the services in that State.

Related Provisions: Reg. 8308.1(2.1) — Pension credit under tax treaty; Art. XVIII:9 — Limit on benefits; Art. XVIII:16 — Where distribution deemed to arise; Art. XVIII:17 — Partners treated as employees.

Notes: See Dept. of Finance news release 2007-070 (Sept. 21, 2007), under "Pensions & other registered plans"; Cardarelli, "The Fifth Protocol to the Canada-US Income Tax Convention", 2008 conference report at 26:26-28; VIEWS doc 2009-0319221E5.

A 401(k) is a qualifying retirement plan: VIEWS doc 2012-0432281E5.

Art. XVIII:8 added by 2007 Protocol, effective for taxable years beginning after 2008, but in respect of taxes withheld at source, for amounts paid or credited after Jan. 2009.

Definitions: "employee", "employer" — Art. XVIII:17, ITCIA 3, ITA 248(1); "individual" — ITCIA 3, ITA 248(1); "month" — ITCIA 3, *Interpretation Act* 35(1); "qualifying retirement plan" — Art. XVIII:15; "related" — ITCIA 3, ITA 251; "resident" — Art. IV; "State" — Art. III:1(i); "taxable income" — ITCIA 3, ITA 248(1); "taxation year" — ITCIA 3, ITA 249, 250.1.

Technical Explanation [2007 Protocol]: Paragraph 3 of Article 13 of the Protocol adds paragraphs 8 through 17 to Article XVIII to deal with cross-border pension contributions. These paragraphs are intended to remove barriers to the flow of personal services between the Contracting States that could otherwise result from discontinuities in the laws of the Contracting States regarding the deductibility of pension contributions.

Such discontinuities may arise where a country allows deductions or exclusions to its residents for contributions, made by them or on their behalf, to resident pension plans, but does not allow deductions or exclusions for payments made to plans resident in another country, even if the structure and legal requirements of such plans in the two countries are similar.

There is no comparable set of rules in the OECD Model, although the issue is discussed in detail in the Commentary to Article 18 (Pensions). The 2006 U.S. Model deals with this issue in paragraphs 2 through 4 of Article 18 (Pension Funds).

Workers on short-term assignments in the other Contracting State

Paragraphs 8 and 9 of Article XVIII address the case of a short-term assignment where an individual who is participating in a "qualifying retirement plan" (as defined in paragraph 15 of Article XVIII) in one Contracting State (the "home State") performs services as an employee for a limited period of time in the other Contracting State (the "host State"). If certain requirements are satisfied, contributions made to, or benefits accrued under, the plan by or on behalf of the individual will be deductible or excludible in computing the individual's income in the host State. In addition, contributions made to the plan by the individual's employer will be allowed as a deduction in computing the employer's profits in the host State.

In order for paragraph 8 to apply, the remuneration that the individual receives with respect to the services performed in the host State must be taxable in the host State. This means, for example, that where the United States is the host State, paragraph 8 would not apply if the remuneration that the individual receives with respect to the services performed in the United States is exempt from taxation in the United States under Code section 893.

The individual also must have been participating in the plan, or in another similar plan for which the plan was substituted, immediately before he began performing services in the host State. The rule regarding a successor plan would apply if, for example, the employer has been acquired by another corporation that replaces the existing plan with its own plan, transferring membership in the old plan over into the new plan.

In addition, the individual must not have been a resident (as determined under Article IV (Residence)) of the host State immediately before he began performing services in the host State. It is irrelevant for purposes of paragraph 8 whether the individual becomes a resident of the host State while he performs services there. A citizen of the United States who has been a resident of Canada may be entitled to benefits under paragraph 8 if (a) he performs services in the United States for a limited period of time and (b) he was a resident of Canada immediately before he began performing such services.

Benefits are available under paragraph 8 only for so long as the individual has not performed services in the host State for the same employer (or a related employer) for more than 60 of the 120 months preceding the individual's current taxable year. The purpose of this rule is to limit the period of time for which the host State will be required to provide benefits for contributions to a plan from which it is unlikely to be able to tax the distributions. If the individual continues to perform services in the host State beyond this time limit, he is expected to become a participant in a plan in the host State. Canada's domestic law provides preferential tax treatment for employer contributions to foreign pension plans in respect of services rendered in Canada by short-term residents, but such treatment ceases once the individual has been resident in Canada for at least 60 of the preceding 72 months.

The contributions and benefits must be attributable to services performed by the individual in the host State, and must be made or accrued during the period in which the individual performs those services. This rule prevents individuals who render services in the host State for a very short period of time from making disproportionately large contributions to home State plans in order to offset the tax liability associated with the income earned in the host State. In the case where the United States is the host State, contributions will be deemed to have been made on the last day of the preceding taxable year if the payment is on account of such taxable year and is treated under U.S. law as a contribution made on the last day of the preceding taxable year.

If an individual receives benefits in the host State with respect to contributions to a plan in the home State, the services to which the contributions relate may not be taken into account for purposes of determining the individual's entitlement to benefits under any trust, company, organization, or other arrangement that is a resident of the host State, generally exempt from income taxation in that State and operated to provide pension or retirement benefits. The purpose of this rule is to prevent double benefits for contributions to both a home State plan and a host State plan with respect to the same services. Thus, for example, an individual who is working temporarily in the United States and making contributions to a qualifying retirement plan in Canada with respect to services performed in the United States may not make contributions to an individual retirement account (within the meaning of Code section 408(a)) in the United States with respect to the same services.

Paragraph 8 states that it applies only to the extent that the contributions or benefits would qualify for tax relief in the home State if the individual were a resident of and performed services in that State. Thus, benefits would be limited in the same fashion as if the individual continued to be a resident of the home State. However, paragraph 9 provides that if the host State is the United States and the individual is a citizen of the United States, the benefits granted to the individual under paragraph 8 may not exceed the benefits that would be allowed by the United States to its residents for contributions to, or benefits otherwise accrued under, a generally corresponding pension or retirement plan established in and recognized for tax purposes by the United States. Thus, the lower of the two limits applies. This rule ensures that U.S. citizens working temporarily in the United States and participating in a Canadian plan will not get more favorable U.S. tax treatment than U.S. citizens participating in a U.S. plan.

Where the United States is the home State, the amount of contributions that may be excluded from the employee's income under paragraph 8 for Canadian purposes is limited to the U.S. dollar amount specified in Code section 415 or the U.S. dollar amount specified in Code section 402(g)(1) to the extent contributions are made from the employee's compensation. For this purpose, the dollar limit specified in Code section 402(g)(1) means the amount applicable under Code section 402(g)(1) (including the age 50 catch-up amount in Code section 402(g)(1)(C)) or, if applicable, the parallel dollar limit applicable under Code section 457(e)(15) plus the age 50 catch-up amount under Code section 414(v)(2)(B)(i) for a Code section 457(g) trust.

Where Canada is the home State, the amount of contributions that may be excluded from the employee's income under paragraph 8 for U.S. purposes is subject to the limitations specified in subsections 146(5), 147(8), 147.1(8) and (9) and 147.2(1) and (4) of the *Income Tax Act* and paragraph 8503(4)(a) of the *Income Tax Regulations*, as applicable. If the employee is a citizen of the United States, then the amount of contributions that may be excluded is the lesser of the amounts determined under the limitations specified in the previous sentence and the amounts specified in the previous paragraph.

The provisions described above provide benefits to employees. Paragraph 8 also provides that contributions made to the home State plan by an individual's employer will be allowed as a deduction in computing the employer's profits in the host State, even though such a deduction might not be allowable under the domestic law of the host State. This rule applies whether the employer is a resident of the host State or a permanent establishment that the employer has in the host State. The rule also applies to contributions by a person related to the individual's employer, such as contributions by a parent corporation for its subsidiary, that are treated under the law of the host State as contributions by the individual's employer. For example, if an individual who is participating in a qualifying retirement plan in Canada performs services for a limited period of time in the United States for a U.S. subsidiary of a Canadian company, a contribution to the Canadian plan by the parent company in Canada that is treated under U.S. law as a contribution by the U.S. subsidiary would be covered by the rule.

The amount of the allowable deduction is to be determined under the laws of the home State. Thus, where the United States is the home State, the amount of the deduction that is allowable in Canada will be subject to the limitations of Code section 404 (including the Code section 401(a)(17) and 415 limitations). Where Canada is the home State, the amount of the deduction that is allowable in the United States is subject to the limitations specified in subsections 147(8), 147.1(8) and (9) and 147.2(1) of the *Income Tax Act*, as applicable.

Cross-border commuters

Paragraphs 10, 11, and 12 of Article XVIII address the case of a commuter who is a resident of one Contracting State (the "residence State") and performs services as an employee in the other Contracting State (the "services State") and is a member of a "qualifying retirement plan" (as defined in paragraph 15 of Article XVIII) in the services State. If certain requirements are satisfied, contributions made to, or benefits accrued under, the qualifying retirement plan by or on behalf of the individual will be deductible or excludible in computing the individual's income in the residence State.

In order for paragraph 10 to apply, the individual must perform services as an employee in the services State the remuneration from which is taxable in the services State and is borne by either an employer who is a resident of the services State or by a permanent establishment that the employer has in the services State. The contributions and benefits must be attributable to those services and must be made or accrued during the period in which the individual performs those services. In the case where the United States is the residence State, contributions will be deemed to have been made on the last day of the preceding taxable year if the payment is on account of such taxable year and is treated under U.S. law as a contribution made on the last day of the preceding taxable year.

Paragraph 10 states that it applies only to the extent that the contributions or benefits qualify for tax relief in the services State. Thus, the benefits granted in the residence State are available only to the extent that the contributions or benefits accrued qualify for relief in the services State. Where the United States is the services State, the amount of contributions that may be excluded under paragraph 10 is the U.S. dollar amount specified in Code section 415 or the U.S. dollar amount specified in Code section 402(g)(1) (as defined above) to the extent contributions are made from the employee's compensation. Where Canada is the services State, the amount of contributions that may be excluded from the employee's income under paragraph 10 is subject to the limitations specified in subsections 146(5), 147(8), 147.1(8) and (9) and 147.2(1) and (4) of the *Income Tax Act* and paragraph 8503(4)(a) of the *Income Tax Regulations*, as applicable.

However, paragraphs 11 and 12 further provide that the benefits granted under paragraph 10 by the residence State may not exceed certain benefits that would be allowable under the domestic law of the residence State.

Paragraph 11 provides that where Canada is the residence State, the amount of contributions otherwise allowable as a deduction under paragraph 10 may not exceed the individual's deduction limit for contributions to registered retirement savings plans (RRSPs) remaining after taking into account the amount of contributions to RRSPs deducted by the individual under the law of Canada for the year. The amount deducted by the individual under paragraph 10 will be taken into account in computing the individual's deduction limit for subsequent taxation years for contributions to RRSPs. This rule prevents double benefits for contributions to both an RRSP and a qualifying retirement plan in the United States with respect to the same services.

Paragraph 12 provides that if the United States is the residence State, the benefits granted to an individual under paragraph 10 may not exceed the benefits that would be allowed by the United States to its residents for contributions to, or benefits otherwise accrued under, a generally corresponding pension or retirement plan established in and recognized for tax purposes by the United States. For purposes of determining an individual's eligibility to participate in and receive tax benefits with respect to a pension or retirement plan or other retirement arrangement in the United States, contributions made to, or benefits accrued under, a qualifying retirement plan in Canada by or on behalf of the individual are treated as contributions or benefits under a generally corresponding pension or retirement plan established in and recognized for tax purposes by the United States. Thus, for example, the qualifying retirement plan in Canada would be taken into account for purposes of determining whether the individual is an "active participant" within the meaning of Code section 219(g)(5), with the result that the individual's ability to make deductible contributions to an individual retirement account in the United States would be limited.

Paragraph 10 does not address employer deductions because the employer is located in the services State and is already eligible for deductions under the domestic law of the services State.

U.S. citizens resident in Canada

Paragraphs 13 and 14 of Article XVIII address the special case of a U.S. citizen who is a resident of Canada (as determined under Article IV (Residence)) and who performs services as an employee in Canada and participates in a qualifying retirement plan (as defined in paragraph 15 of Article XVIII) in Canada. If certain requirements are satisfied, contributions made to, or benefits accrued under, a qualifying retirement plan in Canada by or on behalf of the U.S. citizen will be deductible or excludible in computing his or her taxable income in the United States. These provisions are generally consistent with paragraph 4 of Article 18 of the U.S. Model treaty.

In order for paragraph 13 to apply, the U.S. citizen must perform services as an employee in Canada the remuneration from which is taxable in Canada and is borne by an employer who is a resident of Canada or by a permanent establishment that the employer has in Canada. The contributions and benefits must be attributable to those services and must be made or accrued during the period in which the U.S. citizen performs those services. Contributions will be deemed to have been made on the last day of the preceding taxable year if the payment is on account of such taxable year and is treated under U.S. law as a contribution made on the last day of the preceding taxable year.

Paragraph 13 states that it applies only to the extent the contributions or benefits qualify for tax relief in Canada. However, paragraph 14 provides that the benefits granted under paragraph 13 may not exceed the benefits that would be allowed by the United States to its residents for contributions to, or benefits otherwise accrued under, a generally corresponding pension or retirement plan established in and recognized for tax purposes by the United States. Thus, the lower of the two limits applies. This rule ensures that a U.S. citizen living and working in Canada does not receive better U.S. treatment than a U.S. citizen living and working in the United States. The amount of contributions that may be excluded from the employee's income under paragraph 13 is the U.S. dollar amount specified in Code section 415 or the U.S. dollar amount specified in Code section 402(g)(1) (as defined above) to the extent contributions are made from the employee's compensation. In addition, pursuant to Code section 911(d)(6), an individual may not claim benefits under paragraph 13 with respect to services the remuneration for which is excluded from the individual's gross income under Code section 911(a).

For purposes of determining the individual's eligibility to participate in and receive tax benefits with respect to a pension or retirement plan or other retirement arrangement established in and recognized for tax purposes by the United States, contributions made to, or benefits accrued under, a qualifying retirement plan in Canada by or on behalf of the individual are treated as contributions or benefits under a generally corresponding pension or retirement plan established in and recognized for tax purposes by the United States. Thus, for example, the qualifying retirement plan in Canada would be taken into account for purposes of determining whether the individual is an "active participant" within the meaning of Code section 219(g)(5), with the result that the individual's ability to make deductible contributions to an individual retirement account in the United States would be limited.

Paragraph 13 does not address employer deductions because the employer is located in Canada and is already eligible for deductions under the domestic law of Canada.

Definition of "qualifying retirement plan"

Paragraph 15 of Article XVIII provides that for purposes of paragraphs 8 through 14, a "qualifying retirement plan" in a Contracting State is a trust, company, organization, or other arrangement that (a) is a resident of that State, generally exempt from income taxation in that State and operated primarily to provide pension or retirement benefits; (b) is not an individual arrangement in respect of which the individual's employer has no involvement; and (c) the competent authority of the other Contracting State agrees generally corresponds to a pension or retirement plan established in and recognized for tax purposes in that State. Thus, U.S. individual retirement accounts (IRAs) and Canadian registered retirement savings plans (RRSPs) are not treated as qualifying retirement plans unless addressed in paragraph 10 of the General Note (as discussed below). In addition, a Canadian retirement compensation arrangement (RCA) is not a qualifying retirement plan because it is not considered to be generally exempt from income taxation in Canada.

Paragraph 10 of the General Note provides that the types of Canadian plans that constitute qualifying retirement plans for purposes of paragraph 15 include the following and

any identical or substantially similar plan that is established pursuant to legislation introduced after the date of signature of the Protocol (September 21, 2007): registered pension plans under section 147.1 of the *Income Tax Act*, registered retirement savings plans under section 146 that are part of a group arrangement described in subsection 204.2(1.32), deferred profit sharing plans under section 147, and any registered retirement savings plan under section 146, or registered retirement income fund under section 146.3, that is funded exclusively by rollover contributions from one or more of the preceding plans.

Paragraph 10 of the General Note also provides that the types of U.S. plans that constitute qualifying retirement plans for purposes of paragraph 15 include the following and any identical or substantially similar plan that is established pursuant to legislation introduced after the date of signature of the Protocol (September 21, 2007): qualified plans under Code section 401(a) (including Code section 401(k) arrangements), individual retirement plans that are part of a simplified employee pension plan that satisfies Code section 408(k), Code section 408(p) simple retirement accounts, Code section 403(a) qualified annuity plans, Code section 403(b) plans, Code section 457(g) trusts providing benefits under Code section 457(b) plans, the Thrift Savings Fund (Code section 7701(j)), and any individual retirement account under Code section 408(a) that is funded exclusively by rollover contributions from one or more of the preceding plans.

If a particular plan in one Contracting State is of a type specified in paragraph 10 of the General Note with respect to paragraph 15 of Article XVIII, it will not be necessary for taxpayers to obtain a determination from the competent authority of the other Contracting State that the plan generally corresponds to a pension or retirement plan established in and recognized for tax purposes in that State. A taxpayer who believes a particular plan in one Contracting State that is not described in paragraph 10 of the General Note nevertheless satisfies the requirements of paragraph 15 may request a determination from the competent authority of the other Contracting State that the plan generally corresponds to a pension or retirement plan established in and recognized for tax purposes in that State. In the case of the United States, such a determination must be requested under Revenue Procedure 2006-54, 2006-49 I.R.B. 655 (or any applicable analogous provision). In the case of Canada, the current version of Information Circular 71-17 provides guidance on obtaining assistance from the Canadian competent authority.

Source rule

Paragraph 16 of Article XVIII provides that a distribution from a pension or retirement plan that is reasonably attributable to a contribution or benefit for which a benefit was allowed pursuant to paragraph 8, 10, or 13 of Article XVIII will be deemed to arise in the Contracting State in which the plan is established. This ensures that the Contracting State in which the plan is established will have the right to tax the gross amount of the distribution under subparagraph 2(a) of Article XVIII, even if a portion of the services to which the distribution relates were not performed in such Contracting State.

Partnerships

Paragraph 17 of Article XVIII provides that paragraphs 8 through 16 of Article XVIII apply, with such modifications as the circumstances require, as though the relationship between a partnership that carries on a business, and an individual who is a member of the partnership, were that of employer and employee. This rule is needed because paragraphs 8, 10, and 13, by their terms, apply only with respect to contributions made to, or benefits accrued under, qualifying retirement plans by or on behalf of individuals who perform services as an employee. Thus, benefits are not available with respect to retirement plans for self-employed individuals, who may be deemed under U.S. law to be employees for certain pension purposes. Paragraph 17 ensures that partners participating in a plan established by their partnership may be eligible for the benefits provided by paragraphs 8, 10, and 13.

Relationship to other Articles

Paragraphs 8, 10, and 13 of Article XVIII are not subject to the saving clause of paragraph 2 of Article XXIX (Miscellaneous Rules) by reason of the exception in subparagraph 3(a) of Article XXIX.

9. For the purposes of United States taxation, the benefits granted under paragraph 8 to a citizen of the United States shall not exceed the benefits that would be allowed by the United States to its residents for contributions to, or benefits otherwise accrued under, a generally corresponding pension or retirement plan established in and recognized for tax purposes by the United States.

Related Provisions: Art. XVIII:17 — Partners treated as employees.

Notes: Art. XVIII:9 added by 2007 Protocol, effective on the same basis as para. 8.

Definitions: "employee", "employer" — Art. XVIII:17, ITCIA 3, ITA 248(1); "individual" — ITCIA 3, ITA 248(1); "resident" — Art. IV; "State" — Art. III:1(i); "United States" — Art. III:1(b).

Technical Explanation [2007 Protocol]: See under para. 8 above.

10. Contributions made to, or benefits accrued under, a qualifying retirement plan in a Contracting State by or on behalf of an individual who is a resident of the other Contracting State shall be deductible or excludible in computing the individual's taxable income in that other State, where:

(a) the individual performs services as an employee in the first-mentioned state the remuneration from which is taxable in that State and is borne by an employer who is a resident of that State or by a permanent establishment which the employer has in that State; and

(b) the contributions and benefits are attributable to those services and are made or accrued during the period in which the individual performs those services.

This paragraph shall apply only to the extent that the contributions or benefits qualify for tax relief in the first-mentioned State

Related Provisions: ITA 146(1)"unused RRSP deduction room"(b)D(ii) — Reduction in RRSP deduction room; Art. XVIII:11, 12 — Limits to deductions; Art. XVIII:16 — Where distribution deemed to arise; Art. XVIII:17 — Partners treated as employees.

Notes: Art. XVIII:10 added by 2007 Protocol, effective on the same basis as para. 8. For discussion see Notes to para. 8.

Definitions: "employee", "employer" — Art. XVIII:17, ITCIA 3, ITA 248(1); "permanent establishment" — Art. V; "qualifying retirement plan" — Art. XVIII:15; "related" — ITCIA 3, ITA 251; "resident" — Art. IV.

Technical Explanation [2007 Protocol]: See under para. 8 above.

11. For the purposes of Canadian taxation, the amount of contributions otherwise allowed as a deduction under paragraph 10 to an individual for a taxation year shall not exceed the individual's deduction limit under the law of Canada for the year for contributions to registered retirement savings plans remaining after taking into account the amount of contributions to registered retirement savings plans deducted by the individual under the law of Canada for the year. The amount deducted by an individual under paragraph 10 for a taxation year shall be taken into account in computing the individual's deduction limit under the law of Canada for subsequent taxation years for contributions to registered retirement savings plans.

Related Provisions: ITA 146(1)"unused RRSP deduction room"(b)D(ii) — Reduction in RRSP deduction room.

Notes: Art. XVIII:11 added by 2007 Protocol, effective on the same basis as para. 8.

Definitions: "deduction limits" — ITA 146(1)"RRSP deduction limit"; "individual" — ITCIA 3, ITA 248(1); "registered retirement savings plan" — ITCIA 3, ITA 146(1), 248(1).

Technical Explanation [2007 Protocol]: See under para. 8 above.

12. For the purposes of United States taxation, the benefits granted under paragraph 10 shall not exceed the benefits that would be allowed by the United States to its residents for contributions to, or benefits otherwise accrued under, a generally corresponding pension or retirement plan established in and recognized for tax purposes by the United States. For purposes of determining an individual's eligibility to participate in and receive tax benefits with respect to a pension or retirement plan or other retirement arrangement established in and recognized for tax purposes by the United States, contributions made to, or benefits accrued under, a qualifying retirement plan in Canada by or on behalf of the individual shall be treated as contributions or benefits under a generally corresponding pension or retirement plan established in and recognized for tax purposes by the United States.

Notes: Art. XVIII:12 added by 2007 Protocol, effective on the same basis as para. 8.

Definitions: "qualifying retirement plan" — Art. XVIII:15; "resident" — Art. IV; "United States" — Art. III:1(b).

Technical Explanation [2007 Protocol]: See under para. 8 above.

13. Contributions made to, or benefits accrued under, a qualifying retirement plan in Canada by or on behalf of a citizen of the United States who is a resident of Canada shall be deductible or excludible in computing the citizen's taxable income in the United States, where:

(a) the citizen performs services as an employee in Canada the remuneration from which is taxable in Canada and is borne by an employer who is a resident of Canada or by a permanent establishment which the employer has in Canada; and

(b) the contributions and benefits are attributable to those services and are made or accrued during the period in which the citizen performs those services.

This paragraph shall apply only to the extent that the contributions or benefits qualify for tax relief in Canada.

Related Provisions: Art. XVIII:14 — Limit on benefits; Art. XVIII:16 — Where distribution deemed to arise; Art. XVIII:17 — Partners treated as employees.

Notes: See Peter Megoudis, "The Impact of the New Canada-United States Treaty Protocol on Cross-border Executives", 18(7) *Taxation of Executive Compensation & Retirement* (Federated Press) 795 (March 2007) at 801-05.

Art. XVIII:13 added by 2007 Protocol, effective on the same basis as para. 8.

Definitions: "employee", "employer" — Art. XVIII:17, ITCIA 3, ITA 248(1); "permanent establishment" — Art. V; "qualifying retirement plan" — Art. XVIII:15; "resident" — Art. IV.

Technical Explanation [2007 Protocol]: See under para. 8 above.

14. The benefits granted under paragraph 13 shall not exceed the benefits that would be allowed by the United States to its residents for contributions to, or benefits otherwise accrued under, a generally corresponding pension or retirement plan established in and recognized for tax purposes by the United States. For purposes of determining an individual's eligibility to participate in and receive tax benefits with respect to a pension or retirement plan or other retirement arrangement established in and recognized for tax purposes by the United States, contributions made to, or benefits accrued under, a qualifying retirement plan in Canada by or on behalf of the individual shall be treated as contributions or benefits under a generally corresponding pension or retirement plan established in and recognized for tax purposes by the United States.

Notes: Art. XVIII:14 added by 2007 Protocol, effective on the same basis as para. 8.

Definitions: "qualifying retirement plan" — Art. XVIII:15; "resident" — Art. IV; "United States" — Art. III:1(b).

Technical Explanation [2007 Protocol]: See under para. 8 above.

15. For purposes of paragraphs 8 to 14, a **qualifying retirement plan** in a Contracting State means a trust, company, organization or other arrangement:

(a) that is a resident of that State, generally exempt from income taxation in that State and operated primarily to provide pension or retirement benefits;

(b) that is not an individual arrangement in respect of which the individual's employer has no involvement; and

(c) which the competent authority of the other Contracting State agrees generally corresponds to a pension or retirement plan established in and recognized for tax purposes by that other State.

Notes: Fifth Protocol (2007), Annex B, states:

10. Qualifying retirement plans

For purposes of paragraph 15 of Article XVIII (Pensions and Annuities) of the Convention, it is understood that

(a) In the case of Canada, the term "qualifying retirement plan" shall include the following and any identical or substantially similar plan that is established pursuant to legislation introduced after the date of signature of the Protocol: registered pension plans under section 147.1 of the *Income Tax Act*, registered retirement savings plans under section 146 that are part of a group arrangement described in subsection 204.2(1.32), deferred profit sharing plans under section 147, and any registered retirement savings plan under section 146 or registered retirement income fund under section 146.3 that is funded exclusively by rollover contributions from one or more of the preceding plans; and

(b) In the case of the United States, the term "qualifying retirement plan" shall include the following and any identical or substantially similar plan that is established pursuant to legislation introduced after the date of signature of the Protocol: qualified plans under section 401(a) of the *Internal Revenue Code* (including section 401(k) arrangements), individual retirement plans that are part of a simplified employee pension plan that satisfies section 408(k), section 408(p) simple retirement accounts, section 403(a) qualified annuity plans, section 403(b) plans, section 457(g) trusts providing benefits under section 457(b) plans, the Thrift Savings Fund (section 7701(j)), and any individual retirement account under section 408(a) that is funded exclusively by rollover contributions from one or more of the preceding plans.

Art. XVIII:15 added by 2007 Protocol, effective on the same basis as para. 8.

Definitions: "resident" — Art. IV; "trust" — ITCIA 3, ITA 104(1), 248(1), (3).

Technical Explanation [2007 Protocol]: See under para. 8 above.

16. For purposes of this Article, a distribution from a pension or retirement plan that is reasonably attributable to a contribution or benefit for which a benefit was allowed pursuant to paragraph 8, 10 or 13 shall be deemed to arise in the Contracting State in which the plan is established.

Notes: Art. XVIII:16 added by 2007 Protocol, effective on the same basis as para. 8.

Technical Explanation [2007 Protocol]: See under para. 8 above.

17. Paragraphs 8 to 16 apply, with such modifications as the circumstances require, as though the relationship between a partnership that carries on a business, and an individual who is a member of the partnership, were that of employer and employee.

Notes: Art. XVIII:17 added by 2007 Protocol, effective on the same basis as para. 8.

Definitions: "individual" — ITCIA 3, ITA 248(1); "partnership" — see Notes to ITA 96(1).

Technical Explanation [2007 Protocol]: See under para. 8 above.

Article XIX — Government Service

Remuneration, other than a pension, paid by a Contracting State or a political subdivision or local authority thereof to a citizen of that State in respect of services rendered in the discharge of functions of a governmental nature shall be taxable only in that State. However, the provisions of Article VII (Business Profits), XV (Income from Employment) or XVI (Artistes and Athletes), as the case may be, shall apply, and the preceding sentence shall not apply, to remuneration paid in respect of services rendered in connection with a trade or business carried on by a Contracting State or a political subdivision or local authority thereof.

Related Provisions: ITA 149(1)(a) — Exemption from Canadian tax; Art. XXVIII — Diplomatic agents and consular officials.

Notes: "Functions of a governmental nature" means those carried on solely by government (e.g., military, diplomatic service, tax administrators), and does not include functions commonly found in the private sector (e.g., education, health care, utilities), so Art. XXIX did not cover a public school teacher: *Cloutier*, 2003 TCC 58. Funding from a non-profit org that is funded by the US government does not qualify: VIEWS doc 2005-0153901E5.

ITA 250(1)(c) and 115(2)(b) tax Canadians working in embassies and consulates outside Canada. See Notes to those provisions and VIEWS doc 2011-0415151E5. See also Remission Orders annotation below.

Art. XIX amended by 2007 Protocol, for tax years beginning after 2008, but in respect of taxes withheld at source, for amounts paid or credited after Jan. 2009.

Definitions: "business" — ITCIA 3, ITA 248(1); "pension" — Art. XVIII:3, ITCIA 5; "State" — Art. III:1(i).

Remission Orders: *Locally Engaged Employees of the Canadian Embassy and Consulates in the United States Remission Order*, P.C. 2018-345 (remission of tax under ITA 120(1) and US state tax).

Technical Explanation [2007 Protocol]: Consistent with Articles 9 and 10 of the Protocol, Article 14 of the Protocol amends Article XIX (Government Service) of the Convention by deleting the reference to "Article XIV (Independent Personal Services)" and replacing such reference with the reference to "Article VII (Business Profits)" and by reflecting the new name of Article XV (Income from Employment).

Technical Explanation [1984]: Article XIX provides that remuneration, other than a pension, paid by a Contracting State or political subdivision or local authority thereof to a citizen of that State in respect of services rendered in the discharge of governmental functions shall be taxable only in that State. (Pursuant to paragraph 5 of Article IV (Residence), other income of such a citizen may also be exempt from tax, or subject to reduced rates of tax, in the State in which he is performing services, in accordance with other provisions of the Convention.) However, if the services are rendered in connection with a trade or business, then the provisions of Article XIV (Independent Personal Services), Article XV (Dependent Personal Services), or Article XVI (Artistes and Athletes), as the case may be, are controlling. Whether functions are of a governmental nature may be determined by a comparison with the concept of a governmental function in the State in which the income arises.

Pursuant to paragraph 3(a) of Article XXIX (Miscellaneous Rules), Article XIX is an exception to the "saving clause." As a result, a U.S. citizen resident in Canada and performing services in Canada in the discharge of functions of a governmental nature for the United States is taxable only in the United States on remuneration for such services.

This provision differs from the rules of Article VI of the 1942 Convention. For example, Article XIX allows the United States to impose tax on a person other than a citizen of Canada who earns remuneration paid by Canada in respect of services rendered in the discharge of governmental functions in the United States. (Such a person may, however, be entitled to an exemption from U.S. tax as provided in Code section 893.) Also, under the provisions of Article XIX Canada will not impose tax on amounts paid by the United States in respect of services rendered in the discharge of governmental functions to a U.S. citizen who is ordinarily resident in Canada for purposes other than rendering governmental services. Under paragraph 1 of Article VI of the 1942 Convention, such amounts would be taxable by Canada.

Article XX — Students

Payments received by an individual who is a student, apprentice, or business trainee, and is, or was immediately before visiting a Contracting State, a resident of the other Contracting State, and who is present in the first-mentioned State for the purpose of the individual's full-time education or full-time training, shall not be taxed in that State, provided that such payments arise outside that State, and are for the purpose of the maintenance, education or training of the individual. The provisions of this Article shall apply to an apprentice or business trainee only for a period of time not exceeding one year from the date the individual first arrives in the first-mentioned State for the purpose of the individual's training.

Notes: Art. XX amended by 2007 Protocol, for taxable years beginning after 2008, but in respect of taxes withheld at source, for amounts paid or credited after Jan. 2009.

Definitions: "individual" — ITCIA 3, ITA 248(1); "resident" — Art. IV; "State" — Art. III:1(i).

Technical Explanation [2007 Protocol]: Article 15 of the Protocol replaces Article XX (Students) of the Convention. Article XX provides rules for host-country taxation of visiting students and business trainees. Persons who meet the tests of Article XX will be exempt from tax in the State that they are visiting with respect to designated classes of income. Several conditions must be satisfied in order for an individual to be entitled to the benefits of this Article.

First, the visitor must have been, either at the time of his arrival in the host State or immediately before, a resident of the other Contracting State.

Second, the purpose of the visit must be the full-time education or training of the visitor. Thus, if the visitor comes principally to work in the host State but also is a part-time student, he would not be entitled to the benefits of this Article, even with respect to any payments he may receive from abroad for his maintenance or education, and regardless of whether or not he is in a degree program. Whether a student is to be considered full-time will be determined by the rules of the educational institution at which he is studying.

The host State exemption in Article XX applies to payments received by the student or business trainee for the purpose of his maintenance, education or training that arise outside the host State. A payment will be considered to arise outside the host State if the payer is located outside the host State. Thus, if an employer from one of the Contracting States sends an employee to the other Contracting State for full-time training, the payments the trainee receives from abroad from his employer for his maintenance or training while he is present in the host State will be exempt from tax in the host State. Where appropriate, substance prevails over form in determining the identity of the payer. Thus, for example, payments made directly or indirectly by a U.S. person with whom the visitor is training, but which have been routed through a source outside the United States (e.g., a foreign subsidiary), are not treated as arising outside the United States for this purpose.

In the case of an apprentice or business trainee, the benefits of Article XX will extend only for a period of one year from the time that the individual first arrives in the host country for the purpose of the individual's training. If, however, an apprentice or trainee remains in the host country for a second year, thus losing the benefits of the Article, he would not retroactively lose the benefits of the Article for the first year.

Relationship to other Articles

The saving clause of paragraph 2 of Article XXIX (Miscellaneous Rules) does not apply to Article XX with respect to an individual who neither is a citizen of the host State nor has been admitted for permanent residence there. The saving clause, however, does apply with respect to citizens and permanent residents of the host State. Thus, a U.S. citizen who is a resident of Canada and who visits the United States as a full-time student at an accredited university will not be exempt from U.S. tax on remittances from abroad that otherwise constitute U.S. taxable income. However, an individual who is not a U.S. citizen, and who visits the United States as a student and remains long enough to become a resident under U.S. law, but does not become a permanent resident (*i.e.*, does not acquire a green card), will be entitled to the full benefits of the Article.

Technical Explanation [1984]: Article XX provides that a student, apprentice, or business trainee temporarily present in a Contracting State for the purpose of his full-time education or training is exempt from tax in that State with respect to amounts received from outside that State for the purpose of his maintenance, education, or training, if the individual is or was a resident of the other Contracting State immediately before visiting the first-mentioned State. There is no limitation on the number of years or the amount of income to which the exemption applies.

The Convention does not contain provisions relating specifically to professors and teachers. Teachers are treated under the Convention pursuant to the rules established in Articles XIV (Independent Personal Services) and XV (Dependent Personal Services), in the same manner as other persons performing services. In Article VIII A of the 1942 Convention there is a 2-year exemption in the Contracting State of source in the case of a professor or teacher who is a resident of the other Contracting State.

Article XXI — Exempt Organizations

1. Subject to the provisions of paragraph 4, income derived by a religious, scientific, literary, educational or charitable organization shall be exempt from tax in a Contracting State if it is resident in the other Contracting State, but only to the extent that such income is exempt from tax in that other State.

Related Provisions: Art. XXI:4 — Exceptions.

Notes: A detailed list of exempt U.S. organizations operating in Canada is in CRA publication T4016, "Exempt U.S. Organizations". See also Notes to para. 7 below.

A Canadian charity receiving over $50,000 annually from the US (including donations) may need to file Form 990 with the IRS: Catherine Eberl, "Cross-Border Charitable Activities", 23(11) *Canadian Tax Highlights [CTH]* (ctf.ca) 11 (Nov. 2015). Where a charity has US investment income, see Bienvenue, "Charitable Organizations Investing into the United States", 5(3) *Tax for the Owner-Manager* (ctf.ca) 5-6 (July 2005); Waiss, "IRS Reporting for a Foreign Charity", 23(8) *CTH* 5-6 (Aug. 2015).

For CRA interpretation see VIEWS docs 2009-0330491E5 (where income earned through fiscally-transparent entity under Art. IV:6), 2009-0344201E5 (US charity receiving income from Canadian-resident unlimited-liability corporation).

Art. XXI:1 amended by 2007 Protocol to change reference from para. 3 to para. 4, effective on the same basis as the renumbering of that paragraph.

Definitions: "State" — Art. III:1(i).

Technical Explanation [2007 Protocol]: Paragraph 2 replaces paragraphs 1 through 3 of Article XXI with four new paragraphs. In general, the provisions of former paragraphs 1 through 3 have been retained.

New paragraph 1 provides that a religious, scientific, literary, educational, or charitable organization resident in a Contracting State shall be exempt from tax on income arising in the other Contracting State but only to the extent that such income is exempt from taxation in the Contracting State in which the organization is resident.

Technical Explanation [1984]: Paragraph 1 provides that a religious, scientific, literary, educational, or charitable organization resident in a Contracting State shall be exempt from tax on income arising in the other Contracting State but only to the extent that such income is exempt from taxation in the Contracting State in which the organization is resident. Since this paragraph, and the remainder of Article XXI, deal with entities that are not normally taxable, the test of "resident in" is intended to be similar — but cannot be identical — to the one outlined in paragraph 1 of Article IV (Residence). Paragraph 3 provides that paragraph 1 does not exempt from tax income of a trust, company, or other organization from carrying on a trade or business, or income from a "related person" other than a person referred to in paragraph 1 or 2.

2. Subject to the provisions of paragraph 4, income referred to in Articles X (Dividends) and XI (Interest) derived by a trust, company, organization or other arrangement that is a resident of a Contracting State, generally exempt from income taxation in a taxable year in that State and operated exclusively to administer or provide pension, retirement or employee benefits shall be exempt from income taxation in that taxable year in the other Contracting State.

Related Provisions: Art. XXI:3 — Rule formerly in Art. XXI:2(b); Art. XXI:4 — Exceptions.

Notes: See Notes to ITA 146(4) re requirements for U.S. filers to report RRSPs and RRIFs as foreign trusts.

A detailed list of exempt U.S. organizations operating in Canada is in CRA publication T4016, "Exempt U.S. Organizations". See also Notes to para. 7 below.

For the meaning of "derived by" see VIEWS doc 2005-0140291E5. In 2011-0417531I7, a Retirement Medical Benefits trust exempt under Internal Revenue Code §501(c)(9) was exempt under para. 2 on interest and dividend income.

See US private letter ruling 200810013, discussed in Probus & Jackson, "Canadian Plans US Withholding Exempt", 16(6) *Canadian Tax Highlights* (ctf.ca) 10 (June 2008).

This exemption applies only to dividends and interest, not to distributions from an income trust. See Kevin Kelly, "Income Trusts: US Pensions", 11(6) *Canadian Tax Highlights* (ctf.ca) 6 (June 2003).

Art. XXI:2 amended by 2007 Protocol, effective on the same basis as new para. 3. Earlier amended by 1995 Protocol, generally effective 1996.

Definitions: "company" — Art. III:1(f); "pension" — Art. XVIII:3, ITCIA 5; "resident" — Art. IV; "State" — Art. III:1(i); "trust" — ITCIA 3, ITA 104(1), 248(1).

Technical Explanation [2007 Protocol]: New paragraph 2 retains the provisions of former subparagraph 2(a), and provides that a trust, company, organization, or other arrangement that is resident in a Contracting State and operated exclusively to administer or provide pension, retirement or employee benefits or benefits for the self-employed under one or more funds or plans established to provide pension or retirement benefits or other employee benefits is exempt from taxation on dividend and interest income arising in the other Contracting State in a taxable year, if the income of such organization or other arrangement is generally exempt from taxation for that year in the Contracting State in which it is resident.

New paragraph 3 replaces and expands the scope of former subparagraph 2(b). Former subparagraph 2(b) provided that, subject to the provisions of paragraph 3 (new paragraph 4), a trust, company, organization or other arrangement that was a resident of a Contracting State, generally exempt from income taxation in that State and operated exclusively to earn income for the benefit of one or more organizations described in subparagraph 2(a) (new paragraph 2) was exempt from taxation on dividend and interest income arising in the other Contracting State in a taxable year. The Internal Revenue Service concluded in private letter rulings (PLR 200111027 and PLR 200111037) that a pooled investment fund that included as investors one or more organizations described in paragraph 1 could not qualify for benefits under former subparagraph 2(b). New paragraph 3 now allows organizations described in paragraph 1 to invest in pooled funds with trusts, companies, organizations, or other arrangements described in new paragraph 2.

Former subparagraph 2(b) did not exempt income earned by a trust, company or other arrangement for the benefit of religious, scientific, literary, educational or charitable organizations exempt from tax under paragraph 1. Therefore, the Protocol expands the scope of paragraph 3 to include such income.

As noted above with respect to Article X (Dividends), paragraph 3 of the General Note explains that distributions from Canadian income trusts and royalty trusts that are treated as dividends as a result of changes to Canada's law regarding taxation of income and royalty trusts shall be treated as dividends for the purposes of Article X. Accordingly, such distributions will also be entitled to the benefits of Article XXI.

Technical Explanation [1995 Protocol]: Article 10 of the Protocol amends Article XXI (Exempt Organizations) of the Convention. Paragraph 1 of Article 10 amends paragraphs 2 and 3 of Article XXI. The most significant changes are those that conform the language of the two paragraphs to the revised definition of the term "pension" in paragraph 3 of Article XVIII (Pensions and Annuities). The revision adds the term "arrangement" to "trust, company or organization" in describing the residents of a Contracting State that may receive dividend and interest income exempt from current income taxation by the other Contracting State. This clarifies that IRAs, for example, are eligible for the benefits of paragraph 2, subject to the exception in paragraph 3, and makes Canadian RRSPs and RRIFs, for example, similarly eligible (provided that they are operated exclusively to administer or provide pension, retirement, or employee benefits).

The other changes, all in paragraph 2, are intended to improve and clarify the language. For example, the reference to "tax" in the present Convention is changed to a reference to "income taxation." This is intended to clarify that if an otherwise exempt organization is subject to an excise tax, for example, it will not lose the benefits of this paragraph. In subparagraph 2(b), the phrase "not taxed in a taxable year" was changed to "generally exempt from income taxation in a taxable year" to ensure uniformity throughout the Convention; this change was not intended to disqualify a trust or other arrangement that qualifies for the exemption under the wording of the present Convention.

Technical Explanation [1984]: Paragraph 2 provides that a trust, company, or other organization that is resident in a Contracting State and constituted and operated exclusively to administer or provide employee benefits or benefits for the self-employed under one or more funds or plans established to provide pension or retirement benefits or other employee benefits is exempt from taxation on dividend and interest income arising in the other Contracting State, in a taxable year, if the income of such organization is generally exempt from taxation for that year in the Contracting State in which it is resident. In addition, a trust, company, or other organization resident in a Contracting State and not taxed in a taxable year in that State shall be exempt from taxation in the other State in that year on dividend and interest income arising in that other State if it is constituted and operated exclusively to earn income for the benefit of an organization described in the preceding sentence. Pursuant to paragraph 3 the exemption at source provided by paragraph 2 does not apply to dividends or interest from carrying on a trade or business or from a "related person," other than a person referred to in paragraph 1 or 2. The term "related person" is not necessarily defined by paragraph 2 of Article IX (Related Persons).

3. Subject to the provisions of paragraph 4, income referred to in Articles X (Dividends) and XI (Interest) derived by a trust, company, organization or other arrangement that is a resident of a Contracting State, generally exempt from income taxation in a taxable year in that State and operated exclusively to earn income for the benefit of one or more of the following:

    (a) an organization referred to in paragraph 1; or

    (b) a trust, company, organization or other arrangement referred to in paragraph 2;

shall be exempt from income taxation in that taxable year in the other Contracting State.

Related Provisions: Art. XXI:4 — Exceptions.

Notes: Art. XXI:3(a) is essentially the former Art. XXI:2(b). See Notes to Art. XXI:2.

Art. XXI:3 added by 2007 Protocol, for taxable years beginning after 2008, but in respect of taxes withheld at source, for amounts paid or credited after Jan. 2009.

Definitions: "company" — Art. III:1(f); "resident" — Art. IV; "State" — Art. III:1(i); "trust" — ITCIA 3, ITA 104(1), 248(1), (3).

Technical Explanation [2007 Protocol]: New paragraph 4 replaces paragraph 3 and provides that the exemptions provided by paragraphs 1, 2, 3 do not apply with respect to the income of a trust, company, organization or other arrangement from carrying on a trade or business or from a related person, other than a person referred to in paragraph 1, 2 or 3. The term "related person" is not necessarily defined by paragraph 2 of Article IX (Related Person).

4. The provisions of paragraphs 1, 2 and 3 shall not apply with respect to the income of a trust, company, organization or other arrangement from carrying on a trade or business or from a related person other than a person referred to in paragraphs 1, 2 or 3.

Notes: For a ruling that a U.S. corporation conducting fundraising activities is not carrying on business in Canada for purposes of Art. XXI:4, see VIEWS doc 2005-0149681R3. When an LLC is used (see Art. IV:6), the determination of "related" for para. 4 is made at the shareholder level: doc 2009-0319411C6; and see also doc 2009-0330491E5.

Art. XXI:3 renumbered as 4 and amended to refer to para. 3 by 2007 Protocol, effective on the same basis as new para. 3. Former Art. XXI:3 amended by 1995 Protocol, generally effective 1996.

Definitions: "business" — ITCIA 3, ITA 248(1); "company" — Art. III:1(f); "person" — Art. III:1(e), ITCIA 3, *Interpretation Act* 35(1); "related" — ITCIA 3, ITA 251(2)–(6); "trust" — ITCIA 3, ITA 104(1), 248(1).

Technical Explanation [2007 Protocol]: See under para. 3.

Technical Explanation [1995 Protocol]: See under para. 2.

Technical Explanation [1984]: See under para. 1.

5. A religious, scientific, literary, educational or charitable organization which is resident in Canada and which has received substantially all of its support from persons other than citizens or residents of the United States shall be exempt in the United States from the United States excise taxes imposed with respect to private foundations.

Notes: Art. XXI:4 renumbered as 5 by 2007 Protocol, effective on the same basis as new para. 3.

Definitions: "person" — Art. III:1(e), ITCIA 3, *Interpretation Act* 35(1); "private foundation" — ITCIA 3, ITA 248(1); "resident in Canada" — ITCIA 3, ITA 250; "United States" — Art. III:1(b).

Technical Explanation [2007 Protocol]: Paragraph 1 amends Article XXI by renumbering paragraphs 4, 5, and 6 as 5, 6, and 7, respectively.

Technical Explanation [1984]: [Former] Paragraph 4 provides an exemption from U.S. excise taxes on private foundations in the case of a religious, scientific, literary, educational, or charitable organization which is resident in Canada but only if such organization has received substantially all of its support from persons other than citizens or residents of the United States.

6. For the purposes of United States taxation, contributions by a citizen or resident of the United States to an organization which is resident in Canada, which is generally exempt from Canadian tax and which could qualify in the United States to receive deductible contributions if it were resident in the United States shall be treated as charitable contributions; however, such contributions (other than such contributions to a college or university at which the citizen or resident or a member of his family is or was enrolled) shall not be deductible in any taxable year to the extent that they exceed an amount determined by applying the percentage limitations of the laws of the United States in respect of the deductibility of charitable contributions to the income of such citizen or resident arising in Canada. The preceding sentence shall not be interpreted to allow in any taxable year deductions for charitable contributions in excess of the amount allowed under the percentage limitations of the laws of the United States in respect of the deductibility of charitable contributions. For the purposes of this paragraph, a company that is a resident of Canada and that is taxable in the United States as if it

were a resident of the United States shall be deemed to be a resident of the United States.

Notes: Art. XXI:5 renumbered as 6 by 2007 Protocol, effective on the same basis as new para. 3. The last sentence of former Art. XXI:5 added by 1995 Protocol, generally effective 1996.

Definitions: "Canada" — Art. III:1(a), ITCIA 5; "Canadian tax" — Art. III:1(c); "company" — Art. III:1(f); "resident" — Art. IV; "resident in Canada" — ITCIA 3, ITA 250; "United States" — Art. III:1(b).

Registered Charities Newsletters: 6a (Canadian charities and their U.S. donors).

Technical Explanation [2007 Protocol]: See under para. 5.

Technical Explanation [1995 Protocol]: Paragraph 2 of Article 10 adds a sentence to [former] paragraph 5 of Article XXI of the Convention. The paragraph in the present Convention provides that a U.S. citizen or resident may deduct, for U.S. income tax purposes, contributions made to Canadian charities under certain circumstances. The added sentence makes clear that the benefits of the paragraph are available to a company that is a resident of Canada but is treated by the United States as a domestic corporation under the consolidated return rules of section 1504(d) of the *Internal Revenue Code*. Thus, such a company will be able to deduct, for U.S. income tax purposes, contributions to Canadian charities that are deductible to a U.S. resident under the provisions of the paragraph.

Technical Explanation [1984]: [Former] Paragraph 5 provides that contributions by a citizen or resident of the United States to an organization which is resident in Canada and is generally exempt from Canadian tax are treated as charitable contributions, but only if the organization could qualify in the United States to receive deductible contributions if it were resident in (i.e., organized in) the United States. [Former] Paragraph 5 generally limits the amount of contributions made deductible by the Convention to the income of the U.S. citizen or resident arising in Canada, as determined under the Convention. In the case of contributions to a college or university at which the U.S. citizen or resident or a member of his family is or was enrolled, the special limitation to income arising in Canada is not required. The percentage limitations of Code section 170 in respect of the deductibility of charitable contributions apply after the limitations established by the Convention. Any amounts treated as charitable contributions by [former] paragraph 5 which are in excess of amounts deductible in a taxable year pursuant to [former] paragraph 5 may be carried over and deducted in subsequent taxable years, subject to the limitations of [former] paragraph 5.

7. For the purposes of Canadian taxation, gifts by a resident of Canada to an organization that is a resident of the United States, that is generally exempt from United States tax and that could qualify in Canada as a registered charity if it were a resident of Canada and created or established in Canada, shall be treated as gifts to a registered charity; however, no relief from taxation shall be available in any taxation year with respect to such gifts (other than such gifts to a college or university at which the resident or a member of the resident's family is or was enrolled) to the extent that such relief would exceed the amount of relief that would be available under the *Income Tax Act* if the only income of the resident for that year were the resident's income arising in the United States. The preceding sentence shall not be interpreted to allow in any taxation year relief from taxation for gifts to registered charities in excess of the amount of relief allowed under the percentage limitations of the laws of Canada in respect of relief for gifts to registered charities.

Related Provisions: ITA 118.1(9) — Commuter's charitable donations.

Notes: Art. XXI:6 renumbered as 7 by 2007 Protocol, effective on the same basis as new para. 3.

Para. 7 allows a Canadian to claim a donation to a US charity for Canadian tax purposes, up to 75% of US-source income, such as dividends on US stocks (even if held in a Canadian brokerage account) or consulting to US clients. The words "arising in" are broad and arguably include indirect income, e.g. consulting to a Canadian client who is using the services to earn income from the US. CRA interprets "arising" using the foreign tax credit sourcing rules in Income Tax Folio S5-F2-C1 ¶1.53-1.65; and taxable capital gains qualify if they are US-source under these rules: doc 2015-0614251C6 [2015 TEI q.7]. (CRA's interpretation may be too narrow. See for example the discussion of "source" in *Ardmore Construction*, [2018] EWCA Civ 1438 (UK).) The 5-year carryforward of donations applies to donations to US charities: same doc. Capital gains on a Canadian resident's donation of US securities to a US charity are considered by CRA to arise in Canada: VIEWS doc 1999-0009715. The treaty does not generally define "arising" other than for purposes of specific Articles (see Art. XI:4, XII:6, XXIV:3, XXIV:6); except that "arising" is defined for the entire treaty for annuity income (Art. XVIII:4(b)) and for pension or retirement plan distributions (Art. XVIII:16). *Income Tax Conventions Interpretation Act* 6.3 defines it only with respect to gains on taxable Canadian property. See also *Garcia*, 2007 TCC 548, para. 35: "arise" means to have as a source or originate from (for purposes of Art. XV:1). See also Notes to Art. XXII:1 on "arising".

Para. 7 did not apply for Quebec provincial tax purposes to allow a corporation a deduction, despite *Taxation Act* s. 488 which provides an exemption for amounts exempt under a treaty: *Emballages Starflex*, 2015 QCCQ 7455 (aff'd on other grounds 2016 QCCA 1856). In other provinces, CRA automatically matches the federal assessment, e.g. Ontario *Taxation Act, 2007*, s. 113(1).

Receipts are not always issued by US charities; under IRS regulations, acknowledgment letters must be sent to donors who contribute US$250 or more, confirming that no goods or services were provided in exchange for the donation (Reg. §1-170A-13(f); IRS Publication 1771 on irs.gov).

CRA accepts that any organization that qualifies under s. 501(c)(3) of the U.S. *Internal Revenue Code* will meet the test in this section (VIEWS docs 9900795, 2011-0408401E5). For a complete list of all 800,000 such organizations see irs.gov/charities > "Search for charities". However, this rule does not necessarily apply to para. 1, under an undisclosed Canada-US agreement: see Paul Carenza, "Competent Authority Agreement?" 10(10) *Canadian Tax Highlights* (ctf.ca) 78 (Oct. 2003).

Para. 7 allows a credit for tuition paid to a US religious school that otherwise qualifies under the policy in Information Circular 75-23. This was accepted by CRA Appeals for tuition paid by the author: Robert Hayhoe, "CRA Now Accepts Gifts to US Religious Schools", xxviii(3) *The Canadian Taxpayer* (Carswell) 20 (Jan. 31, 2006).

Canadian charities can arguably make gifts to US charities as though they were qualified donees (ITA 149.1(2)(c)(ii), (3)(b.1)(ii), (4)(b.1)(ii)), due to para. 7: Hayhoe, "A Critical Description of the Canadian Tax Treatment of Cross-Border Charitable Giving", 49(2) *Canadian Tax Journal* 320-44 (2001) at 333-34. CRA disagrees: doc 2012-0451231C6. The FCA unfortunately refused to rule on this issue in *Prescient Foundation*, 2013 FCA 120; leave to appeal denied 2013 CarswellNat 4462 (SCC) (since a gift to a foreign charity was not otherwise prohibited), and in *Public Television Assn of Quebec*, 2015 FCA 170 (since it upheld the charity's revocation on other grounds).

For more on para. 7 see Hayhoe article (above). See also VIEWS docs 2009-0322801E5, 2010-0380811E5.

Relief for donations to specific US charities is also available via ITA 149.1(1) "qualified donee"(a)(iv) (universities in Schedule VIII) and (a)(v) (charities to which the Canadian government has donated; and for commuters under ITA 118.1(9)).

Before May 2020, US residents could donate online to some Canadian charities through the American Fund for Charities, americanfund.info.

Former Art. XXI:6 amended by 1995 Protocol, generally effective 1996.

Definitions: "Canada" — Art. III:1(a), ITCIA 5; "registered charity" — ITCIA 3, ITA 248(1); "resident" — Art. IV; "taxation year" — ITCIA 3, ITA 249; "United States" — Art. III:1(b); "United States tax" — Art. III:1(d).

Information Circulars: 75-23: Tuition fees and charitable donations paid to privately supported secular and religious schools.

Registered Charities Newsletters: 6a (U.S. charities and their Canadian donors).

Technical Explanation [2007 Protocol]: See under para. 5.

Technical Explanation [1995 Protocol]: Paragraph 3 of Article 10 amends [former] paragraph 6 of Article XXI of the Convention to replace references to "deductions" for Canadian tax purposes with references to "relief" from tax. These changes clarify that the provisions of [former] paragraph 6 apply to the credit for charitable contributions allowed under current Canadian law. The Protocol also makes other nonsubstantive drafting changes to [former] paragraph 6.

Technical Explanation [1984]: [Former] Paragraph 6 provides rules for purposes of Canadian taxation with respect to the deductibility of gifts to a U.S. resident organization by a resident of Canada. The rules of [former] paragraph 6 parallel the rules of [former] paragraph 5. The current limitations in Canadian law provide that deductions for gifts to charitable organizations may not exceed 20% of income. Excess deductions may be carried forward for one year.

The term "family" used in [former] paragraphs 5 and 6 is defined in paragraph 2 of the Exchange of Notes accompanying the Convention to mean an individual's brothers and sisters (whether by whole or half-blood, or by adoption), spouse, ancestors, lineal descendants, and adopted descendants. Paragraph 2 of the Exchange of Notes also provides that the competent authorities of Canada and the United States will review procedures and requirements for organizations to establish their exempt status under paragraph 1 of Article XXI or as an eligible recipient of charitable contributions or gifts under [former] paragraphs 5 and 6 of Article XXI. It is contemplated that such review will lead to the avoidance of duplicative administrative efforts in determining such status and eligibility.

The provisions of [former] paragraph 5 and 6 generally parallel the rules of Article XIII D of the 1942 Convention. However, [former] paragraphs 5 and 6 permit greater deductions for certain contributions to colleges and universities than do the provisions of the 1942 Convention.

Information Circulars [Art. XXI]: 77-16R4: Non-resident income tax.

Forms [Art. XXI]: NR602: Non-resident ownership certificate — no withholding tax.

Article XXII — Other Income

1. Items of income of a resident of a Contracting State, wherever arising, not dealt with in the foregoing Articles of this Convention shall be taxable only in that State, except that if such income arises in the other Contracting State it may also be taxed in that other State.

Notes: This rule allows the US to tax Canadians' gambling winnings at US casinos, but only net of losses deductible under US law (Art. XXII:3): US letter ruling 8714055, and see "Gambling" in Notes to ITA 9(1).

Capital gains on the disposition of US securities on the winding-up of a Canadian trust are generally considered to be income "arising" in Canada for purposes of Art. XXII: VIEWS doc 9632715.

Definitions: "resident" — Art. IV; "State" — Art. III:1(i).

Technical Explanation [1984]: Paragraph 1 provides that a Contracting State of which a person is a resident has the sole right to tax items of income, wherever arising, if such income is not dealt with in the prior Articles of the Convention. If such income arises in the other Contracting State, however, it may also be taxed in that State. The determination of where income arises for this purpose is made under the domestic laws of the respective Contracting States unless the Convention specifies where the income arises (e.g., paragraph 6 of Article XI (Interest)) for purposes of determining the right to tax, in which case the provisions of the Convention control.

2. To the extent that income distributed by an estate or trust is subject to the provisions of paragraph 1, then, notwithstanding such provisions, income distributed by an estate or trust which is a resident of a Contracting State to a resident of the other Contracting State who is a beneficiary of the estate or trust may be taxed in the first-mentioned State and according to the laws of that State, but the tax so charged shall not exceed 15 per cent of the gross amount of the income; provided, however, that such income shall be exempt from tax in the first-mentioned State to the extent of any amount distributed out of income arising outside that State.

Notes: For examples of this 15% limit on ITA 212(1)(c) withholding tax on trust or estate income payments to US beneficiaries, see VIEWS docs 2009-0327001C6 (capital dividend); 2013-0497381E5 (REIT distribution to US IRA); 2013-0504641E5 (educational assistance payment from RESP that is a trust); 2013-0509431R3 (mutual fund distribution).

For examples of the same rule applying in other treaties see docs 9108375 (Israel), 2008-0302321E5 (Israel), 2016-0672941E5 (Norway); Cepparo, "Reduced Withholding: Canadian REIT Distributes to Foreign Exempt Entity", 26(8) *Canadian Tax Highlights* (ctf.ca) 6-7 (Aug. 2018).

See also Notes to para. 1 above.

Definitions: "estate" — ITCIA 3, ITA 248(1); "resident" — Art. IV; "State" — Art. III:1(i); "trust" — ITCIA 3, ITA 104(1), 248(1).

Interpretation Bulletins: IT-465R: Non-resident beneficiaries of trusts.

Technical Explanation [1984]: Paragraph 2 provides that to the extent that income distributed by an estate or trust resident in one Contracting State is deemed under the domestic law of that State to be a separate type of income "arising" within that State, such income distributed to a beneficiary resident in the other Contracting State may be taxed in the State of source at a maximum rate of 15% of the gross amount of such distribution. Such a distribution will, however, be exempt from tax in the State of source to the extent that the income distributed by the estate or trust was derived by the estate or trust from sources outside that State. Thus, in a case where the law of Canada treats a distribution made by a trust resident in Canada as a separate type of income arising in Canada, Canadian tax is limited by paragraph 2 to 15% of the gross amount distributed to a U.S. resident beneficiary. Although the Code imposes a tax on certain domestic trusts (e.g., accumulation trusts) and such trusts are residents of the United States for purposes of Article IV (Residence) and paragraph 2 of Article XXII, paragraph 2 does not apply to distributions by such trusts because, pursuant to Code sections 667(e) and 662(b), these distributions have the same character in the hands of a non-resident beneficiary as they do in the hands of the trust. Thus, a distribution by a domestic accumulation trust is not a separate type of income for U.S. purposes. The taxation of such a distribution in the United States is governed by the distribution's character, the provisions of the Code and the provisions of the Convention other than the provision in paragraph 2 limiting the tax at source to 15%.

3. Losses incurred by a resident of a Contracting State with respect to wagering transactions the gains on which may be taxed in the other Contracting State shall, for the purpose of taxation in that other State, be deductible to the same extent that such losses would be deductible if they were incurred by a resident of that other State.

Notes: See Notes to Art. XXII:1. Art. XXII:3 added by 1995 Protocol, generally effective 1996.

Definitions: "resident" — Art. IV; "State" — Art. III:1(i).

Technical Explanation [1995 Protocol]: Article 11 of the Protocol adds a new paragraph 3 to Article XXII (Other Income) of the Convention. This Article entitles residents of one Contracting State who are taxable by the other State on gains from wagering transactions to deduct losses from wagering transactions for the purposes of taxation in that other State. However, losses are to be deductible only to the extent that they are incurred with respect to wagering transactions, the gains on which could be taxable in the other State, and only to the extent that such losses would be deductible if incurred by a resident of that other State.

This Article does not affect the collection of tax by a Contracting State. Thus, in the case of a resident of Canada, this Article does not affect, for example, the imposition of U.S. withholding taxes under section 1441 or section 1442 of the *Internal Revenue Code* on the gross amount of gains from wagering transactions. However, in computing its U.S. income tax liability on net income for the taxable year concerned, the Canadian resident may reduce its gains from wagering transactions subject to taxation in the United States by any wagering losses incurred on such transactions, to the extent that those losses are deductible under the provisions of new paragraph 3. Under U.S. domestic law, the deduction of wagering losses is governed by section 165 of the *Internal Revenue Code*. It is intended that the resident of Canada file a nonresident income tax return in order to substantiate the deduction for losses and to claim a refund of any overpayment of U.S. taxes collected by withholding.

4. Notwithstanding the provisions of paragraph 1, compensation derived by a resident of a Contracting State in respect of the provision of a guarantee of indebtedness shall be taxable only in that State, unless such compensation is business profits attributable to a permanent establishment situated in the other Contracting State, in which case the provisions of Article VII (Business Profits) shall apply.

Notes: This exemption takes priority over Art. XI:1; VIEWS doc 2011-0416261E5.

Art. XXII:4 added by 2007 Protocol, effective for taxable years beginning after 2008, but in respect of taxes withheld at source, for amounts paid or credited after Jan. 2009.

Definitions: "permanent establishment" — Art. V; "resident" — Art. IV; "State" — Art. III:1(i).

Technical Explanation [2007 Protocol]: Article 17 of the Protocol amends Article XXII (Other Income) of the Convention by adding a new paragraph 4. Article XXII generally assigns taxing jurisdiction over income not dealt with in the other articles (Articles VI through XXI) of the Convention.

New paragraph 4 provides a specific rule for residence State taxation of compensation derived in respect of a guarantee of indebtedness. New paragraph 4 provides that compensation derived by a resident of a Contracting State in respect of the provision of a guarantee of indebtedness shall be taxable only in that State, unless the compensation is business profits attributable to a permanent establishment situated in the other Contracting State, in which case the provisions of Article VII (Business Profits) shall apply. The clarification that Article VII shall apply when the compensation is considered business profits was included at the request of the United States. Compensation paid to a financial services entity to provide a guarantee in the ordinary course of its business of providing such guarantees to customers constitutes business profits dealt with under the provisions of Article VII. However, provision of guarantees with respect to debt of related parties is ordinarily not an independent economic undertaking that would generate business profits, and thus compensation in respect of such related-party guarantees is, in most cases, covered by Article XXII.

Article XXIII — Capital

1. Capital represented by real property, owned by a resident of a Contracting State and situated in the other Contracting State, may be taxed in that other State.

Related Provisions: ITCIA 5 — Definition of "immovable property" and "real property".

Definitions: "real property" — Art. VI:2, ITCIA 5; "resident" — Art. IV; "State" — Art. III:1(i).

Technical Explanation [1984]: Although neither Canada nor the United States currently has national taxes on capital, Article XXIII provides rules for the eventuality that such taxes might be enacted in the future. Paragraph 1 provides that capital represented by real property (as defined in paragraph 2 of Article VI (Income From Real Property)) owned by a resident of a Contracting State and situated in the other Contracting State may be taxed in that other State.

2. Capital represented by personal property forming part of the business property of a permanent establishment which a resident of a Contracting State has in the other Contracting State may be taxed in that other State.

Notes: Art. XXIII:2 amended by 2007 Protocol, effective for taxable years beginning after 2008, but in respect of taxes withheld at source, for amounts paid or credited after Jan. 2009. Before the amendment, read (before "may be taxed"): "or by personal property pertaining to a fixed base available to a resident of a Contracting State in the other Contracting State for the purpose of performing independent personal services,".

Definitions: "permanent establishment" — Art. V:1; "property" — ITCIA 3, ITA 248(1); "resident" — Art. IV; "State" — Art. III:1(i).

Technical Explanation [2007 Protocol]: Article 18 of the Protocol amends paragraph 2 of Article XXIII (Capital) of the Convention by deleting language contained in that paragraph consistent with the changes made by Article 9 of the Protocol.

Technical Explanation [1984]: Paragraph 2 provides that capital represented by either personal property forming part of the business property of a permanent establishment or personal property pertaining to a fixed base in a Contracting State may be taxed in that State.

3. Capital represented by ships and aircraft operated by a resident of a Contracting State in international traffic, and by personal property pertaining to the operation of such ships and aircraft, shall be taxable only in that State.

Definitions: "international traffic" — Art. III:1(h); "property" — ITCIA 3, ITA 248(1); "resident" — Art. IV; "State" — Art. III:1(i).

Technical Explanation [1984]: Paragraph 3 provides that capital represented by ships and aircraft operated by a resident of a Contracting State in international traffic and by personal property pertaining to the operation of such ships and aircraft are taxable only in the Contracting State of residence.

4. All other elements of capital of a resident of a Contracting State shall be taxable only in that State.

Notes: CRA's view is that the RRSP overcontribution tax in ITA 204.2(1.1) is not a "tax on capital": VIEWS doc 2009-0308711E5.

Definitions: "resident" — Art. IV; "State" — Art. III:1(i).

Technical Explanation [1984]: Paragraph 4 provides that all elements of capital other than those covered by paragraphs 1, 2, and 3 are taxable only in the Contracting State of residence. Thus, capital represented by motor vehicles or railway cars, not pertaining to a permanent establishment or fixed base in a Contracting State, would be taxable only in the Contracting State of which the taxpayer is a resident.

Article XXIV — Elimination of Double Taxation

Notes: See Notes to Art. XV:1 for the 2007 Protocol Annex B, s. 6 agreement on treatment of stock options.

1. In the case of the United States, subject to the provisions of paragraphs 4, 5 and 6, double taxation shall be avoided as follows: In accordance with the provisions and subject to the limitations of the law of the United States (as it may be amended from time to time without changing the general principle hereof), the United States shall allow to a citizen or resident of the United States, or to a company electing to be treated as a domestic corporation, as a credit against the United States tax on income the appropriate amount of income tax paid or accrued to Canada; and, in the case of a company which is a resident of the United States owning at least 10 per cent of the voting stock of a company which is a resident of Canada from which it receives dividends in any taxable year, the United States shall allow as a credit against the United States tax on income the appropriate amount of income tax paid or accrued to Canada by that company with respect to the profits out of which such dividends are paid.

Definitions: "Canada" — Art. III:1(a), ITCIA 5; "company" — Art. III:1(f); "dividend" — ITCIA 3, ITA 248(1); "income tax paid or accrued" — Art. XXIV:7; "national" — Art. III:1(k); "resident" — Art. IV; "United States" — Art. III:1(b); "United States tax" — Art. III:1(d).

Technical Explanation [1984]: Paragraph 1 provides the general rules that will apply under the Convention with respect to foreign tax credits for Canadian taxes paid or accrued. The United States undertakes to allow to a citizen or resident of the United States, or to a company electing under Code section 1504(d) to be treated as a domestic corporation, a credit against the Federal income taxes imposed by the Code for the appropriate amount of income tax paid or accrued to Canada. In the case of a company which is a resident of the United States owning 10% or more of the voting stock of a company which is a resident of Canada (which for this purpose does not include a company electing under Code section 1504(d) to be treated as a domestic corporation), and from which it receives dividends in a taxable year, the United States shall allow as a credit against income taxes imposed by the Code the appropriate amount of income tax paid or accrued to Canada by the Canadian company with respect to the profits out of which such company paid the dividends.

The direct and deemed-paid credits allowed by paragraph 1 are subject to the limitations of the Code as they may be amended from time to time without changing the general principle of paragraph 1. Thus, as is generally the case under U.S. income tax conventions, provisions such as Code sections 901(c), 904, 905, 907, 908, and 911 apply for purposes of computing the allowable credit under paragraph 1. In addition, the United States is not required to maintain the overall limitation currently provided by U.S. law.

The term "income tax paid or accrued" is defined in paragraph 7 of Article XXIV to include certain specified taxes which are paid or accrued. The Convention only provides a credit for amounts paid or accrued. The determination of whether an amount is paid or accrued is made under the Code. Paragraph 1 provides a credit for these specified taxes whether or not they qualify as creditable under Code section 901 or 903. A taxpayer who claims credit under the Convention for Canadian taxes made creditable solely by paragraph 1 is not, as a result of the Protocol, subject to a per-country limitation with respect to Canadian taxes. Thus, credit for such Canadian taxes would be computed under the overall limitation currently provided by U.S. law. (However, see the discussion below of the source rules of paragraphs 3 and 9 for a restriction on the use of third country taxes to offset the U.S. tax imposed on resourced income.)

A taxpayer claiming credits for Canadian taxes under the Convention must apply the source rules of the Convention, and must apply those source rules in their entirety. Similarly, a taxpayer claiming credit for Canadian taxes which are creditable under the Code and who wishes to use the source rules of the Convention in computing that credit must apply the source rules of the Convention in their entirety.

2. In the case of Canada, subject to the provisions of paragraphs 4, 5 and 6, double taxation shall be avoided as follows:

(a) subject to the provisions of the law of Canada regarding the deduction from tax payable in Canada of tax paid in a territory outside Canada and to any subsequent modification of those provisions (which shall not affect the general principle hereof)

(i) income tax paid or accrued to the United States on profits, income or gains arising in the United States, and

(ii) in the case of an individual, any social security taxes paid to the United States (other than taxes relating to unemployment insurance benefits) by the individual on such profits, income or gains

shall be deducted from any Canadian tax payable in respect of such profits, income or gains;

(b) in the case of a company which is a resident of Canada owning at least 10 percent of the voting stock of a company which is a resident of the United States from which it receives dividends in any taxable year, Canada shall allow as a credit against the Canadian tax on income the appropriate amount of income tax paid or accrued to the United States by the second company with respect to the profits out of which the dividends are paid.

(c) notwithstanding the provisions of subparagraph (a), where Canada imposes a tax on gains from the alienation of property that, but for the provisions of paragraph 5 of Article XIII (Gains), would not be taxable in Canada, income tax paid or accrued to the United States on such gains shall be deducted from any Canadian tax payable in respect of such gains.

Related Provisions: ITA 126 — Foreign tax credit; Art. X:2 — Withholding tax on dividends.

Notes: Double tax includes *economic* double tax as well as direct double tax, and thus includes income attributed under ITA 75(2): *Sommerer*, 2012 FCA 207, para. 66.

"Social security taxes" includes Tier 1 but not Tier 2 railroad retirement taxes under the US *Railroad Retirement Tax Act*: VIEWS doc 2005-0125471E5.

For examples of Art. XXIV:2 applying (Canadian foreign tax credit available if US tax paid) see *Garcia*, 2007 TCC 548, paras. 50-52; VIEWS docs 2010-0369311E5, 2011-039874117. In CRA's view, "tax paid or accrued to the United States" must actually have been *paid*, because para. 2 is subject to ITA s. 126: VIEWS docs 2015-0601781E5, 2019-0824381C6 [2019 CTF q.2].

In *4145356 Canada*, 2011 TCC 220 (Crown's appeal to FCA discontinued on settlement A-193-11), Art. XXIV:2 was argued but the TCC decided the case on other grounds (see Notes to ITA 126(7)"non-business-income tax").

In *FLSmidth Ltd.*, 2012 TCC 3; aff'd 2013 FCA 160, no 20(12) deduction was allowed on a tower structure that included a US limited partnership, Nova Scotia ULC and an LLC. The TCC ruled that this result did not violate Art. XXIV:2 and 3; this point was not appealed to the FCA.

See also Tsatsas & Gagné, "U.S. social security contributions are eligible for Quebec foreign tax credit", 1(5) *It's Personal* (Carswell) 6-7 (Nov. 2008).

Art. XXIV:2(b) amended by 2007 Protocol, for taxable years beginning after 2008, but in respect of taxes withheld at source, for amounts paid or credited after Jan. 2009.

Art. XXIV:2 amended by 1995 Protocol, generally effective 1996.

Definitions: "Canada" — Art. III:1(a), ITCIA 5; "Canadian tax" — Art. III:1(c); "company" — Art. III:1(f); "dividend" — ITCIA 3, ITA 248(1); "income tax paid or accrued" — Art. XXIV:7; "individual", "property" — ITCIA 3, ITA 248(1); "resident" — Art. IV; "United States" — Art. III:1(b).

Interpretation Bulletins: IT-173R2: Capital gains derived in Canada by residents of the United States.

Technical Explanation [2007 Protocol]: Article 19 of the Protocol deletes subparagraph 2(b) of Article XXIV (Elimination of Double Taxation) of the Convention and replaces it with a new subparagraph.

New subparagraph 2(b) allows a Canadian company receiving a dividend from a U.S. resident company of which it owns at least 10% of the voting stock, a credit against Canadian income tax of the appropriate amount of income tax paid or accrued to the United States by the dividend paying company with respect to the profits out of which the dividends are paid. The third Protocol to the Convention, signed March 17, 1995, had amended subparagraph (b) to allow a Canadian company to deduct in computing its Canadian taxable income any dividend received by it out of the exempt surplus of a foreign affiliate which is a resident of the United States. This change is consistent with current Canadian tax treaty practice: it does not indicate any present intention to change Canada's "exempt surplus" rules, and those rules remain in effect.

Technical Explanation [1995 Protocol]: Article 12 of the Protocol amends Article XXIV (Elimination of Double Taxation) of the Convention. Paragraph 1 of Article 12 amends the rules for Canadian double taxation relief in subparagraphs (a) and (b) of paragraph 2 of Article XXIV. The amendment to subparagraph (a) obligates Canada to give a foreign tax credit for U.S. social security taxes paid by individuals. The amendment to subparagraph (b) of paragraph 2 does not alter the substantive effect of the rule, but conforms the language to current Canadian law. Under the provision as amended, Canada generally continues to allow an exemption to a Canadian corporation for direct dividends paid from the exempt surplus of a U.S. affiliate.

3. For the purposes of this Article:

(a) profits, income or gains (other than gains to which paragraph 5 of Article XIII (Gains) applies) of a resident of a Contracting State which may be taxed in the other Contracting State in accordance with the Convention (without regard to paragraph 2 of Article XXIX (Miscellaneous Rules)) shall be deemed to arise in that other State; and

(b) profits, income or gains of a resident of a Contracting State which may not be taxed in the other Contracting State in accordance with the Convention (without regard to paragraph 2 of Article XXIX (Miscellaneous Rules)) or to which paragraph 5 of Article XIII (Gains) applies shall be deemed to arise in the first-mentioned State.

Notes: Where a US citizen in Canada pays double tax on a US-source dividend because the Canadian relief is limited to 15% credit (ITA 126(7)"non-business-income tax"(b)) plus ITA 20(11) deduction, Art. XXIV allows the US-source dividend to be treated as Canadian-source so that it is eligible for US foreign tax credit. See also Notes to Canada-UK treaty Art. 21:3.

For detailed analysis of Art. XXIV:3-6 see VIEWS doc 8M18146, "Foreign tax credit on United States amount" (Oct. 19, 1998, 50pp), outlining CRA's position on granting a Canadian FTC for US minimum tax and the impact of the US credit for prior year minimum tax on the computation of US tax otherwise payable for Canadian FTC purposes. See also docs 9524810, 2014-0525681E5.

For foreign tax credit for US citizens in Canada, see also *Glen Taylor*, [2000] 3 C.T.C. 456 (FCTD); *Arsove*, 2016 TCC 283, paras. 11-14; and VIEWS doc 2010-0355551E5, 2013-0480301C6 [2013 STEP conf. q.4].

See also Notes to para. 2 above.

Definitions: "resident" — Art. IV; "State" — Art. III:1(i).

Technical Explanation [1984]: Paragraph 3 provides source rules for purposes of applying Article XXIV. Profits, income or gains of a resident of a Contracting State which may be taxed in the other Contracting State in accordance with the Convention, for reasons other than the saving clause of paragraph 2 of Article XXIX (Miscellaneous Rules) (e.g., pensions and annuities taxable where arising pursuant to Article XVIII (Pensions and Annuities)), are deemed to arise in the latter State. This rule does not, however, apply to gains taxable under paragraph 5 of Article XIII (Gains) (i.e., gains taxed by a Contracting State derived from the alienation of property by a former resident of that State). Gains from such an alienation arise, pursuant to paragraph 3(b), in the State of which the alienator is a resident. Thus, if in accordance with paragraph 5 of Article XIII, Canada imposes tax on certain gains of a U.S. resident such gains are deemed, pursuant to paragraphs 2 and 3(b) of Article XXIV, to arise in the United States for purposes of computing the deduction against Canadian tax for the U.S. tax on such gain. Under the Convention such gains arise in the United States for purposes of the United States foreign tax credit. Paragraph 3(b) also provides that profits, income, or gains arise in the Contracting State of which a person is a resident if they may not be taxed in the other Contracting State under the provisions of the Convention (e.g., alimony), other than the "saving clause" of paragraph 2 of Article XXIX.

4. Where a United States citizen is a resident of Canada, the following rules shall apply:

(a) Canada shall allow a deduction from the Canadian tax in respect of income tax paid or accrued to the United States in respect of profits, income or gains which arise (within the meaning of paragraph 3) in the United States, except that such deduction need not exceed the amount of the tax that would be paid to the United States if the resident were not a United States citizen; and

(b) for the purposes of computing the United States tax, the United States shall allow as a credit against United States tax the income tax paid or accrued to Canada after the deduction referred to in subparagraph (a). The credit so allowed shall not reduce that portion of the United States tax that is deductible from Canadian tax in accordance with subparagraph (a).

Notes: See Notes to para. 3 above.

Definitions: "Canada" — Art. III:1(a), ITCIA 5; "Canadian tax" — Art. III:1(c); "income tax paid or accrued" — Art. XXIV:7; "resident" — Art. IV; "United States" — Art. III:1(b); "United States tax" — Art. III:1(d).

5. Notwithstanding the provisions of paragraph 4, where a United States citizen is a resident of Canada, the following rules shall apply in respect of the items of income referred to in Article X (Dividends), XI (Interest) or XII (Royalties) that arise (within the meaning of paragraph 3) in the United States and that would be subject to United States tax if the resident of Canada were not a citizen of the United States, as long as the law in force in Canada allows a deduction in computing income for the portion of any foreign tax paid in respect of such items which exceeds 15 per cent of the amount thereof:

(a) the deduction so allowed in Canada shall not be reduced by any credit or deduction for income tax paid or accrued to Canada allowed in computing the United States tax on such items;

(b) Canada shall allow a deduction from Canadian tax on such items in respect of income tax paid or accrued to the United States on such items, except that such deduction need not exceed the amount of the tax that would be paid on such items to the United States if the resident of Canada were not a United States citizen; and

(c) for the purposes of computing the United States tax on such items, the United States shall allow as a credit against United States tax the income tax paid or accrued to Canada after the deduction referred to in subparagraph (b). The credit so allowed shall reduce only that portion of the United States tax on such items which exceeds the amount of tax that would be paid to the United States on such items if the resident of Canada were not a United States citizen.

Notes: See Notes to para. 3 above.

Art. XXIV:5 amended by 1995 Protocol, generally effective 1996.

Definitions: "Canada" — Art. III:1(a), ITCIA 5; "Canadian tax" — Art. III:1(c); "income tax paid or accrued" — Art. XXIV:7; "resident" — Art. IV; "United States" — Art. III:1(b); "United States tax" — Art. III:1(d).

Technical Explanation [1995 Protocol]: Paragraphs 4 and 5 of Article XXIV of the Convention provide double taxation relief rules, for both the United States and Canada, with respect to U.S. source income derived by a U.S. citizen who is resident in Canada. These rules address the fact that a U.S. citizen resident in Canada remains subject to U.S. tax on his worldwide income at ordinary progressive rates, and may, therefore, be subject to U.S. tax at a higher rate than a resident of Canada who is not a U.S. citizen. In essence, these paragraphs limit the foreign tax credit that Canada is obliged to allow such a U.S. citizen to the amount of tax on his U.S. source income that the United States would be allowed to collect from a Canadian resident who is not a U.S. citizen. They also oblige the United States to allow the U.S. citizen a credit for any income tax paid to Canada on the remainder of his income. Paragraph 4 deals with items of income other than dividends, interest, and royalties and is not changed by the Protocol. Paragraph 5, which deals with dividends, interest, and royalties, is amended by paragraph 2 of Article 12 of the Protocol.

The amendments to paragraph 5 of the Article make that paragraph applicable only to dividend, interest, and royalty income that would be subject to a positive rate of U.S. tax if paid to a Canadian resident who is not a U.S. citizen. This means that the rules of paragraph 4, not paragraph 5, will apply to items of interest and royalties, such as portfolio interest, that would be exempt from U.S. tax if paid to a non-U.S. citizen resident in Canada. Under paragraph 4, Canada will not allow a credit for the U.S. tax on such income, and the United States will credit the Canadian tax to the extent necessary to avoid double taxation.

Paragraph 2 of Article 12 of the Protocol makes further technical amendments to paragraph 5 of Article XXIV of the Convention. The existing Technical Explanation of

paragraphs 5 and 6 of Article XXIV of the Convention should be read as follows to reflect the amendments made by the Protocol:

Paragraph 5 provides special rules for the elimination of double taxation in the case of dividends, interest, and royalties earned by a U.S. citizen resident in Canada. These rules apply notwithstanding the provisions of paragraph 4, but only as long as the law in Canada allows a deduction in computing income for the portion of any foreign tax paid in respect of dividends, interest, or royalties which exceeds 15% of the amount of such items of income, and only with respect to those items of income. The rules of paragraph 4 apply with respect to other items of income; moreover, if the law in force in Canada regarding the deduction for foreign taxes is changed so as to no longer allow such a deduction, the provisions of paragraph 5 shall not apply and the U.S. foreign tax credit for Canadian taxes and the Canadian credit for U.S. taxes will be determined solely pursuant to the provisions of paragraph 4.

The calculations under paragraph 5 are as follows. First, the deduction allowed in Canada in computing income shall be made with respect to U.S. tax on the dividends, interest, and royalties before any foreign tax credit by the United States with respect to income tax paid or accrued to Canada. Second, Canada shall allow a deduction from (credit against) Canadian tax for U.S. tax paid or accrued with respect to the dividends, interest, and royalties, but such credit need not exceed the amount of income tax that would be paid or accrued to the United States on such items of income if the individual were not a U.S. citizen after taking into account any relief available under the Convention. Third, for purposes of computing the U.S. tax on such dividends, interest, and royalties, the United States shall allow as a credit against the U.S. tax the income tax paid or accrued to Canada after the credit against Canadian tax for income tax paid or accrued to the United States. The United States is in no event obliged to give a credit for Canadian income tax which will reduce the U.S. tax below the amount of income tax that would be paid or accrued to the United States on the amount of the dividends, interest, and royalties if the individual were not a U.S. citizen after taking into account any relief available under the Convention.

The rules of paragraph 5 are illustrated by the following examples.

Example B

A U.S. citizen who is a resident of Canada has $100 of dividend income arising in the United States. The tentative U.S. tax before foreign tax credit is $40.

Canada, under its law, allows a deduction for the U.S. tax in excess of 15% or, in this case, a deduction of $25 ($40 - $15). The Canadian taxable income is $75 and the Canadian tax on that amount is $35.

Canada gives a credit of $15 (the maximum credit allowed is 15% of the gross dividend taken into Canadian income) and collects a net tax of $20.

The United States allows a credit for the net Canadian tax against its tax in excess of 15%. Thus, the maximum credit is $25 ($40 - $15). But since the net Canadian tax paid was $20, the usable credit is $20.

To be able to use a credit of $20 requires Canadian source taxable income of $50 (50% of the U.S. tentative tax of $40). Under paragraph 6, $50 of the U.S. dividend is resourced to be of Canadian source. The credit of $20 may then be offset against the U.S. tax of $40, leaving a net U.S. tax of $20.

The combined tax paid to both countries is $40, $20 to Canada and $20 to the United States.

Example C

A U.S. citizen who is a resident of Canada receives $200 of income with respect to personal services performed within Canada and $100 of dividend income arising within the United States. Taxable income for U.S. purposes, taking into account the rules of Code section 911, is $220. U.S. tax (before foreign tax credits) is $92. The $100 of dividend income is deemed to bear U.S. tax (before foreign tax credits) of $41.82 ($100/$200 x $92). Under Canadian law, a deduction of $26.82 (the excess of $41.82 over 15% of the $100 dividend income) is allowed in computing income. The Canadian tax on $273.18 of income ($300 less the $26.82 deduction) is $130. Canada then gives a credit against the $130 for $15 (the U.S. tax paid or accrued with respect to the dividend, $41.82 but limited to 15% of the gross amount of such income, or $15), leaving a final Canadian tax of $115. Of the $115, $30.80 is attributable to the dividend:

$$\frac{\$73.18\ (\$100\ \text{dividend less }\$26.82\ \text{deduction})}{\$273.18\ (\$300\ \text{income less }\$26.82\ \text{deduction})} \times \$115$$

Of this amount, $26.82 is creditable against U.S. tax pursuant to paragraph 5. (Although the U.S. allows a credit for the Canadian tax imposed on the dividend, $30.80, the credit may not reduce the U.S. tax below 15% of the amount of the dividend. Thus, the maximum allowable credit is the excess of $41.82, the U.S. tax imposed on the dividend income, over $15, which is 15% of the $100 dividend). The remaining $3.98 (the Canadian tax of $30.80 less the credit allowed of $26.82) is a foreign tax credit carryover for U.S. purposes, subject to the limitations of paragraph 5. (An additional $50.18 of Canadian tax with respect to Canadian source services income is creditable against U.S. tax pursuant to paragraphs 3 and 4(b). The $50.18 is computed as follows: tentative U.S. tax (before foreign tax credits) is $92; the U.S. tax on Canadian source services income is $50.18 ($92 less the U.S. tax on the dividend income of $41.82); the limitation on the services income is:

$$\frac{\$120 \text{ (taxable income from services)}}{\$220 \text{ (total taxable income)}} \times \$92$$

or $50.18. The credit for Canadian tax paid on the services income is therefore $50.18; the remainder of the Canadian tax on the services income, or $34.02, is a foreign tax credit carryover for U.S. purposes, subject to the limitations of paragraph 5.)

Paragraph 6 is necessary to implement the objectives of paragraphs 4(b) and 5(c). Paragraph 6 provides that where a U.S. citizen is a resident of Canada, items of income referred to in paragraph 4 or 5 are deemed for the purposes of Article XXIV to arise in Canada to the extent necessary to avoid double taxation of income by Canada and the United States consistent with the objectives of paragraphs 4(b) and 5(c). Paragraph 6 can override the source rules of paragraph 3 to permit a limited resourcing of income. The principles of paragraph 3 have effect, pursuant to paragraph 3(b) of Article XXX (Entry Into Force) of the Convention, for taxable years beginning on or after January 1, 1976. See the discussion of Article XXX below.

The application of paragraph 6 is illustrated by the following example.

Example D

The facts are the same as in Example C. The United States has undertaken, pursuant to paragraph 5(c) and paragraph 6, to credit $26.82 of Canadian taxes on dividend income that has a U.S. source under both paragraph 3 and the *Internal Revenue Code*. (As illustrated in Example C, the credit, however, only reduces the U.S. tax on the dividend income which exceeds the amount of income tax that would be paid or accrued to the United States on such income if the individual were not a U.S. citizen after taking into account any relief available under the Convention. Pursuant to paragraph 6, for purposes of determining the U.S. foreign tax credit limitation under the Convention with respect to Canadian taxes,

$$\$64.13 \,(\frac{A}{\$220} \times \$92 = \$26.82; A = \$64.13)$$

of taxable income with respect to the dividends is deemed to arise in Canada.

6. Where a United States citizen is a resident of Canada, items of income referred to in paragraph 4 or 5 shall, notwithstanding the provisions of paragraph 3, be deemed to arise in Canada to the extent necessary to avoid the double taxation of such income under paragraph 4(b) or paragraph 5(c).

Notes: See Notes to para. 3 above.

Definitions: "Canada" — Art. III:1(a), ITCIA 5; "resident" — Art. IV; "United States" — Art. III:1(b).

7. For the purposes of this Article, any reference to **"income tax paid or accrued"** to a Contracting State shall include Canadian tax and United States tax, as the case may be, and taxes of general application which are paid or accrued to a political subdivision or local authority of that State, which are not imposed by that political subdivision or local authority in a manner inconsistent with the provisions of the Convention and which are substantially similar to the Canadian tax or United States tax, as the case may be.

Notes: A US state franchise tax that applies even though the Canadian company has no permanent establishment in the US is "imposed . . . in a manner inconsistent with . . . this Convention", so para. 7 does not apply, but a foreign tax credit is available under 126(2): VIEWS doc 2011-0428791E5.

Art. XXIV:7 amended by 1995 Protocol, generally effective 1996, to change "the taxes of that State referred to in paragraphs 2 and 3(a) of Article II (Taxes Covered)" to "the Canadian tax or United States tax, as the case may be", at the end of the paragraph.

Definitions: "Canadian tax" — Art. III:1(c); "State" — Art. III:1(i); "United States tax" — Art. III:1(d).

Technical Explanation [1995 Protocol]: Paragraph 3 of Article 12 of the Protocol makes a technical amendment to paragraph 7 of Article XXIV. It conforms the reference to U.S. and Canadian taxes to the amended definitions of "United States tax" and "Canadian tax" in subparagraphs (c) and (d) of paragraph 1 of Article III (General Definitions). No substantive change in the effect of the paragraph is intended.

8. Where a resident of a Contracting State owns capital which, in accordance with the provisions of the Convention, may be taxed in the other Contracting State, the first-mentioned State shall allow as a deduction from the tax on the capital of that resident an amount equal to the capital tax paid in that other State. The deduction shall not, however, exceed that part of the capital tax, as computed before the deduction is given, which is attributable to the capital which may be taxed in that other State.

Definitions: "resident" — Art. IV; "State" — Art. III:1(i).

9. The provisions of this Article relating to the source of profits, income or gains shall not apply for the purpose of determining a credit against United States tax for any foreign taxes other than income taxes paid or accrued to Canada.

Definitions: "Canada" — Art. III:1(a), ITCIA 5; "income tax paid or accrued" — Art. XXIV:7; "United States" — Art. III:1(b).

10. Where in accordance with any provision of the Convention income derived or capital owned by a resident of a Contracting State is exempt from tax in that State, such State may nevertheless, in calculating the amount of tax on other income or capital, take into account the exempted income or capital.

Notes: Art. XXIV:10 added by 1995 Protocol, generally effective 1996. This provision in effect confirms the interpretation of the Supreme Court of Canada in *Swantje*, [1996] 1 C.T.C. 355 for U.S. residents. The Tax Court of Canada had ruled ([1994] 1 C.T.C. 2559) that the clawback of old age security payments under ITA 180.2 was in effect a tax on exempt German pension income because it took that income into account. That decision was reversed by the higher courts.

Definitions: "resident" — Art. IV; "State" — Art. III:1(i).

Technical Explanation [1995 Protocol]: Paragraph 4 of Article 12 of the Protocol adds a new paragraph 10 to Article XXIV of the Convention. This paragraph provides for the application of the rule of "exemption with progression" by a Contracting State in cases where an item of income of a resident of that State is exempt from tax in that State by virtue of a provision of the Convention. For example, where under Canadian law a tax benefit, such as the goods and services tax credit, to a Canadian resident individual is reduced as the income of that individual, or the individual's spouse or other dependent, increases, and any of these persons receives U.S. social security benefits that are exempt from tax in Canada under the Convention, Canada may, nevertheless, take the U.S. social security benefits into account in determining whether, and to what extent, the benefit should be reduced.

New Article XXIX B (Taxes Imposed by Reason of Death), added by Article 19 of the Protocol, also provides relief from double taxation in certain circumstances in connection with Canadian income tax imposed by reason of death and U.S. estate taxes. However, subparagraph 7(c) of Article XXIX B generally denies relief from U.S. estate tax under that Article to the extent that a credit or deduction has been claimed for the same amount in determining any other tax imposed by the United States. This restriction would operate to deny relief, for example, to the extent that relief from U.S. income tax is claimed under Article XXIV in respect of the same amount of Canadian tax. There is, however, no requirement that relief from U.S. tax be claimed first (or exclusively) under Article XXIV. Paragraph 6 of Article XXIX B also prevents the claiming of double relief from Canadian income taxation under both that Article and Article XXIV, by providing that the credit provided by Article XXIX B applies only after the application of the credit provided by Article XXIV.

Technical Explanation [1984]: Paragraph 9 provides clarification that the source rules of this Article shall not be used to determine the credit available against U.S. tax for foreign taxes other than income taxes paid or accrued to Canada (i.e., taxes of third countries). Thus, creditable third country taxes may not offset the U.S. tax on income treated as arising in Canada under the source rules of the Convention. A person claiming credit for income taxes of a third country may not rely upon the rules of paragraphs 3 and 6 for purposes of treating income that would otherwise have a U.S. source as having a foreign source. Thus, if the taxpayer elects to compute the foreign tax credit for any year using the special source rules set forth in paragraphs 3 and 6, paragraph 9 requires that a separate limitation be computed for taxes not covered by paragraph 1 without regard to the source rules of paragraphs 3 and 6, and the credit for such taxes may not exceed such limitation. The credit allowed under this separate limitation may not exceed the proportion of the Federal income taxes imposed by the Code that the taxpayer's taxable income from foreign sources (under the Code) not included in taxable income arising in Canada (and not in excess of total foreign source taxable income under the Code) bears to the taxpayer's worldwide taxable income. In any case the credit for taxes covered by paragraph 1 and the credit for other foreign taxes is limited to the amount allowed under an overall limitation computed by aggregating taxable income arising in Canada and other foreign source taxable income.

If creditable Canadian taxes exceed the proportion of U.S. tax that taxable income arising in Canada bears to the entire taxable income, such taxes may qualify to be absorbed by any excess in the separate limitation computed with respect to other taxes.

In a case where a taxpayer has different types of income subject to separate limitations under the Code (e.g., section 904(d)(1)(B) DISC dividends) the Convention rules just described apply in the context of each of the separate Code limitations.

A taxpayer may, for any year, claim a credit pursuant to the rules of the Code. In such case, the taxpayer would be subject to the limitations established in the Code, and would forego the rules of the Convention that determine where taxable income arises. In addition, any Canadian taxes covered by paragraph 1 which are not creditable under the Code would not be credited.

Thus, where a taxpayer elects to use the special source rules of this Article to compute the foreign tax credit for any year, the following computations must be made:

Step 1(a): Compute a hypothetical foreign tax credit limitation for Canadian income and taxes using the source rules of the Convention.

Step 1(b): Compute a hypothetical foreign tax credit limitation for third country income and taxes using the source rules of the Code.

Step 1(c): Compute an overall foreign tax credit limitation using the source rules of the Convention to the extent they resource Canadian source income as U.S. source income or U.S. source income as Canadian source income, and using the source rules of the Code with respect to any other income.

Step 2: Allocate the amount of creditable Canadian taxes to the amount of the limitation computed under step 1(a), and allocate the amount of creditable third country taxes to the amount of the limitation computed under step 1(b). The amount of credit to be so allocated may not exceed the amount of the respective limitation.

Step 3: (1) If the total credits allocated under step 2 exceed the amount of the limitation computed under step 1(c), the amount of allowable credits must be reduced to that limitation (see Rev. Rul. 82-215, 1982-2 Cum. Bull. 153 for the method of such reduction).

(2) If the total credits allocated under step 2 are less than the amount of the limitation computed under step 1(c), then (a) any amount of creditable Canadian taxes in excess of the amount of the step 1(a) limitation may be credited to the extent of the excess of the step 1(c) limitation over the total step 2 allocation, and (b) any amount of third country taxes in excess of the amount of the step 1(b) limitation may not be credited.

The following examples (in which the taxpayer's U.S. tax rate is presumed to be 46%) illustrate the application of the source rules of Article XXIV:

Example 1.

(a) A U.S. corporate taxpayer has for the taxable year $100 of taxable income having a U.S. source under both the Convention and the Code; $100 of taxable income having a Canadian source under both the Convention and the Code; $50 of taxable income having a Canadian source under the Convention but a U.S. source under the Code (see, for example, paragraph 1 of Article VII (Business Profits) and paragraph 3(a) of Article XXIV); and $80 of taxable income having a foreign (non-Canadian) source under the Code. The taxpayer pays $75 of Canadian income taxes and $45 of third country income taxes. All the foreign source income of the taxpayer constitutes "other" income described in Code section 904(d)(1)(C).

The source rules of the Convention are applied as follows to compute the taxpayer's foreign tax credit:

Step 1(a):

$$\frac{\$150 \quad \text{(Canadian source taxable income under Convention)}}{\$330 \quad \text{(total taxable income)}} \times \$151.80$$

$$= \$69 \text{ limit for Canadian taxes.}$$

Step 1(b):

$$\frac{\$80 \quad \text{(third country source taxable income under Code)}}{\$330 \quad \text{(total taxable income)}} \times \$151.80$$

$$= \$36.80 \text{ limit for third country taxes.}$$

Step 1(c):

$$\frac{\$230 \quad \text{(overall foreign taxable income under source rules described above)}}{\$330 \quad \text{(total taxable income)}} \times \$151.80$$

$$= \$105.80 \text{ total limit.}$$

Step 2: The taxpayer may tentatively credit $69 of the $75 Canadian income taxes under the step 1(a) limitation, and $36.80 of the third country income taxes under the step 1(b) limitation.

Step 3: Since the total amount of taxes credited under step 2 equals the taxpayer's total limitation of $105.80 under step 1(c), no additional taxes may be credited. The taxpayer has a $6 Canadian income tax carryover and an $8.20 third country income tax carryover for U.S. foreign tax credit purposes.

(b) If the taxpayer had paid only $30 of third country taxes, he would credit that $30 in step 2. Since the total amount of credits allowed under step 2 ($99) is less than the taxpayer's total limit of $105.80, and since the taxpayer has $6 of excess Canadian taxes not credited under step 2, he may also claim a credit for that $6 of Canadian income taxes, for a total credit of $105.

(c) If the taxpayer had paid $45 of third country income taxes and $65 of Canadian income taxes, the computation would be as follows:

Step 2: The taxpayer would credit the $65 of Canadian income taxes, and would also credit $36.80 of the $45 of third country income taxes.

Step 3: Although the total amount of credits computed under step 2 ($101.80) is less than the taxpayer's total limitation of $105.80, no additional credits can be claimed since the taxpayer has only excess third country income taxes. The excess third country income taxes are thus not permitted to offset U.S. tax on income that is Canadian source income under the Convention. The taxpayer would have $8.20 of third country income taxes as a carryover for U.S. foreign tax credit purposes.

Example 2.

A United States corporate taxpayer has for the taxable year $100 of taxable income having a Canadian source under the Convention but a U.S. source under the Code; $100 of taxable income having a U.S. source under both the Convention and the Code; $80 of taxable income having a foreign (non-Canadian) source under the Code; and $50 of loss allocated or apportioned to Canadian source income. The taxpayer pays $50 of foreign (non-Canadian) income taxes, and $20 of Canadian income taxes.

The source rules of the Convention are applied as follows to compute the taxpayer's foreign tax credit:

Step 1(a):

$$\frac{\$50 \quad \text{(Canadian source taxable income under Convention)}}{\$230 \quad \text{(total taxable income)}} \times \$105.80$$

$$= \$23 \text{ limit for Canadian taxes.}$$

Step 1(b):

$$\frac{\$80 \quad \text{(third country source taxable income under Code)}}{\$230 \quad \text{(total taxable income)}} \times \$105.80$$

$$= \$36.80 \text{ limit for third country taxes.}$$

Step 1(c):

$$\frac{\$130 \quad \text{(overall foreign taxable income under source rules described above)}}{\$230 \quad \text{(total taxable income)}} \times \$105.80$$

$$= \$59.80 \text{ limit for Canadian taxes.}$$

Step 2: Since the taxpayer paid $20 of Canadian income taxes, he may credit that amount in full since the step 1(a) limit is $23. Since the step 1(b) limit is $36.80, the taxpayer may credit $36.80 of the $50 foreign income taxes paid.

Step 3: Although the total taxes credited under step 2 ($56.80) is less than the taxpayer's total limit of $59.80, no additional credits may be claimed since the only excess taxes are third country income taxes, and those may not be used to offset any excess limitation in step 3. The $13.20 of foreign taxes not allowed as a credit is available as a foreign tax credit carryover.

Example 3.

The facts are the same as in Example 2, except that foreign (non-Canadian) operations result in a loss of $30 rather than taxable income of $80, and no foreign (non-Canadian) income taxes are paid. The taxpayer's credit is computed as follows:

Step 1(a):

$$\frac{\$50}{\$120} \times \$55.20 \quad = \quad \text{limit for Canadian taxes.}$$

Step 1(b): Since there is no third country source taxable income under the Code, the limit for third country income taxes is zero.

Step 1(c):

$$\frac{\$20}{\$120} \times \$55.20 \quad = \quad \$9.20 \text{ total limit.}$$

Step 2: Since the taxpayer paid $20 of Canadian income tax, he may tentatively credit that amount in full since the step 1(a) limit is $23.

Step 3: Since the total taxes credited under step 2 ($20) exceeds the taxpayer's total limit of $9.20, the taxpayer must reduce the total amount claimed as a credit to $9.20. The remaining $10.80 of Canadian income taxes are available as a foreign tax credit carryover.

Example 4.

The facts are the same as in Example 2, except that the first $100 of taxable income mentioned in Example 2 has a Canadian source under both the Convention and the Code.

Step 1(a):

$$\frac{\$50}{\$230} \times \$105.80 \quad = \quad \$23 \text{ limit for Canadian taxes.}$$

Step 1(b):

$$\frac{\$80}{\$230} \times \$105.80 \quad = \quad \$36.80 \text{ limit for third country income taxes.}$$

Step 1(c):

$$\frac{\$130}{\$230} \times \$105.80 \quad = \quad \$59.80 \text{ total limit.}$$

Step 2: The taxpayer credits the $20 of Canadian income tax and $36.80 of third country income tax.

Step 3: As explained in Example 2, the taxpayer's total credit is limited to $56.80. In this case, however, if the Canadian taxes covered by the Convention are creditable under the Code, the taxpayer could elect the Code limitation of $59.80 ($130/$230 × $105.80), which is more advantageous than the Convention limitation because that limitation does not permit third country income taxes to be credited against the U.S. tax on income arising in Canada under the Convention.

Example 5.

The facts are the same as in Example 2, except that the corporation pays $25 of Canadian income taxes and $12 of foreign (non-Canadian) income taxes. Under step 2, the taxpayer would credit $23 of the $25 of Canadian income taxes and the full $12 of third country income taxes. Since the total amount of income taxes credited under step 2 is $35, which is less than the taxpayer's total limit of $59.80, the taxpayer may credit an amount of Canadian income taxes up to the $24.80 excess. Here, the taxpayer may claim a credit for the additional $2 of Canadian income taxes not credited under step 2, and has a total credit of $37.

Example 6.

(a) A U.S. corporate taxpayer has for the taxable year $100 of taxable income having a Canadian source under the Convention and the Code; $50 of taxable income having a Canadian source under the Convention but a U.S. source under the Code; $80 of taxable income having a foreign (non-Canadian) source under the Code; and $50 of loss allocated or apportioned to U.S. source income. The taxpayer pays $65 of Canadian income taxes, and $45 of third country income taxes.

Step 1(a):

$$\frac{\$150}{\$230} \times \$82.80 = \$69 \text{ limit for Canadian income taxes.}$$

Step 1(b):

$$\frac{\$80}{\$180} \times \$82.80 = \$36.80 \text{ limit for third country income taxes.}$$

Step 1(c):

$$\frac{\$180}{\$180} \times \$82.80 = \$82.80 \text{ total limit.}$$

Step 2: The taxpayer tentatively credits the $65 of Canadian income taxes against the $69 limit of step 1(a), and $36.80 of the $45 of third country income taxes against the $36.80 limit of step 1(b).

Step 3: Since the total amount of credits tentatively allowed under step 2 ($101.80) exceeds the taxpayer's total limit of $82.80 under step 1(c), the taxpayer's allowable credit is reduced to $82.80 under the method provided by Rev. Rul. 82-215.

(b) If the taxpayer had paid only $40 of Canadian income taxes, the total credits tentatively allowed under step 2 is $76.80. Although that amount is less than the $82.80 total limit under step 1(c), no additional taxes may be credited since the taxpayer only has excess third country income taxes. The $8.20 of excess third country income taxes would be allowed as a foreign tax credit carryover.

The general rule for avoiding double taxation in Canada is provided in paragraph 2. Pursuant to paragraph 2(a) Canada undertakes to allow to a resident of Canada a credit against income taxes imposed under the *Income Tax Act* for the appropriate amount of income taxes paid or accrued to the United States. Paragraph 2(b) provides for the deduction by a Canadian company, in computing taxable income, of any dividend received out of the exempt surplus of a U.S. company which is an affiliate. The provisions of paragraphs 2(a) and (b) are subject to the provisions of the *Income Tax Act* as they may be amended from time to time without changing the general principle of paragraph 2. Paragraph 2(c) provides that where Canada imposes a tax on the alienation of property pursuant to the provisions of paragraph 5 of Article XIII (Gains), Canada will allow a credit for the income tax paid or accrued to the United States on such gain.

The rules of paragraph 1 are modified in certain respects by rules in paragraphs 4 and 5 for income derived by United States citizens who are residents of Canada. Paragraph 4 provides two steps for the elimination of double taxation in such a case. First, paragraph 4(a) provides that Canada shall allow a deduction from (credit against) Canadian tax in respect of income tax paid or accrued to the United States in respect of profits, income, or gains which arise in the United States (within the meaning of paragraph 3(a)); the deduction against Canadian tax need not, however, exceed the amount of income tax that would be paid or accrued to the United States if the individual were not a U.S. citizen, after taking into account any relief available under the Convention.

The second step, as provided in paragraph 4(b), is that the United States allows as a credit against United States tax, subject to the rules of paragraph 1, the income tax paid or accrued to Canada after the Canadian credit for U.S. tax provided by paragraph 4(a). The credit so allowed by the United States is not to reduce the portion of the United States tax that is creditable against Canadian tax in accordance with paragraph 4(a).

The following example illustrates the application of paragraph 4.

Example A

- A U.S. citizen who is a resident of Canada earns $175 of income from the performance of independent personal services, of which $100 is derived from services performed in Canada and $75 from services performed in the United States. That is his total world-wide income.

- If he were not a U.S. citizen, the United States could tax $75 of that amount under Article XIV (Independent Personal Services). By reason of paragraph 3(a), the $75 that may be taxed by the United States under Article XIV is deemed to arise in the United States. Assume that the U.S. tax on the $75 would be $25 if the taxpayer were not a U.S. citizen.

- However, since the individual is a U.S. citizen, he is subject to U.S. tax on his worldwide income of $175. After excluding $75 under section 911, his taxable income is $100 and his U.S. tax is $40.

- Because he is a resident of Canada, he is also subject to Canadian tax on his worldwide income. Assume that Canada taxes the $175 at $75.

- Canada will credit against its tax of $75 the U.S. tax at source of $25, leaving a net Canadian tax of $50.

- The United States will credit against its tax of $40 the Canadian tax net of credit, but without reducing its source basis tax of $25; thus, the allowable credit is $40 - $25 = $15.

- To use a credit of $15 requires Canadian source taxable income of $37.50 ($37.50/$100 - $40 = 15). Without any special treaty rule, Canadian source taxable income would be only $25 ($100 less the section 911 exclusion of $75). Paragraph 6 provides for resourcing an additional $12.50 of income to Canada, so that the credit of $15 can be fully used.

Paragraph 5 provides special rules for the elimination of double taxation in the case of dividends, interest, and royalties earned by a U.S. citizen resident in Canada. These rules apply notwithstanding the provisions of paragraph 4, but only as long as the law in Canada allows a deduction in computing income for the portion of any foreign tax paid in respect of dividends, interest, or royalties which exceeds 15% of the amount of such items of income, and only with respect to those items of income. The rules of paragraph 4 apply with respect to other items of income; moreover, if the law in force in Canada regarding the deduction for foreign taxes changes, the provisions of paragraph 5 shall not apply and the U.S. foreign tax credit for Canadian taxes and the Canadian credit for U.S. taxes will be determined solely pursuant to the provisions of paragraph 4.

The calculations under paragraph 5 are as follows. First, the deduction allowed in Canada in computing income shall be made with respect to U.S. tax on the dividends, interest, and royalties before any foreign tax credit by the United States with respect to income tax paid or accrued to Canada. Second, Canada shall allow a deduction from (credit against) Canadian tax for U.S. tax paid or accrued with respect to the dividends, interest, and royalties, but such credit need not exceed 15% of the gross amount of such items of income that have been included in computing income for Canadian tax purposes. (The credit may, however, exceed the amount of tax that the United States would be entitled to levy under the Convention upon a Canadian resident who is not a U.S. citizen.) Third, for purposes of computing the U.S. tax on such dividends, interest, and royalties, the United States shall allow as a credit against the U.S. tax the income tax paid or accrued to Canada after the 15% credit against Canadian tax for income tax paid or accrued to the United States. The United States is in no event obliged to give a credit for Canadian income tax which will reduce the U.S. tax below 15% of the amount of the dividends, interest, and royalties.

The rules of paragraph 5 are illustrated by the following examples.

Example B

- A U.S. citizen who is a resident of Canada has $100 of royalty income arising in the United States. The tentative U.S. tax before foreign tax credit is $40.

- Canada, under its law, allows a deduction for the U.S. tax in excess of 15% or, in this case, a deduction of $25 ($40 - $15). The Canadian taxable income is $75 and the Canadian tax on that amount is $35.

- Canada gives a credit of $15 (the maximum credit allowed is 15% of the gross royalty taken into Canadian income) and collects a net tax of $20.

- The United States allows a credit for the net Canadian tax against its tax in excess of 15%. Thus, the maximum credit is $25 ($40 - $15). But since the net Canadian tax paid was $20, the usable credit is $20.

- To be able to use a credit of $20 requires Canadian source taxable income of $50 (50% of the U.S. tentative tax of $40). Under paragraph 6, $50 of the U.S. royalty is resourced to be of Canadian source. The credit of $20 may then be offset against the U.S. tax of $40, leaving a net U.S. tax of $20.

- The combined tax paid to both countries is $40, $20 to Canada and $20 to the United States.

Example C

A U.S. citizen who is a resident of Canada receives $200 of income with respect to personal services performed within Canada and $100 of royalty income arising within the United States. Taxable income for U.S. purposes, taking into account the rules of Code section 911, is $220. U.S. tax (before foreign tax credits) is $92. The $100 of royalty income is deemed to bear U.S. tax (before foreign tax credits) of $41.82 ($100/$220 × $92). Under Canadian law, a deduction of $26.82 (the excess of $41.82 over 15% of the $100 royalty income) is allowed in computing income. The Canadian tax on $273.18 of income ($300 less the $26.82 deduction) is $130. Canada then gives a credit against the $130 for $15 (the U.S. tax paid or accrued with respect to the royalty, $41.82, but limited to 15% of the gross amount of such income, or $15), leaving a final Canadian tax of $115. Of the $115, $30.80 is attributable to the royalty

$$\frac{\$73.18 \ (\$100 \ \text{royalty less} \ \$26.82 \ \text{deduction})}{\$273.18 \ (\$300 \ \text{income less} \ \$26.82 \ \text{deduction})} \times \$115.$$

Of this amount, $26.82 is creditable against U.S. tax pursuant to paragraph 5. (Although the U.S. allows a credit for the Canadian tax imposed on the royalty, $30.80, the credit may not reduce the U.S. tax below 15% of the amount of the royalty. Thus, the maximum allowable credit is the excess of $41.82, the U.S. tax imposed on the royalty income, over $15, which is 15% of the $100 royalty). The remaining $3.98 (the Canadian tax of $30.80 less the credit allowed of $26.82) is a foreign tax credit carryover for U.S. purposes, subject to the limitations of paragraph 5. (An additional $50.18 of Canadian tax with respect to Canadian source services income is creditable against U.S. tax pursuant to paragraphs 3 and 4(b). The $50.18 is computed as follows: tentative U.S. tax (before foreign tax credits) is $92; the U.S. tax on Canadian source services income is $50.18 ($92 less the U.S. tax on the royalty income of $41.82); the limitation on the services income is:

$$\frac{\$120 \ (\text{taxable income from services})}{\$220 \ (\text{total taxable income})} \times \$92,$$

or $50.18. The credit for Canadian tax paid on the services income is therefore $50.18; the remainder of the Canadian tax on the services income, or $34.02, is a foreign tax credit carryover for U.S. purposes, subject to the limitations of paragraph 5).

Paragraph 6 is necessary to implement the objectives of paragraphs 4(b) and 5(c). Paragraph 6 provides that where a U.S. citizen is a resident of Canada, items of income referred to in paragraph 4 or 5 are deemed for the purposes of Article XXIV to arise in Canada to the extent necessary to avoid double taxation of income by Canada and the United States consistent with the objectives of paragraphs 4(b) and 5(c). Paragraph 6 can override the source rules of paragraph 3 to permit a limited resourcing of income. The principles of paragraph 6 have effect, pursuant to paragraph 3(b) of Article XXX (Entry Into Force), for taxable years beginning on or after January 1, 1976. See the discussion of Article XXX below.

The application of paragraph 6 is illustrated by the following example.

Example D

The facts are the same as in Example C. The United States has undertaken, pursuant to paragraph 5(c) and paragraph 6, to credit $26.82 of Canadian taxes on royalty income that has a U.S. source under both paragraph 3 and the *Internal Revenue Code*. (As illustrated in Example C, the credit, however, only reduces the U.S. tax on the royalty income which exceeds 15% of the amount of such income included in computing U.S. taxable income.) Pursuant to paragraph 6, for purposes of determining the U.S. foreign tax credit limitation under the Convention with respect to Canadian taxes, $64.13 (A/$220 × $92 = $26.82; A = $64.13) of taxable income with respect to the royalties is deemed to arise in Canada.

Paragraph 7 provides that any reference to "income tax paid or accrued" to Canada or the United States includes Canadian tax or United States tax, as the case may be. The terms "Canadian tax" and "United States tax" are defined in paragraphs 1(c) and 1(d) of Article III (General Definitions). References to income taxes paid or accrued also include taxes of general application paid or accrued to a political subdivision or local authority of Canada or the United States which are not imposed by such political subdivision or local authority in a manner inconsistent with the provisions of the Convention and which are substantially similar to taxes of Canada or the United States referred to in paragraphs 2 and 3(a) of Article II (Taxes Covered).

In order for a tax imposed by a political subdivision or local authority to fall within the scope of paragraph 7, such tax must apply to individuals, companies, or other persons generally, and not only to a particular class of individuals or companies or a particular type of business. The tax must also be substantially similar to the national taxes referred to in paragraphs 2 and 3(a) of Article II. Finally, the political subdivision or local authority must apply its tax in a manner not inconsistent with the provisions of the Convention. For example, the political subdivision or local authority must not impose its tax on a resident of the other Contracting State earning business profits within the political subdivision or local authority but not having a permanent establishment there. It is understood that a Canadian provincial income tax that satisfied the conditions of paragraph 7 on September 26, 1980 also satisfied the conditions of that paragraph on June 14, 1983 — i.e., no significant changes have occurred in the taxes imposed by Canadian provinces.

Paragraph 8 relates to the provisions of Article XXIII (Capital). It provides that where a resident of a Contracting State owns capital which, in accordance with the provisions of Article XXIII, may be taxed in the other Contracting State, the State of residence shall allow as a deduction from (credit against) its tax on capital an amount equal to the capital tax paid in the other Contracting State. The deduction is not, however, to exceed that part of the capital tax, computed before the deduction, which is attributable to capital which may be taxed in the other State.

Article XXV — Non-Discrimination

1. Nationals of a Contracting State shall not be subjected in the other Contracting State to any taxation or any requirement connected therewith that is more burdensome than the taxation and connected requirements to which nationals of that other State in the same circumstances, particularly with respect to taxation on worldwide income, are or may be subjected. This provision shall also apply to individuals who are not residents of one or both of the Contracting States.

Notes: In *Chaumont*, 2009 TCC 493, the taxpayer argued that the parallel provision of the Canada-France treaty meant that his interest income from France that would not have been taxable in France should not be taxable in Canada. This argument was rejected on the basis that the provisions of the Act governed, and that Art. 11 permitted the interest to be taxed. In *Bhachu*, 2021 FCA 12, the parallel Canada-Egypt treaty rule did not cancel instalment interest on income that was subject to Egyptian source deductions.

Saipem UK, 2011 FCA 243, held that the non-discrimination clause in the Canada-UK treaty does not prohibit discrimination on the basis of residency, so a non-resident corporation can be treated differently than a Canadian corporation. The same would apply to this treaty: VIEWS doc 2017-0685651E5.

Disclosure of US persons' bank accounts to the IRS under FATCA (see Notes to ITA 269) does not violate Art. XXV: *Hillis (Deegan)*, 2015 FC 1082 (FCA appeal discontinued A-407-15), para. 73.

The pre-2009 version of Art. XXV:1 did not apply in *Luscher*, 2012 TCC 151, as the taxpayer was a US citizen but not resident in Canada.

Art. XXV:1 amended by 2007 Protocol, for taxable years beginning after 2008, but in respect of taxes withheld at source, for amounts paid or credited after Jan. 2009.

Definitions: "individual" — ITCIA 3, ITA 248(1); "national" — Art. III:1(k); "resident" — Art. IV; "State" — Art. III:1(i).

I.T. Technical News: 38 (anti-discrimination provisions).

Technical Explanation [2007 Protocol]: Article 20 of the Protocol revises Article XXV (Non-Discrimination) of the existing Convention to bring that Article into closer conformity to U.S. tax treaty policy.

Paragraph 1 replaces paragraph 1 of Article XXV of the existing Convention. New paragraph 1 provides that a national of one Contracting State may not be subject to taxation or connected requirements in the other Contracting State that are more burdensome than the taxes and connected requirements imposed upon a national of that other State in the same circumstances. The OECD Model would prohibit taxation that is "other than or more burdensome" than that imposed on U.S. persons. Paragraph 1 omits the words "other than or" because the only relevant question under this provision should be whether the requirement imposed on a national of the other Contracting State is more burdensome. A requirement may be different from the requirements imposed on U.S. nationals without being more burdensome.

The term "national" in relation to a Contracting State is defined in subparagraph 1(k) of Article III (General Definitions). The term includes both individuals and juridical persons. A national of a Contracting State is afforded protection under this paragraph even if the national is not a resident of either Contracting State. Thus, a U.S. citizen who is resident in a third country is entitled, under this paragraph, to the same treatment in Canada as a national of Canada in the same or similar circumstances (*i.e.*, one who is resident in a third State).

Whether or not the two persons are both taxable on worldwide income is a significant circumstance for this purpose. For this reason, paragraph 1 specifically refers to taxation or any requirement connected therewith, particularly with respect to taxation on worldwide income, as relevant circumstances. This language means that the United States is not obliged to apply the same taxing regime to a national of Canada who is not resident in the United States as it applies to a U.S. national who is not resident in the United States. U.S. citizens who are not resident in the United States but who are, nevertheless, subject to U.S. tax on their worldwide income are not in the same circumstances with respect to U.S. taxation as citizens of Canada who are not U.S. residents. Thus, for example, Article XXV would not entitle a national of Canada residing in a third country to taxation at graduated rates on U.S.-source dividends or other investment income that applies to a U.S. citizen residing in the same third country.

Technical Explanation [1984]: Paragraphs 1 and 2 of Article XXV protect individual citizens of a Contracting State from discrimination by the other Contracting State in taxation matters. Paragraph 1 provides that a citizen of a Contracting State who is a resident of the other Contracting State may not be subjected in that other State to any taxation or requirement connected with taxation which is other or more burdensome than the taxation and connected requirements imposed on similarly situated citizens of the other State.

2. In determining the taxable income or tax payable of an individual who is a resident of a Contracting State, there shall be allowed as a deduction in respect of any other person who is a resident of the other Contracting State and who is dependent on the individual for support the amount that would be so allowed if that other person were a resident of the first-mentioned State.

Notes: This applies to the credit for a disabled dependant: VIEWS doc 2006-018246I7.

The pre-2009 version of Art. XXV:2 did not assist the taxpayer in *Luscher*, 2012 TCC 151, as ITA s. 118.94 applied equally to all non-residents of Canada.

Former Art. XXV:3 renumbered as para. 2 by 2007 Protocol, with the repeal of former para. 2.

Former Art. XXV:3 amended by 1995 Protocol, generally effective 1996, to add the words "or tax payable" near the beginning. This change recognizes Canada's change in 1988 from personal exemptions (ITA 109) to personal credits (ITA 118).

Former Art. XXV:2 repealed by 2007 Protocol, effective on the same basis as the amendment to para. 1. (See now para. 1 instead.)

Definitions: "individual" — ITCIA 3, ITA 248(1); "person" — Art. III:1(e), ITCIA 3, *Interpretation Act* 35(1); "resident" — Art. IV; "State" — Art. III:1(i); "taxable income" — ITCIA 3, ITA 248(1).

Technical Explanation [1995 Protocol]: Article 13 of the Protocol amends Article XXV (Non-Discrimination) of the Convention. Paragraph 1 of Article 13 amends [former] paragraph 3 of Article XXV to conform the treaty language to a change in Canadian law. The paragraph is intended to allow the treatment of dependents under the income tax law of a Contracting State to apply with respect to dependents who are residents of the other Contracting State. As drafted in the present Convention, the rule deals specifically only with deductions; the amendments made by the Protocol clarify that it also applies to the credits now provided by Canadian law.

Technical Explanation [1984]: [Former] Paragraph 3 assures that, in computing taxable income, an individual resident of a Contracting State will be entitled to the same deduction for dependents resident in the other Contracting State that would be allowed if the dependents were residents of the individual's State of residence. The term "dependent" is defined in accordance with the rules set forth in paragraph 2 of Article III (General Definitions). For U.S. tax purposes, [former] paragraph 3 does not expand the benefits currently available to a resident of the United States with a dependent resident in Canada. See Code section 152(b)(3).

3. Where a married individual who is a resident of Canada and not a citizen of the United States has income that is taxable in the United States pursuant to Article XV (Income from Employment), the United States tax with respect to such income shall not exceed such proportion of the total United States tax that would be payable for the taxable year if both the individual and his spouse were United States citizens as the individual's taxable income determined without regard to this paragraph bears to the amount that would be the total taxable income of the individual and his spouse. For the purposes of this paragraph,

> (a) the "total United States tax" shall be determined as if all the income of the individual and his spouse arose in the United States; and

> (b) a deficit of the spouse shall not be taken into account in determining taxable income.

Notes: Former Art. XXV:4 renumbered as para. 3 by 2007 Protocol, with the repeal of former para. 2.

Definitions: "Canada" — Art. III:1(a), ITCIA 5; "individual" — ITCIA 3, ITA 248(1); "resident" — Art. IV; "taxable income" — ITCIA 3, ITA 248(1); "United States" — Art. III:1(b); "United States tax" — Art. III:1(d).

Technical Explanation [2007 Protocol]: Paragraph 3 makes changes to renumbered paragraph 3 of Article XXV in order to conform with Article 10 of the Protocol by deleting the reference to "Article XV (Dependent Personal Services)" and replacing it with a reference to "Article XV (Income from Employment)."

Technical Explanation [1984]: [Former] Paragraph 4 allows a resident of Canada (not a citizen of the United States) to file a joint return in cases where such person earns salary, wages, or other similar remuneration as an employee and such income is taxable in the United States under the Convention. [Former] Paragraph 4 does not apply where the resident of Canada earns wages which are exempt in the United States under Article XV (Dependent Personal Services) or earns only income taxable by the United States under provisions of the Convention other than Article XV.

The benefit provided by [former] paragraph 4 is available regardless of the residence of the taxpayer's spouse. It is limited, however, by a formula designed to ensure that the benefit is available solely with respect to persons whose U.S. source income is entirely, or almost entirely, wage income. The formula limits the United States tax with respect to wage income to that portion of the total U.S. tax that would be payable for the taxable year if both the individual and his spouse were United States citizens as the individual's taxable income (determined without any of the benefits made available by [former] paragraph 4, such as the standard deduction) bears to the total taxable income of the individual and his spouse. The term "total United States tax" used in the formula is total United States tax without regard to any foreign tax credits, as provided in [former] subparagraph 4(a). (Foreign income taxes may, however, be claimed as deductions in computing taxable income, to the extent allowed by the Code.) In determining total taxable income of the individual and his spouse, the benefits made available by [former] paragraph 4 are taken into account, but a deficit of the spouse is not.

The following example illustrates the application of [former] paragraph 4.

> A, a Canadian citizen and resident, is married to B who is also a Canadian citizen and resident. A earns $12,000 of wages taxable in the U.S. under Article XV (Dependent Personal Services) and $2,000 of wages taxable only in Canada. B earns

$1,000 of U.S. source dividend income, taxed by the United States at 15% pursuant to Article X (Dividends). B also earns $2,000 of wages taxable only in Canada. A's taxable income for U.S. purposes, determined without regard to [former] paragraph 4, is $11,700 ($12,000 - $2,000 (Code sections 151(b) and 873(b)(3)) + $1,700 (Code section 63)). The U.S. tax (Code section 1(d)) with respect to such income is $2,084.50. The total U.S. tax payable by A and B if both were U.S. citizens and all their income arose in the United States would be $2,013 under Code section 1(a) on taxable income of $14,800 ($17,000 - $200 (Code section 116) - $2,000 (Code section 151)). Pursuant to [former] paragraph 4, the U.S. tax imposed on A's wages from U.S. sources is limited to $1,591.36 ($11,700/$14,800 × $2,013). B's U.S. tax liability with respect to the U.S. source dividends remains $150.

The provisions of [former] paragraph 4 may be elected on a year-by-year basis. They are purely computational and do not have either or both spouses residents of the United States for the purpose of other U.S. income tax conventions. The rules relating to the election provided by U.S. law under Code section 6013(g) (see section 1.6013–6 of the Treasury Regulations) do not apply to the election described in this paragraph.

4. Any company which is a resident of a Contracting State, the capital of which is wholly or partly owned or controlled, directly or indirectly, by one or more residents of the other Contracting State, shall not be subjected in the first-mentioned State to any taxation or any requirement connected therewith which is other or more burdensome than the taxation and connected requirements to which other similar companies of the first-mentioned State, the capital of which is wholly or partly owned or controlled, directly or indirectly, by one or more residents of a third State, are or may be subjected.

Notes: Former Art. XXV:5 renumbered as para. 4 by 2007 Protocol, with the repeal of former para. 2.

Definitions: "company" — Art. III:1(f); "resident" — Art. IV; "State" — Art. III:1(i).

Technical Explanation [1984]: [Former] Paragraph 5 protects against discrimination in a case where the capital of a company which is a resident of one Contracting State is wholly or partly owned or controlled, directly or indirectly, by one or more residents of the other Contracting State. Such a company shall not be subjected in the State of which it is a resident to any taxation or requirement connected therewith which is other or more burdensome than the taxation and connected requirements to which are subjected other similar companies which are residents of that State but whose capital is wholly or partly owned or controlled, directly or indirectly, by one or more residents of a third State.

5. Notwithstanding the provisions of Article XXIV (Elimination of Double Taxation), the taxation on a permanent establishment which a resident of a Contracting State has in the other Contracting State shall not be less favourably levied in the other State than the taxation levied on residents of the other State carrying on the same activities. This paragraph shall not be construed as obliging a Contracting State:

> (a) to grant to a resident of the other Contracting State any personal allowances, reliefs and reductions for taxation purposes on account of civil status or family responsibilities which it grants to its own residents; or

> (b) to grant to a company which is a resident of the other Contracting State the same tax relief that it provides to a company which is a resident of the first-mentioned State with respect to dividends received by it from a company.

Notes: Former Art. XXV:6 renumbered as para. 5 by 2007 Protocol, with the repeal of former para. 2.

Definitions: "company" — Art. III:1(f); "permanent establishment" — Art. V:1; "State" — Art. III:1(i).

Technical Explanation [1984]: [Former] Paragraph 6 protects against discrimination in the case of a permanent establishment which a resident of one Contracting State has in the other Contracting State. The taxation of such a permanent establishment by the other Contracting State shall not be less favorable than the taxation of residents of that other State carrying on the same activities. The paragraph specifically overrides the provisions of Article XXIV (Elimination of Double Taxation), thus ensuring that permanent establishments will be entitled to relief from double taxation on a basis comparable to the relief afforded to similarly situated residents. [Former] Paragraph 6 does not oblige a Contracting State to grant to a resident of the other Contracting State any personal allowances, reliefs, and reductions for taxation purposes on account of civil status or family responsibilities which it grants to its own residents. In addition, [former] paragraph 6 does not require a Contracting State to grant to a company which is a resident of the other Contracting State the same tax relief that it grants to companies which are resident in the first-mentioned State with respect to intercorporate dividends. This provision is merely clarifying in nature, since neither the United States nor Canada would interpret [former] paragraph 6 to provide for granting the same relief in the absence of a specific denial thereof. The principles of [former] paragraph 6 would apply with respect to a fixed base as well as a permanent establishment. [Former] Paragraph 6 does not, however, override the provisions of Code section 906.

6. Except where the provisions of paragraph 1 of Article IX (Related Persons), paragraph 7 of Article XI (Interest) or paragraph 7 of Article XII (Royalties) apply, interest, royalties and other disbursements paid by a resident of a Contracting State to a resident of the other Contracting State shall, for the purposes of determining the taxable profits of the first-mentioned resident, be deductible under the same conditions as if they had been paid to a resident of the first-mentioned State. Similarly, any debts of a resident of a Contracting State to a resident of the other Contracting State shall, for the purposes of determining the taxable capital of the first-mentioned resident, be deductible under the same conditions as if they had been contracted to a resident of the first-mentioned State.

Notes: Former Art. XXV:7 renumbered as para. 6 by 2007 Protocol, with the repeal of former para. 2.

Definitions: "resident" — Art. IV; "State" — Art. III:1(i).

Technical Explanation [1984]: [Former] Paragraph 7 concerns the right of a resident of a Contracting State to claim deductions for purposes of computing taxable profits in the case of disbursements made to a resident of the other Contracting State. Such disbursements shall be deductible under the same conditions as if they had been made to a resident of the first-mentioned State. Thus, this paragraph does not require Canada to permit a deduction to a Canadian trust for disbursements made to a non-resident beneficiary out of income derived from a business in Canada or Canadian real property; granting such a deduction would result in complete exemption by Canada of such income and would put Canadian trusts with non-resident beneficiaries in a better position than if they had resident beneficiaries. These provisions do not apply to amounts to which paragraph 1 of Article IX (Related Persons), paragraph 7 of Article XI (Interest), or paragraph 7 of Article XII (Royalties) apply. [Former] Paragraph 7 of Article XXV also provides that, for purposes of determining the taxable capital of a resident of a Contracting State, any debts of such person to a resident of the other Contracting State shall be deductible under the same conditions as if they had been contracted to a resident of the first-mentioned State. This portion of [former] paragraph 7 relates to Article XXIII (Capital).

7. The provisions of paragraph 7 *[now 6 — ed.]* shall not affect the operation of any provision of the taxation laws of a Contracting State:

(a) relating to the deductibility of interest and which is in force on the date of signature of this Convention (including any subsequent modification of such provisions that does not change the general nature thereof); or

(b) adopted after such date by a Contracting State and which is designed to ensure that a person who is not a resident of that State does not enjoy, under the laws of that State, a tax treatment that is more favorable than that enjoyed by residents of that State.

Related Provisions: ITA 18(4) — Thin capitalization rule.

Notes: Former Art. XXV:8 renumbered as para. 7 by 2007 Protocol, with the repeal of former para. 2. The reference in the opening words to "paragraph 7" should have been changed to "paragraph 6", but this was overlooked.

Definitions: "person" — Art. III:1(e), ITCIA 3, *Interpretation Act* 35(1); "resident" — Art. IV; "State" — Art. III:1(i).

Technical Explanation [1984]: [Former] Paragraph 8 provides that, notwithstanding the provisions of [former] paragraph 7, a Contracting State may enforce the provisions of its taxation laws relating to the deductibility of interest, in force on September 26, 1980, or as modified subsequent to that date in a manner that does not change the general nature of the provisions in force on September 26, 1980; or which are adopted after September 26, 1980, and are designed to ensure that non-residents do not enjoy a more favorable tax treatment under the taxation laws of that State than that enjoyed by residents. Thus Canada may continue to limit the deductions for interest paid to certain non-residents as provided in section 18(4) of Part I of the *Income Tax Act*.

8. Expenses incurred by a citizen or resident of a Contracting State with respect to any convention (including any seminar, meeting, congress or other function of a similar nature) held in the other Contracting State shall, for the purposes of taxation in the first-mentioned State, be deductible to the same extent that such expenses would be deductible if the convention were held in the first-mentioned State.

Notes: Former Art. XXV:9 renumbered as para. 8 by 2007 Protocol, with the repeal of former para. 2.

Definitions: "resident" — Art. IV; "State" — Art. III:1(i).

Interpretation Bulletins: IT-131R2: Convention expenses.

Technical Explanation [1984]: [Former] Paragraph 9 provides that expenses incurred by citizens or residents of a Contracting State with respect to any convention, including any seminar, meeting, congress, or other function of similar nature, held in the other Contracting State, are deductible for purposes of taxation in the first-mentioned State to the same extent that such expenses would be deductible if the convention were held in that first-mentioned State. Thus, for U.S. income tax purposes an individual who is a citizen or resident of the United States and who attends a convention held in Canada may claim deductions for expenses incurred in connection with such convention without regard to the provisions of Code section 274(h). Section 274(h) imposes special restrictions on the deductibility of expenses incurred in connection with foreign conventions. A claim for a deduction for such an expense remains subject, in all events, to the provisions of U.S. law with respect to the deductibility of convention expenses generally (e.g., Code sections 162 and 212). Similarly, in the case of a citizen or resident of Canada attending a convention in the United States, [former] paragraph 9 requires Canada to allow a deduction for expenses relating to such convention as if the convention had taken place in Canada.

9. Notwithstanding the provisions of Article II (Taxes Covered), this Article shall apply to all taxes imposed by a Contracting State.

Notes: Former Art. XXV:10 renumbered as para. 9 by 2007 Protocol, with the repeal of former para. 2.

Former Art. XXV:10 amended by 1995 Protocol, generally effective 1996.

Technical Explanation [1995 Protocol]: Paragraph 2 of Article 13 of the Protocol amends [former] paragraph 10 of Article XXV of the Convention to broaden the scope of the non-discrimination protection provided by the Convention. As amended, Article XXV will apply to all taxes imposed by a Contracting State. Under the present Convention, non-discrimination protection is limited in the case of Canadian taxes to taxes imposed under the *Income Tax Act*. As amended by the Protocol, non-discrimination protection will extend, for example, to the Canadian goods and services tax and other Canadian excise taxes.

Technical Explanation [1984]: [Former] Paragraph 10 provides that, notwithstanding the provisions of Article II (Taxes Covered), the provisions of Article XXV apply in the case of Canada to all taxes imposed under the *Income Tax Act*; and, in the case of the United States, to all taxes imposed under the Code. Article XXV does not apply to taxes imposed by political subdivisions or local authorities of Canada or the United States.

Article XXV substantially broadens the protection against discrimination provided by the 1942 Convention, which contains only one provision dealing specifically with this subject. That provision, paragraph 11 of the Protocol to the 1942 Convention, states that citizens of one of the Contracting States residing within the other Contracting State are not to be subjected to the payment of more burdensome taxes than the citizens of the other State.

The benefits of Article XXV may affect the tax liability of a U.S. citizen or resident with respect to the United States. See paragraphs 2 and 3 of Article XXIX (Miscellaneous Rules).

10. [Repealed]

Notes: See Notes to para. 9.

Article XXVI — Mutual Agreement Procedure

1. Where a person considers that the actions of one or both of the Contracting States result or will result for him in taxation not in accordance with the provisions of this Convention, he may, irrespective of the remedies provided by the domestic law of those States, present his case in writing to the competent authority of the Contracting State of which he is a resident or, if he is a resident of neither Contracting State, of which he is a national.

Notes: See Notes to ITA 115.1 re the Canadian competent authority. See Art. XXVI:6 re arbitration.

Definitions: "competent authority" — Art. III:1(g); "person" — Art. III:1(e), ITCIA 3, *Interpretation Act* 35(1); "State" — Art. III:1(i); "writing" — ITCIA 3, *Interpretation Act* 35(1).

Information Circulars: 71-17R6: Competent authority assistance under Canada's tax conventions.

Technical Explanation [1984]: Paragraph 1 provides that where a person considers that the actions of one or both of the Contracting States will result in taxation not in accordance with the Convention, he may present his case in writing to the competent authority of the Contracting State of which he is a resident or, if he is a resident of neither Contracting State, of which he is a national. Thus, a resident of Canada must present to the Minister of National Revenue (or his authorized representative) any claim that such resident is being subjected to taxation contrary to the Convention. A person who requests assistance from the competent authority may also avail himself of any remedies available under domestic laws.

2. The competent authority of the Contracting State to which the case has been presented shall endeavor, if the objection appears to it to be justified and if it is not itself able to arrive at a satisfactory solution, to resolve the case by mutual agreement with the competent authority of the other Contracting State, with a view to the avoidance of taxation which is not in accordance with the Convention. Except where the provisions of Article IX (Related Persons) apply, any agreement reached shall be implemented notwithstanding any time or other procedural limitations in the domestic law of the Contracting States, provided that the competent authority of the other Contracting State has received notification that such a case exists within six years from the end of the taxable year to which the case relates.

Notes: See Notes to ITA 115.1.

Definitions: "competent authority" — Art. III:1(g).

Information Circulars: 71-17R6: Competent authority assistance under Canada's tax conventions.

Technical Explanation [1984]: Paragraph 2 provides that the competent authority of the Contracting State to which the case is presented shall endeavor to resolve the case by mutual agreement with the competent authority of the other Contracting State, unless he believes that the objection is not justified or he is able to arrive at a satisfactory unilateral solution. Any agreement reached between the competent authorities of Canada and the United States shall be implemented notwithstanding any time or other procedural limitations in the domestic laws of the Contracting States, except where the special mutual agreement provisions of Article IX (Related Persons) apply, provided that the competent authority of the Contracting State asked to waive its domestic time or procedural limitations has received written notification that such a case exists within six years from the end of the taxable year in the first-mentioned State to which the case relates. The notification may be given by the competent authority of the first-mentioned State, the taxpayer who has requested the competent authority to take action, or a person related to the taxpayer. Unlike Article IX, Article XXVI does not require the competent authority of a Contracting State to grant unilateral relief to avoid double taxation in a case where timely notification is not given to the competent authority of the other Contracting State. Such unilateral relief may, however, be granted by the competent authority in its discretion pursuant to the provisions of Article XXVI and in order to achieve the purposes of the Convention. In a case where the provisions of Article IX apply, the provisions of paragraphs 3, 4, and 5 of that Article are controlling with respect to adjustments and corresponding adjustments of income, loss, or tax and the effect of the Convention upon time or procedural limitations of domestic law. Thus, if relief is not available under Article IX because of fraud, the provisions of paragraph 2 or Article XXVI do not independently authorize such relief.

3. The competent authorities of the Contracting States shall endeavor to resolve by mutual agreement any difficulties or doubts arising as to the interpretation or application of the Convention. In particular, the competent authorities of the Contracting States may agree:

(a) to the same attribution of profits to a resident of a Contracting State and its permanent establishment situated in the other Contracting State;

(b) to the same allocation of income, deductions, credits or allowances between persons;

(c) to the same determination of the source, and the same characterization, of particular items of income;

(d) to a common meaning of any term used in the Convention;

(e) to the elimination of double taxation with respect to income distributed by an estate or trust;

(f) to the elimination of double taxation with respect to a partnership;

(g) to provide relief from double taxation resulting from the application of the estate tax imposed by the United States or the Canadian tax as a result of a distribution or disposition of property by a trust that is a qualified domestic trust within the meaning of section 2056A of the *Internal Revenue Code*, or is described in subsection 70(6) of the *Income Tax Act* or is treated as such under paragraph 5 of Article XXIX-B (Taxes Imposed by Reason of Death), in cases where no relief is otherwise available; or

(h) to increases in any dollar amounts referred to in the Convention to reflect monetary or economic developments.

They may also consult together for the elimination of double taxation in cases not provided for in the Convention.

Related Provisions: Art. II:2(b)(iv) — Application to U.S. estate taxes.

Notes: See *Memorandum of Understanding Between the Competent Authorities of Canada and the United States Regarding Factual Disagreements Under the Mutual Agreement Procedure* (signed by Frederick O'Riordan for CRA and Robert Green for the IRS on December 8, 2005), on *TaxPartner* or *Taxnet Pro*. In 2014-15, CRA negotiated 115 cases with other tax administrations and obtained full relief in 109 of them; its inventory as of March 31, 2015 was 521 pending cases: CRA *Mutual Agreement Procedure Program Report 2014-2015*.

For para. (g), see VIEWS doc 2002-0124145 and comment on it in Wolfe Goodman, "Avoidance of Double Taxation Under Article XXVI, Paragraph 3(g)", XI(2) *Goodman on Estate Planning* (Federated Press) 871-72 (2002).

To request competent authority assistance in resolving a double taxation problem, see Information Circular 71-7R5 and Notes to ITA 115.1. Note that one might need to file a waiver under ITA 152(4) to ensure that the Canadian return remains open for reassessment (see also ITA 152(4)(b)(iii), which extends the deadline by 3 years for non-arm's length transactions with non-residents, and 152(4.2) for individuals). Note also the deadline in para. 2 for competent authority referrals.

Art. XXVI:3 amended by 1995 Protocol, generally effective 1996.

Definitions: "Canadian tax" — Art. III:1(c); "competent authority" — Art. III:1(g); "estate" — ITCIA 3, ITA 248(1); "permanent establishment" — Art. V:1; "person" — Art. III:1(e), ITCIA 3, *Interpretation Act* 35(1); "property" — ITCIA 3, ITA 248(1); "qualified domestic trust" — *Internal Revenue Code* s. 2056A(a); "resident" — Art. IV; "trust" — ITCIA 3, ITA 104(1), 248(1); "United States" — Art. III:1(b).

Information Circulars: 71-17R6: Competent authority assistance under Canada's tax conventions.

I.T. Technical News: 34 (Canada-U.S. competent authority Memorandum of Understanding).

Technical Explanation [1995 Protocol]: Article 14 of the Protocol makes two changes to Article XXVI (Mutual Agreement Procedure) of the Convention. First, it adds a new subparagraph 3(g) specifically authorizing the competent authorities to provide relief from double taxation in certain cases involving the distribution or disposition of property by a U.S. qualified domestic trust or a Canadian spousal trust, where relief is not otherwise available.

Technical Explanation [1984]: Paragraph 3 provides that the competent authorities of the Contracting States shall endeavor to resolve by mutual agreement any difficulties or doubts arising as to the interpretation or application of the Convention. In particular, the competent authorities may agree to the same attribution of profits to a resident of a Contracting State and its permanent establishment in the other Contracting State; the same allocation of income, deductions, credits, or allowances between persons; the same determination of the source of income; the same characterization of particular items of income; a common meaning of any term used in the Convention; rules, guidelines, or procedures for the elimination of double taxation with respect to income distributed by an estate or trust, or with respect to a partnership; or to increase any dollar amounts referred to in the Convention to reflect monetary or economic developments. The competent authorities may also consult and reach agreements on rules, guidelines, or procedures for the elimination of double taxation in cases not provided for in the Convention.

The list of subjects of potential mutual agreement in paragraph 3 is not exhaustive; it merely illustrates the principles set forth in the paragraph. As in the case of other U.S. tax conventions, agreement can be arrived at in the context of determining the tax liability of a specific person or in establishing rules, guidelines, and procedures that will apply generally under the Convention to resolve issues for classes of taxpayers. It is contemplated that paragraph 3 could be utilized by the competent authorities, for example, to resolve conflicts between the domestic laws of Canada and the United States with respect to the allocation and apportionment of deductions.

4. Each of the Contracting States will endeavor to collect on behalf of the other Contracting State such amounts as may be necessary to ensure that relief granted by the Convention from taxation imposed by that other State does not enure to the benefit of persons not entitled thereto. However, nothing in this paragraph shall be construed as imposing on either of the Contracting States the obligation to carry out administrative measures of a different nature from those used in the collection of its own tax or which would be contrary to its public policy (ordre public).

Definitions: "person" — Art. III:1(e), ITCIA 3, *Interpretation Act* 35(1); "State" — Art. III:1(i).

Technical Explanation [1984]: Paragraph 4 provides that each Contracting State will endeavor to collect on behalf of the other State such amounts as may be necessary to ensure that relief granted by the Convention from taxation imposed by the other State does not enure to the benefit of persons not entitled to such relief. Paragraph 4 does not oblige either Contracting State to carry out administrative measures of a different nature from those that would be used by Canada or the United States in the collection of its own tax or which would be contrary to its public policy.

5. The competent authorities of the Contracting States may communicate with each other directly for the purpose of reaching an agreement in the sense of the preceding paragraphs.

Definitions: "competent authority" — Art. III:1(g).

Technical Explanation [1984]: Paragraph 5 confirms that the competent authorities of Canada and the United States may communicate with each other directly for the purpose of reaching agreement in the sense of paragraphs 1 through 4.

6. Where, pursuant to a mutual agreement procedure under this Article, the competent authorities have endeavored but are unable to reach a complete agreement in a case, the case shall be resolved through arbitration conducted in the manner prescribed by, and subject to, the requirements of paragraph 7 and any rules or procedures agreed upon by the Contracting States by notes to be exchanged through diplomatic channels, if:

(a) tax returns have been filed with at least one of the Contracting States with respect to the taxable years at issue in the case;

(b) the case:

(i) is a case that:

(A) involves the application of one or more Articles that the competent authorities have agreed in an exchange of notes shall be the subject of arbitration; and

(B) is not a particular case that the competent authorities agree, before the date on which arbitration proceedings would otherwise have begun, is not suitable for determination by arbitration; or

(ii) is a particular case that the competent authorities agree is suitable for determination by arbitration; and

(c) all concerned persons agree according to the provisions of subparagraph 7(d).

Related Provisions: ITA 115.1 — Competent authority agreements; Art. XXVI:7 — Rules and definitions.

Notes: In *CGI Holding*, 2016 FC 1086, CRA and the IRS did not agree on a solution, but CRA refused to refer it to arbitration, on the basis that arbitration is only for "very specific narrow cases" (this is not in the Court's reasons).

For detailed arbitration procedures see 2007 Protocol Annex A (reproduced at the end of the Treaty), with diplomatic notes JLAB-0111 (from Canada) and 1015 (from the US); these are agreed to be "an integral part of the Convention". For the CRA-IRS Memorandum of Understanding on arbitration procedures see tinyurl.com/cra-irs-mou. For the Arbitration Board Operating Guidelines see tinyurl.com/arb-board-guidelines. See also CRA Round Table, 2010 Cdn Tax Foundation conference report, qq.29-31, p. 4:27-28.

See Joseffer, "Treaty Dispute Final Arbitration", 16(8) *Canadian Tax Highlights* (ctf.ca) 1-2 (Aug. 2008); Cannon et al., "The Fifth Protocol", 2007 Cdn Tax Foundation conference report at 24:64-72; Love, "Memorandum of Understanding Re Arbitration", 57 *McCarthy Tétrault on Tax Disputes* (CCH) 2-4 (Jan. 2011).

See also Notes to Art. IX:3 re *Teletech Canada* case.

Art. XXVI:6 amended by 2007 Protocol, effective for cases under consideration by the competent authorities as of Dec. 15, 2008 or later.

Art. XXVI:6 added by 1995 Protocol, generally effective 1996.

See Notes to ITA 115.1.

Definitions: "competent authority" — Art. III:1(g); "concerned person" — Art. XXVI:7(a); "State" — Art. III:1(i); "taxpayer" — ITCIA 3, ITA 248(1); "writing" — ITCIA 3, *Interpretation Act* 35(1).

Technical Explanation [2007 Protocol]: Paragraph 1 of Article 21 of the Protocol replaces paragraph 6 of Article XXVI (Mutual Agreement Procedure) of the Convention with new paragraphs 6 and 7. New paragraphs 6 and 7 provide a mandatory binding arbitration proceeding (Arbitration Proceeding). The Arbitration Note details additional rules and procedures that apply to a case considered under the arbitration provisions.

New paragraph 6 provides that a case shall be resolved through arbitration when the competent authorities have endeavored but are unable through negotiation to reach a complete agreement regarding a case and the following three conditions are satisfied. First, tax returns have been filed with at least one of the Contracting States with respect to the taxable years at issue in the case. Second, the case (i) involves the application of one or more Articles that the competent authorities have agreed in an exchange of notes shall be the subject of arbitration and is not a case that the competent authorities agree before the date on which an Arbitration Proceeding would otherwise have begun, is not suitable for determination by arbitration; or (ii) is a case that the competent authorities agree is suitable for determination by arbitration. Third, all concerned persons and their authorized representatives agree, according to the provisions of subparagraph 7(d), not

to disclose to any other person any information received during the course of the Arbitration Proceeding from either Contracting State or the arbitration board, other than the determination of the board (confidentiality agreement). The confidentiality agreement may also be executed by any concerned person that has the legal authority to bind any other concerned person on the matter. For example, a parent corporation with the legal authority to bind its subsidiary with respect to confidentiality may execute a comprehensive confidentiality agreement on its own behalf and that of its subsidiary.

The United States and Canada have agreed in the Arbitration Note to submit cases regarding the application of one or more of the following Articles to mandatory binding arbitration under the provisions of paragraphs 6 and 7 of Article XXVI: IV (Residence), but only insofar as it relates to the residence of a natural person, V (Permanent Establishment), VII (Business Profits), IX (Related Persons), and XII (Royalties) (but only (i) insofar as Article XII might apply in transactions involving related persons to whom Article IX might apply, or (ii) to an allocation of amounts between royalties that are taxable under paragraph 2 thereof and royalties that are exempt under paragraph 3 thereof). The competent authorities may, however, agree, before the date on which an Arbitration Proceeding would otherwise have begun, that a particular case is not suitable for arbitration.

New paragraph 7 provides six subparagraphs that detail the general rules and definitions to be used in applying the arbitration provisions.

Subparagraph 7(a) provides that the term "concerned person" means the person that brought the case to competent authority for consideration under Article XXVI (Mutual Agreement Procedure) and includes all other persons, if any, whose tax liability to either Contracting State may be directly affected by a mutual agreement arising from that consideration. For example, a concerned person does not only include a U.S. corporation that brings a transfer pricing case with respect to a transaction entered into with its Canadian subsidiary for resolution to the U.S. competent authority, but also the Canadian subsidiary, which may have a correlative adjustment as a result of the resolution of the case.

Subparagraph 7(c) provides that an Arbitration Proceeding begins on the later of two dates: two years from the "commencement date" of the case (unless the competent authorities have previously agreed to a different date), or the earliest date upon which all concerned persons have entered into a confidentiality agreement and the agreements have been received by both competent authorities. The "commencement date" of the case is defined by subparagraph 7(b) as the earliest date the information necessary to undertake substantive consideration for a mutual agreement has been received by both competent authorities.

Paragraph 16 of the Arbitration Note provides that each competent authority will confirm in writing to the other competent authority and to the concerned persons the date of its receipt of the information necessary to undertake substantive consideration for a mutual agreement. In the case of the United States, this information is (i) the information that must be submitted to the U.S. competent authority under Section 4.05 of Rev. Proc. 2006-54, 2006-49 I.R.B. 1035 (or any applicable successor publication), and (ii) for cases initially submitted as a request for an Advance Pricing Agreement, the information that must be submitted to the Internal Revenue Service under Rev. Proc. 2006-9, 2006-2 I.R.B. 278 (or any applicable successor publication). In the case of Canada, this information is the information required to be submitted to the Canadian competent authority under Information Circular 71-17 (or any applicable successor publication). The information shall not be considered received until both competent authorities have received copies of all materials submitted to either Contracting State by the concerned person(s) in connection with the mutual agreement procedure. It is understood that confirmation of the "information necessary to undertake substantive consideration for a mutual agreement" is envisioned to ordinarily occur within 30 days after the necessary information is provided to the competent authority.

The Arbitration Note also provides for several procedural rules once an Arbitration Proceeding under paragraph 6 of Article XXVI ("Proceeding") has commenced, but the competent authorities may modify or supplement these rules as necessary. In addition, the arbitration board may adopt any procedures necessary for the conduct of its business, provided the procedures are not inconsistent with any provision of Article XXVI of the Convention.

Paragraph 5 of the Arbitration Note provides that each Contracting State has 60 days from the date on which the Arbitration Proceeding begins to send a written communication to the other Contracting State appointing one member of the arbitration board. Within 60 days of the date the second of such communications is sent, these two board members will appoint a third member to serve as the chair of the board. It is agreed that this third member ordinarily should not be a citizen of either of the Contracting States.

In the event that any members of the board are not appointed (including as a result of the failure of the two members appointed by the Contracting States to agree on a third member) by the requisite date, the remaining members are appointed by the highest ranking member of the Secretariat at the Centre for Tax Policy and Administration of the Organisation for Economic Co-operation and Development (OECD) who is not a citizen of either Contracting State, by written notice to both Contracting States within 60 days of the date of such failure.

Paragraph 7 of the Arbitration Note establishes deadlines for submission of materials by the Contracting States to the arbitration board. Each competent authority has 60 days from the date of appointment of the chair to submit a Proposed Resolution describing the proposed disposition of the specific monetary amounts of income, expense or taxation at issue in the case, and a supporting Position Paper. Copies of each State's submissions are to be provided by the board to the other Contracting State on the date the later of the submissions is submitted to the board. Each of the Contracting

States may submit a Reply Submission to the board within 120 days of the appointment of the chair to address points raised in the other State's Proposed Resolution or Position Paper. If one Contracting State fails to submit a Proposed Resolution within the requisite time, the Proposed Resolution of the other Contracting State is deemed to be the determination of the arbitration board. Additional information may be supplied to the arbitration board by a Contracting State only at the request of the arbitration board. The board will provide copies of any such requested information, along with the board's request, to the other Contracting State on the date the request is made or the response is received.

All communication with the board is to be in writing between the chair of the board and the designated competent authorities with the exception of communication regarding logistical matters.

In making its determination, the arbitration board will apply the following authorities as necessary: (i) the provisions of the Convention, (ii) any agreed commentaries or explanation of the Contracting States concerning the Convention as amended, (iii) the laws of the Contracting States to the extent they are not inconsistent with each other, and (iv) any OECD Commentary, Guidelines or Reports regarding relevant analogous portions of the OECD Model Tax Convention.

The arbitration board must deliver a determination in writing to the Contracting States within six months of the appointment of the chair. The determination must be one of the two Proposed Resolutions submitted by the Contracting States. The determination shall provide a determination regarding only the amount of income, expense or tax reportable to the Contracting States. The determination has no precedential value and consequently the rationale behind a board's determination would not be beneficial and shall not be provided by the board.

Paragraph 11 of the Arbitration Note provides that, unless any concerned person does not accept the decision of the arbitration board, the determination of the board constitutes a resolution by mutual agreement under Article XXVI and, consequently, is binding on both Contracting States. Each concerned person must, within 30 days of receiving the determination from the competent authority to which the case was first presented, advise that competent authority whether the person accepts the determination. The failure to advise the competent authority within the requisite time is considered a rejection of the determination. If a determination is rejected, the case cannot be the subject of a subsequent MAP procedure on the same issue(s) determined by the panel, including a subsequent Arbitration Proceeding. After the commencement of an Arbitration Proceeding but before a decision of the board has been accepted by all concerned persons, the competent authorities may reach a mutual agreement to resolve the case and terminate the Proceeding.

For purposes of the Arbitration Proceeding, the members of the arbitration board and their staffs shall be considered "persons or authorities" to whom information may be disclosed under Article XXVII (Exchange of Information). The Arbitration Note provides that all materials prepared in the course of, or relating to, the Arbitration Proceeding are considered information exchanged between the Contracting States. No information relating to the Arbitration Proceeding or the board's determination may be disclosed by members of the arbitration board or their staffs or by either competent authority, except as permitted by the Convention and the domestic laws of the Contracting States. Members of the arbitration board and their staffs must agree in statements sent to each of the Contracting States in confirmation of their appointment to the arbitration board to abide by and be subject to the confidentiality and nondisclosure provisions of Article XXVII of the Convention and the applicable domestic laws of the Contracting States, with the most restrictive of the provisions applying.

The applicable domestic law of the Contracting States determines the treatment of any interest or penalties associated with a competent authority agreement achieved through arbitration.

In general, fees and expenses are borne equally by the Contracting States, including the cost of translation services. However, meeting facilities, related resources, financial management, other logistical support, and general and administrative coordination of the Arbitration Proceeding will be provided, at its own cost, by the Contracting State that initiated the Mutual Agreement Procedure. The fees and expenses of members of the board will be set in accordance with the International Centre for Settlement of Investment Disputes (ICSID) Schedule of Fees for arbitrators (in effect on the date on which the arbitration board proceedings begin). All other costs are to be borne by the Contracting State that incurs them. Since arbitration of MAP cases is intended to assist taxpayers in resolving a governmental difference of opinion regarding the taxation of their income, and is merely an extension of the competent authority process, no fees will be chargeable to a taxpayer in connection with arbitration.

Technical Explanation [1995 Protocol]: Article 14 also adds a new paragraph 6 to Article XXVI (Mutual Agreement Procedure). Paragraph 6 provides for a voluntary arbitration procedure, to be implemented only upon the exchange of diplomatic notes between the United States and Canada. Similar provisions are found in the recent U.S. treaties with the Federal Republic of Germany, the Netherlands, and Mexico. Paragraph 6 provides that where the competent authorities have been unable, pursuant to the other provisions of Article XXVI, to resolve a disagreement regarding the interpretation or application of the Convention, the disagreement may, with the consent of the taxpayer and both competent authorities, be submitted for arbitration, provided the taxpayer agrees in writing to be bound by the decision of the arbitration board. Nothing in the provision requires that any case be submitted for arbitration. However, if a case is submitted to an arbitration board, the board's decision in that case will be binding on both Contracting States and on the taxpayer with respect to that case.

The United States was reluctant to implement an arbitration procedure until there has been an opportunity to evaluate the process in practice under other agreements that allow for arbitration, particularly the U.S.-Germany Convention. It was agreed, therefore, as specified in paragraph 6, that the provisions of the Convention calling for an arbitration procedure will not take effect until the two Contracting States have agreed through an exchange of diplomatic notes to do so. This is similar to the approach taken with the Netherlands and Mexico. Paragraph 6 also provides that the procedures to be followed in applying arbitration will be agreed through an exchange of notes by the Contracting States. It is expected that such procedures will ensure that arbitration will not generally be available where matters of either State's tax policy or domestic law are involved.

Paragraph 2 of Article 20 of the Protocol provides that the appropriate authorities of the Contracting State will consult after three years following entry into force of the Protocol to determine whether the diplomatic notes implementing the arbitration procedure should be exchanged.

7. For the purposes of paragraph 6 and this paragraph, the following rules and definitions shall apply:

   (a) the term "**concerned person**" means the presenter of a case to a competent authority for consideration under this Article and all other persons, if any, whose tax liability to either Contracting State may be directly affected by a mutual agreement arising from that consideration;

   (b) the "**commencement date**" for a case is the earliest date on which the information necessary to undertake substantive consideration for a mutual agreement has been received by both competent authorities;

   (c) arbitration proceedings in a case shall begin on the later of:

      (i) two years after the commencement date of that case, unless both competent authorities have previously agreed to a different date, and

      (ii) the earliest date upon which the agreement required by subparagraph (d) has been received by both competent authorities;

   (d) the concerned person(s), and their authorized representatives or agents, must agree prior to the beginning of arbitration proceedings not to disclose to any other person any information received during the course of the arbitration proceeding from either Contracting State or the arbitration board, other than the determination of such board;

   (e) unless a concerned person does not accept the determination of an arbitration board, the determination shall constitute a resolution by mutual agreement under this Article and shall be binding on both Contracting States with respect to that case; and

   (f) for purposes of an arbitration proceeding under paragraph 6 and this paragraph, the members of the arbitration board and their staffs shall be considered "persons or authorities" to whom information may be disclosed under Article XXVII (Exchange of Information) of this Convention.

Notes: Art. XXVI:7 added by 2007 Protocol, effective for cases under consideration by the competent authorities as of Dec. 15, 2008 (the "commencement date" for such a case is Dec. 15, 2008). See Notes to para. 6.

Definitions: "commencement date" — Art. XXVI:7(b); "concerned person" — Art. XXVI:7(a).

Technical Explanation [2007 Protocol]: See under para. 6.

Article XXVI-A — Assistance in Collection

1. The Contracting States undertake to lend assistance to each other in the collection of taxes referred to in paragraph 9, together with interest, costs, additions to such taxes and civil penalties, referred to in this Article as a "**revenue claim**".

Notes: This overrides the rule that a court judgment based on a tax debt is not enforceable in a foreign jurisdiction (see ITA 223(3) Notes). However, it does not let CRA use the IRS to collect a tax debt from a US citizen or US-incorporated company; see para. 8. The assistance provided under this Article can reach back to revenue claims determined since Nov. 10, 1985; see Notes at end of Art. XXVI-A.

Art. XXVI-A does not let CRA collect "FBAR" penalties from US persons failing to report non-US bank accounts (see Notes to ITA 233.3(3)): VIEWS docs 2011-0427221E5, 2011-0431621M4; *Hillis (Deegan)*, 2015 FC 1082, para. 55 (FCA appeal discontinued A-407-15); Bonham, "FATCA and FBAR Reporting", 60(2) *Canadian*

Tax Journal 305-54 (2012). The IRS agrees, according to a statement by the Minister of National Revenue in Parliament: Berg, "Dateline — Canada", *Journal of International Taxation* (Dec. 2012), p. 53.

Disclosure of US persons' bank accounts to the IRS under FATCA (see Notes to ITA 269) is not "assistance in collection" for Art. XXVI-A: *Hillis* (above), para. 72.

This is the first general inter-country "collection assistance" provided in any of Canada's tax treaties. Since then, others have been signed:

- Canada-Germany treaty, Art. 27 (April 19, 2001)
- Canada-Netherlands treaty, Art. 26A (Protocol, August 25, 1997)
- Canada-New Zealand treaty, Art. 25 (May 3, 2012)
- Canada-Norway treaty, Art. 28 (July 12, 2002)
- Canada-Spain treaty, Art. XXVI-A (Nov. 18, 2014 Protocol)
- Canada-UK treaty, Art. 24A Protocol, July 21, 2014

A similar "assistance in collection" provision in the UK-South Africa treaty was applied in *Ben Nevis*, [2013] EWCA Civ 578 (England CA).

Canada-Austria treaty Art. XXVI(5) (Protocol, June 15, 1999) provides a much more limited collection assistance, limited to ensuring treaty relief "does not enure to the benefit of persons not entitled thereto" (presumably a reference to treaty shopping; see Notes to Art. X:2). See also Notes to the similar, now repealed, Art. 27:5 in the Canada-UK treaty.

The provision is based on a 1988 OECD convention: Morgan, "Mutual Assistance in Tax Matters", 36(4) *Canadian Tax Journal* 974-91 at 986 (July-Aug. 1988). (Canada signed that International Tax Convention in 2004 and ratified it on Nov. 21, 2013, but is not adopting the collection-assistance provisions, preferring to do this only in bilateral treaties: see Notes to "Current Status of Tax Treaties", after the Canada-U.K. treaty.) The treaties other than with the US do not prevent the foreign country from asking Canada to collect a foreign tax debt from a Canadian citizen, or vice-versa.

Constitutionality: It has been argued that Art. XXVI-A is invalid as outside federal jurisdiction, since the provinces have sole jurisdiction over property and civil rights: Goodman, IV(2) *Goodman on Estate Planning* (Federated Press) 187 (1995); Lemons et al., "Changes in US-Canadian Tax Treaty Resolve Conflicts and Present Planning Opportunities", 82(1) *Journal of Taxation* 42 (1995). However, *Chua*, [2000] 4 C.T.C. 159 (FCTD), held Art. XXVI-A is within federal jurisdiction, though it violated the *Charter* in applying to C, who was not a Canadian citizen when the debt arose but later became one. *US law*: Art. XXVI-A was held valid in *Retfalvi*, (2019, 4th Circuit Court of Appeals, tinyurl.com/retfalvi) [IRS collecting for CRA]; and *Dewees* (2017, DC District Court, tinyurl.com/dewees-tax) [CRA collecting IRS non-filing penalties].

For CRA interpretation and procedures see *National Collections Manual* (2015, on *TaxPartner* or *Taxnet Pro*), "Treaty Collections — Tax programs". CRA will refer only accounts owing $10,000 or more, according to past information released; the threshold is suppressed in the current manual.

From 1995-99, there were 177 referrals by Revenue Canada to the IRS for $47 million in debts (amount collected not disclosed), and 87 referrals from the IRS to RC (amount at stake and amount collected not disclosed). Extracting even this minimal information from CRA under the *Access to Information Act* required tortuous litigation by the author: *Sherman v. MNR*, 2002 FCT 586; rev'd 2003 FCA 202; costs award 2004 FCA 29; access redetermined 2004 FC 1423; rev'd 2005 FCA 375. (CRA claimed no statistics should be released because the IRS did not want them released, and that releasing them would irreparably harm Canada-US relations.)

A later request for data from 1999 through 2004, initially rejected by CRA, was partly fulfilled after a complaint to the Information Commissioner: 422 referrals from CRA (94 in 2003, 90 in 2004), for total $96 million ($16.8m in 2003, $18.9m in 2004) (amounts collected not disclosed). CRA maintained that disclosure of the number of requests from the IRS "could be injurious to the conduct of international affairs", and the Information Commissioner, on March 27, 2008, supported this decision.

For 2008-12, 64 to 115 requests annually were made by CRA to the IRS, for assistance in collecting from $13m to $69m per year. 100% of the requests were accepted by the IRS, but no information on amounts collected was released. No information was released about collection requests made by the IRS to CRA. No information was released about the parallel provisions in the Canada-Netherlands and Canada-Norway treaties. There were 0 requests in either direction under the Canada-Austria and Canada-Germany treaties.

See also Doobay & Ruchelman, "Collecting Another Country's Taxes", tinyurl.com/doobay-ruchel (Nov. 2019, 23pp); Arnold et al., "Judicial Approaches to Treaty Interpretation", 2012 Cdn Tax Foundation conference report, at 29:3-7; Shane, "Collecting Taxes Across International Borders", 82(8) *Tax Notes International* (taxnotes.com) 783-85 (May 23, 2016); De Troyer, "Implementation of Agreements on International Assistance in Collection", *Bulletin for International Taxation* (ibfd.org) 424-29 (Aug. 2017).

Technical Explanation [1995 Protocol]: Article 15 of the Protocol adds to the Convention a new Article XXVI A (Assistance in Collection). Collection assistance provisions are included in several other U.S. income tax treaties, including the recent treaty with the Netherlands, and in many U.S. estate tax treaties. U.S. negotiators initially raised with Canada the possibility of including collection assistance provisions in the Protocol, because the Internal Revenue Service has claims pending against persons in Canada that would be subject to collection under these provisions. However, the ultimate decision of the U.S. and Canadian negotiators to add the collection assistance article was attributable to the confluence of several unusual factors.

Of critical importance was the similarity between the laws of the United States and Canada. The Internal Revenue Service, the Justice Department, and other U.S. negotiators were reassured by the close similarity of the legal and procedural protections afforded by the Contracting States to their citizens and residents and by the fact that these protections apply to the tax collection procedures used by each State. In addition, the U.S. negotiators were confident, given their extensive experience in working with their Canadian counterparts, that the agreed procedures could be administered appropriately, effectively, and efficiently. Finally, given the close cooperation already developed between the United States and Canada in the exchange of tax information, the U.S. and Canadian negotiators concluded that the potential benefits to both countries of obtaining such assistance would be immediate and substantial and would far outweigh any cost involved.

Under paragraph 1 of Article XXVI A, each Contracting State agrees, subject to the exercise of its discretion and to the conditions explicitly provided later in the Article, to lend assistance and support to the other in the collection of revenue claims. The term "revenue claim" is defined in paragraph 1 to include all taxes referred to in paragraph 9 of the Article, as well as interest, costs, additions to such taxes, and civil penalties. Paragraph 9 provides that, notwithstanding the provisions of Article II (Taxes Covered) of the Convention, Article XXVI A shall apply to all categories of taxes collected by or on behalf of the Government of a Contracting State.

2. An application for assistance in the collection of a revenue claim shall include a certification by the competent authority of the applicant State that, under the laws of that State, the revenue claim has been finally determined. For the purposes of this Article, a revenue claim is finally determined when the applicant State has the right under its internal law to collect the revenue claim and all administrative and judicial rights of the taxpayer to restrain collection in the applicant State have lapsed or been exhausted.

Notes: This paragraph has been carefully worded so that where there is no restriction on collection, the enforcement of collection by the other jurisdiction may begin even though the taxpayer's rights of appeal may not have expired. Thus, payroll source deductions and GST net tax remittances, the collection of which are not restricted by ITA 225.1, can be collected by the IRS on behalf of CRA (subject to para. 8) even if the assessments are under appeal.

Definitions: "competent authority" — Art. III:1(g); "revenue claim" — Art. XXVI-A:1; "State" — Art. III:1(i); "taxpayer" — ITCIA 3, ITA 248(1).

Technical Explanation [1995 Protocol]: Paragraph 2 of the Article requires the Contracting State applying for collection assistance (the "applicant State") to certify that the revenue claim for which collection assistance is sought has been "finally determined." A revenue claim has been finally determined when the applicant State has the right under its internal law to collect the revenue claim and all administrative and judicial rights of the taxpayer to restrain collection in the applicant State have lapsed or been exhausted.

3. A revenue claim of the applicant State that has been finally determined may be accepted for collection by the competent authority of the requested State and, subject to the provisions of paragraph 7, if accepted shall be collected by the requested State as though such revenue claim were the requested State's own revenue claim finally determined in accordance with the laws applicable to the collection of the requested State's own taxes.

Definitions: "competent authority" — Art. III:1(g); "revenue claim" — Art. XXVI-A:1; "State" — Art. III:1(i).

Technical Explanation [1995 Protocol]: Paragraph 3 of the Article clarifies that the Contracting State from which assistance was requested (the "requested State") has discretion as to whether to accept a particular application for collection assistance. However, if the application for assistance is accepted, paragraph 3 requires that the requested State grant assistance under its existing procedures as though the claim were the requested State's own revenue claim finally determined under the laws of that State. This obligation under paragraph 3 is limited by paragraph 7 of the Article, which provides that, although generally treated as a revenue claim of the requested State, a claim for which collection assistance is granted shall not have any priority accorded to the revenue claims of the requested State.

4. Where an application for collection of a revenue claim in respect of a taxpayer is accepted

(a) by the United States, the revenue claim shall be treated by the United States as an assessment under United States laws against the taxpayer as of the time the application is received; and

(b) by Canada, the revenue claim shall be treated by Canada as an amount payable under the *Income Tax Act*, the collection of which is not subject to any restriction.

Notes: See Notes to para. 1 above.

Definitions: "assessment" — ITCIA 3, ITA 248(1); "Canada" — Art. III:1(a), ITCIA 5; "revenue claim" — Art. XXVI-A:1; "taxpayer" — ITCIA 3, ITA 248(1); "United States" — Art. III:1(b).

Technical Explanation [1995 Protocol]: Paragraph 4 of Article XXVI A provides that, when the United States accepts a request for assistance in collection, the claim will be treated by the United States as an assessment as of the time the application was received. Similarly, when Canada accepts a request, a revenue claim shall be treated as an amount payable under the *Income Tax Act*, the collection of which is not subject to any restriction.

5. Nothing in this Article shall be construed as creating or providing any rights of administrative or judicial review of the applicant State's finally determined revenue claim by the requested State, based on any such rights that may be available under the laws of either Contracting State. If, at any time pending execution of a request for assistance under this Article, the applicant State loses the right under its internal law to collect the revenue claim, the competent authority of the applicant State shall promptly withdraw the request for assistance in collection.

Definitions: "competent authority" — Art. III:1(g); "revenue claim" — Art. XXVI-A:1; "State" — Art. III:1(i).

Technical Explanation [1995 Protocol]: Paragraph 5 of the Article provides that nothing in Article XXVI A shall be construed as creating in the requested State any rights of administrative or judicial review of the applicant State's finally determined revenue claim. Thus, when an application for collection assistance has been accepted, the substantive validity of the applicant State's revenue claim cannot be challenged in an action in the requested State. Paragraph 5 furthers provides, however, that if the applicant State's revenue claim ceases to be finally determined, the applicant State is obligated to withdraw promptly any request that had been based on that claim.

6. Subject to this paragraph, amounts collected by the requested State pursuant to this Article shall be forwarded to the competent authority of the applicant State. Unless the competent authorities of the Contracting States otherwise agree, the ordinary costs incurred in providing collection assistance shall be borne by the requested State and any extraordinary costs so incurred shall be borne by the applicant State.

Definitions: "competent authority" — Art. III:1(g); "State" — Art. III:1(i).

Technical Explanation [1995 Protocol]: Paragraph 6 provides that, as a general rule, the requested State is to forward the entire amount collected to the competent authority of the applicant State. The ordinary costs incurred in providing collection assistance will normally be borne by the requested State and only extraordinary costs will be borne by the applicant State. The application of this paragraph, including rules specifying which collection costs are to be borne by each State and the time and manner of payment of the amounts collected, will be agreed upon by the competent authorities, as provided for in paragraph 11.

7. A revenue claim of an applicant State accepted for collection shall not have in the requested State any priority accorded to the revenue claims of the requested State.

Definitions: "revenue claim" — Art. XXVI-A:1; "State" — Art. III:1(i).

8. No assistance shall be provided under this Article for a revenue claim in respect of a taxpayer to the extent that the taxpayer can demonstrate that

(a) where the taxpayer is an individual, the revenue claim relates either to a taxable period in which the taxpayer was a citizen of the requested State or, if the taxpayer became a citizen of the requested State at any time before November 9, 1995 and is such a citizen at the time the applicant State applies for collection of the claim, to a taxable period that ended before November 9, 1995; and

(b) where the taxpayer is an entity that is a company, estate or trust, the revenue claim relates to a taxable period in which the taxpayer derived its status as such an entity from the laws in force in the requested State.

Notes: Under 8(a), CRA will not collect US tax from a Canadian citizen (at the time the debt arose) even if the person is also a US citizen: VIEWS doc 2011-0431621M4.

Where a US citizen living in Canada dies and the executors distribute the assets without paying US estate taxes or back income taxes, CRA states that it will collect the US debt (presumably even though the persons being collected from are Canadian citizens): VIEWS doc 2000-0003915. See also ITA 160(1) Notes re the *Montreuil* case.

Art. XXVI-A:8(a) amended by 2007 Protocol, retroactive to its introduction (revenue claims finally determined after Nov. 9, 1985 — see Notes at end of Art. XXVI-A).

Definitions: "company" — Art. III:1(f); "estate", "individual" — ITCIA 3, ITA 248(1); "revenue claim" — Art. XXVI-A:1; "State" — Art. III:1(i); "taxpayer" — ITCIA 3, ITA 248(1); "trust" — ITCIA 3, ITA 104(1), 248(1).

Technical Explanation [2007 Protocol]: Article 22 of the Protocol amends Article XXVI A (Assistance in Collection) of the existing Convention. Article XXVI A sets forth provisions under which the United States and Canada have agreed to assist each other in the collection of taxes.

Paragraph 1 replaces subparagraph 8(a) of Article XXVI A. In general, new subparagraph 8(a) provides the circumstances under which no assistance is to be given under the Article for a claim in respect of an individual taxpayer. New subparagraph 8(a) contains language that is in substance the same as subparagraph 8(a) of Article XXVI A of the existing Convention. However, the revised subparagraph also provides that no assistance in collection is to be given for a revenue claim from a taxable period that ended before November 9, 1995 in respect of an individual taxpayer, if the taxpayer became a citizen of the requested State at any time before November 9, 1995 and is such a citizen at the time the applicant State applies for collection of the claim.

The additional language is intended to avoid the potentially discriminating application of former subparagraph 8(a) as applied to persons who were not citizens of the requested State in the taxable period to which a particular collection request related, but who became citizens of the requested State at a time prior to the entry into force of Article XXVI A as set forth in the third protocol signed March 17, 1995. New subparagraph 8(a) addresses this situation by treating the citizenship of a person in the requested State at anytime prior to November 9, 1995 as comparable to citizenship in the requested State during the period for which the claim for assistance relates if 1) the person is a citizen of the requested state at the time of the request for assistance in collection, and 2) the request relates to a taxable period ending prior to November 9, 1995. As is provided in subparagraph 3(g) of Article 27, this change will have effect for revenue claims finally determined after November 9, 1985, the effective date of the adoption of collection assistance in the third protocol signed March 17, 1995.

Technical Explanation [1995 Protocol]: Paragraph 8 provides that no assistance is to be given under this Article for a claim in respect of an individual taxpayer, to the extent that the taxpayer can demonstrate that he was a citizen of the requested State during the taxable period to which the revenue claim relates. Similarly, in the case of a company, estate, or trust, no assistance is to be given to the extent that the entity can demonstrate that it derived its status as such under the laws in force in the requested State during the taxable period to which the claim relates.

9. Notwithstanding the provisions of Article II (Taxes Covered), the provisions of this Article shall apply to all categories of taxes collected, and to contributions to social security and employment insurance premiums levied, by or on behalf of the Government of a Contracting State.

Notes: The Canadian taxes covered include provincial income taxes, CPP contributions and EI premiums collected by CRA, as well as goods and services tax (GST) and Harmonized Sales Tax (HST) imposed and collected under the *Excise Tax Act*.

Art. XXVI-A:9 amended by 2007 Protocol to add reference to social security contributions and EI premiums, retroactive to its introduction (revenue claims finally determined after Nov. 9, 1985 — see Notes at end of Art. XXVI-A).

Technical Explanation [2007 Protocol]: Paragraph 2 replaces paragraph 9 of Article XXVI A of the Convention. Under paragraph 1 of Article XXVI A, each Contracting State generally agrees to lend assistance and support to the other in the collection of revenue claims. The term "revenue claim" is defined in paragraph 1 to include all taxes referred to in paragraph 9 of the Article, as well as interest, costs, additions to such taxes, and civil penalties. New paragraph 9 provides that, notwithstanding the provisions of Article II (Taxes Covered) of the Convention, Article XXVI A shall apply to all categories of taxes collected, and to contributions to social security and employment insurance premiums levied, by or on behalf of the Government of a Contracting State. Prior to the Protocol, paragraph 9 did not contain a specific reference to contributions to social security and employment insurance premiums. Although the prior language covered U.S. federal social security and unemployment taxes, the language did not cover Canada's social security (*e.g.*, Canada Pension Plan) and employment insurance programs, contributions to which are not considered taxes under Canadian law and therefore would not otherwise have come within the scope of the paragraph.

10. Nothing in this Article shall be construed as:

(a) limiting the assistance provided for in paragraph 4 of Article XXVI (Mutual Agreement Procedure); or

(b) imposing on either Contracting State the obligation to carry out administrative measures of a different nature from those used in the collection of its own taxes or that would be contrary to its public policy (ordre public).

Technical Explanation [1995 Protocol]: Subparagraph (a) of paragraph 10 clarifies that Article XXVI A supplements the provisions of paragraph 4 of Article XXVI (Mutual Agreement Procedure). The Mutual Agreement Procedure paragraph, which is more common in U.S. tax treaties, provides for collection assistance in cases in which a Contracting State seeks assistance in reclaiming treaty benefits that have been granted to a person that is not entitled to those benefits. Subparagraph (b) of paragraph 10 makes clear that nothing in Article XXVI A can require a Contracting State to carry out administrative measures of a different nature from those used in the collection of its own taxes, or that would be contrary to its public policy (ordre public).

11. The competent authorities of the Contracting States shall agree upon the mode of application of this Article, including agreement to ensure comparable levels of assistance to each of the Contracting States.

Definitions: "competent authority" — Art. III:1(g).

Technical Explanation [1995 Protocol]: Paragraph 11 requires the competent authorities to agree upon the mode of application of Article XXVI A, including agreement to ensure comparable levels of assistance to each of the Contracting States.

Paragraph 3 of Article 21 of the Protocol allows collection assistance under Article XXVI A to be sought for revenue claims that have been finally determined at any time within the 10 years preceding the date on which the Protocol enters into force.

Notes [Art. XXVI-A]: Art. XXVI-A added by 1995 Protocol, effective for revenue claims finally determined after November 9, 1985 (Art. 21(3) of the 1995 Protocol, reproduced up to PITA 34th ed.). Similar retroactivity in the UK-South Africa treaty was held valid in *Ben Nevis*, [2013] EWCA Civ 578 (England CA).

Article XXVII — Exchange of Information

1. The competent authorities of the Contracting States shall exchange such information as may be relevant for carrying out the provisions of this Convention or of the domestic laws of the Contracting States concerning taxes to which this Convention applies insofar as the taxation thereunder is not contrary to this Convention. The exchange of information is not restricted by Article I (Personal Scope). Any information received by a Contracting State shall be treated as secret in the same manner as information obtained under the taxation laws of that State and shall be disclosed only to persons or authorities (including courts and administrative bodies) involved in the assessment or collection of, the administration and enforcement in respect of, or the determination of appeals in relation to the taxes to which this Convention applies or, notwithstanding paragraph 4, in relation to taxes imposed by a political subdivision or local authority of a Contracting State that are substantially similar to the taxes covered by this Convention under Article II (Taxes Covered). Such persons or authorities shall use the information only for such purposes. They may disclose the information in public court proceedings or in judicial decisions. The competent authorities may release to an arbitration board established pursuant to paragraph 6 of Article XXVI (Mutual Agreement Procedure) such information as is necessary for carrying out the arbitration procedure; the members of the arbitration board shall be subject to the limitations on disclosure described in this Article.

Notes: For CRA provision of information to the IRS under FATCA (*Foreign Account Tax Compliance Act*) about US citizens and other US persons in Canada, see ITA 263-269 and the Canada-US Enhanced Tax Information Exchange Agreement reproduced after this treaty, and Notes to ITA 269. This disclosure does not violate Art. XXVII: *Hillis (Deegan)*, 2015 FC 1082, para. 68 (FCA appeal discontinued A-407-15).

For Canada-US exchange of Country-by-Country reports from multinational groups, see ITA 233.8.

Automatic information exchange between countries (rather than by specific request) was approved by the OECD and G20 on Oct. 29, 2014 (Global Forum on Transparency and Exchange of Information for Tax Purposes, oecd.org), and 100 countries are committed to start by 2018. See ITA 270-281.

Fifth Protocol (2007), Annex B, states:

13. Exchange of Information

It is understood that the standards and practices described in Article XXVII (Exchange of Information) of the Convention are to be in no respect less effective than those described in the Model Agreement on Exchange of Information on Tax Matters developed by the OECD Global Forum Working Group on Effective Exchange of Information.

In *David M. Sherman*, 2003 FCA 202, the Court stated that para. 1 applies only to information received by Canada from the IRS, and does not extend to information sent by Canada to the IRS unless it also contains information received from the IRS. Furthermore, para. 1 "does not require that statistical information that the minister compiled relating to the functioning of the tax collection assistance regime be treated as secret, provided the statistics contain no information received under the Convention by Canada" (para. 27). The Court also noted that para. 1 is much more limited in scope than *Internal Revenue Code* §6105, which prevents disclosure of any information exchanged under a tax treaty: "If Parliament intended to provide this kind of blanket secrecy and confidentiality, it should have said so" (para. 32).

Canada can demand information under ITA 231.2 on behalf of the IRS for purposes of Art. XXVII. See *Pacific Network Services*, 2002 FCT 1158, interpreting the parallel Article in the Canada-France treaty.

For discussion of the scope and volume of exchanges of information, see CCRA Q&A, IFA seminar of May 13, 2002 (search for "xxvii" on ifacanada.org); OECD, *Automatic Exchange of Information* (oecd.org, 2012), reviewed at 60(3) *Canadian Tax Journal* 768-69 (2012).

See also Notes to ITA 95(1)"non-qualifying country" re the *Ludmer* case.

Art. XXVII:1 amended by 2007 Protocol, for taxable years beginning after 2008, but in respect of taxes withheld at source, for amounts paid or credited after Jan. 2009; and by 1995 Protocol.

Definitions: "assessment" — ITCIA 3, ITA 248(1); "competent authority" — Art. III:1(g); "person" — Art. III:1(e), ITCIA 3, *Interpretation Act* 35(1); "State" — Art. III:1(i).

Technical Explanation [2007 Protocol]: New paragraph 1 of Article XXVII is substantially the same as paragraph 1 of Article XXVII of the existing Convention. Paragraph 1 authorizes the competent authorities to exchange information as may be relevant for carrying out the provisions of the Convention or the domestic laws of Canada and the United States concerning taxes covered by the Convention, insofar as the taxation under those domestic laws is not contrary to the Convention. New paragraph 1 changes the phrase "is relevant" to "maybe relevant" to clarify that the language incorporates the standard in Code section 7602 which authorizes the Internal Revenue Service to examine "any books, papers, records, or other data which may be relevant or material." (Emphasis added.) In *United States v. Arthur Young & Co.*, 465 U.S. 805, 814 (1984), the Supreme Court stated that "the language 'may be' reflects Congress's express intention to allow the Internal Revenue Service to obtain 'items of even *potential* relevance to an ongoing investigation, without reference to its admissibility.'" (Emphasis in original.) However, the language "may be" would not support a request in which a Contracting State simply asked for information regarding all bank accounts maintained by residents of that Contracting State in the other Contracting State, or even all accounts maintained by its residents with respect to a particular bank.

The authority to exchange information granted by paragraph 1 is not restricted by Article I (Personal Scope), and thus need not relate solely to persons otherwise covered by the Convention. Under paragraph 1, information may be exchanged for use in all phases of the taxation process including assessment, collection, enforcement or the determination of appeals. Thus, the competent authorities may request and provide information for cases under examination or criminal investigation, in collection, on appeals, or under prosecution.

Any information received by a Contracting State pursuant to the Convention is to be treated as secret in the same manner as information obtained under the tax laws of that State. Such information shall be disclosed only to persons or authorities, including courts and administrative bodies, involved in the assessment or collection of, the administration and enforcement in respect of, or the determination of appeals in relation to, the taxes covered by the Convention and the information may be used by such persons only for such purposes. (In accordance with paragraph 4, for the purposes of this Article the Convention applies to a broader range of taxes than those covered specifically by Article II (Taxes Covered)). Although the information received by persons described in paragraph 1 is to be treated as secret, it may be disclosed by such persons in public court proceedings or in judicial decisions.

Paragraph 1 also permits, however, a Contracting State to provide information received from the other Contracting State to its states, provinces, or local authorities, if it relates to a tax imposed by that state, province, or local authority that is substantially similar to a national-level tax covered under Article II (Taxes Covered). This provision does not authorize a Contracting State to request information on behalf of a state, province, or local authority. Paragraph 1 also authorizes the competent authorities to release information to any arbitration panel that may be established under the provisions of new paragraph 6 of Article XXVI (Mutual Agreement Procedure). Any information provided to a state, province, or local authority or to an arbitration panel is subject to the same use and disclosure provisions as is information received by the national Governments and used for their purposes.

The provisions of paragraph 1 authorize the U.S. competent authority to continue to allow legislative bodies, such as the tax-writing committees of Congress and the Government Accountability Office to examine tax return information received from Canada when such bodies or offices are engaged in overseeing the administration of U.S. tax laws or a study of the administration of U.S. tax laws pursuant to a directive of Congress. However, the secrecy requirements of paragraph 1 must be met.

It is contemplated that Article XXVII will be utilized by the competent authorities to exchange information upon request, routinely, and spontaneously.

Technical Explanation [1995 Protocol]: Article 16 of the Protocol amends Article XXVII (Exchange of Information) of the Convention. Paragraph 1 of Article 16 amends paragraph 1 of Article XXVII. The first change is a wording change to make it clear that information must be exchanged if it is "relevant" for carrying out the provisions of the Convention or of the domestic laws of the Contracting States, even if it is not "necessary." Neither the United States nor Canada views this as a substantive change. The second amendment merely conforms the language of the paragraph to the language of Article II (Taxes Covered), as amended, by referring to the taxes "to which the Convention applies" rather than to the taxes "covered by the Convention."

The Protocol further amends paragraph 1 to allow a Contracting State to provide information received from the other Contracting State to its states, provinces, or local authorities, if it relates to a tax imposed by that state, province, or local authority that is substantially similar to a national-level tax covered under Article II (Taxes Covered). However, this provision does not authorize a Contracting State to request information on behalf of a state, province, or local authority. The Protocol also amends paragraph 1 to authorize the competent authorities to release information to any arbitration panel that may be established under the provisions of new paragraph 6 of Article XXVI (Mutual Agreement Procedure). Any information provided to a state, province, or local authority or to an arbitration panel is subject to the same use and disclosure provisions as is information received by the national Governments and used for their purposes.

Technical Explanation [1984]: Paragraph 1 authorizes the competent authorities to exchange the information necessary for carrying out the provisions of the Convention or the domestic laws of Canada and the United States concerning taxes covered by the Convention, insofar as the taxation under those domestic laws is not contrary to the Convention. The authority to exchange information granted by paragraph 1 is not restricted by Article I (Personal Scope), and thus need not relate solely to persons otherwise covered by the Convention. It is contemplated that Article XXVII will be utilized by the competent authorities to exchange information upon request, routinely, and spontaneously.

Any information received by a Contracting State pursuant to the Convention is to be treated as secret in the same manner as information obtained under the taxation laws of that State. Such information shall be disclosed only to persons or authorities, including courts and administrative bodies, involved in the assessment or collection of, the administration and enforcement in respect of, or the determination of appeals in relation to, the taxes covered by the Convention and the information may be used by such persons only for such purposes. (In accordance with paragraph 4, for the purposes of this Article the Convention applies to a broader range of taxes than those covered specifically by Article II (Taxes Covered).)

In specific cases a competent authority providing information may, pursuant to paragraph 3, impose such other conditions on the use of information as are necessary. Although the information received by persons described in paragraph 1 is to be treated as secret, it may be disclosed by such persons in public court proceedings or in judicial decisions.

The provisions of paragraph 1 authorize the U.S. competent authority to continue to allow the General Accounting Office to examine tax return information received from Canada when GAO is engaged in a study of the administration of U.S. tax laws pursuant to a directive of Congress. However, the secrecy requirements of paragraph 1 must be met.

2. If information is requested by a Contracting State in accordance with this Article, the other Contracting State shall use its information gathering measures to obtain the requested information, even though that other State may not need such information for its own tax purposes. The obligation contained in the preceding sentence is subject to the limitations of paragraph 3 but in no case shall such limitations be construed to permit a Contracting State to decline to supply information because it has no domestic interest in such information.

Notes: See Notes to para. 1 re FATCA.

In *Blue Bridge*, 2021 FCA 62 (leave to appeal to SCC requested; stay of judgment denied 2021 FCA 114), CRA was entitled to information sought by France under the parallel provision in the Canada-France treaty. It did not matter that a resulting French assessment *might* contravene the treaty: paras. 27, 41, 44, 48 [Morier & Wilson, "Blue Bridge", XXV(1) *International Tax Planning* (Federated Press) 8-12 (2021)].

In *Levett*, 2021 FC 295 (under appeal to FCA), CRA was entitled to ask Switzerland for information about the taxpayers under the Canada-Switzerland treaty.

On whether Art. XXVII permits one country to ask another to use its treaty network to obtain information from a *third* country, see Tonkovich, "The Treaty Network Theory", 61(4) *Canadian Tax Journal* 875-92 (2013).

Art. XXVII:2 amended by 2007 Protocol, effective on the same basis as the amendment to Art. XXVII:1.

Definitions: "competent authority" — Art. III:1(g); "State" — Art. III:1(i).

Technical Explanation [2007 Protocol]: New paragraph 2 conforms with the corresponding U.S. and OECD Model provisions. The substance of the second sentence of former paragraph 2 is found in new paragraph 6 of the Article, discussed below.

Paragraph 2 provides that if a Contracting State requests information in accordance with Article XXVII, the other Contracting State shall use its information gathering measures to obtain the requested information. The instruction to the requested State to "use its information gathering measures" to obtain the requested information communicates the same instruction to the requested State as the language of former paragraph 2

that stated that the requested State shall obtain the information "in the same way as if its own taxation was involved." Paragraph 2 makes clear that the obligation to provide information is limited by the provisions of paragraph 3, but that such limitations shall not be construed to permit a Contracting State to decline to obtain and supply information because it has no domestic tax interest in such information.

In the absence of such a paragraph, some taxpayers have argued that subparagraph 3(a) prevents a Contracting State from requesting information from a bank or fiduciary that the Contracting State does not need for its own tax purposes. This paragraph clarifies that paragraph 3 does not impose such a restriction and that a Contracting State is not limited to providing only the information that it already has in its own files.

Technical Explanation [1984]: If a Contracting State requests information in accordance with Article XXVII, the other Contracting State shall endeavor, pursuant to paragraph 2, to obtain the information to which the request relates in the same manner as if its own taxation were involved, notwithstanding the fact that such State does not need the information. In addition, the competent authority requested to obtain information shall endeavor to provide the information in the particular form requested, such as depositions of witnesses and copies of unedited original documents, to the same extent such depositions and documents can be obtained under the laws or administrative practices of that State with respect to its own taxes.

3. In no case shall the provisions of paragraph[s] 1 and 2 be construed so as to impose on a Contracting State the obligation:

    (a) to carry out administrative measures at variance with the laws and administrative practice of that State or of the other Contracting State;

    (b) to supply information which is not obtainable under the laws or in the normal course of the administration of that State or of the other Contracting State; or

    (c) to supply information which would disclose any trade, business, industrial, commercial or professional secret or trade process, or information the disclosure of which would be contrary to public policy (ordre public).

Related Provisions: Art. XXVII:5 — Exception.

Notes: Art. XXVII:3 amended by 2007 Protocol, effective on the same basis as the amendment to Art. XXVII:1.

Technical Explanation [2007 Protocol]: New paragraph 3 is substantively the same as paragraph 3 of Article XXVII of the existing Convention. Paragraph 3 provides that the provisions of paragraphs 1 and 2 do not impose on Canada or the United States the obligation to carry out administrative measures at variance with the laws and administrative practice of either State; to supply information which is not obtainable under the laws or in the normal course of the administration of either State; or to supply information which would disclose any trade, business, industrial, commercial, or professional secret or trade process, or information the disclosure of which would be contrary to public policy.

Thus, a requesting State may be denied information from the other State if the information would be obtained pursuant to procedures or measures that are broader than those available in the requesting State. However, the statute of limitations of the Contracting State making the request for information should govern a request for information. Thus, the Contracting State of which the request is made should attempt to obtain the information even if its own statute of limitations has passed. In many cases, relevant information will still exist in the business records of the taxpayer or a third party, even though it is no longer required to be kept for domestic tax purposes.

While paragraph 3 states conditions under which a Contracting State is not obligated to comply with a request from the other Contracting State for information, the requested State is not precluded from providing such information, and may, at its discretion, do so subject to the limitations of its internal law.

As discussed with respect to paragraph 2, in no case shall the limitations in paragraph 3 be construed to permit a Contracting State to decline to obtain information and supply information because it has no domestic tax interest in such information.

Technical Explanation [1984]: Paragraph 3 provides that the provisions of paragraphs 1 and 2 do not impose on Canada or the United States the obligation to carry out administrative measures at variance with the laws and administrative practice of either State; to supply information which is not obtainable under the laws or in the normal course of the administration of either State; or to supply information which would disclose any trade, business, industrial, commercial, or professional secret or trade process, or information the disclosure of which would be contrary to public policy. Thus, Article XXVII allows, but does not obligate, the United States and Canada to obtain and provide information that would not be available to the requesting State under its laws or administrative practice or that in different circumstances would not be available to the State requested to provide the information. Further, Article XXVII allows a Contracting State to obtain information for the other Contracting State even if there is no tax liability in the State requested to obtain the information. Thus, the United States will continue to be able to give Canada tax information even if there is no U.S. tax liability at issue.

4. For the purposes of this Article, this Convention shall apply, notwithstanding the provisions of Article II (Taxes Covered):

(a) to all taxes imposed by a Contracting State; and

(b) to other taxes to which any other provision of this Convention applies, but only to the extent that the information may be relevant for the purposes of the application of that provision.

Notes: Art. XXVII:4 amended by 2007 Protocol, effective on the same basis as the amendment to Art. XXVII:1; and by 1995 Protocol.

Technical Explanation [2007 Protocol]: The language of new paragraph 4 is substantially similar to former paragraph 4. New paragraph 4, however, consistent with new paragraph 1, discussed above, replaces the words "is relevant" with "may be relevant" in subparagraph 4(b).

Paragraph 4 provides that, for the purposes of Article XXVII, the Convention applies to all taxes imposed by a Contracting State, and to other taxes to which any other provision of the Convention applies, but only to the extent that the information may be relevant for the purposes of the application of that provision.

Article XXVII does not apply to taxes imposed by political subdivisions or local authorities of the Contracting States. Paragraph 4 is designed to ensure that information exchange will extend to taxes of every kind (including, for example, estate, gift, excise, and value added taxes) at the national level in the United States and Canada.

Technical Explanation [1995 Protocol]: Paragraph 2 of Article 16 amends paragraph 4 of Article XXVII, which describes the applicable taxes for the purposes of this Article. Under the present Convention, the Article applies in Canada to taxes imposed by the Government of Canada under the *Income Tax Act* and on estates and gifts and in the United States to all taxes imposed under the *Internal Revenue Code*. The Protocol broadens the scope of the Article to apply to "all taxes imposed by a Contracting State". This change allows information to be exchanged, for example, with respect to Canadian excise taxes, as is the case with respect to U.S. excise taxes under the present Convention. Paragraph 4 is also amended to authorize the exchange of information with respect to other taxes, to the extent relevant to any other provision of the Convention.

Technical Explanation [1984]: Paragraph 4 provides that, for the purposes of Article XXVII, the Convention applies, in the case of Canada, to all taxes imposed by the Government of Canada on estates and gifts and under the *Income Tax Act* and, in the case of the United States, to all taxes imposed under the *Internal Revenue Code*. Article XXVII does not apply to taxes imposed by political subdivisions or local authorities of the Contracting States. Paragraph 4 is designed to ensure that information exchange will extend to most national level taxes on both sides, and specifically to information gathered for purposes of Canada's taxes on estates and gifts (not effective for deaths or gifts after 1971). This provision is intended to mesh with paragraph 8 of Article XXX (Entry Into Force), which terminates the existing estate tax convention between the United States and Canada.

5. In no case shall the provisions of paragraph 3 be construed to permit a Contracting State to decline to supply information because the information is held by a bank, other financial institution, nominee or person acting in an agency or a fiduciary capacity or because it relates to ownership interests in a person.

Notes: Art. XXVII:5 added by 2007 Protocol, effective on the same basis as the amendment to Art. XXVII:1.

Definitions: "bank", "person" — ITCIA 3, ITA 248(1); "State" — Art. III:1(i).

Technical Explanation [2007 Protocol]: New paragraph 5 conforms with the corresponding U.S. and OECD Model provisions. Paragraph 5 provides that a Contracting State may not decline to provide information because that information is held by a financial institution, nominee or person acting in an agency or fiduciary capacity. Thus, paragraph 5 would effectively prevent a Contracting State from relying on paragraph 3 to argue that its domestic bank secrecy laws (or similar legislation relating to disclosure of financial information by financial institutions or intermediaries) override its obligation to provide information under paragraph 1. This paragraph also requires the disclosure of information regarding the beneficial owner of an interest in a person.

6. If specifically requested by the competent authority of a Contracting State, the competent authority of the other Contracting State shall provide information under this Article in the form of depositions of witnesses and authenticated copies of unedited original documents (including books, papers, statements, records, accounts, and writings).

Notes: Art. XXVII:6 added by 2007 Protocol, effective on the same basis as the amendment to Art. XXVII:1.

Definitions: "competent authority" — Art. III:1(g); "State" — Art. III:1(i).

Technical Explanation [2007 Protocol]: The substance of new paragraph 6 is similar to the second sentence of paragraph 2 of Article XXVII of the existing Convention. New paragraph 6 adopts the language of paragraph 6 of Article 26 (Exchange of Information and Administrative Assistance) of the U.S. Model. New paragraph 6 provides that the requesting State may specify the form in which information is to be pro-

vided (*e.g.*, depositions of witnesses and authenticated copies of original documents). The intention is to ensure that the information may be introduced as evidence in the judicial proceedings of the requesting State. The requested State should, if possible, provide the information in the form requested to the same extent that it can obtain information in that form under its own laws and administrative practices with respect to its own taxes.

7. The requested State shall allow representatives of the requesting State to enter the requested State to interview individuals and examine books and records with the consent of the persons subject to examination.

Notes: Art. XXVII:7 added by 2007 Protocol, effective on the same basis as the amendment to Art. XXVII:1.

Definitions: "competent authority" — Art. III:1(g); "State" — Art. III:1(i).

CRA Audit Manual: 10.3.2: Conducting audits outside Canada; 10.11.17: Requests for information — countries with tax treaties; 15.10.11: International audit issues — other tax administrations.

Technical Explanation [2007 Protocol]: New paragraph 7 is consistent with paragraph 8 of Article 26 (Exchange of Information and Administrative Assistance) of the U.S. Model. Paragraph 7 provides that the requested State shall allow representatives of the requesting State to enter the requested State to interview individuals and examine books and records with the consent of the persons subject to examination. Paragraph 7 was intended to reinforce that the administrations can conduct consensual tax examinations abroad, and was not intended to limit travel or supersede any arrangements or procedures the competent authorities may have previously had in place regarding travel for tax administration purposes.

Paragraph 13 of General Note

As is explained in paragraph 13 of the General Note, the United States and Canada understand and agree that the standards and practices described in Article XXVII of the Convention are to be in no respect less effective than those described in the Model Agreement on Exchange of Information on Tax Matters developed by the OECD Global Forum Working Group on Effective Exchange of Information.

Article XXVIII — Diplomatic Agents and Consular Officers

Nothing in this Convention shall affect the fiscal privileges of diplomatic agents or consular officers under the general rules of international law or under the provisions of special agreements.

Related Provisions: ITA 149(1)(a) — Exemption from Canadian tax; Art. XIX — Government service.

Notes: See Notes to ITA 149(1)(a).

Definitions: "diplomatic agents or consular officers" — ITCIA 3, *Interpretation Act* 35(1)"diplomatic or consular officer".

Technical Explanation [1984]: Article XXVIII states that nothing in the Convention affects the fiscal privileges of diplomatic agents or consular officers under the general rules of international law or under the provisions of special agreements. However, various provisions of the Convention could apply to such persons, such as those concerning exchange of information, mutual agreement, and non-discrimination.

Article XXIX — Miscellaneous Rules

1. The provisions of this Convention shall not restrict in any manner any exclusion, exemption, deduction, credit or other allowance now or hereafter accorded by the laws of a Contracting State in the determination of the tax imposed by that State.

Notes: Art. XXIX:1 is known as the "domestic tax benefit" provision. It provides, in effect, that a taxpayer can choose between the treaty and the domestic tax law and pick the one that offers better treatment. For a discussion of the extent to which this allows "cherry picking" of different items see Arnold, "The Relationship Between Tax Treaties and the *Income Tax Act*", 43(4) *Canadian Tax Journal* 869-905 (1995).

Definitions: "State" — Art. III:1(i).

Technical Explanation [1984]: Paragraph 1 states that the provisions of the Convention do not restrict in any manner any exclusion, exemption, deduction, credit, or other allowance accorded by the laws of a Contracting State in the determination of the tax imposed by that State. Thus, if a deduction would be allowed for an item in computing the taxable income of a Canadian resident under the Code, such deduction is available to such person in computing taxable income under the Convention. Paragraph 1 does not, however, authorize a taxpayer to make inconsistent choices between rules of the Code and rules of the Convention. For example, if a resident of Canada desires to claim the benefits of the "attributable to" rule of paragraphs 1 and 7 of Article VII (Business Profits) with respect to the taxation of business profits of a permanent establishment, such person must use the "attributable to" concept consistently for all items of income and deductions and may not rely upon the "effectively connected" rules of the Code to avoid U.S. tax on other items of attributable income. In no event are the rules of the Convention to increase overall U.S. tax liability from what liability would be if there were no convention.

2. (a) Except to the extent provided in paragraph 3, this Convention shall not affect the taxation by a Contracting State of its residents (as determined under Article IV (Residence)) and, in the case of the United States, its citizens and companies electing to be treated as domestic corporations.

(b) Notwithstanding the other provisions of this Convention, a former citizen or former long-term resident of the United States, may, for the period of ten years following the loss of such status, be taxed in accordance with the laws of the United States with respect to income from sources within the United States (including income deemed under the domestic law of the United States to arise from such sources).

Notes: Both countries have the right to tax former US green-card holders on income from services performed in the US, and Canada will grant the foreign tax credit: VIEWS doc 2011-0391751E5. For application to US tax on a pension, triggered by renouncing US citizenship, see doc 2013-0477121E5.

Fifth Protocol (2007), Annex B, states:

11. Former long-term residents

The term "long-term resident" shall mean any individual who is a lawful permanent resident of the United States in eight or more taxable years during the preceding 15 taxable years. In determining whether the threshold in the preceding sentence is met, there shall not count any year in which the individual is treated as a resident of Canada under the Convention, or as a resident of any country other than the United States under the provisions of any other U.S. tax treaty, and, in either case, the individual does not waive the benefits of such treaty applicable to residents of the other country.

12. Special source rules relating to former citizens and long-term residents

For purposes of subparagraph 2(b) of Article XXIX (Miscellaneous Rules) of the Convention, "income deemed under the domestic law of the United States to arise from such sources" shall consist of gains from the sale or exchange of stock of a U.S. company or debt obligations of a U.S. person, the United States, a State, or a political subdivision thereof, or the District of Columbia, gains from property (other than stock or debt obligations) located in the United States, and, in certain cases, income or gain derived from the sale of stock of a non-U.S. company or a disposition of property contributed to such non-U.S. company would be a controlled foreign corporation with respect to the person if such person had continued to be a U.S. person. In addition, an individual who exchanges property that gives rise or would give rise to U.S.-source income for property that gives rise to foreign-source income shall be treated as if he or she had sold the property that would give rise to U.S. source income for its fair market value, and any consequent gain shall be deemed to be income from sources within the United States.

(Art. XXIX:2(b) contains the only reference to "long-term resident" in the Treaty.)

Art. XXIX:2 amended by 2007 Protocol, for taxable years beginning after 2008, but in respect of taxes withheld at source, for amounts paid or credited after Jan. 2009.

Definitions: "Canada" — Art. III:1(a), ITCIA 5; "company" — Art. III:1(f); "resident" — Art. IV; "United States" — Art. III:1(b).

Technical Explanation [2007 Protocol]: Paragraph 1 replaces paragraph 2 of Article XXIX of the existing Convention. New paragraph 2 is divided into two subparagraphs. In general, subparagraph 2(a) provides a "saving clause" pursuant to which the United States and Canada may each tax its residents, as determined under Article IV (Residence), and the United States may tax its citizens and companies, including those electing to be treated as domestic corporations (*e.g.* under Code section 1504(d)), as if there were no convention between the United States and Canada with respect to taxes on income and capital. Subparagraph 2(a) contains language that generally corresponds to former paragraph 2, but omits certain language pertaining to former citizens, which are addressed in new subparagraph 2(b).

New subparagraph 2(b) generally corresponds to the provisions of former paragraph 2 addressing former citizens of the United States. However, new subparagraph 2(b) also includes a reference to former long-term residents of the United States. This addition, as well as other changes in subparagraph 2(b), brings the Convention in conformity with the US taxation of former citizens and long-term residents under Code section 877.

Similar to subparagraph 2(a), new subparagraph 2(b) operates as a "saving clause" and provides that notwithstanding the other provisions of the Convention, a former citizen or former long-term resident of the United States, may, for a period of ten years following the loss of such status, be taxed in accordance with the laws of the United States with respect to income from sources within the United States (including income deemed under the domestic law of the United States to arise from such sources).

Paragraphs 11 and 12 of the General Note provide definitions based on Code section 877 that are relevant to the application of paragraph 2 of Article XXIX. Paragraph 11 of the General Note provides that the term "long-term resident" means any individual

who is a lawful permanent resident of the United States in eight or more taxable years during the preceding 15 taxable years. In determining whether the eight- year threshold is met, one does not count any year in which the individual is treated as a resident of Canada under this Convention (or as a resident of any country other than the United States under the provisions of any other U.S. tax treaty), and the individual does not waive the benefits of such treaty applicable to residents of the other country. This understanding is consistent with how this provision is generally interpreted in U.S. tax treaties.

Paragraph 12 of the General Note provides that the phrase "income deemed under the domestic law of the United States to arise from such sources" as used in new subparagraph 2(b) includes gains from the sale or exchange of stock of a U.S. company or debt obligations of a U.S. person, the United States, a State, or a political subdivision thereof, or the District of Columbia, gains from property (other than stock or debt obligations) located in the United States, and, in certain cases, income or gain derived from the sale of stock of a non-U.S. company or a disposition of property contributed to such non-U.S. company where such company would be a controlled foreign corporation with respect to the individual if such person had continued to be a U.S. person. In addition, an individual who exchanges property that gives rise or would give rise to U.S.-source income for property that gives rise to foreign-source income will be treated as if he had sold the property that would give rise to U.S.-source income for its fair market value, and any consequent gain shall be deemed to be income from sources within the United States.

Technical Explanation [1984]: Paragraph 2 provides a "saving clause" pursuant to which Canada and the United States may each tax its residents, as determined under Article IV (Residence), and the United States may tax its citizens (including any former citizen whose loss of citizenship had as one of its principal purposes the avoidance of tax, but only for a period of 10 years following such loss) and companies electing under Code section 1504(d) to be treated as domestic corporations, as if there were no convention between the United States and Canada with respect to taxes on income and capital.

3. The provisions of paragraph 2 shall not affect the obligations undertaken by a Contracting State:

(a) under paragraphs 3 and 4 of Article IX (Related Persons), paragraphs 6 and 7 of Article XIII (Gains), paragraphs 1, 3, 4, 5, 6(b), 7, 8, 10 and 13 of Article XVIII (Pensions and Annuities), paragraph 5 of Article XXIX (Miscellaneous Rules), paragraphs 1, 5, and 6 of Article XXIX-B (Taxes Imposed by Reason of Death), paragraphs 2, 3, 4, and 7 of Article XXIX-B (Taxes Imposed by Reason of Death) as applied to estates of persons other than former citizens referred to in paragraph 2 of this Article, paragraphs 3 and 5 of Article XXX (Entry into Force), and Articles XIX (Government Service), XXI (Exempt Organizations), XXIV (Elimination of Double Taxation), XXV (Non-Discrimination) and XXVI (Mutual Agreement Procedure);

(b) under Article XX (Students), toward individuals who are neither citizens of, nor have immigrant status in, that State.

Notes: Art. XXIX:3(a) amended to add reference to Art. XVIII:8, 10 and 13 by 2007 Protocol, effective on the same basis as the amendment to para. 2.

Art. XXIX:3(a) amended by 1995 Protocol, generally effective 1996.

Definitions: "individual" — ITCIA 3, ITA 248(1); "State" — Art. III:1(i).

Technical Explanation [2007 Protocol]: Paragraph 2 replaces subparagraph 3(a) of Article XXIX of the existing Convention. Paragraph 3 provides that, notwithstanding paragraph 2 of Article XXIX, the United States and Canada must respect specified provisions of the Convention in regard to certain persons, including residents and citizens. Therefore, subparagraph 3(a) lists certain paragraphs and Articles of the Convention that represent exceptions to the "saving clause" in all situations. New subparagraph 3(a) is substantially similar to former subparagraph 3(a), but now contains a reference to paragraphs 8, 10, and 13 of Article XVIII (Pensions and Annuities) to reflect the changes made to that article in paragraph 3 of Article 13 of the Protocol.

Technical Explanation [1995 Protocol]: Article 17 of the Protocol amends Article XXIX (Miscellaneous Rules) of the Convention. Paragraph 1 of Article 17 modifies paragraph 3(a), the exceptions to the saving clause, to conform the cross-references in the paragraph to changes in other parts of the Convention. The paragraph also adds to the exceptions to the saving clause certain provisions of Article XXIX B (Taxes Imposed by Reason of Death). Thus, certain benefits under that Article will be granted by a Contracting State to its residents and, in the case of the United States, to its citizens, notwithstanding the saving clause of paragraph 2 of Article XXIX.

Technical Explanation [1984]: Paragraph 3 provides that, notwithstanding paragraph 2, the United States and Canada must respect certain specified provisions of the Convention in regard to residents, citizens, and section 1504(d) companies. Paragraph 3(a) lists certain paragraphs and Articles of the Convention that represent exceptions to the "saving clause" in all situations; paragraph 3(b) provides a limited further exception for students who have not acquired immigrant status in the State where they are temporarily present.

4. With respect to taxable years not barred by the statute of limitations ending on or before December 31 of the year before the year in which the Social Security Agreement between Canada and the United States (signed in Ottawa on March 11, 1981) enters into force, income from personal services not subject to tax by the United States under this Convention or the 1942 Convention shall not be considered wages or net earnings from self-employment for purposes of social security taxes imposed under the *Internal Revenue Code.*

Definitions: "Canada" — Art. III:1(a), ITCIA 5; "the 1942 Convention" — Art. III:1(j); "United States" — Art. III:1(b).

Technical Explanation [1984]: Paragraph 4 provides relief with respect to social security taxes imposed on employers, employees, and self-employed persons under Code sections 1401, 3101, and 3111. Income from personal services not subject to tax by the United States under the provisions of this Convention or the 1942 Convention is not to be considered wages or net earnings from self-employment for purposes of the U.S. social security taxes with respect to taxable years of the taxpayer not barred by the statute of limitations relating to refunds (under the Code) ending on or before December 31 of the year before the year in which the Social Security Agreement between Canada and the United States (signed in Ottawa on March 11, 1981) enters into force. Thus, if that agreement enters into force in 1986, a resident of Canada earning income from personal services and such person's employer may apply for refunds of the employee's and employer's shares of U.S. social security tax paid attributable to the employee's income from personal services that is exempt from U.S. tax by virtue of this Convention or the 1942 Convention. In this example, the refunds would be available for social security taxes paid with respect to taxable years not barred by the statute of limitations of the Code ending on or before December 31, 1985. For purposes of Code section 6611, the date of overpayment with respect to refunds of U.S. tax pursuant to paragraph 4 is the later of the date on which the Social Security Agreement between Canada and the United States enters into force and the date on which instruments of ratification of the Convention are exchanged.

Under certain limited circumstances, an employee may, pursuant to paragraph 5 of Article XXX (Entry Into Force), claim an exemption from U.S. tax on wages under the 1942 Convention for one year after the Convention comes into force. The provisions of paragraph 4 would not, however, provide an exemption from U.S. social security taxes for such year.

Paragraph 4 does not modify existing U.S. statutes concerning social security benefits or funding. The *Social Security Act* requires the general funds of the Treasury to reimburse the social security trust funds on the basis of the records of wages and self-employment income maintained by the Social Security Administration. The Convention does not alter those records. Thus, any refunds of tax made pursuant to paragraph 4 would not affect claims for U.S. quarters of coverage with respect to social security benefits. And such refunds would be charged to general revenue funds, not social security trust funds.

5. Where a person who is a resident of Canada and a shareholder of a United States S corporation requests the competent authority of Canada to do so, the competent authority may agree, subject to terms and conditions satisfactory to such competent authority, to apply the following rules for the purposes of taxation in Canada with respect to the period during which the agreement is effective:

(a) the corporation shall be deemed to be a controlled foreign affiliate of the person;

(b) all the income of the corporation shall be deemed to be foreign accrual property income;

(c) for the purposes of subsection 20(11) of the *Income Tax Act*, the amount of the corporation's income that is included in the person's income shall be deemed not to be income from a property; and

(d) each dividend paid to the person on a share of the capital stock of the corporation shall be excluded from the person's income and shall be deducted in computing the adjusted cost base to the person of the share.

Notes: For guidelines on applying under Art. XXIX:5, see VIEWS doc 2015-0581931C6 [2015 STEP q.4]; 2017-0697901C6 [2017 STEP q.9].

See Michael Colborne, "Article XXIX(5) and the Draft Competent Authority Circular", XI(4) *International Tax Planning* (Federated Press) 819-20 (2003).

Art. XXIX:5 replaced by 1995 Protocol, generally effective 1996. The former Art. XXIX:5 was broadened and moved to Art. XVIII:7.

Definitions: "adjusted cost base" — ITCIA 3, ITA 248(1); "Canada" — Art. III:1(a), ITCIA 5; "controlled foreign affiliate" — ITA 95(1); "corporation", "dividend" — ITCIA 3, ITA 248(1); "foreign accrual property income" — ITA 95(1); "foreign affiliate" — ITCIA 3, ITA 248(1); "person" — Art. III:1(e), ITCIA 3, *Interpretation Act* 35(1); "share" — ITCIA 3, ITA 248(1); "United States" — Art. III:1(b).

Technical Explanation [1995 Protocol]: Paragraph 2 of Article 17 replaces paragraphs 5 through 7 of Article XXIX of the present Convention with three new paragraphs. (Paragraph 5 in the present Convention was moved to paragraph 7 of Article XVIII (Pensions and Annuities), and paragraphs 6 and 7 were deleted as unnecessary.) New paragraph 5 provides a rule for the taxation by Canada of a Canadian resident that is a shareholder in a U.S. S corporation. The application of this rule is relatively limited, because U.S. domestic law requires that S corporation shareholders be either U.S. citizens or U.S. residents. Therefore, the rule provided by paragraph 5 would apply only to an S corporation shareholder who is a resident of both the United States and Canada (i.e., a "dual resident" who meets certain requirements), determined before application of the "tie-breaker" rules of Article IV (Residence), or a U.S. citizen resident in Canada. Since the shareholder would be subject to U.S. tax on its share of the income of the S corporation as it is earned by the S corporation and, under Canadian statutory law, would be subject to tax only when the income is distributed, there could be a timing mismatch resulting in unrelieved double taxation. Under paragraph 5, the shareholder can make a request to the Canadian competent authority for relief under the special rules of the paragraph. Under these rules, the Canadian shareholder will be subject to Canadian tax on essentially the same basis as he is subject to U.S. tax, thus eliminating the timing mismatch.

Technical Explanation [1984]: Paragraph 5 provides a method to resolve conflicts between the Canadian and U.S. treatment of individual retirement accounts. Certain Canadian retirement plans which are qualified plans for Canadian tax purposes do not meet Code requirements for qualification. As a result, the earnings of such a plan are currently included in income, for U.S. tax purposes, rather than being deferred until actual distributions are made by the plan. Canada defers current taxes on the earnings of such a plan but imposes tax on actual distributions from the plan. Paragraph 5 is designed to avoid a mismatch of U.S. taxable income and foreign tax credits attributable to the Canadian tax on such distributions. Under the paragraph a beneficiary of a Canadian registered retirement savings plan may elect to defer U.S. taxation with respect to any income accrued in the plan but not distributed by the plan, until such time as a distribution is made from the plan or any substitute plan. The election is to be made under rules established by the competent authority of the United States. The election is not available with respect to income accrued in the plan which is reasonably attributable to contributions made to the plan by the beneficiary while he was not a Canadian resident.

6. For purposes of paragraph 3 of Article XXII (Consultation) of the General Agreement on Trade in Services, the Contracting States agree that:

(a) a measure falls within the scope of the Convention only if:

(i) the measure relates to a tax to which Article XXV (Non-Discrimination) of the Convention applies; or

(ii) the measure relates to a tax to which Article XXV (Non-Discrimination) of the Convention does not apply and to which any other provision of the Convention applies, but only to the extent that the measure relates to a matter dealt with in that other provision of the Convention; and

(b) notwithstanding paragraph 3 of Article XXII (Consultation) of the General Agreement on Trade in Services, any doubt as to the interpretation of subparagraph (a) will be resolved under paragraph 3 of Article XXVI (Mutual Agreement Procedure) of the Convention or any other procedure agreed to by both Contracting States.

Notes: Art. XXIX:6 replaced by 1995 Protocol, generally effective 1996. The former Art. XXIX:6 was deleted as unnecessary.

Technical Explanation [1995 Protocol]: The Protocol adds to Article XXIX a new paragraph 6, which provides a coordination rule for the Convention and the General Agreement on Trade in Services ("GATS"). Paragraph 6(a) provides that, for purposes of paragraph 3 of Article XXII (Consultation) of the GATS, a measure falls within the scope of the Convention only if the measure relates to a tax (1) to which Article XXV (Non-Discrimination) of the Convention applies, or (2) to which Article XXV does not apply and to which any other provision of the Convention applies, but only to the extent that the measure relates to a matter dealt with in that other provision. Under paragraph 6(b), notwithstanding paragraph 3 of Article XXII of the GATS, any doubt as to the interpretation of subparagraph (a) will be resolved under paragraph 3 of Article XXVI (Mutual Agreement Procedure) of the Convention or any other procedure agreed to by both Contracting States.

GATS generally obliges its Members to provide national treatment and most-favored-nation treatment to services and service suppliers of other Members. A very broad exception from the national treatment obligation applies to direct taxes. An exception from the most-favored-nation obligation applies to a difference in treatment resulting from an international agreement on the avoidance of double taxation (a "tax agreement") or from provisions on the avoidance of double taxation in any other international agreement or arrangement by which the Member is bound.

Article XXII(3) of GATS specifically provides that there will be no access to GATS procedures to settle a national treatment dispute concerning a measure that falls within the scope of a tax agreement. This provision preserves the exclusive application of nondiscrimination obligations in the tax agreement and clarifies that the competent authority mechanism provided by the tax agreement will apply, instead of GATS procedures, to resolve nondiscrimination disputes involving the taxation of services and service suppliers.

In the event of a disagreement between Members as to whether a measure falls within the scope of a tax agreement that existed at the time of the entry into force of the Agreement establishing the World Trade Organization, Article XXII(2), footnote 11, of GATS reserves the resolution of the dispute to the Contracting States under the tax agreement. In such a case, the issue of the scope of a tax agreement may be resolved under GATS procedures (rather than tax treaty procedures) only if both parties to the existing tax agreement consent. With respect to subsequent tax agreements, GATS provides that either Member may bring the jurisdictional matter before the Council for Trade In Services, which will refer the matter to arbitration for a decision that will be final and binding on the Members.

Both Canada and the United States agree that a protocol to a convention that is grandfathered under Article XXII(2), footnote 11, of GATS is also grandfathered. Nevertheless, since the Protocol extends the application of the Convention, and particularly the nondiscrimination article, to additional taxes (e.g., some non-income taxes imposed by Canada), the negotiators sought to remove any ambiguity and agreed to a provision that clarified the scope of the Convention and the relationship between the Convention and GATS.

The purpose of new paragraph 6(a) of the Convention is to provide the agreement of the Contracting States as to the measures considered to fall within the scope of the Convention in applying Article XXII(3) of GATS between the Contracting States. The purpose of new paragraph 6(b) is to reserve the resolution of the issue of the scope of the Convention for purposes of Article XXII(3) of GATS to the competent authorities under the Convention rather than to settlement under GATS procedures.

Technical Explanation [1984]: Paragraph 6 provides rules denying the benefits of the Convention in certain situations where both countries believed that granting benefits would be inappropriate. Paragraph 6(a) provides that Articles VI (Income from Real Property) through XXIV (Elimination of Double Taxation) shall not apply to profits, income or gains derived by a trust which is treated as the income of a resident of a Contracting State (see paragraph 1 of Article IV (Residence)), if a principal purpose of the establishment, acquisition or maintenance of the trust was to obtain a benefit under the Convention or the 1942 Convention for persons who are not residents of that State. For example, the provision could be applied to a case where a non-resident of the United States created a United States trust to derive dividend income from Canada and a principal purpose of the establishment or maintenance of the trust was to obtain the reduced rate of Canadian tax under Article X (Dividends) for the non-resident. Paragraph 6(b) provides that Articles VI through XXIV shall not apply to Canadian non-resident owned investment companies, as defined in section 133 of the *Income Tax Act*, or under a similar provision that is subsequently enacted. This provision operates to deny the benefits of the Convention to a Canadian non-resident owned investment company, and does not affect the grant of benefits to other persons. Thus, for example, a dividend paid by such a company to a shareholder who is a U.S. resident is subject to the reduced rates of tax provided by Article X. The denial of the benefits of Articles VI through XXIV in such cases applies notwithstanding any other provision of the Convention. A Canadian non-resident owned investment company may, however, be entitled to claim the benefits of the 1942 Convention for an additional one-year period, pursuant to paragraph 5 of Article XXX (Entry into Force). Where the provisions of this paragraph apply, the Contracting State in which the income arises may tax such income under its domestic law.

7. The appropriate authority of a Contracting State may request consultations with the appropriate authority of the other Contracting State to determine whether change to the Convention is appropriate to respond to changes in the law or policy of that other State. Where domestic legislation enacted by a Contracting State unilaterally removes or significantly limits any material benefit otherwise provided by the Convention, the appropriate authorities shall promptly consult for the purpose of considering an appropriate change to the Convention.

Notes: Art. XXIX:7 replaced by 1995 Protocol, generally effective 1996. The former Art. XXIX(7) was deleted as unnecessary.

Definitions: "State" — Art. III:1(i).

Technical Explanation [1995 Protocol]: The Protocol also adds to Article XXIX a new paragraph 7, relating to certain changes in the law or treaty policy of either of the Contracting States. Paragraph 7 provides, first, that in response to a change in the law or policy of either State, the appropriate authority of either State may request consultations with its counterpart in the other State to determine whether a change in the Convention is appropriate. If a change in domestic legislation has unilaterally removed or significantly limited a material benefit provided by the Convention, the appropriate authorities are instructed by the paragraph to consult promptly to consider an appropriate amendment to the Convention. The "appropriate authorities" may be the Contracting States themselves or the competent authorities under the Convention. The consultations may be initiated by the authority of the Contracting State making the change in law or policy or by the authority of the other State. Any change in the Convention recommended as a result of this process can be implemented only through the negotiation, signature, ratification, and entry into force of a new protocol to the Convention.

Technical Explanation [1984]: Paragraph 7 provides rules for the U.S. taxation of Canadian social security benefits paid to a resident of Canada who is a U.S. citizen. These rules are described in the discussion of paragraph 5 of Article XVIII (Pensions and Annuities).

Article XXIX-A — Limitation on Benefits

1. For the purposes of the application of this Convention by a Contracting State,

(a) a qualifying person shall be entitled to all of the benefits of this Convention; and

(b) except as provided in paragraphs 3, 4 and 6, a person that is not a qualifying person shall not be entitled to any benefits of this Convention.

Notes: Art. XXIX-A is an "anti-treaty-shopping" provision that appears in most recent US treaties, and denies treaty protection to taxpayers from other countries that try to set up operations in Canada in order to make use of treaty provisions. It also applies in the other direction, to avoidance of Canadian tax. See also Notes to Art. X:2 re "beneficial ownership". In general CRA may accept "simple" restructurings to take advantage of treaties, e.g. VIEWS doc 2008-0284551R3. For CRA experience on the use of Art. XXIX-A see 2013-0507961C6 [2013 CTF conf].

See Colborne & Porter, "The Limitation-on-Benefits Article", 2008 CTF conference report, 25:1-75; Selby, "Navigating the New Bilateral Limitation-on-Benefits Rule", 57(1) *Canadian Tax Journal* 86-118 (2009); Suarez, "Thoughts on the New LOB Clause in The Canada-US Treaty", 56(1) *Tax Notes International* (Tax Analysts) 39-53 (Oct. 5, 2009); Richardson & Wong, "Cross-border Financing Into Canada More Difficult Under Canada's New LOB Provision", XVI(1) *Corporate Finance* 1734-46 (2009); Darmo & Nikolakakis, "The New Rules on Limitation on Benefits and Fiscally Transparent Entities", 2009 conference report, 26:1-80.

For CRA interpretation since the 2007 Protocol see *Income Tax Technical News* 41 (2008 Cdn Tax Foundation conference report, Roundtable qq.29-33 at 3:23-26); *Guidelines for Taxpayers Requesting Treaty Benefits Pursuant to Paragraph 6 of Article XXIX A*, tinyurl.com/cra-xxixa-6; Round Table, 2010 conference report, qq.2-3, p. 4:3-4. For a ruling requiring that Art. XXIX-A be complied with see doc 2008-0284551R3. The US does not publish guidance on its limitation-on-benefits treaty provisions (O'Donnell, 2009 conference report, 16:6-7). See also Notes to ITA 115.1.

Canada had considered adding a general anti-treaty-shopping rule to the ITA (see PITA 45th-52nd ed.), but that was dropped in light of the MLI (see the pages before this Treaty), which effectively amends most of Canada's treaties (but not this one). CRA may also apply GAAR to treaty-shopping arrangements: doc 2015-0581551C6 [IFA 2015 q.2]; and see the back-to-back rules in ITA 212(3.1)-(3.94), for interest and royalties.

Art. XXIX-A:1 opening words amended by 2007 Protocol to change "by the United States" to "by a Contracting State", for taxable years beginning after 2008, but in respect of taxes withheld at source, for amounts paid or credited after Jan. 2009.

Definitions: "qualifying person" — Art. XXIX-A:2; "State" — Art. III:1(i).

I.T. Technical News: 41 (5th protocol to the Canada-US Tax Convention — limitation on benefits).

Forms: NR301: Declaration of eligibility for benefits under a tax treaty for a non-resident taxpayer.

Technical Explanation [2007 Protocol]: Article 25 of the Protocol replaces Article XXIX A (Limitation on Benefits) of the existing Convention, which was added to the Convention by the Protocol done on March 17, 1995. Article XXIX A addresses the problem of "treaty shopping" by residents of third States by requiring, in most cases, that the person seeking benefits not only be a U.S. resident or Canadian resident but also satisfy other tests. For example, a resident of a third State might establish an entity resident in Canada for the purpose of deriving income from the United States and claiming U.S. treaty benefits with respect to that income. Article XXIX A limits the benefits granted by the United States or Canada under the Convention to those persons whose residence in the other Contracting State is not considered to have been motivated by the existence of the Convention. As replaced by the Protocol, new Article XXIX A is reciprocal, and many of the changes to the former paragraphs of Article XXIX A are made to effectuate this reciprocal application.

Absent Article XXIX A, an entity resident in one of the Contracting States would be entitled to benefits under the Convention, unless it were denied such benefits as a result of limitations under domestic law (*e.g.*, business purpose, substance-over-form, step transaction, or conduit principles or other anti-avoidance rules) applicable to a particular transaction or arrangement. As noted below in the explanation of paragraph 7, general anti-abuse provisions of this sort apply in conjunction with the Convention in both the United States and Canada. In the case of the United States, such anti-abuse provisions complement the explicit anti-treaty-shopping rules of Article XXIX A. While the anti-treaty-shopping rules determine whether a person has a sufficient nexus to Canada to be entitled to benefits under the Convention, the anti-abuse provisions under U.S. domestic law determine whether a particular transaction should be recast in accordance with the substance of the transaction.

New paragraph 1 of Article XXIX A provides that, for the purposes of the application of the Convention, a "qualifying person" shall be entitled to all of the benefits of the

Convention and, except as provided in paragraphs 3, 4, and 6, a person that is not a qualifying person shall not be entitled to any benefits of the Convention.

Technical Explanation [1995 Protocol]: *In general*

Article 18 of the Protocol adds a new Article XXIX A (Limitation on Benefits) to the Convention. Article XXIX A addresses the problem of "treaty shopping" by requiring, in most cases, that the person seeking U.S. treaty benefits not only be a Canadian resident but also satisfy other tests. In a typical case of treaty shopping, a resident of a third State might establish an entity resident in Canada for the purpose of deriving income from the United States and claiming U.S. treaty benefits with respect to that income. Article XXIX A limits the benefits granted by the United States under the Convention to those persons whose residence in Canada is not considered to have been motivated by the existence of the Convention. Absent Article XXIX A, the entity would be entitled to U.S. benefits under the Convention as a resident of Canada, unless it were denied benefits as a result of limitations (e.g., business purpose, substance-over-form, step transaction, or conduit principles or other anti-avoidance rules) applicable to a particular transaction or arrangement. General anti-abuse provisions of this sort apply in conjunction with the Convention in both the United States and Canada. In the case of the United States, such anti-abuse provisions complement the explicit anti-treaty-shopping rules of Article XXIX A. While the anti-treaty-shopping rules determine whether a person has a sufficient nexus to Canada to be entitled to treaty benefits, general anti-abuse provisions determine whether a particular transaction should be recast in accordance with the substance of the transaction.

The present Convention deals with treaty-shopping in a very limited manner, in paragraph 6 of Article XXIX, by denying benefits to Canadian residents that benefit from specified provisions of Canadian law. The Protocol removes that paragraph 6 from Article XXIX, because it is superseded by the more general provisions of Article XXIX A.

The Article is not reciprocal, except for paragraph 7. Canada prefers to rely on general anti-avoidance rules to counter arrangements involving treaty-shopping through the United States.

The structure of the Article is as follows: Paragraph 1 states that, in determining whether a resident of Canada is entitled to U.S. benefits under the Convention, a "qualifying person" is entitled to all of the benefits of the Convention, and other persons are not entitled to benefits, except where paragraphs 3, 4, or 6 provide otherwise. Paragraph 2 lists a number of characteristics, any one of which will make a Canadian resident a qualifying person. These are essentially mechanical tests. Paragraph 3 provides an alternative rule, under which a Canadian resident that is not a qualifying person under paragraph 2 may claim U.S. benefits with respect to those items of U.S. source income that are connected with the active conduct of a trade or business in Canada. Paragraph 4 provides a limited "derivative benefits" test for entitlement to benefits with respect to U.S. source dividends, interest, and royalties beneficially owned by a resident of Canada that is not a qualifying person. Paragraph 5 defines certain terms used in the Article. Paragraph 6 requires the U.S. competent authority to grant benefits to a resident of Canada that does not qualify for benefits under any other provision of the Article, where the competent authority determines, on the basis of all factors, that benefits should be granted. Paragraph 7 clarifies the application of general anti-abuse provisions.

2. For the purposes of this Article, a **qualifying person** is a resident of a Contracting State that is:

(a) a natural person;

(b) a Contracting State or a political subdivision or local authority thereof, or any agency or instrumentality of any such State, subdivision or authority;

(c) a company or trust whose principal class of shares or units (and any disproportionate class of shares or units) is primarily and regularly traded on one or more recognized stock exchanges;

(d) a company, if five or fewer persons each of which is a company or trust referred to in subparagraph (c) own directly or indirectly more than 50 percent of the aggregate vote and value of the shares and more than 50 percent of the vote and value of each disproportionate class of shares (in neither case including debt substitute shares), provided that each company or trust in the chain of ownership is a qualifying person;

(e)

(i) a company, 50 percent or more of the aggregate vote and value of the shares of which and 50 percent or more of the vote and value of each disproportionate class of shares (in neither case including debt substitute shares) of which is not owned, directly or indirectly, by persons other than qualifying persons; or

(ii) a trust, 50 percent or more of the beneficial interest in which and 50 percent or more of each disproportionate inter-

est in which, is not owned, directly or indirectly, by persons other than qualifying persons;

where the amount of the expenses deductible from gross income (as determined in the State of residence of the company or trust) that are paid or payable by the company or trust, as the case may be, for its preceding fiscal period (or, in the case of its first fiscal period, that period) directly or indirectly, to persons that are not qualifying persons is less than 50 percent of its gross income for that period;

(f) an estate;

(g) a not-for-profit organization, provided that more than half of the beneficiaries, members or participants of the organization are qualifying persons;

(h) a trust, company, organization or other arrangement described in paragraph 2 of Article XXI (Exempt Organizations) and established for the purpose of providing benefits primarily to individuals who are qualifying persons, or persons who were qualifying persons within the five preceding years; or

(i) a trust, company, organization or other arrangement described in paragraph 3 of Article XXI (Exempt Organizations) provided that the beneficiaries of the trust, company, organization or other arrangement are described in subparagraph (g) or (h).

Related Provisions: Art. XXIX-A:4 — Alternate tests to qualify for relief under Art. X, XI, XII.

Notes: See Notes to para. 1. Fifth Protocol (2007), Annex B, states:

14. Limitation on Benefits

The United States and Canada are part of the same regional free trade area and, as a result, the Convention reflects the fact that publicly traded companies resident in one country may be traded on a stock exchange of the other country. Nevertheless, the Contracting States agree that in making future amendments to the Convention, they shall consult on possible modifications to subparagraph 2(c) of Article XXIX A (Limitation on Benefits) of the Convention (including, modifications necessary to discourage corporate inversion transactions).

For interpretation of para. 2(c) where a corporation has multiple classes of shares, see VIEWS doc 2009-0347701C6, stating that each class of shares must be considered separately; as para. 6 is not a very satisfactory solution, CRA was discussing further relief with the US Competent Authority. See also Yu & Loh, "Dual-Class Canadian Pubco: US Treaty Benefits", 18(12) *Canadian Tax Highlights* (ctf.ca) 5-6 (Dec. 2010).

CRA will "look through" a fiscally-transparent entity (per Art. IV:6) when applying the ownership and base erosion tests in paras. 2(d)-(e): VIEWS docs 2008-0272361C6 (2008 IFA conference), 2008-0278801C6 q.17 (2008 STEP conference), 2009-0317941E5, 2009-0329511E5, 2010-0361251E5. On applying 2(e)(i) where a partnership is interposed, see 2007-0262141E5.

For an example of para. 2(g) applying see doc 2009-0344201E5. A US IRA qualifies under para. 2(h): 2013-0497381E5.

See also doc 2011-0429261R3 (corporation is qualifying person).

Art. XXIX-A:2 amended by 2007 Protocol, effective on the same basis as the amendment to para. 1.

Definitions: "company" — Art. III:1(f); "debt substitute share" — Art. XXIX-A:5(a); "disproportionate class" — Art. XXIX-A:5(b); "disproportionate interest" — Art. XXIX-A:5(c); "individual" — ITCIA 3, ITA 248(1); "not-for-profit organization" — Art. XXIX-A:5(d); "person" — Art. III:1(e), ITCIA 3, *Interpretation Act* 35(1); "principal class" — Art. XXIX-A:5(e); "recognized stock exchange" — Art. XXIX-A:5(f); "share" — ITCIA 3, ITA 248(1); "State" — Art. III:1(i); "trust" — ITCIA 3, ITA 104(1), 248(1).

I.T. Technical News: 41 (5th protocol to the Canada-US Tax Convention — limitation on benefits).

Technical Explanation [2007 Protocol]: New paragraph 2 lists a number of characteristics any one of which will make a United States or Canadian resident a qualifying person. The "look-through" principles introduced by the Protocol (*e.g.* paragraph 6 of Article IV (Residence)) are to be applied in conjunction with Article XXIX A. Accordingly, the provisions of Article IV shall determine the person who derives an item of income, and the objective tests of Article XXIX A shall be applied to that person to determine whether benefits shall be granted. The rules are essentially mechanical tests and are discussed below.

Individuals and governmental entities

Under new paragraph 2, the first two categories of qualifying persons are (1) natural persons resident in the United States or Canada (as listed in subparagraph 2(a)), and (2) the Contracting States, political subdivisions or local authorities thereof, and any agency or instrumentality of such Government, political subdivision or local authority (as listed in subparagraph 2(b)). Persons falling into these two categories are unlikely to be used, as the beneficial owner of income, to derive benefits under the Convention on behalf of a third-country person. If such a person receives income as a nominee on behalf of a third-country resident, benefits will be denied with respect to those items of income under the articles of the Convention that would otherwise grant the benefit, because of the requirements in those articles that the beneficial owner of the income be a resident of a Contracting State.

Publicly traded entities

Under new subparagraph 2(c), a company or trust resident in a Contracting State is a qualifying person if the company's principal class of shares, and any disproportionate class of shares, or the trust's units, or disproportionate interest in a trust, are primarily and regularly traded on one or more recognized stock exchanges. The term "recognized stock exchange" is defined in subparagraph 5(f) of the Article to mean, in the United States, the NASDAQ System and any stock exchange registered as a national securities exchange with the Securities and Exchange Commission, and, in Canada, any Canadian stock exchanges that are "prescribed stock exchanges" or "designated stock exchanges" under the *Income Tax Act*. These are, at the time of signature of the Protocol, the Montreal Stock Exchange, the Toronto Stock Exchange, and Tiers 1 and 2 of the TSX Venture Exchange. Additional exchanges may be added to the list of recognized exchanges by exchange of notes between the Contracting States or by agreement between the competent authorities.

If a company has only one class of shares, it is only necessary to consider whether the shares of that class meet the relevant trading requirements. If the company has more than one class of shares, it is necessary as an initial matter to determine which class or classes constitute the "principal class of shares." The term "principal class of shares" is defined in subparagraph 5(e) of the Article to mean the ordinary or common shares of the company representing the majority of the aggregate voting power and value of the company. If the company does not have a class of ordinary or common shares representing the majority of the aggregate voting power and value of the company, then the "principal class of shares" is that class or any combination of classes of shares that represents, in the aggregate, a majority of the voting power and value of the company. Although in a particular case involving a company with several classes of shares it is conceivable that more than one group of classes could be identified that account for more than 50% of the voting power and value of the shares of the company, it is only necessary for one such group to satisfy the requirements of this subparagraph in order for the company to be entitled to benefits. Benefits would not be denied to the company even if a second, non-qualifying, group of shares with more than half of the company's voting power and value could be identified.

A company whose principal class of shares is regularly traded on a recognized stock exchange will nevertheless not qualify for benefits under subparagraph 2(c) if it has a disproportionate class of shares that is not regularly traded on a recognized stock exchange. The term "disproportionate class of shares" is defined in subparagraph 5(b) of the Article. A company has a disproportionate class of shares if it has outstanding a class of shares which is subject to terms or other arrangements that entitle the holder to a larger portion of the company's income, profit, or gain in the other Contracting State than that to which the holder would be entitled in the absence of such terms or arrangements. Thus, for example, a company has a disproportionate class of shares if it has outstanding a class of "tracking stock" that pays dividends based upon a formula that approximates the company's return on its assets employed in the United States. Similar principles apply to determine whether or not there are disproportionate interests in a trust.

The following example illustrates the application of subparagraph 5(b).

Example. OCo is a corporation resident in Canada. OCo has two classes of shares: Common and Preferred. The Common shares are listed and regularly traded on a designated stock exchange in Canada. The Preferred shares have no voting rights and are entitled to receive dividends equal in amount to interest payments that OCo receives from unrelated borrowers in the United States. The Preferred shares are owned entirely by a single investor that is a resident of a country with which the United States does not have a tax treaty. The Common shares account for more than 50% of the value of OCo and for 100% of the voting power. Because the owner of the Preferred shares is entitled to receive payments corresponding to the U.S.-source interest income earned by OCo, the Preferred shares are a disproportionate class of shares. Because the Preferred shares are not primarily and regularly traded on a recognized stock exchange, OCo will not qualify for benefits under subparagraph 2(c).

The term "regularly traded" is not defined in the Convention. In accordance with paragraph 2 of Article III (General Definitions) and paragraph 1 of the General Note, this term will be defined by reference to the domestic tax laws of the State from which benefits of the Convention are sought, generally the source State. In the case of the United States, this term is understood to have the meaning it has under Treas. Reg. section 1.884-5(d)(4)(i)(B), relating to the branch tax provisions of the Code, as may be amended from time to time. Under these regulations, a class of shares is considered to be "regularly traded" if two requirements are met: trades in the class of shares are made in more than de minimis quantities on at least 60 days during the taxable year, and the aggregate number of shares in the class traded during the year is at least 10% of the average number of shares outstanding during the year. Sections 1.884-5(d)(4)(i)(A), (ii) and (iii) will not be taken into account for purposes of defining the term "regularly traded" under the Convention.

The regularly-traded requirement can be met by trading on one or more recognized stock exchanges. Therefore, trading may be aggregated for purposes of this requirement. Thus, a U.S. company could satisfy the regularly traded requirement through trading, in whole or in part, on a recognized stock exchange located in Canada. Authorized but unissued shares are not considered for purposes of this test.

The term "primarily traded" is not defined in the Convention. In accordance with paragraph 2 of Article III (General Definitions) and paragraph 1 of the General Note, this term will have the meaning it has under the laws of the State concerning the taxes to which the Convention applies, generally the source State. In the case of the United States, this term is understood to have the meaning it has under Treas. Reg. section 1.884-5(d)(3), as may be amended from time to time, relating to the branch tax provisions of the Code. Accordingly, stock of a corporation is "primarily traded" if the number of shares in the company's principal class of shares that are traded during the taxable year on all recognized stock exchanges exceeds the number of shares in the company's principal class of shares that are traded during that year on all other established securities markets.

Subject to the adoption by Canada of other definitions, the U.S. interpretation of "regularly traded" and "primarily traded" will be considered to apply, with such modifications as circumstances require, under the Convention for purposes of Canadian taxation.

Subsidiaries of publicly traded entities

Certain companies owned by publicly traded corporations also may be qualifying persons. Under subparagraph 2(d), a company resident in the United States or Canada will be a qualifying person, even if not publicly traded, if more than 50% of the vote and value of its shares, and more than 50% of the vote and value of each disproportionate class of shares, is owned (directly or indirectly) by five or fewer persons that are qualifying persons under subparagraph 2(c). In addition, each company in the chain of ownership must be a qualifying person. Thus, for example, a company that is a resident of Canada, all the shares of which are owned by another company that is a resident of Canada, would qualify for benefits of the Convention if the principal class of shares (and any disproportionate classes of shares) of the parent company are regularly and primarily traded on a recognized stock exchange. However, such a subsidiary would not qualify for benefits under subparagraph 2(d) if the publicly traded parent company were a resident of a third state, for example, and not a resident of the United States or Canada. Furthermore, if a parent company qualifying for benefits under subparagraph 2(c) indirectly owned the bottom-tier company through a chain of subsidiaries, each subsidiary in the chain, as an intermediate owner, must be a qualifying person in order for the bottom-tier subsidiary to meet the test in subparagraph 2(d).

Subparagraph 2(d) provides that a subsidiary can take into account ownership by as many as five companies, each of which qualifies for benefits under subparagraph 2(c) to determine if the subsidiary qualifies for benefits under subparagraph 2(d). For example, a Canadian company that is not publicly traded but that is owned, one-third each, by three companies, two of which are Canadian resident corporations whose principal classes of shares are primarily and regularly traded on a recognized stock exchange, will qualify under subparagraph 2(d).

By applying the principles introduced by the Protocol (*e.g.* paragraph 6 of Article IV) in the context of this rule, one "looks through" entities in the chain of ownership that are viewed as fiscally transparent under the domestic laws of the State of residence (other than entities that are resident in the State of source).

The 50-percent test under subparagraph 2(d) applies only to shares other than "debt substitute shares." The term "debt substitute shares" is defined in subparagraph 5(a) to mean shares defined in paragraph (e) of the definition in the Canadian *Income Tax Act* of "term preferred shares" (see subsection 248(1) of the *Income Tax Act*), which relates to certain shares received in debt-restructuring arrangements undertaken by reason of financial difficulty or insolvency. Subparagraph 5(a) also provides that the competent authorities may agree to treat other types of shares as debt substitute shares.

Ownership/base erosion test

Subparagraph 2(e) provides a two-part test under which certain other entities may be qualifying persons, based on ownership and lack of "base erosion." A company resident in the United States or Canada will satisfy the first of these tests if 50% or more of the vote and value of its shares and 50% or more of the vote and value of each disproportionate class of shares, in both cases not including debt substitute shares, is not owned, directly or indirectly, by persons other than qualifying persons. Similarly, a trust resident in the United States or Canada will satisfy this first test if 50% or more of its beneficial interests, and 50% or more of each disproportionate interest, is not owned, directly or indirectly, by persons other than qualifying persons. The wording of these tests is intended to make clear that, for example, if a Canadian company is more than 50% owned, either directly or indirectly (including cumulative indirect ownership through a chain of entities), by a U.S. resident corporation that is, itself, wholly owned by a third-country resident other than a qualifying person, the Canadian company would not pass the ownership test. This is because more than 50% of its shares is owned indirectly by a person (the third-country resident) that is not a qualifying person.

It is understood by the Contracting States that in determining whether a company satisfies the ownership test described in subparagraph 2(e)(i), a company, 50% of more of the aggregate vote and value of the shares of which and 50% or more of the vote and value of each disproportionate class of shares (in neither case including debt substitute shares) of which is owned, directly or indirectly, by a company described in subparagraph 2(c) will satisfy the ownership test of subparagraph 2(e)(i). In such case, no further analysis of the ownership of the company described in subparagraph 2(c) is required. Similarly, in determining whether a trust satisfies the ownership test described in subparagraph 2(e)(ii), a trust, 50% or more of the beneficial interest in which and 50% or more of each disproportionate interest in which, is owned, directly or indirectly, by a trust described in subparagraph (2)(c) will satisfy the ownership test of subparagraph (2)(e)(ii), and no further analysis of the ownership of the trust described in subparagraph 2(c) is required.

The second test of subparagraph 2(e) is the so-called "base erosion" test. A company or trust that passes the ownership test must also pass this test to be a qualifying person under this subparagraph. This test requires that the amount of expenses that are paid or payable by the entity in question, directly or indirectly, to persons that are not qualifying persons, and that are deductible from gross income (with both deductibility and gross income as determined under the tax laws of the State of residence of the company or trust), be less than 50% of the gross income of the company or trust. This test is applied for the fiscal period immediately preceding the period for which the qualifying person test is being applied. If it is the first fiscal period of the person, the test is applied for the current period.

The ownership/base erosion test recognizes that the benefits of the Convention can be enjoyed indirectly not only by equity holders of an entity, but also by that entity's obligees, such as lenders, licensors, service providers, insurers and reinsurers, and others. For example, a third-country resident could license technology to a Canadian-owned Canadian corporation to be sub-licensed to a U.S. resident. The U.S.-source royalty income of the Canadian corporation would be exempt from U.S. withholding tax under Article XII (Royalties) of the Convention. While the Canadian corporation would be subject to Canadian corporation income tax, its taxable income could be reduced to near zero as a result of the deductible royalties paid to the third-country resident. If, under a convention between Canada and the third country, those royalties were either exempt from Canadian tax or subject to tax at a low rate, the U.S. treaty benefit with respect to the U.S.-source royalty income would have flowed to the third-country resident at little or no tax cost, with no reciprocal benefit to the United States from the third country. The ownership/base erosion test therefore requires both that qualifying persons substantially own the entity and that the entity's tax base is not substantially eroded by payments (directly or indirectly) to nonqualifying persons.

For purposes of this subparagraph 2(e) and other provisions of this Article, the term "shares" includes, in the case of a mutual insurance company, any certificate or contract entitling the holder to voting power in the corporation. This is consistent with the interpretation of similar limitation on benefits provisions in other U.S. treaties. In Canada, the principles that are reflected in subsection 256(8.1) of the *Income Tax Act* will be applied, in effect treating memberships, policies or other interests in a corporation incorporated without share capital as representing an appropriate number of shares.

The look-through principles introduced by the Protocol (*e.g.* new paragraph 6 of Article IV) are to be taken into account when applying the ownership and base erosion provisions of Article XXIX A. Therefore, one "looks through" an entity that is viewed as fiscally transparent under the domestic laws of the residence State (other than entities that are resident in the source State) when applying the ownership/base erosion test. Assume, for example, that USCo, a company incorporated in the United States, wishes to obtain treaty benefits by virtue of the ownership and base erosion rule. USCo is owned by USLLC, an entity that is treated as fiscally transparent in the United States. USLLC in turn is wholly owned in equal shares by 10 individuals who are residents of the United States. Because the United States views USLLC as fiscally transparent, the 10 U.S. individuals shall be regarded as the owners of USCo for purposes of the ownership test. Accordingly, USCo would satisfy the ownership requirement of the ownership/base erosion test. However, if USLLC were instead owned in equal shares by four U.S. individuals and six individuals who are not residents of either the United States or Canada, USCo would not satisfy the ownership requirement. Similarly, for purposes of the base erosion test, deductible payments made to USLLC will be treated as made to USLLC's owners.

Other qualifying persons

Under new subparagraph 2(f), an estate resident in the United States or Canada is a qualifying person entitled to the benefits of the Convention.

New subparagraphs 2(g) and 2(h) specify the circumstances under which certain types of not-for-profit organizations will be qualifying persons. Subparagraph 2(g) provides that a not-for-profit organization that is resident in the United States or Canada is a qualifying person, and thus entitled to benefits, if more than half of the beneficiaries, members, or participants in the organization are qualifying persons. The term "not-forprofit organization" of a Contracting State is defined in subparagraph 5(d) of the Article to mean an entity created or established in that State that is generally exempt from income taxation in that State by reason of its not-for-profit status. The term includes charities, private foundations, trade unions, trade associations, and similar organizations.

New subparagraph 2(h) specifies that certain trusts, companies, organizations, or other arrangements described in paragraph 2 of Article XXI (Exempt Organizations) are qualifying persons. To be a qualifying person, the trust, company, organization or other arrangement must be established for the purpose of providing pension, retirement, or employee benefits primarily to individuals who are (or were, within any of the five preceding years) qualifying persons. A trust, company, organization, or other arrangement will be considered to be established for the purpose of providing benefits primarily to such persons if more than 50% of its beneficiaries, members, or participants are such persons. Thus, for example, a Canadian Registered Retirement Savings Plan ("RRSP") of a former resident of Canada who is working temporarily outside of Canada would continue to be a qualifying person during the period of the individual's absence from Canada or for five years, whichever is shorter. A Canadian pension fund established to provide benefits to persons employed by a company would be a qualifying person only if most of the beneficiaries of the fund are (or were within the five preceding years) individual residents of Canada or residents or citizens of the United States.

New subparagraph 2(i) specifies that certain trusts, companies, organizations, or other arrangements described in paragraph 3 of Article XXI (Exempt Organizations) are qualifying persons. To be a qualifying person, the beneficiaries of a trust, company, organization or other arrangement must be described in subparagraph 2(g) or 2(h).

The provisions of paragraph 2 are self-executing, unlike the provisions of paragraph 6, discussed below. The tax authorities may, of course, on review, determine that the taxpayer has improperly interpreted the paragraph and is not entitled to the benefits claimed.

Technical Explanation [1995 Protocol]: *Individuals and governmental entities*

Under paragraph 2, the first two categories of qualifying persons are (1) individual residents of Canada, and (2) the Government of Canada, a political subdivision or local authority thereof, or an agency or instrumentality of that Government, political subdivision, or local authority. It is considered unlikely that persons falling into these two categories can be used, as the beneficial owner of income, to derive treaty benefits on behalf of a third-country person. If a person is receiving income as a nominee on behalf of a third-country resident, benefits will be denied with respect to those items of income under the articles of the Convention that grant the benefit, because of the requirements in those articles that the beneficial owner of the income be a resident of a Contracting State.

Publicly traded entities

Under subparagraph (c) of paragraph 2, a Canadian resident company or trust is a qualifying person if there is substantial and regular trading in the company's principal class of shares, or in the trust's units, on a recognized stock exchange. The term "recognized stock exchange" is defined in paragraph 5(a) of the Article to mean, in the United States, the NASDAQ System and any stock exchange registered as a national securities exchange with the Securities and Exchange Commission, and, in Canada, any Canadian stock exchanges that are "prescribed stock exchanges" under the *Income Tax Act*. These are, at the time of signature of the Protocol, the Alberta, Montreal, Toronto, Vancouver, and Winnipeg Stock Exchanges. Additional exchanges may be added to the list of recognized exchanges by exchange of notes between the Contracting States or by agreement between the competent authorities.

Certain companies owned by publicly traded corporations also may be qualifying persons. Under subparagraph (d) of paragraph 2, a Canadian resident company will be a qualifying person, even if not publicly traded, if more than 50% of the vote and value of its shares is owned (directly or indirectly) by five or fewer persons that would be qualifying persons under subparagraph (c). In addition, each company in the chain of ownership must be a qualifying person or a U.S. citizen or resident. Thus, for example, a Canadian company that is not publicly traded but that is owned, one-third each, by three companies, two of which are Canadian resident corporations whose principal classes of shares are substantially and regularly traded on a recognized stock exchange, will qualify under subparagraph (d).

The 50-percent test under subparagraph (d) applies only to shares other than "debt substitute shares." The term "debt substitute shares" is defined in paragraph 5 to mean shares defined in paragraph (e) of the definition in the Canadian *Income Tax Act* of "term preferred shares" (see section 248(1) of the *Income Tax Act*), which relates to certain shares received in debt-restructuring arrangements undertaken by reason of financial difficulty or insolvency. Paragraph 5 also provides that the competent authorities may agree to treat other types of shares as debt substitute shares.

Ownership/base erosion test

Subparagraph (e) of paragraph 2 provides a two-part test under which certain other entities may be qualifying persons, based on ownership and "base erosion." Under the first of these tests, benefits will be granted to a Canadian resident company if 50% or more of the vote and value of its shares (other than debt substitute shares), or to a Canadian resident trust if 50% or more of its beneficial interest, is not owned, directly or indirectly, by persons other than qualifying persons or U.S. residents or citizens. The wording of these tests is intended to make clear that, for example, if a Canadian company is more than 50% owned by a U.S. resident corporation that is, itself, wholly owned by a third-country resident other than a U.S. citizen, the Canadian company would not pass the ownership test. This is because more than 50% of its shares is owned indirectly by a person (the third-country resident) that is not a qualifying person or a citizen or resident of the United States.

For purposes of this subparagraph (e) and other provisions of this Article, the term "shares" includes, in the case of a mutual insurance company, any certificate or contract entitling the holder to voting power in the corporation. This is consistent with the interpretation of similar limitation on benefits provisions in other U.S. treaties.

The second test of subparagraph (e) is the so-called "base erosion" test. A Canadian company or trust that passes the ownership test must also pass this test to be a qualifying person. This test requires that the amount of expenses that are paid or payable by the Canadian entity in question to persons that are not qualifying persons or U.S. citizens or residents, and that are deductible from gross income, be less than 50% of the gross income of the company or trust. This test is applied for the fiscal period immediately preceding the period for which the qualifying person test is being applied. If it is the first fiscal period of the person, the test is applied for the current period.

The ownership/base erosion test recognizes that the benefits of the Convention can be enjoyed indirectly not only by equity holders of an entity, but also by that entity's obligees, such as lenders, licensors, service providers, insurers and reinsurers, and others. For example, a third-country resident could license technology to a Canadian-owned Canadian corporation to be sub-licensed to a U.S. resident. The U.S. source royalty income of the Canadian corporation would be exempt from U.S. withholding tax under Article XII (Royalties) of the Convention (as amended by the Protocol). While the Canadian corporation would be subject to Canadian corporation income tax, its taxable income could be reduced to near zero as a result of the deductible royalties paid to the third-country resident. If, under a Convention between Canada and the third country, those royalties were either exempt from Canadian tax or subject to tax at a low rate, the U.S. treaty benefit with respect to the U.S. source royalty income would have flowed to the third-country resident at little or no tax cost, with no reciprocal benefit to the United States from the third country. The ownership/base erosion test therefore requires both that qualifying persons or U.S. residents or citizens substantially own the entity and that the entity's deductible payments be made in substantial part to such persons.

Other qualifying persons

Under subparagraph (f) of paragraph 2, a Canadian resident estate is a qualifying person, entitled to the benefits of the Convention with respect to its U.S. source income.

Subparagraphs (g) and (h) specify the circumstances under which certain types of not-for-profit organizations will be qualifying persons. Subparagraph (g) of paragraph 2 provides that a not-for-profit organization that is a resident of Canada is a qualifying person, and thus entitled to U.S. benefits, if more than half of the beneficiaries, members, or participants in the organization are qualifying persons or citizens or residents of the United States. The term "not-for-profit organization" of a Contracting State is defined in subparagraph (b) of paragraph 5 of the Article to mean an entity created or established in that State that is generally exempt from income taxation in that State by reason of its not-for-profit status. The term includes charities, private foundations, trade unions, trade associations, and similar organizations.

Subparagraph (h) of paragraph 2 specifies that certain organizations described in paragraph 2 of Article XXI (Exempt Organizations), as amended by Article 10 of the Protocol, are qualifying persons. To be a qualifying person, such an organization must be established primarily for the purpose of providing pension, retirement, or employee benefits to individual residents of Canada who are (or were, within any of the five preceding years) qualifying persons, or to citizens or residents of the United States. An organization will be considered to be established "primarily" for this purpose if more than 50% of its beneficiaries, members, or participants are such persons. Thus, for example, a Canadian Registered Retirement Savings Plan ("RRSP") of a former resident of Canada who is working temporarily outside of Canada would continue to be a qualifying person during the period of the individual's absence from Canada or for five years, whichever is shorter. A Canadian pension fund established to provide benefits to persons employed by a company would be a qualifying person only if most of the beneficiaries of the fund are (or were within the five preceding years) individual residents of Canada or residents or citizens of the United States.

The provisions of paragraph 2 are self-executing, unlike the provisions of paragraph 6, discussed below. The tax authorities may, of course, on review, determine that the taxpayer has improperly interpreted the paragraph and is not entitled to the benefits claimed.

3. Where a person is a resident of a Contracting State and is not a qualifying person, and that person, or a person related thereto, is engaged in the active conduct of a trade or business in that State (other than the business of making or managing investments, unless those activities are carried on with customers in the ordinary course of business by a bank, an insurance company, a registered securities dealer or a deposit-taking financial institution), the benefits of this Convention shall apply to that resident person with respect to income derived from the other Contracting State in connection with or incidental to that trade or business (including any such income derived directly or indirectly by that resident person through one or more other persons that are residents of that other State), but only if that trade or business is substantial in relation to the activity carried on in that other State giving rise to the income in respect of which benefits provided under this Convention by that other State are claimed.

Notes: This is known as the "active trade or business" exception.

See Notes to para. 1. For interpretation see VIEWS docs 2007-0257021E5 (in-force date); 2008-0272371C6 and 2009-0336401C6 (meaning of "in connection with or incidental to"); 2009-0315151C6 (whether activities carried on by bank or insurer with affiliates are with "customers"); 2009-0317941E5 (shareholders of LLC not considered to be carrying on its business); 2009-0319161I7 ("registered securities dealer" is broader than the ITA 248(1) definition); 2009-0343641R3 (dividend paid by ULC to Dutch resident); 2009-0344711R3 (ruling that para. 3 applies); 2009-0345881C6 (no safe harbour in the "substantial" test); 2009-0348041R3 (interest paid by Canadian-resident ULC to US-resident corp whose subsidiary is sole shareholder of the ULC); 2009-0348181R3 (interest paid by Canadian resident corp to US resident corp); 2009-0349701R3 (capital gains on windup of US sub qualifies under para. 3); 2010-0387001C6 [2010 CTF conf. p.4:13, q.12] (meaning of "active conduct"); 2012-0435211R3 (bankruptcy — dividends qualify under para. 3); 2012-0444151C6 (hybrid partnerships and branch tax liability); 2011-0424211R3 and 2012-0458361R3 (cross-border financing: para. 3 applies); 2013-0496401I7 (requirement that income be "derived" from Canada in connection with US trade or business can be met with "funding approach" of interest funded from business cash flow); 2013-0511761R3 (para. 3 applies to interest payments); 2014-0526711C6 [2014 IFA q.2] (para. 3 applies to gain on US Holdco shares that are taxable Canadian property); 2014-0549621C6 [2014 CTF q.7] (interpretation of "substantial"); 2014-0549771E5 (trust is related to beneficiary corp that is controlled by trustee); 2019-0798841C6 [2019 IFA q.8] (para. 3 does not apply where Canco pays dividend to US parent from income derived from FA in a third country); Baker & McCracken, "IFA Round Table", 17(6) *Canadian Tax Highlights* (ctf.ca) 3-4 (June 2009).

Art. XXIX-A:3 amended by 2007 Protocol, effective on the same basis as the amendment to para. 1.

Definitions: "bank", "business" — ITCIA 3, ITA 248(1); "person" — Art. III:1(e), ITCIA 3, *Interpretation Act* 35(1); "qualifying person" — Art. XXIX-A:2; "registered securities dealer" — ITCIA 3, ITA 248(1); "resident" — Art. IV; "State" — Art. III:1(i).

I.T. Technical News: 41 (5th protocol to the Canada-US Tax Convention — limitation on benefits).

Technical Explanation [2007 Protocol]: Paragraph 3 provides an alternative rule, under which a United States or Canadian resident that is not a qualifying person under paragraph 2 may claim benefits with respect to those items of income that are connected with the active conduct of a trade or business in its State of residence.

This is the so-called "active trade or business" test. Unlike the tests of paragraph 2, the active trade or business test looks not solely at the characteristics of the person deriving the income, but also at the nature of the person's activity and the connection between the income and that activity. Under the active trade or business test, a resident of a Contracting State deriving an item of income from the other Contracting State is entitled to benefits with respect to that income if that person (or a person related to that person under the principles of Code section 482, or in the case of Canada, section 251 of the *Income Tax Act*) is engaged in an active trade or business in the State where it is resident, the income in question is derived in connection with, or is incidental to, that trade or business, and the size of the active trade or business in the residence State is substantial relative to the activity in the other State that gives rise to the income for which benefits are sought. Further details on the application of the substantiality requirement are provided below.

Income that is derived in connection with, or is incidental to, the business of making or managing investments will not qualify for benefits under this provision, unless those investment activities are carried on with customers in the ordinary course of the business of a bank, insurance company, registered securities dealer, or deposit-taking financial institution.

Income is considered derived "in connection" with an active trade or business if, for example, the income-generating activity in the State is "upstream," "downstream," or parallel to that conducted in the other Contracting State. Thus, for example, if the U.S. activity of a Canadian resident company consisted of selling the output of a Canadian manufacturer or providing inputs to the manufacturing process, or of manufacturing or selling in the United States the same sorts of products that were being sold by the Canadian trade or business in Canada, the income generated by that activity would be treated as earned in connection with the Canadian trade or business. Income is considered "incidental" to a trade or business if, for example, it arises from the short-term investment of working capital of the resident in securities issued by persons in the State of source.

An item of income may be considered to be earned in connection with or to be incidental to an active trade or business in the United States or Canada even though the resident claiming the benefits derives the income directly or indirectly through one or more other persons that are residents of the other Contracting State. Thus, for example, a Canadian resident could claim benefits with respect to an item of income earned by a U.S. operating subsidiary but derived by the Canadian resident indirectly through a wholly-owned U.S. holding company interposed between it and the operating subsidiary. This language would also permit a resident to derive income from the other Contracting State through one or more residents of that other State that it does not wholly own. For example, a Canadian partnership in which three unrelated Canadian companies each hold a one-third interest could form a wholly-owned U.S. holding company with a U.S. operating subsidiary. The "directly or indirectly" language would allow otherwise unavailable treaty benefits to be claimed with respect to income derived by the three Canadian partners through the U.S. holding company, even if the partners were not considered to be related to the U.S. holding company under the principles of Code section 482.

As described above, income that is derived in connection with, or is incidental to, an active trade or business in a Contracting State, must pass the substantiality requirement to qualify for benefits under the Convention. The trade or business must be substantial in relation to the activity in the other Contracting State that gave rise to the income in respect of which benefits under the Convention are being claimed. To be considered substantial, it is not necessary that the trade or business be as large as the income-generating activity. The trade or business cannot, however, in terms of income, assets, or other similar measures, represent only a very small percentage of the size of the activity in the other State.

The substantiality requirement is intended to prevent treaty shopping. For example, a third-country resident may want to acquire a U.S. company that manufactures television sets for worldwide markets; however, since its country of residence has no tax treaty with the United States, any dividends generated by the investment would be subject to a U.S. withholding tax of 30%. Absent a substantiality test, the investor could establish a Canadian corporation that would operate a small outlet in Canada to sell a few of the television sets manufactured by the U.S. company and earn a very small amount of income. That Canadian corporation could then acquire the U.S. manufacturer with capital provided by the third-country resident and produce a very large number of sets for sale in several countries, generating a much larger amount of income. It might attempt to argue that the U.S.-source income is generated from business activities in the United States related to the television sales activity of the Canadian parent and that the dividend income should be subject to U.S. tax at the 5% rate provided by Article X (Dividends) of the Convention. However, the substantiality test would not be met in this example, so the dividends would remain subject to withholding in the United States at a rate of 30%.

It is expected that if a person qualifies for benefits under one of the tests of paragraph 2, no inquiry will be made into qualification for benefits under paragraph 3. Upon satisfaction of any of the tests of paragraph 2, any income derived by the beneficial owner from the other Contracting State is entitled to treaty benefits. Under paragraph 3, however, the test is applied separately to each item of income.

Technical Explanation [1995 Protocol]: *Active trade or business test*

Paragraph 3 provides an eligibility test for benefits for residents of Canada that are not qualifying persons under paragraph 2. This is the so-called "active trade or business" test. Unlike the tests of paragraph 2, the active trade or business test looks not solely at the characteristics of the person deriving the income, but also at the nature of the activity engaged in by that person and the connection between the income and that activity. Under the active trade or business test, a resident of Canada deriving an item of income from the United States is entitled to benefits with respect to that income if that person (or a person related to that person under the principles of *Internal Revenue Code* section 482) is engaged in an active trade or business in Canada and the income in question is derived in connection with, or is incidental to, that trade or business.

Income that is derived in connection with, or is incidental to, the business of making or managing investments will not qualify for benefits under this provision, unless those investment activities are carried on with customers in the ordinary course of the business of a bank, insurance company, registered securities dealer, or deposit-taking financial institution.

Income is considered derived "in connection" with an active trade or business in the United States if, for example, the income-generating activity in the United States is "upstream," "downstream," or parallel to that conducted in Canada. Thus, if the U.S. activity consisted of selling the output of a Canadian manufacturer or providing inputs to the manufacturing process, or of manufacturing or selling in the United States the same sorts of products that were being sold by the Canadian trade or business in Canada, the income generated by that activity would be treated as earned in connection with the Canadian trade or business. Income is considered "incidental" to the Canadian trade or business if, for example, it arises from the short-term investment of working capital of the Canadian resident in U.S. securities.

An item of income will be considered to be earned in connection with or to be incidental to an active trade or business in Canada if the income is derived by the resident of Canada claiming the benefits directly or indirectly through one or more other persons that are residents of the United States. Thus, for example, a Canadian resident could claim benefits with respect to an item of income earned by a U.S. operating subsidiary but derived by the Canadian resident indirectly through a wholly-owned U.S. holding company interposed between it and the operating subsidiary. This language would also permit a Canadian resident to derive income from the United States through one or more U.S. residents that it does not wholly own. For example, a Canadian partnership in which three unrelated Canadian companies each hold a one-third interest could form a wholly-owned U.S. holding company with a U.S. operating subsidiary. The "directly or indirectly" language would allow otherwise available treaty benefits to be claimed with respect to income derived by the three Canadian partners through the U.S. holding company, even if the partners were not considered to be related to the U.S. holding company under the principles of *Internal Revenue Code* section 482.

Income that is derived in connection with, or is incidental to, an active trade or business in Canada, must pass an additional test to qualify for U.S. treaty benefits. The trade or business in Canada must be substantial in relation to the activity in the United States that gave rise to the income in respect of which treaty benefits are being claimed. To be considered substantial, it is not necessary that the Canadian trade or business be as large as the U.S. income-generating activity. The Canadian trade or business cannot, however, in terms of income, assets, or other similar measures, represent only a very small percentage of the size of the U.S. activity.

The substantiality requirement is intended to prevent treaty-shopping. For example, a third-country resident may want to acquire a U.S. company that manufactures television sets for worldwide markets; however, since its country of residence has no tax treaty with the United States, any dividends generated by the investment would be subject to a U.S. withholding tax of 30%. Absent a substantiality test, the investor could establish a Canadian corporation that would operate a small outlet in Canada to sell a few of the television sets manufactured by the U.S. company and earn a very small amount of income. That Canadian corporation could then acquire the U.S. manufacturer with capital provided by the third-country resident and produce a very large number of sets for sale in several countries, generating a much larger amount of income. It might attempt to argue that the U.S. source income is generated from business activities in the United States related to the television sales activity of the Canadian parent and that the dividend income should be subject to U.S. tax at the 5% rate provided by Article X of the Convention, as amended by the Protocol. However, the substantiality test would not be met in this example, so the dividends would remain subject to withholding in the United States at a rate of 30%.

In general, it is expected that if a person qualifies for benefits under one of the tests of paragraph 2, no inquiry will be made into qualification for benefits under paragraph 3. Upon satisfaction of any of the tests of paragraph 2, any income derived by the beneficial owner from the other Contracting State is entitled to treaty benefits. Under paragraph 3, however, the test is applied separately to each item of income.

4. A company that is a resident of a Contracting State shall also be entitled to the benefits of Articles X (Dividends), XI (Interest) and XII (Royalties) if:

(a) its shares that represent more than 90 percent of the aggregate vote and value of all of its shares and at least 50 percent of the vote and value of any disproportionate class of shares (in neither case including debt substitute shares) are owned, directly or indirectly, by persons each of whom is a qualifying person or a person who:

(i) is a resident of a country with which the other Contracting State has a comprehensive income tax convention and is entitled to all of the benefits provided by that other State under that convention;

(ii) would qualify for benefits under paragraphs 2 or 3 if that person were a resident of the first-mentioned State (and, for the purposes of paragraph 3, if the business it carried on in the country of which it is a resident were carried on by it in the first-mentioned State); and

(iii) would be entitled to a rate of tax in the other Contracting State under the convention between that person's country of residence and that other State, in respect of the particular class of income for which benefits are being claimed under this Convention, that is at least as low as the rate applicable under this Convention; and

(b) the amount of the expenses deductible from gross income (as determined in the company's State of residence) that are paid or payable by the company for its preceding fiscal period (or, in the case of its first fiscal period, that period) directly or indirectly to persons that are not qualifying persons is less than 50 percent of the company's gross income for that period.

Notes: See Notes to para. 1. See Brebber & Guedikian, "The Fifth Protocol to the Canada-US Treaty: Derivative Benefits for Canadian Businesses", 2008 Cdn Tax Foundation conference report, 18:1-23; VIEWS docs 2009-0317941E5, 2012-0471921R3.

Art. XXIX-A:4 amended by 2007 Protocol, effective on the same basis as the amendment to para. 1.

Definitions: "business" — ITCIA 3, ITA 248(1); "company" — Art. III:1(f); "debt substitute share" — Art. XXIX-A:5(a); "disproportionate class" — Art. XXIX-A:5(b); "fiscal period" — ITCIA 3, ITA 249.1; "person" — Art. III:1(e), ITCIA 3, *Interpretation Act* 35(1); "qualifying person" — Art. XXIX-A:2; "resident" — Art. IV; "share" — ITCIA 3, ITA 248(1); "State" — Art. III:1(i).

Technical Explanation [2007 Protocol]: Paragraph 4 provides a limited "derivative benefits" test that entitles a company that is a resident of the United States or Canada to the benefits of Articles X (Dividends), XI (Interest), and XII (Royalties), even if the company is not a qualifying person and does not satisfy the active trade or business test of paragraph 3. In general, a derivative benefits test entitles the resident of a Contracting State to treaty benefits if the owner of the resident would have been entitled to the same benefit had the income in question been earned directly by that owner. To qualify under this paragraph, the company must satisfy both the ownership test in subparagraph 4(a) and the base erosion test of subparagraph 4(b).

Under subparagraph 4(a), the derivative benefits ownership test requires that the company's shares representing more than 90% of the aggregate vote and value of all of the shares of the company, and at least 50% of the vote and value of any disproportionate class of shares, in neither case including debt substitute shares, be owned directly or indirectly by persons each of whom is either (i) a qualifying person or (ii) another person that satisfies each of three tests. The three tests of subparagraph 4(a) that must be satisfied by these other persons are as follows:

First, the other person must be a resident of a third State with which the Contracting State that is granting benefits has a comprehensive income tax convention. The other person must be entitled to all of the benefits under that convention. Thus, if the person fails to satisfy the limitation on benefits tests, if any, of that convention, no benefits would be granted under this paragraph. Qualification for benefits under an active trade or business test does not suffice for these purposes, because that test grants benefits only for certain items of income, not for all purposes of the convention.

Second, the other person must be a person that would qualify for benefits with respect to the item of income for which benefits are sought under one or more of the tests of paragraph 2 or 3 of Article XXIX A, if the person were a resident of the Contracting State that is not providing benefits for the item of income and, for purposes of paragraph 3, the business were carried on in that State. For example, a person resident in a third country would be deemed to be a person that would qualify under the publicly-traded test of paragraph 2 of Article XXIX A if the principal class of its shares were primarily and regularly traded on a stock exchange recognized either under the Convention between the United States and Canada or under the treaty between the Contracting State granting benefits and the third country. Similarly, a company resident in a third country would be deemed to satisfy the ownership/base erosion test of paragraph 2 under this hypothetical analysis if, for example, it were wholly owned by an individual resident in that third country and the company's tax base were not substantially eroded by payments (directly or indirectly) to nonqualifying persons.

The third requirement is that the rate of tax on the item of income in respect of which benefits are sought must be at least as low under the convention between the person's country of residence and the Contracting State granting benefits as it is under the Convention.

Subparagraph 4(b) sets forth the base erosion test. This test requires that the amount of expenses that are paid or payable by the company in question, directly or indirectly, to persons that are not qualifying persons under the Convention, and that are deductible from gross income (with both deductibility and gross income as determined under the tax laws of the State of residence of the company), be less than 50% of the gross income of the company. This test is applied for the fiscal period immediately preceding the period for which the test is being applied. If it is the first fiscal period of the person, the test is applied for the current period. This test is qualitatively the same as the base erosion test of subparagraph 2(e).

Technical Explanation [1995 Protocol]: *Derivative benefits test*

Paragraph 4 of Article XXIX A contains a so-called "derivative benefits" rule not generally found in U.S. treaties. This rule was included in the Protocol because of the special economic relationship between the United States and Canada and the close coordination between the tax administrations of the two countries.

Under the derivative benefits rule, a Canadian resident company may receive the benefits of Articles X (Dividends), XI (Interest), and XII (Royalties), even if the company is not a qualifying person and does not satisfy the active trade or business test of paragraph 3. To qualify under this paragraph, the Canadian company must satisfy both (i) the base erosion test under subparagraph (e) of paragraph 2, and (ii) an ownership test.

The derivative benefits ownership test requires that shares (other than debt substitute shares) representing more than 90% of the vote and value of the Canadian company be owned directly or indirectly by either (i) qualifying persons or U.S. citizens or residents, or (ii) other persons that satisfy each of three tests. The three tests that must be satisfied by these other persons are as follows:

First, the person must be a resident of a third State with which the United States has a comprehensive income tax convention and be entitled to all of the benefits under that convention. Thus, if the person fails to satisfy the limitation on benefits tests, if any, of that convention, no benefits would be granted under this paragraph. Qualification for benefits under an active trade or business test does not suffice for these purposes, because that test grants benefits only for certain items of income, not for all purposes of the convention.

Second, the person must be a person that would qualify for benefits with respect to the item of income for which benefits are sought under one or more of the tests of paragraph 2 or 3 of this Convention, if the person were a resident of Canada and, for purposes of paragraph 3, the business were carried on in Canada. For example, a person resident in a third country would be deemed to be a person that would qualify under the publicly-traded test of paragraph 2 of this Convention if the principal class of its shares were substantially and regularly traded on a stock exchange recognized either under the treaty between the United States and Canada or under the treaty between the United States and the third country. Similarly, a company resident in a third country would be deemed to satisfy the ownership/base erosion test of paragraph 2 under this hypothetical analysis if, for example, it were wholly owned by an individual resident in that third country and most of its deductible payments were made to individual residents of that country (i.e., it satisfied base erosion).

The third requirement is that the rate of U.S. withholding tax on the item of income in respect of which benefits are sought must be at least as low under the convention between the person's country of residence and the United States as under this Convention.

5. For the purposes of this Article,

(a) the term "**debt substitute share**" means:

(i) a share described in paragraph (e) of the definition "term preferred share" in the Income Tax Act, as it may be amended from time to time without changing the general principle thereof; and

(ii) such other type of share as may be agreed upon by the competent authorities of the Contracting States.

(b) the term "**disproportionate class of shares**" means any class of shares of a company resident in one of the Contracting States that entitles the shareholder to disproportionately higher participation, through dividends, redemption payments or other-

wise, in the earnings generated in the other State by particular assets or activities of the company;

(c) the term "**disproportionate interest in a trust**" means any interest in a trust resident in one of the Contracting States that entitles the interest holder to disproportionately higher participation in, or claim to, the earnings generated in the other State by particular assets or activities of the trust;

(d) the term "**not-for-profit organization**" of a Contracting State means an entity created or established in that State and that is, by reason of its not-for-profit status, generally exempt from income taxation in that State, and includes a private foundation, charity, trade union, trade association or similar organization;

(e) the term "**principal class of shares**" of a company means the ordinary or common shares of the company, provided that such class of shares represents the majority of the voting power and value of the company. If no single class of ordinary or common shares represents the majority of the aggregate voting power and value of the company, the "principal class of shares" are those classes that in the aggregate represent a majority of the aggregate voting power and value of the company; and

(f) the term "**recognized stock exchange**" means:

(i) the NASDAQ System owned by the National Association of Securities Dealers, Inc. and any stock exchange registered with the Securities and Exchange Commission as a national securities exchange for purposes of the Securities Exchange Act of 1934;

(ii) Canadian stock exchanges that are "prescribed stock exchanges" or "designated stock exchanges" under the *Income Tax Act*; and

(iii) any other stock exchange agreed upon by the Contracting States in an exchange of notes or by the competent authorities of the Contracting States.

Notes: For designated stock exchanges, see ITA 262. Before Dec. 14/07, the term "prescribed stock exchange" was used (see Reg. 3200, 3201).

Art. XXIX-A:5 amended by 2007 Protocol, effective on the same basis as the amendment to para. 1.

Definitions: "competent authority" — Art. III:1(g); "designated stock exchange" — ITA 248(1), 262, ITCIA 3; "private foundation" — ITCIA 3, ITA 248(1); "State" — Art. III:1(i); "term preferred share" — ITCIA 3, ITA 248(1).

Technical Explanation [2007 Protocol]: Paragraph 5 defines certain terms used in the Article. These terms were identified and discussed in connection with new paragraph 2, above.

6. Where a person that is a resident of a Contracting State is not entitled under the preceding provisions of this Article to the benefits provided under this Convention by the other Contracting State, the competent authority of that other State shall, upon that person's request, determine on the basis of all factors including the history, structure, ownership and operations of that person whether:

(a) its creation and existence did not have as a principal purpose the obtaining of benefits under this Convention that would not otherwise be available; or

(b) it would not be appropriate, having regard to the purpose of this Article, to deny the benefits of this Convention to that person.

The person shall be granted the benefits of this Convention by that other State where the competent authority determines that subparagraph (a) or (b) applies.

Notes: Although the opening words use "shall", it is unclear whether the competent authority can be forced to act by Federal Court judicial review application.

See Notes to Art. XXIX-A:1 for CRA guidelines.

Art. XXIX-A:6 amended by 2007 Protocol, effective on the same basis as the amendment to para. 1, to apply to both countries.

Definitions: "competent authority" — Art. III:1(g); "person" — Art. III:1(e), ITCIA 3, *Interpretation Act* 35(1); "resident" — Art. IV; "State" — Art. III:1(i).

I.T. Technical News: 41 (5th protocol to the Canada-US Tax Convention — limitation on benefits).

Technical Explanation [2007 Protocol]: Paragraph 6 provides that when a resident of a Contracting State derives income from the other Contracting State and is not entitled to the benefits of the Convention under other provisions of the Article, benefits may, nevertheless be granted at the discretion of the competent authority of the other Contracting State. This determination can be made with respect to all benefits under the Convention or on an item by item basis. In making a determination under this paragraph, the competent authority will take into account all relevant facts and circumstances relating to the person requesting the benefits. In particular, the competent authority will consider the history, structure, ownership (including ultimate beneficial ownership), and operations of the person. In addition, the competent authority is to consider (1) whether the creation and existence of the person did not have as a principal purpose obtaining treaty benefits that would not otherwise be available to the person, and (2) whether it would not be appropriate, in view of the purpose of the Article, to deny benefits. If the competent authority of the other Contracting State determines that either of these two standards is satisfied, benefits shall be granted.

For purposes of implementing new paragraph 6, a taxpayer will be permitted to present his case to the competent authority for an advance determination based on a full disclosure of all pertinent information. The taxpayer will not be required to wait until it has been determined that benefits are denied under one of the other provisions of the Article. It also is expected that, if and when the competent authority determines that benefits are to be allowed, they will be allowed retroactively to the time of entry into force of the relevant provision of the Convention or the establishment of the structure in question, whichever is later (assuming that the taxpayer also qualifies under the relevant facts for the earlier period).

Technical Explanation [1995 Protocol]: *Competent authority discretion*

Paragraph 6 provides that when a resident of Canada derives income from the United States and is not entitled to the benefits of the Convention under other provisions of the Article, benefits may, nevertheless be granted at the discretion of the U.S. competent authority. In making a determination under this paragraph, the competent authority will take into account all relevant facts and circumstances relating to the person requesting the benefits. In particular, the competent authority will consider the history, structure, ownership (including ultimate beneficial ownership), and operations of the person. In addition, the competent authority is to consider (1) whether the creation and existence of the person did not have as a principal purpose obtaining treaty benefits that would not otherwise be available to the person, and (2) whether it would not be appropriate, in view of the purpose of the Article, to deny benefits. The paragraph specifies that if the U.S. competent authority determines that either of these two standards is satisfied, benefits shall be granted.

For purposes of implementing paragraph 6, a taxpayer will be expected to present his case to the competent authority for an advance determination based on the facts. The taxpayer will not be required to wait until it has been determined that benefits are denied under one of the other provisions of the Article. It also is expected that, if and when the competent authority determines that benefits are to be allowed, they will be allowed retroactively to the time of entry into force of the relevant treaty provision or the establishment of the structure in question, whichever is later (assuming that the taxpayer also qualifies under the relevant facts for the earlier period).

7. It is understood that this Article shall not be construed as restricting in any manner the right of a Contracting State to deny benefits under this Convention where it can reasonably be concluded that to do otherwise would result in an abuse of the provisions of this Convention.

Notes: Art. XXIX-A:7 amended by 2007 Protocol, effective on the same basis as the amendment to para. 1.

Definitions: "State" — Art. III:1(i).

Technical Explanation [2007 Protocol]: New paragraph 7 is in substance similar to paragraph 7 of Article XXIX A of the existing Convention and clarifies the application of general anti-abuse provisions. New paragraph 7 provides that paragraphs 1 through 6 of Article XXIX A shall not be construed as limiting in any manner the right of a Contracting State to deny benefits under the Convention where it can reasonably be concluded that to do otherwise would result in an abuse of the provisions of the Convention. This provision permits a Contracting State to rely on general anti-avoidance rules to counter arrangements involving treaty shopping through the other Contracting State.

Thus, Canada may apply its domestic law rules to counter abusive arrangements involving "treaty shopping" through the United States, and the United States may apply its substance-over-form and anti-conduit rules, for example, in relation to Canadian residents. This principle is recognized by the OECD in the Commentaries to its Model Tax Convention on Income and on Capital, and the United States and Canada agree that it is inherent in the Convention. The statement of this principle explicitly in the Protocol is not intended to suggest that the principle is not also inherent in other tax conventions concluded by the United States or Canada.

Technical Explanation [1995 Protocol]: *General anti-abuse provisions*

Paragraph 7 was added at Canada's request to confirm that the specific provisions of Article XXIX A and the fact that these provisions apply only for the purposes of the application of the Convention by the United States should not be construed so as to limit the right of each Contracting State to invoke applicable anti-abuse rules. Thus, for example, Canada remains free to apply such rules to counter abusive arrangements involving "treaty-shopping" through the United States, and the United States remains free to apply its substance-over-form and anti-conduit rules, for example, in relation to Canadian residents. This principle is recognized by the Organization for Economic Co-operation and Development in the Commentaries to its Model Tax Convention on Income and on Capital, and the United States and Canada agree that it is inherent in the Convention. The agreement to state this principle explicitly in the Protocol is not intended to suggest that the principle is not also inherent in other tax conventions, including the current Convention with Canada.

Notes [Art. XXIX-A]: Art. XXIX-A added by 1995 Protocol, generally effective 1996.

Article XXIX-B — Taxes Imposed by Reason of Death

1. Where the property of an individual who is a resident of a Contracting State passes by reason of the individual's death to an organization that is referred to in paragraph 1 of Article XXI (Exempt Organizations) and that is a resident of the other Contracting State,

(a) if the individual is a resident of the United States and the organization is a resident of Canada, the tax consequences in the United States arising out of the passing of the property shall apply as if the organization were a resident of the United States; and

(b) if the individual is a resident of Canada and the organization is a resident of the United States, the tax consequences in Canada arising out of the passing of the property shall apply as if the individual had disposed of the property for proceeds equal to an amount elected on behalf of the individual for this purpose (in a manner specified by the competent authority of Canada), which amount shall be no less than the individual's cost of the property as determined for purposes of Canadian tax and no greater than the fair market value of the property.

Related Provisions: See at end of Art. XXIX-B.

Notes: Art. XXIX-B:1 amended by 2007 Protocol, for taxable years beginning after 2008; but for taxes withheld at source, for amounts paid or credited after Jan. 2009.

The amendment is a substantive negative change. See Kevin Gluc, "US Estate Tax Charitable Deduction", 15(11) *Canadian Tax Highlights* (ctf.ca) 2-3 (Nov. 2007); Beth Webel, "Estate Tax Update", 157 *The Estate Planner* (CCH) 4 (Feb. 2008).

See also Notes to para. 3.

Definitions: "individual", "property" — ITCIA 3, ITA 248(1); "resident" — Art. IV; "State" — Art. III:1(i); "United States" — Art. III:1(b).

Technical Explanation [2007 Protocol]: Article 26 of the Protocol replaces paragraphs 1 and 5 of Article XXIX B (Taxes Imposed by Reason of Death) of the Convention. In addition, paragraph 7 of the General Note provides certain clarifications for purposes of paragraphs 6 and 7 of Article XXIX B.

Paragraph 1 of Article XXIX B of the existing Convention generally addresses the situation where a resident of a Contracting State passes property by reason of the individual's death to an organization referred to in paragraph 1 of Article XXI (Exempt Organizations) of the Convention. The paragraph provided that the tax consequences in a Contracting State arising out of the passing of the property shall apply as if the organization were a resident of that State.

The Protocol replaces paragraph 1, and the changes set forth in new paragraph 1 are intended to specifically address questions that have arisen about the application of former paragraph 1 where property of an individual who is a resident of Canada passes by reason of the individual's death to a charitable organization in the United States that is not a "registered charity" under Canadian law. Under one view, paragraph 1 of Article XXIX B requires Canada to treat the passing of the property as a contribution to a "registered charity" and thus to allow all of the same deductions for Canadian tax purposes as if the U.S. charity had been a "registered charity" under Canadian law. Under another view, paragraph 6 of Article XXI (Exempt Organizations) of the Convention continues to limit the amount of the income tax charitable deduction in Canada to the individual's income arising in the United States. The changes set forth in new paragraph 1 are intended to provide relief from the Canadian tax on gain deemed recognized by reason of death that would otherwise give rise to Canadian tax when the individual passes the property to a charitable organization in the United States, but, for purposes of the separate Canadian income tax, do not eliminate the limitation under paragraph 6 of Article XXI on the amount of the deduction in Canada for the charitable donation to the individual's income arising in the United States.

As revised, paragraph 1 is divided into two subparagraphs. New subparagraph 1(a) applies where property of an individual who is a resident of the United States passes by reason of the individual's death to a qualifying exempt organization that is a resident of Canada. In such case, the tax consequences in the United States arising from the passing of such property apply as if the organization were a resident of the United States. A bequest by a U.S. citizen or U.S. resident (as defined for estate tax purposes under the Code) to an exempt organization generally is deductible for U.S. federal estate tax purposes under Code section 2055, without regard to whether the organization is a U.S. corporation. Thus, generally, the individual's estate will be entitled to a charitable deduction for Federal estate tax purposes equal to the value of the property transferred to the organization. Generally, the effect is that no Federal estate tax will be imposed on the value of the property.

New subparagraph 1(b) applies where property of an individual who is a resident of Canada passes by reason of the individual's death to a qualifying exempt organization that is a resident of the United States. In such case, for purposes of the Canadian capital gains tax imposed at death, the tax consequences arising out of the passing of the property shall apply as if the individual disposed of the property for proceeds equal to an amount elected on behalf of the individual. For this purpose, the amount elected shall be no less than the individual's cost of the property as determined for purposes of Canadian tax, and no greater than the fair market value of the property. The manner in which the individual's representative shall make this election shall be specified by the competent authority of Canada. Generally, in the event of a full exercise of the election under new subparagraph 1(b), no capital gains tax will be imposed in Canada by reason of the death with regard to that property.

New paragraph 1 does not address the situation in which a resident of one Contracting State bequeaths property with a situs in the other Contracting State to a qualifying exempt organization in the Contracting State of the decedent's residence. In such a situation, the other Contracting State may impose tax by reason of death, for example, if the property is real property situated in that State.

Technical Explanation [1995 Protocol]: *In general*

Article 19 of the Protocol adds to the Convention a new Article XXIX B (Taxes Imposed by Reason of Death). The purpose of Article XXIX B is to better coordinate the operation of the death tax regimes of the two Contracting States. Such coordination is necessary because the United States imposes an estate tax, while Canada now applies an income tax on gains deemed realized at death rather than an estate tax. Article XXIX B also contains other provisions designed to alleviate death taxes in certain situations.

For purposes of new Article XXIX B, the term "resident" has the meaning provided by Article IV (Residence) of the Convention, as amended by Article 3 of the Protocol. The meaning of the term "resident" for purposes of Article XXIX B, therefore, differs in some respects from its meaning under the estate, gift, and generation-skipping transfer tax provisions of the *Internal Revenue Code*.

Charitable bequests

Paragraph 1 of new Article XXIX B facilitates certain charitable bequests. It provides that a Contracting State shall accord the same death tax treatment to a bequest by an individual resident in one of the Contracting States to a qualifying exempt organization resident in the other Contracting State as it would have accorded if the organization had been a resident of the first Contracting State. The organizations covered by this provision are those referred to in paragraph 1 of Article XXI (Exempt Organizations) of the Convention. A bequest by a U.S. citizen or U.S. resident (as defined for estate tax purposes under the *Internal Revenue Code*) to such an exempt organization generally is deductible for U.S. estate tax purposes under section 2055 of the *Internal Revenue Code*, without regard to whether the organization is a U.S. corporation. However, if the decedent is not a U.S. citizen or U.S. resident (as defined for estate tax purposes under the *Internal Revenue Code*), such a bequest is deductible for U.S. estate tax purposes, under section 2106(a)(2) of the *Internal Revenue Code*, only if the recipient organization is a U.S. corporation. Under paragraph 1 of Article XXIX B, a U.S. estate tax deduction also will be allowed for a bequest by a Canadian resident (as defined under Article IV (Residence)) to a qualifying exempt organization that is a Canadian corporation. However, paragraph 1 does not allow a deduction for U.S. estate tax purposes with respect to any transfer of property that is not subject to U.S. estate tax.

2. In determining the estate tax imposed by the United States, the estate of an individual (other than a citizen of the United States) who was a resident of Canada at the time of the individual's death shall be allowed a unified credit equal to the greater of

   (a) the amount that bears the same ratio to the credit allowed under the law of the United States to the estate of a citizen of the United States as the value of the part of the individual's gross estate that at the time of the individual's death is situated in the United States bears to the value of the individual's entire gross estate wherever situated; and

   (b) the unified credit allowed to the estate of a nonresident not a citizen of the United States under the law of the United States.

The amount of any unified credit otherwise allowable under this paragraph shall be reduced by the amount of any credit previously allowed with respect to any gift made by the individual. The credit otherwise allowable under subparagraph (a) shall be allowed only if all information necessary for the verification and computation of the credit is provided.

Related Provisions: See at end of Art. XXIX-B.

Notes: Note that this provides relief from estate tax, but not from the US gift tax that is otherwise harmonized with the estate tax.

See Wolfe Goodman, "Effect of U.S. Tax Reform on Canadians Owning U.S. Property", *Goodman on Estate Planning* (Federated Press) 808-09 (2001).

See also Notes to para. 3.

Definitions: "Canada" — Art. III:1(a), ITCIA 5; "estate", "individual", "non-resident" — ITCIA 3, ITA 248(1); "resident" — Art. IV; "United States" — Art. III:1(b).

Technical Explanation [1995 Protocol]: *Unified credit*

Paragraph 2 of Article XXIX B grants a "pro rata" unified credit to the estate of a Canadian resident decedent, for purposes of computing U.S. estate tax. Although the Congress anticipated the negotiation of such pro rata unified credits in *Internal Revenue Code* section 2102(c)(3)(A), this is the first convention in which the United States has agreed to give such a credit. However, certain exemption provisions of existing estate and gift tax conventions have been interpreted as providing a pro rata unified credit.

Under the *Internal Revenue Code*, the estate of a nonresident not a citizen of the United States is subject to U.S. estate tax only on its U.S. situs assets and is entitled to a unified credit of $13,000, while the estate of a U.S. citizen or U.S. resident is subject to U.S. estate tax on its entire worldwide assets and is entitled to a unified credit of $192,800. (For purposes of these *Internal Revenue Code* provisions, the term "resident" has the meaning provided for estate tax purposes under the *Internal Revenue Code*.) A lower unified credit is provided for the former category of estates because it is assumed that the estate of a nonresident not a citizen generally will hold fewer U.S. situs assets, as a percentage of the estate's total assets, and thus will have a lower U.S. estate tax liability. The pro rata unified credit provisions of paragraph 2 increase the credit allowed to the estate of a Canadian resident decedent to an amount between $13,000 and $192,800 in appropriate cases, to take into account the extent to which the assets of the estate are situated in the United States. Paragraph 2 provides that the amount of the unified credit allowed to the estate of a Canadian resident decedent will in no event be less than the $13,000 allowed under the *Internal Revenue Code* to the estate of a nonresident not a citizen of the United States (subject to the adjustment for prior gift tax unified credits, discussed below). Paragraph 2 does not apply to the estates of U.S. citizen decedents, whether resident in Canada or elsewhere, because such estates receive a unified credit of $192,800 under the *Internal Revenue Code*.

Subject to the adjustment for gift tax unified credits, the pro rata credit allowed under paragraph 2 is determined by multiplying $192,800 by a fraction, the numerator of which is the value of the part of the gross estate situated in the United States and the denominator of which is the value of the entire gross estate wherever situated. Thus, if half of the entire gross estate (by value) of a decedent who was a resident and citizen of Canada were situated in the United States, the estate would be entitled to a pro rata unified credit of $96,400 (provided that the U.S. estate tax due is not less than that amount). For purposes of the denominator, the entire gross estate wherever situated (i.e., the worldwide estate, determined under U.S. domestic law) is to be taken into account for purposes of the computation. For purposes of the numerator, an estate's assets will be treated as situated in the United States if they are so treated under U.S. domestic law. However, if enacted, a technical correction now pending before the Congress will amend U.S. domestic law to clarify that assets will not be treated as U.S. situs assets for purposes of the pro rata unified credit computation if the United States is precluded from taxing them by reason of a treaty obligation. This technical correction will affect the interpretation of both this paragraph 2 and the analogous provisions in existing conventions. As currently proposed, it will take effect on the date of enactment.

Paragraph 2 restricts the availability of the pro rata unified credit in two respects. First, the amount of the unified credit otherwise allowable under paragraph 2 is reduced by the amount of any unified credit previously allowed against U.S. gift tax imposed on any gift by the decedent. This rule reflects the fact that, under U.S. domestic law, a U.S. citizen or U.S. resident individual is allowed a unified credit against the U.S. gift tax on lifetime transfers. However, as a result of the estate tax computation, the individual is entitled only to a total unified credit of $192,800, and the amount of the unified credit available for use against U.S. estate tax on the individual's estate is effectively reduced by the amount of any unified credit that has been allowed in respect of gifts by the individual. This rule is reflected by reducing the amount of the pro rata unified credit otherwise allowed to the estate of a decedent individual under paragraph 2 by the amount of any unified credit previously allowed with respect to lifetime gifts by that individual. This reduction will be relevant only in rare cases, where the decedent made gifts subject to the U.S. gift tax while a U.S. citizen or U.S. resident (as defined under the *Internal Revenue Code* for U.S. gift tax purposes).

Paragraph 2 also conditions allowance of the pro rata unified credit upon the provision of all information necessary to verify and compute the credit. Thus, for example, the estate's representatives will be required to demonstrate satisfactorily both the value of the worldwide estate and the value of the U.S. portion of the estate. Substantiation requirements also apply, of course, with respect to other provisions of the Protocol and the Convention. However, the negotiators believed it advisable to emphasize the substantiation requirements in connection with this provision, because the computation of the pro rata unified credit involves certain information not otherwise relevant for U.S. estate tax purposes.

In addition, the amount of the pro rata unified credit is limited to the amount of U.S. estate tax imposed on the estate. See section 2102(c)(4) of the *Internal Revenue Code*.

3. In determining the estate tax imposed by the United States on an individual's estate with respect to property that passes to the surviving spouse of the individual (within the meaning of the law of the United States) and that would qualify for the estate tax marital deduction under the law of the United States if the surviving spouse were a citizen of the United States and all applicable elections were properly made (in this paragraph and in paragraph 4 referred to as "qualifying property"), a non-refundable credit computed in accordance with the provisions of paragraph 4 shall be allowed in addition to the unified credit allowed to the estate under paragraph 2 or under the law of the United States, provided that

(a) the individual was at the time of death a citizen of the United States or a resident of either Contracting State;

(b) the surviving spouse was at the time of the individual's death a resident of either Contracting State;

(c) if both the individual and the surviving spouse were residents of the United States at the time of the individual's death, one or both was a citizen of Canada; and

(d) the executor of the decedent's estate elects the benefits of this paragraph and waives irrevocably the benefits of any estate tax marital deduction that would be allowed under the law of the United States on a United States Federal estate tax return filed for the individual's estate by the date on which a qualified domestic trust election could be made under the law of the United States.

Related Provisions: See at end of Art. XXIX-B.

Notes: For discussion of Art. XXIX-B see Park & Gandhi, "Review of US-Canada Income Tax Treaty Art. XXIX B", 11(2) *BorderCrossings* (Carswell) 1-6 (Oct. 2018).

Art. XXIX-B cannot create a provincial foreign tax credit: VIEWS doc 2010-0379381E5.

Definitions: "Canada" — Art. III:1(a), ITCIA 5; "estate", "individual", "property" — ITCIA 3, ITA 248(1); "qualified domestic trust" — *Internal Revenue Code* s. 2056A(a); "resident" — Art. IV; "surviving spouse" — *Internal Revenue Code* s. 2(a); "United States" — Art. III:1(b).

Technical Explanation [1995 Protocol]: *Marital credit*

Paragraph 3 of Article XXIX B allows a special "marital credit" against U.S. estate tax in respect of certain transfers to a surviving spouse. The purpose of this marital credit is to alleviate, in appropriate cases, the impact of the estate tax marital deduction restrictions enacted by the Congress in the *Technical and Miscellaneous Revenue Act* of 1988 ("TAMRA"). It is the firm position of the U.S. Treasury Department that the TAMRA provisions do not violate the non-discrimination provisions of this Convention or any other convention to which the United States is a party. This is because the estate — not the surviving spouse — is the taxpayer, and the TAMRA provisions treat the estates of nonresidents not citizens of the United States in the same manner as the estates of U.S. citizen and U.S. resident decedents. However, the U.S. negotiators believed that it was not inappropriate, in the context of the Protocol, to ease the impact of those TAMRA provisions upon certain estates of limited value.

Paragraph 3 allows a non-refundable marital credit in addition to the pro rata unified credit allowed under paragraph 2 (or, in the case of a U.S. citizen or U.S. resident decedent, the unified credit allowed under U.S. domestic law). However, the marital credit is allowed only in connection with transfers satisfying each of the five conditions set forth in paragraph 3. First, the property must be "qualifying property," i.e., it must pass to the surviving spouse (within the meaning of U.S. domestic law) and be property that would have qualified for the estate tax marital deduction under U.S. domestic law if the surviving spouse had been a U.S. citizen and all applicable elections specified by U.S. domestic law had been properly made. Second, the decedent must have been, at the time of death, either a resident of Canada or the United States or a citizen of the United States. Third, the surviving spouse must have been, at the time of the decedent's death, a resident of either Canada or the United States. Fourth, if both the decedent and the surviving spouse were residents of the United States at the time of the decedent's death, at least one of them must have been a citizen of Canada. Finally, to limit the benefits of paragraph 3 to relatively small estates, the executor of the decedent's estate is required to elect the benefits of paragraph 3, and to waive irrevocably the benefits of any estate tax marital deduction that would be allowed under U.S. domestic law, on a U.S. Federal estate tax return filed by the deadline for making a qualified domestic trust election under *Internal Revenue Code* section 2056A(d). In the case of the estate of a decedent for which the U.S. Federal estate tax return is filed on or before the date on which this Protocol enters into force, this election and waiver must be made on any return filed to claim a refund pursuant to the special effective date applicable to such estates (discussed below).

4. The amount of the credit allowed under paragraph 3 shall equal the lesser of

(a) the unified credit allowed under paragraph 2 or under the law of the United States (determined without regard to any credit al-

lowed previously with respect to any gift made by the individual), and

(b) the amount of estate tax that would otherwise be imposed by the United States on the transfer of qualifying property.

The amount of estate tax that would otherwise be imposed by the United States on the transfer of qualifying property shall equal the amount by which the estate tax (before allowable credits) that would be imposed by the United States if the qualifying property were included in computing the taxable estate exceeds the estate tax (before allowable credits) that would be so imposed if the qualifying property were not so included. Solely for purposes of determining other credits allowed under the law of the United States, the credit provided under paragraph 3 shall be allowed after such other credits.

Definitions: "estate", "individual" — ITCIA 3, ITA 248(1); "qualifying property" — Art. XXIX-B:3; "United States" — Art. III:1(b).

Technical Explanation [1995 Protocol]: Paragraph 4 governs the computation of the marital credit allowed under paragraph 3. It provides that the amount of the marital credit shall equal the lesser of (i) the amount of the unified credit allowed to the estate under paragraph 2 or, where applicable, under U.S. domestic law (before reduction for any gift tax unified credit), or (ii) the amount of U.S. estate tax that would otherwise be imposed on the transfer of qualifying property to the surviving spouse. For this purpose, the amount of U.S. estate tax that would otherwise be imposed on the transfer of qualifying property equals the amount by which (i) the estate tax (before allowable credits) that would be imposed if that property were included in computing the taxable estate exceeds (ii) the estate tax (before allowable credits) that would be imposed if the property were not so included. Property that, by reason of the provisions of paragraph 8 of this Article, is not subject to U.S. estate tax is not taken into account for purposes of this hypothetical computation.

Finally, paragraph 4 provides taxpayers with an ordering rule. The rule states that, solely for purposes of determining any other credits (e.g., the credits for foreign and state death taxes) that may be allowed under U.S. domestic law to the estate, the marital credit shall be allowed after such other credits.

In certain cases, the provisions of paragraphs 3 and 4 may affect the U.S. estate taxation of a trust that would meet the requirements for a qualified terminable interest property ("QTIP") election, for example, a trust with a life income interest for the surviving spouse and a remainder interest for other family members. If, in lieu of making the QTIP election and the qualified domestic trust election, the decedent's executor makes the election described in paragraph 3(d) of this Article, the provisions of *Internal Revenue Code* sections 2044 (regarding inclusion in the estate of the second spouse of certain property for which the marital deduction was previously allowed), 2056A (regarding qualified domestic trusts), and 2519 (regarding dispositions of certain life estates) will not apply. To obtain this treatment, however, the executor is required, under paragraph 3, to irrevocably waive the benefit of any marital deduction allowable under the *Internal Revenue Code* with respect to the trust.

The following examples illustrate the operation of the marital credit and its interaction with other credits. Unless otherwise stated, assume for purposes of illustration that H, the decedent, and W, his surviving spouse, are Canadian citizens resident in Canada at the time of the decedent's death. Assume further that all conditions set forth in paragraphs 2 and 3 of this Article XXIX B are satisfied (including the condition that the executor waive the estate tax marital deduction), that no deductions are available under the *Internal Revenue Code* in computing the U.S. estate tax liability, and that there are no adjusted taxable gifts within the meaning of *Internal Revenue Code* section 2001(b) or 2101(c). Also assume that the applicable U.S. domestic estate and gift tax laws are those that were in effect on the date the Protocol was signed.

Example 1. H has a worldwide gross estate of $1,200,000. He bequeaths U.S. real property worth $600,000 to W. The remainder of H's estate consists of Canadian situs property. H's estate would be entitled to a pro rata unified credit of $96,400 (= $192,800 x (600,000/1,200,000)) and to a marital credit in the same amount (the lesser of the unified credit allowed ($96,400) and the U.S. estate tax that would otherwise be imposed on the property transferred to W ($192,800 [tax on U.S. taxable estate of $600,000])). The pro rata unified credit and the marital credit combined would eliminate all U.S. estate tax with respect to the property transferred to W.

Example 2. H has a worldwide gross estate of $1,200,000, all of which is situated in the United States. He bequeaths U.S. real property worth $600,000 to W and U.S. real property worth $600,000 to a child, C. H's estate would be entitled to a pro rata unified credit of $192,800 (= $192,800 x 1,200,000/1,200,000) and to a marital credit of $192,800 (the lesser of the unified credit ($192,800) and the U.S. estate tax that would otherwise be imposed on the property transferred to W ($235,000, i.e., $427,800 [tax on U.S. taxable estate of $1,200,000] less $192,800 [tax on U.S. taxable estate of $600,000])). This would reduce the estate's total U.S. estate tax liability of $427,800 by $385,600.

Example 3. H has a worldwide gross estate of $700,000, of which $500,000 is real property situated in the United States. H bequeaths U.S. real property valued at $100,000 to W. The remainder of H's gross estate, consisting of U.S. and Canadian situs real property, is bequeathed to H's child, C. H's estate would be entitled to a pro rata unified credit of $137,714 ($192,800 x $500,000/$700,000). In addition, H's estate would be entitled to a marital credit of $34,000, which equals the lesser of the unified credit ($137,714) and $34,000 (the U.S. estate tax that would otherwise be imposed on the property transferred to W before allowance of any credits, i.e., $155,800 [tax on U.S. taxable estate of $500,000] less $121,800 [tax on U.S. taxable estate of $400,000]).

Example 4. H has a worldwide gross estate of $5,000,000, $2,000,000 of which consists of U.S. real property situated in State X. State X imposes a state death tax equal to the federal credit allowed under *Internal Revenue Code* section 2011. H bequeaths U.S. situs real property worth $1,000,000 to W and U.S. situs real property worth $1,000,000 to his child, C. The remainder of H's estate ($3,000,000) consists of Canadian situs property passing to C. H's estate would be entitled to a pro rata unified credit of $77,120 ($192,800 x $2,000,000/$5,000,000). H's estate would be entitled to a state death tax credit under *Internal Revenue Code* section 2102 of $99,600 (determined under *Internal Revenue Code* section 2011(b) with respect to an adjusted taxable estate of $1,940,000). H's estate also would be entitled to a marital credit of $77,120, which equals the lesser of the unified credit ($77,120) and $435,000 (the U.S. estate tax that would otherwise be imposed on the property transferred to W before allowance of any credits, i.e., $780,000 [tax on U.S. taxable estate of $2,000,000] less $345,800 [tax on U.S. taxable estate of $1,000,000]).

Example 5. The facts are the same as in Example 4, except that H and W are Canadian citizens who are resident in the United States at the time of H's death. Canadian Federal and provincial income taxes totalling $500,000 are imposed by reason of H's death. H's estate would be entitled to a unified credit of $192,800 and to a state death tax credit of $300,880 under *Internal Revenue Code* sections 2010 and 2011(b), respectively. Under paragraph 6 of Article XXIX B, H's estate would be entitled to a credit for the Canadian income tax imposed by reason of death, equal to the lesser of $500,000 (the Canadian taxes paid) or $1,138,272 ($2,390,800 (tax on $5,000,000 taxable estate) less total of unified and state death tax credits ($493,680) x $3,000,000/$5,000,000). H's estate also would be entitled to a marital credit of $192,800, which equals the lesser of the unified credit ($192,800) and $550,000 (the U.S. estate tax that would otherwise be imposed on the property transferred to W before allowance of any credits, i.e., $2,390,800 [tax on U.S. taxable estate of $5,000,000] less $1,840,800 [tax on U.S. taxable estate of $4,000,000]).

5. Where an individual was a resident of the United States immediately before the individual's death, for the purposes of subsections 70(5.2) and (6) of the *Income Tax Act*, both the individual and the individual's spouse shall be deemed to have been resident in Canada immediately before the individual's death. Where a trust that would be a trust described in subsection 70(6) of that Act, if its trustees that were residents or citizens of the United States or domestic corporations under the law of the United States were residents of Canada, requests the competent authority of Canada to do so, the competent authority may agree, subject to terms and conditions satisfactory to such competent authority, to treat the trust for the purposes of that Act as being resident in Canada for such time and with respect to such property as may be stipulated in the agreement.

Notes: See VIEWS doc 2009-0345911I7 (para. 5 not available on particular facts).

Art. XXIX-B:5 amended by 2007 Protocol, effective on the same basis as the amendment to para. 1, to add reference to ITA 70(5.2).

Definitions: "Canada" — Art. III:1(a), ITCIA 5; "competent authority" — Art. III:1(g); "individual" — ITCIA 3, ITA 248(1); "resident" — Art. IV; "trust" — ITCIA 3, ITA 104(1), 248(1); "United States" — Art. III:1(b).

Interpretation Bulletins: IT-305R4: Testamentary spouse trusts.

Technical Explanation [2007 Protocol]: Paragraph 2 of Article 26 of the Protocol replaces paragraph 5 of Article XXIX B of the existing Convention. The provisions of new paragraph 5 relate to the operation of Canadian law. Because Canadian law requires both spouses to have been Canadian residents in order to be eligible for the rollover, these provisions are intended to provide deferral ("rollover") of the Canadian tax at death for certain transfers to a surviving spouse and to permit the Canadian competent authority to allow such deferral for certain transfers to a trust. For example, they would enable the competent authority to treat a trust that is a qualified domestic trust for U.S. estate tax purposes as a Canadian spousal trust as well for purposes of certain provisions of Canadian tax law and of the Convention. These provisions do not affect U.S. domestic law regarding qualified domestic trusts. Nor do they affect the status of U.S. resident individuals for any other purpose.

New paragraph 5 adds a reference to subsection 70(5.2) of the Canadian *Income Tax Act*. This change is needed because the rollover in respect of certain kinds of property is provided in that subsection. Further, new paragraph 5 adds a clause "and with respect to such property" near the end of the second sentence to make it clear that the trust is treated as a resident of Canada only with respect to its Canadian property.

For example, assume that a U.S. decedent with a Canadian spouse sets up a qualified domestic trust holding U.S. and Canadian real property, and that the decedent's execu-

tor elects, for Federal estate tax purposes, to treat the entire trust as qualifying for the Federal estate tax marital deduction. Under Canadian law, because the decedent is not a Canadian resident, Canada would impose capital gains tax on the deemed disposition of the Canadian real property immediately before death. In order to defer the Canadian tax that might otherwise be imposed by reason of the decedent's death, under new paragraph 5 of Article XXIX B, the competent authority of Canada shall, at the request of the trustee, treat the trust as a Canadian spousal trust with respect to the Canadian real property. The effect of such treatment is to defer the tax on the deemed distribution of the Canadian real property until an appropriate triggering event such as the death of the surviving spouse.

Technical Explanation [1995 Protocol]: *Canadian treatment of certain transfers*

The provisions of paragraph 5 relate to the operation of Canadian law. They are intended to provide deferral ("rollover") of the Canadian tax at death for certain transfers to a surviving spouse and to permit the Canadian competent authority to allow such deferral for certain transfers to a trust. For example, they would enable the competent authority to treat a trust that is a qualified domestic trust for U.S. estate tax purposes as a Canadian spousal trust as well for purposes of certain provisions of Canadian tax law and of the Convention. These provisions do not affect U.S. domestic law regarding qualified domestic trusts. Nor do they affect the status of U.S. resident individuals for any other purpose.

6. In determining the amount of Canadian tax payable by an individual who immediately before death was a resident of Canada, or by a trust described in subsection 70(6) of the *Income Tax Act* (or a trust which is treated as being resident in Canada under the provisions of paragraph 5), the amount of any Federal or state estate or inheritance taxes payable in the United States (not exceeding, where the individual was a citizen of the United States or a former citizen referred to in paragraph 2 of Article XXIX (Miscellaneous Rules), the amount of estate and inheritance taxes that would have been payable if the individual were not a citizen or former citizen of the United States) in respect of property situated within the United States shall,

(a) to the extent that such estate or inheritance taxes are imposed upon the individual's death, be allowed as a deduction from the amount of any Canadian tax otherwise payable by the individual for the taxation year in which the individual died on the total of

(i) any income, profits or gains of the individual arising (within the meaning of paragraph 3 of Article XXIV (Elimination of Double Taxation)) in the United States in that year, and

(ii) where the value at the time of the individual's death of the individual's entire gross estate wherever situated (determined under the law of the United States) exceeded 1.2 million U.S. dollars or its equivalent in Canadian dollars, any income, profits or gains of the individual for that year from property situated in the United States at that time, and

(b) to the extent that such estate or inheritance taxes are imposed upon the death of the individual's surviving spouse, be allowed as a deduction from the amount of any Canadian tax otherwise payable by the trust for its taxation year in which that spouse dies on any income, profits or gains of the trust for that year arising (within the meaning of paragraph 3 of Article XXIV (Elimination of Double Taxation)) in the United States or from property situated in the United States at the time of death of the spouse.

For purposes of this paragraph, property shall be treated as situated within the United States if it is so treated for estate tax purposes under the law of the United States as in effect on March 17, 1995, subject to any subsequent changes thereof that the competent authorities of the Contracting States have agreed to apply for the purposes of this paragraph. The deduction allowed under this paragraph shall take into account the deduction for any income tax paid or accrued to the United States that is provided under paragraph 2(a), 4(a) or 5(b) of Article XXIV (Elimination of Double Taxation).

Related Provisions: See at end of Art. XXIX-B.

Notes: Fifth Protocol (2007), Annex B, states:

7. Taxes imposed by reason of death

It is understood that,

(a) Where a share or option in respect of a share is property situated in the United States for the purposes of Article XXIX B (Taxes Imposed by Reason of Death) of the Convention, any employment income in respect of the share or option shall be, for the purpose of clause 6(a)(ii) of that Article, income from property situated in the United States;

(b) Where property situated in the United States for the purposes of Article XXIX B (Taxes Imposed by Reason of Death) of the Convention is held by an entity that is a resident of Canada and that is described in subparagraph 1(b) of Article IV (Residence) of the Convention, any income out of or under the entity in respect of the property shall be, for the purpose of subparagraph 6(a)(ii) of Article XXIX B (Taxes Imposed by Reason of Death), income from property situated in the United States; and

(c) [Reproduced under para. 7 below].

Para. 6 may not work for US estate tax paid on US investments held in an RRSP on the annuitant's death: VIEWS doc 2005-0132441C6.

There is no provincial (B.C.) foreign tax credit for US estate tax: VIEWS doc 2003-0003087.

Definitions: "arising" — Art. XXIV:3; "Canada" — Art. III:1(a), ITCIA 5; "Canadian tax" — Art. III:1(c); "estate", "individual", "property" — ITCIA 3, ITA 248(1); "resident" — Art. IV0; "trust" — ITCIA 3, ITA 104(1), 248(1); "United States" — Art. III:1(b).

Technical Explanation [2007 Protocol]: In addition to the foregoing, paragraph 7 of the General Note provides certain clarifications for purposes of paragraphs 6 and 7 of Article XXIX B. These clarifications ensure that tax credits will be available in cases where there are inconsistencies in the way the two Contracting States view the income and the property.

Subparagraph 7(a) of the General Note applies where an individual who immediately before death was a resident of Canada held at the time of death a share or option in respect of a share that constitutes property situated in the United States for the purposes of Article XXIX B and that Canada views as giving rise to employment income(for example, a share or option granted by an employer). The United States imposes estate tax on the share or option in respect of a share, while Canada imposes income tax on income from employment. Subparagraph 7(a) provides that for purposes of clause 6(a)(ii) of Article XXIX B, any employment income in respect of the share or option constitutes income from property situated in the United States. This provision ensures that the estate tax paid on the share or option in the United States will be allowable as a deduction from the Canadian income tax.

Subparagraph 7(b) of the General Note applies where an individual who immediately before death was a resident of Canada held at the time of death a registered retirement savings plan (RRSP) or other entity that is a resident of Canada and that is described in subparagraph 1(b) of Article IV (Residence) and such RRSP or other entity held property situated in the United States for the purposes of Article XXIX B. The United States would impose estate tax on the value of the property held by the RRSP or other entity (to the extent such property is subject to Federal estate tax), while Canada would impose income tax on a deemed distribution of the property in the RRSP or other entity. Subparagraph 7(b) provides that any income out of or under the entity in respect of the property is, for the purpose of subparagraph 6(a)(ii) of Article XXIX B, income from property situated in the United States. This provision ensures that the estate tax paid on the underlying property in the United States (if any) will be allowable as a deduction from the Canadian income tax.

Subparagraph 7(c) of the General Note applies where an individual who immediately before death was a resident or citizen of the United States held at the time of death an RRSP or other entity that is a resident of Canada and that is described in subparagraph 1(b) of Article IV (Residence). The United States would impose estate tax on the value of the property held by the RRSP or other entity, while Canada would impose income tax on a deemed distribution of the property in the RRSP or other entity. Subparagraph 7(c) provides that for the purpose of paragraph 7 of Article XXIX B, the tax imposed in Canada is imposed in respect of property situated in Canada. This provision ensures that the Canadian income tax will be allowable as a credit against the U.S. estate tax.

Technical Explanation [1995 Protocol]: *Credit for U.S. taxes*

Under paragraph 6, Canada agrees to give Canadian residents and Canadian resident spousal trusts (or trusts treated as such by virtue of paragraph 5) a deduction from tax (i.e., a credit) for U.S. Federal or state estate or inheritance taxes imposed on U.S. situs property of the decedent or the trust. This credit is allowed against the income tax imposed by Canada, in an amount computed in accordance with subparagraph 6(a) or 6(b).

Subparagraph 6(a) covers the first set of cases — where the U.S. tax is imposed upon a decedent's death. Subparagraph 6(a)(i) allows a credit for U.S. tax against the total amount of Canadian income tax payable by the decedent in the taxable year of death on any income, profits, or gains arising in the United States (within the meaning of paragraph 3 of Article XXIV (Elimination of Double Taxation)). For purposes of subparagraph 6(a)(i), income, profits, or gains arising in the United States within the meaning of paragraph 3 of Article XXIV include gains deemed realized at death on U.S. situs real property and on personal property forming part of the business property of a U.S. permanent establishment or fixed base. (As explained below, these are the only types of property on which the United States may impose its estate tax if the estate is worth $1.2 million or less.) Income, profits, or gains arising in the United States also include income and profits earned by the decedent during the taxable year of death, to the extent

that the United States may tax such amounts under the Convention (e.g., dividends received from a U.S. corporation and wages from the performance of personal services in the United States).

Where the value of the decedent's entire gross estate exceeds $1.2 million, subparagraph 6(a)(ii) allows a credit against the Canadian income tax on any income, profits, or gains from any U.S. situs property, in addition to any credit allowed by subparagraph 6(a)(i). This provision is broader in scope than is the general rule under subparagraph 6(a)(i), because the United States has retained the right to impose its estate tax on all types of property in the case of larger estates.

Subparagraph 6(b) provides rules for a second category of cases — where the U.S. tax is imposed upon the death of the surviving spouse. In these cases, Canada agrees to allow a credit against the Canadian tax payable by a trust for its taxable year during which the surviving spouse dies on any income, profits, or gains (i) arising in the United States on U.S. situs real property or business property, or (ii) from property situated in the United States. These rules are intended to provide a credit for taxes imposed as a result of the death of the surviving spouse in situations involving trusts. To the extent that taxes are imposed on the estate of the surviving spouse, subparagraph 6(a) would apply as well. In addition, the competent authorities are authorized to provide relief from double taxation in certain additional circumstances involving trusts, as described above in connection with Article 14 of the Protocol.

The credit allowed under paragraph 6 is subject to certain conditions. First, where the decedent was a U.S. citizen or former citizen (described in paragraph 2 of Article XXIX (Miscellaneous Rules)), paragraph 6 does not obligate Canada to provide a credit for U.S. taxes in excess of the amount of U.S. taxes that would have been payable if the decedent had not been a U.S. citizen or former citizen. Second, the credit allowed under paragraph 6 will be computed after taking into account any deduction for U.S. income tax provided under paragraph 2(a), 4(a), or 5(b) of Article XXIV (Elimination of Double Taxation). This clarifies that no double credit will be allowed for any amount and provides an ordering rule. Finally, because Canadian domestic law does not contain a definition of U.S. situs property for death tax purposes, such a definition is provided for purposes of paragraph 6. To maximize coordination of the credit provisions, the Contracting States agreed to follow the U.S. estate tax law definition as in effect on the date of signature of the Protocol and, subject to competent authority agreement, as it may be amended in the future.

7. In determining the amount of estate tax imposed by the United States on the estate of an individual who was a resident or citizen of the United States at the time of death, or upon the death of a surviving spouse with respect to a qualifed domestic trust created by such an individual or the individual's executor or surviving spouse, a credit shall be allowed against such tax imposed in respect of property situated outside the United States, for the federal and provincial income taxes payable in Canada in respect of such property by reason of the death of the individual or, in the case of a qualified domestic trust, the individual's surviving spouse. Such credit shall be computed in accordance with the following rules:

(a) a credit otherwise allowable under this paragraph shall be allowed regardless of whether the identity of the taxpayer under the law of Canada corresponds to that under the law of the United States;

(b) the amount of a credit allowed under this paragraph shall be computed in accordance with the provisions and subject to the limitations of the law of the United States regarding credit for foreign death taxes (as it may be amended from time to time without changing the general principle hereof), as though the income tax imposed by Canada were a creditable tax under that law;

(c) a credit may be claimed under this paragraph for an amount of federal or provincial income tax payable in Canada only to the extent that no credit or deduction is claimed for such amount in determining any other tax imposed by the United States, other than the estate tax imposed on property in a qualified domestic trust upon the death of the surviving spouse.

Notes: Fifth Protocol (2007), Annex B, states:

7. Taxes imposed by reason of death

It is understood that,

(a)-(b) [Reproduced under para. 6 above]; and

(c) Where a tax is imposed in Canada by reason of death in respect of an entity that is a resident of Canada and that is described in subparagraph 1(b) of Article IV (Residence) of the Convention, that tax shall be, for the purpose of paragraph 7 of Article XXIX B (Taxes Imposed by Reason of Death) of the Convention, imposed in respect of property situated in Canada.

Definitions: "Canada" — Art. III:1(a), ITCIA 5; "estate", "individual", "property" — ITCIA 3, ITA 248(1); "qualified domestic trust" — *Internal Revenue Code* s.

2056A(a); "surviving spouse" — *Internal Revenue Code* s. 2(a); "taxpayer" — ITCIA 3, ITA 248(1); "United States" — Art. III:1(b).

Technical Explanation [2007 Protocol]: See under Art. XXIX-B:6 above.

Technical Explanation [1995 Protocol]: *Credit for Canadian taxes*

Under paragraph 7, the United States agrees to allow a credit against U.S. Federal estate tax imposed on the estate of a U.S. resident or U.S. citizen decedent, or upon the death of a surviving spouse with respect to a qualified domestic trust created by such a decedent (or the decedent's executor or surviving spouse). The credit is allowed for Canadian Federal and provincial income taxes imposed at death with respect to property of the estate or trust that is situated outside of the United States. As in the case under paragraph 6, the competent authorities also are authorized to provide relief from double taxation in certain cases involving trusts (see discussion of Article 14, above).

The amount of the credit generally will be determined as though the income tax imposed by Canada were a creditable tax under the U.S. estate tax provisions regarding credit for foreign death taxes, in accordance with the provisions and subject to the limitations of *Internal Revenue Code* section 2014. However, subparagraph 7(a) clarifies that a credit otherwise allowable under paragraph 7 will not be denied merely because of inconsistencies between U.S. and Canadian law regarding the identity of the taxpayer in the case of a particular taxable event. For example, the fact that the taxpayer is the decedent's estate for purposes of U.S. estate taxation and the decedent for purposes of Canadian income taxation will not prevent the allowance of a credit under paragraph 7 for Canadian income taxes imposed by reason of the death of the decedent.

In addition, subparagraph 7(c) clarifies that the credit against the U.S. estate tax generally may be claimed only to the extent that no credit or deduction is claimed for the same amount of Canadian tax in determining any other U.S. tax. This makes clear, for example, that a credit may not be claimed for the same amount under both this provision and Article XXIV (Elimination of Double Taxation). To prevent double taxation, an exception to this restriction is provided for certain taxes imposed with respect to qualified domestic trusts. Subject to the limitations of subparagraph 7(c), the taxpayer may choose between relief under Article XXIV, relief under this paragraph 7, or some combination of the two.

8. Provided that the value, at the time of death, of the entire gross estate wherever situated of an individual who was a resident of Canada (other than a citizen of the United States) at the time of death does not exceed 1.2 million U.S dollars or its equivalent in Canadian dollars, the United States may impose its estate tax upon property forming part of the estate of the individual only if any gain derived by the individual from the alienation of such property would have been subject to income taxation by the United States in accordance with Article XIII (Gains).

Definitions: "Canada" — Art. III:1(a), ITCIA 5; "estate", "individual", "property" — ITCIA 3, ITA 248(1); "United States" — Art. III:1(b).

Technical Explanation [1995 Protocol]: *Relief for small estates*

Under paragraph 8, the United States agrees to limit the application of its estate tax in the case of certain small estates of Canadian resident decedents. This provision is intended to eliminate the "trap for the unwary" that exists for such decedents, in the absence of an estate tax convention between the United States and Canada. In the absence of sophisticated estate tax planning, such decedents may inadvertently subject their estates to U.S. estate tax liability by holding shares of U.S. corporate stock or other U.S. situs property. U.S. resident decedents are already protected in this regard by the provisions of Article XIII (Gains) of the present Convention, which prohibit Canada from imposing its income tax on gains deemed realized at death by U.S. residents on such property.

Paragraph 8 provides relief only in the case of Canadian resident decedents whose entire gross estates wherever situated (i.e., worldwide gross estates determined under U.S. law) have a value, at the time of death, not exceeding $1.2 million. Paragraph 8 provides that the United States may impose its estate tax upon property forming part of such estates only if any gain on alienation of the property would have been subject to U.S. income taxation under Article XIII (Gains). For estates with a total value not exceeding $1.2 million, this provision has the effect of permitting the United States to impose its estate tax only on real property situated in the United States, within the meaning of Article XIII, and personal property forming part of the business property of a U.S. permanent establishment or fixed base.

Saving clause exceptions

Certain provisions of Article XXIX B are included in the list of exceptions to the general "saving clause" of Article XXIX (Miscellaneous Rules), as amended by Article 17 of the Protocol. To the extent that an exception from the saving clause is provided for a provision, each Contracting State is required to allow the benefits of that provision to its residents (and, in the case of the United States, its citizens), notwithstanding the saving clause. General saving clause exceptions are provided for paragraphs 1, 5, and 6 of Article XXIX B. Saving clause exceptions are provided for paragraphs 2, 3, 4, and 7, except for the estates of former U.S. citizens referred to in paragraph 2 of Article XXIX.

Effective dates

Article 21 of the Protocol contains special retrospective effective date provisions for paragraphs 2 through 8 of Article XXIX B and certain related provisions of the Proto-

col. Paragraphs 2 through 8 of Article XXIX B and the specified related provisions generally will take effect with respect to deaths occurring after the date on which the Protocol enters into force (i.e., the date on which the instruments of ratification are exchanged). However, the benefits of those provisions will also be available with respect to deaths occurring after November 10, 1988, provided that a claim for refund due as a result of these provisions is filed by the later of one year from the date on which the Protocol enters into force or the date on which the applicable period for filing such a claim expires under the domestic law of the Contracting State concerned. The general effective dates set forth in Article 21 of the Protocol otherwise apply.

It is unusual for the United States to agree to retrospective effective dates. In this case, however, the negotiators believed that retrospective application was not inappropriate, given the fact that the TAMRA provisions were the impetus for negotiation of the Protocol and that the negotiations commenced soon after the enactment of TAMRA. The United States has agreed to retrospective effective dates in certain other instances (e.g., in the case of the U.S.-Germany estate tax treaty). The retrospective effective dates apply reciprocally, so that they will benefit the estates of U.S. decedents as well as Canadian decedents.

Notes [Art. XXIX-B]: Art. XXIX-B added by 1995 Protocol, generally effective for deaths after November 10, 1988, provided refund claims that would otherwise be too late are filed by November 9, 1996.

Related Provisions [Art. XXIX-B]: ITA 60(d) — Deduction for interest accruing on estate taxes; Art. II:2(b)(iv) — Application to U.S. estate taxes; Art. XXVI:3(g) — Competent authority agreement to eliminate double taxation.

Article XXX — Entry Into Force

1. This Convention shall be subject to ratification in accordance with the applicable procedures of each Contracting State and instruments of ratification shall be exchanged at Ottawa as soon as possible.

Technical Explanation [1984]: Paragraph 1 provides that the Convention is subject to ratification in accordance with the procedures of Canada and the United States. The exchange of instruments of ratification is to take place at Ottawa as soon as possible.

2. The Convention shall enter into force upon the exchange of instruments of ratification and, subject to the provisions of paragraph 3, its provisions shall have effect:

    (a) for tax withheld at the source on income referred to in Articles X (Dividends), XI (Interest), XII (Royalties) and XVIII (Pensions and Annuities), with respect to amounts paid or credited on or after the first day of the second month next following the date on which the Convention enters into force;

    (b) for other taxes, with respect to taxable years beginning on or after the first day of January next following the date on which the Convention enters into force; and

    (c) notwithstanding the provisions of subparagraph (b), for the taxes covered by paragraph 4 of Article XXIX (Miscellaneous Rules) with respect to all taxable years referred to in that paragraph.

Notes: Exchange of instruments of ratification took place on August 16, 1984. See Notes at beginning of the treaty.

Technical Explanation [1984]: Paragraph 2 provides, subject to paragraph 3, that the Convention shall enter into force upon the exchange of instruments of ratification. It has effect, with respect to source State taxation of dividends, interest, royalties, pensions, annuities, alimony, and child support, for amounts paid or credited on or after the first day of the second calendar month after the date on which the instruments of ratification are exchanged. For other taxes, the Convention takes effect for taxable years beginning on or after January 1 next following the date when instruments of ratification are exchanged. In the case of relief from United States social security taxes provided by paragraph 4 of Article XXIX (Miscellaneous Rules), the Convention also has effect for taxable years before the date on which instruments of ratification are exchanged.

3. For the purposes of applying the United States foreign tax credit in relation to taxes paid or accrued to Canada:

    (a) notwithstanding the provisions of paragraph 2(a) of Article II (Taxes Covered), the tax on 1971 undistributed income on hand imposed by Part IX of the *Income Tax Act* of Canada shall be considered to be an income tax for distributions made on or after the first day of January 1972 and before the first day of January 1979 and shall be considered to be imposed upon the recipient of a distribution, in the proportion that the distribution out of undistributed income with respect to which the tax has been paid bears to 85 per cent of such undistributed income;

(b) the principles of paragraph 6 of Article XXIV (Elimination of Double Taxation) shall have effect for taxable years beginning on or after the first day of January 1976; and

(c) the provisions of paragraph 1 of Article XXIV shall have effect for taxable years beginning on or after the first day of January 1981.

Any claim for refund based on the provisions of this paragraph may be filed on or before June 30 of the calendar year following that in which the Convention enters into force, notwithstanding any rule of domestic law to the contrary.

Definitions: "calendar year" — ITCIA 3, *Interpretation Act* 37(1)(a); "Canada" — Art. III:1(a), ITCIA 5; "United States" — Art. III:1(b).

Technical Explanation [1984]: Paragraph 3 provides special effective date rules for foreign tax credit computations with respect to taxes paid or accrued to Canada. Paragraph 3(a) provides that the tax on 1971 undistributed income on hand imposed by Part IX of the *Income Tax Act* of Canada is considered to be an "income tax" for distributions made on or after January 1, 1972 and before January 1, 1979. Any such tax which is paid or accrued under U.S. standards is considered to be imposed at the time of distribution and on the recipient of the distribution, in the proportion that the distribution out of undistributed income with respect to which the tax has been paid bears to 85% of such undistributed income. A person claiming a credit for tax pursuant to paragraph 3(a) is obligated to compute the amount of the credit in accordance with that paragraph.

Paragraph 3(b) provides that the principles of paragraph 6 of Article XXIV (Elimination of Double Taxation), which provides for resourcing of certain dividend, interest, and royalty income to eliminate double taxation of U.S. citizens residing in Canada, have effect for taxable years beginning on or after January 1, 1976. The paragraph is intended to grant the competent authorities sufficient flexibility to address certain practical problems that have arisen under the 1942 Convention. It is anticipated that the competent authorities will be guided by paragraphs 4 and 5 of Article XXIV in applying paragraph 3(b) of Article XXX. Paragraph 3(c) provides that the provisions of paragraph 1 of Article XXIV (and the source rules of that Article) shall have effect for taxable years beginning on or after January 1, 1981.

Any claim for refund based on the provisions of paragraph 3 may be filed on or before June 30 of the calendar year following the year in which instruments of ratification are exchanged, notwithstanding statutes of limitations or other rules of domestic law to the contrary. For purposes of Code section 6611, the date of overpayment is the date on which instruments of ratification are exchanged, with respect to any refunds of U.S. tax pursuant to paragraph 3.

4. Subject to the provisions of paragraph 5, the 1942 Convention shall cease to have effect for taxes for which this Convention has effect in accordance with the provisions of paragraph 2.

Technical Explanation [1984]: Paragraph 4 provides that, subject to paragraph 5, the 1942 Convention ceases to have effect for taxes for which the Convention has effect under the provisions of paragraph 2. For example, if under paragraph 2 the Convention were to have effect with respect to taxes withheld at source on dividends paid as of October 1, 1984, the 1942 Convention will not have effect with respect to such taxes.

5. Where any greater relief from tax would have been afforded by any provision of the 1942 Convention than under this Convention, any such provision shall continue to have effect for the first taxable year with respect to which the provisions of this Convention have effect under paragraph 2(b).

Definitions: "the 1942 Convention" — Art. III:1(j).

Technical Explanation [1984]: Paragraph 5 modifies the rule of paragraph 4 to allow all of the provisions of the 1942 Convention to continue to have effect for the period through the first taxable year with respect to which the provisions of the Convention would otherwise have effect under paragraph 2(b), if greater relief from tax is available under the 1942 Convention than under the Convention. Paragraph 5 applies to all provisions of the 1942 Convention, not just those provisions of the Convention for which the Convention takes effect under paragraph 2(b) of this Article. Thus, for example, assume that the Convention has effect, pursuant to paragraph 2(b), for taxable years of a taxpayer beginning on or after January 1, 1985. Further assume that a U.S. resident with a taxable year beginning on April 1 and ending on March 31 receives natural resource royalties from Canada which are subject to a 25% tax under Article VI (Income from Real Property) of the Convention, as amended by the Protocol, and Canada's internal law, but which would be subject to a 15% tax under Article XI of the 1942 Convention. Pursuant to paragraph 5, the greater benefits of the 1942 Convention would continue to apply to royalties paid or credited to the U.S. resident through March 31, 1986.

6. The 1942 Convention shall terminate on the last date on which it has effect in accordance with the preceding provisions of this Article.

Definitions: "the 1942 Convention" — Art. III:1(j).

Technical Explanation [1984]: Paragraph 6 provides that the 1942 Convention terminates on the last of the dates on which it has effect in accordance with the provisions of paragraphs 4 and 5.

7. The Exchange of Notes between the United States and Canada dated August 2 and September 17, 1928, providing for relief from double income taxation on shipping profits, is terminated. Its provisions shall cease to have effect with respect to taxable years beginning on or after the first day of January next following the date on which this Convention enters into force.

Definitions: "Canada" — Art. III:1(a), ITCIA 5; "United States" — Art. III:1(b).

Technical Explanation [1984]: Paragraph 7 terminates the Exchange of Notes between the United States and Canada of August 2 and September 17, 1928 providing for relief from double taxation of shipping profits. The provisions of the Exchange of Notes no longer have effect for taxable years beginning on or after January 1 following the exchange of instruments of ratification of the Convention. The 1942 Convention, in Article V, had suspended the effectiveness of the Exchange of Notes.

8. The provisions of the Convention between the Government of Canada and the Government of the United States of America for the Avoidance of Double Taxation and the Prevention of Fiscal Evasion with Respect to Taxes on the Estates of Deceased Persons signed at Washington on February 17, 1961 shall continue to have effect with respect to estates of persons deceased prior to the first day of January next following the date on which this Convention enters into force but shall cease to have effect with respect to estates of persons deceased on or after that date. Such Convention shall terminate on the last date on which it has effect in accordance with the preceding sentence.

Definitions: "Canada" — Art. III:1(a), ITCIA 5; "estate" — ITCIA 3, ITA 248(1); "person" — Art. III:1(e), ITCIA 3, *Interpretation Act* 35(1); "United States" — Art. III:1(b).

Technical Explanation [1984]: Paragraph 8 terminates the Convention between Canada and the United States for the Avoidance of Double Taxation with Respect to Taxes on the Estates of Deceased Persons signed on February 17, 1961. The provisions of that Convention cease to have effect with respect to estates of persons deceased on or after January 1 of the year following the exchange of instruments of ratification of the Convention.

Interpretation Bulletins [Art. XXX]: IT-173R2: Capital gains derived in Canada by residents of the United States.

Article XXXI — Termination

1. This Convention shall remain in force until terminated by a Contracting State.

Technical Explanation [1984]: Paragraph 1 provides that the Convention shall remain in force until terminated by Canada or the United States.

2. Either Contracting State may terminate the Convention at any time after 5 years from the date on which the Convention enters into force provided that at least 6 months' prior notice of termination has been given through diplomatic channels.

Technical Explanation [1984]: Paragraph 2 provides that either Canada or the United States may terminate the Convention at any time after 5 years from the date on which instruments of ratification are exchanged, provided that notice of termination is given through diplomatic channels at least 6 months prior to the date on which the Convention is to terminate.

3. Where a Contracting State considers that a significant change introduced in the taxation laws of the other Contracting State should be accommodated by a modification of the Convention, the Contracting States shall consult together with a view to resolving the matter; if the matter cannot be satisfactorily resolved, the first-mentioned State may terminate the Convention in accordance with the procedures set forth in paragraph 2, but without regard to the 5 year limitation provided therein.

Definitions: "State" — Art. III:1(i).

Technical Explanation [1984]: Paragraph 3 provides a special termination rule in situations where Canada or the United States changes its taxation laws and the other Contracting State believes that such change is significant enough to warrant modification of the Convention. In such a circumstance, the Canadian Ministry of Finance and the United States Department of the Treasury would consult with a view to resolving the matter. If the matter cannot be satisfactorily resolved, the Contracting State requesting an accommodation because of the change in the other Contracting State's taxation laws may terminate the Convention by giving the 6 months' prior notice required by paragraph 2, without regard to whether the Convention has been in force for 5 years.

4. In the event the Convention is terminated, the Convention shall cease to have effect:

(a) for tax withheld at the source on income referred to in Articles X (Dividends), XI (Interest), XII (Royalties), XVIII (Pensions and Annuities) and paragraph 2 of Article XXII (Other Income), with respect to amounts paid or credited on or after the first day of January next following the expiration of the 6 months' period referred to in paragraph 2; and

(b) for other taxes, with respect to taxable years beginning on or after the first day of January next following the expiration of the 6 months' period referred to in paragraph 2.

Technical Explanation [1984]: Paragraph 4 provides that, in the event of termination, the Convention ceases to have effect for tax withheld at source under Articles X (Dividends), XI (Interest), XII (Royalties), and XVIII (Pensions and Annuities), and under paragraph 2 of Article XXII (Other Income), with respect to amounts paid or credited on or after the first day of January following the expiration of the 6 month period referred to in paragraph 2. In the case of other taxes, the Convention shall cease to have effect in the event of termination with respect to taxable years beginning on or after Jan. 1 following the expiration of the 6 month period referred to in paragraph 2.

APPENDIX — EXECUTION AND COMPETENT AUTHORITIES LETTER

[From Canada — ed.]   September 26, 1980

Excellency: I have the honor to refer to the Convention between the United States of America and Canada with Respect to Taxes on Income and on Capital, signed today, and to confirm certain understandings reached between the two Governments with respect to the Convention.

1. In French, the term **"société"** also means a "corporation" within the meaning of Canadian law.

2. The competent authorities of each of the Contracting States shall review the procedures and requirements for an organization of the other Contracting State to establish its status as a religious, scientific, literary, educational or charitable organization entitled to exemption under paragraph 1 of Article XXI (Exempt Organizations), or as an eligible recipient of the charitable contributions or gifts referred to in paragraphs 5 and 6 of Article XXI, with a view to avoiding duplicate application by such organizations to the administering agencies of both Contracting States. If a Contracting State determines that the other Contracting State maintains procedures to determine such status and rules for qualification that are compatible with such procedures and rules of the first-mentioned Contracting State, it is contemplated that such first-mentioned Contracting State shall accept the certification of the administering agency of the other Contracting State as to such status for the purpose of making the necessary determinations under paragraphs 1, 5 and 6 of Article XXI.

It is further agreed that the term **"family"**, as used in paragraphs 5 and 6 of Article XXI, means an individual's brothers and sisters (whether by whole or half-blood, or by adoption), spouse, ancestors, lineal descendants and adopted descendants.

3. It is the position of Canada that the so-called "unitary apportionment" method used by certain states of the United States to allocate income to United States offices or subsidiaries of Canadian companies results in inequitable taxation and imposes excessive administrative burdens on Canadian companies doing business in those states. Under that method the profit of a Canadian company on its United States business is not determined on the basis of arm's-length relations but is derived from a formula taking account of the income of the Canadian company and its worldwide subsidiaries as well as the assets, payroll and sales of all such companies. For a Canadian multinational company with many subsidiaries in different countries to have to submit its books and records for all of these companies to a state of the United States imposes a costly burden. It is understood that the Senate of the United States has not consented to any limitation on the taxing jurisdiction of the states by a treaty and that a provision which would have restricted the use of unitary apportionment in the case of United Kingdom corporations was recently rejected by the Senate. Canada continues to be concerned about this issue as it affects Canadian multinationals. If an acceptable provision on this subject can be devised, the United States agrees to reopen discussions with Canada on this subject.

APPENDIX — FIFTH PROTOCOL (2007), ANNEX A

[Diplomatic] Note No. JLAB-0111 [from Canada — ed.] September 21, 2007

Excellency,

I have the honor to refer to the Protocol (the "Protocol") done today between Canada and the United States of America amending the Convention with Respect to Taxes on Income and on Capital done at Washington on 26 September 1980, as amended by the Protocols done on 14 June 1983, 28 March 1984, 17 March 1995, and 29 July 1997 (the "Convention"), and to propose on behalf of the Government of Canada the following:

In respect of any case where the competent authorities have endeavored but are unable to reach a complete agreement under Article XXVI (Mutual Agreement Procedure) of the Convention regarding the application of one or more of the following Articles of the Convention: IV (Residence) (but only insofar as it relates to the residence of a natural person), V (Permanent Establishment), VII (Business Profits), IX (Related Persons), and XII (Royalties) (but only (i) insofar as Article XII might apply in transactions involving related persons to whom Article IX might apply, or (ii) to an allocation of amounts between royalties that are taxable under paragraph 2 thereof and royalties that are exempt under paragraph 3 thereof), binding arbitration shall be used to determine such application, unless the competent authorities agree that the particular case is not suitable for determination by arbitration. In addition, the competent authorities may, on an ad hoc basis, agree that binding arbitration shall be used in respect of any other matter to which Article XXVI applies. If an arbitration proceeding (the "Proceeding") under paragraph 6 of Article XXVI commences, the following rules and procedures shall apply:

1. The Proceeding shall be conducted in the manner prescribed by, and subject to the requirements of, paragraphs 6 and 7 of Article XXVI and these rules and procedures, as modified or supplemented by any other rules and procedures agreed upon by the competent authorities pursuant to paragraph 17 below.

2. The determination reached by an arbitration board in the Proceeding shall be limited to a determination regarding the amount of income, expense or tax reportable to the Contracting States.

3. Notwithstanding the initiation of the Proceeding, the competent authorities may reach a mutual agreement to resolve a case and terminate the Proceeding. Correspondingly, a concerned person may withdraw a request for the competent authorities to engage in the Mutual Agreement Procedure (and thereby terminate the Proceeding) at any time.

4. The requirements of subparagraph 7(d) of Article XXVI shall be met when the competent authorities have each received from each concerned person a notarized statement agreeing that the concerned person and each person acting on the concerned person's behalf, shall not disclose to any other person any information received during the course of the Proceeding from either Contracting State or the arbitration board, other than the determination of the Proceeding. A concerned person that has the legal authority to bind any other concerned person(s) on this matter may do so in a comprehensive notarized statement.

5. Each Contracting State shall have 60 days from the date on which the Proceeding begins to send a written communication to the other Contracting State appointing one member of the arbitration board. Within 60 days of the date on which the second such communication is sent, the two members appointed by the Contracting States shall appoint a third member, who shall serve as chair of the board. If either Contracting State fails to appoint a member, or if the members appointed by the Contracting States fail to agree upon the third member in the manner prescribed by this paragraph, a Contracting State shall ask the highest ranking member of the Secretariat at the Centre for Tax Policy and Administration of the Organisation for Economic Co-operation and Development (OECD) who is not a citizen of either Contracting State, to appoint the remaining member(s) by written notice to both Contracting States within 60 days of the date of such failure. The competent authorities shall develop a non-exclusive list of individuals with familiarity in international tax matters who may potentially serve as the chair of the board.

6. The arbitration board may adopt any procedures necessary for the conduct of its business, provided that the procedures are not inconsistent with any provision of Article XXVI or this note.

7. Each of the Contracting States shall be permitted to submit, within 60 days of the appointment of the chair of the arbitration board, a proposed resolution describing the proposed disposition of the specific monetary amounts of income, expense or taxation at issue in the case, and a supporting position paper, for consideration by the arbitration board. Copies of the proposed resolution and supporting position paper shall be provided by the board to the other Contracting State on the date on which the later of the submissions is submitted to the board. In the event that only one Contracting State submits a proposed resolution within the allotted time, then that proposed resolution shall be deemed to be the determination of the board in that case and the Proceeding shall be terminated. Each of the Contracting States may, if it so desires, submit a reply submission to the board within 120 days of the appointment of its chair, to address any points raised by the proposed resolution or position paper submitted by the other Contracting State. Additional information may be submitted to the arbitration board only at its request, and copies of the board's request and the Contracting State's response shall be provided to the other Contracting State on the date on which the request or the response is submitted. Except for logistical matters such as those identified in paragraphs 12, 14 and 15 below, all communications from the Contracting States to the arbitration board, and vice versa, shall take place only through written communications between the designated competent authorities and the chair of the board.

8. The arbitration board shall deliver a determination in writing to the Contracting States within six months of the appointment of its chair. The board shall adopt as its determination one of the proposed resolutions submitted by the Contracting States.

9. In making its determination, the arbitration board shall apply, as necessary: (1) the provisions of the Convention as amended; (2) any agreed commentaries or explanations of the Contracting States concerning the Convention as amended; (3) the laws of the Contracting States to the extent they are not inconsistent with each other; and (4) any OECD Commentary, Guidelines or Reports regarding relevant analogous portions of the OECD Model Tax Convention.

10. The determination of the arbitration board in a particular case shall be binding on the Contracting States. The determination of the board shall not state a rationale. It shall have no precedential value.

11. As provided in subparagraph 7(e) of Article XXVI, the determination of an arbitration board shall constitute a resolution by mutual agreement under this Article. Each concerned person must, within 30 days of receiving the determination of the board from the competent authority to which the case was first presented, advise that competent authority whether that concerned person accepts the determination of the board. If any concerned person fails to so advise the relevant competent authority within this time frame, the determination of the board shall be considered not to have been accepted in that case. Where the determination of the board is not accepted, the case may not subsequently be the subject of a Proceeding.

12. Any meeting(s) of the arbitration board shall be in facilities provided by the Contracting State whose competent authority initiated the mutual agreement proceedings in the case.

13. The treatment of any associated interest or penalties shall be determined by applicable domestic law of the Contracting State(s) concerned.

14. No information relating to the Proceeding (including the board's determination) may be disclosed by the members of the arbitration board or their staffs or by either competent authority, except as permitted by the Convention and the domestic laws of the Contracting States. In addition, all material prepared in the course of, or relating to, the Proceeding shall be considered to be information exchanged between the Contracting States. The Contracting States shall ensure that all members of the arbitration board and their staffs sign and send to each Contracting State notarized statements, prior to their acting in the arbitration proceeding, in which they agree to abide by and be subject to the confidentiality and nondisclosure provisions of Articles XXVI and XXVII of the Convention and the applicable domestic laws of the Contracting States. In the event those provisions conflict, the most restrictive condition shall apply.

15. The fees and expenses of members of the arbitration board shall be set in accordance with the International Centre for Settlement of Investment Disputes (ICSID) Schedule of Fees for arbitrators, as in effect on the date on which the arbitration proceedings are initiated, and shall be borne equally by the Contracting States. Any fees for language translation shall also be borne equally by the Contracting States. Meeting facilities, related resources, financial management, other logistical support, and general administrative coordination of the Proceeding shall be provided, at its own cost, by the Contracting State whose competent authority initiated the mutual agreement proceedings in the case. Any other costs shall be borne by the Contracting State that incurs them.

16. For purposes of paragraphs 6 and 7 of Article XXVI and this note, each competent authority shall confirm in writing to the other competent authority and to the concerned person(s) the date of its receipt of the information necessary to undertake substantive consideration for a mutual agreement. Such information shall be:

(a) in the United States, the information required to be submitted to the U.S. competent authority under Revenue Procedure 2006-54, section 4.05 (or any applicable analogous provisions) and, for cases initially submitted as a request for an Advance Pricing Agreement, the information required to be submitted to the Internal Revenue Service under Revenue Procedure 2006-9, section 4 (or any applicable analogous provisions), and

(b) in Canada, the information required to be submitted to Canadian competent authority under Information Circular 71-17 (or any applicable successor publication).

However, this information shall not be considered received until both competent authorities have received copies of all materials submitted to either Contracting State by the concerned person(s) in connection with the mutual agreement procedure.

17. The competent authorities of the Contracting States may modify or supplement the above rules and procedures as necessary to more effectively implement the intent of paragraph 6 of Article XXVI to eliminate double taxation.

If the above proposal is acceptable to your Government, I further propose that this Note, which is authentic in English and in French, and your reply Note reflecting such acceptance shall constitute an agreement between our two Governments which shall enter into force on the date of entry into force of the Protocol and shall be annexed to the Convention as Annex A thereto and shall therefore be an integral part of the Convention.

Please accept, Excellency, the assurance of my highest consideration.

Maxime Bernier, Minister of Foreign Affairs [Canada]

[Diplomatic] Note No. 1015 [from U.S. — ed.]

Excellency,

I have the honor to acknowledge receipt of your Note No. JLAB-0111 dated September 21, 2007, which states in its entirety as follows:

[Reproduces in its entirety Note JLAB-0111 above — ed.]

I am pleased to inform you that the Government of the United States of America accepts the proposal set forth in your Note. The Government of the United States of America further agrees that your Note, which is authentic in English and in French, together with this reply, shall constitute an Agreement between the United States of America and Canada, which shall enter into force on the date of entry into force of the Protocol amending the Convention between the United States of America and Canada with Respect to Taxes on Income and on Capital done at Washington on 26 September 1980, as amended by the Protocols done on 14 June 1983, 28 March 1984, 17 March 1995, and 29 July 1997 (the "Convention"), and shall be annexed to the Convention as Annex A thereto, and shall therefore be an integral part of the Convention.

Accept, Excellency, the renewed assurances of my highest consideration.

Embassy of the United States of America

Ottawa, September 21, 2007
Terry Breese

APPENDIX — FIFTH PROTOCOL (2007), ANNEX B

[Diplomatic] Note No. JLAB-0112 [from Canada — ed.] September 21, 2007

Excellency,

I have the honor to refer to the Protocol (the "Protocol") done to-day between Canada and the United States of America amending the Convention with Respect to Taxes on Income and on Capital done at Washington on 26 September 1980, as amended by the Protocols done on 14 June 1983, 28 March 1984, 17 March 1995, and 29 July 1997 (the "Convention").

In the course of the negotiations leading to the conclusion of the Protocol done today, the negotiators developed and agreed upon a common understanding and interpretation of certain provisions of the Convention. These understandings and interpretations are intended to give guidance both to the taxpayers and to the tax authorities of our two countries in interpreting various provisions contained in the Convention.

I, therefore, have the further honor to propose on behalf of the Government of Canada the following understandings and interpretations:

1. Meaning of undefined terms — [See Art. III:2 Notes.]

2. Meaning of connected projects — [See Art. V:9 Notes.]

3. Definition of the term "dividends" — [See Art. X:3 Notes.]

4. Deletion of Article XIV (Independent Personal Services) — [See Notes to repealed Art. IV.]

5. Former permanent establishments and fixed bases — [See Art. VII:2 Notes.]

6. Stock options — [See Art. XV:1 Notes.]

7. Taxes imposed by reason of death — [See Notes to Art. XXIX-B:6 and 7.]

8. Royalties — information in connection with franchise agreement — [See Art. XII:3 Notes.]

9. With reference to Article VII (Business Profits) — [See Art. VII:1 Notes.]

10. Qualifying retirement plans — [See Art. XVIII:15 Notes.]

11. Former long-term residents — [See Art. XXIX:2 Notes.]

12. Special source rules relating to former citizens and long-term residents — [See Art. XXIX:2 Notes.]

13. Exchange of Information — [See Art. XXVII:1 Notes.]

14. Limitation on Benefits — [See Art. XXIX-A:2 Notes.]

If the above proposal is acceptable to your Government, I further propose that this Note, which is authentic in English and in French, and your reply Note reflecting such acceptance shall constitute an agreement between our two Governments which shall enter into force on the date of entry into force of the Protocol and shall be annexed to the Convention as Annex B thereto and shall therefore be an integral part of the Convention.

Please accept, Excellency, the assurance of my highest consideration.

Maxime Bernier, Minister of Foreign Affairs [Canada]

[Diplomatic] Note No. 1014 [from U.S. — ed.]

Excellency,

I have the honor to acknowledge receipt of your Note No. JLAB-0112 dated September 21, 2007, which states in its entirety as follows:

[Reproduces in its entirety Note JLAB-0112 above — ed.]

I am pleased to inform you that the Government of the United States of America accepts the proposal set forth in your Note. The Government of the United States of America further agrees that your Note, which is authentic in English and in French, together with this reply, shall constitute an Agreement between the United States of America and Canada, which shall enter into force on the date of entry into force of the Protocol amending the Convention between the United States of America and Canada with Respect to Taxes on Income and on Capital done at Washington on 26 September 1980, as amended by the Protocols done on 14 June 1983, 28 March 1984, 17 March 1995, and 29 July 1997 (the "Convention"), and shall be annexed to the Convention as Annex B thereto, and shall therefore be an integral part of the Convention.

Accept, Excellency, the renewed assurances of my highest consideration.

Embassy of the United States of America

Ottawa, September 21, 2007
Terry Breese

CANADA-UNITED STATES ENHANCED TIEA (FATCA)

Agreement between the Government of Canada and the Government of the United States of America to Improve International Tax Compliance through Enhanced Exchange of Information under the Convention between Canada and the United States of America with Respect to Taxes on Income and on Capital

Enacted in Canada by S.C. 2014, c. 20, Part 5

Notes: This Canada-US Enhanced Tax Information Exchange Agreement (ETIEA), or InterGovernmental Agreement (IGA), is unrelated to the TIEAs Canada has reached with tax havens (see ITA 95(1)"non-qualifying country" Notes), and is not part of the automatic exchange of financial information with other countries under ITA ss. 270-281, though the general principles are the same. This IGA accommodates FATCA (the US *Foreign Account Tax Compliance Act*), so that instead of Canadian financial institutions having to send information on US persons' accounts to the IRS, they send it to CRA (ITA ss. 263-269) and CRA will pass it on to the IRS. See ITA 269 Notes.

This IGA was signed on Feb. 5, 2014. It is enacted in Canada by the *Canada-United States Enhanced Tax Exchange Information Act*, by Part 5 (s. 99) of 2014 budget bill #1:

AN ACT TO IMPLEMENT THE CANADA–UNITED STATES ENHANCED TAX INFORMATION EXCHANGE AGREEMENT

1. Short title — This Act may be cited as the *Canada–United States Enhanced Tax Information Exchange Agreement Implementation Act*.

2. Definition of "Agreement" — In this Act, "Agreement" means the Agreement between the Government of Canada and the Government of the United States of America set out in the schedule [to this Act — ed.], as amended from time to time.

3. Agreement approved — The Agreement is approved and has the force of law in Canada during the period that the Agreement, by its terms, is in force.

4. (1) Inconsistent laws — general rule — Subject to subsection (2), in the event of any inconsistency between the provisions of this Act or the Agreement and the provisions of any other law (other than Part XVIII of the *Income Tax Act*), the provisions of this Act and the Agreement prevail to the extent of the inconsistency.

(2) Inconsistent laws — exception — In the event of any inconsistency between the provisions of the Agreement and the provisions of the *Income Tax Conventions Interpretation Act*, the provisions of that Act prevail to the extent of the inconsistency.

5. Regulations — The Minister of National Revenue may make any regulations that are necessary for carrying out the Agreement or for giving effect to any of its provisions.

6. (1) Entry into force of Agreement — The Minister of Finance must cause a notice of the day on which the Agreement enters into force to be published in the *Canada Gazette* within 60 days after that day.

(2) Amending instrument — The Minister of Finance must cause a notice of the day on which any instrument amending the Agreement enters into force to be published, together with a copy of the instrument, in the *Canada Gazette* within 60 days after that day.

(3) Termination — The Minister of Finance must cause a notice of the day on which the Agreement is terminated to be published in the *Canada Gazette* within 60 days after that day.

The TIEA came into force on June 27, 2014, as announced by Dept. of Finance news release, July 2/14.

See also Notes to ITA 233.3(3) and ITA 263–269.

Table of Contents

Whereas, the Government of Canada and the Government of the United States of America (each, a "Party," and together, the "Parties") have a longstanding and close relationship with respect to mutual assistance in tax matters and desire to conclude an agreement to improve international tax compliance by further building on that relationship;

Whereas, Article XXVII of the Convention Between Canada and the United States with Respect to Taxes on Income and on Capital done at Washington on September 26, 1980, as amended by the Protocols done on June 14, 1983, March 28, 1984, March 17, 1995, July 29, 1997, and September 21, 2007 (the "Convention") authorizes the exchange of information for tax purposes, including on an automatic basis;

Whereas, the United States of America enacted provisions commonly known as the *Foreign Account Tax Compliance Act* ("FATCA"), which introduce a reporting regime for financial institutions with respect to certain accounts;

Whereas, the Governments of Canada and the United States of America are supportive of applying the underlying policy goal of FATCA on a reciprocal basis to improve tax compliance;

Whereas, FATCA has raised a number of issues, including that Canadian financial institutions may not be able to comply with certain aspects of FATCA due to domestic legal impediments;

Whereas, the Government of the United States of America collects information regarding certain accounts maintained by U.S. financial institutions held by residents of Canada and is committed to exchanging such information with the Government of Canada and pursuing equivalent levels of exchange;

Whereas, the Parties are committed to working together over the longer term towards achieving common reporting and due diligence standards for financial institutions;

Whereas, the Government of the United States of America acknowledges the need to coordinate the reporting obligations under FATCA with other U.S. tax reporting obligations of Canadian financial institutions to avoid duplicative reporting;

Whereas, an intergovernmental approach to FATCA implementation would facilitate compliance by Canadian financial institutions while protecting the ability of Canadians to access financial services;

Whereas, the Parties desire to conclude an agreement to improve international tax compliance and provide for the implementation of FATCA based on domestic reporting and reciprocal automatic exchange pursuant to the Convention and subject to the confidentiality and other protections provided for therein, including the provisions limiting the use of the information exchanged under the Convention;

Now, therefore, the Parties have agreed as follows:

Article 1 — Definitions

1. For purposes of this agreement and any annexes thereto ("Agreement"), the following terms shall have the meanings set forth below:

Related Provisions: ITA 263(5) — Terms in agreement apply to ITA ss. 263-269.

(a) The term **"United States"** has the same meaning as in the Convention. Any reference to a **"State"** of the United States includes the District of Columbia.

(b) The term **"U.S. Territory"** means American Samoa, the Commonwealth of the Northern Mariana Islands, Guam, the Commonwealth of Puerto Rico, or the U.S. Virgin Islands.

(c) The term **"IRS"** means the U.S. Internal Revenue Service.

(d) The term **"Canada"** has the same meaning as in the Convention.

Notes: See Canada-US treaty Art. III:1(a) for the definition in the Convention.

(e) The term **"Partner Jurisdiction"** means a jurisdiction that has in effect an agreement with the United States to facilitate the implementation of FATCA. The IRS shall publish a list identifying all Partner Jurisdictions.

(f) The term **"Competent Authority"** means:

(1) in the case of the United States, the Secretary of the Treasury or the Secretary's delegate; and

(2) in the case of Canada, the Minister of National Revenue or the Minister of National Revenue's authorized representative.

(g) The term **"Financial Institution"** means a Custodial Institution, a Depository Institution, an Investment Entity, or a Specified Insurance Company.

(h) The term **"Custodial Institution"** means any Entity that holds, as a substantial portion of its business, financial assets for the account of others. An entity holds financial assets for the account of others as a substantial portion of its business if the entity's gross income attributable to the holding of financial assets and related financial services equals or exceeds 20 percent of the entity's gross income during the shorter of:

(1) the three-year period that ends on December 31 (or the final day of a non-calendar year accounting period) prior to the year in which the determination is being made; or

(2) the period during which the entity has been in existence.

(i) The term **"Depository Institution"** means any Entity that accepts deposits in the ordinary course of a banking or similar business.

(j) The term **"Investment Entity"** means any Entity that conducts as a business (or is managed by an entity that conducts as a business) one or more of the following activities or operations for or on behalf of a customer:

(1) trading in money market instruments (cheques, bills, certificates of deposit, derivatives, etc.); foreign exchange; exchange, interest rate and index instruments; transferable securities; or commodity futures trading;

(2) individual and collective portfolio management; or

(3) otherwise investing, administering, or managing funds or money on behalf of other persons.

This subparagraph 1(j) shall be interpreted in a manner consistent with similar language set forth in the definition of "financial institution" in the Financial Action Task Force Recommendations.

(k) The term **"Specified Insurance Company"** means any Entity that is an insurance company (or the holding company of an insurance company) that issues, or is obligated to make payments with respect to, a Cash Value Insurance Contract or an Annuity Contract.

(l) The term **"Canadian Financial Institution"** means

(1) any Financial Institution that is resident in Canada, but excluding any branch of such Financial Institution that is located outside Canada, and

(2) any branch of a Financial Institution that is not resident in Canada, if such branch is located in Canada.

Related Provisions: ITA 263(2) — Definition of "Canadian financial institution" for Canadian reporting purposes.

(m) The term **"Partner Jurisdiction Financial Institution"** means

(1) any Financial Institution that is established in a Partner Jurisdiction, but excluding any branch of such Financial Institution that is located outside the Partner Jurisdiction, and

(2) any branch of a Financial Institution that is not established in the Partner Jurisdiction, if such branch is located in the Partner Jurisdiction.

(n) The term **"Reporting Financial Institution"** means a Reporting Canadian Financial Institution or a Reporting U.S. Financial Institution, as the context requires.

(o) The term **"Reporting Canadian Financial Institution"** means any Canadian Financial Institution that is not a Non-Reporting Canadian Financial Institution.

Related Provisions: ITA 263(2) — Definition of "reporting Canadian financial institution" for Canadian reporting purposes.

(p) The term **"Reporting U.S. Financial Institution"** means

(1) any Financial Institution that is resident in the United States, but excluding any branch of such Financial Institution that is located outside the United States, and

(2) any branch of a Financial Institution that is not resident in the United States, if such branch is located in the United States,

provided that the Financial Institution or branch has control, receipt, or custody of income with respect to which information is required to be exchanged under subparagraph (2)(b) of Article 2 of this Agreement.

(q) The term **"Non-Reporting Canadian Financial Institution"** means any Canadian Financial Institution, or other Entity resident in Canada, that is identified in Annex II as a Non-Reporting Canadian Financial Institution or that otherwise qualifies as a deemed compliant FFI or an exempt beneficial owner under relevant U.S. *Treasury Regulations* in effect on the date of signature of this Agreement.

(r) The term **"Nonparticipating Financial Institution"** means a nonparticipating FFI, as that term is defined in relevant U.S. *Treasury Regulations*, but does not include a Canadian Financial Institution or other Partner Jurisdiction Financial Institution other than a Financial Institution treated as a Nonparticipating Financial Institution pursuant to subparagraph 2(b) of Article 5 of this Agreement or the corresponding provision in an agreement between the United States and a Partner Jurisdiction.

(s) The term **"Financial Account"** means an account maintained by a Financial Institution, and includes:

(1) in the case of an Entity that is a Financial Institution solely because it is an Investment Entity, any equity or debt interest (other than interests that are regularly traded on an established securities market) in the Financial Institution;

(2) in the case of a Financial Institution not described in subparagraph 1(s)(1) of this Article, any equity or debt interest in the Financial Institution (other than interests that are regularly traded on an established securities market), if

(A) the value of the debt or equity interest is determined, directly or indirectly, primarily by reference to assets that give rise to U.S. Source Withholdable Payments, and

(B) the class of interests was established with a purpose of avoiding reporting in accordance with this Agreement; and

(3) any Cash Value Insurance Contract and any Annuity Contract issued or maintained by a Financial Institution, other than a noninvestment-linked, nontransferable immediate life annuity that is issued to an individual and monetizes a pension or disability benefit provided under an account, product, or arrangement identified as excluded from the definition of "Financial Account" in Annex II.

Notwithstanding the foregoing, the term **"Financial Account"** does not include any account, product, or arrangement identified as excluded from the definition of Financial Account in Annex II. For purposes of this Agreement, interests are "regularly traded" if there is a meaningful volume of trading with respect to the interests on an ongoing basis, and an **"established securities market"** means an exchange that is officially recognized and supervised by a governmental authority in which the market is located and that has a meaningful annual value of shares traded on the exchange. For purposes of this subparagraph 1(s), an interest in a Financial Institution is not "regularly traded" and shall be treated as a Financial Account if the holder of the interest (other than a Financial Institution acting as an intermediary) is registered on the books of such Financial Institution. The preceding sentence will not apply to interests first registered on the books of such Financial Institution prior to July 1, 2014, and with respect to interests first registered on the books of such Financial Institution on or after July 1, 2014, a Financial Institution is not required to apply the preceding sentence prior to January 1, 2016.

Related Provisions: ITA 263(3) — Application of definition for Canadian reporting purposes.

(t) The term **"Depository Account"** includes any commercial, checking, savings, time, or thrift account, or an account that is evidenced by a certificate of deposit, thrift certificate, investment certificate, certificate of indebtedness, or other similar instrument maintained by a Financial Institution in the ordinary course of a banking or similar business. A Depository Account also includes an amount held by an insurance company pursuant to a guaranteed investment contract or similar agreement to pay or credit interest thereon.

(u) The term **"Custodial Account"** means an account (other than an Insurance Contract or Annuity Contract) for the benefit of another person that holds any financial instrument or contract held for investment (including, but not limited to, a share or stock in a corporation, a note, bond, debenture, or other evidence of indebtedness, a currency or commodity transaction, a credit default swap, a swap based upon a nonfinancial index, a notional principal contract, an Insurance Contract or Annuity Contract, and any option or other derivative instrument).

(v) The term **"Equity Interest"** means, in the case of a partnership that is a Financial Institution, either a capital or profits interest in the partnership. In the case of a trust that is a Financial Institution, an Equity Interest is considered to be held by any person treated as a settlor or beneficiary of all or a portion of the trust, or any other natural person exercising ultimate effective control over the trust. A Specified U.S. Person shall be treated as being a beneficiary of a foreign trust if such Specified U.S. Person has the right to receive directly or indirectly (for example, through a nominee) a mandatory distribution or may receive, directly or indirectly, a discretionary distribution from the trust.

(w) The term **"Insurance Contract"** means a contract (other than an Annuity Contract) under which the issuer agrees to pay an amount upon the occurrence of a specified contingency involving mortality, morbidity, accident, liability, or property risk.

(x) The term **"Annuity Contract"** means a contract under which the issuer agrees to make payments for a period of time determined in whole or in part by reference to the life expectancy of one or more individuals. The term also includes a contract that is considered to be an Annuity Contract in accordance with the law, regulation, or practice of the jurisdiction in which the contract was issued, and under which the issuer agrees to make payments for a term of years.

(y) The term **"Cash Value Insurance Contract"** means an Insurance Contract (other than an indemnity reinsurance contract between two insurance companies) that has a Cash Value greater than $50,000.

(z) The term **"Cash Value"** means the greater of (i) the amount that the policyholder is entitled to receive upon surrender or termination of the contract (determined without reduction for any surrender charge or policy loan), and (ii) the amount the policyholder can borrow under or with regard to the contract. Notwithstanding the foregoing, the term **"Cash Value"** does not include an amount payable under an Insurance Contract as:

(1) a personal injury or sickness benefit or other benefit providing indemnification of an economic loss incurred upon the occurrence of the event insured against;

(2) a refund to the policyholder of a previously paid premium under an Insurance Contract (other than under a life insurance contract) due to policy cancellation or termination, decrease in risk exposure during the effective period of the Insurance Contract, or arising from a redetermination of the premium due to correction of posting or other similar error; or

(3) a policyholder dividend based upon the underwriting experience of the contract or group involved.

(aa) The term **"Reportable Account"** means a U.S. Reportable Account or a Canadian Reportable Account, as the context requires.

(bb) The term **"Canadian Reportable Account"** means a Financial Account maintained by a Reporting U.S. Financial Institution if:

(1) in the case of a Depository Account, the account is held by an individual resident in Canada and more than $10 of interest is paid to such account in any given calendar year; or

(2) in the case of a Financial Account other than a Depository Account, the Account Holder is a resident of Canada, including an Entity that certifies that it is resident in Canada for tax purposes, with respect to which U.S. source income that is subject to reporting under chapter 3 of subtitle A or chapter 61 of subtitle F of the U.S. *Internal Revenue Code* is paid or credited.

(cc) The term **"U.S. Reportable Account"** means a Financial Account maintained by a Reporting Canadian Financial Institution and held by one or more Specified U.S. Persons or by a Non-U.S. Entity with one or more Controlling Persons that is a Specified U.S. Person. Notwithstanding the foregoing, an account shall not be treated as a U.S. Reportable Account if such account is not identified as a U.S. Reportable Account after application of the due diligence procedures in Annex I.

(dd) The term **"Account Holder"** means the person listed or identified as the holder of a Financial Account by the Financial Institution that maintains the account. A person, other than a Financial Institution, holding a Financial Account for the benefit or account of another person as agent, custodian, nominee, signatory, investment advisor, or intermediary, is not treated as the Account Holder for purposes of this Agreement, and such other person is treated as the Account Holder. For purposes of the immediately preceding sentence, the term **"Financial Institution"** does not include a Financial Institution organized or incorporated in a U.S. Territory. In the case of a Cash Value Insurance Contract or an Annuity Contract, the Account Holder is any person entitled to access the Cash Value or change the beneficiary of the contract. If no person can access the Cash Value or change the beneficiary, the Account Holder is any person named as the owner in the contract and any person with a vested entitlement to payment under the terms of the contract. Upon the maturity of a Cash Value Insurance Contract or an Annuity Contract, each person entitled to receive a payment under the contract is treated as an Account Holder.

(ee) The term **"U.S. Person"** means

(1) a U.S. citizen or resident individual,

(2) a partnership or corporation organized in the United States or under the laws of the United States or any State thereof,

(3) a trust if

(A) a court within the United States would have authority under applicable law to render orders or judgments concerning substantially all issues regarding administration of the trust, and

(B) one or more U.S. persons have the authority to control all substantial decisions of the trust, or

(4) an estate of a decedent that is a citizen or resident of the United States.

This subparagraph 1(ee) shall be interpreted in accordance with the U.S. *Internal Revenue Code*.

(ff) The term **"Specified U.S. Person"** means a U.S. Person, other than:

(1) a corporation the stock of which is regularly traded on one or more established securities markets;

(2) any corporation that is a member of the same expanded affiliated group, as defined in section 1471(e)(2) of the U.S. *Internal Revenue Code*, as a corporation described in clause (1);

(3) the United States or any wholly owned agency or instrumentality thereof;

(4) any State of the United States, any U.S. Territory, any political subdivision of any of the foregoing, or any wholly owned agency or instrumentality of any one or more of the foregoing;

(5) any organization exempt from taxation under section 501(a) of the U.S. *Internal Revenue Code* or an individual retirement plan as defined in section 7701(a)(37) of the U.S. *Internal Revenue Code*;

(6) any bank as defined in section 581 of the U.S. *Internal Revenue Code*;

(7) any real estate investment trust as defined in section 856 of the U.S. *Internal Revenue Code*;

(8) any regulated investment company as defined in section 851 of the U.S. *Internal Revenue Code* or any entity registered with the U.S. Securities and Exchange Commission under the U.S. *Investment Company Act of 1940*;

(9) any common trust fund as defined in section 584(a) of the U.S. *Internal Revenue Code*;

(10) any trust that is exempt from tax under section 664(c) of the U.S. *Internal Revenue Code* or that is described in section 4947(a)(1) of the U.S. *Internal Revenue Code*;

(11) a dealer in securities, commodities, or derivative financial instruments (including notional principal contracts, futures, forwards, and options) that is registered as such under the laws of the United States or any State thereof;

(12) a broker as defined in section 6045(c) of the U.S. *Internal Revenue Code*; or

(13) any tax exempt trust under a plan that is described in section 403(b) or section 457(b) of the U.S. *Internal Revenue Code*.

(gg) The term **"Entity"** means a legal person or a legal arrangement such as a trust.

(hh) The term **"Non-U.S. Entity"** means an Entity that is not a U.S. Person.

(ii) The term **"U.S. Source Withholdable Payment"** means any payment of interest (including any original issue discount), dividends, rents, salaries, wages, premiums, annuities, compensations, remunerations, emoluments, and other fixed or determinable annual or periodical gains, profits, and income, if such payment is from sources within the United States. Notwithstanding the foregoing, a U.S. Source Withholdable Payment does not include any payment that is not treated as a withholdable payment in relevant U.S. *Treasury Regulations*.

(jj) An Entity is a **"Related Entity"** of another Entity if either Entity controls the other Entity, or the two Entities are under common control. For this purpose control includes direct or indirect ownership of more than 50 percent of the vote or value in an Entity. Notwithstanding the foregoing, Canada may treat an Entity as not a Related Entity of another Entity if the two Entities are not members of the same expanded affiliated group as defined in section 1471(e)(2) of the U.S. *Internal Revenue Code*.

(kk) The term **"U.S. TIN"** means a U.S. federal taxpayer identifying number.

(ll) The term **"Canadian TIN"** means a Canadian taxpayer identifying number.

Related Provisions: ITA 263(4) — Meaning of "Canadian TIN" for Canadian reporting purposes.

(mm) The term **"Controlling Persons"** means the natural persons who exercise control over an Entity. In the case of a trust, such term means the settlor, the trustees, the protector (if any), the beneficiaries or class of beneficiaries, and any other natural person exercising ultimate effective control over the trust, and in the case of a legal arrangement other than a trust, such term means persons in equivalent or similar positions. The term "Controlling Persons" shall be interpreted in a manner consistent with the Financial Action Task Force Recommendations.

Definitions [Art. 1:1]: "Account Holder" — 1:1(dd); "Annuity Contract" — 1:1(x); "Canada" — 1:1(d), Canada-US Treaty Art:III:1(a); "Canadian Financial Institution" — 1:1(l); "Canadian Reportable Account" — 1:1(bb); "Cash Value" — 1:1(z); "Cash Value Insurance Contract" — 1:1(y); "Custodial Institution" — 1:1(h); "Depository Account" — 1:1(t); "Depository Institution" — 1:1(i); "Entity" — 1:1(gg); "Equity Interest" — 1:1(v); "Financial Account" — 1:1(s); "Financial Institution" — 1:1(g); "Insurance Contract" — 1:1(w); "IRS" — 1:1(c); "Non-Reporting Canadian Financial Institution" — 1:1(q); "Nonparticipating Financial Institution" — 1:1(r); "Partner Jurisdiction" — 1:1(e); "Partner Jurisdiction Financial Institution" — 1:1(m); "Related Entity" — 1:1(jj); "Reportable Account" — 1:1(aa); "Reporting Canadian Financial Institution" — 1:1(o); "Specified Insurance Company" — 1:1(k); "State", "United States" — 1:1(a).

2. Any term not otherwise defined in this Agreement shall, unless the context otherwise requires or the Competent Authorities agree to a common meaning (as permitted by domestic law), have the meaning that it has at that time under the law of the Party applying this Agreement, any meaning under the applicable tax laws of that Party prevailing over a meaning given to the term under other laws of that Party.

Definitions [Art. 1:2]: "Competent Authority" — 1:1(f); "Party" — Preamble.

Article 2 — Obligations to Obtain and Exchange Information with Respect to Reportable Accounts

1. Subject to the provisions of Article 3 of this Agreement, each Party shall obtain the information specified in paragraph 2 of this Article with respect to all Reportable Accounts and shall annually exchange this information with the other Party on an automatic basis pursuant to the provisions of Article XXVII of the Convention.

Definitions [Art. 2:1]: "Party" — Preamble; "Reportable Account" — 1:1(aa).

2. The information to be obtained and exchanged is:

(a) In the case of Canada with respect to each U.S. Reportable Account of each Reporting Canadian Financial Institution:

(1) the name, address, and U.S. TIN of each Specified U.S. Person that is an Account Holder of such account and, in the case of a Non-U.S. Entity that, after application of the due diligence procedures set forth in Annex I, is identified as having one or more Controlling Persons that is a Specified U.S. Person, the name, address, and U.S. TIN (if any) of such Entity and each such Specified U.S. Person;

(2) the account number (or functional equivalent in the absence of an account number);

(3) the name and identifying number of the Reporting Canadian Financial Institution;

(4) the account balance or value (including, in the case of a Cash Value Insurance Contract or Annuity Contract, the Cash Value or surrender value) as of the end of the relevant calendar year or other appropriate reporting period or, if the account was closed during such year, immediately before closure;

(5) in the case of any Custodial Account:

(A) the total gross amount of interest, the total gross amount of dividends, and the total gross amount of other income generated with respect to the assets held in the account, in each case paid or credited to the account (or with respect to the account) during the calendar year or other appropriate reporting period; and

(B) the total gross proceeds from the sale or redemption of property paid or credited to the account during the calendar year or other appropriate reporting period with respect to which the Reporting Canadian Financial Institution acted as a custodian, broker, nominee, or otherwise as an agent for the Account Holder;

(6) in the case of any Depository Account, the total gross amount of interest paid or credited to the account during the calendar year or other appropriate reporting period; and

(7) in the case of any account not described in subparagraph 2(a)(5) or 2(a)(6) of this Article, the total gross amount paid or credited to the Account Holder with respect to the account during the calendar year or other appropriate reporting period with respect to which the Reporting Canadian Financial Institution is the obligor or debtor, including the aggregate amount of any redemption payments made to the Account Holder during the calendar year or other appropriate reporting period.

(b) In the case of the United States, with respect to each Canadian Reportable Account of each Reporting U.S. Financial Institution:

(1) the name, address, and Canadian TIN of any person that is a resident of Canada and is an Account Holder of the account;

(2) the account number (or the functional equivalent in the absence of an account number);

(3) the name and identifying number of the Reporting U.S. Financial Institution;

(4) the gross amount of interest paid on a Depository Account;

(5) the gross amount of U.S. source dividends paid or credited to the account; and

(6) the gross amount of other U.S. source income paid or credited to the account, to the extent subject to reporting

under chapter 3 of subtitle A or chapter 61 of subtitle F of the U.S. *Internal Revenue Code*.

Definitions [Art. 2:2]: "Account Holder" — 1:1(dd); "Annuity Contract" — 1:1(x); "Canada" — 1:1(d), Canada-US Treaty Art:III:1(a); "Canadian Reportable Account" — 1:1(bb); "Canadian TIN" — 1:1(ll); "Cash Value" — 1:1(z); "Cash Value Insurance Contract" — 1:1(y); "Custodial Account" — 1:1(u); "Depository Account" — 1:1(t); "Entity" — 1:1(gg); "Financial Institution" — 1:1(g); "Reportable Account" — 1:1(aa); "Reporting Canadian Financial Institution" — 1:1(o); "United States" — 1:1(a).

Article 3 — Time and Manner of Exchange of Information

1. For purposes of the exchange obligation in Article 2 of this Agreement, the amount and characterization of payments made with respect to a U.S. Reportable Account may be determined in accordance with the principles of Canada's tax laws, and the amount and characterization of payments made with respect to a Canadian Reportable Account may be determined in accordance with principles of U.S. federal income tax law.

Definitions [Art. 3:1]: "Canada" — 1:1(d), Canada-US Treaty Art:III:1(a); "Canadian Reportable Account" — 1:1(bb); "Reportable Account" — 1:1(aa).

2. For purposes of the exchange obligation in Article 2 of this Agreement, the information exchanged shall identify the currency in which each relevant amount is denominated.

3. With respect to paragraph 2 of Article 2 of this Agreement, information is to be obtained and exchanged with respect to 2014 and all subsequent years, except that:

(a) In the case of Canada:

(1) the information to be obtained and exchanged with respect to 2014 is only the information described in subparagraphs 2(a)(1) through 2(a)(4) of Article 2 of this Agreement;

(2) the information to be obtained and exchanged with respect to 2015 is the information described in subparagraphs 2(a)(1) through 2(a)(7) of Article 2 of this Agreement, except for gross proceeds described in subparagraph 2(a)(5)(B) of Article 2 of this Agreement; and

(3) the information to be obtained and exchanged with respect to 2016 and subsequent years is the information described in subparagraphs 2(a)(1) through 2(a)(7) of Article 2 of this Agreement;

(b) In the case of the United States, the information to be obtained and exchanged with respect to 2014 and subsequent years is all of the information identified in subparagraph 2(b) of Article 2 of this Agreement.

Definitions [Art. 3:3]: "Canada" — 1:1(d), Canada-US Treaty Art:III:1(a); "United States" — 1:1(a).

4. Notwithstanding paragraph 3 of this Article, with respect to each Reportable Account that is maintained by a Reporting Financial Institution as of June 30, 2014, and subject to paragraph 4 of Article 6 of this Agreement, the Parties are not required to obtain and include in the exchanged information the Canadian TIN or the U.S. TIN, as applicable, of any relevant person if such taxpayer identifying number is not in the records of the Reporting Financial Institution. In such a case, the Parties shall obtain and include in the exchanged information the date of birth of the relevant person, if the Reporting Financial Institution has such date of birth in its records.

Definitions [Art. 3:4]: "Canadian TIN" — 1:1(ll); "Party" — Preamble; "Reportable Account" — 1:1(aa); "Reporting Canadian Financial Institution" — 1:1(n).

5. Subject to paragraphs 3 and 4 of this Article, the information described in Article 2 of this Agreement shall be exchanged within nine months after the end of the calendar year to which the information relates.

6. The Competent Authorities of Canada and the United States shall enter into an agreement or arrangement under the mutual agreement procedure provided for in Article XXVI of the Convention, which shall:

(a) establish the procedures for the automatic exchange obligations described in Article 2 of this Agreement;

(b) prescribe rules and procedures as may be necessary to implement Article 5 of this Agreement; and

(c) establish as necessary procedures for the exchange of the information reported under subparagraph 1(b) of Article 4 of this Agreement.

Definitions [Art. 3:6]: "Canada" — 1:1(d), Canada-US Treaty Art:III:1(a); "Competent Authority" — 1:1(f); "Convention" — Preamble; "United States" — 1:1(a).

7. All information exchanged shall be subject to the confidentiality and other protections provided for in the Convention, including the provisions limiting the use of the information exchanged.

Definitions [Art. 3:7]: "Convention" — Preamble.

Article 4 — Application of FATCA to Canadian Financial Institutions

1. Treatment of Reporting Canadian Financial Institutions — Each Reporting Canadian Financial Institution shall be treated as complying with, and not subject to withholding under, section 1471 of the U.S. *Internal Revenue Code* if Canada complies with its obligations under Articles 2 and 3 of this Agreement with respect to such Reporting Canadian Financial Institution, and the Reporting Canadian Financial Institution:

(a) identifies U.S. Reportable Accounts and reports annually to the Canadian Competent Authority the information required to be reported in subparagraph 2(a) of Article 2 of this Agreement in the time and manner described in Article 3 of this Agreement;

(b) for each of 2015 and 2016, reports annually to the Canadian Competent Authority the name of each Nonparticipating Financial Institution to which it has made payments and the aggregate amount of such payments;

(c) complies with the applicable registration requirements on the IRS FATCA registration website;

(d) to the extent that a Reporting Canadian Financial Institution is

(1) acting as a qualified intermediary (for purposes of section 1441 of the U.S. *Internal Revenue Code*) that has elected to assume primary withholding responsibility under chapter 3 of subtitle A of the U.S. *Internal Revenue Code*,

(2) a foreign partnership that has elected to act as a withholding foreign partnership (for purposes of both sections 1441 and 1471 of the U.S. *Internal Revenue Code*), or

(3) a foreign trust that has elected to act as a withholding foreign trust (for purposes of both sections 1441 and 1471 of the U.S. *Internal Revenue Code*),

withholds 30 percent of any U.S. Source Withholdable Payment to any Nonparticipating Financial Institution; and

(e) in the case of a Reporting Canadian Financial Institution that is not described in subparagraph 1(d) of this Article and that makes a payment of, or acts as an intermediary with respect to, a U.S. Source Withholdable Payment to any Nonparticipating Financial Institution, the Reporting Canadian Financial Institution provides to any immediate payor of such U.S. Source Withholdable Payment the information required for withholding and reporting to occur with respect to such payment.

Notwithstanding the foregoing, a Reporting Canadian Financial Institution with respect to which the conditions of this paragraph 1 are not satisfied shall not be subject to withholding under section 1471 of the U.S. *Internal Revenue Code* unless such Reporting Canadian Financial Institution is treated by the IRS as a Nonparticipating Financial Institution pursuant to subparagraph 2(b) of Article 5 of this Agreement.

Definitions [Art. 4:1]: "Canada" — 1:1(d), Canada-US Treaty Art:III:1(a); "Canadian Financial Institution" — 1:1(l); "Competent Authority" — 1:1(f); "IRS" — 1:1(c); "Nonparticipating Financial Institution" — 1:1(r); "Reportable Account" — 1:1(aa); "Reporting Canadian Financial Institution" — 1:1(o).

2. Suspension of rules relating to recalcitrant accounts — The United States shall not require a Reporting Canadian Financial Institution to withhold tax under section 1471 or 1472 of the U.S. *Internal Revenue Code* with respect to an account held by a recalcitrant account holder (as defined in section 1471(d)(6) of the U.S. *Internal Revenue Code*), or to close such account, if the U.S. Competent Authority receives the information set forth in subparagraph 2(a) of Article 2 of this Agreement, subject to the provisions of Article 3 of this Agreement, with respect to such account.

Definitions [Art. 4:2]: "Competent Authority" — 1:1(f); "Reporting Canadian Financial Institution" — 1:1(o); "United States" — 1:1(a).

3. Specific treatment of Canadian retirement plans — The United States shall treat as deemed-compliant FFIs or exempt beneficial owners, as appropriate, for purposes of sections 1471 and 1472 of the U.S. *Internal Revenue Code*, Canadian retirement plans identified in Annex II. For this purpose, a Canadian retirement plan includes an Entity established or located in, and regulated by, Canada, or a predetermined contractual or legal arrangement, operated to provide pension or retirement benefits or earn income for providing such benefits under the laws of Canada and regulated with respect to contributions, distributions, reporting, sponsorship, and taxation.

Definitions [Art. 4:3]: "Canada" — 1:1(d), Canada-US Treaty Art:III:1(a); "Entity" — 1:1(gg); "United States" — 1:1(a).

4. Identification and treatment of other deemed-compliant FFIs and exempt beneficial owners — The United States shall treat each Non-Reporting Canadian Financial Institution as a deemed-compliant FFI or as an exempt beneficial owner, as appropriate, for purposes of section 1471 of the U.S. *Internal Revenue Code*.

Definitions [Art. 4:4]: "Non-Reporting Canadian Financial Institution" — 1:1(q); "United States" — 1:1(a).

5. Special rules regarding Related Entities and branches that are Nonparticipating Financial Institutions — If a Canadian Financial Institution, that otherwise meets the requirements described in paragraph 1 of this Article or is described in paragraph 3 or 4 of this Article, has a Related Entity or branch that operates in a jurisdiction that prevents such Related Entity or branch from fulfilling the requirements of a participating FFI or deemed-compliant FFI for purposes of section 1471 of the U.S. *Internal Revenue Code* or has a Related Entity or branch that is treated as a Nonparticipating Financial Institution solely due to the expiration of the transitional rule for limited FFIs and limited branches under relevant U.S. *Treasury Regulations*, such Canadian Financial Institution shall continue to be in compliance with the terms of this Agreement and shall continue to be treated as a deemed-compliant FFI or exempt beneficial owner, as appropriate, for purposes of section 1471 of the U.S. *Internal Revenue Code*, provided that:

(a) the Canadian Financial Institution treats each such Related Entity or branch as a separate Nonparticipating Financial Institution for purposes of all the reporting and withholding requirements of this Agreement and each such Related Entity or branch identifies itself to withholding agents as a Nonparticipating Financial Institution;

(b) each such Related Entity or branch identifies its U.S. accounts and reports the information with respect to those accounts as required under section 1471 of the U.S. *Internal Revenue Code* to the extent permitted under the relevant laws pertaining to the Related Entity or branch; and

(c) such Related Entity or branch does not specifically solicit U.S. accounts held by persons that are not resident in the jurisdiction where such Related Entity or branch is located or accounts held by Nonparticipating Financial Institutions that are not established in the jurisdiction where such branch or Related Entity is located, and such branch or Related Entity is not used by the Canadian Financial Institution or any other Related Entity to circumvent the obligations under this Agreement or under section 1471 of the U.S. *Internal Revenue Code*, as appropriate.

Definitions [Art. 4:5]: "Canadian Financial Institution" — 1:1(l); "Nonparticipating Financial Institution" — 1:1(r); "Related Entity" — 1:1(jj).

6. Coordination of timing — Notwithstanding paragraphs 3 and 5 of Article 3 of this Agreement:

(a) Canada shall not be obligated to obtain and exchange information with respect to a calendar year that is prior to the calendar year with respect to which similar information is required to be reported to the IRS by participating FFIs pursuant to relevant U.S. *Treasury Regulations*;

(b) Canada shall not be obligated to begin exchanging information prior to the date by which participating FFIs are required to report similar information to the IRS under relevant U.S. *Treasury Regulations*;

(c) the United States shall not be obligated to obtain and exchange information with respect to a calendar year that is prior to the first calendar year with respect to which Canada is required to obtain and exchange information; and

(d) the United States shall not be obligated to begin exchanging information prior to the date by which Canada is required to begin exchanging information.

Definitions [Art. 4:6]: "Canada" — 1:1(d), Canada-US Treaty Art:III:1(a); "IRS" — 1:1(c); "United States" — 1:1(a).

7. Coordination of definitions with U.S. *Treasury Regulations* — Notwithstanding Article 1 of this Agreement and the definitions provided in the Annexes to this Agreement, in implementing this Agreement, Canada may use, and may permit Canadian Financial Institutions to use, a definition in relevant U.S. *Treasury Regulations* in lieu of a corresponding definition in this Agreement, provided that such application would not frustrate the purposes of this Agreement.

Definitions [Art. 4:7]: "Canada" — 1:1(d), Canada-US Treaty Art:III:1(a); "Canadian Financial Institution" — 1:1(l).

Article 5 — Collaboration on Compliance and Enforcement

1. Minor and administrative errors — A Competent Authority shall notify the Competent Authority of the other Party when the first-mentioned Competent Authority has reason to believe that administrative errors or other minor errors may have led to incorrect or incomplete information reporting or resulted in other infringements of this Agreement. The Competent Authority of such other Party shall endeavor, including where appropriate by applying its domestic law (including applicable penalties), to obtain corrected and/or complete information or to resolve other infringements of this Agreement.

Definitions [Art. 5:1]: "Competent Authority" — 1:1(f); "Party" — Preamble.

2. Significant non-compliance —

(a) A Competent Authority shall notify the Competent Authority of the other Party when the first-mentioned Competent Authority has determined that there is significant non-compliance with the obligations under this Agreement with respect to a Reporting Financial Institution in the other jurisdiction. The Competent Authority of such other Party shall apply its domestic law (including applicable penalties) to address the significant non-compliance described in the notice.

(b) If, in the case of a Reporting Canadian Financial Institution, such enforcement actions do not resolve the non-compliance within a period of 18 months after notification of significant non-compliance is first provided, the United States shall treat the Reporting Canadian Financial Institution as a Nonparticipating Financial Institution pursuant to this subparagraph 2(b).

Definitions [Art. 5:2]: "Competent Authority" — 1:1(f); "Nonparticipating Financial Institution" — 1:1(r); "Party" — Preamble; "Reporting Canadian Financial Institution" — 1:1(o); "Reporting Financial Institution" — 1:1(n); "United States" — 1:1(a).

3. Reliance on third party service providers — Each Party may allow Reporting Financial Institutions to use third party service providers to fulfill the obligations imposed on such Reporting Financial Institutions by a Party, as contemplated in this Agreement, but these obligations shall remain the responsibility of the Reporting Financial Institutions.

Definitions [Art. 5:3]: "Party" — Preamble; "Reporting Financial Institution" — 1:1(n).

4. Prevention of avoidance — The Parties shall implement as necessary requirements to prevent Financial Institutions from adopting practices intended to circumvent the reporting required under this Agreement.

Definitions [Art. 5:4]: "Financial Institution" — 1:1(g); "Party" — Preamble.

Article 6 — Mutual Commitment to Continue to Enhance the Effectiveness of Information Exchange and Transparency

1. Reciprocity — The Government of the United States acknowledges the need to achieve equivalent levels of reciprocal automatic information exchange with Canada. The Government of the United States is committed to further improve transparency and enhance the exchange relationship with Canada by pursuing the adoption of regulations and advocating and supporting relevant legislation to achieve such equivalent levels of reciprocal automatic information exchange.

Definitions [Art. 6:1]: "Canada" — 1:1(d), Canada-US Treaty Art:III:1(a); "United States" — 1:1(a).

2. Treatment of passthru payments and gross proceeds — The Parties are committed to work together, along with Partner Jurisdictions, to develop a practical and effective alternative approach to achieve the policy objectives of foreign passthru payment and gross proceeds withholding that minimizes burden.

Definitions [Art. 6:2]: "Partner Jurisdiction" — 1:1(e); "Party" — Preamble.

3. Development of common reporting and exchange model — The Parties are committed to working with Partner Jurisdictions and the Organisation for Economic Co-operation and Development on adapting the terms of this Agreement and other agreements between the United States and Partner Jurisdictions to a common model for automatic exchange of information, including the development of reporting and due diligence standards for financial institutions.

Definitions [Art. 6:3]: "Partner Jurisdiction" — 1:1(e); "Party" — Preamble; "United States" — 1:1(a).

4. Documentation of accounts maintained as of June 30, 2014 — With respect to Reportable Accounts maintained by a Reporting Financial Institution as of June 30, 2014:

(a) The United States commits to establish, by January 1, 2017, for reporting with respect to 2017 and subsequent years, rules requiring Reporting U.S. Financial Institutions to obtain and report the Canadian TIN of each Account Holder of a Canadian Reportable Account as required pursuant to subparagraph 2(b)(1) of Article 2 of this Agreement; and

(b) Canada commits to establish, by January 1, 2017, for reporting with respect to 2017 and subsequent years, rules requiring Reporting Canadian Financial Institutions to obtain the U.S. TIN of each Specified U.S. Person as required pursuant to subparagraph 2(a)(1) of Article 2 of this Agreement.

Definitions [Art. 6:4]: "Account Holder" — 1:1(dd); "Canada" — 1:1(d), Canada-US Treaty Art:III:1(a); "Canadian Reportable Account" — 1:1(bb); "Canadian TIN" — 1:1(ll); "Financial Institution" — 1:1(g); "Reportable Account" — 1:1(aa); "Reporting Canadian Financial Institution" — 1:1(o); "Reporting Financial Institution" — 1:1(n); "United States" — 1:1(a).

Article 7 — Consistency in the Application of FATCA to Partner Jurisdictions

1. Canada shall be granted the benefit of any more favorable terms under Article 4 or Annex I of this Agreement relating to the application of FATCA to Canadian Financial Institutions afforded to another Partner Jurisdiction under a signed bilateral agreement pursuant to which the other Partner Jurisdiction commits to undertake the same obligations as Canada described in Articles 2 and 3 of this Agreement, and subject to the same terms and conditions as described therein and in Articles 5 through 9 of this Agreement.

Definitions [Art. 7:1]: "Canada" — 1:1(d), Canada-US Treaty Art:III:1(a); "Canadian Financial Institution" — 1:1(l); "Partner Jurisdiction" — 1:1(e).

2. The United States shall notify Canada of any such more favorable terms, and such more favorable terms shall apply automatically under this Agreement as if such terms were specified in this Agreement and effective as of the date of signing of the agreement incorporating the more favorable terms, unless Canada declines the application thereof.

Definitions [Art. 7:2]: "Canada" — 1:1(d), Canada-US Treaty Art:III:1(a); "United States" — 1:1(a).

Article 8 — Consultations and Amendments

1. In case any difficulties in the implementation of this Agreement arise, either Party may request consultations to develop appropriate measures to ensure the fulfillment of this Agreement.

Definitions [Art. 8:1]: "Party" — Preamble.

2. This Agreement may be amended by written mutual agreement of the Parties. Unless otherwise agreed upon, such an amendment shall enter into force through the same procedures as set forth in paragraph 1 of Article 10 of this Agreement.

Definitions [Art. 8:2]: "Party" — Preamble.

Article 9 — Annexes

The Annexes form an integral part of this Agreement.

Article 10 — Term of Agreement

1. This Agreement shall enter into force on the date of Canada's written notification to the United States that Canada has completed its necessary internal procedures for entry into force of this Agreement.

Definitions [Art. 10:1]: "Canada" — 1:1(d), Canada-US Treaty Art:III:1(a); "United States" — 1:1(a).

2. Either Party may terminate this Agreement by giving notice of termination in writing to the other Party. Such termination shall become effective on the first day of the month following the expiration of a period of 12 months after the date of the notice of termination.

Definitions [Art. 10:2]: "Party" — Preamble.

3. The Parties shall, prior to December 31, 2016, consult in good faith to amend this Agreement as necessary to reflect progress on the commitments set forth in Article 6 of this Agreement.

Definitions [Art. 10:3]: "Party" — Preamble.

IN WITNESS WHEREOF, the undersigned, being duly authorized thereto by their respective Governments, have signed this Agreement.

DONE in duplicate, at ...., this .... day of .... 2014, in the English and French languages, each version being equally authentic.

FOR THE GOVERNMENT OF CANADA:

FOR THE GOVERNMENT OF THE UNITED STATES OF AMERICA:

ANNEX I — DUE DILIGENCE OBLIGATIONS FOR IDENTIFYING AND REPORTING ON U.S. REPORTABLE ACCOUNTS AND ON PAYMENTS TO CERTAIN NONPARTICIPATING FINANCIAL INSTITUTIONS

Table of Contents [paraphrased]

E. Alternative procedures for Financial Accounts held by individual beneficiaries of a cash value insurance contract

F. Reliance on third parties

I. GENERAL

A. [Canada to require due diligence procedures.] Canada shall require that Reporting Canadian Financial Institutions apply the due diligence procedures contained in this Annex I to identify U.S. Reportable Accounts and accounts held by Non-participating Financial Institutions.

Definitions [Annex I:I:A]: "Canada" — 1:1(d), Canada-US Treaty Art:III:1(a); "Nonparticipating Financial Institution" — 1:1(r); "Reportable Account" — 1:1(aa); "Reporting Canadian Financial Institution" — 1:1(o).

B. [Interpretation rules.] For purposes of the Agreement,

1. All dollar amounts are in U.S. dollars and shall be read to include the equivalent in other currencies.

2. Except as otherwise provided herein, the balance or value of an account shall be determined as of the last day of the calendar year or other appropriate reporting period.

3. Where a balance or value threshold is to be determined as of June 30, 2014, under this Annex I, the relevant balance or value shall be determined as of that day or the last day of the reporting period ending immediately before June 30, 2014, and where a balance or value threshold is to be determined as of the last day of a calendar year under this Annex I, the relevant balance or value shall be determined as of the last day of the calendar year or other appropriate reporting period.

4. Subject to subparagraph E(1) of section II of this Annex I, an account shall be treated as a U.S. Reportable Account beginning as of the date it is identified as such pursuant to the due diligence procedures in this Annex I.

5. Unless otherwise provided, information with respect to a U.S. Reportable Account shall be reported annually in the calendar year following the year to which the information relates.

Definitions [Annex I:I:B]: "Reportable Account" — 1:1(aa).

C. [Alternative — Canada may permit reliance on US Treasury Regulations.] As an alternative to the procedures described in each section of this Annex I, Canada may permit Reporting Canadian Financial Institutions to rely on the procedures described in relevant U.S. *Treasury Regulations* to establish whether an account is a U.S. Reportable Account or an account held by a Nonparticipating Financial Institution. Canada may permit Reporting Canadian Financial Institutions to make such election separately for each section of this Annex I either with respect to all relevant Financial Accounts or, separately, with respect to any clearly identified group of such accounts (such as by line of business or the location of where the account is maintained).

Definitions [Annex I:I:C]: "Canada" — 1:1(d), Canada-US Treaty Art:III:1(a); "Financial Account" — 1:1(s); "Nonparticipating Financial Institution" — 1:1(r); "Reportable Account" — 1:1(aa); "Reporting Canadian Financial Institution" — 1:1(o).

II. PREEXISTING INDIVIDUAL ACCOUNTS

The following rules and procedures apply for purposes of identifying U.S. Reportable Accounts among Preexisting Accounts held by individuals ("Preexisting Individual Accounts").

Definitions [Annex I:II opening words]: "Preexisting Account" — Annex I:VI:B:5; "Reportable Account" — 1:1(aa).

A. Accounts Not Required to Be Reviewed, Identified, or Reported. Unless the Reporting Canadian Financial Institution elects otherwise, either with respect to all Preexisting Individual Accounts or, separately, with respect to any clearly identified group of such accounts, where the implementing rules in Canada provide for such an election, the following Preexisting Indivi-

dual Accounts are not required to be reviewed, identified, or reported as U.S. Reportable Accounts:

1. Subject to subparagraph E(2) of this section, a Preexisting Individual Account with a balance or value that does not exceed $50,000 as of June 30, 2014.

2. Subject to subparagraph E(2) of this section, a Preexisting Individual Account that is a Cash Value Insurance Contract or an Annuity Contract with a balance or value of $250,000 or less as of June 30, 2014.

3. A Preexisting Individual Account that is a Cash Value Insurance Contract or an Annuity Contract, provided the law or regulations of Canada or the United States effectively prevent the sale of such a Cash Value Insurance Contract or an Annuity Contract to U.S. residents (e.g., if the relevant Financial Institution does not have the required registration under U.S. law, and the law of Canada requires reporting or withholding with respect to insurance products held by residents of Canada).

4. A Depository Account with a balance of $50,000 or less.

Definitions [Annex I:II:A]: "Annuity Contract" — 1:1(x); "Canada" — 1:1(d), Canada-US Treaty Art:III:1(a); "Cash Value Insurance Contract" — 1:1(y); "Depository Account" — 1:1(t); "Financial Institution" — 1:1(g); "Preexisting Individual Account" — Annex I:II; "Reportable Account" — 1:1(aa); "Reporting Canadian Financial Institution" — 1:1(o); "United States" — 1:1(a).

B. Review Procedures for Preexisting Individual Accounts With a Balance or Value as of June 30, 2014, that Exceeds $50,000 ($250,000 for a Cash Value Insurance Contract or Annuity Contract), But Does Not Exceed $1,000,000 ("Lower Value Accounts").

1. *Electronic Record Search*. The Reporting Canadian Financial Institution must review electronically searchable data maintained by the Reporting Canadian Financial Institution for any of the following U.S. indicia:

a) Identification of the Account Holder as a U.S. citizen or resident;

b) Unambiguous indication of a U.S. place of birth;

c) Current U.S. mailing or residence address (including a U.S. post office box);

d) Current U.S. telephone number;

e) Standing instructions to transfer funds to an account maintained in the United States;

f) Currently effective power of attorney or signatory authority granted to a person with a U.S. address; or

g) An "in-care-of" or "hold mail" address that is the sole address the Reporting Canadian Financial Institution has on file for the Account Holder. In the case of a Preexisting Individual Account that is a Lower Value Account, an "in-care-of" address outside the United States or "hold mail" address shall not be treated as U.S. indicia.

2. If none of the U.S. indicia listed in subparagraph B(1) of this section are discovered in the electronic search, then no further action is required until there is a change in circumstances that results in one or more U.S. indicia being associated with the account, or the account becomes a High Value Account described in paragraph D of this section.

3. If any of the U.S. indicia listed in subparagraph B(1) of this section are discovered in the electronic search, or if there is a change in circumstances that results in one or more U.S. indicia being associated with the account, then the Reporting Canadian Financial Institution must treat the account as a U.S. Reportable Account unless it elects to apply subparagraph B(4) of this section and one of the exceptions in such subparagraph applies with respect to that account.

4. Notwithstanding a finding of U.S. indicia under subparagraph B(1) of this section, a Reporting Canadian Financial

Institution is not required to treat an account as a U.S. Reportable Account if:

a) Where the Account Holder information unambiguously indicates a U.S. place of birth, the Reporting Canadian Financial Institution obtains, or has previously reviewed and maintains a record of:

(1) A self-certification that the Account Holder is neither a U.S. citizen nor a U.S. resident for tax purposes (which may be on an IRS Form W-8 or other similar agreed form);

(2) A non-U.S. passport or other government-issued identification evidencing the Account Holder's citizenship or nationality in a country other than the United States; and

(3) A copy of the Account Holder's Certificate of Loss of Nationality of the United States or a reasonable explanation of:

(a) The reason the Account Holder does not have such a certificate despite relinquishing U.S. citizenship; or

(b) The reason the Account Holder did not obtain U.S. citizenship at birth.

b) Where the Account Holder information contains a current U.S. mailing or residence address, or one or more U.S. telephone numbers that are the only telephone numbers associated with the account, the Reporting Canadian Financial Institution obtains, or has previously reviewed and maintains a record of:

(1) A self-certification that the Account Holder is neither a U.S. citizen nor a U.S. resident for tax purposes (which may be on an IRS Form W-8 or other similar agreed form); and

(2) Documentary evidence, as defined in paragraph D of section VI of this Annex I, establishing the Account Holder's non-U.S. status.

c) Where the Account Holder information contains standing instructions to transfer funds to an account maintained in the United States, the Reporting Canadian Financial Institution obtains, or has previously reviewed and maintains a record of:

(1) A self-certification that the Account Holder is neither a U.S. citizen nor a U.S. resident for tax purposes (which may be on an IRS Form W-8 or other similar agreed form); and

(2) Documentary evidence, as defined in paragraph D of section VI of this Annex I, establishing the Account Holder's non-U.S. status.

d) Where the Account Holder information contains a currently effective power of attorney or signatory authority granted to a person with a U.S. address, has an "in-care-of" address or "hold mail" address that is the sole address identified for the Account Holder, or has one or more U.S. telephone numbers (if a non-U.S. telephone number is also associated with the account), the Reporting Canadian Financial Institution obtains, or has previously reviewed and maintains a record of:

(1) A self-certification that the Account Holder is neither a U.S. citizen nor a U.S. resident for tax purposes (which may be on an IRS Form W-8 or other similar agreed form); or

(2) Documentary evidence, as defined in paragraph D of section VI of this Annex I, establishing the Account Holder's non-U.S. status.

Definitions [Annex I:II:B]: "Account Holder" — 1:1(dd); "Annuity Contract" — 1:1(x); "Cash Value Insurance Contract" — 1:1(y); "High Value Account" — Annex I:I:D; "IRS" — 1:1(c); "Lower Value Account" — Annex I:I:B; "Preexisting Indivi-

dual Account" — Annex I:II; "Reportable Account" — 1:1(aa); "Reporting Canadian Financial Institution" — 1:1(o); "United States" — 1:1(a).

C. Additional Procedures Applicable to Preexisting Individual Accounts That Are Lower Value Accounts.

1. Review of Preexisting Individual Accounts that are Lower Value Accounts for U.S. indicia must be completed by June 30, 2016.

2. If there is a change of circumstances with respect to a Preexisting Individual Account that is a Lower Value Account that results in one or more U.S. indicia described in subparagraph B(1) of this section being associated with the account, then the Reporting Canadian Financial Institution must treat the account as a U.S. Reportable Account unless subparagraph B(4) of this section applies.

3. Except for Depository Accounts described in subparagraph A(4) of this section, any Preexisting Individual Account that has been identified as a U.S. Reportable Account under this section shall be treated as a U.S. Reportable Account in all subsequent years, unless the Account Holder ceases to be a Specified U.S. Person.

Definitions [Annex I:II:C]: "Account Holder" — 1:1(dd); "Depository Account" — 1:1(t); "Lower Value Account" — Annex I:I:B; "Preexisting Individual Account" — Annex I:II; "Reportable Account" — 1:1(aa); "Reporting Canadian Financial Institution" — 1:1(o).

D. Enhanced Review Procedures for Preexisting Individual Accounts With a Balance or Value That Exceeds $1,000,000 as of June 30, 2014, or December 31 of 2015 or Any Subsequent Year ("High Value Accounts").

1. *Electronic Record Search.* The Reporting Canadian Financial Institution must review electronically searchable data maintained by the Reporting Canadian Financial Institution for any of the U.S. indicia described in subparagraph B(1) of this section.

2. *Paper Record Search.* If the Reporting Canadian Financial Institution's electronically searchable databases include fields for, and capture all of the information described in, subparagraph D(3) of this section, then no further paper record search is required. If the electronic databases do not capture all of this information, then with respect to a High Value Account, the Reporting Canadian Financial Institution must also review the current customer master file and, to the extent not contained in the current customer master file, the following documents associated with the account and obtained by the Reporting Canadian Financial Institution within the last five years for any of the U.S. indicia described in subparagraph B(1) of this section:

a) The most recent documentary evidence collected with respect to the account;

b) The most recent account opening contract or documentation;

c) The most recent documentation obtained by the Reporting Canadian Financial Institution pursuant to AML/KYC Procedures or for other regulatory purposes;

d) Any power of attorney or signature authority forms currently in effect; and

e) Any standing instructions to transfer funds currently in effect.

3. *Exception Where Databases Contain Sufficient Information.* A Reporting Canadian Financial Institution is not required to perform the paper record search described in subparagraph D(2) of this section if the Reporting Canadian Financial Institution's electronically searchable information includes the following:

a) The Account Holder's nationality or residence status;

b) The Account Holder's residence address and mailing address currently on file with the Reporting Canadian Financial Institution;

c) The Account Holder's telephone number(s) currently on file, if any, with the Reporting Canadian Financial Institution;

d) Whether there are standing instructions to transfer funds in the account to another account (including an account at another branch of the Reporting Canadian Financial Institution or another Financial Institution);

e) Whether there is a current "in-care-of" address or "hold mail" address for the Account Holder; and

f) Whether there is any power of attorney or signatory authority for the account.

4. *Relationship Manager Inquiry for Actual Knowledge.* In addition to the electronic and paper record searches described above, the Reporting Canadian Financial Institution must treat as a U.S. Reportable Account any High Value Account assigned to a relationship manager (including any Financial Accounts aggregated with such High Value Account) if the relationship manager has actual knowledge that the Account Holder is a Specified U.S. Person.

5. *Effect of Finding U.S. Indicia.*

a) If none of the U.S. indicia listed in subparagraph B(1) of this section are discovered in the enhanced review of High Value Accounts described above, and the account is not identified as held by a Specified U.S. Person in subparagraph D(4) of this section, then no further action is required until there is a change in circumstances that results in one or more U.S. indicia being associated with the account.

b) If any of the U.S. indicia listed in subparagraph B(1) of this section are discovered in the enhanced review of High Value Accounts described above, or if there is a subsequent change in circumstances that results in one or more U.S. indicia being associated with the account, then the Reporting Canadian Financial Institution must treat the account as a U.S. Reportable Account unless it elects to apply subparagraph B(4) of this section and one of the exceptions in such subparagraph applies with respect to that account.

c) Except for Depository Accounts described in subparagraph A(4) of this section, any Preexisting Individual Account that has been identified as a U.S. Reportable Account under this section shall be treated as a U.S. Reportable Account in all subsequent years, unless the Account Holder ceases to be a Specified U.S. Person.

Definitions [Annex I:II:D]: "Account Holder" — 1:1(dd); "AML/KYC Procedures" — Annex I:VI:B:1; "Depository Account" — 1:1(t); "Financial Account" — 1:1(s); "Financial Institution" — 1:1(g); "High Value Account" — Annex I:I:D; "Preexisting Individual Account" — Annex I:II; "Reportable Account" — 1:1(aa); "Reporting Canadian Financial Institution" — 1:1(o).

E. Additional Procedures Applicable to High Value Accounts.

1. If a Preexisting Individual Account is a High Value Account as of June 30, 2014, the Reporting Canadian Financial Institution must complete the enhanced review procedures described in paragraph D of this section with respect to such account by June 30, 2015. If based on this review such account is identified as a U.S. Reportable Account on or before December 31, 2014, the Reporting Canadian Financial Institution must report the required information about such account with respect to 2014 in the first report on the account and on an annual basis thereafter. In the case of an account identified as a U.S. Reportable Account after December 31, 2014, and on or before June 30, 2015, the Reporting Canadian Financial Institution is not required to report information about such account with respect to 2014, but must report information about the account on an annual basis thereafter.

2. If a Preexisting Individual Account is not a High Value Account as of June 30, 2014, but becomes a High Value Ac-

count as of the last day of 2015 or any subsequent calendar year, the Reporting Canadian Financial Institution must complete the enhanced review procedures described in paragraph D of this section with respect to such account within six months after the last day of the calendar year in which the account becomes a High Value Account. If based on this review such account is identified as a U.S. Reportable Account, the Reporting Canadian Financial Institution must report the required information about such account with respect to the year in which it is identified as a U.S. Reportable Account and subsequent years on an annual basis, unless the Account Holder ceases to be a Specified U.S. Person.

3. Once a Reporting Canadian Financial Institution applies the enhanced review procedures described in paragraph D of this section to a High Value Account, the Reporting Canadian Financial Institution is not required to re-apply such procedures, other than the relationship manager inquiry described in subparagraph D(4) of this section, to the same High Value Account in any subsequent year.

4. If there is a change of circumstances with respect to a High Value Account that results in one or more U.S. indicia described in subparagraph B(1) of this section being associated with the account, then the Reporting Canadian Financial Institution must treat the account as a U.S. Reportable Account unless it elects to apply subparagraph B(4) of this section and one of the exceptions in such subparagraph applies with respect to that account.

5. A Reporting Canadian Financial Institution must implement procedures to ensure that a relationship manager identifies any change in circumstances of an account. For example, if a relationship manager is notified that the Account Holder has a new mailing address in the United States, the Reporting Canadian Financial Institution is required to treat the new address as a change in circumstances and, if it elects to apply subparagraph B(4) of this section, is required to obtain the appropriate documentation from the Account Holder.

Definitions [Annex I:II:E]: "Account Holder" — 1:1(dd); "High Value Account" — Annex I:I:D; "Preexisting Individual Account" — Annex I:II; "Reportable Account" — 1:1(aa); "Reporting Canadian Financial Institution" — 1:1(o); "United States" — 1:1(a).

F. Preexisting Individual Accounts That Have Been Documented for Certain Other Purposes. A Reporting Canadian Financial Institution that has previously obtained documentation from an Account Holder to establish the Account Holder's status as neither a U.S. citizen nor a U.S. resident in order to meet its obligations under a qualified intermediary, withholding foreign partnership, or withholding foreign trust agreement with the IRS, or to fulfill its obligations under chapter 61 of Title 26 of the United States Code, is not required to perform the procedures described in subparagraph B(1) of this section with respect to Lower Value Accounts or subparagraphs D(1) through D(3) of this section with respect to High Value Accounts.

Definitions [Annex I:II:F]: "Account Holder" — 1:1(dd); "High Value Account" — Annex I:I:D; "IRS" — 1:1(c); "Lower Value Account" — Annex I:I:B; "Preexisting Individual Account" — Annex I:II; "Reporting Canadian Financial Institution" — 1:1(o); "United States" — 1:1(a).

III. NEW INDIVIDUAL ACCOUNTS

The following rules and procedures apply for purposes of identifying U.S. Reportable Accounts among Financial Accounts held by individuals and opened on or after July 1, 2014 ("New Individual Accounts").

Definitions [Annex I:III opening words]: "Financial Account" — 1:1(s); "Reportable Account" — 1:1(aa).

A. Accounts Not Required to Be Reviewed, Identified, or Reported. Unless the Reporting Canadian Financial Institution elects otherwise, either with respect to all New Individual Accounts or, separately, with respect to any clearly identified group of such accounts, where the implementing rules in Canada provide for such an election, the following New Individual Accounts are not required to be reviewed, identified, or reported as U.S. Reportable Accounts:

1. A Depository Account unless the account balance exceeds $50,000 at the end of any calendar year or other appropriate reporting period.

2. A Cash Value Insurance Contract unless the Cash Value exceeds $50,000 at the end of any calendar year or other appropriate reporting period.

Definitions [Annex I:III:A]: "Canada" — 1:1(d), Canada-US Treaty Art:III:1(a); "Cash Value" — 1:1(z); "Cash Value Insurance Contract" — 1:1(y); "Depository Account" — 1:1(t); "New Individual Account" — Annex I:III; "Reportable Account" — 1:1(aa); "Reporting Canadian Financial Institution" — 1:1(o).

B. Other New Individual Accounts.

1. With respect to New Individual Accounts not described in paragraph A of this section, upon account opening (or within 90 days after the end of the calendar year in which the account ceases to be described in paragraph A of this section), the Reporting Canadian Financial Institution must obtain a self-certification, which may be part of the account opening documentation, that allows the Reporting Canadian Financial Institution to determine whether the Account Holder is resident in the United States for tax purposes (for this purpose, a U.S. citizen is considered to be resident in the United States for tax purposes, even if the Account Holder is also a tax resident of another jurisdiction) and confirm the reasonableness of such self-certification based on the information obtained by the Reporting Canadian Financial Institution in connection with the opening of the account, including any documentation collected pursuant to AML/KYC Procedures.

2. If the self-certification establishes that the Account Holder is resident in the United States for tax purposes, the Reporting Canadian Financial Institution must treat the account as a U.S. Reportable Account and obtain a self-certification that includes the Account Holder's U.S. TIN (which may be an IRS Form W-9 or other similar agreed form).

3. If there is a change of circumstances with respect to a New Individual Account that causes the Reporting Canadian Financial Institution to know, or have reason to know, that the original self-certification is incorrect or unreliable, the Reporting Canadian Financial Institution cannot rely on the original self-certification and must obtain a valid self-certification that establishes whether the Account Holder is a U.S. citizen or resident for U.S. tax purposes. If the Reporting Canadian Financial Institution is unable to obtain a valid self-certification, the Reporting Canadian Financial Institution must treat the account as a U.S. Reportable Account.

Definitions [Annex I:III:B]: "Account Holder" — 1:1(dd); "AML/KYC Procedures" — Annex I:VI:B:1; "IRS" — 1:1(c); "New Individual Account" — Annex I:III; "Reportable Account" — 1:1(aa); "Reporting Canadian Financial Institution" — 1:1(o); "United States" — 1:1(a).

IV. PREEXISTING ENTITY ACCOUNTS

The following rules and procedures apply for purposes of identifying U.S. Reportable Accounts and accounts held by Nonparticipating Financial Institutions among Preexisting Accounts held by Entities ("Preexisting Entity Accounts").

Definitions [Annex I:IV opening words]: "Entity" — 1:1(gg); "Nonparticipating Financial Institution" — 1:1(r); "Preexisting Account" — Annex I:VI:B:5; "Reportable Account" — 1:1(aa).

A. Entity Accounts Not Required to Be Reviewed, Identified or Reported. Unless the Reporting Canadian Financial Institution elects otherwise, either with respect to all Preexisting Entity Accounts or, separately, with respect to any clearly identified group of such accounts, where the implementing rules in Canada provide for such an election, a Preexisting Entity Account with an account balance or value that does not exceed $250,000 as of June 30, 2014, is not required to be reviewed, identified, or re-

ported as a U.S. Reportable Account until the account balance or value exceeds $1,000,000.

Definitions [Annex I:IV:A]: "Canada" — 1:1(d), Canada-US Treaty Art:III:1(a); "Entity" — 1:1(gg); "Preexisting Entity Account" — Annex I:IV; "Reportable Account" — 1:1(aa); "Reporting Canadian Financial Institution" — 1:1(o).

B. Entity Accounts Subject to Review. A Preexisting Entity Account that has an account balance or value that exceeds $250,000 as of June 30, 2014, and a Preexisting Entity Account that does not exceed $250,000 as of June 30, 2014, but the account balance or value of which exceeds $1,000,000 as of the last day of 2015 or any subsequent calendar year, must be reviewed in accordance with the procedures set forth in paragraph D of this section.

Definitions [Annex I:IV:B]: "Entity" — 1:1(gg); "Preexisting Entity Account" — Annex I:IV.

C. Entity Accounts With Respect to Which Reporting Is Required. With respect to Preexisting Entity Accounts described in paragraph B of this section, only accounts that are held by one or more Entities that are Specified U.S. Persons, or by Passive NFFEs with one or more Controlling Persons who are U.S. citizens or residents, shall be treated as U.S. Reportable Accounts. In addition, accounts held by Nonparticipating Financial Institutions shall be treated as accounts for which aggregate payments as described in subparagraph 1(b) of Article 4 of the Agreement are reported to the Canadian Competent Authority.

Definitions [Annex I:IV:C]: "Competent Authority" — 1:1(f); "Entity" — 1:1(gg); "Nonparticipating Financial Institution" — 1:1(r); "Passive NFFE" — Annex I:VI:B:3; "Preexisting Entity Account" — Annex I:IV; "Reportable Account" — 1:1(aa).

D. Review Procedures for Identifying Entity Accounts With Respect to Which Reporting Is Required. For Preexisting Entity Accounts described in paragraph B of this section, the Reporting Canadian Financial Institution must apply the following review procedures to determine whether the account is held by one or more Specified U.S. Persons, by Passive NFFEs with one or more Controlling Persons who are U.S. citizens or residents, or by Nonparticipating Financial Institutions:

1. *Determine Whether the Entity Is a Specified U.S. Person.*

a) Review information maintained for regulatory or customer relationship purposes (including information collected pursuant to AML/KYC Procedures) to determine whether the information indicates that the Account Holder is a U.S. Person. For this purpose, information indicating that the Account Holder is a U.S. Person includes a U.S. place of incorporation or organization, or a U.S. address.

b) If the information indicates that the Account Holder is a U.S. Person, the Reporting Canadian Financial Institution must treat the account as a U.S. Reportable Account unless it obtains a self-certification from the Account Holder (which may be on an IRS Form W-8 or W-9, or a similar agreed form), or reasonably determines based on information in its possession or that is publicly available, that the Account Holder is not a Specified U.S. Person.

2. *Determine Whether a Non-U.S. Entity Is a Financial Institution.*

a) Review information maintained for regulatory or customer relationship purposes (including information collected pursuant to AML/KYC Procedures) to determine whether the information indicates that the Account Holder is a Financial Institution.

b) If the information indicates that the Account Holder is a Financial Institution, or the Reporting Canadian Financial Institution verifies the Account Holder's Global Intermediary Identification Number on the published IRS FFI list, then the account is not a U.S. Reportable Account.

3. *Determine Whether a Financial Institution Is a Nonparticipating Financial Institution Payments to Which Are Subject*

to Aggregate Reporting Under Subparagraph 1(b) of Article 4 of the Agreement.

a) Subject to subparagraph D(3)(b) of this section, a Reporting Canadian Financial Institution may determine that the Account Holder is a Canadian Financial Institution or other Partner Jurisdiction Financial Institution if the Reporting Canadian Financial Institution reasonably determines that the Account Holder has such status on the basis of the Account Holder's Global Intermediary Identification Number on the published IRS FFI list or other information that is publicly available or in the possession of the Reporting Canadian Financial Institution, as applicable. In such case, no further review, identification, or reporting is required with respect to the account.

b) If the Account Holder is a Canadian Financial Institution or other Partner Jurisdiction Financial Institution treated by the IRS as a Nonparticipating Financial Institution, then the account is not a U.S. Reportable Account, but payments to the Account Holder must be reported as contemplated in subparagraph 1(b) of Article 4 of the Agreement.

c) If the Account Holder is not a Canadian Financial Institution or other Partner Jurisdiction Financial Institution, then the Reporting Canadian Financial Institution must treat the Account Holder as a Nonparticipating Financial Institution payments to which are reportable under subparagraph 1(b) of Article 4 of the Agreement, unless the Reporting Canadian Financial Institution:

(1) Obtains a self-certification (which may be on an IRS Form W-8 or similar agreed form) from the Account Holder that it is a certified deemed-compliant FFI, or an exempt beneficial owner, as those terms are defined in relevant U.S. *Treasury Regulations*; or

(2) In the case of a participating FFI or registered deemed-compliant FFI, verifies the Account Holder's Global Intermediary Identification Number on the published IRS FFI list.

4. *Determine Whether an Account Held by an NFFE Is a U.S. Reportable Account.* With respect to an Account Holder of a Preexisting Entity Account that is not identified as either a U.S. Person or a Financial Institution, the Reporting Canadian Financial Institution must identify (i) whether the Account Holder has Controlling Persons, (ii) whether the Account Holder is a Passive NFFE, and (iii) whether any of the Controlling Persons of the Account Holder is a U.S. citizen or resident. In making these determinations the Reporting Canadian Financial Institution must follow the guidance in subparagraphs D(4)(a) through D(4)(d) of this section in the order most appropriate under the circumstances.

a) For purposes of determining the Controlling Persons of an Account Holder, a Reporting Canadian Financial Institution may rely on information collected and maintained pursuant to AML/KYC Procedures.

b) For purposes of determining whether the Account Holder is a Passive NFFE, the Reporting Canadian Financial Institution must obtain a self-certification (which may be on an IRS Form W-8 or W-9, or on a similar agreed form) from the Account Holder to establish its status, unless it has information in its possession or that is publicly available, based on which it can reasonably determine that the Account Holder is an Active NFFE.

c) For purposes of determining whether a Controlling Person of a Passive NFFE is a U.S. citizen or resident for tax purposes, a Reporting Canadian Financial Institution may rely on:

(1) Information collected and maintained pursuant to AML/KYC Procedures in the case of a Preexisting Entity Account held by one or more NFFEs with an account balance or value that does not exceed $1,000,000; or

(2) A self-certification (which may be on an IRS Form W-8 or W-9, or on a similar agreed form) from the Account Holder or such Controlling Person in the case of a Preexisting Entity Account held by one or more NFFEs with an account balance or value that exceeds $1,000,000.

d) If any Controlling Person of a Passive NFFE is a U.S. citizen or resident, the account shall be treated as a U.S. Reportable Account.

Definitions [Annex I:IV:D]: "Account Holder" — 1:1(dd); "Active NFFE" — Annex I:VI:B:4; "AML/KYC Procedures" — Annex I:VI:B:1; "Canadian Financial Institution" — 1:1(l); "Entity" — 1:1(gg); "Financial Institution" — 1:1(g); "IRS" — 1:1(c); "NFFE" — Annex I:VI:B:2; "Nonparticipating Financial Institution" — 1:1(r); "Partner Jurisdiction Financial Institution" — 1:1(m); "Passive NFFE" — Annex I:VI:B:3; "Preexisting Entity Account" — Annex I:IV; "Reportable Account" — 1:1(aa); "Reporting Canadian Financial Institution" — 1:1(o).

E. Timing of Review and Additional Procedures Applicable to Preexisting Entity Accounts.

1. Review of Preexisting Entity Accounts with an account balance or value that exceeds $250,000 as of June 30, 2014 must be completed by June 30, 2016.

2. Review of Preexisting Entity Accounts with an account balance or value that does not exceed $250,000 as of June 30, 2014, but exceeds $1,000,000 as of December 31 of 2015 or any subsequent year, must be completed within six months after the last day of the calendar year in which the account balance or value exceeds $1,000,000.

3. If there is a change of circumstances with respect to a Preexisting Entity Account that causes the Reporting Canadian Financial Institution to know, or have reason to know, that the self-certification or other documentation associated with an account is incorrect or unreliable, the Reporting Canadian Financial Institution must redetermine the status of the account in accordance with the procedures set forth in paragraph D of this section.

Definitions [Annex I:IV:E]: "Preexisting Entity Account" — Annex I:IV; "Reporting Canadian Financial Institution" — 1:1(o).

V. NEW ENTITY ACCOUNTS

The following rules and procedures apply for purposes of identifying U.S. Reportable Accounts and accounts held by Nonparticipating Financial Institutions among Financial Accounts held by Entities and opened on or after July 1, 2014 ("New Entity Accounts").

Definitions [Annex I:V opening words]: "Entity" — 1:1(gg); "Financial Account" — 1:1(s); "Nonparticipating Financial Institution" — 1:1(r); "Reportable Account" — 1:1(aa).

A. Entity Accounts Not Required to Be Reviewed, Identified or Reported. Unless the Reporting Canadian Financial Institution elects otherwise, either with respect to all New Entity Accounts or, separately, with respect to any clearly identified group of such accounts, where the implementing rules in Canada provide for such election, a credit card account or a revolving credit facility treated as a New Entity Account is not required to be reviewed, identified, or reported, provided that the Reporting Canadian Financial Institution maintaining such account implements policies and procedures to prevent an account balance owed to the Account Holder that exceeds $50,000.

Definitions [Annex I:V:A]: "Account Holder" — 1:1(dd); "Canada" — 1:1(d), Canada-US Treaty Art:III:1(a); "Entity" — 1:1(gg); "New Entity Account" — Annex I:V; "Reporting Canadian Financial Institution" — 1:1(o).

B. Other New Entity Accounts. With respect to New Entity Accounts not described in paragraph A of this section, the Reporting Canadian Financial Institution must determine whether the Account Holder is:

1. a Specified U.S. Person;

2. a Canadian Financial Institution or other Partner Jurisdiction Financial Institution;

3. a participating FFI, a deemed-compliant FFI, or an exempt beneficial owner, as those terms are defined in relevant U.S. *Treasury Regulations*; or

4. an Active NFFE or Passive NFFE.

Definitions [Annex I:V:B]: "Account Holder" — 1:1(dd); "Active NFFE" — Annex I:VI:B:4; "Canadian Financial Institution" — 1:1(l); "New Entity Account" — Annex I:V; "Partner Jurisdiction Financial Institution" — 1:1(m); "Passive NFFE" — Annex I:VI:B:3; "Reporting Canadian Financial Institution" — 1:1(o).

C. [Determining that account holder is Active NFFE, Canadian FI or other Partner Jurisdiction FI.] Subject to paragraph D of this section, a Reporting Canadian Financial Institution may determine that the Account Holder is an Active NFFE, a Canadian Financial Institution, or other Partner Jurisdiction Financial Institution if the Reporting Canadian Financial Institution reasonably determines that the Account Holder has such status on the basis of the Account Holder's Global Intermediary Identification Number or other information that is publicly available or in the possession of the Reporting Canadian Financial Institution, as applicable.

Definitions [Annex I:V:C]: "Account Holder" — 1:1(dd); "Active NFFE" — Annex I:VI:B:4; "Canadian Financial Institution" — 1:1(l); "Partner Jurisdiction Financial Institution" — 1:1(m); "Reporting Canadian Financial Institution" — 1:1(o).

D. [Where account holder is Canadian FI or other Partner Jurisdiction FI treated by the IRS as Nonparticipating FI.] If the Account Holder is a Canadian Financial Institution or other Partner Jurisdiction Financial Institution treated by the IRS as a Nonparticipating Financial Institution, then the account is not a U.S. Reportable Account, but payments to the Account Holder must be reported as contemplated in subparagraph 1(b) of Article 4 of the Agreement.

Definitions [Annex I:V:D]: "Account Holder" — 1:1(dd); "Canadian Financial Institution" — 1:1(l); "IRS" — 1:1(c); "Nonparticipating Financial Institution" — 1:1(r); "Partner Jurisdiction Financial Institution" — 1:1(m); "Reportable Account" — 1:1(aa).

E. [All other cases: self-certification required.] In all other cases, a Reporting Canadian Financial Institution must obtain a self-certification from the Account Holder to establish the Account Holder's status. Based on the self-certification, the following rules apply:

1. If the Account Holder is a Specified U.S. Person, the Reporting Canadian Financial Institution must treat the account as a U.S. Reportable Account.

2. If the Account Holder is a Passive NFFE, the Reporting Canadian Financial Institution must identify the Controlling Persons as determined under AML/KYC Procedures, and must determine whether any such person is a U.S. citizen or resident on the basis of a self-certification from the Account Holder or such person. If any such person is a U.S. citizen or resident, the Reporting Canadian Financial Institution must treat the account as a U.S. Reportable Account.

3. If the Account Holder is:

a) a U.S. Person that is not a Specified U.S. Person;

b) subject to subparagraph E(4) of this section, a Canadian Financial Institution or other Partner Jurisdiction Financial Institution;

c) a participating FFI, a deemed-compliant FFI, or an exempt beneficial owner, as those terms are defined in relevant U.S. *Treasury Regulations*;

d) an Active NFFE; or

e) a Passive NFFE none of the Controlling Persons of which is a U.S. citizen or resident,

then the account is not a U.S. Reportable Account and no reporting is required with respect to the account.

4. If the Account Holder is a Nonparticipating Financial Institution (including a Canadian Financial Institution or other

Partner Jurisdiction Financial Institution treated by the IRS as a Nonparticipating Financial Institution), then the account is not a U.S. Reportable Account, but payments to the Account Holder must be reported as contemplated in subparagraph 1(b) of Article 4 of the Agreement.

Definitions [Annex I:V:E]: "Account Holder" — 1:1(dd); "Active NFFE" — Annex I:VI:B:4; "AML/KYC Procedures" — Annex I:VI:B:1; "Canadian Financial Institution" — 1:1(l); "IRS" — 1:1(c); "Nonparticipating Financial Institution" — 1:1(r); "Partner Jurisdiction Financial Institution" — 1:1(m); "Passive NFFE" — Annex I:VI:B:3; "Reportable Account" — 1:1(aa); "Reporting Canadian Financial Institution" — 1:1(o).

VI. SPECIAL RULES AND DEFINITIONS

The following additional rules and definitions apply in implementing the due diligence procedures described above:

A. Reliance on Self-Certifications and Documentary Evidence. A Reporting Canadian Financial Institution may not rely on a self-certification or documentary evidence if the Reporting Canadian Financial Institution knows or has reason to know that the self-certification or documentary evidence is incorrect or unreliable.

Definitions [Annex I:VI:A]: "Reporting Canadian Financial Institution" — 1:1(o).

B. Definitions. The following definitions apply for purposes of this Annex I.

1. *AML/KYC Procedures.* "AML/KYC Procedures" means the customer due diligence procedures of a Reporting Canadian Financial Institution pursuant to the anti-money laundering or similar requirements of Canada to which such Reporting Canadian Financial Institution is subject.

2. *NFFE.* An "NFFE" means any Non-U.S. Entity that is not an FFI as defined in relevant U.S. *Treasury Regulations* or is an Entity described in subparagraph B(4)(j) of this section, and also includes any Non-U.S. Entity that is resident in Canada or another Partner Jurisdiction and that is not a Financial Institution.

3. *Passive NFFE.* A "Passive NFFE" means any NFFE that is not

a) an Active NFFE or

b) a withholding foreign partnership or withholding foreign trust pursuant to relevant U.S. *Treasury Regulations*.

4. *Active NFFE.* An "Active NFFE" means any NFFE that meets any of the following criteria:

a) Less than 50 percent of the NFFE's gross income for the preceding calendar year or other appropriate reporting period is passive income and less than 50 percent of the assets held by the NFFE during the preceding calendar year or other appropriate reporting period are assets that produce or are held for the production of passive income;

b) The stock of the NFFE is regularly traded on an established securities market or the NFFE is a Related Entity of an Entity the stock of which is regularly traded on an established securities market;

c) The NFFE is organized in a U.S. Territory and all of the owners of the payee are bona fide residents of that U.S. Territory;

d) The NFFE is a government (other than the U.S. government), a political subdivision of such government (which, for the avoidance of doubt, includes a state, province, county, or municipality), or a public body performing a function of such government or a political subdivision thereof, a government of a U.S. Territory, an international organization, a non-U.S. central bank of issue, or an Entity wholly owned by one or more of the foregoing;

e) Substantially all of the activities of the NFFE consist of holding (in whole or in part) the outstanding stock of, or providing financing and services to, one or more subsidiaries that engage in trades or businesses other than the business of a Financial Institution, except that an NFFE shall not qualify for this status if the NFFE functions (or holds itself out) as an investment fund, such as a private equity fund, venture capital fund, leveraged buyout fund or any investment vehicle whose purpose is to acquire or fund companies and then hold interests in those companies as capital assets for investment purposes;

f) The NFFE is not yet operating a business and has no prior operating history, but is investing capital into assets with the intent to operate a business other than that of a Financial Institution, provided that the NFFE shall not qualify for this exception after the date that is 24 months after the date of the initial organization of the NFFE;

g) The NFFE was not a Financial Institution in the past five years, and is in the process of liquidating its assets or is reorganizing with the intent to continue or recommence operations in a business other than that of a Financial Institution;

h) The NFFE primarily engages in financing and hedging transactions with, or for, Related Entities that are not Financial Institutions, and does not provide financing or hedging services to any Entity that is not a Related Entity, provided that the group of any such Related Entities is primarily engaged in a business other than that of a Financial Institution;

i) The NFFE is an "excepted NFFE" as described in relevant U.S. *Treasury Regulations*; or

j) The NFFE meets all of the following requirements:

(1) It is established and operated in its jurisdiction of residence exclusively for religious, charitable, scientific, artistic, cultural, athletic, or educational purposes; or it is established and operated in its jurisdiction of residence and it is a professional organization, business league, chamber of commerce, labor organization, agricultural or horticultural organization, civic league or an organization operated exclusively for the promotion of social welfare;

(2) It is exempt from income tax in its jurisdiction of residence;

(3) It has no shareholders or members who have a proprietary or beneficial interest in its income or assets;

(4) The applicable laws of the NFFE's jurisdiction of residence or the NFFE's formation documents do not permit any income or assets of the NFFE to be distributed to, or applied for the benefit of, a private person or non-charitable Entity other than pursuant to the conduct of the NFFE's charitable activities, or as payment of reasonable compensation for services rendered, or as payment representing the fair market value of property which the NFFE has purchased; and

(5) The applicable laws of the NFFE's jurisdiction of residence or the NFFE's formation documents require that, upon the NFFE's liquidation or dissolution, all of its assets be distributed to a governmental entity or other non-profit organization, or escheat to the government of the NFFE's jurisdiction of residence or any political subdivision thereof.

5. *Preexisting Account.* A "Preexisting Account" means a Financial Account maintained by a Reporting Financial Institution as of June 30, 2014.

Definitions [Annex I:VI:B]: "Canada" — 1:1(d), Canada-US Treaty Art:III:1(a); "Entity" — 1:1(gg); "Financial Account" — 1:1(s); "Financial Institution" — 1:1(g);

"Partner Jurisdiction" — 1:1(e); "Related Entity" — 1:1(jj); "Reporting Canadian Financial Institution" — 1:1(o); "Reporting Financial Institution" — 1:1(n).

C. Account Balance Aggregation and Currency Translation Rules.

1. *Aggregation of Individual Accounts.* For purposes of determining the aggregate balance or value of Financial Accounts held by an individual, a Reporting Canadian Financial Institution is required to aggregate all Financial Accounts maintained by the Reporting Canadian Financial Institution, or by a Related Entity, but only to the extent that the Reporting Canadian Financial Institution's computerized systems link the Financial Accounts by reference to a data element such as client number or taxpayer identification number, and allow account balances or values to be aggregated. Each holder of a jointly held Financial Account shall be attributed the entire balance or value of the jointly held Financial Account for purposes of applying the aggregation requirements described in this paragraph 1.

Related Provisions: ITA 263(4) — Meaning of "taxpayer identification number" for Canadian reporting purposes.

2. *Aggregation of Entity Accounts.* For purposes of determining the aggregate balance or value of Financial Accounts held by an Entity, a Reporting Canadian Financial Institution is required to take into account all Financial Accounts that are maintained by the Reporting Canadian Financial Institution, or by a Related Entity, but only to the extent that the Reporting Canadian Financial Institution's computerized systems link the Financial Accounts by reference to a data element such as client number or taxpayer identification number, and allow account balances or values to be aggregated.

Related Provisions: ITA 263(4) — Meaning of "taxpayer identification number" for Canadian reporting purposes.

3. *Special Aggregation Rule Applicable to Relationship Managers.* For purposes of determining the aggregate balance or value of Financial Accounts held by a person to determine whether a Financial Account is a High Value Account, a Reporting Canadian Financial Institution is also required, in the case of any Financial Accounts that a relationship manager knows, or has reason to know, are directly or indirectly owned, controlled, or established (other than in a fiduciary capacity) by the same person, to aggregate all such accounts.

4. *Currency Translation Rule.* For purposes of determining the balance or value of Financial Accounts denominated in a currency other than the U.S. dollar, a Reporting Canadian Financial Institution must convert the U.S. dollar threshold amounts described in this Annex I into such currency using a published spot rate determined as of the last day of the calendar year preceding the year in which the Reporting Canadian Financial Institution is determining the balance or value.

Definitions [Annex I:VI:C]: "Entity" — 1:1(gg); "Financial Account" — 1:1(s); "High Value Account" — Annex I:I:D; "Related Entity" — 1:1(jj); "Reporting Canadian Financial Institution" — 1:1(o).

D. Documentary Evidence. For purposes of this Annex I, acceptable documentary evidence includes any of the following:

1. A certificate of residence issued by an authorized government body (for example, a government or agency thereof, or a municipality) of the jurisdiction in which the payee claims to be a resident.

2. With respect to an individual, any valid identification issued by an authorized government body (for example, a government or agency thereof, or a municipality), that includes the individual's name and is typically used for identification purposes.

3. With respect to an Entity, any official documentation issued by an authorized government body (for example, a government or agency thereof, or a municipality) that includes the name of the Entity and either the address of its principal office in the jurisdiction (or U.S. Territory) in which it claims

to be a resident or the jurisdiction (or U.S. Territory) in which the Entity was incorporated or organized.

4. With respect to a Financial Account maintained in a jurisdiction with anti-money laundering rules that have been approved by the IRS in connection with a QI agreement (as described in relevant U.S. *Treasury Regulations*), any of the documents, other than a Form W-8 or W-9, referenced in the jurisdiction's attachment to the QI agreement for identifying individuals or Entities.

5. Any financial statement, third-party credit report, bankruptcy filing, or U.S. Securities and Exchange Commission report.

Definitions [Annex I:VI:D]: "Entity" — 1:1(gg); "Financial Account" — 1:1(s); "IRS" — 1:1(c).

E. Alternative Procedures for Financial Accounts Held by Individual Beneficiaries of a Cash Value Insurance Contract. A Reporting Canadian Financial Institution may presume that an individual beneficiary (other than the owner) of a Cash Value Insurance Contract receiving a death benefit is not a Specified U.S. Person and may treat such Financial Account as other than a U.S. Reportable Account unless the Reporting Canadian Financial Institution knows, or has reason to know, that the beneficiary is a Specified U.S. Person. A Reporting Canadian Financial Institution has reason to know that a beneficiary of a Cash Value Insurance Contract is a Specified U.S. Person if the information collected by the Reporting Canadian Financial Institution and associated with the beneficiary contains U.S. indicia as described in subparagraph (B)(1) of section II of this Annex I. If a Reporting Canadian Financial Institution knows, or has reason to know, that the beneficiary is a Specified U.S. Person, the Reporting Canadian Financial Institution must follow the procedures in subparagraph B(3) of section II of this Annex I.

Definitions [Annex I:VI:E]: "Cash Value Insurance Contract" — 1:1(y); "Financial Account" — 1:1(s); "Reportable Account" — 1:1(aa); "Reporting Canadian Financial Institution" — 1:1(o).

F. Reliance on Third Parties. Regardless of whether an election is made under paragraph C of section I of this Annex I, Canada may permit Reporting Canadian Financial Institutions to rely on due diligence procedures performed by third parties, to the extent provided in relevant U.S. *Treasury Regulations*.

Definitions [Annex I:VI:F]: "Canada" — 1:1(d), Canada-US Treaty Art:III:1(a); "Party" — Preamble; "Reporting Canadian Financial Institution" — 1:1(o).

ANNEX II — NON-REPORTING CANADIAN FINANCIAL INSTITUTIONS AND PRODUCTS

Table of Contents [paraphrased]

I. GENERAL

A. [How Annex II can be amended.] This Annex may be modified by a mutual written decision entered into between the Competent Authorities of Canada and the United States:

1. To include additional Entities, accounts, and products that present a low risk of being used by U.S. Persons to evade U.S. tax and that have similar characteristics to the Entities, accounts, and products identified in this Annex as of the date of signature of the Agreement; or

2. To remove Entities, accounts, and products that, due to changes in circumstances, no longer present a low risk of being used by U.S. Persons to evade U.S. tax.

Any such addition or removal shall be effective on the date of signature of the mutual decision unless otherwise provided therein.

Definitions [Annex II:I:A]: "Canada" — 1:1(d), Canada-US Treaty Art:III:1(a); "Competent Authority" — 1:1(f); "Entity" — 1:1(gg); "United States" — 1:1(a).

B. [Procedures for amendment.] Procedures for reaching a mutual decision described in paragraph A of this section may be included in the mutual agreement or arrangement described in paragraph 6 of Article 3 of the Agreement.

II. EXEMPT BENEFICAL OWNERS

The following Entities shall be treated as Non-Reporting Canadian Financial Institutions and as exempt beneficial owners for the purposes of sections 1471 and 1472 of the U.S. *Internal Revenue Code*:

Definitions [Annex II:II opening words]: "Entity" — 1:1(gg); "Non-Reporting Canadian Financial Institution" — 1:1(q).

A. Central Bank

1. The Bank of Canada.

Definitions [Annex II:II:A]: "Canada" — 1:1(d), Canada-US Treaty Art:III:1(a).

B. International Organizations

1. A Canadian office of an international organization as defined under paragraph (1) of Section 2 of the *Foreign Missions and International Organizations Act*.

C. Retirement Funds

1. Any plan or arrangement established in Canada and described in paragraph 3 of Article XVIII (Pensions and Annuities) of the Convention, including any plan or arrangement that the Competent Authorities may agree under subparagraph 3(b) of Article XVIII is similar to a plan or arrangement under that subparagraph.

Definitions [Annex II:II:C]: "Canada" — 1:1(d), Canada-US Treaty Art:III:1(a); "Competent Authority" — 1:1(f); "Convention" — Preamble.

D. Investment Entity Wholly Owned by Exempt Beneficial Owners

1. An Entity that is a Canadian Financial Institution solely because it is an Investment Entity, provided that each direct

holder of an Equity Interest in the Entity is an exempt beneficial owner, and each direct holder of a debt interest in such Entity is either a Depository Institution (with respect to a loan made to such Entity) or an exempt beneficial owner.

Definitions [Annex II:II:D]: "Canadian Financial Institution" — 1:1(l); "Depository Institution" — 1:1(i); "Entity" — 1:1(gg); "Equity Interest" — 1:1(v); "Investment Entity" — 1:1(j).

III. DEEMED-COMPLIANT FINANCIAL INSTITUTIONS

The following Financial Institutions are Non-Reporting Canadian Financial Institutions that shall be treated as deemed-compliant FFIs for the purposes of section 1471 of the U.S. *Internal Revenue Code*.

Definitions [Annex II:III opening words]: "Financial Institution" — 1:1(g); "Non-Reporting Canadian Financial Institution" — 1:1(q).

A. Financial Institution with a Local Client Base.

A Financial Institution that qualifies as a local FFI as described in relevant U.S. *Treasury Regulations*, applying subparagraphs A(1), A(2) and A(3) of this section in lieu of the relevant paragraphs in those regulations:

1. Beginning on or before July 1, 2014, the Financial Institution must have policies and procedures, consistent with those set forth in Annex I, to prevent the Financial Institution from providing a Financial Account to any Nonparticipating Financial Institution and to monitor whether the Financial Institution opens or maintains a Financial Account for any Specified U.S. Person who is not a resident of Canada (including a U.S. Person that was a resident of Canada when the Financial Account was opened but subsequently ceases to be a resident of Canada) or any Passive NFFE with Controlling Persons who are U.S. residents or U.S. citizens who are not residents of Canada;

2. Such policies and procedures must provide that if any Financial Account held by a Specified U.S. Person who is not a resident of Canada or by a Passive NFFE with Controlling Persons who are U.S. residents or U.S. citizens who are not residents of Canada is identified, the Financial Institution must report such Financial Account as would be required if the Financial Institution were a Reporting Canadian Financial Institution (including by following the applicable registration requirements on the IRS FATCA registration website) or close such Financial Account;

3. With respect to a Preexisting Account held by an individual who is not a resident of Canada or by an Entity, the Financial Institution must review those Preexisting Accounts in accordance with the procedures set forth in Annex I applicable to Preexisting Accounts to identify any Financial Account held by a Specified U.S. Person who is not a resident of Canada, by a Passive NFFE with Controlling Persons who are U.S. residents or U.S. citizens who are not residents of Canada, or by a Nonparticipating Financial Institution, and must report such Financial Account as would be required if the Financial Institution were a Reporting Canadian Financial Institution (including by following the applicable registration requirements on the IRS FATCA registration website) or close such Financial Account;

Definitions [Annex II:III:A]: "Canada" — 1:1(d), Canada-US Treaty Art:III:1(a); "Entity" — 1:1(gg); "Financial Account" — 1:1(s); "Financial Institution" — 1:1(g); "IRS" — 1:1(c); "Nonparticipating Financial Institution" — 1:1(r); "Reporting Canadian Financial Institution" — 1:1(o).

B. Local Bank.

A Financial Institution that qualifies as a nonregistering local bank as described in relevant U.S. *Treasury Regulations*, using the following definitions where applicable:

1. The term "bank" shall include any Depository Institution to which the *Bank Act* or the *Trust and Loan Companies Act* applies, or which is a trust or loan company regulated by a provincial Act; and

2. The term "credit union or similar cooperative credit organization that is operated without profit" shall include any credit union or similar cooperative credit organization that is entitled to tax-favored treatment with respect to distributions to its members under Canadian law, including any credit union as defined in subsection 137(6) of the *Income Tax Act*.

Definitions [Annex II:III:B]: "Depository Institution" — 1:1(i); "Financial Institution" — 1:1(g).

C. Financial Institution with Only Low-Value Accounts.

A Canadian Financial Institution satisfying the following requirements:

1. The Financial Institution is not an Investment Entity;

2. No Financial Account maintained by the Financial Institution or any Related Entity has a balance or value in excess of $50,000, applying the rules set forth in Annex I for account aggregation and currency translation; and

3. The Financial Institution does not have more than $50 million in assets on its balance sheet, and the Financial Institution and any Related Entities, taken together, do not have more than $50 million in total assets on their consolidated or combined balance sheets.

Definitions [Annex II:III:C]: "Canadian Financial Institution" — 1:1(l); "Financial Account" — 1:1(s); "Financial Institution" — 1:1(g); "Investment Entity" — 1:1(j); "Related Entity" — 1:1(jj).

D. Sponsored Investment Entity and Controlled Foreign Corporation.

A Financial Institution described in subparagraph D(1) or D(2) of this section having a sponsoring entity that complies with the requirements of subparagraph D(3) of this section.

1. A Financial Institution is a sponsored investment entity if:

   a. It is an Investment Entity established in Canada that is not a qualified intermediary, withholding foreign partnership, or withholding foreign trust pursuant to relevant U.S. *Treasury Regulations*; and

   b. An Entity has agreed with the Financial Institution to act as a sponsoring entity for the Financial Institution.

2. A Financial Institution is a sponsored controlled foreign corporation if:

   a. The Financial Institution is a controlled foreign corporation* organized under the laws of Canada that is not a qualified intermediary, withholding foreign partnership, or withholding foreign trust pursuant to relevant U.S. *Treasury Regulations*;

   *A "controlled foreign corporation" means any foreign (i.e., non-U.S.) corporation if more than 50 percent of the total combined voting power of all classes of stock of such corporation entitled to vote, or the total value of the stock of such corporation, is owned, or is considered as owned, by "United States shareholders" on any day during the taxable year of such foreign corporation. The term a "United States shareholder" means, with respect to any foreign corporation, a United States person who owns, or is considered as owning, 10 percent or more of the total combined voting power of all classes of stock entitled to vote of such foreign corporation.

   b. The Financial Institution is wholly owned, directly or indirectly, by a Reporting U.S. Financial Institution that agrees to act, or requires an affiliate of the Financial Institution to act, as a sponsoring entity for the Financial Institution; and

   c. The Financial Institution shares a common electronic account system with the sponsoring entity that enables the sponsoring entity to identify all Account Holders and payees of the Financial Institution and to access all account and customer information maintained by the Financial Institution including, but not limited to, customer identification information, customer documentation, account balance, and all payments made to the Account Holder or payee.

3. The sponsoring entity complies with the following requirements:

a. The sponsoring entity is authorized to act on behalf of the Financial Institution (such as a fund manager, trustee, corporate director, or managing partner) to fulfill applicable registration requirements on the IRS FATCA registration website;

b. The sponsoring entity has registered as a sponsoring entity with the IRS on the IRS FATCA registration website;

c. If the sponsoring entity identifies any U.S. Reportable Accounts with respect to the Financial Institution, the sponsoring entity registers the Financial Institution pursuant to applicable registration requirements on the IRS FATCA registration website on or before the later of December 31, 2015 and the date that is 90 days after such a U.S. Reportable Account is first identified;

d. The sponsoring entity agrees to perform, on behalf of the Financial Institution, all due diligence, reporting, and other requirements (including providing to any immediate payor the information described in subparagraph 1(e) of Article 4 of the Agreement), that the Financial Institution would have been required to perform if it were a Reporting Canadian Financial Institution;

e. The sponsoring entity identifies the Financial Institution and includes the identifying number of the Financial Institution (obtained by following applicable registration requirements on the IRS FATCA registration website) in all reporting completed on the Financial Institution's behalf; and

f. The sponsoring entity has not had its status as a sponsor revoked.

Definitions [Annex II:III:D]: "Account Holder" — 1:1(dd); "Canada" — 1:1(d), Canada-US Treaty Art:III:1(a); "Entity" — 1:1(gg); "Financial Institution" — 1:1(g); "Investment Entity" — 1:1(j); "IRS" — 1:1(c); "Reportable Account" — 1:1(aa); "Reporting Canadian Financial Institution" — 1:1(o); "State", "United States" — 1:1(a).

E. Sponsored, Closely Held Investment Vehicle. A Canadian Financial Institution satisfying the following requirements:

1. The Financial Institution is a Financial Institution solely because it is an Investment Entity and is not a qualified intermediary, withholding foreign partnership, or withholding foreign trust pursuant to relevant U.S. *Treasury Regulations*;

2. The sponsoring entity is a Reporting U.S. Financial Institution, Reporting Model 1 FFI, or Participating FFI, and is authorized to act on behalf of the Financial Institution (such as a professional manager, trustee, or managing partner);

3. The Financial Institution does not hold itself out as an investment vehicle for unrelated parties;

4. Twenty or fewer individuals own all of the debt interests and Equity Interests in the Financial Institution (disregarding debt interests owned by Participating FFIs and deemed-compliant FFIs and Equity Interests owned by an Entity if that Entity owns 100 percent of the Equity Interests in the Financial Institution and is itself a sponsored Financial Institution described in this paragraph E); and

5. The sponsoring entity complies with the following requirements:

a. The sponsoring entity has registered as a sponsoring entity with the IRS on the IRS FATCA registration website;

b. The sponsoring entity agrees to perform, on behalf of the Financial Institution, all due diligence, reporting, and other requirements (including providing to any immediate payor the information described in subparagraph 1(e) of Article 4 of the Agreement), that the Financial Institution

would have been required to perform if it were a Reporting Canadian Financial Institution and retains documentation collected with respect to the Financial Institution for a period of six years;

c. The sponsoring entity identifies the Financial Institution in all reporting completed on the Financial Institution's behalf; and

d. The sponsoring entity has not had its status as a sponsor revoked.

Definitions [Annex II:III:E]: "Canadian Financial Institution" — 1:1(l); "Entity" — 1:1(gg); "Equity Interest" — 1:1(v); "Financial Institution" — 1:1(g); "Investment Entity" — 1:1(j); "IRS" — 1:1(c); "Reporting Canadian Financial Institution" — 1:1(o).

F. Restricted Fund. A Financial Institution that qualifies as a restricted fund as described in relevant U.S. *Treasury Regulations*, applying the procedures set forth in, or required under, Annex I in lieu of the procedures set forth in, or required under, *Treasury Regulation* section 1.1471-4, and applying references to "report" or "reports" in lieu of references in relevant paragraphs in those regulations to "withhold and report" or "withholds and reports", provided that the Financial Institution provides to any immediate payor the information described in subparagraph 1(e) of Article 4 of the Agreement, or fulfills the requirements described in subparagraph 1(d) of Article 4 of the Agreement, as applicable.

Definitions [Annex II:III:F]: "Financial Institution" — 1:1(g).

G. [Labour-sponsored venture capital corporation.] Labour-Sponsored Venture Capital Corporations prescribed under section 6701 of the *Income Tax Regulations*.

H. [Central cooperative credit society.] Any Central Cooperative Credit Society as defined in section 2 of the *Cooperative Credit Associations Act* and whose accounts are maintained for member financial institutions.

I. [Exempt organization.] Any entity described in paragraph 3 of Article XXI (Exempt Organizations) of the Convention.

Definitions [Annex II:III:I]: "Convention" — Preamble.

J. [Certain regulated investment entities.] An Investment Entity established in Canada that is regulated as a collective investment vehicle, provided that all of the interests in the collective investment vehicle (including debt interests in excess of $50,000) are held by or through one or more exempt beneficial owners, Active NFFEs described in subparagraph B(4) of section VI of Annex I, U.S. Persons that are not Specified U.S. Persons, or Financial Institutions that are not Nonparticipating Financial Institutions.

Definitions [Annex II:III:J]: "Canada" — 1:1(d), Canada-US Treaty Art:III:1(a); "Financial Institution" — 1:1(g); "Investment Entity" — 1:1(j); "Nonparticipating Financial Institution" — 1:1(r).

K. Special Rules. The following rules apply to an Investment Entity:

1. With respect to interests in an Investment Entity that is a collective investment vehicle described in paragraph J of this section, the reporting obligations of any Investment Entity (other than a Financial Institution through which interests in the collective investment vehicle are held) shall be deemed fulfilled.

2. With respect to interests in:

a. An Investment Entity established in a Partner Jurisdiction that is regulated as a collective investment vehicle, all of the interests in which (including debt interests in excess of $50,000) are held by or through one or more exempt beneficial owners, Active NFFEs described in subparagraph B(4) of section VI of Annex I, U.S. Persons that are not Specified U.S. Persons, or Financial Institutions that are not Nonparticipating Financial Institutions; or

b. An Investment Entity that is a qualified collective investment vehicle under relevant U.S. *Treasury Regulations*;

the reporting obligations of any Investment Entity that is a Canadian Financial Institution (other than a Financial Institution through which interests in the collective investment vehicle are held) shall be deemed fulfilled.

3. With respect to interests in an Investment Entity established in Canada that is not described in paragraph J or subparagraph K(2) of this section, consistent with paragraph 3 of Article 5 of the Agreement, the reporting obligations of all other Investment Entities with respect to such interests shall be deemed fulfilled if the information required to be reported by the first-mentioned Investment Entity pursuant to the Agreement with respect to such interests is reported by such Investment Entity or another person.

Definitions [Annex II:III:K]: "Canada" — 1:1(d), Canada-US Treaty Art:III:1(a); "Canadian Financial Institution" — 1:1(l); "Financial Institution" — 1:1(g); "Investment Entity" — 1:1(j); "Nonparticipating Financial Institution" — 1:1(r); "Partner Jurisdiction" — 1:1(e).

IV. ACCOUNTS EXCLUDED FROM FINANCIAL ACCOUNTS

The following accounts and products established in Canada and maintained by a Canadian Financial Institution shall be treated as excluded from the definition of Financial Accounts, and therefore shall not be treated as U.S. Reportable Accounts under the Agreement:

Definitions [Annex II:IV opening words]: "Canada" — 1:1(d), Canada-US Treaty Art:III:1(a); "Canadian Financial Institution" — 1:1(l); "Financial Account" — 1:1(s); "Reportable Account" — 1:1(aa).

A. [RRSP.] Registered Retirement Savings Plans (RRSPs) — as defined in subsection 146(1) of the *Income Tax Act*

B. [RRIF.] Registered Retirement Income Funds (RRIFs) — as defined in subsection 146.3(1) of the *Income Tax Act*

C. [PRPP.] Pooled Registered Pension Plans (PRPPs) — as defined in subsection 147.5(1) of the *Income Tax Act*

D. [RPP.] Registered Pension Plans (RPPs) — as defined in subsection 248(1) of the *Income Tax Act*

E. [TFSA.] Tax-Free Savings Accounts (TFSAs) — as defined in subsection 146.2(1) of the *Income Tax Act*

F. [RDSP.] Registered Disability Savings Plans (RDSPs) — as defined in subsection 146.4(1) of the *Income Tax Act*

G. [RESP.] Registered Education Savings Plans (RESPs) — as defined in subsection 146.1(1) of the *Income Tax Act*

H. [DPSP.] Deferred Profit Sharing Plans (DPSPs) — as defined in subsection 147(1) of the *Income Tax Act*

I. [AgriInvest account.] AgriInvest accounts — as defined under "NISA Fund No. 2" and "net income stabilization account" in subsection 248(1) of the *Income Tax Act* including Quebec's Agri-Quebec program as prescribed in section 5503 of the *Income Tax Regulations*

J. [Eligible funeral arrangement.] Eligible Funeral Arrangements — as defined under subsection 148.1 of the *Income Tax Act*

K. Escrow Accounts. An account maintained in Canada established in connection with any of the following:

1. A court order or judgment.

2. A sale, exchange, or lease of real or immovable property or of personal or movable property, provided that the account satisfies the following requirements:

a. The account is funded solely with a down payment, earnest money, deposit in an amount appropriate to secure an obligation directly related to the transaction, or a similar payment, or is funded with a financial asset that is deposited in the account in connection with the sale, exchange, or lease of the property;

b. The account is established and used solely to secure the obligation of the purchaser to pay the purchase price for the property, the seller to pay any contingent liability, or the lessor or lessee to pay for any damages relating to the leased property as agreed under the lease;

c. The assets of the account, including the income earned thereon, will be paid or otherwise distributed for the benefit of the purchaser, seller, lessor, or lessee (including to satisfy such person's obligation) when the property is sold, exchanged, or surrendered, or the lease terminates;

d. The account is not a margin or similar account established in connection with a sale or exchange of a financial asset; and

e. The account is not associated with a credit card account.

3. An obligation of a Financial Institution servicing a loan secured by real or immovable property to set aside a portion of a payment solely to facilitate the payment of taxes or insurance related to the property at a later time.

4. An obligation of a Financial Institution solely to facilitate the payment of taxes at a later time.

Definitions [Annex II:IV:K]: "Canada" — 1:1(d), Canada-US Treaty Art:III:1(a); "Financial Institution" — 1:1(g).

L. [Other agreed accounts.] An account maintained in Canada and excluded from the definition of Financial Account under an agreement between the United States and another Partner Jurisdiction to facilitate the implementation of FATCA, provided that such account is subject to the same requirements and oversight under the laws of such other Partner Jurisdiction as if such account were established in that Partner Jurisdiction and maintained by a Partner Jurisdiction Financial Institution in that Partner Jurisdiction.

Definitions [Annex II:IV:L]: "Canada" — 1:1(d), Canada-US Treaty Art:III:1(a); "Financial Account" — 1:1(s); "Partner Jurisdiction" — 1:1(e); "Partner Jurisdiction Financial Institution" — 1:1(m); "United States" — 1:1(a).

CANADA–UNITED KINGDOM TAX CONVENTION

Convention Between the Government of Canada and the Government of the United Kingdom of Great Britain and Northern Ireland for the Avoidance of Double Taxation and the Prevention of Fiscal Evasion With Respect to Taxes on Income and Capital Gains, as Amended by the Protocols Signed on April 15, 1980, October 16, 1985, May 7, 2003 and July 21, 2014

Enacted in Canada by S.C. 1980-81-82-83, c. 44, Part X (1980 Protocol enacted by Part XI); 1985 Protocol enacted in Canada by SI/86-47 (April 16, 1986), in force Dec. 23, 1985; 2003 Protocol enacted in Canada by P.C. 2003-1374 (Sept. 18, 2003), in force May 4, 2004; 2014 Protocol in force Dec. 18, 2014.

Notes: The Canada-United Kingdom Income Tax Convention was signed on Sept. 8, 1978 [in force Dec. 17, 1980] and amended by four Protocols signed on April 15, 1980 [in force Dec. 18, 1980], Oct. 16, 1985 [in force Dec. 23, 1985], May 7, 2003 [in force May 4, 2004], and July 21, 2014 [in force Dec. 18, 2014]. For the Nov. 26, 2015 "Agreement Concerning the Application of the Arbitration Provisions of the Canada-United Kingdom Tax Convention", see Notes to Art. 23:6.

Both Canada and the UK have signed and ratified the MLI, the Multilateral Instrument that effectively amends tax treaties worldwide. See before the Canada-US Treaty for the MLI. The MLI effects on this treaty are shown in shaded boxes below.

For discussion of this treaty see: Krishna and Cross, *The Canada-U.K. Tax Treaty: Text and Commentary* (LexisNexis, 2005); Bowman, "Canada-United Kingdom Income Tax Convention — Third Protocol Signed", XI(1) *Corporate Finance* (Federated Press) 1018-22 (2003); Bowman & Tyler, "Tax Treaty Update", 2014 Cdn Tax Foundation conference report at 21:12-20 (re 2014 Protocol). For interpretation of tax treaties generally see Notes to *Income Tax Conventions Interpretation Act*, before the Canada-US treaty. See also Notes at beginning of the Canada-US treaty.

UK income tax is administered by Her Majesty's Revenue & Customs. See hmrc.gov.uk.

Exchange of Letters between the Governments of the United Kingdom and Canada, May 7, 2003

[from the UK] Excellency:

I have the honour to refer to the Protocol amending the Convention between the Government of the United Kingdom of Great Britain and Northern Ireland and the Government of Canada for the Avoidance of Double Taxation and the Prevention of Fiscal Evasion with Respect to Taxes on Income and Capital Gains, signed at London on 8 September 1978, as amended by the Protocol signed at Ottawa on 15 April 1980 and as further amended by the Protocol signed at London on 16 October 1985, which has been signed today and to make on behalf of the Government of the United Kingdom of Great Britain and Northern Ireland the following proposals:

With reference to Articles IV, V and VI:

It is understood that, in the event that, pursuant to an agreement or convention concluded after the date of signature of this Protocol with a country that is a member of the Organisation for Economic Co-operation and Development, Canada agrees to a rate of tax on dividends, interest, or royalties lower than that provided for in the Convention, the appropriate authorities of the Contracting States shall consult at the earliest opportunity with respect to further reductions in the withholding taxes provided for in the Convention.

With reference to paragraph 1 of Article VII:

It is understood that an individual who becomes a resident of the United Kingdom and is treated as resident for any year of assessment from the date of arrival shall be charged to capital gains tax only in respect of chargeable gains from the alienation of property made after the date of arrival, provided that the individual has not been resident or ordinarily resident in the United Kingdom at any time during the six years immediately preceding the alienation of the property and that the gain in question is not one that is chargeable on the individual as the settlor of a settlement under sections 77-79 or section 86 and Schedule 5 of the Taxation of Chargeable Gains Act 1992.

With reference to Article XII:

It is understood that the provisions of Article 24 (Exchange of Information) of the Convention, as amended by Article XII of the Protocol signed today, shall have effect from the date of entry into force of the Protocol, without regard to the taxable or chargeable period to which the request for information relates.

If the foregoing proposals are acceptable to the Government of Canada, I have the honour to suggest that the present note and Your Excellency's reply to that effect shall be regarded as constituting an agreement between the two Governments in this matter, which shall enter into force at the same time as the Protocol.

I avail myself of this opportunity to extend to Your Excellency the assurance of my highest consideration.

Dawn Primarolo

[from Canada] Excellency:

I have the honour to refer to your note dated 7 May 2003 which reads as follows: [see Letter from the Government of the United Kingdom above — ed.]

The foregoing proposals being acceptable to the Government of Canada, I have the honour to confirm that your note and this reply shall be regarded as constituting an agreement between the two Governments in this matter which shall enter into force at the same time as the Protocol.

Please accept the renewed assurance of my highest consideration.

Mel Cappe

In-force rules for 2014 Protocol

The July 21, 2014 Protocol, Art. XVI, provides:

1. Each Contracting State shall notify the other Contracting State, by diplomatic notes, of the completion of its internal procedures required to bring this Protocol into force. This Protocol shall enter into force on the date of the later of these notes and its provisions shall have effect:

    (a) in Canada:

        (i) in respect of tax withheld at the source, on amounts paid or credited to non-residents on or after the first day of January in the calendar year next following the date that this Protocol enters into force; and

        (ii) in respect of other Canadian tax, for taxation years beginning on or after the first day of January in the calendar year next following the date that this Protocol enters into force;

    (b) in the United Kingdom:

        (i) in respect of tax withheld at the source, on amounts paid or credited to non-residents on or after the first day of January in the calendar year next following the date that this Protocol enters into force;

        (ii) in respect of income tax and capital gains tax, for any year of assessment beginning on or after 6th April next following the date that this Protocol enters into force; and

        (iii) in respect of corporation tax, for any financial year beginning on or after 1st April next following the date that this Protocol enters into force.

2. Notwithstanding the provisions of paragraph 1, the provisions of Article 23 (Mutual agreement procedure), Article 24 (Exchange of information) and Article 24A (Assistance in the collection of taxes) of the Convention, introduced by Articles XII, XIII and XIV of this Protocol, shall have effect from the date of entry into force of this Protocol, without regard to the taxable period to which the matters relate. However, paragraphs 6 and 7 of Article 23 (Mutual agreement procedure) of the Convention introduced by Article XII of this Protocol shall have effect from the date specified through an exchange of diplomatic notes, and Article 24A (Assistance in the collection of taxes) introduced by Article XIV of this Protocol shall not apply to revenue claims in respect of taxation years ending more than five years before the date on which this Protocol enters into force.

Interpretative Protocol for 2014 Protocol

At the signing of the Protocol amending the *Convention between the Government of Canada and the Government of the United Kingdom of Great Britain and Northern Ireland for the avoidance of double taxation and the prevention of fiscal evasion with respect to taxes on income and capital gains*, signed at London on 8 September 1978, as amended by the Protocol signed at Ottawa on 15 April 1980, by the Protocol signed at London on 16 October 1985 and by the Protocol signed at London on 7 May 2003 (hereinafter referred to as the "Convention"), the undersigned have agreed upon the following provisions which shall form an integral part of the Convention:

1. In relation to the application of the Convention to United Kingdom Limited Liability Partnerships:

    It is understood that for the purpose of providing benefits under the Convention in respect of income or gains derived by or through a Limited Liability Partnership which is established under the laws of the United Kingdom, has its place of effective management in the United Kingdom, and is treated as fiscally transparent under the tax laws of the United Kingdom, the income or gains shall be considered to be income or gains of the members of the Limited Liability Partnership, but only to the extent that the income or gains are treated, for purposes of taxation by the United Kingdom, as the income or gains of a resident of the United Kingdom. In no case shall the provisions of this paragraph be construed so as to restrict in any way a Contracting State's right to tax the residents of that State. The competent authorities of the Contracting States may consult to determine the application of this paragraph.

2. In relation to paragraph 1 of Article 4 of the Convention:

It is understood that the word "instrumentality" includes a person that is wholly owned, directly or indirectly, by a Contracting State or a political subdivision or local authority of a Contracting State.

3. For the purposes of paragraph 3(c) of Article 11 of the Convention, it is understood that:

(a) in the case of Canada, whether persons are considered to be dealing at arm's length with each other, or not, is determined by subsection 251(1) of the *Income Tax Act*;

(b) in the case of the United Kingdom, persons are considered not to be dealing at arm's length where:

(i) one person is treated as having control of another person as defined in section 450 or section 1124 of *Corporation Tax Act 2010*;

(ii) persons are associates or connected persons as defined by section 448 or section 1122 of *Corporation Tax Act 2010;* or

(iii) neither subparagraph (i) nor subparagraph (ii) applies and conditions are made or imposed between those persons which does not reflect ordinary commercial dealing between persons acting in their separate interests.

IN WITNESS WHEREOF the undersigned, duly authorised thereto, have signed this Interpretative Protocol.

DONE in duplicate at London, this 21st day of July 2014, in the English and French languages, each version being equally authentic.

The Government of Canada and the Government of the United Kingdom of Great Britain and Northern Ireland, desiring to conclude a Convention for the avoidance of double taxation and the prevention of fiscal evasion with respect to taxes on income and capital gains, have agreed as follows:

Enacted Addition — Treaty Preamble (MLI Art. 6:1)

Intending to eliminate double taxation with respect to the taxes covered by this agreement without creating opportunities for non-taxation or reduced taxation through tax evasion or avoidance (including through treaty-shopping arrangements aimed at obtaining reliefs provided in this agreement for the indirect benefit of residents of third jurisdictions).

Application: The Multilateral Instrument (MLI), Art. 6:1, adds the above text to the Preamble, effective (per MLI Art. 35) Jan. 1, 2020 for withholding taxes; and otherwise, for taxable periods beginning March 1, 2020 or later. For the MLI, see the pages before the Canada-US Treaty.

Article 1 — Personal Scope

This Convention shall apply to persons who are residents of one or both of the Contracting States.

Notes: For the treaty's application to a UK limited liability partnership (LLP) see 2014 Interpretative Protocol (before Art. 1), para. 1; ITA 248(1)"corporation" Notes.

Definitions: "person" — Art. 3:1(c); "resident" — ITCIA 3, ITA 250.

Article 2 — Taxes Covered

1. The taxes which are the subject of this Convention are:

(a) in Canada:

the income taxes which are imposed by the Government of Canada, (hereinafter referred to as **"Canadian tax"**);

(b) in the United Kingdom of Great Britain and Northern Ireland:

the income tax, the corporation tax, the capital gains tax, the petroleum revenue tax and the development land tax (hereinafter referred to as **"United Kingdom tax"**).

Definitions: "Canada" — Art. 3:1(a)(i), ITCIA 5; "company" — Art.3:1(d); "tax" — Art. 3:1(g); "United Kingdom" — Art. 3:1(a)(ii).

2. The Convention shall apply also to any identical or substantially similar taxes which are imposed after the date of signature of this Convention in addition to, or in place of, the existing taxes by either Contracting State or by the Government of any territory to which the present Convention is extended under Article 26. The Contracting States shall notify each other of changes which have been made in their respective taxation laws.

Definitions: "tax" — Art. 3:1(g).

Article 3 — General Definitions

1. In this Convention, unless the context otherwise requires:

(a)

(i) the term **"Canada"** used in a geographical sense, means the territory of Canada, including any area beyond the territorial waters of Canada which is an area where Canada may, in accordance with its national legislation and international law, exercise sovereign rights with respect to the sea-bed and sub-soil and their natural resources;

(ii) the term **"United Kingdom"** means Great Britain and Northern Ireland, including an area outside the territorial sea of the United Kingdom which in accordance with international law has been or may be hereafter designated, under the laws of the United Kingdom concerning the Continental Shelf, as an area within which the rights of the United Kingdom with respect to the sea-bed and sub-soil and their natural resources may be exercised;

(b) the terms **"a Contracting State"** and **"the other Contracting State"** means, as the context requires, Canada or the United Kingdom;

(c) the term **"person"** includes an individual, a trust, a company, a partnership and any other body of persons;

(d) the term **"company"** means any body corporate or any other entity which is treated as a body corporate for tax purposes; in French, the term **"société"** also means a "corporation" within the meaning of Canadian law;

(e) the terms **"enterprise of a Contracting State"** and **"enterprise of the other Contracting State"** mean respectively an enterprise carried on by a resident of a Contracting State and an enterprise carried on by a resident of the other Contracting State;

(f) the term **"competent authority"** means:

(i) in the case of Canada, the Minister of National Revenue or the Minister's authorised representative;

(ii) in the case of the United Kingdom, the Commissioners for Her Majesty's Revenue and Customs or their authorised representative;

(g) the term **"tax"** means Canadian tax or United Kingdom tax, as the context requires;

(h) the term **"national"** means:

(i) in relation to the United Kingdom, any British citizen, or any British subject not possessing the citizenship of any other Commonwealth country or territory, provided that citizen or subject has the right of abode in the United Kingdom; and any legal person, partnership, association or other entity deriving its status as such from the law in force in the United Kingdom;

(ii) in relation to Canada, all citizens of Canada and all legal persons, partnerships and associations deriving their status as such from the law in force in Canada;

(i) the term **"international traffic"** means any transport by a ship or aircraft operated by an enterprise of a Contracting State, except when the ship or aircraft is operated solely between places in the other Contracting State.

Notes: See also the provisions of the *Income Tax Conventions Interpretation Act*, reproduced before the Canada-US Treaty.

See Notes to ITA 115.1 re the designated Canadian "competent authority".

1(c) amended, 1(f) amended to change "Inland Revenue" to HMRC, and 1(i) added by 2014 Protocol, effective 2015 as per Protocol Art. XVI (reproduced before Art. 1).

Art. 3:1(c) and (h)(i) amended by 2003 Protocol, effective 2005.

Definitions: "a Contracting State" — Art. 3:1(b); "Canada" — Art. 3:1(a)(i), ITCIA 5; "Canadian tax" — Art. 2:1(a); "company" — Art. 3:1(d); "corporation", "individual" — ITCIA 3, ITA 248(1); "partnership" — ITCIA 3, ITA 96(1); "person" — Art. 3:1(c); "resident of a Contracting State" — Art. 4; "tax" — Art. 3:1(g); "the other Contracting State" — Art. 3:1(b); "trust" — ITCIA 3, ITA 104(1), 248(1), (3); "United Kingdom" — Art. 3:1(a)(ii); "United Kingdom tax" — Art. 2:1(b).

2. As regards the application of the Convention by a Contracting State any term not otherwise defined shall, unless the context otherwise requires, have the meaning which it has under the laws of that Contracting State relating to the taxes which are the subject of the Convention.

Related Provisions: Art. 2 — Taxes that are the subject of the Convention.

Notes: For detailed discussion see Michael Kandev, "Tax Treaty Interpretation: Determining Domestic Meaning Under Article 3(2) of the OECD Model", 55(1) *Canadian Tax Journal* 31-71 (2007).

Definitions: "a Contracting State" — Art. 3:1(b); "tax" — Art. 3:1(g).

Article 4 — Fiscal Domicile

1. For the purposes of this Convention, the term **"resident of a Contracting State"** means any person who, under the laws of that State, is liable to taxation therein by reason of his domicile, residence, place of management, place of incorporation or any other criterion of a similar nature. This term also includes that State and any political subdivision or local authority thereof, or any agency or instrumentality of that State, subdivision or local authority. But this term does not include any person who is liable to tax in that Contracting State in respect only of income from sources therein.

Related Provisions: ITCIA 4.3 — Residence of trust; ITCIA 6.2 — Residence of partnership.

Notes: See Notes to Canada-US Tax Treaty Art. IV:1.

For the meaning of "instrumentality" see para. 2 of the Interpretative Protocol, reproduced before Art. 1.

Art. 4:1 amended by 2014 Protocol to add "place of incorporation" and the sentence "This term also includes", effective 2015 as per Protocol Art. XVI (reproduced before Art. 1).

Definitions: "person" — Art. 3:1(c); "tax" — Art. 3:1(g).

I.T. Technical News: 34 (treaty interpretation and the meaning of "liable to tax"); 35 (treaty residence — resident of convenience).

2. Where by reason of the provisions of paragraph 1 an individual is a resident of both Contracting States, then his status shall be determined as follows:

(a) he shall be deemed to be a resident of the Contracting State in which he has a permanent home available to him. If he has a permanent home available to him in both Contracting States, he shall be deemed to be a resident of the Contracting State with which his personal and economic relations are closer (centre of vital interests);

(b) if the Contracting State in which he has his centre of vital interests cannot be determined, or if he has not a permanent home available to him in either Contracting State, he shall be deemed to be a resident of the Contracting State in which he has an habitual abode;

(c) if he has an habitual abode in both Contracting States or in neither of them, he shall be deemed to be a resident of the Contracting State of which he is a national;

(d) if he is a national of both Contracting States or of neither of them, the competent authorities of the Contracting States shall settle the question by mutual agreement.

Notes: See Notes to Canada-US Tax Treaty Art. IV:2, and Notes to ITA 250(5) re the *Conrad Black* case.

Definitions: "competent authority" — Art. 3:1(f); "individual" — ITCIA 3, ITA 248(1); "national" — Art. 3:1(h); "resident" — ITCIA 3, ITA 250; "resident of a Contracting State" — Art. 4.

3. Where by reason of the provisions of paragraph 1 of this Article a person other than an individual is a resident of both Contracting States, the competent authorities of the Contracting States shall endeavour to determine by mutual agreement the State of which the person shall be deemed to be a resident, having regard to its place of effective management, the place where it is incorporated or otherwise constituted and any other relevant factors. If the competent authorities are unable to determine the matter by mutual agreement, they shall endeavour to determine by mutual agreement the mode of application of the Convention to that person.

Enacted Replacement Rule — Treaty Art. 4:3 (MLI Art. 4)

Article 4 — Dual Resident Entities

1. Where by reason of the provisions of a Covered Tax Agreement a person other than an individual is a resident of more than one Contracting Jurisdiction, the competent authorities of the Contracting Jurisdictions shall endeavour to determine by mutual agreement the Contracting Jurisdiction of which such person shall be deemed to be a resident for the purposes of the Covered Tax Agreement, having regard to its place of effective management, the place where it is incorporated or otherwise constituted and any other relevant factors. In the absence of such agreement, such person shall not be entitled to any relief or exemption from tax provided by the Covered Tax Agreement except to the extent and in such manner as may be agreed upon by the competent authorities of the Contracting Jurisdictions.

2. Paragraph 1 shall apply in place of or in the absence of provisions of a Covered Tax Agreement that provide rules for determining whether a person other than an individual shall be treated as a resident of one of the Contracting Jurisdictions in cases in which that person would otherwise be treated as a resident of more than one Contracting Jurisdiction. Paragraph 1 shall not apply, however, to provisions of a Covered Tax Agreement specifically addressing the residence of companies participating in dual-listed company arrangements.

Definitions: "Contracting Jurisdiction" — MLI 2:1(c); "Covered Tax Agreement" — MLI 2:1(a).

Application: The Multilateral Instrument (MLI), Art. 4, provides the above rules effectively replacing Treaty Art. 4:3, effective (per MLI Art. 35) Jan. 1, 2020 for withholding taxes; and otherwise, for taxable periods beginning March 1, 2020 or later. For the MLI, see the pages before the Canada-US Treaty.

Announced Administrative Change — COVID-19 — Place of effective management

CRA notice (tinyurl.com/cra-internat, April 27, 2021): See under ITA 250(1)(a), sections I.B "Income Tax Residency: Corporations" and VII.B "Permanent establishment".

Related Provisions: ITA 115.1 — Competent authority agreements.

Notes: The term "place of effective management" means the same as "central management and control" (Notes to ITA 250(4)): *Smallwood*, [2010] EWCA Civ 778 (UK).

The term "relevant factor" is defined in ITA 248(1), but that definition is clearly not intended to apply to this para., so presumably the "context otherwise requires" (*Income Tax Conventions Interpretation Act* s. 3) that that definition not be applied here.

Art. 4:3 amended by 2003 Protocol, effective 2005.

Definitions: "competent authority" — Art. 3:1(f); "individual" — ITCIA 3, ITA 248(1); "person" — Art. 3:1(c); "resident" — ITCIA 3, ITA 250.

Article 5 — Permanent Establishment

1. For the purposes of this Convention, the term **"permanent establishment"** means a fixed place of business in which the business of the enterprise is wholly or partly carried on.

Related Provisions: Reg. 5906(2)(a)(i), 5906(2)(b)(i) — Treaty definition applies for certain purposes; Art. 5, ss. 2–6 — Extensions to definition of "permanent establishment".

Notes: See Notes to Canada-US tax treaty Art. V:2.

Definitions: "business" — ITCIA 3, ITA 248(1).

I.T. Technical News: 25 (e-commerce — whether web site is permanent establishment); 33 (permanent establishment — the *Dudney* case update); 34 (permanent establishments — *Toronto Blue Jays* case).

2. The term "permanent establishment" shall include especially:

(a) a place of management;

(b) a branch;

(c) an office;

(d) a factory;

(e) a workshop;

(f) a mine, quarry or other place of extraction of natural resources;

(g) a building site or construction or assembly project which exists for more than 12 months.

Announced Administrative Change — COVID-19 — Permanent Establishment

CRA notice (tinyurl.com/cra-internat, April 27, 2021): [CRA will generally not consider a PE to be created by a foreign company's employees who are forced by COVID-19 to remain in Canada. See under ITA 250(1)(a), sections II "Carrying on business in Canada/Permanent establishment" and VII.B "Permanent establishment" — ed.]

Proposed Amendment — Digital Services Tax on large non-resident businesses

Federal Budget, Annex 7, April 19, 2021: See under ITA 115(1) for this proposal, which starting in 2022 will tax certain non-resident businesses on revenue from digital services, even if they have no permanent establishment in Canada.

Notes: See Notes to Canada-US tax treaty Art. V:2, 3.

3. The term "permanent establishment" shall not be deemed to include:

(a) the use of facilities solely for the purpose of storage, display or delivery of goods or merchandise belonging to the enterprise;

(b) the maintenance of a stock of goods or merchandise belonging to the enterprise solely for the purpose of storage, display or delivery;

(c) the maintenance of a stock of goods or merchandise belonging to the enterprise solely for the purpose of processing by another enterprise;

(d) the maintenance of a fixed place of business solely for the purpose of purchasing goods or merchandise, or for collecting information, for the enterprise;

(e) the maintenance of a fixed place of business solely for the purpose of advertising, for the supply of information, for scientific research, or for similar activities which have a preparatory or auxiliary character, for the enterprise.

Definitions: "business" — ITCIA 3, ITA 248(1).

4. A person — other than an agent of independent status to whom paragraph 5 applies — acting in a Contracting State on behalf of an enterprise of the other Contracting State shall be deemed to be a permanent establishment in the first-mentioned State if he has, and habitually exercises in that first-mentioned State, an authority to conclude contracts in the name of the enterprise, unless his activities are limited to the purchase of goods or merchandise for the enterprise.

Definitions: "a Contracting State" — Art. 3:1(b); "enterprise of the other Contracting State" — Art. 3:1(e); "person" — Art. 3:1(c).

5. An enterprise of a Contracting State shall not be deemed to have a permanent establishment in the other Contracting State merely because it carries on business in that other State through a broker, general commission agent or any other agent of an independent status, where such persons are acting in the ordinary course of their business.

Definitions: "enterprise of a Contracting State" — Art. 3:1(e); "business" — ITCIA 3, ITA 248(1); "person" — Art. 3:1(c); "the other Contracting State" — Art. 3:1(b).

6. The fact that a company which is a resident of a Contracting State controls or is controlled by a company which is a resident of the other Contracting State, or which carries on business in that other State (whether through a permanent establishment or otherwise), shall not of itself constitute either company a permanent establishment of the other.

Definitions: "business" — ITCIA 3, ITA 248(1); "company" — Art. 3:1(d); "resident" — ITCIA 3, ITA 250; "resident of a Contracting State" — Art. 4; "the other Contracting State" — Art. 3:1(b).

Article 6 — Income from Immovable Property

1. Income from immovable property, including income from agriculture or forestry, may be taxed in the Contracting State in which such property is situated.

Definitions: "immovable property" — Art. 6:2, ITCIA 5, Quebec *Civil Code* art. 900-907; "property" — ITCIA 3, ITA 248(1).

2. For the purposes of this Convention, the term **"immovable property"** shall be defined in accordance with the law of the Contracting State in which the property in question is situated. The term shall in any case include property accessory to immovable property, livestock and equipment used in agriculture and forestry, rights to which the provisions of general law respecting landed property apply, usufruct of immovable property and rights to variable or fixed payments as consideration for the working of, or the right to work, mineral deposits, sources and other natural resources; ships, boats and aircraft shall not be regarded as immovable property.

Notes: See also the definition of "immovable property" in s. 5 of the *Income Tax Conventions Interpretation Act*. In Quebec, "immovable" is defined in the *Civil Code*, art. 900-907.

Definitions: "immovable property" — Art. 6:2, ITCIA 5, Quebec *Civil Code* art. 900-907; "mineral", "property" — ITCIA 3, ITA 248(1).

3. The provisions of paragraph 1 shall apply to income derived from the direct use, letting, or use in any other form of immovable property and to profits from the alienation of such property.

Definitions: "immovable property" — Art. 6:2, ITCIA 5, Quebec *Civil Code* art. 900-907; "property" — ITCIA 3, ITA 248(1).

4. The provisions of paragraphs 1 and 3 shall also apply to income from immovable property of an enterprise and to income from immovable property used for the performance of professional services.

Definitions: "immovable property" — Art. 6:2, ITCIA 5, Quebec *Civil Code* art. 900-907.

Article 7 — Business Profits

1. Profits of an enterprise of a Contracting State shall be taxable only in that State unless the enterprise carries on business in the other Contracting State through a permanent establishment situated therein. If the enterprise carries on business as aforesaid, the profits that are attributable to the permanent establishment in accordance with the provisions of paragraph 2 may be taxed in that other State.

Related Provisions: Art. 7:2 — Profits attributable to PE.

Notes: See Notes to Canada-US Treaty Art. VII:1.

For CRA interpretation see VIEWS doc 2004-0078321E5 (branch profits of UK bank in Canada).

For 2014 amendments to all of Art. 7 see Notes at end of Art. 7.

Definitions: "business" — ITCIA 3, ITA 248(1); "enterprise of a Contracting State" — Art. 3:1(e); "permanent establishment" — Art. 5; "the other Contracting State" — Art. 3:1(b).

2. For the purposes of this Article and Article 21, the profits that are attributable in each Contracting State to the permanent establishment referred to in paragraph 1 are the profits it might be expected to make, in particular in its dealings with other parts of the enterprise, if it were a separate and independent enterprise engaged in the same or similar activities under the same or similar conditions, taking into account the functions performed, assets used and risks assumed by the enterprise through the permanent establishment and through the other parts of the enterprise.

Related Provisions: Art. 7:3 — Where one state adjusts profits.

Definitions: "permanent establishment" — Art. 5.

3. Where, in accordance with paragraph 2, a Contracting State adjusts the profits that are attributable to a permanent establishment of an enterprise of one of the Contracting States and taxes accordingly profits of the enterprise that have been charged to tax in the other State, the other State shall, to the extent necessary to eliminate double taxation on these profits, make an appropriate adjustment to the amount of the tax charged on those profits. In determining such adjustment, the competent authorities of the Contracting States shall if necessary consult each other.

Definitions: "a Contracting State" — Art. 3:1(b); "permanent establishment" — Art. 5; "tax" — Art. 3:1(g).

4. Where profits include items of income or gains which are dealt with separately in other Articles of this Convention, then the provisions of those Articles shall not be affected by the provisions of this Article.

Notes: Art. 7 amended by 2014 Protocol, effective 2015 as per Protocol Art. XVI (reproduced before Art. 1). These amendments bring the treaty into line with the OECD Model Treaty.

Article 8 — Shipping and Air Transport

1. Profits derived by an enterprise of a Contracting State from the operation of ships or aircraft in international traffic shall be taxable only in that State.

Definitions: "enterprise of a Contracting State" — Art. 3:1(e); "international traffic" — Art. 3:1(i).

2. Notwithstanding the provisions of paragraph 1 and Article 7, profits derived by an enterprise of a Contracting State from the carriage by a ship or aircraft of passengers or goods taken on board at a place in the other Contracting State for discharge at another place in that other Contracting State may be taxed in that other Contracting State, unless all or substantially all of the passengers or goods carried to that other place were taken on board at a place outside that other Contracting State.

Notes: Art. 8:2 amended by 2014 Protocol, effective 2015 as per Protocol Art. XVI (reproduced before Art. 1).

Definitions: "a Contracting State" — Art. 3:1(b); "the other Contracting State" — Art. 3:1(b).

3. Notwithstanding the provisions of Article 7, profits of an enterprise of a Contracting State from the use, maintenance or rental of containers (including trailers and related equipment for the transport of containers) used for the transport of goods or merchandise in international traffic shall be taxable only in that State.

Definitions: "enterprise of a Contracting State" — Art. 3:1(e); "international traffic" — Art. 3:1(i).

4. The provisions of this Article shall also apply to profits derived by an enterprise of a Contracting State from its participation in a pool, a joint business or an international operating agency.

Definitions: "enterprise of a Contracting State" — Art. 3:1(e).

Article 9 — Associated Enterprises

1. Where:

(a) an enterprise of a Contracting State participates directly or indirectly in the management, control or capital of an enterprise of the other Contracting State; or

(b) the same persons participate directly or indirectly in the management, control or capital of an enterprise of a Contracting State and an enterprise of the other Contracting State;

and in either case conditions are made or imposed between the two enterprises in their commercial or financial relations which differ from those which would be made between independent enterprises, then any profits which would, but for those conditions, have accrued to one of the enterprises, but, by reason of those conditions, have not so accrued, may be included by a Contracting State in the profits of that enterprise and taxed accordingly.

Notes: See Notes to Canada-US treaty Art. IX:1.

Art. 9 renumbered as 9:1 and closing words amended by 2003 Protocol, effective 2005.

Definitions: "enterprise of a Contracting State", "enterprise of the other Contracting State" — Art. 3:1(e); "person" — Art. 3:1(c).

2. Where a Contracting State includes in the profits of an enterprise of that State — and taxes accordingly — profits on which an enterprise of the other Contracting State has been charged to tax in that other State and the profits so included are profits which would have accrued to the enterprise of the first-mentioned State if the conditions made between the two enterprises had been those which would have been made between independent enterprises, then, subject to the provisions of paragraph 3 of this Article, that other State shall (notwithstanding any time limits in the domestic law of that other State) make an appropriate adjustment to the amount of tax charged therein on the profits. In determining such adjustment, due regard shall be had to the other provisions of this Convention and the competent authorities of the Contracting States shall if necessary consult each other.

Related Provisions: Art. 9:4 — Exception.

Notes: Art. 9:2 added by 2003 Protocol, effective 2005.

Definitions: "a Contracting State" — Art. 3:1(b); "enterprise of the other Contracting State" — Art. 3:1(e); "tax" — Art. 3:1(g).

3. A Contracting State shall not make a primary adjustment to the profits of an enterprise in the circumstances referred to in paragraph 1 after the expiry of the time limits provided in its domestic laws and, in any case, after eight years from the end of the taxable year in which the profits which would be subject to such an adjustment would, but for the conditions referred to in paragraph 1, have been attributed to that enterprise.

Related Provisions: Art. 9:4 — Exception.

Notes: Art. 9:3 amended by 2014 Protocol, effective 2015 as per Protocol Art. XVI (reproduced before Art. 1).

Art. 9:3 added by 2003 Protocol, effective 2005.

Definitions: "a Contracting State" — Art. 3:1(b); "Canada" — Art. 3:1(a)(i), ITCIA 5; "the other Contracting State" — Art. 3:1(b); "United Kingdom" — Art. 3:1(a)(ii).

4. The provisions of paragraphs 2 and 3 shall not apply in the case of fraud, wilful default or where a person's obligations have not been fulfilled owing to careless or deliberate behaviour.

Notes: For "careless" see Notes to ITA 152(4) on "careless or neglect".

Art. 9:4 amended by 2014 Protocol, effective 2015 as per Protocol Art. XVI (reproduced before Art. 1). Added by 2003 Protocol, effective 2005.

Article 10 — Dividends

1. Dividends paid by a company which is a resident of a Contracting State to a resident of the other Contracting State may be taxed in that other State.

Notes: See under Art. 10:2 below.

Definitions: "a Contracting State" — Art. 3:1(b); "company" — Art. 3:1(d); "dividends" — Art. 10:5; "resident" — Art. 4; "the other Contracting State" — Art. 3:1(b).

2. However, such dividends may also be taxed in the Contracting State of which the company paying the dividends is a resident and according to the laws of that State, but if the beneficial owner of the dividends is a resident of the other Contracting State the tax so charged shall not exceed:

(a) 5 per cent of the gross amount of the dividends if the beneficial owner is a company which controls, directly or indirectly, at least 10 per cent of the voting power in the company paying the dividends;

(b) 15 per cent of the gross amount of the dividends in all other cases.

The provisions of this paragraph shall not affect the taxation of the company in respect of the profits out of which the dividends are paid.

Enacted Anti-Treaty-Shopping Rule — MLI Art. 7

[See under Art. 10:8.]

Non-Amendment for this treaty — 365-day shareholding rule (MLI Art. 8)

Notes: See the pages before the Canada-US Treaty for the Multilateral Instrument (MLI), which effectively amends most of Canada's tax treaties starting 2020 or later. Canada accepts MLI Article 8, which would add a 365-day holding period requirement to Art. 10:2(a) of this treaty (i.e., would require such holding period for determining whether a shareholder controls at least 10% of the voting power of the paying corporation to obtain the reduced 5% withholding tax rate). However, the UK has stated in its MLI "reservations and notifications" that it "reserves the right for the entirety of Article 8 not to apply". This means that MLI Art. 8 does not apply to this treaty, unless the UK drops this "reservation" in the future.

Related Provisions: Art. 10:3 — Exception; Art. 27:2 — For non-domiciled UK resident, relief from Canadian tax applies only if dividend is remitted to the UK.

Notes: The 10% rate (instead of 25% under ITA 212(2)) applies only if the principal-purpose test in the MLI is satisfied. See under Art. 10:8 below. See also Notes to Canada-US treaty Art. X:2.

Limited partners do not indirectly *control* shares owned by the LP for 10:2(a), but do indirectly *own* them for Art. 10:3: VIEWS doc 2014-0563781E5 [Pantry & Korkh, "Canada-UK Treaty and UK Partnerships", 25(7) *Canadian Tax Highlights* (ctf.ca) 2-4 (July 2017)]. See also ITA 17.1(1) Notes re "indirectly".

Art. 10:1 and 2 amended by 2003 Protocol, effective 2005.

Definitions: "company" — Art. 3:1(d); "dividends" — Art. 10:5; "resident" — Art. 4; "the other Contracting State" — Art. 3:1(b).

Forms: NR301: Declaration of eligibility for benefits under a tax treaty for a non-resident taxpayer.

3. Notwithstanding the provisions of paragraph 2, dividends arising in a Contracting State and beneficially owned by an organisation that was constituted and is operated in the other Contracting State exclusively to administer or provide benefits under one or more recognized pension plans shall be exempt from tax in the first-mentioned State if:

(a) the organisation is the beneficial owner of the shares on which the dividends are paid, holds those shares as an investment and is generally exempt from tax in the other State;

(b) the organisation does not own directly or indirectly more than 10 per cent of the capital or 10 per cent of the voting power of the company paying the dividends; and

(c) each recognized pension plan provides benefits primarily to individuals who are resident of the other Contracting State.

Related Provisions: Art. 10:4 — Meaning of "recognized pension plan".

Notes: See Notes to Art. 10:2.

Art. 10:3 added by 2014 Protocol, effective 2015.

Former Art. 10:3 repealed by 2003 Protocol, effective 2005.

Definitions: "a Contracting State" — Art. 3:1(b); "dividends" — Art. 10:4; "recognized pension plan" — Art. 10:4; "resident" — Art. 4; "the other Contracting State" — Art. 3:1(b).

4. For the purposes of paragraph 3, the term **"recognized pension plan"** means:

(a) in the case of Canada, a retirement or employee benefits plan described in paragraph (a) of the definition of "pension" under Article 5 of the *Income Tax Conventions Interpretation Act*;

(b) in the case of the United Kingdom, a pension scheme (other than a social security scheme) registered under Part 4 of the *Finance Act 2004*, including pension funds or pension schemes arranged through insurance companies and unit trusts where the unit holders are exclusively pension schemes; and

(c) any other pension plan agreed by the competent authorities of both Contracting States.

Notes: Art. 10:4 added by 2014 Protocol, effective 2015.

5. The term **"dividends"** as used in this Article means income from shares, "jouissance" shares or "jouissance" rights, mining shares, founders' shares or other rights, not being debt-claims, participating in profits, as well as income assimilated to or treated in the same way as income from shares by the taxation law of the State of which the company making the payment is a resident.

Notes: A "dividend" includes an ITA 84(1) deemed dividend: VIEWS docs 2009-0341681R3, 2009-0348581R3.

Art. 10:4 renumbered 10:5 by 2014 Protocol, effective 2015.

Definitions: "company" — Art. 3:1(d); "resident" — ITCIA 3, ITA 250; "share" — ITCIA 3, ITA 248(1).

6. The provisions of paragraphs 1 and 2 of this Article shall not apply if the beneficial owner of the dividends, being a resident of a Contracting State, carries on business in the other Contracting State of which the company paying the dividends is a resident, through a permanent establishment situated therein, or performs in that other State professional services from a fixed base situated therein, and the holding in respect of which the dividends are paid is effectively connected with such permanent establishment or fixed base. In such a case, the provisions of Article 7 or Article 14, as the case may be, shall apply.

Notes: Art. 10:5 renumbered 10:6 by 2014 Protocol, effective 2015.

Former Art. 10:5 amended by 2003 Protocol, effective 2005.

Definitions: "business" — ITCIA 3, ITA 248(1); "dividend" — Art. 10:4; "permanent establishment" — Art. 5; "resident of a Contracting State" — Art. 4; "the other Contracting State" — Art. 3:1(b).

7. Where a company is a resident of only one Contracting State, the other Contracting State may not impose any tax on the dividends paid by the company, except insofar as such dividends are paid to a resident of that other State or insofar as the holding in respect of which the dividends are paid is effectively connected with a permanent establishment or a fixed base situated in that other State, nor subject the company's undistributed profits to a tax on undistributed profits, even if the dividends paid or the undistributed profits consist wholly or partly of profits or income arising in such other State.

Notes: Art. 10:6 renumbered 10:7 by 2014 Protocol, effective 2015.

Definitions: "a Contracting State" — Art. 3:1(b); "dividend" — Art. 10:4; "permanent establishment" — Art. 5; "the other Contracting State" — Art. 3:1(b); "tax" — Art. 3:1(g).

8. The provisions of this Article shall not apply if it was the main purpose or one of the main purposes of any person concerned with the creation or assignment of the shares or other rights in respect of which the dividend is paid to take advantage of this Article by means of that creation or assignment.

Enacted Replacement Rule — Art. 10:8, 11:9, 12:8 (MLI Art. 7)

Article 7 — Prevention of Treaty Abuse

1. Notwithstanding any provisions of a Covered Tax Agreement, a benefit under the Covered Tax Agreement shall not be granted in respect of an item of income or capital if it is reasonable to conclude, having regard to all relevant facts and circumstances, that obtaining that benefit was one of the principal purposes of any arrangement or transaction that resulted directly or indirectly in that benefit, unless it is established that granting that benefit in these circumstances would be in accordance with the object and purpose of the relevant provisions of the Covered Tax Agreement.

2. Paragraph 1 shall apply in place of or in the absence of provisions of a Covered Tax Agreement that deny all or part of the benefits that would otherwise be provided under the Covered Tax Agreement where the principal purpose or one of the principal purposes of any arrangement or transaction, or of any person con-

cerned with an arrangement or transaction, was to obtain those benefits.

3–14. [Reproduced with the MLI, before the Canada-US Treaty]

15. A Party may reserve the right:

a) [Reproduced with the MLI];

b) for paragraph 1 (and paragraph 4, in the case of a Party that has chosen to apply that paragraph) not to apply to its Covered Tax Agreements that already contain provisions that deny all of the benefits that would otherwise be provided under the Covered Tax Agreement where the principal purpose or one of the principal purposes of any arrangement or transaction, or of any person concerned with an arrangement or transaction, was to obtain those benefits;

c) [Reproduced with the MLI].

Definitions: "Covered Tax Agreement" — MLI 2:1(a); "Party" — MLI 2:1(b).

Application: The Multilateral Instrument (MLI), Article 7, provides the above rules effectively amending Art. 10:8, 11:9 and 12:8, effective (per MLI Art. 35) Jan. 1, 2020 for withholding taxes. For the MLI, see the pages before the Canada-US Treaty.

Notes: Tinyurl.com/canada-mli states that this treaty is *not* subject to a reservation under MLI Art. 7:15(b) and contains a provision described in MLI Art. 7:2 (specifically, Art. 10:8, 11:9 and 12:8). As a result, MLI Art. 7:1 above applies in place of Art. 10:8 for dividends, in place of Art. 11:9 for interest and in place of Art.12:8 for royalties.

Notes: This rule is replaced by the MLI. See shaded box above. Before 2020, this is a specific anti-treaty-shopping rule, parallel to Art. 11:11 and 12:8. See Canada-US treaty Art. X:2 Notes. For the meaning of "one of the main purposes" see ITA 83(2.1) Notes.

Art. 10:7 renumbered 10:8 by 2014 Protocol, effective 2015. Former Art. 10:7 amended by 2003 Protocol.

Definitions: "Canada" — Art. 3:1(a)(i), ITCIA 5; "Canadian tax"Art. 2:1(a); "company" — Art. 3:1(d); "dividend" — Art. 10:4; "person" — Art. 3:1(c); "resident" — ITCIA 3, ITA 250; "share" — ITCIA 3, ITA 248(1); "United Kingdom" — Art. 3:1(a)(ii).

Information Circulars [Art. 10]: 76-12R6: Applicable rate of part XIII tax on amounts paid or credited to persons in countries with which Canada has a tax convention.

Article 11 — Interest

1. Interest arising in a Contracting State and paid to a resident of the other Contracting State may be taxed in that other State.

Related Provisions: Art. 11:2 — Exception.

Notes: Art. 11 replaced by 2014 Protocol, effective 2015 as per Protocol Art. XVI (reproduced before Art. 1), but 11:1 was unchanged.

Definitions: "arising" — Art. 11:7; "a Contracting State" — Art. 3:1(b); "interest" — Art. 11:5; "resident" — ITCIA 3, ITA 250; "the other Contracting State" — Art. 3:1(b).

2. However, such interest may also be taxed in the Contracting State in which it arises and according to the laws of that State, but if the beneficial owner of the interest is a resident of the other Contracting State, the tax so charged shall not exceed 10 per cent of the gross amount of the interest.

Enacted Anti-Treaty-Shopping Rule — MLI Art. 7

[See under Art. 10:8.]

Related Provisions: Art. 11:2 — Exception; Art. 27:2 — For non-domiciled UK resident, relief from Canadian tax applies only if interest is remitted to the UK.

Notes: The 10% rate (instead of 25% under ITA 212(1)(b), where it applies) applies only if the principal-purpose test in the MLI is satisfied. See under Art. 10:8 above.

Art. 11:2 amended by 2014 Protocol, effective 2015 as per Protocol Art. XVI (reproduced before Art. 1), effectively to add the "resident" condition.

Definitions: "arises" — Art. 11:7; "interest" — Art. 11:5; "resident" — Art. 4; "tax" — Art. 3:1(g).

Forms: NR301: Declaration of eligibility for benefits under a tax treaty for a non-resident taxpayer.

3. Notwithstanding the provisions of paragraph 2:

(a) interest arising in the United Kingdom and paid to a resident of Canada shall be taxable only in Canada if it is paid in respect of a loan made, guaranteed or insured, or a credit extended, guaranteed or insured by Export Development Canada;

(b) interest arising in Canada and paid to a resident of the United Kingdom shall be taxable only in the United Kingdom if it is paid in respect of a loan made, guaranteed or insured, or a credit extended, guaranteed or insured by the United Kingdom Export Credits Guarantee Department; and

(c) interest arising in a Contracting State and paid to a resident of the other Contracting State shall not be taxable in the first-mentioned State if the beneficial owner of the interest is a resident of the other Contracting State and is dealing at arm's length with the payer.

Related Provisions: Art. 11:4 — Exception to para. 3(c).

Notes: For the meaning of "arm's length" see para. 4 of the Interpretative Protocol, reproduced before Art. 1, and VIEWS doc 2014-0563781E5. For a ruling applying para. 3(c) see 2017-0712731R3 [Pantry & Korkh, "Interest Earned by UK Partners Through a Non-Resident Partnership", 27(2) *Canadian Tax Highlights* (ctf.ca) 13-14 (Feb. 2019)].

3(c) amended by 2014 Protocol, effective 2015. Art. 11:3 amended by 2003 Protocol, effective 2005.

Definitions: "arising" — Art. 11:7; "Canada" — Art. 3:1(a)(i), ITCIA 5; "interest" — Art. 11:5; "resident" — ITCIA 3, ITA 250; "United Kingdom" — Art. 3:1(a)(ii).

4. Paragraph 3(c) shall not apply to interest, all or any portion of which is contingent or dependent on the use of or production from property or is computed by reference to revenue, profit, cash flow, commodity price or any other similar criterion or by reference to dividends paid or payable to shareholders of any class of shares of the capital stock of a company.

Notes: See Notes to ITA 18(1)(e) and 12(1)(g) for the meaning of "contingent" and "dependent on the use of or production from property".

Art 11:4 replaced by 2014 Protocol, effective 2015 as per Protocol Art. XVI (reproduced before Art. 1).

Definitions: "interest" — Art. 11:5.

5. The term **"interest"** as used in this Article means income from debt-claims of every kind, whether or not secured by mortgage, and in particular, income from government securities and income from bonds or debentures, including premiums and prizes attaching to such securities, bonds or debentures, as well as income which is subjected to the same taxation treatment as income from money lent by the laws of the State in which the income arises. However, the term "interest" does not include income dealt with in Article 8 or Article 10.

Notes: Art 11:5 amended by 2014 Protocol, effective 2015 as per Protocol Art. XVI (reproduced before Art. 1).

Definitions: "arises" — Art. 11:7.

6. The provisions of paragraphs 1, 2 and 3 shall not apply if the beneficial owner of the interest, being a resident of a Contracting State, carries on business in the other Contracting State in which the interest arises through a permanent establishment situated therein, or performs in that other State professional services from a fixed base situated therein, and the debt-claim in respect of which the interest is paid is effectively connected with such permanent establishment or fixed base. In such case the provisions of Article 7 or Article 14, as the case may be, shall apply.

Notes: Art 11:6 amended to change "1, 2, 3 and 4" to "1, 2 and 3" by 2014 Protocol, effective 2015 as per Protocol Art. XVI (reproduced before Art. 1).

Art. 11:6 amended by 2003 Protocol, effective 2005.

Definitions: "arises" — Art. 11:7; "interest" — Art. 11:5; "permanent establishment" — Art. 5; "resident of a Contracting State" — Art. 4; "the other Contracting State" — Art. 3:1(b).

7. Interest shall be deemed to arise in a Contracting State when the payer is a resident of that State. Where, however, the person paying the interest, whether the payer is a resident of a Contracting State or not, has in a Contracting State a permanent establishment or a fixed base in connection with which the indebtedness on which the interest is paid was incurred, and such interest is borne by such permanent establishment or fixed base, then such interest shall be deemed to arise in the State in which the permanent establishment or fixed base is situated.

Notes: Art 11:7 amended by 2014 Protocol, effective 2015 as per Protocol Art. XVI (reproduced before Art. 1).

Definitions: "a Contracting State" — Art. 3:1(b); "interest" — Art. 11:5; "permanent establishment" — Art. 5; "person" — Art. 3:1(c); "resident of a Contracting State" — Art. 4.

8. Where, by reason of a special relationship between the payer and the beneficial owner or between both of them and some other person, the amount of the interest exceeds for whatever reason the amount which would have been agreed upon by the payer and the beneficial owner in the absence of such relationship, the provisions of this Article shall apply only to the last-mentioned amount. In such case, the excess part of the payments shall remain taxable according to the laws of each Contracting State, due regard being had to the other provisions of this Convention.

Related Provisions: ITA 247 — Transfer pricing adjustments.

Notes: Art 11:8 amended by 2014 Protocol, effective 2015.

Definitions: "interest" — Art. 11:5; "person" — Art. 3:1(c).

9. The provisions of this Article shall not apply if it was the main purpose or one of the main purposes of any person concerned with the creation or assignment of the debt-claim in respect of which the interest is paid to take advantage of this Article by means of that creation or assignment.

Enacted Replacement Rule — Art. 11:9 (MLI Art. 7)

[See under Art. 10:8.]

Notes: This rule is replaced by the MLI. See under Art. 10:8. Before 2020, this is a specific anti-treaty-shopping rule, parallel to Art. 10:7 and 12:8. See Notes to Canada-US treaty Art. X:2. For the meaning of "one of the main purposes" see Notes to ITA 83(2.1).

Former Art. 11:9 and 11:10 repealed, and 11:11 renumbered 11:9, by 2014 Protocol, effective 2015 as per Protocol Art. XVI (reproduced before Art. 1).

Former Art. 11:11 added by 2003 Protocol, effective 2005.

Information Circulars [Art. 11]: 76-12R6: Applicable rate of part XIII tax on amounts paid or credited to persons in countries with which Canada has a tax convention.

Article 12 — Royalties

1. Royalties arising in a Contracting State and paid to a resident of the other Contracting State may be taxed in that other State.

Definitions: "arising" — Art. 12:6; "a Contracting State" — Art. 3:1(b); "royalties" — Art. 12:4; "the other Contracting State" — Art. 3:1(b).

2. However, such royalties may be taxed in the Contracting State in which they arise, and according to the laws of that State, but if the beneficial owner of the royalties is a resident of the other Contracting State, the tax so charged shall not exceed 10 per cent of the gross amount of the royalties.

Enacted Anti-Treaty-Shopping Rule — MLI Art. 7

[See under Art. 10:8.]

Related Provisions: Art. 27:2 — For non-domiciled UK resident, relief from Canadian tax applies only if royalty is remitted to the UK.

Notes: The 10% rate (instead of 25% under ITA 212(1)(d)) applies only if the principal-purpose test in the MLI is satisfied. See under Art. 10:8 above.

Art. 12:2 amended by 2014 Protocol, effective 2015, effectively to add the "resident" condition.

Definitions: "arise" — Art. 12:6; "resident" — Art. 4; "royalties" — Art. 12:4; "tax" — Art. 3:1(g); "the other Contracting State" — Art. 3:1(b).

I.T. Technical News: 23 (computer software).

Forms: NR301: Declaration of eligibility for benefits under a tax treaty for a non-resident taxpayer.

3. Notwithstanding the provisions of paragraph 2 of this Article,

(a) copyright royalties and other like payments in respect of the production or reproduction of any literary, dramatic, musical or artistic work (other than payments in respect of motion pictures, and payments in respect of works on film, videotape or other means of reproduction for use in connection with television broadcasting);

(b) payments for the use of, or the right to use, any patent or for information concerning industrial, commercial or scientific experience (but not including any such payment provided in connection with a rental or franchise agreement);

(c) payments for the use of, or the right to use, computer software;

arising in a Contracting State and beneficially owned by a resident of the other Contracting State shall be taxable only in that other State.

Notes: Para. 3(b) can exempt payments for customer lists: VIEWS doc 2014-0525501E5. CRA says streamed movies are "broadcast" (despite *Interpretation Act* 35(1)) and not exempt: 2017-0715561E5.

Art. 12:3(a) amended by 2014 Protocol, effective 2015.

Art. 12:3(b), (c) added by 2003 Protocol, effective 2005.

Definitions: "a Contracting State" — Art. 3:1(b); "arising" — Art. 12:6; "royalties" — Art. 12:4; "the other Contracting State" — Art. 3:1(b).

4. The term **"royalties"** as used in this Article means payments of any kind received as a consideration for the use of, or the right to use, any copyright, patent, trade mark, design or model, plan, secret formula or process, or for the use of, or the right to use, industrial, commercial or scientific equipment, or for information concerning industrial, commercial or scientific experience, and includes payments of any kind in respect of motion pictures and works on film, videotape or other means of reproduction for use in connection with television broadcasting.

Definitions: "broadcasting" — ITCIA 3, *Interpretation Act* 35(1).

I.T. Technical News: 23 (computer software); 25 (e-commerce — payments for digital products not royalties).

5. The provisions of paragraphs 1, 2 and 3 of this Article shall not apply if the beneficial owner of the royalties, being a resident of a Contracting State, carries on business in the other Contracting State in which the royalties arise through a permanent establishment situated therein, or performs in that other State professional services from a fixed base situated therein, and the right or property in respect of which the royalties are paid is effectively connected with such permanent establishment or fixed base. In such a case, the provisions of Article 7 or Article 14, as the case may be, shall apply.

Notes: Art. 12:5 amended by 2003 Protocol, effective 2005.

Definitions: "arise" — Art. 12:6; "business" — ITCIA 3, ITA 248(1); "permanent establishment" — Art. 5; "property" — ITCIA 3, ITA 248(1); "resident of a Contracting State" — Art. 4; "royalties" — Art. 12:4; "the other Contracting State" — Art. 3:1(b).

6. Royalties shall be deemed to arise in a Contracting State when the payer is a resident of that State. Where, however, the person paying the royalties, whether he is a resident of a Contracting State or not, has in a Contracting State a permanent establishment or a fixed base in connection with which the obligation to pay the royalties was incurred, and those royalties are borne by that permanent establishment or fixed base, then such royalties shall be deemed to arise in the Contracting State in which the permanent establishment or fixed base is situated.

Notes: Art. 12:6 amended by 2014 Protocol, effective 2015.

Definitions: "a Contracting State" — Art. 3:1(b); "permanent establishment" — Art. 5; "person" — Art. 3:1(c); "resident of a Contracting State" — Art. 4; "royalties" — Art. 12:4.

7. Where, owing to a special relationship between the payer and the person deriving the royalties or between both of them and some other person, the amount of the royalties paid exceeds for whatever reason the amount which would have been paid in the absence of such relationship, the provisions of this Article shall apply only to the last-mentioned amount. In that case, the excess part of the payments shall remain taxable according to the law of each Contracting State, due regard being had to the other provisions of this Convention.

Definitions: "person" — Art. 3:1(c); "royalties" — Art. 12:4.

8. The provisions of this Article shall not apply if it was the main purpose or one of the main purposes of any person concerned with the creation or assignment of the rights in respect of which the royalties are paid to take advantage of this Article by means of that creation or assignment.

Enacted Replacement Rule — Art. 12:8 (MLI Art. 7)

[See under Art. 10:8.]

Notes: This rule is replaced by the MLI. See under Art. 10:8 above. Before 2020, this is a specific anti-treaty-shopping rule, parallel to Art. 10:7 and 11:11. See Canada-US treaty Art. X:2 Notes. For "one of the main purposes" see ITA 83(2.1) Notes.

Art. 12:8 added by 2003 Protocol, effective 2005.

Definitions: "person" — Art. 3:1(c); "royalties" — Art. 12:4.

Article 13 — Capital Gains

1. Gains derived by a resident of a Contracting State from the alienation of immovable property situated in the other Contracting State may be taxed in that other State.

Related Provisions: ITA 126(2.21), (2.22) — Foreign tax credit to emigrant for tax payable on gain accrued while resident in Canada; ITA 128.1(4)(b)(i) — Real property in Canada excluded from deemed disposition on emigration.

Definitions: "immovable property" — Art. 6:2, ITCIA 5; "resident of a Contracting State" — Art. 4; "the other Contracting State" — Art. 3:1(b).

2. Gains from the alienation of movable property forming part of the business property of a permanent establishment which an enterprise of a Contracting State has in the other Contracting State or of movable property pertaining to a fixed base available to a resident of a Contracting State in the other Contracting State for the purpose of performing professional services, including such gains from the alienation of such a permanent establishment (alone or with the whole enterprise) or of such fixed base, may be taxed in that other State.

Definitions: "a Contracting State" — Art. 3:1(b); "business" — ITCIA 3, ITA 248(1); "permanent establishment" — Art. 5; "property" — ITCIA 3, ITA 248(1); "resident of a Contracting State" — Art. 4; "the other Contracting State" — Art. 3:1(b).

3. Gains derived by a resident of a Contracting State from the alienation of ships or aircraft operated in international traffic or movable property pertaining to the operation of such ships or aircraft, shall be taxable only in that Contracting State.

Definitions: "international traffic" — Art. 3:1(i); "property" — ITCIA 3, ITA 248(1); "resident of a Contracting State" — Art. 4.

4. Gains from the alienation of:

(a) any right, licence or privilege to explore for, drill for, or take petroleum, natural gas or other related hydrocarbons situated in a Contracting State, or

(b) any right to assets to be produced in a Contracting State by the activities referred to in sub-paragraph (a) above or to interests in or to the benefit of such assets situated in a Contracting State,

may be taxed in that State.

Notes: For the meaning of "right, licence or privilege" in 4(a), see ITA 66(15)"Canadian resource property" Notes.

Definitions: "a Contracting State" — Art. 3:1(b).

5. Gains from the alienation of:

(a) shares, other than shares quoted on an approved stock exchange, deriving their value or the greater part of their value directly or indirectly from immovable property situated in a Con-

tracting State or from any right referred to in paragraph 4 of this Article, or

(b) an interest in a partnership or trust the assets of which consist principally of immovable property situated in a Contracting State, of rights referred to in paragraph 4 of this Article, or of shares referred to in sub-paragraph (a) above,

may be taxed in that State.

Non-Amendment for this treaty — 365-day look-back rule (MLI Art. 9)

Notes: See the pages before the Canada-US Treaty for the Multilateral Instrument (MLI), which effectively amends most of Canada's tax treaties starting 2020 or later. Canada accepts MLI Article 9:1, which would add a 365-day look-back rule to Art. 13:5 of this treaty; in other words, if the value of the shares (or partnership or trust interests) was primarily attributable to Canadian real property *at any time* in the past 365 days, Canada would be able to tax the gain (and vice versa for the UK taxing a gain on UK real property). However, the UK has stated in its MLI "reservations and notifications" that it "reserves the right for the entirety of Article 9:1 not to apply". This means that MLI Art. 9:1 does not apply to this treaty, unless the UK drops this "reservation" in the future.

Notes: For CRA interpretation see VIEWS doc 2017-0695131C6 [2017 CPTS q.3].

Definitions: "a Contracting State" — Art. 3:1(b); "an approved stock exchange" — Art. 13:7(a); "immovable property" — Art. 6:2, 13:7(b), ITCIA 5; "partnership", "share" — ITCIA 3, ITA 248(1); "trust" — ITCIA 3, ITA 104(1), 248(1).

6. The provisions of paragraph 5 of this Article shall not apply:

(a) in the case of shares, where immediately before the alienation of the shares, the alienator owned, or the alienator and any persons related to or connected with him owned, less than 10 per cent of each class of the share capital of the company; or

(b) in the case of an interest in a partnership or trust, where immediately before the alienation of the interest, the alienator was entitled to, or the alienator and any persons related to or connected with him were entitled to, an interest of less than 10 per cent of the income and capital of the partnership or trust.

Definitions: "company" — Art. 3:1(d); "person" — Art. 3:1(c); "partnership", "share" — ITCIA 3, ITA 248(1); "trust" — ITCIA 3, ITA 104(1), 248(1).

7. For the purposes of paragraph 5 of this Article:

(a) the term **"an approved stock exchange"** means a stock exchange prescribed for the purposes of the Canadian *Income Tax Act* or a recognised stock exchange within the meaning of the United Kingdom Corporation Tax Acts; and

(b) the term **"immovable property"** does not include any property (other than rental property) in which the business of the company, partnership or trust was carried on.

Notes: In *Alta Energy Luxembourg*, 2018 TCC 152; aff'd 2020 FCA 43 (leave to appeal to SCC granted Aug. 6/20), "in which the business of the company ... was carried on" (in the Canada-Luxembourg treaty) applied to an *entire* exploration property that had only a small number of wells drilled (due to slow ramp-up of the exploration) [see Notes to ITA 245(2) for commentary]. See also VIEWS doc 2000-0015753.

Definitions: "business" — ITCIA 3, ITA 248(1); "company" — Art. 3:1(d); "partnership", "prescribed", "property" — ITCIA 3, ITA 248(1); "trust" — ITCIA 3, ITA 104(1), 248(1); "United Kingdom" — Art. 3:1(a)(ii).

8. Gains from the alienation of any property, other than that referred to in paragraphs 1, 2, 3, 4 and 5 of this Article shall be taxable only in the Contracting State of which the alienator is a resident.

Notes: See Notes to Canada-US treaty Art. XIII:4.

For a ruling that shares are exempt see VIEWS doc 2011-0429961R3.

Definitions: "property" — ITCIA 3, ITA 248(1); "resident" — ITCIA 3, ITA 250.

9. The provisions of paragraph 8 of this Article shall not affect the right of a Contracting State to levy according to its law a tax on or in respect of gains from the alienation of any property on a person who is a resident of that State at any time during the fiscal year in which the property is alienated, or has been so resident at any time during the six years immediately preceding the alienation of the property.

Notes: Art. 13:9 amended by 2003 Protocol, effective 2005.

Definitions: "a Contracting State" — Art. 3:1(b); "individual" — ITCIA 3, ITA 248(1); "national" — Art. 3:1(h); "person" — Art. 3:1(c); "property" — ITCIA 3, ITA 248(1); "resident" — Art. 4; "the other Contracting State" — Art. 3:1(b).

10. Where an individual ceases to be a resident of a Contracting State and by reason thereof is treated under the laws of that State as having alienated property before ceasing to be a resident of that State and is taxed in that State accordingly and at any time thereafter becomes a resident of the other Contracting State, the other Contracting State may tax gains in respect of the property only to the extent that such gains had not accrued while the individual was a resident of the first-mentioned State. However, this provision shall not apply to property, any gain from which that other State could have taxed in accordance with the provisions of this Article, other than this paragraph, if the individual had realized the gain before becoming a resident of that other State. The competent authorities of the Contracting States may consult to determine the application of this paragraph.

Related Provisions: ITA 128.1(1)(c) — Same rule applies in Canada anyway.

Notes: Art. 13:10 added by 2003 Protocol, effective 2005.

Definitions: "a Contracting State" — Art. 3:1(b); "individual" — ITCIA 3, ITA 248(1); "property" — ITCIA 3, ITA 248(1); "resident" — ITCIA 3, ITA 250; "the other Contracting State" — Art. 3:1(b).

Article 14 — Professional Services

1. Income derived by a resident of a Contracting State in respect of professional services or other independent activities of a similar character shall be taxable only in that State unless he has a fixed base regularly available to him in the other Contracting State for the purpose of performing his activities. If he has such a fixed base, the income may be taxed in the other Contracting State but only so much of it as is attributable to that fixed base.

Notes: See Notes to repealed Art. XIV of Canada-US treaty re the meaning of "fixed base". See also Manu Kakkar, "Back to the Future: The 'Dependent Personal Services' Treaty Provision", 14(3) *Tax for the Owner-Manager* (ctf.ca) 9 (July 2014).

Definitions: "a Contracting State" — Art. 3:1(b); "professional services" — Art. 14:2; "resident" — ITCIA 3, ITA 250; "the other Contracting State" — Art. 3:1(b).

2. The term **"professional services"** includes independent scientific, literary, artistic, educational or teaching activities as well as the independent activities of physicians, lawyers, engineers, architects, dentists and accountants.

Notes: Payments from the Public Lending Right Program of the Canada Council for the Arts fall under the same definition in the Canada-Ireland treaty, as being for independent literary and artistic activities rather than royalties under Art. 12: VIEWS doc 2014-052790117 (but note ITA 212(1)(d)(vi), which could exempt them before considering the treaty).

Definitions: "lawyer" — ITCIA 3, ITA 248(1).

Article 15 — Dependent Personal Services

1. Subject to the provisions of Articles 17 and 18, salaries, wages and other similar remuneration derived by a resident of a Contracting State in respect of an employment shall be taxable only in that State unless the employment is exercised in the other Contracting State. If the employment is so exercised, such remuneration as is derived therefrom may be taxed in that other State.

Notes: In *Hale*, [1992] 2 C.T.C. 379 (FCA), a taxpayer who had been employed in Canada, moved to England, then exercised stock option rights, was taxed under ITA 2(3) and 7(1). His claimed exemption under Art. 15:1, because he was no longer employed in Canada, was denied.

Definitions: "employment" — ITCIA 3, ITA 248(1); "resident of a Contracting State" — Art. 4; "the other Contracting State" — Art. 3:1(b).

2. Notwithstanding the provisions of paragraph 1, remuneration derived by a resident of a Contracting State in respect of an employment exercised in the other Contracting State shall be taxable only in the first-mentioned State if:

    (a) the recipient is present in the other State for a period or periods not exceeding in the aggregate 183 days in any 12 month period commencing or ending in the fiscal year concerned, and

    (b) the remuneration is paid by, or on behalf of, an employer who is not a resident of the other State, and

    (c) the remuneration is not borne by a permanent establishment or a fixed base which the employer has in the other State.

Announced Administrative Change — Art. 15:2 — COVID-19

CRA notice (tinyurl.com/cra-internat, April 27, 2021): See under ITA 250(1)(a), sections III and VII.C "Cross-border employment income".

Notes: See Notes to Canada-US treaty Art. XV:2, but note that Art. 27A:4 overrides Art. 15: VIEWS doc 2009-031995117.

Art. 15:2(a) amended by 2014 Protocol, effective 2015.

Definitions: "employer", "employment" — ITCIA 3, ITA 248(1); "permanent establishment" — Art. 5; "person" — Art. 3:1(c); "resident" — ITCIA 3, ITA 250; "resident of a Contracting State" — Art. 4; "the other Contracting State" — Art. 3:1(b).

3. Notwithstanding the preceding provisions of this Article, remuneration derived in respect of an employment exercised aboard a ship or aircraft operated in international traffic by an enterprise of a Contracting State may be taxed in that State.

Notes: For application of this rule where a UK airline is subcontracted to transport Canadian passengers, see VIEWS doc 2013-0515431E5. For the meaning of "place of effective management" see Notes to Art. 4:3.

Art. 15:3 amended by 2014 Protocol, effective 2015.

Definitions: "employment" — ITCIA 3, ITA 248(1); "international traffic" — Art. 3:1(i).

4. In relation to remuneration of a director of a company derived from the company the preceding provisions of this Article shall apply as if the remuneration were remuneration of an employee in respect of employment, and as if reference to employer were references to the company.

Definitions: "company" — Art. 3:1(d); "employee", "employer", "employment" — ITCIA 3, ITA 248(1).

5. [Repealed]

Notes: Art. 15:5 repealed by 2014 Protocol, effective 2015.

Article 16 — Artistes and Athletes

1. Notwithstanding the provisions of Articles 7, 14 and 15, income derived by entertainers, such as theatre, motion picture, radio or television artistes, and musicians, and by athletes, from their personal activities as such may be taxed in the Contracting State in which these activities are exercised.

2. Where income in respect of personal activities as such of an entertainer or athlete accrues not to that entertainer or athlete himself but to another person, that income may, notwithstanding the provisions of Articles 7, 14 and 15, be taxed in the Contracting State in which the activities of the entertainer or athlete are exercised.

Definitions: "person" — Art. 3:1(c).

3. The provisions of paragraphs 1 and 2 shall not apply:

    (a) to income derived from activities performed in a Contracting State by entertainers or athletes if the visit to that Contracting State is wholly or substantially supported by public funds;

    (b) to a non-profit making organization no part of the income of which is payable, or is otherwise available for the personal benefit of, any proprietor, member or shareholder thereof; or

    (c) to an entertainer or athlete in respect of services provided to an organization referred to in sub-paragraph (b).

Definitions: "a Contracting State" — Art. 3:1(b); "shareholder" — ITCIA 3, ITA 248(1).

Article 17 — Pensions and Annuities

1. Periodic pension payments arising in a Contracting State and paid to a resident of the other Contracting State who is the beneficial owner thereof shall be taxable only in that other State.

Notes: See Notes to ITCIA 5 "periodic pension payment" (reproduced before the Canada-US treaty). For taxation (under ITA 56(1)(a)(i)) of UK pension received by a Canadian resident see VIEWS docs 2005-0156471E5, 2005-0157981E5, 2010-0371131E5, 2011-0413601E5, 2012-0439641E5, 2012-0458481E5, 2012-0468271E5; 2014-0553001E5 (self-funded personal pension scheme); 2015-0588521E5 (Widowed Parent's Allowance); 2018-0782381E5, 2019-0824281E5 (depends on whether plan is pension plan or employee benefit plan). In *Ruparel*, 2012 TCC 268, a UK pension was taxable to a Canadian resident, with no deduction for National Insurance contributions required to qualify for it. See Notes to ITA 147.2(4) re deductions for contributions.

Transfer from a Personal Pension Scheme: see docs 2014-0543091E5, 2016-0640281E5 (taxable if contributions made by employer). Transfer from workplace pension plan to self-invested personal pension (SIPP) is taxable, but SIPP to SIPP is not: 2019-0809641E5.

Interest earned in a UK Individual Savings Account (similar to a TFSA) is taxable (even if it was opened for retirement purposes), as there is no treaty relief: 2013-0478241E5, 2013-0485661E5.

Art. 17:1 amended by 2003 Protocol, effective 2005.

Definitions: "a Contracting State" — Art. 3:1(b); "periodic pension payment" — ITCIA 5; "pension" — Art. 17:3, ITCIA 5; "the other Contracting State" — Art. 3:1(b).

2. Annuities arising in a Contracting State and paid to a resident of the other Contracting State may be taxed in that other State. However, such annuities may also be taxed in the Contracting State in which they arise and according to the laws of that State, but if the recipient is the beneficial owner of the annuities the tax so charged shall not exceed 10 per cent of the portion thereof that is subject to tax in that State.

Definitions: "a Contracting State" — Art. 3:1(b); "annuity" — Art. 17:4, ITCIA 5; "tax" — Art. 3:1(g).

3. For the purposes of this Convention, the term **"pension"** includes any payment under a superannuation, pension or retirement plan, Armed Forces retirement pay, war veterans' pensions and allowances, and any payment under a sickness, accident or disability plan, as well as any payment made under the social security legislation in a Contracting State.

Notes: Art. 17:3 amended by 2003 Protocol, effective 2005.

Definitions: "a Contracting State" — Art. 3:1(b); "income-averaging annuity contract" — ITCIA 3, ITA 248(1).

4. For the purposes of this Convention, the term **"annuity"** means a stated sum payable periodically at stated times during life or during a specified or ascertainable period of time under an obligation to make the payments in return for adequate and full consideration in money or money's worth, but does not include any payment under a superannuation, pension or retirement plan or any payment under an income-averaging annuity contract.

Notes: See sections 5 and 5.1 of the *Income Tax Conventions Interpretation Act*, reproduced preceding the Canada-US Convention.

Art. 17:4 amended by 2003 Protocol, effective 2005.

Definitions: "pension" — Art. 17:3, ITCIA 5; "income-averaging annuity contract" — ITCIA 3, ITA 248(1).

5. Notwithstanding any other provision of this Convention, alimony and similar payments arising in a Contracting State and paid to a resident of the other Contracting State who is the beneficial owner thereof shall be taxable only in that other State.

Definitions: "a Contracting State" — Art. 3:1(b).

Article 18 — Government Service

1. (a) Remuneration, other than a pension, paid by a Contracting State or a political subdivision or a local authority thereof to any individual in respect of services rendered to that State or subdi-

vision or local authority thereof shall be taxable only in that State.

(b) However, such remuneration shall be taxable only in the other Contracting State if the services are rendered in that State and the recipient is a resident of that State who:

(i) is a national of that State; or

(ii) did not become a resident of that State solely for the purpose of performing the services.

Notes: An employee of the Ontario Securities Commission on secondment to the UK Financial Services Authority did not fall under 18(1)(a) because he did not render services to the OSC, nor under 18(1)(b) because he remained a resident of Canada: VIEWS doc 2004-0065821E5.

Definitions: "a Contracting State" — Art. 3:1(b); "national" — Art. 3:1(h); "pension" — Art. 17:3, ITCIA 5; "political subdivision" — Art. 18:3; "the other Contracting State" — Art. 3:1(b).

2. This Article shall not apply to remuneration in respect of services rendered in connection with any trade or business carried on by one of the Contracting States or a political subdivision or a local authority thereof.

Definitions: "business" — ITCIA 3, ITA 248(1); "political subdivision" — Art. 18:3.

3. [Repealed]

Notes: Art. 18:3 repealed by 2014 Protocol, effective 2015 as per Protocol Art. XVI (reproduced before Art. 1). It defined "political subdivision" to include Northern Ireland.

Definitions: "United Kingdom" — Art. 3:1(a)(ii).

Article 19 — Students

Payments which a student, apprentice or business trainee who is or was immediately before visiting one of the Contracting States a resident of a Contracting State and who is present in the other Contracting State solely for the purpose of his education or training receives for the purpose of his maintenance, education or training shall not be taxed in that other State, provided that such payments are made to him from sources outside that other State.

Definitions: "resident of a Contracting State" — Art. 4; "the other Contracting State" — Art. 3:1(b).

Article 20 — Estates and Trusts

1. Income received from an estate or trust resident in Canada by a resident of the United Kingdom who is the beneficial owner thereof may be taxed in Canada according to its law, but the tax so charged shall not exceed 15 per cent of the gross amount of the income.

Notes: See Notes to Canada-US treaty Art. XXII:2.

Definitions: "Canada" — Art. 3:1(a)(i), ITCIA 5; "estate" — ITCIA 3, ITA 248(1); "resident in Canada" — ITCIA 3, ITA 250; "tax" — Art. 3:1(g); "trust" — ITCIA 3, ITA 104(1), 248(1); "United Kingdom" — Art. 3:1(a)(ii).

2. The provisions of paragraph 1 of this Article shall not apply if the recipient of the income, being a resident of the United Kingdom, carries on business in Canada through a permanent establishment situated therein, or performs in Canada professional services from a fixed base situated therein, and the right or interest in the estate or trust in respect of which the income is paid is effectively connected with such permanent establishment or fixed base. In such a case, the provisions of Article 7 or Article 14, as the case may be, shall apply.

Definitions: "business" — ITCIA 3, ITA 248(1); "Canada" — Art. 3:1(a)(i), ITCIA 5; "estate" — ITCIA 3, ITA 248(1); "permanent establishment" — Art. 5; "professional services" — Art. 14:2; "trust" — ITCIA 3, ITA 104(1), 248(1); "United Kingdom" — Art. 3:1(a)(ii).

3. For the purposes of this Article, a trust does not include an arrangement whereby the contributions made to the trust are deductible for the purposes of taxation in Canada.

Definitions: "trust" — ITCIA 3, ITA 104(1), 248(1).

Article 20A — Other Income

1. Items of income beneficially owned by a resident of a Contracting State, wherever arising, not dealt with in the foregoing Articles of this Convention shall be taxable only in that State.

Notes: See at end of Art. 20A.

Definitions: "resident of a Contracting State" — Art. 4.

2. The provisions of paragraph 1 of this Article shall not apply to income, other than income from immovable property, if the beneficial owner of such income, being a resident of a Contracting State, carries on business in the other Contracting State through a permanent establishment situated therein, or performs in that other State independent personal services from a fixed base situated therein, and the right or property in respect of which the income is paid is effectively connected with such permanent establishment or fixed base. In such case the provisions of Article 7 or Article 14 of this Convention, as the case may be, shall apply.

Definitions: "business" — ITCIA 3, ITA 248(1); "immovable property" — Art. 6:2, 13:7(b), ITCIA 5; "permanent establishment" — Art. 5; "property" — ITCIA 3, ITA 248(1); "resident of a Contracting State" — Art. 4.

3. Notwithstanding the provisions of paragraphs 1 and 2 of this Article, items of income of a resident of a Contracting State not dealt with in the foregoing Articles of this Convention and arising in the other Contracting State may also be taxed in that other State.

Definitions: "resident of a Contracting State" — Art. 4; "the other Contracting State" — Art. 3:1(b).

Notes: Art. 20A added by 2003 Protocol, effective 2005.

Article 21 — Elimination of Double Taxation

1. In the case of Canada, double taxation shall be avoided as follows:

(a) subject to the existing provisions of the law of Canada regarding the deduction from tax payable in Canada of tax paid in a territory outside Canada and to any subsequent modification of those provisions — which shall not affect the general principle hereof — and unless a greater deduction or relief is provided under the laws of Canada, tax payable in the United Kingdom on profits, income or gains arising in the United Kingdom shall be deducted from any Canadian tax payable in respect of such profits, income or gains;

(b) subject to the existing provisions of the law of Canada regarding the allowance as a credit against Canadian tax of tax payable in a territory outside Canada and to any subsequent modification of those provisions — which shall not affect the general principle hereof — where a company that is a resident of the United Kingdom pays a dividend to a company that is a resident of Canada that controls directly or indirectly at least 10 per cent of the voting power in the first-mentioned company, the credit shall take into account the tax payable in the United Kingdom by that first-mentioned company in respect of the profits out of which such dividend is paid;

(c) where in accordance with any provision of this Convention income derived by a resident of Canada is exempt from tax in Canada, Canada may nevertheless, in calculating the amount of tax on other income take into account the exempted income.

Notes: See Notes to Art. 10:2 re the meaning of "controls ... indirectly" in para. (b).

CRA's view (doc 2019-0824381C6 [2019 CTF q.2]) is that "tax payable in the United Kingdom" must actually have been *paid*, because Art. 21:1 is subject to ITA s. 126.

Art. 21:1(b) amended and (c) added by 2003 Protocol, effective 2005.

Definitions: "arising" — Art. 21:3; "Canada" — Art. 3:1(a)(i), ITCIA 5; "Canadian tax" — Art. 2:1(a); "company" — Art. 3:1(d); "dividend" — ITCIA 3, ITA 248(1); "resident in Canada" — ITCIA 3, ITA 250; "taxable income" — ITCIA 3, ITA 248(1); "United Kingdom" — Art. 3:1(a)(ii).

2. Subject to the provisions of the law of the United Kingdom regarding the allowance as a credit against United Kingdom tax of tax payable in a territory outside the United Kingdom or, as the case may be, regarding the exemption from United Kingdom tax of a dividend arising in a territory outside the United Kingdom or of the profits of a permanent establishment situated in a territory outside the United Kingdom (which shall not affect the general principle of this Article):

(a) Canadian tax payable under the laws of Canada and in accordance with this Convention, whether directly or by deduction, on profits, income or chargeable gains from sources within Canada (excluding in the case of a dividend tax payable in respect of the profits out of which the dividend is paid) shall be allowed as a credit against any United Kingdom tax computed by reference to the same profits, income or chargeable gains by reference to which the Canadian tax is computed;

(b) a dividend which is paid by a company which is a resident of Canada to a company which is a resident of the United Kingdom shall be exempted from United Kingdom tax, when the exemption is applicable and the conditions for exemption under the law of the United Kingdom are met;

(c) the profits of a permanent establishment in Canada of a company which is a resident of the United Kingdom shall be exempted from United Kingdom tax when the exemption is applicable and the conditions for exemption under the law of the United Kingdom are met;

(d) in the case of a dividend not exempted from tax under subparagraph (b) which is paid by a company which is a resident of Canada to a company which is a resident of the United Kingdom and which controls directly or indirectly at least 10 per cent of the voting power in the company paying the dividend, the credit mentioned in subparagraph (a) shall also take into account the Canadian tax payable by the company in respect of its profits out of which such dividend is paid.

Related Provisions: Art. 7:2 — Profits attributable to permanent establishment.

Notes: See Notes to Art. 10:2 re the meaning of "controls ... indirectly" in para. (d).

Art. 21:2 amended by 2014 Protocol, effective 2015.

Definitions: "arising" — Art. 21:3; "Canada" — Art. 3:1(a)(i), ITCIA 5; "Canadian tax" — Art. 2:1(a); "company" — Art. 3:1(d); "dividend" — ITCIA 3, ITA 248(1); "United Kingdom" — Art. 3:1(a)(ii); "United Kingdom tax" — Art. 2:1(b).

3. For the purposes of paragraphs 1 and 2 of this Article, income, profits and capital gains owned by a resident of a Contracting State which are taxed in the other Contracting State in accordance with this Convention shall be deemed to arise from sources in that other Contracting State.

Notes: For an example of this rule see VIEWS doc 2020-0838001C6 [2020 STEP q.4]: Canadian taxpayer sells shares of UK corp whose value comes from Australian real property. Under the Canada-Australia treaty, Australia can tax the gain (like Art. 13(5)(a) of this treaty). Art. 23:2(a) of that treaty (like this Art. 21:3) deems the gain to arise in Australia so as to be eligible for foreign tax credit in Canada.

Definitions: "capital gain" — ITCIA 3, ITA 248(1); "resident of a Contracting State" — Art. 4; "the other Contracting State" — Art. 3:1(b).

4. [Repealed]

Notes: Art. 21:4 repealed by 2003 Protocol, effective 2005.

Article 22 — Non-Discrimination

1. The nationals of a Contracting State shall not be subjected in the other Contracting State to any taxation or any requirement connected therewith which is other or more burdensome than the taxation and connected requirements to which nationals of that other State in the same circumstances are or may be subjected.

Notes: In *Saipem UK*, 2011 FCA 243, the Court rejected the argument that Art. 22:1 or 22:2 should permit a non-resident corp to be treated as a "Canadian corporation" for ITA 88(1.1). Discrimination on the basis of residency is permitted. See Russell, "Saipem", 8(2) *Tax Hyperion* (Carswell, Feb. 2011).

In *Addy*, [2020] FCAFC 135 (Australia, Full Federal Court), this rule did not prevent Australia from applying its "working holiday worker" tax to a UK citizen [Mackey & Sigalet, "Australian Backpacker Tax", XXIV(3) *International Tax Planning* (Federated Press) 8-14 (2020)].

2. The taxation on a permanent establishment which an enterprise of a Contracting State has in the other Contracting State shall not be less favourably levied in that other State than the taxation levied on enterprises of that other State carrying on the same activities. This provision shall not be construed as obliging either Contracting State to grant to individuals not resident in its territory those personal allowances and reliefs for tax purposes which are by law available only to individuals who are so resident.

Notes: See Notes to Art. 22:1 above.

Definitions: "enterprise of a Contracting State" — Art. 3:1(e); "individual" — ITCIA 3, ITA 248(1); "permanent establishment" — Art. 5; "taxation" — Art. 22:5; "the other Contracting State" — Art. 3:1(b).

3. Nothing in this Convention shall be construed as preventing a Contracting State from imposing on the earnings attributable to permanent establishments in that State of a company which is a resident of the other Contracting State, tax in addition to the tax which would be chargeable on the earnings of a company which is a resident of the first-mentioned State, provided that the rate of any additional tax so imposed shall not exceed 5 per cent of the amount of such earnings which have not been subjected to such additional tax in previous taxation years.

Related Provisions: ITA 219 — Branch tax.

Notes: Art. 22:3 amended by 2003 Protocol, effective 2005.

Definitions: "a Contracting State" — Art. 3:1(b); "company" — Art. 3:1(d); "earnings" — Art. 22:4; "permanent establishment" — Art. 5; "taxation year" — ITCIA 3, ITA 249.

4. For the purpose of paragraph 3 of this Article, the term **"earnings"** means the profits attributable to permanent establishments in a Contracting State (including gains from the alienation of property forming part of the business property of such permanent establishments) in a year and previous years after deducting therefrom:

(a) business losses attributable to such permanent establishments (including losses from the alienation of property forming part of the business property of such permanent establishments) in such year and previous years; and

(b) all taxes, other than the additional tax referred to in paragraph 3 of this Article, imposed on such profits in that State; and

(c) the profits reinvested in that State, provided that where that State is Canada, the amount of such deduction shall be determined in accordance with the existing provisions of the law of Canada regarding the computation of the allowance in respect of investment in property in Canada, and any subsequent modification of those provisions which shall not affect the general principle thereof; and

(d) five hundred thousand Canadian dollars ($500,000) or two hundred and fifty thousand pounds sterling (£250,000), whichever is the greater, less any amount deducted in that State under this subparagraph (d) by the company or a company associated therewith; for the purposes of this subparagraph (d) a company is associated with another company if one of them directly or indirectly has control of the other or both are directly or indirectly under the control of the same person, or if the two companies deal with each other not at arm's length.

Definitions: "a Contracting State" — Art. 3:1(b); "arm's length" — ITCIA 3, ITA 251(1); "associated" — ITCIA 3, ITA 256; "business" — ITCIA 3, ITA 248(1); "Canada" — Art. 3:1(a)(i), ITCIA 5; "permanent establishment" — Art. 5; "person" — Art. 3:1(c); "property" — ITCIA 3, ITA 248(1); "tax" — Art. 3:1(g).

5. In this Article, the term **"taxation"** means taxes which are the subject of this Convention.

Definitions: "tax" — Art. 3:1(g).

Article 23 — Mutual Agreement Procedure

1. Where a person considers that the actions of one or both of the Contracting States result or will result for that person in taxation not in accordance with the provisions of this Convention, that person may, irrespective of the remedies provided by the domestic law of those States, address to the competent authority of the Contracting State of which that person is a resident an application in writing stating the grounds for claiming the revision of such taxation. To be admissible, the application must be submitted within three years from the first notification of the action resulting in taxation not in accordance with the provisions of this Convention.

Enacted Mutual Agreement Procedure Rules — Art. 23 (MLI Art. 16)

Notes: See the pages before the Canada-US Treaty for the Multilateral Instrument (MLI), which effectively amends most of Canada's tax treaties starting 2020 or later. MLI Article 16 provides detailed rules for dispute resolution. However, not all of Art. 16 will apply. See tinyurl.com/canada-mli. The OECD Matching Database (tinyurl.com/oecd-match) states that, for purposes of the Canada-UK treaty, the first and second sentences of each of Art. 16:1, 2 and 3 will not apply. See Notes to MLI Art. 16:1 and 16:2.

See also MLI Art. 17, which applies when a transfer pricing adjustment is made in one country and requires "corresponding adjustments" in the other country; and MLI Art. 18-26, which provide for arbitration of disputes.

Notes: For the application of the treaty to UK limited liability partnerships (LLPs) see para. 2 of the Interpretative Protocol, reproduced before Art. 1.

For 2014 amendments to all of Art. 23 see Notes at end of Art. 23.

Definitions: "competent authority" — Art. 3:1(f); "person" — Art. 3:1(c); "resident" — Art. 4; "resident of a Contracting State" — Art. 4; "writing" — ITCIA 3, *Interpretation Act* 35(1).

2. The competent authority referred to in paragraph 1 shall endeavour, if the objection appears to it to be justified and if it is not itself able to arrive at a satisfactory solution, to resolve the case by mutual agreement with the competent authority of the other Contracting State, with a view to the avoidance of taxation not in accordance with this Convention. Any agreement reached shall be implemented notwithstanding any time limits in the domestic law of the Contracting States.

Related Provisions: ITA 115.1 — Competent authority agreements.

Definitions: "competent authority" — Art. 3:1(f); "the other Contracting State" — Art. 3:1(b).

3. For the purposes of Articles 6, 7 and 14 of this Convention, a Contracting State shall not, after the expiry of the time limits provided in its domestic laws and, in any case, after eight years from the end of the taxable period to which the income concerned was attributed, make a primary adjustment to the income of a resident of one of the Contracting States where that income has been charged to tax in the other Contracting State in the hands of that resident. The foregoing shall not apply in the case of fraud or wilful default or where a person's obligations have not been fulfilled owing to careless or deliberate behaviour.

Definitions: "a Contracting State" — Art. 3:1(b); "resident" — Art. 4; "tax" — Art. 3:1(g).

4. The competent authorities of the Contracting States shall endeavour to resolve by mutual agreement any difficulties or doubts arising as to the interpretation or application of this Convention. They may also consult together for the elimination of double taxation in cases not provided for in this Convention.

Definitions: "competent authority" — Art. 3:1(f).

Information Circulars: 71-17R6: Competent authority assistance under Canada's tax conventions.

5. The competent authorities of the Contracting States may communicate with each other directly for the purpose of applying this Convention.

Definitions: "competent authority" — Art. 3:1(f).

6. Where,

(a) under paragraph 1, a person has presented a case to the competent authority of a Contracting State on the basis that the actions of one or both of the Contracting States have resulted for that person in taxation not in accordance with the provisions of this Convention, and

(b) the competent authorities are unable to reach an agreement to resolve that case pursuant to paragraph 2 within a period of three years from the date on which the information necessary to undertake substantive consideration for a mutual agreement has been received by both competent authorities or such other period from that date as is agreed by both competent authorities,

any unresolved issues arising from the case shall be submitted to arbitration. The arbitration shall be conducted in the manner prescribed by the rules and procedures agreed upon by the Contracting States through an exchange of diplomatic notes. These unresolved issues shall not, however, be submitted to arbitration if a decision on these issues has already been rendered by a court or administrative tribunal of either State. Unless a person whose taxation is directly affected by the arbitration decision does not accept that decision, the decision shall be binding on both States and shall constitute a resolution by mutual agreement under this Article.

Notes: The Dept. of Finance announced on Nov. 26, 2015 an "Agreement Concerning the Application of the Arbitration Provisions of the Canada-United Kingdom Tax Convention", to establish the rules and procedures for the arbitration process under paras. 6-7; and announced on Feb. 8, 2017 that the agreement entered into force on Dec. 21, 2016. It can be found at tinyurl.com/cda-uk-arb.

Definitions: "a Contracting State" — Art. 3:1(b); "competent authority" — Art. 3:1(f); "person" — Art. 3:1(c).

Information Circulars: 71-17R6: Competent authority assistance under Canada's tax conventions.

7. The provisions of paragraph 6 shall apply only with respect to issues arising under Article 4 (but only insofar as the issue relates to the residence of an individual), Article 5, Article 7, Article 9, Article 12 (but only insofar as Article 12 might apply in transactions involving related persons to which Article 9 might apply), Article 14, and any other Articles subsequently agreed by the Contracting States through an exchange of diplomatic notes.

Notes: See Notes to para. 6.

Notes [Art. 23]: Art. 23 amended by 2014 Protocol, effective 2015 as per Protocol Art. XVI (reproduced before Art. 1). These amendments bring the treaty into line with the OECD Model Treaty.

Article 24 — Exchange of Information

1. The competent authorities of the Contracting States shall exchange such information as is foreseeably relevant for carrying out the provisions of this Convention or to the administration or enforcement of the domestic laws concerning taxes of every kind and description imposed on behalf of the Contracting States, insofar as the taxation thereunder is not contrary to this Convention. The exchange of information is not restricted by Articles 1 and 2.

Notes: Automatic exchange of information is now provided under the Common Reporting Standard. See ITA 270-281. See also Notes to Canada-US treaty Art. XXVII:2.

For 2014 amendments to all of Art. 24 see Notes at end of Art. 24.

Art. 24 renumbered as 24:1 and amended by 2003 Protocol, effective 2005.

Definitions: "competent authority" — Art. 3:1(f); "tax" — Art. 3:1(g).

CRA Audit Manual: 10.3.2: Conducting audits outside Canada; 10.11.17: Requests for information — countries with tax treaties; 15.10.11: International audit issues — other tax administrations.

2. Any information received under paragraph 1 by a Contracting State shall be treated as secret in the same manner as information obtained under the domestic laws of that State and shall be disclosed only to persons or authorities (including courts and administrative bodies) concerned with the assessment or collection of, the enforcement or prosecution in respect of, the determination of appeals in relation to taxes of every kind and description imposed by or on behalf of the Contracting States or of their political subdivi-

sions, or the oversight of the above. Such persons or authorities shall use the information only for such purposes. They may disclose the information in public court proceedings or in judicial decisions. Notwithstanding the foregoing, information received by a Contracting State may be used for other purposes when such information may be used for such other purposes under the laws of both States and the competent authority of the supplying State authorises such use.

Definitions: "a Contracting State" — Art. 3:1(b); "person" — Art. 3:1(c); "tax" — Art. 3:1(g).

3. In no case shall the provisions of paragraphs 1 and 2 be construed so as to impose on a Contracting State the obligation

(a) to carry out administrative measures at variance with the laws and the administrative practice of that or of the other Contracting State;

(b) to supply information which is not obtainable under the laws or in the normal course of the administration of that or of the other Contracting State;

(c) to supply information which would disclose any trade, business, industrial, commercial or professional secret or trade process, or information the disclosure of which would be contrary to public policy (*ordre public*).

Definitions: "a Contracting State" — Art. 3:1(b); "the other Contracting State" — Art. 3:1(b).

4. If information is requested by a Contracting State in accordance with this Article, the other Contracting State shall use its information gathering measures to obtain the requested information, even though that other State may not need such information for its own tax purposes. The obligation contained in the preceding sentence is subject to the limitations of paragraph 3 but in no case shall such limitations be construed to permit a Contracting State to decline to supply information solely because it has no domestic interest in such information.

Notes: See Notes to Canada-US treaty Art. XXVII:2.

Definitions: "a Contracting State" — Art. 3:1(b).

5. In no case shall the provisions of paragraph 3 be construed to permit a Contracting State to decline to supply information solely because the information is held by a bank, other financial institution, nominee or person acting in an agency or a fiduciary capacity or because the information relates to ownership interests in a person.

Definitions: "a Contracting State" — Art. 3:1(b); "bank" — ITCIA 3, ITA 248(1), *Interpretation Act* 35(1); "person" — Art. 3:1(c).

6. Authorized representatives of a Contracting State shall be permitted to enter the other Contracting State to interview individuals or examine a person's books and records with their consent, in accordance with procedures mutually agreed upon by the competent authorities.

Notes: Art. 24 amended by 2014 Protocol, effective 2015 as per Protocol Art. XVI (reproduced before Art. 1). Former Art. 24:2, 3 added by 2003 Protocol, effective 2005.

Definitions: "a Contracting State" — Art. 3:1(b).

Article 24A — Assistance in the Collection of Taxes

1. The Contracting States shall lend assistance to each other in the collection of revenue claims. This assistance is not restricted by Articles 1 and 2. The competent authorities of the Contracting States shall by mutual agreement settle the mode of application of this Article, including agreement to ensure comparable levels of assistance.

Notes: See Notes to Canada-US treaty Art. XXVI-A:1. See also Notes at end of Art. 24A for in-force date.

Definitions: "competent authority" — Art. 3:1(f); "revenue claim" — Art. 24A:2.

2. The term **"revenue claim"** as used in this Article means an amount owed in respect of taxes of every kind and description collected by or on behalf of the Contracting States, or on behalf of the political subdivisions of the Contracting States, insofar as the taxation thereunder is not contrary to this Convention or any other instrument to which the Contracting States are parties, as well as interest, administrative penalties and costs of collection or conservancy related to such amount.

3. When a revenue claim of a Contracting State is enforceable under the laws of that State and is owed by a person who, at that time, cannot, under the laws of that State, prevent its collection, that revenue claim shall, at the request of the competent authority of that State made in accordance with the mode of application referred to in paragraph 1, be accepted for purposes of collection by the competent authority of the other Contracting State. That revenue claim shall be collected by that other State in accordance with the provisions of its laws applicable to the enforcement and collection of its own taxes as if the revenue claim were a revenue claim of that other State.

Definitions: "a Contracting State" — Art. 3:1(b); "competent authority" — Art. 3:1(f); "person" — Art. 3:1(c); "revenue claim" — Art. 24A:2; "the other Contracting State" — Art. 3:1(b).

4. Notwithstanding the provisions of paragraph 3, a revenue claim accepted by a Contracting State for purposes of paragraph 3 shall not, in that State, be accorded any priority applicable to a revenue claim under the laws of that State by reason of its nature as such. In addition, a revenue claim accepted by a Contracting State for the purposes of paragraph 3 shall not, in that State, have any priority applicable to that revenue claim under the laws of the other Contracting State.

Definitions: "a Contracting State" — Art. 3:1(b); "revenue claim" — Art. 24A:2; "the other Contracting State" — Art. 3:1(b).

5. Proceedings with respect to the existence, validity or the amount of a revenue claim of a Contracting State shall not be brought before the courts or administrative bodies of the other Contracting State.

Definitions: "a Contracting State" — Art. 3:1(b); "revenue claim" — Art. 24A:2; "the other Contracting State" — Art. 3:1(b).

6. Where, at any time after a request has been made by a Contracting State under paragraph 3 and before the other Contracting State has collected and remitted the relevant revenue claim to the first-mentioned State, the relevant revenue claim ceases to be a revenue claim of the first-mentioned State that is enforceable under the laws of that State and is owed by a person who, at that time, cannot, under the laws of that State, prevent its collection, the competent authority of the first-mentioned State shall promptly notify the competent authority of the other State of that fact and, at the option of the other State, the first-mentioned State shall either suspend or withdraw its request.

Definitions: "a Contracting State" — Art. 3:1(b); "competent authority" — Art. 3:1(f); "person" — Art. 3:1(c); "revenue claim" — Art. 24A:2; "the other Contracting State" — Art. 3:1(b).

7. In no case shall the provisions of this Article be construed so as to impose on a Contracting State the obligation:

(a) to carry out administrative measures at variance with the laws and administrative practice of that or of the other Contracting State;

(b) to carry out measures which would be contrary to public policy (*ordre public*);

(c) to provide assistance if the other Contracting State has not pursued all reasonable measures of collection available under its laws or administrative practice;

(d) to provide assistance in those cases where the administrative burden for that State is clearly disproportionate to the benefit to be derived by the other Contracting State;

(e) to provide administrative assistance if and insofar as it considers the taxation in the other State to be contrary to generally accepted taxation principles.

Notes: Art. 24A added by 2014 Protocol, effective 2015 as per Protocol Art. XVI (reproduced before Art. 1).

Definitions: "a Contracting State" — Art. 3:1(b); "the other Contracting State" — Art. 3:1(b).

Article 25 — Diplomatic and Consular Officials

1. Nothing in this Convention shall affect the fiscal privileges of members of diplomatic or consular missions under the general rules of international law or under the provisions of special agreements.

2. This Convention shall not apply to International Organizations, to organs or officials thereof and to persons who are members of a diplomatic or permanent mission or consular post of a third State, being present in a Contracting State and not treated in either Contracting State as residents in respect of taxes on income or capital gains.

Definitions: "a Contracting State" — Art. 3:1(b); "capital gain" — ITCIA 3, ITA 248(1); "person" — Art. 3:1(c); "tax" — Art. 3:1(g).

Article 26 — Extension

1. This Convention may be extended, either in its entirety or with modifications to any territory for whose international relations either of the Contracting States is responsible, and which imposes taxes substantially similar in character to those which are the subject of this Convention and any such extension shall take effect from such date and subject to such modifications and conditions (including conditions as to termination) as may be specified and agreed between the Contracting States in notes to be exchanged for this purpose.

Definitions: "tax" — Art. 3:1(g).

2. The termination of this Convention under Article 29 shall, unless otherwise expressly agreed by both Contracting States, terminate the application of this Convention to any territory to which it has been extended under this Article.

Article 27 — Miscellaneous Rules

1. The provisions of this Convention shall not be construed to restrict in any manner any exclusion, exemption, deduction, credit or other allowance now or hereafter accorded by the law of a Contracting State in the determination of the tax imposed by that Contracting State.

Definitions: "a Contracting State" — Art. 3:1(b); "tax" — Art. 3:1(g).

2. Where under any provision of this Convention any income is relieved from tax in a Contracting State and, under the law in force in the other Contracting State a person, in respect of that income, is subject to tax by reference to the amount thereof which is remitted to or received in that other Contracting State and not by reference to the full amount thereof, then the relief to be allowed under this Convention in the first-mentioned Contracting State shall apply only to so much of the income as is taxed in the other Contracting State.

Notes: This rule applies to income of a UK non-domiciled resident that is not received in the UK, and so not taxed by the UK. If the Canadian tax is "relieved" by the treaty (e.g. because the income is profit from carrying on business in Canada without a PE in Canada: Art. 7:1), Art. 27:2 says that such relief does not apply to income not taxed by the UK. It is uncertain whether this rule applies to provisions limiting the withholding tax rate under Art. 10:2, 11:2 or 12:2, as tax is arguably not "relieved" if it still applies at a lower rate. CRA says that "relieved" includes a reduction of tax that does not eliminate tax: VIEWS doc 2017-0723051E5 (answering the author).

In *Conrad Black*, 2014 FCA 275 (leave to appeal denied 2015 CarswellNat 1274 (SCC)), this rule permitted Canada to tax non-UK income (arising in the US), not just income that arose in Canada.

Art. 27:2 amended by 2003 Protocol, effective 2005.

Definitions: "a Contracting State" — Art. 3:1(b); "person" — Art. 3:1(c); "tax" — Art. 3:1(g); "the other Contracting State" — Art. 3:1(b).

3. Nothing in this Convention shall be construed as restricting the right of a Contracting State to tax a resident of that State on that resident's share of any income or capital gains of a partnership, trust or controlled foreign affiliate in which that resident has an interest.

Notes: For the application of the treaty to UK limited liability partnerships (LLPs) see para. 2 of the Interpretative Protocol, reproduced before Art. 1.

Art 27:3 amended to change "Canada to tax a resident of Canada" to "a Contracting State to tax a resident of that State" by 2014 Protocol, effective 2015 as per Protocol Art. XVI (reproduced before Art. 1).

Art. 27:3 amended by 2003 Protocol, effective 2005.

Definitions: "Canada" — Art. 3:1(a)(i), ITCIA 5; "resident" — ITCIA 3, ITA 250; "tax" — Art. 3:1(g).

4. The competent authorities of the Contracting States may communicate with each other directly for the purpose of applying this Convention.

Notes: Art. 27:6 renumbered 27:4 by 2014 Protocol, effective 2015 as per Protocol Art. XVI (reproduced before Art. 1).

Former Art. 27:4 repealed by 2003 Protocol, effective 2005.

Definitions: "competent authority" — Art. 3:1(f).

5. Contributions paid in a year by, or on behalf of, an individual who exercises employment in a Contracting State in that year to a pension arrangement established in the other Contracting State (including an arrangement created under the social security legislation in that other State) and in which the individual participates in order to secure retirement benefits in respect of those services shall, during a period not exceeding in the aggregate 60 months, and if the contributions to the arrangement would qualify for tax relief if they had been made in that other State, be treated in the same way for tax purposes in the first-mentioned State as contributions paid to a pension arrangement that is recognised for tax purposes in the first-mentioned State, provided that:

(a) immediately before the individual began to exercise employment in the first-mentioned State, that individual was not a resident of that State and contributions had been paid by or on behalf of that individual to the pension arrangement; and

(b) the pension arrangement is accepted by the competent authority of the first-mentioned State as generally corresponding to a pension arrangement recognised as such for tax purposes by that State.

Notes: See CRA "Guidance for Taxpayers Requesting Tax Treaty Relief for Cross-Border Pension Contributions" (March 15, 2011).

Art. 27:5 does not apply to a Canadian resident whose employment and pension were both in the UK: *Zong*, 2019 TCC 270, para. 17.

Art. 27:7 renumbered 27:5 and former 27.5 repealed by 2014 Protocol, effective 2015 as per Protocol Art. XVI (reproduced before Art. 1). Former 27:5 provided limited collection assistance. It would appear to apply if, say, a dividend was paid by a Canadian company to a UK company, only 5% tax was withheld due to Art. 10(2)(a), CRA determined that the tax should have been 25%, but the Canadian company had no assets. CRA would be able to ask UK Inland Revenue to collect the extra 20%. The Canada-Austria treaty has a similar provision.

Former Art. 27:7 added by 2003 Protocol, effective 2005.

Definitions: "a Contracting State" — Art. 3:1(b); "employment", "individual" — ITCIA 3, ITA 248(1); "pension" — Art. 17:3; "resident" — Art. 4; "the other Contracting State" — Art. 3:1(b).

6. [Repealed]

Notes: See Notes to Art. 27:4.

7. [Repealed]

Notes: See Notes to Art. 27:5.

Article 27A — Miscellaneous Rules Applicable to Certain Offshore Activities

1. The provisions of this Article shall apply notwithstanding any other provision of this Convention.

2. A person who is a resident of a Contracting State and carries on activities in the other Contracting State in connection with the exploration or exploitation of the sea bed and sub-soil and their natural resources situated in that other Contracting State shall, subject to paragraph 3 of this Article, be deemed to be carrying on a business in that other Contracting State through a permanent establishment situated therein.

Notes: Art. 27A:2 was applied in *Gulf Offshore*, 2006 TCC 246, where a ship was deemed to be a PE [Russell, "Gulf Offshore — Offshore Permanent Establishment", 4(11) *Tax Hyperion* (Carswell, Nov. 2007)].

Definitions: "business" — ITCIA 3, ITA 248(1); "permanent establishment" — Art. 5; "person" — Art. 3:1(c); "resident of a Contracting State" — Art. 4; "the other Contracting State" — Art. 3:1(b).

3. The provisions of paragraph 2 of this Article shall not apply where the activities referred to therein are carried on for a period or periods not exceeding in the aggregate 30 days in any 12 month period. For the purposes of this paragraph:

(a) where a person carrying on activities referred to in paragraph 2 of this Article is associated with an enterprise carrying on substantially similar activities, that person shall be deemed to be carrying on those substantially similar activities of the enterprise with which he is associated, in addition to his own activities;

(b) two enterprises shall be deemed to be associated if one enterprise participates directly or indirectly in the management or control of the other enterprise or if the same persons participate directly or indirectly in the management or control of both enterprises.

Definitions: "associated" — ITCIA 3, ITA 256; "person" — Art. 3:1(c).

4. Salaries, wages and similar remuneration derived by a resident of a Contracting State in respect of an employment connected with the exploration or exploitation of the sea bed and sub-soil and their natural resources situated in the other Contracting State may, to the extent that the duties are performed offshore in that other Contracting State, be taxed in that other Contracting State.

Notes: For CRA interpretation see VIEWS doc 2009-0319951I7.

Definitions: "employment" — ITCIA 3, ITA 248(1); "resident of a Contracting State" — Art. 4; "the other Contracting State" — Art. 3:1(b).

Article 28 — Entry into Force

1. The Convention shall come into force on the date when the last of all such things shall have been done in Canada and the United Kingdom as are necessary to give the Convention the force of law in Canada and the United Kingdom respectively and shall thereupon have effect:

(a) in Canada:

(i) in respect of tax withheld at the source on amounts paid or credited to non-residents on or after 1 January 1976;

(ii) in respect of other Canadian taxes, for the 1976 taxation year and subsequent years;

(b) in the United Kingdom:

(i) in relation to any dividend to which paragraph 3 of Article 10 applied in respect of income tax and payment of tax credit, for any year of assessment beginning on or after 6 April 1973. A dividend paid on or after 1 April 1973 but before 6 April 1973 shall be treated for tax credit purposes as paid on 6 April 1973;

(ii) in relation to any other provision of this Convention, in respect of income tax and capital gains tax, for any year of assessment beginning on or after 6 April 1976;

(iii) in respect of corporation tax, for any financial year beginning on or after 1 April 1976;

(iv) in respect of petroleum revenue tax for any chargeable period beginning on or after 1 January 1976;

(v) in respect of development land tax, for any realised development value accruing on or after 1 August 1976.

Definitions: "assessment" — ITCIA 3, ITA 248(1); "Canada" — Art. 3:1(a)(i), ITCIA 5; "capital gain", "dividend", "non-resident" — ITCIA 3, ITA 248(1); "taxation year" — ITCIA 3, ITA 249; "United Kingdom" — Art. 3:1(a)(ii).

2. The Governments of the Contracting States shall, as soon as possible, inform one another in writing of the date when the last of all such things have been done as are necessary to give the Convention the force of law in Canada and the United Kingdom respectively. The date specified by the last Government to fulfil this requirement, being the date on which the Convention shall come into force in accordance with paragraph 1, shall be confirmed in writing by the Government so notified.

Definitions: "Canada" — Art. 3:1(a)(i), ITCIA 5; "United Kingdom" — Art. 3:1(a)(ii); "writing" — ITCIA 3, *Interpretation Act* 35(1).

3. Subject to the provisions of paragraph 4 of this Article the existing Agreement shall cease to have effect as respects taxes to which this Convention applies in accordance with the provisions of paragraph 1 of this Article.

Definitions: "tax" — Art. 3:1(g); "the existing agreement" — Art. 28:7.

4. Where, however, any greater relief from tax would have been afforded by any provision of the existing Agreement than is due under this Convention, any such provision as aforesaid shall continue to have effect

(a) in the United Kingdom for any year of assessment, chargeable period or financial year;

(b) in Canada for any taxation year;

beginning before the entry into force of this Convention.

Definitions: "Canada" — Art. 3:1(a)(i), ITCIA 5; "tax" — Art. 3:1(g); "taxation year" — ITCIA 3, ITA 249; "the existing agreement" — Art. 28:7; "United Kingdom" — Art. 3:1(a)(ii).

5. The existing Agreement shall terminate on the last date on which it has effect in accordance with the foregoing provisions of this Article.

Definitions: "the existing agreement" — Art. 28:7.

6. The termination of the existing Agreement as provided in paragraph 5 of this Article shall not revive the Agreement between the Government of Canada and the Government of the United Kingdom of Great Britain and Northern Ireland for the Avoidance of Double Taxation with respect to certain classes of Income signed at Ottawa on 6 December 1965. Upon the entry into force of this Convention that Agreement shall terminate.

Definitions: "Canada" — Art. 3:1(a)(i), ITCIA 5; "the existing agreement" — Art. 28:7; "United Kingdom" — Art. 3:1(a)(ii).

7. In this Article the term **"the existing Agreement"** means the Agreement between the Government of Canada and the Government of the United Kingdom of Great Britain and Northern Ireland for the Avoidance of Double Taxation and the Prevention of Fiscal Evasion with respect to taxes on Income and Capital Gains signed at Ottawa on 12 December 1966.

Definitions: "Canada" — Art. 3:1(a)(i), ITCIA 5; "tax" — Art. 3:1(g); "United Kingdom" — Art. 3:1(a)(ii).

8. Notwithstanding any provisions of the respective domestic laws of the Contracting States imposing time limits for applications for relief from tax, an application for relief under the provisions of this Convention shall have effect, and any consequential refunds of tax made, if the application is made to the competent authority concerned within one year of the end of the calendar year in which this Convention enters into force.

Definitions: "competent authority" — Art. 3:1(f); "tax" — Art. 3:1(g).

Article 29 — Termination

This Convention shall continue in effect indefinitely but the Government of either Contracting State may, on or before 30 June in any calendar year after the year 1980 give notice of termination to the Government of the other Contracting State and, in such event, this Convention shall cease to be effective:

(a) in Canada

(i) in respect of tax withheld at the source on amounts paid or credited to non-residents on or after 1 January in the calendar year next following that in which the notice is given; and

(ii) in respect of other Canadian taxes for any taxation year ending in or after the calendar year next following that in which the notice is given;

(b) in the United Kingdom

(i) in respect of income tax and capital gains tax for any year of assessment beginning on or after 6 April in the calendar year next following that in which such notice is given;

(ii) in respect of corporation tax, for any financial year beginning on or after 1 April in the calendar year next following that in which such notice is given;

(iii) in respect of petroleum revenue tax for any chargeable period beginning on or after 1 January in the calendar year next following that in which such notice is given;

(iv) in respect of development land tax, for any realised development value accruing on or after 1 April in the calendar year next following that in which such notice is given.

Definitions: "assessment" — ITCIA 3, ITA 248(1); "Canada" — Art. 3:1(a)(i), ITCIA 5; "capital gain", "non-resident" — ITCIA 3, ITA 248(1); "tax" — Art. 3:1(g); "taxation year" — ITCIA 3, ITA 249; "the other Contracting State" — Art. 3:1(b); "United Kingdom" — Art. 3:1(a)(ii).

IN WITNESS WHEREOF the undersigned, duly authorized thereto, have signed this Convention.

DONE in duplicate at London, this 8th day of September 1978, in the English and French languages, both texts being equally authoritative.

FOR THE GOVERNMENT OF CANADA: Paul Martin

FOR THE GOVERNMENT OF GREAT BRITAIN AND NORTHERN IRELAND: Frank Judd

CURRENT STATUS OF TAX TREATIES

T-1 — Tax treaties in force

Notes: Bilateral tax treaties are in force between Canada and the countries in the Table below (in some cases replacing an earlier treaty). See tinyurl.com/cra-comp-auth for competent authority agreements affecting these treaties.

For the *Multilateral Convention to Implement Tax Treaty Related Measures to Prevent Base Erosion and Profit Shifting* (MLI), see the pages before the Canada-US treaty. The MLI effectively amends Canada's tax treaties with countries that have also ratified the MLI (most treaty partners, but not the US, Germany or Switzerland), generally starting in 2020 or later.

For questions about CRA administrative policy with respect to treaties, contact the International Tax Services Office at 1-800-267-5177.

For information regarding the status of treaty negotiations with any country, see Tables T-2 and T-3 below, and Dept. of Finance web site at tinyurl.com/treaty-status.

Canada signed the Convention on Mutual Administrative Assistance in Tax Matters (tinyurl.com/oecd-mutu) on April 28, 2004, and ratified it on Nov. 21, 2013 (see Finance news release of that day). Canada and Switzerland exchanged notes in Dec. 2016 to permit administrative assistance starting Jan. 1, 2017 for purposes of ITA 270–281. See ITA 270–281 for automatic exchange of financial information (for US taxpayers, 263–269 and Canada-US ETIEA).

For inter-country assistance in collecting tax debts, see Notes to ITA 223(3) and to Canada-US Treaty Art. XXVI-A:1.

For countries with which Canada has a tax information exchange agreement (TIEA), see Notes to ITA 95(1)"non-qualifying country".

Country	Date Signed	MLI Ratification*	Notes (see tinyURL.com/cra-agreements for Agreements and Notices cited)
Algeria	February 28, 1999		
Argentina	April 29, 1993		See also Agreement on Argentina's Certificate of Residency Form.
Armenia	June 29, 2004		
Australia	May 21, 1980; and Protocol of January 23, 2002	September 26, 2018	Negotiations are underway for a revised treaty or amending protocol. See Table T-3 below.
Austria	December 9, 1976; and Protocols of June 15, 1999 and March 9, 2012	September 22, 2017	
Azerbaijan	September 7, 2004		
Bangladesh	February 15, 1982		
Barbados	January 22, 1980; and Protocol of November 8, 2011	December 21, 2020	See McCracken, "Protocol Amends Canada-Barbados Tax Treaty", XVII(2) *International Tax Planning* (Federated Press) 1164-69 (2011); Bowman & Tyler, "Tax Treaty Update", 2014 Cdn Tax Foundation conf. report, 21:20-25; Agreement increasing Art. XVI:2(a) amount to $10,000, and Agreement regarding Art. XIII.
Belgium	May 23, 2002	June 26, 2019	Tax information exchange Protocol signed April 1, 2014, not yet in force. See also Agreement on institutions exempt under Art. 11:3(c).
Brazil	June 4, 1984		Negotiations to update the treaty began November 2018.
Bulgaria	March 3, 1999		
Cameroon	May 26, 1982		
Chile	January 21, 1998	November 26, 2020	See also 3 Agreements re withholding rates, and independent personal services.
China (People's Republic of)	May 12, 1986		The Canada-China Convention does not apply to Hong Kong since unification in 1997: *Edwards*, 2003 FCA 378. A treaty with Hong Kong, signed in 2012, came into force in 2013. See also Notes to China in Table T-3 below; and Agreements listing institutions exempt under Art. 11.
Colombia	November 21, 2008		
Croatia	December 9, 1997	February 18, 2021	
Cyprus	May 2, 1984	January 23, 2020	
Czech Republic	May 25, 2001	May 13, 2020	
Denmark	September 17, 1997	September 30, 2019	
Dominican Republic	August 6, 1976		
Ecuador	June 28, 2001		
Egypt	May 30, 1983	September 30, 2020	
Estonia	June 2, 1995	January 15, 2021	See also Notice re royalties.
Finland	July 20, 2006	February 25, 2019	
France	May 2, 1975 and Protocols of January 16, 1987, November 30, 1995 and February 2, 2010	September 26, 2018	See also 3 Agreements re Art. 12, payments to Canadian mutual funds and payments to Canadian pension plans.

Country	Date Signed	MLI Ratification*	Notes (see tinyURL.com/cra-agreements for Agreements and Notices cited)
Gabon	November 14, 2002		
Germany	April 19, 2001	* [MLI will not apply to this treaty]	Negotiations to update the treaty began June 2017. See 3 Notices re social security pensions.
Greece	June 29, 2009	March 30, 2021	
Guyana	October 15, 1985		
Hong Kong	November 11, 2012		HK is treated as a "country" when applying the treaty: see Notes to ITA 219.2. See also Lee & Radelet, "Canada-Hong Kong Income Tax Agreement", 2013 British Columbia Tax Conf. (ctf.ca), 6:1-33; Bowman & Tyler, "Tax Treaty Update", 2014 Cdn Tax Foundation conf. report, 21:2-12; and Agreement re exchange of country-by-country reports.
Hungary	April 15, 1992 and Protocol of May 3, 1994	March 25, 2021	
Iceland	June 19, 1997	September 26, 2019	
India	January 11, 1996	June 25, 2019	
Indonesia	April 1, 1998	April 28, 2020	
Ireland	October 8, 2003	January 29, 2019	
Israel	September 21, 2016	September 13, 2018	
Italy	June 3, 2002		See 2 Agreements, on institutions exempt under Art. 11:3(c) and on pension payments and social security benefits.
Ivory Coast	June 16, 1983		
Jamaica	March 30, 1978		
Japan	May 7, 1986; amended by Protocol of February 19, 1999	September 26, 2018	
Jordan	September 6, 1999	September 29, 2020	
Kazakhstan	September 25, 1996	June 24, 2020	
Kenya	April 27, 1983		
Korea (Republic of)	September 5, 2006	May 13, 2020	See also Agreement on institutions exempt under Art. 11:4.
Kuwait	January 28, 2002		
Kyrgyzstan (Kyrgyz Republic)	June 4, 1998		
Latvia (Republic of)	April 26, 1995	October 29, 2019	
Lithuania (Republic of)	August 29, 1996	September 11, 2018	
Luxembourg	September 10, 1999 and Protocol of May 8, 2012	April 9, 2019	
Madagascar	November 24, 2016		Effective Jan. 2021 for withholding taxes, and for tax years beginning after 2020 otherwise.
Malaysia	October 15, 1976	February 18, 2021	Negotiations are underway for a revised treaty or amending protocol. See Table T-3 below.
Malta	July 25, 1986	December 18, 2018	
Mexico	September 12, 2006		
Moldova	July 4, 2002		
Mongolia	May 27, 2002		
Morocco	December 22, 1975		
Netherlands	May 27, 1986 and Protocols of same date, March 4, 1993, and August 25, 1997	March 29, 2019	See Agreement on withholding tax on closed fonds voor gemene rekening (FGR).
New Zealand	May 3, 2012 and Protocol of September 12, 2014	June 27, 2018	See Notice re application of Art. 10.
Nigeria	August 4, 1992		
Norway	July 12, 2002	July 17, 2019	A Competent Authority Agreement regarding Professors and Teachers provides that Article 18 of the 1966 Canada-Norway treaty continues to apply in certain cases: CCRA, Nov. 28, 2003. See also Agreements re Art. 10 and 11.

Country	Date Signed	MLI Ratification*	Notes (see tinyURL.com/cra-agreements for Agreements and Notices cited)
Oman	June 30, 2004	July 7, 2020	
Pakistan	February 24, 1976	December 18, 2020	
Papua New Guinea	October 16, 1987		
Peru	July 20, 2001		
Philippines	March 11, 1976		
Poland	May 14, 2012	January 23, 2018	
Portugal	June 14, 1999	February 28, 2020	
Romania	April 8, 2004		
Russia	October 5, 1995	June 18, 2019	
Senegal	August 2, 2001		
Serbia	April 27, 2012	June 5, 2018	Treaty negotiations were announced in December 2003 with "Serbia and Montenegro", but Montenegro became a separate country in 2006 and is not part of the treaty negotiated with Serbia. No negotiations are underway with Montenegro.
Singapore	March 6, 1976 and Protocols of that date and November 29, 2011	December 21, 2018	
Slovak Republic	May 22, 2001	September 20, 2018	
Slovenia	September 15, 2000	March 22, 2018	
South Africa (Republic of)	November 27, 1995		
Spain	November 23, 1976 and Protocol of November 18, 2014		
Sri Lanka	June 23, 1982		
Sweden	August 27, 1996	June 22, 2018	
Switzerland	May 5, 1997 and Protocol of October 22, 2010	* [MLI will not apply to this treaty]	Negotiations to update the treaty began June 2017. See also 3 Agreements, re refunding Swiss tax on investment vehicle, social security arrangements, and pension and retirement plans for Art. 10:3(b)(v).
Taiwan	January 15, 2016		Titled an "arrangement" but is treated as a "treaty" with a "country": see Notes to ITA 219.2.
Tanzania (United Republic of)	December 15, 1995		
Thailand	April 11, 1984		
Trinidad and Tobago (Republic of)	September 11, 1995		
Tunisia	February 10, 1982		
Turkey	July 14, 2009		
Ukraine	March 4, 1996	August 8, 2019	
United Arab Emirates	June 9, 2002	May 29, 2019	
United Kingdom of Great Britain and Northern Ireland	September 8, 1978 and Protocols of April 15, 1980, October 16, 1985, May 7, 2003 and July 21, 2014	June 29, 2018	See treaty reproduced above.
United States of America	September 26, 1980 and Protocols of June 14, 1983, March 28, 1984, March 17, 1995, July 29, 1997 and September 21, 2007	[The US is not signing the MLI]	See 6 Agreements, and see treaty reproduced above.
Uzbekistan (Republic of)	June 17, 1999		
Venezuela	July 10, 2001		
Vietnam	November 14, 1997		See also agreement on institution exempt under Art. 11:3(b).
Zambia (Republic of)	February 16, 1984		
Zimbabwe	April 16, 1992		

* Date of deposit of instrument of ratification of the Multilateral Instrument (MLI), per tinyurl.com/oecd-mli; see before the Canada-US Treaty for the annotated text. Once 3 calendar months have passed from this date, as well as 3 calendar months from Canada's deposit (Aug. 29, 2019), the MLI is in force on the first date of the following month to amend the treaty between Canada and the indicated country. (Germany and Switzerland have signed the MLI but are excluded from Canada's MLI deposit, as Canada is renegotiating these treaties and will include the necessary provisions in the new treaties. The US is not signing the MLI.)

T-2 — Tax treaties or protocols signed but not yet in force (not yet ratified by both countries)

Country	Date Signed	Notes
Belgium	April 1, 2014	Amending Protocol re tax information exchange.
Lebanon	December 29, 1998	Enacted in Canada by S.C. 2000, c. 11 (Bill S-3), Royal Assent June 29, 2000.
Namibia	March 25, 2010	Enacted in Canada by S.C. 2013, c. 27 (Bill S-17), Royal Assent June 19, 2013.

T-3 — Tax treaties or protocols under negotiation (re-negotiation)

Country	Notes
Australia	Negotiations to update the treaty began July 2012.
Brazil	Negotiations to update the treaty announced Oct. 24, 2018.
China	This will eventually replace the 1986 treaty. Prime Minister Harper announced on Feb. 9, 2012 that an agreement in principle had been reached on an updated Canada-China treaty, which "will include modernized provisions that conform to current Canadian and international tax treaty policies, which is based on the Model Tax Convention on Income and on Capital developed by the Organisation for Economic Co-operation and Development (OECD)". The new treaty will "further reduce tax barriers in order to encourage trade and investment between Canada and China; reduce the rates of withholding taxes that apply on certain cross-border payments; and eliminate double taxation for individuals and companies doing business or earning income in the other country." It is subject to approval by both governments before it can be signed. (Backgrounder, reproduced in 2012(4) *Tax Times* (Carswell) p. 5 (Feb. 24, 2012))
Germany	Negotiations to update the treaty announced June 7, 2017.
Malaysia	Will eventually replace the existing treaty. A declaration of intent to conclude a new treaty was signed on October 6, 2013.
Netherlands	Will eventually replace the existing treaty.
San Marino	Negotiations announced Oct. 7, 2016.
Switzerland	Negotiations to update the treaty announced June 7, 2017.

Notes: See Notes before Table T-1.

INTERPRETATION ACT

An Act respecting the Interpretation of Statutes and Regulations

REVISED STATUTES OF CANADA 1985, CHAPTER I-21, as am. R.S.C. 1985, c. 11 (1st Supp.), s. 2; R.S.C. 1985, c. 27 (1st Supp.), s. 203; SOR/86-532; R.S.C. 1985, c. 27 (2nd Supp.), s. 10; S.C. 1990, c. 17, s. 26; 1992, c. 1, ss. 87–91; 1992, c. 47, s. 79; 1992, c. 51, s. 56; SOR/93-140; 1993, c. 28, s. 78 (Sched. III, item 82) [Amended 1998, c. 15, s. 28; 1999, c. 3, (Sched., item 18).]; 1993, c. 34, s. 88; 1993, c. 38, s. 87; 1995, c. 39, s. 174; SOR/95-366; 1996, c. 31, ss. 86–87; 1997, c. 39, s. 4; 1998, c. 30, s. 15(i); 1999, c. 3, s. 71; 1999, c. 28, s. 168; 1999, c. 31, ss. 146, 147 (Fr.); 2001, c. 4, s. 8; 2002, c. 7, s. 188; 2002, c. 8, s. 151; 2003, c. 22, s. 224(z.43); 2014, c. 2, s. 14; 2015, c. 3, s. 124.

Short Title

Notes: The *Interpretation Act* applies to all federal statutes: see 3(1) and 2(1)"enactment" below. Each province has an *Interpretation Act* or similar for interpreting its legislation (Ontario: *Legislation Act, 2006*, Part VI).

For digests of cases interpreting the provisions of this Act, especially in a tax context, see McMechan & Bourgard, *Tax Court Practice* (Carswell, 2 vols. looseleaf or *Taxnet Pro* Reference Centre), Appendix B.

1. Short title — This Act may be cited as the *Interpretation Act*.

Interpretation

2. (1) Definitions — In this Act,

"Act" means an Act of Parliament;

"enact" includes to issue, make or establish;

"enactment" means an Act or regulation or any portion of an Act or regulation;

"public officer" includes any person in the federal public administration of Canada who is authorized by or under an enactment to do or enforce the doing of an act or thing or to exercise a power, or on whom a duty is imposed by or under an enactment;

Notes: "Public service of Canada" changed to "federal public administration" by *Public Service Modernization Act* (S.C. 2003, c. 22), in force Apr. 1, 2005 (P.C. 2005-375).

"regulation" includes an order, regulation, rule, rule of court, form, tariff of costs or fees, letters patent, commission, warrant, proclamation, by-law, resolution or other instrument issued, made or established

(a) in the execution of a power conferred by or under the authority of an Act, or

(b) by or under the authority of the Governor in Council;

"repeal" includes revoke or cancel.

(2) Expired and replaced enactments — For the purposes of this Act, an enactment that has been replaced is repealed and an enactment that has expired, lapsed or otherwise ceased to have effect is deemed to have been repealed.

Notes: 2(2) amended by *Miscellaneous Statutes Law Amendment Act* (S.C. 1999, c. 31), effective June 17, 1999.

Application

3. (1) Application — Every provision of this Act applies, unless a contrary intention appears, to every enactment, whether enacted before or after the commencement of this Act.

Notes: See Notes to 33(2).

(2) Application to this Act — The provisions of this Act apply to the interpretation of this Act.

(3) Rules of construction not excluded — Nothing in this Act excludes the application to an enactment of a rule of construction applicable to that enactment and not inconsistent with this Act.

Enacting Clause of Acts

4. (1) Enacting clause — The enacting clause of an Act may be in the following form:

"Her Majesty, by and with the advice and consent of the Senate and House of Commons of Canada, enacts as follows:".

(2) Order of clauses — The enacting clause of an Act shall follow the preamble, if any, and the various provisions within the purview or body of the Act shall follow in a concise and enunciative form.

Operation

Royal Assent

5. (1) Royal Assent — The Clerk of the Parliaments shall endorse on every Act, immediately after its title, the day, month and year when the Act was assented to in Her Majesty's name and the endorsement shall be a part of the Act.

(2) Date of commencement — If no date of commencement is provided for in an Act, the date of commencement of that Act is the date of assent to the Act.

(3) Commencement provision — Where an Act contains a provision that the Act or any portion thereof is to come into force on a day later than the date of assent to the Act, that provision is deemed to have come into force on the date of assent to the Act.

(4) Commencement when no date fixed — Where an Act provides that certain provisions thereof are to come or are deemed to have come into force on a day other than the date of assent to the Act, the remaining provisions of the Act are deemed to have come into force on the date of assent to the Act.

Day Fixed for Commencement or Repeal

6. (1) Operation when date fixed for commencement or repeal — Where an enactment is expressed to come into force on a particular day, it shall be construed as coming into force on the expiration of the previous day; and where an enactment is expressed to expire, lapse or otherwise cease to have effect on a particular day, it shall be construed as ceasing to have effect upon the commencement of the following day.

(2) When no date fixed — Every enactment that is not expressed to come into force on a particular day shall be construed as coming into force

(a) in the case of an Act, on the expiration of the day immediately before the day the Act was assented to in Her Majesty's name;

(b) in the case of a regulation, on the expiration of the day immediately before the day the regulation was registered pursuant to section 6 of the *Statutory Instruments Act* or, if the regulation is of a class that is exempted from the application of subsection

5(1) of that Act, on the expiration of the day immediately before the day the regulation was made.

(3) Judicial notice — Judicial notice shall be taken of a day for the coming into force of an enactment that is fixed by a regulation that has been published in the *Canada Gazette*.

Regulation Prior to Commencement

7. Preliminary proceedings — Where an enactment is not in force and it contains provisions conferring power to make regulations or do any other thing, that power may, for the purpose of making the enactment effective on its commencement, be exercised at any time before its commencement, but a regulation so made or a thing so done has no effect until the commencement of the enactment, except in so far as may be necessary to make the enactment effective on its commencement.

Territorial Operation

8. (1) Territorial operation — Every enactment applies to the whole of Canada, unless a contrary intention is expressed in the enactment.

(2) Amending enactment — Where an enactment that does not apply to the whole of Canada is amended, no provision in the amending enactment applies to any part of Canada to which the amended enactment does not apply, unless it is provided in the amending enactment that it applies to that part of Canada or to the whole of Canada.

(2.1) Exclusive economic zone of Canada — Every enactment that applies in respect of exploring or exploiting, conserving or managing natural resources, whether living or non-living, applies, in addition to its application to Canada, to the exclusive economic zone of Canada, unless a contrary intention is expressed in the enactment.

Related Provisions: ITA 37(1.3) — SR&ED performed in exclusive economic zone deemed done in Canada.

Notes: See Notes to 8(2.2). "Exclusive economic zone" is defined in 35(1).

(2.2) Continental shelf of Canada — Every enactment that applies in respect of exploring or exploiting natural resources that are

(a) mineral or other non-living resources of the seabed or subsoil, or

(b) living organisms belonging to sedentary species, that is to say, organisms that, at the harvestable stage, either are immobile on or under the seabed or are unable to move except in constant physical contact with the seabed or subsoil

applies, in addition to its application to Canada, to the continental shelf of Canada, unless a contrary intention is expressed in the enactment.

Notes: 8(2.1), (2.2) added by *Oceans Act* (Bill C-26, 1996, c. 31), proclaimed in force January 31, 1997 (SI/97-21).

(3) Extra-territorial operation — Every Act now in force enacted prior to December 11, 1931 that expressly or by necessary or reasonable implication was intended, as to the whole or any part thereof, to have extra-territorial operation shall be construed as if, at the date of its enactment, the Parliament of Canada had full power to make laws having extra-territorial operation as provided by the *Statute of Westminster, 1931.*

Rules of Construction

Property and Civil Rights

8.1 Duality of legal traditions and application of provincial law — Both the common law and the civil law are equally authoritative and recognized sources of the law of property and civil rights in Canada and, unless otherwise provided by law, if in interpreting an enactment it is necessary to refer to a province's rules, principles or concepts forming part of the law of property and civil rights, reference must be made to the rules, principles and concepts in force in the province at the time the enactment is being applied.

I.T. Technical News: No. 22 (international taxation).

Notes: 8.1 and 8.2 added by S.C. 2001, c. 4 and proclaimed in force June 1, 2001 by P.C. 2001-956. The Department of Justice is, under a "bijuralism" project, redrafting all federal legislation for "four audiences": English and French, common-law and civil law (previously, the English version used common-law terms such as "real property" and "mortgage" and the French used *Civil Code* terms such as "immeuble" (immovable) and "hypothèque" (hypothec)). The new drafting accommodates English speakers in Quebec and French speakers in New Brunswick and other common-law provinces. See tinyurl.com/bijuralism; and two books *The Harmonization of Federal Legislation with Quebec Civil Law and Canadian Bijuralism: Collection [Second Collection] of Studies in Tax Law* (2002, 2005), on apff.org ("Publications" > "Autres publications"). See also Notes to ITA 248(3). Extensive amendments were made to the *Income Tax Act* by 2002-2013 technical bill (Part 4 — bijuralism) (see, e.g., ITA 12(9)).

See 51(1) *Canadian Tax Journal* (2003), including David Duff, "The Federal *Income Tax Act* and Private Law in Canada" (pp. 1-63), and "Symposium on Canadian Bijuralism and Harmonization of Federal Tax Legislation" (pp. 133-513). See also Aline Grenon, "The Interpretation of Bijural or Harmonized Federal Legislation: *Schreiber v. Canada*", 84(1) *Canadian Bar Review* 131-50 (2005); David Duff, "Canadian Bijuralism and the Concept of an Acquisition of Property in the Federal Income Tax Act", 55 *McGill Law Review* (2009), ssrn.com/abstract=1526325; Robert Décary, "The Federal Court of Appeal to the Rescue of Civil Law", 61(Supp.) *CTJ* 71-80 (2013).

The Courts have confirmed that provincial law applies to determine legal relationships before tax law is applied to those relationships, and thus that a provincial superior court can issue an order that has the effect of changing the tax consequences: *Dale*, [1997] 2 C.T.C. 286 (FCA); *Sussex Square Apartments Ltd.*, [1999] 2 C.T.C. 2143 (TCC); aff'd [2000] 4 C.T.C. 203 (FCA); *Juliar*, [2001] 4 C.T.C. 45 (Ont. CA); leave to appeal to SCC denied 2001 CarswellOnt 1805. See Notes to ITA 169(1) re rectification.

Common law vs civil law: In the past, if the *Civil Code* resulted in different tax effects than the common law, then "for the sake of uniformity, the common law approach should prevail even in Quebec": *Hewlett Packard*, 2004 FCA 240, para. 62. In *Larocque*, 2016 QCCA 556 (overturning the Court of Quebec; leave to appeal to SCC requested), *Civil Code* art. 2904 (limitation period does not apply if it is impossible for a person to act) did not apply to a Quebec Sales Tax objection because it should be consistent with the GST, and under federal tax legislation, statutory limitation periods are binding. However, "uniformity is not sufficient reason for disregarding the applicable private law": *French*, 2016 FCA 64, para. 43 (but non-Quebec taxpayers claiming charitable donations were still allowed to plead that the *Civil Code* was relevant to their appeals in determining the meaning of "gift", since it was arguable that Parliament intended the civil law meaning to apply). Quebec law does not recognize a constructive trust or implied trust for purposes of federal bankruptcy law: *Groupe Sutton-Royal Inc.*, 2015 QCCA 1069, paras. 90-91 (leave to appeal denied 2016 CarswellQue 3452 (SCC)). Similarly, in Quebec a partnership formed to carry on illegal acts is void, so its partners are not partners and not jointly liable for its tax liabilities, though this is not the law in other provinces: *Raposo*, 2019 FCA 208. There must be a need to refer to private law rules, principles or concepts in interpreting federal legislation, or 8.1 does not apply: *Quebec v. Canada (Human Resources)*, 2011 SCC 60.

The Tax Court applied 8.2 in *Vallée*, 2004 TCC 320, ruling that a Quebec "fiducie" should be treated as a trust and thus ineligible for a GST new housing rebate.

The Courts apply the *Civil Code* to determine whether a Quebec worker is an employee or independent contractor. See Notes to ITA 248(1)"employee".

On whether a company can claim CCA when it builds a garage on property owned by its shareholder, based on the Quebec *Civil Code* rules for surface rights, see VIEWS doc 2011-0409671E5. As to whether a "counter letter" (undisclosed agreement) affects CRA's rights, see VIEWS doc 2012-0471151E5; *ZT22 Holding*, [2013] G.S.T.C. 9 (TCC); *Abdulnour*, [2013] G.S.T.C. 18 (TCC).

French vs English: Under *Official Languages Act* s. 13, both versions of federal legislation are equally authoritative. However, this is not an "absolute" rule overriding "all other canons of construction": *Cie. Imm. BCN*, 1979 CanLII 12 (SCC). Seek the "shared meaning" between the two versions (*Daoust*, 2004 SCC 6), and if the difference is irreconcilable, the right interpretation is that which better accords with Parliament's intent: *Medovarski*, 2005 SCC 51, paras. 24-26; *Perrier Group*, [1996] 1 C.T.C. 167 (FCA); *Irwin*, [1962] C.T.C. 572 (Exch. Ct.; rev'd on other grounds [1964] C.T.C. 362 (SCC)); *McLaughlin*, [1978] C.T.C. 602 (FCTD); *Nima v. McInnes*, 1988 CanLII 3201 (BCSC); *Conocophillips*, 2016 FC 98, para. 45 (rev'd on other grounds 2017 FCA 243); *Roode*, [1987] 1 C.T.C. 2418 (TCC); *Hlopina*, [1998] 2 C.T.C. 2669 (TCC); *Genex Communications*, 2009 TCC 583, paras. 24-26; *Sommerer*, 2011 TCC 212, para. 96 (aff'd on other grounds 2012 FCA 207); *Bolduc*, 2013 TCC 77; *Hughes*, 2017 TCC 95, paras. 39-41; *Filiatrault*, 2017 TCC 232, para. 36; *506913 N.B.*, 2016 TCC 286, para. 8. See also Couzin, "What Does it Say in French?", 33(2) *Canadian Tax Journal* 300-08 (March-April 1985); Bastarache, *The Law of Bilingual Interpretation* (LexisNexis, 2008); Gadbois & Gentile, "The Quebec Runaway Bride", 2016 Commodity Tax Symposium (CPA Canada), slides 1-6. Where tax treaty French/English texts differ, see Notes to *Income Tax Conventions Interpretation Act* (before the Canada-US treaty).

8.2 Terminology — Unless otherwise provided by law, when an enactment contains both civil law and common law terminology, or terminology that has a different meaning in the civil law and the common law, the civil law terminology or meaning is to be adopted in the Province of Quebec and the common law terminology or meaning is to be adopted in the other provinces.

Notes: See Notes to 8.1.

Private Acts

9. Provisions in Private Acts — No provision in a private Act affects the rights of any person, except as therein mentioned or referred to.

Law Always Speaking

10. Law always speaking — The law shall be considered as always speaking, and where a matter or thing is expressed in the present tense, it shall be applied to the circumstances as they arise, so that effect may be given to the enactment according to its true spirit, intent and meaning.

Imperative and Permissive Construction

11. "Shall" and "may" — The expression "shall" is to be construed as imperative and the expression "may" as permissive.

Notes: "Shall" used in its normal grammatical sense is presumptively imperative unless such an interpretation would render the legislative enactment irrational or meaningless: *Manitoba Language Rights*, 1985 CanLII 33 (SCC), para. 27; *Billard Fisheries*, [1995] 2 C.T.C. 2505 (TCC), para. 90.

Federal government legislative drafting standards changed in 2011 to use "must" in place of "shall" generally, with no change in meaning, as directed by the Chief Legislative Counsel.

Enactments Remedial

12. Enactments deemed remedial — Every enactment is deemed remedial, and shall be given such fair, large and liberal construction and interpretation as best ensures the attainment of its objects.

Notes: See *Canada Trustco*, 2005 SCC 54, for the "textual, contextual and purposive" method to be used in interpreting tax legislation, and the interpretive principles of "certainty, predictability and fairness". See also Alan Schwartz, "Understanding what the Supreme Court of Canada Said in *Canada Trustco*", 2006 Cdn Tax Foundation conference report, at 3:12-21.

Parliament in enacting legislation "is presumed to know all that is necessary to produce rational and effective legislation", including "mastery of existing law, common law and the *Civil Code* of Quebec as well as ordinary statute law, and the case law interpreting statutes": *Triple M Metal*, 2016 TCC 293, para. 70.

For discussion of the history of this section back to 1849, see *High-Crest*, 2017 TCC 210, para. 74, footnote 35.

Preambles and Marginal Notes

13. Preamble — The preamble of an enactment shall be read as a part of the enactment intended to assist in explaining its purport and object.

14. Marginal Notes and historical references — Marginal notes and references to former enactments that appear after the end of a section or other division in an enactment form no part of the enactment, but are inserted for convenience of reference only.

Notes: The "marginal notes", which are printed down the left margin in the official legislation as published by Parliament, are shown in this publication as titles to the provision (i.e., for this section, the bold-face words "Marginal Notes and historical references").

S. 14 is acknowledged but often ignored. Courts use marginal notes (and actual headings, not covered by s. 14) to interpret the ITA and other statutes: *Wigglesworth*, [1987] 2 S.C.R. 541 at 556-7; *Law Society v. Skapinker*, [1984] S.C.R. 357 (*Charter of Rights* headings "must be examined and some intent made to discern the intent of the makers of the document from the language of the heading"); *Imperial Oil (Inco)*, 2006 SCC 46,

para. 57 ("Although marginal notes are not entirely devoid of usefulness, their value is limited"); *Corbett*, [1997] 1 C.T.C. 2 (FCA); *Brill*, 1996 CarswellNat 1856 (FCA); *Lawyers' Professional Indemnity*, 2020 FCA 90, para. 54 (leave to appeal denied 2021 CarswellNat 865 (SCC)); *Cameco*, 2020 FCA 112, paras. 58-60 (applying both a sub-section marginal note and a Part heading without seeing them as different) [leave to appeal to SCC requested by Crown]; *Loewen*, 2003 TCC 101, paras. 34-40 ("marginal notes should be used with caution... I do not think that s. 14 of the *Interpretation Act* can be totally ignored"); *Fleck Manufacturing*, 1997 CanLII 12007 (CITT).

"Section 14 ... does not specifically exclude headings and titles, and as such, these elements form part of the interpretative context of the [Income Tax] Act" (and so the term "*bona fide* arrangements for repayment" should not be interpreted under the heading "Special Rules Applicable in Certain Circumstances", meaning tax shelters, the same as under "Computation of Income", for shareholder benefits): *Tolhoek*, 2006 TCC 681, para. 32; aff'd 2008 FCA 128.

Application of Interpretation Provisions

15. (1) Application of definitions and interpretation provisions — Definitions or rules of interpretation in an enactment apply to all the provisions of the enactment, including the provisions that contain those definitions or rules of interpretation.

(2) Interpretation sections subject to exceptions — Where an enactment contains an interpretation section or provision, it shall be read and construed

(a) as being applicable only if a contrary intention does not appear, and

(b) as being applicable to all other enactments relating to the same subject-matter unless a contrary intention appears.

16. Words in regulations — Where an enactment confers power to make regulations, expressions used in the regulations have the same respective meanings as in the enactment conferring the power.

Her Majesty

17. Her Majesty not bound or affected unless stated — No enactment is binding on Her Majesty or affects Her Majesty's rights or prerogatives in any manner, except as mentioned or referred to in the enactment.

Related Provisions: ITA 27 — Application of ITA to Crown corporations.

Notes: "Her Majesty" in s. 17 includes the provincial Crown: *Nova Scotia Power*, 2004 SCC 51.

Proclamations

18. (1) Proclamation — Where an enactment authorizes the issue of a proclamation, the proclamation shall be understood to be a proclamation of the Governor in Council.

(2) Proclamation to be issued on advice — Where the Governor General is authorized to issue a proclamation, the proclamation shall be understood to be a proclamation issued under an order of the Governor in Council, but it is not necessary to mention in the proclamation that it is issued under such an order.

(3) Effective day of Proclamations — A proclamation that is issued under an order of the Governor in Council may purport to have been issued on the day of the order or on any subsequent day and, if so, takes effect on that day.

Oaths

19. (1) Administration of oaths — Where, by an enactment or by a rule of the Senate or House of Commons, evidence under oath is authorized or required to be taken, or an oath is authorized or directed to be made, taken or administered, the oath may be administered, and a certificate of its having been made, taken or administered may be given by

(a) any person authorized by the enactment or rule to take the evidence; or

(b) a judge of any court, a notary public, a justice of the peace or a commissioner for taking affidavits, having authority or jurisdiction within the place where the oath is administered.

(2) Where justice of peace empowered — Where power is conferred on a justice of the peace to administer an oath or solemn affirmation or to take an affidavit or declaration, the power may be exercised by a notary public or a commissioner for taking oaths.

Related Provisions: ITA 220(5) — Administration of oaths.

Reports to Parliament

20. Reports to Parliament — Where an Act requires a report or other document to be laid before Parliament and, in compliance with the Act, a particular report or document has been laid before Parliament at a session thereof, nothing in the Act shall be construed as requiring the same report or document to be laid before Parliament at any subsequent session.

Corporations

21. (1) Powers vested in Corporations — Words establishing a corporation shall be construed

(a) as vesting in the corporation power to sue and be sued, to contract and be contracted with by its corporate name, to have a common seal and to alter or change it at pleasure, to have perpetual succession, to acquire and hold personal property for the purposes for which the corporation is established and to alienate that property at pleasure;

(b) in the case of a corporation having a name consisting of an English and a French form or a combined English and French form, as vesting in the corporation power to use either the English or the French form of its name or both forms and to show on its seal both the English and French forms of its name or have two seals, one showing the English and the other showing the French form of its name;

(c) as vesting in a majority of the members of the corporation the power to bind the others by their acts; and

(d) as exempting from personal liability for its debts, obligations or acts individual members of the corporation who do not contravene the provisions of the enactment establishing the corporation.

(2) Corporate name — Where an enactment establishes a corporation and in each of the English and French versions of the enactment the name of the corporation is in the form only of the language of that version, the name of the corporation shall consist of the form of its name in each of the versions of the enactment.

(3) Banking business — No corporation is deemed to be authorized to carry on the business of banking unless that power is expressly conferred on it by the enactment establishing the corporation.

Majority and Quorum

22. (1) Majorities — Where an enactment requires or authorizes more than two persons to do an act or thing, a majority of them may do it.

(2) Quorum of board, court, commission, etc. — Where an enactment establishes a board, court, commission or other body consisting of three or more members, in this section called an "association",

(a) at a meeting of the association, a number of members of the association equal to,

(i) if the number of members provided for by the enactment is a fixed number, at least one-half of the number of members, and

(ii) if the number of members provided for by the enactment is not a fixed number but is within a range having a maximum or minimum, at least one-half of the number of members in office if that number is within the range,

constitutes a quorum;

(b) an act or thing done by a majority of the members of the association present at a meeting, if the members present constitute a quorum, is deemed to have been done by the association; and

(c) a vacancy in the membership of the association does not invalidate the constitution of the association or impair the right of the members in office to act, if the number of members in office is not less than a quorum.

Appointment, Retirement and Powers of Officers

23. (1) Public officers hold office during pleasure — Every public officer appointed by or under the authority of an enactment or otherwise is deemed to have been appointed to hold office during pleasure only, unless it is otherwise expressed in the enactment, commission or instrument of appointment.

(2) Effective day of appointments — Where an appointment is made by instrument under the Great Seal, the instrument may purport to have been issued on or after the day its issue was authorized, and the day on which it so purports to have been issued is deemed to be the day on which the appointment takes effect.

(3) Appointment or engagement otherwise than under great seal — Where there is authority in an enactment to appoint a person to a position or to engage the services of a person, otherwise than by instrument under the Great Seal, the instrument of appointment or engagement may be expressed to be effective on or after the day on which that person commenced the performance of the duties of the position or commenced the performance of the services, and the day on which it is so expressed to be effective, unless that day is more than sixty days before the day on which the instrument is issued, is deemed to be the day on which the appointment or engagement takes effect.

(4) Remuneration — Where a person is appointed to an office, the appointing authority may fix, vary or terminate that person's remuneration.

(5) Commencement of appointments or retirements — Where a person is appointed to an office effective on a specified day, or where the appointment of a person is terminated effective on a specified day, the appointment or termination is deemed to have been effected immediately on the expiration of the previous day.

24. (1) Implied powers respecting public officers — Words authorizing the appointment of a public officer to hold office during pleasure include, in the discretion of the authority in whom the power of appointment is vested, the power to

(a) terminate the appointment or remove or suspend the public officer;

(b) re-appoint or reinstate the public officer; and

(c) appoint another person in the stead of, or to act in the stead of, the public officer.

(2) Power to act for ministers — Words directing or empowering a minister of the Crown to do an act or thing, regardless of whether the act or thing is administrative, legislative or judicial, or otherwise applying to that minister as the holder of the office, include

(a) a minister acting for that minister or, if the office is vacant, a minister designated to act in the office by or under the authority of an order in council;

(b) the successors of that minister in the office;

(c) his or their deputy; and

(d) notwithstanding paragraph (c), a person appointed to serve, in the department or ministry of state over which the minister presides, in a capacity appropriate to the doing of the act or thing, or to the words so applying.

Notes: See Notes to ITA 244(13) for case law on the validity of documents signed by or on behalf of various CRA officials.

(3) Restriction as to public servants — Nothing in paragraph (2)(c) or (d) shall be construed as authorizing the exercise of any authority conferred on a minister to make a regulation as defined in the *Statutory Instruments Act*.

(4) Successors to and deputy of public officer — Words directing or empowering any public officer, other than a minister of the Crown, to do any act or thing, or otherwise applying to the public officer by his name of office, include his successors in the office and his or their deputy.

(5) Powers of holder of public office — Where a power is conferred or a duty imposed on the holder of an office, the power may be exercised and the duty shall be performed by the person for the time being charged with the execution of the powers and duties of the office.

Evidence

25. (1) Documentary evidence — Where an enactment provides that a document is evidence of a fact without anything in the context to indicate that the document is conclusive evidence, then, in any judicial proceedings, the document is admissible in evidence and the fact is deemed to be established in the absence of any evidence to the contrary.

(2) Queen's printer — Every copy of an enactment having printed thereon what purports to be the name or title of the Queen's Printer and Controller of Stationery or the Queen's Printer is deemed to be a copy purporting to be printed by the Queen's Printer for Canada.

Computation of Time

26. Time limits and holidays — Where the time limited for the doing of a thing expires or falls on a holiday, the thing may be done on the day next following that is not a holiday.

Notes: "Holiday" is defined in 35(1) to mean Sunday as well as statutory holidays and "non-juridical days" under provincial legislation or regulations. The *Holidays Act* states that Canada Day (July 1, or July 2 if July 1 is a Sunday), Remembrance Day (Nov. 11) and Victoria Day (Monday before May 25) are legal holidays. See also 35(1)"holiday" below. Thus, when a 90-day objection deadline expired on a Sunday, an objection filed the next day was valid: *Leibovich*, 2016 TCC 6, para. 6. In all provinces other than British Columbia, Saturday is a holiday due to provincial rules re time limits in civil cases (Quebec: *Code of Civil Procedure* s. 83), so a Saturday deadline (whether the taxpayer's or CRA's) is extended to the next business day: *Canada (Human Rights Commission) v. Canada (Armed Forces) (re Lagacé)*, 1996 CarswellNat 655 (FCA). "For administrative purposes, the Agency has adopted the position that Saturday will be considered a non-work day in all provinces and territories" (tinyurl.com/rpd-consults, 2003 q. 10 (now removed)); Transfer Pricing Memorandum TPM-05R, para. 19; and VIEWS doc 2015-0598291C6 [2015 APFF q. 21].

As well, if a filing deadline expires on a Saturday or other day when CRA offices are closed, the deadline may be judicially extended: *P.F. Collier & Son Ltd.*, [1986] 2 C.T.C. 375 (FCA). (For Tax Court appeals under ITA 169(1), this might not be true given that appeals can now be filed over the Internet.) See the commentary in the *Canada GST Service* or *GST Partner* to ETA s. 306. In *Barrington Lane Developments*, 2010 TCC 388, para. 3, the parties agreed that when a CRA reassessment date expired on a Saturday, the deadline was extended to Monday.

For CRA's list of public holidays for which an extension applies, see tinyurl.com/cra-holidays.

For Quebec legislative deadlines, the same rule as s. 26 applies under Quebec *Interpretation Act* s. 52. For Ontario, see ss. 88–89 of the *Legislation Act, 2006*.

See also Notes to 35(1)"holiday" re municipal holidays, and to ITA 150(1)(d).

Transfer Pricing Memoranda: TPM-05R, para. 19.

27. (1) Clear days — Where there is a reference to a number of clear days or "at least" a number of days between two events, in calculating that number of days the days on which the events happen are excluded.

(2) Not clear days — Where there is a reference to a number of days, not expressed to be clear days, between two events, in calculating that number of days the day on which the first event happens is excluded and the day on which the second event happens is included.

Notes: As to whether "30 days" is measured by the time of day on the start and end days, see Benjamin Arkin, "If you Survive me by 30 Days", 28(1) *Money & Family Law* (Carswell) 3-5 (Jan. 2013), discussing *Barbeau Estate*, 2012 ONSC 3249.

The reassessment deadline that is 3 years from (say) May 15, 2014 is May 15, 2017. See Notes to ITA 152(4).

(3) Beginning and ending of prescribed periods — Where a time is expressed to begin or end at, on or with a specified day, or to continue to or until a specified day, the time includes that day.

(4) After specified day — Where a time is expressed to begin after or to be from a specified day, the time does not include that day.

Notes: In *Brunette*, [2001] 1 C.T.C. 2008 (TCC) the Court held that 27(4) applies to exclude the day of the initial assessment from the calculation of the 3-year reassessment limit.

In *TD Bank*, 2017 BCCA 159 (reversing the BCSC), a BC statute's filing deadline "within 18 months after the end of the taxation year", for an Oct. 31, 2012 year-end, was not met by a return filed May 1, 2014.

(5) Within a time — Where anything is to be done within a time after, from, of or before a specified day, the time does not include that day.

Related Provisions: 26 — Extension of time when deadline expires on weekend or holiday.

Notes: For interpretation see Notes to ITA 227.1(4).

28. Calculation of a period of months after or before a specified day — Where there is a reference to a period of time consisting of a number of months after or before a specified day, the period is calculated by

(a) counting forward or backward from the specified day the number of months, without including the month in which that day falls;

(b) excluding the specified day; and

(c) including in the last month counted under paragraph (a) the day that has the same calendar number as the specified day or, if that month has no day with that number, the last day of that month.

Notes: See VIEWS docs 2009-0343331I7 (calculation of SR&ED filing deadline); 2011-0411831C6 (calculation of 2-year holding period for capital gains exemption on small business shares). See also Notes to 27(2) and (4) above.

Transfer Pricing Memoranda: TPM-05R, para. 17.

29. Time of the day — Where there is a reference to time expressed as a specified time of the day, the time is taken to mean standard time.

Notes: This rule is somewhat counterintuitive during the summer months in provinces that use Daylight Savings Time. See 35(1) for the definition of "standard time". One exception to this rule is *Canada Elections Act* s. 2(4).

30. Time when specified age attained — A person is deemed not to have attained a specified number of years of age until the commencement of the anniversary, of the same number, of the day of that person's birth.

Miscellaneous Rules

31. (1) Reference to magistrate, etc. — Where anything is required or authorized to be done by or before a judge, magistrate, justice of the peace, or any functionary or officer, it shall be done by or before one whose jurisdiction or powers extend to the place where the thing is to be done.

(2) Ancillary powers — Where power is given to a person, officer or functionary, to do or enforce the doing of any act or thing, all such powers as are necessary to enable the person, officer or functionary to do or enforce the doing of the act or thing are deemed to be also given.

(3) Powers to be exercised as required — Where a power is conferred or a duty imposed, the power may be exercised and the duty shall be performed from time to time as occasion requires.

(4) Power to repeal — Where a power is conferred to make regulations, the power shall be construed as including a power, exercisable in the same manner and subject to the same consent and conditions, if any, to repeal, amend or vary the regulations and make others.

32. Forms — Where a form is prescribed, deviations from that form, not affecting the substance or calculated to mislead, do not invalidate the form used.

Notes: "S. 32 is concerned with variations in the form itself and not with its content.... as long as the required information is provided, the fact that the form used differs from the one prescribed does not affect its validity. In the present case, the form used by the Appellant is the one prescribed, without any deviations. S. 32 does not apply": *Robertson*, [1996] 2 C.T.C. 2269 (TCC). Based on s. 32, a proof of claim in bankruptcy need not be on a prescribed form to establish a director's liability: VIEWS doc 2009-0311441I7.

S. 32 applied in *Mitchell*, 2002 FCA 407: a letter saying the taxpayers "will not object to ... reassessment, regardless of whether it is before or after the statute-bar period" was held to be an ITA 152(4)(a)(ii) "waiver in prescribed form".

S. 32 did not apply in *Easy Way Cattle*, 2016 FCA 301, or *AFD Petroleum*, 2016 FC 547 (FCA appeal discontinued A-215-16), para. 25, where SR&ED claims were missing information on Form T661 or T2 Schedule 31, required by ITA 37(11). Having provided the information on another form or in another year's claim was not enough.

33. (1) Gender — Words importing female persons include male persons and corporations and words importing male persons include female persons and corporations.

(2) Number — Words in the singular include the plural, and words in the plural include the singular.

Notes: Since the singular extends to include the plural, a reference to records of "a lawyer" applied to records of a law firm: *Heath*, 1989 CarswellBC 683 (BCSC), paras. 57-61.

The phrase "child support amount" in ITA 56.1(4) includes an award of support for two children, due to 33(2): *Whelan*, 2006 FCA 384.

In *Abdalla*, 2011 TCC 329, 33(2) allowed two foreign university courses totalling 16 consecutive weeks to meet the ITA 118.5(1)(b) requirement that a "course" be at least 13 consecutive weeks, to qualify for the tuition credit.

Due to 33(2), the words "all the beneficiaries of which" in ITA 149(1)(o.2)(iv)(B), (C) are satisfied by a trust with only one beneficiary: VIEWS doc 2015-0582901E5.

For an example of CRA stating that 33(2) does not apply because a contrary intention appears in the ITA (*Interpretation Act* s. 3(1)), see VIEWS doc 2004-0065441C6. In *Sheldon Inwentash and Lynn Factor Charitable Foundation*, 2012 FCA 136, the requirement in ITA 149.1(1)"public foundation" that more than 50% of the directors or trustees deal with each other at arm's length was a "contrary intention", so a public foundation cannot have only one trustee.

(3) Parts of speech and grammatical forms — Where a word is defined, other parts of speech and grammatical forms of the same word have corresponding meanings.

Notes: In *Qit-Fer*, [1996] 2 C.T.C. 30 (FCA), "manufactured and processed" was held to have the meaning given by the ITA to "manufacturing and processing", "the gerund forms of the same verbs".

Offences

34. (1) Indictable and summary conviction offences — Where an enactment creates an offence,

    (a) the offence is deemed to be an indictable offence if the enactment provides that the offender may be prosecuted for the offence by indictment;

    (b) the offence is deemed to be one for which the offender is punishable on summary conviction if there is nothing in the context to indicate that the offence is an indictable offence; and

    (c) if the offence is one for which the offender may be prosecuted by indictment or for which the offender is punishable on summary conviction, no person shall be considered to have been convicted of an indictable offence by reason only of having been convicted of the offence on summary conviction.

(2) *Criminal Code* to apply — All the provisions of the *Criminal Code* relating to indictable offences apply to indictable offences created by an enactment, and all the provisions of that Code relating to summary conviction offences apply to all other offences created by an enactment, except to the extent that the enactment otherwise provides.

Notes: For an example of this rule applying in considering whether an accused should be imprisoned in default of payment of a fine, see *Diamond*, 2004 ABPC 156.

In *Nagel*, 2008 SKPC 117; aff'd 2009 SKQB 502; aff'd 2010 SKCA 118, this rule was used as authority for the Provincial Court to hear a summary-conviction prosecution for GST evasion.

(3) Documents similarly construed — In a commission, proclamation, warrant or other document relating to criminal law or procedure in criminal matters

    (a) a reference to an offence for which the offender may be prosecuted by indictment shall be construed as a reference to an indictable offence; and

    (b) a reference to any other offence shall be construed as a reference to an offence for which the offender is punishable on summary conviction.

Powers to Enter Dwelling-houses to Carry out Arrests

34.1 Authorization to enter dwelling house — Any person who may issue a warrant to arrest or apprehend a person under any Act of Parliament, other than the *Criminal Code*, has the same powers, subject to the same terms and conditions, as a judge or justice has under the *Criminal Code*

    (a) to authorize the entry into a dwelling-house described in the warrant for the purpose of arresting or apprehending the person, if the person issuing the warrant is satisfied by information on oath that there are reasonable grounds to believe that the person is or will be present in the dwelling-house; and

    (b) to authorize the entry into the dwelling-house without prior announcement if the requirement of subsection 529.4(1) is met.

Definitions

35. (1) General definitions — In every enactment,

"Act", in respect of an Act of a legislature, includes a law of the Legislature of Yukon, of the Northwest Territories or for Nunavut;

Notes: 35(1)"Act" amended by *Northwest Territories Devolution Act* (2014, c. 2), effective April 2014 (per P.C. 2014-305), to change from "an ordinance of the Northwest Territories" so it is "a law" as for the other territories. Earlier amended by 2002, c. 7, effective April 2003 (P.C. 2003-394), and by 1993, c. 28, to add reference to Nunavut effective April 1999.

"bank" means a bank listed in Schedule I or II to the *Bank Act*;

Notes: "Bank" added by 1999, c. 28, s. 168, in force June 28, 1999.

"British Commonwealth" or **"British Commonwealth of Nations"** has the same meaning as "Commonwealth";

"broadcasting" means any radiocommunication in which the transmissions are intended for direct reception by the general public;

Notes: CRA says streamed movies are "broadcast" despite this definition, so payments to a non-resident are subject to withholding tax: VIEWS doc 2017-0715561E5.

"Canada", for greater certainty, includes the internal waters of Canada and the territorial sea of Canada;

Notes: "Canada" added by *Oceans Act* (S.C. 1996, c. 31), proclaimed in force January 31, 1997 (SI/97-21).

"Canadian waters" includes the territorial sea of Canada and the internal waters of Canada;

Notes: "Canadian waters" added by *Oceans Act* (1996, c. 31), proclaimed in force January 31, 1997 (SI/97-21).

"Clerk of the Privy Council" or **"Clerk of the Queen's Privy Council"** means the Clerk of the Privy Council and Secretary to the Cabinet;

"commencement", when used with reference to an enactment, means the time at which the enactment comes into force;

"Commonwealth" or **"Commonwealth of Nations"** means the association of countries named in the schedule;

"Commonwealth and Dependent Territories" means the several Commonwealth countries and their colonies, possessions, dependencies, protectorates, protected states, condominiums and trust territories;

"contiguous zone",

(a) in relation to Canada, means the contiguous zone of Canada as determined under the *Oceans Act*,

(b) in relation to any other state, means the contiguous zone of the other state as determined in accordance with international law and the domestic laws of that other state;

Notes: "Contiguous zone" added by *Oceans Act* (1996, c. 31), proclaimed in force January 31, 1997 (SI/97-21).

"continental shelf",

(a) in relation to Canada, means the continental shelf of Canada as determined under the *Oceans Act*, and

(b) in relation to any other state, means the continental shelf of the other state as determined in accordance with international law and the domestic laws of that other state;

Notes: "Continental shelf" added by *Oceans Act* (S.C. 1996, c. 31), proclaimed in force January 31, 1997 (SI/97-21).

"contravene" includes fail to comply with;

"corporation" does not include a partnership that is considered to be a separate legal entity under provincial law;

"county" includes two or more counties united for purposes to which the enactment relates;

"diplomatic or consular officer" includes an ambassador, envoy, minister, chargé d'affaires, counsellor, secretary, attaché, consul-general, consul, vice-consul, pro-consul, consular agent, acting consul-general, acting consul, acting vice-consul, acting consular agent, high commissioner, permanent delegate, adviser, acting high commissioner, and acting permanent delegate;

"exclusive economic zone",

(a) in relation to Canada, means the exclusive economic zone of Canada as determined under the *Oceans Act* and includes the seabed and subsoil below that zone, and

(b) in relation to any other state, means the exclusive economic zone of the other state as determined in accordance with international law and the domestic laws of that other state;

Related Provisions: ITA 37(1.3) — SR&ED performed in exclusive economic zone deemed done in Canada.

Notes: See Notes to ITA 37(1.3) for the *Oceans Act* definition (200 nautical miles offshore). "Exclusive economic zone" added by *Oceans Act* (1996, c. 31), proclaimed in force January 31, 1997 (SI/97-21).

"Federal Court" — [Repealed]

Notes: Definition "Federal Court" repealed by 2002 courts administration bill, effective July 2, 2003. It defined "Federal Court" as the Federal Court of Canada. Under the new *Federal Courts Act*, the former Federal Court–Trial Division is now the "Federal Court", and there is no longer a "Federal Court of Canada".

"Federal Court–Appeal Division" or **"Federal Court of Appeal"** — [Repealed]

Notes: Definition repealed by 2002 courts administration bill, effective July 2, 2003. Under the *Federal Courts Act*, the Federal Court of Appeal is now a separate court rather than a division of the Federal Court of Canada, which no longer exists under that name.

"Federal Court–Trial Division" — [Repealed]

Notes: Definition repealed by 2002 courts administration bill, effective July 2, 2003 (see Notes to "Federal Court" above).

"Governor", **"Governor General"**, or **"Governor of Canada"** means the Governor General of Canada or other chief executive officer or administrator carrying on the Government of Canada on behalf and in the name of the Sovereign, by whatever title that officer is designated;

"Governor General in Council" or **"Governor in Council"** means the Governor General of Canada acting by and with the advice of, or by and with the advice and consent of, or in conjunction with the Queen's Privy Council for Canada;

Notes: This means the federal Cabinet.

"Great Seal" means the Great Seal of Canada;

"Her Majesty", **"His Majesty"**, **"the Queen"**, **"the King"** or **"the Crown"** means the Sovereign of the United Kingdom, Canada and Her or His other Realms and Territories, and Head of the Commonwealth;

Notes: Definition amended to change "Her other Realms" to "Her or His other Realms" by S.C. 2015, c. 3, effective Feb. 26, 2015.

"Her Majesty's Realms and Territories" or **"His Majesty's Realms and Territories"** means all realms and territories under the sovereignty of Her or His Majesty;

Notes: Definition amended to change "Her" to "Her or His" by S.C. 2015, c. 3, effective Feb. 26, 2015.

"herein" used in any section shall be understood to relate to the whole enactment, and not to that section only;

"holiday" means any of the following days, namely, Sunday; New Year's Day; Good Friday; Easter Monday; Christmas Day; the birthday or the day fixed by proclamation for the celebration of the birthday of the reigning Sovereign[1]; Victoria Day; Canada Day; the first Monday in September, designated Labour Day; Remembrance Day; any day appointed by proclamation to be observed as a day of general prayer or mourning or day of public rejoicing or thanksgiving[2]; and any of the following additional days, namely:

> ### Enacted Amendment — 35(1)"holiday" opening words — National Day for Truth and Reconciliation (Sept. 30)
>
> **Application**: S.C. 2021, c. 11 (Bill C-5, Royal Assent June 3, 2021), s. 3, has amended the opening words of the definition "holiday" in subsec. 35(1) to change "Labour Day" to "Labour Day; National Day for Truth and Reconciliation, which is observed on September 30", in force on Aug. 3, 2021.
>
> **Notes**: Bill C-5 s. 1 states: "The purpose of this Act is to respond to the Truth and Reconciliation Commission of Canada's call to action number 80 by creating a holiday called the National Day for Truth and Reconciliation, which seeks to honour First Nations, Inuit and Métis Survivors and their families and communities and to ensure that public commemoration of their history and the legacy of residential schools remains a vital component of the reconciliation process."
>
> The same proposal was passed by the House of Commons as Private Member's Bill C-369 and received First Reading in the Senate on April 2, 2019, but expired because it had not been enacted when Parliament was prorogued for the 2019 election.

(a) in any province, any day appointed by proclamation of the lieutenant governor of the province to be observed as a public holiday or as a day of general prayer or mourning or day of pub-

---

[1] The Monday immediately preceding May 25 (SOR/57-55, *Canada Gazette*, Part II, February 27, 1957).

[2] The second Monday in October (SOR/57-56, *Canada Gazette*, Part II, February 27, 1957).

lic rejoicing or thanksgiving within the province, and any day that is a non-juridical day by virtue of an Act of the legislature of the province, and

(b) in any city, town, municipality or other organized district, any day appointed to be observed as a civic holiday by resolution of the council or other authority charged with the administration of the civic or municipal affairs of the city, town, municipality or district;

Notes: "Holiday" includes Saturday in all provinces except B.C. See Notes to s. 26.

CRA does not have a list of municipal holidays, and there is a question as to which municipality's or province's holidays should apply for purposes of s. 26 (taxpayer's residence? business? tax services office? bank?). See VIEWS doc 2011-0394691I7.

National Day for Truth and Reconciliation added by S.C. 2021, c. 11, effective Aug. 3, 2021. S. 1 of the bill says this holiday "seeks to honour First Nations, Inuit and Métis Survivors and their families and communities and to ensure that public commemoration of their history and the legacy of residential schools remains a vital component of the reconciliation process."

"internal waters",

(a) in relation to Canada, means the internal waters of Canada as determined under the *Oceans Act* and includes the airspace above and the bed and subsoil below those waters, and

(b) in relation to any other state, means the waters on the landward side of the baselines of the territorial sea of the other state;

Notes: "Internal waters" added by *Oceans Act* (Bill C-26, 1996, c. 31), proclaimed in force January 31, 1997 (SI/97-21).

"legislative assembly", "legislative council" or "legislature" — [Repealed]

Notes: Definition amended by *Northwest Territories Devolution Act* (2014, c. 2), effective April 2014 (per P.C. 2014-305), now that NWT has a legislature like the other territories.

Earlier amended by 2002, c. 7, effective April 2003 (per P.C. 2003-394), and by 1993, c. 28, to add reference to Nunavut effective April 1999.

"legislative assembly" or "legislature" includes the Lieutenant Governor in Council and the Legislative Assembly of the Northwest Territories, as constituted before September 1, 1905, and the Legislature of Yukon, of the Northwest Territories or for Nunavut;

"lieutenant governor" means the lieutenant governor or other chief executive officer or administrator carrying on the government of the province indicated by the enactment, by whatever title that officer is designated, and in Yukon, the Northwest Territories and Nunavut means the Commissioner;

Notes: The definition "lieutenant governor" amended by 2002, c. 7, subsec. 188(1), proclaimed in force April 1, 2003 (P.C. 2003-394). Amended by 1993, c. 28, Sch. III, s. 82, to add reference to Nunavut, in force April 1, 1999.

"lieutenant governor in council" means

(a) the lieutenant governor of the province indicated by the enactment acting by and with the advice of, by and with the advice and consent of, or in conjunction with, the executive council,

(b) in Yukon, the Commissioner of Yukon acting with the consent of the Executive Council of Yukon,

(c) in the Northwest Territories, the Commissioner of the Northwest Territories acting with the consent of the Executive Council of the Northwest Territories, and

(d) in Nunavut, the Commissioner;

Notes: Definition amended by *Northwest Territories Devolution Act* (2014, c. 2), effective April 2014 (per P.C. 2014-305).

Earlier amended by 2002, c. 7, effective April 2003 (per P.C. 2003-394), and by 1993, c. 28, to add reference to Nunavut effective April 1999.

"local time", in relation to any place, means the time observed in that place for the regulation of business hours;

"military" shall be construed as relating to all or any part of the Canadian Forces;

"month" means a calendar month;

"oath" includes a solemn affirmation or declaration when the context applies to any person by whom and to any case in which a solemn affirmation or declaration may be made instead of an oath, and in the same cases the expression "sworn" includes the expression "affirmed" or "declared";

"Parliament" means the Parliament of Canada;

"person" or any word or expression descriptive of a person, includes a corporation;

"proclamation" means a proclamation under the Great Seal;

"province" means a province of Canada, and includes Yukon, the Northwest Territories and Nunavut;

Notes: Due to 33(3), this definition should apply to the word "provincial" as well.

The definition "province" amended by 2002, c. 7, subsec. 188(1), proclaimed in force April 1, 2003 (P.C. 2003-394). Amended by 1993, c. 28, Sch. III, s. 82, to add reference to Nunavut, in force April 1, 1999.

"radio" or "radiocommunication" means any transmission, emission or reception of signs, signals, writing, images, sounds or intelligence of any nature by means of electromagnetic waves of frequencies lower than 3000 GHz propagated in space without artificial guide;

"regular force" means the component of the Canadian Forces that is referred to in the *National Defence Act* as the regular force;

"reserve force" means the component of the Canadian Forces that is referred to in the *National Defence Act* as the reserve force;

"security" means sufficient security, and "sureties" means sufficient sureties, and when those words are used one person is sufficient therefor, unless otherwise expressly required;

"standard time", except as otherwise provided by any proclamation of the Governor in Council that may be issued for the purposes of this definition in relation to any province or territory or any part thereof, means

(a) in relation to the Province of Newfoundland and Labrador, Newfoundland standard time, being three hours and thirty minutes behind Greenwich time,

(b) in relation to the Provinces of Nova Scotia, New Brunswick and Prince Edward Island, that part of the Province of Quebec lying east of the sixty-third meridian of west longitude, and that part of Nunavut lying east of the sixty-eighth meridian of west longitude, Atlantic standard time, being four hours behind Greenwich time,

(c) in relation to that part of the Province of Quebec lying west of the sixty-third meridian of west longitude, that part of the Province of Ontario lying between the sixty-eighth and the ninetieth meridians of west longitude, Southampton Island and the islands adjacent to Southampton Island, and that part of Nunavut lying between the sixty-eighth and the eighty-fifth meridians of west longitude, eastern standard time, being five hours behind Greenwich time,

(d) in relation to that part of the Province of Ontario lying west of the ninetieth meridian of west longitude, the Province of Manitoba, and that part of Nunavut, except Southampton Island and the islands adjacent to Southampton Island, lying between the eighty-fifth and the one hundred and second meridians of west longitude, central standard time, being six hours behind Greenwich time,

(e) in relation to the Provinces of Saskatchewan and Alberta, the Northwest Territories and that part of Nunavut lying west of the one hundred and second meridian of west longitude, mountain standard time, being seven hours behind Greenwich time,

(f) in relation to the Province of British Columbia, Pacific standard time, being eight hours behind Greenwich time, and

(g) in relation to Yukon, Yukon standard time, being nine hours behind Greenwich time;

Notes: Para. (a) amended to change "Newfoundland" to "Newfoundland and Labrador" by S.C. 2015, c. 3, effective Feb. 26, 2015.

Para. (g) amended by 2002, c. 7, subsec. 188(2), proclaimed in force April 1, 2003 (P.C. 2003-394), to change "the Yukon Territory" to "Yukon".

Order in Council SOR/2001-182, May 23, 2001 (*Canada Gazette*, Part II, Vol. 135, No. 12, June 6, 2001) provides:

Whereas "standard time", in relation to any province or territory, has the meaning set out in subsection 35(1) of the *Interpretation Act*, except as otherwise provided by a proclamation of the Governor in Council;

And Whereas the Government of Nunavut has expressed the desire to change the definition of standard time in relation to Nunavut;

Now Know You that We, by and with the advice of Our Privy Council for Canada, and pursuant to Order in Council P.C. 2001-804 of May 2, 2001, do by this Our Proclamation provide that, for the purpose of the definition "standard time" in subsection 35(1) of the *Interpretation Act*, "standard time" means

(a) in relation to that part of Nunavut that is east of the 85th meridian of west longitude, and in Southampton Island and the islands adjacent to Southampton Island, Eastern Standard Time, being five hours behind Greenwich time;

(b) in relation to that part of Nunavut that is between the 85th meridian of west longitude and the 102nd meridian of west longitude, except Southampton Island and the islands adjacent to Southampton Island and all areas lying within the Kitikmeot Region, Central Standard Time, being six hours behind Greenwich time; and

(c) in relation to that part of Nunavut that is west of the 102nd meridian of west longitude, and all areas lying within the Kitikmeot Region, Mountain Standard Time, being seven hours behind Greenwich time.

Before this proclamation, Order in Council SOR/99-408, October 20, 1999 (*Canada Gazette*, Part II, Vol. 133, No. 23, November 10, 1999) provided that all of Nunavut was 6 hours behind Greenwich time.

Paragraphs (b) to (e) amended by 1993, c. 28, Sch. III, s. 82, to add references to Nunavut, in force April 1, 1999.

"statutory declaration" means a solemn declaration made pursuant to section 41 of the *Canada Evidence Act*;

"superior court" means

(a) in the Province of Newfoundland and Labrador, the Supreme Court,

(a.1) in the Province of Ontario, the Court of Appeal for Ontario and the Superior Court of Justice,

(b) in the Province of Quebec, the Court of Appeal and the Superior Court in and for the Province,

(c) in the Province of New Brunswick, Manitoba, Saskatchewan or Alberta, the Court of Appeal for the Province and the Court of Queen's Bench for the Province,

(d) in the Provinces of Nova Scotia, British Columbia and Prince Edward Island, the Court of Appeal and the Supreme Court of the Province, and

(e) the Supreme Court of Yukon, the Supreme Court of the Northwest Territories and the Nunavut Court of Justice,

and includes the Supreme Court of Canada, the Federal Court of Appeal, the Federal Court and the Tax Court of Canada;

Notes: PEI moved from para. (a) to (d), and (a) amended to change "Newfoundland" to "Newfoundland and Labrador", by S.C. 2015, c. 3, effective Feb. 26, 2015.

Closing words of 35(1)"superior court" amended by 2002 courts administration bill, effective July 2, 2003, to change "Federal Court of Canada" to "Federal Court of Appeal, the Federal Court".

Definition previously amended by S.C. 1999, c. 3 and 1993, c. 28.

"telecommunications" means the emission, transmission or reception of signs, signals, writing, images, sounds or intelligence of any nature by wire, cable, radio, optical or other electromagnetic system, or by any similar technical system;

"territorial sea",

(a) in relation to Canada, means the territorial sea of Canada as determined under the *Oceans Act* and includes the airspace above and the seabed and subsoil below that sea, and

(b) in relation to any other state, means the territorial sea of the other state as determined in accordance with international law and the domestic laws of that other state;

Notes: "Territorial sea" added by *Oceans Act* (Bill C-26, 1996, c. 31), proclaimed in force January 31, 1997 (SI/97-21).

"territory" means Yukon, the Northwest Territories and Nunavut;

Notes: The definition "territory" amended by 2002, c. 7, subsec. 188(1), proclaimed in force April 1, 2003 (P.C. 2003-394), to change "the Yukon Territory" to "Yukon".

"two justices" means two or more justices of the peace, assembled or acting together;

"United Kingdom" means the United Kingdom of Great Britain and Northern Ireland;

"United States" means the United States of America;

"writing", or any term of like import, includes words printed, typewritten, painted, engraved, lithographed, photographed or represented or reproduced by any mode of representing or reproducing words in visible form.

Notes: This definition applies to the word "written" as well. See subsec. 33(3).

(2) Governor in Council may amend schedule — The Governor in Council may, by order, amend the schedule by adding thereto the name of any country recognized by the order to be a member of the Commonwealth or deleting therefrom the name of any country recognized by the order to be no longer a member of the Commonwealth.

36. Construction of "telegraph" — The expression "telegraph" and its derivatives, in an enactment or in an Act of the legislature of any province enacted before that province became part of Canada on any subject that is within the legislative powers of Parliament, are deemed not to include the word "telephone" or its derivatives.

37. (1) Construction of "year" — The expression "year" means any period of twelve consecutive months, except that a reference

(a) to a "calendar year" means a period of twelve consecutive months commencing on January 1;

(b) to a "financial year" or "fiscal year" means, in relation to money provided by Parliament, or the Consolidated Revenue Fund, or the accounts, taxes or finances of Canada, the period beginning on April 1 in one calendar year and ending on March 31 in the next calendar year; and

(c) by number to a Dominical year means the period of twelve consecutive months commencing on January 1 of that Dominical year.

(2) Governor in Council may define year — Where in an enactment relating to the affairs of Parliament or the Government of Canada there is a reference to a period of a year without anything in the context to indicate beyond doubt whether a financial or fiscal year, any period of twelve consecutive months or a period of twelve consecutive months commencing on January 1 is intended, the Governor in Council may prescribe which of those periods of twelve consecutive months shall constitute a year for the purposes of the enactment.

38. Common names — The name commonly applied to any country, place, body, corporation, society, officer, functionary, person, party or thing means the country, place, body, corporation, society, officer, functionary, person, party or thing to which the name is commonly applied, although the name is not the formal or extended designation thereof.

39. (1) Affirmative and negative resolutions — In every Act

(a) the expression "subject to affirmative resolution of Parliament", when used in relation to any regulation, means that the regulation shall be laid before Parliament within fifteen days after it is made or, if Parliament is not then sitting, on any of the first fifteen days next thereafter that Parliament is sitting and shall not come into force unless and until it is affirmed by a resolution of both Houses of Parliament introduced and passed in accordance with the rules of those Houses;

(b) the expression "subject to affirmative resolution of the House of Commons", when used in relation to any regulation, means that the regulation shall be laid before the House of Commons within fifteen days after it is made or, if the House is not then sitting, on any of the first fifteen days next thereafter that the House is sitting and shall not come into force unless and until it is affirmed by a resolution of the House of Commons introduced and passed in accordance with the rules of that House;

(c) the expression "subject to negative resolution of Parliament", when used in relation to any regulation, means that the regulation shall be laid before Parliament within fifteen days after it is made or, if Parliament is not then sitting, on any of the first fifteen days next thereafter that Parliament is sitting and may be annulled by a resolution of both Houses of Parliament introduced and passed in accordance with the rules of those Houses; and

(d) the expression "subject to negative resolution of the House of Commons", when used in relation to any regulation, means that the regulation shall be laid before the House of Commons within fifteen days after it is made or, if the House is not then sitting, on any of the first fifteen days next thereafter that Parliament is sitting and may be annulled by a resolution of the House of Commons introduced and passed in accordance with the rules of that House.

(2) Effect of negative resolution — Where a regulation is annulled by a resolution of Parliament or of the House of Commons, it is deemed to have been revoked on the day the resolution is passed and any law that was revoked or amended by the making of that regulation is deemed to be revived on the day the resolution is passed, but the validity of any action taken or not taken in compliance with a regulation so deemed to have been revoked shall not be affected by the resolution.

References and Citations

40. (1) Citation of enactment — In an enactment or document

(a) an Act may be cited by reference to its chapter number in the Revised Statutes, by reference to its chapter number in the volume of Acts for the year or regnal year in which it was enacted or by reference to its long title or short title, with or without reference to its chapter number; and

(b) a regulation may be cited by reference to its long title or short title, by reference to the Act under which it was made or by reference to the number or designation under which it was registered by the Clerk of the Privy Council.

(2) Citation includes amendment — A citation of or reference to an enactment is deemed to be a citation of or reference to the enactment as amended.

41. (1) Reference to two or more parts, etc. — A reference in an enactment by number or letter to two or more parts, divisions, sections, subsections, paragraphs, subparagraphs, clauses, subclauses, schedules, appendices or forms shall be read as including the number or letter first mentioned and the number or letter last mentioned.

(2) Reference in enactments to parts, etc. — A reference in an enactment to a part, division, section, schedule, appendix or form shall be read as a reference to a part, division, section, schedule, appendix or form of the enactment in which the reference occurs.

(3) Reference in enactment to subsections, etc. — A reference in an enactment to a subsection, paragraph, subparagraph, clause or subclause shall be read as a reference to a subsection, paragraph, subparagraph, clause or subclause of the section, subsection, paragraph, subparagraph or clause, as the case may be, in which the reference occurs.

(4) Reference to regulations — A reference in an enactment to regulations shall be read as a reference to regulations made under the enactment in which the reference occurs.

(5) Reference to another enactment — A reference in an enactment by number or letter to any section, subsection, paragraph, subparagraph, clause, subclause or other division or line of another enactment shall be read as a reference to the section, subsection, paragraph, subparagraph, clause, subclause or other division or line of such other enactment as printed by authority of law.

Repeal and Amendment

42. (1) Power of repeal or amendment reserved — Every Act shall be so construed as to reserve to Parliament the power of repealing or amending it, and of revoking, restricting or modifying any power, privilege or advantage thereby vested in or granted to any person.

(2) Amendment or repeal at same session — An Act may be amended or repealed by an Act passed in the same session of Parliament.

(3) Amendment part of enactment — An amending enactment, as far as consistent with the tenor thereof, shall be construed as part of the enactment that it amends.

Notes: For an example of amending legislation relying on 42(3) so that terms it uses are those terms as defined in the ITA, consider every amendment that takes effect for the "2017 and later taxation years". Under ITA 249(1.1), this means a taxation year ending in 2017.

In *Fedak*, [1999] G.S.T.C. 65 (TCC), a GST amendment applied to supplies "made after" a given date. This phrase was interpreted based on *Excise Tax Act* s. 133, which determines when a supply is "made", though the Court did not cite 42(3).

43. Effect of repeal — Where an enactment is repealed in whole or in part, the repeal does not

(a) revive any enactment or anything not in force or existing at the time when the repeal takes effect,

(b) affect the previous operation of the enactment so repealed or anything duly done or suffered thereunder,

(c) affect any right, privilege, obligation or liability acquired, accrued, accruing or incurred under the enactment so repealed,

(d) affect any offence committed against or contravention of the provisions of the enactment so repealed, or any punishment, penalty or forfeiture incurred under the enactment so repealed, or

(e) affect any investigation, legal proceeding or remedy in respect of any right, privilege, obligation or liability referred to in paragraph (c) or in respect of any punishment, penalty or forfeiture referred to in paragraph (d),

and an investigation, legal proceeding or remedy as described in paragraph (e) may be instituted, continued or enforced, and the punishment, penalty or forfeiture may be imposed as if the enactment had not been so repealed.

Notes: S. 43 applies only to a repeal, not to the typical ITA repeal-and-replacement, to which s. 44 applies instead: *Agazarian*, [2003] 1 C.T.C. 2323 (TCC) (rev'd on other grounds 2004 FCA 32, leave to appeal denied 2004 CarswellNat 4638 (SCC)). See also *742190 Ontario [Van Del Manor]*, 2009 FC 985 (rev'd on other grounds 2010 FCA 162), re objection rights "acquired" before an amendment.

44. Repeal and substitution — Where an enactment, in this section called the "former enactment", is repealed and another enactment, in this section called the "new enactment", is substituted therefor,

(a) every person acting under the former enactment shall continue to act, as if appointed under the new enactment, until another is appointed in the stead of that person;

(b) every bond and security given by a person appointed under the former enactment remains in force, and all books, papers, forms and things made or used under the former enactment shall continue to be used as before the repeal in so far as they are consistent with the new enactment;

(c) every proceeding taken under the former enactment shall be taken up and continued under and in conformity with the new enactment in so far as it may be done consistently with the new enactment;

(d) the procedure established by the new enactment shall be followed as far as it can be adapted thereto

(i) in the recovery or enforcement of fines, penalties and forfeitures imposed under the former enactment,

(ii) in the enforcement of rights, existing or accruing under the former enactment, and

(iii) in a proceeding in relation to matters that have happened before the repeal;

(e) when any punishment, penalty or forfeiture is reduced or mitigated by the new enactment, the punishment, penalty or forfeiture if imposed or adjudged after the repeal shall be reduced or mitigated accordingly;

(f) except to the extent that the provisions of the new enactment are not in substance the same as those of the former enactment, the new enactment shall not be held to operate as new law, but shall be construed and have effect as a consolidation and as declaratory of the law as contained in the former enactment;

(g) all regulations made under the repealed enactment remain in force and are deemed to have been made under the new enactment, in so far as they are not inconsistent with the new enactment, until they are repealed or others made in their stead; and

(h) any reference in an unrepealed enactment to the former enactment shall, with respect to a subsequent transaction, matter or thing, be read and construed as a reference to the provisions of the new enactment relating to the same subject-matter as the former enactment, but where there are no provisions in the new enactment relating to the same subject-matter, the former enactment shall be read as unrepealed in so far as is necessary to maintain or give effect to the unrepealed enactment.

Notes: See Notes to s. 43.

45. (1) Repeal does not imply enactment was in force — The repeal of an enactment in whole or in part shall not be deemed to be or to involve a declaration that the enactment was previously in force or was considered by Parliament or other body or person by whom the enactment was enacted to have been previously in force.

(2) Amendment does not imply change in law — The amendment of an enactment shall not be deemed to be or to involve a declaration that the law under that enactment was or was considered by Parliament or other body or person by whom the enactment was enacted to have been different from the law as it is under the enactment as amended.

Notes: This does not mean that amendments do not change the law, but only that there is no presumption that they must change the law: *HSC Research*, [1995] 1 C.T.C. 2283 (TCC), paras. 31-37; *Silicon Graphics*, 2002 FCA 260, para. 43.

(3) Repeal does not declare previous law — The repeal or amendment of an enactment in whole or in part shall not be deemed to be or to involve any declaration as to the previous state of the law.

(4) Judicial construction not adopted — A re-enactment, revision, consolidation or amendment of an enactment shall not be deemed to be or to involve an adoption of the construction that has by judicial decision or otherwise been placed on the language used in the enactment or on similar language.

Demise of Crown

46. (1) Effect of demise — Where there is a demise of the Crown,

(a) the demise does not affect the holding of any office under the Crown in right of Canada; and

(b) it is not necessary by reason of such demise that the holder of any such office again be appointed thereto or, having taken an oath of office or allegiance before the demise, again take that oath.

(2) Continuation of proceedings — No writ, action or other process or proceeding, civil or criminal, in or issuing out of any court established by an Act is, by reason of a demise of the Crown, determined, abated, discontinued or affected, but every such writ, action, process or proceeding remains in full force and may be enforced, carried on or otherwise proceeded with or completed as though there had been no such demise.

SCHEDULE
(section 35 "Commonwealth")

Antigua and Barbuda	Australia
The Bahamas	Bangladesh
Barbados	Belize
Botswana	Brunei Darussalam
Canada	Cyprus
Dominica	Fiji
Gambia	Ghana
Grenada	Guyana
India	Jamaica
Kenya	Kiribati
Lesotho	Malawi
Malaysia	Maldives
Malta	Mauritius
Nauru	New Zealand
Nigeria	Pakistan
Papua New Guinea	St. Christopher and Nevis
St. Lucia	St. Vincent and the Grenadines
Seychelles	Sierra Leone
Singapore	Solomon Islands
South Africa	Sri Lanka
Swaziland	Tanzania
Tonga	Trinidad and Tobago
Tuvalu	Uganda
United Kingdom	Vanuatu
Western Samoa	Zambia
Zimbabwe	

Note: References are to sections of the *Income Tax Act*. "Reg." references are to the *Income Tax Regulations*. "Reg. Sch. II:Cl." are references to the capital cost allowance Classes in Schedule II of the *Income Tax Regulations*, reproduced at the end of the Regulations. "ITAR" references are to the *Income Tax Application Rules*, reproduced after the text of the *Income Tax Act*.

Alberta Stock Exchange
- prescribed stock exchange, Reg. 3200(a) [repealed]

Alcatel **case overruled**, 143.3

Alex Parallel Computers **case overruled**, 220(2.2)

Algoa Trust **case overruled**, 160(1) closing words, 160(1.1) closing words

Alimony, *see* Support payments (spousal or child)

All or substantially all
- not defined (CRA treats it as meaning "90% or more")

Allied war veterans
- death or disability pension exempt, 81(1)(e)

Allocable amount (for preferred beneficiary election)
- defined, 104(15)
- election to include in beneficiary's income, 104(14)

Allocation, *see also* Apportionment
- allocation in proportion to patronage, *see* Patronage
- borrowing, in proportion to, *see also* Borrowing
- by Minister, where associated corporations do not file agreement
- • base level deduction, for soft costs on land, 18(2.4)
- • dividend allowance, for Part VI.1 tax, 191.1(5)
- • expenditure limit, for investment tax credit, 127(10.4)
- coal mine depletion allowance, 65(3)
- consideration, where combined transfer of property, 13(33), 68
- credits between spouses, *see* Splitting, sharing or apportionment
- foreign tax credit, by trust to beneficiary, 104(22)–(22.4)
- income of trust, to beneficiaries
- • capital gains, 104(21)–(21.7)
- • dividends, 104(19), (20)
- • preferred beneficiary election, 104(13)
- liability for debt obligation, 80(2)(o)
- partnership income among partners, 103
- patronage, in proportion to, *see* Patronage
- proceeds
- • between land and building, 13(21.1), 70(5)(d)
- • between property and services, 68

Allowable business investment loss, *see also* Business investment loss
- capital gains exemption, interaction with, 39(9), 110.6(1)"annual gains limit"B(b), 110.6(1)"cumulative gains limit"(b)
- carryforward, 111(1)(a), 111(8)"non-capital loss"
- • reduction on debt forgiveness, 80(4)(a)
- deduction, 3(d)
- defined, 38(c)
- partnership, of, 96(1.7)

Allowable capital loss, *see* Capital loss

Allowable disposition
- defined, for agricultural cooperatives, 135.1(1)

Allowable refund
- defined
- • for tax on registered plans, 207.01(1)

Allowance
- capital cost, *see* Capital cost allowance
- clergyman's, not taxable, 6(1)(b)(vi)
- defined
- • capital cost, 20(1)(a), Reg. 1100, *see also* Capital cost allowance
- • for alimony, maintenance, child support, 56(12)
- • for employee benefits, reasonable, 6(1)(b)(x), (xi)
- • retiring, 248(1), *see also* Retiring allowance
- depletion, *see* Depletion allowances
- depreciable property, *see* Capital cost allowance
- disabled employee: transportation and attendant, 6(16)
- employee, 6(1)(b)
- • child's schooling, 6(1)(b)(ix)

- exempt, 81(1)(d)
- family, *see* Canada Child Benefit
- inventory, repealed [was 20(1)(gg)]
- investment in property in Canada, 219(1)(j), Reg. 808
- Member of Legislative Assembly, 81(2)
- members of Canadian Forces, 6(1)(b)(ii)
- mines, Reg. Part XII
- motor vehicle, employee's, 6(1)(b)(vii.1)
- • where deemed not reasonable, 6(1)(b)(x), (xi)
- municipal officer's, 81(3)
- not income, 6(1)(b)(i)–(ix)
- oil or gas wells, Reg. Part XII
- parking, for disabled employee, not income, 6(16)
- received, as income, 6(1)(b)
- representation, not income, 6(1)(b)(iii), (iv)
- resource [repealed], 20(1)(v.1)
- resource and processing, Reg. Part XII
- retiring, *see* Retiring allowance
- support payments, defined with respect to, 56(12)
- transportation
- • disabled employee, 6(16)
- • remote work site, 6(6)(b)
- travelling, not income, 6(1)(b)(i), (ii), (v)–(vii)
- volunteer firefighters and emergency workers
- • not income, 81(4)

Alter ego trust
- deduction from income, 104(6)(b)B(i)
- defined, 104(4)(a)(iv)(A), 248(1)
- distribution of property to person other than taxpayer, 107(4)(a)(ii)
- preferred beneficiary election by, 104(15)(a)
- principal residence exemption, 54"principal residence"(c.1)(iii.1)(A)
- transfer by, to another trust, 104(5.8)
- transfer to, rollover, 73(1.01)(c)(ii)

Alterations to driveway
- medical expense credit, 118.2(2)(l.6)

Altered auditory feedback device
- medical expense credit, Reg. 5700(z.1)

Alternative basis for assessment
- Minister allowed to raise, 152(9)

Alternative Minimum Tax, *see* Minimum tax

Amalgamation, 87, *see also* Merger
- accrual rules, 87(2)(j.4)
- affiliated corporations, 251.1(2)
- agricultural cooperative corporation, 87(2)(s)
- associated corporations, 256(7)(b)
- balance-due day, 87(2)(oo.1)
- balance of tax for year, when due, 87(2)(oo.1)
- Canadian film or video tax credit, 87(2)(j.94)
- Canadian resource property, 66.7(10)(j), 66.7(10.1)
- capital dividend account, 87(2)(z.1)
- capital dividends, 87(2)(x)(ii)
- capital property, 53(6), 87(2)(e)
- carryback of losses, 87(2.11)
- charitable gifts, 87(2)(v)
- computation of income, 87(2)(c)
- continuation of predecessors, 87(2)(g.1), (j.6)–(j.95), (qq)
- • butterfly reorganizations, 55(3.2)(b)
- contributed surplus, 87(2)(y)
- corporation beneficiary under life insurance policy, 89(2)
- corporations deemed related, 251(3.1), (3.2)
- credit unions in Quebec, 87(2.3)
- cross-border, 128.2
- cumulative eligible capital, 87(2)(f) [before 2017]
- cumulative offset account, computation, 87(2)(pp)
- debt obligation acquired, 87(2)(e.2)
- debts

Anti-avoidance rules *(cont'd)*
- life insurer using foreign branch to insure Canadian risks, 138(2.1)–(2.6)
- loan from corporation, 15(2)–(2.6), 90(6)–(15)
- loan not at arm's length, 56(4.1)–(4.3)
- loan to non-resident, 17
- • through partnership, 17(4)
- • through trust, 17(5)
- look-through for trusts and partnerships, on non-arm's length sale of shares, 212.1(7)
- loss carryover rules, on change of corporate control, 111(5.5)(b)
- losses imported by partnership by acquiring Canadian partner, 96(8), (9)
- misuse of the Act, 245(4)
- mutual fund trust election for December 15 year-end, where beneficiaries change, 132.11(8)
- newspaper or periodical, control by non-resident, 19(8)
- non-resident trust, indirect transfer to, 94(2)
- non-resident trust transfer to another trust, 94(11)–(13)
- offshore trusts, 94
- 150-investor rule for non-resident trusts, 94(15)(a)
- partnership acquiring capital properties to avoid debt forgiveness rules, 80(18)
- partnership, by, 103
- partnership capital contribution where other partner withdraws funds, 40(3.13)
- partnership interest disposition, 100(1.4), (1.5)
- partnership with non-resident partners importing losses, 96(8), (9)
- payment of capital dividend through trust to non-resident, 212(1)(c)(i)
- penalties, *see* Penalty
- pension adjustment, artificial reduction of, Reg. 8503(14)
- pension, past service employer contributions in lieu of salary, Reg. 8503(15)
- pregnant losses, *see* Pregnant loss
- private foundations, 149.2(2), 188.1(3.2)–(3.5)
- purchase butterfly, 55(1)"permitted exchange", (3.1), (3.2)
- registered disability savings plan (RDSP)
- • advantage, prohibited investment or non-qualified investment, 207.01–207.07
- registered education savings plan (RESP)
- • advantage, prohibited investment or non-qualified investment, 207.01–207.07
- • replacement of beneficiary, 204.9(4)
- registered pension plan phased retirement rules, Reg. 8503(22)
- registered pension plan, replacement of money purchase benefits, Reg. 8304(2)(f)
- reportable transaction rules, 237.3
- residence of corporation, 250(5)
- retirement compensation arrangement
- • disposition for less than fair market value, 56(11)
- "right to reduce" an expenditure, 143.4
- royalty reimbursements, 80.2
- SIFT rollovers, 248(1)"SIFT trust wind-up event"(e)
- sale of shares by non-resident, 212.1
- sale of shares for dividend stripping, 84.1
- securities lending arrangement, 260(1)"securities lending arrangement" closing words
- selling property and donating proceeds to charity, 248(39)
- share acquired to obtain dividend refund, 129(1.2)
- share repurchase transaction, 112(5.2)B(a)
- small business deduction limit, 125(9)
- • corporate partners, 34.2, 125(6), 125(7)"specified partnership income"
- small business investment rollover, 44.1(12)
- specified member of partnership, 40(3.131), 127.52(2.1)
- stapled securities, 12.6
- stop-loss rules, *see* Stop-loss rules

- straddle transactions, 18(17)–(23)
- surplus stripping, *see* Surplus stripping
- synthetic equity arrangements, 112(2.3)–(2.34)
- TFSA, 207.01–207.07
- testamentary trust, 108(1)"testamentary trust"(d)
- transfer of insurance business by non-resident insurer, 138(11.7)
- transfer of property between trusts to delay deemed disposition rules, 104(5.8)
- transfer of property by tax debtor, 160
- transfer of property for low or no consideration, 69(1)(b), 74.1, 160(1)
- transfer of property with pregnant loss, 13(21.2), 40(3.3), (3.4)
- transfer pricing, 247
- treaty shopping, Canada-U.S. Tax Treaty:Art. XXIX-A
- trust distributing assets before death, 104(4)(a.2)
- trust, excessive capital interest, 104(7.1), (7.2)
- trust receiving assets before emigration, 104(4)(a.3)
- trust with accrued loss, acquisition of interest in, 107(6)
- trusts, allocation of income and capital to different beneficiaries, 104(7.1), (7.2)
- underlying foreign tax, Reg. 5907(1.03)
- unreasonable consideration, 247
- withholding tax on dividends, Canada–U.K. Tax Treaty Art. 10:7
- withholding tax on interest, Canada–U.K. Tax Treaty Art. 11:11
- withholding tax on royalties, Canada–U.K. Tax Treaty Art. 12:8

Anti-dumping duties or countervailing duties
- deductible, 20(1)(vv)
- included in UCC of depreciable property, 13(21)"undepreciated capital cost"D.1
- refund of
- • deducted from UCC of depreciable property, 13(21)"undepreciated capital cost"K
- • taxable, 12(1)(z.6)

Anti-money laundering and know your customer procedures
- defined, for Common Reporting Standard, 270(1)

Antiques, CCA disallowed, Reg. 1102(1)(e)

***Antoine Guertin Ltée* case overruled**, 20(1)(e.2)

Appeal, *see also* Tax Court of Canada
- bifurcation, 171(2)
- books and records, 230(6)
- disposal of
- • Minister's duty after, 164(4.1)
- • reassessment, on consent, 169(3)
- • Tax Court, by, 171
- ecological property valuation, 169(1.1)
- expense of making, deduction, 60(o)
- extension of time for making, 167
- Federal Court of Appeal, to, *see* Federal Court of Appeal
- frivolous, 10% penalty, 179.1
- general procedure, 175
- grounds for, whether raised in Notice of Objection, 169(2.1)
- *in camera* proceedings in Federal Court, 179
- informal procedure, 170
- large corporation by, only on grounds raised in objection, 169(2.1)
- legal costs of, 152(1.2)
- limitation on grounds for filing, 169(2), (2.1)
- Minister may change grounds for assessment, 152(9)
- notice of, Tax Court to Commissioner, 170(1)
- Part IV.1 tax, 187.6
- Part VI.1 tax, 191.4(2)
- Part XII.2 tax, 210.2(7)
- Part XII.3 tax, 211.5
- Part XII.4 tax, 211.6(5)
- Part XII.5 tax, 211.82

Index

Index

Canadian oil and gas property expense *(cont'd)*
- successor corporation, rules, 66.7(5)
- • application, 66.6(2)
- unitized oil or gas field, 66(12.5)

Canadian option interest note
- prepaid interest not deductible, 18(9.2)–(9.8)

Canadian outstanding premiums
- defined, Reg. 2400(1)

Canadian Pacific Ltd. case overruled, 20.3

Canadian partnership, *see also* **Canadian resident partnership**
- defined, 102(1), 248(1)
- eligible, defined, 80(1)

Canadian premiums
- defined, Reg. 8600

Canadian property, *see also* Foreign property
- mutual fund investment, *see* Canadian property mutual fund investment
- taxable, *see* Taxable Canadian property

Canadian property mutual fund investment
- defined, 218.3(1)

Canadian property mutual fund loss
- defined, 218.3(1)

Canadian Radio-television and Telecommunications Commission
- disclosure of information to, 241(4)(d)(xvi)

Canadian real, immovable or resource property
- defined, 248(1)

Canadian renewable and conservation expense
- capital cost allowance disallowed, Reg. 1102(1)(a.1)
- defined, 66.1(6), Reg. 1219
- included in CEE, 66.1(6)"Canadian exploration expense"(g.1)

Canadian reserve liabilities
- of financial institution, defined, 181(2), 190(1)
- of insurer, Reg. 2400(1)
- • Large Corporations Tax, Reg. 8600

Canadian resident partnership, *see also* **Canadian partnership**
- defined, 248(1)
- taxation year of, 249(1)(a)

Canadian resource expenses
- reduction of, on change of control, 66.7(12)

Canadian resource profits
- defined, Reg. 5202

Canadian resource property
- acquisition from exempt person, 66.6
- amalgamation — partnership property, 66.7(10)(j), 66.7(10.1)
- amount designated re
- • "outlay" or "expense", 66(15)"outlay" or "expense"
- constitutes taxable Canadian property for certain purposes, 248(1)"taxable Canadian property"(n)(i)
- defined, 66(15)
- disposition of
- • by non-resident
- • • certificate, 116(5.2)
- • • purchaser liable for tax, 116(5.2)
- • • rules, 116(5.1)
- • • treaty-protected property, 116(5.01), (5.02)
- • effect on successor rules, 66.7(14)
- • no capital gain, 39(1)(a)(ii)
- • no capital loss, 39(1)(b)(ii)
- "eligible property" for transfer to corporation by shareholder, 85(1.1)(c)
- in corporation, share is taxable Canadian property, 248(1)"taxable Canadian property"(e)(i)(B), (ii)(B)
- in partnership, constitutes taxable Canadian property, 248(1)"taxable Canadian property"(g)(ii)

- non-resident's income earned on, 115(4)
- non-successor acquisitions, 66.7(16)
- original owner, defined, 66(15)
- predecessor owner, defined, 66(15)
- production from, defined, 66(15)
- refund or rebate of Crown royalties, 12(1)(x.2)
- reserve amount, defined, 66(15)
- rules for trusts, 104(5.2)
- successor rules, 66.7(14)

Canadian security
- defined, 39(6)
- disposition of, 39(5)
- • election re, 39(4)
- owned by partnership, 39(4.1)

Canadian Security Intelligence Service
- provision of charity information to, for security purposes, 241(9), (9.1)

Canadian service provider
- defined, re non-resident investment or pension fund, 115.2(1)

Canadian tax
- defined, Canada-U.S. Tax Treaty:Art. III:1(a)

Canadian tax results
- defined, for functional currency rules, 261(1)

Canadian Venture Exchange
- prescribed securities exchange investment, Reg. 9002.2(e)
- prescribed stock exchange, Reg. 3200(a) [repealed]

Canadian Vessel Construction Assistance Act
- conversion cost deemed separate class, 13(17)
- deduction under, deemed depreciation, 13(13)
- disposition of deposit under, 13(19), (20)

Canadian waters
- defined, *Interpretation Act* 35(1)

Canadian Wheat Board
- defined, 135.2(1)
- Farmers' Trust, 135.2(1)"eligible trust"
- • unit of, ineligible for TFSA, 135.2(4)(g)
- paid-up capital on issuing shares to trust, 135.2(3)(c)
- tax consequences of privatization, 135.2

Canadian Wheat Board Act, 76(5)

Canadian Wheat Board continuance
- defined, 135.2(1)

Canals
- capital cost allowance, Reg. Sch. II:Cl. 1(b)

Cancellation of interest, penalty or tax, *see* Waiver

Cancellation of lease, *see* Lease cancellation payment

Canoes
- capital cost allowance, Reg. Sch. II:Cl. 7

Canterra Energy Ltd. case overruled, 257

Capacity test
- for shareholder loans, 15(2.4)(e)

Cape Breton
- defined, 127(9)
- Development Corporation, subject to tax, 27(2), Reg. 7100

Capital
- contribution of, addition to adjusted cost base, 53(1)(c)
- cost, *see* Capital cost; Capital cost allowance
- cost of, defined, Reg. 5204
- cumulative eligible, defined, 14(5) [before 2017], *see also* Cumulative eligible capital
- deemed contribution of, 53(1.1)
- defined, Reg. 5202, 5203, 5204
- • for financial institutions tax, 190.13
- • for large corporations tax, 181.2(3), 181.3(3)
- element, *see* Capital element
- "eligible capital expenditure" defined, 14(5) [before 2017]
- expenditure, not deductible, 18(1)(b)

Capital deduction
- for financial institutions tax
- - deducted in computing amount subject to tax, 190.1(1)
- - defined, 190.15
- for large corporations tax, defined, 181.5

Capital dividend, 83(2)
- account, *see* Capital dividend account
- amalgamation, on, 87(2)(x)(ii)
- election to treat dividend as, 83(2), (2.2)–(2.4)
- - form and manner of making, Reg. 2101
- - where not available, 83(2.1)
- paid to non-resident, 212(2)(b)
- - through trust, 212(1)(c)(ii)
- private corporation, Reg. 2101

Capital dividend account
- amalgamation, on, 87(2)(z.1)
- corporation ceasing to be exempt, 89(1.2)
- defined, 89(1)
- "designated property" defined, 89(1)
- dividend payable before May 7, 1974, ITAR 32.1(4)
- gift by corporation, 89(1)"capital dividend account"(a)(i)(A)
- life insurance proceeds
- - after May 23, 1985, 89(1)"capital dividend account"(d)
- - before May 24, 1985, 89(1)"capital dividend account"(e)
- - exclusion from anti-avoidance rule, 83(2.3)
- payment out of, *see* Capital dividend
- prescribed labour-sponsored venture capital corporation, of, deemed nil, 131(11)(e)
- where control acquired, 89(1.1)

Capital element
- annuity, of, deductible, 60(a)
- blended payment, 16(1), (4), (5); 20(1)(k) [repealed]

Capital gain, *see also* Capital gains and losses
- allocation of
- - credit union, by, 137(5.1), (5.2)
- convertible property, 51
- deduction, *see* Capital gains deduction
- deemed
- - capital gains stripping, 55(2)–(5)
- - debt forgiveness, 80(12)
- - negative adjusted cost base, 40(3)
- - - of passive partnership interest, 40(3.1)
- defined, 39(1)(a), 40(1)(a)
- dividend instead of, on disposition of share of foreign affiliate, 93(1)
- donation of publicly traded shares, 38(a.1)
- - partnership interests exchangeable for, 38(a.3)
- exchanges of property, 44
- failure to report, 110.6(6)
- foreign affiliate, of
- - election re, Reg. 5902
- income, 3
- income-splitting tax, 120.4(4), (5)
- life insurer's pre-1969 property, 138(11.2)
- listed personal property
- - taxable net gain, 41
- non-resident, 115(1)(b)
- - prorating for gains before May 1995, 40(9)
- not included in income from property, 9(3)
- principal residence
- - exemption, 40(2)(b)
- - farmer's, 40(2)(c)
- recovery of bad debt, 39(11)
- reserve, *see* Reserve: capital gain
- rollover, *see* Rollover
- shares or exchangeable partnership interests, donation of, 38(a.1), (a.3)
- specified, deductions for, 126(5.1)

- split income, 120.4(4), (5)
- stripping, 55(2)–(5)
- taxable
- - beneficiary's, designated by trust, 104(21.2)
- - defined, 38(a), 248(1)
- - definitions, 54
- - excluded from income of certain exempt organizations, 149(2)
- - foreign affiliate, of, 95(2)(f)
- - insurer's, 138(2)(b), 142
- - net, of trust, 104(21.3)
- - partnership, of, 96(1.7)
- - trust's, designation to beneficiary, 104(21)
- taxed
- - defined, 130(3)
- treaty rules, Canada-U.S. Tax Treaty:Art. XIII

Capital gains and losses, *see also* Capital gain; Capital loss
- adjusted cost base of property owned on Dec. 31/71, ITAR 26(3), (4)
- application of subdivision c, ITAR 26(1)
- becoming resident, on, 128.1(1)(b)
- ceasing to be resident, on, 128.1(4)(b)
- deemed, from property transferred to spouse, 74.2(2)
- deemed acquisition or disposal of property, 45
- disposition after June 18/71 where not at arm's length, ITAR 26(5)
- disposition before 1972, ITAR 26(5)
- disposition subject to warranty, 42
- disposition to corporation controlling or controlled by taxpayer, 40(2)(a)(ii)
- dividend in kind, cost of, 52(2)
- election re cost of property owned on Dec. 31/71, ITAR 26(7)
- employees profit sharing plan, allocated under, 144(4)–(4.2)
- exempt person, of, 40(2)(a)(i)
- fair market value of securities, ITAR 26(11)
- foreign affiliate, of, 95(2)(f)
- foreign exchange, 39(1.1), (2)
- identical properties, 47
- "listed-personal-property loss" defined, 41(3)
- lottery prize, 40(2)(f)
- meaning of, 39(1)
- negative adjusted cost base deemed gain, 40(3), (3.1)
- non-resident taxpayer, 40(2)(a)(i)
- options, *see* Option
- partial dispositions, 43
- personal-use property, 46
- - corporation, 46(4)
- prizes, 52(4)
- property whose value included in income, cost of, 52(1)
- purchase of bond etc. by issuer, 39(3)
- reacquired property, ITAR 26(6)
- rollover, *see* Rollover
- stock dividends, 52(3)
- Valuation Day, ITAR 24, 25

Capital gains deduction, 110.6
- allowable business investment loss, interaction with, 39(9), 110.6(1)"annual gains limit"B(b), 110.6(1)"cumulative gains limit"(b)
- anti-avoidance rules, 110.6(7)–(11)
- beneficiary of trust, 104(21.2)
- definitions, 110.6(1)
- determination of income while not resident, 110.6(13)
- double-dipping restriction, *see* Cumulative net investment loss
- election to trigger gain before corporation goes public, 48.1
- election to trigger gain on Feb. 22/94, 110.6(19)–(30); ITAR 26(29)
- - cumulative eligible capital, 14(9) [before 2017]
- - depreciable capital property
- - - cost, 13(7)(e.1)

Cash flow adjustment
- insurance corporation, Reg. 2412

Cash method of computing income
- becoming non-resident, on, 28(4), (4.1)
- COVID-19 Canada Emergency Wage Subsidy qualification, 125.7(4)(e)
- changing from, 28(3)
- defined, 28(1), 248(1)
- farming or fishing business, 28(1)–(3)
- non-resident ceasing to carry on business in Canada, 28(4), (4.1)

Cash-out of employee stock option, 7(1)(b.1), (d.1)

Cash purchase ticket
- grain, for
- • when amount included in income, 76(4)

Cash register, electronic, *see* **Electronic cash register**

Cash surrender value
- of insurance policy, defined, 148(9), Reg. 310, 1408(1)

Cash value
- defined, for Common Reporting Standard, 270(1)

Cash value insurance contract
- defined, for Common Reporting Standard, 270(1)

Casino
- defined, for international electronic funds transfer reporting, 244.1

Catalyst
- capital cost allowance for, Reg. Sch. II:Cl. 26

Catch
- defined, Reg. 105.1(1)

Catheters and related products
- medical expense credit, 118.2(2)(i.1)

Cattle
- basic herd maintained since 1971, deduction, 29
- breeding, 80.3(1)"breeding animals"
- dairy farming, 248(1)"farming"
- exhibiting and raising, 248(1)"farming"
- inventory, valuation of, 28(1.2)

Ceasing to act as agent of beneficiary
- constitutes disposition, 248(1)"disposition"(b)(v)

Ceasing to be a financial institution, 142.6(1)(a), (c)

Ceasing to be qualifying environmental trust, 107.3(3)

Ceasing to be resident in Canada, *see also* Former resident
- attribution rule, application to deemed disposition, 74.2(3)
- corporation, *see* Continuance outside Canada
- deemed disposition of property, 128.1(4)(b)
- • election for, 128.1(4)(d)
- • instalment obligation not increased, 128.1(5)
- • returning former resident, 128.1(6), (7)
- • stock option income excluded, 7(1.6)
- demand for payment of taxes owing, 226(1)
- departure tax, 128.1(4)
- • additional tax on corporations, 219.1(1), 219.3
- • security for, 220(4.5)–(4.54)
- employee life and health trust, 128.1(4)(b.1)
- farmer or fisherman, 28(4), (4.1)
- fiscal period end, 128.1(4)(a.1)
- foreign tax credit after emigration, 126(2.21)
- • trust beneficiary, 126(2.22)
- Home Buyers' Plan income inclusion, 146.01(5)
- information return, 128.1(9)
- Lifelong Learning Plan income inclusion, 146.02(5)
- loss after emigration, 128.1(8)
- moving to United Kingdom, Canada–U.K. Tax Convention Art. 13:9
- moving to the United States, Canada-U.S. Tax Treaty:Art. XIII:6

- negative cumulative eligible capital balance, 14(8)(a) [before 2017]
- payment of tax
- • election to defer, 220(4.5)–(4.54), Reg. 1301
- post-emigration loss, 128.1(8)
- reporting of assets, 128.1(9)
- rollovers of shares after emigration ignored, 128.3
- security for departure tax, 220(4.5)–(4.54)
- seizure of goods and chattels for non-payment of tax, 226(2)
- to pursue research under grant, 115(2)(b.1)
- trust, deemed, 94(5)–(5.2)
- trust deemed to dispose of property on transferor's emigration, 104(4)(a.3)

Ceasing to carry on business, *see also* Death of taxpayer; Sale: business, of; Winding-up
- accounts receivable, 28(5)
- business income of individual, effect on, 34.1(8)(a)
- disposition of depreciable property after, 13(8), 20(16.3)
- eligible capital property, 24(1) [before 2017]
- farming business, 28(4), (5)
- general rules, 22–25
- information returns to be filed, Reg. 205(2)
- non-resident, 10(12), (14)
- subsequent transactions
- • repayment of assistance, deduction relating to eligible capital expenditure, 20(1)(hh.1)
- • sale of inventory, 23(1)

Ceasing to use eligible capital property in business
- non-resident, 14(14) [before 2017]

Ceasing to use inventory in business
- non-resident, 10(12), (14)

Ceasing to use property in Canadian business
- non-resident financial institution, 142.6(1.1)

Celiac disease patients, medical expense credit for gluten-free food costs, 118.2(2)(r)

Cemetery arrangements, *see* Eligible funeral arrangement; Funeral services

Cemetery care trust
- defined, 148.1(1), 248(1)
- emigration of individual, no deemed disposition, 128.1(10)"excluded right or interest"(e)(iii)
- excluded from various trust rules, 108(1)"trust"(e.1)
- rollover to new trust, 248(1)"disposition"(f)(vi)

Cemetery services
- defined, 248(1)
- provision of under eligible funeral arrangements, 148.1(2)(b)(i)

Central bank
- defined, for Common Reporting Standard, 270(1)

Central paymaster
- provincial allocation of corporate income, Reg. 402.1

Certificate
- accredited film or video production, 125.5(1), (6)
- amount payable, re, 223(2)
- • application of, 223(1)
- • charge on land, 223(5), (6)
- • costs, 223(4)
- • registration in Court, 223(3)
- • • binding under provincial laws, 223(8)
- • • proceedings re, 223(7)
- • • sale of property, 223(9)
- • sale of property
- • • application by Minister for Federal Court order, 223(11)
- • • requirements re documentation, 223(10)
- • total amount, "prescribed rate" sufficient details, 223(12)
- before distribution of estate etc., 159(2)
- • failure to obtain, 159(3)
- Canadian film or video production, 125.4(1)
- change of ownership, Reg. 502

Index

Index

Index

Employment insurance *(cont'd)*
- • repayment of overpayment, deduction for, 60(n)(iv)
- • right to, no disposition on emigration, 128.1(10)"excluded right or interest"(h)
- • self-employment (Part VII.1), taxable, 56(1)(a)(iv)
- • taxable, 56(1)(a)(iv)
- • withholding tax, 153(1)(d.1), Reg. 100(1)"remuneration"(g)
- income replacement benefits under temporary program, 56(1)(r)
- premium
- • collection of debt by US Internal Revenue Service, Canada-U.S. Tax Treaty:Art. XXVI-A:9
- • paid by employee
- • • as employee, credit, 118.7:B(a)
- • • as employer, deduction, 8(1)(l.1)
- • paid by employer, deduction, 9(1) (general accounting principles)
- • paid by self-employed person, credit, 118.7:B(a)
- Program for Older Worker Adjustment, *see* Older Worker Adjustment, Program for
- tips and gratuities covered by, Reg. 100(1)"remuneration"(a.1)

Employment Insurance Act
- benefits under, *see* Employment insurance: benefit
- costs of appealing decision under, deductible, 60(o)
- • recovery of, income, 56(1)(l)(ii)
- financial assistance under, 56(1)(r)

Enactment, *see also* Amendment; Legislation
- defined, ITAR 12"enactment"

End of taxation year
- defined, Reg. 1104(1)

Endowment date
- of exemption test policy, defined, Reg. 310

Endowment (to charity), *see* Enduring property [repealed]

Enduring property [repealed]
- of registered charity
- • defined, 149.1(1)

Energy
- conservation property, Reg. 8200.1, Reg. Sch. II:Cl. 43.1
- • determination of, 13(18.1)
- • disclosure of information to Energy, Mines & Resources, 241(4)(d)(vi.1)
- conversion grant
- • included in income, 12(1)(u), 56(1)(s)
- • information return re, Reg. 224
- • non-resident taxable on, 212(1)(s)
- • prescribed program, Reg. 5501
- distribution of, 66(15)"principal-business corporation"(h)
- electrical
- • combustion turbine for, separate class, Reg. 1101(5t)
- • corporation distributing or generating
- • • equipment for, Reg. 1102(8), (9), Sch. II:Cl. 1(m), Sch. II:Cl. 2(c)
- • • • exclusion from CCA restrictions, Reg. 1100(26)(a)
- • • • information return, Reg. 213(1)
- • • • municipal corporation, exemption, 149(1.2)
- • • equipment for processing in prescribed area, 127(9)"qualified property"(c.1)
- • • generating equipment, capital cost allowance, Reg. Sch. II:Cl. 17(a.1)
- • • generating, manufacturing & processing credit, 125.1(2)
- • • producing or processing, 125.1(3)"manufacturing or processing"(h), Reg. 1104(9)(h)
- generation of, 66(15)"principal-business corporation"(h)
- property, *see* Specified energy property
- renewable, generation of, Reg. Sch. II:Cl. 43.1

Energy Cost Benefit
- disclosure of taxpayer information to enable payment, 241(4)(d)(vii.2)
- payments non-taxable, 81(1)(g.5)

Energy, Mines & Resources, *see* Department of Energy, Mines and Resources

Enforcement of Act, 220–244, *see also* Collection of tax

Engineer, *see* **Professional practice**

England, *see* United Kingdom

Enhanced combined cycle system
- defined, Reg. 1104(13)

Enhanced garnishment, 224(1.2), (1.3)

Enhanced recovery equipment, Reg. 1206(1)
- proceeds of disposition, 59(3.3)(d)

Enquiry, *see* Inquiry

Entering Canada, *see* Becoming resident in Canada

Entertainer
- U.S. resident, Canada-U.S. Tax Treaty:Art. XVI

Entertainment expenses (and meals)
- airplane, train, bus travel, 67.1(4)
- Christmas party exemption, 67.1(2)(f)
- club dues and facilities, 18(1)(l)
- construction work camp exemption, 67.1(2)(e.1)
- "entertainment" meaning of, 67.1(4)
- general limitation on deduction for, 67.1(1)
- • exceptions, 67.1(2)
- included in convention fee
- • limitation on deductibility, 67.1(3)
- interpretation, 67.1(4)

Entity
- defined
- • for Common Reporting Standard, 270(1)
- • for electronic funds transfer reporting, 244.1
- • for foreign affiliates, 95(1)
- • for SIFT trust and partnership distributions, 122.1(1)
- • • for stapled-security rules, 18.3(1), 122.1(1)
- • for third-party civil penalty, 163.2(1)

Entrant bank
- defined, for conversion of foreign bank affiliate to branch, 142.7(1)

Entrusted shares percentage [repealed], *see* Exempt shares percentage

Entry
- Canada, into, *see* Becoming resident in Canada
- dwelling-house, into, for audit, 231.1(3), *see also* Search warrant
- • compliance required, 231.5(2)

Environment
- conservation of, *see* Ecological gifts

Environmental law
- compliance with
- • required for certain Canadian renewable and conservation expenses, Reg. 1219(5)
- • required for clean-energy CCA, Reg. 1104(17)

Environmental Quality Act **(Quebec)**
- trust required by, no tax on, 149(1)(z.1)

Environmental trust, *see* Qualifying environmental trust

Environmentally hypersensitive person
- equipment qualifying for medical expense credit, Reg. 5700(c)–(c.2)

Equalization payments (family law)
- rules on partition of property, 248(20)

Equipment
- administering oxygen, for, 118.2(2)(k)
- automotive, CCA, Reg. Sch. II:Cl. 10(a), *see also* Automobile
- bituminous sands
- • defined, 59(6), Reg. 1206(1)
- • proceeds of disposition, 59(3.3)(c)
- cable systems interface, CCA, Reg. Sch. II:Cl. 10(v)

Exempt earned income *(cont'd)*
- defined, for pooled registered pension plan, 147.5(1)

Exempt earnings (of foreign affiliate)
- defined, Reg. 5907(1)

Exempt foreign trust
- defined, 94(1)

Exempt gains balance, *see also* Exempt capital gains balance (re flow-through entity)
- defined, 14(5) [before 2017]
- effect of excessive election, 14(9) [before 2017]

Exempt income
- defined, 248(1)
- under treaty, used in calculating clawback, Canada-U.S. Tax Treaty:Art. XXIV:10

Exempt-income contribution amount
- defined, for pooled registered pension plan, 147.5(1)
- reduces unused RRSP deduction room, 146(1)"unused RRSP deduction room"(b)D(iv)

Exempt loan of transfer
- defined, re loans to non-residents, 17(15)

Exempt loss (of foreign affiliate)
- defined, Reg. 5907(1)

Exempt person, *see also* Exempt corporation
- capital gains and losses, 40(2)(a)(i)
- exchanges of property, determination of gain, 44(7)
- for investments by deferred income plans
- - defined, Reg. 4901(2)"connected shareholder"(b), 4901(2)"designated shareholder"(a)(ii)
- for non-resident trust (NRT) rules
- - defined, 94(1)
- - excluded from NRT rules, 94(1)"contributor", 94(1)"resident beneficiary"
- no reserve for amount not due until later year, 20(8)
- obligation issued at discount by, 16(2), (3)
- partnership of, effect where taxable partner joins, 96(8)
- sale of Canadian resource property by, 66.6
- U.S. charitable organization, Canada-U.S. Tax Treaty:Art. XXI

Exempt policy
- defined, 12.2(11), Reg. 306

Exempt property
- for specified leasing property CCA rules
- - defined, Reg. 1100(1.13), (1.14)
- - excluded from specified leasing property, Reg. 1100(1.11)
- for trusts' 21-year deemed disposition rule
- - defined, 108(1)
- - excluded from deemed disposition, 104(4), (5), (5.2)

Exempt service
- defined, for non-resident trust rules, 94(1)
- excluded from service being a deemed transfer of property, 94(2)(f)

Exempt shares percentage
- defined, for private foundations, 149.1(1)

Exempt surplus (of foreign affiliate)
- adjustment where gain deemed due to negative adjusted cost base, 93(1)(b)(ii)
- deduction for dividend paid out of, 113(1)(a), 113(4), Reg. 5900(1)(a)
- defined, 113(1)(a), Reg. 5907(1)
- portion of dividend deemed paid out of, Reg. 5900(1)(a)

Exempt trust
- defined, for FAPI rules, 95(1)
- defined, foreign reporting rules, 233.2(1), *see also* Exempt foreign trust

Exemption test policy
- defined, Reg. 306(3)

Exemption threshold
- deemed capital gain on donation of flow-through share, 40(12)

- defined, 54

Exemption-end time
- defined, for TFSA, 146.2(9)(a)

Exemptions, 81, 149, *see also* Grandfathering
- agricultural organizations, 149(1)(e), 149(2)
- apportionment rule, 149(6)
- Association of Universities and Colleges of Canada, 149(1)(h.1)
- basic, re minimum tax, 127.53
- benevolent or fraternal benefit society, 149(4)
- - limitation, 149(4)
- benevolent society, 149(1)(k)
- boards of trade, 149(1)(e), 149(2)
- capital gains, 110.6, *see also* Capital gains deduction
- chambers of commerce, 149(1)(e), 149(2)
- charitable organization, 149(2)
- compensation by Federal Republic of Germany, 81(1)(g)
- Crown corporations, 149(1)(d)–(d.4)
- - exception, 27(1), (2)
- employee of foreign country, 149(1)(a)
- - family and servants of, 149(1)(b)
- expenses of gaining exempt income not deductible, 18(1)(c)
- fraternal benefit society/order, 149(1)(k)
- funeral arrangements, 148.1(2), 149(1)(s.1)
- general, 149
- Governor General's stipend, 81(1)(n)
- Halifax disaster pension, 81(1)(f)
- housing corporation, 149(1)(i), 149(2)
- income from aircraft operated by non-resident, 81(1)(c)
- income from ship operated by non-resident, 81(1)(c)
- insurer of farmers and fishermen, 149(1)(t), 149(4.2)
- - limitation, 149(4.1)
- labour organizations, 149(1)(k)
- master trust, 149(1)(o.4)
- mines, Reg. Part XIX [Revoked]
- municipal authorities, 149(1)(c)
- municipal corporations, 149(1)(d.6)
- mutual insurance corporations, 149(1)(m)
- non-profit corporation for scientific research, 149(1)(j), 149(2)
- non-profit organizations, 149(1)(l), 149(2)
- - deemed trust, 149(5)
- pension corporation, 149(1)(o.1), (o.2)
- pension trust, 149(1)(o)
- personal, *see* Personal credits
- personal injury award, income from, 81(1)(g.1), (g.2)
- prisoners of war, compensation paid to, 81(1)(d)
- prospecting, 81(1)(l)
- provincial corporations, 149(1)(d)–(d.4)
- provincial indemnity, 81(1)(q)
- RCA trust, 149(1)(q.1)
- RCMP pensions, 81(1)(i)
- registered charities, 149(1)(f)
- scholarships, *see* Scholarship exemption
- scientific research corporation (non-profit), 149(1)(j), 149(2)
- - control, rules re, 149(8)
- - rules as to income, 149(9)
- service and other pensions, 81(1)(d)
- service pension from other country, 81(1)(e)
- small business investment corporation, 149(1)(o.3)
- social assistance payments, 110(1)(f)(ii)
- societies, 149(1)(l), 149(2)
- - deemed a trust, 149(5)
- statutory, 81(1)(a)
- trust
- - deferred profit sharing plan, 149(1)(s)
- - employees profit sharing plan, 149(1)(p)
- - registered disability savings plan, 146.4(5), 149(1)(u.1)
- - registered education savings plan, under, 149(1)(u)

Expropriation

- amount paid constitutes proceeds of disposition, 13(21)"proceeds of disposition"(d), 54"proceeds of disposition"(d)
- foreign assets, *see* Expropriation assets
- resource properties, 59.1
- rollover where property replaced, 13(4), (4.1), 44

Expropriation assets

- acquired from foreign affiliate, 80.1(4)–(6)
- adjusted cost base of, 80.1(2)(b)
- adjusted principal amount, 80.1(7)
- • currency in which computed, 80.1(8)
- cost base, addition to, 53(1)(k)
- • deductions from, 53(2)(n)
- election re, 80.1(1), Reg. 4500
- income from, computation of, 80.1(2)(a)
- interest and capital amounts received at same time, 80.1(3)
- interest on
- • election re, 80.1(2)
- sale of foreign property, for, 80.1

Extended motor vehicle warranty

- defined (insurance policy reserves), Reg. 1408(1)

Extension of time

- to file appeal
- • by Tax Court, 167
- to file election or application, 220(3.2)
- to file notice of objection
- • by Minister, 166.1
- • by Tax Court, 166.2
- • deadline for requesting, 166.1(7)(a)
- to file notice of qualified dependant for Canada Child Benefit, 122.62(2)
- to file return, 220(3)
- to invest in labour–sponsored venture capital corporation, 127.4(5.1)
- to make or revoke election or designation, 220(3.2)
- to make RRSP contribution, 146(22)
- to post security for departure tax, 220(4.54)

Extinct shellfish, *see* Ammonite gemstone

Eyeglasses, as medical expense, 118.2(2)(j)

F

FACL, *see* Foreign accrual capital loss

FAD, *see* Foreign affiliate dumping

FAPI, *see* Foreign accrual property income

FAPL, *see* Foreign accrual property loss

FAPI year

- defined, Reg. 5907(1.5)

FATCA, *see* Foreign Account Tax Compliance Act (U.S.)

FEDE, *see* Foreign exploration and development expenses

FIE, *see* Foreign investment entity

FINTRAC, *see also* Financial Transactions and Reports Analysis Centre (FINTRAC)

- provision of information by CRA to, for limited purposes, 241(4)(d)(xv)

FMV, *see* Fair market value

FRE, *see* Foreign resource expenses

FTC, *see* Foreign tax credit

FTS, *see* Flow-through shares

Facsimile machine, *see* Fax machine

Factoring of accounts

- income of foreign affiliate from, 95(1)"investment business"
- • accounts arising in active business of related corporation, 95(2)(a)(iii), Reg. 5907(1)"exempt earnings"(d)(ii)(J)

Failure to file return, *see* Returns: failure to file, penalty

Failure to keep records, 230(3)

Failure to remit withheld taxes, 227(9)

- penalty applicable only on amounts over $500, 227(9.1)
- salary or wages, from, 227(9.5)

Failure to withhold tax, 227(8)

- assessment for, 227(10)
- salary or wages, from, 227(8.5)

Fair market value

- charitable donation of property, limited to cost, 248(35)–(38)
- cultural property, donated, 118.1(10)
- deemed disposition at, *see* Disposition: deemed
- defined, 69(1) (Notes)
- ecological gift, 118.1(10.1)–(10.5)
- • certificate, 118.1(10.5)
- inadequate considerations deemed to be, 69
- • exceptions re pre-1972 property, ITAR 32
- inventory property, of, 10(1), (4)
- meaning of, 69(1) (Notes)
- property donated or contributed, limited to cost, 248(35)–(38)
- property of deceased, 70(5.3)
- publicly-traded securities held since before 1972, ITAR 26(11)
- share
- • disposed of on death, 70(5.3)
- • foreign affiliate, of, ITAR 26(11.1), (11.2)
- • that is not capital property, 112(4.1)
- transfer at, to spouse or minor, 74.5(1)
- trust, capital interest in, 107.4(4)
- • held as inventory, 107(1.2)
- trust for benefit of spouse, 70(8)(a)
- undivided interest in property transferred by tax debtor, 160(3.1)
- V-day election, Reg. 4700, Reg. Sch. VII

Fair value property

- defined, for mark-to-market rules, 142.2(1)

Fairness package (1991), *see* Taxpayer relief

False statement, *see also* Penalty: false statement

- defined, for third-party penalty, 163.2(1)
- offence, 239(1), (1.1)
- penalty, 163(2)
- • charity receipt, 188.1(9), (10)
- • third-party penalty, 163.2

Family allowances, *see* Canada Child Benefit

Family Caregiver credit

- additional amount, 118(1)B(a)(ii)C(A), 118(1)B(b)(iv)D(A), 118(1)B(b.1)
- base amount for infirm adult relative, 118(1)(B)(d)

Family farm or fishing corporation/partnership

- capital gains exemption on disposition, 110.6(2), (31)
- farm or fishing property leased to
- • transfer of, 70(9.8)
- interest in partnership, defined, 70(10)"interest in a family farm or fishing partnership"
- share of corporation, defined, 70(10)"share of the capital stock of a family farm or fishing corporation" 110.6(1)
- transfer of
- • *inter vivos*, 73(4), (4.1)
- • on death, 70(9.2), (9.21), (9.3), (9.31)
- • to parent, 70(9.6)

Family law, *see* Province: laws of; Spouse

Family Orders and Agreements Enforcement Assistance Act

- Canada Child Benefit payments not garnishable under, 122.61(4)(e)
- disclosure of taxpayer information for purposes of, 241(4)(e)(vii)

Family Support Plan

- payroll deduction reduces source withholding, Reg. 100(3)(d)

Family Tax Cut (2014–15 only), 119.1

Index

Index

Flared gas, *see* Solution gas

Flat benefit provision (of pension plan)
- defined, Reg. 8300(1)

Flood region, *see* Drought or flood region

Floorcovering installer
- apprenticeship job creation credit, 127(9)"investment tax credit"

Flow-through
- adjusted cost base of option, to share, partnership interest or trust interest, 49(3.01)
- Canadian development expense, to shareholder, 66(12.62)
- Canadian exploration expense, to shareholder, 66(12.6)
- Canadian oil and gas property expense, to shareholder, 66(12.64)
- corporate income to shareholder, *see* Integration
- corporation's capital gain, untaxed portion, 83(2)
- death benefit, through trust or estate, 104(28)
- entity, *see* Flow-through entity (re capital gains exemption)
- intercorporate dividends, 82(1)(a), (a.1), 112(1)
- investment tax credits on windup, 88(1)(e.3)
- paid-up capital deficiency, on conversion of shares, 51(3), 86(2.1)
- partnership income to partner, 96(1)
- • limited to amount at risk, 96(2.1)–(2.7)
- qualifying environmental trust income to beneficiary, 107.3(1)
- shares, *see* Flow-through shares
- trust capital gains to beneficiary, 104(21)
- trust income to preferred beneficiary, 104(14)
- trust pension benefits to beneficiary, 104(27)

Flow-through entity (re capital gains exemption)
- adjusted cost base, addition to, 53(1)(p)
- amalgamation of, 87(2)(bb.1)
- defined, 39.1(1)
- distribution of property to beneficiary, 107(2.2)
- reduction in capital gain, 39.1(2)–(6)
- sale of interest in, 39.1(7)

Flow-through mining expenditure
- defined, 127(9)
- • reduction for assistance received, 127(11.1)(c.2)
- investment tax credit for, 127(5)(a)(i), 127(9)"investment tax credit"(a.2)
- • carryforward or carryback, 127(9)"investment tax credit"(c)
- reduces CCEE, 66.1(6)"cumulative Canadian exploration expense"L

Flow-through share class of property
- deemed capital gain on donation of, 40(12)
- defined, 54

Flow-through shares, 66(12.6)–(12.75)
- amalgamation, effect of, 87(4.4)
- COVID-19 extensions, 66(12.6001), (12.731), 211.91(2.1)
- class of property, *see* Flow-through share class of property
- cost of, 66.3(3)
- defined, 66(15), 248(1)
- donation to charity, deemed capital gain, 40(12)
- • capital dividend account impact, 89(1)"capital dividend account"(a)(i)(A), (B.1)
- • subsequent rollover, 38.1
- information return, Reg. 228
- interest on renunciation for previous year, 211.91(1)
- minimum tax, 127.52(1)(e), (e.1)
- mining exploration expenses in first 60 days of year, 66.1(8)
- not "tax shelter", 237.1(1)
- one-year look-back rule, 66(12.66)(a.1), 211.91
- paid-up capital, 66.3(4)
- prescribed, Reg. 6202.1
- renunciation of, 66(12.6), (12.62), (12.64), 66(12.73)
- • Canadian development expenses
- • • conversion to CEE before 2019, 66(12.601), (12.602)

- • Canadian exploration expenses, 66(12.6)
- • Canadian oil and gas property expenses, 66(12.64)
- • expenses in first 60 days of the year, 66(12.66)
- • member of partnership, by, 66(19)
- • mining properties excluded, 66(12.62)(b.1)
- • restrictions, 66(12.67), (12.71), (19)
- selling instrument
- • defined, 66(15)
- • filing of, 66(12.68)
- • late filing, 66(12.74), (12.75)

Fluctuations in currency, *see* Foreign exchange

Fondaction
- prescribed as labour-sponsored venture capital corporation, Reg. 6700(f), 6701(g)

Food, *see also* Entertainment expenses (and meals); Meals
- delivered after the end of the year, reserve for, 20(6)

Food and animal waste
- defined, Reg. 1104(13)

Food waste
- defined, Reg. 1104(13) [repealed]

Football players, *see* Athlete

Foreclosure, *see* Surrender: of property to creditor

Foreign Account Tax Compliance Act (U.S.)
- intergovernmental agreement for exchange of information, *see at end of Canada-U.S. Tax Convention*
- reporting required by Canadian financial institutions, 263–269
- • information return of accounts held by U.S. persons, 266(1)
- • records to be kept for 6 years, 267(3)
- U.S. taxpayer identifying number must be provided to financial institution, 162(6)

Foreign accrual capital loss
- application to FAPI, 95(1)"foreign accrual property income"F.1, Reg. 5903.1(1)
- defined, Reg. 5903.1(3), (4)

Foreign accrual property income, *see also* Foreign affiliate
- banks, rules for, 95(2.31), (2.43)–(2.45), (3.01)
- contract manufacturing, 95(3.2)
- currency hedging, 95(2)(g.01)
- defined, 95(1), 95(2), 248(1)
- definitions, 95(1), (4)
- foreign affiliate purchasing goods for use in Canada, 95(2)(a.1)
- fresh start rule, 95(2)(k)
- included in income, 91(1)
- insurance of risks in Canada, 95(2)(a.2)
- loss carryback, 152(6.1), Reg. 5903(1)(b)
- loss carryforward, Reg. 5903(1)(a)
- partnership, of, 93.1(5), (6)
- partnerships and trusts, 95(3.6)
- regulated foreign financial institution exception, 95(2.11)
- stub period, 91(1.1)–(1.5)
- transparent affiliate, Reg. 5907(1.091), (1.092)

Foreign accrual property loss
- carryback 3 years, Reg. 5903(1)(b)
- • reassessment to permit, 152(6.1)
- carryforward 20 years, Reg. 5903(1)(a)
- defined, Reg. 5903(3)

Foreign accrual tax
- deduction from income, 91(4)
- defined
- • for foreign accrual property income, 95(1)

Foreign affiliate, *see also* Controlled foreign affiliate; Foreign accrual property income
- absorptive merger of, 87(8.2)
- active business income, 95(2)(a), Reg. 5907(2)–(2.6)
- acquisition of shares of
- • from partnership, 91(7)
- assets acquired from

2414

Foreign business corporation
- deemed resident in Canada, 250(4)(b)
- defined, 213(3)
- no withholding tax on dividend from, 213(1)

Foreign charitable organization
- designation of, for donations to qualify, 149.1(26)

Foreign charity
- qualifying for Canadian donations
- • charity that received gift from Canada, 149.1(1)"qualified donee"(a)(v), 149.1(26)
- • US charity, where donor has US-source income, Canada-U.S. Tax Treaty:Art. XXI:7
- US charity, no Canadian tax on, Canada-U.S. Tax Treaty:Art. XXI:1

Foreign corporation, *see* Foreign affiliate; Non-resident

Foreign country, *see* Foreign government; Foreign investment entity; Prescribed countries

Foreign currency, *see also* Foreign exchange
- defined, 248(1)
- election to use for tax reporting, 261(3)

Foreign currency debt
- defined, 111(8), 248(1)
- gain or loss on, after change of control, 40(10), (11), 111(12), (13)

Foreign divisive reorganization
- effect on shareholders, 15(1.5)

Foreign exchange, *see also* Foreign currency
- adjustment, re specified debt obligation, Reg. 9104
- calculating currency defined, 95(1)
- calculation of income where foreign assets expropriated, 80.1(8)
- change of control of corporation, effect of, 111(12), (13)
- debt obligation denominated in
- • application of debt forgiveness rules, 80(2)(k), 80.01(11)
- • assumed by non-resident in Canadian business, 76.1(2)
- • moved by non-resident from Canadian business, 76.1(1)
- • surrender of property to creditor, calculation of proceeds, 79(7)
- exchange rate defined, 111(8), 248(1)
- fluctuations in
- • capital gain or loss, 39(1.1), (2)
- • debt parking and statute-barred debt rules to be ignored, 80.01(11)
- • foreign affiliate's capital gain or loss from, 95(2)(g)–(g.02)
- • ignored in determining employee stock option deduction, 110(1)(d)(iii)
- • loan or lending asset, 248(1)"amortized cost"(c.1), (f.1)
- • revenue to real estate investment trust, 122.1(1.3)
- • specified debt obligation of financial institution, 142.4(1)"tax basis"(f), (o)
- income in blocked currency, waiver of interest on tax, 161(6)
- restriction, reserve where, 91(2), (3)

Foreign exploration and development expenses, *see also* Exploration and development expenses; Resource expenses
- borrowed money
- • capitalization of interest, 21(2), (4)
- • • reassessment, 21(5)
- country-by-country allocation, 66(4.1), (4.2)
- • successor rules, 66.7(2.1), (2.2)
- deduction for, 66(4)
- • short taxation year, 66(13.1)
- defined, 66(15)
- individual ceasing to be resident in Canada, 66(4.3)
- limitation, 66(12.4)
- reduction of, on debt forgiveness, 80(8)(e)
- short taxation year, 66(13.1)
- specified, *see* Specified foreign exploration and development expense
- successor corporation, rules, 66.7(2)

- • application, 66.6(1)

Foreign government, *see also* United States
- bonds of, eligible for RRSP investment, 204"qualified investment"(c.1) (formerly Reg. 4900(1)(o))
- bribery of officials non-deductible, 67.5
- diplomats, exempt, 149(1)(a), Canada-U.S. Tax Treaty:Art. XXVIII
- employees of, exempt, 149(1)(a), Canada-U.S. Tax Treaty:Art. XIX, XXVIII
- expropriation by, 80.1
- social security plan of, excluded from RCA, Reg. 6802(g)
- stock exchanges recognized, 262
- tax paid to, *see* Foreign tax credit; Foreign taxes

Foreign immigration trust, *see* Immigration trust

Foreign income, *see also* Foreign accrual property income
- Canadian resident, generally taxable, 3(a)
- employment, tax credit for (pre-2016), 122.3
- foreign affiliate, of, *see* Foreign accrual property income
- non-resident, not taxable, 115(1)
- taxed by foreign country, *see* Foreign tax credit

Foreign insurance subsidiary
- defined, Reg. 8605(4)

Foreign investment entity, 94.1–94.4 [former draft, not implemented]

Foreign investment income
- defined, 129(4)
- refund to private corporation in respect of, 129(1), (3)

Foreign merger
- absorptive merger, 87(8.2)
- defined, 87(8.1)
- effect of, 87(8)
- taxable Canadian property rollover, 87(8.4), (8.5)

Foreign Missions and International Organizations Act
- employment income from international organization, tax credit, 126(3)

Foreign mutual fund trust
- exemption from reporting requirement, 233.2(1)"exempt trust"(c)
- reporting requirement, 233.3

Foreign non-profit organization
- defined, Reg. 6804(1)

Foreign oil and gas business
- defined
- • for foreign tax credit, 126(7)
- • for FAPI, Reg. 5910(4)
- foreign tax credit for, 126(5)

Foreign plan (pension plan)
- contributions made to, Reg. 6804(4)–(6)
- defined, Reg. 6804(1), 8308.1(1)
- electing employer with respect to, Reg. 6804(2), (3)
- PSPA of, Reg. 8308.1(5), (6)
- • information return, Reg. 8402(2)
- pension adjustment, prescribed amount, Reg. 8308.2
- pension credit of, Reg. 8308.1(2)–(4)

Foreign policy loan
- defined, Reg. 2400(1)

Foreign policy pool
- defined, for FAPI on insurance swaps, 95(2)(a.21)

Foreign property, *see also* Foreign reporting requirements
- investments in, annual information return, 233.3
- sale of, expropriation assets for, 80.1

Foreign reporting requirements, 233.1–233.7
- foreign affiliates, 233.4
- foreign property, 233.3
- • reassessment deadline extended if return not filed accurately, 152(4)(b.2)
- foreign trusts

Interest (money) *(cont'd)*
- income from business or property, 12(1)(c)
- - whether specified investment business, 125(7)"specified investment business"
- increasing rates, income accrual, Reg. 7000(2)(c.1)
- instalments of tax, late or insufficient, 161(2)
- - additional 3% payable, 161(3)
- - limitation, 161(4), (4.1)
- - not deductible, 18(1)(t)
- - offset, 161(2.2)
- - scientific research tax credit, when deemed paid, 161(10)
- - share-purchase tax credit, when deemed paid, 161(10)
- - where not payable, 161(2.1)
- interest repaid, on, 164(4)
- loss carryback, effect of, 161(7)
- loss of source of income, 20.1(1)
- obligation issued at a discount, 16(3)
- offset
- - arrears interest against refund interest, 161.1
- - early instalments against late instalments, 161(2.2)
- paid on death duties, deduction, 60(d)
- - paid or payable, deduction for, *see* deductible *(above)*
- paid to non-resident, withholding tax, 212(1)(b)
- - by wholly-owned subsidiary, 218
- - to U.S. resident, Canada-U.S. Tax Treaty:Art. XI
- participating debt, *see* Participating debt interest
- payable
- - carryback re minimum tax, no effect, 161(7)
- penalty, on, 161(11)
- penalty or bonus, treated as interest expense, 18(9.1)
- prepaid, deduction for, 18(9), (9.2)–(9.8)
- prescribed rate, Reg. 4301
- property transferred from spouse, 74.1
- rate of, Reg. 4301
- rate reduction payments, treated as interest expense, 18(9.1)
- refunds and repayments, on, 164(3)–(4)
- repayment of, deduction for, 20(1)(ll)
- spouse, property transferred to, 74.1, *see also* Attribution rules
- student loan, paid, credit for, 118.62
- tax withheld but not remitted, on, 227(9.3)
- unclaimed at year-end
- - withholding tax, 153(4)
- - - effect of remittance, 153(5)
- unpaid tax, on, 161(1), 227(9.3)
- - adjustment of foreign tax, 161(6.1)
- - grace period to pay balance, 161.2
- - income in blocked currency, 161(6)
- - loss carryback, effect of, 164(5), (5.1)
- - none, re participation certificate, 161(5)
- - not deductible, 18(1)(t)
- - offset
- - - arrears interest against refund interest, 161.1
- - - early instalments against late instalments, 161(2.2)
- - Part III, 185(2)
- - Part III.1, 185.2(2)
- - Part IV, 187(2)
- - Part V, 189(7)
- - Part X, 202(5)
- - Part XII.3, 211.5
- - Part XII.4 tax, 211.6(5)
- - Part XII.5 tax, 211.82
- - retroactive to application date of provision, 221.1
- - up to $25, may be cancelled, 161.3
- - waiver of, 220(3.1)
- withholding tax, 212(1)(b)

Interest-free loan, *see* Loan: interest-free

Interest gross-up period
- defined, for non-resident trust rules, 94(15)(c)(ii)C

Interest in a family farm or fishing partnership
- defined, 70(10)
- rollover, 70(9)-(9.31), 73(3)-(4.1)

Interference with remittances of tax withheld, 227(5.2)–(5.4) (1995 draft, abandoned)

Intergenerational transfers
- attribution of income or loss, 74.1(2)
- farm or fishing property
- - *inter vivos*, 73(3)–(4.1)
- - on death, 70(9)–(9.31)

Interim receiver
- withholding tax, liability for, 227(5), (5.1)(d)

Internal Revenue Service (U.S.), *see also* United States
- collection of Canadian tax, Canada-U.S. Tax Treaty:Art. XXVI A
- competent authority procedures, Canada-U.S. Tax Treaty:Art. XXVI
- exchange of information with CRA, Canada-U.S. Tax Treaty:Art. XXVII

Internal waters
- defined, *Interpretation Act* 35(1)

International agencies, prescribed, Reg. 806.1

International Air Transport Association
- employment income of non-Canadians, deduction for, 110(1)(f)(iv)

International Bank for Reconstruction and Development
- bonds of, qualified investment for RRSP etc., 204"qualified investment"(c.1) (formerly Reg. 4900(1)(l)(i))

International banking centre until 2013, 33.1

International development assistance programs
- person working on deemed resident in Canada, 250(1)(d)
- prescribed, Reg. 3400

International Finance Corporation
- bonds of, qualified investment for RRSP etc., 204"qualified investment"(c.1) (formerly Reg. 4900(1)(l)(i.1))

International Financial Reporting Standards
- effect of, 9(1) (Notes)
- insurers, application to, 138(17.1)
- - liabilities and reserves to be computed gross of reinsurance, Reg. 2400(1)"Canadian reserve liabilities"
- - transition year, 138(12)"transition year"(b)

International organization
- defined, for Common Reporting Standard, 270(1)
- employment income from
- - deduction, 110(1)(f)(iii)
- - tax credit, 126(3)
- interest paid to, withholding tax exemption, Reg. 806

International shipping
- aircraft used in
- - lease payments exempt from withholding tax, 212(1)(d)(xi)
- corporation, residence of, 250(6)
- defined, 248(1)
- income of non-resident from, exempt, 81(1)(c)
- non-resident's income from, exempt, 81(1)(c)
- residence of shipping corporation, 250(6)–(6.04)
- service provider deemed to have international shipping as principal business, 250(6.02), (6.03)

International sport federation, eligibility requirements of, *see* Amateur athlete trust

International tax
- advisory panel, *see* Advisory Panel on International Taxation
- conventions, *see* Tax treaty
- dividends received from foreign corporations, 90, 113
- foreign accrual property income, 91, 95
- foreign tax credit, 126, *see also* Foreign tax credit
- treaties, *see* Tax treaty
- United States, rules re, *see* United States

Mute person
- speech synthesizer
- - disability supports deduction, 64(a)A(ii)(E)
- - medical expense credit, Reg. 5700(p)

Mutual agreement procedure, Canada-U.S. Tax Treaty:Art. XXVI

Mutual corporation
- provincial life insurance corporation converted into, 139

Mutual fund, *see also* Mutual fund corporation; Mutual fund trust
- defined, for non-resident trust rules, 94(1)

Mutual fund corporation, 131
- amalgamation, 87(2)(bb)
- capital gains dividends, election, 131(1)–(1.4), Reg. 2104
- - interest on, 131(3.1), (3.2)
- capital gains on Canadian securities, 39(5)
- capital gains redemptions, defined, 131(6)
- deemed private corporation, 131(5)
- defined, 131(8), (8.1), 248(1)
- distributions to non-residents, tax on, 218.3
- dividend refund to, 131(5)
- election not to be restricted financial institution, 131(10)
- increase in paid-up capital not deemed dividend, 131(4)
- information return where share claimed to be qualified investment, Reg. 221
- non-residents, distributions to, tax on, 218.3
- non-residents, for benefit of, 131(8.1)
- not subject to mark-to-market rules, 142.2(1)"financial institution"(c)(iii)
- payment of tax, 157(3)
- qualified investment for RRSP, RRIF, etc.
- - bond or debenture of trust, Reg. 4900(1)(c.1)
- - unit of trust, Reg. 4900(1)(c)
- refund to, re capital gains dividend, 131(2), (3)
- refundable capital gains tax on hand, 131(6)
- - reduction of, 131(9)
- rollover of property to mutual fund trust, 132.2
- shares of
- - transferred in exchange for units of mutual fund trust, 132.2(3)(l)
- switch fund
- - conversion to mutual fund trusts tax-free, 132.2(1)"qualifying exchange"
- - no rollover of shares allowed, 131(4.1)
- taxable Canadian property, gains distributed to non-residents, 131(5.1), (5.2)
- taxed capital gains, 131(7)
- transitional election to be MFC for 2016–17, 131(8.01)

Mutal fund limited partnership
- financing, restrictions on, 18.1

Mutual fund trust, 132
- allocation to redeemers, 132(5.3)
- amounts designated by, 132.1
- - adjusted cost base of unit, 132.1(2)
- - deduction for, 132.1(1)(c)
- - - carryover, 132.1(4)
- - - limitation, 132.1(3)
- - inclusion in taxpayer's income, 132.1(1)(d)
- - where designation of no effect, 132.1(5)
- capital gains on Canadian securities, 39(5)
- capital gains redemptions, defined, 132(4)
- capital gains refund to, 132(1), (2)
- - interest on, 132(2.1), (2.2)
- defined, 132(6)–(7), 248(1)
- - election to be from beginning of first taxation year, 132(6.1)
- - following rollover of assets in qualifying exchange, 132.2(3)(k)
- - retention of status to end of calendar year, 132(6.2)
- distributions to non-residents, tax on, 218.3

- election for December 15 year-end, 132.11
- - allocation or designation of amount to be included in income, 132.11(6)
- - - late filing of allocation or designation, 220(3.21)(b)
- exemption from Part XII.2 tax, 210(2)(c)
- information return, Reg. 204, 204.1
- - that trust is qualified investment, Reg. 221
- instalment payments of tax, 156(2)
- interest received by, on behalf of non-residents, exemption, 212(9)(c)
- minimum tax not payable by, 127.55(f)(ii)
- non-residents, distributions to, tax on, 218.3
- non-residents, for benefit of, 132(7)
- not subject to mark-to market rules, 142.2(1)"financial institution"(d)
- obligation guaranteed by, qualified investment for deferred income plan, Reg. 4900(1)(i)
- qualified investment for RRSP, RRIF, etc.
- - bond or debenture of, Reg. 4900(1)(d.1)
- - unit of trust, Reg. 4900(1)(d)
- real estate investment trust as, 132(6)(b)(ii)
- redemptions, allocation to redeemers, 132(5.3)
- refundable capital gains tax on hand
- - defined, 132(4)
- rollover of property to another mutual fund trust, 132.2
- SIFT conversion to corporation
- - exchange of employee stock options, 7(1.4)(b)(vi)
- taxable Canadian property, gains distributed to non-residents, 132(5.1), (5.2)
- taxable capital gains
- taxation year, election for December 15, 132.11
- taxed capital gains, 132(5)
- transfer of property from mutual fund corporation or trust, 132.2
- unit of
- - adjusted cost base of, 53(1)(d.2)
- - "Canadian security", 39(6)
- - deemed to be a share for rollover purposes, 132.2(1)"share"
- - employee option to acquire, 7(1), 110(1)(d)
- - transferred in course of qualifying exchange, 132.2(3)(a.1), (f)
- year-end, election for December 15, 132.11

Mutual holding corporation
- deemed dividend on distribution by, 139.2
- defined, for insurance demutualization, 139.1(1)

Mutual insurance corporations
- exemption for, 149(1)(m)

Mutual life insurance corporation
- provincial corporation converted into, 139

Mutualization proposal (for insurer), 139

N

NDDA, *see* Non-deductible distributions amount

NERDTOH, *see* Non-eligible refundable dividend tax on hand

NFE
- defined, for Common Reporting Standard, 270(1)"non-financial entity"

NFFE
- defined, for certain purposes (re FATCA), 265(4)(b)

NISA, *see* Net income stabilization account

NISA Fund No. 2, *see also* Net income stabilization account
- amount credited to, not taxed, 12(10.3)
- deemed paid on acquisition of control of corporation, 12(10.4)
- deemed paid on death, 70(5.4)
- defined, 248(1)
- disposition of, 73(5)
- paid to non-resident, withholding tax, 212(1)(t), 214(3)(l)
- - information return required, Reg. 202(2.1)

Post-1971 spousal or common-law partner trust *(cont'd)*
- preferred beneficiary election by, 104(15)(a)
- transfer by, to another trust, 104(5.8)

Post-1995 life insurance policy
- defined, Reg. 1408(1)

Post-1995 non-cancellable or guaranteed renewable accident and sickness policy
- defined, Reg. 1408(1)

Post-secondary school level
- defined, for RESP purposes, 146.1(1)

Poultry
- raising, constitutes farming, 248(1)"farming"

Poverty, vow of, 110(2)

Powerline technician
- apprenticeship job creation credit, 127(9)"investment tax credit"

Pre-acquisition surplus
- election for dividend to come out of (return of capital), Reg. 5901(2)(b)

Pre-acquisition surplus (of foreign affiliate)
- deduction for dividend paid out of, 113(1)(d), Reg. 5900(1)(c)
- dividend received by partnership, 92(4)–(6)

Preexisting account
- defined, for Common Reporting Standard, 270(1)

Preexisting entity account
- defined, for Common Reporting Standard, 270(1)

Preexisting individual account
- defined, for Common Reporting Standard, 270(1)

Pre-funded group life insurance policy

Pre-1972 capital surplus on hand
- amalgamation, on, 87(2)(t)
- on windup of corporation, 88(2)–(2.3)

Pre-1972 spousal trust
- deemed disposition by, 104(4)(a.1)
- defined, 108(1)

Pre-1986 capital loss balance
- defined, 111(8)
- usable, $2,000 per year, 111(1.1)

Pre-1996 life insurance policy
- defined, Reg. 1408(1), (7)

Pre-1996 non-cancellable or guaranteed renewable accident and sickness policy
- defined, Reg. 1408(1), (7)

Pre-production mining expenditure
- Canadian exploration expense, 66.1(6)"Canadian exploration expense"(f)(v.1), (g)
- defined, 127(9)
- - reduction for assistance received, 127(11.1)(c.3)
- investment tax credit for, 127(5)(a)(i), 127(5)(a)(ii)(A), 127(9)"investment tax credit"(a.3)
- - carryforward or carryback, 127(9)"investment tax credit"(c)
- - specified percentage, 127(9)"specified percentage"(j)
- reduces CCEE, 66.1(6)"cumulative Canadian exploration expense"L

Pre-reversion debt (for functional currency rules)
- defined, 261(1)
- rules for, 261(13), (14)

Pre-transition debt (for functional currency rules)
- defined, 261(1)
- rules for, 261(8)–(10), (12)(f)

Precious metals
- eligible for RRSP, RRIF etc. investment, Reg. 4900(1)(t)
- purchase of, information return required, Reg. 230(5)

Predecessor corporation, *see* Amalgamation

Predecessor employer
- defined, Reg. 8500(1)

- - definition applies to *Income Tax Act*, 147.2(8), Reg. 8500(1.2)
- former employee of, for pension plan rules, 147.2(8)
- pensionable service counts towards member's benefits, Reg. 8504(2.1)

Predecessor owner
- defined, for resource allowance, Reg. 1206(1)

Preferred beneficiary
- defined, 108(1)
- election, 104(14), Reg. 2800
- - allocable amount, 104(15)
- - filing deadline, 104(14)–(14.02)

Preferred-rate amount, for credit union
- deduction based on, 137(3)
- defined, 137(4.3)

Preferred share, *see also* Short-term preferred share; Taxable preferred share; Term preferred share
- consideration for property transferred to corporation, 85(1)(g)
- deemed interest on, 258(3)
- defined, 248(1)
- issued by loss corporation
- - where dividends on not deductible, 112(2.4)–(2.9)
- tax-deferred series, Reg. 2107
- tax on payment of dividends on, 191.1
- tax on receipt of dividends on, 82(1), 187.2, 187.3
- taxable, *see* Taxable preferred share

Pregnant loss, *see also* Superficial loss
- rules preventing transfer of,
- - capital property, 40(3.3), (3.4)
- - depreciable property, 13(21.2)
- - eligible capital property, 14(12), (13) [before 2017]
- - share or debt owned by financial institution, 18(13), (15)

Preliminary work activity
- defined, for oil sands mine development project, 66.1(6)
- defined, for oil sands project, Reg. 1104(2)

Premium
- defined
- - Home Buyers' Plan, 146(1)"premium", 146.01(1)"premium"
- - life insurance as taxable benefit, Reg. 2700(2)
- - life insurance policy, 148(9)"premium"
- - Lifelong Learning Plan, 146(1)"premium", 146.02(1)"premium"
- - obligation owned since before 1972, ITAR 26(12)
- - registered retirement savings plan, 146(1)"premium"
- group term life insurance policy
- - limitation on deductibility, 18(9.01)
- - taxable benefit to employee, 6(4), Reg. 2700–2704
- health care insurance, deductible, 20.01
- home insurance, deduction after moving away, 62(3)(g)
- life insurance used as collateral, deductible, 20(1)(e.2)
- outstanding, *see* Outstanding premiums
- prescribed, Reg. 309(1)
- RRSP, under, 146(1)"premium"
- refund of, *see* Registered retirement savings plan: refund of premiums

Premium category
- defined, Reg. 2700(1)

Premium paid by the policyholder
- defined, Reg. 1408(4)

Prepaid amounts, taxable when received, 12(1)(a)

Prepaid expenses
- amalgamation, 87(2)(j.2)
- farming or fishing (cash-basis) business, 28(1)(e), (e.1)
- limitation re deductibility, 18(9)

Prepaid insurance benefit
- defined, Reg. 2703

Index

Qualifying payment
- defined, Reg. 809(4)

Qualifying performance income (for amateur athlete trust)
- defined, 143.1(1)
- included in RRSP earned income, 146(1)"earned income"(b.2)

Qualifying period
- defined, for COVID-19 Canada Emergency Wage Subsidy, 125.7(1)
- defined, for phased retirement rules, Reg. 8503(16)
- defined, for SIFT trust wind-up event, 248(1)"SIFT trust wind-up event"(c)(ii)

Qualifying person
- defined
- - re eligible funeral arrangement, 148.1(1)
- - re registered disability savings plan, 146.4(1)
- - re stock option rules, 7(7)
- - re treaty shopping, Canada-U.S. Tax Treaty:Art. XXIX-A:2

Qualifying portion of a capital gain
- defined, for small business investment capital gain rollover, 44.1(1)

Qualifying portion of a distribution
- defined, 207.01(1)"excess TFSA amount"E

Qualifying portion of the proceeds of disposition
- defined, for small business investment capital gain rollover, 44.1(1)

Qualifying property
- defined, for COVID-19 Canada Emergency Rent Subsidy, 125.7(1)

Qualifying recovery entity
- defined, for Canada Recovery Hiring Program, 125.7(1)

Qualifying relation
- defined, for public transit pass credit, 118.02(1) [pre-2018]

Qualifying renovation
- defined
- - for home acessibility tax credit, 118.041(1)

Qualifying rent expense
- defined, for COVID-19 Canada Emergency Rent Subsidy, 125.7(1)

Qualifying renter
- defined, for COVID-19 Canada Emergency Rent Subsidy, 125.7(1)

Qualifying retirement plan
- defined, Canada-U.S. Tax Treaty:Art. XVIII:15
- tax treatment of, Canada-U.S. Tax Treaty:Art. XVIII:8–17

Qualifying return of capital
- defined, for upstream loans, 90(3)
- reduction of ACB, 53(2)(b)(i)(B)(II)

Qualifying revenue
- defined, for COVID-19 Canada Emergency Wage Subsidy, 125.7(1)

Qualifying services
- benefits in respect of, 94(1)"exempt foreign trust"(f)(ii)(C)
- defined, for non-resident trust rules, 94(1)

Qualifying share
- defined
- - RRSP or RRIF investment in cooperative corporation, Reg. 4901(2)
- prescribed, Reg. 6203

Qualifying site
- in respect of qualifying environmental trust, defined, 211.6(1)

Qualifying student
- defined, 118.6(1)

Qualifying subscription expense
- credit for, 118.02(2)
- defined, 118.02(1)

Qualifying substitute corporation
- defined, for foreign affiliate dumping rules, 212.3(4)

Qualifying survivor
- defined, for pooled registered pension plan rules, 147.5(1)

Qualifying transfer
- defined, for merger of segregated funds, 138.2(1)

Qualifying transfers
- re past service event, Reg. 8303(6), (6.1), Reg. 8304(2)(h)

Qualifying transitional income
- defined (for corporate inclusion of partnership income), 34.2(1)
- reserve, deduction for, 34.2(11)

Qualifying trust
- acquisition of shares for labour-sponsored funds tax credit, 127.4(3)
- defined, 127.4(1), 211.7(1)

Qualifying trust annuity
- attribution of amount paid out from, 75.2(a)
- - joint and several liability, 160.2(2.1), (5)
- death of taxpayer, effect of, 75.2(b)
- defined, 60.011(2), 248(1)

Qualifying withdrawals
- defined, Reg. 8307(3)

Quebec, *see also* Province
- accord with Canada for oil exploration, *see* Gulf of St. Lawrence oil exploration
- application of civil law to federal Acts, *Interpretation Act* 8.1, 8.2
- *Environmental Quality Act*, trust required by, exempt, 149(1)(z.1)
- Gaspé, *see* Gaspé Peninsula
- gift of succession in, deemed to be release or surrender, 248(9)
- labour-sponsored venture capital corporation of
- - prescribed, Reg. 6700(a)(i), (vii)
- logging tax, credit for, 127(1), (2), Reg. 700
- matrimonial regime, 248(22), (23)
- Montreal, international banking centre until 2013, 33.1(3)
- northern, *see* Northern Canada
- Office de professions, dues deductible, 8(1)(i)(vii)
- Pension Plan, *see* Canada Pension Plan/Quebec Pension Plan
- qualifying arrangement, 248(3), (3.2)
- RRSP, RRIF, RDSP, RESP or TFSA set up in, deemed to be trust, 248(3)(c), 248(3.2)(d)
- renunciation of succession in, deemed to be disclaimed, 248(9)
- residents, federal tax abatement, 120(2)
- *Supplemental Pension Plans Act*, Reg. 8502(d)(ix), 8510(9)
- tax on failing to acquire replacement LSVCC share, matching federal tax, 211.81
- tax rates, *see* introductory pages
- usufructs, rights of use or habitation, and substitutions, deemed to be trusts, 248(3)

Quebec North Shore Paper Co. case overruled, 12(1)(r)

Quebec Parental Insurance Plan
- deduction for premiums paid by self-employed person, 8(1)(l.2)
- benefit
- - repayment of overpayment, deduction for, 60(n)(v.1)
- - taxable, 56(1)(a)(vii)
- - withholding tax, 153(1)(d.1)
- premium
- - paid by employee
- - - as employee
- - - - credit, 118.7:B(a.1), (a.2)
- - - - deduction, 60(g)
- - - as employer, deduction, 8(1)(l.2)
- - paid by employer, deduction, 9(1) (general accounting principles)

Quebec Pension Plan, *see* Canada Pension Plan/Quebec Pension Plan

Index

Real property *(cont'd)*
- donation after sale of, capital gain exempt, 38(a.4), 38.3, 38.4 (abandoned)
- income from, Canada-U.S. Tax Treaty:Art. VI
- interest in, defined, 248(4)
- leasehold interest in, *see* Leasehold interest
- life estate in, 43.1
- non-qualifying real property, defined, 110.6(1)
- outside Canada
- • foreign tax credit to emigrant on disposition, 126(2.21)
- • foreign tax credit to trust, 126(2.21)
- • reporting of to CRA, 233.3
- principal-business corporations
- • associated, base level deduction, 18(2.3)–(2.5)
- • base level deduction, 18(2)(f), 18(2.2)
- rent paid before acquisition, deemed CCA, 13(5.2)
- trust owing, whether a unit trust, 108(2)(c)

Real right in an immovable
- meaning of, 248(4.1)

Real-time captioning services, *see* Captioning services

Reality television
- ineligible for Canadian film/video credit, Reg. 1106(1)"excluded production"(b)(vii)
- ineligible for film/video production services credit, Reg. 9300(2)(g)

Reappropriations of amounts, 221.2

Reasonable efforts
- to determine transfer prices
- • defined, 247(4)
- • required, 247(3)(a)(ii)(B)

Reasonable expectation of profit
- not required to deduct loss from business or property, 9(2) (Notes)
- personal or living expenses, 18(1)(h), 248(1)
- required for loss carryforward after change in control, 111(5)(a)(i), 111(5)(b)(i)

Reasonable return
- defined, for income-splitting tax, 120.4(1)

Reasonableness
- criterion for expenses, 67

Reassessment, *see also* Assessment
- after normal reassessment period, 152(4)–(5)
- • disposition of vessel, after, 13(18)
- consequential on other change, 152(4.3)
- constitutes an assessment, 248(1)"assessment"
- deceased's estate, election re losses, 152(6)
- election to capitalize interest, on, 21(5)
- exercise of option, on, 49(4), (5)
- extended reassessment period, 152(4)(b)
- Minister, by, 152(4), (4.1), (6), 165(3)
- • after filing notice of objection, 165(5)
- • disposing of appeal, on consent, 169(3)
- normal reassessment period, defined, 152(3.1)
- second notice of objection not required, 165(7)
- time for, 152(4); 231.8
- time to object to, 165(1)
- unused Part I.3 tax credit, 152(6)(f)
- validity, 165(5), (6)
- waiver of limitation period by taxpayer, 152(4)(a)(ii), 152(4)(c)
- within normal reassessment period, 152(4)

Recapture, *see also* Clawback; Negative amounts
- capital cost allowance, *see* Capital cost allowance: recapture
- eligible capital property, 14(1) [before 2017]
- goodwill, 14(1) [before 2017]
- investment tax credit, 127(27)–(36)
- SR&ED expenditures, 37(6)

Receivables
- in later year, reserve for, 20(1)(n), 20(8)
- • where property repossessed by creditor, 79.1(4)
- 1971, ITAR 23(5)"1971 receivables"

Receiver or receiver-manager, *see also* Legal representative
- clearance certificate before distributing property, 159(2)
- deemed to be legal representative, 248(1)"legal representative"
- obligations of, 159
- return to be filed, 150(3)
- withholding tax, liability for, 227(5), 227(5.1)

Recipient
- defined, re royalty reimbursements, 80.2(1)(a)

Reclamation obligations
- no reserve for, 20(7)(d)

Reclamation of mines, *see* Qualifying environmental trust

Reclassification
- depreciable property, change in class, 13(5)
- expenditures, R&D claims, 37(12)

Recognized derivatives exchange
- defined, for synthetic equity arrangement rules, 248(1)

Recognized forestry professional
- defined, Reg. 7400(3)

Recognized stock exchange
- defined, 248(1)

Record, *see also* Books and records
- defined, 248(1)

Record suspension
- defined, 149.1(1.01)
- effect on entitlement to operate charity, 149.1(1)"ineligible individual"(a)(ii)

Recovery
- labour-sponsored funds tax credit, *see* Labour-sponsored funds tax credit: recovery
- limit, *see* Recovery limit

Recovery limit
- defined, for non-resident trusts, 94(8)

Recovery wage subsidy rate
- defined, for Canada Recovery Hiring Program, 125.7(1)

Recreation program
- youth boarding allowance non-taxable, 6(1)(b)(v.1)

Recreation vehicle service technician
- apprenticeship job creation credit, 127(9)"investment tax credit"

Recreational club
- non-profit, exempt, 149(1)(l), 149(5)

Recreational facilities
- use of, expense not deductible, 18(1)(l)(i)

Recreational program for children, *see* Children's Arts Tax Credit (pre-2017)

Recreational property
- capital cost allowance, Reg. 1102(17)

Rectification, 169(1) (Notes)

Record suspension
- defined, 149.1(1.01)
- effect on entitlement to operate charity, 149.1(1)"ineligible individual"(a)(ii)

Red Seal trades
- prescribed, for apprenticeship credit, Reg. 7310

Redeeming entity
- defined, 135.1(7)

Redemption of shares by corporation
- capital loss denied, 40(3.6)
- deemed dividend of excess over paid-up capital, 84(3)

Redetermination, *see* Determination

Reduction of tax, *see* Abatement of tax

2480

Reed Stenhouse Companies Ltd.
- Class I shares, no deemed dividend on redemption, 84(8), Reg. 6206

Reference security
- defined, 18.3(1)"stapled security"(a)

Refinery
- capital cost allowance, Reg. Sch. II:Cl. 10(u), Sch. II:Cl. 41

Refrigeration and air conditioning mechanic
- apprenticeship job creation credit, 127(9)"investment tax credit"

Refugee
- entitled to Canada Child Benefit, 122.6"eligible individual"(e)(iii)

Refund
- after normal reassessment period, 152(4.2), 164(1.5)
- assignment of, by corporation, 220(6), (7)
- capital gains
- • mutual fund corporation, to, 131(2), (3)
- • mutual fund trust, to, 132(1), (2)
- Crown royalty, income inclusion, 12(1)(x.2)
- dividend
- • mutual fund corporation, to, 131(5)
- • private corporation, to, 129(1)
- duty of Minister, 164(4.1)
- employees profit sharing plan, to former beneficiary, 144(9)
- fraudulently obtained, offence, 239(1.1)
- included in income, 12(1)(x)(iv)
- interest on, 164(3)–(4)
- labour-sponsored funds tax credit clawback, 211.82
- non-resident tax, of, 227(6)–(7)
- of payments, *see* Refund of payments
- overpayment of tax, of, 164
- • application to other taxes, 164(2)
- Part I tax, 164
- partial refundable investment tax credit re scientific research and development, 164(1)
- premiums, of, *see* Registered retirement savings plan: refund of premiums
- provincial portion of income tax, 164(1.4)
- RRSP premiums, of, 146(1)"refund of premiums"
- • deemed receipt of, 146(8.1)
- reassessment to give rise to, 152(4.2)
- refundable dividend tax, 129
- • application to other liability, 129(2)
- repayment on objections and appeals, 164(1.1)
- returns must be filed before payable by Minister, 164(2.01)
- tax, of
- • deferred profit sharing plan, to, 202(2)
- • • application to other taxes, 203
- • • excessive, 160.1(1)
- tax on non-qualified investment, of
- • on disposition, 198(4), 199(2)
- • on recovery of security, 198(5)

Refund benefit
- defined, Reg. 8300(1)

Refund interest
- defined
- • for M&P credit on resource income, Reg. 5203(4)
- • for corporate interest offset, 161.1(1)
- payable to taxpayer, 164(3)
- • rate of interest, Reg. 4301(b)

Refund of payments
- defined, for education savings plan, 146.1(1)

Refund of premiums, *see* Registered retirement savings plan: refund of premiums

Refund Set-Off program, 164(2)

Refundable capital gains tax on hand
- mutual fund corporation, of, 131(6)"refundable capital gains tax on hand"
- • carryover to mutual fund trust on qualifying exchange, 132.2(3)(i)
- • reduction of, 131(9)
- mutual fund trust of, 132(4)"refundable capital gains tax on hand"
- • addition to following reorganization, 132.2(3)(i)

Refundable credits
- Canada Child Benefit, 122.61(1)
- Canada Workers Benefit (former Working Income Tax Benefit), 122.7
- Canadian film/video production credit, 125.4
- carbon tax rebate, 122.8
- child fitness credit (2015-2016), 122.8
- Climate Action Incentive, 122.8
- dividend refund, 129(1)
- film or video production services credit, 125.5
- GST credit, 122.5(3)
- greenhouse gas tax rebate, 122.8
- individual resident in Quebec, 120(2)
- investment tax credit, 127.1(1)
- journalism labour credit, 125.6
- medical expenses, 122.51
- qualifying environmental trust credit, 127.41(3)
- teacher school-supplies credit, 122.9
- U.S. social security tax adjustment due to treaty amendment, Canada-U.S. Tax Treaty:Art. XVIII:5

Refundable dividend tax on hand, *see also* Dividend refund
- aggregate investment income, defined, 129(4), 248(1)
- amalgamation, on, 87(2)(aa)
- deemed, 186(5)
- defined, 129(3) [repealed], 129(4)"eligible refundable dividend tax on hand", "non-eligible refundable dividend tax on hand"
- foreign investment income, defined, 129(4)
- "income" or "loss" defined, 129(4)
- meaning of certain expressions, 129(8)
- parent's, after subsidiary wound up, 87(2)(aa), 88(1)(e.2)
- refund of, 129(1)
- taxable dividend, defined, 129(7)

Refundable federal sales tax credit, 122.4 [repealed]

Refundable goods and services tax credit, 122.5, *see also* Goods and services tax (GST): refundable credit

Refundable investment tax credit
- deemed deduction from tax otherwise payable, 127.1(3)
- defined, 127.1(2)
- partial refund in respect of, 164(1)

Refundable medical expense credit, 122.51

Refundable Part IV tax, 186
- refund of, 129(1)

Refundable Part VII tax
- defined, 192(3), 248(1)

Refundable Part VIII tax on hand
- defined, 194(3), 248(1)

Refundable taxes
- investment income of CCPC, 123.3, *see also* Dividend refund
- Part IV tax, 186(1)
- prohibited investments for RRSP, RRIF, TFSA, RESP or RDSP, 207.04
- retirement compensation arrangement arrangement, 207.5(1)

Registered animal
- defined, Reg. 1802(5)

Registered Canadian amateur athletic association
- business activities of, 149.1(6.01)
- constitutes qualified donee for donations, 149.1(1)"qualified donee"(c)
- defined, 248(1)

Registration *(cont'd)*
- registered pension plan, *see* pension plan (above)
- registered retirement income fund, *see* retirement income fund (below)
- registered retirement savings plan, *see* retirement savings plan (below)
- retirement income fund, 146.3(2)
- retirement savings plan, 146(2), (3), (13.1)
- revocation of, *see* Revocation of registration
- tax shelter, 237.1, *see also* Tax shelter

Registration information
- defined, re disclosure of taxpayer information, 241(10)
- disclosure of, 241(4)(l)

Regular adjustment period
- defined, re indexed debt obligation, Reg. 7001(7)

Regular customers
- defined, for FAPI rules, 95(2.4)(b)

Regular eligible amount
- defined, for Home Buyers' Plan, 146.01(1)

Regulated foreign financial institution, *see* Offshore regulated bank

Regulated innovative capital
- defined, 122.1(1)
- excluded in determining whether trust is SIFT trust, 122.1(1)"investment"(b)(ii)

Regulated Investment Company (U.S.)
- dividend paid to Canadian resident, Canada-U.S. Tax Treaty:Art. X:7(b)

Regulations
- definitions in, *Interpretation Act* s. 16
- failure to comply with, penalty, 162(7)
- incorporating material amended from time to time, 221(4)
- Income Tax, reproduced after the *Income Tax Act* and *Income Tax Application Rules*
- judicial notice to be taken of, 244(12)
- meaning, 248(1)
- provision for, 147.1(18), 214(13), 215(5), 221(1)
- publication of, in *Canada Gazette*, 221(2)
- reducing amount of non-resident withholding tax, 215(5)
- residents in Canada, re, 214(13)
- retroactive effect, limitation on, 221(2)
- whether binding on Her Majesty, 221(3)

Regulatory innovative capital, *see* Regulated innovative capital

Rehabilitative therapy
- for hearing/speech loss, medical expense, 118.2(2)(l.3)

Reimbursement
- alimony or maintenance payments, 56(1)(c.2), 60(c.2)
- disability insurance top-up paid by employer, 8(1)(n.1)
- election to offset against outlay or expense, 12(2.2)
- housing loss, by employer, 6(19)–(22)
- included in income, 12(1)(x)
- - prescribed amount, Reg. 7300
- inducements, 20(1)(hh)
- legal expenses of collecting salary etc., re
- - included in employee's income, 6(1)(j)
- loss in value of home, for, 6(19)–(22)
- medical expenses, 118.2(3)(b)
- motor vehicle expenses, in respect of, 6(1)(b)(xi)
- payments as
- - election re adjusted cost base, 53(2)(s), 53(2.1)
- petroleum/natural gas etc. royalties included in income, for, 80.2
- received by beneficiary of trust, or partner, 12(2.1)
- salary or wages, of, 8(1)(n)
- support payments, 56(1)(c.2), 60(c.2)

Reimbursement payment
- defined (re top-up disability payments), 8(1)(n.1)(i)

Reinsurance arrangement
- defined, 211(1)

Reinsurance commission
- defined, Reg. 1408(1)
- exclusion from matchable expenditure rules, 18.1(15)
- whether deductible, 18(9.02)

Reinsurance recoverable
- defined, Reg. 2400(1)

Reinsurance recoverable amount
- defined, Reg. 1408(1)

Reinsurance trust
- exemption from withholding tax, 212(9)(d)

Reinsurer
- sales commissions, excluded from matchable expenditure rules, 18.1(15)

Related, *see* Related persons

Related business
- defined, for income-splitting tax, 120.4(1)
- income derived from, income-splitting tax, 120.4(1)"split income"(b)(ii), (c)(ii)(C)
- of charity
- - defined, 149.1(1)
- - revocation of registration for carrying on other business, 149.1(2)(a)

Related entity
- defined, for Common Reporting Standard, 270(1)

Related group, defined, 251(4)

Related persons, *see also* Associated corporations
- deemed not to deal at arm's length, 251(1)(a)
- defined, 251(2)
- extensions to definition
- - for butterfly transactions, 55(5)(e)
- - for debt forgiveness rules, 80(2)(j)
- - for financial institutions tax, 190.15(6)
- - for foreign affiliates, 95(2.2)(b), 95(6)(a)(i)
- - for loans to non-residents, 17(11), (11.1), (11.3)
- - for transfer pricing, Canada-U.S. Tax Treaty:Art. IX:2

Related segregated fund trust, 138.1
- adjusted cost base of, 53(1)(l), 53(2)(q)
- application on qualifying disposition to trust, 107.4(3)(g)
- defined, 138.1(1)(a)
- minimum tax not payable by, 127.55(f)(i)
- rollover to new trust, 248(1)"disposition"(f)(vi)

Related transactions
- defined, for foreign tax credit, 126(7)

Relationship, defined, 251(6)
- for certain Part I.3 purposes, 181.5(6)

Relationship deposits
- defined, for FAPI of banks, 95(2.43)

Release or surrender, defined, 248(9)

Relevant assumption
- defined, FAPI partnership rules, 93.1(6)(b)

Relevant authority, *see also* Competent authority
- defined
- - for policy reserves in insurance business, Reg. 1408(1)
- - for prescribed amount and recovery rate, Reg. 8006

Relevant contribution (re eligible funeral arrangement)
- defined, 148.1(1)

Relevant conversion benefit
- defined, for insurance demutualization, 139.1(16)(a)

Relevant criminal offence, *see also* Relevant offence
- causing person to be ineligible to manage charity, 149.1(1)"ineligible individual"(a)
- defined, 149.1(1)

To install, click Start and click Run. Enter d:\setup.exe (where d: is your DVD drive) and click OK. That's it! Good luck with your research!

Take this short tour to familiarize yourself with the new features of Folio 4.

New Functionality -- the print document button

We have introduced a new print document button that greatly simplifies printing. If you wish to just print the document that you are currently viewing, ensure that the cursor is placed within the document and click on the Print Document button.

- Click in the infobase whose table of contents you want to view. The text infobase is on the left side of your screen. The find infobase, which contains valuable cross-reference information for all the documents in the text infobase, is on the right. Click in the text infobase.

- Click on the Contents View button on the toolbar. You could also click on the Contents/Document View to get a split screen. Try both buttons now to see the difference.

- Navigate through the contents by clicking on the plus and minus signs. No need to double click!

- Notice the small boxes on each branch of the table of contents. Click on these boxes to put a checkmark in them in order to restrict a search to just these branches of the infobase. For now, put a checkmark just on the Case Law branch.

- On the toolbar is a search field where you can enter search terms. Click in the box and type: bank mortgage

- Click on the Find button or simply hit enter to initiate the search. You will note that you now have a number of hits under case law that you can review.

- Click on either the Full Document View button or the Contents/Document View to see your first hit. Use the next hit button to navigate through your hits. Is the first document clearly not relevant? Jump to the next document by hitting the Next Document with Hits button.

- Begin a new search now by clicking on the Template 1 button. Immediately you should notice something different which is the One-Kad Branches box. Note it has a checkmark in it. That is because you have checked branches on the table of contents. If you leave this box checked, your template search will be restricted to just those branches of the infobase. Leave the box checked so for now. In the "Within Same Paragraph" field type: bank mortgage. Click on OK. If you haven't got the table of contents in view, click on the Contents View button. Do you notice something different? In all likelihood, the number of hits you have is much fewer. That is because you restricted the search so that bank and mortgage had to be in the same paragraph. The other search field only required them to be within the same document.

- Click on the Synchronize Contents button to open the Table of Contents to see where your first hit is. You can now simply double click on the documents in order to automatically bring up the Full Document View.

- Click on the Next Hit button to see where your first hit is in the document. You can now tag that record for the purposes of printing or saving to a file by clicking on the Tag button on the toolbar. You could also tag the record by typing ctrl+t.

- Click on the Print button to bring up the Print dialogue box. Note that "tagged records" is selected because we have tagged records. Click on OK to print the tagged records. To save them to a file, select Export from the File menu. Let's now see some of the enhanced flexibility of the print function in Folio 4. If necessary, click on the Contents View button to bring up the table of contents. Go to the View menu and click on Clear all Checks to start fresh. Now find a number of documents that you would like to print and put checkmarks in their boxes. Now click on the Print button. Click on the Section ratio button. Note the mini table of contents that will show the documents you have checked. Click on the OK button to batch print all the documents you selected in the table of contents.

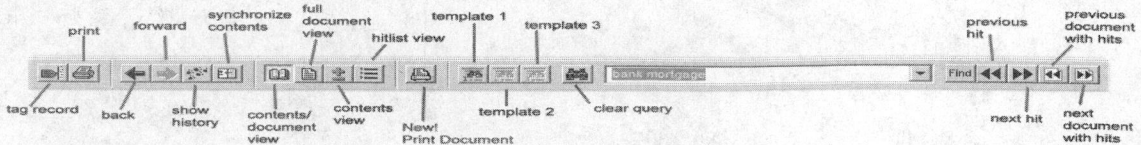

IF YOU PURCHASED THE DVD, LET'S GET STARTED!

To install, click **Start** and click **Run**. Enter **d:\setup.exe** (where d is your DVD drive) and click **OK. That's it! Good luck with your research!**

Take this short tour to familiarize yourself with the new features of Folio 4:

New Functionality — the print document button

We have introduced a new print document button that greatly simplifies printing. If you wish to just print the document that you are currently viewing, ensure that the cursor is placed within the document and click on the Print Document button.

➤ Click in the infobase whose table of contents you want to view. The text infobase is on the left side of your screen. The find infobase, which contains valuable cross-reference information for all the documents in the text infobase, is on the right. Click in the text infobase.

➤ Click on the Contents View button on the toolbar. You could also click on the Contents/Document View to get a split screen. Try both buttons now to see the difference.

➤ Navigate through the contents by clicking on the plus and minus signs. No need to double click!

➤ Notice the small boxes on each branch of the table of contents? Click on these boxes to put a checkmark in them in order to restrict a search to just these branches of the infobase. For now, put a checkmark just on the Case Law branch.

➤ On the toolbar is a search field where you can enter search terms. Click in the box and type: bank mortgage

➤ Click on the Find button or simply hit enter to initiate the search. You will note that you now have a number of hits under case law that you can review.

➤ Click on either the Full Document View button or the Contents/Document View to see your first hit. Use the next hit button to navigate through your hits. Is the first document clearly not relevant? Jump to the next document by hitting the Next Document with Hits button.

➤ Begin a new search now by clicking on the Template 1 button. Immediately you should notice something different which is the Checked Branches box. Note it has a checkmark in it. That is because you have checked branches on the table of contents. **If you leave this box checked, your template search will be restricted to just those branches of the infobase.** Leave the box checked for now. In the "Within Same Paragraph" field type: bank mortgage. Click on OK. If you haven't got the table of contents in view, click on the Contents View button. Do you notice something different? In all likelihood, the number of hits you have is much fewer. That is because you restricted the search so that bank and mortgage had to be in the same paragraph. The other search field only required them to be within the same document.

➤ Click on the Synchronize Contents button to open the Table of Contents to see where your first hit is. You can now simply double click on the document in order to automatically bring up the Full Document View.

➤ Click on the Next Hit button to see where your first hit is in the document. You can now tag that record for the purposes of printing or saving to a file by clicking on the Tag button on the toolbar. You could also tag the record by typing ctrl + t.

➤ Click on the Print button to bring up the Print dialogue box. Note that "tagged records" is selected because we have tagged records. Click on OK to print the tagged records. To save them to a file, select Export from the File menu. Let's now see some of the enhanced flexibility of the print function in Folio 4. If necessary, click on the Contents View button to bring up the table of contents. Go to the View menu and click on Clear all Checks to start fresh. Now find a number of documents that you would like to print and put checkmarks in their boxes. Now click on the Print button. Click on the Section radio button. Note the mini table of contents that will show the documents you have checked. Click on the OK button to batch print all the documents you selected in the table of contents.